THE
GRAMOPHONE
CLASSICAL
MUSIC
GUIDE
2010

INTRODUCTION

Our partner in publishing *The Gramophone Classical Music Guide* this year is an independent UK-based classical record retailer whose philosophy chimes with our own. Presto Classical's approach to selling classical discs is underpinned by an evident love of the music and the world of recordings. There's a knowledge that emerges on every page of Presto Classical's website and a good old-fashioned belief in quality customer service. You know you are dealing with a business that talks the same language as its customers – ask for a recording and you won't be greeted with a blank expression. Knowledge and enthusiasm are the qualities that make us perfect partners – and both of us are in the business of uniting music lovers with great music and great music-making.

Published by haymarket consumer media

Teddington Studios
Broom Road
Teddington
Middlesex TW11 9BE
United Kingdom

EDITOR James Jolly
PRODUCTION EDITOR Antony Craig
ART EDITOR Charlotte Chandler
PRODUCTION MANAGER Ailsa Donovan

PUBLISHER Simon Temlett
BRAND MANAGER Rachael Butler

PUBLISHING DIRECTOR Bob McDowell
GROUP DESIGN DIRECTOR Paul Harpin
GROUP EDITORIAL DIRECTOR Mel Nichols
CHAIRMAN & MANAGING DIRECTOR Kevin Costello

© haymarket media group 2009
ISBN 9 780860 249221

ACKNOWLEDGEMENT

Material from **GROVE**music reproduced from
The Concise Grove Dictionary of Music
under licence from Oxford
University Press, New York, USA

SALES AND DISTRIBUTION

North America
Omnibus Press
Music Sales Distribution Center
455 Bellvale Road
Chester, NY 10918 USA
Telephone 800 438 6874 or 845 469 4699
Fax 800 345 6842 or 845 469 7544

UK and Rest of World
Music Sales Ltd
Newmarket Road
Bury St Edmunds, Suffolk IP33 3YB
Great Britain
Telephone +44 (0)1284 702600 **Fax** +44 (0)1284 768301
e-mail trade.enquiries@musicsales.com

Printed in the UK by
CPI William Clowes Beccles NR34 7TL

CONTRIBUTORS

Andrew Achenbach
Nicholas Anderson
Nalen Anthoni
Mike Ashman
Mary Berry
Alan Blyth
Joan Chissell
Philip Clark
Robert Cowan
Peter Dickinson
Jed Distler
Duncan Druce
John Duarte
Adrian Edwards
Richard Fairman
David Fallows
David Fanning
Andrew Farach-Colton
Iain Fenlon
Hilary Finch
Fabrice Fitch
Jonathan Freeman-Attwood
Edward Greenfield
David Gutman
Martyn Harry
Stephen Johnson
Lindsay Kemp
Tess Knighton
Andrew Lamb
Richard Lawrence
Robert Layton
Ivan March
Ivan Moody
Bryce Morrison
Jeremy Nicholas
Christopher Nickol
Patrick O'Connor
Michael Oliver
Richard Osborne
Tim Parry
Stephen Plaistow
Peter Quantrill
Nicholas Rast
Guy Rickards
Malcolm Riley
Marc Rochester
Julie-Anne Sadie
Stanley Sadie
Lionel Salter
Alan Sanders
Michael Scott Rohan
Edward Seckerson
Robert Seeley
Pwyll ap Siôn
Harriet Smith
Ken Smith
John Steane
Michael Stewart
Jonathan Swain
David Vickers
John Warrack
Richard Whitehouse
Arnold Whittall
Richard Wigmore
Barry Witherden
William Yeoman

CONTENTS

Foreword   **VI**

Downloading   **VIII**

100 New Recordings   **XIV**

Gramophone Records of the Year   **XVIII**

Suggested Basic Library   **XX**

1000 Years of Music   **XXII**

Abbreviations   **XXXV**

The Reviews
A-Z by composer   **1**
Collections   **1311**

Indexes   **1362**

FOREWORD

By James Jolly, Editor-in-Chief of *Gramophone*

Compiling *The Gramophone Classical Music Guide* each summer is a wonderful reminder of the extraordinary riches music lovers are offered. There has never been so much music available from so many different sources. And though the classical wing of the record industry has been subject to as much turmoil and uncertainty as the rock and pop sectors, there's one area of creativity that has carried on, virtually unchanged: inspired A&R. In the pages that follow you'll encounter recordings from across the entire spectrum of the recorded music business, and each one has been produced with the same philosophy – a shared belief that the artist has something worthwhile to say about the music he or she is performing, and that the public will enjoy that interpretation. Of course, with so much of the repertoire re-recorded so often you might be forgiven for asking whether we really need a new set of the Brahms symphonies or another Liszt B minor Sonata. And yes, if those works were suddenly banned from the recording studio we'd still have a huge selection to choose from. But recordings – to take that word at its most literal – are snapshots of a style of performing at a given moment.

When the new Millennium dawned many of us wondered whether any company would risk the major investment of a complete Beethoven symphony cycle, and for a couple of years it seemed as if no one was prepared to make the first move. But in the years since 2000 we have had cycles from Sir Simon Rattle, Osmo Vänskä, Jos van Immerseel and Sir Charles Mackerras, to pick out a handful of the most impressive. And yes, they each have something special to say, in a language that an early 21st-century music lover responds to and – and I don't think this can be underestimated – by performers who are part of our world and can be heard live. Historic performances are fascinating, rewarding and often have a magic all their own, but for classical music to live and thrive, we need to engage with the artists of our own time. And Beethoven isn't the only beneficiary – think of all the Brahms and Mahler symphonies, Schubert songs and Chopin piano works…

The major companies still continue to make recordings that are beyond the reach of most independents – starrily cast opera recordings of the core works of the repertoire. This year Cecilia Bartoli and Juan Diego Flórez brought us a new Bellini *Sonnambula*, Angela Gheorghiu and Jonas Kaufmann rewarded us with a new studio recording of Puccini's *Madama Butterfly*, and Anna Netrebko and Elina Garanča delivered Bellini's *I Capuleti e i Montecchi* in a performance that captured imaginations across the globe. All three sets have taken their rightful place in the recorded canon – and in this guide. And the same could be said of recordings by major artists of the calibre of Sir Simon Rattle, Claudio Abbado, Bernard Haitink, Mariss Jansons and Esa-Pekka Salonen (though many of these maestri are now being cared for by their orchestras' own labels).

The Gramophone Classical Music Guide has been evolving and growing for more than two decades, drawing not only on the hundreds of new reviews published in *Gramophone* over the course of each year but also building on a tradition of informed, quality criticism that goes back to 1923 when the magazine was founded by the writer Compton Mackenzie. His philosophy back then was to search out the finest writers in their field and build a panel of reviewers who were experts in the own areas – and that's a philosophy that remains all these years later. (The launch this year of *Gramophone*'s entire history at **www.gramophone.net** allows anyone to read every page of every issue from April 1923 onwards.)

In selecting the reviews for the guide I've not aimed at a comprehensive coverage of every single recording of every single work. Instead I've been guided by *Gramophone*'s critics to the best version, and where possible offered alternatives at different price points and also a historic version and one on DVD. For some of most popular works of the repertoire a box of at-a-glance comments is offered.

Recordings are discussed as they are coupled on the disc so you will find, say, the piano concertos of Grieg and Schumann (one of the most popular pairings on disc) discussed under Grieg – so if you fail to find a particular work a quick look at the index to couplings will reveal if that work is to be found elsewhere in the book.

The biggest problem in compiling this guide has been the availability of recordings. Long gone are the days when a disc was either available or had been deleted. Nowadays discs inhabit a strange grey world of limited availability, even restricted by territory (not to mention availability as a download). If a disc appears not to be available where you live, take to the internet – you'll almost certainly find it! Top of the list of recordings that slip quietly into this grey world are Collections and Recitals – as a result I have tended to focus the various Collection sections at the back of the book on releases from the past 12 months (with, of course, some of the undisputed classics retained). It also means that they should be relatively easy to obtain.

All that remains to say is happy listening and I hope you make some rewarding and enjoyable discoveries.

DOWNLOADING

Downloading has become the norm for a new generation of music lovers: there are numerous teenagers who haven't even played a CD. Classical music fans are starting to dip their toes into this new world – and enjoying the experience. **James Jolly** offers an introduction to the sites and the music available for download.

A couple of years ago, *Gramophone* readers – hard-core music lovers to a fault – were asked whether they downloaded music. Twice as many said yes when compared with those who replied to the same question two years earlier. That's not an overwhelming constituency but it definitely marks a sizeable interest in the new format. The CD, though, isn't going to disappear overnight but it will become just one of a number of formats on offer. Already a vast array of recordings are available as downloads – one glance through this guide will reveal the extent of the catalogue: the ⟿ symbol alongside a disc's details shows that the recording is also available as a download. But first, let's dispel a few concerns.

'I don't want to walk round with little white headphones on...' You don't have to! The millions of iPod users (and listeners to other kinds of MP3 players) are merely making portable a medium that is essentially a new form of delivery – down the phone line, straight into your PC or Mac. But there is no denying the allure that instant, portable music has, and how it has driven the music market.

'I don't want to listen to my music in my study...' OK, you don't want to transport your music around in an iPod or sit at your computer to listen either. There are now numerous, wireless ways of transmitting your music from your PC to your hi-fi. Or there are an increasing number of systems that allow you to insert your player (more often than not an iPod) and offer remarkably good sound quality. It's also pretty easy to link your iPod/MP3 player using its cradle and a good old-fashioned cable. I regularly plug my iPod into my kitchen mini-system and am more than satisfied with the results (and a phono-to-headphones cable is a mandatory holiday accessory now that many hotels and apartments have hi-fi as standard).

With the advent of a new generation of Network Music Players, freedom and quality go hand in hand. The audiophile listener can listen to downloaded (and no doubt lossless) music with no degradation of sound quality. And with companies such as Linn, Gimell and Chandos offering studio-quality downloads, there is no reason that your music should not sound as good as (and in some cases better then) the equivalent CD. A good introduction to Network Music Players can be found on the Gimell website (**gimell.com**) and on the various manufacturers' sites (**logitech.com** and **linn.co.uk** among the market leaders).

'I don't have a broadband connection to the internet...' It's not absolutely necessary, but it does take considerably longer to download an album's worth of music if you don't have a broadband connection (on iTunes it takes about three minutes to download a CD's worth via a 2 megabyte modem). But broadband packages are becoming increasingly attractive – and standard.

'I'm worried about sound quality...' This is one of the biggest concerns voiced about downloaded music. No one has ever claimed that MP3 is a hi-fi medium. But if you're happy with FM-quality sound (say BBC Radio 3) played back through high-end equipment, you are unlikely to be disappointed with the quality of the sound of the music you download. However, there are a growing number of digital retailers (often record labels themselves) who are seriously addressing this issue and offering lossless sound (in other words, no degradation in sound quality over the equivalent CD). Sites to check out for lossless formats are Linn, Gimell and the **classicalshop.net** (Chandos's download site). The abbreviation to look out for is FLAC, now the preferred lossless file type – you can be sure of sound of the highest quality combined with manageable file sizes. The site that offers more FLAC files than anyone else is Chandos's, and you can guarantee great sound to start with!

'I've a huge CD collection which I still want to listen to...' Most people's MP3 players contain a combination of music that they've ripped (ie transferred from CD to their computer's hard-drive) and music that has been downloaded (the proportion is invariably a single-figure percentage of downloaded music). It makes sense to load your computer (especially if you are planning to take your music with you) with your favourite recordings and then supplement them with downloads as necessary. If you've a laptop, why not store some music there – then you'll always have something for those unplanned-for delays when music is the only balm!

'I like to read the notes that come with the CD...' Again this is being fast addressed by the independent sector. Chandos, via its **classicalshop.net**, is assiduously adding sleeve-notes to all of its downloadable offerings. Some of the high-profile major company releases are also being offered with downloadable PDF notes. This embarrassment of material, though, brings with it its own problem: where do you store it? It's also worth trawling the web for programme notes – an increasing number of orchestras are making their material available on their websites. It's also worth searching *Gramophone*'s own archive site for information. With over 85 years' worth of commentary on recordings you might well find everything you're looking for (**www.gramophone.net**).

'I see that certain recordings are only being made available as a download...' True, and that's clearly the way things will start to go. Universal has been exploring download-only productions under the DG and Decca Concerts brand. These offer live concert recordings with minimal editing.

The one genre that would seem ideally suited to download-only music is new music, where sales are invariably low. It's an option being explored by a number of orchestras, allowing people to capture the quality and experience of the ensemble performing in its own concert hall. The St Louis Symphony, under its dynamic music director David Robertson, has already embarked on an imaginative series that offers live recordings of works central to each season's music-making. And there's a complete Mahler cycle from the New York Philharmonic under Lorin Maazel available only as a download. With the cost savings made by not having to press CDs and print booklets, this could greatly benefit new music ventures.

Where?

For the purposes of this explanatory section, let's assume you are buying your music to transport around on an MP3 player – most people do and it's a staggeringly easy way of guaranteeing that you can hear pretty well whatever you want, whenever you want it. (But as already noted in the introductory questions and answers, you need go no further than downloading it onto your computer and leaving it there to listen to.) However you choose to listen to your music, you will need to store it. Many DSPs (Digital Service Providers – basically download stores) offer a player that works with their offerings. The most widespread and probably the easiest to use is the iTunes version. It's better than most at coping with the sort of information that a classical music consumer will need: it's certainly visually appealing – clean and intuitive in the typical Apple house-style – but it also easily allows you to alter the various information columns to suit your musical tastes. For example, with pop and rock music you may prefer a hierarchy that gives artist, album and song the dominant position. With classical music, you may prefer a line-up that works something like: composer / work / movement or subsection / artist / genre (chamber, instrumental, song, etc).

Searching for music on the various sites is still a far-from-ideal manoeuvre. Most sites are geared up to the rock/pop consumer for whom an artist's name is probably all that is necessary to home in on their various albums and from there the selection is simple. Imagine typing in Herbert von Karajan – the choice is immense and the whole process is like shooting in the dark. One of the best search engines is found on the **classicsonline.com** site – it allows a number of fields to be entered and invariably locates what you're looking for immediately. If the big DSPs want to be taken seriously by the classical consumer they will have to address the 'search-ability' of their sites (though this presumes that the data on each recording is in some kind of useable form to start with – mention the word 'metadata' to anyone working in this field and they tend to roll their eyes in a state of horror).

So, you want to dip a toe into the fresh waters of downloading. What do you do?

How?

Until recently there weren't many options for the download enthusiast to organise and play his or her music. Apple's Jukebox has the enormous advantage in being part of the iTunes eco-system where music can be seamlessly acquired, stored and synchronised to your iPod. Get it at **apple.com/itunes**. There are versions for Mac and PC, so everyone is catered for. Once installed, the set-up process is very easy: you simply follow the instructions on the screen.

Sound quality is an important issue for many classical music enthusiasts, so before you start you need to decide what bit-rate you are happiest with. Apple's 128kbps (and for iTunes Plus recordings 192) is starting to look rather parsimonious for classical collectors. Many classical stores – Passionato and theclassicalshop among them – start at 320kbps, more than acceptable for all but the 'golden eared'.

I suggest you try ripping a few of your favourite CDs simply to get a feel for the quality you are happy with. On a PC go to 'Edit', then 'Preferences', click on 'Importing' and you will be offered a number of file-format options. Once the disc is ready for ripping, go to the 'iTunes' prompt at the top left of your screen. Click on it, and then on Preferences. Then in the centre of the tab which opens, click on 'Importing'. You will then be given the option for Setting. The default will probably be 128kbps AAC. Try importing using this setting. Next, using 'Get Info' (the Control-click/right-click option as described above), add 192 to the composer's name (say, Mozart192) and, using the Import option, import at 192kbps. You can do this as many times as you want with all permutations of file type and bit-rate – just make sure you label your files so that you can compare later. And of course you can go as high as loss-less, but the file size will be substantially larger.

Now, choosing the usual way you'll be listening to your music – headphones or speakers – play each of the different imported options and be critical! Once you've decided on the amount of compression you can cope with (I would be hesitant to go below 192kbps AAC – piano music tends to fray a little at the edges), you're ready to load some music onto your computer. Of course if you've a laptop then you're pretty close to starting a portable music collection.

Now you are set up to download. Further on in this section I suggest some of the different sites to visit to find your music, but before you go mad and start downloading an entire new music collection it's worth pausing to consider how you'll find all the music you've bought.

You will be amazed at how quickly you can amass a substantial collection of music on your PC (usually through a combination of ripping CDs and downloading) so it's a good idea to create a 'house style' for cataloguing the music. The information that accompanies a music file – whether acquired automatically on the web using a service like Gracenote (which is supplied largely by fellow enthusiasts in a kind of collective responsibility) or as supplied by the DSP – can arrive in a variety of styles. Decide early on how you are likely to sort though your music when you are looking for something to listen to. (One example of the inconsistency of web-based metadata services is the difference you will encounter between discs if you are ripping an opera: each CD can attract a completely different style of information that can waste an enormous amount of time if you then edit it manually. You can even get the information in different languages between discs – not exactly conducive to easy listening.)

If you listen to classical as well as other genres (pop, rock, jazz, world and so on), the chances are that you will sort your classical music initially by composer and your non-classical music by artist or album. For the eclectic music consumer I would recommend that you remove composer details from all kinds of music other than classical: this makes searching far quicker; and besides, the chances are that you've never heard of half the people who compose pop tunes. Relying on the genre column is one option but I've yet to encounter anyone who does this.

Simplicity is the keynote: pare the details down to the minimum.

Ludwig van Beethoven
Symphony No 3 in C minor, Op 55, 'Eroica'
Allegro con brio
Berlin Philharmonic Orchestra /
Herbert von Karajan

may satisfy the completist (or the librarian), but that's an awful lot of information to contain in the small window of an iPod (which actually has a larger window than many MP3 players). Why not settle for:

Beethoven
Symphony No 3
I (or first movt)
BPO / Karajan

It says exactly what is playing and gets the message across with economy and clarity. The best advice is to experiment and decide how much information you need to find your music quickly and efficiently. (Do be careful that you don't oversimplify your system – there is a risk that you could end up being offered all the first movements, followed by all the second movements and so on – and that risk is increased when you start adding multiple versions of a particular work to your collection. And if you're especially completist you'll almost certainly run into trouble when you add a different version of a particular work by a single performer – say, Brendel's *Hammerklavier* Sonata, but that's probably not going to happen too often!)

Another decision that needs to be taken is whether to keep your music in its original album form (do you want the Bruch Violin Concerto always to deliver the Mendelssohn as well?) or to store your music as individual pieces.

There are strong arguments to be made for both approaches: on a purely practical level you'd be amazed how quickly you seem to be re-programming your iPod if you have broken up albums into individual pieces (though you can easily make a special playlist that includes all your favourite violin concertos, so you can have a feast of Maxim Vengerov in great concertos if you want).

Where to find your music

There are various different 'business models' in operation for purchasing music. There is the simple, pay for what you buy (the most traditional and still most popular): the average price for a new 'full-price' album is about £8. This is the model used by iTunes, Passionato, theclassicalshop, classicsonline and numerous others. A second model is the subscription, where a monthly payment allows you either unlimited access to music (though with certain restrictions) or a fixed number of downloads (the eMusic model – see below). Here, for the classical music enthusiast, is a guide to some of the best sites for acquiring music.

iTunes

The mother of all DSPs is iTunes: it's the biggest source of downloads across the entire range of genres and in the classical arena it carries an impressive selection. And, like a traditional retailer, you pay for what you download – but don't expect much in the way of special offers.

There is a lot of music here – from majors to independents – though the ability to search easily, given the somewhat primitive engine on offer, is a bit frustrating. And iTunes' pretty low bit-rate (128, or 192 for the iTunes Plus titles – EMI included) might not be to all tastes (piano and choral music tends to suffer most).

Of course if you have an iPod then iTunes is a perfect fit with seamless transfer from search to purchase to synchronisation with iPod. However, downloads from the site carry Apple's proprietory DRM and cannot be transferred to other players or computers without restrictions (though iTunes Plus recordings are DRM-free and at a slightly higher bit-rate).

eMusic

Second only in size to iTunes comes eMusic (it has both .com and .co.uk sites). It operates a payment system that allows you a certain number of download tracks for a fixed fee (at the time of writing, 24 tracks for £9.99; £13.99 for 35 and £17.99 for 50). If you consider that most symphonies have just four movements and concertos have three, that's potentially a lot of music for very little money. If you add in the free 25 tracks eMusic gives you as an incentive to join (and which you can keep even if you don't stay with them), then this might be a good first destination to see if you enjoy acquiring your music in this new way. All eMusic downloads are DRM-free, which means that once you've bought it you can do whatever you like with it. (Incidentally, eMusic's recently upgraded Download Manager allows you store your music and control the audio files on your PC before you import them into your iTunes jukebox or preferred player. And it's very easy to use.)

The site focuses exclusively on independent companies – it contains recordings from Naxos, LSO Live, BIS, Ondine, SDG, Guild, Naïve, Chandos, Danacord and numerous others, and also does rather more editorialising than other sites, containing artist profiles, reviews and so on. The eMusic site does contain many gems, though finding them is always slightly difficult – you tend to to stumble over them when you

least expect it (and a sense of serendipity is still nice to encounter in this too-often-streamlined world!). That said though, the search engine is infinitely superior to that offered by iTunes which simply is not up to the task of locating classical music easily (or indeed logically).

Classical Archives

Re-launched in a stylish new livery and with a hugely enhanced functionality in 2009 is the US-based (and for the moment only US-serving) Classical Archives (**www.classicalarchives.com**). This is a formidable destination for classical music lovers containing a wealth of recordings from many of the leading labels in 320kbps DRM-free sound. The site claims to house over 620,000 recorded tracks representing 6,600 composers, 21,000 artists and over 100 record labels representing a cross-section of the majors (Universal, EMI and Sony Classical) and independent labels. The site allows you to stream music for a subscription fee of $9.95 per month or $99.50 per year.

Passionato

Passionato, launched in late 2008, like iTunes offers major-company recordings as well as independents (Universal, EMI, Chandos and Naxos are among the many labels on offer). Quality is a guiding principle, so 320kbps downloads are the norm and many files are offered in lossless FLAC sound – if you have a Network Music Player then you can enjoy CD-quality music through your hi-fi direct from your PC or laptop.

Passionato's player not only stores purchased music but it will transfer across all your existing music files (though not those purchased from iTunes). Once there, the player will offer you recommendations and ideas for future expansion of your music collection. The metadata is not the clearest: once into the contents of an album it's quite hard to relate the composer and performers to individual tracks.

theclassicalshop

One destination that has been steadily growing in size and confidence is theclassicalshop, a digital store with an increasingly broad catalogue. Chandos, the site's host, launched this download site early in 2006 and suddenly we were offered over 6000 MP3 files of the company's deleted recordings. The range is too immense to list but if you're attracted to Chandos's unequalled catalogue of rarer British orchestral music this could well be the place for you. There are gems such as Bryden Thomson's *Gramophone* Award-winning Bax Fourth, works by Finzi, Kenneth Leighton and Rubbra, and more standard fare such as the complete Rachmaninov piano concertos played by Earl Wild, with Jascha Horenstein conducting. The remainder of the catalogue followed and now all new releases are offered digitally alongside the CD.

Labels other than Chandos to be found at theclassicalshop include Avie, Amon Ra, Brana, Coro, CRD, Doyen, Guild, LSO Live, Naxos, Nimbus, NMC, Onyx, Priory, Pristine, Quartz, Signum, Somm and Wigmore Hall Live. Again, everything is DRM-free and an increasing number of recordings are being offered in Lossless formats (**theclassicalshop.net**).

classicsonline.com

Naxos, despite being well represented on the larger sites like iTunes and eMusic, also has its own website, which also contains music from the labels the company distributes around the world (**classicsonline.com**). It's worth checking out, though you might find that acquiring Naxos material via eMusic is a more cost-effective method. The search engine, however, is probably the best around – so finding your music is no problem here.

Another destination within Naxos's world is the Naxos Music Library (**naxosmusiclibrary. com**), a website with a mine of information that contains biographies, sleeve-notes, histories of music and the ability to listen to everything in the Naxos catalogue as well as a host of distributed label. All this comes for a modest annual fee and is an invaluable resource for the inquisitive as well as the professional consumer of fine music.

eclassical.com

Based in Sweden, this download store has been around since 1999 and so has a fair amount of experience. There is some helpful 'editorial' material to support the downloads (biographies, introductory notes on the music and so on) and a good selection of music. Performances are a little variable but there are some treasures to be found, so it's a site that's worth exploring when you've time on your hands (**eclassical.com**). Not surprisingly, there's good representation of the (Swedish) BIS label, and also a large quantity of recordings from Hänssler Classic.

pristineclassical.com

Pristine Audio (**pristineclassical.com**) has a dual role as remastering experts who offer their very fine transfers on custom-made CD or as downloads. Focusing on out-of-copyright recordings (in other words, public domain music recorded before 1957), it has amassed a large catalogue full of the great names of 20th-century music-making. One wonderful series is the restoration of the entire HMV Haydn Quartet Society discs from the Pro Arte Quartet recorded in the 1930s.

Pristine has been exploring new transfer methods recently and has been achieving some very impressive results. Some of the highlights of the Music & Arts catalogue have been treated this way and are sounding better than ever! And the arrival this year of the doyen of transfer engineers Mark Obert-Thorn, who provides a monthly downloadable album, is yet another incentive.

Another powerful reason to visit this site is that it offers the recordings issued in the late 1920s and early 1930s on *Gramophone*'s own label, the National Gramophonic Society. Fascinating chamber music releases – including Sir John Barbirolli's first recording – have been cleaned up with remarkable success.

Own-label websites

Why rely on others when you can do it yourself? This is a philosophy that has always fostered innovation and imagination – and, in the world of classical music, has been the biggest force for advance. A number of labels have launched their own digital stores. Top of the list must be Linn Records, not only because it's a classy little label in its own right, but also because its technical instructions and usability are second to none. In fact, I'd suggest anyone interested in downloading should spend some time on the Linn site reading the FAQ section. The answers are level-headed and honest – and extremely helpful (**linnrecords.com**).

The UK wing of the vast Universal Music company, Universal Classics and Jazz, has launched its own site (**classicsandjazz.co.uk**) which is a useful destination for the gems of the Decca, DG and Philips catalogues, as well as a growing amount of jazz material. And since its launch, DRM has been dropped and the music is compatible with just about every MP3 player on the market.

If you're a fan of Deutsche Grammophon – the Yellow Label, and for many the classical music brand *par excellence* – then check out its own webshop (**dgwebshop.com**). It's a rhapsody in yellow that offers the entire DG catalogue in the environment of the company's activities, both present and past. Music here is DRM-free and competitively priced.

Toccata Classics, the record-company arm of Toccata Press, furthers the aim of exploring the byways of classical music. As a label it has turned up some real treats: encountering Donald Tovey as composer rather than as the author of a series of splendid analytical essays on music has been a real ear-opener. Well, Toccata Classics has grasped the nettle and launched a download service that works well. If exotica from the Baroque to the present day appeals, log on to **toccataclassics.com**.

Mention of new music brings us to NMC, a record company that has been doing a unique service for new British music for many years. Having built up an impressive catalogue – and gained a few *Gramophone* Awards on the way – logic demanded that NMC make it available for downloading. And it's a splendid place to go for challenging and invariably deeply rewarding musical experiences (**nmc.greedbag.com**). Rather charmingly, you search by the composers using their first name rather than their surname – but I guess that just adds a touch of familiarity. There are also some excellent samplers that are great ways to see whether a particular composer appeals to you.

The Gramophone Listening Room

Launched in July 2009, The Gramophone Listening Room is a subscription service that allows music lovers to sample recordings before they're released and then purchase them quickly and easily. Free content is often offered alongside the subscriber-only music, and audio and video programmes are featured in the bespoke music player that sits on your desktop. Check it out and sign up at **gramophone.telljack.com**.

Podcasting

Podcasting has suddenly become the buzzword in the media world – everyone is podcasting, even *Gramophone*! A podcast is, essentially, a series of mini radio programmes (they tend to be about 20 minutes long, though there's no time limit) that you subscribe to, usually at no cost, and when a new podcast is ready, it automatically downloads onto your MP3 player. iTunes created a vast podcast offering, and most people with a podcast to offer house it at iTunes. The search engine isn't great for tracking down classical music podcasts since they tend to be stirred in with every other sort of music, but if you're persistent you can find a few gems.

BBC Radio dominates the UK-originated podcasts and many of Radio 3's programmes have podcast equivalents. *Gramophone* readers should definitely sign up for the weekly *Building a Library* podcast, and *Music Matters*, with the estimable Tom Service doing the honours, invariably has much to fascinate and entertain. *Discovering Music*, usually presented by Charles Hazlewood and Stephen Johnson, is another must. (And of course the BBC iPlayer offers pretty well every programme for a week.)

A new addition to the burgeoning podcast scene is a subscription service from Archive Classics that explores the wonderful world of historic recordings with Stephen Johnson the urbane guide. A weekly podcast finds him introducing great music in often magnificent performances from musicians of the middle years of the last century (**archiveclassics.co.uk**).

There are countless podcasts on offer – most orchestras and opera companies offer something, even if only a season preview. But some are works of art in their own right. A short search using Google will unearth the treasures very quickly.

To the future

These are exciting times for music lovers: there has never been so much music available, and now the ways to get at it have become even easier. If you live miles from a record store (provided that store even stocks classical music), then downloading is an option you should explore. It will inevitably become the obvious way for record companies to keep their back-catalogues available – a truly appealing prospect. Welcome to a world of infinite choice – the head spins!

100 NEW RECORDINGS

The following list offers a quick guide to 100 notable recordings that have entered *The Gramophone Classical Music Guide* this year.

Adams Doctor Atomic
Netherlands Opera cast
(Opus Arte DVD)
Reviewed on page 6

Adès The Tempest
Royal Opera cast
(EMI)
Reviewed on page 10

Bach Flute Sonatas
Emmanuel Pahud, Trevor Pinnock
(EMI)
Reviewed on page 48

Bach Solo Sonatas and Partitas
Viktoria Mullova
(Onyx)
Reviewed on page 52

Bach Cantatas Vol 17
John Eliot Gardiner
(SDG)
Reviewed on page 78

Balfe Falstaff
Marco Zambelli
(RTÉ Lyric FM)
Reviewed on page 96

Bax Symphonic Variations
Ashley Wass, James Judd
(Naxos)
Reviewed on page 114

Beethoven
Piano Concertos Nos 1-5
Evgeny Kissin, Sir Colin Davis
(EMI)
Reviewed on page 125

Beethoven Symphonies Nos 1-9
Claudio Abbado
(DG)
Reviewed on page 135

Beethoven
Symphonies Nos 4 & 7
Douglas Boyd
(Avie)
Reviewed on page 140

Beethoven Cello Sonatas Nos 1-3
Daniel Müller-Schott, Angela Hewitt
(Hyperion)
Reviewed on page 153

Beethoven Piano Sonatas Nos 9, 10, 12 & 15
Murray Perahia
(Sony Classical)
Reviewed on page 159

Beethoven Diabelli Variations
Stephen Kovacevich
(Onyx)
Reviewed on page 163

Bellini I Capuleti e i Montecchi
**Anna Netrebko, Elina Garanča,
Fabio Luisi**
(DG)
Reviewed on page 173

Bellini La Sonnambula
**Cecilia Bartoli, Juan Diego Flórez,
Alessandro de Marchi**
(L'Oiseau-Lyre)
Reviewed on page 177

Berg Kammerkonzert
(coupled with Mozart's Gran Partita)
**Mitsuko Uchida, Christian Tetzlaff,
Pierre Boulez**
(Decca)
Reviewed on page 182

Bernstein Mass
Marin Alsop
(Naxos)
Reviewed on page 205

Birtwistle The Minotaur
Antonio Pappano
(Opus Arte DVD)
Reviewed on page 216

Bowen Piano Concertos Nos 3 & 4
**Danny Driver,
Martyn Brabbins**
(Hyperion)
Reviewed on page 236

Brahms Symphony No 1
John Eliot Gardiner
(SDG)
Reviewed on page 246

Brahms Piano Sonata No 2 etc
Libor Novacek
(Landor)
Reviewed on page 259

Brahms Piano Pieces Opp 116-119
Markus Groh
(Avie)
Reviewed on page 260

Britten Piano Concerto etc
Steven Osborne, Ilan Volkov
(Hyperion)
Reviewed on page 270

Britten War Requiem
Helmuth Rilling
(Hänssler Classic)
Reviewed on page 276

Britten
Owen Wingrave
Richard Hickox
(Chandos)
Reviewed on page 284

Bruckner Symphony No 3
Roger Norrington
(Hänssler Classic)
Reviewed on page 293

Byrd Edition, Vol 11
The Cardinall's Musick
(Hyperion)
Reviewed on page 313

Carter String Quartets
Pacifica Quartet
(Naxos)
Reviewed on page 321

Chopin Piano Sonatas Nos 2 & 3 etc
Marc-André Hamelin
(Hyperion)
Reviewed on page 332

Copland Early symphonies
Marin Alsop
(Naxos)
Reviewed on page 345

Debussy Jeux. Préludes (orch Matthews)
Mark Elder
(Hallé)
Reviewed on page 360

Debussy. Fauré. Ravel String Quartets
Quatuor Ebène
(Virgin Classics)
Reviewed on page 363

Debussy
Complete Piano Works, Vol 4
Jean-Efflam Bavouzet
(Chandos)
Reviewed on page 365

Debussy Préludes Book 1
Nelson Freire
(Decca)
Reviewed on page 366

Dufay Missa Se la face y pale
Binchois Consort
(Hyperion)
Reviewed on page 388

Eccles The Judgement of Paris
Christian Curnyn
(Chandos)
Reviewed on page 412

Elgar Violin Concerto
Gil Shaham, David Zinman
(Canary Classics)
Reviewed on page 416

Elgar The Dream of Gerontius
Mark Elder
(Hallé)
Reviewed on page 424

Fauré Requiem
Accentus
(Naïve)
Reviewed on page 434

Feldman The Viola in my Life
Marek Konstantynowicz
(ECM New Series)
Reviewed on page 439

Foerster Violin Concertos
Iván Zenaty, Jiří Bělohlávek
(Supraphon)
Reviewed on page 441

Gershwin Complete works for piano and orchestra
Anne-Marie McDermott, Justin Brown
(Bridge)
Reviewed on page 455

Glazunov Symphony No 6 etc
José Serebrier
(Warner Classics)
Reviewed on page 467

Grieg. Schumann. Saint-Saëns Piano concertos
Howard Shelley
(Chandos)
Reviewed on page 489

Grieg Lyric Pieces
Katya Apekisheva
(Quartz)
Reviewed on page 493

Handel Water Music.
Music for the Royal Fireworks
Federico Guglielmo
(CPO)
Reviewed on page 504

Handel Coronation Anthems
The Sixteen
(Coro)
Reviewed on page 511

Handel Acis and Galatea
The Dunedin Consort
(Linn)
Reviewed on page 513

Handel Messiah
The Sixteen
(Coro)
Reviewed on page 517

Handel 'Furore'
Joyce DiDonato, Christophe Rousset
(Virgin Classics)
Reviewed on page 531

Haydn. Hummel. Neruda Trumpet Concertos
Alison Balsom
(EMI)
Reviewed on page 549

Haydn Piano Trios Nos 24-27
Florestan Trio
(Hyperion)
Reviewed on page 561

Haydn Opera arias
Thomas Quasthoff
(DG)
Reviewed on page 571

Holst The Perfect Fool
Richard Hickox
(Chandos)
Reviewed on page 588

Ives Psalms
South West German Radio Vocal Ensemble
(Hänssler Classic)
Reviewed on page 610

Janáček String Quartets
Quatuor Diotima
(Alpha)
Reviewed on page 614

Janáček From the House of the Dead
Pierre Boulez
(DG DVD)
Reviewed on page 617

Lindberg Concerto for Orchestra
Sakari Oramo
(Ondine)
Reviewed on page 659

Liszt Piano Concertos
Eldar Nebolsin
(Naxos)
Reviewed on page 661

Liszt Années de pèlerinage
Daniel Grimwood
(SFZ Music)
Reviewed on page 667

Łukaszewski Choral works
Trinity College Choir, Cambridge
(Hyperion)
Reviewed on page 673

Mahler Symphony No 4
Miah Persson, Iván Fischer
(Channel Classics)
Reviewed on page 697

Martinů Violin Concertos
**Bohuslav Matoušek,
Christopher Hogwood**
(Hyperion)
Reviewed on page 713

Martinů
Julietta Fragments
**Magdalena Koženà,
Charles Mackerras**
(Supraphon)
Reviewed on page 716

D Matthews The Music of Dawn etc
Rumon Gamba
(Chandos)
Reviewed on page 724

Mazzocchi Vespro della Beata Vergine
Konrad Junghänel
(Harmonia Mundi)
Reviewed on page 728

Mendelssohn Songs without words
Sebastian Knauer

(Berlin Classics)
Reviewed on page 737

Messiaen Préludes etc
Pierre-Laurent Aimard
(DG)
Reviewed on page 743

Mozart Violin Concertos
**Giuliano Carmignola,
Claudio Abbado**
(Archiv Produktion)
Reviewed on page 772

Padilla 'Streams of Tears'
The Sixteen
(Coro)
Reviewed on page 835

Puccini Madama Butterfly
**Angela Gheorghiu,
Jonas Kaufmann,
Antonio Pappano**
(EMI)
Reviewed on page 877

Purcell Keyboard works
Richard Egarr
(Harmonia Mundi)
Reviewed on page 887

Rachmaninov Preludes
Steven Osborne
(Hyperion)
Reviewed on page 902

Ravel Daphnis et Chloé
Jun Märkl
(Naxos)
Reviewed on page 913

Schnittke Concerto for Choir
Prague Philharmonic Choir
(Praga Digitals)
Reviewed on page 979

Schubert Lieder
**Elizabeth Watts,
Roger Vignoles**
(RCA Red Seal)
Reviewed on page 1010

Schubert Schwanengesang etc
**Christoph Prégardien,
Andreas Staier**
(Challenge Classics)
Reviewed on page 1014

Schumann Works for cello and piano
**Steven Isserlis,
Dénes Várjon**
(Hyperion)
Reviewed on page 1024

Schumann
Das Paradies und die Peri
Nikolaus Harnoncourt
(RCA Red Seal)
Reviewed on page 1029

Schumann Dichterliebe etc
Gerald Finley, Julius Drake
(Hyperion)
Reviewed on page 1032

Shchedrin
The Sealed Angel
David Trendell
(Delphian)
Reviewed on page 1046

Sibelius Night Ride and Sunrise
Pietari Inkinen
(Naxos)
Reviewed on page 1075

Smetana Orchestral works Vol 2
Gianandrea Noseda
(Chandos)
Reviewed on page 1086

R Strauss An Alpine Symphony
Mariss Jansons
(RCO Live)
Reviewed on page 1102

R Strauss Der Rosenkavalier
Carlos Kleiber
(Orfeo)
Reviewed on page 1120

Szymanowski
Symphonies Nos 1 & 4
Antoni Wit
(Naxos)
Reviewed on page 1142

Tchaikovsky Symphony No 5
Gustavo Dudamel
(DG)
Reviewed on page 1165

Tchaikovsky Manfred Symphony
Vasily Petrenko
(Naxos)
Reviewed on page 1165

Wagner Parsifal
Reginald Goodall
(Royal Opera House)
Reviewed on page 1271

Wagner The Ring
Royal Danish Opera
(Decca DVD)
Reviewed on page 1279

Wagner Tristan und Isolde
Daniel Barenboim
(DG DVD)
Reviewed on page 1286

Weber Overtures
Antoni Wit
(Naxos)
Reviewed on page 1295

Stephen Hough in Recital
(Hyperion)
Reviewed on page 1328

Yuja Wang Debut Album
(DG)
Reviewed on page 1337

'Music from the Chirk Castle Partbooks'
Brabant Ensemble
(Hyperion)
Reviewed on page 1340

'A Spotless Rose'
Paul McCreesh
(DG)
Reviewed on page 1343

'Song of Songs'
Stile Antico
(Harmonia Mundi)
Reviewed on page 1346

'Opium'
Philippe Jaroussky,
Jérôme Ducros
(Virgin Classics)
Reviewed on page 1355

'Songs My Mother Taught Me'
Magdalena Kožená,
Malcolm Martineau
(DG)
Reviewed on page 1356

'Midsummer Night'
Kate Royal
(EMI)
Reviewed on page 1358

RECORDS OF THE YEAR

The annual *Gramophone* Awards celebrate the best in recorded music –
listed below are the best of the best, the winners of the Records of the Year

1977 (Opera)
Janáček
Kát'a Kabanová
**Vienna State Opera Chorus; Vienna Philharmonic
Orchestra / Sir Charles Mackerras**
Decca ⑨ 475 6872DC9   *Reviewed page 619*

1978 (Opera)
Puccini
La fanciulla del West
**Soloists; Royal Opera House Chorus and
Orchestra, Covent Garden / Zubin Mehta**
DG ② 474 840-2GOR2   *Reviewed page 875*

1979 (Chamber)
Haydn
Piano Trios
Beaux Arts Trio
Philips ⑨ 454 098-2PB9   *Reviewed page 561*

1980 (Opera)
Janáček
From the House of the Dead
**Soloists; Vienna State Opera Chorus; Vienna
Philharmonic Orchestra / Sir Charles Mackerras**
Decca ② 430 375-2DH2   *Reviewed page 617*

1981 (Opera)
Wagner
Parsifal
**Soloists; Chorus of the Deutsche Oper, Berlin;
Berlin Philharmonic Orchestra / Herbert von Karajan**
DG ④ 413 347-2GH4   *Reviewed page 1271*

1982-83 (Concerto)
Tippett
Triple Concerto
**György Pauk; Nobuko Imai; Ralph Kirshbaum;
London Symphony Orchestra / Sir Colin Davis**
Philips ⑥ 475 6750DC6

1984 (Orchestral)
Mahler
Symphony No 9
**Berlin Philharmonic Orchestra /
Herbert von Karajan**
DG ② 453 040-2GTA2   *Reviewed page 703*

1985 (Concerto)
Elgar
Violin Concerto
Nigel Kennedy *vn*
**London Philharmonic
Orchestra / Vernon Handley**
EMI 575139-2   *Reviewed page 418 (In brief)*

1986 (Opera)
Rossini
Il viaggio a Reims
**Soloists; Prague Philharmonic Chorus;
Chamber Orchestra of Europe /
Claudio Abbado**
DG ② 415 498-2GH2

1987 (Early music)
Josquin Desprez
Masses – Pange lingua; La sol fa re mi
The Tallis Scholars / Peter Phillips
Gimell CDGIM009   *Reviewed page 622*

1988 (Orchestral)
Mahler
Symphony No 2, 'Resurrection'
**Soloists; City of Birmingham Symphony
Orchestra and Chorus / Sir Simon Rattle**
EMI ② 345794-2   *Reviewed page 694*

1989 (Chamber)
Bartók
String Quartets Nos 1-6
Emerson Quartet
DG ② 423 657-2GH2   *Reviewed page 109 (In brief)*

1990 (Opera)
Prokofiev
The Love for Three Oranges
**Soloists; Chorus and Orchestra of
Lyon Opéra / Kent Nagano**
Virgin Classics ② 358694-2

1991 (Choral)
Beethoven
Mass in D, 'Missa solemnis'
**Soloists; Monteverdi Choir; English Baroque
Soloists / Sir John Eliot Gardiner**
Archiv Produktion 429 779-2AH   *Reviewed page 167*

1992 (Orchestral)
Beethoven
Symphonies Nos 1-9
**Chamber Orchestra of Europe /
Nikolaus Harnoncourt**
Teldec ⑤ 0927-49768-2   *Reviewed page 134*

1993 (Solo vocal)
Grieg
Songs
Anne Sofie von Otter *mez*
Bengt Forsberg *pf*
DG 477 6326GGP   *Reviewed page 494*

1994 (Instrumental)
Debussy
Préludes
Krystian Zimerman *pf*
DG ② 435 773-2GH2   *Reviewed page 365*

1995 (Concerto)
Prokofiev Violin Concerto No 1*
Shostakovich Violin Concerto No 1**
Maxim Vengerov *vn*
**London Symphony Orchestra /
Mstislav Rostropovich**
*Warner Elatus 0927 49567-2, **Warner Elatus
0927 46742-2   ***Reviewed page 1050*

1996 (Concerto)
Sauer. Scharwenka
Piano Concertos
Stephen Hough *pf* **City of Birmingham
Symphony Orchestra / Lawrence Foster**
Hyperion CDA66790   *Reviewed page 975*

1997 (Opera)
Puccini
La rondine
**Soloists; London Voices;
London Symphony Orchestra / Antonio Pappano**
EMI ② 556338-2   *Reviewed page 879*

1998 (Choral)
Martin
Mass for Double Choir. Passacaille.
Pizzetti Messa di Requiem. De profundis
Westminster Cathedral Choir / James O'Donnell
Hyperion CDA67017   *Reviewed page 711*

1999 (Opera)
Dvořák
Rusalka
**Soloists; Kühn Mixed Choir;
Czech Philharmonic Orchestra /
Sir Charles Mackerras**
Decca ③ 460 568-2DHO3   *Reviewed page 409*

2000 (Orchestral)
Mahler
Symphony No 10 (ed Cooke)
Berlin Philharmonic Orchestra / Sir Simon Rattle

EMI 556972-2   *Reviewed page 705*

2001 (Orchestral)
Vaughan Williams
A London Symphony (original 1913 version)
Butterworth
The Banks of Green Willow
London Symphony Orchestra / Richard Hickox
Chandos CHAN9902; ⊛ CHSA5501
          Reviewed page 1198

2002 (Concerto)
Saint-Saëns
Piano Concertos Nos 1-5. Wedding Cake.
Rapsodie d'Auvergne. Africa
Stephen Hough *pf* **City of Birmingham
Symphony Orchestra / Sakari Oramo**
Hyperion ② CDA67331/2   *Reviewed page 963*

2003 (Chamber)
Schumann
String Quartets Nos 1 and 3
Zehetmair Quartet
ECM 472 169-2   *Reviewed page 1022*

2004 (Opera)
Mozart
Le nozze di Figaro
**Soloists; Collegium Vocale; Concerto Köln /
René Jacobs**
Harmonia Mundi HMC90 1818/20;
⊛ HMC80 1818/20   *Reviewed page 806*

2005 (Baroque vocal)
JS Bach
Cantatas Vol 1
**Soloists; Monteverdi Choir; English Baroque
Soloists / Sir John Eliot Gardiner**
SDG ② SDG101   *Reviewed page 76*

2006 (Orchestral)
Mahler
Symphony No 6
**Berlin Philharmonic Orchestra /
Claudio Abbado**
DG ② ⊛ 477 5684GSA2   *Reviewed page 700*

2007 (Orchestral)
Brahms
Piano Concertos Nos 1 & 2
**Nelson Freire; Gewandhaus Orchestra /
Riccardo Chailly**
Decca ② 475 7637DX2   *Reviewed page 241*

2008 (Instrumental)
Beethoven
Piano Sonatas Vol 4
Paul Lewis
Harmonia Mundi ③ HMC90 1909/11
          Reviewed page 160

Suggested Basic Library

ORCHESTRAL

Bach Brandenburg Concertos
Bach Concerto for two violins
Bach Orchestral Suites
Barber Adagio for strings
Barber Violin Concerto
Bartók Concerto for Orchestra
Bartók The Miraculous Mandarin
Bartók Violin Concerto No 2
Beethoven Complete symphonies
Beethoven Piano Concertos Nos 4 and 5
Beethoven Violin Concerto
Berg Violin Concerto
Berlioz Symphonie fantastique
Brahms Complete symphonies
Brahms Piano Concerto No 1
Brahms Violin Concerto
Britten Young Person's Guide to the Orchestra
Bruch Violin Concerto No 1
Bruckner Symphonies Nos 4, 5, 8 and 9
Chopin Piano Concertos
Copland Appalachian Spring
Copland Fanfare for the Common Man
Corelli 12 Concerti grossi, Op 6
Delibes Coppélia
Debussy Jeux
Debussy La mer
Debussy Prélude à L'après-midi d'un faune
Dvořák Cello Concerto
Dvořák Symphony No 9, 'New World'
Elgar Cello Concerto
Elgar Enigma Variations
Elgar String music
Elgar Symphonies Nos 1 and 2
Elgar Violin Concerto
Falla Noches en los jardines de España
Gershwin Rhapsody in Blue
Górecki Symphony No 3
Grieg Peer Gynt Suite
Grieg Piano Concerto
Handel Fireworks Music
Handel Water Music
Haydn Cello Concerto in C
Haydn London Symphonies
Haydn Trumpet Concerto
Holst The Planets
Ives Three Places in New England
Mahler Symphonies Nos 5 and 9
Mendelssohn A Midsummer Night's Dream
Mendelssohn Hebrides Overture
Mendelssohn Symphony No 4 , 'Italian'
Mendelssohn Violin Concerto
Messiaen Turangalîla Symphony
Mozart Clarinet Concerto
Mozart Horn Concerto No 4
Mozart Piano Concertos Nos 20-27
Mozart Serenade for 13 Winds
Mozart Symphonies Nos 40 and 41
Mussorgsky Pictures at an Exhibition
Pärt Tabula rasa
Prokofiev Lieutenant Kijé
Prokofiev Peter and the Wolf
Prokofiev Piano Concerto No 3
Prokofiev Romeo and Juliet
Prokofiev Symphonies Nos 1 and 5
Rachmaninov Paganini Rhapsody
Rachmaninov Piano Concertos Nos 2 and 3
Rachmaninov Symphony No 2
Ravel Boléro
Ravel Daphnis et Chloé
Ravel Piano Concerto in G
Respighi Roman Trilogy
Rimsky-Korsakov Scheherazade
Rodrigo Concierto de Aranjuez
Rossini Overtures
Saint-Saëns Le carnaval des animaux
Saint-Saëns Piano Concerto No 2
Saint-Saëns Symphony No 3
Schoenberg Five Orchestral Pieces, Op 16
Schoenberg Variations for Orchestra, Op 31
Schubert Symphony No 8, 'Unfinished'
Schumann Piano Concerto
Shostakovich Cello Concerto No 1
Shostakovich Piano Concerto No 2
Shostakovich Symphonies Nos 5 and 10
Sibelius Finlandia
Sibelius Symphonies Nos 2 and 5
Sibelius Tapiola
Sibelius Violin Concerto
Smetana Má vlast
Strauss J II Waltzes
Strauss R Alpine Symphony
Strauss R Also sprach Zarathustra
Strauss R Till Eulenspiegel
Stravinsky Agon
Stravinsky The Rite of Spring
Stravinsky The Firebird
Tchaikovsky Romeo and Juliet
Tchaikovsky 1812 Overture
Tchaikovsky Ballets – The Nutcracker,
Sleeping Beauty and Swan Lake
Tchaikovsky Piano Concerto No 1
Tchaikovsky Symphonies Nos 4-6
Tchaikovsky Violin Concerto
Vaughan Williams Symphony No 2, 'London'
Vaughan Williams Symphony No 5
Vaughan Williams Tallis Fantasia
Vaughan Williams The Lark Ascending
Vivaldi The Four Seasons
Walton Violin and Viola Concertos

CHAMBER

Bartók String Quartets
Beethoven Piano Trio in B flat, Op 97, 'Archduke'
Beethoven String Quartets [late]
Beethoven Violin Sonatas
Borodin String Quartet No 2
Brahms Clarinet Quintet
Debussy Sonata for Flute, Viola and Harp
Debussy String Quartet
Dvořák String Quartet No 12
Franck Violin Sonata
Haydn String Quartets, Opp 20 and 76
Mendelssohn Octet
Mozart Clarinet Quintet
Mozart String Quartet in C, K465, 'Dissonance'
Mozart String Quintet in G minor, K516
Ravel String Quartet

Reich Different Trains
Schubert Piano Quintet, 'Trout'
Schubert Piano Trios
Schubert Arpeggione Sonata in A minor, D821
Schubert String Quartet No 14
Schubert String Quintet
Shostakovich String Quartet No 8

INSTRUMENTAL

Bach Cello Suites
Bach Das wohltemperierte Klavier
Bach Goldberg Variations
Bach Solo Violin Sonatas and Partitas
Beethoven Complete piano sonatas
Beethoven Diabelli Variations
Biber Mystery Sonatas
Brahms Variations on a Theme of Paganini
Chopin Nocturnes
Chopin Piano Sonata No 2
Chopin Preludes
Debussy Children's Corner Suite
Debussy Préludes
Grieg Lyric Pieces
Haydn Piano Sonata E flat major, HobXVI/52
Liszt Piano Sonata
Mozart Piano Sonata No 11 in A, K331
Paganini 24 Caprices
Prokofiev Piano Sonata No 7
Ravel Gaspard de la nuit
Satie Piano works
Schubert Impromptus
Schubert Piano Sonata in B flat, D960
Schubert Wandererfantasie
Schumann Carnaval
Schumann Kinderszenen
Schumann Kreiserleriana

VOCAL

Allegri Miserere
Bach Cantatas – No 82 'Ich habe genug' and
    140 'Wachet auf'
Bach Magnificat
Bach Mass in B minor
Bach St Matthew Passion
Beethoven Missa solemnis
Berlioz Grande messe des morts
Berlioz L'enfance du Christ
Berlioz Les nuits d'été
Brahms Ein deutsches Requiem
Britten Serenade
Britten War Requiem
Bruckner Motets
Byrd Masses for 3, 4 and 5 voices
Canteloube Chants d'Auvergne
Duruflé Requiem
Elgar The Dream of Gerontius
Fauré Requiem
Handel Coronation Anthems
Handel Dixit Dominus
Handel Messiah
Haydn Nelson Mass
Haydn The Creation
Howells Hymnus Paradisi

Mahler Das Lied von der Erde
Mahler Kindertotenlieder
Mendelssohn Elijah
Monteverdi 1610 Vespers
Monteverdi Madrigals, Book 8
Mozart Mass in C minor
Mozart Requiem
Orff Carmina burana
Palestrina Missa Papae Marcelli
R Strauss Four Last Songs
Rachmaninov Vespers
Ravel Shéhérazade
Schubert Winterreise
Schumann Dichterliebe
Tallis Spem in alium
Vaughan Williams Serenade to Music
Verdi Requiem
Victoria Requiem
Vivaldi Gloria in D, RV589
Walton Belshazzar's Feast

OPERA, OPERETTA & STAGE WORKS

Bartók Duke Bluebeard's Castle
Beethoven Fidelio
Bellini Norma
Berg Wozzeck
Bernstein West Side Story
Bizet Carmen
Bizet Les pêcheurs de perles
Britten Peter Grimes
Britten Turn of the Screw
Debussy Pelléas et Mélisande
Gershwin Porgy and Bess
Gluck Orfeo ed Euridice
Handel Alcina
Handel Giulio Cesare
Handel Rinaldo
Janáček The Cunning Little Vixen
Lehár Die lustige Witwe
Leoncavallo Pagliacci
Mascagni Cavalleria rusticana
Monteverdi L'Orfeo
Mozart Die Zauberflöte
Mozart Don Giovanni
Mozart Le nozze di Figaro
Mussorgsky Boris Godunov
Puccini La bohème
Puccini Madama Butterfly
Puccini Tosca
Puccini Turandot
R Strauss Der Rosenkavalier
Rossini Il barbiere di Siviglia
Strauss J II Die Fledermaus
Sullivan The Pirates of Penzance
Tchaikovsky Eugene Onegin
Verdi Aida
Verdi Il trovatore
Verdi La traviata
Verdi Otello
Verdi Rigoletto
Wagner Der Ring des Nibelungen
Wagner Tristan und Isolde
Weber Der Freischütz

1OOO YEARS OF MUSIC

The story of classical music is a long and complex one, but **Jeremy Nicholas**

has risen to the challenge of telling it once again. Here he offers a guided

tour of the key players and movements that have made classical music

the rich art-form that today still entrances, moves and uplifts.

Fixing a date for 'the beginning of music' is as elusive as pin-pointing the millennium in which dinosaurs became extinct. 1000 AD merely provides a convenient starting point for the birth of modern Western music. It was around that date when the idea first occurred of combining several voices to sing a melody; it was the time, too, when the Church, for so long the most important influence and inspiration on the development of music, recognised a need to standardise the single-line unaccompanied chants that had been used for centuries in sacred ceremonies.

This early Christian music, derived from Greek songs and from the chanting used in synagogues, had evolved into what we now call plainsong, plainchant or Gregorian chant, the traditional music of the Western Church – a single melodic line, usually sung without accompaniment. (The Gregorian chant melodies sung today date from after the death of Pope Gregory in 604 AD.) Without any accepted written system to denote the pitch or length of a note, the scoring of music was inevitably a haphazard affair.

Guido d'Arezzo, a Benedictine monk whose life as a teacher and musical theorist usefully coincided with the Church's need for musical unification, is generally credited with the introduction of a stave of horizontal lines by which one could accurately record the pitch of notes. He also came up with what we now call the tonic sol-fa system, used by singers, in which notes are named by their position in the scale, as opposed to being named after letters of the alphabet (a practice derived from the ancient Greeks).

Still there was no method of notating the length of a note. Without this, it is difficult to see how any sense of rhythm could be measured. Some scholars say that this was defined by the natural accentuation and emphasis of speech patterns and that therefore no special device was needed – the singers (without a conductor, of course) provided their own 'flow' and expression.

With two of the three main elements of music – i.e. Melody and Rhythm – in the process of being codified, the idea of Harmony came into the world. Naturally, not all the singers in a choir would have the same vocal range, a problem for the comfortable unison singing of the psalms. So voices began to be divided according to natural range, chanting the Plainsong in parallel lines at two pitches, five notes apart (C-G for example) The gap between the two notes is called an interval, thus the singers sang the interval of a perfect fifth. From this apparently simple concept, but which took so long to implement, the idea grew that while one line sang the Plainsong (the 'tenor' or 'holding' part), others could weave another tune around it.

Rules were drawn up as to which part of the service could use which type of intervals. Gradually, the interval of a third (C-E), for long considered to be a dischord, was allowed. Within the moderately short time-scale of a century, we have Pérotin of Notre Dame – one of the early masters of Polyphony – writing music for three and four voices.

Parallel to the development of liturgical (Church) music ran the flowering of the secular music of the troubadours, the poet-musicians who sang of beautiful ladies, chivalry, spring and suchlike. These were the successors of the court minstrels, employed to sing the great sagas and legends, who themselves had their less-educated counterparts in the jongleurs, itinerant singers and instrumentalists. Nobly-born for the most part, the troubadours came from Provence and Aquitaine (the trouvères, their northern counterparts, and the minnesingers of Germany were almost contemporary). Only about 60 manuscripts of troubadour and trouvère poetry survive today and few of them contain musical notation which, again, have indications only of pitch but not of note length.

These 200 years witnessed the birth of harmony, of modern musical notation, the dance and song craze which pervaded Europe during the time of the Crusades and the complex structure of the troubadours' poetry – more than enough to ignite the imagination of Renaissance man.

From melody to harmony

The study and use of chords is what we call Harmony. Diaphony – 'two-voiced' music – dominated all musical composition till the 13th century; this two-part singing as applied to plainchant was also called organum. Voices would sing an octave apart (C-C), a perfect fifth (C-G), a perfect fourth (C-F) or a major third (C-E) apart. Polyphony is also concerned with the sounding of more than one note, but through melody – the word means 'many-sounds', 'many-voiced'. The addition of a third, fourth or more independent musical lines sung or sounded together was the next obvious development, and it was the extraordinary Philippe de Vitry, a French bishop, musical theorist, composer, poet and diplomat, who showed the way forward in a famous book called The New Art – *Ars Nova* (as opposed to the *Ars Antiqua* of Guido d'Arezzo). Time-signatures indicated a rhythm for the music and improvements in notation symbolised note lengths – the ancestors of our minim, breve and semibreve. Guillaume de Machaut (another French priest, poet and composer) took de Vitry's ideas a stage further and wrote both secular songs and settings of the Mass (1364 – the earliest known complete setting by one composer) with three and four polyphonic voices.

Though France was the musical centre of Europe at this time, Italy was developing its own *ars nova* independently with music that reflected the warmth and sensuality of the country, in contrast to the more intellectual Gallic writing. England, less affected by *ars nova*, did not make a significant contribution to any musical development until the arrival of John Dunstable. Living in France as the court composer to the Duke of Burgundy (the younger brother of Henry V), Dunstable used rhythmic phrases, traditional plainchant and added other free parts, combining them into a flowing, mellifluous style. Nearly 60 pieces of his music still survive.

Dunstable in turn influenced the Burgundian composers Guillaume Dufay and Gilles Binchois, whose music can be said to be the stylistic bridge between *ars nova* and the fully developed polyphony of the 15th century. The technical aspects of musical composition and the almost mathematical fascination with note combination began slowly to open the door to the personality of a composer being reflected in his music.

Out of the church

By the middle of the 15th century, the royal palaces and the great houses of the noblemen had usurped the Church as the single most important influence on the course of music (in 1416, Henry V of England employed more than 30 voices in the Chapel Royal while the Papal Chapel had only nine). One by-product was the closer relationship between secular music and the music of the Church, a cross-pollination which benefited the development of both. The musicians who passed through the Burgundian court disseminated its style and learning to all points of the European compass.

The most noticeable advances during this period were the increased freedom composers gave to their vocal lines and the difference in the treatment of the texts they set. Previously, words had to fit the music; now the reverse was the case and this is no better illustrated than by the work of one of the next generation of composers to become renowned throughout Europe, Josquin Desprez. His music incorporates a greater variety of expression than any previously – there are even flashes of quirky humour – and includes attempts at symbolism where the musical ideas match those of the text. With various voices singing in polyphony, it is difficult to follow the words; where the subject called for the words to be heard clearly, Josquin wrote music that had the different voices singing different notes but the same words at the same time – chordal music, in other words. Not surprisingly, Josquin has been called 'the first composer whose music appeals to our modern sense of art'. After him, it is easy for our ears to follow the development of music into the language which is familiar to us today through the works of the great classical composers of two centuries later.

The 16th century witnessed four major musical phenomena: the polyphonic school reached its zenith, the tradition of instrumental music was founded, the first opera was produced and music began to be printed for the first time. For most people, the opportunity to see and read music had simply not been there; musicians could now, for the first time, stand around a score printed in a book and sing or play their part. Limited and expensive though it was, music was now available. No wonder it flourished so rapidly.

It's hard to conceive now of the central importance of the Christian Church at this time. The buildings which the men of the Renaissance erected with such splendour and confidence symbolised the age of 're-birth' and the music of the time rose to fill the naves of the great European cathedrals. Palestrina in Italy, Lassus in the Netherlands and Byrd in England carried on from where Josquin had left off to produce complex and richly expressive works which took the art of polyphonic writing for the voice to new heights and demonstrated man's ability to express his faith with a glory and fervour that no previous century had matched.

How was this rich cloth of musical gold woven? One distinguished writer on music, Percy Scholes, drew an illuminating analogy on musical 'fabric' when discussing the music of Palestrina. 'Woven' he felt, was an appropriate word for this kind of composition. 'The music consists of the intertwining of a fixed number of strands. And as [the composer] weaves he is producing a 'woof' as well as a 'warp'. Looked at as warp the composition is a horizontal combination of melodies; looked at as woof it is a perpendicular collection of chords. The composer necessarily has both aspects in his mind as he pens his piece, but the horizontal (or 'warp') aspect is probably uppermost with him. Such music as this we speak of as 'Contrapuntal' or as 'in Counterpoint'. The 'woof' (= perpendicular, ie 'Harmonic') element is there, but is less observable than the 'warp' (= horizontal, i.e. 'Contrapuntal'). A moment's thought will show that all Contrapuntal music must also be Harmonic, and a second moment's thought that not all Harmonic music need be Counterpoint.'

It had taken 1000 years from the earliest Plainsong for the tradition to develop into the elaborate, highly sophisticated art form, which produced such masterpieces as Palestrina's *Stabat mater*, Victoria's *Ave verum Corpus* and Byrd's *O Quam Gloriosum*.

Now, new preoccupations challenged composers. The reverent, lush choral works of the Church, mainly from Northern Europe, became fertilised by the lively, sunny dances and songs of the south. The secular counterparts of the church musicians led to the madrigal, a contrapuntal setting of a poem, usually about 12 lines in length, and whose subject was usually amorous or pastoral. The emphasis was on the quality of word-setting and the form proved remarkably popular if short-lived – especially in England (perhaps because of our great literary heritage) where the likes of Gibbons, Weelkes and Morley were the madrigal's finest exponents.

The madrigal and the birth of opera

The madrigals, like the liturgical motets and settings of the Mass, were all for unaccompanied voices – that was how the vast majority of music produced up to this time was conceived. It wasn't until the end of the 14th century that instrumental music began to emerge as an art-form in its own right. The recorder, lute, viol and spinet had played their part in dance music and in accompanying voices (occasionally replacing them) but now composers such as Byrd, Gibbons, Farnaby and Frescobaldi began to write music for specific instruments, though it must be said that the art form did not truly flourish until the Baroque era. Musicians would join together to play a series of varying dance tunes, forming a loosely-constructed suite; or a player might improvise his own tune round another's – a 'fancy' or 'fantasia'; or they might compose variations on a tune played over the same repeating bass line – 'variations on a ground' as it's called. Other innovations were by the Italians Andrea Gabrieli (*c*1510-86) – the first to combine voices with brass instruments – and his nephew Giovanni (1557-1612), whose antiphonal effects for choirs of brass instruments might have written for our modern stereo systems.

And it was from Italy that the next important step in musical history was taken. Indeed Italy was the country – actually a collection of small independent states at the time, ruled by a number of affluent and cultured families – which would dominate the musical world for a century and a half from 1600. Such was the power of Italian influence at this time that music adopted the language as its lingua franca. To this day, composers almost universally write their performance directions in Italian. One particular word, opera, described a new art form: that of combining drama and music. No one had thought of the concept till the end of the 16th century.

In the late 16th century, artists, writers and architects became interested in the ancient cultures of Greece and Rome. In Florence, a group of the artistic intelligentsia became interested in how the ancient Greek dramas were performed. Experimenting with declaiming the more poetic passages and using a few chords of instrumental music to accompany other passages in natural speech rhythm, the idea of music reflecting, supporting and commenting upon dramatic action was born: *dramma per musica* ('drama by means of music'), a play with a musical setting.

Into the ring then came one of the supreme musicians of history, Claudio Monteverdi. He did not write the first opera (that honour goes to Jacopo Peri and his *Dafne*, now lost, of 1594 or 1597) but with one work, *Orfeo* (1607) he drew up the future possibilities of the medium. Solo singers were given a dramatic character to portray and florid songs to sing, there were choruses, dances, orchestral interludes, scenery. Opera was a markedly different entertainment to anything that had gone before but, more importantly, it was a completely new way of using music.

The right instruments

Monteverdi's successors such as Pier Cavalli and Marc'Antonio Cesti developed a type of flowing, lyrical song inspired by the flow of spoken Italian – *bel canto* ('beautiful singing') which in turn encouraged the prominence of the singer. Dramatic truth soon went out of the window in favour of the elaborate vocal displays of the opera soloists – composers were only too happy to provide what their new public wanted – and no class of singers were more popular than the castrati. Feted wherever they appeared, the castrati, who had had their testicles removed as young boys to preserve their high voices, were highly paid and immensely popular, a not dissimilar phenomenon to The Three Tenors of today (with two small differences). The practice of castration to produce an entertainer, an extraordinarily barbaric concept, was only halted in the early 19th century. The last castrato, Alessandro Moreschi, actually survived until 1922 and made a dozen or so records in 1902.

St Paul had written that women should keep silent in church. They were therefore not available for the taxing high lines in church music. If the origins of the castrati could be laid firmly at the door of the Church, similar dogma can also be held responsible for the slow progress of instrumental composition. From the earliest times the Church had voiced its disapproval of the practice. St Jerome had declared that no Christian maiden should know what a lyre or flute looked like (let alone hear what they sounded like). The weakening of the Church's authority after the Reformation encouraged composers in the writing of instrumental music for groups, music moreover that took into account the relative strengths and colours of the different instruments, another new concept. The same change of emphasis led also to a flood of brilliant instrumental soloists. Among them was a brilliant Italian-born violinist named Jean-Baptiste Lully who went to France in 1646. Here he worked for King Louis XIV, the extravagant builder of Versailles who employed 120 musicians in various bands. An orchestra of 'Twenty-four Violins' provided music at the French court; with Lully's addition of flutes, oboes, bassoons, trumpets and timpani, the modern orchestra began to emerge.

Another important by-product of the Italian opera was the introduction of the sonata – the term originally simply meant a piece to be sounded (played), as opposed to sung (cantata). Although it quickly took on a variety of forms, the sonata began with the Italian violinists imitating the vocal display elements of opera – a single melody played against a harmonised background or, if you like, accompanied by chords. This was a huge difference from the choral works of a century before driven by their polyphonic interweavings. Now there was music which, even if there was no background accompaniment, the listener's ears could supply the harmony mentally – you could tell where the tune was going to resolve, you could sense its shape and destination more easily. With the musical emphasis on harmony – a key feature of the coming century and a half – rhythm began to take an increasingly important part. Chordal patterns naturally fall in sequences, in regular measures or bars. Listen to a chaconne by Purcell or Handel and you realise that the theme is not a tune but a sequence of chords. Measuring the beats in a bar (*one*-two or *one*-two-three or *one*-two-three-four – the emphasis always on the first beat) gives the music a sense of form and helps its onward progress. Phrases lead the ear to the next sequence like the dialogue between two people, exchanging thoughts in single words, in short sentences or in long paragraphs. Sing a simple hymn tune like *All people that on earth do dwell* and you are aware of what music had now acquired – a strong tonal centre.

Makers of musical instruments responded by adapting and improving instruments: the great Italian violin makers Stradivari, Amati and Guarneri, the Ruckers family of Antwerp with its harpsichords and the Harris family of England building organs.

A final contribution to this period was made by Italian opera. The use of the orchestra in opera naturally led to the expression of dramatic musical ideas – one reason why the Italian orchestra developed faster than elsewhere. Round about the start of the 18th century composers began to write overtures in three sections (fast-slow-fast), providing the model for the classical sonata form used in instrumental pieces, concertos and symphonies for the next 200 years and more.

Thus this 'homophonic' period, emphasising music with a single melody and harmonic accompaniment, melted seamlessly during the 17th century into the Baroque era of Vivaldi, Bach and Handel.

The concerto is born

The concerto developed from the dance suites popular in Italy at the beginning of the 17th century, known as the *sonata da camera*. Originally a composition that contrasted two groups of instrumentalists with each other, the form developed into the *concerto grosso* ('great concerto') of which the first leading exponent was Arcangelo Corelli. Here a group of solo string instrumentalists alternate with the main body of strings in a work, usually of three or four movements. Geminiani, Albinoni, Torelli, Handel and others contributed to the form. The solo concerto was but a short step from here where a soloist is contrasted with (later pitted against) the orchestra. No concertos of this period have achieved the popularity of Vivaldi's whose 500 essays in the genre (mainly for strings but sometimes for wind instruments) are the product of one of the most remarkable musical minds of the early 18th century. *The Four Seasons*, among the best known and most frequently-played pieces of classical music, illustrates the new concept.

Northern Europe provided the springboard for the rapid development of keyboard music: the North German school of organ music, founded by Frescobaldi and Sweelinck a century before, with its interest in contrapuntal writing, laid the way for the likes of Pachelbel and Buxtehude whose line reached its peak in the great works of Bach. Meanwhile Rameau and Couperin in France were producing short descriptive harpsichord pieces (as well as operas) in a style that is called 'rococo' – from the

French *rocaille*, a term originally alluding to fancy shell and scroll work in art. It was predominantly diverting rather than elevating and rococo usefully defines the character of lighter music written in the Baroque period, especially when contrasted with the works of the two musical heavyweights of the time, Johann Sebastian Bach and George Frideric Handel.

Bach in his own time was considered old-fashioned, a provincial composer from central Germany. But his music contains some of the noblest and most sublime expressions of the human spirit and with him the art of contrapuntal writing reached its zenith. The 48 Preludes and Fugues for *The Well-Tempered Clavier* explore all the permutations of fugal writing in all the major and minor keys; his final work, *The Art of Fugue* (left incomplete at his death) takes a mathematical delight in the interweaving of contrapuntal variations on the same theme. Yet the technical brilliance of Bach's music is subsumed in the expressive power of his compositions, in particular his organ music, church cantatas and the great *St Matthew Passion* and Mass in B minor. His instrumental music is evidence that he was by no means always the stern God-fearing Lutheran – the exuberant six *Brandenburg Concertos* show that he was well acquainted with the sunny Italian way of doing things and many of his most beautiful and deepest thoughts are reserved for the concertos and orchestral suites. His influence on composers and musicians down the years has been immeasurable. For many he remains the foundation stone of their art.

Bach's great contemporary, Handel, also came from Germany but in contrast was a widely travelled, man-of-the-world who settled in England and became a shrewd entrepreneur and manipulator of musical affairs. In instrumental forms, such as the *concerto grosso*, Handel was equally at home writing in homophonic or polyphonic style and introduced a variety of wind/string combinations in his colourful scoring. He developed the typical 17th-century dance suite into such famous (and still immensely popular) occasional works as *The Water Music* and *Royal Fireworks Music*. Opera was a field into which Bach never ventured but Handel – between 1711 and 1729, – produced nearly 30 operas in the Italian style until the public tired of these when, ever the pragmatist, he turned to oratorio. An oratorio is an extended setting of a (usually) religious text in dramatic form but which does not require scenery or stage action. Handel's have an immense dramatic and emotional range and often employ daring harmonies, never mind the unending stream of glorious melodies and uplifting choruses

Bach was the last great composer to be employed by the church, fittingly, for the church had been the mainspring for the progress

of polyphonic music and Bach was the *ne plus ultra* of the style. Henceforward, musical patronage came from the nobility and the nobility preferred music that was elegant, entertaining and definitely not smacking of anything 'churchy'. Following the 17th century's example of the French court and Italian principalities, every European duke worth his salt aspired to his own orchestra and music director. One such was the court of Mannheim where an orchestra under the direction of Johann Stamitz raised orchestral playing to a standard unheard of previously. A new era, breaking away from the contrapuntal writing of the later Baroque, was ushered in.

The Classical Era

The term 'Classical Music' has two meanings: used to describe any music which is supposedly 'heavy' (as opposed to pop or jazz as in 'I can't stand classical music') and also a certain period in the development of music, the Classical era. This can be summarised as music which is notable for its masterly economy of form and resources and for its lack of overt emotionalism. If Bach and Handel dominated the first half of the 17th century, Haydn and Mozart are their counterparts for the latter half and represent all the virtues of the Classical style.

This can be traced back to a generation or so before the birth of Haydn to the rococo style of Couperin and Rameau and, more powerfully, in the invigorating keyboard works of Domenico Scarlatti whose more than 500 short sonatas composed in his sixties demonstrate a brilliance that only Bach equalled. Scarlatti, though, writing on a smaller scale, had the specific intent of delighting and instructing his pupil, the Queen of Spain. His near-contemporary Georg Philipp Telemann brought the rococo style to Germany. Lighter and even more fecund than Bach, Telemann was held in far greater esteem in his lifetime than Johann Sebastian. Despite his stated credo ('He who writes for the many does better work than he who writes only for the few... I have always aimed at facility. Music ought not to be an effort, an occult science') the two greatly admired each other to such an extent that Bach named his son Carl Philipp Emanuel after Telemann and chose him as godfather.

CPE Bach's music represents a cross-roads between the Franco-Italian rococo and the emerging classical schools – indeed, in some of his keyboard music he seems to anticipate Beethoven. His piano sonatas, making use of the expressive powers of the newly invented pianoforte, lead us to redefine the term 'sonata' as used in the previous century. Now the sonata became a formalised structure with related keys and themes. These Bach developed into extended movements, as opposed to the short movements of the Baroque form. Listening to CPE, perhaps the most original and daring composer of the mid-18th century, one becomes aware of the serious and comical, the inspired and the routine, lying side by side with engaging unpredictability.

Parallel to this was the work of Johann Stamitz. His music is rarely heard today yet he and his son Carl (1746-1801) were pioneers in the development of the symphony. This form had grown out of the short quick-slow-quick one-movement overtures or sinfonias of Italian opera. Stamitz, in the employ of the Mannheim court, had one of the most distinguished orchestras in Europe under his direction. The symphonies he wrote were to be the pattern for those of Haydn and Mozart – in them we can see, as in CPE Bach's sonatas, use of related keys, two contrasted first movement subjects (themes) and the graceful working out and development of material. He was the first to introduce the clarinet into the orchestra (and was probably the first to write a concerto for the instrument), also allowing the brass and woodwind greater prominence. His orchestral crescendos, a novel effect at this time, were said to have excited audiences to rise from their seats.

Italy had dominated the musical world of the 17th and early 18th centuries with its operas and great violinists. From the middle of the 18th century, the centre of musical pre-eminence moved to Vienna, a position it would retain until the last of the Hapsburg emperors in the early years of the 20th century. The Hapsburgs loved music and imported the best foreign musicians to court; the imperial chapel became a second centre of musical excellence. Equally important was Vienna's location at the centre of Europe. With the Viennese court as its focus, all kinds of influences met and mingled from nearby Germany, Bohemia and Italy.

Sonata form and the symphony

There is less than half a century between the death of Handel (1759) and the first performance of Beethoven's *Fidelio* (1809). Bach and Handel were still composing when Haydn was a teenager. To compare the individual 'sound world' of any of these four composers is to hear amazingly rapid progress in musical thinking. Without doubt, the most important element of this was the development of the sonata and symphonic forms. During this period, a typical example generally followed the same basic pattern: four movements – 1) the longest, sometimes with a slow introduction, 2) slow movement, 3) minuet, 4) fast, short and light in character. Working within this formal structure, each movement in turn had its own internal structure and order of progress. Most of Haydn's and Mozart's sonatas, symphonies and chamber music are written in

accordance with this pattern and three-quarters of all Beethoven's music conforms to 'sonata form' in one way or another.

Haydn's contribution to musical history is immense, he was nicknamed 'the father of the symphony' (despite Stamitz's prior claim) and was progenitor of the string quartet. Like all his well-trained contemporaries, Haydn had a thorough knowledge of polyphony and counterpoint (and, indeed, was not averse to using it) but his music is predominantly homophonic. His 104 symphonies cover a wide range of expression and harmonic ingenuity. The same is true of the string quartets. With its perfect balance of string sound (two violins, viola and cello), the implicit economy in the scoring, the precision and elegance in the handling of the medium, the string quartet is the quintessential Classical art form.

Mozart composed 41 symphonies and in the later ones (try the famous opening of No 40 in G minor) enters a realm beyond Haydn's – searching, moving and far from impersonal. This is even more true of the great series of piano concertos, among music's most sublime creations, where the writing becomes deeply involved – the slow movement of the A major Concerto (K488) is grief-stricken, anticipating the writing of a future generation. It was Mozart, too, who raised opera to new heights. Gluck had single-handedly broken away from the ossified, singer-dominated Italian opera and shown in works such as *Orfeo ed Euridice* (1762) that music must correspond to the mood and style of the piece, colour and complement the stage action; arias should be part of the continuous action and not merely stuck in to display the singer's vocal talents. Mozart went further and in his four masterpieces *The Marriage of Figaro, Così fan tutte, Don Giovanni* and *The Magic Flute* revealed more realistic characters, truer emotions (and, of course, incomparably greater music) than anything that had gone before. Here, for the first time, opera reflected the foibles and aspirations of mankind, themes on which the Romantic composers were to dwell at length.

The Age of Revolution

'The Old Order Changeth': for the first half of the 19th century, Europe, taking its cue from the French Revolution and American War of Independence, was imbued with a spirit of general political unrest, culminating in the 1848 uprisings. Nationalism, the struggle for individual freedom and self-expression were reflected and indeed created by all the arts – the one fed off the other. The neat, well-ordered regime of the periwig and minuet gave way to the impetuous, passionate world of the tousle-headed revolutionary.

Ludwig van Beethoven coupled his genius for

music with profoundly held political beliefs and an almost religious certainty about his purpose. With the possible exception of Wagner, no other composer has, single-handedly, changed the course of music so dramatically and continued to develop and experiment throughout his entire career. His early music, built on the Classical paths trod by Haydn and Mozart, demonstrates his individuality in taking established musical structures and re-shaping them to his own ends. Unusual keys and harmonic relationships are explored, while as early as the Third Symphony (*Eroica*), the music is vastly more inventive and cogent than anything Mozart achieved even in a late masterpiece like the *Jupiter*. Six more symphonies followed, all different in character, all attempting new goals of human expression, culminating in the great *Choral* Symphony (No 9) with its ecstatic final choral movement celebrating man's existence. No wonder so many composers felt daunted by attempting the symphonic form after Beethoven and that few ever attempted more than the magic Beethovenian number of nine.

His chamber music tells a similar story, building on the classical form of the string quartet, gradually making it his own (listen to the Middle Period *Razumovsky* quartets) until the final group of late quartets which contain music of profound spirituality and deeply felt personal statements – light years from the recent world of his illustrious predecessors. The cycle of 32 piano sonatas reflect a similar portrait of his life's journey; the final three of his five piano concertos and the sublime Violin Concerto are on a par with the symphonies and quartets. His single opera *Fidelio*, while not a success as a piece of theatre, seems to express all the themes that Beethoven held most dear – his belief in the brotherhood of man, his disgust at revolutionaries-turned-dictators, the redeeming strength of human love. All this was achieved, romantically enough, while he himself struggled with profound deafness. Beethoven's unquenchable spirit and his ability to use music to express himself places him in the forefront of man's creative achievements. 'Come the man, come the moment' – Beethoven's lifespan helpfully delineates the late classical period and the early Romantics. His music is the titanic span between the two.

Those who followed revered him as a god. Schubert, the next great Viennese master, 27 years younger but who survived him by a mere 18 months, was in awe of Beethoven. He did not progress the symphonic or sonata forms, there was no revolutionary zeal in his make-up. What he gave was the gift of melody. Schubert is arguably the greatest tunesmith the world has ever known and in his more than 600 songs established the German song (or Lied) tradition. From his *Erlkönig* (1815) onwards, Schubert unerringly caught the heart of a poem's meaning and reflected it in his setting. For the first time, too, the piano assumed equal importance with the vocal part, painting a tone picture or catching the mood of the piece in its accompaniment.

And it was the new iron-strung pianos which came to be the favoured instrument of the first part of the Romantic era. A bewildering number of composer-pianists were born just after the turn of the century, the most prominent of whom were Liszt, Chopin, Schumann and Mendelssohn. Of these, Mendelssohn relied on the elegant, traditional structures of Classicism in which to wrap his refined poetic and melodic gifts. Many of his piano works (his *Songs Without Words*, for example) and orchestral pieces (*Hebrides* Overture and *Italian* Symphony, No 4) describe nature, places, emotions and so forth. Schumann, too, favoured such short musical essays with titles like *Traümerei* and *Des Abends* to evoke a mood or occasion – 'characteristic pieces' they were called, 'programme music' later on. The undisputed master of the romantic keyboard style was Frédéric Chopin. Almost his entire oeuvre is devoted to the piano in a string of highly individual and expressive works composed in the short period of 20 years. Fifty years after his early death in 1849, composers were still writing pieces heavily influenced by him. Chopin rarely used descriptive titles for his work (beyond such labels as Nocturne, Berceuse or Barcarolle). The technical and lyrical possibilities of the instrument were raised to new heights in such masterpieces as the Four Ballades, the final two (of three) piano sonatas and the many short dance-based compositions. Most of these derived from his homeland of Poland and, as a self-imposed exile living in Paris, Chopin was naturally drawn to expressing his love of his country. Nationalism of a much more fervent kind was to be a key factor in the music of composers writing later in the Romantic tradition (Chopin himself, incidentally, disliked being labelled 'a Romantic').

But to truly define 'the Romantic era' in music, we have to look at the three composers who dominated the musical world for the second and third quarters of the 19th century and who pushed music onward to the dawn of the next: Liszt, Berlioz and Wagner.

The Romantics

Rebellion and freedom of expression lie at the heart of the Romantic movement in music, literature, painting and architecture, a self-conscious breaking of the bonds and belief in the right of the artist. Liszt, Byronic in looks and temperament, the greatest pianist of the day, gave us the solo piano recital, the 'symphonic poem' – the extended orchestral equivalent of Schumann's 'characteristic pieces' – and a bewildering variety of music in all shapes and forms. The B minor Piano Sonata, in which all the elements of traditional sonata form are subsumed into an organic whole, is one of the cornerstones of the repertory; his final piano works anticipate the harmonies of Debussy, Bartók and beyond. While all of his music is by no means profound – there's a great deal of gloss and glitter – his adventurous scores and his patronage and encouragement of any young composer who came to him made him one of the most influential musical geniuses of the entire century.

Berlioz was not a pianist. Perhaps that is why he is the most important composer of the period in terms of orchestral writing. He based his music on 'the direct reaction of feeling' and could summon up with extraordinary vividness the supernatural, say, or the countryside or ardent lovers. Like Liszt, he never wrote a formal symphony: Liszt's *Faust Symphony* and Berlioz's *Symphonie fantastique* are 'programmatic' and rely on their literary inspiration for their structure. Berlioz wrote on an epic scale, employing huge forces to convey his vision: the *Grande Messe des Morts*, for example, requires a tenor solo, brass bands and a massive chorus as well as an expanded orchestra. Théophile Gautier, whose *Nuits d'été* Berlioz set to music, summed Berlioz up thus: '[He] represents the romantic musical idea, the breaking up of old moulds, the substitution of new forms for unvaried square rhythms, a complex and competent richness of orchestration, truth of local colour, unexpected effects in sound, tumultuous and Shakespearean depth of passion, amorous or melancholy dreaminess, longings and questionings of the soul, infinite and mysterious sentiments not to be rendered in words, and that something more than all which escapes language but may be divined in music.' Technical improvements in the manufacture of orchestral instruments – the brass and woodwind especially – helped composers like Berlioz achieve their ends, for the modern instruments provided a wider range and variety of sound. This additional colour in the composer's orchestral palette encouraged more extended (sometimes seemingly formless) works. The prop of the symphonic structure was needed less, though, writing this at the beginning of the 21st century, many still enjoy the challenges of composing in that form.

The third Titan of the Romantics was the most written- and talked-about composer of all time: Richard Wagner. As intelligent and industrious as he was ruthless and egocentric, Wagner's great achievement was *The Ring of the Nibelungen*, a cycle of four operas which took opera from the realm of entertainment to a quasi-religious experience. Influenced by Beethoven, Mozart (held to be the first truly German operatic composer) and Meyerbeer (whose sense of epic theatre, design and orchestration impressed him), Wagner's vision was to create a work that was a fusion of all the arts – literature, painting and music. He called his vision 'music-drama'.

Some of his ideas had been anticipated 40 years earlier by Carl Maria von Weber, one of the first to insist on total control of all aspects of the production of his work and who, as early as 1817, wrote of his desire to fuse all art forms into one great new form. Weber's opera *Der Freischütz*, the first German Romantic opera, was a milestone in the development of these ideas, using German mythology as its subject.

Wagner decided that the music must grow from the libretto (he supplied his own), that there must be no display arias for their own sake, inserted just to please the public; the music, like the opera's narrative flow, must never cease, for the music is equally important in the telling of the story and commenting on the action and characters; leitmotivs, short musical phrases associated with different characters and moods, would recur throughout the score to underpin and bind the whole work. The orchestral contribution was at least as important as the vocal element. But Wagner was more than just an operatic reformer. He opened up a new harmonic language, especially in the use of chromaticism (see page XXXI). This had not only a profound influence on succeeding generations of composers but led logically to the atonal music of the 20th century.

Not all composers fell under Wagner's spell. Brahms was the epitome of traditional musical thought. His four symphonies are far nearer the style of Beethoven than those of Mendelssohn or Schumann, and the first of these was not written until 1875, when Wagner had all but completed *The Ring*. Indeed Brahms is by far the most classical of the German Romantics. He wrote little programme music and no operas. It's a curious coincidence that he distinguished himself in the very musical forms that Wagner chose to ignore – the fields of chamber music, concertos, variation writing and symphonies.

Verdi v Wagner

It was only in old age that Giuseppe Verdi adopted some of Wagner's musical ideas. The Italian represents the culmination of the different school of opera. Wagner's operas are the descendants of Beethoven and Weber; Verdi's developed from the comic masterpieces of Rossini and the Romantic dramas by Bellini and Donizetti. With the famous trilogy of *Rigoletto* (1851), *Il trovatore* (1853) and *La traviata* (1853), Verdi combined his mastery of drama with a flow of unforgettable lyrical melodies, creating masterpieces of the genre of which the public has never tired. *Don Carlos* (1867), *Aida* (1871), *Otello* (1887) and *Falstaff* (1893) show a development and tirelessly searching mind that remain among the great miracles of music.

One thing that Wagner and Verdi had in common was their fierce patriotism. In his own lifetime, Verdi was held as a potent symbol of Italian independence, while Wagner espoused the dubious theories which made him such hero of the Third Reich. During the course of the century, Western music, now dominated by German tradition and forms, began to be more and more influenced by the rise of nationalism. Composers wanted to reflect the character and cultural identity of their native lands by using material and forms which derived from their own country. Russia was the foremost in the surge of nationalism that now fertilised the Late Romantic era. Glinka was the first important Russian composer to use Russian subjects and folk tunes in his opera A Life for the Tsar. Influenced by the Italian tradition, it nevertheless succeeded in conveying typical Russian song and harmony and had a profound effect on Borodin, Balakirev, Cui, Mussorgsky and Rimsky-Korsakov – the so-called 'Mighty Five' (or 'Mighty Handful' – though Cui is hardly 'mighty' compared with the genius of his peers).

Tchaikovsky, the most accomplished of all his Russian contemporaries, paid lip-service to the Nationalists, composing largely in the German tradition. Elsewhere in Europe, nationalist schools of music arose: in Bohemia there were Smetana, Dvořák and Janáček; in Scandinavia, Nielsen, Grieg and Sinding; in Finland, Sibelius, whose seven symphonies developed the medium in a highly arresting and individual way; in Spain, Albéniz, Granados and de Falla. Britain and the United States were slow in developing a nationalist school: Parry and Elgar wrote firmly in the German manner and it was not until the later arrival of Vaughan Williams and Holst that a 'British' (or at any rate 'English') sound began to emerge. America was a curious case. Its first native composer of any note, Gottschalk, used indigenous native rhythms for his (mainly) piano works as early as the 1850s – South American, New Orleans and Cuban elements are boldly to the fore. It took another half century before any music directly derived from American folk material began to assert itself in the form of jazz.

The dates for each period of music must be treated flexibly. The Romantic period embraces a wide divergence of personal styles and represents a long and rapid period in Western music's development. In common with every aspect of life, the art developed at an ever-increasing pace. Parallel to the growth of Nationalism, came the Italian *verismo* school of opera, the school of Realism or Naturalism epitomised by the works of Puccini, Leoncavallo and Mascagni, whose subjects were drawn from contemporary life presented with heightened violence and emotions. During the closing years of the period, emerging under the influence of Wagner, came the neo-Romantics whose use of massive symphonic structures and elaborate orchestration is heard in the music of Bruckner, Mahler, Scriabin and the early works of Richard Strauss.

The Nationalists

Towards the end of the century there was a reaction against the excesses of the Romantics – the too-obvious heart-on-sleeve approach, the emotional over-indulgence, the extra-musical programmes and philosophies began to pal. Just as the Baroque period had melted into the Classical period, the Classical drifted into the early Romantic era, so the close of the 19th century saw a tendency toward bold experimentation in new styles and techniques. Coinciding with the French Impressionist movement in painting and poetry, came Impressionist music, epitomised by the daring (at the time), personal harmonic idiom of Claude Debussy. Here emphasis was put not on the subject of a piece of music but on an emotion or sensation aroused by the subject. His music is just as closely organised as anything in the classical German manner but, using the whole-tone scale and fresh harmonies, Debussy conjures up a sensuous, atmospheric spell in his piano music and orchestral works. The fastidious Maurice Ravel followed in his footsteps with exotic evocations of light and colour, later tinged with jazz references.

By the turn of the century, it was no longer possible to define a dominant general musical trend. Under its many fragmented divisions we can only label the successor of the Classical and Romantic periods somewhat lamely 'Modern Music'.

Igor Stravinsky studied with one of music's great orchestrators, Rimsky-Korsakov. He orchestrated some of Beethoven's piano sonatas as an exercise; he worked at counterpoint and learnt about classical forms – in other words, a sound, traditional conservatoire training. In less than a decade, we find Stravinsky writing music that is a world away from that of his mentor. *The Firebird* (1909), *Petrushka* (1911) and *The Rite of Spring* (1913), his three ballet masterpieces, became progressively more adventurous: in *Petrushka* we find bitonal passages (ie music written in two keys simultaneously), dissonant chords, a new rhythmic freedom and a percussive orchestral quality; in *The Rite of Spring*, a score which provoked a riot at its première, Stravinsky reduced all the elements of music to reinforce rhythm. Debussy and Schoenberg in certain of their works reduced music to the vertical effect of simultaneously sounding notes, so Stravinsky reduced melody and harmony to rhythm. As Alec Harman and Wilfred Mellers put it in their *Man and His Music*: 'Harmony without melody and rhythm, rhythm without melody and harmony, are static. Both the pandemonium of Stravinsky's *Rite of Spring* and Debussy's *Voiles* deprive music of the sense of motion from one point to another. Though they started from diametrically opposed points, both composers mark a radical departure from the traditions of European music since the Renaissance.'

Stravinsky went on to write in a number of other styles throughout his remarkable career, dominating the musical world for 50 years, in the same way that his almost exact contemporary Pablo Picasso dominated his field. Arguably, no other composer this century has exercised a greater influence than Stravinsky – Debussy and Ravel were less wide-ranging, Sibelius and Bartók less daring, Schoenberg and Webern less accessible.

Arnold Schoenberg is Stravinsky's only rival as the musical colossus of the age – to some he opened the door on a whole new world of musical thought that is as exciting as it is challenging; to others he is the bogey man of music, who sent it spiralling out of reach to the ordinary man in the street until, nearly one hundred years later, it has revealed itself as a cul de sac.

Since the Renaissance, all music had a tonal centre. No matter how far away from the tonic – the basic key – the music wandered, the listener was always conscious of the inevitability of a final return to that centre. Increasingly towards the end of the 19th century, music began to incorporate intervals outside the prevailing diatonic scale with the result that a work would feature an extraordinary amount of modulation. This is known as chromatic writing, since intervals from the chromatic scale (not the diatonic scale) are used to harmonise a piece. Listen, for instance, to Wagner's later works and to those of Mahler and Richard Strauss which followed closely on their heels. Hearing them, it becomes less clear as to which key the piece is written in, its tonal centre less obvious. What Schoenberg did was follow logically on from this and ask 'If I can introduce these chromatic notes into my music, can a particular key be said to exist at all? Why should any note be foreign to any given key? Harmony is simply the sounding together of notes, so why shouldn't the 12 semitones of the chromatic scale be accorded equal significance?'

The Second Viennese School

The theories and music of the so-called Second Viennese School – in succession to the First Viennese School of Haydn, Mozart et al – put the listener's expectations on a wrong footing.

There are none of the familiar features of chords we recognise, tunes we can hum or rhythms we can tap our feet to. Only the traditional manner of indicating on the score individual notes, time-signatures and expression marks remain. Because the vast majority of the music we are exposed to when growing up is tonal, it is fairly easy to assimilate a Beethoven symphony on a first hearing. Because serial music is written in a completely foreign language with which most of us have no reference points, its effect is like listening to a Scandinavian epic poem spoken in Japanese. The music lover has to acquire a knowledge of the language – in other words, the musical technique involved in the composition – before it can be appreciated. There are comparatively few who have the time to study Scandinavian poetry in Japanese translation, as it were.

Not all composers were attracted to the new technique but dissonance, atonality and the abandonment of melody are strong features of many composers' work this century. Very little serial or atonal music has established itself in the regular concert repertoire; still less has found its way into the hearts and affections of the ordinary music-loving public. This, to jump forward in time, is especially true of music written since the Second World War. A list of works from the pens of world-famous contemporary composers will elicit a blank response form the majority of people. The avant-garde of today is taking far longer to become assimilated than the avant-garde of previous centuries. Opinions are deeply divided over the merits of a composer like Charles Ives, for example, whose polyrhythmic, polytonal works are far too complex for them ever to achieve popularity; Stockhausen, Birtwistle, Cage, Carter, Berio, Nono (the list is endless) will remain a closed book for most people. Yet each of these composers have a huge and fanatical following in certain quarters. Musical development will always, hopefully, have daring, fantastical innovators, examining new possibilities, expressing themselves in new and original ways. Whether they will ever find a broad, responsive and appreciative audience, only time will tell. Most new commissions have a première, a broadcast (if they're lucky) and are then consigned to oblivion – in whatever musical language they're written.

The other path taken by music this century is the one which retains its link with tonality and (increasingly, nowadays) with melody. Harsh and acid though some of Prokofiev's music may be, his style is a tangible descendant of the Romantics. Shostakovich too, sharing Prokofiev's love of the spiky, humorous and satirical, as well as the sombre and introspective, follows on from the same tradition. Rachmaninov to an even greater degree wrote in the late-Romantic vein, producing some of the most popular symphonies and concertos written this century. In France, the most important composers after Ravel and Debussy were Honegger, Milhaud and Poulenc, three disparate composers un-usefully grouped together as Les Six (the other three made negligible contributions) and all influenced by the whimsical and eccentric Eric Satie. The most significant French composer since the Impressionists is Oliver Messiaen who introduced elements of Indian music and bird-song into the language of Western music. Pierre Boulez, whose complex works are often based on mathematical relationships, and Karlheinz Stockhausen, whose scores for his innovative electronic music are represented by charts and diagrams, are both pupils of Messiaen.

No longer does one school of musical thought prevail. There seems little to link the socio-political operas of Kurt Weill and their brittle, haunting melodies with his contemporary Paul Hindemith and his dense, contrapuntal neo-classical idiom. Far less does Aaron Copland, born only five years later in 1900, have any connection with either. The first conspicuously great American-born composer, Copland used in his music folk material, the sixths and sevenths intervals of the blues, echoes of cowboy songs, jazz and the memory of Jewish synagogues. His *Appalachian Spring* (1944) has been compared by one critic to Vaughan Williams's *Pastoral Symphony*.

The British legacy

And what has happened to British music this century? The Purcell centenary of 1895 stimulated interest in the great heritage of England's musical past; the English Folk Song Society was founded in 1898; the London Promenade Concerts were inaugurated in 1895 and suddenly, 'the land without music' found itself in the midst of a musical renaissance. No one deserves more credit for the revival of the nation's musical fortunes than Ralph Vaughan Williams and Gustav Holst. Vaughan Williams took as his creed the belief that 'The Art of Music above all other arts is the expression of the soul of the nation'. English Tudor music, medieval tonalities and folk song attracted him, composing in what might loosely be called a romantic neo-classical style, using counterpoint, classical forms (such as the symphony and the fugue) and modern harmony. Holst was inspired similarly but also drew inspiration from the east – his most famous piece, *The Planets*, from the ideas of Chaldean astrology. Of the succeeding generation, the most important have been Benjamin Britten, Michael Tippett and William Walton. Britten especially, with his many stage works, established English music on the international stage, writing for a wide variety of mediums including an opera for television (*Owen Wingrave*). *Peter Grimes, Billy Budd, War Requiem, Serenade for Tenor, Horn and Strings, The Young Person's Guide to the Orchestra* – the list of works he composed since the Second World War now in the regular concert repertoire is remarkably high. Walton's outstanding contributions were made before the war with *Façade, Belshazzar's Feast*, the Viola Concerto and the First Symphony. Tippett has had less lasting success compared with his two contemporaries but *A Child of Our Time* (1941), the Concerto for Double String Orchestra (1939) and the *Fantasia Concertante on a Theme of Corelli* (1953) will undoubtedly stay the course.

Of the more recent generations of British composers, it is still too early to say with any certainty who and what will be remembered in the great scheme of things 50 years hence. Elizabeth Lutyens, Humphrey Searle and the so-called Manchester School of Peter Maxwell Davies, Harrison Birtwistle and Alexander Goehr have their champions and devoted admirers; they do not always mix comfortably with the likes of Richard Rodney Bennett, Malcolm Arnold and George Lloyd – to name those born prior to the War and who each enjoy a loyal following.

A contemporary postscript

Music written in our own time, *writes James Jolly*, remains a divisive art-form, with battle lines drawn up by its partisans. Here are some guides for exploring new music.

One of the strongest 'schools' – and one which drew people in from 'outside' the classical world – were the so-called Minimalists. Steve Reich (b1936), Philip Glass (b1936) and John Adams (b1947) are the three leading representatives, writing music that relies on repeated notes or phrases and which creates wave-like patterns as the phrases interact. All three have developed musical voices that won audience's hearts. Philip Glass has moved effortlessly between the opera-house, concert-hall and film studio, though latterly he has returned to purely abstract composition. John Adams has successfully managed to woo the critics as well as his public. Works such as his recent opera *Doctor Atomic* have an assured place in the repertoire, and his orchestral works are performed with regularity. One of Steve Reich's latest composition, his *Daniel Variations*, a work who impetus was the murder by Islamic extremists of the journalist Daniel Pearl, is a powerful and imaginative response to contemporary events. As *The New Yorker* put it, 'In the most recent pieces Reich has consolidated four decades of invention. Neon-lit textures have given way to dense, dusky landscapes, with tender lyrical passages at the heart of each piece. It's as if Reich were finally letting himself look back in time, perhaps even indulging a secret Romantic urge.'

Currently enjoying huge popularity on both sides of the Atlantic is the Argentinian-Jewish composer Osvaldo Golijov. His music represents 'fusion' at a very high level of sophistication and crosses boundaries with ease. His Lorca opera *Ainadamar*, recorded by DG (and included in this guide) is a magical creation, beautifully presented. His boundary-crossing music has touched a contemporary chord and the reverberations have filled concert-halls the world over.

Henryk Górecki (b1933), Arvo Pärt (b1935) and John Tavener (b1944) sprang to huge popularity during the 1980s with their individual and often gentle voices enhanced by a strong spiritual dimension. Górecki's Third Symphony was one of the musical phenomena of the day – a work of enormous popularity, made a virtual cult by its air-play on Classic FM. John Tavener looks to his deeply held Greek Orthodox beliefs for inspiration and has created a stream of haunting works. His cello concerto *The Protecting Veil* achieved enormous popularity and very quickly chalked up five recordings. Most recently he has written a *concertante* work for violinist Nicola Benedetti.

Oliver Knussen (b1952) grew up under the influence of Benjamin Britten, the then dominant voice in British music. His best known works are his two one-act operas *Higglety Pigglety Pop!* and *Where the Wild Things Are*; his *Ophelia Dances* and Symphonies Nos 2 and 3 reveal the work of a master craftsman. Born less than a decade later, George Benjamin (b1960) established his credentials while still a child. A pupil of Messiaen and Goehr, and friend of Boulez, his first work of significance was *Ringed by the Flat Horizon*. His fine ear for colour has created some wonderfully translucent scores, an approach no doubt enhanced by his skill as a conductor.

Benjamin's contemporary Mark-Anthony Turnage (b1960) enjoys popularity and patronage on both sides of the Atlantic – he is a composer in residence with both the London Philharmonic and the Chicago Symphony. His high-octane earlier works like *Greek*, *Blood on the Floor* and *Three Screaming Popes* (after Francis Bacon's disturbing triptych) have been succeeded by a more lyrical musical language. Many of his LPO commissions have been recorded and give a valuable insight into a the development of a major compositional voice.

Marc-André Dalvabie (b1961) is a French composer worth listening out for – his studies with Boulez and Murail clearly unleashed a fascination with texture and colour, and sometimes it's hard to reconcile Dalbavie's musical training with the actual sound of his music. It can be lush in the extreme but it is beautifully crafted.

Back in the UK, though he has taught in the US for the past few years, Julian Anderson (b1967) has been collecting a loyal following. His fascinating for and love of folk-music gives his works a dimension often lacking in new music – and he is not afraid of melody: his can strikingly beautiful music. His *Book of Hours* (2005) weaves electronics into an orchestral palette to rewarding effect and *Eden*, from 2005, explores the potential of non-tempered tuning.

The golden boy of music in the English-speaking world is the prodigiously gifted Thomas Adès (b1971) whose grasps of musical forms as diverse as an opera and a piano quintet has stunned his audiences. His orchestral *Asyla* (1999) was selected by Simon Rattle for his inaugural concert with the Berlin Philharmonic and the same performers have since given the premiere of *Tevot* (2007): the work was lauded by critics in London and New York. His operas *Powder Her Face* (1995) and *The Tempest* (2004) have both entered the operatic repertory – the Met has announced performances in its 2012-3 of *The Tempest*. His Violin Concerto was premiered at the BBC Proms and a subsequent London performance was recorded and released as a download by EMI.

The contemporary music scene is a rich and vibrant one – there is no shortage of talent and there is a loyal audience for new music. And it is also good to see so many high-profile musicians devoting their energies to performing new music. Vladimir Jurowski regularly conducts Turnage's music, Marin Alsop champions the music of Christopher Rouse, John Corigliano and Jennifer Higdon, Simon Rattle ensures that new music features prominently in Berlin. Conductors such as David Robertson, Esa-Pekka Salonen, Daniel Barenboim, Michael Tilson Thomas, Claudio Abbado and Riccardo Chailly all display a passion for the new. And with instrumentalists such as Anne-Sophie Mutter, Pierre-Laurent Aimard and Emanuel Pahud commissioning new works, the art form's profile stays visible at a very high level. Filter down through the world of music and the levels of passion and commitment increase even more... and the audiences come to listen.

HOW TO USE THE GUIDE

The presentation and design of this *Guide* is similar to that of its parent publication, *Gramophone*. Reviews of works generally appear in the following sequence: Orchestral, Chamber, Instrumental, Vocal/Choral and Opera.

The title for each review contains the following information: composer(s), work(s), artist(s), record company or label, price range, catalogue number and recording date. The circled numeral before the catalogue number indicates the number of discs (if there is more than one), while the timing and mode of recording are given in brackets afterwards. (The abbreviations AAD/ADD/DDD denote analogue or digital stages in the recording/editing or mixing/mastering or transcription processes in CD manufacture.) All other abbreviations used in this *Guide* are given below.

Where three or more composers are represented on a single disc, the review generally appears in the Collections section which starts on page 1311.

The indexes are divided into an artists' index and an index to couplings – an index of works reviewed under other composers. For example, you'll find Prokofiev's Third Piano Concerto with Martha Argerich reviewed under its Bartók Concerto No 3 coupling; to find the page number simply look in the couplings index under Prokofiev.

All recordings are flagged with one or more of the symbols explained below.

KEY TO SYMBOLS

Ⓕ Full price £11 and over
Ⓜ Medium price £8-£10·99
Ⓑ Budget price £6-£7·99
Ⓢ Super-budget price £5·99 and below

Ⓗ Denotes a Historic recording and generally applies to pre-1960 recordings. It can also be an indication that the recording quality may not be up to the highest standards

Ⓟ Denotes recordings where period instruments are used

⮑ Denotes recordings that are available as downloads

Simply the best
An unrivalled version, a cornerstone of the catalogue. A real gem!

●●● **Classic**
Gramophone Award-winners and recordings of legendary status

●● **Outstanding**
Outstanding performance and fine sound/transfer

● **Strongly recommended**
Not a top choice but nonetheless a fine recording

No disc
Recommended
Good performance with the odd reservation

(S/N/T/t)
(after the recording details)
Synopsis, notes, texts and translation if included in the CD package

ABBREVIATIONS

aas	all available separately	**mndl**	mandolin
alto	countertenor/male alto	**narr**	narrator
anon	anonymous	**oas**	only available separately
arr	arranged	**ob**	oboe
attrib	attributed	**Op**	opus
b	born	**orig**	original
bar	baritone	**org**	organ
bass-bar	bass-baritone	**perc**	percussion
bn	bassoon	**pf**	piano
c	circa (about)	**picc**	piccolo
cl	clarinet	**pub**	publisher/published
clav	clavichord	**rec**	recorder
compl	completed	**recons**	reconstructed
cont	continuo	**rev**	revised
contr	contralto	**sax**	saxophone
cor ang	cor anglais	**sngr**	singer
cpsr	composer	**sop**	soprano
cpte(d)	complete(d)	**spkr**	speaker
d	died	**stg**	string
db	double bass	**synth**	synthesizer
dig pf	digital piano	**tbn**	trombone
dir	director	**ten**	tenor
ed	edited (by)/edition	**timp**	timpani
exc	excerpt	**tpt**	trumpet
fl	flute	**trad**	traditional
fl	flourished	**trans**	transcribed
fp	fortepiano	**treb**	treble
gtr	guitar	**va**	viola
harm	harmonium	**va da gamba**	viola da gamba
hn	horn	**vars**	variations
hp	harp	**vc**	cello
hpd	harpsichord	**vib**	vibraphone
keybd	keyboard	**vn**	violin
lte	lute	**voc**	vocal/vocalist
mez	mezzo-soprano	**wds**	words

THE
GRAMOPHONE
CLASSICAL
MUSIC
GUIDE
2010

Carl Friedrich Abel   German 1723-1787

He was no doubt a pupil of his father's, especially for the bass viol; but on his father's death in 1737 Carl Friedrich may have turned to the former relationship with the Bach family and gone to Leipzig to study, as Burney, who knew Abel, stated. By 1743 Abel was a player in the court orchestra under Hasse in Dresden. During the 1758–9 season Abel went to London, the city where he was to spend most of his remaining years. Abel was primarily a composer of instrumental music; his few vocal pieces are relatively unimportant. The symphonies, sonatas and bass viol pieces form the largest groups among his output.   GROVEmusic

---

Mr Abel's Fine Airs
Susanne Heinrich *va da gamba*
Hyperion CDA67628 (78' · DDD)   Ⓕ**OO**

Carl Friedrich Abel is usually thought of as a genial symphonist much in the mould of his London concert-promoting business partner JC Bach, but this delightful release shows that anyone considering on that basis not to delve further into Abel's output is missing not only an important side of the man, but indeed his very core. Abel was one of the last masters of the viola da gamba, and in these unaccompanied pieces he reveals an intimate art which instantly makes sense of the affection and reverence in which he was held by his friends, they being the ones who got to hear him improvising at home in front of the fire and left touching accounts of his power to stir their emotions. 'He was the Sterne of music' is how one described him, which is saying something.

Susanne Heinrich has chosen 24 solo gamba pieces from the 30 contained in a manuscript in the New York Public Library which surely represent the kind of music Abel played in those domestic musical occasions. Unencumbered by showy virtuosity, they are never less than supremely elegant, yet at their best exhibit profound sentiment in the word's exquisite 18th-century sense. Four of the pieces are grouped together to make a sonata, but the others are free-standing and range from deeply felt adagios to lightly arpeggiated preludes, and from suave minuets to the occasional faintly rustic dance. Heinrich brings to them exactly the right blend of emotional involvement and earnest good taste, and finds pleasing resonance and smoothness in her instrument, such that even nearly 80 minutes of solo gamba never tires the ear. An unsuspected and atmospheric gem.

The Drexel Manuscript – Suite in D major; Suite in D minor; Suite in D major; Two Pieces in A major
Paolo Pandolfo *va da gamba*
Glossa GCD920410 (79' · DDD)   Ⓕ**OO**

Carl Friedrich Abel was a close friend of Johann Christian Bach, with whom he later appeared in London in the celebrated Bach-Abel Concerts (1774-82). Among his other friends was the painter Thomas Gainsborough, a passionate amateur violist, whose portrait of Abel hangs in London's National Portrait Gallery. Gainsborough was the owner of the Drexel Manuscript, containing 29 pieces for solo bass viol.

We are treated on this CD to all but one – a fragment. Paolo Pandolfo has arranged them, appropriately, into two suites in D major and one in D minor, concluding with two pieces in A major. Anyone familiar with the elder Bach's solo cello suites will immediately appreciate the influences as well as the originality and relative modernity of Abel's music. Pandolfo, considered by many to be the finest violist of our day, has already recorded several of the cello suites on the viol. But whereas the Suites present the modern player with awkward challenges (the Sixth in particular), Abel's music (like that of Marais) is supremely crafted for his instrument.

In Pandolfo's hands, Abel's music is highly communicative – packed with ideas, oft-repeated and always varied. His strong sense of overall form, both in freely expressed (preludes and slow movements) and more structured movements (dances and rondos), allows him to indulge in dynamic moments of silence, heightening the impression of monologue, and even dialogue. Technically wondrous, few could perform these delightful pieces with the skill, eloquence and sheer panache Pandolfo brings to them.

Adolphe Adam   French 1803-1856

Adam studied at the Paris Conservatoire with Reicha (counterpoint) and Boieldieu (composition). A prolific composer, he wrote more than 80 stage works, some of which, especially those produced for the Opéra-Comique such as Le châlet (1834) and Le postillon de Lonjumeau (1836), had considerable and lasting success. Other notable works, showing a natural sense of theatre, fresh invention and graceful melody. include the opera Si j'étais roi (1852) and the well-known ballet Giselle (1841).
                                          GROVEmusic

Giselle

Giselle
Royal Opera House Orchestra, Covent Garden / Richard Bonynge
Double Decca ② 452 185-2DF2 (126' · DDD)   Ⓜ**O**Ⓑ+

Giselle has drawn harsh words from the more superior music critics, but the public has taken it to heart for its atmospheric writing and tender and haunting themes. The text used here is the complete original score; Bonynge's desire to re-record it lies in matters of performance and interpretation. Reviews of his previous version, made with the Monte Carlo Opera Orchestra in 1970, spoke of the limitations of the woodwind and brass, and suggested that a little more rehearsal time might have brought benefits. Here the musicians of the Royal Opera House bring both a confidence of attack and a refinement that aren't quite achieved by the Monte Carlo players. That same extra confidence of attack is displayed by Bonynge himself. Each of the discs of this issue is between one-and-a-half and two minutes longer than the older recording, but the dramatic moments are more vigorously attacked and the slower ones more lovingly caressed – always to considerable effect. Add recorded sound that's warmer and more spacious, and there's no hesitation in acknowledging the superiority of this version over the old. Without a doubt, this represents the first-choice version of Adam's complete score.

Further listening

Le postillon de Lonjumeau
Stuttgart Choristers; Kaiserslautern Radio Symphony Orchestra / Arp
Capriccio ② 60 040-2 (97' · DDD)   Ⓕ
Celebrated for the fiendishly difficult tenor solo 'Mes amis, écoutez l'histoire', Adam's opera has a lot of charm. This German language recording must be considered a stop-gap until a French version returns to the catalogue.

John Adams   American b1947

Adams studied at Harvard with Kirchner, Kim, Del Tredici and Sessions, and in 1972 began teaching at the San Francisco Conservatory. He became interested in electronics (Onyx, 1976), then, influenced by Reich, turned to minimalism. His works, in an elegant minimalist style, include Shaker Loops for strings (1978), Harmonium for orchestra with choir (1981), the exuberant, parodistic Grand Pianola Music (1982), the opera Nixon in China (1987) – summary of his musical languages over 10 years – and a violin concerto (1994). His most recent opera, Doctor Atomic (2005), is again based on true events; the story concerns the creation of the atomic bomb; the work was premiered in San Francisco.
                                        GROVEmusic

Violin Concerto

Adams Violin Concerto
Corigliano The Red Violin – Chaconne
Enescu Romanian Rhapsody No 1 (arr Waxman)
Wagner/Waxman Tristan and Isolde Fantasia[a]
Chloë Hanslip vn [a]**Charles Owen** pf
Royal Philharmonic Orchestra / Leonard Slatkin
Naxos 8 559302 (64' · DDD)   Ⓢ🅓➤

As an overall concept this album is a mess. Franz Waxman's arrangement of Enescu's *First Romanian Rhapsody* is positioned before the Adams Concerto and sounds like an encore before the main event. Waxman's *Tristan and Isolde Fanta-*

sia pushes Wagner towards Cecil B DeMille histrionics, while John Corigliano's hacked-together Chaconne is episodic and rhetorical and is severely lacking in the material department.

This is a pity because nothing should hide the fact that Chloë Hanslip is the sort of musician every teenager forced to practise their scales dreams of becoming. The richness and clarity of her tone is beyond learning, and she demonstrates such profound empathy for John Adams's 1993 Violin Concerto that Gidon Kremer (Nonesuch) can consider himself completely outplayed. This is the sort of performance that secures a reputation for life.

The first movement is a particular challenge, as an unwinding melodic line generates itself over a quarter-hour span. Kremer plays the notes mechanically but Hanslip deconstructs their meaning and pieces together a cogent narrative direction that's a bona fide interpretation. The sing-song ballad quality of the slow middle movement unlocks her lyrical imagination, while the tricky *moto perpetuo* of the violin part zigzags and breakdances across occasional Nancarrow-like rhythmic overlays in an exuberant finale. Assertive and enthused accompaniment from Slatkin and the RPO, too – everybody's doing Adams the greatest of service.

The Dharma at Big Sur

The Dharma at Big Sur[a].
My Father Knew Charles Ives[b]
[a]**Tracy Silverman** elec vn [b]**Bill Houghton** tpt
BBC Symphony Orchestra / John Adams
Nonesuch ② 7559 79857-2 (54' · DDD)   Ⓕ

Both Charles Ives and John Adams composers grew up in New England and both have a healthy magpie attitude to their source material. Adams begins *My Father Knew Charles Ives* with the trademark solo trumpet writing he regularly deploys whenever he wants to evoke Ives: here it's like a camera slowly panning towards an Ivesian landscape far below. Brass-band music marches onwards and the famous 'false' last chord of Ives's Second Symphony flashes by. It's difficult to say what exactly Adams has created. It falls somewhere between direct quotation and constructivist allusion, like hearing deconstructed 'picture postcard' Ives. It's fun for sure, and the BBC Symphony Orchestra relish its follies.

Borrowing the experimental composer Lou Harrison's ideas about non-tempered tuning – as Adams does in his Jack Kerouac-inspired electric violin concerto *The Dharma at Big Sur* – gives another spin to a familiar Adams sound world. Tracy Silverman's folksy material in the concerto partly evolved from his own improvisations, and I fear a one-size-fits-all world-music patois is just around the corner. Nevertheless, the opening section is quite beautiful as non-tempered chords sensuously ebb and flow, and Adams integrates Silverman into his developing argument with a strategic sense of purpose. In the cathartic second section harmonic impetus races ahead, as gong-like sounds in the orchestra suggest inner stillness – a trademark Adams hook reborn.

Chamber Symphony

Chamber Symphony. Grand Pianola Music
London Sinfonietta / John Adams
Nonesuch 7559-79219-2 (53' · DDD)   Ⓕ●

A loud bash on an old tin can, and they're off – yelping, tapping, chattering, chasing to and fro, like a barn-yard full of loopy professors. And to think that the prime mover for John Adams's madcap Chamber Symphony (1992) was its 'eponymous predecessor', Schoenberg's Op 9. Even the instrumentation is similar, save that Adams has added synthesizer, jazz-style percussion, trumpet and trombone. It's a raw piece, with the merest suggestion of repose in the central 'Aria with Walking Brass' and a 'Roadrunner' finale that includes a manic violin cadenza followed by an ingenious passage where synthesizer, bass clarinet, bassoon and horn crank up for the panic-stricken home straight. It might not be exactly rich in tunes, but it's maddeningly moreish, a high-speed comedy where all the characters are temporarily on holiday from their more serious selves.

In complete contrast, the far gentler *Grand Pianola Music* (1971) provides a relatively 'easy' listen, with its smooth-driving motor rhythms, sensual female voices, warming waves of brass tone and occasional bouts of thumping excitement. Clichés there certainly are, especially the 'big tune' that crowns the third section, 'On the Dominant Divide', which is probably most effective when, towards the end of the work, it slims down to basic harmonic constituents. *Grand Pianola Music* is a sort of aural truck ride, with smooth tarmac, plenty of scenic incident, a glowing sunset on the far horizon and a closing cadence that rather unexpectedly recalls Sibelius. Both performances are fine and the recordings are superb.

El Dorado

Adams El Dorado **Busoni** Berceuse élégiaque, Op 42 (arr Adams)[a] **Liszt** La lugubre gondola, S200 No 1 (arr Adams)[a]
Hallé Orchestra / Kent Nagano; [a]**London Sinfonietta / John Adams**
Nonesuch 7559-79359-2 (47' · DDD)   Ⓕ●

El Dorado is a dramatic commentary on irreconcilable opposites: chromaticism versus pure modalities, malignancy versus rude health, and man's destructive impulses versus the unspoiled glory of unpopulated landscapes. Adams claims to have composed the second movement, 'Soledades' – the one 'without man' – in seven days. Indeed, the whole work appeared to him as a sort of apparition, 'alarmingly complete in its details, even before I wrote down a single sketch'.

The first movement, 'A Dream of Gold', opens to sinister held chords, pensive shufflings and rising clouds of string tone. The last section charges forth like some maniacal spectre, racing out of control then stopping dead. By contrast, 'Soledades' weaves a delicate web of sound, at least initially, with unmistakably Sibelian undertones. The ending, however, suggests a tranquil death. Overall, the recording of *El Dorado* reproduces a dynamic sound curve. The performance itself is deft and well paced, very much on a par with Adams's own performances of his Busoni and Liszt arrangements.

The *Berceuse élégiaque* is beautifully realised, while the richly coloured orchestration of Liszt's late *La lugubre gondola* is in total contrast to other, more austere, readings. Winds and solo strings are used to sensitive effect and the playing is uniformly excellent.

Gnarly Buttons

Gnarly Buttons. John's Book of Alleged Dances
Michael Collins *cl* **Kronos Quartet** (David Harrington, John Sherba *vns* Hank Dutt *va* Joan Jeanrenaud *vc*)
London Sinfonietta / John Adams
Nonesuch 7559-79465-2 (61' · DDD)   Ⓕ●

John's Book of Alleged Dances (the equivocation in the title refers to dance steps that have yet to be invented) is prime-cut Adams – fidgety, tuneful, teeming with invention and all but tactile in its aural variety; its use of the prepared piano is fascinating. We start by following a streetcar from town to coast and back again, then visit 'Toot Nipple' with 'chainsaw triads on the cello'. There's a raw-edged 'Hoe-Down' for leader David Harrington, a 'Pavane' for cellist Joan Jeanrenaud and a doleful Habanera. 'Hammer & Chisel' are contractor friends who construct to a knotty toccata; a slithery 'Alligator Escalator' employs reptilian harmonics and a chirpy 'Serenade' pays subtle homage to Beethoven and Schubert. These and more are kept on a high flame by the Kronos Quartet, whereas *Gnarly Buttons* calls on the combined talents of Michael Collins and the London Sinfonietta. A more intense piece by far, its dry but colourful demeanour occasionally recalls Schoenberg's similarly spice-flavoured Serenade. The first movement is based on a Protestant shape-note hymn; the second is a 'Mad-Cow' hoe-down; and the third is a warming song of sure-fire hit potential. Collins does Adams proud, and so does the London Sinfonietta. The recordings are first-rate.

Harmonielehre

Harmonielehre. The Chairman Dances. Two Fanfares – Tromba lontana; Short Ride in a Fast Machine
City of Birmingham Symphony Orchestra /

Sir Simon Rattle
EMI 555051-2 (62' · DDD)   Ⓜ️Ⓞ🅓➔

Harmonielehre was inspired by a dream vision of a massive tanker that suddenly took flight, displaying a 'beautiful brownish-orange oxide on the bottom part of its hull'; the setting was just off San Francisco Bay Bridge. 'Those pounding E minor chords are like a grinding of gears,' says John Adams of its violent, gunshot opening. Scored for a huge orchestra and structured in three contrasted sections, *Harmonielehre* is probably the nearest thing on offer to a minimalist symphony, and for that reason alone it could well appeal beyond the élite coterie of minimalist-fanciers.

Rattle's recording has great heft and dynamic range, an informative balance and a vivid sense of aural perspective. The brass components of those opening chords have enormous weight and presence, and the ringing marimbas thereafter a bright complexion. Adams's frequent requests for subtle tempo transitions are subtly honoured by the conductor.

Naive and Sentimental Music

Naive and Sentimental Music
Los Angeles Philharmonic Orchestra / Esa-Pekka Salonen
Nonesuch 7559-79636-2 (44' · DDD)   Ⓕ🅞🅞

The title is adapted from *On Naïve and Sentimental Poetry*, a 1795 essay by Schiller, who regarded the naïve artist as one for whom art is a natural form of expression, and who creates without concern for historical significance; the sentimental artist is all too aware that he and his art stand apart, and what he creates reflects this chasm. 'This particular piece,' Adams writes, 'perhaps more than any of my others, attempts to allow the naïve in me to speak, to let it play freely.' A symphony in all but name, *Naïve and Sentimental Music* (1999) is cast in three movements. The first is an 'essay on melody,' built around an expansive theme that unfolds in long strands. Adams' harmonic sensitivity and structural control are breathtaking. And the entire movement unfolds as organically as the melody that's its *idée fixe*. Adams titled the finale 'Chain to the Rhythm'. Melody takes a back seat to what quickly becomes a dazzling and increasingly ominous *moto perpetuo*. *Naïve and Sentimental Music* is dedicated to Esa-Pekka Salonen and the Los Angeles Philharmonic, who premièred it in February 1999. Though the fiendishly difficult finale could perhaps be played more tautly, the overall interpretation is very persuasive indeed.

China Gates

China Gates. Phrygian Gates.
American Berserk. Hallelujah Junction[a]
Ralph Van Raat, [a]Maarten Van Veen pfs

Naxos American Classics 8 559285 (52' · DDD)   Ⓢ🅞🅞➔

China Gates and *Phrygian Gates* from 1977-78 show Adams defining his own style as opposed to the classical minimalists such as Riley, Reich and Glass. *China Gates* is under six minutes and consistently delicate, while *Phrygian Gates* is a blockbuster of nearly 25. In *Phrygian Gates* the repetition is constant but there are also abrupt dislocations which function like film cuts – or the electronic gate which is meant by these titles. The technique is the same in the larger concert works as well as the operas that have made Adams famous. There seems to be no obvious reason why one texture ends and another begins, but that's the point of the discontinuity – and it goes back to Satie and Stravinsky.

American Berserk (2000) is the most recent piece and both words in the title are justified. From an early age Adams was surrounded by popular music and jazz on equal terms with classical composers. That background figures here with the crazier improvisational Ives and – very obviously – the swinging mechanical complexities of Conlon Nancarrow's studies for player piano. As in *Grand Pianola Music*, it's extravagantly entertaining.

In the exhilarating two-piano *Hallelujah Junction* (1996) Nancarrow again stands as godfather and you can hear the rhythmic hallelujahs as it belts on to its hilarious climax.

The Dutch pianists, cleanly recorded, deliver everything with consistent aplomb.

El niño

El niño
Dawn Upshaw sop **Lorraine Hunt Lieberson** mez **Willard White** bass **London Voices; Theatre of Voices; Deutsches Symphony Orchestra, Berlin / Kent Nagano**
Nonesuch ② 7559 79634-2 (111' · DDD · T/t)   Ⓕ🅞🅞

El niño is an ecstatic celebration of Christ's birth, at once ethereal and fiercely driven, and as remote from homely 'Seasonal' images as Greenland is from Bethlehem. The pain and alienation of birth is as much a part of Adams's ground plan as the Holy child whose universal significance has kept the legend alive.

Maybe it's coincidence that the score opens like a robust relation of Reich's *The Desert Music*, but given the Biblical setting, the idea of desert isn't exactly inappropriate. Bach is another probable reference point. And yet any influences are absorbed among the pages of a score that, aside from its melodic appeal and considerable rhythmic (ie, quasi-minimalist) vitality, can toy delicately with guitar and harpsichord or breathe fire through trombones and low woodwinds. Adams's facility for musical word-painting at times levels with Benjamin Britten's. Voices and characters intertwine or juxtapose with a skill that only a seasoned opera composer could summon.

Countertenors echo ancient church modes, initially as Gabriel in dialogue with Mary, sweetly sung by Dawn Upshaw, then reporting on the Babe 'that leaped in her womb' and standing by as Joseph (a grainy-voiced Willard White) struggles with the concept of Mary's pregnancy. The choice of texts, many written by Hispanic women, was selected in collaboration with Peter Sellars. The overall aim seems less to tell a consistent story than to create narrative images within a spiritual context. The episodes, whether inwardly lyrical or outwardly aggressive, have an urgency, or relevance, that reaches beyond religious edification. It brings the Christmas story alive. But, be warned – this is no starlit Cosy Encounter. The performance can't be faulted, and the recording achieves a true aural perspective. Very strongly recommended.

El Niño
Dawn Upshaw sop **Lorraine Hunt Lieberson** mez **Willard White** bar **Maîtrise de Paris Children's Choir; London Voices; Theatre of Voices; Deutsches Symphony Orchestra, Berlin / Kent Nagano**
Stage director **Peter Sellars**
Video director **Peter Maniura**
ArtHaus **DVD** 100 220 (147' · 16:9 · 2.0 · 0 · N) Includes 'Making Of' documentary   Ⓕⵔ

'An opera by John Adams' says the packaging. Not quite. This is the composer's multi-cultural, post-feminist, quasi-minimalist take on Handel's *Messiah*, drawing on sources ranging from the pre-Christian prophets to 20th-century Hispanic women writers. While designed to allow fully staged productions, the concept and its musical realisation bring us closer to oratorio. Adams's musical language is predictably inclusive. There's a prominent role for three Brittenish countertenors, Broadway and popular idioms are more or less willingly embraced, and the use of repetition is sometimes reminiscent of Philip Glass in his heyday. *El Niño*'s sound world is delicate and lustrous, and, although Part 1 can seem a mite static with a surfeit of vocal recitative, there are fewer longueurs in Part 2. If not perhaps the unqualified masterpiece acclaimed by some critics, this is an effective and often truly affecting score: derivative, to be sure, yet obstinately fresh.

The performance as such is pretty much beyond criticism. The main characters are on top form, combining absolute vocal assurance with dramatic flair – and none more so than Lorraine Hunt Lieberson. The crisp DVD images certainly help explain the sensational impact of the European première, a multimedia extravaganza from Peter Sellars' top drawer in which dance and film interact quirkily with the exertions of chorus and soloists. If you haven't yet acquired a player, the remarkable success of *El Niño* is as good a reason as any to take the plunge. Strongly recommended.

The Death of Klinghoffer

The Death of Klinghoffer
Sanford Sylvan bar Leon Klinghoffer **Stephanie Friedman** mez Omar **James Maddalena** bar First Officer **Thomas Hammons** bar First Officer **Thomas Young** sngr Molqui **Eugene Perry** bar Mamoud **Sheila Nadler** mez Marilyn Klinghoffer **London Opera Orchestra Chorus; Lyon Opera Orchestra / Kent Nagano**
Nonesuch ② 7559-79281-2 (135' · DDD · N/T)   Ⓕ

How many living composers do you suppose would happily watch their scores lead a short life, relevant but finite? Not many; but John Adams might be one. First *Nixon in China*, then *The Death of Klinghoffer*: rarely before has a composer snatched subjects from yesterday's news and made operas out of them. Admittedly, themes of lasting significance lurk beneath this work's immediate surface: conflict between cultures and ideologies, rival claims to ancestral lands, human rights in general. Specifically, however, it takes us back no further than October 1985, when Palestinian terrorists hijacked the Italian cruise liner *Achille Lauro* and murdered wheelchair-bound passenger Leon Klinghoffer. The opera guides us through those events, albeit in an oblique fashion. Whatever the long-term fate of the opera, Alice Goodman's libretto certainly deserves to be spared from oblivion. It's eloquent and beautiful, compassionate and humanitarian, rich in imagery and spacious in its sentence-structure. If *The Death of Klinghoffer* finally disappoints, it's because the marriage of words and music is so fragile. The opera's musical language is firmly rooted in tradition, but it's doubtful if anyone will come away from it with a memorable lyric moment lodged in the mind. The recording uses the cast of the original production, and contains no weak links. As you expect from Adams, the score has been superbly orchestrated, and it's done full justice by the Lyon Opera Orchestra.

The Death of Klinghoffer
Sanford Sylvan bar Klinghoffer **Christopher Maltman** bar Captain **Yvonne Howard** mez Marilyn Klinghoffer **Tom Randle** ten Molqi **Kamel Boutros** bar Mamoud **Leigh Melrose** bar Rambo **Emil Marwa** act Omar (sung by **Susan Bickley** mez) **London Symphony Chorus and Orchestra / John Adams** Video director **Penny Woolcock**
Decca **DVD** 074 189-9 (166' · DDD; NTSC · 16:9 · PCM stereo & 5.1 · 0) Includes a 'Making of…' documentary   Ⓕ

Klinghoffer has yet to be performed in the US, and Penny Woolcock's live-action film, shot on location, won't do much to quieten the controversies that have kept it off the stage. She fleshes out the opera's philosophies, inasmuch as the composer conducted and discussed production details with Woolcock, and was thereby at least complicit in the choice of images. *Klinghoffer* is more an oratorio than an opera, and she uses the choruses and non-dramatic stretches to fill out the characters with flashbacks to 1940s Palestine and even historical footage of Nazi Germany.

This is Adams's slowest stage piece, and Woolcock's close, hand-held camerawork tests severely the singers' acting, particularly when they aren't singing. The singers were actually recorded live during the on-location filming, after the orchestra was recorded. The payoff is immense: synchronisation is perfect, and what we hear goes believably with what we see. Even in these trying circumstances, the vocalism and acting are outstanding.

So, does the film show librettist Alice Goodman and stage director Peter Sellars's scenario to be anti-Semitic and sympathetic to terrorism, as some of its American critics claim? The film does round out the terrorists' characters, but there's a balanced portrayal, showing the good and the bad of both Jews and Palestinians. The terrorists show regret after the killing, but there is also a stoning where a Palestinian mob gets drunk on its own brutality. Some of the Jewish tourists are parodies early on, but Marilyn Klinghoffer comes to take on towering dignity and strength. Most of those who've criticised the politics are responding to what they want to see in the opera than what's actually there. ·

Woolcock has turned *Klinghoffer* into a fairly gripping visual drama; but her success shows up the musical deficiencies: encountered as an opera rather than a film, it may be of no more than topical interest.

Doctor Atomic

Doctor Atomic
Gerald Finley *bar* J Robert Oppenheimer **Jessica Rivera** *sop* Kitty Oppenheimer **Eric Owens** *bass* General Leslie Groves **Richard Paul Fink** *bar* Edward Teller **James Maddalena** *bar* Jack Hubbard **Thomas Glenn** *ten* Robert Wilson **Jay Hunter Morris** *ten* Captain James Nolan **Ellen Rabiner** *mez* Pasqualita **Netherlands Opera Chorus; Netherlands Philharmonic Orchestra / Lawrence Renes**
Stage and video director **Peter Sellars**
Opus Arte **DVD** OA0998D (3h 50' · NTSC · 16:9 · PCM stereo and DTS 5.1 · 0). Includes bonus interview with Peter Sellars, mini documentary, cast gallery and illustrated synopsis Ⓕ**❍❍❍**

Doctor Atomic is the most dramatic subject matter of any John Adams opera and musically the most inconsistent. Indeed, as subject matter goes, *Doctor Atomic* could hardly be more apocalyptic. The work's principal character is J Robert Oppenheimer, the scientist who developed the atomic bomb during the Second World War from its earliest prototype through to the test bomb that was detonated in 1945 at a secret site in New Mexico. The opera's First Act takes place a month before the test; the Second Act is set on the day itself, with a finale that strategically plays with our perception of time as the bomb is about to be detonated.

Adams's first opera, *Nixon in China*, rattled along with a note-specific clarity that flickered like newsreel; he paints *Doctor Atomic* in broader brushstrokes, using post-Bernard Herrmann suspense tactics and angsty chromatic swells to portray charged emotions. But an underlying weakness is the stubbornly unmemorable and melodically colourless vocal writing, leading to one-dimensional characterisations. Adams's and librettist Peter Sellars's decision to incorporate poetry by John Donne and Muriel Rukeyser into the opera only highlights the functional flavour of Sellars's own words as the balance is flipped towards contrived artifice. No complaints about the performance though. Gerald Finley carries the problems of the world on his shoulders as Oppenheimer and the Netherlands Philharmonic and Lawrence Renes play like it's the best score since *Fidelio*.

I Was Looking at the Ceiling...

I Was Looking at the Ceiling and Then I Saw the Sky
Martina Mühlpointner *sngr* Consuelo Kimako
Xavier Trotman *sngr* Dewain Markus **Alexander Neisser** *sngr* Rick **Jeannette Friedrich** *sngr* Leila
Darius de Haas *sngr* David **Lilith Gardell** *sngr* Tiffany **Jonas Holst** *sngr* Mike **Freiburg Young Opera Company; The Band of Holst-Sinfonietta / Klaus Simon**
Naxos ② 8 669003/4 (116' · DDD · S/N) Ⓢ▷

John Adams's stylistic range is vast, yet even in such a diverse output, *I Was Looking at the Ceiling and Then I Saw the Sky* (1995) stands apart. Conceived, in the composer's words, as 'a Broadway-style show', it draws its musical inspiration from popular song, moving from doo-wop to gospel, from pop ballad to the blues. The text, a poetic piece of social and political commentary by June Jordan, introduces us to seven young Angelenos whose intertwined lives are transformed by the 1994 Northridge earthquake. There's no recitative, no spoken dialogue; the story is told through song and ensemble. This posed a problem when Nonesuch issued a composer-conducted recording of excerpts in 1998, cutting seven of the 22 vocal numbers. Here, Naxos gives us the complete score.

It hard to state that the narrative flows a whole lot more smoothly when the show is heard in its entirety. There are still quite a few jarring gaps, although one certainly gets a better sense of the characters as well as a heightened sense of drama. Missing from the Nonesuch recording, for example, was the crucial post-earthquake scene involving Tiffany, Mike and Rick – the score's longest number.

As for the performance: the Freiburg-based Holst-Sinfonietta Band plays its intricate part with tightly coiled energy for conductor Klaus Simon; the mostly German cast copes reasonably well with the different American dialects (only Lilith Gardell's Tiffany fails to convince); and although the women's voices can turn shrill when pressed, all the singers sound fresh and youthful. Indeed, Martina Mühlpointner may not have the extraordinary tonal richness of Audra McDonald (Nonesuch) but her wide-eyed rendition of 'Consuelo's Dream' – one of the piece's prettiest and most effective numbers – is also deeply affecting. Not all the songs in *Ceiling/Sky* are as successful as this one but I'd guess that there's enough here to make this daring experiment in American musical theatre attractive to more than just Adams's fans.

Nixon in China

Nixon in China
Sanford Sylvan *bar* Chou en-Lai **James Maddalena** *bar* Richard Nixon **Thomas Hammons** *bar* Henry Kissinger **Mari Opatz** *mez* Nancy T'ang First Secretary to Mao **Stephanie Friedman** *mez* Second Secretary to Mao **Marion Dry** *mez* Third Secretary to Mao **John Duykers** *ten* Mao Tse-Tung **Carolann Page** *sop* Pat Nixon **Trudy Ellen Craney** *sop* Chiang Ch'ing
St Luke's Chorus and Orchestra / Edo de Waart
Nonesuch ② 7559-79177-2 (144' · DDD · T)   Ⓕ

Whatever its weaknesses, there's no denying that *Nixon in China* is striking. Structured curiously, its three acts reduce from three scenes to two, and then to one, and they diminish proportionally in duration from more than an hour in Act 1 to the unbroken 30-minute span of Act 3. This last act played out in the statesmen's bedrooms, is a weary sequence of dialogues and soliloquies, ending in a curious but calculated state of anticlimax. Preceding this, though, is a run of colourful scenes that symbolise the main events without imposing any artificial sense of dramatic shape. By the end of the work, the public faces have given way to private lives; even Nixon and Chairman Mao emerge as mere mortals rather than mythical demi-gods.

The music serves the libretto deftly in fast-moving dialogue but the reflective and rhapsodic portions of text seem to leave Adams baffled, the melodic lines wandering aimlessly, short on intrinsic musical interest and rarely moving the singers to expressive performances. In the handling of spectacle and scene-setting, by contrast, Adams is in his element. He freely avails himself of any idiom, any oblique references or musical quotation that serves as a means to an end. Some passages would be unthinkable without the operas of Philip Glass; elsewhere lie uncanny ghosts of 1930s Stravinsky. Magpie just about sums this score up. The singing is sympathetic, with James Maddalena as an aptly volatile Nixon and Trudy Ellen Craney coping admirably with the coloratura lines of Madam Mao.

Further listening

The Wound-dresser
Coupled with: Short Ride on a Fast Machine.

Shaker Loops. Berceuse elegiaque
Gunn *bar* **Bournemouth Symphony Orchestra / Alsop**
Naxos 8 559031 (62' · DDD)   ⑤▶
A near-perfect Adams Primer containing his tender and powerful meditation, to words by Walt Whitman, on the subject of those lost to AIDS. Touchingly performed by Nathan Gunn.

Richard Addinsell   British 1904-1977

After study at the Royal College of Music, London, and in Vienna, Addinsell visited the USA (1933), where he wrote for films. Most of his music was for the theatre and cinema; his hugely popular Warsaw Concerto, in the style of Rachmaninov, was used in the film Dangerous Moonlight (1941).
                                        GROVEmusic

Warsaw Concerto

Warsaw Concerto (arr Douglas)[b].The Admirable Crichton[a] – Polka and Galop; Waltz Sequence ([a]reconstructed by P Lane) The Black Rose – Suite[a]. Blithe Spirit[a] – Prelude; Waltz. Goodbye Mr Chips – Suite[ac]. Love on the Dole – Suite[a]. Out of the Clouds – Flame Tango (arr Sharples). Scrooge – Suite (arr S Bernstein)[c]. Tom Brown's Schooldays – Overture[a]
[b]**Martin Roscoe** *pf* [c]**Manchester Cathedral Choir;** [c]**Chetham's Chamber Choir; BBC Philharmonic Orchestra / Rumon Gamba**
Chandos CHAN10046 (80' · DDD)   Ⓕ●

None of the modern versions of the *Warsaw Concerto* seems to have the freshness, urgency and lack of self-indulgence of this very fine version. That's a pointer to the high level of playing and interpretation to be found throughout this ever fascinating and altogether quite delightful selection of Addinsell's film music. Though Rachmaninov comes so immediately and vividly to mind in the most celebrated of Addinsell's creations, that was strictly for the purposes of its film context. Elsewhere you're more likely to be reminded of Vaughan Williams, Ravel or Eric Coates. Pastiche was an inevitable part of a film composer's armoury, but the very real inventive gifts displayed in the *Warsaw Concerto* are also evident throughout this collection. About half the music has already been recorded in other Addinsell collections, but not with the chorus that's especially effective here in the 'School Song' from *Goodbye Mr Chips*. Of the new items the sumptuously lyrical finale to the music for *The Black Rose* is particularly fine (expertly reconstructed, like much else here, by Philip Lane), as are the dances from the 1957 film *The Admirable Crichton*.

It's by no means just nostalgia that makes Addinsell's film music well worth exploring, and this generously filled CD is undoubtedly the best single-CD selection available.

Addinsell Orchestral

Additional recommendation

Warsaw Concerto
Coupled with: **Beaver** Portrait of Isla **Rózsa**
Spellbound Concerto. **Rota** The Legend of the Glass
Mountain **RR Bennett** Murder on the Orient Express
– excs. **Bath** Cornish Rhapsody **Herrmann** Concerto
Macabre **Williams** The Dream of Olwen **Pennario**
Midnight on the Cliffs
Fowke pf RTE Concert Orchestra / O'Duinn
Naxos 8 554323 (74' · DDD)   Ⓢ☞

Fowke plays all the pieces with affection and
panache. If you've always wished that the
Warsaw Concerto were longer, this is for you.

Film Music

Blithe Spirit – Prelude; Waltz. Encore – Miniature
Overture. Gaslight – Prelude. Parisienne – 1885.
Southern Rhapsody. Waltz of the Toreadors – March;
The General on Parade; Waltz (all arr. Lane). Fire
over England – Suite (arr. Zalva). Passionate Friends
– Lover's Moon. South Riding – Prelude. A Christmas
Caro – Suite (arr S Bernstein). WRNS March
Robert Gibbs vn **Peter Lawson** pf **Royal Ballet
Sinfonia / Kenneth Alwyn**
ASV White Line CDWHL2115 (68' · DDD)   Ⓜ❍

Nobody should imagine that the *Warsaw Concerto* is all that's worth hearing from this fine
composer. Addinsell had a natural feel for richly
tuneful, romantic music in the best tradition of
British light music. The diverse commissions he
fulfilled served to turn these gifts to contrasted
musical styles; these provide a rewardingly varied programme.

The most familiar music will probably be the
swaggering march and haunting waltz from the
Waltz of the Toreadors. Others will know the
prelude and waltz from David Lean's film of
Blithe Spirit or the suite from *A Christmas Carol*.
Perennial favourites are the invigorating *WRNS
March*, the delightfully mysterious prelude to
the 1939 film of *Gaslight* and the waltz from the
stage play *Parisienne*.

The last has been given a splendid Glazuno-
vian orchestration by compiler, producer,
arranger and annotator Philip Lane, who
again leaves us in his debt, as do conductor Kenneth Alwyn and the admirable Royal Ballet
Sinfonia.

Additional recommendation

Film music

Goodbye Mr Chips – exc. Ring around the moon –
exc. Smokey Mountains Concerto. The Isle of
Apples. The Prince and the Showgirl – exc. Tune in
G. Tom Brown's Schooldays – exc. Festival. Journey
to Romance. Fire over England – exc. A Tale of Two
Cities – exc
Martin, Elms pfs **BBC Concert Orchestra / Alwyn**
Marco Polo 8 223732 (68' · DDD)   Ⓕ

A most attractive release. Much of the orchestral
material for this recording was prepared by Philip

Lane, who also provides the informative notes.
Fine performances, too.

Thomas Adès   British b1971

*One of the leading lights in contemporary classical
music, pianist/conductor/composer Adès's meteoric rise
to international musical prominence has been phenomenal. He gained early success as a pianist, winning Second Prize in the 1989 BBC Young Musician
of the Year, then read music at King's College, Cambridge (1989-92). Among the works from his student
years are his first opus, Five Eliot Landscapes (1990)
and the Chamber Symphony (1990) – his first work
to receive a professional performance. In 1993 he
became Composer in Association to the Hallé Orchestra for whom he wrote The Origin of the Harp (1994)
and These Premises Are Alarmed (1996). His most
performed work, Living Toys (1993), brought him
widespread critical acclaim, though it was the chamber
opera Powder Her Face (1995) that earned him an
international reputation.*

*In 1998 he became artistic director of the Bir-
mingham Contemporary Music Group and the following year, for his first large-scale orchestral work,
Asyla (1997), he received the Ernst von Siemens
Prize and the Grawemeyer Award. Also in 1999 he
became joint artistic director of the Aldeburgh Festival. Recent commissions include operas for the Royal
Opera House, Covent Garden (The Tempest), and
Glyndebourne. Adès's compositions showed exceptional assurance of style and technique from the start,
and his success had much to do with the umistakable
presence of a personal accent in music which blends
vividness of detail with a clear sense of compelling
overall design. His most recent work is a piano
concerto, 'In Seven Days', a collaboration with his
partner, the Israeli video-artist, Tal Rosner. It was
premiered in London in April 2008.* GROVEmusic

Asyla

Asyla[bc]. ... but all shall be well[bd]. Chamber
Symphony[ad]. Concerto conciso[ae]. These Premises
are Alarmed[bd]
[a]**Birmingham Contemporary Music Group;** [b]**City
of Birmingham Symphony Orchestra /** [c]**Sir Simon
Rattle,** [d]**Thomas Adès** [e]pf
EMI 556818-2 (61' · DDD)   Ⓕ❍☞

This CD includes the *Chamber Symphony*, the
work that first aroused interest in Adès's work
when he was 18, set alongside *Asyla*, a recent
un-chamber symphony and his first work for
full orchestra. The progression between them is
remarkable: the *Chamber Symphony* has both
real invention and real economy, and its use of
jazz elements is neither patronising nor culinary. Maybe its last movement adds little of
consequence to the preceding three, but *Asyla*
genuinely grows from the grave, rather Brittenish horn line that sets it going through the
strong drama of the central movements to the

almost Sibelian climax of the finale. Adès's own voice is clearly audible throughout, elegant, coolly intelligent but urgent.

These Premises are Alarmed, a sinewy toccata of bright colour and urgent energy, was written for the opening of the Bridgewater Hall, Manchester. In the *Concerto conciso* Adès perhaps takes his pleasure in simple intervals and brief motives a little too far. However, ... *but all shall be well* is something else again. It develops abundant, earnest melody from a pair of simple phrases in an impressively sustained argument that reaches a powerful and satisfying climax. Fine performances, admirably recorded.

Chamber Concerto

Adès Chamber Symphony **Higdon** Percussion Concerto[a] **MacMillan** The Confession of Isobel Gowdie
[a]**Colin Currie** *perc*
London Philharmonic Orchestra / Marin Alsop
LPO LPO0035 (61′ · DDD) Ⓜ

Not the least notable aspects of this CD are the two works, both dating from 1990, that launched their composers' careers. In Thomas Adès's *Chamber Symphony*, an often oblique musical syntax binds fragmentary ideas and textures into a cumulative whole; its motifs moving purposefully through a 'slow movement' and 'scherzo' before finding repose in an exquisite coda. All the more pity, then, that this vivid but fallible reading does not quite match that by the composer.

Where Adès intrigues listeners, James MacMillan fairly bludgeons them into submission with *The Confession of Isobel Gowdie*, though this depiction of a 17th-century Scottish woman tortured then burnt at the stake for witchcraft could hardly afford to be self-effacing. And the initial accumulation of intensity, spilling over into an extended onslaught then recalling the opening in expressively heightened terms before the accusatory final *crescendo*, is nothing if not powerful. Marin Alsop has its measure, while the LPO give everything in an account that should convince those hearing the piece for the first time.

Jennifer Higdon's Percussion Concerto (2005) might also be found engaging on first hearing. The solo part, dispatched with aplomb by Colin Currie, is disappointingly limited in its invention and rhythmic profile, while the orchestral part – a mild distillation of Stravinskian and Coplandesque gestures – is unlikely to set the pulse racing. The sound and booklet are on a par with earlier LPO releases, however, making this disc well worth investigating for the MacMillan alone.

Violin Concerto

Violin Concerto, 'Concentric Paths'
Anthony Marwood *vn*
Chamber Orchestra of Europe / Thomas Adès
EMI ⊳ available from iTunes (20′ · DDD) Ⓑ●●●⊳

EMI's coverage of the music of Thomas Adès continues with this download (available DRM-free from iTunes for £3.49/$9.99) of his Violin Concerto, composed in 2005. Subtitled *Concentric Paths*, the work consists of three movements. 'Rings' has something of a preludial function – focusing on harmonic and rhythmic asymmetry and with a Ligeti-cum-Adams synthesis that unfolds in an engaging if provisional manner. 'Paths' then expands across two layers of musical activity – the soloist's constant and intensifying lyricism underpinned and, at crucial points, offset by the orchestra's violent interjections and volatile textures. 'Rounds' ends the work with its deft polyrhythmic interplay and sense of closure that is conclusive if peremptory.

Adès's previous large-scale instrumental work, the Piano Quintet, left one admiring but uninvolved – something that the Violin Concerto, in the sheer diversity and expressive richness of its material and the evident virtuosity of its writing, certainly avoids; not least when the solo part is unerringly geared to the strengths of Anthony Marwood, and the response of the Chamber Orchestra of Europe lacks nothing in keenness or commitment. If lacking a degree of perspective, the sound has a lustre and fullness that otherwise presents the work to best advantage: indeed, the Barbican acoustic is all but unrecognisable here. Which only goes to show that today's post-production is capable of the same alchemical feats as is Adès in his music.

Living Toys
Arcadiana, Op 12[a]. The Origin of the Harp, Op 13[b]. Sonata da caccia, Op 11[c]. Living Toys, Op 9[d]. Gefriolsae me, Op 3b[e] [c]**Michael Neisemann** *ob* [c]**Andrew Clark** *hn* [c]**Thomas Adès** *hpd* [a]**Endellion Quartet** (Andrew Watkinson, Ralph de Souza *vns* Garfield Jackson *va* David Waterman *vc*) [e]**King's College Choir, Cambridge / Stephen Cleobury;** [b]**instrumental ensemble / Thomas Adès;** [d]**London Sinfonietta / Markus Stenz**
EMI Debut 572271-2 (64′ · DDD · T/t) Ⓑ●●●⊳

These five pieces suggest a composer as delightedly surprised by his prodigal inventiveness as we are. *Arcadiana*, for example, is a seven-movement string quartet whose central and longest movement (four minutes) contains an extraordinary range of precisely imagined, highly original textures and yet in its penultimate section can settle to a serene and wonderfully beautiful *adagio* whose sound and mood be conveyed only by the adjective 'Beethovenian'. Far more overtly, the engaging *Sonata da caccia* uses elements that are very directly derived from Couperin, but the sensibility is entirely modern, even when you strongly suspect that this or that phrase is a note-for-note quotation. However, as with Adès's first collection, his is an imagination that you can trust. *Living Toys* has a quite Birtwistle-like sense of ritual to it, although more lyrical, quite frequently with a tangible jazz element. *The Origin of the Harp* is a dark, dramatic chamber tone-poem. *Gefriolsae me*, for male voices and organ, is a brief but impressive motet to Middle English words. All five pieces are finely performed. *Arcadiana*, with its exquisite textures and melodic richness, is perhaps Adès's finest achievement so far, a work constantly aware of the musical past but renewing that past with astonishing freshness.

Life story

Catch, Op 4. Darknesse visible. Still sorrowing, Op 7. Under Hamelin Hill, Op 6. Five Eliot Landscapes, Op 1. Traced overhead, Op 15. Life story, Op 8b
Valdine Anderson, Mary Carewe *sops* **Lynsey Marsh** *cl* **Anthony Marwood** *vn* **Louise Hopkins** *vc* **Thomas Adès** *pf/org* **David Goode, Stephen Farr** *orgs*
EMI Debut 569699-2 (77' · DDD · T)   Ⓑ**OO**▷

Adès has the gift of seizing your attention with strange but ravishingly beautiful sonorities and then holding it with entrancingly mysterious inventions that allure the ear. Yet he also has the much rarer quality of inspiring utter confidence. His style can't be defined by simply describing any one of these pieces. Each solves a new problem or investigates a new scenario with such adroitness and completeness that it seems a quite new and delightful adventure. In *Still sorrowing* the starting point is a piano whose central register is muted with a strip of plastic adhesive. The effect on those pitches is obvious: they are dulled to a sort of subdued drumming, but by observing the new light that this casts on the undamped upper and lower registers Adès effectively invents a new and alluring instrument, or rather three of them. And he plays them with poetry and wonder.

Catch is a game in which a piano trio tempt and tease an off-stage clarinet; he eventually joins them in sober homophony, for this is a game with serious and lyrical substance as well as a jest. A similar but more ambiguous game is played in *Under Hamelin Hill*, where the piping toccata of one organist attracts two others to join him in co-operative apparent improvisation, but he's left alone for a shadowy soliloquy filled with shudders. *Darknesse visible* is a haunting meditation in which the presence of John Dowland is clearest where the music seems least like him; a magical illusion as well as a moving homage. In *Life story* the soprano is asked to imitate the manner of Billie Holiday in her wry reflection on a casual one-night encounter; it's the dark, searching piano that adds pity and bleakness to turn this into a riveting miniature opera. *Traced overhead* is filled with mysterious, glancing references to remembered piano music, but is grippingly coherent. And as if this weren't enough, in the Eliot settings, Op 1, the 17-year-old Adès already proved himself a song-writer of rare talent. The performances are first-rate.

Piano Quintet

Adès Piano Quintet[a]
Schubert Piano Quintet, 'Trout'[b]
Thomas Adès *pf* [b]**Corin Long** *db*
[a]**Arditti Quartet** (Irvine Arditti, Graeme Jennings *vns* Dov Scheindlin *va* Rohan de Saram *vc*);
[b]Members of the **Belcea Quartet** (Corina Belcea *vn* Krzysztof Chorzelski *va* Alasdair Tait *vc*)
EMI 557664-2 (62' · DDD)   Ⓕ**OO**▷

Thomas Adès features both as composer and pianist on this release: two piano quintets which, though composed 182 years apart, are equally alive with formal and expressive provocations. That said, expression per se is not really an issue in Adès's Piano Quintet (2001). The single movement places its sonata-form emphasis so the near-literal repeat of an already evolving exposition takes on a strongly developmental feel, with the development then assuming the guise of a varied reprise, and the brief recapitulation becoming almost a transition that anticipates the coda.

It all amounts to an intriguing rethink of an age-old medium, though one whose musical material is so geared up to the unfolding of the formal process as to evince little intrinsic memorability beyond the pervasive opening motif. Adès and the Ardittis ensure a reading of unremitting clarity, with perhaps a didactic element such as seems more than appropriate to the work itself.

Outwardly, nothing could be less didactic than the near-effortless spontaneity of Schubert's *Trout* Quintet – though its often unpredictable formal transitions confirm the benign influence of Haydn and early Beethoven, while its taciturn tonal progressions anticipate the composer's instrumental works of the 1820s. These are qualities to which Adès and the Belcea Quartet are responsive: listen to the hushed intensity going into the codetta of the first movement's exposition, the tellingly unquiet repose which opens the *Andante*'s second half, or the lucidly drawn contrast between the last two variations of the fourth movement – making the return of *Die Forelle* itself the more arresting.

As an overall reading, it lacks the unforced naturalness of Clifford Curzon and members of the Vienna Octet, or the sense of discovery which Alfred Brendel et al manage to convey with an even greater communicative zeal. Recorded sound, with the instrumental interplay palpably defined if lacking the final degree of spatial depth, is well suited to the interpretative stance that these performances bracingly convey.

The Tempest

The Tempest
Simon Keenlyside *bar* Prospero Kate Royal *sop* Miranda Toby Spence *ten* Ferdinand Ian Bostridge *ten* Caliban Cyndia Sieden *sop* Ariel Philip Langridge *ten* King of Naples Donald Kaasch *ten*

Antonio **Jonathan Summers** *bar* Sebastian **David Cordier** *counterten* Trinculo **Stephen Richardson** *bass-bar* Stefano **Graeme Danby** *bass* Gonzalo **Chorus and Orchestra of the Royal Opera House, Covent Garden / Thomas Adès**
EMI ② 695234-2 (118' · DDD · S/T/N)
Recorded live in 2007   Ⓕ❍❍❍❏➙

🅖 Thomas Adès's 'ism'-defying output gains in variety all the time, but whatever he comes up with in the future it is likely that *The Tempest* will remain one of his most significant achievements. Premiered at Covent Garden in 2004, and recorded there at the 2007 revival, Adès's second opera succeeds where most *Tempest* adaptations have failed: in adding something to Shakespeare's magical and inherently lyrical scenario. From the tornado-like prelude to Ariel's stratospheric yet ethereal 'Five fathoms deep' the music illuminates rather than merely illustrates the drama. It may not be a flawless masterpiece Meredith Oakes's otherwise musical libretto relies on some clunky rhythms, and Adès could occasionally have tightened his writing, notably in Act 3 but it is one of the most viable and stageworthy of modern British operas. Most of this recording's cast created their roles, and the performances have a lived-in feel.

Yet even the newcomer, Kate Royal as Miranda, is fully inside her part and sings alluringly. For many, the most memorable writing in *The Tempest* comes attached to Ariel's vocal high-wire act. Few coloratura sopranos are able to dispatch it like Cyndia Sieden, whose sound lends special colour to the performance, and it is hardly her fault that her stratospheric flights leave the words almost unintelligible.

Simon Keenlyside, on the young side as Prospero, mixes brain and baritonal brawn in his characteristically charismatic way. Ian Bostridge sings unstintingly as a wonderfully weird Caliban and his Peter Pears-ish voice strengthens the impression of the character as an outsider. His younger tenor colleague, Toby Spence, is a fine Ferdinand. Philip Langridge's King of Naples and Jonathan Summers's Sebastian represent luxury casting in a recording made under the composer's own baton. The playing of the Covent Garden orchestra is another luxury no, a necessity, given the brilliantly conceived and demanding orchestral aspect of this piece.

Alexander Agricola
Franco-Flemish 1446-1506

Agricola's career centred mainly on Italian courts (Milan, Florence, Naples) and the French court – from 1498 until his death he served Philip the Handsome of Burgundy at home and abroad. His travels brought him renown as a singer and composer. His works include eight Masses, over 20 motets and other sacred pieces, nearly 50 chansons and c25 instrumental works. His style is predominantly northern, akin to Ockeghem's, using long,

rhythmically complex contrapuntal lines built from short, decorative motifs and linked with frequent yet unobtrusive cadences.   **GROVE**music

Vocal works

A la mignonne de fortune. Adieu m'amour.   🅟
Adieu m'amour II. Allez, regretz. Ay je rien fait. Cecsus non iudicat de coloribus. De tous biens plaine. De tous biens plaine II. De tous biens plaine III. Et qui la dira. Fortuna desperata. Guarde vostre visage. Guarde vostre visage II. Guarde vostre visage III. J'ay beau huer. S'il vous plaist. Soit loing ou pres. Sonnes muses melodieusement

Ensemble Unicorn (Bernhard Landauer *counterten* Johannes Chum *ten* Colin Mason *bass-bar* Marco Ambrosini *fiddle* Nora Kallai *vihuela d'arco* Thomas Wimmer *vihuela d'arco/lte* Riccardo Delfino *hp/snare hp*) / **Michael Posch** *rec*
Naxos 8 553840 (65' · DDD)   Ⓢ❍❍❏➙

Agricola was praised by his contemporaries for the bizarre turn of his inspiration, and his music likened to quicksilver. By the standards of the period this is a highly unusual turn of phrase, but remains spot-on. The Ferrara Ensemble anthology, the first ever devoted to the composer, focused on the secular music, both instrumental and vocal, precisely the area covered by Michael Posch and Ensemble Unicorn in this most satisfying disc. Where there's duplication (surprisingly little, in fact) the performances compare with those of the Ferrara Ensemble, although the style of singing is very different. The voices are more up front and less inflected, perhaps the better to match the high instruments with which they're sometimes doubled. But the tensile quality of Agricola's lines comes through none the less, as does the miraculous inventiveness and charm of his music. Further, much of what's new to the catalogue really is indispensible, for example Agricola's most famous song, *Allez, regretz*. Unicorn keeps its improvisations and excursions to a minimum, and the music is the better for it. This disc would be indispensable at full price, let alone super-budget. It really is a must-have.

'Chansons'
Agricola De tous biens plaine I. De tous biens plaine II. Pater meus agricola est. En actendant. Fortuna desparata. Je n'ay dueil. De tous biens plaine III. Dung aultre amer I. De tous biens plaine IV. Comme femme desconfortee I. Comme femme desconfortee II. Comme femme desconfortee III. Se je fais bien. Tout a part moy I. De tous biens plaine V. Vostre hault bruit. Dung aultre amer II. Dung aultre amer III **Fitch** Agricologies – Agricola I: Comme femme a 2/4; Agricola III/Obrecht canon I: De tous biens plaine a 4 **Isaac** Si dormiero **Ninot le Petit** Si bibero crathere pleno
Michael Chance *counterten* **Fretwork** (Richard Boothby, Richard Campbell. Wendy Gillespie,

Susanna Pell, Asako Morikawa, Richard Tunnicliffe viols)
Harmonia Mundi HMU90 7421 (75' · DDD · T/t) Ⓕ

Alexander Agricola, the quincentenary of whose death fell in 2006, is not over-represented in the catalogue so this disc, then, is very welcome.

Fretwork take hold of this frequently unpredictable music (all but one of the pieces are performed in new editions by composer Fabrice Fitch) with confidence. They produce performances of exuberance, proving that what a contemporary of the composer called his 'bizarre and crazy manner', as Fitch notes, can either be subverted or assumed to be, in fact, less crazy than it might appear and give impressive musical results. The chansons also prove that Agricola was a fine melodist: his contrapuntal strangeness elsewhere (perhaps best shown here in the freely composed *Pater meus agricola est*) is probably no greater than that of Ockeghem or Obrecht, both of whose counterpoint is frequently thoroughly eccentric.

A unique feature of this anthology is that it includes two parts from Fitch's cycle of *Agricologies*, a work in several movements for Fretwork and the Kreutzer Quartet. The material for the work comes from Agricola, or material used by him, and Fitch makes a point of working, in the first, with his melodic quirkiness and, in the very brief second, with his counterpoint, a remarkable texture being produced by the performers tapping on the strings rather than plucking or bowing. An impressive disc on all counts, which should do much to restore Agricola's obscure profile to the light.

Kalevi Aho   Finnish b1949

Aho studied at the Sibelius Academy in Helsinki under Einojuhani Rautavaara and with Boris Blacher in West Berlin. He has taught at Helsinki University and the Sibelius Academy, but since 1993 has been a freelance composer. His extensive output includes much orchestral music and several operas.

Clarinet Concerto

Aho Clarinet Concerto **Nielsen** Clarinet Concerto
Martin Fröst cl
Lahti Symphony Orchestra / Osmo Vänskä
BIS ⊛ BIS-SACD1463 (54' · DDD)   Ⓕ ❶❷❸ ▸

Kalevi Aho's Concerto starts arrestingly but without a trace of the attention-seeking that afflicts certain other clarinet concertos of recent times. There is something in Aho's five continuous movements that recalls Nielsen's directness and free-flowing succession of ideas, and the cadenza that forms the second movement even brings momentary echoes of Nielsen's uncompromising skirls and flourishes. But the Finn's sights are set more on the starkly elemental than on the quirkily personal.

For Aho the *Vivace con brio* third movement is the 'centre and culmination', and it is certainly exuberant – dangerous, even – in its restless virtuosity, rather like Strauss's *Till Eulenspiegel* driven mad by inner demons. After this a sad slow movement brings sober reflection, and an Epilogue concludes the work on a note of mystery. There can have been few equally impressive head-on engagements with the concerto medium in recent years.

There are eight or so modern accounts of the Nielsen Clarinet Concerto in the catalogue. Most have fine qualities. Yet for sureness of idiomatic touch none dislodges Ib Erikson's classic 1954 Danish accounts (now available on Dutton Labs).

Closer to the mark than any modern rivals is this new issue from Martin Fröst, the clarinettist of the moment for all-round artistry allied to adventurous approach to repertoire. He seems to have Nielsen's irascible masterpiece in his bloodstream, as surely as he has its technical contortions under his fingers. Vänskä ensures that the Lahti players are never fazed by the exposed edges in the accompaniment, and only the very drawn-out final bars come across as slightly self-conscious. Detail for detail, phrase for phrase, this team takes the palm over the old Danish recording, even before considering BIS's immeasurably superior sound quality. Even so, Erikson and Wöldike remain a benchmark for insight into the character of the piece.

In sum, a CD of rare distinction.

Orchestral music

Symphony No 11[a]. Symphonic Dances
[a]**Kroumata Percussion Ensemble** (John Eriksson, Anders Holdar, Leif Karlsson, Anders Loguin, Ulrik Nilsson, Johan Silvmark perc) **Lahti Symphony Orchestra / Osmo Vänskä**
BIS BIS-CD1336 (61' · DDD)   Ⓕ Ⓑ▸

Aho's *Symphonic Dances* (2001) bear the subtitle 'Hommage à Uuno Klami' – and therein lies the clue to the work's genesis. Klami (1900-1961), one of the leading Finnish composers of the last century, had high hopes for his large-scale, *Kalevala*-inspired ballet *Pyrörteitä*, but by the time of his death had managed to orchestrate only the second of its three acts. Aho orchestrated Act 1 in 1988. During 2000, no material having come to light for the final act, he embarked on completing Klami's *magnum opus*, bolstered by the prospect of a production at the Finnish National Ballet. In the event, that belated premiere never materialised, and it was left to Osmo Vänskä and the Lahti SO to champion Aho's 'Third Act' in the concert hall. A thoroughly approachable, 27-minute creation of exhilarating drive and colour, its four movements take their names from Klami's original synopsis. It's stunningly well served here by artists and production crew alike.

Symphony No 11 is almost as rewarding. It grew out of a commission for an orchestral work involving the Kroumata Percussion Ensemble, and is cast in three movements, the last of which distils a wondrous stillness and inner calm. It also serves as a perfect foil to the first two movements, both of which demonstrate Aho's comprehensive mastery of rhythm, timbre and drama. Again, the performance is a definitive one and BIS's engineering breathtaking in its realism.

Concert for Chamber Orchestra – The Book of Questions[a]; Viola Concerto[b]; Symphony No 14, 'Rituals'[c]
[a]**Monica Groop** *mez* [b]**Anna Kreetta Gribajcevic** *va*
[c]**Herman Rechberger** *darabuka/djembe*
[c]**Jukka Koski** *gong/tam* **Chamber Orchestra of Lapland / John Storgårds**
BIS BIS-CD1686 (80' · DDD)   Ⓕ

Following the *Luosto* Symphony's premiere, Aho wanted to write on a smaller scale, for chamber orchestra. In the event, however, he produced a concert full of three interlinked works (2006-07) that, while performable separately, taken together 'form some sort of great "meta-symphony"'.

The concert opens with *The Book of Questions*, a half-hour-long song-cycle to lines from Neruda's final collection. Absent is the lushness of the *Chinese Songs*: the opening and closing sections are spoken and not until the fourth section does anything like their radiance of vocal writing emerge; by the 10th there is a hint of Aho's old teacher Rautavaara. Monica Groop sings as beautifully as she may, but the cycle's restraint is all-pervasive. Not so in the Viola Concerto which starts from the same chord with which the cycle concludes (in concert the soloists play tag while the music is still sounding); this is the more familiar Aho, dramatic, lyric, rhythmically vital.

The Fourteenth Symphony (*Rituals*) forms the concert's second half, exchanging singer and viola-player for two percussionists, the first performing on the Arabian darabuka and African djembe (Aho confesses he is 'bored' with Western drums). Their special timbres infuse the three main sections called 'Incantation', separated by two interludes and a Procession in which the second percussionist takes centre stage with an array of gongs. At a few points the spirit of Hovhaness hovers dimly over proceedings but Aho's personal voice is too strong to succumb to pastiche. The performances here are strong and compelling, the soloists at the top of their game and BIS's recording (made in Rovaniemi Church) superb as always.

Jehan Alain   French 1911-1940

Alain studied with Dupré and Dukas at the Paris Conservatoire (1927-39) and was organist of St Nicolas de Maisons Lafitte in Paris (1935-39); he was killed in action. He shared Messiaen's enthusiasms for Debussy and Asian music, reflected in the modalities, rhythmic irregularities and ecstatic osti- *natos of his works, which are mostly for the organ or the Catholic Mass. His organ works include Deux danses à Agni Yavishtra (1934), two Fantaisies (1934, 1936), Litanies (1937) and Trois danses (1937-39).*   **GROVE**music

---

Organ Works

Suite. Climat. Prélude et Fugue. Choral dorien. Choral phrygien. Aria. Variations sur 'Lucis créator'. Berceuse sur deux notes qui cornent. Deux préludes profanes. Monodie. Ballade en mode phrygien. Choral cistercian pour une élévation. Variations sur un thème de Clément Janequin. Le jardin suspendu. Litanies. Fantasmagorie. Trois danses. Quatre pièces. Grave. Petite pièce. Intermezzo. Lamento. Premiere fantaisie. Deuxième fantaisie. Deux dances à Agni Yavishta. Cinque pièces faciles – Complainte à la mode ancienne; Fugue en mode de Fa; Verset-Choral; Berceuse. Postlude pour l'office de Complies. Page 21 du huitième cahier de notes de Jehan Alain
Kevin Bowyer *org*
Nimbus ② NI5551/2 (146' · DDD). Recorded on the Marcussen Organ, Chapel of St Augustine, Tonbridge School, Kent   Ⓕ❶❷❸▷

Ⓖ   This is the most comprehensive and impressive recording yet of Alain's organ music. Bowyer offers nine pieces not included on Eric Lebrun's two-disc survey from Naxos. These may not be among the composer's most substantial creations, but Alain enthusiasts wouldn't like to be without any of them, least of all the intensely moving page from one of Alain's notebooks setting out his musical reactions to the death, in a mountaineering accident, of his sister, Marie-Odile. Bowyer's performances are thought-provoking, stimulating and often inspired. His tempos aren't especially quick, though he does turn out the fastest performance ever recorded of the *Intermezzo*. Yet even here the choice of speed is symptomatic of his approach; nobody could deny that when played so rapidly the work takes on a new dimension. Nimbus achieves a near-perfect balance between clarity and atmosphere on the new Marcussen in Tonbridge School's rebuilt Chapel. When the disarming dialogue between a single reed and the flutes of the charming *Petite pièce* can be revealed in such detail nobody could realistically ask for a better setting for this magical music. Bowyer proves to be an unusually perceptive and persuasive advocate of Alain's music. It will probably be a long time before a serious contender to this outstanding release comes along.

Alain Trois danses. Le jardin suspendu. Aria. Litanies, Op 79. Variations sur 'Lucis creator'. Deux dances à Agni Yavishta **Duruflé** Danses pour orchestre, Op 6 – Danse lente (arr Whitehead). Prélude et fugue sur le nom d'Alain, Op 7
William Whitehead *org*

Chandos CHAN10315 (74' · DDD)
Played on the Oberthür organ of Saint-Etienne
Cathedral, Auxerre　　　　　　　Ⓕ❍❍↦

With its futuristic console and its aurally shattering battery of chamade reeds, this astonishing 1986-built Oberthür organ is the perfect
vehicle for this programme.

One is acutely aware of the terrible loss to
French music when Jehan Alain was killed by a
German sniper at the Battle of Saumur in 1940.
His best known organ pieces are all here, including *Litanies*, *Le jardin suspendu* and the masterful
Trois danses, completed just before his death.
With his fondness for ostinati, Eastern-
influenced modes and irregular rhythms, Alain is
almost a proto-minimalist. The little-known *Aria*
is a gem worthy of greater exposure. Although the
recordings of the composer's sister, Marie-Claire
Alain, have long remained the benchmark,
Whitehead's more spacious approach reveals
greater clarity. His sense of rhythmic bounce,
coupled with a fastidious choice of colour, creates
a strongly atmospheric performance. The recording, too, is outstanding.

Duruflé's music, while less experimental, is
just as compelling. Whitehead's transcription of
the *Danse lente* works well and should become a
repertoire regular. The final track, the memorial *Prélude et fugue sur le nom d'Alain* bobs and
weaves with a dramatic fervour. A winning disc.

Isaac Albéniz　　　　　Spanish 1860-1909

*Albéniz is one of the most important figures in
Spanish musical history; he helped create a national
idiom and an indigenous school of piano music. He
studied at the Brussels Conservatory and with Liszt,
Dukas and d'Indy; other important influences were
Felipe Pedrell (who inspired him to turn to Spanish
folk music), 19th-century salon piano music and
impressionist harmony. But he was not simply a follower of the French school and exchanged ideas with
Debussy and Ravel in Paris. Most of his many works
are for piano solo, the best known being the suite
Iberia (1906-08), distinguished by its complex technique, bold harmony and evocative instrumental
effects. He also wrote a notable opera, Pepita Jiménez
(1896). Albéniz was also a virtuoso pianist with a
highly personal style.*　　　　　GROVEmusic

Guitar Works

Albéniz Mallorca, Op 202. Suite española, Op 47.
Cantos de España, Op 232 – Córdoba **Granados**
Cuentos de la juventud – Dedicatoria. 15 Tonadillas
– El majo olvidado. 12 Danzas españolas, Op 37 –
Villanesca; Andaluza (Playera). 7 Valses poéticos
Rodrigo Tres Piezas españolas
Julian Bream *gtr*
RCA Navigator 74321 17903-2 (77' · DDD)　　Ⓢ❍❍

This recital offers playing of extraordinary

magnetism and an almost total illusion of the
great guitarist seated in the room making music
just beyond your loudspeakers; this effect is
particularly striking in Albéniz's *Córdoba* and
the *pianissimo* reprise of the central section of
the Granados *Danza española* No 5, which is
quite magical. The other works included are all
played with comparable spontaneity.

RCA here reissues this disc at super-bargain
price on its enterprising Navigator label; moreover, they have added Rodrigo's *Tres Piezas
españolas*, recorded a year later. The second of
these, a seven-minute 'Passacaglia', is quite
masterly, while the final 'Zapateado' brings
characteristically chimerical virtuosity from the
soloist. It's difficult to identify another recital of
Spanish guitar music that surpasses this, and it's
now one of the great bargains in the catalogue.

Piano Works

Iberia. Navarra. España: Souvenirs.
La Vega. Yvonne en visite! – La révérence!;
Joyeuse rencontre et quelques...
Marc-André Hamelin *pf*
Hyperion ② CDA67476/7 (126' · DDD)　　Ⓕ❍❍↦

Ⓖ　Here's the most immaculate, effortless
　　and refined of all *Iberias*. Where others
　　fight to stay afloat, Marc-André Hamelin rides the crest of every formidable wave with
nonchalant ease and poetry. Did Albéniz, as
Rubinstein once claimed, need a helping hand
in *Iberia*, simplifying textures for greater clarity,
brilliance and accessibility? Hamelin's musical
grace mocks the very question. His 'Evocación',
audaciously free and perfumed, makes you hang
on every note, and although characteristically
cool, elegant and supple, he's true to the heart of
Albéniz's incomparable tapestry of southern
Spain. Try 'Almeria' and you'll hear playing of
jewelled perfection, a mesmerising dream-
world rudely interrupted by 'Lavapiés', where
every one of the composer's torrents of notes is
made crystal clear.

Again, when has 'Málaga' been played with
greater fluency and imaginative delicacy?
Perhaps such playing is a compensation for
Rubinstein's legendary but never recorded performance. Certainly in its suppleness and transparency it has a Chopinesque rather than Lisztian bias, but Hamelin gives us all the notes and
he's recorded in sound as natural and refined as
his playing.

After *Iberia* there's *La Vega*, inspired by the
plains surrounding Granada, by a 'land of flowers and sapphire skies'. This surely ranks among
the greatest recordings of a Spanish piano work.
Limpid, haunting and evocative, it resolves
every complexity in rapt poetry. For added
measure he gives us 'Yvonne en visite', a hilarious imitation of a pianist who stumbles from
note to note, tenacious but incompetent. Finally,
there is 'Navarra', complete with William Bolcom's coda, a lengthy and witty résumé and
cadenza rather than de Sévérac's brief conclu-

sion. Comparison with Larrocha's benchmark Albéniz is inevitable. But Hamelin's is radically different in both execution and character, and she, for all her magisterial command, is no match for him in musical grace and fluency.

Hamelin's Albéniz proudly but nonchalantly raises a new and astonishing standard.

Merlin

Merlin
David Wilson-Johnson bar Merlin **Eva Marton** sop Morgan le Fay **Stuart Skelton** ten King Arthur **Carol Vaness** sop Nivian **Ángel Ódena** bar Mordred **Victor Garcia Sierra** bass King Lot of Orkney **Ángel Rodriguez** ten Gawain **Juan Tomás Martinez** bar Sir Ector de Maris **Federico Gallar** bar Sir Pellinore **Eduardo Santamaria** ten Kay **Stephen Morscheck** bass Archbishop of Canterbury **Madrid Community Children's Choir; Madrid Symphony Chorus and Orchestra / José De Eusebio** Stage director **John Dew** Video director **Toni Bargalló**
BBC/Opus Arte ② ⦾ OA0888D (184' · 16:9 · 2.0 & 5.1 · 0 · N) Recorded live at the Teatro Real, Madrid, 9 June 2003. Includes interviews with José de Eusebio, Eva Marton and David Wilson-Johnson
Ⓕ⦿

Decca's release of its outstanding recording of Albéniz's *Merlin* marked a turning-point in our appreciation of this Spanish composer, best known for his colourful nationalistic piano music. José de Eusebio, conductor and force behind that project, followed it with a full staging of the opera in Madrid; this DVD is the result.

The staging certainly adds to one's involvement. When you can see the young Arthur drawing Excalibur from the stone, the Wagnerian echoes become clearer, even if Albéniz is much more diatonic. John Dew's direction sets out the story clearly, and the stylised sets and costumes are medieval enough to create the right atmosphere, but with a touch of science fiction.

Though the cast isn't as starry as that on disc (with Plácido Domingo as King Arthur), there's obvious benefit in having English speakers in three of the principal parts, David Wilson-Johnson commanding and noble as Merlin, with the American tenor, Stuart Skelton as Arthur, powerful rather than subtle, and Carol Vaness, also American, as Nivian. The big snag is the singer who might have been counted the star, Eva Marton as the evil Morgan le Fay. The unsteadiness of her voice, so extreme that one can hardly tell what pitch she's aiming at, may convey the wickedness of the character. She acts convincingly, but is painful on the ear. Ángel Odena characterises her son Mordred well but also has bouts of unsteadiness; Victor Garcia Sierra, as King Lot of Orkney, is another wobbler.

Happily, the chorus work is first-rate, and Eusebio draws warmly committed playing from the Madrid Symphony Orchestra. With so rare an opera it's a pity that the booklet contains no synopsis, though there's compensation in having English· subtitles available, even if that underlines the banality and incomprehensibility of the doggerel verses of Francis Burdett Money-Coutts's libretto. Outweighing any flaws, though, what shines out is the richness and variety of Albéniz's musical inspiration.

Tomaso Albinoni   Italian 1671-1751

Born of wealthy parents, Albinoni was a dilettante musician, never seeking a church or court post, though he had contact with noble patrons. He concentrated on instrumental and secular vocal music and had early successes with his opera Zenobia (1694, Venice) and 12 Trio Sonatas, Op 1 (1694). His reputation grew, with operas staged in other cities, beginning with Rodrigo in Algeri (1702, Naples); later operas, such as I veri amici (1722, Munich), were staged abroad. In all he wrote over 50 operas, several other stage works and over 40 solo cantatas; few works date from after 1730.

Albinoni's instrumental works, mostly for strings, were especially popular; 10 sets were published in his lifetime. Bach based four keyboard fugues on subjects from the Op 1 sonatas. While Albinoni's concertos were less adventurous and soloistic than Vivaldi's, they were probably the earliest consistently in three movements, and his Oboe Concertos, Op 7 (1715) were the first by an Italian to be published. The sonatas (for one to six instruments with continuo) are mostly in four movements. His music is individual, with a strong melodic character and, especially in the early works, formally well balanced. **GROVE**music

Concerti a cinque, Opp 5, 7 & 9

Op 5 – No 1 in B flat **No 2** in F **No 3** in D **No 4** in G **No 5** in A minor **No 6** in A **No 7** in D minor **No 8** in F **No 9** in E minor **No 10** in A **No 11** in G minor **No 12** in C

Op 7 – No 1 in D **No 2** in C **No 3** in B flat **No 4** in G **No 5** in C **No 6** in D **No 7** in A **No 8** in D **No 9** in F **No 10** in B flat **No 11** in C **No 12** in C **Op 9 – No 1** in B flat **No 2** in D minor **No 3** in F **No 4** in A **No 5** in C **No 6** in G **No 7** in D **No 8** in G minor **No 9** in C **No 10** in F **No 11** in B flat **No 12** in D

Concerti a cinque, Op 5   Ⓟ
Collegium Musicum 90 / Simon Standage vn
Chandos Chaconne CHAN0663 (76' · DDD) Ⓕ⦿⦾➔

Albinoni might be described as a specialist in the medium of the Concerto *a cinque*, of which he composed 54, published at intervals during almost half his productive life. The first six appeared in his Op 2 (1700), together with six sonatas from which they inherited some structural features, and were followed in 1707 by the 12 of Op 5. They were 'halfway houses' on the road to the violin concerto *per se* as we know it – and as Vivaldi established it four years later.

Virtuoso passages for a solo violin appear only *en passant* in flanking movements and 'symmetrically' in the *Adagios* of Nos 3, 6, 9 and 12. Each Concerto is in three-movement form and all the finales are fugal, as they are in the Op 2, though in their simplicity they sound rather like rondos.

There was little by way of innovation in Albinoni's concertos, which leant on past examples and stressed some of their most durable features, but the lyricism of the *Adagios* of Nos 2, 5, 8 and 11 (again symmetrically placed) was indeed new. Their strength is in his gift of melodic invention, their clearly defined form and thematic material, their conciseness – a virtue that didn't survive in some of his later concertos – and their vitality and freshness. The recording and annotation are of the highest standard, and of the performances it might be said that if they're ever bettered in any respect, we and Albinoni will indeed be fortunate.

CHAN0579 – Op 7 Nos 3, 6, 9 & 12.　　　　Ⓟ
Op 9 Nos 2, 5, 8 & 11
CHAN0602 – Op 7 Nos 1, 2, 4 & 5.
Op 9 Nos 1, 3, 4 & 6. Sinfonia in G minor
CHAN0610 – Op 7 Nos 7, 8, 10 & 11.
Op 9 Nos 7, 9, 10 & 12
Anthony Robson, Catherine Latham obs
Collegium Musicum 90 / Simon Standage vn
Chandos Chaconne CHAN0579/0602/0610
(oas: 72', 63' & 65' · DDD)　　　　Ⓕ Ⓞ➜

Albinoni's Op 7 and Op 9 consist of four concertos *with* (rather than *for*, as the composer insisted) one oboe, four with two oboes and four for strings only. Overall, the last show a strong family resemblance, with vivacious outer movements and suave slow movements that tend to be more chromatic; but the Op 9 string concertos include a solo violin part, at times very elaborate. The first volume contains the works for solo oboe and strings. Albinoni treats the oboe like a voice and the slow movements have tunes that stay in the mind. The second volume contains the string and double-oboe concertos. All are three-movement *da chiesa* works, with cheerful outer movements and slow ones that often remind you that Albinoni wrote a good deal of vocal music. The two oboes 'sing' together for the most part, either in thirds or in unison. The concertos on Vol 3 for two oboes display rather more individuality – the joyous finale of Op 7 No 11 intriguingly sharpens the fourth of the scale, Op 9 No 9 allows the oboes more independence of each other, while in the outer movements of Op 9 No 12 the oboes put up a good pretence at being trumpets.

Anthony Robson and Catherine Latham contribute deftly to the spirit of enjoyment that emanates from the whole of this disc. Collegium Musicum 90 is one of the very best Baroque bands around and here the players are in their element. The recorded balance is just right, keeping soloists and strings in equal perspective.

Hugo Alfvén　　　　Swedish 1872-1960

Alfvén studied at the Stockholm Conservatory (1887-91) and privately with Lindegren, also training as a painter. Thereafter he worked as a choirmaster and Director Musices at Uppsala University (1910-39). His music is distinguished by orchestral subtlety and a painterly exploitation of harmony and timbre. It is almost all programmatic, often seeking to evoke the landscapes and seascapes of southern Sweden (eg Midsummer Vigil, 1903; Shepherd-girl's Dance, 1923). His main works include five symphonies, much choral music and songs.

GROVEmusic

Swedish Rhapsodies

Swedish Rhapsodies – No 1, Op 19, 'Midsummer Vigil'; No 2, Op 24, 'Upsala-rapsodi'; No 3, 'Dalarapsodi'. A Legend of the Skerries, Op 20. Gustav Adolf II, Op 49 – Elegy
Iceland Symphony Orchestra / Petri Sakari
Chandos CHAN9313 (70' · DDD)　　　　Ⓕ Ⓑ➜

Petri Sakari gives us the most natural, unaffected and satisfying *Midsummer Vigil* to be heard on disc. He's light in touch, responsive to each passing mood and every dynamic nuance, self-effacing and completely at the service of the composer. Moreover, in the *Upsala-rapsodi* and its later companion he's fresher and more persuasive than any of his rivals on record. Even the Wagnerian-Straussian echoes from the skerries sound convincing. The only reservation concerns the *Elegy* from the incidental music to Ludwig Nordström's play about Gustav Adolf II, which might have benefited from greater reticence. Unusually for Sakari, he doesn't tell the tale simply or let the music speak for itself. The recorded sound is refreshingly free from analytical point-making; everything is there in the right perspective, although listeners whose first response is to find the recording recessed will find that a higher level of playback than usual will produce impressively natural results on high-grade equipment.

Charles-Valentin Alkan
French 1813-1888

Alkan was a leading piano virtuoso and an unusual composer, remarkable in technique and imagination yet largely ignored by his own and succeeding generations. A child prodigy, he studied at the Paris Conservatoire. Although he held no official appointment and rarely played publicly, he was known for the brilliance of his playing, his wide repertory of earlier music and as a champion of the pedal piano (for which he composed). His complex works include extra-musical elements; he favoured obscure titles and subject matter (often with a satanic, childish or mystical tone), bold tonal structures and unusual metres. He exploited brilliantly the keyboard's resources, often making great demands of technique and stamina, and used scrupulously exact notation. Many of his some 70 opus numbers are organised in long schemes of harmonic studies, such as the 25 Préludes in all the major and minor keys, Op 31 (1847) and the 12 Etudes, Op 39 (1857); his most famous and demanding works are his Grande Sonate, Op 33, and the Concerto for Piano Solo from Op 39. He was greatly admired by Liszt and Busoni.

GROVEmusic

Sonate de concert

Alkan Sonate de concert, Op 47 **Chopin** Cello Sonata, Op 65
Alban Gerhardt vc **Steven Osborne** pf
Hyperion CDA67624 (63' · DDD)   Ⓕ Ⓞ

Alkan's Sonata has been recorded several times before, yet it has remained obstinately in the wings of the cello repertoire. This new version must surely drag it centre-stage. It is a masterpiece: meaty, melodic and, as with most of Alkan's music, extremely demanding to play – Mendelssohn with balls. The *Allegretto* second movement with its sly, pungent harmonies and the mystical, almost impressionistic slow movement especially are further proof, if it were needed, of Alkan's genius.

Chopin's Cello Sonata, his final major work and the last published in his lifetime, has never lacked champions, despite the notorious problems of balance in the first movement. Here the musical line is focused and unambiguous, though the *da capo* repeat turns what is by far the longest movement (usually about 10 minutes) into one approaching 15, making it quite disproportionate to the scale of the other three. However, it offers the chance to hear twice the heart-catching little motif at 2'42" which has rarely been played so affectingly. Both performances from this outstanding partnership are out of the top drawer, fresh, spontaneous and beautifully recorded.

Concerto for Solo Piano

Concerto for Solo Piano, Op 39 Nos 8-10.
Troisième recueil de chants – Book 3, Op 65
Marc-André Hamelin pf
Hyperion CDA67569 (68' · DDD)   Ⓕ ⦿⦿⦿

This is Marc-André Hamelin's second recording of the Alkan Concerto for Solo Piano (the first for Music & Arts dates from 1992) and he now trumps his previous ace with a performance of the Concerto of such brilliance and lucidity that one can only listen in awe and amazement. Scaling even the most ferocious hurdles with yards to spare, he is blessedly free to explore the

very heart of Alkan's bewildering interplay of austerity and monstrous elaboration. In the gigantic first movement you can hear avalanches of notes given with the rarest focus and trenchancy. And whether you turn to the finale's helter-skelter pages (with their curious Eastern underpinnings) or the baleful central *Adagio*, you can only marvel at such a unique mix of blazing if nonchalantly deployed virtuosity and poetic conviction.

For his substantial encore Hamelin gives us Alkan's *Troisième recueil de chants* where outward convention vies with that sinister and pervasive oddity so central to this composer's nature. No 3 is a near bitonal canon, No 4 a polonaise with memories of the Etudes from which the Concerto is drawn and a crazy, race-away coda, while the concluding Barcarolle contains ironic echoes of Liszt's *Au lac de Wallenstadt*.

All this is superbly recorded and presented, prompting some not unreasonable conjecture: if Liszt feared Alkan's mastery as a pianist he may well have feared Hamelin's.

Grand duo concertante, Op 21

Grand duo concertante in F sharp minor, Op 21. Sonate de concert in E, Op 47. Trio in G minor, Op 30
Trio Alkan (Kolja Lessing vn Bernhard Schwarz vc Rainer Klaas pf)
Naxos 8 555352 (75' · DDD)   Ⓢ ⮞

As this disc so persuasively reveals, there are a number of Alkan's chamber works that are long overdue for serious consideration. His violin sonata, the *Grand duo concertante*, for instance, is so thoroughly original and masterly in invention that it should have acquired for itself a prominent place in the French violin sonata repertoire. The somewhat unconventional tonal layout of the bold and memorable first movement suggests, at times, the harmonic world of Berlioz, but perhaps more strikingly looks forward, both here and in the final movement, to the melodic, Gallic charm of the Fauré sonatas.

The *Sonate de concert* for cello and piano is perhaps Alkan's finest and most important contribution to chamber music. Although clearly rooted in the classical tradition, it shouts Alkan from every page. The second movement, in *siciliano* style, is a fine example of Alkan whimsy; in the slow movement, Alkan draws musical inspiration from his Jewish faith to create a serene and somewhat mystical oasis of calm before launching into the helter-skelter activity of the finale. The earlier Piano Trio of 1841 is perhaps even more classical in design and utterance, and is certainly more terse and economical in its use of material. However, it's no easy ride for the performers. The *Scherzo* is strangely prophetic of Tchaikovsky in places and is graced with a fiendishly difficult finale. The performances are quite superb. Klaas copes admirably with all the keyboard pyrotechnics thrown at him, and Lessing and Schwarz provide performances of dedication and great under-standing. Recording is full-bodied and close.

---

48 Esquisses, Op 63

48 Esquisses, Op 63
Steven Osborne pf
Hyperion CDA67377 (75' · DDD)   Ⓕ

Here's a superlative record of music to confound the sceptics, including the soloist himself, who, in a witty, concentrated essay, expresses his surprise at discovering Alkan's *Esquisses* and their journey into intimacy rather than gargantuan bravura. Not that these 48 fragments, many of them of a teasing and enigmatic brevity, could be by any other composer. Gnomic, introspective, full of odd twists and turns of phrase and expression, they invariably catch you unawares.

In 'Confidence', a Field-like innocence is countered by enough surprises to declare the composer's identity. 'Les soupirs' is so much more than a foretaste of Debussyan impression-ism. 'Inflexibilité' holds the listener in a vice-like grip and the change from charm ('Petite marche villageoise') to grimness ('Morituri te salutant') is typical of Alkan's volatile yet rigor-ous command of the widest variety of ideas and pastiches. 'Le frisson', 'Pseudo-naïveté', 'Délire', 'Fais Dodo', 'L'homme aux sabots' – the titles predict an eccentricity that's nonethe-less qualified by a formidable intellectual focus.

Osborne's performances are of a sensitivity, radiance and finesse rarely encountered from even the finest pianists. He floats the opening of 'La vision' in a magical haze or nimbus of sound, peppers the keyboard with an immaculate virtu-osity in 'La staccatissimo', relishes the Norweg-ien tang of 'Début de quatuor' and brings a wicked *frisson* to 'Les diablotins', where Alkan's little devils are hustled from the field almost as if the composer had lost patience with his own grotesque creation.

Misha Donat's notes are as affectionate as they are perceptive, and Hyperion's sound is of demonstration quality. An invaluable disc, particularly for those drawn to music's byways.

Organ works

11 grands préludes et un transcription. Benedictus, Op 54. 12 études pour les pieds seulement – Nos 1-6
Kevin Bowyer org
Toccata Classics TOCC0030 (76' · DDD)
Played on the organ of Blackburn Cathedral   Ⓕ

This disc scores top marks in every department. Kevin Bowyer displays his customary polish, felicity and technical mastery, playing with an assurance made all the more astounding since this programme – none of it previously recorded – is hardly standard repertoire, cer-tainly outside France.

By all accounts Alkan's organ technique equalled his command of the piano. In 1834 he gained the premier prix d'orgue at the Paris Conservatoire and he maintained close friend-ships with César Franck and Lefébure-Wély, dedicatees respectively of the *Grands préludes* and the *Douze études*. The first half-dozen of the *Etudes* – played on the pedals alone – are strik-ingly original and much more than mere techni-cal exercises. Dupré considered them to be 'the complete and indispensable foundation of pedal technique'. The *Grands préludes* are equally engrossing and entertaining, especially the fiendish 10th, which Ronald Smith termed a 'Cossack Dance'. As the final notes of the tran-scription of Handel's 'Behold, and See' hover, teasingly, on a half close, succeeding volumes are eagerly awaited.

Blackburn Cathedral's magnificent Walker/Wood organ (superbly captured by sound engineer Lance Andrews) combined with Bowyer's effortless artistry and Malcolm MacDonald's masterful notes make this a must-have recommendation.

Pro organo. 12 Etudes pour les pieds seulement – Nos 7-12. 11 Pièces dans le style réligieux, et un transcription du Messie de Handel, Op 72
Kevin Bowyer org
Toccata TOCC0031 (74' · DDD)
Played on the organ of Blackburn Cathedral   Ⓕ

Pro Organo, two minutes' worth of harmless and innocent tranquillity, opens this second volume of Kevin Bowyer's Alkan cycle, but it is a false dawn. You have to wait until the final track for anything so soothing to crop up again. Every-thing else is as challenging to the listener as it must be to the performer, but luckily in Bowyer we have a performer who not only guides us through the music with the assurance of one who sees nothing out of the ordinary in Alkan's musical language but who cuts through the immense technical difficulties like a hot knife through butter.

Bowyer's breathtaking footwork in the final six of the *Etudes pour les pieds seulement* doesn't diminish the slightly circus-like melodrama of these astonishing pieces which range from the tempestuous No 7 to the dark No 11 by way of the jaunty (but, as Malcolm MacDonald's excellent booklet-notes point out, fiendishly difficult) Ninth.

The remainder of the disc is given over to all 12 pieces in Alkan's Op 72, an opus with a typi-cally unambiguously wordy title. Handel informs the first of these, majestically striding along, at once pompous and celebratory, both characteristics (as well as the vivid final echo effects) magnificently highlighted by the regal splendour of Blackburn Cathedral's matchless Walker/Wood, the cathedral's heady acoustic and a superlative recording from Toccata Clas-sics. There then follows a series of increasingly complex and demanding pieces which, were it not for the amazing intensity of Bowyer's interpretative vision and his wonderful use of organ colour, would prove insurmountably daunting to most listeners. As it is we are treated to some of the most vividly focused and technically fluent organ-playing imaginable.

It seems curious that Alkan rounded his Op 72 off with a simple transcription of the 'Pastoral Symphony' from *Messiah*. But it turns out to be a stroke of genius, restoring calm after so much, as MacDonald puts it, 'tortured and sardonic' writing.

Gregorio Allegri   Italian c1582-1652

Allegri was a singer and composer at the cathedrals of Fermo and Tivoli and later maestro di cappella of Spirito in Sassia, Rome, and a singer in the papal choir. He composed many of his works for this choir and that of S Maria in Vallicella. His reputation rests on his Miserere, a psalm-setting traditionally sung every Holy Week by the papal choir: it is basically a simple five-part chant, transformed by interpolated ornamented passages for a four-part solo choir which reaches top C (rare at that time). These passages were a closely guarded secret for many years; Mozart wrote out the work from memory when he was 14. Allegri was at his best in the a cappella style, as in his five Masses; he also published three books of more up-to-date small-scale concertato church music.   GROVEmusic

---

Miserere mei

Allegri Miserere mei (two versions). **Palestrina** Missa Papae Marcelli. Stabat mater. Tu es Petrus
The Tallis Scholars / Peter Phillips
Gimell CDGIM041 (76' · DDD · T/t)   Ⓕ **OO**

It's about 25 years since The Tallis Scholars' debut recording, which included the *Pope Marcellus* Mass and Allegri's *Miserere*; and in 1994 they issued a video (also available as a CD) of a concert in the Sistine Chapel commemorating the 400th anniversary of Palestrina's death. This third recording has far more in common with the latter interpretation than with the first, and in essentials little seems to have changed in 10 years, but the wholly ethereal approach a quarter-century ago is now changed into something more robust. That's attributable as much to the difference in the singers' timbres as to a change in Peter Phillips's view of these works.

This new recording's principal innovation is the inclusion of two different readings of the Allegri (or rather, the modern-day elaboration of it that bears his name – a distinction that Phillips's booklet-notes don't acknowledge): one sung quite 'straight', and the other with embellishments to the famous top line evolved over many years (and countless live performances) by soprano Deborah Roberts. This is the main reason for recommending the disc,

even though the ornaments to the opening verses are a little slow to get off the ground. By the end, the excitement is undeniable.

Miserere mei (two versions). Missa Vidi turbam magnam. De ore prudentis. Repleti sunt omnes. Cantate domino
A Sei Voci / Bernard Fabre-Garrus
with **Dominique Ferran** .org
Naïve E8524 (62' · DDD · T/t)   Ⓕ

Allegri's setting of the psalm *Miserere mei* is presented in two versions. The first is sung with ornamentation added by the French musicologist Jean Lionnet following 17th-century models, while the second presents the Burney-Alfieri version familiar from the classic 1963 Willcocks recording above. A Sei Voci produce a rather varied sound, which is at times somewhat flat and white but at its best is embued with an appropriate Italianate edge. For the most part the embellishments are negotiated with style and verve; just occasionally they're fuzzy or insecure. *Miserere mei* apart, hardly any of Allegri's music is heard either liturgically or in the concert hall. By training a pupil of Nanino, a distinguished follower of Palestrina, his best music is written confidently in the High Renaissance contrapuntal manner. The six-voice *Missa Vidi turbam magnam*, composed on one of his own motets, is a fine work, and shows that the *stile antico*, far from being a mere academic exercise, could still be vividly sonorous and dramatic, qualities which are brought out in this reading. The disc is nicely rounded out with a selection of short continuo motets in the popular new manner, well established in Northern Italy, which was becoming fashionable in Rome.

Allegri Miserere mei **Palestrina** Stabat mater a 8. Hodie beata virgo. Senex puerem portabat. Magnificat a 8. Litanie de Beata Virgine Maria l
Roy Goodman *treb* **King's College Choir, Cambridge / Sir David Willcocks**
Decca Legends 466 373-2DM (56' · ADD)
Recorded 1963-4   Ⓜ **OOO**▷

Ⓖ It's doubtful if any recording made by the choir of King's College, Cambridge, in the fertile Willcocks era, will prove more enduring than this celebrated performance of Allegri's *Miserere*. Admittedly there are more authentic versions in the catalogue, authentic not only in that they use the original Latin words where Willcocks opts for an English translation, but also in the sense that they search for a style less obviously redolent of choral evensong and the Anglican tradition. At the farthest extreme from King's, other versions strip Allegri's score of its various 18th- and 19th-century accretions – a nice piece of musical archaeology which, ironically, reveals the utter plainness of the *Miserere* when denied its familiar jewels, and sounds like an imposter when dressed up in even more garish baubles. For many the richly communicative singing of King's remains the ideal, however far removed it may be from the orginal intentions of Allegri. The *Miserere* is accompanied here by some classic Palestrina performances, which are still as fresh as when they were recorded in 1964. Some tape hiss intrudes, but otherwise the sound is excellent. A fabulous disc.

Eyvind Alnæs   Norwegian 1872-1932

Alnæs studied with Peter Lindeman and Iver Holter at the Christiana Music and Organ School; he later studied with Reinecke. An organist as well as conductor, he founded the Norsk Komonistforening. Among his output are numerous songs and choral works, as well as two symphonies.

Piano Concerto

Alnæs Piano Concerto, Op 27
Sinding Piano Concerto, Op 6
Piers Lane pf **Bergen Philharmonic Orchestra /**
Andrew Litton
Hyperion CDA67555 (65' · DDD)   Ⓕ ●

For the 42nd issue in its 'Romantic Piano Concerto' series, Hyperion turns for inspiration to Norway and, in a first recording of Eyvind Alnæs's Concerto, they light up the sky like an aurora borealis. Here is music very much for those in love with the most succulent romanticism, with lush, lavishly decorated melodies and a fin-de-siècle array of props. The opening *Allegro moderato* follows one sumptuous gesture with another and in the central *Lento* the pianist weaves starry figuration around the orchestra's full-blooded outcry. In the finale all fashionable gloom is cast aside for a rollicking waltz guaranteed to sweep its dancers off the floor. So for those wishing to venture beyond the Grieg or MacDowell concertos such music is heaven-sent, particularly when played by Piers Lane with such enviable poetry, fluency and aplomb.

Few pianists could have entered into the romantic spirit more infectiously, though even he is hard-pressed to make a convincing case for Sinding's less heart-warming Concerto. Here, the music remains more effortful than inspired, huffing and puffing its way through one inflated gesture after another. Yet listening to Lane in the finale is to be reminded of playing as to the romantic manner born. Andrew Litton and the Bergen Philharmonic are a perfect foil for their scintillating and indefatigable soloist, and Hyperion's sound balance is impeccable.

William Alwyn   British 1905-1985

Alwyn studied with McEwen at the Royal Academy of Music (1920-23) and later taught there (1926-

55*); in 1961 he retired to Suffolk to compose. He disowned everything he wrote before the Divertimento for flute (1939), which opened a neo-classical phase, followed in the 1950 by a personal vein of English Romanticism. His music is characterised by precise workmanship. It includes five symphonies (1949, 1953, 1956, 1959, 1973) and two string quartets, opera (Miss Julie, 1976) and songs (often to his own words: he also published poems and essays); he wrote over 60 film scores, too.*   GROVEmusic

Piano concertos

Piano Concertos[ab] – No 1; No 2. Sonata alla toccata[a]. Derby Day[b] [a]**Peter Donohoe** pf
[b]**Bournemouth Symphony Orchestra / James Judd**
Naxos 8 557590 (60' · DDD)   Ⓢ●●🅑➤

Alwyn (whose centenary year fell in 2005) is a composer of strong communicative gifts and the best of his music exhibits a disarming emotional candour, generous lyricism, powerful sense of argument and superior craftsmanship.

If not as tautly constructed as, say, the Second, Third or Fifth Symphonies, the Second Piano Concerto undoubtedly makes pleasurable listening. It was commissioned for the 1960 Proms, where its big-boned theatricality and unabashed ardour would surely have gone down a treat had the dedicatee, the Dutch virtuoso Cor de Groot, not been struck down by sudden paralysis of his right arm. As a consequence, the work remained unheard until Howard Shelley's passionate 1993 Chandos recording with Hickox and the LSO. If anything, Peter Donohoe proves an even more dashing soloist and he is supported to the hilt by James Judd and an audibly fired-up Bournemouth SO. An airy, tastefully balanced production, too. Similarly, these accomplished newcomers set out a most persuasive case for the much earlier, single-movement First Concerto, a likeable offering with echoes of Ireland and Walton, written in 1930 for Alwyn's fellow RAM graduate and good friend, Clifford Curzon.

Canny programming allows us to hear the bustling 1960 overture *Derby Day* that Alwyn fashioned as a replacement for the ill-starred Second Concerto. Judd's spry performance is in every way the equal of both its fine predecessors, and the disc concludes with the exuberant *Sonata alla toccata*. This was composed in 1945-46 for Denis Matthews and Donohoe dispatches it with purposeful aplomb and dazzling technical prowess. Yet another Naxos winner.

Piano Concerto No 2. Symphony No 5, 'Hydriotaphia'. Sinfonietta for Strings
Howard Shelley pf
London Symphony Orchestra / Richard Hickox
Chandos CHAN9196 (74' · DDD)   Ⓕ ●

Piano Concerto No 2 opens heroically and contains a good deal of rhetoric, yet the string writing has a romantic sweep and the *Andante* proves to be the highlight of the piece.

Howard Shelley plays with bravura and appealing sensitivity. The Fifth Symphony is a cogent argument distilled into one movement with four sub-sections. The energetically kaleidoscopic first section is sharply contrasted by a melancholy *Andante*. A violent *Scherzo* is followed by a curiously ambivalent finale which provides a moving and compelling, if equivocal, apotheosis. The richly expansive Sinfonietta, almost twice as long as the symphony, is very much in the English tradition of string writing. It's vigorous in the first movement and hauntingly atmospheric in the beautiful but disconsolate *Adagio*. The unpredictable finale begins impulsively before the mood changes completely and becomes altogether more subdued and muted in feeling. The obviously dedicated LSO is particularly responsive in the masterly *Sinfonietta*.

Symphonies

Symphonies – No 1; No 3
Royal Liverpool Philharmonic Orchestra / David Lloyd-Jones
Naxos 8 557648 (69' · DDD)   ⓈⒹ►

Completed in 1956 and premiered that year by Beecham, the third of William Alwyn's five symphonies won approval for its taut logic from no less an authority than Hans Keller, while John Ireland declared it the finest British symphony since Elgar's Second. The work's cogent drive registers to the full in Lloyd-Jones's thrusting conception, which clocks in at just over half an hour (the composer takes nearly 33 minutes, Hickox more than 34). At the same time, this score's lyrical ardour, giddy beauty and serene poetry are more potently conveyed on Alwyn's 1972 recording, where the combination of a less clinical acoustic (Watford Town Hall), Kenneth Wilkinson's superbly integrated balance and the LPO's richer body of string-tone makes for more involving listening.

When it comes to the the First Symphony of 1949, honours are more evenly divided. Dedicated to Barbirolli (who gave the first performance with the Hallé), this is a rather more effusive and looser-limbed statement than the Third; but its heart is always in the right place and there's plenty of red-blooded melodic appeal (the playful *Scherzo* is especially fetching). Again, Lloyd-Jones's clear-headed, muscular account shaves a couple of minutes off both his rivals' and the RLPO respond with unstinting spirit. To be honest, each of the three versions satisfies, though Hickox and the LSO sound particularly fired up (audibly revelling in the wide-screen splendour of Alwyn's sumptuous orchestration).

Overall, another eminently enjoyable disc in this useful series.

Symphonies – No 2; No 5, 'Hydriotaphia'.
Harp Concerto, 'Lyra angelica'[a]

[a]**Suzanne Willison** hp
Royal Liverpool Philharmonic Orchestra / David Lloyd-Jones
Naxos 8 557647 (70' · DDD)   ⓈⒹ►

All three works here show the composer at the height of his powers. The Second Symphony (1953) was Alwyn's own favourite of his five. Economically argued and cast in two parts, it's a stirring, heartfelt creation, full of striking invention and resplendently scored. Impressive, too, is the Fifth from 1973 (dedicated 'to the immortal memory of Sir Thomas Browne', from whose 1658 elegiac discourse *Hydriotaphia* the work derives its inspiration), a tightly organised single-movement essay of considerable emotional impact and touching sincerity. Lloyd-Jones provides a tauter, more convincingly paced view than either of the earlier recordings but the RLPO, enthusiastically though they respond, can't quite match Richard Hickox's LSO (Chandos, only available as a download) in terms of tonal sheen.

Sandwiched between the symphonies comes *Lyra angelica*, the ravishing concerto for harp and string orchestra that Alwyn penned in 1953-54. Inspired by lines from *Christ's Victorie and Triumph* (1610) by the English metaphysical poet Giles Fletcher, it's a work of unbounded lyrical beauty and leaves an indelibly rapt impression here.

The immaculate soloist, Suzanne Willison, is placed well forward in the sound picture without any undue masking of detail. In the symphonies, on the other hand, the orchestral balance is neither as effortlessly natural nor helpfully transparent as that struck by the Lyrita engineers three decades earlier – and the distant toot of a car horn breaks the spell after the *diminuendo a niente* conclusion of No 2's first half. Small niggles but not enough to withhold a solid recommendation.

Additional recommendations

Symphonies Nos 2, 3 and 5
London Philharmonic Orchestra / Alwyn
Lyrita SRCD228 (77' · ADD)   ⒻⒹ►
   A must if you've caught the Alwyn bug: three very different symphonies given superb performances.

Elizabethan Dances. Festival March. The Magic Island. Concerto for Oboe, Harp and Strings[a]. The Innumerable Dance – An English Overture. Aphrodite in Aulis
Small ob **Hudson** hp
Royal Liverpool Philharmonic Orchestra / Lloyd-Jones
Naxos 8 570144 (71' · DDD)   ⓈⒹ►
   A delightful pendant to Naxos's Alwyn series with nimble performances by the RLPO.

Film Music

The Crimson Pirate – Overture. Green Girdle – excerpts. Take my Life – Aria[a]. A Night to Remember

Alwyn Orchestral

– Main Title. Suite from The Card. Suite from Desert Victory – excerpts. Svengali – Aria: Libera mea[b.] Suite from The Winslow Boy. In Search of the Castaways – excerpts. Suite from State Secret – excerpts.
[a]**Susan Bullock** sop [b]**Canzonetta; BBC Philharmonic Orchestra / Rumon Gamba**
Chandos CHAN9959 (77' · DDD)   Ⓕ

With vintage British films of the 1940s and '50s you expected a major orchestral film score. William Alwyn, alongside Malcolm Arnold, supplied some of the finest examples. His orchestral flair and the ready lyrical flow of his themes brought much that was memorable, and Philip Lane's reconstructions from the original soundtracks continually remind us of his melodic gifts, never more effectively than in the opening pot-pourri from *The Crimson Pirate*, which is teeming with lively ideas and nautical colour. In *Take my Life* Alwyn composed a pastiche aria for the operatic heroine, and wrote yet another for *Svengali*, both powerfully sung here by Susan Bullock.

The delectably light-hearted score for *The Card* is a quite perfect, whimsical portrayal of the engagingly resourceful hero (played by Alec Guinness) of one of Arnold Bennett's most endearing lighter novels. It opens, appropriately, with a (human) whistle, but includes both a lively ball sequence and a nice touch of sentimental romantic nostalgia, exquisitely scored; the 'Coachride to Bursley' is a delightful *moto perpetuo scherzando*, and the finale is equally charming and capricious. There's a fine 'Ship's Waltz' and a rumbustious 'Rumba' for *In Search of the Castaways*, while the wartime epic *Desert Victory* opens *nobilmente*, and closes in similarly patriotic mood with a grandiloquent march. As shown by the main title for *A Night to Remember* Alwyn wasn't a purveyor of flamboyant Hollywoodian theme tunes, but his music always added much to the background atmosphere, and for the most part stands up very well on its own, especially when it's as superbly played and recorded as it is here.

Chamber music

String Quartets –
No 1; No 2, 'Spring Waters'; No 3. Novelette
Maggini Quartet (Lorraine McAslan, David Angel vns Martin Outram va Michal Kaznowski vc)
Naxos 8 570560 (69' · DDD)   ⓈⓄ↦

Between 1920 and 1936 Alwyn wrote no fewer than 13 string quartets, but it was not until 1953 that the 48-year-old composer produced what he regarded as his official No 1. A splendid achievement it is, too, as consummately crafted, organically integrated and emotionally involving as the mighty Second and Third Symphonies flanking it, and reaching genuine heights in the *Adagio* slow movement (literally so, in fact, as the first violin climbs into the stratosphere to heart-stoppingly beautiful effect).

Completed in September 1975, the Second Quartet is a much darker beast and derives its subtitle *Spring Waters* from Turgenev's eponymous novel. The composer's description of the central *Allegro scherzando* as recalling 'the lost turbulence of youth and young love, but seen "as through a glass darkly"' strikes to the heart of this gritty, uncommonly terse essay, which ends in a mood of hard-won triumph. The two-movement Third Quartet of 1984 proved to be Alwyn's swansong and if anything boasts the most idiomatically assured writing of the three. It's also a deeply moving work, with a rapt lyrical flow, clear-sighted logic and exquisite refinement of which Ravel himself would have been proud.

The *Novelette* (a winsome miniature from 1938-39) rounds off yet another absorbing anthology from the Magginis, who play with the utmost perception and have been vividly recorded.

Concerto for Flute and Eight Wind Instruments[a]. Flute Sonata[b]. Trio for Flute, Cello and Piano[c]. Naiades[d]. Divertimento[e]. French Suite[f]
Philippa Davies fl **Nash Ensemble** ([a]Gareth Hulse, [a]Katie Clemmow obs [a]Richard Hosford, [a]Marie Lloyd cls [a]Gareth Newman, [a]Robin Kennard bns [a]Richard Watkins, [a]Tim Anderson hns [e]Malin Broman vn [e]Louise Williams va [c]Paul Watkins vc [de]Lucy Wakeford hp bclan Brown pf)
Dutton Digital Epoch CDLX7176 (77' · DDD)   Ⓜ

The Dutton anthology centres around Alwyn's ouptut for flute. Indeed, it was as a flautist that the 15-year-old Alwyn gained admission to the Royal Academy of Music in 1920, later joining the ranks of the LSO (with whom he frequently performed under Elgar's baton), so it comes as no surprise that he writes with such fluency and understanding for the instrument. Of the six works here particularly appealing is *Naiades*, a pellucid, often ravishing fantasy-sonata for flute and harp composed in 1971 for Christopher Hyde-Smith and Marisa Robles. William Bennett was the lucky dedicatee of the engaging 1980 Concerto, while the distinguished French virtuoso René Le Roy premiered the resourceful (and technically demanding) *Divertimento* that Alwyn wrote for the 1941 ISCM Festival in New York.

Ten years later, Alwyn fashioned his two-movement Trio for Le Roy, pianist Jacques Février and composer-cellist Roger Albin. It's a most fetching creation, as is the compact Sonata from 1948. The *French Suite* (1937) is a graceful reworking of 18th-century airs for flute, violin, viola and harp. Needless to say, Philippa Davies performs with phenomenal control, sensitivity and panache throughout, and her colleagues in the Nash Ensemble tender immaculate support. Strongly recommended.

Rhapsody[a]. Sonata Impromptu[b]. Ballade[c]. Two Songs[d]. Three Songs[e]. Sonatina[f]. Three Winter Poems[g]. Chaconne for Tom[h]
[de]**Jeremy Huw Williams** bar

[h]**John Turner** rec [bc]**Roger Chase** va
[cf]**Andrew Ball**, [adeh]**Iain Burnside** pfs
[g]**Bridge Quartet**
([abdf]Madeleine Mitchell, Catherine Schofield vns
[a]Michael Schofield va [a]Lucy Wilding vc)
Naxos 8 570340 (72' · DDD)   Ⓢ ⮕

Having surveyed William Alwyn's orchestral output with such conspicuous success, Naxos now turns its attention to the chamber and vocal music. Just three of the eight items on this useful anthology have previously been recorded: the urgently expressive Rhapsody for piano quartet and strikingly resourceful *Sonata Impromptu* for violin and viola were completed in 1939, the latter written for (and premiered by) Frederick Grinke and Watson Forbes, while the ravishing *Three Winter Poems* for string quartet date from early in 1948 and bear a dedication to Alwyn's teacher at the RAM, Sir John McEwen (who died that same year aged 80). All are well worth getting to know and display the fastidious craft and generosity of feeling that are characteristic of their creator.

Of the music new to the catalogue, the 1939 *Ballade* for viola and piano combines full-throated ardour and wistfulness in a manner which suggests a more than passing acquaintance with Bax's powerful Viola Sonata. The 1933 Sonatina for violin and piano wears a sunnier demeanour, and we're also treated to five exquisite settings of poetry by Trevor Blakemore (1879-1953) and the composer himself (Alwyn was an accomplished flautist and painter to boot). The disc concludes with the pithy (and witty) *Chaconne for Tom* (1982), part of an 80th-birthday tribute devised by recorder player John Turner for the Lancastrian composer Thomas Pitfield (1903-99).

Performances throughout reflect great credit on all concerned in their scrupulous preparation and unquenchable conviction. Sound and balance, too, give no real cause for complaint. Alwyn's growing band of admirers needn't hold back.

Julian Anderson   British b1967

Early study with John Lambert, Alexander Goehr and Tristan Murail was supplemented by summer courses in composition by Oliver Knussen, Per Nørgard and György Ligeti. He won the Royal Philharmonic Society's Young Composer Prize in 1993 and has held composer-in-residence posts with Sinfonia 21 (1997-2000), the CBSO (2001-) and the Cleveland Orchestra (2005-07). His music is characterised by an unashamed use of melody allied to a strongly rhythmic drive. He draws on folk traditions, particularly from Eastern Europe and is also fascinated by the modality of Indian ragas. Major works include Diptych (1990), The Crazed Moon (1997), a moving memorial to a fellow composer, The Stations of the Sun (1998) and Alhambra Fantasy (2000). His Symphony of 2004 won him a British Composer Award. His work Alleluia was

premiered at the re-opening of London's Royal Festival Hall in June 2007

Alhambra Fantasy

Alhambra Fantasy[a]. Khorovod[a]. The Stations of the Sun[b]. The Crazed Moon[b]. Diptych[b]
[a]**London Sinfonietta;** [b]**BBC Symphony Orchestra /**
[ab]**Oliver Knussen**
Ondine ODE1012-2 (77' · DDD)   Ⓕ **OOO**⮕

For more than a decade British composer Julian Anderson has been consolidating his reputation as a leading talent. This first CD shows that talent at full stretch. The music is always direct in its tone of voice and unfailingly approachable without turning its back on all contact with progressive modernism. It has the benefit here of superbly prepared and executed performances, recorded with fine responsiveness to instrumental colour and textural balance.

The earliest work, *Diptych*, is already formidably accomplished in its control of gradually intensifying formal design but it is in *Khorovod*, Anderson's first London Sinfonietta commission, that his feeling for balancing resonant harmonic densities and spontaneous melodic flow comes into its own. Anderson filters his admiration for such powerful contemporary presences as Per Nørgård and Tristan Murail through aspects of folk and popular music which are most immediately evident in the rhythmic and motivic profile of the piece. The result of such conjunctions could be mindlessly disparate but Anderson's knack for dramatising unexpected compatibilities makes for an enthralling structure of genuine substance, and this kind of process is replicated on the more ambitious scale of his 1998 Proms commission *The Stations of the Sun*, as well as in a second, no less rewarding Sinfonietta piece, *Alhambra Fantasy*.

The Stations of the Sun is complemented by *The Crazed Moon*, written slightly earlier, whose much darker, dance-free character indicates that Anderson is well able to inhabit quite different emotional spheres with equal success. With this release Ondine has made an impressive start to the Anderson discography; it is high time that Anderson was given his due.

Book of Hours

Eden[a]. Imagin'd Corners[b]. Four American Choruses[c]. Symphony[d]. Book of Hours[e]
[e]**Lamberto Coccioli,** [e]**Scott Wilson** elecs
[e]**Birmingham Contemporary Music Group /**
[e]**Oliver Knussen; City of Birmingham Symphony**
[c]**Chorus and** [abd]**Orchestra /** [a]**Martyn Brabbins,**
[c]**Simon Halsey,** [bd]**Sakari Oramo**
NMC NMCD121 (80' · DDD)   Ⓕ⮕

This, the magnificent follow-up to the Ondine Julian Anderson disc (see above), contains the five works he wrote for Birmingham forces during his years as CBSO composer-in-association

(2001-5). The recordings were made at different times in different places but the strongest impression is of a group of compositions exploring closely related ideas and beliefs.

The opening of the Symphony is emblematic, evolving from attenuated noises to the trills, arabesques and fanfares of a pastoral dawn-music. You might pick up hints of Tippett's *Ritual Dances*, Nicholas Maw's *Odyssey*, even of Ravel's *Daphnis et Chloé*.

But the music never falls back on simple imitation, and while it seems to share Tippett's modern construction of Utopia – of aspiration inseparable from uncertainty and doubt – the subtle intricacy of Anderson's approach to harmony, and to the interplay between tempered and non-tempered tunings, reinforces its strongly personal, authentically contemporary quality. Similar images are powerfully projected at the end of *Book of Hours* for instrumental ensemble and live electronics, when an artless, folklike tune is challenged by much darker, denser materials, and again in the shorter orchestral works *Eden* and *Imagin'd Corners*. In all these scores the luminous yet abrasive resonance of the textures counters the risks of old-style pastoral complacency.

As John Fallas's well-informed notes point out, Anderson's is not an escapist vision of Utopia. Hope is always 'uncertain', and in the *Four American Choruses*, setting verses from Ira Sankey's evangelical hymns collection, the music seems to question as much as to endorse the simple religious sentiments of the texts.

Even if these works receive more polished performances in future years, the present recordings are all special in the imagination and excitement they convey.

Leroy Anderson
American 1908-75

He studied with Piston and Enescu (composition) at Harvard where, from 1930 to 1934, he pursued studies in German and Scandinavian languages. In the early 1930s he tutored at Radcliffe College (1930–32), directed the Harvard University Band (1931–5), and conducted and arranged music for dance bands. In 1936 he composed an arrangement of Harvard songs for the conductor of the Boston Pops, Arthur Fiedler. The growth of Pops concerts around the nation consolidated his popularity, and a 1953 study named him the American composer most frequently performed by native orchestras.
GROVEmusic

Orchestral works

'Orchestral Music, Vol 3'
Harvard Sketches. Melody on Two Notes. Mother's Whistler. The Penny-Whistle Song. The Phantom Regiment. Plink, Plank, Plunk! Promenade. Sandpaper Ballet. Sarabande. Serenata. Old MacDonald had a Farm. Sleigh Ride. Suite of Carols. The Typewriter[b]. A Trumpeter's Lullaby[a]. The

Syncopated Clock **Gershwin** (arr Anderson)
Wintergreen for President **M Willson** (arr Anderson)
Seventy-Six Trombones
[a]**Catherine Moore** *tpt* [b]**Alasdair Malloy** *typewriter*
BBC Concert Orchestra / Leonard Slatkin
Naxos American Classics 8 559357 (62' · DDD)
Ⓢ**⊙**▸

This volume has its quota of favourites – *Plink, Plank, Plunk!*, *Sandpaper Ballet*, *Sleigh Ride*, *The Typewriter* and *The Syncopated Clock* among them, though there are also several pieces never before recorded. *Mother's Whistler* especially is so immediately engaging that one can only wonder why. Though the charm of other pieces such as *Melody on Two Notes* may be less immediate, it is ultimately hardly less real.

Of the rest, *Harvard Sketches* is a successor to the *Harvard Fantasy* that first attracted Arthur Fiedler to Anderson's gifts in 1936. Like Vol 2, this also has its share of Anderson adaptations, including one of his suites of carols – this time for brass – and three straight arrangements. Perhaps "straight" is not an apt description, though, in so far as Anderson was ever one to add his own distinctive twist. In *Old MacDonald Had a Farm* he introduces some distinctly comical additional effects, while in *Seventy-Six Trombones* he cleverly highlights the debt Meredith Willson owed to the marches of Sousa.

Performances are technically and interpretatively outstanding, with utmost fidelity to the style and tempi of Anderson's own recordings. Richard S Ginell's notes add to our appreciation of a composer too readily taken for granted.

'Orchestral Music, Vol 4'
Irish Suite. Summer Skies. Scottish Suite.
Blue Tango[a]. Forgotten Dreams[a]. Belle of the Ball[ab].
Alma mater. A Christmas Festival
MacDowell To a Wild Rose (orch L Anderson)
[a]**Kim Criswell** *sop* [b]**William Dazeley** *bar*
BBC Concert Orchestra / Leonard Slatkin
Naxos American Classics 8 559381 (60' · DDD)   Ⓢ▸

'Orchestral Music, Vol 5'
Goldilocks – selection[a]. Suite of Carols (version for woodwinds)
[a]**Kim Criswell** *sop* [b]**William Dazeley** *bar*
BBC Concert Orchestra / Leonard Slatkin
Naxos American Classics 8 559382 (52' · DDD)   Ⓢ▸

On Volume 4 of this Naxos series, only the delightful *Summer Skies* falls into the familiar format of Anderson orchestral miniature. The rest constitutes arrangements, including Anderson's exquisitely wrought orchestration of MacDowell's *To a Wild Rose*. If the inclusion of vocal arrangements of *Blue Tango*, *Forgotten Dreams* and *Belle of the Ball* in a collection of orchestral works seems strange, few will object to the chance to hear Tin Pan Alley's attempts to capitalise on Anderson's successes.

The *Irish Suite* (the main item on this disc) – a clever compilation of Irish folk tunes – has already been recorded by Fiedler, Anderson himself (four movements only) and Fennell, and is done here with no less grace, charm and excitement. On the back of its success, Anderson conceived his *Scottish Suite*, but he completed only four of the planned six movements, recorded only two, and then withdrew the suite altogether. Though overall nowhere near as clever a piece as its predecessor, it's good to have the whole included here; 'Turn ye to me' is especially beautifully done.

Previous volumes in this series have included suites of carols; however, the arrangement of less devotional melodies within the Christmas overture heard here seems to me much the most attractive of such seasonal offerings.

Another of Anderson's Christmas selections (this time for woodwind) appears on Volume 5, a CD that's otherwise given over wholly to music from the only Anderson theatre score ever to reach Broadway. We have here a good proportion of *Goldilocks* (a misleading title, for the show is about a quarrelling actress and a millionaire who eventually acknowledge their love), though it's by no means as comprehensive as the original Broadway cast version. It's not made clear why – in a less than overfilled CD – the selection is so restricted. In fact, it's less a representation of the show per se than a concert suite – an ad hoc compilation of show extracts and Anderson's own concert arrangements. Thus it offers something different for those who know the show as much as for those who don't. Kim Criswell and William Dazeley do the vocal items justice, and as ever Leonard Slatkin and the BBC Concert Orchestra provide performances full of panache which are absolutely in the authentic Anderson orchestral style.

Those who have followed the series so far will find these successors no less superbly performed, recorded and annotated.

Volkmar Andreae   Swiss 1879-1962

Swiss conductor and composer. He was a pupil of Wüllner in Cologne (1897-1900). Following a one-year engagement as répétiteur at the Munich Hofoper, in 1902 he settled in Zürich where he dominated musical life for the next half-century, as a conductor, musical director and teacher; he also worked extensively abroad. He was president of the Schweizerische Tonkünstlerverein from 1920 to 1925. Like most of his output, his operas date from the early part of his career: Ratcliff op.25, after Heine's tragedy, was first staged in Duisburg (25 May 1914), and Abenteuer des Casanova op.34, a group of four one-act works to a libretto by Ferdinand Lion, in Dresden (17 June 1924). They are rooted in the Romantic tradition, with Straussian orchestration.

Piano Trios – No 1, Op 1; No 2, Op 14
Locrian Ensemble (Rita Manning vn
Justin Pearson vc Kathy Rockhill pf)

Guild GMCD7307 (65' · DDD)   Ⓕ

The Swiss musician Volkmar Andreae was répétiteur at the Munich Opera when his First Piano Trio appeared in 1901. He went on to direct the Zürich Tonhalle Orchestra for 43 years. His Second Trio arrived in 1914.

Like much music written by conductors, the works have undeservedly fallen by the wayside. Both trios open with an immediately endearing main theme and their invention throughout is consistently memorable. The influence of Brahms is strong (especially in the richly scored slow movements) but in the central *scherzando* section of the *Adagio* of No 1 there is a lighter mood that reminds one a little of the easier-going Dvořák. The attractive lilting finale, too, has similar reminders. The *Adagio* of the Second Trio, whose first movement is obviously more mature, has a profound expressive depth and its gentle ending is wonderfully serene. The third movement moves swiftly at first but its lyricism predominates in a yearning middle section; then the opening theme dances back and combines with the lyrical material. The finale gallops into action and is essentially lighthearted, but again the richly lyrical melody is at its core. Both works deserve to be in the performing repertoire.

Accomplished and warm-hearted performances by the ideally balanced Locrian Trio, and the recording is first class. If you enjoy the chamber music of Brahms and Dvořák, do try this coupling; you won't be disappointed.

George Antheil   American 1900-1959

Antheil studied privately with Sternberg and with Bloch (1920) before moving to Berlin in 1922 to make his name as a modernist. Jazz, noise and ostinato were the means, worked into brutally simple designs in the Airplane Sonata (1922) and Sonata sauvage (1923), written after his move from Berlin to Paris. There he wrote the Ballet mécanique (1925) for an ensemble of pianos and percussion including electric bells and propellers. In 1926 he turned to neo-classicism, then to opera: Transatlantic (1930, Frankfurt) was a satire on American political life. In 1936 he settled in Los Angeles, where he wrote symphonies, operas vocal, chamber and piano music along more conventional lines. GROVEmusic

Symphonies

Symphonies – No 1, 'Zingareska'; No 6,
'after Delacroix'. Archipelago
Frankfurt Radio Symphony Orchestra / Hugh Wolff
CPO CPO999 604-2 (63' · DDD)   ⒻⒺ

In 1923 Antheil gave a piano recital of his own music at the Théâtre des Champs-Elysées in Paris which created the kind of sensation not seen since *The Rite of Spring* 10 years earlier.

Erik Satie was there and applauded vigorously, refusing to be deterred by Milhaud. You can see why. His Symphony No 1, *Zingareska* (*Gypsy Song*), comes from the same year as that spectacular piano recital and Antheil was uncertain about it. The gypsy element perhaps covers his own unsettled existence between the USA, Berlin and Paris, but it also symbolises his own kind of style-modulation long before he could have heard anything by Ives. We're now starting to enjoy Antheil's bare-faced kleptomania on its terms. Indeed, there are some lovely things in this young man's music, often beautifully scored and hovering hazardously between *Petrushka* and *Parade*; you never quite know what's going to happen next. In spite of his bravado Antheil had soul – take the delicious opening of the *Doloroso* third movement with celesta background to the oboe or the melodies over ostinato patterns in the middle of the final ragtime – the one which starts at 1'26" gets so close to the first of Stravinsky's *Five Easy Pieces* for piano duet as to be actionable.

It's a pity that Symphony No 6 (partly based on Delacroix's picture *Liberty leading the people*) duplicates the National Symphony Orchestra of the Ukraine under Kuchar on Naxos, since both are strong performances of this substantial piece from 1948. Antheil pays another debt to Satie since the *Larghetto* is a slow *Gymnopédie*, an oasis of calm between patriotic war music. The riotous *Archipelago*, subtitled 'Rhumba', is in the tradition of Gottschalk but, via Gershwin's *Cuban Overture*, is pure 1930s and ends a most impressive and enjoyable case for orchestral Antheil from three different decades.

Symphony No 3 'American'. McKonkey's Ferry.
Capital of the World – Suite. Tom Sawyer. Hot-Time
Dance
Frankfurt Radio Symphony Orchestra /
Hugh Wolff
CPO 777 040-2 (61' · DDD)   Ⓕ

George Antheil is doing well on disc and he is lucky here to have a conductor of the calibre of Hugh Wolff taking up his cause and reviving a Frankfurt connection going back to the premiere of *Transatlantic*, the opera acclaimed there in 1930 but not seen in his native US for another 50 years.

Antheil was hesitant about his Third Symphony, written during the 1930s when he was returning from a decade spent mostly in Europe and exploring his own country. He broke off to write film scores and fulfil other commitments so it was picked up and put down, then revised in 1945. In its first recording, the Third is more successful than commentators have suggested, but as attractive tableaux rather than a symphonic entity. Antheil wanted to write American music and the breezy syncopations of the third movement show common ground with Copland, who in 1926 regarded Antheil as having 'the greatest gift of any young American now writing'.

If the Third Symphony is transitional, Antheil was very much in his stride during the 1940s. The short overture *Tom Sawyer* is an endearing evocation of Mark Twain's hero, and *Hot-Time Dance*, premiered at the Boston Pops in 1949, is characteristically swaggering and irrepressible – Antheil's orchestration can stand up with the most blatant Shostakovich; either would be a smash-hit encore. *Capital of the World*, a ballet based on Hemingway's short story, was premiered on television then staged at the Met in 1953. This is the suite, a suave and polished example of Antheil's late style. Wolff once again makes the most of everything.

Symphonies – No 4, '1942'; No 5, 'Joyous'.
Decatur at Algiers
Frankfurt Radio Symphony Orchestra /
Hugh Wolff
CPO CPO999 706-2. (63' · DDD)   Ⓕ

Symphony No 4, written in the worst years of the war, gets an ebullient performance which has the edge over the Ukrainians since the recorded sound is richer. The music employs juxtapositions, exactly like cinematic cuts, that have little to do with symphonic development and are less dominated by Stravinsky than some of Antheil's earlier works. The tunes are memorable. The novelty here is *Decatur at Algiers*, called a nocturne although it's based on Stephen Decatur conquering the Barbary pirates in the early 1800s. There's an attractive Arabic flavour about the spooky principal theme on the oboe. This release also brings the Fifth Symphony – first recorded by the Vienna Philharmonia under Herbert Haefner in 1952 – back into the catalogue. This is a war symphony too. Antheil lost his brother in the conflict and dedicated the symphony to 'the young dead of all countries who sacrificed everything'.

The first movement is continuously bustling in an idiom which crosses Stravinsky with jazz: it works. The *Adagio molto* is an elegiac siciliano, and the finale is a pot-pourri which raises constant echoes – that's how musical kleptomania operates. Almost at the start Antheil recalls the opening of Shostakovich's Fifth in homage to America's wartime ally. These are fine performances, well recorded too – another impressive case for later Antheil on his own terms.

Ballet mécanique

Ballet mécanique (rev 1953). Serenade for Strings
No 1. Symphony for Five Instruments.
Concert for Chamber Orchestra
Philadelphia Virtuosi Chamber Orchestra /
Daniel Spalding
Naxos 8 559060 (61' · DDD)   ⓈⒹ⇨

Although *Ballet mécanique* is the inevitable selling point here, the 1953 revision eschews many of the sonic and rhythmic excesses that give the work its infamy and, to be honest, its musical appeal. Spalding secures a zestful performance from the Philadelphia Virtuosi, less frenetic than the Ensemble Modern, with the interlocking ostinatos of pianos and percussion readily invoking *Les noces* in sound if not substance. The other works give a good overview of Antheil's changing idiom over the greater part of his career. From 1948, the First Serenade might seem a continuation of his inter-war neo-classicism, yet the chromatic unease that permeates the brusque outer movements, and the plaintive solos and chill *sul ponticelli* of the *Andante* intimate deeper emotions. The Symphony of 1923 offers a statement of stylistic intent to rival Stravinsky's Octet, though the astringent polytonal writing is more akin to Milhaud's Chamber Symphonies. Nine years on, and the *Concert* finds the eclipsed composer pursuing understated yet intriguing directions. The succession of mini-ensembles, linked by a varied *ritornello* for the whole group, may have its basis in Stravinsky's *Symphonies of Wind Instruments*, but Antheil's piece is formally open-ended and emotionally anything but cathartic. Characterful and well-prepared performances, cleanly recorded, and informative notes.

Anton Arensky   Russian 1861-1906

After study in St Petersburg with Rimsky-Korskov, Arensky, a pianist as well as a composer, became professor of harmony at the Moscow Conservatoire where his pupils included Rachmaninov, Scriabin and Glière. His musical influences were highly eclectic and his output included three operas, two symphonies and a number of concertos, as well as choral and chamber music. GROVEmusic

Violin Concerto

Arensky Violin Concerto, Op 54 **Taneyev** Suite de concert, Op 28
Ilya Gringolts vn **BBC Scottish Symphony Orchestra / Ilan Volkov**
Hyperion CDA67642 (60' · DDD) Ⓕ

Arensky's Concerto is a continuous, four-in-one, 20-minute movement, Mendelssohnian in style, elegantly turned at every stage, and with a relatively undemanding solo part that would be perfect for students looking for something other than Bruch to limber up on. Taneyev's Suite is far more ambitious, not to say hybrid in form, encompassing a neo-Baroque Prelude and Gavotte, a Schumannesque 'folktale', a Theme with seven variations and coda, and a final Tarantella, all in a 40-minute structure that needs a soloist of outstanding technical command and expressive range.

Ilya Gringolts is fine advocate for both works, combining brilliance and idiomatic sensitivity, and enjoying fine support from Volkov and the

BBC Scottish. In short, another superbly conceived and truthfully recorded addition to Hyperion's 'Romantic Violin Concerto' series.

Thomas Arne   British 1710-1778

Arne, the son of an upholsterer, was probably encouraged in his musical career by his violin teacher Michael Festing. In 1732-33 he and his sister Susanna (later Mrs Cibber) were associated with musicians who aimed to establish an Italian-style English opera. After the success of his masque Dido and Aeneas (1734), Arne was engaged at Drury Lane Theatre, where he was to produce his works until 1775. In 1737 he married the singer Cecilia Young, who appeared in his next production, Comus (1738); influenced by Handel's Acis and Galatea, it was his most individual and successful work. Also popular was the masque Alfred (1740) (including 'Rule, Britannia'). While in Dublin in 1742-44 Arne produced his oratorio The Death of Abel (1744) and music by Handel. His dialogue Colin and Phoebe established him as a leading composer at the London pleasure gardens; during the next 20 years he published annual song collections. Among his next major works were a miniature English opera buffa, Thomas and Sally (1760), the oratorio Judith (1761) and an English opera seria to a Metastasio libretto, Artaxerxes (1762), the first and only such work to achieve lasting fame. After his masque The Arcadian Nuptials (1764) Arne's career declined; L'Olimpiade (1765; now lost), his only Italian opera, was a failure. But his last years saw the production of many of his best works, notably Shakespeare Ode (1769), the masque The Fairy Prince (1771) and the afterpiece May-day (1775); he also wrote catches and glees for concerts at Ranelagh House. One of the most significant English composers of his century, Arne wrote over 80 stage works and contributed to some 20 others. His essentially lyrical genius is obvious also in his instrumental music. GROVEmusic

Eight Overtures

Eight Overtures in 8 Parts. Alfred – Overture.   Ⓟ
Thomas and Sally – Overture
Collegium Musicum 90 / Simon Standage vn
Chandos Chaconne CHAN0722 (70' · DDD)   ⒻⓄ

Collegium Musicum 90 rarely get the adulation they deserve. This anthology of overtures by Arne, featuring a who's who of the English period-instrument scene, is a charming disc of beautifully played and brightly executed performances. Simon Standage nurtures affectionate interpretations and his violin-playing still perpetuates the impeccable stylishness and musical taste that made his pioneering recordings with Pinnock and Hogwood so enduring.

The Overture to the English comic opera *Thomas and Sally* (1760) gets things off to a splendid start; its Scotch gavotte features masterful, witty playing from bassoonist Sally Jackson. The bulk of the disc is devoted to 'Eight Overtures in 8 Parts' that Arne published in 1751. Peter Holman's informative booklet-notes say these overtures were probably extracted from introductions to vocal works, many of which are now lost. Among the finest moments are the vivacious opening *Presto* of Overture No 3 and the invigorated horn blasts and chuckling oboes in the middle movement of No 4. Trumpeters Crispian Steele-Perkins and David Blackadder provide grandeur in the bright Overture to Arne's setting of Milton's *Comus* (No 7). Although those devoted to pleading Arne's cause would love to hear a recording of such fine quality of *Comus*, or the oratorio *Judith*, this collection is comfortably among the strongest advocacies of Arne's merits on CD.

Artaxerxes

Artaxerxes   P
Christopher Robson *counterten* Artaxerxes
Ian Partridge *ten* Artabanes **Patricia Spence** *mez* Arbaces **Richard Edgar-Wilson** *ten* Rimenes
Catherine Bott *sop* Mandane **Philippa Hyde** *sop* Semira **The Parley of Instruments / Roy Goodman**
Hyperion CDA67051/2 (140' · DDD· T/N)   F O B

This is a work of great historical importance and musically fascinating. Arne, the leading English composer of his time for the theatre, wanted to write serious as well as comic English operas, and decided that Italian *opera seria* should serve, on the literary side, as his model; he chose the most famous of all the Metastasio librettos, *Artaserse*, as the basis for his first (and last) attempt at the genre. It's generally supposed that the translation was his own work. He performed the opera at Covent Garden in 1762 with considerable success, and it remained a favourite for many years. He never followed up that success, and nor, regrettably, did anyone else. English vocal music of this period has quite a distinctive manner, being tuneful, rather short-breathed, often with a faintly 'folky' flavour. It doesn't naturally reflect the exalted emotional manner of an *opera seria* text. Nevertheless, the music is enormously enjoyable, full of good melodies, richly orchestrated, never (unlike Italian operas of the time) long-winded. Several of its numbers became popular favourites in Arne's time, and for long after.

Much of the best and most deeply felt music goes to Arbaces, very finely and expressively sung by Patricia Spence. She uses more vibrato than anyone else in the cast but her warmth of tone and expressive power are ample justification. Mandane, Arbaces's beloved, composed for Arne's mistress Charlotte Brent, is another rewarding part and is finely sung here by Catherine Bott, who can encompass both the charming English ditties and the more Italianate virtuoso pieces. Christopher Robson makes an excellent Artaxerxes, although this castrato part is bound to be testing for a countertenor and he's often covered by the orchestra. Arne's

orchestral style here is very rich, with much prominent wind writing; sometimes the singers don't ride the full textures very comfortably. Roy Goodman's accompaniments aren't generally very subtle. The original score doesn't survive complete, a victim (like so many) of the frequent theatre fires of the time; Peter Holman has done an unobtrusive and stylish job of reconstructing some of the lost recitatives. This recording is recommended warmly to anyone curious about this byway of 18th-century opera, and to anyone drawn to Arne's very appealing melodic style.

Richard Arnell   British b1917

English composer and conductor. He studied at the RCM (1936–9) with Ireland (composition) and Dykes Bower (piano), winning the Farrar composition prize in 1938. He was music consultant to the North American service of the BBC (1939–45). In 1948 he became a professor of composition at Trinity College of Music. He made extended visits to the USA as a Fulbright Visiting Lecturer (1967-70). Arnell's music has an immediately recognizable style. As a composer, he is known mainly for his instrumental music, including six symphonies: but he has also written distinctive stage and film music. Ireland's influence is largely absent from Arnell's music, except for an occasional burgeoning Romanticism, as in the Third String Quartet's second movement.   GROVEmusic

Symphonies

Symphonies – No 1, Op 31; No 6, 'The Anvil', Op 171. Sinfonia quasi variazioni, Op 13
Royal Scottish National Orchestra / Martin Yates
Dutton Epoch CDLX7217 (58' · DDD)   M

Dutton's revelatory cycle of Richard Arnell's symphonies reaches a fitting culmination with this highly stimulating anthology. It's launched in arresting fashion by the *Sinfonia quasi variazioni* of 1941, an economical and inventive canvas of considerable dramatic and emotional scope premiered by Beecham in March of the following year.

By contrast, the First (1943) of Arnell's six numbered symphonies wears an altogether more restrained, urbane and finely chiselled demeanour. This, too, dates from Arnell's prolific New York sojourn, and both Beecham and Bernard Herrmann were early exponents of a work which Arnell initially designated as a 'Chamber Symphony' on the manuscript but which is surely rather more deserving of the epithet 'Classical Symphony'.

Over half a century separates it and the completion of the Sixth Symphony (1992-94). Lasting just under 14 minutes, this is an enigmatic, often uncompromisingly gritty statement, with something of the bare-faced agitation and autobiographical resonance of Malcolm Arnold's symphonic output. Its four parts run without a break and there are key roles for anvil (best heed the warning on the rear sleeve about replay levels!) and piano.

As on previous volumes, Martin Yates's clearheaded interpretations fairly crackle with conviction, and the Dutton microphones capture the RSNO's spirited and eloquent contribution to extremely vivid, if occasionally raw effect.

Symphonies – No 4, Op 52; No 5, Op 77
Royal Scottish National Orchestra / Martin Yates
Dutton Epoch CDLX7194 (64' · DDD)   Ⓜ

Written in London between 1955 and 1957 and revised seven years later, Richard Arnell's Fifth Symphony is an enormously sincere, patiently argued statement, full of rhetorical grandeur and unapologetically epic in countenance. Its centrepiece comprises a memorable conflation of slow movement and scherzo which is flanked in turn by two imposing *Andante*s, the second of which builds impressively to a jubilant peroration. One could easily imagine the piece going down a treat at the Proms, where it would make a refreshing alternative to, say, a Mahler or Shostakovich symphony.

The Fourth is more concise and no less involving. Begun in New York in the spring of 1948 and finished in London that July, it was premiered in a BBC studio broadcast under Charles Groves and soon taken up by dedicatee Leon Barzin, Barbirolli and Beecham. Its subsequent, almost wholesale neglect is hard to fathom, such is the communicative fervour of those arching lyrical lines in the eloquent central *Andante con moto* in particular. Nor is there an ounce of flab in the substantial first movement or enviably terse finale.

As in the Fifth, Yates and a fired-up RSNO give their all, and the sound is immensely full-blooded to boot, though the comparatively unflattering acoustic of Glasgow's Henry Wood Hall imparts a touch of steeliness when the decibels rise. No matter; if you enjoyed Naxos's recent Alwyn cycle, chances are you'll feel right at home here too.

Sir Malcolm Arnold   British 1921-2006

Arnold studied with Jacob at the Royal College of Music, London, and in 1941 joined the LPO as a trumpeter, leaving in 1948 to devote himself to composition. His most important works are orchestral (nine symphonies, 1951-82; numerous light and serious pieces). His language is diatonic, owing something to Walton and Sibelius, and the scoring is dramatically brilliant, Berlioz being his acknowledged model. A fluent, versatile composer, he has written scores for nearly 100 films. Perhaps because of his long involvement in films, Arnold never wrote a full-length opera. He claimed never to have found the ideal subject or librettist. By all accounts, though,

despite his lack of formal education, he was exceptionally well-read, and it is possible that far from being insensitive to words he was if anything over-responsive.   **GROVE**music

---

Concertos

Arnold Clarinet Concerto No 2, Op 115 **Copland** Concerto for Clarinet and String Orchestra with Harp and Piano **Hindemith** Clarinet Concerto
Martin Fröst *cl* **Malmö Symphony Orchestra / Lan Shui**
BIS CD893 (57' · DDD)   Ⓕ❶❶➔

All three of these concertos were written for Benny Goodman but, not surprisingly, it's the Arnold work which most fully exploits his dedicatee's jazz background. The first movement is a typical Arnoldian *scherzando*, with an irrepressible *Tam O'Shanter/Beckus the Dandipratt* audacity. Fröst and Lan Shui clearly relish its verve and energy, and then bring a seductive richness to the main theme of the slow movement. Yet they don't miss the plangent emotional ambivalence later, for there are characteristic moments of Arnold-like darkness here too. The outrageous showstopper finale, with its rooty-tooty clarinet tune and orchestral whoops, also has a surprise up its sleeve in its sudden lyrical interlude; but one and all let their hair down for the boisterous reprise.

At the haunting opening of the Copland concerto, Martin Fröst's clarinet steals in magically on a half-tone. Lan Shui's sympathetic and flexible support contributes to a memorable performance of Copland's masterly first movement, with the coda gently fading into the cadenza. The Hindemith concerto which follows produces a characteristic sinewy lyricism in the first of its four movements, with some nicely touched-in brass and woodwind comments. Again Fröst cajoles the ear with his pliable line and the effect is unexpectedly mellow. With extremely fine recording and marvellous solo playing, this triptych will be hard to surpass.

Concerto for Piano Duet and Strings, Op 32ª.
Concerto for Two Pianos, Three Hands, and Orchestra, Op 104ª. Beckus the Dandipratt, Op 5.
Fantasy on a Theme of John Field, Op 116
ª**Phillip Dyson**, ª**Kevin Sargent** *pfs*
Ulster Orchestra / Esa Heikkilä
Naxos 8 570531 (67' · DDD)   Ⓢ➔

The three major *concertante* works here reflect in a moving way the strange contradictions in Arnold's character, the mixture of lyrical warmth, popular inspiration and, in complete contrast, the darkness of Arnold's deeply depressive side, which at times had him consigned to psychiatric hospitals.

The longest work is the *Fantasy on a Theme of John Field*, the theme being one of the Nocturnes, a favourite work with Arnold's mother. Field, like Arnold, was alcoholic and depressive, and that made him a sympathetic figure to

Arnold when the composer was living in Dublin. In effect, it is a set of variations which for the most part are dark but which end with a lyrical Rachmaninov-like passage.

The Concerto for Piano Duet and Strings dates from 1951, a time of frenetic activity which in a very short while produced a whole sequence of works including several film scores but which also resulted in distressing treatment for his depression. The work brings busy and brilliant passagework for the soloists in the first movement, a still and intense passacaglia slow movement and a relentlessly high-spirited finale.

The Concerto for Two Pianos was written for Cyril Smith and Phyllis Sellick after Smith lost the use of his left hand, and represents Arnold's lighter side, notably in the big tune of the central slow movement, first cousin to the great surging second subject theme in the Fifth Symphony. The work ends with a delightful rumba full of cross-rhythms.

The overture *Beckus the Dandipratt* is an exuberant comedy overture, with particularly brilliant writing for the brass – Arnold at the time was first trumpet in the LPO.
Phillip Dyson and Kevin Sargent are brilliant and alert piano soloists, with the young Finnish conductor Esa Heikkilä drawing dazzling playing from the Ulster Orchestra, vividly recorded.

Symphonies

Symphonies – No 1, Op 22; No 2, Op 40
London Symphony Orchestra / Richard Hickox
Chandos CHAN9335 (61' · DDD)   Ⓕ**O▷**

Here's an entirely appropriate coupling of the first two symphonies, superbly played by the LSO and given demonstration sound in what's surely an ideal acoustic for this music, with striking depth and amplitude and a wholly natural brilliance. The dynamic range is wide but the moments of spectacle – and there are quite a few – bring no discomfort. Richard Hickox shows himself to be thoroughly at home in both symphonies and the readings have a natural flow and urgency, with the two slow movements bringing haunting, atmospheric feeling.

The three-movement First Symphony opens with thrusting confidence on strings and horns, and at its climax, where the strings soar against angry brass ostinatos, the playing generates great intensity; then at the start of the slow movement the purity of the flute solo brings a calm serenity, which returns at the close. The plangent lyrical melancholia of the expansive march theme of the finale is filled out by some superb horn playing, which is enormously compelling. The first movement of Symphony No 2 brings a most winning clarinet solo (Arnold's fund of melodic ideas seems to be inexhaustible). There's an energetic, bustling *Scherzo* to follow, but again it's the slow movement that you remember, for its elegiac opening, its arresting climax and its lovely epilogue-like close. Above all, these are real performances without any of the inhibitions of 'studio' recording.

Symphonies – No 3, Op 63; No 4, Op 71
National Symphony Orchestra of Ireland / Andrew Penny
Naxos 8 553739 (69' · DDD)   Ⓢ**O▷**

These recordings of two of Arnold's finest symphonies carry the composer's imprimatur (he attended the sessions). Penny is clearly right inside every bar, and the orchestra play with impressive ensemble and feeling, and above all great freshness and spontaneity.

The Naxos recording's concert-hall ambience has been beautifully caught. One of the finest players in Dublin is the principal oboe, whose solos often bring a specially plangent quality, particularly in the slow movement of No 3, where there's a real sense of desolation. The finale then lightens the mood with its kaleidoscope of wind and brass and a wispy string melody that soon becomes more fulsome. Penny's momentum and characterisation here are superb, as is the orchestral response. Similarly the winningly scored opening of the Fourth Symphony flashes with colour: that marvellous tune (2'44") is played with captivating delicacy by the violins. The exquisitely fragile *Scherzo* is etched with gossamer lightness and the slow movement is shaped by Penny with fine lyrical feeling and the most subtle use of light and shade. Its romanticism is heart-warming, yet is also balanced by Arnold's underlying unease. The boisterous fugal finale has some of the best playing of all.

Symphonies – No 5, Op 74; No 6, Op 95
London Symphony Orchestra / Richard Hickox
Chandos CHAN9385 (58' · DDD)   Ⓕ**O▷**

Arnold's Fifth is one of his most accessible and rewarding works. The inspiration for the work was the early deaths of several of Arnold's friends and colleagues: Dennis Brain, Frederick Thurston, David Paltenghi and Gerard Hoffnung. They are all remembered in the first movement and Hoffnung's spirit pops up in the third and fourth. The Chandos recording is richly resonant and reinforces the impression that in Hickox's hands the *Andante* has an added degree of acceptance in its elegiac close, while the last two movements are colourfully expansive. The Sixth Symphony is nothing like as comfortable as the Fifth, with a bleak unease in the unrelenting energy of the first movement, which becomes even more discomfiting in the desolate start to the *Lento*. This leads to a forlorn suggestion of a funeral march, which then ironically quickens in pace but is suddenly cut down; the drum strokes become menacingly powerful and the despairing mood of the movement's opening returns. Hickox handles this quite superbly and grips the listener in the music's pessimism, which then lifts completely with the energetic syncopated trumpet theme of the rondo finale. Although later there are moments of ambiguity, and dissonant reminders of the earlier music, these are eclipsed by the thrilling life-asserting coda.

Symphonies – No 7, Op 113; No 8, Op 124;
No 9, Op 128. Oboe Concerto, Op 39ᵃ
ᵃ**Jennifer Galloway** ob
BBC Philharmonic Orchestra / Rumon Gamba
Chandos ② CHAN9967 (116' · DDD)   Ⓜ🅑➤

In No 7 Gamba takes a more urgent approach
than does Andrew Penny in his account for
Naxos. With weightier orchestral sound,
helped by a full, atmospheric Chandos recording, Gamba is even more compelling, though
in that first movement the ragtime march
halfway through loses some of its grotesquerie
at a faster speed. At a more flowing speed in
the slow movement Gamba is warmer than
Penny, less chilly. One consistent advantage
of Gamba's faster speeds is that the extra challenge to the orchestra brings out an element
of daring, almost always an advantage in writing that's surreal in its sharp juxtapositions of
ideas and mood, with Mahlerian references to
popular music. That's specially true of the
Giubiloso third movement of No 9. Penny and
his Irish players by comparison seem almost
too well-behaved, though the transparency of
the sound lets you hear the heaviest textures
clearly.

The final Mahlerian slow movement of the
Ninth is also warmer, weightier and more measured with Gamba than with Penny, though both
sustain the slow, spare writing superbly, with
Gamba bringing an extra velvety warmth to the
final movements of consolation. The Oboe
Concerto makes a welcome supplement on that
second disc, with Gamba and his excellent soloist, Jennifer Galloway, bringing out the wit and
biting jauntiness of earlier Arnold.

Additional recommendations

Symphonies Nos 5 and 6
National Symphony Orchestra of Ireland / Penny
Naxos 8 552000 (57' · DDD)   Ⓢ🅑➤
A good bargain alternative worth considering.

Overtures

Anniversary Overture. Beckus the Dandipratt. The
Fair Field. A Flourish for Orchestra. A Grand, Grand
Festival Overture. Peterloo. Robert Kett. The Smoke.
A Sussex Overture. Tam O'Shanter
BBC Philharmonic Orchestra / Rumon Gamba
Chandos CHAN10293 (76' · DDD)   Ⓕ🅞

Arnold's genius was particularly suited to
smallscale orchestral works, and every one of
these examples shows his orchestral personality
at its exuberant best. *Beckus the Dandipratt* came
first, in 1943, a portrait which has the wit of
Strauss's *Till* and the harum-scarum quality of
Walton's *Scapino*. *Tam O'Shanter*, a brilliantly
droll portrayal drawing on the Burns poem, has
a spectacular climax bringing an orchestral
realisation of bagpipes. The *Grand, Grand Festival Overture*, written for a 1956 Gerard Hoff-

nung festival, is remembered for including
parts for four vacuum cleaners and the floor
polisher. But this piece isn't just about high
spirits; it has a really good tune, too. There's
another memorable tune in the vivid *Peterloo*,
which is more of a Lisztian tone-poem.

The brief *Anniversary Overture* was for a
Hong Kong fireworks spectacular, while
The Smoke brings a sultry atmosphere in its
middle section.

The Fair Field celebrates the Croydon Concert Hall (with its superb acoustics), *A Sussex
Overture* is jauntily characteristic, while the
Orchestral Flourish, not surprisingly, brings
resplendent brass. The lively *Robert Kett* Overture is a recording premiere. The Chandos
recording is of the demonstration class.

Dances

English Dances – Set 1, Op 27; Set 2, Op 33.
Four Scottish Dances, Op 59. Four Cornish
Dances, Op 91. Four Irish Dances, Op 126.
Four Welsh Dances, Op 138
**Queensland Symphony Orchestra /
Andrew Penny**
Naxos 8 553526 (55' · DDD)   Ⓢ🅞➤

This set includes the *Four Welsh Dances*,
not otherwise available on CD. These were the
last to be written, and their mood follows on
naturally from the ambivalence of the *Irish
Dances*. Penny's tempos are very like Arnold's
own in his superb set made with the LPO for
Lyrita. Where there's a difference, Penny
is slightly faster, but the effect is marginal.
The greater character of the LPO under
Arnold shows in the very first of the *English
Dances*, notably at the reprise, which is more
warmly positive.

The Queensland Hall is reverberant, and
detail is generally less well focused than on the
Lyrita disc; yet so vivid is Arnold's scoring that
not much is missed. The lovely *Mesto* third
English Dance is beautifully done in Queensland, and in the second set of *English Dances*,
the *Con brio* and *Giubiloso* have all the necessary
colour and flair. The Australian orchestra has
obviously warmed up for the Scottish set and
the inebriated Glaswegian is nicely observed.
For some the lyrical third *Scottish Dance* is one
of the most beautiful and memorable of all
Arnold's many fine tunes.

Penny treats it gently; his coda is particularly
delicate, but at its appearance on the full
strings the composer is that little bit more
romantic. However, Penny's closing dance,
a Highland fling, is superb in its drunken
abandon.

In the opening *Cornish Dance* that follows,
Penny captures the mysterious evocation of
deserted copper mines well, and in the *Irish
Dances*, written some 20 years later, he captures the fragile mood of the central *Commodo*
and *Piacevole* tenderly. This is altogether an
excellent and inexpensive collection.

Ballet music

Homage to the Queen, Op 42a – Ballet Suite
Rinaldo and Armida, Op 49. Little Suite No 2, Op 78.
Organ Concerto, Op 47[a]
[a]**Ulrik Spang-Hanssen** *org* **Royal Aarhus Academy
of Music Symphony Orchestra / Douglas Bostock**
Classico CLASSCD424 (65' · DDD)   Ⓕ

No fewer than three first recordings adorn this
set, in which some of Denmark's finest young
musicians lend spirited advocacy to three
appealing Arnold scores from the 1950s.

Bostock's first recording of the 20-minute
concert suite from the 1953 Coronation-ballet
Homage to the Queen is all the more welcome
given that Robert Irving's superbly stylish 1954
Philharmonia recording of the complete work is
now deleted. Hailed by Dame Ninette de Valois
as 'the finest ballet composer since Tchaikovsky', Arnold penned a further three scores for
the Royal Ballet. First staged in 1955 and choreographed (like *Homage to the Queen*) by Frederick Ashton, *Rinaldo and Armida* packs a wealth
of colourful and touching invention into its
tight-knit 22-minute span. Elsewhere, Ulrik
Spang-Hanssen is a nimble soloist in the Organ
Concerto written in 1954 for Denis Vaughan
(the central *Lento* casts quite a spell), and we
also get the bright-eyed, impeccably crafted
Little Suite No 2 that Arnold fashioned for the
1963 Farnham Festival.

Nicely prepared, committed performances one
and all; reasonably vivid sound. Sir Malcolm's
many fans will love this enterprising collection.

Film Music

Trapeze – Suite. No Love for Johnnie – Suite. David
Copperfield – Suite. Stolen Face – Ballade or Piano and
Orchestra[b]. The Belles of St Trinian's – Comedy Suite[c].
The Captain's Paradise – Postcard from the Med (all
arr Lane). You Know What Sailors Are – Scherzetto[a].
The Holly and The Ivy – Fantasy on Christmas Carols
(both arr Palmer). The Roots of Heaven – Overture.
Symphonic Study, 'Machines', Op 30
[a]**John Bradbury** *cl* [b]**Phillip Dyson,** [c]**Paul Janes** *pfs*
BBC Philharmonic Orchestra / Rumon Gamba
Chandos CHAN9851 (79' · DDD)   Ⓕ**OOᗕ**

Almost all the film music here comes from the
1950s, when memorable ideas were pouring out
of Arnold, and his unique orchestral palette was
already glowing luminously.

The suite arranged by Philip Lane from
Trapeze is quite outstanding in the quality of
its invention, including a swinging tune for
the horns in the Prelude, an engaging blues for
saxophone and guitar to follow, an ebullient
circus march, and a deliciously lugubrious 'Elephant waltz' for tuba duet, while the closing
sequence opens hauntingly and then introduces
an accordion to remind us we're in Paris. The
suite from *David Copperfield* has a fine lyrical
opening sweep, then introduces a delightfully
quirky, syncopated *moto perpetuo* representing
'The Micawbers'. This features a solo clarinet,
and Christopher Palmer has arranged another
witty clarinet *Scherzetto* from an equally winning
theme used in *You Know What Sailors Are*.

The *concertante* Ballade for Piano and Orchestra adeptly arranged by Lane from *Stolen Face* is
less memorable, but the overture from *The Roots
of Heaven* (provided for the film's New York
premiere) opens with a splendid Hollywood/
Waltonesque flourish, then follows with more
catchy syncopation and a lilting waltz tune. Perhaps the most tender, romantic writing comes in
No Love for Johnnie (after another rousing
march). The irrepressible score for *The Belles of
St Trinian's* (the composer's favourite film) has
something of the audacious sparkle of Ibert's
Divertissement, and if *The Holly and the Ivy* brings
a rather predictable collection of familiar carols,
for the most part fully scored and not particularly individual, the jaunty samba from *The
Captain's Paradise*, which memorably had Alec
Guinness in the bigamous title-role, makes a
splendid finale.

The performances have plenty of zest, and the
flow of bittersweet lyrical writing is poignantly
caught by Rumon Gamba and the excellent BBC
Philharmonic in a recording of top Chandos
quality. If you enjoy film music, it doesn't come
any better than this.

String quartets

String Quartets – No 1, Op 23; No 2, Op 118.
Phantasy for String Quartet, 'Vita abundans'
Maggini Quartet (Laurence Jackson, David Angel
vns Martin Outram va Michal Kaznowski vc)
Naxos 8 557762 (57' · DDD)   Ⓢᗕ

Here's a disc to demonstrate Arnold's gift of
bringing out from whatever medium he is using
sounds that are utterly original. Even in the
very early *Phantasy*, he was using quartet writing with a confidence and originality which
rightly won him a prize in the Cobbett competition in 1941.

In both of the numbered quartets Arnold
opens abrasively, almost as though he is seeking
to demonstrate his modernity before relaxing
into a more approachable, lyrical idiom. In No 1
(1949) the opening brings high entries for all
four instruments, and if later there are one or
two indications that he was influenced by the
quartets of Bartók, particularly in the *Scherzo*,
the echoes are only peripheral and in no way
obscure the composer's originality. The *Andante*
brings a poignant melody, leading into the energetic finale.

The Second Quartet (1975) is generally sparer,
with the bold opening involving the instruments
in pairs, leading to a sequence of bold and striking ideas, well contrasted. For all the profusion
of material, there is nothing perfunctory about
the result. Nor is there in the opening solo violin
passage, leading to an *Allegro vivace* main section
like a Celtic dance.

The *Andante* is spare and dark in its 'desolate polyphony', deeply meditative in the Maggini's superb performance, leading to a powerful climax and a hushed close. The finale opens with a violin melody over tremolos, a piece full of elusive shifts linked by the main theme, resolving in a warm, broad melody, and final emphatic chords. The Maggini performances achieve new standards and their bargain disc offers a valuable supplement in the *Phantasy*.

Piano works

Arnold Two Piano Pieces – Prelude; Romance. Piano Sonata. Variations on a Ukrainian Folksong **Lambert** Elegiac Blues. Elegy. Piano Sonata. Suite in Three Movements
Mark Bebbington pf
Somm New Horizons SOMMCD062 (77' · DDD)   Ⓕ

Mark Bebbington's 85th-birthday tribute to the late Sir Malcolm Arnold starts with his first substantial piano composition, the Piano Sonata in B minor from 1942. After a concise opening movement, a wistful *Andante con moto* leads without a break into the *Alla marcia* finale, whose element of ironic burlesque suggests an acquaintance with Prokofiev and Shostakovich. The Piano Pieces, completed the following year, already possess that bittersweet tang characteristic of the composer. However, the meatiest Arnold offering here is the absorbing 1944 *Variations on a Ukrainian Folksong*. Bebbington is a splendidly intrepidly communicative and an unruffled advocate. He also benefits from a superbly rounded, firmly focused sound-picture.

Bebbington proves equally at home in the music of Constant Lambert. His interpretation of the magnificent 1929 Sonata that bridges the gap between *The Rio Grande* (1927) and the Piano Concerto (1930-31) has all the stylish aplomb, improvisatory freedom and infectious swagger one could wish for, yet with a touch more introspection and poignancy in the bluesy slow movement than either Ian Brown or John McCabe locate. The finale hurtles menacingly towards its grim apotheosis, after which the skies darken further still for the inconsolable *Elegy* that Lambert wrote in 1938. The three-movement Suite from 1925 is full of daring, ear-tickling invention (sample the hallucinatory opening *Andante*) and a striking achievement for someone barely out of their teens. The sweetly touching *Elegiac Blues* of 1927 (written within days of the news of the early death of singer Florence Mills) rounds off another high-class collection from this intelligent and tasteful performer.

Samuel Arnold   British 1740-1802

A hugely prolific composer, Arnold was also an organist, conductor, editor and musical entrepreneur who mounted stage works in Marylebone Gardens which he owned. Arnold was composer and music director of the Little Theatre in London for 25 years writing numerous operas and stage works. In addition to that post he was also organist at the Chapen Royal, at Westminster Abbey and was in charge of the Lenten oratorios at Drury Lane. He was also a great champion of Handel's music, overseeing a complete Handel edition. GROVEmusic

Six Overtures

Six Overtures, Op 8. Macbeth. Polly – Overture
Toronto Camerata / Kevin Mallon
Naxos 8 557484 (76' · DDD)   Ⓢ⊕▸

Samuel Arnold's Op 8 Overtures are in fact three-movement symphonies, and in truth pretty light fare, their standardised *galant* clichés presenting the amiable countenance of a JC Bach or an early Mozart without capturing their more refined features or finding their kind of momentum.

Of more interest is the stage music. Like many a theatre man, he is not afraid to make the odd pragmatic borrowing, and in his incidental music to *Macbeth* he bypasses the play's supernatural element and emphasises its Scottishness by importing several authentic folk tunes, each given a pleasingly sensitive orchestral arrangement. His own original music includes a rattling military march and an ever-so-slightly Scottish-sounding Minuet for the Banquet scene. In the overture to *Polly*, sequel to *The Beggar's Opera*, Arnold again shows his theatrical nous by conjuring up the past in a medley of some of the earlier work's well known tunes. Under Kevin Mallon the modern instruments of Toronto Camerata play with style, accuracy and commitment.

Thomas Ashewell   English c1478-1513

He was admitted as a chorister to St George's Chapel, Windsor, on October 29, 1491 and remained there until January 14, 1493. The roll of accounts of the stewards of Tattershall College, Lincolnshire, for Michaelmas 1502 to Michaelmas 1503 lists him as one of the singing clerks (clerici conducticii). An entry dated January 29, 1508 in the chapter acts of Lincoln Cathedral shows that at that time he was informator choristarum there but the date of his appointment is unknown. In 1513 he was cantor at Durham Cathedral. Ashewell's presence at Tattershall College is particularly interesting for its support of a suspected teacher-pupil relationship between him and Taverner, who is supposed to have been a chorister at Tattershall at about this time. The only two works by Ashewell surviving complete are the six-voice Missa 'Ave Maria' and Missa 'Jesu Christe' in the Forrest-Heyther Partbooks copied by or for Taverner when he assumed his duties as choirmaster at the new Cardinal College, Oxford, in 1526. GROVEmusic

'La quinta essencia'
Ashewell Missa 'Ave Maria' **Lassus** Missa 'Tous les regretz' **Palestrina** Missa 'Ut me re fa sol la' – Kyrie, Gloria, Sanctus, Agnus dei
Huelgas Ensemble / Paul van Nevel
Harmonia Mundi ② HMC90 1922 (77' · DDD) Ⓕ Ⓞ ▣

This is a typically imaginative programme from Paul van Nevel. The two acknowledged Renaissance masters do very well: the Huelgas have a long-standing affinity with Lassus, and van Nevel's reading of the *Missa Tous les regretz* is very fine. That of the Palestrina is perhaps not quite so lucid, and it is here shorn of its *Credo* for reasons of space.

The real discovery here, and the work that earns this disc the highest recommendation, is Thomas Ashewell, whose *Missa Ave Maria* is something of a minor masterpiece, full of fine detail and the kaleidoscopic sonority that makes early Tudor polyphony so absorbing. It has also a focus sometimes lacking in this repertory. Ashewell may well have taught the young John Taverner, but even so, the extent to which the work appears to be a dress rehearsal (though by no means a mere dry run) for the younger man's more famous *Missa Gloria tibi Trinitas* is astounding: the way the plainchant is presented in the top voice to set the words 'In nomine' in the *Sanctus* is surely a dead giveaway. Worth hearing? Most definitely.

Georges Auric   French 1899-1983

Auric studied at the Paris Conservatoire and with d'Indy at the Schola Cantorum (1914-16), becoming acquainted with Satie, Milhaud and Honegger. He was a member of Les Six, wrote ballets for Diaghilev (Les fâcheux, 1923) and film scores for Cocteau and was also a music critic. In the 1950s and '60s he held administrative posts while maintaining his musical curiosity: some of his later pieces are serial.
GROVEmusic

Film Music

Suites – Caesar and Cleopatra; Dead of Night; Father Brown; The Innocents[a]; It always rains on a Sunday; The Lavender Hill Mob; Moulin Rouge[b]; Passport to Pimlico; The Titfield Thunderbolt; Hue and Cry – Overture
BBC Philharmonic Orchestra / Rumon Gamba with [a]**Anthea Kempston**, [b]**Mary Carewe** sops
Chandos CHAN9774 (74' · DDD) Ⓕ Ⓞ ▣

All the scores here (expertly reconstructed by Philip Lane) are from British films, for which Auric wrote some 30; but he also wrote another 100 or so for French, German, Italian and American movies. It was in fact by a French film – René Clair's delightful satire *A nous la liberté* – that he first won our hearts in 1932; it wasn't until the end of the war that he was taken up by Denham and Ealing. Auric, not one for the 'hit tune' score beloved by commercial exploiters, nevertheless showed in his *Moulin Rouge* waltz that he too could command the popular style. On this disc he's heard running the gamut through the grandiose or the dramatic (*It always rains on a Sunday*, one of his finest pieces), the menacing (the unforgettably scary *Dead of Night*) and the atmospheric ('At the Sphinx' in *Caesar and Cleopatra*) to the swirling gaiety of *The Titfield Thunderbolt*, the perky *Passport to Pimlico* and the ebullient high spirits of *Hue and Cry*. From the gusto of the playing throughout, it seems clear that the BBC Philharmonic enjoyed making this disc: understandably so.

Further listening

The Ladykillers
Royal Ballet Sinfonia / Alwyn
Silva Screen FILMCD177 (61' · DDD)   Ⓕ
A splendid collection of scores for Ealing comedies splayed with lashings of gusto and a great feeling for this now sadly lost idiom. A 1997 *Gramophone* Award winner.

Carl Philipp Emanuel Bach
German 1714-1788

Carl Philipp Emanuel Bach, second son of Johann Sebastian Bach, studied music under his father at the Leipzig Thomasschule and law at university. In 1738 he became harpsichordist to the Prussian crown prince, moving to Berlin when his employer became King Frederick in 1740. There he was accompanist to the royal chamber music, and had the particular task of accompanying the king's flute solos. His most important compositions of this period were his keyboard sonatas; he also wrote his famous Essay on the True Art of Keyboard Playing (1753-62), which established him as the leading keyboard teacher and theorist of his time. He was however discontented in Berlin, because of the poor salary, the want of opportunity and the narrow scope of his duties. In 1767 Frederick reluctantly released him and he then succeeded Telemann as Kantor and music director in Hamburg, with responsibility for teaching, for some 200 performances of music each year at five churches and for ceremonial music on civic occasions. At this time he produced much church music as well as keyboard music, sets of symphonies and concertos.

CPE Bach, the best-known member of his family in his lifetime, was greatly respected for his treatise – which summarised the musical philosophy and the musical practices in north Germany at the middle of the 18th century – as well as for his music. His keyboard sonatas (he composed c150 as well as countless miscellaneous pieces) above all break new ground in their treatment of form and material; he also wrote improvisatory fantasias of intense expressiveness. His symphonies – he wrote c20 – are in the fiery, energetic manner favoured in north Germany, with dramatic breaks, modulations and changes of mood or texture; usually the movements run continuously.

There are twice as many concertos (and more concerto-like sonatinas), also vigorous in style; all were written for harpsichord and some were adapted for other instruments. His chamber works are numerous; there are many songs, as well as choral works from his late years, including two fine oratorios (Die Israeliten in der Wüste, Die Auferstehung und Himmelfahrt Jesu), Passion settings and other church works which often include adaptations of his own and other composers' music. GROVEmusic

Cello Concertos

Cello Concertos – A minor, H432; B flat, H436;   Ⓟ
A, H439
Bach Collegium Japan / Hidemi Suzuki *vc*
BIS CD807 (68' · DDD)   Ⓕ

Why is it that cellists who bemoan their lack of concerto repertory continue to neglect CPE Bach's three essays in the genre? It's a mystery; they're excellent pieces, full of infectious nervous energy in their outer movements and tender lyricism in central ones. They aren't unknown to the recording catalogues, however, not least because they also exist in alternative versions which the composer made for flute and harpsichord. Though there are times when the low-lying cello has difficulty making itself heard against the orchestra, Suzuki makes light of the matter with performances whose agility, lightness and textural clarity make those of Bylsma and the larger-sounding Orchestra of the Age of Enlightenment sound heavy-handed. But while Suzuki – thanks to a generally thinner sound – is the more successful in the way he transmits the surface excitement and energy of the quick movements, he can't match Bylsma's vocal inspiration in the eloquent poetry of the slow movement. Suzuki's, nevertheless, are refreshing, enlivening performances of attractive and substantial music.

Cello Concertos – A minor, H432; B flat, H436;
A, H439
Timothy Hugh *vc* **Bournemouth Sinfonietta /
Richard Studt**
Naxos 8 553298 (71' · DDD)   ⓈⒹ

Timothy Hugh's bow dances in the flanking movements and is matched by those of the Bournemouth Sinfonietta, alert to every nuance and disposed to throw their weight around only as much as is fitting. However, it's the slow movements that are the heart of these works. All are tinged with sadness, but none more than the *Largo* of the A major Concerto, where Hugh's abated vibrato, attenuated lines and resistance to the excessive squeezing of *appoggiaturas* express a sadness that's held within, not spilt in salt tears.

Keyboard Concertos

Harpsichord Concertos – G minor, H409;   Ⓟ

A, H411; D, H421
Miklós Spányi *hpd* **Concerto Armonico / Péter Szüts**
BIS CD767 (68' · DDD)   ⒻⒹ

These concertos demonstrate the emerging inventiveness of CPE's musical personality within the trend towards public concerts in the mid-18th century. In fits and starts there are those sparsely etched landscapes which at their best can captivate us. If decorum is sometimes overworked, Bach's originality is even more remarkable given that the ritornello structure inherited from his father's generation, with its alternating solo and string sections, is less easy to sustain in a relatively uncontrapuntal style. Contrast is therefore a key element, and Bach needs a soloist who can discern how the relationship between the harpsichord and the orchestra can be manipulated to good effect. Miklós Spányi and Concerto Armonico, led by Péter Szüts, give wonderfully lucid, flexible and clearly articulated readings. The shading in the finale of the G minor and middle movement of the D major concertos is also energised by a naturally discursive balance, a deft textural palette for which artist and engineer can take equal credit. With such eloquent playing, this volume of world premiere recordings will give the listener more than just an opportunity to refine his perspective on Bach's achievements. It deserves a welcoming audience.

Keyboard Concertos – D, H414;   Ⓟ
E, H417; A, H422
Concerto Armonico / Miklós Spányi *fp*
BIS CD785 (74' · DDD)   ⒻⒹ

With his fifth volume of CPE Bach's complete keyboard concertos, Miklós Spányi comes to three works composed in the mid-1740s, which he plays on a copy of a Silbermann fortepiano of that period. The choice isn't only determined by the existence of such instruments at Frederick the Great's court, where Carl Philipp was employed, but also because the keyboard layout is more suited to the fortepiano than the harpsichord, and because the A major work here – a first recording, like that of the D major – includes the marking *pianissimo*. The present instrument is light and silvery in tone, which makes for some difficulties of proportion in the D major, performed with additional manuscript parts found in Brussels for trumpets and drums. The more embellished version of the A major Concerto is adopted here. The first movement displays some particularly athletic passagework for the piano. The E major Concerto is musically the most inventive and unusual of the three works, and harmonically certainly the most adventurous – a splendid concerto that deserves to be better known. The recording has occasional problems with balance but the performances are praiseworthy.

Keyboard Concertos – E minor, H418;   Ⓟ
B flat, H429; G minor, H442

Miklós Spányi *fp* Concerto Armonico /
Péter Szüts *vn*
BIS CD786 (73' · DDD)   Ⓕ

On this recording Miklós Spányi has exchanged
his previous harpsichord or fortepiano for a
tangent piano: it's like a fortepiano but has the
strings struck vertically by tangents (as in the
clavichord) rather than at an angle by hammers.
Its tone could also be modified by raising the
dampers completely or only in the treble,
employing only one of each note's two strings
(*una corda*), inserting a leather strip ('moderator') between tangents and strings, or creating a
harp-like effect by damping the strings with
small pieces of cloth.

The boldness and unusual style of CPE Bach's
concertos took his contemporaries aback, and
even now they can surprise. The extrovert
E minor work, for example, begins with
dramatic energy but is interrupted by extraordinary, tentative-sounding broken phrases at the
soloist's first entry before being allowed to
continue on its way: the *Adagio*, which includes
striking chromatic progressions, has imitative
interplay between the solo instrument and the
violins. The finale of the otherwise more
'normal' *galant* G minor Concerto generates
very vehement chordal attacks – or are these
being overdone here? Spányi's playing throughout has vitality and neatness, although his lifting
of the dampers in running passages inevitably
causes them to become blurred.

Symphonies

CPE Bach Sinfonias, H663-66 – No 1 in D; No 2 in
E flat; No 3 in F; No 4 in G **WF Bach** Sinfonia in F
**Salzburg Chamber Philharmonic Orchestra /
Yoon K Lee**
Naxos 8 553289 (52' · DDD)   Ⓢ▶

The exhilarating CPE Bach symphonies
presented here aren't the more frequently
recorded, surprise-filled string symphonies of
1773 (H657-62), but the set of four for strings,
flutes, oboes, bassoons and horns which Bach
wrote a couple of years later. They are no less
astonishing. Bewildering changes of direction,
disorientating rhythmic games and unexpected
solos all turn up in this nervous, excitable
music, which for originality and life-force could
surely only have been matched in its day by
that of Haydn.

The Salzburg Chamber Philharmonic, under
its founder Yoon K Lee, turns in crisp, spirited
and (the odd moment of slack tuning apart) disciplined performances which do the music full
justice. They aren't timid about making the
most of Bach's strong contrasts, although they
produce them more by the release of some thunderous *forte* passages than by the pursuit of too
many unearthly *pianissimos*.

The overall effect is wholly convincing, and
only in the symphony by Emanuel's older
brother Wilhelm Friedemann – more old-

fashioned and less successful as a piece – does
the use of modern instruments begin to get in
the way of the spirit of music. An undeniably
good buy.

Symphonies Nos 1-4, Wq183. Cello Concerto, H439
Wq172ᵃ
ᵃ**Alison McGillivray** *vc*
The English Concert / Andrew Manze   Ⓟ
Harmonia Mundi HMU90 7403 (64' · DDD)   Ⓕ▶

These four symphonies from 1775 emerge from
their performances by The English Concert
sounding like the work of a forceful and original
master, one perhaps out to shock with his sudden changes of direction, jagged melody lines
and surprise silences, but whose expressive
integrity never seems under threat. Andrew
Manze, as is to be expected, revels in their
extremes, not just at the local level but over
wider spans too, as in the first minute of Wq183
No 4, when he rides the swell from opening
nervy string unison to triumphant orchestral
tutti with great aplomb.

These are performances full of life which,
while not always matching the perfections of
ensemble and intonation attained by some of
this orchestra's top European counterparts, certainly leave a strong image of CPE Bach as a
creative force. The sequence is broken up by a
cello concerto, an earlier and less forward-looking work (as concertos often are), but a fine one
nevertheless, with a hauntingly emotional slow
movement. Soloist Alison McGillivray plays
with the silver-toned elegance of some smooth-
voiced tenor.

Chamber Works

Quartet for Keyboard, Flute, Viola and Continuo   Ⓟ
in D, H538. Viola da gamba Sonata in G minor, Wq88
– Larghetto. Trio Sonatas – Two Violins and Continuo
in C minor, H579; Flute, Violin and Continuo in C,
H571. Solo Flute Sonata in A minor, H562
Florilegium (Ashley Solomon *fl* Rachel Podger *vn/va*
Lucy Russell *vn* Daniel Yeadon *vc/va da gamba* Neal
Peres da Costa *hpd/fp*)
Channel Classics CCS11197 (59' · DDD)   Ⓕ⦿▶

More than half a century separates the earliest
and the latest of the works here. The C major
Trio Sonata was one of Bach's earliest compositions, written at the age of 17 more or less under
his father's supervision, and the D major Quartet was composed in the last year of his life, while
he was Music Director in Hamburg. The
remaining items date from his time at the court
of Frederick the Great. The C minor Sonata is
extraordinary, a programmatic work 'portraying
a conversation between a Sanguineus and a Mel-
ancholicus' who disagree throughout the first
two movements, but the former's outlook prevails in the finale. The talented Florilegium
players bring out to the full the bewilderingly
diverse character of this sonata.

If the Sonata for unaccompanied flute was written for Frederick, as seems likely, he must have been quite skilled, able to cope with some virtuoso passagework. Ashley Solomon's performance is most persuasive. How far Carl Philipp developed is shown by the late quartet, an attractive composition which, besides promoting the keyboard (fortepiano here) from a mere continuo to prominent solo status, is already in the style of the Viennese classics in form, and links the first two movements. The whole disc is strongly recommended.

Die Auferstehung und Himmelfahrt Jesu

Die Auferstehung und Himmelfahrt Jesu   ℗
Uta Schwabe sop **Christoph Genz** ten **Stephan Genz** bar **Ex Tempore; La Petite Bande / Sigiswald Kuijken**
Hyperion CDA67364 (73' · DDD· T/t)   Ⓕ⊙

CPE Bach is much better known for his instrumental works, which are numerous, than his vocal, which are few: but his short oratorio *Die Auferstehung und Himmelfahrt Jesu* ('The Resurrection and Ascension of Jesus'), a late work which was written in the 1770s, has a strong claim to be reckoned among his most original and his finest. It certainly proclaims his originality in its opening bars, a sombre and mysterious passage for cellos and basses alone, and the ensuing chorus at least hints at the grandeur and sense of the momentous that distinguishes his father's great choral works.

The narrative is sung by a tenor in a series of recitatives, mostly starting *secco* but increasingly coloured by orchestral textures as they gather emotional force. Here they're impressively done by Christoph Genz, with subtle and refined shading of the tone and a quiet intensity of expression. The soprano aria, warmly and touchingly done by Uta Schwabe, with a mournful first part and a joyous second, is a particularly expressive piece, although arguably it's outshone by the duet that follows, with its attractive use of two flutes to accompany the soprano and its typical use of appoggiaturas and the dissonances they create to heighten the expression.

Sigiswald Kuijken's lively but sensitive and thoughtful direction, and his attention to details of the instrumental texture, ensure that the work gets the performance it merits.

Johann Christian Bach

German 1735-1782

Johann Christian Bach, the youngest son of JS Bach, probably studied first under his father, then on his death with his half-brother Carl Philipp Emanuel in Berlin. In 1754 he left for Italy, where he became a Roman Catholic and organist at Milan Cathedral. He also embarked on an operatic career, with operas staged in Turin and Naples. He was then invited to compose for the King's Theatre in London, where he settled in 1762; his operatic career was patchy, but he was soon appointed royal music master and was successful as a teacher. He also promoted and played in a prominent concert series with his friend CF Abel, bringing the newest and best European music to Londoners' notice. Many of his works were published, including songs written for Vauxhall Pleasure Gardens. In 1772 and 1774 he visited Mannheim for performances of his operas Temistocle and Lucio Silla and in 1779 he wrote Amadis de Gaule for the Paris Opéra, but the success of these works, like that of his London operas, was limited. His popularity faded in the late 1770s, and after financial troubles his health declined; he died at the beginning of 1782, and was soon forgotten.

JC Bach's music blends sound German technique with Italian fluency and grace; hence its appeal to, and influence upon, the young Mozart. His symphonies follow the Italian three-movement pattern: the light, Italian manner of his earlier ones gave way to richer-textured and more fully developed writing by the mid-1760s. The peak of his output comes in the six symphonies of his Op 18, three for double orchestra and exploiting contrasts of space and timbre. His interest in orchestral colour gave rise to several symphonies concertantes, for various soloists and orchestra, suitable material for his London concerts. At these he also played his piano concertos, attractive for their well-developed solo-tutti relationship though still modest in scale.   **GROVE**music

---

Keyboard concertos

Six Concertos for Keyboard and Strings, Op 7 –   ℗
No 1 in C; No 2 in F; No 3 in D; No 4 in B flat;
No 5 in E flat; No 6 in G
Members of the **Hanover Band** (Graham Cracknell, Anna McDonald vns Sebastian Comberti vc) /
Anthony Halstead fp
CPO CPO999 600-2 (73' · DDD)   Ⓕ⊙

On Halstead's previous disc of JC Bach's keyboard concertos, he employed nine strings from the Hanover Band; but the present Op 7 concertos, like those of Op 1, call for only two violins and cello. He played the Op 1 work on the harpsichord, as specified on the title-page of the original edition: here he plays a fortepiano on the grounds that not only does the title-page of Op 7 designate 'Harpsichord or Piano Forte', but also that the fortepiano had made considerable headway in London in the seven years since the Op 1 appeared in 1763. The most interesting of these concertos are the last two of the set, each in three movements. No 5 is particularly fine, not merely because of its brilliant keyboard writing (notably in its finale) but because the sturdy initial *Allegro di molto* is more mature in style, with fresh material appearing in the development, and because of its deeply expressive, almost Mozartian, *Andante*. No 6 is distinguished by its central movement's long cantilena lines and for an extraordinary key-move near the end of the finale. Halstead's playing is a model of neatness and crisp rhythmicality: his decorations are in good taste, and in No 5 he adopts the composer's own cadenzas. His string colleagues are excellent. In short, a very pleasing disc.

Harpsichord Concertos – D minor; B flat; F minor   **P**
Hanover Band / Anthony Halstead hpd
CPO CPO999 393-2 (57' · DDD)   (F)

The works of JC Bach's Berlin years are almost indistinguishable from those of his brother, CPE, and anyone putting on this disc could be excused for thinking the first movement of the D minor Concerto – with its purposeful, energetic scales, its stark textures, its heavily used motifs, its rushing harpsichord writing, its sombre minor key and its total lack of lyricism – to be wholly CPE's work. In fact it's a very accomplished piece for a composer less than 20 years old and there are glimmerings of JC's own voice in the *Adagio affettuoso* that follows; it still sounds like North German music, untouched by Italian softness and sunshine, but the harpsichord cantilena certainly has a more personal expressive character and so does some of the string writing in the ritornellos and accompaniment. The slow movements throughout seem individual and appealing in a sense that CPE's aren't. The quick movements, especially in the B flat Concerto, contain gestures of the abrupt and musically violent kind that CPE so often used. The finale of the D minor has a curious element of fantasy and an imaginative use of *pizzicato* behind the first solo entry.

Halstead uses a small orchestra, strings only, 3.3.1.1.1, which is quite sufficient and very alert. The solo playing is extremely fluent and indeed brilliant; Halstead plays with ample energy and rhythmic precision and realises the elaborate melodic lines effectively.

Symphonies concertantes

Symphonies concertantes – F, T287 No 2;   **P**
B flat, T287 No 7; D
Anthony Robson ob **Jeremy Ward** bn **Graham Cracknell, Anna McDonald** vns **Sebastian Comberti** vc **Hanover Band / Anthony Halstead**
CPO CPO999 537-2 (52' · DDD)   (F)●

The *symphonie concertante*, predominantly lighthearted, allotted a more prominent role to the solo instruments than did the *concerto grosso*. The earliest of the present three works is that in F, and the JC Bach scholar Ernest Warburton speculates that the choice of a solo oboe and bassoon suggests that it may have been written in 1761 for Naples, where Bach's opera *Catone in Utica* called for outstanding players of just these instruments. It's a cheerfully engaging two-movement work that takes the bassoon up into the tenor register: its first movement is unorthodox in shape. The D major work, in three movements, likewise ends in a minuet, with a trio in the minor for a change. Overall, the writing places more emphasis on

virtuosity for the two soloists, and both in the energetic first movement and the more formal second there's a lengthy cadenza. The most notable *symphonie concertante* here, however, is that in B flat, long considered lost and rediscovered only in 1996: this is its first recording. Probably composed for JC's London concerts in the late 1770s, it allows the orchestra greater say; the initial ritornellos in the first two movements are unusually long. In the *Larghetto* the solo cello drops out, leaving the violin long, sweetly pungent cantilenas – a strikingly fine movement. Halstead secures neat performances of finesse of all three works, which also benefit from skilful soloists and well-balanced recording. Delightful.

Symphonies

Six Symphonies, Op 6 – No 1 in G; No 2 in D;   **P**
No 3 in E flat; No 4 in B flat; No 5 in E flat;
No 6 in G minor
Hanover Band / Anthony Halstead
CPO CPO999 298-2 (56' · DDD)   (F)

In the Op 6 Symphonies the frothy Italianate music of the composer's Italian and early London years was behind him; these pieces, dating from the late 1760s, while still Italian-influenced in their formal clarity and melodic style, are sturdier, more carefully composed, more symphonic. Both the E flat works have something of the solidity and warmth associated with that key, and each has a C minor *Andante*. The G major's first movement has the confident ring and thematic contrasts of his mature music, and the D major contains Mannheim *crescendos* and some delightful textures, with flutes and divided violas, in its charming, slightly playful middle movement.

The set ends with Bach's single minor-key symphony in G minor, very similar in spirit to Mozart's No 25; this piece, often recorded before, shows an unfamiliar side to his musical personality. Anthony Halstead and his players convey the music's strength and spirit convincingly. The lively finales all go with a swing, and the opening movements have plenty of energy. The slow movements aren't always quite so persuasive: the third C minor slow movement of the G minor Symphony is a little overly deliberate and becomes detached and modest in expressive impact. Generally, though, these are strong and appealing performances of attractive and unfamiliar music, clearly, slightly drily recorded. Admirers of the London Bach and his music needn't hesitate.

Symphonies – Op 9: No 1 in B flat; No 2 in E flat;   **P**
No 3 in B flat; B flat, Sieber No 1; E flat, Sieber No 2;
E flat (ed Warburton)
Hanover Band / Anthony Halstead
CPO CPO999 487-2 (60' · DDD)   (F)●

This disc offers the Op 9 Symphonies published in The Hague in 1773, two of them in two versions, along with a little-known symphony.

Ernest Warburton explains in his notes that the usual texts for these works, with oboes and horns, are in his view arrangements of originals calling for clarinets – still rarities in most European orchestras at the time – and bassoon, in which form one of them was published in Paris. Here, then, Op 9 Nos 1 and 2 are done twice over to allow comparison; and certainly the versions differ markedly in flavour with clarinets and bassoon. The E-flat work, No 2, one of Bach's finest and most vigorously argued symphonies, comes out particularly well, with quite a different ring to its tuttis.

The E flat Symphony is an attractive work, with an eloquent violin line in the *Andante*, and a charming final gavotte. Of the works played twice, the B flat is lightish, probably originally an opera overture; the E flat has more substance and notably a C minor slow movement with a melody of a haunting, graceful beauty. The third Op 9 Symphony is a brisk little piece which again started life as an overture. Halstead directs with his usual style and shapeliness.

Overtures

Overtures – Gioas, re di Giuda; Adriano in Siria;   P
Zanaida; Orione. La clemenza di Scipione – Overture;
No 5, March in G; No 22, March in E flat. Carattaco–
-Overture; No 20, March in B flat; No 26, March in G.
Symphony in D, Schmitt Op 18 No 1
Hanover Band / Anthony Halstead
CPO CPO999 488-2 (58' · DDD)   Ⓕ Ⓞ

Small-scale but elegantly fashioned, melodious and pleasurable music: it's no wonder that the London public in the 1760s and 1770s took JC to their hearts. Here we have the overtures to six works of his that were performed at the King's Theatre in the Haymarket – from his first opera there, *Orione* in 1763, to his last, *La clemenza di Scipione* in 1778, and the 1770 oratorio, *Gioas*, plus a symphony which is a *pasticcio* of the *Clemenza* overture with additional trumpets and drums and a revised version of the *Andante* from the overture to his only completed French opera, the 1779 *Amadis de Gaule*. The most striking feature about all these works, apart from their vigorous openings, is the freedom in the use of wind instruments: *Zanaida* has *soli* clarinets, and the trio of *Orione*'s minuet is for wind band only, as are passages in *Adriano*, the E flat March in *Clemenza* and the brilliant final *Presto* of *Carattaco*.

The Hanover Band's playing is vital and fresh, rhythmically crisp and tonally clean-cut; the recording is first rate.

Johann Sebastian Bach

German 1685-1750

*Johann Sebastian was the youngest son of Johann Ambrosius Bach, a town musician, from whom he probably learnt the violin and the rudiments of musi-*cal theory. When he was 10 he was orphaned and went to live with his elder brother Johann Christoph, organist at St Michael's Church, Ohrdruf, who gave him lessons in keyboard playing. From 1700-1702 he attended St Michael's School in Lüneburg, where he sang in the church choir and probably came into contact with organist and composer Georg Böhm. He also visited Hamburg to hear JA Reincken at the organ of St Catherine's Church.

After competing unsuccessfully for an organist's post in Sangerhausen in 1702, Bach spent the spring and summer of 1703 as 'lackey' and violinist at the court of Weimar and then took up the post of organist at the Neukirche in Arnstadt. In June 1707 he moved to St Blasius, Mühlhausen, and four months later married his cousin Maria Barbara Bach in nearby Dornheim. Bach was appointed organist and chamber musician to the Duke of Saxe-Weimar in 1708, and in the next nine years he became known as a leading organist and composed many of his finest works for the instrument. During this time he fathered seven children, including Wilhelm Friedemann and Carl Philipp Emanuel. When, in 1717, Bach was appointed Kapellmeister at Cöthen he was at first refused permission to leave Weimar and was allowed to do so only after being held prisoner by the duke for almost a month.

Bach's new employer, Prince Leopold, was a talented musician who loved and understood the art. Since the court was Calvinist, Bach had no chapel duties and instead concentrated on instrumental composition. From this period date his violin concertos and the six Brandenburg Concertos, as well as numerous sonatas, suites and keyboard works, including several (eg the Inventions and Book I of the '48') intended for instruction. In 1720 Maria Barbara died while Bach was visiting Karlsbad with the prince; in December of the following year Bach married Anna Magdalena Wilcke, daughter of a court trumpeter at Weissenfels. A week later Prince Leopold also married, and his bride's lack of interest in the arts led to a decline in the support given to music at the Cöthen court. In 1722 Bach entered his candidature for the prestigious post of Director musices at Leipzig and Kantor of the Thomasschule there. In April 1723 after the preferred candidates, Telemann and Graupner, had withdrawn, he was offered the post and accepted it.

Bach remained as Thomaskantor in Leipzig for the rest of his life, often in conflict with the authorities, but a happy family man and a proud and caring parent. His duties centred on the Sunday and feast-day services at the city's two main churches, and during his early years in Leipzig he composed prodigious quantities of church music, including four or five cantata cycles, the Magnificat and the St John and St Matthew Passions. He was by this time renowned as a virtuoso organist and in constant demand as a teacher and an expert in organ construction and design. His fame as a composer gradually spread more widely when, from 1726 onwards, he began to bring out published editions of some of his keyboard and organ music.

From about 1729 Bach's interest in composing church music sharply declined, and most of his sacred works after that date including the B minor Mass and the Christmas Oratorio consist mainly of 'parodies' or arrangements of earlier music. At the same time he took over the direction of the collegium musicum that Telemann had founded in Leipzig in 1702 – a mainly amateur society which gave regular public concerts. For these Bach arranged harpsichord concertos and composed several large-scale cantatas, or serenatas, to impress the Elector of Saxony, by whom he was granted the courtesy title of Hofcompositeur in 1736.

Bach's eyesight began to deteriorate during his last year, and in March and April 1750 he was twice operated on by the itinerant English oculist John Taylor. The operations and the treatment that followed them may have hastened Bach's death. He took final communion on 22 July and died six days later. On 31 July he was buried at St John's cemetery. His widow survived him for 10 years, dying in poverty in 1760.

Bach's output embraces practically every musical genre of his time except for the dramatic ones of opera and oratorio (his three 'oratorios' being oratorios only in a special sense). He opened up new dimensions in virtually every department of creative work to which he turned, in format, musical quality and technical demands. As was normal at the time, his creative production was mostly bound up with the external factors of his places of work and his employers, but the density and complexity of his music are such that analysts and commentators have uncovered in it layers of religious and numerological significance rarely to be found in the music of other composers. Many of his contemporaries, notably the critic JA Scheibe, found his music too involved and lacking in immediate melodic appeal, but his chorale harmonisations and fugal works were soon adopted as models for new generations of musicians. The course of Bach's musical development was undeflected (though not entirely uninfluenced) by the changes in musical style taking place around him. Together with his great contemporary Handel (whom chance prevented his ever meeting), Bach was the last great representative of the Baroque era in an age which was already rejecting the Baroque aesthetic in favour of a new, 'enlightened' one. **GROVE**music

Keyboard Concertos

D minor, **BWV1052**; E, **BWV1053**; D, **BWV1054**; A, **BWV1055**; F minor, **BWV1056**; F, **BWV1057**; G minor, **BWV1058**; D minor, **BWV1059**
Harpsichord Concertos – D minor, BWV1052;   **P**

D, BWV1054. Concerto for Flute, Violin, Harpsichord and Strings in A-minor, BWV1044. Das wohltemperierte Klavier, BWV846-93 – Preludes and Fugues: F, BWV880; B, BWV892
Le Concert Français / Pierre Hantaï hpd
Naïve E8837 (70' · DDD)   **Ⓜ OO**

The concertos come over well. Ensembles are tautly controlled, and the string playing effectively articulated, although on occasion the first violin is a little too favoured in the recorded balance. However, the string playing is so unanimous in sound and purpose that there's little to worry about in this department. Hantaï himself is impressive for his wonderfully rhythmic playing, the clarity with which he interprets both his

own keyboard textures and those which support and punctuate it, and not least for his supple, muscular concept of the music. These are extraordinarily invigorating performances, which draw the listener deep into the harmonic and contrapuntal complexities and conceits of Bach's art. Take for instance the elusive *Adagio* of BWV1052, where careful punctuation and sensitive interaction between solo and *tutti* make for a rewarding coherence. In the A minor Triple Concerto, Hantaï is joined by his flautist brother, Marc, and François Fernandez, the violinist leader of the ensemble. The work is a Leipzig arrangement of movements from earlier pieces not in concerto form. The opening *Allegro* is a little too heavy, but the essentially three-part texture of the middle movement is realised with affection. A stimulating disc.

Keyboard Concertos, Vol 1 – No 1, BWV1052;
No 7, BWV1058. Triple Concerto, BWV1044[a].
Brandenburg Concerto No 5, BWV1050[a]
Angela Hewitt pf
[a]**Alison Mitchell** fl **Australian Chamber Orchestra /
Richard Tognetti** [a]vn
Hyperion CDA67307 (77' · DDD)   **Ⓟ OOO**
Keyboard Concertos, Vol 2 – No 2, BWV1053;
No 3, BWV1054; No 4, BWV1055; No 5, BWV1056;
No 6, BWV1057[a]
Angela Hewitt pf
[a]**Alison Mitchell** fl, [a]**Emma Sholl** fls **Australian
Chamber Orchestra / Richard Tognetti** vn
Hyperion CDA67308 (76' · DDD)   **Ⓟ OOO**
Also available as a two-CD set CDA67607/8

These are not entirely modern-instrument performances. Angela Hewitt includes, as she says, 'a harpsichord in its traditional role as continuo'. Combining old and new isn't unusual because in the early years of period performing practices, the likes of Thurston Dart, Raymond Leppard and George Malcolm married a harpsichord to modern strings and wind. What's unusual here is the melding of two different types of keyboard, one sharply transient, the other ductile; and just how their functions dovetail with one another may be heard in the slow movement of the *Brandenburg* Concerto No 5. Hewitt also adds a cello to the continuo while contributing *notes inégales*, *appogiature* and other embellishments to her own line. The result is a potent artistic synergy between the musicians.

Hewitt doesn't slavishly follow a formula, though. In the *Adagio* of No 1 and the *Adagio e piano sempre* of No 3 (where she is most intense because both remind her of Passion music), she omits the keyboard's bass notes for the exposition of the theme but only in No 1 does she play them for its return at the end. In these instances, in the *Andante* of No 7 and elsewhere, she also varies the prominence of her left hand to give the *ripieno* string bass a strong presence too, while delineating the right hand melody most feelingly.

Interpretative decisions are intelligently applied; and Hewitt is at her best in the slow movements, all of which are played with the finest sensibility. If a more sinewy approach to a few of the outer movements might not have come amiss, her ability to gauge the critical notes of phrases so as to maintain an elastically accented rhythm so offers ample compensation; and the consummate Australian Chamber Orchestra is with her every step of the way. The flute is placed backward in BWV1044 but otherwise recorded balance and sound ensure unimpeded concentration on the performances. Small changes in level between some works are easily adjusted. A superb pair of discs.

Keyboard Concertos – D minor, BWV1052;
E, BWV1053; A, BWV1055
Academy of St Martin in the Fields /
Murray Perahia *pf*
Sony Classical 509970 89245-2 (53' · DDD)   (F)**OO**D→

Soloist-conducted piano concertos can sometimes mean compromise, even chaos… but not in this case. As soloist, Perahia is his usual stylish, discreet and pianistically refined self. He takes the D minor Concerto's opening at a fair lick, a hot-foot sprinter embellishing the line with taste and affecting a little *ritardando*, just as the mood momentarily brightens, *à la* Edwin Fischer. Elsewhere, he's very much his own man, intensifying his tone for rising sequences or softening it to the most rarefied murmur. His command of colour is as striking here as it is on his CD of the *Goldberg* Variations, especially in the *Adagio*, which approaches cantorial heights of intensity.

As for the E major and A major Concertos, elegance is more of the essence than fire, but there too Perahia delivers. He has a way of accenting without jabbing the keys, tracing counterpoint while keeping the top line well to the fore. And how nice to hear the warming tone of a theorbo (bass lute) in the E major Concerto's central Siciliano, a beautiful performance, more ornamental than cantorial, in keeping with the more decorative nature of the music.

Rivals are plentiful, but credible contenders at this level of interpretation are rare. Sviatoslav Richter plays with incredible control while keeping every note alive, but some might find his manner too austere. And while Edwin Fischer is consistently spontaneous, he's rather less elegant than Perahia – and his version of the A major Concerto sounds as if it's 'Busonified'. András Schiff, like Perahia, commands a wide range of colours, though the binding force of Perahia's concentration – always a boon in his latest recordings – leaves the stronger impression. The carefully balanced Sony recordings keep the sound frame tight and lively.

Keyboard Concertos – D, BWV1054; F minor,
BWV1056; F, BWV1057; G minor, BWV1058
Academy of St Martin in the Fields /
Murray Perahia *pf*
Sony Classical 509970 89690-2 (54' · DDD)   (F)**OO**D→

BACH BRANDENBURG CONCERTOS – IN BRIEF

European Brandenburg Ensemble / Trevor Pinnock
Avie ② AV2119 (94' · DDD)   (M)**OOO**D→
A triumphant return 25 years on with some classy playing from Pinnock's ensemble. This is chamber-music-making writ large.

Concerto Italiano / Rinaldo Alessandrini
Naïve ② OP30412 (100' · DDD)   (F)**OOO**
Bach's concertos given a truly 21st-century make-over courtesy of these imaginative Italian musicians. Sensational!

Il Giardino Armonico
Warner Elatus ② 2564-61773-2 (95' · DDD)   (M)D→
Another Italian set of the concertos – full of life and imagination. Continuo work is a constant joy and there are some notable solo contributions. A fun set.

Orchestra of the Age of Enlightenment
Virgin Classics ② 561552-2 (93' · DDD)   (B)**O**
Often taken at quite a lick, these period performances never sound rushed but rather imbued with a spirit of dance.

Tafelmusik / Jeanne Lamon
Sony Classical ② 07464 66289-2 (93' · DDD)   (M)**O**
One of the finest period performances with a broad extrovert flair that occasionally flirts with danger but excites as a result.

Boston Baroque / Martin Pearlman
Telarc CD80368/54 (93' · DDD)   (F)**O**
Not quite on the level of their Bach Suites, these are highly enjoyable performances with plenty to marvel at and superbly recorded.

ASMF / Sir Neville Marriner
Philips ② 468 549-2PM2 (98' · ADD)   (M)**O**
Middle-of-the-road performances that show the Marriner/ASMF style at its best: *de luxe* soloists add to the allure of the set.

English CO / Benjamin Britten
Decca ② 443 847-2DF2 (128' · ADD)   (B)
A historic set, made in 1968, and one great composer's take on another. Slightly dated in approach but still worth sampling.

Brandenburg Consort / Roy Goodman
Hyperion ② CDD22001 (96' · DDD)   (M)
There are sleeker period performances around but few that have as much character or charm.

The English Concert / Trevor Pinnock
DG Blue 471 720-2ABL (Nos 1-3), 474 220-2ABL (Nos 4-6) (99' · DDD)   (M)**O**D→
Something of a modern classic, but only available on two single CDs, Pinnock's period performance interpretations are swift but never rushed, and magnificently played.

As well as being immensely vital, Perahia's Bach is profoundly pianistic, not in any exhibitionistic sense, but in the way tempo, dynamics and nuance register without undue exaggeration. Perahia's *staccato* never loses quality, even when soft – try the opening movement of the Sixth Concerto. And yet he's just as capable of increasing the pressure as he sees fit: listen out for his brightening tone at 5'16" into the same movement, or the extraordinary dexterity of his finger work from around 1'45" into the finale, a fair match for any fiddler tackling the same passage in the parallel Fourth *Brandenburg* Concerto. The counterpoint-crazy Glenn Gould is the benchmark here, wonderfully absorbing as ever, but this warmer, more discreet and more overtly decorative version is preferable. The sound is beautifully clear (violin desks are antiphonally placed) with impressive richness in the bass. Nothing much more to say except, don't hesitate – life's too short.

Violin Concertos, Double Concertos

Violin Concertos – A minor, **BWV1041**; E, **BWV1042**. Double Concertos – Two Violins and Strings in D minor, **BWV1043**; Oboe, Violin and Strings in C minor, **BWV1060**

Violin Concertos – BWV1041-42.
Double Concertos – BWV1043[b]; BWV1060[a]
[a]**Albrecht Mayer** *ob* [b]**Daniel Stabrawa** *vn* **Berlin Philharmonic Orchestra / Nigel Kennedy** *vn*
EMI 557016-2 (59' · DDD) Ⓕ🅞➔

Bach isn't a composer you generally associate with Nigel Kennedy, but this recording of the four most popular concertos is far more than a dutiful 250th anniversary offering. Kennedy is nothing if not characterful, taking a positive, often robust view of Bach. It isn't just his breath-takingly fast speeds in finales and in some first movements, too, that will have listeners pricking up their ears, but often a fierceness of manner which can initially take you aback. With brilliant playing not just from the soloist but from the Berlin Philharmonic, the results are certainly exciting. The power of Bach's writing is reinforced thanks also to the rather close recorded balance in the Jesus-Christus Kirche.

However fast Kennedy's speeds in *Allegros*, he counters any feeling of breathlessness not just in his clean articulation, but in his fine detailing. The Berlin players respond sympathetically, but aren't always quite so adept at springing rhythms at such fast speeds. By contrast, slow movements tend to be taken broadly, but there again Kennedy has thought through his expressive phrasing in detail, consciously pointing rhythms, shading dynamics and colouring tone. Any reservations over Kennedy's readings don't detract their positive strength.

In the Double Concerto Daniel Stabrawa makes a perfectly matched partner, and in the Concerto for oboe and violin there's no question of his seeking to overshadow the fine art-istry of the warm-toned Berlin oboist Albrecht Mayer. These are the visions of an exceptional artist, helped by warm, full sound.

Violin Concertos – BWV1041-42. Double Concerto, BWV1043[b]. Brandenburg Concerto No 5[ab].
Daniel Hope *vn* with [a]**Jaime Martin** *fl*
[b]**Marieke Blankestijn** *vn* **Kristian Bezuidenhout** *hpd*
Chamber Orchestra of Europe
Warner Classics 2564 62545-2 (64' • DDD) Ⓕ➔

First impressions suggest a high-energy, tightly accented approach, 'period'-schooled while retaining an element of modern-instrument intensity, mostly in the slow movements. Daniel Hope sees to it that the bass-line is firm and prominent, which tends to underline the sense of urgency. The Double Concerto's *Largo* focuses two well-matched players responding to, rather than mirroring, each other, invariably with one using more vibrato than the other. Outer movements are fast and buoyant (the A minor's gigue-allegro really whizzes along) and in the E major, Hope whirls into the first movement's second idea like a dervish possessed. Embellishment is legion, both along the solo line and in the discreetly balanced but lavishly stated continuo. The results approximate, more than usual with this music, dance models of the day, yet Hope always allows the slower music to breathe.

Plenty of air around the notes in the Fifth *Brandenburg* Concerto, too. Again the spirit of the dance is all-pervasive, but come the solo harpsichord cadenza, although Kristian Bezuidenhout plays brilliantly, the intrusive bending of tempo isn't entirely convincing. This sort of approach has become fairly popular: Rinaldo Alessandrini's set of *Brandenburgs* for Naïve is similarly individualistic. In most other respects this is a refreshing, often enlightening programme, very well recorded.

Violin Concertos – BWV1041-42[a]. Double Concertos – BWV1043[b]; BWV1060 (arr Fischer)[c]
[abc]**Ryo Terakado**, [b]**Natsumi Wakamatsu** *vns*
[c]**Marcel Ponseele** *ob* **Bach Collegium Japan / Masaaki Suzuki**
BIS CD961 (59' · DDD) Ⓕ🅞➔

These aren't just 'authentic' performances, they're also outstandingly musical ones. There's happy animation in the flanking movements – bows are lifted from or stopped on the strings to ensure the cleanest of textures – and a warmth of expression in the slow ones which comes from a deeper source than mere academic study.

The admirable soloist in the A minor and E major concertos, Ryo Terakado, and his partner in the Double Concerto, Natsumi Wakamatsu, both studied with Sigiswald Kuijken in The Hague and served with various Baroque ensembles in Europe before returning to Japan. It shows in the beautifully 'vocalised' shaping of their lines. Not once do they or their ripieno colleagues jar the ear with acidic sounds, and in the *Andante* of the A minor Concerto Terakado achieves a *pianissimo* that's near-miraculous in its quality. Marcel Ponseele, the only European on parade, has a comparably distinguished pedigree. In the reconstructed Concerto BWV1060 his fluency, rounded tone and clean articulation are second to none, and he makes the *Adagio* one of the serenely lovely high spots of the entire programme. As for the ripieno, you couldn't ask for better, and they're recorded in excellent balance with the soloists. Suzuki directs the whole with sure hands.

Additional recommendation

Violin Concertos – BWV1041-42.
Double Concertos – BWV1043; 1060
Podger *vn* **Academy of Ancient Music / Manze** *vn* Ⓟ
Harmonia Mundi HMU90 7155 (57' · DDD)　　Ⓕ
　Manze projects a highly developed sense of fantasy in his interpretations and, for the most part, it proves immensely effective.

Brandenburg Concertos

No 1 in F, BWV1046; **No 2** in F, BWV1047;
No 3 in G, BWV1048; **No 4** in G, BWV1049;
No 5 in D, BWV1050; **No 6** in B flat, BWV1051

Brandenburg Concertos Nos 1-6.　　　　　　Ⓟ
Cantata No 174 – Sinfonia
Concerto Italiano / Rinaldo Alessandrini
Naïve ③ (2 CDs +,1 📀) OP30412 (100' · DDD)
　　　　　　　　　　　　　　　　Ⓕ**OOO**
Also includes DVD 'Rinaldo Alessandrini and Concerto Italiano record the Brandenburg Concertos', a film by Phillippe Béziat

How do you embark on a new addition to the vast pile of *Brandenburg* Concerto recordings? Do you go for a radical interpretation set to make people jump, laugh or recoil in surprise? Or do you perform them more or less as other good performers have but just try to do it better? Rinaldo Alessandrini and Concerto Italiano have gone for the latter approach and succeeded brilliantly. There is perhaps no Baroque group around today that can do the simple and obvious things to such exciting effect.

This is not to say that their *Brandenburg*s have no distinguishing features – just that, where they do, they spring from eminent good sense, as, for instance, in No 3 when the two central link chords come attached to a harpsichord flourish which has arisen directly from the first movement's final chord; or the abrupt ending of No 2; or any number of places where an inner part is brought out with the help of a generously drawn *legato* so that you are left wondering why you never noticed it before.

Indeed, clarity of texture is one of this recording's most glorious virtues, offering a view of the contrapuntal wonders of the music that has

---

BACH ORCHESTRAL SUITES – IN BRIEF

(Nos 1-3) English Baroque Soloists / Sir John Eliot Gardiner
Erato 8573-82931-2 (97' · DDD)　　　Ⓕ**OOⒷ**
Gardiner has a wonderful way with Bach and he and his fine players float this music with a real lightness and flair. Only Nos 1-3.

The English Concert / Trevor Pinnock
Archiv ② 477 6348 (76' · DDD)　　　　　ⓂⒷ
A most enjoyable romp through Bach's suites with some delicious solo work and always an engaging rhythmic drive and flair.

Boston Baroque / Martin Pearlman
Telarc CD80619 (74' · ADD)　　　　　　Ⓜ**O**
A set of performances that pays great attention to detail and nuance. Pearlman is a Bach conductor of imagination and flair.

Brandenburg Consort / Roy Goodman
Hyperion ② CDD22002 (113' · DDD)　　　　Ⓜ
Sometimes Goodman's players are hard pressed by the speeds he chooses but they cope manfully and deliver the suites with great flair and sparkle.

Freiburg Baroque Orchestra / Gottfried von der Goltz
Euroarts 📀 205 0316 (95' · NTSC · 16:9 · 5.1 · 0)
　　　　　　　　　　　　　　　　　　Ⓕ
Never mind the serious faces, this is a fine set of the suites to rival the best audio-only versions. The film is dutiful but not thrilling!

Philharmonia Orchestra / Otto Klemperer
Testament ② SBT2131 (138' · ADD)　　　　Ⓕ
From 1954, the very grand post-war Bach style is displayed by Klemperer and the great Philharmonia Orchestra. Some stunning solo work but it's all very large scale.

Concert des Nations / Jordi Savall
Naïve Astree ES9958 (61' · DDD)　　　　　Ⓜ
A breath of Mediterranean warmth adds an appealing glow to the suites. A fine reminder of one of Spain's leading period ensembles and its charismatic music director.

ASMF / Neville Marriner
EMI Encore 586083-2 (72' · ADD)　　　　　Ⓑ
Marriner's 1984 set of the suites also fits onto a single disc and conveys much of the spirit if not the letter of the authentic movement. A stylish undertaking.

AAM / Christopher Hogwood
Double Decca ② 458 069-2OF2 (118' · DDD)　　Ⓑ
A reading great refinement but also full of vibrant detail. With swift tempi and a keen alertness to rhythmic variety, this is a fine period instrument version. Coupled now with the Double Harpsichord Concerto.

not always been available. This is particularly striking in the potentially murky, homogeneous textures of Nos 3 and 6; but the other, more colourfully scored concertos are just as lucidly done – a triumph of the balancer's art, obviously, but surely just as much a result of clear-headed thinking on the part of the performers. Equally enlivening is a tight attention to articulative detail and tasteful ornamentation which keeps the music bouyant and forward-moving at all times.

Technically, things are not always perfect: the horn players struggle sometimes to keep up in No 1 and the solo trumpet part in No 2 is a bit harum-scarum. But the performances are so joyous and fresh that, in their straightforward but deeply musical way, they are the most invigorating newcomers to the *Brandenburg* fold since Musica Antiqua Köln's provocative recording of the mid-1980s.

Bonuses come in the form of the Sinfonia to Cantata 174 (a version of the first movement of Concerto No 3 to which lusty oboes and horns have been added) and a curious 'patch take' of the shorter, swirling first version of the harpsichord cadenza to No 5. There is also a pleasingly unhyperbolic DVD of the sessions including interviews with Alessandrini.

Brandenburg Concertos Nos 1-6   🅿
**European Brandenburg Ensemble /
Trevor Pinnock**
Avie ② AV2119 (94' · DDD)   Ⓜ❶❶❶❶🅑→

When Trevor Pinnock first recorded the *Brandenburg*s with The English Concert for Archiv in 1982, period performances of these works were relatively rare; today they abound, and it has become harder to make a mark in music that does not readily admit a wide range of interpretations. Not that Pinnock need worry about that at this point in his career. This new recording, made with an ensemble hand-picked for the job, is a 60th-birthday present to himself, and is just what such a project should be: talented musicians relishing each other's company in music of truly inspiring greatness.

Unsurprisingly, it reflects the increased playing standards of 25 years of period-instrument growth. Only Pinnock himself remains from that first line-up, and while the players then were a high-class team, the players of the European Brandenburg Ensemble include some of the finest of today's Baroque chamber players, and there is a relaxed expertise about their performances which seems to allow them to communicate directly and without technical or ideological hindrance. A hint of over-exuberant thickness in the texture of Concerto No 1 is perhaps a reflection of this, but elsewhere it is good to hear playing from the likes of violinist Kati Debretzeni, flautist Katy Bircher and the excellent David Blackadder on trumpet that is bold and confident without straying into coarseness. The clarity achieved in Nos 4, 5

and 6 also has a more natural air than the 'studio-y' balance of the Archiv set, no doubt helped by the decision to use a violone at pitch rather than the more usual octave below. The pensive violin improvisation which links the two movements of No 3 is surely a miscalculation, feeling like more of a hold-up than it need be; more lastingly refreshing to my ears were the subtle relaxations of tension in the first movement of No 6, these days so often given the hard-drive treatment.

This is not a *Brandenburg* set that seeks to score points, and all that is needed from us is to sit back and enjoy its relaxed, celebratory spirit.

Brandenburg Concertos Nos 1-6   🅿
Tafelmusik / Jeanne Lamon vn
Sony Classical ② 07464 66289-2 (93' · DDD)   Ⓜ❶

Tafelmusik's *Brandenburgs* come straight from the heart and as such they're performances that invite repeated listening, and are easy and enjoyable to live with. There are no startling novelties here and nothing which attempts to impede the natural course of musical flow. Tempos are sensibly chosen and, once chosen, consistently adhered to. That isn't to say that there's an absence of affective gesture or a lack of rhetorical awareness. Everything in fact is punctuated in a way that allows the listener to follow the subtly shaded nuances of Bach's dialogue. Some readers may feel that these interpretations lack the stamp of a strong personality but any such fears of interpretative neutrality are largely dispelled by the sensibility of the players and their skill at reaching the heart of the music without the assistance either of pretension or muddled intellectual clutter.

Reservations chiefly concern minutiae of tuning, and to a much lesser extent, ensemble. Neither these weaknesses, nor the occasional blip or thwack, hindering the production of clean notes from oboe, horns or trumpet, spoil enjoyment of Nos 1 and 2. It's a pity that the first movement of No 3 is marred by indifferent tuning and, more disturbingly, by a marked acceleration in speed beginning at bar 84 (3'26"); but the second *Allegro* of the work is so well done that you're inclined to forgive them. Tafelmusik's account of this brilliant binary movement isn't to be missed.

CD80368 – Brandenburg Concertos Nos 1-3   🅿
CD80354 – Brandenburg Concertos Nos 4-6
Boston Baroque / Martin Pearlman hpd
Telarc CD80368/54 (52 & 41' · DDD)   🅕❶

Boston Baroque is a close-knit group of highly accomplished and stylish instrumentalists. On their discs their enthusiasm is clear in the bustling outer movements; it's a wise leader who knows his team, in this case Martin Pearlman, who no doubt set the tempos. In the slow movements there's the breathing-space which is often found lacking. The soloists are first-class (though Friedemann Immer's trumpet trills in Concerto No 2 sound a mite uncomfortable) and the multi-talented Daniel Stepner (violone piccolo in No 2, violin soloist in Nos 4 and 5, and viola soloist in No 6) and Pearlhan himself (harpsichord) are especially impressive. However, it's the ensemble, supported by a finely balanced recording, that makes these accounts so outstanding, and those who are allergic to thin or nasal string sounds will find nothing to cringe from in the warmth of tone that characterises these performances.

The annotation states (but without explanation) that Concerto No 6 'must remain a chamber piece with one player to a part': whether it must or not, the recording shows it to be wholly effective played in that way. We are also told that 'it includes the transparent sounds of gambas' and so it does, but we're left to guess who their players might be. There can be no clear 'best' in the *Brandenburgs*, but this set is likely to remain among those which will prove to be enduring.

Brandenburg Concerto No 5 in D, BWV1050ª.
Concerto for Flute, Violin, Harpsichord in A minor, BWV1044ª. Concerto in the Italian style, 'Italian Concerto', BWV971
ªJaime Martin *fl* ªKenneth Sillito *vn*
ªJakob Lindberg *theo*
ªAcademy of St Martin in the Fields /
Murray Perahia *pf*
Sony Classical SK87326 (55' · DDD)   Ⓕ❍❍❍

 Murray Perahia is first among equals in the concertos, and the whole production is infused with a sense of spontaneous musical interplay. The sense of engagement is infectious. The cadenza of the *Brandenburg* is reminiscent of Alfred Cortot in its bell-like voicing, elegance and, just before the orchestra's return, cumulative excitement.

There are, in a sense, two Perahias at work: the first a non-percussive front-man whose evenly deployed runs are a joy, unlike some who more approximate a hard stick being drawn past iron railings. And then there's the keyboard poet within the orchestra, who even when playing *mezzoforte* or *piano* manages to project a full tone. The presence of a theorbo helps flavour the two concerto slow movements, the Triple Concerto especially. Superb solo playing, too, flautist Jaime Martin producing a memorably plangent tone.

As on previous Perahia Bach concerto recordings, the overriding impression is of intelligence, sensitivity and drama tempered by humility. The *Italian Concerto* begs the by-now familiar question as to how one pair of hands can command so many simultaneous dynamic grades without sounding strained or self-conscious. The outer movements are colourful but never prettified, the principal melody of the central *Andante* like a memory of classic *bel canto*. An exceptional CD.

Six Brandenburg Concertos
Orchestra Mozart / Claudio Abbado
Video director **Andreas Morell**
Medici Arts Ⓕ 🆅 205 6738 (100' · NTSC · 16:9 · PCM stereo, 5.1 and DTS 5.1 · 0)
Recorded live at the Teatro Municipale Romolo Valli, Reggio Emilia in 2007   Ⓕ❍❍

Here Claudio Abbado is gambolling among the *Brandenburg Concertos* in this straightforward TV-style concert film, recorded in the classic 19th-century opera house at Reggio Emilia during an Italian tour in spring 2007.

The orchestra is at first glance a curious gathering, mixing 'Baroque' players such as violinist Giuliano Carmignola and harpsichordist Ottavio Dantone with 'modern' names such as trumpeter Reinhold Friedrich and 'un-Baroque' recorder-player Michala Petri. Furthermore, a look round the instruments reveals mostly modern models, some hybrids (for instance Jacques Zoon's wooden, multi-keyed flute) and a sprinkling of Baroque bows. Mind you, most younger players these days are well versed in Baroque style whatever they play on, and the tenor of these performances is firmly consistent with current ideas of what Baroque music ought to sound like.

So what, then, does Abbado bring to pieces that these days are rarely considered to require a conductor? Well, in the performance itself, not a lot; his batonless beating is minimal, at times barely perceptible, and in Concerto No 6 he is not even on stage. But these are Bach interpretations very much in his image, as detailed and humane as in any Mahler symphony, and infused with a musical sensitivity that is ever-present yet refuses to draw attention to itself. In music that is surely more for players than conductors, he allows fine soloists such as Carmignola, Zoon and the two yearningly exquisite viola soloists in No 6 to shine, yet has clearly worked hard to ensure that every note is in precisely the right place, every tempo convinces, and the texture is always deliciously transparent.

Miscellaneous concertos

Flute Concerto, BWV1050a. Orchestral Suite No 2, BWV1067. Flute Concerto (after BWV209/1, BWV173a/2 & BWV207/3, ed Zimei)
Marcello Gatti *fl* **Aurora Ensemble** (Rossella Croce *vn* Joanna Huszcza *va* Judith-Maria Olofsson *vc* Riccardo Coelati *vion* Michele Barchi *hpd*) /
Enrico Gatti *vn*
Glossa GCD921204 (56' · DDD)   Ⓕ

Three pieces: a new concerto, an old friend in a (not very) different guise, and a repertory staple. The 'new concerto' is a reconstruction by Francesco Zimei based on movements from three of Bach's secular cantatas. In his booklet-note, Zimei sets out the reasoning behind his choice: it reads convincingly and, more important, the result sounds convincing as well.

The 'old friend', billed as a Triple Concerto, is none other than the Fifth *Brandenburg Concerto* in an earlier version, BWV1050*a*. Most of us would be hard pressed to spot the difference – minor variations of figuration, mostly in the harpsichord part, and four bars less in the third movement – with two exceptions: there's no satisfying chord to herald the reprise in that movement, and the famous harpsichord cadenza consists of only 18 bars.

The 'repertory staple' is, of course, the Second Orchestral Suite. Marcello Gatti, Michele Barchi and the single strings of Ensemble Aurora are all superb, playing with grace and style. This disc is very warmly recommended.

Orchestral Suites

C, **BWV1066**; B minor, **BWV1067**; D, **BWV1068**; D, **BWV1069**

Orchestral Suites, BWV1066-9
Boston Baroque / Martin Pearlman
Telarc CD80619 (74 '·DDD)   Ⓕ Ⓞ

Scholars are now sure that Bach did not plan his four orchestral suites as a set – unlike the six *Brandenburg Concertos*. It seems likely, then, that the stylistic diversity exhibited in the suites is inadvertent, not, as in the case of the *Brandenburgs*, an overt display of compositional virtuosity. On recordings, however, the suites are usually presented as an entity, so the fact that each has its own identifiable personality actually has taken on interpretive significance.

On this Telarc disc, Martin Pearlman effectively delineates the unique character of each work. The C major Suite is essentially lyrical, its phrases unfolding in long, florid arcs; the B minor suite is more fidgety, particularly in the Overture, with its tense trills; and the two D major suites combine grandeur and gaiety. Yet Pearlman remains true to the specific nature of each dance form, as well – listen to the four bourées in succession (the only dance that appears in every suite), for example, and you will find a remarkable consistency of tempo and spirit.

Special attention has also been paid to details of instrumental balance, with admirably transparent results. Some might prefer a bit more thrust and bite from the trumpets in the D major works, where Pearlman prefers to blend the brass into the orchestral fabric, but the sound is still exhilaratingly brilliant.

The crystalline quality of Telarc's recording reveals a few slight imperfections in the strings' intonation; otherwise Boston Baroque's virtuosity and élan leaves little to be desired. Indeed, the Bostonians' interpretation is a strong contender in a crowded field.

Orchestral Suites – No 1 in C, BWV1066; No 4 in D, BWV1069. Sonata for Violin and Harpsichord No 4 in C minor, BWV1017. Cantata No 21, 'Ich hatte viel Bekümmernis', BWV21 - Sinfonia

Amandine Beyer *vn*
Le Concert Français / Pierre Hantaï *hpd*
Mirare MIR017 (69' · DDD)   Ⓕ

Converting a reputation as a distinguished solo harpsichordist into one as an orchestral director is not an obvious path these days. Performances of Bach's Suites are usually led from the continuo keyboard, though Pierre Hantaï would argue that greater control of detail can be best effected with a dedicated conductor at the helm. We know from Hantaï's thoughtful and challenging performances (his *Goldbergs* as prime examples) that each part of a journey needs appropriate attention with a view to its contribution to the whole. It is this, above all, which provides us with two suites where the dances cannot have felt more mutually integrated than here.

The curtain-raising Fourth Suite is a case in point after a blisteringly incisive, restless and punchy overture – one which both here and in the First Suite carries its Gallic ostentation to heights which Bach may have witnessed in the faux French courts of early-18th-century Germany. Instead of presenting diversely stylised vignettes, Hantaï brings a consistently infectious *réjouissance* to each movement until the final dance of that name. The scope is one of contained characterisation, carefully chiselled and fleet-of-foot articulation counterbalanced by delicately nuanced *legatos* and natural resonance.

The great C major First Suite is no less considered and polished. If generally rather clipped and fey, it comes as a welcome release after a hard, edgy, metronomic and small-scale performance of the C minor Sonata for violin and obbligato harpsichord, a work which deserves far greater expressive exploration than we hear from Hantaï and violinist Amandine Beyer.

In sum, here are interesting alternative readings of two great orchestral suites, lovingly nurtured but strangely ephemeral in effect – as perhaps these recreational works should be.

Trio Sonatas

E flat, **BWV525**; C minor, **BWV526**; D minor, **BWV527**; E minor, **BWV528**; C, **BWV529**; G, **BWV530**

Trio Sonatas, BWV525-30.
Purcell Quartet (Catherine Weiss vn, Catherine Mackintosh vn, Robert Woolley hpd, Richard Boothby va da gamba)
Chandos Chaconne CHAN0654 (73' · DDD)   Ⓕ Ⓑ→

'Too good to be left only to organists' is how Richard Boothby cheekily describes Bach's six delightful 'organ trios', in which the organist's two hands play one of the upper lines each, while the bass is played on the pedals. Such is the integrity of this texture in Bach's writing that transferral of this music to a 'true' trio sonata line-up of two melody instruments and continuo is a relatively simple and satisfactory task, and there seems to have been no shortage in recent years of musicians who would agree with Boothby to the point of making their own arrangements for various small ensembles. On disc, these have often served as filler items. Recordings of all six are rarer.

Boothby's arrangements for the Purcell Quartet differ from the others currently available in involving no wind instruments. He shows considerable imagination, however, in convincingly varying the scoring between just two violins, viola da gamba and harpsichord, transferring the melodic line to his own viola da gamba whenever the tessitura demands in some movements, making it a full-blown partner in the dialogue in others, and also awarding the harpsichord a melodic role in BWV530.

Typically for the Purcell Quartet, the performances offer a sweet sound and a clarity of texture which is all to the good in such intricately and ingeniously contrapuntal music. Generally speaking, however, these performances are enjoyable for their lightness and tenderness (try the slow movement of BWV529). If you want something livelier, and do not necessarily require all six sonatas, you may just favour the Palladian Ensemble's characteristically alert recording of four of them on Linn (see below).

Additional recommendation

Trio Sonatas, BWV525, 527, 529, 530   **P**
Coupled with: Four Duets, BWV802-5.
14 Verschiedene Canones, BWV1087
Palladian Ensemble
Linn Records CKD036 (75' · DDD)   ⓕ
  Refreshingly committed performances which stray from old paths in stimulating ways and show off the corporate style of the Palladian Ensemble.

Flute Sonatas

B minor, **BWV1030**; E flat, **BWV1031**; A, **BWV1032**; C, **BWV1033**; E minor, **BWV1034**; E, **BWV1035**

Flute Sonatas – B minor, BWV1030;   **P**
C, BWV1033; E minor, BWV1034; E, BWV1035.
Solo Flute Partita in A minor, BWV1013.
Ashley Solomon *fl* **Terence Charlston** *hpd*
Channel Classics CCS15798 (71' · DDD)   ⓕ**OO**

This is an impressive and enjoyable CD that easily bears repeated listening. There's a soothing quality to the Baroque flute, and its gentle, slightly reedy tone is captured very well here. It's closely recorded in a church acoustic to give a brilliant tone with added depth. Today's makers of the Baroque flute are producing highly refined instruments, exemplified here by the Rod Cameron copy of a Denner, which has a strong, even tone and good balance of register, allowing highly accomplished performers like Ashley Solomon complete technical freedom.

This recording isn't merely music therapy, however, but a genuine musical experience. His performance of the unaccompanied A minor

BACH CELLO SUITES – IN BRIEF

Mstislav Rostropovich
EMI ② 555363-2 (147' · DDD)   ⓕ**O**ⓑ➛
Big-hearted, bold-gestured Bach from one of the greatest cellists of our time. Here is emotion writ large but done with such passion it's hard not to be won over.

Heinrich Schiff
EMI ② 586534-2 (124' · DDD)   ⓑ**OO**ⓑ➛
One of the finest modern-instrument performances that takes academic advances into account, making for a delightfully buoyant set of the suites. Quite a bargain.

Pablo Casals
EMI mono ② 562611-2 (130' · ADD)   Ⓜ**O**ⓑ➛
or Naxos mono ② 8 110915/6 (149')   Ⓢ**O**ⓑ➛
A historic set from the 1930s which shows off the integrity and artistry of the man who rescued these works for posterity. Warts and all, these have to be heard.

Pierre Fournier
DG ② 449 711-2GOR2 (139' · ADD)   Ⓜ**OOO**ⓑ➛
For many the classic performances: expressive, full-bodied yet never threatening to overwhelm the music. Fournier clearly adores this music and it shows.

Yo-Yo Ma
Sony Classical ② 82876 78751-2 (143' · DDD) Ⓜ**O**ⓑ➛
The first of Ma's two cycles of the suites and at the price well worth considering for this fine cellist's innate musicality.

Pieter Wispelwey
Channel Classics ② CCS12298 (140' · DDD) ⓕ**OO**
Another cellist with two sets to his name offers a period approach that positively dances with a lightness of touch and songfulness. A real *tour de force*.

Truls Mørk
Virgin Classics ② 545650-2 (141' · DDD)   ⓕⓑ➛
A modern interpretation that brings many lessons from the period-instrument movement. It has a terrific 'rightness' about it and really dances.

Steven Isserlis
Hyperion ② CDA67541/2 (137' · DDD)   ⓕ**OOO**
He bided his time before taking these works into the studio, but the wait has been worth it because these are wonderfully lived-in ans thought-about interpretations. Experience shines from every note. A modern classic?

Mischa Maisky
DG ③ 463 314-2GH3 (136' · DDD)   ⓕⓑ➛
Another cellist who felt the need to return to these infinitely rewarding pieces. He has so much more to say, albeit in a big, quasi-romantic style. Also has a fascinating CD-ROM extra.

Partita, for example, is nothing short of commanding: the control in articulation and breathing allows the phrasing to be flexible and unfussy. It's the directness of his interpretations that's so telling; there's almost none of that slightly coy *rubato* that some other flautists use to disguise the need to breathe. Rather, Solomon ensures that the phrases are neither choppy nor fragmented. He has an excellent sense of the longer line and the harmonic pull beneath Bach's wonderfully melodic writing. The faster movements are perhaps the most successful, full of buoyancy and energy without seeming rushed or pushed. Try the second movement of the E minor Sonata, for example, or that of the C major. Slow movements are far from inexpressive, but again refreshingly direct: he never wallows (a good example is the introductory movement of the E major Sonata).

Solomon is well partnered by Terence Charlston on a rich-toned Ruckers-copy harpsichord. Even if you already have a version of Bach's flute works on CD this can be strongly recommended, and it makes an equally good first-time buy too. Prepare to be uplifted.

Six Sonatas, BWV1030-35ª. Sonata, BWV1020.
Trio Sonata, BWV1039ᵇ
Emmanuel Pahud *fl* **Trevor Pinnock** *hpd*
with ᵃᵇ**Jonathan Manson** *vc* ᵇ**Silvia Careddu** *fl*
EMI ② 217443-2 (101' · DDD)　　　Ⓜ❍➔

Bach flute sonata recordings on modern instruments are not unknown but a 'complete' set of all seven authentic and doubtful works, plus the Sonata for two flutes and continuo (better known as the G major Gamba Sonata), is bit of a rarity. That said, we can be glad that the excellent Emmanuel Pahud is the one to have taken up the challenge, for this is a recording of great skill and refinement which should give considerable pleasure. He has teamed up with distinguished Baroque-specialising partners to achieve results that are technically assured and stylistically confident.

The most immediately attractive feature of these performances is their touching and gentle beauty; Pahud never forces the sound and maintains an evenly controlled tone at all times, with no tightening on high notes or straining on low ones. It is true that he is without the constant subtle shadings possible on a Baroque wooden flute, but for the most part Pahud's playing shows a sensitive concern for detailed and enlivening articulation without being slave to it, and a keen sense of the music's greater rise and fall, revealed in some drowsily relaxed slow movements.

The recording is not generous to the harpsichord, which, while crisply caressed as ever by Pinnock, is too far back to contribute as meaningfully as it should in the sonatas where it has an obbligato role equal to the flute's, and neither is there any great sweetening of sound for compensation. But this is fine stuff nevertheless.

Lute Works

Suites – G minor, **BWV995**; E minor, **BWV996**;
C minor, **BWV997**; E, **BWV1006a**
Prelude, Fugue and Allegro in E flat, **BWV998**
Prelude in C minor, **BWV999**
Fugue in G minor, **BWV1000**
Lute Suites – BWV995-97, 1006a. Prelude, Fugue and Allegro in E flat, BWV998. Prelude in C minor, BWV999. Fugue in G minor, BWV1000
Stephan Schmidt *gtr*
Naïve ② V4861 (98' · DDD)　　　Ⓟ❍❍❍

Whether or not the description of these as 'lute' works is justified has long been a matter for debate, and in their annotation Stephan Schmidt and Claude Chauvel inevitably fail to resolve the matter, though they lean more in the direction of 'yes' than most. In a sense it matters little, for the works have been performed and recorded on a variety of other plucked-string instruments – harpsichord and lute-harpsichord as well as guitar – in exemplary fashion. The 'standard' six-string guitar is a baritone instrument, but its lowest register isn't extended enough to avoid the need for compromises; accordingly guitars with more strings (the extra ones at the bass end) have been in use for over 30 years. Now Schmidt, using 10 strings, sets a new benchmark with this magnificent set. The extra four strings give firmer bass and more resonant bass lines, as did Söllscher's five, and free the player's left hand from the restriction of having to hold many of them down.

Schmidt's touch is happily light in the *galanteries* and in the Loure of BWV1006a, but there's gravity in the unhurried sarabandes – such variations apply not only to pace but to spirit, too. He knows when to embellish (which he does with elegance) and when not. His *rubato* 'bends' a little more than Söllscher's and he's less conservative in his approach to embellishment – but attitudes to such matters have since eased. If there's a better version of these works on any kind of guitar in terms of content and recording quality we have yet to hear it.

Viola da gamba Sonatas

Bach Three Viola da gamba Sonatas, BWV1027-29
CPE Bach Viola da gamba Sonata, H559 Wq137
Daniel Müller-Schott *vc* **Angela Hewitt** *pf*
Orfeo C693 071A (55' · DDD) Ⓕ

From the moment the cello starts its suave tread over the piano's gently rising bass and sustained right-hand trill at the beginning of the G major Sonata, you know this is going to be a disc to sit back and enjoy. Daniel Müller-Schott and Angela Hewitt may have substituted modern instruments for the viola da gamba and harpsichord Bach had in mind but nothing in this superb music's original character has been lost – this is as clear-textured and as vividly articulated a performance as you could hope to hear. Indeed, it has gained much by the sheer musical feeling and intelligence that these two players have put into it, aided by extra warmth from Müller-Schott's cello (achieved without resorting to excessive vibrato) and from the delicate dynamic subtleties of Hewitt's piano-playing.

There are some memorable moments here. Architecturally, too, they consistently get things just right. With a perfect balance between instruments, this is playing which gives nothing but a glow of pleasure, that not even what sounds like some weary tuning at the piano's top end can dispel.

All Bach gamba sonata discs need a filler, and the choice here is a sonata by CPE Bach, rather more romantically drawn by Müller-Schott and with a continuo accompaniment less well suited to the piano. But then this disc is worth your money for the JS alone.

Additional recommendation

Viola da gamba Sonatas, BWV1027-29
Coupled with: Trio Sonata in C, BWV529   ℗
Savall *va da gamba* **Koopman** *hpd*
Alia Vox AV9812 (59' · DDD)   Ⓕ

A significant Bach gamba release. Savall and Koopman conjure performances whose sheer rightness and creative warmth make the music sound invigoratingly fresh.

Violin Sonatas

No 1 in B minor, BWV1014; **No 2** in A, BWV1015; **No 3** in E, BWV1016; **No 4** in C minor, BWV1017; **No 5** in F, BWV1018; **No 6** in G, BWV1019

Violin Sonatas Nos 1-6, BWV1014-19   ℗
Sonata for Violin and Continuo in G, BWV1019*a*ᵃ.
Cantabile, BWV1019a/2. Sonatas for Violin and Continuoᵃ – No 2 in G, BWV1021; No 4 in E minor, BWV1023
Rachel Podger *vn* ᵃ**Jonathan Manson** *va da gamba*
Trevor Pinnock *hpd*
Channel Classics ② CCS14798 (139' · DDD)   ○○○

A recording of Bach's violin sonatas that really hits the spot. Rachel Podger has already attracted much praise for her recordings of the solo violin music, but is heard here to even better advantage in the Six Sonatas for violin and obbligato harpsichord, BWV1014-19, for which she's joined by Trevor Pinnock.

The two make a fine match. Both are uncomplicated, instinctive musicians with a sure technical command and sound stylistic sense, and in works as robust and complete as these, that's most of the battle already won. But this is also music of great poetry, and, without straining unduly to make their points, Podger and Pinnock bring this out superbly; Pinnock's harpsichord is gently resonant and softly voiced, and Podger coaxes a lyrical flexibility out of her violin, its singing qualities enhanced thanks to a

restrained but telling use of vibrato – one which also enables her to play more consistently and blessedly in tune than almost any other Baroque fiddler currently in business.

It's difficult to single out details of this recording for comment; there just seems to be such a tremendous feeling of overall 'rightness' to it. Maybe the finale of Sonata No 2 seems rather frantic and the wonderful *Adagio ma non tanto* of No 3 a touch lumpy, but there really isn't much else to criticise. And there are true gems to be enjoyed in the opening movement of BWV1014, where the violin makes an almost imperceptible initial entry, or the warm embrace of BWV1017's *Adagio*, or practically any of the sparkling fast movements, played with invigorating rhythmic drive and clarity.

This recording's closest period rival, that of Andrew Manze and Richard Egarr, shows a typical wealth of new ideas and inspired moves but is less satisfying as a whole, and suffers from some intonationally hairy moments and a less precisely pointed sound. The only period recording to touch Podger and Pinnock for technical assurance is that of Fabio Biondi and Rinaldo Alessandrini, but in both sound and interpretation it's heavy-handed compared with the spontaneous musicianship and airy texture on display here, and rather meanly it gives the six obbligato sonatas only. Though all the recent recordings of these sonatas have had their merits, this – two discs for the price of one – is, quite simply, the best yet.

Solo Cello Suites

No 1 in G, BWV1007; **No 2** in D minor, BWV1008; **No 3** in C, BWV1009; **No 4** in E flat, BWV1010; **No 5** in C minor, BWV1011; **No 6** in D, BWV1012

Solo Cello Suites Nos 1-6
Pierre Fournier *vc*
DG The Originals ② 449 711-2GOR2 (139' · ADD)
Recorded 1961-63   Ⓜ○○○↩

Of all the great cellists, Pierre Fournier came closer to the heart of the music than almost any other. He seems to have possessed all the virtues of his fellow cellists without yielding to any of their self-indulgences. He could be brilliant in execution – his technique was second to none, as he proves throughout this set – profound in utterance, aristocratic in poise and wonderfully coherent in his understanding of Bach's articulation and phrases.

We need look no further than the *Prelude* of the First Suite in G major to find the supreme artistry which characterises each and every moment of these performances. There are very occasionally notes which fail to reach their centre but they're few and far between, and Fournier's intonation compares favourably with that of some of his virtuoso companions. Fournier's *rubato* is held tightly in rein and when he does apply it, it's in the interests of enlivening aspects of Bach's formal writing. He can sparkle too, as he does in many of the faster dance-orientated movements such as courantes, gavottes and bourrées; in the sarabandes, he invariably strikes a note of grandeur coupled with a concentration amounting at times almost to abstraction. Above all, his Bach playing is crowned with an eloquence, a lyricism and a grasp of the music's formal and stylistic content which will not easily be matched. Fine recorded sound and strongly commended on virtually all counts.

Solo Cello Suites Nos 1-6*.   **H**
English Suite No 6 in D, BWV811 – Gavotte I;
Gavotte II (arr Pollain). Musicalisches Gesangbuch –
Komm, süsser Tod, BWV478 (arr Siloti). Violin Sonata,
BWV1003 – Andante (arr Siloti). Orchestral Suite No 3
in D, BWV1068 – Air (arr Siloti). Toccata, Adagio and
Fugue in C, BWV564 – Adagio
Pablo Casals vc with **Nikolai Mednikoff,**
Blas-Net, Otto Schulf pfs
*EMI mono 562611-2 (132' · ADD)   ⓂⒶ➔

Naxos Historical mono ② 8 110915/6 (149' · ADD)
Recorded 1927-39   ⓈⒶ➔

When these recordings first appeared back in the 1930s and 40s, Bach for solo cello was a singular and esoteric concept. Casals had rediscovered the Suites for modern ears and his probing, albeit highly idiosyncratic, playing was a mandatory recommendation. Indeed, in those days it was the only recommendation. Nowadays, his achievement is still beyond question, but there will be some listeners who won't like what they hear.

After, say, the elegantly tapered playing of János Starker, Casals can initially sound wilful and ungainly. His bow seems to slice through chords like a meat cleaver. His intonation wanders, and his fingers press down on the strings so forcefully that a note 'pings' even before the bow is drawn. Casals reels and rhapsodises as if blind drunk on expressive freedom.

However, this impression is only transitory. What at first sounds gruff, even off-hand soon registers as boldly assertive. The intonation isn't so much 'faulty' as expressively employed, and as for those pre-echoing 'pings', they soon cease to matter – much as Glenn Gould's mumbling did years later. Time teaches you that the speaking tone, the poetic *tenutos*, the irresistible lilt in faster dance movements and the varied approach to vibrato were part of a grand musical plan, one that's now cherishable.

Casals makes a singular musical experience out of every movement. Try the Courante and Sarabande of the Fifth Suite – muscular resolve followed by profound self-communing.

Transfer-wise, things could hardly have gone better. True, there's some surface noise, but the sound has considerable realism and the broad contours of Casals's tone are untroubled by excessive filtering. A rival package from Pearl (identical couplings plus a transcription from a Bach-Vivaldi Concerto) reports a fatter cello sound with less well-focused contours. EMI's set offers only the Suites in transfers that, while admirably clear, are rather less natural than Ward Marston's for Naxos.

Solo Cello Suites Nos 1-6
Traditional The Song of the Birds (arr Beamish)
Steven Isserlis vc
Hyperion ② CDA67541/2 (137' · DDD)   Ⓕ●●●

Steven Isserlis clearly venerates Casals as an important figure in the suites' history, even paying touching homage to him by appending a performance of a Catalan folksong. Like Casals, Isserlis bided his time before committing them to disc, and he has looked for interpretative guidance to extra-musical ideas. Isserlis proposes a detailed concept. For him the Suites suggest a meditative cycle on the life of Christ, rather like Biber's Mystery Sonatas. He points out that this is 'a personal feeling, not a theory', but it has to be said that once you know that he is thinking of the Agony in the Garden during the darkly questioning Second Suite (the five stark chords towards the end of the Prélude representing the wounds of Christ), the Crucifixion in the wearily troubled Fifth or the Resurrection in the joyous Sixth, it adds immense power and interest to his performances.

But then, this is also the most wonderful cello-playing, surely among the most consistently beautiful to have been heard in this demanding music, as well as the most musically alert and vivid. Not everyone will like the brisk tempi (though the Allemandes, for instance, gain in architectural coherence), but few will fail to be charmed by Isserlis's sweetly singing tone, his perfectly voiced chords and superb control of articulation and dynamic – the way the final chord of the First Prélude dies away is spellbinding. There are so many other delights: the subtle comings and goings of the Third Prélude, the nobly poised Fifth Allemande, the swaggering climax that is the Sixth Gigue – to name but a few. Suffice to say that Isserlis's Bach is a major entrant into an already highly distinguished field, and a disc many will want to return to again and again.

Solo Cello Suites Nos 1-6   **P**
Pieter Wispelwey vc
Channel Classics ② CCS12298 (140' · DDD)   Ⓕ●●

Pieter Wispelwey is equally at home on Baroque and modern instruments. These performances are carefully prepared, beautifully executed and most eloquently expressed. The instruments, too, sound well, Wispelwey having chosen an early 18th-century cello by Barak Norman for the first five Suites, and a five-stringed *violoncello piccolo* by an unidentified craftsman for the special requirements of the Sixth.

Wispelwey is an imaginative player with a highly developed sense of fantasy. These qualities are as welcome in his performances of Bach as they're to be treated with circumspection in his almost entirely fanciful written introduction to the music. Preludes come across especially well since it's in these wonderfully varied opening movements, with their rhetorical diversity, that the performer can give rein most freely to his or her most natural conversational inflexions. And he makes the most of that thrilling climax at the peak of a chromatic accent through a full scale and a half. Sarabandes are profound and reflective without being weighty, and allemandes graceful and substantial. The *galanteries*, by contrast, are lightly bowed and redolent of playful and demonstrative gestures. That, to an extent, is true also of the courantes, while the gigues are firmly projected, full-toned and splendidly robust.

Wispelwey's set of Bach's Cello Suites, then, is deserving of praise. If you're familiar with the gruff grandeur of Pablo Casals, or the aristocratic nobility of Fournier, then these performances will throw an entirely different light on the music, more conversational and with airier discourse. You may never want to be without the two earlier sets, but Wispelwey's version sits comfortably on the uppermost range of the period-instrument performance ladder.

Solo Violin Sonatas & Partitas

Sonatas – **No 1** in G minor, BWV1001; **No 2** in A minor, BWV1003, BWV1005; **No 3** in C.
Partitas – **No 1** in B minor, BWV1002; **No 2** in D minor, BWV1004; **No 3** in E, BWV1006

CCS12198: Sonata No 1. Partitas Nos 1 & 2   ℗
CCS14498: Sonatas Nos 2 & 3. Partita No 3
Rachel Podger vn
Channel Classics ② CCSSEL2498 (142' · DDD)
℗ ○○○

Hitherto we have heard Rachel Podger only in early chamber works and as Andrew Manze's partner in Bach double concertos: here now, at last, is an opportunity to hear her on her own. And you couldn't be more on your own than in Bach's mercilessly revealing Solo Sonatas and Partitas, perhaps the ultimate test of technical mastery, expressiveness, structural phrasing and deep musical perception for a violinist. Playing a Baroque instrument, Podger challenges comparison with the much praised and individual reading by Monica Huggett: she has many of the same virtues – flawless intonation, warm tone, expressive nuances, clear understanding of the proper balance of internal strands – but her approach is sometimes markedly different. This is most obvious in the great D minor Chaconne, in which Huggett's rhythmical flexibility worried some people, but in which Podger, here as else-

where, while fully characterising the varied repetitions of the ground, is intent on building up the cumulative effect. One pleasing general feature of her playing, indeed, is her firm but unassertive rhythmic sense; others are the absence of any suspicion that technical difficulties exist (instead a calm control, as in the G minor's Siciliano), her subtle phrasing (as in the B minor Corrente, with the fleetest of *doubles*), the cross-rhythms of her G minor *Presto* and, most strikingly, the poetic feeling with which she imbues the initial *Adagio* of the G minor Sonata. She touches in chords lightly: though some might have been split downwards rather than upwards so as to preserve the continuity of a lower part (for example, in bar 5 of the B minor Allemande, bar 10 of the Chaconne and in the 18th and 19th bars of its major section). Her D minor Giga is stunning. Altogether a most impressive and rewarding disc.

As a matter of tactics disregarding the printed order of the works, the second disc opens in the most effective way with a joyous performance of the ever-invigorating E major *Preludio*. At once we can recognise Podger's splendid rhythmic and tonal vitality (not merely Bach's marked terraced dynamics but pulsatingly alive gradations within phrases), her extremely subtle accentuations and harmonic awareness (note her change of colour at the move from E to C sharp major in bar 33), are all within total technical assurances. The Gavotte en Rondeau is buoyantly dance-like, and in the most natural way she elaborates its final statement (throughout the Partita her ornamentation is stylish and convincing). She takes the Giga at a restrained pace that allows of all kinds of tiny rhythmic nuances. Only a rather cut-up performance of the Loure detracts.

In the sonatas she shows other sterling qualities. She preserves the shape in the A minor Grave's ornate tangle of notes; she judges to a nicety the balance of the melodic line against the plodding accompanimental quavers of the *Andante*; she imbues the C major's *Adagio* with a hauntingly poetic musing atmosphere, and her lucid part-playing of its Fuga could scarcely be bettered. In the Fuga of the A minor Sonata, however, she unexpectedly allows herself considerable rhythmic freedom in order to point the structure. The final track is a stunning performance of the C major's closing *Allegro assai* which would bring any audience to its feet.

Violin Sonatas and Partitas, BWV1001-6
Gidon Kremer vn
ECM New Series ② 476 7291 (131' · DDD)   ℗

Are a beautiful sound and a warm, singing tone as important to you as intelligent, stylish interpretation in Bach's Sonatas and Partitas? If so, you probably won't sympathise with Gidon Kremer's seeming determination to bypass his instrument in pursuit of musical truths, nor the hard-hitting, raw, squeezed-out quality of many notes above the stave and loud broken chords (although Kremer's intonation is, for the most part, absolutely dead-on).

The utterly unprettified G minor and C major Sonatas' *adagios*, for example, are brisker and grittier than what one usually hears. While many treat the B minor Partita's opening Allemande as an expansive aria, Kremer's headlong tempo, emphatic double-dotting and pronounced dynamic contrasts realise the music's French ouverture implications, making it easy to slip into the following Double movement unnoticed. Following a dazzling sprint through the *Presto* Double Kremer reduces the Sarabande and Double to a studied and rather precious whisper.

Kremer shapes the three sonatas' fugues in large, dramatic arcs, intensified by subtle tempo fluctuations. His unusually soft playing of the D minor Chaconne's most virtuoso passages convinces more than his dynamic exaggerations in bars 32-33. Similarly, the E major Partita's archly phrased Gavotte and Rondeau contrast with Kremer's imaginatively inflected, tough, driving dispatch of the Preludio.

With Kremer's earlier solo Bach set unavailable, his equally controversial yet more evolved (and better engineered) remakes offer ample food for thought, if not quite a first choice.

Solo Violin Sonatas and Partitas, BWV1001-06
Viktoria Mullova vn
Onyx ② ONYX4040 (132' · DDD)　　　　　Ⓕ

Viktoria Mullova plays a gut-strung Guadagnini (in modern set-up) at low pitch, using a Baroque-style bow, so it's with the period instrument Bach recordings that Mullova can be most usefully compared.

These are outstanding performances, however, whatever category they belong to. Mullova brings together several ideal qualities for a Bach player. Firstly, there's a secure sense of style, apparent equally in the rhythm and character of each of the Partitas' dances, and in the ornamented introductory movements of the first two Sonatas. Then there's her superior, virtuoso's technique, producing beautifully precise tuning and, in the fugal movements, finely controlled, varied and euphonious playing of the most densely polyphonic passages. To this we can add her deep musical understanding; by means of subtle emphasis and natural dynamic contrasts, she draws our attention to the beauty of Bach's harmonic progressions and to the balance and grandeur of his designs. Even on the few occasions where Mullova isn't entirely convincing the poise and sheer quality of the playing remains extremely persuasive.

There have been many fine recent recordings of these works, but this one is definitely not to be missed.

Violin Sonatas and Partitas, BWV1001-06
Christian Tetzlaff vn
Hänssler Classic ② CD98 250 (130' · DDD)　Ⓕ⒪Ⓞ➔

Christian Tetzlaff, always one of the most thoughtful, imaginative violinists, has obviously found Bach's solo works a stimulating and rewarding challenge. Technically, he's most impressive: using a modern bow, he can achieve, with each phrase, the kind of subtle give and take that's normally the preserve of the best Baroque violinists. His chord playing, too, shows wonderful control; in the more densely polyphonic pieces – the Chaconne and the fugues in the three sonatas – it seems there's often little choice between aggressive accentuation and rhythmic distortion caused by spreading the chords. Tetzlaff, however, manages to avoid both pitfalls, with varied arpeggiation that never fails to take account of the music's rhythmic requirements.

The performances have a remarkable air of spontaneity, the result of a pervasive *rubato*, especially notable in the ornamented opening movements of the first two sonatas, and in the freer sections of the Chaconne. There's a sense of line and balance that ensures that each departure from metronomic regularity sounds entirely natural, unlocking the music's expressive potential. This is even felt when, in a few movements in the partitas, the dance character suggests a more regular, metrical pulse. Apart from this, it's notable how Tetzlaff realises the virtuosity of Bach's violin writing – the *moto perpetuo* finales of the sonatas sound truly thrilling, full of temperament and fire. Do investigate this outstanding set.

Violin Sonatas and Partitas, BWV1001-6
Itzhak Perlman vn
EMI ② 476811-2 (143' · DDD)　　　ⓂⓄ⒪➔

These works are brutally difficult to play, not least in securing accurate intonation and in minimising the disruptive effect of hacking out the three- and four-note chords but, given today's Olympian standards, technical shortcomings may be tolerated only in performances that are musically relevatory.

Technically Perlman is beyond reproach; chords are traversed deftly and in the *Adagio* of Sonata No 3 skilfully subjugated to the melodic line, and his differentiation between marked *pianos* and *fortes* is very clear. There's brilliance in the faster movements, delicacy in the *galanteries*, and except perhaps for the Allemande of Partita No 2, grave expressiveness in the slower ones; stylistic misfits are far fewer than those of, say, Sándor Végh or Nathan Milstein (1971), and all repeats are offered – usually with some changes of dynamics.

Bach with a fair degree of gloss maybe, but a version by one of today's greatest violinists that's justly popular.

Solo Violin Partita No 2 in D minor, BWV1004.
Two-part Inventions, BWV772-86. Three-part Inventions, BWV787-801.
Janine Jansen vn **Maxim Rysanov** va
Torleif Thedéen vc
Decca 475 9081DH (79' · DDD)　　　　Ⓕ➔

Bach tends to sound well in any arrangement, and the Two- and Three-part Inventions certainly make entirely convincing string music, but it seems slightly odd to play the two-part pieces as violin/viola duos when violin and cello could play them with minimal alteration to the original text. Jansen and Rysanov are finely matched, however, and the necessary octave transpositions don't impair the sense of the music in any way. Both sets of Inventions receive exceptional performances, bursting with spirit and imagination. The fifth Three-part Invention is a delight, with *pizzicato* cello and beautifully stylish ornamentation in the upper parts, and the lightness and brilliance of the penultimate Two-part Invention would lift anyone's spirits. Some pieces (eg Nos 9 and 15 of the Two-part) are played throughout in an ultra-quiet, spectral style – very striking, though it's an approach that tends to iron out Bach's expressive gestures. But throughout there's a sense of enjoyment that's most inspiriting.

Coming between the sets of short pieces, the Partita appears the more expansive. Janine Jansen makes the most of this – her playing is remarkable for its sense of continuity and feeling for the long line. Her interpretations may lack something of the compelling detail of Christian Tetzlaff's more closely recorded performance (see page 49), but, with her powerful yet flexible rhythmic sense, she gives us something just as impressive. Her Corrente and Giga have a joyful élan, and the Ciaccona builds in long paragraphs, giving the listener a memorable tour of Bach's grand design.

Lute works

Suites – BWV995; BWV1006a. Sonata No 1, BWV1001
Paul O'Dette *lte*
Harmonia Mundi HMU90 7438 (68' · DDD)   Ⓔ ▶

Bach never wrote directly for lute; his works for the instrument are transcriptions from his pre-existing music or were written for the lute-harpsichord (Lautenwerk), an instrument designed to imitate the lute. The A minor Suite, BWV995, *Pièces pour la Luth à Monsieur Schouster*, is an arrangement of the Cello Suite BWV1011; the Partita in E major is an arrangement of the Partita BWV1006 for solo violin, transposed to F major. The Sonata in G minor is an arrangement by O'Dette of the Sonata in G minor for solo violin BWV1001, modelled after the arrangement of its fugue for lute by Johann Christian Weyrauch, a friend of Bach's.

A direct comparison with Hopkinson Smith's magisterial readings (Astrée) is revealing. He treats the dance in the abstract. His pulse is flexible, his expressive shading copious. O'Dette is determined to restore the dance proper. The rhythmic outlines are sharply defined by a judicious use of *staccato* bass notes and extensive employment of notes *inégales* and other French-style embellishments. That's not to say that O'Dette isn't alive to a more improvisatory

quality, especially in the preludes and the Sonata in G minor. But in short, with his readings, the body dances; with Smith's, the soul. Neither approach is superior to the other – it's merely a matter of emphasis.

English Suites, BWV806-11

Six English Suites, BWV806-11
Glenn Gould *pf*
Sony Classical Glenn Gould Edition ② 07464 52606-2 (112' · ADD). Recorded 1971-73   Ⓜ●
BWV806-8 also available on Glenn Gould Anniversary Edition 69699 87765-2;
BWV809-11 on 69699 87766-2   ●

There has been no more original genius of the keyboard than Glenn Gould, but this has drawbacks as well as thrilling advantages. He can sacrifice depth of feeling for a relentless and quixotic sense of adventure. Yet love it or deride it, every bar of these lovingly remastered discs tingles with *joie de vivre* and an unequalled force and vitality. Try the opening of the First Suite. Is such freedom glorious or maddening, or is the way the odd note is nonchalantly flicked in the following sustained argument a naughty alternative to Bach's intention? The *pizzicato* bass in the second Double from the same Suite is perhaps another instance of an idiosyncrasy bordering on whimsy, an enlivenment or rejuvenation that at least remains open to question. But listen to him in virtually any of the sarabandes and you'll find a tranquillity and equilibrium that can silence such criticism. Even at his most piquant and outrageous his playing remains, mysteriously, all of a piece. The fiercely chromatic, labyrinthine argument concluding the Fifth Suite is thrown off with a unique brio, one of those moments when you realise how he can lift Bach out of all possible time-warps and make him one of music's truest modernists.

English Suites, BWV806-11
Murray Perahia *pf*
Sony Classical ② 88697 31050-2 (128' · DDD)   Ⓜ●●●▶

Murray Perahia's *English Suites* (his first Bach recordings) originally appeared as full-price individual releases, beginning with Nos 1, 3 and 6 in 1997, followed by Nos 2, 4 and 5 in 1998. Now programmed in numerical order, the performances have more than worn well. No matter how full-bodied and luminous his sonority, Perahia is a line player first and foremost, achieving clear, colourfully diversified textures mainly through finger power and hand balance. Perahia's Sarabandes are firmly etched and the Courantes propulsive. Ornaments are adventurous and he brings rhythmic drive to the quicker movements. The superb sound adds further value to an attractively priced reissue that collectors seeking the *English Suites* on the piano ought to seriously consider.

Bach English Suites – No 2, BWV807ᵃ; No 3, BWV808.
Italian Concerto, BWV971. Toccata, BWV911ᵃ.
Capriccio, BWV992ᵃ **Gulda** Prelude and Fugue
Friedrich Gulda pf
DG ᵃmono 477 8020GH (72' · ADD)   Ⓕ▶

Lovingly compiled from a mix of live and studio
recordings by his son Paul, all these performances tell us that Gulda's legendary eccentricity was countered by an acutely economic and
disciplined style and uncompromising musical
integrity. For Gulda, Bach was 'a pillar of moral
support' but for Paul Gulda, his father's life was
full of foibles and oddities rather than airs and
graces, and his lifelong attempt to reconcile the
Apollonian and Dionysian elements in music
were shown in his special reverence for Mozart
and Beethoven. But here, his Bach is of a crystalline clarity combined with an innate musicality
that erases all possible dryness or pedantry. The
Italian Concerto's opening *Allegro* is both sturdy
and magnificently assured, the central *Andante*
magically fine-spun while the final *Presto* is a
marvel of exuberant virtuosity. Gulda's way with
the *English Suites* just possibly tells us the source
of Martha Argerich's dazzling Bach (Gulda was
a guiding force and mentor to her) and throughout all these performances you are made gloriously aware of Bach as a contemporary, a composer for all time. The *Aria de postiglione* is
springy and piquant while for his final offering,
his own *Prelude and Fugue*, Gulda whisks us to
New York's Birdland, the jazz club where, after
playing Beethoven recitals at Carnegie Hall, he
would jam away with his esteemed colleages into
the small hours.
  Excellently recorded and lavishly illustrated,
this special disc is part of 'an ocean of music'
(Argerich) left by a very special pianist.

Toccata in C minor, BWV911. Partita No 2 in C minor,
BWV826. English Suite No 2 in A minor, BWV807
Martha Argerich pf
DG The Originals 463 604-2GOR (50' · ADD)
Recorded 1979   Ⓜ❍▶

This recital, first issued in 1980, has an
extraordinary authority and panache. Argerich's
attack in the C minor Toccata could hardly be
bolder or more incisive, a classic instance of virtuosity all the more clear and potent for being so
firmly but never rigidly controlled. Here, as
elsewhere, her discipline is no less remarkable
than her unflagging brio and relish of Bach's
glory. Again, in the Second Partita, her playing
is quite without those excesses or mannerisms
that too often pass for authenticity, and in the
Andante immediately following the Sinfonie
she's expressive yet clear and precise, her following *Allegro* a marvel of high-speed yet always
musical bravura. True, some may question her
way with the Courante from the Second English
Suite, finding it hard-driven, even overbearing,
yet her eloquence in the following sublime Sarabande creates its own hypnotic authority. The
dynamic range of these towering, intensely

musical performances has been excellently
captured by DG.

French Suites, BWV812-17

Six French Suites, BWV812-17. Sonata in D minor,
BWV964. Five Preludes, BWV924-28. Prelude in
G minor, BWV930. Six Preludes, BWV933-38.
Five Preludes, BWV939-43. Prelude in C minor,
BWV999. Prelude and Fugue in A-minor, BWV894
Angela Hewitt pf
Hyperion ② CDA67121/2 (151' · DDD)   Ⓕ❍

Even the most out-and-out purists who blench
at the thought of Bach on the piano will find it
hard not to be won over by Angela Hewitt's
artistry. Eschewing all hieratic pretentiousness
on the one hand and self-regarding eccentricities on the other, she gives us Bach performances that aren't only admirable in style but
marked by poise, and what used to be called a
'quiet hand': 'chaste' might not be too fanciful a
term, so long as that does not suggest any lack of
vitality. There's intelligence in her carefully
thought-out phrasing and subtle variety of
articulation: gradations of sound are always
alive without their becoming precious. The
bulk of this recording is devoted to the *French
Suites*. Particularly enjoyable is the lightness of
her treatment of the Airs of Nos 2 and 4, the
vigour of No 5's Bourrée and the freshness of
No 6's Allemande; the extra decorations she
adds in repeats everywhere sound properly
spontaneous and are in the best of taste; ornaments are always cleanly played and matched up
in imitative voices.

Keyboard Partitas, BWV825-30

B flat, **BWV825**; C minor, **BWV826**; A minor, **BWV827**;
D, **BWV828**; G, **BWV829**; E minor, **BWV830**

Six Keyboard Partitas, BWV825-30   ℗
Trevor Pinnock hpd
Hänssler Classic ② 92 115 (149' · DDD)   Ⓜ❍❍❍

Ⓖ The six Partitas are virtually a
compendium of Bach's keyboard
styles, with toccatas and French overtures, fugues and fantasies and all manner of
dances. Trevor Pinnock rises to a new level of
mastery in his new recording of them. We all
know about the brilliance of his fingerwork
and his beautifully sprung, ebullient rhythms;
but here he goes further, showing a true grandeur of manner that embraces Bach at his
most serious and pensive, his most learned,
and – above all – his most vividly rhetorical.
Pinnock takes his time over the music: these
are measured readings of the partitas, thought
through, viewed whole. The natural and spontaneous musicianship of old is still there, but
now it's given extra depth and meaning
through the carefully judged articulation,

the tiny moments of hesitation, all within a fluent larger rhythm, that lend extra point and shape to a phrase, a group of phrases, an entire musical paragraph.

The warm, rather resonant recording beautifully captures the rich sound of his instrument – a David Way copy from 1983 of a Hemsch original – as well as the detail of his playing. There could hardly have been a happier return to the recording studio for Pinnock than this fine set.

Six Keyboard Partitas, BWV825-30
Angela Hewitt pf
Hyperion ② CDA67191/2 (143' · DDD) Ⓕ Ⓞ Ⓓ

If Bach is to be played on the piano, this is the kind of way to do it. Inherent in all Hewitt's playing is a rhythmic vitality, always under control, that sweeps you along with its momentum, subtly varied articulation, dynamics that follow the natural rise or fall of phrases without exaggerations, an appreciation of Bach's harmonic tensions, an ability to differentiate between the strength of contrapuntal lines, and an unfailing clarity of texture.

This is a sane and sensible interpretation, deeply musicianly and devoid of eccentricity. Her attitude, rather like Toscanini's, is to accept the text com' è scritto and then to make legitimate adjustments, so we get double-dotting and assimilation of rhythms. Technically she's immaculate, with the cleanest possible ornaments. In the great E minor Sarabande Hewitt is justifiably emotional, without becoming soggy: only in the first half of the A minor Allemande is there a hint of coyness. No, the whole disc gives unalloyed pleasure.

Keyboard Partitas – No 2; No 3; No 4
Cédric Tiberghien pf
Harmonia Mundi HMC90 1869 (78' · DDD) Ⓕ

No double-dotting in the Sinfonia of No 2 or the Overture of No 4; and that alone might be a bone of contention. But there is no consensus on the use of this unwritten Gallic custom. Couperin, for instance, felt it ought to apply only to French music. Muffat disagreed, and included German music in a French style as well. Cédric Tiberghien doesn't challenge his illustrious compatriot. He obeys the text; and while the searing introduction to the Sinfonia might have gained from a compact, incisive rhythm (the swifter third part would certainly have gained from a slower traversal), the corresponding introduction to the Overture is grand indeed. And here the succeeding section is taken at a credible tempo. The result is a lucid yet animated exposé of an imposing movement.

Tiberghien doesn't attempt to imitate a harpsichord, and, apart from a few spread chords, doesn't add embellishments. Again he might be thought of as not adhering to Baroque

performing practices. But, with the exception of the Rondeaux in No 2 and No 3's Fantasia, he does observe repeats, though he prefers to vary them through articulation and dynamics rather than decoration. He uses the piano – tonally a touch strident as recorded – mostly wisely, to offer interpretations of Bach that stretch the expressive envelope, particularly so in deeply felt allemandes and sarabandes. Tiberghien may not please everybody; but his emotional involvement with the music is so high, it is a pleasure to recommend this disc.

Keyboard Partitas – No 2, No 3, No 4
Murray Perahia pf
Sony Classical 88697 22695-2 (60' · DDD) Ⓕ Ⓞ Ⓓ

In Murray Perahia's hands, Bach's Partitas not only work well on the modern concert grand but also sound completely at home. The pianist's vibrant and variegated sonority perpetually sings, while his contrapuntal acumen leaves no detail unconsidered nor unduly fussed over. His tempi always seem right for what the music has to express, as opposed to what Perahia wants to express in the music.

A few examples should suffice to pinpoint what makes these performances special. For instance, the C minor No 2's Allemande and A minor No 3's Corrente's two-part textures gorgeously showcase Perahia's fluent, utterly natural conversational give and take between the hands. The C minor Rondeaux's dance-like profile acquires uncommon and welcome gravitas due to Perahia's measured pulse and a non-legato touch that avoids any hint of percussive residue. The D major Partita No 4 easily takes its place alongside versions by Kapell, Gould, Weissenberg, Hewitt, Tureck and Goode. Strong melodic projection, inner "swing" and a sense of air in between the notes characterise the Corrente, Aria and Menuet. In both the Allemande and Sarabande he gives the decorative righthand lines their full lyrical due, while his left hand provides a strong, decisive underpinning. Even at a brisk tempo, the Gigue speaks clearly and eloquently, with every accent, syncopation and cross-rhythmic gesture perfectly placed. Stylish, well considered and discreet embellishments flavour the repeats in all three works. A release to savour and cherish as we await Partitas Nos 1, 5 and 6.

Keyboard Partitas – No 1, No 3; No 6
Richard Goode pf
Nonesuch 7559-79698-2 (65' · DDD) Ⓕ Ⓞ Ⓞ Ⓞ

 In this second volume of Richard Goode's complete set of Bach Partitas there's the sense of a distinguished lineage, a tradition of Bach piano playing with a Classical-Romantic bent that reaches back to Harold Samuel via Borowsky, Horszowski, Schnabel and Serkin. Like them (though not specifically in the Partitas) Goode treats line as paramount, stressing counterpoint only where and when it serves an expressive end, as in the First Partita's Allemande. Like Schnabel, Goode can occasionally accelerate a phrase to focus its place in the larger context. The use of *crescendo* is subtle yet telling (the Corrente) and the way phrases breathe, suggests hours spent focusing on a precise *rubato*.

This is glorious music, and there's barely a second when you aren't aware of that. Everything flows from the logic of the line, and when perspectives do change (at around 46 seconds into the A minor Partita's opening two-part Fantasia, for example, where the lower voice takes the lead) the option seems inevitable.

Everything essential to the spirit is here: dance and reverie, clarity and form, digital brilliance. Goode never forces his tone and although he has a secure sense of rhythm – the faster dances trip along rather than rush – there's no hint of the obsessive drive indulged by the post-Gould school. That, too, can be exciting, but Goode's inner explorations of Bach will probably yield longer-term satisfaction. This is an exceptionally fine set.

Disc 1: 'Bach Performance on the Piano' –
An Illustrated Lecture. Disc 2: Chromatic Fantasia and Fugue, BWV903. Concerto in the Italian Style, BWV971. Partita No 4, BWV828
Angela Hewitt *pf*
Video director **Uli Aumüller**
Hyperion Ⓕ ② 📀 DVDA68001 (3h 30' · NTSC · 16:9 · PCM stereo, 2.0, 5.1 and DTS 5.1 · 0)

Angela Hewitt has been giving illustrated lecture recitals on Bach performance for some time but not, on this showing, direct to camera. Though she becomes more fluent and confident over the 148 minutes, for most of the time she resembles the Queen delivering her Christmas message to the Commonwealth. Is she reading off an autocue? Her measured and articulated delivery with nary an 'um' or 'er' suggests that she is; if she isn't, then it sounds as though she is, and reading a script which, moreover, has been written to be published in a book rather than spoken aloud.

Its seven chapters are divided into 36 sections, each one fading to black-out and up again: usefully cued but tiresome to watch. The whole exercise would have been better on CD. What Hewitt has to say is full of wisdom and perspicacity, liberally illustrating the talk at her Fazioli piano (it is filmed in the Fazioli factory). But who is it aimed at? The conservatory student (useful), the teacher (instructive), the amateur Bach player (daunting) or the general public (illuminating but esoteric)?

Disc two is a live recital filmed in the Fazioli concert hall where Hewitt puts into practice what she has been preaching: her poise, clarity of voicing, spontaneity, wonderful finger *legato* and palpable joy in performing these works is a masterclass in itself.

Das wohltemperierte Clavier

48 Preludes and Fugues –
Book 1 BWV846-69; **Book 2** BWV870-93

Das wohltemperierte Clavier   Ⓗ
8 110651/2: Book 1
8 110653/4: Book 2
Edwin Fischer *pf*
Naxos Historical mono ② (107' & 126' · ADD)
Recorded 1933-36   Ⓢ❶❶❶

 Edwin Fischer's recording of the '48' was the first by a pianist of the set, and probably remains the finest of all. Fischer might have agreed with András Schiff that Bach is the 'most romantic of all composers', for his superfine musicianship seems to live and breathe in another world. His sonority is as ravishing as it's apt, never beautiful for its own sake, and graced with a pedal technique so subtle that it results in a light and shade, a subdued sparkle or pointed sense of repartee that eludes lesser artists. No matter what complexity Bach throws at him, Fischer resolves it with a disarming poise and limpidity. All this is a far cry from, say, Glenn Gould's egotism in the '48'. Fischer showed a deep humility before great art, making the singling out of one or another of his performances an impertinence.

In Book 2, you could hardly imagine a more seraphic utterance in No 3, later contrasted with the most skittish *allegro* reply. He possessed a touch with 'the strength and softness of a lion's velvet paw', and there are few recordings from which today's generation of pianists could learn so much; could absorb his way of transforming a supposedly learned tome into a fountain of limitless magic and resource. Here he is, then, at his most sublimely poised and unruffled, at bargain price in beautifully restored sound.

Das wohltemperirte Clavier, BWV846-893
Angela Hewitt *pf*
Hyperion ④ CDA67741/4 (4h 31' · DDD)
Recorded live   Ⓕ❶❶❶

Listening to Angela Hewitt's latest thoughts on Bach's *Well-Tempered Clavier* alongside her late-1990s Hyperion cycle (reviewed below), it appears that her interpretations haven't changed so much as evolved, intensified and, most important, internalised. This perception is enhanced by a closer sonic image, plus the leaner, more timbrally diverse qualities of Hewitt's Fazioli concert grand that contrast with her earlier recording's mellower, more uniform Steinway. Yet one readily credits Hewitt's pianistic prowess for more acutely differentiated *legato* and detached articulation this time around, together with a wider range of melodic inflection. This adds considerable textural dimension to fugues whose close counterpoint is extremely difficult to voice and clarify.

Hewitt's uncommonly brisk and elegantly poised G sharp minor Book 2 Fugue has acquired conversational light and shade. Rubati hinted at earlier re-emerge in fuller, more purposeful bloom: compare both readings of the E flat major Book 1 Prelude and the E major Book 2 Fugue, for example. Perhaps one could pigeonhole Hewitt I as characterised by dance, while Hewitt II mainly celebrates song. While both versions hold equal validity and stature, Hewitt's remake ultimately digs deeper, with more personalised poetry. Perhaps she'll revisit the *Goldberg Variations* next?

Das wohltemperierte Clavier
CDA67301/2 – Book 1
CDA67303/4 – Book 2
Angela Hewitt *pf*
Hyperion ④ CDA67301/2 and CDA67303/4
(117' & 148' · DDD)   Ⓕ**OO**

Admirers of Canadian pianist Angela Hewitt's lightly articulated and elegantly phrased Bach playing won't be disappointed by this recording. These qualities characterise the playing of each and every one of these profoundly didactic yet sublimely poetic pieces. Her restrained use of the sustaining pedal, her consequently clearly spoken articulation, and the resultant lucidity of musical thought, bring to mind the recorded performances of Edwin Fischer. Hewitt certainly sounds more comfortable in a studio than Fischer ever did, and her technique is more consistently disciplined than his was under these circumstances. Her reflective view of the more inward-looking fugues, such as the lyrical one in E flat minor, is most attractive. Taut, but with a suppleness that's entirely devoid of stiffness, this is indeed cogent and gracefully beautiful playing of a high order. You may sense, from time to time, an overtly intense element of subjective thought in her understanding of the music, a quality which seems to be endorsed by occasional references in her lively, illuminating and detailed introduction, to Bach's 'sense of inner peace', and so on. However, to conclude on a thoroughly positive and enthusiastic note, these are performances of Book 1 that you'll want to hear many times over. The recording and instrument sound well, too.

Hewitt's Book 2 is a delight to both ear and mind. Everything is in the best taste and free of exhibitionism. There are subtle tonal nuances, natural rises and falls of dynamics, well-defined differentiation of contrapuntal lines and appreciation of the expressive implications of Bach's chromaticisms. Throughout her playing of these preludes and fugues – several longer, more mature and more demanding than those of Book 1 – there's a sense of unhurried poise, with flowing rhythm. The air of tranquillity is underlined by her frequent adoption of very quiet openings, many of which then take on a warmer tone towards the end – even the E major Fugue, which Landowska labelled 'combative', is handled quietly, yet she's able to sound contempla-

BACH GOLDBERG VARIATIONS – IN BRIEF

Murray Perahia *pf*
Sony Classical 5099708924324 (73' · DDD)
    Ⓕ**OOO**D➔

💎 A magnificent achievement combining superb control of the piano with a probing intellect that's also deeply moving. This is an outstanding modern performance.

Angela Hewitt *pf*
Hyperion CDA67305 (72' · DDD)   Ⓕ**OO**
The Bach player of our day brings to the *Goldbergs* every quality that makes her approach to this composer so appealing – a commandingly wide dynamic range and a palette full of colours. A very fine and judiciously subtle achievement.

Glenn Gould *pf*
Sony Classical 074645259420 (78' · ADD)   Ⓜ**OO**
Sony Classical 5099709307027 (72' · ADD)   Ⓜ**OO**
Sony Classical offer both Gould's 1955 recording (listed first) and his 1981 re-make (second). The 1955 version has the freshness of youth and Gould's historic approach to Bach pianism. The 1981 version has a more meditative quality that is equally fascinating. (For a fascinating lesson in developing interpretation try hunting for the twin-pack that combines both versions – 696998770324)

Wanda Landowska *hpd*
EMI mono 567200-2 (73' · ADD)   Ⓜ**O**
A historic document of the woman who put the harpsichord back on the map. Her Pleyel instrument makes a fine sound and she plays with great taste and spirit. It *does* sound its age.

Wilhelm Kempff *pf*
DG 439 978-2GGA (63' · ADD)   Ⓕ**O**
A great pianist heard in 1969 in a version that sounds pretty romantic in approach, but which just drips with irresistible musicality and intelligence.

Kenneth Gilbert *hpd*
Harmonia Mundi HMA195 1240 (77' · DDD) Ⓕ**OO**
A deeply impressive performance from a very serious musician and a very fine harpsichordist: this is not a reading laden with display but it has an appealing honesty.

András Schiff *pf*
ECM New Series 472 185-2 (71' · DDD)   Ⓕ**O**
A piano version of these boundlessly fruitful variations that has much to say and does so with an appealing style and a greater sense of danger than on his previous set for Decca.

Julian Rachlin *vn* **Nobuko Imai** *va* **Mischa Maisky** *vc*
DG 477 6378GH (80' · DDD)   Ⓕ🅑➔
An intriguing piano trio version from three fine chamber musicians. Worth trying…

tive (as in the E major Fugue) without lapsing into Tureckian reverentiality.

Just occasionally Bach's more intense movements tempt her into emotional *rubatos* which, though musically affecting, take Bach out of his century, and not everyone will care for the big *allargandos* she makes at the ends of some of the earlier movements. Otherwise these are musicianly and imaginative performances.

Das wohltemperierte Clavier, Book 1
Evgeni Koroliov pf
Tacet ② TACET93 (129' · DDD)   Ⓕ ⦿

No music is more impervious to the vagaries of interpretation than Bach's. Play his keyboard music on a piano and it remains obstinately in character. Proponents of the harpsichord may disagree, but musicologist Eva Badura-Skoda has thrown a spanner in the works by arguing that Bach, in his Leipzig years, extensively used fortepianos in an effort to help Silbermann perfect these instruments. So a pianoforte was the next step, after all. Edwin Fischer used it in the first recording of the '48', but his approach and emendations have their detractors.

What intrigues and impresses is that Koroliov largely ignores the sustaining pedal. He often prefers to let fingers, rather than feet, dictate colour; and his fingers are capable of a variety of touch. They can also project the notes with pinpoint velocity, which, when wrongly applied, turns the G major Fugue into a mechanical exercise. This is a serious miscalculation, but it's the only one. The instrument is closely miked, which can lead to moments of discomfort, for instance in the starkly presented A minor Fugue. But he isn't always uncompromising, and the B flat minor Prelude offers an example of his sensitivity to the changes within a single work, from rigorous beginnings to a resigned ending. He reserves his best for the last pair, for which, unusually, Bach added markings *Andante* and *Largo* respectively. His performance of the Fugue marries tension to an inexorable flow that portrays the structure as an imposing edifice. Purists may quibble at the very slow tempo, but this is a *tour de force*.

Das Wohltemperierte Klavier – Book 2, BWV870-893
Masaaki Suzuki hpd
BIS ② BIS-CD1513/4 (160' · DDD)   Ⓕ ⦿⦿⦿

More than a decade has lapsed between instalments of Masaaki Suzuki's *Well-Tempered Clavier*. However, Book 2 was worth the wait. It lives up to Book 1's high artistic and sonic standards, and possibly surpasses them.

Suzuki's intelligent virtuosity operates on several levels. A vocal sensibility consistently determines how phrases begin, end and follow one another to their ultimate destinations. No matter what the basic tempo may be, breath pauses and agogic adjustments naturally mesh into the flow of Bach's lines, rather than work against them. Textural variety also manifests itself through Masaaki's subtle fingerwork. One also senses that Suzuki seriously pondered when and how to arpeggiate chords for maximum expressive and structural purpose, as the C sharp major, F minor and F sharp minor Preludes revealingly display. Yet the D major and B minor Fugues prove that Suzuki can deliver straightforward, even brash vitality when he choses.

As before, Suzuki plays an attractive and vibrantly recorded Willem Kroesbergen harpsichord modelled on a period Ruckers instrument, and Yo Tomita provides fascinating, informative booklet-notes. In all, Suzuki's heartfelt synthesis of scholarship and musicality will provide repeated listening pleasure in one of the finest harpsichord recordings of Book 2 available.

Das wohltemperierte Clavier, Book 2
Daniel Barenboim pf
Warner Classics ③ 2564 61940-2 (164' · DDD)   Ⓕ Ⓑ➤

There have been times when Barenboim's omnivorous musical appetite has threatened his musical stability and reflection but here, revisiting Bach – a childhood 'friend' – his individuality and poetic richness erase all stale notions of pedantry or aridity. There is no sense of received wisdom, only a vital act of recreation that captures Bach's masterpiece in all its first glory and magnitude; no simple-minded notions of period style or strict parameters but a moving sense of music of a timeless veracity.

The romantic influences of Furtwängler and Edwin Fischer can be sensed throughout. What a triumphant sense of homecoming he achieves in the Fugue from No 2, what musical rather than academic authenticity in the doubling or filling-out of the Sixth Prelude. His flight through the 15th Prelude is a marvel of lightness and vivacity and in the Fugue from No 17 every voice is given its due without a trace of that heavy underlining beloved by those intent on explaining their explanation.

Purists may quibble over this or that phrase or detail (and few performances of the 48 have been so richly coloured or inflected) but that is surely their loss. For Barenboim, Bach is the most 'romantic' of composers and his imaginative fullness and delicacy laugh to scorn a less bold or inclusive view. How Jacqueline du Pré, Barenboim's late wife, would have warmed to such performances; this is music-making after her own heart. Superb sound.

Das wohltemperierte Clavier – Book 1: Nos 1-12[a];
Nos 13-24[b]; Book 2: Nos 1-12[c]; Nos 13-24[d]
[a]**Andrei Gavrilov**, [b]**Joanna MacGregor**, [c]**Nikolai Demidenko**, [d]**Angela Hewitt**
Video directors [ab]**Karen Whiteside**,
[cd]**Peter Mumford**
Euroarts ② 𝐃𝐕𝐃 205 0309 (260' · 16:9 · PCM stereo & 5.1 · 0)   Ⓕ

In February 2000 BBC Wales and Euroarts Music co-produced Bach's complete *Well-Tempered Clavier* for television, dividing the work between four very different pianists filmed in four visually distinct venues. Rather than impart a concert performance continuity between the pieces, the directors treat each Prelude and Fugue as a separate entity in terms of lighting, camera angles, placement of the piano, extramusical imagery (kept to a minimum), as well as the pianists' wardrobe and hairstyles.

Collectors familiar with Andrei Gavrilov's romantically tinged, pianistic Bach *French* Suites won't register much surprise as to how he treats Book 1's first 12 Preludes and Fugues. Contrapuntal rigour takes a back seat to melodic nuance and tone colour in his languid, slightly sedate way. It's interesting how his pianism contrasts with the stark visual impact of Walsall's Art Gallery. Conversely, the gothic, shadowy detail Whiteside conveys in Barcelona's Güell Palace differs from Joanna McGregor's leaner propulsion throughout the rest of Book 1.

While she and Gavrilov use the printed score, Nikolai Demidenko and Angela Hewitt play Book 2 from memory. The plangent clarity of Demidenko's Fazioli concert grand stands out in Nos 1-12 (the other pianists perform on Steinways). Several tempo choices are wayward, such as an over-fast and flippant F minor Prelude. However, his linear clarity in the difficult-to-balance C sharp major Prelude and rhythmic swagger in the D major Prelude greatly impress.

Of the four pianists, Angela Hewitt commands the widest variety of articulations and inner dynamics, together with her finely honed ability to follow Bach's lines through to their final destination without sounding the least bit studied. Cogent examples include the long-lined refinement of the G sharp minor Prelude and Fugue, the G major Prelude's lilting, conversational trajectory, and the B major Prelude's delicate yet firmly centred fingerwork. In the B flat minor Prelude the camera zooms in on Hewitt from above, allowing one to observe how she achieves her superior *legato* through fingers and hand balance alone. Aside from optional titles, the menu offers no bells and whistles to supplement the programme, but the audio engineering boasts ample warmth and presence.

Bach Das wohltemperirte Clavier – BWV847; BWV851; BWV852; BWV854; BWV855; BWV856; BWV857; BWV860; BWV862; BWV864; BWV866 **Bach/Busoni** Nun komm' der Heiden Heiland, BWV659. Ich ruf' zu dir, Herr Jesu Christ, BWV639. Wachet auf, ruft uns die Stimme, BWV645 **Brahms** Schmücke dich O liebe Seele, Op 122 No 5
Edna Stern pf
Zig Zag Territoires ZZT090104 (65' · DDD)   Ⓕ

If you prefer Bach on the piano served up in heaping Romantic portions, accompanied by dollops of creamy tone, tapered phrases and languishing tenutos, Edna Stern's ravishing pianism will turn your ears to jelly. Few modern

pianists can pull off this approach, but Stern's sincerity, conviction and masterful control of the instrument prove utterly disarming. Her wide array of *legato* pedallings in the Busoni and Brahms choral prelude arrangements spill over into a selection of Preludes and Fugues from *The Well-Tempered Clavier*, Book 1, without ever obscuring the profile and direction of Bach's contrapuntal lines. Her unpressured fluidity in the F minor Fugue is a case in point. Likewise, the A major Fugue's cross-rhythmic phrases take on a curvaceous, playful character, while the B flat major Prelude's arpeggiated patterns unsystematically alternate between blurry and dry. Stern's *rubato* in the E minor Fugue dismantles the work's toccata-like drive, as if Pablo Casals's cello bow was guiding her fingers. And in contrast to more overtly virtuoso, incisive renditions of the G major Prelude and Fugue, Stern relaxes within her chosen fast tempi. Perhaps her ordering the programme according to key relationships explains how easily each work slips into the next. In short, a disc that will cause unrepentant pianophiles to jump for joy while historically informed performance mavens duck for cover.

Toccatas, BWV910-16

F sharp minor, **BWV910**; C minor, **BWV911**; D, **BWV912**; D minor, **BWV913**; E minor, **BWV914**; G minor, **BWV915**; G, **BWV916**

Toccatas, BWV910-16
Angela Hewitt pf
Hyperion CDA67310 (69' · DDD)   ⒻOOO

As Angela Hewitt tells us in her exemplary accompanying essay, Bach's Toccatas were inspired by Buxtehude's '*stylus fantasticus* – a very unrestrained and free way of composing, using dramatic and extravagant rhetorical gestures'. For Wanda Landowska, they seemed initially 'incoherent and disparate' and it takes an exceptional artist to make such wonders both stand out and unite. Yet Angela Hewitt – always responsive to such a teasing mix of discipline and wildness – presents even the most audacious surprises with a superb and unfaltering sense of balance and perspective. Time and again she shows us that it's possible to be personal and characterful without resorting to self-serving and distorting idiosyncrasy. Everything is delightfully devoid of pedantry or over-emphasis; few pianists have worn their enviable expertise in Bach more lightly. In the F sharp minor Toccata everything is meticulously graded, and in the dazzling D major Toccata, which so fittingly closes her programme, not even Bach's most ebullient virtuosity can induce her to rush; everything emerges with a clarity that never excludes expressive beauty. Her performances could hardly be more stylish or impeccable, more vital or refined; and, as a crowning touch, Hyperion's sound is superb.

Goldberg Variations, BWV988

Goldberg Variations
Murray Perahia pf
Sony Classical SK89243 (73' · DDD)   Ⓕ**OOOO**▸

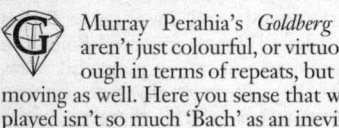 Murray Perahia's *Goldberg* Variations aren't just colourful, or virtuoso, or thorough in terms of repeats, but profoundly moving as well. Here you sense that what's being played isn't so much 'Bach' as an inevitable musical sequence with a life of its own, music where the themes, harmonies and contrapuntal strands await a mind strong enough to connect them.

Rosalyn Tureck was the first recorded Goldbergian to take the structural route, and her EMI/Philips set remains among the most cogent of older alternatives. And while Glenn Gould achieves formidable levels of concentration, his gargantuan personality does occasionally intrude. Perahia brooks neither distraction nor unwanted mannerism. Yes, there are fine-tipped details and prominent emphases, but the way themes are traced and followed through suggests a performance where the shape of a phrase is dictated mostly by its place in the larger scheme of things. Perahia never strikes a brittle note, yet his control and projection of rhythm are impeccable. He can trace the most exquisite *cantabile*, even while attending to salient counterpoint, and although clear voicing is a consistent attribute of his performance, so is flexibility. Like Hewitt, he surpasses himself. It's just that in his case the act of surpassing takes him that little bit further. A wonderful CD.

Goldberg Variations
Angela Hewitt pf
Hyperion CDA67305 (72' · DDD)   Ⓕ**OO**

Name your leading interpretative preferences in the *Goldberg* Variations, and there's bound to be someone on disc who expresses them. Leaving aside numerous harpsichord versions, the current catalogue is notably rich in colourful piano alternatives. Two things strike you about Hewitt's *Goldbergs* from the start: first, that she can summon many dynamic grades simultaneously; and second, that her variations between repeats aren't restricted to matters of voicing. For example, in Variation 13, she accelerates her phrases as if caught on a spontaneous impulse, then relaxes for the response. When she plays the variation's first half again she significantly modifies her tone and *rubato*, then opts for a more formal approach to the second half. All this in just over four and a half minutes!

Her mastery of the keyboard is exemplary. She can launch an elegant *staccato* or allow one voice to weave an ivy-like thread, while others argue above it. Beyond a seamless account of the pivotal Variation 25, Hewitt rattles off manic trills in Var 23 and favours a grand, free-wheeling approach for Var 29. This disc is strongly recommended.

Goldberg Variations
Glenn Gould pf
Sony Classical SK93070 (51' · DDD). Recorded 1981   Ⓕ**OOO**

Also available coupled with 1955 Variations on Sony SM2K87703   Ⓕ

 This astonishing performance was recorded 26 years after Gould's legendary 1955 disc (see below). Gould was not in the habit of re-recording but a growing unease with that earlier performance made him turn once again to a timeless masterpiece and try, via a radically altered outlook, for a more definitive account.

By his own admission he had, during those intervening years, discovered 'slowness' or a meditative quality far removed from flashing fingers and pianistic glory. And it's this 'autumnal repose' that adds such a deeply imaginative dimension to Gould's unimpeded clarity and pin-point definition. The Aria is now mesmerically slow. The tremulous confidences of Variation 13 in the 1955 performance give way to something more forthright, more trenchantly and determinedly voiced, while Var 19's previously light and dancing measures are humorously slow and precise. Var 21 is painted in the boldest of oils, so to speak and, most importantly of all, Var 25 is far less romantically susceptible than before and has an almost confrontational assurance. The Aria's return, too, is overwhelming in its profound sense of solace and resolution. This is surely the finest of Gould's recordings.

Goldberg Variations[a]   **H**
Das wohltemperierte Clavier, Book 2 – No 33 in E;
No 38 in F sharp minor
Glenn Gould pf
Sony Classical mono SMK52594 (46' · ADD) [a]Recorded 1955   **MO**

Also available coupled with 1981 Variations on Sony SM2K87703   Ⓕ

Gould's pianistic skills have been universally and freely acknowledged, but his musical vision has elicited a range of critical response that has few parallels in this century. The view that Bach was a mere mathematical genius and little more has long passed, but it has its echoes in Gould's approach; he was fascinated by the structure of the music and was supremely skilful in showing the Jacquard-loom patterns woven by its contrapuntal threads. Every structural detail is exposed with crystal clarity, but, switching metaphors, what's revealed is a marvellously designed and executed building, inhabited only by a caretaker. An overall time of 38 minutes doesn't seem unreasonable for the *Goldberg* Variations (here shorn of every repeat) but the statistic is misleading: many variations pass at breakneck speeds. As an exposition of the music's mechanism this is a remarkable performance but, despite occasional intrusions of sing-along and sparing use of the pedals (music first, pianism second), it says little of Bach's humanity.

Two Fugues from the '48' extend the playing time to the lower limit of respectability. Neither is hurried and No 33 proceeds with the solemnity that some others perceived to be its due. The sound quality of the recordings is impressive, but overall this is probably of archival rather than definitive interest.

Goldberg Variations
András Schiff pf
ECM New Series 472 185-2 (71' · DDD)   Ⓕ◗

Whatever your likes or dislikes in the *Goldbergs*, Schiff will surely elicit a positive reaction, more so than with his 1982 Decca recording, which, though similarly felicitous, had little of the daring, imagination and scale of this live remake. After Perahia's probing intellect, Hewitt's sense of fantasy and Tureck's sepulchral *gravitas*, Schiff is the master colourist who, like Gould in his later Sony recording, achieves impressive continuity between variations. Contrasts, too, and never more so than in the sequence of variations Nos 20-22, taking us from brilliantly realised syncopations, to a glowering canon in sevenths, then dipping suddenly for the intimate *stile antico* of the four-part Variation 22. As for overall style, repeats are often embellished, sometimes radically varied. He has an occasional tendency to spread chords (Var 15), obviously loves to dance (the irresistibly lilting Var 18), relishes an elegant turn of phrase (Var 13) and has a keen ear for Bach's wit (the tripping exuberance of Var 23). This is a fascinating, beautiful, deeply pondered and profoundly pianistic account. While not 'authentic' in the scholarly sense, it's appreciative of Baroque manners and ornamentation. It's also beautifully recorded on a mellow, finely tuned Steinway.

Goldberg Variations, BWV988.
Fourteen Canons, BWV1087
Sylvain Blassel with **Fabrice Pierre** hps
Lontano 2564 69199-6 (55' · DDD)   Ⓕ

Goldberg Variations, BWV988 (arr Finch)
Catrin Finch hp
DG 477 8097GH (64' · DDD)   Ⓕ▣

Bach's *Goldberg Variations* have been arranged for everything from string orchestra to accordion with varying degrees of success – but never (complete, at any rate) for the harp. Suddenly we have two very different interpretations on that instrument released simultaneously.

Blassel's is an exquisite reading: the Aria is played almost with a surfeit of warmth and delicacy, as if to impress the potential of its material upon the listener from the outset so as to allow a fuller savouring of the ensuing variations – which are all, without exception, played with a great feeling for overall architecture and interior

expressiveness that recalls Hewitt and Tureck in equal measure.

Welsh harpist Catrin Finch observes most of the repeats; tempi are generally on the brisk side; tonal and dynamic variation is minimal but telling when it occurs. Blassel observes no repeats (thus leaving room on the disc for the 14 *Goldberg Canons*, which Blassel performs with his former teacher Fabrice Pierre); tempi are generally measured, especially in the canonic variations; tonal and dynamic variation is maximal, as is the variety of articulation.

Perhaps it's to do with the differences between the instruments – Finch's modern harp is bright and thickly resonant; Blassel's 1904 Erard delicate and muted – but Finch's playing is more extrovert and forthright (although sometimes, as in Var 25, disappointingly prosaic), Blassel's more introvert and nuanced (you'll never hear a more magically delicate account of Var 28). Either way, both versions have much to recommend them.

Keyboard Works

15 Two-Part Inventions, BWV772-86. 15 Three-Part Inventions, BWV787-801. Chromatic Fantasia and Fugue in D minor, BWV903. Fantasia in C minor, BWV906
Angela Hewitt pf
Hyperion CDA66746 (63' · DDD)   Ⓕ◗▣

Angela Hewitt's approach may be gleaned from her refreshingly lucid annotation, or simply by listening to what she does. 'A skilful player can [bring out the different voices] with different colours' and 'To be capable of producing a true *legato* without using the pedal will serve a pianist well in any repertoire.' She puts her fingers where her thoughts are. She never upsets the balance of the lines that it's in the nature of the harpsichord to yield, and her economy with the sustaining pedal helps preserve their clarity.

The two- and three-part Inventions are treated as music in their own right, not simply as invaluable exercises; each is given its distinctive character, with a wonderful variety of sensitive touch and shapely rubato that never threatens to become anachronistic. Her readings of the C minor Fantasia and the *Chromatic* Fantasia and Fugue are as eloquent and stimulating as any yet recorded by a harpsichordist.

Duets, BWV802-5. French Overture in B minor, BWV831. Concerto in the Italian Style in F, 'Italian Concerto', BWV971. Capriccios – in B flat, BWV992; in E, BWV993
Angela Hewitt pf
Hyperion CDA67306 (69' · DDD)   Ⓕ◗◗▣

Here is an attractive recital of five varied pieces or suites of pieces, familiar and not so familiar, played with Hewitt's expected intelligence and finish and not a little verve. In her very readable introduction, Hewitt quotes a contemporary review of the *Italian* Concerto describing Bach not only as a great master but as someone 'who has almost alone taken possession of the clavier', and whose compositions are exceedingly difficult to play 'because the efficiency of his own limbs sets his standards'.

They still are, and Hewitt conveys the feeling that the challenges aren't just to be met but should be sensed as integral to successful performance. By giving the quick numbers plenty of pace she makes the music sound difficult in the right way. No question of hustling them along, but rather of touching the core of the rhythmic energy and of making all the lines, throughout the texture, directional and lively. Hewitt's isn't a monumental Bach, rooted to the spot, but one that makes us curious as to what lies around the next corner. The brilliant outer movements of the *Italian Concerto*, the long fugal section of the *French Overture*, the second and fourth of the Duets (those extraordinary studies in two-part writing) are all successes of her musical dynamic and high-stepping style. And the Echo movement of the *French Overture* (track 28) has a positively theatrical allure, like something out of Rameau – wonderful!

What she can't disguise, however, is that some of the movements in this great suite 'in the French style' lie uneasily on the piano, especially when the sonorities characteristic of a two-manual harpsichord are transcribed as if for a piano without sustaining pedal. If only she'd allow herself a dab of it now and then; the music needs to hang in the air a bit, and the 18th-century harpsichord was, after all, an instrument of mass as well as point, richer in colour and weight of sound than Hewitt's pencil-lines and sometimes rather brittle and over-articulated manner suggest.

On the other hand, her characterisation of the two early Capriccios in terms of the modern piano is a *tour de force* – sparky, fresh, as if improvised. The greatness of the rest of the music here may put them in the shade, a little, but they're delightful. Bach aged 17, trying his hand at programme music? Well, the Capriccio 'on the departure of his beloved brother' remained his only example of it, but it's a reminder too that there was nothing he couldn't do. A stimulating disc, and beautiful sound.

'Per cembalo solo...'   **P**
Chromatic Fantasia and Fugue in D minor, BWV903. Fantasia and Fugue in A minor, BWV904. Fantasia in C minor, BWV906. Sonata in A minor, BWV965. Concerto in the Italian Style in F, 'Italian Concerto', BWV971. Concerto in D, BWV972 (after Vivaldi: Concerto, Op 3 No 9 RV230). Concerto in G, BWV973 (after Vivaldi's Concerto, Op 7 No 8 RV299).
Richard Egarr *hpd*
Harmonia Mundi HMU90 7329 (79' · DDD)   Ⓕ**O**

Richard Egarr is the doyen of English harpsichordists at present, displaying uninhib-

ited virtuosity, rhetorical and dramatic sensibilities, and an ear for refinement of sound. This discriminating recital combines the familiar (including a marvellously dapper *Italian Concerto*) with more pragmatic and intimate Bachian creations which are too often lost in the crevices of the expert's discography. The two Vivaldi concertos are idiomatic, thrilling and revealing exposés of Bach's hands-on approach to mastering new styles. Perhaps more diverting still is the Fantasia and Fugue in A minor, where Egarr shrewdly considers the intense coexistence of contrapuntal and textural relationships in the fantasia, before a fugue of extraordinary clarity of interpretative design. This is playing of real stature.

The remarkable Sonata in A minor, after Bach's aged spiritual mentor Reinken, might have been arranged as early as 1703; it's a masterful demonstration of a young man in full creative flow. Egarr has the edge on Staier's penetrating but relatively dry execution; here we have a quasi-Toccata and Fugue of dazzling colour and affirmation before an Allemande portrayed with somewhat looser stitching, a highly affecting manipulation of rhythm. This exquisite recital ends with the mature, unfinished Fantasia and Fugue in C minor, with Egarr's own reworking of the fugue.

French Suite No 5 in G, BWV816. Partita No 1   **P**
in B flat, BWV825. Three Minuets, BWV841-43. Clavier-Büchlein for WF Bach – Preludes: C, BWV924; D, BWV925; D minor, BWV926; F, BWV927; F, BWV928; G minor, BWV930. Preludes, BWV939-43. Fugue in C, BWV953. Fughetta in C minor, BWV961. Concerto in the Italian Style in F, 'Italian Concerto', BWV971. Prelude in C minor, BWV999. Anna Magdalena Notenbuch – Minuets: G,-BWVAnh114; G minor, BWVAnh115
Richard Egarr *hpd*
EMI Debut 569700-2 (78' · DDD)   Ⓑ**OO**⤸

Richard Egarr's programme is an attractive one in which three major solo harpsichord works – the Partita (BWV825), the *French Suite* (BWV816), and the *Italian Concerto* (BWV971) – are interspersed with Preludes, Minuets and two Fugues from the Kellner Collection, the *Clavier-Büchlein* for Wilhelm Friedemann Bach, 'the son I love, the one who fills me with joy', and the *Notenbuch* for Bach's second wife, Anna Magdalena. The character of Egarr's instrument, a copy by Joel Katzman of a 1638 Ruckers, has been effectively recorded, capturing its warm timbre in an intimate, domestic-sounding ambience.

Egarr's B flat Partita is an unhurried affair, reflective in its Prelude and Allemande and rhythmically supple. Some readers may not at once respond to the extent to which he leans on notes, thereby breaking up that strict regularity of pulse that used to be the order of the day. His articulation and rhythmic flexibility are both illuminating and communicative. The music breathes, and with each breath comes a natural pause in the declamation allowing for rhetorical gesture and a feeling for scansion. Just occasionally in the Sarabande phrases are a little too clipped and skimped over, but such instances, both here and in the *French Suite*, are both few and far between. Each of the little Preludes and Minuets is lovingly shaped and played with a sense of affection for, and understanding of, the music's poetry. In short this is an outstanding disc, both for Egarr's technically accomplished playing and for his delicacy of feeling.

'The Secret Bach'   Ⓟ
Partite diverse sopra 'O Gott, du frommer Gott', BWV767. Klavierbüchlein für WF Bach – Menuet in G, BWV841; Menuet in G, BWV843; Allemande in G minor, BWV836. Chromatic Fantasia and Fugue in D minor, BWV903a. Adagio in G, BWV968. Fugue in G minor, BWV1000. Violin Partita No 2 in D minor, BWV1004 (arr Mortensen)
Christopher Hogwood *clav*
Metronome METCD1056 (72' · DDD)   Ⓕ

Christopher Hogwood's incisive mind regularly leads to strong and imaginative concepts: this, the first of a series of clavichord discs dedicated to Bach, Handel, Haydn, Mozart and Beethoven, is a perfect example. The clavichord has a history of domestic usage, the intimate nature of its utterances seeming both exquisite and slightly enigmatic. Its main mechanical feature of stretching strings gives the player the 'touch' to grade dynamics, alter pitch through vibrating and other idiomatic colouring. We know that Bach loved the instrument. Hogwood uses three clavichords of very particular tonal quality. In his thoughtful and devotional reading of *O Gott, du frommer Gott*, he plays a Schmahl copy from Finchcocks with a lovely cushioned and even tone. A Bodechtel clavichord provides contrast for the shorter vignettes, while a larger Hass is used for the *Chromatic* Fantasia and the Partita in A minor (a transcription of the violin Partita in D minor) – it's as extrovert and bold as you get with a clavichord. The chaconne, arranged by Lars Ulrik Mortensen, contains a few questionable harmonic and figurative quirks, but Hogwood glides through them fluidly and genially. It leads the mind and ears into revitalised pastures of how this music can be experienced afresh.

The Art of Fugue, BWV1080

The Art of Fugue
Pierre-Laurent Aimard *pf*
DG 477 7345GH (79' · DDD)   Ⓕ Ⓞ ➔

This is Bach-playing to listen to every day, fresh, spry and well modulated. If spirituality is to be found in *The Art of Fugue*, Aimard seems to say, it will not be through slow tempi, dynamic extremes or the quasi-religious trappings arrayed

by the likes of Sokolov, Kocsis, Koroliov and Nikolaieva. The tripping, French swagger of Contrapuncti 2 and 6 and the smart Italian cut of No 9 fit neatly under the fingers. Freedom is found within the interplay of voices rather than any fancy phrasing: in fact the mirror fugues and canons are so unfussily done that you'd never guess without a score to hand how much a single musician can look and sound like Mr Messy while playing them.

This is not to imply dryness or inflexibility on Aimard's part. He follows Tovey in finding No 3 to be 'one of Bach's most beautiful pieces of quiet chromatic slow music', after which the extraordinary cadences of No 4 are necessarily pedalled and clipped, even chirpy: the envoi of a true Kapellmeister. The great unfinished fugue is especially fascinating, gradually accumulating kinesis until the surge of B-A-C-H pulls us towards its unattained apotheosis with colossal force. Applied with more plain-spoken authority, such emphatic strength of wrist and will rather chews up the Tenth's preludial bars and the expansive, chorale-fantasia conclusion of the Fifth, though with equal force one senses that, in this case, they had to be so. Perhaps no pianist since Charles Rosen has so persuasively demonstrated that this contrapuntal encyclopedia is to be heard as well as read.

Bach The Art of Fugue – Contrapuncti 1-11;   Ⓟ
Fuga **Mozart** Five Fugues, K405. Fugue in G minor, K401/K375e
Phantasm (Laurence Dreyfus, Wendy Gillespie, Jonathan Manson, Markku Luolajan-Mikkola *viols*)
Simax PSC1135 (65' · DDD)   Ⓕ Ⓞ

Seeing that we enjoy Bach and Mozart on a modern piano, should we demur at their music being played on an equally anachronistic consort of viols? Leaving aside the argument advanced in Laurence Dreyfus's note that much viol consort music was fugal in texture anyway, the fact is that the contrapuntal lines here emerge with great clarity and with a subtlety of timbre, articulation and dynamics beyond even the ablest keyboard player, thanks to Phantasm's accomplished and expressive performances.

The group offers the first 11 Contrapuncti, without the canons or mirror fugues, but plus the final uncompleted *chef d'oeuvre* that was to have crowned the project; Phantasm's playing offers new insights into Bach's prodigious mind. In his transcriptions for string quartet of fugues from the '48', Mozart – who, it's reported, constantly had Bach's volume lying open on his piano – made a few small adjustments to details of rhythm and part-writing; and the process also fired him to write several fugues of his own, including the one in G minor (for piano solo or duet) here. Phantasm, despite a slight tendency to hurry, brings a smile to the lips by its intonation, precision and, above all, musicality.

The Art of Fugue   P
Fretwork (Richard Boothby, Richard Campbell,
Wendy Gillespie, Julia Hodgson, William Hunt,
Susanna Pell *viols*)
Harmonia Mundi HMU90 7296 (76' · DDD)   F●●

Though *The Art of Fugue* is usually considered a composition for keyboard, the timbre of strings, especially viols played and reproduced this way, does give the music another dimension.

Though there are no tempo directions for the 20 pieces that comprise this work – performers are expected to relate speed to time signatures without other guidance – Fretwork's judgements are difficult to fault. Turn to the Canon alla Duodecima, or alternatively Contrapunctus 9, where the required swift pulse does not preclude expressive articulation; and then to Contrapunctus 10, where four-in-a-bar is reflected in a slower pace that also allows more space for a keener, but not overt, subjective response. Indeed, throughout their idiomatically phrased, impressively cohesive and clean-textured exploration of the work, these thoughtful musicians don't italicise anything.

In sum, Fretwork opt for a quiet, controlled intensity that perhaps needs extended listening to be fully appreciated. The recording certainly won't stand in your way. It's expertly balanced, the acoustic giving both ambience and intimacy.

Organ Trio Sonatas, BWV525-30

No 1 in E flat, BWV525 **No 2** in C minor, BWV526
No 3 in D minor, BWV527 **No 4** in E minor, BWV528
No 5 in C, BWV529 **No 6** in G, , BWV530

Trio Sonatas Nos 1-6
Kay Johannsen *org*
Hänssler Classic 92 099 (78' · DDD).
Recorded on the Metzler organ of the Stadtkirche,
Stein am Rhein, Switzerland   F●●

Kay Johannsen's performance is distinguished by uniformly stylish, immaculately tailored readings of the Trio Sonatas. Johannsen has verve, spirit and musical persuasiveness, the organ is ideal both for these sparkling performances and the transparency of the musical textures (and Johannsen has chosen a glorious Swiss Metzler – this time the 1992 instrument in the Municipal Church of Stein am Rhein), and Hänssler Classic's recording has exceptional presence and clarity.

Schübler Chorales, BWV645-50

Preludes and Fugues – C, BWV545; E flat, BWV552, 'St Anne'. Trio Sonata in E minor, BWV528. Largo in A minor, BWV529. Fantasia in C minor, BWV562. Schübler Chorales, BWV645-50
Piet Kee *org*
Chandos Chaconne CHAN0590 (66' · DDD)
Recorded on the Schnitger organ of the

Martinikerk, Groningen, Netherlands   F●▶

This is playing of heart-warming humanity and spiritual equilibrium, combining deep thought with complete spontaneity. Kee's control of the long, singing line goes hand in hand with a poetic command of Baroque instrumental articulation. Dip anywhere into the Schübler Chorales or to either of the Trio Sonata slow movements and you can hear the separate melodic lines not only given individual character, shape and direction but also combined with ease and gentle authority. Tempos in extrovert movements are unusually moderate, Bach's markings of *Vivace* and *Allegro* being taken by Kee as indications of mood rather than velocity, and yet the musical discourse is involving and full of wit, helped by registrations that are both simple and wise. The disc is crowned by a magnificent performance of the Prelude and Fugue in E-flat, one that fully exploits the vivid contrasts of theme and texture and yet binds the work into a structural unity without a hint of haste or stiffness. Rightly, the recording presents this refined, robust organ as heard within its natural acoustic habitat and Kee has subtly absorbed the church's acoustic into his interpretations.

Clavier-Übung III, BWV669-89

Clavier-Übung III, BWV669-89. Duets, BWV802-5.
Fugue in E flat, BWV552 No 2
Kay Johannsen *org*
Hänssler Edition Bachakademie ② 92 101 (100' · DDD)
Recorded on the Erasmus-Bielfeldt organ,
St Wilhadi, Stade   F●

These discs transport the listener back to 1736, the date of the Erasmus-Bielfeldt organ recorded here. Three years later Bach published the third part of his *Clavier-Übung*, an academically austere title which disguises one of his most symbolic and liturgically important cycles. He had high hopes for the commercial success of the volume and its successor, the *Goldberg Variations*. The *Clavier-Übung* features the so-called Organ Mass. A Hymn Mass, it uses Lutheran texts and melodies in one major and several minor arrangements.

The two discs open and close with the Prelude and Fugue in E flat, BWV552. From the Prelude's first notes it's clear that Johannsen's playing is of the highest calibre. There's emotional involvement without a superfluity of ornamentation and *rubato*. Here, too, is tenderness, flamboyance, attack and rhythmic drive. In Johannsen's hands the listener is subtly drawn to the core of the music, its complexity simplified through his beautifully balanced registrations. Highlights include the extended prelude on *Vater unser im Himmelreich*, BWV682, and those on *Aus tiefer Not*, BWV686/687.

The Four Duets are stylistically related and unified through an ascending key sequence which, as the notes mention, represent the

Passion, Easter, Ascension and Pentecost. The superb booklet includes notes on the individual registrations employed. First-rate recording quality.

Chorale Preludes, BWV1090-1120

Chorale Preludes – Neumeister Collection, BWV1090-1120; Ach Gott und Herr, BWV714; Der Tag, der ist freudenreich, BWV719; Vater unser im Himmelreich, BWV737; Ach Herr, mich armen Sünder, BWV742; Machs mit mir, Gott, nach deiner Güt, BWV957
Christopher Herrick org
Hyperion CDA67215 (80' · DDD)   Ⓕ

These 38 chorale preludes come from a collection of 83 pieces compiled in the 18th century by Johann Gottfried Neumeister that eventually made its way to Yale University, where it was discovered by the Bach scholar Christoph Wolff. Bach's preludes are early works, and as Wolff so aptly wrote: 'Already there is innovation. There's a degree of originality and sophistication that is really quite remarkable.' Herrick gives clear, attractive performances with rhythmic articulation and lively ornamentation. Some listeners may find his playing too calculated and self-conscious, but these are sprightly readings, free of excessive mannerism. The most enjoyable aspect of the CD is the way Herrick gives each chorale prelude its own distinct sound world, despite having only a nine-stop, one-manual Metzler organ. This instrument is one of the most beautiful organs imaginable, and Herrick achieves a pleasing variety of colour. Some may find the organ a little too closely miked.

Organ Works

Trio Sonata No 1 in E flat, BWV525. Fantasia and Fugue in G minor, BWV542. Toccata and Fugue in D minor, BWV565. Pastorale in F, BWV590. Organ Concerto No 1 in G, BWV592. Erbarm' dich mein, O Herre Gott, BWV721. Aus tiefer Not schrei ich zu dir, BWV1099
Kevin Bowyer org
Nimbus NI5280 (67' · DDD). Recorded on the Marcussen organ of St Hans Kirke, Odense, Denmark   Ⓕ

This disc includes the best-known of all Bach's organ pieces – although some would dispute that it's an organ piece or even that Bach wrote it; Bowyer's account of the *Toccata and Fugue* in D minor is invigorating, exciting and very fast. It sets the scene for a CD of virtuoso performances and sound musicianship. The whole is a well-chosen, self-contained programme which also includes an indisputably 'great' organ work, a Trio Sonata, a transcription Bach made of an effervescent concerto by Ernst, a youthful chorale prelude as well as one from a collection only discovered in 1985 and one real oddity. Much

thought has gone into the choice of organ and this instrument serves its purpose admirably; roaring magnificently in the *Fantasia* and emulating the tranquil sounds so characteristic of the *Pastorale*.

Short Preludes and Fugues, BWV553-60. Fantasia con imitazione in B minor, BWV563. Fugue in C minor, BWV575. Toccatas – G minor, BWV915; G,-BWV916. Fugues on themes of Albinoni – A, BWV950; B minor, BWV951
Kevin Bowyer org
Nimbus NI5377 (74' · DDD)
Recorded on the Marcussen organ of St Hans Kirke, Odense, Denmark   Ⓕ

Critical opinion and academic argument may deter others, but Bowyer is content to let the music speak for itself, whether it's 'by JS Bach, JL Krebs or AN Other'. The music here speaks with absolute conviction. A gloriously dramatic rhetoric is brought to the two toccatas (BWV915 and 916). Harpsichordists may claim these as their own, but who could deny this lovely Odense organ the opportunity to glitter with such flamboyant music? The eight 'short' Preludes and Fugues have a muscular, clean-shaven feel to them underlined by plain and simple registrations. While other recordings of such indefinable pieces seem like scraps from the cutting-room floor, Bowyer sets them firmly in the mainstream of high Baroque organ music.

Prelude and Fugue in A minor, BWV551. Trio in C minor, BWV585. Canzona in D minor, BWV588. Wo soll ich fliehen hin, BWV694. Christum wir sollen loben schon, BWV696. Nun komm, der Heiden Heiland, BWV699. Gottes Sohn ist kommen, BWV703. In dich hab' ich gehoffet, BWV712. Fantasia: Jesu, meine Freude, BWV713. Ach Gott und Herr, BWV714. Gelobet seist du, Jesu Christ, BWV723. Lobt Gott, ihr Christen gmein, BWV732. Nun freut euch, lieben Christen g'mein, BWV734. Wie schön leucht' der Morgenstern, BWV739. Ach Gott, vom Himmel sieh' darein, BWV741. Auf meinen lieben Gott, BWV744. Herr Jesu Christ, mein's Lebens Licht, BWV750. O Vater, allmächtiger Gott, BWV758. Vater unser im Himmelreich, BWV762. Wie schön leuchtet der Morgenstern, BWV763. Prelude and Fugue in A minor, BWV894. Toccatas – D, BWV912; D minor, BWV913. Concerto in D minor, BWV974.
Kevin Bowyer org
Nimbus ③ NI566970 (3h 19' · DDD)
Recorded on the Marcussen Organ at Hanskirche, Odense, Denmark   ⒻⒶ

This is probably by far and away the best release so far in this comprehensive survey of Bach's organ works. What distinguishes it is, first of all, the recorded sound, which has lost that underlying feeling of artificiality in its mix between instrument and acoustic which has occasionally surfaced in previous Nimbus recordings from the Hanskirche in Odense. Most of all, however, the outstanding feature is Bowyer's own playing. Always able to come up with enjoyable and eminently listenable performances as a result of his phenomenal technique and intense musicianship, his playing here has real authority. There may be stylistic quibbles (Bowyer's ornamentation can be a little too sparing), but few would argue that the playing lacks real understanding of the music's essential spirit. You sense here a level of empathy with the world of Bach which has been missing from earlier releases. The chorale preludes are sweet sounding but really do sound like the musings of a great master on both the chorale melodies and their texts, while the handful of large-scale display works here seem to look beyond superficial virtuosity and into the mind of a composer for whom every note of music (good or mediocre) was of real intrinsic value. Those not so far tempted to explore this gargantuan series could do a lot worse than invest in this release.

Allein Gott in der Höh sei Ehr: BWV715; BWV717; BWV711; BWV260. Christ lag in Todesbanden: BWV4[a]; BWV695. Fugue on a theme by Corelli in B minor, BWV579. Herr Jesu Christ, dich zu uns wend: BWV332[a]; BWV655. Jesus Christus unser Heiland: BWV363[a]; BWV688. Preludes and Fugues – C minor, BWV549; G, BWV550; E flat, BWV552. Prelude in A minor, BWV569. O Lamm Gottes, unschuldig: BWV401[a]; BWV618. Schmücke dich, o-liebe Seele: BWV180[a]; BWV654. Trio Sonata No 1 in E flat, BWV525. Valet will ich dir geben: BWV415[a]; BWV736

[a]**Caroline Magalhaes** mez [a]**Philippe Froeliger** ten **Francis Jacob** org

Zig-Zag Territoires ② ZZT001001 (90' · DDD) Recorded on the Aubertin organ of the Parish Church, Saessolsheim, Alsace 2000 Ⓕ🌑

This might look like just another organ recital, but in reality it celebrates the remarkable philanthropy of a small Alsatian community who have collectively funded, over nine years, a beautiful organ in Saessolsheim in the north of Alsace. Here it's played by a local son, Francis Jacob, an accomplished young player whose programme is an imaginative cross-section of Bach's organ works. He's not afraid to play a fugue without a prelude if he feels it serves the greater architectural good of the programme. Indeed, his ideals of passing through carefully ordered genres, keys and colourific possibilities are engaging and perceptive.

The performances are striking for the ebullience and vitality of Jacob's fast playing, which is rhythmically assured and with a strong feel for instrumental timbre, not just organ sound – the key to discovering allusions and subtexts as the Bach player must. Lift and immediacy of articulation prevail over endless swathes of *legato*. How refreshing it is to hear such glowing colours in the opening chorale prelude, *Valet will ich dir geben*.

However invigorating Jacob's playing though, there's a tendency to resist the poetic instinct, as if he's mistaking it for indulgence. *Schmücke dich*

sounds unyielding, calculated and even wearing. He produces an idiosyncratic equivalent in the middle movement of the Trio Sonata in C major (what possessed him to break this restful melody up into little squares?), and yet all is forgiven in a deeply touching *O Lamm Gottes*, a chorale marvellously disguised as a taut canonic web irradiating ethereal harmonic consequences – this is where the expressive effect of dissonance is more at consonance with the underlying conceit than consonance could ever be! Jacob rattles off *Allein Gott* with supreme dexterity, and the dazzling upper partials are further evident in a compellingly neurotic reading of the A minor Prelude.

The programme of two short CDs ends with the E flat *St Anne* Fugue, not as grand or mature in conception as some, but carefully considered and, like most of this recording, it conveys a notably immediate, 'one-off' and animated musical presence.

Preludes and Fugues – E minor, BWV533; G minor, BWV535; D minor, BWV539; D minor, BWV549a; G, BWV550. Prelude in A minor, BWV551. Fantasia in A minor, BWV561. Fantasia con imitazione in B minor, BWV563. Toccata and Fugue in E, BWV566. Preludes – in G, BWV568; A minor, BWV569. Fantasia in C, BWV570. Fugues – C minor, BWV575; G, BWV576; G, BWV577, 'Jig Fugue'; G minor, BWV578. Trios – D minor, BWV583; C minor, BWV585; G, BWV586. Aria in F, BWV587. Canzona in D minor, BWV588. Allabreve in D, BWV589. Pastorale in F, BWV590. Four Duets, BWV802-5. Trio Sonata in G, BWV1027a. Musikalisches Opfer, BWV1079 – Ricercar a 3; Ricercar a 6

Christopher Herrick org

Hyperion ③ CDA67211/2 (156' · DDD) Recorded on the organ of the Stadtkirche, Rheinfelden, Switzerland Ⓕ🌑🌑

Some might be tempted to describe what we have here as the 'scrapings from the barrel', for when you've taken out the chorale-based works, the trio sonatas, the concertos and the b   i   g preludes, fantasias, toccatas, passacaglias and fugues this is what's left. However, you could be tempted almost to prefer these crumbs from the table of great genius to those stupendous musical feasts which are everybody's idea of the real JS Bach. And when you have those crumbs seasoned with such loving care, such elegance and such finesse as Christopher Herrick gives to, say, the G minor fugue (BWV578) or the enchanting Trio Sonata (BWV1027a), you realise that here's music every bit as worthy of close attention as anything Bach wrote for the organ. In matters of registration, tempo, articulation and phrasing, Herrick displays immaculate taste.

This is playing of the very highest order. The modest two-manual Metzler, built in 1992, makes an enchanting sound, and the recording fully supports the superlative artistry of the playing.

Sacred Cantatas

No 1 Wie schön leuchtet der Morgenstern; **No 2** Ach Gott, vom Himmel sieh darein; **No 3** Ach Gott, wie manches Herzeleid; **No 4** Christ lag in Todes Banden; **No 5** Wo soll ich fliehen hin; **No 6** Bleib bei uns; **No 7** Christ unser Herr zum Jordan kam; **No 8** Liebster Gott, wenn werd ich sterben?; **No 9** Es ist das Heil uns kommen her; **No 10** Meine Seel erhebt den Herren; **No 11** Lobet Gott in seinen Reichen (Ascension Oratorio); **No 12** Weinen, Klagen, Sorgen, Zagen; **No 13** Meine Seufzer, meine Tränen; **No 14** Wär Gott nicht mit uns diese Zeit; **No 15** (spurious); **No 16** Herr Gott, dich loben wir; **No 17** Wer Dank opfert, der preiset mich; **No 18** Gleichwie der Regen und Schnee; **No 19** Es erhub sich ein Streit; **No 20** O Ewigket, du Donnerwort

No 21 Ich hatte viel Bekümmernis; **No 22** Jesus nahm zu sich die Zwölfe; **No 23** Du wahrer Gott und Davids Sohn; **No 24** Ein ungefärbt Gemüte; **No 25** Es ist nich Gesundes an meinem Liebe; **No 26** Ach wie flüchtig, ach wie nichtig; **No 27** We weiss, wie nahe mir mein Ende; **No 28** Gottlob! nun gebt das Jahr zu Ende; **No 29** Wir danke dir, Gott; **No 30** Freue dich, erlöste Schar; **No 31** Der Himmel lacht! die Erde jubilieret; **No 32** Liebster Jesu, mein Verlangen; **No 33** Allein zu dir, Herr Jesu Christ; **No 34** O ewiges Feuer, O Ursprung der Liebe; **No 35** Geist und Seele wird verwirret; **No 36** Schwingt freudig euch empor; **No 37** Wer da gläubet und getauft wird; **No 38** Aus tiefer Not schrei ich zu dir; **No 39** Brich dem Hungrigen dein Brot; **No 40** Dazu ist erschienen der Sohn Gottes

No 41 Jesu, nun sei gepreiset; **No 42** Am Abend aber desselbigen Sabbats; **No 43** Gott fähret auf mit Jauchzen; **No 44** Sie werden euch in die Bann tun; **No 45** Es ist dir gesagt, Mensch, was gut ist; **No 46** Schauet doch und sehet; **No 47** Wer sich selbst erhöhet; **No 48** Ich elender Mensch, wer wird mich erlösen; **No 49** Ich geh und suche mit Verlangen; **No 50** Nun ist das Heil und die Kraft; **No 51** Jauchzet Gott in allen Landen!; **No 52** Falsche Welt, dir trau ich nicht; **No 53** (spurious); **No 54** Widerstehe doch der Sünde; **No 55** Ich armer Mensch, ich Sündenknecht; **No 56** Ich will den Kreuzstab gerne tragen; **No 57** Selig ist der Mann; **No 58** Ach Gott, wie manches Herzeleid; **No 59** Wer mich liebet, der wird mein Wort halten; **No 60** O Ewigkeit, du Donnerwort

No 61 Nun komm, der Heiden Heiland; **No 62** Nun komm, der Heiden Heiland; **No 63** Christen, ätzet diesen Tag; **No 64** Sehet, welch eine Liebe; **No 65** Sie werden aus Saba alle kommen; **No 66** Erfreut euch, ihr Herzen; **No 67** Halt im Gedächtnis Jesum Christ; **No 68** Also hat Gott die Welt geliebt; **No 69** Lobe den Herrn, meine Seele; **No 70** Wachet! betet! betet! wachet!; **No 71** Gott ist mein König; **No 72** Alles nur nach Gottes Willen; **No 73** Herr, wie du willt, so schicks mit mir; **No 74** Wie mich liebet, der wird mein Wort halten; **No 75** Die Elenden sollen essen; **No 76** Die Himmel erzählen die Ehre Gottes; **No 77** Du sollt Gott, deinen Herren, lieben; **No 78** Jesu, der du meine Seele; **No 79** Gott der Herr ist

Sonn und Schild; **No 80** Ein feste Burg ist unser Gott **No 81** Jesus schläft, was soll ich hoffen?; **No 82** Ich habe genug; **No 83** Erfreute Zeit im neuen Bunde; **No 84** Ich bin vergnügt mit meinem Glücke; **No 85** Ich bin ein guter Hirt; **No 86** Wahrlich, wahrlich, ich sage euch; **No 87** Bisher habt ihr nichts gebeten; **No 88** Siehe, ich will viel Fischer aussenden; **No 89** Was soll ich aus dir machen, Ephraim?; **No 90** Es reisset euch ein schrecklich Ende; **No 91** Gelobet seist du, Jesu Christ; **No 92** Ich hab in Gottes Herz und Sinn; **No 93** Wer nur den lieben Gott lässt walten; **No 94** Was frag ich nach der Welt; **No 95** Christus, der ist mein Leben; **No 96** Herr Christ, der einge Gottessohn; **No 97** In allen meinene Taten; **No 98** Was Gott tut, das ist wohlgetan; **No 99** Was Gott tut, das ist wohlgetan; **No 100** Was Gott tut, das ist wohlgetan

No 101 Nimm von uns, Herr, du treuer Gott; **No 102** Herr, deine Augen sehen nach dem Glauben; **No 103** Ihr werdet weinen und heulen; **No 104** Du Hirte Israel, höre; **No 105** Herr, gehe nicht ins Gericht; **No 106** Gottes Zeit ist die allerbeste Zeit, 'Actus tragicus'; **No 107** Was willst du dich betrüben; **No 108** Es ist euch gut, dass ich hingehe; **No 109** Ich glaube, lieber Herr, hilf meinem Unglauben!; **No 110** Unser Mund sei voll Lachens; **No 111** Was mein Gott will, das g'scheh allzeit; **No 112** Der Herr ist mein getreuer Hirt; **No 113** Herr Jesu Christ, du höchstes Gut; **No 114** Ach, lieben Christen, seid getrost; **No 115** Mache dich, mein Geist, bereit; **No 116** Du Friedefürst, Herr Jesu Christ; **No 117** Sei Lob und Ehr dem höchsten Gut; **No 118** O Jesu Christ, mein Lebens Licht; **No 119** Preise Jerusalem, den Herrn; **No 120a** Herr Gott, Beherrscher aller Dinge; **No 120b** Gott, man lobet dich in der Stille

No 121 Christum wir sollen loben schon; **No 122** Das neugeborne Kindelein; **No 123** Liebster Immanuel, Herzog der Frommen; **No 124** Meinen Jesum lass ich nicht; **No 125** Mit Fried und Freud ich fahr dahin; **No 126** Erhalt uns, Herr, bei deinem Wort; **No 127** Herr Jesu Christ, wahr' Mensch und Gott; **No 128** Auf Christi Himmelfahrt allein; **No 129** Gelobet sei der Herr, mein Gott; **No 130** Herr Gott, dich loben alle wir; **No 131** Aus der Tiefen rufe ich, Herr, zu dir; **No 132** Bereitet die Wege, di Bahn!; **No 133** Ich freue mich in dir; **No 134** Ein Herz, das seinen Jesum lebend weiss; **No 135** Ach Herr, mich armen Sünder; **No 136** Erforsche mich, Gott, und erfahre mein Herz; **No 137** Lobe den Herren, den mächtigen König der Ehren; **No 138** Warum berübst du dich, mein Herz?; **No 139** Wohl dem, der sich auf seinen Gott; **No 140** Wachet auf, ruft uns die Stimme

Nos 141-42 (spurious); **No 143** Lobe den Herr, meine Seele; **No 144** Nimm, was dein ist, und gehe hin; **No 145** Ich lebe, mein Herze, zu deinem Ergötzen; **No 146** Wir müssen durch viel Trübsal; **No 147** Herz und Mund und Tat und Leben; **No 148** Bringet dem Herrn Ehre seines Namens; **No 149** Man singet mit Freuden vom Sieg; **No 150** Nach dir, Herr, verlanget mich; **No 151** Süsser Trost, mein Jesus kömmt; **No 152** Tritt auf die Glaubensbahn; **No 153** Schau, lieber Gott, wie meine Feind; **No 154** Mein liebster Jesus ist verloren; **No 155** Mein Gott, wie lang, ach lange; **No 156** Ich steh mit einem Fuss im Grabe; **No 157** Ich lasse dich nicht, du segnest mich denn; **No 158** Der Friede sei mit dir; **No 159** Sehet, wir gehn hinauf gen Jerusalem

No 160 (spurious); **No 161** Komm, du süsse Todesstunde; **No 162** Ach! ich sehe, jetzt, da ich zur Hochzeit gehe; **No 163** Nur jedem das Seine; **No 164** Ihr, die ihr euch von Christo nennet; **No 165** O heiges Geist- und Wasserbad; **No 166** Wo gehest du hin?; **No 167** Ihr Menschen, rühmet Gottes Liebe; **No 168** Tue Rechnung! Donnerwort; **No 169** Gott soll allein mein Herze haben; **No 170** Vergnügte Ruh', beliebte Seelenlust; **No 171** Gott, wie dein Name, so ist auch dein Ruhm; **No 172** Erschallet, ihr Lieder; **No 173** Erhöhtes Fleisch und Blut; **No 174** Ich liebe den Höchsten von ganzem Gemüte; **No 175** Er rufet seinen Schafen mit Namen; **No 176** Es ist ein trotzig, und verzagt Ding; **No 177** Ich ruf zu dir, Herr Jesu Christ; **No 178** Wo Gott der Herr nicht bei uns hält; **No 179** Siehe zu, dass deine Gottesfurcht; **No 180** Schmücke dich, o liebe Seele

No 181 Leichtgesinnte Flattergeister; **No 182** Himmelskönig, sei willkommen; **No 183** Sie werden euch in den Bann tun; **No 184** Erwünschtes Freudenlicht; **No 185** Barmherziges Herze der ewigen Liebe; **No 186** Ärgre dich, o Seele, nicht; **No-187** Es wartet alles auf dich; **No 188** Ich habe meine Zuversicht; **No 189** (spurious); **No 190** Singet dem Herrn ein neues Lied!; **No 191** Gloria in excelsis Deo; **No 192** Nun danket alle Gott; **No 193** Ihr Tore zu Zion; **No 194** Höchsterwünschtes Freudenfest; **No 195** Dem Gerechten muss das Licht; **No 196** Der Herr denket an uns; **No 197** Gott ist unsre Zuversicht; **No 197a** Ehre sei Gott in der Höhe; **No 198** Lass Fürstin, lass noch einen Strahl, 'Trauer Ode'; **No 199** Mein Herze schwimmt im Blut; **No 200** Bekennen will ich seinen Namen

Volume 1 – Nos 16, 33, 37, 42, 56, 61, 72, 80,   🅟
82, 97, 113, 132, 133, 170. **Volume 2** – Nos 22, 23, 44, 54, 57, 85, 86, 92, 98, 111, 114, 135, 155, 159, 165, 167, 188. **Volume 3** – Nos 17, 35, 87, 90, 99, 106, 117, 123, 153, 161, 168, 172, 173, 182, 199. **Volume 4** – Nos 7, 13, 45, 69, 81, 102, 116, 122, 130, 138, 144, 149, 150, 169, 196. **Volume 5** – Nos 6, 26, 27, 46, 55, 94, 96, 107, 115, 139, 156, 163, 164, 178, 179. **Volume 6** – Nos 2, 3, 8, 60, 62, 78, 93, 103, 128, 145, 151, 154, 171, 185, 186, 192. **Volume 7** – Nos 9, 36, 47, 73, 91, 110, 121, 125, 129, 152, 157, 166, 184, 198. **Volume 8** – Nos 18, 30, 40, 49, 79, 84, 88, 89, 100, 108, 136, 140, 176, 187, 194. **Volume 9** – Nos 1, 5, 14, 20, 32, 38, 50, 51, 58, 63, 83, 104, 109, 162, 183, 195. **Volume 10** – Nos 21, 25, 28, 39, 43, 48, 52, 59, 65, 75, 119, 137, 143, 146, 175, 180, 197. **Volume 11** – Nos 4, 10, 12, 64, 70, 71, 74, 76, 95, 101, 105, 124, 127, 131, 134, 158, 177. **Volume 12** – Nos 19, 24, 29, 31, 34, 41, 66, 67, 68, 77, 112, 120, 126, 147, 148, 174, 181
Ruth Holton, Marjon Strijk sops **Sytse Buwalda** counterten **Marcel Beekman, Martinus Leusink, Nico van der Meel, Knut Schoch** tens **Bas Ramselaar** bass **Holland Boys Choir; Netherlands Bach Collegium / Pieter Jan Leusink**
Brilliant Boxes (12 five-disc sets) 99363/99364/ 99367/99368/99370/99371/99373/99374/99377-80 (61h 31' · DDD · T)   Ⓢ⬤

Brilliant Classics, through licensing and creative plundering of old catalogues, has contrived its own Bach Edition. Rather more surprising is that within this patchwork of miscellaneous performances comes a brand new set of the complete cantatas. How on earth can such a project be viable as a realistic competitor to the meticulously prepared work of leading exponents, or even prudent financially? The answer lies in the spirit of the task, one clearly designed to provide a large audience with the opportunity to experience all these masterworks on period instruments, at an affordable price. A ridiculous price actually. The practice of speed-recording represents quite an art in itself, attempting to engender inspiration while also ensuring acceptable standards of performance and recording – all within an intensive low-budget schedule. Unsurprisingly then, Pieter Jan Leusink's standard-sized Holland Boys Choir and Netherlands Bach Collegium deliver a rather uneven collection of performances with highs and lows in close proximity.

Volumes 1-8: Some readings are simply too indistinct to warrant comparison with more considered and glamorous competition, doubtless in those cases where not enough time has been allowed for the performers to find their interpretative feet beyond merely 'getting it together'. Some, like that of the 'Trauer Ode', miss the point with overt force dispatching fragrant delicacy, while a healthy number constitute refreshing accounts disarmingly caught at the point of discovery. You take the rough with the smooth in this roller-coaster enterprise.

If there's one overriding Achilles heel, it's the unreliability of the solo singing. The tenor contributions, in particular, too often undermine Leusink's generally bright and well-judged conceptions. Volume 5 is a case in point, where Knut Schoch, in the solo tenor cantata, No 55, is simply not up to the task. Judging by the qualities the less ubiquitous Marcel Beekman demonstrates in a beautifully executed No 164, he would have been a better first choice throughout. The most seasoned of the tenors, Nico van der Meel, becomes more authoritative as the set progresses. Soprano Marjon Strijk often finds Bach's taxing melisma a squiggle too far, in marked contrast to the expert if somewhat recessed singing of Ruth Holton and the excellent bass contributions of Bas Ramselaar (they also combine well in their many duets, such as the rollicking No 49). Ramselaar is the best singer on the set and would, for the most part, grace any of the current series; he has the grainy intimacy of Klaus Mertens, and also a burly resonance when it suits him. His reading of *Ich will den Kreuzstab*, No 56, is a commendable achievement by any standards, and there are fine arias in the splendid Ascension works, Nos 37 and 128, as well as in 36, 100 and 108.

Further on the credit side, the boy-led choruses can irradiate a compellingly sure-footed and unmannered perspective of Bach, as in Nos 33 and 97 and in the refreshing and unselfconscious clarity of intent sweetly imparted in Nos 94, 6 and 117; the chorales are also luminously immediate and affecting.

Other cantatas are rather down-played, such as Nos 139 and 62, but are still worthy and enjoyable as honest performances in an unpretentious Kappellmeister mould. If there's a shortage of refinement and blend in No 133 or spit and polish in the rhythmically exacting Nos 26 and 33, bright and energetic declamation is agreeably more the rule than the exception in Leusink's no-airs-and-graces approach. In the general firmament of new cantata recordings, these spontaneous performances stand comparison more in terms of individual movements (many, including several mentioned above, of real conviction and distinction) than complete pieces. Of the handful of cantatas where a special vision of the whole work is unanimously conveyed, with the performers firing on all cylinders, highlights are (in no particular order) Nos 57, 87, 33, 42, 192, 45, 88, 176, 125 and 129. If the choral movements are the best things in these sets, there are still some memorable arias (to counter an abundance of ropey ones) with which Volumes 1, 2, 4, 6, and 8 are particularly well endowed.

Volumes 9-12: Here, Leusink traverses the final peak with far more consistently enduring accounts than the comparative 'hit or miss' of the earlier readings, though unsurprisingly for an enterprise designed around tight rehearse-record schedules, there will always be scrappy moments.

More encouragingly, there's also a striking and rare quality here that shines through more strongly than in most of the earlier volumes, and gives Leusink and his Dutch colleagues genuine credentials. It's the unmannered and straightforward approach to delivering the essence of the work, the honesty and means to get directly to its heart through real 'performance', often at the point of discovery. In this respect it recalls the earlier recordings from Leonhardt/Harnoncourt, a set that should be increasingly revisited for that very reason. For all the 'al dente' movements here, there are as many refreshingly uninhibited and distinguished readings, notably Nos 119, 43, 74, 197, 127, 104 and 148. There's a keen ear for the fundamental 'conceit' of the music upon which spontaneous music-making happens 'as if live'; unassuming, common sensical and unegotistical, the earthy Kappellmeister approach reminds one of the unspectacular (and occasionally a touch unimaginative) but free-breathing performances by the likes of Karl Ristenpart, Wolfgang Gönnenwein, Fritz Lehmann, Felix Prohaska and Fritz Werner in the 1950s and '60s.

Ears attuned to the refined and homogeneous textures of the top Baroque orchestras will find the grainy and sometimes rather thin violins altogether too disturbing. Others may find this more acceptable and, at times, even liberating, especially when joined by the wonderfully colourful wind playing and robust brass playing; the oboe of Peter Frankenberg, in particular, is one of the set's greatest qualities, though not far behind is the trumpet consort, led by Susan

Williams. Notable again is the outstanding bass singing of Bas Ramselaar, whose resonant warmth and musicianly response to text is the most significant vocal strength in the set. Also to be admired are the two main sopranos, Ruth Holton and Marjon Strijk. Both have a vocal timbre of the effervescent and light variety though they bring much radiance and projection to their music-making, and far more accuracy in matters of tuning than in the earlier boxes. Holton sings splendidly in the two demanding arias in No 75, with breeziness in No 52 and loving understanding in the stunning *cantabile* of No 120 (which Bach used in a later version of the G major Violin Sonata), and with great cultivation in BWV31. She sails through the treacherous No 51 with great élan. Strijk brings considerable fluency to her arias in both Nos 25 and 28.

The alto part is less appealingly taken. Sytse Buwalda should not have been lumbered with the responsibility for all the alto arias, several movements of which represent some of Bach's most treasured examples of reflective ardour (why not use mezzos, contraltos and even boy altos for these parts, rather than the often excellent but over-used countertenor?). Despite Buwalda's unsteadiness, he occasionally delivers something reasonable though, such as in Nos 148 and 83. Exactly the same complaint can be levelled at Knut Schoch, a courageous tenor but one without the capacity for variation of colour in his sound, as you hear and expects from both Paul Agnew for Koopman (Erato) or Gerd Türk for Suzuki (BIS). Too often, the upper tessitura just isn't there or else he can't control it. Luckily, Nico van der Meel is wheeled out for the big ones and he's splendid in both 'Ja, tausendmal tausend' in No 43, as well as No 74. In No 31, he's redolent of the deeply touching singing of Helmut Krebs for Werner. Also used is Marcel Beekman, who shines in No 48 and projects a palpable *joie de vivre* with Ramselaar in the fine duet, 'Wie will ich mich freuen' from No 146, as does Holton with Ramselaar in the duet of No 32.

The boy-led Holland Choir and 'period' band, Netherlands Bach Collegium, are again central to the success and distinctive essence of this series. The teamwork in the choir is admirably demonstrated in some of the most difficult pieces, such as the large 'da capo' chorus of No 34, the fervent No 197 and infectiously crackling No 70, resulting in white-hot expositions of thrilling proportions. Leusink's success elsewhere comes largely through his admirably well-judged feeling for tempos and a means of accentuation which drives the music forward inexorably. But there's a fine line here between luminous vitality and panic; the latter afflicts control in some choruses where Bach just can't be learnt in a rush: Nos 65, 48 and 137 are examples where phrases are snatched, or over-sung, to the detriment of both textural cohesion and intonation, as well as general quality of sound.

In sum, these readings deserve to be recognised, primarily for their attractive and well measured strides, but also for a lack of dogma or self-importance. Hard-driven and intermittently rough in places (especially string intonation), they're nevertheless consistently honest, rarely disastrous, and occasionally illuminating statements. Bachians, old and new, should investigate the series with an eager circumspection, taking the rough with the smooth but relishing the open-hearted spirit of the enterprise. The best performances will bring the listener close to the solar plexus of Bach's 'Kantatenwelt'.

'Cantatas Volume 34' Ⓟ
Cantatas – Nos 1, 126 & 127
Carolyn Sampson sop **Robin Blaze** counterten
Gerd Türk ten **Peter Kooij** bass
Bach Collegium Japan / Masaaki Suzuki
BIS ⊚ BIS-SACD1551 (60' · DDD · T/t)   Ⓕ

On March 25, 1725, Bach celebrated the Feast of the Annunciation and Palm Sunday with a special cantata, *Wie schön leuchtet der Morgenstern* ('How beautifully shines the morning star'), a work of breathtaking atmosphere and delicate ardour. Masaaki Suzuki's poised grandeur brings considerable richness to this marvellous score, a sparkling duo of solo violins offset deftly against the full ivory texture of high horns and low oboes in the chorus, and joined by top-drawer solo singing. If Gardiner brings more immediate emotion and Koopman a little more élan, Suzuki captures the moment with sustained warmth and intensity.

Equally striking in this volume of pieces from the unfinished chorale-cantata cycle (the second 'Jahrgang') is the graphic immediacy of Bach Collegium Japan; there have been occasions recently when rhetorical projection has become rather too smoothed over, neutral and objectivised. Not so in Nos 126 and 127, the former leaving no stone unturned in its spiky outbursts (trumpet fanfares in wrathful and unusual minor keys) to reflect the 'murderous intent of Pope and Turks'!

The evocative Quinquagesima work *Herr Jesu Christ, wahr' Mensch und Gott* is a pre-Passiontide lament of sublime quality and, again, Suzuki hits the mark with heightened characterisation and, especially, meticulous care with 'Die Seele ruht'. There are not many extended arias here but this masterpiece for soprano, solo oboe and two punctuating recorders and *pizzicato* continuo (for 'Sterbeglocken' – knells of death) is exquisitely performed by Carolyn Sampson. All in all, a disc to be cherished.

'Cantatas, Volume 29' Ⓟ
Cantatas – Nos 2, 3, 38, & 135
Dorothee Mields sop **Pascal Bertin** counterten
Gerd Türk ten **Peter Kooij** bass **Bach Collegium,
Japan / Masaaki Suzuki**
BIS ⊚ BIS-SACD1461 (72' · DDD/DSD · T/t)   Ⓕ

The theme of these four works from Bach's second cycle of cantatas at Leipzig is almost universally concerned with the journey from despair towards longed-for reconciliation and the victory over sin. Masaaki Suzuki has chosen three works from the Trinity season of 1724, and the Epiphany cantata, *Ach Gott, wie manches Herzeleid* (No 3) from early 1725. Again, no Japanese soloists appear in this volume, yet the singers all produce worthy contributions in arias which mainly provide solace after the gloomy sentiments of the opening movement.

The chorus of No 2 is a case in point, a chorale fantasia whose austere and semi-inspired (it's all comparative) motet style can appear, in less capable hands, dour to the point of inertia. The work is soon lifted by the revelation of God's cross in 'Fire purifies silver', a strikingly contrasting *à la mode* aria sung with compelling involvement from Gerd Türk. The patience of Suzuki's glowing chorus with its doubling trombones builds with sustained gravitas here and in the highly suggestive contours of No 38, *Aus tiefer Not*, a work inspired by Luther's Phrygian hymn and where succour is harder to unearth.

One really can't but admire Suzuki's judgement when confronted with the contemplative. There are high-points in all the choruses: No 3 arches with eloquence, the hopeful but long-suffering oboe sequences countering the biting, dissonant language. Likewise, the pacing of *Ach Herr, mich armen Sünder* (No 135) results in a naturally incremental voyage of genuine discovery. Occasionally the arias pursue generic smoothness over greater articulation of sentiment. Such is the case in the fine duet 'Wenn Sorgen' (from No 3), where the strings never make the most of the wonderful 'leap' of joyful praise to Jesus. In sum, another serious addition to this most consistent of Bach series.

'Cantatas, Volume 5' Ⓟ
Cantatas Nos 18, 143, 152, 155 & 161
Midori Suzuki, Ingrid Schmithüsen sops **Yoshikazu
Mera** counterten **Makoto Sakurada** ten **Peter Kooij**
bass **Bach Collegium Japan / Masaaki Suzuki** org
BIS BIS-CD841 (78' · DDD · T/t)   ⒻⓄⓄ

The fifth volume of Bach's sacred cantatas performed by the Bach Collegium Japan continues their Weimar survey with five pieces written between c1713 and 1716. It begins with No 18, performed in its Weimar version – Bach later revived it for Leipzig, adding two treble recorders to the purely string texture of the upper parts of the earlier composition. The scoring of No 152 is more diverse, featuring in its opening Sinfonia a viola d'amore, viola da gamba, oboe and recorder.

A conspicuous feature of No 155 is its melancholy duet for alto and tenor with bassoon obbligato. While the vocal writing sustains something of the character of a lament the wonderfully athletic, arpeggiated bassoon solo provides a magical third voice. The accompanying essay is confused here, emphasising the importance of a solo oboe which in fact has no place at all in this work. No 161 is a piece of sustained beauty, scored for a pair of treble recorders, obbligato organ, strings and continuo. Bach's authorship of No 143 has sometimes been questioned. Much of it is un-Bach-like, yet at times it's hard to envisage another composer's hand.

The performances are of unmatched excellence. Suzuki's direction never falters and his solo vocalists go from strength to strength as the series progresses. Suzuki makes a richly rewarding contribution with beautifully poised singing, a crystal-clear voice and an upper range that only very occasionally sounds at all threatened. Mera and Sakurada sustain a delicately balanced partnership in the elegiac duet of No 155, the limpid bassoon-playing completing this trio of outstanding beauty. Kooij is a tower of strength, a sympathetic partner to Suzuki in the dance-like duet between Jesus and the Soul (No 152), and resonantly affirmative in his aria from the same cantata. But the highest praise should go to Mera and Sakurada for their affecting performance in No 161. All the elements of this superb cantata are understood and deeply felt by all concerned. The disc is admirably recorded and, apart from the aforementioned confusion, painstakingly and informatively documented.

'Cantatas, Volume 6'   ℗
Cantatas Nos 21 & 31
Monika Frimmer sop **Gerd Türk** ten **Peter Kooij** bass **Bach Collegium Japan / Masaaki Suzuki**
BIS BIS-CD851 (68' · DDD · T/t)   Ⓕ

Both of these are Weimar compositions, dating from c1713 and 1715 respectively, and both were later sung at Leipzig. Where No 21 is concerned, the performance history is complex since Bach, who clearly and understandably set great store by this extended and profoundly expressive piece, made no fewer than four versions of it. Following what was probably its second Weimar performance, in 1714, Bach produced a new version which he used as a test-piece in Hamburg's Jacobikirche, when applying for an organist's post there in 1720. It's this version, for soprano and bass soloists only, in which the parts are transposed from C minor to D minor that forms the basis of the present recording. Suzuki offers listeners an opportunity, by way of an appendix, of hearing Bach's alternative thoughts on certain sections of the cantata. These are meticulously prepared and affectingly declaimed performances. Listen, for instance, to the beautifully articulated and delicately placed bassoon quavers in the poignant opening Sinfonia of No 21. This is most sensitively done and an auspicious beginning to the work. String playing isn't always quite as clean as it could be but the instrumental expertise is impressive. The solo line-up is strong, with Monika Frimmer sustaining several demanding soprano arias with eloquence and tonal warmth. Gerd Türk and Peter Kooij are secure and expressive, and the singing of the 18-voice choir

of women's and men's voices is impressive, though tenors sound strained in the first chorus of No 21.

'Cantatas, Volume 8'   ℗
Cantatas Nos 22, 23 & 75
Midori Suzuki sop **Yoshikazu Mera** counterten
Gerd Türk ten **Peter Kooij** bass **Bach Collegium Japan / Masaaki Suzuki** org
BIS BIS-CD901 (64' · DDD · T/t)   Ⓕ ⓞⓞ

This eighth volume of Bach Collegium Japan's Bach cantata series bridges the period between Bach's departure from Cöthen and his arrival at Leipzig, early in 1723. *Du wahrer Gott und Davids Sohn* (No 23) was mainly written at Cöthen, while *Jesus nahm zu sich die Zwölfe* (No 22) must have been composed almost immediately on Bach's reaching Leipzig. The remaining cantata, *Die Elenden sollen essen* is on an altogether grander scale, in two parts, each of seven movements. The performances maintain the high standards of singing, playing and scholarship set by the previous issues in this series. There are little insecurities here and there – the oboes, which play a prominent role in each of the three pieces, aren't always perfectly in agreement over tuning – but the careful thought given to the words, their significance and declamation, and the skill with which they're enlivened by the realisation of Bach's expressive musical vocabulary, remain immensely satisfying. The disciplined, perceptively phrased and beautifully sustained singing of the two choral numbers of No 23 illuminate the words at every turn, savouring the seemingly infinite expressive nuances of the music. As for No 75, we can only imagine the astonishment with which Leipzig ears must have attuned to its music. In this absolutely superb piece Bach entertains us with a breathtaking stylistic diversity. Polyphony, fugue, chorale fantasia, *da capo* aria, instrumental sinfonia, varied recitative, wonderful oboe writing and a rhythmic *richesse* all contribute to the special distinction both of this cantata and No 76.

Lose no time in becoming acquainted with this one. It reaches, you might say, those parts that other performances do not.

'Cantatas, Volume 28'   ℗
Cantatas – Nos 26, 62, 116 & 139
Yukari Nonoshita sop **Robin Blaze** counterten
Makoto Sakurada ten **Peter Kooij** bass
Bach Collegium Japan / Masaaki Suzuki

BIS 🎞 BIS-SACD1451 (69' · DDD · T/t)   ⒻⓞⒹ
This volume takes its name from Bach's second and least-established setting based on the great Advent hymn *Nun komm, der Heiden Heiland* (No 62), composed in 1724 to inaugurate the new church year in Leipzig. If not quite boasting the magisterial imagery of his earlier effort from Weimar, the spirit of Luther's celebrated purloining of 'Veni redemptor gentium' lives on, especially in a brilliant opening concerto-style

chorus whose unambiguous thematic character perfectly inhabits the hopes of the new season.

Masaaki Suzuki delivers a less visceral performance than some but derives a most effective contrast between the ecstatic fragrance of the first aria and the 'militant, tumultuous continuo theme of the second,' as Dürr puts it. The latter, 'Streite, siege', is sung with considerable gusto by Peter Kooij but it is the contemplative elements to which Suzuki is most naturally drawn. The opening of *Wohl dem, der sich auf seinen Gott* (No 139) is a case in point, where the affectionate oboi d'amore provide a tender backdrop to a particularly reassuring treatment of Bach's most elegant of harmonic strategies. The return of Robin Blaze to the series brings a similarly involved and reflective musicianship to the anguished strains in 'Ach, unaussprechlich ist die Not' in No 116.

Elsewhere there is an urgent account of the graphic and succinct *Ach wie flüchtig* (No 26) in which Bach alights gleefully on the triviality and materialism of man's life; images of time and opportunity flash past us with striking immediacy here. This was a popular cantata in the pre-period era but few recordings maintain the focus of the conceit as effectively as Suzuki.

Less telling is the opening chorus of No 116 (*Du Friedefürst*) which, for all its tidy articulation and refined shaping, contains little of the rich repository of nuances, large and small, which Nikolaus Harnoncourt so effortlessly instills. For all the many beauties bestowed on us from Bach Collegium Japan over the past 27 volumes, that ageing series soberingly reminds us of a kind of musical assumption which oxygenated the best cantata performances then – qualities somehow less easily uncovered these days. The Super Audio option, used in the series for the first time, offers an even more luminous presence to the sound than the extant stereo picture.

'Cantatas, Vol 39'   Ⓟ
Cantatas – Nos 28, 68, 85, 175 & 183
Carolyn Sampson *sop* **Robin Blaze** *counterten* **Gerd Türk** *ten* **Peter Kooij** *bass* **Bach Collegium, Japan / Masaaki Suzuki**
BIS ⓢ BIS-SACD1641 (78' · DDD · T/t)   Ⓕ

None of these five cantatas extends beyond a quarter of an hour and yet the wealth of material is brilliantly compressed in a manner which followers of Bach's chorale cantata *Jahrgang*, his second cycle from Trinity 1724, would have come to expect. Before the following Easter, the composer had abandoned the cycle – at least partly, one imagines, as a result of some upset with the church authorities – and resumed with the conventional model where the music takes the gospel as catalyst for poetic inspiration.

Vol 39 from Masaaki Suzuki introduces us initially to the outstanding Whit Monday cantata, No 68, *Also hat Gott die Welt geliebt* ('God so loved the world') in a performance of uncharacteristically ruddy complexion by Collegium

Bach Japan. The *siciliana* rhythm is elegantly turned here but lacks intensity. Likewise, the bubbling radiance of 'Mein gläubiges Herze' ('My heart ever faithful', as early English arrangers have known it) is short of the genial *joie de vivre* which Agnes Giebel famously brings to Fritz Werner's performance (Erato).

If the texts of Marianne von Ziegler for Nos 68, 175 and 183 (sadly, she collaborated with Bach on only nine works) afford a special luminosity of imagery which Bach clearly found profoundly arresting, Suzuki is equally committed to Neumeister's effervescent representation of God's gifts of the past year in the Christmas Cantata *Gottlob!*, No 28. After Carolyn Sampson's authoritative opening aria, the great motet movement on the chorale, 'Nun lob, mein Seel, den Herren', finds a happy balance between textural refinement and declamatory zeal.

These are, indeed, fine performances with notable contributions from all the soloists (and obbligato instruments – apart from some laboured violoncello piccolo playing in BWV183, albeit played on the shoulder, "da spalla"), though no single one falls into that special category where an association between work and performer is formed for instant recall.

'Cantatas, Volume 30'   Ⓟ
Cantatas No 51. Cantata No 210, O holder Tag, erwünschte Zeit – Aria: Spielet, ihr beseelten Lieder. Alles mit Gott und nichts ohn' ihn, BWV1127
Carolyn Sampson sop
Bach Collegium Japan / Masaaki Suzuki
BIS ⓢ BIS-SACD1471 (74' · DDD/DSD · T/t)   ⒻⓄ

Of Bach's 12 sacred solo cantatas, *Jauchzet Gott* stands as a virtuoso concert piece without peer. No other work – with the possible exception of the secular cantata *O holder Tag* – pushes the soprano voice to such dazzling limits of coloratura. While Bach is thought to have used the work for a Trinity Sunday, perhaps in 1730, its provenance would appear to lie in the same celebratory context as *O holder Tag* (an aria of which is included as a 'bonus' track here), where courtly entertainment and panegyric often encouraged Bach to impress a potentially influential audience.

Carolyn Sampson joins a notable and plentiful list of fine sopranos who have tackled the work on record. She sails through it with controlled authority, encouraged by Masaaki Suzuki's spacious approach to tempi until, that is, the Choral and Alleluja where she and the admirable solo trumpeter (Toshio Shimada) pick off each fiendish run with a brilliant, almost nonchalant ease. Still, this is not a performance where Suzuki seeks to liberate the musicians towards true exultance: perfection is all but achieved, but rather as a geometric proof than the kind of genuine uplift we get from Stich-Randall, Giebel or Stader. Sampson's performance still remains highly accomplished and her natural poetic instincts are wonderfully realised in the recitative 'Wir beten' and the delectable but slight *Alles mit Gott.* Suzuki presents all 12 verses in a 48-minute marathon which no manner of variation and embellishment can sustain: maybe it's rather too much of a good thing.

'Cantatas, Volume 19'　　　　　　　P

Cantatas Nos 37, 86, 104 & 166

Yukari Nonoshita sop **Robin Blaze** counterten
Makoto Sakurada ten **Stephan MacLeod** bass
Bach Collegium Japan / Masaaki Suzuki
BIS BIS-CD1261 (64' · DDD · T/t)　　　　F

The first work on this CD is a little-known gem, No 86, *Wahrlich, wahrlich, ich sage euch* ('Verily, I say unto you'). Succinct and imploring, the listener follows the doctrinal and attentive tone set so marvellously by a composer arrested by the intensity of Christ's promise: 'Whatsoever ye shall ask the Father in my name, he will give it you.' Suzuki, as ever, chooses exceptionally well-judged tempi throughout, leaves no stone unturned in his confident preparedness and also introduces a fine new bass to the series, Stephan MacLeod, as the 'vox Christi'.

Of the other three works here, none is particularly long but each contains a central movement of special significance. In No 37 it's the chorale duet of a stanza from 'How brightly shines the morning star', sung with disarming fluency by Yukari Nonoshita and Robin Blaze, and in No 166, the tidy tenor Makoto Sakurada gives a sensitive, if somewhat under-nourished, account of 'Ich will an den Himmel denken'. This cantata also boasts a ravishing and peerless 'Man nehme sich in Acht' from Blaze.

In the great bass aria 'Beglückte Herde', MacLeod gives a gentle and soft-grained performance (very much in the spirit of Suzuki's usual bass, Peter Kooij) as Christ's sheep are offered the rewards of faith. Some will wish for a more involving performance of this highly original work, as Richter provides (from 1973) – with a majestic Fischer-Dieskau – and the radiant spontaneity of Pieter Jan Leusink, which arguably boasts the best bass singing in recent years from Bas Ramselaar.

Suzuki's volume will, however, satisfy many tastes. These are consistently impressive performances, beautifully recorded and Suzuki communicates Bach with unalloyed joy.

'Cantatas, Volume 15'　　　　　　　P

Cantatas Nos 40, 60, 70 & 90

Yukari Nonoshita sop **Robin Blaze** counterten
Gerd Türk ten **Peter Kooij** bass **Bach Collegium Japan / Masaaki Suzuki**
BIS BIS-CD1111 (68' · DDD · T/t)　　　　F

Masaaki Sukuki here brings us four more fine cantatas, of which *Wachet! betet! betet! wachet!* (No 70) stands apart as one of Bach's most graphically dramatic and cohesive choral achievements. The first movement is justly celebrated, its tautness, forbidding fanfares and diminished chords representing the coming of Christ and the Last Judgement. The apocalyptic backdrop fascinated early interpreters of Bach in the 1950s and '60s, notably Felix Prohaska with his menacing pacing and sepia-like textures offset against a Viennese elegance.

Suzuki's direction is more pressing and urgent in style; his less theatrical, more meticulous approach allows the filigree in the instrumental writing to emerge in a way too rarely heard. Koopman (Erato) has the edge in conveying a more harrowing perspective to the first movement, but the remainder of the cantata is beautifully crafted by Suzuki, demonstrating the artistic conviction and vocal bravura of Robin Blaze in 'Wenn kommt' (though his soaring tones are heard to even better effect in No 60). The pivotal aria in No 70 is the radiant 'Hebt euer Haupt empor', a succinct piece whose openheartedness requires something more than Gerd Türk and Suzuki can give.

The most compelling performances on this disc are in the busy counterpoint, such as the opening chorus of No 40, 'Dazu ist erschienen', the vibrant tenor aria 'Christenkinder', which shows off BCJ's exemplary wind section, and (to return to the horror of Judgement) the peerlessly executed bass aria of No 90, where Peter Kooij and the obbligato trumpet of Toshio Shimada find the perfect synergy. But it's in the stirring and decidedly prescient *Sturm und Drang* quality of No 60, *O Ewigkeit, du Donnerwort*, that Suzuki's infectious grasp of pulse, biting accentuation and luminous textures take fullest flight: he entertains no half-measures in the opening chorus. All round, yet another prestigious addition to the series.

'Cantatas, Volume 14'　　　　　　　P

Cantatas Nos 48, 89, 109 & 148

Midori Suzuki sop **Robin Blaze** counterten
Gerd Türk ten **Chiyuki Urano** bass **Bach Collegium Japan / Masaaki Suzuki**
BIS BIS-CD1081 (66' · DDD · T/t)　　　　F

Masaaki Suzuki's considered approach to this oeuvre is what marks him out as a distinctive voice in current Bach performance. This volume reveals much of the best in the series so far: consistently good singing, a sustained familiarity with the music (not always to be taken for granted in the studio) beyond mere pristine executancy, and Suzuki's guiding hand which is especially attentive to the textual motivation in Bach's music.

A broader approach seems to win the day for much in this disc, as can be admired in the defining logic of the fine opening fugal chorus of *Bringet dem Herrn* (No 148), whose resplendent contrapuntal bravura takes thrilling flight in the chapel's ringing acoustic. Here, and rather less so in the relatively unpolished Leusink reading, the paragraphs connect in a way which ensures an inexorable momentum and sustained uplift – which was rarely achieved in performances of this work from the early days of Bach cantata recordings. The instrumental and obbligato playing throughout is of a high order (if not perhaps boasting the depth of string quality of Koopman), doubtless inspired by the alto and tenor of Robin Blaze and Gerd Türk respectively – who are the main soloists in all four works. Both sing with delectation and authority. In No 109 Suzuki eschews over-characterisation and instead accentuates the instrumental profile as the means of gathering the disparate melodic ideas. There are many other highlights here. The plangent opening lament-chorus of No 48 is slower than Koopman's, but it's a remarkably controlled, even and luminous creation. If not always emotionally exhaustive, Bach Collegium Japan explore the naked emptiness in this work, leaving you feeling properly wrung out. A notable achievement.

'Cantatas, Volume 38'   **P**
Cantatas – Nos 52, 55, 58 & 82
Carolyn Sampson sop **Gerd Türk** ten **Peter Kooij** bass **Bach Collegium Japan / Masaaki Suzuki**
BIS ⬚ BIS-SACD1631 (66' · DSD · T/t)   Ⓕ

As the honeymoon period of Bach's appointment began to wear off, two or three years after his arrival in Leipzig, the composer's cantatas became less central to his creative life. More works by other composers began to appear in the church calendar as energy was increasingly focused towards new large-scale projects, of which the *St Matthew Passion* was the most pressing at the time these four solo cantatas were composed.

Smaller resources may also suggest a shortage of adequate forces in Leipzig in the months between late 1726 and early 1727 but there is no let-up in quality. This latest Bach Collegium volume includes one of the most celebrated of all bass-baritone works, *Ich habe genug*, in a reading of profoundly felt utterance by the experienced Peter Kooij. This is an even and fluent version, if in 'Schlummert ein' a touch too objective and laid-back. Yet the world-weariness of this great slumber aria is beautifully caught by Masaaki Suzuki in both the textural sensibility and rhythmic nuance of the ensemble. Unforced and natural, this is a reading reminding us of the simplicity of the work's unalloyed beauty.

Carolyn Sampson grows in stature as a Bachian in her exquisite musical judgement and technical assurance, not least in the outstanding tuning and allure of 'Ich halt es mit lieben Gott' (from *Falsche Welt*, No 52, which includes a rather sleepy performance of its Sinfonia, from the earliest version of *Brandenburg* No 1). *Ich armer Mensch* is the only extant solo tenor cantata, a piece for whom man's inherent sinfulness is prevalent in supplicatory chromaticism, but hampered here by a tired-sounding Gerd Türk and some uncharacteristically sour intonation from the flautist, Liliko Maeda.

Sampson and Kooij share the delights of No 58, *Ach Gott, wie manches*, a symmetrical and passionately conceived work framed by splendid duets in which the bass paraphrases the soprano chorale (the symbol of Soul and God) – transformed from a tortured chaconne in a cathartic concerto romp. This is a fine close to another largely successful addition to this distinguished series.

'Cantatas, Volume 21'   **P**
Cantatas Nos 65, 81, 83 & 190**Robin Blaze** counterten **James Gilchrist** ten **Peter Kooij** bass **Bach Collegium Japan / Masaaki Suzuki**
BIS BIS-CD1311 (70' · DDD · T/t)   Ⓕ ⬤

Another meticulously prepared volume in this distinguished series comprises the late festivities of Christmas 1724 and two Epiphany works from a few weeks later. Taken from the first of Bach's annual cantata cycles, these four works reveal the astonishing variety and textual (and textural) coloration which the composer exercised in this period of free-wheeling creativity from his early months of employment in Leipzig.

While the instrumentation of horns, recorders, oboes da caccia and strings in No 65 captures the spiciness of eastern promise, Suzuki imbues the whole with a relaxed and soft-grained pastoral regality. This is further exemplified in the easy delivery of the aria 'Nimm mich dir zu eigen' in which James Gilchrist performs with supreme awareness, beckoning the listener to inhabit his world: this is exceptionally characterised singing by any standards and Suzuki shouldn't look back.

No less successful is the way Bach Collegium Japan embraces the Christmas message in the incomplete Cantata No 190. Imaginative reconstruction can bring this work to life and Masaaki Suzuki has found a majestic solution to the opening chorus, which his namesake realises with abandon.

Cantata No 81 is a mesmerisingly compact piece in which St Matthew's account of Jesus calming the storm provides arresting imagery for three fine arias. The middle movement is the set-piece *par excellence*, truly operatic in its posturing bravura and burning focus of conceit. Gilchrist again brings tremendous commitment and open-heartedness with the kind of cultivated vocal élan of great Bach tenors in the Helmut Krebs and Anton Dermota mould. Both Robin Blaze and Peter Kooij perform their arias with customary distinction. Altogether, an extremely fine volume, finer than any rival.

'Cantatas, Volume 2'   **P**
Cantatas Nos 71, 106 & 131
Midori Suzuki, Aki Yanagisawa sops **Yoshikazu Mera** counterten **Gerd Türk** ten **Peter Kooij** bass **Bach Collegium Japan / Masaaki Suzuki**
BIS BIS-CD781 (63' · DDD · T/t)   Ⓕ

Here these artists are abreast of current thinking concerning Baroque style, yet sometimes you find yourself longing for a little more expression and a little less fashionable orthodoxy. The three cantatas included here are among Bach's earliest essays in the form. Nos 106 and 131 (c1707) belong to the Mühlhausen period, while No 71 was written in 1708. By and large, Suzuki has chosen effective tempos, though there are notable exceptions. One of these affects the beautiful Sonatina for recorders and viola da gamba that introduces the *Actus tragicus* (No 106), a funeral piece of startling intensity. Suzuki feels too slow here, adding a full 40 seconds on to performances by virtually all his rivals. Elsewhere, and above all in his choice of soloists, Suzuki fields an exceptional team. We can feel this especially in the effortlessly projected singing of Midori Suzuki (Nos 71 and 131) and Aki Yanagisawa (No 106), the uncluttered declamation of Gerd Türk, and the resonant contributions by Peter Kooij. The countertenor here lacks either conviction or consistent aural charm. The choir is well drilled and, as with the solo element, the voices respond urgently to the spirit of the text. Listen to the thrice supplicatory 'Israel' in the concluding chorus of No 131 for one such example.

'Cantatas, Volume 26'   P
Cantatas – No 96, 122 & 180
Yukari Nonoshita *sop* Timothy Kenworthy-Brown *counterten* Makoto Sakurada *ten* Peter Kooij *bass*
Bach Collegium Japan / Masaaki Suzuki *hpd*
BIS BIS-CD1401 (53' · DDD · T/t)   (F)

Although Bach never completed the second cycle of cantatas, he left us with an extraordinary range of solutions for how the chorale can inspire fantasy and invention. Some pieces are magnificent, others darned good and a few (dare one say) a touch severe. Such an example of 'magnificent' is the highly wrought *Schmücke dich* from October 1724, the *ne plus ultra* cantata for many, where the invitation to the feast provided Bach with radiant images of the hospitality of God's kingdom.

Masaaki Suzuki brings an especially balletic prospect to the opening chorus with strong, driving bass-lines and a dazzling sense of expectancy. One has never felt so sure of Bach's delight in an exceptional melody. This is counterbalanced by a soft-grained and lucid reading of the tenor aria 'Ermuntre dich' by Makoto Sakurada and then, fleetingly, an accompanied recitative introducing yet another countertenor to the series in the attractive and polished warmth of Timothy Kenworthy-Brown.

More heartening than anything is to hear soprano Yukari Nonoshita developing into a Bach singer of real stature. Both in *Schmücke dich* and the startlingly original inner movements of *Das neugeborne Kindelein* she conveys the gentle, compassionate honesty of Agnes Giebel.

Cantata No 96 is a less integrated piece but boasts some dazzling sopranino recorder playing in the opening chorus which Suzuki imbues with indulgent delight in Bach's glorious

orchestration. Peter Kooij's 'Bald zur Rechten' deftly imparts the timid and halting steps of the Christian's human vulnerability. Another success chalked up in this riveting series.

'Cantatas, Volume 10'   P
Cantatas Nos 105[a], 179 & 186[b]
Miah Persson *sop* [ab]Robin Blaze *counterten* Makoto Sakurada *ten* Peter Kooij *bass* Bach Collegium Japan / Masaaki Suzuki
BIS BIS-CD951 (63' · DDD · T/t)   (F)O

Bach Collegium Japan's eloquent advance into the rich repository of cantatas composed during Bach's first year at Leipzig is distinguished in Vol 10 by Masaaki Suzuki's remarkable instinct for the emotional core of each of these three works. Experiencing *Herr, gehe nicht ins Gericht* (No 105) reveals a sense of open-hearted fervour and contemplation, never for a minute cloying or self-regarding at the expense of vibrant expression. This is a work embued with a rich discography, yet what Suzuki uniquely achieves, compelling in the opening chorus, is an intensity born of subtle contrast in vocal and instrumental articulation, underpinned by his uncanny ability to choose a tempo which provides for lyrical intimacy and organic gesture, as the respective texts demand. Suzuki grasps the magnificent nobility of the composer's inspired musical commentary on the human soul in No 105. Miah Persson exhibits sustained control and delectable purity of tone in the continuo-less 'Wie zittern und wanken' and 'Liebster Gott' from No 179. With Peter Kooij's cathartic recitative singing (preparing the spirit of salvation) and the beautifully balanced tenor aria and final chorale, Herreweghe's elegant and fragrant 1990 account, a clear leader until now, has a companion on the top rung.

The bipartite Trinity cantata, *Ärgre dich, o Seele, nicht* (No 186), revised from a Weimar version of 1716, conveys equally Suzuki's assurance and vision. Perhaps the choruses which frame Part 1 are a touch short on gravitas (and tuning is intermittently awry in the first) but here, and in the formidable opening movement of No 179 rhythmic incision is the order of the day. This is another first-rate achievement (the soloists are slightly recessed but the recorded sound is excellent). Arguably the most complete and mature offering in the series so far.

'Cantatas, Volume 32'   P
Cantatas – No 111, 123, 124, & 125
Yukari Nonoshita *sop* Robin Blaze *counterten*
Andreas Weller *ten* Peter Kooij *bass*
Bach Collegium Japan / Masaaki Suzuki *hpd*
BIS BIS-SACD1501 (74' · DDD · T/t)   (F)

Masaaki Suzuki takes us further into the second year of Bach's post in Leipzig with four fine cantatas which sit at the solar plexus of the second cycle in New Year 1725 – the unfinished series of works whose primary catalyst was the hymn of the week and not the usual gospel reading. The quality and maturity of Bach's vocal writing is revealed here in works which are still fighting for recognition. No 111 is the exception, with Bach's taut representation of God's might and also celebrated for the great duet, 'So geh ich mit behertzen Schritten' ('So I go with heartened steps') which Robin Blaze and Andreas Weller perform with exultant esprit.

Bach Collegium Japan are at their most persuasive in the superficially dour but incrementally magisterial opening choruses of both Nos 125 and 123, the latter a brilliant slow-burn contemplation of faith (and hope) with predominant falling motifs from the tender opening of the hymn. Suzuki paces this with as much warmth and understanding as he does in No 124, where a sweetly running oboe d'amore line threads its way through the galant minuet.

With *Mit Fried und Freud* we enter into another meditation on death, one in which Suzuki traverses Bach's extraordinary tonal excursions in the opening chorus, matched only by the succeeding aria where the blind disciple seeks Christ. Robin Blaze is quite exquisite here, as are the poignant oboe and flute obbligati which reflect the fragile human condition in a way strikingly akin to the mysteries and musical language of the *St Matthew Passion*. Suzuki and his musicians can be content that they have pulled out all the stops for one of Bach's most mesmerising creations.

'Cantatas, Vol 16' **P**
Cantatas Nos 119[b] & 194[a]
[b]**Yoshie Hida**, [a]**Yukari Nonoshita** *sops*
[b]**Kirsten Sollek-Avella** *contr* [a]**Makoto Sakurada** *ten*
[a]**Jochen Kupfer** *bar* [b]**Peter Kooij** *bass*
Bach Collegium Japan / Masaaki Suzuki
BIS BISCD1131 (63' · DDD · T/t)   **F**

Masaaki Suzuki gives No 194 a fittingly airy charm, heard most infectiously in 'Hilf, Gott' where an underlying Gavotte (with resonances of the final movement of the *Wedding* Cantata, No 202) finds bright-eyed soprano, Yukari Nonoshita, in confident and beguiling voice. She's most accomplished throughout and delectably joins the gentle and receptive baritone Jochen Kupfer in 'O wie wohl' ist uns geschehn', a bucolic minuet-style duet. This is, all told, the most persuasive reading on disc, and supersedes both Rilling's stiff reading and even Harnoncourt's cultivated (if slightly hit-and-miss) performance, notable also for the presence of a young Thomas Hampson.

Harnoncourt, however, comes out better in one of the grandest French-overture cantatas Bach was to write, 'Preise Jerusalem' (No 119). Composed to honour the new Leipzig town council, Bach really pushed the boat out. Suzuki never quite boasts either the grand sonic cohesion of Philippe Herreweghe's urgent account or the thrilling characterisation of Harnoncourt. Strongly recommended nevertheless for Suzuki's superb reading of No 194.

'Cantatas, Volume 1: London'   **P**
Cantatas – Nos 7, 20, 30, 39, 75 & 167
Gillian Keith, Joanne Lunn *sops* **Wilke te Brummelstroete** *contr* **Paul Agnew** *ten* **Dietrich Henschel** *bass* **Monteverdi Choir; English Baroque Soloists / Sir John Eliot Gardiner**
Soli Deo Gloria ② SDG101 (149' · DDD · T/t)
Recorded live at St Giles Cripplegate, London,
June 23-26, 2000   Ⓜ **●●●**↦

'Cantatas, Volume 8: Bremen/Santiago de Compostela'   **P**
Cantatas Nos 8, 27, 51, 95, 99, 100, 138 & 161
Katharine Fuge, Malin Hartelius *sops* **William Towers, Robin Tyson** *countertens* **James Gilchrist, Mark Padmore** *tens* **Thomas Guthrie, Peter Harvey** *basses* **Monteverdi Choir; English Baroque Soloists / Sir John Eliot Gardiner**
Soli Deo Gloria ② SDG104 (145' · DDD · T/t)
Recorded live at the Unser Lieben Frauen, Bremen, Germany, 28 September 2000, and Santo Domingo de Bonaval, Santiago de Compostela, Spain, October 7, 2000   Ⓜ **●●●**↦

In 2000 John Eliot Gardiner commemorated the 250th anniversary of Bach's death with the Bach Cantata Pilgrimage, a year-long European tour by the English Baroque Soloists and Monteverdi Choir that presented all of Bach's extant cantatas on the appropriate liturgical feast days. Here are the first two instalments of the complete cycle. Soli Deo Gloria's presentation is first class. The CDs are cased in a handsomely designed hardbound book, complete with texts, translations and Gardiner's extensive, informative notes based on a journal he kept during the pilgrimage.

The interpretations are consistently fine – often superb, in fact – with surprisingly few wrong steps or disappointments, especially given the unusually gruelling performance schedule that produced them. Among the many mind-blowing, beautiful moments is the deliciously syncopated contralto aria from No 30, sung with poise by Wilke te Brummelstroete and graced by playing of magical delicacy from the EBS. And there's the extraordinary opening chorus of No 8, with its seemingly endless melodic tendrils, chiming flute part and plucked strings, sounding like a celestial dance. Special mention must be made of the artistry of tenor Mark Padmore, who maintains his sweet, ringingly clear tone even in the demanding leaps and roulades of his aria in No 95.

It's in delicate or intimate music that Gardiner shines most luminously, and some may find that he unduly emphasises the contemplative. His thoughtful, refined approach is strikingly similar to Suzuki's cycle on BIS, though Gardiner's versions sound just a bit warmer. Although his interpretations offer the finest attributes of period practice – transparency and litheness – there's a long-breathed musicality here that can be lacking in other accounts.

'Cantatas – Volume 3: Tewkesbury/Mühlhausen' Ⓟ
Cantatas – Nos 24ᵃ, 71ᵇ, 88ᵇ, No 93ᵇ, 131ᵇ, 177ᵃ, 185ᵃ
Joanne Lunn *sop* **Magdalena Kožená** *mez* **Nathalie
Stutzmann** *contr* **William Towers** *counterten* **Paul
Agnew, Kobie van Rensburg** *tens* **Peter Harvey,
Nicolas Testé** *basses* **Monteverdi Choir; English
Baroque Soloists / Sir John Eliot Gardiner**
Soli Deo Gloria ② SDG141 (138' · DDD · T/t)
Recorded live at ᵃTewkesbury Abbey, ᵇBlausiuskirche,
Mühlhausen in 2000   ⒻⒹ➤

'Cantatas – Volume 27: Blythburgh/Kirkwall' Ⓟ
Cantatas – Nos 129ᵇ, 165ᵇ, 175ᵃ, 176ᵇ, 184ᵃ & No 194ᵇ.
Brandenburg Concerto No 3, BWV1048ᵃ
Ruth Holton, Lisa Larsson *sops* **Nathalie Stutzmann**
contr **Daniel Taylor** *counterten* **Christoph Genz** *ten*
Peter Harvey, Stephan Loges *basses* **Monteverdi
Choir; English Baroque Soloists / Sir John Eliot
Gardiner**
Soli Deo Gloria ② SDG138 (111' · DDD · T/t)
Recorded live at the ᵃHoly Trinity, Blythburgh, ᵇSt
Magnus Cathedral in 2000   ⒻⒹ➤

The spread of locations – from Mühlhausen to
Kirkwall – complements and intensifies the
extraordinary range of cantatas in these rich and
varied offerings from Sir John Eliot Gardiner.
Those who thought that, perhaps, the best fruits
of the Pilgrimage had already been tasted, can
think again with these two latest volumes.

One is reminded here – in works mainly for the
extended summer months of the Trinity season
– that the experience of touring so many masterpieces in such a short space of time obviated all
dangers of homogeneity, comfort zones or complacency. Some exhaustion and rough-edged-
ness, yes, and just occasionally there's not quite
enough time for the performers to get under the
skin of a particular work, yet such instances are
impressively infrequent.

Gardiner and his forces rise here to each
challenge (as the Pilgrimage had now passed the
halfway point) with, it seems, a creative regimen
of Bachian proportions: just as Bach efficiently
identified how to react with supreme concentration and speed according to the compositional
demands of the week, so these 21st-century performers adapt robustly to the seasonal implications within this pattern of ever-changing
locales.

The proof is in the imagination and wide compass of these performances – objectively assessed
after nearly eight years – where the intense
archaic idioms of *Aus der Tiefen* (No 131) and the
municipal bravura of *Gott ist mein König* (No 71),
performed in the Mühlhausen church for which
they were written, are accentuated in quiet, contemplative dignity and surface finery, respectively. For Gardiner the emotional stakes are
high and this possible memorial cantata for a
horrific town fire is especially moving.

Bach's own engagement with a text or liturgical 'problem' depended largely on personal circumstances and this means that some cantatas
make for challenging listening. Gardiner recognises this in his note for the austere *Ein ungefärbt
Gemüte* (No 24), where the Gospel paraphrase

of 'ye would that men should do to you, do ye
even so to them' is reflected in a fiddly chorus of
contrapuntal finger-wagging, a caveat of hypocrisy which then implores us to constancy.

Gardiner is a master of delivering these hard
enigmatic pieces with renewed logic and understanding, aided in No 185 by the fine duet of
Magdalena Kožená and Paul Agnew and, then,
alto Nathalie Stutzmann in the delectable 'Sei
bemüht in dieser Zeit' (where the successful
sower reaps a splendid harvest). This is, in fact,
far from enigmatic but one of those courtly
Weimar arias whose inimitable generosity of
spirit, not least in its ordered periodic phrasing,
requires assiduous refinement in voicing, which
is exactly what the beautiful oboe-and-strings
blend provides.

If the cantatas discussed this far are included in
the unusually rich Vol 3, Vol 27 from Blythburgh and Kirkwall is only marginally less uniformly good. Both volumes are characterised by
choral and instrumental contributions of the
most imploring and thrilling extremes (for
instance, the glowing chorus to No 177, Bach's
provocative take on Marianne von Ziegler's
text in No 176 and the ecstatic trumpetings of
Gelobet, No 129).

Many of the arias for Whit Tuesday and Trinity Sunday comprise reused material from secular cantatas at Cöthen and hence the bright-eyed
and bushy-tailed gavottes, minuets and bourrées, which appear regularly. Nothing better
captures Bach's endless capacity for exuding
inner succour than the luminous, gentle melodic
contours of 'Was des Höchsten' (from No 194),
although it's only one example in another treasure chest of cantatas, whose jewels continue to
glisten for the new pilgrim-collectors.

'Cantatas, Vol 5: Rendsburg/Braunschweig' Ⓟ
Cantatas – Nos 45, 46, 101, 102, 136 & 178
Joanne Lunn *sop* **Daniel Taylor, Robin Tyson**
countertens **Christoph Genz** *ten* **Gotthold Schwarz,
Brindley Sherratt** *basses* **Monteverdi Choir; English
Baroque Soloists / Sir John Eliot Gardiner**
Soli Deo Gloria ② SDG147 (119' · DDD)
Recorded live in August 2000   Ⓕ

Our Pilgrimage travels to Rendsburg and
Braunschweig for a selection from Bach's
'golden years' of vocal writing, 1723-25. The
immediacy of the sound in the former seems
almost ideal for the intensity of *Wo Gott der
Herr*, which thrusts us into an unyielding para-
noia about God's indifference to our plight.
Gardiner summons an impressive, generative
agitation that illuminates the imagery of shipwreck in the bass aria, as well as the tenor aria
with its declamatory 'Schweig, schweig' (Be
silent) which, despite its final consolation, reeks
of dissembling. Brindley Sherratt and Christophe Genz deliver exceptional realisations.

The short journey to the resonant Braunschweig involves a new solo team and performances
which are altogether more transporting. If one
reveres the 'Qui tollis' from the B minor Mass,

doesn't the opening of *Schauet doch* in its original context of dissolute lamentation say even more? Certainly, Gardiner uses it brilliantly to take off with one of Bach's most jarring fugal exegeses. Equally breathtaking is the traumatic opening chorus, on Luther's hymn 'Vater unser', of No 101 with its almost flagellatory appoggiaturas to depict the breaking of Satan's hold.

In Nos 46 and 102 (with another sensational opening chorus), the arias and obbligato contributions are remarkable. Gardiner calls No 102's 'Dein Wetter' one of Bach's rare 'tsunami' arias: bass Gotthold Schwarz carries this image ideally, accompanied by the fine trumpet-playing of Gabriele Cassone.

If not flawless compared to the studio series, this Pilgrimage encourages a heart-warming depth of engagement with the music.

'Cantatas, Volume 23: Arnstadt/Echternach' [P]
Cantatas – Nos 42[a], 67[a], 85[b], 104[b], 112[b], 150[a] & 158[a]
Gillian Keith, Katharine Fuge *sops* **Daniel Taylor,
William Towers** *countertens* **Charles Daniels,
Norbert Meyn** *tens* **Stephen Varcoe** *bass*
**Monteverdi Choir; English Baroque Orchestra /
Sir John Eliot Gardiner**
Soli Deo Gloria ② SDG131 (111' · DDD · T/t)
Recorded live at [a]Johann-Sebastian-Bach-Kirch,
Arnstadt, in April 2000; [b]Basilique St Willibrord,
Echternach, in May 2000   Ⓕ Ⓞ ➧

The seven cantatas here, nominally representing the works for the two Sundays after Easter, cover an unusual range from No 150 to the dazzling maturity of three pastoral cantatas from three different cycles in Leipzig. As Gardiner reminds us in his entertaining diary, the Neue Kirche in Arnstadt is now named after its teenage protégé organist and it seems appropriate that the early cantata *Nach dir, Herr, verlangen mich* should appear at the very place in which it probably received its premiere. One observes the ostentation of youth where Bach rolls out his command of past and current *musica lingua* as an advertisement of his ability.

The performances from Arnstadt are generally fresh and satisfying, and in No 150 there is a real sense of occasion. There are significant challenges in the burly orchestral concerto movement which opens *Am Abend* (No 42) and its long meandering aria 'Wo zwei und drei', bravely negotiated by Daniel Taylor but which, for me, cries out for the embracing security of a fine mezzo or contralto. The bold *Halt im Gedächtnis* (No 67) receives a committed reading but the extraordinarily dramatic scene with bass and chorus (where Christ brings peace and assurance to his ostracised disciples) fails to resonate with special moment.

The more durable performances come from Echternach in Luxembourg. *Du Hirte Israel* (No 104) is a gloriously poised work, unassuming on the surface and yet requiring the judgement to 'lift' each balletic movement without pushing the pace. Gardiner is only thwarted from hitting the spot by generally uneventful solo singing.

Ich bin ein guter Hirt (No 85), on the other hand, conveys the delicate and subtle pastoral conceits of 'Christ, the good shepherd' with endlessly alluring dialogues between on-form singers and instrumentalists, notably some disarmingly beautiful oboe playing, a performance of real distinction. The concise No 112 (following Psalm 23 to the letter) glows with the same ardour. It is indeed the second disc which establishes the longer-term credentials in this richly endowed and unique series.

'Cantatas, Volume 10: Potsdam/Wittenberg' [P]
Cantatas – No 5[a]; No 48[a]; No 56[a]; No 79[b]; No 80[b];
No 90[a]; No 192[b]
Joanne Lunn *sop* **William Towers** *counterten*
James Gilchrist *ten* **Peter Harvey** *bass*
**Monteverdi Choir; English Baroque Soloists /
Sir John Eliot Gardiner**
Soli Deo Gloria ② SDG110 (122' · DDD · T/t)
Recorded live at [a]the Erlöserkirche, Potsdam,
on October 29, 2000; [b]the Schlosskirche, Wittenberg,
on October 31, 2000   Ⓕ Ⓞ ➧

There is unpredictable excitement in the random way the fruits of John Eliot Gardiner's Bach Pilgrimage are being released, as the next steps of that memorable year are retraced with autumn cantatas from Leipzig (19th Sunday after Trinity) and three Reformation pieces. Volume 10 represents another compelling reminder of what Gardiner can achieve in Bach when he has the wind behind him – 'living' these works appears to have fired the imagination.

The largest work here is *Ein feste Burg* (No 80) whose gothic arches of sound find rasping advocacy in the Schlosskirche on the site where Luther preached. His famous hymn is most effectively fortified with a rousing bass sackbut in the first chorus. Here and in the outstanding sister-piece *Gott, der Herr* (No 79), the performances are distinguished by a palpable immediacy. The cathartic duet 'Wie selig' (No 80) from William Towers and James Gilchrist is a treasure.

The quality of music never lets up in Potsdam. *Wo soll ich fliehen hin* (No 5) is one of the finest of Bach's chorale cantatas, its hymn nurtured by an arresting concerto style which conveys the gnawing presence of sin and the yearning to escape its insidious influence. The contrast between its opening fantasia and the radiant tenor aria 'Ergiesse' is skilfully negotiated: James Gilchrist relishes the transformation of the chorus's 'flight' motif into one of tactile pleasure as the divine spring washes away all man's blemishes.

Mention must be made of Peter Harvey's cultivated and flexible bass. Joanne Lunn is perhaps not ideal but the chorus and orchestra are in stirring form and the recorded sound is captivating.

'Cantatas, Volume 17: Berlin' [P]
Cantatas – No 16, 41, 58, 143, 153 & 171
Ruth Holton *sop* **Lucy Ballard, Sally Bruce-Payne**

contrs **Charles Humphries** *counterten*
James Gilchrist *ten* **Peter Harvey** *bass*
Monteverdi Choir; English Baroque Soloists /
Sir John Eliot Gardiner
Soli Deo Gloria ② SDG150 (96' · DDD · T/t)
Recorded live at the Gethsemanekirche, Berlin, on
January 1 & 2, 2000   Ⓜ️Ⓞ❍➔

Performed on the first days of the new millennium, this Pilgrimage volume has an especially candid coherence about it. These six New Year cantatas consistently speak of new prospect and a consolidated ambition to serve God's purpose.

If trumpets predominate in the festive exulting of the first four cantatas, the forces diminish markedly in Nos 153 and 58, partly because the theme of joy is startlingly checked by the fear of evil influence but, also, because Bach's hard-working troupe would have been sung-out after a busy Christmas. The resonant Gethsemanekirche in Berlin is beautifully handled throughout by both Gardiner and his engineers.

Most stirring perhaps is the bold canvas of *Jesu, nun sei gepreiset*, whose energetic climbs (with, in the opening chorus, one exceptional break to wave farewell on the words 'that we in prosperous peace have completed the old year') are negotiated with exceptional bravura. Then, later, there's a pastoral aria with oboe contours of shepherding solace that one recognises from the *Christmas Oratorio*.

If pickings are rich here, the 'guardian' arias are most illuminatingly realised by James Gilchrist, notably in 'Woferne' from the same cantata, whose piccolo cello circumnavigates the all-encompassing grace of the vocal line. Possibly even more beguiling is the conceit of untainted bliss in 'Geliebter Jesu' in No 16 with its stunning oboe da caccia accompaniment. Bach instils an innocence and trust here which Peter Harvey virtuosically sets up in the great solo nestling between the exhortations of the maverick aria-chorus, 'Lasst uns jauchzen'.

The opening cantata, No 143, may be a spurious work: there's something of the apprentice about it. This could not be further from the truth in the concise masterpieces No 153 and 58. In the former, there's something touching about Sally Bruce-Payne emerging from the Monteverdi Choir to sing her cathartic 'Soll ich meinen' after the mental breakdown of 'Stürmt nur' (a fine 'rage' aria). *Ach Gott, wie manches Herzeleid* is given a slightly brittle reading here.

Gardiner reminds us again here that his hit-rate is exceptionally high.

'Cantatas Volume 19: Greenwich/Romsey'   🅟
Cantatas – No 3[a], 13[a], 14[b], 26[b], 81[b], 155[a]. Motet: Jesu, meine Freude, BWV227[b]
[ab]**Joanne Lunn,** [a]**Katharine Fuge** *sops* [a]**William**
Towers, [a]**Richard Wyn Roberts** *countertens* [a]**Julian**
Podger, [a]**Paul Agnew** *tens* [a]**Gerald Finley,**
[a]**Peter Harvey** *basses* **Monteverdi Choir; English**
Baroque Soloists / Sir John Eliot Gardiner

Soli Deo Gloria ② SDG115 (128' · DDD · T/t)
Recorded live at the [a]Old Royal Naval College, Greenwich, London, on January 16-17 and [b]Romsey Abbey, Hampshire, on January 30, 2000   Ⓕ️Ⓞ❍➔

Gardiner's performance of *Ach Gott, wie manches Herzeleid* bends the ear towards the power of doleful dissonance, as the opening chorus wends its way through the 'narrow path of sorrow' with all the emblematic trappings of the operatic chaconne. Equally compelling is the taut, cathartic duet 'Wenn Sorgen', where Joanne Lunn and Richard Wyn Roberts chase each other in canonic bliss – in what Gardiner describes as Bach's 'Singin' in the Rain'.

Indeed, it is the naturalness of the solo singing that marks out this latest volume. Not always smoothed out or glamorous, the response is always fresh, engaged and alive to text. Roberts proclaims his consoling chorale in Meine Seufzer with a fervour encapsulated in the opening aria by the passionate angst of Julian Podger's exhortation and – if it seemed possible – yet greater despair from the slightly uneven but characterful Gerald Finley in 'Ächzen und erbärmlich Weinen'.

William Towers brings a telling control and declamation to the fine opening aria of *Jesus schläft*. Gardiner rightly asserts that few places reveal the operatic Bach more triumphantly than the peerlessly graphic aria 'Die schäumenden Wellen' – especially in the slightly more forgiving space of Romsey Abbey, allowing Paul Agnew to let rip brilliantly. Bach is not just profoundly arrested by the raging sea but also by the implications of faith following Jesus's calming miracle in Peter Harvey's authoritative 'Vox Christi' scena. The bonus of the great motet *Jesu, meine Freude*, performed with customary vividness if not polish by the Monteverdi Choir, completes another memorable addition to the series.

'Cantatas, Vol 20: Naarden/Southwell'   🅟
Cantatas – No 18, 84, 92, 126, 144 & 181
Angharad Gruffydd Jones, Gillian Keith, Miah
Persson *sop* **Wilke te Brummelstroete, Robin**
Tyson *countertens* **James Gilchrist, James Oxley**
tens **Jonathan Brown, Stephan Loges** *basses*
Monteverdi Choir; English Baroque Soloists / Sir
John Eliot Gardiner
Soli Deo Gloria ② SDG153 (95' · DDD · T/t)
Recorded live at the Grote Kerk, Naarden, and
Southwell Minster in 2000   Ⓜ️Ⓞ➔

The weeks leading up to Lent carry a preparatory message which unifies these latest Pilgrimage cantatas: namely, one of expressing gratitude for spiritual blessings and – as specifically articulated in the wonderful minuet alto aria of the first work, BWV144 – the robust exhortation to 'be happy with your lot and get going'.

Gardiner's rapt performances launch themselves magnificently from the 'standing start' (as he aptly calls it) of the above-mentioned piece, whose opening chorus is stripped of all indulgence, in both setting and rendering, to the unequivocal aggression of 'Erhalt uns', via the emotional extremes in the chorale cantata, *Ich hab in Gottes Herz und Sinn*, whose muscular hymn by Paul Gerhardt is worked over by Bach in juxtapositions of extraordinary range.

Then, on a more reflective note, comes the solo soprano cantata *Ich bin vernügt*, receiving a measured, rhetorically questing reading from Miah Persson. If not instantly radiant, this is terrific Bach-singing and Persson extends her fine contribution with a wonderfully moving 'Meinem Hirten', the last aria in No 92: one of those irresistible vignettes of unswerving discipleship in pastoral mode.

Likewise, there are outstanding contributions from the compellingly focused James Oxley in the 'rage' aria 'Seht, seht!' ('See, see how all things snap, break, fall'), almost Schreier-like in its onomatopoeic designs, Stephan Loges's suitably avaricious and pettifogging representation of those who 'devour the seed' in No 181 and the invigorated Monteverdi Choir extending the conceit, in No 126, in perhaps the most angry piece Bach ever composed. Spoiling for a fight, 'fending off murderous Papists and Turks' – an odd sentiment to be conveying in these ecumenical times – Gardiner's forces are on splendid form in another exceptional volume.

'Cantatas, Volume 28: Eisenach'   P
Cantatas – No 4, 6, 31, 66, 134 & 145
Angharad Gruffydd Jones, Gillian Keith sops
Daniel Taylor counterten **James Gilchrist** ten
Stephen Varcoe bass **Monteverdi Choir; English Baroque Soloists / Sir John Eliot Gardiner**
Soli Deo Gloria ② SDG128 (121' · DDD · T/t)
Recorded live at the Georgenkirche, Eisenach, in April 2000   M O O D+

Easter 2000 had strong historical resonances for Sir John Eliot Gardiner's cantata pilgrims, as these outstanding works were performed in St George's, Eisenach, where Bach was baptised, and only a stone's throw from Wartburg Castle where Luther completed his New Testament translations.

One can only guess what inspired an unusually visceral reading of *Christ lag in Todesbanden* (arguably Bach's first great creation), with a plethora of extremes from the Monteverdi Choir. One might quibble with moments where orchestral gestures are a little exaggerated but this is a performance where the sinuous lines and the momentum of liturgical ritual allow Luther's great hymn to take us tantalisingly to the brink of Christ's victory.

The Easter cantatas receive some ebullient readings. Erfreut euch boasts one of Bach's longest choral movements and the composer (and Gardiner) demands vigilance from his virtuoso ensemble, whose roulades of quicksilver scales shed all the fear of the preceding weeks. Despite a few uncertainties in the chromatic solos of the middle section, this is a powerful account whose spiritual core is found in the central recitative-

duet between the allegorical characters Hope and Fear.

The presence of James Gilchrist in any Bach recording raises the stakes and his singing in the little-known pearl *Ein Herz* is an infectious display of the new believer's ecstatic joy, expressed disarmingly in his first aria and reinforced in the duet with alto 'Wir danken and preisen'.

This volume continues to present the riches of the Pilgrimage with admirable consistency; rough edges aside, there is a unique sense of exploration and devotion to the music which comes from the palpable adrenalin of live performance in an oeuvre which has, historically, been studio-bound. *Bleib' bei uns*, with its strong *St John Passion* undertones, is an embodiment of the best in the millennial journey and receives one of the most concentrated and telling performances on disc.

'Cantatas, Volume 21: Cambridge/Norfolk'   P
Cantatas – No 1[b]; No 22[a]; No 23[a]; No 54[a];
No 127[a]; No 159[a]; No 18[b]
[a]**Ruth Holton,** [b]**Malin Hartelius** sops
[a]**Claudia Schubert,** [b]**Nathalie Stutzmann** contrs
[b]**James Gilchrist,** [a]**James Oxley** tens
[ab]**Peter Harvey** bass **Monteverdi Choir;**
[a]**Trinity College Choir, Cambridge;**
English Baroque Soloists / Sir John Eliot Gardiner
Soli Deo Gloria ② SDG118 (135' · DDD · T/t)
Recorded live at [a]King's College Chapel, Cambridge, on March 5 and [b]Walpole St Peter, Norfolk, on March 26, 2000   M O D+

This eclectic selection covers works for Quinquagesima, the Annunciation, Palm Sunday and Oculi (the third Sunday in Lent) in arguably the least even of the seven releases so far. Yet there are significant contributions smattered throughout, not least Nathalie Stutzmann's purple-clad *Widerstehe* (No 54). This true contralto imparts a captivating resilience in the face of sin's devious tricks.

Inspired by the chamber-like ecclesiastical works of Bach's Weimar period, the reduced string ensemble lends a similar intimacy to No 182, though both works suffer from some scrappy playing that clearly could not be rectified simply by dropping in 'patches' from before or after. Stutzmann, however, projects just the right sense of involvement without forcing the issue.

Wie schön leuchtet der Morgenstern (No 1) is the major work here – a masterpiece of understated majesty and gentle celebration (for the Annunciation) where Bach appears to alight on the morning star as a direct resonance of Epiphany; such musical connections within the cantata oeuvre, throughout the church calendar, provide listeners with endless sources of fascination. Gardiner's performance is more an example of a splendid occasion captured rather than a notable addition to a distinguished discography.

Cantatas Nos 22 and 23 were Bach's first to have been performed at Leipzig, audition pieces for the post of Thomascantor before his eventual appointment. Both were performed in the same service on the morning of February 7, 1723. Given the Lenten context, Bach hardly had a chance to flex his muscles in opulent displays of orchestration but he makes up for this with two pieces of subtle stylistic range. *Jesus nahm zu sich die Zwölfe* (No 22) is strikingly prescient of Passion narrative as Christ prepares for his death with melismas of distilled sadness and acceptance of destiny. Peter Harvey's is an affecting performance, as is the incrementally impressive *Du wahrer Gott* (No 23), of which Gardiner completely has the measure.

One special movement to bottle? 'Es ist vollbracht' from No 159 – arguably even better than the setting of the words at the end of the *St John Passion*. Heartfelt singing from Harvey is adorned by playing from oboist Marcel Ponseele which is as exquisite as you'll ever hear.

'Jesu, deine Passion'   **P**
Cantatas – No 22, 23, 127 & 159
Dorothee Mields *sop* **Matthew White** *counterten*
Jan Kobow *ten* **Peter Kooy** *bass* **Collegium Vocale, Ghent / Philippe Herreweghe**
Harmonia Mundi HMC90 1998 (64' · DDD· T/t)   Ⓕ

'Jesu, deine Passion' represents one of Collegium Vocale Gent's most outstanding Bach projects for quite a while. Not least the power of the Quinquagesima (the start of the fasting before Easter) message – the preparation and prescience for all things 'Passion' – gathers Herreweghe into a contemplative world in which he feels most responsive.

The four works here are all masterpieces (sure, No 22 was probably composed in a hurry as a pre-Sermon accompaniment to No 23 as the dual audition pieces for Leipzig), rich in imagery and beguiling in the pure intricacy and invention of Bach's emotional world. Where does one begin? *Du wahrer Gott is*, at last, establishing itself as one of Bach's most profoundly crafted creations; Herreweghe asserts his luminous *a cappella* principles with an almost galant turn.

Elsewhere we hear Peter Kooy, mostly in good voice. Es ist vollbracht from No 159 is a restrained affair but effective nonetheless, especially with the exquisite oboe-playing of Marcel Ponseele. This aria would grace the *St Matthew Passion* with its Picander-esque sensibility (not least the setting of the words 'Welt, gute Nacht!', redolent of 'Mache dich').

This is, above all, a highly atmospheric programme, often overwhelming in content. *Herr Jesu Christ, wahr' Mensch und Gott* (No 127) is another corker: the opening chorus sublime in its incandescent contrapuntal mastery and then the main aria, 'Die Seele ruht', whose funeral bells (through recorders and *pizzicato*) are beautifully portrayed in Dorothee Mield's brittle but awestruck delivery.

Cantatas Nos 49, 58 & 82   **P**
Nancy Argenta *sop* **Klaus Mertens** *bass* **La Petite**

Bande / Sigiswald Kuijken *vn*
Accent ACC9395 (63' · DDD · T/t)   ⒻⓄⓄ

Few readers will be disappointed either by the music or the performances on this disc. It features one of Bach's very finest cantatas, *Ich habe genug* (No 82) for solo baritone, and two 'Dialogue' cantatas for soprano and bass. Leaving out for the moment such issues as instrumental timbre, Sigiswald Kuijken is among the most thoughtful of present-day practitioners of Baroque music. That isn't to say you'll always like what he does, but that he always has a good reason for doing it, and is prepared to defend it to the end. Here, there are no complaints whatsoever: tempos are beautifully judged, the string sound is warmer than usual and the overall approach to the music expressive and eloquently shaped. Mertens gives a fine performance of *Ich habe genug*, clearly articulated and resonantly declaimed. Kuijken has opted for the first of several versions of this cantata which Bach made subsequently for various voice pitches and with small instrumental adjustments.

Mertens is joined in the two 'Dialogue' cantatas by Nancy Argenta. Both voices are tonally well focused and project the music in a manner admirably free from needless affectation or contrivance. An expressive peak is reached in Argenta's aria, 'Ich bin herrlich, ich bin schön' (No 49), a ravishing quartet movement with oboe d'amore and a violoncello piccolo beautifully played by Hidemi Suzuki. Add to this a first-rate performance of the organ obbligatos in the opening Sinfonia and final duo of the same cantata and you've a performance of distinction. An outstanding achievement.

Cantatas Nos 51 (arr W F Bach), 202 & 210   **P**
Christine Schäfer *sop* **Musica Antiqua Köln / Reinhard Goebel** *vn*
DG 459 621-2GH (62' · DDD · T/t)   ⒻⓄⒹ

Of the two wedding cantatas, *Weichet nur, betrübte Schatten* (No 202) ranks among Bach's best-loved, but the other, *O holder Tag, erwünschte Zeit* (No 210), is much less heard. To these, Christine Schäfer adds another Bach favourite, *Jauchzet Gott in allen Landen!* (No 51) which, although not specifically for a wedding, confirms propriety in a nuptial context.

The partnership of Schäfer and Reinhard Goebel with his Musica Antiqua Köln is an interesting one, and rewarding more often than not. Schäfer is a spirited singer with a bright tone and an agile technique. Her clearly articulated phrases accord well with Goebel's well-defined instrumental contours and colourfully characterised rhythms – the fourth aria of No 210, in the rhythm of a polonaise, is admirably enlivened in these respects – and her well-controlled vibrato is a pleasure throughout.

If Emma Kirkby's performance of this piece and No 202 is more understated than the present one there's still an underlying expressive subtlety and a warmth of vocal timbre in her singing which may prove the more rewarding and enduring. The opening aria of No 202, a sublime piece of musical imagery, points up some of the essential differences between the two approaches: Schäfer declamatory, demonstrative and bright toned, with an edge to the voice, Kirkby, warm toned, alluring and exercising superb control throughout. On the other hand Schäfer's even technique, with its easier access to the highest notes of the range, often has the edge over Kirkby in more virtuoso movements. And in No 210 Schäfer's vocal brilliance and unfailing security, together with Goebel's lively if on occasion provocative gestures, make one of the most alert and interesting performances of the piece. Schäfer also rises brilliantly to the occasion in No 51. A stimulating and often satisfying release.

Cantatas Nos 63[a], 91, 121 & 133. Magnificat, BWV243[a]
Dorothee Mields, [a]Carolyn Sampson sops   ℗
Ingeborg Danz contr **Mark Padmore** ten **Peter Kooij, [a]Sebastian Noack** basses **Collegium Vocale, Ghent / Philippe Herreweghe**
Harmonia Mundi ② HMC90 1781/2; SACD
HMC80 1781/2 (117' · DDD · T/t)   Ⓕ

Bach composed Christmas music for more than 30 years of his professional life, but none in such a short a space of time as when he arrived at Leipzig in 1723. He used the relatively quiet Advent period to prepare for the onslaught of commitments around Christmas. This recording celebrates his vibrant representation of all the major themes of the season.

The *Magnificat* was his major contribution in his first year, as it was needed for Christmas Day. One his few works in Latin, this grandiloquent 16-movement canticle enabled the new Cantor to make his mark with a supreme exhibition of compositional mastery and acoustical opulence. Today's audiences usually hear the *Magnificat* in D, but it was originally composed in E flat, with four interpolated movements reflecting the special seasonal context. Philippe Herreweghe presents as tailored and tonally refined a reading as you are likely to find, as indeed he did in his more intimate but prosaic account of the D major version from 1990. This new performance also ranks with the best in terms of varied coloration and sonic choral brilliance.

Bach's Christmas cantatas from 1723 and 1724 comprise works of fascinating range. 'Christen, ätzet diesen Tag' (No 63) is another extrovert celebration, with trumpets and drums, originally conceived in Weimar and smartened up for its new surroundings. Most interesting is 'Christen wir sollen', which presents the idea of thanksgiving as coming from within the dark recesses of Advent, preparation and expectation; Collegium Vocale are supreme in austerity, and the distilled *stilo antico*.

Herreweghe can be a touch anodyne, but this is a mild gripe for what is, overall, an outstand-

ing collection of performances to celebrate a Bach Christmas – beyond the great Oratorio.

Cantatas Nos 82 & 199[a]   ℗
Concerto for Oboe, Violin and Strings, BWV1060
[a]**Emma Kirkby** sop **Katharina Arfken** ob **Freiburg Baroque Orchestra / Gottfried von der Goltz** vn
Carus 83 302 (62' · DDD · T/t)   ⒻⓄⓄ

One of the world's brightest Baroque ensembles performing with one of the world's most admired Baroque sopranos is an enticing proposition. What's more, the solo cantatas on offer here are two of Bach's most moving: No 82, *Ich habe genug*, that serene contemplation of the afterlife; and No 199, *Mein Herze schwimmt im Blut*, a relatively early work with a text that moves from the wallowing self-pity of the sinner to joyful relief in God's mercy. Each contains music of great humanity and beauty, and each, too, contains an aria of aching breadth and nobility – the justly celebrated 'Schlummert ein' in the case of *Ich habe genug*, and in *Mein Herze* the humble but assured supplication of 'Tief gebückt'.

Both could have been written for Emma Kirkby, who's perhaps at her best in this kind of long-breathed, melodically sublime music, in which pure beauty of vocal sound counts for so much. The support of the Freiburg Baroque Orchestra is total, combining tightness of ensemble with such flexibility and sensitivity to the job of accompaniment that you really feel they're 'playing the words'. The Freiburgers also give one of the most satisfyingly thoroughbred accounts of the Violin and Oboe Concerto on disc. Add a recorded sound which perfectly combines bloom, clarity and internal balance, and you've a CD to treasure.

Cantatas Nos 82 & 199
Lorraine Hunt Lieberson mez **Peggy Pearson** ob
Orchestra of Emmanuel Music / Craig Smith
Nonesuch 7559 79692-2 (51' · DDD · T/t)   ⒻⓄⓄ

Lorraine Hunt Lieberson's performances of these two cantatas are like deeply personal, supplicatory confessionals. The American mezzo-soprano has a dark and well-focused sound, and brings words and music to life through a wealth of imaginative detail. The Orchestra of Emmanuel Music (a Boston-based church that incorporates the Bach cantata cycle into its regular liturgy) provides warm-hearted, rich-toned support from 11 strings plus bassoon, and Peggy Pearson shapes the obbligato oboe d'amore parts with exquisite sensitivity. A stunning and remarkably affecting achievement all around.

Cantatas Nos 80 & 147
Ingrid Kertesi sops **Judit Nemeth** mez **Jozsef Mukk** ten **István Gáti** bar **Hungarian Radio Chorus; Failoni Chamber Orchestra, Budapest / Mátyás Antál**
Naxos 8 550642 (54' · DDD)   Ⓢ

Cantatas Nos 51 & 208
Ingrid Kertesi, Julia Pászthy sops **Judit Nemeth**
mez **Jozsef Mukk** ten **István Gáti** bar **Hungarian**
Radio Chorus; Failoni Chamber Orchestra, Buda-
pest / Mátyás Antál
Naxos 8 550643 (50' · DDD)   ⓈD→

Naxos include here four of Bach's most celebrated and accessible cantatas. The performances are far removed in character from the
complete Harnoncourt and Leonhardt edition
on Teldec; women rather than boys sing all the
soprano and alto solos, the Hungarian Radio
Chorus is a mixed male and female ensemble
and the Failoni Chamber Orchestra of Budapest
plays modern rather than period instruments.
However, for much of the time this is enjoyable
spirited music-making which, in its choice of
tempos, its understanding of recitative and its
feeling for the lyricism of Bach's writing compares favourably with rival modern instrument
versions. The disappointment lies partly in the
choice of edition and solution to instrumentation. *Sheep may safely graze* (No 208) is without
the treble recorders which Bach specifically
asked for and which intensify the pastoral idyll.
Here, furthermore the flutes are rather distantly
balanced giving them a somewhat irrelevant role
which is far from Bach's intention.

More serious is the decision to follow the
inflated version of the first and fifth movements
of *Ein feste Burg* (No 80) penned by Bach's eldest
son, Wilhelm Friedemann shortly after his
father's death. Here Friedemann added three
trumpets and a kettledrum to the original texture
of oboes and strings, and though some may prefer
the more overt sense of occasion and the emphasis of the church militant, that this achieves, the
scoring of the original is unquestionably effective
and in keeping with the piece as a whole. Much
else here is sensitively and unsentimentally performed. 'Jesu, joy of man's desiring' (from No
147) is perhaps a shade on the slow side.

Most affecting of all though, is the canonic
alto/tenor duet from No 80 whose tender writing for oboe da caccia and violin has long been
for some one of the purplest of all passages in the
entire Bach cantata canon. The soprano Ingrid
Kertesi negotiates the many difficulties of
Jauchzet Gott in allen Landen! fluently and with a
youthful zeal and few will be disappointed by her
spirited artistry. These are two mainly very
enjoyable discs which can be confidently recommended. Clear recorded sound.

Cantata No 198, Lass, Fürstin, lass noch einen. Mass,
BWV234. Prelude and Fugue, BWV544. Herzlich tut
mich verlangen, BWV727
Katharine Fuge sop **Carlos Mena** counterten
Jan Kobow ten **Stephan MacLeod** bass **Francis**
Jacob org **Ricercar Consort / Philippe Pierlot**
Mirare MIR030 (78' · DDD · T/t)   Ⓕ

Rather gentler than the reconstruction culture
of recent years, the Ricercar Consort ask the
listener to contemplate the mourning for the

Queen of Poland, Princess Christiane Eberhar-
dine – in 1727, through a 'funerary monument'
conceived around Bach's *Trauer* or Funeral
Ode, the Mass in A major and contemporaneous
organ pieces. We have no evidence that the
Mass or the instrumental music appeared in the
'catalfalque in sound' (to quote Gilles Can-
tagrel), the memorial ceremony which occurred
a month after the Queen's death and for which
Bach was commissioned to write his exquisite
Ode, but that is of little matter.

Whatever one's view on single-voiced Bach,
the performances here are among the most persuasive in this medium. Philippe Pierlot understands the music from the thorough bass up –
which one imagines should be common enough;
yet so often a properly directed bass in Bach is
traded for contrapuntal panache and facile
rhythmic gesture. The Mass may lack a certain
dramatic presence in the stunningly original
exchanges in the *Gloria*, reconstituted from
Cantata No 67 with its memorable Vox Christi
'scena' of Jesus's blessing bestowed on mankind.
However, the vitality, interest and warmth of
the opening, as in all the choruses on the disc,
are determined above all by textural definition
and characterful instrumental playing, the flutes
beautifully appointed throughout.

The Ode is a remarkable example of a Bachian
synergy between a carefully selected palette of
light pastels (lutes, gambas, recorders, oboes
d'amores and strings) and a melodic flavour and
nostalgic intensity drawn from a Passion-
inspired language, ideally crafted around the
Enlightenment poetry of the young Leipzig
humanist, Johann Christoph Gottshed. Its
unique atmosphere is captured here, though as
so often in single-voiced readings, the solo
voices don't always have as much to say out of
the collective realm. Francis Jacob's organ playing is both searchingly fluid and articulated.
With the odd misgiving, this is a compelling and
instinctive new Bach recording.

Additional recommendation

Cantatas Nos 39, 73, 93, 105, 107 & 131   Ⓟ
Collegium Vocale, Ghent / Herreweghe
Virgin Veritas ② 562025-2 (120' · DDD)   ⓂD→
This is a veritable treasure trove. The pick of the
bunch is No 105, *Herr gehe nicht ins Gericht*, delivered with glowing intensity, led by the shimmering
Barbara Schlick. Herreweghe and his beautifully
blended ensemble give deeply considered
performances.

Secular Cantatas, BWV201-16

No 201 Der Streit zwischen Phoebus und Pan;
No 202 Weichet nur, betrübte Schatten; **No 203**
(doubtful); **No 204** Ich bin in mir vergnügt; **No 205**
Der zufriedengestellte Äolus; **No 206** Schleicht,
spielende Wellen; **No 207** Vereinigte Zwietracht der
wechselnden; **No 208** Was mir behagt, ist nur die
muntre Jagd; **No 209** Non sa che sia dolore; **No 210**

O holder Tag, erwünschte Zeit; **No 211** Schweigt stille, plaudert nicht, 'Coffee'; **No 212** Mer hahn en neue Oberkeet, 'Peasant'; **No 213** Hercules auf dem Scheidewege; **No 214** Tönet, ihr Pauken!; **No 215** Preise dein Glücke, gesegnetes Sachsen; **No 216** Vergnügte Pleissenstadt

---

Cantatas – Nos 207 & 214   P
Carolyn Sampson *sop* **Ingeborg Danz** *contr*
Mark Padmore *ten* **Peter Kooij** *bass* **Collegium Vocale, Ghent / Philippe Herreweghe**
Harmonia Mundi HMC90 1860 (56' · DDD · T/t)   F

Whether parody or prototype, Bach's handful of secular cantatas present the face of a municipal composer who often sought to enhance his reputation by rising to special occasions. These two works are exceptional examples.

In *Vereinigte Zwietracht*, the subject is a popular professor named Kortte, whose inauguration in late 1726 encouraged his devoted students to commission a congratulatory work. For *Tönet, ihr Pauken!* from 1733 the purpose is more openly self-promotional as Bach sought, as he did in the dedication of his Mass of the same year, to ingratiate himself with the King of Poland and Elector of Saxony. This is, quite coincidentally, a brilliantly conceived homage cantata to the Elector's wife.

As usual, allegorical figures convey prized human qualities in various degrees of panegyric and yet the sensibilities in the music are far from obsequious. In recasting the third movement of the third *Brandenburg* Concerto for No 207, the tone is set for something compelling and moving. Philippe Herreweghe is equal to both with a performance of elegance and due restraint. Collegium Vocale – as their name suggests – relish the lines, the textural possibilities (note the mellow, dignified oboe sound) and the rhetorical detail. Mark Padmore's aria on 'Diligence' is a beautifully poetic and fluent reading and the later duet between Honour (Carolyn Sampson) and Happiness (Peter Kooij) trips with an effortless glee.

Tönet is the original source for movements which Bach was to recondition for the *Christmas Oratorio*. The opening movement is all but identical to the equivalent in the Oratorio but others present fascinating textual deviations which require, especially in the bass aria that was to become 'Grosser Herr', an adaptable ear for music so familiar.

Again, Herreweghe pitches the work just right, with consummate performances from the radiant Sampson (probably her best Bach work to date) and the soft-grained focus of contralto Ingeborg Danz. Her sincere and unsolicitous 'Gratitude', from No 207, with its winning obbligato flutes and mesmerising bass-line (it arches, hovers, rises and sinks), is exquisite. Kooij has rather less edge and character to his voice than in recent years but that's a small gripe in a release of considerable aplomb and exceptional vitality.

Cantatas Nos 211 & 212   P
Emma Kirkby *sop* **Rogers Covey-Crump** *ten*
David Thomas *bass* **Academy of Ancient Music / Christopher Hogwood**
L'Oiseau-Lyre 417 621-2OH (52' · DDD · T/t)   F O

These two most delightful of Bach's secular cantatas here receive sparkling performances fully alive to the humour and invention of the music. The *Coffee* Cantata illustrates a family altercation over a current enthusiasm, the drinking of coffee. A narrator tells the story while the soprano and bass soloists confront each other in a series of delightful arias. Thomas brings out the crabby dyspeptic side of Schlendrian's character imaginatively and Kirkby makes a charming minx-like Lieschen. Covey-Crump's sweet light tenor acts as a good foil. The *Peasant* Cantata also takes the form of a dialogue, here between a somewhat dull and simple young man and his sweetheart Mieke, a girl who intends to better herself. Through the 24 short movements Bach conjures up a wonderfully rustic picture with some vivid dance numbers and rumbustious ritornellos. The soloists' nicely rounded characterisations emerge with great humour and Hogwood directs with vitality and sprightly rhythmic control. The recording is excellent.

Mass in B minor, BWV232

Mass in B minor   P
Carol Hall, Lynne Dawson, Nancy Argenta, Patrizia Kwella *sops* **Mary Nichols** *mez* **Michael Chance** *alto*
Howard Milner, Wynford Evans *tens* **Stephen Varcoe** *bar* **Richard Lloyd Morgan** *bass*
English Baroque Soloists; Monteverdi Choir / Sir John Eliot Gardiner
Archiv Produktion ② 415 514-2AH2 (106' · DDD · T/t)   F

Gardiner bases his forces on the famous memorandum which Bach handed to the Leipzig town council in 1730 outlining the vocal and instrumental requirements for performances of his church music. This results in a larger ripieno group. Gardiner also includes a harpsichord as well as an organ, the simultaneous playing of which, in Wolff's words, was 'a practice that can probably be assumed to be normative in the great majority of Bach's church music'. Gardiner uses women's voices for the soprano solo and ripieno lines and also a male alto soloist and male alto ripieno singers.

This is a fine achievement. Here the many strong points of his direction – a vital rhythmic understanding, a clear and positive sense of purpose, and a naturally affective response to Bach's music, combine in forming a concept of the work which not only explores its eneffable mysteries but also savours the magnificence of its architecture. The solo vocal line-up is a strong one and there are few weak moments; most of the soloists sing in the ripieno group as well, though Patrizia Kwella and Lynne Dawson appear to be exceptions to the rule. Nancy

Argenta's 'Laudamus te', in which she is lightly partnered by Elizabeth Wilcock's sensitive violin playing is very fine and the singing of Mary Nichols who provides an expressive and well-balanced partnership with Patrizia Kwella in the 'Et in unum Dominum' deserves special mention. Michael Chance gives a beautifully controlled account of the 'Agnus Dei' and there are assured contributions elsewhere from Wynford Evans and Stephen Varcoe.

The crowning achievement of Gardiner's recording lies in the vitality, accuracy and homogeneity of the ripieno singing it is in no sense intended to underplay the considerable virtues of the soloists and the orchestra; but this, after all, is first a vocal work and foremost a choral one. The ripieno singing at its very best – as it is for example, in the 'Et resurrexit' – is thrilling and gives a fervent imprint to the entire work. There is a spontaneity about this singing to which few listeners could remain indifferent. Gardiner's choruses are immediately striking and handled with such skill and rigorous discipline that repeated hearing in no sense diminishes their impact.

Mass in B minor   Ⓟ
Carolyn Sampson, Rachel Nicholls *sops*
Robin Blaze *counterten* **Gerd Türk** *ten* **Peter Kooij**
bass **Bach Collegium Japan / Masaaki Suzuki**
BIS ② 🔊 BIS-SACD1701/2 (108' · DDD/DSD · T/t)
                Ⓕ🔁

This is, as you would expect from Masaaki Suzuki, a B minor performance of extraordinary devotional weight, as its resonant surround sound irradiates the score in a patiently constructed explication. The reflective objectivity may seem a little too tantalising as the strangely uncharacterised 'Christe eleison' duet is dogged by the kind of over-regulated articulations in the strings from which Bach Collegium Japan can still suffer.

Yet, after the somewhat lugubrious *Kyrie*, the *Gloria* fairly crackles and Suzuki's careful voicing between singers and instrumentalists generates extraordinary revelations (such as the consoling beauty of the 'Qui tollis' and, later, a remarkable reading of the *Sanctus*). The choral movements are admirably unhurried but purposeful. The solo movements are more variable: intonation takes time to settle early on, especially in the 'Laudamus te', and the 'Quoniam' is shorn of its eloquent grandeur in a prosaic romp, but 'Et in unum Dominum' reveals its expectant delights, as does Blaze's heart-stopping *Agnus Dei*.

Comparing this to Frieder Bernius's vital account with his Stuttgart forces (see below), the over-riding feeling with Suzuki is that generic beauty of sound, 'good judgement' and expert production (though the stereo picture is preferable to the undefined Super Audio) are collectively not quite enough. Preference remains with Bernius whose reverence for Bach's consummate compendium brings greater inner

---

BACH B MINOR MASS – IN BRIEF

Soloists; Monteverdi Ch; English Baroque Soloists / Sir John Eliot Gardiner
Archiv ② 415 514-2AH2 (106' · DDD)   Ⓕ🅞🅞🅞🔁
🅖 Stunning choral singing with fine solo work drawn from the choir. A performance that successfully captures the majesty of the work, but also uncovers its intimacy.

Soloists; Tölz Boys' Choir; The Kings' Consort / Robert King
Hyperion ② CDD22051 (110' · DDD)   Ⓑ🅞🅞
A light-filled, fresh approach to the great Mass, the South German boys blend well with the English men's voices and the whole performance has an uplifting, celebratory feel.

Soloists; New Philharmonic Choir and Orchestra / Carlo Maria Giulini
BBC Legends BBCL4062-2 (77' · ADD)   Ⓕ
Recorded in St Paul's Cathedral in 1972, this is a performance on a large scale with broad tempi. The soloists and orchestra are superb, though the choir is rather indistinct.

Soloists; Viennensis Chorus; Concentus Musicus Wien / Nikolaus Harnoncourt
Teldec ② 4509-95517-2 (107' · ADD)   Ⓜ
Harnoncourt always has something fascinating and powerful to impart when he conducts Bach. His fine team of soloists does him proud in this recording from 1968.

Soloists; Bavarian Radio Chorus and Orchestra / Eugen Jochum
EMI ② 586537-2 (122' · DDD)   Ⓑ🅞🅞
If you're looking for modern instruments, superb soloists and a conductor totally in sympathy with this piece, Eugen Jochum's 1980 performance is well worth considering.

Soloists; Bach Collegium Japan / Masaaki Suzuki
BIS ② 🔊 BIS-SACD1701/2 (108' · DDD)   Ⓕ🔁
A moving, devotionally poised reading from this tried-and-trusted line-up.

Stuttgart Chamber Choir; Stuttgart Baroque Orchestra / Frieder Bernius
Carus ② 83 211 (101' · DDD)   Ⓕ🅞
A very striking and satisfying version of Bach's great Mass. Full of the spirit of discovery.

Soloists; Maîtrise de Notre-Dame, Paris; Ensemble Orchestral de Paris / John Nelson
Virgin Classics 📀 370636-9
(153' · NTSC · 16:9 · 2.0 and 5.0 · 0)   Ⓕ
By no means perfect – there are some silly editing mishaps and awkward entries – but this performance is very much John Nelson's vision of the work. He has clearly thought long and hard about the B minor Mass and his passion and dedication shows. There is a real sense of occasion here.

dialogue, colour and emotional risk and – apart from the expert soloists here – just a touch more quality. Still, this is a rounded and impressive reading whose 'Dona nobis pacem' encapsulates the best of Suzuki: committed, life-affirming and generous.

Mass in B minor   P

Mechthild Bach *sop* **Daniel Taylor** *counterten*
Marcus Ullmann *ten* **Raimund Nolte** *bass*
Stuttgart Chamber Choir; Stuttgart Baroque Orchestra / Frieder Bernius
Carus ② 83 211 (101' · DDD · T/t)   F O

Frieder Bernius gives us a B minor Mass which neither sits obediently in the groove of seasoned reverence nor resorts to well-worn and predictable period reflexes. It is a reading whose invigorating momentum is underpinned by a confident bass presence and an immediacy which resolutely ignores the heavy burden of posterity from which performances regularly suffer.

To say that the buoyant, syncopated *concertante*-like second *Kyrie* heralds an iconoclastic journey would be an exaggeration but Bernius knowingly approaches the Latin text as a means of liberating the abstract brilliance and lyricism inherent in Bach's great edifice. The 'Et in terra pax' is exquisitely judged with every one of those aspiring figures each yielding a little more ambition, as is the case in the urgent 'Gratias agimus' – though perhaps too driven for some. The same is true in both the 'Qui sedes' and *Agnus Dei* (despite the introduction being alarmingly faster than the initial vocal strains), sung by the refined Daniel Taylor, where both are approached with an easy and open-ended fluidity which avoids the obvious pit-falls of 'stop-start' between solo movements and the virtuoso ensemble 'concerti'.

Bernius repeatedly seeks a close alliance between his singers and instrumentalists with eloquent arched lines and yet without an obsession for homogeneity at the expense of individual character in the ensemble. The 'Crucifixus' is given an unselfconscious and gently accentuated reading, the chromatic ground and the flute and string 'pointings' instinctively realised. If the 'Confiteor' falls slightly short, the large choruses are open-breathed and thrilling. The Stuttgart Chamber Choir are full of vim and alertness and the trumpet playing is cataclysmically brilliant throughout. Of the solo singers, special mention must be made of the bass, Raimund Nolte, whose soft-grained 'Et in Spiritum Sanctum' stands out, though it is the effect of the combined ingredients which makes this the most striking and satisfying Mass in B minor to have appeared in years.

Mass in B minor

Jenny Hill *sop* **Dame Janet Baker** *contr* **Peter Pears** *ten* **John Shirley-Quirk** *bass* **New Philharmonia Chorus and Orchestra / Carlo Maria Giulini**
BBC Legends/IMG Artists ② BBCL4062-2

(138' · ADD) Recorded live at St Paul's Cathedral, London 1972   M ▶

In these days of period-instrument hegemony in the performance of Bach, this 'old-fashioned' B minor Mass may be considered an anachronism among younger collectors, but it has its own validity in terms of Giulini's absolute commitment to the work in hand and in the thoroughness of the execution. The downside of the large-scale approach can be heard in the somewhat lumbering account of 'Qui tollis', its upside in the grave, measured 'Gratias agimus' where the successive entries of the same idea are unerringly propelled. 'Et incarnatus est' and 'Crucifixus' in the *Credo* have a wonderful inwardness, the 'Sanctus' a power unavailable to a smaller choir.

When it comes to the soloists this performance wins hands down over authenticity. Janet Baker, on top form, is warm, vibrant, above all communicative with her words. Shirley-Quirk, in both his solos, is confident and bold in his vocal projection, secure and full in tone. There's no one to match them today. Jenny Hill sings purely and with fresh feeling. Only Peter Pears, already in his sixties, disappoints. The recording catches both the St Pauls' reverberation and the sense of a notable occasion.

Mass in B minor

Ruth Ziesak *sop* **Joyce DiDonato** *mez*
Daniel Taylor *counterten* **Dietrich Henschel** *bar*
Maîtrise de Notre-Dame, Paris; Ensemble Orchestral de Paris / John Nelson
Video director **Olivier Simonnet**
Virgin Classics **DVD** 370636-9
(153' · NTSC · 16:9 · 2.0 and 5.0 · 0)   F
Recorded live at the Cathedral of Notre-Dame, Paris, in March 2006.

In a short interview before this concert in Notre-Dame Cathedral, John Nelson calls this performance 'a culmination of my experience with Bach' and it is one which is characterised by the conductor's highly considered and distilled understanding of the score. This is evident in his decisive direction, which is a model of clarity. The tempi are beautifully judged, the monumental choruses are chiselled lovingly and the image-laden and reflective movements – reaching a tortured sadness and composed dignity in a superbly judged 'Crucifixus' – all conspire towards a magisterial and logical conclusion in the 'Dona nobis pacem', where heart and head seem happily entwined.

What prevents this from being as memorable are both the capability of the forces, beyond a certain level, and the flawed filming – random and quick-fire shots from all manner of angles. The results are profoundly restless. There are far too many occasions where dubbing is ineptly handled, not least in the 'Laudamus te', where the admirable Joyce DiDonato is suddenly out of kilter with proceedings with an edit (26'39") using a patch where the tempo is far too fast. Comedy is the order of the day at the end of the

'Cum Sanctu Spiritu', where Nelson is filmed bringing off the ensemble at least two beats after the music has ended.

The Ensemble Orchestral de Paris perform in a fairly prosaic fashion by today's 'informed' standards and Nelson has a habit of accentuating appoggiaturas into submission; only the vibrant personality of the bassoons (notable in both bass 'arias') and the slick trumpeting ring out with complete confidence. The choir are committed and well drilled and Ruth Ziesak is the pick of the soloists, apart from an 'Et in unum' which is full of gratuitous accents – maybe in an attempt to encourage Daniel Taylor to take his head out of his copy. This DVD is not quite what it promises, though John Nelson's motivation and vision certainly bring a real sense of occasion.

Lutheran Masses, BWV233-36

F, **BWV233**; A, **BWV234**; G minor, **BWV235**; G, **BWV236**

Masses,[a] BWV233 & 236. Trio Sonata in C, BWV529 (arr Boothby)   **P**
[a]**Nancy Argenta** sop [a]**Michael Chance** counterten
[a]**Mark Padmore** ten [a]**Peter Harvey** bass
Purcell Quartet (Catherine Mackintosh, Catherine Weiss vns Richard Boothby vc Robert Woolley org)
Chandos Chaconne CHAN0653 (65' · DDD · T/t) Ⓟ Ⓞ�

The absurd prejudice that long deprived us of adequate recordings of Bach's four Lutheran Masses (or short Masses, as they're also known because, in accordance with Lutheran usage, they set only the *Kyrie* and *Gloria*) seems finally to have died a death. The Masses' crime has been to be made up almost entirely of paraphrases of cantata movements from the 1720s, yet Bach is Bach, whatever the circumstances, and this is wonderful music which, like the B minor Mass, offers sober old-style polyphonic choral movements of impressive cumulative power alongside choruses of almost physical excitement and clamour and some first-rate arias with instrumental obbligato.

As with volume 1, a one-to-a-part approach is taken, with the four vocal soloists also forming the choir and the Purcell Quartet being augmented by whatever extra instruments are needed. The result doesn't sound at all underpowered, and gains considerably over Herreweghe's typically well-turned but more traditional choral approach in vividness of texture and harmony, crispness of attack and a madrigalian litheness of expressive response.

The recording allows just the right amount of bloom without becoming washy. There are times when the two higher voices sound further forward than the others, and Michael Chance occasionally disappears a bit towards the bottom of his range, but in general this release brings nothing but pleasure both in the music and in the stylish and lively performances.

Magnificat in D, BWV243

Bach Magnificat in D   **P**
Vivaldi Ostro picta, RV642. Gloria in D, RV589
Emma Kirkby, Tessa Bonner sops **Michael Chance** counterten **John Mark Ainsley** ten **Stephen Varcoe** bar **Collegium Musicum 90 Chorus and Orchestra / Richard Hickox**
Chandos CHAN0518 (64' · DDD · T/t)   Ⓕ Ⓞ➡

Hickox sets effective tempos in Bach's *Magnificat* and points up the many striking contrasts in colour and texture with which the piece abounds. From among the many successful features of the recording Stephen Varcoe's 'Quia fecit mihi magna' and the 'Et misericordia' sung by Michael Chance and John Mark Ainsley stand out. Vivaldi's *Gloria*, RV589 is the better known of two settings by the composer in D major. In this programme it's prefaced by an introductory motet *Ostro picta*, which may well in fact belong to the *Gloria* and is here sung with warmth and radiance by Emma Kirkby. Hickox's performance of this evergreen vocal masterpiece comes over with conviction. It's gracefully phrased, sensitively sung and affectingly paced with an admirable rapport between vocalists and instrumentalists. The sound is first rate.

Magnificat in D. Cantata No 21   **P**
Greta de Reyghere sop **René Jacobs** counterten
Christoph Prégardien ten **Peter Lika** bass
Netherlands Chamber Choir; La Petite Bande / Sigiswald Kuijken
Virgin Classics The Classics 561833-2 (73' · DDD · T/t)   Ⓑ Ⓞ

The first of this batch of The Classics, coupling performances of Bach's *Magnificat* with Cantata No 21, is in every way recommendable. Indeed Nicholas Anderson's original review commented that in the *Magnificat* Sigiswald Kuijken and La Petite Bande 'reach the heart of Bach's music more convincingly than almost any other [version] currently available'. He went on to comment that he found Kuijken's performance of *Ich hatte viel Bekümmernis* 'profoundly affecting', although he also noticed some instrumental insecurity. Certainly the lovely solo and choral singing in both works, coupled to a superbly atmospheric recording, make this a Bach CD to treasure.

Magnificat in D. Cantata No 51   **P**
Nancy Argenta, Patrizia Kwella, Emma Kirkby sops **Charles Brett** counterten **Anthony Rolfe Johnson** ten **David Thomas** bass **English Baroque Soloists / Sir John Eliot Gardiner**
Philips 50 Great Recordings 464 672-2PM
(41' · DDD · T/t)   Ⓜ Ⓞ

Bach's *Magnificat* is a work full of contrasts – contrasts of texture, of colour and of temperament – few of which escape the attention of Gardiner, his choir, orchestra and fine group of soloists. The choruses are sung with great vigour and precision; articulation is crisp and diction excellent. The solo singing is of a uniformly high standard with some outstanding contributions from Charles Brett, Anthony Rolfe Johnson and David Thomas. Notable are the 'Quia fecit', in which Thomas is admirably accompanied by a perfectly balanced continuo texture, and the 'Et misericordia' duet for alto and tenor, which is sung with great tenderness and restraint by these artists. Among the obbligato contributions that can be singled out is the oboe d'amore in the 'Quia respexit', which is sensitively played and hauntingly beautiful.

The cantata *Jauchzet Gott in allen Landen!* is one of three for solo soprano which Bach wrote at Leipzig during the 1730s. The spirit of the text, as its title implies, is one of rejoicing. It's a spirit which the soloist, Emma Kirkby, captures well. Her solo partner in the colourful opening movement and in the fugal 'Alleluia' at the close is Crispian Steele-Perkins who manages Bach's exacting trumpet parts with precision. Less enjoyable is the exaggerated acceleration in tempo for the 'Alleluia' section of the final movement, but it's a dazzling display without a doubt. These are fine performances of two of Bach's best-known church compositions, with admirably clear recordings.

St Matthew Passion, BWV244

St Matthew Passion   **P**
Anthony Rolfe Johnson ten Evangelist **Andreas Schmidt** bar Christus **Barbara Bonney, Ann Monoyios** sops **Anne Sofie von Otter** mez **Michael Chance** counterten **Howard Crook** ten **Olaf Bär** bar **Cornelius Hauptmann** bass **London Oratory Junior Choir; Monteverdi Choir; English Baroque Soloists / Sir John Eliot Gardiner**
Archiv Produktion ③ 427 648-2AH3 (167' · DDD · T/t)
Ⓕ**OOOO➷**

What makes Gardiner's *St Matthew Passion* stand out in the face of stiff competition is, more than anything, his vivid sense of theatre. Bach's score is, after all, a sacred drama and Gardiner interprets this aspect of the work with lively and colourful conviction. That in itself isn't sufficient to ensure a fine performance, but here we have a first-rate group of solo voices, immediately responsive choral groups and refined obbligato and orchestral playing. Anthony Rolfe Johnson declaims the Evangelist's role with clarity, authority and the subtle inflexion of an accomplished story-teller. Ann Monoyios, Howard Crook and Olaf Bär also make strong contributions but it's Michael Chance's 'Erbarme dich', tenderly accompanied by the violin obbligato, which sets the seal of distinction on the performance. Singing and playing of this calibre deserve to win many friends and Gardiner's deeply felt account of Bach's great Passion does the music considerable justice. Clear recorded sound.

St Matthew Passion   **P**
Christoph Prégardien ten Evangelist **Matthias Goerne** bar Christus **Christine Schäfer, Dorothea Röschmann** sops **Bernarda Fink, Elisabeth von Magnus** contrs **Michael Schade, Markus Schäfer** tens **Dietrich Henschel, Oliver Widmer** basses **Vienna Boys' Choir; Arnold Schoenberg Choir; Concentus Musicus Wien / Nikolaus Harnoncourt**
Teldec ③ 2564-64347-2 (163' · DDD · T/t) Includes enhanced CD with full autograph score   Ⓕ**OOO**

Harnoncourt waited over 30 years to return to the 'Great Passion', which, but for his live Concertgebouw recording, he last recorded in 1970 when he had completed only a handful of cantatas in Teldec's defining series. Harnoncourt's revisitation presents a unique statement, one that can't fail to make an impression. Recorded in the sumptuous acoustic of the Jesuitenkirche in Vienna, there's a detectable flavour of southern European oratorio, ebulliently theatrical, immediate and free-breathing, and without the austerity of North German rhetoric. What's recognisably perceived as 'spiritual' in the carefully coiffured renderings of Suzuki (BIS) and Herreweghe (Harmonia Mundi) has no place here. Harnoncourt's religiosity isn't imposed but stands rather in a lifetime of musical distillation. This is instantly obvious in the opening chorus, where bridal imagery (in the music's secular, balletic lift) is juxtaposed with the physical imagery of what's at stake (in the broad, enduring bow strokes). While Suzuki's visceral chorale is more spine-tingling, the refinement here of 'Sehet, Wohin?' amid inexorable, paradoxically unquestioning direction, is masterful.

Pacing Part 1 is no easy task, and many a tank has been emptied before reaching what the great Bach scholar Friederich Smend called 'the central message of the work' (encompassing Nos 46-49). Harnoncourt neither dallies unduly with the chorales nor charges through them; they skilfully counterbalance the remarkably incandescent narrative of Prégardien's Evangelist. The tenor shows a supreme attention to detail (even if his singing is sometimes effortful), and his dialogue with Matthias Goerne's vital Christus is especially compelling. Harnoncourt gives 'Blute nur' a touch of characteristic melodrama, but none can doubt how Dorothea Röschmann and the orchestra, between them, project its expressive core.

The strikingly cultivated crowd scenes of the well-drilled, medium-sized Arnold Schoenberg Choir make a strong contrast with the relatively brazen chorus in Harnoncourt's 1970 version. Unlike the specialists of the pioneering years, Harnoncourt hand-picks his soloists from the widest possible pool. Apart from the excellent Röschmann, Christine Schäfer impresses here far more than in her rather harried solo Bach disc (DG). More relaxed and controlled, she sings with acute coloration and stillness in 'Aus Liebe'. With Bernarda Fink's beguiling 'Erbarme dich' and Michael Schade's resplendent 'Geduld', only Oliver Widmer (who sings

'Gebt mir') gives less than unalloyed pleasure. The pick of the crop is Dietrich Henschel, who sings with great warmth and penetration with a 'Mache dich' to stand alongside (if not to rival) Fischer-Dieskau for Karl Richter. But with even these wonderful contributions, it still takes clarity of vision to graphically propel the drama yet also ponder it reverentially. Again, Harnoncourt leaves his mark with his unerring compassion at most of the critical points.

Finally, mention should be made of Concentus Musicus, grainy and luminous in ensemble, the obbligato wind a far cry from the softer-edged and rounded tonal world of almost all other 'period' groups. In short, this is the most culturally alert reading in years and a truly original and illuminating experience.

St Matthew Passion
Nicholas Mulroy *ten* The Evangelist **Matthew Brook** *bar* Christus **Susan Hamilton, Cecilia Osmond** *sops* **Clare Wilkinson, Annie Gill** *contr* **Nicholas Mulroy, Malcolm Bennett** *tens* **Matthew Brook, Brian Bannatyne-Scott** *basses* **Dunedin Consort and Players / John Butt**
Linn ② ⌂ CKD313 (161' · DDD)   Ⓕ◐➾

Having swept the board with their Award-winning *Messiah*, John Butt and the Dunedin Consort and Players proceed headlong into the *summa* of dramatic religious masterpieces. One imagines, however, that this highly singular approach has been marinating in Butt's mind for years. This is a reading (the first to draw on the 1742 performing version with its re-allocation of continuo instruments) where scholarly and musical penetration is indivisible in the strength of the approach and the unswerving commitment of the 'players'.

And 'players' they are – except that Butt argues here for a new dramatic understanding of the *Matthew* (note the curious de-sanctification) where the work challenges the notion of 'parts' in an opera, towards various 'voices' which reflect the listener's absorption of the conflicting positions – both biographical and emotional – of the main protagonists and the most far-flung thresholds of human experience. This is achieved using the main singers, from the eight principal voices, in different contexts. Hence, as Butt explains in his illuminating note, the Evangelist may rally us to lament as an allegorical 'Daughter of Zion' in the opening chorus before darting in and out of the story in recitatives, chorus, aria and chorales, mixing up the past and present, first person and third person, in a web of intense and coherent narrative and reflection.

All of this presupposes a one-to-a-part troupe where all these subtle character combinations can be perceived. With such a spectacularly clear and balanced sound from Philip Hobbs, these ambitious perspectives are powerfully realised; refreshingly, too, Bach's 'novel in sound' is presented in a small inter-reliant ensemble without the need for tiresome dog-

---

BACH ST MATTHEW PASSION – IN BRIEF

Soloists; Monteverdi Choir; English Baroque Soloists / Sir John Eliot Gardiner
Archiv ③ 427 648-2AH3 (167' · DDD) Ⓕ◐◐◐➾
Ⓖ A stunning achievement from 1989 projected with powerful conviction. (Also available coupled with the B minor Mass and *St John Passion* – 469 769-2X9: a real bargain.)

Soloists; Arnold Schonberg Choir; Concentus Musicus Wien / Nikolaus Harnoncourt
Teldec ③ 2564-64347-2 (163' · DDD) Ⓕ◐◐◐➾
Ⓖ With its ROM-capabilities offering the full autograph score, and Harnoncourt's long experience and sympathy for the work, this is one of the triumphs of recent times.

Soloists; Gabrieli Players / Paul McCreesh
Archiv ③ 474 200-2AH2 (161' · DDD) Ⓕ◐◐➾
There's a brightness and lightness that comes from a one-to-a-part approach, but you must decide whether it sacrifices some of the work's nobility.

Soloists; Choir and Orchestra of the Eighteenth Century / Frans Brüggen
Philips ② 473 263-2PH2 (160' · DDD) Ⓕ◐◐➾
A wonderfully human and humane approach from Brüggen, who eloquently brings out the heart of the work, with its powerful emotional currents.

Soloists; Bach Collegium Japan / Masaaki Suzuki
BIS ② BIS-CD1000/2 (164' · DDD) Ⓕ◐➾
Suzuki touches the deep spiritual core of this universal drama and inspires his colleagues to scale truly dizzying heights. Beautifully recorded.

Soloists; Philharmonia Chorus and Orchestra / Otto Klemperer
EMI ③ 567538-2 (223' · ADD) Ⓜ◐
Bach on a large canvas from 1962 with fine soloists and the great Philharmonia Chorus. A strong devotional reading with broad tempi – light years away from today's approach.

Soloists; Dunedin Consort and Players / John Butt
Linn ② ⌂ CKD313 (161' · DDD) Ⓕ◐➾
A superb follow-up to their *Messiah*, and carrying the same conviction and passion. This is a Matthew Passion with a sense of being pu on by a 'company'. It has drama but it also has tremendous intimacy.

Soloists; Hungarian Festival Choir and State Symphony Orchestra / Géza Oberfrank
Naxos ③ 8 550832/4 (163' · DDD) Ⓢ
Don't overlook this fine, modern-instrument set. There are no musical compromises, and these fine Hungarian musicians sing and play with real conviction.

matic mantras on historical rectitude. Indeed, often so entwined are the textures that singers' vowels are shadowed by instruments in a close-knit rapport of exceptional immediacy.

For those steeped in both recent and old schools, this performance will resonate with both, though it is not always so easy to summarise how. The thread of intensity is achieved largely by the focus and roundness of the Dunedin Consort's palette, the thrusting legatos (when called for) and the welcome presence of a strong, directed bass-line.

Such responses are relatively superficial because Butt's *St Matthew* is truly original in spheres resonating beyond established parameters. As his story-teller, Nicholas Mulroy brings his own striking naturalness of delivery, clarity of diction and honesty. At the start of Part 2, especially, there are moments of disarming reportage, such as the encounter with the High Priest where the Evangelist conveys a sickened response to Christ's humiliation and a gutting catch in his voice at the emptiness of Peter's denial. Yet it is Mulroy's identification with the outstanding Christus of Matthew Brook which raises the stakes in this performance. The timing between the two and the realism of the musical choreography is both remarkably patient and animated.

The only downside of a single-part *St Matthew* is that, while the singers – in Butt's words – 'become familiar to us as the piece progresses', this only works to advantage if they have the tonal and musical range to sustain such an extended and exposed vision. For all the stylistic nuancing and deft ensemble work of the sopranos, their arias rarely lift themselves beyond the generic. 'Ich will dir' sounds unsure and snatched and 'So ist mein Jesus gefangen' fails to demarcate the almost cosmic mystery ('moon and light have set in their anguish') alongside the admirable discipline of the crowd's graphic interjections.

No recorded *St Matthew Passion* comes without its blemishes but few parade such a compellingly fresh and raw realism, one so strongly identifiable by its wilful clarity of intent that it asks new questions about what this great work can say to us.

St Matthew Passion   Ⓟ

Mark Padmore ten Evangelist **Peter Harvey** bass
Christus **Julia Gooding, Deborah York** sops
Magdalena Kožená, Susan Bickley mezs **James**
Gilchrist ten **Stephan Loges** bass **Gabrieli Players /**
Paul McCreesh

Archiv Produktion ② 474 200-2AH2 (161' · DDD · T/t)
ⒻⓄⓄ▸

In the distinguished performance history of the Great Passion, this is a dynamic and powerful reading. What we have here, primarily, is a compelling directorial vision, a dramatically cohesive whole. The only 'controversial' aspect is the use of single voices in the chorus, thereby applying the research presented in the last two dec-

ades by Joshua Rifkin and Andrew Parrott. However, as it happens, Paul McCreesh sees this option as a flexible way of enhancing the rich expressive possibilities of the *St Matthew*, a means to a somewhat greater end, thankfully, than joining the band of zealots who seek world domination in Bach vocal performance. And there can be no denying that McCreesh uses the single voices to great and encouraging effect. The warm intimacy of expression in the chorales is often spellbinding, the lucid realism of the madrigalian commentaries touchingly palpable and the crowd scenes almost crazed, as if you were among the mob. McCreesh's pragmatism also ensures that his quality singers produce a rich tonal body rather than a pushed, squawking consort.

There's some outstandingly characterised singing to be heard here, and a few missed opportunities too. Deborah York sounds somewhat *al dente* in her soprano arias, a limited emotional range partly accentuated by the colour and subtlety of expression of Magdalena Kožená's 'Buss und Reu' as well as the enraptured and troubled 'Ach, nun ist mein Jesus hin!'. Mark Padmore's Evangelist is highly charged and responsive: at times he hovers, regaling the facts of the matter with disarming poise; at others he becomes agitated, even manic. He seems somehow implicated in Peter's denial in a tableau performed with quite remarkable dramatic power, setting up Kožená's 'Erbarme dich'. Hers is one of the most painfully beautiful performances in years, even if the violin obbligato bulges rather too much.

Of the two basses, the Christus of Peter Harvey conveys neither gilded halo nor testosterone-fired ruddiness but he remains an effective and constant companion. Stephan Loges is rhetorically imploring in timbre, unafraid to take risks and a singer you listen to attentively.

There's yet to be a clear leader in *St Matthew Passion* recordings, even if that were desirable. The quality of the production is mainly first-rate, though there are the usual dips and troughs you expect from such a challenging undertaking. 'Können Tränen' is a scrappy and flat affair with a strangely below-par Susan Bickley, and the strings aren't always universally impressive. Overall, if not as culturally resonant as Harnoncourt's remarkably mature and poetic reading, McCreesh's interpretation has an unremitting singularity of purpose, as aesthetically Protestant as Harnoncourt's is Catholic. A memorable and vitally conceived account.

St John Passion, BWV245

St John Passion   Ⓟ

Gerd Türk ten Evangelist **Chiyuki Urano** bass
Christus **Ingrid Schmidthüsen, Yoshie Hida** sops
Yoshikazu Mera counterten **Makoto Sakurada** ten
Peter Kooij bass **Bach Collegium Japan /**
Masaaki Suzuki

BIS ② BIS-CD921/2 (110' · DDD · T/t)   ⒻⓄⓄ▸

Bach seems to have performed his *St John Passion* on four Good Fridays during his tenure as Thomaskantor at Leipzig. However, he continued to make significant revisions right up to the last performance under his direction, on April 4, 1749. Of the four versions, the second, dating from 1725, contains the most distinctive revisions, the first version (1724) and the last bearing close affinity with one another. Masaaki Suzuki and his talented Bach Collegium Japan have chosen Bach's latest version. All has evidently been carefully prepared and deeply considered: what's refreshing about their approach is the importance afforded to the relationship between text and music, to the theological source of Bach's inspiration, and the emotional impact of the story and music on its audience. Some of their thoughts may strike readers as simplistic, even perhaps a shade sentimental, but on the strength of this fervent performance we can hardly question their sincerity.

The role of the Evangelist is sung with clarity and lightness of inflexion by Gerd Türk. His performance is eloquently measured, his phrasing well shaped and his articulation engagingly varied. All this makes him a riveting story-teller. The role of Jesus is taken by Chiyuki Urano, warm-toned and resonant. Ingrid Schmidthüsen and Yoshikazu Mera make strongly appealing contributions and Peter Kooij is satisfying and affecting.

Excellent, too, are the contributions of the Collegium's choir of women's and men's voices. Choral and instrumental articulation is incisive, propelling the rhythms with energy. The performance draws you in from the start. This is a major recording event, and an eminently satisfying one.

St John Passion (sung in English)
Sir Peter Pears *ten* Evangelist **Gwynne Howell** *bass* Christus **Heather Harper, Jenny Hill** *sops* Alfreda **Hodgson** *contr* **Robert Tear, Russell Burgess, John Tobin, Adrian Thompson** *tens* **John Shirley-Quirk** *bar* Wandsworth School Boys' Choir; English Chamber Orchestra / Benjamin Britten
Double Decca ② 443 859-2DF2 (130' · ADD)
Recorded 1971   Ⓜ🅾🅾↦

Britten's recording of the *St John Passion* is very special indeed. Apparently he preferred to perform this Bach choral work because of its natural potential for drama. This account takes over the listener completely. The soloists are all splendid, though Heather Harper must be singled out, and the choral response is inspirational in its moments of fervour. Peter Pears is a superb Evangelist; Britten's direction is urgent and volatile; the Wandsworth School Boys' Choir sings out full-throatedly and the English Chamber Orchestra underpins the whole performance with gloriously rich string textures. The analogue recording offers a demonstration of ambient fullness, vividness of detail and natural balance. In fact, it's as if a live performance at The Maltings, Snape, has been transported to the area just beyond your speakers.

St John Passion   🅿
James Gilchrist *ten* Evangelist **John Bernays** *bass* Christus **Eamonn Dougan** *bass* Pilatus **Joe Littlewood** *sop* **James Bowman** *counterten* **Matthew Beale** *ten* **Colin Baldy** *bass*
New College Choir, Oxford; Collegium Novum / Edward Higginbottom
Naxos ② 8 557296/7 (110' · DDD · T/t)   Ⓢ↦

When you hear the ominous first chorus of Bach's *St John Passion* sung and played like this, liturgical ritual and visceral human drama make for an unusually intense experience. The bass line pulsates, the boys articulate the words with supreme clarity and the steady speed provides the movement with just the right length – a consideration too often neglected.

Recorded in New College, Oxford, the resident choristers, choral scholars and lay clerks appear to be entirely at ease with the special juxtaposition of quicksilver action and warm reflection which Bach demands in his choruses and chorales. Edward Higginbottom delivers a palpable sense of narrative, unfussy, as if habit lies at the root of its being. Just listen to the searing choral chromaticisms as Christ is brought before Caiaphas, the startlingly urgent declamations as the crowd bays for blood or the distraught tenderness of James Bowman in 'Es ist vollbracht'.

The Evangelist is the established tenor James Gilchrist, whose alert and straightforward singing makes his performance wholly believable. Of the current generation of choristers, Joe Littlewood reminds us that English choirboys can sing German music beautifully and convey the emotional essence of the text with maturity and purpose. His 'Ich folge' is a delight.

There's the odd strain in Matthew Beale's testing tenor arias but a pleasing timbre, as indeed there is in John Bernays' proud but unblustering Christus. If there's a general tendency, it's to allow the music to speak in its own time within a relaxed beat. The rest is instinct, experience and letting what will be, be. In such light comes this refreshing and captivating new interpretation.

St John Passion   🅿
Ruth Holton *sop* **Bogna Bartosz** *contr* **Markus Brutscher** *ten* **Thomas Laske** *bar* **Tom Sol** *bass*
Cologne Chamber Choir; Collegium Cartusianum / Peter Neumann
Dabringhaus und Grimm ② MDG332 0983-2 (114' · DDD · T/t)   Ⓕ🅾

Bach never entirely settled on a single view of the *St John* and there are at least four known versions, from Good Friday 1724 (Bach's first Easter in Leipzig) to a performance the year before he died. Peter Neumann expounds here on the virtues of the second, dating from a year after the first. The differences are neither extensive nor merely cosmetic; such is Bach's skilful pacing of the narrative that the original conception can shift markedly with an ever-so-slight nudge. The most immediate difference is the replacement of the austere, imagery-laden opening chorus, 'Herr, unser Herrscher', with the chorale fantasy 'O Mensch, bewein', later employed to conclude Part 1 of the *St Matthew*.

To the unsuspecting, this is the St John Passion that can have you thinking you're playing the beginning of the second disc of the St Matthew; this and two further movements demonstrate Bach's obsession – as with the cantatas of the period – with employing chorales as integral raw material. Yet perhaps more striking still is the interpolation of new arias, possibly derived from an earlier Passion setting conceived in Weimar. These arias, 'Himmel reisse' and 'Zerschmettert mich', are far more animated and graphic than anything in the earlier version. More remarkable still is 'Zerschmettert', performed with dazzling immediacy by Evangelist and tenor soloist Markus Brutscher. This is a superb piece of theatrical posturing of the sort that Handel and Telemann would have filched for their opera, had they only known. The one casualty in this version is 'Erwage', a perennial favourite.

Given that the majority of the work remains common to all, this account should not be judged merely on its special properties. Neumann conveys strong musical ideas throughout: the choruses are wonderfully attentive to contrapuntal detail, and mesmerisingly varied in articulation. You can forget how beautifully crafted and selected the chorale tunes are in this work, and Neumann allows the music to breathe so that they represent a kind of caesura in the otherwise intense narrative.

Brutscher is a reliable, if somewhat monochrome Evangelist. His technical ease and superb intonation are noteworthy, but often he chooses to remain studiously uninvolved. Ruth Holton is made for the bright-eyed discipleship of 'Ich folge', but there's more to her Bach than youthful piping, as we can hear in her sensitive account of 'Zerfliesse, mein Herze'. However, the soloists individually aren't what marks out this recording; rather it's Neumann's corporate, controlled and intimate concept. He moves skilfully between incandescence and emotionally charged intensity. This is, then, a persuasive testament to Bach's most radically different version of the St John.

St John Passion   Ⓟ
Caroline Stam *sop* **Peter de Groot** *counterten*
Charles Daniels, Gerd Türk *tens* **Stephan MacLeod,**
Bas Ramselaar *basses* **Netherlands Bach Society /**
Jos van Veldhoven
Channel Classics ② 💿 CCSSA22005 (112' · DDD/
DSD · T/t)   ⒻⓄ

This is the most beautifully packaged account of the *St John Passion* on the market. The performance is cushioned by informative essays and sharp reproductions of paintings and objects from the Museum Catharijneconvent, Utrecht. Such extras can illuminate an understanding of the music so long as the performance lives up to expectations. Thankfully it does.

Veldhoven brings his distinctive angle to the *St John* by presenting it as a notional 'first version'. Among some judicious tinkering, he ignores Bach's last-minute addition of flutes, made before the premiere in April 1724, and promotes an atmosphere of private devotion where the one-to-a-part ensemble allows for a distilled immediacy in the arias and flexible and varied choral contributions. This is a reading that shows that the argument for size in Bach's chorus – large or small – is better fought on musical grounds than musicological ones.

The Netherlands Bach Society, and Veldhoven especially, are more drawn to rhetorical effect than poetic instinct. The chorales are sometimes over-pointed and even precious, and string articulation rather unyielding, but little detracts from a profoundly luminous sense throughout, led by the supremely clear-sighted Evangelist of Gerd Türk. The other voices, soloists and ripienists alike, make a fine and colourful impression, especially in the crowd scenes, where Veldhoven presents them as a more questing, equivocal and three-dimensional group than the incessant hectoring of an uncompromising lynch mob.

This *St John* holds a special place in a notable catalogue of which, in their different ways, Gardiner, Fasolis, Higginbottom and Suzuki are all leading lights. Veldhoven is thoughtful and effective, even if he never quite takes flight and allows the music to be expressed on the widest emotional canvas. The Super Audio sound is suitably rich and all-embracing.

St John Passion
Gerd Türk *ten* Evangelist **Stephen MacLeod** *bass*
Christus **Midori Suzuki** *sop* **Robin Blaze** *counterten*
Chiyuki Urano *bass-bar*; **Bach Collegium Japan /**
Masaaki Suzuki *Video director* **Shokichi Amano**
TDK 📀 DV-BAJPN (120' · 16:9 · 2.0 · 0)   Ⓕ

With his outstanding series of choral recordings for BIS, Masaaki Suzuki has rightly established a high reputation for stylish interpretations of Bach. As he explains in a brief interview which comes as a supplement on this DVD, he had intensive training in period performance in Holland. Certainly, his vigour and sensitivity in Bach defies any idea that Japanese culture has been a barrier in authentically interpreting Bach. Suzuki recorded the *St John Passion* for BIS back in 1998. This DVD version marks a special performance recorded on the anniversary on 28 July 2000 of Bach's birth 250 years earlier. In essence the interpretation remains the same, with fresh, light textures and generally brisk speeds which yet allow for depth of feeling, and the sense of occasion is irresistible.

Gerd Türk gives an achingly beautiful performance, with his profound involvement all the more evident when seen as well as heard. Türk also sings the tenor arias, and the other soloists also have double roles, singing in the 16-strong choir before stepping forward when needed as soloists: Stephen MacLeod singing Christus as well as the bass arias, Chiyuki Urano singing Pilate and other incidental solos, Robin Blaze a superb alto soloist and the ravishing Midori Suzuki in the two soprano arias.

First-rate sound too. The leaflet offers minimal information and no text, though one can plumb into subtitles, either the original German or the English translation, but not both together.

St Luke Passion, BWV246 (attrib)

St Luke Passion (attrib)   Ⓟ
Mona Spägele sop **Christiane Iven** contr
Rufus Müller, Harry van Berne tens **Stephan
Schreckenberger, Marcus Sandmann** basses **Alsfeld
Vocal Ensemble; Bremen Baroque Orchestra /
Wolfgang Helbich**
CPO ② CPO999 293-2 (106' · DDD · T/t)   ⒻⓄ

Though it isn't a genuine Bach work, those who love his music will want to investigate the *St Luke Passion*. In terms of scale, rhetorical intensity, structural and stylistic sophistication, musical invention and artistic ambition generally, it finds no common ground with his two extant Passions. But there's much that's intimate and touching about it. The meditative element comes less from contemplative arias than from a continuous and freshly fashioned narrative, although the arias, with their favoured wind obbligato parts, are often skilled and affecting. Wolfgang Helbich and his Bremen forces pitch the dramatic climate just about right throughout. Smoothly articulated, unmannered and technically accomplished, the chorales and *turba* scenes are especially well judged. The Evangelist, Rufus Müller, conveys the Gospel with soft-grained clarity and understated dignity and the other soloists do more than justice to the six arias.

Christmas Oratorio, BWV248

Christmas Oratorio   Ⓟ
Monika Frimmer sop **Yoshikazu Mera** counterten
Gerd Türk ten **Peter Kooij** bass **Bach Collegium
Japan / Masaaki Suzuki**
BIS ② BIS-CD941/2 (145' · DDD · T/t)   ⒻⓄ⇨

The six cantatas that make up Bach's *Christmas Oratorio* are part of a unified work celebrating not just Christmas itself but also the New Year and Epiphany. Masaaki Suzuki faces plentiful if not invariably stiff competition in this work. In fact, it outstrips most of its rivals, in respect both of vocal and instrumental considerations. A notable quality in Masaaki Suzuki's direction is his feeling for naturally expressive contours, allowing the music to breathe freely. Best of all, perhaps, is his refusal to pay even lip service to Bach's supposed predilection for fast tempos. Everything here seems to be excep-

tionally well judged, which isn't to say that the pace of individual movements is necessarily slower than those in competing versions but that it's more interrelated with a concept of each section as a whole, and more textually conscious than some.

The soloists are generally very good indeed. Yoshikazu Mera makes a distinctive contribution and Gerd Türk is a communicative singer whose light articulation suits his partly narrative role. Peter Kooij never puts a foot wrong, while Monika Frimmer makes a favourable impression in her duet with Kooij, 'Herr, dein Mitleid, dein Erbarmen'. A small, well-balanced choir of technical agility and an accomplished quorum of instrumentalists set the seal on an outstanding achievement. The finest all-round performance of the *Christmas Oratorio* on disc.

Christmas Oratorio
Sibylla Rubens sop **Ingeborg Danz** contr
James Taylor, Marcus Ullmann tens **Hanno Müller-
Brachmann** bass **Gächinger Kantorei;
Stuttgart Bach Collegium / Helmuth Rilling**
Hänssler Classic ② 92 076 (144' · DDD · T/t)   ⓂⓄ⇨

Energetic director Helmut Rilling is more fired up than ever here. The choruses crackle with thrilling fervour and a blistering attack and shine to notes which, alongside a forthright Gächinger Kantorei, carry the day persuasively on modern instruments. There will always be those for whom Rilling represents an inflexibility of phrasing and unyielding articulation in Bach, paradoxically more reminiscent of the least alluring elements of period performance than the 'ebb and flow' of mainstream consciousness. This recording doubtless reinforces the odd prejudice, though the habitually hard-edged orchestral textures of the Bach Collegium Stuttgart seem more mollifying and warm hearted in movements such as the pastoral Sinfonia at the beginning of Part 2 and the divinely inspired 'Schlafe, mein Liebster' later in the same cantata (it must be said now, flawed by a tiresomely repeated pull-up before the second phrase).

James Taylor is a natural Evangelist: articulate, discriminating, exacting if not emotionally candid. He also retains focus throughout the events of each tableau and gives clearly etched readings. Yet much of the credit must also go to the outstanding solo singing. Sibylla Rubens and Hanno Müller-Brachmann are stunning in the pivotal duet of Part 3, 'Herr, dein Mitleid', and Ingeborg Danz sings with exquisite and gentle poise in the scene-setting 'Bereite dich, Zion'. If her 'Schlafe' is a touch disappointing, then that reflects the weight of expectation which surrounds this central aria. If you prefer a mezzo to a countertenor, then only Anne Sofie von Otter for Gardiner or Christa Ludwig for Richter can better her largely satisfying contribution. Müller-Brachmann is a fine bass soloist in 'Grosser Herr' and as movingly intimate as Michael George for Philip Pickett in the recitative with chorale, 'Immanuel, O süsses Wort'. Rubens is on really terrific form throughout, and her 'Nur in Wink' in Part 6 is a model of outstanding Bach singing.

There's a spiritual containment which serves its purpose here – there's absolutely no sentimental guff – and yet it perhaps trespasses into the clinical too readily. Rilling, as ever, raises hopes and only intermittently fulfils them, but this is still a distinguished reading.

Wilhelm Friedemann Bach

German 1710-1784

Wilhelm Friedemann, the eldest son of JS Bach, studied under his father at the Leipzig Thomasschule; his father put together a 'Clavier-Büchlein' for him and may have written book 1 of the '48' with him in mind. Friedemann also studied the violin with JG Graun. After university study, he became organist at the Dresden Sophienkirche in 1733; he moved to the Liebfrauenkirche, Halle, in 1746 but his years there were turbulent and he left in 1764. He later lived in Brunswick and then in Berlin, but with his difficult temperament and perhaps dissolute character found no regular employment though his organ playing was admired.

The volatility of his musical style is of a piece with his life. In his early years he wrote mainly for keyboard; at Dresden, for instruments; at Halle, church cantatas and some instrumental music; and in his late years, chiefly chamber and keyboard works. He vacillated in style between old and new, with galant elements alongside conservative Baroque ones, intense north German expressiveness alongside more formal writing. His keyboard music includes fugues and deeply felt polonaises. His gifts are unmistakable here and in such works as the Concerto for two solo harpsichords or the often suite-like Sinfonia in F, but the final impression is of a composer whose potential was never fully realised. GROVEmusic

Keyboard works

Eight Fugues, F31. 12 Polonaises, F12
Paul Simmonds clav
London Independent Records LIR014 (80' · DDD) Ⓕ

Bach's oldest and most doted-on son Wilhelm Friedemann has seldom been credited with being an 'even' composer. Not only do his works show widely varying levels of inspiration and originality, they also make little attempt to reconcile the older Baroque manners of his father with the newer, mid-18th-century developments of the *galant* and *empfindsamer* styles, often 'solving' the problem by simply throwing them all in together to make a crazy mix.

Most commentators have also agreed, however, that in the 12 Polonaises, composed in the 1750s and '60s, we have some of his finest and most personal creations. Though their titles

suggest that they might be little more than fripperies, they are in fact considered and sophisticated compositions whose deep expression was much admired by the Romantic generation. No two are greatly alike: there is the anguished poetry of the E minor, or the more cheerful atmosphere of the G major and D major, while the contemplative and plangent E flat minor contrasts with the more robust C major and E flat major. Their generally introspective nature suits them well to the clavichord, and Paul Simmonds's tidily controlled and sensitive playing on a large Swedish instrument serves them well. Particularly enjoyable are his singing tone, helped by exquisitely generated vibrato on longer notes, and his touchingly quiet, almost disappearing endings to a number of these pieces.

Friedemann's Fugues are less individual, though you would not mistake any of them for the work of his father. Again, though, they are delivered by Simmonds with a sure and caressing touch. For the best results, make sure that you play this CD at a low dynamic level.

Cantatas

Cantatas – Lasset uns ablegen die Werke der Finsternis, F80. Es ist eine Stimme eines Predigers in der Wüste, F89 Ⓟ
Barbara Schlick sop **Claudia Schubert** contr **Wilfried Jochens** ten **Stephan Schreckenberger** bass **Rheinische Kantorei; Das Kleine Konzert / Hermann Max**
Capriccio 10 425 (54' · DDD · T/t) ⒻⓄ

This disc makes a valuable contribution towards a fuller understanding of this highly gifted but complex member of the Bach clan. In the mid-1740s Wilhelm Friedemann was appointed Director of Music and organist at the Liebfrauenkirche at Halle. He remained in the post for almost 20 years, a period which witnessed the composition and performance of all the cantatas represented here. Among the many delights to be found in this music are those occasioned by Friedemann's disparate, even opposing terms of reference. In other words the stylistic vocabulary is both rich and varied, often harking back to a strong paternal influence – what better one has there ever been? JS Bach's idiom, for instance, is startlingly apparent in the opening chorus of the Advent cantata, F80 ('Let us cast off the works of darkness'). Both the arias of this fine cantata are of high quality, the first, for soprano with obbligato flute ably demonstrating how carefully Friedemann thought out his declamation.

For the most part the performances are excellent. The four soloists are first-rate, Barbara Schlick and Wilfried Jochens in particular; and the singing of the Rheinische Kantorei is effective, though just occasionally its component 16 voices sound under threat from Bach's sometimes exacting requirements.

Imaginative programming and sympathetic performances add to this musical revelation.

Simon Bainbridge

English 1952

Bainbridge studied at the Royal College of Music, London, and Tanglewood; American music, in particular Ives and Reich, has been a formative influence. There is a spatial element in some of his music, which is largely instrumental. Among his most characteristic pieces are the Viola Concerto (1976), Concertante in moto perpetuo (1983) and Fantasia for two orchestras (1984). GROVEmusic

Ad ora incerta

Ad ora incerta (Four orchestral songs from Primo Levi)[a]. Four Primo Levi Settings[b]
Susan Bickley *mez* [a]**Kim Walker** *bn* [b]**Nash Ensemble;** [a]**BBC Symphony Orchestra / Martyn Brabbins**
NMC NMCD059 (54' · DDD · T/t) Ⓕ❹❹☊

At the beginning of the fourth Primo Levi setting in *Ad ora incerta* (a depiction of the ghastly chemical factory attached to Auschwitz that Levi miraculously survived) there's a slow orchestral *crescendo*, like the panning of a camera to reveal the full horror of the scene. What follows isn't a shout of protest but sober lyricism, and when that *crescendo* returns it introduces an eloquently poignant melody. Simon Bainbridge is an uncommonly fine musical dramatist. He lets the words speak, and distils his music so as to clarify them. In *Ad ora incerta* the vocalist has a companion, a solo bassoon. Because that fourth poem repeatedly speaks of a dead companion, of course, but also in the way the bassoon shadows or reflects the voice, there's also a subtle and moving suggestion that after Auschwitz Levi lacked and longed for a companion, a fellow survivor who would understand his memories in ways that none of us can. It's scarcely believable that these beautiful but painful poems could be set to music; certainly not with the delicate and imaginative sympathy that Bainbridge shows here.

The four chamber settings are still sparer but no less gravely beautiful. In the seven brief lines of the first of them Levi distils the impossibility of communicating his experiences yet the imperative need to try. Bainbridge's setting conveys that, but adds the most restrained and loving pity. It's a remarkable and a deeply moving achievement. Both performances are fine, that of the chamber settings beyond praise in its quiet intimacy.

Edgar Bainton

English 1880-1956

English composer, pianist and teacher. He studied at the RCM under Stanford and Franklin Taylor. In 1901 he was appointed to teach the piano and composition at the Newcastle Conservatory of which he became principal a few years later. He was on the Continent at the outbreak of World War I and was

interned at Ruhleben. On his return to Newcastle he resumed his activities as teacher, pianist, conductor and composer until the end of 1933, when he was appointed director of the New South Wales State Conservatorium, Sydney. His symphony 'Before Sunrise' won a Carnegie Award in 1917. Bainton was less affected by the modality of English folksong than were many contemporaries, although much of his work has a pastoral tone. He was drawn to late-Romantic harmony, yet even his richest writing never obscures the direct lyrical impulse. His works have clarity of form and show a high degree of craftsmanship. One of his major works, The Pearl Tree, was produced with great success in Sydney in 1944. GROVEmusic

Orchestral works

Three Pieces for Orchestra. Pavane, Idyll and Bacchanal. The Golden River, Op 16. Concerto fantasia[a]
[a]**Margaret Fingerhut** *pf*
BBC Philharmonic Orchestra / Paul Daniel
Chandos CHAN10460 (69' · DDD) Ⓕ❹☊

All four works were composed prior to Bainton's permanent move to Australia in 1934, by far the most ambitious being the *Concerto fantasia* for piano and orchestra which won Bainton his second Carnegie Award. It is cast in four movements, launched by a solo cadenza destined to reappear at salient points throughout the work's half-hour course. Margaret Fingerhut's limpid pianism proves tailor-made for such a gorgeously lyrical, tenderly poetic and subtly integrated offering, which bids farewell in the sunset glow of a somewhat Baxian epilogue.

Bainton himself was the soloist for the 1921 world premiere of the *Concerto fantasia* in Bournemouth, where it shared a programme with the extremely fetching *Three Pieces for Orchestra* (1916-20). These grew out of incidental music for two Shakespeare productions in Ruhleben Camp near Berlin, where Bainton was held during the First World War, and are followed here by another most attractive triptych, the *Pavane, Idyll and Bacchanal* that Bainton wrote in 1924 for amateur groups but which requires a high level of technical expertise.

Unheard for the best part of a century, the four-movement suite *The Golden River* (1908, but revised four years later) derives its inspiration from a short story by John Ruskin and packs plenty of touching and colourful invention into its 16-minute span.

The BBC Philharmonic under the sympathetic baton of Paul Daniel seem to enjoy the experience. Excellent sound.

Sir Edward Bairstow

English 1874-1946

English organist, composer and conductor. He studied with John Farmer of Balliol College, Oxford, and

was articled to Frederick Bridge at Westminster Abbey, where he received organ tuition from the assistant organist Walter Alcock. In 1893 Bairstow became organist of All Saints, Norfolk Square, and in 1899 of Wigan parish church. On being appointed to Leeds parish church in 1907, he became organist to the Leeds Festival of that year and of 1910 and, later, conductor of the Leeds Philharmonic Society (from 1917 until his death). In 1913 he was appointed organist at York Minster. In 1929 he was appointed professor of music at Durham. An accomplished performer and accompanist, he was also in frequent demand as a lecturer and guest speaker, proving an avid supporter in particular of the competitive festival movement. Bairstow's compositions are mainly for the church.

Choral works

Blessed City, heavenly Salem. Evening Services – in D; in G. If the Lord had not helped me. Jesu, the very thought of Thee. Let all mortal flesh keep silence. Lord, Thou hast been our refuge. Save us, O Lord. Five Poems of the Spirit[a]
St John's College Choir, Cambridge; Britten Sinfonia / David Hill with [a]**Roderick Williams** bar **Paul Provost** org
Hyperion CDA67497 (63' · DDD · T/t)　　　Ⓕ●

An excellent disc in regard both to the standard of performance and to the selection of Bairstow's music. And to that should be added straight away the quality of recorded sound, for in choral music of this type it is particularly important to allow for enough reverberance and sense of space without loss of clarity; also to balance choir and organ so as to keep a focus upon the singers and their words while enabling the organist to exploit the full range of the instrument in tone and volume. The recommendation for this new issue is confirmed most decisively by the inclusion of the *Five Poems of the Spirit*. Completed in 1944, it remained unpublished till after Bairstow's death. The orchestration was provided by Sir Ernest Bullock, and with its baritone solos and (largely) early-17th-century texts it stands, not unworthily, alongside Vaughan Williams's *Five Mystical Songs*. Particularly memorable is the fourth, Raleigh's 'Give me my scallop-shell of quiet', but all are attractive. Roderick Williams is the ideally suited soloist and the Britten Sinfonia do justice to a delightful score. In the accompanied anthems and services the organ parts are played with skilful registration by Paul Provost, and the choir sing throughout with their customary expressiveness and variety of colour: exquisitely (for instance) in the unaccompanied *Jesu, the very thought of Thee*.

Michael William Balfe　　Irish 1808-70

Balfe was the most successful composer of operas in English in the 19th century, a reputation grounded on his hugely popular work, The Bohemian Girl. He started his profesional career as a violinist in the Drury Lane orchestra before discovering his voice, a fine baritone (he made his stage debut in Weber's Der Freischütz). He studied composition with Paer in Rome where his first opera was premiered. His reputation was sealed with The Siege of Rochelle (1835). During his career he composed dozens of operas, all revealing an innate understanding of the voice. Characterisation was not a strong suit of his writing, the success of his works relying more on the 'hit' numbers he could invariably be relied upon to produce. In addition to singing and composing, Balfe developed quite a reputation as a conductor, taking charge of the Italian Opera at Her Majesty's Theatre in London fron 1846 until 1852.

Falstaff

Falstaff
Marcel Vanaud bar Falstaff **Majella Cullagh** sop Mrs Ford **Sam McElroy** bar Ford **Barry Banks** ten Fenton **Tara Erraught** sop Annetta **Nyle Wolfe** bar Mr Page **Victoria Massey** mez Mrs Smith **Brendan Collins** bar Giorgio **Edel O'Brien** mez Mrs Quickly
National Chamber Choir of Ireland; RTÉ Concert Orchestra / Marco Zambelli
RTÉ Lyric FM ② CD119 (143' · DDD)　　　Ⓕ●●

This mighty impressive recording of a public performance in Dublin of Balfe's 1838 Italian opera *Falstaff* is no more likely to shift allegiance of fans of Verdi's or Vaughan Williams's operatic treatment of Shakespeare's *Merry Wives of Windsor* to Balfe than to Nicolai. However, it should have surer and wider appeal today than the melodramatic 'with one bound our heroine was free' operas such as *The Bohemian Girl* for which Balfe is most famed.

It's a score full of good tunes. From the joyous overture onwards, it's also a score full of skilfully worked numbers, several of which enjoyed favour on both sides of the English Channel for some years afterwards. The splendid trio for the ladies who receive a love letter from Falstaff (three in this version) has already been recorded; but others are no less impressive, including a duet for Ford and Falstaff and solos for Fenton and Mrs Ford. The latter two roles, written for Rubini and Grisi, contain fiendishly challenging writing that at times threatens to defeat Majella Cullagh. However, her final solo – along with that of the wholly admirable Barry Banks – justly receives the most enthusiastic applause of the evening. Altogether the recording is strongly sung and conducted, and it should be essential listening for any lover of Italian opera of its period.

The Maid of Artois

The Maid of Artois
Kay Jordan sop Isoline, Maid of Artois **Stephen Anthony Brown** ten Jules de Montangon **Jonathan Pugsley** bass-bar Marquis de Chateau-Vieux **John Molloy** bass Sans Regret **Rebecca Rudge** sop

Coralie **George Hulbert** bar Synnelet **Annette Reis-Dunne** sop Ninka **Adrian Lawson** bar Martin **Geoffrey Brocklehurst** bass Count Saulnier **John Elliott** ten Centinel **Victorian Opera Chorus and Orchestra / Philip Mackenzie**
Campion ② CAMEO2042/3 (148' · DDD · S/T/N) Ⓕ

All credit, then, to Victorian Opera for undertaking the huge task of preparing performing material to record and document another Balfe opera as ably as they have here. In quality of composition, performance and recording alike, this is the most convincing exposition of Balfe's abilities to date – *The Bohemian Girl* not excluded.

Here in *The Maid of Artois*, with a libretto based on *Manon Lescaut*, there are winning melodies, flowing sub-Donizettian arias and ensembles, and imaginative orchestral scoring. Only infrequently does the piece lapse into mere British balladry. The work was composed for the celebrated Malibran, and it would be misleading to pretend that either Kay Jordan or Stephen Anthony Brown has complete control of the sometimes fiendishly high extremes of the heroine's and hero's music. Yet, within more comfortable range, both sing hugely impressively, and they get admirable support in key roles from Jonathan Pugsley and John Molloy, as well as from a strong chorus and orchestra under the inspired conducting of Philip Mackenzie.

On this showing Balfe deserves to be heard, and this set is commended warmly to lovers of early-19th-century opera.

Sir Granville Bantock British 1868-1946

Bantock studied with Corder at the Royal Academy of Music (1889-93), then worked as a conductor and teacher (professor at Birmingham, 1908-34). He did much to promote the music of his English contemporaries and produced a large output of orchestral and large-scale choral works, influenced by early Wagner, a taste for the exotic, and Hebridean folksong. Though much performed at the beginning of the century, when he was at his most productive and a prominent figure in the English musical renaissance, his music has all but disappeared from the repertory; the oratorio Omar Khayyám (1906-9), the overture The Pierrot of the Minute (1908), the Hebridean Symphony (1915) and the Pagan Symphony (1928) have been admired for their undemanding lyricism.
GROVEmusic

Pagan Symphony

Pagan Symphony. Fifine at the Fair.
Two Heroic Ballads
Royal Philharmonic Orchestra / Vernon Handley
Hyperion CDA66630 (80' · DDD · T/t) Ⓕⵔ

This collection confirms Bantock as a composer of real achievement whose music has been unde-servedly neglected. He was a superb technician, and his impressively large-scale structures have a real urgency. Or perhaps we should say, a real enjoyment. Despite the potentially tragic undertones of *Fifine at the Fair*, both works are almost untroubled, filled instead with the geniality of a craftsman joyfully exercising a craft of which he's master. The cleverness of the thematic transformations can make you smile with pleasure once you've worked out what he's doing – and then smile again at the realisation that the result of the transformation isn't an arid piece of technique for technique's sake, but another jolly good tune. And it's all very beautifully scored. He was a master of the orchestra. Can he be just a bit too clever, forever finding yet another ingenious and delightful thing to do with a scale-figure? Possibly, but he's never dull. Is real emotional depth lacking, despite hints of it whenever the wronged wife appears in *Fifine*? Maybe; possibly he was more given to enjoying than to pondering. The performances are stunning, the recordings most sumptuous. The two *Heroic Ballads*, for all that they're concerned with Cuchullan and his ilk, have not a shred of Irish Sea mist hanging around them: they're bold, colourful and stirring.

Pierrot of the Minute

Christ in the Wilderness – The Wilderness and the Solitary Place[a]. Overture to a Greek Tragedy. Pierrot of the Minute. Three scenes from 'The Song of Songs'[ab]
[ab]**Elizabeth Connell** sop [b]**Kim Begley** ten
RPO / Vernon Handley
Hyperion CDA67395 (78' · DDD) Ⓕ

Written quickly over the summer of 1908 and premièred at that year's Three Choirs Festival in Worcester, Bantock's comedy overture *Pierrot of the Minute* enjoyed much success before the First World War. It's a charming work, and Vernon Handley and the RPO deliver a performance of atmospheric delicacy and wit. Three years later Worcester also played host to the first performance of the *Overture to a Greek Tragedy*, an imposing curtain-raiser. Handley extracts every ounce of drama and lyricism from Bantock's ripely colourful inspiration; the majestically paced reading attains a moving nobility in the radiant, rather Straussian peroration.

From Bantock's two-and-a-half-hour setting of *The Song of Songs* (1912-26) come excerpts from three of the five scenes (or 'Days'). The Second Day and love duet from the Fifth Day are thematically related, and frame a purely orchestral sequence from the Third Day. In their respective roles of the Shulamite and her Shepherd lover, Elizabeth Connell and Kim Begley rise admirably to the wide-ranging vocal challenges. Connell also makes an affectionate showing in 'The Wilderness and the Solitary Place', a pretty, gently exotic six-minute aria from the 1907 oratorio *Christ in the Wilderness*. Excellent sound.

Sonatas

Cello Sonatas[a] – No 1 in B minor; No 2 in F sharp minor. Solo Cello Sonata in G minor. Hamabdil[b]. Pibroch[b]. Elegiac Poem[a]
Andrew Fuller vc with [a]**Michael Dussek** pf [a]**Lucy Wakeford** hp
Dutton Laboratories Epoch CDLX7107 (75' · DDD) Ⓜ

There are some rewarding discoveries here, not least the two sonatas for cello and piano. Both were penned during the first half of the 1940s, though the sketches for the B minor Sonata date back to 1900. The latter is a finely sculpted, generously lyrical creation, boasting a particularly lovely slow movement. For the *scherzo* Bantock pressed into service his earlier *Fantastic Poem* of 1925, and the whole work ends in a mood of autumnal nostalgia. The impulse for the unaccompanied G minor Sonata appears to have been Kodály's magnificent example in the genre: Bantock had heard Beatrice Harrison give the British première in 1924. Cast in four compact movements, it's an uncommonly well-knit essay and a demanding workout for any aspiring virtuoso (as the giddy *moto perpetuo* of the finale attests). We also get two offerings for cello and harp: particularly striking is *Pibroch*, a wonderfully affecting 'Highland lament' .

Andrew Fuller is an accomplished artist, mellow of tone and technically secure; he enjoys sympathetic support from Michael Dussek. Lucy Wakeford, too, contributes most beautifully. With eminently truthful sound and balance throughout, this enterprising collection deserves a warm welcome.

Violin Sonatas – No 1 in G; No 2 in D. Coronach (Pro Patria Mori). Salve Regina, 'Hail Queen of Heaven'
Lorraine McAslan vn **Michael Dussek** pf
Dutton Epoch CDLX7119 (64' · DDD) Ⓜ

Dedicated to that great British violinist Albert Sammons, the first of Bantock's three violin sonatas was penned in 1928-9, and appeared in print a year before its first performance (a BBC broadcast in June 1930, with Sammons accompanied by the composer). It's a work of strong appeal, whose clean-cut, songful demeanour would seem tailor-made for its legendary dedicatee's wonderfully sweet timbre; but somewhat surprisingly, given its lyricism and thematic resourcefulness, it failed to secure a place in the repertoire. The opening movement of its D major successor followed quickly in April 1929, but it was another three years before the two remaining movements were completed. It was finally premiered on the BBC in July 1940, but subsequently sank into oblivion – a great pity in view of its bright-eyed vigour, deftness of touch and impeccable craftsmanship.

Two shorter pieces bring up the rear: originally conceived for strings, organ and harp, *Coronach* (1918) is a wistful elegy in memory of a friend who had perished in the trenches three years previously; the contemplative *Salve Regina* is based on a plainsong melody Bantock had heard in Canada during the summer of 1923.

These interpretations from Lorraine McAslan and Michael Dussek are consistently compelling and sure-footed.

Vocal works

Atalanta in Calydon. Vanity of Vanities
BBC Singers / Simon Joly
Albany TROY180 (66' · DDD · T) Ⓕ

In 1911 Bantock embarked on the first of his two unaccompanied 'choral symphonies', a half-hour setting of texts from Swinburne's 1865 verse drama, *Atalanta in Calydon*. Written for the amateur Hallé Choir, it's an extraordinarily ambitious offering. Bantock's luxuriant 20-part writing (the composer envisaged 'not less than 10 voices to each part') exhibits a prodigious technical facility allied to a remarkable fluency and poetic sensibility.

By comparison, the 35-minute *Vanity of Vanities* (based on Bantock's own selection of verses from the Book of Ecclesiastes) is a model of restraint, being laid out for a mere 12 parts. It was completed in September 1913. Again, the sounds created exhibit a ravishing variety of texture, colour and harmony, further testament to Bantock's fantastically vivid aural imagination. Both works impose great technical demands which are easily surmounted in these incisive, dedicated performances, admirably captured by the recording team.

Omar Khayyám
Olivia Robinson sop **Catherine Wyn-Rogers**, **Siân Menna** mezs **Toby Spence** ten **Roderick Williams** bar **Edward Price** bass **BBC Symphony Chorus and Orchestra / Vernon Handley**
Chandos ③ 💿 CHSA5051 (172' · DDD) ⒻⓄⓄⒹ⁺

The London-born Granville Bantock used his early championship of contemporaries – Strauss, Debussy and especially Sibelius, who became a close friend and correspondent – to enrich his own Wagner-nourished sonorities and dramatic ambitions. Because he was British, he fought shy of opera, channelling his gift for theatre into song-cycles (he wrote 40), symphonic tone-poems (he once planned a 24-work cycle), forward-looking multi-media events (*Apollo and the Seaman* for film projection and orchestra) and oratorios (a 700-page score of *Christus*).

Writing in the age of Mahler's Eighth and Elgar's three major oratorios, Bantock found 101 quatrains of 12th-century Persian philosophical poetry – in the then widely read (and very free) rendering of Pre-Raphaelite poet Edward Fitzgerald – an irresistible challenge. He set Fitzgerald's work by feeding his natural gift for effective scoring and mood illustration with his own first-hand impressions of the Middle East. It is to his credit that, throughout the nearly three-hour performance span, genuine symphonic interest rarely flags. His large orchestra calls for two complete, antiphonally placed, string sections, as well as the extra wind and brass that his European heroes were deploying. The choral part becomes virtuoso in its frequent use of unaccompanied, tricky-to-pitch passages, while three named soloists, the Beloved (mezzo), the Poet (tenor) and the Philosopher (baritone) are continually 'onstage' in roles of operatic length.

This first recording reflects the detail and passion of Vernon Handley's championing of Bantock's kaleidoscopic output, and Stephen Jackson ensures that the choral input is similarly lively and fresh. Toby Spence brings a bright mix of Italianate slancio and English declamation to the Poet, combining well with Catherine Wyn-Rogers's more controlled reading of the Beloved in substantial (and *Parsifal*-like) duets in Parts 1 and 3 (a highlight and a good starting-point for samplers). Chandos's sound is suitably lush, occasionally at the expense of the chorus's diction. It's what recordings should be for, and should encourage future festival performances.

Samuel Barber   American 1910-1981

Barber studied as a baritone and composer (with Scalero) at the Curtis Institute (1924-32) and while there began to win acclaim with such works as Dover Beach (1931), written for himself to sing with string quartet. His opulent yet unforced Romanticism struck a chord and during the 1930s he was much in demand: his overture The School for Scandal (1933), First Symphony (1936), First Essay (1937) and Adagio (originally the second movement of his String Quartet, 1936) were widely performed, the lyrical, elegiac Adagio remaining a popular classic. In the 1940s he began to include more 'modern' features of harmony and scoring. Of his operas, Vanessa (1958), praised as 'highly charged with emotional meaning', was more successful than Antony and Cleopatra (1966, for the opening of the new Met).
GROVEmusic

Violin Concerto

Barber Violin Concerto **Bloch** Baal Shem **Walton** Violin Concerto
Joshua Bell vn **Baltimore Symphony Orchestra / David Zinman**
Decca 476 1723DGR (68' · DDD)   Ⓕ❍❍❍🅑

Bell's coupling of the Barber Violin Concerto with Walton and Bloch brings together three highly romantic *concertante* works. Bell is placed less forward in the Barber than in the rich-sounding recordings of Gil Shaham and Itzhak Perlman, but if anything the results are even more intense. In the central slow movement the opening oboe solo leads to a magi-

BARBER VIOLIN CONCERTO – IN BRIEF

Joshua Bell; Baltimore SO / Zinman
Decca 476 1723DGR   Ⓜ❍❍❍🅑
An intense, beautifully conceived performance, with the violin naturally balanced. Zinman is a hugely sympathetic partner. Coupled with Walton and Bloch. A *Gramophone* Award winner.

Hilary Hahn; St Paul CO / Wolff
Sony Classical 509970 89029-2   Ⓕ❍❍
A more transparent, smaller-scale performance that finds Hilary Hahn on fine form, brigning out the lyricism of the work. Coupled with Edgar Meyer's concerto

Gil Shaham; LSO / Previn
DG 439 886-2GH   Ⓕ❍🅑
A rich, luxurious, Hollywood-style performance that makes the work sound bigger than usual. Coupled, appropriately, with Korngold's wonderfully high-cholesterol Violin Concerto and some violin and piano works.

James Buswell; RSNO / Alsop
Naxos 8 559044   Ⓢ🅑
A strong, muscular performance, fresh and spontaneous sounding and the RSNO, nearing the end of their Barber cycle with Marin Alsop, have the measure of the idiom.

Isaac Stern; NYPO / Bernstein
Sony Classical SMK63088   Ⓑ
One of the first recordings of the work and still one of the best. Isaac Stern's unique sound and personality shine through the somewhat dated sound.

Elmar Oliviera; St Louis SO / Slatkin
EMI 586561-2   Ⓢ❍
A very fine budget-price version and a welcome return to the catalogue, especially as it comes in a superb two-disc Barber compilation that makes an perfect introduction.

Itzhak Perlman; Boston SO / Slatkin
EMI 562600-2   Ⓑ❍❍🅑
Itzhak Perlman's elegant and honeyed performance returns at budget price as part of a most appealing all-American programme (Bernstein and Foss). Ozawa is a superb accompanist.

Transcribed for flute and orchestra
Stinton; Philharmonia / Bedford
Regis RRC1100   Ⓢ
Really no more than a curiosity because the Violin Concerto was so evidently conceived for a string instrument that a transcriptions seems unnecessary but Stinton makes a brave stab at the work and the last movement, it must be admitted, does work rather well on the flute.

cally hushed first entry for the violin, and the balance of the soloist also allows a quicksilver lightness for the rushing triplets in the *moto perpetuo* finale. Shaham may find more humour in that brief movement, but Bell's view is equally valid.

From an American perspective, Walton can well be seen as Barber's British counterpart. The playing of this American orchestra is warmly idiomatic, defying the idea that non-British orchestras find Walton difficult. Bell gives a commanding account – his expansive treatment of the central cadenza of the first movement, making it more deeply reflective – is most appealing. Not just there but in many gentle moments the rapt intensity of his playing is magnetic. Bell's is among the finest versions ever, with Bloch's own 1939 orchestration of *Baal Shem* offering a fine, unusual makeweight.

Barber Violin Concerto **E Meyer** Violin Concerto
Hilary Hahn vn **Saint Paul Chamber Orchestra /**
Hugh Wolff
Sony Classical 509970 89029-2 (50′ · DDD)   ⓕⓄⓄ▶

The 19-year-old Hilary Hahn once again shows her natural feeling for the American brand of late Romanticism, bringing out heartfelt emotion without overplaying it. There have been a number of outstanding versions of the Barber Concerto in recent years and Hahn's is among the finest ever. She stands between the urgently, fullbloodedly romantic Shaham and the more meditative Bell. It's partly a question of recording balances. The latter has the advantage of a recording which, setting him a little further back, allows *pianissimos* to be registered in a genuine hush. Hahn, like Shaham, is placed well forward, and it's hardly her fault that dynamic contrasts are reduced. The use of a chamber orchestra also affects the balance. The extra weight in the orchestral sound on the DG and Decca discs is here compensated by the incisiveness of the St Paul Chamber Orchestra under Hugh Wolff, with textures a fraction clearer in detail. Even so, in the long introduction to the *Andante* a smaller body of strings, however refined, can't quite match in ear-catching beauty the bigger string sections of the LSO and Baltimore Symphony. What Hahn and Wolff nicely achieve between them, though, is a distinction between the first two movements, both of them predominantly lyrical. Deceptively, the first is marked *Allegro* (hardly sounding it), but here it's registered as a taut first movement leading to a powerful climax. Speeds in both the first two movements are a fraction broader than with either rival, but Hahn reserves her big coup for the *Presto* finale which is noticeably faster than either rival's, offering quicksilver brilliance and pinpoint articulation.

Meyer's Concerto makes an apt coupling. Unashamedly tonal and freely lyrical, it opens with a yearning folk-like melody that echoes Vaughan Williams, and there's also a folk-like,

pentatonic cut to some of the writing in both of the two substantial movements. It's amazing what variety Meyer achieves (a string player himself), considering that conscious limitation of having a sustained drone underlying his argument. Hahn plays with passionate commitment, amply justifying her choice of so approachable a new piece for this important issue.

Barber Violin Concerto **Korngold** Violin Concerto,
Op 35. Much ado about nothing, Op 11 – The maiden
in the bridal chamber; Dogberry and Verges; Intermezzo; Hornpipe
Gil Shaham vn **London Symphony Orchestra /**
André Previn pf
DG 439 886-2GH (71′ · DDD)   ⓕⓄ▶

This performance of the Barber, warm and rich with the sound close and immediate, brings out the work's bolder side, allowing moments that aren't too distant from the world of Hollywood music (no disparagement there) and aptly the Korngold emerges as a central work in that genre. There have been subtler readings of Barber's lovely concerto, with the soloist not always helped by the close balance, but it's good to have a sharp distinction drawn between the purposeful lyricism of the first movement, marked *Allegro*, and the tender lyricism of the heavenly *Andante*. In the finale Shaham brings out the fun behind the movement's manic energy, with Previn pointing the Waltonian wit.

In the Korngold, Gil Shaham may not have quite the flair and panache of the dedicatee, Jascha Heifetz, in his incomparable reading (reviewed under Korngold), but he's warm and committed. What emerges again and again is how electric the playing of the LSO is under Previn, rich and full as well as committed. The recording helps, clear and immediate.

The suite from Korngold's incidental music to *Much ado about nothing*, dating from his early precocious period in Vienna, provides a delightful and apt filler, with Previn, as pianist, just as understanding and imaginative an accompanist, and Shaham yearningly warm without sentimentality, clean and precise in attack.

Additional recommendations

Violin Concerto
Coupled with: Souvenirs, Op 28. Serenade for Strings,
Op 1. Music for a Scene from Shelley, Op 7
Buswell vn **Royal Scottish National Orchestra /**
Alsop
Naxos 8 559044 (64′ · DDD)   Ⓢ▶
  A fine performance, notable for its easy
  spontaneity and unforced eloquence.

Symphonies Nos 1 and 2

Symphonies – No 1, Op 9; No 2, Op 19.
First Essay for Orchestra, Op 12. The School
for Scandal Overture, Op 5

Royal Scottish National Orchestra / Marin Alsop
Naxos 8 559024 (70' · DDD)   Ⓢ●🅑➔

That Marin Alsop is a musician of outstanding
gifts is amply reinforced by this all-Barber
anthology. In her red-blooded rendering of the
wartime Second Symphony, she shows just what
a powerfully inspired creation it is, extracting
every ounce of sinewy logic from its fraught
outer movements, while distilling wonder and
atmosphere in the haunting central *Andante, un
poco mosso*. No less convincing is her reading of
the magnificent First Symphony, always acutely
responsive to the music's daring expressive
scope and building climaxes of riveting cumulative intensity. In its unhurried authority, big
heart and epic thrust, it's the kind of interpretation you could have imagined from Bernstein in
his NYPO heyday. Elsewhere, she brings an
aptly bardic quality to the outer portions of the
First Essay, while few could fail to respond to the
twinkling affection and gentle wit she lavishes
on the irresistible *School for Scandal* Overture.
Were the orchestral contribution just a fraction
more polished, this would be a world-beater.
Zinman's stylish 1991 anthology with the Baltimore SO tends to throw into sharper relief the
relative shortcomings of Alsop's hard-working
Scots (their fiddles especially lack something in
silk-spun refinement and tone when playing
above the stave). The expert engineering can't
quite disguise the acoustical shortcomings of
Glasgow's Henry Wood Hall, but the result is
tonally truthful and conveys plenty of impact
when required.

Adagio for Strings, Op 11

Barber Adagio for Strings **Bernstein** Candide –
Overture **Copland** Appalachian Spring – Ballet
W Schuman American Festival Overture
**Los Angeles Philharmonic Orchestra /
Leonard Bernstein**
DG Galleria 439 528-2GGA (54' · DDD) Recorded live
1982   Ⓜ●🅑➔

This is a beautiful collection of American music,
lovingly and brilliantly performed. With Barber's lovely *Adagio* you might fear that Bernstein
would 'do a Nimrod' and present it with exaggerated expressiveness. Although the tempo is
very slow indeed, the extra hesitations aren't
excessive and the Los Angeles strings play with
angelic refinement and sweetness, as they do
also in the many hushed sequences of the Copland ballet. There the live recording made in
San Francisco in a dryish acoustic brings a
degree of constriction at heavy *tutti*s, but the
advantages of digital recording in this beautiful
score are obvious, not least at the climax of the
haunting variations on the Shaker hymn, *Simple
Gifts*. To the three favourite works here is added
William Schuman's brazenly extrovert overture
with its virtuoso opening section, its quiet
fugato, ominously introduced, and a brazen conclusion to match the opening. It's a splendid

work, almost as joyously inspired as Bernstein's
Candide Overture, with the composer here
adopting a fairly relaxed speed, though with a
wild coda.

Piano Sonata, Op 26

Piano Sonata, Op.26. Excursions, Op 20. Nocturne,
Op 33, 'Homage to John Field'. Three Sketches.
Ballade, Op 46. Interludes —No 1, Intermezzo.
Souvenirs, Op 28
Daniel Pollack pf
Naxos 8 550992 (72' · DDD)   Ⓢ🅑➔

Daniel Pollack studied with (among others)
Rosina Lhévinne and Wilhelm Kempf. His
playing exudes confidence, especially in the
more rhythmic and forthright passages. In his
hands the Sonata is powerfully driven and
crisply articulated, creating a palpable sense of
raw energy and excitement. His full sonorities
and sense of shape in the *Interlude* and the *Ballade* are also impressive, and while his tempo in
the latter may seem a shade fast, it adds to the
essential restlessness of the piece. In the more
lyrical works, notably the *Nocturne*, however,
Pollack's handling is too brusque, trampling
roughshod over the contrast between passion
and delicacy. The dance pieces of the *Excursions* and *Souvenirs* are generally more sensitive, and he effectively captures the diversity of
distinctive flavours, from the slow blues
(*Excursions*) to the Schottische (*Souvenirs*).
Horowitz inevitably remains the benchmark in
the Sonata, and his virtuoso fire is in a class of
its own. Nevertheless, despite the poor
recorded sound from Naxos's problematic
Santa Rosa studio, this is an enjoyable disc and
quite a bargain.

Knoxville: Summer of 1915, Op 24

Knoxville: Summer of 1915, Op 24ᵃ. Essays for
Orchestra – No 2, Op 17; No 3, Op 47. Toccata
Festiva, Op 36ᵇ
ᵃ**Karina Gauvin** sop ᵇ**Thomas Trotter** org
Royal Scottish National Orchestra / Marin Alsop
Naxos 8 559134 (57' · DDD · T)   Ⓢ●●🅑➔

Karina Gauvin and Marin Alsop take a nostalgic
view of *Knoxville: Summer of 1915*. Theirs is an
adult's bittersweet reminiscence rather than a
child's innocent view. The outer sections sway
slowly, the phrases longingly caressed as if
soprano and orchestra were loath to let them go.
Gauvin sings smoothly, generally emphasising
song over text, though she's alive to James
Agee's fragrant imagery, and varies the colour of
her voice appropriately. With deeply expressive
playing from the Royal Scottish National
Orchestra, the result is ravishing; this is one of
the finest versions of *Knoxville* to date.
Alsop's tautly argued Second Essay is equally
satisfying. She resists the temptation to stretch
the tempo at climactic moments, creating a

strong sense of momentum; you're swept along by the music's powerful current.

Knoxville and the Essays pack a nice sonic punch. If only Thomas Trotter's brilliant execution of the solo organ part in the *Toccata Festiva* were recorded with greater presence than the acoustic of Paisley Abbey allows. The *Toccata* may not be top-drawer Barber, but it has its moments. Nevertheless, Alsop's ear-opening Barber series reaches a new high-point with this instalment. Strongly recommended.

Additional recommendation

Knoxville: Summer of 1915
Coupled with: works by Menotti, Harbison and Stravinsky
Upshaw sop **Orchestra of St Luke's / Zinman**
Nonesuch 7559 79187-2 (44' · DDD)   Ⓕ🅱➔
　　Dawn Upshaw captures the childish innocence of Barber's gorgeous scena in a programme of comparable vocal treats.

Songs

Dover Beach, Op 3[a]. Hermit Songs, Op 29.
Mélodies passagères, Op 27. Three Songs,
Op 2. Three Songs, Op 10. Four Songs, Op 13 –
No 3, Sure on this shining night; No. 4, Nocturne.
In the dark pinewood. The Beggar's Song. There's
nae lark
Gerald Finley bar **Julius Drake** pf
[a]**Aronowitz Ensemble** (Magnus Johnston, Nadia
Wijzenbeek vns Jennifer Stumm va Guy Johnston vc)
Hyperion CDA67528 (62' · DDD · T)   Ⓕ🅞🅞🅞🅞🅱➔

🅖　Performances of this calibre emphasise Barber's stature in the mainstream of 20th-century song composers. The tradition is Anglo-American and *There's nae lark*, written when Barber was 16 to a poem by Swinburne in imitation Scots, could even be by Quilter. But Barber soon gets into his stride and by the time he reached his Three Songs, Op 10, there's a rare kind of intensity as impressive as anything on this CD. The poems are from James Joyce's *Chamber Music*; Barber set a few more, such as *In the dark pinewood* included here; but what a tragedy he never set the whole cycle that could have been an American *Winterreise*. The *Hermit Songs*, fey and whimsically amusing, are probably the best-known set.

'Sure on the shining shore' is vintage Barber, and Finley and Drake are impeccable (as are the Aronowitz Quartet in *Dover Beach*). The French songs, to poems by Rilke, who did write in French, have less character, but the single songs are all gems. An outstanding release.

Agnus Dei, Op 11

Barber Twelfth Night, Op 42 No 1. To be sung on the water, Op 42 No 2. Reincarnations, Op 16. Agnus Dei, Op 11. Heaven-Haven. Sure on this shining night. The monk and his cat. The Virgin Martyrs, Op 8 No 1. Let down the bars, O Death, Op 8 No 2. God's Grandeur
Schuman Perceptions. Mail Order Madrigals
Anthony Saunders pf **The Joyful Company of Singers / Peter Broadbent**
ASV CDDCA939 (66' · DDD · T)   Ⓕ🅞

Newcomers should make haste to track 6 for a pleasant surprise. Here they will encounter Samuel Barber's indestructible *Adagio* in its alternative and mellifluous 1967 vocal guise, set to the text of the *Agnus Dei*. Peter Broadbent's Joyful Company of Singers acquit themselves extremely well. Also to be particularly relished are the exquisite Op 42 pairing of *Twelfth Night* and *To be sung on the water*, the carefree lilt of *The monk and his cat* and, above all, the majestic, strikingly ambitious 1938 setting of Gerald Manley Hopkins's sonnet, *God's Grandeur* (perhaps the single most impressive achievement on the disc). Further delights are provided by Barber's countryman and contemporary, William Schuman. The concise, beautifully sculpted *Perceptions* (1982) are settings of choice aphorisms from the pen of Walt Whitman, while the *Mail Order Madrigals* (1972) wittily utilise the flowery prose drawn from advertisements contained within a Sears and Roebuck catalogue of 1897. A most attractive issue, in short, excellently produced and engineered.

Vanessa, Op 32

Vanessa
Christine Brewer sop Vanessa **Susan Graham** mez
Erika **Catherine Wyn-Rogers** mez Baroness **William
Burden** ten Anatol **Neal Davies** bass-bar The Old
Doctor **BBC Singers; BBC Symphony Orchestra /
Leonard Slatkin**
Chandos ② 🎵 CHSA5032
(123' · DDD/DSD · S/T/t/N)   Ⓕ🅞

Gian Carlo Menotti took as his starting-point for the libretto of *Vanessa* the atmosphere of Isak Dinesen's *Seven Gothic Tales*. His story is original, but the ideas that fired him can be found in the stories. One of Dinesen's heroines lives a secluded life, and although beautiful, she's forlorn – 'she knew that she did not exist, for nobody ever looked at her'. Vanessa, too, has lived her adult life waiting for the return of her faithless admirer, Anatol. When he does come, it's an impostor.

For an opera that's so seldom performed, *Vanessa* has been accorded a generous three complete recordings. This new one, recorded in London's Barbican after a concert in 2003, has splendidly vivid sound. Leonard Slatkin draws full-blooded playing from the BBC Symphony Orchestra, accentuating Barber's use of yearning, Puccini-inspired melodies, laced with a few nods to Berg and Strauss. The weirdest music, that for the ball in Act 3, sounds like some kind of Western barn dance, even though the setting is northern Europe.

Excellent though Susan Graham is as Erika, Christine Brewer is so much in command, and in such splendid voice, there's no doubt it's Vanessa's story. One problem is that the three female voices sound a little similar: Catherine Wyn-Rogers is a youthful old Baroness.

Anatol, the greatest cad in opera since Pinkerton, is made almost sympathetic by William Burden. Neal Davies does what he can with the rather stock figure of the Doctor.

But listening at home one is conscious of an awful lot of generalised mood music. *Vanessa* was the last gasp of American *verismo*: its Met première in 1958 was in the same season as Bernstein's *West Side Story* on Broadway, and we all know what that led to.

Additional recommendations

Vanessa
Steber Vanessa **Elias** Erika **Resnik** Baroness **Gedda** Anatol **Tozzi** Old Doctor **New York Metropolitan Opera Chorus & Orchestra / Mitropoulos**
Sony Classical ② 88497 72400-1 (114' · ADD) Ⓜ
The original-cast recording on RCA will always be irreplaceable. Brilliantly cast, it has the real feel of theatre. It is also Barber's first version, with four acts, and includes Vanessa's skating aria.

Richard Barrett
British b1959

Early studies in genetics were abandoned in favour of composition after an encounter with Michael Finnissy's work Alongside. *He then studied with Brian Ferneyhough and Hans-Joachim Hespos at the Darmstadt Ferienkurse to which he returned later as a teacher. Barrett's music is characterised by an intensely fragmented, texture-focused approach. It is also notable for its extreme difficulty. He often employs electronics and leaves many decisions to the performers.*

interference

interference[a]. transmission[b]. basalt[c]. air[d]. abglanzbeladen/auseinandergeschrieben[e]. knospend-gespaltener[f]
Elision ([b]Richard Barrett *elecs* [b]Daryl Buckley *elec gtr* [a][f]Carl Rosman *cl* [c]Benjamin Marks *tbn* [a][e]Peter Neville *perc* [d]Susan Pierotti *vn*)
NMC NMCD117 (64' · DDD) ⒻⒹ

The violent end of the world is perhaps dark enough matter for Richard Barrett. His *interference* for contrabass clarinet, male voice and pedal bass drum firmly punctuates the piece with short, titanic stabs, played in true one-man-band style with the foot. Simultaneously, contrabass clarinettist Carl Rosman uses multiphonics, throat-flutter and slap-tongue techniques while vocalising a Latin text fragment from Lucretius' apocalyptic poem *De rerum natura*. *interference* is

part of Barrett's larger *Dark Matter* work for voices, ensemble and electronics but stands well alone as a vehicle for extended technique on the contrabass clarinet.

What sets Barrett apart is his unswerving internal logic and consistency of style. While others use extended technique to impress, the works on this release use these in a natural and unforced manner. The present disc carries this through into a more intimate world of solo performances with members of new-music ensemble Elision. The impressive *transmission* closes the disc with a *tour de force* for solo electric guitar and live electronics, using a hybrid sound that mixes acoustic and electric guitar output. Guitarist Daryl Buckley had a hand in devising the guitar timbres that slide effortlessly from dense electronic structures to fast, distorted passages reminiscent of jazz-rock guitarist John McLaughlin. The work ends with the sparse, unamplified sound of the electric guitar. Buckley is to be congratulated on his near note-perfect interpretation of a difficult, many-layered score.

Béla Bartók
Hungarian 1881-1945

Bartók began lessons with his mother, who brought up the family after his father's death in 1888. In 1894 they settled in Bratislava, where he attended the Gymnasium (Dohnányi was an elder schoolfellow), studied the piano with László Erkel and Anton Hyrtl, and composed sonatas and quartets. In 1898 he was accepted by the Vienna Conservatory, but following Dohnányi he went to the Budapest Academy (1899-1903), where he studied the piano with Liszt's pupil István Thomán and composition with János Koessler. There he deepened his acquaintance with Wagner, though it was the music of Strauss, which he met at the Budapest premiere of Also sprach Zarathustra in 1902, that had most influence. He wrote a symphonic poem, Kossuth (1903), using Strauss's methods with Hungarian elements in Liszt's manner.

In 1904 Kossuth was performed in Budapest and Manchester; at the same time Bartók began to make a career as a pianist, writing a Piano Quintet and two Lisztian virtuoso showpieces (Rhapsody Op 1, Scherzo Op 2). Also in 1904 he made his first Hungarian folksong transcription. In 1905 he collected more songs and began his collaboration with Kodály: their first arrangements were published in 1906. The next year he was appointed Thomán's successor at the Budapest Academy, which enabled him to settle in Hungary and continue his folksong collecting, notably in Transylvania. Meanwhile his music was beginning to be influenced by this activity and by the music of Debussy that Kodály had brought back from Paris: both opened the way to new, modal kinds of harmony and irregular metre. The 1908 Violin Concerto is still within the symphonic tradition, but the many small piano pieces of this period show a new, authentically Hungarian Bartók emerging, with the 4ths of Magyar folksong, the rhythms of peasant dance and the scales he had dis-

covered among Hungarian, Romanian and Slovak peoples. The arrival of this new voice is documented in his String Quartet No 1 (1908), introduced at a Budapest concert of his music in 1910.

There followed orchestral pieces and a one-act opera, Bluebeard's Castle, dedicated to his young wife. Influenced by Mussorgsky and Debussy but most directly by Hungarian peasant music (and Strauss, still, in its orchestral pictures), the work, a grim fable of human isolation, failed to win the competition in which it was entered. For two years (1912-14) Bartók practically gave up composition and devoted himself to the collection, arrangement and study of folk music, until World War I put an end to his expeditions. He returned to creative activity with the String Quartet No 2 (1917) and the fairytale ballet The Wooden Prince, whose production in Budapest in 1917 restored him to public favour. The next year Bluebeard's Castle was staged and he began a second ballet, The Miraculous Mandarin, which was not performed until 1926 (there were problems over the subject, the thwarting and consummation of sexual passion). Rich and graphic in invention, the score is practically an opera without words.

While composing The Miraculous Mandarin Bartók came under the influence of Stravinsky and Schoenberg, and produced some of his most complex music in the two violin sonatas of 1921-2. At the same time he was gaining international esteem: his works were published by Universal Edition and he was invited to play them all over Europe. He was now well established at home, too. He wrote the confident Dance Suite (1923); there was then another lull until the sudden rush of works in 1926 designed for himself to play, including the Piano Concerto No 1, the Piano Sonata and the suite Out of Doors. These exploit the piano as a percussion instrument, using its resonances as well as its xylophonic hardness. The search for new sonorities and driving rhythms was continued in the next two string quartets (1927-8), of which No 4, like the concerto, is in a five-section palindromic pattern (ABCBA).

Similar formal schemes, with intensively worked counterpoint, were used in the Piano Concerto No 2 (1931) and String Quartet No 5 (1934), though now Bartók's harmony was becoming more diatonic. The move from inward chromaticism to a glowing major (though modally tinged) tonality is basic to the Music for Strings, Percussion and Celesta (1936) and the Sonata for Two Pianos and Percussion (1937), both written for performance in Switzerland at a time when the political situation in Hungary was growing unsympathetic.

In 1940 Bartók and his second wife (he had divorced and remarried in 1923) left war-torn Europe to live in New York, which he found alien. They gave concerts and for a while he had a research grant to work on a collection of Yugoslav folksong, but their finances were precarious, as increasingly was his health. It seemed that his last European work, the String Quartet No 6 (1939), might be his pessimistic swansong, but then came the exuberant Concerto for Orchestra (1943) and the involuted Sonata for Solo Violin (1944). Piano Concerto No 3, written to provide his widow with an income, was almost finished when he died, a Viola Concerto left in sketch.

GROVEmusic

Piano Concertos

No 1 Sz83; **No 2** Sz95; **No 3** Sz119

Piano Concertos Nos 1-3   Ⓗ
Géza Anda pf **Berlin Radio Symphony Orchestra /
Ferenc Fricsay**
DG The Originals 447 399-2GOR (78' · ADD)
Recorded 1959-60   Ⓜ❶❶❶➪

Much as you'd like to tout the new as the best, there are some older recordings where a very special chemistry spells 'definitive', and that pose an almost impossible challenge to subsequent rivals. Such is this 1959 recording of Bartók's Second Piano Concerto, a tough, playful, pianistically aristocratic performance where dialogue is consistently keen and spontaneity is captured on the wing (even throughout numerous sessions). The first movement is relentless but never tires the ear; the second displays two very different levels of tension, one slow and mysterious, the other hectic but controlled; and although others might have thrown off the finale's octaves with even greater abandon, Anda's performance is the most successful in suggesting savage aggression barely held in check.

The Third Concerto is again beautifully moulded and carefully thought through. Moments such as the loving return from the second movement's chirpy central episode are quite unforgettable, while the finale is both nimble and full toned. The First Concerto was the last to be recorded and is perhaps the least successful of the three: here ensemble is occasionally loose, and characterisation less vivid than with some. Still, it's a fine performance and the current transfer has been lovingly effected.

Bartók Piano Concerto No 2, Sz95[a] **Mozart** Piano Concertos – No 16, K451[b]; No 17, K453[c]
Géza Anda pf [a]**BBC Symphony Orchestra / Pierre Boulez**; [bc]**English Chamber Orchestra**
BBC Legends BBCL4247-2 (81' · ADD)
Recorded live at [b]BBC Studios, London, on Novmber 27, 1968; Royal Festival Hall, London,
on [a]December 5, 1973, and [c]April 9, 1975   Ⓕ❶

Géza Anda's all-too-brief 30-year career (he died in 1976 at the age of 54) left us with a string of fine recordings including one of the first complete cycles of Mozart's concertos (for DG) and benchmark versions of all three of Bartók's. It is with these two vastly dissimilar composers featured here that Anda is indelibly linked.

From the first bar of K451, the least-played of all Mozart's mature keyboard concertos, you know you are in for something special. Anda, directing from the keyboard, launches the ECO into a true allegro assai, exuberantly matched by the piano's entry. This is Mozart-playing of a refined order, robust, sparkling and fully in tune with the entertainment character of the work. The sublime K453 is a live performance from over six years later, no less successful in its precision, stylishness and general high spirits, though the piano tone is slightly glassy compared to the more rounded studio sound of K451. In Pierre Boulez, Anda, who had been playing the Bartók concertos since the 1950s, had a sympathetic and experienced collaborator. This live 1973 performance of No 2 is played at a cracking pace, rich in detail and, in the treacherously difficult outer movements, simply thrilling. Yet few pianists (not even Pollini) have found on disc quite the same mesmerising, unsettling atmosphere as Anda does here in the central *Adagio*. This is a valuable and well-filled disc.

Bartók Piano Concerto No 3
Prokofiev Piano Concertos – No 1 & 3
Martha Argerich pf
Montreal Symphony Orchestra / Charles Dutoit
EMI 556654-2 (70' · DDD)   Ⓕ**O**🅑➤

As always with this most mercurial of virtuosos, Martha Argerich's playing is generated by the mood of the moment and many listeners may well be surprised at her relative geniality with Dutoit. Personal and vivacious throughout, she always allows the composer his own voice. This is particularly true in Bartók's Third Concerto where her rich experience in chamber music makes her often *primus inter pares*, a virtuoso who listens to her partners with the greatest care. In the *Adagio religioso* she achieves a poise that has sometimes eluded her in the past and her finale is specially characterful, her stealthy start to the concluding *Presto* allowing the final pages their full glory. Dutoit and the Montreal Symphony achieve a fine unity throughout, a sense of like-minded musicians at work.

All true musicians will recognise performances of a special magic and integrity. In the Prokofiev First Concerto, her opening is arguably more authentically *brioso* than ferocious, her overall view a refreshingly fanciful view of Prokofiev's youthful iconoclasm. The central *Andante assai* is inflected with an improvisatory freedom she probably wouldn't have risked earlier in her career and in the *Allegro scherzando* she trips the light fantastic, reserving a suitably tigerish attack for the final octave bravura display. Her performance of the Third Concerto is less fleet or nimble-fingered than in her early days but is more delectably alive to passing caprice. The recordings are clear and naturally balanced.

Additional recommendation

Piano Concertos Nos 1ᵃ; 2ᵇ & 3ᶜ
ᵃ**Zimerman**, ᵇ**Andsnes**, ᶜ**Grimaud** pfs ᵃ**Chicago SO;**
ᵇ**BPO;** ᶜ**LSO / Boulez**
DG download 447 5330GH (76' · DDD)   Ⓕ**OO**🅑➤

Grimaud's Third is a winner; the Second with Andsnes has a fabulous finale, and Zimerman's First is brilliant in parts, if not quite a meeting of minds.

Viola Concerto, Sz120

Bartók Viola Concerto **Eötvös** Replica
Kurtág Movement for Viola and Orchestra
Kim Kashkashian va **Netherlands Radio Chamber Orchestra / Peter Eötvös**
ECM New Series 465 420-2 (50' · DDD)   Ⓕ**O**🅑➤

Kashkashian's superbly engineered recording of the Bartók Viola Concerto bears witness to a total identification between performer and composer. Even the tiny pause bridging the opening and the secondary idea growing out of it, is perfectly judged. Kashkashian makes this music dance, not just in the finale but also in the way that she phrases and articulates the entire piece. Eötvös's conducting offers many parallel insights, not least towards the end of the first movement where a growing sense of agitation throws the succeeding *Adagio religioso* into a particularly favourable light. Eötvös employs Tibor Serly's completion, revising odd details and accommodating a few articulations and phrasings that Kashkashian has herself instigated. If you need convincing that Bartók's Viola Concerto is a great work, then Kashkashian and Eötvos should, between them, do the trick.

Of the other pieces, Eötvös's *Replica* for viola and orchestra is astonishing music in which foggy harmonies hover between startled highs and raucous lows, then mutate into a strange, sickly pulsing. By contrast, György Kurtág's early *Movement for Viola and Orchestra* – two-thirds of a concerto Kurtág completed in 1953-4 – is relatively conventional, with plenty of virtuoso viola writing.

Bartók Viola Concerto **Hindemith** Trauermusik
Martinů Rhapsodie-concerto for Viola and Orchestra
Vladimír Bukač va **Czech Radio Symphony Orchestra / Vladimír Válek**
Calliope CAL9364 (47' · DDD)   Ⓕ

The combination of three fairly sombre viola pieces by major composers in exile hits the spot exactly: one extra work would have thrown the whole project out of kilter. Vladimír Bukač is violist of the Talich Quartet and it's interesting that rather than opt for the familiar Tibor Serly completion of Bartók's Viola Concerto, he appears to have used Peter Bartók's revision (one of several that have appeared since the 'original' was published in 1950). If you want to check Serly against Bartók *fils*, there's a give-away in the first two bars where Serly answers the solo viola on *pizzicato* cellos and basses, and Peter Bartók opts for timpani. Thereafter differences between the two are both plentiful (many passages are completely rescored) and musically fascinating, the newer version claiming a far wider range of colours than its spartan predecessor.

Bukač offers a warm, emotionally committed performance of the Bartók, flexible, dusky-brown in tone and sensitively accompanied by

BARTÓK'S CONCERTO FOR ORCHESTRA – IN BRIEF

Hungarian Festival Orchestra / Iván Fischer
Philips 476 7255 (67' · DDD)   Ⓜ❶❶❶❶➔

A tremendous modern performance with lashings of character and some really stunning orchestral work. Fischer negotiates all the changes of tempo and rhythm with his customary panache.

Chicago SO / Fritz Reiner
RCA 09026 61504-2 (76' · ADD)   Ⓜ❶❶

Recorded in 1956, this still sounds stunning and Reiner's interpretation has the idiomatic feel of someone who has really lived with the score. This is Bartók with an iron grip, but thrilling none the less. Coupled with the *Music for strings, percussion and celesta*.

Chicago SO / Sir Georg Solti
Decca ② 470 516-2DF2 (138' · DDD)   Ⓜ➔

This powerful recording from another great Hungarian conductor comes as part of a most appealing Bartók collection. Rather brightly recorded though!

Concertgebouw Orchestra / Eduard van Beinum
Dutton mono CDK1206 (69' · ADD)   Ⓜ

A wonderfully vital and exciting performance from one of The Netherlands' greatest conductors – the ex-Decca sound is remarkable for the early 1950s.

Boston SO / Serge Koussevitzky
Naxos mono 8 110105 (59' · DDD)   Ⓢ❶

A radio relay of the first Boston performance under the man who commissioned the work. This has all the energy, excitement and sense of discovery of a creator's recording (it even has the original ending).

Chicago SO / Pierre Boulez
DG 437 826-2GH (60' · DDD)   Ⓕ➔

A master Bartók conductor with one of the great Bartók orchestras in a reading that shows off both the work's and the players' virtuosity. This is a very exciting modern account of this extraordinary creation.

Berlin PO / Herbert von Karajan
DG 457 890-2GGA (71' · ADD)   Ⓜ➔

This is one of a number of recordings Karajan made of the work. His quest to seek out the beautiful did somewhat take the pungency out of much of the writing.

Philadelphia Orchestra / Christoph Eschenbach
Ondine ⏣ ODE1072-5 (69' · DDD)   Ⓕ❶

With playing as beautiful as on the Karajan version, Eschenbach offers more grit and bite. Enterprisingly coupled with Klein and Martinů, this is a very fine version in very well-engineered (live) sound.

Válek and the Czech Radio Symphony. The Hindemith *Trauermusik* for viola and string orchestra was famously written at breakneck speed while the viola player-composer was on a performing visit to London. George V had died the previous day, which meant that Hindemith's relatively upbeat *Schwanendreher* Concerto was deemed inappropriate for the occasion and the new piece, all seven minutes of it, was played in its place. Brief though it is, Hindemith's *Trauermusik* is one of his loveliest works, the poignant two-minute finale based on Bach's last chorale. Again, the performance radiates warmth but for me the highlight of this excellent disc is the *Rhapsodie-concerto* that Martinů wrote to a commission from the principal viola of George Szell's Cleveland Orchestra (Szell himself conducted the premiere in 1953). Martinů came up with a work cast in his most lyrical vein, music that while deeply nostalgic and mostly slow-moving does allow for a dash of dancing in the second of its two movements. Bukač's new recording is very persuasive and very well engineered. Again the orchestral playing is idiomatic and the conducting sympathetic and intelligent.

Violin Concertos Nos 1 & 2

Violin Concertos Nos 1 & 2
György Pauk vn
National Polish Radio Symphony Orchestra of Katowice / Antoni Wit
Naxos 8 554321 (62' . DDD)   Ⓢ➔

The strongest aspect of these performances is soloist Gyorgy Pauk's supremely idiomatic playing. He may not have the virtuosity of a Mullova or Midori, but there are only one or two moments when he sounds uncomfortable with the technical demands, and the Hungarian idioms of Concerto No 2 flow naturally from his bow, unexaggerated yet full of character. He's strikingly successful, too, at seeing each movement as a whole. It's so easy for the first movement of Concerto No 2, with its dramatic mood-swings, to sound disjointed, but here the march-tread of the opening remains somewhere in the background through most of the movement, giving it real coherence. Rob Cowan, reviewing a recent Shaham/Boulez recording, commented that performances of this concerto which elongate Bartók's meticulous timings tend to miss something of the music's fiery spirit, and this version might also be thought rather easygoing by the side of Mullova, who stays close to Bartók's suggested tempos. She benefits, too, from a more sharply-focused recording. Though well balanced, this one lacks the last degree of definition and perspective – essential if Bartók's marvellously detailed orchestration is to make its full effect. The orchestral playing is accurate and spirited, but doesn't have the refinement that allows an orchestra like the Berlin Philharmonic to give such a strong sense of direction to the first movement of the First Concerto, and to accentuate the grotesque features of its second movement.

Pauk's interpretations, thoughtful and strongly felt, are essential listening for Bartók enthusiasts.

Additional recommendations

Violin Concertos Nos 1 and 2
Coupled with: Piano Concertos
Chung vn **Ashkenazy** pf **Chicago Symphony Orchestra, London Philharmonic Orchestra / Solti**
Decca Double ② 473 271-2DF2 (137' · DDD)　　Ⓜ🅑➔

Highly extrovert, likeable performances from Chung with Solti a like-minded collaborator. The piano concertos make a great package – Ashkenazy is on superb form.

Concerto for two pianos , percussion and orchestra

Concerto for Two Pianos, Percussion and Orchestra, Sz115ᵃ. Violin Concerto No 1, Sz36ᵇ. Viola Concerto, Sz120ᶜ
ᵇ**Gidon Kremer** vn ᶜ**Yuri Bashmet** va
ᵃ**Pierre-Laurent Aimard**, ᵃ**Tamara Stefanovich** pfs
ᵃ**Neil Percy**, ᵃ**Nigel Thomas** perc ᵇᶜ**Berlin Philharmonic Orchestra;** ᵃ**London Symphony Orchestra / Pierre Boulez**
DG 477 7440GH (70' · DDD)　　Ⓕ🅞➔

And so Pierre Boulez's DG survey of Bartók's major orchestral works draws to a close. This final instalment opens with an Abbey Road taping of a masterpiece (the two-piano Sonata-turned-Concerto) then alternates two four-year-old Berlin Philharmonic recordings – the richly scored and erotically charged First Violin Concerto and the pared-down, largely ascetic Viola Concerto, an incomplete last testament rendered performable by the viola-player Tibor Serly. Yuri Bashmet treats the opening with considerable freedom and is consistently responsive to the score's more lyrical passages, though both he and Boulez bring a touch of menace to the closing moments of the slow movement.

Gidon Kremer sounds equally unfettered at the start of the Violin Concerto's gorgeous first movement but come the dizzy antics of the *Allegro giocoso* he engages more with play than with reverie. In fact from around 2'20" he sounds positively bored – very unlike him (he's a favourite player of mine).

Boulez has spoken about the 'Concerto' orchestration of the Sonata for Two Pianos and Percussion as adding 'a different dimension' to the Sonata, especially in the first movement, and he substantiates his claim with a performance that is typically transparent and attentive in matters of balancing, the brass fanfares at around 9'16" in the first movement so vividly reminiscent of parallel passages in the Second Piano

Concerto. Pierre-Laurent Aimard and Tamara Stefanovich, although technically brilliant, keep a relatively low profile, which makes for added intimacy in the first movement's busy, often humorous badinage but rather mutes the rhythmic impact of the finale's opening. Greatly preferable is the stark, demonically driven spirit of the original – the Concerto pulls punches that the Sonata delivers in full – but Boulez's performance states a strong case for the plusher concerto alternative.

Concerto for Orchestra, Sz116

Concerto for Orchestra. Kossuth. 5 Village Scenes.
Budapest Festival Orchestra / Iván Fischer
Philips 476 7255 (67' · DDD)　　Ⓜ🅞🅞🅞➔

It is the flavour of this *Concerto for Orchestra* that wins the day. Just sample the subtle *portamento* that spices the string line at bars 52-3 (2'36") of the first movement, and the sombre colouring near the end of the movement, at 8'58". Fischer is a dab hand at shaping and inflecting the musical line, and his characterisation of the 'Giuoco delle coppie' – paced, incidentally, at the prescribed crotchet=94 – is second to none. He invests the 'Elegia' with the maximum respectable quota of passion and the 'Intermezzo interrotto' dances to a few added accents and the finale is a riot of sunshine and swirling skirts, except for the mysterious – and notoriously tricky – *più presto* coda, with its rushing *sul ponticello* string choirs, which Fischer articulates with great care. One senses that the players are being driven to the very limits of their abilities, which only serves to intensify the excitement.

Additional recommendations

Concerto for Orchestra
Coupled with: Music for Strings, Percussion and Celesta. Hungarian Sketches

Chicago Symphony Orchestra / Reiner
RCA 09026 61504-2 (67' · ADD) Recorded 1956　Ⓜ🅞🅞

A classic recording by one of the master Bartók conductors. With staggering playing by the Chicago Symphony and recording that simply dones't sound its age, this is a magnificent achievement. RCA's sound reportage of the *Concerto for Orchestra* has uncanny realism, and if the climaxes are occasionaly reined in, the fervour of Reiner's direction more than compensates. His couplings are excellent too.

The Miraculous Mandarin, Sz73

The Miraculous Mandarin. Hungarian Peasant Songs, Sz100. Hungarian Sketches, Sz97. Romanian Folkdances, Sz68. Transylvanian Dances, Sz96. Romanian Dance, Sz47
Hungarian Radio Chorus; Budapest Festival Orchestra / Iván Fischer

Philips Gramophone Awards Collection 476 1799
(67' · DDD)   Ⓜ ⦿⦿⦿⦿☞

As *Mandarins* go, they don't come more miraculous than this – a vivid, no-holds-barred
performance. Everything tells: the flavour is
right, the pacing too, and the sound has a tough-
ened, raw-edged quality that's an essential constituent of Bartók's tonal language. Although
lurid, even seedy, in narrative detail, this is ultimately a tale of compassion, and Fischer never
forgets that. Observable detail, all of it musically
significant, occurs virtually by the minute. Delicacy trails bullish aggression, forcefulness alternates with almost graphic suggestiveness: it's all
there in the score. Fischer never vulgarises, brutalises or overstates the case; most important, he
underlines the quickly flickering, folkish elements in Bartók's musical language that other
conductors barely acknowledge.

The strongly individual character of the Budapest Festival Orchestra is delightful. The strings
have a biting edge, the woodwinds a gypsy-style
reediness, while brass and percussion are forceful and incisive but never raucous. This is Hun-
garian-grown Bartók that actually *sounds* Hungarian; if only other European orchestras would
reclaim parallel levels of individuality.

The Wooden Prince, Sz60

The Wooden Prince. Kossuth, Sz21
**Hungarian National Philharmonic Orchestra /
Zoltán Kocsis**
Hungaroton ⏺ HSACD32502 (72' · DDD/DSD)   Ⓕ

Kocsis's account of *Kossuth* is terrific – the best
we now have. The budding composer's youthful
essay has rarely sounded more engaging,
for example in the tangy portrait at the start
of the piece, the Wagnerian picture of 'The
Battlefield', and the cynical minor-key distortion of the Austrian Hymn in the eighth section,
the bizarre way Hungarian and Austrian motives
collide. *Heldenleben* is an obvious forebear
and Kocsis directs a performance that suggests
a paprika-flavoured variant on Straussian
exuberance.

The Wooden Prince ballet has enjoyed a rather
more distinguished recorded history than Kossuth, with Fischer, Boulez and, from the analogue era, Dorati offering the best versions thus
far. As with Bartók's piano music, Kocsis is a
master of idiomatic *rubato*, of holding the crest
of a phrase (the first dance) and of course he fully
understands, even relishes, the rustic element
(ie, the fourth dance with its spicy *col legno*
strings). Like Fischer, he knows how to focus a
narrative, for example the drooping brass
glissandi when the prince is 'in greatest despair'.
And there's the humour – the tipsy-sounding
bassoon as the disorderly prince unsuccessfully
attempts to dance with the princess. Swathes of
post-impressionist tone-painting (the enchantment scene) alternate with passages of great
delicacy and Hungaroton's fairly close-set

recording captures it all vividly. If you already
have Fischer's equally fine *Wooden Prince* stick
with it, but if you haven't and the present
coupling appeals then I would wholeheartedly
recommend this new CD.

The Wooden Prince
Bournemouth Symphony Orchestra / Marin Alsop
Naxos 8 570534 (53' · DDD)   Ⓢ☞

Bartók's tonally effulgent second stage work
suits the warm, texture-sensitive conducting
style of Marin Alsop, who coaxes some stylish
solos from her accomplished Bournemouth
players. Three minutes into the teasing 'Dance
of the Princess and the Wooden Prince' and
you'll hear nicely pointed woodwinds set within
an ambient, realistically balanced sound frame.
The solo clarinet in the 'Dance of the Princess in
the Forest' is also very charterful: Alsop's feel
for the ballet's romantic narrative – basically
about love overcoming a series of obstacles – is
at its most productive where the line is slow and
expressive, for example the 'The Prince in
Despair' and the final embrace, both of which
have an almost filmic quality to them. Another
good sampling-point, more an illustration of the
score's humour this time, is the droll bassoon
solo at the start of the fifth dance where the
Princess 'prods and encourages the Wooden
Prince to dance'.

Alsop's most recent rival is Zoltán Kocsis with
the Hungarian National Philharmonic (see
above), an unforgettable performance and a distinguished production that tops all rivals in at
least two specific episodes: 'The Fairy Enchanting the stream' and the tangy dance where 'The
Princess Spies the Wooden Prince', the score's
most Hungarian-sounding music. Here the
Bournemouth performance is rather low on
energy and 'bite', at least initially. But then
you'd expect a Hungarian band to latch onto the
national element.

All in all, Alsop and her orchestra do justice to
Bartók's most overtly romantic large-scale
score; it's a performance that will surely appeal
beyond the ranks of Bartók devotees to balleto-
manes generally, not to mention lovers of *fin
de siècle* musical excess. Good notes too, by
Carl Leafstedt.

String Quartets

No 1 Sz40; **No 2** Sz67; **No 3** Sz85; **No 4** Sz91;
No 5 Sz102; **No 6** Sz114

String QuartetsNos 1-6
Belcea Quartet (Corina Belcea, Lara Samuel *vns*
Krzysztof Chorzelski *va* Alasdair Tait *vc*)
EMI ② 394400-2 (157' · DDD)   Ⓕ⦿⦿⦿⦿☞

Bartók's quartets are one of the great musical
collision points between modernism and romanticism. How to handle the tension between their
expressive gestures and constructivist designs is

one of the abiding issues for performers and one reason why even the plethora of fine available recordings cannot remotely exhaust their riches. Getting the best of all worlds interpretatively is hardly a realistic aim. Even so, there are long stretches where the Belceas come as close to the ideal as any ensemble on disc.

Try the first few minutes of Quartets Nos 2 and 3, and marvel at the gradation of *forte* and *fortissimo*, of *piano* and *pianissimo*, which helps to give entire movements far more convincing shape than less precisely observant ensembles achieve. Try the outer movements of No 5 and marvel at the gear-changes negotiated smoothly, instantly and unanimously, yet never as ends in themselves, always accompanied by a sense of expressive-dramatic purpose. Try virtually every movement in fact, and revel, as the Belceas do, in the interplay of the lines, even in passages where others seem thankful just to come through unscathed.

Clearly immense thought has been given to tone quality. In the first movement of No 1, for instance, the Belceas point the periodic arrivals on consonant harmonies by withdrawing vibrato, and instantly the as yet not fully mature Bartók's straggly structure gains sharpness of profile. They apply the same ploy in the much tauter environment of the first movement of No 5, and with similarly revelatory results. At the other extreme, their sustained tonal intensity makes the most barbaric onrushes exhilarating rather than exhausting, neither too streamlined nor too effortful. When the score is bare of instructions, as in the first slow movement of No 5, they take it at its word and uncover a hypnotic, staring blankness. And when the invitation to humour is extended, as in the finale of the same quartet, they seize it with full-blooded, yet never self-serving, relish.

Before surrendering to the power of these performances, one wondered if there was going to be enough ethnic tang and zest, enough wildness and strangeness, enough sultry longing. We've certainly heard more of those qualities in the first two quartets. Yet the central movement of No 2 is marked *molto capriccioso*, not *barbaro*, and that's exactly what comes across, while the coda is pushed daringly close to the edge, sounding like the distant fluttering of giant moths – not as precisely by the book as the Emersons but vastly more imaginative and emotionally telling – while the slow finale has a superbly intense accumulation at its heart.

Pushed for a general reservation, perhaps when a 'speaking' quality is needed in the quasi-recitatives, the first violin's colleagues don't quite match her for idiomatic insight. And do the Belceas get to the heart of the matter in the trauma-shaded No 6? Not quite – not by comparison with The Lindsays, anyway, who are generally more prepared to tolerate rough edges for the sake of emotional revelation.

In short, the Belceas are more than worthy rivals to the best on disc and EMI's recording quality is just right.

BARTÓK STRING QUARTETS – IN BRIEF

Many of the classics sets of the Bartók string quartets are currently unavailable on CD in the local catalogue, but are available for download or through international distribution.

Belcea Quartet
EMI ② 394400-2 (157' · DDD)
Ⓕ ⦿⦿⦿↦

A set of real distinction: the Belcea show flair and imagination aplenty. Their playing is first rate and their feeling for Bartók's language total.

Emerson Quartet
DG ② download *423 657-2GH2* (149' · DDD)
Ⓑ ⦿⦿⦿↦

One of the three *Gramophone* Award-winning sets of these seminal 20th-century quartets. High-powered and totally accurate – this is one of the most virtuoso recordings.

Tokyo Quartet
DG ② download *476 1833* (159' · ADD) Ⓜ⦿⦿↦
Recently reissued as part of Universal's *Gramophone* Award series, these are gentler but infinitely subtle performances with great attention to colour and texture.

Takács Quartet
Decca ② 455 297-2DH2 (152' · DDD) Ⓕ⦿⦿⦿↦
The most recent award-winning set and possibly the finest all-round set of the six quartets. The Takács Quartet play every note as if it were their last – the conviction positively crackles from the speakers.

Hagen Quartet
DG ② download *463 576-2GH2* (154' · DDD)
Ⓕ⦿⦿⦿↦

Adventurous, imaginative performances from one of the younger quartets with a lovely consistency of approach throughout. There's real fire in their playing, as well as a truly songful lyricism.

Juilliard Quartet
Pearl mono ② GEMS0147 (156' · ADD) Ⓜ⦿
This 1950s set originally from CBS is mightily impressive. As the first cycle to be recorded as a cycle it was something of a milestone, and that quality of novelty and discovery shines through magnificently.

Keller Quartet
Warner Apex ② 2564-62686-2 (149' · DDD)
Ⓑ⦿⦿↦

A fine bargain cycle well worth considering if you're on a tight budget. As Hungarians the Kellers have an innate feel for the idiom, and the digital recording is beautifully handled.

String Quartets Nos 1-6
Takács Quartet (Edward Dusinberre, Károly Schranz
vns Roger Tapping *va* András Fejér *vc*)
Decca ② 455 297-2DH2 (152' · DDD)   ⓕ**OOOO**▷

Ⓖ These performances provide more impressive sampling points than can be enumerated in a single review. The First Quartet's oscillating tempo-shifts work wonderfully well, all with total naturalness. Characterisation is equally strong elsewhere, not least the first movement of the Debussian arpeggios of the Second Quartet, and the second movement where Fejér races back into the rustic opening subject. The nightmare climax in the last movement has rarely sounded more prophetic of the great *Divertimento*'s central movement. The middle quartets work very well, with prominent inner voices in the Third and plenty of swagger in the Fourth. The high spots of No 4 are Fejér's improvisational cello solo in the third movement and a finale where the violent opening is a hefty *legato* to compare with the sharper, more Stravinskian attack of, say, the Tokyo Quartet. Likewise, the sudden dance-like episode in the first movement of the Fifth Quartet, savage music played from the pit of the stomach, while the third movement's bleary-eyed viola melody over teeming violin triplets suggests peasants in caricature.

The Takács are responsive to Bartók's sardonic humour – the 'barrel-organ' episode at the end of the Fifth Quartet, and the corny 'Burletta' in the third movement of the Sixth. The Sixth itself has some of the saddest, wildest and wisest music written in the last 100 years: the opening viola solo recalls Mahler's Tenth and the close fades to a mysterious question. Throughout the cycle, Bartók's metronome markings are treated more as guidelines than literal commands. The playing imparts Bartók's all-embracing humanity. If the greatest string quartets after Beethoven are still unknown to you, this set may well prove the musical journey of a lifetime. The recording has ambient, full-bodied sound that's more reminiscent of the concert hall than the studio.

Bartók String Quartet No 5
Hindemith String Quartet No 4, Op 22
Zehetmair Quartet (Thomas Zehetmair, Kuba
Jakowicz *vns* Ruth Killius *va* Ursula Smith *vc*)
ECM New Series 476 5779 (51' · DDD)   ⓕ**OO**

A few seconds into the first movement of this extraordinary version of the Fifth Quartet check whether the dynamics are being played as written – many aren't. The Zehetmairs career around the notes like bikers on a zig-zag course, tracing arches at speed with what sounds like the least effort. At the fervid build-up nearly three minutes in they lunge at the music *fortissimo* though for the starkly syncopated passage a few seconds later their *legato* handling of the viola/cello lines tends to soften the argument's impact. It'll take some getting used to, but persevere.

There's savagery, too – for example where Bartók asks the leader to play *ff stridente* and Zehetmair all but saws through his fiddle.

Don't expect either a comfortable or a familiar ride. The two symmetrically placed slow movements embrace vivid, often rough-hewn textures, from a quiet chalky treble to fierce full chords. Perhaps the most satisfying movements are the *Scherzo alla bulgarese* and the finale: both suggest an element of rustic dance, the finale's quieter music sounding eerily effective, especially at speed.

Hindemith's somewhat drier Fourth Quartet (1921) predates Bartók's Fifth by some 13 years. Like the Bartók it is cast in five rather than the usual four movements, the first opening to a slow, shadowy fugato which soon flares to near-rage. Both here and in the ferocious *Scherzo* the Zehetmair Quartet capture the music's radical spirit, much as they do for the equivocal, gently marching slow movement.

This is a fascinating CD. With the Zehetmairs you're rarely aware of bar-lines, more a constant flow of ideas, a compelling journey with a stated destination but with little need of pedantic signposting en route. You sense that the written notes have been fully absorbed and that the playing has become, in a sense, pure instinct.

String Quartets – No 5, Sz102; No 6, Sz114
Arcanto Quartet (Antje Weithaas, Daniel Sepec *vns*
Tabea Zimmermann *va* Jean-Guihen Queyras *vc*)
Harmonia Mundi HMC90 1963 (60' · DDD)   ⓕ**OO**

Quite exceptional, this…and on many levels. For one, the playing is superb, the biting attack of the Fifth Quartet's opening, its precision, energy and tempered rhythmic momentum, not to mention the accuracy of intonation throughout. Everything tells, nothing sounds rushed. Just as remarkable are the gentler episodes in the two interrupted slow movements, barely sighing in the first, scarily building to a maelstrom in the second. Humour is a priority in the *Scherzo*, which wafts in quietly then, towards the end, after a sudden snap, scurries back into the night. The finale often proves a stumbling block but not here, again strongly driven, the two madcap minuet episodes raising a smile, the first toying with atonalism (the timing here is crucially spot-on), the other a dazed minuet. No doubt about it, this is one of the most impressive, the most human accounts of Bartók No 5 to have appeared for a long time.

Though merely five years old as an ensemble, the Arcanto Quartet have clocked up considerable pooled experience. And they didn't enter into quartet playing lightly, having previously tried out other instrumental formations. What's for sure is that any internal disharmony would have surfaced in Bartók's fragile last quartet, another memorable performance. Again, everything is well articulated, tiny motifs that otherwise go for nothing are made clear, curving glissandi shaped as if carefully planed and the haunting motif that prefaces each movement and dominates the last is sustained with maximum expressive intensity. Echoes of folk music tail rarefied abstract invention, and the alternation of slapstick comedy and implied tragedy is underlined, though never too heavily. It's another winner, purposeful yet refined.

Violin Sonatas, Rhapsodies, Contrasts

Violin Sonatas – No 1 Sz75; **No 2** Sz76
Rhapsodies – No 1 Sz86 **No 2** Sz89
Contrasts Sz111. **Solo Violin Sonata** Sz117
Violin Sonatas Nos 1 & 2. Solo Violin Sonata
Christian Tetzlaff vn **Leif Ove Andsnes** pf
Virgin Classics 545668-2 (79' · DDD) (F)❍❍❍❍➤

Would it be too fanciful to divide interpreters of Bartók's violin music into two approximate categories: Szigeti-Végh and Menuhin-Stern? In other words, cerebral-rustic and emotive-universal? Listen to Thomas Zehetmair's Bartók or Isabelle Faust's, Gidon Kremer's or, indeed, Christian Tetzlaff's and the spirit of Végh in particular seems prominent. Whereas Eugene Drucker, György Pauk and Robert Mann (on Bartók Records) are more aligned with Menuhin and Stern.

Tetzlaff's tone is grainy and lightly-brushed, his inward approach most evident in the Solo Sonata, a work he plays with sovereign command – and with greater freedom than on his more straightlaced 1991 recording (Virgin, nla), which veered less towards the Végh axis than this new version does. Here Tetzlaff makes more of the fugue's shifting perspectives and relishes Bartók's bold chord constructions. Other players may at times employ a richer tone palette but few take a more thoughtful interpretative standpoint on what is after all the finest unaccompanied violin sonata since Bach.

The two duo sonatas are also beautifully done. Tezlaff again proves both focused and expressive, though among modern rivals you might prefer Faust's questing expressiveness, and György Pauk's Naxos coupling offers honest musical reportage. But what makes these performances more or less indispensable is the character and control of Leif Ove Andsnes's piano playing, its fastidious deployment of tone and immaculate timing. The clarion alarms in the outer movements of the First Sonata, where tonality is stretched to its limits, ring out without percussive overkill. The Second Sonata's folksy *Allegretto* is strong and tidy but with the unmistakable sense of earth under foot. Andsnes is the stronger personality, Tetzlaff the more confidential, yielding presence (wonderful in the First Sonata's *Adagio*); an ideal anima-animus performing relationship.

This is chamber music playing of the highest order, candid and straightforward enough for a basic library recommendation but also rich enough in subtleties to satisfy even the most discerning connoisseur.

Violin Sonatas Nos 1 & 2. Contrasts, Sz111
Kálmán Berkes cl **György Pauk** vn **Jenö Jandó** pf
Naxos 8 550749 (75' · DDD) (S)(B)➤

Readers who habitually fight shy of Bartók's provocatively astringent piano writing might at first find these endlessly fascinating works rather unpalatable, the First Sonata especially. But careful scrutiny reveals manifold beauties which, once absorbed, tend to haunt the memory and prompt repeated listening. Jenö Jandó's piano playing is fairly forthright yet without the naked agression of, say, Sviatoslav Richter. And it provides an effective foil for György Pauk's warm tone and fluid solo line, especially in the First Sonata, where ungainly tone production could so easily compound the listener's discomfort. Here, however, the interpretation is at once thoughtful and well shaped, and fully appreciative of the mysterious 'night music' that sits at the heart of the *Adagio*.

The Second Sonata is both gentler and more improvisatory, its language and structure – although still pretty formidable – somewhat in the manner of a rhapsody. Pauk and Jandó again hit the target, and the full-bodied recording makes for a homogeneous sound picture. To have a spirited performance of the multi-faceted *Contrasts* (with Kálmán Berkes on clarinet) as a bonus certainly helps promote this well-annotated CD to the front line of competition. A confident mainstream recommendation, then, and superb value for money.

Rhapsodies Nos 1 & 2. Contrasts. Solo Violin Sonata. Six Romanian Folk Dances, Sz56 (arr Székely)
Michael Collins cl **Krysia Osostowicz** vn **Susan Tomes** pf
Helios CDH55149 (72' · DDD) (F)❍

Unusually for a composer who wrote so much fine chamber music Bartók wasn't himself a string player. But he did enjoy close artistic understanding with a succession of prominent violin virtuosos, including the Hungarians Jelly d'Arányi, Joseph Szigeti and Zoltán Székely, and, towards the end of his life, Yehudi Menuhin. It was Menuhin who commissioned the Sonata for solo violin, but Bartók died before he could hear him play it – Menuhin was unhappy with the occasional passages in quarter-tones and the composer had reserved judgement on his proposal to omit them. It was Menuhin's edition which was later printed and which has been most often played and recorded; but Krysia Osostowicz returns to the original and, more importantly, plays the whole work with intelligence, imaginative flair and consummate skill.

The Sonata is the most substantial work on this disc, but the rest of the programme is no less thoughtfully prepared or idiomatically delivered. There's the additional attraction of an extremely well balanced and natural-sounding recording. As a complement to the string quartets, which are at the very heart of Bartók's output, this is a most recommendable disc.

Violin Duos

Bartók 44 Duos for Two Violins, Sz98
Kurtág Ligatura – Message to Frances-Marie, Op 31b
Ligeti Ballad and Dance
András Keller, János Pilz vns
ECM New Series 465 849-2 (58' · DDD)   Ⓕ❍

Hearing top-grade quartet violinists tackle these flavoured educational duos is a delight, though not an original one. (The Emerson's co-leaders Eugene Drucker and Philip Setzer have already done likewise, albeit to quite different effect.) All, or virtually all, is revealed right from the opening 'Transylvanian Dance' where the newcomers' phrasing and rhythm are appropriately unbuttoned, their combined tone full but unforced. (Note: Keller and Pilz actually start at the end with Duo 'No 44'.) Bartók's original plan had been to place the easiest pieces first, then gradually pile on the challenges as the series progressed. However, for concert purposes he sanctioned the idea of not playing them in order.

Their chosen sequence is very well planned. The interpretative axis centres principally on harmony and rhythm, and characterisation is always vivid. In general the slower pieces leave the strongest impression: that's where these players harbour their most personal responses, but then the slowest pieces probably are the best. Though Sándor Végh's accounts with Alberto Lysy are rather more earthy, the advantage of this version is that it seems to have been conceived with continuous listening in mind: the ear never tires.

It would be easy to pigeonhole this set as veering in the general direction of the Végh's Bartók, just as the Keller's Bartók quartet cycle does, then make a parallel observation of Drucker and Setzer as representing the less stylised manner of their own Emerson Quartet. Which would be fairly accurate and explain a preference for this disc, where an extra shot of interpretative re-creativeness ultimately wins the day. The sound quality is spacious and pleasingly full bodied.

Piano Works

For Children, Sz42. The First Term at the Piano, Sz53. 15 Hungarian Peasant Songs, Sz71. Three Hungarian Folksongs from the Csík District, Sz35a. Hungarian Folktunes, Sz66. Eight Improvisations on Hungarian Peasant Songs, Sz74. Three Rondos on (Slovak) Folktunes, Sz84. Romanian Christmas Carols, Sz57. Six Romanian Folkdances, Sz56. Two Romanian Dances, Sz43. Suite, Sz62, with original Andante. Piano Sonata, Sz80. Sonatina, Sz55. 14 Bagatelles, Sz38. Four Dirges, Sz45. Petite Suite, Sz105. Violin Duos, Sz98 (arr Sándor) – No 1, Teasing Song; No 17, Marching Song; No 35, Ruthenian kolomejka; No 42, Arabian Song; No 44, Transylvanian Dance. 10 Easy Pieces, Sz39. Allegro barbaro, Sz49. Out of doors, Sz81. Seven Sketches, Sz44. Two Elegies, Sz41. Three Burlesques, Sz47. Nine Little Pieces, Sz82. Three

Studies, Sz72
György Sándor pf
Sony Classical ④ SB4K87949 (287' · DDD)   Ⓑ❍

There can't be many pianists on the current circuit whose fund of experience extends to working with a major 20th-century master; but of those still recording, György Sándor must surely take pride of place. Sándor prepared Bartók's first two piano concertos under the composer's guidance and gave the world premières of the Third Concerto and the piano version of the Dance Suite. The present collection is Sándor's second survey of Bartók's piano music and contains all the major works apart from Mikrokosmos.

Many of these performances are exceptionally fine, even though the passage of time has witnessed something of a reduction in Sándor's pianistic powers, mostly where maximum stamina and high velocity fingerwork are required (as in the first Burlesque). However, you may be astonished at the heft, energy and puckish humour of Sándor's 1994 recording of the Piano Sonata, a more characterful rendition than its predecessor, with a particularly brilliant account of the folkish Allegro molto finale. The Allegro barbaro is similarly 'on the beam', while Sándor brings a cordial warmth to the various collections of ethnic pieces, the Romanian Christmas Carols especially.

His phrasing, rubato, expressive nuancing, attention to counterpoint and command of tone suggest the touch of a master, while his imagination relishes the exploratory nature of the Improvisations, Bagatelles and Miraculous Mandarin-style Studies. Sándor connects with all the music's abundant qualities: harmonic or rhythmic innovation, powerful emotion, humour, introspection, ethnic variety and the scope and complexity of Bartók's piano writing in general. Intuitive interpreters, especially those who knew and understand the composers they perform, are becoming a rare breed. In that respect alone, Sándor's Bartók deserves an honoured place in every serious CD collection of 20th-century piano music.

Bartók Kossuth, Sz21 – Funeral March. Mikrokosmos, Book 6, Sz107 – Dance in Bulgarian rhythm Nos 1-6. Three Rondos on Slovak Folktunes, Sz84. Seven Sketches, Sz44 **D Scarlatti** Keyboard Sonatas – Kk3; Kk9; Kk17; Kk58; Kk82; Kk135; Kk159; Kk380; Kk430; Kk420; Kk491
Dejan Lazic pf
Channel Classics ⌖ CCSSA23407 (79' · DDD)   Ⓕ

An exciting idea this…and it works! After all, Bartók greatly admired Scarlatti: he even recorded a couple of his sonatas. Both composers were innovators and combined a strong feeling for rhythm with an audacious sense of harmony.

Dejan Lazic wastes no time in establishing his credentials as a Scarlatti player. He opens the programme with a somewhat militaristic-sounding C major piece, K420, and already it's all there – the light, resilient touch, the crisp (and often free) approach to rhythm, nimble passagework and an obvious appreciation of subsidiary material. The last of that particular Scarlatti trio, a filigree piece in F, segues beautifully with the first of Bartók's *Three Rondos on Slovak Folktunes* (in C), the principal common denominator here, as so often elsewhere, the dance element.

Lazic has a very individual Bartók style; he's no literalist, as illustrated by his emphatic handling of the syncopated main motif of the last Rondo. Again the segue from Bartók (third Rondo) to Scarlatti (the processional D major Sonata, K491) is imaginative, though the switch from the gaily skipping D major Sonata (K159) to the first of Bartók's haunting *Seven Sketches* is more surprising. Lazic personalises the sequence in a most compelling way. He then gently breaks their spell with Scarlatti's D minor ('Pastoral') and interestingly sandwiches a dramatic piano version (Bartók's own) of the *Kossuth* Funeral March between lively sonatas in F major and A minor. Perhaps the most effective segue finds the flamenco strumming of Scarlatti's K135 (E major) acting as a prelude to the first of six *Dances in Bulgarian Rhythm* which conclude Bartók's Mikrokosmos. Here Lazic underlines the individual character of each dance, tenderising the fourth (a tribute to Gershwin) with expressive arpeggios, and focusing the fifth's dizzying rhythmic ambiguities.

You reach the journey's end eager to start all over again – or maybe work out another Scarlatti-Bartók sequence. The potential is limitless and let's hope that that this first volume of a series called 'Liaisons' doesn't preclude a second Scarlatti-Bartók sequence.

Additional recommendation

Solo piano works etc   **H**
Bartók *pf*
Pearl mono GEMMCD9166 (69' · ADD)   Ⓜ
    This Bartók-plays-Bartók compilation offers full-bodied transfers of some fascinating commercial recordings, including the first *Romanian Dances*, *Allegro barbaro* and Liszt's 'Sursum corda'.

Duke Bluebeard's Castle

John Tomlinson *bass* Bluebeard **Anne Sofie von Otter** *mez* Judith **Sándor Elès** *spkr* Berlin **Philharmonic Orchestra / Bernard Haitink**
EMI 556162-2 (63' · DDD · N/T/t)   Ⓕ**OOⒹ**

Bernard Haitink's poetic axis is vividly anticipated in the rarely recorded spoken prologue where Sándor Elès bids us search beneath the story's surface. Elès's timing and his sensitivity to word-colouring and the rhythmic inflexions of his native language greet the Gothic imagery of Bartók's solemn opening bars. The main characters soon establish very definite personalities, Bluebeard/Tomlinson as commanding, inscrutable and just a little arrogant, von Otter/ Judith as profoundly frightened but filled with curiosity. Haitink and the Berlin Philharmonic

paint a rich aural backdrop that's neither too slow nor overly lugubrious and that shows due appreciation of Bartók's seamless scoring, especially in terms of the woodwind. The disembodied sighs that greet Judith's violent hammering on the first door mark a momentary retreat from the Philharmonie's ambient acoustic (or so it seems) and in so doing suggest – quite appropriately – a chilling 'world beyond'. Judith's shock as she recoils in horror is conveyed in clipped, halting tones by von Otter (note too how seductively she manipulates Bluebeard into opening the first door).

Beyond the expansive introduction come the doors themselves, and here too Haitink balances the 'outer' and 'inner' aspects of Bartók's score to perfection – whether in the torture chamber, the glowing textures of 'The Secret Garden' or the Brucknerian expanses of the fifth door, 'Bluebeard's Kingdom' (the opera's structural apex), launched here on a series of epic *crescendos*. Von Otter's stunned responses suggest lonely disorientation within a vast space, whereas the sullenness of the 'Lake of Tears' prompts an exquisite blending of instrumental timbres, most particularly between brass and woodwind. Haitink draws an aching curve to the string writing, but when Judith rushes panic-stricken towards the seventh door, fearful of Bluebeard's secret murders, he effects a gradual but cumulatively thrilling *accelerando*. The internment itself is devastating, while Bluebeard's helpless retreat marks a slow journey back to the questioning void. Recording live can have its pitfalls, but here the atmosphere is electric, the grasp of Bartók's sombre tone-painting – whether sung or played – absolute.

EMI's engineering favours a full sound stage rather than picking out specific instrumental details, but the overall effect remains comprehensively satisfying.

Duke Bluebeard's Castle
Gustáv Beláček *bass* Duke Bluebeard
Andrea Meláth *mez* Judith
Bournemouth Symphony Orchestra / Marin Alsop
Naxos 8 660928 (58' · DDD)   Ⓢ**Ⓓ**

Duke Bluebeard's Castle is in many ways the ideal opera for CD; stage action is less of the essence than a highly descriptive orchestral score, and the 'plot' provides as much mental as visual stimulation. There are plenty of good *Bluebeards* on disc, and this new Naxos production is a welcome addition to the ranks. Imaginative moments are in generous supply. For example, Judith's blasé, low-key response to Bluebeard's pride as he throws open the Castle's fifth door, her implied rolling eyes at his 'spacious country', a passage thrillingly prepared by Marin Alsop and the orchestra. There's the feverish orchestral build-up approaching the sixth door, the lake of tears, and at the moment when Judith asks Bluebeard to tell her who he had loved before her – less 'asks' in this context than dares to enquire in the thrall of a terrible fear. Andrea Meláth sounds stunned, even terror-stricken, and Alsop draws a sickly-grey backdrop from her Bournemouth players. Best of all is the faltering path to the seventh door: 'I have guessed your secret,' cries Judith, and Alsop charts the tortuous course of this terrible moment to perfection. In context it proves the drama's high-point, more overwhelming in fact than the internment which isn't quite as effective as on some rivals.

Less impressive is Meláth's response to the 'mountains of gold' beyond the third door. The voices here are good but uneven, Meláth often impressive in the higher registers but lacking in colour (and tonal quality) at mid-range and with a tendency to excessive vibrato. Gustáv Beláček's Bluebeard is theatrically characterful but vocally grey, though his animated singing of the opening sequence is appealing. Alsop has the measure of the score. Certainly this *Bluebeard* is more than good enough to introduce a great and compelling work but if pressured to choose while ignoring of the price-tag John Tomlinson's Bluebeard under Bernard Haitink (see above) is still the one to go for.

Duke Bluebeard's Castle (sung in English)
John Tomlinson bar Duke Bluebeard
Sally Burgess mez Judith
Opera North Orchestra / Richard Farnes
Chandos CHAN3133 (63' · DDD)   ⓕⒹ▶

This recording grew from performances by Opera North but the absence of a visual element hardly matters. Nor in this instance does the language issue either. *Bluebeard* is perfect food for the mind's theatre, the tale of a man alone (as John Tomlinson reminds us in the cryptic spoken prologue) and while under normal circumstances Hungarian would win over any translation, here vivid vocal acting and clarity of diction more than compensate. And there's Farnes's conducting, which even from as early as the introduction counters the pervading darkness with deftly pointed woodwind phrases and a light, expressive curve to the string lines.

Tomlinson's Bluebeard is godlike, cautioning and doleful, the voice hugely resonant. Sally Burgess sounds old enough to know better than to stray thoughtlessly from her father's home. When Judith first views the castle's interior she sounds suitably tremulous and awestruck, though when she blurts out the words 'tell me why the doors are bolted?' an air of petulance spells trouble: her command to 'open!' cues forceful thwacks on timps and bass drum. And so the drama unfolds, Burgess's Judith, shrewish and fatally curious, Tomlinson's Bluebeard, inwardly tortured but fired by Judith's dark beauty. The instruments of torture, the armaments, mountains of gold, tender flowers and spacious kingdom, all are graphically tone-painted, Farnes delivering with distinction every time – though when Burgess gasps at the kingdom newly revealed she keeps her high C fairly short. Tomlinson's most sensitive moment, as so often with him in this work, comes when he

recalls his former wives, and Farnes's comes at the 'lake of tears', the perfect dovetailing of winds and strings, mournful but also extremely beautiful. The later climactic moments are delivered with enormous power, the sum effect very moving.

For a thoroughly sympathetic, theatrically effective English-language *Bluebeard's Castle*, this new release is about as good as it's likely to get.

Additional recommendation

Duke Bluebeard's Castle
Berry bass-bar Bluebeard **Ludwig** mez Judith **LSO / Kertész**
Decca Legends download 466 377-2DM (59' · ADD · T/t) Ⓜ❶▶
> Recorded in 1965, the husband-and-wife team of Walter Berry and Christa Ludwig convey more the sense of a woman discovering sinister aspects of the man she loves than an inquisitive shrew intent on plundering Bluebeard's every secret.

Sir Arnold Bax   British 1883-1953

Bax studied at the Royal College of Music, London, (1900-1905). After discovering the poetry of Yeats, with which he was deeply impressed, he strongly identified with Irish Celtic culture. Drawing on many sources (Strauss, Debussy, Ravel, Elgar) he created a style of luxuriant chromatic harmony, rich ornament and broad melody, notably deployed in his tone poems The Garden of Fand *(1916),* November Woods *(1917) and* Tintagel *(1919). Other important works of this period include his First Quartet (1918) and Second Piano Sonata (1919). In the 1920s his music became clearer in outline and more contrapuntal, though without losing its wide range of harmonic resource: Sibelius became an influence. His main works were now symphonies, seven written 1922-39, though he remained a prolific composer in all non-theatrical genres. In 1942 he was made Master of the King's Music, after which he composed little.*
GROVEmusic

Symphonic Variations

Symphonic Variations. Concertante for Piano (Left Hand) and Orchestra
Ashley Wass pf
Bournemouth Symphony Orchestra / James Judd
Naxos 8 570774 (68' · DDD)   Ⓢ❶❶▶

Composed between 1916 and 1918, the *Symphonic Variations* for piano and orchestra bear a dedication to Bax's muse and lover, Harriet Cohen. It's an expansive and highly virtuoso work in two parts, whose six sections are apportioned titles ('The Temple' being the most eye-catching) that tantalisingly suggest some underlying programme. Borrowings from Bax's own First Violin Sonata and (more crucially) his 1916 setting of George 'AE' Russell's poem *Parting*, add a further layer of autobiographical intrigue. Best to sit back and let the piece weave its uniquely potent spell, for it contains page after page as raptly beautiful and ecstatically sensuous as even Bax ever conceived.

James Judd keeps a firm hand on the structural and motivic tiller and there's no disputing that Ashley Wass is the most stylish, characterful and charismatic of the three soloists to have recorded the work: the way he shapes the spellbinding opening paragraph of the final section ('Triumph', one of Bax's symphonic epilogues in all but name) is sheer magic and betokens a true poet of the keyboard.

The 1949 *Concertante*, written (again) for Harriet Cohen after she had lost the use of her right hand in a domestic accident, is smaller fry – but it can boast an absolute gem of a slow movement. Again, the performance is a very persuasive one. A hearty welcome for this conspicuously successful pairing.

Complete symphonies

Symphonies Nos 1-7. Rogue's Comedy Overture. Tintagel
BBC Philharmonic Orchestra / Vernon Handley
Chandos ⑤ CHAN10122 (5 hours 55' · DDD)
Includes an interview with Vernon Handley by Andrew McGregor ⓜ❶❶❶↪

This Bax symphony cycle comes under the baton of the composer's doughtiest champion, and superlatives are in order. Even seasoned Baxians will be startled by the propulsive vigour and sinewy strength of these performances.

In its uncompromising thrust and snarling tragedy, Handley's account of the First Symphony packs an almighty punch, but also quarries great detail from Bax's darkly opulent orchestration. In the closing pages the motto theme's sanguine tread is soon snuffed out, as the shredded nerve-ends of this music are exposed as never before.

The wild and brooding Second generates less heady sensuality than either the Thomson or Myer Fredman's pioneering Lyrita version, but there's ample compensation in the chaste beauty and enviable authority of Handley's conception. Scrupulous attention is paid to thematic unity and the many contrapuntal and harmonic felicities that bind together the progress of this extraordinary canvas. The BBC Philharmonic respond with such eager application that it's easy to forgive some slight loss of composure in the build-up to the cataclysmic pinnacle.

There can be no reservations about the Third, an interpretation that's by far the finest since Barbirolli's 1943-4 world première recording with the Hallé. Bax's iridescent textures shimmer and glow, bass lines stalk with reassuring logic and solidity, and these exemplary artists distil all the poetry and mystery in the ravishing slow movement and epilogue. Deeply moving is Handley's tender, unforced handling of the first movement's *Lento moderato* secondary material.

Handley's previous recording of the Fourth is comprehensively outflanked by this bracing remake. If you've ever regarded the Fourth as something of a loose-limbed interloper in the Bax canon, this will make you think again, such is the muscular rigour Handley locates in this lovable creation. At the same time, there's playful affection, rhythmic bite and pagan splendour of both outer movements.

Revelations abound, too, in the Fifth. Handley plots a superbly inevitable course through the first movement. At the start of the slow movement the glinting brilliance and sheen of the orchestral playing take the breath away, as does the richness of the lower strings in the first subject. The finale is stunning, its whirlwind *Allegro* a veritable bevy of cackling demons.

The bass ostinato that launches the Sixth picks up where the epilogue of the Fifth left off. A taut course is steered through this stormy first movement, though in some ways Norman Del Mar's recording got closer still to the essence of Bax's driven inspiration. The succeeding *Lento* has a gentle radiance that's very affecting. However, it's in the innovatory finale where Handley pulls ahead of the competition, cannily keeping some power in reserve, and locating a transcendental wonder in the epilogue.

Handley's Seventh is wonderfully wise and characterful music-making, the first movement in particular sounding for all the world as if it was set down in a single take. There's bags of temperament about the performance, as well as an entrancing freedom, flexibility and purposefulness that proclaim an intimate knowledge of and total trust in the composer's intentions. The BBC Philharmonic respond with unflagging spirit and tremendous body of tone.

A majestic *Tintagel* and rollicking account of the 1936 *Rogue's Comedy Overture* complete the feast. Disc 5 houses an hour-long conversation about Bax the symphonist between the conductor and Andrew McGregor. Stephen Rinker's engineering does fabulous justice to Bax's imaginative and individual orchestration, particularly towards the lower end of the spectrum. The set is magnificent; its insights copious.

Symphonies – selected

Symphony No 2. November Woods
Royal Scottish National Orchestra / David Lloyd-Jones
Naxos 8 554093 (57' · DDD) Ⓢ❶↪

From the grinding dissonances at the outset through to the inconsolable coda, Lloyd-Jones and his orchestra bring out the unremitting toughness of Bax's uncompromising, breathtakingly scored Second Symphony; even the gorgeous secondary material in the first movement offers an occasional shaft of pale, wintry sunlight. It helps, too, that Lloyd-Jones has clearly thought hard about the task in hand. How lucidly, for example, he expounds the arresting introduction, where the symphony's main building-blocks are laid out before us, and how well he brings out the distinctive tenor of Bax's highly imaginative writing for low wind and brass. The Scottish brass have a field-day.

Lloyd-Jones proves an equally clear-sighted navigator through the storm-buffeted landscape of *November Woods*, for many people, Bax's greatest tone-poem. Thoroughly refreshing in its enthusiasm and exhilarating sense of orchestral spectacle, this recording has a physical impact and emotional involvement that genuinely compel. A veritable blockbuster.

Symphonies – No 2ª; No 5ᵇ
London Philharmonic Orchestra / ªMyer Fredman, ᵇRaymond Leppard
Lyrita SRCD233 (78' · ADD)

Here's a majestic (and long overdue) return to currency for two cornerstones of the Lyrita catalogue. The LPO respond with all the edge-of-seat excitement of new discovery, particularly so in the turbulent Second Symphony, where an impassioned and inspired Myer Fredman secures playing of terrific fire, dedication and spontaneity. If Raymond Leppard's account of the Fifth operates at a slightly lower voltage, his cannily paced, sensitive and meticulously prepared reading none the less remains a most distinguished contribution to the Bax discography.

Both these vintage displays were marvellously engineered by Decca personnel working within the benign acoustic of Walthamstow Town Hall. The eloquent original sleeve-notes by Lewis Foreman and Robert Layton have sensibly been retained, and Simon Gibson's remasterings are first class (No 2 sounding a tad more clinical than it did on LP). A hugely rewarding reissue.

Symphony No 3. The Happy Forest
Royal Scottish National Orchestra / David Lloyd-Jones
Naxos 8 553608 (54' · DDD)

Dedicated to Sir Henry Wood, Bax's Symphony No 3 boasts arguably the richest store of memorable melodic invention to be found in any of the composer's cycle of seven, culminating in an inspired epilogue of wondrous, jaw-dropping beauty. David Lloyd-Jones's clear-headed, purposeful conducting of this intoxicating repertoire is the most judiciously paced and satisfyingly cogent Bax Third we've had since Barbirolli's pioneering 1943-4 Hallé account. Moreover, not only does Lloyd-Jones keep a firm hand on the tiller, he also draws some enthusiastic playing from the RSNO, which responds throughout with commendable polish and keen application.

Finely poised, affectingly full-throated solo work from principal horn and trumpet illuminates the progress of the ensuing Lento, whose ravishing landscape Lloyd-Jones surveys in less lingering fashion than either Barbirolli or Thomson. The first half of the finale, too, is a great success, Lloyd-Jones negotiating the

fiendish twists and turns dictated by Bax's copious tempo markings with impressive aplomb. Only in the epilogue do you feel a need for a touch more rapt poetry. Tim Handley's excellently balanced recording is rich and refined, though the perspective is perhaps fractionally closer than ideal for The Happy Forest, which receives a performance of bounding vigour, gleeful mischief and muscular fibre; just that last, crucial drop of enchantment remains elusive. No matter, a disc not to be missed.

Symphony No 4. Nympholept.
Overture to a Picaresque Comedy
Royal Scottish National Orchestra / David Lloyd-Jones
Naxos 8 555343 (65' · DDD)

David Lloyd-Jones and the RSNO continue their stimulating championship of Bax with this extremely persuasive account of the Fourth Symphony. It's at once the most exuberantly inventive and most colourful of the cycle (the instrumentation includes six horns and organ). Lloyd-Jones steers a tauter, more athletic course through the eventful first movement than his *Gramophone* Award-winning rival (Bryden Thomson on Chandos), yet there's no want of playful affection, and the orchestral playing satisfyingly combines polish and eagerness. In the gorgeous central *Lento moderato* Lloyd-Jones perceptively evokes a bracing, northerly chill wafting across Bax's dappled seascape. The unashamedly affirmative finale is a great success, its festive pomp and twinkling sense of fun conveyed with personable panache and swagger. If the symphony's jubilant closing pages reverberate in Thomson's version with just that crucial bit of extra weight and splendour in Belfast's Ulster Hall, Tim Handley's expert sound and balance do ample justice to Bax's distinctive scoring and his writing for low woodwind in particular. The *Overture to a Picaresque Comedy* makes an apt and boisterous curtain-raiser, Lloyd-Jones's rip-roaring rendering knocking Thomson's limp LPO version into a cocked hat. *Nympholept* could hardly form a greater contrast: a ravishing nature-poem in Bax's most enchanted Celtic vein. Again, this sensitive account is far preferable to Thomson's curiously laboured conception. Altogether a superb release.

Symphony No 5.
The Tale the Pine Trees Knew
Royal Scottish National Orchestra / David Lloyd-Jones
Naxos 8 554509 (58' · DDD)

The Fifth is perhaps the most characteristic of Bax's symphonies. For all the music's powerful range of emotion and its seemingly bewildering profusion of material and countless moments of bewitching beauty, its resourceful symphonic processes aren't easy to assimilate on first hearing. Lloyd-Jones's intelligent and purposeful direction pays handsome dividends, and a well-drilled RSNO responds with sensitivity and enthusiasm. Lloyd-Jones excels in the opening movement's tightly knit canvas, its epic ambition matched by a compelling sense of momentum, architectural grandeur and organic 'wholeness'. In the slow movement Lloyd-Jones paints a chillier, more troubled landscape than does Bryden Thomson (Chandos). The finale's main *Allegro* sets out with gleeful dash and a fine rhythmic snap to its heels. Lloyd-Jones judges that tricky, crisis-ridden transition into the epilogue well, and the apotheosis is a hard-won, grudging victory. The 1931 tone-poem *The Tale the Pine Trees Knew* makes an ideal bedfellow, foreshadowing as it does the bracingly 'northern' (to quote the composer) demeanour of the Fifth. Lloyd-Jones's comparatively extrovert treatment of the work's exultant final climax works perfectly convincingly within the context of his overall conception. Another eminently truthful, judiciously balanced sound picture from producer/engineer Tim Handley.

Symphony No 6[a]. Irish Landscape[b]. Overture to Adventure[c]. Rogue's Comedy Overture[c]. Overture: Work in Progress[c]
[a]**New Philharmonia Orchestra / Norman Del Mar**;
[bc]**Royal Philharmonic Orchestra / Vernon Handley**
Lyrita SRCD296 (76' · [ab]ADD/DDD) Ⓕ❶❶🅑▸

Here's yet another valuable reissue from Lyrita's vaults. Norman Del Mar's pioneering 1966 account of Bax's Sixth Symphony has held up extremely well. Occupying an interpretative middle ground between the thrilling thrust and narrative coherence of Vernon Handley's much-praised recording (part of his *Gramophone* Award-winning cycle – see page 115) and the colourfully expressive languor of Bryden Thomson's, Del Mar may be the most satisfying of the lot. Like Handley, Del Mar makes sense of the symphony's unusual structure (the finale is a fierce scherzo positioned between a dark introduction and elegiac epilogue) while allowing one to savour more of the details. The result remains the most emotionally potent on disc. Note, for instance, how warmly the New Philharmonia strings sing their opening cantilena at the beginning of the slow movement. And although he is not as graceful as Handley, Del Mar brings far more character and incident to the finale's scherzo section.

The CD is rounded out with shorter works performed by Handley and the RPO, including a succinctly passionate, though somewhat rough-edged, reading of the atmospheric *Irish Landscape* (1913). The conductor's recording of the *Rogue's Comedy Overture* (1936), on the above-mentioned Chandos set, is slightly more frisky than this one – but only slightly. And while neither the *Overture to Adventure* (1936) nor the *Overture: Work in Progress* (1943) is top-drawer Bax, both are attractively vivacious and dispatched with élan.

Symphony No 6. Into the Twilight. Summer Music
Royal Scottish National Orchestra / David Lloyd-Jones
Naxos 8 557144 (58' · DDD) Ⓢ❶🅑▸

David Lloyd-Jones's Bax series goes from strength to strength with this clear-headed interpretation of the exhilarating Sixth Symphony (arguably the last work to show the composer at creative white heat).

Lloyd-Jones rides the tempest of the opening movement with particular success, while still allowing himself plenty of expressive leeway for the ravishing secondary material. In the central *Lento* he paints a bleakly beautiful, snow-flecked landscape. As for the ambitious finale (a *tour de force* of structural innovation and thematic integration), the conductor steers a superbly confident course, and the RSNO respond with unflagging spirit and no mean skill.

Both Lloyd-Jones's fill-ups are sensitively done, although *Into the Twilight* doesn't equal the fragrant beauty and haunting allure of Thomson's intoxicating Ulster version. Unfortunately, the sound, while enormously vivid and wide ranging, is neither quite as natural in timbre nor judiciously blended as on previous instalments (bigger *tutti*s tend towards an aggressive blur). None the less, a firm recommendation.

Additional recommendations

Symphony No 3
Coupled with: Violin Concerto 🄷
Kersey *vn* **Hallé Orchestra / Barbirolli; BBC Symphony Orchestra / Boult**
Dutton Laboratories Epoch CDLX7111 (73' · ADD)
Recorded 1943-4 Ⓜ❶
Barbirolli's recording of Bax's Third was the first of any Bax symphony and is a spellbinding achievement. No account on disc since can match it for authority and depth of feeling. The transfer boasts remarkable body and miraculously quiet surfaces.

Tone Poems

In Memoriam. Concertante for Piano (Left-Hand) and Orchestra[a]. The Bard of the Dimbovitza[b]
[b]**Jean Rigby** *mez* [a]**Margaret Fingerhut** *pf*
BBC Philharmonic Orchestra / Vernon Handley
Chandos CHAN9715 (77' · DDD) Ⓕ❶❶🅑▸

The glorious tune that dominates the 1916 tone-poem *In Memoriam* will be familiar to many Bax enthusiasts from its use in his 1948 film score for David Lean's *Oliver Twist*, and to hear it in its original surroundings is both a moving and thrilling experience. It had long been assumed that the 32-year-old composer never got round to scoring this deeply felt elegy so it's pleasing to find that Vernon Handley and the BBC Philharmonic do full justice to its opulent yet iridescent sound world, with its strong echoes of *The Garden of Fand* and *Nympholept*.

The *Concertante* for left-hand piano and orchestra, written for Harriet Cohen after a domestic accident had disabled her right hand, isn't top-drawer Bax, but remains a most appealing creation, with a central *Moderato tranquillo* in the composer's sweetest lyrical vein. Margaret Fingerhut is a deft, sympathetic soloist.

The five orchestral songs that make up *The Bard of the Dimbovitza*, setting poems allegedly based on Romanian folk-songs, contain not a hint of local colour but are purest Bax, the harmonic idiom and overall mood strikingly similar to his *Enchanted Summer*. Jean Rigby vividly characterises the dialogue in the last two songs ('My girdle I hung on a tree-top tall' and 'Spinning Song'), while bringing plenty of drama to the almost operatic scena that's 'The Well of Tears'. Some typically lustrous Chandos engineering adorns this valuable triptych of recorded premières, and the issue as a whole deserves the heartiest of welcomes.

The Garden of Fand. In the Faery Hills. November Woods. Sinfonietta
BBC Philharmonic Orchestra / Vernon Handley
Chandos CHAN10362 (76' · DDD)　　　Ⓕ🅑➔

In the Faery Hills and *The Garden of Fand* are among Bax's loveliest and most loveable creations, and though the windswept *November Woods* is far less tuneful, its emotional undercurrents run unfathomably deep. Bryden Thomson's shimmering, sensuous interpretations of these scores, recorded for Chandos some 20 years ago, laid bare the music's Impressionist roots; Vernon Handley (in an encore to his *Gramophone* Award-winning set of Bax's symphonies – see page 115) takes a tougher, more vigorous view. The only place he's notably slower than Thomson is in *November Woods*, yet how much darker and more ominous are the leaden skies that Handley paints. Indeed, even in such sensitive hands as Boult's, some of the stormier passages sound rather like film music, while Handley's deliberate focus on motivic clarity brings out a Wagnerian grandeur and gravity that strengthen the work's narrative backbone.

In *The Garden of Fand* and *In the Faery Hills* Handley adopts brisk tempi, occasionally pushing the music into a kind of giddy ecstasy that makes Thomson's fragrant, graceful readings sound downright languorous. If only the BBC Philharmonic were as flatteringly recorded as Thomson's Ulster Orchestra or, for that matter, the RSNO in David Lloyd-Jones's superb Naxos cycle. Lloyd-Jones's dynamic direction is similar in spirit to Handley's, in fact, and almost as arrestingly characterised – but not quite. This restless, syncopated score may not be top-drawer Bax but the Manchester musicians play it with the fervour of true believers.

Three Northern Ballads. Nympholept. Red Autumn. The Happy Forest. Into the Twilight
BBC Philharmonic Orchestra / Vernon Handley

Chandos CHAN10446 (77' · DDD)　　　Ⓕ🅞🅞🅑➔

Vernon Handley's revelatory Bax odyssey for Chandos comes up trumps once again with this generous feast spanning a quarter of a century from the enchanted Donegal glens of the youthful *Into the Twilight* (1908) to the rugged, wintry seascape of the Second *Northern Ballad*, completed in 1934. The latter is flanked by its roistering and plaintive predecessor and the darkly opulent *Prelude for a Solemn Occasion* (also known as *Northern Ballad* No 3). Whether Bax ever envisaged them as a self-contained entity is pure conjecture but, when presented with such swaggering commitment, they do comprise a deeply stirring and evocative sequence.

Elsewhere, *Into the Twilight* receives ideally radiant, heartfelt treatment – and you'll wait a lifetime to hear the ecstatic *Nympholept* better done. *The Happy Forest* raises the bar in its lightness of touch, iridescent glow and twinkling fun. The gale-tossed *Red Autumn* (more familiar in its two-piano garb) is clad in a remarkably idiomatic new orchestration by Graham Parlett.

So, gloriously assured music-making from first measure to last, and it's a relief to be able to report that Chandos's spectacularly ample and informative sound has all the natural bloom and crucial mid-range warmth that the companion disc (above) lacked. An unmissable treat.

Bax Tintagel **Rachmaninov** Symphony No 3, Op 44
London Philharmonic Orchestra / Osmo Vänskä
LPO LPO0036 (53' · DDD)
Recorded live at the Royal Festival Hall, London, on December 8, 2007　　　🅜🅞🅑➔

Vänskä's *Tintagel* has real fire in its belly allied to a surging momentum, and he uncovers many a fleck of exquisite detail within Bax's endlessly resourceful and wondrously evocative scoring. The ecstatic B major sunburst that heralds the second subject's unforgettable return has all the thrusting ardour one could wish for. The justly enthusiastic applause bursts in somewhat too precipitately for comfort.

The Rachmaninov (complete with exposition repeat in the first movement) is just as involving, not quite as volatile or heart-on-sleeve as some but intensely refreshing all the same in its zestful swagger, scrupulous preparation, limpid beauty and concern for the bigger scheme (how shrewd of Vänskä to keep in reserve such a scintillating burst of energy for the headlong closing pages). The engineering does ample justice to some splendidly selfless and thoroughly invigorating music-making, though in the Bax you might need to crank up the volume a notch higher than usual. A strongly recommendable issue.

Additional recommendations

November Woods
Coupled with: Northern Ballad No 1. Mediterranean. The Garden of Fand. Tintagel

LPO / Boult
Lyrita SRCD231 (62' · ADD) Ⓕ Ⓓ▸
Boult's performance of this tone-poem is masterly and he generates a great deal of tension, atmosphere and drama.

The Truth about the Russian Dancers. From Dusk till Dawn
LPO / Thomson
Chandos CHAN10457X (67' · DDD) Ⓜ Ⓞ Ⓑ▸
Not top-drawer Bax, admittedly, but the LPO under Bryden Thomson relish both scores' undeniable period charm and they have been sumptuously served by Chandos. A really enjoyable disc.

Tintagel
Coupled with: **Vaughan Williams** Symphony No 5
Philharmonia Orchestra; London Symphony Orchestra / Barbirolli
EMI British Composers 565110-2 (54' · ADD) Ⓑ
Bax's rugged, wind-swept seascape finds Barbirolli in his element, and his reading is on the whole more passionately involving than either Boult's or Thomson's.

String Quartets

String Quartets Nos 1 & 2
Maggini Quartet (Laurence Jackson, David Angel vns Martin Outram va Michal Kaznowski vc)
Naxos 8 555282 (54' · DDD) Ⓢ Ⓓ▸

Had Dvořák written an *Irish* Quartet to sit alongside his delectable *American*, it might well have sounded like the start of Bax's First String Quartet. Completed in 1918, this is one of Bax's most endearing and approachable scores. The clean-cut opening *Allegretto semplice* positively beams with happiness, and it's succeeded by a wistfully intimate slow movement. The finale begins and finishes in a mood of pagan revelry, though there's time for a ravishing episode in Bax's sweetest lyrical vein, its indelible tune a close cousin to the folksong *The Fair Hills of Ireland*. The Second Quartet of 1924-5 proves an altogether tougher nut to crack. Conceived at the same time as the Second Symphony, it's a knotty, densely plotted creation, as harmonically daring as Bax ever ventured and demanding formidable concentration from performers and listeners alike.

The Maggini Quartet do Bax absolutely proud, their performances striking an ideal balance between urgent expression and purposeful clarity. Both rival readings on Chandos have considerable strengths, but the Maggini's scrupulously dedicated advocacy will captivate both seasoned Baxians and newcomers alike. An outstanding coupling in every way.

String Quartet No 3. Adagio ma non troppo, 'Cathaleen-ni-Hoolihan'. Lyrical Interlude for String Quintet[a]
Maggini Quartet (Laurence Jackson, David Angel vn Martin Outram va Michal Kaznowski vc) with

[a]**Garfield Jackson** va
Naxos 8 555953 (57' · DDD) Ⓢ Ⓞ Ⓞ Ⓑ▸

Bax composed the last of his three mature string quartets between May and September 1936, inscribing it to the Griller Quartet who gave the first performance on the BBC National Programme the following May. An appealing, cogently structured 37-minute work, it's cast (unusually for Bax) in four movements, the joyous first of which 'was probably influenced by the coming of spring in beautiful Kenmare' (to quote the composer's own descriptive notes in *The Radio Times*). An Irish flavour also permeates the bardic *Poco lento*, while the third movement's 'dreamy, remotely romantic' trio melody is eventually cleverly welded to the 'rather sinister and malicious' *scherzo* material. The vigorous finale builds up a fine head of steam and incorporates a wistful backward glance just before the close that's entirely characteristic of its creator.

The Maggini Quartet forge a well-paced and concentrated interpretation, playing with assurance, infectious rhythmic snap and heartwarming dedication. They are joined by violist Garfield Jackson for the haunting *Lyrical Interlude* from 1922 (a reworking of the slow movement from Bax's ambitious String Quintet of 1908), and there's another rarity in the shape of the lovely *Adagio ma non troppo* centrepiece from the 1903 String Quartet in E major that Bax orchestrated two years later as his first tone-poem, *Cathaleen-ni-Hoolihan*.

Throughout, the sound is faithful in timbre and the balance most musically judged.

Violin Sonatas

Violin Sonatas – in G minor; No 1 in E. Ballad. Legend
Robert Gibbs vn **Mary Mei-Loc Wu** pf
ASV CDDCA1127 (61' · DDD) Ⓕ

The First Sonata is a passionate, deeply personal outpouring, essayed here with rapt understanding and tender intimacy. The rival Chandos performance may exhibit rather more in the way of commanding projection and urgent expression, but these newcomers' keen poetic instincts are never in doubt. Both the *Legend* and *Ballad* date from the First World War years (of the broodingly elegiac *Legend* – much liked by Vaughan Williams, apparently – Bax later recalled to violinist May Harrison that it 'came straight out of the horror of that time'), whereas the single-movement Sonata in G minor is an amiable, confidently argued student effort from November 1901. Again, Gibbs and Wu lend consistently idiomatic and warm-hearted advocacy to this material. A very appealing collection, in short, and a mandatory purchase for confirmed Baxians.

Violin Sonatas – No 2 in D; No 3; [No 4] in F
Robert Gibbs vn **Mary Mei-Loc Wu** pf
ASV CDDCA1098 (72' · DDD) Ⓕ Ⓞ

Robert Gibbs may not command the projection or outsize personality of some of his more illustrious, globe-trotting colleagues, but his neat technique, soft-spoken eloquence and attractively husky tone give enormous pleasure, while Mary Mei-Loc Wu tenders ideally deft support. Theirs is a less 'public', more thoughtfully intimate reading of Bax's turbulent Second Sonata than either of their rivals', an approach well suited to this most autobiographical of Bax's utterances. Their reading of the Third Sonata exhibits similar interpretative and poetic insights. Completed in 1927, it's a two-movement work of strong appeal, comprising a wondrously beautiful *Moderato* in this composer's most wistfully Celtic vein and a dashing *Allegro* whose exuberantly dancing outer portions frame a more poignantly reflective central episode. Gibbs and Wu also do full justice to the F major Sonata, which Bax subsequently recast as his bewitching Nonet. The sound picture is beguilingly warm and the disc as a whole earns the heartiest of welcomes.

Violin Sonata No 2. Ballad for Violin and Piano. Legend for Violin and Piano. Allegro appassionato. Sonata in F.
Laurence Jackson *vn* **Ashley Wass** *pf*
Naxos 8 570094 (74' · DDD)   ⓢ🅑➔

Cast in four linked movements and held together by a motto theme which also appears in the 1917 tone-poem *November Woods*, Bax's storm-tossed Second Violin Sonata was conceived during the summer of 1915 at a time of great personal upheaval for the 31-year-old composer and comprehensively overhauled six years later. Be it in the seductive sway of the second movement (a ghostly waltz enigmatically entitled 'The Grey Dancer in the Twilight') or hair-raising final climax prior to the ecstatically serene epilogue, these dashingly poised newcomers give of their considerable best, with CBSO leader Laurence Jackson formidably secure in the solo part's more scarily vertiginous exploits. No one coming to this music for the first time will be left unstirred by its piercing beauty, urgency of expression and vaulting ambition.

In any case, what lifts this collection into the indispensable category are the spellbinding performances of the darkly smouldering *Legend* and *Ballad* from 1915 and 1916 respectively, as well as the *Allegro appassionato* in G minor (a likeable student effort from 1901) and unpublished F major Sonata of 1928 (which Bax subsequently recast as his captivating Nonet). The Potton Hall sound in these last four items (emanating from sessions a year after those for the Second Sonata) is particularly handsome and true, and the disc as a whole represents yet another 'must have' within this extensive series.

Viola Sonata

Legend. Viola Sonata. Concert Piece. Trio[a]
[a]**Laurence Jackson** *vn* **Martin Outram** *va*

Julian Rolton *pf*
Naxos 8 557784 (61' · DDD)   ⓢ🅑➔

Here is a stunningly coordinated reading of urgent drive, bold contrasts and edge-of-seat drama reminiscent of dedicatee Lionel Tertis's even fleeter 1929 recording with the composer and manages to knock more than four minutes off that of their transatlantic rivals. It's sensationally exciting in its way, but there's no escaping the fact that others convey the greater bardic poetry and affectionate warmth. Although a tad dry, Naxos's sound is accommodating.

Reservations evaporate in the flamboyant *Concert Piece* (1904) and wintry *Legend* from 1929, both convincingly done, and proceedings conclude with the 1906 Trio in one movement for piano, violin and viola. In his autobiography *Farewell, My Youth*, Bax witheringly refers to it as 'a derivative and formless farrago', but the 'Irish' skip some five minutes in is characteristic. This dashing performance has real fire in its belly and strikes me as every bit the equal of Naxos's own rival version (see below) from Robert Plane and colleagues where the viola part is assigned to the clarinet (an option authorised by the composer).

Don't let my minor niggles concerning the sonata deter you. Expertly annnotated by Lewis Foreman, here's a release that all Baxians should check out.

Clarinet Sonatas

Clarinet Sonatas[ad] – in E (1901); in D (1934). Folk-Tale[cd]. Piano Trio[abd]. Romance[ad]. Trio[abd]
[a]**Robert Plane** *cl* **Gould Piano Trio**
([b]Lucy Gould *vn* [c]Alice Neary *vc* [d]Benjamin Frith *pf*)
Naxos 8 557698 (77' · DDD)   ⓢ🅑➔

Bax's engaging Clarinet Sonata of 1934 has been lucky on disc, with distinguished versions from Janet Hilton, Emma Johnson and Michael Collins happily still adorning the catalogue. Robert Plane's irreproachably alert and stylish account with Benjamin Frith leaves a similarly delightful impression. Plane's timbre could hardly be more alluring and he strikes up a tangible rapport with Frith. The pleasures continue with the 1945-46 Piano Trio, Bax's final chamber offering, which finds him at his most economical and relaxed.

It gets a first-rate performance from the Gould Trio, who bring plenty of bite and sparkle to the rhythmically buoyant finale. In the wistful and brooding *Folk-Tale* (first performed in 1918) Alice Neary and Frith do full justice to what is an unexpectedly powerful eight-minute essay.

But what makes this generously timed Naxos CD essential listening are three world-premiere recordings. Both the one-movement Sonata in E and Romance for clarinet and piano date from 1901 (Bax's first year at the Royal Academy) and may well have been conceived as parts of a larger work. The 1906 'Trio in one movement for piano, violin and viola' was the first extended score Bax deemed worthy for publication, a decision he later regretted (he described it as a 'derivative and formless farrago'); it is performed here with the viola part taken by the clarinet, an option sanctioned by the composer.

Neither of the clarinet pieces is likely to set the world alight, whereas the fluent and predominantly extrovert 17-minute Trio contains tantalising glimpses of greater achievements to come. Enthusiasts can rest assured that these admirably agile and idiomatic performers give Bax's youthful inspiration every chance to shine; indeed, it's impossible to imagine a more convincing account of the Trio.

Chamber Works

Nonet. Oboe Quintet. Elegiac Trio. Clarinet Sonata. Harp Quintet
Nash Ensemble (Philippa Davies *fl* Gareth Hulse *ob* Michael Collins *cl* Marcia Crayford, Iris Juda, Elizabeth Wexler *vns* Roger Chase *va* Christopher van Kampen *vc* Duncan McTier *db* Skaila Kanga *hp* Ian Brown *pf*)
Hyperion CDA66807 (73' · DDD)   ⓕ**OO**

A truly first-rate modern recording of Bax's Nonet. What a bewitching creation it is, overflowing with invention and breathtakingly imaginative in its instrumental resource (the sounds created are often almost orchestral). Bax worked on the Nonet at the same time (1929-30) as he was composing his Third Symphony and there are striking similarities between the two. The Nash Ensemble gives a masterly, infinitely subtle reading.

The remainder of the disc brings comparable pleasure. The delightful Oboe Quintet (written for Leon Goossens in 1922) receives immensely characterful treatment, especially the jaunty, Irish-jig finale (such richly communicative playing). The same is true of the lovely Harp Quintet, essayed here with rapt intensity and delicious poise. In the hands of these stylish artists, the *Elegiac Trio* possesses a delicacy and poignancy that are really quite captivating. That just leaves the engaging Clarinet Sonata, a work that has fared well in the recording studio over the last few years. Suffice to report, Michael Collins and Ian Brown are compelling advocates, and theirs is a performance to set beside (if not supersede) all rivals. Beautiful sound throughout.

Octet. String Quintet. Concerto. Threnody and Scherzo. In Memoriam
Margaret Fingerhut *pf* **Academy of St Martin in the Fields Chamber Ensemble**
Chandos CHAN9602 (72' · DDD)   ⓕ**O**

This is a beautiful and enterprising collection of works by Bax. *In Memoriam* for cor anglais, harp and string quartet probably dates from 1917. It's subtitled 'An Irish Elegy'; like the *Elegiac Trio* from the same period, its poignant mood reflects Bax's despair at the tragic events of the Easter Rising. In the single-movement String Quintet

(completed in January 1933) he draws some luscious, almost orchestral sonorities from his chosen forces. Scored for horn, piano and string sextet, the 1934 Octet (labelled 'Serenade' on the short score) is a two-movement work of strong appeal and engaging charm: the magically evocative opening brings echoes of those unforgettable horn solos in the Third Symphony's central *Lento*, while the icy glitter of the piano part from 1'53" in the second-movement *Scherzo* momentarily conjures up the far-Northern landscape of *Winter Legends*.

The *Threnody and Scherzo* for bassoon, harp and string sextet of 1936 is perhaps less immediately striking. The writing is as fluent and accomplished as ever but the melodic material isn't as fresh as might have been wished. By contrast, the Concerto for flute, oboe, harp and string quartet is one of Bax's most likeable chamber offerings. This is a captivating transcription for septet of a Sonata for flute and harp from 1928 and proves an exquisite gem, its deft and joyous outer movements framing a lovely central 'Cavatina'. The sound is warm and transparent.

Elegiac Trio[a]. Fantasy Sonata[b]. Quintet for Harp and Strings[c]. Sonata for Flute and Harp[d]
Mobius ([ad]Lorna McGhee *fl* [c]Kanako Ito, [c]Philippe Honoré *vns* [abc]Ashan Pillai *va* [c]Martin Storey *vc* Alison Nicholls *hp*)
Naxos 8 554507 (65' · DDD)   Ⓢ**OO**➔

Mobius is a gifted young London-based ensemble of seven prize-winning instrumentalists from four different countries, and their scrupulously shaded, fervent playing betokens a very real empathy with this gorgeous repertoire. In both the *Elegiac Trio* and Harp Quintet these artists favour a more boldly etched, less delicately evanescent approach than that of the Nash Ensemble (which is perhaps marginally more successful in distilling the poignant heartache of two works indissolubly associated with the tragic events of the 1916 Easter Rising). Especially valuable is the impassioned rendering of the marvellous *Fantasy Sonata* for harp and viola of 1927. Certainly, harpist Alison Nicholls (a beguiling presence throughout) copes heroically with the daunting technical demands of Bax's writing (tailored for the virtuosity of the great Russian harpist, Maria Korchinska); moreover, she's splendidly partnered by violist Ashan Pillai. Likewise, the engagingly relaxed Sonata for Flute and Harp emerges with delightful freshness, its plangent central 'Cavatina' as haunting as ever. Sound and balance are just fine. Terrific value and strongly recommended.

Piano Sonatas

Piano Sonatas – No 1 in F sharp minor; No 2 in G. Burlesque. In a Vodka Shop. Nereid. Dream in exile
Ashley Wass *pf*
Naxos 8 557439 (77' · DDD)   Ⓢ**OOO**➔

Not only does this gifted young pianist possess a rock-solid technique and striking keyboard finesse, his penetrating accounts of both these large-scale, single-movement sonatas make you sit up and listen. So it is that in the bracing First Sonata (written in 1910 during Bax's sojourn in Russia and Ukraine) Ashley Wass finds the balance between epic and introspective. More than that, he brings out the music's brazen Slavic fervour with its echoes of Scriabin and Rachmaninov (the coda's pealing bells toll with magnificent cumulative impact). He paces its turbulent successor of 1919 with cogency and concentration. Even more than the magisterial John McCabe, Wass takes us on a genuine voyage of discovery: the control, sense of colour and dynamic range are remarkable, and his tone never hardens under pressure.

Of the four couplings, *Dream in Exile* stands out. The sound throughout is vividly truthful.

Songs

Far in a Western Brookland[b]. The Market Girl[b]. A Milking Sian[a]. The Song in the Twilight[a]. To Eire[b]. The White Peace[b]. A Celtic Song Cycle[a]. The Fairies[b]. Youth[b]. Parting[b]. A Lullaby[a]. Roundel[b]. When I was one and twenty[b]. The Enchanted Fiddle[b]. When We Are Lost[b]

[a]**Jean Rigby** *mez* [b]**Ian Partridge** *ten*
Michael Dussek *pf*
Dutton Laboratories Epoch CDLX7136 (78' · DDD) Ⓜ

With the exception of *The White Peace* (a favourite of John McCormack), Bax's songs have been largely and undeservedly neglected. Ian Partridge sings with his customary sensitivity and intelligence, responding with particular eloquence to the grateful melodic lines of *To Eire* (1910) and the yearningly ecstatic *Parting*. The latter appeared in the aftermath of the 1916 Easter Uprising, and its haunting strains are heard again in the epilogue of the Symphonic Variations completed two years later. Likewise, the opening phrase of the 1914 Chaucer-setting *Roundel* will already be familiar to listeners to the tone-poem *Nympholept*. Jean Rigby works wonders with the youthful *Celtic Song Cycle*, and imparts almost operatic scope to the quietly intense *Song in the Twilight*. She's impressive, too, in *A Lullaby*, a 1910 setting of one of Bax's own poems, conceived in the middle of an unrequited love-affair with a Ukrainian girl, Natalia Skarginska. Michael Dussek's accompaniments are a model of scrupulous musicality.

Antonio Bazzini   Italian 1818-1897

Italian violinist, composer and teacher. He was a pupil of a Brescian violinist, Faustino Camisani (Camesani); encouraged by Paganini, he began his concert career at an early age and became one of the most highly regarded artists of his time. Written in the classic forms of the German school Bazzini's chamber

works earned him a central place in the Italian instrumental renaissance of the 19th century.

GROVEmusic

Works for violin and piano

La ronde des lutins, Op 25. Trois morceaux lyriques, Op 41. Calabrese, Op 34 No 6. Le carillon d'Arras, Op 36. Deux morceaux de salon, Op 12. Deux grande études, Op 49. Trois morceaux en forme de sonate, Op 44
Chloë Hanslip *vn* **Caspar Frantz** *pf*
Naxos 8 570800 (71' · DDD)

Among 19th-century violinist/composers, Antonio Bazzini was probably the most successful in escaping from exclusive specialisation in the virtuoso repertoire. His compositions include operas, sacred music, orchestral works and chamber music, so it's rather sad that he should be remembered today by a single piece, the scintillating *Ronde des lutins* ('Dance of the Goblins'). Chloë Hanslip demonstrates most persuasively that, even among his violin showpieces, it isn't a one-off. The items in her recital may make for fairly undemanding listening, the idiom may not be strikingly original, but Bazzini has the knack of integrating post-Paganini virtuoso features into a romantic style that's sophisticated, subtle and tasteful. The *cantabile* items are very appealing – the central Romance in the *Trois morceaux en forme de sonate* could rival the ubiquitous Massenet *Méditation* were it to become better known – and the Op 49 Etudes are particularly interesting, the first a *moto perpetuo* with very original accented dissonances, the second a delightful scherzo with elegant double-stopping and lively cross accents, and an unexpectedly lyrical central section.

Hanslip certainly has the confidence and technique for this repertoire: more importantly, she's able to engage with each piece, bringing out its particular expressive character. For the Romance in Op 44, for instance, she produces a soft, sensuous tone, quite different from her sound in the plaintive, ornate Nocturne from Op 41. Caspar Frantz accompanies very stylishly throughout, and Hanslip's musical personality, graceful and with spontaneous verve, brings everything to life. It's lovely violin-playing!

Amy Beach   American 1867-1944

Amy Marcy Cheney Beach was born in New Hampshire in the United States. Musically precocious, she sang improvised harmony parts at the age of two, composed aged four, and began piano studies with her mother, Clara Imogene Marcy Cheney, at six, giving her first public recitals at seven. In 1885 she made her piano debut with the Boston Symphony. That same year she married Dr Henry Beach, a Harvard professor and amateur musician. In accordance with his wishes, she limited her public appearances and concen-

trated on composition until after his death in 1910.

Beach compsed works in many genres, including a Mass, a symphony, a piano concerto, and works for chamber ensembles, piano, mixed chorus, and solo voice. Her 30 works for women's chorus, including several cantatas, are well-crafted in a Romantic idiom, always with intelligent text setting.

GROVEmusic

Piano Concerto

Piano Concerto in C sharp minor, Op45[a]. Symphony in E minor, Op 32, 'Gaelic'
[a]**Alan Feinberg** pf **Nashville Symphony Orchestra / Kenneth Schermerhorn**
Naxos 8 559139 (79' · DDD)   Ⓢ➔

Composed in 1898-9, Amy Beach's ambitious, singularly impressive Piano Concerto is at long last coming in from the cold. An expansively rhetorical Allegro moderato launches the work before a playful *perpetuum mobile* Scherzo and moody Largo (described by its creator as a 'dark, tragic lament'); the finale goes with a delightful swing. In fact, it's a rewarding achievement all round, full of brilliantly idiomatic solo writing (Beach was a virtuoso pianist herself and performed the work many times) and lent further autobiographical intrigue by its assimilation of thematic material from three early songs.

Alan Feinberg brings more charisma to bear than Joanne Polk on her rival account for Arabesque, without any loss of delicacy or poetry, and his collaboration with Kenneth Schermerhorn and the Nashville Symphony undoubtedly generates greater thrust and spontaneity. The recording, too, is more pleasingly spacious, if a little lacking in body.

Following the success of her 1889 Mass in E flat, Beach knew that she needed to produce a large-scale symphony to cement her reputation; it was the Boston premiere of Dvořák's *New World* that finally spurred her into action. Responding to the Czech master's exhortation that American composers should turn to spirituals, plantation songs and minstrel-show music for inspiration, Beach selected four Irish melodies of 'simple, rugged and unpretentious beauty', moulding any additional themes 'in the same idiom and spirit'.

That the *Gaelic* Symphony (1894-6) won golden opinions from the outset comes as no surprise, given its big heart, irresistible charm and confident progress. Schermerhorn and his eager Nashville band give a convincingly paced, tidy performance with real fire in its belly and plenty of character. A thoroughly enjoyable issue.

Sally Beamish   English b1956

English composer and viola player, active in Scotland. Though drawn to composition, she studied the violin and the viola at the RNCM and worked for around ten years as a viola player with several London ensembles. In 1986 she received her first professional commission, for Dances and Nocturnes; in 1989 she moved to Scotland where, aided by an Arts Council bursary, she began to concentrate on composition. She founded the Chamber Group of Scotland with James MacMillan and her husband Robert Irvine. Her distinctive music draws on many different sources. Motherhood has been an important inspiration

Viola Concerto No 2, 'The Seafarer'[a]. Whitescape. Sangsters
[a]**Tabea Zimmermann** va
Swedish Chamber Orchestra / Ola Rudner
BIS BIS-CD1241 (59' · DDD)   Ⓕ

From 1998 to 2002 Sally Beamish enjoyed a four-year dual residency with the Swedish and Scottish chamber orchestras. The compositional results included this trio of orchestral works, which are among her best: there's the kind of creative confidence and certainty, couched in unmistakable personal tones, which, in assured performances, well recorded, makes for a first-rate CD.

The common factor lies in the way all three works respond to the chilly essences of very northern landscapes. The earliest, *Whitescape* (2000), is particularly bold in suggesting the monstrous in nature (it has links with Beamish's Mary Shelley opera), and is also impressively direct in expression, regularly cutting back on tendencies to elaborate its material and setting its strong, stark climax in a forbidding but never merely austere context.

More impressively still, the Second Viola Concerto (2001) takes a fresh look at the genre's standard three-movement form. Beamish makes reference to an Anglo-Saxon poem which sets the travails of seafarers, aware of storms and the cries of birds, alongside visions of heavenly life after death. Against this background she charts a progression from brooding, rhapsodic material, within which quirky contrasts, percussion prominent, make highly effective incursions, towards a kind of repose – not exactly serene in spirit, but founded in rich, lucid harmony. This fine work has the added benefit of Tabea Zimmermann's marvellously characterful performance.

Sangsters (2002) is also rooted in a poem – a modern one in Scots – which shows how birds, seals and humans adapt to nature and celebrate their different worlds. The second of the three movements is marginally less characterful and cogent than the rest, but for the most part Beamish sustains the high level of invention and imagination which the disc as a whole embodies. No praise is too great for the excellence of the Swedish Chamber Orchestra and their conductor Ola Rudner: never has musical northern-ness seemed more inviting!

Ludwig van Beethoven

German 1770-1827

Beethoven studied first with his father, Johann, a singer and instrumentalist in the service of the Elector of Cologne at Bonn, but mainly with CG Neefe, court organist. At 11 he was able to deputise for Neefe; at 12 he had some music published. In 1787 he went to Vienna, but quickly returned on hearing that his mother was dying. Five years later he went back to Vienna, where he settled.

He studied first with Haydn, though there was some clash of temperaments, and also with Schenk, Albrechtsberger and Salieri. Until 1794 he was supported by the Elector at Bonn, but he found patrons among the music-loving Viennese aristocracy and soon enjoyed success as a piano virtuoso, playing at private houses or palaces rather than in public. His public début was in 1795; about the same time his first important publications appeared, three piano trios Op 1 and three piano sonatas Op 2. As a pianist, it was reported he had fire, brilliance and fantasy as well as depth of feeling. It is naturally in the piano sonatas, writing for his own instrument, that he is at his most original in this period; the Pathétique belongs to 1799, the Moonlight ('Sonata quasi una fantasia') to 1801, and these represent only the most obvious innovations in style and emotional content. These years also saw the composition of his first three piano concertos, first two symphonies and a set of six string quartets Op 18.

1802, however, was a year of crisis for Beethoven, with his realisation that the impaired hearing he had noticed for some time was incurable and sure to worsen. That autumn, at a village outside Vienna, Heiligenstadt, he wrote a will-like document, addressed to his two brothers, describing his bitter unhappiness over his affliction in terms suggesting that he thought death was near. But he came through with his determination strengthened and entered a new creative phase, generally called his 'middle period'. It is characterised by a heroic tone, evident in the 'Eroica' Symphony (No 3, originally to have been dedicated not to a noble patron but to Napoleon), in Symphony No 5, where the sombre mood of the C minor first movement ('Fate knocking on the door') ultimately yields to a triumphant C major finale with piccolo, trombones and percussion added to the orchestra, and in his opera Fidelio. Here the heroic theme is made explicit by the story, in which (in the post-French Revolution 'rescue opera' tradition) a wife saves her imprisoned husband from murder at the hands of his oppressive political enemy. The three string quartets of this period – Op 59, are similarly heroic in scale: the first, lasting some 45 minutes, is conceived with great breadth, and it too embodies a sense of triumph as the intense F minor Adagio gives way to a jubilant finale in the major, embodying (at the request of the dedicatee, Count Razumovsky) a Russian folk melody.

Fidelio, unsuccessful at its premiere, was twice revised by Beethoven and his librettists and successful in its final version of 1814. Here there is more emphasis on the moral force of the story. It deals not only with freedom and justice, and heroism, but also with married love, and in the character of the heroine Leonore, Beethoven's lofty, idealised image of womanhood is to

be seen. He did not find it in real life: he fell in love several times, usually with aristocratic pupils (some of them married), and each time was either rejected or saw that the woman did not match his ideals.

With his powerful and expansive middle-period works, which include the Pastoral Symphony (No 6, conjuring up his feelings about the countryside, which he loved), Symphonies Nos 7 and 8, Piano Concertos Nos 4 (a lyrical work) and 5 (the noble and brilliant 'Emperor') and the Violin Concerto, as well as more chamber works and piano sonatas (such as the 'Waldstein' and the 'Appassionata') Beethoven was firmly established as the greatest composer of his time. His piano-playing career had finished in 1808 (a charity appearance in 1814 was a disaster because of his deafness). That year he had considered leaving Vienna for a secure post in Germany, but three Viennese noblemen had banded together to provide him with a steady income and he remained there, although the plan foundered in the ensuing Napoleonic wars in which his patrons suffered and the value of Austrian money declined.

The years after 1812 were relatively unproductive. He seems to have been seriously depressed, by his deafness and the resulting isolation, by the failure of his marital hopes and (from 1815) by anxieties over the custodianship of the son of his late brother, which involved him in legal actions. But he came out of these trials to write his profoundest music. There are seven piano sonatas in this, his 'late period', including the turbulent 'Hammerklavier' Op 106, with its dynamic writing and its harsh, rebarbative fugue, and Op 110, which also has fugues and much eccentric writing at the instrument's extremes of compass; there is a great Mass and a Choral Symphony, No 9 in D minor, where the extended variation-finale is a setting for soloists and chorus of Schiller's Ode to Joy; and there is a group of string quartets, music on a new plane of spiritual depth, with their exalted ideas, abrupt contrasts and emotional intensity. The traditional four-movement scheme and conventional forms are discarded in favour of designs of six or seven movements, some fugal, some akin to variations (these forms especially attracted him in his late years), some song-like, some martial, one even like a chorale prelude. For Beethoven, the act of composition had always been a struggle, as the tortuous scrawls of his sketchbooks show; in these late works the sense of agonising effort is a part of the music.

Musical taste in Vienna had changed during the first decades of the 19th century; the public were chiefly interested in light Italian opera (especially Rossini) and easygoing chamber music and songs, to suit the prevalent bourgeois taste. Yet the Viennese were conscious of Beethoven's greatness: they applauded the Choral Symphony, even though, understandably, they found it difficult, and though baffled by the late quartets they sensed their extraordinary visionary qualities. His reputation went far beyond Vienna: the late Mass was first heard in St Petersburg, and the initial commission that produced the Choral Symphony had come from the Philharmonic Society of London. When he died 10,000 are said to have attended the funeral. He had become a public figure, as no composer had done before. Unlike composers of the preceding generation, he had never been a purveyor of music to the nobility: he had lived *into the age, indeed helped create it, of the artist as hero and the property of mankind at large.* GROVEmusic

Piano Concertos

No 1 in C, Op 15; **No 2** in B flat, Op 19;
No 3 in C minor, Op 37; **No 4** in G, Op 58;
No 5 in E flat, Op 73, 'Emperor'

Complete Piano Concertos

Piano Concertos Nos 1-5
Pierre-Laurent Aimard pf **Chamber Orchestra of Europe / Nikolaus Harnoncourt**
Teldec ③ 0927-47334-2 (184' · DDD) Ⓜ ❍❍❍❍⊕

The freshness of this set is remarkable. You do not have to listen far to be swept up by its spirit of renewal and discovery, and in Pierre-Laurent Aimard as soloist Harnoncourt has made an inspired choice. Theirs aren't eccentric readings of these old warhorses – far from it. But they could be called idiosyncratic – from Harnoncourt would you have expected anything else?

These are modern performances which have acquired richness and some of their focus from curiosity about playing styles and sound production of the past. Harnoncourt favours leaner string textures than the norm and gets his players in the excellent COE to command a wide range of expressive weight and accent; this they do with an immediacy of effect that's striking. Yet there's a satisfying body to the string sound, too.

The playing seems to have recourse to eloquence without having to strive for it, and that's characteristic of Aimard's contribution as well. Strong contrasts are explored and big moments encompassed as part of an unforced continuity in which nothing is hurried. The big moments do indeed stand out: one of them is the famous exchange of dramatic gestures between piano and orchestra in the development of the E flat Concerto's (No 5's) first movement; another the equally dramatic but very different exchange when the piano re-enters at the start of the development in the first movement of the G major Concerto (No 4). At these junctures, conductor and pianist allow the gestures to disrupt the rhythmic continuity. Over the top? No, but risky maybe, and if you've strong views about what Beethoven's rubrics permit, or have swallowed a metronome, you may react strongly. For make no mistake, Aimard is as intrepid an explorer here as Harnoncourt – by conviction, not simply by adoption.

Technically he's superbly equipped. This is evident everywhere, but especially in the finales, brimful of spontaneous touches and delight in their eventfulness and in the pleasure of playing them. The finale of the *Emperor* tingles with a continuously vital, constantly modulated dynamic life that it rarely receives; so many players make it merely rousing. And among the first movements, that of the G major Concerto is a quite exceptional achievement for the way Harnoncourt and his soloist find space for the fullest characterisation of

the lyricism and diversity of the solo part – Aimard begins almost as if improvising the opening statement, outside time – while integrating these qualities with the larger scheme. It's the most complex movement in the concertos and he manages to make it sound both directional and free as a bird.

The first movement of the E flat Concerto is nearly as good, lacking only the all-seeing vision and authority Brendel brings to it, and perhaps a touch of Brendel's ability to inhabit and define its remoter regions. In general, Aimard imposes himself as a personality less than Brendel. In spite of being different exercises, their distinction touches at several points and is comparable in degree. What Aimard doesn't match is the variety of sound and the amplitude of Brendel's expressiveness in the first two concertos' slow movements. Balances are good, with the piano placed in a concert-hall perspective.

This set balances imagination and rigour, providing much delight and refreshment, and playing that will blow you away.

Piano Concertos Nos 1-5
Evgeny Kissin pf
London Symphony Orchestra / Sir Colin Davis
EMI ③ 206311-2 (180' · DDD) Ⓑ ❍❍⊕

It has been clear for some time that Evgeny Kissin is a Beethoven player of rare pedigree and distinction, the finest Russian-born Beethovenian since Emil Gilels. Twelve years ago he recorded the Second and Fifth concertos in performances of flair and élan with the Philharmonia under James Levine (Sony Classical – reveiewed below). His own playing was vital and fluent, the technique awesome, not least his ability to refine tone and taper dynamics in those high-lying passages where Beethoven's expressive powers are at their most rarefied.

The new recordings were made in the autumn of 2007 at Abbey Road and it must be said that the piano sound is a thing of quite exceptional beauty, well forward though not unpleasingly so. Doubts linger about the handling of the difficult-to-judge orchestral *ritornelli* that launch the three earliest concertos. The playing has a slightly sullen feel to it, set back on its heels rhythmically, that Kissin's arrival decisively transforms. Was there at the outset a gap in expectation between the orchestra and its soloist? If so, it quickly dissolves as the real music-making gets under way.

Nowadays Sir Colin is more in love with the music's lyric aspect, audibly so at times. The unfurling of the strings' rapt eight-bar rejoinder to the piano's opening statement in the Fourth Concerto can rarely have been more memorably realised. After such an opening, Kissin has every right to spend the next 20 minutes contemplating the heavens in his own uniquely affecting way, ably abetted by his attentive accompanists.

BEETHOVEN THE FIVE PIANO CONCERTOS – IN BRIEF

Daniel Barenboim; New Philharmonia / Otto Klemperer
EMI 763360-2   Ⓑ●▷
Youth and experience combine for a set of the concertos that constantly reveals new facets of the works. Klemperer draws playing of fierce commitment from the orchestra. The coupling is the *Choral Fantasy*.

Pierre-Laurent Aimard; COE / Nikolaus Harnoncourt
Teldec 0927-47334-2   Ⓑ●●●▷
An inspirational set with a truly impressive freshness and spontaneity (partly due to the set's having been recorded live). This is very much a Beethoven set for the new century.

Maurizio Pollini; BPO / Claudio Abbado
DG 439 770-2GH3   Ⓕ▷
Pollini's second cycle (the first with the VPO remains available) is a fine achievement with Abbado a sympathetic partner. Pollini may shy away from Beethoven's jokes but he thrives on the majesty and grandeur.

Murray Perahia: Concertgebouw Orchestra / Bernard Haitink
Sony Classical 07464 44575-2   Ⓕ●●▷
Limpid, spontaneous and wonderfully poetic, Perahia is a magnificent interpreter. With glorious sound, this is one of the most 'complete' of all concerto cycles.

Alfred Brendel; VPO / Simon Rattle
Philips 462 781-2PH3   Ⓢ●▷
Two musicians completely in tune with each and an orchestra that really understands this music makes for a richly rewarding encounter. The slow movements are magnificent. A set of probing intellectual rigour married to years of Beethoven experience.

Wilhelm Kempff; BPO / Paul van Kempen   Ⓗ
DG 474 024-2GOM5   Ⓢ●●▷
A classic set (Kempff's first) withstands the passing of years remarkably well. Kempff's lucid yet poetc way with Beethoven is enormously satisfying. There's a real sense of delight here. (It forms part of a set focusing on Kempff's complete concerto recordings for DG.)

Radu Lupu; Israel PO / Zubin Mehta
Decca ④ 475 4065DC4 (4h 50' · ADD)   Ⓜ●▷
A new recording from Lupu seems unlikely so all the more reason to cherish these supreme interpretations form the 1970s. Lupu's lyricism is illustrated on every page and he brings myriad detail to these very fine performances. They form part of four-disc Beethoven set that also includes sonatas and a superb Quintet for Piano and Winds.

Despite Davis's slowish tempo, Kissin announces himself in the Second Concerto with playing of great brilliance and vernal loveliness. The entire performance is a success, not least the finale where Kissin throws down the gauntlet to the orchestra with a driving molto allegro that sets up to perfection a typically Beethovenian jest in which high seriousness is made to crook its knee to the life-affirming power of play.

Kissin also sets a cracking pace in the Rondo of the rather grander First Concerto, though is this a true *allegro scherzando*? Beethoven loved to shock but after a slowish albeit beautifully articulated opening movement (where Kissin aptly and intriguingly uses Beethoven's shorter second cadenza) and a sublime account of the *Largo*, this rabid assault on the finale rather unbalances the whole.

There is no such lack of balance in the Third Concerto on which many a pianist-conductor combination has come to grief. Once past that rather dourly played *ritornello*, Kissin and Davis realise the concerto as well as some and better than many.

We know from their earlier recordings how fine both soloist and conductor are in the *Emperor* Concerto and this new version does not disappoint. Kissin's realisation of the big opening cadenza is broadly phrased in the Russian manner, subtler and less extreme than Pletnev in his recent DG recording.

As in the Fourth Concerto, the agogic freedom Kissin allows himself in moments of visionary meditation is underwritten both by the orchestra and his own capacity to return swiftly and pointedly to the *tempo primo*.

A sterner producer might have persuaded Davis to provide a grunt-free start to the string recitative that begins the slow movement of the Fourth Concerto. The exchanges, stilted at first, shed self-consciousness as the dialogue evolves and quietens. And the finale is a delight, the scherzando and visionary elements held in perfect balance. (An unlooked-for bonus is the fact that the set is being offered at budget price!)

Piano Concertos Nos 1-5
Richard Goode pf
Budapest Festival Orchestra / Iván Fischer
Nonesuch ③ 7559 79928-3 (168' · DDD)   Ⓕ

This is not a set that immediately fires the imagination, nor is it in all respects a perfectly 'finished' production. That said, it contains fine accounts of the elusive Third Concerto and the imperturbably splendid Fifth.

The two early concertos receive disappointing performances. Though Fischer and his Budapest players provide brisk, no-nonsense support, soloist Richard Goode appears to be in the grip of a self-denying ordinance, happy to provide an accurate tally of the notes but not much inclined to report upon them. Narrowness of dynamic and expressive range is complemented by a similar narrowness of dramatic vision.

In the Third Concerto the clouds lift. Here is freshness and attack, real poetry in the first movement development, a recapitulation that matters and a superbly calibrated account of Beethoven's built-in cadenza. In the finale of the Third, there is nothing daemonic. Rather, there is a sense of an uncomplicated dance to the music of time. Richard Goode's way with the opening of the Fourth Concerto also has a somewhat balletic feel to it. His reading has a gracious, clean-cut quality which deserves a more aurally sensitive, less matter-of-fact accompaniment than it receives here from the Budapest players. In the slow movement, the orchestral summonses are given a strangely militaristic character.

After which, everything comes right in the Fifth Concerto. This is a straightforward performance of the old school, with clean symphonic lines and classy articulation from the soloist; one of those readings of the *Emperor* that manages to combine lightness of spirit with a proper sense of heroic endeavour.

The piano sound, dull-toned in the two early concertos, is brighter and more robust in the later works without being absolutely in the first flight of excellence.

Piano Concertos Nos 1-5
Murray Perahia pf
Concertgebouw Orchestra / Bernard Haitink
Sony Classical ③ 07464 44575-2
(178' · DDD)   Ⓜ︎🅾️🅾️🅱️➔

Perahia's account of the C minor Concerto (No 3) is a joy from start to finish, wonderfully conceived, executed conducted and recorded. The single issue, coupled with this account of the G major Concerto (No 4), began life by winning the 1986 *Gramophone* Concerto Award. In these two concertos, and in the two earlier ones, Perahia and Haitink are difficult to fault. The First Concerto is especially well done with a quick first movement and the apt and delightful inclusion in the finale of a cadenza that Beethoven sketched in 1800. If Perahia is anywhere slightly below par it's in the *Emperor* Concerto. The reading gives us an emergent view of the work, undiscursive but perhaps at times lacking in a certain largeness of vision and purpose. For that we must return to Kempff or Arrau, which only confirms the pitfalls of buying cycles rather than separate performances. However, the Perahia cycle is one of the most consistently accomplished of those currently available; the recordings are a joy to listen to.

Piano Concertos Nos 1-5. Choral Fantasia in C minor, Op 80
Daniel Barenboim pf **John Alldis Choir;**
New Philharmonia Orchestra / Otto Klemperer
EMI ④ 763360-2 (211' · ADD) Recorded 1967 Ⓜ︎🅾️➔

Klemperer had done concert cycles, perhaps most memorably in London in the 1950s with Claudio Arrau but his decision to record the piano concertos at the age of 82 came as a result of his admiration for the most precociously talented of all young Beethoven pianists at the time, Daniel Barenboim. Barenboim was 25 and about to embark on what was to be an exceptionally fine cycle of the Beethoven piano sonatas. He was steeped in Beethoven and perhaps peculiarly well suited to the concertos which, we should not forget, are essentially a young man's music. It was a fascinating pairing, Klemperer and Barenboim contrasted in age and to some extent in temperament but at the same time symbiotically at one musically. Had this not been the case, Barenboim would have been swamped, lost in the wash of Klemperer's accompaniments which deliver the orchestral argument and the orchestral detail with an articulacy and authority unique in the history of these works on record.

The performance of the B flat Concerto, the first historically if not numerically, is a typical joy, full of fire and grace and unstoppably vital. Given Klemperer's propensity for taking slow tempos in Beethoven, you might imagine him being taken for a ride by the young Barenboim in the B flat and C major finales. But not a bit of it. It's Klemperer, as much as his youthful soloist, who seems to be the driving force here. Rarely on record has the slow movement of the C major Concerto been played with so natural a sense of concentrated calm, the whole thing profoundly collected on the spiritual plane. One of the joys of the Barenboim/Klemperer cycle is its occasional unpredictability: rock-solid readings that none the less incorporate a sense of 'today we try it this way'.

Ensemble is mostly first rate during the cycle. The tricky coda of the first movement of the C minor Concerto is both rapt and dramatic. But in the coda of the first movement of the G major there's little doubt that Klemperer drags the pulse. And elsewhere there are some occasionally awkward adjustments to be made between soloist and orchestra. At the time of its initial appearance, the *Emperor* performance was generally adjudged a success. Again it's broadly conceived. At first the finale seems a little staid; but later the 6/8 rhythms are made to dance and the performance has a burning energy by the end. So does the account of the *Choral Fantasia*. Given Klemperer's magisterial style and authority, this set could have emerged as five symphonies with piano obbligato. In fact, it's a set of rare authority and spontaneity, and given the slightly unconventional idea of the soloist as *primus inter pares*, it's probably unique.

Piano Concertos Nos 1-5
Alfred Brendel pf **Vienna Philharmonic Orchestra /**
Sir Simon Rattle
Philips ③ 462 781-2PH3 (178' · DDD)   Ⓕ🅾️➔

Happily, Alfred Brendel's fourth recorded cycle of the Beethoven piano concertos shares with the previous three qualities of energy, sensibility, intellectual rigour and high pianistic finish which made the earlier recordings so interesting. Brendel has always played all five slow movements supremely well, drawing the orchestra around him like a celebrant at the communion table and here we have even finer performances than previously.

In the two early concertos the Vienna Philharmonic's playing has a sweetness and allure, in the grander, later works a black-browed power, that's specially its own. Brendel's playing in the early concertos recalls his fine recordings of the early sonatas and the early and late *Bagatelles*, but it's as a private person impatient with the conventions and frock-coated formalities of the concertos as 'public' works. With No 3 we move into a different world. This is a marvellous performance from all three partners, purposeful and robust, the tonic C minor the cue for a reading full of darkness and menace, basses to the fore, drums at the ready. The finale is particularly ominous (relieved only by a lustrous clarinet solo) after an account of the slow movement, full toned yet deeply quiet, the like of which is rarely heard. The C minor Concerto's heroic antitype, the *Emperor* in E flat, fares less well. Not the slow movement or finale, but the first movement which is slower than previously, to no very good effect. Perhaps interpreters nowadays are less happy than their predecessors were with Beethoven's heroic persona. Back in the private world of the Fourth Concerto, soloist, orchestra and conductor are at their inspired best. Brendel's glittering, wonderfully propelled account of the solo part is superbly backed by playing of real fire and sensitivity. The recordings are first rate.

Piano Concertos Nos 1[a] & 2[b]   H
Solomon pf **Philharmonia Orchestra / [a]Herbert Menges, [b]André Cluytens**
Testament [b]mono SBT1219 (63' · ADD)   Ⓕ☉

Piano Concertos Nos 3[a] & 4[b]   H
Solomon pf **Philharmonia Orchestra / [a] Menges, [b]Cluytens**
Testament [b]mono SBT1220 (70' · ADD)   Ⓕ☉

Beethoven Piano Concerto No 5 **Mozart** Piano   H
Sonatas – No 11 in A, K331; No 17 in D, K576
Solomon pf **Philharmonia Orchestra / Menges**
Testament mono SBT1221 (74' · ADD)
All recorded 1952-6   Ⓕ☉

Here on three CDs are Solomon's legendary 1952-6 recordings of the Beethoven piano concertos and two Mozart piano sonatas, a felicitous coupling. Time and again Beethoven's exuberant, unpredictable nature is qualified by playing of a supreme poise and equanimity that omits so little of his essential character. It's also one of Solomon's cardinal qualities that he makes it impertinent to single out this or that detail, offering instead a seamless argument as supple and natural as it's understated.

Solomon makes the slow movements the expressive centres of each concerto, and here his

ability to sustain an *Adagio* or *Largo* is without equal. This is notably true of the first two concertos, where such writing becomes music to soothe the savage breast rather than awake more immediate emotions. In the outer movements his superfine technique and musicianship make light of every difficulty, and at 6'55" in the Second Concerto, after an impatient if very Beethovenian entry, he re-creates a magical sense of stillness and repose.

In the Third Concerto the *Largo* is impeccably controlled and so, too, is the central *Andante con moto* from the Fourth Concerto. Solomon's momentary lack of control in the first movement at 9'37" is, perhaps, an indication of problems caused by Cluytens' less than vital or stimulating partnership. And yet the finale could hardly be more *vivace*, with all the clarity and grace for which Solomon was celebrated.

In the *Emperor* Concerto Solomon somehow bridges the gap between the Fourth and Fifth Concertos. His immaculate ease and buoyancy in the double-note descent just before the first movement's conclusion, his limpid and serene traversal of the central *Adagio* are pure Solomon, and his finale is among the least opaque on record. Surprises include the shorter cadenza in the First Concerto, Clara Schumann's cadenza in the Third (enterprising if less distinguished than Beethoven's own magnificent offering) and a few teasing elaborations in the two cadenzas from the Fourth.

The recordings come up well (though the sound in the Fifth needs some opening out; it lacks ring and brilliance), and the Mozart sonatas are a delectable bonus. Listening to Solomon's peerless pianism and musicianship, the critic discards pen and paper and listens in awe, wonder and affection.

Piano Concertos – selected

Piano Concertos Nos 1 & 2
Murray Perahia pf **Concertgebouw Orchestra / Bernard Haitink**
Sony Classical 07464 42177-2 (70' · DDD)   Ⓕ☉

It's a pleasure here to salute such all-round excellence: a very remarkable soloist, superb orchestral playing and direction, and a recording which gets everything right, offering the kind of sound picture and natural perspective of solo piano with orchestra as we might experience them from a good seat in the Concertgebouw itself, where these performances were recorded.

Precision, clarity of expression, variety of character, beauty of sound: these are the qualities Haitink and Perahia sustain, and through which their readings gain an illuminating force. And it's perhaps in the slow movements that the illumination brings the most distinguished results. Their raptness and distinctive colouring are established from the first notes, and the inward quality of the expression takes breath as if there was nothing to the business of delineating these great set-pieces, so special among the achievements of Beethoven's first maturity, except to sing them through. Perahia has the gift of reducing his voice to the quietest level and still remaining eloquent. The poise of the playing is classical, his authority unblemished by any hint of exaggeration or false emphasis.

Piano Concertos Nos 1 & 2
Yefim Bronfman pf
Tonhalle Orchestra, Zürich / David Zinman
Arte Nova 82876 82587-2 (67' · DDD) Ⓢ❍❍❍

This Zurich performance of the First Concerto is beautifully articulated. True, there are moments of grandeur but the overall impression is of a poised, at times chamber-like traversal, with sculpted pianism and crisply pointed orchestral support. The sensation of shared listening, between Bronfman and the players and between the players themselves, is at its most acute in the First Concerto's *Largo*, which although kept on a fairly tight rein is extremely supple (the woodwinds in particular excel). In the finale, Bronfman and the Tonhalle provide a clear, shapely aural picture.

Bronfman's B flat Concerto (No 2) has the expected composure, the many running passages in the first movement polished if relatively understated. Again the slow movement is full of unaffected poetry and the finale (with the odd added embellishment) is appropriately buoyant – has Bronfman ever played better?

Piano Concertos Nos 2 & 5
Evgeny Kissin pf
Philharmonia Orchestra / James Levine
Sony Classical 07464 39814-2 (69' · DDD) Ⓕ

From his very first entry, in the B flat Concerto, Kissin is revealed as a Beethoven player of great articulacy, brilliance and sensitivity after the manner of such pianists as Kempff, Solomon, and Gilels. The playing is vital and fluent, the technique awesome, not least in the way Kissin is able to refine his tone and taper dynamics in the high-lying coloratura passages where Beethoven's writing is at its most inspired and rarefied. The recitative at the end of the slow movement is predictably beautiful: intense and otherworldly. Levine draws from the Philharmonia playing that's both spirited and engaged. The recorded sound is admirable, too: strong and clean yet appropriately intimate.

The performance of the *Emperor* Concerto is also very fine. If you take the view that this is essentially a symphony with piano obbligato, you may hanker after a grander kind of musical theatre than that provided by Levine. He directs with decision and accompanies superbly. Kissin, too, plays with great flair and technical security. If there's a problem, it's with the articulation of the simple-seeming lyric statements where a degree of self-consciousness occasionally creeps in: where the flow is arrested and music suddenly seems to be walking on stilts. There's an element

of this in the slow movement, though Kissin's playing of the bleak, trailing 24-bar-long *diminuendo* close is masterly. This is very much a young man's view of the music, but weighty too, such is the power of his technique.

Piano Concertos Nos 3 & 4
Murray Perahia pf
Concertgebouw Orchestra / Bernard Haitink
Sony Classical 07464 39814-2 (70' · DDD) Ⓜ❍❍❍

 These performances have rightly been described as exceptional. They were directly compared to Alfred Brendel's accounts with James Levine (on Philips) but in the event, there's little to choose between these two distinguished soloists. The first movements are brilliantly and sensitively etched (Perahia uses Beethoven's bigger first cadenza in the first movement of the G major Concerto). Tempos are steady but with a fine degree of forward projection. Once past the daunting opening solo, Perahia plays the C minor's slow movement with great sureness and subtlety of touch; and with Haitink as his partner the exchanges in the G major's slow movement are memorably brought off. Note the superior quality of the Sony recordings and the wonderfully judicious accompaniments prepared for Perahia by the Concertgebouw Orchestra under Haitink, who's exemplary.

Piano Concertos Nos 4 & 5
Emil Gilels pf **Philharmonia Orchestra /**   Ⓗ
Leopold Ludwig
Testament SBT1095 (73' · ADD) Recorded 1957 Ⓕ❍❍

This is one of the – perhaps *the* most – perfect accounts of the Fourth Concerto recorded. Poetry and virtuosity are held in perfect poise, with Ludwig and the Philharmonia providing a near-ideal accompaniment. The recording is also very fine, though be sure to gauge the levels correctly by first sampling one of the *tutti*s. If the volume is set too high at the start, you'll miss the stealing magic of Gilels's and the orchestra's initial entries and you'll be further discomfited by tape hiss.

The recording of the *Emperor* Concerto is also pretty good, not quite on a par with that of the Fourth. Ludwig and the orchestra tend to follow Gilels rather than always integrate with him and there are times, too, especially in the slow movement, when Gilels's playing borders on the self-indulgent. This isn't, however, sufficient reason for overlooking this fine and important reissue.

Piano Concerto No 5
Murray Perahia pf
Concertgebouw Orchestra / Bernard Haitink
Sony Classical 07464 42330-2 (42' · DDD) Ⓜ❍❍❍

This is a superb performance though not as generous as in its previous coupling where it came with Perahia's Award-winning Fourth.

(G) This is an excellent *Emperor*, on a level with the best. Comparisons with other pianists, at this level, can be rather futile. It's a splendidly engineered recording, with a natural concert-hall type of balance, and there's good presence to the sound and depth to the perspective. The presentation of the orchestral detail allows you to delight in it, and perhaps to discover new subtleties, without a moment of unease as to whether anything has been forced into the wrong kind of relief. Perahia's performance has the freshness and natural authority we have come to expect of him in Beethoven. His reading might be described as uncomplicated if that didn't risk implying that it's in some way lightweight, or that he plays like a child of nature. The weight is certainly there, in sound (when he wants it) as in expression.

Perahia himself has spoken of the happy experience of making this Beethoven cycle with Haitink (the other concertos including the complete set are reviewed above). It has indeed been a successful collaboration, and a joyous quality about the music-making communicates itself quite strongly from the beginning.

Piano Concerto No 5
Arturo Benedetti Michelangeli pf
Vienna Symphony Orchestra / Carlo Maria Giulini
DG 419 249-2GH (42' · ADD) Recorded live 1979 Ⓕ**O**

There has, over the years, been mixed reactions to Michelangeli's Beethoven. He was a most perplexing artist, perplexing because he liked to keep his musical personality well hidden – or at any rate mysterious – behind the armour-plated magnificence of his playing; disconcerting too because it's hard to arrive at a reasoned assessment of readings of classical music by someone who evidently isn't a man of balance. To interpret texts of the classical masters in a way which will give them the most vivid life doesn't seem to be his principal concern. There could be an intellectual *froideur* about his playing of Beethoven which verges on the disdainful and which was sometimes more than off-putting.

Not here though. This performance was recorded at a public performance in the Musikverein. He drives the opening flourishes hard, and thereafter responds keenly to Giulini's exposition, grand but always moving forward, matching it with a purpose that seems to derive from just that long-range musical thinking which is so often missing in his accounts of the other concertos. There's spaciousness, and time for everything, and always that rock-like strength of rhythm. The detailing could hardly be bettered but isn't allowed to deflect attention from our perception of the form. The security of the technique is enough to make most other pianists attempting an Olympian view of the concerto seem clumsy; but it doesn't draw attention to itself. Since the depth of his sonority is perfectly matched to the orchestra's, it makes for some especially exciting listening in the finale. Great playing by a great pianist.

Piano Concerto No 5[a]. Choral Fantasia[ab].
Meeresstille und glückliche Fahrt[b]
[a]**Yefim Bronfman** pf [b]**Swiss Chamber Choir;**
Tonhalle Orchestra, Zürich / David Zinman
Arte Nova 82876 82585-2 (64' · DDD) Ⓑ**OO**

Rather than opt for superficial barnstorming, Yefim Bronfman and David Zinman offer us a discreet, subtly voiced and above all durable *Emperor*, that rewards listening with increasing musical dividends. Bronfman plays with a light, precise though never brittle touch, always phrasing elegantly and dipping his tone whenever important instrumental lines need to be heard. There are numerous details that reveal how minutely all the participants are listening to each other. The slow movement unfolds in a mood of unruffled calm, Bronfman's first entry gentle, delicate, with an appropriate, even touching simplicity. The finale is brisk and energetic and the way Bronfman keeps accompanying rhythmic figurations light and well buoyed is most appealing.

The fill-ups are worthwhile, the *Choral Fantasy*'s long solo opening more thoughtful than usual and with a bright, easy-going contribution from the chorus. Nothing is ever forced or overstated and the contrast in the seven-minute *Calm Sea and Prosperous Voyage* between worrying stillness and the first signs of a redeeming breeze, ingeniously painted by slowly swirling triplets, is superbly handled.

It is hard to imagine anyone being less than satisfied with Bronfman and Zinman, the Tonhalle Orchestra scoring top marks for teamwork, their woodwinds sounding fully on a par with Europe's best. Superbly balanced sound helps clinch an unmissable bargain.

Piano Concerto No 5. Triple Concerto in C, Op 56[a]
Leon Fleisher, Eugene Istomin pfs **Isaac Stern** vn
Leonard Rose vc **Cleveland Orchestra / George**
Szell; [a]**Philadelphia Orchestra / Eugene Ormandy**
Sony Classical 69699 89961-2 (74' · ADD) Recorded
1961, [a]1964 Ⓑ**O**

Leon Fleisher's recording of the *Emperor* is very powerful indeed. He was relatively young at the time and obviously George Szell had a considerable influence on the reading, but the solo playing is remarkably fresh and its pianistic authority is striking. That great octave passage in the first movement, just before the recapitulation, is enormously commanding, and Fleisher's lyrical playing, in the slow movement especially, has striking poise. Szell keeps the voltage high throughout, but for all its excitement this is by no means a hard-driven, unfeeling interpretation. The recording is bright, bold and forward in the CBS 1960s manner, and the Severance Hall acoustic prevents any ugliness.

A splendid *Emperor*, then, but what makes this disc even more enticing is the inclusion of an equally distinguished version of the Triple Concerto, recorded in Philadelphia Town Hall (a much more successful venue than many used over the years for this great orchestra). The very gentle opening by the orchestra is full of anticipatory tension, and at the beginning of the slow movement Ormandy's preparation for Rose's glorious cello solo demonstrates what a superb accompanist he is. Indeed, this is no mere accompaniment, but a complete partnership. Although Stern's personality dominates marginally, the three soloists play together like a chamber-music team, without in any way submerging their individuality. The sound is very good for its time.

Additional recommendation

Piano Concertos Nos 2 & 3
Argerich pf **Mahler CO / Abbado**
DG download 477 5026GH (64' · DDD)   (F)**OO**(B→)

Martha Argerich's long-awaited recording of Beethoven's Third Concerto appears with the Second, music she's relished over the years. But whether novel or familiar, both performances are of a quality rarely encountered.

Violin Concerto in D, Op 61

Violin Concerto. Romances
Christian Tetzlaff vn
Tonhalle Orchestra, Zürich / David Zinman
Arte Nova 82876 76994-2 (56' · DDD   (F)**OOO**

This superb Beethoven disc from Christian Tetzlaff is a real winner. The main stumbling-block on so many rival recordings of this work is a sort of romantic reverence, a trend challenged by Zehetmair, Kremer and others – and now Tetzlaff. For all its many moments of profound 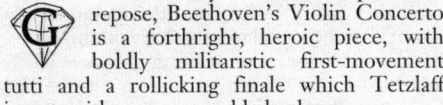 repose, Beethoven's Violin Concerto is a forthright, heroic piece, with boldly militaristic first-movement tutti and a rollicking finale which Tetzlaff invests with numerous added colours.

Following on the heals of Zehetmair, Kremer and Schneiderhan, Tetzlaff performs the violin version of the cadenza that Beethoven wrote for his piano transcription of the work, a playful excursion and a snug fit for his overall interpretation. Tempi are brisk without hurrying, the slow movement has an unruffled serenity and a lively added cadenza in the finale helps accentuate the pervading sense of play. Excellent booklet-notes explain the work's genesis and the basic drift of Tetzlaff's approach and the two Romances that complete the programme are performed with the same chaste lyricism.

Violin Concerto
Itzhak Perlman vn **Philharmonia Orchestra /
Carlo Maria Giulini**
EMI Great Recordings of the Century 566900-2
(44' · DDD)   (M)**OOO**(B→)

This is a very distinguished performance, as much from Giulini as from Perlman. Early on Giulini

BEETHOVEN PIANO CONCERTO NO 5, 'EMPEROR' – IN BRIEF

**Murray Perahia; Concertgebouw Orchestra /
Bernard Haitink**
Sony Classical SMK89711 (73' · DDD)   (M)**OOO**
 A superb performance of real authority but above all of true poetry. Beautifully accompanied by the great Dutch orchestra. Coupled with an equally fine No 4.

Wilhelm Kempff; Berlin PO / Ferdinand Leitner
DG 447 402-2GOR (70' · ADD)   (M)**OO**
A magnificent, aristocratic interpretation from Kempff's second (stereo) cycle (with No 4). Still sounding very good for its 1962 vintage.

Evgeny Kissin; Philharmonia / James Levine
Sony Classical SK62926 (69' · DDD)   (F)**OO**
The young Russian pianist reveals himself to be an artist of great articulacy, brilliance and sensitivity. Coupled with a lively No 1.

Emil Gilels; Philharmonia / Leopold Ludwig   (H)
Testament SBT1095 (73' · DDD)   (F)
A fine *Emperor* coupled with a superb Fourth. Gilels was a commanding Beethoven interpreter. There is some hiss from the 1957 tape, otherwise fine at reasonable levels.

Maurizio Pollini; Vienna PO / Karl Böhm
DG download 439 483-2GCL (71' · ADD)   (B)(B→)
A cooler Beethoven than Pollini later gave with Abbado, but certainly spontaneous and fresh sounding (coupled with No 4).

**Leon Fleisher; Cleveland Orchestra /
George Szell**
Sony Classical SBK46549 (74' · DDD)   (B)**O**
High-octane Beethoven from Fleisher and Szell: commanding, virtuoso and iron-willed. Not for the faint hearted! Coupled with a fine Triple Concerto.

Solomon; Philharmonia / Herbert Menges   (H)
Testament mono SBT1221 (74' · ADD)   (F)**O**
A stunning *Emperor* for its classical poise, ease and limpid fingerwork. A reminder of one of the UK's greatest pianists. Coupled with two Mozart piano sonatas.

Robert Levin fp **Orchestre Révolutionnaire
et Romantique / Sir John Eliot Gardiner**
Archiv download 447 771-2AH (71' · DDD)   (F)(B→)
A most successful period-instrument *Emperor*: the combination of Levin's fantasy and Gardiner's drama pays dividends. The coupled *Choral Fantasy* with Gardiner's superb Monteverdi Choir is magnificent.

**Edwin Fischer; Philharmonia / Wilhelm
Furtwängler**   (H)
EMI mono 574800-2 (78' · ADD)   (F)**OO**
A great *Emperor* for its sense of grandeur and majesty. A superb collaboration from 1951.

makes clear the importance of recognising the difference between *forte* and *fortissimo* in Beethoven – for example the *ff* of bars 73 and 74 and the which surrounds them; and the marvellous way he gets the Philharmonia to play *sfp* is a pleasure in itself. The liquid smoothness of the winds is another joy.

The slow movement has the utmost calm beauty from both soloist and orchestra, while Perlman plays the finale at an admirably swift speed, yet with all the flexibility it needs, so that it really dances lightly. The clarity of the orchestral texture is outstanding too. The bassoon, for example, sings its solos in the finale easily and without the least forcing. A real Great Recording of the Century!

Violin Concerto. Romances
Gidon Kremer vn **Chamber Orchestra of Europe / Nikolaus Harnoncourt**
Warner Elatus 0927-49773-2 (57' · DDD) Recorded live 1992 Ⓜ️Ⓞ➡️

Gidon Kremer offers one of his most commanding performances, both polished and full of flair, magnetically spontaneous from first to last. Rarely do you hear such consistently pure tone in this work and the orchestral writing too is superbly realised. It has become customary to treat the long first movement as expansively as possible but Kremer takes a more urgent view, and after his thoughtful and dedicated, slightly understated reading of the slow movement, he and Harnoncourt round the performance off magically with a finale that skips along the more infectiously thanks to light, clean articulation and textures. Traditional performances seem heavyweight by comparison. The controversial point for some will be the cadenza in the first movement where he uses a transcription of the big cadenza which Beethoven wrote for his piano arrangement of the work. However, this is altogether one of the most refreshing versions of the concerto ever committed to record, backed up by crisp, unsentimental readings of the two *Romances*.

Beethoven Violin Concerto[a] Ⓗ
Mendelssohn Violin Concerto in E minor, Op 64[b]
Yehudi Menuhin vn [a]**Philharmonia Orchestra,** [b]**Berlin Philharmonic Orchestra / Wilhelm Furtwängler**
EMI Great Recordings of the Century mono 566975-2 (71' · ADD) Recorded 1952-3 Ⓜ️

Furtwängler and Menuhin recorded the Beethoven Concerto on two occasions, and this second version has an extraordinary quality of spirituality and profundity. Furtwängler's conducting of the opening *tutti* has a magnificently arresting, weighty quality, and Menuhin's response, profound and rich in re-creative imagination shows the two great artists in perfect accord. Their account of this movement is on the largest scale, yet they convey Beethoven's vision in a humane, approachable fashion. The slow movement has a highly concentrated yet serene character, with Menuhin's rapt, singing tone achieving rare eloquence, and the finale is superbly balanced, with an affecting sense of a shared, joyful experience. The recording sounds quite similar to the original LP issue, but the quality is quite acceptable.

The Mendelssohn was recorded a year earlier, and here remastering has brought a slight roughening in an orchestral sound which was never very ingratiating, though the defect isn't serious. Menuhin and Furtwängler float the first movement in an unhurriedly serene, elegantly shaped fashion. In the slow movement they achieve a touchingly tender, almost innocent quality and the finale, taken at a moderate tempo, has lightness and an appealingly eager character.

Beethoven Violin Concerto[a] Ⓗ
Brahms Violin Concerto in D, Op 77[b]
Jascha Heifetz vn [a]**NBC Symphony Orchestra / Arturo Toscanini;** [b]**Boston Symphony Orchestra / Serge Koussevitzky**
Naxos Historical mono 8 110936 (77' · AAD) Recorded [a]1939, [b]1940 Ⓢ️ⓄⓄⓄ

 'An old diamond in the rough' is how Robert C Marsh (*Toscanini and the Art of Orchestra Performance*; London: 1956) recalled the original Victor 78s of this 1940 Heifetz Studio 8-H recording of the Beethoven. Of the LP reissue he wrote: 'On the whole, the recording is so dead and artificial that at times the thin line of violin sound reminds one of something from the golden age of Thomas Edison's tinfoil cylinder rather than 1940.' Early CD transfers suggested that all wasn't lost but even they barely anticipated the extraordinary fineness of the sound we now have on this transfer by archivist and restorer Mark Obert-Thorn.

The performance itself is one of the most remarkable the gramophone has ever given us. The visionary, high *tessitura* violin writing is realised by Heifetz with a technical surety which is indistinguishable, in the final analysis, from his sense of the work as one of Beethoven's most sublime explorations of that world (in Schiller's phrase) 'above the stars where He must dwell'. Those who would query the 'depth' of Heifetz's reading miss this point entirely. To adapt Oscar Wilde, it is they who are in the gutter, Heifetz who is looking at the stars.

As for Toscanini's contribution, it, too, is masterly. Now that we can actually hear the performance, the orchestral *tutti*s seem beautifully balanced both within themselves and *vis-à-vis* the soloist. As for the actual accompaniment, it's discreet and self-effacing, fiery yet refined, and always wondrously subtle.

In the case of the Brahms, it's more reasonable to argue that there are other ways of playing the concerto. Heifetz's isn't a Romantic reading. It's lean, athletic, classical, aristocratic, finely drawn, an approach which wears exceptionally well on record. The Brahms enjoys another impeccable transfer. Musically and technically, this is a real thoroughbred of a release, unignorable at any price.

Beethoven Violin Concerto[a]   **H**
Tchaikovsky Violin Concerto in D, Op 35[b]
Bronislaw Huberman vn [a]**Vienna Philharmonic Orchestra / George Szell;** [b]**Staatskapelle Berlin / William Steinberg**
Naxos Historical mono 8 110903 (67' · AAD) Recorded
[a]1934, [b]1928   Ⓢ❶❶↪

Virtuoso violinist Bronislaw Huberman was an idealist, an ardent Pan-European and co-founder (with William Steinberg) of the Israel Philharmonic. He was, in a sense, the prototype for such present-day fiddling mavericks as Kremer, Zehetmair, Tetzlaff and Kennedy. Huberman's open letter to the conductor Wilhelm Furtwängler, in which he pledged support of the persecuted, and refused to perform in Nazi Germany, has become famous, and his astringent though frequently dazzling playing translates that steely resolve into musical terms.

This Naxos coupling is very nearly the answer to a prayer. Huberman's interpretation is more in line with, say, Zehetmair and Brüggen than the stately readings of Kreisler, Szigeti, Men-uhin or David Oistrakh. His lively speeds and darting inflections spin silver beams where others opt for (for some misplaced) 'Olympian' heights. The luminosity of the reading, its radiance and refusal to dawdle, run counter to the languid sweetness favoured by various of his peers and successors.

The 1929 Tchaikovsky recording is peerless. Huberman's first entry reveals all: elastic phrasing, sweeping *portamento*s and generous *rubato* stamp a giant personality. Thereafter, quicksilver bowing and a steely *spiccato* level with the best of the period. Brahms loved Huberman's playing (he promised the budding youngster a *Fantasy* but never lived to compose it), and no wonder, given the veiled beauty of his tone (*Canzonetta*) and the uninhibited swagger of his bravura style (finale).

You simply have to hear Huberman's recording, and Naxos's give-away price makes it a mandatory purchase. However, the transfer of the Beethoven, although perfectly adequate, is rather spoiled by excessive digital noise reduction. On one occasion in the first movement, the violinist momentarily disappears; in the second movement two chords inadvertently become one. But these technical reservations will likely prove trifling for anyone who has never heard Huberman before. There are no greater violin recordings in existence.

Additional recommendation

Violin Concerto. Romances   Ⓟ
Zehetmair vn **Orchestra of the 18th Century / Brüggen**

Philips download *462 123-2PH* (54' · DDD)   Ⓕ❶❶↪

This is a great performance, one that simply has to be heard. The use of period instruments adds extra fibre to the aural mix, and Brüggen's conducting has a pressing urgency about it that, again, intensifies the drama. Limited availability on CD.

Triple Concerto in C, Op 56

Beethoven Triple Concerto[a] **Brahms** Double Concerto in A minor, Op 102[b]
David Oistrakh vn **Mstislav Rostropovich** vc
Sviatoslav Richter pf [a]**Berlin Philharmonic Orchestra / Herbert von Karajan;**
[b]**Cleveland Orchestra / George Szell**
EMI Great Recordings of the Century mono 566902-2 (70' · ADD) Recorded 1969   Ⓜ❶❶↪

These are illustrious performances and make a splendid coupling. EMI planned for a long time to assemble this starry line-up of soloists, conductor and orchestra for Beethoven's Triple Concerto, and the artists don't disappoint, bringing sweetness as well as strength to a work which in lesser hands can sound clumsy and long winded. The recording, made in a Berlin church in 1969, is warm, spacious and well balanced, placing the soloists in a gentle spotlight. The account of Brahms's Double Concerto is perhaps the most powerful recorded performance since the days of Heifetz and Feuermann or Thibaud and Casals. The recording has come up extremely well in this remastering: although the sound isn't as smooth as can be achieved nowadays, this is soon forgotten, and you're caught up in the magnificent music-making.

Triple Concerto. Choral Fantasia in C minor, Op 80. Rondo in B flat, WoO6
Pierre-Laurent Aimard pf **Thomas Zehetmair** vn
Clemens Hagen vc **Arnold Schoenberg Choir; Chamber Orchestra of Europe / Nikolaus Harnoncourt**
Warner Classics 2564 60602-2 (66' · DDD) Recorded live   Ⓕ❶❶

Listening to the opening tutti on this joyful new Triple Concerto, you can just picture Nikolaus Harnoncourt cueing his strings, perched slightly forwards, impatiently waiting for that first, pregnant *forte*. This is a big, affable, blustery Triple, the soloists completing the sound canvas rather than dominating it, a genuine collaborative effort. So beside the Beethovenian strut to this performance there's poetry too. Yet thoughtfulness never spells timidity; Hagen and Thomas Zehetmair throw caution to the winds near the end of the first movement. The Concerto's *Largo* is simplicity itself, rather like a song without words, but it's the finale that is likely to raise the most smiles, a rumbustious affair, uninhibited without coursing out of control. Harnoncourt and his team go for the burn, always brilliant but, more importantly, full of character and humour.

The fill-ups (like the Concerto, recorded at concerts in Graz) are hardly less engaging. The little B flat Rondo is bubbly from the start, Aimard and the orchestra maintaining a feeling of chamber collaboration. And then the *Choral Fantasia*, so often clunky on disc but here aided by Aimard's sense of style – his arpeggios in the long opening solo have so much colour – and by Harnoncourt's relaxed approach to the music that follows, each variation imaginatively tended within a larger framework. The singing is excellent, the sound both warm and realistic. As 'feel-good' Beethoven programmes go, this is about as enjoyable as it gets, though a high level of musical insight further enhances one's pleasure.

Additional recommendation

Triple Concerto
Coupled with: Choral Fantasia in C minor, Op 80
Perlman vn **Ma** vc **Chorus of the Deutsche Oper, Berlin; Berlin Philharmonic Orchestra / Barenboim** pf
EMI 555516-2 (55' · DDD)   Ⓕ☒➤

Superb live performances which grab you with their refreshing spontaneity. Choice between this and Masur's comes down to a preference for crisp co-ordination and the inspiration of the moment.

Symphonies

No 1 in C, Op 21; **No 2** in D, Op 36; **No 3** in E flat, Op 55, 'Eroica'; **No 4** in B flat, Op 60; **No 5** in C minor, Op 67; **No 6** in F, Op 68, 'Pastoral'; **No 7** in A, Op 92; **No 8** in F, Op 93; **No 9** in D minor, Op 125, 'Choral'

Complete Symphonies

Symphonies Nos 1-9
Charlotte Margiono sop **Birgit Remmert** mez
Rudolf Schasching ten **Robert Holl** bass **Arnold Schoenberg Choir; Chamber Orchestra of Europe / Nikolaus Harnoncourt**
Warner Elatus ⑤ 0927-49768-2 (358' · DDD) Recorded live 1990-91   ⓂⒶOOO

Brimful of intrepid character and interpretative incident, this is surely one of the most stimulating Beethoven symphony cycles of recent times. As Harnoncourt himself states in the booklet: 'It has always been my conviction that music is not there to soothe people's nerves…but rather to open their eyes, to give them a good shaking, even to frighten them.' So it transpires that there's a re-creative daring about Harnoncourt's conducting – in essence an embracement of recent scholarly developments and his own pungent sense of characterisation – which is consistently illuminating, thus leaving the listener with the uncanny sensation that he or she is encountering this great music for the first time. In all this Harnoncourt is backed to the hilt by some superbly responsive, miraculously assured playing from the COE: their personable, unforced assimilation of his specific demands, allied to his intimate knowledge of the inner workings of these scores, make for wonderfully fresh, punchy results. In this respect Nos 6-8 in particular prove immensely rewarding, but the Eroica and the Fourth, too, are little short of superb. This is a cycle which excitingly reaffirms the life-enhancing mastery of Beethoven's vision for many years to come.

Symphonies Nos 1-9
Gundula Janowitz sop **Hilde Rössel-Majdan** contr **Waldemar Kmentt** ten **Walter Berry** bass **Vienna Singverein; Berlin Philharmonic Orchestra / Herbert von Karajan**
DG Collectors Edition ⑤ 463 088-2GB5 (332' · ADD · T/t) Recorded 1961-2   ⓂⒶ

This was the first set of the Nine to be planned, recorded and sold as an integral cycle. It was also a set that had been extremely carefully positioned from the interpretative point of view. Where Karajan's 1950s Philharmonia cycle had elements in it that owed a certain amount to the old German school of Beethoven interpretation, the new-found virtuosity of the Berliners allowed him to approach more nearly the fierce beauty and lean-toned fiery manner of Toscanini's Beethoven style as Karajan had first encountered it in its halcyon age in the mid-1930s. Nothing demonstrates this better than the 1962 recording of the Fourth Symphony, fiery and radiant as Karajan's reading had not previously been, and never would be again. The old shibboleth among writers and musicians that the even-numbered symphonies were somehow less dramatic than the odd-numbered ones meant nothing to Karajan. His accounts of the Second, Fourth, Sixth and Eighth Symphonies were every bit as intense as their allegedly sturdier neighbours. Only in the Seventh Symphony's third movement Trio and the Menuetto of the Eighth Symphony – where he continued to follow Wagner's idea of this as an essentially stately dance, a kind of surrogate slow movement – did he deviate significantly from the Toscanini model. And it worked. True, the first movement of the *Pastoral* Symphony was a touch airless, lacking some of the easy wonderment of Karajan's old Philharmonia recording. But, then, Toscanini himself had never managed to replicate the unique charm of his pre-war English recording with the BBC SO.

The original review of the cycle entered a number of caveats, some of which still pertain, though it's the lack of certain repeats and the non-antiphonal dispensation of the violins that may worry some most nowadays. What so enthused us back then was the urgency of the music-making, its vitality and, ultimately, a fierce sense of joy that had its natural point of culmination in a thrillingly played and eloquently sung account of the finale of the Ninth. The playing of the new rejuvenated BPO dazzled throughout, as did Günther Hermanns recordings: clean and clear, and daringly 'lit' with a bright shimmer of reverberation. The recordings have always transferred effortlessly to CD and the present reissue is no exception.

Symphonies Nos 1-9
Karita Mattila sop **Violeta Urmana** mez **Thomas Moser** ten **Thomas Quasthoff** bass-bar **Eric Ericson Chamber Choir; Swedish Radio Choir; Berlin Philharmonic Orchestra / Claudio Abbado**
DG ⑤ 477 5864 (5h 46' · DDD)   ⓑ❍❍⤷
Nos 1-8 from TDK and EuroArts DVD originals

The finest of fine lines can divide routine and revelation. Seven years on from the release of a studio set of the nine, Abbado reveals doubts of his own. The Ninth excepted, the original DG set has been consigned to history, its place taken on CD by live performances given by Abbado and the Berliners in Renzo Piano's acclaimed new Santa Cecilia hall in Rome in February 2001. Originally recorded for DVD, this Rome cycle now emerges as Abbado's 'legacy' choice.

Hindsight tells us that the original set was premature, recorded before the project had established a purpose beyond that of providing the obligatory Beethoven cycle Abbado owed the orchestra; recorded, too, before players or engineers were conversant with the soundscapes needed to create Abbado's vision of a vital yet at the same time properly autochthonous Beethoven manner.

Where the Berlin set lacked emotional intensity and sonic immediacy, the Rome cycle provides both. As early as the slow movement of the First Symphony, it is evident that the warmer, more intimate Rome sound is helping concentrate our minds; the performance too is more strongly characterised, the finale markedly so.

The First, Third, Fifth and Seventh symphonies are the principal beneficiaries here. An examination of the relative timings tells us little beyond the fact that the Rome performances may occasionally be a touch broader. In practice, this has little to do with tempo, everything to do with shape and commitment – with concentration of tone and intensity of phrasing.

Abbado's claim that the Rome performances 'marked a significant advance in terms of style, spirit, and technique' is best illustrated in the Seventh Symphony. In Berlin, the finale seemed driven and over-quick; in Rome, everything is absorbed and of a piece. The more closely focused sound also helps. The individual string sections, the violins in particular, are far more clearly defined, an important factor when Abbado's retention of non-antiphonal layouts might be thought (wrongly as it turns out) to take the edge off the drama.

With the even-numbered symphonies it is more a case of swings and roundabouts. The Rome *Pastoral* is less vernal, the Eighth fiercer and more monumental, albeit not entirely settled rhythmically in the outer movements. The Fourth is again outstanding, though fuller-bodied and more overtly songful. The Berlin Ninth

---

BEETHOVEN SYMPHONIES – IN BRIEF

CO of Europe / Nikolaus Harnoncourt
Teldec ⑤ 3984 28144-2 (10 hr 40' · DDD)
Ⓑ❍❍❍⤷

Ⓖ A ground-breaking set which harnessed fresh ideas, totally committed playing and a *Gramophone* Record of the Year now economically coupled with more Beethoven works. It should be seriously considered.

Zurich Tonhalle / David Zinman
Arte Nova ⑤ 74321 65410-2 (5 hr 36' · DDD)
Ⓢ❍❍

Another set that blends modern instruments and a historically aware approach. There's a freshness and sparkle here that's very hard to resist. Only the Ninth slightly disappoints.

BPO / Claudio Abbado
DG ⑤ 477 5864 (5 hr 46' · DDD)   Ⓑ❍❍
Caught live in Rome and original issued as the soundtrack to the DVD, Abbado's second Berlin cycle in magnificent, a superb memento of his years with the BPO.

London Classical Players / Sir Roger NorringtonⓅ
Virgin Classics ⑤ 561943-2 (5 hr 53' · DDD) Ⓑ❍❍
A fine period-instrument cycle – Nos 2 and 8 won a *Gramophone* Award – with a fine sense of excitement and an intoxicating feeling for the adventure of such a project.

Orchestre Révolutionaire et Romantique /   Ⓟ
Sir John Eliot Gardiner
Archiv ⑤ 439 900-2AH5 (5 hr 28' · DDD)   Ⓕ❍❍
A superb, carefully considered and very theatrical cycle: this is Beethoven straight off the stage. The playing on period instruments is very fine and the recording nicely handled.

Berlin PO / Herbert von Karajan
DG ⑤ 463 088-2 (5 hr 32' · ADD)   Ⓑ❍❍
Dating from 1961-2, Karajan's second cycle was the first cycle recorded and released as such. It's still fresh and imaginative, boasting a real sense of discovery and excitement.

Vienna PO / Sir Simon Rattle
EMI ⑤ 557445-2 (5 hr 42' · DDD)   Ⓜ
Recorded live, this is a controversial set. Much admired in some quarters, it's lacking in the joy that's so central to this music. Rattle's 'period' approach sits uneasily with the lush, romantic style of the VPO. Sample first...

Scottish CO, Philharmonia /
Sir Charles Mackerras
Hyperion ⑤ CDS44301/5 (5h 36' · DDD) Ⓑ❍❍❍
Ripeness is all! Mackerras, caught live at the 2006 Edinburgh, offers a magnificent cycle (the only regret is a change of orchestra for the Ninth). This is historically informed Beethoven, but so full of humanity and life.

remains. It is a pretty good performance with an outstandingly well realised finale. What happened to the Rome Ninth is not explained. Ever since student days in Vienna with Toscanini fanatic Hans Swarowsky, Abbado has been in semi-permanent revolt against the Italian school of Beethoven interpretation. In these vibrant Rome performances he achieves an intensity of effect his hero Furtwängler just might have approved.

Symphonies Nos 1-9   ☐
Luba Orgonasova sop **Anne Sofie von Otter** mez
Anthony Rolfe Johnson ten **Gilles Cachemaille** bar
Monteverdi Choir; Orchestre Révolutionnaire et Romantique / Sir John Eliot Gardiner
Archiv Produktion ⑤ 439 900-2AH5 (328' · DDD)
Ⓕ🅞🅞▷

This set is remarkable and many will rate it as Mr Knightley rates Emma Woodhouse 'faultless in spite of her faults'. In his booklet essay, Peter Czorny tells us that the recordings are offered in the hope of transporting the listener back 'to that moment when this music burst forth into a world of heroes, wars and revolution, creating its own world of the sublime and ineffable'. This theme is developed by Gardiner in a robust 20-minute talk on the project that comes free on a sixth CD. Gardiner's opinion that Beethoven wanted his musicians to live dangerously has some peculiar consequences.

Symphony No 1: The opening is superbly judged. Gardiner doesn't overplay the *Adagio molto*, and the *Allegro con brio*, often played with a fatal languor by members of the old German School, is pretty quick. After his absurdly brisk reading of the second movement, Gardiner goes on to conduct dazzlingly successful accounts of the *Scherzo* and finale. Symphony No 2: This is very fine throughout. By following the written tempo markings and his own musical instincts Gardiner produces a perfomance of the first movement that opens out the drama most compellingly. Symphony No 3: More *révolutionnaire* than *romantique*. A very fast first movement gets within spitting distance of an impossible metronome mark. That and keen texturing make for tremendous dramatic urgency. Unfortunately, there's also too little accommodation *en route* of the rich cargo of ideas that Beethoven has shipped into this movement. In his haste to get to the recapitulation itself, Gardiner and his players are decidedly unpoised. He's superb in the last two movements; but these are considerably less than half the story where the *Eroica* is concerned. Symphony No 4: An unusually quick introductory and brisk *Allegro vivace*. Gardiner treats the pivotal drum entry before the recapitulation atmospherically. Glorious slow movement, impossibly quick finale.

Symphony No 5: Here is the stuff of which revolutions are made. Gardiner plays the piece pretty straight, and at white heat. The orchestra is superb, helped by the Francophone bias of its sound base. That said, the *Scherzo* (with repeat)

is surely too fast. It starts briskly and not especially quietly. The pace drops back for the Trio, which is just as well since the strings are hard-pressed to articulate clearly. The finale is also very fast, again ahead of what's generally regarded as a good metronome. There's a grandeur to the Scherzo-cum-finale that could be seen to reflect a vision that transcends the politics of revolution. Still, for its *éclat terrible*, this is unbeatable. The slow movement is also superbly shaped and directed.

Symphony No 6: Despite some lovely playing in the slow movement and an air of brisk efficiency, this is a rather joyless *Pastoral*. Nor is it a spiritually uplifting one. The *Scherzo* – 'A merry gathering of country folk' – is a very high-speed affair. At such a pace the various amusing false entries rather lose their point; to play in this village band you would need to be a virtuoso, and teetotal to boot.

Symphony No 7: A glorious performance. The introduction sets the scene with an ideal blend of weight and anticipation. The *Vivace* has a splendid dance feel and a power that's wholly unforced. *Scherzo* and finale are also superbly paced. The *Allegretto* is eloquent with a sense of barely sublimated grieving. The recording is magnificent. Symphony No 8: In general, the symphony thrives on the Gardiner approach, though in the finale the emphasis is again on high-speed locomotion.

Symphony No 9: The first movement has never been dispatched as rapidly as here. In fact, Gardiner doesn't get the bit between the teeth until bar 51, so the celebrated introduction has room to breathe. But he isn't entirely inflexible, and he and his players show remarkable skill in making busy detail tell. Yet a lot does go by the board. The slow movement is also played very quickly. However, the finale is superb. Tempos are unerringly chosen, the choral singing is beyond criticism, and there's a rare expressive quality to the singing of the solo quartet. High quality playing from the orchestra and often exceptional Archiv sound. At best, the physical and intellectual vitality of this music-making brings us close to the *Ding an sich*'. It's a best that occurs only intermittently. That it occurs at all is perhaps a sufficient miracle.

Symphonies Nos 1-9
Ruth Ziesak sop **Birgit Remmert** contr **Steve Davislim** ten **Detlef Roth** bar **Swiss Chamber Choir; Zurich Tonhalle Orchestra / David Zinman**
Arte Nova Classics ⑤ 74321 65410-2 (336' · DDD)
Ⓢ🅞🅞

Also available separately
74321 63645-2 – Nos 1 & 2 (54')
74321 59214-2 – Nos 3 & 4 (75')
74321 49695-2 – Nos 5 & 6 (74')
74321 56341-2 – Nos 7 & 8 (61')
74321 65411-2 – No 9 (73')

Viewed overall, the performances of Nos 1, 4, 6 and 8 are the best in this set, though there's a certain levelling of dynamics in the Eighth. In the Seventh and the Fifth, the finales might have benefited from a wider curve of dynamics and a little more in the way of tonal weight. On the other hand, Zinman's fleet-footed *Eroica* grows on you, and the Fourth is among the most vivacious accounts available. As to the Ninth, the *Scherzo*'s super-fast Trio makes particular sense at the very end of the movement where Trio and outer section engage in a brief comic tussle. The fast first movement is suitably dangerous and while the finale will no doubt court controversy (primarily for some unusual tempo relations), the *Adagio* sounds matter-of-fact, even a little impatient. Indeed, it's the one movement in this cycle that seems to misfire.

Zinman has used Bärenreiter's new edition of Beethoven's texts, although the extra appoggiaturas and ornaments, invariably sewn along the woodwind lines – were inserted by the conductor, based on sound musicological principles. All repeats are observed, and so are the majority of Beethoven's metronome markings. What matters most is the overall character of Zinman's Beethoven which is swift, lean, exhilarating and transparent. The Tonhalle copes bravely, often with exceptional skill, and the recordings easily compare with their best full-price rivals.

And the best bargain alternatives? Günter Wand's sense of structure (RCA) draws a sympathetic response, while Leinsdorf's solid, strong-arm Beethoven also has much to commend it (RCA). Karajan's 1962 cycle is surely the best of four (see above) and although Mackerras (Classics for Pleasure), like Zinman, sheds revealing beams of light here and there, this Zurich set has the greater impact. Those who favour the darker, weightier, more obviously 'heroic' Beethoven known (wrongly, perhaps) as 'old school' will probably not respond quite so readily, but they should still give Zinman a try. On balance, his cycle remains the best bargain digital option. Besides, Arte Nova's asking price is so ludicrously cheap that it's worth buying on impulse, if only for the sake of a refreshing change. Just try to have someone else's *Choral* in reserve.

Additional recommendations

Symphonies Nos 1-9

Wiens *sop* **Hartwig** *contr* **Lewis** *ten* **Hermann** *bar* **Hamburg State Opera Chorus; North German Radio Chorus; North German RSO / Wand**
RCA Red Seal ⑤ 74321 20277-2 　　Ⓜ
(356' · DDD) also available separately
　Consistently inspired: Wand's tempos are superbly judged, the orchestral balance ideal, and in the Ninth the soloists make a first-rate team.

Symphonies Nos 1-9ᵃ. Overtures – Coriolan, Op 62; Egmont, Op 84
Die Geschöpfe des Prometheus, Op 43
ᵃ**The Schütz Choir of London; London Classical Players / Sir Roger Norrington**
Virgin Classics ② 561943-2 (DDD) Recorded 1986-8

BEETHOVEN SYMPHONY NO 5 – IN BRIEF

Vienna Philharmonic Orchestra / Carlos Kleiber
DG The Originals 447 400-2GOR　　Ⓜ❍❍❍▷
　This is one of those legendary recordings that everyone knows about, but which quite takes the breath every time it's played. Kleiber paces the work magnificently and draws from the great VPO playing of an unparalleled intensity and beauty. Also available as a single download from iTunes.

Minnesota Orchestra / Osmo Vänskä
BIS　　BIS-SACD1416　　Ⓕ❍❍❍▷
　This disc, coupled with the Fourth Symphony, launched a new cycle and what a start! Vänskä's keen ear for orchestral texture and rhythmic bite makes for a thrilling ride: the sound may occasionally coarsen, but that's an effect he's probably after.

New York Philharmonic Symphony Orchestra / Arturo Toscanini
Naxos Historical mono 8 110840　　Ⓢ❍❍❍▷
If you can cope with the 1936 sound, here's a Fifth that positively blazes. Other Toscanini performances are better drilled but few achieved this incendiary quality when the music catches light. Thrilling.

London Classical Players / Sir Roger Norrington
Virgin Veritas 562489-2　　Ⓜ❍▷
One of the first 'period' Fifths and still a performance to take note of – Norrington manages very successfully to concey that coiled-spring intensity right from the start. When the finale finally explodes, the punch of the LCP is really impressive

Zurich Tonhalle / David Zinman
Arte Nova 74321 49695-2　　Ⓜ❍
Zinman's Beethoven – fleet of foot and with a zestful spring in its step – has gathered a substantial following. In the Fifth, his 'period' informed approach makes for a reading of agility but with an appealing dramatic bite.

Concertgebouw Orchestra / Wolfgang Sawallisch
EMI ② 573326-2　　Ⓑ❍
Coupled with Nos 4, 6 and 7, Sawallisch offers a traditional big-band approach, but a sane and very rewarding one. Don't expect any surprises from the interpretation – but then they are supplied in plenty by this extraordinary score.

Royal Liverpool Philharmonic Orchestra / Sir Charles Mackerras
Classics for Pleasure 572849-2　　Ⓢ❍❍
A richly rewarding pairing with No 7 that finds Sir Charles inspiring his players to performers of agility and intensity, though with a nice period feel.

Ⓢ⒪Ⓞ┅

This was a trail-blazing set that collected a Gramophone Award for Symphonies Nos 2 and 8. Norrington made much of Beethoven's metronome marks but also brought great drama and excitment to these well=known scores.

Symphonies – selected

Symphonies Nos 1 & 4. Egmont Overture, Op 84[a]
Berlin Philharmonic Orchestra / Herbert von Karajan
DG Galleria 419 048-2GGA (64' · ADD) Recorded
[a]1969, 1975-6
ⓂⓄ┅

The opening of the First, perfectly timed and chorded, announces playing of rare pedigree, though the *Allegro* itself, taken at a gently ruminative pace, is a surprise. The autumnal side of Karajan's make-up is one we don't often see. It's a beautifully shaped reading, with glorious wind playing and a nobly sustained through-rhythm. The mellow *Andante*, like the Minuet and Trio, emerges as a miracle of instrumental ensemble, a reminder of how, summer by summer, Karajan encouraged his players to make chamber music together on vacation. After so gentle a start, the finale seems strangely quick. Orchestrally, it's the finest quick Beethoven playing imaginable and for all the aerial excitement the final *fortissimo* peaks are compelling placed.

Karajan's instinctively dynamic approach to Beethoven is modified in the Fourth by a contrasted but equally strong feel for the German symphonic tradition. The performance strikes deepest at the points of stasis midway through each of the first three movements. Indeed, the sonority of the performance is remarkable throughout, with great use made of bass and cello colourings (something which the BPO had perfected by this time) and a huge dynamic range – implicit in the score from massive *tutti* chords down to the most perfectly regulated quiet drum rolls. It's in such playing, as subtle as it is creatively alive, that the flame of Beethoven's genius can be seen to burn brightly on. The *Egmont* Overture, played superbly and surprisingly swiftly, makes a welcome filler.

Symphonies – No 2, Op 36; No 7, Op 92
Minnesota Orchestra / Osmo Vänskä
BIS ⓢ BIS-SACD1816 (76' · DDD/DSD)
ⒻⓄ┅

This coupling of the Second and Seventh symphonies points up what Rob Cowan has called Vänskä's ability to 'focus the music's rhythmic profile with unwavering control'. Not that the performances are control-orientated. Even where the metronomes are good and speed is of the essence, as in the finale of the Second Symphony, quickness does not preclude ease.

In the Seventh Symphony, Vänskä keeps the harmonic drama in as sharp a focus as the rhythmic. The pulse may be quicker, the sound tauter, but the epic first movement breathes here much

as Klemperer would have allowed it to breathe. With Vänskä, old insights are not necessarily invalid insights. In the *Allegretto* and third-movement Trio there is a reversion, not to old-fashioned Teutonic slowness, but to thoughtful tempi that are on the measured side of quick.

What is truly outstanding here is the transparency of the texturing and the meticulous integration of phrase shape and accent within the rhythmic continuum. Everything is audible but since Vänskä is not a didactic conductor nothing is italicised or underlined. That said, the violins' extraordinarily precise articulation of the Second Symphony's notorious seventh bar, with its arch of double-dotted trilled quavers and interior grace notes, may shock collectors used to the old pre-Bärenreiter fudges.

The BIS recording has exceptional clarity, with finely judged reverberation times, and a dynamic range that catches every gradation of the orchestra's scrupulously judged sound profile right down to *pianissimi* of quite astonishing beauty and restraint.

Symphonies No 2 & 6, 'Pastoral'
London Symphony Orchestra / Bernard Haitink
LSO Live LSO0082 (76' · DDD); ⓢ LSO0582.
Recorded live 2005
Ⓢ ┅

Very appealing, this – the punchy, neatly packed sound; the way the timps thwack away at the right-hand side of the stage, the antiphonally placed fiddles busying to and fro, Haitink's unmannered, high-energy but essentially non-aggressive approach to both symphonies. The first thing that strikes you about the *Pastoral* is its sensitive shaping. The second is the lively pacing, but never breathless or unduly hurried. The 'Scene by the brook' ebbs and flows at roughly the prescribed speed and yet the LSO's playing, ever warm-hearted, never adopts 'period' affectations: it's as if the laudable old guard has had a wash, a brush-up and a slight change of heart regarding tempo and articulation. The 'Peasants' Merrymaking' enjoys something of Toscanini's bacchanalian drive, the storm a measure of his dynamism.

The Second Symphony is formal but fun. The opening *Adagio molto* is pretty powerful, the principal *allegro* light on its feet but rock-steady and with an imposing and firmly held bass-line. Again, Haitink keeps the slow movement on the move without sacrificing gravitas.

Both readings are profoundly satisfying, the work of musicians who know the scores backwards, love playing them and know what not to do. To say that they provide a new benchmark would be crass; but Haitink and the LSO seem set to provide one of the top Beethoven symphony cycles of the digital era.

Symphonies – No 3, 'Eroica', Op 55; No 4, Op 60
Basle Chamber Orchestra / Giovanni Antonini
Sony Classical ② ⓢ 88697 19252-2 (79' · DDD/DSD)
ⓂⓄ┅

It is rare nowadays, even in the daredevil world of period performance, to come across a performance of Beethoven's *Eroica* Symphony that makes this revolutionary piece seem new-minted. Here though is just such a performance. Giovanni Antonini has been mentioned in the same breath as Toscanini, which may seem odd given Antonini's origins as a recorder- and Baroque flute-player and founder member of Il Giardino Armonico. Yet one can see how the comparison arose. The mix of drive and acumen is indeed extraordinary.

Not that the Maestro could, or would, have approved of Antonini's megalomaniac account of the Fourth Symphony where tempi, always a notch faster than Toscanini's own, are driven to extremes and where there is barely a *cantabile* in sight, even in the slow movement. This is the Fourth Symphony on a war-footing, brutal and unreflecting, with some odd sonorities to boot. The *pianissimo* timpani rolls, to whose care Beethoven entrusts the first movement's most magical transitions, rattle like rain on a corrugated iron roof.

Period performers like to live dangerously. Even so, it is difficult to reconcile the conductor who so brutalises the Fourth Symphony with the sure-footed interpreter of the *Eroica*. Here is a musician who understands the *Eroica* from within, dramatically, logistically and imaginatively. A musician, moreover, who can project that understanding into an orchestral performance that glows white in the furnace. The *Marcia funebre* is particularly fine with a characteristically forward-moving pulse, finely chiselled phrasing and strikingly 'French' sonorities.

Symphony No 3. Overtures – Leonore Nos 1 & 2
Philharmonia Orchestra / Otto Klemperer Ⓗ
EMI Great Recordings of the Century mono 567740-2
(76' · ADD) Recorded 1954-5 ⓂⓄⓄ➔

In 1955 the Philharmonia Orchestra was at the peak of its powers. And what cogency there is sustaining and feeding the drama. Where other orchestras and conductors whip themselves into a terrible lather at the start of the finale, Klemperer and the Philharmonia sail majestically on. This is a great performance, steady yet purposeful, with textures that seem hewn out of granite. There's no exposition repeat, and the trumpets blaze out illicitly in the first movement coda, but this is still one of the great *Eroicas* on record. As Karajan announced to Klemperer after flying in to a concert performance around this time: 'I have come only to thank you, and say that I hope I shall live to conduct the Funeral March as well as you have done'. In the *Leonore* Overtures, recorded in 1954, the playing is a bit more rough-edged.

'Eroica'
A film by Simon Cellan Jones
Ian Hart Beethoven **Tim Piggott-Smith** Count

Dietrichstein **Jack Davenport** Prince Lobkowitz
Fenella Woolgar Princess Lobkowitz **Claire Skinner**
Josephine **Lucy Akhurst** Therese **Frank Finlay**
Haydn **Leo Bill** Ferdinand Ries
Music performed by the **Orchestre Révolutionnaire et Romantique / Sir John Eliot Gardiner**
Opus Arte ⒹⓋⒹ OA0908D (129' · 16:9 · PCM stereo and DTS 5.1 · 0) Includes a complete performance of Symphony No 3, 'Eroica' Ⓕ

'June 1804' says the legend at the film's opening. Denis Matthews (in his Master Musicians volume) thought it was six months later that the *Eroica* was given a first run-through in the palace of Prince Lobkowitz, but had that been so we should have been denied Beethoven and his pupil Ferdinand Ries tramping river banks, and Beethoven and the object of his unrequited love lazing idly in the palace courtyard, so June it is. Let's not complain: historical verisimilitude is always going to be at a premium in such reconstructions, and the makers of this BBC film do not take us for fools. They use what we know of the people and places concerned to invent a plausible narrative of politics, love and anger that, most importantly, centres on the music.

In fact the domestic scale of the setting is a powerful reminder of the work's vast reach and capacity to shock. Potential purchasers will have to judge for themselves whether they are likely to be bothered by the soundtrack being palpably separate from the visuals, or the orchestra being visibly smaller than the sum of its excellent parts. The recording is instrumental in bringing film and symphony to life: winds to the fore, bassoons and growly double-basses balefully ever-present.

In the *Eroica* itself, Gardiner's first movement (without its repeat) has a bare and remorseless intensity; his own previous DG recording is nearer Beethoven's metronome mark and some distance further from the expressive force of this new recording. The *Scherzo* is a little plainly phrased but Gardiner springs his surprise with the finale. A tempo that seems at first tepid grows around the music, allowing the fugue its due weight, the flute solo its pathos and the horns their full measure of glory.

The film's producers think the performance worth hearing on a separate set of tracks, without noises off: there are only so many times that you will want to hear Beethoven tell Ries to 'piss off' after his pupil has interrupted halfway through the first movement. In a further act of charity, Opus Arte spares us the otherwise ubiquitous musical excerpt over the title menus. The enterprise is probably a one-off but it's tempting to imagine what this team could do with the Fifth, or even the Ninth.

Symphonies Nos 4 & 5
Minnesota Orchestra / Osmo Vänskä
BIS BIS-SACD1416 (67' · DDD/DSD) ⒻⓄⓄⓄ➔

It was during Osmo Vänskä's time with the BBC Scottish SO that his Beethoven began winning golden opinions. His reading of the Fourth is fiery but not relentless. Metronome marks are important but not mandatory. Transparent textures and a rigorous way with dynamics also feature. Of particular interest is the skill with which he continuously keeps in view the bass line, and thus the music's harmonic contour, never easy, given the 'open' nature of Beethoven's scoring.

The Minnesota Orchestra are extraordinarily proficient: fleet-footed and articulate, though tonally they have less in reserve than the Berlin or Vienna orchestras. This can be a limitation in the Fifth, where the sound occasionally edges towards coarseness but it makes little or no difference in the Fourth, even in the *Adagio*. What Vänskä sacrifices in lyric poetry he makes up for in justness of rhythm and chasteness of texture. Skilful as BIS's engineers are in dealing with the quietest passages, finding an optimum playback level for the vibrant but *pianissimo*-strewn Fourth takes time and patience.

The performance of the dynamically less problematic Fifth also also bristles with character. Typically, *Scherzo* and finale are bound to one another structurally but not tamed emotionally.

Symphonies – No 4, Op 60; No 7, Op 92
Manchester Camerata / Douglas Boyd
Avie AV2169 (74' · DDD)   Ⓕ **OOD**

Thirty years ago, 'chamber orchestra' Beethoven was considered to be a mildly interesting eccentricity; nowadays it is practically *de rigueur*. The Chamber Orchestra of Europe blazed the trail. Douglas Boyd was its principal oboe for many years, though more recently his widely recognised drive and musical acumen have been put at the service of the long-established and nowadays upwardly mobile Manchester Camerata. This, surely, is one of their finest records.

The Camerata do not use period instruments (under Boyd they do not even use period layouts), nor is Boyd an interpretative absolutist. Harnoncourt and Abbado, his old bosses at the COE, have probably helped determine his approach, yet there is no sense that these are hand-me-down readings. The switch of roles has clearly refocused his interest in the music and rekindled it: an experience the orchestra evidently shares.

There is aggression in the performances, but it is an artistically contained aggression. The playing, with its gutsy, tensile strings and characterful lead woodwinds, has a powerfully communicative quality. Both readings are rhythmically strong, though the delayed string entry at the start of the hushed return to the dominant in the second subject group of the first movement of the Seventh (bars 141-42) is still a surprise. As this happens three times, twice in the exposition and again in the recapitulation, it is clearly no accident.

The recordings are superb. For once we have an in-house, orchestra-live product that actually works on record, with a sharply focused bespoke production (no applause) that vividly conveys the no-holds-barred immediacy of the music-making.

Symphonies Nos 5 & 7
Vienna Philharmonic Orchestra / Carlos Kleiber
DG The Originals 447 400-2GOR (72' · ADD) Recorded 1974   Ⓜ **OOOD**

The recording of the Fifth, always very fine, comes up superbly in this transfer. What, though, of the Seventh, an equally distinguished performance though always perceptibly greyer-sounding on LP, and on CD? The result is a performance of genius that now speaks to us freely and openly for the first time. In some ways this is a more important document than the famous Fifth.

Great recordings of the Seventh, greatly played and conducted, but with first and second violins divided left and right, are as rare as gold dust. Freshly refurbished, this Kleiber Seventh would go right to the top of any short list of recommendable Sevenths. It's wonderful to have these two legendary performances so expertly restored.

Symphonies Nos 5ᵃ & 7ᵇ   Ⓗ
New York Philharmonic Symphony Orchestra / Arturo Toscanini
Naxos Historical mono 8 110840 (77' · ADD) Recorded at Carnegie Hall, New York ᵇ1936, ᵃlive 1933   Ⓢ **OOOD**

Toscanini is a near-impossible act to follow. But then in a sense he was fortunate. He didn't have a fat record catalogue full of Rostrum Greats to live up to and he wasn't under pressure to say something new, or at least something different. On the contrary, Toscanini's avowed mission was to clean up where others had indulged in interpretative excess. And he could as well have been cleaning up for the future.

There are numerous Toscanini Fifths in public or private circulation, at least four of them dating from the 1930s. This one is lithe, dynamic and consistently commanding. Comparing it with Toscanini's 1952 NBC recording finds numberless instances where a natural easing of pace helps underline essential transitions, such as the quiet alternation of winds and strings that holds the tension at the centre of the first movement. The glow of the string playing towards the close of the second movement has no parallel with the 1952 version and while the NBC *Scherzo* is better drilled, this finale really blazes. Mark Obert-Thorn has done a first-rate job with the sound, focusing the orchestra's whispered *pianissimo*s while keeping surface noise to a minimum.

The commercially released 1936 New York Seventh has already been hailed as a classic. As with the Fifth, Toscanini's ability to gauge pauses to the nth degree – in this case the rests that separate the finale's opening *fortissimo* rallying calls – is truly inimitable. The nobility and the visceral thrill of Toscanini's pre-war version remains unchallenged. The transfer is excellent.

Beethoven Symphony No 6
Schubert Symphony No 5 in B flat, D485
Vienna Philharmonic Orchestra / Karl Böhm
DG The Originals 447 433-2GOR (74' · ADD)
Recorded 1971, 1979   Ⓜ❍❍❍❍➔

Ⓖ Karl Böhm's Beethoven is a compound of earth and fire. His VPO recording of Beethoven's Sixth of 1971 dominated the LP catalogue for over a decade, and has done pretty well on CD on its various appearances. His reading is generally glorious and it remains one of the finest accounts of the work ever recorded. It still sounds well and the performance (with the first-movement exposition repeat included) has an unfolding naturalness and a balance between form and lyrical impulse that's totally satisfying. The brook flows untroubled and the finale is quite lovely, with a wonderfully expansive climax.

The Schubert dates from the end of Böhm's recording career. It's a superb version of this lovely symphony, another work that suited Böhm especially well. The reading is weighty but graceful, with a most beautifully phrased *Andante* (worthy of a Furtwängler), a bold Minuet and a thrilling finale. The recording is splendid. If you admire Böhm this is a worthy way to remember his special gifts.

Symphonies Nos 5 & 6   Ⓟ
London Classical Players / Sir Roger Norrington
Virgin Veritas 562489-2 (74' · DDD)   Ⓜ❍➔

Norrington conducts an enjoyable, memorable account of the Fifth. He throws off the introduction to the first movement with crisp brilliance, and the *Allegro* conveys enormous underlying energy. His *Andante* is beautifully phrased and flows most delicately; in the bustling double bass theme at the centre of the *Scherzo* the bowing is light, the effect refined and offering easy virtuosity. Norrington's finale is strongly accented, his horns broadly sonorous, partly as a result of the resonant EMI sound.

The *Pastoral* is also a revelation. Norrington adopts a swift tempo in the joyous first movement but there's no hint of that relentless, driven quality we've sometimes had on record. He's fully up to tempo in the vibrant *tuttis*; elsewhere he's most careful to allow the music to dance and breathe, the transitions always most sensitively moulded. It's also a joy to hear this symphony on period instruments. This *Pastoral* is a real voyage of aural discovery. Sometimes the wind tuning isn't 100 per cent true, at others it's simply a matter of Norrington teasing us with the timing of a trill's release or pointing up dissonances that usually get smoothed over. The sound is wonderfully clear and trenchant.

Symphony No 7. Triple Concerto
Gordan Nikolitch *vn* **Tim Hugh** *vc*
Lars Vogt *pf*
London Symphony Orchestra / Bernard Haitink
LSO Live 🄂 Ⓜ LSO0578 (75' · DDD)   Ⓜ➔

Nothing like having your expectations challenged, especially in Beethoven where interpretative templates tend to settle for good. Past experience of Bernard Haitink in the symphonies left an impression of worthiness and generalised musicality; but the first instalment of the conductor's projected live Beethoven symphony cycle with the London Symphony Orchestra witnesses a significantly increased adrenalin count. As well as being vital and intelligently thought through, Haitink's new Seventh honours all repeats and has the inestimable advantage of spatially divided violin desks, particularly telling in the clear but relatively dry Barbican Hall acoustic. The first movement's bracing rhythms gambol rather than storm and there's genuine tenderness in the Allegretto. The *Scherzo*'s dancing gait and the unforced momentum of the finale is very attractive.

What's strong about the Haitink's excellent Triple Concerto is its sense of architecture, the way Haitink builds the opening tutti so that the climactic passage where winds alternate with strings (2'04") establishes a real sense of arrival. Interesting Haitink's soloists seem more integrated within the rest of the band than sopme versions, less in terms of sound than overall playing-style: inspired moments include Tim Hugh's rapt opening phrases in the second movement. And James Mallinson's integrated sound-picture for LSO Live is very pleasing.

Symphony No 9
Helena Juntunen *sop* **Katarina Karnéus** *mez*
Daniel Norman *ten* **Neal Davies** *bass*
Minnesota Chorale and Orchestra / Osmo Vänskä
BIS 🄂 BIS-SACD1616 (66' · DDD · T/t)   Ⓕ❍➔

Vänskä offers a radical re-think of Beethoven's *Choral* Symphony, a youthful, brave statement, free of iconic influences. Considered in purely musical terms, his version would better fit the idea of revolution through renewal.

The opening of Vänskä's *Choral*, though deathly quiet, is chiselled and precise, the first *tutti* like a fireball from the heavens, much aided by a hugely dynamic recording. Within a mere minute or two, one quality has made its mark with maximum force, namely rhythm, tight as a drum – that, and an astonishing power of projection. But what is really striking is the muscularity of the playing, its clipped, propulsive phrasing, quite unlike any other modern-instrument version of the Ninth. Suddenly this quirky first movement sounds like tough-grained middle-period Beethoven, the fugal writing at its centre granitic and purposeful, the music's many calculated repetitions unnervingly obsessive. The contrast with the Bacchanalian *Scherzo* is more marked than usual, Vänskä again focusing the music's rhythmic profile with unwavering control. The *Adagio*'s quiet opening is breathtaking and although the variations that follow are seamlessly interwoven, the effect is anything but rigid.

Vänskä's finale returns us to the shock and awe of his first moment, with a decisive, tight-lipped opening (the fast tempo held absolutely firm), warmly phrased counterpoint surrounding the 'Ode to Joy' build-up and then, with the unleashing of the voices, an excellent group of soloists and a well drilled chorus who sing as if they really know (and mean) what they're singing. The tenor's March episode is fairly swift, leading to a razor-sharp fugue. And when the chorus enters, well... In a word, Vänska's finale is full of zeal.

Symphony No 9 **H**
Aase Nordmo-Løvberg sop **Christa Ludwig** mez
Waldemar Kmentt ten **Hans Hotter** bass-bar **Philharmonia Chorus and Orchestra / Otto Klemperer**
Testament SBT1177 (71' · ADD) Recorded live 1957
Ⓕ**OO**

This is a revelatory live recording by EMI's engineers of Klemperer's performance of the Ninth Symphony at the Royal Festival Hall, immediately before his 1957 EMI recording. Where the studio recording gives us a frontal, ground-level view of the players spread out across the spaces of the Kingsway Hall, this live Festival Hall recording offers us that special Klemperer balance which gave particular prominence to the winds and the timpani. Strings, and in the finale the chorus, are nicely focused; but from where we sit, somewhere above the first oboe, it's winds and timpani that are the centre of interest. No one would have dared balance a studio recording this way, yet this is far closer to what a Klemperer performance really sounded like.

There are a couple of oddities in the finale. In the preliminary orchestral statement of the 'joy' theme, the bassoon descant drowns out the violas and cellos; then, later on, we get a less than clear view of the tenor. (A blessed relief, perhaps, given Kmentt's thin, dried-out sound here.) Interpretatively, the two performances are identical, though the live performance is just that bit more intense. The first movement does not benefit greatly but the Scherzo is transformed; what rather lumbers in the studio is here a thrilling dance of the Titans. The finale is wonderfully performed, thrillingly articulated by the newly founded Philharmonia Chorus and the Philharmonia players. Detail after detail shines out, etched into the imagination by the playing and the persistently enquiring recording.

Symphony No 9 **H**
Elisabeth Schwarzkopf sop **Elisabeth Höngen** mez
Hans Hopf ten **Otto Edelmann** bass **Bayreuth Festival Chorus and Orchestra / Wilhelm Furtwängler**

EMI Great Recordings of the Century mono 566901-2
(75' · ADD) Recorded live 1951 Ⓜ**OO**▷

This performance has become legendary, as much for the occasion as for the music-making itself. The reopening of Wagner's Festival Theatre in Bayreuth in 1951 after the catastrophe of war was nothing if not symbolic. If anything could lay the ghost of Bayreuth's immediate past, the years from 1930 to 1944 when the theatre was run by the English-born, Nazi-worshipping Winifred Wagner, it might be a performance of the Ninth Symphony under the most celebrated of the German conductors who had lived through Nazi rule without being, in any real sense, morally or artistically party to it. Certainly, it isn't difficult to think of the slow movement's second subject, unfolded here in a way that has never been bettered, as an atonement and a benediction.

Not everyone will respond to this vision of the Ninth: as an interpretation it's broadly based, with some slow tempos and some quirky adjustments of pace; though beneath everything – beneath the gear changes and failures in ensemble – a great current massively flows. The solo vocal and choral work in the finale is electric after the *fugato* but is breezily, bumpily Teutonic before that; Hans Hopf is his usual restless, hectic self. The CD transfer provides some added clarity of image for the generally excellent mono recording; and it also provides an all-important continuity. Instrumental bass frequencies are rather wooden but the recording reproduces higher frequency string, wind, and vocal sound more smoothly than was often the case at this time.

Many collectors will be looking to a stereo, digital recording of the Ninth as a CD library acquisition; yet this performance has a prior, if not absolute, claim on collectors' attention.

Symphony No 9 **H**
Elisabeth Schwarzkopf sop **Elsa Cavelti** mez
Ernst Haefliger ten **Otto Edelmann** bass **Lucerne Festival Chorus; Philharmonia Orchestra / Wilhelm Furtwängler**
Tahra mono FURT1054/7(78' · ADD) Recorded live 1954
Ⓕ**OOO**

Ⓖ The 40th anniversary of Furtwängler's death on November 30, 1954 brought forth a rich crop of reissues and remasterings, most notably on the French label Tahra, which secured the rights to publish limited editions of some of Furtwängler's most important (and, it must be said, most frequently pirated) live recordings. Some of Furtwängler's finest performances of Beethoven's music were given in the last months of his life, an odd paradox given his failing health, and by November the apparent extinction of his will to live. Yet this Lucerne Ninth is a seismic utterance, the final heroic regrouping of musical and psychic powers that in certain works of the repertory have this gangling figure towering over all his rivals. This is arguably the greatest of all Furtwängler's recordings of the symphony. Walter Legge wanted to acquire the performance as EMI's official replacement for the momentous 1951 Bayreuth account, but it wasn't to be. Since then, there have been various 'unofficial' editions. The Tahra differs in being 'official', well transferred, and further enhanced by a few introductory remarks made by Furtwängler himself.

Here, the most significant section is that in which Furtwängler sees the problem of interpreting the Ninth as one that effectively postdates the performing culture into which it was born. Furtwängler understood the Ninth as well as any conductor in the 20th century. You can argue this way or that over the pacing of the slow movement (though we defy anyone to say that his performance is anything other than deeply eloquent) or the leisurely speed of the second movement Trio. In the all-important first movement, though, there's no doubt that Beethoven's written tempo markings and frequent subsequent modifications clearly presuppose the kind of uniquely singing, flexible, harmonically searching (but by no means too slow) reading Furtwängler invariably gave us.

Additional recommendation

Symphony No 9
Wiens sop **Hartwig** mez **Lewis** ten **Hermann** bass
**Hamburg State Opera Chorus; North German
Radio Symphony Orchestra and Chorus / Wand**
RCA Red Seal 74321 68005-2 (66' · DDD) Ⓢ
A real bargain. Wand's 1986 recording enshrines a wonderfully wise and humane Ninth, unerringly paced and always intensely refreshing in its lean purposefulness, if at times lacking that last ounce of lump-in-the-throat universality.

Septet, Op 20

Septet in E flat, Op 20. Piano Quintet in E flat, Op 16. Sextet in E flat, Op 81b
Ottó Rácz ob **József Balogh** cl **József Vajda** bn **Jenő Keveházi, János Keveházi, Sándor Berki** hns **Ildikó Hegyi, Péter Popa** vns **Győző Máthé** va **Peter Szabó** vc **István Toth** db
Naxos 8 553090 (74' · DDD) Ⓢ▸

These talented Hungarian players offer a fluent, responsive account of the Septet that highlights the music's intimate chamber character – delight in the music's elegance and perfect balance of instrumental forces. In the present instance, vivid recording creates a clear, natural ambience for this alert, sensitively blended ensemble. In the Sextet, horn players, Jenő and János Keveházi play with subtlety and panache as required, their tone spontaneous and free. This excellent, value-for-money Naxos disc also offers an elegant, well-turned performance of Beethoven's E flat Quintet.

Piano Quintet, Op 16

Beethoven Piano Quintet in E flat, Op 16 Ⓗ
Mozart Piano Quintet in E flat, K452. Sinfonia concertante in E flat, K297b[a]
Walter Gieseking pf **Philharmonia Wind Quartet** (Sidney Sutcliffe ob Bernard Walton cl Dennis Brain hn Cecil James bn) [a]**Philharmonia Orchestra / Herbert von Karajan**
Testament mono SBT1091 (80' · ADD) Recorded 1955 ⒻOO

There have never been any doubts about these performances. The horn playing in the *Sinfonia concertante* is unsurpassable and in the quintets Gieseking's lightness and his clarity and sense of style is simply beyond praise. The tempos are on the slow side in the first movement of the Mozart and the finale of the Beethoven but somehow with Gieseking, slow tempos have a way of seeming to be just about right. Richard Osborne's excellent notes quote a letter from Sidney Sutcliffe of touching modesty. Speaking of their run-through of the Mozart, he says, 'On reaching the *Allegro moderato*, the great man played two bars at an absolutely perfect tempo and then stopped and asked in the most gentle and hesitant manner, "Will that be all right for you?" So it was a most happy occasion although I found it a grave responsibility matching the artistry of my colleagues when Bernard [Walton], Cecil [James] and Dennis [Brain] were producing sounds of breath-taking beauty.' Breathtaking is the right word for all concerned here on one of the great chamber music records of the LP era. Considerable pains have been taken with the transfers, which now sound fresh and full bodied. Thoroughly recommended.

String Quartets

Op 18: No 1 in F; No 2 in G; No 3 in D;
No 4 in C minor; No 5 in A; No 6 in B flat
Op 59 'Rasumovsky': No 1 in F;
No 2 in E minor; No 3 in C
Op 74 in E flat, 'Harp'; Op 95 in F minor, 'Serioso'
'Late' Quartets: Op 127 in E flat; Op 130 in B flat;
Op 131 in C sharp; Op 132 in A minor; Op 135 in F
Grosse Fuge in B flat, Op 133

Complete String Quartets

Complete String Quartets. Grosse Fuge
Quartetto Italiano (Paolo Borciani, Elisa Pegreffi vns Piero Farulli va Franco Rossi vc)
Philips ⑩ 454 062-2PB10 (544' · ADD) Recorded 1967-75 ⒷOO

It goes without saying that no one ensemble can unlock all the secrets contained in these quartets. The Quartetto Italiano's claims are strongest in the Op 18 Quartets. They offer eminently civilised, thoughtful and aristocratic readings. Their approach is reticent but they also convey a

BEETHOVEN STRING QUARTETS OP 18 – IN BRIEF

Tokyo Quartet
Harmonia Mundi ② HMU90 7436/7   Ⓜ❍❍❍
A superb achievement that manages wonderfully to combine the wisdom of years with the ability to convey the startling originality of these six quartets. The actualy sound these four players make is stunning.

Takács Quartet
Decca ② 470 848-2DH2   Ⓜ❍❍
The Takács bring tremendous intensity to these six quartets: this is playing of enormous consrasts, with barely audible pianissimi turing to sledge-hammer fortissimi with amazing control. Listening to this sense you follow the music in a way that few of other groups permit.

Alban Berg Quartet
EMI ② 562778-2   Ⓑ❍
Elegant, aristocratic playing from one of the great European ensembles. You rarely find playing of this cultivation that digs so deeply into the music. A real bargain drawn from the ABQ's first (studio) cycle.

The Lindsays
ASV ③ CDDCA1111/3   Ⓑ❍❍
The UK's greatest string quartet returned to the Beethoven for a second recorded cycle and offered readings that are even more satisfying than their first cycle. Speeds have quickened, the textures have lightened but nothing of the intensity is sacrificed. They add the String Quintet which takes the set onto a third disc.

Leipzig Quartet
MDG 307 0853-2, 0855-2 & 0856-2   Ⓕ❍❍
Deeply rewarding musicianship and a complete lack of showmanship make these performances well worth hearing. There's a lovely sheen to their sound and they are constantly alive to Beethoven's imaginative world.

Talich Quartet
Calliope CAL9633, CAL9634   Ⓜ
If you are drawn to the Talich's very individual approach this set might be worth conisdering, though it's not at the level we have come to expect in the later, greater works. They still sound wonderful inspired by this music. The sound could benefit from a little more space around it.

Miro Quartet
Vanguard Classics ② ATMCD1655   Ⓕ
A set of lively, dancing playing from one of the shooting stars on the US chmaber music scene. These Op 18 quartets have a fizzing, modern feel to them that make them very appealing.

strong sense of making music in domestic surroundings. Quite frankly, you couldn't do very much better than this set. In the middle-period quartets the Italians are hardly less distinguished, even though there are times when the Végh offer deeper insights, as in the slow movement of Op 59 No 1. Taken in isolation, however, the Quartetto Italiano remain eminently satisfying both musically and as recorded sound. As far as sound quality is concerned, it's rich and warm. In Opp 74 and 95, they more than hold their own against all comers. These are finely proportioned readings, poised and articulate.

The gain in clarity because of the remastering entails a very slight loss of warmth in the middle register, but as recordings the late quartets, made between 1967 and 1969, can hold their own against their modern rivals. Not all of these received universal acclaim at the time of their first release. The opening fugue of Op 131 is too slow at four-in-the-bar and far more *espressivo* than it should be, but, overall, these performances still strike a finely judged balance between beauty and truth, and are ultimately more satisfying and searching than most of their rivals.

Complete String Quartets
Végh Quartet (Sándor Végh, Sándor Zöldy vns
Georges Janzer va Paul Szábo vc)
Astrée Naïve ⑩ V4871 (8 hours 46' · ADD) Recorded
1974   Ⓑ❍❍

The Végh's classic accounts of the String Quartets are in a completely different league from any of their rivals: there's no cultivation of surface polish but there's no lack of elegance and finesse. Above all, there's no attempt to glamorise their sound. In Op 18 No 1 they find the *tempo giusto* right at the beginning and they find more depth in the slow movement than anyone else on record. Végh himself floats the melodic line in this movement in a most imaginative way and is wonderfully supported. In the civilised exchanges that open Op18 No 2 the Végh brings alight touch to bear, and has an elegance and wit that's almost unmatched and great refinement of tone. There were complaints of the bottom-heavy recording when it appeared on LP, and it's less transparent and lifelike than more modern recordings.

The *Rasumovsky* set is admirable for its alertness of articulation, rhythmic grasp and flexibility and its subtle range of tone-colour. The effortlessness with which the dialogue proceeds silences criticism. The Végh brings special insights to this inexhaustible music. The style and the quality of perception seem so remarkable and so well sustained here that any deficiencies can be overlooked. There are lapses in tone and intonation, most of them on the part of the leader, yet what a musician he is, and what a remarkable guide to the visionary content of these quartets. Where the music demands most in such matters he's never wanting. These are neither the most 'perfect' nor the most sumptuously recorded accounts available, yet they are the deepest and most searching.

When listening to them you're conscious only of Beethoven's own voice. The transfers give a slightly firmer focus and sharper detail, though that slight bottom-heaviness still remains.

String Quartets Op 18

CDDCA1111: String Quartets, Op 18 Nos 1-3
CDDCA1112: String Quartets, Op 18 Nos 4 & 5.
String Quartet in F, H34
CDDCA1113: String Quartet, Op 18 No 6.
String Quintet in C, Op 29ª
The Lindsays (Peter Cropper, Ronald Birks *vns*
Roger Bigley *va* Bernard Gregor-Smith *vc*) with
ª**Louise Williams-***va*
ASV CDDCA1111-3 (oas: 78', 66', 58' · DDD) Ⓕ**O**

It's wonderful how The Lindsays, after a career of more than 30 years, could still sound so fresh and spontaneous. From the start of Op 18 No 1 we feel that every phrase is shaped individually, the music felt as it's being played. The dynamics are beautifully differentiated; *pianissimo* always has an altered sound compared with *piano*. Presenting the sense of the music and its emotions is always a priority, which leads to some daring interpretative decisions. The fast and fantastical finale of the Op 29 Quintet, with its scary *tremolos* and wild-sounding *rubato* in the first violin arpeggios is one example of a no-holds-barred approach that gets into the character of the music in a way that a more measured style couldn't. It's a splendid idea to include this neglected quintet as well as Beethoven's brilliant arrangement of the Op 14 No 1 Piano Sonata; the Quintet's rich, often complex, textures are relished, helping us to hear this work as a half-way house between the C major Quintets of Mozart and Schubert.

Despite the air of spontaneity, The Lindsays' interpretations of Op 18 remain very similar to those they offered us 20 years ago. The new recordings are certainly crisper and more immediate than their analogue predecessors, yet the sound has a warmth that enhances the often very atmospheric playing to be found, for instance, in the mysterious *pianissimo* passages at the ends of the slow movements of Nos 3 and 6. The main difference in the playing is that the new performances are generally faster, brighter and rhythmically lighter, with clearer articulation. The earlier version of No 2's highly ornamented *Adagio* has a beautiful sustained sound; in this recording Peter Cropper plays the melody with more fantasy, giving a powerful, rhetorical expression to each phrase. The slight increase in speed of most of the *allegros* brings them more into line with Beethoven's often challenging metronome marks: as a result there's more sparkle and excitement, and the light touch means there's rarely any sense of strain. The two Minuets, in Nos 4 and 5, benefit from being played faster; the passionate C minor character in No 4 is brought out most persuasively. For the *Adagio* of No 6 The Lindsays, in common with most other groups, adopt a more flowing speed than Beet-

BEETHOVEN LATE STRING QUARTETS – IN BRIEF

Quartetto Italiano
Philips ③ 464 684-2PM3 (216' · ADD) Ⓜ**OO**▷
'Civilised', 'aristocratic', 'thoughtful' are some of the words often used to describe this great Italian ensemble's approach. Their late quartets were recorded in the late 1960s, and still sound very fine. A notable achievement.

Talich Quartet
Calliope CAL9637/8/9 (213' · DDD) Ⓕ**O**
A powerfully intimate set which conveys the impression of four outstanding chamber musicians playing for each other – music-making eavesdropped upon, rather than projected to an imagined audience. A fine set.

Busch Quartet
Pearl mono ③ GEMS0053 (220' · ADD) Ⓜ**O**
A wonderfully human and humane experience: this is quartet-playing of towering achievement that satisfies at every level. The sound, from the 1930s, is evidently somewhat antique, but the passion and understanding shines down the years.

Lindsay Quartet
ASV ③ CDDCS403 (220' · DDD) Ⓜ**O**
A *Gramophone* Award-winner back in the 1980s and deservedly so, for this is very impressive quartet playing. The Lindsays have lived long with this music and, though their newer cycle may plumb deeper, this first set is still a notable achievement.

Hollywood Quartet Ⓗ
Testament ③ SBT3082 (193' · ADD) Ⓕ**O**
A very fine set from the late 1950s featuring the superb Los Angeles-based quartet. Their technical address is considerable and, unlike some American quartets from later generations, they don't overproject this music – it remains appropriately and rightly 'chamber music'.

Takács Quartet
Decca ③ 470 849-2DH3 (200' · DDD) Ⓕ**OOO**▷
Ⓖ A staggering achievement to crown a magnificent cycle: the Takács evidently appreciate this music both as musical argument and as sound and it shows in every bar of these beautifully recorded performances.

Alban Berg Quartet
EMI ③ 768230-2 (193' · ADD) Ⓕ**O**▷
A quartet that has always divided opinion: can their playing be *too* beautiful? This set from their second (live) cycle has am extraordinary sense of concentration. There may not be the anger and anguish of the Takács's performances but they have clearly thought long and hard about this amazing music.

hoven's very slow suggestion, and their new recording is noticeably faster than the old. Yet, this is one of the most finely played movements in the set, with soft, sensuous tone, delicate ornamentation, and mysterious, tenuous unisons.

For the *Adagio* of No 1, on the other hand, Beethoven provides what seems a very fast tempo). The Lindsays play it a good deal slower – their earlier version has a particularly impressive, concentrated atmosphere. The 1933 Busch Quartet recording, however, shows how it's possible for the movement to sound even more impressive at a speed close to Beethoven's mark; the fiercely dramatic interruptions lose the somewhat ponderous effect they have when taken more slowly.

With these much-recorded quartets – in their way just as challenging to the performers as the later works – but there is no group that brings out better the startling range of the youthful Beethoven's imagination.

String Quartets, Op 18
Tokyo Quartet (Martin Beaver, Kikuei Ikeda *vns* Kazuhide Isolmura *va* Clive Greensmith *vc*)
Harmonia Mundi ② HMU90 7436/7 (146' · DDD)
Ⓕ**OOO**

Enjoyable as other digital recordings of Beethoven's first quartets by (for example) the Takács and Lindsay Quartets are, this new Tokyo set just about pips all rivals to the post. The reason is primarily one of balance, not only within the group itself but also in terms of overall musical judgement – whether relating to tempo, dynamics or emphases, or simply the way the players combine a sense of classical style with an appreciation of Beethoven's startling originality. Even as early as No 1's pensive opening, you notice how skilfully rests are being gauged, contrasts in colour and inflection, too: the way the clipped first motif leads into its sweetly imploring extension a couple of bars later. The *Scherzo*'s skipping gait, incisive but lightly dispatched, is another source of pleasure, and so is the seemingly effortless swirl of the closing *Allegro*. The old quartet cliché about 'leaning together' is here a principal attribute. At times it could be just one person playing.

The qualifying *ma non tanto* of the C minor's opening *Allegro* is pointedly observed: dramatic impact is sustained while composure is maintained. The crispness of the *Andante scherzoso* and the cannily calculated crescendi at the start of the finale is oustanding. Few ensembles have characterised the A major's cantering first idea as happily as the Tokyos do here, while the ethereal and texturally variegated middle movements anticipate the very different world of Beethoven's 'late' quartets. Beautifully blended recordings, too: if you're after a top-ranking digital set of Op 18, you couldn't do better.

String Quartets, Op 18
Takács Quartet (Edward Dusinberre, Károly Schranz

vns Roger Tapping *va* András Fejér *vc*)
Decca ② 470 848-2DH2 (148' · DDD)
Ⓕ**OOᗒ**

Robert Simpson disagreed with writers who believed that Beethoven's backward glances to Haydn and Mozart in his Op 18 set were so obvious as to distract attention from his own individuality. The Takács disagree, too. They concede the tradition, but those glances are far from obvious. From the beginning this is Beethoven through and through. The opening bars of Op 18 No 1 are soft yet terse. The answering calls are conciliatory, but the suspense is palpable. And, in a trenchant *Allegro con brio*, every *sforzando* is used to raise the tension, especially in the development. There are no concessions to surface beauty, and the message isn't subdued.

The Takács are particular about dynamics. The *fortissimo* chord near the finish of the slow movement is startling, and the build up from *pianissimo* is as impressive as the drop back to the end. The *Adagio*, though directed to be both impassioned and tender, tends to be fervent, while fine inflections to the line ensure that the fairly swift tempo doesn't appear hurried. Conversely, the *Adagio ma non troppo* of No 6 is compassionately slow, but continuously mobile: these musicians don't overlay textures with fatty tissue. Despite wide separation, ensemble is always close-knit. Just how close may be appreciated in the Scherzos, which are tight and cohesive. That of No 4 has, in addition, precise give and take between the contrapuntal lines. The Takács play them in a way that leads the ear on without ignoring the expressive demands of the unusual marking *Andante scherzoso quasi Allegretto*.

String Quartets, Op 18 Nos 3 & 6
Leipzig Quartet (Andreas Seidel, Tilman Büning *vn* Ivo Bauer *vc* Matthias Moosdorf *vc*)
Dabringhaus und Grimm MDG307 0856-2 (51' · DDD)
Ⓕ**O**

These are performances of exceptional finesse and integrity. Such qualities are immediately apparent at the opening of No 6 where, amid the splendidly vigorous, bustling atmosphere, they manage to give the answering phrases in violin and cello a gentler articulation. The second movement of this Quartet, though marked *Adagio ma non troppo*, has a surprisingly slow metronome mark, which the Leipzigers observe, their fine sense of line allowing the music to flow easily even at this spacious tempo, and they impart an especially chilling aspect to the sinister minor-key middle section.

The D major Quartet starts sweetly and gently, gradually and effortlessly picking up more liveliness as the movement progresses. The *Andante* flows easily, with notably rich, dark-hued tone in the passages in low register, and the third movement winningly combines a lively tempo with a slightly wistful manner.

In short, these must be among the most persuasively played, finely recorded Op 18 performances available. There are places where you might prefer other versions – The Lindsays' spontaneity in the finale of No 6, or the joyful virtuosity of the Emerson in the last movement of No 3 – but, overall, the Leipzig Quartet is as satisfying as any.

'String Quartets, Volume 1'
String Quartets – Op 18 No 2; Op 95, 'Serioso'; Op 135. Satz (Allegretto), WoO
Endellion Quartet (Andrew Watkinson, Ralph de Souza vns Garfield Jackson va David Waterman vc)
Warner Classics 2564 62161-2 (74' · DDD)   Ⓕ Ⓑ➔

Three works, reflecting different stages in Beethoven's artistic life, mark an auspicious return to the recording studio. Tony Faulkner's engineering handsomely honours their playing, as secure as their interpretative acumen is keenly honed. How so is heard in the slow movement of Op 135, *Lento assai, cantante e tranquillo*, to which Beethoven in one of his sketches added the words 'Sweet song of rest or of peace'. And that is what we get, the call for profundity expressed through absolute control of tempo, tone, balance, phrasing and dynamics, the pathos of the coda particularly moving.

At the other extreme is the opening movement of Op 95 (*Quartetto serioso* is Beethoven's title), an *Allegro con brio* of tightly packed invention where the Endellions' pacing reflects both stony determination and the sardonic humour implicit in the mad modulations. Their view may lack the terse concision of the Takács or the concentrated drive of The Lindsays, yet it is just as trenchant and cohesive.

So, too, is their performance of the Second Quartet as exemplified by the lyrically played slow movement, with its incisive yet nicely shaded fast section and chiselled *Scherzo*, the Trio a tad slower to emphasise its barer fabric.

A small point: *pianissimi* could be softer and *mezza voce* more of an undertone. But there is no questioning the assiduity of these musicians, even in the recently discovered 34-second B minor *Allegretto*. Welcome back.

'String Quartets, Volume 2'
String Quartets – Op 18 No 3; Op 132
Endellion Quartet (Andrew Watkinson, Ralph de Souza vns Garfield Jackson va David Waterman vc)
Warner Classics 2564 62196-2 (67' · DDD)   Ⓕ

One of the greatest moments in the classical repertoire occurs 31 bars into the slow movement of Beethoven's late A minor Quartet (that's at around 3'12" into track 7 on this particular recording). After the solemnly archaic sounds of music cast 'in the Lydian Mode', the sun suddenly breaks through, *adagio molto* turns to *andante* and the sick composer sings a prayer of thanksgiving. He'd at last recovered – and surely no music before or since so vividly expresses the sensation of an emotional weight being lifted. The Endellion Quartet do a nice

job, pacing the *Adagio* judiciously then, come the chirping birdsong of the *Andante*, effortlessly easing into the new tempo. 'Nicely', but not especially movingly.

This is the second volume of the Endellions' projected complete set of the quartets (plus string quintets and fragments), conscientious playing, a little reserved at times perhaps, but musical and, at the mysterious onset of the development section of the A minor's first movement, memorable. The D major Quartet from Op 18 is another fine example of considered ensemble playing where phrases 'lift' with just the right degree of emphasis: try the sparring between paired upper and lower strings near the start of the finale. Sensible and sensitive, but not earth-shattering.

Both recordings use texts 'based on the latest research into all known surviving sources', which means mistakes put right – not big mistakes but significant notational errors. The scholar Jonathan Del Mar offers chapter and verse in the CD booklet, and there will no doubt be some readers for whom the Urtext angle alone will make purchase mandatory.

String Quartets, Op 18 No 3; Op 59 No 1
Orpheus Quartet (Charles-André Linale, Emilian Piediçuta vns Emile Cantor va Laurentiu Sbarcea vc)
Channel Classics CCS6094 (68' · DDD)   Ⓕ

The Orpheus Quartet doesn't use this music as a vehicle for its virtuosity; and they don't draw attention to their spot-on ensemble, immaculate intonation and tonal finesse, though they possess all these qualities. Take the *Presto* finale of Op 18 No 3. The sense of pace is in harmony with the horse-drawn rather than the jet-driven; every note speaks, every phrase tells and the overall effect is all the more exhilarating. Generally speaking, the Orpheus find the *tempo giusto* throughout. They remain attuned to the sensibility of the period and relate their pace to a dance movement in a manner that their rivals have lost. There's something very natural about the players' music-making. They're inside these scores and convey their involvement; no auto pilot, no *ersatz* feeling, no exaggerated or mechanised *sforzatos*. What a relief! The recording is bright and clean.

String Quartets Op 59, 'Rasumovsky'

String Quartets Op 59 Nos 1-3. String Quartet Op 74
Takács Quartet (Edward Dusinberre, Károly Schranz vns Roger Tapping va András Fejér vc)
Decca ② 470 847-2DH2 (144' · DDD)   Ⓕ ❶❷❸

The Takács do a fine job here: controlled, well paced and impeccably balanced. They manage to balance the music's vertical and horizontal aspects beautifully, long-breathed contrapuntal lines gliding serenely above a sharp, occasionally dramatic accompaniment – masterful playing indeed and typical of this first lap of the Takács' projected Beethoven cycle.

The Takács hold both line and rhythm in Op 59 No 1 with imposing control. Their manner of badinage in the mischievously hocketing second movement is more intense than the rival account by The Lindsays, and their tempos consistently swifter. In Op 59 No 3 the Takács approximate the Busch in a broad, soulful *Andante con moto*. And in the fugal finale they're almost on a par with the Emersons, whose demonic DG account is one of the most viscerally exciting quartet recordings around. The finale of Op 59 No 2 is a tautly braced canter whereas in the *Scherzo* of the *Harp*, Op 74, taken at a hair-raising lick, the Takács make obsessive music of the dominating four-note idea – and there's absolutely no let up in tension for the cello-led trio. Indeed, the Takács' *Harp* is one of the finest ever recorded, with fiery reportage of the first movement's central development and a delightfully playful account of the finale, the 'tipsy' first variation especially.

The jewel, then, is Op 59 No 2, though you'd be hard pressed to find a rival digital set of Opp 59 and 74 that's better overall. Andrew Keener's recording (St George's, Bristol) reports a realistic 'edge' within a sympathetic acoustic. You won't find a finer quartet recording anywhere.

String Quartets, Op 59 – Nos 2 & 3
Brodsky Quartet (Andrew Haveron, Ian Belton vns Paul Cassidy va Jacqueline Thomas vc)
Brodsky Records BRD3502 (71' · DDD)   Ⓕ

This isn't just another *Rasumovsky* recording: the Brodskys manage to sound thoroughly individual without ever seeming eccentric or one-sided. They pay close attention to detail – balance, articulation and accentuation are all carefully controlled – but as part of a performance full of conviction. One might argue that the interpretation is in places excessively literal: in the second quartet's first movement, for instance, where Beethoven writes *staccato* dots only at the start of a passage, it seems likely he intended the same articulation to persist. But the Brodsky performance, becoming smoother after the first bar, is convincing enough to prompt one to question such an assumption.

For the majority of movements the Brodskys stay close to Beethoven's metronome indications: the extraordinarily swift *Presto* finale of No 2 is revelatory and, in No 3, the flowing *Andante con moto quasi allegretto*, and the following Minuet, spacious and truly *grazioso*, would surely have pleased the composer. No 2's *Molto adagio* moves serenely onwards at Beethoven's suggested 60 beats per minute: it's a lovely performance, but there's no doubt that groups adopting a slower speed – the Takács or the Busch, for example – achieve greater intensity.

The Brodskys don't always observe the metronome marks, however. For No 3's finale the tempo is slower than in many versions; but

what's lost in brilliance is gained in dramatic power. And in No 2's opening *Allegro*, moderate and unhurried, we may miss something of the music's impulsive, disturbed character but can focus on a wealth of expressive detail. So it's well worth hearing this, however many *Rasumovsky*s you have on your shelves.

Late String Quartets

String Quartets, Opp 95, 127, 130, 131, 132 & 135. Grosse Fuge.
Takács Quartet (Edward Dusinberre, Károly Schranz vns Roger Tapping va András Fejér vc)
Decca ③ 470 849-2DH3 (3h 40' · DDD)   Ⓕ ●●●●▷

Interpreters of the late quartets have to convey what at times sounds like a stream of musical consciousness while respecting the many written markings. The Takács do better than most. For openers, they had access to the new Henle Edition and have made use of some textual changes – nothing too drastic but encouraging evidence of a good musical conscience. In Op 130 they take the long first-movement exposition repeat, using the *Grosse Fuge* as the rightful finale (Beethoven's original intention) which, in the context of their fiery reading of the fugue, works well. Contemporary incredulity at the sheer scale and complexity of the fugue caused Beethoven to offer a simpler alternative finale, in which they again play the repeat, which helps balance the 'alternative' structure.

The Takács evidently appreciate this music both as musical argument and as sound. Try their glassy *sul ponticello* at the end of Op 131's *Scherzo*, or the many instances where plucked and bowed passages are fastidiously balanced. Attenuated inflections are honoured virtually to the letter, textures carefully differentiated, musical pauses intuitively well-timed and inner voices nearly always transparent.

This set completes one of the best available Beethoven quartet cycles, possibly the finest in an already rich digital market, more probing than the pristine Emersons or Alban Bergs (live), more refined than the gutsy and persuasive Lindsays, and less consciously stylised than the Juilliards (and always with the historic Busch Quartet as an essential reference).

String Quartets, Opp 95; Op 132
Talich Quartet (Petr Messiereur, Jan Kvapil vns Jan Talich va Evzen Rattai vc)
Calliope Approche CAL5639 (68' · ADD) Recorded 1977-9   Ⓜ ●

After the expansive canvas of the Op 59 quartets and the *Eroica*, Beethoven's F minor Quartet, Op 95, displays musical thinking of the utmost compression. The first movement is a highly concentrated sonata design, which encompasses in its four minutes almost as much drama as a full-scale opera. With it comes one of the greatest masterpieces of his last years, the A minor, Op 132. The isolation wrought first by his deafness and secondly, by the change in fashion of which he complained in the early 1820s, forced Beethoven on in himself. Op-132 with its other-worldly *Heiliger Dankgesang*, written on his recovery from an illness, is music neither of the 1820s nor of Vienna, it belongs to that art which transcends time and place. Though other performances may be technically more perfect, these are interpretations that come closer to the spirit of this great music than any other on CD.

The Talich Quartet's readings bring a total dedication to this music: their performances are innocent of artifice and completely selfless. There's no attempt to impress with their own virtuosity or to draw attention to themselves. The recordings are eminently faithful and natural, not overbright but the effect is thoroughly pleasing.

String Quartets, Opp 95 & 127
The Lindsays (Peter Cropper, Ronald Birks vns Robin Ireland va Bernard Gregor-Smith vc)
ASV CDDCA1116 (59' · DDD)   Ⓕ**ⓄⓄⓄ**

The prospect of actually listening to Beethoven never loses its appeal. It's also clear that The Lindsays approach Beethoven's quartets with undiminished enthusiasm. This is immediately apparent in the physical energy with which they attack the opening of Op 95. Along with enthusiasm comes a deep understanding, expressed most strikingly in the way their fine internal balance is adapted to allow important subsidiary lines to make their effect. Nothing as crude as making a decision to 'bring out' an inner part; just the feeling that each player knows how much pressure is needed to fulfil a line's potential. Such expressive detail allied to a lovely *dolce* sound makes a contrapuntal movement like Op 95's *Allegretto* especially memorable.

The Lindsays aren't the smoothest, slickest ensemble to have recorded this music. In the *Scherzo* of Op 95 the Quartetto Italiano's tone is more blemish-free, and the fast coda to this quartet's finale sees the Emerson Quartet create a more brilliant, sparkling impression. But such things only become noticeable with comparative listening; if you stick with The Lindsays what will impress you is the splendid rhythm and drive of the Op 95 *Scherzo*, the magnificent, rich sound, without any sense of aggressiveness or strain, at the start of Op 127, the way the expression is sustained throughout the great *adagio* variations of Op 127, and the delicate, magical atmosphere established at the beginning of this quartet's final section. A hugely compelling set.

String Quartets, Op 59 No 2; Op 130
Talich Quartet (Petr Messiereur, Jan Kvapil vns Jan Talich va Evzen Rattai vc)
Calliope CAL5637 (73' · ADD) Recorded 1977-80   Ⓕ

The advantage of this Talich recording is that it couples a masterpiece from Beethoven's middle period, the great E minor Quartet, Op 59 No 2, with one of the greatest of his last years. The B flat, Op 130, was the third of the late quartets to be composed and at its first performance in 1826 its last movement, the *Grosse Fuge*, baffled his contemporaries. Later that same year, he substituted the present finale. The Talich Quartet has a no less impressive technical command than other ensembles but theirs are essentially private performances, which are a privilege to overhear, rather than the overprojected 'public' accounts that so often appear on record nowadays.

String Quartets, Op 18 No 4; Op 132
Petersen Quartet (Conrad Muck, Gernot Süssmuth vns Friedemann Weigle va Hans-Jakob Eschenburg vc)
Capriccio 10 722 (63' · DDD)   Ⓕ**Ⓞ**

The Petersen Quartet possesses impeccable technical address, immaculate ensemble, flawless intonation and tonal finesse. Tempos are judged with real musicianship, and dynamic markings are observed without being exaggerated. The C minor Quartet, Op 18 No 4, has dramatic tension without loss of lyrical fervour and the *Scherzo* has wit. When we move to the first movement of the A minor Quartet the sound world changes as if youth has given way to wisdom and experience.

They hardly put a foot wrong here and their *Heiliger Dankgesang* is rapt and inward-looking. They press ahead fractionally in one or two places – on the reprise of the main section in the second movement and when the main theme returns in the finale. But one or two minor reservations apart, theirs is quite simply the most satisfying late Beethoven to have appeared in recent years. Above all the Petersen do not invite you to admire their prowess. They appear to be untouched by the three 'g's (Gloss, Glamour and Glitz) and their concern is with truth rather than beauty.

String Quartets, Opp 132 & 135
Cleveland Quartet (William Preucil, Peter Salaff vns James Dunham va Paul Katz vc)
Telarc CD80427 (69' · DDD)   Ⓕ

The Cleveland Quartet are upholders of tradition, rather than seekers after new truths. One of this ensemble's most notable characteristics is its rich, warm tone, well captured here. The first movement of the A minor Quartet, Op 132, has a level of emotional commitment that's quite compelling – all the details of this complex music fall into place and contribute to the overall effect.

If the rest isn't quite so outstanding it's still very good, with a lovely swinging rhythm to the second movement, and delightfully sprightly accounts of the *Andante* episodes in the slow movement – absolutely 'feeling new strength', as Beethoven's caption puts it. Their Op 135 is also very impressive. The *Lento* is deeply felt, their rich sound coming into its own. And the finale must be one of the best versions on record – spirited, touching, playful, as the music's mood demands.

Beethoven String Quartet Op 135
(arr Prooijen) **Walton** Sonata for Strings
Amsterdam Sinfonietta
Channel Classics CCSSA23005 (55' · DDD/DSD)   Ⓕ

As the booklet asks, why Beethoven and Walton? The answer is, the Walton has become a favourite work with this superb Dutch ensemble and it was felt appropriate to couple it with another arrangement of a string quartet, the last Beethoven wrote. Walton made the imaginative arrangement of his A minor Quartet at the prompting of Neville Marriner, who wanted a work for the Academy of St Martin in the Fields. The arrangement of the Beethoven by Marijn van Prooijen similarly adapts the original without inflating it.

As the booklet-note says, the Amsterdam Sinfonietta aim to preserve the intimate character of the works. In this they contrast their approach to that of Bernstein and the VPO (DG), in which he uses a full body of strings. With the Amsterdam players showing the give-and-take, ebb-and-flow of small chamber groups, they achieve rare refinement and natural warmth.

The bite and precision of the Amsterdam account is most impressive, with the rhythmic lift of the *Scherzo* and of the finale after the ominous opening bringing a joyful lightness. Yet it is the sublime *Lento* slow movement which achieves the greatest heights in playing of hushed dedication. This new version of the Walton is more intimate than the LPO full-strings Chandos rival. It is true that Walton freely sets the full ensemble in contrast with passages for solo strings, as at the very start, but the Amsterdam performance brings out that terracing of sound more clearly, helped by the refined recording. As in the Beethoven, the heart of the performance comes in the lovely *Lento* movement.

The Sonata emerges as a fair match for other great British string pieces – Elgar's *Introduction and Allegro* and Vaughan Williams's *Tallis* Fantasia, for example. It's a work which neatly spans the gap between the early Walton, passionate and electrifying, and his later refined and carefully considered style.

Piano Trios

Op 1: No 1 in E flat; **No 2** in G; **No 3** in C minor
Op 11 in B flat
Op 38 in E flat
Op 70: No 1 in D, 'Ghost'; **No 2** in E flat
Op 97 in B flat, 'Archduke'

Complete Piano Trios
Piano Trios. Opp 1, 11, 38, 70, 97; WoO38 & 39.
Variations, Opp 44, 121a. Trio in D (after Symphony

No 2). Triosatz
Beaux Arts Trio (Isidore Cohen *vn* Bernard Greenhouse *vc* Menahem Pressler *pf*)
Philips ⑤ 468 411-2 (356' · DDD/ADD) Recorded 1980   Ⓜ Ⓞ

Growing older doesn't always mean growing wiser, though in the case of the Beaux Arts Trio and Beethoven the passage of some 20-odd years signalled a rare and fruitful broadening of musical vision. In the period between their two recordings of the Beethoven Piano Trios there had been just one personnel change – Daniel Guilet was replaced by ex-Juilliard Quartet second violin Isidore Cohen. The principal route of the Beaux Arts' interpretative development was forged by the pianist, Menahem Pressler, whose increased tonal subtlety and willingness to widen expressive dynamics lent the trio a whole new palette of colours. Just listen to the opening of Op 1 No 2's ineffably deep *Largo con espressione*.

Heard superficially, there's not that much in it between the Pressler of the 1960s and of 1980, but labour the comparison and you'll soon hear the benefits of a more variegated touch and a freer approach to phrasing. There are many other plus-points. The *Archduke*, for example, is at once softer-grained and more wistful than its energetic predecessor and you couldn't hope for a happier rendition of the Septet transcription (the E flat Trio, Op 38).

Philips' sound quality is just as good as the original: clear, full-bodied and well balanced. Given the price, the superior sound quality, the comprehensive coverage of repertoire and the profundity of the Beaux Art's later interpretative standpoint, this new reissue justifies a front-ranking recommendation. So much is said with so much feeling – and so little fuss – that you're drawn back again and again.

Piano Trios – Op 1 Nos 1-3; Op 11; WoO39
The Kalichstein-Laredo-Robinson Trio (Joseph Kalichstein *pf* Jaime Laredo *vn* Sharon Robinson *vc*)
Koch International Classics ② 37724-2 (119' · DDD)   Ⓕ

Piano Trios – Op 70 No 1, 'Ghost'; Op 70 No 2; Op 97, 'Archduke'. Variations, Op 44. Variations on Müller's Ich bin der Schneider Kakadu, Op 121a
The Kalichstein-Laredo-Robinson Trio
Koch International Classics ② 37722-2
(134' · DDD)   Ⓕ Ⓞ

This set is copyrighted 2000 and offers a clear, warm-textured sound frame for performances that are memorable above all for their thoughtfulness, nimble execution and a shared sense of musical purpose.

The jewel of the enterprise, musically, is the perennially fresh and at times startlingly original E flat Trio, Op 70 No 2, the main body of the first movement imbued by the players with subtle colouring and impressive tonal variety, while the *Allegretto* that follows alternates whimsicality with typically offbeat humour. Laredo's violin glows brightest in the third movement, especially in the opening measures…and how can one fail to gape at the piano's weird 'off-key' descent soon afterwards – a truly astonishing piece of writing? The finale is one of those outgoing romps (the Seventh Symphony's finale is another) that suggests unrealisable levels of energy and Laredo and Co do it proud.

They also measure up well in the *Archduke*, their turns of phrase invariably as flexible as their team interplay (especially in the first two movements) though the neatest example of their poetically unfettered playing style is the lovely 'teaching' piece, WoO39, that Beethoven wrote for Maxmiliane Brentano. This element of quiet caprice suits the three Op 1 Trios well, the *Presto* finale of the second piece a *tour de force*, though they also focus the drama in the third of the trios (in C minor).

There have been more unsettling and more urgently driven accounts of the *Ghost* Trio but few that can claim as much sensitivity to the modulating phrase. Good to hear the relatively extrovert Op 11 (the violin standing in for the more familiar clarinet) and two sets of variations. Previous benchmarks in the Beethoven trios have tended to be the early Beaux Arts set and the Stern-Rose-Istomin set for Sony, both still treasured for their robust spirit and unfailing intelligence; but these newer recordings for their intimate insights and, especially, for Joseph Kalichstein's superbly articulated piano-playing will also demand attention.

Piano Trios – selected

Piano Trios Op 1 Nos 1 & 2; WoO38
Florestan Trio (Susan Tomes *pf*
Anthony Marwood *vn* Richard Lester *vc*)
Hyperion CDA67393 (72' · DDD)   Ⓕ Ⓞ ▶

The Florestan Trio seems determined to extract every last ounce of energy, wit and spirit from these early works. Op 1 No 2's finale, for example, fizzes along; all Beethoven's surprising inventions and transformations grab our attention, and the whole piece is evidently as much fun to play as to listen to.

The principal vehicle for conveying the music's brightness and verve is Susan Tomes's fingerwork, wonderfully precise and rhythmical, though Anthony Marwood and Richard Lester also play with fine spirit and character. The two Op 1 slow movements are taken at flowing speeds, and allow for some relaxation of mood – Marwood's entry at the start of No 2's *Largo* is particularly poetic – but it's the bouncy, extrovert character of the *Allegro*s and *Presto*s that leaves the strongest impression.

Piano Trios – Op 1 No 3; Op 11. Variations in E flat, Op 44
Florestan Trio
Hyperion CDA67466 (61' · DDD)   Ⓕ Ⓞ Ⓞ ▶

This completes the Florestan Trio's Beethoven series. Their thoughtfulness throughout has been impressive; their overall style avoids heaviness, keeping the textures light and airy, and giving every phrase individual life and character. Occasionally the liveliness can seem relentless, but their bubbling vitality is a natural response to Beethoven's inventiveness. And their care for detail makes the early and not fully characteristic Variations in E flat (Op 44) into an absorbing, thoroughly entertaining piece.

It's interesting to compare Op 1 No 3 with the version by the Kempf Trio (BIS), which is finely played but less searching as an interpretation. The contrast is especially noticeable in the *Andante*, treated by Kempf and friends as a poetic, hymn-like slow movement, while the Florestans give us a true 18th-century *Andante*; much faster, and, in places, light and playful.

Op 11 is often more enjoyable in the version with clarinet instead of violin. But this is another Florestan triumph. By modifying the usual robust, jolly character of the outer movements, and introducing more delicate tones, Anthony Marwood can interpret his part in violinistic terms, establishing a close rapport with the cello, yet, at the start of the finale, proving he can be as bright and perky as any clarinettist.

Piano Trios, Op 70 Nos 1 & 2. Allegretto, WoO39
Florestan Trio
Hyperion CDA67327 (60' · DDD)   Ⓕ Ⓞ ▶

Here's a recording that immediately, from the first, impetuous bars of Op 70 No 1, feels just right. In this movement the Florestan makes the long second repeat, but there's such a sense of momentum that no one could find it too extended or repetitious. Indeed, the reiterated chords that precede the lead-back reignite our concentration with their air of tense mystery. And when we reach this point for the second time, the G major harmony at the start of the coda has a wonderful, dense tranquillity. The famous 'Ghost' movement creates a powerful, chilling effect, with stark, *senza vibrato* string tone and the extraordinary writing in the piano's deep bass register exploited by Susan Tomes with superb control and sensitivity.

Op 70 No 2 is something of a Cinderella work, but the Florestan performance helps us to see it as a major achievement of Beethoven's middle period. Although they're a thoughtful, highly controlled group, there's room for moments of the most intense expression. And the finale, one of Beethoven's most prodigiously inventive pieces, has in this performance a feeling of uninhibited enjoyment. The recorded sound and balance are equally fine.

String Trios

Op 3 in E flat. Op 9: No 1 in G; No 2 in D; No 3 in C minor

String Trio, Op 3; Serenade in D, Op 8
Leopold String Trio (Marianne Thorsen vn
Sarah-Jane Bradley va Kate Gould vc)
Hyperion CDA67253 (73' · DDD) Ⓕ Ⓞ➔

String Trios Op 9
Leopold String Trio
Hyperion CDA67254 (77' · DDD) Ⓕ Ⓞ➔
Both discs available through Hyperion's Archive Service

The Leopold String Trio demonstrate the kind
of virtues that come from long study together:
polished ensemble, excellent intonation and
notably consistent and well-conceived interpretations. Just occasionally the viola is
swamped by the outer voices, but overall it's a
particularly well-balanced and recorded set.
They show that a restrained style can bring out
the inward aspect to the music. On the fourth
track of Op 8, where Beethoven alternates a
sombre *Adagio* with a facetiously jolly *Scherzo*,
the stark yet gentle Leopold playing of the slow
music expresses more pathos and melancholy
than the intensity of other versions. And the
Leopold's care and respect for the text also tips
the balance in its favour – in Op 3's second
Minuet, for example, Marianne Thorsen's
beautiful and exact interpretation is winning.
In Op 9 No 1's *Scherzo*, another splendidly
poised and spirited reading, there's a special
bonus – a second Trio, omitted from most editions. It's an attractive bit of music and gives
the movement a new dimension.

String Quintets

String Quintets – Op 4; Op 29
Nash Ensemble (Marianne Thorsen, Malin Broman
vns Lawrence Power, Philip Dukes vas Paul Watkins
vc)
Hyperion CDA67693 (63' · DDD) Ⓕ Ⓞ

The Nash Ensemble here give flawless, superbly
disciplined performances of Beethoven's two
string quintets. Op 4 is the composer's transcription of the wind octet that he wrote in
emulation of Mozart's great examples of *Harmoniemusik*, the wind octets in E flat and C minor.
Op 29, on the other hand, is Beethoven's first
completely original exploitation of the genre.

It is fascinating to find how Beethoven developed his arguments by rewriting wind music for
strings, as Richard Wigmore explains in his
excellent note. Key modulations are more
adventurous and textures lightened, making this
by far the finer work. The Nash players, carefully balanced and helped by the transparent
recording, bring out the inner lines with admirable clarity. The slow movement, marked simply andante, is free-flowing with a warmly lyrical
violin solo, while the mis-titled *Menuetto più
allegretto* is the most dashing scherzo, full of wit,
and the finale is a dance-like rondo. The performance of Op 29 in C brings similar qualities,
with clean separation and well chosen speeds on
the fast side. What especially comes out is the

originality of the finale, with its bizarre opening,
chromatic passages and striking dynamic contrasts. Warmly welcomed for its first-rate sound
and immaculate performances.

Cello Sonatas

No 1 Op 5 No 1 in F; **No 2** Op 5 No 2 in G minor;
No 3 Op 69 in A;
No 4 Op 102 No 1 in C; **No 5** Op 102 No 2 in D

Cello Sonatas, Op 102 Nos 1 & 2. Duo in E flat,
WoO32. Variations on 'See the conqu'ring hero
comes'
Maria Kliegel vc **Tabea Zimmermann** va
Nina Tichman pf
Naxos 8 555787 (59' · DDD) Ⓢ Ⓞ➔

Complete Works for Cello and Piano
Miklós Perényi vc **András Schiff** pf
ECM New Series ② 472 401-2 (151' · DDD) Ⓕ Ⓞ Ⓞ➔

Maria Kliegel and Nina Tichman conclude their
three-volume Beethoven exploration with fine-
toned, vigorous performances of the last two
sonatas. Most sets of the cello- and-piano music
fit onto two CDs; Naxos's more liberal allowance permits the inclusion of extra items, in this
case the Duo, with 'Two Obbligato Eyeglasses',
for viola and cello; not, perhaps, one of the
young Beethoven's finest achievements, but
most imaginatively written for the two instruments. Tabea Zimmermann's spirited playing
prompts regret that Beethoven never wrote a
concertante work for viola.

In the sonatas and variations Tichman and
Kliegel make a well-matched pair. They favour
firm, rounded tone and strong, expressive projection, and are equally convincing in the passionate A minor *Allegro* that forms the second
part of the Fourth Sonata's first movement, and
in the preceding *Andante*, where warm sound
and soaring lines perfectly express the music's
romantic spirit. What's missing, perhaps, is a
range of tone colour that can suggest mystery or
solemnity. And in the variations, Kliegel is
inclined to phrase in a smooth, somewhat bland
way, where a more articulated, 18th-century
style would be more in order. The passages in
dialogue between the instruments, however, are
most beautifully realised.

Turning to András Schiff and Miklós Perényi,
the first impression is of a much lighter sound.
The piano, indeed, might seem quite brittle, if it
weren't for Schiff's beautiful *cantabile* touch and
his exceptional ability to balance chords – Beethoven's gruffest harmonies form part of a texture that's richly coloured and always clear. It's
the kind of thing we normally only experience
with the best period-instrument players.

In contrast to the finely matched pairing of
Tichman and Kliegel, Perényi and Schiff appear
as distinct, contrasting characters – Perényi suave
and elegant, and though demonstrating a wide
expressive range, always staying within the

boundaries of what is polished and unexaggerated, Schiff much more volatile and extreme. In the high-spirited finales of the first two sonatas you can easily imagine the tempestuous young composer performing before the King of Prussia.

But this contrast of styles doesn't result in unbalanced performances. There are, maybe, one or two places (in the Third Sonata's first movement, for example) where where you might welcome more intensity from Perényi, but overall his playing has all the vigour and commitment one could wish for. And where it's necessary to achieve perfect unity, the two come together in the most inspiring way. The most remarkable instance of this is Op 102's fugal finale, a movement that's often been perceived as impressive rather than attractive, but these two artists match articulation, note-lengths, volume and tone colour in such a way as to make the music seem beautiful as well as uplifting. An outstanding set.

Complete Works for Cello and Piano
Adrian Brendel vc **Alfred Brendel** pf
Philips ② 475 379-2PX2 (148' · DDD)   Ⓕ**OOO**▷

(G) The Brendels, father and son, give us Beethoven's complete works for piano and cello. You'll have to search long and hard to hear performances of a comparable warmth and humanity or joy in music-making. Sumptuously recorded and lavishly presented (including engaging family photographs), the sonatas are offered in a sequence that gives the listener an increased sense of Beethoven's awe-inspiring scope and range.

CD 1 juxtaposes early, middle and late sonatas with a joyous encore in the Variations on Mozart's 'Ein Mädchen oder Weibchen'. CD 2 gives us the Variations on 'See the conqu'ring hero comes' from Handel's *Judas Maccabaeus*, continues with the remaining two sonatas and ends with the other *Magic Flute* Variations, on 'Bei Männern'.

Pianist and cellist are united by a rare unity of purpose and stylistic consistency, whether in strength and exuberance, an enriching sense of complexity or in other-worldly calm (often abruptly terminated). What eloquence they achieve in the opening *Adagio* of the Second Sonata, what musical energy in the following *Allegro molto tanto presto*, instances where Beethoven's volatility is always tempered by the Brendels' seasoned musicianship.

In Op 102 No 2 Beethoven's far-reaching and still bewildering utterance, there is a quiet strength and lucidity; time and again a direction such as *Allegro vivace* is exactly that and not stretched, as in more urgently, even neurotically, propelled performances. Their glowing expressiveness at 10'57" in Sonata No 3 is 'interior' yet never at the expense of impetus, and Adrian Brendel's *ad libitum* lead into the concluding *Allegro* is memorable – improvisatory and relaxed. Both players display rhythmic resilience in the final Rondo from Sonata No 1, and

what open-hearted delight and *joie de vivre* there is in the sets of variations.

The Brendels offer an invaluable additions to the recordings of these masterpieces.

Complete Works for Cello and Piano
Antonio Meneses vc **Menahem Pressler** pf
Avie ② AV2103 (154' · DDD)   Ⓕ**OOO**▷

Between them, Menahem Pressler and Antonio Meneses offer us a rare listening privilege, with playing that is at once intimate, conversational, reposeful, intelligent and, above all, simple in its musical intentions, which are, or seem to be, to present the music without excessive interpretative intervention. Not that these are in any way bland performances: Pressler may now be a venerable 84 but his wisdom isn't at a high premium, either mentally or physically: both his mind and to a large extent his fingers are still remarkably agile. Maybe the call to arms in the first movement of the Third Sonata, Op 69, sounds less forceful than on some rival versions, but it certainly doesn't drag and the crucial virtue is concentration: throughout this set both players hold the line without letting it flag and although moments of rapt intensity are far too plentiful to catalogue in detail.

The outer movements of both Op 102 sonatas achieve clarity without clatter (some pianists force an excessively hard tone here) but if you fancy a prime sampling of Meneses/Pressler magic, then sample the *Conqu'ring Hero Variations*, starting with the chorale-like piano variation then picking up the tempo before relaxing again for some slow-breathing dialogue. There's nothing sensational about it, no showing off or theatrical arching of eyebrows, just the joy of hearing two seasoned players getting it absolutely right. A rare privilege, and a credible, gently stated alternative to more forthright sets.

Cello Sonatas – No 1, Op 5 No 1;
No 2, Op 5 No 2; No 3, Op 69
Daniel Müller-Schott vc **Angela Hewitt** pf
Hyperion CDA67633 (78' · DDD)   Ⓕ**O**▷

Daniel Müller-Schott and Angela Hewitt give Beethoven's first three cello sonatas a nimble and colourful outing. Their musical 'dress' sense is immaculate, with never so much as a quaver out of place, no hint of ungainliness or aggression and a cultivated sound world which, whether presented singly or in duet, is consistently smooth. Their duo engagement is compelling and their repertoire of gestures – vivid dynamics, tiny instances of expressive *rubato*, suspended breathing and so on – is exceedingly broad. Sometimes the reverie might be considered a little overplayed. At the opening of the A major Third Sonata's brief *Adagio* third movement Hewitt's dreamily sculpted phrasing verges on sounding Chopinesque, though poetic in effect and poignantly responded to by Müller-Schott.

These performances are full of interesting ideas: there's rarely a bar without a subtle bend somewhere along the line and yet the various *allegros* are sparky in the best sense of the term, rhythmically crisp and alert, especially the rondo finale of the G minor Sonata, which is deliciously pointed by Hewitt. Those in search of a more overtly masculine approach to Beethoven would probably be better off elsewhere but Müller-Schott and Hewitt provide a bright, decorative antidote to their more austere rivals. The recorded sound is beautifully balanced.

Additional recommendation

Cello Sonata, Op 69
Coupled with: Sonata in E flat, Op 64; 12 Variations on 'Ein Mädchen oder Weibchen', Op 66
Kliegel vc **Tichman** pf
Naxos 8 555786 (77' · DDD)   ⑤➡

A sound recommendation, both for the rare Op 64 (an arrangement of the Op 3 String Trio) and as an excellent bargain version of the more familiar items. Kliegel and Tichman give highly sympathetic performances; in the A major their playing has a breadth and confidence that easily encompasses the music's great emotional range.

Variations for Cello

12 Variations on Handel's 'See the conqu'ring   ℗
hero comes', WoO45. 12 Variations on Mozart's 'Ein Mädchen oder Weibchen', Op 66. Seven Variations on Mozart's 'Bei Männern, welche Liebe fühlen', WoO46. Horn Sonata, Op 17 (arr vc)
Pieter Wispelwey vc **Lois Shapiro** fp
Channel Classics CCS6494 (45' · DDD)   ℗○

There are only 45 minutes of it, but this recital teems with fresh insights in the irresistible serendipity of its playing. Lois Shapiro partners Wispelwey's 1701 cello on a 1780 Viennese fortepiano whose wiry energies she unleashes in an attention-grabbing opening theme for Handel's *See the conqu'ring hero comes*. Her bright-eyed first variation glints as phrases dart from dynamic shadow to light and back again. Then the cello's lean, slightly astringent voice makes itself felt in no uncertain terms before the keyboard gets its own back in mercurial scale passages. The players' delight in teasing, sparring and debating with each other comes into its own in the variations on *Ein Mädchen oder Weibchen*. The theme itself struts forward cheekily, only to peck its way through the first variation, before the cello makes the most of the wry harmonic subtext of the second. In the seventh, one half of a shared phrase caresses and preens the other; the 10th casts the shadow of Papageno's noose. Each player's imagination and technique is tested to the full in an absorbing account of the more abstracted *Bei Männern* variations. The world of *Singspiel* isn't far away, either, in this performance of the Sonata, Op 17: Wispelwey

and Shapiro summon up the nascent world of Marzelline and Jacquino in their quick, ardent responses to the music and to each other.

Violin Sonatas

Op 12: No 1 in D; **No 2** in A; **No 3** in E flat
Op 23 in A minor **Op 24** in F, 'Spring'
Op 30: No 1 in A; **No 2** in C minor; **No 3** in G
Op 47 in A, 'Kreutzer' **Op 96** in G

Complete Violin Sonatas
Itzhak Perlman vn **Vladimir Ashkenazy** pf
Decca Ovation ④ 421 453-2DM4 (239' · ADD)
Recorded 1973-5   Ⓜ○○➡

Although Beethoven designated these works as 'for piano and violin', following Mozart's example, it's unlikely that he thought of the piano as leading the proceedings, or the violin either, for that matter: both instruments are equal partners, and in that sense this is true chamber music. Perlman and Ashkenazy are artists of the first rank and there's much pleasure to be derived from their set. Such an imaginative musician as Ashkenazy brings great subtlety to these works composed by a supreme pianist-composer. And the better the pianist is in this music, the better does the violinist play. Discernment is matched by spontaneity and the whole series is remarkably fine, while their celebrated performance of the *Kreutzer* Sonata has quite superb eloquence and vitality.

The recording boasts unusually truthful violin sound capturing all the colour of Perlman's playing.

Complete Violin Sonatas   Ⓗ
Wolfgang Schneiderhan vn **Wilhelm Kempff** pf
DG The Originals ③ 463 605-2GOR3 (236' · ADD)
Recorded 1952   Ⓜ○➡

In the 1950s these recordings would have probably given a very up-to-date impression; the playing is extremely clean – there's never a hint of sentimental violin slides or over-use of the sustaining pedal. But nearly half a century later, perhaps we're more conscious of the old-world virtues – Schneiderhan's beautiful *legato* bowing and gentle vibrato, Kempff's full, unforced tone, and a flexible approach from both artists, with finely graded *ritardandos* and subtle variations of tempo.

Though not regular sonata partners, Kempff and Schneiderhan have an admirable collective sense of rhythm. They favour moderate, poised speeds, and so tend to miss something of the impulsive quality of early Beethoven. And, in the same way, their dedication to pure, well-balanced, unforced tone means that the grotesque element in such a movement as the finale of Op 30 No 2 is underplayed. It's a delight to hear them find so many ways of interpreting Beethoven's frequent *sforzando* markings, from sharp accents to the expressive melodic emphasis they give to the theme of the *Kreutzer* Sonata's variations. But quite often Kempff downgrades or ignores these accents, smoothing away any angular corners, and this tendency towards blandness occasionally leads to disappointingly inexpressive playing, at the start of the *Spring* Sonata, for instance, where Schneiderhan's beautifully lyrical opening doesn't elicit a comparable response from the piano.

If there are a few let-downs, however, there are far more moments where the characteristically moderate, unexaggerated approach bears rich dividends. Schneiderhan's beautiful singing tone is a constant delight; witness the intensely vocal style of Op 24's finale and the luminous sound of his high register in the last of the *Kreutzer* variations. Similarly, Kempff's continual care for clear textures and his finely balanced chordal playing seem to offer glimpses into the essence of Beethoven's thought. The mono sound is beautifully clear and well balanced.

Violin Sonatas – No 4, Op 23; No 7, Op 30 No 2. Variations on 'Se vuol ballare' from Mozart's 'Le nozze di Figaro', WoO40
Daniel Sepec vn **Andreas Staier** pf
Harmonia Mundi HMC90 1919 (55' · DDD)   Ⓕ

The novel feature here is that Daniel Sepec's violin is one of a set presented to Beethoven in 1800 by Prince Lichnowsky. Made in Salzburg around 1700 and restored to its original condition, its whereabouts were unknown until 10 years ago, when it was presented to the Beethoven-Haus in Bonn. In Sepec's hands it has a sweet, expressive tone, an important element in these remarkably imaginative, stimulating performances. Andreas Staier plays a Graf pianoforte from the 1820s, of a type Beethoven was familiar with, though not at the time he wrote these sonatas. But if it has a smoother sound and wider dynamic range than earlier instruments, it's still able to present Beethoven's keyboard textures with perfect clarity. Staier's enthusiastic approach occasionally swamps the violin – but one can easily imagine the young Beethoven doing the same.

Staier and Sepec take us a long way beyond the concept of historically informed playing as simply avoiding anachronism. In the first movement of Sonata No 7, Sepec introduces expressive *portamenti*, as well as the kind of *rubato* where he momentarily lags behind the piano's rhythm. In the following *Adagio*, Staier makes highly expressive use of spread chords, and throughout the CD there are instances of subtle tempo variation and added dynamics, for example the beautiful shaping of the main theme in No 4's second movement. In the Variations, Staier makes full use of the Graf's range of sonorities, including a remarkable percussive surprise! Yet these 'authentic' features all stem from a clear view of the music's expressive qualities and result in performances of unusual verve and spontaneity.

Additional recommendation

Complete Violin Sonatas
Oistrakh vn **Oborin** pf
Philips ④ 468 406-2PB4 (229' · ADD)   ⒻⓄ
The most striking asset of this famous set is David Oistrakh's fabulous tone. The other great virtue is the close unity of style and purpose between the pair, both players striving to present a beautifully shaped, unexaggerated picture of the music.

Piano Sonatas

No 1 in F minor, Op 2 No 1 **No 2** in A, Op 2 No 2 **No 3** in C, Op 2 No 3 **No 4** in E flat, Op 7 **No 5** in C, Op 10 No 1 **No 6** in F, Op 10 No 2 **No 7** in D, Op 10 No 3 **No 8** in C minor, Op 13, 'Pathétique' **No 9** in E, Op 14 No 1 **No 10** in G, Op 14 No 2 **No 11** in B flat, Op 22 **No 12** in A flat, Op 26 **No 13** in E flat, Op 27 No 1, 'Quasi una fantasia' **No 14** in C sharp minor, Op 27 No 2, 'Moonlight' **No 15** in D, Op 28, 'Pastoral' **No 16** in G, Op 31 No 1 **No 17** in D minor, Op 31 No 2 'Tempest' **No 18** in E flat, Op 31 No 3 **No 19** in G minor, Op 49 No 1 **No 20** in G, Op 49 No 2 **No 21** in C minor, Op 53, 'Waldstein' **No 22** in F, Op 4 **No 23** in F minor, Op 57 'Appassionata' **No 24** in F sharp, Op 78 **No 25** in G, Op 79 **No 26** in E flat, Op 81a, 'Les adieux' **No 27** in E minor, Op 90 **No 28** in A, Op 101 **No 29** in B flat, Op 106, 'Hammerklavier' **No 30** in E, Op 109 **No 31** in A flat, Op 110 **No 32** in C minor, Op 111

Piano Sonatas Nos 1-32
Richard Goode pf
Nonesuch ⑩ 7559-79328-2 (608' · DDD)   ⓂⓄⓄ

You may have a doubt as to whether all the playing represents everything Goode is capable of: sometimes he disappoints, slightly, by appearing to hold back from the listener the boldness and fullness of communication the greatest players achieve. You might say that, for all their insight and illumination, some of the performances lack the final leap and a degree of transcendence. But his playing is so very likeable: the finish, technical and musical, is immaculate, but on top of that he's exciting. His sound always makes you listen. His feeling for it and for fine gradations of sound from one end of his wide dynamic range to the other are those of a virtuoso, and inform everything he does. When he's more obviously on virtuoso territory, he responds to the demands for brilliance and thrilling projection as to the manner born. He's constantly inside the music, and what a lively, cultivated, lucid and stimulating guide he is. There's nothing diffident or half-hearted about the way he makes this cycle of Beethoven resound wonderfully, the earlier sonatas appearing no less masterly or characteristic of their composer than the later. His interpretation of the A major Sonata, Op 101, is one of the finest ever put on record.

Piano Sonatas Nos 1-32
Friedrich Gulda pf
Brilliant Classics ⑨ 92773 (9h 58' · ADD)   Ⓢ❍

Friedrich Gulda's stereo Beethoven sonata cycle from the late 1960s differs from his 1950s mono/stereo Beethoven cycle in that the rhythms are tighter, tempi are generally faster, the sonority is more astringent, and the composer's fingerprint accents are harder-hitting. Tonal warmth, geniality and spacious introspection play little part in Gulda's expressive game plan, and that may not sit well with collectors who gravitate towards Arrau's full-bodied rhetoric or Kempff's intimately scaled, multi-hued conceptions. Perhaps the Op 10 triumvirate best typifies Gulda's chosen Beethoven style: the C minor Sonata's finale truly takes the composer's controversial *Prestissimo* at face value. The three Op 31 works and the Op 26 'Funeral March' Sonata receive unusual and refreshingly stark, headlong readings. Yet Gulda is anything but predictable. If the *Appassionata*'s unyielding drive and gaunt patina are positively Brechtian, he pulls the *Waldstein* apart to a fault.

Among the late sonatas, tension and severity serve Gulda's Opp 109 and 110 less well than in his remarkably concentrated *Hammerklavier*. And who'd have expected such an affectionately nuanced Op 54, Op 28 or *Pathétique* slow movement? All told, the pianist's occasional idiosyncracies and misfired moments are but a tiny price to pay for a stimulating, absorbing Beethoven cycle whose virtues proudly stand the test of time. The recording is closely miked, slightly dry yet decidedly impactful.

Piano Sonatas Nos 1-32   Ⓗ
Artur Schnabel pf
EMI Références mono ⑩ 763765-2 (605' · ADD)
Recorded 1932-8   Ⓜ❍❍

Schnabel was almost ideologically committed to extreme tempos; something you might say Beethoven's music thrives on, always provided the interpreter can bring it off. By and large he did. There are some famous gabbles in this sonata cycle, notably at the start of the *Hammerklavier*, with him going for broke. In fact, Schnabel also held that 'It is a mistake to imagine that all notes should be played with equal intensity or even be clearly audible. In order to clarify the music it is often necessary to make certain notes obscure.' If it's true, as some contemporary witnesses aver, that Schnabel was a flawless wizard in the period pre-1930, there's still plenty of wizardry left in these post-1930 Beethoven recordings. They are virtuoso readings that demonstrate a blazing intensity of interpretative vision as well as breathtaking manner of execution. Even when a dazzlingly articulate reading like that of the *Waldstein* is home and dry, the abiding impression in its aftermath is one of Schnabel's (and Beethoven's) astonishing physical and imaginative daring. And if this suggests recklessness, well, in many other instances the facts are quite other, for Schnabel has a great sense of decorum. He can, in many of the smaller sonatas and some of the late ones, be impeccably mannered, stylish and urbane. Equally he can be devilish or coarse. At the other extreme, he's indubitably the master of the genuinely slow movement.

For the recorded sound, there's nothing that can be done about the occasional patch of wow or discoloration but, in general, the old recordings come up very freshly.

Piano Sonatas Nos 1-32   Ⓗ
Wilhelm Kempff pf
DG Dokumente mono ⑧ 447 966-2GDO8 (511'· ADD) Includes bonus disc, 'Wilhelm Kempff –
An All-Round Musician'. Recorded 1951-6   Ⓜ❍❍❍

Ⓖ   Wilhelm Kempff was the most inspirational of Beethoven pianists. Those who have cherished his earlier stereo cycle for its magical spontaneity will find Kempff's qualities even more intensely conveyed in this mono set, recorded between 1951 and 1956. Amazingly the sound has more body and warmth than the stereo, with Kempff's unmatched transparency and clarity of articulation even more vividly caught, both in sparkling *Allegros* and in deeply dedicated slow movements. If in places he's even more personal, some might say wilful, regularly surprising you with a new revelation, the magnetism is even more intense, as in the great *Adagio* of the *Hammerklavier* or the final variations of Op-111, at once more rapt and more impulsive, flowing more freely. The bonus disc, entitled 'An All-Round Musician', celebrates Kempff's achievement in words and music, on the organ in Bach, on the piano in Brahms and Chopin as well as in a Bachian improvisation, all sounding exceptionally transparent and lyrical. Fascinatingly, his pre-war recordings of the Beethoven sonatas on 78s are represented too. Here we have his 1936 recording of the *Pathétique*, with the central *Adagio* markedly broader and more heavily pointed than in the mono LP version of 20 years later.

Complete Piano Sonatas
Daniel Barenboim pf
Video directors **Andy Sommer** and **Alan Miller**
EMI ⑥ 📀 368993-9
(10h 20' · NTSC · 16:9 · PCM stereo and 5.1 · 0)
Recorded live at the Deutsche Staatsoper, Berlin in June and July 2005   Ⓕ❍❍

For those seeking a home-video Beethoven cycle featuring an established, internationally acclaimed artist, Barenboim's is the only game in town for now. The musical results synthesise the best qualities of Barenboim's two earlier (audio only) cycles (the EMI from the 1960s and the DG from the early 1980s). More than 20 years on, the 62-year-old pianist revisits many of the rhetorical nuances he favoured in his youth, but now applies them within a context of greater expressive economy and structural cohesion. This particularly holds true in difficult-to-sustain slow movements such as those in Op 2 No 3, Op 7, the *Tempest* and the *Hammerklavier*, along with movements in variation form (Op 26's first movement, the *Appassionata*'s *Andante con moto* and Op 111's majestically unfolding Arietta).

Notwithstanding tiny inaccuracies, imbalances and occasional pounding in louder moments that are inevitable in a live, minimally edited concert, Barenboim's technique remains never less than solid and world-class. His body language isn't particularly eye-catching, except that he often raises his hands high at the end of big, declamatory phrases, and makes conducting gestures with the left hand while the right hand plays alone. However, the set's most provocative revelations appear on the final two discs in the form of masterclasses in Chicago in 2005. Six young pianists (including familiar names such as Lang Lang, Jonathan Biss and Alessio Bax) each play a movement from a sonata. Barenboim acknowledges the performances' positive attributes, then gets down to work. He guides the pianists through details of articulation, tempo relationships, dynamics, pedalling and harmonic motion, helping their interpretations attain greater clarity and specificity. Judging from the post-session questions, it's clear that the audience has been listening nearly as well as the teacher. We then return to Barenboim in Berlin and replay that recently dissected sonata movement with the benefit of newly enlightened ears and sharpened insights. Does the pianist practise what he preaches? Well, maybe 90 per cent of the time, yes.

SBT1188 – Piano Sonatas – Nos 1; 3; 32   H
SBT1189 – Piano Sonatas – Nos 7; 8; 13; 14
SBT1190 – Piano Sonatas – Nos 17; 18; 21; 22
SBT1191 – Piano Sonatas – Nos 26; 27; 29
SBT1192 – Piano Sonatas – Nos 23; 28; 30; 31
Solomon pf
Testament mono/°stereo SBT1188-92 (oas: 73', 78', 80', 78' & 79' · ADD) Recorded 1951-6   F

By the autumn of 1956, when a stroke ended Solomon's career at the absurdly early age of 54, he'd recorded 18 of the Beethoven piano sonatas, 12 of which had been released. Had his career continued, the cycle would almost certainly have been revised and completed. The immediate rivals would have been the two cycles Wilhelm Kempff recorded for Deutsche Grammophon (mono 1951-6, stereo 1964-5) and the pre-war Schnabel recordings which EMI reissued in its series Great Recordings of the Century in 1963-4. In the event, Solomon's cycle remained incomplete, as did later Emil Gilels's not dissimilar DG cycle.

Some will fret over this but sanguine folk will reflect that all the 'important' sonatas are here in performances that can generally be reckoned

BEETHOVEN'S COMPLETE PIANO SONATAS – IN BRIEF

Paul Lewis
Harmonia Mundi ⑩ HMC90 1902, 1903/5, 1906/8, 1909/11   F O O ►
Spread over four volumes, Paul Lewis offers a sonata cycle of great intellectual strength but also of real poetry and imagination. This is Beethoven playing that doesn't smile that often, but it has an integrity that jumps out of every bar. Here's a young artist not afraid to throw down the gauntlet to his elders.

Artur Schnabel   H
EMI Références mono ⑩ 763765-2   M O O ►
Also availably singly from Naxos
This was the first Beethoven piano sonata cycle ever recorded: Schnabel went into the studio for HMV during the 1930s and recorded a cycle that for many remains the greatest. Technically fallible he may be from time to time, but he offers the real Beethoven: a man of contrasts, of contradictions even, but someone with poetry in his every fibre.

Wilhelm Kempff   H
DG Dokumente mono ⑧ 447 966-2   M O O O
Though Kempff recorded a stereo cycle a decade later this mono set from the 1950s has an intensity married to his characteristic intensity that makes it the preferred cycle. There is a transparency to his sound that remains undimmed all these years later.

Friedrich Gulda
Brilliant Classics ⑨ 92773   S O
Gulda's second sonata cycle is a real bargain: performances of flair and imagination. Accents are forceful and there's a really bracing sense of re-discovery about these interpretations. A fascinating document from a fascinating musician.

Stephen Kovacevich
EMI ⑨ 562700-2   B O O ►
The most recent of piano sonata cycles (it wa recorded between 1992 and 2003), Kovacevich's is a magnificent achievement (and it is particularly well priced). Kovacevich is not a comfortable pianist – he never lets you relax into the music – and he constantly draws attention to the challenges Beethoven makes to his interpreters and to his listeners. A triumphant success crowned by some outstanding individual intertations (such as the *Hammerklavier*).

Alfred Brendel
Philips ⑩ download 446 909-2PH10   F O O ►
An intellectually rigorous yet deeply poetic response to these extraordinary works. Brendel has devoted a lifetime to these sonatas and brings that experience to bear in way that will guarantee hours of rewards. (Not currently listed on CD, but available to download.)

'representative'. Testament's Paul Baily has done a first-rate job on the transfers and the layouts: five CDs, each packed to the gunnels, each logically planned. The only sonata that's significantly out of sequence is Op 111 (No 32), yet curiously, that's the one performance from among the late, great sonatas which isn't entirely up to scratch. Here you might think back to Schnabel. Alongside Schnabel's reading, Solomon's sounds scampered (in the first movement), lacking in depth (in the second), and oddly unspontaneous, as though haunted by the knowledge of the older reading. The rather hollow-sounding 1951 recording doesn't help.

Op 111 is coupled here (SBT1188) with two of the Op 2 sonatas (Nos 1 and 3), the playing by turns fiery and lucid, gracious and gay. If anything's missing, it's the sense of tragic pathos Schnabel finds in the slow movement of the C major Sonata and his radical recklessness of spirit in the two finales.

The second disc contains celebrated readings of the *Moonlight* (No 14) and the *Pathétique* (No 8). Solomon's reading of the opening movement of the *Moonlight* is famously longbreathed, his reading of the opening movement of the *Pathétique*, and the *Moonlight*'s finale, wonderfully tense and austere.

The remaining three discs are, quite simply, indispensable, Solomon at the peak of his powers as a Beethoven player. In sonata after sonata, we hear virtuosity of the finest and most discriminating kind put at the service of some of the loftiest yet most physically beautiful and physically exciting music known to man. Solomon was famous for the Cistercian clarity of his quick playing (the *Waldstein* – No-21, and *Appassionata* – No 23, sonatas *passim*) and for the concentrated calm of his playing of the great slow movements (this 1952 recording of the *Hammerklavier* – No 29, as fine an example as any). Underpinning both these phenomena is a quality of dynamic control that both gratifies the eye (Beethoven's text lifted off the page with rare precision) and bewitches the ear. It's this latter point which gives Solomon his special ability to define for us that element of unalloyed wonder in Beethoven's writing, those moments when we're brought to what TS Eliot called 'the still point of the turning world'.

There are minor disappointments on each of these three final discs. The 1951 recording of Op 54 (SBT1190) is dowdily recorded and would almost certainly have been remade had circumstances allowed. Both the 1956 Op 90 (SBT1191) and the 1954 Op 101 (SBT1192) are good without being a match for what we have elsewhere on the discs. In the case of Op 90, this is Solomon's legendary elucidation of the *Hammerklavier* Sonata and his well-nigh definitive account of *Les adieux*, a performance, humane and vivid, that's fine almost beyond belief.

Piano Sonatas – Nos 3, 8, 'Pathétique' & 15, 'Pastoral'
Angela Hewitt pf
Hyperion 🌐 SACDA67605 (74' · DDD)   Ⓕ

The *Pastoral* Sonata leads off Angela Hewitt's second Beethoven sonata cycle instalment, and she taps into the music's overall geniality while also paying heed to its darker corners. In the first movement, her accompaniments are full and resonant, yet convey a murmuring, disembodied aura, while she gauges the development section's silences and transitions to particularly dramatic effect. She also plays the central movements well, although the *Andante*'s *staccato* left-hand lines are more characterfully bassoon-like in Stephen Kovacevich's hands, and some might prefer Richard Goode's more impetuous, angular fingerwork in the *Scherzo*. Yet Hewitt's conversational give-and-take between the droning left-hand ostinato and the main theme at the Rondo finale's outset is quite wonderful.

Having enjoyed Hewitt's edgy, fervent *Appassionata*, her *Pathétique* seems underplayed and studio-bound by comparison. Her fastidious, occasionally rounded-off execution softens the outer movements' ardour and momentum.

Hewitt's way with the C major Sonata, Op 2 No 3, boasts considerable profile and personality. Her tempo fluctuations in the first movement (the lyrical G major theme, for example) illuminate rather than detract from the structure, while the *Andante* appears more internally animated than one would guess from its nearly eight-minute timing. The contrapuntal acumen that distinguishes Hewitt's Baroque interpretations brilliantly comes to the fore in the *Scherzo*. In contrast to the pouncing scintillation Kovacevich and Richter bring to the *Allegro assai*, Hewitt evokes Rubinstein's urbane poise and patrician control, and treats the display passages in the manner of rapid melodies. Small wonder that Hewitt considers this one of Beethoven's most fulfilling sonatas to perform. In addition to Hyperion's superb sound, Hewitt, as usual, provides her own penetrating, vividly articulate annotations.

Piano Sonatas Nos 4, 7 & No 23, 'Appassionata'
Angela Hewitt pf
Hyperion 🌐 SACDA67518 (77' · DDD)   Ⓕ

Angela Hewitt's first instalment in a projected Beethoven sonata cycle for Hyperion offers intelligent, stylish and often illuminating interpretations. The contrapuntal acumen she regularly brings to Bach suits Beethoven's linear trajectory, as borne out by Hewitt's astute (yet never fussy) care over inner voices and bass-lines. She takes Beethoven's characteristic dynamic contrasts on faith but not to extreme, discontinuous ends, while her ear for uncovering melodic outlines of rapid arpeggios ensures that these figurations don't sound 'notey'. In addition, Hewitt's strong left hand lends uncommon clarity and direction to passages such as the double notes in No 4's first movement, or the motoric sequences in No 7's Rondo.

Occasional telltale signs of pre-planning include Hewitt's tendency to hesitate a split second before Beethoven's trademark *subito piano*s, thereby softening one's sense of surprise.

Her protracted treatment of No 4's *Largo* might have benefited from Claudio Arrau's gravitas and sustaining power. Fusing poetry and passion, Hewitt lets her long hair down and her fingers run wild in the *Appassionata*'s first movement. She continues with a brisk and well unified account of the central variations, and suffuses her powerful, headlong finale with cutting accents and perceptive modifications of the basic pulse. The Fazioli piano's lean bass and bright treble characterise the kind of timbral differentiation one often associates with instruments of Beethoven's time. Hyperion's SACD surround sound better absorbs the engineering's resonant ambience than conventional two-channel playback's relatively flatter sound-stage.

Piano Sonatas – Nos 5, 6, 7, 8, 'Pathétique'
András Schiff pf
ECM New Series 476 3100 (77' · DDD) Ⓕ

András Schiff's sharp attention to detail spills over from the first volume in his projected Beethoven cycle into this recital, although he sometimes crosses the thin line separating astute perception and finicky mannerism. The exaggerated quality of his clipped chords and staccato passages proves mincing and ultimately monotonous in No 6's outer movements, although some of the intricate left-hand runs attain uncommon clarity.

Surprisingly, Schiff holds back in No 5's finale, maintaining a comfortable *allegro*, whereas Beethoven marks *prestissimo*, in contrast to the thrust and momentum Glenn Gould, Stephen Kovacevich and, more recently, Gerhard Oppitz generate. Although Schiff makes the most of No 7's finale's questioning silences, others bring more gravity and desolation to the sonata's great slow movement (Arrau and Schnabel, for example).

Yet Schiff's subtle tempo modifications in the first movement add expressive dimension to the hurling octaves, while numerous left-hand counterlines zoom to the forefront. He similarly modifies the *Pathétique*'s first movement's basic tempo so that the bass tremolos have enough room to resonate and breathe, and follows the Rudolf Serkin tradition of repeating the introduction. Intense right- and left-hand interplay vibrantly unhinges the slow movement from its comfort zone, while Schiff's adherence to Beethoven's careful dynamic differentiations restores the Rondo's long lost thematic spice.

Heed these reservations: but respect Schiff's forethought, integrity and utter lack of routine.

Piano Sonatas – Nos 9, 10, 12 & 15, 'Pastoral'
Murray Perahia pf
Sony Classical 88697 32646-2 (71' · DDD) ⒻⓄⓄ➔

Perahia is a quiet Beethovenian, referring not to his dynamics but his utterly unhistrionic approach. Though you might want higher voltages running through some works, the sonatas here respond well to such a temperament. The opening of the variation set in Op 26, for instance, is simplicity itself, and Perahia's swiftly flowing second movement is beautifully judged. If anything is missing from these readings, it's a certain irreverent humour. Perahia's playing is so well honed that sometimes that last aspect seems to have been tamed, though he brings an effective sense of unease to the finale of the work.

His *Pastoral*, on the other hand, is a joyous balance of warmth of sound (how he makes the piano sing) in the outer movements, both simultaneously anchored by, and tensing against, a pedal note of D, and the shadowy *Andante*. A thought-provoking essay by Jeremy Siepmann and a well balanced recording match the quality of the playing.

'Piano Sonatas, Volume 1'
Piano Sonatas – Nos 16, 17, 'Tempest' & 18
Paul Lewis pf
Harmonia Mundi HMC90 1902 (74' · DDD) ⒻⓄⓄ➔

Paul Lewis launches his cycle of the 32 Beethoven sonatas with a triptych of richly varied middle-period masterpieces, the Op 31 set. A more auspicious start would be hard to imagine. True, others may characterise the first and third sonatas more playfully or show themselves more obviously attuned to Beethoven's scintillating wit and whimsy, but Lewis's unalloyed musicianship and overall mastery are worth their weight in gold; every bar declares his calibre and generosity of spirit.

Sometimes his warmth and flexibility suggest Beethoven seen, as it were, through Schubert's eyes (the finale to Op 31 No 1) and he often suggests a darker, more serious side to the composer's laughter and high jinks. But he plays Beethoven's humorous afterthought at the close of the Op 31 No 1's *Allegro vivace* as to the manner born and his *presto* coda to the finale becomes a joyous chase.

His way with the so-called *Tempest* Sonata is a reminder, too, of his outwardly relaxed mastery, quite without a sign of a skewed or telescoped phrase and with page after page given with a quiet but superbly focused intensity. His *Adagio* is gravely processional, his finale (that agitated, teasingly enigmatic *moto perpetuo*) acutely yet subtly and unobtrusively characterised. Again, while others may offer a swifter trajectory through No 3's finale, Lewis's wish to give substance to every note carries its own unswerving conviction. Harmonia Mundi's sound is excellent.

'Piano Sonatas, Volume 2'
Piano Sonatas – Nos 8, 'Pathétique', 9, No 10, 11, 21, 'Waldstein', 24, 25, 27, 28 & 29, 'Hammerklavier'
Paul Lewis pf
Harmonia Mundi ③ HMC90 1903/5 (3h 27' · DDD) ⒻⓄⓄ➔

Throughout all 10 sonatas Lewis's unswerving authority thinly veils his profound immersion in the very wellspring of Beethoven's creative genius. Even the composer's relatively carefree or lightweight gestures are invested with a drama and significance that illuminate them in a novel but wholly natural light. Here is one of those rare pianists who can charge even a single note or momentary pause with drama and significance and convince you, for example, that his lyrical, often darkly introspective way with Beethoven's pulsing *con brio* brilliance in the *Waldstein* Sonata is a viable, indeed, memorable alternative to convention.

So, too, is his way with the *Hammerklavier*, that most daunting of masterpieces, where he tells us that even when the composer is at his most elemental he remains deeply human and vulnerable. Not for him Schnabel's headlong attempt to obey Beethoven's wild first-movement metronome mark; nor does he view the vast spans of the *Adagio* as 'like the icy heart of some remote mountain lake' (JWN Sullivan) but rather a place of ineffable sadness. And here as elsewhere he is able to relish every detail of the composer's ever-expanding argument while maintaining a flawless sense of line and continuity.

Faced with such excellence a mere critic can only abandon paper and pencil and listen to this heroic but deeply moving young artist with awe and amazement. These are early days but Paul Lewis's superbly recorded and presented Beethoven may well turn out to be the most musicianly and ultimately satisfying of all recorded Beethoven piano sonata cycles.

'Piano Sonatas, Volume 3'
Piano Sonatas – Nos 1-4, 12, 13, 'quasi una fantasia', 14, 'Moonlight', 22 & 23, 'Appassionata'
Paul Lewis *pf*
Harmonia Mundi ③ HMC90 1906/8 (189' · DDD)
Ⓕ❍❍❍❍▷

Paul Lewis's third volume of his Beethoven sonata cycle once more shows him playing down all possible roughness and angularity in favour of a richly humane and predominantly lyrical beauty. Again, here is nothing of that glossy, impersonal sheen beloved of too many young pianists, but a subtly nuanced perception beneath an immaculate surface.

His technique, honed on many ultra-demanding areas of the repertoire allows him an imaginative and poetic latitude only given to a musical elite. Telescoped phrasing, rapid scrambles for security, waywardness and pedantry he gladly leaves to others, firmly but gently guiding you to the very heart of the composer. His *Appassionata* is characterised by muted gunfire, as if the sonata's warlike elements were heard from a distance. Yet the lucidity with which he views such violence easily makes others' more rampant virtuosity become sound and fury, signifying little. His way, too, with the teasing toccata-like finales of Nos 12 and 22 is typical of his lyrical restraint, a far cry, indeed, from a

more overt brilliance. How superbly he captures Beethoven's over-the-shoulder glance at Haydn, his great predecessor, yet gives you all of his forward-looking Romanticism in the early F minor Sonata (No 1). Again, how many pianists could achieve such unfaltering poise and sensitivity in No 4's *Largo, con gran espressione*?

These performances are a transparent act of musical love and devotion. Nothing is exaggerated yet virtually everything is included. Of all the modern versions of the sonatas, Lewis's is surely the most eloquent and persuasive. And, as in previous issues, Harmonia Mundi's sound is of demonstration quality.

'Piano Sonatas, Volume 4'
Nos 5, 6, 7, 15, 'Pastoral', 19, 20, 26, 'Les adieux', 30, 31 & 32
Paul Lewis *pf*
Harmonia Mundi ③ HMC90 1909/11 (3h 4' · DDD)
Ⓕ❍❍❍❍▷

Only an extended essay could do justice to the fourth and final volume of Paul Lewis's Beethoven sonata cycle… You may well cherish your beloved sets by Schnabel, Kempff and Brendel (to name but three), but Lewis surely gives you the best of all possible worlds; one devoid of idiosyncrasy yet of a deeply personal musicianship.

Where else can you hear Op 10 No 2's madcap finale given with such unfaltering lucidity and precision? Try Op 28's finale for an ultimate pianistic and musical finesse or the opening *Allegro* where Lewis makes you conscious of how the music's gracious and mellifluous unfolding is momentarily clouded by mystery and energised by drama. In such hands the final pages of Op 111 do indeed become 'a drift towards the shores of Paradise' (Edward Sackville-West) and throughout all these performances you sense how 'the great effort of interpretation' (Michael Tippett) is resolved in playing of a haunting poetic commitment and devotion. Such playing is hardly for lovers of histrionics or inflated rhetoric, but rather for those in search of other deeper, more refreshing attributes, for Beethoven's inner light and spirit.

Somehow Lewis's quiet and distinctive voice can lift even the most familiar phrase on to another sphere and his playing throughout, shorn of accretion, makes all these sonatas shine with their first radiance and eloquence. Admirably recorded, this three-disc set is crowned with a scholarly and illuminating essay by Jean-Paul Montagnier.

Beethoven Piano Sonatas Nos 8, 23 & 31.　Ⓗ
Handel Keyboard Suite in D minor, HWV428 – Prelude; Air and Variations; Presto. Chaconne and Variations in G, HWV435
Edwin Fischer *pf*
APR Signature mono APR5502 (72' · AAD) Recorded 1931-8
Ⓜ❍❍

On this invaluable disc are some of Fischer's finest and most legendary performances. His very first published recording (1931) of the Handel Chaconne, for example, was made at a time when his matchless *leggiero* and radiant tone were unimpeded by obvious blemishes or erratic pianism. Both this performance and that of the pieces from the Suite No 3 are endowed with an improvisatory magic, a strength and grace and supreme assurance. Fischer commences the *Pathétique* with a scrupulous adherence to Beethoven's *fp* marking, a sudden shift of sound that's fascinatingly modernist or prophetic. The *Allegro di molto e con brio* is exactly that, dancing with an irrepressible lightness and urgency; in the slow octave descent just before the final outburst there's a rapt 'all-passion-spent' quality, something that Fischer was able to achieve with supreme naturalness, without even a hint of artifice or calculated effect.

All past vicissitudes are finally resolved in Sonata, Op 110 (No 31) in a blaze of heroic glory, and time and time again he makes you pause to consider key points and details that have somehow eluded others. There's a richness and humanity here that was uniquely Fischer's.

Piano Sonatas Nos 8, 'Pathétique', 14, 'Moonlight', 15, 'Pastoral', 17, 'Tempest', 21, 'Waldstein', 23, 'Appassionata' & 26, 'Les adieux'
Alfred Brendel pf
Philips Duo ② 438 730-2PM2 (152' · ADD)
Recorded 1970-77   ⓜⓞ➔

The Philips reissue, with seven of Beethoven's most popular sonatas admirably played by Alfred Brendel, is in every way an outstanding bargain, and is well worth obtaining, even if duplication is involved. All the performances are authoritative and offer consistently distinguished playing, while the recording is very realistic indeed. The *Tempest* resonates in the memory and the central movements of the *Pastoral* are most beautifully shaped. The *Pathétique, Moonlight* and *Appassionata* all bring deeply satisfying readings that are compellingly conceived and freshly executed. This set can be recommended without any reservations.

Piano Sonatas – No 14, 'Moonlight', 21, 'Waldstein', 26, 'Les adieux' & No 31
Nelson Freire pf
Decca 475 8155DH (69' · DDD)   ⓕⓞ➔

What's not to admire about Nelson Freire's brilliantly virtuoso, heartfelt and utterly alive Beethoven interpretations? They're pianistically oriented in terms of tone colour and symmetry, yet never feel the least bit four-square, and convey vivid communicative immediacy, even when Freire tends to hurry in hot anticipation of a dramatic build that lies just a few steps ahead. Freire takes the *Waldstein* first movement's *Allegro con brio* directive to scintillating heart, as the

sweeping scales jump out of your loudspeakers like white lightning and the development section's relentless left-hand arpeggios gain urgency through unusual accentuations. He also generates plenty of tonal magic from the *Rondo*'s unconventional long pedal markings and galvanic momentum in the prestissimo coda. Some may prefer a more austere, contained *Adagio molto*, yet one could make a case for Freire's unfolding animation as being true to this music's intended introductory function.

In *Les adieux*, Freire fuses Solomon's incredibly poised fingerwork and Schnabel's passionate sweep into his own individualised *tour de force*. Other Op 110 performances may offer more breadth and spirituality, yet Freire's carefully gauged tempo relationships in the hard-to-pace Fugue pay no less expressive dividends. Also notice that Freire, like Claudio Arrau, takes trouble to make the first movement's rapid left-hand figurations clear and distinct. The *Moonlight*'s *Adagio sostenuto* is beautifully sung out, while the *Allegretto*'s varied articulations sound as how they read on the page. So do those of the finale. You won't find Kovacevich's shock and awe, but rather a masterclass in steady cumulation that should reveal more with each listening.

Beethoven Piano Sonatas – Nos 15, 'Pastoral' & 23, 'Appassionata' **Schubert** Piano Sonata No 21, D960
Andreas Haefliger pf
Avie ② AV2148 (91' · DDD)   ⑧➔

Haefliger's innate affinity for Beethoven's largely lyrical *Pastoral* Sonata manifests itself via the pianist's relaxed tempi and ample tone. Taste and proportion govern his penchant for rhetorical broadenings and tenuti. Although Haefliger tempers Beethoven's characteristic *subito* dynamics more than he ought to, he pays special heed to matters of articulation. You'll notice how he distinguishes the slurs and staccati in the *Scherzo*'s main theme, whereas many pianists treat these notes equally. The *Appassionata*'s outer movements achieve a happy fusion of drama, cumulative sweep and textural clarity. Haefliger's keen attention to the *Andante con moto*'s left-hand lines rivets the attention to the point that one barely notices how he bumps up the variations' tempi in bite-size increments.

With exposition repeat in tow, Haefliger sculpts the Schubert B flat's lengthy first movement in long arcs propelled more by songful than symphonic impulses (the way he pulls back from certain high notes, for instance). And here's the surprise: for some reason, Haefliger races through the first ending nearly twice as fast as it's written. Strange. Similar breadth and vocally informed phrasing inform the *Andante sostenuto*. The *Scherzo*'s Trio expands and contracts as Haefliger magnifies the bass-note syncopations, while the finale convinces entirely. You get a strong sense of concert-hall realism if you play these discs at a loud volume.

'Complete Works for Solo Piano, Vol 6'
Piano Sonatas – Nos 21-25
Ronald Brautigam fp
BIS ⓜ BIS-SACD1573 (73' · DDD/DSD)　　ⒻOᎱ

Volume 6 in Ronald Brautigam's Beethoven cycle offers stunning performances that are technically breathtaking, stylistically astute, emotionally intense and musically alive in every moment. What is more, they make the most compelling case on disc for period instruments in this repertoire. Go to the *Waldstein*'s Rondo, for example, to hear uncommon textural differentiation from register to register, where Beethoven's controversial long pedal markings make sense, the left-hand figurations emerge with rare shape and purpose, and the octave glissandi in the coda are light as feathers.

In both the *Waldstein*'s and *Appassionata*'s first movements, Brautigam's fast tempi generate drama and tension, not so much through sheer speed as by way of characterful thematic contrasts, pointed accents and subtle yet expressively powerful modifications of the basic pulse. The slightly militant edge with which Brautigam phrases the graceful main theme in the Op 54 Sonata's first movement makes the subsequent octaves in triplets sound less jarring in context. At first one fears that his brisk pace for the second movement leaves Beethoven's humbler *Allegretto* directive at the starting-gate, but the clarity of the toccata-like part writing and off-beat accents make Brautigam's conception work. By contrast, the little Op 79 Sonata's outer movements are comparatively sedate and graceful.

Wonderful sound quality too, in both SACD and conventional two-channel formats. Don't pass up this amazing release!

Piano Sonatas Nos 27-32　　Ⓗ
Solomon pf
EMI Références mono/stereo ② 764708-2
(141' · ADD) Recorded 1951-6　　ⓜOOO

Solomon's 1952 recording of the *Hammerklavier* Sonata is one of the greatest of the century. At the heart of his performance there's as calm and searching an account of the slow movement as you're ever likely to hear. And the outer movements are also wonderfully well done. Music that's so easy to muddle and arrest is here fiercely played; Solomon at his lucid, quick-witted best.

The CD transfer is astonishing. It's as though previously we have merely been eavesdropping on the performance; now, decades later, we're finally in the presence of the thing itself. It's all profoundly moving. What's more, EMI has retained the juxtaposition of the 1969 LP reissue: Solomon's glorious account of the A major Sonata, No 28 as the *Hammerklavier*'s proud harbinger. We must be grateful that Solomon had completed his recording of these six late sonatas before his career was abruptly ended by a stroke in the latter part of 1956.

The Sonatas Nos 27 and 31, were recorded in August 1956. In retrospect the warning signs were already there; yet listening to these edited tapes you'd hardly know anything was amiss. There's the odd fumble in the *Scherzo* of No 31; but, if anything, the playing has even greater resolve, both in No 31 and in a songful (but never sentimental) account of No 27. The recordings of Nos 30 and 32 date from 1951. Sonata No 30, is very fine; No 32 is, by Solomon's standards, a shade wooden in places, both as a performance and as a recording.

Still, this is a wonderful set, and very much a collectors' item.

Piano Sonatas Nos 28-32
Maurizio Pollini pf
DG The Originals ② 449 740-2GOR2 (126' · ADD)
Recorded 1975-7　　ⓜOOO

This reissued DG Originals set makes an exceptionally neat package. Consistent praise has been heaped on these recordings since they won the Instrumental Record Award in 1977. One of Pollini's greatest strengths is his ability to stand up to the accumulated momentum of Beethoven's structure, but he can also build on it so as to leave the impression of one huge exhalation of creative breath. In the first movement of the Hammerklavier the astonishing technical assurance has you on the edge of your seat with excitement. His controlled vehemence is without rival in the outer movements, and though he doesn't get right to the bottom of No 29's poetry, his far-sighted phrasing and paragraphing is again remarkable.

In the last three sonatas there are others who stop to peer deeper into some of the psychic chasms, but Pollini's mastery of integration and continuous growth, and his ability to hold potentially conflicting musical demands in balance, are again sources of wonderment. In terms of the qualities just mentioned, who is Pollini's equal? Other than small touches of pre-echo in No 32, there's nothing here to distract from the exalted quality of both the music and the playing.

'The Piano Sonatas, Vol 7'
Piano Sonatas – Nos 27, 28 & 29, 'Hammerklavier'
András Schiff pf
ECM New Series 476 6189 (77' · DDD)　　ⒻᎱ
Recorded live at the Tonhalle, Zürich

'The Piano Sonatas, Vol 8'
Piano Sonatas – Nos 30, 31 & 32
András Schiff pf
ECM New Series 476 6192 (65' · DDD)　　ⒻᎱ

Imagine a fortepiano's clipped, biting quality of note attacks, acute timbral distinctions between registers and widely varying resonances available from the sustain pedal. Fortify these attributes with the modern concert grand's lung-power and potential for large-scale projection, and you've got the essence of András Schiff's Beethoven cycle, which remains as provocative as ever throughout its final two instalments.

If you've followed the cycle to date, you'll notice that Schiff's fondness for breaking of hands is more pronounced this time around. Sometimes the effect magnifies felicities of voice-leading or expression; other times it comes off as arch and mannered. Schiff's variegated touch and tonal control impress in Op 101's first movement, yet he sidesteps the second-movement march's obsessive ferocity. He is fastidious in the fugal finale at the expense of forward momentum. This comment also applies to the *Hammerklavier*'s challenging outer movements, although Schiff's detailed inflections leave none of the oddball gestures of the little *Scherzo* unscrutinised. The easy ebb and flow of his intimately scaled *Adagio sostenuto* belies its relatively short playing-time.

Schiff's strengths and quirks make their marks throughout the last three sonatas. He plays Op 109 directly and simply, absorbing finely tuned details of balance, voicing and articulation within a big picture (such as the *Scherzo*'s rarely observed non-legato phrasings). The long cantabiles of Op 110's *Adagio ma non troppo* lend themselves better to Schiff's hand-breaking than the first movement's gentle, rapid figurations. However, the pianist assiduously navigates the fugue's tricky tempo relationships.

Schiff begins Op 111's *Maestoso* promisingly (note the impeccably gauged trills, for example), only to tread gingerly in a rather four-square, underprojected *Allegro con brio*. Only a few fussy distensions break Schiff's long-lined focus and concentration in the expansively conceived *Arietta*, where the long chains of trills fill the room at even their softest point. ECM's sound is remarkably lifelike.

Piano Sonatas – Nos 29, 'Hammerklavier'[a] & 31[b]
Rudolf Serkin pf
BBC Legends [a]mono BBCL4241-2 (66' · ADD)
Recorded live at the Royal Festival Hall, London, on [a]May 13, 1968 and [b]June 16, 1971   Ⓕ❍

Rudolf Serkin was one of music's greatest over-reachers, at his finest lifting his capacity audiences into the most exalted regions of the mind and imagination. And here, in two incomparable performances taken from two London recitals, his candour and intensity are of a searing force and conviction. Others may plough a smoother furrow but smooth furrows have little to do with the *Hammerklavier* Sonata's epic and intimidating utterance. Caressing *pianissimi* or magical, multicoloured nuance were hardly Serkin's way, even when he chose less obviously daunting repertoire, and as he himself put it, 'the piano has always been less interesting to me than the music'. In this sense he was Horowitz's polar opposite and here in late Beethoven nothing stands between you and the composer.

In the first movement of the *Hammerklavier* there is no question of emulating Schnabel's ill-advised attempt at Beethoven's supposed metronome markings so that the music's force and eloquence have rarely been more powerfully paced and unfolded. Again, whether storming the heavens or making time stand still (and you will hear both in the *Adagio sostenuto*'s closing pages) Serkin makes you aware that beneath the mask of the benignly smiling 'Rudy' lay a ferocious missionary zeal. Once more, in Op 110 everything is achieved by essentially gritty musical rather than pianistic means so that what can initially seem literal and forbidding takes on a sublime perspective. Serkin was, quite simply, a unique voice and presence and, as these excellently transferred recordings tell us, true musical stature is only achieved by unfaltering commitment and an awareness that you can never do enough for music.

Diabelli Variations, Op 120

Beethoven Diabelli Variations
Bach Partita No 4, BWV828
Stephen Kovacevich pf
Onyx ONYX4035 (78' · DDD)   Ⓕ❍❍❍▣►

Ⓖ Kovacevich writes in his introduction to this new set that it was the *Diabelli Variations* – via the Serkin recording – that first made him love Beethoven. It's a reading that still holds its head high today, and just a decade later, in 1968, Kovacevich set down his own recording, rightly acclaimed and something of a calling-card for the young pianist. But what of this new performance, made 40 years later? What is immediately striking is the sense of a cumulative whole, the tension and indeed speed with which he approaches the work. The work's juxtapositions of the sublime and the ridiculous are presented with a vividness that sounds more live than studio-bound.

Kovacevich emphasises the sense of continuous development with a certain fleetness of finger: his opening theme sets quite a pace, and dances more lightly than many rival versions. It's certainly faster than his own earlier recording. But more important is the sense that Kovacevich has now encompassed the extremes of the work more fully. His understanding of Beethoven's juxtapositions of beauty and crudity, reflection and action, and the sheer dynamic range, are fully exposed in this new version, which captures the piano sound beautifully.

Kovacevich has, in the intervening decades between his first and second *Diabelli*s, recorded a complete sonata cycle and again that familiarity with Beethoven's language in the final years shows and, again and again, Kovacevich reveals how that humour can tip over into something far more menacing. Perhaps in his younger days Beethoven would have ended the set with the fugue, but instead we get a final addition: a switch to C major and an utter change in mood, with a graceful, quasi-Mozartian idea, whirled ever higher. It's as enigmatic and undefinable as anything Beethoven wrote and a transcendent ending to this remarkable performance.

Kovacevich might be less associated with Bach, but let's not forget that his teacher was that consummate Bachian, Myra Hess. He treads a middle path between the tonally slimline, rhythmically motivated readings of Angela Hewitt and the more obviously romantic ones of Cédric Tiberghien. And it's an enlightening partner to the *Diabelli* Variations, not only in its basis in dance rhythms but also in its scope and its extrovert demeanour, whose tone is set with the grand Ouverture. Altogether, a disc to treasure.

Diabelli Variations
Piotr Anderszewski pf
Virgin Classics 545468-2 (63' · DDD) ⓕ❶❷➔

This is the most intelligent, searching and delightful account of the *Diabelli Variations* to have reached us since Brendel's. It gives opportunities everywhere to admire a superfine control of every aspect of piano playing, but that isn't the great thing about it, splendid though the finish is. The performance is entirely composer-led, driven by the music, not by ideas *about* the music, and in that sense you hardly notice the means to the end at all. It's an account of the *Diabelli* based on a much closer reading of the text than you usually get, and you've only to hear the theme and the first variation to perceive an exceptional balance of rigour and imagination: rigour in the way Anderszewski has thought about every inflection marked by Beethoven; imagination, evident here and throughout, in the quality with which he has realised them in terms of expression and vividness of character. His rhythm is tremendous.

More remarkable still is his feeling for dynamics, so copiously prescribed in this work and yet treated with approximation by so many players. He's not one to play the daredevil, and you could say his tempos in the quick numbers are sometimes surprisingly moderate; but he isn't a sober-sides. He has fingers which are always saying something, a varied and attractive sound, usually built from the bass up, and that rare ability to get from one thing to another with pinpoint accuracy, expressively speaking, as if forging sonority and character with a laser. A fine recording, and the sound is at an apt distance. An outstanding issue.

Piano Variations

32 Variations on an Original Theme in C minor, WoO80.
Six Variations on an Original Theme in F,
Op 34. Fifteen Variations and a Fugue on an Original Theme in E flat, 'Eroica', Op 35. Six Variations on an Original Theme, 'Die Ruinen von Athen', Op 76.
Six Variations on an Original Theme in G, WoO77.
Seven Variations in C on 'God save the King', WoO78. Five Variations in D on 'Rule Britannia', WoO79.
Cédric Tiberghien pf
Harmonia Mundi HMC90 1775 (76' · DDD) ⓕ❶❷

Cédric Tiberghien commences the *Eroica* Variations with a meticulous weight and balance of

textures and although exceptionally delicate and precise, rarely misses the force and energy underlining one of Beethoven's lithest, most vigorous arguments. He sinks gratefully into reflection in Variation 8 and his musicianship in the richly ornamented *Largo* of Variation 15 is at once individual but unsullied by personal idiosyncrasy. Again, in the *32 Variations* in C minor – that compendium of classical virtuosity – Tiberghien is meticulous but never severe, precisely yet generously registering the mood and character of each brief Variation in a manner that may well have caused Beethoven to alter his unfavourable opinion of his work ('Beethoven, what a fool you have been!'). His *stretto* in Variations 21-2 makes the dark place of Variation 23 sound unusually mysterious while Variations 10-11 show an unfaltering assurance and style.

Tiberghien is no less outstanding in less demanding fare, relishing the explosive whimsy of the *Rule Britannia* and *God save the King* Variations, with their mock solemnity and affectionate digs at British assumptions of superiority. Here, clearly, is a pianist to watch. Harmonia Mundi's sound is excellent, making this an altogether exceptional disc.

Bagatelles

Bagatelles – Op 33; Op 119; C minor, WoO52;
C, WoO56. Rondos – Op 51: No 1 in C; No 2 in G;
C, WoO48; A, WoO49. Six Minuets, WoO10.
Polonaise in C, Op 89. Andante favori in F, WoO57.
Variations – Six in F on an Original Theme, Op 34;
Nine in C minor on a March by Dressler, WoO63; Six in F on a Swiss Song, WoO64; 24 in D on Righini's 'Venni amore', WoO65; 12 in C on Haibel's 'Menuet à la Viganò', WoO68; Six in G on Paisiello's 'Nel cor più non mi sento', WoO70
Mikhail Pletnev pf
DG ② 457 493-2GH2 (152' · DDD) ⓕ❶❷➔

From the very first notes of the *Dressler* Variations – Beethoven's first-known composition, dating from 1782 – it's clear that Pletnev is a master of piano texture, and that he's going to use his mastery not only to ravish the ear but to delight the mind. His nuances in the simple Swiss theme and its artless variations are quite delicious. At the opposite extreme, the grand set of 24 Variations on Righini's 'Venni amore' come across as a dry run for later cycles such as the *Eroica* or even the *Diabelli* Variations, both in overall design and in certain idiosyncratic details. Technical *tours de force* abound; Pletnev negotiates them all not only with phenomenal pianistic aplomb but, where appropriate, dry wit. It's a fascinating glimpse into the laboratory of the 20-year-old Beethoven's mind.

In the two early Rondos Pletnev is freer than some might wish with the notated dynamics, phrasing and articulation, and his touch suggests at times that he's thinking more of Scarlatti than of Beethoven. Nevertheless the most startling moments of whimsy in these pieces aren't his but the composer's. By contrast, in the Vienna-period Rondos of Op 51 he seems to be thinking forward to the age of Lisztian rhetoric. But the fact that he's never satisfied with the default response to the surface of the music is much to be welcomed, and almost always his initiatives are stylish and effective. Similarly the bagatelles radiate openness to all sorts of possibilities. In some instances Brendel finds more of a rough-and-tumble edginess; but Pletnev's range of touch and tonal nuance outstrips them both and brings rewards of its own, as in the proto-Schubertian touches of Op 119.

Instrument and recording quality are near to ideal. An outstanding issue.

Cantatas

Cantata on the death of the Emperor Joseph II, WoO87. Cantata on the accession of the Emperor Leopold II, WoO88. Opferlied, Op 121b. Meeresstille und glückliche Fahrt, Op 112
Janice Watson, Judith Howarth sops **Jean Rigby** mez **John Mark Ainsley** ten **José van Dam** bass-bar
Corydon Singers and Orchestra / Matthew Best
Hyperion CDA66880 (80' · DDD· T/t)   Ⓕ

Beethoven was only 19 when he was commissioned to write this 40-minute cantata on the emperor's death. It was never performed, the musicians claiming it was too difficult, and remained buried for almost a century. Arguably Beethoven's first major masterpiece, it was one of his few early unpublished works of which he approved. When he came to write *Fidelio*, he used the soaring theme from the first of the soprano arias here, 'Da stiegen die Menschen an's Licht', for Leonore's sublime moment in the finale, 'O Gott! Welch' ein Augenblick'. The tragic C minor power of the choruses framing the work is equally memorable. Dramatic tension is kept taut through all seven sections, with recitatives indicating the young composer's thirst to write opera. Matthew Best conducts a superb performance, fresh, incisive and deeply moving, with excellent soloists as well as a fine chorus. In this first cantata the solo quartet simply contribute to the opening and closing choruses.

The second cantata, only a little more than half the length of the first, was written soon after, when Leopold II had succeeded as emperor. This second work is less ambitious, expressing less deep emotions, yet it anticipates later masterpieces. Much more specific is the way that the finale of the cantata, 'Heil! Stürzet nieder, Millionen', clearly looks forward to the finale of the Ninth Symphony, a point reinforced by the key of D major. The two shorter pieces, both dating from Beethoven's difficult interim period between middle and late, with Jean Rigby as soloist in the *Opferlied*, make a generous fill-up, performed with equal dedication. With plenty of air round the chorus, the recording has ample weight yet is transparent enough to clarify even the heaviest textures. A revelatory issue.

Songs

Sechs Gellert Lieder, Op 48. Lieder – Op 52: No 3, Das Liedchen von der Ruhe; No 4, Mailied; Op 75: No 2, Neue Liebe, neues Leben; No 3, Aus Goethes Faust; Op 83:-No 1, Wonne der Wehmut; No 2, Sehnsucht. Adelaide, Op 46. An die Hoffnung, Op 94. An die ferne Geliebte, Op 98. Klage, WoO113. Der Liebende, WoO139. An die Geliebte, WoO140
Stephan Genz bar **Roger Vignoles** pf
Hyperion CDA67055 (69' · DDD · T/t)   ⒻⓄⓄⓄ

 The young baritone Stephan Genz is in the first bloom of his youthful prime. Beethoven's setting of Goethe's 'Mailied', with its lightly breathed, springing words, could have been written with Genz in mind. Roger Vignoles, Genz's regular accompanist, contributes an irresistible bounding energy and even a sense of mischief to one of Beethoven's most spontaneous yet subtle settings, 'Neue Liebe, neues Leben'; and an elusive sense of yearning is created as the voice tugs against the piano line in 'Sehnsucht'. The six *Gellert Lieder* form the centrepiece of this recital: Beethoven's song cycle, *An die ferne Geliebte*, its grand finale. The intensity of Genz's cry 'Is there a God?' in *An die Hoffnung*, at the start of the disc, gives some indication of the *gravitas* he brings to his firmly enunciated 'spiritual songs' of Gellert. Genz and Vignoles have here reinstated a number of the original verses omitted by Beethoven in the first printed edition, creating a greater sense of balance and proportion within the set. The concluding song cycle is quite simply one of the best performances currently available. Fresh and bright of tone, awe-filled and beautifully paced and scaled, Genz's singing is modulated exquisitely from song to song by Vignoles's sentient piano accompaniment.

Beethoven An die ferne Geliebte
Schubert Schwanengesang
Matthias Goerne bar **Alfred Brendel** pf
Decca 475 6011DH (72' · DDD · T/t)
Recorded live 2003   ⒻⓄⓄⒹ

Matthias Goerne and Alfred Brendel form one of the great Lieder partnerships of the day. The sympathy between them goes beyond skilful ensemble, and beyond shared enjoyment of the wealth of illustration in Schubert, into a deep understanding of the poetry as he composed it. There is no surprise that these two thoughtful artists should produce powerful performances of the most inward-looking Heine songs – the suffering power of 'Der Atlas', the misery from which the harmony allows no escape in 'Die Stadt', the terror of 'Der Doppelgänger'. In its beauty, their shared phrasing springs from an understanding of the meaning of each poem, so that the lighter ones are scarcely less affecting. 'Das Fischermädchen' has a slightly knowing lilt, catching Heine's typical irony in the girl's false wooing. In 'Der Abschied' Goerne's young man sings happily as he sets off while Brendel's merry trot tells us that the horse has caught his mood. Their mutual understanding completely solves such a difficult song as 'Kriegers Ahnung'. And the Beethoven cycle moves in a steady progress not into the usual triumphant assertion but into a warmth of belief that song may truly join the parted lovers. Music-making of genius.

Als die Geliebte sich trennen wollte, WoO132. An die Geliebte, WoO140. Vier Arietten und ein Duett, Op 82. Das Geheimnis, WoO145. In questa tomba oscura, WoO133. Der Kuss, Op 128. Sechs Lieder von Gellert, Op 48. Acht Lieder, Op 52. Sechs Lieder, Op 75. Der Mann von Wort, Op 99. Sehnsucht, WoO134. Sehnsucht, WoO146. Seufzer eines Ungeliebten und Gegenliebe, WoO188
Ann Murray mez **Roderick Williams** bar **Iain Burnside** pf
Signum Classics ② SIGCD139 (87' · DDD)　　Ⓜ➔

Beethoven was a reluctant song composer, avowedly frustrated by the limitations of the human voice – and, one suspects, the genre's limited scope for motivic-symphonic development. Yet he still left over 80 songs, ranging from agreeable trifles and Italianate scenas to the gravely majestic Gellert Lieder and the song-cycle *An die ferne Geliebte*. Mirroring Beethoven's life, the distant, unattainable beloved is a recurrent obsession here, whether in three settings of 'An die Geliebte' or four of Mignon's yearning 'Nur wer die Sehnsucht kennt', the last surely in Schubert's mind when he composed his famous setting of 1826. Elsewhere we have ingenuous quasi folksongs, the sombre 'In questa tomba oscura', and a clutch of comic songs, by turns lusty, viciously satirical (Mephistopheles's 'Song of the Flea' from *Faust*) or coyly erotic ('Der Kuss').

Two thirds of the numbers on this pair of CDs go to Roderick Williams, whose clean, mellifluous timbre, firm legato and expressive diction are well nigh ideal. The Gellert Lieder can be a bit of a bore when performed as lofty hymns: Williams sings them as personal dramas of the soul. At the other end of the spectrum he sings a slyly lubricious 'Der Kuss', colouring and timing to perfection, characterises the 'Song of the Flea' with gusto, and even brings off the potentially tedious 'Urians Reise um die Welt', a 14-verse travelogue related by a blinkered bore.

Ann Murray is, as ever, a thoughtful interpreter; and when she sings softly – as in her touching performances of the 'Nur wer die Sehnsucht kennt' settings or 'An den fernen Geliebten' – she gives pleasure. At *mezzo forte* and above her tone tends to grow squally – marring, say, her deeply felt 'Kennst du das Land' and 'Liebes-klage'. This proviso aside, these discs offer many unsuspected delights, enhanced throughout by Iain Burnside's vividly imagined and, where appropriate, witty keyboard commentaries and epilogues.

Irish, Welsh and Scottish Songs

Irish Songs, WoO152 – No 1, The Return to Ulster[b]; No 5, On the Massacre of Glencoe[b]; No 6, What shall I do to shew how much I love her[b]; No 8, Come draw we round a cheerful ring[b]; No 9, The Soldier's Dream[c]; No 19, Wife, Children and Friends[abc]; WoO153 – No 4, Since greybeards inform us that youth will decay[b]; No 9, The kiss, dear maid, thy lip has left[c]; WoO154 – No 3, The Farewell Song[b]; No 4, The Pulse of an Irishman[c]. Welsh Songs, WoO155 – No 2, The Monks of Bangor's March[bc]; No 9, To the Aeolian Harp[a]; No 14, The Dream[ab]; No 19, The Vale of Clwyd[a]; No 22, Constancy[bc]; No 25, The Parting Kiss[b]. Scottish Songs, Op 108 – No 5, The sweetest lad was Jamie[a]; No 8, The lovely lass of Inverness[a]; No 11, Oh! thou art the lad of my heart, Willy[a]; No 13, Come fill, fill, my good fellow[abc]; No 20, Faithfu' Johnie[a]; No 24, Again, my Lyre[b]; WoO156 – Womankind[abc]. God save the King!, WoO157[abc]
[a]**Sophie Daneman** sop [b]**Paul Agnew** ten [c]**Peter Harvey** bar **Alessandro Moccia** vn **Alix Verzier** vc **Jérôme Hantaï** fp
Astrée Naïve E8850 (71' · DDD · N/T/t)　　Ⓕ

Here's an excellent selection of Beethoven's 140 folksong arrangements, performed with all due care and accomplishment, spirit and affection. They're a joy: the songs in themselves, for a start, but more especially Beethoven's work on them. Or put it another way: 'work' is exactly what it does not sound like. It sounds as though he met these tunes (sent him, mostly, by George Thomson of Edinburgh), took to them like magic, found something in each that warmed his heart or set him dancing, and eventually, sorry when the verses had run out, made him add a ritornello or coda like a pat on the back to send each on its way.

Each number is a delight, but among the favourites are *Faithfu' Johnie*, with its deep cello underlining the heart's affections, *The Pulse of an Irishman*, both rumbustious and delicate in its fun, and, unexpectedly, *God save the King*, in which, in spite of its two peremptory calls to attention, Beethoven seems to be doing anything but. A special feature is the use of period instruments, effective in the more dramatic arrangements such as *The Return to Ulster* and the jovial party-pieces, *Come, fill, fill, my good fellows* and *Since greybeards inform us*. All three singers contribute ably, and the occasional collaborations in duet and trio are welcome.

Mass in C, Op 86

Mass in C. Ah! perfido, Op 65.　　Ⓟ
Meeresstille und glückliche Fahrt, Op 112
Charlotte Margiono sop **Catherine Robbin** mez **William Kendall** ten **Alastair Miles** bar Monteverdi Choir; Orchestre Révolutionnaire et Romantique / **Sir John Eliot Gardiner**
Archiv Produktion 435 391-2AH (62' · DDD · T/t)
　　　　Ⓕ❶❷➔

Gardiner's genius is in evidence here. The *Kyrie eleison*, is a plea for mercy, but its opening bars speak of comfort: there's almost the simple good faith of a quiet, very Germanic carol about them. Gardiner sets a mood of deliberate seriousness, with lowered period, pitch and a tempo rather slower than that suggested by Beethoven's direction: *Andante con moto, assai vivace, quasi allegretto ma non troppo*. He also appears to have encouraged the soloists, especially the soprano, to shape and shade the phrases, so intensifying the feeling of seriousness and deliberation. Happily, this policy prevails for only a short time, and to some extent the music itself goes out to meet it. As the second *Kyrie* (following the *Christe*) moves towards its climax, the *fortissimo* brings suspensions where the alto part grinds against the soprano, and then come sudden *fortissimos* with intense modulations and momentary discords, all of which are particularly vivid in this performance. What follows has the same exhilarating quality as that which was so applauded in Gardiner's *Missa solemnis* and, just as he did there, Gardiner is constantly illuminating detail while maintaining an apparently easy natural rightness throughout.

Again, an outstanding contribution is made by the Monteverdi Choir. Splendidly athletic, for instance, are the leaps of a seventh in the fugal 'Hosanna'. The tone-painting of *Meeresstille* finds them marvellously alert and vivid in articulation. *Ah! perfido* brings a similar sense of renewal: there isn't even a momentary suspicion of concert routine, but rather as though it's part of an exceptionally intense performance of *Fidelio*. Charlotte Margiono sings the angry passages with the concentration of a Schwarzkopf, and brings to those that are gentler-toned a special beauty of her own. Other soloists in the Mass sing well if without distinction. Distinction is certainly a word to use of the disc as a whole.

Mass in C[a]. Meeresstille und glückliche Fahrt, Op 112. Elegischer Gesang, Op 118
[a]Rebecca Evans sop [a]Pamela Helen Stephen mez [a]Mark Padmore ten [a]Stephen Varcoe bar Collegium Musicum 90 / Richard Hickox
Chandos Chaconne CHAN0703 (56' · DDD · T/t) ⓕⒹ➔

Beethoven's Mass in C, like Haydn's late masterpieces and the Masses of Hummel, was written on commission from Prince Esterházy for the nameday of the Princess. Puzzlingly, Beethoven's 1807 contribution was counted a failure: the prince described the music as 'totally ridiculous'. Beethoven starts his setting more conventionally than Haydn did in his late masses. Where Haydn brilliantly gave his *Kyrie*s a symphonic flavour, Beethoven is devotional in a simpler, more innocent style. That's surely apt in a prayer for mercy, even if you note the Beethovenian modulations and dissonances, individual touches well brought out in Richard Hickox's performance.

Hickox, with an excellent quartet of soloists, gives full-blooded performances that bring out the exuberance of the inspiration. Where Gardiner brings out the work's drama with phenomenally crisp singing and playing, there's an infectious joy to Hickox's reading, in which, with a choir of 24 singers, a closer focus and a marginally more intimate acoustic, the words can be heard more clearly.

Throughout the liturgy one Beethoven took nothing on trust, thinking afresh rather than relying on convention, as when the *Credo*'s first eight bars are quiet before the full outburst of affirmation from the choir, and the setting of 'Et resurrexit' begins with a baritone solo, not with a choral or orchestral outburst. The setting of 'passus' just before it has extraordinary intensity, just it does in the later *Missa*. Hickox brings out such points with clarity, with period forces making the music sound not just more vital but more modern.

The Mass is coupled with the lovely Goethe setting *Meeresstille und glückliche Fahrt*, and the *Elegischer Gesang*, written in a simple, homophonic style to commemorate the passing of a noble friend's wife.

Mass in D, 'Missa solemnis', Op 123

Missa solemnis
Charlotte Margiono sop **Catherine**   Ⓟ
Robbin mez **William Kendall** ten **Alastair Miles** bass
**Monteverdi Choir; English Baroque Soloists /
Sir John Eliot Gardiner**
Archiv Produktion 429 779-2AH (72' · DDD· T/t)
ⒻⓄⓄⓄ➔

The *Missa solemnis* is one of the supreme masterpieces of the 19th century, but attempts to record a genuinely great performance have over many years run into difficulties. Usually the greatness itself is flawed, perhaps in the quality of the solo singers or in passages where the conductor's approach is too idiosyncratic or momentarily not up to the challenge of Beethoven's inspiration. The strain on the choir, especially its sopranos, is notorious; similarly the technical problems of balance by producer and engineers. This performance mixes discipline and spontaneous creativity; the rhythms are magically alive and the intricate texture of sound is made wonderfully clear. The great fugues of the *Gloria* and *Credo* achieve their proper Dionysiac sense of exalted liberation. Gardiner uses a choir of 36 and an orchestra of 60 playing on period instruments, aiming at a 'leaner and fitter' sound. The exceptional clarity of his smaller body of singers and players, their meticulous responsiveness to direction and concentrated attention to detail is impressive; yet you're aware of it *as* a performance. Sometimes, as in the first sounding of drums and trumpets signifying war, Gardiner's additional intensity brings a real gain.

Missa solemnis   Ⓟ
Eva Mei sop **Marjana Lipovšek** contr **Anthony Rolfe Johnson** ten **Robert Holl** bass **Arnold Schönberg Choir; Chamber Orchestra of Europe / Nikolaus Harnoncourt**

BEETHOVEN'S MISSA SOLEMNIS – IN BRIEF

Margiono; Robbin; Kendall; Miles; Monteverdi Choir; English Baroque Soloists / Sir John Eliot Gardiner Ⓟ
Archiv Produktion 429 779-2AH (72' · DDD)
Ⓕ**OOO**

Ⓖ *Gramophone*'s 1991 Record of the Year. Magnificent choral singing, four superb soloists and the fervent committed playing of the EBS under Gardiner's incandescent direction. Lean and lithe and terrifically powerful.

Mei; Lipovšek; Rolfe Johnson; Holl; Arnold Schoenberg Choir; CO of Europe / Nikolaus Harnoncourt
Teldec Ultima ② 0630-18945-2 (81' · DDD)   Ⓑ**OO**
Period manners and modern instruments combined to great effect: it may lack the dynamism of the Gardiner or the monumental quality of the Levine, but there's binding integrity that makes this a very powerful experience. The soloists are well matched and the COE play their hearts out.

Studer; Norman; Domingo; Moll; Leipzig Radio Chorus; Swedish Radio Choir; Vienna PO / James Levine
DG ② 435 770-2GH2 (83' · DDD)   Ⓕ**O**
A truly festive performance in memory of Karajan recorded at the Salzburg Festival. This is grand, majestic Beethoven that's mighty impressive and deeply moving.

Orgonasova; Larsson; Trost; Selig; Swiss Chamber Choir; Zurich Tonhalle Orchestra / David Zinman
Arte Nova 74321 87074-2 (66' · DDD)   Ⓢ**O**
A *Missa solemnis* for the 21st century – the lessons of the period-instrument movement have been well and truly absorbed into this thrillingly vital and low-calorie performance.

Mannion; Remmert; Taylor; Hauptmann; La Ⓟ **Chapelle Royale Collegium Vocale; Orchestre des Champs-Elysées / Philippe Herreweghe**
Harmonia Mundi ② HMC90 1557 (140' · DDD)   Ⓕ
Another successful period-instrument version, recorded live, that captures the questing spirituality at the heart of this great Mass. Four light-voiced, young soloists add to the performance's considerable appeal.

Milanov; Thorborg; von Pataky; Moscona; Ⓗ **BBC Choral Society; BBC SO / Arturo Toscanini**
BBC Legends ② BBCL4016-2 (145')   Ⓕ
Milanov; Castagna; Björling; Kipnis; Westminster Choir; NBC SO / Arturo Toscanini
Istituto Discografico Italiano IDIS6365 (79')   Ⓜ**OO**
Beethoven at white heat in 1939 and 1940, both with more humanity than the classic RCA set. This was a work that Toscanini adored – and it shows in every bar.

Teldec ② 9031-74884-2 (81' · DDD · T/t) Recorded live 1992.   Ⓑ**OO**

There are many marvellous performances in the catalogue of Beethoven's great Mass. Gardiner catches the greatness, rises to it with his uncanny freshness of perception, and secures a performance virtually without fault. Levine (DG, and currently out of the catalogue), with conventional forces, presents a large-scale performance, not universally liked, but which impresses you almost unequivocally on every hearing. Harnoncourt is very different from either of the others, but brings at least equally the stamp of devotion and high attainment. Choir and orchestra achieve wonderful precision and clarity of articulation; they're sensitive to the needs of shading, to the ever-shifting balance of the parts, and to the purpose of cross-rhythms which at first may look like anarchy.

The soloists, who all meet their immense individual challenges, work intelligently as a quartet. It might be good simply to stop there and say, 'Enjoy it'. But once comparisons start, such simplicity begins to melt. Gardiner's performance is recorded more brightly and sharply. Returning to Harnoncourt after listening to that for a few minutes you feel a relative remoteness of contact with the sound. Moving then to Levine, there's again a more immediate presence in the sound. Yet in this three-way comparison Harnoncourt emerges as a kind of halfway-house between Gardiner and Levine, and not quite as colourful as either. You might opt for Gardiner because his performance is confined to a single disc. Yet, listening again to the *Credo*, there's something almost military in the way his people march along, and, as Harnoncourt stresses, the whole Mass is above all 'an appeal for peace'. This is a performance of great integrity: that is, it's a complete, consistent whole, and all its parts are sound.

Missa solemnis   Ⓗ
Zinka Milanov *sop* **Bruna Castagna** *contr*
Jussi Björling *ten* **Alexander Kipnis** *bass*
Westminster Choir; NBC Symphony Orchestra / Arturo Toscanini
Istituto Discografico Italiano mono IDIS6365 (79' · ADD) Recorded 1940   Ⓜ**OO**

A very fine line separates Toscanini's triumphant 1939 performance from this 1940 reading. On the other hand, John Steane in his chapter on the work in *Choral Music on Record* (CUP: 1991) heaped praise on 1940, commenting that 'all elements seem in equilibrium' and that 'the total effect…is not adequately represented by references to "electricity"'. The two readings are of such overwhelming conviction and power that either will come as a revelation to the newcomer either to the work or the conductor.

If the preference is ever so slightly for the 1940 account, it's because the sound is marginally better, the singing of the Westminster

Choir even more inspired than that of the BBC Choral Society and the Carnegie Hall soloists by a small margin superior to their Queen's Hall counterparts, mainly because of the presence of the irreplaceable Björling and Kipnis. Zinka Milanov is common to both, but in more confident form on the later occasion. Listen to this quartet at 'Et incarnatus' in the *Credo* or in the whole of the *Benedictus* and you'll hear singing fit for the gods both in tone and expression, not forgetting the subtle use of *portamento*, out of fashion today. As for the chorus, hear the end of the *Gloria* and you must realise why Toscanini, in this work, is supreme.

Although this Italian issue has fairly primitive sound, it's worth every penny for anyone wanting to encounter what must be one of the greatest accounts ever of this challenging work.

Additional recommendation

Missa solemnis[a] **H**
Coupled with: Symphony No 7
Cherubini Anacréon – Overture. **Mozart** Symphony No 35 in D, 'Haffner', K385
[a]**Milanov** sop [a]**Thorborg** mez [a]**Pataky** ten [a]**Moscona** bass [a]**BBC Choral Society; BBC Symphony Orchestra / Toscanini**
BBC Legends/IMG Artists mono ② BBCL4016-2 (145' · ADD) Recorded live 1939 Ⓜ**OO**

This is an absolute triumph – a hair's breadth separates this from the 1940 account reviewed above; both are equally gripping. The transfer eschews excessive de-hissing for a quiet sea of surface noise that soon ceases to matter.

Fidelio

Fidelio
Inga Nielsen sop Leonore **Gösta Winbergh** ten Florestan **Alan Titus** bar Don Pizarro **Kurt Moll** bass Rocco **Edith Lienbacher** sop Marzelline **Herwig Pecoraro** ten Jaquino **Wolfgang Glashof** bass Don Fernando **Péter Pálinkás** ten First Prisoner **József Moldvay** bass Second Prisoner **Hungarian Radio Chorus; Nicolaus Esterházy Sinfonia / Michael Halász**
Naxos ② 8 660070/1 (114' · DDD· D) Ⓢ**OO**

Naxos has an uncanny knack for choosing the right artists for its operatic ventures. On this occasion, four of the singers are among the better known in the field, each judiciously cast. Halász projects every facet of the score, inspiring his forces to live every moment of the plot in words and music. This isn't an interpretation in the romantic, quasi-philosophical mode of Furwängler or Klemperer, rather one that alerts the mind and ear to the human agony of it all.

Nielsen's Leonore is no projection of subservient femininity but a tormented wife seeking to save her husband, her plight expressed in every key phrase. She doesn't provide the heroic sounds of a Nilsson (Maazel) or all the warmth of

Rysanek (Fricsay), but her slimmer, more compact tone exactly fits this performance. Winberg is a Florestan equal to his Leonore in vocal and interpretative assets. Not even Heppner (Davis) or Seiffert (Harnoncourt), among modern interpreters, sings the role better. His voice poised between the lyrical and the heroic, his tone warm, his technique firm, Florestan's scene can seldom have been so satisfyingly sung and enacted. As Marzelline, Edith Lienbacher is something of a discovery, catching the eagerness, also the sense of nerves a-jangle predicated by the part.

The dialogue, rather drastically foreshortened, is well spoken by all and intelligently directed. The orchestral and choral singing need fear no comparisons, and the recording has plenty of presence, no tricks. This is a performance that fulfils almost all the demands made on its principals and at the price should be eagerly sought after: its most notable predecessors are matched, if not surpassed.

Fidelio
Sena Jurinac sop Leonore **Jon Vickers** ten Florestan **Hans Hotter** bass-bar Don Pizarro **Gottlob Frick** bass Rocco **Elsie Morison** sop Marzelline **John Dobson** ten Jaquino **Forbes Robinson** bass Don Fernando **Chorus and and Orchestra of the Royal Opera House Chorus, Covent Garden / Otto Klemperer**
Testament mono ② SBT21328 (143' · ADD T/t) Ⓟ**OOO**

Here is the first night of Otto Klemperer's legendary 1961 *Fidelio*, from the Royal Opera House, to challenge his noted studio set from a year later.This confirms the Achilles' heel of Walter Legge, EMI's leading mogul at the time, in his unwillingness to record live occasions, probably because he liked to have every aspect of a recording under his control. In this case there is more to it than that. Klemperer wanted, in the studio, to retain his Covent Garden cast; Legge preferred to make changes with two exceptions (Jon Vickers and Gottlob Frick). On the evidence of this magnificent issue, Klemperer was right. Not only are the singers, by and large, better equipped for their roles, but given the electricity of the occasion the conductor's interpretation is more vital (often faster tempi) and even more eloquent. For his own staging, Klemperer decided to include far more dialogue than is usually heard so that we have as much a play with music as an opera. The singers speak and act with such feeling and immediacy, most particularly Jurinac, Hotter and Frick, as to justify the added text. Add to that the dedication on all sides to Klemperer, and you can imagine why this was such a special occasion.

Compared to Christa Ludwig on Klemperer's studio version, Sena Jurinac creates a more believable and vulnerable Leonore. Her heartfelt sympathy with the role is evident in every line she speaks and sings, most notably in key phrases in her duet with Rocco near the end of Act 1 and the melodrama in Act 2. Once past

BEETHOVEN'S FIDELIO – IN BRIEF

Inga Nielsen Leonore **Gösta Windbergh** Florestan
Alan Titus Don Pizarro **Hungarian Radio Chorus,**
Nicolaus Esterházy Sinfonia / Michael Halász
Naxos ② 8 660070/1 (114' · ADD)   Ⓢ**OO**
At bargain price, a good place to start: a vivid
performance with stellar leading singers, and
good dramatic conducting.

Christa Ludwig Leonore **Jon Vickers** Florestan
Walter Berry Don Pizarro **Philharmonia Chorus**
and Orchestra / Otto Klemperer
EMI download 567364-2 (143' · ADD)   Ⓜ**OO**
Often considered a definitive recording,
Klemperer's is a massive, granitic reading
harking back to symphonic Beethoven, with a
cast of heroic stature. Ludwig is a dark-toned,
dramatic soprano Leonore, but Vickers is
unforgettable in Florestan's suffering. Great
value now it's at mid-price (if you can still find
it on CD), but don't overlook the live Klemperer set of Testament noted below…

Charlotte Margiono Leonore **Peter Seiffert**
Florestan **Sergei Leiferkus** Don Pizarro
Arnold Schoenberg Choir, CO of Europe /
Nikolaus Harnoncourt
Teldec ② 4509 94560-2 (119' · ADD)   Ⓕ
An attempt at an intimate interpretation,
with a lighter-voiced cast in which Seiffert's
vigorous Florestan stands out. Harnoncourt's
eccentric tempi and the deliberately under-
stated drama won't suit everyone.

Hildegard Behrens Leonore **James King**
Florestan **Donald McIntyre** Don Pizarro
Bavarian State Opera Chorus and Orchestra /
Karl Böhm
Orfeo ② C560012I (141' · ADD)   Ⓜ**O**
A 1978 theatre performance, well recorded
but with some resultant noise and stagey
dialogue delivery, this is an intense, dramatic
reading with a brilliant Leonora in Hilde-
garde Behrens.

Sena Jurinac Leonore **Jon Vickers** Florestan
Hans Hotter Don Pizarro **Royal Opera House**
Chorus and Orchestra / Otto Klemperer
Testament ② SBT21328 (143' · ADD)   Ⓕ**OOO**
A performance of tremendous authority and
stature taken live from the stage of Covent
Garden. A superb cast headed by Jurinac's
deeply moving Leonore.

Anja Kampe Leonore **Torsten Kerl** Florestan
Peter Coleman-Wright Don Pizarro
Glyndebourne Chorus; London Philharmonic
Orchestra / Sir Mark Elder
Glyndebourne Festival Opera ② GFOCD004/6
(121' · DDD)   Ⓕ**O**
A very fine memento of a thrillingly dramatic
Glyndebourne performance. Paced to per-
fection, it unfolds with colossal theatricality
and poetry, and strongly cast, too.

some first night nerves evident in 'Abscheulicher!' she proves an ideal Leonore. Vickers,
even in these early days of his career, is inclined
to sentimentalise his Florestan with scoops and
lachrymose effects, but all is forgiven when he
provides the heroic thrust and inner feeling
which the part demands and which is so notably
absent from the Florestan on the recent Rattle
version. Frick's Rocco is, if possible, even more
admirable than on the studio set, expressing the
jailor's terrible dilemma in the kind of incisive,
warm tones few other basses on disc match.

It is incomprehensible that Legge preferred as
Pizarro the too-comfortable sounding Walter
Berry to Hans Hotter. Hotter, usually known for
his noble roles, is here the epitome of evil, a
threatening force of nature, his voice and diction
full of menace so that he can be forgiven one or
two wobbles in his aria. The young lovers are
personably sung and enacted by Elsie Morison
and John Dobson, and another Royal Opera stalwart, Forbes Robinson, is a dignified Don Fernando. There was a fuss at the time about Klemperer's inclusion of *Leonore* III, but he fully
justifies it by his electrifying interpretation. He
insisted on placing the wind in the middle of the
orchestra spectrum, and the balance is improved
throughout as a result. His reading overall has the
stature and sense of the work's philosophical basis
which will be familiar to those who know his discs
of the symphonies.

Fidelio
Charlotte Margiono sop Leonore **Peter Seiffert** ten
Florestan **Sergei Leiferkus** bar Pizarro **László Polgár**
bass Rocco **Barbara Bonney** sop Marzelline **Deon**
van der Walt ten Jaquino **Boje Skovhus** bar Don
Fernando **Reinaldo Macias** ten First Prisoner **Robert**
Florianschütz bass Second Prisoner **Arnold**
Schoenberg Choir; Chamber Orchestra of Europe
/ Nikolaus Harnoncourt
Teldec ② 4509-94560-2 (119' · DDD· T/t)   Ⓕ**OO**
Highlights available on Warner Apex 0927-401374-2
          Ⓢ

Everything Harnoncourt touches leaves a sense
of a country rediscovered: we listen to the piece
in hand with new ears. So it is again here. Beethoven's sole but intractable opera has seldom
emerged from the recording studio, or indeed
the theatre, with such clarity of texture, such
promptness of rhythm, such unity of purpose on
all sides. This is a reading that gives full play to
winds and horns, making you aware, whether it's
in the Overture, Pizarro's aria, Leonore's big
scene or the Prelude to Act-2, just how important they are to the structure and character of
each movement. Where tempos are concerned,
Harnoncourt is almost bound to be controversial somewhere. If many speeds are to their
advantage just on the measured side of the customary, as in the Dungeon quartet, allowing us
for once to hear every strand of the argument,
that for 'O namenlose Freude' is uncommonly
moderate. At this pace, Leonore and Florestan
seem to be conducting a gentle exchange of
deeply felt emotions on an interior level rather

than allowing their pent-up emotions to burst forth in an explosion of joy, as is more usual.

The dialogue is delivered in an understated fashion. Two vocal interpretations stand out for excellent singing and pungent characterisation. Once Leiferkus's Pizarro takes centre-stage the action lifts on to a new, more tense plane. This vicious little dictator with his incisive diction, spoken and sung, and his biting, vital voice is a commanding presence. But Evil is up against an equally arresting advocate of Good in Margiono's gloriously sung and read Leonore. Hers isn't the quasi-dramatic soprano usually associated with the part, but she never sounds strained in the context of a more lyrical, smaller-scale performance. Seiffert fills Florestan with more refulgent tone than any other tenor on recent recordings – the high tessitura of his aria's close causes him no distress at all – but it must be admitted that there's little of the *Schmerz* in the tone found, quite differently, in the recording of Vickers (Klemperer). In that sense, though, he fits into Harnoncourt's well-ordered scheme of things. The only piece of miscasting is Don Fernando: a role that needs a solid bass with strong low notes has been given to a high baritone who sounds anything but authoritative. Harnoncourt has opted for a professional chamber choir to second the superb Chamber Orchestra of Europe. By the side of the superb Teldec recording, the Klemperer and Maazel sound less than immediate.

Fidelio
Anja Kampe *sop* Leonore **Lisa Milne** *sop* Marzelline **Brindley Sherratt** *bass* Rocco **Peter Coleman-Wright** *bar* Don Pizarro **Andrew Kennedy** *ten* Jaquino **Torsten Kerl** *ten* Florestan **Henry Waddington** *bass* Don Fernando **Nathan Vale** *ten* First Prisoner **Anthony Cleverton** *bass* Second Prisoner **Glyndebourne Chorus; London Philharmonic Orchestra / Sir Mark Elder**
Glyndebourne Festival Opera ② GFOCD004/6 (121' · DDD · T/t). Recorded live in August 2006   Ⓕ**O**

Fidelio, so difficult to bring off in the theatre, is an ideal opera for listening to at home. In this recording we have the best of both worlds: all the intensity of stage performances without the irritations of Deborah Warner's production.

As one expects from Glyndebourne performances, the teamwork of the singers is impeccable. But the highest praise must be reserved for Sir Mark Elder. Whereas his predecessor, when the production was first staged in 2001, raced through the score as though he had a train to catch, Elder paces it almost to perfection. He instils confidence from the start with a weighty account of the Overture. The opening scene, before Fidelio appears, has the right lightness of touch. The mood darkens when Don Pizarro enters (after much stage clatter). His vengeance aria works up to a terrific climax, albeit with understated horns at 'in seiner letzten Stunde' (compare Klemperer's Philharmonia!). Elder's steady speeds, his close attention to *crescendos*

and *sforzandos*, reflect the drama in the most wonderful way. There are just two places where it seems that his instinct deserted him: the lingering at the beginning of 'Euch werde Lohn' (and at the reprise), and the speedy, almost perfunctory response to the first trumpet-call. Against that, one could cite numerous examples of his sensitivity, such as the dying fall of the Act 1 finale.

That finale, of course, includes the Prisoners' Chorus: the Glyndebourne Chorus sing it beautifully and it's Beethoven's fault, not theirs, if they sound improbably robust. The Act 2 finale, where the prisoners are joined by 'the people', is another matter: a jubilant outburst, gloriously sung.

The cast is excellent: especially Torsten Kerl, deeply moving in his aria. Minor drawbacks include an editing slip that adds a half-bar to the Act 2 quartet and a not wholly accurate translation of the libretto. The competition is formidable, but Elder can hold his head high in their company.

Fidelio
Hildegard Behrens *mez* Leonore **James King** *ten* Florestan **Donald McIntyre** *bass-bar* Don Pizarro **Kurt Moll** *bass* Rocco **Lucia Popp** *sop* Marzelline **Norbert Orth** *ten* Jaquino **Nikolaus Hillebrand** *bass* Don Fernando **Friedrich Lenz** *ten* First Prisoner **Hans Wilbrink** *bar* Second Prisoner **Bavarian State Orchestra and Opera Chorus / Karl Böhm**
Orfeo d'Or ② C560012I (141' · ADD) Recorded live 1978   Ⓜ**OO**

At 84 this was to be Böhm's last *Fidelio*, and he knew it. Yet absolutely no allowances have to be made for his age in this life-enhancing, dramatically alert reading, quite on a par with his earlier versions of the work on disc. Indeed this now joins those other legendary live performances by great conductors of the past – Böhm himself in 1944 in Vienna, Bruno Walter at the Met in the same year, Toscanini at a concert in New York in 1945 and Furtwängler at Salzburg in 1950. But, of course, this one is vastly superior in sound. Everyone seems determined to give of their best. None more than Hildegard Behrens, the very epitome of the dedicated, highly strung wife on a rescue mission and singing her heart out at all the important moments, not least in her 'Abscheulicher!'. She far surpasses her performance for Solti on Decca a year later. By her side throughout is the sterling, warm, authoritative Rocco of Kurt Moll in a reading that surpasses his own high standards on other versions. James King, though his voice had dried out a little by 1978, sings a Florestan imbued with anguish.

As Pizarro, McIntyre, in powerful voice, is evil personified. For all the vocal glories, Böhm remains the evening's hero. Above all, he makes the opera living drama. Were this *Fidelio* his only work that survived for us to judge him by, it would be enough to clinch his reputation as a great conductor. There's more dialogue than we usually hear either in the theatre or on disc. There's also a deal of stage action. None of that should deter you from hearing such a truthful enactment of this masterpiece, few if any better on CD.

Fidelio

Gabriela Beňačková sop Leonore **Josef Protschka** ten Florestan **Monte Pederson** bar Don Pizarro **Robert Lloyd** bass Rocco **Marie McLaughlin** sop Marzelline **Neill Archer** ten Jaquino **Hans Tschammer** bass-bar Don Fernando **Lynton Atkinson** ten First Prisoner **Mark Beesley** bar Second Prisoner **Royal Opera House Chorus and Orchestra, Covent Garden / Christoph von Dohnányi**
Stage director **Adolf Dresen**
Video director **Derek Bailey**
ArtHaus Musik 🔵 100 074 (129' · Regions 2 & 5) Ⓕ ⬤

'Triumph! Triumph! Triumph!' as nasty Pizarro exultantly cries. He's in for a disappointment, of course. Not so the listener and viewer of this performance, which is caught in fine sound and skilfully filmed. Pizarro will, for instance, have no place in the great festival of light that is the finale. Here the rejoicing is so powerful that we switch off the DVD player and go to bed with the surge and sequence of inspired creation fully in possession, convinced that in the whole of opera there's nothing to match it. That's the sign of a great *Fidelio*, and it means that, throughout, the proportions, structure and balance of the work have been rendered with clarity and conviction. That in turn means that the opening scene – the Marzelline-Jaquino duet and the solos which might seem to be from some other opera – has been integrated, so that the work is a journey from light into the blackest tunnel and out again into an infinitely greater light.

A prime contribution to the success of this process is made by the portrayal of Rocco, the gaoler. Instead of the bumbling, coarse-grained character of convention, Robert Lloyd presents a full human being, a man with a rueful-realistic twinkle, and above all a loving father. This of itself guards against the alien introduction of comic opera, and helps to fashion the role so that even here our concern is with real humanity. Leonore is the radiant Beňačková, and she presents a problem. The camera reveals unsparingly a disguise which just possibly might pass in the theatre. It says much for her singing, and for something in the spirit of her performance, that the willing suspension of disbelief can prevail as well as it does. In all other respects the visual element satisfies well; and musically, under Dohnányi's direction, this is a memorable and moving *Fidelio*.

Fidelio

Gundula Janowitz sop Leonore **René Kollo** ten Florestan **Hans Sotin** bass Don Pizarro **Manfred Jungwirth** bass Rocco **Lucia Popp** sop Marzelline **Adolf Dallapozza** ten Jaquino **Hans Helm** bass Don Fernando **Karl Terkal** ten First Prisoner **Alfred Sramek** bass Second Prisoner

Vienna State Opera Chorus and Orchestra / Leonard Bernstein
Stage and video director **Otto Schenk**
DG Ⓕ 🔵 073 4159GH (147' · NTSC · 4:3 · PCM stereo, 5.0 and DTS 5.0 · 0). Recorded at the Staatsoper, Vienna, on January 29, 1978

Bernstein conducts with all his heart – and with the occasional eccentricities as regards tempo that went with the package. By 1978 Bernstein was God in Vienna and receives here an almost too effusive welcome at start and finish. Indeed, the public applaud far too often, wrecking the end of Florestan's aria with seemingly endless clapping when all one craves is silence.

The Vienna Philharmonic play superbly for a conductor they had come to love. Otto Schenk's staging remains a marvel of sensible action, pertinent handling of the singers and clarity of action – no updating, no silly ideas, just straightforward, unobtrusive direction.

Gundula Janowitz has a lovely voice, which she uses intelligently, but her acting, as so often, is unconvincing. One never for a moment believes in her as the vulnerable, courageous rescuing wife, a fatal flaw. René Kollo sings with strength and conviction as Florestan, and acts effectively, but he does have a tendency to maul his line. Hans Sotin as Pizarro is not half as terrifying as he could be, though he sings securely. By contrast, Manfred Jungwirth's stalwart Rocco is involved and involving. Lucia Popp offers an unforgettably moving and clearly sung Marzelline; Adolf Dallapozza is an average Jaquino.

Dialogue is cut to the minimum. Sound and video direction (by Schenk himself) are both excellent. There are no extras – unless you include Bernstein's tense account of *Leonore* No 3 which he leads into from the end of 'O namenlose Freude'. On the whole, though, preference remains for the Harnoncourt performance (see below) with Camilla Nylund providing the kind of Leonore who is truly moving.

Fidelio

Camilla Nylund sop Leonore **Jonas Kaufmann** ten Florestan **Alfred Muff** bass Don Pizarro **László Polgár** bass Rocco **Elizabeth Magnuson** sop Marzelline **Christoph Strehl** ten Jaquino **Günther Groissböck** bass Don Fernando **Bogusław Bidzinski** ten First Prisoner **Gabriel Bermúdez** bass Second Prisoner **Zurich Opera House Chorus and Orchestra / Nikolaus Harnoncourt**
Stage director **Jürgen Flimm**
Video director **Felix Breisach**
TDK 🔵 DV-OPFID (134' · 16:9 · PCM stereo, 5.1 & DTS 5.1 · 0). Recorded live at the Opernhaus, Zürich, 15 February 2004 Ⓕ ⬤ ⬤

Harnoncourt's predominantly light but dramatic reading harks back to the 18th century rather than forward to the 19th, with romantic feeling at a premium. The orchestra foretells the rest in its crisply accented rhythms, clean sound and sense of the impending drama: they play splendidly. However, the thrust of Beethoven's universal message sometimes goes missing by comparison with the Dohnányi version on DVD from Covent Garden.

The simple, somewhat geometric sets, sensitively lit, house a direction that's sometimes fussy in detail. Jürgen Flimm offers a fairly minimalist production concentrating on the characters of the principals. Marzelline (the bright-voiced Elizabeth Magnuson) and Jaquino are preparing guns and ammunition for the troops. She is bossy, he slightly sadistic. By contrast, Rocco – a wonderfully moving, warm and eloquent performance from László Polgár – is kindly, cowed by his surroundings, and alert to every nuance of feeling in those around him. His body language and his eyes tell us everything about the jailer's torment.

Leonore, in the arresting figure of Camilla Nylund, is slim and appealing, truly believable as a young man. Her singing, in the modern way, is lighter than one would have expected of yore. Every note is well placed, united into a real *legato* projected on a compact, firm tone. Jonas Kaufmann's Florestan, also a more youthful portrayal than usual, sings with accuracy and feeling, though he may find more in the words and notes in years to come. He and Nylund make 'O namenlose Freude', taken at an extraordinarily slow tempo, more an inward expression of release than the usual excited one. Alfred Muff's Pizarro, more conventional, is always a hateful presence, as he should be.

The sound could be a bit more immediate; the video direction is for the most part perceptive.

Vincenzo Bellini   Italian 1801-1835

Bellini was given piano lessons by his father, and could play well when he was five. At six he wrote a Gallus cantavit and began studying composition with his grandfather. After a few years his sacred pieces were being heard in Catania churches and his ariettas and instrumental works in the salons of aristocrats and patricians. In 1819 he went to Naples to study at the conservatory, entering the class of the director, Nicola Zingarelli, in 1822. In 1825 his opera semiseria, Adelson e Salvini, was produced at the conservatory. Its success led to commissions from the Teatro S Carlo and from La Scala, Milan.

Bellini's first opera for Milan, Il pirata (1827), instantly laid the foundation of his career, and with it began his fruitful collaborations with the librettist Felice Romani and the tenor GB Rubini. From 1827 to 1833 Bellini lived mostly in Milan, and during this time his operas, including La sonnambula and Norma, earned him an international reputation, while he himself went through a passionate love affair with Giuditta Cantù, the wife of a landowner and silk manufacturer, Ferdinando Turina. Bellini's amatory entanglements have been romanticised in popular literature but the realities are less creditable.

In 1833 Bellini visited London, where four of his operas were performed with great success at the King's Theatre and Drury Lane. He then proceeded to Paris, where he was commissioned to write I puritani for the Théâtre-Italien and formed a close acquaintance with Rossini and got to know Chopin and other musicians. I puritani enjoyed a genuine triumph in January 1835, and Bellini was appointed a Chevalier de la Légion d'honneur. He decided to remain in Paris and formulated several projects for his future there, but in August 1835 he fell ill and the following month he died, from 'an acute inflammation of the large intestine, complicated by an abscess of the liver' according to the post-mortem report.

Bellini's importance to posterity is as a composer of opera, especially opera seria; his other works can be ignored without great loss. His first influences were the folksong of Sicily and Naples, the teaching of Zingarelli and, above all, the music of Rossini. The Naples performance of Rossini's Semiramide in 1824 was one of the most decisive musical experiences of his student years, and the novel lyrical style of his early operas represented a sentimentalisation and heightening of Rossinian lyricism, which in Il pirata broadens to include forceful and dramatic emotions. With this opera Bellini became one of Italy's most influential composers; Donizetti and Pacini, Mercadante and Verdi all learnt from him.

The quintessential feature of Bellini's operatic music is its close relationship with the text. He did not look for musical delineation of character, but the content and mood of each scene are given thoroughgoing musical interpretation and the text is precisely declaimed. His melodic style, of which the famous 'Casta diva' in Norma is a perfect example, is characterised by the building of broad melodic curves from small (usually two-bar) units. While his treatment of rhythm is more conventional, his melodies are supported by some colourful harmony and reticent though effective orchestration. More than any other Italian composer of the years around 1830, Bellini minimised the difference between aria and recitative by introducing a large number of cantabile, aria-like passages into his recitative. His expressive range goes far beyond the delicate, elegiac aspects of his art, which have been frequently overemphasised.

GROVEmusic

I Capuleti ed i Montecchi

I Capuleti e i Montecchi
Anna Netrebko sop Giulietta **Elīna Garanča** mez
Romeo **Joseph Calleja** ten Tebaldo **Robert
Gleadow** bass Lorenzo **Tiziano Bracci** bass-bar
Capellio **Vienna Singakademie; Vienna Symphony
Orchestra / Fabio Luisi**
DG ② 477 8031GH2 (128' · DDD · S/T/t/N) Ⓕ❌❌➡

Bellini's version of the Romeo and Juliet story has notched up quite an impressive discography considering that is not performed that often. This new set boasts three of the most admired singers of the moment, all of them in fine form. The performance is dominated by Elīna Garanča's Romeo; she easily suggests both the swaggering duellist and the lovelorn youth. There are times when her rich, velvety tones sound almost like a soprano, and in the duets with Anna Netrebko's Juliet, the two voices seem naturally to complement each other. The slow section of their Act 1 'Ah, crudel, d'onor ragioni' develops into an almost Norma-like blend of scales and trills. Netrebko sings the beautiful lament 'Oh! Quante volte' with considerable feeling, although the voice is beginning to sound a bit mature now for the innocent daughter of the Capulets. This is all to her advantage in the more tragic Act 2 'Morte io non temo' as she contemplates taking the poison.

I Capuleti e i Montecchi was one of the last important operas to employ a mezzo as the masculine lead. The tenor who sings Tebaldo needs to be of equal strength to balance the drama, and Joseph Calleja rises to the challenge of his two-part Act 1 aria, 'È serbata a questo acciaro' with virile strength. The duet in Act 2, when Tebaldo and Romeo are about to fight but then learn of Juliet's death, finds Garanča and Calleja striking sparks off each other; despite the beauty of the final tomb-scene duet, this confrontation is the highlight of the proceedings.

Robert Gleadow makes a strong impression as Friar Laurence, and Tiziano Bracci is impressive as Capellio. Fabio Luisi leads the Vienna forces in a performance which, though obviously sympathetic to the voices, manages to accentuate the drama. It's certainly a star vehicle but also a satisfying account of Bellini's near-masterpiece, and one which now leads the field.

I Capuleti e i Montecchi
Patrizia Ciofi sop Giulietta **Clara Polito** mez Romeo **Danilo Formaggia** ten Tebaldo **Federico Sacchi** bass Capellio **Nicola Amodio** bass Lorenzo **Orchestra Internazionale d'Italia** / **Luciano Acocella**
Stage director **Denis Krief**
Video director **Marco Scalfi**
Dynamic 📀 DV33504 (136' · NTSC · 16:9 · 2.0, DTS 5.1 and ODS · 0). Recorded live at the Martina Franca Festival, Italy in August 2005 ⒻOO

This *Capuleti e i Montecchi* is one of the best versions of this opera on disc. The edition used is the one Bellini made for La Scala a few months after the Venice premiere in 1830. The main difference is that Friar Lawrence here is a tenor (the excellent Nicola Amodio), and Juliet's solo in Act 2 is a continuous aria, rather than being punctuated by interjections from her father. Patrizia Ciofi gives this a really passionate performance: she is an ideal Juliet, youthful in appearance, in no way over-extended by Bellini's long vocal lines. Clara Polito makes a tremendous Romeo, adding some effective flourishes in the cabaletta to her Act 1 aria and joining Danilo Formaggia as Tybalt in an exciting account of their fight duet in Act 2. Federico Sacchi is a thunderous Capulet, and the chorus makes an always positive contribution.

Luciano Acocella and the Orchestra Internazionale d'Italia make the opera sound quite the equal of Bellini's later, more famous works, but as Wagner wrote of it, 'there is true passion and emotion there'. Denis Krief's production is

straightforward and always concentrated on the drama. It is played in modern dress, the Montagues and Capulets obviously on opposite sides in some unforgiving sectarian civil war, the men brandishing machine guns and revolvers. It works extremely well on its own terms, and the setting of the Ducal Palace in Martina Franca makes a perfect backdrop: recommended.

Norma

Norma
Maria Callas sop Norma **Christa Ludwig** mez Adalgisa **Franco Corelli** ten Pollione **Nicola Zaccaria** bass Oroveso **Piero De Palma** ten Flavio **Edda Vincenzi** sop Clotilde **Chorus and Orchestra of La Scala, Milan** / **Tullio Serafin**
EMI ③ 566428-2 (161' · ADD· T/t) Recorded 1960 ⓂOO➔

Norma ⚥
Maria Callas sop Norma **Ebe Stignani** mez Adalgisa **Mario Filippeschi** ten Pollione **Nicola Rossi-Lemeni** bass Oroveso **Paolo Caroli** ten Flavio **Rina Cavallari** sop Clotilde **Chorus and Orchestra of La Scala, Milan** / **Tullio Serafin**
EMI Callas Edition mono ② 556271-2 (160' · ADD· T/t) Recorded 1954. ⒻOO➔

Norma may be considered the most potent of Bellini's operas, in its subject – the secret love of a Druid priestess for a Roman general – and its musical content. It has some of the most eloquent music written for the soprano voice. The title-role has always been coveted by dramatic sopranos, but there have been few in the history of the opera who have completely fulfilled its considerable vocal and histrionic demands: in recent times the leading exponent has been Maria Callas.

Is the 1960 recording better or worse than the 1954 recording? The answer can't be put in a word. But those who heard Callas sing Norma at Covent Garden in 1953-4, and then again, slim, in 1957, will know the difference. The facts are that in 1954 the voice above the stave was fuller, more solid and more certain, but that in 1960 the middle timbres were more beautiful and more expressive; and, further, that an interpretation which was always magnificent had deepened in finesse, flexibility and dramatic poignancy.

The emphasis you give to these facts must be a matter of personal opinion. Certainly Callas's voice lets her down again and again, often when she essays some of her most beautiful effects. The F wobbles when it should crown a heart-rending 'Oh rimembranza'; the G wobbles in an exquisitely conceived 'Son io' – and yet how much more moving it is than the simpler, if steadier *messa di voce* of the earlier set. There are people who have a kind of tone-deafness to the timbres of Callas's later voice, who don't respond to one of the most affecting and eloquent of all sounds. They'll stick to the earlier set. But ardent Callas collectors will probably find that it's the later one to which they will be listening again and again, not unaware of its faults, but still more keenly responsive to its beauties. 'Casta Diva', by the way, is sung in F, as in 1954 – not in the original G, as in the Covent Garden performances of June 1953. The big duet with Adalgisa is again down a tone, 'Deh! con te' in B flat, 'Mira, o Norma' in E flat, and the change is once again effected in the recitative phrase 'nel romano campo'. Callas doesn't decorate the music. Adalgisa, a soprano role, is as usual taken by a mezzo. Ludwig blends beautifully with Callas in the low-key 'Mira, o Norma' (though her downward scales are as ill-defined as her colleague's). She's no veteran Adalgisa, but youthful and impetuous except when she lets the rhythm get heavy, and Serafin does nothing to correct her.

On the earlier set, Stignani is a worthy partner, while Filippeschi is rough but quite effective. On both sets, Serafin restores the beautiful quiet coda to the 'Guerra' chorus, and on both sets, Callas disappointingly doesn't float over the close of that slow rising *arpeggio*. In the later set, the conducting is spacious, unhurried, elevated and eloquent. Only in his handling of the mounting tension and the two great climaxes and releases of the finale, might you prefer the earlier version. The La Scala playing is superlative, and the recording is excellent.

Norma
Edita Gruberová *sop* Norma **Elina Garanča** *sop* Adalgisa **Aquiles Machado** *ten* Pollione **Alastair Miles** *bass* Oroveso **Judith Howarth** *mez* Clotilde **Ray M Wade** *ten* Flavio **Rastatt Vocal Ensemble; Rhineland Palatinate Philharmonic Orchestra / Friedrich Haider**
Nightingale Classics ② NC040245 (145' · DDD · S/T/ t/N) Recorded live 2004   Ⓕ**O**

'Nothing is played for as willed theatrical pathos or as melodrama, but simply as the predicament of a woman whose emotional being is totally real and whose singing voice is its unique and irreplaceable expression.' That was the verdict on Maria Callas's Norma from a *Gramophone* survey in 2002. Something very similar can now be said of Edita Gruberová's Norma, and to it will have to be added notice of the extraordinary radiance of her voice.

That requires a further note of wonder, for Gruberová was in her 58th year at the time of these performances. Her voice, as recorded recently, had begun to show its age – which this singing does not do. The purity and Tetrazzini-like radiance of tone seem scarcely diminished; the years have brought an underlying maturity to the voice and have enabled her to acquire the rare art of infusing her high, bright soprano with warmth and depth of feeling; and the occasionally intrusive unfocused tones which we have known in the past are hardly in evidence at all. 'Casta diva' is sung in the high, original key of G, the decorations in verse two being ingenious, neat and natural. The pain of those crucial

'debate' recitatives ('Vanne, e li cela entrambi', 'Dormono entrambi!', 'Ei tornerà') is marvellously actual and the climax of the great role is reached with vocal and emotional reserves still to draw on.

The Adalgisa, Elina Garanča, is also an exceptional singer: pure and rich in tone, extensive in range, accomplished in technique and intelligently expressive. Aquiles Machado makes a sturdy, resonant Pollione: no brute but not very interesting either. Alastair Miles brings an authoritative manner to support his true *basso cantante* singing. And Judith Howarth is luxury casting as Clotilde. The Rastatt Vocal Ensemble give the Druids more life (young and responsive to rhythm) than usual.

The Rhineland Palatinate State Philharmonic play with relish and Haider conducts with firmness and an effective feeling for tempo (sometimes refreshingly brisk). Recording is clear and well balanced, and the only textual grumble is that the lovely 'Sun-god' chorus ('A mirare il trionfo dei figli') is omitted, as regrettably and by this time inexcusably it still generally is.

Norma
Montserrat Caballé *sop* Norma; **Josephine Veasey** *sop* Adalgisa **Jon Vickers** *ten* Pollione **Agostino Ferrin** *bass* Oroveso **Gino Sinimberghi** *ten* Flavio **Marisa Zotti** *mez* Clotilde **Teatro Regio di Torino Chorus and Orchestra / Giuseppe Patanè** *Stage director* **Sandro Sequi** *Video director* **Pierre Jourdan**
Hardy Classic Video **DVD** HCD4003 (161' · 4:3 · 1.0 · 0) Recorded live 1974   Ⓕ**OOO**

Here in Orange, France, on a windswept, night in 1974, they had greatness itself. Pierre Jourdan's film of the event is a priceless document, first of all, in the history of the opera. Stage-settings of *Norma* are usually hopeless: an offence to the eye, a chafing confutation of the spirit by gross matter. The ancient Roman amphitheatre is at any rate worthy and appropriate, and the Mistral, which threatened to close down the whole show and turn away an audience estimated at 10,000, adds a fine reminder of the power of Nature as it sets the druidical robes billowing and attacks the microphones.

The vastness of the stage provides a further challenge to the man in charge, and although conductor Giuseppe Patanè's star is somewhat eclipsed in the general view of things, he deserves congratulation for two contrary achievements – holding the ensemble together and giving the soloists freedom. But it's their night, and particularly Caballé's. She called it the greatest single performance of her career. In certain passages it's hard to think of any voice we've known that could sound more lovely; but, more than that, the great role is sung and acted with such well-founded assurance that for once it fulfils its own legend, the embodiment of musical-dramatic sublimity in 19th-century opera. Of the others in the cast it must for now suffice to say that they're worthy partners.

Norma

Edita Gruberová *sop* Norma **Sonia Ganassi** *sop*
Adalgisa **Zoran Todorovich** *ten* Pollione **Roberto
Scandiuzzi** *bass* Oroveso **Markus Herzog** *ten* Flavio
Cynthia Jansen *mez* Clotilde
**Bavarian State Opera Chorus and Orchestra /
Friedrich Haider**
Stage director **Jürgen Rose**
Video director **Brian Large**
DG ② *DVD* 073 4219GH2
(155' · NTSC · 16:9 · PCM stereo & DTS 5.0 · 0)
Includes a 'Making Of' documentary and
Gruberová Discography.　　　　　　　　　Ⓕ Ⓞ

Edita Gruberová waited until 2006 to sing
Norma on stage for the first time. In this production from Munich she is revealed as the
greatest Norma of today. Her singing and acting bring out the complete portrait of the guilt-
ridden priestess, trapped between her sense of
duty to her religion and country, and the sick-
ening prospect of losing her lover and her
children. Gruberová brings a lifetime's experience of singing *bel canto* opera and caresses
Bellini's vocal lines with many subtle touches.
Almost entirely absent is that mannerism of
sliding between notes which has marred some
of her singing in the past. Every phrase is
moulded with the feeling and reticence of a
great artist.

　Jürgen Rose, in total control of the production
– stage direction, lighting, costumes and sets –
succeeds where many have failed in the past.
The action seems to be taking place in the aftermath of some terrible conflict. The middle-east-
ern costumes suggest the Iraq war, but the whole
concept is more ambitious than merely to rely
on familiar signs. Norma's tribe seems to have
returned to its ancient religion as a refuge from
the surrounding chaos. The semi-abstract sets
are beautiful, the costumes simple. The priest-
esses' hands are stained with symbolic woad.
The men carry machine guns and wear black
woollen masks. Norma's dwelling is an underground bunker.

　Sonia Ganassi makes a sympathetic Adalgisa,
and she and Gruberová sing both the great
duets with exquisite tenderness. There is a
touching moment when Adalgisa first confesses
her love and Norma removes the girl's veil, as if
to free her from her vows. Zoran Todorovich is
a charismatic and virile Pollione. In the first act
his singing seems rather over-loud at moments,
but he is a fine actor and rises to the challenge
of the final scene, where Gruberová begins 'In
mia man' while he is bound to the altar with
ropes.

　Roberto Scandiuzzi makes the most of the
somewhat ungrateful part of Oroveso. He too is
very moving in the closing ensemble, as he forgives Norma and agrees to care for her children.
Friedrich Haider conducts the Munich forces
with fine urgency and an impeccable understanding of the grand sweep of this notoriously
tricky work. The whole undertaking is a triumph for all concerned, above all Gruberová
and Jürgen Rose.

I Puritani

Eduardo Valdes *ten* Bruno **Franco Vassallo** *bar*
Riccardo **Anna Netrebko** *sop* Elvira **John Relyea**
bass Giorgio **Eric Cutler** *ten* Arturo **Valerian
Ruminski** *bass* Gualtiero **Maria Zifchak** *mez*
Enrichetta **Metropolitan Opera Ballet, Chorus and
Orchestra, New York / Patrick Summers**
Stage director **Sandro Sequi**
Video director **Gary Halvorson**
DG ② *DVD* 073 4421GH2 (149' · NTSC · HD ·
16:9 · PCM stereo and DTS 5.1 · 0)
Includes 'Backstage at the Met with Anna Netrebko,
Renée Fleming and Beverly Sills'　　　Ⓕ Ⓞ Ⓞ

Although *I Puritani* was performed during the
Metropolitan Opera's first season in 1883, it had
not been seen there for decades until this production by Sandro Sequi was unveiled in 1976. It
was one of the greatest triumphs for the partnership of Joan Sutherland and Luciano Pavarotti,
and it is to the credit of all concerned in this
recent revival that one soon forgets names from
the past and enjoys what is a spirited attempt to
evoke mid-19th-century style.

　Although it is very much an opera for four singers – the original 'Puritani quartet' of Grisi,
Rubini, Tamburini and Lablache entered into
legend – this is essentially Anna Netrebko's evening. In her tightly waisted costumes, her pale face
framed by a dark wig, she succeeds in dominating
the action both by her singing and by her physical
presence, using sudden, jerky movements to suggest Elvira's unhinged state. At the climax of the
mad scene in Act 2, she flings herself on the floor
and, with her head hanging over the orchestra pit,
launches the second verse of 'Vien, diletto'. She
negotiates both 'Son vergin vezzosa' and 'Oh vieni
al tempio' with brilliance in Act 1, and has more
than enough stamina left in Act 3 to match Eric
Cutler as Arturo in the vertiginous 'Vieni fra
queste braccia'. If there is something missing from
her singing it is the ability to invest Carlo Pepoli's
verses with an edge of pathos beyond what is
already there in Bellini's languid melodies.

　Cutler makes a good cavalier hero, especially
in the desperate plea of 'Credeasi, misera!'. As
usual, the baritone and bass, Franco Vassallo
and John Relyea, bring down the house with
'Suoni la tromba' at the end of Act 2. After more
than 30 years, the sets and costumes by Ming
Cho Lee and Peter J Hall look very handsome.
Whether you consider the production quaint or
merely traditional, it is something of a relief not
to have to battle with an elaborate political concept. Patrick Summers conducts the Met forces
always with consideration for the singers. The
photography is excellent, and there are some
intriguing glimpses of the singers backstage,
including an interval feature in which Renée
Fleming is the interviewer, chatting to Netrebko
in her dressing-room.

La sonnambula

La sonnambula　　　　　　　　　　　　　　Ⓗ
Maria Callas *sop* Amina **Cesare Valletti** *ten* Elvino

Giuseppe Modesti *bass* Rodolfo **Eugenia Ratti** *sop*
Lisa **Gabriella Carturan** *mez* Teresa **Pierluigi**
Latinucci *bass* Alessio **Giuseppe Nessi** *ten* Notary
La Scala, Milan Chorus and Orchestra / Leonard
Bernstein
EMI mono ② 567906-2 (141' · ADD · N/T/t) Recorded
live in 1955   Ⓜ ⚫⚫

This important historical document comes
from live performances at La Scala in 1955
when the diva was at the height of her powers.
Callas gives a more vital performance here than
on the set recorded in the studio. The only
drawback is the intrusive distortion at climactic
moments.

It was Callas's particular genius to find exactly
the appropriate mode of expression for every
role she tackled. Here Callas gives us Amina,
the shy, vulnerable sleepwalker. Bernstein and
Callas join forces (having performed *Médée*
together the previous year) for an utterly
charming account of *Sonnambula*. The conductor's feeling for rhythm and colour and Callas's
subtle responses to her fragile role are everywhere felt. And it isn't only Callas and Bernstein who make this set so unmissable. Cesare
Valletti – a still underrated artist – is as sensitive and involved an Elvino as any on disc and
he duets to perfection with Callas, Bernstein
giving them the space to phrase as only they
can phrase. And Giuseppe Modesti is a warm
Rodolfo. Not to be missed.

La sonnambula
Cecilia Bartoli *mez* Amina **Juan Diego Flórez** *ten*
Elvino **Ildebrando D'Arcangelo** *bass* Rodolfo
Gemma Bertagnolli *sop* Lisa **Liliana Nikiteanu** *mez*
Teresa **Peter Kálmán** *bass* Alessio **Zürich Opera**
House Chorus; La Scintilla Orchestra, Zürich /
Alessandro De Marchi
L'Oiseau-Lyre ② 478 1087 (134' · DDD)   Ⓕ ⚫➤

In this first recording of the new critical edition of
Bellini's pastoral romance Juan Diego Flórez and
Cecilia Bartoli are well matched. Bellini composed the role of Amina for Giuditta Pasta, who
was also the first Norma and Beatrice di Tenda. As
the 19th century progressed the roles were generally assigned to different kinds of voices – Norma
becoming the province of heavier, dramatic
sopranos, Amina a favourite with lighter coloratura sopranos, Jenny Lind, Patti and Tetrazzini
among them. Pasta, though, was basically what we
would think of as a mezzo-soprano nowadays, and
the new edition has realigned the part in a slightly
lower tessitura. Although the booklet says that this
is the longest version of the score yet recorded, in
its text it does not differ significantly from existing
recordings. So the difference in the new edition is
more in the general texture, and played as it is here
on period instruments by the Orchestra La Scintilla conducted by Alessandro De Marchi, the
sound is warmer, more in keeping with the mood
of *opera semi-seria*.

The problem with *La sonnambula* is the lack
of action during the first hour. The characters

introduce themselves in arias and duets but
nothing happens, the only hint of drama being
provided by the arrival of the Count, the new
master of the castle. The bass aria 'Vi ravisso'
became a great favourite with Victorian soloists, and it is given an elegant performance
here by Ildebrando D'Arcangelo. The other
significant subsidiary role is that of Lisa, the
flirty innkeeper, and Gemma Bertagnolli sings
both her arias with spirit. *Sonnambula*, though,
stands or falls on the *bel canto* expertise of its
two main protagonists, and on this occasion
they are both on great form. Bartoli's decorations in the second verse of 'Sovra il sen la
mano', the cabaletta of her entrance aria, are
delivered in that typical, slightly hushed 'confidential' manner of hers. De Marchi lets her
have a *rallentando* towards the end, with a couple of dips down into the contralto range that
make about as extreme a contrast as possible
with the brilliant effects above the stave that
Callas, Sutherland and more recently Dessay
achieve in their various recordings. The highlight of the first scene, and indeed of the whole
recording, is the duet 'Son geloso del zefiro'
which gives Flórez and Bartoli an opportunity
to demonstrate both exquisite piano passagework and some welcome passionate utterance.

It is the ensemble in the second scene of Act 1,
'D'un pensiero', that provides the moment of
high drama. Flórez is in his element as the
apparently betrayed lover, and Bartoli's distress
is convincing, even though she cannot quite
equal – who could? – Callas's sense of outrage as
she realises her predicament. In Act 2 Florez
sings the vehement aria 'Ah! perchè non posso
odiarti' with all his accustomed vigour.

What, though of the most famous passage in
the whole opera, the sleepwalking aria, 'Ah, non
credea'? Bartoli maintains a beautiful line
throughout the aria, without any intrusive
'expressive' elements that can sometimes distort
this, perhaps the ultimate Bellinian cantilena.
'Ah, non giunge' is joyful, with many pretty
decorations but the quieter atmosphere here is
in keeping with the whole conception of this,
very much a new view of *La Sonnambula*. It is
highly enjoyable, and one to sit alongside the
1962 Sutherland-Bonynge set, and of Callas's
recordings, although it is in poor sound, the
1955 live La Scala version conducted by Bernstein.

La sonnambula
Dame Joan Sutherland *sop* Amina **Nicola Monti** *ten*
Elvino **Fernando Corena** *bass* Count Rodolfo
Margreta Elkins *mez* Teresa **Sylvia Stahlman** *sop*
Lisa **Giovanni Foiani** *bass* Alessio **Angelo Mercuriali**
ten Notary **Chorus and Orchestra of the Maggio**
Musicale Fiorentino / Richard Bonynge
Decca ② 448 966-2DMO2 (136' · ADD ·
T/t) Recorded 1962   Ⓜ ⚫⚫➤

La sonnambula was Bonynge's and Sutherland's
first Bellini recording. Sutherland's Amina in the
early 1960s was sung with extraordinary freedom

and exuberance. It's difficult to describe her in the role: it's felt. She doesn't touch a thrilling nerve of passion as Callas can; but in the final scene – a wonderfully sustained and imaginative piece of dramatic, as well as delicate and brilliant singing – she's very moving. Far more so, in fact, than Callas, who overloaded 'Ah! non credea' and made 'Ah non giunge' too artful. It's no good comparing Sutherland with Callas at this late stage, though it's inevitable here, especially as the Elvino, Nicola Monti, sings the role on both sets. Callas does superb things in the coloratura of 'Sovra il sen', Sutherland is full of dramatic fire in the scene in the inn – the tone, the note-shaping is simply exquisite. And Bonynge excels in conducting the choruses. (Currently not listed on CD, but available to download.)

La straniera
Patrizia Ciofi sop Alaide **Mark Stone** bar The Baron of Valdeburgo **Dario Schmunck** ten Arturo **Enkelejda Shkosa** mez Isoletta **Graeme Broadbent** bass The Prior of the Knights Hospitallers **Roland Wood** bass-bar The Lord of Montolino **Aled Hall** ten Osburgo **Geoffrey Mitchell Choir; London Philharmonic Orchestra / David Parry**
Opera Rara ② ORC38 (141' · DDD)　　　　Ⓕ**O**

La straniera was Bellini's fourth opera, first performed at La Scala in February 1829. During the composer's lifetime, and for a few years after his death in 1835, it enjoyed considerable international success, though contemporary reviewers were sometimes hostile, criticising its lack of set-piece arias and complaining of the 'continual interruptions' to the musical line. It is this that strikes the modern listener as one of the most interesting aspects of the score. Bellini was experimenting with something, if not exactly through-composed, then sacrificing vocal fireworks for the sake of the dramatic structure.

The libretto concerns the woes of the exiled Queen of France, Agnese, who is obliged to live incognito in Brittany as Alaide – 'The Stranger'. She spends the whole opera refusing to tell anyone, including her beloved Arturo, who she really is. When he at last finds out – at his wedding to another woman – he stabs himself to death at the Queen's feet. It is a blood-and-thunder piece of gothic melodrama, with the inevitable courtroom scene in which the heroine is wrongly accused.

Renata Scotto, Montserrat Caballé and Elena Souliotis have sung the work but this set is the first studio recording of the work, and Opera Rara has done it proud. David Parry leads the LPO in a gripping account of a tricky piece. Patrizia Ciofi is meltingly pathetic and then imperious when necessary. Dario Schmunck makes a virile and ardent Arturo, and in the crucial role of Valdeburgo (also in disguise, he is Agnese's brother), Mark Stone is suitably warrior-like. In the rather ungrateful role of the 'other woman', Enkelejda Shkosa gets quite a jolly little rondo towards the end of Act 2. Among the other highlights are a catchy hunters' chorus

and the trio in which the two men fight for the stranger's affection. The scene in Act 1, when they both end up in the lake apparently drowning, is a rousing finale. The contributions of the Geoffrey Mitchell Choir are splendid. A must for lovers of the bel canto repertory.

George Benjamin　　　　British 1960

Benjamin studied at the Paris Conservatoire with Messiaen and at Cambridge with Goehr: Ligeti and Boulez have been other influences. He first came to attention with the vividly imagined orchestral piece Ringed by the Flat Horizon *(1980); this was consolidated with* A Mind of Winter *(1981) for soprano and small orchestra and* At First Light *for chamber ensemble (1982).* GROVEmusic

---

Antara

Ringed by the flat horizon[a]. A Mind of Winter[b]. At first light[c]. Panorama[d]. Antara[e]
[b]**Penelope Walmsley-Clark** sop [e]**Sebastian Bell**, [e]**Richard Blake** fls [c]**Gareth Hulse** ob [b]**Paul Archibald** tpt [a]**Ross Pople** vc [e]**Pierre-Laurent Aimard**, [e]**Ichiro Nodaira** pfs [a]**BBC Symphony Orchestra / Mark Elder**, [bce]**London Sinfonietta / George Benjamin** [d]electronics
Nimbus NI5643 (71' · DDD · T)　　　Ⓕ**OO**➔

Between March 1979, when *Ringed by the flat horizon* was begun, and March 1987, when *Antara* was completed, foundations of remarkable potential were well and truly laid, and it's fascinating to be able to trace that process through four such different George Benjamin works. There are, of course, five items on the disc, but the 2'24" of *Panorama* – a beguiling, all-too-brief indication of Benjamin's work using pre-recorded tape – form a study for *Antara* rather than a wholly independent conception. The overall impression is certainly one of progress, in that the accomplished but in some ways rather stiff procedures to be heard in *Ringed by the flat horizon* led directly to the magnificently fluent setting of Wallace Stevens in *A Mind of Winter*, in which lucid instrumental textures provide the ideal foil for a brilliantly resourceful vocal line. In *At first light*, the stylistic spectrum opens up further, with clear hints of Varèse and even Xenakis. This disc is an essential document of the music of our time.

Sudden Time

Sudden Time[a]. Upon Silence[b]. Upon Silence[c]. Octet[d]. Three Inventions[d]
[bc]**Susan Bickley** mez [a]**London Philharmonic Orchestra**, [bd]**London Sinfonietta**, [c]**Fretwork / George Benjamin**
Nimbus NI5505 (65' · DDD · T)　　　Ⓕ**OO**

Sudden Time, originally issued as a CD single, is here reissued in the context of a range of other works which underline its distinctive textural refinement and expressive conviction. *Upon Silence* (1993) is a setting for mezzo-soprano and five viols of a poem by Yeats in which textures of exceptional subtlety reflect a response to the text which is captivating in its blend of spontaneity and stylisation. The alternative version, with the viols replaced by a septet of violas, cellos and double basses is no less imaginative, while obviously lacking the unique quality – old instruments used in an entirely viable modern way – of the original.

Three Inventions (1994) has ear-opening instrumental effects on every page, but these never detract from the essential processes of argument and cogent form-building in music perhaps more urgently expressive (especially in the third piece) than anything else of Benjamin's. With the astonishingly precocious *Octet*, written in 1979, when the composer was 18, and with highly effective recordings of definitive performances, this disc is an outstanding success.

In the Little Hill

Into the Little Hill[a]. Dance Figures[b]. Sometime Voices[c]
[a]**Anu Komsi** *sop* [a]**Hilary Summers** *contr* [c]**Dietrich Henschel** *bar* [b]**BBC Symphony Orchestra / Oliver Knussen**; [c]**Deutsches Symphony Orchestra, Berlin / Kent Nagano**; [a]**Ensemble Modern / Franck Ollu**
Nimbus NI5828 (63' · DDD)
Recorded live Ⓕ

George Benjamin's 36-minute 'lyric tale' *Into the Little Hill* taps into the rich vein of English music theatre stemming from Benjamin Britten's church parables, Alexander Goehr's *Triptych* and Harrison Birtwistle's smaller-scale dramas, such as *The Io Passion*. Martin Crimp's concise text, made even more concise by Benjamin's omissions (shown in the admirably detailed booklet) shapes a version of the Pied Piper story to highlight contemporary anxieties about fragile political and social structures.

But fragile is exactly what Benjamin's music is not. The drama's rituals are far from reassuring, and the music's eerie colours (cornets, basset-horns, cimbalom) are the stuff of rat-infested nightmare. As always with Benjamin at his best, sonic refinement and formal lucidity lay the foundations for a uniquely involving musical experience, and having the story enacted and narrated by just two singers fits the sinister expressionism of the musical style to perfection. Instead of expansive melodic lyricism the tale demands a vocal idiom that shifts disconcertingly between fearful reticence and shrill ferocity. The recorded sound is not in itself especially vivid, but with Anu Komsi, Hilary Summers and the 15-strong Ensemble Modern all responding to Franck Ollu's direction with razor-sharp alacrity, this unsettling piece exerts a vice-like grip.

The scene for *Into the Little Hill* is set by Benjamin's daringly economical portrait of Shakespeare's Caliban (*Sometime Voices*) and the haunting sequence of orchestral miniatures comprising *Dance Figures*. Both these performances are also from live concerts, and both get to the heart of Benjamin's finely balanced and powerfully sculpted sound images. This is an outstanding release.

Richard Rodney Bennett

British b1936

Richard Rodney Bennett studied at the Royal Academy of Music (1953-7) and with Boulez in Paris (1957-9), though his public career as a composer had begun before this. At 16 he was writing 12-note music, and the period with Boulez encouraged him towards Darmstadt techniques. But in the 1960s he recovered more conventional aspects to develop a style of Bergian expressionism (e.g. in his opera The Mines of Sulphur, 1965); his opera Victory was given at Covent Garden in 1970. His subsequent output is large, including many concertos, settings of English poetry, chamber music, and, notably, big Romantic film scores. A musician of great versatility, he has worked as a jazz pianist (several of his scores of the 1960s are in a sophisticated jazz style) and has played and arranged American popular music.

GROVEmusic

Film Music

Murder on the Orient Express – Suite. Far from the Madding Crowd – Suite. Lady Caroline Lamb – Elegy[a]. Tender is the Night – Nicole's Theme. Enchanted April – Suite[b]. Four Weddings and a Funeral – Love Theme
[a]**Philip Dukes** *va* [b]**Cynthia Miller** *ondes martenot*
BBC Philharmonic Orchestra / Rumon Gamba
Chandos Movies CHAN9867 (70' · DDD) Ⓕ●

Richard Rodney Bennett possesses a natural flair for composing for both big screen or small. The concept of presenting the music in suites (no credit here for the arrangers) makes the best possible case for it, circumventing the problems encountered on the original soundtracks where fragmentation sometimes marrs enjoyment.

It's a measure of his standing in the film world that all these scores were issued on disc concurrently with the film. The earliest, *Far from the Madding Crowd* (1967), belongs to another era sonically speaking, but on this sumptuously recorded disc you can imagine yourself back in that state-of-the-art Odeon, Marble Arch, as the curtains parted to reveal Hardy's Dorset landscape on its giant curved screen, with Bennett's wistful unaccompanied theme for flute answered by oboe on the soundtrack.

Like that film, *Lady Caroline Lamb* was presented on its initial run as a road-show attraction, with an Overture, Entr'acte and Exit Music on the soundtrack, played respectively before the showing, during the intermission and after the film.

The Suite reveals Bennett's fondness for a lyrical line at its most impassioned, with Philip Duke's eloquent viola-playing going to the heart of the story of this aristocratic lady's doomed affair with Byron. *Enchanted April* moves us to the sunshine of Italy, where the colours of the percussion and ondes martenot lend a sweet fragrance to the scene. Elgar's *Chanson de matin* makes an unexpected but entrancing appearance.

When concentrating on the music without visual distractions it's easier to note the discreet Love Theme for *Four Weddings and a Funeral*. Beginning on low flute with broken chords on the harp, it subtly underlines the weddings and the funeral where John Hannah reads Auden's poem *Stop all the Clocks*.

From television comes *Tender is the Night – Nicole's Theme*, a popular foxtrot, 20s style, representing Scott Fitzgerald's ill-fated character Nicole Diver, inspired by his wife Zelda. Period dance music plays a part, too, in *Murder on the Orient Express*, where Yuri Torchinsky, leader of the BBC Philharmonic, catches to a tee that sweet sound so characteristic of Oscar Grasso, leader of Victor Silvester's ballroom orchestra.

Conductor Rumon Gamba knows just how to levitate Bennett's celebrated train waltz theme, and the response of his orchestra throughout this disc suggests that they can turn their hand to the idiom of this music at the flick of a wrist.

Partita. Reflections on a Sixteenth Century Tune. Songs before Sleep[a]. Reflections on a Scottish Folk Song[b]
[a]**Jonathan Lemalu** *bar* [b]**Paul Watkins** *vc*
Philharmonia Orchestra / Richard Hickox
Chandos CHAN10389 (76' · DDD)   Ⓕ

It's hard to imagine a more beguiling start to this series or a more appealing introduction to Richard Rodney Bennett than this CD. It begins with a Partita that has a spring in its step and the breeze of the countryside blowing through it. Bennett's way with fashioning long strands of melody is a special feature of his lyrical writing. It's a gift he may owe, in part, to the songwriters he admires, like Kern and Arlen. In the Lullaby second movement there's a glorious outpouring of instrumental song ravishingly realised by the Philharmonia under Hickox's fervent direction. The finale has players paired off in the manner of a concerto for orchestra.

A chanson by Josquin provides the theme for the *Reflections on a Sixteenth Century Tune*, which enshrines a homage to Peter Warlock, whose *Capriol Suite* similarly drew on Renaissance music. The scoring is breathtaking, with soloists highlighted against the muted string ensemble. Jonathan Lemalu characterises *Before Sleep* well with colour, dynamics and some exquisite quiet singing in the upper voice, notably in Bennett's memora-

ble setting of 'Twinkle, twinkle, little star'.

Reflections on a Scottish Folk Song ('Ca' the yowes') was written in memory of the Queen Mother. It's the most substantial piece here, with a formidable cello part played with great feeling by Paul Watkins. There is a Scottish lilt in some of the variations, a beautiful Interlude, and a brilliant finale that concludes *pianissimo*, like a Scottish mist enclosing by stealth. It's hard to imagine anyone not being enraptured by this CD.

Choral Works

Sea Change[a]. Verses. Out of Your Sleep. Puer nobis. A Good-Night. Susanni. A Farewell to Arms[b]. Missa brevis. There is no rose. That younge child. Sweet was the song. Lullay mine liking. What sweeter music
Cambridge Singers / John Rutter with [a]**Charles Fullbrook** *bells* [b]**Sue Dorey** *vc*
Collegium Records ⓢ CSACD901 (75' · DDD · T/t)
Ⓕ ⓞ ⓞ ⓓ

Hard to believe, but this is the first CD devoted solely to Sir Richard Rodney Bennett's extensive choral output. That it's a richly rewarding body of work is nowhere better exemplified than in the curtain-raiser, *Sea Change* (1984) a marvellously effective, 17-minute cycle to texts by Shakespeare, Andrew Marvell and Edmund Spenser. The Spenser setting thrillingly evokes the terrible monsters encountered by Sir Guyon during a stormy sea voyage by employing a technique akin to *Sprechgesang*, while the concluding 'Full fathom five' is a worthy successor to Vaughan Williams's setting in his *Three Shakespeare Songs*.

Whereas *Sea Change* minimally and subtly deploys tubular bells, *A Farewell to Arms* (2001) memorably incorporates an extensive role for solo cello and sets the same poems by Ralph Knevet and George Peele that Finzi first brought together for his 1945 diptych. It's a tenderly moving creation, as is the part-song 'A Good-Night' (1999) from the sequence *A Garland for Linda*. If Britten's shadow looms large over the *Missa brevis* (1990) for Canterbury Cathedral Choir, it's a no less appealing creation for all that.

Bouquets all round to John Rutter and his Cambridge Singers; theirs is *a cappella* singing of a very high order. Exemplary presentation and admirable sound, tastefully balanced within the comparatively intimate acoustic of the LSO's home, St Luke's in the City of London. A delightful anthology.

Additional recommendation

The Mines of Sulphur
Soloists; Glimmerglass Opera Orchestra / Stewart Robertson
Chandos ② ⓢ CHSA5036 (107' · DDD)   Ⓕ ⓓ

The Mines of Sulphur was a Sadler's Wells commission premiered in 1965. It was a considerable success. *The Mines* is a gripping thriller set in an isolated, decaying country house. The oscillation between lyrical arioso and violence is compelling; there are countless examples of evocative scoring; and the word-setting is realistic and well enunciated. Everyone is well cast and directed in this astonishingly assured first full-length opera.

Alban Berg
Austrian 1885-1935

Berg wrote songs as a youth but had no serious musical education before his lessons with Schoenberg, which began in 1904. Webern was a pupil at the same time, a crucial period in Schoenberg's creative life, when he was moving rapidly towards and into atonality. Berg's Piano Sonata Op 1 (1908) is still tonal, but the Four Songs Op 2 (1910) move away from key and the Op 3 String Quartet (1910) is wholly atonal; it is also remarkable in sustaining, through motivic development, a larger span when the instrumental works of Schoenberg and Webern were comparatively momentary. Berg dedicated it to his wife Helene.

Then came the Five Songs for soprano Op 4 (1912), miniatures setting poetic instants by Peter Altenberg. This was Berg's first orchestral score, and though it shows an awareness of Schoenberg, Mahler and Debussy, it is brilliantly conceived and points towards Wozzeck – and towards 12-note serialism, notably in its final passacaglia. More immediately Berg produced another set of compact statements, the Four Pieces for clarinet and piano Op 5 (1913), then returned to large form with the Three Orchestral Pieces Op 6 (1915), a thematically linked sequence of prelude, dance movement and funeral march. The prelude begins and ends in the quiet noise of percussion; the other two movements show Berg's discovery of how traditional forms and stylistic elements (including tonal harmony) might support big structures.

In May 1914 Berg saw the Vienna premiere of Büchner's Woyzeck and formed the plan of setting it. He started the opera in 1917, while he was in the Austrian army (1915-18), and finished it in 1922. He made his own selection from the play's fragmentary scenes to furnish a three-act libretto for formal musical setting.

The close musical structuring, extending to small details of timing, may be seen as an analogue for the mechanical alienness of the universe around Büchner's central characters, though Berg's music crosses all boundaries, from atonal to tonal (there is a Mahlerian interlude in D minor), from speech to song, from café music to sophisticated textures of dissonant counterpoint. Wozzeck had its premiere in Berlin in 1925 and thereafter was widely produced, bringing Berg financial security.

His next work, the Chamber Concerto for violin, piano and 13 wind (1925), moves decisively towards a more classical style: its three formally complex movements are still more clearly shaped than those of the op.6 set and the scoring suggests a response to Stravinskian objectivity. The work is also threaded through with ciphers and numerical conceits, making it a celebration of the triune partnership of Schoenberg, Berg and Webern.

Then came the Lyric Suite for string quartet (1926), whose long-secret programme connects it with Berg's intimate feelings for Hanna Fuchs-Robettin – feelings also important to him in the composition of his second opera, Lulu (1929-35). The suite, in six movements of increasingly extreme tempo, uses 12-note serial along with other material in projecting a quasi-operatic development towards catastrophe and annulment.

The development of Lulu was twice interrupted by commissioned works, the concert aria Der Wein on poems by Baudelaire (1929) and the Violin Concerto (1935), and it remained unfinished at Berg's death: his widow placed an embargo on the incomplete third act, which could not be published or performed until 1979. As with Wozzeck, he made his own libretto out of stage material, this time choosing two plays by Wedekind, whom he had long admired for his treatment of sexuality. Dramatically and musically the opera is a huge palindrome, showing Lulu's rise through society in her successive relationships and then her descent into prostitution and eventual death at the hands of Jack the Ripper. Again the score is filled with elaborate formal schemes, around a lyricism unloosed by Berg's individual understanding of 12-note serialism. Something of its threnodic sensuality is continued in the Violin Concerto, designed as a memorial to the teenage daughter of Mahler's widow.   GROVEmusic

Violin Concerto

Berg Violin Concerto **Stravinsky** Violin Concerto in D **Ravel** Tzigane[a]
Itzhak Perlman vn **Boston Symphony Orchestra / Seiji Ozawa;** [a]**New York Philharmonic Orchestra / Zubin Mehta**
DG The Originals download 447 445-2GOR (57' · ADD/[a]DDD) Recorded 1978   Ⓜ❍❍▷

Perlman's account of the Berg Violin Concerto with the Boston orchestra under Ozawa has long occupied a respected place in the catalogue. The original reviewer in *Gramophone* in March 1980 was completely convinced by Perlman's 'commanding purposefulness'. As to the recording, he wrote that 'though Perlman's violin – beautifully caught – is closer than some will like, there's no question of crude spotlighting'.

Twenty years later and in a different competitive climate, his favourable verdict still holds good. Perlman is also a little too close in the *Tzigane*, the recording of which sets him very firmly front-stage again. But this is playing of stature and still among the best available versions. There are more desirable recordings now available of the Stravinsky.

Violin Concerto. Lyric Suite (original version)   Ⓗ
Louis Krasner vn **Galimir Quartet** (Felix Galimir, Adrienne Galimir vns Renee Galimir va Marguerite Galimir vc) **BBC Symphony Orchestra / Anton Webern**
Testament mono SBT1004 (57' · ADD) Recorded 1936
Ⓕ❍❍❍

This is an extraordinary issue of more than mere documentary interest. Krasner commissioned the Violin Concerto and had just given the first performance at the 1936 ISCM Festival in Barcelona (with Hermann Scherchen conducting) only three months after Berg's death. Webern was to have conducted,but withdrew at the last moment much to the consternation of the BBC who had booked him for the following month with some misgivings. Fortunately adequate rehearsal time had been allotted, and the players of the BBC Symphony Orchestra proved more expert in coping with the score than their Barcelona colleagues. Webern had appeared on a number of occasions with the orchestra, but no recording of him survives in the BBC Archives. Berg's death had shocked the musical world, though not as much as the death of the 18-year-old Manon Gropius had shaken the composer, who wrote the concerto as a memorial to her.

What's most striking about this performance is its glowing intensity. There's no sense of the bar-line or of the music ever being 'moved on'; time seems to stand still, yet there's also a natural sense of musical pace. The surface noise on this recording, made before an invited audience in the Concert Hall of Broadcasting House, London, can't disguise the care with which the textures are balanced and the finesse of the wind players. This was only the work's second performance, yet the players sound as if they'd lived with the music all their lives. It has all the anguish and poignancy the music demands, and Krasner is an eloquent exponent. The opening bars suffer from some minor audience coughs and the surface noise and moments of distortion call for a tolerance that's well worth extending.

The Galimir Quartet specialised in contemporary music and its playing has commendable ensemble and dedication. Unfortunately its pioneering account of the *Lyric Suite*, recorded shortly before the performance of the Violin Concerto, was hampered by a very dry acoustic that must have deterred many listeners. It was the only version for many years, and in spite of its musical excellence can't have made many new friends for the work. But this shouldn't deter collectors from acquiring this remarkable issue.

Berg Violin Concerto[a] **Janáček** Sinfonietta[b]
Tippett Concerto for Double String Orchestra[c]
[a]**Edith Peinemann** vn
BBC Symphony Orchestra / Rudolf Kempe
BBC Legends BBCL4215-2 (78' · ADD)
Recorded live at the Royal Festival Hall, London in
[ac]1976, [b]Fairfield Hall, Croydon in 1975 Ⓕ

Did his mastery of mainstream European orchestral music leave Rudolf Kempe at a loss when confronted with Tippett's Utopian synthesis of Tudor polyphony and English folksong in the Concerto for Double String Orchestra? Not a bit of it. There may be a bustling, Hindemithian weight to the first movement's busy textures, an unexpected but not inapposite touch of Straussian opulence in the slow movement,

and a lack of truly sprung rhythm in the finale. But this reading never sells Tippett short, and even in a rather airless recording, the symphonic ambitions that underpin the music's pastoral and pictorial elements are very well realised.

The sound quality in the Berg Concerto is similarly constrained, yet the strengths of the performance cannot be denied. By some standards Edith Peinemann may appear self-effacing, but her technique is secure, her commitment to the piece absolute: in music which has ample flamboyance built in she is never timid or tentative. Kempe ensures that the first movement flows effortlessly around its evocations of the dance, and even if you prefer the later stages of the second movement to move on a bit more than they do here, Kempe's flair for balancing the music's intricate moods and even more intricate strands of texture is admirable. With a lively and eloquent account of Janáček's *Sinfonietta* thrown in, clear as a bell despite the limitations of the recording, this is a refreshing disc: a reminder of the all-round virtues of the BBC SO in its post-Boulez phase, and of Kempe's special ability to bring not just care but a degree of charisma to performances of 20th-century classics.

Additional recommendation

Berg Violin Concerto
Coupled with: **Rihm** Gesungene Zeit
Mutter vn **Chicago SO / Levine**
DG download *437 093-2GH* (52' · DDD) F

Mutter fusing ice and fire to powerful results in music she is perfectly suited to. Levine is a superb partner. Terrific sound too – try and track down th CD, but the download is always available.

Kammerkonzert

Berg Chamber Concerto[a] **Mozart** Serenade, 'Gran partita', K361
[a]**Christian Tetzlaff** vn [a]**Mitsuko Uchida** pf
Ensemble Intercontemporain / Pierre Boulez
Decca 478 0316DH (80' · DDD)   ⒻⓄⓄⓄⒹ

Lucky number 13: Boulez has come up with a characteristically inventive pairing of Mozart's great wind serenade with Berg's *Chamber Concerto*. OK, he's cheated slightly, in that Mozart's original stipulation was for a double bass rather than a contrabassoon (though it's a common enough substitution), and the wind instruments used by Berg and Mozart are not identical. But conceptually it's a winner; and musically too, with Old Vienna coming face to face with its more turbulent post-First World War self.

The sheer scale of the work, too, suggests that this was an august occasion. Within the seven movements of the *Gran Partita*, Mozart deftly moves between the worlds of the military band, traditional Harmoniemusik and, of course, opera, both *seria* and *buffa*. The (sadly uncredited) members of Ensemble Intercontemporain clearly relish the opportunity to venture into earlier territory, and the playing, as you'd expect, is supremely accomplished and in perfect accord. But much more than that, there's a sense of fun, of genial affection for the music. Whether in the fluid lines of the tender *Adagio* or the yearning *Andante*, or in the bustling, concise finale, where everything – in the true spirit of *opera buffa* – seems to come right, Boulez makes plain his relish for the work. This serenade, he reminds us, is so much more than merely an attractive backdrop for the goings-on of Viennese life.

Berg's *Chamber Concerto* was written for the 50th birthday of his friend and mentor Arnold Schoenberg. It's a work that has endlessly fascinated theorists, not just for Berg's very particular way of using Schoenberg's serial methods, but also for his obsessive interest in numerology, which is touched on with great lucidity by Boulez in the booklet. But although it's useful for the performers to be able to dissect the piece in such a manner, for the listener it is hardly any more essential than an in-depth knowledge of fugal techniques is for the enjoyment of late Beethoven quartets. Boulez has been here before, of course, memorably recording the concerto with Barenboim and Zukerman, and he knows his way round the piece's stickier points and its occasionally intransigently dense wind textures. But what makes Mitsuko Uchida and Christian Tetzlaff outstanding is their feeling for the piece's inherent theatricality.

The writing for wind instruments is hardly less original, whether in sustained, organ-like chords or the extreme sonorities at the end of the movement, where textures are sunk as low as can be against a heaven-bound violin. Finally the soloists come face to face for the *Rondo ritmico*, which begins with a swirling cadenza. The freedom of the two players here is extraordinary, undoubtedly helped by the fact that they toured the work before taking it into the studio.

The real achievement here is that most people will buy the disc for either the Mozart or the Berg, not both. But in listening to it, they'll discover something new and utterly remarkable. Lucky 13 indeed.

Piano Sonata, Op 1

Berg Piano Sonata, Op 1 **Schoenberg** Drei Klavierstücke, Op 11. Sechs Klavierstücke, Op 19. Fünf Klavierstücke, Op 23. Piano Suite, Op 25. Klavierstücke, Op 33a & Op 33b **Webern** Variations, Op 27
Peter Hill pf
Naxos 8 553870 (79' · DDD)   Ⓢ**OO**▷

When interviewed by *Gramophone* back in September 1989, Peter Hill said he felt he had things to say about the Schoenberg piano works which had not been said on record. Here is the complete vindication of that statement. These are scrupulously prepared performances, with all the polyphonic strands clarified and all the

myriad articulation marks respected. In order to accommodate that detail and let it speak musically, Hill takes tempos on the relaxed side of Schoenberg's frequently rather manic metronome indications. The first two of the Op 11 pieces gain a gravity that might have surprised the composer, and the fourth piece of Op 23 loses some of the suggested *schwungvoll* character. Yet there's no lack of brilliance and velocity in such pieces as the Gigue from Op 25, and time and again Hill's thoughtfulness and search for expressiveness and beauty of sound justify his spacious approach.

Hill probes with equal subtlety, sympathy and high intelligence in the Webern Variations, while in the Berg Sonata, Hill's unforced lyricism, inwardness and flexibility of phrasing are again immensely appealing. Apart from its amazing value for money, Naxos's first-rate recording quality, Peter Hill's own lucid booklet-essay, and what sounds like an ideally regulated instrument, all contribute to the outstanding success of this issue.

Seven Early Songs

Seven Early Songs. Three Orchestral Pieces, Op 6. Der Wein
Anne Sofie von Otter *mez* **Vienna Philharmonic Orchestra / Claudio Abbado**
DG 445 846-2GH (49' · DDD · T/t)   Ⓕ**O**▷

Anne Sofie von Otter included the *Seven Early Songs* on a recital disc (no longer available on CD). Singing with orchestra, von Otter naturally works on a larger scale. The words are more firmly bound into the vocal line; there isn't the detailed give-and-take that's possible with a pianist. But the outline of her interpretation remains that of a true Lieder singer, always lighting upon unexpected subtleties of colour and emphasis to inflect the poetry. In all this Abbado is an equal partner. Von Otter needs careful accompaniment in the concert hall if she's to dominate an orchestra and Abbado, in co-operation with DG's technical team, has produced a balance that never drowns her, but still sounds fairly natural. In *Der Wein*, Berg's late concert aria, von Otter and Abbado catch the lilt of the jazz rhythms. In the *Seven Early Songs* are they a touch too cool? Perhaps, but in the final song, 'Sommertage', they throw caution to the winds and end the cycle on a passionate high.

Abbado has recorded the *Three Orchestral Pieces* before and his 1970s recording has long been one of the standard versions of this work. The opportunity to see how his thoughts have developed since then brings more surprises than might have been expected.

In short, his outlook is progressing from the Italianate to the Germanic. No doubt the influence of the Vienna Philharmonic Orchestra has much to do with this and their marvellously eloquent playing is one of the prime attractions of the disc.

In their company Abbado finds more depth and complexity in the music than before, although that does mean that the March loses the Bartókian attack and driving rhythms that made his first version so exciting.

Lulu

Lulu (Orchestration of Act 3 completed by Friedrich Cerha)

Teresa Stratas sop Lulu **Franz Mazura** bar Dr-Schön, Jack **Kenneth Riegel** ten Alwa **Yvonne Minton** mez Countess Geschwitz **Robert Tear** ten The Painter, A Negro **Toni Blankenheim** bar Schigolch, Professor of Medicine, The Police Officer **Gerd Nienstedt** bass An Animal-tamer, Rodrigo **Helmut Pampuch** ten The Prince, The Manservant, The Marquis **Jules Bastin** bass The Theatre Manager, The Banker **Hanna Schwarz** mez A-Dresser in the theatre, High School Boy, A Groom **Jane Manning** sop A 15-year-old girl **Ursula Boese** mez Her Mother **Anna Ringart** mez A Lady Artist **Claude Meloni** bar A Journalist **Pierre-Yves Le-Maigat** bass A Manservant **Paris Opéra Orchestra / Pierre Boulez**

DG ③ download 476 2524GGR3 (172' · ADD · S/T/t/N) Recorded 1979.

Ⓜ ➍➍➍➍➲

This is a masterpiece that fulfils all the requirements for a commercial smash hit – it's sexy, violent, cunning, sophisticated, hopelessly complicated and emotionally draining. The meaningful but gloriously over-the-top story-line, after two tragedies by Frank Wedekind, deserves acknowledgement, but what matters is that Berg's music is magnificent, Romantic enough to engage the passions of listeners normally repelled by 12-tone music, and cerebral enough to keep eggheads fully employed.

It's opulent yet subtle (saxophone and piano lend the score a hint of jazz-tinted decadence), with countless telling thematic inter-relations and much vivid tonal character-painting. Berg left it incomplete (he orchestrated only 390 of the Third Act's 1326 bars), but Friedrich Cerha's painstaking reconstruction is a major achievement, especially considering the complicated web of Berg's musical tapestry. This recording first opened our ears to the 'real' Lulu in 1979.

The performance is highly distinguished. Teresa Stratas is an insinuating yet vulnerable Lulu, Yvonne Minton a sensuous Gräfin Geschwitz and Robert Tear an ardent artist. Dr Schön is tellingly portrayed by Franz Mazura, Kenneth Riegel is highly creditable as Schön's son and that Boulez himself is both watchful of detail and responsive to the drama, hardly needs saying. It's not an easy listen, but it'll keep you on your toes for a stimulating, even exasperating evening.

Lulu (sung in English)

Lisa Saffer sop Lulu **Robert Hayward** bar Dr Schön; Jack the Ripper **John Graham-Hall** ten Alwa **Susan Parry** mez Countess Geschwitz **Gwynne Howell** bass

Schigolch **Graeme Danby** bass Professor of Medicine; Theatre Manager; Banker **Robert Poulton** bar Animal Tamer; Athlete **Alan Oke** ten Manservant; Prince; Marquis **Roger Begley** spkr Police Commissioner **Claire Mitcher** sop Girl **Jane Powell** mez Her Mother **Moira Harris** sop Lady Artist **Toby Stafford-Allen** bar Journalist **Anna Burford** mez Dresser; School Boy **English National Opera Orchestra / Paul Daniel**

Chandos ③ CHAN3130 (166' · DDD · S/T/N) Ⓜ Ⓞ➲

The 2002 production of Berg's Lulu by Richard Jones is generally agreed to be one of the best things to come from troubled English National Opera in recent years. Chandos has done everyone a favour by transferring its 2005 revival lock, stock and smoking revolver from the opera house to the studio.

This is important for several reasons. Lulu can seem forbidding to the uninitiated. Its amoral characters, its sordid plot, its enigmatic anti-heroine, its complex (and masterful) formal design: all these aspects repel some as much as they attract others. Yet cabaret burlesque is as integral to the opera's make-up as high operatic tragedy. Paul Daniel and the Chandos engineers don't let us forget it. Piano, saxophone and vibraphone get the prominence they deserve. The farcical comings and goings in Parisian salon and London garret alike spring to life without the inevitable noises-off and dropouts of an in-house recording.

Richard Stokes has rendered Wedekind's demotic text aptly and brilliantly enough for anyone who will not wrinkle their noses at (say) the Acrobat's refrain of 'Bugger, bugger, bugger it!' And the ENO orchestra swing where the Paris Opéra for Boulez are stiff. It should come as no surprise that Böhm and the Viennese know their way around a quickstep and a tango; likewise Daniel and his players really get under the skin of Berg's 'English Waltz' in Act 3.

So consistent an overall vision is perhaps bound to reduce the starring role of Lulu herself. In Jones's production, Lisa Saffer projected her onstage as a fantasy-u-like for her many admirers. Without the sublime confidence of an Anja Silja, the vulnerability of a Constance Haumann or the hauteur of a Teresa Stratas, she brings unruffled poise and a shapely, silken tone that would not be out of place in Wolf. Nor is it here; as Dr Schön observes, after Lulu has shot him and poured herself a glass of champagne, 'You never change'. Robert Hayward's Schön is gruff, like his Wotan: a bully reduced to bluster. It is Countess Geschwitz who must convey whatever redemptive transformation Berg (not Wedekind) has to offer, and Susan Parry is equal to the task, moving from mannish suavity to an intensely moving Liebestod. John Graham-Hall is no more of a cipher than most Alwas – a Wunderlich or a Bostridge may be too much to hope for.

The many smaller parts are well taken and distinctly enunciated but the most definitive portrayal here is Gwynne Howell's Schigolch, weary and pervy and always with the emphasis on the *gesang*, not the *sprech*.

Original-language recordings will hardly go out of fashion, nor ones with more Mahlerian breadth and depth of feeling; for both, Christine Schäfer needs to be seen in Graham Vick's production on DVD (see below). But for *Lulu* in the raw, a *Rosenkavalier* with no underwear, this is one to go for.

Lulu

Christine Schäfer *sop* Lulu **Wolfgang Schöne** *bar* Dr Schön, Jack the Ripper **David Kuebler** *ten* Alwa **Kathryn Harries** *mez* Countess Geschwitz **Stephan Drakulich** *ten* Painter, Negro **Norman Bailey** *bass* Schigolch **Jonathan Veira** *bass* Professor of Medicine, Banker, Theatre Manager **Donald Maxwell** *bass* Animal tamer, Athlete **Neil Jenkins** *ten* Prince, Manservant, Marquis **Patricia Bardon** *contr* Dresser, High-School Boy, Groom **London Philharmonic Orchestra / Sir Andrew Davis**
Stage director **Graham Vick**
Video director **Humphrey Burton**
Warner Music Vision/NVC Arts 🔲 0630 15533-2 (183' · NTSC · 4:3 · PCM stereo · 2-6)　　Ⓕ**OO**

Warner has reissued Glyndebourne's 1996 staging of all three acts of *Lulu*, a much-lauded affair that won the *Gramophone* Award for Best Video in 1997. Graham Vick's direction is admirable not only for what it achieves but also for what it avoids. With its redbrick interior, upward-curving staircase and minimal furnishings, the stage-set has a spartan air, enlivened by a central hole in the floor through which characters disappear and emerge according to the needs of the drama. Costumes have a generalised present-day feel, and the recourse to mobile phones was a prescient touch. Crucially, this staging doesn't encumber the opera with a specious extra-musical concept or smother it with designer cleverness. The filmed interlude in Act 2 is both a pragmatic realisation of Berg's concept and faithful to the spirit of his intentions: a triumph of dramatic common sense.

Schäfer's Lulu is the best sung and most beautifully voiced yet recorded: diffident, even distanced at the outset, yet assuredly in control as she closes down Dr Schön's emotional space at the end of Act 1 and evincing real expressive pain at her degradation in Acts 2 and 3. Wolfgang Schöne has the right hollow authority for Dr Schön, and brings an appropriately Mr Hyde-like demeanour to his Jack the Ripper *alter ego*, while David Kuebler's fantasising Alwa is the most complete rendition since Kenneth Riegel's for Boulez. Aloof in her initial emotional exchanges, Kathryn Harries goes on to to find quiet strength and nobility in Countess Geschwitz. Stephan Drakulich's seedy-looking Painter is unusually accurate, Donald Maxwell's Athlete over-acted to the point of caricature, while Norman Bailey's Schigolch has a wiliness that makes the part more substantial than usual.

Davis conducts with a sure awareness of short-term incident and long-term tension. His sense of dramatic pace makes the best case yet for the first scene of Act 3, its mosaic-like succession of exchanges throwing the the second scene's seamless intensity into greater relief. Friedrich Cerha's realisation of this act has come in for its share of criticism, but makes for a musical and dramatic whole such as Berg is unlikely to have altered appreciably had he lived to complete the work.

As directed for video, Humphrey Burton goes to town on facial asides and long-range stares. The picture reproduces with the expected sharpness of focus, though the sound throws the orchestra a little too far forward – giving voices a slightly distanced, though never unfocused quality. Subtitles are clear and to the point, and the 33 chapter selections well-placed for ease of access. On DVD this performance is now a clear first choice.

Wozzeck

Wozzeck
Franz Grundheber *bar* Wozzeck **Hildegard Behrens** *sop* Marie **Heinz Zednik** *ten* Captain **Aage Haugland** *bass* Doctor **Philip Langridge** *ten* Andres **Walter Raffeiner** *ten* Drum-Major **Anna Gonda** *mez* Margret **Alfred Sramek** *bass* First Apprentice **Alexander Maly** *bar* Second Apprentice **Peter Jelosits** *ten* Idiot **Vienna Boys' Choir; Vienna State Opera Chorus; Vienna Philharmonic Orchestra / Claudio Abbado**
DG ② download *423 587-2GH2* (89' · DDD · T/t)
Recorded live 1987.　　Ⓕ**O➔**

A live recording, in every sense of the word. The cast is uniformly excellent, with Grundheber good both at the wretched pathos of Wozzeck's predicament and his helpless bitterness, and Behrens as an outstandingly intelligent and involving Marie, even the occasional touch of strain in her voice heightening her characterisation. The Vienna Philharmonic responds superbly to Abbado's ferociously close-to-the-edge direction.

It's a live recording with a bit of a difference, mark you: the perspectives are those of a theatre, not a recording studio. The orchestra is laid out as it would be in an opera-house pit and the movement of singers on stage means that voices are occasionally overwhelmed. The result is effective: the crowded inn-scenes, the arrival and departure of the military band, the sense of characters actually reacting to each other, not to a microphone, makes for a grippingly theatrical experience. This version has a raw urgency, a sense of bitter protest and angry pity that are quite compelling and uncomfortably eloquent. (Currently not listed on CD; well worth tracking down internationally or downloading.)

Wozzeck (sung in English)
Andrew Shore *bar* Wozzeck **Dame Josephine**

Barstow sop Marie **Alan Woodrow** ten Drum Major
Peter Bronder ten Andres **Stuart Kale** ten Captain
Clive Bayley bass Doctor **Jean Rigby** contr Margret
Leslie John Flanagan, Iain Paterson bass
Apprentices **John Graham-Hall** ten Idiot **Susan
Singh** Choristers; **Geoffrey Mitchell Choir;
Philharmonia Orchestra / Paul Daniel**
Chandos/Peter Moores Foundation Opera in English
② CHAN3094 (92' · DDD · N/L)   Ⓜ➔

This is a fine *Wozzeck*; the perfect complement
to the outstanding Abbado version which has
been the top recommendation for so long.
Abbado's was recorded live in Vienna, and any
studio recording of an opera risks sounding
score-bound when compared with a real, live
performance in the theatre. But with *Wozzeck* a
studio ambience can bring real advantages, especially if it underlines the kind of claustrophobic
intimacy and obsessiveness which theatrical
histrionics inevitably broaden and – in some
instances – coarsen. Ranting and raving are
kept to a minimum in Paul Daniel's interpretation, and the result is intensely moving without
in any way underplaying the music's visceral
dramatic power.

One result of Daniel's concentrated yet
warmly expressive moulding of the score is a
strong sense of its late-Romantic background in
Strauss and also in Mahler. The Philharmonia
play superbly throughout, and the recording
successfully balances a spacious orchestral canvas of the widest dynamic range while placing
the voices effectively. Nor are there any weak
links in the cast, with three tenors, John Graham-Hall, Stuart Kale and Alan Woodrow,
making particularly telling contributions. Josephine Barstow has one or two squally moments
in delineating Marie's bewilderment and fear,
but her voice remains in remarkably good shape,
and the character's conflicting impulses are brilliantly conveyed. Shore is one of the best operatic baritones of our time, and he dominates the
drama with an utterly convincing blend of the
menacing and the pathetic. Moreover, his way
with the text is exemplary.

This performance proves that an English
Wozzeck can easily match the impact of the best
German performances. Its virtues are such that
it makes as powerful a case for this extraordinary
work as any other version.

Wozzeck
Toni Blankenheim bar Wozzeck **Sena Jurinac** sop
Marie **Richard Cassilly** ten Drum Major
Peter Haage ten Andres **Gerhard Unger** ten
Captain **Hans Sotin** bass Doctor
Kurt Marschner ten Idiot **Kurt Moll** bass Apprentice
Franz Grundheber bar Apprentice II
Elisabeth Steiner contr Margret
**Hamburg State Opera Chorus;
Hamburg State Philharmonic Orchestra /
Bruno Maderna**
Video director **Rolf Liebermann**
ArtHaus Musik 🎥 101 277
(106' · NTSC · 4:3 · PCM mono · 0)   Ⓕ

Wozzeck is perfect for the small screen, as the
composer and intendant Rolf Liebermann
intuited when he made his seventh and, he
thought, best TV opera film by decamping the
Hamburg State Opera to a castle in southern
Germany.

The many short scenes, abrupt shifts of perspective and concentrated dialogue are no more
or less macabre, pitiful and comic than a month
in the life of Weatherfield's Coronation Street.
Willi Reich points out in his monograph on the
composer that *Wie arme Leut* ('We Poor People') 'summarises the whole social milieu of the
work'. Just so, the orchestra squeezes into your
sitting room like a busy night at the Rovers
Return.

Liebermann could not have picked a better
conductor for the job. Bruno Maderna's studies with Hermann Scherchen, his uneasy
blood-brotherhood with Boulez and the
Darmstadt bunch and his own creative analysis of Renaissance music in performance and
composition make him ideally equipped to
eschew the broad strokes of an opera-house
production, even one as finely tuned as Abbado's, for a more expansive, analytical approach
that zeros in on the structural fundamentals of
Berg's score just as the camera registers every
flicker of naivety (Andres), lust (Marie) and
uncomprehending despair (Wozzeck) in
relentless close-up.

Toni Blankenheim presents a noble,
wretched Everyman, one who only at the last
buckles under torment into insanity. Sena
Jurinac plays Marie in the tradition of lighter
voices such as Danco and Seefried, more agile
and believably seductive-pathetic than the
Wagnerian assumptions by (say) Polaski or
Behrens. The remainder of the cast has
strength in depth, and they all heed Berg's
injunction to treat their lines as though singing *Il trovatore* instead of his *Sprechstimme*
instructions in the score: even Gerhard Unger's hysterically admonishing Captain is sung
rather than shrieked.

The considerable problems of the TV opera
enterprise are overcome, triumphantly so:
synchronisation is almost perfect, and the
total commitment of all the singers is such as
to suspend disbelief when their voices are
coming from a generous studio acoustic while
we see them outdoors – often with breath visible in the chill. It is an oppressively claustrophobic, deeply sobering experience, and so it
should be.

Wozzeck
Franz Grundheber bar Wozzeck **Hildegard Behrens**
sop Marie **Walter Raffeiner** ten Drum Major **Philip
Langridge** ten Andres **Heinz Zednik** ten Captain
Aage Haugland bass Doctor **Anna Gonda** contr
Margret **Alfred Sramek** bass Apprentice I **Alexander
Maly** bar Apprentice II **Peter Jelosits** ten Madman
**Vienna State Opera Chorus and Orchestra /
Claudio Abbado**
Stage director **Adolf Dresen**

Video director **Brian Large**
ArtHaus Musik **DVD** 100 256 (97' · 4:3, 2.0 · 2 & 5)   Ⓕ

Coarse conducting and highly approximate singing have been so readily excused in 'difficult' idioms such as *Wozzeck*'s that they became almost expected, obscuring the music's beauty and emotional intensity. Not so, in this welcome DVD appearance of an appropriately Viennese production. Abbado recognises the late Romantic lyricism that unifies the score, but emphasises translucent textures rather than Teutonic density, while still unleashing Berg's nascent Expressionist snarls with vividly theatrical force. The singers, too, treat the vocal line with greater respect than was once the norm, especially Grundheber's memorable Wozzeck. Behrens sings Marie's anguished, tender lines with intense beauty and keen characterisation, suggesting a sluttishness almost sanctified by her capacity for love. Zednik's steely-toned, neurotic Captain becomes unusually sinister, a sort of hellish Laurel to the late Aage Haugland's Hardy. Adolf Dresen, sometimes a dull producer, here creates a quite effective world whose derelict interiors and expansively desolate marshlands reflect its alienation of human feeling. Sliding sets keep the short scenes moving crisply, but lowering the curtain during interludes leaves Brian Large's excellent visual direction with only conductor and orchestra, to the detriment of tension. Striking and involving none the less.

Additional recommendation

Wozzeck
Falkman Wozzeck **Dalayman** Marie **Qvale** Captain
Swedish Opera Chorus & Orchestra / Segerstam
Naxos ② 8 660076/7 (100' · DDD)   Ⓢ▷

A few minor quibbles apart – both the Captain and the Doctor are portrayed as being more 'normal' than usual, and the orchestral balance is a little skewed in places – this is close to being a giant among *Wozzeck* recordings.

Luciano Berio
Italian 1925-2003

Berio studied with his father and grandfather, both organists and composers, and with Ghedini at the Milan Conservatory in the late 1940s. In 1950 he married the American singer Cathy Berberian, and the next year at Tanglewood he met Dallapiccola, who influenced his move towards and beyond 12-note serialism in such works as his Joyce cycle Chamber Music for voice and trio (1953). Further stimulus came from his meetings with Maderna, Pousseur and Stockhausen in Basle in 1954, and he became a central member of the Darmstadt circle. He directed an electronic music studio at the Milan station of Italian radio (1955-61), at the same time producing Sequenza I for flute (1958, the first of a cycle of solo explorations of performing gestures), Circles (1960, a loop of *Cummings settings for voice, harp and percussion) and* Epifanie *(1961, an aleatory set of orchestral and vocal movements designed to show different kinds of vocal behaviour). These established his area of interest: with the means and archetypes of musical communication.*

For most of the next decade he was in the USA, teaching and composing, his main works of this period including the Dante-esque Laborintus II for voices and orchestra (1965), the Sinfonia for similar resources (1969, with a central movement whirling quotations round Mahler and Beckett) and Opera (1970), a study of the decline of the genre and of Western bourgeois civilisation. Two more operas, La vera storia (1982) and Un re in ascolto (1984), came out of his collaboration with Calvino. Other works include Coro (1976), a panoply of poster statements and refracted folksongs for chorus and orchestra, and numerous orchestral and chamber pieces.

GROVEmusic

Sinfonia

Sinfonia. Eindrücke
Regis Pasquier vn **New Swingle Singers; French National Orchestra / Pierre Boulez**
Erato 2564-69707-5 (45' · DDD)   Ⓢ●

This was the first complete recording of Berio's *Sinfonia*. Previously this absorbing and bewilderingly complex work was available only in the four-movement version that Berio himself prepared in 1969 for the first performance with the Swingle Singers and the New York Philharmonic Orchestra. Within a few months, he'd completed a fifth and final movement which, though ostensibly an appendix, arguably stands as the apotheosis of the entire work; for it's genuinely a 'sounding together' (sinfonia) of the preceding movements, a rich sequence of reminiscences, just as the celebrated third movement leads us through memories of the standard orchestral repertoire in a kind of stream of subconsciousness. To hear the work in its completed form is a revelation, and for this reason alone Boulez's performance must be said to supersede Berio's own. To complete the disc he chose one of Berio's less-familiar orchestral works, *Eindrücke* ('Impressions', 1973-4). This is a complete contrast: a vast monody, projected by the string orchestra against the stuttering interjections and lingering trills of the wind and percussion, a stark and uncompromising conception. Again, the reading is a powerful one. This is a most important issue, far too good to miss.

Chamber Works

Notturno. Quartetto. Sincronie. Glosse
Arditti Quartet (Irvine Arditti, Graeme Jennings vns
Dov Scheindlin va Rohan de Saram vc)
Naïve Montaigne MO782155 (62' · DDD)   Ⓕ

Berio's music for string quartet, if hardly central to his composing life, contains much that's characteristic and impressive. The two pairs of compositions are separated by a 30-year gap, yet it's fascinating to hear how clearly *Sincronie* (1963-4) anticipates the manner of *Notturno* (1993) in the wide range of its materials, from simple to complex, and the skill with which a large-scale single-movement structure is balanced and sustained. *Sincronie* and *Notturno* give us Berio at his best. Just as *Sincronie* uses its initial perception about the homogeneity of the four string instruments as the starting point for an enthrallingly spontaneous journey which never loses its sense of direction, so *Notturno* ventures well beyond the connotations of tranquil repose into the kind of dark, concentrated volatility which Berio has made his own. *Notturno* was recorded some years ago by the Alban Berg Quartet (EMI), the Arditti's all-Berio programme is more persuasive. These new performances are no less persuasive, bringing the music to fascinating life, with the help of a recording that's well-nigh ideal.

Stanze

Stanze[a] **Schubert/Berio** Rendering
[a]**Dietrich Henschel** bar [a]**French Army Chorus;
Orchestre de Paris / Christoph Eschenbach**
Ondine ODE1059-2 (64' · DDD · T/t)
[a]Recorded live 2004   (F)(→)

Stanze, a sequence of five songs for baritone, male chorus and orchestra, was Berio's last completed work, premiered after his death in 2003. Though the title is Italian – and means 'rooms', not 'verses', indicating the distinct character of each individual movement – only the texts for movements two and three are in that language. The third movement sets an English version of a whimsical poem by Alfred Brendel and the outer movements are both to German texts – the first Paul Celan's *Tenebrae*, the last translated from the Hebrew of Dan Pagis.

The movements are indeed diverse and it could be that, after hearing them, Berio would have had second thoughts, if not about the order then about some details of the balance between voice and orchestra. Even the admirable Dietrich Henschel has difficulty adhering to the dynamics as marked in the score – perhaps he should have been more forwardly balanced. But this is a live recording of the premiere. Given the work's importance, it's a pity that it couldn't have been taken into the studio and worked on more intensively. Yet this Ondine release captures the emotional power of a special occasion, all five movements coloured by the brooding atmosphere established at the outset in Celan's great threnody.

Christoph Eschenbach has recorded *Rendering* before and although his new reading of Berio's idiosyncratic filling-out of the sketches for Schubert's Tenth Symphony is excellent in its way, it seems a pity that a different and more substantial orchestral work, not otherwise available, couldn't have been included instead.

Folk Songs

Berio Recital I for Cathy[a]. 11 Folk Songs[b] **Weill** (arr Berio. Sung in English) Die Dreigroschenoper – Ballade von der sexuellen Hörigkeit. Marie Galante – Le grand Lustucru. Happy End – Surabaya-Johnny
Cathy Berberian *mez* [a]**London Sinfonietta;**
[b]**Juilliard Ensemble / Luciano Berio**
RCA Victor Gold Seal 09026 62540-2 (65' · ADD · T)
Recorded 1972.   (M)(O)(O)

These are classic recordings that no contemporary music enthusiast or Berberian/Berio admirer will want to be without. This disc could be regarded as a fitting tribute to Cathy Berberian and her inimitable vocal genius. As an artist she was unique. As a champion of contemporary music (particularly that of Berio, her ex-husband) she was second to none – not only for her interpretative prowess but also the inspirational quality of her highly individual style. These pieces were all composed, or arranged for her, by Berio. *Recital I for Cathy* makes use of Berberian's dramatic training in a composition in which the vocalist, frustrated by the non-appearance of her pianist, struggles through the programme while sharing a Beckett-like stream-of-consciousness monologue with her audience. her performance here is a monumental *tour de force*. Another example of the extraordinary qualities of Berberian's voice can be found in the celebrated *Folk Songs* of 1964. The three Weill songs reveal Berberian as a natural interpreter of his music (perhaps the best since Lotte Lenya). A wonderful tribute to a phenomenal talent.

Additional recommendations:

Berio Folk Songs[a]
Coupled with: **Golijov** Ayre[b]
Upshaw *sop* [a]**O'Connor** *fl* [a]**Palmer** *cl* [a]**Gottlieb,**
[a]**Poland** *perc* [a]**Ljova** *va* [a]**Friedlander** *vc* [a]**Kibbey** *hp*
[b]**Andalucian Dogs**
DG download *477 5414GH* (62' · DDD · T/t   (F)(O)(O)(→)
Dawn Upshaw taps into the core of each song with an intensity and abandon that is likely to astonish many listeners. She is less playful than Berberian but she is in some ways more expressive, and her deeply felt interpretation offers its own joys and revelations. (Not universally listed on CD.)

Sequenzas – I-VIII, IXa, IXb & X-XIII, 'Chanson'
Castellani *sop* **Cherrier** *fl* **Hadady** *ob* **Damiens** *cl*
Gallois *bn* **Wirth** *alto sax* **Cassone** *tpt* **Sluchin** *tbn*
Conquer *vn* **Desjardins** *va* **Cambreling** *hp* **Fisk** *gtr*
Boffard *pf* **Anzellotti** *accordion*
DG (3) download *457 038-2GH3* (158' · DDD)
                                                  (F)(O)(O)(O)(→)
Berio's sequence of solo compositions complements his larger-scale vocal and orchestral works in various productive ways. These discs are a definitive document and a wonderful reminder of why Berio's music matters. (Not available on CD in all countries, but always downloadable.)

Lennox Berkeley
British 1903-1989

Berkeley studied at Oxford and with Boulanger in Paris (1927-32), where he met Stravinsky and became friendly with Poulenc. In 1928 he became a Roman Catholic. Back in London he worked for the BBC (1942-5) and taught at the RAM (1946-68). His official Op 1 dates from after he was 30, but his output is large, including a full-length opera (Nelson, 1954), three one-acters (including the comedy A Dinner Engagement, 1954), four symphonies, sacred music (Missa brevis with organ, 1960), songs (Four Poems of St Teresa of Avila for contralto and strings, 1947; Five Auden Poems with piano, 1958), chamber and piano music. The earlier music looks towards Paris, with its suave neo-classicism, though his acquaintance with the young Britten was also important. In the 1960s his work became more complex and darker, including elements of 12-note serialism. GROVEmusic

String Quartets

String Quartets Nos 1-3
Maggini Quartet (Lorraine McAslan, David Angel vns Martin Outram va Michal Kaznowski vc)
Naxos 8 570415 (63' · DDD)　　　　Ⓢ▶

The Maggini turn their attention to Sir Lennox Berkeley, giving us all three of these landmarks in 20th-century British chamber music with the first recordings of Nos 1 and 3.

The First, the longest of the three, is a revelation. Virtually unknown, it has usually been regarded as just an early work from 1935. Nothing could be more wrong since it's teeming with ideas and ingenious string quartet textures. There are plenty of Berkeley fingerprints, such as the regular pulse of the second movement supporting diatonic melodies in counterpoint; the high spirits of the *Scherzo*; and the final theme and variations, which anticipates examples later in the Two-Piano Concerto and the Violin and Piano Sonatina.

The Second (1942) has an eloquent slow movement in what the composer called free form is a fine example of Berkeley's completely individual melodic and harmonic style. By the time of No 3 (1970) Berkeley was in his slightly tougher, final phase. But it is recognisably the same composer and his spiritual roots emerge in the connections between a simple setting of *Hail, Holy Queen* and the slow movement.

These performances are simply magnificent. Clean and immediate sound, perhaps slightly shrill. But the main thing is that at last these outstanding chamber works are available. A legacy comparable to Britten's? See what you think – at a bargain price.

Additional recommendation

String Quartet No 2
Coupled with: **M Berkeley** Abstract Mirror[a].

Magnetic Field
Chilingirian Quartet with [a]**Thomas Carroll** vc
Chandos CHAN10364 (55' · DDD)　　　　Ⓕ

A fine performance coupled with two pieces by Berkeley's son, Michael. *Magnetic Field* of 1995 explores, *à la* Purcell, a single middle-register F and in the quintet *Abstract Mirror* there's a special richness about the two cellos.

Choral music

Missa brevis, Op 57[ae]. A Festival Anthem, Op 21 No 2[cde]. Three Latin Motets, Op 83 No 1. Magnificat and Nunc Dimittis, Op 99[be]. Crux Fidelis, Op 43[d] No 1. Three Pieces, Op 72 – No 1, Toccata[e]. Look up sweet Babe, Op 43 No 2[ce]. The Lord is my Shepherd, Op 91 No 1[be]
[a]**Julian Gregory**, [b]**Benjamin Durrant**, [c]**James Geidt** trebs [d]**Allan Clayton** ten [e]**Johnny Vaughan** org
St John's College Choir, Cambridge / Christopher Robinson
Naxos 8 557277 (75' · DDD)　　　　Ⓢ▶

Lennox Berkeley's church music has now entered the cathedral lists – both Anglican and Roman – to an extent unthinkable even 10 years ago. He was a pious Catholic, and much of his music is rooted in his deep spiritual convictions His personal kind of melody and harmony sounds like nobody else. This is particularly evident in the most familiar of his religious works here – the 1960 *Missa Brevis* for Westminster Cathedral, which Britten much admired, and *The Lord is my shepherd* for Chichester. Just as typical are *Look up sweet babe* and the ecstatic George Herbert setting which forms the central section of the expansive *Festival Anthem*. Once heard, these tunes are difficult to forget.

The Mass for five voices and Three Latin Motets, written for this choir in 1972, are more austere but, like the eloquent sacred works of his friend Poulenc, they clearly come from the same imagination as the composer's other works. And quite late in life Berkeley boldly brings the discoveries of his more advanced later music into the *Magnificat* and *Nunc Dimittis*.

This is an impressive collection which merits repeated hearings. The choir sounds well and boasts fine soloists.

Operas

A Dinner Engagement
Roderick Williams bar Earl of Dunmow **Yvonne Kenny** sop Countess of Dunmow **Claire Rutter** sop Susan **Jean Rigby** mez Mrs Kneebone **Anne Collins** mez HRH The Grand Duchess of Monteblanco **Robin Leggate** ten HRH Prince Philippe **Blake Fischer** ten Errand Boy **City of London Sinfonia / Richard Hickox**
Chandos CHAN10219 (60' · DDD · N/T)　　　　ⒻⒶ

A Dinner Engagement (Aldeburgh, 1954) was written for Britten's English Opera Group, suited their resources and philosophy admirably and was much admired by Britten himself. This jewel of a one-act comic opera has somehow escaped the record catalogue for half a century.

The period is that of British kitchen-sink theatre in the 1950s; however, this kitchen is an aristocratic one. Lord and Lady Dunmow, living in desperately reduced circumstances, have invited the Grand Duchess of Monteblanco to dinner. The Dunmows ardently hope that the Duchess's batchelor son, Prince Philippe, might be interested in their daughter Susan. Paul Dehn's libretto abounds in amusing incidents *en route* to a happy ending. The layout of the opera is an impeccable blend of aria and recitative; the scoring is colourful and effective; and the piece is full of memorable tunes.

Anne Collins as the Duchess is magnificent; Claire Rutter as Susan is enchanting; Robin Leggate makes a mellifluously charming Prince. This is an all-star cast, and the Mozartian ensembles are scintillating. Once again enormous credit to Richard Hickox, whose total understanding of Berkeley's music gives him unrivalled authority in this long-delayed début. Well recorded, too.

Ruth

Jean Rigby *mez* Ruth **Mark Tucker** *ten* Boaz **Yvonne Kenny** *sop* Naomi **Clare Rutter** *sop*
Orpah **Roderick Williams** *bar* Head Reaper **Joyful Company of Singers; City of London Sinfonia / Richard Hickox**
Chandos CHAN10301 (79' · DDD · S/T/N)   Ⓕ

Much has changed for Lennox Berkeley on disc in the past couple of years thanks to the superb advocacy of Richard Hickox. When *A Dinner Engagement* was released (see above) we wondered how this scintillating jewel of a comic opera could have escaped the catalogue for 50 years. Now *Ruth* – just as fine – shows the religious side of Berkeley, stemming from his *Four Teresa of Avila Poems* written nine years earlier.

Ruth is based on the biblical story and was adapted by Eric Crozier. At the opening of the first of the three scenes, Naomi is returning dejected to her homeland with her two daughters-in-law after all have lost their husbands. Ruth stays to support Naomi; after some resistance to Ruth as a foreigner, the workers on the estate of Boaz, a distant kinsman, are persuaded to allow her to work with them. The climax comes in the last scene, in which Ruth, urged by Naomi, cautiously offers herself to Boaz in marriage. He accepts her, announces his decision to the people, and all ends with rejoicing.

Every detail of this touching story is depicted with typical Berkeley finesse; the set-piece arias are precisely focused and memorable, and the scoring is masterly. Hickox's pacing is consistently right. Jean Rigby as Ruth is charming but firm in resolve when needed and Yvonne Kenny is a dignified and vocally imposing Naomi. Much of the drama is carried by these two women but all the roles are well cast and effec-

tive. There are plenty of lively choruses for the reapers, projected with panache.

Hector Berlioz   French 1803-1869

As a boy Berlioz learnt the flute, guitar and, from treatises alone, harmony (he never studied the piano); his first compositions were romances and small chamber pieces. After two unhappy years as a medical student in Paris (1821-3) he abandoned the career chosen for him by his father and turned decisively to music, attending Le Sueur's composition class at the Conservatoire. He entered for the Prix de Rome four times (1827-30) and finally won. Among the most powerful influences on him were Shakespeare, whose plays were to inspire three major works, and the actress Harriet Smithson, whom he idolised, pursued and, after a bizarre courtship, eventually married (1833). Beethoven's symphonies too made a strong impact, along with Goethe's Faust and the works of Moore, Scott and Byron. The most important product of this time was his startlingly original, five-movement Symphonie fantastique (1830).

Berlioz's 15 months in Italy (1831-2) were significant more for his absorption of warmth, vivacity and local colour than for the official works he wrote there; he moved out of Rome as often as possible and worked on a sequel to the Symphonie fantastique (Le retour à la vie, renamed Lélio in 1855) and overtures to King Lear and Rob Roy, returning to Paris early to promote his music. Although the 1830s and early 1840s saw a flow of major compositions – Harold en Italie, Benvenuto Cellini, Grande messe des morts, Roméo et Juliette, Grande symphonie funèbre et triomphale, Les nuits d'été – his musical career was now essentially a tragic one. He failed to win much recognition, his works were considered eccentric or 'incorrect' and he had reluctantly to rely on journalism for a living; from 1834 he wrote chiefly for the and the Gazette musicale and the Journal des débats .

As the discouragements of Paris increased, however, performances and recognition abroad beckoned: between 1842 and 1863 Berlioz spent most of his time touring, in Germany, Austria, Russia, England and elsewhere. Hailed as an advanced composer, he also became known as a leading modern conductor. He produced literary works (notably the Mémoires) and another series of musical masterpieces – La damnation de Faust, the Te Deum, L'enfance du Christ, the vast epic Les troyens (1856-8; partly performed, 1863) and Béatrice et Bénédict (1860-62) – meanwhile enjoying happy if short-lived relationships with Liszt and Wagner. The loss of his father, his son Louis (1834-67), two wives, two sisters and friends merely accentuated the weary decline of his last years, marked by his spiritual isolation from Parisian taste and the new music of Germany alike.

A lofty idealist with a leaping imagination, Berlioz was subject to violent emotional changes from enthusiasm to misery; only his sharp wit saved him from morbid self-pity over the disappointments in his private and professional life. The intensity of the personality is inextricably woven into the music: all his works reflect something in himself expressed through poetry, literature, religion or drama. Sincere expression is the key – matching means to expressive ends, often to the point of mixing forms and media, ignoring pre-set schemes. In Les troyens, his grand opera on Virgil's Aeneid, for example, aspects of the monumental and the intimate, the symphonic and the operatic, the decorative and the solemn converge. Similarly his symphonies, from the explicitly dramatic Symphonie fantastique with its idée fixe (the theme representing his beloved, changed and distorted in line with the work's scenario), to the picturesque Harold en Italie with its concerto element, to the operatic choral symphony cum tone poem Roméo et Juliette, are all characteristic in their mixture of genres. Of his other orchestral works, the overture Le carnaval romain stands out as one of the most extrovert and brilliant. Among the choral works, Faust and L'enfance du Christ combine dramatic action and philosophic reflection, while the Requiem and Te Deum exploit to the full Berlioz's most spacious, ceremonial style.

Though Berlioz's compositional style has long been considered idiosyncratic, it can be seen to rely on an abundance of both technique and inspiration. Typical are expansive melodies of irregular phrase length, sometimes with a slight chromatic inflection, and expressive though not tonally adventurous harmonies. Freely contrapuntal textures predominate, used to a variety of fine effects including superimposition of separate themes; a striking boldness in rhythmic articulation gives the music much of its vitality. Berlioz left perhaps his most indelible mark as an orchestrator, finding innumerable and subtle ways to combine and contrast instruments (both on stage and off), effectively emancipating the procedure of orchestration for generations of later composers. As a critic he admired above all Gluck and Beethoven, expressed doubt about Wagner and fought endlessly against the second-rate.   GROVEmusic

Symphonie fantastique, Op 14

Symphonie fantastique. Béatrice et Bénédict – Overture
London Symphony Orchestra / Sir Colin Davis
LSO Live LSO0007CD (65' · DDD)   ⓢⓞⓞ🅑

This LSO performance of the *Symphonie fantastique* is in many ways the subtlest of Davis's four accounts to date, conveying more mystery, with *pianissimos* of extreme delicacy beautifully caught. There's an overall gain, too, from having a live recording of a work with such an individual structure, with its hesitations and pauses. In overall timings it's marginally longer than earlier versions, maybe also reflecting the conditions of a live performance, even though some of this must have been put together from rehearsal tapes as there's no applause at the end.

The *Béatrice et Bénédict* Overture is taken from the complete recording of the opera on the same label, and makes both a welcome bonus and a tempting sampler. Though the disc comes at super-budget price, it offers splendid notes by David Cairns, author of the definitive, prize-winning biography of the composer.

Berlioz Symphonie fantastique **Mozart** Symphony No 35, 'Haffner', K385 **Sibelius** Finlandia
Philharmonia Orchestra / Charles Dutoit
Decca Concerts   Ⓜ🅑·only
Recorded live 2006

Historically informed performances really are 'informing' the most conventional of Romantic symphony concerts. Even 10 years ago would the *Andante* of Mozart's *Haffner*, given here with conventional, albeit reduced forces, have moved on at this light, swift tread, woodwinds at the back of the orchestra rightly given parity with the string band. In the opening *Allegro*, too, the winds rightly have their say as the main motivators of rhythmic interest. This reading makes a subtle contrast to the 19th-century weight at either end of the programme. *Finlandia* also goes well – alert, not as gloomy and raspy as some, a tone-poem rather than nationalistic stomping.

The Berlioz, too, has picked up some period sonorities. Dutoit finds more drama in the tricky opening movement (and its exposition repeat) than he did in his perfect but prim Montreal recording (Decca), and plays the Ball scene as a story rather than a mere dance movement. His cor anglais and oboe soloists have taken on some French tang and really act out in sound the parts of Romeo and Juliet (or Hector and Harriet) in the country. The Scaffold begins with promising roughness in the brass but, on the whole, these last two movements feel too beautiful, too purely symphonic: no nasty slithering basses nor eardrum-damaging winds in this Witches' Sabbath.

Closely recorded but with real presence, this is a concert to be appreciated as an effective programme in itself, rather than to be matched off against comparative recordings.

Symphonie fantastique
RAI Symphony Orchestra, Turin / Sergiu Celibidache
Opus Arte 📀 OA0977D
(58' · NTSC · 4:3 black & white · PCM mono · 0)   Ⓕ

1969 is long enough ago in the history of sound and vision to feel primitive compared to today's technology, but Opus Arte has buffed up this black-and-white Italian TV original to some purpose. As has Maestro Celibidache Turin's RAI orchestra, whose every section shows off the care of his characteristically detailed rehearsal. It translates into a reading whose tempi and dynamics have been tailored with the care of a wonderful listener to the band and the hall at hand.

This *Fantastique* is not an especially dramatic or grandstanding performance – only the final pages of the 'Witches' Round' put the players

BERLIOZ'S SYMPHONIE FANTASTIQUE – IN BRIEF

Lamoureux Orchestra / Igor Markevitch
DG 447 406-2GOR (71' · ADD)   Ⓜ▷
Of the many recordings with French orchestras, Igor Markevitch's extraordinarily characterful 1961 version with is perhaps the most tangily idiomatic. A bonus is the remarkably undated sound.

French National Radio Orchestra / Sir Thomas Beecham   Ⓗ
EMI 567971-2 (75' · ADD)   Ⓜ
Sir Thomas at his inimitable best: an elegant and exciting interpretation, full of panache. Beecham's thrilling 1958 *Le corsaire* with the RPO provides a cherishable bonus.

Mahler CO / Marc Minkowski
DG download *474 209-2GH* (81' · DDD)   Ⓕ▷
A daring and characterful *Symphonie fantastique* that blends period sensibility with the bite of modern instruments. His approach makes the drama of the work more daring than usual, even though he inclines towards slower speeds en route. Well worth hearing…

ORR / Sir John Eliot Gardiner
Philips download *434 402-2PH* (53' · DDD)   Ⓕ●▷
Gardiner brings out the daring originality of Berlioz's visionary inspiration and draws hugely spirited, yet refined playing from his period-instrument band. Exemplary sound and balance, too.

Hallé Orchestra / Sir John Barbirolli   Ⓗ
Dutton CDEA5504 (69' · ADD)   Ⓑ
Dating from 1947, a splendidly combustible reading from this magnetic partnership. Barbirolli had a particular affection for this score, and it shows.

London Symphony Orchestra / Sir Colin Davis
LSO Live LSO0007CD (65' · DDD)   Ⓢ●●▷
The *Symphonie fantastique* has long been a Davis speciality. Captured live at the Barbican in September 2000, this is Sir Colin's fourth recording of it and arguably his most masterly yet.

Philharmonia Orchestra / Charles Dutoit
Decca Concerts Download only   ▷
Less suave than his Montreal performance, Dutoit find more bite and excitement in this download-only Decca Concert. Doesn't oust the Davis performances, but it is elegant and Gallic none the less.

RAI SO, Turin / Sergiu Celibidache
Opus Arte 📀 OA0977D (58' · NTSC · 0)   Ⓕ
A fascinating glimpse of a master-magician at work. Filmed in black and white this is gem of observation as Celibidache creates an elegant performance of Berlioz's symphony.

under stress. But it is one where everyone has time and space to play with comfort and expression, to live fully in the rits of Celibidache's graceful, rather miniaturist waltz, to enjoy the pulsing, guitar-like accompaniments as the *idée fixe* gets under way for the first time in 'Passions', or to dig in with force (but never crudity) to a serious, steady 'March to the Scaffold'.

As an interpretation though per se this performance remains, intentionally perhaps, on the page, with the notes and the music viewed through an essentially 20th-century brain, as played smoothly by a 'modern' orchestra. Celibidache is totally uninterested in the dirtiness of some of Berlioz's bass and brass writing, or the Weber-like shrieks of the high wind, or the orchestral opera going on within the symphony.

A stylish, detailed note by Misha Donat and sensitive work by RAI's camera director – following the score's high-points without indulging in visual ping-pong – add to the value of a release that promises to be the first of a series.

Additional recommednations

Symphonie fantastique   Ⓟ
ORR / Gardiner
Philips download *434 402-2PH* (53' · DDD)   Ⓕ●▷
Endless fascination and enjoyment here! A period instrument performanve to set beside other well-loved interpretations with a modern orchestra. Worth trying to track down a CD, or downloading.

Symphonie fantastique.
Coupled with: Herminie[a].
[a]**Legay** sop **Les Musiciens du Louvre; Mahler CO / Minkowski**
DG download *474 209-2GH* (81' . DDD)   Ⓕ▷

Recorded live, this characterful version breaks new ground in bringing together the talented performers of the Mahler CO, using modern instruments, and wind-players from Minkowski's period orchestra, Les Musiciens du Louvre. Some listeners will find themselves jumping up to change volume levels, such is the dynamic range of DG's all-embracing recording. (Restricted availability on CD.)

Harold in Italy, Op 16

Harold en Italie. Les troyens – Ballet Music
Tabea Zimmermann *va* **London Symphony Orchestra / Sir Colin Davis**
LSO Live LSO0040 (52' · DDD)   Ⓢ●▷

Yet again Sir Colin Davis demonstrates his mastery as a Berlioz interpreter. It's fascinating to compare this latest version of *Harold en Italie* with his 1975 Philips version with Nobuko Imai as soloist, and the 1962 HMV one, no longer available, with Yehudi Menuhin.

Most noticeable is the extra tautness of Davis's interpretation, with speeds consistently faster, sometimes markedly so. The textures are sparer, sharper and lighter, bringing an extra incisiveness all round. The soloist, the magnificent Tabea Zimmermann, is balanced as part of the orchestra instead of being spotlit. The beauty of her tone, with its nut-brown colours on the C-string, is never masked, but at the other end of the spectrum the balance allows *pianissimo*s of a delicacy never achieved by the excellent Nobuko Imai, even though she may well have been playing just as quietly, or by the relaxed and rich-toned Menuhin, who prefers lyrical expansion to urgency.

The fierceness of the *Allegro*s, with their quirky bursts of high dynamic contrasts, is enhanced on the new disc. The first movement, 'Harold in the Mountains', is markedly faster and tauter this time (some 2'30" shorter than with Menuhin), and the more flowing speed for the second movement, 'Pilgrims' March', establishes the feeling of a procession, with the surprisingly gentle dynamic markings meticulously observed. Though the third movement 'Serenade' the skipping rhythms are infectious, with dotted rhythms sparklingly pointed by the oboists at the start, and the 'Brigands' Orgy' of the finale clearly gains in dramatic flair from the extra incisiveness.

The Ballet Music, taken from Davis's prize-winning LSO Live version of *Les troyens* makes an atmospheric bonus.

Harold in Italy. Le corsaire – Overture. ⊞
King Lear – Overture[a]. Trojan March
Frederick Riddle *va* **Royal Philharmonic Orchestra;**
[a]**BBC Symphony Orchestra / Sir Thomas Beecham**
BBC Legends/IMG Artists mono BBCL4065-2
(72' · ADD) Recorded live [a]1956, [b]1951,[c]1954, [d]1951
Ⓜ 🟠🟠

These radio recordings of Beecham in full flight could not be more welcome. The mono sound is limited but beefy and immediate, with fine transfers by Paul Baily, even though the opening *Corsaire* Overture is taken from an acetate disc, not a tape. What above all hits you hard from first to last is that Beecham in such live performances of Berlioz conveyed a manic intensity, a red-blooded thrust that brings out to the full the characterful wildness in this ever-original composer, making almost any rival seem cool.

So, the *Corsaire* Overture has a fierceness and thrust entirely apt to the Byronic subject, culminating in a swaggering climax that verges on the frenetic. It will have you laughing with joy. You find a similar approach in Beecham's studio performances of this overture, but this is even more uninhibited in its excitement. *King Lear* – with the BBC Symphony Orchestra, not the RPO – surges with warmth in the lyrical first half, before similarly building excitement in the *Allegro*.

Harold in Italy, recorded in 1956 in the dry acoustic of the Usher Hall, Edinburgh, with the dynamic range compressed so as to magnify *pianissimo*s, as at the very start, is specially valuable for having as soloist Beecham's chosen leader of his viola section, Frederick Riddle. It was Riddle who

made the first recording of the Walton Viola Concerto in 1937 with the composer conducting, arguably still the finest ever interpretation, and here his expressive warmth and responsiveness to Beecham's volatile inspiration make up for the sort of intonation problems that the viola at that period always seemed to invite, even with players of this calibre. The pauseful tenderness of the *Adagio* section just after the start of the finale, is similarly magnetic, thanks to both conductor and soloist, bringing out the parallel in the review of themes with the finale of Beethoven's Ninth. The *Trojan March* makes a swaggering encore, a performance the more electrifying for being recorded at the opening concert of the Colston Hall in Bristol in 1951.

Overtures

Overtures – Les francs-juges, Op 3. Waverley, Op 1.
King Lear, Op 4. Le carnaval romain, Op 9. Béatrice
et Bénédict. Le corsaire, Op 21. Benvenuto Cellini
Staatskapelle Dresden / Sir Colin Davis
RCA Victor Red Seal 09026 68790-2 (74' · DDD)Ⓕ🟠🟠

Berlioz's seven overtures fit comfortably into an hour and a quarter, in performances that reflect Sir Colin's long absorption with music that remains difficult, original, surprising. The most extrovert, the Ball Scene in *Le carnaval romain*, is exhilaratingly played, but done so without the strenuous attempts after excitement at all costs, through speed and volume, which are all too familiar. The music is more interesting than that, its tensions more dramatic. What are perhaps the two hardest overtures to play successfully, *Waverley* and *King Lear*, benefit from some understatement, especially in the quieter sections when, particularly in *Lear*, a sense of trouble animates the music. As elsewhere, Berlioz's melodies made out of awkward rhythms and uneven metres call for a skilled hand: nowhere is this more evident than at the opening of *Benvenuto Cellini*, whose oddity doesn't immediately strike the listener but whose 'rightness' is proved by its wonderful verve. Davis handles this superbly, as in different vein he does the soft music answering the opening of *Le carnaval romain*, in which he's given some beautiful playing (especially from the cor anglais) by the Dresden orchestra. It responds to his understanding of the different levels of tension and expression, as well as different dynamic levels, at which Berlioz can make his effects, such as at the start of *Les francs-juges*. Sometimes a slight emphasis in the accompaniment, even the touch of warmth on a single note, can illuminate much in the melody. It's all beautifully done.

Benvenuto Cellini – Overture. Le carnaval romain.
Le corsaire. Béatrice et Bénédict – Overture.
Harold en Italie[a]
[a]**William Primrose** *va* **Boston Symphony Orchestra
/ Charles Munch** ⊞
RCA 88888 01525-3 (65' · ADD) Recorded 1955-62 Ⓜ

Benvenuto Cellini – Overture. Le carnaval romain.
Le corsaire. Béatrice et Bénédict – Overture.
Les troyens – Chasse royale et orage. Roméo et
Juliette – Queen Mab Scherzo. Le rouet d'Omphale
Boston Symphony Orchestra / Charles Munch
RCA 09026 61400-2 (57' · ADD) Recorded 1955-62 Ⓜ

Munch's Berlioz is something to cherish. *Harold
in Italy* is played with wonderful style, poetry
and elegance by William Primrose at the heart
of this still fine-sounding programme. As for the
overtures, the performances are electric with
energy, and dispatched with an élan that's at
once French in spirit but emphatically transatlantic in execution. The alternative coupling
replaces *Harold* with some equally enticing
orchestral 'bleeding chunks'.

Additional recommendation

Overtures: Le carnaval romain. Le corsaire. Les   Ⓗ
francs-juges. King Lear. Les Troyens – Act 3 Prelude;
March. Waverley
RPO / Beecham
Sony Classical SMK89807 (69' · ADD) Recorded 1950s
                                                    Ⓜ
Astonishing performances. All are played with a
wonderful shaping of phrases and with a fiery
attack and zest that are utterly satisfying.

Roméo et Juliette, Op 17

Roméo et Juliette
Daniela Barcellona *mez* **Kenneth Tarver** *ten* **Orlin
Anastassov** *bass* **London Symphony Chorus and
Orchestra / Sir Colin Davis**
LSO Live LSO0003CD (99' · DDD)   ⓈⓄⓄ➟

This recording of Berlioz's masterpiece builds
in important ways on what Sir Colin has revealed
to us in his two previous versions, both for
Philips, and preserves what by any reckoning
was an electrifying event at the Barbican. The
recording was edited from two separate concerts, so ironing out irritating flaws of the
moment, while offering the extra dramatic
thrust of a live performance. That's most strikingly illustrated in the concluding chorus, a passage that has often been felt to let the rest of the
work down, but which here provides an incandescent climax, silencing any doubts. That said,
the differences between this live recording and
Davis's two studio ones are less a question of
interpretation than of recording balance and
quality. Davis's view of the work has remained
fundamentally unchanged, though his speeds at
the Barbican are marginally broader until the
concluding sections from Juliet's funeral
onwards, which now flow more easily. The live
recording may not match in opulence either the
1993 one with the Vienna Philharmonic or the
1968 one with the LSO, for the Barbican acoustic is drier. Yet the refinement of the sound this
time, with orchestra and chorus set at a slight
distance, brings *pianissimos* of breathtaking deli-

cacy, focused in fine detail. Not only the Love
scene but the choral recitatives gain greatly from
that, as does the lovely passage before the Love
scene where the Capulets return home after the
party. The three young soloists are first-rate,
characterising strongly. A fine modern recording at such a reasonable price.

Grande messe des morts, Op 5

Grande messe des morts, Op 5[a]. Te Deum, Op 22[b]
[a]**Ronald Dowd**, [b]**Franco Tagliavini** *tens* [b]**Nicolas
Kynaston** *org* **Wandsworth School Boys' Choir;
London Symphony Chorus and Orchestra /
Sir Colin Davis**
Philips 50 Great Recordings ② 464 689-2PM2
(144' · ADD · T/t) Recorded 1969.   ⓂⓄⓄ

The similarities between these two great choral
works – the monumental style and blend of austerity and brilliance – make them an ideal coupling. Both are tremendous sonic showpieces,
and although Sir Colin Davis's Berlioz cycle
dates back over 30 years, the performances
remain among the front runners.
  The key is Davis's ability to concentrate on the
inner meaning of the music, rather than its outward effects. In the *Grande messe des morts*, conductors as various as Maazel, Levine and Ozawa
have failed to see any more than generalised
beauty and grandeur, but Davis is always alive to
the specific emotion of the moment, whether it's
the pleading of the 'Quaerens me' or the angular
pain of the 'Lacrymosa'. His chorus is stretched,
especially in the underweight tenor section
(Berlioz prescribes 60 tenors, adding helpfully
that the numbers may be doubled or tripled if
space permits) and Ronald Dowd isn't entirely
comfortable in the solo part of the 'Sanctus'. But
in all other respects this is a high-quality performance of vision and imagination.
  The splendid *Te Deum* is given a performance
of comparable virtues, and Philips' natural
sound stands up well to recent competition.

Grande Messe des morts, Op 5
Keith Ikaia-Purdy *ten* **Saxon State Opera Choir;
Dresden Symphony Chorus; Dresden
Singakademie; Staatskapelle Dresden /
Sir Colin Davis**
Profil ② PH07014 (90' · DDD). Recorded live in 1994
                                              ⒻⓄ
The *Grande Messe des morts* was recorded one year
short of the 50th anniversary of the day that
dawned to reveal to Dresdeners the devastation of
their city. For many years, Dresden was not an
easy city for Englishmen to visit; but attitudes
change, and it was certainly a moving gesture for
Davis to conduct this performance. The Kreuz-
kirche has been beautifully reconstructed, and it
has beautiful acoustics that welcome Berlioz's
wide-ranging demands.
  The quieter moments fare best here: the
strange chords in the *Hostias*, with a firm trom-

bone seeming to project overtones in the flutes; the soft cor anglais and bassoon lines over cellos and basses in the *Quid sum miser*; the unaccompanied choral *Quarens me*, which the Dresden choirs sing most sensitively; the high sounds of the *Sanctus*, with Keith Ikaia-Purdy an elegant if slightly operatic tenor. The acoustic seems positively to welcome these, and it can well accommodate, though not without some loss of verbal clarity, the great clamour of the *Dies irae* and the snapping rhythms of the *Lacrymosa*, which have a cut that Davis achieves more sharply than any other conductor. This is his only recording of the work since his classic 1969 version, and his grasp of the music remains supreme.

Grande messe des morts   Ⓗ
Richard Lewis *ten* **Royal Philharmonic Chorus and Orchestra / Sir Thomas Beecham**
BBC Music Legends mono BBCL4011-2
(78' · ADD · T/t) Recorded live 1959.   Ⓜ●

Almost 60 years to the day since his first Berlioz performance, Beecham conducted the *Grande messe des morts* in the Albert Hall. Though the *Dies irae* thunders out tremendously, and the 'Lachrymosa' has a wonderful snap on the off-beat chords, it's the quieter movements that characterise what's, after all, a Requiem Mass. Beecham's response to them is with a lifetime's devotion to one of the composers who had been closest to his heart. The 'Quid sum miser' has an enchanting clarity; the long, hushed end of the 'Offertoire', as Berlioz lingers over the gently alternating notes that suffuse the invention, is finely judged; the *Sanctus* is eloquently sung by Lewis and the splendid chorus; the return of the opening 'Te decet hymnus', near the close of the whole work, is sublime. Such things aren't achieved without the attention to detail with which Beecham used to complain people did not credit him. How wrong. His orchestral parts were always covered with powerful blue pencil marks and the signature 'TB', so that it was impossible to mistake intentions which players would then shape for him in rehearsal. Here, the detail is exquisite. Occasionally he takes his own view, not Berlioz's, about phrasing; and the orchestra contains not a whiff of an ophicleide. No matter. This is a recording of a great occasion – full in recording, scarcely bothered by audience noise – but also of a marvellous performance.

Te Deum, Op 22

Te Deum
Roberto Alagna *ten* **Marie-Claire Alain** *org*
European Union and Maîtrise d'Antony Childrens Choirs; Orchestre de Paris Chorus; Orchestre de Paris / John Nelson
Virgin Classics 545449-2 (58' · DDD)   Ⓕ●◗

The Berlioz *Te Deum* has been relatively neglected on disc in comparison with his other major works. This latest version has John Nel-

son as an incisive, understanding conductor of Berlioz, revelling in the weight of choral sound, balancing his forces beautifully. He's helped here by fuller, more detailed digital sound than on previous versions.

The organ sound may be less transparent than it might be, but the authentic French timbre of the Cavaillé-Coll organ of the Madeleine in Paris blends beautifully in the ensemble, and Marie-Claire Alain, as you might expect, is the most idiomatic soloist, making her non-French rivals seem rather square by comparison. It makes for luxury casting, too, to have Roberto Alagna as an imaginative, idiomatic tenor soloist in the prayer, 'Te ergo quaesumus', warmly persuasive and full of temperament.

An additional plus-point for the new issue, even in relation to Sir Colin Davis's now classic version for Philips (see below), isn't only the fuller, more open recorded sound but the interesting bonus provided. The two extra instrumental movements included here were written by Berlioz expressly for performances celebrating victory, both with military overtones. On CD either can easily be left out, yet Berlioz, even at his most populist, never fails to grab the listener's attention.

Additional recommendation

Coupled with: Grande messe des morts
Dowd, Tagliavini *tens* **Kynaston** *org* **Wandsworth School Boys' Choir; LSO & Chor / C Davis**
Philips 50 Great Recordings ② 464 689-2PM2
(144' · ADD) Recorded 1969   Ⓜ●●◗
A classic recording and an ideal coupling: these performances remain among the front-runners, though the chorus sounds rather stretched at times. Philips' natural sound quality stands up well (reviewed opposite under *Grande messe*).

La damnation de Faust, Op 24

La damnation de Faust
Enkelejda Shkosa *mez* **Giuseppe Sabbatini** *ten* **David Wilson-Johnson** *bar* **Michele Pertusi** *bass*
London Symphony Orchestra and Chorus / Sir Colin Davis
LSO Live ② LSO0008CD (132' · DDD · T/t)   Ⓢ●●◗

This *Damnation de Faust* matches and even outshines previous sets at whatever price, not least in the gripping drama of the performance, the more intense for being recorded live. Even more than in his classic 1973 recording for Philips, Davis involves you in the painful quandry obsessing Faust, never letting tension slip for a moment.

There may be different views over Giuseppe Sabbatini's portrayal of the central character. He's more overtly emotional than any of his immediate rivals. In the heat of the moment he tends to resort to an Italianate style, with the hint of a half-sob or the occasional phrase which is only half vocalised. Purists may resist, yet with his firm, golden, finely shaded tone and his radiant treatment of the highest-lying passages the impact is intensely characterful and involving.

As for Davis, the differences between his reading here and in 1973 are ones of detail and refinement, for there's an extra lightness and resilience in the playing of the current LSO, as in Mephistopheles' Flea song, which is more wittily pointed than before. The little snarling flourishes which herald Mephistopheles' arrival have you sitting up immediately, while the excitement generated in a number such as the Trio at the end of Part 3 leaves you breathless.

Michele Pertusi as Mephistopheles matches Sabbatini in the red-blooded fervour of his singing, weighty yet agile, and Enkelejda Shkosa is a warm, vibrant Marguerite, with a flicker in the voice giving a hint of the heroine's vulnerability. Not just the LSO but the London Symphony Chorus, too, are in searing form, and the recording brings out the detail of Berlioz's orchestration with ideal transparency, though the transfer is at rather a low level, needing fair amplification for full impact. Davis is given wonderfully refined sound, with any problems from the Barbican acoustic completely eliminated. An astonishing bargain.

La damnation de Faust
Susan Graham sop **Thomas Moser** ten **José van Dam** bass-bar **Frédéric Caton** bass; **Chorus and Orchestra of Opéra de Lyon / Kent Nagano**
Erato ② 0630-10692-2 (122' · DDD · T/t) Ⓜ**O**

New versions of *Faust* appear regularly, but one as good this is rare. At its centre is a perception of Berlioz's extraordinary vision, in all its colour and variety and humour and pessimism, and the ability to realise this in a broad downward sweep while setting every detail sharply in place. It's a work about the steady failure of consolations in a romantic world rejecting God, until all Faust's sensations are numbed and Mephistopheles has him trapped in the hell of no feeling. Every stage of the progress is mercilessly depicted here. The chorus is brilliant in all its roles, offering in turn the lively charms of peasant life, raptures of faith in the Easter Hymn, beery roistering in Auerbach's Cellar that grows as foul as a drunken party, cheerful student Latin bawls; later they sing with delicacy as Mephistopheles's spirits of temptation and finally become a vicious pack of demons. Nagano takes the Hungarian March at a pace that grows hectic as the dream of military glory turns hollow. It's all brilliantly realised.

There's the same care for orchestral detail. Nagano seems to be conducting from the New Berlioz Edition score, and he uses his imagination with it. He has an unerring sense of tempo, balancing weight of tone against speed, and he can light upon the telling contrapuntal line, or point a detail of instrumental colour or even a single note (like the snarl in the Ride to the Abyss), elements that give Berlioz's marvellous orchestration its expressive quality.

José van Dam is outstanding as Mephistopheles, curling his voice round phrases with hideous elegance, relishing the mock-jollity of the Serenade and the Song of the Flea, taunting Faust with lulling sweetness on the banks of the Elbe, yet also disclosing the sadness of the fallen spirit. Thomas Moser sings gravely and reflectively as he's first discovered on the plains of Hungary, and rises nobly to the challenge of the Invocation to Nature, but is almost at his finest in the many recitative passages as he twists and turns in Mephistopheles' grasp.

Susan Graham doesn't match these two superb performances but sings her two arias simply and well. This version sets Nagano among the outstanding Berlioz conductors of the day.

La damnation de Faust
Vesselina Kasarova mez **Paul Groves** ten **Willard White** bass **Andreas Macco** bass **San Sebastian People's Choral Society; Tölz Boys' Choir; Staatskapelle Berlin / Sylvain Cambreling**
Stage directors **Alex Olle, Carlos Pedrissa**
Video director **Alexandre Tarta**
ArtHaus Musik **DVD** 100 003 (146' · DDD)   Ⓕ**OOO**

 This production was the sensation of the 1999 Salzburg Festival, and this riveting DVD captures most of the excitement that must have been felt at the time in the evocative Felsenreitschule. The staging is a joint venture. The spectacular scenic realisation of Berlioz's 'Légende dramatique' originated with the Spanish theatre troupe La Fura dels Baus; the staging itself is the work of Olle and Pedrissa. The sets and costumes were conceived by the Spanish sculptor Jaume Piensa.

The results were described in the press as 'extreme theatre' – and one can see why when viewing the virtuoso treatment of the vast stage area. It's dominated by a transparent cylinder which serves all sorts of purposes, depicting in particular the soul-searching struggles of Faust and Méphistophélès; while the complex choral movements and an elaborate lighting plot are all carried out without a hint of a hitch.

The producer certainly managed to inspire all the participants to heights of interpretative skill. Cambreling and the Berlin Staatskapelle perform with discipline and fire, wanting only that extra dedicated vision evinced by Colin Davis and the LSO on CD. Kasarova and Willard White, stage beings to their fingertips, sing and act with total conviction. Kasarova is the vulnerable, insecure, beautiful Marguerite to the life, every gesture and facial expression supporting her intense reading of the glorious music Berlioz wrote for her. Her vision of the great Romance is idiosyncratic to say the least, but a triumph of erotic communication on its own account, a cross between Callas and Ewing at their most individual. White is commanding throughout – at once demonic, cynical, relaxed and satirical, his huge voice absolutely in command of the role. Groves isn't quite on his colleagues' level of accomplishment, but acts and sings with the awe and sense of identity-seeking which this production requires of its Faust. The sound, as on most DVDs, is exemplary. Highly recommended.

L'enfance du Christ, Op 25

L'enfance du Christ
Jean Rigby mez **John Aler, Peter Evans** tens **Gerald Finley, Robert Poulton** bars **Alastair Miles, Gwynne Howell** basses **St Paul's Cathedral Choir; Corydon Singers and Orchestra / Matthew Best**
Hyperion Dyad ② CDD22067 (101' · DDD · T/t) ⒷⓄ

Best treats *L'enfance du Christ* as overtly operatic, not so much by cast movements or varied microphone placings as by his pacing of the action and by encouraging his artists to throw themselves wholeheartedly into the emotions of the story. He gets off to a tremendous start with a superb reading by a black-voiced Alastair Miles as a Herod haunted by his dream and startled into belligerent wakefulness by the arrival of Polydorus. Later, there's desperate urgency in the appeals for shelter by Joseph (an otherwise gently lyrical Gerald Finley), harshly rebuffed by the chorus. And, throughout, there are spatial perspectives – the soldiers' patrol advancing (from practically inaudible pizzicatos) to centre-stage and going off again; and a beautifully hushed and atmospheric faraway 'Amen' at the end. Balance in general is excellent.

The clear enunciation (in very good French) of nearly everyone is a plus point. The chorus's response to the mood and meaning of words is always alert and sensitive, matched by the nuanced orchestral playing. The scurrying of the Ishmaelite family to help, played really *pianissimo*, is vividly graphic; and their home entertainment on two flutes and a harp, which can mark a drop in the interest, here has great charm. But overall it's Best's pacing which makes this recording distinctive. This recording stands comparison well with its much-praised predecessors.

Messe solennelle

Messe solennelle (also includes revised version Ⓟ of Resurrexit)
Donna Brown sop **Jean-Luc Viala** ten **Gilles Cachemaille** bar **Monteverdi Choir; Orchestre Révolutionnaire et Romantique / Sir John Eliot Gardiner**
Philips 464 688-2PM (61' · DDD · T/t) Recorded live 1993. ⓂⓄⓄ➛

The reappearance of Berlioz's lost Mass of 1824 is the most exciting musical discovery of modern times. To an incredulous meeting of the New Berlioz Edition in 1992 the General Editor, Hugh Macdonald, announced that a Belgian choirmaster, Frans Moors, had made contact with news of an improbable find in an Antwerp organ loft. A few days later, Prof Macdonald reported back from Antwerp that this was indeed the *Messe solennelle* which Berlioz claimed

to have burnt after a couple of performances. Gardiner with his Monteverdi Choir and Orchestre Révolutionnaire et Romantique gave performances in Bremen, Vienna, Madrid, Rome and Westminster Cathedral. This is a live recording of that last, thrilling occasion.

Why did Berlioz abandon the work? Only the *Resurrexit* was retained, though it was rewritten: both versions are included here. Some of it, but not much, is dull: the *Offertory* and *Sanctus* sit rather stolidly with the rest. He was unfair on what he denounced in an angry scribble on the MS as an 'execrable' fugue. Some is disconcertingly awkward, and Gardiner tells in the notes to this record of his and the singers' and players' confusion – until they all came together and suddenly the music made sense. The best of the work is superb: among this one may count the *Incarnatus*, the *O Salutaris* and the lovely *Agnus Dei*. The latter was too good to lose, and survives in another form in the *Te Deum*. So do other ideas: it was at first disconcerting to hear the chorus singing 'Laudamus te. Benedicimus te' to the Carnival music from *Benvenuto Cellini*, more so than to hear the slow movement of the *Symphonie fantastique* in the beautiful *Gratias*.

Once these and other associations are overcome, the work coheres remarkably well. Yet perhaps it did not do so well enough for Berlioz, and perhaps he was dissatisfied with the conjunction of some rather academic music with ideas that were too original, indeed too beautiful, to make a satisfying whole. Who knows whether he might have been made to think twice about abandoning the work had he heard a performance such as this? In any case, this is a recording of a great musical event, not to be missed.

Cantatas

Herminie[a]. La mort de Cléopâtre[b]. La mort d'Orphée[c]. La mort de Sardanapale[c]
[a]**Michèle Lagrange** sop [b]**Béatrice Uria-Monzon** mez [c]**Daniel Galvez Vallejo** ten **Choeur Régional Nord, Pas de Calais; Lille National Orchestra / Jean-Claude Casadesus**
Naxos 8 555810 (61' · DDD) ⓈⒹ➛

To have on a single disc Berlioz's four attempts at the Prix de Rome, or at least as much of them as survives, was one of the most enjoyable fruits of the bicentenary year. Together they present a vivid portrait of the composer in his twenties, a Janus figure looking at once back to Gluck and forward to the more highly coloured, Romantic products of the mid-19th century. These four works are all the more extraordinary for being based on a format devised by someone else – something Berlioz preferred to avoid after *Benvenuto Cellini*; even here he couldn't resist adding at times to the texts provided.

He tried to destroy *La mort de Sardanapale*, his prize-winning cantata of 1830, and only its end has survived by accident. Like its predecessors, it deals with an extreme situation. To that extent they all chimed in with Berlioz's natural propensities for shaking and stirring audiences, even to the point of aural discomfort. It's fascinating to find so many features of the mature Berlioz already in place: the ubiquitous diminished sevenths, the hitching up of tonalities by semitones, the love of descending scales (as in the wonderful line for Cléopâtre's 'Il n'en est plus pour moi que l'éternelle nuit', which could be Dido in *Les troyens* some 30 years later). The poetic Berlioz is also in evidence, notably in the beautiful Nature-music that opens *La mort d'Orphée*, his earliest attempt from 1827.

The contribution of the solo singers on this disc belongs more to the 19th century than to the 18th, which is possibly what Berlioz would have wanted. That's to say, all three voices are dramatic in size and style. There's some spreading at the top of all three above *mezzo forte*, but in giving their all they're merely taking a cue from Berlioz's orchestra, which, under Casadesus's firm direction, miraculously already sounds like the Berlioz we know. In softer passages all three are excellent.

Les nuits d'été, Op 7

Les nuits d'été. Herminie
Mireille Delunsch *sop* **Brigitte Balleys** *mez*
**Orchestre des Champs-Elysées, Paris /
Philippe Herreweghe**
Harmonia Mundi HMC90 1522 (54' · DDD · T/t)
Ⓕ**OO**

It isn't fanciful to hear decided pre-echoes in *Herminie* of Cassandra's fateful, searing music (quite apart from the dry-run for the *Symphonie fantastique*'s main motif). This extraordinary work of 1828, almost as arresting as its near-contemporary *Cléopâtre*, receives a grand rendering from Mireille Delunsch, who sings it in a compact, direct manner. Her tone is narrow and focused, her French diction clear. Herreweghe and his orchestra adopt a lean sound, surely close to that of Berlioz's time. Delunsch enters into the inner agony of the distraught, frustrated Herminie with a will. Her interpretation is absorbing from start to finish.

The recording imparts a slight glare to her tone as it does to that of Balleys in the much more familiar *Nuits d'été*, but that's hardly enough to detract from an idiomatic, unfussy reading. Her voice doesn't luxuriate in the more sensual moments of the cycle as does Régine Crespin's in her famous version (currently unavailable on CD, listed 'In Brief') but it has a clarity of profile and a definition of phrase and, where strength of feeling is called for, Balleys provides it, as in 'Au cimetière' and 'Absence'. This makes a sensible pairing with the cantata. What may also influence your choice is, again, Herreweghe's lean, well-pointed support which often emphasises, rightly, the striking originality of Berlioz's scoring.

Les nuits d'été. Benvenuto Cellini – Tra la la ... Mais qu'ai-je donc?. Les Troyens – Je vais mourir ... Adieu, fière cité. Béatrice et Bénédict – Dieu! Que vien-je d'entendre? ... Il m'en souvient. La damnation de Faust – D'amour l'ardente flamme
Susan Graham *mez*
**Royal Opera House Orchestra,
Covent Garden / John Nelson**
Sony Classical 07464 62730-2 (61' · DDD · T/t) Ⓕ**OO**

It would be hard to imagine a more inspiriting and rewarding display of Berlioz singing than this from a singer who has the composer's style in her voice and heart. Graham manages to explore and deliver the soul of each of her chosen pieces, her voice – firm yet vibrant, clear yet warm – responding interpretatively and technically to the appreciable demands placed on it. In *Les nuits d'été*, she faces the greatest challenge from revered favourites and meets it head on, catching in almost every respect the varied moods of each song. Her French pronunciation is excellent and she uses the language to evoke the atmosphere of each song without a hint of exaggeration.

The noble dignity of her account of Dido's farewell, in particular at the recollection of the love duet, is deeply moving, and Béatrice's equivocal thoughts about her lover are another triumph. The fleeter, lighter side of Graham's art is caught in the rapturous cabaletta to Béatrice's aria and in Ascanio's excitable aria from *Benvenuto Cellini*, both dispatched securely. Nelson and the LSO provide idiomatic support, and the recording catches the full colour of the singer's performances.

Berlioz Les nuits d'été, Op 7[a]
Chausson Poème de l'amour et de la mer, Op 19[b]
Schoenberg Gurrelieder – Song of the Wood Dove[c]
Dame Janet Baker *mez* [a]**London Philharmonic Orchestra / Carlo Maria Giulini;** [bc]**London Symphony Orchestra /** [b]**Evgeny Svetlanov,** [c]**Norman del Mar**
BBC Legends/IMG Artists BBCL4077-2 (75' · ADD · N)
Recorded live [a]1975, [b]1975, [c]1963.   Ⓕ**O**

These three absorbing interpretations are a welcome addition to the growing discography of Dame Janet in live performances, where the *frisson* of a 'real' occasion adds an extra immediacy to her readings. Dame Janet recorded *Nuits d'étés* some 10 years earlier with Barbirolli, when speeds were on the slow side. Here they're even more deliberate, possibly the longest 'Le spectre de la rose' on disc. The extra time allows the singer to bring an even deeper sense of mystery and longing to the four middle songs. Has 'Absence' ever sounded so sad and eloquent? Her ability to control a wide range of dynamic effects is astonishing. Giulini and the LPO couldn't be more supportive.

All the recordings are a tribute to the BBC's recording expertise, giving more presence to the voice than is often the case today. Apart from one disfiguring cough in the Berlioz, the presence of an audience is hardly intrusive.

Additional recommendation

Les nuits d'été[a]
Coupled with: Songs by Ravel, Debussy and Poulenc
Crespin sop [b]**Wustman** pf
[a]**Suisse Romande Orchestra / Ansermet**
Decca download 460 973-2DM (68' · ADD · T/t)

Ⓜ**ⒺⒺⒺ**➔

Scandalously available only as a download in many countries, Crespin's *Nuits dété* has always been the interpretation by which others have been assessed and, listening to it again, there's no reason to challenge the verdict.

Les nuits d'été   Ⓗ
Coupled with: Symphonie fantastique. Roméo et Juliette – Queen Mab Scherzo. Overtures – Benvenuto Cellini; Béatrice et Bénédict. Le carnaval romain. Le corsaire. Les Troyens – Chasse royale et orage
De los Angeles sop **Boston SO / Munch**
RCA Red Seal Artistes et Répertoires
② 74321 84587-2 (129' · ADD)   Ⓜ**ⒺⒺ**

De los Angeles' *Nuits d'été* still remains a benchmark by which all others are judged; she has all the vocal range and variety of expression needed for these songs. It's a shame, though, that no stereo tapes exist for these 1955 sessions. The performances of the overtures are electric.

Songs

Mélodies, Op 19 – No 2, Les champs; No 6, Le Chasseur danois. Mélodies, Op 13 – No 1, Le matin; No 2, Petit oiseau, chant de paysan; No 4, Le Jeune pâtre breton[c]; No 5, Le Chant des Bretons. Mélodies, 'Irlande', Op 2 – Le coucher du soleil; Chant guerrier[b]; La belle voyageuse; Chanson à boire[b]; Chant sacré[a]; L'origine de la harpe; Adieu Bessy; Elégie en prose. Roméo et Juliette, Op 17 – Premiers transports[d]
Jérôme Corréas bass-bar **Arthur Schoonderwoerd** pf with [a]**Claire Brua**, [a]**Marie-Bénénedicte Souquet** sops [b]**Alain Gabriel**, [a]**Jean-Francois Novelli**, [a]**Jean-Francois Lombard** tens [a]**Vincent Deliau** bar [c]**Claude Maury** hn [d]**Christophe Coin** vc
Alpha ALPHA024 (58' · DDD · T/t)   Ⓕ

It's surprising that Berlioz's songs aren't better known. Anyone who thinks *Les nuits d'été* constitutes a summary of his vocal production need only listen to this disc to be disabused. Jérôme Corréas has so far tended to specialise in Baroque music and his dark, warm bass-baritone is surprisingly flexible in its articulation, with an especially tender *mezza voce*. Berlioz's roots aren't generally thought to extend further back than Gluck, but Corréas's well-focused tone and shapely phrasing is ideal for this music. Certainly Berlioz's vocal lines, asymmetrical and often plain weird, have little to do with Viennese Classicism. Corréas embraces the asymmetry, but is ingenious in finding some logic in the composer's most outlandish effusions, and you can hear every word. Arthur Schoonderwoerd draws wonderful sounds from an 1836 Pleyel and in a song like *Elégie en prose*

BERLIOZ LES NUITS D'ÉTÉ – IN BRIEF

Régine Crespin; SRO / Ernest Ansermet
Decca download 460 973-2DM (69' · ADD)

Ⓜ**ⒺⒺⒺ**➔

The classic recording in which every nuance has been scrupulously articulated. Gorgeous.

Janet Baker; New Philharmonia / Sir John Barbirolli
EMI 562788-2 (78' · ADD)   Ⓜ**ⒺⒺⒺ**

The version that for many vies with the Crespin. Baker in 1967 is on top form and her rapport with Barbirolli conjures some moments of breathtaking allure.

Janet Baker; LPO / Carlo Maria Giulini
BBC Legends BBCL4077-2 (75' · ADD)   Ⓕ**ⒺⒺⒺ**

A live recording from 1975 shines a light on different areas than her earlier version – speeds here tend to be quite slow.

Anne Sofie von Otter; Berlin PO / James Levine
DG 445 823-2GH (63' · DDD)   Ⓕ➔

An early von Otter foray into the French repertoire – it's good, but nowhere as full of the insight she customarily brings to the French repertoire these days.

Susan Graham; ROH Orchestra / John Nelson
Sony Classical 07464 62730-2 (61' · DDD)   Ⓕ**ⒺⒺ**

A wonderfully imaginative, carefully moulded performance: perhaps the most complete interpretation since the celebrated Régine Crespin version. A modern classic.

Diana Montague; Catherine Robbin; Howard Crook; Gilles Cachemaille; Lyon Opera Orchestra / Sir John Eliot Gardiner
Apex 0927 49583-2 (63' · ADD)   Ⓑ**Ⓔ**➔

The most successful of the multi-voice recordings and a set that showed early on (1989) Gardiner's wonderful way with Berlioz. A real bargain, too.

David Daniels; Ensemble Orchestral de Paris / John Nelson
Virgin Classics 545646-2 (69' · DDD)   Ⓕ➔

A reasonably successful countertenor version, but the mezzos generally find more to say in these magical songs.

Isabel Vernet; Laurent Martin pf
Ligia LIDI0201032 (57' · ADD)   Ⓑ

One of the handful of recordings with piano uncovers many subtleties and insights.

Brigitte Balleys; Champs-Elysées Orchestra / Philippe Herreweghe
Harmonia Mundi HMC90 1522 (54' · ADD)   Ⓕ**ⒺⒺ**

Fine singing from Brigitte Balleys, but Philippe Herreweghe's control of his French orchestra is a thing of wonder.

you can sense Duparc in the making. The other supporting artists are all excellent – a particularl joy is Christophe Coin's cello playing in the marvellous 'Premiers transports'. The spacious church acoustic, with up to a three-second echo, isn't ideal, but then traffic-free venues in Paris are hard to find.

Béatrice et Bénédict

Béatrice et Bénédict
Susan Graham sop Béatrice **Jean-Luc Viala** ten
Bénédict **Sylvia McNair** sop Héro **Catherine Robbin**
mez Ursule **Gilles Cachemaille** bar Claudio **Gabriel**
Bacquier bar Somarone **Vincent Le Texier** bass Don
Pedro **Philippe Magnant** spkr Léonato **Lyon Opera**
Chorus and Orchestra / John Nelson
Erato MusiFrance ② 2292-45773-2 (111' · DDD · T/t)
ⒻⓄ

We have to note that the title isn't a French version of *Much Ado about Nothing*. Berlioz takes the two principal characters of Shakespeare's play and constructs an opera around them. The comedy centres on the trick that is played on the pair by their friends, producing love out of apparent antipathy. Much of the charm lies in the more incidental matters of choruses, dances, the magical 'Nocturne' duet for Béatrice and Héro, and the curious addition of the character Somarone, a music-master who rehearses the choir in one of his own compositions. There's also a good deal of spoken dialogue. Perhaps surprisingly, the extra dialogue is a point in its favour, for it's done very effectively by good French actors and it makes for a cohesive, Shakespearian entertainment. John Nelson secures a well-pointed performance of the score, and with excellent playing by the Lyon Orchestra. Susan Graham and Jean-Luc Viala are attractively vivid and nimble in style, and Sylvia McNair makes a lovely impression in Héro's big solo. The veteran Gabriel Bacquier plays the music-master with genuine panache and without overmuch clownage. There's good work by the supporting cast and the chorus and the recording is finely produced.

Benvenuto Cellini

Benvenuto Cellini
Gregory Kunde ten Benvenuto Cellini **Laurent**
Naouri bass Balducci **Jean-François Lapointe** bass
Fieramosca **Patrizia Ciofi** sop Teresa **Joyce Di**
Donato mez Ascanio **Radio France Chorus; French**
National Orchestra / John Nelson
Virgin Classics ③ 545706-2 (3h 8' · DDD · S/T/t/N).
Recorded live 2003
ⒻⓄ

Thanks to to Hugh Macdonald's brilliant work for the *New Berlioz Edition* the 1838 Paris Opéra version of *Benvenuto Cellini* is once again performable; this adds almost half an hour's music to the Colin Davis recording of 1972 (Philips, nla). It's a splendid achievement. Macdonald's notes are an exemplary guide to the music's youthful genius, and David Cairns's original translation for the Davis recording is augmented by Lisa Hobbs, alongside the French.

Each of the singers responds with a quick understanding to the unexpected, eloquent contours of the recitatives, none more so than Gregory Kunde, who can phrase elegantly Cellini's wistful aria longing for a shepherd's simple life, but also prove an ardent suitor for Teresa, and challenge his adversaries with an heroic, defiant *brio*. Patrizia Ciofi can sound a little timid for him, and for Teresa's light vivacity, though she sings fluently and gracefully. Jean-François Lapointe characterises the devious Fieramosca wittily, and joins the the other two cleverly in the brilliant *tour de force* of their trio. There's a high-spirited performance of Ascanio from Joyce Di Donato that includes witty imitations of the men, and Laurent Naouri vigorously struts his hour on the stage as Teresa's father Balducci.

Berlioz's reckless demands on the orchestra are brilliantly answered. The recording engineers have done extraordinarily well in conveying so much detail even when matters are hurtling full tilt in the Roman Carnival scene and in the final casting of the Perseus. John Nelson steers it all with a sure hand and total conviction.

Les Troyens

Les Troyens
Ben Heppner ten Enée **Michelle DeYoung** mez
Didon **Petra Lang** mez Cassandre **Sara Mingardo**
mez Anna **Peter Mattei** bar Chorèbe **Stephen**
Milling bass Narbal **Kenneth Tarver** ten Iopas **Toby**
Spence ten Hylas **Orlin Annastassov** bass Ghost of
Hector **Tigran Martirossian** bass Panthée **Isabelle**
Cals mez Ascagne **Alan Ewing** bass Priam **Guang**
Yang mez Hécube **Andrew Greenan** bass First
sentry **Roderick Earle** bass Second sentry **Bülent**
Bezdüz ten Hélénus **Leigh Melrose** bass A-Trojan
soldier/Mercure **Mark Stone** bar A Greek Chieftain
London Symphony Chorus and Orchestra /
Sir-Colin Davis
LSO Live ④ LSO0010 (240' · DDD)
ⓈⓄⓄⓄ↦

Colin Davis's 1969 recording remains a landmark event, the first time this grand opera of Meyerbeerian length, spectacular *éclat* and Wagnerian artistic ambition had found its way complete onto LP. It effectively changed views about Berlioz the opera composer and orchestral genius and has for many remained the yardstick by which all later performances have been judged. Although studio recorded, it was based on the Covent Garden casting of the day – Jon Vickers' heroic Enée and Josephine Veasey's voluptuous Didon – with a couple of Frenchmen to boost the ranks of lesser Trojans and Carthaginians.

The tantalising glimpses of Régine Crespin's Cassandre and Didon belong to a now lost tradition which none of the singing on the new LSO disc quite emulates – with the possible exception of the delightful young French mezzo Isabelle Cals as Ascagne. Part for part, however, the LSO have assembled a cast which challenges without comprehensively surpassing that of the earlier Davis recording. Some of the *comprimario* singers are without doubt their predecessors' superiors: the handsome-voiced Peter Mattei is a nobler-toned, more youthful and romantic-sounding Chorèbe in his fraught interview with his 'vierge adorée', Cassandre; Sara Mingardo's sumptuous contralto is luxury casting for Didon's sister beside the admirable but plain Heather Begg. And as the Carthaginian court poet, Iopas, Kenneth Tarver's tone catches the microphone just that bit more sweetly than Ian Partridge's.

Any account of *Les Troyens*, however, stands or falls by the casting of the three central characters – Cassandre, Enée and Didon – and this the LSO has done with exceptional results. Michelle DeYoung was originally assigned Cassandre, but was 'promoted' to Didon when Olga Borodina fell ill. Her replacement as Cassandre, the German dramatic mezzo Petra Lang, was a revelation at the Barbican, a passionate prophetess, thrilling in her imprecations against the Greeks and heroic in her suicide as Troy is consumed in flames at the close of Act 2.

Her French has a slightly 'thick' Germanic flavour, but she makes every word tell and she has the grand rhetorical manner Berlioz learned from Gluck and Cherubini to the manner born.

It's hard to imagine today – vocally at least –a more musical, more romantic, more impetuous Enée than Ben Heppner who brings real stylish distinction and heroic bravura to bear. Michelle DeYoung's Didon isn't quite so successful. Her big, bright-toned voice is less warm than Veasey's and she has a tendency to 'yowl' on climactic notes. She doesn't really convey Didon's regal bearing either: her imperiousness is that of a bossy housekeeper rather than a great founding Queen. That said, she rises to a magnificent 'Adieu, fier cité' and works herself into a Medea-like rage when she threatens to serve a dismembered Ascagne as her perjured lover's dinner.

What really makes this issue indispensable is Davis's conducting of an LSO on incandescent form. The 'world's greatest Berlioz conductor' seems to become ever more convinced of the greatness of this astonishing score and revels, with greater conviction than ever, in its magical orchestral effects and its grand theatrical rhetoric. For Davis and his orchestra – and the splendid immediacy of the live recording – this account of *Les Troyens* is first choice at any price. This set is a must-buy.

Additional recommendations

Ferrer Didon, Cassandre **Giraudeau** Enée   H
Cambon Chorèbe, Narba **BBC Theatre Chorus;**
Royal Philharmonic Orchestra / Beecham

Malibran-Music mono ④ CDRG162 (226' · ADD)
Broadcast 1947   Ⓟ❶❶❶

One of the most important documents ever to appear from previously unavailable archives. Beecham is at least Davis's peer here. An arresting, inspiriting performance, which has the benefit of a superb French cast.

Les Troyens
Susan Graham *mez* Dido **Gregory Kunde** *ten*
Aeneas **Anna Caterina Antonacci** *sop* Cassandra
Ludovic Tezier *bar* Choroebus **Renata Pokupic**
contr Anna **Laurent Naouri** *bass* Narbal **Nicolas**
Testé *bass* Pantheus **Stéphanie d'Oustrac** *mez*
Ascanius **Mark Padmore** *ten*-Iopas **Topi Lehtipuu**
ten Hylas, Helenus **Monteverdi Choir;**
Théâtre du Châtelet Chorus, Paris;
Orchestre Révolutionnaire et Romantique /
Sir John Eliot Gardiner
Stage director **Yannis Kokkos**
Video director **Peter Maniura**
BBC/Opus Arte ② 𝐃𝐕𝐃 OA0900D (312' · NTSC · S/s/
N · 16:9 · PCM Stereo, DTS 5.1 · 0) Recorded live.
Includes documentary, cast gallery   Ⓟ❶❶❶

Les Troyens hasn't fared well on DVD, but this superb authentic-instrument performance of October 2003 from the Théâtre du Châtelet, Paris, equals Sir Colin Davis's pioneering original. Orchestrally it's everything we've come to expect from Gardiner's Berlioz, his tempi swift and dynamic, sharing the composer's delight in complex rhythmic interplay, yet always propelling the drama. Passages like Andromache's entrance and Hector's ghost nevertheless have their proper gravitas and sombre hues against the brighter shades of Carthage. Colour is the great gift of the period instruments, revealing a wide range of sonorities, and creating a sense of freshness and discovery. The effect is sometimes rawer, sometimes more classical, but almost always more complex and dramatic than the homogenised modern sound.

Gardiner's singers, too, could hardly be more committed. Anna Caterina Antonacci is a fiery Cassandra, superbly classical-looking, so wrung and tormented that some moments of strain scarcely matter. Gregory Kunde tackles Aeneas with ringing tone, looks and acts pretty well, and brings a welcome *bel canto* touch to the gorgeous duet. Susan Graham, though, needs no caveats: a radiant Dido, queenly yet youthful, lyrical and lighter-toned than Janet Baker, but in her final despair no less tragically moving. Other roles are generally excellent. The mostly youthful chorus sounds marvellous, and is a constant force in Yannis Kokkos's moderately modern production.

The stage is plain and bare, capped by a reflector in which most of the décor appears: an Italian Renaissance cityscape for Troy, and the Horse only as a menacing head. Carthage is a classical vision of white walls and blue sea with stylised ships. The Trojans wear the inescapable greatcoats the brutal Greeks, inevitably, American combat gear, and the Carthaginians vaguely

North African whites and pastels. This is a mostly straightforward, lively staging which lets characters and drama speak for themselves, and so works well on screen. The magnificent high-definition recording does it ample sonic and visual justice.

For anyone who loves *Les Troyens*, this is a revelatory and essential performance.

Lord Berners
British 1883-1950

English composer, writer and painter Lord Berners was essentially self-taught. He was honorary attaché in Rome (1911-19), where he came to know Stravinsky and Casella. In 1919 he succeeded to the barony, and thereafter was an eccentric English gentleman. His early works are mostly small and ironical (chiefly songs and piano pieces), close to Les Six; later he wrote ballets, including The Triumph of Neptune (1926), Luna Park (1930) and A Wedding Bouquet (1936). GROVEmusic

Songs / Solo piano works

Polka. Le poisson d'or. Dispute entre le papillon et le crapaud. Trois petites marches funèbres. Fragments psychologiques. March. The expulsion from Paradise. Valse. Lieder Album[a]. Trois chansons[a]. Three English Songs[a]. Dialogue between Tom Filuter and his man by Ned the Dog Stealer[a]. Three Songs[a]. Red Roses and Red Noses[a]. Come on Algernon[a]
[a]**Ian Partridge** ten **Len Vorster** pf
Marco Polo 8 225159 (52' · DDD · T/t)   Ⓕ🅑➔

The minuscule, dejected, lovelorn *Le poisson d'or*, based on Lord Berners' own poem, has a distant Debussian inheritance, while the *Trois petites marches* and *Fragments psychologiques* are Satie-esque, and not just for their bizarre titles. Yet they, too, have a distinct avant-garde precocity, and 'Un soupir' (the third of the *Fragments*) brings a pensive dolour all its own. Berners' sense of fun erupts in the simulated German *Lieder Album* (the seriousness underpinned with a twinkle), and the French *Trois chansons* are naturally idiomatic, with 'La fiancée du timbalier' engagingly light-hearted. The English songs are most winning. *Tom Filuter*'s dialogue changes mood chimerically, and the *Three Songs* of 1921 are like a re-discovery of the English folksong idiom, while the sentimental *Red Roses and Red Noses* has an endearingly flowing lyrical line. It's followed by the irrepressible *Come on Algernon*. It makes a delightful pay-off to end the recital.

Ian Partridge obviously relishes all the stylistic changes like a vocal chameleon, while Len Vorster backs him up splendidly and is completely at home in the solo piano music.

Le carrosse du Saint-Sacrement

Le carrosse du Saint-Sacrement[a]. Fanfare[b] Caprice péruvien[c]

[a]**Ian Caddy** bass Viceroy; [a]**Alexander Oliver** ten Martinez; [a]**John Winfield** ten Balthasar; [a]**Cynthia Buchan** mez La Périchole; [a]**Thomas Lawlor** bar Thomas d'Esquivel; [a]**Anthony Smith** bass Bishop of Lima; [a]**BBC Scottish Symphony Orchestra / Nicholas Cleobury**; [b]**Royal Ballet Sinfonia / Gavin Sutherland**; [c]**RTE Sinfonietta / David Lloyd-Jones**
Marco Polo 8 225155 (79' · DDD · T/t)   Ⓕ🅑➔

Berners' one-act was neglected after its 1924 Paris premiere under Ansermet until the BBC Radio 3 revival in 1983, which is issued here for the first time. The libretto is adapted from a short story by Mérimée, also used in Offenbach's *La Périchole*. The attractive score has such Berners fingerprints as the rhythms of his cynical 'Funeral March for a Rich Aunt' and Spanish effects, daringly close to Chabrier, to suit the Peruvian setting. The leading lady, La Périchole, is a young actress carrying on with the jealous, gout-ridden Viceroy. Their extended duet in Scene 4 develops as a fascinating alliance of scoundrels. At the end of it, she prises the Viceroy's brand-new coach out of him so she can parade in it to the cathedral and eclipse her rivals in Lima. After a spectacular ride, including a collision, she upstages everyone by giving the carriage to the church to take the sacrament to the dying. Chris de Souza's excellent radio production used a translation by Adam Pollock of the French libretto. The diction of all the characters is clear: everyone is well cast, especially Cynthia Buchan and Ian Caddy. The *Caprice péruvien* is a later compilation based on music from the opera. Both orchestras are adequate, decently recorded, but above all *Le carrosse* is an enchanting discovery in British comic opera.

Leonard Bernstein
American 1918-1990

Bernstein studied at Harvard and the Curtis Institute and was a protégé of Koussevitzky. In 1944 he made his reputation as a conductor when he stepped in when Bruno Walter was ill; thereafter he was associated particularly with the Israel PO (from 1947), the Boston SO and the New York PO (musical director, 1958-69), soon achieving an international reputation, conducting in Vienna and at La Scala. During his tenure the New York PO flourished as never before. A gifted pianist, he often performed simultaneously as soloist and conductor. At the same time, he pursued a career as a composer, cutting across the boundaries between high and popular culture in his mixing of Mahler and Broadway, Copland and Bach. His theatre works are mostly in the Broadway manner: they include the ballet Fancy Free (1944) and the musicals Candide (1956) and West Side Story (1957). His more ambitious works, many of them couched in a richly chromatic, intense post-Mahlerian idiom, often have a religious inspiration, for example the 'Jeremiah' Symphony with mezzo (1942), 'Kaddish', with soloists and choirs (1963) and the theatre piece Mass (1971). GROVEmusic

Symphonies

Symphony No 1, 'Jeremiah'[a]. Concerto for Orchestra, 'Jubilee Games'[b]
[a]**Helen Medlyn** *mez* [b]**Nathan Gunn** *bar* **New Zealand Symphony Orchestra / James Judd**
Naxos 8 559100 (55' · DDD)   Ⓢ↦

In life, Leonard Bernstein ran into criticism for programming his own concert music. Now he's gone, it seems we can't get enough of it – and in a variety of performance styles. Latterday champions such as Michael Tilson Thomas and Marin Alsop still go for the idiomatic jugular. Less extrovert interpreters – David Zinman and Kent Nagano spring to mind – downplay the bravado to discover a fresher transparency. On this disc James Judd, British-born but for many years Florida-based, seems closer to the second camp while remaining remarkably faithful to the composer's own overall timings in both pieces.

Keeping a stiff upper lip isn't an option in the Concerto for Orchestra, one of Bernstein's most exploratory and frankly uneven scores. Some of its music is very beautiful, though it isn't easy to see what it has to do with the rest. Judd sometimes trumps the composer's own wilder performance with his paler, more neutral tone.

Competition is fiercer in the coupling. The *scherzo* of the *Jeremiah*, rowdy, raw and rhetorical in the composer's New York recording, is brought that much closer to the symphonic mainstream here, the New Zealand winds relatively polite and in tune. The portentous, hieratic tendencies of the last movement may even be less apparent when the singer is an Australasian crossover artist rather than the customary *grande dame*. The sonorities are lighter and the voltage a little lower than you might be used to. A genuine bargain even so, with recorded sound way ahead of the super-budget norm. There are full if not always felicitously expressed notes. Newcomers needn't hesitate.

Bernstein Symphony No 2, 'The Age of Anxiety'
Bolcom Piano Concerto
Marc-André Hamelin *pf* **Ulster Orchestra / Dimitry Sitkovetsky**
Hyperion CDA67170 (59' · DDD)   ⒻↃ↦

After Hamelin's fantastic virtuosity in the outrageously difficult Godowsky *Studies on Chopin's Etudes* (for which he won the *Gramophone* Instrumental Award 2000) these two works for piano and orchestra are – for him – mere bagatelles. But this is an impressive release since it contains the most convincing account of Bernstein's Symphony No 2 (1949) in recent years.

The whole piece is Bernstein's obsessive response to Auden's poem *The Age of Anxiety*, published the year before, about four characters struggling to sort themselves out in New York City. Even though Auden apparently disliked it, you can increasingly hear Bernstein's Symphony as saturated with the poem,

its ideas and atmosphere. Often programmatic, it represents a particularly original approach to piano and orchestra and is personal in countless ways – the gentleness of the soft opening and its mystical descending scale, the precisely engineered variations, memorable tunes, a splendid jazzy *Scherzo* and so on. Hamelin and the Ulster Orchestra in fine form under Sitkovetsky deliver a well-paced and cogent performance right up to the deliberately inflated, optimistic ending.

Bolcom is one of the most idiosyncratic American composers of the next generation. His 1976 Piano Concerto draws widely on various types of popular music, which he's always performed superbly. The Concerto was written in memory of his teacher, Darius Milhaud, who'd have loved it. The opening movement is captivatingly serene until the blue notes get out of hand; the slow movement is more stable and serious; but the finale comes over as a riotous celebration of Americana. Unfortunately Bolcom intended it to be ironic, as a kind of anti-bicentennial tribute. But tunes like these have a habit of occupying centre-stage on their own terms. Hamelin is again utterly scrupulous and idiomatic, and delivers all the musical styles with supreme confidence – nobody could have mixed them up like Bolcom.

Symphony No 3, 'Kaddish'[a]. Chichester Psalms[b]
[a]**Yvonne Kenny** *sop* [b]**Michael Small** *treb* [a]**Willard White** *spkr* **Liverpool Metropolitan Cathedral Choir Liverpool Philharmonic Youth Choir; Royal Liverpool Philharmonic Choir and Orchestra / Gerard Schwarz**
Naxos American Classics/Milken Archive 8 559456 (56' · DDD)   Ⓢ↦

The word 'chutzpah' might have been invented for Leonard Bernstein's *Kaddish* Symphony. Not content with challenging the great deity in the sky, Bernstein also takes on the credo of 1960s 12-tone orthodoxies in his third symphony – a far greater sin in the eyes of some. 'Every son defies his father, fights him…only to return to him closer and more secure than before,' Bernstein wrote as he explained how Jewish theology informed his score. And as his speaker rages against God, down in the orchestra there's a furious debate about what Bernstein perceived as the crisis in modern music.

The raw material of Bernstein's score is a dialectical clash between paternal tonality and 'errant' 12-tone music, although it's hard to imagine a more hummable tone-row. This centrifugal tension powers the symphony on, and Gerard Schwarz conveys the unfolding drama with strategic clarity. Ironically in the circumstances, Bernstein's own pull-no-punches 1977 DG recording with the Israel PO must hang heavy over any conductor approaching the piece. One giant tick in Schwarz's plus-column is Willard White, a less mannered speaker than Bernstein's Michael Wager. The orchestra and voices, too, sound as if they're taking pleasure in Bernstein's highly inventive scoring, running the spectrum of his jazzy big-band swagger and post-Darmstadt atonal webs with ease.

In comparison to Kaddish's angst, *Chichester Psalms* is a cathartic work that, to paraphrase, requires little more than reading the lines without tripping over the lopsided time signatures. Schwarz energises the Technicolor opening movement, although choral vulnerabilities detract from the work's conclusion. None the less, a disc Bernstein fans will relish.

Fancy Free

Candide – Overture. West Side Story – Symphonic Dances. On the Waterfront – Symphonic Suite. Fancy Free
New York Philharmonic Orchestra / Leonard Bernstein
Sony Classical Bernstein Century 82796 92728-2
(69' · ADD) Recorded 1960-63　　　　Ⓜ**OO**

These performances have long been considered definitive. All but *Fancy Free* were taped in New York's Manhattan Center in the early 1960s, a problematic venue in which the original sound engineers sought to reconcile the close-miking of individual sections and sometimes individual players with a substantial reverberation period. The results have a synthetic, larger-than-life quality which suits most of the music here. The exception is the Overture to *Candide*, a high driven sort of reading, the brashness of Broadway insufficiently tempered by the rapid figurations of Rossini, the academicism of Brahms, the *joie de vivre* of Offenbach: subtler details tend to disappear into a fog of resonance. In the Symphonic Dances from *West Side Story*, the players eschew the customary shouts in the 'Mambo' but it's doubtful whether there will ever be a more idiomatic reading of what was then essentially 'new music'. The score, by no means a straightforward 'greatest hits' selection, had only recently been unveiled, with Lukas Foss conducting, at a gala concert intended to raise funds for the NYPO pension fund. Here certainly was the 'aura of show business' which so irked Harold Schonberg, the influential music critic of the *New York Times*: Bernstein's own recording from March 6th has the quality of an unanswerable rejoinder. *On the Waterfront* is if anything even more intense, its lyrical core dispatched with an overwhelming ardour. Last up is what's almost the best of all possible *Fancy Frees*. It was originally sung in inimitable style by Billie Holiday.

Chichester Psalms

Bernstein Chichester Psalms **Barber** Agnus Dei, Op 11 **Copland** In the Beginning. Four Motets – Help us, O Lord; Have mercy on us, O my Lord; Sing ye praises to our King
Dominic Martelli *treb* **Catherine Denley** *mez* **Rachel Masters** *hp* **Gary Kettel** *perc* **Thomas Trotter** *org*
Corydon Singers / Matthew Best
Hyperion CDA66219 (54 minutes · T · DDD)　　　　Ⓕ

Half of this programme is devoted to unaccompanied choral music by Copland: *In the Beginning*, a striking 15-minute 'Creation' for mixed four-part chorus and solo mezzo (which is eloquently executed by Catherine Denley) written in 1947, and three of four short motets he composed in 1921, while studying with Nadia Boulanger in Paris. The performance of the *Chichester Psalms* recorded here uses Bernstein's own reduced (but very effective) instrumentation of organ, harp and percussion, but follows the composer's New York precedent in employing a mixed chorus – although the illusion of a cathedral choir is persuasively conveyed. It's very impressive.

The singing of the Corydon Singers under Matthew Best is very fine, and the vivid recording, which gives the voices a pleasant bloom while avoiding the resonance of King's College Chapel, reproduces the instrumental accompaniment, notably the percussion, with electrifying impact. Best's soloist is Dominic Martelli, and very sweetly he sings too. The disc is completed by Barber's setting of the *Agnus Dei* from 1967 and is an arrangement of the famous *Adagio for Strings*.

This imaginative and enterprising programme is extremely well sung and vividly recorded.

Chichester Psalms[a] On the Waterfront – Symphonic Suite. On the Town – Three Dance Episodes.
[a]**Thomas Kelly** *treb* [a]**Elizabeth Franklin-Kitchen** *sop* [a]**Victoria Nayler** *contr* [a]**Jeremy Budd** *ten* [a]**Paul Charrier** *bass* **Bournemouth Symphony** [a]**Chorus and Orchestra / Marin Alsop**
Naxos 8 559177 (49' · DDD)　　　　Ⓢ**OO**Ⓓ+

Some years ago Andrew Litton presided over a memorable all-Bernstein concert for Virgin Classics that showed that the Bournemouth orchestra could swing with the best of them; now it's the turn of new principal conductor Marin Alsop to put them through their paces. Very sassily they strut, too, in the exuberant outer numbers of *On the Town*. It's a similar tale in the symphonic suite from *On the Waterfront*. Alsop displays a special sympathy for this score's intimate undertow, investing softer music with a tingling atmosphere and lyrical poetry that consistently ignite the imagination, and moulding the love theme with a warmth and vulnerability that all but match the composer's NYPO version. Not that there's any lack of red-blooded drama or brazen spectacle, even though Mike Clements's otherwise excitingly dynamic sound-frame exposes some slight thinness of violin tone. The account of the *Chichester Psalms* is polished, communicative and beautifully sprung, attaining eloquent heights in the soothing setting of Psalm 23 for boy treble and mixed choir, as well as the strings' impassioned plea that launches the last movement.

A conspicuous success. The playing-time is comparatively stingy, but, given the superior quality of the music-making and the low Naxos price-tag, not many should complain.

Mass

Mass
Jubilant Sykes bar **Peabody Children¹s Chorus;
Morgan State University Choir and Marching
Band; Baltimore Symphony Orchestra / Marin
Alsop**
Naxos American Classics ② 8 559622/3
(104' · DDD · T)   Ⓢ❍❍❍▶

 Bernstein's relationship with God is
dangerous, probing, transformational.
There are those, of course, who proffer
that Bernstein thought he was God, that's why he
could stand in defiance against Him. But *Mass*
reveals a man thirsting for faith but petrified of
blind acceptance. Bernstein's religion was muscular and intellectualised, and the experience of
Mass expands, rather than contracts, the further
you travel towards the essence of its cosmology.

Alsop's Jubilant Sykes is the best of all possible
Celebrants. There can be few roles in contemporary music theatre that demand so many sides
of a performer. He must disentangle music of
gnarly complexity; he needs an operatic sensibility, but must also swing like a hipster jazzer and
declaim with authentic rockist swank. Sykes's
voice shakes with James Brown's ecstasy, snarls
with Janis Joplin-like indigence and projects
through the labyrinth of Bernstein's tricky
melodic contours like any trained voice would.
He was born to play this part.

Although she doesn't drive things quite as far
as Bernstein, Alsop is pacey, creating a dramatic
slipstream that is powered relentlessly onwards
by the awkward discontinuities and jagged narrative. Even if the atheist cannot quite love the
God-fearing D major affirmation of the final
scene, it doesn't matter. The journey, the process of discovery, counts for more.

Candide (1988 final version)

Candide
Jerry Hadley ten Candide **June Anderson** sop
Cunegonde **Adolph Green** ten Dr Pangloss, Martin
Christa Ludwig mez Old lady **Nicolai Gedda** ten
Governor, Vanderdendur, Ragotski **Della Jones** mez
Paquette **Kurt Ollmann** bar Maximilian, Captain,
Jesuit father **Neil Jenkins** ten Merchant, Inquisitor,
Prince Charles Edward **Richard Suart** bass Junkman,
Inquisitor, King Hermann Augustus **John Treleaven**
ten Alchemist, Inquisitor, Sultan Achmet, Crook
Lindsay Benson bar Doctor, Inquisitor, King
Stanislaus **Clive Bayley** bar Bear-Keeper, Inquisitor,
Tsar Ivan **London Symphony Chorus and Orchestra
/ Leonard Bernstein**
DG ② 734205 (112' · DDD · N/T)   Ⓜ❍❍❍▶

 Here's-musical comedy, grand opera,
operetta, satire, melodrama, all rolled
into one. We can thank John Mauceri
for much of the restoration work: his 1988 Scottish Opera production was the spur for this
recording and prompted exhaustive reappraisal.

Numbers like 'We Are Women', 'Martin's
Laughing Song' and 'Nothing More Than This'
have rarely been heard, if at all. The last mentioned, Candide's 'aria of disillusionment', is
one of the enduring glories of the score, reinstated where Bernstein always wanted it (but
where no producer would have it), near the very
end of the show. Bernstein called it his 'Puccini
aria', and that it is – bittersweet, long-breathed,
supported, enriched and ennobled by its inspiring string counterpoint. And this is but one of
many forgotten gems.

It was an inspiration on someone's part
(probably Bernstein's) to persuade the great
and versatile Christa Ludwig and Nicolai
Gedda (in his sixties and still hurling out top
Bs) to fill the principal character roles. To say
they do so ripely is to do them scant justice.
Bernstein's old sparring partner Adolph Green
braves the tongue-twisting and many-hatted
Dr Pangloss with his own highly individual
form of *Sprechstimme*, Jerry Hadley sings the
title role most beautifully, *con amore*, and June
Anderson has all the notes, and more, for the
faithless, air-headed Cunegonde. It's just a pity
that someone didn't tell her that discretion is
the better part of comedy. 'Glitter and Be Gay'
is much funnier for being played straighter,
odd as it may sound. Otherwise, the supporting roles are all well taken and the London
Symphony Chorus has a field-day in each of its
collective guises.

Having waited so long to commit every last
note (or thereabouts) of his cherished score to
disc, there are moments here where Bernstein
seems almost reluctant to move on. His tempos are measured, to say the least, the score
fleshier now in every respect: even that raciest
of Overtures has now acquired a more deliberate gait, a more opulent tone. But Bernstein
would be Bernstein, and there are moments
where you're more than grateful for his indulgence: the grandiose chorales, the panoramic
orchestra-scapes (sumptuously recorded), and
of course, that thrilling finale – the best of all
possible Bernstein anthems at the slowest of all
possible speeds – and why not (prepare to hold
your breath at the choral *a cappella*). You're
unlikely to be disappointed by this disc.

West Side Story

West Side Story
Dame Kiri Te Kanawa sop Maria (Nina Bernstein)
José Carreras ten Tony (Alexander Bernstein)
Tatiana Troyanos mez Anita **Kurt Ollmann** bar Riff
Marilyn Horne mez Off-stage voice **chorus and
orchestra / Leonard Bernstein**
DG 457 199-2GH (77' · DDD · N/t)   Ⓕ❍❍▶

If the job of a 'crossover' record is to shatter
preconceptions on both sides of any musical
fence, then this is the greatest ever. Not all the
aficionados of Broadway musicals are going to
warm to de facto operatic treatment of *West Side
Story*: not all opera-lovers or devotees of Bern-

stein as star conductor are going to rate *West Side Story* as an equivalent to opera. But any listener who keeps any sort of open mind, forgetting the constriction of barriers, must recognise this historic disc as superb entertainment and great music-making on every level, with an emotional impact closely akin to that of a Puccini opera. That of course is the doing of Leonard Bernstein as conductor as well as composer. It's astonishing that before this recording he had never conducted his most famous work.

Te Kanawa may not be a soprano you'd cast as Maria on stage, yet the beauty of the voice, its combination of richness, delicacy and purity, brings out the musical strengths of Bernstein's inspiration. Similarly, with Carreras as Tony, it's self-evident to point out how such a voice brings out the pure beauty of the big melodies like 'Maria' or 'Tonight', but even a sharp number like his first solo, 'Something's coming', with floated *pianissimos* and subtly graded *crescendos* allied to sharp rhythms, makes it more clearly a question-mark song, full of expectation, more than just a point number. Marilyn Horne is in glorious voice, while Tatiana Troyanos will surprise you as Anita with the way she could switch her naturally beautiful operatic voice into a New York throaty snarl. Troyanos, it appears, was brought up in exactly the area of the West Side, where the story is supposed to be set, which makes her natural affinity with the idiom less surprising. Kurt Ollmann, American too, as Riff equally finds a very confident balance between the traditions of opera and those of the musical. Diction may not always be so clear as with less rich-toned singers, but Carreras manages a very passable American accent and Dame Kiri a creditable Spanish-American one. The speed with which the piece moves is astounding, not just as superb entertainment but as a Shakespearean tragedy modernised and intensified.

West Side Story
Tinuke Olafimihan Maria **Paul Manuel** Tony **Caroline O'Connor** Anita **Sally Burgess** Off-stage voice **Nicholas Warnford** Riff **Julie Paton** Rosalia **Elinor Stephenson** Consuela **Nicole Carty** Francisca **Kieran Daniels** Action **Mark Michaels** Diesel **Adrian Sarple** Baby John **Adrian Edmeads** A-rab **Garry Stevens** Snowboy **Nick Ferranti** Bernardo **Chorus and National Symphony Orchestra / John Owen Edwards**
TER ② CDTER2 1197 (101' · DDD)   Ⓕ

This recording of *West Side Story* is something of an achievement. The set starts with the major advantage of being inspired by a production at the Haymarket, Leicester, so that many of the cast are really inside their roles. They have youth on their side, too. Paul Manuel from that company may not have a large voice, but his sympathetic portrayal of Tony, both in his solos and duets with Maria, makes you feel that he identifies totally with the part. Moreover, the way in which he can float a high note, as at the end of the alternative film version of 'Something's Coming' puts him on a par with Carreras (for Bernstein). His Maria,

Tinuke Olafimihan, is a gem. Her ability to interact with him and express the laughter and the tragedy of the heroine is very real. At the heart of the 'Somewhere' ballet, Sally Burgess voices the lovers' plea for peace with a magnificent rendition of its famous soaring tune. Nicholas Warnford as leader of the Jets gives no less than his rival in the tricky 'Cool' sequence and Jet song. John Owen Edwards directs Bernstein's score as if he believes in every note. He has imparted to his players the very pulse that sets this music ticking.

West Side Story – The Making of the Recording
Kiri Te Kanawa sop **Tatiana Troyanos** mez **José Carreras** ten **Kurt Ollman** bar orchestra and chorus / **Leonard Bernstein**
Film director **Christopher Swann**
DG 🟤 073 017-9GH (89' · NTSC · 4:3 · 2.0 · 0)
Filmed during the recording sessions in 1984   Ⓕ⬤

This is the famous – or notorious – documentary about the 'operatic' recording of Bernstein's best-loved work (reviewed on page 187), a considerable popular and critical success that overrode the rather silly crossover controversy it aroused. Seeing it again in this excellent DVD transfer emphasises both the strengths and weaknesses of Bernstein's approach. Unquestionably the music is fine enough to stand the weight of the operatic treatment, and it's a pleasure to watch him rejuvenated by rediscovering his own score. However, the visual element shows that, despite his denials, even the youngest and freshest trained voices do add an extra layer of artificiality. Kurt Ollmann and the other Jets sound altogether too mannered, for all the heavy accents, and the chattering teenyboppers more like housewives. Te Kanawa, with her popular background, is at least at home in the idiom, and her songs benefit from the richer colour and *legato*; but Troyanos, for all her authentically comic West-Sidese, sounds inescapably middle-aged and blowsy for a girlish role. And Carreras is ludicrously condemned to play the all-American boy. This miscasting causes him painful struggles with diction and tempo, especially in the fiendishly difficult 'Something's Coming!' number, and Bernstein's refusal to allow for this clearly provokes the ugly scenes in which the composer petulantly humiliates him – not his finest moment. But Carreras and the others obviously love the music so much that, while they can't obscure these handicaps, they largely transcend them. A fascinating record of a great composer/conductor.

Wonderful Town

Wonderful Town
Kim Criswell sop Ruth **Audra McDonald** sop Eileen **Thomas Hampson** bar Baker **Brent Barrett** sngr Wreck **Rodney Gilfry** bar Guide, First Editor, Frank **Carl Daymond** bar Second Editor, Chick Clark **Timothy Robinson** ten Lonigan **Michael Dore** bass First Man, Cadet, Third Cop, Villager **Lynton**

Atkinson *ten* Second Man, Second Cop **Simone
Sauphanor** *sngr* First Girl **Melanie Marshall** *mez*
Second Girl **Kimberly Cobb** *sngr* Violet **Robert
Fardell** *sngr* First Cop **London Voices; Birmingham
Contemporary Music Group / Sir Simon Rattle**
EMI 518175-2 (67' · DDD · N/t)   Ⓜ**ⓄⓄ**→

The Birmingham Contemporary Music Group,
with key brass and sax personnel bumped in from
the West End, play the Overture with great
attitude, trumpets with the throttle full out and a
bevy of saxes licking everyone into shape. Check
out the Original Cast album (on Sony) and you'll
find it's faster, tighter – not much, but enough to
sound like NYC in the fast lane; crude and sassy
with plenty of grime in the mix. Accept the fact
that Rattle's is a pristine *Wonderful Town*, temporarily divorced from its smart book (Joseph
Fields and Jerome Chodorov), out of context,
and, to some extent, out of its element, and you'll
have a good time. No one in the Original Broadway Cast can come within spitting distance of the
vocal talent assembled here. Kim Criswell's Ruth
has to live with Rosalind Russell's keys – in the
bass-baritone range. Where Russell had about
three notes in her voice – all dubious – Criswell
has them all but doesn't have too much occasion
to use them. So she works the lyric of 'One Hundred Easy Ways' a little harder than Russell – a
piranha to Russell's shark. Audra McDonald as
Sister Eileen uses every part of her versatile
voice, wrapping it round a lyric like the two are
inseparable, and sings 'A Little Bit in Love' with
such contentment that it's as if she's giving herself a big, well-deserved hug. It's a gorgeous
voice and the microphone loves her. It loves
Hampson, too, and though he will never quite
erradicate the 'formality' from his delivery he's
rarely sounded quite so unassuming as here
imagining his 'Quiet Girl'.

Of the big set-pieces, 'Conversation Piece'
sounds as if it could have been lifted from a performance of the show. When the village kids get
in on the action that's quite a stretch for Simon
Halsey's London Voices. Now and again you
catch their English choral tradition, but not
long enough for it to get in the way. 'Conga!'
sounds sufficiently inebriated and they sound
right at home on 'Christopher Street'. You get
slightly more *Wonderful Town* for your money
with Rattle (a couple of reprises for a start). Don
Walker's feisty orchestrations get more of an
airing with the addition of 'Conquering New
York', a dance number which demonstrates how
ready Lenny was to raid his bottom drawer by
reusing *Prelude, Fugue and Riffs*.

Thomas Beveridge

American b1938

*After study at Harvard with Randall Thompson and
Walter Piston, Beveridge travelled to Paris to join
Nadia Bouanger's class. He has enjoyed a considera-
ble reputation as a singer, conductor, instrumentalist*

*and teacher. His output numbers some 450 works
including three symphonies and numerous vocal compositions.*

Yizkor Requiem

Yizkor Requiem
Ana María Martínez *sop* **Elizabeth Shammash** *mez*
Robert Brubaker *ten* **Rodney Mariner** *narr*
**Academy of St Martin in the Fields Chorus and
Orchestra / Sir Neville Marriner**
Naxos American Classics/Milken Archive 8 559453
(53' · DDD · T/t)   Ⓢ→

If Leonard Bernstein could write his theatrical
Mass and an ecumenical *Chichester Psalms*,
what's to stop a nice Episcopalian boy like
Thomas Beveridge from writing his *Yizkor
Requiem*, a musical juxtaposition of the Jewish
and Catholic memorial services? Indeed, the
spirit of Bernstein hovers over the proceedings,
with a few sprinkles of Verdi, Fauré, Stravinsky
and Shostakovich to taste. But no matter how
many voices clutter the background, the guiding
personality is still Beveridge, who conceived the
piece as a tribute to his choirmaster father.

Musically as well as theologically, the piece
focuses less on mere juxtaposition than on actual
integration. The text goes right to the source of
the respective traditions, finding relationships
and commonality in the roots of the Latin and
Hebrew languages, which are extensively illuminated in the booklet-notes. Although he avoids
any traditional tunes, Beveridge draws heavily
on a handful of intervallic motifs, spinning an
unapologetically tonal web where both traditions remain recognisable even as they point
towards something new.

A former student of both Randall Thompson
and Walter Piston, Washington-based Beveridge clearly knows how to put both orchestra
and chorus in their best light. Rabbi Rodney
Mariner offers a commanding presence, and Sir
Neville Marriner (no relation) conducts his
musical forces not just with musical respect but
apparent love.

Unlike a lot of compositions released under
the umbrella of the Milken Archive series, this
work is strong enough to stand alone without
the programmatic context of 'American Jewish
Music'. Really, though, any excuse to hear the
piece performed with this level of musicianship
is fine.

Franz Adolf Berwald

Swedish 1796-1868

*Swedish composer and violinist Berwald is the most
individual and commanding musical personality
Sweden has produced. He was the son of CFG Berwald (1740-1825), a violinist of German birth
who studied with F. Benda and played in the Stockholm court orchestra. Franz was a violinist or viol-*

ist in the orchestra (1812-28) and probably studied composition with its conductor, JBE Dupuy. He disowned all his early works, which in their bold modulations show Spohr's influence, except a Serenade for tenor and six instruments (1825) and the fine Septet (?1828). He cherished operatic ambitions but failed to stir much interest in any of his works except Estrella de Soria (1841, performed 1862); The Queen of Golconda was not staged until 1968. In fact he was never properly recognised in his own country.

He made his greatest contribution to the repertory in his orchestral compositions of the 1840s, above all the four symphonies: the Sinfonie singulière (1845) is the most original, but all share vigorous freshness, formal originality (he sometimes used cyclic forms) and warm harmony and textures, especially in slow movements. His chamber works (two piano quintets, four piano trios and two string quartets), which occupied his main attention from 1849 to 1859, are often Mendelssohnian in style and show real command of form and idiom. Berwald pursued several business interests (he ran an orthopedic institute, a glassworks and a sawmill) and was active as a polemical writer on social issues from 1856. Although he was made professor of composition at the Swedish Royal Academy in 1867, the discovery of his work was a 20th-century phenomenon. His brother August (1798-1869) was also a violinist and composer, and a granddaughter, Astrid, a leading Swedish pianist.

GROVEmusic

Symphonies

Symphonies – No 1 in G minor, 'Sinfonie sérieuse'; No 2 in D, 'Sinfonie capricieuse'; No 3 in C, 'Sinfonie singulière'; No 4 in E flat. Konzertstück for Bassoon and Orchestra
Christian Davidsson bn **Malmö Symphony Orchestra / Sixten Ehrling**
BIS ② BIS-CD795/6 (131' · DDD)　　　　Ⓕ❶➔

As might be expected, given Sixten Ehrling's excellent account of the *Singulière* and the E flat Symphonies with the LSO for Decca way back in the late 1960s and his no less impressive 1970 Swedish Radio version of the *Sérieuse*, the performances are *echt*-Berwald. Ehrling gives us plenty of space without ever lingering too lovingly. Even apart from the *tempo giusto*, you feel rather more comfortable with Ehrling's handling of phrasing and balance. He's very attentive to dynamic markings and sometimes, as at the beginning of the *Sinfonie singulière*, pianissimo becomes *pianopiano-pianissimo*!

The recording reproduces these dynamic extremes flawlessly. The Malmö Concert Hall, where this set was made, has a good acoustic. The recordings are generally excellent, though there seems to be more back-to-front perspective and air around the players in the *Singulière* and E flat Symphonies than in the *Sérieuse*. In short, Ehrling and his fine players bring us closer to the spirit of this music than do any of the current rivals.

Heinrich Biber　　Bohemian 1644-1704

Biber is important for his works for the violin, of which he was a virtuoso. In the mid-1660s he entered the service of the Prince-Bishop of Olomouc who maintained an excellent Kapelle at his Kroměříz castle. By 1670 Biber had moved to the Salzburg court Kapelle, becoming Kapellmeister in 1684. His formidable violin technique is best seen in the eight Sonatae violino solo with continuo (1681), where brilliant passage-work (reaching 6th and 7th positions) and multiple stopping abound in the preludes, variations and elaborate finales. Most of the Mystery (or Rosary) Sonatas (c1676, for violin and bass) require scordatura tuning: by linking the open strings to the key the sonority and polyphonic possibilities of the violin were increased. The unaccompanied Passacaglia here, built on 65 repetitions of the descending tetrachord, is the outstanding work of its type before Bach. Besides other violin works (which include a Battalia, with strings and continuo), Biber composed sacred music (in a cappella style as well as large-scale concertato works for solo and ripieno voices), 15 school dramas, three operas (only Chi la dura la vince, 1687, survives) and much instrumental ensemble music (often for unusual combinations including brass). Especially notable are the Requiem in F minor, the Missa Sancti Henrici (1701), the 32-part Vesperae (1693), the motet Laetatus sum (1676), and the Sonata S Polycarpi for eight trumpets and timpani. Biber may have composed the 53-part Missa salisburgensis (1628) formerly attributed to Benevoli.

GROVEmusic

Balletti

Arias a 4 in A. Ballettae a 4 violettae. Balletti a 6 in C. Balletti lamentabili a 4 in E minor. Harmonia Romana. Trombet undt musicalischer Taffeldienst
Ars Antiqua Austria / Gunar Letzbor vn
Symphonia SY95143 (75' · DDD)　　　　Ⓕ

The Baroque palace of Kremsier was the summer residence of Prince-Bishop Karl Liechtenstein-Kastelkorn of Olmütz, an ardent music lover. During his rule, 1664-95, the palace library acquired what's a precious collection of manuscripts. This programme features some of the ensemble music by Biber from that source, though the authenticity of the *Harmonia Romana* anthology, some of whose dances are on the disc, hasn't been established. In any case, the sequence put together by violinist and director Gunar Letzbor is entertaining and very well executed. Most is for strings, but there are contributions from variously sized recorders, too, as well as some splendidly gruff, earthy and inebriate interjections from bass, Michael Oman, as the Nightwatchman.

Letzbor has built his programme around an idea of a Carnival feast at the bishop's court: the bishop enters to a fanfare; dance music greets the guests; a nightwatchman passes by; table music during dinner; dancing; the nightwatchman passes by again, this time drunk; peasant dancing; midnight, the end of Carnival and the beginning of Lent. The revelry is concluded by the 12 strokes of midnight sounded on what sounds like a school bell. The notion comes off well, for the scheme allows for a degree of musical contrast, both of sound and mood. Biber's dances are enchanting for the fullness of their character and for their rhythmic bite, and Ars Antiqua bring them to life with vigour, imagination and style. The group offers us well over an hour of first-class entertainment in which only the Bishop's festive board and the contents of his cellar aren't shared with us. The disc is superbly recorded.

Mensa sonora

Mensa sonora seu musica instrumentalis.
Sonata in A for Violin and Continuo
Purcell Quartet (Catherine Mackintosh, Catherine Weiss vns Richard Boothby vion Robert Woolley hpd) with Jane Rogers va
Chandos Chaconne CHAN0748 (59' · DDD)   Ⓕ Ⓑ➤

Mensa sonora, published in Salzburg in 1680, is scored for four-part strings and basso continuo. It consists of six suites of mainly very short dance movements and could be seen as the least substantial of Biber's instrumental collections. But the consistently high level of craftsmanship and imagination transforms what might have been purely functional music. We're continually delighted by Biber's contrapuntal dexterity, by the beautiful sonorities and by the way he introduces a deeper level of expression into the longer movements. There are moments, too, of startling originality – the pointillist treatment of the arpeggio motif at the start of Suite No 3, and the astonishing ending to the last suite, where the musical discourse is broken into smaller and smaller fragments.

The Purcell Quartet bring out these and many more facets of the music with playing that's always lively and sweetly tuned. The many decisions on tempo and character are well taken – even the more surprising ones, such as the very moderate, smooth first Gigue in Suite No 5, sound entirely convincing in context.

The Violin Sonata comes at the disc's midpoint; its broader canvas, with improvisatory passagework over static bass notes, a toccata-like episode in dotted rhythms and a substantial set of variations, makes an excellent contrast with *Mensa sonora*'s miniature movements. Catherine Mackintosh has this demanding music at her fingertips. Her manner avoids the extravagance of some Baroque violinists but she can be relied on to project the expressive, rhetorical character that's always present in Biber's figuration. Strongly recommended.

Violin Sonatas

Eight Sonatas for Violin and Continuo   Ⓟ
(1681). Sonata violino solo representativa in A.

Sonata, 'La Pastorella'. Passacaglia for Solo Lute.
Mystery Sonatas – Passacaglia in G-minor
Romanesca (Andrew Manze vn Nigel North lte/ theorbo John Toll hpd/org)
Harmonia Mundi ② HMX290 7344/45 (127' · DDD)
Ⓜ Ⓞ Ⓞ Ⓞ

While the more famous *Mystery Sonatas* have quickly found friends, the 1681 set is still largely unknown. Yet what's immediately noticeable from this premiere recording of the sonatas is that Biber isn't only a legendary virtuoso, probably never bettered in the 17th or 18th centuries, but one of the most inventive composers of his age: bold and exciting, certainly, but also elusive, mercurial and mysterious. Most of the works are preludes, arias and variations of an unregulated nature: improvisatory preludes over naked pedals and lucid arias juxtaposing with eccentric rhetorical conceits are mixed up in an unpredictable phantasm of contrast, and yet at its best it all adds up to a unified structure of considerable potency. Andrew Manze is the player *par excellence* for music that requires a considered response to complement the adventurous spirit of the virtuoso. This is masterful playing in which he doesn't overcharacterise Biber's volatile temperament. The preludes are sweet and restrained, yet there's also a held-back, almost smouldering quality, skilfully pitched against the free-wheeling energy of the fast music.

Eight Sonatas for Violin and Continuo – Nos 3, 4, 6-7
Sonata No 81 in A. Sonata No 84 in E
John Holloway vn **Aloysia Assenbaum** org
Lars Ulrik Mortensen hpd
ECM New Series 472 084-2 (77' · DDD)   Ⓕ Ⓞ Ⓞ Ⓞ ➤

 John Holloway has contributed as much as anyone to modern-day recognition of Biber's status as one of the greatest of all violinist-composers. In his notes he draws attention to the difference in character between the sonatas in normal tuning and those that asl for *scordatura* or altered tunings, citing the latter (Nos 4 and 6 from the published set) as 'more intimate, more personal'. But actually this is the side which comes across most strongly in these performances anyway, at the expense of the extrovert maybe, but with no shortage of effective musical moments nevertheless; the point halfway through the Sixth Sonata when the violin re-emerges retuned and with a veiled new sound is managed with ghostly beauty.

With the violin resonating pleasingly through the many double- and triple-stoppings, and Holloway's bowing demonstrating a delicious lightness and freedom, these fundamentally inward, tonally aware performances also seem to have more of the smell of the 17th century about them than their current rivals (including Manze's, reviewed above), which push the violin's sound out a bit more. A respectfully resonant recording is a help here, as is the gentle but effectively unfussy continuo support of harpsichord and organ.

Anyone who already has the Manze need have no qualms about adding this one to their collection.

Violin Sonatas – Nos 2, 3, 5, 7. Nisi Dominus. Ⓟ
Passacaglia[a]
Sonnerie (Monica Huggett *vn/dir* Emilia Benjamin *va da gamba* Gary Cooper *hpd/org* Elizabeth Kenny *theo/gtr*) [a]**Thomas Guthrie** *bass*
ASV Gaudeamus CDGAU 203 (65' · DDD)   Ⓕ❍❍❍

Monica Huggett's arrival at these marvels of the 17th-century violin repertoire has the authority of a player to the manner born. She has a strong but fluent technique, and produces from her violin a sweet sound at all times, rarely forcing the tone into stridency (as Manze does, for instance in the clashing dissonances of the Variation of Sonata No 5). Rather, her navigation of what Charles Burney, writing in the 1770s, called the 'most difficult and most fanciful music of any I have seen of the period' is characterised, not by Manze's energetic interpretative gestures, but by her own rather aristocratic brand of easy poise and balance, proving that these sonatas can work as pure music, without the need for urgent drama. It's an alternative view of Biber from that of the fiery virtuoso (though virtuosity is certainly needed to achieve it), and rather a seductive one it is, too. Those who find Manze's fantasies a little over the top may well prefer Huggett's gentler readings; lovers of Biber's music will relish them both.

Mystery Sonatas   Ⓟ
John Holloway *vn* **Davitt Moroney** *org/hpd*
Tragicomedia (Stephen Stubbs *lte/chitarrone* Erin Headley *va da gamba/ lirone* Andrew Lawrence-King *hp/regal*)
Virgin Classics Veritas ② 562062-2 (131' · DDD)
                                Ⓜ❍❍❍

Biber's 15 *Mystery Sonatas* with their additional *Passacaglia* for unaccompanied violin were written in about 1678 and dedicated to his employer, the Archbishop of Salzburg. Each Sonata is inspired by a section of the Rosary devotion of the Catholic Church which offered a system of meditation on 15 Mysteries from the lives of Jesus and the Virgin Mary. The music isn't, strictly speaking, programmatic, though often vividly illustrative of events which took place in the life of Christ.

All but two of the 16 pieces require *scordatura* or retuning of the violin strings; in this way Biber not only facilitated some of the fingerings but also achieved sounds otherwise unavailable to him. The Sonatas are disposed into three groups of five: Joyful, Sorrowful and Glorious Mysteries whose contrasting states are affectingly evoked in music ranging from a spirit reflecting South German Baroque exuberance to one of profound contemplation. John Holloway plays with imaginative sensibility. He's supported by a first-rate continuo group whose instruments include Baroque lute, chitarrone,

viola da gamba, a 15-string lirone, double harp and regal.

Additional recommendations

Les Veilleurs de Nuit / Piérot *vn*
Alpha ② ALPHA038 (120' · DDD)   Ⓕ
A wonderful combination of virtuosity and poise characterise this set and her colleagues repsond with great imagination

Beznosiuk *vn* **Tunnicliffe** *va da gamba*
Roblou *hpd* with **T West** *spkr*
Avie ② AV0038 (157' · DDD)   Ⓕ❍Ⓑ⟶
Timothy West reads from the Jesuit Rosary psalter before each sonata. Again, great imagination is employed to bring these powerful works to life for a new generation.

Manze *vn* **Egarr** *org/hpd* with **McGillivray** *vc*
Harmonia Mundi ② HMU90 7321/2 (141' · DDD)
                                   Ⓕ❍❍
Andrew Manze offers a rapt and intimate version of these pieces and his virtusoty and flair in this repetroire is never in question

---

'Der Türken Anmarsch'
Biber Eight Violin Sonatas – No 1 in A; No 2 in D minor (Dorian); No 5 in E minor; No 8 in A **Muffat** Violin Sonata in D **Biber/A Schmelzer** Violin Sonata in A minor 'Victory of the Christians over the Turks'
John Holloway *vn* **Aloysia Assenbaum** *org*
Lars Ulrik Mortensen *hpd*
ECM New Series 472 432-2 (63' · DDD)   Ⓕ Ⓑ⟶

John Holloway plays four sonatas from the set of eight Biber published in 1681 and also dedicated to the archbishop. First, however, comes a curiosity: an adaptation by Andreas Anton Schmelzer (son of the better-known Johann Heinrich) of Biber's 'Crucifixion' sonata, transposed up a tone and retitled as a representation of the siege of Vienna in 1683. It's difficult, though, to detect any difference other than some small changes to the Praeludium and an extra movement at the end.

The 1681 sonatas show Biber's propensity for rhapsodic flights over a pedal point and for variations on a ground bass. In the imitative writing of No 8 the double-stopping is so skilfully done that it's hard to believe that Holloway hasn't cloned himself. In this sonata especially, there's some nicely pointed continuo playing. The Muffat is a *sonata da chiesa*, with a return to the first movement at the end. Here and throughout the disc Holloway plays with a most appealing warmth and a faultless technique.

Masses

Missa Bruxellensis   Ⓟ
La Capella Reial de Catalunya;
Le Concert des Nations / Jordi Savall

Alia Vox AV9808 (52' · DDD · T) Ⓕ**OO**

Modern technology and expert engineering allow us to bask in Biber's magnificent-sounding and spaciously conceived masses, complete with all the glistening attention to detail, the visceral *tutti* impact and the delicate textural contrasts which constitute some of Baroque music's most opulent expressions of earthly potency. Salzburg Cathedral provided exceptional acoustical possibilities. Biber, in his mass, could satisfy the potentate by adorning the unique status of Salzburg as the court with everything. The problem, however, with the *Missa Bruxellensis* – so called since it was discovered in Brussels – is that it appears to serve its purpose more as a professional job than as a vehicle for extended inspiration. Even so, a world premiere recording of a monumental work by a major composer isn't to be sniffed at, especially when directed by Jordi Savall. He lets Biber's score roll out unassumingly; even if at the expense of fine tuning and exacting ensemble, the final sections of the *Credo* are immensely stylish, and the 'Miserere' from the *Gloria* has the dignity of a spontaneous event rather than a contrived vignette.

The recorded sound has a mixed success, taken from sessions held in the original location; there's a natural sense of the cathedral acoustic, though not, happily, at the expense of immediacy in the solo sections. Less satisfactory are the strident upper frequencies, in particular the solo sopranos. Gripes aside, this will delight collectors who relish fortress-like recordings.

Missa Christi resurgentis*a*. Sonatae tam aris quam aulis servientes – Fanfare No 1; Fanfare No 4. 12 Sonatas, 'Fidicinium sacro-profanum' – I; III; V; VII; XI. Sonata a 6. JH Schmelzer 13 Sonatas, 'Sacro-profanus concentus musicus' – XII
*a***Choir of The English Consort;**
The English Concert / Andrew Manze
Harmonia Mundi HMU90 7397 (78' · DDD · T/t) Ⓕ

Missa Christi resurgentis. Mystery Sonatas – The Resurrection*a*
New York Collegium / Andrew Parrott with
*a***Ingrid Matthews** vn *a***Eric Milnes** org
Kleos Classics 🔊 KL5135 (74' · DDD/DSD · T/t) Ⓕ

The *Missa Christi resurgentis* seems to have lain in obscurity for centuries, known about but otherwise ignored, until brought to life by James Clements and published by A-R Editions in the US. The New York Collegium gave the first modern performance in 2003 and The English Concert followed a year later with the European premiere. The recordings differ in the way the music is presented: both are very welcome.

After perhaps descending to the crypt to sneer at the tomb of Prince-Archbishop Hieronymus Colloredo, Mozart's employer, the visitor to the Baroque cathedral of Salzburg cannot fail to be impressed by the interior

with its four galleries. Biber, who had joined the service of the Archbishop Maximilian Gandolph in 1670, made full use of the cathedral's spatial opportunities: two four-part choirs are complemented by string and brass groups used, like Venetian *cori spezzati*, both antiphonally and in combination.

The Mass was probably written for Easter 1674. It begins with a sonata, the strings answering the brass. Andrew Manze takes it straight; while Andrew Parrott, by slurring the second and third notes, adds an appealing rakishness to the phrase. 'Christe eleison' sees the first of several appearances by three basses, a difficult ensemble to balance. The Americans, with a light first bass, make it sound quite airy. The English Concert, at a slower speed and a lower pitch, tend to growl away in their boots. The 'Et expecto' section of the *Credo* finds Manze's sopranos singing high with a real sense of awe. In general, the singing of the Choir of The English Concert is the more accomplished: some of the solo work in Parrott's choir sounds tentative and the boy alto causes moments of unease for the listener. The orchestral playing is first-rate on both recordings.

Which to choose must depend on the supplementary pieces. Manze includes five sonatas for strings. The tonal palette is limited, as is usual for the time, to the home key with occasional excursions to the relative major or minor. The first movement of the Sonata a 6 for trumpet and strings reappears on the American disc. Here, however, the context is that of an actual service. It starts with an alternatim setting of the introit *Resurrexi* by Johann Stadlmayr and includes, as well as the chanting of the epistle and gospel, organ pieces by Kerll and Poglietti. There are also two string sonatas from the *Sonatae tam aris* collection, one of which includes a fugue theme that anticipates the *Allegro* of Handel's *Concerto grosso*, Op 3 No 2.

Gilles Binchois French c1400-1460

Binchois was one of the three leading musical figures of the first half of the 15th century (with Dufay and Dunstable). Organist at Ste Waudru, Mons, from 1419, he was granted permission to move to Lille in 1423 and apparently entered the service of William Pole, Earl of Suffolk, soon after. Later in the 1420s he joined the Burgundian court chapel where he was much honoured and appointed a secretary to the court (c1437). He held prebends in Bruges, Mons, Cassel and Soignies, where he finally retired; there he was appointed provost of the collegiate church of St Vincent (1452), though he continued to receive a pension from the Burgundian court.

Although Binchois name was mentioned in contemporary literature only alongside Dufay's, his works had a more independent reputation and, though less widely circulated than Dufay's, were very popular. Six of his songs survive in keyboard arrangements; tenor lines of two or three were used to make basse danses, and numerous compositions from the mid- and late 15th century, including three mass cycles (Ockeghem's Missa 'De plus en plus', Bedyngham's Missa 'Dueil angoisseux' and the anonymous mass-motet cycle 'Esclave puist il devenir'), were based on his works. The fact that many of his compositions survive in only one source, and that most of those were compiled in southern Europe, far from the Burgundian court, suggests that much of his work may be lost or survive only anonymously. His songs, mostly rondeaux, remain within the conventions of refined courtly tradition. They are nearly all for a single-texted upper voice supported by an untexted tenor in longer notes a fifth lower in range and a contratenor in the same range or a little lower. They are characterised by effortless, graceful melodies, uncomplicated rhythms and carefully balanced phrases. His sacred music tends to be more conservative. No complete mass cycle by him has survived, though some of the mass movements can be paired on the basis of similarity. He wrote only one isorhythmic motet, and many of his smaller sacred works are purely functional. GROVEmusic

Sacred works

Binchois Nove cantum melodie. Domitor Hectoris. Kyrie. Sanctus. Agnus Dei **Dufay** Mass for St Anthony Abbot
Binchois Consort (Mark Chambers, William Towers countertens Edwin Simpson, Nick Todd, Matthew Vine, Christopher Watson tens) / Andrew Kirkman
Hyperion CDA67474 (71' · DDD)   Ⓕ

The Binchois Consort finally turn their attentions to the composer whose name they bear. The contrast between Dufay and Binchois is every bit as striking in sacred music as in the secular. Binchois's Mass movements trip along very un-solemnly, a worthy foil to the stately Dufay; but the high-point is his single surviving isorhythmic motet, here seamlessly reconstructed by Philip Weller.

It is fascinating to hear a familiar voice like Binchois's speaking in a language one's not used to from him. If the tempo chosen for the piece stretches the singers more than usually (albeit exhilaratingly), in the rest of the Dufay programme they are masterful. The verse of the Offertory has one of those spine-tingling moments (a high countertenor f' conjured out of nowhere) that hits the bull's eye every time you hear it.

Judith Bingham   British b1952

Bingham has always been attracted to the voice and its musical possibilities. Early study with Alan Bush, Eric Fenby and John Hall led to two years of tutorials with Hans Keller whom Bingham counts as a major influence. In 1977 she won the BBC Young Composer of the Year Award which lead to BBC commissions as well as for works for brass band. She has been widely performed by British orchestras.
GROVEmusic

Choral works

'Remoter Worlds'
Gleams of a Remoter World. The Shepheardes Calender. Water Lilies. Irish Tenebraea. Unpredictable but Providential. Beneath these Alien Starsb. Ghost Towns of the American West
BBC Singers / David Hill with ªOlivia Robinson sop
ªKrysia Osostowicz vn ªbIain Farrington org
ªRichard Benjafield, ªChris Brannick perc
Signum Classics SIGCD144 (71' · DDD)   Ⓕ

Judith Bingham's discography is slowly catching up with her increasingly impressive body of work. Unsurprisingly, the releases to date have concentrated on her choral music and it is heartening to see the BBC Singers – with whom she sang as a permanent member for 12 years and has been Associate Composer for the past four – perform a whole disc's worth of repertoire mostly unavailable otherwise.

The Shepheardes Calender, a triptych written in 2006 for the St Louis Chamber Choir receives a polished and refined account, with great bite and drive. There is an expressive resonance to the central setting of Psalm 23 (in a variant textual version) and the opening 'Winter' is icy as befits the words. *Unpredictable but Providential* (1992, rev 2007) is a delightful skit on Elizabethan word-setting and *Beneath these Alien Stars* (2001), like the larger *Ghost Towns of the American West* (2005), sets poems by the Mormon poet Vesta Pearce Crawford.

The major item is *Irish Tenebrae* (1990, rev 1992 and 2007), a remarkable cantata in seven sections for solo and choral voices, violin, organ and percussion. Inspired by the composer's part-Irish origins, the Troubles and a love of Irish folksong, the work is a tremendous achievement, Britten-like in its range and variety – and expressive acuity – yet distinctly Binghamian in its sound (though quite unlike its couplings). The performances by all concerned are superb, from the opening *Gleams of a Remoter World* (1997) and *Water Lilies* (1999) to the larger pieces. Strongly recommended.

The Secret Gardenª. Salt in the Blood. First Light. The Darkness is no Darkness. The Snow Descendsb
Thomas Trotter org **BBC Symphony Chorus;**
bFine Arts Brass / Stephen Jackson
Naxos 8 570346 (68' · DDD)   ⓈⒹ▸
ªRecorded live

Judith Bingham is a composer with a special gift for vocal setting and a wealth of experience in what can be sung: for 13 years she was a permanent member of the BBC Symphony Chorus and BBC Singers (for whom she is Associate Composer).

All five works on this new disc reveal a distinctive voice writing in a recognisably modern idiom which combines clarity of thought and complexity of vision. Bingham's music draws audiences in, without alienating them or compromising her expressive integrity. *Salt in the Blood* (1995) is a prime example, a large musical – at times theatrical – tapestry of British sea-song, weaving in existing shanties and invented hornpipes to retell the tale of two sailors' rivalry as to who was the better dancer. Bingham thinks convincingly in long spans, as her 2004 Prom commission *The Secret Garden* confirms (given here in a live performance). *First Light* (2001) and the brief *The Darkness is no Darkness* (1993) engage with the English choral tradition to an unusual degree, the latter – a reinterpretation of a Wesley hymn – in particular.

The performances all round are first rate and the recorded sound is excellent, which is no less than Bingham deserves. The BBC Symphony Chorus sing with gusto and Fine Arts Brass relish some fine brass writing, not least in *The Snow Descends* (1997), an atmospheric paraphrase for brass of one of Bingham's choral works. Recommended.

Sir Harrison Birtwistle   British b1934

Birtwistle studied at the Royal Manchester College of Music (1952-5), where Davies and Goehr were fellow students, interesting themselves in contemporary and medieval music. He then worked as a clarinettist and schoolteacher for brief periods; in 1975 he was appointed music director at the National Theatre. His works suggest comparison with Stravinsky in their ritual form and style, and sometimes with Varèse in the violence of their imagery (as in the opera Punch and Judy, 1968, a savage enactment of pre-social behaviour). In the 1970s, however, he began to work musical blocks into long, gradual processes of change (The Triumph of Time for orchestra, 1972), then to develop networks of interconnected pulsings beneath such processes (Silbury Air for small orchestra, 1977; agm for voices and orchestral groups, 1979). His biggest work of this period was the opera The Mask of Orpheus (1973-83, performed 1986), a multi-layered treatment of the myth.
GROVEmusic

Orchestral works

Secret Theatre. Silbury Air. Carmen Arcadiae Mechanicae Perpetuum
London Sinfonietta / Elgar Howarth
NMC Ancora NMCD148 (58' · DDD)   Ⓜ

When these recordings first appeared Birtwistle enthusiasts were still absorbing the impact of three 1986 premieres, *Earth Dances*, *The Mask of Orpheus* and *Yan Tan Tethera* – works which helped to catapult a highly regarded composer into something as close to superstardom as contemporary classical music can provide. *Secret Theatre*, the longest of the three works, was itself a mere three years old in 1987: more than two decades on, its elaboration and refinement of

basic formal and textural elements present in *Silbury Air* and *Carmen Arcadiae Mechanicae Perpetuum* (both from 1977) is ever more striking. Written between *The Mask of Orpheus* and the no less epic enterprise of *Earth Dances*, *Secret Theatre* really does mark a great leap forward, and this performance captures the special, pioneering dedication and enthusiasm which Elgar Howarth and the London Sinfonietta were able to summon up in those days. The recording, even with sensitive remastering, can't give a full picture of the spatial processes at work, involving the tension and interaction between separated individuals and groups, but it is still a highly charged, eloquent account of one of the composer's most powerful and most personal scores.

The more starkly differentiated mechanisms of the other pieces now seem like relatively unelaborated blueprints for the riches to follow, and despite the very different connotations of their titles – the Wiltshire landscape in *Silbury Air*, a Paul Klee canvas in *Carmen Arcadiae* – there are evident similarities, as well as moments which now sound unexpectedly derivative (for example, of Ligeti at the opening of *Silbury Air*). But that simply reinforces Birtwistle's importance as part of the European modernist mainstream, something to which his substantial and distinctive contribution remains a thing to wonder at as he approaches his 75th birthday.

Pulse Shadows

Pulse Shadows
Claron McFadden *sop* **Arditti Quartet** (Irvine Arditti, Graeme Jennings *vns* Dov Scheindlin *va* Rohan de Saram *vc*) **Nash Ensemble / Reinbert de Leeuw**
Teldec 3984-26867-2 (64' · DDD)   Ⓕⓞⓞⓞ

From Schoenberg's *Pierrot lunaire* to Boulez's *Le marteau sans maître* and Kurtág's *Messages of the late RV Troussova*, modernist composers have used the medium of voice with mixed instrumental ensemble for their most allusive and personal utterances. Birtwistle's *Pulse Shadows* (1991-6) belongs in this company. While not easy listening, it deals with some of the most elemental and profound topics in contemporary culture, and this recording rises to the score's many challenges, both technically and interpretatively.

Pulse Shadows is subtitled 'Meditations on Paul Celan', acknowledging the poet-author of the texts for the nine vocal movements, and indicating that the nine movements for string quartet with which the vocal movements are interleaved reflect on – shadow – the emotions that setting Celan (mainly in Michael Hamburger's English translations) created in the composer. The poems are oblique rituals, meditations on the state of human consciousness after the Holocaust, and Birtwistle's music links that quality with the kind of innately melancholic, stoical, intensely humane spirit that informs most of his finest works. Claron McFadden proves herself the most mellifluous singer of this music. Together with the precision and empathy of the Arditti Quartet and Reinbert de Leeuw, not to mention the admirable recorded sound, this is a disc to live with, and be haunted by, for years to come.

Additional recommendation

Theseus Game[a]. Earth Dances[b]
[a]**Ensemble Modern / Brabbins, Valade; [b]Ensemble Modern / Boulez**
DG download 477 070-2GH (67' · DDD) Recorded live
ⓅⓄ➔

Theseus Game (2002-3) offers clear visual contrasts: an ensemble of 30 players has two conductors, and there's a central space at the front of the platform for the succession of soloists who emerge from the ensemble. *Earth Dances* (1985-6) demands total surrender; as the music unwinds to its end, spasms of the seismic dance stand in the way of any comforting sense of fulfilment, or resolution.

Five Distances

Five Distances[a]. The Silk House Tattoo[b]. 17 Tate Riffs[c]
[b]**John Wallace,** [b]**Adam Wright** tpts [b]**Sam Walton** perc [a]**Gallimaufry Ensemble** (Louisa Dennehy fl Holly Fawcett ob Peter Sparks cl Siona Crosdale bn Nicholas Wolmark hn) [c]**Royal Academy of Music Chamber Ensemble**
Royal Academy of Music RAM019 (29' · DDD)　　Ⓜ

To coincide with the composer's 70th birthday, the Royal Academy of Music released a sequence of Birtwistle recordings made by staff and students in 2001. *Five Distances* for wind quintet (1992) has been recorded before, and this version risks substituting a generalised resonance for a strong sense of actual separation between the players. Yet it's very well played and persuasively shaped. Distance and resonance are even more basic to *The Silk House Tattoo* (1993) with its circling, echoing trumpets kept in line by a peremptory drummer, and to *17 Tate Riffs* (2000), Birtwistle's characteristically ritualised response to a commission for the opening ceremony of Tate Modern, with 15 players spread around the cavernous Turbine Hall. No recording can match the far-flung aural vistas of the original location, but this one is well worth having as a reminder of how – even on the smallest timescale – Birtwistle can hint at the wider formal perspectives and grander mythic themes which form his usual terrain.

Piano Works

The Axe Manual[a]. Harrison's Clocks. Hector's Dawn. Berceuse de Jeanne. Précis. Sad Song. Oockooing Bird. Ostinato with Melody. Betty Freeman: Her

Tango. Saraband: The King's Farewell
Nicolas Hodges pf [a]**Claire Edwardes** perc
Metronome METCD1074 (71' · DDD)　　Ⓕ

Though most of the items in this indispensable collection of Birtwistle's keyboard music last five minutes or less, two are on a scale commensurate with the orchestral *Triumph of Time* or *Secret Theatre*.

In *Harrison's Clocks* (1997-8) simultaneously unfolding strata demonstrate that 'interdependent independence' of which Birtwistle often speaks. On one level, the music is potently mechanical, welded together from clearly defined rhythmic patterns which recur and collide like meshing cogs. Yet lying behind these mechanics is that background of complex associations with myth and ritual that's never far away in any Birtwistle composition, even the shortest and simplest.

The first recording of *The Axe Manual* (2000), reveals it as an exuberant, and, in its central stages, delicate essay in 'extending' piano sound by means of metal and wood percussion. It turns fascination with tone-colour and texture into an absorbing musical drama, a battle with and against time that has an intensely human urgency and passion. It's a tribute to the quality of the WDR Cologne recording, excellent throughout, that the balance between the two performers seems so effortlessly right.

Nicolas Hodges is an accomplished guide to these varied perspectives, never over-nuancing the understated poetry of the miniatures, but meeting with total authority all the technical and interpretative challenges of the larger works.

Harrison's Clocks
Joanna MacGregor pf
SoundCircus SC004 (26' · DDD)　　Ⓜ

Even if Harrison Birtwistle was not knowingly named after John Harrison, the 18th-century clockmaker discussed in Dava Sobel's recent best-seller *Longitude*, his recurrent concern with musical mechanisms whose 'ticking' regularity is the perfect foil for other, much less predictable elements, makes him the ideal composer to celebrate the pioneer of navigational chronometers. The recurring patterns which dominate the first of these five pieces (composed in 1998) are deceptive in that they create a relatively mild-mannered, even static effect, with contrast confined to brief episodes marking the movement's main formal divisions. But if this leads you to expect a sequence of neo-classical toccatas, the explosive fragmentation of the second piece will soon disabuse you, and in the hair-raisingly intense third movement the implacable power of the composer's invention takes the breath away.

Joanna MacGregor meets the demands with interest, bringing the music vividly to life, and the recording is excellent. Indispensable.

Vocal works

The Field of Sorrow[ac]. Verses for Ensembles[c].
Nenia: The Death of Orpheus[ab]
[a]Jane Manning sop [b]The Matrix / Alan Hacker;
[c]London Sinfonietta / David Atherton
Lyrita SRCD306 (56' · ADD) Recorded 1975   Ⓕ

This trio of compositions charts Harrison Birtwistle's transition from the brutal mechanics and plaintive lyricism of his first opera *Punch and Judy* (1967) to the more subtle expressive qualities and more expansive forms of his second, *The Mask of Orpheus*, begun in 1973. The recordings, especially of *Verses* (1969), show their age, but the performances remain uniquely arresting, unsurpassed in their eager response to the challenges and rewards these scores offered to David Atherton, Alan Hacker and their colleagues.

Listening to *Verses* today, its well-nigh half hour of improvisatory drumming interspersed with woodwind and brass riffs recalling Varèse and Tippett, you can see why Birtwistle felt the need to open himself up to the kind of mythic subject matter that the *Orpheus* pieces explore. *Verses* has its quieter moments but they tend to sound drained of expression, and the strategy of moving the players around the platform makes little impact in a parched analogue recording. The great leap forward in *Nenia: The Death of Orpheus* (1972) is obvious and profound. Birtwistle might not have been immediately confident enough in his vocal writing to dispense with a battery of effects close to the kind of thing Berio had devised for Cathy Berberian, but Jane Manning's brilliant account, especially in the soft yet intense speech of the final section, helps to underline that newfound mastery of slow but certain pacing – drifting with a purpose – that would be a Birtwistle feature from then on.

The Field of Sorrow (1972) further concentrates form and expression with consistent, complementary textural layering and richly focused lyricism. That Birtwistle has remained faithful to such principles ever since is evidence not of a lack of fresh ideas but of his awareness that he had found a winning, infinitely adaptable formula. This disc is valuable above all in reminding today's listeners of where and when that formula was first deployed.

The Woman and The Hare[a]. Nine Settings of Lorine Niedecker[b]. Duets for Storab[c]. An Interrupted Endless Melody[d]. Entr'actes and Sappho Fragments[e]
[abe]Claron McFadden sop [a]Julia Watson spkr Nash Ensemble ([ace]Philippa Davies, [ac]Helen Keen fls [a]Richard Hosford cl [de]Gareth Hulse ob [e]Skaila Kanga hp Ian Brown [d]pf/[a]cels [ae]Simon Limbrick perc [ae]Marianne Thorsen, [a]Elizabeth Wexler vns [ae]Lawrence Power va [ab]Paul Watkins vc) / [ae]Martyn Brabbins
Black Box BBM1046 (77' · DDD· N/T)   Ⓕ

The Woman and the Hare (1999) shares its sound world with such close contemporaries as *Pulse*

Shadows, *The Last Supper* and (near the end, in particular) with Birtwistle's music for the 2002 Royal National Theatre production of *The Bacchae*. The composer's genius for moving swiftly and imperceptibly between austerity and warmth is evident in both works, his characteristically fragmentary forms generating more than enough expressive continuity to ensure a powerful dramatic charge. This is equally true of the recent settings for soprano and cello of Lorine Niedecker, whose aphoristic poems about the threats and rituals of interactions between nature and humanity might have been written expressly for Birtwistle.

The vocal compositions gain greatly from the assured direction of Martyn Brabbins and the effortless yet characterful singing of Claron McFadden. Birtwistle's decision to divide David Harsent's text for *The Woman and the Hare* between a narrator and a singer, coupled with some particularly graphic instrumental writing, make this one of his most unambiguously theatrical concert pieces, and this account emphasises the claustrophobic aura of Harsent's text. The cumulative impact of the whole is remarkable, with a visceral thrust that complements the more withdrawn lyricism of the *Sappho Fragments* and the Niedecker settings.

The instrumental works, *Duets for Storab* and *An Interrupted Endless Melody* are performed with the Nash Ensemble's special flair, and the sound, throughout, has admirable presence. Both compositions are already available on a valuable Deux-Elles release from the Galliard Ensemble, but the two discs complement each other well enough to make both essential purchases.

Operas

Punch and Judy
Stephen Roberts bar Punch **Jan DeGaetani** mez Judy; Fortune-teller **Phyllis Bryn-Julson** sop Pretty Polly; Witch **David Wilson-Johnson** bar Choregos; Jack Ketch **Philip Langridge** ten Lawyer **John Tomlinson** bass Doctor
London Sinfonietta / David Atherton
NMC Ancora ② NMCD138 (103' · ADD)   Ⓜ❶❶❶❶➔

It's almost 40 years since the 1968 premiere of *Punch and Judy*, celebrated in legend as a rude gesture in the face of Aldeburgh primness, and with hindsight as one of the finest achievements by Britten's most gifted British successor in the field of opera composition.

Good though it would be to have a new performance, the chances of something recent outclassing this 1979 version are remote. David Atherton has total empathy with the tricky blend of short numbers and culminative intensity, and draws brilliantly polished and characterful playing from the London Sinfonietta. The dream cast is headed by Stephen Roberts's stunning portrayal of Mr Punch as a demented Oxbridge choral scholar, and by David Wilson-Johnson's suave, sinister Master of Ceremonies, while Philip Langridge and John Tomlinson make telling contributions. This, it need hardly be said, is not 'slice of life' opera, but the characters are animated and individualised, as they should be, through music which fits Stephen Pruslin's hilariously concise word-games like a glove. And if all this weren't enough, the fabulous Phyllis Bryn-Julson comes into her own in the final stages, a succession of vivid, poignant musical moments which Birtwistle has never bettered. And given NMC's no-deletion policy, this classic set is here to stay. No collection should be without it.

The Mask of Orpheus

The Mask of Orpheus
Jon Garrison ten Orpheus: Man Peter Bronder ten Orpheus: Myth, Hades Jean Rigby mez Euridice: Woman Anne-Marie Owens mez Euridice: Myth, Persephone Alan Opie bar Aristaeus: Man Omar Ebrahim bar Aristaeus: Myth, Charon; Marie Angel sop Aristeus: Oracle of the Dead, Hecate; Arwel Huw Morgan bar Caller; Stephen Allen ten Priest, First Judge; Nicholas Folwell bar Priest, Second Judge; Stephen Richardson bass Priest, Third Judge; Juliet Booth sop Woman, First Fury; Philippa Dames-Longworth sop Woman, Second Fury; Elizabeth McCormack mez Woman, Third Fury; Ian Dearden sound diffusion BBC Singers; BBC Symphony Orchestra / Sir Andrew Davis, Martyn Brabbins
NMC NMCD050 ③ (162' · DDD · N/T)   Ⓜ❍❍❍

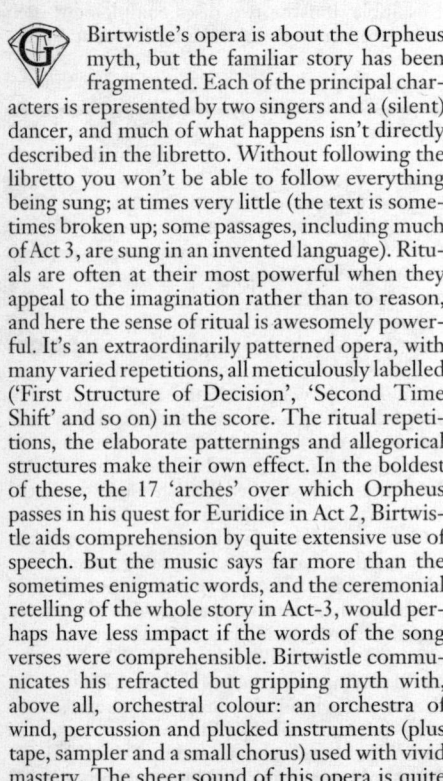Birtwistle's opera is about the Orpheus myth, but the familiar story has been fragmented. Each of the principal characters is represented by two singers and a (silent) dancer, and much of what happens isn't directly described in the libretto. Without following the libretto you won't be able to follow everything being sung; at times very little (the text is sometimes broken up; some passages, including much of Act 3, are sung in an invented language). Rituals are often at their most powerful when they appeal to the imagination rather than to reason, and here the sense of ritual is awesomely powerful. It's an extraordinarily patterned opera, with many varied repetitions, all meticulously labelled ('First Structure of Decision', 'Second Time Shift' and so on) in the score. The ritual repetitions, the elaborate patternings and allegorical structures make their own effect. In the boldest of these, the 17 'arches' over which Orpheus passes in his quest for Euridice in Act 2, Birtwistle aids comprehension by quite extensive use of speech. But the music says far more than the sometimes enigmatic words, and the ceremonial retelling of the whole story in Act-3, would perhaps have less impact if the words of the song verses were comprehensible. Birtwistle communicates his refracted but gripping myth with, above all, orchestral colour: an orchestra of wind, percussion and plucked instruments (plus tape, sampler and a small chorus) used with vivid mastery. The sheer sound of this opera is quite

haunting and moving. *The Mask of Orpheus* is a masterpiece, and this performance is fully worthy of it. There are no weak links at all in the extremely fine cast. Although it's unfair to single out any singer for special mention, Jon Garrison's portrayal of Orpheus the Man is outstanding. The recording, direct and pungent but by no means lacking in atmosphere, leaves nothing to be desired.

The Minotaur
John Tomlinson bass The Minotaur Johan Reuter bar Theseus Christine Rice mez Ariadne Andrew Watts counterten Snake Priestess Philip Langridge ten Hiereus Chorus and Orchestra of the Royal Opera House, Covent Garden / Antonio Pappano
Stage director Stephen Langridge
Video director Jonathan Haswell
Opus Arte 📀 OA1000D (175' · NTSC · 16:9 · PCM stereo and DTS 5.1 · 0). Extra features include the documentary 'Myth Is Universal'   Ⓕ❍❍

Birtwistle's latest large-scale music drama, written for Covent Garden, is a quite different experience on DVD: what might have been planned by composer and stage director to be witnessed from a distance is shown in unsparing close-up. But this seething, monumental reinvention of one of the most disquieting Greek myths – with a pithy libretto by David Harsent – is neither betrayed nor diminished by this excellent film.

Only in its final stages does the opera's focus shift decisively to the doomed Minotaur from the scheming Ariadne, and the drama's most essential point is that this Ariadne – as different from Strauss's as Birtwistle's Orpheus is different from Gluck's – is in her own way as much of a monster as the half-man/half-bull. These demanding roles are projected with maximum musical eloquence by Christine Rice and Sir John Tomlinson, no doubt because – as Rice makes clear in the absorbing 30-minute documentary that accompanies the performance – what is demanding is also intensely rewarding to singers prepared to commit themselves to a steep learning curve. Equal commitment is evident in Johan Reuter's Theseus, the conventions of heroic posturing given new depth and relevance in text, music and vocal acting alike.

The filming reinforces the strengths of Stephen Langridge's tightly controlled, potently expressive production in an economical yet atmospheric setting, with the whole ensemble totally engaged in the drama's dark enterprise. We see little of Antonio Pappano and his orchestra, but the excellent sound never lets us escape the inexorable magnetism of the instrumental continuum. As Stephen Langridge says in the documentary, this is 'a very dark piece', and a first hearing might not reveal its subtlety of pacing, the care it takes to avoid being merely unremitting. Repeated hearings underline that, in the end, this tragedy is the more convincing for the way its turn towards pathos does not involve any false consolation.

Georges Bizet
French 1838-1875

Bizet was trained by his parents, who were musical, and admitted to the Paris Conservatoire just before his tenth birthday. There he studied counter-point with Zimmerman and Gounod and composition with Halévy, and under Marmontel's tuition he became a brilliant pianist. Bizet's exceptional powers as a composer are already apparent in the products of his Conservatoire years, notably the Symphony in C, a work of precocious genius dating from 1855 (but not performed until 1935). In 1857 Bizet shared with Lecocq a prize offered by Offenbach for a setting of the one-act operetta Le Docteur Miracle; later that year he set out for Italy as holder of the coveted Prix de Rome.

During his three years in Rome Bizet began or projected many compositions; only four survive, including the opera buffa, Don Procopio (not performed until 1906). Shortly after his return to Paris, in September 1861, his mother died; the composer consoled himself with his parents maid, by whom he had a son in June 1862. He rejected teaching at the Conservatoire and the temptation to become a concert pianist, and completed his obligations under the terms of the Prix de Rome. The last of these, a one-act opéra comique, La guzla de l'emir, was rehearsed at the Opéra-Comique in 1863 but withdrawn when the Théâtre-Lyrique director, who had been offered 100 000 francs to produce annually an opera by a Prix de Rome winner who had not had a work staged, invited Bizet to compose Les pêcheurs de perles .

Bizet completed it in four months. It was produced in September 1863, but met with a generally cool reception: an uneven work, with stiff characterisation, it is notable for the skilful scoring of its exotic numbers. In the ensuing years Bizet earned a living arranging other composers' music and giving piano lessons. Not until December 1867 was another opera staged – La jolie fille de Perth, which shows a surer dramatic mastery than Les pêcheurs. It received a good press but had only 18 performances.

1868 was a year of crisis for Bizet, with more abortive works, attacks of quinsy and a re-examination of his religious stance; and his attitude to music grew deeper. In June 1869 he married Geneviève, daughter of his former teacher, Halévy, and the next year they suffered the privations caused by the Franco-Prussian war (Bizet enlisted in the National Guard). Bizet found little time for sustained composition, but in 1871 he produced the delightful suite for piano duet, Jeux d'enfants (some of it scored for orchestra as the Petite Suite), and he worked on a one-act opera, Djamileh. Both the opera and Daudet's play L'arlésienne, for which Bizet wrote incidental music, failed when produced in 1872, but in neither case did this have anything to do with the music.

Bizet was convinced that in Djamileh he had found his true path, one which he followed in composing his operatic masterpiece, Carmen. Here Bizet reaches new levels in the depiction of atmosphere and character. The characterisation of José, his gradual decline from a simple soldier's peasant honesty through insurbordination, desertion and smuggling to murder is masterly; the colour and vitality of Carmen herself are remarkable, involving the use of the
harmonic, rhythmic instrumental procedures of Spanish dance music, to which also the fate-laden augmented 2nds of the Carmen motif may owe their origin. The music of Micaela and Escamillo may be less original, but the charm of the former and the coarseness of the latter are intentional attributes of the characters. The opera is the supreme achievement of Bizet and of opéra comique, a genre it has transformed in that Bizet extended it to embrace passionate emotion and a tragic end, purging it of artificial elements and embuing it with a vivid expression of the torments inflicted by sexual passion and jealousy. The work, however, was condemned for its 'obscene' libretto, and the music was criticised as erudite, obscure, colourless, undistinguished and unromantic. Only after Bizet's death was its true stature appreciated, and then at first only in the revised version by Guiraud in which recitatives replace the original spoken dialogue (it is only recently that the original version has been revived). The reception of Carmen left Bizet acutely depressed; he fell victim to another attack of quinsy and, in June 1875, to the two heart attacks from which he died. GROVEmusic

Orchestral works

Symphony in Cª. L'Arlésienneᵇ – Suites Nos 1 & 2 **H**
ªFrench National Radio Symphony Orchestra;
ᵇ**Royal Philharmonic Orchestra / Sir Thomas Beecham**
EMI 5672312 (65' · ADD) Recorded 1956-9 Ⓕ🅾🅾🅱➡

In Beecham's hands the Symphony in C is made to sound wonderfully songful and although the French orchestral playing is less than ideally polished, the *joie de vivre* of Beecham's performance is irresistible. What makes this disc doubly desirable are the marvellous RPO wind solos (and, of course, the haunting strings in the *Adagietto*) in *L'Arlésienne*. The performances of these two suites stand head and shoulders above present CD competition, their loving finesse mixes evocative magic (the 'Intermezzo' of No 2) with wonderful rhythmic vivacity (the closing 'Farandole'). The refurbishing of the recordings is remarkably successful, especially *L'Arlésienne*.

Carmen – Prélude; Entractes 1, 2 and 3. L'Arlésienne – Suites Nos 1 and 2; Incidental Music
Lyon Opera Chorus; Les Musiciens du Louvre-Grenoble / Marc Minkowski
Naïve V5130 (59' · DDD) Ⓕ🅾🅾🅾

Couplings of the *Carmen* and *L'Arlésienne* suites have long been a favourite, and Minkowski's new disc has the best of all worlds in demonstrating a Beechamesque flair (the opening cymbal crash of the *Carmen* Suite is immediately arresting) and in including three suites from *L'Arlésienne*, their content well thought out and lovingly prepared. They consist of the familiar First Suite (as Bizet designed it), the Second, arranged after the composer's death by Ernest Guiraud, including the borrowed Menuet from *La jolie fille de Perth*, and a third

BIZET'S CARMEN – IN BRIEF

Leontyne Price Carmen **Franco Corelli** Don José
Mirella Freni Micaëla **Robert Merrill** Escamillo;
VPO / **Herbert von Karajan**
RCA ③ 74321 39495-2 (160' · ADD)   ⓂⓄⓄ
One of Price's greatest studio achievements,
one of Corelli's richest, and Freni at her most
charming. Conducted a little effortlessly.

Angela Gheorghiu Carmen **Roberto Alagna**
Don José **Inva Mula-Tchako** Micaëla **Thomas
Hampson** Escamillo; **Toulouse Capitole
Orchestra / Michel Plasson**
EMI ③ 557434-2 (157' · DDD)   ⒻⓄ▷
The husband-and-wife team of Gheorghiu
and Alagna really strike sparks off each other,
and the tenor has rarely done anything better
on disc.

Jessye Norman Carmen **Neil Shicoff** Don José
Mirella Freni Micaëla **Simon Estes** Escamillo;
French National Orchestra / Seiji Ozawa
Philips ③ 470 417-2 (161' · DDD)   Ⓑ▷
A surprise success – Jessye Norman might
not appear to be a natural Carmen, but she
sings with real insight and intelligence.
Shicoff's José, too, is magnificent.

Victoria de los Angeles Carmen **Nicolai Gedda**
Don José **Janine Micheau** Micaëla **Ernst Blanc**
Escamillo **French National Radio Orchestra /
Sir Thomas Beecham**
EMI ③ 567357-2 (162' · DDD)   ⒻⓄⓄⓄ▷
A classic recording, superbly cast and con-
ducted with a lightness of touch by Beecham
that has rarely been equalled.

Teresa Berganza Carmen **Plácido Domingo**
Don José **Ileana Cotrubas** Micaëla **Sherill Milnes**
Escamillo; **LSO / Claudio Abbado**
DG ② 477 5342GOR2 (157' · DDD)   ⓂⓄ
Even the sluggishly delivered dialogue
can't detract from the theatricality of this
much-loved recording. Berganza is an aristocratic Carmen, and Cotrubas one of the
loveliest Micaëlas.

Maria Callas Carmen **Nicolai Gedda** Don José
Andrea Guiot Micaëla **Robert Massard**
Escamillo; **Orchestre de Paris / Georges Prêtre**
EMI ② 556281-2 (146' · ADD)   Ⓜ▷
Callas is Callas and demands to be heard: this
isn't conventional but, wow, it works. Gedda
sounds more comfortable chez Beecham…

Julia Migenes Carmen **Plácido Domingo** Don
José **Faith Esham** Micaëla **Ruggero Raimondi**
Escamillo **French National Orchestra / Lorin
Maazel**
Erato ② 2292-45207-2 (151' · DDD)   ⓂⓄ
The soundtrack to a successful film version
finds Migenes a fiery, earthy Carmen and
Domingo once again proves his worth as a
singing-actor of real class.

suite of excerpts from the original score. The
collection is a delight, not least because of the
beautifully elegant orchestral playing.
Minkowski's choice of tempi and crisp pointing
of the woodwind are admirable – in the first
Entr'acte from Carmen, for instance, and the
Minuet which follows. The Farandole too, is
given a splendid lift by Minkowski's virtual
double-dotting, while the flute solos in both
Carmen and L'Arlésienne all have a delicious
delicacy. There is much pleasure too, from the
sensitive phrasing and the light and shade of
the playing. L'Arlésienne's famous Adagietto is
very affecting at the slower pacing, and it
touchingly returns before the final reprise of
the exuberant Farandole, heard first with men's
voices and then full choir in imitation.

The choral singing is splendid and the playing
of Les Musiciens du Louvre-Grenoble alternates sparkle with delicacy of colour and feeling,
while the recording and sumptuous packaging
are first-class. This is now a clear first choice on
virtually all counts for those wanting a disc combining music from Carmen and L'Arlésienne.

Carmen

Carmen
Angela Gheorghiu sop Carmen; **Roberto Alagna**
ten Don José; **Inva Mula** sop Micaëla; **Thomas
Hampson** bar Escamillo; **Elizabeth Vidal** sop
Frasquita; **Isabelle Cals** sop Mercédès; **Nicolas
Rivenq** ten Dancaïre; **Yann Beuron** ten Remendado;
Ludovic Tézier bar Moralès; **Nicolas Cavallier** bass
Zuniga; **Toulouse Children's Choir; Les Eléments;
Toulouse Capitole Orchestra / Michel Plasson**
EMI ② 557434-2 (157' · DDD · N/T/t)   ⒻⓄ

Michel Plasson draws some very fine playing
indeed from the Toulouse orchestra, and his
choice of speeds seems just right, never resorting to extreme effects. The one moment when
things get a bit sluggish is in the Card scene, but
he is, perhaps rightly, more concerned with letting Gheorghiu have as much breathing space as
she needs; the chest tone she uses for the cries of
'La mort!' is amazingly forceful. Her portrayal
has little of the easy sensuality of such celebrated
interpreters as Grace Bumbry or Teresa Berganza. But Gheorghiu and Roberto Alagna have
obviously worked very hard to achieve some fine
moments, a beautifully soft ending to 'Là-bas,
dans la montagne', and an almost visible change
of mood towards the end of the Séguedille, as
Carmen begins to work her charms. Gheorghiu
can't help sounding rather imperious at times,
and there's no exchange of remarks at the
moment when she throws the flower.

Alagna has done nothing better recently: he's
really inside the character, and portrays the
man's descent into degradation. There's little
sense of him pushing the tone – as in his Manrico – although his voice is much lighter than
many other famous Don Josés. This is all in his
favour, though, for moments such as the beautifully realised ending to 'Parle-moi de ma mère'.

Other roles are well taken: Thomas Hampson presents Escamillo as a very jovial sort of fellow, Inva Mula as Micaëla is better in the Act 1 duet than she is in her aria. The sound is uncomplicated, though Carmen's castanets (some very classy playing) seem to be coming from quite a distance away from her.

With dozens of *Carmen*s available on disc, it's impossible to recommend only one. This will be a pleasure for the many admirers of Plasson, Gheorghiu and Alagna. Once you get to the final duet in this 21st-century *Carmen*, you should find yourself completely gripped – by Alagna, who, while sounding distraught, still manages to produce some lovely tone, and by Gheorghiu, who, though she may never sing the role on stage, is a remarkably dramatic lady-in-distress for the microphone.

Carmen　　　　　　　　　　　　　　　　　　Ⓗ
Victoria de los Angeles *sop* Carmen; **Nicolai Gedda** *ten* Don José; **Janine Micheau** *sop* Micaëla; **Ernst Blanc** *bar* Escamillo; **Denise Monteil** *sop* Frasquita; **Marcelle Croisier** *mez* Mercédès; **Monique Linval** *sop* Mercédès; **Jean-Christophe Benoit** *bar* Dancaïre; **Michel Hamel** *ten* Remendado; **Bernard Plantey** *bass* Moralès; **Xavier Depraz** *bass* Zuniga; **Les Petits Chanteurs de Versailles; French National Radio Choir and Symphony Orchestra / Sir Thomas Beecham**
EMI Great Recordings of the Century ③ 567357-2 (162' · ADD) Recorded 1958/9　　　Ⓜ❍❍❍➲

🄶　This classic Beecham set stands the test of time, sparkling, swaggering and seducing in a way that's uniquely Beecham's. It now comes in the EMI Great Recordings of the Century series, with brightened, freshened and clarified sound. As Richard Osborne points out in his brilliant, informative note, there were serious problems at the sessions – a second series was organised 15 months after the first (hence the two Mercédès) – but you would never realise there had been difficulties, either from the performance or the firmly focused, spacious recording in which the atmospheric off-stage effects are vividly caught.

What's so individual is the way that Beecham points rhythms to captivate the ear, as well as his persuasive moulding of phrases. Witness the sensuous way he coaxes the string phrase leading into the second half of the Don José/Micaëla duet in Act 2, 'Parle-moi de ma mère!' (disc 1, track 9, 3'47"). In those qualities Beecham is matched by Victoria de los Angeles in the title-role.

Osborne reveals that Beecham's original choice of heroine was the Swedish mezzo Kerstin Meyer. After all, de los Angeles – Mimì in Beecham's *Bohème* recording – is hardly an obvious candidate for such a fire-eating role. But there's far more to Carmen than is conveyed in that conventional approach, and de los Angeles instantly establishes her as a seductive, provocative character with wickedly sparkling eyes. In her opening solo, the Habanera, her delicious downward *portamento* on 'Je t'aime' is irresistible. The Carmen quality which de los Angeles doesn't have in her regular armoury, though, is a snarl. Instead she consistently uses her golden tone to tantalise and provoke, as in the magically sultry moment leading into 'Là-bas dans la montagne' in her Act 2 duet with José just after the Flower song (disc 2, track 13). At that point Beecham, too, subtly pressing the music forward, is a fellow magician. Then at the very end, in Act 4, de los Angeles does finally muster a snarl in the culminating phrase 'laisse-moi passer' ('Well stab me then, or let me pass').

In a way, Nicolai Gedda's portrait of Don José is just as remarkable. He was at his peak, and sings not just with refinement and imagination but with deep passion, leading you on in the widest expressive range in the Flower song. Janine Micheau makes a bright, clear Micaëla, very French in tone, and Ernst Blanc, if not the most characterful Escamillo, makes the bullfighter a forthright, heroic character, singing with firm, clear tone.

The rest of the cast, all French, make an excellent team, as is clear in ensembles: the sparkling account of the Act 2 Quintet or the opening of the Card scene, or the swaggering march ensemble as the smugglers depart in Act 3 (disc 3, track 6). A magic set now made all the more enticing in this mid-price reissue.

Carmen
Teresa Berganza *sop* Carmen; **Plácido Domingo** *ten* Don José; **Ileana Cotrubas** *sop* Micaëla; **Sherrill Milnes** *bar* Escamillo; **Yvonne Kenny** *sop* Frasquita; **Alicia Nafé** *mez* Mercédès; **Robert Lloyd** *bass* Zuniga; **Stuart Harling** *bar* Moralès; **Gordon Sandison** *bar* Dancaïre; **Geoffrey Pogson** *ten* Remendado; **Ambrosian Singers; London Symphony Orchestra / Claudio Abbado**
DG ② 477 5342GOR2 (157' · ADD · N/T/t)　Ⓜ❍❍➲

This notable recording followed immediately on from the famous Faggioni production at the 1977 Edinburgh Festival, a staging finely observed enough still to remain with those who were there. In it Berganza declared her aim of rescuing the role from bad traditions and from its insults to Spanish womanhood. Her reading was restrained, haughty, but no less attractive and haunting for that. She developed the character, as she does on the recording, from carefree gypsy to tragic woman and, in doing so, is scrupulous in her obedience to Bizet's notes, rhythms and dynamics. Nothing is exaggerated yet nothing is left out in this sensuous but never overtly sensual portrayal, bewitchingly sung. Maybe you don't feel the full engagement of her emotions in her entanglement with José, but better a slight reticence than overacting. Migenes, on the Maazel set, is more immediately seductive, and occasionally more varied in tonal colouring, but Berganza is the more subtle artist. She works in keen rapport with Abbado, who brings clarity of texture, Mediterranean fire and intense concentration to the score.

You may find more elegance, more Gallic wit in, say, Beecham's famous EMI set, but only Maazel of other conductors comes near Abbado's emphasis on close-knit ensemble and histrionic strength – and both their sets come as the result of experience of 'real' performances. Domingo benefits here, as on the Maazel in the same way, being more involved in affairs. Like his Carmen, he sometimes lacks variety of colour in his singing, but its sheer musicality and, in the last two acts, power, count for much. Sherrill Milnes is at once virile and fatuous as Escamillo should be. Cotrubas makes a vulnerable, touching Micaëla. The dialogue is heavily foreshortened compared to rival sets. Abbado chooses some of the questionable Oeser alternatives, but – apart from the one in the finale – they aren't disturbing. The recording is first-rate.

Carmen

Christa Ludwig mez Carmen **James King** ten Don José **Eberhard Waechter** bar Escamillo **Jeanette Pilou** sop Micaëla **Lucia Popp** sop Frasquita **Margarita Lilova** bar Mercédès **Oskar Czerwenka** bar Zuniga **Reid Bunger** bar Moralès **Murray Dickie** ten Remendado **Erich Kunz** ten Le Dancaïre **Vienna State Opera Chorus; Vienna State Opera Orchestra / Lorin Maazel**
Orfeo ② C733 082I (145' · ADD · T/t)
Recorded live at the Staatsoper, Vienna, on February 19, 1966 Ⓜ

In this 1966 live recording conductor Lorin Maazel adopts some rather extreme tempi, for instance rather stately in the introduction to the Toreador's song, but elsewhere seeming a bit rushed. As the evening progresses, however, the performance gains considerably in dramatic fervour.

Christa Ludwig was fond of the title-role; she made a complete recording of it in German for EMI, conducted by Horst Stein, but as she explained in her autobiography: 'I'm personally the exact opposite of Carmen…I made her shameless, fearless, amoral and high-spirited.' Hers is a gypsy in the Viennese tradition of Maria Jeritza; in Acts 1 and 2 it's very much a star turn, but once things turn nasty in Act 3, Ludwig rises to the challenge and makes a tragic, proud figure. Her French is pretty good, although she has a bit of trouble with 'tu' and 'tout'.

James King recorded very little outside the German repertory for which he was best known. He overdoes the emotion a bit at the end of Act 1, but this is a valuable souvenir of this great trouper in one of his favourite parts. Jeanette Pilou was a lovely soprano, not well enough represented on disc, although she also made a studio recording as Micaëla under Jean Martinon. Lucia Popp is luxury casting as Frasquita, her unmistakable voice riding over the quintet, with Erich Kunz, no less, as Le Dancaïre. Eberhard Waechter must have cut a glamorous figure as Escamillo, and he too is impressive in his command of the original language. As Gottfried Kraus explains in the booklet, until this production by Otto Schenk the opera had often been given in polyglot performances, principals singing in French or Italian, chorus and comprimarios in German!

The mono sound is adequate, the stage noises atmospheric rather than distracting, and at the centre a pair of great singers, Ludwig and King, inhabiting their roles, aided by the dynamic leadership provided by Maazel: a heady dose of nostalgia.

Carmen

Julia Migenes mez Carmen; **Plácido Domingo** ten Don José; **Faith Esham** sop Micaëla; **Ruggero Raimondi** bass Escamillo; **Lilian Watson** sop Frasquita; **Susan Daniel** mez Mercédès; **Jean-Philippe Lafont** bar Dancaïre; **Gérard Garino** ten Remendado; **François Le Roux** bar Moralès; **John Paul Bogart** bass Zuniga; **French Radio Chorus; French Radio Children's Chorus; French National Orchestra / Lorin Maazel**
Erato ② 2292-45207-2 (151' · DDD · T/t) Ⓕ🔘🔘

Too many recordings of *Carmen* have blown up the work to proportions beyond its author's intentions but here Maazel adopts a brisk, lightweight approach that seems to come close to what Bizet wanted. Similarly Julia Migenes approaches the title part in an immediate, vivid way, exuding the gipsy's allure and suggesting Carmen's fierce temper and smouldering eroticism; she develops the character intelligently into the fatalistic person of the card scene and finale. Her singing isn't conventionally smooth but it's compelling throughout. Plácido Domingo has made Don José very much his own, and here he sings with unstinting involvement and finesse. Ruggero Raimondi is a macho Toreador though Faith Esham is a somewhat pallid Micaëla.

Carmen

Maria Ewing mez Carmen **Jacques Trussell** ten Don José **Miriam Gauci** sop Micaëla **Rosemary Ashe** sop Frasquita **Ludmilla Andrew** sop Mercédès **Alain Fondary** bar Escamillo **Emile Belcourt** ten Remendado **David Hamilton** bar Dancaïre **Rodney McCann** bass-bar Zuniga **Christopher Blades** bass Moralès **Ambrosian Opera Chorus; National Philharmonic Orchestra / Jacques Delacôte**
Stage director **Steven Pimlott**
Video director **Gavin Taylor**
Stax Entertainment 📀 MAWA131 (165' · 4:3 · 5.1 · 0) Recorded live 1989 Ⓕ🔘🔘

This DVD derives from a television relay from Earl's Court in June 1989, an unexpectedly successful staging in the barn-like venue. The triumph of the event was almost entirely due to Steven Pimlott's highly imaginative use of the huge space, presenting the work in the round on a large dais with a kind of moving platform surrounding it.

Maria Ewing's Carmen, as on her other two video interpretations of the role (Glyndebourne and Covent Garden), is an earthily mesmeric, wholly sensual and elemental gypsy, conceived perfectly for her own character yet marching with Bizet's concept. She's in wonderful voice, with many subtle emphases of word and tone to bring her solos to life. Trussell is a good foil, at once fiery, vulnerable, tetchy, and he sings with a combination of plangency and power. Fondary delivers his native French and the character of Escamillo with unerringly economic strength as to the manner born. Gauci is a limpid, lyrical, properly ingenuous Micaëla.

Delacôte is a near-ideal conductor of this score, an elegant, sensitive, vibrant reading that hits all the right spots. The work is played superbly by the National Philharmonic, who are heard to far better effect here than in the original venue. The sound-enhancement occasionally produces odd effects, but they hardly detract from enjoyment of the riveting performance. Subtitles are provided, but in the last two acts they're out of synch with the action.

U-Carmen eKhayelitsha (Sung and spoken in Xhosa) **Pauline Malefane** sngr Carmen **Zweilungile 'Zorro' Sidloyi** sngr Lulamile Nkomo **Andiswa Kedama** sngr Amanda **Andries Mbali** sngr Bra Nkomo **Sibulele Mjali** sngr Kayza **Andile Tshoni** sngr Jongikhaya **Andile Kosi** sngr Sargeant Kosi **Lungelwa Blou** sngr Nomakhaya **Zamile Christopher Gantana** sngr Captain Gantana **Dimpho di Kopane Theatre Ensemble; orchestra / Charles Hazlewood** Film director **Mark Dornford-May** Tartan ◉ **DVD** TVD3646 (120' · 1.85:1 · 2.0, 5.1 and DTS 5.1 · 0) Ⓕ

This is hardly the first retelling of Bizet's *Carmen*. It's not even the first to feature an all-black cast, with productions as diverse as the Broadway musical *Carmen Jones* and the more recent 'hip-hopera' with Beyoncé Knowles already lurking on the shelves. Still, *U-Carmen eKhayelitsha*, the cinematic rendering of the South African theatre company Dimpho Di Kopane's highly acclaimed stage production, loses no points for originality. This is not merely a successful retelling of a famous operatic tale; it's a compelling piece of film-making by any standard.

Part of that success relies on what remains unchanged, namely Bizet's score, which receives no more liberties than your average repertory production. But what is most memorable in this account, which won the Golden Bear for Best Film at the 2005 Berlin International Film Festival, is how well the production transcends its original language and culture while retaining Bizet's original spirit.

Setting the story in a South African township and translating the libretto into Xhosa, one of country's 'click' languages, presents some obvious challenges. Cigarette factories may be part of the landscape, but bullfights are rather less common, leaving Escamillo to be reinvented as a returning opera singer who sets the hearts of women in the local chorus aflutter. The country's indigenous vocal tradition dictates a rougher, less stylised sound than is usually heard in this music, though it does justify large groups of people spontaneously bursting into song.

Some of the recontextualisations are worth a few chuckles if compared with the original ('In the hottest part of the township with my friend Bra Nkomo – that's where I dance the Twalasta and drink sputla') but taken on its own terms the new libretto never distracts. In fact, trading the socially disenfranchised gypsies in the original Seville slums for more contemporary victims of racial repression makes the original point all the more apparent. When this Carmen sings her climactic 'Free I was born, and free I will die', it can't help but make a dramatic personal and political statement.

The fact that so few of the performers look like 'actors' is a mark of this production's roots. Most had originally lined up not specifically for casting auditions, the director admits in a telling interview included in the special features, but merely to get a job. Most had never even been in a theatre before, much less a production. In this case, the story behind the scenes is at least as dramatic as the one on camera.

Les pêcheurs de perles

Les pêcheurs de perles **Barbara Hendricks** sop Leïla; **John Aler** ten Nadir; **Gino Quilico** bar Zurga; **Jean-Philippe Courtis** bass Nourabad **Toulouse Capitole Chorus and Orchestra / Michel Plasson** EMI ② 749837-2 (127' · DDD · T/t) Ⓕ⬤

Let a tenor and a baritone signify that they're willing to oblige with a duet, and the cry will go up for *The Pearl Fishers*. It's highly unlikely that many of the company present will know what the duet is about – it recalls the past, proclaims eternal friendship and nearly ends up in a quarrel – but the melody and the sound of two fine voices blending in its harmonies will be quite sufficient. In fact there's much more to the opera than the duet; and the EMI recording goes further than previous versions in giving a complete account of a score remarkable for its unity as well as for the attractiveness of individual numbers.

It's a lyrical opera, and the voices need to be young and graceful. Barbara Hendricks and John Aler fulfil those requirements, she with a light, silvery timbre, he with a high tenor admirably suited to the tessitura of his solos. The third main character, the baritone whose role is central to the drama, assumes his rightful place here: Gino Quilico brings true distinction to the part, and his aria in Act 3 is one of the highlights. Though Plasson's direction at first is rather square, the performance grows in responsiveness. It's a pity the accompanying notes aren't stronger in textual detail, for the full score given here stimulates interest in its history. One of the changes made in the original score of 1863 concerns the celebrated duet itself, the first version of which is given in an appendix. It ends in a style you'd swear owed much to the 'friendship' duet in Verdi's *Don Carlos* – except that Bizet came first.

Sir Arthur Bliss   British 1891-1975

Bliss Studied with Wood at Cambridge and served in the army in France. Immediately after World War I he made a mark with works using nonsense texts and brittle Les Six-style irony (Rout, 1920), but successive orchestral works (A Colour Symphony, 1922; Introduction and Allegro, 1926; Music for Strings, 1935) established him as Elgar's successor. His three ballets (Checkmate, 1937 ; Miracle in the Gorbals, 1944 ; Adam Zero, 1946), a notable score for the film Things to Come (1935) and his opera The Olympians (1949) express his feelings for high drama and atmosphere. Among his other works are concertos for piano (1938), violin (1955) and cello (1970), songs, chamber and piano music, and choral works (notably the choral symphony Morning Heroes, 1930). In 1953 he was appointed Master of the Queen's Music. **GROVE**music

Cello Concerto, T120

Cello Concerto, T120. Music for Strings, T54. Two Studies, T16
Tim Hugh vc **English Northern Philharmonia / David Lloyd-Jones**
Naxos 8 553383 (64' · DDD)   Ⓢ Ⓞ ➔

This is a first-rate performance of Bliss's Cello Concerto from Tim Hugh, stylishly and sympathetically partnered by David Lloyd-Jones and the English Northern Philharmonia. The work is a delightful creation, ideally proportioned, impeccably crafted and full of the most beguiling invention. Hugh plays with commanding assurance, great beauty of tone and rapt commitment, and the accompaniment is sprightly and sensitive to match. What makes this release indispensable to all Bliss admirers is the inclusion of the *Two Studies*. These date from 1921 and were believed lost until they turned up in the composer's papers after his death in 1975. The first is a memorably chaste, coolly serene affair, scored with delicious poise, whereas the second is an energetic, good-humoured and occasionally face-pulling romp.

That just leaves the tremendous *Music for Strings*, which is where, alas, reservations must be raised. This superb score displays and demands a formidable technical facility, and Bliss's exhilaratingly well-judged writing would surely test any string section. It would be idle to pretend that the hard-working strings of the English Northern Philharmonia are ideally secure exponents. The work is well served by

Lloyd-Jones's clear-headed, expressive interpretation, but in the finale's crucial introductory bars his approach is oddly perfunctory. The Cello Concerto and the *Two Studies* alone though, will probably be enticement enough for many listeners. The recorded sound is excitingly realistic.

Piano Concerto, T58

Piano Concerto in B flat. Concerto for Two Pianos and Orchestra[a]. Sonata for Piano
Peter Donohoe, [a]**Martin Roscoe** pfs **Royal Scottish National Orchestra / David Lloyd-Jones**
Naxos 8 557146 (73' · DDD)   Ⓢ ➔

In recent times Bliss's swaggering Piano Concerto (written in 1938-9 for Solomon) has found a champion in Peter Donohoe, and it's good that he's been able to set down his powerful interpretation as part of Naxos's British Piano Concertos series. As those thunderous octaves at the outset demonstrate, Bliss's bravura writing holds no terrors for Donohoe and he generates a satisfying rapport with David Lloyd-Jones and the RSNO. Theirs is a beautifully prepared and attentive reading which grips from start to finish. The bittersweet central *Adagietto* casts an especially potent spell, while both outer movements harness blistering virtuosity to supple affection. All told, a worthy modern counterpart to the thrilling historic displays from Solomon and Mewton-Wood.

No less compelling is the buoyant account of the Concerto for Two Pianos: an infectiously enjoyable, single-movement work that began life in 1921 as a Concerto for Piano, Tenor and Strings (that same year, Bliss embarked on his *Colour* Symphony, of which there are fleeting echoes here). The present revision dates from 1950; 18 years later, Bliss overhauled the piece one last time for the three-hand partnership of Phyllis Sellick and Cyril Smith. As in the Piano Concerto, the recording's a touch bright and clangorous, but the ear soon adjusts.

No such technical qualms surround Donohoe's intelligent and accomplished performance of the Sonata composed in 1952 for Noel Mewton-Wood. With his commanding presence and rich tonal palette, Donohoe again exhibits a remarkable empathy with Bliss's red-blooded inspiration. This rewarding Naxos disc deserves every success.

Additional recommendation

Piano Concerto in B flat, T58[a]. Adam Zero, T67[b]
Solomon pf [a]**NYPSO / Boult;** [b]**Royal Opera House Orchestra, Covent Garden / Lambert**   Ⓗ
APR mono APR5627 (61' · DDD) Recorded [a]1939 (live), [b]1946   Ⓜ
  Solomon, for whose sovereign technique the Concerto was designed, plays like a man possessed. His partnership with Boult operates at the highest level of excitement, eloquence and dedication.

A Colour Symphony

A Colour Symphony. Adam Zero
English Northern Philharmonia / David Lloyd-Jones
Naxos 8 553460 (74' · DDD)   Ⓢ**OO**⮕

David Lloyd-Jones's exciting and idiomatic account of *A Colour Symphony* proves more than a match for all current competition, including the composer's own 1955 recording so spectacularly transferred by Dutton Laboratories. Speeds are judged to perfection – nicely flowing for the first and third movements, not too hectic for the flashing *Scherzo* – and countless details in Bliss's stunning orchestral canvas are deftly attended to. Phrasing is sensitive and affectionate, solo work is consistently excellent (the slow movement's delicate woodwind arabesques are exquisitely voiced), and *tuttis* open out superbly in a technically fine recording from Naxos (magnificently keen-voiced horns throughout).

Whereas *A Colour Symphony* was inspired by the heraldic associations of four different colours (one for each movement), the theme of *Adam Zero* is the inexorable life-cycle of humankind. In its entirety, this 1946 ballet score does admittedly have its occasional *longueurs*, but for the most part Bliss's invention is of high quality. Certainly, the vivid exuberance and theatrical swagger of numbers like 'Dance of Spring' and 'Dance of Summer' have strong appeal. Equally, the limpid beauty of both the 'Love Dance' and the hieratic 'Bridal Ceremony' which immediately ensues isn't easily banished, while the darkly insistent 'Dance with Death' distils a gentle poignancy which is most haunting.

Checkmate & Checkmate Suite

Bliss Checkmate – Suite. **Lambert** Horoscope – Suite. **Walton** Façade – Suites Nos 1 & 2
English Northern Sinfonia / David Lloyd-Jones
Hyperion Helios CDH55099 (74' · DDD)   Ⓑ

What a joy to welcome on CD, a major British ballet score (comparable in appeal to Walton's *Façade* with which, happily, it's coupled). Constant Lambert's *Horoscope* is a highly individual score that's somehow very English. It's played here with striking freshness and expansiveness. Lloyd-Jones responds to Bliss's lyricism very warmly. What makes this disc particularly enticing is the inclusion of the two *Façade* suites, welcome away from the spoken poems. This is music that in a witty performance can make you smile and even chuckle. So it is here, especially the 'Tango Pasodoble' with a delicious lilt for 'I do like to be beside the seaside' contrasting with its Offenbachian gusto, the 'Swiss Yodelling Song' with its droll Rossini quotation and refined mock-melancholy, and the irresistibly humorous 'Polka' that just manages not to be vulgar. All are ideally paced and the solo wind playing a delight. The recording is near perfect.

Checkmate. Mêlée fantasque
Royal Scottish National Orchestra / David Lloyd-Jones
Naxos 8 557641 (65' · DDD)   Ⓢ⮕

Bliss composed *Checkmate* at the behest of dancer and choreographer Ninette de Valois to mark the Vic-Wells Ballet's inaugural visit to Paris in June 1937. A keen chess player, Bliss devised the scenario himself, the original idea having germinated some 14 years before in a dinner conversation with the Russian ballerina Tamara Karsavina. Lasting some 53 minutes, it's a mightily impressive achievement, scored with sumptuous skill and crammed full of first-rate, colourful invention, much of which will already be familiar from the six-movement concert suite.

Now comes a compelling account of the complete ballet from David Lloyd-Jones and the RSNO, who respond with commendable polish and ebullient swagger. Lloyd-Jones's characteristically lucid conception possesses just that crucial bit more dramatic tension, expressive scope and thrust – and how pliantly he moulds those ravishing melodic tendrils in 'Entry of the Black Queen' (where there's some particularly disarming wind playing). Some occasionally raucous brass sonorities aside, the engineering is enormously vivid, the slightly unflattering acoustic appropriately akin to that of the theatre-pit.

The *Mêlée fantasque* (written in 1921 in memory of the painter Claude Lovat Fraser) makes a delightful curtain-raiser, with Lloyd-Jones extracting just that bit more vitality from this by turns exuberant and touching dance-poem than the composer (always an accomplished interpreter of his own music). A real bargain.

Chamber Works

Piano Quartet in A minor, T6a. Viola Sonata. Oboe Quintet, T44
Maggini Quartet (Laurence Jackson, David Angel *vns* Martin Outram *va* Michal Kaznowski *vc*) with **Peter Donohoe** *pf* Nicholas Daniel *ob*
Naxos 8 555931 (62' · DDD)   Ⓢ⮕

The Maggini Quartet and Peter Donohoe give a commanding performance of the Piano Quartet, locating an underlying toughness of argument and urgency of expression in both outer movements to make one regret all the more forcefully the budding composer's decision to withdraw the piece following his demobilisation in 1919.

Otherwise unrepresented in the domestic catalogue, the Viola Sonata was written in 1933 for Lionel Tertis. If Bliss's inspiration lacks the distinctive melodic profile and organic mastery of, say, Walton's Viola Concerto of four years previously, the work as a whole is still worth getting to know. The Maggini's violist, Martin Outram, makes commendably light of the solo part's at times hair-raising demands and Dono-hoe offers exemplary support.

But the jewel in this anthology is the Oboe Quintet that Bliss composed in 1927 for Leon Goossens. Elegance and resourcefulness are the watchwords in the first two movements, whose bitter-sweet lyricism forms an effective contrast with the exuberant festivities of the finale. Nicholas Daniel and the Maggini give a spry, ideally proportioned reading. Production-values throughout are of a high order. Very warmly recommended.

A Knot of Riddles

Two American Poems[ag]. Seven American Poems[cg]. Angels of the Mind[ag]. The Ballads of the Four Seasons[ag]. A Knot of Riddles[chi]. Two Love Songs[cg]. Two Nursery Rhymes[aef]. Three Romantic Songs[bg]. Three Songs[bg]. Four Songs[adf]. At the Window[bg]. Auvergnat[bg]. A Child's Prayer[ag]. Elegiac Sonnet[bhi]. The Fallow Deer at the Lonely House[bg]. The Hammers[bg]. Rich or Poor[cg]. Simples[bg]. Three Jolly Gentlemen[ag]. 'Tis time, I think, by Wenlock Town[bg]. The Tramps[cg]. When I was one-and-twenty[cg]. The Tempest[bcg] – The Storm; Overture and Act 1, Scene 1
[a]**Geraldine McGreevy** sop [b]**Toby Spence** ten [c]**Henry Herford** bar [d]**Leo Phillips** vn [e]**Michael Collins** cl [f]**John Lenehan** pf [g]**Kathron Sturrock** pf [h]**Nash Ensemble** / [i]**Martyn Brabbins**
Hyperion ② CDA67188/9 (123' · DDD · T)   ⒻO

Nearly all Bliss's songs are here (only a few orchestral ones are omitted) but they're of uneven quality and are presented in almost random order, with no sense given of Bliss's development as a songwriter. It was a mistake to include the *Two Love Songs*, which are in fact the vocal movements of Bliss's beautiful *Serenade* for baritone and orchestra. Kathron Sturrock, throughout a wonderfully musical and responsive accompanist, does her best to make Bliss's piano reductions seem pianistic; but despite her they just sound clumpy.

The finest songs here are mostly on the second disc. Kathleen Raine's poems drew the best from the composer – simple eloquence, bold, shining gestures and memorable images including a fine nocturne: they're masterly, and would alone make investigating this pair of discs worthwhile. Geraldine McGreevy sings them simply, purely and very movingly, as she does the progression from lyric charm to bare strength of *The Ballads of the Four Seasons*. Also on CD2 is *The Tempest*; this vivid storm scene is all that survives of some 1921 incidental music to Shakespeare's play, set with striking originality for two voices, trumpet, trombone and five percussion players. Things of such quality are rarer on CD1, though the *Three Songs* to poems by W H Davies are all strong, Bliss's setting of *When I was one-and-twenty* has a blithe insouciance, and several of the other sets contain pleasing discoveries, like the elegantly witty 'A Bookworm' from *A Knot of Riddles* or the charming 'Christmas Carol' that opens *Four*

Songs. McGreevy is the best of the singers, but both Herford and Spence are committed advocates. The best of these songs (about half) are of a quality to make their present neglect seem inexplicable.

Ernest Bloch   Swiss/American 1880-1959

Bloch studied with Dalcroze in Geneva, in Brussels (1897-9) and with Knorr in Frankfurt (1900). In 1916 he went to the USA, thereafter spending most of his time there (he took citizenship in 1924). He also taught at Cleveland (1920-25), San Francisco (1925-30) and Berkeley (1940-52). His early works are eclectic: the opera Macbeth (1910) draws on Strauss, Musorgsky and Debussy. Then came a period of concern mostly with Jewish subjects (Schelomo for cello and orchestra, 1916), followed by a vigorous neo-classicism (Piano Quintet No 1, 1923; Concerto grosso No 1 for strings and piano, 1925). He returned to epic compositions in the 1930s with the Sacred Service (Avodath hakodesh, 1933) and the Violin Concerto (1937). His last works represent a summation of his career and lean towards a less subjective style. GROVEmusic

Symphony in C sharp minor

Symphony in C sharp minor. Schelomo
Torleif Thedéen vc **Malmö Symphony Orchestra /
Lev Markiz**
BIS CD576 (78' · DDD)   Ⓕ

Bloch's early symphony is an endearing and at times impressive showcase for a young composer (he was 23) endowed by nature and nurture with all the gifts save individuality (though there are hints in the later movements that that too is on the way). He can write impressively strong, expansive melodies, develop them with real ingenuity and build them into monumental climaxes. Climax-building, indeed, is what young Bloch seems most interested in at this stage, that and a love for all the rich contrasts of colour and texture that a big orchestra can provide. He's so adept at pulling out still more stops when you thought there could hardly be any left that you're scarcely ever made impatient by the occasional feeling that this or that movement could have ended two or three minutes earlier.

It's a pleasure, too, to listen for fulfilled echoes of that youthful exuberance in the mature 'biblical rhapsody' *Schelomo*. Just as Lev Markiz adroitly avoids any impression of overpadded grossness in the symphony, so he and his fine soloist find more than richly embroidered oriental voluptuousness in this portrait of King Solomon; there's gravity and even poignancy to the music as well, and Thedéen's subtle variety of tone colour provides shadow and delicacy as well as richness. The recording is excellent.

Violin Sonatas

Violin Sonatas – No 1; No 2, 'Poème mystique'.
Suite hébraïque. Abodah. Melody
Miriam Kramer vn **Simon Over** pf
Naxos 8 554460 (75' · DDD)   ⑤Ⓞ↪

Miriam Kramer's programme might usefully serve as a sort of 'Bloch starter-pack', with the delightful *Suite hébraïque* as its tuneful opener. 'Rapsodie', the Suite's first movement, harbours a noble melody reminiscent of top-drawer Max Bruch and Kramer's performance of it could hardly be more heartfelt. Both violin sonatas are given extremely good performances, that of the Second particularly fine especially in the ecstatic, double-stopped statements of the central theme. The combination of Kramer's musicianship and Naxos's price will be irresistible to most repertory explorers.

Bloch Baal Shem. Suite hébraïque. Solo Violin Suites
– No 1; No 2 **Ben-Haim** Berceuse sfaradite. Solo
Violin Sonata. Improvisation and Dance
Hagai Shaham vn **Arnon Erez** pf
Hyperion CDA67571 (74' · DDD)   Ⓕ

Bloch's two unaccompanied suites date from 1958, the year before his death; they combine a chromatic idiom with a strong sense of tonality. Occasionally the music seems to lack individuality – the third movement of the First Suite is almost like pastiche Bach and its final cadence is academically predictable – but more often one's attention is caught and held by the expressive melodic writing and, in both suites, by a compelling sense of continuity. Shaham revels in Bloch's demanding yet imaginatively idiomatic violin writing. In the solo suites, as well as the more extravagantly emotional pieces with piano on Jewish themes, he enters wholeheartedly into the feeling of the music yet retains a measure of balance and restraint – the vibrato isn't exaggerated and a feeling of rhapsodic freedom is achieved without sacrificing natural flow.

Bloch's popularity has waned somewhat in recent decades, and the Israeli composer Paul Ben-Haim (1897–1984) is even more poorly represented in the CD catalogue. His Solo Sonata, written for Yehudi Menuhin, is, however, a masterly work, not at all original in form and idiom, perhaps, but full of memorable ideas. Shaham's playing of the central *Lento e sotto voce* is stunningly beautiful. And the *Improvisation and Dance*, a folk-style showpiece after the manner of the Bartók rhapsodies, inspires both Shaham and Erez to brilliant feats of virtuosity.

Piano Quintets

Piano Quintets[a] – No 1; No 2. Landscapes. Night.
Two Pieces
[a]**Piers Lane** pf **Goldner Quartet** (Dene Olding,
Dimity Hall vns Irina Morozova va Julian Smiles vc)

Hyperion CDA67638 (70' · DDD)   Ⓕ ❍❍❍

A fabulous CD this, easily the best recording of Bloch's chamber music in years. The First Quintet, a product of the early 1920s, seems to combine the acerbic drive of middle-period Bartók with the kind of veiled sensuality one associates more with Chausson or Fauré. Bloch's use of quarter-tones, aimed at intensifying the work's already heightened emotional atmosphere, requires careful handling, and the Goldner Quartet make them sound both musically striking and entirely natural. If you need a sampling-point, try the finale's opening, where the sense of urgency will hold you riveted.

The real revelation here is the Second Piano Trio (1957). The language recalls the First Quintet's stronger elements, with tone-rows this time rather than quarter-tones, though again their employment is musical rather than 'political'. Amazing to think that this was Bloch's last chamber work (he was already suffering from cancer when he wrote it), the combination of raw energy and mysticism suggesting the mind of a much younger man, much as Janáček's late chamber music does. The Quintet's quiet coda is rapturously beautiful and the blending of voices between Piers Lane and the Goldners simply could not be bettered. The short quartet bonuses suggest that a Goldner Bloch quartet cycle would be a good idea. But that's one for the future; as for this current release, the music is truly wonderful, the playing entirely sympathetic and the sound perfectly balanced.

John Blow   British 1649-1708

Blow was trained as a Chapel Royal chorister and then worked as organist of Westminster Abbey, 1668-79. In 1674 he both became a Gentleman of the Chapel Royal and succeeded Pelham Humfrey as Master of the Children; from 1676 he was also an organist there. Henry Purcell served an apprenticeship under him and many others were influenced by his teaching. The 1680s and 1690s were his most productive years as a composer. While still active at the Chapel Royal (where he was named official composer in 1700), he was Almoner and Master of the Choristers at St Paul's Cathedral in 1687-1703, and in 1695 he returned to Westminster Abbey as organist, succeeding Purcell.

Blow was the most important figure in the school of musicians surrounding Purcell and a composer of marked individuality. His music uses a wide range of idioms and reflects his interest in structure. Foremost in his sacred output are c100 anthems, mostly verse anthems (some with instrumental movements); the powerful coronation work God spake sometime in visions (1685) combines features of both types. Blow also wrote several services and Latin sacred works. Most of his odes were written for court occasions; among the others are works for St Cecilia's Day such as Begin the song (1684). The highly original and poignant miniature opera Venus and Adonis (1685), also for the court, was his only dramatic work. A well-known part of his output was his secular vocal music, comprising songs and duets, catches etc; the Ode on the Death of Mr Henry Purcell (1696), a duet with instruments, is notable for its expressiveness. GROVEmusic

Ode on the Death of Purcell

Blow Sonata in A. Ground in G minor. 🅟
Fugue in G minor. Suite in G. Ground in C minor.
An Ode on the Death of Mr Henry Purcell[ab]
Purcell Birthday Ode, Z331 – Sweetness of Nature[ab].
Here let my life[a]. Oedipus – Music for a while[a]. St
Cecilia's Day Ode, Z328 – In vain the am'rous flute
[ab]**Gérard Lesne**, [b]**Steve Dugardin** countertens
La-Canzona (Pierre Hamon, Sébastien Marq recs
Elisabeth Joyé clav Philippe Pierlot va da gamba
Vincent Dumestre theorbo)
Virgin Veritas 545342-2 (64' · DDD · T/t)   Ⓕ🅾➸

The teacher who has even one pupil who becomes even more distinguished than himself is fortunate; in Purcell, Blow had one such. And when that pupil's death precedes his own he has cause for genuine grief, as Blow did. One of Purcell's songs, here alternated with instrumental pieces by Blow, contains the line 'Nor let my homely death embroider'd be with scutcheon or with elegy', but it's one with which Blow and others could not concur. In a programmatic tour de force Blow's profoundly beautiful vocal tribute to Purcell comes at the end. Few countertenors are as finely matched in artistry and vocal quality as Lesne and Dugardin who, in both the solo songs and duets, wring every drop of emotion from the texts with sincerity, technically effortless *messa di voce* and admirably clear diction. In Blow's *Ode on the death of Mr Henry Purcell*, the risk that the recorders may cover the singers is avoided. The instrumental support faithfully shadows every vocal nuance throughout. Much of Blow's instrumental music was unpublished in his time and has remained unrecorded – some first-time pieces here. Where violins were originally specified, as in the A major Trio Sonata, in this recording they're replaced by recorders, and the harpsichord Suite in G minor is a modern compilation from various sources. Altogether this album is pure, unalloyed delight.

Luigi Boccherini   Italian 1743-1805

The son of a cello or double bass player, Boccherini made his public début as a cellist at 13. After studying in Rome, he worked intermittently at the Viennese court, 1757-64. In 1760 he began to catalogue his compositions (though excluding cello sonatas, vocal music and certain other works). In 1764-6 he worked in Lucca, where he composed vocal music and in 1765 reputedly arranged the first string quartet performances in public. On tour with the violinist Filippo

Manfredi in Paris, 1767-8, he had his six string quartets op.1 and six string trios Op 2 published. In 1769 the duo arrived in Madrid, where Boccherini became composer and performer to the Infante Don Luis. Up to the time of Luis death in 1785 he composed chamber music for his court, notably string quintets for two violins, viola and two cellos. From 1786, as chamber composer to Prince (later King) Friedrich Wilhelm of Prussia, he sent string quartets to the Prussian court, though probably never went there.

The chief representative of Latin instrumental music during the Viennese Classical period, Boccherini was especially prolific in chamber music: he wrote well over 120 string quintets, nearly 100 string quartets and over 100 other chamber works. At first he used a standard Italian idiom, but with unusually ornate melodies and frequent high cello writing. Later, reflecting his isolated position, his style became more personal, with delicate detail, syncopated rhythms and rich textures; he sometimes used cyclic forms. The orchestral music includes several virtuoso cello concertos and over 20 symphonies; the vocal works include an opera, two oratorios and a Stabat mater (1781). GROVEmusic

Cello Concertos

Cello Concertos – No 4 in C, G477; No 6 in D, G479;
No 7 in G, G480; No 8 in C, G481
Tim Hugh vc **Scottish Chamber Orchestra /
Anthony Halstead**
Naxos 8 553571 (74' · DDD)   Ⓢ🅾➸

This disc is a winner, the first of a series of all 12 Boccherini cello concertos, beautifully performed on modern instruments but with concern for period practice and superbly recorded. Each concerto has its individual delights, but the formula in all four works is similar, with strong, foursquare first movements, slow movements that sound rather Handelian, and galloping finales in triple time.

Many collectors will be concerned about the Boccherini Cello Concerto beloved of generations in Grützmacher's corrupt edition. Many years ago Jacqueline du Pré was questioned about choosing it for her recording: she promptly justified herself, saying, 'But the slow movement is so lovely.' She was quite right, as her classic recording makes clear, but that movement was transferred from another work, in fact No 7 in G, one of the four works here. Tim Hugh's dedicated account of this lovely G minor movement is a high spot of this issue, with rapt, hushed playing not just from the soloist but also from the excellent Scottish Chamber Orchestra under Anthony Halstead. Hugh offers substantial cadenzas not just in the first movements of each work, but in slow movements and finales too, though none is as extended as the almost two minute meditation in the G minor slow movement. Halstead, as a period specialist and a horn virtuoso as well as a conductor, matches his soloist in the dedication of these performances, clarifying textures and encouraging Hugh to choose speeds on the fast side, with easily flowing slow movements and outer movements which test the soloist's virtuosity to the very limit, without sounding breathless. Not just for those who know only the old Grützmacher concerto, all this will be a delightful discovery.

'Simply Baroque' Ⓟ
Boccherini Cello Concertos – No 5 in D, G478; No 7 in G, G480 **Bach** Cantatas: No 22, Jesus nahm zu sich die Zwölfe: Choral – Ertöt' uns durch dein' Güte; No 136, Erforsche mich, Gott, und erfahre mein Herz: Choral – Dein Blut, der edle Saft; No 147, Herz und Mund und Tat und Leben: Choral – Jesu bleibet meine Freude; No 163, Nur jedem das Seine: Aria – Lass mein Herz die Münze sein; No 167, Ihr Menschen, rühmet Gottes Liebe: Choral – Sei Lob und Preis mit Ehren. St Matthew Passion, BWV244 – Erbarme dich. Orgel-Büchlein – Ich ruf' zu dir, BWV639. Schübler Chorales – Kommst du nun, Jesu, von Himmel herunter, BWV650. Orchestral Suite No 3 in D, BWV1068 – Air (all arr Koopman)
Yo-Yo Ma *vc* **Amsterdam Baroque Orchestra / Ton Koopman** *hpd/org*
Sony Classical SK60680 (69' · DDD) Ⓕ●➔

This appealing compilation is extremely imaginative: nine movements from Bach sensitively arranged for cello and chamber orchestra, plus an attractive pair of Boccherini cello concertos. Yo-Yo Ma's Stradivarius was altered for the occasion by luthier Charles Beare, and Ma uses a Baroque bow. As superior 'light' listening goes, it's difficult to think of a happier 70 minutes' worth. It also provides an ideal 'soft-option' introduction to the sound of period instruments. The *St Matthew Passion*'s 'Erbarme dich' becomes a cleverly worked duet for violin and cello, always flowing and discreet, aided by responsive strings and a tactile lute continuo. Ton Koopman's harpsichord brushes *Jesu Joy of Man's Desiring* into action with a flourish, answered by a mellifluous mix of solo cello, strings and winds. Bassoon and cello join forces for a swaggering 'Lass mein Herz die Münze sein', before the brief chorale 'Dein Blut, der edle Saft'. Last comes the inevitable 'Air' from the Third Orchestral Suite, tellingly arranged (as a duet for cellos) and superbly played. In fact, Koopman's 'second' cello – his lead cellist Jaap ter Linden – is every bit as eloquent as the star act.

Listening to the two Boccherini works on this marvellous CD reminds you again of Ma's uncanny technical facility, at once elegant and unselfconsciously virtuosic. Ton Koopman provides the cadenzas and the performances are pure delight.

String Quintets

String Quintets, Op 25 – No 1 in D minor, G295; No 4 in C, G298; No 6 in A minor, G300. String Quintet, Op 11 No 5 – Minuet Ⓟ
Europa Galante (Fabio Biondi, Enrico Casazza *vns* Ernesto Braucher *va* Maurizio Naddeo, Antonio Fantinuoli *vcs*)
Virgin Veritas 545421-2 (60' · DDD) Ⓕ●●●➔

The frustration of those who seek to identify Boccherini's works by their opus numbers may end in their being taken into care by sympathetic men in white coats. The first three of the six string sextets listed in his own catalogue as Op 25 were first published as Op 36, No 4, as Op 47 No 9, and No 6 as Op 47 No 5. The six of his Op 11, from the Fifth of which the 'amputated' and very famous Minuet is taken, appeared as Op 13 and his own Op 13 became Op 20.

Thank goodness for Gérard, here also the annotator, by whom be guided when in any doubt! Given that Boccherini wrote 100 string quintets it isn't surprising that none of the three from Op 25 on this disc has any other listed recording. These three quintets serve as a persuasive introduction to his music, full of melodic invention, harmony that knows when and for how long to remain static or flowing, or ready to spring surprises, great variety of form, and a kaleidoscope of sounds that could have been imagined only by an accomplished and venturesome virtuoso – which Boccherini was of the cello.

If the music itself is persuasive it becomes irresistible in these performances on period instruments (or copies thereof) at slightly lower pitch than today's standard, wielded by players of the highest calibre and sensitivity. The Font family quartet with whom Boccherini played at the Madrid court of Don Luis must have revelled in these quintets; in these recordings we come as close to sharing that experience as it's possible to get. An absolute must.

String Quintets – in E, G275; in F minor, G348; in G minor, G351
Richard Lester *vc* **Vanbrugh Quartet** (Gregory Ellis, Keith Pascoe *vns* Simon Aspell *va* Christopher Marwood *vc*)
Hyperion CDA67287 (62' · DDD) Ⓕ●

With more than 100 Boccherini cello quintets to choose from, the problem for anyone wanting to make recordings is which to choose. The E major G275 (formerly Op 13 No 5) makes an obvious first choice, when the third movement is the music universally associated with the very name of Boccherini, his Minuet. It's particularly refreshing in the Vanbrugh performance to hear it set in context against the work's other three movements, with their approach, light and crisp, paying obvious tribute to period practice in the choice of tempo – far faster than one usually associates with 'Boccherini's Minuet'.

The format of a string quintet with two cellos instead of two violas was very much Boccherini's special genre. Himself a cellist, it allowed him to free at least one of the cellos from following the bass line, so as to soar lyrically. To have this fascinating music vividly recorded in such fine performances, both polished and refreshing, with Richard Lester a perfect partner for the prize-winning Vanbrugh Quartet, makes an ideal sampler disc.

String Quartets

String Quartets, Op 32 – No 3 in D, G203; No 4 in C, G204; No 5 in G minor, G205; No 6 in A, G206
Quartetto Borciani (Fulvio Luciani, Elena Ponzoni vns Roberto Tarenzi va Claudia Ravetto vc)
Naxos 8 555043 (79' · DDD) ⓈⒹ⊳

Boccherini was a little less indulgent in his string quartets than in his string quintets, which are more numerous: here he couldn't allow so many fanciful flights for the cello into the upper reaches of the treble clef, nor could he create textures of quite such luxuriance. But the range of invention in these four works, composed in his compositional prime in 1780, is extraordinarily wide. The gem of this group is the A major work, with its graceful 6/8 opening, its pathetic, chromatic *Andantino lentarello*, its haunting little minuet with its echoing open E strings, and its brilliant and ebullient finale. This was recorded many, many years ago by the Carmirelli Quartet (for Decca), whose Boccherini style was a model. The present group, the Quartetto Borciani, probably play it more perfectly in a sense, but the magic isn't quite so well captured. Named after the leader of the much admired Quartetto Italiano, this group play in a manner close to their model, with passion, intensity and accuracy, and their soft playing is wonderfully smooth and controlled, with a fine, veiled sound. In the quick movements they're a little sharper, more incisive in articulation than sometimes seems ideal for this music (they use modern instruments), but certainly the result is enormously spirited. This is very fine quartet playing and immensely endearing music; you can hardly ask for more.

Stabat mater, G532

Boccherini Stabat mater, G532 (1800 vers)ᵃ
Astorga Stabat materᵇ
Susan Gritton, ᵃ**Sarah Fox** sops **Susan Bickley** mez
Paul Agnew ten ᵇ**Peter Harvey** bass ᵇ**The King's Consort Choir; The King's Consort / Robert King**
Hyperion 🎧 SACDA67108 (73' · DDD · T/t) ⒻⓄ⊳

These settings of the same text by two Italian composers (more exactly, Sicilian in the case of Astorga), who spent much of their lives in Spain, vary from each other both by the different groupings of the lines into movements and by the stylistic changes that had taken place in music in the course of the at least half century that separates them. Astorga's earlier setting has a good deal more contrapuntal writing, especially in three of its four choruses, as well as some diversity of style: more ornate in the

double duet 'Quis est homo' and, in particular, the extremely florid, almost operatic, final 'Amen', but gently pathetic in the instrumental introduction and the soprano solo 'Sancta mater'. Intensity of feeling is heard in the duet stanza voicing the desire to weep with the distraught Mary, and the chorus sings expressively throughout, though 'Virgo virginum praeclara' sounds altogether too cheerful, and in the initial chorus the tenor line obtrudes rather edgily. Boccherini's is by far the more remarkable and beautiful setting. Originally written in 1781 for solo soprano, it was expanded in 1800 for three solo voices: fears that this could lead to a more 'symphonic' sound are dispelled by King's use of only seven instrumentalists. Robert King has a fine team of vocalists who on the whole blend well, an important consideration since only four of the 11 sections of the work are single-voice settings. The anguished melancholy of the opening and the grave serenity of the ending enclose a finely planned diversity of treatments, from the intense 'Quae moerebat' or the lyrical 'Fac ut portem' (both admirably sung by Sarah Fox) to the vigorous 'Tui nati' or the vehemently passionate 'Fac me plagis vulnerari' (for all three singers). The performance is accomplished and polished, but the recording venue tends to amplify singers' higher notes out of proportion.

Antoine Boësset   French 1586–1643

Boësset held various appointments at the French court from 1613 and was widely recognized as the leading composer of airs de cour (nine books, 1617-42). He also wrote vocal music for ballets de cour and some sacred music. **GROVE**music

Airs de cour

Je meurs sans mourir
Anonymous Nos esprits libres et contents. Ballet des fous et des estropiés de la cervelle – Entrée de l'Embabouinée; Entrée des demy-fous; Entrée des fantasques. Ballet des vaillans combattans. Entrée des Laquais **Boësset** Frescos ayres del prado. Dove ne vai, crudele. A la fin cette bergère. Je meurs sans mourir. Départ que le devoir me fait précipiter. O Dieu, ce ne sont point vos armes. Una musiqua. Quel soleil hors de saison. Quels doux supplices. Quel beautés, Ô mortels. Quelle merveilleuse advanture. Ballet des voleurs – Récit: Bien que je vole toutes choses; Chorus: Aux voleurs, au secours, accourez tous **Briçeño** La gran chacona **Constantin** La Pacifique
Le Poème Harmonique / Vincent Dumestre bqtr
Alpha ALPHA057 (57' · DDD · T/t) ⒻⓄⓄ

This CD completes a trilogy devoted to the *airs de cour* which help redefine one's perception of French court song. The first two were devoted to Guédron and Moulinié, and this last one to Antoine Boësset, who succeeded Guédron at the French royal court on his death in 1620. In many ways it's the most diverse and complex of the three.

Some songs appear in a four-voice version with continuo accompaniment, departing from the voice-plus-lute format that once pervaded recordings of this repertory. Interspersed with the songs are instrumental *entrées* from *ballets de cour* to which Boësset contributed in the 1620s. (Louis XIII was an avid dancer.) The composer didn't confine himself to French texts; the fraught relations between the Bourbons and the Spanish Habsburgs wrought a certain fascination with Iberian idioms, and an Italian text is thrown in for good measure. These complex links and political undercurrents are explained in an informative booklet-note.

This diverse mixture of languages and ensemble may appear unsettling at first, but later it becomes clear how well managed is that diversity, and one begins to trace the threads in common. *Dove ne vai, crudele* is thoroughly Italianate, and wonderfully sung. Claire Lefilliâtre, in particular, continues to impress: the title track, *Je meurs sans mourir*, combines artifice and a restrained but genuine emotional depth.

Georg Böhm
German 1661-1733

Böhm was organist of the Johanniskirche, Lüneburg, from 1698. He is important for his influence on JS Bach and for his development of the organ chorale partita (and variations) in which he used different compositional techniques in a synthesis of national styles. Böhm's keyboard works display his strongest gifts: among them are 11 suites and a Prelude, Fugue and Postlude in G minor which is one of the finest organ works of the period, combining French grace and charm with north German intensity. He also composed motets, cantatas, sacred songs, and a St John Passion (1704) formerly attributed to Handel. **GROVE**music

Keyboard Music

11 Keyboard Suites. Prelude, Fugue and Postlude in G minor
Mitzi Meyerson hpd
Glossa ② GCD921801/2 (96' · DDD)   Ⓕ

Bach knew a good thing when he heard it and Georg Böhm was one. Based in Luneburg (where Bach was, to all intents and purposes, a sixth-former at St Michael's School) Böhm had mastered the flamboyant keyboard styles prevalent in northern Germany while taking a particular interest in adapting French keyboard sensibility and technique to the high emotional stakes beloved of Germans. These discs are, above all, a celebration of sonority; you notice this in Böhm's splendid organ music too, where his

command of the textural impact of strong harmonic movement has as much to offer as the actual progressions themselves.

Mitzi Meyerson brings considerable colour and suavity to these 11 Suites and the miscellaneous 'triptych' piece, the very original 'scena', Prelude, Fugue and Postlude (which Schumann described as an 'eerie caprice'). Playing on a responsive and lyrical 1998 double-manual harpsichord by Keith Hill, Meyerson homes in on the essential *Affekt* of each prelude and treads a fine line between those occasions when the specific dance is to be articulated and when it's plainly a servant to another expressive end. She's especially successful in the movements requiring incisive execution and portentous nobility. She does Böhm a great service here, and reminds us why Bach justly rated him in the top division of senior contemporaries.

William Bolcom
American b1938

Bolcom studied with Milhaud at Mills College (1958-61) and Leland Smith at Stanford (1961-4) and began teaching at the University of Michigan in 1973. As a pianist he has taken a leading part in the revival of ragtime and other American vernacular music. His works are polystylistic and concerned with momentous philosophical and religious themes: they include a monumental setting of Blake's Songs of Innocence and Experience for soloists, choirs and orchestra (1956-81). **GROVE**music

Violin Sonatas

Complete Violin Sonatas
Solomia Soroka vn **Arthur Greene** pf
Naxos 8 559150 (77' · DDD)   Ⓢ⮕

These four violin and piano sonatas cover a period of almost 40 years. Bolcom gave up violin lessons with relief at the age of about 10 when his instrument was stolen from his father's car, but he has retained a strong affection for the fiddle and the sonatas represent his more serious side rather than the rumbustious ragtimer.

The First Sonata comes from 1956, Bolcom's freshman year at the University of Washington, Seattle, but was revised later. The Second Sonata arose 20 years later, after he met jazz violinist Joe Venuti, and it was completed in memoriam. In the first movement the violin sings in a gentle bluesy manner over regular patterns in the piano: 'Brutal', which follows, is as tough as anything in Ives. There are conventional triads in both the last two movements and the whole piece affectionately recalls some of Venuti's own licks.

The other two sonatas come from the mid-1990s. The Third is subtitled *Stamba* ('Weird') and, admittedly, you never quite know what is going to happen next. A mini-scherzo is a scrap of tarantella, then the finale fuses tangos and

Arab music,. The last one is another virtuoso piece, at times hyperactive, where everything is confidently delivered by this brilliant duo.

Songs of Innocence and Experience

Songs of Innocence. Songs of Experience
Christine Brewer, Measha Brueggergosman, Ilana Davidson, Linda Hohenfeld, Carmen Pelton sops **Joan Morris** mez **Marietta Simpson** cont **Thomas Young** ten **Nmon Ford** bar **Nathan Lee Graham** sngr **Peter 'Madcat' Ruth** harc/sngr **Michigan State University Children's Choir; Orpheus Singers; Choir, Chamber Choir, Musical Society Choral Union, Contemporary Directions Ensemble and Symphony Orchestra of Michigan University / Leonard Slatkin**
Naxos American Classics ② 8 559216/8
(138' · DDD · T)   ⑤➔

This is a *magnum opus* that occupied Bolcom for 25 years, starting as early as 1956. He's drawn on a wide range of musical styles to parallel Blake's method of moving from sophisticated to almost folk idioms. In some features – diatonic writing, English text and children's voices – Britten's *Spring* Symphony is in the background, but Bolcom is defined by the styles he juxtaposes with carefully calculated transitions in between. Some of the most memorable moments involve popular idioms, evoking his ragtime performances or the songs he recorded so vividly with his wife Joan Morris. The word-setting is straightforward, reflecting the strophic poems, and refreshingly free from elaboration. The *Songs of Innocence* are charming and pastoral but in the *Songs of Experience* there's real anger at the human predicament.

This recording is based on a live performance with massive forces comprising 10 soloists, three choirs totalling almost 350 singers and a full symphony orchestra plus a harmonica and various extra electronic players and percussion. Nathan Lee Graham is an actor-singer who can project his catchy tunes and spoken poems; Joan Morris exercises all her magic in a range of styles, but Thomas Young seems too consistently declamatory. Christine Brewer is magisterial in numbers that reflect the modernistic side of Bolcom, and Carmen Pelton has a rare purity of sound.

This unique Blake spectacular makes a cumulative impact that represents Bolcom's wide stylistic embrace at its most ambitious.

Songs

I will breathe a mountain. Casino Paradise – Night make my day; My father the gangster. Greatshot – You cannot have me now (or The Military Orgy). The Digital Wonder Watch. The Last Days of Mankind. Mary. Songs to Dance. Tillinghast Duo. Three Songs from The Wind in the Willows. Dynamite Tonite – When we built the church

Carole Farley sop **William Bolcom** pf
Naxos American Classics 8 559249 (64' · DDD · T)

Bolcom has always exemplified his eclectic American heritage in a distinctly personal way. As a pianist he's known for superb LPs of ragtime, Gershwin, Milhaud and songs with his wife Joan Morris. This collection of his songs with piano with Carole Farley, another performer of remarkable versatility, covers a range of styles from various periods; there are cycles and single songs.

Most of the accompaniments are hyperactively virtuoso, drawing on the full compass of the piano – a refreshing change from so much of the literature, but you're left wondering who else could play them like this. There are moments of repose, some in the witty mini-cycle *Songs to Dance* from 1989. *I will breathe a mountain* (1990) sets 10 American women poets, each song reflecting their personalities in a different style. 'The Fish' is an amusing poem by Elizabeth Bishop, a helter-skelter ride as dizzy as some of Sondheim's patter-songs. 'Messing about in boats', one of three poems based on *The Wind in the Willows*, makes an easy-going habanera.

This is a fascinating collection from one of the most individual American composers, who shouldn't be forgotten in the minimalist onslaught. Full texts of songs are an asset, it's vividly recorded and is delivered with effervescent enthusiasm by both performers.

Laci Boldemann   Swedish 1921-69

Swedish composer. He studied conducting with Wood and the piano at the Royal Academy of Music, London; then in 1939 he moved to Sweden and there took piano lessons with de Frumerie. As a composer he aimed at simplicity, purity and expressiveness, finding vocal music his ideal medium.
GROVEmusic

Boldemann Four Epitaphs, Op 10 **Gefors** Lydia's Songs **Hillborg** ...lontana in sonno...
Anne Sofie von Otter mez
Gothenburg Symphony Orchestra / Kent Nagano
DG 477 7439GH (63' · DDD)   Ⓕ➔

This exemplary release finds Anne Sofie von Otter again stamping her distinctive mark on a disc. Two of these works were written for her, and with her special qualities in mind, so right from the start of Anders Hillborg's *...lontana in sonno...* von Otter's dusky voice traces a lonely line with supreme musical concentration. Hillborg's setting of Petrarch features an orchestra including glass harmonica, which weaves otherworldly textures around the singer, and her voice soars with purity.

The musical result occasionally recalls Sibelius's *Luonnotar*, but of course the subject matter is entirely different. The threads here are love and death, and Hans Gefors's *Lydia's Songs* (the second world premiere recording) is inspired by one of Sweden's greatest and most tragic love stories, Hjalmar Söderberg's novel *The Serious Game*. The unhappy affair between Lydia and the music critic Arvid is outlined in settings in Swedish, French and German, and the eclectic style is Gefors's tribute to von Otter's versatility: the music, which moves from slow-burning passion to sardonic cabaret, is another example of how von Otter has enriched the repertory.

She also dusts off the *Four Epitaphs* of Laci Boldemann (1921-69), a fascinating figure in Swedish music. Composed in 1952, five years after his release from an American PoW camp, this cycle for mezzo and string orchestra takes poems from Edgar Lee Masters's *Spoon River Anthology* and sets them with a simple intensity that is perhaps the key to everything here.

Alexander Borodin   Russian 1833-1887

As a youth Borodin developed parallel interests in music and chemistry, teaching himself the cello and qualifying in medicine (1856); throughout his life music was subordinated to his research and his activities as a lecturer (from 1862) at the Medico-Surgical Academy in St Petersburg. His predilection for the music of Mendelssohn and Schumann, together with his acquaintance with Mussorgsky, Cui, Rimsky-Korsakov, Liszt and above all Balakirev gave shape to his compositional efforts. It was mainly through Balakirev's influence that he turned towards Russian nationalism, using Russian folksong in his music; he was one of 'The Five', the group eager to create a distinctive nationalist school.

Borodin's earliest completed works include the First Symphony in E flat (1867), showing a freshness and assurance that brought immediate acclaim, and No 2 in B minor (1876) which, though longer in the making, is one of the boldest and most colourful symphonies of the century, in the Russian context a mature, symphonic counterpart to Glinka's Ruslan and Lyudmila. The piece contributing most to his early fame, however, especially in western Europe, was the short orchestral 'musical picture' On the Steppes of Central Asia (1880; dedicated to Liszt). Among the important chamber pieces, including those works which give the lie most clearly to charges of inspired dilettantism still sometimes brought against him, are the early Piano Quintet in C minor (1862) and the two string quartets, the second famous for its beautiful Nocturne, with their craftsmanship and latent muscularity. His most substantial achievement was undoubtedly the opera Prince Igor (written over the period 1869-87; completed and partly orchestrated by Rimsky-Korsakov and Glazunov). Despite its protracted creation and weak, disjointed libretto (Borodin's own), it contains abundant musical richness in its individual arias, in its powerfully Russian atmosphere and its fine choral scenes crowned by the barbaric splendour of the Polovtsian Dances. GROVEmusic

Symphonies

Symphony No 2 (two performances)   Ⓗ
[a]**NBC Symphony Orchestra / Erich Kleiber;**
[b]**Stuttgart Radio Symphony Orchestra / Carlos Kleiber**
Hänssler Classic 93 116 (52' · ADD) Recorded live
[a]1947, [b]1972   Ⓕ

Keen collectors may have acquired these off-air recordings in previous, more or less illicit incarnations but, in placing them back to back, Hänssler's authorised release allows us to make instructive comparison between Kleiber father and son. It's obvious here that Carlos has lifted key interpretative features from his father's marked-up score, and, in all probability, the recording too. Even so, his is the more remarkable of the two performances. He takes the music seriously, imparting a unique level of intensity to the argument, without moulding melodic lines with what we think of as idiomatic 'Russian' warmth.

In the first movement, both Kleibers eschew the grandiose rhetoric; Carlos has the edge in the development, hurtling forward with astonishing power. Surprisingly, perhaps, he makes more of the second movement, too, even relaxing a little for the trio's local colour where Erich stiffens up. Neither *Andante* can boast a truly Russian-sounding horn but Carlos comes closer. He's also a notch faster than Erich; even if the Stuttgart players aren't always quite on top of his demands, they struggle manfully with his no doubt fanatical insistence on crisp and resilient rhythms at high speed. When everything comes together, as in the finale's dash for the finishing line, the results are sensational.

The SWR studio relay has come up reasonably well, whereas the 1947 NBC broadcast (with audience) is inevitably rather dry and limited. Enthusiasts shouldn't hesitate.

Additional recommendations

Symphony No 2[a]
Coupled with: Symphony No 3 (unfinished)[b]. Prince Igor – Overture; Polovtsian Dances[c]
[a]**London Symphony Orchestra / Martinon** [b]**Suisse Romande Orchestra / Ansermet** [c]**LSO / Solti**
Decca Eloquence 467 482-2 (66' · ADD) Recorded 1961-6)   ⒷⓄ▷
Martinon draws a thrilling performance from the LSO, an orchestra on top form. Solti's contributions are equalling thrilling – what playing!

String Quartets

String Quartets – No 1 in A; No 2 in D. String Sextet in D minor[a]
The Lindsays (Peter Cropper, Ronald Birks *vns* Robin Ireland *va* Bernard Gregor-Smith *vc*) [a]**Louise Williams** *va* [a]**Raphael Wallfisch** *vc*
ASV CDDCA1143 (73' · DDD)   ⒻⓄ

Borodin's two string quartets have been coupled several times, and for a long time the most idiomatic versions were those made by the Borodin Quartet, who set the standard and persuaded many that they should be heard more often. The Lindsays don't ape these interpretations: for instance, they take the *Scherzo* of No 1 much more steadily than the fleeting performance of the Borodins, more as a dance than a *scherzo*, and they tackle the rather problematic finale of No 2 after their own fashion, by means of well-judged structural emphases, making a strong and just conclusion to the work. It isn't an easy movement, and like some other parts of the quartet, such as the spectral central section of the *Scherzo*, they manage the textures beautifully.

There's a less easy flow to the opening of No 2, and sensitively as The Lindsays play the much-traduced *Andante*, it's difficult not to feel the well-loved melody coming more instinctively, less lavishly, from the Borodins. Nevertheless, these are characteristically sensitive, thoughtful interpretations from a quartet whose fine work has brought us so much.

Unusually, they find room for the two surviving movements of Borodin's String Sextet, a lively *Allegro* in which, as is often remarked, Borodin seems to be taking Mendelssohn on at his own game, and a pleasant *Andante*. It's an agreeable addition to an attractive coupling.

Prince Igor

Prince Igor
Mikhail Kit *bar* Igor **Galina Gorchakova** *sop* Yaroslavna **Gegam Grigorian** *ten* Vladimir **Vladimir Ognovenko** *bass* Prince Galitzky **Bulat Minjelkiev** *bass* Khan Kontchak **Olga Borodina** *mez* Kontchakovna **Nikolai Gassiev** *ten* Ovlour **Georgy Selezniev** *bass* Skula **Konstantin Pluzhnikov** *ten* Eroshka **Evgenia Perlasova** *mez* Nurse **Tatyana Novikova** *sop* Polovtsian Maiden **Kirov Opera Chorus and Orchestra / Valery Gergiev**
Philips ③ download *442 537-2PH3* (209' · DDD · N/T/ t)   ⓕⓄ▷

Prince Igor, even after 18 years of work, remained unfinished at Borodin's death in 1887, and it was finally completed by Rimsky-Korsakov and Glazunov. Borodin's main problem with *Prince Igor* was the daunting task of turning what was principally an undramatic subject into a convincing stage work. In many ways he never really succeeded in this and the end result comes over more as a series of epic scenes rather than a musical drama.

Despite this, however, the impression is given of a rounded whole, and it contains some of Borodin's most poignant and moving music, rich in oriental imagery and full of vitality. Curious things happen long before the official surprises of this vitally fresh *Prince Igor*, not least in the Overture, where Gergiev takes the horn's beautiful melody at a very slow pace. Gergiev is anxious to prepare us for the weighty events which follow and his particular point with the theme is to relate it to its place in the opera as the heart of Igor's great aria. There, in league with the bass-baritonal timbre of Gergiev's prince, Mikhail Kit, it solemnly underlines the fact that this is an aria of potency frustrated, sung by a hero who spends most of the opera in captivity; and that's further emphasised by a second aria which no listener will ever have heard before. It's the most significant of the passages discovered among Borodin's papers, rejected by Rimsky-Korsakov in his otherwise sensitive tribute to Borodin's memory but specially orchestrated for this recording by Yuri Faliek.

The other problem with the *Prince Igor* we already know is the way that Act 3 rather weakly follows its much more imposing Polovtsian predecessor. Gergiev obviates both that, and the problem of too much time initially spent in Igor's home town of Putivl, by referring to a structural outline of Borodin's dating from 1883 which proposes alternating the Russian and Polovtsian acts. In the theatre, we might still want the famous Polovtsian *divertissement* as a centrepiece; but on the recording the new order works splendidly, not least because Gergiev is at his fluent best in the scenes of Galitzky's dissipation and Yaroslavna's despair, now making up the opera's Second Act. While Borodina executes Kontchakovna's seductive chromaticisms with astonishing breath control and focus of tone, Bulat Minjelkiev's Kontchak is a little too free and easy, at least next to Ognovenko's perfectly gauged Galitzky, a rogue who needs the extra rebellion music of the more recent version to show more threatening colours. There's just the right degree of relaxation, too, about his drunken supporters Skula and Eroshka. It takes two Russian character-singers to make sense of this pair – 'with our wine and our cunning we will never die in Russia', they tell us truthfully – and their comical capitulation on Igor's return wins respect for Borodin's daring happy-end transition here.

It's beautifully paced by Pluzhnikov, Selezniev and their conductor, and crowned by a choral cry of joy which brings a marvellous rush of tearful adrenalin. That leaves us with Gorchakova, so touching in Yaroslavna's first aria but not always projecting the text very vividly and clearly not at her best in the big scena of the last act. Still, in terms of long-term vision, orchestral detail and strength of ensemble, Gergiev is ahead of the competition.

Dmitry Bortnyansky

Ukrainian 1751-1825

Bortnyansky studied in Italy from 1769; his first operas were given there, 1776-8. Returning to Russia in 1779, he became Kapellmeister at the St Petersburg court and in 1796 director. His many Russian sacred pieces (later edited by Tchaikovsky) are notable for their Italianate lyricism and skilful counterpoint. He also wrote operas, cantatas and instrumental pieces, notably a Sinfonia concertante (1790). **GROVE**music

Sacred Concertos

Sacred Concertos – No 17, How amiable are thy tabernacles, O Lord of hosts!; No 18, It is a good thing to give thanks unto the Lord; No 19, The Lord said unto my Lord: sit thou at my right hand; No 20, In thee, O Lord, do I put my trust; No 21, He that dwelleth in the secret place of the most high; No 22, The Lord is my light and my salvation; No 23, Blessed is the people that know the joyful sound
Russian State Symphonic Cappella / Valéry Polyansky
Chandos CHAN9840 (66' · DDD · T/t) ⓕⓞ

Bortnyansky has been mostly ignored in the West until quite recently. Tchaikovsky's disparaging comments on editing his sacred concertos also show he was not universally appreciated in his native Russia, but he has never lost his place in the repertoire of the Russian Orthodox Church and, as this series shows, these works are finely crafted pieces with an endless variety of invention.

This is Volume 3, and it contains some real gems. Concerto No 19 is a *locus classicus* of Bortnyansky's considerable lyrical power, though he also employs his neo-Baroque fugal writing to impressive effect, but No 20 is even more convincing, each movement containing a sub-structure characterised by different musical moods. Tchaikovsky complained that the concertos used 'stagey or even operatic' techniques, and that's quite true, but it's done with consummate elegance, as you may hear in No 22. The Russian State Symphonic Cappella understand this music, in all its manifestations, completely, responding to its subtlest nuances.

Rutland Boughton   British 1878-1960

Boughton studied briefly at the RCM but was mostly self-taught. While teaching in Birmingham (1905-11) he developed his ideas on the basis of Wagner and William Morris socialism, and put them into practice at his Glastonbury festivals (1914-27), where several of his operas were first produced, including The Immortal Hour (1914); this had immense success when staged in London in 1922. After the collapse of the Glastonbury venture he retired to farm, write and compose, and in 1945 completed his Arthurian cycle of five operas, in which Wagnerianism gives way to a simpler folk-song manner. **GROVE**music

Songs

Four Songs, Op 24. Five Celtic Love Songs. Songs of Womanhood, Op 33. Three Songs, Op 39. Symbol Songs. Sweet Ass
Louise Mott *mez* **Alexander Taylor** *pf*
British Music Society BMS431CD (71' · DDD · T) ⓕ

None of Rutland Boughton's more than 100 songs is listed in the current catalogue, so this (at very least) breaks new ground and fills a gap. With one exception (Eleanor Farjeon's nativity poem *Sweet Ass*), the programme draws on sets rather than single songs, so that one has some assurance that the composer is being represented in sustained work, likely to carry the personal flavour and provide a fair sample of his style. As the note-writer for this recital, Michael Hurd, says, the songs have had little attention.

Fiona Macleod (aka William Sharp) is the author of the texts for *Five Celtic Love Songs*, likeable though ultimately unsatisfying as the music runs its rather loose, improvisatory course. This is so with most of the earlier songs. A strong initial impulse often seems to give way to an unsure sense of development and a tendency to overload. Much firmer in control and more assured in technique are the later *Symbol Songs* (1920) and *Sweet Ass* (1928), already mentioned. These are attractive and could prove useful additions to the singer's repertoire.

The mezzo Louise Nott brings a voice of fine quality, not always quite even in its production but expressively used. The accompaniments are expansive and eventually become more genuinely pianistic: Alexander Taylor makes the best of them.

The Immortal Hour

The Immortal Hour
Roderick Kennedy *bass* Dalua **Anne Dawson** *sop* Etain **David Wilson-Johnson** *bar* Eochaidh **Maldwyn Davies** *ten* Midir **Geoffrey Mitchell Choir; English Chamber Orchestra / Alan G Melville**
Hyperion ② CDD22040 (125' · DDD · N/T) Ⓜ

The Immortal Hour is part of theatrical folklore: in London in the early 1920s it ran, unprecedentedly, for 216 consecutive performances and, shortly afterwards, for a further 160 at the first of several revivals. Within a decade it had been played a thousand times. Many in those audiences returned repeatedly, fascinated by the otherworldly mystery of the plot (it concerns the love of a mortal king, Eochaidh, for the faery princess Etain and the destruction of their happiness by her nostalgic longing for the Land of the Ever Young) and by the gentle, lyrical simplicity of its music. In the bleak aftermath of 1918, with civil war in Ireland, political instability at home and the names of Hitler, Mussolini and Stalin emerging from obscurity into the headlines, what blessed escapism this blend of Celtic myth and folk-tinged pentatonic sweetness must have been. Boughton's score still has the power to evoke that world, immediately and effortlessly.

It's quiet, sweet music, muted in colour and softly plaintive, and whenever the plot demands more than this the opera sags. Midir, the visitant from the Land of the Ever Young who lures Etain away from the mortal world, really needs music of dangerously heady, Dionysiac incandescence, but Boughton's vocabulary can run to nothing more transported than the prettily lilting Faery Song and some pages of folksy lyricism with a few showy high notes. No less seriously the music has little dramatic grip. Despite all this, *The Immortal Hour* does have a quality, difficult to define, that's genuinely alluring. It's there in the touching purity of Étain's music (and how movingly Anne Dawson sings the role). It's there in the moments of true darkness that the music achieves: Dalua, the tormented Lord of Shadow conjures up something of the sombre shudder of the supernatural world.

The performance could hardly speak more eloquently for the opera. Alan G Melville allows the music to emerge from and retreat into shadowy silences; all the principal singers are accomplished and the superb chorus has been placed so as to evoke a sense of space.

Lili Boulanger   French 1893-1918

Boulanger studied at the Paris Conservatoire and won the Prix de Rome before her 20th birthday. Her composing life was short but productive: most important are her psalm settings and other large-scale choral works in a strong, subtle style. GROVEmusic

Psalms

Psalms – 24[b]; 129[d]; 130, 'Du fond de l'abîme'[abd]. Pour les funérailles d'un soldat[cd]. D'un soir triste. D'un matin du printemps. Vieille prière bouddhique[bd]
[a]**Sonia de Beaufort** *mez* [b]**Martial Defontaine** *ten* [c]**Vincent le Texier** *bar* [d]**Namur Symphonic Chorus; Luxembourg Philharmonic Orchestra / Mark Stringer**
Timpani 1C1046 (67' · DDD · T/t)   Ⓕ❶

The name of the remarkable teacher and conductor Nadia Boulanger is famous throughout the musical world, but her sister Lili (six years younger), phenomenally gifted – she was the first woman to win the Premier Prix de Rome (while Nadia had attained only a Second Prix) – showed promise of at least equal distinction. Always of delicate health, her death at the age of 24 was a tragedy for music. Apart from works written in her early teens, which she later destroyed, her composing career lasted a mere seven years; but the quality of these compositions is arresting.

Except for parts of *D'un matin du printemps* (originally for violin and piano, and orchestrated only two months before her death), a grave, even sombre air permeates her works, which are heavily tinged with modal thinking. Her idiom is strong, with a bold harmonic sense and an individual feeling for scoring (her stirring Psalm 24, for example, has the unusual combination of brass, timpani, harp and organ with the male voices): the beatific ending of Psalm 129 is heart-easing after the earlier harshness of 'Hard as they have harried me, they have not overcome me' (words significantly applicable to her own determined spirit). Her choral works are compa-

rable to the best of Roussel or Honegger, but her Psalm 130 (dedicated to her father's memory), with its exotic scale and chromaticisms, has more affinity with Bloch and is, without much doubt, a masterpiece. A disc not to be missed.

Faust et Hélène

D'un matin du printemps. D'un soir triste. Faust et Hélène[a]. Psalm 24[b]. Psalm 130, 'Du fond de l'abîme'[c]
[a]**Lynne Dawson** *sop* [c]**Ann Murray** *mez* [a]**Bonaventura Bottone**, [b,c]**Neil MacKenzie** *tens* [a]**Jason Howard** *bar* [b,c]**City of Birmingham Symphony Orchestra Chorus; BBC Philharmonic Orchestra / Yan Pascal Tortelier**
Chandos CHAN9745 (74' · DDD · T/t)   Ⓕ❶❶❶❷

This disc largely duplicates Mark Stringer's programme on the Timpani label mentioned above (inevitably, since in her mere 24 years of life Lili's output was limited). The performances here are first class, and splendidly recorded too. The eloquent sombreness of *D'un soir triste* tugs at the heart, *D'un matin du printemps* is deliciously airy and optimistic, Psalm 24 is given tremendous attack by orchestra and chorus and the powerful Psalm 130 is presented as the masterly, heartfelt work it is. The major work here, though, is the 30-minute cantata *Faust et Hélène* in its first recording. No wonder that it won the 1913 Premier Prix de Rome: the jury must have been thunderstruck by the maturity of this entry from a 19-year-old. It blends lyricism of striking beauty, rapturous fervour, emotional anguish and tense drama with, for a young composer, an astonishing sureness of touch in overall structure, freshness of invention, technical brilliance and imaginative scoring. It seems to have inspired the present performers, among whom it's almost invidious to praise Bonaventura Bottone.

Pierre Boulez   French b1925

Boulez studied with Messiaen at the Paris Conservatoire (1942-5) and privately with Andrée Vaurabourg and René Leibowitz, inheriting Messiaen's concern with rhythm, non-developing forms and extra-European music along with the Schoenberg tradition of Leibowitz. The clash of the two influences lies behind such intense, disruptive works as his first two piano sonatas (1946, 1948) and Livre pour quatuor for string quartet (1949). The violence of his early music also suited that of René Char's poetry in the cantatas Le visage nuptial (1946) and Le soleil des eaux (1948), though through this highly charged style he was working towards an objective serial control of rhythm, loudness and tone colour that was achieved in the Structures for two pianos (1952). At this time he came to know Stockhausen, with whom he became a leader of the European avant garde, teaching at Darmstadt (1955-67) and elsewhere, and creating one of the key postwar works in his Le marteau sans maître (1954). Once more to poems by

Char, the work is for contralto with alto flute, viola, guitar and percussion: a typical ensemble of middle-range instruments with an emphasis on struck and plucked sounds. The filtering of Boulez's earlier manner through his 'tonal serialism' produces a work of feverish speed, unrest and elegance.

In the mid-1950s Boulez extended his activities to conducting. He had been Barrault's musical director since 1946 and in 1954 under Barrault's aegis he set up a concert series, the Domaine Musical, to provide a platform for new music. By the mid-1960s he was appearing widely as a conductor, becoming chief conductor of the BBC SO (1971-4) and the New York PO (1971-8). Meanwhile his creative output declined. Under the influence of Mallarmé he had embarked on three big aleatory works after Le marteau, but of these the Third Piano Sonata (1957) remains a fragment and Pli selon pli for soprano and orchestra (1962) has been repeatedly revised; only a second book of Structures for two pianos (1961) has been definitively finished. Other works, notably Eclat/Multiples for tuned percussion ensemble and orchestra, also remain in progress, as if the open-endedness of Boulez's proliferating musical world had committed him to incompleteness. Only the severe memorial Rituel for orchestra (1975) has escaped that fate.

Since the mid-1970s Boulez has concentrated on his work as director of the Institut de Recherche et Coordination Acoustique/Musique, a computer studio in Paris where his main work has been Répons for orchestra and digital equipment. **GROVE**music

Rituel in memoriam Bruno Maderna

Rituel in memoriam Bruno Maderna[a]. Eclat/Multiples[b]
[a]**BBC Symphony Orchestra,** [b]**Ensemble Intercontemporain / Pierre Boulez**
Sony Classical 07464 45839-2 (52' · ADD/DDD)
Recorded 1976-82   Ⓜ

Whatever's involved in the 20-bit technology used by Sony Classical to enhance the original CBS recordings of these works, the result is a very immediate and clear sound-picture. The sound does justice to a disc that can be recommended without reservation: magisterial performances by fine musicians of two masterworks by a leading contemporary composer. Boulez's casting off of post-Debussian refinements in *Eclat/Multiples* is enormously invigorating, and there's little of the stately, Messiaen-like processional writing that dominates *Rituel*. Here, two very different facets of Boulez's musical personality come into mutually illuminating confrontation, and this recording is frustrating only to the extent that the work itself remains unfinished. Maybe what's most radical about Boulez is that Western music's traditional concern with preparing and achieving a definitive ending has ceased to be necessary. In which case, of course, the way in which *Rituel* draws to a close could represent a concession to convention he now regrets.

In its CD transfer *Rituel* seems more than ever in thrall to the chiming, clattering percussion spread through the orchestra, which shepherds the various instrumental groups like so many anxious guardians. The source of *Rituel* lies in Boulez's tribute to Stravinsky, and the music – a massive public act of mourning, not a private expression of grief – is in some respects more appropriate as a memorial for the great Russian than for the genial Maderna. Solemn, hieratic, carved from blocks of harmonic marble by a master musical sculptor, *Rituel* is a fitting homage for a composer who learned to keep his emotions under strict control.

Piano Sonatas

Piano Sonatas Nos 1-3
Idil Biret pf
Naxos 8 553353 (64' · DDD)

It sometimes seems as if Boulez has spent a lifetime paying the penalty for having found composition so easy as a young man. The first two piano sonatas, works of his early twenties, are formidably assured in technique and tremendously rich in ideas. Those sections of the Third Sonata released for performance sound cold and tentative by comparison. Or is it that the Third Sonata's much more extreme rejection of tradition is itself a triumph, an authentic modernity that stands out the more prominently for its individualism? Such thoughts are inspired by Idil Biret's absorbing disc. In the first movement of the First Sonata the broader picture proves to be well fleshed out, the argument kept on the move, the young composer's impatience and arrogance palpable in Biret's steely touch and the rather dry but never harsh recorded sound.

The Second Sonata is no less confidently played. Its power suggests why such experiments as No 3 represents could never be a last word for Boulez. This disc isn't the first to bring us the three sonatas together, but Biret's musical persuasiveness, and the up-to-date sound, earn it a strong recommendation.

Pli selon pli

Pli selon pli
Christine Schäfer sop **Ensemble InterContemporain / Pierre Boulez**
DG download 471 344-2GH (70' · DDD · N/T/t)

This is the third recording of *Pli selon pli*, with the Ensemble InterContemporain expanded to 57 players, fitting the composer's definitive conception of the work as enhanced chamber music. Moreover, this is in effect a first recording, since it incorporates the revisions which Boulez made to the first and fourth movements during the 1980s. The recording was, as he wryly notes, the result of assiduous preparation, with no insecurity or 'panic'. It's a remarkably polished, gravely expressive account, as if he now sees his 'portrait of Mallarmé' more as a ritual homage to the radical 19th-century poet than as a multivalent, urgent, even angry sketch of the kind of intransigent creativity that few of Boulez's contemporaries were committed to at the time of the work's genesis (1957-60). But, even without panic, there can be no such thing as a sanitised, lushly comforting *Pli selon Pli*. The music remains Boulez's most extended engagement with the modernist aesthetic.

The recording is technically immaculate, with the intricate tapestry woven around guitar, mandolin and harps and the labyrinthine interactions between families of flutes, horns and lower strings especially well managed. Christine Schäfer sings serenely and securely, with an admirable poetic presence. Although you can imagine other performances recapturing more of the score's original fire and fury, this is an imposing representation of a work which sums up the composer's vision of art and life in the years before he found his way to a viable electro-acoustic technique and a more stable view of musical structure.

Pli selon pli[a]. Les soleil des eaux[b]. Le visage nuptial[c].
Figures, Doubles, Prismes
[abc]**Phyllis Bryn-Julson** *sop* [c]**Elisabeth Laurence** *mez*
[bc]**BBC Singers; BBC Symphony Orchestra / Pierre Boulez**
Warner Classics Apex ② 2564 62083-2
(129' · DDD · T/t)   ⒷOOOⴹ

This is a super-budget-price reissue of four of Boulez's most imposing earlier works. True, the 1981 *Pli selon pli* doesn't give you his most recent thoughts on his endlessly evolving Mallarmé portrait – for that you need the DG account reviewed above. But this BBC version, a *Gramophone* award-winner in 1983, remains a very satisfying document of its time. A special strength of the set as a whole is the vividness with which it demonstrates what has been lost in Boulez's complete abandonment of writing for the voice since the 1980s.

The large-scale cantata *Le visage nuptial*, originally composed in 1946, but performed here in the revised version from 1988-9, has an expressive incandescence and a sustained dramatic power that not only reconcile you to René Char's convoluted verse but provoke the thought that Boulez might, after all, be contemporary music's greatest opera composer manqué. The BBC Singers have have probably never done anything finer on disc.

More subversive dynamism can be heard in the expansive, eruptive monumentality of the orchestral *Figures, Doubles, Prismes*, strikingly enigmatic in its commitment to strongly sustained oppositions, and bringing back the composer's own 1985 reading. Add to all this the fascinating feline glitter of *Le soleil des eaux* and you have a 'portrait de Boulez' of exceptional quality.

Additional recommendation

Le Marteau sans maître[a]. Dérive 1 & 2
[a]**Summers** *contr* **EIC / Pierre Boulez**
DG download 477 5327 (69' · DDD · T/t)   ⒫OOⴹ

This is notable for a new recording of *Le Marteau sans maître*: a score now half a century old and sounding more urgently volatile than ever in this superbly crafted performance. With the finest present-day sound quality, this DG release is outstanding in every way: try and find a CD version!

York Bowen
British 1884-1961

Bowen studied at the Royal College of Music, London, played the violin and horn and became known as a fine pianist and a productive composer who wrote in a Romantic style and in many forms: as well as numerous chamber works and works for solo piano he also wrote three piano concertos.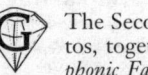

Concertos

Piano Concertos[a] – No 2, 'Concertstück', Op 17;
No 3, 'Fantasia', Op 23. Symphonic Fantasia, Op 16
[a]**Michael Dussek** *pf*
BBC Concert Orchestra / Vernon Handley
Dutton Laboratories Epoch CDLX7187 (75' · DDD) Ⓜ

The Second and Third Piano Concertos, together with the ambitious *Symphonic Fantasia*, make a fine follow-up to the coupling of the First Piano Concerto and Violin Concerto. Such largesse deserves the highest praise and it is easy to see a wry if grateful smile crossing Bowen's face if he were alive as he remembered his dismissal by modernists who viewed him as little better than a seashell washed ashore in a ruthlessly unaccommodating age.

Today, Bowen's unapologetic romanticism has found several champions taken by his warmth and sincerity and an open-hearted nostalgia for less brittle, over-sophisticated times. How hard it is to resist the appeal of the Second Concerto's *Lento espressivo*. How easy to imagine an elegantly attired audience greeting the finale's virtuoso close with gloved plaudits, sighing with delight over present if fast-receding conservative values. The rippling charm of the Third Concerto's central *Andante grazioso* and the finale's sunlit capers are sure to please.

So, too, is the *Symphonic Fantasia*, an ideal ballet score where the third movement's nodal and expressive centre is countered by the fifth movement's proud ceremonial stance. All this is superbly performed by Vernon Handley while Michael Dussek plays with brilliant facility and the warmest musical commitment. Dutton's sound is excellent.

Piano Concertos – No 3, 'Fantasia', Op 23; No 4,
Op 88
Danny Driver *pf*
BBC Scottish Symphony Orchestra / Martyn Brabbins
Hyperion CDA67659 (61' · DDD)   ⒫OO

Sorabji, in the final essay of *Mi Contra Fa*, declared York Bowen to be 'at the present time [1947], the one English composer whose work can justly be said to be that of a great Master of the [piano]'. Hearing these two works, it's hard to deny that Sorabji had a point.

It takes a particular kind of pianistic sensibility to take up Bowen's virtuoso challenges and 'sell' them. Danny Driver certainly lives up to his surname. He, Brabbins and the punchy Scottish players play Bowen as if he were standard repertoire with the added zest of a live performance. The 1908 four-movements-in-one Third Concerto (aka *Fantasia*), with its surging climaxes and soaring themes, offers 17 minutes of instant gratification, though it's a pity Hyperion did not provide separate tracks for the work's distinct sections.

The much longer (42'53") Fourth Concerto (1937) is generally darker in character, no less attractive but even more rewarding. The writing veers between magical impressionism and passionate bravura outbursts couched in Straussian orchestral textures. Thrilling stuff. Driver, again, is firmly in the spotlight. This is his first recording for Hyperion. Here's to many more, including his planned complete York Bowen sonatas.

Bowen Viola Concerto **C Forsyth** Viola Concerto
Lawrence Power *va* **BBC Scottish Symphony
Orchestra / Martyn Brabbins**
Hyperion CDA67546 (63' · DDD)　　　Ⓕ❍❍❍

During the decade leading up to the First World War, York Bowen, one of the brightest and most prolific young talents in British music, produced no fewer than three piano concertos, two symphonies, a concert overture, Symphonic Fantasia, *Concertstücke* for piano and orchestra and a tone-poem, *The Lament of Tasso*. His exquisitely polished and sure-footed Viola Concerto in C minor was written for Lionel Tertis (viola professor at the Royal Academy of Music), who first performed it in March 1908. Lasting nearly 36 minutes, each of its three movements serves up a heady flow of intoxicating melody, all clothed in the deftest orchestral garb (there's a definite Russian tang to proceedings – Bowen clearly knew and loved his Tchaikovsky, Borodin and Rimsky-Korsakov). This new performance is beyond criticism. Not only does Lawrence Power effortlessly surmount every technical challenge, he forms a scintillating partnership with Martyn Brabbins and an uncommonly well-prepared BBC Scottish SO.

A pupil of Stanford, Greenwich-born Cecil Forsyth (1870-1941) played the viola in Henry Wood's Queen's Hall Orchestra (as, indeed, did Bowen) before emigrating to the USA in 1914. His G minor Concerto (in all likelihood the first for viola by a British composer) was premiered in 1903 by the French virtuoso (and its dedicatee) Emile Férir. Beside its its present companion it strikes a rather more conventional note, but remains an appealingly lyrical and sturdily

crafted achievement. The performance is everything one could desire, and the recording is wonderfully ripe and glowing.

Violin Concerto[a]. Piano Concerto No 1[b]
[a]**Lorraine McAslan** *vn* [b]**Michael Dussek** *pf*
BBC Concert Orchestra / Vernon Handley
Dutton Digital Epoch CDLX7169 (64' · DDD)　　Ⓜ

York Bowen's Viola Concerto was quite a discovery last year so getting to know his Violin Concerto was an intriguing prospect. Finished in 1913 but not performed until 1920, it was briefly taken up by May Harrison but failed to establish itself. This exemplary first commercial recording reveals another substantial, exquisitely scored and unjustly forgotten Bowen gem which lovers of the Tchaikovsky, Elgar and Delius concertos should waste no time in seeking out.

The slow movement proves especially fetching, evincing a most engaging poetry and warm-hearted lyricism, while the finale serves up many opportunities for virtuoso display and ends with the clinching return of the horns' rousing call to arms. Lorraine McAslan gives a technically brilliant, sweet-toned account. Vernon Handley, too, well and truly in his element, secures memorably responsive, glowingly affectionate playing from the BBC Concert Orchestra.

The First Piano Concerto was written a decade earlier and first performed by the 19-year-old composer at London's Queen's Hall in December 1903. If less distinctive than its bedfellow, it's a thoroughly attractive piece, whose cheeky central *Scherzo* (which nods towards Saint-Saëns) precedes an extended, at times unashamedly Tchaikovskian, finale (with an exceedingly catchy main theme). This performance is outstanding, with Michael Dussek admirably stylish and Handley offering the most malleable support. The Watford Town Hall production marries amplitude and warmth to realistic balance.

String Quartets

String Quartets – No 2 in D minor, Op 41;
No 3 in G, Op 46b. Phantasy Quintet, Op 93[a]
[a]**Timothy Lines** *bcl* **Archaeus Quartet** (Ann Hooley,
Bridget Davey *vns* Elizabeth Turnbull *va* Martin
Thomas *vc*)
British Music Society BMS426CD (70' · DDD)　　Ⓕ

Published in 1922 after scooping a Carnegie Trust Award, York Bowen's Second String Quartet proves a most endearing discovery. Brimful of sweet-toothed yet never cloying melodic charm and written with consummate virtuosity for the medium, it's a fluent, poised and readily assimilable creation which merits immediate investigation by anyone with a penchant for, say, Bax or Korngold. Its unpublished successor was probably conceived about the same time and again boasts a wealth of big-hearted, felicitous invention. Both works follow the same Classical ground-plan, comprising two soundly constructed, sonata-form outer movements which frame a tenderly reflective slow movement in straightforward ternary form, and both certainly merit their resuscitation here. A similar technical mastery, harmonic pungency and generously lyrical cast inform Bowen's later *Phantasy Quintet* for the unusual combination of bass clarinet and string quartet, a single-movement essay of considerable imagination and frequently haunting beauty.

The Archaeus Quartet are sterling advocates of all this rewarding material. Timothy Lines, too, contributes most sensitively in the Quintet, and the sound is vivid to match. A stimulating and enjoyable release.

Viola Sonatas

Viola Sonatas – No 1 in C minor; No 2 in F. Phantasy, Op 54
James Boyd va **Bengt Forsberg** pf
Dutton Laboratories Epoch CDLX7126 (72' · DDD) Ⓜ

A valuable survey of three early Bowen offerings fashioned for that great British violist, Lionel Tertis (1876-1975). Not surprisingly, given Tertis's phenomenal technique and tone-production, each piece here makes exceptional demands. Happily, James Boyd is fully equal to the task. What's more, he forges a marvellously eloquent alliance with Bengt Forsberg, their playing brimful of affectionate understanding while retaining a sense of freshness in discovery.

Both sonatas date from 1905 and were premiered at London's Aeolian Hall by Tertis, with the 21-year-old composer at the piano, in May 1905 and February 1906 respectively. Described by its dedicatee as 'a vivacious and light-hearted work', the First Sonata comprises an expansive and confident *Allegro moderato*, a songful slow movement in ternary form (whose principal melody hints at Lowell Mason's 1856 hymn-tune for *Nearer, my God, to Thee*) and an unusually meaty finale, where sheer high spirits win out in the end. Its F major successor follows pretty much the same pattern, though the slow movement now quarries a darker vein of expression, while the concluding *Allegro giocoso* yields plenty of opportunity for cheeky display. Boasting admirable sound and balance, this is a gem of a disc.

Viola Sonatas – No 1; No 2. Romances – in D flat major; in A major. Fantasia, Op 41 No 1ª. Phantasy. Allegro de concert. Melody for the G string. Melody for the C string. Rhapsody **Beethoven/Bowen** Piano Sonata, 'Moonlight', Op 27 No 2 – I
Lawrence Power va **Simon Crawford-Phillips** pf with ªPhilip Dukes, ªJames Boyd, ªScott Dickinson vas
Hyperion ② CDA67651/2 (123' · DDD) ⒻО

Inspired by the incomparable Lionel Tertis, his friend and colleague at the Royal Academy of Music, Bowen wrote music for the viola of such richness and fantasy that its long neglect is one of music's saddest mysteries. True, Bowen's

delight in resurrecting the glamour of the past and archaisms too long uncherished, sat uneasily with the engulfing modernism of his age. Bowen, like Medtner, had little wish to move with the times, and yet if his music is endearingly old-fashioned it is also full of surprises and of a harmonic language and idiom peculiarly his own. Only a puritan could fail to respond to Bowen's warmth and exquisite craftsmanship in, for example the *Fantasia*, two *Romances* and the two *Melodies* where his sense of elegy takes on a double meaning: the aftermath of the war and the loss of what he saw as the departure of civilised creativity.

Both discs are beautifully planned, opening with sizeable sonatas and continuing with shorter works before ending with more large-scale offerings, and the performances could hardly be more glowing. Bowen's writing for both instruments is more than demanding yet nothing detracts from Lawrence Power's and Simon Crawford-Phillips's enviable fluency and achievement. Once again Hyperion has hit the jackpot in a much-needed revival and the sound and balance are exemplary.

Piano works

Piano Sonata No 5, Op 72. Fantasia, Op 132. Nocturne, Op 78. Four Bagatelles, Op 147. Siciliano e Toccatina, Op 128. Two Intermezzi, Op 141. Two Preludes. Ripples, Op 100 No 1. Evening Calm
Joop Celis pf
Chandos CHAN10410 (74' · DDD) Ⓕ

The major offering here is York Bowen's Fifth Sonata, music on a heroic scale, heavily indebted to Rachmaninov's Second Sonata, music that had clearly got under Bowen's skin. Yet the cross-fertilisation of Russian and English idioms is richly personal and such superbly crafted writing is a constant reminder of a composer in love with the piano. Again, as old-timers will recall, Bowen was a master pianist in his own and other people's music. The central *Andante* broods with a wholly Russian sense of romantic darkness and despondency, and the finale's dazzling rhetoric includes a ghostly recall of the first movement's fanfares before ending in a blaze of virtuoso glory. Not everything speaks with this level of inspiration yet all this music is composed with an innate understanding of a sheerly pianistic magic.

Bowen's *Fantasia* is hugely ambitious and *Evening Calm* also outstays its welcome. But the First Intermezzo's Schumannesque charm is beguiling and so is the delightfully off-centre *Siciliano e Toccatina*. However, not a single piece on this excellently recorded disc could be in more sensitive or magisterial hands. Joop Celis confirms his stature at every point.

Further listening

Bowen Flute Sonata
Coupled with: **Arnold** Flute Sonata **L Berkeley** Sona-

tina **Hamilton** Spring Days **D Matthews** Duet Variations **Maw** Sonatina
Khaner fl **Abramovic** pf
Avie AV0016 (65' · DDD)   Ⓕ

The Bowen Sonata is a real discovery; a strong and characterful piece full of Gallic lyricism, underpinned with ample, and always interesting, keyboard writing. A fascinating programme.

William Boyce   British 1711-1779

Boyce was a St Paul's Cathedral chorister and an organ pupil of Maurice Greene, also studying with Pepusch. From 1734 he held organist's posts in London and from 1736 was a composer to the Chapel Royal, writing anthems and services. His oratorio David's Lamentation over Saul and Jonathan (1736) was followed by his first dramatic works, including a short opera, Peleus and Thetis (by1740), The Secular Masque (1746) and the highly successful pastoral The Chaplet (1749), the first of a series of works for Drury Lane theatre. Increasing deafness hindered him – his last stage work was Heart of Oak (1759) – but his output in other vocal genres continued, and as Master of the King's Musick from 1757 he composed over 40 court odes. Among his few instrumental works are 12 trio sonatas (1747), Eight Symphonys (from ode and opera overtures, 1735-41, published 1760) and Twelve Overtures (1770). Boyce was among the finest and most respected English composers of his time, though his Baroque idiom had become old-fashioned by the end of his life. His music has a fresh vigour, especially evident in fugues, dance movements and expressive vocal writing. The owner of a valuable music library, he gained lasting fame for his Cathedral Music (1760-73), an edition of earlier English services by Orlando Gibbons, Purcell and others.   **GROVE**music

Eight Symphonys, Op 2

Eight Symphonys, Op 2   ℗
The English Concert / Trevor Pinnock hpd
Archiv Produktion 419 631-2AH (60' · DDD)   Ⓕ Ⓞ ➤

William Boyce's eight Symphonys (his own spelling) aren't symphonies in the modern sense, but a collection, issued for concert use, of overtures he had composed over nearly 20 years for theatre pieces and court odes. They represent English 18th-century music at its unpretentious best, notably in their formal unorthodoxy. The performances are a delight – cleanly articulated, decisive in rhythm, just in tempo. The French overture-like movements that open Nos 6 and 7 are crisp and brilliant; the more Italianate first movements, like those of Nos 2 and 4, have a splendid swing. And the tone of gentle melancholy behind the fine, expansive D minor first movement of No 8 is particularly well caught. Three of the symphonies have middle movements marked *Vivace*,

which often leads conductors into unsuitably quick tempos; but Pinnock obviously knows that, in 18th-century England, *Vivace* meant a speed not much above *Andante*, and for once these movements make proper sense: they're lively, to be sure, but not fast. This disc comfortably surpasses any rivals in both style and accomplishment. The sound of the modest-sized band is brightly and truly reproduced.

Eight Symphonys
Aradia Ensemble / Kevin Mallon
Naxos 8 557278 (62' · DDD)   Ⓢ ➤

While Trevor Pinnock (see above) or Christopher Hogwood might justifiably retain benchmark status, Kevin Mallon and his Canadian period-instrument Aradia Ensemble offer a nicely judged and pleasantly played alternative, vibrantly conveying the difficult blend of dance-like wit and muscular energy in Boyce's music.
Apart from the list of participants being wildly incorrect (a choir where none exists, horns overlooked, no organ and uncredited harpsichord) the only mild reservation is that the over-reverberant recorded sound conceals occasional problems with intonation and washes everything in a mushy soup that does not always assist transparency and clarity. However, the acoustic lends an attractive bloom to the horns in Symphony No 4, and the effect of the resonant trumpets and timpani in Symphony No 5 is invigorating. If you are curious about Boyce's orchestral music, then this is an ideal place to start.

David's Lamentation

David's Lamentation over Saul and Jonathan   ℗
(Dublin vers[a] and London vers excs[b]). Ode for St Cecilia's Day[c]
[c]**Patrick Burrowes** treb **William Purefoy**, [a]**Andrew Watts** countertens [ab]**Richard Edgar-Wilson** ten [c]**Michael George** bar **New College Choir Oxford; Hanover Band / Graham Lea-Cox**
ASV Gaudeamus CDGAU208 (80' · DDD)   Ⓕ

This third disc in ASV's excellent Boyce series offers an unfamiliar work that shows an unfamiliar side of the composer. In *David's Lamentation over Saul and Jonathan*, written in 1736, when he was 24, Boyce is in elegiac vein. It starts with a sombre G minor overture, using the typical 'lamentation' bass, falling chromatically; this is followed by a succession of choruses and airs, in sorrowful tone and minor keys, telling the tale of Israel's defeat and the deaths of Saul and Jonathan – and the slaying of the Amalekite. Of course, it's hardly on the emotional or dramatic scale of Handel's oratorio of three years later (of which the action of this work forms an episode), but Boyce's musical language is, on its more modest canvas, telling, and the work is full of moving and affecting ideas.

The version given here, as the main text, incorporates Boyce's revisions for a Dublin performance in 1744. Boyce in more familiar vein is represented by the Cecilian ode. Graham Lea-Cox directs with authority and obvious affection; the rhythms are sturdy, and the particular flavour of the music of perhaps the greatest English 18th-century composer is happily captured. He's helped by a capable band, the admirable choir of New College, and an accomplished team of soloists. Michael George is in good voice and gets his best chance in the ode, with his energetic account of 'In war's fierce alarms'; and Richard Edgar-Wilson shows a full, elegant tenor in his airs in the cantata. Of the two high men's voices William Purefoy produces some soft and sweet-toned, uncommonly even singing, and Andrew Watts, higher in tessitura, fine in line, excels in the poignant numbers. Overall, then, a most enjoyable disc.

Johannes Brahms   German 1833-1897

Brahms studied the piano from the age of seven and theory and composition (with Eduard Marxsen) from 13, gaining experience as an arranger for his father's light orchestra while absorbing the popular alla zingarese style associated with Hungarian folk music. In 1853, on a tour with the Hungarian violinist Reményi, he met Joseph Joachim and Liszt and Joachim, who became a lifelong friend, encouraged him to meet Schumann. Brahms's artistic kinship with Robert Schumann and his profound romantic passion (later mellowing to veneration) for Clara Schumann, 14 years his elder, never left him. After a time in Düsseldorf he worked in Detmold, settling in Hamburg in 1859 to direct a women's chorus. Though well known as a pianist he had trouble finding recognition as a composer, largely owing to his outspoken opposition – borne out in his D minor Piano Concerto Op 15 – to the aesthetic principles of Liszt and the New German School. But his hopes for an official conducting post in Hamburg (never fulfilled) were strengthened by growing appreciation of his creative efforts, especially the two orchestral serenades, the Handel Variations for piano and the early piano quartets. He finally won a position of influence in 1863-64, as director of the Vienna Singakademie, concentrating on historical and modern a cappella works. Around this time he met Wagner, but their opposed stances precluded anything like friendship. Besides giving concerts of his own music, he made tours throughout northern and central Europe and began teaching the piano. He settled permanently in Vienna in 1868.

Brahms's urge to hold an official position (connected in his mind with notions of social respectability) was again met by a brief conductorship – in 1872-3 of the Vienna Gesellschaftskonzerte – but the practical demands of the job conflicted with his even more intense longing to compose. Both the German Requiem (first complete performance, 1869) and the Variations on the St Antony Chorale (1873) were rapturously acclaimed, bringing international renown and financial security.

Honours from home and abroad stimulated a spate of masterpieces, including the First (1876) and Second (1877) Symphonies, the Violin Concerto (1878), the songs of Opp 69-72 and the C major Trio. In 1881 Hans von Bülow became a valued colleague and supporter, 'lending' Brahms the fine Meiningen court orchestra to rehearse his new works, notably the Fourth Symphony (1885). At Bad Ischl, his favourite summer resort, he composed a series of important chamber works. By 1890 he had resolved to stop composing but nevertheless produced in 1891-4 some of his best instrumental pieces, inspired by the clarinettist Richard Mühlfeld. Soon after Clara's death in 1896 he died from cancer, aged 63, and was buried in Vienna.

Fundamentally reserved, logical and studious, Brahms was fond of taut forms in his music, though he used genre distinctions loosely. In the piano music, for example, which chronologically encircles his vocal output, the dividing lines between ballade and rhapsody, and capriccio and intermezzo, are vague; such terms refer more to expressive character than to musical form. As in other media, his most important development technique in the piano music is variation, whether used independently (simple melodic alteration and thematic cross-reference) or to create a large integrated cycle in which successive variations contain their own thematic transformation (as in the Handel Variations).

If producing chamber works without piano caused him difficulty, these pieces contain some of his most ingenious music, including the Clarinet Quintet and the three string quartets. Of the other chamber music, the eloquent pair of string sextets, the serious C minor Piano Quartet Op 60 (known to be autobiographical), the richly imaginative Piano Quintet and the fluent Clarinet Trio Op 114 are noteworthy. The confidence to finish and present his First Symphony took Brahms 15 years for worries over not only his orchestral technique but the work's strongly Classical lines at a time when programmatic symphonies were becoming fashionable; his closely worked score led him to be hailed as Beethoven's true heir. In all four symphonies he is entirely personal in his choice of material, structural manipulation of themes and warm but lucid scoring. All four move from a weighty opening movement through loosely connected inner movements to a monumental finale. Here again his use of strict form, for example the ground bass scheme in the finale of the Fourth Symphony, is not only discreet but astonishingly effective. Among the concertos, the four-movement Second Piano Concerto in B flat – on a grandly symphonic scale, demanding both physically and intellectually – and the Violin Concerto (dedicated to Joachim and lyrical as well as brilliant) are important, as is the nobly rhetorical Double Concerto.

Brahms's greatest vocal work, and a work central to his career, is the German Requiem (1868), combining mixed chorus, solo voices and full orchestra in a deeply felt, non-denominational statement of faith. More Romantic are the Schicksalslied and the Alto Rhapsody. Between these large choral works and the many a cappella ones showing his informed appreciation of Renaissance and Baroque polyphony (he was a diligent collector, scholar and editor of old music) stand the justly popular Zigeunerlieder (in modified gypsy style) and the ländler-like Liebeslieder waltzes with piano accompaniment. His best-loved songs include, besides the narrative Magelone cycle and the sublime Vier ernste Gesänge, Mainacht, Feldein-samkeit and Immer leiser wird mein Schlummer.

GROVEmusic

Piano Concertos

No 1 in D minor, Op 15; **No 2** in B flat, Op 83

Piano Concertos Nos 1 & No 2
Nelson Freire pf **Gewandhaus Orchestra, Leipzig / Riccardo Chailly**
Decca ② 475 7637DX2 (95' · DDD) Recorded live
ⓂOOO☐→

This is the Brahms piano concerto set we've been waiting for. Nelson Freire and Riccardo Chailly offer interpretations that triumphantly fuse immediacy and insight, power and lyricism, and incandescent virtuosity that leaves few details unturned, yet always with the big picture in clear sight. The D minor No 1's headlong opening tutti updates Szell/Cleveland's patented fire and brimstone with a warmth of tone that manages to convey both line and mass as few others do. Timpani and brass proudly step up to the fore in both concertos, while frequently buried lines emerge from the gnarly textures with uncommon clarity and specificity. In Chailly's hands, a genuine chamber music aesthetic consistently governs the lustrous warmth of Brahms's underrated orchestrations, to say nothing of the heights to which the conductor has led his revitalised Leipzig Gewandhaus ensemble.

Balanced within the orchestra as an equal partner, Freire is completely on top of and inside both works' solo parts, from No 1's fervent yet cogently shaped octave outbursts and the B flat's graceful, light-footed finale to both slow movements' unforced simplicity, organic flow, and freedom from sentimentality. No doubt that the presence of an audience fuels the palpable give and take between soloist and conductor. Just as the Szell/Cleveland cycles with Serkin and Fleisher, and Gilels/Jochum (reviewed below) were benchmarks in their day, these gorgeously engineered, stunningly executed and temperamentally generous performances will stand as points of reference for generations to come.

Piano Concertos Nos 1 & 2.
Seven Piano Pieces, Op 116
Emil Gilels pf **Berlin Philharmonic Orchestra / Eugen Jochum**
DG The Originals ② 447 446-2GOR2 (125' · ADD)
Recorded 1972-5
ⓂOO☐→

The booklet-notes make reference to the original *Gramophone* review, in which Gilels and Jochum were praised for 'a rapt songfulness that in no way detracts from Brahms's heroism, and so comes closer to that unique and complex combination of attitudes that for me is Brahms more than any other performances of these concertos I have ever heard, on records or otherwise'. It might be added

that Jochum and the Berlin Philharmonic make plain sailing where others struggle with choppy cross-currents (admittedly sometimes to Brahms's advantage) and that the recordings don't sound their age. Other interpreters have perhaps probed a little deeper here and there; neither concerto rests content with a single interpretation, the Second especially. As for the Seven Piano Pieces, Gilels viewed the opus as a single piece, a musical novella in several chapters.

Violin Concerto in D, Op 77

Brahms Violin Concerto[a]
Schumann Violin Concerto[a] **Tchaikovsky** Violin Concerto[b] **Wieniawski** Violin Concerto No 2[b]
Joshua Bell vn
Cleveland Orchestra / [a]Christoph von Dohnányi, [b]Vladimir Ashkenazy
Decca ② 475 6703-5DF2 (134' · DDD) ⓂO☐→

Bell's first entry in the Brahms instantly reveals the soloist's love of bravura display, his gift for turning a phrase individually in a way that catches the ear, always sounding spontaneous, never self-conscious. Regularly one registers moments of new magic, not least when, in the most delicate half-tones, *pianissimos* seem to convey an inner communion, after which the impact of bravura *fortissimos* is all the more dramatic. He rounds off the movement with his own big cadenza and a magically hushed link into the coda, rapt and intense. The slow movement, sweet and songful, gains too from Bell's love of playing really softly, not least in stratospheric registers. In the finale the vein of fantasy is less apparent. Next to others this can seem a little plain. Dohnányi and the Cleveland Orchestra provide weighty and sympathetic support and the generous Schumann, Tchaikovsky, Wieniawski couplings in commanding performance adds to the attractions of the set.

In the Schumann Dohnányi and the Cleveland Orchestra add to the weight and dramatic impact of a performance that defies the old idea of this as an impossibly flawed piece, with Bell bringing out charm as well as power. With full and atmospheric Cleveland sound, well-balanced, the Tchaikovsky makes an excellent choice, particularly if you fancy the Wieniawski Second Concerto for coupling. Bell may not quite match Perlman in either of his recordings for his individual poetry, but within its less searching compass Bell's is a masterly performance, full of flair.

Brahms Violin Concerto
Tchaikovsky Violin Concerto in D, Op 35
Jascha Heifetz vn **Chicago Symphony Orchestra / Fritz Reiner** Ⓗ
RCA Victor Living Stereo 88888 03034-2 (64' · ADD)
Recorded 1955, 1957 ⓂO☐→

This combination appears unbeatable. You may think that Reiner starts the opening *tutti* at an extraordinarily quick speed – until you remember that he's going to accompany no less

BRAHMS PIANO CONCERTOS – IN BRIEF

Nelson Freire; Gewandhaus Orchestra, Leipzig / Riccardo Chailly
Decca ② 475 7637DX2 (95' · DDD)   ⓂⓄⓄⓄⒹ→
A magnificent achievement that finds a pianist of enormous integrity supported by a conductor with excellent Brahms credentials at the helm of a newly re-invigorated orchestra. This set – a Brahms concerto set for the new millennium – took *Gramophone*'s Record of the Year Award

Emil Gilels; Berlin PO / Eugen Jochum
DG ② 447 446-2GOR2 (125' · ADD)   ⓂⓄⓄⒹ→
This is a modern classic: awe-inspiring piano playing and accompaniments of weight, power and great sympathy. Unmissable.

Rudolf Serkin; Cleveland Orchestra / George Szell
Sony Classical ② 82796 93447-2, 07464 48166-2 (64' & 67' · ADD)   Ⓑ
A fine memento of a great partnership and one of the glories of the US orchestra scene, the Cleveland Orchestra. These are wonderfully intense performances but the sound takes a bit of getting used to. Available in various couplings: here Mendelssohn and solo Brahms.

Stephen Hough; BBC SO / Sir Andrew Davis
Virgin Classics ② 561412-2 (100' · DDD)   ⒷⒹ→
Hough's set of these two mightly concertos is remarkably successful with delicacy matched by considerable power, but there's a luminosity here that's very attractive.

Daniel Barenboim; Philharmonia, Vienna PO / Sir John Barbirolli
EMI ② 572649-2 (146' · ADD)   Ⓜ
An often overlooked pair of performances but a superb one none the less. The First Concerto is magnficent, with the partnership of piano and conductor at its most inspired. There's a wonderful freshness about both finales, and the 1960s sound is excellent.

Emanuel Ax; Chicago SO / James Levine, Boston SO / Bernard Haitink
Sony Classical ② 88697 03510-2 (134' · DDD)   Ⓑ
A recoupling that finds Ax purveying poetry and passion in equal measure. The First, with Levine in charge, is magnificent, and though Haitink can be a little generalised there is much to win the heart in the performance of No 2.

a virtuoso than Heifetz, so he's merely taking it to match his soloist's performance. You'll like this if you think that this concerto is too often played in the kind of 'autumnal' manner often attributed to Brahms's compositions but which really shouldn't apply to many of them. With Heifetz it's played with respect but without any kind of reverent hushed awe. The slow movement is lovely and the finale is a winner, the playing of an exuberant young man, yet Heifetz was over 50 when he made this record. Reiner conducts the fast movement with a fiery rhythmic impetus that incandescently matches the exhilarating, yet unforced bravura of his great soloist. It's confident throughout – and just listen to his real *staccato*, a rare thing from violinists.

The RCA recording comes up extraordinarily well – although the soloist is balanced forwardly, he's naturally focused and the Chicago acoustic ensures a convincing concert-hall balance. If anything, the remastering of the Tchaikovsky is even more remarkable, considering that originally Heifetz was apparently placed right up against the microphone. You soon adapt to the closeness when the fiddle-playing is so peerless; and Heifetz colours Tchaikovsky's melodies ravishingly.

Violin Concerto, Op 77. Double Concerto, Op 102[a]
Julia Fischer vn [a]**Daniel Müller-Schott** vc
Netherlands Philharmonic Orchestra / Yakov Kreizberg
Pentatone 🅂 PTC5186 066 (73' · DDD/DSD)   ⒻⓄ

Julia Fischer offers this ideal Brahms coupling in strong and sympathetic readings, joined in the Double Concerto by her brilliant young compatriot, cellist Daniel Müller-Schott. In the Violin Concerto, Fischer takes an expansive view of the first movement, freely varying the tempo as she did in her outstanding version of the Tchaikovsky Concerto. The 23-minute timing even underestimates her spaciousness, as she uses an unidentified cadenza rather shorter than the usual Joachim one (the booklet incorrectly says it's the Joachim).

Others offer tauter and brisker accounts of the first movement but Fischer amply justifies her spacious and flexible speeds in the feeling of spontaneity. Her performance never feels self-conscious or too studied and her range of tone and dynamic is extreme, bringing *pianissimi* of breathtaking delicacy. Fischer's slow movement, too, is expansive while in the finale she lets the tempo relax just enough to allow a persuasive spring in the rhythms, bringing out the Hungarian dance flavour.

The Double Concerto is not nearly as expansive: no doubt the influence of Müller-Schott was important here as the cello takes the lead in introducing each theme, with the cellist matching his partner in warmth and brilliance. Fischer and Müller-Schott are relaxed and easily lyrical in the slow movement, brilliant and thrusting in the finale. An outstanding disc which stands high on the list of this perfect coupling.

Double Concerto, Op 102

Double Concerto, Op 102[a]. Clarinet Quintet, Op 115[b]
Renaud Capuçon *vn* **Gautier Capuçon** *vc*
[b]**Paul Meyer** *cl*
[b]**Aki Saulière** *vn* [b]**Béatrice Muthelet** *va*
[a]**Gustav Mahler Jugendorchester / Myung-Whun Chung**
Virgin Classics 395147-2 (72' · DDD)   Ⓕ Ⓞ ➔

The stellar young Capuçon brothers seem incapable of setting a foot wrong on disc and they put their considerable chamber-music experience to great use in Brahms's final orchestral work, with cellist Gautier Capuçon proving an eloquent lead in the vehement first movement.

The other striking aspect about this performance is the sheer range of colour, not only from the soloists but also from the Gustav Mahler Youth Orchestra, who play their hearts out for Myung-Whun Chung in this most symphonic of concertos. If Oistrakh and Fournier are still irresistible in the slow movement, offering a perfect balance of melodic lines that are lovingly cherished but never saccharine, the Capuçons are still very impressive, and their finale is full of vitality, making much of the folk-tinged inflections and achieving a seemingly telepathic unanimity in their shared passages.

For a change from the usual concerto companion we get Brahms's Clarinet Quintet, written in 1891, four years after the Double Concerto. In this coupling it's easy to hear the Quintet's famous autumnal quality prefigured in the outer sections of the concerto's *Andante*. Paul Meyer is an ideal protagonist, producing a wide array of mellow shadings in the opening movement, yet never underplaying the more agitated passages within the piece, notably the *Presto* of the third movement. The quartet are minutely responsive to Meyer's every move and even seasoned Brahms aficionados will find new detail to relish in both the performances here.

Brahms Double Concerto
Schumann Cello Concerto in A minor, Op 129
Ilya Kaler *vn* **Maria Kliegel** *vc* **National Symphony Orchestra of Ireland / Andrew Constantine**
Naxos 8 550938 (59' · DDD)   Ⓢ ➔

The Brahms and Schumann concertos make an excellent and apt coupling, here given warmly spontaneous-sounding performances, very well recorded. The violinist, Ilya Kaler, is as clean in attack and intonation as Maria Kliegel. Kliegel in her opening cadenza allows herself full freedom, but any feeling that this is to be an easygoing, small-scale reading is dispelled in the main *Allegro*, which is clean and fresh, sharp in attack, helped by full-bodied sound. Kaler and Kliegel make the second subject tenderly expressive without using exaggerated rubato. Similarly there's no self-indulgence in the soar-

BRAHMS VIOLIN CONCERTO – IN BRIEF

Joshua Bell; Cleveland Orchestra / Christoph von Dohnányi
Decca 475 6703-5DF2   Ⓕ Ⓞ ➔
Sweet-toned and subtle, Bell is an appealing soloist with a winning spontaneity that reveals great depths of feeling. Dohnányi displays his Brahmsian credentials to fine effect. (Coupled with the Schumann, Tchaikovsky and Wieniawski No 2.)

Jascha Heifetz; Chicago SO / Fritz Reiner   Ⓗ
RCA mono 88888 03034-2   Ⓕ Ⓞ ➔
This is a high-octane, high-velocity performance in which Heifetz's legendary virtuosity is matched by some staggering playing by the Chicago orchestra under Reiner. This is no autumnal vision of the work but an athletic, graceful display. (Coupled with the Tchaikovsky.)

Gil Shaham; Berlin Philharmonic Orchestra / Claudio Abbado
DG 469 529-2GH   Ⓕ ➔
Coupled with the Double Concerto, this is one of the most impressive of modern versions, intensity and full of imagination. Recorded live, it shows Shaham at his spontaneous best.

David Oistrakh; London Philharmonic Orchestra / Norman Del Mar
BBC Legends BBCL4102-2   Ⓕ ➔
This is great violin playing: Oistrakh is on superb form, playing with his customary warmth. Well accompanied by Norman Del Mar, this builds up to a finale of thrilling power. Inevitably, the 1960 recording shows its years.

Julia Fischer; Netherlands Philharmonic Orchestra / Yakov Kreizberg
Pentatone PTC 5186 066   Ⓕ Ⓞ
A hugely impressive reading of this huge concerto from one of the brightest of the new generation of violin stars. Kreizberg is a model accompanist and together with his characterful young soloist gives a performance that demands to be heard.

Ginette Neveu; Philharmonia Orchestra / Issay Dobrowen   Ⓗ
Dutton mono CDBP9710   Ⓜ
Dutton improves on EMI's own transfer of this magnificent performance, giving it a winning warmth and body. Neveu was a commanding violinist and there's never a moment's doubt that she has the measure (and beyond) of this great work. Her technique is astounding and the accuracy of her playing an object lesson in great musicianship.

ing main melody of the central *Andante*, but no lack of warmth or tenderness either. The finale is then unhurried but has dance-rhythms so beautifully sprung and such delicate pointing of phrases that any lack of animal excitement is amply replaced by wit and a sense of fun.

In the Schumann Kliegel takes a spacious, lyrical view of the first movement, using a soft-grained tone at the start with wide vibrato. She then builds up the power of the performance, and with Constantine providing sympathetic accompaniment, the spontaneous expression is most compelling. So, too, is the simple, dedicated playing in the central Langsam, and, as in the Brahms, Kliegel brings witty pointing to the finale, not least in the second subject. The balance of the soloists is good.

Double Concerto[a]. Symphony No 2 in D, Op 73
[a]**Gordan Nikolitch** *vn* [a]**Tim Hugh** *vc*
London Symphony Orchestra / Bernard Haitink
LSO Live LSO0043 (75' · DDD)　　　Ⓢ**OO**▷

Labels such as LSO Live bring altered priorities and fresh perspectives. When did a studio-based company last contemplate recording Brahms's Double Concerto with soloists drawn from within the orchestra? Brahms wrote the work with Joachim and his colleague in the Joachim Quartet, Robert Hausmann, in mind. It has a chamber-music dimension to it, yet it's also a work of real symphonic power. Haitink's accompaniment is superb, allowing the soloists the space for the lyric outpourings at the heart of the work. The sweet-toned Gordan Nikolitch and the burlier-sounding, though endlessly responsive Tim Hugh are perfectly matched, and grow ever closer and more eloquent as the romantic, at times almost operatic, colloquy of the two opening movements unfolds. After which, slippered ease and remembered passion is the order of the day in a sweetly judged reading of the finale. The recording, rich and immediate, brings out the tactile quality of Brahms's writing.

Haitink's 1990 Boston recording of the symphony has a certain Mediterranean glow to it. In this imposing and beautifully shaded new LSO performance, we return north again with a reading that's weightier and even more cleanly articulated than his 1973 Amsterdam version.

Symphonies

No 1 in C minor **No 2** in D **No 3** in F **No 4** in E minor

---

Symphonies Nos 1-4. Variations on a Theme by Haydn. Tragic Overture
Staatskapelle Dresden / Kurt Sanderling
RCA ③ 09478 69220-2
(197' · ADD) Recorded 1971-2　　　Ⓑ**OO**

Kurt Sanderling has recorded the Brahms symphonies twice (his first set, with the Berlin Sym-

phony Orchestra, is available on Capriccio), but what started out as solid, patient and well built broadened significantly, and in doing so stressed the epic element that was always implicit in the first recordings: the first movement of the later First Symphony is slower than its predecessor by over two minutes. Sanderling's great strength is in the way he handles Brahms's choppy, obdurate string writing, whether in the First Symphony's strutting first movement *Allegro* or the opening *Allegro non troppo* of the Fourth. Tempos are consistently held firm, the lyrical passages allowed their due only within a solid structural frame (the Third Symphony's middle movement, for example) and first-movement repeats omitted. As ever, it's the Third Symphony that underlines specific interpretative differences between conductors – the first movement especially, a vigorous *Allegro con brio* that, for some reason or other, defeats even the greatest maestros. Sanderling takes a majestic, even marmoreal option that seems misguided: the gestures are grand, certainly, but the music remains rooted to earth. And if ever a piece said 'come fly with me', it's the first movement of Brahms's Third Symphony.

In short, Sanderling is sturdy, intelligently phrased, warmly played, fairly well recorded (the strings are a little grainy) and supplemented by equally well-considered accounts of the *Haydn* Variations and *Tragic Overture*.

Symphonies Nos 1-4. Variations on a Theme by Haydn. Tragic Overture, Op 81. Academic Festival Overture, Op 80. Hungarian Dances – No 1 in G minor; No 3 in F; No 10 in F. Serenades – No 1 in D, Op 11; No 2 in A, Op 16
Concertgebouw Orchestra / Bernard Haitink
Philips Bernard Haitink Symphony Edition ④
442 068-2PB4 (291' · ADD) Recorded 1970-80　Ⓑ**O**

Concertgebouw standards at the time of Haitink's survey (1970-80) left little to be desired. Perhaps the clarinets don't always overcome reservations about their tone and intonation with the sensitivity of their phrasing; but the horns invariably do, and more often than not Brahms's favourite instrument is a source of joy in these recordings, blazing gloriously at appropriate moments (especially in the Fourth Symphony), or opening up and sustaining huge vistas in the 'dawn' of the First's finale. As to the strings, Haitink's insistence on firmly defined (though never over-emphatic) rhythms from the bass lines up is altogether exceptional; there are countless examples, but most memorable of all is the cellos' and basses' ostinato that sees the Second Symphony's finale in the home straight. What an articulate, integrated Brahms sound this is, too; a case of conductor and engineers easily achieving their aims working in a familiar acoustic. The only movement you may initially find overly sober is the first of the Third Symphony, taken very broadly, though it's determined and imposing, and the launching of the coda is stupendously powerful. There's no better way of getting to know Brahms's orchestral works on a budget.

Symphonies Nos 1-4. Variations on a Theme by
Haydn. Academic Festival Overture. Tragic Overture
**Berlin Philharmonic Orchestra / Nikolaus
Harnoncourt**
Teldec ③ 0630-13136-2 (214' · DDD)　　Ⓕ❍❍

Any fears that Nikolaus Harnoncourt's Brahms
will be quirky, provocative or abrasive can be
dispelled. There are interpretative novelties
(freshly considered articulation and clarified
counterpoint) and the Berlin strings project
a smooth, curvaceous profile. Harnoncourt
makes a beeline for the brass, and the horns in
particular. The live recordings have remarkable
presence and are mostly cough-free.

The First Symphony's opening *Un poco sostenuto* seems a trifle soft-grained but the pounding
basses from bar 25 are beautifully caught and the
first-movement *Allegro* is both powerful and
broadly paced. The *Andante sostenuto* slow movement is both limpid and conversational, with
trance-like dialogue between oboe and clarinet
and sparing use of vibrato among the strings.
Harnoncourt makes real chamber music of
the third movement, though he drives the trio
section to a fierce climax, and the finale's first
accelerating pizzicatos are truly *stringendo poco a
poco* – the excitement certainly mounts, but only
gradually.

The Second Symphony's first movement is
relatively restrained. Harnoncourt's strategy
is to deliver a sombre exposition and a tough-
ened development. Again, the slow movement
is fluid and intimate, with some tender string
playing. The third movement's rustling trio
is disarmingly delicate and the finale, tightly
held, keenly inflected and heavily accented: the
coda threatens to break free and the effect
is thrilling.

First impressions of the Third suggest a marginal drop in intensity, yet the first movement's
peroration is so powerful that there's a retrospective suspicion that all the foregoing was mere
preparation. The middle movements work well
but the rough-hewn, flexibly phrased finale
really makes the performance.

Like the Third, the Fourth opens with less
import than some of its older rivals, yet the
development intensifies perceptibly, the recapitulation's hushed *piano dolce* opening bars are
held on the edge of a breath and the coda is
recklessly headstrong. The slow movement has
some heartfelt moments, the top-gear *Scherzo*
is quite exhilarating and the finale, forged with
the noble inevitability of a Baroque passacaglia.
Ultimately, Harnoncourt delivers a fine and
tragic Fourth.

Harnoncourt's Brahms is the perfect antidote
to predictability and interpretative complacency.

Symphonies Nos 1-4. Tragic Overture, Op 81.　Ⓗ
Variations on a Theme by Haydn, 'St Antoni Chorale',
Op 56a
Philharmonia Orchestra / Arturo Toscanini
Testament mono ④ SBT3167 (200' · ADD)　Recorded
live 1952　　Ⓕ❍❍

BRAHMS SYMPHONIES – IN BRIEF

Hallé Orchestra / James Loughran
CfP ③ 575753-2 (279' · ADD)　　Ⓑ❍
A longtime favourite: honest, muscular, with
a fine sweep and sense of architecture. The
Second Symphony is magnificent

Berlin PO / Nikolaus Harnoncourt
Teldec ③ 0630 13136-2 (214' · DDD)　Ⓕ❍❍▷
A fresh approach to four classics played with
total conviction by a band with a tradition.

Berlin PO / Herbert von Karajan
DG ② 453 097-2GTA2 (156' · ADD)　　Ⓜ❍▷
From the late 1970s, the BPO's Brahms
sound glows under Karajan's total command.
(Don't confuse this with his later, more
expensive, very similar digital recordings.)

Philharmonia / Otto Klemperer
EMI ② 562742-2 (156' · ADD)　　Ⓜ❍▷
A set that shows Klemperer at his finest: there
is a power and strength that inspires real
admiration. The Philharmonia plays with
burning passion.

Staatskapelle Dresden / Kurt Sanderling
RCA ② 09478 69220-2 (197' · ADD)　Ⓑ❍❍
Perfectly proportioned, sturdy readings from
a master conductor and great ensemble.

Concertgebouw Orchestra / Bernard Haitink
Philips ④ 442 068-2PB4 (291' · ADD)　　Ⓑ❍
Exquisitely phrased, elegant Brahms from
one of the world's great orchestras.

Berlin PO, Vienna PO / Wilhelm Furtwängler　Ⓗ
EMI mono ④ 565513-2 (219' · ADD)　　Ⓜ❍
Perhaps *the* historic choice (1948-52) and a fine
example of Furtwängler's incandescent art: the
Fourth positively drips with tragedy.

Philharmonia Orchestra / Arturo Toscanini　Ⓗ
Testament ② SBT3167 (200' · ADD)　　Ⓕ❍❍
From 1952, the Italian maestro's singing way
with Brahms is gloriously conveyed.

Berlin PO / Claudio Abbado
DG ④ 435 683-2GH4 (246' · DDD)　　Ⓕ❍▷
One of the finest of modern Brahms cycles
with stylish, sleek orchestral work.

North German RSO / Günter Wand
RCA ③ 74321 89103-2 (158' · DDD)　　Ⓕ❍
Wonderfully wise, beautifully prepared performances that speak of a lifetime's love of
this music and thorough familiarity with it.

Scottish CO / Sir Charles Mackerras
Telarc ③ CD80450 (199' · DDD)　　Ⓕ
An interesting historic approach that uses an
orchestra of the same size as the one Brahms
had at Meiningen – fresh and light on its
feet.

The concerts recorded here preserve the two legendary occasions in the autumn of 1952 when in a Brahms cycle at the Royal Festival Hall Toscanini conducted the Philharmonia Orchestra, then only six years old but already the front runner among London orchestras. The recording itself, now legendary, has generated pirated versions, but never before has the original made by EMI, under the supervision of Walter Legge, been officially released. Testament's remastering is a revelation. This new set brings the clearest of demonstrations that the RCA recordings of Toscanini and the NBC Symphony Orchestra made during the last years of his life (including his Brahms cycle of the very same 12-month period) give only an imperfect picture of a conductor who at the time, and for a generation or so previously, was almost universally counted the greatest in the world. That reputation has been eroded over the years, but this issue may help to put the record straight.

Take for example the quite different NBC version of No 3 that he recorded in New York barely a month after this performance: as Alan Sanders says in his note, a 'rhythmically staid recording which entirely lacked the lyricism and eloquence of the Philharmonia performance'. His description points to the marked contrasts, not only in No 3 but in all four symphonies. Whereas the New York performances, resonant and superbly drilled, have a hardness and rigidity, with the dynamic contrasts ironed out, thus eliminating *pianissimos* (partly a question of recording balance), the Philharmonia's consistently bring a moulding of phrase and subtlety of rubato which bears out the regular Toscanini instructions to 'Sing!'. And in contrast with most Toscanini recordings, the hushed playing is magical. The New York players, by comparison, seem to have forgotten how to respond to the finer subtleties of this notorious taskmaster among conductors. The extra flexibility of the Philharmonia performances over the NBC has an interesting effect on tempo too. Whereas in No 1 the NBC speeds of 1951 are faster, not just than those of the Philharmonia but of the 1941 NBC performance, in the other three symphonies the Philharmonia timings tend to be a degree quicker, notably in No 3, where for example the *Andante* flows far better.

Walter Legge fought hard to get these live recordings officially released – now we can understand why.

Additional recommendation

Symphonies Nos 1-4
Coupled with: Violin Concerto[a]. Alto Rhapsody[b].
Hungarian Dances
[a]**Hasson** vn [b]**Greevy** mez [a]**LPO; Hallé Orchestra /
Loughran**
Classics for Pleasure ④ 575753-2
(279' · ADD) Recorded mid-1970s   Ⓑ
  Loughran's cycle had a very loyal following on LP.
It still sounds pretty good some 25 years on. He
knows how to build a Brahms symphony not only

towards its climax but from its bass line; his choice of tempo rarely falters. And No 2 is a sheer delight. Add a glorious *Alto Rhapsody* and a cultivated Violin Concerto and you've a real bargain.

Brahms Symphony No 1
Schumann Symphony No 1 in B flat, Op 38, 'Spring'
**Berlin Philharmonic Orchestra /
Herbert von Karajan**
DG The Originals 447 408-2GOR (76' · ADD)
Recorded 1964, 1971   Ⓜ▷

The first of Karajan's three Berlin Brahms cycles was, by general consent, his finest for DG. Which was his finest 'phase' in general, only time will tell. Few would deny that this C minor Symphony has a 'halcyon days' feel. It's certainly present in the first two movements, the drive established in the main *Allegro* of the first (no repeat) allowing Karajan to relax for the second theme without loss of purpose. The second movement, ideally mobile, evolves freely and seamlessly, with masterfully graded wide dynamic contrasts felt rather than fashioned. This orchestra's tone production is even, rich and rounded. So far, so good. In the third movement bar-by-bar dynamic contrasts are smoothed out, with the route to the Trio's climax taken as one very gradual *crescendo*. The finale's 'daybreak' is broad and awe-inspiring. Karajan here has gauged tempo, dynamics and accentuation so the strings can articulate without strain; all very impressive, but his *Allegro*'s progress is thus relatively short on attack, energy and the ability to fly.

The more you hear Karajan's Schumann First Symphony, the more convinced you may be that it's spring cultivated and monitored under laboratory conditions. The most unsettling of those conditions is an effect common to a number of his 1970s DG Berlin recordings, namely, for a fairly closely balanced orchestra (particularly the strings, which aren't entirely glare-free), as dynamic levels drop, to walk off several paces into a glowing Berlin sunset. This also exaggerates the conductor's own contrasts, neither exactly redolent of the vitality and freshness of spring: the resolutely robust and measured delivery of the rustic *forte*, and the carefully crafted confection of his *dolce piano*.

Brahms Symphony No 1, Op 68. Begräbnisgesang,
Op 13[a]. Schicksalslied, Op 54[a]
Mendelssohn Mitten wir in Leben sind, Op 23[a]
[a]**Monteverdi Choir; Orchestre Révolutionnaire et
Romantique / Sir John Eliot Gardiner**
Soli Deo Gloria SDG702 (75' · DDD)   Ⓕ ⚫⚫▷

Part of a project whose purpose is to contextualise Brahms's four symphonies and *German Requiem*, this is a record that needs to be heard chronologically and complete, not cherry-picked for individual items.

Sir John Eliot Gardiner's project promises to bring into play the work of Schütz, Palestrina, and Bach, along with choral pieces by admired contemporaries. Here Felix Mendelssohn is the representative 'other', his superb *Mitten wir*, composed three years before Brahms's birth. It is flanked by Brahms's *Begräbnisgesang* (1858), a threnody for chorus, winds and timpani that openly anticipates the second movement of the *German Requiem*, and the sublime yet troubled Hölderlin-inspired *Schicksalslied* ('Song of Destiny', 1868-71) which can be seen as a pendant to the Requiem.

Brahms's setting of Hölderlin's poem was controversial. Where Hölderlin supplants his opening vision of celestial quiet with images of the hell of earthly existence, Brahms ends by revisiting that celestial vision in a ruefully beautiful orchestral coda in C major. *Schicksalslied* tells us a good deal about the First Symphony. In Gardiner's powerful juxtaposition, the descent from that rueful C major coda to the C minor of the symphony's tumultuous opening is a true *coup de théâtre*, the terrible enactment of another Fall.

These are intensely dramatic performances, powerful and unmanicured. The gathering drama of the three choral pieces is channelled and unleashed in a towering account of the First Symphony's opening movement. When Klemperer conducted the symphony in Los Angeles in 1941 a player recalled: "He drove, as in a huge chariot, to the highest planes of expression." There is something of that spirit here in Gardiner's gaunt, no-holds-barred account of the work.

The use of period instruments and their deployment in the brooding acoustic of Paris's Salle Wagram are clearly factors in the performance's wider impact. It has to be said that the playing in the symphony's middle movements is rather rough and ready. In the third movement, which under Gardiner is neither *allegretto* nor *grazioso*, Sir Charles Mackerras's historically informed Scottish Chamber Orchestra version (Teldec) is much to be preferred. Not that comparisons matter. This is a mighty Brahms First which, like the programme it inhabits, is a thing sufficient unto itself.

Brahms Symphony No 1 **Wagner** Siegfried Idyll. H
Siegfried – Siegfried's horn-call
Dennis Brain hn
Philharmonia Orchestra / Guido Cantelli
Testament mono SBT1012 (62' · ADD) Recorded
1947-53 　　　　　　　　　　　　　　　　　Ⓕ●

Cantelli conducts an interpretation which is free of any idiosyncrasy. Yet there's an extraordinary electricity in his conducting, a sense of concentration and conviction which lifts the performance into one of the greatest ever set down on record. The fiery young Italian makes the vintage Philharmonia play in an inspired fashion, and the 1953 mono recording is very acceptable.

A slightly edgy string sound betrays the 1951 origin of the *Siegfried Idyll* recording, but the performance has a tenderness, warmth and eloquence which has never been surpassed. Dennis

Brain's exuberant horn-call completes a very desirable Testament disc.

Brahms Symphony No 1[a]
Mozart Symphony No 36, 'Linz', K425[b]
Philharmonia Orchestra / Carlo Maria Giulini
BBC Legends/IMG Artists [a]mono BBCL4175-2 (76' ·
ADD) Recorded live [a]1962; [b] 1982 　　　　　Ⓕ

Giulini appears to have taken Mozart's festive and eloquent *Linz* Symphony into his repertory when he was in his mid-50s, though as we know from his unsurpassed recording of *Don Giovanni*, his interpretations which arrived, as it were, out of the blue, always came fully formed. This live 1982 Proms performance (Giulini made no commercial recording of the *Linz*) is a joy to hear: vital, companionable, generous-spirited.

The celebrated recording which Bruno Walter made, with attendant rehearsal sequences, with the Columbia SO in 1955 for CBS was very similar. Indeed, that may well have been Giulini's model (he had greatly admired Walter's conducting when he played under him in Rome's Augusteo Orchestra in the 1930s). 'Authenticists' will no doubt sniff at the full-bodied sonorities here (did Mozart dream of anything less?) and the non-antiphonal disposition of the violins, though they would be ill-advised to do so. Rarely has the symphony's important second violin part been as carefully, or as eloquently, attended to as here.

And, of course, Giulini knows the symphony's anatomical make-up as well as anyone. At the technical level, this is a wonderfully articulated performance, with clean yet pliant rhythms (the work's trade-mark trills tautly but expressively attended to), and well terraced wind and string sonorities. The only thing to be regretted is an exposition repeat in the finale.

The Brahms could not be more different. Recorded at the 1962 Edinburgh Festival in dry, immediate, somewhat acidulous mono sound, it bears about as much relation to the Mozart as a Fragonard landscape does to a grainy black-and-white photograph of Berlin after the blitz. This is a quite literally terrific performance. The physiognomy is recognisably that of Giulini's three studio recordings: powerful, imposing, superbly sculpted. What those recordings don't have is the sense of a performance taking shape in the shadow of an apocalypse. So great is the tension, Giulini even moves the finale's big tune on at a half-decent pace, something he was generally loath to do.

Symphonies Nos 1 and 2
**West German Radio Symphony Orchestra,
Cologne / Semyon Bychkov**
Video director **Hans Hadulla**
ArtHaus Musik DVD 101 243 (98' · NTSC · 16:9 · PCM
stereo, 5.1 and DTS 5.1 · 0) Also includes 'The
Horizon Moves With You' – a portrait of Semyon
Bychkov 　　　　　　　　　　　　　　　　　Ⓕ

It's a long time since we've had such satisfying accounts of either work, free of any idiosyncrasies, adeptly paced and in a clear, warm acoustic. The oboe(s), clarinet(s) and horns make outstanding contributions. Visually, Hans Hadulla (director) and Lothar Mattner (editor) are classy and imaginative without being intrusive (except, arguably, at the end of the First Symphony); they make the most of the medium and eschew any gimmickry. Particularly fine are the long steadicam shots that introduce and end each performance.

The documentary on Bychkov also comes highly recommended – international locations, crisply and atmospherically shot, eloquent contributions from the conductor, and a particularly touching sequence as he celebrates the 95th birthday of his teacher, Ilya Musin.

Symphony No 2. Hungarian Dances – Nos 1, 3, 10, 17, 18, 19, 20 & 21
London Philharmonic Orchestra / Marin Alsop
Naxos 8 557429 (65' · DDD)   ⓈⒹ→

This is a late-summer idyll of a performance, easily paced, nicely judged and warmly played. For first-time buyers it will provide unalloyed pleasure; for older hands it will satisfy without necessarily enlightening or surprising.

It is one of those Brahms performances whose centre of gravity is in the violas, cellos and horns. This is apt to the symphony's lyrical, ruminative character, though there are times when the music is robbed of its light and shade. In the finale, for example, one rather misses the chill-before-dawn mood of the lead-in to the recapitulation; and one needs a keener differentiation of horn and trumpet tone to catch the final page's incomparable D major blaze. Alsop's account of the third movement is strong in contrast, the oboe-led *Allegretto grazioso* strangely muted, the quicker 2/4 section done more or less to perfection. That said, you might think the slow movement under-characterised: insufficiently distinct in tone and temper from the first.

The symphony was recorded in Blackheath Concert Hall, the Hungarian Dances in Watford's Colisseum: a bigger, brawnier acoustic that doesn't suit the music quite so well. In dance No 18 in D, one of Dvořák's orchestrations, there is a noisy, cluttered feel to the performance. By contrast, the alfresco No 3 in F, winningly and economically orchestrated by Brahms himself, is played with real charm and style.

Brahms Symphony No 2 in D, Op 73ᵃ   Ⓗ
Beethoven Symphony No 2 in D, Op 36ᵇ
Royal Philharmonic Orchestra / Sir Thomas Beecham
BBC Legends/IMG Artists mono BBCL4099-2
(70' · ADD) Recorded live in ᵇ1956, ᵃ1956   ⒻⓄ

Beecham was no Brahmsian but he loved the Second Symphony and was one of its most persuasive interpreters. In 1936 he made a much-admired recording with the newly founded LPO. Reviewing Beecham's stereo remake in *The*

Gramophone in June 1960, William Mann recalled: 'I grew up with his 78 set and remember it with keen pleasure. It was light and sunny and full of charm, though perfectly strong; some people probably thought it a reading that lacked nobility.' The remake, recorded in 1958-9, wasn't as well liked as the 78rpm original. This live 1956 Edinburgh Festival performance is superior in almost every respect to that laboriously assembled studio version, and left the festival audience flabbergasted, walking on air.

In the studio the rip-roaring conclusion seemed contrived, but here it electrifies sense. If there's a whiff of the circus about the Edinburgh performance – Beecham audibly urging his players on like a shiny-hatted ringmaster, the final chord sounding defiantly on even as it drowns in a sea of applause – it's largely to do with the fact that the performance is live. The actual reading is exemplary: a thrilling denouement thrillingly realised.

And in the earlier movements Beecham's reading is everything William Mann remembered it as – sunny and full of charm but also, by 1956, wise and wondering, too. The mono sound is first-rate.

The Beethoven is less interesting, though this Maida Vale broadcast is every bit as vital as the generally well-respected EMI studio recording which Beecham and the RPO made that same winter. Buy it for the Brahms.

Symphony No 3. Tragic Overture. Schicksalslied
Ernst-Senff Choir; Berlin Philharmonic Orchestra / Claudio Abbado
DG 429 765-2GH (68' · DDD)   ⒻⓄ→

This disc is gloriously programmed for straight-through listening. It gets off to a cracking start with an urgently impassioned *Tragic Overture* in which the credentials of the Berlin Philharmonic to make a richly idiomatic, Brahmsian sound are substantially reaffirmed. A wide-eyed, breathtaking account of the *Schicksalslied* ('Song of Destiny') follows to provide sound contrast before the wonders of the Third Symphony are freshly explored. This is a reading of the Symphony to be savoured; it's underpinned throughout by a rhythmic vitality which binds the four movements together with a forward thrust, making the end inevitable right from the opening bars. Even in the moments of repose and, especially, the warmly felt *Andante*, Abbado never lets the music forget its ultimate goal. Despite this, there are many moments of wonderful solo and orchestral playing along the way in which there's time to delight, and Abbado seems to bring out that affable, Bohemian-woods, Dvořák-like element in Brahms's music to a peculiar degree in this performance. The Symphony is recorded with a particular richness and some may find the heady waltz of the third movement done too lushly, emphasised by Abbado's lingering tempo. Nevertheless, this is splendid stuff, and not to be missed.

Symphony No 3. Variations on a Theme by Haydn,
'St Antoni Chorale'
London Philharmonic Orchestra / Marin Alsop
Naxos 8 557430 (56' · DDD)   ⑤◐◑🅑➔

Brand-new budget-price recordings which can
rub shoulders with the best are rarer than one
imagines but this fine new Brahms disc probably
comes into that category. Finding a recommendable Brahms Third is more difficult than
one might suppose. Since Felix Weingartner
made his very fine LPO recording in 1938, the
number of great, or even successful, Thirds can
probably be listed on the fingers of two hands.

Marin Alsop's reading is certainly fine: dark of
hue, lyrical and long drawn, though never, even
for a moment, comatose. Rhythm is good,
articulation keen, phrasing exquisite, the reading's crepuscular colours glowingly realised by
the LPO. The reading has a quality of melancholy, a wistfulness crossed with a sense of
incipient tragedy, which is almost Elgarian
(Elgar's fascination with the piece is well
attested).

Readings such as Furtwängler's and Sanderling's, which are more inclined to tower and
course, may not have allowed themselves to be
overtopped by the *St Antoni* Variations, yet
there is something rather wonderful about the
transition we have here from dark to light. It is a
long time since we had a performance of the
Variations as well grounded and as keenly profiled as this. Winds are splendidly to the fore:
skirling flutes, songful oboes, grumbling descants on the horns 'in deep B'. It is, above all, a
reading of great character: the horn-led sixth
variation a burgherly jaunt, the seventh variation a handsome galliard, the finale a *Meistersinger*-like revel.

Symphonies Nos 1a & 3b   🅗
ᵃ**London Symphony Orchestra / Hermann
Abendroth;** ᵇ**Vienna Philharmonic Orchestra /
Clemens Krauss**
Biddulph WHL052 (75' · ADD) Recorded ᵃ1928, ᵇ1930
                                                Ⓜ

Symphonies Nos 2ᵃ & 3ᵇ   🅗
ᵃ**New York Symphony Orchestra / Walter
Damrosch;** ᵇ**London Symphony Orchestra /
Hermann Abendroth**
Biddulph WHL053 (79' · ADD) Recorded ᵃ1928, ᵇ1927
                                                Ⓜ

Much as we prize the Brahms of Furtwängler,
Toscanini, Klemperer and Walter, anyone with
active critical faculties – and the ability to listen
'through' old sound – is likely to enjoy Krauss,
Abendroth or Damrosch virtually as much. All
three conductors reflect a performing style that
might well have been recognised by the composer
himself. Flexibility is a constant attribute, though
the three orchestras featured produce very different pooled sonorities. A good many of Abendroth's post-war East German recordings have latterly found their way on to CD, but most

collectors will have first encountered the conductor through these Brahms 78s with the LSO. The
original sound quality – although generally well
balanced – is cramped and mono-dimensional,
but the transfers make the best of a difficult job.

The First Symphony opens magisterially. The
main body of the first movement is pliable but
energetic, whereas the *Andante sostenuto* second
movement flows nicely and the finale generates
considerable visceral excitement. Abendroth
leans on the initial upbeat of the big string tune
then pushes forwards. Occasionally the tempo
seems too fast, but the effect of Abendroth's
approach is rugged and impulsive. The LSO's
strings are more expressive than its rather acid
woodwinds, the cellos being especially fine. As
in the First Symphony, wide tempo fluctuations
are conspicuous but convincing, save perhaps in
the Passacaglia where the flow is sometimes
impeded. Most of Brahms's dynamics are faithfully observed and Abendroth's treatment of the
interrelationship of the movements perceptive.

Clemens Krauss was even more celebrated as an
opera conductor than Abendroth, and his symphonic records are few and far between. This
Vienna Philharmonic account of the Third is
distinguished by taut string playing, glorious contributions from the horn section and an unselfconscious approach to rubato. You could easily
imagine that anyone who learned the *Andante*
from this recording will have found all subsequent
versions pallid and unconvincing. Krauss's handling of the opening bars – where violas, cellos and
basses answer woodwinds and horns – suggests
the intimacy of chamber music. Rarely has the
writing breathed more naturally, or the underlying sentiment been more precisely gauged.
Although some of the finale's faster passages are a
little uncoordinated, the driving force of Krauss's
approach marks a telling contrast with the
symphony's reflective coda.

Among Walter Damrosch's many claims to
musical fame are the first American performances of Brahms's Third and Fourth Symphonies, and his New York recording of the Second
is in some respects the most interesting of the
set. The second subject is very broadly paced,
but the highlight of the performance is the *Adagio non troppo* slow movement, a minutely
observed reading full of tender incident. On the
debit side, violins tend to lack body at anything
above *mezzo-forte* and some will question the
finale's very fast speeds (especially later on in the
movement). But viewed as a whole, Damrosch's
Brahms Two is both lyrical and lively, a quietly
individual reading that repays close scrutiny.
With fine transfers and expert annotation, these
CDs provide an invaluable historical supplement to existing recommendations. You may
not always agree with what you hear, and yet all
four performances should significantly extend
your knowledge of these fine works.

Symphony No 4
Vienna Philharmonic Orchestra / Carlos Kleiber
DG The Originals 457 706-2GOR (40' · DDD) Ⓜ◐◑➔

Kleiber's charismatic 1981 Vienna recording, a classic of sorts and still sounding exceptionally well, continues to stand its ground. From the beginning, he keeps the speed fairly steady. In the first movement's coda, he scores over many of his rivals with prominent horns and a particularly exciting conclusion. He opens the second movement in a rather perfunctory manner, but the Vienna cellos make a beautiful sound in the *piano dolce* second subject. In the *Scherzo*, Kleiber pulls back for the two accented notes that dominate the first theme, an interesting gesture that lends the music an appropriately swaggering gait. This, arguably, is his finest movement – also from 4'48", where he keeps the timpani's triplets crystal-clear, then pushes his horns very much to the fore. Overall, Kleiber in the Fourth is the knight with shining breast-plate, bold, handsome, outgoing, relatively straightforward and (this will court controversy) perhaps just a little superficial.

Symphony No 4, Op 98. Hungarian Dances –
No 2; No 4; No 5; No 6; No 7; No 8; No 9 (orch Breiner)
London Philharmonic Orchestra / Marin Alsop
Naxos 8 570233 (65' · DDD)   Ⓢ❶➔

The LPO, London's finest Brahms ensemble, has been in vintage form during this cycle under Marin Alsop's measured and thoughtful direction. Not since the classically incisive Loughran/ Hallé recordings of the mid-1970s has there been a more obviously collectable budget-price Brahms set.

Alsop's reading of the Fourth Symphony is not dissimilar to Sir Adrian Boult's 1972 LPO recording. Like Boult, Alsop is happy to establish a tempo and emotional trajectory for each movement and leave it at that – a plausible view given the astonishing degree of thematic integration that underpins the work.

As elsewhere in the cycle, tempi tend to be measured. The *Andante moderato* is downright slow, though Alsop manages to maintain line and interest. The *Scherzo*, happily, is a true *Allegro giocoso*, which is important. By acting out the role of a conventional finale, the *Scherzo* leaves the actual finale free to enact its own tragic destiny.

The recording sounds well if played at a decent level. In the *Scherzo*, the triangle (deliciously placed and recorded in the *Hungarian Dances*) is more an impression than a presence. There is also an editing glitch midway through the movement, not the first in this series. The seven *Hungarian Dances*, unorchestrated by Brahms, are heard in newly commissioned orchestrations by Peter Breiner. The thudding fairground timpani in No 6 doesn't appeal. Elsewhere, piquancy is the watchword, with stylish playing from the LPO, gamesomely led.

Symphony No 4. Hungarian Dances – selection
(orch Brahms; Dvořák)
Pittsburgh Symphony Orchestra / Marek Janowski

Pentatone ⟲ PTC5186 309 (57' · DDD/DSD) Ⓕ❶➔

It's been true for many years now that American orchestras have been sounding more middle-European, but the Pittsburgh Symphony could easily be mistaken for a top German orchestra, like Leipzig or Dresden, in this music. Listen to the slow movement of the Fourth Symphony where Marek Janowski really has his players leaning into the harmonic radiance of the writing. All those wondrous transfigurations evolve so naturally and so dreamily that the brawny exuberance of the *Scherzo* – tough and resilient in Janowski's hands – really does come as an unexpected blast.

Approaches differ greatly with regard to the highly innovative first movement, the whole of which constitutes a development of sorts. So, how soon do the darkening clouds descend? For some they cannot descend soon enough. But here it's as if Janowski is delaying the inevitable right through to the high anxiety of the final pages. He tightens the screw relatively late in the movement. The slow movement then restores some sense of prior well-being and inner calm, as does the still centre of the finale with its tranquil flute and trombone-led chorale variation. The refulgence of the playing is a constant source of pleasure.

The Hungarian Dances come in Brahms and Dvořák's orchestrations, their kinship self-evident. They are earthy and sinewy with plenty of surge factor in the lower strings and the requisite cheekiness in the phrasing exemplified by those traditionally tantalising hesitations and stomping downbeats.

Serenade No 1, Op 11

Brahms Serenade No 1 **Schumann** Cello Concerto[a]
[a]**Natalia Gutman** vc
Mahler Chamber Orchestra / Claudio Abbado
DG download 476 5786GH (73' · DDD)   Ⓕ❶❶➔
Recorded live

The most enjoyable feature of this superbly engineered CD is the high level of musical interrelation that it more or less consistently conveys, between Natalia Gutman and the orchestra in the Schumann, and between Abbado and his young players in both works. Gutman's playing, like Abbado's conducting, is communicative and conversational, earnestly so at times, her tone mostly warm in texture, her bowing seamless and in the quieter sections quite ravishing although she's also capable of muscular attack. For a sustained sense of musical line, try the opening minute or so of the slow movement – note how easily the music breathes, even at a relatively slow tempo. The effect is of poignancy beyond words. The finale is playful and fairly genial, and the clarity of Gutman's articulation means that the solo line never sounds merely 'busy'. The orchestra is there with her every bar of the way, ever responsive, attentive and affectionate.

Schumann's Cello Concerto is a late work whereas Brahms's First Serenade is relatively early. Abbado's performance is chamber-like, modestly individual and for the most part beautifully played by the Mahler CO. Just listen to the easeful charm of the opening and the adoring way Abbado draws the first movement's second subject, gradually slowing the tempo before picking it up again for a return to the otherwise pervasive ebullience. No single movement anticipates the later, equivocal Brahms more tellingly than the whimsical *Scherzo*, thoughtfully played here, while the tripping finale is both assertive and delicate – though, again, the second set is poetically underlined. This is prime-quality Abbado: points are made but never overstated, and there's always the sense that quality musicians are working together with a common musical aim. Who could possibly ask for more?

String Sextets

No 1 in B flat, Op 18; **No 2** in G, Op 36

String Sextets Nos 1 & 2
Raphael Ensemble (James Clark, Elizabeth Wexler vns Sally Beamish, Roger Tapping vas Andrea Hess, Rhydian Shaxson vcs)
Hyperion CDA66276 (74' · DDD)   Ⓕ**OO**

Completed after the First Piano Concerto, but still comparatively early works, the Sextets are typified by lush textures, ardent emotion, and wonderfully memorable melodic lines. The first is the warmer, more heart-on-the-sleeve piece, balancing with complete naturalness a splendidly lyrical first movement, an urgent, dark set of intricate variations, a lively rustic dance of a *Scherzo*, and a placidly flowing finale. The second inhabits at first a more mysterious world of half-shadows, occasionally rent by glorious moments of sunlight. The finale, however, casts off doubt and ends with affirmation. Both works are very susceptible to differing modes of interpretation, and the Raphael Ensemble has established distinctive views of each, allowing the richness of the texture its head without obscuring the lines, and selecting characteristically distinct tone qualities to typify the two works. The recording is clear and analytic without robbing the sound of its warmth and depth. An impressive recording début for this ensemble.

String Sextets – No 1, Op 18; No 2, Op 36
Nash Ensemble (Marianne Thorsen, Malin Broman vns Lawrence Power, Philip Dukes vas Paul Watkins, Tim Hugh vcs)
Onyx ONYX4019 (77' · DDD)   Ⓕ**O**➜

The Nash Ensemble, with a particularly strong line-up of violas and cellos, offer superb new versions, crisp and clear, beautifully coordinated, with plenty of light and shade, and infectious springing of rhythms.

There is real precision and polish of ensemble here that marks the Nash performances out.

The players appear to be listening keenly and responding to one another. The Nash omit exposition repeats in the first movement of each sextet, unlike the older versions. As a sampler try the delectable third movement *Scherzo* of No 1, which with the Nash Ensemble is beautifully and wittily sprung, one of the gems of Brahms's chamber music.

Clarinet Quintet in B minor, Op 115

Clarinet Quintet. Clarinet Trio in A minor, Op 114
Thea King cl **Karina Georgian** vc **Clifford Benson** pf
Gabrieli Quartet (Kenneth Sillito, Brendan O'Reilly vns Ian Jewel va Keith Harvey vc)
Hyperion CDA66107 (65' · DDD)   Ⓕ**O**

These players' tempo in the Clarinet Quintet is more leisurely than most of their rivals. In the faster flanking movements of the trio, a stronger forward drive mightn't have come amiss. On the other hand, they allow themselves time to savour every bar to the full. Strinking in both these performances is their underlying warmth of heart. You'll respond easily to their quality of good-natured, unforced civility. The ensemble is excellent, with the clarinet very much one of the team, never assuming the role of soloist in a quasi-chamber concerto.

Thea King's phrasing is unfailingly perceptive and stylish, and her undemonstrative, wise artistry in both works is most appealing. In the Trio, the sumptuous-sounding cello is impressive, which at times makes you feel that Brahms could just as well have called the work a cello trio. This is a disc which will bear frequent repetition. Playing such as this, committed and serious, yet at the same time relaxed and spontaneous, isn't easy to contrive in the recording studio, and Hyperion has done well to capture these interpretations on the wing. The sound is very good indeed, mellow and natural.

Clarinet Quintet. String Quartet No 2 in A minor, Op 51 No 2
Karl Leister cl **Leipzig Quartet** (Andreas Seidel, Tilman Büning vns Ivo Bauer va Matthias Moosdorf vc)
Dabringhaus und Grimm MDG307 0719-2 (71' · DDD)   Ⓕ

One of the most attractive qualities of this version of a well-loved quintet is the skill with which the artists, abetted by the record producer, have integrated the clarinet into the string textures. Having listened more creatively than any other composer to Mozart's example, Brahms allows the clarinet to become part of the tone colour in the string ensemble; and he has also followed the implications, as not all his interpreters seem to understand. Here, the little falling third theme, one of his lifelong obsessions, moves in and out of the musical texture with wonderful subtlety, so that the return of the opening figure at the very end needs no special emphasis but is a natural conclusion.

Leister is an artist of long skill and experience, and also of great musical intelligence; the qualities tell. They also mean that there's no need to confer upon the performance anything approaching the sentimentality which can afflict it, in the name of 'nostalgia' as the old composer looks affectionately back on his life's work. This is quite a robust performance, clearly appreciated by the enthusiastic young string quartet, who give a suitably matching account of the Op 51 work. There are, of course, any number of performances of the quintet, but this is unique.

Clarinet Quintet. Trio for Horn, Violin and Piano [H] in E flat, Op 40
Reginald Kell *cl* **Aubrey Brain** *hn* **Rudolf Serkin** *pf*
Busch Quartet (Adolf Busch, Gosta Andreasson *vns*
Karl Doktor *va* Hermann Busch *vc*)
Pearl mono GEMMCD0007 (63' · ADD) or Testament
SBT1001 (63' · ADD)   Ⓜ/Ⓕ ⓞⓞ

There's no need, at this remove of time, for further praise to be lavished on these performances. This account of the Horn Trio remains at, or very near, the top of any list of recorded rivals. HMV's recording of this somewhat idiosyncratic combination of instruments survives well and has been cleanly, honestly transferred. However, the performance of the Clarinet Quintet will give you even deeper pleasure. Where nowadays do we hear playing of such emotional range, such probing intensity? Here the Busch Quartet and Reginald Kell out-sing and out-search most rivals in the work's autumnal aspect but also make everything seem alive and doubly intense with their fierce and intense response to the music's wild mood-swings. It helps to have a clarinettist who can coo like a dove and exult like a gipsy; but, in the end, the performance's genius rests in the players' profound and unflinching identification with Brahms's shifting moods.

Clarinet/Viola Sonatas, Op 120 Nos 1 & 2

Clarinet Sonatas. Clarinet Trio, Op 114ᵃ
Martin Fröst *cl* ᵃ**Torleif Thedéen** *vc*
Roland Pöntinen *pf*
BIS ⊕ BIS-SACD1353 (67' · DDD/DSD)   Ⓕ ➔

The Trio tends to be the neglected one among the great clarinet works from Brahms's mellow last period, usually coupled with the Clarinet Quintet as though a poor relation. That is grossly unfair to a work which, while maybe not on such a grand scale as the Quintet, has over its four compact movements both profundity and charm. BIS, however, has put it with the sonatas, works on a scale closer to the Trio, and an excellent and successful coupling it is.

Young Swedish clarinettist Martin Fröst has established himself as a leading soloist, appearing with many of the most important European orchestras and inspiring works from composers including Penderecki. He tends to favour speeds on the fast side in the Trio, which means that the second movement *Andante* may lack the meditative depth one finds elsewhere but which has an easy flow. The dramatic bite and thrust of the outer movements is enhanced by relatively urgent speeds, with the coda of the first fading away on a ghostly scalic passage.

Cellist Torleif Thedéen matches Fröst in imaginative playing but pianist Roland Pöntinen, placed backward in the recording balance, is less individual. None the less this is a generously filled CDs and the couplings are apt.

Clarinet Sonatas (trans flute and piano)
Schumann Drei Romanzen, Op 94
C Schumann Drei Romanzen, Op 22 (all arr Khaner)
Jeffrey Khaner *fl* **Charles Abramovic** *pf*
Avie AV2075 (62' · DDD)   Ⓕ ➔

With the poignant flute solo in the middle of the passacaglia finale of the Fourth Symphony among the most tenderly reflective passages in all Brahms, it is sad that he did not write any work specifically for the flute. That, no doubt among other considerations, was what led Jeffrey Khaner, the distinguished principal flute of the Philadelphia Orchestra, to make his transcriptions of the two Brahms clarinet sonatas.

As one would expect, his alterations to the solo parts are discreet, involving occasional octave transpositions upwards and, more rarely, downwards. In many of the changes it seems that Khaner has been concerned not so much whether the flute can actually play Brahms's written notes but what is more effective on the lighter instrument.

Naturally the replacement of the clarinet by the flute brings a marked change of character. While these late chamber works in their clarinet versions – or in the viola alternatives which the composer himself suggested – have an autumnal quality, the freshness of flute tone brings more of a spring-like feeling. Khaner also demonstrates that though flute tone in its lightness is fresher and brighter than clarinet tone, it is also generally gentler, with such passages as the running quavers in the finale of the First Sonata made more delicate. Yet sensitive as Khaner's arrangements are, it is hard to imagine many people actually preferring these flute versions to the originals: they simply make a splendid showpiece for an outstanding flautist.

Much the same can be said of the Romances by Robert and Clara Schumann, though there is a stronger case for flute transcriptions of Robert's pieces: he suggested the violin or clarinet as an alternative to the oboe which he originally had in mind. The charming Clara pieces were written specifically for violin but again Khaner's transcriptions could not be more sensitive, nor the playing more inspired. In all these works he is greatly helped by the brilliant, warmly understanding accompaniment of Charles Abramovic.

Viola Sonatas, Op 120. Trio, Op 114ᵃ
Lawrence Power va ᵃ**Tim Hugh** vc
Simon Crawford-Phillips pf
Hyperion CDA67584 (65' · DDD)   Ⓕ

Viola players have reason to be grateful to Brahms for giving them the chance to perform the two Op 120 sonatas, originally for clarinet. It's less well known that he similarly provided a viola part as alternative to clarinet for the Op 114 Trio. For the sonatas he reworked the part, adding a few chords and double stops, as well as transposing some of it downwards (to exploit the instrument's generally lower tessitura) but in the Trio he contented himself with a simple transcription. In Lawrence Power's hands the extensive use of the viola's upper register poses no problem; he commands a wide tonal spectrum throughout his range, and there's no sense of strain. The Trio does lose something without clarinet, sounding more monochrome as the viola and cello blend together. This blending can, of course, be an advantage – the two string instruments in octaves, in the *Adagio*, make a wonderful sound. And this is a very fine performance, of exceptional expressive range, from extreme delicacy to thrilling power.

The sonatas as played here will surely demonstrate (even to clarinettists) that the viola version is in no way second best. Particularly enjoyble in the Second Sonata, is the second movement's dark passion, relieved by glowing intensity in the middle section, where Simon Crawford-Phillips manages exactly to convey Brahms's *forte ma dolce e ben cantando*. The final variations are just as impressive, each one so well characterised yet perfectly paced so that the coda seems an inevitable climax to the whole work.

Trios – Op 40ᵃ; Op 114ᵇ. Viola Sonatas, Op 120 – No 1ᶜ; No 2ᵈ. Violin Sonata No 1, Op 78 (arr Klengel/Rysanov)ᵉ
Maxim Rysanov va ᵃ**Boris Brovtsyn** vn
ᵇ**Kristine Blaumane** vc ᵃᶜᵉ**Katya Apekisheva**,
ᵇᵈ**Jacob Katsnelson** pfs
Onyx Classics ② ONYX4033 (125' · DDD)   ⓂⓄ➔

Brahms was the first to admit that he hadn't entirely solved the new problems of balance in the works that replace the clarinet with a viola (the clarinet sonatas and the Op 114 Trio). With recording, of course, some help can be given. The viola is well forward in the performances by Rysanov, and this suits the music's extrovert, eloquent manner. In the First Sonata, in which Rysanov is accompanied by the excellent Katya Apekisheva, the music is more freely phrased, with a humorous sense of the latent waltz in the

Allegretto and plenty of vigour in the finale. In the Op 114 Trio, the outside movements benefit from the vivid sense of melodic direction provided by Rysanov and Katsnelson.

The G major Violin Sonata was also written for Joachim, and arranged for viola not by Brahms but by his publisher Simrock's editor Paul Klengel. Transposing it from G down a fourth to D to accommodate the viola loses the music something of its elegance, but this is a persuasive performance. Persuasiveness is also needed in Op 40, which began life as the Horn Trio. Not all the cheerful vigour that Rysanov and Apekisheva provide can make the finale seem anything but a piece of hunting exuberance, but they do splendidly with the *Scherzo* and the *Adagio mesto*.

Piano Quintet in F minor, Op 34

Brahms Piano Quintet, Op 34
Schumann Piano Quintet, Op 44
Leif Ove Andsnes pf **Artemis Quartet**
Virgin Classics 395143-2 (69' · DDD)   ⒻⓄⓄ➔

Leif Ove Andsnes has an uncanny knack of revealing the inner truth of the music he plays without recourse to excessive gimmickry. He also has exquisite taste when it comes to choosing his chamber music collaborators, as this pairing of the two cornerstones of the piano quintet repertoire demonstrates.

Schumann's Quintet has become the most famous of his chamber works, with its boundless energy and melodic generosity. Andsnes and the Artemis let the notes speak for themselves, never lingering too lovingly on mere details. It's an approach that serves the work well, and an ideal instrumental balance helps illuminate the work's compelling textures throughout.

It's a similar story in the Brahms. Andsnes and the Artemis are alive to all the possibilities in the pregnant opening phrases of each movement and maintain the intensity of the impetuous passion implicit in this youthful music. The Brahms hasn't fared as well on disc as the Schumann and this recording of it can certainly take its place among the finest. As for the Schumann, it's undoubtedly up there with the best.

Piano Quintet, Op 34ᵃ. String Quartet No 2, Op 51 No 2
ᵃ**Stephen Hough** pf
Takács Quartet (Edward Dusinberre, Károly Schranz vns Geraldine Walther va András Fejér vc)
Hyperion CDA67551 (73' · DDD)   Ⓕ

In the Brahms Second Quartet the Takács find a most appealing lightness of touch. They reveal anew the extraordinarily imaginative way in which the work begins, and breathe air into the intricate textures which precede the vacillating second theme. There's an absolute unanimity to their playing, but a fetching liveliness too. Compared to such groups as the Alban Berg, who revel in the lushness of Brahms's writing, the Takács are more febrile and transparent. Their third movement creeps in, skittering, but there's no lack of sweetness of tone when required. And the fugal section has a spring in its step. Brahms isn't all seriousness, they remind us.

The other major selling-point of this disc is the Piano Quintet, for which the Takács are joined by Stephen Hough. There's nothing cosy about this latest reading, which has fire and passion aplenty, and the recording places Hough pleasingly within the overall texture rather than unduly spotlighting him. There's a feeling of coming together of ideas, with these artists – masters of colour all of them – sparking off one another in a very unstudio-ish way. And throughout, Hough's virtuosity makes light of Brahms's unforgiving textures.

Brahms Piano Quintet. **Schubert** Piano Quintet in A, D667, 'Trout'
Sir Clifford Curzon pf **Amadeus Quartet** (Norbert Brainin, Siegmund Nissel vns Peter Schidlof va Martin Lovett vc) **James Edward Merrett** db
BBC Legends ② BBCL4009-2 (82' · ADD) Recorded live 1974, 1971   Ⓜ**OO**

The 1971 recording of the Schubert sounds marginally better than the 1974 Brahms, but the visceral excitement generated by the Brahms Quintet has to be heard to be believed. It would be fairly easy to imagine a tidier performance, but not one that's more spontaneous or inspired. Sir Clifford Curzon's grand vision registers within a few bars of the opening movement and heats to near boiling-point by the start of the recapitulation. The emotional temperature rises even higher for the second movement.

The distinction of the performance resides in the co-operation of all five players, which reaches unprecedented heights in the finale. No wonder the audience explodes: it's doubtful that anyone present has heard a finer performance since. The *Trout*'s repeated exposition is even more exciting than its first statement, and there's some gentle tempo acceleration during the development. True, the strings make a fractionally late entrance at the beginning of the *Andante*, but the vitality of the *Scherzo* would be hard to beat, while the Theme and Variations features notable playing from Lovett. There's an amusing spot of premature congratulation when applause momentarily breaks in at the end of the *Allegro giusto*'s exposition, but it soon withers to silence for a joyous finale. Here the recording rather favours the strings, but better that than have the piano drown everyone else out. Wonderful stuff, all of it.

Piano Quintet
Andreas Staier pf **Leipzig Quartet** (Andreas Seidel, Tilmann Büning vns Ivo Bauer va Matthias Moosdorf vc)
Dabringhaus und Grimm MDG307 1218-2 (39' · DDD)   Ⓜ**OO**

Here's something quite unusual! Andreas Staier is playing a Steinway model-D dating from 1901; not exactly contemporary with the Quintet (1865), but producing a noticeably lighter sound than its modern counterpart, and taking us closer to what would have been familiar to Brahms.

On this excellent recording we're aware that the dominating resonance of the present-day concert grand is missing; the balance shifts in favour of the strings, making the work seem more colourful, less sombre. The first movement and the *Scherzo* are especially successful, with full, resonant *tutti*s contrasting dramatically with the more tenuous, atmospheric music. The Leipzig Quartet maintain a notably pure sound, without excessive vibrato, adding to the feeling of transparency.

Other performers, such as Peter Serkin and the Guarneri Quartet, have delved more searchingly into the Quintet's emotional content, bringing out the moments of deep pathos or soaring lyricism. But Staier and the Leipzigers will expand your view of this great work.

Piano Quartets

No 1 in G minor, Op 25; **No 2** in A, Op 26; **No 3** in C minor, Op 60
Piano Quartets Nos 1-3ª. Three Pieces, Op 117
Marc-André Hamelin pf
ªⁿ**Leopold String Trio** (Marianne Thorsen vn Lawrence Power va Kate Gould vc)
Hyperion ② CDA67471/2 (142' · DDD)   Ⓕ**OO**

Brahms's three piano quartets sometimes exhibit this tendency but in performances as fine as these it is triumphantly surmounted with a combination of brisk speeds and an extraordinary collective *joie de vivre*.

The G minor Quartet (No 1) opens simply, with Hamelin shaping the line beautifully but unaffectedly, the Leopold players gradually entering, their playing filled with ardour. The *Zigeuner*-finale is irresistibly ebullient, with a jaw-dropping ending. The other aspect that is so impressive about these readings is the sense of absolute precision, which lightens the textures and keeps edges crisp. Sample, for instance, the *Scherzo* of the C minor (No 3) which can, in some hands, sound positively elephantine. Not here though, Hamelin dealing with Brahms's dense chords as easily as if they were single lines.

The epic A major Quartet (No 2), more a symphony than a quartet, is a considerable challenge to players and audience. Hamelin and the Leopold get to the heart of the matter in the soulful *Poco adagio* and while they in no way lack heft when it's needed, particularly in the opening movement, there's always a dancing quality to their playing which does much to illuminate textures. This music certainly benefits from their defiantly un-Germanic approach.

Hamelin signs off with the Op 117 *Intermezzi*, as well recorded as the rest of the disc. They're elegantly played, but the main reason for buying this CD lies firmly with the quartets.

Piano Quartet No 1. Four Ballades, Op 10
Emil Gilels pf members of the **Amadeus Quartet**
(Norbert Brainin vn Peter Schidlof va Martin Lovett vc)
DG The Originals 447 407-2GOR (65' · ADD)
Recorded 1970, 1975　　　　　　　　　ⓂⓄ☞

This is an outstanding performance of Brahms's G minor Piano Quartet, unforgettable for its spontaneity and uninhibited Romantic warmth and verve. The booklet reminds us that this 1971 recording made history since 'a contract between an artist from the Soviet Union and a Western label was a sensational event in cultural diplomacy'. Reproduced with respect for the sound quality of its time, the playing has a glowing strength and intensity throughout. Only in the first movement's opulent textures does the keyboard occasionally dominate. From Emil Gilels we're also given a maturely unhurried, essentially 'inward' recording of Brahms's youthful *Ballades*.

Piano Quartets No 3ᵃ. Double Concertoᵇ
Isaac Stern vn ᵃ**Jaime Laredo** va Yo-Yo Ma vc
ᵃ**Emanuel Ax** pf ᵇ**Chicago Symphony Orchestra /
Claudio Abbado**
Sony Classical 509970 90405-2 (68' · DDD)　Ⓕ❍❍❍

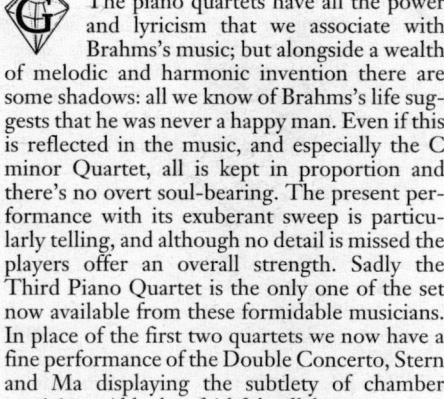

The piano quartets have all the power and lyricism that we associate with Brahms's music; but alongside a wealth of melodic and harmonic invention there are some shadows: all we know of Brahms's life suggests that he was never a happy man. Even if this is reflected in the music, and especially the C minor Quartet, all is kept in proportion and there's no overt soul-bearing. The present performance with its exuberant sweep is particularly telling, and although no detail is missed the players offer an overall strength. Sadly the Third Piano Quartet is the only one of the set now available from these formidable musicians. In place of the first two quartets we now have a fine performance of the Double Concerto, Stern and Ma displaying the subtlety of chamber musicians; Abbado a faithful collaborator.

String Quartets

No 1 in C minor, Op 51 No 1; **No 2** in A minor, Op 51; **No 3** in B flat, Op 67

String Quartets – Nos 1 & 3
Takács Quartet (Edward Dusinberre, Károly Schranz vns Geraldine Walther va Andras Fejér vc)
Hyperion CDA67552 (65' · DDD)　　　　Ⓕ❍❍

Viola to the fore in the third movement, *Agitato*, of No 3; and Geraldine Walther, firm-toned

and assertive, rises to the occasion as the only un-muted instrumentalist here. Agitation isn't consistently maintained though because the Takács Quartet tend to ease the tension in places. Yet there is no slack in the other movements. This close-knit group unanimously stretch or tighten the rhythm, achieving evenly matched dynamics such as the *sotto voce* sequences in the opening *Vivace*, the hushed *dolce e grazioso* in the recapitulation of the *Andante* and the stilled peace of the G flat sixth variation in the finale. Walther is well in the picture in this movement too whereas elsewhere she appears occasionally to lose focus.

Not so in No 1. Her place on the right of the ensemble is firmly assured here. The work is 'commonly held to be representative of Brahms's austerity and asceticism' (Edwin Evans), and these epithets are apposite for the Takács, spare of style and tone. The players' control over the first movement doesn't preclude a range of *rubato* that serves to sharpen the musical argument. Nor does it preclude a linear drive that knits the six themes of the last movement into a coherent whole, while they do not let up on the melancholy of the middle movements, the third particularly dark. The recording is tonally credible but is widely separated.

String Quartets Nos 1 & 2
Cleveland Quartet (William Preucil, Peter Salaff vns James Dunham va Paul Katz vc)
Telarc CD80346 (68' · DDD)　　　　　　　Ⓕ

Though the Cleveland Quartet has changed both its leader and viola player in recent years, all the old tonal opulence is still very much there. So is all the old fire, and equally, the determination to wring the last drop of expression from even the most intimate confession. In short, you'd be unlikely to meet a more overtly romantic composer than the Brahms you meet here. In the C minor Quartet's *Romanze* some might in fact prefer the very mellow but more emotionally reticent Borodin Quartet, or the Alban Berg with their ethereally withdrawn *pianissimo*. In the bolder flanking movements it's as compulsive as the highly strung, impressionable Alban Berg while often finding a broader, suaver, melodic sweep. Opulent sound.

Clarinet Trio in A minor, Op 114

Brahms Clarinet Trio **Holbrooke** Clarinet Quintet　Ⓗ
　No 1 in G, Op 27 No 1 **Weber** Clarinet Concertino in E flat, J109
Reginald Kell cl **Anthony Pini** vc **Louis Kentner** pf
Willoughby Quartet (Louis Willoughby, Kenneth Skeaping vns Aubrey Appleton va Vivian Joseph vc)
orchestra / Walter Goehr
Testament mono SBT1002 (54' · ADD)
Recorded 1941　　　　　　　　　　　　　Ⓕ

In the rapturous love-duet between clarinet and cello in the *Adagio* of the Clarinet Trio, Reginald

Kell's tonal warmth and beauty seem more than ever appropriate. Elsewhere in this work, though, despite his liquid sound and finesse of dynamics he's all but outshone by the eloquent lyricism and passion of that superb player Anthony Pini. Together with Kentner's understanding collaboration, never over-assertive but always supportive, an admirably cohesive team is formed, alive to Brahms's interplay of interest and changes of mood. Kell is the star of the Quintet by Josef Holbrooke which has fallen into total neglect; frankly the present diffuse work (concocted out of previous compositions) will not prompt much revaluation of his status. Nevertheless, it offers great opportunities for *cantabile* clarinet playing in the central Canzonet and for fluent virtuosity in the finale: Kell excels in both. Not unexpectedly the Weber *Concertino*, every clarinettist's party-piece, finds him displaying, besides an easy technical brilliance, beauty of tone, a charming sense of phrase and sensitive dynamic nuances. Goehr's orchestral accompaniment is clean and alert.

Piano Trios

No 1 in B, Op 8; **No 2** in C, Op 87; **No 3** in C minor, Op 101

Piano Trios Nos 1-3. Horn Trio in E flat, Op 40
Clarinet Trio in A minor, Op 114
Richard Hosford *cl* **Stephen Stirling** *hn* **Florestan Trio** (Anthony Marwood *vn* Richard Lester *vc* Susan Tomes *pf*)
Hyperion ② CDA67251/2 (137' · DDD)　　ⒻⓄ

Aided by an especially clear, vivid, yet spacious recording, the Florestan Trio and their two colleagues allow us to hear far more of this music than usual – the elaborate decoration of Op 114's *Adagio*, or the sinister detail of the more delicate passages in Op 8's *Scherzo*. Much of the credit for this goes to Susan Tomes; her playing is an object-lesson in sensitivity and in matching the other voices. Balance and blend are a special feature of these performances. Anthony Marwood and Richard Lester match their sounds perfectly for the lovely duet passages in the slow movements of Opp 8 and 101. Less expected, and less usual, is the matching of violin and horn, cello and clarinet. But perhaps the single outstanding feature of all the performances is the way the music is shaped. It's not only that the phrases are projected clearly and expressively – the approach moves outwards to encompass the music's larger paragraphs and, indeed, whole movements. These are very desirable recordings, then.

Additional recommendation

Piano Trios Nos 1 & 2
Augustin Dumay *vn* **Jian Wang** *vc*
Maria João Pires *pf*
DG download 447 055-2GH (67' · DDD)　　ⒻⓄ
　The duo of Augustin Dumay and Maria João Pires

have found themselves a true soul mate in the Chinese cellist Jian Wang, as this, their first disc of piano trios, engagingly shows. Poetic and powerful, this is glorious chamber-music making.

Cello Sonatas

No 1 in E minor, Op 38; **No 2** in F, Op 99

Cello Sonatas Nos 1 & 2
Mstislav Rostropovich *vc* **Rudolf Serkin** *pf*
DG 410 510-2GH (58' · DDD)　　

Our younger generation of cello soloists seems to favour a tone production which balances a refined upper range with a middle and lower register that's strong and well focused, rather than expansively rich and resonant. Readers will not need to be told that Rostropovich's solo image is definitely not of this ilk: his musical personality is in every sense larger than life and in this magnificent coupling of the cello sonatas, in partnership with Rudolf Serkin, the very forward balance of the recording exaggerates this impression in the most vivid way. By comparison the piano image – to the right of and behind the cello – is more reticent in timbre and seldom matches Rostropovich's rich flood of sound, which isn't, of course, to suggest that Serkin fails to project the music, merely that the microphone placing makes Rostropovich very much the dominating artist. This passionately warm-hearted and ripely Brahmsian music-making almost overwhelms the listener in its sheer impact. But with playing of this calibre, with both artists wonderfully attuned to each other's responses, every nuance tells and Brahms's bold melodic lines soar out from the speakers to capture the imagination, and provide an enthralling musical experience in each and every work.

Cello Sonatas – Nos 1 & 2 **Dvořák** Silent Woods.
Rondo **Suk** Ballade, Op 3 No 1. Serenade, Op 3 No 2
Steven Isserlis *vc* **Stephen Hough** *pf*
Hyperion CDA67529 (74' · DDD)　　ⒻⓄⓄ

In 1984 Steven Isserlis made excellent recordings for Hyperion of the Brahms sonatas with Peter Evans; this time he's added some substantial extra items – the two Suk pieces, wonderfully played, are particularly welcome. The new recording is fuller in sound and more realistic; Stephen Hough's commanding playing of Brahms's 'big' piano parts could, one feels, overpower the cello but, thanks to his sensitivity, this never happens.

　In the sonatas, the timings are in nearly every case slightly shorter, due not to any very different tempi but because the music now flows more easily, with less sense of effort. Some listeners may miss the intensity of Evans's involvement with the music but the new versions have a wonderful sense of line, and Hough's more detached approach comes with vivid characterisation – seen in the sinister colours of No 2's *Allegro passionato*, for example, or the limpid, elegant playing of No 1's *Allegretto quasi menuetto*.

Only in one place, the finale of No 2, is there the feeling that Hough's fluency creates a problem: repeating the opening theme, he pushes on in a way that detracts from the sunny, contented atmosphere at the start. These are deeply considered, immensely satisfying accounts. Isserlis and Hough make a formidable team.

Cello Sonatas – No 1, Op 38; No 2, Op 99.
Anklänge, Op 7 No 3. Die Mainacht, Op 43 No 2
Anthony Leroy *vc* **Sandra Moubarak** *pf*
Zig Zag Territoires ZZT070202 (63' · DDD)   Ⓕ**O**

Brahms's cello sonatas tackle head on the real problem of balancing the cello's potentially gruff lowest register and singing high tones with the orchestra, but he does not make matters easy for himself. Some of the piano textures are very thick and there are places in this recording where the problems are barely solved: the start of the F major Second Sonata and the finale of the E minor No 1 are cases in point. He is at least considerate enough to refine the piano textures when he risks asking the cello to play the flowing theme of this finale with the tricky slurred *pizzicato*, and this comes off excellently here.

The performances are exceptional. Anthony Leroy and Sandra Moubarak have a real understanding of Brahms's unusually long phrases. In the great sweeping melody of the opening of the E minor Sonata they begin pensively and are not afraid to use considerable freedom of tempo change at the peak of the exposition before returning to this inwardness. The *Adagio*, another very long and varied melody, is beautifully phrased, as is the middle section of the third movement, its marking dolce espressivo contrasting with the general *Allegro passionato*. The E minor Sonata's Minuet has a delightful lilt, and they go with a will at the difficult final fugue. There are also charming performances of the two songs included as fill-ups.

Violin Sonatas

No 1 in G, Op 78; **No 2** in A, Op 100;
No 3 in D minor, Op 108

Violin Sonatas Nos 1-3
Itzhak Perlman *vn* **Vladimir Ashkenazy** *pf*
EMI Great Recordings of the Century 566893-2
(70' · DDD)   Ⓜ**OO**➛

If anyone doubts that these three sonatas represent Brahms at his most blissfully lyrical, then this is an essential set to hear. The trouble-free happiness of these mellow inspirations, all written after the main body of Brahms's orchestral music had been completed, comes over richly and seductively in these fine performances. In their sureness and flawless confidence, they

carry you along cocooned in rich sound. Perlman consistently produces rich, full-bodied tone, an excellent illustration being the way that he evokes a happy, trouble-free mood in the melody which opens the second movement *Adagio* of No 3. The obverse of this is that with such consistent richness and warmth, the three sonatas come to sound more alike than they usually do, or maybe should, a point which comes out the more from playing them in sequence. It's true that Perlman does quite often play softly, but for some tastes it's placed too close to the microphone, and the actual dynamic level stays rather high, however gently he's playing. This isn't to say that with sharp imagination and superbly clean articulation from the pianist, these performances lack range of expression – in particular, there's the rhythmic pointing, which gives a Hungarian or a Slavonic tang to such passages as the first contrasting episode in the 'raindrop' finale of No 1 or the contrasting *Vivace* passages in the second movement of No-2, where the last pizzicato reprise is made totally delectable. These performances are both distinctive and authoritative. The recording is bright, with a good sense of atmosphere to give bite to the piano tone without diminishing the warmth of Perlman's violin.

Violin Sonatas Nos 1- 3. Sonata 'FAE' – Scherzo
Renaud Capuçon *vn* **Nicholas Angelich** *pf*
Virgin Classics 545731-2 (79' · DDD)   Ⓕ**O**➛

Capuçon and Angelich make a wonderfully well-matched team, with a command of genuine *rubato* (pressing forward in order to make room for subsequent holding back) that gives a truly authentic impression. Each detail of the music is expressively convincing: it seems that it's a priority for Angelich and Capuçon to feel the music. This can lead them sometimes to go against Brahms's expressed intentions. The theme at 3'18" in the first movement of Op 78 is marked to be in tempo (after a *ritardando*) but here the speed suddenly becomes faster, the dynamic much louder than the written *pianissimo*. Similarly, in the *Presto agitato* finale of Op 108 the quieter passages are taken more slowly.

These are occasional lapses: overall the performances are beautifully considered, tending towards an expansive, romantic view of Brahms, but with a care for balance and proportion. The *FAE* Scherzo, for example, has all the necessary youthful exuberance, but it's coupled with a fine feeling for balance between the parts and for rhythmic character. And, throughout, there's a magnificent sense of line: Capuçon plays the great G-string melodies in Op 108's *Adagio* and Op 100's finale with rich, opulent sound but his vibrato is never too prominent – the most important thing is the shape of the melody.

Violin Sonatas Nos 1- 3. Sonata 'FAE' – Scherzo
Nikolaj Znaider *vn* **Yefim Bronfman** *pf*
RCA Red Seal 88697 06106-2 (71' · DDD)   Ⓕ**O**➛

Brahms's Op 78 Violin Sonata, the first of his three, comes closer to a work of some wistfulness, the opening phrase taking on, with Nikolaj Znaider and Yefim Bronfman, a gentle melancholy that suits the music well. The hesitancy of this dotted phrase marks the whole of the sonata's invention, and is picked up with touching effect, as Clara Schumann was moved to find, when Brahms quotes an earlier song in the finale. This is all sensitively done.

So is the Second Sonata, with delightful touches: when the *Andante* gives way to a faster section, it is here played as gaily as a Brahms waltz, one that turns faintly spectral on its return with the *pizzicato* violin. Perhaps the finale, *Presto agitato*, deserves more extrovert agitation, but these are most thoughtful and sympathetic performances. There is also room on the disc for the lively scherzo which, as a young man, Brahms wrote for a composite sonata, with movements by Schumann and Albert Dietrich.

Sonata for two pianos

Sonata for Two Pianos, Op 34b. Waltzes, Op 39 – Nos 1, 2, 11, 14, 15 and 16. Hungarian Dances – No 5; No 17 **Saint-Saëns** Variations on a Theme of Beethoven
Güher Pekinel, Süher Pekinel pfs
Warner Classics 2564 61959-2 (67' · DDD)

A quick glance at Warner Classics's note reminds us that the twin sisters Güher and Süher Pekinel studied with Serkin, Arrau, Yvonne Loriod and Horszowski, a formidable pedigree reflected in performances of rare brilliance and pinpoint definition. Their crystalline clarity and verve erase the very real threats of strenuousness, opacity and coagulated textures in the Brahms Sonata, music exposed to severe criticism from Clara Schumann before its final reincarnation as the Piano Quintet.

The Pekinels achieve exactly the right note of foreboding at the start of the first movement development. They also give us a true oasis of calm in the *Andante* before racing through the *Scherzo* at a tempo sufficiently precipitate to tempt fate. But their command and control win the day at every point and never more so than in the finale's concluding *Presto non troppo*, whirled to an exhilarating close with total assurance.

After such a weighty offering the Waltzes and Hungarian Dances provide charming and scintillating relief, and, moving from Germany to France, the Pekinels' performance of Saint-Saëns's *Variations on a Theme of Beethoven* is of an enchanting vivacity and lightness. The rapid chording of Variation 3 holds no terrors for them and, throughout, their virtuosity is as fearless as it is musical. This is a fine and well recorded addition to the sisters' discography.

Piano Works

Piano Sonatas – No 1 in C, Op 1; No 2 in F sharp minor, Op 2; No 3 in F minor, Op 5 Variations on a

Theme by Paganini, Op 35. Variations and Fugue on a Theme by Handel, Op 24. Four Ballades, Op 10b. Variations on a Theme by Schumann, Op 9. Variations on an Original Theme, Op 21 No 1. Variations on a Hungarian Song, Op 21 No 2. Waltzes, Op 39. Two Rhapsodies, Op 79. Scherzo in E flat minor, Op 4. Piano Pieces – Op 76; Op 116; Op 117; Op 118; Op 119. Hungarian Dances[a]
Julius Katchen, [a]**Jean-Pierre Marty** pfs
Decca London ⑥ 455 247-2LC6 (388' · ADD)
Recorded 1962-6

The American pianist Julius Katchen made his name in the early 1950s and died in 1969, but although he's generally though of as a distinguished figure from the last generation, it's salutary to realise that he would probably be performing today if his career had not ended when he was only 42. Even so, his legacy of recordings reminds us of his gifts and the breadth of his repertory, and the present Brahms cycle has distinction. It begins with an account of the *Paganini* Variations that gives ample proof of his assured technique: the playing tells us at once that the challenging variations in sixths (Nos 1 and 2 in Book 1) held no terrors for him, and the athleticism here is matched by a fluency in the *leggiero* writing of the variation that follows. In this work, though, you're generally made more aware of a keyboard virtuoso than a poet; there are other performances which balance these two qualities more finely. Tempos tend to rapidity, too, and the piano sound tends to have a hardish brilliance. However, he does bring a gentler quality to the three other sets of variations here, not least in his freer use of rubato and tonal nuance, as witness (say) the serene Variations Nos 11-12 in the big *Handel* set, where the recording from three years earlier is easier on the ear. Here, as elsewhere, there's a little tape hiss, but not enough to distract.

Poetry is to be found in good measure in Katchen's playing of the *Four Ballades*, Op 10. These pieces belie the composer's youth in their deep introspection, though the pianist takes a brisk view of the *Andante con moto* tempo in No 4. The 16 Waltzes of Op 39 are attractive too in their crispness and charm, and the early *Scherzo* in E flat minor has the right dour vigour. The three sonatas are also impressive in their strong, energetic interpretative grasp, though you could wish that the first-movement repeat of No 1 had been observed. Also, slow movements could have a still more inward quality to convey that brooding self-communion which is so characteristic of this composer (though that of Sonata No 3 in F minor is pretty near it). But the great F minor Sonata is spacious and thoughtful as well as leonine, and this is a noble performance, well recorded in 1966.

The shorter pieces are finely done also. Katchen is in his element in the Two Rhapsodies of Op 79, balancing the stormy and lyrical qualities to perfection. The *Fantasias*, Op 116, aren't so well recorded (the sound is a bit muffled). However, the playing is masterly, with tragedy, twilight mystery and storm and stress fully playing their part and giving a golden glow to such pieces as the lovely E major *Intermezzo* which is No 6 of the set and the A major *Intermezzo*, Op 118 No 2. Possibly more sensuous gipsy charm could be found in, say, the B minor *Capriccio* of Op 76, but it's very attractive playing and the playful C major *Intermezzo* in Op 119 is delightful, as is the tender lullaby that begins Op 117.

Only the first 10 of the 21 Hungarian Dances exist in the composer's own (very difficult) version for piano solo, and in the others, written for piano duet, Katchen is joined by Jean-Pierre Marty; there's plenty of fire here and much to enjoy. Altogether, this Brahms set is a fine memorial to Katchen and a worthy issue.

Piano Sonata No 2, Op 2. Three Pieces, Op 117. Eight Pieces, Op 76
Libor Novacek pf
Landor LAN285 (76' · DDD)　　　　　Ⓕ**O**

Libor Novacek shows himself deeply sensitive to the interior light burning beneath the surface of Brahms's often dark-hued later masterpieces. What unfaltering poise and tonal translucence he achieves throughout Opp 76 and 117. Less ebullient than, say, Rubinstein or Perahia in the second *Capriccio* from Op 76, his playing is so finely 'worked' and controlled that even here he captures a reflection and nostalgia at the heart of such music. His poetic refinement in No 6 is exquisite and if Novacek dims the radiance of No 8, keeping its exultance on a tight rein, he remains musicianly to his fingertips. Here once more he locates an underlying poetry denied to less subtle or less engaging pianists.

A master of inwardness, he also sets the storm clouds scudding menacingly across No 6 and shows that he's as swashbuckling as the best of them in the early F sharp minor Sonata, resolving every thorny and perverse difficulty with ease and lucidity. The Landor sound (Potton Hall in Suffolk) is of demonstration quality.

Piano Sonata No 3. Hungarian Dances – No 1 in G minor; No 2 in D minor; No 3 in F; No 6 in D flat; No 7 in A. Eight Pieces, Op 76 – No 2, Capriccio in B minor; No 7, Intermezzo in A minor
Evgeny Kissin pf
RCA Red Seal 82876 52737-2 (56' · DDD)　　Ⓕ➡

Kissin opens the F minor Sonata with an imperious thrust, and in the octave outburst at 4'46" again proves himself a fearless virtuoso; few pianists of any generation would even consider such a whirlwind tempo. For some, his *rubato*, heated and intense, will seem overbearing, yet he finds the still centre at the heart of the *Andante*. He thunders to the heavens the final climax (*molto appassionata*) and launches the *Scherzo* as though with a rush of blood to the head. He may be a less subtle poet of the keyboard in this sonata than, say, Radu Lupu, but his searing projection carries its own rewards,

and every bar of Brahms's early and rhetorical masterpiece is marked by his overwhelming technique and magisterial temperament.

In Op 76 No 2 you'd hardly mistake the pressure he exerts for Rubinstein's or Perahia's patrician grace, but it says much for his conviction that in No 7 he can so audaciously replace the composer's *semplice* direction with his own more elaborate notion of style. But it's in five of the *Hungarian Dances* that his extrovert nature finds its truest outlet: in No 6 his performance is of an astounding verve and resilience. Here's virtuosity in the grandest of grand manners, and RCA's sound, for once, is as red-blooded as the playing.

Piano Sonata No 3. 16 Waltzes, Op 39
Antti Siirala pf
Ondine ODE1044-2 (62' · DDD)　　　　Ⓕ**OO**➡

Antti Siirala has been a serial entrant of piano competitions. He wins most of them, including the Beethoven, London, Dublin and Leeds (2003) events but Siirala is a great deal more than a jury-pleaser. This is a strikingly good disc, notable both for the full-bodied, golden tone of the piano (superbly recorded) and his ability to hold together both long movements and large structures with playing of refined musicality. After the first two pages of the F minor Sonata other mighty performances spring to mind – Katchen, Solomon, of course, Grainger and Bauer from an even earlier era. After the leonine first movement comes the long nocturnal narrative of the second. To hear Siirala at his most expressive, try the final section (*andante molto*) from 9'02", sensitive to every nuance, deeply felt and aching with regret. He characterises the rumbustious *Scherzo* and its chorale-like Trio equally well, and builds to the impassioned climax of the finale with abandon.

Siirala brings colour and imagination to the Op 39 Waltzes. He makes subtle use of all the repeats, and the sighing falls of No 12 are beautifully done, though it's debatable whether almost all the left hand of the famous A flat waltz (No 15) should be played *staccato* (only the first four bars and six towards the end are so marked). It's a detail, to be sure, an aspect of the music to which Siirala, otherwise, pays admirable attention.

Two Rhapsodies, Op 79. Three Intermezzos, Op 117. Six Piano Pieces, Op 118. Four Piano Pieces, Op 119
Radu Lupu pf
Decca 417 599-2DH (71' · ADD) Recorded 1970s　Ⓕ

Here are 71 minutes of the finest Brahms piano music, played by one of the outstanding Brahms exponents of our day. What's most treasurable about it is the quiet rapture of some of the most quintessentially Brahmsian moments; for example, the way Lupu sleepwalks into the last section of Op 117 No 3 and the revelation in Op 118 No 2 that the inversion of the theme is even more beautiful than its original statement. The Op 79 *Rhapsodies* are perhaps a fraction less memorable.

Decca's recording sounds a little bottom-heavy, in the manner of certain Ashkenazy records of this vintage, and in the heavier textures of the *Rhapsodies* Lupu compounds the problem by reinforcing the bass with octaves and even fifths. Still, this remains as fine a selection of Brahms's piano works as you're likely to find on one disc.

Brahms Piano Sonata No 3 🄷
Liszt La leggierezza, S144 No 2a. Années de pèlerinage, Première Année, S160, 'Suisse' – Au bord d'une source^a. Hungarian Rhapsody No 15 in A minor, S244^b **Schumann** Carnaval, Op 9
Solomon pf
Testament mono SBT1084 (79' · ADD) Recorded 1952; ^a1930, ^b1932   Ⓕ❍❍

Solomon's 1952 recordings of Schumann's *Car-naval* and the Brahms Sonata in F minor are essential for the desert island, so this well-produced compilation, generously filled out with Liszt, recommends itself. If you've heard tell of Solomon's reputation but don't know his work, or perhaps know only his Beethoven, snap it up. The sound has come up astonishingly well, also in the Liszt pieces which were made in 1930 and 1932. Solomon's performance of 'Au bord d'une source' is a match for Liszt's poetic inspiration, as few recordings of it are. Technical address and refinement on this level constitute a small miracle.

Piano Pieces – Op 116; Op 117; Op 118; Op 119
Markus Groh pf
Avie ⟨⟩ AV2136 (79' · DDD)   Ⓕ❍ᗏ

Markus Groh's supreme control of the instrument and sensitivity regarding timbre and texture enable him convincingly to stretch the Op 117 No 1 Intermezzo's middle section to its arguable breaking-point. The same goes for his full-throated, polyphonically aware conceptions of the A major and G minor Capriccios from Op 116. The Intermezzi, Op 118 No 6 and Op 119 No 1, elicit brooding, weighty interpretations that still manage to convey shape and sustaining power. Notable too are Groh's slightly agitated take on Op 117 No 3's con moto directive, with more varied *legato* articulation than one commonly hears. The pianist's ample tone and deft delineation of the Op 116 No 7 Capriccio's gnarly textures are all the more impressive once you realise how discreetly he employs the sustain pedal. To be certain, some selections meet with less success: for example, the little C major Intermezzo, Op 119 No 3 (made famous by Myra Hess), is voiced to perfection yet never takes wing; nor does the cycle's closing Rhapsody break out from Groh's four-square shell.

Still, for a single-disc release that includes all four 'late' Brahms piano works, Groh more than holds his own alongside moreseasoned performances. The dryish room ambience characterising Avie's engineering via conventional two-

channel and headphone playback appreciably opens up when experienced in surround-sound.

---

16 Waltzes, Op 39. 10 Hungarian Dances
Idil Biret pf
Naxos 8 550355 (52' · DDD)   Ⓢᗏ

Both the *Waltzes* and the *Hungarian Dances* are extremely demanding in their two-hand form, and in the latter collection you could often believe that the 20 fingers of two duettists must be involved, so many notes are being played in all registers (for an example, try No 8 in A minor). However, the technical problems hold no terrors for this pianist and her performances are convincing and attractive. What more need be said about this playing of music in which Brahms portrayed, in turn, sophisticated Vienna and untamed Hungary? Well, not a great deal. The quicker *Waltzes* have plenty of vivacity, and the slower ones are lyrical in an aptly Viennese manner. Tempos, textures, phrasing, rubato and pedalling are well managed and the playing has a very convincing blend of subtlety and simplicity. She treats these 16 pieces as a sequence, as Brahms's key structure allows, and leaves relatively little gap between them. The *Hungarian Dances* have a darkly surging Magyar energy and sound that are very pleasing: indeed, Biret seems totally at home in this music. The recording is a bit larger than life, but perfectly acceptable.

Brahms Choral Preludes, Op 122 (arr Mandyczewski)
Febel Seven Choral Arrangements after JS Bach
Reger Choral Fantasia on 'Rejoice My Soul', Op 30
Yaara Tal, Andreas Groethuysen pfs
Sony Classical 88697 12146-2 (65' · DDD)   Ⓕ

Brahms's 11 Chorale Preludes for organ have been arranged for solo piano by a number of composers including Busoni and Paul Juon, but here we have the world premiere of versions for four-hands-one-piano by Brahms's friend Eusebius Mandyczewski (1857-1929). Brahms knew he was dying when he wrote them and most of the chosen chorales are concerned with death, so the music is not exactly calculated to put a spring in your step, but these faithful translations are welcome discoveries. In fact, I'm not sure I don't prefer them to the originals, at least when played by this superb duo. Listen to the best known of the set, the haunting harmonisation of *Es is ein Ros entsprungen*, to which Tal and Groethuysen bring an affecting simplicity, reminding us of the art that conceals art.

The Reger Fantasy in the composer's arrangement (1899) of his organ original (1898) was unearthed by the duo and premiered by them in 2004. Seven of the chorale's nine verses, notated throughout the score by Reger, inspire a sequence of seven variations culminating in a complex three-part canon.

Reinhard Febel (b1952), on the other hand, takes six different Bach chorale preludes (*Wo soll ich fliehen hin?* is treated twice) and leaves the originals intact for one pianist while the other supplements additional layers using contemporary devices. I found these quite mesmerising, especially the barely audible overtones in the first version of *Wo soll ich fliehen hin?* and the disconcerting dissonant chords that float above *Allein Gott in der Höh sei Her*.

Ein deutsches Requiem, Op 45

Ein deutsches Requiem
Elisabeth Schwarzkopf *sop* **Dietrich Fischer-Dieskau** *bar* **Philharmonia Chorus and Orchestra / Otto Klemperer**
EMI Great Recordings of the Century 566903-2
(69' · ADD · T/t) Recorded 1961   Ⓜ❶❶❶➔

Brahms's *German Requiem*, a work of great concentration and spiritual intensity, is rather surprisingly, the creation of a man barely 30 years old. Klemperer's reading of this mighty work has long been famous: rugged, at times surprisingly fleet and with a juggernaut power. The superb Philharmonia is joined by its excellent chorus and two magnificent soloists – Schwarzkopf offering comfort in an endless stream of pure tone and the superb solo contribution from Fischer-Dieskau, still unequalled, taking us closer to the work's emotional, theological and musical sources than any other. Digital remastering hasn't entirely eliminated tape noise, but the engineers appear to have encountered few problems with the original tapes. A uniquely revealing account of the work.

Ein deutsches Requiem
Dorothea Röschmann *sop* **Thomas Quasthoff** *bar* **Berlin Radio Chorus; Berlin Philharmonic Orchestra / Sir Simon Rattle**
EMI 365393-2 (67' · DDD · T/t)   Ⓕ❶❶➔

This is a lovely performance, sensitive to the work's consolatory mood, free-moving and sweetly sung. Rattle's reading does not obscure Brahms's debt to Schütz, Bach and the other great pre-classical German Protestant composers, but it stresses more the work's roots in the new German school: to the influence, above all, of Brahms's cherished and much mourned mentor, Robert Schumann.

This is not a period performance in the sense of attempting to conjure forth period sounds. The opening colloquy for violas and divided cellos is pure Berlin (Nikisch would have recognised the sound, as would the young Karajan). The singing is awed and reverential, with ravishing *pianissimi* from the superb Berlin Radio Chorus. What we have here is not authenticity of sound but authenticity of feeling and effect. Has there ever been a swifter performance of the fourth movement, 'Wie lieblich sind deine Wohnungen', or a more calming one? A flowing tempo which creates a sense of deep repose suggests that most sought-after of all qualities in an interpreter, the art that disguises art.

BRAHMS'S EIN DEUTSCHES REQUIEM – IN BRIEF

Schwarzkopf; Fischer-Diekau; Philharmonia Chorus and Orchestra / Otto Klemperer
EMI 566903-2 (69' · DDD)   Ⓜ❶❶❶➔
💎 A genuine Great Recording of the Century: two superb soloists, a great choir and orchestra, and a conductor whose rugged feeling for the music pays colossal dividends.

Margiono; Gilfry; Monteverdi Choir; Orchestre Révolutionnaire et Romantique / Sir John Eliot Gardiner
Philips 432 140-2PH (66' · DDD)   Ⓕ❶❶➔
Gardiner's magnificent choir cover themselves in glory here: this is a performance charactersied by great clarity and transparency that makes this a wonderfully light-filled spiritual experience. Beautiful playing from the period strings.

Röschmann; Quasthoff; Berlin Radio Chorus; Berlin Philharmonic Orchestra / Sir Simon Rattle
EMI 365393-2 (67' · DDD)   Ⓕ❶❶➔
Rattle has long cherished this work and the BPO has a long tradition of performing it. It is a beautiful burnished interpretation with choral singing to match thr wondrous playing of the Berlin orchestra. Only Quasthoff's rather flappy singing detracts a little.

Grümmer; Fischer-Dieskau; St Hedwig's Cathedral Choir; Berlin PO / Rudolf Kempe Ⓗ
EMI mono 764705-2 (76')   Ⓜ
The earliest of Fischer-Dieskau's numerous recordings of the work finds him, in 1955, in glorious voice – as is Elisabeth Grümmer. Kempe's interpretation is deeply moving.

Janowitz; Waechter; Vienna Singverein; Berlin Philharmonic Orchestra / Herbert von Karajan
DG 463 661-2GOR (77' · ADD)   Ⓜ
DG 📀 073 4398GH (79' · NTSC · 0)
Two glorious soloists – Waechter's mellow toned and wonderfully humane, Janowitz almost instrumental in her purity – add to Karajan's soft-grained performance. A long-time favourite that still sounds good. Karajan's video version is also worth considering: same line-up except for José van Dam as the (excellent) baritone soloist.

Bonney; Terfel; Swedish Radio Choir; Eric Ericson Chamber Choir; Berlin PO / Claudio Abbado
TDJ 📀 DV-MUSIK (140')   Ⓕ❶
Though the CD version of this performance is currently available, the DVD makes a fine alternative. Made in Vienna's striking Musikverein, this has been sensitively filmed by Bob Coles and presents a deeply impressive reading in a beautifully understated way. Excellent performances.

Throughout, Rattle strikes a shrewd balance between the work's affective nature and its narrative power. Tempi are brisk in the two movements with baritone solo which carry much of the work's doctrine. The great choral codas to the second, third and sixth movements are also superbly judged. In the great choral peroration to the penultimate movement, space is provided for the words to tell, as Brahms clearly intends.

Thomas Quasthoff, who seems a little out of sorts, is no match for Fischer-Dieskau on Klemperer's unignorably splendid recording (reviewed above); and Dorothea Röschmann's reedy tone and tight vibrato in 'Ihr habt nun Traurigkeit' may not appeal either. Still, the movement is so persuasively shaped that, heard in context, it, too, 'speaks' to us through the sonic squall. Internal balances between choir, soloists, and orchestra are generally well judged: apt to a performance which treats this great memorial prose poem with a mixture of acumen and affection that is entirely special.

Ein deutsches Requiem   Ⓟ
Charlotte Margiono sop **Rodney Gilfry** bar
Monteverdi Choir; Orchestre Révolutionnaire et Romantique / Sir John Eliot Gardiner
Philips 432 140-2PH (66' · DDD· T/t)   Ⓕ ❶❶❶➤

Gardiner's performance is notable for its intensity and fervour, and for the superb singing of his choir: splendidly firm and secure attacks and phrasing, always with fine tonal quality, meticulous attention to dynamic nuances, and alertness to verbal meaning and nuance. The solo baritone is a real find: an admirably focused voice with cleanly projected words and sensitive tonal gradations: if the soprano, pure-voiced and consoling, seems slightly less distinguished, it may be that she's set a trifle too far from the microphone. Pains have been taken to bring out contrapuntal strands with clarity, in both the chorus and the orchestra; and here the employment of period instruments and of selective string vibrato makes a significant contribution. In the past Gardiner has been accused of minimising the spiritual quality of religious works; but not in this outstanding performance.

Ein deutsches Requiem (London Version)
Sandrine Piau sop **Stéphane Degout** bar **Boris Berezovsky, Brigitte Engerer** pfs **Accentus Chamber Choir / Laurence Equilbey**
Naïve V4956 (65' · DDD · T/t)   Ⓕ

It was in Wimpole Street in 1871, at the home of a leading surgeon and his musical wife, that the London first performance of Brahms's *Deutsches Requiem* was given, two years before it was introduced to the British public at large and with orchestral scoring. The arrangement for piano duet was the composer's own, made at the urgent request of his publisher. The occasion was essentially a domestic one, with a small invited audience, piano duettists and singers who, having sung of all flesh being grass, would doubtless have found cold meats laid out for them in the dining room and a glass of wine to refresh the spirits.

This recording successfully presents the Requiem as chamber music. An earlier performance on Opus 111 suggested a final piano rehearsal, the orchestra being expected next week. Here the piano part is played on two instruments, achieving a far more satisfying musical finish. The playing is sensitive, with a singing tone most of the time, and a keen ear for the differentiation between parts or melodic strands. Sandrine Piau is clear-toned and well in control after a very slightly tremulous start; Stéphane Degout, a fine baritone, isn't particularly expressive here but admirable in quality and phrasing. The choir sing with fresh, well-matched tones and care for detail. Choice of tempo seems unerringly right: that is but one of many reasons we have to be grateful to Laurence Equilbey, the conductor.

Ein deutsches Requiem
Gundula Janowitz sop **José van Dam** bass-bar
Vienna Singverein; Berlin Philharmonic Orchestra / Herbert von Karajan
Video director **Herbert von Karajan**
DG 𝔻𝕍𝔻 073 4398GH
(79' · NTSC · 4:3 · PCM stereo and DTS 5.1 · 0)
Recorded live in Salzburg in March 1978   Ⓕ❶

You can see the Vienna Singverein in this Easter Festival performance spaced across the back of the Felsenreitschule, but the sound mix – supervised by Karajan – mingles them with the orchestra to an intriguing and unprecedented extent. The result is quite different from the closely communicative *German Requiem* recently recorded by Simon Rattle.

Sometimes one feels it has been done to spare the chorus, or spare us from them. There are too many occasions on which the orchestra comes in after an *a cappella* section and finds the chorus has dropped by a fraction to take the performance entirely seriously. But there is also much to admire and even love here: the relatively swift outer movements, the genuinely awe-ful Marschmässig at the start of 'Denn alles Fleisch', and the genteel, beneficent relaxation of its interlude, like peasants by Poussin – and you could feel the character of text, sound and interpretation even with the sound off, just as Karajan's hands build, mould and then smother a conflagration on the same movement's final chord.

The tempo for the third movement is slow for the vocal lines – José van Dam is nobly stentorian – but perfect for the minatory dialogue between timpani and horns and its subsequent, syncopated fragmentation. Janowitz achieves the communion in her movement that had been shaped with these performers many times, but, as ever in Karajan's interpretation of the Requiem, the sixth movement never recovers from its pedantic opening trudge, and is not improved by a cussedly obtrusive electric organ.

Stepping over this Achilles heel, however, this is a loving document of a work, time and place.

Choral Works

Two Motets, Op 74. Fest- und Gedenksprüche,
Op 109. Three Motets, Op 110. Missa Canonica. Two
Motets, Op 29
RIAS Chamber Choir, Berlin / Marcus Creed
Harmonia Mundi HMC90 1591 (61' · DDD · T/t) Ⓕ

These are wonderful pieces, which, hearing, you would suppose to be all heart, looking at, you think must be all brain, and in fact are compounded of both, the one feeding upon and stimulating the other. In no other area of his work is Brahms quite so conscious of his heritage. Writing in the midday of Romanticism, he finds the great formal, contra-puntal tradition not a weight upon him but a refreshment. He draws upon Schütz as upon Bach, and from the Italian polyphonists and masters of the double choir as well as from his own German background. The innocent ear would never suspect the mathematical intricacies, the musical logic, and yet it tells, even without conscious recognition: the workmanship is clear, and the emotion which would in any case go out to greet such strong, vivid word-setting is immeasurably enhanced. A striking example is provided by the three movements, all that survive, from the *Missa Canonica*. The *Sanctus* is set in deeply reverential mood and, like the flowing triple-time *Benedictus*, betrays nothing of its origin as an academic exercise. The *Agnus Dei* is overtly polyphonic, yet that too gives way to a gently lyrical mode, in the 'Dona nobis pacem'. They were published in 1984 and this is their first recording. The motets, of course, have been recorded many times and very well too, yet, on balance, no more satisfyingly than they are here. The RIAS Chamber Choir produces a fine quality of homogeneous tone and, under Marcus Creed, shows itself fully responsive to both words and music. This disc carries a strong recommendation, especially for its inclusion of the surviving *Missa Canonica* fragments.

Gesänge – Op 17; Op 42; Op 104. Sieben Lieder, Op
62. Deutsche Volkslieder, WoO33 – In stiller Nacht
Stefan Jezierski, Manfred Klier hns ª**Marie-Pierre
Langlamet** hp **RIAS Chamber Choir, Berlin /
Marcus Creed**
Harmonia Mundi HMC90 1592 (62' · DDD · T/t) Ⓕ

The RIAS Chamber Choir's blend of voices is impeccable and the tone-quality perfectly lovely. They're sensitive to word and phrase, responding as one to their conductor's shading and shaping. The performances give pleasure and complete satisfaction. The sheer beauty of sound preserves the gentle, romantic qualities of the music faithfully; and there's never any question of dullness, for text and music are both lovingly tendered. The pieces themselves always have more to them than you think at first, and the sureness of Brahms's feeling for choral

sound impresses immediately. All are unaccompanied save Op 17, where the harp and horns bring a delightful enrichment. This is quiet, late-night listening, of the kind that helps to ease the day into retrospective contentment.

Liebeslieder, Op 52

Liebeslieder. Neue Liebeslieder, Op 65.
Three Quartets, Op 64
Edith Mathis sop **Brigitte Fassbaender** mez
Peter Schreier ten **Dietrich Fischer-Dieskau** bar
Karl Engel, Wolfgang Sawallisch pfs
DG 423 133-2GH (55' · DDD · T/t) ⒻⓄ➜

These delightful works will be eagerly snapped up by lovers of these seemingly simple but, in fact, quite complex settings for one, two or four voices. The performances are thoroughly idiomatic, both as regards the singers and pianists, with full value given to the words and their meaning. It isn't merely a question of fine singing, which with this quartet can be more or less taken for granted: the subtlety and charm of the interpretations makes what can all too often be a dreary sequence of three-four numbers into a poetic response to the nature of the waltz. There's an intelligent give-and-take between the soloists, so that voices move in and out of the limelight, as the skilful recording allows, and an extra dimension of the music is disclosed here that's too often obscured. The immediate sound is here a great advantage. This is a very worthwhile and welcome reissue of a most attractive individual record.

Songs

Vier ernste Gesänge, Op 121. Neun Lieder, Op 69.
Sechs Lieder, Op 86. Zwei Lieder, Op 91ª
Marie-Nicole Lemieux contr ª**Nicolò Eugelmi** va
Michael McMahon pf
Analekta AN29906 (68' · DDD · T/t) ⒻⓄ➜

The absorbing six songs that make up Op 86 are all easily encompassed by Marie-Nicole Lemieux, not least because her technique is so secure that she can pay attention to the meaning of each song. *Feldeinsamkeit*, so inwardly sung, and *Todessehnen* receive particularly thoughtful readings, all supported finely by Michael McMahon's perceptive playing.

The nine songs of Op 69 are expressly designed for a woman and have their moments, but they're among the less inspired in Brahms's large output of Lieder. Not so, of course, the two songs with viola – the admirable Nicolò Eugelmi here. To these gently lulling, timeless pieces, Lemieux brings the sovereign virtues of firm line and apt phrasing.

The CD reaches its zenith in Brahms last and greatest Lieder, his *Vier ernste Gesänge*. Lemieux rises to their challenge. The interpretations are properly earnest, but intimate, never overblown. Her partner is again exemplary in his discreet yet positive playing.

A natural acoustic adds to the pleasure to be gained from this sensibly planned recital, which is highly recommended.

Liebestreu, Op 3 No 1. Spanisches Lied, Op 6 No 1. Anklänge, Op 7 No 3. Der Schmied, Op 19 No 4. Vier Lieder, Op 43 – No 1, Von ewiger Liebe; No 2, Die Mainacht. An die Nachtigall, Op 46 No 4. Sonntag, Op 47 No 3. Der Gang zum Liebchen, Op 48 No 1. Fünf Lieder, Op 49 – No 1, Am Sonntag Morgen; No 4, Wiegenlied. Dein blaues Auge, Op 59 No 8. Geheimnis, Op 71 No 3. Fünf Lieder, Op 72 – No 1, Alte Liebe; No 4, Verzagen. Vergebliches Ständchen, Op 84 No 4. Mädchenlied, Op 85 No 3. Sechs Lieder, Op 86 – No 1, Therese; No 2, Feldeinsamkeit. Sapphische Ode, Op 94 No 4. Sieben Lieder, Op 95 – No 1, Das Mädchen; No 2, Bei dir sind meine Gedanken; No 4, Der Jäger; No 6, Mädchenlied. Der Tod, das ist die kühle Nacht, Op 96 No 1. Nachtigall, Op 97 No 1. Fünf Lieder, Op 105 – No 1, Wie Melodien zieht es mir; No 4, Auf dem Kirchhofe. Ständchen, Op 106 No 1. Fünf Lieder, Op 107 – No 3, Das Mädchen spricht; No 5, Mädchenlied
Bernarda Fink mez **Roger Vignoles** pf
Harmonia Mundi HMC90 1926 (63' · DDD · T/t) Ⓕ

'Bei dir sind meine Gedanken', one of Brahms's happiest songs, makes an inviting aperitif. Buoyed by the evanescent shimmer of Roger Vignoles's accompaniment, Bernarda Fink is all confiding eagerness, phrasing deftly and gracefully and showing a natural feeling for Brahmsian rubato. One would expect Fink's warm, luminous mezzo, flecked by darker, deeper tints, to be near ideal for, say, the nostalgia of 'Alte Liebe' or the many songs of elegiac loss and heartbreak, all touchingly done here. But having thought of her as an essentially 'serious' singer, dignified, eloquent, the vivacity and 'face' she brings to 'Bei dir sind meine Gedanken' and other lighter songs is sheer delight. 'Ständchen', here more sunlit than moonlit, is charmingly characterised, with an affectionate caress on the dreaming girl's 'Vergiss nicht mein'. Fink is playfully coquettish without archness in the delicious 'Spanisches Lied', and sings 'Vergebliches Ständchen' with an outgoing boldness and witty touches of timing – and the tender lingering on the penultimate 'Mein Knab' suggests that the boy's luck may soon be about to change.

Other singers have brought a more intense yearning to 'Die Mainacht' and found greater mystery amid the slumberous balm of 'Feldeinsamkeit'. But Fink's flowing performances, sensitively shaped and inflected, are never less than satisfying. It is good to be reminded, too, that, for all its melancholy, 'Die Mainacht' is also a song of spring, suffused by warm major-key harmonies, with a hint of excited anticipation at the line 'Wann, o lächelndes Bild'. On the face of it, Fink's lyric mezzo would seem to be on the light side for 'Von ewiger Liebe'. But with Vignoles imaginatively 'orchestrating' the keyboard part, she gives a finely graded, deeply moving performance, vividly contrasting the contained passion of the boy's words with the girl's gentle candour. The glowing climactic avowal of eternal love is truly overwhelming, setting the seal on a Brahms recital of rare distinction.

Von ewiger Liebe, Op 43 No 1[b]. An die Nachtigall, Op 46 No 4c. Herbstgefühl, Op 48 No 7c. Neun Lieder, Op 63 – No 5, Junge Lieder I , 'Meine Liebe ist grün'c; No 8, Heimweh II , 'O wüsst ich doch den Weg zur'a. Abendregen, Op 70 No 4c. Geheimnis, Op 71 No 3a. Fünf Lieder, Op 72 – No 2, Sommerfädenc; No 3, O kühler Walda; No 4, Verzagenc. Vergebliches Ständchen, Op 84 No 4c. Sechs Lieder, Op 86c – No 2, Feldeinsamkeit; No 3, Nachtwandler. Vier Lieder, Op 96 – Der Tod, das ist die kühle Nachtc; Wir wandeltena; Meerfahrta. Komm bald, Op 97 No 5c. Auf dem Kirchhofe, Op 105 No 4a. Fünf Lieder, Op 106a – No 1, Ständchen; No 5, Ein Wanderer. Fünf Lieder, Op 107a – No 3, Das Mädchen spricht; No 5, Mädchenlied. Mondnachta. Regenlieda
Dame Janet Baker mez
abErnest Lush, cPaul Hamburger pfs
BBC Legends/IMG Artists acmono BBCL4200-2 (70' · ADD). Recorded in b1960; a1961; c1968 Ⓕ

Listening to these Brahms songs culled from BBC broadcasts one realises just why Dame Janet's reputation continues to remain so high and why so many of her successors don't quite match her standards. To every song here, familiar or unfamiliar, she brings her special ability of making it her own and reaching to its heart. It's an almost uncanny gift, and not one easy to explain, but it makes every song in this programme momentous. Wondrous is the sustained half-voice with which she invests *Nachtwandler* with its intimate, sad feeling.

Then there's the outpouring of joy that is *Meine Liebe ist grün* to which she brings the most lustrous tone and an outgoing manner, and finally the gentle sense of fun, never overdone, which she brings to the very familiar *Vergebliches Ständchen*.

If Brahms had written no other songs than *Feldeinsamkeit*, *Der Tod, das ist die kühle Nacht* and *Von ewiger Liebe*, he would surely be hailed as a great Lieder composer. Baker obviously understands their astonishing high quality. The first is sung, as it should be, with a kind of inner wonder, each amazing line given its full due. In the second, a Liebestod *avant la lettre*, she sings with the proper impassioned feeling, while the last, a happier statement of eternal love, is sung with the rugged conviction that always showed the singer at her very best.

Lush and Hamburger, especially the latter, are fully cognisant of what to do with Brahms's intricate writing for the piano. The sound is admirable, catching early Baker in full flow.

Neun Gesänge, Op 69. Vier Gesänge, Op 70. Fünf Gesänge, Op 71. Fünf Gesänge, Op 72
Juliane Banse sop **Andreas Schmidt** bar
Helmut Deutsch pf

CPO CPO999 446-2 (56' · DDD · T/t) Ⓜ

Of all the leading composers of Lieder, Brahms suffers more than any other through neglect, with so little of his output in the field ever appearing on recital programmes. There's some reason for this, given that his contribution to the genre is uneven, as you can judge listening to the uninspired settings of minor poets comprising Op 69. But just when you think the composer might have been on auto-pilot in his songs of the mid-1870s, along come the four pieces of Op 70 to make you revise your opinion. The impressionistic 'Lerchengesang', the reflective 'Serenade' and the better-known 'Abendregen', all show the composer in his most imaginative mode, alive to words and their inner meaning. The inspiration is more intermittent in Opp 71 and 72, but the better of the songs here – the Hölty 'Minnelied' and Bretano 'O kühler Wald' – rank with the finest in Brahms's output.

Both Banse and Schmidt are at their appreciable best as regards voice and interpretation, Banse always inside her readings, Schmidt producing tone that's consistently warm and appealing. She alternates convincingly between passion and lighter emotions. He's particularly well suited by the whole of Op 72, giving a nicely ebullient account of 'Unüberwindlich', a Goethe setting that ends the programme. Deutsch is fully up to the exigent demands of the piano parts, often almost like solos in themselves.

Tomás Bretón Spanish 1850-1923

Spanish composer and conductor. At the age of 12 he was earning his living as a violinist in Madrid. He studied the violin at the conservatory and took part in zarzuela and circus orchestras. Bretón struggled tirelessly for the establishment of a sophisticated Spanish lyric drama, but his own operas met with little favour. **GROVE**music

La verbena de la paloma

La verbena de la paloma
José Antonio López *bar* Julián **Amparo Navarro** *sop* Susana **Maria José Suárez** *sop* Casta **David Rubiera** *bass* Don Hílarión **Emilio Sánchez** *ten* Don Sebastián **Marina Pardo** *mez* Señá Rita **Federico Gallar** *ten* Antonia **Chorus and Orchestra of the Comunídad de Madrid / Miguel Roa**
Decca 🄳🅅🄳 074 3262DH (87' · NTSC · 16:9 · PCM stereo and DTS 5.1 · 0) Ⓕ

La verbena de la paloma is one of the masterpieces of the shorter *género chico zarzuela*. First performed in Madrid in 1894, it has never fallen out of favour, though like the rest of this essentially Spanish repertory it has never caught on in other countries. Set in the Lavapiès district of Madrid, the libretto by Ricardo de la Vega tells of the amorous complications involving a couple of sisters, their aunt, and their suitors, one rich, one poor. Various neighbours and passers-by contribute more or less irrelevant local colour, and of course there are the all-important flamenco-style dancers and singers.

Many collectors know the 1930 recording of the big duet 'Ya estás frente a la casa' by Conchita Supervia and Marcos Redondo (recently reissued on Marston) and the work has had several complete recordings, including versions with Alfredo Kraus and Plácido Domingo as the poor lover, Julián. Marina Bollain's production updates the action to the present day, from a city square to a block of flats, the action spread over four levels so that individuals can be singled out – for instance the wealthy Don Hílarión, who sings his solo about his attachment to two girlfriends while taking a bath. David Rubiera displays some impressive muscles but draws the shower curtain discreetly. As Julián, José Antonio López has a nice line in sulky charm, and he joins Marina Pardo in the famous duet.

Amparo Navarro and Maria José Suárez are irresistible as the two sisters. Miguel Roa conducts the Madrid forces with tremendous verve. Despite initial doubts concerning the all-out updating – not to mention the casting of a baritone, Federico Gallar, as the aunt, it's a real winner.

Havergal Brian British 1876-1972

Despite his lack of any formal musical education, Havergal Brian dedicated his life to music, creating numerous vast symphonies and large-scale choral works. He received encouragement from Elgar and Henry Wood who conducted the English Suite and For Valour. His primary sopurce of income was as a journalist and critic – he was assistant editor of Musical Opinion from 1927 until 1940 – and he championed many then-unfashionable composers like Bruckner, Mahler and Schoenberg. His musical language is late-romantic and lush, and invariably expressed on a colossal scale. He tended increasingly to explore his ideas through motivic development and contrrapuntal means rather than rely on traditional techniques such as sonata form. **GROVE**music

Orchestral Works

Violin Concerto[a]. Symphony No 18. The Jolly Miller.
[a]**Marat Bisengaliev** *vn*
BBC Scottish Symphony Orchestra / Lionel Friend
Naxos 8 557775 (55' · DDD) Ⓢ🄾🄾➤

The late Robert Simpson once referred to Havergal Brian as the 'Original Awkward Cuss raised to the level of genius'. A highly misunderstood composer, one either loves (sadly the minority) or hates his music. Michael Oliver clearly liked it, as his review of the original release shows, where he waxed lyrical over the kind of compositional processes, games even, that Brian played in his Violin Concerto (1934-

35). He described the performance of Kazakh virtuoso Marat Bisengaliev as 'jaw-droppingly' good; hearing it again it really does sound like one of the finest British violin concertos, worthy of comparison with Elgar's, Walton's, Britten's, Stevens's and McCabe's. Tony Kime's excellent recording catches all the subtle detail of the solo writing – especially when so wonderfully well played – along with the tuttis' massive splendour.

The best is saved until last, however, with the Symphony No 18 (1961), long a personal favourite. Written in gratitude for Bryan Fairfax, conductor of *The Gothic*'s premiere that year, it is one of Brian's most beguiling march-fantasies, scored for a fairly standard orchestra. All the typical late Brian fingerprints are present, the bold, craggy harmonies, expressive dislocations and haunting melody. Lionel Friend directs a crisp and crystal clear account of this quarter-hour gem. Very strongly recommended.

Brian Symphonies[a] – No 6, 'Sinfonia tragica'; No 16
Cooke Symphony No 3[b]
London Philharmonic Orchestra / [a]Myer Fredman;
[b]Nicholas Braithwaite
Lyrita SRCD295 (60' · ADD) Ⓕ🅑➡

Havergal Brian's Sixth and Sixteenth Symphonies were recorded in April 1973. The Sixth (1948), incorporating material from an abandoned opera on Synge's *Deirdre of the Sorrows*, is highly illustrative with atmospheric orchestration, a gorgeous, full-blooded romantic melody in the slow central section and a dramatic finale. Completely convincing symphonically, it plays continuously in an effective three-in-one design.

A marvellous example of Brian's late polyphony, the Sixteenth (1960) is the finest of a group of five single-movement symphonies that signalled the start of his final compositional phase (1959-68), in which he completed no fewer than 20 symphonies. It too has its dramatic and evocative aspects, possibly derived from his reading of Herodotus while composing the work. But it is as absolute music that the work succeeds brilliantly. These performances, directed by Myer Fredman, still sound excellent.

It is a shame that No 24 was not available to complete an all-Brian disc, but the inclusion of Arnold Cooke's Third (1967) will not disappoint. Certainly, there are stylistic differences; not for nothing was Cooke described (or derided?) as the 'English Hindemith', but the influence of his German teacher never hampered his expressive mission. The Third's outer movements are brisk and vigorous but its heart is the central *Lento*, which opens like a missing interlude from *Mathis der Maler*. Another first-class performance, too. Full marks to Lyrita for its remastering, especially in dealing with Brian's singular orchestral soundscapes. Strongly recommended.

Frank Bridge
British 1879-1941

Bridge studied with Stanford at the RCM (1899-1903) and made a reputation as a chamber musician (a violist) and conductor. His early works, including the orchestral suite The Sea (1911), the symphonic poem Summer (1914) and much chamber music, are close to Bax and Delius, but after World War 1 he developed rapidly. His Third (1926) and Fourth (1937) Quartets are highly chromatic, reflecting his admiration for Berg, though his music remained distinctively English. Also remarkable is the contrapuntal vigour and energy of his later orchestral works, which include the rhapsody Enter Spring (1927), Oration with solo cello (1930) and Phantasm with solo piano (1931). None of his more adventurous music was much regarded until the 1970s, his fame resting largely on his having been Britten's teacher. **GROVE**music

Orchestral Works

Lament, H117. Oration (Concerto elegiaco), H180[a].
Rebus, H191. Allegro moderato, H192. A Prayer[b]
[a]**Alban Gerhardt** vc BBC National [b]**Chorus and
Orchestra of Wales / Richard Hickox**
Chandos CHAN10188 (77' · DDD) Ⓕ🅞🅑➡

Here's probably the most appealing and varied instalment in Richard Hickox's Frank Bridge series for Chandos. The disc's highlight is a superb performance of the 1930 'Concerto elegiaco' *Oration*, in which Hickox teams up with the gifted German cellist Alban Gerhardt. High drama and emotional candour are the keynotes to a riveting display. But there's no want of intimacy or compassion in the more contemplative passages, and the result is a trenchant interpretation that does justice to one of the towering masterpieces of British music.

The 1940 *Rebus* overture is as invigorating and impeccably crafted a concert-opener as any British composer has yet produced. The touching *Lament* (1915) is sensitively done, but Hickox and company seem less comfortable in Anthony Pople's completion of the patiently argued opening *Allegro moderato* from a projected symphony for strings upon which Bridge was working at the time of his death in 1941. Fortunately, there's a glowing account of *A Prayer*, Bridge's only composition for chorus and orchestra, a moving and often hauntingly beautiful setting from 1916-18 of words from *The Imitation of Christ* by Thomas à Kempis. Minor strictures notwithstanding, this is an essential purchase for *Oration* alone – and the music itself deserves the widest dissemination.

Adoration, H57[b]. Berceuse, H8. Berceuse, H9[a]. Blow out, you bugles, H132[b]. Chant d'espérance, H18 No 2. Love went a-riding, H114[b]. Mantle of Blue, H131[a]. The Pageant of London, H98. A Royal Night of Variety, H184. Serenade, H23. Three Tagore Songs, H164[a] – Day after Day; Speak to me, my love! Thy hand in mine, H124[b]. Where she lies asleep, H113[b]

[a]**Sarah Connolly** *mez* [b]**Philip Langridge** *ten* **BBC National Orchestra of Wales / Richard Hickox**
Chandos CHAN10310 (62' · DDD · T/t) Ⓕ

No fewer than 10 first recordings adorn this, the last instalment in Hickox's valuable Bridge series. Philip Langridge is in ardent voice for the first five tracks, the fourth of which, *Love went a-riding*, remains the composer's best-known song. It sounds exhilaratingly new-minted in its sumptuous orchestral garb and is framed here by two companion settings of words by Mary Coleridge, *Where she lies asleep* and *Thy hand in mine*. Particularly striking is the big-scale treatment afforded to Rupert Brooke's *Blow out, you bugles*, written in 1918 for the tenor Gervase Elwes and whose incorporation of the Last Post movingly anticipates Bridge's own towering *Oration* for cello and orchestra of a dozen years later.

Sarah Connolly is wonderfully eloquent in the haunting and often inspired 1922-24 Tagore diptych for mezzo and orchestra and also excels in the very early *Berceuse* (a remarkably assured setting of Dorothy Wordsworth from 1901) and affecting *Mantle of blue* (1918, and orchestrated 16 years later, to words by the Irish poet Padraic Colum). The programme concludes with five purely instrumental items, the most extended of which is the 1911 suite for wind band, *The Pageant of London*. Expertly fashioned, it makes for a diverting enough quarter of an hour (the 'Pavane' in the middle movement was destined to reappear 15 years later in Warlock's *Capriol Suite*). The tuneful *Serenade* exudes plenty of sepia-tinted charm, as does the wistful little *Berceuse* (1901).

Throw in some spick and span orchestral playing from the BBC NOW and Chandos's commendably natural engineering, not to mention Paul Hindmarsh's scholarly notes, and you have a job well done.

Allegro moderato, H192. Dance Poem, H111. Dance Rhapsody, H84. Two Poems, H118. Rebus, H191
London Philharmonic Orchestra / Nicholas Braithwaite
Lyrita SRCD243 (72' · DDD) ⒻⓄ🔊

How, one wonders, can such a rapturously tuneful work as Bridge's *Dance Rhapsody* (1908) be so shamefully neglected: it deserves to be as popular as, say, Ravel's *La valse*! The intense songfulness of the strings' inner voices and the general fervour of the London Philharmonic's playing is thrilling throughout. In the more elusive (yet still alluring) *Dance Poem* (1913), Braithwaite unflinchingly explores the music's darker corners, finding a tragic vein that Hickox misses, though the newer account moves with admirable grace.

Braithwaite is magically sensitive, too, in the vaguely Delian world of the *Two Poems* (1916); 'The Open Air' sustains a fragile atmosphere of mystery and 'The Story of my Heart' is simultaneously passionate and mercurial. The extreme contrasts of character contained in the *Rebus* overture (1940) are crisply delineated – and note how the LPO revel in the passages of glittering,

Straussian opulence. As for the *Allegro moderato* (a loose-limbed movement that Bridge left unfinished at his death in 1941), Hickox's taut, focused reading provides a semblance of symphonic cohesion, while Braithwaite elicits the stronger emotional charge. It's hard to imagine being without either recording.

Additional recommendation

The Sea, H100. Summer, H116. Two Poems, H118. Enter Spring, H174
New Zealand Symphony Orchestra / James Judd
Naxos 8 557167 (63' · DDD) Ⓢ🔊
A hearty, sensibly paced account of *Enter Spring*, a gorgeous *Summer*. Despite any minor reservations, an enjoyable concert and very decent value.

String Quintet, H7 / String Sextet, H107

String Quintet in E minor, H7[a]. String Sextet in E flat, H107[b]. Lament[c]
[b]**Raphael Ensemble** ([a]James Clark, [a]David Adams *vns* [ac]Louise Williams, [ac]Adsis Valdimarsdottír *vas* [a]Andrea Hess, Tim Gill *vcs*)
Hyperion CDA67426 (66' · DDD) Ⓕ🔊

Bridge was a star student at the RCM, and his E minor String Quintet from 1901, one of four chamber offerings he wrote at that time, reveals a burgeoning talent. Cast in four movements and lasting just over half an hour, it's an accomplished achievement. A scrupulous craft and pleasing sense of proportion attest to lessons well learnt under Stanford's tutelage, yet there's already a strongly emergent personality in pages such as the third-movement trio section. The finale, too, shows enviable skills, the poignant backward glance to the work's opening just before the close being particularly effective. It's preceded by a powerfully wrought Lament for two violas first performed by Lionel Tertis and the composer at London's Aeolian (now Wigmore) Hall in March 1912. Both works are worthy of resuscitation and both are superbly served here.

So too is the Sextet (1906-12) in an even more persuasive performance than that by the Academy of St Martin in the Fields Chamber Ensemble on Chandos. The Raphael Ensemble produce a leaner, more subtly shaded sonority, allied to an extra re-creative spark and expressive urgency (witness the edgy anxiety they locate in the *scherzo* at the heart of the work). And the opening *Allegro moderato* is surveyed with due appreciation of its lyrical grace and elegant architecture; likewise, the finale combines pliancy and thrust.

A delightful anthology, highly recommended.

String Quartets

String Quartets No 1 in E minor, 'Bologna', H70; No 3, H175
Maggini Quartet (Laurence Jackson, David Angel,

vns Martin Outram va Michal Kaznowski vc)
Naxos 8 557133 (60' · DDD)　　　　Ⓢ℗➔

Even by the high standards of previous Maggini/
Naxos offerings, this is an exceptionally fine disc.
If you don't know Frank Bridge's First Quartet of
1906, its ardour and melodic fecundity compel
investigation. The Maggini Quartet give a performance to match, of sweep, assurance and affection. At the same time, their rapt concentration
and daring range of expression (especially in the
slow movement) banish for good any vestige of
salon-room cosiness; the return of the opening
material at the quartet's close has never seemed
more wistfully inevitable.

That the Magginis are no less attuned to the far
more challenging sound world of the 1926 Third
Quartet is at once evident from the articulate
authority and thrust they impart to the introductory bars (which sow the seeds for so much that
follows). Both this work and the searching Piano
Sonata, completed the previous year, represent
the first wholly convincing examples of Bridge's
liberating brand of English expressionism.

The Magginis are scrupulously alive to anguished
introspection which runs through the work: the
ghostly visions that stalk the central *Andante con
moto* and finale's twilit coda linger long in the
memory here. A superb coupling, impeccably
captured by the Walton/Thomason production
team and well annotated by Andrew Burn.

String Quartets – No 2; No 4. Phantasy[a]
Maggini Quartet ([a]Laurence Jackson, David Angel
vns [a]Martin Outram va [a]Michal Kaznowski vc)
with [a]**Martin Roscoe** pf
Naxos 8 557283 (60' · DDD)　　　Ⓢ❶❶❶❶➔

Ⓖ　Bridge's glorious Second Quartet, writ-
　　ten in 1915 and winner of that year's
　　Cobbett Prize, is arguably his first true
chamber masterwork, superbly realised on every
level (the finale is a *tour de force* of motivic integration) and full of the most engagingly fresh
invention and invigorating part-writing. The
last of his four quartets (completed in 1937)
represents more of a challenge, but strong emotions stir beneath its uncompromising surface.
Once again, the finale proves a fitting summation, and Bridge's technical command of the
medium is absolute. Leaner and more 'classically' compact than its towering predecessor
from 1926, this searching score will afford the
patient listener plentiful long-term rewards.

The Brindisi Quartet's coupling has served us
handsomely over the past dozen years but must
now yield to this Naxos release. These are exemplary, scrupulously prepared readings from the
Magginis, who play with unquenchable fire,
keen intelligence and immaculate polish
throughout. Joined by the admirable Martin
Roscoe, they also offer a considerable bonus in
the shape of the lovely Phantasy Piano Quartet
of 1909-10.

With vividly realistic, beautifully balanced
sound from the experienced Walton/Thomason

production-team and succinct annotation by
Andrew Burn, this is an unmissable disc.

Piano Trio No 2

Piano Trio No 2, H178. Phantasie Trio, H79.
Miniatures – Set 1, H87; Set 2, H88; Set 3, H89.
Jack Liebeck vn **Alexander Chaushian** vc
Ashley Wass pf
Naxos 8 570792 (73' · DDD)　　　Ⓢ●℗➔

How encouraging to see Ashley Wass branching
into Bridge's chamber output – and with such
gifted colleagues, too. This Naxos version of the
adorable, Cobbett Prize-winning *Phantasie Trio*
is an adroit and boldly characterised affair. The
three sets of *Miniatures* probably date from the
following year and comprise nine exquisitely
crafted and tuneful morsels originally intended
for domestic use. They're best dipped into
rather than played at one stretch, but all are dispatched with sizzling panache and evident relish
by these elegant performers.

Of course, the masterpiece here is the epic
Second Piano Trio of 1929, one of Bridge's
most cogent, questing and durable utterances,
whose radical language so bamboozled the
largely conservative British critics of the
period. Wass and company lend it exhilarating
advocacy in a realisation of enviable security,
unswerving concentration and burning
conviction. Tip-top production values and
exemplary notes set the seal on an irresistible
bargain.

Additional recommednation

Phantasy Trio in C minor, H79. Piano Trio No 2, H178.
Miniatures – H88: Romance; Intermezzo; H89: Valse
russe; Hornpipe
Bernard Roberts Trio
Black Box BBM1028 (57' · DDD)　　　Ⓕ
These are utterly sympathetic, beautifully prepared
performances from this fine family group. The
centrepiece is the Second Piano Trio, a work of
searing intensity and astounding individuality.

Piano Quintet

Piano Quintet, H49a[a]. Three Idylls, H67. String
Quartet No 4, H188
[a]**Piers Lane** pf **Goldner Quartet**
(Dene Olding, Dimity Hall vns Irini Morozova va
Julian Smiles vc)
Hyperion CDA67726 (65' · DDD)　　　Ⓕ

Frank Bridge's comprehensive 1912 revision of
his D minor Piano Quintet from seven years
before remains the sole comparative dud in his
early chamber output – and not even this splendidly articulate rendering from Piers Lane and
the Goldners can persuade otherwise. The
original work's four movements are condensed

to three, its centrepiece a gratefully lyrical amalgam of slow movement and scherzo enclosed within one of Bridge's arch-like 'phantasy'structures. Alas, the opening movement (after a promising start) soon drifts into a worryingly humdrum, sequential lassitude, and the finale fails to provide sufficient ballast to counterbalance what has preceded it.

The *Three Idylls* of 1906 are an infinitely more enticing proposition – exquisitely crafted, keenly proportioned and supremely touching miniatures for string quartet, the second of which later provided the 23-year-old Britten with the theme for his Op 10 Variations for string orchestra. The Fourth Quartet is utterly different again. Completed in 1937 after a near-fatal bout of bronchitis, this is arguably Bridge's most rivetingly cogent and harmonically bracing statement, evincing a deftness, compassion and unerring intellectual scope that beg comparison with the greatest 20th-century examples in the medium.

These unfailingly sympathetic, flexible and exhilaratingly assured performances have been most truthfully captured. So, despite reservations surrounding the Quintet, this is clearly a release to investigate.

Cello Sonata in D minor, H125

Bridge Cello Sonata. Meditation. Spring Song. Serenade. Berceuse. Scherzo. Elégie. Mélodie. Cradle Song **Britten** Cello Sonata in C, Op 65
Øystein Birkeland vc **Vebjørn Anvik** pf
Simax PSC1160 (70' · DDD)   Ⓕ

The Norwegian duo of Øystein Birkeland and Vebjørn Anvik lend gloriously unaffected and formidably lucid advocacy to Bridge's masterwork, his Cello Sonata, the strength and nobility of their playing always ideally counterbalanced by tender restraint and songful intimacy. These superbly stylish performers prove no less responsive to the poetic charms of Bridge the miniaturist.

The winsome *Serenade* of 1903 is a fresh-faced delight here, while the 1902 *Scherzo* fairly twinkles with humour. How memorably, too, they sustain the long-breathed ardour of both the *Elégie* (1904) and *Mélodie* (written in 1911 and dedicated to the cellist Felix Salmond).

Sandwiched between the Bridge Sonata and a sequence of miniatures comes a really fine account of the Cello Sonata that Britten penned for Rostropovich in 1960-61. Here, too, Birkeland and Anvik form an intelligent, scrupulously observant partnership, their playing as thoughtful as it's intense, though not even they can match the extraordinary fluidity that Rostropovich and Britten bring to the work's opening bars on their inspirational premiere recording for Decca.

Among digital contenders, however, this beautifully engineered and sensitively balanced recording is as good as any and more imposing than most. Calum MacDonald contributes the exemplary booklet essay. All told, a very positive recommendation.

Benjamin Britten   British 1913-1976

Britten studied with Frank Bridge as a boy and in 1930 entered the RCM. In 1934 he heard Wozzeck and planned to study with Berg, but opposition at home stopped him. The next year he began working for the GPO Film Unit, where one of his collaborators was Auden: together they worked on concert works as well, Auden's social criticism being matched by a sharply satirical and virtuoso musical style (orchestral song cycle Our Hunting Fathers, 1936). Stravinsky and Mahler were important influences, but Britten's effortless technique gave his early music a high personal definition, notably shown in orchestral works (Bridge Variations for strings, 1937; Piano Concerto, 1938; Violin Concerto, 1939) and songs (Les illuminations, setting Rimbaud for high voice and strings, 1939).

In 1939 he left England for the USA, with his lifelong companion Peter Pears; there he wrote his first opera, to Auden's libretto (Paul Bunyan, 1941). In 1942 he returned and, partly stimulated by Purcell, began to concentrate on settings of English verse (anthem Rejoice in the Lamb and Serenade for tenor, horn and strings, both 1943). His String Quartet No 2 (1945), with its huge concluding chaconne, also came out of his Purcellian interests, but the major work of this period was Peter Grimes (1945), which signalled a new beginning in English opera. Its central character, the first of many roles written for Pears, struck a new operatic tone: a social outcast, he is fiercely proud and independent, but also deeply insecure, providing opportunities for a lyrical flow that would be free but is not. Britten's gift for characterisation was also displayed in the wide range of sharply defined subsidiary roles and in the orchestra's sea music.

However, his next operas were all written for comparatively small resources (The Rape of Lucretia, 1946; Albert Herring, 1947; a version of The Beggar's Opera, 1948; The Little Sweep, 1949), for the company that became established as the English Opera Group. At the same time he began writing music for the Aldeburgh Festival, which he and Pears founded in 1948 in the Suffolk town where they had settled (cantata St Nicolas, 1948; Lachrymae for viola and piano, 1949). And in this prolific period he also composed large concert works (The Young Person's Guide to the Orchestra, 1946; Spring Symphony with soloists and choir, 1949) and songs.

The pattern of his output was thus set, though not the style, for the operas show an outward urge to ever new subjects: village comedy in Albert Herring, psychological conflict in Billy Budd (1951), historical reconstruction in Gloriana (1953), a tale of ghostly possession in The Turn of the Screw (1954), nocturnal magic in A Midsummer Night's Dream (1960), a struggle between family history and individual responsibility in Owen Wingrave (1971) and, most centrally, obsession with a doomed ideal in Death in Venice (1973), the last three works being intermediate in scale between the chamber format of Herring and The Screw, and the symphonic fullness of Budd and

Gloriana, both written for Covent Garden. But nearly all touch in some way on the themes of the individual and society and the violation of innocence. Simultaneous with a widening range of subject matter was a widening musical style, which came to include 12-note elements (Turn of the Screw) and a heterophony that owed as much to oriental music directly as it did to Mahler (cycle of 'church parables', or ritualised small-scale operas: Curlew River, The Burning Fiery Furnace, The Prodigal Son, 1964-8).

Many of these dramatic works were written for the Aldeburgh Festival, as were many of the instrumental and vocal works Britten produced for favoured performers. For Rostropovich he wrote the Cello Symphony (1963) as well as a sonata and three solo suites; for Pears there was the Hardy cycle Winter Words (1953) among many other songs, and also a central part in the War Requiem (1961). His closing masterpiece, however, was a return to the abstract in the String Quartet No 3 (1975).

Britten was appointed a Companion of Honour in 1952, to the Order of Merit in 1965, and was awarded a life peerage in 1976.

Piano Concerto in D, Op 13

Piano Concerto. Violin Concerto, Op 15
Mark Lubotsky *vn* **Sviatoslav Richter** *pf* **English Chamber Orchestra / Benjamin Britten**
Decca British Music Collection 473 715-2 (67' · ADD)
Recorded 1970   ⓂÐ➤

Just after Britten's performances were released on LP in 1971, the composer admitted with some pride that Sviatoslav Richter had learned his Piano Concerto 'entirely off his own bat', and had revealed a Russianness that was in the score. Britten was attracted to Shostakovich during the late 1930s, when it was written, and the bravado, brittleness and flashy virtuosity of the writing, in the march-like finale most of all, at first caused many to be wary of it, even to think it somehow outside the composer's style. Now we know his music better, it's easier to accept, particularly in this sparkling yet sensitive performance.

The Violin Concerto dates from the following year, 1939, and it, too, has its self-conscious virtuosity, but it's its rich nostalgic lyricism which strikes to the heart and the quiet elegiac ending is unforgettable. Compared to Richter in the other work, Mark Lubotsky isn't always the master of its hair-raising difficulties, notably in the *Scherzo*, which has passages of double artificial harmonics that even Heifetz wanted simplified before he would play it (Britten refused), but this is still a lovely account. Fine recordings.

Piano Concerto, Op 13 (incl both versions of the third movement). Young Apollo, Op 16. Diversions, Op 21
Steven Osborne *pf* **BBC Scottish Symphony Orchestra / Ilan Volkov**
Hyperion CDA67625 (71' · DDD)   Ⓕⵔ

Commissioned as a 24-year-old to compose and perform a piano concerto for the 1938 Proms,

Britten played safe. None of the edginess he might have filched from Bartók or Stravinsky, no Bergian angst: instead, the models are Prokofiev, Shostakovich and Ravel, and in these terms he doesn't miss a trick, at least before the finale's rather perfunctory final gallop. Most of the piece takes a genuinely fresh look at pianistic conventions, and Steven Osborne yields nothing to the great Sviatoslav Richter in the punchiness and fine-tuned filigree of his playing. No skating over the surface here, with Ilan Volkov and the BBC Scottish SO adept at teasing out the music's symphonic subtext, as well as its piquant orchestral effects.

Britten replaced the original slow movement in 1945, possibly because it spent too much time in waltz-like regions already visited in the second movement. This disc adds it anyway, alongside two other scores for piano and orchestra. *Young Apollo* (1939) was not heard for half a century after its premiere, perhaps discarded by Britten because its fanfare-like material was more effectively deployed in *Les illuminations* (also 1939). It's a quirky piece, difficult to programme, a euphorically unguarded response to Keats's vision of male beauty in Hyperion.

Diversions is on a much grander scale, its style making even clearer those debts to Mahler which Britten had allowed to surface now and again in the concerto. The multifarious challenges to the single-handed soloist create moments of strong emotional depth and, as throughout the disc, Osborne and his colleagues make the best possible case for pieces which have tended to be placed on the outer fringes of the Britten canon. The recordings, made in Glasgow's Henry Wood Hall, have ample depth of sonority and vividness of colour.

Violin Concerto in D minor, Op 15

Britten Violin Concerto **Walton** Viola Concerto
Maxim Vengerov *vn/va* **London Symphony Orchestra / Mstislav Rostropovich**
EMI 557510-2 (64' · DDD)   Ⓕ Ð➤

When artists of the stature of Vengerov and Rostropovich tackle English music it's often a revelation, and here's some of the most ravishing string-playing ever heard in either of these masterpieces. But these readings don't always follow convention, let alone metronome markings, and there's at least one choice of tempo that may have traditionalists spluttering in protest. As you might expect with Rostropovich as conductor, the Britten is the less controversial of the two readings. The soloist's first entry over crisply sprung ostinato repetitions on bassoon and harp is marked *dolcissimo*, and the sweetness of Vengerov's playing in the high-lying cantilena is nothing short of heavenly. Here and throughout the work his free expressiveness, his use of *rubato*, far from sounding forced, reflects a seemingly spontaneous understanding, the creative insight of a major artist, rapt and intense. Rostropovich and the LSO match him in their warm expressiveness. The full-blooded recording not only covers the widest dynamic range throughout, but brings out many inner details in the orchestral writing normally obscured.

That's also true of the Russians' reading of the Walton Viola Concerto, with Vengerov evidently just as much at ease on the viola as the violin. Yet the timings alone will bear witness to the individuality of the reading. Vengerov is even more expansive than Kennedy or Bashmet, and the wonder is that, with Rostropovich in total sympathy, he sustains the slow tempo with rapt intensity, pure and tender with no hint of soupiness of the kind that mars the Kennedy version. Unconventional as it is, this is a reading that demands to be heard, even if Waltonians won't want it as their only choice.

Violin Concerto[a]. Symphony for Cello and Orchestra, Op 68[b]
[a]**Rebecca Hirsch** vn [b]**Tim Hugh** vc **BBC Scottish Symphony Orchestra / Takuo Yuasa**
Naxos 8 553882 (68' · DDD)　　　　Ⓢ🄓➔

Not only does Rebecca Hirsch (for the most part) make light of the solo part's fiendish technical difficulties, her playing evinces a beguiling lyrical beauty that's breathtaking. By the side of both Ida Haendel and Lorraine McAslan, she perhaps lacks the last ounce of fiery temperament (and there are a handful of tiny misreadings), but generally she's convincing and characterful.

In the *Cello Symphony*, Tim Hugh displays a profound musicality, great subtlety of tone and affecting lyrical ardour that puts in mind Steven Isserlis's account with Richard Hickox, though not quite achieving the dark-hued individuality and unremitting logic of that distinguished 1987 production. Nor does it displace dedicatee Rostropovich's blisteringly intense, composer-directed versions of this gritty masterpiece, but Hugh's achievement is considerable and he more than holds his own alongside the formidable roster of current rivals.

Takuo Yuasa draws an eloquent response from his forces. However, at the Violin Concerto's opening *Moderato con moto*, some leisurely tempos tend to undermine the purposeful thrust of the whole. Sound and balance are generally very good indeed.

Double Concerto in B minor

Double Concerto[b]. Young Apollo[a]. Two Portraits[c].
Sinfonietta, Op 1[d]
[b]**Gidon Kremer** vn [bc]**Yuri Bashmet** va [a]**string quartet** (Lyn Fletcher, Dara De Cogan vns Tim Pooley va Peter Worrall vc) [a]**Nikolai Lugansky** pf **Hallé Orchestra / Kent Nagano**
Warner Elatus 0927-46718-2 (59' · DDD)　　Ⓜ🄞➔

This release contains three world-premiere recordings. Most striking is the Double Con-

certo, the short score of which the gifted 18-year-old completed by the early autumn of 1932. That same summer Britten also produced his 'official' Op 1, the dazzlingly inventive *Sinfonietta* for 10 instruments. The two works have plenty in common both formally and stylistically. The 'orchestral' version of the *Sinfonietta* heard here incorporates a full complement of strings as well as a second horn part.

Colin Matthews fashioned a performing edition of the Double Concerto from Britten's helpfully detailed sketches, the piece receiving its premiere at the 1987 Aldeburgh Festival. While not quite showing the effortless fluency and innovative thematic guile of the *Sinfonietta*, it remains an astonishing work for one so young, with numerous examples of sparky, head-turning inspiration. Likewise, the *Two Portraits* make intriguing listening. Composed in August 1930, the first is a 'sketch for strings describing David' (David Layton, a close friend of the 16-year-old Britten at Gresham's School), whose emotional vehemence and harmonic restlessness nod towards Janáček and even Berg.

Nagano directs a set of performances which are beyond praise in their luminous refinement and blistering commitment; all three distinguished soloists are on unimpeachable form. Warners' sound quality is sumptuously realistic to match.

Cello Symphony, Op 68

Cello Symphony[a]. Sinfonia da Requiem, Op 20[b].
Cantata misericordium, Op 69[c]
Mstislav Rostropovich vc **Sir Peter Pears** ten **Dietrich Fischer-Dieskau** bar [a]**English Chamber Orchestra**, [b]**New Philharmonia Orchestra**, [c]**London Symphony Chorus and Orchestra / Benjamin Britten**
Decca London 425 100-2LM (75' · ADD · T/t)
Recorded 1964　　　　　　　　　　Ⓜ🄞➔

The Cello Symphony, written in 1963 as part of a series for the great Russian cellist Mstislav Rostropovich, was the first major sonata-form work written since the *Sinfonia*. The idea of a struggle between soloist and orchestra, implicit in the traditional concerto, has no part here; it's a conversation between the two. Rostropovich plays with a depth of feeling that has never quite been equalled in other recordings and the playing of the English Chamber Orchestra has great bite. The recording, too, is extraordinarily fine for its years.

From the opening drumbeat the *Sinfonia* employs a sonata form with dramatic power, although the tone is never fierce or savage; it has an implacable tread and momentum. The central movement, 'Dies irae', however, has a real sense of fury, satirical in its biting comment – the flutter-tongued wind writing rattling its defiance. The closing 'Requiem aeternam' is a movement of restrained beauty. The New Philharmonia play superbly. The *Cantata misericor-*

dium was written in 1962 as a commission from the Red Cross. It takes the story of the Good Samaritan and is scored for tenor and baritone soloists, chorus, string quartet and orchestra. It's a universal plea for charity and receives a powerful reading. A must for any Britten enthusiast.

Additional recommendations

Cello Symphony[a]
Coupled with: Elgar Cello Concerto
Mørk *vc* **City of Birmingham Symphony Orchestra / Rattle**
Virgin Classics 545356-2   Ⓜ︎●●

Truls Mørk plays this powerful work as if his life depended on it: it's his second recording of the work and long familiarity has clearly paid off. In Rattle and the CBSO he has truly supportive partners. (And the Elgar as coupling is a refreshingly unsentimental performance that never, alas, quite takes wing as it might, fine though it is.)

'Frank Bridge' Variations, Op 10

Variations on a theme of Frank Bridge, Op 10.
The Young Person's Guide to the Orchestra, Op 34.
Four Sea Interludes, Op 33a. Passacaglia, Op 33b
BBC Symphony Orchestra / Sir Andrew Davis
Warner Apex 8573 89082-2 (68' · DDD)   Ⓢ︎➔

The real reason for investing in this bargain reissue is Davis's exceptionally insightful account of the *Variations*. After a deceptively low-key 'Introduction and Theme', this quickly develops into a reading of striking application and abundant character, plumbing genuine depths in the 'Funeral March' and 'Chant', and conveying an overwhelming sense of pathos towards the close. Of course, no home should be without the composer's uniquely authoritative 1966 account with the ECO on Decca (still unsurpassed and perhaps unsurpassable), but, as 'big-band' contenders go, there's no more perceptive rendering than Davis's.

The couplings include a thoroughly professional, no-frills *Young Person's Guide*, finely played and with a delectable rhythmic snap in the variation for percussion in particular. What's missing is harder to define: that sense of playfulness, fun even, you hear in, say, Hickox's excellent account for Chandos, which remains the pick of the digital crop, though Britten's own classic LSO recording is also an absolute must. Davis's *Four Sea Interludes* are agreeable enough in their comparatively breezy, uncomplicated manner, and it's always a pleasure to hear the imposing *Passacaglia* given with such intensity. Overall, well worth its modest outlay.

The Young Person's Guide ..., Op 34

The Young Person's Guide to the Orchestra. Simple Symphony, Op 4[a]. A Spring Symphony, Op 44 –

Spring, the sweet spring. Noyes Fludde[b] – Noye, Noye, take thou thy company ... Sir! heare are lions. Serenade for Tenor, Horn and Strings, Op 31 – Nocturne. Folk Songs – The Plough Boy; Early One Morning. Billy Budd – Interlude and Sea Shanties. A Ceremony of Carols, Op 28 – Adam lay i-bounden. A Hymn to the Virgin. War Requiem – Lacrimosa. Peter Grimes – Interlude (Dawn)
Sir Peter Pears *ten* **Barry Tuckwell** *hn* **various soloists; choirs, choruses and orchestras, London Symphony Orchestra,** [ab]**English Chamber Orchestra / Benjamin Britten** *pf* [b]**Norman Del Mar**
Decca 436 990-2DWO (74' · ADD) Recorded 1963-8
                                            Ⓜ︎●➔

This reissue includes the composer's own 1963 recording of *The Young Person's Guide to the Orchestra* with the LSO and his complete 1968 ECO version of the *Simple Symphony*. The latter is delightfully fresh and is unforgettable for the joyful bounce of the 'Playful Pizzicato', helped by the resonant acoustic of The Maltings, Snape. In *The Young Person's Guide*, without the now somewhat rather dated text, he adopts quick, demanding tempos, with more spacious ones for the more introspective sections. This is beautiful playing, possessing wit and brilliance, with all kinds of memorable touches. Even if this transfer is a little dry in sonority, this disc is invaluable for these two performances alone. As a bonus we're offered ten short excerpts from other major Britten works.

Film music

'Britten on Film'

Britten When you're feeling like expressing your affection[ad]. Night Mail[dg]. Way to the Sea[dg]. The Tocher (Rossini Suite)[fg]. The King's Stamp[g]. Negroes[abcg]. Telegrams[fg]. Peace of Britain[g]. Men Behind the Meters[g]. Coal Face[bcdeg]
[a]**Mary Carewe** *sop* [b]**Daniel Auchincloss** *ten* [c]**Adam Green** *bar* [d]**Simon Russell Beale** *narr* [d]**Malcolm Wilson** *pf* [e]**City of Birmingham Symphony Orchestra Chorus;** [f]**Choir of King Edward's School, Birmingham;** [g]**Birmingham Contemporary Music Group / Martyn Brabbins**
NMC NMCD112 (79' · DDD)   Ⓕ➔

In the mid-1930s, in his early twenties, Britten wrote film scores, giving him an unrivalled opportunity to hear his own music immediately after it had been composed. He learnt to apply his imagination to visual effects and drama – this was the genesis of the great opera composer. His colleagues included WH Auden, intimidatingly erudite and sometimes bullying, who was a formative influence on Britten at this impressionable period.

This generous 79-minute collection consists of the film music without the film, so if you have once seen some of the better known ones such as *Night Mail* or *Coal Face* your visual memory fills the gap. An excellent feature is the provision of Auden's texts as well as thorough documentary material from Philip Reed.

There are familiar elements in *The Tocher (Rossini Suite)*, which overlaps with Britten's *Soirées musicales* based on Rossini, and it's odd to find Britten arranging Balfe's 'I dreamt that I dwelt in marble halls' in a film about the gas industry. Surprisingly often the musical ideas are strong enough on their own but some extracts such as *The King's Stamp* (commemorating the George V Silver Jubilee issue of 1935) consist of bits and pieces that weren't meant to cohere and don't. Simon Russell Beale is the narrator and his rather low-pitched voice is sometimes drowned by the instruments: he also drops his voice at the end of sentences. The track listing has gone awry at the start of *The Negroes*, which begins with a passage very close to Kurt Weill. But most of this material is well worth having at least for its pre-echoes and is admirably performed.

String Quartets

No 1 in D, Op 25; **No 2** in C, Op 36; **No 3** Op 94

String Quartets Nos 1-3. Three Divertimentos
Belcea Quartet (Corina Belcea, Lara Samuel *vns*
Krzysztof Chorzelski *va* Alasdair Tait *vc*)
EMI ② 557968-2 (115' · DDD)　　　Ⓕ❍❍❍Ⓑ➔

The Belcea Quartet have become prominent players on the chamber-music scene. In the concert hall, their rather balletic style of performance can be alienating, but in these Britten recordings you can appreciate their high level of technical accomplishment without the risk of visual distraction.

Collectors familiar with any of the earlier sets of the quartets may not warm immediately to the Belcea's exceptionally dramatic way with the music's contrasting materials. But almost nothing is forced or eccentric here. The hell-for-leather tempo adopted for the First's finale is genuinely exciting, not a scramble, and although there are a few obtrusive, fussy details in the outer movements of No 2 the overall impression is powerfully convincing. No 3 is even better, at least in the earlier movements, bringing a sense of barely suppressed anger to some of Britten's most personal and allusive music. In the last movement the phrasing is occasionally over-pointed: yet, despite tempi that make this account significantly faster than the excellent Magginis and considerably faster than the stately Brodskys, the effect reinforces the true consistency of tone and character which underpins this notably diverse score. This is one of the best-engineered quartet discs you might hope to hear.

String Quartets – Nos 2 & 3
Brodsky Quartet (Andrew Haveron, Ian Belton *vns*
Paul Cassidy *va* Jacqueline Thomas *vc*)
Challenge Classics CC72099 (61' · DDD)　　Ⓕ

The Brodsky are the Britten team for the new century, and at full price they take advantage of

the super-refined Snape Maltings acoustic to offer performances of great intelligence and expressive power. No other recording of No 2 manages to convey the dramatic passion and lyric sweep of Britten's marvellously idiomatic string writing more persuasively than this one does. At two points during the long finale, the inner voices don't sound, to these ears, sufficiently distinct, the presentation of the all-pervading chaconne theme under-articulated. But these are momentary quibbles rather than sustained reservations, and it can certainly be argued that the overall interpretation of the movement benefits from the kind of contrasts which these effects represent.

In general, No 3 unfolds at slightly broader tempi than those chosen by the Maggini (on Naxos), and the episodic recitative that opens the finale seems a shade too expansive for its own good. Otherwise, this is exemplary, with immaculate ensemble and a sense of spontaneous expressive engagement bringing out the full stature of this deeply felt, valedictory music. A memorable disc, then, and an outstanding Britten cycle.

String Quartet No 3. Alla marcia. Quartettino. Simple Symphony, Op 4
Maggini Quartet (Laurence Jackson, David Angel *vns* Martin Outram *va* Michal Kaznowski *vc*)
Naxos 8 554360 (65' · DDD)　　　　　　Ⓢ➔

This second volume of the Maggini Quartet's Britten series amply fulfils the promise of the first. As before, the recording favours blend and immediacy: the leading full-price alternative, recorded at Snape by the Sorrel Quartet for Chandos, has a richer atmosphere and a stronger sense of space, but, as interpretations, the Maggini's versions need fear nothing from the current competition. The major work here is the late Third Quartet, a score whose extreme contrasts of mood and texture, ranging from rapt serenity to explosive bitterness, are the more difficult to make convincing for the extraordinary economy of means which the ailing Britten summoned. The Maggini are hard to beat in the conviction they bring to all aspects of a notably well-focused, technically polished account. Their choice of basic tempos for the tricky outer movements is ideal, and they relish the elements of parody elsewhere without descending into caricature. This disc also provides the only currently available version of the early but radical *Quartettino*, and the quartet version of the *Simple Symphony*.

String Quartet No 2; String Quartets – in D (1931); in F (1928)
Sorrel Quartet (Gina McCormack, Catherine Yates *vns* Vicci Wardman *va* Helen Thatcher *vc*)
Chandos CHAN9664 (74' · DDD)　　　　　Ⓕ❍

The Sorrel Quartet can claim a significant 'first' in its account of the recently resurrected F major

Quartet from 1928. At 15 Britten was nothing if not precocious, and although the ideas in this substantial piece offer few hints of his mature style, he was already using the medium to excellent effect. Three years later, in the D major Quartet which has been a repertory item since Britten revised it in 1974, there are signs of a more individual voice; this is an attractive performance, well shaped and effectively characterised. Nevertheless, it's on the interpretation of the Quartet No 2 that the disc must be judged. The Sorrel's naturalness and feeling for line are much in evidence. Tempos for the first movement are broader than most rivals, but they serve an approach which makes a virtue of reticence, and still manages to be quite gripping. It has just about the best sound currently available (with The Maltings, Snape, providing an ideal acoustic), and the otherwise unrecorded F major Quartet adds strength to the recommendation of this noteworthy disc.

Phantasy Quartet

Britten Phantasy Quartet, Op 2[acde] **Dohnányi** Serenade, Op 10[cde] **Mozart** Oboe Quartet, K370[acde]. Die Zauberflöte[ac] – Der Vogelfänger bin ich ja; Ach, ich fühl's; Der Hölle Rache. Adagio, K580[abcde]
François Leleux [a]ob/[b]cor ang [c]**Lisa Batiashvili** vn [d]**Lawrence Power** va [e]**Sebastian Klinger** vc
Sony Classical 88697 28585-2 (64' · DDD)   (F)

Distinguished soloists do not always make distinguished chamber musicians. Here they do; and unsuspected depths in the music are plumbed. A measure of daring seems implicit in their control of fine *pianissimi* and tonal halflights at the beginning of Britten's *Phantasy Quartet*. The initial notes marked to be played on the fingerboard of a muted cello emanate from an inky nothingness, to be gradually joined by the viola and violin playing in a similar fashion. And there is no rude awakening from oboist François Leleux; his softly reedy tone steals in to reinforce the delicate texture.

This is no flash in the pan. Technique, both individual and corporate, is consummate, a vehicle for a penetrating intelligence that reaches beyond the limitations of musical notation. Leleux avoids a narrow dynamic range and blunt attack, instead producing within the scope of his instrument a ductile expressiveness of the sort that is usually heard from strings. The interpretation of Mozart's Oboe Quartet is sure to meet the expectations of many a dream, as will the C minor *Adagio* where an eloquent case is made for a piece not often heard. Ditto Dohnányi's Trio, Lisa Batiashvili as unobtrusively cogent a leader here as she is the duo partner in the arias from *Die Zauberflöte*. Bewitching performances!

Solo Cello Suites

No 1, Op 72; **No 2**, Op 80; **No 3**, Op 87

Solo Cello Suites Nos 1 & 2. Cello Sonata, Op 65
Mstislav Rostropovich vc **Benjamin Britten** pf
Decca London 421 859-2LM (68' · ADD)   Recorded 1961-9   Ⓜ ⓄⓄⓄ

 This is a classic recording of the Cello Sonata, with Rostropovich and Britten playing with an authority impossible to surpass, and is here coupled with the unaccompanied First and Second Cello Suites. The suggestive, often biting humour, masks darker feelings. However, Britten manages, just, to keep his devil under control. Rostropovich's and Britten's characterisation in the opening *Dialogo* is stunning and their subdued humour in the *Scherzo-pizzicato* also works well. In the *Elegia* and the final *Moto perpetuo*, again, no one quite approaches the passion and energy of Rostropovich. This work, like the two Suites, was written for him and he still remains the real heavyweight in all three pieces. Their transfer to CD is remarkably successful; it's difficult to believe that these recordings were made in the 1960s.

Solo Cello Suites Nos 1-3
Jean-Guihen Queyras vc
Harmonia Mundi Les Nouveaux Interprètes
HMN91 1670 (65' · DDD)   Ⓑ Ⓞ

Britten's three Cello Suites have all the strength of musical character to sustain a permanent place in the repertory. Inspired by the personality, and technique, of Mstislav Rostropovich, they're remarkable for the way in which they acknowledge yet at the same time distance themselves from the great precedent of Bach's Cello Suites. The best performers (like Rostropovich himself, though he has never recorded No 3) are equally at ease with the music's Bach-like contrapuntal ingenuity and its lyric intensity, where Britten's own most personal voice is heard. Queyras has such a fine sense of phrase that his slower speeds do not sound unconvincing, and his technically superbplaying has an impressive consistency of style. The quality of the recording is another plus, with the close focus needed to ensure that all the details tell. The only disappointment came in the final track, with the Russian Prayer for the Dead that ends Suite No 3. Here, of all places, Queyras is simply too fast. Nevertheless, this lapse isn't so great as to deprive the disc of a place in this guide.

War Requiem, Op 66

War Requiem[a]. Sinfonia da Requiem, Op 20. Ballad of Heroes, Op 14[b]
Heather Harper sop [a]**Philip Langridge**, [b]**Martyn Hill** tens **John Shirley-Quirk** bar [a]**St Paul's Cathedral Choir; London Symphony Chorus and Orchestra / Richard Hickox**
Chandos ② CHAN8983/4 (125' · DDD · T/t)
(F) ⓄⓄⓄⓄ→

Britten's *War Requiem* is the composer's most public statement of his pacifism. The work is cast in six movements and calls for massive forces: full chorus, soprano soloist and full orchestra evoke mourning, supplication and guilty apprehension; boys' voices with chamber organ, the passive calm of a liturgy which points beyond death; tenor and baritone soloists with chamber orchestra, the passionate outcry of the doomed victims of war. The most recent challenger to the composer's classic Decca version offers up-to-date recording, excellently managed to suggest the various perspectives of the vast work, and possibly the most convincing execution of the choral writing to date under the direction of a conductor, Richard Hickox, who's a past master at obtaining the best from a choir in terms of dynamic contrast and vocal emphasis. Add to that his empathy with all that the work has to say and you've a cogent reason for acquiring this version even before you come to the excellent work of the soloists. In her recording swan-song, Harper at last commits to disc a part she created. It's right that her special accents and impeccable shaping of the soprano's contribution have been preserved for posterity.

Shirley-Quirk, always closely associated with the piece, sings the three baritone solos and duets with rugged strength and dedicated intensity. He's matched by Langridge's compelling and insightful reading, with his notes and words more dramatic than Pears's approach. The inclusion of two additional pieces, neither of them short, helps to give this version an added advantage even if the *Ballad of Heroes* is one of Britten's slighter works.

War Requiem
Stefania Woytowicz sop **Sir Peter Pears** ten **Hans Wilbrink** bar **Wandsworth School Boys' Choir; Melos Ensemble; New Philharmonia Orchestra and Chorus / Carlo Maria Giulini**
BBC Legends/IMG Artists BBCL4046-2 (79' · ADD · T)
Recorded live 1969   Ⓜ︎ⒶⒶ

This performance is a revelation. As the authoritative note makes clear, Britten and Giulini had a mutual respect for and an admiration of each other's work. Here they combine to give a performance that's a true Legend, as this BBC series has it. Giulini's reading is as dramatic and viscerally exciting as any rival version. The music leaps from the page new-minted in his histrionically taut hands, the rhythmic tension at times quite astonishing. For instance, the sixth movement, 'Libera me', is simply earth-shattering in its effect, every bar, every word, every instrument sung and played to the hilt – and so it's throughout, with the live occasion added to the peculiar, and in this case peculiarly right, acoustics of the Albert Hall adding its own measure of *verité* to the inspired occasion.

The performance of the New Philharmonia forces, under the man who was at the time their favourite conductor after Klemperer, is at once

Vishnevskaya; Pears; Fischer-Dieskau; Bach Choir; Highgate School Ch; London Symphony Chorus; Melos Ens; LSO / Benjamin Britten
Decca 4757511 (132': ADD)   ⒻⓄⓄⓄⒹ▸
Ⓖ A true recording classic, sounding more resplendent than ever in its latest 24-bit remastering. It also now contains a fascinating 50-minute rehearsal sequence.

Brewer; Griffey; LP Choir; LPO / Kurt Masur
LPO LPO0010 (83': DDD)   Ⓕ
With moments of searing insight and power this is a fine if not outstanding reading. Masur's soloists were better on his Teldec recording, though Finley, as always, brings superior musicianship and intelligence to the baritone solos.

Curtin; Di Virgilio; Krause; Chorus Pro Musica; Columbus Boychoir; Boston SO / Leinsdorf
VAI 📀 VAIDVD4429 (89' · PAL · 4:3 black and white · 1.0 · 0).   Ⓜ︎Ⓞ
The *War Requiem*'s US premiere is a genuine moment in history and captured for posterity on this excellent film. Leinsdorf is superb and holds the entire work together, and also draws from his fine soloists performances of genuine distinction.

Harper; Langridge; Shirley-Quirk; St Paul's Cathedral Choir; London Symphony Chorus & Orchestra / Richard Hickox
Chandos CHAN8983/4 (125': DDD)   ⒻⓄⓄⓄⒹ▸
Now available at mid-price, Richard Hickox's admirably incisive and dedicated realisation rightly triumphed in both the Choral and Engineering categories at the 1992 *Gramophone* Awards. Generously coupled with the *Sinfonia da Requiem* and *Ballad of Heroes*.

Woytowicz; Pears; Wilbrink; Wandsworth School Boys' Choir; Melos Ensemble / Britten; New Philharmonia Chorus & Orchestra / Carlo Maria Giulini
BBC Legends BBCL4046-2 (79': ADD)   Ⓜ︎ⓄⓄ
An unmissable live recording from April 1969. Giulini's thrustingly intense and superbly sung account fits snugly onto a single disc. Britten himself directs the chamber forces in the Wilfred Owen settings. A remarkable document.

Dasch; Taylor; Gerhaher; Aurelius Sängerknaben Calw; Stuttgart Festival Ensemble / Robin Engelen, Helmuth Rilling
Hänssler Classic ② 💿 CD98 507 (83' · DDD)   ⒻⓄⓄⓄⒹ▸
A wonderful new recording with three superb soloists, excellent choral work and a fine control of the different orchestral perspectives. The SACD recording makes it well worth considering.

technically assured and wholly dedicated. Only perhaps the classic Decca recording comes near equalling it in this respect, and that doesn't quite have the electrifying atmosphere, found on this astonishing occasion. Nor have the Wandsworth Boys' Choir, placed up in the Hall's gallery, been surpassed.

The soloists also seem to realise the special quality of the occasion. Pears surpasses even his own creator's reading on the Decca set, singing with the sustained concentration and vocal acuity that were so much his hallmarks in Britten's music. The soprano Stefania Woytowicz, who at the time made something of a speciality of this work, has very much the vocal timbre of Vishnevskaya, for whom the part was written, and perhaps a shade more sensitivity. She's certainly the best soprano on any version, and Wilbrink comes near being the best baritone. He may not be quite as varied or subtle as Decca's Fischer-Dieskau, nor as confident as Chandos's Shirley-Quirk, but he has a more beautiful voice than either, with a plangency in his tone that's so right for this music.

Most of all it's the sum of the parts that so impresses here, as does the truthfulness of the sound, preferable to that on the Chandos set.

War Requiem
Galina Vishnevskaya sop **Sir Peter Pears** ten
Dietrich Fischer-Dieskau bar **Simon Preston** org
Bach Choir; Highgate School Choir; Melos Ensemble; London Symphony Orchestra / Benjamin Britten
Decca ② 4757511 (132' · DDD · T/t) Recorded 1963.
Includes previously unreleased rehearsal sequence
Ⓕ❶❶❶❶↦

Decca has used the most recent digital and Cedar technology to improve the original sound, under the overall supervision of veteran technician James Lock. This is one of the great performances of recording history. As an imaginative bonus, Decca gives us the first issue of a long rehearsal tape made by the producer John Culshaw without Britten's approval. When Culshaw presented it to the composer on his 50th birthday, Britten was 'appalled', considering it 'an unauthorised invasion of a territory exclusively his own and his performers', as Donald Mitchell relates in the booklet. Now Mitchell believes that we should be allowed 'to assess the tape as a contribution to our knowledge of him [Britten] as a performer and interpreter of his own music and to our understanding of the *War Requiem* itself.'

Throughout this fascinating document you hear evidence of Britten's vision of his own music, his astonishing ear for timbre and intimate details, above all his wonderful encouragement of all his forces, culminating in his heart-warming words of thanks at the end of the sessions, not to mention his tension-breaking humour and a couple of sharp comments from Vishnevskaya, who's unsurpassed as soprano soloist. The merit of this ground-breaking performance is that it so arrestingly conveys Britten's intentions. We're lucky to have not only Britten's irreplaceable reading refurbished, but also his commentary suggested by the rehearsal sequences.

War Requiem
Annette Dasch sop **James Taylor** ten **Christian Gerhaher** bar **Aurelius Sängerknaben Calw; Stuttgart Festival Ensemble / Robin Engelen, Helmuth Rilling**
Hänssler Classic ② ⓢ CD98 507 (83' · DDD)
Recorded live
Ⓕ❶❶❶❶↦

A wonderful performance and a most moving experience. Critically, one must keep the experience (subjective) as distant from the relatively objective facts of the performance as possible: on this occasion that wasn't very easy, or even desirable. Certainly all the elements in this complex organisation are well served. The soloists are admirable, Annette Dasch pure in tone, powerfully concentrated in style, James Taylor a tenor whose voice can respond to what is gentle and compassionate in his music as to the unsparing harshness, and Christian Gerhaher authoritative, humane and (like the others) entirely firm in his singing. The choir is fine in blend, precision and enunciation; the boys' choir, too, ideal in its embodiment of unsanctimonious sanctity. For the chamber ensemble and full orchestra, only admiration, as for the recording's producer and engineer who have dealt so well with the difficult task of keeping these elements distinct and unifying them at the same time. Above all, we must honour their conductor, whose mature guidance is everywhere in evidence.

It's the sense of unity that has distinguished this experience of the *War Requiem* most especially. Rarely has it moved with such logic. That seems a strange word to use in the description of what was so deeply emotional, yet it's right. For the first time the work moved with the single-minded force of a geometrical theorem. Darkness and light, war and peace, noise and quiet are the unifying opposites throughout. The selection and sequence of Owen's poems are so well-fitting that the line – can you call it 'of argument'? – is unbroken and all goes forward to the almost painful easement of 'Let us sleep now'. Do to try it for yourself.

War Requiem
Phyllis Curtin sop **Nicholas Di Virgilio** ten
Tom Krause bar **Chorus Pro Musica; Columbus Boychoir; Boston Symphony Orchestra / Erich Leinsdorf**
VAI *DVD* VAIDVD4429 (89' · PAL · 4:3 black and white · 1.0 · 0). Recorded live at the Tanglewood Festival, USA, on July 27, 1963
Ⓕ❶

'It makes criticism impertinent,' thought Peter Shaffer of the *War Requiem*, and for all Stravinsky's grousing that any such criticism would be 'as if one had failed to stand up for *God Save the Queen*' the piece still carries as much sense of occasion as it evidently did at this, its American premiere in 1963, a year after its fraught first performance. What a contrast. The *al fresco* acoustic of the Tanglewood Music Shed may have been no more favourable in its way than that of Coventry Cathedral, though, you might think miraculously, there is no trace of indistinctness or inadequacy about the stereo sound preserved by WGBH Boston to accompany its telecast.

Nor is there about the performance, which was evidently prepared with all the care that such an occasion merited. The hero of the hour is pre-eminently Leinsdorf, who picked the work as the centrepiece of his first season as Tanglewood's music director. Whatever else the *War Requiem* stands for, its performance here serves as a conducting masterclass. Leinsdorf stands ramrod-straight, no baton, and his timing and pacing are equally impeccable, honed by his years in the pit at the Met. When he raises his left hand, infrequently, it is either to conduct the chamber ensemble to his left or to indicate 'too loud'. When both arms are aloft and the eyes blaze at the climax of the *Sanctus*, on the upbeat to the 'Hosanna', the response is electrifying, as though all heaven's angels had joined the already excellent Chorus Pro Musica.

It would be easy but misleading to equate the unyielding body language with the interpretation: a strict, dry-eyed tempo for the 'Lacrymosa' makes all the more sense when it eventually contrasts so poignantly with the tenor's desperate cry of 'Was it for this the clay grew tall', as though the ancient liturgy was cracking under the strain of expressive necessity.

The booklet-note accurately summarises Nicholas Di Virgilio's contribution as having 'a robust and honest American style', though he rises to the challenge in the brief but crucial *Agnus Dei* and is less troubled by the *passaggio* between D and F than many Britten tenors past and present. As Di Virgilio does elsewhere, the Finnish baritone Tom Krause perhaps responds more to Britten's setting than to Owen's poetry in 'Be slowly lifted up', though the trumpet obbligato is something of a highlight, and the singer ratchets up the tension for the apocalyptic recapitulation of the *Dies irae*. Phyllis Curtin's soprano matches Leinsdorf for unobtrusive clarity – and she never scoops, despite every Verdian invitation to do so. A one-off event invites excuses for slips of all kinds, but there are none, and the breathless hush from the 11,000-strong audience suggests that the stoic power latent in Britten's testament affected them as it might anyone watching 44 years hence.

AMDG

AMDG. Choral Dances from 'Gloriana'. Chorale after an Old French Carol. Five Flower Songs, Op 47. A-Hymn to the Virgin. Sacred and Profane, Op 91

Polyphony / Stephen Layton
Hyperion CDA67140 (62' · DDD)   Ⓕ**OOO**

The programme is delightful and the choir excellent. *AMDG* presents as formidable a challenge to its singers as any of Britten's compositions for unaccompanied choir. In fact that's sometimes suggested as the reason why, having written it for an expert group in 1939 and realising that its chances of frequent performance were slim, Britten never prepared the work for publication. It's a pity he couldn't have heard Stephen Layton's Polyphony! Even more than the Finzi Singers, their predecessors on record, they've worked it into the system so that they have the sense of it clearly in their mind and can make the word-setting fresh and spontaneous. 'God's Grandeur' (*allegro con fuoco*) has the fire: the Finzis seem almost cautious by comparison. In 'The Soldier' Polyphony catch the swing of the triplets and dotted notes with more panache and make more of the words. They also bring out the tender lyricism in 'Prayer II' and grasp more decisively the *con moto*, *Vivace* and *Avanti!* markings in 'O Deus, ego amo te'.

In the *Five Flower Songs* Polyphony have a young tone and their numbers allow them to convey a sense of round-the-table intimacy. In the *Choral Dances* from 'Gloriana', Polyphony improve on the Finzi Singers' performance with crisper rhythms and a clearer acoustic. *Sacred and Profane*, like *AMDG* a work for virtuosos, is given with wonderful confidence and imagination. A wonderful disc.

Additional recommendation

AMDG
Coupled with: Hymns – to St Peter, Op 56a; of St Columba; to the Virgin; to St Cecilia, Op 27. Rejoice in the Lamb, Op 30. Choral Dances from 'Gloriana'
Finzi Singers / Spicer with **Lumsden** *org*
Chandos CHAN9511 (67' · DDD · T)   Ⓕ
    Very enjoyable performances from this expert choir, successfully directed by Paul Spicer.

The World of the Spirit

An American Overture. King Arthur – Suite (arr Hindmarsh). The World of the Spirit (arr Hindmarsh)
Susan Chilcott *sop* **Pamela Helen Stephen** *mez*
Martyn Hill *ten* **Stephen Varcoe** *bar* **Hannah Gordon, Cormac Rigby** *spkrs* **Britten Singers; BBC Philharmonic Orchestra / Richard Hickox**
Chandos CHAN9487 (79' · DDD · T)   ⒻⒹ▸

Hickox's performance of the Coplandesque *An American Overture* has exemplary polish, commitment and dash. The remaining items owe their revival to the efforts of Paul Hindmarsh. Britten wrote his incidental music for a BBC radio dramatisation of the King Arthur legend in 1937. It was the first of his 28 radio commissions and contains much high-quality invention.

Hindmarsh has fashioned the 23-year-old composer's inventive inspiration into a terrific four-movement orchestral suite lasting some 25 minutes, which Hickox and the BBC PO devour with audible relish.

The 'radio cantata' *The World of the Spirit* dates from May 1938. Commissioned by the BBC as a successor to *The Company of Heaven* (1937), it intersperses sung and spoken texts chosen by R Ellis Roberts. Again, Britten's fertile compositional powers are much in evidence. The work contains a whole string of memorable numbers, from the lilting barca-rolle-like treatment of Emily Brontë's 'With wide-embracing love', via the joyful strut and swagger of Part-2's concluding 'The Spirit of the Lord' with its unmistakable echoes of Walton's *Belshazzar's Feast*, to a strikingly imaginative setting of Gerard Manley Hopkins's *God's Grandeur*. Framing the 42-minute edifice are two radiant settings of the Whitsuntide plainsong, *Veni Creator Spiritus* – an idea possibly inspired by a recent encounter with Mahler's Eighth Symphony at the Queen's Hall under Sir Henry Wood.

The recording is superbly wide in its range and offers a realistic quality.

A Ceremony of Carols, Op 28

A Ceremony of Carols. Missa brevis in D, Op 63. A Hymn to the Virgin. A Hymn of St Columba, 'Regis regum rectissimi'. Jubilate Deo in E flat. Deus in adjutorum meum
Sioned Williams hp **Westminster Cathedral Choir / David Hill** with **James O'Donnell** org
Hyperion CDA66220 (49' · DDD · T)   ⓕ◐

A Ceremony of Carols sets nine medieval and 16th-century poems between the 'Hodie' of the plainsong Vespers. The sole accompanying instrument is a harp, but given the right acoustic, sensitive attention to the words and fine rhythmic control the piece has a remarkable richness and depth. The Westminster Cathedral Choir performs this work beautifully; diction is immaculate and the acoustic halo surrounding the voices gives a festive glow to the performance. A fascinating *Jubilate* and *A Hymn to the Virgin*, while lacking the invention and subtlety of *A Ceremony*, intrigue with some particularly felicitous use of harmony and rhythm. *Deus in adjutorum meum* employs the choir without accompaniment and has an initial purity that gradually builds up in texture as the psalm (No 70) gathers momentum.

The *Missa brevis* was written for this very choir and George Malcolm's nurturing of a tonal brightness in the choir allowed Britten to use the voices in a more flexible and instrumental manner than usual. The effect is glorious. St Columba founded the monastery on the Scottish island of Iona and Britten's hymn sets his simple and forthright prayer with deceptive simplicity and directness. The choir sings beautifully and the recording is first rate.

Hymn to St Cecilia, Op 27

Rejoice in the Lamb, Op 30. Te Deum in C. Jubilate Deo in C. Antiphon, Op 56b. A Hymn to the Virgin. Festival Te Deum, Op 32. Missa brevis in D, Op 63. Hymn to St Peter, Op 56a. A Hymn of St Columba. Prelude and Fugue on a Theme of Vittoria. Hymn to St Cecilia
St John's College Choir, Cambridge / Christopher Robinson with **Ian Farrington** org
Naxos 8 554791 (74' · DDD)   Ⓢ▷

As with other recent records from St John's, there's a freshness, almost a feeling of adventure and a sense that all this choral discipline is an easy yoke. These are excellent performances, the opening item setting a standard which is to be maintained throughout. Buoyant rhythms, precise accentuations and well-pointed contrasts are features of the singing; and the playing of Ian Farrington in accompaniments that are often difficult and always demanding of maximum alertness, is outstanding. Outstanding, too, is the contribution of the trebles. In tone they preserve the traditional John's sound, without exaggerating its so-called continental element. But what impresses most is the sense of imaginative involvement. It's there, for instance, in the *Kyrie* of the *Missa brevis*, and most of all in the 'I cannot grow' section of *A Hymn to St Cecilia*. To this they bring a distinctive excitement, a wide-eyed, breathlessly playful feeling of childlike wonder. The programme itself is highly attractive. The 'hymns' are fully developed compositions, and the canticles are notably independent of tradition (for instance, a quietly meditative note of praise is struck at the start of both Te Deums). The *Missa brevis* makes inventive use of its forces; and *Rejoice in the Lamb*, a masterly expression of the liberal spirit, never ceases to amaze with its evocation of the cat Jeoffry, valiant mouse and staff-struck poet. Recorded sound isn't as vivid as the performances, but this remains a very likeable disc.

Serenade, Op 31

Serenade for Tenor, Horn and Strings, Op 31[a]   Ⓗ
Folksongs[b] – The Bonny Earl o' Moray; Avenging and Bright; The Last Rose of Summer; Sally in our Alley
Walton Façade[c]
[abc]**Sir Peter Pears** ten/spkr [c]**Dame Edith Sitwell** spkr [a]**Dennis Brain** hn [b]**Benjamin Britten** pf [a]**Boyd Neel String Orchestra / Benjamin Britten;** [c]**English Opera Group Ensemble / Anthony Collins**
Decca 468 801-2DM (74' · ADD/DDD) Recorded 1953-4   Ⓜ◐◐

This disc includes one of the great highlights of the whole Britten discography, that first magical recording of the *Serenade*, with Pears in fresh, youthful voice and Dennis Brain's marvellous horn obbligatos, creating *frisson*-making echoes in Tennyson, dark melancholy in Blake, and rippling away exuberantly in Johnson's 'Hymn to

Diana'. What playing! The transfer is faithful; but why on earth couldn't Decca have removed the surface rustle, and above all, the clicks? The coupled Walton *Façade*, however, was a consummate technical and artistic miracle of Decca's mono era. Edith Sitwell and Pears deliver the engagingly preposterous words with bravura insouciance, Collins conducting the English Opera Group Ensemble with matching wit and flair, and even today the 1953 recording sounds almost like stereo.

Serenade. Les Illuminations, Op 18. Nocturne, Op 60.
Ian Bostridge ten **Radek Baborák** hn **Berlin Philharmonic Orchestra / Sir Simon Rattle**
EMI 558049-2 (75' · DDD · T/t)   Ⓕ ❶ ❶ ➔

This recording offers a profoundly considered and technically immaculate traversal of Britten's three great and varied cycles for tenor and orchestra, conceived with Pears's voice in mind. Authoritative as the recordings by composer and tenor may be, there is plenty of room for new insights into such complex and inspired scores.

Bostridge's particular gift for lighting texts from within, and projecting so immediately their images, comes into its own arrestingly in the *Nocturne*. With his vocal agility and vital word-painting at their most assured – allied to surely the most virtuoso account of the obbligato parts yet heard, and Rattle supremely alert – this reading sets a standard hard to equal. Add a perfectly balanced recording and you have an ideal result.

Not that the accounts of the earlier cycles are far behind in going to the heart of the matter. Bostridge catches all the fantasy and irony of *Les illuminations* and projects the text with a biting delivery that stops just the right side of caricature. Rattle and his orchestra are once again aware of Britten's subtleties of rhythm and instrumentation.

The Serenade, most easily accessible of the three works, demonstrates the advantages of recording after live performances. Everything seems fresh-minted and immediate, nowhere more so than in Radek Baborák's bold yet sensitive horn playing. Some of the verbal overemphases that are now part of Bostridge's vocal persona might not have been approved by the composer but for the most part they second the plangent beauty of his voice, which is evident throughout these very personal and satisfying interpretations. Bostridge writes illuminating notes in the booklet, too, adding to the disc's value.

Songs

Harmonia Sacra – Lord! I have sinned; Hymn to God the Father; A Hymn on Divine Musick. This way to the Tomb – Evening; Morning; Night. Night covers up the rigid land. Fish in the unruffled lakes. To lie flat on the back with the knees flexed. A poison tree. When you're feeling like expressing your affection. Not

even summer yet. The red cockatoo. Wild with passion. If thou wilt ease thine heart. Cradle song for Eleanor. Birthday song for Erwin. Um Mitternacht. The Holy Sonnets of John Donne, Op 35
Ian Bostridge ten **Graham Johnson** pf
Hyperion CDA66823 (65' · DDD · T)   Ⓕ

Bostridge is in the royal line of Britten's tenor interpreters. Indeed his imaginative response to words and music may come closer than any to Pears himself. He's heard here in a veritable cornucopia of mostly unfamiliar and unknown songs (the Donne cycle apart), mainly from the earliest period of Britten's song-writing career when his inspiration was perhaps at its most free and spontaneous. The three settings from Ronald Duncan's *This way to the Tomb* nicely match that poet's florid, vocabulary-rich style as Britten was to do again two years later in *Lucretia*, with 'Night', based on a B-minor ground bass, a particularly arresting piece. The Auden settings, roughly contemporaneous with *On this Island*, all reflect Britten's empathy with the poet at that time. The third, *To lie flat on the back*, evinces Britten's gift for writing in racy mode, as does *When you're feeling like expressing your affection*, very much in the style of *Cabaret Songs*. Much deeper emotions are stirred by the two superb Beddoes settings (*Wild with passion* and *If thou wilt ease thine heart*), written when the composer and Pears were on a ship returning home in 1942. *The red cockatoo* itself is an early setting of Waley to whom Britten returned in *Songs from the Chinese*.

All these revelatory songs are performed with full understanding and innate beauty by Bostridge and Johnson, who obviously have a close artistic rapport. The *Donne* Sonnets are as demanding on singer and pianist as anything Britten wrote, hence their previously small representation in the catalogue. Both artists pierce to the core of these electrifying songs, written after, and affected by, Britten's visit to Belsen with Menuhin in 1945. The recording catches the immediacy of these riveting performances. A richly satisfying issue.

'Britten Abroad'
Six Hölderlin Fragments, Op 61[a]. Seven Sonnets of Michelangelo, Op 22[a]. The Poet's Echo, Op 76[a]. Um Mitternacht[b]. Eight French Folksongs[b]
[b]**Susan Gritton** sop [a]**Mark Padmore** ten
Iain Burnside pf
Signum Classics SIGCD122 (74' · DDD)   Ⓕ ❶

Britten is 'abroad' here in the sense that he is occupied with foreign texts. He is also away in time. The breadth of cultural reference is large, involving four languages, none of them his own. The recital, then, challenges its listeners as well as its performers.

And how these two singers have grown, both in voice and artistry. The languages assist in the sense we have of them as being transformed. Mark Padmore in Italian, Susan Gritton in Russian show themselves in new guises. Each is inescapably performing in the shadow of a great original; but even as (in our minds) we hear Pears and Vishnevskaya, recognising that their voices are written into these songs, we can acknowledge these younger artists as worthy successors, and (to be honest) part of us is glad to be hearing them instead. Padmore has now quite a full-bodied ring to his voice at a *forte* (hear him in the strong affirmations of the last sonnet), and Gritton commands an aristocratic concentration of tone, unshakeably firm and precise in its placing.

Iain Burnside more than copes with the formidable technical difficulties, and in many songs (for instance, the last of the Pushkin poems with its ticking clock, or the spinning-wheel in 'File-use' mingling past and present in the old woman's thoughts) we bless the imaginative touch. Recorded sound is fine, as are John Evans's introductory notes.

Albert Herring, Op 39

Albert Herring
Christopher Gillett *ten* Albert Herring **Dame Josephine Barstow** *sop* Lady Billows **Felicity Palmer** *contr* Florence Pike **Peter Savidge** *bar* Mr-Gedge **Robert Lloyd** *bass* Superintendent Budd **Stuart Kale** *ten* Mr Upfold **Susan Gritton** *sop* Miss Wordsworth **Della Jones** *mez* Mrs Herring **Gerald Finley** *bar* Sid **Ann Taylor** *mez* Nancy **Yvette Bonner** *sop* Emmie **Témimé Bowling** *sop* Cis **Matthew Long** *treb* Harry **Northern Sinfonia / Steuart Bedford**
Naxos ② 8 660107/8 (142' · DDD) Libretto available with UK copies only ⑤❍❍➔

Vivid as Hickox's traversal of the score for Chandos may be, Bedford's is just that much more alert, crisper. With his long experience of Britten in the theatre, dating back to *Death in Venice* under the composer's aegis, his timing carries unique authority and, in better sound than the old Decca set can now offer, he even has the edge over the composer's obviously definitive reading. Bedford's players are at least as accomplished as Hickox's, and are caught in a more immediate, less reverberant acoustic.

As for the singers, in almost every case Bedford's are the equal of, or superior to, Hickox's and several surpass Britten's. For instance, Albert was never one of Peter Pears's happiest assumptions; Christopher Gillett makes a more credible mother's boy and does well when he decides to break loose. Where the crucial role of Lady Billows is concerned, Josephine Barstow's commanding performance may not quite be on a par with Sylvia Fisher for Britten, but the difference is small. Susan Gritton gives us a dotty and cleanly sung Miss Wordsworth (Margaret Ritchie, the role's creator must have sounded like this), Robert Lloyd is a simpleton of a Budd (as well sung as any), and Felicity Palmer makes a wonderfully fussy Florence Pike.

It only remains to laud once again the score's many delights as regards technical mastery and subtle characterisation, and to suggest you hurry off to enjoy a real bargain.

Albert Herring   Ⓗ
Peter Pears *ten* Albert Herring **Sylvia Fisher** *sop* Lady Billows **Johanna Peters** *contr* Florence Pike **John Noble** *bar* Mr George **Owen Brannigan** *bass* Mr Budd **Edgar Evans** *ten* Mr Upford **April Cantelo** *sop* Mrs Wordsworth **Sheila Rex** *mez* Mrs Herring **Joseph Ward** *ten* Sid **Catherine Wilson** *mez* Nancy **English Chamber Orchestra / Benjamin Britten**
Decca London ② 421 849-2LH2 (138' · ADD · N/T) Recorded 1964.   Ⓕ❍Ⓞ➔

Also available in the Complete Britten Operas volume 1, also containing Owen Wingrave, Billy Budd and Peter Grimes (475 6020DC8 – eight discs)

Having shown us the grim and nasty side of Aldeburgh life at the beginning of the 19th century in *Peter Grimes*, Britten had fun with its parochial aspects at the end of the century in his comic opera *Albert Herring*, a tale of a mother-dominated shop assistant elected May King because of his virtue, and who's is slipped a laced drink at his crowning and goes off for a night on the tiles, after which he asserts himself. For some tastes, it's proved too parochial; some who otherwise admire the composer are repelled by its self-regarding whimsicality. The possible cure for these people is to listen to Britten's own recording, here marvellously transferred to CD and showing again what a genius the producer John Culshaw was. Britten finds all the humour in the piece, but he gives it a cutting-edge and is totally successful in conveying the proximity of comedy to tragedy in the remarkable ensemble where Albert is thought to have been killed. With the English Chamber Orchestra on peak form, all kinds of Bergian echoes in the score are revealed and some, too, of Verdi's *Falstaff* (Act 3). There's also Sir Peter Pears's brilliant performance as Albert, a genuine piece of perceptive singing-acting. The cast is well-nigh ideal. If only Britten had written more comic operas.

Albert Herring   Ⓗ
Peter Pears *ten* Albert Herring **Nancy Evans** *mez* Nancy **Joan Cross** *sop* Lady Billows **Gladys Parr** *contr* Florence Pike **Margaret Ritchie** *sop* Miss Wordsworth **Otakar Kraus** *bar* Mr Gedge **Roy Ashton** *ten* Mr Upfold **Norman Lumsden** *bass* Superintendent Budd **Denis Dowling** *bar* Sid **Catherine Lawson** *mez* Mrs Herring **English Opera Group / Benjamin Britten**
Nimbus ③ NI5824/6 (133' · ADD · N/T) Recorded live at the Theatre Royal, Copenhagen, on September 15, 1949   Ⓑ

This recording of *Albert Herring* is of considerable historical interest. By the time Benjamin Britten conducted the Decca studio version in 1964, both he and Peter Pears were finding it difficult to recapture the guileless comic spirit so evident here. Plenty of tenors have been able to suggest Albert's blithe gormlessness more naturally than Pears, but in September 1949 (two years after the opera's first performance at Glyndebourne) there was a lightness and flexibility to his voice which could modulate effortlessly into the more dramatic vein the role also calls for.

Nimbus provides a complete version of Eric Crozier's spick-and-span libretto, which comes as close as any Britten set to being self-sufficient as a performable stage play. Some verbal details get lost in a recording that initially seems to be favouring the pit at the expense of the stage, but ears soon adjust to the balance, and the ensemble's experience with, and relish for, this tricky score (all but two were members of the Glyndebourne cast) shines out. The line-up includes particularly characterful contributions from Margaret Ritchie and Otakar Kraus, but there are no weak links, and none of the singers sinks into caricature – something which can easily happen in less tightly knit performances. Britten conducts with immense vitality and needle-sharp attention to shifting moods, evoking frequent but never distracting laughter from an attentive audience. He rewards them with a brief speech at the end, quoting Albert's crucial line: 'Thank you very much!'

A 1949 recording of an opera set in 1900 is a period piece twice over, and the cut-glass vowels of Joan Cross and Nancy Evans suggest degrees of gentility that help to highlight the satirical social nuances of the story, and its knife-edge avoidance of mere cosiness. The booklet gives full details of how the original tapes were made, and the CD transfers and edits have been well done. Tape changes lead to two brief gaps in the opera. The second, near the start of Act 2 scene 2, is the more regrettable, but even this can't honestly be said to damage the special value of this splendid performance.

Billy Budd, Op 50

Billy Budd.
The Holy Sonnets of John Donne, Op 35[a].
Songs and Proverbs of William Blake, Op 74[a]
Peter Glossop bar Billy Budd [a]**Sir Peter Pears** ten Captain Vere **Michael Langdon** bass John Claggart **John Shirley-Quirk** bar Mr Redburn **Bryan Drake** bar Mr Flint **David Kelly** bass Mr Ratcliffe **Gregory Dempsey** ten Red Whiskers **David Bowman** bar Donald **Owen Brannigan** bass Dansker **Robert Tear** ten Novice **Robert Bowman** ten Squeak **Delme Bryn-Jones** bar Bosun **Eric Garrett** bar First Mate **Nigel Rogers** ten Maintop **Benjamin Luxon** bar Novice's Friend **Geoffrey Coleby** bar Arthur Jones [a]**Dietrich Fischer-Dieskau** bar; **Ambrosian Opera Chorus; London Symphony Orchestra / Benjamin Britten** [a]pf
Decca London ③ 417 428-2LH3 (205' · ADD · N/T)
Recorded 1961   Ⓟ**❍❍**➪

Billy Budd is remarkable in having been composed for male voices, yet not once is there any lack of colour or variety. Britten marvellously supports the tenor, baritone and bass voices with extraordinary flair in the use of brass and woodwind. This was the last operatic recording John Culshaw produced for Decca and he again showed himself unsurpassed at creating a theat-

rical atmosphere in the studio. Although there have been several striking and brilliant stage productions of this opera in recent years, not to mention Nagano's recording, it must also be said that both technically and interpretatively this Britten/Culshaw collaboration represents the touchstone for any that follows it, particularly in the matter of Britten's conducting. Where Britten is superb is in the dramatic tautness with which he unfolds the score and his unobtrusive highlighting of such poignant detail as the use of the saxophone after the flogging. But most of all, he focuses with total clarity on the intimate human drama against the background of life aboard the ship.

And what a cast he had, headed by Peter Pears as Vere, conveying a natural authoritarianism which makes his unwilling but dutiful role as 'the messenger of death' more understandable, if no more agreeable. Peter Glossop's Billy Budd is a virile performance, with nothing of the 'goody-goody' about him. Nor is there any particular homo-eroticism about his relationship with Michael Langdon's black-voiced Claggart: it's a straight conflict between good and evil, and all the more horrifying for its stark simplicity. Add to these principals John Shirley-Quirk, Bryan Drake and David Kelly as the officers, Owen Brannigan as Dansker and Robert Tear and Benjamin Luxon in the small roles of the novice and his friend, and the adjective 'classic' can be applied to this recording with a clear conscience. Also on the discs are two of Britten's most sombre song cycles, the *Donne Sonnets* and the *Blake Songs and Proverbs*, the former with Pears, the latter with Fischer-Dieskau, and both incomparably accompanied by Britten. They make ideal complements to *Billy Budd*. This is without doubt a vintage set.

Billy Budd
Simon Keenlyside bar Billy Budd **Philip Langridge** ten Captain Vere **John Tomlinson** bass John Claggart **Alan Opie** bar Mr Redburn **Matthew Best** bass-bar Mr Flint **Alan Ewing** bass Lt Ratcliffe **Francis Egerton** ten Red Whiskers **Quentin Hayes** bar Donald **Clive Bayley** bass Dansker **Mark Padmore** ten Novice **Richard Coxon** ten Squeak **Timothy DuFore** bar Bosun **Christopher Keyte** bar Bosun **Richard Whitehouse** bar Second Mate, Gunner's Mate **Daniel Norman** ten Maintop **Roderick Williams** bar Novice's Friend, Arthur Jones **Alex Johnson** treb Cabin Boy **Tiffin Boys' Choir; London Symphony Chorus and Orchestra / Richard Hickox**
Chandos ③ CHAN9826 (165' · DDD · N/T)   Ⓟ**❍**➪

Britten's score is so often praised that we tend to neglect the distinction of Forster and Crozier's libretto, sung in this set with unerring conviction by its three principals. Keenlyside and Langridge deserve special mention for their arresting sensitivity throughout the final scenes, when they make the utterances of Billy and Vere so poetic and moving: refined tone allied to eloquent phrasing – the epitome of English singing at its very best. Keenlyside has a voice of just the right weight and an appreciation of how Billy must be at once sympathetic and manly. From first to last you realise the lad's personal magnetism in vocal terms alone, explaining the crew's admiration for his qualities. Langridge is the complete Vere, suggesting the man's easy command of men, his poetic soul, his agony of mind at the awful decision placed in his hands to sacrifice Billy. At the opposite end of the human spectrum, Claggart's dark, twisted being and his depravity of thought are ideally realised by Tomlinson, give or take one or two moments of unsteadiness when his voice comes under pressure. In supporting roles there's also much to admire. Mark Padmore conveys all the Novice's terror in a very immediate, tortured manner. Clive Bayley's Dansker is full of canny wisdom. Alan Opie is a resolute Mr Redburn. Matthew Best's is an appropriately powerful Mr Flint, though his large, gritty bass-baritone records uneasily.

Hickox conducts with all his old zest for marshalling large forces, searching out every cranny of the score, and the London Symphony forces respond with real virtuosity. Speeds now and again sound a shade too deliberate, and there's not always quite that sense of an ongoing continuum you feel in both of Britten's readings, which are by and large tauter. But the Chandos, using the revised two-act version, comes into most direct competition with Britten's later Decca set. The latter still sounds well, though inevitably it hasn't the aural range of the Chandos recording. Yet nobody will ever quite catch the creative tension the composer brings to his own work. For all that, the Chandos set benefits from this trio of imaginative singers, and most newcomers will be satisfied with its appreciable achievement.

Billy Budd (original four-act version)
Thomas Hampson bar Billy Budd **Anthony Rolfe Johnson** ten Captain Vere **Eric Halfvarson** bass-bar John Claggart **Russell Smythe** bar Mr Redburn **Gidon Saks** bass Mr Flint **Simon Wilding** bass Mr Ratcliffe **Martyn Hill** ten Red Whiskers **Christopher Maltman** bar Donald **Richard Van Allan** bass Dansker **Andrew Burden** ten Novice **Christopher Gillett** ten Squeak **Matthew Hargreaves** bass Bosun **Ashley Holland** bass First Mate **Simon Thorpe** bar Second Mate, Arthur Jones **Robert Johnston** ten Maintop **William Dazeley** bar Novice's Friend **Manchester Boys' Choir; Northern Voices; Hallé Choir and Orchestra / Kent Nagano**
Erato ② 3984-21631-2 (148' · DDD · N/T)　Ⓜ🄳➤

This recording is an exciting achievement; it restores to circulation the original, four-act version of the score. The crucial difference between this and Britten's two-act revision is a scene at the close of what's here Act 1, in which 'Starry' Vere addresses his crew and is hailed by them as the sailors' champion, thus establishing the relationship between captain and foretopman. It's an important scene, though musically not particularly distinguished. You can quite see why Britten wanted a tauter two-act drama. Nagano gives us a wonderfully full-bodied and detailed account of the score. There are electrifying moments, not least the battle scene, where the listener feels very much in the middle of things, and the end of Act 3 where those tremendous and ominous series of chords represent Vere telling Budd of the sentence of death. Britten, in his studio recording, prefers a leaner sound and a slightly tauter approach all-round – in his hands you feel the tension of the personal relationships even more sharply than with Nagano.

Hampson is very good, singing with all his customary beauty of voice and intelligence of style, though he imparts a touch of self-consciousness that goes against the grain of the writing. Halfvarson, as Budd's antagonist, the evil Claggart, gives us a mighty presence, singing with power and bite, though not always a steady tone. Rolfe Johnson sings his heart out as he presents Vere's tormented soul. For the rest, Gidon Saks makes a dominant Mr Flint, the sailing-master, Richard Van Allan, is here, predictably, a characterful Dansker, and Andrew Burden stands out as a properly scared Novice, far preferable to Tear's placid reading on Decca. The sum here is greater than the parts, and this set can be heartily recommended.

The recording possesses an amazingly wide spectrum of sound: indeed, sometimes the orchestra is simply too loud.

Curlew River, Op 71

Curlew River
Sir Peter Pears ten Madwoman **John Shirley-Quirk** bar Ferryman **Harold Blackburn** bass Abbot **Bryan Drake** bar Traveller **Bruce Webb** treb Voice of the Spirit **English Opera Group / Benjamin Britten** and **Viola Tunnard**
Decca London 421 858-2LM (69' · ADD · T) Recorded 1965.　Ⓜ🄞🄞🄳➤

Curlew River captured completely the composer's fascination with the Japanese Noh play on which it was based. The recording, produced by John Culshaw, was made in Orford Church, and the atmosphere of this unforgettable occasion is preserved. The procession of monks at the beginning and end comes towards us and recedes, just as if we were sitting in a pew. Pears's performance as the Madwoman is one of his finest and most touching, while Shirley-Quirk and Drake are equally authoritative. The voice of the Madwoman's dead son is devoid of the sentimentality that might have been a peril if any treble other than Bruce Webb had sung it, and the inventive and beguiling orchestral score is marvellously played. With the composer and Viola Tunnard directing the performance, this is in a class of its own.

Death in Venice, Op 88

Death in Venice
Sir Peter Pears ten Gustav von Aschenbach **John Shirley-Quirk** bar Traveller, Elderly Fop, Old

Gondolier, Hotel Manager, Hotel Barber, Leader of the Players, Voice of Dionysus **James Bowman** *countertenor* Voice of Apollo **Kenneth Bowen** *ten* Hotel Porter **Peter Leeming** *bass* Travel Clerk **Neville Williams** *bass-bar* **Penelope MacKay** *sop* Strolling Players **Iris Saunders** *sop* Strawberry-seller **English Opera Group Chorus; English Chamber Orchestra / Steuart Bedford**
Decca London ② 425 669-2LH2 (145' · ADD · N/T) Recorded 1973 ⓕ 🔘🔘▶

Also available in the Complete Britten Operas volume 2, also containing A Midsummer Night's Dream, The Rape of Lucretia, The Turn of the Screw and Gloriana (475 60296CD10 – 10 discs)

In his insert-notes, Christopher Palmer has pertinent things to say about the sexual climate of Britten's last opera, *Death in Venice*; but these seem to become of less consequence as you listen to the music. Its potency and inventiveness create this opera's disturbing and intense atmosphere, each episode heightened dramatically by instrumental colouring. Under Bedford's direction each scene is fully integrated into a fluent and convincing whole. This recording was made while Britten was very ill; it omits Aschenbach's first recitative ('I have always kept a close watch over my development as a writer ...'), given as an optional cut in the vocal score, which was published after the recording was made, by which time Britten had changed his mind about this cut and wished it had been included in the recording. Pears's Aschenbach, a very English conception, is a masterly performance, matched by John Shirley-Quirk's assumption of the six characters who are Aschenbach's messengers of death and the Voice of Dionysus.

Death in Venice

Philip Langridge *ten* Gustav von Aschenbach **Alan Opie** *bar* Traveller, Elderly Fop, Old Gondolier, Hotel Manager, Hotel Barber, Leader of the Players, Voice of Dionysus **Michael Chance** *counterten* Voice of Apollo **BBC Singers; City of London Sinfonia / Richard Hickox**
Chandos ② CHAN10280 (152' · DDD · S/T/t/N) ⓕ 🔘🔘▶

This recording in Richard Hickox's Britten series is beautifully played and recorded, and in its all-important central role reunites Hickox with Philip Langridge, so compelling in their earlier set of *Peter Grimes*. Britten tailored the role of Aschenbach so perfectly for Peter Pears's inimitable tenor that it's unlikely any other singer will find it an easy fit. A few years ago Langridge might have been more adept than he is now at handling some of the high-lying lyrical lines, but the compromises in this department are worth making for a singer who's so penetrating in dramatic insight. Hardly a page of the score passes without his vivid delivery opening up some new dimension of the role. As the drama deepens he progressively strips the soul of Aschenbach bare.

His two main colleagues perform to an equally high level. Alan Opie is still in his vocal prime and all seven of his multifarious Dionysiac characters are sharply delineated. The excellent Michael Chance is more ethereal as the Voice of Apollo than James Bowman, and for that reason is preferable by a whisker.

As always, Hickox takes his time over the score, but there's less sense of self-indulgence than in some of his earlier Britten recordings. He raws playing of high quality and generosity of feeling from the City of London Sinfonia. Add an exemplary choral contribution from the BBC Singers and a typically atmospheric Chandos recording, and there's no reason to resist.

Gloriana, Op 53

Gloriana
Sarah Walker *sop* Queen Elizabeth I **Anthony Rolfe Johnson** *ten* Earl of Essex **Jean Rigby** *mez* Countess of Essex **Neil Howlett** *bar* Lord Mountjoy **Alan Opie** *bar* Sir Robert Cecil **Elizabeth Vaughan** *sop* Lady Rich **Richard Van Allan** *bass* Sir Walter Raleigh **Malcolm Donnelly** *bar* Henry Cuffe
ENO Chorus and Orchestra / Mark Elder
Stage director **Colin Graham**
Video director **Derek Bailey**
ArtHaus Musik ⓕ 📀 102 097
(147' · NTSC · 4:3 · PCM stereo · 0). ⓕ
Recorded live at the Coliseum, London, in 1984

It was this staging that conclusively restored the work to the repertory when directed with such utter conviction in Alix Stone's and Colin Graham's evocative sets, and Stone's proud costumes. Many fine singers graced the title-part over the years. Sarah Walker is among the foremost of them. Barstow is, of course, unforgettable, but Walker's portrayal stands up to the comparison and, though a mezzo, she has no trouble with high-line passages.

At the time ENO still boasted fine ensembles. Every other member of the cast surpasses its Opera North counterpart: Rolfe Johnson's manly, hot-headed and finely sung Essex, Richard Van Allan's menacing Raleigh, Jean Rigby's moving Frances Essex, Alan Opie's sly Cecil. Over all presides Mark Elder, projecting a grandly conceived yet subtle account of the whole score, played with acumen by the ENO orchestra. This is an experience of a great company in full flight and should not be missed; it gives the score in its entirety, allowing us to hear what a dramatically varied and superbly crafted piece of work Britten's opera has proved to be.

Noye's Fludde / The Golden Vanity

Noye's Fludde
Owen Brannigan *bass* Noye **Sheila Rex** *mez* Mrs Noye **David Pinto** *treb* Sem **Darian Angadi** *treb* Ham **Stephen Alexander** *treb* Jaffett **Trevor**

BRITTEN'S PETER GRIMES – IN BRIEF

Peter Pears *Peter Grimes* **Claire Watson** *Ellen Orford* **James Pease** *Balstrode* **ROH Chorus & Orchestra / Benjamin Britten**
Decca Legends ② 467 682-2DL2 (142 mins: ADD)
Ⓕ❶❷❸❹▶

💎 A uniquely authoritative set. Britten's Covent Garden forces respond magnificently, and Pears is simply unforgettable in the title-role specially written for him. John Culshaw's newly remastered 1958 production barely begins to show its years.

Jon Vickers *Peter Grimes* **Heather Harper** *Ellen Orford* **Jonathan Summers** *Balstrode*
ROH Chorus & Orchestra / Sir Colin Davis
Philips ② 462 847-2PM2 (146 mins: ADD)   Ⓜ▶
Davis conducts an intensely refreshing performance, dominated by Jon Vickers's searingly passionate Grimes. Heather Harper, too, is quite superb as Ellen Orford.

Anthony Rolfe Johnson *Peter Grimes* **Felicity Lott** *Ellen Orford* **Thomas Allen** *Balstrode*
ROH Chorus & Orchestra / Bernard Haitink
EMI ② 754832-2 (145 mins: DDD)   Ⓕ
Haitink's 1993 set boasts a strong cast, most notably Felicity Lott's outstandingly sympathetic and secure Ellen Orford. Anthony Rolfe Johnson's Grimes is not always as involving as one might wish, and the whole venture lacks the whiff of grease-paint that marks out the composer's own classic version.

Philip Langridge *Peter Grimes* **Janice Watson** *Ellen Orford* **Alan Opie** *Balstrode* **Opera London, London Sym Chorus, City of London Sinfonia / Richard Hickox**
Chandos ② CHAN9447/8 (147 mins: DDD) Ⓕ❶❷
Philip Langridge's Grimes is one of the glories of our age, and Alan Opie's Balstrode is another triumphant assumption. Hickox is in his element.

Glenn Winslade *Peter Grimes* **Janice Watson** *Ellen Orford* **Anthony Michaels-Moore** *Balstrode*
London Symphony Chorus and Orchestra / Sir Colin Davis
LSO Live ② LSO0054 (143 mins: DDD)   Ⓢ▶
A stunning achievement for conductor, chorus and orchestra, and while the performances of the soloists may not match those of Davis's earlier recording, the strikingly powerful LSO forces demand to be heard.

Christopher Ventris *Peter Grimes* **Emily Magee** *Ellen Orford* **Alfred Muff** *Balstrode* **Zurich Opera Chorus and Orchestra / Franz Welser-Möst**
EMI ② **DVD** 500971-9 (150′ · NTSC · 16:9 · PCM stereo, 5.1 and DTS 5.1 · 0)
Quite simply phenomenal! A vision that steps outside the tradition and triumphs!

Anthony *spkr* The Voice of God **Caroline Clack** *sop* Mrs Sem **Maria-Thérèse Pinto** *sop* Mrs Ham **Eileen O'Donnovan** *sop* Mrs Jaffett **Chorus; English Opera Group Orchestra; An East Suffolk Children's Orchestra / Norman Del Mar**

The Golden Vanity
Mark Emney *treb* Captain **John Wojciechowski** *treb* Bosun **Barnaby Jago** *treb* Cabin-boy **Adrian Thompson** *treb* Captain **Terry Lovell** *treb* Bosun **Benjamin Britten** *pf* **Wandsworth School Boys' Choir / Russell Burgess**
Decca London 436 397-2LM (66′ · ADD · T) Recorded 1961, 1966.   Ⓕ

Britten wrote these two works for children, but don't imagine that they're cosy and childish. Many of his friends thought that there remained much of the child in him, and this clearly comes out in the boisterous high spirits of some of this music. By and large, *Noye's Fludde* and *The Golden Vanity* are happy works. *Noye's Fludde* makes invigorating listening. This 1961 performance is immensely vivid, and the enthusiasm of the young singers and instrumentalists is infectious. All the children of East Suffolk seem to be involved in the enterprise: consorts of recorders, bands of bugles, peals of handbell-ringers, plenty of violins, a few lower strings, seven percussion players, child soloists, and a choir as big as you like, enough to give full representation to the 49 different species of animal mentioned in the text. Then three grown-ups, and the English Chamber Orchestra. The skill and imaginative power with which Britten has used these forces defy adequate description. There are inevitably rough edges in the singing and playing, but the spirit is there in abundance.

The same is true of *The Golden Vanity*, and although there's more conscious vocal skill in the singing of the Wandsworth School Boys' Choir, it never gets in the way of the presentation, which bubbles with life.

Owen Wingrave, Op 85

Owen Wingrave
Peter Colman-Wright *bar* Owen Wingrave **Alan Opie** *bar* Spencer Coyle **James Gilchrist** *ten* Lechmere **Elizabeth Connell** *sop* Miss Wingrave **Janice Watson** *sop* Mrs Coyle **Sarah Fox** *sop* Mrs Julian **Pamela Helen Stephen** *mez* Kate **Robin Leggate** *ten* Sir Philip Wingrave; Narrator **Tiffin School Boys' Choir; City of London Sinfonia / Richard Hickox**
Chandos ② CHAN10473 (107′ · DDD · S/T/N)   Ⓕ▶

After experimenting with smaller-scale forms of musical theatre throughout the 1960s, Britten returned to 'grand' opera in *Owen Wingrave*, based on Henry James's pacifist debate about following the flag or one's conscience. Premiered as a TV commission, *Wingrave* enjoyed unmerited Cinderella status among Britten's stage works until the recent TV film conducted by Kent Nagano (with Gerald Finley in the title-role – see below) and an innovative stage production by Tim Hopkins at Covent Garden's Linbury Studio in 2007.

Over the years Richard Hickox has used his studio skills to telling effect in the vocal works of Britten. In this new recording following concert performances, Peter Coleman-Wright is most adept at conveying Owen's pain and troubled conscience, the while never giving way to an over-emotionalism untrue to anyone brought up in a soldier's family. Alan Opie, in what is in many ways the beau role of the military tutor Spencer Coyle, achieves both a superb neutrality and an evident empathy with Owen's decision to quit the military life. Robin Leggate avoids caricature (or simple Peter Pears homage) in the small but essential role of the family termagant, General Sir Philip Wingrave. The women are no less characterful, with an especially sympathetic reading of Coyle's wife from Janice Watson.

Throughout *Wingrave*, Britten's cunning reworking of rhythmic structures and harmonic devices pioneered as early as *Peter Grimes* reaches a new level of plasticity and sophistication. The shimmer of orchestral sound – sometimes impressionistic, sometimes Gamelan-influenced, sometimes wholly percussive – is a still insufficiently appreciated wonder of 1970s operatic writing. The core duets of Coyle/Wingrave, Wingrave/Lechmere and Wingrave/Kate (in which she sets the reluctant soldier the challenge of spending a night alone in the haunted room) are anchored on a sophisticated version of the tonal atonal structures on which Britten had once based *The Turn of the Screw*. It lends the drama an amazing tensile strength, closely parallel to the Berg operas which Britten wanted to get to know better in the 1930s but was discouraged by his teachers from approaching too closely.

The new set, in Chandos's customary natural comfortable sound, becomes the first recording in any medium to do the work full musical and dramatic justice. It should also satisfy the curiosity of those who wonder why its devotees hail *Wingrave* as Britten's greatest completed opera.

Owen Wingrave

Gerald Finley bar Owen Wingrave **Peter Savidge** bar Spencer Coyle **Hilton Marlton** ten Lechmere **Josephine Barstow** sop Miss Wingrave **Anne Dawson** sop Mrs Coyle **Elizabeth Gale** sop Mrs Julian **Charlotte Hellekant** mez Kate **Martyn Hill** ten Sir Philip Wingrave **Andrew Burden** nar **Deutsches Symphony Orchestra, Berlin / Kent Nagano** Video director Margaret Williams ArtHaus Musik ⑩ 100 372 (150' · 16:9 · PCM stereo · 2 & 5) Includes 'Benjamin Britten: The Hidden Heart' – a film directed by Teresa Griffiths Ⓕ**OO**

Britten's penultimate opera was planned to be equally effective on television or in the opera house, but it was its first stage production at Covent Garden that made the bigger impact,. Now this film version, imaginatively directed by Margaret Williams and tautly conducted by Kent Nagano, helps swing the balance the other way.

There's almost nothing stagey about the opera here. The camera roams freely indoors and out, using cleverly executed angles to follow members of the fearsome Wingrave family at their ancestral home, and throwing in flashbacks and voice-overs wherever they might be apposite – much as one might expect of an adaptation of a literary classic. In fact, the period has been updated to the 1950s, which necessitates some minor changes to Myfanwy Piper's libretto (no need to escort the ladies to their bedchambers by candlelight any more) but this handsome version in all other respects stays close to Britten's intentions.

Gerald Finley is a tower of strength as Owen Wingrave, completely believable as the sturdy but sensitive scion of an upper-crust family. The other singers are well cast, and play expertly to the camera.

The 'special feature' on the disc, Teresa Griffiths's three-part biographical film, *Benjamin Britten: The Hidden Heart*, lasts as long as the opera. It focuses on three major works – *Peter Grimes*, the *War Requiem* and *Death in Venice* – and, while its message is somewhat diffuse and the editorial style jumps irritatingly from image to image as if afraid to let the camera come to rest, it does include a wealth of fleeting extracts showing Britten and Pears in performance. Those alone are enough to make it a desirable collector's item.

Peter Grimes, Op 33

Peter Grimes Ⓗ

Sir Peter Pears ten Peter Grimes **Claire Watson** sop Ellen Orford **James Pease** bass Captain Balstrode **Jean Watson** contr Auntie **Raymond Nilsson** ten Bob Boles **Owen Brannigan** bass Swallow **Lauris Elms** mez Mrs Sedley **Sir Geraint Evans** bar Ned Keene **John Lanigan** ten Rector **David Kelly** bass Hobson **Marion Studholme** sop First Niece **Iris Kells** sop Second Niece **Chorus and Orchestra of the Royal Opera House, Covent Garden / Benjamin Britten** Decca ② 467 682-2DL2 (142' · ADD · N/T) Recorded 1958 Ⓕ**OOO**⤇

Also available in the Complete Britten Operas volume 1, also containing Albert Herring, Owen Wingrave, Billy Budd (475 6020DC8 – eight discs)

Ⓖ The Decca set, which in 1958 introduced this opera to many listeners, has never been superseded in its refinement or insight. Britten's conducting, lithe and lucid, reveals his work as a complex, ambiguous drama. Peter Pears, in the title-role written for him, brings unsurpassed detail of nuance to Grimes's words while never losing sight of the essential plainness of the man's speech. The rest of the cast form a vivid portrait gallery of characters. The recording is as live and clear as if it had been made yesterday, and takes the listener right onto the stage. The bustle of activity and sound effects realise nicely Britten's own masterly painting of dramatic foreground and background.

Peter Grimes
Philip Langridge ten Grimes **Janice Watson** sop Ellen Orford **Alan Opie** bar Captain Balstrode **Ameral Gunson** mez Auntie **John Graham-Hall** ten Bob Boles **John Connell** bass Swallow **Anne Collins** contr Mrs Sedley **Roderick Williams** bar Ned Keene **John Fryatt** ten Rector **Matthew Best** bass Hobson **Yvonne Barclay** sop First Niece **Pamela Helen Stephen** mez Second Niece **London Symphony Chorus; City of London Sinfonia / Richard Hickox**
Chandos ② CHAN9447/8 (147' · DDD · N/T)Ⓕ**OO**➸

Any reading that so potently confirms the genius of this piece must have a distinguished place in the discography. In the first place there's Langridge's tense, sinewy, sensitive Grimes. Predictably he rises to the challenge of the Mad Scene; this is a man hugely to be pitied, yet there's a touch of resignation, of finding some sort of peace at last, after all the agony of the soul. His portrayal is tense and immediate, and a match for that of Pears in personal identification – listen to the eager touch at 'We strained in the wind'. The next composite heroes are the members of the chorus. Electrifying as their rivals are, the LSO singers, trained by Stephen Westrop, seem just that much more arresting, not least in the hue-and-cry of Act 3, quite terrifying in its immediacy as recorded by Chandos. Hickox's interpretation has little to fear from the distinguished competition. Many details are placed with special care, particularly in the Interludes and the parodistic dances in Act 3, and whole episodes, such as the Grimes-Balstrode dispute in Act 1, have seldom sounded so dramatic. Once or twice one would have liked a firmer forward movement, as in the fifth Interlude, but the sense of total music-theatre is present throughout.

Of the other soloists, the one comparative disappointment is Janice Watson's Ellen Orford. She sings the part with tone as lovely as any of her rivals on disc and with carefully wrought phrasing, but doesn't have the experience to stand out from the village regulars. Britten's set remains *hors concours*, but that recording stretches over three CDs. Hickox is the finest of the modern recordings: as sound it's quite spectacular, vast in range, with well-managed perspectives and just enough hints of stage action to be convincing.

Peter Grimes
Christopher Ventris ten Peter Grimes **Emily Magee** sop Ellen Orford **Alfred Muff** bar Balstrode **Liliana Nikiteanu** contr Auntie **Sandra Trattnigg** sop Niece I **Liuba Chuchrova** sop Niece II **Rudolf Schasching** ten Bob Boles **Richard Angas** bass Swallow **Cornelia Kallisch** mez Mrs Sedley **Martin Zysset** ten Rev Horace Adams **Cheyne Davidson** bar Ned Keene

Valeriy Murga bass Hobson
Zurich Opera House Chorus and Orchestra / Franz Welser-Möst
Stage director **David Pountney**
Video director **Felix Breisach**
EMI ② 𝗗𝗩𝗗 500971-9 (150' · NTSC · 16:9 · PCM stereo, 5.1 and DTS 5.1 · 0)
Recorded live in December 2005   Ⓕ**OO**

Peter's line 'Where the walls themselves gossip of inquest' – his cry of pain to Ellen after the coroner's open verdict on the loss of his first apprentice – cues the scenery and concept. The Borough, some of its citizens mounted on chairs and pillars permanently suspended above an unchanging set, is never absent from this stylised, Brechtian (and Weillian) production. Pountney's stage has no room for naturalistic clutter – no real boats, no fishing nets, no beach.

The English director's characters step out of years of 'English' ambiguity into a light of glaring every-man (and woman)-for-himself selfishness. Balstrode listens to Grimes (Christopher Ventris, riveting) but only once (the capstan ensemble) does anything to help him; in the pub he gropes the women as much as Boles. Auntie, a red-headed Widow Begbick played with Oscar-winning charisma by Liliana Nikiteanu, and her Nieces are, quite openly, a Madame and her whores. Hobson, another terrifyingly intense portrayal, is a lazy, uncooperative psychopath, roused only by drink and the prospect of violence. Ellen is allowed more intimacy with Peter than one often sees but, as soon as she realises his obsessive work methods will never change, her 'Peter – we've failed' is final, provoking Grimes to inevitable self-destruction. In a penultimate Mad Scene of haunting, almost religious (or sacrilegious) beauty, she and Balstrode sit with a dead boy each draped across their laps, either side of the constantly see-sawing Peter on a stylised boat platform with a cross-like mast. Unforgettable.

Welser-Möst's reading of the score is hardly less innovative, reminding one with its forward, motoric winds of some great, lost Shostakovich score and, in the dance music so present in the pub scenes, of contemporaries Weill and Gershwin.

No *Grimes* on film is without some distinctive merit but this new EMI issue is carried by its cast, phenomenal chorus contribution, director and conductor to an important new interpretative level.

Additional recommendation

Peter Grimes
Vickers Peter Grimes **Harper** Ellen Orford **Royal Opera House Chorus and Orchestra / C Davis**
Philips 462 847-2PM2 (146' · ADD)   Ⓜ➸
A mid-price alternative which enshrines the wonderfully drawn Grimes of Jon Vickers and the touching, immensely human Ellen of Heather Harper. Colin Davis's conducting, too, displays his love of the score.

The Turn of the Screw, Op 54

The Turn of the Screw   H
Sir Peter Pears *ten* Prologue, Peter Quint **Jennifer Vyvyan** *sop* Governess **David Hemmings** *treb* Miles **Olive Dyer** *sop* Flora **Joan Cross** *sop* Mrs Grose **Arda Mandikian** *sop* Miss Jessel **English Opera Group Orchestra / Benjamin Britten**
Decca London mono ② 425 672-2LH2
(105' · ADD · N/T) Recorded 1955   ⒻOO

Also available in the Complete Britten Operas volume 2, also containing A Midsummer Night's Dream, The Rape of Lucretia, Death in Venice, Gloriana (475 60296DC10 – 10 discs)

As Sir Colin Davis has shown on Philips, there's room for an alternative interpretation of this remarkable work, but this superb first recording will remain as documentary-historical evidence of the highest importance and value. Will there ever be a better performance, let alone recording, of *The Turn of the Screw* than this by the original cast, recorded less than four months after the 1954 Venice premiere?

This score is Britten at his greatest, expressing good and evil with equal ambivalence, evoking the tense and sinister atmosphere of Bly by inspired use of the chamber orchestra and imparting vivid and truthful life to every character in the story. As one listens, transfixed, all that matters is Britten's genius as a composer. Jennifer Vyvyan's portrayal of the Governess is a classic characterisation, her vocal subtleties illuminating every facet of the role and she has the perfect foil in Joan Cross's motherly and uncomplicated Mrs Grose. The glittering malevolence of Pears's Quint, luring David Hemmings's incomparable Miles to destruction; the tragic tones of Arda Mandikian's Miss Jessel; Olive Dyer's spiteful Flora – how fortunate we are that these performances are preserved. As with all the Decca/Britten reissues, the transfer is a triumph.

The Turn of the Screw
Ian Bostridge *ten* Prologue, Peter Quint **Joan Rodgers** *sop* Governess **Vivien Tierney** *sop* Miss Jessel **Julian Leang** *treb* Miles **Caroline Wise** *sop* Flora **Jane Henschel** *sop* Mrs Grose **Gustav Mahler Chamber Orchestra / Daniel Harding**
Virgin Classics ② 545521-2 (106' · DDD · N/T/t)
     ⒻOOO

Ⓖ This absorbing version of Britten's arresting masterpiece, derived from Henry James's ever-mysterious short story, is based on the stage performances given by London's Royal Opera in Deborah Warner's controversial staging. It offers a considerable challenge to both the premiere recording, conducted by the composer, and the more recent version conducted by Steuart Bedford. The new recording catches all the sinister fascination of Britten's most tautly composed opera score, so

aptly matched to James's tale and to Myfanwy Piper's evocative libretto.

Daniel Harding extracts the greatest tension from both the finely wrought writing for the chamber ensemble and from the well-balanced and, by and large, exemplary cast. He's helped by the clearest and most detailed recording the work has yet received.

When discussing the merits of the casts one is comparing three teams of undoubted excellence. Nevertheless there are distinctions to be made. As on stage, Joan Rodgers nicely balances the need to suggest the ingenuous and the excitable side of the Governess's nature, which she conveys in a performance that combines clarity of diction with the vocal verities. Bostridge's ethereal, other-worldly, eerily magnetic Quint provides an interesting contrast with Philip Langridge's more forceful and present assumption for Bedford. Both are preferable to Pears's more mannered singing on the pioneering set, but that, needless to say, has its own authority. On the other hand neither Vivian Tierney nor Nadine Secunde (Bedford) quite match the searing sadness of Arda Mandikian's dark-hued Miss Jessel for Britten. In the case of Mrs Grose, Jane Henschel, imposingly as she sings, sounds a trifle too stock-operatic in her responses to words and notes beside the particular gentility of Joan Cross (Britten) or the marvellously detailed and intensely uttered interpretation of Phyllis Cannan (Bedford).

This is an utterly absorbing version. Given its masterly engineering and sense of atmosphere it's, by a hair's-breadth, preferable to the Bedford among stereo recordings. The composer's set remains both a historic document and the tautest reading, but most will prefer and be satisfied with the conviction and the sound of this newcomer.

The Turn of the Screw
Helen Field *sop* Governess **Menai Davies** *mez* Mrs Grose **Richard Greager** *ten* Peter Quint / Prologue **Phyllis Cannan** *sop* Miss Jessel **Machiko Obata** *sop* Flora **Samuel Linay** *treb* Miles **Stuttgart Radio Symphony Orchestra / Steuart Bedford**
Stage director **Michael Hampe**
Video director **Claus Viller**
ArtHaus Musik 🎦 100 198 (114' · 4:3 · 2.0 · 2-8)
Recorded live 1990   ⒻO

Michael Hampe clearly places the audience in the expected quandary as to whether the ghosts are 'real' or a product of the Governess's vivid imagination. The concept is underlined by Helen Field, who makes the role very much her own by her intelligent acting and fine singing of it. The young Samuel Linay could hardly be bettered as Miles, suggesting the boy's innocence and his devilment while singing purely and accurately. Menai Davies brings out all Mrs Grose's generous character and her slight befuddlement at events beyond her ken. Phyllis Cannan is at once a menacing and unearthly Miss Jessel. Richard Greager sings splendidly as Quint but rather misses out on the character's menace. The Flora, as so often with this part, looks too mature. The instrumental playing is superb. The sound balance and video direction faultless. Along with the fine rival version (below), this opera is very lucky on DVD.

The Turn of the Screw
Mark Padmore ten Peter Quint **Lisa Milne** sop
Governess **Catrin Wyn-Davies** sop Miss Jessel
Diana Montague sop Mrs Grose **Nicholas Kirby**
Johnson treb Miles **Caroline Wise** sop Flora City of
London Sinfonia / Richard Hickox
Video director **Katie Mitchell**
Opus Arte **DVD** OA0907D (117' · 16:9 · PCM stereo ·
0) Extra features include Synopsis and Cast Gallery

Ⓕ**OOO**

This film was much lauded when shown on BBC2. Katie Mitchell's arresting production opens up the story, taking it into the countryside and producing spooky and louring images to create the mysterious and dangerous aura of Bly, which does no harm to the intentions of Henry James and Benjamin Britten. Mitchell allows the characters' interior monologues to be heard while the singers' mouths remain closed – especially apt for the role of the Governess.

For about two-thirds of the work the director keeps within the boundaries stipulated by Britten and librettist Myfanwy Piper, making us fully aware of the ambiguities of the participants and their relationships. But in the third part she rather allows her ideas to get out of hand, the nightmarish images becoming too surreal, especially for the ghosts and the children, although she recovers in time to make the final struggle between the Governess and Quint for Miles's soul an arresting close. We're left, as we should be, uncertain at the state of the Governess's mind and the exact powers of the ghosts.

Richard Hickox commands every aspect of the tricky score, lovingly executed by members of his City of London Sinfonia, even if the balance with the singers sometimes goes awry. The cast is splendid. Nicholas Kirby Johnson as Miles achieves just the right balance between innocence and knowingness. His singing is fluent and pointed, as is that of Caroline Wise, a teenage Flora with a lively presence, expressive eyes and a malleable voice. Lisa Milne, unflatteringly garbed, is rather too confident of voice and mien as the Governess. Although she sings with her customary clarity of line and word, she doesn't suggest the nervous vulnerability of Jennifer Vyvyan, who created the role. Diana Montague is a gratifyingly sympathetic Mrs Grose, using body language to convey just the right feeling of apprehension and concern over the fate of her charges. Mark Padmore is among the best of Quints, vocally and histrionically. Catryn Wyn-Davies is a properly wild and scary Miss Jessel. All in all, this is the version to have.

Leo Brouwer
Cuban 1939

Cuban composer and guitarist. He studied in New York (1960-61) but was most influenced by the new music he heard at the 1961 Warsaw Autumn Festival. He has been occupied with being an artist in a revolutionary society; his early works are nationalist, the later ones adopting avant-garde techniques.

GROVEmusic

Guitar Concerto

Guitar Concerto No 5, 'Helsinki' **Albéniz/Brouwer**
Iberia Suite **Lennon-McCartney/Brouwer** From
Yesterday to Penny Lane
Timo Korhonen gtr **Tampere Philharmonic**
Orchestra / Tuomas Ollila
Ondine ODE979-2 (66' · DDD)

Ⓕ**O**

The Concerto No 5, *Helsinki*, was commissioned for the Helsinki Festival but contains no musical reference to that city. As Brouwer explains: 'I compose in Space or in Lightness and Heaviness,' referring to the titles of the first two movements, but whether he ever does so in 'Luminosity', the title of the third, we aren't told. It's a substantial work that's none the worse for its lack of memorable tunes – except to those who regard them as essential. Brouwer's fingerprints abound, especially in the first movement's gestures, made familiar in other (solo) pieces. He has an intimate knowledge of the guitar, and uses the orchestra skilfully and imaginatively. Renaissance composers didn't hesitate to use popular and folk tunes, so why shouldn't today's do likewise? Brouwer describes The Beatles' tunes as 'folk songs of today' and the seven in this recording are set in a variety of pastiche forms, *à la* Wagner, Hindemith, Stravinsky *et al*, a pleasing counterbalance to the serious business of the Concerto. Timo Korhonen is a superb guitarist who takes everything in his clean-fingered stride. The Tampere orchestra shares his zest, and the recording is first-class.

John Browne
English fl c1490

Browne may have been the John (or William) Browne, clerk of Windsor, who died in 1479 or the lawyer and rector of West Tilbury who died in 1498. The Eton Choirbook originally contained 11 antiphons and four Magnificats by him, of which only nine antiphons (two incomplete) and a fragment of a Magnificat remain.

Motets

Music from the Eton Choirbook
O Maria Salvatoris mater. Salve regina. Stabat iuxta Christi crucem. Stabat mater dolorosa. O regina mundi clara

The Tallis Scholars / Peter Phillips
Gimell CDGIM036 (71' · DDD · T/t)   Ⓕ**OOO**⯈

By any other name, John Browne would surely
be recognised as one of the very greatest English composers. The fact that fewer than 10
works survive intact in the Eton Choirbook
(practically the only source transmitting his
music anyway) only adds to his mysterious
aura; the music sends normally dispassionate
specialists reaching for superlatives. He stands
head and shoulders above the other Eton composers, and it's high time he was accorded an
anthology of his own. The discography of
early polyphonic music has made such great
strides that 'landmark' recordings are fewer
and further between; yet this can hardly be
described as anything else.

An index of Browne's stature is the variety of
scorings he deploys. His eight-voice *O Maria
Salvatoris mater* was considered extraordinary
enough to be given pride of place in the Eton
Choirbook, and each of the three six-voice
pieces included here is scored differently. No
other Eton composer wrote so much six-voice
music excluding trebles. Two of his pieces in
this mould (*Stabat iuxta Christi crucem* and *O
regina mundi*) are here recorded convincingly for
the first time. Phillips's line-up of men's voices
(especially on the top lines) is as superb as
Browne's must have been, for an exceptional
keenness of focus is needed to prevent the thick
texture from becoming stodgy; as it is, the sound
of six parts jostling in a compass of under two
octaves is thrilling.

But the pieces with trebles have long been
reckoned Browne's masterpieces; as such, they
have been recorded several times before. Phillips sees Browne as a mystical figure, and his
choice of tempi in the *Stabat mater* and *O Maria*
reflects this. His singers articulate it so convincingly as to suspend disbelief absolutely. The
Tallis Scholars are to be heard at their best in
this repertory; this recording confirms that. If
you don't know Browne's music, you simply
must hear this.

Max Bruch   German 1838-1920

*Bruch studied with Hiller and Reinecke and had
some success with his cantata Frithjof Op 23 (1864)
before taking posts in Koblenz, Sondershausen, Liverpool and Breslau. Official recognition came in 1891
when he became professor at the Berlin Academy.
Although he composed three operas, his talent lay in
epic expression; during his lifetime the secular choral
works Odysseus and Das Feuerkreuz, with their solid
choral writing and tuneful style, sometimes showing
affinities with folk music, were considered particularly significant. Only his violin concertos (especially
the appealing No 1 in G minor), the Scottish Fantasy
for violin and orchestra and the Kol nidrei for cello
and orchestra Op 47 have remained in the repertory.*
GROVEmusic

Clarinet and Viola Concerto, Op 88

Clarinet and Viola Concerto in E minor, Op 88.
Romance, Op 85. Eight Pieces, Op 83
Paul Meyer *cl* **Gérard Caussé** *va* **François-René
Duchâble** *pf* **Orchestra of the Opéra National
de Lyon / Kent Nagano**
Apex 8573-89229-2 (65' · DDD)   Ⓢ

The Double Concerto and the Eight Pieces
both stem from Bruch's later years as a composer, by which time he was ill and tiring, also
embittered and resentful of the successes being
enjoyed by Strauss and Debussy (the latter 'an
unqualified scribbler'). His Concerto isn't only
a backward-looking and inward-looking work:
it's the music of a weary composer with little
more to say but the habit of a lifetime in saying
it. The technique doesn't fail, though the last
movement is thinly stretched; the manner is
still lyrical, and makes graceful use both of the
solo instruments and of the accompaniments.
This is unusually disposed so that the chamber
orchestra of the first movement gradually
swells in numbers until it's virtually a full symphony orchestra for the finale. Some problems
ensue for the viola, which is in any case cast in a
secondary role to the clarinet.

Parity is restored with the *Eight Pieces*, though
Bruch wrote them for the talents of his son Max
Felix, a gifted clarinettist whose performance of
these pieces earned him favourable comparison
with the great Richard Mühlfeld from the conductor Fritz Steinbach. They are pleasant
pieces, sometimes drawing on the tonal companionship which Mozart discovered the instruments to have in his *Kegelstatt* Trio, sometimes
contrasting them with opposing kinds of music.

Violin Concerto No 1, Op 26

Bruch Violin Concerto No 1
[a]**Beethoven** Violin Concerto in D, Op 61[b]
Kyung Wha Chung *vn* [a]**Royal Concertgebouw
Orchestra;** [b]**London Philharmonic Orchestra /
Klaus Tennstedt**
EMI 503410-2 (70' · DDD) [b]Recorded live 1989 Ⓜ**OO**

Kyung Wha Chung has recorded both of these
concertos before, but these performances not
only have the benefit of more modern sound but
are more spontaneous in their expressive
warmth. The Bruch was recorded in the studio
and reflects Chung's growing ease in a recording
environment. Notoriously, she dislikes the constraints of recording, when she's so essentially
spontaneous in her expressiveness. Here her
rubato is freer, so that in the first movement the
opening theme is more impulsive, and her freedom in the second subject conveys the sort of
magic you find in her live performances. The
slow movement brings extreme contrasts of
dynamic and expression from orchestra as well
as soloist, and the finale is again impulsive in its
bravura.

BRUCH'S VIOLIN CONCERTO NO 1 – IN BRIEF

Nathan Milstein; NYPSO / Sir John Barbirolli Ⓗ
Biddulph LAB096 (77' · ADD) ⓂⓄ
Milstein captured on peak form in this memorable 1942 alliance with Barbirolli. A generous sequence of assorted bon-bons make up the remainder.

Jascha Heifetz; New SO of London / Ⓗ
Sir Malcolm Sargent
RCA 09026 61745-2 (65' · ADD) ⓂⓄ
A delectable souvenir of Jascha Heifetz's incomparable gifts. Similarly superlative accounts of Bruch's *Scottish Fantasy* and Vieuxtemps's Fifth Concerto make for ideal bedfellows.

Josef Suk; Czech Philharmonic Orchestra /
Karel Ančerl
Supraphon SU3663-2 (79' · ADD) ⓂⓄ
An irresistibly songful, warm-hearted performance. Suk's sweet, silky tone gives much pleasure, and he generates a profoundly satisfying rapport with Ančerl.

Nigel Kennedy; English Chamber Orchestra /
Jeffrey Tate
EMI 518173-2 (69' · DDD) ⓂⓄⒹ
A powerful reading that's also full of poetry from a youthful Kennedy. It's not been out of the catalogue in 18 years and it's not surprising: this is Kennedy at his most poetic.

Kyung Wha Chung; London Philharmonic
Orchestra / Klaus Tennstedt
EMI 503410-2 (70' · DDD) ⒻⓄⓄ
A freer, more impulsive account than Chung's own earlier Decca recording with Kempe. Tennstedt and the LPO tender powerful support.

Itzhak Perlman; Concergebouw Orchestra /
Bernard Haitink
EMI 356523-2 (77' · DDD) ⓂⒹ
Sweetness and poetry characterise this likeable performance by one of the fiddle's greats. Haitink is a sympathetic accompanist.

Maxim Vengerov; Leipzig Gewandhaus
Orchestra / Kurt Masur
Teldec 4509-90875-2 (51' · DDD) ⓂⓄ
The 19-year-old Vengerov's first concerto disc is a winner all the way. Wonderfully vital, raptly expressive playing that never fails to lift the spirits.

SCO / Jaime Laredo
Regis RRC1152 (54' · DDD) ⓈⓄ
A lovely, sweet-toned version if you're on a budget. Directed from violin by Laredo, the Scottish CO are wonderfully fleet of foot, but also capable of power too (as at the start of the first movement).

The Beethoven is a live recording. Chung sustains spacious speeds very persuasively indeed. She's freely flexible in her approach to Beethoven, as Tennstedt is too, but magnetically keeping an overall command. The element of vulnerability in Chung's reading adds to the emotional weight, above all in the slow movement, which in its wistful tenderness is among the most beautiful on disc. As for the outer movements, they're full of flair, with a live event bringing few if any flaws of ensemble. Altogether, an exceptionally attractive release.

Serenade, Op 75

Serenade, Op 75. Scottish Fantasy, Op 46.
Maxim Fedotov vn
Russian Philharmonic Orchestra /
Dmitry Yablonsky
Naxos 8 557395 (73' · DDD) ⓈⒹ

Though the *Scottish Fantasy*, with its wealth of traditional melodies, ripely presented, is firmly based in the repertory, most of Bruch's other *concertante* works for violin are largely unknown. Here's one of the most ambitious, the Serenade, dating from 1900, 20 years after the Fantasy. Its breadth and weight belies the lightweight title. It's a warm and fluent work in Bruch's high-Romantic style, built on clearly defined themes that lack only the last degree of memorability of the Fantasy. The third of the four movements, a dreamy, lyrical *Notturno*, comes nearest to matching the Fantasy's natural glow, but the other movements have striking moments, too. Bruch had the idea of putting this substantial work among his numbered concertos but changed his mind.

Maxim Fedotov gives a warm, thrusting performance of both the Serenade and the Fantasy. He may be a little short on the mystery and tenderness, but his bravura playing, helped by full-blooded accompaniment from Dmitry Yablonsky, makes the results consistently compelling.

Anton Bruckner   Austrian 1824-1896

Bruckner was the son of a village schoolmaster and organist, with whom he first studied and for whom he could deputise when he was 10. His father died in 1837 and he was sent at 13 as a chorister to the St Florian monastery where he could study organ, violin and theory. He became a schoolmaster-organist, holding village posts, but in 1845 went to teach at St Florian, becoming organist there in 1851. During these years he had written masses and other sacred works. In 1855 he undertook a counterpoint course in Vienna with the leading theorist, Simon Sechter; the same year he was appointed organist at Linz Cathedral. He continued his studies almost to the age of 40, but more crucial was his contact, in 1863, with Wagner's music – first Tannhäuser, then Tristan und Isolde; these pointed to new direc-

tions for him, as the Masses in D minor, E minor and F minor, and Symphony No 1, all written in 1864-8, show.

In 1868, after Sechter's death, he was offered the post of theory teacher at the Vienna Conservatory, which he hesitantly accepted. In the ensuing years he travelled to Paris and London as an organ virtuoso and improviser. In Vienna, he concentrated on writing symphonies; but the Vienna PO rejected No 1 as 'wild', No 2 as 'nonsense' and 'unplayable' and No 3 as 'unperformable'. When No 3 was given, it was a fiasco. No 4 was successfully played, but No 5 had to wait 18 years for a performance and some of No 6 was never played in Bruckner's lifetime. He was criticised for his Wagnerian leanings during the bitter Brahms-Wagner rivalries. His friends urged him to make cuts in his scores (or made them for him); his lack of self-confidence led to acquiescence and to the formal distortion of the works as a result. Late in his life he revised several of his earlier works to meet such criticisms.

Bruckner taught at a teacher-training college, 1870-74, and at Vienna University – after initial opposition – from 1875. Only in the 1880s did he enjoy real success, in particular with Symphony No 7; his music began to be performed in Germany and elsewhere, and he received many honours as well as grants from patrons and the Austrian government. Even in his last years, he was asked to rewrite Symphony No 8, and when he died in 1896 No 9 remained unfinished.

Bruckner was a deeply devout man, and it is not by chance that his symphonies have been compared to cathedrals in their scale and their grandeur and in their aspiration to the sublime. The principal influences behind them are Beethoven and Wagner. Beethoven's Ninth provides the basic model for their scale and shape, and also for their mysterious openings, fading in from silence. Wagner too influenced their scale and certain aspects of their orchestration, such as the use of heavy brass (from No 7 Bruckner wrote for four Wagner tubas) and the use of intense, sustained string cantabile for depth of expression. His musical forms are individual: his vast sonata-type structures often have three rather than two main tonal areas, and he tends to present substantial sections in isolation punctuated by pregnant silences. Huge climaxes are attained by remorseless reiterations of motifs, or, in the Adagios, by the persistent use of swirling figural patterns in the violins against which a huge orchestral tutti is inexorably built up, often with ascending phrases and enriching harmonies. Secondary themes often have a chorale-like character, sometimes counterpointed with music in dance rhythms. Slow movements are often planned (as in Beethoven's Ninth) around the alternation of two broad themes. Scherzos are in 3/4, often with the kind of elemental drive of that in Beethoven's Ninth; they carry hints of Austrian peasant dances, and some of the trios show ländler-like characteristics. From No 3 onwards, Bruckner's symphonies each end with a restatement of the work's opening theme. Because of their textual complications, Bruckner's symphonies have mostly been published in two editions: the Sämtliche Werke series (ed R Haas and others) usually give the work as first written, the Gesamtausgabe (ed L Nowak and others) the revised and cut versions. GROVE music

Symphonies

No 00 in F minor, 'Study Symphony'; **No 0** in D minor, 'Die Nullte'; **No 1** in C minor; **No 2** in C minor; **No 3** in D minor; **No 4** in E flat, 'Romantic'; **No 5** in B flat; **No 6** in A; **No 7** in E; **No 8** in C minor; **No 9** in D minor

Symphonies – Nos 1 (Linz version), 2, 3 (1889 version, ed Nowak), 4-7, 8 (ed Haas) & 9
Berlin Philharmonic Orchestra /
Herbert von Karajan
DG ⑨ Karajan Symphony Edition 4777580
(520' · ADD/DDD) Recorded 1975-81   Ⓜ❍❍❍➔

Karajan's understanding of the slow but powerful currents that flow beneath the surfaces of symphonies like the Fifth or Nos 7-9 has never been bettered, but at the same time he shows how much more there is to be reckoned with: strong emotions, a deep poetic sensitivity (a Bruckner symphony can evoke landscapes as vividly as Mahler or Vaughan Williams) and a gift for singing melody that at times rivals even Schubert. It hardly needs saying that there's no such thing as a perfect record cycle, and Karajan's collection of the numbered Bruckner symphonies (unfortunately he never recorded 'No 0') has its weaknesses. The early First and Second Symphonies can be a little heavy-footed and, as with so many Bruckner sets, there's a suspicion that more time might have been spent getting to know the fine but elusive Sixth.-However, none of these performances is without its major insights, and in the best of them – particularly Nos 3, 5, 7, 8 and 9 – those who haven't stopped their ears to Karajan will find that whatever else he may have been, there was a side to him that could only be described as 'visionary'. As for the recordings: climaxes can sound a touch overblown in some of the earlier symphonies, but overall the image is well focused and atmospheric. A valuable set, and a landmark in the history of Bruckner recording.

Additional recommendation

Symphonies Nos 1-9
Berlin Philharmonic Orchestra; Berlin Radio SO /
Jochum
DG ⑨ 469 810-2GB9 (9 hours 12' · ADD) Recorded 1958-68   Ⓑ➔
If you're used to Karajan's Bruckner, Jochum's approach can appear rather stop-start. But he was a great Brucknerian, and his highly charged, romantically intense, seemingly spontaneous approach will appeal to many. This is a great set with few real weaknesses, except for the Eighth.

Symphonies Nos 1 (ed Carragan) & 3 – Bewegt, quasi Andante (1876 version)
Royal Scottish National Orchestra / Georg Tintner
Naxos 8 554430 (76' · DDD)   Ⓢ❍➔

Some of the outstanding performances in the late Georg Tintner's Naxos Bruckner series have been of the early symphonies. 'Your young men shall see visions,' says the Prophet Joel. It has been Tintner's skill to conjure vision by marrying sharpness of detail and youthful diction with a daring breadth of utterance. He did this in his recording of the Symphony No 3 and he does it again here in a fine account of the First recorded in Glasgow's Henry Wood Hall with the RSNO at the top of its considerable form.

Timings of individual movements confirm a broad reading, as broad as Václav Neumann's on his old Leipzig set. But where Neumann's performance ended up sounding soulful and ponderous, Tintner's is as fresh as could be. Bruckner called this a 'cheeky little minx' of a symphony. Tintner shows it to be that, and more. (Bruckner's own generally unavailing pursuit of cheeky post-pubescent minxes clearly fed a rich and lively fantasy life which the symphony vividly charts. Or so Freudians might have us believe.)

The announcement that this is the 'world premiere recording' of the 'unrevised Linz version' shouldn't cause seasoned collectors to throw out cherished extant recordings of the 1866 'Linz' (as opposed to 1890-91 'Vienna') version. The emendations Bruckner made in 1877 to the 1866 text are fairly minor. That said, future interpreters may want to follow Tintner in using this plainer Haas/Carragan edition rather than the 1955 Nowak edition which, in typically meddling style, incorporates the 1877 changes into the original text. The plainness of the orchestration at the very end of the symphony is absolutely right for a peroration that's both prompt and ingenious.

The fill-up is rather more intriguing textually. It's the largely forgotten 1876 revision of the original 1873 version of the *Adagio* of the Third Symphony. The changes include a quicker tempo, a gentle elaboration of the violin figurations near the start, and a disastrous attempt to underpin the lead to the final climax with a new *Tannhäuser*-like violin accompaniment. Since this is funny in the wrong way, it could be said nicely to complement the main work on the disc which is funny (and fun) in all the right ways.

Symphony No 2 (ed Carragan)
National Symphony Orchestra of Ireland /
Georg Tintner
Naxos 8 554006 (71' · DDD)   Ⓢ ❶❷❸➔

This exceptional recording by veteran Austrian conductor Georg Tintner is in a league of its own. It's a beautifully shaped performance, characterfully played and vividly recorded. What's more, it's, in effect, a gramophone 'first', for though the original, 1872 version of Bruckner's Second Symphony has been recorded elsewhere this is the first to reach a wider market. Not that the differences between editions are hugely significant. What the earlier 1872 version principally offers is the reversal of the order of the two inner movements (the *Scherzo* now

comes before the *Andante*), a full clutch of repeats in the *Scherzo* and Trio, a rather longer development section in the finale, various small changes to the orchestration and the absence of some of the more meretricious tempo markings. What's appealing about the 'full monty' is the feeling it gives of the symphony's Schubertian pedigree: heavenly length joining hands with a deep sense of melancholy and melodic *Angst*. Which brings us to Tintner's reading of the symphony, which is shrewd and affectionate, tellingly phrased and beautifully paced, the moves away from and back to the basic pulse nicely handled. This is Bruckner conducting of the old school. There's also something reassuringly old-fashioned about the playing of the National Symphony Orchestra of Ireland. The entire orchestra has the character of a well-to-do country cousin who's blessedly innocent of the more tiresome aspects of metropolitan life. This is an exceptional recording.

Symphony No 2 (1877 Novak edition)
Vienna Symphony Orchestra / Carlo Maria Giulini
Testament SBT1210 (59' · ADD) Recorded 1974   Ⓕ

Perhaps the greatest of all recordings of the work, spacious, involved, profoundly human. So persuasive is Giulini's interpretation, it makes it almost impossible to take seriously the attempt at a more detached, monumental approach found in Daniel Barenboim's relatively recent Teldec performance. Giulini's ability to convey fervour without sentimentality is little short of miraculous, and it's clear from the way the early stages of the first movement effortlessly project an ideal balance between the lyrical and the dramatic that this reading will be exceptional. The recording might not have the dynamic range of current digital issues, and resonance can sound rather artificial in louder passages. There's also an obtrusive extension of the trumpet triplets seven bars before the end of the first movement. But such things count for less than nothing in the face of a performance which culminates in a finale of such glowing spontaneity you could almost believe that the orchestra are playing it for the first time, and that neither they (nor any other orchestra) will ever play it better.

A fuller and more authentic text of the symphony is available at super-bargain price in Georg Tintner's fine account of the 1872 edition (on Naxos; reviewed above). Serious collectors will need both. Yet the last thing you're likely to feel after hearing Giulini is that there's something inauthentic about this Bruckner. Matters musicological fade to vanishing point, given such communicative genius.

Symphony No 3 (1877/78 version)
Wagner Lohengrin – Act 1, Prelude; Act 3, Prelude
South West German Radio Symphony Orchestra /
Michael Gielen
Hänssler Faszination Musik 93 031 (67' · DDD)
Ⓕ ❶❷❸

The Bruckner is the thing here. This is a truly inspired performance, keenly argued, swift and clean-limbed, yet one that's also sensitive to the characteristic Brucknerian musings in lyric subjects and at points of transitions. Haitink may create more space in the finale's polka-cum-chorale in his 1988 Vienna recording but his account of the finale runs into gearing problems of its own later on.

The Gielen was made over three days in May 1999 in the Festspielhaus in Baden-Baden. It was evidently made with care; yet it sounds live. It even 'settles' as a real performance might, the orchestra shifting focus a few minutes into the first movement as the players begin to illuminate the drama from within rather than merely sounding it from without. Like Haitink, Gielen includes the scampering coda to the third movement which Bruckner added to this 1877 revision in January 1878. It's a curious afterthought which can sound trite. Not so here. Gielen's performance of the *Scherzo* and Trio is so lithe and fiery you half expect the music to race on beyond its accredited end.

Brucknerians who lust after the weight and unfailing security of the Berlin or Vienna string ensembles may have a few reservations about this Gielen version. The Gielen is *hors concours* principally because of the intuitive brilliance of a reading which profiles so vividly the ardent, aspiring mood of a provincial musician, intoxicated by his craft, giving his all in the service of the god Wagner to whom the work was dedicated.

Symphony No 3 (1873 version)
**Stuttgart Radio Symphony Orchestra /
Sir Roger Norrington**
Hänssler Classic CD93 217 (61' · DDD)   Ⓕ Ⓞ↱

Since he first recorded the symphony in 1995, Sir Roger has modified his tempo in the first movement. His brisk though no longer over-quick tempo works superbly with and through the spare, pellucid, finely honed texturing he draws from the Stuttgart orchestra, an ensemble which under his guidance has brought the art of playing modern instruments in old ways to a new pitch of excellence. There are wind and string sonorities here such as you would expect to hear in music of the Baroque period, something that suits early Bruckner especially well.

The vibrato-free Stuttgart strings play with a purity and simplicity that merits the epithet Cistercian. There are spellbinding moments of quiet at the start and finish of the first movement development and throughout the slow movement (a requiem, in part, for Bruckner's lately deceased mother). The all-in-one *Scherzo* and Trio is also betwitchingly done, fiery but with grace and charm to spare.

One thing Sir Roger has not modified is his quick-fire treatment of the finale's second theme: the counterpointing of polka and chorale inspired by Bruckner's experience of hearing dance music issuing from a house while nearby a revered colleague lay in his coffin. Karl Böhm in

his wonderfully idiomatic VPO recording of the 1889 version takes this at a leisurely 52 bars per minute, the usual pace for a *Polka française* (as opposed to *Schnell-Polka*) in Viennese ballrooms at the time. That reservation aside, this is a touching and exhilarating new account of the Third.

Symphony No 3 (1889 version, ed Nowak)
Mozarteum Orchestra, Salzburg / Ivor Bolton
Oehms OC722 (58' · DDD)   Ⓕ

Though you might wonder at the idea of the Salzburg Mozarteum Orchestra playing Bruckner, they have been doing so for many years. Joseph Schröcksnadel's history of the orchestra reproduces a poster from July 1928 advertising a performance of the Fifth Symphony conducted by Bernhard Paumgartner in the Cathedral Square. In 2004 Ivor Bolton took over as music director, and judging by this excellent 2007 Bruckner Third, it would seem that he has made a difference.

The deftness and buoyancy with which the opening string ostinatos are realised indicate qualities of grace and manoeuvrability that more than make up for the fact that the orchestra will never command the weight or fire-power of, say, Böhm's Vienna Philharmonic, an ensemble that also brings to the third- and fourth-movement dance subjects a properly Austrian tread.

There have been outstanding versions of this 1889 version from Wand, Karajan, Böhm (the latter currently available as a two-CD set that also includes a fabulous Fourth – see above) and others besides. However, with few, if any, of these surviving as single-CD releases, this admirable new Oehms CD might be said to have the market at its mercy.

Symphony No 4
Berlin Philharmonic Orchestra / Günter Wand
RCA Victor Red Seal 09026 68839-2
(69' · DDD) Recorded live 1997   Ⓕ Ⓞ Ⓞ Ⓞ

The pacing of each movement is majestic. Not too fast in the first movement; a slow, contemplative tread in the second; animated, but capable of opening out into something more leisurely in the Scherzo; varied, but with the sense of an underlying slow pulse in the finale. Wand allows himself some fairly generous rubato from time to time, halting slightly on the high unaccompanied cello phrase in the first movement second subject. From the start there's something about his performance that puts it in a different league from rivals. There's the depth and richness of the string sound in the opening tremolo. A few seconds later the Berlin Philharmonic's principal horn intones the opening phrases so magically and majestically that it's hard to believe you aren't listening to a real voice – a superhuman larynx, not just a contraption of brass and valves. The sound is, to some extent, the orchestra's own, but there's a feeling that the players are giving

BRUCKNER SYMPHONY NO 4 – IN BRIEF

Vienna PO / Karl Böhm
Decca 446 374-2DM (68' · ADD) Ⓜ❶❶❶❶🅑➔

💎 A classic performance from 1973, in which both orchestra and conductor rise to the challenge with one of the freshest, most endearing interpretations ever recorded. (Also coupled with a fine No 3 on an excellent Double Decca, 448 098-2DM2.)

Berlin PO / Günter Wand
RCA 09026 68839-2 (69' · DDD) Ⓕ❶❶❶

💎 Recorded live at the Philharmonie, Berlin in 1997, and taking a *Gramophone* Award on its release, this is a fine souvenir of the Wand way with Bruckner: thoughful, structurally as safe as houses and beautifully phrased, every note lavished with attention. Truly inspired.

Berlin PO / Herbert von Karajan
EMI 768872 (70 mins: ADD) Ⓜ❶🅑➔
Berlin PO / Herbert von Karajan
DG 439 522-2GGA (64' · ADD) Ⓜ🅑➔

The EMI was Karajan's first recording of the work (1970) and demonstrates his credentials as a Brucknerian. Beautifully recorded, it still sounds splendid. The DG version dates from five years later. Both show an innate grasp of the work's architecture.

Royal Concertgebouw Orchestra / Nikolaus Harnoncourt
Warner Elatus 2564-60129-2 (65' · DDD) Ⓜ🅑➔
A fresh and refreshing view of Bruckner's Fourth, more exciting than is usual with a delightful rustic gait and very light on its toes. Well worth considering for a slightly unconventional approach to Bruckner.

Royal Scottish National Orchestra / Georg Tintner
Naxos 8 554128 (73' · DDD) Ⓢ🅑➔
A CD that matches value with musical insight: Tintner was an experienced Brucknerian and gives a reading full of poetry and delightful incident. Good playing from the RSNO. A real bargain.

Philharmonia Orchestra / Lovro von Matačić Ⓗ
Testament mono SBT1050 (76' · ADD) Ⓕ
Coupled with a stereo recording of the rarely encountered Overture in G minor, von Matačić's 1954 Bruckner Fourth is a fine one, though for many the Schalk edition used, with its substantial cuts, may count against it.

Staatskapelle Dresden / Herbert Blomstedt
Dal Segno DSPRC045 (76' · ADD) Ⓜ❶❶
Originally issued on the Denon label, this is a very fine, beautifully judged and, above all, musical performance. The sound is still mighty fine.

extra for Wand, something with more inner life; and the unaffected eloquence and shapeliness of the phrasing is all Wand. It carries you along even when the rubato ought to jar, as it does sometimes in other versions.

This is a concert performance, and feels like one. Things that work in concert aren't always ideal solutions on a repeatable commercial recording. Take Wand's big *ritardando* at the fleeting reference to Brünnhilde's Magic Sleep motif in the finale – the effect might pall after a couple of playings. But then he does ease very effectively into the weird *pianissimo* cello and bass figures that follow, triplet quavers gradually becoming triplet crotchets. The sound quality is excellent.

Symphony No 4
Vienna Philharmonic Orchestra / Karl Böhm
Decca Legends 466 374-2DM (68' · ADD) Recorded 1973 Ⓜ❶❶❶❶🅑➔

Böhm's VPO account of the Fourth Symphony has the unmistakable stamp of greatness. It was made in the Sofiensaal in Vienna with its helpful acoustic; for though you can detect a whisper of tape-hiss if you put your ear against the loudspeaker, in almost every other way the sound is realistic and warm. There's a roundness in the brass tone with plenty of bite and fullness but no unwanted rasp – especially important in this symphony. Böhm's Fourth is at the head of the field irrespective of price. The warmth as well as the mystery of Bruckner are far more compellingly conveyed in Böhm's spacious view than with any other conductor.

Symphony No 4
London Philharmonic Orchestra / Klaus Tennstedt
LPO LPO0014 (71' · DDD) Ⓜ
Recorded live in 1989

The physical and psychological variables of live music-making can lead musicians to adopt stratagems which are disagreeable and distracting when repeated on record. Tennstedt, curiously, was not such a musician. For all that his performances are vibrant and alive, they tend to be of a piece. There was never anything manufactured or self-conscious about his music-making.

This live Bruckner Fourth is certainly a performance sufficient unto itself. Most conductors worth their fee can make an effect with the glowingly atmospheric first movement and hunting *Scherzo*. It is quite another thing to be able to make sense of the fallibly drafted finale and trickier still to give the impression that the two outer movements are of a piece, culminating in a coda that truly 'arrives'. Tennstedt achieves all this. As to the inner movements, his tempo for the *Andante* is unnecessarily broad, though the playing itself is poetic and precise, the climax finely achieved. The *Scherzo*, by contrast, is rather quick. The horns, led by Nicholas Busch in whose honour the recording is released, retain their composure at this driving pace; the trumpets are inclined to shout.

The Royal Festival Hall was never a good Bruckner venue. The acoustic shows chordal sonority to advantage but tends to be unforgiving in soaring climaxes and sudden *fortissimi*. For that reason alone, this is not a 'library' Fourth to set beside the classic versions. Not that admirers of Tennstedt, an under-recorded conductor, are going to lose much sleep over such a caveat.

Symphony No 4
Royal Concertgebouw Orchestra /
Nikolaus Harnoncourt
Warner Elatus 2564-60129-2 (65' · DDD)　　Ⓜ🅱➔

If you're expecting something controversial here you'll probably be disappointed. Harnoncourt's Bruckner Fourth is nothing like as provocative as his Beethoven. It's relatively fast, but not startlingly so. If Harnoncourt's first movement is more gripping, more like a symphonic drama than usual, that has more to do with the crisp, clear rhythmic articulation than with the number of crotchets per minute. The solo woodwind and horn playing that follows is lovely, expansive enough; what else would you expect from the Concertgebouw in Bruckner? This is an unusually compelling Bruckner Fourth – exciting throughout the first movement and *Scherzo*, and in passages like the problematical Brucknerian Ride of the Valkyries that erupts after the finale's bucolic second theme. In many more traditional Bruckner performances the bass often seems to move in sustained, undifferentiated pedal points. In Harnoncourt's version you're often aware of a deep pulsation – like the throbbing repeated notes that open the finale – continuing, however discreetly, while the tunes unfold above. To hear the finale's second theme in this version is to be reminded that Bruckner was an excellent dancer, light on his feet until he was nearly 70. Of course, you shouldn't confuse the man with the musical personality, but why should Bruckner always sound heavy, sedentary, as though slowly digesting a gigantic meal? Harnoncourt provides us with the light-footedness, while allowing the music to unfold at its own speed, to take time. There's no question that Harnoncourt must be considered a serious contender in Bruckner.

Symphony No 5
Philharmonia Orchestra / Benjamin Zander
Telarc ② 2CD80706 (149' · DDD)　　Ⓜ❍❍❍🅱➔
Includes bonus disc of Benjamin Zander discussing Bruckner Symphony No 5

Yet another Bruckner Fifth? Not exactly. The performance, which has its own distinction, comes with an 80-minute bonus disc of unusual quality and interest. Not since the halcyon days of Antony Hopkins 'Talking About Music' has there been a commentary as lucid, as approachable and yet as musically satisfying as this.

Devised by Zander and his co-producer David St George, it is a multifaceted essay. Mapping the symphony has pride of place and is superbly done. It also thrives on a rich array of music examples tucked with consummate skill in, around and beneath the narrative.

Another distinctive touch is his breathing new life into the old cathedral analogy. The CD comes with a foldaway leaflet. On one side is a cathedral floor-plan, on the other the structure of the Fifth Symphony laid over that same plan. Nor does Zander stop there. His profound and often moving remarks on time, space, spiritual struggle and spiritual renewal grow naturally out of this.

His trump card is his father Walter Zander, who died in 1993 at the age of 95. In the summer of 1918, while fighting on the Russian front, Walter was sent a score of Bruckner's Fifth Symphony by his mother. His letters home with their comments on what the music meant to him have only recently reappeared. These, too, have been woven into the narrative, and very remarkable they are.

Despite his father's urging, Zander did not study the symphony until he was past 60. Antony Hopkins once said that some of his best scripts were written on works he knew little about before writing. Zander seems to have been similarly blessed, creating a remarkable narrative and complementing it with a performance of great lucidity and drive. If the finely geared playing seems a touch lightweight in places, turning up the level of the beautifully judged Watford Coliseum recording helps bulk out the vertical dimension.

Symphony No 5 (ed Haas/Nowak)
Vienna Philharmonic Orchestra /
Nikolaus Harnoncourt
RCA Red Seal 🔊 82876 60749-2 (73' · DDD/DSD)
Recorded live 2004. Includes a disc of rehearsal excerpts　　Ⓕ❍❍

Nikolaus Harnoncourt's Fifth is more a realisation than an interpretation, musically vivid but spiritually serene. Serene but now slow. By the clock, this is one of the quickest Fifths on record, though only the *Adagio* is taken more swiftly than usual. It was here that Bruckner began the symphony in the pit of despair in 1875 with a keening oboe melody he marked 'Sehr langsam' but scored *alla breve*. Harnoncourt treats it *allegretto* after the manner of a threnody by Bach or Mozart, whose Requiem is quoted during the course of the movement. Furtwängler, surprisingly, took a similar view of the movement.

The 'liveness' of the live performance owes much to Harnoncourt – his persona fuelling the music-making not the concept, which is as it should be – though the superlative playing of the Vienna Philharmonic is also a factor. The light-fingered realisation of the exquisite string traceries is a constant source of wonder; *tutti*s are glowing and unforced. The hall of the Musikverein helps, too; with an audience present it offers a uniquely natural-sounding Bruckner acoustic. This is a performance of rare vision and strength.

Symphony No 6
Stuttgart Radio Symphony Orchestra /
Sir Roger Norrington
Hänssler Classic ② CD93 219 (52' · DDD)
Recorded live   ⒡❶❷▸

Bruckner's Sixth has always been the most elusive of the composer's mature symphonies. Treat it 'as a kind of music we have never heard before' wrote an admiring Donald Tovey in 1935. But few have. Only that grand old iconoclast Otto Klemperer, and now Sir Roger, have had the courage to recognise the piece as an epic off-the-wall revel.

Not that Norrington downplays the symphony's moments of introspection. No symphony, not even Beethoven's revel in A, can be a total knees-up. Norrington is aware where the outer movement song-subjects and their attendant harmonic adventures are going to land us. Even more than Klemperer (see below), he takes the main themes of these movements at quite a lick (the finale especially so, at some cost to orchestral equanimity in the lyric countersubject) though as with Klemperer the pulse of the lyric subjects remains proportionate. Where Norrington is fearless is in Bruckner's on-the-spot shifts of tempo or key. But, then, he has always rather relished the shock of the obvious.

It is difficult to outsmart Klemperer in the *Adagio* since he too divides his fiddles and deploys minimal vibrato. He is also a touch quicker than Norrington and has a more keenly recorded first oboe. That said, Norrington generates real tension in the harmonically indeterminate climax before the recapitulation. And Norrington's is the more gamesome third movement, the downbeats in the *Scherzo's* plodding string ostinato cheekily accented. With its rustic vigour and devil-may-care insouciance, this is a performance that really does tell it as it is.

Symphony No 6
Deutsches Symphony Orchestra, Berlin /
Kent Nagano
Harmonia Mundi HMC90 1901 (57' · DDD)   ⒡▸

'Bruckner's Sixth Symphony is not easy to play,' says Habakuk Traber in his fine booklet essay. Nor is it easy to conduct; witness the fact that no one these past 40 years has seriously challenged Klemperer's sublimely direct account of the work (see below). In fact, Kent Nagano's reading is not unlike Klemperer's: purposeful and big-boned. Even in the finale, where Nagano takes too brisk an opening tempo and thereafter does too much stopping and starting for comfort, the performance coheres inasmuch as he appears to have an overview of the work, and the will to enforce it.

In a symphony where, as Traber suggests, the home key of A major is easier to perceive on the printed page than to hear in performance, conductors often end up not seeing the wood for the trees. Nagano, happily, appears to have moved to higher ground. Like Klemperer, he establishes moments of real gravitational pull, ensuring that the first movement's critical passages – the exposition, the glorious transition to the recapitulation, and the celebrated coda which sent Sir Donald Tovey into such raptures – are commandingly done. The slow movement, the work's epicentre, is played with great solemnity, serious and fine, and the *Scherzo* is more or less perfectly judged.

The recording, made in the Berlin Philharmonie, is clear and robust with woodwind and brass well in the picture.

Additional recommendation

Symphony No 6
Coupled with: **Gluck/Wagner** Iphigénie en Aulide Overture **Humperdinck** Hänsel und Gretel Overture
New Philh, Philh / Klemperer
EMI download 562621-2 (80' · ADD)   Ⓜ❶❷❸❹▸
    Klemperer's performance is masterly from first note to last. It is a performance by turns lofty tender and serene, but it is, above all, a structurally cogent performance and within the compass of its steady-treading tempos an intensely exciting one. (Not currently listed, but worth tracking down.)

Symphony No 7 (ed Haas)
Vienna Philharmonic Orchestra / Herbert von Karajan
DG Karajan Gold 439 037-2GHS (66' · DDD)   ⒡❶

The Vienna Philharmonic features on what was Karajan's last recording, an idiomatic account of Bruckner's Seventh Symphony, lighter and more classical in feel than either of his two Berlin recordings yet loftier, too. As for the Original-image bit-processing you need go no further than the first fluttered violin *tremolando* and the cellos' rapt entry in the third bar to realise how ravishingly 'present' the performance is in this reprocessing. Or go to the end of the symphony and hear how the great E major peroration is even more transparent than before, the octave drop of bass trombone and bass tuba 13 bars from home the kind of delightfully euphoric detail that in 1989 only the more assiduous score-reader would have been conscious of hearing. This remastered Seventh is definitely pure gold.

Symphony No 7
Sinfonia Varsovia / Jerzy Semkow
Dux DUX0668 (65' · DDD)   ⒡❶❷

Once in a while a performance of Bruckner's Seventh Symphony will descend from on high like a benediction. This performance recorded in 2005 in the cathedral of St Mary Magdalene in Warsaw is one such, which may explain why it was singled by Dux to mark the 80th birthday of the Polish-born Jerzy Semkow.

Semkow studied with Mravinsky in Leningrad before beginning his professional career at the Bolshoi. The reference books also speak of work with Bruno Walter, whose 1961 CBS recording of the symphony this to some extent resembles. Though the opening movement is as contemplative as it can reasonably afford to be, it is sustained by a single pulse, subtly flexed. With individual themes nicely characterised and points of arrival expertly prepared across all four movements, this is a benign and beautiful reading, well judged as to both pacing and architecture.

As with many such Bruckner performances, the work appears to be rooted in its inner string parts – the violas, cellos and second violins. In this respect it is also a somewhat Giulini-like reading. If the first violins seem a little sparse of tone, the horns are superb, as are the light-toned Warsaw trumpets. Semkow's old-fashioned skills with orchestral balance have clearly helped the engineers: it's hard to recall a better-made cathedral recording, the sound focused and warm.

The recording is based on a live performance. There are some minor glitches and one major one – a sudden unannounced jump in dynamic level in the final three bars of the first movement. Be that as it may, this birthday tribute to Semkow is rich in musical interest. Collectors of conducting memorabilia might well be drawn to it.

Symphony No 7 (ed Haas)
Royal Scottish National Orchestra / Georg Tintner
Naxos 8 554269 (66′ · DDD)   ⓈⒹ▸

In the absence of recommendable budget or super-budget recordings of Bruckner's Seventh Symphony, this will do nicely. It's a finely schooled performance, chaste and discreet, with a notable reading of the *Adagio* which lies at the heart of the work. Tintner sees this very much as a piece, the first (G major) climax finely achieved, the later, greater climax splendidly 'placed'. The coda, Bruckner's lament for the dead Wagner, is played relatively swiftly, touchingly and without bombast. In general, his reading of the score is loyal without being in any sense dull or hidebound. In an ideal world, the playing of the first violins would be more consistently secure *in alt*. In particular, you have the feeling that both the players and the engineers (the engineering is generally excellent) would have benefited from a chance to refine and tidy parts of the performance of the first movement. A notable bargain, none the less.

Symphony No 7 (ed Haas)
Aarhus Symphony Orchestra / James Loughran
Danacord DACOCD655 (67′ · DDD)

BRUCKNER'S SYMPHONY NO 8 – IN BRIEF

Vienna PO / Herbert von Karajan
DG download only (83 mins: DDD)   ⒻⓄⓄⓄⒹ▸
Bruckner's longest *Adagio* has perhaps never radiated such warmth as in Karajan's last and most integrated recording of the Eighth, with the Vienna Philharmonic more flexible than their Berlin rivals for the conductor.

Hallé Orchestra / Sir John Barbirolli
BBC Legends BBCL4067-2 (74 mins: ADD)   ⒻⓄⓄ
An electric live performance – the last Barbirolli gave in London – in which the tragic first movement casts a baleful shadow over the rest. Not for the faint-hearted, or for those who like their Bruckner opulent.

Vienna PO / Carlo Maria Giulini
DG ② 445 529-2GMA2 (88 mins: DDD)   ⓂⓄⓄ
Giulini takes such loving, paternal care over inner parts that his spacious tempi rarely register as such. Opulence never obscures the sure-footed journey from C minor to major.

Berlin PO / Günter Wand
RCA ② 74321 82866-2 (87 mins: DDD)   ⒻⓄⓄⓄ
The last of Günter Wand's recordings of the work, but one which shows an ever-deepening desire to present all of its many sides, from the unrelieved tension of the first movement, through the Olympian dance of the *Scherzo* to the finale's unifying triumph.

North German RSO / Günter Wand
RCA 09026 68047-2 (88 mins: DDD)   ⒻⓄⓄ
Wand's second recording of the work with 'his' orchestra, and many would say his finest of all. Lubeck Cathedral's acoustic bestows its own benediction – the audience is understandably awed into silence.

Vienna PO / Boulez
DG 459 678-2GH (76 mins: DDD)
TDK 🅓🅥🅓 DV-VOPBR (95 mins)   ⒻⓄ
Boulez's famed clarity of ear results not in the antiseptic traversal some might expect but lends a startling clarity and sense of purpose to Bruckner's symphonic argument. A superbly 'terraced' orchestral balance in the best Bruckner tradition.

Vienna PO / Furtwängler   Ⓗ
Music & Arts CD-764 (77 mins: ADD)   ⓂⓄⓄ
Furtwängler judged this work as the finest of all symphonies. Hear this terror-filled, midwar performance and you understand why.

Munich PO / Celibidache
EMI ② 556696-2 (107 mins: DDD)   Ⓕ
Bruckner never sounds the same again once heard through Celibidache's patient, prismatic analysis. You'll love it or you'll hate it.

Recorded live at Aarhus Cathedral in 2005　Ⓕ

During his time with the Hallé (he succeeded Barbirolli, though since the early 1980s he has worked mostly abroad, in Germany, Japan, and in Denmark where he was principal conductor of the Aarhus SO from 1996 until 2003), James Loughran made some memorable recordings of the Beethoven symphonies (including a ground-breaking *Eroica*) and a set of the Brahms symphonies which even now would wipe the floor with most rival budget-price sets. It is no surprise, then, to hear him conducting a fine live Bruckner Seventh which the Aarhus orchestra has seen fit to preserve on record. The first two movements are especially successful, Loughran showing real mastery in commuting between the first movement's lyrical and giocoso elements within the context of a larger overall vision.

The orchestra's manager freely admits that it is rare for recordings to be made in the 'acoustically difficult' Aarhus Cathedral. If that is the case, sound engineer Clemens Johansen is something of a miracle-worker. A slightly backward woodwind sound notwithstanding, the sound doesn't seem at all cathedral-like. One does wonder, however, to what extent the acoustic was a problem for the orchestra in the *Scherzo* and those parts of Bruckner's tellingly brief finale which are unusually quick-moving and closely argued.

Symphony No 8 (ed Haas)
London Philharmonic Orchestra / Klaus Tennstedt
LPO LPO0032 (74' · ADD)　　　　　Ⓜ〇〇

Tennstedt's performance of Bruckner's mighty Eighth Symphony is high on adrenalin from the very first minute and remains so for the next 73. There were times during the performance when, had the law of physics permitted it, the speakers would have glowed white. Not all Brucknerians will approve of so unremittingly intense a performance – the *Scherzo*, for example, treated as a rip-roaring festive joust – though it is impossible to fault Tennstedt on the cogency and long-term reach of the reading. When it comes to seeing the symphony whole, hewn as it were from a single block of marble, he is up there with the best: Barbirolli, Furtwängler, Karajan, Klemperer. The players, the brass in particular, are also high on adrenalin. Given the dry, bright, somewhat unaccommodating Festival Hall acoustic, this doesn't always make for easy listening. The audience greets the performance with its own ecstatic yawp. But, then, they heard the real thing, not this all too brazen aural précis.

Symphony No 8 in C minor (ed Haas)
Hallé Orchestra / Sir John Barbirolli
BBC Legends BBCL4067-2 (74' · ADD) Recorded live 1970　　　　　　　　　　　　Ⓕ〇〇

At the time of this concert in May 1970 there were just three recordings of Bruckner's Eighth

Symphony in the catalogue; now there are more than 50, and counting. This performance is that rare thing, an intensely dramatic Bruckner Eighth. It isn't often that you hear an account of the turbulent first movement as thrilling as this. The jagged downward slashes of the trumpets are terrible to experience, yet the space that opens up after the vast and glorious E flat cadence 40 bars later is the very reverse, a way to heaven even from the gates of hell. The odd stumble in the brass, the occasional cough are immaterial. This isn't a performance for those who measure out their life in coffee spoons. The *Scherzo* is ferociously quick with a Trio of compensating loftiness. The loftiness returns in the *Adagio* which Barbirolli again projects urgently and with a full heart. Plaintive winds, trenchant brass, and speaking strings, full-bodied and emotionally intent, build the heaven on earth that Bruckner envisions. To hear why this is great music-making, listen to the coda and the gloriously articulated long string recitative that underpins it. The finale, too, is fairly gripping, though there's a brief tired patch midway.

The Festival Hall's fierce acoustic suits the performance well and the engineering is spectacular for its day. Barbirolli was mortally ill when this concert took place. He died just 10 weeks later. 'This might be the old man's last, so let's make it a good one,' the players were saying at the time. By all accounts, Karajan's last live Bruckner Eighth was a lofty, out-of-life experience. Barbirolli's is the very opposite, a case of 'Do not go gentle into that good night/Rage, rage against the dying of the light.' It's a one-off, eloquent beyond measure: the boldest, bravest Bruckner Eighth on record.

Symphony No 8 in C minor (ed Haas)
Berlin Philharmonic Orchestra / Günter Wand
RCA Red Seal ② 74321 82866-2 (87' · DDD) Recorded live 2001　　　　　　　　Ⓕ〇〇〇

Few readings have been more assiduously toured or generally acclaimed than Wand's Bruckner Eighth yet Wand himself struggled to better on record the exact and far-seeing account of the symphony he made with the Cologne RSO in 1979. In January 2001 he harnessed the Berlin Bruckner sound to his own particular ends, a potentially Sisyphean task for a man then nearing his 90th birthday.

And the rewards are here. This Eighth is exceptionally fine. When in the *Scherzo* you sense that the mountains themselves are beginning to dance, you know you're onto a good thing; on this occasion, Olympus itself seems to have caught the terpsichorean bug. Not that anything is exaggerated or overblown. Wand knows where each peak is and how best to approach it. His reading is broader than it was 20 years ago, yet nowhere is there any sense of unwanted stasis. Wand draws from the orchestra, the brass and strings in particular, sound of great power and transparency which the engineers have translated in a recording of uncommon reach and splendour. This is a grand and worthy memento for the tens of thousands who heard Wand conduct the symphony in the concert hall.

Symphony No 9
Berlin Philharmonic Orchestra / Daniel Barenboim
Elatus 0927-46746-2 (63' · DDD) Recorded live   Ⓜ️Ⓞ

This is an outstanding version of Bruckner's Ninth Symphony. Like Karajan's reading on DG, it's essentially a 'central' account of the score that attempts neither extreme breadth of utterance nor sharp-edged drama. Rather it's a reading that combines long lines, flowing but astutely nuanced, and sonorities that are full-bodied yet always finely balanced. The outer movements have great rhetorical and emotional power; the *Scherzo* is thunderous and glinting by turns. The *Adagio* begins very slowly but, for once, Barenboim gets away with it, the movement growing organically rather than remaining still-born near the start. This is a live performance and, as you would expect, it's superbly executed, the playing every bit as fine as it is on the Karajan recording. But even that doesn't compete with the natural splendours of this issue. This is superb Bruckner sound, spacious and clear, with strings, woodwind and brass at once unerringly 'placed' and finely matched. Given good engineering and the kind of astute playing we have from Barenboim and the Berliners, the Philharmonie is far from being the acoustic lemon it's sometimes said to be. This is a front-runner for this symphony.

Symphony No 9
Vienna Philharmonic Orchestra / Nikolaus Harnoncourt
RCA Red Seal SACD/CD hybrid ② 82876 54332-2 (131' · DDD) Includes a workshop concert with commentary by Harnoncourt   Ⓕ

Harnoncourt's flirtations with Bruckner haven't always impressed. He didn't seem to 'know' the symphonies as the old master Brucknerians did. But this live Salzburg Ninth is glorious. There's no sense here of fallible rhythms or a conductor not being able to see the wood for the trees. Like all great interpreters of the Ninth, Harnoncourt treats the opening movement as a vast tripartite structure – exposition, countervailing statement, and coda – which can be taken in a single glance. Nor is there any falling off in the *Scherzo* or the great concluding *Adagio*, both of which are beautifully paced and expertly realised in terms of each new harmonic salient. In beauty of sound and accuracy and articulacy of ensemble, the Vienna Philharmonic matches, even occasionally surpasses, its own high standards in this work. All of which must have helped the Teldex engineers, who make the acoustically problematic Grosses Festspielhaus sound like one of the great Bruckner halls.

Additional recommendations

Symphony No 9
Saarbrücken Radio Symphony Orchestra / Skrowaczewski
Arte Nova Classics 74321 80781-2 (61' · DDD)   Ⓢ
A very closely controlled performance. Skrowaczewski has taken enormous care over the preparation of the performance and the results tell in orchestral playing of a quality and articulacy that few ensembles could rival.

Symphony No 9
Stuttgart Radio Symphony Orchestra / Carlo Maria Giulini
Video director **Agnes Meth**
ArtHaus Musik 📀 101 065 (123' · 4:3 · PCM stereo · 0)   Ⓕ

'My intention always has been to arrive at human contact without enforcing authority … The great mystery of music-making requires real friendship among those who work together.' So said Carlo Maria Giulini, now living in seclusion in Milan. From the first few moments of the rehearsal, you know that he practises what he preaches, a gracious, spiritual presence whose stature doesn't preclude him from apologising at one point to the solo horn for suggesting a misleading dynamic: 'Sorry, that is my mistake – it sounds too much like Debussy.' If you're unfamiliar with Bruckner's Ninth (the one he left incomplete at his death), then this absorbing hour-long sequence will prove a stimulating, unmissable introduction; for aspiring conductors and Brucknerphiles, this and the live concert performance as an essential purchase for repeated viewing.

Masses

No 1 in D minor; **No 2** in E minor; **No 3** in F minor

Masses – Nos 1[a], 2 & 3[ba]
Edith Mathis, [b]**Maria Stader** *sops* [a]**Marga Schiml,** [b]**Claudia Hellmann** *mezzos* [a]**Wiesław Ochman,** [b]**Ernst Haefliger** *tens* [a]**Karl Ridderbusch,** [b]**Kim Borg** *basses* **Bavarian Radio Chorus and Symphony Orchestra / Eugen Jochum**
DG ② The Originals 447 409-2GOR2 (148' · ADD · T/t) Recorded [a]1963, [b]1971, [c]1972.   Ⓜ️ⒶⒾ↦

Like Bruckner, Eugen Jochum came from a devout Catholic family and began his musical life as a church organist. He would have known the Mass texts more or less inside out, which explains why his readings focus not on the sung parts – which, for the most part, present the text in a relatively four-square fashion – but on the orchestral writing which, given the gloriously full-bodied playing of the Bavarian orchestra, so lusciously illuminates familiar words. He approaches the Masses with many of the same ideas he so eloquently propounds in his recordings of the symphonies and the music unfolds with a measured, almost relaxed pace which creates a sense of vast spaciousness. This can have its drawbacks: you can be so entranced by the beautifully moulded orchestral introduction to the *Benedictus* from the D minor Mass that the entry of a rather full-throated Marga Schiml comes as a rude interruption. DG's transfers are extraordinarily good – they really seem to have produced a sound which combines the warmth of the original LP with the clarity of detail we expect from CD.

Mass No 2ª. Ave Maria. Christus factus est. Locus iste. Os justi. Pange lingua, 'Tantum ergo'. Vexilla regis. Virga Jesse floruit
Polyphony; ªBritten Sinfonia / Stephen Layton
Hyperion CDA67629 (70' · DDD · T/t)   Ⓕ Ⓞ

Hyperion long ago paid signal service to Bruckner's mature settings of the Mass with recordings by Matthew Best's Corydon Singers of all three (see review of the F minor below). Interestingly, their 1985 recording of the E minor Mass has just been re-reissued on the budget Helios label, providing pretty powerful opposition to any new release, let alone one at full price. But while the Corydons were the choir *par excellence* on Hyperion in the 1980s and '90s, the torch has been passed to Polyphony, whose sound is, if anything, even more smoothly rounded, more fully blended and more sumptuous. In Stephen Layton, too, they have a director who is every bit as openly communicative, and while Best reveals the soul of Bruckner's sacred utterings more intensely, Layton (who also uses the 1882 version), produces such gorgeous sound from his singers that the overall listening experience is infinitely satisfying.

There's no doubt that the latest Hyperion recording, made in Ely Cathedral, has more presence and atmosphere than that made over 20 years earlier in St Alban's Church, Holborn. That certainly helps produce an ideal balance between wind ensemble and singers, the delicate woodwind flutterings of the *Benedictus* providing a delicious undercurrent to the broad, spacious choral lines. The rare moments of climax are nicely restrained and never impinge on the overall calmness of Bruckner's setting.

Splendid as the performance of the Mass is, the seven unaccompanied motets which surround it on this disc are absolute gems. An ethereal account of *Ave Maria* has a breadth and grandeur which belies its short time-span; as the vocal lines crowd in on each other, the effect is nothing short of electrifying. And popular as it is, if there is to be a 'definitive' interpretation on disc of *Locus iste*, this has to be it. Put simply, we're unlikely to hear choral singing as fine as this for a good few years to come.

Mass No 3. Psalm 150 in C
Juliet Booth sop **Jean Rigby** mez **John Mark**

Ainsley ten **Gwynne Howell** bass **Corydon Singers and Orchestra / Matthew Best**
Helios CDS440713 (68' · DDD · T/t)   Ⓕ

The F minor Mass can certainly be regarded as being among the finest music Bruckner ever created. The intensity of religious feeling is heightened rather than diminished by the sumptuous orchestral support, and the soaring melodies and opulent harmonies are somehow purified and enriched by the devotional character of these familiar texts. Matthew Best's performance, by understating the music's abundant richness, gives tremendous point to the inner conviction of Bruckner's faith. His orchestra, sounding as if it has been playing this music all its days, plays with commendable discretion, balancing admirably with a relatively small choral body. As with everything the Corydon Singers and Best turn their hands to, it's an impeccable performance, infused with real artistry and sensitive musicianship. Enhanced by the glorious solo voices from a high-powered team this is a CD of rare depth and conviction.

Te Deum

Te Deumª. Symphony No 1
ªJessye Norman sop ªYvonne Minton mez
ªDavid Rendall ten ªSamuel Ramey bass
Chicago Symphony ªChorus and Orchestra / Daniel Barenboim
DG download 435 0682 (69' ·DDD)   Ⓜ ➡

The download-only reissue of this 1980 Chicago recording of the boisterous First Symphony (in its original Linz version of 1866) under Barenboim is a very attractive choice, particularly if you don't mind adding to your collection a superb – eloquently sung, expertly played, exceptionally well recorded – account of Bruckner's mighty *Te Deum*. In it, the Chicago Symphony Chorus boasts basses to challenge the magnificent Samuel Ramey himself. The tenor could be better matched, though hardly more ardent. As for Jessye Norman's all-too-brief contribution, it so ravishes the ear as to leave one frustrated that Bruckner did not entrust more of the work to the siren-voiced daughters of Eve.

In the symphony, Barenboim is witty, affectionate and vital and the Chicago playing is sumptuous without in any way being bland or suffocating. Here and there one might long for the countrified tread of Jochum, a German Bruckner conductor of the old school, but one can understand DG's desire to give the best of this Barenboim Bruckner cycle another airing.

Antoine Brumel   French c1460-c1515

A singer at Notre Dame, Chartres, from 1483, Brumel became Master of the Innocents at St Peter's, Geneva, by 1486. He was installed as a canon at

Laon Cathedral by 1497 and the following year took charge of the choirboys at Notre Dame, Paris. In 1501-2 he was a singer at the Duke of Savoy's Court in Chambéry, and from 1506 to 1510 acted as maestro di cappella to Alfonso I d'Este. He was prominent among the composers who ranked, after Josquin Desprez, as the most eminent masters of the late 15th and early 16th centuries. He was primarily a composer of sacred music, notably of Masses (15 survive complete). He also wrote motets. The secular works also frequently use pre-existing melodies; the four-part pieces have texts but those in three parts are purely instrumental. GROVEmusic

---

Missa Et ecce terrae motus

Missa Et ecce terrae motus
Ensemble Clément Janequin; Toulouse Saqueboutiers / Dominique Visse
Harmonia Mundi HMC90 1738 (58' · DDD · T/t) Ⓕ

Until somebody finds Ockeghem's 36-voice motet (which almost certainly did exist) Brumel's so-called 'Earthquake Mass' must count as the earliest seriously large composition – not just in its 12 voices, used together almost throughout, but also in its sheer length.

Another reason it's so long is that Dominique Visse likes to linger over particular passages and bring out some of the inside details. This is most welcome, because the previous two recordings of the cycle (Paul Van Nevel in 1990 and Peter Phillips in 1992) tended to keep a steady tempo and charge past much of the lovely inner writing Visse makes more audible. Especially in the 'Benedictus' and the *Agnus Dei*, he reveals new glories in this enormously complicated score. His flexibility of tempo also makes it possible for the singers to give more value to the texts, which is again a welcome change.

His recording is fundamentally different in other ways, too. Whereas Phillips had 24 voices and no instruments, and Van Nevel had four instruments, Visse has 12 voices and 12 instruments. Whether Brumel is likely to have had such forces around 1500 seems unlikely, but it brings certain advantages: it makes it possible fto pitch the whole thing fairly low without losing clarity on the crucial bottom lines and to have men singing the top line.

The result has a slightly nasal quality that isn't at all in line with what we expect here; those who dislike this may be a lot happier with the direct brilliance of The Tallis Scholars under Peter Phillips. But it's a beautifully balanced ensemble with a coherent and unusual sound; and it brings out unexpectedly different qualities in the music. If you love this work, one of the most fascinating and original of the years around 1500, you'll want this recording alongside the others.

Missa pro defunctis
La Rue Missa pro defunctis
The Clerks' Group / Edward Wickham
Gaudeamus CDGAU352 (56' · DDD · T/t) Ⓕ

This is the first complete recording of Brumel's setting and it makes an interesting contrast to La Rue's, being conceived in a simpler idiom. Brumel seems far less inclined than La Rue to draw out the contrapuntal possibilities inherent in the plainchant, and his setting of the *Dies irae* (the first polyphonic setting that survives) makes little of the text's famously vivid imagery. Is it the less accomplished setting, then? Not necessarily: few of the earliest Requiem settings are particularly striking in their 'response' to the text, and Brumel is in this sense the more typical of its time.

But there are two significant exceptions – those of Ockeghem and La Rue. Though less overtly dramatic than Ockeghem's (on which it is surely modelled), La Rue's Requiem abounds in affecting inflections, especially in the latter movements. It is also scored for remarkably low-pitched voices and there seems no reason for The Clerks' Group not to revel in the depth and lung-power of their basses. Their reading deepens in gravity along with the work itself, and by the end it carries such conviction that one is compelled to return to it. Brumel is well worth hearing, but on balance La Rue deserves top billing.

Gavin Bryars   British b1943

Bryars studied philosophy at Sheffield University and music privately; in the 1960s he played in jazz groups and since 1970 he has lectured at Leicester Polytechnic. A leading experimental composer, influenced by Cage and Satie, he first wrote for indeterminate forces (The Sinking of the Titanic, 1969), but more recently his music has been influenced by theories of literature; it is often repetitive and witty. His opera Medea was staged in 1984. GROVEmusic

---

String Quartets

String Quartets – No 1, 'Between the National and the Bristol'; No 2; No 3
Lyric Quartet (Jonathan Carney, Edmund Coxon *vns* Nick Barr *va* David Daniels *vc*)
Black Box BBM1079 (63' · DDD) Ⓕ

A quiet strain of melancholy passes through all three of Gavin Bryars's string quartets, though the Third and latest – which was commissioned by, and is dedicated to, the Lyric Quartet – has a bardic feel to it that's quite unlike the others. Part of the reason lies in the use of pure intervals which in turn reflects a passing preoccupation with the world of early music.

Bryars' original plan for the First Quartet had been to create a sort of compositional séance where memories of such past masters as Ysaÿe, Hindemith and Schoenberg would be conjured musically. In the event it's the Second Quartet that's more suggestive of musical side references: to John Adams of *Shaker Loops* and the Schoenberg of *Verklärte Nacht*, though these are probably just coincidental similarities.

All that needs to be said about the music Bryars says himself in the booklet-note, much as he did for the Balanescu Quartet's Argo CD of the first two quartets. There the coupling is *Die letzten Tage* for two violins but this disc will hold the greater appeal for those building their quartet repertoire on CD. Comparing the two versions finds the colour-conscious Balanescu employing a subtler range of nuance while the Lyric press for greater emphases and rather more in the way of inner voice detail. Either disc will probably find you returning to this haunting, though by no means immobile, music again and again.

Choral works

Bryars Lauda 22. Lauda 23. Lauda 24. Glorious Hill. Cadman Requiem. **Ešenvalds** Legende de la femme emmurée **Vasks** Zilis zina **Anonymous** Fammi cantar l'amor. Dammi conforto Dio
Latvian Radio Choir / Ieva Ezeriete,
Kaspars Putninž, Sigvards Klava
GB Records BCGBCD09 (78' · DDD)   Ⓟ Ⓓ→

Gavin Bryars's music and the special qualities of the Latvian Radio Choir fit one another like hand and glove. And the glorious acoustic of Riga Cathedral lends its aura to his *Cadman Requiem* and two 13th-century chants (the latter chosen because they relate to, and effectively offset, the three Bryars *Laude*).

All this music has a restrained purity that never admits suspicions of opportunism, in the way some work in this spiritual minimalist field does. There is more floridity to Eriks Ešenvalds's *Legend of the Walled-up Woman*, but this too feels like part of the natural voice of the music and its subject matter. Only in Peteris Vasks's *Zilis zina* does the impression surface of special effects for special effects' sake. And even that can be taken as an effective vehicle for this remarkable choir to display the full range of its talents.

Bryars's 12-minute *Glorious Hill*, which lends its title to this generously filled disc, sets a marvellous Italian Renaissance text that imagines God addressing Adam as He confers free will on mankind. Even more powerful in its inspiration and consistent in its focus is the *Cadman Requiem*, composed in memory of a friend killed in the 1988 Lockerbie disaster. In this new version with organ rather than strings or viols, the music is utterly gripping, and affinities with the Fauré Requiem stand out in ways not previously registered. Overall then, an eminently collectable disc, beautifully sung and recorded from first note to last..

Leichtentritt. From 1924 onwards he completed his training in London. He first became known as a pianist, making his début in London in 1927, and later in Berlin and New York. During the 1930s he was well known in England and was a regular broadcaster. However, composition was his chief interest, and from about 1935 he devoted more and more time to it. For several years before his early death he was a sick man, often unable to work. It was in pursuit of better health that he settled at Woolacombe, in Devon, where his last compositions, mainly elegiac in tone, were written.

Concertos

Cello Concerto[a]. Piano Concerto[b]
[a]**Raphael Wallfisch** vc [b]**Piers Lane** pf
Royal Philharmonic Orchestra / Vernon Handley
Lyrita SRCD320 (52' · DDD)   Ⓟ Ⓓ→

Here's another rewarding discovery courtesy of Lyrita, this time two substantial concertos by a composer born in London in 1901 to naturalised German parents. William Busch initially studied piano in Berlin with Wilhelm Backhaus and Egon Petri in the early 1920s, as well as composition under John Ireland, Alan Bush (his close friend and near-contemporary) and Bernard van Dieren.

Nerves scuppered a promising career on the concert platform, so from the mid-1930s onwards Busch decided to devote himself full-time to composition. He died tragically young, aged just 43, the victim of a brain haemorrhage, shortly after the birth of his daughter, Julia.

The Cello Concerto bears a dedication to Florence Hooton (who first performed it at a 1941 Prom) and proves a beautifully wrought, enviably terse yet warm-hearted score, its modal lyricism and appealingly ruminative manner strikingly prescient of Finzi's gorgeous Cello Concerto (lovers of the latter should most certainly lend an ear). Premiered in January 1939 with the composer as soloist partnered by Sir Adrian Boult and the BBC SO, the Piano Concerto wears a knottier, more harmonically adventurous demeanour which shows a shrewd awareness of continental trends audaciously out of kilter with attitudes prevailing within the British musical establishment of the period, its meaty opening *Allegro* and finale (a resourceful theme and 32 variations) framing a bittersweet central *Allegretto tranquillo*.

As one might expect from the calibre of the artists involved, the performances are all one could wish for. Eminently truthful sound and balance, too for this enterprising coupling, which is definitely worth seeking out.

William Busch   British 1901-1945

Busch studied the piano in Berlin with Leonid Kreutzer – and to some extent with Backhaus and Egon Petri – and harmony and composition with Hugo

Alan Bush   British 1900-1995

Bush studied at the Royal Academy of Music and privately with John Ireland, going on to study musi-

cology and philosophy at Berlin University. In 1925 he began teaching at the RAM and in 1936, already a committed communist, founded the Workers' Music Association. His earlier works (Dialectic for string quartet, 1929; First Symphony in C, 1940) are progressive, using his own 'thematic' method, in which each note must be thematically significant. After the war he simplified his style and began a series of operas expressing his political beliefs: Wat Tyler (1953), Men of Blackmoor (1960), The Sugar Reapers (1966) and Joe Hill (1970), all produced in East Germany.   **GROVE**music

Chamber Works

Three Concert Studies, Op 31[abd]. Two Easy Pieces[ad]. Two Melodies, Op 47[ac]. Sonatina, Op 88[ac]. Concert Piece, Op 17[ad]. Summer Valley, Op 125[ad]
[a]**Catherine Summerhayes** pf **Adam Summerhayes**
[b]vn/[c]va [d]**Joseph Spooner** vc
Meridian CDE84458 (67' · DDD)   Ⓕ

The challengingly rhapsodic *Concert Piece* for cello and piano was written prophetically as war clouds were gathering in Europe. The music's angst expresses real despair, the harmony bleakly astringent. Yet there's a touching central cantilena of the utmost sadness before the malevolent closing section with its march rhythms builds to an urgent and uncompromising climax. One then turns to the balm of the Sonatina for viola with its pastoral atmosphere (the opening and close might almost be by Vaughan Williams) or the lovely, very English evocation of a *Summer Valley* (ravishingly played here). These three artists have obviously lived with this music and play very sympathetically indeed and with fine ensemble.

There's all the expressive power needed in Op 17, while the central 'Nocturne' of the Op 31 *Concert-Studies* for piano trio is haunting in its gentle atmospheric feeling, and the closing 'Alla Bulgaria' great fun. The two charming *Easy Pieces* for cello, and the pair for viola (both with piano) show Bush's disarming melodic gift.

In short, this CD combines excitement and real stimulation, lyrical strength and musical pleasure, in varying measure. Let John Amis, who wrote the booklet notes, have the final word. He tells us that 'Bush was a delightful man' who 'wrote music for head and heart, and many times managed to combine the two elements…these [works] are all masterly and endearing.'

Ferruccio Busoni

Italian/German 1866-1924

Born to musician parents, an Italian father and a German mother, Busoni appeared from the age of eight as a pianist. In 1876 the family settled in Graz, where he had lessons with Wilhelm Mayer and produced his first published works. He then moved to Vienna, where he came to know Goldmark and

Brahms, to Leipzig and eventually Berlin in 1894. Until he was 40 his output consisted mostly of piano and chamber music, including arrangements of Bach (these were eventually published in seven volumes). But in 1902 he began conducting concerts of modern music, including works by Debussy, Bartók, Sibelius and himself, and his music began to open itself to a wider range of influence. He adopted an aesthetic of 'junge Klassizität', by which he intended a return to the clarity and purely musical motivation of Bach and Mozart; yet such works as his Elegien (1907), the virtuoso Fantasia contrappuntistica (1910) and the Second Sonatina (1912), all for piano, show his awareness of the latest developments including Schoenberg's most recent music, along with his reverence of the past. His Sketch of a new Aesthetic of Music (1907) looks forward with enthusiasm to the use of microtones and electronic means.

The unresolved conflicts in his musical mind between futurism and classical recovery, Italian vocality and German substance, Lisztian flamboyance and Mozartian calm all inform his larger works, which include a Piano Concerto with choral finale (1904), several works on American Indian themes and operas – the ETA Hoffmann fantasy Die Brautwahl (1912), a commedia dell'arte double bill of Arlecchino and Turandot (1917) and the unfinished Doktor Faust (1924), where the protagonist's search after knowledge and experience is finally assuaged when he gives birth to a new future.
      GROVEmusic

Piano Concerto, K247

Piano Concerto
Marc-André Hamelin pf Men's Voices of the **City of Birmingham Symphony Chorus and Orchestra / Mark Elder**
Hyperion CDA67143 (72' · DDD)   ⒻⓄⓄ

Busoni's Piano Concerto has never become a repertoire piece. It fits awkwardly into a concert programme, due to its length and its choral finale, and the extreme difficulty of its solo writing can't quite disguise the fact that it's really more of a symphony with an elaborate piano part than a real concerto. This new recording might just change all that, for like no other performance (not even Garrick Ohlsson's stunning account on Telarc) it proves what a richly enjoyable piece it is. Without in the least understating the grandeur of the central movement (or its Faustian pointers to Busoni's later style), it finds humour not only of the gallows kind in the first *Scherzo* (even a touch of irony to its nostalgic centre), while the brilliant tarantella second *Scherzo* is often very funny indeed: Busoni celebrates his Italian ancestry, but at times bursts into helpless laughter at it as well. Hamelin obviously loves the work's opportunities for grand romantic pianism and barnstorming, and he has a fine ear for its stark boldness. Elder is splendidly eloquent, from the nobly Brahmsian introduction to the full-throatedly sung finale. Both are at their best in the central *Pezzo Serioso*, which is grand and grave, but alert to the presence of Chopin as well as Liszt. The recording is warm and spacious, the piano at times just a touch (but forgivably) close. This is a remarkable performance.

Violin Concerto

Violin Concerto[a]. Violin Sonata No 2[b]
Frank Peter Zimmermann vn
[b]**Enrico Pace** pf [a]**RAI National Symphony Orchestra / John Storgårds**
Sony Classical SK94497 (54' · DDD)   Ⓕ

Frank Peter Zimmermann performs an inestimable service by coupling two of the most approachable works by a master too often sidelined as excessively prolix. Prior to hearing this assured and musically persuasive account of the Violin Concerto, only Joseph Szigeti and Adolf Busch have really made it work.

It's an early piece, premiered in Berlin in 1897, a three-movement structure that plays without a break. Busoni himself called the Concerto 'good…if unpretentious', quietly original, too, though near the start you'll hear a short passage that replicates almost to the note the transition from first to second subjects in the first movement of Brahms's Violin Concerto. Busoni's Concerto is at its darkest in the *Quasi andante* where solo and orchestral voices are beautifully integrated. The bustling finale is filled with typically Busonian playfulness, felicitously scored music that's stylishly played by Zimmermann – his tonal polish and technical mastery reminiscent at times of both Milstein and David Oistrakh.

The half-hour Violin Sonata, a seminal piece from 1900, opens more like the Busoni we know and love (or not, as the case may be) and owes an obvious debt to both Beethoven and Schubert. The first movement is mostly sombre and austere, the *Scherzo* a manic tarantella, then after a brief slow movement there's a set of variations based on a chorale-like theme, a world on its own that incorporates elements of dance, fugue and virtuoso display. The transition to the closing *Allegro* unmistakably echoes Schubert's great C major Fantasy. Again Zimmermann comes up trumps with a modern benchmark, matched in spirit and expertise by his pianist Enrico Pace. A marvellous disc, not to be missed on any count.

Orchestral Works

Turandot – concert suite, Op 41. Sarabande und Cortège: Zwei Studien zu Doktor Faust, Op 51. Berceuse élégiaque, Op 42
Hong Kong Philharmonic Orchestra / Samuel Wong
Naxos 8 555373 (71' · DDD)   Ⓢ➍

Of the six works recorded here, two are essential for anyone interested in Busoni: the *Berceuse élégiaque* and the *Sarabande und Cortège*. Samuel Wong, music director of the Hong Kong Phil-

harmonic, is on this reading a very interesting artist. He takes the *Berceuse élégiaque*, for example, at a very slow tempo and indeed its pace suggests mournful sighing rather than the rocking of a cradle. The extraordinary end of the piece, string chords with the dark glow of gong strokes, is quite magical, partly because it's so sombrely slow. In the *Cortège*, also a touch slow, he misses something of Busoni's mercurial quality but imparts a lovely nobility to its string counter-subject.

Every one of the *Turandot* suite's movements is entertaining, two are Busoni at his most imaginative (the strikingly malign fourth and the sinister seventh) and they're all brilliantly and characterfully played. Wong's intriguing musicality and Naxos's bargain price make this a worthwhile issue.

Piano Works

Sieben Elegien. Perpetuum mobile. Prélude et Etude en Arpèges. Sieben Kurze Stücke zur Pflege des polyphonen Spiel
Roland Pöntinen pf
CPO CPO999 853-2 (73' · DDD)   Ⓕ

Few composers have more resolutely avoided popularity than Busoni. Like Rachmaninov and Liszt he took a jaundiced view of his career as a virtuoso pianist, seeing it as a vainglorious alternative to the serious business of composition. Is this why his work so often exudes an atmosphere of dark intellectuality and desolation? Such music, in Alfred Brendel's words, only 'begins to glow when the right eye falls on it', and in Roland Pöntinen it surely has an ideal interpreter. His playing is subtly and brilliantly judged and, whether in the far-reaching Elegies, the more didactic *kurze Stücke* or in the *Perpetuum mobile*, where Busoni temporarily rises from the slough of despond, his sympathy and virtuosity are unfailing. The recordings are excellent; those looking for an uneasy rather than comfortable experience need look no further.

Busoni Fantasia contrappuntistica, K255/6. **Liszt/Busoni** Fantasia and Fugue, 'Ad nos, ad salutarem undam' **Mozart/Busoni** Piano Concerto No 9, K271 – Andantino
Hamish Milne pf
Hyperion CDA67677 (71' · DDD)   ⒻⓄ

This daunting and inspired coupling is played by Hamish Milne with an uplifting musical authority. Indeed, aided by Hyperion's superb sound (rich and resonant throughout the entire register), you are made to realise that the *Ad nos* Fantasy – a massive tribute to Busoni as transcriber – is not only among his finest achievements but (as Milne suggests in his accompanying notes) transcends Liszt's original organ work and seemingly takes on a life of its own. The central *Adagio* in particular has all of Liszt's obsessive and ecstatic wheeling round an idea yet is unmistakably stamped with Busoni's own intimidating power. And it is here in particular that Milne offers playing of the rarest refinement and sensitivity before launching the final fugue in a blaze of virtuosity.

Busoni's *Fantasia contrappuntistica* takes such music to a further extreme. Among the composer's most formidable works, its colossal range and scope tell you that Busoni's music can seem like a mighty mountain range glimpsed behind clouds. Again, Milne's performance is of an unfaltering beauty and lucidity. As an extra he sandwiches Busoni's transcription of the *Andantino* from Mozart's *Jeunehomme* Concerto between these two peaks, a rarity where Mozart's sublimity is coloured by Busoni's altogether more forbidding personality. Milne may playfully claim in his notes that he would 'like to play like Bill Evans and Ahmad Jamal and sing like Flagstad', but we should surely be mightily grateful for his own unmistakable personality.

Die Brautwahl

Die Brautwahl
Siegfried Vogel *bass* Voswinkel **Carola Höhn** *sop* Albertine **Graham Clark** *ten* Thusman **Vinson Cole** *ten* Lehsen **Pär Lindskog** *ten* Baron Bensch **Roman Trekel** *bar* Leonhard **Günter von Kannen** *bar* Manasse **Chorus of the Deutsche Staatsoper, Berlin; Staatskapelle Berlin / Daniel Barenboim**
Teldec ② 3984-25250-2 (116' · DDD · N/T/t) Ⓕ**ⓞ�'t**

Busoni's first mature opera occupied him for seven years (1905-11). He may not have been as natural a man of the theatre as Richard Strauss, but *Die Brautwahl* has plenty of fine music in it – at times foreshadowing the splendours of *Doktor Faust*. This 1992 Berlin production used a version made by Antony Beaumont, whose completion of *Doktor Faust* was a great success. As Beaumont explains in the booklet, we get only about two-thirds of the whole, and all aspects of the opera's subject-matter may not be ideally balanced. This 'fantastic comedy' is based on a story by E T A Hoffmann, with the climactic scene in which a bride is chosen (hence the title) leaning heavily on *The Merchant of Venice*. The action is set in Berlin, but there are echoes of Wagner's Nuremberg in the text and characterisation. Musically, Busoni keeps his distance from Wagner, and the music is attractive, ranging widely in character.

This performance is a strong one, with a certain, untroublesome amount of stage noise. No doubt reflecting the staging, the recording occasionally recesses the singers, but the energy and command of Barenboim's conducting are never in doubt. The energy does not mean that anything is rushed, and the romantic episodes are warmly moulded, the scenes of fantasy properly attentive to matters of colour and texture. Roman Trekel, a warm yet dramatically resonant baritone, makes a strong impression as Leonhard. He's the perfect foil to Graham Clark, who tackles the role of Thusman with relish, and with considerable technical skill in music which demands lyrical sensitivity as well as comic agility.

Doktor Faust

Doktor Faust
Dietrich Henschel *bar* Doktor Faust **Markus Hollop** *bass* Wagner, Master of Ceremonies **Kim Begley** *ten* Mephistopheles **Torsten Kerl** *ten* Duke of Parma **Eva Jenis** *sop* Duchess of Parma **Detlef Roth** *bar* Soldier **William Dazeley** *bar* Natural Philosopher **Eberhard Lorenz** *ten* Lieutenant **Frédéric Caton** *bass* Theologian **Jérôme Varnier** *bass* Jurist **Dietrich Fischer-Dieskau** *spkr* Poet **Geneva Grand Theatre Chorus; Chorus and Orchestra of the Opéra National de Lyon / Kent Nagano**
Erato ③ 3984-25501-2 (196' · DDD · N/T/t) Ⓜ**ⓞ➚**

Finally we have a recording that not only provides the full, uncut text, as completed by Busoni's pupil Philipp Jarnach soon after the composer's death, but also offers as supplements Antony Beaumont's very different realisations of parts of the opera's later stages. So complete is this version, indeed, that it includes the spoken prologues and epilogues, with Dietrich Fischer-Dieskau providing a poignant link to DG's heavily cut 1969 recording.

Given that Beaumont worked from sketches and other information of which Jarnach was unaware (or chose to ignore), there can be no question as to which of the two is the more genuinely Busonian, and the extended closing scene in Beaumont's version has a persuasive gravity and sense of fulfilment quite different from Jarnach's more terse yet slightly melodramatic completion. Nevertheless, it will take a sensibility more refined than most not to be swept away by the sheer visceral power of Jarnach's rendering of the death of Faust.

Dietrich Henschel displays considerable style and stamina during his two extended monologues in the opera's final stages, and although his singing isn't entirely free of straining for effect, or of bluster, the character's tortured humanity is vividly conveyed. Kim Begley makes a considerable success of the other principal role, although, in an ideal world, Mephistopheles would manage more variety. But Begley tackles the many demanding aspects of the part with panache and, in the scintillating ballad, wit and menace are in perfect balance. Other parts are adequately taken, though articulation of the German text varies in clarity and accuracy.

This variability is one reason why the performance takes some time to take wing: another, more fundamental reason concerns the rather dry nature of the recording itself. At times, principal voices are backwardly placed, and, even when they aren't, one suspects that the brilliance of the orchestral sound is being damped down in order to ensure their audibility. Nevertheless, Nagano's shaping of this extremely demanding score is neither inflexible nor inexpressive.

Doktor Faust can at last be heard in a recording, that, in the end, reaches and reveals its essence, and whose documentary value is inestimable.

Doktor Faust
Thomas Hampson *bar* Doktor Faust **Günther Groissböck** *bass* Wagner; Master of Ceremonies **Gregory Kunde** *ten* Mephistopheles **Reinaldo Macias** *ten* Duke of Parma; Soldier **Sandra Trattnigg** *sop* Duchess of Parma **Martin Zysset** *ten* Lieutenant **Andreas Winkler** *ten* 1st Student from Cracow **Thilo Dahlmann** *bass-bar* 2nd Student from Cracow **Matthew Leigh** *bar* 3rd Student from Cracow **Giuseppe Scorsin** *bass* Gravis **Tomasz Slawinski** *bass* Levis **Gabriel Bermúdez** *bar* Asmodus **Randall Ball** *ten* Belzebuth **Miroslav Christoff** *ten* Megäros
Zurich Opera House Chorus and Orchestra / Philippe Jordan
Stage director **Klaus Michael Grüber**
Video director **Felix Breisach**
ArtHaus Musik ② 📀 101 283 (172' · NTSC · 16:9 · PCM stereo, 5.1 and DTS 5.1 · 0)
Recorded live in 2006   Ⓕ

Presented here is Philipp Jarnach's version (completed for the premiere, unaware of the composer's notes for its unfinished sections, realised only by Antony Beaumont 60 years later) which Philippe Jordan prefers on musical grounds, 'whether it really fits with the rest of the work or not'. He approves of Jarnach's use of Wagnerian leitmotif and darker conclusion, finding it 'simply overwhelming' and Beaumont's more positive finale 'drier'. Jarnach's version is – unavoidably – a misrepresentation of Busoni's vision and stylistically jars the moment it starts. Beaumont's may be a musicologist's rather than composer's edition but it gives us more of Busoni's intentions.

That aside, this production has many strengths. Hampson, after seeming ill-at-ease in the first Prelude, audibly grows into the role. Trattnigg is beguiling as the Duchess and Macias shines as the Soldier (Gretchen's grief-stricken brother) and pompous Duke. The show is stolen, however, by Gregory Kunde's Mephistopheles, a portrayal vocally superb throughout and brilliantly acted. The Zurich Opera House Chorus are excellent. Some of Jordan's tempi are a tad measured but the orchestra's playing is assured.

There are minor annoyances: for instance in Prelude 1, why do the Students not bring Faust the book, key and paper they sing about? A major omission is the Students' serenade to Wagner (Faust's former familius) at the start of the final scene. Wagner's replacement of Faust as Rector is included in the sung text and meaningless without its representation onstage. Musically, the cut section provides vital contrast between the defiance of the second scene's close and the denouement. Felix Breisach's video direction is commendably unfussy, catching both the scale of the production's biggest moments as well as Kunde's mischievous expressions. The Devil is truly in the detail.

Martin Butler   English b1960

Butler studied the piano and composition at the RNCM and the University of Manchester (1978-82), following which he undertook postgraduate studies with Babbitt and JK Randall at Princeton University (1983-7). He became a lecturer at the University of Sussex in 1988, and was later appointed reader in music. In 1988 he was awarded the Mendelssohn Scholarship which enabled him to work at Tempo reale, Berio's electro-acoustic studio in Florence, on Graffiti. Butler has forged a distinctive musical identity rooted, on the one hand, in the European tradition of Stravinsky and Berio, and, on the other, in American folk and popular music, and minimalism.

Chamber works

American Rounds. Funérailles[a]. Nathaniel's Mobile[a]. Sequenza notturna[b]. Siward's River Song[c]. Suzanne's River Song[d]. Walden Snow[e] **D Scarlatti** Sonatas (arr Butler) – Kk119; Kk215
Schubert Ensemble of London
([bd]Simon Blendis *vn* [be]Douglas Paterson *va* [bc]Jane Salmon *vc* Peter Buckoke *db* [abde]William Howard *pf*)
NMC NMCD120 (72' · DDD)   Ⓕ🅑➤

Martin Butler's contribution to the chamber domain has been a significant one. All of these pieces were written over the past decade with the Schubert Ensemble in mind: the earliest being *American Rounds* – which combines American folk idioms with a rhythmic impetus whose Stravinskian incisiveness is anything but mindlessly post-minimalist. Equally engaging are the 'River Songs' derived from the chamber opera *A Better Place*, its restrained yet evocative mood distilled in the threnody for Siward and the effulgent lyricism of that for Suzanne. On a lighter note, the two Scarlatti transcriptions – respectively vigorous and poetic – evince a keen ingenuity. The most striking works, however, are the two piano pieces: *Nathaniel's Mobile* – which intercuts linear and harmonised melody so the music evolves, without intensifying, towards its conclusion; and *Funérailles*, which adds a more disruptive element that opens out the music's dynamic and emotional range on the way to its quiet yet restive close. *Sequenza notturna* passes through several expressive vignettes, given focus by the unassuming viola melody that underpins them, while *Walden Snow* is a 'postcard' from New England of touching limpidity.

The performances are as sensitive and assured as one would expect from the Schubert Ensemble, continuing their laudable contribution to British new music, and the sound is a model of chamber balance. Informative notes from John Fallas, and a disc that should extend the audience for a composer whose idiom – distinctive but accessible and never remotely facile – is nowhere better represented than here.

Dietrich Buxtehude German c1637-1707

Buxtehude's first studies were under his father, who held posts as organist in Hälsingburg and Helsingor (Elsinore), as did Buxtehude himself between c1657 and 1668, when he became organist at the Marien-kirche at Lübeck, one of the most important posts in north Germany; he was also appointed Werkmeister (general manager) of the church. Later that year he married Anna Margarethe Tunder, his predecessor's daughter. Besides his normal duties on Sundays and feast days, he reinstated the practice of giving Abend-musik concerts in the church on five Sunday after-noons each year. These events attracted much interest and drew JS Bach from Arnstadt in Advent 1705.

Surviving texts from the Abendmusik perform-ances show that he composed a number of oratorio-like works, but none has survived. The bulk of his known sacred music consists of cantatas or sacred concertos, the latter often settings of psalm texts, consisting of contrasting sections in which each line of the text is treated with a new motif. He used a concer-tato style, for voices and continuo (sometimes with other instruments), in which the motifs are treated in dialogue in a manner related to the Venetian poly-choral style; there are also arioso sections. Buxtehude wrote a number of chorale settings, commonly with the melody in the soprano but with instrumental accompaniment and interludes; in ensemble settings he used the chorale motet style, in the manner of a sacred concerto but with motifs from the chorale melody, and he also set chorales with the melody in one voice and instrumental counterpoints. His sacred arias are mostly in strophic or varied strophic form, with a fluent, sometimes Italianate melodic style. Some extended vocal works, akin to Bach's cantatas, combine movements in the sacred concerto style with others of the aria type.

Most of Buxtehude's instrumental music is for the organ: about half consists of freely composed music, often using a toccata-like section with several fugues and incorporating virtuoso passage-work, while half consists of chorale settings, some of the variation and fantasia types, but mostly highly unified settings of a single stanza of the chorale with a richly ornamented melody. He composed suites and other music for the harpsichord; his courantes are variations of the alle-mandes and the gigues are loosely fugal. French influence is noticeable. Especially in his sacred vocal works and his organ music, Buxtehude represents the climax of the 17th-century north German school, and he significantly influenced Bach. GROVEmusic

Organ works

Complete Organ Works
Bernard Foccroulle org
with **Bernarda Fink** mez **Dirk Snellings** bass
Ricercar ⑤ RIC250 (6h 50' · DDD)　　　　　Ⓕ⦿

What better way to mark the 300th anniversary of Buxtehude's death in 1707 than with this wonderful box-set? Its 77 tracks reaffirm what a central figure Buxtehude was to subsequent generations of Northern European organists working in the German Lutheran tradition.

These recordings (made between 2003 and 2006) are played on two historic Schnitger instruments in the Ludgerikirche, Norden, and the Martinkerk, Groningen, two recent organs in Hoogstraten (near Antwerp) and the German Church, Stockholm, and the recon-structed Lorentz-Frietzsch organ in Helsingor's St Maria Church, parts of which Buxtehude himself played.

The 19 organ praeludia form the core of Buxtehude's organ oeuvre and are considered his most important contributions to the 17th-century literature. Their quasi-improvisatory flair and brilliance always sounds spontane-ous, at times quite extrovert. Foccroulle wisely contrasts them with the much plainer devo-tional chorale settings. He teases endlessly fresh solo timbres from these striking instru-ments. The variety of tuning temperaments keeps the ear alert and the playing is con-stantly inspiring.

The careful juxtaposition of pieces means that each disc makes a highly satisfying programme in its own right. By way of an epilogue the set concludes with the poignant *Klag-Lied* for organ and vocal duet. Other complete Buxtehude organ sets have clearly been superseded by this release.

'Opera omnia VIII – Organ Works III'
Auf meinen lieben Gott, BuxWV179. Canzonetta, BuxWV225. Ciacona, BuxWV159. Durch Adams Fall ist ganz verderbt, BuxWV183. Erhalt uns, Herr, bei deinem Wort, BuxWV185. Es spricht der Unweisen Mund wohl, BuxWV187. Fugue, BuxWV176. Herr Jesu Christ, ich weiss gar wohl, BuxWV193. Komm, heiliger Geist, Herre Gott, BuxWV200. Nun lob mein Seel' den Herren – BuxWV213; BuxWV214; BuxWV215. Prelude and Fugue, BuxWV145 – Prelude. Praeludiums – BuxWV149; BuxWV140; BuxWV137; BuxWV148
Ton Koopman org
Challenge Classics CC72247 (66' · DDD). Played on the Schnitger organ of St Jacobi Kirche, Hamburg　Ⓕ

Koopman's programme displays examples of the five distinct genres of improvisatory styles central to the organist's craft in Lutheran Germany: multi-sectional Pedaliter preludes, freer large-scale preludes in the *stylus fantasti-cus*, ostinato-based pieces and two types of chorale movements. And where better to pres-ent a selection of Buxtehude's broad composi-tional spectrum than the oft-recorded 1693 Schnitger organ in Hamburg's St Jacobi Church?

Koopman's approach remains refreshingly free, radical even, the no-nonsense opening Prelude in G minor setting the tone for that which follows. Ornamentation is tastefully florid and melodic lines are allowed to sing out naturally. Tempo changes seem effortless and Koopman achieves a near-perfect balance of dextral clarity and pace. The warm Hamburg acoustic helps.

Among the many highlights, mention must be made of the Chaconne in C minor. Koopman obviously relishes the piece's innovations (a direct inspiration for JS Bach). In addition, the setting of the chorale *Nun lob mein Seel'* combined with verses 2 and 3 of BuxWV213 makes a logical set of four variations. The Schnitger's wealth of registers never tire the ear. Its soothing, limpid flutes and sparkling and spitting upperwork are superbly captured by sound engineer Adriaan Verstijnen. He presents a deep sound stage, with plenty of ambience and sense of height, an effect enhanced by the floor-wobbling 32-foot registers.

Harpsichord works

'Opera omnia VI – Harpsichord Works, Vol 2'
Aria, BuxWV246. Aria and Three Variations,
BuxWV249. Canzona, BuxWV166. Canzonetta,
BuxWV168. Courante, BuxWVAnh6. Rofilis,
BuxWV248. Toccata and Fugue, BuxWV165. Suites –
BuxWV227; BuxWV229; BuxWV236; BuxWV237;
BuxWV239; BuxWV240; BuxWV241; BuxWV244;
BuxWVdeest
Ton Koopman *hpd*
Challenge Classics ② CC72245 (97' · DDD)   Ⓕ

Performing on two copies of Stefanini and Ruckers harpsichords, Ton Koopman completes the exquisite solo *oeuvre* by Buxtehude with captivating élan. For a musician with somewhat precipitous tendencies, Koopman here delivers a considered programme of mainly standard four-movement suites, interpolated with other contemporaneous genres, from variations to the flamboyance of the 'stylus phantasticus' of toccatas and the like.

Koopman's most significant achievement is the poetry he brings to Buxtehude's cultivated and understated world of pre-Telemann domestic music. This is where the Suites appear as the apogee of a tradition which Froberger honed and which Bach extended in his early works. Indeed, keen ears will notice the prescient melodic seeds of the *English Suites* and, more specifically, the Canzona in C whose turns perhaps inspired the ambitious young Turk in the Capriccio in E (BWV993).

That aside, witness the sheer richness of Buxtehude's luminous textures, as well as the finely drawn and grateful melodic contours. The opening Aria in C (with 10 variations) reveals the warmth of both Buxtehude's hypnotically life-affirming variations and Koopman's concentrated placement and esprit.

Within such compositional calibre and refinement, Koopman also explores a steeliness in the investigative lines of the fine C major Suite which concludes the first disc; as throughout, the tempo relationships between movements are thoughtfully rendered, with the 'gamey' meantone tuning and elegant characterisation all conspiring towards a notable 'world premiere' set of harpsichord recordings. In sum, an outstanding release in this enterprising series.

Membra Jesu nostri, BuxWV75

Membra Jesu nostri   Ⓟ
**The Sixteen; Symphony of Harmony and Invention
/ Harry Christophers**
Linn Records CKD141 (61' · DDD · T/t)   ⒻⒹ▸

Composed in 1680, this group of seven tiny cantatas – each meditating on a part of Christ's body (feet, knees, hands, side, breast, heart and face) – represents an extreme in formal compression. Each cantata has just six movements: an instrumental introduction, a choral setting of the relevant Biblical citation, three short solo arias, and a repeat of the chorus. Few of those movements last more than 90 seconds, and some are a lot shorter. But the real catch is that the solo arias are all on texts consisting of 80-syllable trochaic lines: Buxtehude sets the vast majority of them to four-bar phrases, which can lead to musical predictability. The first task of musicians is to counteract the numbing regularity of those phrases. They approach this by adopting a generally very smooth rhythmic style, benefiting much from the marvellous continuo group of Paul Nicholson (organ), Jane Coe (cello) and Elizabeth Kenny (theorbo): all three superbly resourceful in their range of colours and attacks, without ever interrupting the music's flow. Above this the violins of David Woodstock and Walter Reiter glow or sparkle as the music requires. In line with today's best practice, the choruses are taken just by the five excellent solo singers, led by Carolyn Sampson in luscious form. A wonderfully moving account of Buxtehude's remarkable cycle of cantatas.

Sacred Cantatas

Sacred Cantatas   Ⓟ
Fuga, BuxWV174. Ich habe Lust abzuscheiden, Bux-
WV47ᵃᵇᶜ. Ich halte es dafür, BuxWV48ᵇᶜ. Jesu meine
Freude, BuxWV60ᵃᵇᶜ. Mein herz ist bereit, BuxWV73ᶜᵈ.
Herr, wenn ich nur dich hab, BuxWV38ᵇ. Salve, Jesu,
Patris gnate unigenite, BuxWV94ᵃᵇ.
Jesu dulcis memoria, BuxWV56ᵃᵇ. Cantate Domino,
BuxWV12ᵃᵇᶜ
ᵃ**Emma Kirkby**, ᵇ**Suzie LeBlanc** *sops* ᶜ**Peter Harvey**
bass ᵈ**Clare Salaman** *vn* **Purcell Quartet** (Catherine
Mackintosh *vn/va* Catherine Weiss *vn* Richard
Boothby *bar vio* Robert Woolley *org*)
Chandos Chaconne CHAN0691 (76' · DDD · T/t) ⒻⒹ▸

Setting various German and Latin texts for solo voices, violins and continuo, these sacred cantatas are typical products of the late 17th century in their pragmatic approach to form.

Here are patchworks such as *Jesu dulcis memoria* and *Salve, Jesu, Patris gnate unigenite*; chorale or song variations such as *Jesu, meine Freude*; and others, like *Ich halte es dafür* and *Ich habe Lust abzuscheiden*, which combine the two. *Cantate Domino* is liltingly Italianate, *Mein Herz ist bereit* is an agile showpiece for solo bass, while *Herr, wenn ich nur dich hab* is a set of variations over a ground bass. The Purcell Quartet's essential string sound has always been sweet, airy and lucid, and it's interesting to hear how that has been transferred here from the instrumental sphere to the vocal. To this end the choice of singers is important, and on this occasion they could hardly have picked more shrewdly: Emma Kirkby and Suzie LeBlanc make an excellent pairing, distinguishable from each other in both voice and approach, yet at the same time superbly matched in duet; and Peter Harvey has the friendliest of bass voices, his alert account of *Mein Herz ist bereit*, set against the thrillingly radiant background of three violins, being one of the disc's highlights.

An expert recording in an amenable acoustic completes a release of many refined pleasures.

Fried- und Freudenreiche Hinfart, BuxWV76. Gen Himmel zu dem Vater mein, BuxWV32. Singet dem Herrn ein neues Lied, BuxWV98. Was mich auf dieser Welt betrübt, BuxWV105. Herr, wenn ich nur dich hab, BuxWV38. Sicut Moses exaltavit serpentem, BuxWV97. O dulcis Jesu, BuxWV83. O fröhliche Stunden, BuxWV84. Schaffe in mir, Gott, BuxWV95
Emma Kirkby sop **John Holloway, Manfred Kraemer** vns **Jaap ter Linden** va da gamba
Lars Ulrik Mortensen org/hpd
Naxos 8 557251 (72' · DDD)   Ⓢ

Those enamoured of opulent voices may wonder why Emma Kirkby is the undisputed first lady of early music, but this anthology of Buxtehude's music for solo voice and instruments captures much of what makes her so special: she has acute awareness of dance forms in her delivery of rhythms (even in slower music), a crystal-clear tone, superb agility in quick passages, and a marvellous sense of rhetorical communication. The mournfully sublime *Klaglied* (BuxWV76 No 2) is movingly performed. Also superb is the lovely 12-minute *O dulcis Jesu*.

Ritornelli are beautifully articulated by violinists John Holloway and Manfred Kraemer, and Lars Ulrik Mortensen's organ continuo is delightful. The programme is 100 per cent authentic Buxtehude, spellbindingly performed, with an excellent essay by the leading authority Kerala Snyder (although sung texts are not included). Emma Kirkby and her accomplices do more to illustrate why he is the supreme genius of the generation before JS Bach.

Quemadmodum desiderat cervus, BuxWV92. Singet dem Herrn ein neues Lied, BuxWV98. Lobe den Herren, meine Seele, BuxWV71. Herr, wenn ich nur dich hab, BuxWV38. O fröhliche Stunden, BuxWV84. Herr, nun lässt du deinen Diener, BuxWV37. Fugue, BuxWV175. Toccata and Fugue, BuxWV164
Hans Jörg Mammel ten La Fenice / Jean Tubéry
Alpha ALPHA113 (56' · DDD · T/t)   Ⓕ

This collection of Buxtehude's church concertos (and a few other miscellaneous bits) has been hand-picked and thoughtfully researched

by the outstanding German tenor Hans Jörg Mammel. Any admirers of the warm musicianship of Jean Tubéry and his ensemble La Fenice will not hesitate to investigate this. The richly exotic continuo group (including harp and theorbo) and cornetts put Buxtehude's instrumentation into glorious Technicolor (*Quemadmodum desiderat cervus*, for example). When a more restrained approach to scoring is taken the results are equally sublime. For example, the effect of the solo voice, violin, viola da gamba and keyboard continuo unfurls gloriously without unnecessary additives in *Singet dem Herrn*.

It is not rare to hear Buxtehude's intimately scaled church music sung by sopranos, countertenors and even basses, but it seems that tenors have infrequently got in on the act. Mammel is an assured singer of intelligent quality, and, although he often sounds rooted in his baritonal chest voice, his occasional excursions upwards prove to be particularly well rounded and sweetly judged, and his agile singing is well illustrated by the tricky coloratura in *Herr, nun lässt du deinen Diener*. It seems as if he has genuinely absorbed the meaning of texts and is narrating a story rather than merely singing lovely pious music. Also, full marks to Alpha for yet another lovingly prepared recording with its customary emphasis on fine artwork.

William Byrd   English 1543-1623

Brought up in London, Byrd was a pupil of Tallis. In 1563 he became Organist and Master of the Choristers at Lincoln Cathedral and married there in 1568. Though he remained at Lincoln until c1572 he was a Gentleman of the Chapel Royal from 1570 and its organist from 1575 (at first jointly with Tallis). In London he rapidly established himself as a composer, gaining influential friends and patrons and earning favour with Queen Elizabeth, who granted him a patent (with Tallis) in 1575 for the printing and marketing of part-music and MS paper. After his wife's death in the 1580s he remarried. He and his family were often cited as Catholic recusants, but he continued to compose openly for the Roman church. In 1593 Byrd moved to Essex, where he spent the rest of his life and was frequently involved in property litigation. His reputation was very high: he was described as 'Father of British Music'. Morley and Tomkins were among his pupils.

Much of Byrd's vast and varied output was printed during his lifetime. His sacred music ranges widely in style and mood, from the florid and penitential motets of the Cantiones sacrae to the concise and devotional ones in the Gradualia (motet sections intended to form an impressive scheme of complete Mass Propers). His secular songs predate the true madrigal; they use intricate, flowing counterpoint derived from an earlier English style (eg Tallis, Taverner) and range from solemn lamentations to exuberant jests. His instrumental music is specially important: the many consort songs greatly influenced the later lute ayre, while the virginal pieces are unparalleled in richness of invention and contrapuntal brilliance. In all the genres in which he wrote Byrd was both traditionalist and innovator, channelling continental ideas into a native English tradition, and his expressive range was unusually wide for his day. He wrote for both Catholic and Anglican churches with equal genius. GROVEmusic

Consort works

Byrd Fantasia a 5, BE17/8. Browning a 5, BE17/10. **P**
Fantasias a 6, BE17/13-14. In Nomines a 5, BE17/19-22 **Mico** Fancies a 4 Nos 4a, 5-7, 9, 10, 14, 18 & 19.
Pavans a 4 Nos 2-4
Phantasm (Laurence Dreyfus, Wendy Gillespie, Jonathan Manson, Markku Luolajan-Mikkola, *viols*)
with **Martha McGaughey, Alison McGillivray** *viols*
Simax PSC1143 (60' · DDD) Ⓕ

The odd juxtaposition of Byrd's very finest chamber music with pieces by Richard Mico may seem rather like pairing late Beethoven with Vanhal; but it works extremely well. Though Mico has been little regarded, much of his music shows absolute mastery (his Pavan No 4 is in some ways one of the most perfect and beautiful examples of the simple eight-bar pavane). The Mico selection includes two pieces that are by no means certainly his (*Fancies* Nos 18 and 19); but they're still fine work. Phantasm play this music with immaculate control and balance, finding many telling details that might elude less careful musicians. Some listeners may be a touch less happy with the Byrd, feeling that the honeyed sounds cover certain details, that the speed of *Browning* loses the work's harmonic and contrapuntal magic, that the myriad changes in the grand six-voice *fantasias*-could benefit from greater lightness of touch. But that would be like saying that only the English can perform Elgar idiomatically. What Phantasm brings to this music is a clear and unusual view of the music. Moreover, they present what's absolutely the best of Byrd's consort work, omitting the troublesome first *In Nomine* and the less perfect first six-part *Fantasia*. The four *Fantasias* and the four *In Nomines* on this disc are the core of Byrd's claim to stand among the world's greatest composers of chamber music. The performances convincingly support that claim.

Complete Keyboard Works

23 Pavans and Galliards (with two additional **P**
Pavans and five Galliards). 14 sets of Variations.
11 Fantasias. 11 Grounds. Nine Preludes. Miscellanea and variant versions
Davitt Moroney *chbr org/clav/hpd/muselar virg/org*
Hyperion ⑦ CDA66551/7 (497' · DDD) Ⓜ**OOO**
Selected highlights available on Ⓕ CDA66558

The three volumes of keyboard music added in 1950 as an afterthought to Edmund Fellowes's edition of Byrd have only slowly made their full

Ⓖ impact as containing one of the most remarkable and innovative repertories in the history of music. A much-needed new edition by Alan Brown (1969-71) was followed by Oliver Neighbour's important critical study (1978), which perhaps for the first time made it clear that Byrd wasn't just another of the 'Elizabethan Virginalists' but stood head and shoulders above all his contemporaries – in range, contrapuntal technique, melodic invention and above all formal control and imagination. Davitt Moroney has completed the picture by presenting the entire body of music on seven CDs. The results here are a triumph for all concerned. Moroney has the music in his hands, head and soul. There are so many fine details in his playing that it's hard to know where to begin in its praise: the wonderful clarity of the part-writing; the superb energy of the playing; the glittering virtuosity; the ability to vary the colours and move from the ineffably light and whimsical to the seriously confrontational; the constant delicate flexibility of his metre; or his compelling grasp of Byrd's often difficult formal designs.

Moroney approached this Everest of a project over many years, in constant consultation with Brown and particularly Neighbour (who, appropriately enough, plays the 'third hand' for the duet *Fantasia* on Disc 4). The engineers have coped well with the different recording venues and occasions. Six different instruments are used to vary the colour and to fit the different styles of the music. The most novel is the muselar virginal, a marvellously earthy instrument with a refreshingly noisy action. The others are plainly chosen with loving care. A harpsichord by Hubert Bédard (after Ruckers) tends to be used for the lighter pieces, while he chooses one by Reinhard von Nagel (after Couchet) for some of the more serious works. Neatly enough, the set ends with a prelude already heard on Ahrend's Toulouse organ, now played on four different instruments in turn (omitting only the chamber organ). Alongside all this, Moroney has provided the most detailed set of notes: 200 pages of wide-ranging erudition (in English and French) including a key to the 'BK' numbers of the Brown edition which are used throughout his running prose. So when you've got through the 497 minutes needed to listen to the discs, you still have several hours of reading to do.

Masses

Masses – for Three Voices; for Four Voices; for Five Voices (ed Skinner). Fantasias[a] – in G, 'A Voluntary for My Ladye Nevell'; in D minor; C, 'A Fancie for My Ladye Nevell'
[a]**Patrick Russill** *org* **The Cardinall's Musick /**
Andrew Carwood
ASV Gaudeamus CDGAU206 (79' · DDD · T/t)
Ⓕ**OOO**

This is incomparable music by one of the great

G est English composers and it was high time for someone to take a fresh look at these works in the light of more recent research and of changing attitudes to performance practice.

Byrd had composed his three settings of the Ordinary of the Mass in troubled times for the small recusant Catholic community that still remained in England in spite of persecution. The settings would have been sung, in all probability, during festive, albeit furtive, celebrations of the old time-honoured Roman liturgy, in private chapels in the depths of the country, at places such as Ingatestone, the seat of Byrd's principal patron, Sir John Petre. Andrew Carwood has recorded them in the Fitzalan Chapel of Arundel Castle, a small but lofty building with a clear resonance that enables the inner voices of the part-writing to come through straight and clean. It hasn't the aura of King's College Chapel, but is probably easier to manage than, say, Winchester Cathedral or Merton College Chapel.

Carwood uses two voices to a part in all three Masses. In comparison with rival recordings he's alone in selecting high voices for the three-part Mass, transposed up a minor third, which introduces a note of surprising lightness and grace. He, too, is alone in taking the initiative of using an all-male choir for the four-part Mass – alto, tenor, baritone, bass. This close, low texture, together with the transposition down an augmented fourth, adds a fitting sense of gravity to the performance. In particular, it heightens the poignancy of such passages as the 'dona nobis pacem' in the *Agnus Dei*, with its series of suspensions in the drooping phrases leading to the final cadence.

That dimension of understanding is precisely what this recording by The Cardinall's Musick so keenly demonstrates. Theirs is a simplicity of style that belies simplistic criticism. Vibrato is used sparingly: 40 years on, some listeners might consider its constant use by a King's Choir of the late 1950s almost too overpowering. Carwood chooses his tempos with care, avoiding the modern tendency to speed everything up inordinately.

The interesting historical note on the whole background is a good pointer to what the listener may experience as the music unfolds.

Masses – Three Voices; Four Voices; Five Voices
Motet – Ave verum corpus a 4
The Tallis Scholars / Peter Phillips
Gimell CDGIM345 (67' · DDD · T/t)   Ⓕ**ⓄⓄ**➔

Byrd was a fervently committed Roman Catholic and he helped enormously to enrich the music of the English Church. His Mass settings were made for the many recusant Catholic worshippers who held services in private. They were published between 1593 and 1595 and are creations of great feeling. The contrapuntal writing has a much closer texture and fibre than the Masses of Palestrina and there's an austerity and rigour that's allowed to blossom and expand

with the text. The beautifully restrained and mellow recording, made in Merton College Chapel, Oxford, fully captures the measure of the music and restores the awe and mystery of music that familiarity can dim.

'Playing Elizabeth's Tune'
Ave verum corpus. Great Service – Magnificat. Mass for five voices. Mass for four voices. Mass for three voices. Ne irascaris Domine. O Lord make thy servant. Prevent us, O lord. Tristitia et anxietas. Vigilate. Tribue, Domine. Diffusa est gratia. Nunc dimittis servum tuum
The Tallis Scholars / Peter Phillips
Video directors **Philip George, Rhodri Huw**
Gimell ᴅᴠᴅ GIMDP901 (184' · 16:9 · PCM stereo & 5.0 · 0). Includes a documentary about the life and music of Byrd, presented by Charles Hazlewood   Ⓕ

In 2002 The Tallis Scholars recorded an audio-visual Byrd-fest in three parts: a concert-format sequence of some of his sacred music in the atmospheric setting of Tewkesbury Abbey; a documentary of his life and his relationship to his powerful patroness, Queen Elizabeth I; and, as an 'audio bonus', another outing for the Scholars' outstanding version of the three Byrd Masses, recorded in Merton College Chapel.

Charles Hazlewood fronts the documentary; xasually attired and casually unshaven, he has a degree of ease, if not exactly charm, in front of the camera. He traces adeptly and fluently the different phases of Byrd's career, with stunning visuals of Lincoln Cathedral, the Chapel Royal and Ingatestone Hall as impressive backdrops. The whole is lent authority through the erudite but accessible contributions of experts on Reformation England (Christopher Haigh) and Byrd's music (David Skinner). Hazlewood sums up by talking about the hidden depths of passion in Byrd's music, and its range, though given that the documentary is slanted towards his development as a composer of church music, we get only background snippets of his keyboard and consort music. Nevertheless, the tale is well told, not least with added visual elements such as shots of 16th-century documentation, the original printed editions of Byrd's music and his own beautifully penned autograph.

As to the performances, it's interesting to hear Peter Phillips emphasize the passionate nature of Byrd's sacred music, when this aspect is fairly understated in The Tallis Scholars' performances. This isn't to say that they don't have a high degree of intensity at times: on the whole: they capture the ebb and flow of the music well, but there's a sense of distance. Phillips talks of getting right inside, of 'ticking along with the music', and that's what he does above all. This may not be the only way to perform Byrd's music but it's still very impressive in the ethereal clarity of the overall sound, and in the total commitment and rare understanding resulting from these musicians' years of experience.

The Great Service

The Great Service. My Ladye Nevells Booke – Fancie in C; Voluntary a 3. Christ rising again. O Lord, make thy servant Elizabeth. Prevent us, O lord. Sing joyfully unto God our strength. Out of the deep. How long shall mine enemies?
Westminster Abbey Choir / James O'Donnell with **Robert Quinney** org
Hyperion CDA67533 (76' · DDD · T/t)   Ⓕ⧐

This particular work needs no introduction; indeed, some fine recordings already exist of this set, which has become a particular favourite of modern choirs. The atmosphere one associates with this combination of 'artist and repertoire' is present in abundance: warmth and intimacy combined with a certain reserve. At times the latter quality is perhaps too marked, or could have been leavened with a hint of extroversion: the opening track, perhaps, *O Lord, make thy servant Elizabeth*. On the other hand the final selection, *Sing joyfully* (which, like the opening track, is sung *a cappella*) does indeed sound joyful.

In *The Great Service* itself, the character of the interpretations is entirely appropriate, and the choir may be heard at its best there. Its warmth of tone is due to the admixture throughout *The Great Service* of a chamber organ, sensitively handled by Robert Quinney. In the anthem *Christ rising again* the two treble soloists (accompanied by the organ) alternate with the full choir, a strategy that seems unconvincing because the music doesn't always lend itself to so strongly sectional an approach. Otherwise it's very polished and confident performance. Quinney gives equally fluent renditions of the Voluntary and 'Fancie for My Ladye Nevell', completing a disc that fulfils its brief with distinction.

Cantiones Sacrae

Cantiones Sacrae (1575) – Tribue, Domine. Siderum rector. Domine secundum. Fantasias – C; D. Attollite portas. Miserere mihi. Aspice Domine. Peccantem me quotidie. Salvator mundi II. O lux, beata Trinitas
New College Choir, Oxford / Edward Higginbottom with **Timothy Morris** org
CRD CRD3492 (64' · DDD · T/t)   Ⓜ⧐

There's so much wonderful six-part writing in this attractive selection from the 1575 *Cantiones Sacrae* that such a medium appears in a new light, particularly when performed by the choir and in the acoustic of New College Chapel – where, as Edward Higginbottom reminds us, they 'have been rehearsing for 500 years'. The beauty and balance of the musical architecture is constantly conveyed to the listener, particularly in the six-part writing. It doesn't matter whether these compositions were intended for liturgical or domestic use, or as a noble offering to the Queen: from a purely musical point of view they're superb. To give a single example, the

little Vespers hymn *O lux, beata Trinitas* displays consummate craftsmanship through the ingenious use of the number three – three high, then three low voices, three diverse voices, a canon three-in-one, three strophes, triple time, and so on, building up to a tremendous final 'Amen'. The point made by this recording is that it all sounds natural, uncontrived, magnificent. The three organ pieces are a welcome addition: with their brilliant fingerwork and gentle registrations they present a charming and lively contrast to the vocal settings.

Cantiones Sacrae (1589) – Vigilate; In resurrectione tua; Aspice Domine de sede; Ne irascaris Domine. Propers for the Feast of the Purification – Ave regina caelorum; Adorna thalamum; O quam gloriosum; Tribulationes civitatum; Domine secundum multitudinem; Laetentur caeli
The Cardinall's Musick / Andrew Carwood
ASV Gaudeamus CDGAU309 (71' · DDD · T/t)   Ⓕ

ASV's Byrd Edition presents Propers for Candlemas (also known as the 'Feast of the Purification'), and further motets from the 1589 *Cantiones Sacrae*, many of them composed to strengthen the spirits of the Queen's loyal Catholic subjects in those troubled and highly dangerous times. Which goes to explain the high proportion of sorrowful or penitential texts, the frequent cries for deliverance (*Aspice Domine, Ne irascaris, Tribulationes*), and the mastery with which Byrd sets them. This historical background, vital to an understanding of the music, doesn't exclude the possibility of a joyful outcome: Byrd can also contemplate the ultimate joys of heaven, (*O quam gloriosum, Laetentur caeli*).

The choir enters deeply into an understanding of what lies behind these pieces. And Byrd is never averse to raising his singers' spirits by introducing a jaunty rhythm – the crowing cock in *Vigilate*, for example – or a bright, rising theme to inspire hope. The choir responds with sustained restraint, perfect balance and crisp rhythms.

The settings of the Propers for Candlemas offer a short recital of their own, this time in the full context of the liturgy for this ancient feast, and following the whole course of events as the story unfolds. A thoroughly satisfying disc.

Gradualia

Gradualia – Volume 1: Saturday Lady Masses in Advent. Domine quis habitabit. Omni tempore benedic Deum. Christe redemptor omnium. Sermone blando a 3. Miserere. Ne perdas cum implis. Lamentations of Jeremiah. Christe, qui lux es a 5. Christe qui lux es a 4. Sanctus. Audivi vocem de caelo. Vide Dominum quoniam tribulor. Peccavi super numerum (all ed Skinner)
The Cardinall's Musick; Frideswide Consort
(Caroline Kershaw, Jane Downer, Christine Garratt, Jean McCreery *recs*) / **Andrew Carwood**
ASV Gaudeamus CDGAU170 (70' · DDD · T/t)   Ⓕ

This is a great start to The Cardinall's Musick's project to record Byrd's complete output. On the disc, some of the shorter motets are entrusted to The Cardinall's' habitual instrumental accomplices, finds the Frideswide Consort. A full list of sources is given for each piece, along with appropriate editorial commentary. Since Byrd set certain texts a number of times, such precision seems only sensible. Much of this music is new to the CD catalogue, and even in this selection of largely unpublished motets, there are impressive finds (the nine-voice *Domine quis habitabit*, for instance). This repertory is the mother's-milk of English choristers, and of the younger generation of English vocal ensembles The Cardinall's Musick remains perhaps the closest to that tradition outside of actual choral establishments. So they respond to Byrd with a suavity and confidence born of longstanding acquaintance. The expansive penitential pieces, such as the early *Lamentations*, are far removed from the small-scale forms of the *Gradualia*. The Cardinall's Musick respond effectively to these different functions and moods, and the recording complements them admirably.

Gradualia – Volume 2: Nativity of our Lord Jesus Christ – Puer natus est; Viderunt … omnes fines terrae; Dies sanctificatus; Tui sunt coeli; Viderunt omnes fines terrae; Hodie Christus natus est; O admirabile commercium; O magnum mysterium. Ave regina caelorum. O salutaris hostia. Confitemini DomiNo In exitu Israel (with Sheppard and Mundy). Laudate pueri Dominum. Decantabat populus. Deus in adjutorium. Ad Dominum cum tribularer (all ed Skinner)
The Cardinall's Musick / Andrew Carwood
ASV Gaudeamus CDGAU178 (73' · DDD · T/t) Ⓕ Ⓞ

This second volume of The Cardinall's Musick's Byrd edition is, if anything, more impressive than the first. It may be a matter of programming, for the works recorded here seem to be of a higher overall calibre: even an obviously experimental piece such as *O salutaris hostia* could have been included on merit alone – yet this appears to be its first recording. Complete surveys sometimes turn up items of lesser interest, yet they also allow one to hear pieces that might have difficulty in finding a home elsewhere: witness the responsory, *In exitu Israel*, an intriguing collaborative effort by Byrd and his contemporaries, Mundy and Sheppard. Finally, one can judge for oneself the authenticity of works that modern scholarship has deemed doubtful (such as the opening *Ave regina caelorum*). Most of the pieces here involve male altos on the top line. The centrepiece is a collection of Propers from the *Gradualia* of 1607, this time for the Nativity. As on their first set, Skinner's and Carwood's decision to structure each volume around a set of Propers proves an astute piece of programming, integrating shorter items as it does (such as the various *Alleluia* settings) within a framework that allows them

their own space. The singers are on very fine form indeed. It takes confidence to carry off *O salutaris hostia*, whose fierce false relations could so easily have sounded merely wilful. Only in the final, extended settings does the pace flag: the disc's last moments are rather ponderous. That aside, this is a disc to delight Byrd-lovers everywhere.

Gradualia, Vol 1/ii: Miscellaneous and Office Text – Laetania. Gradualia, Vol 2: Feast of Saints Peter and Paul – Introit: Nunc scio vere; Gradual: Constitues eos…Domine; Alleluia: Solve iubente Deo; Antiphon: Hodie Simon Petrus; Antiphon: Tu es pastor ovium; Antiphon: Quodcunque ligaveris. Liber secundus sacrarum cantionum – Descendit de caelis; Miserere mei, Deus; Circumdederunt me dolores mortis; Recordare, Domine; Exsurge, quare obdormis, Domine?; Levemus corda; Haec dicit Dominus
The Cardinall's Musick / Andrew Carwood
Hyperion CDA67653 (68' · DDD · T/t) Ⓕ Ⓞ

Andrew Carwood's programme-note begins with a comment on the motet *Haec dicit Dominus* with which the programme ends. The lament of Rachel weeping for her children is thematic, if indeed we are to see these *Cantiones sacrae* of 1591 as a cry on behalf of the old, true believers besieged in a Protestant stronghold. As Rachel wept then, so (it is suggested) does the Church now. And yet there is hope ('et est spes') and this is the message reiterated throughout these heartfelt works of a master craftsman.

This is the 11th volume in The Cardinall's Musick's edition of Byrd's Latin settings. Apart from the *Cantiones*, the other major source is the *Gradualia* of 1607, probably written for the Catholics of Ingatestone Hall in Essex. The Litany from Book 2 (1605) is the principal variant in the mode of composition, which is dense in imitative polyphony, usually in six parts, concentrated in the intensity of their utterance. Particularly fine examples are the *Miserere mei, Deus* and the vigorous *Exsurge, quare obdormis, Domine?* with its strong, well defined climax.

The performances are admirably directed, responsive to words, clear in their exposition of counterpoint, carefully blended in the homophonic passages. The Cardinall's Musick is an expert body of singers who know exactly what they are doing. Even so, balance and tone are not everywhere ideal: the bass-line, for instance, though utterly reliable, has been so stripped of natural vibrancy that the tone is dulled. A small point, no doubt, in relation to the riches their work is opening up.

Music for Holy Week and Easter

Plorans plorabit. Passio Domini nostri Jesu Christe secundum Johannem[a]. Adoramus te[bc]. Vespers for Holy Saturday[a]. Mass Propers for Easter Day. Haec dies. Angelus Domini. Mane vobiscum. Post dies octo. Christus resurgens
The Cardinall's Musick / Andrew Carwood [a]ten

with [b]**Robin Tyson** counterten [c]**Patrick Russill** org
ASV Gaudeamus CDGAU214 (76' · DDD · T/t)

Ⓕ**OOO**

The sixth volume of The Byrd Edition is a land-mark recording, covering most of Byrd's Holy Week and Easter music, from the St John's Passion choruses for Good Friday to the Octave day of Easter, and including miniature Vespers at the end of the Easter Vigil, and the whole of the Proper of the Mass for Easter Day.

The opening motet *Plorans plorabit*, recalling the Lamentations chanted earlier in the week, is a stern reminder of the recusant atmosphere in which Byrd lived out his religious beliefs. The straightforward Passion choruses are rightly set into their proper context, an edition of St John's Passion prepared by Byrd's Roman contemporary, Guidetti. Admirably sung, Carwood maintains throughout a remarkable balance between drama and restraint. A gentle consort song, *Adoramos te*, fills the space in the listener's imagination between the burial of Christ and his rising from the dead. The miniature Vespers follow, sung, almost with bated breath, to Byrd's simple three-part settings of the two antiphons, with a correction of Bretts' suggested psalm-tone for the single – and shortest – psalm.

The Mass *Resurrexi* is exhilarating, with surging themes, rhythmic interplay and bursts of joy. Byrd, unable to resist word-painting suggestive of earthquake at the Offertory, introduces here a note of merriment into a particularly serious liturgy, and doesn't entirely avoid it elsewhere. Thankfully it was under- rather than over-played.

The solemn final four-part processional *Christus resurgens* is a triumphant restatement of the Easter: total joy.

Consort Songs

All in a garden green. La volta No 1 in G, 'Lady Ⓟ
Morley'. O mistress mine I must. Wolsey's Wild.
O-Lord, how vain are all our delights. Psalmes, Sonets and Songs – Who likes to love; My mind to me a kingdom is; Farewell, false love. Triumph with pleasant melody. Truth at the First. Ad Dominum cum tribularer. Cantiones sacrae – Attollite portas; da mihi auxilium; Domine secundum actum meum; Miserere mihi, Domine
Sophie Yates virg
I Fagiolini / Robert Hollingworth; Fretwork
Chandos Chaconne CHAN0578 (73' · DDD · T/t) ⒻO

This disc adopts an imaginative approach to programming Byrd's music by presenting works in different genres grouped together to demonstrate a single stage in his development. It includes Latin motets, keyboard dances and variations on popular songs of the day, and sacred and secular songs (and a dialogue) with viols. There's so much here that wins our admiration: the dazzling contrapuntal elaboration of *Attollite portas*, the close-knit texture of *Da mihi auxilium* and the massive *Ad Dominum cum trib-*

ularer; the exuberant variations on *O mistress mine* (neatly played by Sophie Yates) and Byrd's melodic gift in the strophic *O Lord, how vain*. The singers' adoption of period pronunciation – for example, 'rejoice' emerges as 'rejwace' – affects the tuning and the musical sound, it's claimed here, but without rather clearer enunciation the point remains not proven. Probably more upsetting to many will be the Anglicised pronunciation of Latin.

The viol consort gives stylish support and is well balanced, the Fagiolini sopranos occasionally 'catch the mike' on high notes (eg in the passionate pleas of *Miserere mihi, Domine*), and the recorded level of the virginals might have been a little higher without falsifying its tone. But these are minor criticisms of a most rewarding disc.

Rejoice unto the Lord. Ah, silly soul. Come to me, grief, for ever. Constant Penelope. Lullaby my sweet little baby. O dear life. O God that guides the cheerful sun. O that most rare breast. Ye sacred muses. An aged dame. Psalmes, Songs and Sonnets – How vain the toils that mortal men do take; Who likes to love; All as a sea
Robin Blaze counterten **Concordia** (Emilia Benjamin, Reiko Ichise, Joanna Levine, Mark Levy, Alison McGillivray viols Elizabeth Kenny lte)
Hyperion CDA67397 (67' · DDD · T/t)   ⒻⒹ

The subject-matter of these songs is wide ranging, from a triumphant celebration of an Elizabethan anniversary, *Rejoice unto the Lord*, to the two laments on the death of Sir Philip Sidney, the quietly poignant funeral song *Come to me, grief, for ever*, and the deeply felt sonnet *O that most rare breast*, the text attributed to Sir Edward Dyer, one of Sidney's circle of poets. A third lament, *Ye sacred muses*, was Byrd's personal, most moving tribute to his great master: 'Tallis is dead, and music dies'.

The performance brings out two seemingly contradictory points. One is the importance Byrd gives to the soloist's line. He admires the fine natural voice, so rare, he says, 'as there is not one among a thousand, that hath it...' He'd have appreciated the voice and art of Robin Blaze, whose sympathetic interpretation of Byrd's melodic style, the rests, the patterning of the phrases and the syncopation, is remarkable. The second point is the way in which viols and lute become an integral part of 'a carol for New Yeares Day' – *O God that guides the cheerful sun*. Their imitation of the movements of the voice in the little tableau of the old lady tumbling over on top of the hill, spilling her lapful of skulls, is equally delightful (*An aged dame*). And the sprightly rhythms in *All as a sea* brought home the analogy between human life and life on the ocean wave.

Fantasias – a 6 Nos 2 & 3. Pavan and Galliard a 6, BE17/15. Gradualia, Vol 1/ii: Miscellaneous and Office Text – In manus tuas, Domine. Constant Penelope[a]. Content is rich[a]. My mistress had a little

dogᵃ. The Noble famous Queenᵃ. O Lord how vain are all our delightsᵃ. O you that hear this voiceᵃ. Psalmes, Sonets and Songsᵃ – My mind to me a kingdom is; O that most rare breast. Truth at the Firstᵃ. Out of the Orient crystal skieeᵃ. O Lord, bow down thine... He that all earthy pleasure scornsᵃ
ᵃ**Emma Kirkby** sop **Fretwork** (Richard Boothby, Richard Campbell, Wendy Gillespie, Julia Hodgson, William Hunt, Susanna Pell viols)
Harmonia Mundi HMU90 7383 (75' · DDD · T/t)   Ⓕ

Byrd's consort songs reveal a homelier, more personal aspect than his sterner sacred music. Many have texts reflecting the earlier part of his life, the reign of Edward VI, a time of moralising peity: *He that all earthly pleasure scorns* would be an obvious example, or *Content is rich*. But that particular song becomes fast and witty in this performance, almost tongue-in-cheek: it's as if the singer has joining the viols and uses a vocal technique to match their bowing.

Emma Kirkby's versatile performance brings these delightful items to life, and Fretwork fill out the texture with sensitive imitative polyphony. Sometimes the soprano's almost-too-perfect clarity of articulation tends to obscure the subtlety of the musical phrasing: Byrd makes a point of measuring the English text with extreme care, and the gentle cross-rhythms he creates are essential, adding to the life and flow of the composition.

The well-chosen programme is interspersed with five instrumental pieces, three Fantasias for viols, and a delightful pairing and sharing Pavan and Galliard. Fretwork excel here with their vibrant rhythms and gorgeous interplay of parts.

John Cage   American 1912-1992

Cage left Pomona College early to travel in Europe (1930-31), then studied with Cowell in New York (1933-4) and Schoenberg in Los Angeles (1934): his first published compositions, in a rigorous atonal system of his own, date from this period. In 1937 he moved to Seattle to work as a dance accompanist, and there in 1938 he founded a percussion orchestra his music now concerned with filling units of time with ostinatos (First Construction (in Metal), 1939). He also began to use electronic devices (variable-speed turntables in Imaginary Landscape No 1, 1939) and invented the 'prepared piano', placing diverse objects between the strings of a grand piano in order to create an effective percussion orchestra under the control of two hands. He moved to San Francisco in 1939, to Chicago in 1941 and back to New York in 1942, all the time writing music for dance companies (notably for Merce Cunningham), nearly always for prepared piano or percussion ensemble. There were also major concert works for the new instrument: A Book of Music (1944) and Three Dances (1945) for two prepared pianos, and the Sonatas and Interludes (1948) for one.

During this period Cage became interested in Eastern philosophies, especially in Zen, from which he gained a treasuring of non-intention. Working to remove creative choice from composition, he used coin tosses to determine events (Music of Changes for piano, 1951), wrote for 12 radios (Imaginary Landscape No 4, also 1951) and introduced other indeterminate techniques. His 4'33" (1952) has no sound added to that of the environment in which it is performed; the Concert for Piano and Orchestra (1958) is an encyclopedia of indeterminate notations. Yet other works show his growing interest in the theatre of musical performance (Water Music, 1952, for pianist with a variety of non-standard equipment) and in electronics (Imaginary Landscape No 5 for randomly mixed recordings, 1952; Cartridge Music for small sounds amplified in live performance, 1960), culminating in various large-scale events staged as jamborees of haphazardness (HPSCHD for harpsichords, tapes etc, 1969). The later output is various, including indeterminate works, others fully notated within a very limited range of material, and pieces for natural resources (plants, shells). Cage also appeared widely in Europe and the USA as a lecturer and performer, having an enormous influence on younger musicians and artists; he wrote several books.

The Seasons

The Seasons. Suite for Toy Pianoᵃ. Concerto for Prepared Piano and Orchestraᵇ. Seventy-Four (Versions A & B)ᶜ
Margaret Leng Tan ᵃtoy pf/ᵇprepared pf **American Composers Orchestra / Dennis Russell Davies**
ECM New Series 465 140-2 (76' · DDD)   Ⓕ Ⓞ➔

This is an enchanting CD, every item a sheer delight. Margaret Leng Tan worked with Cage in the last decade of his life, and her earlier recordings show a special sympathy for Cage's keyboard music. The second of her New Albion CDs included the piano solo version of *The Seasons*, and Cage was honest enough to admit to her that he had help from Virgil Thomson and Lou Harrison in making the orchestral version recorded here. The result is Cage at his most poetic, evoking each of the four seasons in lovely changing colours.

There are two realisations of one of the last of what are called Cage's 'Number Pieces', *Seventy-Four*, written for the American Composers Orchestra a few months before his death in 1992. This seamless garment of sustained sound in two overlapping parts is an immensely moving document from a unique human being at the end of his life. Anyone who responds to the spiritual minimalism of Pärt, Górecki or Tavener will understand, especially in these dedicated performances.

The *Concerto for Prepared Piano* (1951) takes its rightful place as the major classic for the transformed instrument with orchestra – a status emphasised by this fastidious performance with its delicate sonic tapestry, including discreet radio, all reflecting Cage's absorption with oriental philosophy. Tan has recorded the *Suite for Toy Piano* (1948) before. This time the sound is closer, you can hear her in-breath just before some movements, and we could have done with more precise rhythms. Lou Harrison's orchestration is perfectly in the spirit and makes a fascinating complement – Cage writing memorable tunes!

This disc shows that much of Cage has now entered the mainstream and that his music is unique.

Number Pieces

Three2. Seven. Ten[a]. Fourteen
The Barton Workshop / James Fulkerson [a]tbn
Megadisc MCD7801 (79′ · DDD)   Ⓕ

Cage's late *Number Pieces* transform the act of subversion into a thing of majorly profound beauty. Musicians are given material framed by 'time brackets' that indicate how long each sound lasts. The different instrumental parts aren't meant to coordinate, and the random overlapping of colliding time brackets creates a texture where harmony without function and over-exposed instrumental timbre fuse with clandestine intent.

The Barton Workshop's survey of four *Number Pieces* is dominated by a monumental 30-minute performance of *Ten* (1991). The wind players dig deep into the fervent beauty of a carefully conceived microtonal patois. The piano is deployed to add pointed perspective, with inside-of-the-instrument stabs cutting across the fluidly sustained grid of the wind and strings. The structure is punctuated by wild-card percussion strokes, the whole unfolding construct growing holistically from the DNA of the material and the process the composer has set up.

Three2 (1991) for three percussionists teases by hovering on a precipice of inaudibility, a device that overturns expectations of percussion music. The piece stutters between momentum and interruption, and the coolly abstract process is embedded with unexpectedly potent drama. Two earlier ensemble works – *Fourteen* (1990) and *Seven* (1988) – are perhaps slightly arid in their realisation, but a beautiful and worthy disc nonetheless.

Piano works

Music for Piano – 1; 2; 3; 4-19; 20; 21-36; 37-52; 53-68; 69-84; 85. Music for-… Two Pianos I/II; Three Pianos; Four Pianos; Five Pianos. Electronic Music for Two Pianos
Steffen Schleiermacher *pf*
Dabringhaus und Grimm ② MDG613 0784-2
(153′ · DDD)   Ⓕ

This set is devoted to the *Music for Piano* series almost entirely written in the 1950s, which is neglected and mostly unavailable. You can see

why performers have found these pieces less attractive. After Cage's crisis year of 1952, which saw him produce the so-called silent piece *4'33"*, he was obsessed with removing his own tastes and desires from his compositions. Before he became fully committed to the *I Ching*'s random numbers he marked out imperfections in the manuscript paper he was using as a way of getting the notes. He said he looked at his paper and suddenly realised that all the music was there. This procedure also settled the density of notes on the page. In the whole series the performer is left to decide dynamics and pace in a continuity dominated by single notes. If this sounds austere, we're reckoning without Schleiermacher's ingenuity. Cage specifies various types of sound production, apart from the use of the keys: primarily plucking the strings from inside or muting them. As in Schleiermacher's prepared piano recordings, the quality of sound has been carefully considered. A muted low note or a single plucked string can be marvellously evocative in conjunction with conventionally produced pitches. The ambience of the prepared piano isn't far away. Further, Schleiermacher avails himself of Cage's provision for several of these pieces to be played together, which he does at intervals in the series. Since we've heard the same pieces solo, the superimposed versions bring back familiar material in a fascinating way. Fastidiously researched and performed, Schleiermacher says he's taken the pieces seriously. In so doing he's begun a new chapter of virtually unknown Cage.

In a Landscape. A Metamorphosis. The Seasons. Ophelia. Two Pieces (c1935). Two Pieces (1946). Quest
Herbert Henck *pf*
ECM New Series 476 1515 (69′ · DDD)   ⒻⒹ

The shock here is that this is simply piano music – no preparations, nothing played from the inside, every detail notated. *In a Landscape*, with a dozen recordings already, tops Cage's greatest hits. It was written for dance, can be played on harp or piano, and again exercises its uncanny, mesmeric powers in this performance by Herbert Henck, who takes it much more slowly than the marked tempo. But Henck's performances throughout are fastidious in representing every detail of the scores. The longest work, *The Seasons* (1947), was a ballet for Lincoln Kirstein which, like the *Sonatas and Interludes*, shows Cage's interest in Indian philosophy before he moved on to Zen. At this period, perceptibly under the influence of Satie, Cage would assemble a collection of attractive sounds and then rotate them automatically, a procedure that became his trademark. The *Two Pieces* (1946) use some of the same autonomous sonorities as *The Seasons* in a different context.

Some of these early pieces are not linked to dance but stem from Cage's study with Schoenberg and his development of his own kind of row technique. Late in life Cage liked his early keyboard pieces but found *A Metamorphosis* the least interesting. These are fascinating documents, well recorded, which bring this part of Cage's enormous output quite naturally into the mainstream of 20th-century piano music.

Sonatas and Interludes
Yuji Takahashi *prpf*
Fylkingen Records FYCD1010 (58' · ADD) Recorded 1965   Ⓕ

Written between February 1946 and March 1948, the *Sonatas and Interludes* were, at the time of this recording, still quite new, although already established as core contemporary repertoire. Even when they were premiered they were accepted as among the least controversial of Cage's works: the somewhat conservative journal *Musical America* welcomed them as 'quite enchanting'. Cage had devised the prepared piano in 1940. Wanting a percussion ensemble for a dance piece but having room only for a piano, he began to transform the instrument into a substitute gamelan. In the *Sonatas and Interludes* he explored the timbral possibilities further, here and there extending them by the use of contact mikes.

These pieces, often structured in accordance with complicated mathematical schemes, leave little to chance. The preparation of the piano is a long and meticulous process, and Cage provided precise directions. Nevertheless, performers need to make choices, and the results can be very different.

The benchmark recording by Aleck Karis (on Bridge) is certainly an impressive, powerful, virtuoso performance. Yet, compared with Takahashi's fresh-sounding reading, with its endlessly subtle gradations and reflective approach, evoking the image of a musical archaeologist's brush carefully revealing ancient, magical inscriptions, Karis sounds too burly, sometimes seeming to fall prey to the contemporary tendency to confuse aggression with conviction. Takahashi is a marvellous guide through the mystery and strange beauty of these appealing pieces.

Litany for the Whale

Litany for the Whale. Aria No 2. Five. The Wonderful Widow of Eighteen Springs. Solo No 22. Experiences No 2. Thirty-six Mesostics re and not re Marcel Duchamp. Aria (arr Hillier). The Year Begins to Be Ripe
Theatre of Voices (Paul Elliott, Andrea Fullington, Allison Zelles, Terry Riley *vocs* Alan Bennett *voc/ closed pf* Shabda Owens *voc/electronics*) / **Paul Hillier** *voc*
Harmonia Mundi HMU90 7279 (72' · DDD · T/t)   Ⓜ

This is a landmark for Cage, Paul Hillier's group and everyone else. Hillier says he's been interested in Cage for years and here his own considerable advocacy has turned Cage into a troubadour of our global village. The Theatre of Voices' collection jumps right in at the deep end with *Litany for the Whale* (1980), a 25-minute monody with two uncannily similar voices (Alan Bennett and Paul Elliott) using only five notes in antiphonal phrases. Shut your eyes and this ritual could almost be Gregorian chant. The scope narrows to three notes in *The Wonderful Widow*, where the closed piano part is slightly subdued, and the same three recur in *Thirty-six Mesostics*, spoken by American minimalist Terry Riley and sung by Hillier.

Cage's *Aria* (1958), for Cathy Berberian, has been associated with one voice but this realisation for seven voices and electronic sounds is thoroughly idiomatic. *Experiences* No 2, another monody to a poem by E E Cummings is beautifully sung, but the precisely notated pauses aren't always accurate. *Aria* No 2 is a fastidious mix of extended vocal techniques by Alan Bennett with weather sounds. Cage convinces us of the musical beauty of rainfall, water and thunder. *Five* is a vocal version of one of Cage's late number pieces. This type of sustained writing is ideal for voices and there are meditative qualities in all these performances. The close-microphone breathing in *Solo* No 22 is, like everything else here, artistic and well engineered.

---

49 Waltzes for the Five Boroughs

49 Waltzes for the Five Boroughs
Video director **Don Gillespie**
Mode 📀 MODE204 (127' · NTSC · 4:3 · 2.0 · 0)   Ⓕ

In 1977 Cage devised this do-it-yourself environmental piece based on 147 New York street locations selected by using chance operations. The conception was realised complete only in 1994/95 when Don Gillespie and colleagues decided to visit all these places and video whatever they saw and heard. So the 49 Waltzes (three sections each = 147 places) are simply film with no other soundtrack apart from what is heard at the time. It's a celebration of ordinary life in urban and residential streets. Refreshingly there's no background music, no asinine commentator, and the visual aspect dominates so that it's more film than music. Cage enjoyed the sound of what happens – so here it is for just over two hours.

In each shot the camera swings out and back from a fixed position; and apart from endless ordinary streets there's a subway station, the Bronx Zoological Gardens, Cunningham Park in Queens, and JFK. The random processes often focus on Staten Island and the whole series ends picturesquely with the sound of gulls and waves at Weir Creek Park in the Bronx. Birds are the soloists elsewhere too. As people go about their business there's surprisingly little conventional music, apart from operetta on tap in a record store and the occasional car radio. The team has realised exactly what Cage intended in the most conscientious way; excellent documentation in three languages.

Antonio Caldara   Italian c1670-1736

Caldara was a chorister at St Mark's, Venice, and proficient on the viol, cello and keyboard. In the 1690s he began writing operas, oratorios and cantatas; his trio sonatas opp. 1 and 2 (1693, 1699) are his only known instrumental chamber works. He served as maestro di cappella da chiesa e dal teatro to the Duke of Mantua, 1699-1707, and maestro di cappella to Prince Ruspoli in Rome between 1709 and 1716, meanwhile composing for other cities. From 1716 until his death he was vice-Kapellmeister at the Viennese court. He was much favoured there for his dramatic works, cantatas liturgical music and oratorios; latterly he also composed stage works for the Vienna Carnival, for court celebrations and for Salzburg. His output (over 3000 works, almost all vocal) was one of the largest of his generation. His operas and oratorios make him a central figure in the creation of music drama in the tradition of Metastasio, many of whose texts he was the first to set.

GROVEmusic

Maddalena ai piedi di Cristo

Maddalena ai piedi di Cristo
Maria-Cristina Kiehr, Rosa Dominguez *sops*
Bernarda Fink *contr* **Andreas Scholl** *counterten*
Gerd Türk *ten* **Ulrich Messthaler** *bass* **Schola
Cantorum Basiliensis / René Jacobs**
Harmonia Mundi ② HMC90 5221/2 (126' · DDD · T/t)
Ⓕ🟠🟠🟠

Caldara was the most prolific and famous oratorio composer of his day and this one, written around 1700, is wonderfully rich in fresh and attractive invention. Practically devoid of external action, it's dramatically tense and concentrates on the struggle between the forces of good and evil, the sinner Magdalen being urged towards penitence by her sister Martha; the roles of Christ and a Pharisee are considerably smaller. The work opens arrestingly, with an agitated sinfonia followed by the hypnotic aria 'Dormi, o cara': then come another 27 brief *da capo* arias with their associated recitatives – ensembles scarcely exist. But there's no lack of variety: some arias, flanked by an orchestral ritornello, are accompanied only by a continuo instrument; others are furnished with different usages of the five-part strings.

René Jacobs furthers the dramatic impact by his pacing; and his casting is flawless. He has the highly effective idea of differentiating the parts of Earthly and Celestial Love by allocating the former to a mezzo and the latter to a countertenor. Both are excellent, but so are all the participants. It seems invidious to single out highlights but outstanding are the aria 'Diletti' for Magdalen (Kiehr) and the succeeding ornate 'Vattene' for Martha (Dominguez) and, even more, two florid arias from Scholl rejoicing in the eventual triumph of good, and two passionately delivered by Fink, of fury by evil at its overthrow. You're urged to acquire this disc.

Cantatas

12 Suonate da camera, Op 2 – in B flat; in A; in F; in G minor. 12 Cantate da camera a voce sola, Op 3[a] – Il Silentio; L'anniversario amoroso; La Fama. Vicino a un rivoletto[a]
Four Nations Ensemble ([a]Jennifer Lane *mez* Ryan Brown, Claire Jolivet *vns* Loretta O'Sullivan *vc*) /
Andrew Appel *hpd*
ASV Gaudeamus CDGAU347 (68' · DDD · T/t)   Ⓕ

This very agreeable disc samples the two chamber genres favoured by Caldara, prolific writer of operas and oratorios in Venice, Rome and Vienna. The sonatas are in the Corelli mould of *sonate da camera*, but half a generation on – more regular in their patterns, rather perkier in their manner, their counterpoint always beautifully dovetailed. The voice behind them isn't especially original, but the music is always pleasingly and elegantly formed. Four of the 12 sonatas of Op 2 are recorded here, including the last of the set, which in the Corelli tradition is an extended ground-bass movement, carried off with a lot of ingenuity. There's wit, too, in some of these pieces: try for example the sparkling little Corrente from No 8. The Four Nations Ensemble play them with real feeling for the idiom as well as impeccable technique, and the recorded sound is bright and true.

It's principally as a vocal composer that Caldara is known, and Jennifer Lane, possessor of a full and warmly musical voice, makes the most of his graceful and shapely lines while always giving due weight and sense to the words. There's plenty of appealing, if again not specially distinctive, music in the three cantatas here, but the gem is *Vicino a un rivoletto*, where the first aria has an *obbligato* for violin and the second one for cello, which, exquisitely played by Loretta O'Sullivan, unmistakably represents the heart swooning with pain, and coupled with Lane's singing does so to very moving effect.

Joseph Canteloube   French 1879-1957

Canteloube studied with d'Indy at the Schola Cantorum and collected and arranged folksongs from throughout France, especially from his native province (four volumes of Chants d'Auvergne for voice and orchestra, 1923-30). He also wrote two operas and other works.   GROVEmusic

Chants d'Auvergne

Canteloube Chants d'Auvergne – La pastoura als camps; Baïlèro; Lʼïo de rotso; Ound' onorèn gorda; Obal, din lou Limouzi; Pastourelle; L'Antouèno; La pastrouletta è lo chibaliè; La deliˈssádo; N'aï pas iéu de mio; Lo calhé; Lo fiolaïré; Passo pel prat;

Lou boussu; Brezairola; Maluros qu'o uno fenno.
Jou l'pount d'o Mirabel; Oï, ayaï; Pour l'enfant;
Chut, chut; Pastorale; Lou coucut; Postouro sé
tu m'aymo; Quand z-éyro petituono; Té, l'co tèl;
Uno jionto postouro; Hél beyla-z-y-dau fél;
Obal, din lo combuèlo; Là-haut, sur le rocher;
Lou diziou bé **Villa-Lobos** Bachianas brasileiras
No 5
Dame Kiri Te Kanawa sop **English Chamber
Orchestra / Jeffrey Tate**
Double Decca ② 444 995-2DF2 (111' · DDD · T/t) Ⓜ️🄳➔

Te Kanawa's richly sensuous approach to these
delightful songs is very seductive, especially
when the accompaniments by Jeffrey Tate and
the ECO are so warmly supportive and the
sound so opulent. Her account of the most
famous number, 'Baïlèro', must be the most
relaxed on record, yet she sustains its repetitions
with a sensuous, gentle beauty of line, supported
by lovely wind playing from the orchestra which
seems to float in the air. There's a resonance
given to the sound, which means that certain of
the brighter, more obviously folksy numbers,
lose a little of their rustic sharpness. However,
the overall effect is very appealing, particularly
when her voice (recorded in the early 1980s) is
so young and fresh.

As an encore we are offered the Villa-Lobos
Bachianas brasileiras No 5, an 'Aria' for soprano
and cellos. The result is ravishing, almost decadent at its softly intoned reprise. An enticing
disc.

Chants d'Auvergne – Baïlèro; L'ïo dè rotso; Ound'
onorèn gorda; Obal, din lou Limouzi; L'Antouèno; La
delïssádo; N'aï pas iéu de mio; Lo calhé; Lo fiolaïré;
Passo pel prat; Brezairola; Oï, ayaï; Pour l'enfant;
Chut, chut; Lou coucut; Tè, l'co, tèl; Uno jionto
postouro; La pastoura als camps; Pastourelle; La
pastrouletta è lo chibaliè; Lou boussu; Malurous qu'o
uno fenno; Jou l'pount d'o Mirabel; Pastorale
Frederica von Stade mez **Royal Philharmonic
Orchestra / Antonio de Almeida**
Sony Classical Essential Classics SBK63063
(73' · DDD)   Ⓑ

This Sony selection with Frederica von Stade is
an old friend. Two sets of recordings have been
combined and all the best-known songs are here
in conventional performances.

Von Stade varies her tone according to the
sense of each song, but the overall mood is less
sharp, more comfortable if you like, than with
some. The RPO sounds a rich and, at generally
broad speeds, Antonio de Almeida provides big-
orchestra accompaniments. You'll probably find
that the consoling romanticism of the *Songs of
the Auvergne* on this tried-and-trusted disc is
more what you had in mind.

Chants d'Auvergne – La pastoura als camps; Baïlèro;
L'ïo dè rotso; Ound' onorèn gorda; O bal, din lou
Limousi; Pastourelle; L'Antouèno; La delïssádo; N'aï
pas iéu de mïo; Lo calhé; Passo pel prat; Lou boussu;

Brezairola; Malurous qu'o uno Fenno; Jou l'pount d'o
Mirabel; Oï, ayaï; Lou coucut; Quand z-èyro
petituono; Uno jionto postouro; Là-haut, sur le
rocher; Lou diziou bé
Véronique Gens sop **Lille National Orchestra /
Jean-Claude Casadesus**
Naxos 8 557491 (62' · DDD · T/t)   Ⓢ🄾➔

Each decade finds its favourite soloist for the
Chants d'Auvergne: in the 1960s it was Natania
Devrath, the 70s had Victoria de los Angeles, the
80s Kiri Te Kanawa, the 90s Dawn Upshaw.
They weren't French, whereas Véronique Gens
is quite at home in the dialect, as she comes from
the Auvergne. Her singing is smooth and delicate, with plenty of body in the tone for some of
the earthier moments.

In all, five volumes of Auvergne songs were
published between 1923-54. Each singer naturally includes 'Baïlèro', the most famous, and
Gens doesn't disappoint in this. The 20 other
songs range from the sad 'Uno jionto postouro',
the lament of the girl whose lover has deserted
her, to 'Malurous qu'o ono Fenno', the jaunty
exposé of unhappy couples.

Jean-Claude Casadesus and the Lille Orchestra bring out all the little details in the score,
such as the lovely woodwind solos that link the
three Bourrées. Perhaps this will become the
interpretation for the present decade.

Chants d'Auvergne – La pastrouletta è lo chibaliè; Lo
fiolaïré; Pour l'enfant; Chut, chut; Pastorale; Postouro
sé tu m'aymo; Tè, l'co, tèl; Hé! beyla-z-y-dau fé!;
Obal, din lo combuèlo. Triptyque. Chants de France
– Auprès de ma blonde; Où irai-je me plaindre?; Au
prè de la rose; Délicieuses cimes; Réveillez-vous!;
D'où venez-vous fillette?
Véronique Gens sop
Lille National Orchestra / Serge Baudo
Naxos 8 570338 (57' · DDD)   Ⓢ🄾➔

For her second CD devoted to Joseph Canteloube's vocal music, Véronique Gens has looked
beyond the celebrated, much-recorded *Chants
d'Auvergne*, and back to *Tryptique*, composed in
1913. Canteloube dedicated this to Maggie
Teyte but the First World War interrupted its
progress, and it was not until 1923 that Jane
Campredon gave the premiere, with the Colonne orchestra conducted by Gabriel Pierné.

A setting of three poems by Roger Frêne, its
lush, not to say extravagant orchestration anticipates Canteloube's later folksong settings. The
influence of both Ravel and Debussy is obvious,
maybe also Stravinsky (it was, after all, the year
of *The Rite of Spring*). The first section, 'Offrande
à l'été' is an ardent love song, with some pretty
giddy scoring for harps. The central 'Lunaire'
has a more mysterious, yearning feel, with a
lovely little dissonance at the word 'cendre', as
the poet imagines the leaves turning to ash. The
finale, 'Hymne dans l'aurore' is an ecstatic
prayer to Pan, celebrating every wonder of
nature. The final cry, 'Mon âme s'ouvre ainsi
qu'une aube étincellante! O Pan!' is marked in

the score *crescendo en grandissant*, and Gens, Serge Baudo and the Lille orchestra rise to the moment with splendid force. It is really surprising that this work has not become better known; any soprano wanting to look beyond the obvious repertory should welcome it.

The rest of the disc is taken up with those remaining Auvergne songs not included on the earlier issue, conducted by Jean-Claude Casadesus. Once again, Gens proves that an authentic knowledge of the dialect is a great advantage. The much later group from *Chants de France* makes a pleasant end to the recital, but it is *Tryptique* that has to be heard.

Elliott Carter   American b1908

Carter studied at Harvard (1926-32), at the Ecole Normale de Musique in Paris (1932-5) and privately with Boulanger. Back in the USA he worked as musical director of Ballet Caravan (until 1940) and as a teacher. From boyhood he had been acquainted with the music of Schoenberg, Varèse, Ives and others, but for the moment his works leaned much more towards Stravinsky and Hindemith: they included the ballets Pocahontas (1939) and The Minotaur (1947), the Symphony No 1 (1942) and Holiday Overture (1944). However, in his Piano Sonata (1946) he began to work from the interval content of particular chords, and inevitably to loosen the hold of tonality. The development was taken further in the Cello Sonata (1948), already characteristic of his later style in that the instruments have distinct roles. A period of withdrawal led to the First Quartet (1951), a work of complex rhythmic interplay, long-ranging atonal melody and unusual form, the 'movements' being out of step with the given breaks in the musical continuity: effectively it is a single unfolding of 40 minutes' duration. It was followed by exclusively instrumental works of similar complexity, activity and energy, including the Variations for orchestra (1955), the Second Quartet (1959), the Double Concerto for harpsichord and piano, each with its own chamber orchestra (1961), the Piano Concerto (1965), the Concerto for Orchestra (1969), the Third Quartet (1971) and the Brass Quintet (1974). At that point Carter returned to vocal composition for a triptych of works for soloist and ensemble: A Mirror on which to Dwell (1975), Syringa (1978) and In Sleep, in Thunder (1981), with words by Elizabeth Bishop, John Ashbery and Robert Lowell respectively. But he has also continued the output of large instrumental movements with A Symphony of Three Orchestras (1976), the piano solo Night Fantasies (1980), the Triple Duo (1983) and Penthode for small orchestra (1985). His String Quartet No 4 (1986) is in a simpler style.

GROVEmusic

Piano Concerto

Piano Concerto. Concerto for Orchestra. Three Occasions

Ursula Oppens pf
**South West German Radio Symphony Orchestra /
Michael Gielen**
Arte Nova Classics 74321 27773-2 (62' · DDD)   Ⓢ

Oppens and Gielen have collaborated in a recording of the Piano Concerto before, and their long familiarity with the work brings an air of confidence to an account which is admirable in its feeling for the essential character as well as the formal logic of a score whose shoals of notes will defeat all but the most dedicated of interpreters. Gielen's ability to bring a convincing sense of shape and a persuasive expressive profile to complex music is no less apparent in an admirable reading of the *Concerto for Orchestra*. Again and again, the solo lines marked in the score are brought out, although the recording isn't able to give ideal clarity to the highly detailed string writing (a compositional problem, perhaps). But Gielen's is as compelling a presentation of this turbulent yet strangely affirmative music as one could hope to hear.

In *Three Occasions* Gielen is weighty, perhaps to excess in the often delicate third piece. Nevertheless, the interpretation is full of character, and the orchestra confirms its excellence in this demanding repertory. Recommended, despite the inadequate insert-notes.

Violin Concerto

'The Music of Elliott Carter, Volume 6'
Violin Concerto[a]. Four Lauds[b]. Holiday Overture[c]
[ab]**Rolf Schulte** vn [ac]**Odense Symphony Orchestra /**
[a]**Justin Brown**, [c]**Donald Palma**
Bridge BRIDGE9177 (58' · DDD)   Ⓕ

'The Music of Elliott Carter, Volume 7'
Dialogues[a]. Boston Concerto[b]. Cello Concerto[c].
ASKO Concerto[d]
[a]**Nicolas Hodges** pf [c]**Fred Sherry** vc
[d]**ASKO Ensemble**; [a]**London Sinfonietta**
[bc]**BBC Symphony Orchestra / Oliver Knussen**
Bridge BRIDGE9184 (62' · DDD)   Ⓕ

There are composers who get a second wind late in their career – and then there's Elliott Carter. Late bloomers such as Verdi (to whom he's often compared) usually make a dramatic coda to their careers, but Carter's burst of productivity in his nineties has actually revealed a noticeable change in musical direction. Their respective rate of maturity notwithstanding, a more fitting comparison would be Ginastera, another composer who began in an accessible folkloric style, turned almost excessively complex in middle age, and reconciled the two in his late maturity.

Having these two volumes of Bridge's Elliott Carter series arrive almost concurrently helps put the composer's career in perspective. Despite the pleasing tonality and unapologetic American-ness of Carter's 1945 *Holiday Overture* (the connection with Ives's *Holidays Symphony* worn handily in its title), the dense counterpoint and rhythmic complexity are nonetheless already in place. The aggressively modernist Carter we usually think of came of age shortly afterward and is still going strong in the Violin Concerto (1990), where musical lines remain unrestrained by tonality or conventional rhythmic pulse.

Those lines may not be as individualistic as in the composer's chamber works but they nonetheless need firm guidance from the podium. Justin Brown shows a sure sense of each line and its destination, making instrumental outbursts more purposeful and less impulsive than they might otherwise seem. It provides, in fact, a nearly unified orchestral front against Rolf Schulte's fairly lyrical solo playing, with textural contrasts duly marking emotional contrasts.

Four Lauds for solo violin, part of an ongoing series of short virtuoso works, traces Carter's more recent transition, from the assertive *Riconoscenza per Goffredo Petrassi* (1984) to the more freely 'romantic' (the composer's own description) *Rhapsodic Musings* (2000). Though hardly as prevalent as his chamber works, the inner musical lines remain surprisingly vital, setting up a palpable internal counterpoint that Schulte deftly navigates.

At first glance, *Dialogues* (2003) would seem to be in the old Carter model, where different musical lines unfold with such clearly delineated personalities that they're often compared to characters in a play. Carter describes the piece as a conversation between piano and orchestra, but the lively discourse continues with little of his former abrasiveness. This is civilised cocktail chatter rather than a raucous town meeting, with musical points respecting each other's space rather than yelling each other down. The Cello Concerto (2001), by contrast, is more a solo oration with some periodic cheers from the crowd. A full decade away from the Violin Concerto, the piece falls back much more squarely on traditional string phrasing and playing technique, but under soloist Fred Sherry the rhetoric is less of a crutch than a platform to make the main points clear and fresh.

Without the benefit of soloists, the remaining concerto grosso works here, the *ASKO Concerto* (2000) and the *Boston Concerto* (2002), indeed confirm a change in Carter's musical approach. It might be too much of a stretch to blame this new-found clarity on the composer writing his first opera in 1999 (at the age of 90!) but clearly Carter has started letting his musical ideas sing as well as shout.

Additional recommendation

Symphonia: sum fluxae pretium speia. Clarinet Concerto[b]
[b]Collins *cl* [a]BBC SO, [b]London Sinf/ Knussen
DG download 459 660-2GH (64' · DDD) Ⓕ❶❶❶↝

In Knussen's supremely authoritative interpretation, the sound quality has been meticulously managed in order to help the listener trace the gradually emerging and steadily unfolding arcs of eloquent melody. It takes time to appreciate how *Symphonia*'s extraordinary variety of pace contributes to the music's melodic and harmonic coherence. The performance of the more approachable Clarinet Concerto will leave you breathless with admiration, not only for Carter's inventiveness but also for the brilliance with which the score is realised by these dedicated artists.

String Quartets – No 2; No 3; No 4
Pacifica Quartet (Simin Ganatra, Sibbi Bernhardsson *vns* Masumi Per Rostad *va* Brandon Vamos *vc*)
Naxos 8 559363 (74' · DDD) Ⓢ❶↝

This disc finds the composer exploring the genre's potential for conversation and confrontation. The Second Quartet (1959) sees its members as a divisive, even dysfunctional foursome – compressing the four movements while interspersing them with cadenzas in which the introspection, impulsiveness and exhibitionism of viola, cello and first violin are offset by the uniformity of the second violin. The Pacifica enter into the discourse with relish, while at times evincing Mozartian poise. The Third Quartet (1971) sets up an opposition between duos of first violin and cello, against second violin and viola in a continuous and vivid juxtaposition of movement types always meaningful in context. Adopting a degree of expressive license, the Pacifica rightly give the sheer velocity of the material its head right through to the seismic energy of the closing pages.

The Fourth Quartet (1986) can seem a retrenchment in its more equable dialogue over four outwardly traditional movements, but this does not account for a deft superimposing of elements across movements in a powerfully cumulative argument; any final 'coming together' being undermined by the coda's fragmentation. Not a work likely to yield its secrets easily, yet the Pacifica add appreciably to its understanding. Both sound and booklet-notes are up to the standard of the earlier disc, thus making its successor an equally indispensable acquisition.

Francesco Cavalli   Italian 1602-1676

Cavalli received musical instruction from his father, GB Caletti, and probably sang in Crema Cathedral choir. In 1616 the governor, Federico Cavalli, persuaded Caletti to allow him to take Francesco to Venice, where the boy (who adopted his patron's name) joined the cappella of St Mark's as a soprano and later tenor. In 1630 Cavalli made an advantageous marriage with a Venetian widow, Maria Sozomeno, and in 1639 he was appointed second organist at St Mark's. He began his opera career at the Teatro San Cassiano and in the 1650s was also active in other Venetian theatres and other Italian cities.

In 1660-62 Cavalli was in Paris, where his celebratory opera, Ercole amante, was played to a less than appreciative audience; when he returned to Venice he vowed never to work for the theatre again. In the event he composed six more operas, but his life centred more on St Mark's and in 1668 he succeeded Rovetta as its maestro di cappella. His wife had died in 1652; they had no children.

The modest quantity of Cavalli's extant sacred music is probably only a small part of a continuous production throughout his career. Most of it follows in the tradition of large concerted works for St Mark's, best represented by the Gabrielis and Monteverdi. The Musiche sacrae (1656) includes a mass and Magnificat for double choir with instruments as well as several motets, and the Vesperi (1675) consists of three Vespers services in eight parts with continuo. A requiem and another Magnificat are among other sacred pieces published during Cavalli's lifetime. He also left secular arias and cantatas, but his most important works were the nearly 30 operas composed for Venetian theatres. They run from the tentative beginnings of public opera to the establishment of Venice as the chief centre of Italian opera, and offer the only continuous view of Venetian operatic style over two decades. Modern revivals, notably of Didone, Ormindo, Calisto and Egisto, have shown Cavalli to be the most important opera composer in the quarter-century after Monteverdi.

GROVEmusic

Statira, Principessa di Persia

Statira, Principessa di Persia
Roberta Invernizzi sop Statira **Dionisia di Vico** mez
Cloridaspe **Maria Ercolano** sop Ermosilla, Usimano
Giuseppe de Vittorio ten Elissena **Guiseppe Nav-
iglio** bass Plutone, Nicarico, Dario **Maria Grazia Schi-
avo** sop Floralba **Daniela del Monaco** contr Bri-
monte **Rosario Totaro** ten Vaffrino **Roberta Andalò**
sop Maga, Eurillo **Stefano di Fraia** ten Marcurio,
Brisante **Valentina Varriale** sop Messo **Cappella de'
Turchini / Antonio Florio**
Opus 111 ② OP30382 (139' · DDD · N/T/t)   Ⓕ

The plot of Statira, first produced in Venice in 1656, is a convoluted mixture of supernatural hatred and royal love triangles. It's given here in a revised form that includes comic scenes prob-ably inserted for a performance at Naples ten years later as part of the festivities celebrating the coronation of King Philip IV of Spain. The Cappella de' Turchini present a refined per-formance. The prominent continuo section juggle the busy demands of the music with seeming ease. Ritornelli are consistently infec-tious and irresistibly dance-like. The playing is generally first class, exemplified by the mournful yet tasteful string playing in Ermosilla's aria 'Menfi, mia Patria, Regno'.

There are few moments of intense drama in an opera that seems to have been devised primarily as entertainment rather than a profound experi-ence. The final chorus declares that 'After all sufferings, all joy comes at last', but the preced-ing drama doesn't present a credible exploration of suffering. It's only when the plot grows more desperate in Act 3 that Statira becomes notably

riveting, but there are delectable moments to enjoy. During the prologue the band plays beau-tifully, while a malcontent sorceress plots revenge on the Arabian King Cloridaspe with caustic glee. Meanwhile, the king has fallen in love with Statira, and their love is subsequently challenged and threatened before all ends hap-pily. Roberta Invernizzi in the title-role is more muscular than most 'early music' sopranos, but lacks nothing in finesse and clarity in the raptur-ous night scene that opens the opera. The out-standing aria of the recording is Invernizzi's exuberantly heroic 'La tromba orgogliosa', although her lament 'Lassa che fò' is an equally potent moment.

The opera's plenteous comic scenes are hammed up, but the plain-speaking servant characters have dated worse than the conven-tional opera seria lovers that monopolise the best arias. Mountains of recitative are delivered with sparkle, and Antonio Florio judges each scene effectively. The quality of the recording is indis-putable, and Opus 111 deserves immense credit for continuing to reveal fascinating lesser-known repertoire. This recording is an indis-pensable indication of operatic style in the under-represented period between Monteverdi and Handel, and those interested in buying it shouldn't hesitate.

Friedrich Cerha   Austrian b1926

Cerha studied at the Vienna Music Academy and later attended the Darmstadt summer courses (1956, 1958, 1959); he also studied philosophy and German studies at the University of Vienna. In 1958 he co-founded the ensemble Die Reihe with Schwertsik. Its regular concerts from 1959 gave a platform not only to a wide range of new compositions, but also to the work of the Second Viennese School, especially Webern. After the ensemble's first foreign tour in 1962, Cerha embarked on an international conduct-ing career. He has also been an active champion of early music, founding the ensemble Camerata Fres-cobaldiana in 1960 and producing several editions of 16th- and 17th-century Italian music. He is perhaps best known for completing the orchestration of the third act of Berg's Lulu (1962-78). In 1959 he was appointed to teach at the Vienna Academy (later the Vienna Hochschule), where he later became reader (1969-76) and professor (1976-88).

Beginning in 1980, Cerha frequently returned to earlier projects, resuming work on them from a new perspective. He has remarked that for him innova-tion does not lie in the creation of the material itself as much as in the act of shaping it.

Cello Concerto

Cerha Cello Concerto[a]
Schreker Chamber Symphony
[a]**Heinrich Schiff** vc **Netherlands Radio
Chamber Orchestra / Peter Eötvös**

ECM New Series 476 3098 (61' · DDD) Ⓕ Ⓞ ▶

ECM has performed another valuable service in releasing a major work by Friedrich Cerha who remains best known for completing the third act of Berg's *Lulu*. His own music is poorly represented but the Cello Concerto is certainly representative of his recent output. It began life in 1989 as a 'Phantasiestück' that, seven years on, was made the centrepiece of the present three-movement work. And it is this movement, its serene outer sections enclosing a scherzo of limpid delicacy, that makes the strongest impression. Those either side intensify Cerha's combative post-Romanticism, but their rather dutiful alternation between relative dynamism and stasis does not always generate the momentum needed to power the 35-minute whole, for all that dedicatee Heinrich Schiff is effortlessly in command of its interpretative challenges.

Whether or not Cerha occupies a niche corresponding to that of Franz Schreker at the beginning of the 20th century (as Hans-Klaus Jungheinrich's booklet-note seems to imply), his Chamber Symphony (1916) makes an apposite coupling: a work that both reflects the Straussian opulence of his previous operas and anticipates the impressionistic subtlety of those that followed. Peter Eötvös emphasises the latter and throws the ingenious four-movements-in-one format into constructive relief. With its luminous textures alluringly caught by the superb recording, this is now the version to have and the whole disc offers an unfailingly absorbing listen.

Emmanuel Chabrier   French 1841-1894

Chabrier was trained as a lawyer and worked in the Ministry of the Interior until 1880, meanwhile developing his talents as a pianist and improviser, studying composition, publishing piano pieces and writing light stage works. His friends included Verlaine, Manet, Fauré and Chausson, who encouraged his admiration for Wagner. He produced several imaginative operas, among which the Wagnerian Gwendoline (1885) and the graceful opéra comique Le roi malgré lui (1887) were favourably received in Germany. He is best known for his sparkling orchestral rhapsody España (1883), but his natural talent for the lyric, the comic and the colourful is most apparent in his piano works, notably the Impromptu (1873), the ten Pièces pittoresques (1881), the Bourrée fantasque (1891) and the Valses romantiques (1883); they show free treatment of dissonance, modality, bold harmonic contrasts, rhythmic verve and dynamic inventiveness, and inspired subsequent generations of French composers, particularly Ravel.
GROVEmusic

Piano works

Habañera. Impromptu. 10 Pièces pittoresques. Cinq Pièces posthumes - Aubade; Ballabile; Caprice;

Feuillet d'album; Ronde Champêtre
Angela Hewitt pf
Hyperion CDA67515 (76 '·DDD) Ⓕ Ⓞ Ⓞ

Chabrier's name lives on primarily through *España* and *Marche joyeuse*. His tiny output for piano is far too rarely encountered in the concert hall or on recordings, yet he is a delightful, self-contained original. From his total of a mere 26 titles, Angela Hewitt plays 18 on this little gem of a disc. It sounds as though the piano was recorded in some deserted *fin de siècle* spa hotel – and so it proves, for Hewitt's richly coloured Fazioli was captured in 'Das Kulturzentrum Grand Hotel, Dobbiaco, Italy'. In fact, whenever there is an exposed soft passage in the upper treble in this programme, the same atmospheric effect engages the ear momentarily; in the more robust items, it is hardly noticeable. As to Hewitt's performances, they are as affectionate, warm, lyrical and charming as one could wish, underlining but not exaggerating Chabrier's deliciously predictable unpredictability.

Further recommendation

Suite pastorale. Habanera. España. Larghetto. Prélude pastoral. Joyeuse marche. Gwendoline – Overture. Le roi malgré lui – Fête polonaise
Ronald Janezic vn **VPO / Gardiner**
DG download *447 751-2GH* (66' · DDD) Ⓕ Ⓞ ▶
Gardiner draws some superbly responsive playing from the Vienna Philharmonic and a first-class recording, while warm, leaves all detail clear, and sweeps the board with a set of outstanding, exuberant performances.

Marc-Antoine Charpentier
French 1643-1704

Charpentier studied in Rome, probably with Carissimi, whose oratorios he introduced into France. On his return to Paris he was employed as composer and singer by the Duchess of Guise and also collaborated with Molière in the theatre. In the early 1680s he entered the service of the grand dauphin, for which Louis XIV granted him a pension in 1683, and he was for a time music teacher to Philippe, Duke of Chartres (later Duke of Orleans and Regent of France). Perhaps also in the 1680s Charpentier became attached to the Jesuit church of St Louis in Paris, and from 1698 until his death he held the important post of maître de musique of the Saint-Chapelle, for which he wrote some of his most impressive works.

Charpentier's church music was based initially on mid-century Italian models, but soon incorporated French modes of expression – the 'official' grandeur of the grand motet; the declamatory manner of the court air and Lullian récit; the 'popular' simplicity of noëls; and an often elaborately ornamented melodic line. Charpentier was the only Frenchman of his time to write oratorios of any quality. His theatre composi-

tions are even more indebted to French models, and he was an important composer of airs sérieux and airs à boire. **GROVE**music

---

Mass, H1

Mass, H1. Te Deum, H147. Precatio pro filio regis, 🅟 H166. Panis quem ego dabo, H275. Canticum Zachariae, H345, 'Benedictus Dominus Deus'
Le Concert Spirituel / Hervé Niquet
Naxos 8 553175 (57' · DDD · T/t) Ⓢ🅑▶

This early Mass is a beautiful piece, intimately scored for voices with two melody instruments and continuo. The Mass is harmonically richly inventive with passages of vivid word-painting. Taken as a whole the work is generously endowed with subtle inflexions, a pervasive element of contemplation, and effectively varied rhythmic juxtapositions which enliven the text and hold our attention.

The *Te Deum*, for four soloists, four-part choir and *colla parte* instruments, isn't that one for which Charpentier is renowned but a smaller, later piece belonging to the last years of his life. Modest in scale it may be but musically it's impressive and emotionally satisfying. The choir and instrumentalists of Le Concert Spirituel are on their usual lively form. Some of the solo vocal contributions are more focused than others but the choir maintains a high standard of vocal blend and secure intonation. The recorded sound is very good indeed and Niquet directs with stylistic assurance.

Te Deum, H146

Te Deum, H146. Dixit Dominus, H202. Domine salvum fac regem, H291. In honorem S Ludovici Regis Galliae canticum, H365. Marches pour les trompettes, H547
Le Concert Spirituel / Hervé Niquet
Glossa GCD921603 (55' · DDD) Ⓕ🅞

Hervé Niquet and his ensemble are old hands at the French *grand motet* for choir and instruments by now, and Charpentier in particular has been well served by them. Here they move into familiar ground in the form of the best-known of his *Te Deum* settings, prefaced by two scurrying, delightful little marches and coupled with three motets not currently available elsewhere. These last should be good enough reason to acquire the disc, but even for those who have a *Te Deum* or two in their collection already, Niquet's reading of it is another. With a choir of 12 and a one-to-a-part band, this is as limpid and lithe a performance of the piece as you're likely to hear. Niquet chooses some fleet tempos, but also injects the music with a catchy rhythmic lilt and an attention to declamatory detail that constantly keeps the music alive. And when a smoother arch is required, as in the choral soprano setting of 'te ergo quaesumus', he can

touch the heart too. Good recorded sound and balance make this a disc to have.

Vesper psalms / Magnificat, H72

Charpentier Beatus vir, H221. Laudate pueri, H149. Laetatus sum, H216. Nisi Dominus, H150. Lauda Jerusalem, H210. Ave maris stella, H60. Magnificat, H72. Salve regina, H24 **Nivers** Antiphonarium Monasticum, Antiennes I-VI
Le Concert Spirituel / Hervé Niquet
Naxos 8 553174 (61' · DDD · T/t) Ⓢ🅑▶

This release offers a liturgical reconstruction of the Vespers office. The five Vesper psalms and *Magnificat* belong to different periods in Charpentier's life and the six antiphons are by his organist-composer contemporary, Nivers. The reconstruction works well and Le Concert Spirituel, under Hervé Niquet, demonstrates its rapport with Charpentier's music. The vocal sound is fresh and the wide range of musical *Affekt* shows off a greater diversity of tonal colour. Tenors and basses incline towards a roughness of timbre here and there yet, overall, the bright and full-blooded choral sound is pleasing and vital. Some may find the recording balance of the psalms and canticle a fraction too close, creating the atmosphere of a drawing-room Vespers rather than one in more spacious, ecclesiastical surroundings. The antiphons fare much better in this respect, having a deeper aural perspective. This is a richly rewarding programme of music which never disappoints.

Leçons de Ténèbres du Vendredi Saint

Leçons de Ténèbres de la Semaine Sainte de 1692 – H135; H136; H137. Méditations pour le Carême – H380; H381; H386; H387; H388
Thibaut Lenaerts, Cyril Auvity countertens **Pierre Evreux, Ian Honeyman** tens **Alain Buet, Ronan Nédélec** bars **Le Concert Spirituel / Hervé Niquet**
Glossa GCD921604 (59' · DDD · T/t) Ⓕ

Messe de Monsieur de Mauroy, H6
Marie-Louise Duthoit, Claire Gouton sops **Serge Goubiod** counterten **Pierre Evreux** ten **Christophe Sam** bass **Le Concert Spirituel / Hervé Niquet**
Glossa GCD921602 (66' · DDD · T/t) Ⓕ

It almost goes without saying that a Hervé Niquet recording of Charpentier is going to be a thing of beauty. Whether it's in the long build-up to the top of the grand arch that's the opening *Kyrie* of the *Messe de Monsieur de Mauroy*, or the ardent twists and dissonances with which the first of the *Leçons de Ténèbres* announces itself, it only takes a few moments for Niquet's expert team of singers and instrumentalists to draw us into the achingly expressive world of 17th-century France.

Composed around 1691, this is the longest of his 11 Masses, and its many sections seem to move effortlessly from one to another, creating a constantly shifting range of subtle responses to text – some sweet, some stirring, some lilting and some weighty – while successfully maintaining the work's continuity.

Charpentier composed 31 incomplete sets of *Leçons de Ténèbres*, those intense settings of the Lamentations of Jeremiah that were so popular in Holy Week in France during the mid-Baroque period, and which produced some of its most ravishing musical moments. Scored for six male voices, strings, flutes and continuo, this set moves between straightforward declamation and music of increasing harmonic and dramatic urgency to present a striking evocation of the desolation of the ruined Jerusalem.

These performances are exquisitely judged, showing an unerring feel for the music's expressive ebb and flow. Two releases of thorough desirability.

Dialogus inter angelum et pastores, H406

Dialogus inter angelum et pastores, H406[a]. Mors
Saülis et Jonathae, 'Cum essent congregata ad praelium', H403[b]. Sacrificium Abrahae, H402[c]
[bc]**Jaël Azzaretti**, [bc]**Marie-Louise Duthoit** sops
Gérard Lesne, [bc]**Benjamin Clee** countertens
Jean-François Novelli, [bc]**Nicholas Bauchau** tens
Ronan Nédélec, [bc]**Raimonds Spogis** basses
Il Seminario Musicale / Gérard Lesne
Naïve Astrée E8821 (68' · DDD)   Ⓕ⊙

French countertenor Gérard Lesne and Il Seminario Musicale manage to bring Charpentier's three miniature oratorios vividly to life. The works employ narrators – sometimes a solo voice, sometimes the chorus – in a highly dramatic series of instrumental and vocal movements, carefully tinged with suspensions and chromatic inflections. Both *Mors Saülis et Jonathae* and *Sacrificium Abrahae* rely on tightly constructed dialogues cast in recitative. Lesne intensifies the characterisation by associating particular combinations of continuo instruments and organ stops with each of the interlocutors. Melodic, melismatic movements are reserved for moments of powerful emotion, as when David weeps for his brother Saül.

Although Il Seminario Musicale take pride in performing without a conductor, they wouldn't produce the precision of ensemble so evident in this recording but for the vigilance of the continuo players. The absence of a principal interpreter is audible and here, as in less complex chamber music, the effect is highly desirable. Lesne delivers a string of inspiring performances in a raft of roles – as do Jean-François Novelli as David and Abraham and the bass Raimonds Spogis as Samuel.

Christmas Music

Canticum in nativitatem Domini, 'Usquequo avertis', H416. Dialogus inter angelos et pastores Judeae in nativitatem Domini, H420. Noël: un flambeau, Janette, Isabelle!, H460c

Aradia Ensemble / Kevin Mallon
Naxos 8 557036 (62' · DDD)   Ⓢ⮕

Perhaps few composers have produced as much beautiful Christmas music as Charpentier. Both oratorios recorded here are generously laid out for soloists, chorus and a sweet-toned, atmospherically nocturnal ensemble of recorders and strings, a grand motet-style line-up which Charpentier uses to create a work with clear dramatic pretensions. Thus, in addition to the ravishing choral writing of the kind at which Charpentier excelled, each oratorio has a gentle instrumental number to represent night (an archetype taken straight from the dreamy *sommeil*s of French Baroque opera), followed by a tootly little dance-chorus to represent the 'awakening of the shepherds', and later on a perky march to send them off to Bethlehem. In this way Charpentier's faultless music brings together his own contemporary world and that of the New Testament in an utterly beguiling mixture of richness and simplicity.

The Toronto-based Aradia Ensemble are superbly attuned to the music's atmosphere. Perhaps an extra ounce of vocal refinement could have been drawn from the choir, but more important be that these performances show an unfailing appreciation of style, taste and sheer beauty of sound. The result is a Christmas treat for us all.

Actéon, H481

Actéon   Ⓟ
Dominique Visse counterten Actéon **Agnès Mellon** sop Diane **Guillemette Laurens** mez Junon **Jill Feldman** sop Arthébuze **Françoise Paut** sop Hyale
Les Arts Florissants Vocal Ensemble
La Comtesse d'Escarbagnas/Le Mariage Forcé, H494 – Ouverture
Michel Laplénie ten **Philippe Cantor** ten
Les Arts Florissants Ensemble / William Christie
Harmonia Mundi Musique d'abord HMA195 1095 (47' · ADD) Recorded 1981   Ⓑ⊙⊙⊙

Ⓖ Charpentier's little vignette opera is an astonishingly rich score containing most, if not all, the ingredients of a *tragédie-lyrique*. There's a profusion of fine choruses and dances but an overture which departs somewhat from the standard Lullian pattern. *Actéon* is made up of six well-contrasted short scenes. The first of them is musically the most colourful with appealing evocations of *La chasse* and a riotous dance as the hunters go in search of their quarry. The second scene is much gentler with a tender air for Diana, pastoral reflections from her followers and a recurring chorus of nymphs which recalls passages in Blow's *Venus and Adonis*. Jill Feldman as Arthebuze, one of Diana's attendants, is admirably languid in her air disdaining love's ardour. Scene 3 discloses a pensive Actéon who, while reflecting on matters of the heart, stumbles upon Diana and her retinue in a state of *déshabillé*. Actéon's defence is touching and is delicately portrayed by Dominique Visse. The fourth tableau begins with Acteon's discovery that he has been turned into a stag: 'A horrible fur enwraps me', he cries and, at this point Visse cleverly alters the character of his voice: 'Ma parole n'est plus qu'une confuse voix.' A poignant symphonie follows. In the fifth tableau Actéon is torn to pieces by his own hounds and, in the sixth and final scene, Junon imperious as ever explains to the hunters what they have just done. A chorus of grief mingled with anger sung by Acteon's followers brings this little *opera de chasse* to an end.

Christie directs the work from beginning to end with conviction and assurance. The action is well paced and there's an intensity of expression, a fervour, which gives a touching emphasis to the drama.

Médée, H491

Médée   **P**
Lorraine Hunt sop Médée **Bernard Deletré** bass
Créon **Monique Zanetti** sop Créuse **Mark Padmore**
ten Jason **Jean-Marc Salzmann** bar Oronte **Noémi**
Rime sop Nérine **Les Arts Florissants / William**
Christie
Erato ③ 4509-96558-2 (195' · DDD · T/t)   Ⓕ**OO**

Lorraine Hunt's Medea is something of a *tour de force*. She invests every word with meaning and produces the widest range of colour to express all the emotional nuances in Medea's complex character – jealousy, indignation, tenderness, sorrow, fury, malignity and outright barbarism: she's outstanding in Act 3, one of the most superb acts in all Baroque opera, in which she has no fewer than four great monologues, the first with affecting chromatic harmonies, the second accompanied by feverish rushing strings, the third the sombre 'Noires filles du Styx' with its eerie modulations, the fourth with dark orchestral colours. Charpentier's orchestration and texture, indeed, are wonderfully effective: string writing varies between extreme delicacy (beautifully played here) and savage agitation; the cool sound of the recorders is refreshing and the many dances featuring recorders and oboes are enchanting. As Jason, Mark Padmore, a real *haute-contre*, sings with admirable ease and intelligence and the tragic Creusa, poisoned by the vengeful Medea is the light-voiced Monique Zanetti, the very embodiment of youthful innocence and charm: her death scene, still protesting her love for Jason, is most moving. A notable detail in all the principals, incidentally, is their absorption of *agréments*, with Hunt showing special mastery in this regard. All told, a considerable achievement, and a triumph for Christie.

Ernest Chausson   French 1855-1899

Chausson grew up in comfortable and cultured circumstances but turned to music only after being trained in law. Studying with Massenet at the Paris

Conservatoire, he came under Franck's influence and visited Germany to hear Wagner. His friends in Paris included Mallarmé, Debussy, Albéniz and Cortot. He died prematurely in a cycling accident but his output reflects his growing maturity from dependence on Massenet, Franck and Wagner, seen in the prettiness of early songs and the orchestration of the symphonic poem Viviane (1882), to a more elaborate, intensely dramatic style in the Poème de l'amour et de la mer (1882-93) and the opera Le roi Arthus (1886-95), and finally to a period of serious melancholy which produced the Turgenev-inspired Poème Op 25 for violin and orchestra (1896) and some concise chamber music.   **GROVE**music

Symphony in B flat, Op 20

Symphony in B flat, Op 20. Viviane, Op 5. Soir de fête, Op 32. La têmpete – Air de danse; Danse rustique
BBC Philharmonic Orchestra / Yan Pascal Tortelier
Chandos CHAN9650 (67' · DDD)   Ⓕ**OO**

There are at least two misconceptions to put right about Franck's arguably most gifted pupil. The first, which this disc dispels admirably, is that the majority of Chausson's music, in the manner of his *Poème*, is endlessly melancholic or elegiac. The second, which the disc doesn't dispel quite so well, is that in his orchestral writing never managed to free itself from Wagner's embrace. Never *entirely* perhaps, but by the time the 43-year-old composer came to write his last orchestral piece, the nocturnal *Soir de fête* included here, his escape from Wagner was well under way, and who knows where it might have led, had it not been for his tragically early death the following year? The outer sections of *Soir de fête* have something about them of 'the vibrating, dancing rhythms of the atmosphere' of Debussy's later *Fêtes*. The programme as a whole, the overall richness of the orchestral process – whether Wagnerian, Franckian, Straussian or Chaussonian – is well served by the full-bodied sound of Tortelier's BBC Philharmonic.

The Symphony, like Franck's, is cyclical, but not otherwise as indebted to the older composer as is often suggested. There are none of Franck's organ-loft sonorities anywhere in this wonderfully variegated, open-air orchestration. This is the finest modern recording of the Symphony now available. Each movement is superbly built, and Chandos's recording is truly impressive although in the excerpts from Chausson's incidental music for *The Tempest*, the sound is perhaps a little bulky.

Chausson Symphony, Op 20 **Franck** Symphony
Liège Philharmonic Orchestra / Louis Langrée
Accord 476 8069 (72' · DDD)   Ⓕ**OO**

It is apt that this excellent new version of the Franck Symphony, the most important orchestral work by the greatest of Belgian composers, should come from a Belgian orchestra. It is good, too, that it is coupled with a symphony by a composer closely associated with him, Chausson's Op 20. It may come as a surprise to find what a refined body the Liège orchestra is under Louis Langrée: their Franck could hardly be more idiomatic, with subtle nuances of phrasing and variations of tempo reflecting the players' affection for the music.

The syncopated rhythms of principal themes in the first movement and finale come over with natural ease and affection, and, helped by a well balanced recording, the playing has splendid dramatic bite. Langrée's tempo for the central slow movement keeps the music moving, fairly enough in reflection of the perhaps unexpected tempo marking of *Allegretto*.

The performance of the Chausson is equally persuasive and the result is totally idiomatic. Langrée again opts for a flowing speed in the central slow movement, this time marked *Très lent* – very slow – but never sounds at all rushed. The clarity and immediacy of the sound add to the impact and Chausson's syncopated rhythms are conveyed most persuasively.

Piano Trio in G minor, Op 3

Piano Trio **Ravel** Piano Trio
Pascal Rogé *pf* **Mie Kobayashi** *vn*
Yoko Hasegawa *vc*
Onyx ONYX4008 (58' · DDD)   Ⓕ🅑➤

Pascal Rogé heads up this thoughtful disc of French trios. He has described his gods as Bach, Beethoven and Schumann, with Poulenc, Debussy and Satie as his friends. And so, too, are Ravel and Chausson, to judge by his finely sensitive performances.

Ravel's swaying, insinuating opening theme could hardly be played more lucidly or affectionately and its final return is full of hushed magic, a far cry from smarter, more metropolitan and impersonal readings. The *Pantoum* is vivacious rather than aggressive and the entire performance, even in moments of heightened drama and intensity, is unforced, its sparkle gentle rather than metallic or self-consciously virtuosic.

Chausson's early Trio is remote from such ultra-Gallic refinement and sophistication, its opening Pas trop lent romantically troubled in a style clearly deriving from César Franck's recently completed Piano Quintet. The second movement *Vite*, on the other hand, falls like manna from heaven after so much chromatic turbulence. Both here and in the finale Chausson breaks out into a reassuring lightness which has its origins in Saint-Saëns. Such alternating solace and despair are beautifully realised by Rogé and his colleagues. The warm and fluid Onyx sound reflects performances of a quiet but unmistakable authority.

Additional recommendation

Piano Trio
Coupled with:

Poème, Op 25 (arr cpsr). Andante et Allegro. Pièce, Op 39
Neidich *cl* **Graffin** *vn* **Hoffman** *vc* **Devoyon** *pf*
Chilingirian Qt
Hyperion CDA67028 (62' · DDD)   Ⓕ🅑➤
Opulent sound and wonderfully committed playing makes this is a real winner and an ideal disc if you want an all-Chausson programme.

Poème de l'amour et de la mer, Op 19

Poème de l'amour et de la mer, Op 19
Debussy Cinq poèmes de Charles Baudelaire (arr Adams) – Le balcon; Harmonie du soir; Le jet d'eau; Recueillement **Ravel** Shéhérazade
Susan Graham *sop* **BBC Symphony Orchestra / Yan Pascal Tortelier**
Warner Classics 2564 61938-2 (63' · DDD · T/t)
Ⓕ❶❷❸➤

Ⓖ Only a brave, or foolhardy, composer sets about reorchestrating Debussy. Yet that's what John Adams has done, in 'Le jet d'eau', the third of Debussy's *Cinq poèmes de Charles Baudelaire*, the first four of which Adams has chosen to score for a modern orchestra. He's done an effective job, and if it makes the songs sound more boisterous, less mysterious than in the usual version for voice and piano, he's probably doing his soloist a big favour. By common consent, these are the most difficult of all Debussy's early songs. Susan Graham seems totally in command, her *diminuendo* on the words 'Et le charme des soirs' is tender, and is echoed a few bars later by Adams providing a nostalgic woodwind for the reference to those firelit evenings, 'par l'audeur du charbon'.

There's a lovely photograph, taken in 1893, the year of *Poème de l'amour et de la mer*. It shows Debussy, at Chausson's house, playing the piano. Both composers are in white shirts, surrounded by a peaceful group of family and friends, all in summer clothes, the windows openThis is the sort of mood this disc evokes. Yan Pascal Tortelier and Susan Graham give Chausson's work a well-nigh perfect performance, capturing the sense of quiet regret at the memory of springtime love that has faded, and of a story that is never quite told.

As for Ravel's *Shéhérazade*, like nearly all mezzo-sopranos, Graham is stretched to the limits of her resources by the big climactic phrases in 'Asie'. She sings a hushed, beautiful 'La flûte enchantée' and a rather too sad 'L'indifférent', but it's all done with a fine line, with the BBC Symphony Orchestra playing Ravel's music with a good deal of passion.

Luigi Cherubini   Italian 1760-1842

Cherubini was a dominant figure in French musical life for half a century. At 18, with 36 works (mainly church music) to his credit, he began a period of study with Sarti in Bologna and Milan (1778-80). The resulting Italian operas he produced in Italy and London (1784-5), and his work as an Italian opera director (1789-90) in Paris (where he had settled in 1786), pale in significance next to the triumphant premiere of his second French opera, Lodoïska (Paris, 1791). He was appointed inspector at the new Institut National de Musique (from 1795 the Conservatoire), his status soon being enhanced by the successes of Médée (1797) and Les deux journées (1800). As surintendant de la musique du roi under the restored monarchy, he turned increasingly to church music, writing seven masses, two requiems and many shorter pieces, all well received (unlike his later operas).

Cherubini's importance in operatic history rests on his transformation of merely picturesque or anecdotal opéra comique into a vehicle for powerful dramatic portrayal (eg Médée's depiction of psychological conflict) and for the serious treatment of contemporary topics.

His best church music, notably the C minor Requiem (specially admired by Beethoven, Schumann, Brahms and Berlioz), unites his command of counterpoint and orchestral sonority with appropriate dramatic expression, while his non-vocal works, chiefly the operatic overtures, Symphony in D and six string quartets, make their effect through the creative use of instrumental colour. GROVEmusic

Mass No 1 in C minor

Mass No 1 in C minor. Marche funèbre
**Corydon Singers; Corydon Orchestra /
Matthew Best**
Hyperion CDA66805 (54' · DDD · T/t)   Ⓕ

It would be an oversimplification to suggest that Matthew Best emphasises the Beethoven rather than the Berlioz aspect of the main work here; but he does seem less interested in the fascinating use of colour as an element in the actual invention than in the rugged moral strength and the force of the statements. The recording reflects this emphasis, and is firm and clear without being especially subtle over orchestral detail. The choir delivers the *Dies irae* powerfully, and much dramatic vigour is recalled in the fugue traditionally reserved for 'Quam olim Abrahae'. Berlioz, however, was satirical about Cherubini's fugues, and saved his admiration for the wonderful long *decrescendo* that ends the *Agnus Dei*. This is beautifully controlled here.

Best includes the tremendous *Marche funèbre*, inspiration here again for Berlioz. Best handles this superbly, opening with a merciless percussion crash and sustaining the pace and mood unrelentingly. It sounds more original than ever, a funeral march that, rather than mourn or honour, rages against the dying of the light.

Requiem in C minor

Requiemᵃ. Marche funèbre
ᵃ**Gruppo Vocale Cantemus; Italian Swiss Radio**
ᵃ**Chorus and Orchestra / Diego Fasolis**
Naxos 8 554749 (56' · DDD · T/t)   Ⓢ➔

Cherubini's C minor Requiem was admired by both Berlioz and Beethoven, with good reason, since both owed a great deal to a work that isn't far short of a masterpiece. For Beethoven, the music's rugged strength and the force of the statements held much; Berlioz, often mocking and unfair to Cherubini, responded warmly to the use of instrumental colour as part of the actual invention. To oversimplify, if Christoph Spering and his Cologne artists (Opus 111) give a more colourful, 'Berliozian' performance, Matthew Best and the Corydon Singers (Hyperion) respond to the 'Beethovenian' aspect of the music. Of course, there's much more to it than that. Both are excellent performances.

So is the present one. Certainly it has more of an emotional charge in the 'Dies irae' than Spering's which, once the trump has sounded, gathers the voices with nervous intensity rather than the urgent drama that both Best and Fasolis discover. Best and Fasolis also produce great vigour for the 'Quam olim Abrahae' fugue. No one can make very much of the *Sanctus*, a surprisingly weak movement; all respond sensitively to the strange 'Pie Jesu', Best and Fasolis with rather sharper definition of phrasing.

All three open with the tremendous *Marche funèbre*, another piece that inspired Berlioz when he came to write his *Hamlet* funeral march. Excellent as the new performance is, those who acquired Best, in particular, can rest content.

Fryderyk Chopin   Polish 1810-1849

The son of French émigré father (a schoolteacher working in Poland) and a cultured Polish mother, Chopin grew up in Warsaw, taking childhood music lessons (in Bach and the Viennese Classics) from Wojciech Zywny and Jósef Elsner before entering the Conservatory (1826-9). By this time he had performed in local salons and composed several rondos, polonaises and mazurkas. Public and critical acclaim increased during the years 1829-30 when he gave concerts in Vienna and Warsaw, but his despair over the political repression in Poland, coupled with his musical ambitions, led him to move to Paris in 1831. There, with practical help from Kalkbrenner and Pleyel, praise from Liszt, Fétis and Schumann and introductions into the highest society, he quickly established himself as a private teacher and salon performer, his legendary artist's image being enhanced by frail health (he had tuberculosis), attractive looks, sensitive playing, a courteous manner and the piquancy attaching to self-exile. Of his several romantic affairs, the most talked about was that with the novelist George Sand – though whether he was truly drawn to women must remain in doubt. Between 1838 and 1847 their relationship, with a strong element of the maternal on her side, coincided with one of his most productive creative periods. He gave few public concerts, though his playing was much praised, and he published much of his best music simultaneously in Paris, London and Leipzig. The breach with Sand was followed by a rapid deteriora-

tion in his health and a long visit to Britain (1848). His funeral was attended by nearly 3000 people.

No great composer has devoted himself as exclusively to the piano as Chopin. By all accounts an inspired improviser, he composed while playing, writing down his thoughts only with difficulty. But he was no mere dreamer – his development can be seen as an ever more sophisticated improvisation on the classical principle of departure and return. For the concert-giving years 1828-32 he wrote brilliant virtuoso pieces (eg rondos) and music for piano and orchestra the teaching side of his career is represented by the studies, preludes, nocturnes, waltzes, impromptus and mazurkas, polished pieces of moderate difficulty. The large-scale works – the later polonaises, scherzos, ballades, sonatas, the Barcarolle and the dramatic Polonaise-fantaisie – he wrote for himself and a small circle of admirers. Apart from the national feeling in the Polish dances, and possibly some narrative background to the ballades, he intended notably few references to literary, pictorial or autobiographical ideas.

Chopin is admired above all for his great originality in exploiting the piano. While his own playing style was famous for its subtlety and restraint, its exquisite delicacy in contrast with the spectacular feats of pianism then reigning in Paris, most of his works have a simple texture of accompanied melody. From this he derived endless variety, using wide-compass broken chords, the sustaining pedal and a combination of highly expressive melodies, some in inner voices. Similarly, though most of his works are basically ternary in form, they show great resource in the way the return is varied, delayed, foreshortened or extended, often with a brilliant coda added.

Chopin's harmony however was conspicuously innovatory. Through melodic clashes, ambiguous chords, delayed or surprising cadences, remote or sliding modulations (sometimes many in quick succession), unresolved dominant 7ths and occasionally excursions into pure chromaticism or modality, he pushed the accepted procedures of dissonance and key into previously unexplored territory. This profound influence can be traced alike in the music of Liszt, Wagner, Fauré, Debussy, Grieg, Albéniz, Tchaikovsky, Rachmaninov and many others.

GROVEmusic

Piano Concertos

No 1 in E minor, Op 11; **No 2** in F minor, Op 21

Piano Concertos Nos 1 & 2
Martha Argerich pf
Montreal Symphony Orchestra / Charles Dutoit
EMI 556798-2 (69' · DDD)　　Ⓟ🅖◐➔

 Martha Argerich's first commercially released recordings of the Chopin concertos were for DG; No 1 in 1968, No 2 in 1978. Here she revisits both concertos and offers an act of re-creative daring, of an alternating reverie and passion that flashes fire with a thousand different lights. Indeed, her earlier performances are infinitely less witty,

personal and eruptive, less inclined to explore, albeit with the most spontaneous caprice and insouciance, so many new facets, angles and possibilities. Now, everything is accomplished without a care for studios and microphones and with a degree of involvement that suggests an increase rather than a diminution of her love for these works. The recordings are impressively natural and if Dutoit occasionally seems awed if not cowed into anonymity by his soloist (the opening *tutti*s to the slow movements of both concertos are less memorable than they should be) he sets off Argerich's charisma to an exceptional degree. Argerich's light burns brighter than ever. Rarely in their entire history have the Chopin concertos received performances of a more teasing allure, brilliance and idiosyncrasy.

Piano Concertos Nos 1 & 2
Murray Perahia pf
Israel Philharmonic Orchestra / Zubin Mehta
Sony Classical 07464 44922-2 (76' · DDD)
Recorded live 1989　　🅜◐➔

Perahia has never made any secret of his liking for the 'inspirational heat-of-the-moment' of a live performance as opposed to a studio recording, where 'sometimes things get tame'. As enthusiastic audience applause (discreetly rationed on the disc) makes plain, these two concertos were recorded live at Tel Aviv's Mann Auditorium. Whether they were subsequently 'doctored' we don't know, but the finished product brings us a Perahia miraculously combining exceptional finesse with an equally exceptional urgency. In all but the finale of No 1 (where Pollini on EMI beats him by a minute) his timings throughout both works are considerably faster than most of his rivals on disc. Was this prompted by 'inspirational heat-of-the-moment'? Or was it a deliberate attempt to come closer than others do to the surprisingly briskish metronome markings printed in the Eulenburg scores? The two slow movements are distinguished by exquisitely limpid *cantabile* and superfine delicacy of decorative detail while again conveying urgent undercurrents. But in a guessing-game perhaps it would be the two finales that would most betray the identity of the soloist. Not only are they faster, but also of a more scintillating, *scherzando*-like lightness. The recording is first rate.

Piano Concertos Nos 1 & 2
Polish Festival Orchestra / Krystian Zimerman pf
DG ② 459 684-2GH2 (82' · DDD)　　🅜◐➔

Krystian Zimerman was in his early twenties when he recorded the Chopin concertos for DG two decades ago, with Carlo Maria Giulini conducting the Los Angeles Philharmonic. For his long-anticipated remakes he directs the Polish Festival Orchestra from the keyboard, an ensemble he founded and trained from scratch. Are the results worth all the extraordinary effort (and no doubt expense) that went into this project? In many ways, yes. Helped by DG's exquisite engineering, Chopin's oft-maligned orchestrations emerge with the clarity of a venerable painting scrubbed clean and fully restored. Not one string phrase escapes unaccounted for. Every dynamic indication and accent mark is freshly considered, and each orchestral strand is weighed and contoured in order for each instrument to be heard, or, at least, to make itself felt. Some listeners may find the strings' ardent vibrato and liberal *portamentos* more cloying than heartfelt, yet the vocal transparency Zimerman elicits from his musicians underscores the crucial influence of *bel canto* singing on this composer. If he downplays many of Chopin's dynamic surges and enlivening accents, he compensates with carefully pinpointed climaxes in both concertos' slow movements. The slow timings, incidentally, have less to do with fast versus slow than the pianist's insidiously spaced *ritardandos* and broadening of tempos between sections. More often than not he lets his right hand lead, rather than building textures from the bottom up, or bringing out inner voices as Argerich does in her more forceful, impulsive renditions. By contrast, some of Zimerman's salient expressive points have calcified rather than ripened with age. Having said that, he has clear ideas of what he wants, and commands the formidable means to obtain the desired results, both at the keyboard and in front of his hand-picked musicians. Of the many offerings made to celebrate Chopin's 150th anniversary, Zimerman's achievement stands out.

Piano Concertos – No 1, Op 11[a]; No 2, Op 21[b]
Arthur Rubinstein pf [a]**Los Angeles Philharmonic Orchestra / Alfred Wallenstein**; [b]**NBC Symphony Orchestra / William Steinberg**
Naxos Historical mono 8 111296 (67' · ADD)
Recorded [a]1953, [b]1946   Ⓢ**OO**▷

Mercifully uncut, unlike Rubinstein's previous discs of both concertos with Barbirolli, these are astonishing performances, occasionally, particularly in the Second Concerto, content simply to astonish. Here there is an almost arrogant dismissal of all difficulties and a prima donna stance sometimes hard to square with some of Chopin's more delicate and ornate confidences. In the scintillating coda Rubinstein takes his bravura to a spine-tingling edge, but in, for example, the *Larghetto*'s central storms there is a brusque, streamlined indifference to the music's finer qualities.

In the First Concerto, while recognisably the same pianist, Rubinstein is altogether more subtle, following his characteristic exuberance and extroversion with playing of a rapt magic and delicacy. The music may be sent smartly on its way by both conductor and soloist, but the patrician ease, nonchalant glitter and authority of Rubinstein's playing are uniquely his to command. These are both extraordinary performances by an extraordinary pianist though of

the two, the First Concerto is the more affecting. Mark Obert-Thorn's restoration of the 1953 sound is a model of remastery though even he cannot make the 1946 Second Concerto sound less than cramped.

Piano Concertos Nos 1[a] & 2[b]   Ⓗ
Noel Mewton-Wood pf [a]**Netherlands Philharmonic Orchestra**, [b]**Zurich Symphony Orchestra / Walter Goehr**
Dante Historical Piano Collection HPC105 (69' · ADD)
Recorded c1951, 1948   Ⓕ

Inconsolable after the death of his partner Bill Fredricks, Noel Mewton-Wood (1922-53) committed suicide and robbed the world of a musical genius. Born in Melbourne, he included, in his London-based career, work with Schnabel, a début (in Beethoven's Third Concerto) with Sir Thomas Beecham, the frequent replacement of Benjamin Britten as Peter Pears's musical collaborator and, mercifully for the present generation, the making of several recordings taken from his eclectic and enterprising repertoire.

Amazingly, in his incomparably sensitive and robust hands, the Chopin concertos seem as though heard for the first time, their passions and intimacies virtually re-created on the spot. Who of today's pianists would or could risk such candour or phrase and articulate Chopin's early intricacy with such alternating strength and delicacy? The notes (in French only) suggest parallels with Solomon, Anatole Kitain and Murray Perahia, yet as with all truly great artists, Mewton-Wood's playing defies comparison, however exalted. No more vital or individual performances exist on record. The orchestra is hardly a model of precision or refinement, but the recordings have come up remarkably well.

Piano Concerto No 1. Ballade in G minor, Op 23 . Nocturnes, Op 15 – No 1 in F; No 2 in F sharp minor. Nocturnes, Op 27 – No 1 in C sharp minor; No 2 in D flat. Polonaise No 6 in A flat, Op 53, 'Heroic'
Maurizio Pollini pf **Philharmonia Orchestra / Paul Kletzki**
EMI 567548-2 (73' · ADD) Recorded 1960-68   Ⓜ**OO**

This disc is a classic. The concerto was recorded shortly after the 18-year-old pianist's victory at the Warsaw competition in 1959. Nowadays we might expect a wider dynamic range to allow greater power in the first movement's *tutti*s, but in all other respects the recording completely belies its age, with a near perfect balance between soloist and orchestra. This is very much Pollini's disc, just as the First Concerto is very much the soloist's show, but effacing as the accompaniment is, Pollini's keyboard miracles of poetry and refinement could not have been achieved without one of the most characterful and responsive accounts of that accompaniment ever committed to tape. The expressive range of the Philharmonia on top form under Kletzki is exceptional, as is the accord between soloist and conductor in phrasing and shading. The solo items are a further reminder of Pollini's effortless bravura and aristocratic poise.

Piano Concerto No 2 in F minor, Op 21[a]. Ⓗ
Ballade No 1 in G minor, Op 23. Mazurka in C minor, Op 56 No 3. Etudes, Op 10 – No 6 in E flat minor; No 8 in F; No 9 in F minor. Scherzo No 4 in E, Op 54. Andante spianato and Grande Polonaise, Op 22
Arthur Rubinstein pf [a]**Philharmonia Orchestra / Carlo Maria Giulini**
BBC Legends/IMG Artists mono BBCL4105-2
(78' · ADD) Recorded live 1959; [a]1961 ⒻⓄ

Rubinstein remains the most elegant and life-affirming of all great Chopin pianists, his patrician ease and stylistic distinction the envy and despair of lesser mortals. Above all he understood a central paradox, that Chopin was in love with the human voice yet sensing the limitation of words and a single vocal line confided his deepest, most fiery and intimate thoughts to the piano, an instrument of a supposed percussive limitation. No pianist has played Chopin with a more translucent and uncluttered tone, with a greater sense of singing 'line', of vocal breathing and inspiration. His *rubato* was personal and inimitable, a subtle bending of the phrase, an ebb and flow. Above all there was his sovereign naturalness. Audiences felt transported, indeed transfigured by his playing.

These wondrous performances transport you to another world. True, there are tiny slips of finger and concentration, yet they do nothing to qualify a sense of supreme mastery. In the Concerto, where, despite a once traditional and disfiguring cut in the opening *tutti*, he's memorably partnered by Giulini, Rubinstein achieves a flawless balance between Chopin's ever-elusive mix of poise and intensity. In his recital his reading of the great C minor Mazurka surely numbers among the greatest of all Chopin performances in its play of light and shade, of brio and introspection.

But all these performances are memorable, haunting one over the years and now, thankfully, available in beautifully remastered sound.

Piano Concertos Nos 1 & 2 (chamber versions)
Fumiko Shiraga pf **Jan-Inge Haukås** db **Yggdrasil Quartet** (Fredrik Paulsson, Per Oman vns Robert Westlund va Per Nyström vc)
BIS CD847(72' · DDD) ⒻⓄ

This is one of the most exciting Chopin recordings in recent years because it confronts and deepens the uneasiness that Chopin lovers have with his concertos. They are more comfortable as chamber works, the chamber works he never succeeded in writing when he confronted that form head on. If you find Chopin's ideas inflated when cast in orchestral form, this recording will remove the last traces of doubt. Pianist Fumiko Shiraga has reduced the scope of the music, and wisely so. The heroism and grandeur is of the sort one finds in Schumann's piano-chamber context, the

dynamic and expressive extremes that Shiraga achieves are no less compelling than a pianist unleashed against a large orchestra. Shiraga doubles in some *tutti* passages – a surprise at first, but again a wise decision. She adds gravity and fullness to the Yggdrasil Quartet's excellent accompaniment while remaining hidden, diligently underscoring but never overbearing.

Cello Works

Cello Sonata in G minor, Op 65. Polonaise brillante in C, Op 3 (ed Feuermann). Grande duo concertante in E on themes from Meyerbeer's 'Robert le Diable'. Nocturne in C sharp minor, Op posth (arr Piatigorsky). Etude in E minor, Op 25 No 7 (arr Glazunov). Waltz in A minor, Op 34 No 2 (arr Ginzburg). Etude in D minor, Op 10 No 6 (arr Glazunov)
Maria Kliegel vc **Bernd Glemser** pf
Naxos 8 553159 (64' · DDD) ⓈⒹ

Here are Chopin's complete works for cello and piano complemented by an intriguing garland of encores. Performed with youthful relish, impressively balanced and recorded, this is a notable offering. Clearly, Kliegel and Glemser have few reservations concerning the sonata's surprisingly Germanic overtones. Recognisably Chopin in virtually every bar there remains an oddly Schumannesque bias, particularly in the finale's tortuous argument – an irony when you consider that Chopin had so little time for his adoring colleague. Yet this awkward and courageous reaching out towards a terser form of expression is resolved by both artists with great vitality and, throughout, they create an infectious sense of a live rather than studio performance. Kliegel and Glemser are no less uninhibited in Chopin's earlier show-pieces, written at a time when the composer had a passing passion for grand opera and for what he dismissed as 'glittering trifles'. Their additions (transcriptions by Glazunov, Piatigorsky and Ginzburg) remind us how singers, violinists and cellists beg, borrow or steal Chopin from pianists at their peril. As Chopin put it, 'the piano is my solid ground; on that I stand the straightest', and his muse has proved oddly and magically resistant to change or transcription. Still, even though the selection often suggests an alien opacity, the performances are most warmly committed.

Piano Sonatas

No 1 in C minor, Op 4; **No 2** in B flat minor, Op 35; **No 3** in B minor, Op 58

Piano Sonatas Nos 2[a] & 3[b]. Scherzo No 3 in C sharp minor, Op 39[c]
Martha Argerich pf
DG 419 055-2GGA (56' · ADD) Recorded [a]1975, [b]1967, [c]1961 ⓂⓄⓄⒹ

Here, simply and assuredly, is one of the most magisterial talents in the entire history of piano playing. She's hardly a comfortable companion, confirming your preconceptions. Indeed, she sets your heart and mind reeling so that you positively cry out for respite from her dazzling and super-sensitive enquiry. But she's surely a great musician first and a great pianist second. From her, Chopin is hardly the most balanced or classically biased of the romantics. She can tear all complacency aside. How she keeps you on the *qui vivre* in the Second and Third Sonatas. Is the Funeral March too brisk, an expression of sadness for the death of a distant relative rather than grief for a nation? Is the delicate rhythmic play at the heart of the Third Sonata's *Scherzo* virtually spun out of existence? Such qualms or queries tend to be whirled into extinction by more significant felicities. Who but Argerich, with her subtle half-pedalling, could conjure so baleful and macabre a picture of 'winds whistling over graveyards' in the Second Sonata's finale, or achieve such heart-stopping exultance in the final pages of the Third Sonata (this performance is early Argerich with a vengeance, alive with a nervous brio). And if her free spirit leaves us tantalised, thirsting for Chopin's First, Second and Fourth as well as his Third *Scherzos*, for example, she has also left us overwhelmingly enriched, for ever in her debt.

Piano Sonata No 2, Op 35. Ballade No 2, Op 38. Mazurkas, Op 33. Waltzes, Op 34. Impromptu No 2, Op 36
Maurizio Pollini pf
DG 477 7626GH (57' · DDD)   ⓕⓄ🡒

The programme embraces Chopin's Opp 33-38 with the exception of the two Nocturnes, Op 37, though they're not played in chronological order. Pollini begins with a magnificent account of the Ballade No 2, the maelstrom that erupts after the pastoral first page sounding like a howl of despair. The four Mazurkas, Op 33, and three Waltzes, Op 34, not only form a contrast to the Ballade but are themselves contrasted with each other. The F sharp major Impromptu, almost a mini-ballade, is heard in another refined account, Pollini relishing the *leggiero jeu perlé* scale passagework at the close. In the Second Sonata, Pollini unites what Schumann called 'four of [Chopin's] wildest children' into a family, a feat managed by few pianists, the first movement (with a *da capo* repeat) leading quite naturally into the *Scherzo* and so on.

It'd be difficult for Pollini to produce an ugly sound (and he doesn't here), but while the piano is captured from a slight distance (say the front row of the stalls), the pianist's frequent nasal intakes of breath are recorded in close-up.

Piano Sonata No 2. Four Scherzi
Simon Trpčeski pf
EMI 375586-2 (65' · DDD)   ⓕⓄⓄ🡒

From Simon Trpčeski, a relatively new star in EMI's firmament, Chopin's music boils with a

Heathcliff-like defiance. Here is no drawing-room dandy but a composer who truly rages against the dying of the light. Yet just as awe replaces critical scrutiny when faced with Trpčeski's formidable mastery, you remember how such towering virtuosity is complemented by an equally remarkable refinement. If few pianists have stormed the Second Sonata's first movement more heroically, even fewer have played the Funeral March's central Elysian Trio with such poise and concentration.

The four *Scherzi*, too, offer a similar combination of superlatives, one where a thrusting youthful impetuosity is balanced by lyrical introspection (try Chopin's central *molto più lento* reworking of the Polish carol 'Sleep little Jesus'). Such unfaltering style and assurance are enough to make lesser pianists weep with envy and, more generally, there is an almost palpable sense of Chopin's irony, when he called three of his most savage utterances 'scherzo' (literally meaning a joke). Trpčeski's dizzying voltage and aplomb, superbly recorded, represent the finest modern alternative.

Piano Sonatas Nos 2 & 3. Fantasie in F minor, Op 49
Arthur Rubinstein pf
RCA Victor Red Seal 09026 63046-2 (61' · ADD)
Recorded 1960s   Ⓜ

In the Chopin sonatas it's difficult to think of which performance to choose as the greatest. Aside from the Funeral March itself, Rubinstein's account of the Second Sonata is a bit too imperious; the Third is much more thrilling, with considerable technical risks being taken both in the first movement and the finale. His own feeling for quiet nuances in the *Largo* of this work is quite superb, and here too Pollini on DG achieves an innocence that's disarming. Pollini's disc is the most perfect, both in terms of the pianist's technical accomplishment and the lucid piano sound, with nothing that offends the ear. The middle treble range in Rubinstein's piano sound has a hollow resonance. Rubinstein tackles the F minor *Fantasie* in rather a heavy-handed manner, with more power than searching drama. If you want your Chopin sonatas balanced and formally cohesive, then Rubinstein is for you.

Piano Sonatas – No 2, Op 35; No 3, Op 58. Barcarolle, Op 60. Berceuse, Op 57. Nocturnes – No 7, Op 27 No 1; No 8, Op 27 No 2.
Marc-André Hamelin pf
Hyperion CDA67706 (77' · DDD)   ⓕⓄⓄ

This is a disc that takes you by stealth. Not simply because it opens almost unassumingly, with a finely wrought *Berceuse*, but because it was only after several listenings that one realises just how good it is. This is Hamelin's second recording of the Second Sonata and it shows how much Hamelin's pianism has developed during the intervening time.

Hamelin's playing is refreshingly free from the 'inverted comma' school of profundity, and he lets the music speak through him most eloquently; he doesn't get carried away with the subtext of the Second's Funeral March, keeping it flowing (with desynchronisation of the hands subtly done) and all the more effective as a result. In the slow movement of the Third he finds time to dream without ever becoming portentous, and is every bit the equal of Nelson Freire, whose Chopin sonatas have rightly won considerable praise. Predictably, Hamelin is wonderful in such things as the *Scherzo* of the Third and the visceral finale of the Second, though perhaps slower than you might expect in the neurotic *Scherzo* of No 2. In the finale of the Third he doesn't begin the build-up too soon, as can be a temptation, and even has a skip in his step.

· The addition of two Nocturnes and the sublime Barcarolle simply confirm that though Hamelin has made many fabulous discs, particularly in repertoire of superhuman virtuosity, this is one of his very finest achievements to date.

Piano Sonata No 3. Mazurkas Nos 36-38. Nocturne No 4. Polonaise No 6. Scherzo No 3
Martha Argerich pf
EMI 556805-2 (52' · ADD) Recorded 1965   Ⓕ➲

Argerich's pianism is remarkable for combining seemingly effortless technical resource with temperamental volatility. Yet the vehemence of her playing is seldom to the disadvantage of the extraordinary subtlety of her art. Moreover, despite the limits she places on her repertory, such is the spontaneity of her approach that each of her interpretations, no matter how familiar in broad outline, is characterised by a profusion of contrasting details beneath the surface. In the B minor Sonata she omits the first-movement repeats. Such a formal contraction can contribute to the momentum with which the movement unfolds. Ironically, however, she seems to rein in the propulsive power for which she's renowned, appearing instead to be seeking at every turn to exploit a deeply felt exprssive lyricism to offset the febrile intensity of the most energetic figurational devices. This has the virtue of allowing us a less hectic view of subsidiary elements within the music, which elsewhere can too often be overwhelmed by the sheer turbulance of the action. Some of the most satisfying playing on the disc comes in her account of the Op 59 *Mazurkas*. There's a vulnerability as well as an affecting wistfulness about the playing which captures the elusiveness of the idiom, with its harmonic ambiguities, with rare acuity. At the other end of the scale, the excitement she generates in the A flat *Polonaise* is of an order that goes far beyond mere effect. If these accounts do not necessarily outstrip her other recordings, they nevertheless offer an intriguing insight into ongoing 'work in progress' from a pianistic giant whose artistry continues to fascinate and perplex.

Piano Sonata No 3. Mazurkas – A minor, Op 17 No 4; B flat minor, Op 24 No 4; D flat, Op 30 No 3; D, Op 33 No 2; C sharp minor, Op 50 No 3; C, Op 56 No 2; F sharp minor, Op 59 No 3; B, Op 63 No 1; F minor, Op 63 No 2; C sharp minor, Op 63 No 3; F minor, Op 68 No 4
Evgeny Kissin pf
RCA Victor Red Seal 09026 62542-2 (65' · DDD)
Recorded live 1993   Ⓕ⊙

Kissin is among the master-pianists of our time. What magnificence and assertion he finds in the B minor Sonata's opening, what menace in the following uprush of chromatic scales, his deliberate pedal haze capturing one of Chopin's most truly modernist moments. He may relish left-hand counter-melody in the return of the second subject and elsewhere, yet such detail is offered within the context of the whole. A momentary failure of concentration in the *Scherzo* comes as reassuring evidence of human fallibility but elsewhere one can only marvel at a manner so trenchant, musicianly and resolutely unsentimental. The equestrian finale is among the most lucid on record and concludes in a controlled triumph that has the audience cheering to the heavens.

The 12 *Mazurkas* are no less remarkable for their strength and discretion. Everything unfolds with complete naturalness and authority. The beautifully idiomatic rubato is so stylishly applied that you're only aware of the finest fluctuations of pulse and emotion. Few pianists have gone to the heart of the matter with such assurance (always excepting Arthur Rubinstein). The recording captures Kissin's clear, unnarcissistic sonority admirably and audience noise is minimal.

Four Ballades

No 1 in G minor, Op 23; **No 2** in F, Op 38; **No 3** in A flat, Op 47; **No 4** in F minor, Op 52

Ballades Nos 1-4. Mazurkas – No 7 in F minor, Op 7 No 3; No 13 in A minor, Op 17 No 4; No 23 in D, Op 33 No 2. Waltzes – No 1 in E flat, Op 18; No 5 in A flat, Op 42; No 7 in C sharp minor, Op 64 No 2. Etudes, Op 10 – No 3 in E; No 4 in C sharp minor. Nocturne No 1 in F, Op 15
Murray Perahia pf
Sony Classical 07464 64399-2 (61' · DDD)   Ⓕ🅞🅞🅞🅞➲

 This is surely the greatest, certainly the richest, of Perahia's many exemplary recordings. Once again his performances are graced with rare and classic attributes and now, to supreme clarity, tonal elegance and musical perspective, he adds an even stronger poetic profile, a surer sense of the inflammatory rhetoric underpinning Chopin's surface equilibrium. In other words the vividness and immediacy are as remarkable as the finesse. And here, arguably, is the oblique but telling influence of Horowitz whom Perahia befriended during the

CHOPIN'S PIANO SONATA NO 2 – IN BRIEF

Martha Argerich
DG 419 055-2GGA (56' · ADD)   Ⓜ❍●🅑➼
Coupled with the Third Sonata and the *Scherzo* No 3, this disc shows off Argerich's mastery of this music. You never quite know what will happen next, which only adds to the excitement! Red-blooded Chopin, for sure.

Vladimir Ashkenazy
Decca download 448 123-2DM (76' · ADD)   Ⓜ🅑➼
Ashkenazy's Chopin is wonderfully poetic, and this disc contains all three sonatas. His way with the slow movements – try the Funeral March – is very appealing.

Murray Perahia
Sony Classical 07464 32780-2 (50' · DDD)   Ⓜ❍🅑➼
Beautifully played, intellectually probing Chopin with an great emphasis on detail and incidental delights. Coupled with the Third Piano Sonata – another joy.

Arthur Rubinstein
RCA 09026 63046-2 (61' · ADD)   Ⓜ❍❍
Rubinstein is the Chopin pianist *par excellence* for many people, and listening to him in the Second and Third Sonatas it's easy to agree. Poetry flows from his fingers with ease, and his way with the most subtle nuance is quite breathtaking.

Maurizio Pollini
DG 415 346-2GH (52' · DDD)   Ⓕ❍🅑➼
This is Chopin playing of great power and feeling: there's no hint of the chilliness of which Pollini is occasionally accused.

Ivo Pogorelich
DD download 463 678-2GOR (73' · ADD)   Ⓑ❍🅑➼
Perhaps Pogorelich's most controversial recording, but in 1981, as his recorded début, it established him as a player of quite extraordinary technique and temperament. It's coupled, unusually, with Ravel's *Gaspard de la nuit* and Prokofiev's Piano Sonata No 6.

Simon Trpčeski pf
EMI 375586-2 (65' · DDD)   Ⓜ❍❍🅑➼
Power and poetry fuse magnificently for the yong Macedonian pianist. He wears his considerable virtuosity lightly and gives the sonata a really heroic face: this is not salon Chopin but living drama.

Emil Gilels   Ⓗ
Testament SBT1089 (64' · ADD)   Ⓕ
The great Russian pianist, far too little represented on record in Chopin, proves to be a magnificent interpreter, full of majestic gesture and noble utterance. This is resonant playing (coupled, oddly, with Mozart and Shostakovich).

DGlast months of the old wizard's life. Listen to the First *Ballade*'s second subject and you'll hear rubato like the most subtle pulsing or musical breathing. Try the opening of the Third and you'll note an ideal poise and lucidity, something rarely achieved in these outwardly insouciant pages. From Perahia the waltzes are marvels of liquid brilliance and urbanity. Even Lipatti hardly achieved such an enchanting lilt or buoyancy, such a beguiling sense of light and shade. In the mazurkas, too, Perahia's tiptoe delicacy and tonal irridescence (particularly in Op 7 No 3 in F minor) make the music dance and spin as if caught in some magical hallucinatory haze. Finally, two contrasting *Etudes*, and whether in ardent lyricism (Op 10 No 3) or shot-from-guns virtuosity (Op 10 No 4) Perahia's playing is sheer perfection. The recording beautifully captures his instantly recognisable, glistening sound world.

Ballades Nos 1-4. Barcarolle in F sharp, Op 60. Berceuse in D flat, Op 57. Scherzo No 4 in E, Op 54
Evgeny Kissin pf
RCA Red Seal 09026 63259-2 (62' · DDD)   Ⓕ

Kissin plays Chopin with a rhetorical drama, intensity and power that few could equal. His technique is of an obliterating command, enough to make even his strongest competitors throw up their hands in despair, and yet everything is at the service of a deeply ardent and poetic nature. Listen to his slow and pensive *Andantino* in the Second *Ballade*, its rhythm or thought-pattern constantly halted and checked, the following *presto* storms of such pulverising force that they will make even the least susceptible hackles rise and fists clench as Jove's thunder roars across the universe. The first subject of the First *Ballade* is daringly slow and inward-looking, the start of the glorious Fourth evoking the feelings of a blind man when first granted the gift of sight, while the *Berceuse* is seen through an opalescent pedal haze that creates its own hallucinatory and rarified atmosphere.

The final page of the *Barcarolle* – always among music's most magical homecomings – is given with an imaginative brio known to very few, and the Fourth *Scherzo* is among the most Puckish and highly coloured on record. The recordings are less than ideally beautiful but more than adequate. An astonishing achievement.

Ballades Nos 1-4. Four Scherzos
Stephen Hough pf
Hyperion CDA67456 (72' · DDD)   Ⓕ❍❍

This is astonishing piano playing; Chopin interpretation that, at its best, fully measuring up to the greatness of these pieces. Stephen Hough's accounts offer plenty of refreshment to spirit and senses.

The distribution is interesting, chronological but alternating one of each, which may not make a recital to consume at one go, but helps to point up their diversity and individual character, as well as Chopin's mastery of large forms. Hough is unfailingly thoughtful; there isn't a note that hasn't been cared for. Just a few of them (Third Ballade, for example) are picked out of the texture and strung together for our delectation in a way that might strike you as otiose if you're in a sober-sides kind of mood. The surfaces of his presentations are very 'worked', more indicative of application, maybe, than of organic growth. But this isn't superficial playing – the performances catch fire.

He inclines to the accepted view that Chopin's large forms have a 'plot' that culminates in a tumult or a whirlwind of activity. The tempest in the coda of the Fourth Ballade might have been a mite less furious, to let the ear have more time to register what's going on. The closing pages of No 1, on the other hand, have an exemplary finish and allure. Most distinguished of the Ballades is No 2, where Hough perceives the invasion of one kind of music by another in all its subtlety and lays out a spellbinding seven-minute drama.

He has interesting points to make in the *Scherzos*, too. Where many a player is content to let recurring sections and paragraphs register simply as the music we heard before, with him they sound different in some degree, affected by what's come in between. Hough is always doing something, though sometimes you might wish he were doing less. This is an issue out of the ordinary; welcome, too, for being handsomely recorded and produced.

Ballades – No 3 in A flat, Op 47; No 4 in F minor, Op 52. Mazurkas – No 36 in A minor, Op 59 No 1; No 37 in A flat, Op 59 No 2; No 38 in F sharp minor, Op 59 No 3; No 39 in B, Op 63 No 1; No 40 in F minor, Op 63 No 2; No 41 in C sharp minor, Op 63 No 3; No 49 in F minor, Op 68 No 4. Polonaises – No 5 in F sharp minor, Op 44; No 6 in A flat, 'Heroic', Op 53
Piotr Anderszewski *pf*
Virgin Classics 545619-2 (60' · DDD)   ⓕ**OO**🔊

Following his celebrated earlier discs of Beethoven, Mozart and Bach, 34-year-old Piotr Anderszewski gives us an exceptionally powerful and seductive Chopin recital. He prefers a subtly chosen programme to complete sets of the Mazurkas, Ballades or Polonaises, and his often phenomenally acute and sensitive awareness of Chopin's constantly shifting perspective has you reliving every bar of such incomparable music.

In the three Op 59 Mazurkas (a notably rich part of Chopin's deeply confessional diary) he achieves a rare sense of brooding introspection, close to neurosis, with bittersweet mood swings that shift from resignation to flashes of anger. Then there's the F minor Mazurka, Op 63 No 2, taken for once at a true *lento*, a dark place indeed for Anderszewski, with only relative light in the central idea to lessen the mood of heart-stopping despondency. Again, in both the Ballades his sharply original ideas combine with a total

responsibility to the score; seldom can the letter and spirit of the composer be united so flawlessly.

Eyebrows may be raised in the A flat Polonaise, but this is no obvious celebration of triumph over adversity, rather a re-creation of music which lives again in all its initial audacity. Here, in this great young pianist's incomparable hands, and in Virgin's excellent sound, is living proof that Chopin's music is forever new, forever revelatory.

Ballades Nos 1-4. Nocturnes – No 2, Op 9 No 2 (two recordings); No 4, Op 15 No 1; No 5, Op 15 No 2; No 7, Op 27 No 1; No 15, Op 55 No 1; No 16, Op 55 No 2   🅷
Alfred Cortot *pf*
Naxos Historical mono 8 111245 (62' · ADD)
From HMV originals, recorded 1929-51   Ⓢ🔊

This fifth and final release of Cortot's 78rpm Chopin recordings is surely the jewel in the crown. Here, the 1929 rather than the more familiar 1933 set of the Ballades blazes with a passion, brilliance and poetic audacity that set the pulses racing and the mind reeling. Here is a great artist who seized the opportunity to achieve ever greater heights of eloquence and rhetorical verve. Superbly restored by Mark Obert-Thorn, every performance is charged with a heady and consuming poetry that confirms Daniel Barenboim's claim that 'Cortot discovered the opium in Chopin'. Take the First Ballade's opening, where Cortot is every inch the bardic poet, free, rhapsodic and inimitable; or hear him in the *Presto con fuoco* storms of the Second Ballade, where he plays as if pursued by the furies of hell.

Again, even when inaccuracies fly in all directions in the heat of the chase, no other pianist has approached the Third Ballade's central C sharp minor turbulence with such daring or recreative force. Cortot was never one to hold back in the interests of decorum and in the Fourth Ballade he stretches the parameters of Chopin's poetry to the very edge, his playing close to being consumed in its own ecstasy.

His selection of Nocturnes (sadly his projected Chopin survey was never completed) pulse with the same alluring quality, suggesting the reverse of Rubinstein's more patrician elegance. True, for today's more antiseptic and 'tasteful' practitioners such artistic conviction and originality will seem extravagant or even camp. Yet there is surely no living pianist who could or would attempt to emulate such heart-stopping poetry. Maria Callas herself would have been among the first to pay tribute to Cortot's *cantabile*, an unequalled 'singing' at the piano.

Etudes

Etudes, Opp 10 & 25
Murray Perahia *pf*
Sony Classical 509970 61885-2 (56' · DDD) ⓕ**OOO**🔊

Perahia brings order and lucidity to the heart of Chopin's most audacious firestorms and in, for example, Etudes Nos 1 and 4 from Op 10, you're made aware of an incomparable mix of poetry and precision. Perahia's may be a wholly modern voice yet he truly speaks in the spirit of his revered masters of the past, of Cortot and Fischer in particular, and this, allied with his immaculate infinitely polished and shaded pianism, gives his performances the rarest distinction and quality.

How superb and unfaltering is his mastery in No 1, that magnificent curtain-raiser to Op 10, how magical his improvisatory touch in its closing page. His textural translucency and musical breathing, his *rubato* in No 3, like that of Rubinstein, is that of a great and natural singer of the keyboard. Chopin would surely have cried out once again, 'ah, mon patrie!' if he had heard this performance.

No 8 is delightfully rumbustious and just when you note a touch of evasion in his rapid spin through the morbid near-Wagnerian chromaticism of No 6 you find yourself relishing his cool tempo, a musical ease and flexibility that give new meaning to Chopin's prescribed *con molto espressione*. On the other hand No 7 from Op 25 unfolds with the truest, most memorable sense of its *lento* elegy. And where else have you heard a more impassioned or articulate *Revolutionary* Etude? Perahia's is the finest of all modern discs of the Etudes, and Sony's sound captures all his artistry.

Etudes, Opp 10 & 25
Maurizio Pollini pf
DG 413 794-2GH (56' · ADD) Recorded 1972 Ⓕ Ⓞ Ⓓ➤

The 24 *Etudes* of Chopin's Opp 10 and 25, although dating from his twenties, remain among the most perfect specimens of the genre ever known, with all technical challenges – and they are formidable – dissolved into the purest poetry. With his own transcendental technique (and there are few living pianists who can rival it) Pollini makes you unaware that problems even exist – as for instance in Op 10 No 10 in A flat, where the listener is swept along in an effortless stream of melody. The first and last of the same set in C major and C minor have an imperious strength and drive, likewise the last three impassioned outpourings of Op 25. Lifelong dislike of a heart worn on the sleeve makes him less than intimately confiding in more personal contexts such as No 3 in E major and No 6 in E flat minor from Op 10, or the nostalgic middle section of No 5 in E minor and the searing No 7 in C sharp minor from Op 25. Like the playing, so the recording itself could profitably be a little warmer at times, but it's a princely disc all the same.

Fantasie, Op 49

Fantasie in F minor, Op 49. Waltzes – No 2 in A flat, Op 34 No 1; No 3 in A minor, Op 34 No 2; No 5 in

A flat, Op 42. Polonaise No 5 in F sharp minor, Op 44. Nocturnes – No 1 in C sharp minor, Op 27 No 1; No 2 in D flat, Op 27 No 2; No 10 in A flat, Op 32 No 2. Scherzo No 2 in B flat minor, Op 31
Evgeny Kissin pf
RCA Victor Red Seal 09026 60445-2 (67' · DDD) Recorded live 1993 Ⓕ

Evgeny Kissin's playing at 21 (when these performances were recorded) quite easily outmatches that of the young Ashkenazy and Pollini – and most particularly in terms of the maturity of his musicianship. The programme launches off with a reading of the great F minor *Fantasie*, which, though a bit measured, is integrated to perfection. The power and determination of the performance certainly make one sit up and listen, but at the same time it would be difficult not to be moved by the heartfelt lyricism of the melodic passages. Although Kissin may be a little unsmiling in the three waltzes, at least he has admirable sophistication in being able to add interest to the interpretations. His control in the tricky A flat, Op 42, is quite amazing. The *Nocturne* in C sharp minor is a jewel. This reading is among the most darkly imaginative and pianistically refined on disc. The disc ends with a powerfully glittering performance of the Second *Scherzo*.

Mazurkas

Nos 1-64: Op 6 Nos 1-4 **(1-4)**; Op 7 Nos 1-5 **(5-9)**; Op 17 Nos 1-4 **(10-13)**; Op 24 Nos 1–4 **(14-17)**; Op 30 Nos 1-4 **(18-21)**; Op 33 Nos 1-4 **(22-25)**; Op 41 Nos 1-4 **(26-29)**; Op 50 Nos 1-3 **(30-32)**; Op 56 Nos 1-3 **(33-35)**; Op 59 Nos 1-3 **(36-38)**; Op 63 Nos 1-3 **(39-41)**; Op 67 Nos 1-4 **(42-45)**; Op 68 Nos 1-4 **(46-49)**; Op posth **(50-64)**

Mazurkas Nos 1-51
Arthur Rubinstein pf
RCA Victor Red Seal ② 09026 63050-2 (140' · ADD) Recorded 1960s Ⓑ Ⓞ Ⓞ

Recording in the studio, rather than at a live concert, quite naturally leads to a safe and uniform approach, which doesn't really serve the inspired inventiveness of the music. In some ways these recordings suffer from this. If you compare Rubinstein's readings here with those he recorded on 78rpm discs in 1938-9, you immediately notice that an element of fantasy and caprice has given way to a more sober view of the music. The *Mazurkas* are so intricate in their variety of moods that the successful pianist has to be able to treat each one as an entity, contrasting the emotional content within the context of that particular piece. Rubinstein, with his serious approach, lends the music more weight than is usual and he wholly avoids trivialising it with over-snappy rhythms. With him many of the lesser-known *Mazurkas* come to life, such as the E flat minor, Op 6 No 4, with its insistent little motif that pervades the whole piece. His phrasing is free and flexible and he has utter appreciation of the delicacy of Chopin's ideas. He doesn't, however, take an improvisatory approach. Rubinstein judges to perfection which details to bring out so as to give each piece a special character. He convinces one that he has made this music his own. When you hear Rubinstein tackle the C sharp minor Mazurka, Op 53 No 3, you at once know that he fully comprehends the depth of this, perhaps the greatest of them all. He ranges from the pathos of the opening to a persuasive tonal grandeur in the more assertive parts, and yet is able to relate the two. The recording has a number of blemishes: the piano is too closely recorded, the loud passages are hollow-toned, especially in the bass, and little sparkle to the sound.

Mazurkas Nos 1-52, 55, 56, 59-62
Vladimir Ashkenazy pf
Double Decca 448 086-2DF2 (143' · DDD/ADD)
Recorded 1976-85   ⑧OO

Vladimir Ashkenazy made his integral set of the *Mazurkas* over a decade. He has always played outstandingly. He does so again here, giving complete satisfaction. The set includes all those published posthumously and the revised version of Op 68 No 4; so his is the most comprehensive survey in the current catalogue. Ashkenazy memorably catches their volatile character, and their essential sadness. Consider, for example, the delicacy and untrammelled spontaneity with which he approaches these works. He shows the most exquisite sensibility, each item strongly, though never insistently characterised. His accounts of the Mazurkas, Op 6 and Op 7, for instance, offer a genuine alternative to Rubinstein. Nine pieces in all, they were Chopin's first published sets and their piquancy, the richness of their ideas, is here made very apparent. One is given a sense of something completely new having entered music. Although there are fine things in all the groups, Op 24 is the first Mazurka set of uniformly high quality and No 4 is Chopin's first great work in the genre.

On hearing them together like this one appreciates the cumulative effect which the composer intended, and Ashkenazy makes a hypersensitive response to their quickly changing moods. The recorded sound has the warmth, fullness and immediacy typical of this series, with a nice bloom to the piano tone.

Mazurkas Nos 1-51[a]; No 23 in D, Op 33 No 2[b];   ⓗ
No 35 in C minor, Op 56 No 3[e]; No 41 in C sharp
minor, Op 63 No 3[f]. Waltzes – No 2 in A flat, Op 34
No 1[c]; No 7 in C sharp minor, Op 64 No 2[d]
Arthur Rubinstein pf
Naxos Historical mono ② 8 110656/7
(137' · ADD) Recorded [cd]1928-30, [bef]1930-32, [a]1939
                                                 ⑤O➤

Nocturnes[a] – Opp 9, 15, 27, 32, 37, 48, 55, 62   ⓗ
71. Scherzos[b] – Opp 20, 31, 39 & 54
Arthur Rubinstein pf

Naxos Historical mono ② 8 110659/60
(132' · ADD) Recorded [b]1932, [a]1936-7   ⑤➤

It's controversial to say so, but such playing makes a mockery of present-day standards. All these performances prove that Rubinstein played the piano as naturally as a bird flies or a fish swims. He was simply in his element, and never more so than in Chopin. Who else has given us the Nocturnes with such ravishing inwardness, pianistic sheen and a bel canto to rival the finest singer? Decorative fioriture are spun off like so much silk, and whether or not you consider Op 15 No 2 'inseparable from champagne and truffles' and Op 27 No 1 a portrait of 'a corpse washed ashore on a Venetian lagoon', or hear the nightingales of Nohant in Op 62 No 1 and the chant of the monks of Valdemosa in Op 15 No 3 and Op 37 No 1, you can hardly remain unaffected by Rubinstein's unique artistry. His feline ease in the double-note flow of Op 37 No 2, or the way he lightens the darkness of the great C minor Nocturne without losing an ounce of its tragedy, all form part of the genius that made him the most celebrated of all Chopin pianists.

Rubinstein's Mazurkas are equally the stuff of legends. Chopin's most subtle and confessional diary, they transcend their humble origins and become in Rubinstein's hands an ever-audacious series of miniatures extending from the neurasthenic to the radiant, from Chopin's nagging child (Op 17 No 3) to the unfurling of proud ceremonial colours (Opp 63 No 1). What heartache he conveys in Op 63 No 3; and when has Op 67 No 3 been more intimately confided, its banal association with *Les sylphides* more blissfully resolved? Chopin's final composition, Op 68 No 4, becomes a valediction encouraging rather than forbidding weeping, Rubinstein's rubato the caressing magic that created a furore at his unforgettable recitals.

Finally the Scherzos, played with an outrageous but enthralling disregard for safety. Only a pedant will underline the odd mis-hit or pock-mark in the context of such sky-rocketing bravura and poetic impulse. As an added bonus there are additional recordings of three Mazurkas and two Waltzes, the A flat Op 34 No 1 alive with dizzying virtuoso trickery. The sleeve-note writer may comically mistake the Mazurkas for the Polonaises in referring to Schumann's oft-misquoted description, 'guns [sic] buried in flowers', but that's a mere spot on Naxos's blazing sun. No more life-affirming Chopin exists.

Nocturnes

No 1 in B flat minor, Op 9; **No 2** in E flat, Op 9;
No 3 in B, Op 9; **No 4** in F, Op 15; **No 5** in F sharp,
Op 15; **No 6** in G minor, Op 15; **No 7** in C sharp
minor, Op 27; **No 8** in D flat, Op 27; **No 9** in B flat,
Op 32; **No 10** in A flat, Op 32; **No 11** in G minor, Op
37; **No 12** in G, Op 37; **No 13** in C minor, Op 48; **No
14** in F sharp minor, Op 48; **No 15** in F minor, Op 55;

No 16 in E flat, Op 55; **No 17** in B flat, Op 62; **No 18** in E, Op 62; **No 19** in E minor, Op 72; **No 20** in C sharp minor, Op posth; **No 21** in C minor, Op posth

Nocturnes Nos 1-19
Maria João Pires pf
DG ② 447 096-2GH2 (109' · DDD) Ⓕ❶❶❶❶➔

Passion rather than insouciance is Pires's keynote. Here is an intensity and drama that scorn all complacent salon or drawing-room expectations. How she relishes Chopin's central storms, creating a vivid and spectacular yet unhistrionic contrast with all surrounding serenity or 'embalmed darkness'. The *con fuoco* of Op 15 No 1 erupts in a fine fury and in the first *Nocturne*, Op 9 No 1, Pires's sharp observance of Chopin's *appassionato* marking comes like a prophecy of the coda's sudden blaze. Chopin, she informs us in no uncertain terms, was no sentimentalist. More intimately, in Op-15 No 3 (where the music's wavering sense of irresolution led to the sobriquet 'the Hamlet Nocturne') Pires makes you hang on to every note in the coda's curious, echoing chimes, and in the *dolcissimo* conclusion to No 8 (Op 27 No 2) there's an unforgettable sense of 'all passion spent', of gradually ebbing emotion. Pires with her burning clarity has reinforced our sense of Chopin's stature and created a new range of possibilities (showing us that there's life after Rubinstein). Naturally, Rubinstein's legendary cycles possess a graciousness, an ease and elegance reflecting, perhaps, a long-vanished *belle époque*. Yet moving ahead, one has no hesitation in declaring Maria João Pires among the most eloquent master-musicians of our time.

Complete Nocturnes
Bernard d'Ascoli pf
Athene Minerva ② 23 201 (105' · DDD) Ⓕ❶

Even in a heavily competitive market place this ranks among the most remarkable of Chopin Nocturne recordings. Courting controversy at one level yet burningly sincere at another, Bernard d'Ascoli goes his own heartwarming way unburdened by tradition. From him, the Nocturnes are not a world of sweet dreams but possess a troubled and assertive life. True, simplicity is hardly his byword (in Nos 1, 6 and 11, his intense *rubato* often tugs against the music's natural line) yet such bold and declamatory playing is never less than enlivening, positively forbidding the listener to sink into complacency or repose. An impetuous thrust given to the D flat Nocturne's long-breathed Italianate lines, and the sudden plunge into darkness at the end of Op 32 No 1, are two among many examples of performances of a living, breathing presence, the reverse of studio-bound.

The two extra posthumous Nocturnes are added for good measure and the ever-popular Op 9 No 2 comes complete with flashing variants authorised by the composer. The record-

ings are vivid and immediate and the oustanding notes (a provocative side-swipe at Fauré notwithstanding) are by the pianist himself.

Polonaises

No 1 in C sharp minor, Op 26; **No 2** in E flat minor, Op 26; **No 3** in A, Op 40, 'Military'; **No 4** in C minor, Op 40; **No 5** in F sharp minor, Op 44; **No 6** in A flat, Op 53, 'Heroic'; **No 7** in A flat, Op 61, 'Polonaise-fantaisie'; **No 8** in D minor, Op 71; **No 9** in B flat, Op 71; **No 10** in F minor, Op 71; **No 11** in B flat minor; **No 12** in G flat; **No 13** in G minor; **No 14** in B flat; **No 15** in A flat; **No 16** in G sharp minor

Polonaises Nos 1-7. Andante spianato and Ⓗ
Grande Polonaise in E flat, Op 22
Arthur Rubinstein pf
Naxos Historical mono 8 110661 (64' · ADD) Recorded 1934-5 Ⓢ❶❶❶➔

Here, in all their glory, are Rubinstein's 1934-5 recordings of Chopin's six mature Polonaises framed by examples of his early and late genius (Opp 22 and 61 respectively). Together with his early discs of the Mazurkas, Scherzos and Nocturnes, these performances remain classics of an unassailable calibre, their richness and character increased rather than diminished by the passage of time.

For Schumann, the Polonaises were 'canons buried in flowers' and whether epic or confiding, stark or florid their national and personal fervour is realised to perfection by Rubinstein. Listen to the *Andante spianato* from Op 22 and you'll hear a matchless *cantabile*, a tribute to a *bel canto* so often at the heart of Chopin's elusive and heroic genius. Try the central *meno mosso* from the First Polonaise and witness an imaginative freedom that can make all possible rivals sound stiff and ungainly by comparison. The colours of the A major Polonaise are unfurled with a rare sense of its ceremonial nature, and the darker, indeed tragic, character of its sombre C minor companion is no less surely caught. The two 'big' Polonaises, Opp 44 and 53, are offered with a fearless bravura (you can almost hear the audience's uproar after Rubinstein's thunderous conclusion to the latter), rhythmic impetus and idiomatic command beyond criticism.

The simple truth is that Rubinstein played the piano as a fish swims in water, free to phrase and inflect with a magic peculiarly his own, to make, in Liszt's words, 'emotion speak, weep and sing and sigh'. The sound may seem dated but Naxos's transfers are excellent, and to think that all this is offered at a bargain price…

Polonaises Nos 1-7
Maurizio Pollini pf
DG The Originals 457 711-2GOR (62' · ADD)
Recorded 1975 Ⓜ❶❶➔

This is Pollini in all his early glory, in expertly transferred performances. Shorn of all virtuoso compromise or indulgence, the majestic force of his command is indissolubly integrated with the seriousness of his heroic impulse. Rarely will you be compelled into such awareness of the underlying malaise beneath the outward and nationalist defiance of the *Polonaises*. The tension and menace at the start of No 2 are almost palpable, its storming and disconsolate continuation made a true mirror of Poland's clouded history. The C minor *Polonaise*'s denouement, too, emerges with a chilling sense of finality, and Pollini's way with the pounding audacity commencing at 3'00" in the epic F sharp minor *Polonaise* is like some ruthless prophecy of every percussive, anti-lyrical gesture to come. At 7'59" Chopin's flame-throwing interjections are volcanic, and if there's ample poetic delicacy and compensation (notably in the *Polonaise-fantaisie*, always among Chopin's most profoundly speculative masterpieces), it's the more elemental side of his genius, his 'canons' rather than 'flowers' that are made to sear and haunt the memory. Other pianists may be more outwardly beguiling, but Pollini's magnificently unsettling Chopin can be as imperious and unarguable as any on record. That his performances are also deeply moving is a tribute to his unique status.

Polonaises Nos 1-16. Allegro de concert in A, Op 46. Etudes – F minor, Op posth; A flat, Op posth; D flat, Op posth. Tarantelle in A flat, Op 43. Fugue in A minor. Albumleaf in E. Polish Songs, Op 74 – Spring. Galop marquis. Berceuse. Barcarolle. Two Bourrées
Vladimir Ashkenazy *pf*
Double Decca ② 452 167-2DF2 (145' · DDD/ADD) Recorded 1974-84　Ⓑ🅳

Ashkenazy's Chopin hardly needs any further advocacy. His distinguished and virtually complete survey rests alongside the Rubinstein recordings in general esteem. The 16 *Polonaises* were not recorded in sets but individually, or in small groups, which is one reason why they sound so fresh, with Ashkenazy striking a sensitive artistic balance between poetic feeling and the commanding bravura that one takes for granted in the more extrovert pieces, with their Polish patriotic style. The recordings vary between analogue and digital, and the recording venues are as different as the Kingsway Hall, St-John's, Smith Square, and All Saints, Petersham; but the realism of the piano sound is remarkably consistent. A series of shorter pieces is included on the second disc and the playing is always distinguished. Among the major items, the gentle *Berceuse* is quite melting, while the *Allegro de concert* and *Barcarolle* are hardly less memorable.

Preludes, Op 28

No 1 in C; No 2 in A minor; No 3 in G; No 4 in E minor; No 5 in D; No 6 in B minor; No 7 in A; No 8 in F sharp minor; No 9 in E; No 10 in C sharp minor; No 11 in B; No 12 in G sharp minor; No 13 in F

sharp; No 14 in E flat minor; No 15 in D flat; No 16 in B flat minor; No 17 in A flat; No 18 in F minor; No 19 in E flat; No 20 in C minor; No 21 in B flat; No 22 in G minor; No 23 in F; No 24 in D minor; No 25 in C sharp minor; Op 45; No 26 in A flat, Op posth

Preludes Nos 1-26[a]. Barcarolle[b]. Polonaise No 6[c]. Scherzo No 2 in B flat minor, Op 31[d]
Martha Argerich *pf*
DG Galleria 415 836-2GGA (62' · ADD) Recorded [a]1977, [b]1961, [c]1967, [d]1975　Ⓜ🅾🅳

Professor Zurawlew, the founder of the Chopin Competition in Warsaw, was once asked which one of the prize-winners he would pick as having been his favourite. The answer came back immediately: 'Martha Argerich'. This disc could explain why. There are very few recordings of the 24 Preludes (Op 28) that have such a perfect combination of temperamental virtuosity and compelling artistic insight. Argerich has the technical equipment to do whatever she wishes with the music. Whether it's in the haunting, dark melancholy of No 2 in A minor or the lightning turmoil of No 16 in B flat minor, she's profoundly impressive. It's these sharp changes of mood that make her performance scintillatingly unpredictable. In the *Barcarolle* there's no relaxed base on which the melodies of the right hand are constructed, as is conventional, but more the piece emerges as a stormy odyssey through life, with moments of visionary awareness. Argerich is on firmer ground in the *Polonaise*, where her power and technical security reign triumphant. The CD ends with a rippling and yet slightly aggressive reading of the second *Scherzo*. This is very much the playing of a pianist who lives in the 'fast lane' of life. The sound quality is a bit reverberant, an effect heightened by the fact that Argerich has a tendency to overpedal.

Preludes
Grigory Sokolov *pf*
Opus 111 OP30-336 (47' · DDD) Recorded live 1990 Ⓕ

Grigory Sokolov is an uncompromising, exclusively serious rather than commercial artist and has consequently paid a price. Even today, he remains an awe-inspiring figure to connoisseurs rather than a wider public. His recordings, too, are sadly few, though this reissue reaffirms him as among the most formidable and characterful pianists of our time. So deeply is every bar, indeed, every note, weighed and considered that each Prelude emerges in a new and arresting light. True, he can bear down so intensely that Chopin isn't always allowed his truest or most natural voice. But glories far outweigh queries. Prelude No 2 is authentically *lento* and lugubrious, its morbidity realised quite without a cool and over-familiar evasion. Again, just as you wonder whether No 13, an idyllic Nocturne, needs such strenuous pleading, you find yourself at No 16, played with a thunderous and lavishly pedalled aplomb, and to a reading of No 17 inflected with rare affection. What daring in No 18, what imaginative delicacy in No 19 (that flight into a cloudless azure), what aerial magic in No 23 with its audacious close, and when have you heard a more dramatic dip from *fortissimo* to *pianissimo* in the elegaic and processional C minor Prelude (No 20)?

The sound captures Sokolov's immense dynamic range exceptionally well, and even if you're a lover of understatement or of Cortot's careless and unforgettable rapture you'll surely admit that this is among the most powerfully individual of all Chopin recordings.

Chopin 24 Preludes[a] **Mendelssohn** 　　　　　 Ⓗ
(arr Rachmaninov) A Midsummer Night's Dream[b] –
Scherzo **Prokofiev** Suggestion diabolique, Op 4 No
4[c] **Rachmaninov** Lilacs[d]. Moment musical in E minor,
Op 16 No 4[e] . Preludes – G, Op 32 No 5[f]; B minor, Op
32 No 10[g] **Schumann** Kinderszenen, Op 15[h]
Stravinsky Etude, Op 7 No 4[i] **Vallier** Toccatina[j]
Weber Piano Sonata No 1 in C – Rondo, 'Perpetuum
mobile'[k]
Benno Moiseiwitsch *pf*
Testament SBT1196 (78' · ADD) Recorded [h]1930,
[i]1938, [b]1939, [g]1940, [ad]1948, [cjk]1950, [ef]1956　　Ⓕ🔘🔘

Benno Moiseiwitsch's love affair with the piano spawned numerous fine recordings, though few match this superlative 1948 set of Chopin's Preludes. The first Prelude is candid and forthright, whereas No 4's *Largo* projects an outspoken top line (and note how sensitively Moiseiwitsch negotiates the accompaniment's constantly shifting harmonies). Desynchronised chords mark the opening of Prelude No 6, while the same Prelude's quiet close *segues* almost imperceptibly into the gnomic A major (a parallel sense of transition marries Preludes 10 and 11). Bryce Morrison, in his booklet-notes for Testament, singles out No 16 for its dexterity, but the more oratorical Nos 18 and 22 are particularly notable too for their especially keen sense of narrative.

But the greatness of these performances lies beyond detail. Much of the magic resides in Moiseiwitsch's ability to balance close-up and landscape, cultivating the individual phrase while keeping an eye on whole paragraphs. His touch, pedalling and attention to contrapuntal side-play are remarkable. These are profoundly individual readings that positively teem with incident. But which CD to choose? Testament's transfer achieves a marginally clearer sound frame, APR a touch more warmth but a tad more surface noise. One minor criticism of Testament's disc: there's a very slight drop in pitch between the end of the 14th Prelude and the beginning of the 15th – not a full semitone, but noticeable enough to trouble those with perfect or relative pitch. APR's transfer is spot-on.

Choosing between the two programmes is more problematic. APR's all-Chopin sequence includes fluent accounts of the four Ballades, the Fourth a first-ever release. Odd smudges hardly matter in the face of such compelling musicianship. In the B flat Polonaise it's fascinating to compare Moiseiwitsch with fellow Leschetizky pupil Ignaz Friedman, the one restrained and elegant, the other

(Friedman) pointed and rhythmically fierce. Likewise in the A flat Ballade, where Friedman invests the 'Galloping Horse' second set (Sir Winston Churchill's description) with extra impetus, Moiseiwitsch's musical manners are far milder.

Testament's makeweights highlight Moiseiwitsch's virtuosity, most memorably in Rachmaninov's reworking of the *Scherzo* from the *Midsummer Night's Dream*, which is heard to even better advantage than on the arranger's own recording. So much happens, so quickly and at so many dynamic levels, you can hardly credit the results to a single pair of hands. A Rachmaninov sequence includes a stereo G major Prelude (Op 32 No 5) and a justly famous 1940 account of the sombre B minor Prelude, Op 32 No 10. His primary-coloured 1930 recording of *Kinderszenen* is a joy. In contrast, lightning reflexes benefit textually bolstered Weber and the dry wit of Prokofiev, Stravinsky and John Vallier.

Those fancying an 'Essential Moiseiwitsch' collection should plump for Testament, though Chopin's magnificent Ballades are a significant enough draw to push the scales in APR's direction. It really is a matter of repertory preferences. Both discs are extremely well annotated.

Scherzos

No 1 in B minor, Op 20; **No 2** in B flat minor, Op 31;
No 3 in C sharp minor, Op 39; **No 4** in E, Op 54

Scherzos Nos 1-4
Ivo Pogorelich *pf*
DG 439 947-2GH (42' · DDD)　　　　　　Ⓕ🔘

Love him or hate him, Pogorelich guarantees a response. Chopin for the faint-hearted this isn't; original, provocative, challenging, daring, it emphatically is. Nevertheless, if Pogorelich's most unconventional ideas approach wilful eccentricity, the rewards far outweigh any reservations. True, if they weren't reinforced by such transcendental pianism Pogorelich's interpretations wouldn't carry nearly the same authority or conviction; but it's precisely the marrying of his imaginative scope with his extraordinary technical resource that opens up such startling expressive possibilities.

The first and second *Scherzos* show the juxtaposition of extremes at its most intense, stretching the limits of the musically viable. Predictably, the outer sections of the B minor *Scherzo* are incredibly fast, possessed with an almost demonic drive, while the central Polish carol (*Sleep, little Jesus*) is unusually slow and luxuriously sustained. But such extremes, of character as much as tempo, place enormous tension on the musical structure, and this is most evident in the B flat minor *Scherzo*. Make no mistake, Pogorelich's playing is astounding, from the imperious opening to the lingering and ravishing middle section, where his sublime lyrical simplicity is of the deepest inward poetry.

To sum up, a recording like this isn't easy.

Some may find Pogorelich's probing individualism too overwhelming. There are more ideas crammed into under 42 minutes than on many discs almost twice the length, although most collectors will still feel short-changed by the playing time. This may not be Chopin for every day, but the force of Pogorelich's musical personality subtly and irrevocably shapes one's view of the music. A truly extraordinary disc.

Waltzes

No 1 in E flat, Op 18; **No 2** in A flat, Op 34 No 1; **No 3** in A minor, Op 34 No 2; **No 4** in F, Op 34 No 3; **No 5** in A flat, Op 42; **No 6** in D flat, Op 64 No 1; **No 7** in C sharp minor, Op 64 No 2; **No 8** in A flat, Op 64 No 3; **No 9** in A flat, Op 69 No 1; **No 10** in E minor, Op 69 No 2; **No 11** in G flat, Op 70 No 1; **No 12** in F minor, Op 70 No 2; **No 13** in D flat, Op 70 No 3; **No 14** in E minor, Op posth; **No 15** in E, Op posth; **No 16** in A flat, Op posth; **No 17** in E flat, Op posth; **No 18** in E flat, Op posth; **No 19** in A minor, Op posth

Waltzes Nos 1-14
Arthur Rubinstein pf
RCA Red Seal 09026 63047-2 (50' · ADD) Recorded 1960s ⒷО

There has in recent years been a tendency to take Rubinstein's imposing series of Chopin recordings from the mid-1960s for granted, but to hear them digitally refurbished soon puts a stop to that. His tone doesn't have much luxuriance, being quite chiselled; yet a finely tuned sensibility is evident throughout. This is at once demonstrated by his direct interpretation of Op 18, its elegance explicit. His reading of Op 34 No 1 is *brillante*, as per Chopin's title. In Op 34 No 2 Rubinstein judges everything faultlessly, distilling the sorrowful yet cannily varied grace of this piece. The two finest here are Opp 42 and 64 No 2, and with the former Rubinstein excels in the unification of its diverse elements, its rises and falls of intensity, its hurryings forward and holdings back. This is also true of his reading of Op 64 No 2, the yearning of whose brief *più lento* section is memorable indeed. The sole fault of this issue is that conventional programming leads to the mature Waltzes, which were published by Chopin himself, coming first, the lesser, posthumously printed, items last. Not all of these are early but they have less substance than Opp 18-64, and should come first.

Waltzes Nos 1-14. Mazurka in C sharp minor, Op 50. No 3. Barcarolle. Nocturne in D flat, Op 27 No 2 Ⓗ
Dinu Lipatti pf
EMI Great Recordings of the Century mono 566904-2 (65' · ADD) Recorded 1947-50 ⓂОООⰄ

As a former pupil of Cortot, it wasn't perhaps surprising that Lipatti always kept a special place

Ⓖ in his heart for Chopin. And thanks primarily to the 14 Waltzes, played in a non-chronological sequence of his own choosing, it's doubtful if the disc will ever find itself long absent from the catalogue. Like the solitary *Mazurka*, they were recorded in Geneva during his remarkable renewal of strength in the summer of 1950. The *Nocturne* and *Barcarolle* date back to visits to EMI's Abbey Road studio in 1947 and 1948 respectively. Just once or twice in the Waltzes you might feel tempted to question his sharp tempo changes for mood contrast within one and the same piece – as for instance in No 9 in A flat, Op 69 No 1. However, for the most part his mercurial lightness, fleetness and charm are pure delight. His *Nocturne* in D flat has long been hailed as one of the finest versions currently available. And even though we know he himself (one of the greatest perfectionists) was not completely happy about the *Barcarolle*, for the rest of us this glowing performance has a strength of direction and shapeliness all its own. In fuller contexts there's just a trace of plumminess in the recorded sound.

'Chopin Recordings 1916-27' Ⓗ
Benno Moiseiwitsch pf
Naxos Historical mono 8 111117 (69' · ADD) ⓈⰄ

Ward Marston has done his best with Vol 11 of Naxos's invaluable Moiseiwitsch series where the pianist's legendary magic somehow surfaces through recordings dating from 1916-22 and 1925-27. Moiseiwitsch's Chopin remains indelibly his own, and if his frequent desynchronisation of the hands, expressive dalliance, the odd clinker and a naughty, twinkly delight in tampering with the text are old-fashioned, they are often attributes rather than failings. True, there were days when, overstretched by an unnerving schedule, Moiseiwitsch could sound diffident and workaday, but at his finest he could lighten even the most serious gesture or idea with a nonchalant wit and sparkle. The little B flat Polonaise (a Moiseiwitsch speciality) is spun off with all his charm and virtuosity, and his selection of four Etudes crosses the Rubicon from pragmatism to poetry with a wealth of colour, grace and nuance unknown to all but the finest pianists. The Second Scherzo may bristle with confusions and approximations but it is never less than brilliantly alive and, most generously, there are two performances of both the G flat Waltz and F sharp Impromptu for comparison and enlightenment.

Muzio Clementi   Italian/British 1752-1832

Clementi trained first in Rome, but in 1766-7 went to Dorset, England, to study the harpsichord. Moving to London in 1774, he became conductor at the King's Theatre and from 1770 gave concerts, often including his well-known keyboard sonatas Op 2 (1779).

Clementi travelled widely as a pianist in 1780-85,

and in 1781 took part in a piano contest with Mozart in Vienna. In 1785-1802 he was a frequent piano soloist in London and conductor of his own symphonies, but in the 1790s he was overshadowed by the visiting Haydn. He was in great demand as a teacher. In 1798 he established a music publishing and piano-making firm, touring Europe (initially with his pupil John Field) as its representative in 1802-10. Among the firm's publications were major works by Beethoven. Clementi continued to conduct his symphonies in London and abroad; his last major works were three piano sonatas Op 50 (1821).

Foremost in Clementi's large output are c70 keyboard sonatas, spanning some 50 years. Counterpoint, running figuration and virtuoso passage-work are constant elements. Dramatic writing (which strongly influenced Beethoven) appears increasingly, and works such as Op 13 (1785) feature motivic unity and powerful expression. The sonatas of after c 1800 tend to be more diffuse. Only six of the symphonies and one piano concerto (1796) survive. Clementi also wrote keyboard duets, chamber music and two influential didactic works, Introduction to the Art of Playing on the Piano Forte (1801) and the comprehensive keyboard collection Gradus ad Parnassum (1817-26). GROVEmusic

Keyboard Sonatas

Keyboard Sonatas – F minor, Op 13 No 6; F,   🅟
Op 33 No 2; G minor, Op 34 No 2. Musical
Characteristics, Op 19 – Preludio I alla Haydn;
Preludio I alla Mozart. Capriccio in B flat, Op 17.
Fantasie with Variations, 'Au clair de lune', Op 48
Andreas Staier fp
Teldec Das Alte Werk 2564-69613-6 (68' · DDD)
Ⓜ🅞🅞🅞

One's inclined to think of Clementi as a rather dry composer, however brilliant, but there's nothing remotely dry about this CD, which is full of expressive and often powerful music. Partly it's the instrument: on the fortepiano Clementi's music has a sharpness of impact that it lacks on a modern grand, and also a gently poetic, often almost mysterious ring that carries overtones of early Romanticism, especially in some of the slower music. But the chief responsibility belongs with Andreas Staier, who's clearly fired by the music and discovers so many layers of expression in it.

Essentially he plays three sonatas with a framework of single pieces surrounding them. Two of those pieces come from Clementi's Musical Characteristics, a group of short preludes published in 1787 and imitating Haydn and Mozart as well as Sterkel, Kozeluch and Vaňhal. Interestingly, these lively pieces indicate the features of the two composers that Clementi regarded as distinctive. Then there's a Capriccio, a charming piece demanding (and receiving) crisp and athletic fingerwork. The final item is a brilliant and imaginative fantasy on Au clair de lune, which Clementi varies in some highly inventive ways. This is a late work, from about 1820, and its style is comparable with mature Beethoven.

Of the three sonatas, the last (Op 33 No 2, 1794) is an elegantly written piece, in effect in two movements. Staier is masterly in his command of Clementi's dialectic and of the slightly quirky character of some of his themes, as in the first movement's finale. Op 34 No 2 is a big G minor work: its Adagio draws beautifully shapely and pointed playing from Staier, and the finale, another elaborate and extended movement, is impassioned music, powerfully done. The first of the sonatas, the earlier F minor work (1785), seems in some ways the most 'Romantic' in tone, with its Allegro agitato carrying hints of menace and darkness (enhanced by Staier's sensitive pedalling and misty textures), its eloquent Largo, where the melodic line is enunciated with real pathos, and its stormy final Presto. In all, Staier's reconciliation of the poetic and imaginative content of this music, with his command of its structure and its arguments, makes this one of the most impressive fortepiano discs in memory.

Piano Sonatas – WoO3; Op 13 Nos 4-6; Op 20; Op 23; Op 24
Howard Shelley pf
Hyperion ② CDA67729 (122' · DDD)   🅕🅞

The third volume of Howard Shelley's invaluable survey of Clementi piano sonatas confirms every expectation. Once more you are left to marvel at his unfailing brilliance and musicianship, qualities that can lift and enliven even the most predictable and mechanical gestures. There may be possible thefts from Mozart (who disliked Clementi) and prophecies of Beethoven but, more generally, it would be difficult to imagine all these works, whether slight or distinguished, given with greater skill, zest and affection. Every finger-twisting challenge is met with effortless ease, energy and grace, and Hyperion's sound is, as usual, of demonstration quality.

Eric Coates   British 1886-1957

Coates studied at the Royal Academy of Music, worked as an orchestral viola player (working with both Beecham and Wood), and wrote light orchestral music and c100 songs. He is best known for the suite London (1933) and The Dam Busters march from his film score. He was a founding-member and director of the Performing Rights Society.
GROVEmusic

Light orchestral works

Sweet Seventeen. Summer Afternoon. Impressions of a Princess[a]. Salute the Soldier. Two Light Syncopated Pieces. For Your Delight. The Unknown Singer[a]. I Sing to You. Coquette. Over to You. Idyll. Under the Stars. By the Tamarisk. Mirage. Last Love. The Green Land[a]
[a]**Peter Hughes** sax

BBC Concert Orchestra / John Wilson
ASV White Line CDWHL2107 (79' · DDD)   Ⓜ

The title of these pieces won't ring much of a bell with any but the most avid Coates fans. Indeed, four pieces are here recorded for the first time. But what delights there are! It goes without saying that Coates's craftsmanship is in evidence from start to finish. Yet so often, one wonders just *why* a particular piece never quite made it in the way his most popular works did. Isn't *Summer Afternoon* every bit as delightful as *By the Sleepy Lagoon*? And wouldn't *Salute the Soldier* have served just as well as other marches as a radio signature tune? Most simply, aren't *Under the Stars*, *For Your Delight* and others just simply such utter charmers? The BBC Concert Orchestra plays beautifully, and the conductor seems thoroughly imbued with the Coates style. The recorded sound is crisp and clean, too. You are urged to sample the pleasures of this splendid collection.

The Enchanted Garden. Footlights.
London Bridge. Two Symphonic Rhapsodies – No 1; No 2. The Three Men. Dancing Nights.
Idyll. Four Centuries Suite – 20th Century Rhythm
London Philharmonic Orchestra / Barry Wordsworth
Lyrita SRCD213 (76' · DDD   Ⓕ⮕

'Boult conducts Coates'
Coates The Dam Busters – March[a]. From Meadow to Mayfair[b]. The Merrymakers[b]. Summer Days[b]. The Three Bears[b]. The Three Elizabeths – Youth of Britain: The Princess Elizabeth[b] **Delius** Marche-caprice, RTVI/6[b] **Grainger** Children's March: Over the Hills and Far Away, RMTB4[a] **Holst** Suite No 1, H105 – March[a] **Rossini/Britten** Soirées musicales, Op 9 – March[a] **Vaughan Williams** The Wasps – March-past of the Kitchen Utensils[b] **Walton** Hamlet – Finale (Funeral March)[a]
[a]**London Philharmonic Orchestra;**
[b]**New Philharmonia Orchestra / Sir Adrian Boult**
Lyrita SRCD246 (63' · ADD)   Ⓕ❍❍❍⮕

Fans of Eric Coates and Sir Adrian Boult are in for a field-day as Lyrita at long last restores to currency the 87-year-old maestro's much-loved 1976 concert with the New Philharmonia alongside a previous unreleased collection delivered with polish and enthusiasm by the LPO under Barry Wordsworth. Still, there can be no real grumbles with the production values (though a touch more ventilation and bloom would have been nice), and Wordsworth directs proceedings with chipper ebullience.
Especially valuable here is the 1938 ballet *The Enchanted Garden*, Coates's biggest orchestral canvas, opulently scored and full of the most warm-hearted invention. Other plums include the roistering '20th Century Rhythm' from the 1941 *Four Centuries* suite, glittering concert waltz *Footlights* (1939) and exuberant 1934 march *London Bridge* (the follow-up to the previous year's indelible 'Knightsbridge').

However, there's no disputing the step-up in class when one turns to Boult's famous selection, which radiates a tingling spontaneity and beaming affection that are very special. For evidence of a master at work, just listen to the way Boult caresses the glorious second subject in *The Merrymakers*; and what vernal freshness and unruffled elegance he brings to the witty *Three Bears* fantasy and entrancing *Summer Days* suite (a great favourite of Elgar's, and whose fragrant centrepiece possesses a truly heady beauty). The rest of the CD is filled out with seven treats from Lyrita's 1978 'Sir Adrian Boult conducts Marches' anthology. Grainger's irresistible *Over the Hills and Far Away* in particular fairly bounds along with irrepressible vigour – as, for that matter, does Coates's *The Dam Busters* – and Delius's *Marche-caprice* has a captivating twinkle in its eye. The sound remains crisp and nicely detailed. A joyous tonic indeed – they don't make 'em like this any more!

Samuel Coleridge-Taylor
British 1875-1912

Coleridge-Taylor's father was from Sierra Leone and his mother was English. He studied the violin, singing and composition (with Stanford) at the RCM, producing anthems, chamber music and songs. His fame rests mainly on the cantata Hiawatha's Wedding Feast (1898), once popular for its exotic flavour, and on choral works commissioned for provincial festivals, including further 'Hiawatha' scenes and A Tale of Old Japan (1911). He wrote incidental music for His Majesty's Theatre and was a composition professor and an excellent conductor, making three visits to the USA and maintaining contacts with prominent African-Americans who shared his mission to establish the dignity of blacks.
Stylistically close to the music of his idol Dvořák, some of his works are modelled on African-American subjects and melodies, though some lack harmonic inventiveness. He was at his best in smaller pieces, including the Petite suite de concert for orchestra (1910). GROVEmusic

Violin Concerto in G minor, Op 80

Coleridge-Taylor Violin Concerto
Dvořák Violin Concerto in A minor, B108
Philippe Graffin vn **Johannesburg Philharmonic Orchestra / Michael Hankinson**
Avie AV0044 (63' · DDD)   Ⓕ⮕

The resurgence of interest in the music of Samuel Coleridge-Taylor reaches another milestone with this long-overdue first recording of his Violin Concerto. Coleridge-Taylor completed it in 1911 for the American virtuoso Maud Powell but never lived to hear a note. Abetted by polished and passionate playing from the recently formed Johannesburg PO under its British-born chief Michael Hankinson, Philippe

Graffin triumphantly demonstrates what an effective, endearing work it is, acutely responsive as he is to its bittersweet lyricism while equally relishing the many opportunities for solo display in both outer movements.

The choice of Dvořák's concerto as a coupling would no doubt have pleased Coleridge-Taylor; the Czech master was his favourite composer. Again, there's no missing the wholehearted commitment of all involved. Admittedly, there are times when you're aware that the orchestra isn't in the luxury class, but Graffin plays with such vibrant character and imagination, and the whole venture radiates such a life-affirming spontaneity and joy in music-making that any drawbacks dwindle into insignificance.

Additional recommendation

Violin Concerto
Coupled with: **Somervell** Violin Concerto
Marwood *vn* **BBC Scottish SO / Brabbins**
Hyperion CDA67420 (65' · DDD)   Ⓕ

> The coupling with Arthur Somervell's English pastoral concerto of 1930 is interesting. Marwood's unflashy sweet-toned playing lends the right note of enchantment and authenticity to these forgotten scores.

Chamber works

Clarinet Quintet, Op 10ᵃ.
Piano Quintet, Op 1ᵇ. Ballade, Op 73ᶜ
Nash Ensemble (ᵃRichard Hosford *cl* ᵃᵇᶜMarianne
Thorsen, ᵇMaln Broman, ᵃBenjamin Nabarro *vns*
ᵃᵇLawrence Power *va* ᵃᵇPaul Watkins *vc* ᵇᶜIan Brown *pf*)
Hyperion CDA67590 (69' · DDD)   Ⓕ

Coleridge-Taylor is enjoying a decent innings at present. The performance of the 1895 Clarinet Quintet is superb: it comes as no surprise to learn that these consummate artists had given a memorable live rendering at the Wigmore Hall just a few weeks previously. The work emerges as a quite astonishingly mature achievement for a 19-year-old, its pleasing sense of architecture and ambition reinforced by the inclusion of the first-movement exposition repeat. What's more, the slow movement is now revealed as so much more than just a songful interlude, its 'deepest sensibility' (to quote Lionel Harrison's admirable annotation) and wistful tenderness that recalls the ravishing Air from Parry's *An English Suite*.

The even earlier Piano Quintet (1893) may be marginally less assured but likewise manifests a tumbling lyricism and joyful spontaneity worthy of Dvořák, and well merits the entrancingly poised championship it receives here. The 13-minute Ballade in C minor for violin and piano was written in 1907 for the Anglo-Russian virtuoso Michael Zacherewitsch (1879-1953), who had made his debut at the age of 12 playing the Tchaikovsky Concerto under the composer's baton.

Backed up by a blemish-free production from the Keener/Eadon team and attractively presented, this has to be one of the most engaging releases of the year.

Francesco Bartolomo Conti
Italian 1681/2-1732

A theorbist and composer, Conti was held in high regard for his performances as a theorbist in Florence, Ferrara and Milan. News of his virtuoso playing spread beyond Italy and by 1701 the Habsburg court in Vienna had offered him an appointment as associate theorbist with the same stipend paid to the principal theorbist, Orazio Clementi. Conti served in this capacity from 1701 to 1708. On the death of Clementi in August 1708 he was promoted to principal theorbist, a position which he held until illness forced him to retire in 1726. The court had difficulty selecting his successor; Joachim Sarao from Naples was appointed in January 1727.

David
Marijana Mijanović *contr* David **Simone Kermes** *sop*
Micol **Furio Zanasi** *bar* Saul **Birgit Christensen** *sop*
Gionata **Sonia Prina** *contr* Abner **Vito Priante** *bar*
Falti **Il Complesso Barocco / Alan Curtis**
Virgin Classics ② 378877-2 (154' · DDD)   Ⓕ

The Florentine Francesco Bartolomeo Conti (1682-1732) was the finest theorbo player in early 18th-century Europe, and spent almost his entire career at the Habsburg court in Vienna. He composed sacred and secular vocal works special enough to warrant the attention of both Bach and Handel. Conti's oratorio *David*, a setting of a dramatic libretto by Apostolo Zeno, was first performed at Vienna in March 1724. The cast of singers included the tenor Francesco Borosini, soon afterwards a principal cast member for Handel in *Tamerlano* and *Rodelinda* (Conti's writing for Borosini descends to a low G, hence the decision here to cast baritone Furio Zanasi as Saul). Alan Curtis speculates that Borosini might have shown Conti's score to Handel because Conti's use of the theorbo to portray David playing the harp to soothe the insanely jealous Saul is neatly reflected in Handel's use of solo harp in his oratorio Saul (1738). Conti's difficult obbligato theorbo part in David's 'Quanto mirabile' is entrusted to the safe hands of Jakob Lindberg; the vocal part is sung by Marijana Mijanović, whose tuning and phrasing are better here than in her Handel recordings. Furio Zanasi's top register is stretched a notch too much for comfort at times but this never gets in the way of a convincing performance. Simone Kermes is beautifully emotive as Micol, Birgit Christensen's sparkling soprano is impressive, and Sonia Prina sings with exemplary sense of proportion and melodic line.

Curtis has edited the score himself, and writes an illuminating essay. This labour of love reveals that Conti's arias are strikingly apposite to the dramatic situations and invested with sincere musical depth and richness. This is essential for lovers of Italianate Baroque vocal music.

Arnold Cooke
British 1906-2005

He studied with Dent at Cambridge (1925-8, BA, MusB; MusD 1948) and with Hindemith at the Berlin Hochschule für Musik (1929-32). He spent a year as music director of the Festival Theatre, Cambridge (following Walter Leigh, an earlier Hindemith pupil), and then taught composition at the Manchester College of Music from 1933 to 1938. After war service in the navy he was appointed professor of harmony, counterpoint and composition at the Trinity College of Music, where he remained from 1947 until his retirement in 1978. A pianist and cellist himself, Cooke wrote chamber music and vocal music for soloists, for children and for choirs. His woodwind writing is especially grateful and, like Hindemith, he has written successfully for the organ.

Symphony No 1. Concerto for Strings. Jabez and the Devil – Suite
London Philharmonic Orchestra / Nicholas Braithwaite
Lyrita SRCD203 (70' · DDD) ⒻⒹ➔

The first of Arnold Cooke's five symphonies was completed in 1947 and premiered under Sir Adrian Boult in a BBC broadcast two years later. At first glance both the home tonality and formal plan might imply a nod or two towards Walton's First Symphony from the previous decade. However, it doesn't take very long to discover that the most fruitful influence is that of Hindemith (Cooke's teacher at the Berlin Hochschule für Musik from 1929 to 1932); anyone who responds to the German master's *Mathis der Maler*, Symphony in E flat or *Symphonia serena* should most certainly lend an ear. Closer to home, annotator Calum MacDonald also perceives a timeless, deep-rooted quality in Cooke's fad-free music that suggests a kinship with Rubbra (witness the long-breathed polyphony of the heartfelt slow movement). In sum, a work of impeccable resourcefulness, cogent argument and affecting sincerity that invites and repays repeated listening.

The symphony is flanked by the 1948 Concerto in D for string orchstra (a bracingly assured, big-hearted essay in three movements, which features some grateful writing for the section principals) and a splendidly colourful and diverting 18-minute suite from the 1959 ballet *Jabez and the Devil* (eventually staged at Covent Garden in September 1961). Kenneth Wilkinson's 1974 Kingsway Hall sound in the latter boasts fabulous bite and presence still, but the two other works (taped in 1988-89) have likewise been ripely captured by the microphones, and Nicholas Braithwaite helms the LPO with scrupulous care and infectious commitment throughout. Definitely one for the 'want' list!

Aaron Copland
American 1900-1990

Copland studied with Goldmark in New York and with Boulanger in Paris (1921-4), then returned to New York and took a leading part in composers organisations, taught at the New School for Social Research (1927-37) and composed. At first his Stravinskian inheritance from Boulanger was combined with aspects of jazz (Music for the Theatre, 1925) or with a grand rhetoric (Symphonic Ode, 1929), but then he established an advanced personal style in the Piano Variations (1930) and orchestral Statements (1935). Growing social concerns spurred him towards a popular style in the cowboy ballets Billy the Kid (1940) and Rodeo (1942), but even here his harmony and orchestral spacing are distinctive. Another ballet, Appalachian Spring (1944) – a continuous movement towards a set of variations on a Shaker hymn – brought a synthesis of the folksy and the musically developed.

Other works from the 'Americana' period include the Lincoln Portrait for speaker and orchestra (1942), the Fanfare for the Common Man (1942), the 12 Poems of Emily Dickinson for voice and piano (1950), two sets of Old American Songs (1950-52) and the opera The Tender Land (1954). But there were also more complex developments, especially among the chamber and instrumental works: the Piano Sonata (1941), Violin Sonata (1943), Piano Quartet (1950) and Piano Fantasy (1957). In the orchestral Connotations (1962) and Inscape (1967) he completed a journey into serialism, though again the sound is individual. Other late works, including the ballet Dance Panels (1963), the String Nonet (1960) and the Duo for flute and piano (1971), continue the cool triadic style. He was conductor, speaker and pianist, a generous and admired teacher, and author of several books, among them Music and Imagination (1952). GROVEmusic

Early symphonies

Symphony No 1. Short Symphony. Dance Symphony
Bournemouth Symphony Orchestra / Marin Alsop
Naxos American Classics 8 559359 (59' · DDD) ⓈⓄⒹ➔

There are two attractions here: the only current recording of the *Short Symphony* and a fine recording of Symphony No 1 – at last. It started life as the Symphony for Organ and Orchestra, written for Copland's teacher Nadia Boulanger whose performances launched his career in 1925. Six years later the reworking of the score without organ was first performed but it has never made much headway. Alsop and the Bournemouth players make a fine case for this neglected score with many characteristics of mature Copland.

There are also two versions of Copland's *Short Symphony*. It was first played in Mexico City under Carlos Chávez in 1934 but the rhythmic difficulties were considered so great that the American premiere had to wait 10 years. Meanwhile, despairing of orchestral performances, Copland made the version for sextet. There are no difficulties now for the Bournemouth SO but one might have hoped for more sparkle and a better recording.

There are odd circumstances about the *Dance Symphony* too. It was taken from the ballet *Grohg* – never performed – that Copland wrote during his student years in Paris. In the absence of a full recording of *Grohg*, the *Dance Symphony* completes an essential CD.

Symphony No 3

Symphony No 3. Billy the Kid – Suite
New Zealand Symphony Orchestra / James Judd
Naxos American Classics 8 559106 (64' · DDD) ⓈⓄ

The first of Copland's three popular ballets is coupled here with what's arguably the greatest American symphony. Judd's first movement has more dynamic range than Eiji Oue's performance (below) and the long lines feel better paced. The second movement is the rumbustious *Scherzo* in Copland's most extrovert manner. Judd's interpretation works, and makes Oue seem a trifle pedestrian, closer to Copland's own performances than the dazzle that Bernstein brought to this kind of texture. The New Zealand strings aren't as precise in the taxing high opening as Oue's Minnesota players but, when it eventually comes, the fanfare and the subtle textures surrounding it are completely convincing.

The verdict on this efficient and sympathetic performance will be affected by its being the best buy around now. The suite from *Billy the Kid* gets thoroughly idiomatic treatment too and the coupling will encourage lovers of the most folksy Copland to recognise and enjoy the same composer in the big symphony.

Symphony No 3. Appalachian Spring.
Fanfare for the Common Man
Minnesota Orchestra / Eiji Oue
Reference Recordings RR-93CD (72' · DDD) ⒻⓄ

As an opening salute, the *Fanfare for the Common Man* makes a good centenary tribute and prepares listeners for its appearance in the finale of the Third Symphony. It also shows off the prowess of the Minnesota brass. The version of *Appalachian Spring* here is the suite, not the full ballet, and it's well paced under Oue although occasionally lacking attack in the strings where Copland said he wanted 'bitten out *marcato*'.

Significant earlier versions of the Third Symphony have included Copland's rather understated treatment with the New Philharmonia and Bernstein's much better projected interpretation on DG. Yet Oue's approach is compelling, falling midway between Copland's objectivity and Bernstein's dramatisation. The soft, long lines of the first movement move inexorably towards the first climax, and Copland's translucent scoring tells in its purely personal way. The *scherzo* is a controlled riot, again showing off the brass – the orchestra's best feature – and the finale is convincing. The recorded sound is spectacular too.

Ballets

Appalachian Spring. Billy the Kid. Rodeo
San Francisco Symphony Orchestra / Michael Tilson Thomas
RCA Red Seal 09026 63703-2 (77' · DDD) Ⓜ ❍❍❍

 For *Appalachian Spring* Tilson Thomas boldly opts for the rarely heard full orchestral version of the complete ballet score. This includes an extra 10 or so minutes of fretful, dark-hued music omitted from the familiar suite, after which that glorious final statement of *Simple Gifts* seems to emerge with even greater éclat and emotional release than usual. Elsewhere, these newcomers distil all the tender poetry and dewy freshness you could wish for, while bringing a marvellously supple spring and athletic purpose to any faster music.

Under Tilson Thomas, the suite from *Billy the Kid* opens with a real sense of 'once upon a time' wonder, the illimitable expanses of the prairie stretching out before our very eyes. The ensuing street scene soon generates an infectious rhythmic snap, and there's a wonderfully affecting contribution from the SFSO's principal trumpet during the card game at night. Best of all is 'Billy's death', as poignantly intoned as you've ever heard it. Absolutely no grumbles, either, about the four *Rodeo* dance episodes. Tilson Thomas sees to it that 'Buckaroo Holiday' packs all the requisite punch and high-kicking swagger, while the two middle numbers ravish the ear in their disarming beauty. Moreover, the concluding 'Hoe-Down' goes with terrific, toe-tapping gusto, though the orchestra's delirious whoops of delight may perhaps strike some listeners as too much of a good thing.

Boasting some opulent, exhilaratingly expansive sonics, this is a corker of a release.

El salón México[a]. Danzón cubano[b]. An Outdoor Overture[b]. Quiet City[b]. Our Town[b]. Las agachadas[a]. Fanfare for the Common Man[b]. Lincoln Portrait[b]. Appalachian Spring – suite[b]. Rodeo – Four Dance Episodes[b]. Billy the Kid – orchestral suite[b]. Music for Movies[c]. Letter from Home[b]. John Henry[b]. Symphony No 3[c]. Clarinet Concerto[d]
Benny Goodman *cl* **Henry Fonda** *narr*
[a]**New England Conservatory Chorus;** [b]**London Symphony Orchestra;** [c]**New Philharmonia Orchestra;** [d]**Columbia Symphony Orchestra / Aaron Copland**
Sony Classical ③ 07464 46559-2 (226' · ADD)
Recorded 1963-76 Ⓜ
Single 'Copland conducts Copland' disc available on Sony Classical Ⓜ 09970 90403-2 includes Appalachian Spring, Fanfare for the Common Man, Rodeo – Four Dance Episodes, Old American Songs (with William Warfield) & Billy the Kid – Celebration

This offers a welcome gathering of a lot of Copland's own performances. Only *Las agachadas* ('The shake-down song') for unaccompanied chorus is new to the British catalogue; this is a rather lame performance and nobody would buy the three-CD set for that. The oldest recording is the Clarinet Concerto with Benny Goodman – the second of the two he made under Copland. *Lincoln Portrait* with Henry Fonda is disappointing, but apart from earlier recordings in Spanish and Portuguese, this, made in 1968, is the only one under Copland. He was surprisingly modest about interpretation and wrote (in *Copland on Music*; New York: 1960): 'Composers rarely can be depended upon to know the correct tempi at which their music should proceed'. All the same it's a pleasure to have Copland as both composer and interpreter in some of his most delightful shorter works such as *Letter from Home*, *John Henry*, *Quiet City* and *An Outdoor Overture*. All told, this is an economical way to build up a collection of his performances which provide such an insight into his personality.

The Red Pony – Suite. Rodeo – Four Dance Episodes. Letter from Home. Music for Radio, 'Prairie Journal'
Buffalo Philharmonic Orchestra / JoAnn Falletta
Naxos American Classics 8 559240 (60' · DDD) Ⓢ➤

This attractive anthology represents Copland the Populist, to quote the title of Tilson Thomas's stunning RCA disc of all three ballets with the San Francisco Symphony. There are two suites, one from film and one from ballet, plus a couple of less familiar short pieces written for radio.

The least recorded of these is *Prairie Journal*, which had an odd genesis. It was commissioned by CBS Radio in 1936, premiered simply as *Music for Radio*, and their massive audience was invited to send in suggestions for a better title. A thousand people responded and Copland chose *Saga of the Prairie* – even at this stage listeners thought his music evoked the Western scene. Copland changed the title much later. In both this piece and *Letter from Home* – as he admitted, a slightly sentimental picture of our boys at the front receiving mail in 1944 – he was taking the mass medium of radio seriously.

He did the same with films, as *The Red Pony* shows. The suite was performed in 1948 before the Steinbeck film was released. It's full of diatonic tunes you think you've known all your life, pure triads and Copland's characteristic snappy scoring. These are lively performances in the Copland tradition, although *Letter from Home* seems fast and at times the orchestra lacks finesse.

Piano Quartet

Movement[a]. Two Pieces[a]. Vitebsk[b]. Piano Quartet[c]. Sextet[d]
[d]**Michael Collins** *cl* [bcd]**Martin Roscoe** *pf* [ad]**Vanbrugh Quartet** ([bc]Gregory Ellis, Keith Pascoe *vns* [c]Simon Aspell *va* [bc]Christopher Marwood *vc*)
ASV CDDCA1081 (65' · DDD) Ⓕ

This fine collection of Copland's small output of chamber music offers the first British recording of *Movement*, a characteristically introspective

COPLAND'S APPALACHIAN SPRING – IN BRIEF

San Francisco SO / Michael Tilson Thomas
RCA 09026 63511-2 (77' · DDD) ⒻOOO
The complete 35-minute score in its guise for full orchestra, surveyed with acute perception by Tilson Thomas and his peerlessly refined band. Sensational, spectacularly natural sound.

Los Angeles PO / Leonard Bernstein
DG 439 528-2GGA (54' · DDD) ⓂO➤
The popular 1945 suite in the performance of a lifetime. Lenny at his most charismatic and raptly understanding. Marvellous orchestral playing.

Boston SO / Serge Koussevitzky
Biddulph WHL050 (80' · ADD) Ⓜ
Koussevitzky's 1945 account was the suite's world premiere recording, a blazingly committed display with a coda as touchingly serene as you could hope to hear.

London SO / Aaron Copland
Sony SMK89874 (77' · ADD) Ⓜ
The suite receives an eminently sprightly, forthright performance under Copland's lead, though it's perhaps neither quite as distinctive nor as radiant as his own 1959 RCA Boston predecessor.

Atlanta SO / Robert Spano
Telarc CD80596 (69' · DDD) ⒻO
A beautifully sprung account of the suite from this burgeoning partnership. Barber's tremendous First Symphony and approachable new works by Jennifer Higdon and Christopher Theofanidis complete a varied programme.

Detroit SO / Antál Dorati
Decca 430 705-2DM (74' · DDD) Ⓜ➤
Glowingly caught by the Decca microphones, Dorati's uncomplicated Detroit account of the 1945 suite will give pleasure. Part of a supremely enjoyable all-Copland concert.

Seattle SO / Gerard Schwarz
Delos DE3154 (62' · DDD) Ⓕ
Another lucid, gently perceptive reading of the 1945 suite. Enterprisingly coupled with the Piano Concerto and *Symphonic Ode*, and handsomely engineered by Delos.

Atlanta SO / Lane
Telarc CD80074 (68' · DDD) Ⓜ
Louis Lane offers the ballet suite in a performance that has a real feel of the theatre about it: you could almost imagine that these musicians had played in the pit for a while. Telarc's sound is all you could wish for. Part of an appealing Copland programme.

piece from his student years in Paris which shares a theme with the *Symphony for Organ and Orchestra*. The *Two Pieces* (1928) are also rarities well worth having, the rapid second one embodying to perfection the ideals of Nadia Boulanger's teaching.

Then there are the three major chamber works, starting with *Vitebsk*, the 1929 trio based on a Jewish folk theme. This is a commanding performance, which makes the most of the off-key quarter-tones and is thoroughly adroit in the central *Allegro*. The Sextet is a genuine chamber piece, although it was an arrangement of the *Short Symphony* which was found too difficult for most orchestras in 1933 and had to wait until 1944 for its American premiere. With Collins and Roscoe the Vanbrugh give an accomplished performance of the Sextet's sparklingly affirmative rhythms.

The Piano Quartet (1950) is in the same slow-quick-slow layout as *Vitebsk*. Like the final slow movement of the Piano Sonata its outer movements have a sublime immobility. Written while Copland was working on his great cycle, *Twelve Poems of Emily Dickinson*, the first two movements of this impressive quartet enter new territory, Copland tentatively exploring serial techniques. A few exposed string phrases lack finesse, and some soft details in the piano are almost lost – at the end of the first movement and more seriously at the end of the last movement when the dissonant note in the last chord is inaudible. But this is a valuable collection, well worth acquiring to have all these works together, played – and recorded – like this.

---

12 Poems of Emily Dickinson

Four Piano Blues. 12 Poems of Emily Dickinson. Night. Pastorale. Poet's Song. Old American Songs – Set 1; Set 2
Susan Chilcott *sop* **Iain Burnside** *pf*
Black Box BBM1074 (69' · DDD · T)   Ⓕ●

In this excellent selection Susan Chilcott and Iain Burnside grasp the subtlety of Copland's idiom. The two sets of *Old American Songs* are rightly sung in an American accent in a range of styles from the soulful-nostalgic of 'Long time ago' to the knockabout comedy of 'I bought me a cat'. But 'Simple Gifts', so well known from *Appalachian Spring*, is taken well below the marked tempo.

Copland's settings of Emily Dickinson are given with the commanding authority that this great cycle deserves. The competition on CD consists of Roberta Alexander with Roger Vignoles, where there are minor flaws, and Barbara Bonney with André Previn, which isn't an all-Copland disc. Neither of Copland's own recordings is still available. Even in this company Chilcott is impressive, with an enviable control of the wide leaps from top to bottom. Her breath control is so good that she can easily sustain the last note of 'I could not stop for death' for its full length, symbolising eternity. In each song every mood is right, although the recorded balance varies.

The early songs are interesting. Copland set his friend Aaron Schaffer's poem *Night* when he was only 18 and Debussy's impressionism still avant-garde. But *Pastorale* three years later, just before he went to study with Nadia Boulanger in Paris, shows real personality.

Arcangelo Corelli   Italian 1653-1713

Corelli studied in Bologna from 1666, and was admitted to the Accademia Filarmonica at 17. By 1675 he was in Rome, where he became the foremost violinist and a chamber musician to Queen Christina of Sweden, to whom he dedicated his 12 trio sonatas da chiesa Op 1 (1681). His 12 trio sonatas da camera Op 2 (1685) were dedicated to Cardinal Pamphili; Corelli was his music master, 1687-90. His next patron, Cardinal Pietro Ottoboni, received the dedication of the trio sonatas Op 4 (1694). Corcilli came to dominate Rome musical life, and also directed opera performances there and in Naples. After 1708 he retired from public view.

Corelli was the first composer to derive his fame exclusively from instrumental music. His works were immensely popular during his lifetime and long afterwards, and went through numerous reprints and arrangements (42 editions of the op.5 violin sonatas had appeared by 1800). They were seen as models of style for their purity and poise. His small output – six published sets and a few single pieces – contains innovations of fundamental importance to Baroque style, reconciling strict counterpoint and soloistic violin writing, and using sequential progressions and suspensions to give a notably modern sense of tonality. Distinctions between 'church' (abstract) and 'chamber' (dance) idioms are increasingly blurred in his sonatas. The op.6 concerti grossi (1714) resemble trio sonatas with orchestral reinforcement and echo effects. They were especially popular in England, preferred even to Handel's concertos well into the 19th century. There were many imitations of Corelli's music, notably of the folia variations in the violin sonata Op 5 No 12 (1700), and some composers used his music as a springboard; Bach borrowed a theme from the trio sonata Op 3 No 4 (1689) for an organ fugue. As a violinist Corelli was the finest, most influential teacher of his day; as an ensemble director he imposed high standards of discipline.   **GROVE**music

---

Concerti grossi

12 Concerti grossi, Op 6 – No 1 in D; No 2 in F;   Ⓟ
No 3 in C minor; No 4 in D; No 5 in B flat; No 6 in F;
No 7 in D; No 8 in G minor; No 9 in F; No 10 in C;
No-11 in B flat; No 12 in F
The English Concert / Trevor Pinnock
Archiv Produktion Gramophone Awards Collection
② 474 907-2 (130' · DDD)   Ⓜ●●●❿

In his working life of about 40 years Corelli must have produced a great deal of orchestral music, yet the 12 *Concerti grossi*, Op 6, form the bulk of what's survived. Their original versions are mostly lost; what we know today are those published in Amsterdam by Estienne Roger. These had been assembled from movements Corelli had written over a period of years, and which he'd carefully polished and revised. The first eight are of the *da chiesa* type, the last four the *da camera* type, which essentially means that-the latter have dance movements; the former don't. The number of movements in each varies from four to seven. All feature the interplay of a group of soloists, the *concertino* (two violins and a cello) and the orchestra, the *ripieno*, whose size, as Corelli wrote, could be flexible. These are masterpieces of their genre, much admired in their day, and very influential. The scores leave scope for embellishment, and the players of The English Concert take full advantage of them.

Trio Sonatas

Trio Sonatas, Op 1ª,2ᵇ,3ᶜ,-4ᵈ
Purcell Quartet (Catherine Mackintosh, ᵃᵇᶜElizabeth Wallfisch, ᵈCatherine Weiss *vns* Richard Boothby *vc*)
Jakob Lindberg *theorbo* **Robert Woolley** ᵇᵈ*hpd/*ᵃᶜ*org*
Chaconne Classics ③ CHAN0692/4 (276' · DDD)
Ⓜ**Ⓞ**⊡➛

Corelli's chamber music was reprinted 84 times during his lifetime and 31 more during the rest of the 18th century, a record most composers would envy even today. The Sonatas of Ops 1 and 3 are *da chiesa*, those of Ops 2 and 4 are *da camera* (with dance-titled movements). They are small gems: most have four movements, and their durations range from five and a half to seven and a half minutes, within which they pack a wealth of invention, pure beauty and variety of pace and mood. Surviving evidence suggests that they were played at a much lower pitch than today's standard, the lower string tension adding warmth and opulence to the sound. Catherine Mackintosh takes full advantage of the works' opportunities for pliant phrasing and added embellishments; Elizabeth Wallfisch 'converses' with her in her own characteristic way, while Catherine Weiss follows her example more closely. The Purcell Quartet's oneness of thought and timing is a joy to hear and the recording is superb in all respects.

Violin Sonatas, Op 5

Violin Sonatas, Op 5
Andrew Manze *vn* **Richard Egarr** *hpd*
Harmonia Mundi ② HMU90 7298/9 (131' · DDD)
Ⓜ**ⒸⓄ**⊡➛

Considering the acknowledged status of Corelli's Op 5 violin sonatas, it's surprising how few of today's star Baroque violinists have recorded them. Published as a clear statement of intent on January 1, 1700, they're a benchmark not only in the history of the violin but of chamber music in

general; yet despite being an accepted model of compositional purity and refinement which lasted throughout the 18th century and beyond, for many music-lovers – even Baroque music-lovers – they're still relatively little-known territory. Perhaps it's their finely honed perfection which has counted against them. Maybe they just seem too polite. Accounts of Corelli's violin-playing tell us that his eyes would glow 'red as fire' and his face contort, but evidence of this volatile character has not not always been easy to detect in the written notes of the violin sonatas.

If anyone is going to find him, however, it's Andrew Manze, who has repeatedly demonstrated that the heart of Baroque music lies beyond what's on the printed page. At a time when improvisational flair and spontaneity have never been a more exciting part of Baroque music-making, Manze and his accompanist Richard Egarr are the masters of it, and here they have produced a Corelli recording which is nothing short of revelatory.

Not that it's unthinkingly wild or bizarre. Manze may have adorned the music with his customarily liberal decoration of extra double-stops, flowery arabesques and emphatic gestures – and Egarr may have performed his usual extraordinary feats at the keyboard, devising an array of inventive keyboard textures which ranges from luxurious feather-bed arpeggios and swirls to daring, stabbing left-hand double octaves (no other continuo player manages to sound so much as if his fingers were a direct extension of his imagination) – but this is still Corelli with a measure of north Italian dignity.

The resulting balance between restraint and urgency is compelling, because the performers, you feel, aren't out to shock but to search for something new and real. This really is Corelli as you haven't heard him before. The performances reach a high technical standard, as does the recording, though strangely long gaps are left between some of the movements. This vital, ear-opening disc is in a category of its own, classic music in a classic recording.

John Corigliano   American b1938

After studying at Columbia University, Corigliano worked as a music programmer for the New York Times radio station, WQXR, and as music director for WBAI. He also produced recordings for Columbia Masterworks and worked with Leonard Bernstein on the Young People's Concerts series for CBS. He has taught at the Manhattan School, the Juilliard School and Lehman College, CUNY, where he was named distinguished professor in 1984. During the period 1987-90 he served as the first composer-in-residence of the Chicago SO. Corigliano's first period, which he described as a 'tense, histrionic outgrowth of the "clean" American sound of Barber, Copland, Harris and Schuman', extends from the Violin Sonata (1963) through the choral symphony, A Dylan Thomas Trilogy (1960-76). The Oboe Concerto (1975) and, more definitively, the Clarinet Concerto (1977), introduced by Bernstein and the New York PO, inaugurated a change in style, abandoning an earlier restriction to conventional notation and embracing an 'architectural' method of composition. Many of Corigliano's mature orchestral works have experimented with the physical placement of players: offstage instrumentalists figure prominently in both Troubadours and Symphony No 1; The Ghosts of Versailles features an orchestra onstage as well as in the pit, and both the Flute Concerto and the Clarinet Concerto conclude with dialogue between players onstage and in the auditorium. This concern reached an apotheosis of sorts with Circus Maximus (Symphony No 3, 2005).

Symphony No 3

Symphony No 3, 'Circus Maximus'. Gazebo Dances
University of Texas Wind Ensemble / Jerry Junkin
Naxos 8 559601 (53' · DDD) Ⓢ➋

Just as Corigliano's First Symphony embodied his anger about Aids, this spectacular based on the vast Roman arena the Circus Maximus finds 'parallels between the high decadence of Rome and our present time'. Corigliano rightly slates our entertainment-dominated culture and compares today's ubiquitous obsession with violence to the ancient Romans enjoying the sight of lions devouring human beings for amusement. This is heady stuff and nowhere more so than in the extravagant resources of Circus Maximus itself.

There's a stage band of 37 players plus four to five percussionists; a 'surround band' with 22 players including 11 trumpets and three percussionists; and a marching band that moves down the centre of the auditorium in track 6 and, like everything else, is stunningly caught by the sound engineers. As if that wasn't enough, the work ends with a sustained high note followed by a blast from a 12-bore shotgun! Some sections are as laceratingly violent as Varèse, and there are sirens and whistles too. But there's some repose in 'Night Music I' with its uncanny tapestry of animal sounds even if 'Night Music II' evolves into a nightmare through dotted rhythms. The following 'Prayer' is sustained triadic relief.

The American wind band has a noble tradition and Corigliano has added a substantial work to the repertoire. The *Gazebo Dances*, originally for piano duet, are affable early pieces with a waltz that falls out of step and a hectic tarantella.

The Red Violin Concerto

The Red Violin Concerto[a]. Violin Sonata[b]
Joshua Bell vn [b]**Jeremy Denk** pf [a]**Baltimore Symphony Orchestra / Marin Alsop**
Sony Classical 82876 88060-2 (62' · DDD) Ⓕ❶➋

With his 70th birthday in 2009 and decorated with many awards, John Corigliano is one of the most prominent American composers of his generation. Thirty years ago his Clarinet Concerto made a strong initial impact and the *Red*

Violin is his fifth concerto, with a new one for percussion to follow.

Corigliano's score for François Girard's film *The Red Violin* (1997) was the starting-point for the latest concerto. Even before the film was finished the composer extracted a *Chaconne* for violin and orchestra, which eventually became the first movement of the concerto. He felt that a single movement would get lost compared with a full-scale concerto.

And this is exactly what he has delivered – a romantic, dramatic, lyrical four-movement work with luxuriant orchestral textures that benefited from starting life as a film. In his essay in the booklet Corigliano says this context encouraged him to write with fewer inhibitions; things flowed easily, but he has cunningly adapted the work to the concert hall. Even further the *Red Violin* Concerto is a resourceful vehicle for the eloquence and panache of Joshua Bell, who gave the premiere in 2003. The opening movement now seems long but the ghostly *Scherzo* is concise and throughout passages there is a special rapt atmosphere in *pianissimo* passages.

Bell and Jeremy Denk give a polished performance of the 1963 Violin Sonata that fuses neoclassical and American styles. Ideal performances well recorded.

Violin Sonata / Red Violin Caprices

Corigliano Violin Sonata[a]. The Red Violin Caprices.
V Thomson Five Ladies[a]. Three Portraits[a]. Eight Portraits
Philippe Quint vn [a]**William Wolfram** pf
Naxos 8 559364 (65' · DDD) Ⓢ❶➋

This is another incarnation of John Corigliano's *Red Violin* music. First the film and the *Chaconne* for violin and orchestra derived from it (1997); then the Concerto (2003); and now the composer has extracted a set of caprices for solo violin.

These were originally written as studies and the actors, filmed playing the instrument, had to mime to them. Because of the demands of the film, reflecting the life of a violin at various times and places, the writing has a wider stylistic range than most contemporary works for solo violin.

Corigliano's Sonata for Violin and Piano (1963) is an early piece with ingenious Stravinskian panache in the rapid writing and lyrical charm elsewhere of the kind which led to *The Red Violin* 35 years later. Quint and Wolfram make it sound just as impressive as Bell and Denk (Sony).

Most of Virgil Thomson's *Portraits* were for piano so it's unusual to have three groups for violin, with and without piano. Thomson began with seven of the *Eight Portraits* for solo violin in 1928 and went on to produce about 150. He actually composed in front of the sitter like an artist sketching, and the results are delightfully spontaneous. There's a 'Tango Lullaby' for Mlle Alvarez de Toledo, who must have been quite a character; sketches of Gertrude Stein and Alice B Toklas, both so important in Thomson's life; and composer colleagues like Henri Sauguet. Philippe Quint's panache is stunning and this CD offers some of the most attractive music for solo violin in the entire repertoire.

William Cornysh   English1468-1523

After being at court (from 1494) Cornysh became Master of the Children at the Chapel Royal, a post he held until his death. From 1509 he was the leading figure in the plays and entertainments that enlivened court life. In 1513 he made the first of several visits to France with the Chapel Royal, in Henry VIII's retinue. Several of his sacred vocal works are in the Eton Choirbook; their style ranges from the flamboyance of the Stabat mater to the simplicity of the Ave Maria Mater Dei.   GROVEmusic

Magnificat

Salve regina. Ave Maria, mater Dei. Gaude virgo mater Christi. Magnificat. Ah, Robin. Adieu, adieu, my heartes lust. Adieu courage. Woefully arrayed. Stabat mater
The Tallis Scholars / Peter Phillips
Gimell CDGIM014 (65' · DDD · T)   Ⓕ

Cornysh's music is a riot of abundant, often seemingly wild melody, constantly in search of wanton, abstract, dare-devil ideas. Take, for example, the extraordinary conclusion to the five-part *Magnificat*, where pairs of voices are challenged with music of gradually increasing complexity, peaking in an exchange of quite hair-raising virtuosity between the sopranos – and all this just for the words 'and ever shall be, world without end'! As far as the sacred works are concerned, The Tallis Scholars respond magnificently to Cornysh's audacious imagination. Theirs is a majestic and glorious sound, to be relished in full in the *Stabat mater*, a huge piece that survives incomplete and for which the late Frank Harrison composed treble parts that may even trump Cornysh himself in their sheer bravura. Marginally less striking in The Tallis Scholars' performances are the short partsongs and the carol *Woefully arrayed*, robbed as they are here of some of their latent expressiveness and strength by being sung (admittedly very beautifully) in an inappropriately resonant building, and in rounded modern English vowels. But judged as a whole this disc must be reckoned an outstanding success.

Louis Couperin   French c1626-1661

Louis Couperin was the first important member of a major dynasty of French composers, influential for more than two and a half centuries. He settled in

Paris and by 1653 was organist of St Gervais. He wrote pieces for wind and strings, but most of his music is for keyboard: some 70 fugues, plainchant settings and other pieces for organ, notable for their vigorous counterpoint and expressive force, and some 135 for harpsichord, consisting of preludes and dances, longer than most from this period and remarkable for their lively ideas, their grandeur and their intensity.   GROVEmusic

Suites

L Couperin Suites – in F; in A; in D; in A; in F; in C. · Pavane in F sharp minor **Froberger** Le Tombeau de Monsieur Blancheroche
Skip Sempé hpd
Alpha ALPHA066 (79' · DDD)   ⒻOO

Louis Couperin, less famous than his nephew, François 'Le Grand', was nevertheless one of the greatest harpsichord composers of the 17th century, a creator of suites of beautifully honed miniatures cast predominantly in the standard French dance-forms of the day (Allemande, Courante, Sarabande and so on) exuding all the noble expressiveness and lyrical melancholy of their age.

He finds an ideal interpreter in Skip Sempé, a player who relishes the sheer sound of the harpsichord and knows how to exploit its glorious resonance. Sempé achieves this by means of probably the most exquisite touch you'll ever hear on the instrument, leaving him in control of the tone at every turn. Chords are spread lovingly, ornaments tumble easily into one another, all without a hint of unwelcome percussiveness or jangliness – every note seems to have been deftly caressed into being.

He also shows us just how much he enjoys the bass sonority of his harpsichord (a compliant French copy by Bruce Kennedy) by throwing in a low-lying transcription of a Marais gamba piece; another guest composer is Froberger, who answers Couperin's *Prélude* in explicit imitation of his style, with his sombrely magnificent *Tombeau de Monsieur Blancheroche*. A minute lack of improvisatory flow in the unmeasured *Préludes* is scarcely worth mentioning when so much else in Sempé's playing gives unalloyed pleasure. This is demonstration-class musicianship at the harpsichord.

François Couperin   French 1668-1733

Couperin was the central figure of the French harpsichord school. He came from a long line of musicians, mostly organists, of whom the most eminent was his uncle, Louis Couperin, though his father Charles (1638-79) was also a composer and organist of St Gervais. François succeeded to that post on his 18th birthday; his earliest known music is two organ masses. In 1693 he became one of the four royal organists which enabled him to develop his career as a teacher through his court connections. He was soon recognised as the leading French composer of his day through his sacred works and his chamber music and, from 1713, his harpsichord pieces. In 1716 he published an important treatise on harpsichord playing and the next year he was appointed royal harpsichordist.

Among the music Couperin composed for Louis XIV's delectation were his Concerts royaux, chamber works for various combinations. He had written works in his own elaboration of trio-sonata form in the 1690s following the Italianate style of Corelli but retaining French character in the decorative lines and rich harmony. Later, he published these alongside French-style groups of dances as Les nations; they include some of his emotionally most powerful music. He was much concerned with blending French and Italian styles; he composed programmatic tributes to Lully and Corelli and some under the title Les goûts-réünis. He also wrote intensely expressive pieces for bass viol.

But it is as a harpsichord composer that Couperin is best known. He published four books with some 220 pieces, grouped in 27 ordres or suites. Some movements are in the traditional French dance forms, but most are character pieces with titles that reflect their inspiration: some are portraits of individuals or types, some portray abstract qualities, some imitate the sounds of nature. The titles may also be ambiguous or metaphorical, or even intentionally obscure. Most of the pieces are in rondeau form. All are elegantly composed, concealing a complex, allusive and varied emotional world behind their highly wrought surface. Couperin took immense pains over the notation of the ornaments with which his harpsichord writing is sprinkled and animated. These, and his style generally, are expounded in his L'art de toucher le clavecin.

Couperin's children were also musicians: Nicholas (1680-1748) succeeded his father at St Gervais, and probably composed, while Marie-Madeleine (1690-1742) was probably an abbey organist and Marguerite-Antoinette (1705-c1778) was active as a court harpsichordist, c1729-1741. GROVEmusic

Pièces de clavecin

Quatre Livres de pièces de clavecin
Michael Borgstede hpd
Brilliant Classics ⑪ 93082 (11h 17' · DDD)   Ⓢ

Couperin's creative world can be a difficult one to enter as a listener; not everyone finds its refined expression and intimacy of thought involving, bound up as it is in the Watteau-esque subtleties of early-18th-century French court society, and shot through with enigmatic character pieces named after people and preoccupations long gone and forgotten. Yet once one has put such ephemeral matters out of one's mind – and this set forces one to, since there is little room for explanations in the skinny booklet – then this great music stands revealed as able to speak for itself with all the eloquence of a Chopin ballade or a Debussy prélude.

Michael Borgstede's spruce performances of the four published books of Pièces de clavecin plus the eight Préludes from L'art de toucher le clavecin

keep drawing one back for further doses, to revel not only in the sheer poetry, imagination and individuality of Couperin's musical personality, but also its classical balance and poise. The compact ordres (or suites) of the later books in particular offer meticulously planned sets of varied yet complementary character pieces in perfect 'drop-in'-sized sequences.

Borgstede's two instruments, one Flemish and one German, are not always voiced with perfect precision and their tuning sounds a little tired on occasion. A box of goodies to snap up.

L'art de toucher le clavecin – Prelude No 6 in   Ⓟ
B minor. Troisième livre de pièces de clavecin –
Treizième ordre; Quatorzième ordre; Quinzième
ordre
Robert Kohnen hpd **Barthold Kuijken** fl
Accent ACC9399D (64' · DDD)   Ⓕ

Kohnen's playing is rhythmically incisive, fastidious in detail – Couperin was hot on that – and full of character. If, on first acquaintance, his realisation of Couperin's vignette 'Les lis naissans' (Ordre No-13) seems a shade spiky then his lyrical approach to the flowing 6/8 melody of the rondeau 'Les rozeaux', which follows, reassures us that Kohnen does have the poetry of the music at heart, and intends that it should be so. Less appealing are Kohnen's somewhat intrusive vocal introductions to 'Les folies françoises'. This information is provided in the booklet so it hardly needs to be reiterated. In a concert recital such snatches of actuality can be effective; on a disc, after repeated listening, they become an unwelcome interruption. Occasional departures from the norm in the following two ordres are of an altogether more agreeable nature. In 'Le rossignol-en-amour' (Ordre No-14) Kohnen takes Couperin up on his suggestion to use a transverse flute, played here with a beautifully rounded tone by Barthold Kuijken. Likewise, in the jaunty rondeau, 'La Julliet', the trio texture is realised by flute and harpsichord rather than the more usual two-harpsichord texture. This piece is beautifully done, as is the subtly bell-like 'Carillon de Cithère' which follows it. In short, a stylish and entertaining release which is as likely as any to draw the cautious listener into Couperin's refined, allusory and metaphor-laden idiom.

F Couperin Livres de clavecin, Books I-IV – selection
Duphly La Pothouïn
Alexandre Tharaud pf
Harmonia Mundi HMC90 1956 (65' · DDD)   ⒻⒹ→

Alexandre Tharaud's disc of Rameau keyboard works was a refreshing demonstration that French harpsichord music can be convincingly transferred to the piano, twiddles and all, if its essential character is respected and understood. Now he attempts the seemingly tougher task of doing the same for the more delicate Couperin, and again emerges with honour. Reactions to a disc like this can only be personal, but Tharaud's unapologetically pianistic approach not only yields highly attractive results but also gets closer to Couperin's true spirit.

Mind you, he only chooses works that he considers suitable to the piano, selecting from right across Couperin's output rather than playing whole suites. Arguably, he gets it wrong only twice, in *La visionnaire* and the great B minor Passacaille, fulsome formal pieces both, whose grandeur the piano somehow manages to dull. Yet for the most part the music sounds beautifully at home. Poetic wonders such as *La muse plantine*, *Les ombres errantes* and the iconic *Les baricades mistérieuses* are played with tender sensitivity of mind and touch, while *Le carillon de Cithére* is a glistening vision of a Watteauesque paradise. Elsewhere, *Le tic-toc-choc* and *Les tours de passe-passe* are enlivened by off-beat accents, *Bruit de guerre* thrills with its added drum part, and *Muséte de taverni*, multi-tracked into a work *à 5 mains*, rattles away like some delicious missing movement from *L'arlésienne*. Tharaud closes with a piece by Duphly, relishing its dark melancholy and, not for the first time on this disc, evoking another great keyboard poet, Robert Schumann. This is a release which successfully recognises and celebrates Couperin's genius, and you cannot ask for much more than that.

Armand-Louis Couperin

French c1727-1789

Armand-Louis was a member of the great Couperin dynasty – a son of one of Louis's cousins (see below). Aged 21 he inherited his father's post as organist at St Gervais, Paris. He married Elisabeth-Antionette Blanchet, daughter of the great harpsichord maker. Such was his reputation as an improviser that he was mentioned by Burney. He left a substantial oeuvre at the time of his death which resulted from a traffic accident as he rushed from Vespers at St Gervais.

Harpsichord works

Pièces de clavecin – La victoire; Allemande; Courante: La De Croissy; Les Caqueteuses; La Grégoire; L'Intrépide; Première menuet; Deuxième menuet; L'Arlequine ou la Adam; La Blanchet; La de Boisgelou; La Foucquet; La Semillante, ou La Joly; La Turpin; Première gavotte; Deuxième gavotte; Première menuet; Deuxième menuet; La du Breüil; La Chéron; L'Affligée; L'Enjoué; Les tendres sentimens; Rondeau gracieux
Sophie Yates hpd
Chandos Chaconne CHAN0718 (80' · DDD)   Ⓕ

According to accounts Armand-Louis Couperin was a likeable man whose life was led free from strife and uncorrupted by ambition, and it is not fanciful to say that such are the qualities which inform his harpsichord music. Mostly rather rangy character pieces, though with a sprinkling

of dances, they show the bold textural richness of the later French harpsichordist-composers, if without the galloping imagination of figures such as Rameau, Balbastre or Royer. Instead, they prefer to inhabit a contented rococo world, into which they bring considerable professional polish.

If that makes the pieces sound predominantly 'pleasant', well, so they are… as agreeable a body of solo harpsichord music as any. But they are not vapid and neither are they easy, and we can be grateful that this selection has fallen to a player as technically assured and as musically sympathetic as Sophie Yates. Whether skipping through the wide-spread arpeggios and scales of *La Semillante*, firing out the repeated notes of *Les Caqueteuses* or tumbling down the helter-skelters of *L'Enjoué*, she exudes invigorating virtuosity. Yet she shows delicacy, too, in the little gavottes and minuets, and sensitivity in the melancholy *L'Affligée* (a piece somewhat reminiscent of Rameau's *L'Enharmonique*). Her harpsichord, a copy of a 1749 Goujon, sounds superb, being resonant without boominess and clear-voiced without excessive punchiness of attack. One of Sophie Yates's best yet.

Henry Cowell   American 1897–1965

Before he had had any formal training in composition Cowell wrote piano pieces using clusters and other new effects. He then studied in California and New York (1916-18), though continued an independent path as composer, publisher (through his New Music Edition, founded in 1927 and providing scores of Ives, Ruggles and others) and spokesman (through his book New Muscial Resources, 1930). He taught at the Peabody Conservatory (1951-6) and Columbia University (1949-65). Apart from piano clusters (Advertisement, 1914), he pioneered strumming on the instrument's strings (Aeolian Harp, 1923; The Banshee, 1925), complex rhythms, mobile form (Mosaic Quartet, 1935) and unusual combinations. But from 1936 he composed in a more regular, tonal style influenced by American and Irish folk music (18 Hymns and Fuguing Tunes for various forces, 1943-64). In his last 15 years he returned to clusters and other unconventional means while drawing on non-European musical cultures. His immense output includes over 140 orchestral works (including 21 symphonies and many concertos), c60 choral and c170 chamber works, over 200 piano pieces, and operas, incidental and film music, showing him to have been an indefatigable musical explorer.
GROVEmusic

Miscellaneous Works

Deep Color[a]. Fabrica. Fairy Answer[a]. Tiger[a]. Violin Suite[b]. Quartet for Flute, Oboe, Cello and Harpsichord[c]. Polyphonica[d]. Three Anti-Modernist Songs[e]. Irish Suite[f]
[e]**Ellen Lang** mez [c]**Jayn Rosenfeld** fl [c]**Marsha Heller** ob [b]**Mia Wu** vn [c]**Maria Kitsopoulos** vc **Cheryl**

Seltzer [bef]pf/[c]hpd [d]Continuum /[de]Joel Sachs [a]pf
Naxos American Classics 8 559192 (66' · DDD) ⓢⒹ→

Set of Five[a]. The Banshee[b]. Vestiges[b]. Euphoria[b].
What's This?[b] Elegie[b]. Six Casual Developments[c].
Homage to Iran[d]. Piece for Piano with Strings[e]. Two
Songs[f] – Sunset; Rest
[f]Raymond Murcell bar [c]David Krakauer cl [a]Gordon
Gottlieb perc [d]Mark Steinberg, [a]Marilyn Dubow
vns [bdef]Cheryl Seltzer pf [be]Continuum / Joel Sachs
[a]pf/[d]perc
Naxos American Classics 8 559193 (60' · DDD) ⓢⒹ→

Henry Cowell was an avant-garde pioneer with
his tone-clusters; became a multi-culturalist,
some of whose music falls midway between East
and West; and was an inspiration to younger
American composers such as John Cage and Lou
Harrison. His use of the insides of the piano has
borne fruit in the work of George Crumb. Cowell said he wanted to 'live in the whole world of
music' and wrote almost 1000 works to prove it.
Many of these are unknown but his position in
the record catalogue has been improving steadily since his centenary in 1997.

Cowell recorded three of the group of four
piano pieces on the first CD in 1962; his aggressive *Tiger* is better phrased and slower than Joel
Sachs's and thus more comprehensible but *Deep
Color* is barely known. Both the Suite for Violin
and Piano (1925) and the much later Quartet
for flute, oboe, cello and harpsichord are neo-
Baroque. The Bach-with-clusters approach at
first seems surreal but the *Andante calmato* is
magical. *Polyphonica* is a bracing study in the
kind of dissonant textures fashionable in the late
1920s but the *Irish Suite* is quite different. It's an
expanded version for piano and small orchestra
of three earlier pieces played directly on the
piano strings. The first is *Banshee* (the original
version is on the second CD) named after
the ghost which wails at the time of a death.
The ravishing new sounds in all three pieces –
amazing for 1929 – are uniquely Cowell's.

In 1956 he spent some time in the Middle East;
one result was the *Homage to Iran* for violin, piano
and drums. As elsewhere, he ingeniously adapts
ethnic materials in a manner that falls midway
between the two cultures. The *Six Casual Developments* (1933) for clarinet and piano are vivid
epigrammatic miniatures. The *Set of Five* (1952)
is for violin, piano and varied percussion, used to
provide an ethnic flavour. The final *vigoroso* is
spacious and declamatory with a surprise in the
middle – a duet for celesta and prepared piano.

These two CDs provide a judiciously chosen
sample of Cowell's work on a small scale; the
performances are fine; enthusiasts for Cowell
will certainly want both.

George Crumb American b1929

*The Pulitzer Prize-winning George Crumb has
gathered a cult following, largely due to his string
quartet Black Angels of 1970. He has never distanced himself from the music of the classical and
Romantic eras, and has developed a musical language
that creates an atmospheric chiaroscuro. He oftens
employs musical quotations. Surprisingly, he has
written very little for orchestra, preferring instead
more intimate forces, as well as small vocal ensembles.*
                                                GROVEmusic

Songs, Drones and Refrains of Death[a]. Quest
Ensemble New Art ([a]Nicholas Isherwood bass-bar
Hugo Read sax Alexander Swete gtr Peter
Degenhardt kybds Silke Aichorn hp Carmen Erb,
Hans-Peter Achberger perc Franzisco Obieta db) /
Fuat Kent
Naxos American Classics 8 559290 (55' · DDD) ⓢⒹ→

This disc will bring Crumb to a wider audience
with two substantial works, one early and one
late. *Songs, Drones and Refrains of Death* was completed in 1968 and has all the hallmarks of
Crumb's magical sound world. It's one of several
pieces stemming from the poetry of Federico
García Lorca. Nicholas Isherwood, after many
live performances, is totally in command of this
spooky territory and delivers his lines with great
clarity (full texts of the four poems are available
online). 'The Song of the Rider' is a spine-chilling counterpart to Schubert's *Erlkönig* – both
scenarios end in death, a consistent presence
throughout both in the poems and in the movements called 'Death-Drones'.

Written in 1994, Quest shows Crumb still
finding unusual sonorities for his six players with
prominent guitar. So we hear the Appalachian
hammer dulcimer, the African talking drum, the
Mexican rainstick, and sometimes the guitar and
harp are interwoven. Crumb admits that he had
some trouble in finding a final form for *Quest*:
there is no programme but he pondered a couple
of gloomy phrases from Dante and Lorca.

Alexander Swete plays electric guitar in *Songs,
Drones* and acoustic guitar in *Quest*, which
becomes a showpiece for him (it was written for
David Starobin). It's now good to have both
these works together, well recorded, with notes
by the composer.

Bernhard Crusell Finnish 1775-1839

*Crusell studied the clarinet from the age of eight and
at 12 joined a military band in Sveaborg; in 1791 he
went to Stockholm where he became a court musician
two years later. He studied the clarinet in Berlin in
1798 with Tausch and in 1803 went to Paris to study
composition with Gossec and Berton and the clarinet
with Lefevre. He later held posts as music director in
the Swedish court chapel and royal regiment. His
compositions include three clarinet concertos (1811,
1816, 1829), an air and variations for clarinet and
a Concertante for clarinet, bassoon and horn (1816);
he also wrote chamber music, including three clarinet
quartets (1812, 1816, 1823), an opera Den lilla
Slafvinnan (1824, Stockholm) and 12 songs. He was*

a fluent composer with a fresh vein of melody. He also made Swedish translations of operas by Mozart, Rossini and others. **GROVE**music

---

Clarinet Concertos

Crusell Clarinet Concerto No 2 in F minor, 'Grand'
Baermann Adagio in D flat **Rossini** Introduction and Variations in C minor **Weber** Concerto Concertino in C minor, J109
Emma Johnson *cl* **English Chamber Orchestra /
Sir Charles Groves**
ASV CDDCA559 (55' · DDD)   (F)

It was this Crusell Grand Concerto which Emma Johnson played when she won the BBC Young Musician of the Year competition in 1984. That occasion was the first time she had played a concerto with a full symphony orchestra, and her special affection for the piece, her total joy in each of the three movements, comes over vividly in this performance. The uninhibited spontaneity of her playing, exactly matching a live performance, brings an extra compulsion and immediacy of expression. Emma Johnson in each movement translates the notes with very personal phrasing and expression, always taking risks and bringing them off. This is a daring performance, naughtily lilting in the outer movements, happily songful in the *Andante pastorale* of the slow movement. In the three shorter pieces Johnson may not have the same technical perfection, but the free expressiveness could not be more winning. Her moulding of *legato* melodies in the Weber and Rossini works, as well as the Baermann, brings warm expressiveness, with free rubato and sharp contrasts of tone and dynamic. The orchestral sound is full and bright, with Groves a lively, sympathetic accompanist.

Clarinet Concertos – No 1 in E flat, Op 1; No 2 in F minor, Op 5; No 3 in B flat, Op 11
Kari Kriikku *cl* **Finnish Radio Symphony Orchestra / Sakari Oramo**
Ondine ODE965-2 (64' · DDD)   (F)(D)→

With full, bright, immediate sound, the Finnish clarinettist Kari Kriiku gives dazzling performances of these three delightful clarinet concertos. In many ways he's even more daring than his rivals, regularly choosing speeds that stretch virtuosity to the limit, particularly in the finales. Those of Nos 1 and 2 may be marked *allegretto* merely, but Kriiku, by choosing exceptionally fast speeds, brings out an extra *scherzando* quality, often sharp and spiky, in which Crusell's characteristically dotted rhythms are delightfully crisp. The almost impossibly rapid tonguing never seems to get in the way of detailed characterisation.

Johnson (above) in her recordings is altogether more relaxed, regularly adopting speeds rather broader, extremely so in the *Alla Polacca* which ends No 3. Consistently, her pointing of rhythm brings out the fun in the writing, and in her comparably broad approach to slow movements she finds extra poetry. Partly as a result of the

immediacy of the recording, Kriiku's *pianissimos* aren't as extreme, yet in flair and panache Kriiku is second to none, superbly supported by the crisp, purposeful playing of the Finnish National Radio orchestra under Sakari Oramo.

An excellent disc, guaranteed to win friends for these sparkling works.

Marc-André Dalbavie   French b1961

Dalbavie had his first piano lesson aged six and within two years he had already won his first national competition. He attended the Conservatoire National Supérieure de Musique in Paris and followed this with study with John Cage and at the Academia Chigiana in Siena. Between 1983 and '89 he studied composition with Tristan Murail; he has also worked with Boulez and at IRCAM. His works include a Piano Concerto written for Leif Ove Andsnes and a number of orchestral works, many drawing their inspiration from music of the Middle Ages.

Concertos

Violin Concerto[a]. Color. Ciaccona
[a]**Eiichi Chijiiwa** *vn* **Orchestre de Paris / Christoph Eschenbach**
Naïve MO782162 (64' · DDD)
Recorded live 2001-3   (F)

Marc-André Dalbavie is one of the more visible French composers of his generation and as such he is able to draw upon musicians of real distinction. Indeed, he could hardly hope for better live performances than those on this recording. The latter point is eloquently made by Eiichi Chijiiwa, who handles the many bravura passages of the Violin Concerto's solo part seemingly effortlessly. So it is disconcerting to turn to the music and find so little of substance.

Dalbavie can certainly write for show: in his hands the orchestra has a glitzy patina, at times reminiscent in its allure of film music, and the soloist in the Concerto has much to do. The composer/conductor knows the repertoire of modernist orchestral and ensemble scores very well, and in not a few instances one can even identify specific works that he references; the problem is that this isn't done it seems in any playful spirit of postmodernism. Perhaps his signature (an element that occurs in all three scores) is the unfolding of slow, steady scalar passages, or of chords whose tessituras gradually ascend or descend, expand or contract. These simple gestures may betoken the accessibility to which he aspires (according to the booklet-notes) but the end result is a kind of modernism-lite, likely to frustrate as many listeners as it flatters.

Dalbavie Flute Concerto[a] **Jarrell** Flute Concerto, '...un temps de silence...'[b] **Pintscher** Transir[c]
Emmanuel Pahud *fl* **Radio France Philharmonic**

Orchestra / [a]Peter Eötvös, [b]Pascal Rophé, [c]Matthias Pintscher
EMI 501226-2 (55' · DDD) Ⓟ◉▶

Like other high-profile wind players, Emmanuel Pahud has sought to compensate for the dearth of pre-1900 concertos by commissioning contemporaries. These three works provide a well balanced programme, and high standards of playing and recording combine to make this a release to be reckoned with.

Marc-André Dalbavie has no hang-ups about evoking both the languor and the energy of Ravel's *Daphnis et Chloé* – and the music is all the better for the kind of tongue-in-cheek approach which leads Pahud himself to make comparisons with Ibert. It works because there are no half-measures: both the opulence and the tenderness seem genuine and well judged in terms of Dalbavie's own personal angle on contemporary idioms. After this, Michael Jarrell's *…un temps de silence…* and Matthias Pintscher's *Transir* are a good deal more intense. Jarrell risks over-indulging the defining features of his idiom – fast and febrile at one extreme, quietly whispering at the other. But there's enough drama to keep the piece in focus, and Pahud's way with its intricate flurries and withdrawn musings is mesmerisingly fastidious.

Transir is the most radical of the three works in its addiction to fragmentation, brief expressionistic outbursts articulating what might be heard as an extended modernist mad scene. Even if the work's dedication to the memory of a composer called Dominic Transir is not a joke, 'transir' also happens to be the French verb for 'to paralyse, to chill to the bone'. This is indeed profoundly chilly music, constantly on the verge of freezing solid, never thawing into expansiveness. After it, Dalbavie's unaffected warmth seems even more seductive than it otherwise might.

Luigi Dallapiccola   Italian 1904-1975

Dallapiccola studied at the conservatoire in Florence in 1920s, becoming a professor there in 1931, a post he retained until 1967. He numbered Luciano Berio among his pupils. His early interest in Wagner's music was supplanted by a fascination with the works of Debussy and later works by Busoni, Berg and Webern. His Canti di prigionia, one of his the operas, sealed his reputation after the Second World War and also revealed his strong political views, especially his passionate opposition to Fascism. As he aged his music took on a more sensuous feel, in sharp opposition to the raw intensity of his early works.

Orchestral works

Dialoghi[a]. Variazioni. Due pezzi. Three Questions with Two Answers
[a]Jean-Guihen Queyras *vc* RAI National Symphony Orchestra / Pascal Rophé

Stradivarius STR33698 (61' · DDD) Ⓕ

This new collection of Dallapiccola's later orchestral works is more than welcome. As Mario Ruffi's informative booklet-note points out, their emergence was largely due to the composer's success in the United States, as opposed to the hostility aroused in his native Italy – notably the Milan premiere of *Due pezzi* (1947), an orchestral expansion of violin-and-piano originals whose inspiration in frescos by Piero della Francesca is here made the more explicit.

In the *Pezzi*, Pascal Rophé makes great sense of its subtle timbral continuity and downplays the overtly rhetorical in the 'Fanfara e Fuga'. Rophé shapes the *Variazioni* (1954) into a cohesive and cumulative whole, emphasising the emotional impact that arises out of technical rigour. The new disc includes the first modern recording of *Dialoghi* (1960) – the most hermetic of all Dallapiccola's works in its inwardness and glacial, though never inexpressive, harmonies, played with keen eloquence by Jean-Guihen Queyras. A satellite to the in-progress *Ulisse, Three Questions with Two Answers* (1963) fairly encapsulates the opera's metaphysical concerns in its motivic richness and sense of grand vistas – whether of nature or humanity – aspiring towards the infinite.

Rophé obtains responsive playing from Turin's RAI orchestra, with sound that brings out detail and atmosphere in equal measure. Strongly recommended.

Peter Maxwell Davies   British b1934

Davies studied at the Royal Manchester College of Music (1952-6); his fellow students included Goehr and Birtwistle They studied the music of Boulez, Nono and Stockhausen which, together with early English music, provided him with the roots of a style (Trumpet Sonata, 1955). He then studied with Petrassi in Rome (1957-9) and extended his range to orchestral works (St Michael for 17 wind, 1957; Prolation, 1958). But a period of teaching at Cirencester Grammar School (1959-62) encouraged him to reconsider not only school music (drawing out children's creative potential) but also his own: he began to write in a more expressively focussed, dramatic way and to recover aspects of symphonic largeness, particularly as he found them in Mahler (second In Nomine Fantasia for orchestra, 1964). Much work was done at the universities of Princeton (1962-4) and Adelaide (1966).

Back in England, Davies and Birtwistle formed the Pierrot Players in 1967 (re-formed as the Fires of London, 1970) and Davies began a sequence of music-theatre pieces for them (Eight Songs for a Mad King and Vesalii icones, both 1969). These exploited a fiercely expressionist style that came out of Pierrot lunaire and from work on his opera Taverner (1967), concerning the war between creed and creativity in the mind of the Tudor composer. Another symptom of disintegration was his use of foxtrots in works of desperate seriousness (St Thomas Wake for orchestra, 1969), though at the same time he was working, in the big orchestral movement Worldes Blis (1969), towards a more integrated style.

Since 1970 he has pursued that style, with occasional expressionist throwbacks, while living remotely in Orkney, where in 1977 he founded the St Magnus Festival; there many of his works have been introduced, often reflecting on the landscapes, legend and literature of the islands (e.g. the opera The Martyrdom of St Magnus, 1977, children's operas, choral pieces). At the same time he has been writing large-scale symphonic works (three symphonies, 1976, 1980, 1983; Violin Concerto, 1985).

GROVEmusic

String Quartets

Naxos Quartets Nos 1 & 2
Maggini Quartet (Laurence Jackson, David Angel *vns* Martin Outram *va* Michal Kaznowski *vc*)
Naxos 8 557396 (75 ' · DDD)   ⓈⓄⒺ▸

This first instalment of Sir Peter Maxwell Davies's ambitious series of 10 Naxos Quartets indicates that it's shaping up to be quite a journey. The septuagenarian composer rises superbly to the technical challenges of the medium. The first two movements of the First Quartet evince a formal strength, expressive scope and thematic ingenuity that launch the cycle in sure-footed fashion; both attain a dramatic and emotional resolution in some arresting unison writing. The compact concluding *scherzo* could hardly provide a bolder contrast; its ghostly, Will-'o-the-wisp dialogue will re-emerge in the Third Quartet.

There are four movements in the Second Quartet, the second and third of which comprise a self-contained diptych (and the former's recitative first half harks back to No-1's *Largo* centrepiece). The outer movements are more expansive. An expectant *Lento* introduction leads to a bracing *Allegro*, its progress stimulating and satisfyingly proportioned. The *Lento flessibile* finale is finer still: a memorably serene and utterly inevitable essay.

The Magginis are most accurate and cogent guides, realistically recorded within the sympathetic acoustic of Potton Hall in Suffolk. A most rewarding coupling.

Naxos Quartets Nos 3 & 4
Maggini Quartet (Laurence Jackson, David Angel *vns* Martin Outram *va* Michal Kaznowski *vc*)
Naxos 8 557397 (56' · DDD)   Ⓢ▸

The impression of great things given by the first two quartets in the Naxos cycle is amply confirmed by this no less rewarding second volume. Work on the Third Quartet during the spring of 2003 was profoundly affected, the composer informs us in his booklet-note, by news of the invasion of Iraq. Presumably, then, it's not too fanciful to ascribe certain aspects of the score to

his dismay at that conflict. Sample the development section of the first-movement March (described by its creator as a 'military march of a fatuous and splintered nature'), the queasily wide vibrato that discolours the short hymn marked *stucchevole* (meaning 'cloying' or 'nauseating') towards the end of the third movement ('Four Inventions and a Hymn'), or the questioning demeanour of the finale ('Fuga'). At the same time, the quartet (whose four movements span some 31 minutes) stands up convincingly on its own terms. Impressive is its unerring sense of growth, proportion and contrapuntal ingenuity (Davies states that, before composition, he embarked upon a fruitful re-examination of Bach's Two- and Three-part Inventions), while the slow movement ('In nomine') incorporates the magical return of the ghostly, ethereal dialogue 'left hanging in the air' at the end of the First Quartet.

Cast in a single movement lasting just under 25 minutes, No 4 takes its cue from Bruegel's *Children's Games* (a canvas which also inspired Davies's Sixth Strathclyde Concerto, for flute and orchestra). The composer had originally intended it to be 'lighter and much less fierce than its predecessor', but a fretful mood underpins the relentless logic of this music with its protean motivic transformations and intriguing harmonic byways. The immaculately judged part-writing displays a bracing mastery of the idiom and, needless to say, the Magginis once again play with superlative poise and intelligence. Both sound and balance are first-rate.

Naxos Quartets Nos 9 & 10
Maggini Quartet (Lorraine McAslan, David Angel *vns* Martin Outram *va* Michal Kaznowski *vc*)
Naxos 8 557400 (64' · DDD)   ⓈⓄ▸

Cast in six movements and dedicated to Mancunian mathematician and politician Dame Kathleen Ollerenshaw, the Ninth in Sir Peter Maxwell Davies's cycle of 10 Naxos Quartets is a 36-minute canvas of formidable rigour and accomplishment, positively Beethovenian in its fearless ambition, questing spirit and unremitting concentration. The first two movements – a pugnacious *Allegro* and no less absorbing *Largo flessibile* – grow from the same seed and incorporate some frequently violent contrasts that hark back to childhood memories of war. Next come three shorter movements with a strongly burlesque flavour followed by a taut and driven finale.

Taking its cue from the Baroque suite but employing Scottish dance forms, the Tenth wears a more reflective demeanour, its emotional kernel comprising a central *Adagio flessibile*, which boasts some of the most probingly sincere inspiration in the whole series. The fifth and final movement suddenly stops in mid air – a deliberately inconclusive gesture. 'I needed to leave the door open,' explains the composer. 'I had enjoyed writing the Naxos Quartets so much, and perhaps even learned a thing or two, that more could, in theory, eventually flourish.'

The Maggini perform with the no-holds-barred commitment and jaw-dropping technical acumen we have come to expect from them throughout this massive project. Splendidly rich sound and a most truthful balance, too.

Choral music

Missa parvula^{ab}. Mass^{abc}. Dum complerentur^a. Veni Sancte Spiritus^a. Veni Creator Spiritus^b. Reliqui Domum Meum^b
^a**Westminster Cathedral Choir / Martin Baker,** with
^b**Robert Quinney,** ^c**Robert Houssart** orgs
Hyperion CDA67454 (67' · DDD· T/t)   (F)

Under David Hill and subsequently James O'Donnell the choir of Westminster Cathedral established a tradition of excellent recordings for Hyperion. That tradition is as strong as ever under Martin Baker, who became Master of the Music in 2000. Like his immediate predecessors, Baker is exploring repertoire which isn't just challenging and unusual, but of real value.

The *Missa parvula* for unison boys' voices vividly recalls Britten's *Missa brevis* both in its terse musical language and understated emotion. The opening of the Mass occupies the same sound-world as the *Missa parvula* and it's only with the thrilling and lavishly scored *Gloria* that it's apparent we are now into a work of much greater depth and impact. This is a hugely impressive performance, as much for the astonishing effect of the two organs as for the often magical choral effects. Baker entices some of the most wonderful singing from his choir here while Roberts Quinney and Houssart revel in their virtuoso interplay. Hyperion's recording captures the full effect of Maxwell Davies' astonishing writing.

A revelatory disc for those keen to know what sort of 'establishment' music we might expect from the new Master of the Queen's Music.

Mr Emmet Takes a Walk
Adrian Clarke bar Mr Emmet **Jonathan Best** bass
Mr Todd; Security; Waiter; Heating Engineer; Piano Teacher; Gabor **Rebecca Caine** sop Ka; Woman in Café; Reception; Maid; Housekeeper; Crone; Varoomschka
Psappha / Etienne Siebens
Psappha PSACD1002 (75' · DDD · T/N)   (F)

Sir Peter Maxwell Davies regards *Mr Emmet Takes a Walk* (2000) as his music-theatre swansong, and in the 20-minute discussion with Paul Driver that follows this performance he muses on the various ways in which it can be linked to his earlier operas and dramatic works, from *Taverner* to *The Doctor of Myddfai*. As a chamber opera, or 'dramatic sonata', in which the citation and distortion of earlier musics are prominent, there are even stronger links with *Eight Songs for a Mad King* and *The Martyrdom of St Magnus*. Mr Emmet is a martyr too, driven to suicide by the self-doubt and disorientation

that can so easily afflict middle management in the modern age.

With a pithy libretto by David Pountney, a cast of three and a versatile ensemble of just 10 players, the piece delivers a scary yet ultimately poignant portrait of psychological crack-up. It might not have the universal resonance of a *Wozzeck* or a *Grimes*, but Maxwell Davies is a past master of the economical, vividly expressive gesture. The best music in *Emmet* is instrumental – culminating in the archetypally dreamy yet intense cello solo that accompanies Emmet to his doom. The vocal writing is less characterful but the excellent and versatile cast make sure that it functions potently in the inexorable unfolding of the drama. Psappha and their conductor Etienne Siebens are brilliant in support, and the booklet presents the full text in an admirably clear format. Recorded with maximum attention to clarity and atmosphere, this is an exemplary release.

Walford Davies   English 1869-1941

Davies studied with Parry and Stanford at the RCM, where he joined the staff in 1895, also working as a conductor, organist (of St George's Chapel, Windsor, 1927-32) and broadcaster. His works include church music. In 1934 he became Master of the King's Music.   GROVE music

---

Everyman

Everyman
Elena Ferrari sop **Jennifer Johnston** contr **Andrew Staples** ten **Pauls Putnins** bass **London Oriana Choir; Kensington Symphony Orchestra / David Drummond**
Dutton Laboratories Epoch CDLX7141 (69' · DDD · T)
                                         (M)

Henry Walford Davies's splendid oratorio was written and first heard in 1904, in the shadow of Elgar's *Gerontius*. Yet it was an immediate success and widely performed. But by the end of the First World War it had fallen into oblivion, apart from an isolated revival in 1929. Like *Gerontius*, it's based on a vision of a human soul crossing into the next world, where Everyman has to justify his life to God. It, too, offers dialogues between Everyman and the subsidiary characters, here representing Good Deeds (a particularly lovely duo) and Knowledge (jointly, the equivalent of Elgar's Angel). There's no 'Go forth' at the end of Part 1: here the choral sequences are more lyrical. Instead, Everyman learns that the attributes he's taken for granted in life (friends, possessions, physical attributes) will be left behind when he dies; riches, too, are sneeringly dismissed. The choral Epilogue brings a thrillingly optimistic conclusion. The solo parts must be very grateful to sing, and the soloists here rise to the occasion. The frequently inspired choral writing is at times Elgarian, though there's no hint of plagiarism, and the music is communicative and appealing. David Drummond's direction has a powerful yet lyrical thrust, with the feeling of a live performance. The recording is first class, too.

Claude Debussy
French 1862-1918

Debussy studied with Guiraud and others at the Paris Conservatoire (1872-84) and as prize-winner went to Rome (1885-7), though more important impressions came from his visits to Bayreuth (1888, 1889) and from hearing Javanese music in Paris (1889). Wagner's influence is evident in the cantata La damoiselle élue (1888) and the Cinq, poèmes de Baudelaire (1889) but other songs of the period, notably the settings of Verlaine (Ariettes oubliées, Trois mélodies, Fêtes galantes, set 1) are in a more capricious style, as are parts of the still somewhat Franckian G minor String Quartet (1893); in that work he used not only the Phrygian mode but also less standard modes, notably the whole-tone mode, to create the floating harmony he discovered through the work of contemporary writers: Mallarmé in the orchestral Prélude à 'L'après-midi d'un faune' (1894) and Maeterlinck in the opera Pelléas et Mélisande, dating in large part from 1893-5 but not completed until 1902. These works also brought forward a fluidity of rhythm and colour quite new to Western music.

Pelléas, with its rule of understatement and deceptively simple declamation, also brought an entirely new tone to opera – but an unrepeatable one. Debussy worked on other opera projects and left substantial sketches for two pieces after tales by Poe (Le diable dans le beffroi and La chûte de la maison Usher), but nothing was completed. Instead the main works were orchestral pieces, piano sets and songs.

The orchestral works include the three Nocturnes (1899), characteristic studies of veiled harmony and texture ('Nuages'), exuberant cross-cutting ('Fêtes') and seductive whole-tone drift ('Sirènes'). La mer (1905) essays a more symphonic form, with a finale that works themes from the first movement, though the centrepiece ('Jeux de vagues') proceeds much less directly and with more variety of colour. The three Images (1912) are more loosely linked, and the biggest, 'Ibéria', is itself a triptych, a medley of Spanish allusions. Finally the ballet Jeux (1913) contains some of Debussy's strangest harmony and texture in a form that moves freely over its own field of motivic connection. Other late stage works, including the ballets Khamma (1912) and La boîte à joujoux (1913) and the mystery play Le martyre de St Sébastien (1911), were not completely orchestrated by Debussy, though St Sébastien is remarkable in sustaining an antique modal atmosphere that otherwise was touched only in relatively short piano pieces (e.g. 'La cathédrale engloutie').

The important piano music begins with works which, Verlaine fashion, look back at rococo decorousness with a modern cynicism and puzzlement (Suite

bergamasque, 1890; Pour le piano, 1901). But then, as in the orchestral pieces, Debussy began to associate his music with visual impressions of the East, Spain, landscapes etc, in a sequence of sets of short pieces. His last volume of Etudes (1915) interprets similar varieties of style and texture purely as pianistic exercises and includes pieces that develop irregular form to an extreme as well as others influenced by the young Stravinsky (a presence too in the suite En blanc et noir for two pianos, 1915). The rarefaction of these works is a feature of the last set of songs, the Trois poèmes de Mallarmé (1913), and of the Sonata for flute, viola and harp (1915), though the sonata and its companions also recapture the inquisitive Verlainian classicism The planned set of six sonatas was cut short by the composer's death from rectal cancer.

GROVEmusic

Orchestral Works

Images. Berceuse héroïque[a]. Danse sacrée et danse profane[b]. Jeux. Nocturnes. Marche écossaise sur un thème populaire. Prélude à l'après-midi d'un faune. La mer. Première rapsodiec[b]
Vera Badings hp [c]**George Pieterson** cl
Concertgebouw Orchestra / [a]**Eduard van Beinum, Bernard Haitink**
Philips Duo ② 438 742-2PM (141' · ADD) Recorded [b]1957, 1976-9
Ⓜ︎ ❍❍❍➔

Philips has repackaged Haitink's late-1970s recordings on two CDs for the price of one. Space has also been found for Debussy's last orchestral work, the short *Berceuse héroïque* conducted by Eduard van Beinum (in excellent 1957 stereo). In every respect this package is a bargain. In *La mer*, like the 1964 Karajan on DG Galleria, there's a concern for refinement and fluidity of gesture, for a subtle illumination of texture; and both display a colourist's knowledge and use of an individually apt variety of orchestral tone and timbre. It's the wind playing that you remember in Haitink's *Images*: the melancholy and disconsolate oboe d'amore in 'Gigues'; and from 'Ibéria', the gorgeous oboe solo in 'Les parfums de la nuit', and the carousing clarinets and raucous trumpets in the succeeding holiday festivities. And here, as elsewhere in the set, the Concertgebouw acoustic plays a vital role. Haitink's *Jeux* is slower and freer than average, and possessed of a near miraculous precision, definition and delicacy. The jewel in this set, for many, will be the *Nocturnes*, principally for the purity of the strings in 'Nuages'; the dazzling richness and majesty of the central procession in 'Fêtes'; and the cool beauty and composure of 'Sirènes'. Haitink opts for an ethereal distance; there may be passages where you're unsure if they're singing or not, but the effect is magical.

Debussy La mer. Prélude à l'après-midi d'un faune
Ravel Daphnis et Chloé – Suite No 2. Boléro
Berlin Philharmonic Orchestra / Herbert von Karajan

DG Galleria 427 250-2GGA (64' · ADD) Recorded
1964-5   Ⓜ️ 🔴🔴🔴🔴➔

Ⓖ Beautifully recorded, controlled and
aristocratic, these performances show a
scrupulous regard for the composers'
wishes. The sound of the Berlin strings is sumptuous, with detail well placed and in a generally
natural perspective. It's a joy to relish the beauty
of the playing in such clear, well-defined sound. It
has that indefinable quality that one can more
readily recognise than describe, a magic that
makes one forget the performer and transports
one into the composer's world. You can either be
seduced by some of the most sheerly beautiful
orchestral sound recorded, or appreciate it for its
wide-ranging imagery and its properly mobile
pacing; whichever, it's one of the great recorded
*La mer*s and one of the classics of the gramophone.
Karajan's interpretation of *Prélude à l'après-midi
d'un faune* remains one of the most beautiful readings committed to record – the first flute, Karl-
heinz Zöller, plays like a wizard. *Boléro* is slow and
steady (but Karajan risks floating the early solos).
This is also a ravishing account of the Second
Suite from *Daphnis et Chloé*.

La mer. La boîte à joujoux (arr Caplet).
Prélude-à L'après-midi d'un faune. Three Préludes
(arr C Matthews)
Berlin Philharmonic Orchestra / Sir Simon Rattle
EMI 558045-2 (79' · DDD) Recorded live 2004
                                    Ⓕ 🔴🔴🔴🔴➔

Ⓖ Karajan and the Berlin Philharmonic's
perfumed, pictorial 1964 recordings of
Debussy's *Prélude à L'après-midi d'un
faune* and *La mer* (see above) have come to be
revered – and rightly so, as they possess a remarkable frisson. Rattle's interpretations, recorded
live, are markedly less urgent; with nary a noise
from the audience, one might even mistake them
for studio recordings. Yet these new accounts, too,
have the ability to engross and sometimes even
astonish. Note, for example, the sinuous swoop of
the flutes and clarinets at the beginning of 'Jeux de
vagues' in *La mer*, or the shimmering rustle of
strings at 1'00" in the *Prélude* – both almost tactile
sensations.

Of course, one counts on Rattle to elucidate
detail, and here the clarification of the music's
intricately layered textures is revelatory. Karajan
appears more intent on blending colours, creating
a kind of sonic kaleidoscope that, coupled with a
strong narrative thrust, can make Debussy sound
a little like Rimsky-Korsakov. Subtlety may be
part of the issue. Karajan, for example, heightens
dynamic contrast whereas Rattle grades the
dynamics as per Debussy's instructions (he's one
of the few conductors who seems to have noticed
that there's but one *fortissimo* in the *Prélude*).

The makeweights are especially valuable.
There aren't that many recordings of *La boîte à
joujoux* in the catalogue and this zestful, gracefully droll performance is among the best. As in
the *Prélude* and *La mer*, the conductor's supple

tempo manipulations convey a real feeling of
spontaneity. Colin Matthews's scoring of three
piano *Préludes* evokes Debussy's sound world
with preternatural accuracy.

The turbulence of 'Ce qu'a vu le vent d'Ouest'
and sparkle of 'Feux d'artifice' are most impressive, though 'Feuilles mortes', with its hauntingly desolate atmosphere, is perhaps finer still.
In short, a dazzling disc.

La mer. Préludes (arr C Matthews) – Le vent
dans la plaine; Les sons et les parfums; Ce qu'a vu le
vent d'Ouest; La fille aux cheveux de lin; La danse de
Puck; Minstrels; Brouillards; Feuilles mortes;
La puerta del Vino; Général Lavine; Canope;
Les tièrces alternées
Hallé Orchestra / Mark Elder
Hallé CDHLL7513 (67' · DDD)   Ⓜ️ 🔴🔴

Mark Elder has achieved an astonishing transformation at the Hallé, and there is no better
example of his achievement than in this
immensely compelling account of *La mer*, which
in refinement of detail, warmth of atmosphere
and the sheer brilliance of the playing is comparable with any in the catalogue.

The *pianissimo* opening has an evocative
sense of mystery, reminiscent of Reiner's Chicago version. Elder's control of phrase and
shaping of line has the most subtle *rubato* and
infinitely varied dynamic, always seeming
spontanous. The tension is high but there are
moments of languor – the sunshine on the
water glowing on the horns is magical, and the
closing of the first section moves from sensuous feeling to grandeur.

'Jeux de vagues' glitters, bringing solo instrumental playing of great delicacy and an exotic
colouring, with an underlying rhapsodical feeling that reminds me of Barbirolli, the lustre of
the strings exquisite at the becalmed close. The
spectacular 'Dialogue du vent et de la mer'
opens darkly, even ominously, and has haunting
evocation at its gentle central section, yet Elder
generates exhilaration and ardour at the climax
with the racing waves of the orchestra's virtuosity. The recording is extraordinarily vivid.

What makes this disc unmissable is the equally
fine playing (and lustrous recording) in Colin
Matthews's imaginative orchestration of 12 of
Debussy's piano *Préludes*. Forget the piano
originals, these are far more than 'orchestrations': the music is completely and creatively
rethought in orchestral terms. Altogether a
remarkable achievement.

Debussy Jeux. Préludes (arr C Matthews) –
Danseuses de Delphes; Voiles; Les collines
d'Anacapri; Des pas sur la neige; La sérénade
interrompué; La cathédrale engloutie; Les fées sont
d'exquises; Bruyères; Les terrasses des audiences;
Ondine; Homage à S Pickwick Esq, PPMPC; Feux
d'artifice **C Matthews** Postlude: Monsieur Croche
Hallé Orchestra / Mark Elder
Hallé CDHLL7518 (74' · DDD)   Ⓕ 🔴

The diaphonous atmospheric detail from the strings and subtle wind colouring in *Jeux*, Debussy's *poème dansé*, require great delicacy of feeling and sensuous caressing from the violins in the moments of restrained ecstasy, which are exquisitely realised here. The transparent acoustic of the Bridgewater Hall and the balancing skill of producer Andrew Keener add to the allure of this miraculous score, with the violent climax superbly graduated and the closing pages returning spontaneously to the opening mood.

The programme is completed by 12 more of Colin Matthews's highly imaginative orchestrations of Debussy's piano *Préludes*, and these, to my ears, have even more distinction than the first group, which came in harness with Mark Elder's compelling Hallé account of *La mer* (see above). The shimmering textures Matthews creates from the 'Danseuses de Delphes', 'Des pas sur la neige' and 'Les fées sont d'exquises' are even more translucently exotic, balanced by the luxuriance of 'Bruyères'. If not quite matching Stokowski's famous over-the-top transcription, 'La cathédrale engloutie' produces a splendidly expansive, watery spectacle, tolling bell included, which is sonorously moving. However, 'S Pickwick Esq', with its side drum and mock-solemn national anthem snippet on the brass, feels rather too heavily pompous, not witty enough, and 'Feux d'artifice', too, is a bit of a damp squib – it sounds much more effective in its barer piano original. Moreover, Colin Matthews's own *Monsieur Croche* makes an exuberantly brilliant postlude, even if its helter-skelter progress obviously includes very few crochets. Altogether this is a fascinating and rewarding disc and is well worth aquiring to make a pair, alongside its illustrious companion.

Pelléas et Mélisande – Symphonie (arr Constant).
Suite bergamasque – Clair de lune (orch Caplet).
Nocturnes[a]. Berceuse héroïque. Etudes (orch Jarrell)
– No 9, Pour les notes répétées; No 10, Pour les sonorités opposées; No 12, Pour les accords
[a]**MDR Radio Choir, Leipzig; Orchestre National de Lyon / Jun Märkl**
Naxos 8 570993 (74' · DDD)   Ⓢ⬤🅑➤

The two major items here are the set of three *Nocturnes*, central to Debussy's output, and the substantial symphonic suite from *Pelléas et Mélisande* that Marius Constant put together using almost entirely the opera's evocative orchestral interludes. Märkl's performance is warm and idiomatic, and the only reservation is that almost inevitably there is rather a lack of contrast in music that moves slowly. It is nonetheless a valuable item, adding to the outstanding performance of the three *Nocturnes* which is the high-point of the whole collection. The first, 'Nuages', is supremely evocative with refined strings and a cor anglais solo that stands out in the terracing of textures. 'Fêtes' is richly seductive in its bright colours. The passage where one hears a procession from afar on muted trumpets is wonderfully achieved, with crisply precise

---

DEBUSSY LA MER – IN BRIEF

Concertgebouw Orchestra / Bernard Haitink
Philips 438 742-2PM   Ⓜ⬤⬤⬤🅑➤
🅖 A glorious performance that finds Haitink in masterly control of his magnificent Dutch orchestra: beautifully recorded in the Concertgebouw's near-perfect acoustic, this is a miracle of refinement. A *Gramophone* Award winner.

Berlin PO / Herbert von Karajan
DG 427 250-2GGA   Ⓜ⬤⬤⬤🅑➤
🅖 A classic recording from 1964 proving that a German orchestra and Austrian conductor can get under the skin of this elusive score. Karajan's feeling for the ebb and flow is supreme.

Berlin PO / Simon Rattle
EMI 558045-2   Ⓕ⬤⬤⬤🅑➤
🅖 A modern classic perhaps? Rattle offers a cooler Debussy than Karajan but his generation of Berliners cede nothing to their great predecessors in beauty of tone and virtuosity. A glorious programme

Lucerne Festival Orchestra / Claudio Abbado
DG 477 5082GH2   Ⓕ
Abbado's much-lauded ability to paint with an orchestra is here beautifully confirmed with a reading of iridescent colourings. The Lucerne orchestra plays superbly, and the recording is handled with great skill.

Philharmonia / Guido Cantelli   Ⓗ
Testament SBT1011   Ⓕ
A historic account that shows what a amazing conducting talent was lost to the world with Cantelli's early death. The Philharmonia, at a vintage period in their history, play magnificently.

London PO / Serge Baudo
Classics for Pleasure 586167-2   Ⓢ
A really marvellous Debussy collection at budget price. Baudo sculpts this music with a masterly hand and the LPO play superbly. A Debussy 'primer' well worth considering.

Hallé / Sir Mark Elder
Hallé CDHLL7513   Ⓜ⬤⬤
Yet another snapshot of the reinvigorated Hallé playing with lashings of personality. Elder's is a rhapsodic sea-scape achieving a Barbirolli-like poetry.

NBCSO / Arturo Toscanini   Ⓗ
Naxos mono 8 110811/2
A valuable glimpse of Toscanini in French repertoire – there's an electricity as well as an awareness of light that makes these fascinating performances. The couplings are of Debussy rarities.

DEBUSSY'S STRING QUARTET – IN BRIEF

Belcea Quartet
EMI Debut 574 020-2   ⒷOOOᴰ►

Ⓖ The fast-rising Belcea Quartet serve this enchanting score with exquisite sensitivity and understanding. Like the Juilliard on Sony, they also offer quartets by Ravel and Dutilleux.

Juilliard Quartet
Sony Classical 82796 92622-2   Ⓕ

A wealth of wisdom and interpretative insight informs the Juilliard Quartet's third recording of Debussy's masterpiece. As well as the popular coupling of Ravel's Quartet, we also get Dutilleux's sole contribution to the genre (*Ainsi la nuit*).

Melos Quartet
DG download 463 082-2GGA   ⓂOOᴰ►

Another distinguished account, fastidiously prepared and beautifully balanced by the DG engineers. Likewise, the Ravel Quartet coupling falls ravishingly on the ear.

Hagen Quartet
DG download 437 836-2GH   Ⓕᴰ►

In terms of virtuosity and sumptuous tonal refinement the youthful Hagen Quartet are second to none, though their artistry is perhaps not entirely without a certain self-conscious mastery.

Ebène Quartet
Virgin Classics 519045-2   ⒻOOOᴰ►

Ⓖ A recording that will give enormous pleasure for its subtlety and style – a real winner. (It generously adds the Debussy and the Fauré.)

Kodály Quartet
Naxos 8 550249   Ⓢᴰ►

A slightly curate's eggish pairing of the Debussy and Ravel. When they are good they are tremdendous – but here are moments that seem to ebb from the usual high level of their playing.

Alban Berg Quartet
EMI 567550-2   Ⓑ

Gorgeously played and recorded, there's a tonal glow that is very seductive but these do sounded rather over-rehearsed interpretations that lack a little in freshness.

Formosa Quartet
EMI 366557-2   Ⓑ

A stylish debut on disc for this young quartet: thye may not as yet plumb the depths but they have style and techniqu aplenty. Unusually coupled with Wolf and Mozart (his Quartet No 14, K387).

triplets leading up to a powerful climax before fading away again.

The longest of the three *Nocturnes*, 'Sirènes', brings a vital contribution from the Leipzig choir attached to the other orchestra with which Märkl is associated, the Leipzig Radio Symphony. Their chording and ensemble is flawless. The Caplet orchestration of the piano piece 'Clair de lune' is beautifully wrought and here given a sumptuous performance.

The *Berceuse héroïque* is similarly evocative, with its distant fanfares and its climactic reference to the Belgian National Anthem. The three *Etudes*, orchestrated by Michael Jarrell as recently as 1991, represent a different approach; a degree sharper, appropriate enough for some of Debussy's most advanced music, and pointing forward to a new generation of composers. A richly satisfying collection, immaculately recorded, with its full measure of rarities.

Nocturnes – Nuages; Fêtes   Ⓗ
Prélude à l'après-midi d'un faune. Le martyre de Saint-Sébastien – symphonic fragments. La mer
Philharmonia Orchestra / Guido Cantelli
Testament mono SBT1011 (67' · ADD) Recorded 1954-5   ⒻO

The death of Guido Cantelli in an air crash at the age of 36 in 1956 was a terrible loss. In a career lasting just 13 years he made his way right to the top, although at the end of his life he was still developing and maturing, and would surely have been one of the most important artists of our time. Fortunately he made a number of superlative recordings and this disc, which contains all his Debussy, shows why concert audiences in the 1950s were bowled over by him.

It's a pity that he never conducted all three *Nocturnes*, for 'Nuages' flows beautifully and expressively and he chooses just the right tempo for 'Fêtes'. He doesn't press this piece too hard as most conductors do, and its colour and piquant personality thus flower freshly and easily. *L'après-midi* is also given plenty of room to breathe: the playing cool, elegant, beautifully poised, yet very eloquent. In *La mer* Cantelli avoids the ham-fisted, overdramatic approach of so many conductors, and instead we have a performance with clear, gleaming textures. The first movement ebbs and flows in a movingly poetic fashion: every detail makes its effect and everything is perfectly in scale. The middle movement is taken quite briskly, but phrasing is hypersensitive and appropriately fluid. In the last movement there's plenty of drama and excitement, although climaxes are kept within bounds in a way which paradoxically makes for a greater effect than if they were given Brucknerian proportions, as they often are.

During Cantelli's lifetime *Le martyre de Saint-Sébastien* was strangely regarded as a tired, feeble work, yet he conducted the 'Symphonic fragments' quite frequently. His approach is very much of the concert hall in that he gives the four pieces a life of their own rather than relating them to the unfolding drama. However, he still captures the music's peculiarly fervent, religious-cum-exotic flavour very effectively. The Philharmonia plays with extraordinary subtlety, and the recordings sound very well indeed.

String Quartet

Debussy String Quartet in G minor, Op 10 **Ravel** String Quartet in F **Dutilleux** Ainsi la nuit
Belcea Quartet (Corina Belcea, Laura Samuel *vns* Krzysztof Chorzelski *va* Alasdair Tait *vc*)
EMI Debut 574020-2 (71' · DDD)　Ⓑ ❍❍❍▷

 This CD is the work of a highly talented, exceptionally well-integrated ensemble. Their excellent balance is highlighted by crystal-clear recording. This is quartet-playing of great musicality, with a wonderful sense of interaction. They find a near ideal transparency in the Ravel, its subtleties beautifully articulated.

The denser, less light-filled style of the Debussy, too, is perfectly weighted – this is a work they've clearly played on numerous occasions, and their performance has a feeling of a work truly inhabited by its players. And the Dutilleux is exquisitely observed, its fragmentary structure creatively embraced by these young musicians. And if all that weren't enough, this disc comes at budget price.

Debussy String Quartet, Op 10 **Fauré** String Quartet, Op 121 **Ravel** String Quartet
Quatuor Ebène (Pierre Colombet, Gabriel Le Magadure *vns* Mathieu Herzog *va* Raphaël Merlin *vc*)
Virgin Classics 519045-2 (80' · DDD)　Ⓕ ❍❍❍▷

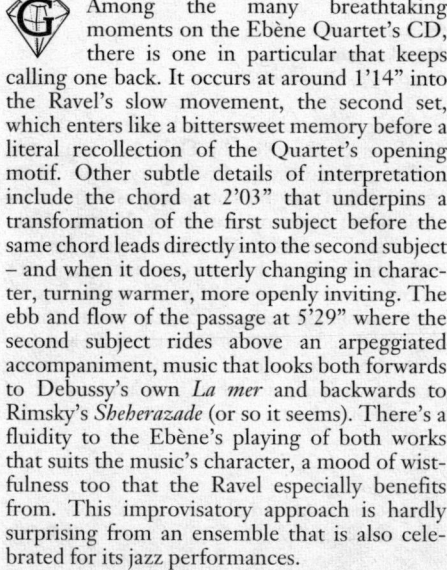 Among the many breathtaking moments on the Ebène Quartet's CD, there is one in particular that keeps calling one back. It occurs at around 1'14" into the Ravel's slow movement, the second set, which enters like a bittersweet memory before a literal recollection of the Quartet's opening motif. Other subtle details of interpretation include the chord at 2'03" that underpins a transformation of the first subject before the same chord leads directly into the second subject – and when it does, utterly changing in character, turning warmer, more openly inviting. The ebb and flow of the passage at 5'29" where the second subject rides above an arpeggiated accompaniment, music that looks both forwards to Debussy's own *La mer* and backwards to Rimsky's *Sheherazade* (or so it seems). There's a fluidity to the Ebène's playing of both works that suits the music's character, a mood of wistfulness too that the Ravel especially benefits from. This improvisatory approach is hardly surprising from an ensemble that is also celebrated for its jazz performances.

It was a brilliant idea to include Fauré's late Quartet which, in a sense, provides the linchpin

for all three works, the Ravel having been composed in Fauré's class to mark the 10th anniversary of Debussy's quartet, and which is dedicated to Fauré. An extraordinary work by any standards, ethereal and other-worldly with themes that seem constantly to be drawn skywards, Fauré's Quartet responds well to the Ebène's sensitised approach.

Anyone requiring this particular trio of works won't be disappointed, which makes the various pairings of the Ravel and Debussy quartets on their own seem somewhat less enticing.

Piano Trio

Debussy Piano Trio in G **Fauré** Piano Trio in D minor, Op 120 **Ravel** Piano Trio in A minor
Florestan Trio (Anthony Marwood *vn* Richard Lester *vc* Susan Tomes *pf*)
Hyperion CDA67114 (66' · DDD)　Ⓕ ❍❍▷

The Florestan Trio has the ability to adapt its style to different kinds of music without any loss of conviction. After Brahms and Schumann comes this French disc showing it equally adept at entering the 1880 salon world of Debussy's youthful Trio, Ravel's brilliant exotic idiom, and the intimate, intense thoughts of Fauré's old age. In the quicker movements Susan Tomes's playing is remarkably light and precise. The finale of the Fauré, for example, has a *scherzando* quality that throws into relief the seriousness of the strings' initial gesture. The string players are always ready to modify their sound to produce special expressive effects – the eerily quiet unison passage in Fauré's *Andante* (track 2, 2'54") or the vibrato-less duet in the Ravel *Passacaille* (track 10, 5'15") – sounding wonderfully remote and antique. The clarity of the Hyperion recording allows the fantastical detail in the Ravel *Pantoum* to emerge. In the Debussy, the Florestan favour elegance rather than trying to search out expressive depths. Their freshness, imagination and purposeful directness makes this a top choice.

Sonata for Flute, Viola and Harp

Sonata for Flute, Viola and Harp[a]. Prélude à l'après-midi d'un faune (arr Samazeuilh)[b]. Syrinx[b]. La flûte de Pan[c]. Chansons de Bilitis[d]
[cd]**Irène Jacob** *spkr* **Philippe Bernold**, [d]**Mathieu Dufour** *fls* [a]**Gérard Caussé** *va* [ad]**Isabelle Moretti**, [d]**Germaine Lorenzini** *hps* **Ariane Jacob** [b]*pf*/[d]*celesta*
Harmonia Mundi HMC90 1647 (50' · DDD · T)　Ⓕ

The high point of this disc is a beautifully sensitive performance of Debussy's elusive late sonata, a 'terribly sad' work according to the composer himself, but also containing in its latter two movements an uneasy kind of high spirits born of desperation. The opening and close of the first movement provide two of those haunting moments at which French composers seem to excel. Philippe Bernold is a player of delicate, refined tone whose descents to the edge of sound are hypnotic in their effect; and with his two partners the performance rivals those recordings hitherto cherished as yard-sticks – the classic Melos of 1962 and the Nash of 1991. Bernold captures the spirit of rapture in *Syrinx*, which is heard both in its usual form as an unaccompanied solo and as it was originally intended, as incidental music to a play, *Psyché*. Unfortunately Irène Jacob, who reads the text admirably, is too distantly placed in relation to the flute. The same criticism applies to the erotic *Chansons de Bilitis* poems. It was Debussy's own idea to make a transcription for flute and piano of the *Prélude à l'après-midi d'un faune*; but imaginatively as Samazeuilh wrote this and Ariane Jacob plays the piano part, the sensuous magic of this score suffers from this reduction of colour.

Cello Sonata

Debussy Sonata for Cello and Piano. Valse 'La plus que lente'. Scherzo. Intermezzo **Poulenc** Sonata for Cello and Piano. Suite française. Bagatelle. Sérénade
Jean-Guihen Queyras vc **Alexandre Tharaud** pf
Harmonia Mundi HMC90 2012 (63' · DDD)   ⒻⒷ⁺

Vividly captured in a warm acoustic, Queyras and Tharaud's is an intimate approach which exactly suits the two short sonatas of Debussy and Poulenc, the former with its abrupt changes of direction and unpredictable mood swings, the latter brimful of Poulencian wit and, not surprisingly as it was sketched in 1940 (completed in 1948), replete with some self-plagiarising from *Babar*.

These are fine accounts, the programme made even more attractive by the inclusion of the seven short movements of Poulenc's *Suite française* (1935) based on 16th-century dances by Claude Gervaise. It's a charmer. Apart from this, there are five other short works by the two composers making a truly delightful whole.

Complete Piano Works

Préludes, Books 1 & 2. Pour le piano.   Ⓗ
Estampes . Images, Sets 1 & 2. Children's Corner. 12 Etudes. D'un cahier d'esquisses. Rêverie. Valse romantique. Masques. L'isle joyeuse. La plus que lente. Le petit nègre. Berceuse héroïque. Hommage à Haydn. Danse bohémienne. Mazurka. Deux Arabesques. Nocturne. Tarantelle styrienne. Ballade. Suite bergamasque. Fantaisie
Walter Gieseking pf **Hessian Radio Orchestra, Frankfurt / Kurt Schröder**
EMI mono ④ 565855-2 (276' · ADD) Recorded 1951-5   ⓂⓄⓄⓄ

The complete Préludes are also available on EMI Great Recordings of the Century 567233-2   ⓂⓄⒷ⁺

 Gieseking's insight and iridescence in Debussy are so compelling and hypnotic that they prompt either a book or a blank page – an unsatisfactory state where criticism is concerned! First and foremost,

there's Gieseking's sonority, one of such delicacy and variety that it can complement Debussy's witty and ironic desire to write music 'for an instrument without hammers', for a pantheistic art sufficiently suggestive to evoke and transcend the play of the elements themselves ('the wind, the sky, the sea…'). Lack of meticulousness seems a small price to pay for such an elemental uproar in 'Ce qu'a vu le vent d'ouest', and Puck's elfin pulse and chatter (*pp aérian*) are caught with an uncanny deftness and precision. The final Debussian magic may not lie in a literal observance of the score, in the unfailing dotting and crossing of every objective and picturesque instruction, yet it's the start or foundation of a great performance.

More domestically, no one (not even Cortot) has ever captured the sense in *Children's Corner* of a lost and enchanted land, of childhood re-experienced through adult tears and laughter, as Gieseking does here. 'Pour les tierces', from the *Etudes*, may get off to a shaky start but, again, in Debussy's final masterpiece, Gieseking's artistry tugs at and haunts the imagination. Try 'Pour les sonorités opposées', the expressive centre of the *Etudes*, and you may well wonder when you've heard playing more subtly gauged or articulated, or the sort of interaction with a composer's spirit that can make modern alternatives seem so parsimonious by comparison. So here's that peerless palette of colour and texture, of a light and shade used with a nonchalant but precise expertise to illuminate every facet of Debussy's imagination.

An added bonus, a 1951 performance of the *Fantaisie* for piano and orchestra, completes an incomparable set of discs. The transfers are a real triumph.

Etudes

Etudes – Books 1 & 2
Mitsuko Uchida pf
Philips 4757559 (47' · DDD)   ⓂⓄⒷ⁺

The harmonic language and continuity of the *Etudes* is elusive even by Debussy's standards, and it takes an artist of rare gifts to play them 'from within', at the same time as negotiating their finger-knotting intricacies. Mitsuko Uchida is such an artist. On first hearing perhaps rather hyperactive, her playing wins you over by its bravura and sheer relish, eventually disarming criticism altogether. This isn't just the finest ever recorded version of the *Etudes*; it's also one of the finest examples of recorded piano playing in modern times, matched by sound quality of outstanding clarity.

Etudes. Images
Pierre-Laurent Aimard pf
Teldec 8573 83940-2 (72' · DDD)   ⒻⓄⓄⒷ⁺

With Pierre-Laurent Aimard the sheer freshness and novelty of this music come across strongly. So does the ardour; whereas some players are content with mood and atmosphere, his communication of feeling is acute. There are passages of extraordinary violence in this music, especially in the Etudes; he makes them still sound modern. Others would favour letting sonorities hang longer in the air. You couldn't ask for more colour, or greater sensibility, but he isn't a charmer. He has edge and likes sonority to work directly on the business in hand. He always goes for the movement and the thrust of what's written; those used to a more spacious and laid-back view of the Images, in particular, may occasionally be disconcerted.

This is a Debussy record of high class, hugely stimulating. Aimard's version of the *Etudes* is up there with the very best. Technically, he's a wizard, without a chink in his armour; but he's the best kind of technician, playing like a composer, and letting the music drive him.

'Complete Works for Solo Piano, Vol 4'
Images. 12 Etudes. Etude retrouvée (ed Howat)
Jean-Efflam Bavouzet pf
Chandos CHAN10497 (76' · DDD) Ⓕ**OOO**▷

Ⓖ Jean-Efflam Bavouzet's flexible virtuosity and innate grasp of Debussy's style and sound world yields ravishing, freshly minted interpretations of the *Images* and *Etudes* that proudly rank with (and sometimes surpass) the catalogue's reference versions. The *Images* gain welcome nourishment from Bavouzet's portfolio of ravishing colour shadings and articulations, while easily absorbing such pianistic liberties as playing one hand before the other, *à la* Michelangeli. His headlong, impulsive 'Hommage à Rameau' contrasts with similarly nuanced yet more austere readings. In 'Poissons d'or', he sneaks a few piranhas into the fishbowl as he modifies Debussy's *aussi léger que possible* directive with volatile dynamic hairpins and witty accents. 'Et la lune descend sur le temple qui fût' also rivets your attention via his seductive *legato* and three-dimensional textures.

Bavouzet's Chandos *Etudes* remake may well be the best yet. As you follow the intelligently contoured left-hand counterlines of 'Pour les tierces' you almost don't notice the fluency and easy evenness of Bavouzet's right-hand double notes. On the other hand, in 'Pour les huit doigts' and 'Pour les degrés chromatiques' he favours melodic inflection and linear motion over Aimard's and Uchida's smoother, scintillating surfaces.

The difficult leaps of 'Pour les accords' have rarely sounded less like technical feats and more like music, and 'Pour les arpèges composés' rivals Horowitz's 1965 reading for harmonic pointing and sexiness.

Bavouzet precedes this étude with a full-bodied, emotionally generous performance of its recently rediscovered earlier version, *Etude retrouvée*. This attractively engineered release will reveal more and more details to savour with each rehearing – guaranteed! If you haven't yet ordered it, what are you waiting for?

Images

Images. Le petit nègre. Children's Corner. La plus que lente. Valse romantique. Tarantelle styrienne. Mazurka. Suite bergamasque. Hommage à Haydn. Elégie. Berceuse héroïque. Page d'album. Etudes. Etude retrouvée
Jean-Yves Thibaudet pf
Decca ② 460 247-2DH2 (151' · DDD) Ⓟ▷

Jean-Yves Thibaudet's Debussy cycle is a cornucopia of delights. The 12 *Etudes* could hardly be presented more personally or vivaciously. Nos 6 and 7 are marvels of bright-eyed irony and humour, while Nos 8 and 9 contrast a haunting alternation of lassitude and hyperactivity with razor-sharp cascades of repeated notes. His timing in the central *lento, molto rubato* of No 12 is memorably acute; throughout, you're aware of a pianist with a penchant for spare pedalling and a refined brilliance, far remote from, say, Gieseking's celebrated, opalescent magic. He takes a brisk hand to the *Children's Corner* suite (*allegro* rather than *allegretto* in 'Serenade for the Doll', hardly *modérément animé* in 'The Snow is Dancing') but even here his spruce technique and vitality are never less than enlivening. In the *Suite bergamasque* he dances the 'Menuet' with an unusual sense of its underlying grace and gravity, and his 'Clair de lune' is exceptionally silvery and transparent. Both books of *Images* are given with a rare sense of epiphany or illumination, of flashing fins and sunlight in 'Poissons d'or' and of a timeless sense of archaism in 'Hommage à Rameau'. Decca's presentation and sound are, respectively, lavish and natural. If you want to hear Debussy new-minted, with air-spun and scintillating textures, Thibaudet is your man.

Préludes

Préludes – Books 1 & 2
Krystian Zimerman pf
DG ② 435 773-2GH2 (84' · DDD) Ⓜ**OOO**▷

 Two discs, retailing at a high mid-price and playing for a total of 84 minutes? The playing and the recording had better be in the luxury class. Fortunately they are. Zimerman is the very model of a modern virtuoso. His overriding aim is vivid projection of character. His quasi-orchestral range of dynamic and attack, based on close attention to textual detail (there are countless felicities in his observation of phrase-markings) and maximum clarity of articulation, is the means to that end. As a result, he draws out the many connections in this music with the romantic tradition, especially in pianistic *tours de force* such as 'Les collines d'Anacapri', 'Ce qu'a vu le vent d'ouest' and 'Feux d'artifice', which are treated to a dazzling Lisztian *élan*.

At the other extreme Zimerman displays an exquisite refinement of touch that makes the

DEBUSSY'S PRÉLUDES – IN BRIEF

Walter Gieseking
EMI 567233-2 (71' · AAD)

Gieseking's classic recording of the *Préludes* dates from 1953-4 and remains unsurpassed in extracting the elusive poetry of the more delicate pieces. This is one of the greatest of all piano recordings, and one of the greatest of Debussy's music.

Krystian Zimerman
DG ② 435 773-2GH2 (84' · DDD)

Larger in scale if perhaps less obviously idiomatic, Zimerman's compelling revivification tips over onto a second disc. This is high-octane playing for our own times, with the widest dynamic range and very tangible digital sound. It took a *Gramophone* Award on its release.

Noriko Ogawa
BIS BIS-CD1205 (76' · DDD)

The second instalment of Ogawa's Debussy survey includes a fine account of the First Book of *Préludes* in unbeatably natural sound.

Martino Tirimo
Regis RRC1111 (78' · DDD)

Complete on one super-bargain CD, Tirimo's set offers excellent value, his sensitive playing enhanced by fine digital sound.

Jean-Yves Thibaudet
Decca ② 452 022-2 (157' · DDD)

Always a crisp and articulate pianist, Thibaudet's *Préludes* display greater freedom and imagination than is sometimes the case with him. The eruptive, lightly pedalled *Feux d'artifice* is a particular highlight. This is volume 1 of his first-rate survey of the complete Debussy piano music.

Jos van Immerseel
Channel Classics CCS4892 (54' · DDD)

This is something of a curiosity and certainly isn't a prime recommendation: van Immerseel uses an 1897 Erard piano for the First Book of *Préludes*, as well as the *Images Oubliées*. It's certainly worth hearing for its special note of authenticity. When not played loudly the piano makes a delightful sound, but Immerseel isn't the most imaginative of players.

Jacques Rouvier
Dal Segno DSPRC043 (78' · DDD)

Rouvier is one of the most stylish and elegant interpreters of this repertoire: wonderfully alive the variety of nuance and colour in these extraordinary pieces. Under his fingers, each prelude becomes a sparkling miniature.

quieter pieces both evocative and touching. Such sensitively conceived and wonderfully executed Debussy playing stands, at the very least, on a level with a classic recording such as Gieseking's. The instrument selected is itself something of a star and DG's recording combines opulence with razor-sharp clarity.

Préludes – Books 1 & 2
Walter Gieseking pf
EMI Great Recordings of the Century 567233-2 (71' · ADD) (in USA: 5 67262-2) Recorded 1953-4

Gieseking's set of both Books of the *Préludes* is one of the great classics of the gramophone. The individual insights are endless, so is the extraordinary feeling for the music's evocation and atmosphere. The 1953-4 recordings just missed the stereo era, but the Abbey Road mono sound is first-class. Don't miss it.

Préludes – Books 1 & 2
Steven Osborne pf
Hyperion CDA67530 (78' · DDD)

Steven Osborne tells us that in preparing this recording he was struck 'by the enormous scope of these preludes. What other collection of pieces manages to create so many utterly distinct and compelling worlds?' But he has prepared well, and every prelude glows, always rich in atmosphere.

The opening 'Danseuses de Delphes' has a commandingly grave serenity and 'Voiles' floats effortlessly. Yet 'Les collines d'Anacapri' dances with sparkling rhythmic vitality and 'La danse de Puck' is deliciously capricious. Osborne's delicacy of feeling (and texture) is at its most magical in the soft footfalls 'sur la neige', although 'Feuilles mortes' has similar moments of evocative quietness. The unpredictability of 'Le vent dans la plaine' is matched by the simulated violence of 'Ce qu'a vu le vent d'Ouest', and the thrilling climax of 'La cathédrale engloutie' has rich depth and sonority. By contrast, 'La fille aux cheveux de lin' has a ravishing simplicity, without sentimentalising. 'S Pickwick' brings a momentary smile but his eccentricity is banished by the calm of 'Canope' and the joyful virtuosity of 'Les tierces alternées'.

Osborne's virtuosity is never for its own sake and always reflects the music's spirit. The obvious comparison is with Zimerman's stunningly vivid recording; but his extraordinarily brilliant playing is at times almost over-projected and Osborne's natural spontaneity and powerful conveying of inner feeling is every bit as telling – less intense but deeply satisfying. The Hyperion recording is very realistic.

Préludes – Book 1. D'un cahier d'esquisses.
Children's Corner. Clair de lune
Nelson Freire pf

Decca 478 1111DH (63' · DDD)　　　Ⓕ⚫▷

Nelson Freire, the legendary Brazilian pianist and longtime musical partner of Martha Argerich, turns to Debussy. In the accompanying notes he confesses to a special empathy for Debussy and you will be hard pressed to find a recital of comparable warmth, affection and finesse. Here, there is no need for spurious gestures and inflections; everything is given with a supreme naturalness and a perfectly accomodated virtuosity that declare Freire a master pianist throughout. When have you heard 'Voiles' given with a greater sense of its mystery or witnessed playing throughout Book 1 of the *Préludes* more delicate, rapt and precise? There is lightly worn fantasy and expertise in 'La sérénade interrompue' and the direction *Profondément calme (dans une brume doucement sonore)* is distilled into something close to perfection. Always Freire 'evokes rather than spells out' and has one every heard a more subtle or engaging way with 'Dr Gradus ad Parnassum' (from the *Children's Corner Suite*). *Clair de lune*, added, as it were, as an encore, is dreamy and magically remote, making you long for further Debussy from this artist. Decca's sound is warm and brilliant.

Préludes – Book 1. D'un cahier d'esquisses. Morceau de concours. La plus que lente. Hommage à Joseph Haydn. The little nigar. Children's Corner
Noriko Ogawa pf
BIS BIS-CD1205 (76' · DDD)　　　Ⓕ⚫⚫

Every bar of these performances confirms Ogawa as a most elegant, scrupulously sensitive interpreter of 'music like a dream from which one draws away the veil' (Debussy). She achieves a magical transparency throughout Book 1 of the *Préludes* with her refined pedalling and cool command of texture and colour. In 'Voiles' she makes you readily recall Cortot's heady description of 'the flight of the white wing on the crooning sea toward the horizon bright with the setting sun' while maintaining her own individuality. Her hushed start before the start of the whirling tarantella in 'Les collines d'Anacapri' is one of many haunting touches; and her playing of 'Des pas sur la neige', the Arctic centre of Book 1 of the *Préludes*, suggests some ultimate desolation. In *Children's Corner* she never turns 'Doctor Gradus', marked *modérément animé*, into a glittering *presto* and finds time to convey its mix of guile and sophistication. You could hardly find a more skilful or sympathetic artist from a younger generation. BIS's demonstration sound quality crowns this superb issue.

Préludes: Book 2. Berceuse héroïque. La boîte à joujoux. Elégie. Pièce pour l'oeuvre du 'Vêtement du blessé'.
Noriko Ogawa pf
BIS BIS-CD1355 (80' · DDD)　　　Ⓕ⚫⚫

Volume 3 of Noriko Ogawa's highly praised Debussy cycle includes a superlative performance of *La boîte à joujoux* that's worth the price of the disc alone. Here, the wildest selection of characters, folk tunes and operas – whether gentle or uncouth, charmers or roustabouts – twirl and tapdance their way through an intricate variety of steps clearly inspired by Stravinsky's *Petrushka*. Ogawa responds to every fleeting whimsicality with such clarity and refinement that you are lost in wonder and almost forget that the piano version finally outstays its welcome.

On more authentic pianistic ground, Ogawa wears her sense of Debussian mystery lightly, taking a sometimes disappointingly open-ended view of some of the composer's most poignant and interior thoughts. Scrupulously modern in her approach, she scorns all sentimental evasion but, while she's never less than musicianly, one would have liked a greater awareness of elegy in the *Berceuse héroïque*, and, in the *Préludes*, more of the whirring evanescence and less of the superficially abstract, étude-like character in 'Les tierces alternées'.

'Brouillards' and 'Canope' are other coolly perceived evocations and Ogawa is surely happier when not confined by so many *pianissimo* demands. 'Feux d'artifice' and 'La puerto del vino' are outstanding examples of her virtuosity at its most superfine and characterful.

These, then, are masterly performances even when they hardly sound like music composed 'for an instrument without hammers'. The sound, like the playing, is close, bright and intense.

Additional recommendation

24 Preludes – Books 1 & 2
Tirimo pf
Regis RRC1111 (78' · DDD)　　　Ⓢ⚫
　It would be hard to find a more quietly stylish or subtle account than that offered by Tirimo. His undemonstrative mastery makes him among the finest Debussy interpreters on disc.

Miscellaneous piano works

Ballade. Berceuse héroïque. Danse bohémienne. Elégie. Six Epigraphes antiques. Trois Estampes. Hommage à Haydn. Trois Images oubliées. Mazurka. Morceau de concours. Nocturne. Page d'album. Le petit nègre. La plus que lente. Pour le piano. Rêverie. Tarantelle styrienne. Valse romantique. Roi Lear, L107 – Le sommeil de Lear. Les soirs illuminés par l'ardeur du charbon
Alain Planès pf
Harmonia Mundi ② HMC90 1947/8 (114' · DDD)　　Ⓕ

Alain Planès at long last concludes his Harmonia Mundi Debussy cycle with a two-disc set that upholds his excellent standards. There's much to savour. Sample the pianist's warm, intelligently modulated sonority and calm sense of line in the first two *Images oubliées* and the Sarabande from *Pour le piano*. Then clear your palate vis-à-vis Planès's vivacious, dry-point articulation in *Jardins sous la pluie* that evokes cascading raindrops of all shapes and sizes. Perhaps it's slightly un-kosher to raid piano duet masterworks for soloistic purposes, yet Planès's sophisticated textural layering in a two-handed transcription of the *Six Epigraphes antiques* nearly made me forget the original. The pianist also lavishes care and consideration over the short pieces. *Le plus que lent* emerges less like a vignette than an epic, whose unexpected moodswings and tempo fluctuations convinced me only after several auditions. But Planès's lush, serious and cannily voiced *Rêverie* conveys a depth of feeling beyond the salonish norm many pianists prefer. The *Mazurka* and *Le petit nègre* gain sharpened rhythmic spring through Plainès's measured, firmly held basic tempi. Aside from a few jangled moments like the climaxes of *Pour le piano*'s *Prélude and Tarentelle styrienne*, Harmonia Mundi's engineering does full justice to the pianist's attractive sounding Steinway.

Deux Arabesques. Children's Corner. Six Images.
Suite bergamasque – Clair de lune
Simon Trpčeski pf
EMI 500272-2 (62' · DDD) Ⓕ🄳▸

Simon Trpčeski turns to Debussy's withdrawn poetry and fantasy with an ease and delicacy that suggest, once more, a wholly exceptional artist. He is, perhaps above all, harmonically aware, with every change of colour and sonority subtly underpinned, making you doubly aware of Debussy's chiaroscuro, his infinite play of light and shade. The First Arabesque could hardly be more charming or insinuating, the Second thrown off with all the requisite perkiness and vivacity.

In *Children's Corner* Trpčeski's 'Dr Gradus' is truly *modérément* and a far cry from a once fashionable virtuoso rush as well as much received French wisdom. His 'Golliwogg' is superbly cantankerous and up-front, though with plenty of sly winks and nudges when required, and in extreme contrast, in 'Et la lune descend sur le temple qui fut' (*Images*, Bk 2) you will hear an ideally balanced chording and a tonal translucency inseparable from great Debussy-playing. The end, too (*pianissimo* and *lointain*) is memorably evocative. True, there is a momentary loss of focus at the end of 'Poissons d'or' where the final shift of emphasis is blurred, but such tiny lapses are like spots on the sun. Trpčeski's way with 'Clair de lune' makes you long to hear him in the complete *Suite bergamasque*.

'Complete Works for Piano, Vol 2'
Ballade. D'un cahier d'esquisses. Estampes. Images
oubliées. L'isle joyeuse. Masques. Pour le piano.
Tarentelle styrienne. Valse romantique
Jean-Efflam Bavouzet pf
Chandos CHAN10443 (66' · DDD) Ⓕ🅾🅾🄳▸

While Bavouzet is no slouch in the tone-colour department, his interpretations do not primarily concern themselves with sound-painting. Instead he focuses upon clarity of textures, rhythmic precision, well differentiated articulation, plus scrupulous balances between the hands and within chords. Timbral variety and tonal allure arise from these elements working together. As you listen to Bavouzet's effortless rhythmic lilt and buoyant sense of line in the *Tarantelle styrienne*, *Masques* and 'Jardins sous la pluie', or his firm bass underpinnings and impeccably calibrated arabesques throughout *L'isle joyeuse*, you don't perceive the 'hammerless' piano of Debussy's dreams. Instead, the piano's innards morph into a finely honed chamber orchestra. Similarly in 'Pagodes', Bavouzet's sharply profiled melodies shed welcome animated light on a piece that's often interpreted too flaccidly. Some might favour a warmer, more curvaceous way with the *Valse romantique* but Bavouzet's shapelier urgency proves more convincing in *Pour le piano*'s central Sarabande, as well as its earlier incarnation in the cycle of 'forgotten' *Images*. The recorded sound is never less than pleasing.

'Complete Works for Piano, Vol 3'
Deux Arabesques. Berceuse héroïque. Children's
Corner. Danse bohémienne. Elégie. Hommage à
Haydn. Mazurka. Morceau de concours. Nocturne.
Page d'album. Le petit nègre. La plus que lente.
Rêverie. Suite bergamasque
Jean-Efflam Bavouzet pf
Chandos CHAN10467 (72' · DDD) Ⓕ🅾🅾🅾🄳▸

'Complete Works for Piano, Vol 3'
Berceuse héroïque. D'un cahier d'esquisses.
Hommage à Haydn. Six Images. L'isle joyeuse. Page
d'album. Pour le piano. Rêverie. Tarentelle styrienne.
Pascal Rogé pf
Onyx ONYX4028 (78' · DDD) Ⓕ🅾🅾🄳▸

Volume 3 of Jean-Efflam Bavouzet's superb Debussy cycle links mostly early miniatures with the *Suite bergamasque* and *Children's Corner*. Once more he turns conventional notions of 'impressionism' topsy-turvy, cleansing Debussy of years of dust and accretion and recreating him in every bar in a sparkling and pristine light. Fiercely energised yet superfine, his performances are not for those with comfortable drawing-room notions of Debussy, and rarely in my experience has a pianist so faultlessly or precisely achieved his aims.

All sentimentality is erased from the *Nocturne*'s enchanting evanescence and just when he momentarily has you wishing that his formidable directness would melt into something more heart-easing, he makes you gasp at his flawless balance of sense and sensibility. He makes something audaciously epic out of *Hommage à Haydn* and the startling hesitancy in the opening of 'The Snow is Dancing' is convincing rather than idiosyncratic. His recital ends on a desolating note with the *Berceuse héroïque*'s phantom battle-cries and bugle-calls memorably evoked. The superbly recorded disc includes his own remarkable essay. This could well be the finest and most challenging of all Debussy piano cycles.

A greater study in contrast in 'composer and interpreter' would be hard to imagine then between Bavouzet and Pascal Rogé. Where Bavouzet breaks out into blazing Mediterranean sunlight, Rogé (radically enriching his earlier Decca Debussy discs) is happy to withdraw into shadow-land. Time and again his playing suggests emotion recollected in tranquillity rather than turmoil; and in, say, 'Hommage à Rameau' or the Sarabande from *Pour le piano* he discovers the mysterious, still centre of Debussy's art. 'Poissons d'or' is a marvellous distillation of indolence and flashing disruption, and 'Mouvement' is a perky and vivacious rejoinder to all former introspection. And so too is the *Toccata*, played with unerring ease and grace, and with many ear-catching details.

To summarise, the ever-elusive truth lies somewhere between Rogé the dreamer, Bavouzet the sinewy but always musical athlete, Thibaudet, the teasing wit and sophisticate and, of course, the legendary Gieseking. You pays your money and you takes your choice…

'Nuit d'étoiles'
Danse sacrée et Danse profaneb. Deux Arabesques. Préludes – Danseuses de Delphes; Voiles; La fille aux cheveux de lin. Rêverie. Suite bergamasque. Valse romantique. Mélodiesa – Apparition; Beau soir; Clair de lune; Fleur des blés; Mandoline; Nuit d'étoiles; Le lilas
Xavier de Maistre hp with ªDiana Damrau sop
ᵇMembers of the **Vienna Philharmonic Orchestra**
RCA Red Seal 88697 22249-2 (73' · DDD)   Ⓕ

In many ways, Debussy's piano music finds its rightful home on the harp. Apart from the distinctive textural and colouristic elements in the writing itself, we have contemporary accounts of Debussy's piano-playing that refer to his ability to make you forget a piano even had hammers. Of course, this doesn't allow for dreamy, 'impressionistic' interpretations; rather, it makes clarity and precision absolute imperatives – which qualities we find in abundance in this recital by Xavier de Maistre and friends.

Perhaps realising that you can have too much of a good thing, de Maistre has chosen to include among the many solo works here a selection of *mélodies* and the two *Danses* for harp and strings. All, with the exception of the *Danses* and the *Deux Arabesques*, were transcribed by de Maistre himself.

De Maistre's playing throughout is both robust and delicate; his ability to recall the percussiveness of the piano when necessary, especially noticeable in the Prélude of the *Suite bergamasque*, the *Valse romantique* and the Second *Arabesque*, is most impressive. Elsewhere, finely cascading scales and glassy, rippling figurations are offset by sensitively brushed chords.

Soprano Diana Damrau is broadly expressive in the *mélodies*, if occasionally strident in tone; her 'Mandoline' is suffused with a playful urgency that contrasts nicely with the earnestness of 'Le lilas'. Some of de Maistre's colleagues

from the Vienna Philharmonic join him in the two dances; the playing is bold and carefree, the well judged crescendo in the *Danse profane* a delightful way to end this magical disc.

Pelléas et Mélisande

Pelléas et Mélisande
Hans Wilbrink bar Pelléas **Denise Duval** sop Mélisande **Michel Roux** bar Golaud **Anne Reynolds** mez Genevieve **Guus Hoekman** bass Arkel **Rosine Brédy** sop Yniold **John Shirley-Quirk** bass-bar A Doctor **Glyndebourne Festival Chorus; Royal Philharmonic Orchestra / Vittorio Gui**
Glyndebourne Festival Opera ③ GFOCD003-63 (164' · ADD) Recorded live 1963   Ⓜ●

If Gui's reading is 'Italianate', this is because it gives considerable though never excessive weight to the drama's emotional intensity. The idea that Debussy's opera is reticent from start to finish is a myth, and in this close-up recording the turbulent anguish of the orchestral interludes is especially vivid. When the focus is on the voices, the orchestra suffers to a degree in the restricted balance. That bright hard edge which is the accursed associate of digital remastering is evident here too, though never to a disabling extent: better a hard edge than a pervasive lack of clarity.

In 1963 Glyndebourne fielded a cast of French, Dutch and English singers whose handling of the French text stands up well in comparison with the best recent recordings. There is the minor incongruity of a very feminine Yniold, and also a Pelléas (Hans Wilbrink) whose occasionally strained moments suggest dramatic engagement rather than musical weakness. Gui's Denise Duval is a persuasive, convincingly youthful Mélisande – although Act 1 scene 2 does rather underline the fact that Anna Reynolds, singing the mother of Golaud and Pelléas, was actually 10 years younger than Duval. The Golaud, Michel Roux, had recorded the role in 1955 and again in 1962 but he was not the first singer to find the Glyndebourne experience uniquely energising, and there is no lack of force in his telling portrayal of this most maddeningly obtuse of operatic characters. Guus Hoekman is an eloquent Arkel, and John Shirley-Quirk has all the necessary gravitas as the Doctor in Act 5. The packaging comes with full text (four languages) and production photographs but no biographies of the performers.

Pelléas et Mélisande
Wolfgang Holzmair bar Pelléas **Anne Sofie von Otter** sop Mélisande **Laurent Naouri** bar Golaud **Alain Vernhes** bass Arkel **Hanna Schaer** mez Geneviève **Florence Couderc** sop Yniold **Jérôme Varnier** bar A Doctor, A Shepherd **Radio France Chorus; French National Orchestra / Bernard Haitink**
Naïve ③ V4923 (160' · DDD · T/t)   Ⓜ●

Bernard Haitink has always had a soft spot for French music, where his control of texture and

DEBUSSY'S PELLÉAS ET MÉLISANDE – IN BRIEF

Jacques Jansen *Pelléas* Iréne Joachim
Mélisande Henri Etcheverry *Golaud* Yvonne
Gouverné Choir / Roger Desormière Ⓗ
EMI ③ 761038-2 (196' · AAD) ⓂⓄⓄ
A truly historic 1941 recording that transcends limited sound with superbly idiomatic
performances by a native French cast, a great
advantage in this opera, with Jacques Jansen's
still youthful Pelléas and Irene Joachim's
glass-clear Mélisande.

Wolfgang Holzmair *Pelléas* Anne Sofie von
Otter *Mélisande* Laurent Naouri *Golaud*
Radio France Chorus, French National
Orchestra / Bernard Haitink
Naïve ③ V4923 (160' · DDD) ⓂⓄ
Though the international cast is quite
impressive, Haitink's conducting, luminous
but highly dramatic, is the star of this concert
recording.

Le Roux *Pelléas* Alliot-Lugaz *Mélisande* Van
Dam *Golaud* Chorus and Orchestra of the Lyon
Opera / Gardiner *Dir* Pierre Strosser
ArtHaus Musik ② 𝗗𝗩𝗗 100 100 (147') Ⓕ
With luminous, diaphanous conducting from
Gardiner and exquisite lighting, this is a won-
derfully atmospheric performance. The cast is
excellent, making this a strong contender not
only for video but also for the music-making.

Richard Sitwell *Pelléas* Frederica von Stade
Mélisande José van Dam *Golaud* Deutsche Oper
Berlin Chorus, Berlin PO / Herbert von Karajan
EMI ③ 567057-2 (162' · ADD) Ⓜ
Pelléas meets *Tristan* in this extraordinary and
– for many – misguided set, with a decent cast
and superb orchestral playing subjected to an
over-romantic, glutinous interpretation.

Neill Archer *Pelléas* Alison Hagley *Mélisande*
Donald Maxwell *Golaud* Welsh National Opera
Chorus and Orchestra / Pierre Boulez
Dir Peter Stein
DG ② 𝗗𝗩𝗗 073 030-9GH2 (158') Ⓕ
A grittier more psychologically acute approach
than the Strosser for Gardiner. Stein and
Boulez are scrupulously faithful to Debusy's
instructions and the eye is perfect led along by
the ebb and flow of the music.

François Le Roux *Pelléas* Maria Ewing *Mélisande*
José van Dam *Golaud* Vienna State Opera
Chorus, Vienna PO / Claudio Abbado
DG ③ 435 344-2GH2 (148' · DDD) Ⓕ
A large-scale but beautifully translucent and
poetic performance, very well recorded, with
probably the best modern cast on disc,
appropriately Francophone except for Maria
Ewing's unconventional and strikingly seduc-
tive Mélisande.

pace often brings out beauties and strengths that
other conductors do not find. *Pelléas et Mélisande*,
for which long-term flow is a crucial require-
ment, is ideally suited to his talents. He has the
ability, like a good games player, to create his
own time and space.

Throughout, the beauty, energy and brilliance
of the orchestral playing ride over an undertow of
melancholy and impending disaster, echoing that
'strange air' Mélisande has of someone who, in
Arkel's words, 'is always waiting for some great
sorrow in the sunshine in a lovely garden'. Haitink
is well served by his singers. Holzmair is a fresh-
voiced, ardent but elegant Pelléas, and innocent
enough to make his entrapment plausible. Even
the slight signs of tiring on his high notes in Act 4
can be heard as portraying vulnerability. Von
Otter plays Mélisande in the traditional way as
timid and fatally seductive. But she brings more
vibrato to her top notes than some other interpreters and this gives her timidity a slightly used,
passive-aggressive colouring, as though she has
employed her don't-touch-me gambit several
times in the past, and has found it works.

Laurent Naouri is a supremely intelligent
Golaud, slow to jealousy and anger, but terrifying when the dam finally bursts. By contrast, in
the final act he's the image of a spiritually lost
soul and his choked cries of 'Mélisande!' are
truly heartrending. Alain Vernhes's Arkel has
that 'goodness' in his tone that the composer
wanted, though his pitching, hitherto perfect,
wanders somewhat in Act 5.

Members of the French National Orchestra are,
apparently, still talking two years later of this *Pelléas* as a high point in their professional lives. It
isn't to be wondered at: Haitink gives us a deeply
serious and powerful interpretation of the opera.

Pelléas et Mélisande
Neill Archer *bar* Pelléas Alison Hagley *sop*
Mélisande Donald Maxwell *bar* Golaud Kenneth
Cox *bass* Arkel Penelope Walker *contr* Geneviève
Samuel Burkey *treb* Yniold Peter Massocchi *bar*
Doctor, Shepherd Welsh National Opera Chorus
and Orchestra / Pierre Boulez
Stage and Video director Peter Stein
DG ② 𝗗𝗩𝗗 073 030-9GH2 (158' · NTSC · 4:3 · 2.0, 5.1
& DTS 5.1 · 0) Includes picture gallery, 'Pelléas at
Welsh National Opera'. Notes included
Recorded live 1992 ⒻⓄⓄⓄ

This is, in every respect, a model of what a DVD
ought to be, a perfect realisation in picture and
sound of Debussy's sole and inspired opera.
Peter Stein staged the work for Welsh National
Opera in 1992 and won universal praise, as did
Pierre Boulez for his conducting.

Within austere, wholly appropriate sets, beautifully lit by Jean Kalman, Stein catches the very
essence of this singular and elusive piece. Each
of the 15 scenes is given its own distinctive décor
in which the action is played out on several levels
– high for the tower scenes, low for the eerie,
subterranean grottoes, for instance. A masterstroke is the subtle evolution from one scene to

another in view of the audience, offering a visual counterpoint to the interludes.

Stein sees that Debussy's instructions are scrupulously observed. In fact, as a whole, this is an object-lesson in modern staging. Stein and his collaborators reflect the ebb and flow of crude realism and fragile dream-life that permeate the score, which Boulez has identified as lying at its heart. Director and conductor worked closely with each other over a six-week rehearsal period, something unlikely to occur today, so Boulez's interpretation is in complete accord with the staging, his musical direction at once direct and luminous, timbres finely balanced one with the other.

The cast also benefited from the long gestation. Alison Hagley catches ideally the paradox that is Mélisande, candour married to duplicity, and sings the enigmatic character with an acute ear for French syllables. Neill Archer, though not quite as responsive to the French language, is a poetic, youthfully ardent Pelléas. Donald Maxwell's Golaud rightly stands at the centre of the production, conveying guilt, jealousy and self-torment in tellingly intense tones. Kenneth Cox is a grave, world-weary Arkel, Penelope Walker a properly dignified, compassionate Geneviève. The treble singing Yniold is remarkably assured. This is a riveting experience.

Pelléas et Mélisande
Le Roux Pelléas **Alliot-Lugaz** Mélisande **Van Dam** Golaud **Chorus and Orchestra of the Lyon Opera / Gardiner**
Stage director **Pierre Strosser**
Video director **Jean-François Jung**
ArtHaus Musik ② *DVD* 100 100 (147' · Regions 2 & 5)
Recorded 1987 ⒻⓄⓄ

On DVD, with superb lighting and camerawork, the results are even more convincing than in the theatre. Gardiner conducts a translucent, firmly shaped account. His interpretation brings the piece even more clearly into a post-Wagnerian world of sound, and the Lyon Orchestra play up to the hilt. The entirely French cast is one of the best to record the work, challenging the hegemony of the audio-only versions.

Additional recommendation

Stilwell *Pelléas* von Stade *Mélisande*
Berlin Philharmonic Orchestra / Karajan
EMI 567057-2 (162' · ADD) Ⓜ🅑➤

A controversial recording: too 'hot-house' for some but full of breathtaking playing and a heartbreakingly touching pair of lovers. This was clearly a labour of love for the great Austrian conductor.

Léo Delibes   French 1836-1891

A church, organist until 1871, Delibes was drawn to the theatre, first writing light operettas in the style of his teacher Adolphe Adam (roughly one a year from 1856 to 1869), then becoming chorus master at the Théâtre-Lyrique and the Opéra. He is best known for his appealing classical ballets Coppélia (1870), with its charming character numbers, and the tuneful but more sophisticated Sylvia (1876), both admired by Tchaikovsky. Meyerbeer's influence is evident in his serious opera Jean de Nivelle (1880), and a gift for witty pastiche in his dances for Hugo's play Le roi s'amuse (1882). His masterpiece is Lakmé (1883), a highly successful opera indebted to Bizet and memorable for its oriental colour, strong characterisation and fine melodies. **GROVE**music

---

Sylvia

Delibes Sylvia **Saint-Saëns** Henry VIII – Ballet-divertissement
Razumovsky Sinfonia / Andrew Mogrelia
Naxos ② 8 553338/9 (114' · DDD) Ⓢ🅑➤

Of Delibes's two full-length ballets, *Coppélia* is the more obviously popular, the one with the bigger tunes and the greater number of recordings. However, *Sylvia* is also a superbly crafted score, full of haunting melodies. Andrew Mogrelia's Naxos series is one to be collected and treasured: there's loving care applied to selection of tempos, shaping of phrases, orchestral balance and refinement of instrumental detail. Here you thrill to *Sylvia*'s Act 1 Fanfare, marvel at the control of tempo and refinement of instrumental detail in the 'Valse lente' and 'Entrée du sorcier', and revel in the sheer ebullience of Sylvia's return in Act 2. The inclusion of the ballet music from Saint-Saëns's *Henry VIII* was an admirably enterprising move, even though it doesn't amount to anything major apart from the 'Danse de la gitane', being essentially a collection of mock 'Olde Britishe' dances. All the same, a quite remarkable bargain.

Lakmé

Lakmé
Natalie Dessay *sop* Lakmé **Gregory Kunde** *ten*
Gérald **José van Dam** *bass-bar* Nilakantha **Delphine Haidan** *mez* Mallika **Franck Leguérinel** *bar* Frédéric **Patricia Petibon** *sop* Ellen **Xenia Konsek** *sop* Rose **Bernadette Antoine** *sop* Mistress Bentson **Charles Burles** *ten* Hadji **Toulouse Capitole Chorus and Orchestra / Michel Plasson**
EMI ② 556569-2 (144' · DDD · T/t) Ⓕ🅞

Opera audiences in 19th-century Paris may never have visited India, but they loved to dream about it. After the successes enjoyed by *Les pêcheurs de perles* and *Le roi de Lahore* Delibes knew what he was doing when he chose to set an adaptation of Pierre Loti's exotic Indian novel *Rarahu* and duly scored a hit with his opera *Lakmé* at the Opéra-Comique in 1883. The opera is nothing without a star in the title-role. Natalie Dessay is certainly that and yet she never fails to remember that Delibes's heroine must be fragile and sensitive. Her Bell Song, brilliantly sung, is also intent on telling a story. Her singing of the death scene, with its delicate *fil de voce* perfectly poised each time the high A comes round, is heartfelt and leaves no doubt that this is a Lakmé who deserves to go to heaven. EMI found a worthy tenor to partner her. Gregory Kunde, as Gérald, is at ease at the top of his voice. At the first entrance of the colonial Brits, Frédéric describes Gérald as a poet and Kunde lives up to the promise by phrasing his opening solo, 'Fantaisie aux divins mensonges', with poetic sensibility. In the duets he and Dessay are tender young love personified. The supporting cast is also a decent one.

Michel Plasson gives the music room to breathe and is able to conjure a dreamy atmosphere in the scenes of romance. His Toulouse orchestra is adequate, if not exceptional, and the recording is of a good standard. What reason is there to resist?

Frederick Delius   British 1862-1934

Delius's father lent him money to set up as a citrus grower in Florida (1884-6), where he had lessons with Thomas Ward; he then studied at the Leipzig Conservatory (1886-8) and met Grieg. He settled in Paris as a man of bohemian habits, a friend of Gauguin, Strindberg, Munch and others, until in 1897 he moved to Grez with Jelka Rosen, later his wife. There he remained.

He had written operas, orchestral pieces and much else before the move to Grez, but nearly all his regularly performed output dates from afterwards while looking back to the musical and other experiences of earlier years: the seamless flow of Wagner, the airier chromaticism of Grieg, the rich colouring of Strauss and Debussy, the existential independence of Nietzsche. His operas A Village Romeo and Juliet (1901) and Fennimore and Gerda (1910) are love stories cast in connected scenes and examining spiritual states within a natural world. Nature is important too in such orchestral pieces as In a Summer Garden (1908), A Song of the High Hills (with wordless chorus, 1911) or A Song of Summer (1930), though there are other works in which the characteristic rhapsodising is made to serve symphonic forms, notably the Violin Concerto (1916) and three sonatas for violin and piano (1914, 1923, 1930). The choral works include two unaccompanied, wordless songs 'to be sung of a summer night on the water' (1917), the large-scale A Mass of Life with words from Nietzsche (1905) and a secular Requiem (1916). In the early 1920s he grew blind and paralysed as a result of syphilitic infection, and his last works were taken down by Eric Fenby.

GROVEmusic

Orchestral Works

Appalachia, RTVII/2[d]. Brigg Fair, RTVI/16[a]. **H**
Koanga[b] – La Calinda (arr Fenby). Hassan[c] – Closing scene. Irmelin Prelude, RTVI/27[b].
[c]**Jan van der Gucht** ten [c]**Royal Opera House Chorus, Covent Garden;** [d]**BBC Chorus;** [a]**Symphony Orchestra;** [bcd]**London Philharmonic Orchestra / Sir Thomas Beecham**
Naxos Historical mono 8 110906 (66' · AAD) Recorded [a]1928-9, 1938 ⑤●▶

There always was a unique alchemy between the art of Sir Thomas Beecham and the music of Frederick Delius, to be heard in every bar of this remarkable January 1938 recording of *Appalachia*. It's a performance of beaming dedication, wistful heartache and rapt wonder leaves the listener in no doubt about Sir Thomas's boundless love for a work that served as his introduction to the composer. (He later recalled how the 1907 London premiere under Fritz Cassirer left him 'startled and electrified'.) By July 1938 Beecham and the LPO had committed to disc the three remaining items that eventually made up The Delius Society's lavishly presented third and final volume of the composer's music issued by Columbia Records; suffice it to say, *La Calinda* skips along entrancingly here, while no true Delian could fail to respond to Beecham's ineffably poignant way with both the closing scene from *Hassan* and the lovely *Irmelin Prelude*.

Naxos's curtain-raiser, *Brigg Fair*, was recorded towards the end of the previous decade. Some seven months separated the two days required to produce a reading of unforgettable tenderness and bewitching poetry (the results of an even earlier session in July 1928 having been rejected altogether), although some will still hold a slight preference for the second of Sir Thomas's three versions (a gloriously intuitive display with the newly formed RPO from November 1946).

David Lennick's transfers have been admirably managed, *Appalachia* now sounding rather more open and full bodied than on a rival Dutton compilation. Throw in a lively and informative booklet-essay from Lyndon Jenkins, not to mention the absurdly low price-tag, and it should be abundantly clear that this is a self-recommending issue.

Fantastic Dance. A Dance Rhapsody No 1[a]. A Dance Rhapsody No 2. A Song of the High Hills. Three Preludes. Zum Carnival
Maryetta Midgley sop **Vernon Midgley** ten **Eric Parkin** pf **Ambrosian Singers**
Royal Philharmonic Orchestra / Eric Fenby, [a]**Norman Del Mar**
Unicorn-Kanchana Souvenir UKCD2071 (65' · DDD)Ⓜ

Irmelin Prelude. A Song of Summer. A Late Lark. Piano Concerto in C minor[a]. Violin Concerto[b]
Anthony Rolfe Johnson ten **Ralph Holmes** vn **Philip Fowke** pf **Royal Philharmonic Orchestra / Eric Fenby,** [a]**Norman Del Mar,** [b]**Vernon Handley**
Unicorn-Kanchana Souvenir UKCD2072 (71' · DDD) Ⓜ

Koanga – La Calinda (arr Fenby). Idyll: Once I passed through a populous city. Songs of Sunset. A Village

Romeo and Juliet – The Walk to the Paradise Garden[a]
Felicity Lott sop **Sarah Walker** mez **Thomas Allen** bar **Ambrosian Singers; Royal Philharmonic Orchestra / Eric Fenby,** [a]**Norman Del Mar**
Unicorn-Kanchana Souvenir UKCD2073 (73' · DDD)
All recorded 1981-90 Ⓜ●

The unique insight that the late Eric Fenby would bring as an interpreter of Delius was the reason for many of these Unicorn recordings, but we owe the idea and its realisation to their producer, Christopher Palmer. As well as providing Delians with some of the most illuminating text on the music, Palmer, in the studio, and especially in a work like *A Song of the High Hills*, was able to put his understanding (and Fenby's, of course) into practice. You don't need the score of *A Song of the High Hills* to tell you that the passage from 9'54" represents 'The wide far distance, the great solitude'. What you're listening to – totally spellbound – couldn't be anything else (or by anyone else).

Ralph Holmes's recording of the Violin Concerto is a warm, leisurely reading. The Piano Concerto, as recorded here, is a grand showstopper in the best Romantic piano concerto tradition, yet Fowke and Del Mar alert you to all the Delian reverie in the making (the dynamic range of Fowke's piano is colossal). But the outlay for Vol 2 is justified by Anthony Rolfe Johnson alone, in the all too brief six-minute *A Late Lark* ('one of Delius's works that is surely entirely without flaw', as Trevor Harvey put it in his original review).

In Vol 3, Fenby's control in *Songs of Sunset* doesn't always match his insight (choral work is often sloppy and too distantly recorded); the recent Hickox, or the 1957 Beecham is to be preferred. But without Fenby in the recording studio (or at Grez!), we would never have had *Idyll*: Whitman texts combined with a late reworking of music from an earlyish opera, *Margot la Rouge*, to provide a reflective then rapturous love duet that looks back to Delius's Paris as well as to his *Paris* – this makes Vol 3 indispensable, especially as sung and played here.

And a very considerable bonus to be found in Vol 3 is Del Mar's previously unissued *Walk to the Paradise Garden*. This isn't the Beecham version for reduced orchestra, though it incorporates many of Beecham's dynamics and tempo indications. Most assuredly, it's a *Walk* on the grandest (11'00" to Beecham's 8'38"), most passionate scale (there's not a barline in earshot, either), and turns out to be yet another of these three discs' memorials to inspired Delians who died in our, but before their, time.

On Hearing the First Cuckoo in Spring. Brigg Fair. In a Summer Garden. Paris: The Song of a Great City. Summer Night on the River. A Village Romeo and Juliet – The Walk to the Paradise Garden
BBC Symphony Orchestra / Sir Andrew Davis
Warner Apex 8573-89084-2 (77' · DDD) Ⓢ🅳➤

This *Brigg Fair* is unique. What a lovely surprise to hear real London sparrows sharing the air space of St Augustine's Church with Delius's translated Lincolnshire larks (flute and clarinet) in the opening minutes of the work, albeit much more distantly. Very effective too are those almost still pools of string sound (early morning mists?), given the extended boundaries of this acoustic, and the familiar warmth and depth of tone Davis draws from the orchestra's strings. In the final magnificently broad climax (pealing bells, for once, very clear), you can't fail to be impressed by the depth, coherence and articulacy of the sound – hallmarks, indeed, of the entire disc.

Davis's strings come into their own in the *Walk to the Paradise Garden*. For *In a Summer Garden*, Davis mutes his strings more often than Delius asks; but the reading's delicacy of texture and hazy, suffusing warmth are difficult to resist.

American Rhapsody. Fantastic Dance. Marche caprice. Three Small Tone Poems. Two Pieces for Small Orchestra. A song before sunrise. A Village Romeo and Juliet – The walk to the Paradise Garden
Royal Scottish National Orchestra / David Lloyd-Jones
Naxos 8 557143 (64' · DDD) Ⓢ🅳➤

A chronologically wide-ranging programme starts with Bizet-meets-Elgar in *Marche caprice* (composed in Paris in 1889) and finishes with the flourishes of the 1931 *Fantastic Dance* that Delius inscribed to his amanuensis Eric Fenby. There are two further rarities: the fragrant *Spring Morning* of 1890, which breathes a distinctly Norwegian air, and the colourful *American Rhapsody* of 1896, an embryonic (and purely orchestral) dry run for the towering *Appalachia* of six years later.

Lloyd-Jones's flowing yet deeply felt way with *The Walk to the Paradise Garden* leaves a less artfully self-conscious impression than Mark Elder's silky Hallé version. The only reservation applies to the Two Pieces for Small Orchestra, *On hearing the first cuckoo in Spring* and *Summer night on the river*, both of which are too robust to work their full magic. (Thomas Beecham and Norman Del Mar remain unsurpassed in this 1911-12 diptych; the same goes for *A song before sunrise*.) Otherwise, the RSNO respond attentively throughout.

Additional recommendations

Brigg Fair – An English Rhapsody. Dance Ⓗ
Rhapsody No 2. On Hearing the First Cuckoo in Spring. Summer Night on the River. A Song Before Summer. Intermezzo (arr Fenby). Irmelin Prelude. Sleighride. Summer Evening (ed & arr Beecham). Florida Suite (rev & ed Beecham) – Daybreak, Dance
RPO / Beecham
EMI download 567552-2 (77' · ADD) Ⓜ🅳➤

373

Brigg Fair A Song Before Sunrise. Songs from
the Norwegian. Hassan – excerpts. Dance Rhapso-
dies Nos 1 & 2. On Hearing the First Cuckoo in
Spring. Summer Night on the River. Danish Songs.
Irmelin Prelude.
Suddaby sop **Thomas** contr **RPO / Beecham**
Dutton CDLX7028 (77' · ADD) Ⓜ

Two superb reissues containing superlative
performances from Beecham and the RPO, both
beautifully remastered and at mid-price. At least
one of these discs of these should be on every
classical enthusiast's shelf (the EMI is not currently
listed on CD, but the download is).

Appalachia. In a Summer Garden.
North Country Sketches
RPO / Beecham
Sony Classical SMK89429 (76' · ADD) Recorded 1950s

Delians will almost certainly want this CD. Ⓜ
Keenly and clearly recorded. Beecham fully demonstrates his sensitivity for Delius's music.

Violin Sonatas

Violin Sonatas Nos 1-3. Cello Sonata
Ralph Holmes vn **Julian Lloyd Webber** vc
Eric Fenby pf
Unicorn-Kanchana Souvenir UKCD2074
(65' · ADD/DDD) Recorded 1972-81 Ⓜ

This is selfless, utterly dedicated music-making,
always spontaneous-sounding yet never losing
the organic thread of Delius's remarkable, free-
flowing inspiration. There's a slight fragility to
Holmes's distinctive, silvery tone that's
extremely moving, and Fenby, though no virtuoso practitioner, accompanies with intuitive
sympathy. The recording of the piano (the
instrument used is the three-quarter Ibach
grand left to Fenby by Delius himself) remains a
touch boxy and wanting in bloom, though the
balance is otherwise natural and the overall
effect nicely intimate. In the Cello Sonata Lloyd
Webber and Fenby adopt a mellow, notably
ruminative approach.

A Mass of Life

A Mass of Life[a]. Requiem[ba]
[a]**Joan Rodgers,** [b]**Rebecca Evans** sops [a]**Jean Rigby**
mez [a]**Nigel Robson** ten **Peter Coleman-Wright** bar
**Waynflete Singers; Bournemouth Symphony
Chorus and Orchestra / Richard Hickox**
Chandos ② CHAN9515 (129' · DDD · T/t) Ⓕ⊞➔

This is only the third commercial recording of *A
Mass of Life*. The previous two recordings were
the 1952 Beecham (no longer available) and the
1971 Groves on EMI. You might imagine modern recording would best place this vast canvas
between your loudspeakers. And yes, Hickox's
dynamic peaks are marginally higher, his perspectives marginally wider and deeper. Actually,
some of this has as much to do with Hickox's
own pacing and shading as the engineering. In

general, this 'idealised' light- and air-filled
sound brings a sharper, bright presence for the
chorus, and such things as the piccolo trilling
atop the final 'Hymn to Joy'. What it doesn't
bring is the sense of performers in a specific
acoustic space. But the chorus shines in the
prominent role which the Chandos balance
gives them, with ringing attack for all entries
where it's needed, and singing as confident as it's
sensitive, even if one has to make the odd allowance for not quite perfect pitching on high
(Delius's demands are extreme) and moments
where they're too loud. The soloists are fine;
Hickox's baritone has a good line in stirring,
virile address, though little of Benjamin Luxon's
nobility, inwardness and true *legato*. What
makes the Hickox *Mass* preferable to the Groves
(but only just) is the conductor's inspired handling of each part's central dance panels. Hickox
makes you believe in them, with a judicious
drive, lift to the rhythms, and really incisive,
eager singing and playing. As a coupling, Hickox
has only the second-ever commercial recording
of the Requiem: more Nietzsche, but this time
dogma not poetry, all the more unpalatable/
embarrassing (regardless of your faith) for being
in English, but containing much unique Delius.

Sea Drift

Sea Drift. Songs of Sunset. Songs of Farewell
Sally Burgess mez **Bryn Terfel** bass-bar **Waynflete
Singers; Southern Voices; Bournemouth Symphony
Chorus and Orchestra / Richard Hickox**
Chandos CHAN9214 (77' · DDD · T) Ⓕ❶❷❸❹➔

Ⓖ *Sea Drift* is a sublime conjunction of
Whitman's poetry and Delius's music
describing love, loss and unhappy
resignation, with the sea (as Christopher Palmer
put it) as 'symbol and agent of parting'. Written
in 1903-4 (the same years as Debussy's *La mer*),
it's surely Delius's masterpiece; right from the
swaying opening bars its spell is enduring and
hypnotic. Hickox in his second recording of the
work now gives us the finest recorded post-Bee-
cham *Sea Drift*. The shaping of the opening
falling woodwind figures at a slow tempo more
than usually (and very beautifully) portends the
sad turn of events; and the climax is broad and
superbly co-ordinated. Terfel's bar-by-bar characterisation (and glorious voice), conveys the
full expressive range of the role from impassioned appeal to gentle call without artifice; and
the choral singing is superb. The whole is
recorded with warmth, spaciousness, depth and
clarity.

Songs

The Song of the High Hills, RTII/6[b] Eventyr, 'Once
upon a time', RTVI/23. Sleigh ride (Winter night),
RTVI/7. Five Songs from the Norwegian, RTV/5[a]
(arr Holten)
[a]**Henriette Bonde-Hansen,** [b]**Helle Høyer Hansen**

sops ᵇ**John Kjøller** ten ᵇ**Aarhus Chamber Choir;**
ᵇ**Aarhus University Choir; Aarhus Symphony**
Orchestra / Bo Holten
Danacord DACOCD592 (66' · DDD · T/t)   Ⓟ**OOO**

 Bo Holten and the excellent Aarhus
Symphony Orchestra include here a collection of Delius works inspired by
Norway, a country to which he was specially
attracted. His first major visit was in 1887 during
a summer vacation while studying at the Leipzig
Conservatory, when he spent more than six weeks
joyfully exploring fjords, moors and mountains.

Later that year his Leipzig contemporary,
Christian Sinding, introduced him to Grieg, for
whom as a Christmas present Delius wrote
Sleigh Ride, a piano piece buried for many years
that finally surfaced in the composer's orchestration in 1946 long after his death. It's a jolly
little piece, not at all Delian in style, that by
rights should have been a popular hit from the
start; here it's given a delightful, lightly sprung
performance.

The *Five Songs from the Norwegian* were written the following year in 1888 in gratitude for
Grieg's intervention with Delius's father over
giving him an allowance so as to devote himself
to composition. Dedicated to Grieg's wife,
they're charming pieces, setting poems by
Bjornsen and others that Grieg himself had set,
and are here made the more seductive in Bo
Holten's sensitive orchestrations, with Henriette Bonde-Hansen the fresh, pure-toned
soprano. The most ambitious Delius work
inspired by Norway is *The Song of the High Hills*,
the most substantial item on the disc. Though
Beecham recorded it in the days of 78, it has
been curiously neglected on disc when over its
25-minute span it offers some of the most
hauntingly atmospheric music that Delius ever
wrote, notably in the passages for wordless
choir. Holten conducts a beautiful, refined performance which keeps the music moving, never
letting it meander, building to powerful climaxes thrillingly recorded. With a wide dynamic
range the sound is evocatively atmospheric, not
least in the offstage choral passages.

Fennimore and Gerda – Intermezzo. Lebenstanz,
RTII/15. An Arabesque, RTII/7ᵇᶜ. Sakuntalaᵇ. The Page
Sat in the Lofty Towerᵃ. In Bliss we Walked with Laugh-
terᵃ. Two Brown Eyesᵃ. I Hear in the Nightᵃ. Two Danish
Songs, RTV/21 – The Violetᵇ; Autumnᵃ. Seven Danish
Songs, RTIII/4ᵃ. Summer Landscape, RTV/24ᵇ
ᵃ**Henriette Bonde-Hansen** sop ᵇ**Johan Reuter** bar
ᶜ**Danish National Opera Chorus;** ᶜ**Aarhus Chamber**
Choir; Aarhus Symphony Orchestra / Bo Holten
Danacord DACOCD536 (70' · DDD · T/t)   Ⓕ

This collection of Delius's Danish inspirations,
beautifully performed and recorded, makes a
delightful disc, including as it does rarities that are
otherwise unavailable. Even if 'masterworks' is a
bit of an exaggeration, the pieces here all show
Delius at his most characteristic, drawing on his
deep sympathy for Scandinavia and its culture.

Significantly, the performances under Bo Holten
tend to be faster and often more passionate than
those on rival recordings, such as in Unicorn's
admirable Delius Collection.

An Arabesque dates from 1911, but all the other
vocal items were written much earlier. In many
ways the conventional picture we have of Delius,
as the blind and paralysed composer of his later
years, is misleading, failing to reflect what we
know of the younger man, active and virile, a
point that Bo Holten has clearly registered. It's
good to have the *Seven Danish Songs* of 1897 as a
group in Delius's own sensuous orchestrations.
The self-quotations in the ballad-like 'Irmelin
Rose' are the more telling in orchestral form,
and the most beautiful song of all, 'Summer
Nights', is magically transformed in its atmospheric evocation of a sunset.

Delius also orchestrated two separate Danish
songs, 'The Violet' and *Summer Landscape* as
well as *Sakuntala*, prompting Holten to orchestrate the five other Danish songs, which here
form another orchestral cycle. These, too, are
more beautiful than with piano, even though
Holten is less distinctive than Delius himself in
his use of orchestral colour, notably in woodwind writing. All these songs are sung in the
original language, where the Unicorn series
opted for the English translations which Delius
either made himself or approved. The two singers here may not be as characterful as such British soloists as Felicity Lott, Sarah Walker or
Thomas Allen (in *An Arabesque*), but they both
have fresh young voices, clear and precise, with
Henriette Bonde-Hansen shading her bright
soprano down to the gentlest *pianissimos*. The
choral singing, too, is excellent in *An Arabesque*.

The *Fennimore and Gerda* 'Intermezzo' is relatively well known, but *Lebenstanz* ('Life's Dance'),
inspired by a play of Helge Rode, is a rarity, otherwise available only on Unicorn conducted by
Norman Del Mar. Here, too, Holten opts for
marginally faster speeds in a piece depicting (in
the composer's words) 'the turbulence, the joy,
energy, great striving of youth'. The dance sections – one of them surprisingly Straussian – are
punctuated by typically reflective passages, and
the depiction of death at the end is peaceful and
not at all tragic.

The Aarhus Symphony Orchestra respond
warmly to Holten's idiomatic direction, and the
refined playing is quite closely balanced in a
helpful acoustic.

Five Partsongs (1887). Her ute skal gildet staa. Irmelin
Rose (arr Lubin). On Craig Dhu. Wanderer's Song.
Midsummer Song. The splendour falls on castle
walls. Two Songs for Children. To be sung of a
summer night on the water. A Village Romeo and
Juliet – The dream of Sali and Vrenchen (arr Fenby).
Appalachia – Oh, Honey, I am going down the river
(arr Suchoff). Irmelin – Away; far away to the woods.
Hassan – Chorus behind the scenes; Chorus of
Beggars and Dancing Girls
Joanna Nolan sop **Stephen Douse** ten **Andrew Ball**
pf **Mark Brafield** org **Elysian Singers of London /**

Matthew Greenall
Somm Recordings SOMMCD210 (50' · DDD · T/t) Ⓕ

Delius had a special relationship with the collective human voice, and the songs here are presented chronologically, which allows us to follow pleasurably the development of his style. The extracts from *A Village Romeo and Juliet* and *Appalachia* prolong what would otherwise be a rather brief encounter and their accompaniments also provide contrast of timbre, but they do need to be heard in context to 'take off'. The 'essential' Delius comes with *On Craig Dhu* – experience of nature not so much tinged by melancholy as perceived through it; a haunting evocation in grey; and the setting of Tennyson's *The splendour falls on castle walls*, as characteristically Delius as Britten's setting of it, in his *Serenade*, is Britten.

Though the singing itself deserves a generally warm welcome, not all Delius's chromatic wanderings are as confidently charted as they might be. The sopranos seem the strongest contingent, and the ones most often in the expressive spotlight. Nor are the soloists ideal, the tenor sounding unhappy in the higher regions of the second of the two songs, *To be sung of a summer night on the water*. And on occasions, as in the first of those two songs, one might have wished for more varied pacing and dynamic shading from the conductor. But the world of Delius performance is one where devotees are used to taking the roundabouts with the swings, and this is the only all-Delius collection of its kind on the market.

Film

'Song of Summer'
Max Adrian Frederick Delius **Maureen Pryor** Jelka Delius **Christopher Gable** Eric Fenby **David Collings** Percy Grainger **Geraldine Sherman** Girl next door **Elizabeth Ercy** Maid **Roger Worrod** Bruder
Film director **Ken Russell**
BFI 🄓🅥🄳 BFIVD518 (72' · 4:3 · 1.0 · 0) Made for the BBC in 1968. Includes director's commentary and on-screen biography. Ⓕ⚪⚪

Ken Russell's extraordinarily compelling and intensely moving *Song of Summer* remains, quite simply, a joy from start to finish, arguably the controversial director's finest achievement to date and a landmark in the history of British television. Based on Eric Fenby's 1936 memoir *Delius as I knew him* (Faber & Faber: 1981), *Song of Summer* tells of Delius's syphilis-wracked final years and the remarkable relationship that develops between the blind, crippled composer and his gifted, tirelessly devoted amanuensis. The screenplay (by Russell and Fenby) fairly teems with intelligent observation, darkly mischievous humour and compassionate warmth. Indeed, the film's chief fascination lies in its subtle exploration of the profoundly contradictory nature of Delius's life and art ('I can't reconcile such hardness with such lovely music,'

says Fenby, just after Delius's wife, Jelka, has filled him in on her unfaithful husband's wanton sexual exploits from years past).

Memorable characterisations abound. As the by-turns irascible yet vulnerable composer, Max Adrian gives a performance of towering eloquence. Christopher Gable, too, is totally believable in the role of Fenby, while Maureen Pryor makes a touching Jelka. There's also a boisterous cameo from David Collings as Percy Grainger. Dick Best's luminous black-and-white photography comes up with pristine freshness, and Russell himself provides a typically candid and personable commentary. All told, a real treat.

Henry Desmarest   French 1661-1741

As a boy chorister in the royal chapel Desmarest became a disciple of Lully. He maintained court links and his first opera was given at Versailles in 1682. Later he was maître de chapelle at a Jesuit college. An amorous imbroglio led to his exile in 1699, and in 1701 he took a court post in Madrid. From 1707 he was surintendant de la musique to the Duke of Lorraine at Lunéville, where he expanded musical activities. He wrote c20 stage works; the tragédies lyriques, such as Iphigénie en Tauride (1704), use more adventurous harmony and more flexible recitative than Lully's. His other works include impressive grands motets, cantatas, airs and sonatas.
GROVEmusic

Grands Motets Lorrains

Grands Motets Lorrains – Usquequo, Domine; Ⓟ
Lauda Jerusalem; Domine, ne in furore
Sophie Daneman, Rebecca Ockenden sops **Paul Agnew** ten **Laurent Slaars** bar **Arnaud Marzorati** bass **Les Arts Florissants / William Christie**
Erato 8573-80223-2 (68' · DDD · T/t) Ⓕ⚪⚪

If Henry Desmarest hasn't yet joined other French Baroque composers among the ranks of the Great Rediscovered, here's a disc which ought to help him on his way. These three *grands motets* were composed between 1708 and 1715, the early years of his time as musical director to the court of the Duke of Lorraine. Scored for soloists, choir and orchestra, each is a multi-sectional psalm-setting lasting about 20 minutes. What's immediately striking isn't only how strong-boned and well-written the music is, but also how contrasted; here are moments of supreme tenderness, powerful intensity, robust grandeur and uplifting rhythmic vigour. And if a tendency towards melancholy is unsurprising given that two of these psalm-texts are penitential, who's to say that we aren't also witnessing a reflection of the unhappy circumstances of this composer's life?

Such music couldn't have fallen into better hands than Christie's. His talent is to see the work as a totality, with the result that the music never fails to punch its full expressive weight. With Sophie Daneman and Paul Agnew excellent among the soloists, and choral singing which remains unfailingly vivid and alert throughout, these are vibrant performances that don't put a foot wrong. The recording is clear and nicely balanced, though an unusual profusion of extraneous noises is an irritant. Even so, this is a must-buy for French Baroque fans.

The Dickinson journey is traced here in supremely well articulated and strongly characterised performances by Jennifer Bate. The three organs involved are recorded with maximum fidelity and no sense of distortion, even in the loudest passages. The disc is a fine birthday tribute to a composer who has escaped the confines of the predictable without ever ceasing to communicate.

Peter Dickinson
English b1934

English composer, pianist and musicologist. As organ scholar at Cambridge, he was a pupil of Philip Radcliffe. He also received advice and encouragement from Berkeley. In 1958 he was given a scholarship to the Juilliard School, where he studied with Bernard Wagenaar. While in the USA he encountered and was influenced by Cage, Cowell and Varèse. If his early work shows affinities with middle-period Stravinsky, the original application of simple material in the experimental and aleatory works of the 1970s recalls Ives and Satie. GROVEmusic

Organ music

Complete Solo Organ Works
Jennifer Bate org
Naxos 8 572169 (78' · DDD)
Played on the organs of St John's, Duncan Terrace, St James's, Muswell Hill, and St Dominic's Priory, London ⓈⓄⒹ

The student pieces that begin this fascinating disc demonstrate the expected ability to identify with the musical worlds of Vaughan Williams and Herbert Howells, though one piece at least – the *Postlude on Adeste fideles* – shows signs of a more abrasive idiom, as if Ives were waiting in the wings. The *Meditation on Murder in the Cathedral* is another, quite different kind of early acknowledgement that the dissonance and a sense of disquiet so common in contemporary concert music by 1958 could be no less relevant to the organ loft.

When Dickinson exchanged Cambridge for New York in the late 1950s, that potential for responding to changes taking place in the wider musical world began to be realised with interest. The organ works from the 1960s which followed his return to the UK reveal the edgy, angular perspectives stemming from Dickinson's familiarity with composers as different as Copland and Cage. However, neither *Three Statements* nor *Paraphrase 1* are pale imitations of such composers – nor, for that matter, of other Dickinson enthusiasms such as Satie and Berners. Only with the exuberant, ebullient absorption of blues and rag music found in *Blue Rose Variations* (1985) do specific stylistic associations emerge, and this piece remains an invigorating blast of fresh air, a kind of secular equivalent to Messiaen's ecstatic spiritual dances.

James Dillon
Scottish b1950

He studied music and linguistics at London University, but was self-taught as a composer. His music, influenced by Ferneyhough and Finnissy, is characterised by wild complexity and extreme instrumental demands. His early works are for solo instruments or small ensembles – Once Upon a Time for eight instruments (1980), East 11th St NY 10003 for six percussionists (1982) – but in Überschreiten for 16 instruments (1986) and his first orchestral score Helle Nacht (1987) he began to extend his techniques to larger forces. GROVEmusic

Chamber Works

String Quartet No 2[a]. Parjanya-vata[b]. Traumwerk[c]. Vernal Showers[d]
[a]**Arditti Quartet** ([cd]Irvine Arditti vn David Alberman vn Garth Knox va [b]Rohan de Saram vc) [c]**Graeme Jennings** vn [d]**Nieuw Ensemble / Ed Spanjaard**
Auvidis Montaigne MO782046 (67' · DDD) Ⓕ

For a composer with James Dillon's avant-garde credentials, the title *Vernal Showers* might lead you to expect a send-up of English pastoralism. In fact, there's nothing the least frivolous or forbidding about this response to Coleridge's *The Nightingale*. The music invokes the glittering cascades of sudden downpours while the sun still shines, and even the nocturnal song of the nightingale, without compromising Dillon's very personal blend of inventiveness and carefully weighted structuring.

Parjanya-vata is an appropriate partner for *Vernal Showers*, its title involving two Sanskrit words for rain and wind. This exhilarating essay for solo cello is executed with charismatic brilliance by Rohan de Saram. That there's far more to his music than mere sound-effects is confirmed by the Second String Quartet, a fizzing firework display as exuberant as it's poetic and a supremely imaginative rethinking of the traditional quartet. In *Traumwerk*, 12 miniatures for two violins, Dillon seizes the opportunity to devise a sequence of sharply drawn character pieces whose variety of mood ranges from sly comedy to unbridled ferocity. As always with this composer, nothing about the medium – like the contrast between playing vibrato and non vibrato – is taken for granted. The persuasive technical and interpretative virtuosity of all the performers on this CD should not be taken for granted either, and the various recordings are all superb.

---

the soadie waste[ac]. Del cuarto elemento[d]. Dillug-Kefitsah[a]. Traumwerk Book III[ad]. black/nebulae[ab].
[a]**Noriko Kawai**, [b]**Hiroaki Takenouchi** pfs
[c]**Arditti Quartet** ([d]Irvine Arditti, Ashot Sarkissjan vns
Ralf Ehlers va Lucas Fels vc)
NMC NMCD131 (76' · DDD)   (F)

The 27-year period covered by this group of compositions, taking James Dillon from his mid-twenties to his early fifties, could hardly fail to outline substantial changes. *Dillug-Kefitsah* (1976) might well be fully representative in its relish for weird titles and joyful technical radicalism, shifting between gentleness and turbulence in thoroughly disconcerting ways. But it gives little sign of the delight in forceful pattern-making and affectionate allusion to a Glaswegian location that makes *the soadie waste* (2003) such a bracing and engaging experience. The more confidently international Dillon's range of reference, the more resourceful his acknowledgement of his native Scots roots becomes.

The two big works here, *black/nebulae* (1994) and *Traumwerk Book III* (completed 2002) belong to a time when Dillon was deep in larger-scale projects. Yet neither sounds remotely like music of reduced ambition or limited scope. The space/time drama underpinning *black/nebulae* promotes a surface that seethes and erupts in 20 effortlessly sustained minutes of duo-pianistic bravura, in which meticulous coordination is as crucial as assertive independence. The 12 miniatures of the *Traumwerk* collection are even more fastidious in their intricacy, yet the result is often playful, even nonchalant, as Irvine Arditti and Noriko Kawai make light (apparently) of the formidable challenges presented. Arditti is also characteristically arresting in the 10-minute solo piece Dillon wrote for him in 1988 and named after the fourth element, water. The music, a miniature drama, is not merely liquid-like in its fluidity but is constantly reaching and retreating from boiling-point.

These performances benefit greatly from the crystal-clear Potton Hall acoustics. With luck, some of Dillon's more substantial works from recent years – even, perhaps, the opera *Philomela* – will turn up on disc before too long.

The Book of Elements

The Book of Elements
Noriko Kawai pf
NMC ② NMCD091 (83' · DDD)   (F)**OO**

There's a marvellously flamboyant spontaneity and exuberance *The Book of Elements*, demonstrating his view of the elements – air, water and so on – as standing for 'different forms of energy'. Energy is life, life is both time and transience, and the composer's over-riding concern is with images of impermanence and flux. These determine musical processes that speak of the inherent fragility of life and the essential sadness of attempts to construct something relatively stable and permanent in sound.

The work, composed between 1996 and 2003, is in five volumes with a clear formal trajectory, comprising 11, 7, 5, 3 and 1 pieces respectively. The listener is kept enthralled, not only by allusions to familiar generic prototypes (*toccata* or *moto perpetuo* at one extreme, nocturne or threnody at the other), but also by a musical language that plays with perceptions about centricity: repeated notes or chords reconfigure traditional, even tonal identities as much as they contradict them. All this is accomplished with a mastery of piano style in which the entire history of keyboard virtuosity from Frescobaldi to Ligeti is thrown into the melting pot.

The Book of Elements began with a commission from Roger Woodward, and Rolf Hind, Nicolas Hodges and Ian Pace have all been associated with individual volumes. But Noriko Kawai has become most closely involved with this music, and she offers an unfailingly persuasive realisation, helped by a recording of exemplary immediacy and atmosphere. While she has ample reserves of strength for the many episodes of turbulence, the delicacy with which she plays the soft yet immensely intricate polyphony of the third piece of Volume 3 is even more remarkable.

Dillon manages to use all the instrument's traditional technical devices for prolonging sound with barely a hint of cliché. The final dispersal of energy at the end of the fifth volume, coming as it does after a positive *Hammerklavier* of trills and tremolos, is one of the great moments of early 21st-century music, simply because it speaks as much of affirmation as of dissolution. It sets the seal on a memorable release.

Ernö Dohnányi   Hungarian 1877-1960

Dohnányi studied with Thomán and Koessler at the Budapest Academy (1894-7) and came quickly to international eminence as both pianist and composer. After teaching at the Berlin Hochschule (1905-15) he returned to Budapest and worked there as pianist, teacher, conductor and composer. His influence reached generations in all spheres of musical life and he is considered one of the chief architects of 20th-century Hungarian musical culture; he championed the music of Bartók and Kodály. He also toured internationally as a pianist, ranking among the greatest of his time, and as a conductor (his pupils included Solti). He left Hungary in 1944 and in 1949 settled in the USA. His works are in a Brahmsian style, crossed with Lisztian virtuosity and thematic transformation; they include two symphonies (1901, 1944), two piano concertos (1898, 1947), two piano quintets (1895, 1914) and two violin concertos (1915, 1950), the popular Variations on a Nursery Song for piano and orchestra (1914) and three string quartets (1899, 1906, 1926). GROVEmusic

Variations on a Nursery Theme, Op 25

Dohnányi Variations on a Nursery Theme
Brahms Piano Concerto No 1 in D minor, Op 15
Mark Anderson pf **Hungarian State Symphony
Orchestra / Adám Fischer**
Nimbus NI5349 (75' · DDD)   Ⓕ

Mark Anderson gives a glittering performance
of the Dohnányi, and a spontaneous one at that;
he's superbly accompanied by Adám Fischer and
the Hungarian State SO. Nimbus's recording is
admirable in everything but the backward placing of the woodwind in general and the bassoons
in particular. One thing that the Dohnányi
Variations share with the D minor Brahms Concerto is a passionate minor key opening. Again
Fischer and his Hungarian orchestra are quite
superb, the playing incisive and gloweringly
vivid. It's a measure, too, of the accord that exists
between conductor and soloist that the pianist
enters the fray with the perfectly groomed musical manners of a soloist in a Baroque concerto.
And it's the logic of Anderson's playing, his
sweet reasonableness, that holds the attention,
even though Brahmsians may find Anderson a
shade light-toned in bravura passages. The
Brahms obviously faces tough competition, but
the Dohnányi is without doubt a fine performance in its own right.

Variations on a Nursery Theme, Op 25[a] Der Schleier
der Pierrette – Pierrot's Love-lament; Waltz-rondo;
Merry Funeral March; Wedding waltz. Suite in F sharp
minor, Op 19.
[a]**Howard Shelley** pf **BBC Philharmonic Orchestra /
Matthias Bamert**
Chandos CHAN9733 (70' · DDD)   Ⓕ⮞

Dohnányi's penchant for quality musical entertainment bore popular fruit with his perennially fresh *Variations on a Nursery Theme*.
Howard Shelley's performance is a model of
wit and style, blending in with the orchestra
whenever the moment seems right and employing an ideal brand of *rubato*. Bamert's conducting is properly portentous in the Introduction
and charming elsewhere, whether in the music-
box delights of the fifth variation, the animated
bustle of the sixth or the seventh's novel scoring (plenty for the bassoons and bass drum).
Kocsis and Fischer's is still marginally the best
version overall, but Shelley and Bamert are no
less musical.

Lovely, too, is the F sharp minor Suite, especially the opening *Andante con variazioni* which
seems to straddle the worlds of Dvořák and
Elgar (try the serene string choirs from 9'35").
The stamping *Scherzo* brings to mind the
Scherzo from Bruckner's Ninth Symphony, and
the tuneful Rondo finale has a striking resemblance to a key passage in the *Rondo-burleske* in
Mahler's Ninth.

Also included is the very first recording of *The
Veil of Pierrette*, four scenes from a mimed

entertainment dating from 1908-9. The best
movement is the exuberant 'Wedding Waltz'
(track 21), rumbustious music, carefree and
beautifully scored. Chandos has come up with a
dazzlingly realistic recording. A peach of a
disc.

Ruralia hungarica

Suite, Op 19. Ruralia hungarica. American Rhapsody
Danubia Symphony Orchestra / Domonkos Héja
Warner Classics 2564 62409-2 (71' · DDD)   Ⓕ⮞

Good to have Dohnányi delivered in bright,
local packaging. The substantial Suite, Op 19,
revisits Brahmsian vistas, the string-writing
especially, and at around the seven-minute
mark into the sizeable theme-and-variations
first movement there's a vivid premonition of
Bartók and Bluebeard's cache of jewels (put
together some 10 years later). Clean, incisive,
light in texture – Héja's still-young orchestra is
all of these and projects a subtly individual
personality, at once grainy and slimline, if not
yet quite the equal of Iván Fischer's more
colourful Budapest Festival band. The Danubia's playing of the Suite's *Scherzo* (echoes of
the Russian late-Romantics) and momentarily
Mahlerian finale is quite brilliant, whereas the
strings do very nicely in the exotic *Romanza*
slow movement.

The somewhat later suite *Ruralia hungarica* is
less 'earth under the fingernails' (which is what
Bartók and Kodály were offering) than peasant
life spied from the business lounge. The suite's
lyrical centrepiece is the dusky, rhapsodic *Adagio
non troppo*, widely known out of context as a
'Gypsy Andante'. If you don't immediately
recognise it, be patient: the big theme sweeps in
at around the two-minute mark. The more
memorable of the fast movements, pungently
played here, is the pentatonic *Presto* with its
coincidental echoes of American-Indian music,
while the finale is charmingly childlike in its
simplicity.

How different the relatively late and infinitely
more complex *American Rhapsody*, a melange of
traditional tunes woven into a contrapuntal
tapestry that would have made even Reger green
with envy. Good to hear once or twice, especially when played with conviction and just a
touch of wistfulness – which is how it's played
here. Good sound.

Piano Quintets

Piano Quintets[a] – No 1 in C minor, Op 1; No 2 in E flat
minor, Op 26. Suite in the Old Style, Op 24 [a]**Vanbrugh
Quartet** (Gregory Ellis, Elizabeth Charleson vns Simon
Aspell va Christopher Marwood vc) **Martin Roscoe** pf
ASV CDDCA915 (70' · DDD)   Ⓕ

Dohnányi's First Piano Quintet, Op 1, written
when the composer was only 18, is a work of
abounding confidence and energy that's played

here with suitable verve and exuberance. Roscoe and the Vanbrugh Quartet luxuriate in lush, romantic textures in the first movement, and delight in the melodic exchanges of the warmly expressive *Adagio*. Moreover, their expression of Hungarian flavour, evident in the *Scherzo*'s jaunty cross-rhythms and the engagingly dance-like finale, has considerable charm.

The Second Quintet, written some 19 years later, shows a striking advance in technique. Sensitive evocation of atmosphere in the first movement by Roscoe and the Vanbrugh Quartet highlights both Dohnányi's more searching harmonic language and his remarkably fresh and imaginative approach to form.

The performers deftly blend the *Intermezzo*'s faintly Viennese character with the flamboyant toccata material, and the final movement's fusion of slow movement and finale is ingeniously turned from sombre minor to radiant major. Both the quintets display Dohnányi's considerable pianistic skills; the *Suite in the Old Style* being a highly effective display of the composer's parody of Baroque keyboard techniques. Roscoe's evident sympathy for his music contributes to this arrestingly persuasive account, which fully exploits the work's rich variety of style and technique.

Gaetano Donizetti Italian 1797-1848

Donizetti was of humble origins but received help and a solid musical education (1806-14) from Mayr, producing apprentice operas and many sacred and instrumental works before establishing himself at Naples with La zingara (1822). Here regular conducting and a succession of new works (two to five operas a year) marked the real start of his career. With the international triumph of Anna Bolena (1830, Milan) he freed himself from Naples; the further successes of L'elisir d'amore and Lucrezia Borgia (1832, 1833, Milan), Marino Faliero (1835, Paris) and the archetype of Italian Romantic opera, Lucia di Lammermoor (1835, Naples), secured his pre-eminence. Some theatrical failures, however, as well as trouble with the censors and disappointment over losing the directorship of the Naples Conservatory to Mercadante, caused him to leave for Paris, where besides successful French versions of his earlier works he brought out in 1840 La fille du régiment and La favorite. His conducting of Rossini's Stabat mater (1842, Bologna) and enthusiasm in Vienna for Linda di Chamounix (1842) led to his appointment as Kapellmeister to the Austrian court. Declining health began to affect his work from this time, but in Don Pasquale (1843, Paris) he produced a comic masterpiece, and in the powerful Maria di Rohan (1843, Vienna), Dom Sébastien, roi di Portugal (1843, Paris) and Caterina Cornaro (1844, Naples) some of his finest serious music.

Donizetti's reputation rests on his operas: in comedy his position has never been challenged but in the tragic genre, though his work sums up a whole epoch, no single opera can be considered an unqualified masterpiece. His works survive through the grace and spontaneity *of their melodies, their formal poise, their effortless dramatic pace, their fiery climaxes and above all the romantic vitality underlying their artifice. Like Bellini, Donizetti epitomised the Italian Romantic spirit of the 1830s. Having imitated Rossini's formal, florid style for ten years (1818-28) he gradually shed heavily embellished male-voice parts, conceiving melodies lyrically and allowing the drama to determine ensemble structures.*

From 1839 his style was further enriched by fuller orchestration and subtler, more varied harmony. If he contributed nothing so distinctive to the post-Rossinian tradition as Bellini's 'heavenly' melody, he still showed a more fluent technique and a wider-ranging invention, from the brilliant to the expressive and sentimental. He was particularly responsive to the individual qualities of his singers, including Persiani (Lucia), Pasta and Ronzi de Begnis (Anna Bolena, Maria Stuarda, Roberto Devereux), the baritone Giorgio Ronconi and the tenors Fraschini and Moriani (L'elisir d'amore, Lucia).

Although his practical facility and readiness to adapt scores themselves constructed of 'spare-part' set forms once brought criticism, since 1950 revivals and reassessment as well as a fuller understanding of the theatrical practices of his day have restored Donizetti to critical and popular favour. GROVEmusic

Anna Bolena

Anna Bolena
Maria Callas sop Anna Bolena **Nicola Rossi-** ⊞
Lemeni bass Enrico VIII **Giulietta Simionato** mez
Giovanna Seymour **Gianni Raimondi** ten Riccardo
Percy **Plinio Clabassi** bass Rochefort **Gabriella
Carturan** mez Smeton **Luigi Rumbo** ten Hervey
**Chorus and Orchestra of La Scala, Milan /
Gianandrea Gavazzeni**
EMI mono ② 566471-2 (140' · ADD · T/t) Recorded
live 1957 Ⓜ↦

One of Callas's unique qualities was to inspire an audience with the sense of a great occasion, and to key-up a sympathetic conductor into the production of something to match her own intensity and the public's expectations. Here she gives one of her finest performances. The first impression is a vocal one, in the sense of the sheer beauty of sound. Then, in the first solo, 'Come innocente giovane', addressing Jane Seymour, she's so clean in the cut of the voice and the style of its usage, delicate in her fioriture, often exquisite in her shading, that anyone, ignorant of the Callas legend, would know immediately that this is an artist of patrician status. There are marvellous incidental moments, and magnificent *crescendos*, into, for instance, 'per pietà delmio spavento' and 'segnata è la mia sorte', culminating in the Tower scene.

Unfortunately, the singers at her side hardly measure up. Simionato has a splendid voice that nevertheless bumps as it goes into the low register and isn't reliably steady in many passages, while the manner is too imperious and unresponsive. The tenor role has been reduced by Gavazzeni's cuts, but Gianni Raimondi makes limited impression in what remains; and, as the King, Rossi-Lemeni produces that big but somewhat woolly tone that became increasingly characteristic. Even so, the great ensembles still prove worthy of the event, and the recording, which is clear without harshness or other distortion, conveys the special quality of this memorable evening with remarkable vividness and fidelity.

For those who insist on a modern recording, there's an imaginatively conducted 1994 performance on Nightingale Classics by Elio Boncompagni, with Edita Gruberová in the title-role. But this Callas/Gavazzeni set is in a different class altogether.

Dom Sébastien, roi de Portugal

Dom Sébastien, roi de Portugal
Vesselina Kasarova mez Zayda **Giuseppe Filianoti** ten Dom Sébastien **Alastair Miles** bass Dom Juam de Sylva **Simon Keenlyside** bar Abayaldos **Carmelo Carrado Caruso** bar Camoëns **Robert Gleadow** bass Dom Henrique **John Upperton** ten Dom Antonio **Andrew Slater** bass Ben-Sélim
Chorus and Orchestra of the Royal Opera House, Covent Garden / Mark Elder
Opera Rara ③ ORC33 (176' · DDD · S/T/t/N) Ⓕ**OO**

As is usual in this series, Jeremy Commons writes a well informed and judicious introductory essay, and he seems convinced. It was, he says, Donizetti's most ambitious opera. But the nature of that ambition is indicated by the remark of Donizetti which he has just quoted: 'If you could see what a frightening spectacle it presents: Portuguese, Arabs, Procession of Inquisitors, Royal Procession with funeral bier, the subterranean chambers of the Inquisition'. In other words, grand entertainment for the Paris Opéra: big, expensive, sensational. Preferable, surely, is the ambition which produced *Lucia di Lammermoor* and *Don Pasquale*.

The performance raises fewer questions, though enough is said about textual revisions for the Vienna premiere to make one wonder whether the Paris original is indeed always the best version. More immediately, some doubts arise about the casting. It seems strange that the major role of Camoëns (who on his return to Lisbon has one of the two best-known arias) should be given to a baritone whose voice-production is so unsteady when at hand is Simon Keenlyside, whose own role, well as he sings it, hardly makes best use of a singer of his quality. Something similar is true of Alastair Miles, whose sympathetic *basso cantante* is not a natural choice for the vindictive Grand Inquisitor. The two principals, however, are truly excellent: Kasarova so rich in voice and vivid in expression, Filianoti a tenor with brilliantly focused tone impressively supporting his place at the centre of the opera. Orchestra and chorus are at all times responsive, and Mark Elder conducts with energy and imagination. If you

need convincing, here are three passages in which opera and recording might be sampled at their best: Zayda's duets with Sébastien (Act 2) and with Abayaldos (Act 3), and the grand ensemble of Act 4.

Don Pasquale

Don Pasquale
Renato Bruson bar Don Pasquale **Eva Mei** sop Norina **Frank Lopardo** ten Ernesto **Thomas Allen** bar Malatesta **Alfredo Giacomotti** bass Notary **Bavarian Radio Chorus; Munich Radio Orchestra / Roberto Abbado**
RCA Victor Red Seal ② 09026 61924-2
(120' · DDD · T/t) Ⓕ

Roberto Abbado balances equably the witty and more serious sides of this score, finding a gratifying lightness in the 'A quel vecchio' section of the Act 1 finale and creating a delightful sense of expectancy as Pasquale preens himself while awaiting his intended bride. Abbado plays the score complete and respects Donizetti's intentions. This set has many strengths and few weaknesses. Pasquale is usually assigned to a veteran singer and with Bruson you hear a voice hardly touched by time and a technique still in perfect repair. Apart from weak low notes, he sings and acts the part with real face, and his vital diction is a pleasure to hear. He works well with Thomas Allen's nimble, wily Malatesta, an inspired piece of casting. Like Bruson, Allen sings every note truly and relishes his words.

Eva Mei's Norina is an ebullient creature with a smile in her tone. The edge to her voice seems just right for Norina though others may find it tends towards the acerbic under pressure. Her skills in coloratura are as exemplary as you would expect from a reigning Queen of Night. Lopardo is that rare thing, a tenor who can sing in an exquisite half-voice, yet has the metal in his tone to suggest something heroic in 'E se fia', the cabaletta to 'Cercherò lontana terra', which in turn is sung in a plangent, loving way, just right. The recording here is exemplary.

L'elisir d'amore

L'elisir d'amore
Mariella Devia sop Adina **Roberto Alagna** ten Nemorino **Pietro Spagnoli** bar Belcore **Bruno Pratico** bar Dulcamara **Francesca Provvisionato** mez Giannetta **Tallis Chamber Choir; English Chamber Orchestra / Marcello Viotti**
Erato ② 4509-98483-2 (129' · DDD) Ⓜ▷

This set is a delight, making one fall in love all over again with this delightful comedy of pastoral life. Roberto Alagna, disciple of Pavarotti, sings Nemorino with all his mentor's charm and a rather lighter tone appropriate to the role. He also evinces just the right sense of vulnerability and false bravado that lies at the heart of Nemorino's predicament. He's partnered by Mariella

Devia who has every characteristic needed for the role of Adina. With a fine sense of buoyant rhythm, she sings fleetly and uses the coloratura to enhance her reading. She can spin a long, elegiac line where it's needed, and her pure yet full tone blends well with that of her colleagues. She also suggests all Adina's high spirits and flirtatious nature. The other principals, though not as amusing in their interpretations as some predecessors, enter into the ensemble feeling of the performance. All are helped by the lively but controlled conducting of Viotti and by the ideal recording.

L'elisir d'amore (sung in English)
Mary Plazas sop Adina **Barry Banks** ten Nemorino
Ashley Holland bass Belcore **Andrew Shore** bar
Dulcamara **Helen Williams** sop Giannetta
**Geoffrey Mitchell Choir; Philharmonia Orchestra /
David Parry**
Chandos Opera in English Series ② CHAN3027
(133' · DDD · T)   Ⓕ🅑▶

'Prima la musica' no doubt, but in this instance the words should perhaps take their share of the credit first. The late Arthur Jacobs, who was an expert on Arthur Sullivan, provides a translation that might almost be the work of W S Gilbert. A resourceful vocabulary and a keen ear for verbal rhythms are its main technical assets, and a natural sense of humour rather than the untiring facetiousness of a self-conscious clever-dick is the source of its wit. Dulcamara is a Gilbertian figure to start with, so the translator isn't forcing an entrance for his hobby-horse, and any inventions are all in the spirit of the thing. The Gilbertian element emerges again when Andrew Shore, in the Barcarolle, sings his part of 'elderly Senator' in the tones of Sir Henry Lytton. Generally his portrayal is well sung and gracefully turned, as is Ashley Holland's Sergeant Belcore. The lovers have light, well-matched voices, Mary Plazas avoiding the pert, hard character-note and vocal tone that can make Adina so unsympathetic, and Barry Banks giving particular pleasure with the freedom and clarity of his upper notes.

The playing of the Philharmonia under David Parry calls for special remark: from the Overture onwards (with its delightfully chirruping woodwind) there are passages in the score that find a flavour, their own by rights but usually lost because not sought-out. The recording is one of the series' best.

L'elisir d'amore
Angela Gheorghiu sop Adina **Roberto Alagna** ten
Nemorino **Roberto Scaltriti** bar Belcore **Simone
Alaimo** bass Dulcamara **Elena Dan** sop Giannetta
**Lyon National Opera Chorus and Orchestra /
Evelino Pidò** Stage director **Frank Dunlop**
Video director **Brian Large**
Decca 📀 074 103-9DH (177' · 16:9 · 2.0 & 5.1 · 0)
Includes documentary 'Love Potion', a behind-the-
scenes look at the making of the production   Ⓕ
Frank Dunlop's witty, unvarnished view of

Donizetti's country comedy, updated to the 1930s, is delightful to see, wondrous to hear. Gheorghiu and Alagna make an ideal partnership as capricious girl and shy bumpkin. They both act and sing their roles to near perfection in a staging that exposes the heart and heartlessness as much as the fun of this work.

Singing with every care for tone and nuance, Gheorghiu presents Adina as by turns, haughty, flighty, concerned, annoyed when the other girls paw him, and finally tender when love at last triumphs, and she finds the vocal equivalent for each mood. Not so versatile vocally, but always tidy and responsive to the text, Alagna makes an attractively naive, emotionally vulnerable Nemorino. Scaltriti's Belcore is made deliberately unsympathetic by Dunlop and at times he seems to be overblowing his basically attractive voice. There need be no reservations about Alaimo's witty yet genial Dulcamara: all the *buffo* elements of the part are there but never exaggerated. Evelino Pidò conducts a trim account of the score, his often fast speeds justified by the way his singers enjoy them in terms of athletic delivery. Brian Large's video direction is predictably exemplary. The sound and widescreen picture make us feel present at an obviously enjoyable night at the opera.

La fille du régiment

La fille du régiment
Joan Sutherland sop Marie **Luciano Pavarotti** ten
Tonio **Spiro Malas** bass Sulpice **Monica Sinclair** contr
Marquise **Edith Coates** contr Duchess **Jules Bruyère**
bass Hortensius **Eric Garrett** bar Corporal **Alan
Jones** ten Peasant **Chorus and Orchestra of the
Royal Opera House, Covent Garden / Richard
Bonynge**
Decca ② 414 520-2DH2 (107' · ADD · T/t) Recorded
1968   Ⓕ🅞🅞▶

Even Joan Sutherland has rarely, if ever, made an opera recording so totally enjoyable and involving as this. With the same cast (including chorus and orchestra) as at Covent Garden, it was recorded immediately after a series of live performances in the Royal Opera House, and both the comedy and the pathos come over with an intensity born of communication with live audiences. That impression is the more vivid on this superb CD transfer. As with some of Decca's early CD transfers, you could do with more bands to separate items and it strikes one as odd not to indicate separately the most spectacular of Luciano Pavarotti's contributions, his brief but important solo in the finale to Act 1, which was the specific piece which prompted the much-advertised boast 'King of the High Cs'. For those who want to find it, it comes at 2'58" in band 13 of the first disc. Dazzling as the young Pavarotti's singing is, it's Sutherland's performance which, above all, gives glamour to the set, for here in the tomboy Marie she found a character through whom she could at once display her vocal brilliance, her ability to convey pathos and equally her sense of fun. The reunion of Marie with the men of her regiment and later with Tonio makes one of the most heartwarming operatic scenes on record.

The recording is one of Decca's most brilliant, not perhaps quite so clear on inner detail as some, but more atmospheric. Though there are one or two deliberately comic touches that approach the limit of vulgarity, the production is generally admirable. The sound at once takes one to the theatre, without any feeling of a cold, empty studio.

Lucia di Lammermoor

Lucia di Lammermoor
Maria Callas sop Lucia **Ferruccio Tagliavini** ten [H] Edgardo **Piero Cappuccilli** bar Enrico **Bernard Ladysz** bass Raimondo **Leonard del Ferro** ten Arturo **Margreta Elkins** mez Alisa **Renzo Casellato** ten Normanno **Philharmonia Chorus and Orchestra / Tullio Serafin**
EMI Callas Edition ② 556284-2 (142 minutes · ADD · T/t) Recorded 1959

Ⓕ❶❶❶❶➔

Callas was certainly more fallible here than in her first Lucia for Serafin in 1953, but the subtleties of interpretation are much greater; she's the very epitome of Scott's gentle, yet ardently intense heroine, and the special way she inflects words and notes lifts every passage in which she's concerned out of the ordinary gamut of soprano singing. In that sense she's unique, and this is certainly one of the first offerings to give to an innocent ear or a doubter to help convince them of Callas's greatness. The earlier part of the Mad scene provides the most convincing evidence of all. Then the pathos of 'Alfin son tua', even more that of 'Del ciel clemente' are here incredibly eloquent, and the coloratura is finer than it was in 1953, if not always so secure at the top. Tagliavini, after a rocky start, offers a secure, pleasing, involving Edgardo. Cappuccilli, then in his early prime, is a forceful but not insensitive Enrico, Bernard Ladysz a sound Raimondo. Serafin is a far more thoughtful, expressive Donizettian than his rivals on other sets, confirming this as the most persuasive account of the opera ever recorded.

Additional recommendations

Lucia di Lamermoor [H]
Callas Lucia **di Stefano** Edgardo **Berlin RIAS Symphony Orchestra / Karajan**
EMI mono ② 566438-2 (119' · ADD) Recorded live Ⓜ
A great event: two great musicians striking sparks off each other. Karajan directs a white-hot performance and Callas sings with huge passion.

Sutherland Lucia **Pavarotti** Edgardo **ROHO / Bonynge**
Decca ② 4781513 (140' · ADD) Recorded 1971

Ⓕ❶❶➔

Sutherland's second commercial recording finds her on great form in one of her signature roles. Pavarotti is a stylish Edgardo and Bonynge is the most sympathetic of conductors.

Maria Stuarda

Maria Stuarda (sung in English)
Janet Baker mez Maria Stuarda **Rosalind Plowright** sop Elisabetta **David Rendall** ten Leicester **John Tomlinson** bass Talbot **Alan Opie** bar Cecil **Angela Bostock** sop Anna **English National Opera Chorus and Orchestra / Sir Charles Mackerras**
Chandos Opera in English Series ② CHAN3017 (136' · ADD · N/t) Recorded live 1982 Ⓜ❶

This revival celebrates the association of Janet Baker and Charles Mackerras within the context of the ENO company and one of its most memorable productions. For those who saw this, the set will call the stage back to mind with wonderful vividness; but the appeal goes well beyond that, preserving a performance stamped with the strong individuality that confers the status of a gramophone classic. This brought a personal triumph for Janet Baker and it impresses afresh by the distinctiveness of her vocal characterisation. It isn't every singer who reflects, or re-creates, the distinctive identities through vocal colour and 'registration'. Everyone who was there will remember the 'Royal bastard!' in confrontation with Elizabeth, but equally powerful, and more regal, is her command – 'Be silent! Leave me!' – to the Lord Chancellor of England who brings to Fotheringay news of her condemnation to death. By contrast, the quieter moments can be immensely moving, as, for instance, in the line in which she acknowledges an unexpected generosity in her great opponent. In that role, Rosalind Plowright gives what surely must have been one of the supreme performances of her career. The writing for Elizabeth makes immense demands of the singer, and in these fearsome opening solos the technical challenges are triumphantly met.

John Tomlinson's massive bass commands attention (which it doesn't then always reward with evenness of production). The male soloists have not the most grateful of roles, but Alan Opie's Cecil shows its quality in the duet with Elizabeth, and David Rendall endows the ineffectual Leicester with plenty of Italianate ardour. The chorus has limited opportunities, and has certainly been heard to better advantage on other occasions.

A word of warning must be added concerning texts which involve cuts and adaptations. The transpositions are defended as standard practice when an exceptional mezzo-soprano (such as Malibran) took a soprano role, in the present instance merely conforming to the lower orchestral pitch of Donizetti's time. However, it's unlikely that at this date the set would be bought or rejected with this kind of consideration foremost.

What remains are the strong positives, most notably the vitality of Mackerras's conducting and the glory of Baker's singing. Also, for those to whom this is a priority, the opera is given in clear English.

Poliuto

Poliuto   **H**
Franco Corelli ten Poliuto **Maria Callas** sop Paolina **Ettore Bastianini** bar Severo **Nicola Zaccaria** bass Callistene **Piero de Palma** ten Nearco **Rinaldo Pelizzoni** ten Felice **Virgilio Carbonari, Giuseppe Morresi** basses Christians **Chorus and Orchestra of La Scala, Milan / Antonino Votto**
EMI mono ② 565448-2 (111' · ADD · T/t) Recorded live 1960   Ⓜ

This is the first appearance of this recording in the official canon, by incorporation into EMI's Callas Edition; and the quality is certainly an improvement on the previous 'unofficial' incarnation. The sound is clear and faithful to the timbre of the voices, which are slightly favoured in the balance at the expense of the orchestra. With it comes unforgettable testimony to what was clearly a great night at La Scala. Its place in the Callas history owes less to the importance of this new role in her repertory than to the triumph of her return to the house she had left in high dudgeon in 1958. The part of Paolina in this Roman tragedy is restricted in opportunities and leaves the centre of the stage to the tenor. In other ways it suits her remarkably well, the Second Act in particular involving the heroine in grievous emotional stress with music that here runs deep enough to give it validity.

There's a big part for the chorus, which sings with fine Italian sonority. Nicola Zaccaria, La Scala's leading *basso cantabile*, has not quite the sumptuous quality of his predecessors, Pasero and Pinza, but is still in their tradition. Ettore Bastianini is rapturously received and, though wanting in polish and variety of expression, uses his firm and resonant voice to exciting effect. The tenor *comprimario*, Piero de Palma cuts a by no means inadequate vocal figure by the side of Corelli, who's mostly stupendous: it isn't just the ring and range of voice that impress, but a genuinely responsive art, his aria 'Lasciando la terra' in Act 3 providing a fine example. It's for his part in the opera, quite as much as for Callas's, that the recording will be valued.

Rosmonda d'Inghilterra

Rosmonda d'Inghilterra
Renée Fleming sop Rosmonda **Bruce Ford** ten Enrico II **Nelly Miricioiu** sop Leonora di Guienna **Alastair Miles** bass Gualtiero Clifford **Diana Montague** mez Arturo **Geoffrey Mitchell Choir; Philharmonia Orchestra / David Parry**
Opera Rara ② ORC13 (150' · DDD · T/t)   Ⓕ

The performance of this, Donizetti's 41st opera,

could hardly be improved. And there's scarcely more than a single item in which Donizetti seems not to be writing with genuine creativity. Parry conducts with what feels like a natural rightness and the playing of the Philharmonia is of unvaryingly high quality – the Overture is one of Donizetti's best, and the orchestral score shares interest on equable terms with the voice-parts. These include two virtuoso roles for sopranos, who in the final scene confront each other in duet. As Rosmonda, Renée Fleming shows once again that not only has she one of the most lovely voices of our time but that she's also a highly accomplished technician and a sympathetic stylist. Nelly Miricioiu is the older woman, the Queen whose music encompasses a wide range of emotions with an adaptable vocal character to match. She fits the Second Act more happily than the First, where for much of the time the tone appears to have lost its familiar incisive thrust. Bruce Ford is an excellent, incisive Enrico, and Alastair Miles makes an authoritative father and councillor as Clifford. The *travesto* role of Arturo is taken by the ever welcome Diana Montague, and it's good to find that a solo has been dutifully included for 'him' in Act 2, even if it's a less than inspired piece of music. The only complaint concerns balance, which sometimes accords prominence and recession in a somewhat arbitrary way. The opera and performance, however, are strong enough to take that on board..

Jonathan Dove   British b1959

Jonathan Dove is best known as a composer of operas and choral music. His output includes a dozen operas, including the successful airport-comedy Flight, which premiered at Glyndebourne; it has since been broadcast on television, and been performed to acclaim in The Netherlands and Belgium, and has recently received its US premiere at the St Louis Opera. He has arranged a number of operas for English Touring Opera and the City of Birmingham Touring Opera (now Birmingham Opera Company), including in 1990 an 18-player two-evening adaptation of Wagner's Der Ring des Nibelungen.

Operas

Siren Song
Brad Cooper ten Davey Palmer **Mattijs van de Woerd** bar Jonathan Reed **Amaryllis Dieltiens** sop Diana Reed **Mark Omvlee** ten Regulator **Marijn Zwitserlood** bass-bar Captain **John Edward Serrano** spkr Wireless Operator
Siren Ensemble / Henk Guittart
Chandos CHAN10472 (78' · DDD · S/T/N) Recorded live at the Grachtenfestival, Amsterdam, in August 2007   ⒻⒷ

Not since Benjamin Britten has a British composer succeeded in writing operas which communicate with such clarity and coherence to their audience as those by Jonathan Dove. The secret to his success lies partly in his experiences of writing 'community' operas, resulting in refreshingly open and accessible works. But there's also plenty of grit and grime beneath the polished veneer of his streamlined style, especially when the plot is as equally compelling and disturbing as it is in *Siren Song*.

The opera recounts the true story of a Royal Navy sailor (Davey) who becomes the victim of an elaborate hoax. Duped by means of letter exchanges into believing that the beautiful and alluring Diana lies waiting for him on terra firma upon completing Navy service, the hapless sailor parts with thousands of pounds in anticipation of marital bliss, all of which lines the pockets of Jonathan, the perpetrator of this ruse.

Dove's dramatic skill lies in his ability to create a seamless continuity by weaving cell-like musical figures from one scene to the next. His subtle manipulation of an undulating pattern first heard in the opening seascape scene is adapted to accompany a whole host of other states and situations. Given the seafaring setting, it's hardly surprising that echoes of Debussy's *La mer*, Britten's *Peter Grimes* and Adams's *The Death of Klinghoffer* rise to the surface. Dove also shares with the latter composer an ability to generate large-scale structures from the simplest of musical means. But it is testimony to the Englishman's eclecticism that he skilfully appropriates such references into a language undeniably his own.

This live recording possesses its fair share of onstage clanks and offstage coughs, but at least they all lend an air of vraisemblance to proceedings, and the opera's rapid descent into the depths of deceit and desperation is effectively portrayed, despite the absence of visuals.

The Adventures of Pinocchio
Victoria Simmonds *mez* Pinocchio **Jonathan Summers** *bar* Geppetto **Mary Plazas** *sop* Blue Fairy **Rebecca Bottone** *sop* Cricket; Parrot **Graeme Broadbent** *bass* Puppeteer; Ape-Judge; Ringmaster; Big Green Fisherman **Allan Clayton** *ten* Lampwick **Mark Wilde** *ten* Cat **James Laing** *counterten* Fox; Coachman **Carole Wilson** *mez* Pigeon; Snail **Chorus and Orchestra of Opera North / David Parry**
Stage director **Martin Duncan**
Opus Arte ② 𝗗𝗩𝗗 OA1005D (3h 33' · NTSC · 16:9 · PCM stereo and DTS 5.1 · 0) Ⓕ
Recorded live at Sadler's Wells Theatre, London, in 2008. Includes Interviews, Synopsis and Cast gallery

The story of Pinocchio, as told by Carlo Collodi, is best known through the Disney cartoon version, an equivocal movie generally less sympathetic than other Disney features, but giving a graphic if partial view of the story. Jonathan Dove with his librettist, Alasdair Middleton, in this operatic version in two substantial acts gives a much fuller idea of the story starting with the moment when Gepetto the woodman finds a talking log in the forest.

Gepetto is about to chop it up when it speaks to him demanding that he preserve it, later demanding that he should bring out the secret it contains, nothing less than the puppet, Pinocchio, who kicks him as his legs appear. Dove tells the story in brief scenes, 12 in Act 1, nine in Act 2, which carry the story on swiftly and effectively, going on to one sequence involving a circus – cue for pastiche circus music – also one when Pinocchio and Gepetto are trapped inside a whale, from which they escape thanks to Pinocchio's cunning in realising that this asthmatic animal is asleep with its mouth open. Generally the scenes follow the development of Pinocchio from rebellious puppet to kind and considerate boy.

Dove's writing characteristically is colourful and vigorous, with inventive instrumentation, as when Pinocchio refuses to pull a cart when asked by a stranger, denying that he is a donkey – at which Dove has the orchestra briefly making a hee-haw sound. Dove's sharp, jazzy syncopations add to the attractions of the writing, which is generally easily lyrical. This, believe it or not, is Dove's 21st opera, though few are as long or ambitious as this one, which was written for Opera North and given its premiere in 2007.

The performance, filmed live, is excellent, with a cast which includes a number of the singers discovered by the Peter Moores Foundation, and conducted very ably by David Parry, the Foundation's regular conductor. A very welcome issue of a most attractive new opera.

John Dowland English c1563-1626

Dowland became a Catholic while serving the English ambassador in Paris (1580-84) and in 1588 graduated at Oxford. In 1592 he played the lute to the queen, then travelled in Europe, visiting the courts of Brunswick, Kassel, Nuremberg and cities in Italy, where he met Marenzio. He was back in London in 1597, then became a lutenist at the Danish court (1598-1603, 1605-6). On his return he served Lord Walden (1609-12) and eventually achieved his ambition, the post of court lutenist, in 1612. He had been awarded a doctorate by 1621 and played at James I's funeral in 1625. He was succeeded by his son Robert (c1591-1641), also known for the lute collections he edited.

Though known in his day as a virtuoso lutenist and singer, Dowland was also a prolific, gifted composer of great originality. His greatest works are inspired by a deeply felt, tragic concept of life and a preoccupation with tears, sin, darkness and death. In the best of his 84 ayres for voice and lute (published mainly in 4 vols., 1597, 1600, 1603, 1612), he markedly raised the level of English song, matching perfectly in music the mood and emotion of the verse; in his best songs, such as In darknesse let mee dwell, he freed himself of almost all conventions, accompanying the singer's strange, beautiful melody with biting discords to express emotional intensity to an extent unsurpassed at the time. His 70-odd pieces for solo lute include intricate polyphonic fantasias, expressive dances and elaborate variation sets; foremost among his other instrumental music is the variation set Lachrimae, which contains the famous 'Semper Dowland semper dolens', characterising his air of melancholy. But he could also write in a lighter vein, as in the ballett-like Fine Knacks for Ladies. He also wrote psalm settings and spiritual songs. GROVEmusic

Lute Works

A fancy, P73. Pavana Dowlandi Angli. Doulands [P] rounde battell galyarde, P39. The Erle of Darbies galiard, P44. Mistris Norrishis delight, P77. A jig, P78. Galliard, P76. Une jeune fillette, P93. Gagliarda, P103. Squires galliard. A fancy, P72. Sir Henry Umptons funerall. Captayne Pipers galliard, P88. A fantasie, P1 **Bacheler** (arr ?) The Earl of Essex galliard, P89 **Moritz, Landgrave of Hessen** (arr Dowland?) Pavin **Joachim Van Den Hove** Pavana Lachrimae **Holborne** Hasellwoods galliard **R Dowland** Sir Thomas Monson, his Pavin and Galliard. Almande
Paul O'Dette *lte*
Harmonia Mundi HMU90 7164 (73' · DDD) [F]

Given the odd transmission of John Dowland's lute music, any 'complete' recording of it's inevitably going to include a fair number of works that can have had little to do with him. Paul O'Dette has boldly put most of these together in his fifth and last volume, adding for good measure the three surviving works of the master's son, Robert Dowland. O'Dette is engagingly candid in expressing his views about the various works and their various degrees of authenticity. The only works he seems to think authentic are the *Sir Thomas Monson* pavan and galliard that survive only under the name of Robert Dowland. The collection is none the less fascinating for all that. They are nearly all thoroughly worthwhile pieces, some of them very good indeed; and he ends with what he considers a late adaptation of one of Dowland's most famous fantasies. O'Dette continues to show that in terms of sheer freedom of technique he's hard to challenge among today's lutenists: the often complicated counterpoint is always crystal clear; and he invariably conveys the strongest possible feeling for the formal design of the works. Anyone who's fascinated by the work of the prince of lutenists will want to have this disc.

Preludium, P98. Fantasias – P6; P71. Pavans – [P] Lachrimae, P15; The Lady Russell's Pavan, P17; Pavana Johan Douland, P94; La mia Barbara, P95. Galliards – Frog Galliard, P23; Galliard (upon a galliard by Dan Bachelar), P28; The Lord Viscount Lisle, his Galliard, P38; The Earl of Essex, his Galliard, P42a; Galliard to Lachrimae, P46; A Galliard, P82; Galliard on 'Awake sweet love', P92. An Almand, P96. My Lord Willoughby's Welcome Home, P66a. Loth to departe, P69. The Shoemakers Wife, a Toy, P58. Coranto, P100. Come away, P60
Paul O'Dette *lte*
Harmonia Mundi HMU90 7163 (64' · DDD) [F]

Cadential trills played on one string are a recurrent problem for performers; the less well equipped use a *rallentando* or slur them, while guitarists tend to play them across two strings. No one is more adept at delivering them cleanly and in tempo than O'Dette. It's in the suppleness of his phrasing, clarity of his contrapuntal lines and attention to the functional purpose of every note, that he's pre-eminent – and has the edge over Lindberg. This disc has all the virtues of its predecessors, and though it's doubtful that the Earl of Essex would have been happy to dance his galliard at O'Dette's pace, you can share the sentiment of its last track – you'll be loath to leave it.

'A Dream'

Almains – Sir John Smith his Almain, P47; My Lady Hunsdons Allmande (Puffe), P54. Settings of Ballads and Other Popular Tunes – Fortune my foe, P62. Fantasies and Other Contrapuntal Pieces – Fantasie, P1; Farwell, P3; A Fancy, P73. Galliards – Melancholy Galliard, P25; Galliard (upon a galliard by Dan Bachelar), P28; The Battle Galliard (The King of Denmarke his Galliard), P40; K Darcyes Galliard, P41; The Earl of Essex his Galliard, P42; The Right Honourable Lady Rich her Galliard, P43; The Right Honourable the Lady Cliftons Spirit, P45. Frogg galliard, P90. Jigs, Corantos, Toys, etc – Mrs Whites Nothing, P56. Pavans – Semper Dowland Semper Dolens, P9; Lachrimae, P15; A Dream, P75; La mia Barbara, P95 **Moritz** Pavan
Hopkinson Smith *lte*
Naïve E8896 (69' · DDD) [F]

Hopkinson Smith's latest collection, 'A Dream', invites the listener '...to penetrate the world of the inner senses that is the domain of the lute'. An elegantly constructed programme (built around groups of Hilliard-like portraits and melancholy flights of fancy) tropes sonnet-like at the wonderful *Farwell*, a magical, troubling fantasy that treats its chromatically rising theme contrapuntally while somehow tying all the preceding emotional strands in the programme together. This propels the listener lachrymoneously (*sic* – Smith's word) into an even darker dwelling-place than was expected. In fact, this is the genius of the disc, and what makes it a genuinely moving experience.

Smith's playing, too, is elegant rather than overtly virtuosic, although he has technique to burn, as anyone who's familiar with his numerous recordings will tell you. He prefers a more suggestive, diffuse approach to Dowland's music (compared with, say, Paul O'Dette). As a result, the numerous diminutions serve to intensify the character of each piece in a profound and subtle way.

Lute Songs

The First Booke of Songes or Ayres – If my [P] complaints could passions moue; Can she excuse my wrongs with vertues cloake; Deare if you change ile neuer chuse againe; Go Cristall teares; Sleepe wayward thoughts; All ye whom loue or fortune hath

betraide; Come againe: sweet loue doth now enuite; Awake sweet loue thou art returnd. The Second Booke of Songs or Ayres – I saw my Lady weepe; Flow my teares fall from your springs; Sorrow sorrow stay, lend true repentant teares; Tymes eldest sonne, old age the heire of ease; Then sit thee down, and say thy 'Nunc Dimitis'; When others sings 'Venite exultemus'; If fluds of tears could clense my follies past; Fine knacks for Ladies, cheap, choise, braue and new; Come ye heavie states of night; Shall I sue, shall I seeke for grace
Paul Agnew ten **Christopher Wilson** lte　　Ⓕ
Metronome METCD1010 (59' · DDD · T)

Paul Agnew is light of step in the quicker songs, and he languishes longer than most over the variously sorrowful ones. Many of his choices now enjoy 'pop' status, but his inclusion of the beautiful trilogy of which 'Tymes eldest sonne' is the first part is particularly welcome. He receives the most sensitive of support from Wilson, clearly articulated, warm in tone, and perfectly complementary in completing the contrapuntal textures – neither intrusively nor coyly balanced with the voice. Dowland's lute songs have generated many fine recordings, as they richly deserve, and here's one more, beautifully presented, with a booklet containing all the texts.

Lachrimae, or Seven Teares

Lachrimae, or Seaven Teares.　　Ⓟ
First Booke of Songs[a] – Come heavy sleepe; Go teares. Second Booke of Songs[a] – Sorrow stay; I saw my Lady weepe; Flow my teares
Paul O'Dette lte **The King's Noyse** ([a]Ellen Hargis sop Robert Mealy, Scott Metcalfe, Margriet Tindemans vas Emily Walhout bvn) **David Douglass**-vn
Harmonia Mundi HMU90 7275 (75' · DDD · T/t) Ⓕ ⓄⓄ

The Seaven Teares are the heart of *Lachrimae*; the purpose of the other 14 items is unknown – were they intended to be played together with the Pavans, and if so, in what order?

This present recording is superb in every way. Ellen Hargis sings in sensitive response to her texts and her diction is almost clear enough to make the printed ones in the inlay booklet redundant. The violins of The King's Noyse have a rounder and less edgy sound than those of The Parley of Instruments, and their dynamic ebb and flow is as eloquent as that of Ellen Hargis's voice. The recording itself and the annotation are superb.

With so many options available you pays your money and you takes your choice. Our choice rests firmly with this recording.

Guillaume Dufay　　French c1400-1474

Dufay was acknowledged by his contemporaries as the leading composer of his day. Having been trained as a choirboy at Cambrai Cathedral, where he probably studied under Loqueville, he seems to have entered the service of the Malatesta family in Pesaro some time before 1420. Several of his works from this period were written for important local events. After returning briefly to Cambrai and establishing links with Laon, where he held two benefices, he was a singer in the papal choir in Rome from 1428 until 1433, when he became associated with the Este family in Ferrara and the Dukes of Savoy. He rejoined the papal choir (1435-7), and composed the famous motet Nuper rosarum flores for the dedication of Brunelleschi's dome of Florence Cathedral in 1436, but spent his later years (apart from 1451-8, when he was again in Savoy) at Cambrai, where he was visited as a celebrity by such musicians as Binchois, Tinctoris and Ockeghem. Although he composed up to his death, most of his late works are lost.

Working in a period of relative stability in musical style, Dufay achieved distinction rather by consummate artistry than bold innovation. More than half his compositions, including most of his antiphons, hymns, Magnificats, sequences and single items of the Mass, are harmonisations of chant, with the melody usually in the upper part. Most of his motets are imposing compositions written to celebrate a political, social or religious event; four- and five-part textures, often alternating with duos, are common, two or more texts may be set simultaneously, and isorhythm is sometimes used. Others, in a three-voice, treble-dominated style, are more direct and intimate expressions of religious sentiment. Moving from early paired mass movements to the developing form of the cyclic tenor mass, he was apparently the first to base a cycle on a secular melody. Outstanding among his masses is the Missa 'Ave regina celorum', perhaps his last composition. He also composed secular songs, three-quarters of them rondeaux. As an artist of international fame, he is represented in some 70 MSS in many countries.　　GROVE music

Sacred Music

Sacred Music from Bologna Q15

O sancte Sebastiane. Supremum est mortalibus bonum. Vasilissa, ergo gaude. O gemma, lux et speculum. Kyrie, 'Fons bonitatis'. O beate Sebastiane. Gloria, Q15 No 107. Credo, Q15 No 108. Sanctus and Benedictus, Q15 No 104. Inclita stella maris. Agnus Dei, Q15 No 105. Gloria, 'Spiritus et alme'
The Clerks' Group (William Missin counterten Lucy Ballard alt Chris Watson, Matthew Vine tens Jonathan Arnold bass) / **Edward Wickham** bass
Signum SIGCD023 (60' · DDD · T/t)　　Ⓕ Ⓞ➔

This recording focuses on sacred works by Dufay from a 15th-century manuscript preserved at Bologna and known as Q15. This is a complex source, compiled over a number of years in northern Italy, and containing a wide range of polyphonic repertory, including diverse works by the great Dufay.

This CD isn't in any sense a reconstruction, but a carefully selected anthology of not necessarily very familiar pieces by Dufay. Indeed, this is a really superb recording: vocal lines are well shaped and the sonorities achieved through accuracy of ensemble and pacing result in performances that are decidedly sensual, even dance-like, at times.

Just try the four-voice *Gloria* or the isorhythmic motet *Supremum est mortalibus bonum*, in praise of peace. This extraordinary work composed to commemorate the signing of a peace treaty between the Pope and Holy Roman Emperorelect in 1433 combines just about every musical technique and idiom available to a composer in the first half of the 15th century, complete with, in this interpretation by The Clerks' Group, improvised vocal flourishes on the block chords declaiming the names of the signatories.

Vocal agility – notably in the faster-moving upper parts of *Inclita stella maris* – and a textcentred intensity of projection are hallmarks of this excellent group: only in the three-voice setting of *O beate Sebastiane*, a plea for delivery from the plague, does the approach seem too cool. Elsewhere, even in familiar texts such as the *Sanctus*, there's a real sense of engagement. If you've yet to discover the delights of Dufay, this is an excellent place to start; Dufay fans can't fail to be delighted.

Missa Se la face ay pale. Venite benedicti. Gloriosus Deus. Iudicabunt sancti. Mirabilis Deus. Gaudete iusti. O très piteulx. Se la face ay pale. Magnanime gentis
Binchois Consort (Mark Chambers, William Towers *altos* George Pooley, Christopher Watson, Edwin Simpson, Matthew Vine *tens* Giles Underwood, William Gaunt *basses*) / **Andrew Kirkman**
Hyperion CDA67715 (72' · DDD)   Ⓕ Ⓞ

Se la face ay pale remains Dufay's most approachable Mass, one that is assembled as though elegance of line was Dufay's main criterion of musical excellence. And Andrew Kirkman chooses to treat it as such: at least, he essentially persuades the singers on the contratenor line to keep well down so that borrowed melody in the tenor can come through while allowing the top line to stand out as it must. What the Binchois Consort do here sounds both transparent and natural. The balance is superb; and all lines are presented in a free and supple manner that projects the music very well. This is easy, effortless musicianship.

Meanwhile Kirkman intersperses the five Ordinary movements with movements for the Proper for St Maurice. Much of the music is in three or two voices only, so sounding different from the *Missa Se la face ay pale* and contrasting with it neatly. Only the glowing Offertory is in four voices. Metrical complexities in the *Alleluia* and in the *Offertory* add neat spice to the music. Special credit here should be given to the soloists who sing the long and exposed duos: these have lines and phrases that seem to go on for ever, so they are astonishingly hard to sing, and these musicians do them marvellously.

To fill out the disc they perform three more Dufay pieces that can be associated with the court of Savoy: the song *Se la face ay pale* is heard

in the rarer four-voice version that may not have anything to do with Dufay but is delightful and eminently worth hearing, especially in a spirited performance like this; the famous *Lament for Constantinople*, a touch less transparent than one might wish; and the motet *Magnanime gentis*, sounding as though it was done in a hurry at the end of an exhausting session.

'The Fall of Constantinople'
Anonymous Hierarchical Entrance Rite for a Byzantine Divine Liturgy. Kyrie **Dufay** Vasilissa ergo gaude. Apostolo glorioso. Ecclesiae militantis. Lamentatio Sanctae Matris Ecclesiae Constantinopolitanae **Manuel Chrysaphes the Lampadarios** Lament for the Fall of Constantinople **Manuel Gazes the Lampadarios** Hymn for Great Compline Plousiadenos Canon in honour of Thomas Aquinas: Ode 1. Communion Verse for Mid-Pentacost. Canon for the Council of Florence: Ode 5
Cappella Romana / Alexander Lingas
Cappella Romana CR402CD (74' · DDD)   Ⓕ

English-speaking audiences commonly associate Greek Orthodox plainchant with the music of John Tavener, whose work draws substantially from its ethos. This recording confronts plainchant with the compositions of another Western composer, albeit one from the 15th century, when the two Christian churches were nearly reunited after a thousand-year split. It's even likely that Dufay's singers and their Eastern counterparts had a chance to hear each other in Florence. But these attempts at reconciliation came to nothing, and in 1453 came the event after which this disc is named, and to which Dufay devoted a commemorative lament, which concludes this recital very movingly.

The performance of Western polyphony with voices trained in, or inflected by, Eastern chant is not unfamiliar – Ensemble Organum have been doing it for years. To do so, it's not necessary to invoke a context within which the two might have commingled; as Alexander Lingas observes in his informative note, it's likely that the Greeks found Dufay's polyphony 'incomprehensible'. But it must have been a fascinating confrontation, and it's that sense of occasion that's conveyed here. The range of performance options for the plainchant itself is surprisingly diverse, and an intriguing new light is shed on Dufay's motets: the five-voice *Apostolo glorioso* is particularly striking, although *Ecclesiae militantis* is a touch less sure. The singers are miked more distantly than is usual nowadays for polyphony, but this only adds to the sense of pleasurable unfamiliarity.

Paul Dukas   French 1865-1935

Dukas studied with Guiraud at the Paris Conservatoire (1881-9) and became a friend of Debussy, d'Indy and Bordes. His Franckian leanings are evident in his first published work, the overture Polyeucte (1891), though Beethoven is also suggested, as again in his Symphony in C (1896). But the symphonic scherzo L'apprenti sorcier (1897) is more individual, not least in its augmented-triad and diminished-7th harmonies, which influenced Stravinsky and Debussy. The next years were devoted to the opera Ariane et Barbe-Bleue (1907), though at the same time he produced two piano works of Beethovenian range and power: the Sonata in E flat minor and the Variations, interlude et final sur un thème de Rameau. Dukas self-criticism constricted his later output. Apart from the exotic ballet La péri (1912) he published only a few occasional works. He cultivated craftsmanship to an extreme degree and his orchestration has been widely admired and imitated. His voluminous criticism reveals an unusual breadth of sympathy and he was a conscientious editor of Beethoven, Couperin, Rameau and Scarlatti and an admired teacher at the Conservatoire. GROVEmusic

The Sorcerer's Apprentice

The Sorcerer's Apprentice **Saint-Saëns** Symphony
No 3 in C minor, Op 78, 'Organ'
Simon Preston org
Berlin Philharmonic Orchestra / James Levine
DG 419 617-2GH (47' · DDD)   Ⓕ Ⓑ➡

Levine's account of Dukas' masterpiece is still the best in the catalogue. Levine chooses a fast basic tempo, but justifies his speed by the lightness of his touch and the clean articulation and rhythmic bounce of the Berlin Phil playing help considerably. The climax is thrilling, but Levine reserves something for the moment when the sorcerer returns to quell the flood. In all, it provides a marvellous finish to an exhilarating listening experience. Levine's performance of Saint-Saëns' Third Symphony is also among the best available. The balance between the orchestra and organ, here played powerfully by Simon Preston, is well judged and the overall acoustic very convincing. Levine directs a grippingly individual reading, full of drama and with a consistently imaginative response to the score's detail. The organ entry in the finale is quite magnificent, the excitement of Preston thundering out the main theme physical in its impact. The music expands and blossoms magnificently, helped by the spectacular dynamic range of the recording.

Piano Sonata

Piano Sonata **Decaux** Clairs de lune
Marc-André Hamelin pf
Hyperion CDA67513 (65' · DDD)   Ⓕ Ⓑ➡

Dukas's E flat minor Sonata (1900) is a rare (the only?) French example of the form from this period. Lasting more than 45 minutes, each of its four movements is underpinned by almost unremitting motion. The chromaticism of the first owes an obvious debt to Franck; the second has prescient touches of Scriabin and Debussy; the outer sections of the

third are an Alkanesque toccata with a haunting *mystérieuse* central section, while the equally virtuosic finale shows that while Dukas remains firmly his own man, he also knew his Schumann and Liszt.

Hamelin, one needs hardly say, makes light of any difficulty, clarifying complex textures and subtly highlighting different voices with myriad keyboard colours. It is this facility that sometimes leads to a certain coolness and lack of (audible) engagement. Not here: this performance has an expressive power and intense emotional involvement that make it one of his most successful recordings – and that is saying something.

For those who have never previously encountered Dukas's companion on this CD, Abel Decaux (1869-1943) – and you'd not be alone – was a French organist (pupil of Widor and Guilmant) who studied composition with Massenet. What the composer of *Manon* and *Werther* would have made of the four pieces that comprise *Clairs de lune* (note the plural), one can only guess. Written between 1900 and 1907, they were not published till a year after Massenet's death in 1912. Listen blindfold and you might think, as Roger Nichols points out in his informative notes, that you were listening to Schoenberg or Debussy – except that Decaux's pieces pre-date both of them. Not for everyday listening, but fascinating nevertheless and a further example of this great pianist's extraordinary musical savoir-faire and his invaluable, unflagging curiosity.

Ariane et Barbe-Bleu

Ariane et Barbe-Bleu
Lori Phillips sop Ariane **Patricia Bardon** mez Nurse
Peter Rose bass Barbe-Bleu **Laura Vlasak Nolen**
mez Sélysette **Ana James** sop Ygraine **Daphne**
Touchais sop Mélisande **Sarah-Jane Davies** sop
Bellangère **Graeme Danby** bass Old Peasant **BBC**
Singers and Symphony Orchestra / Leon Botstein
Telarc ② CD80680 (115' · DDD · S/T/t/N)   Ⓕ ⓞ

If you think the libretto of *Pelléas et Mélisande* is impenetrable, try making sense of this: Maurice Maeterlinck's 'prequel' in which Mélisande is one of Bluebeard's imprisoned wives. They are rescued by his latest victim, Ariane, but refuse to leave their tormentor; they prefer his dark castle to the threat posed by the world outside, to which, at the final curtain, Ariane and faithful nurse return.

Georgette Leblanc, Maeterlinck's longtime companion, had been disappointed not to get the role of Mélisande in Debussy's opera in 1902, and there is some feeling that Maeterlinck was offering her a consolation prize – she sang the title-role at the Opéra-Comique premiere in 1907. Ariane is seldom offstage – conversely, Bluebeard hardly appears, and has only a few lines to sing. There is very little action as such, although the crowd of angry peasants break in occasionally with threats against their monstrous lord.

The effect is more like a symphonic poem. There are wonderful moments: when Ariane unlocks the doors of the rooms containing gems; when she breaks open the window and lets light into the dungeon; and in the long final scene as she slowly leaves Bluebeard and his harem to their fate. The subject matter – sexual abuse, the victim's need for their torturer, and the power of suggestion – ought to make the opera attractive for an imaginative theatre director. Leon Botstein makes the strongest possible case for the opera in this new recording, the BBC SO playing Dukas's elaborate score with great élan.

Lori Phillips sings Ariane with great feeling; her voice is rather too similar to that of Patricia Bardon as the Nurse, who also makes a strong impression. Of the other wives, not all of whom sing, Laura Vlasak Nolen has the most substantial part as Sélysette, who declares 'Oh! Tu es pâle, Mélisande…ta robe est en lambeaux', as if she were anticipating Pelléas's words in Debussy's opera.

It would be easy to ridicule some of the more obvious psychological symbolism with which Maeterlinck has weighed down his story and it was destined to be Dukas's only completed opera. But if you have never encountered *Ariane et Barbe-Bleu* it is an instructive and rewarding experience.

Henry Du Mont   French 1610-1684

Du Mont was organist at Maastricht Cathedral before studying in Liège with Hodemont. In 1638 he moved to Paris as organist at StPaul and later compositeur de musique de la Chapelle Royale (1672) and maître de la musique de la Reine (1673-81). The petits motets in his Cantica sacra (1652), influenced by Italian motets, are the first in France with figures and a separate continuo part. Some of the 30 in the Motets à deux voix avec la basse continue (1668) show Du Mount's exploitation of dramatic monody. The Motets à II, III et IV parties (1671) move closer to French models; italianate dialogues co-exist with French dance rhythms, which also affect his Airs à quatre parties (1663). His 20 grand motets, published 1684-6, show him as a miniaturist, excelling in the more intimate moments.
GROVEmusic

Grands motets

'Grands motets pour la chapelle de Louis XIV au Louvre'
Allemandes. Allemande grave. Dialogus de anima. Super flumina Babylonis. Benedic anima mea. Ecce iste venit. Pavane
Pierre Robert Ensemble / Frédéric Desenclos *org*
Alpha ALPHA069 (73' · DDD · T/t)   Ⓕ**OO**

Henry Du Mont has long been credited as one of the creators, alongside Lully, of the *grand motet*, the opulent style of church composition for soloists, choir and orchestra associated with Louis XIV's chapel at Versailles. The Pierre Robert Ensemble take a different view. Noting

that Du Mont's 20 *Motets pour la Chapelle du Roy*, printed two years after his death in 1684, contain the kind of clumsy viola parts reconcilable with the work of a publisher's hack, they propose that such 'posthumous tawdry' can be dispensed with to reveal the originals as more intimate works for five solo singers, two violins and continuo, probably written for pre-Versailles times at the Louvre palace. It's in this form that they present three of the motets here, emphasising their argument by adding the semi-dramatic *Dialogus de anima*, scored for the same line-up.

When performed and recorded as beautifully and sensitively as they are here, Du Mont's plangent harmonies and dissonances reach into the listener's heart with sensuous clarity. These are near-perfect performances by an ensemble ideal for such ravishing music, and who, in Marcel Beekman, have an *haute-contre* of striking quality. Frédéric Desenclos's tidy organ solos break up the programme nicely, but the motets are the stars.

John Dunstaple   English c1390-1453

Dunstaple is acknowledged as the most eminent of the Englishmen who strongly influenced the generation of Dufay and later continental composers. Little is certainly known about his career; he was probably not the John Dunstavylle who was at Hereford Cathedral, 1419-40, but may have been in the service of the Duke of Bedford before 1427. He was in the service of Queen Joan of Navarre, second wife of Henry IV, 1427-36, and was serviteur et familier domestique in the household of Henry, Duke of Gloucester, in 1438. In the late 1430s he held lands in northern France. There is evidence that he was also an astronomer. He was buried at St Stephen's, Walbrook, where his epitaph described him as 'prince of music'.
GROVEmusic

Sacred Works

Descendi in ortum meum. Ave maris stella. Gloria in canon. Speciosa facta es. Sub tuam protectionem. Veni, Sancte spiritus / Veni creator spiritus. Albanus roseo rutilat / Quoque ferundus eras / Albanus domini laudus. Specialis virgo. Preco preheminencie / Precursor premittitur / textless / Inter natos mulierum. O crux gloriosa. Salve regina mater mire. Missa Rex seculorum
Orlando Consort
Metronome METCD1009 (74' · DDD · T/t)   Ⓕ**OOO**

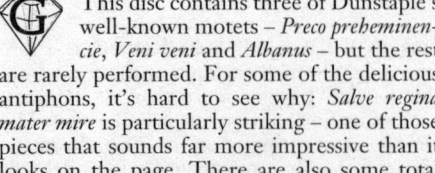 This disc contains three of Dunstaple's well-known motets – *Preco preheminencie*, *Veni veni* and *Albanus* – but the rest are rarely performed. For some of the delicious antiphons, it's hard to see why: *Salve regina mater mire* is particularly striking – one of those pieces that sounds far more impressive than it looks on the page. There are also some total novelties. The canonic *Gloria* was discovered in Russia: it's a massively inventive work that adds

a substantial new dimension to our knowledge of Dunstaple. And *Descendi in ortum meum*, though discovered and published a quarter of a century ago, surely stands as the latest known work of its composer: a magnificent piece that builds an entirely new kind of edifice with the materials of his characteristic style. Most impressive of all, though, is the Mass, *Rex seculorum*, which ends the disc. This may or may not be by Dunstaple – which is probably why it has never been recorded. Whoever the composer, though, it's a key work in the history of the polyphonic mass cycle, brimming with invention. The Orlando Consort has a wonderfully forward style that beautifully matches the music and helps the listener to understand why Dunstaple achieved such an enormous reputation on the continental mainland. If they're occasionally a touch rough, these are classic performances that will be hard to challenge.

Henri Duparc   French 1848-1933

Duparc studied the piano and composition with Franck, writing works that he later destroyed; this loss, together with a crippling psychological condition that caused him to abandon composition at the age of 36, has resulted in a legacy of just 13 songs (composed 1868-84). An important influence is Wagner, seen in the ambitious harmonic structure of Chanson triste and the shifting chromaticism of Soupir. Yet Duparc's feeling for poetic atmosphere and the craftsmanship he used to communicate it, as in the sinister drama of La manoir de Rosemonde, were unique, giving the French mélodie a rare musical substance and emotional intensity. From 1885 he led a quiet life, remaining close to Ernest Chausson and cultivating his aesthetic sensibility through reading and drawing.   **GROVE**music

Mélodies

L'invitation au voyage. Sérénade florentine. Extase. Chanson triste. Le manoir de Rosemonde. Lamento. Au pays où se fait la guerre. La fuite. La vague et la cloche. Sérénade. Testament. Phidylé. Romance de Mignon. Elégie. Le galop. Soupir. La vie antérieure
Danielle Borst sop **François Le Roux** bar
Jeff Cohen pf
REM REM311049 (63' · DDD · T/t)   Ⓕ

If you consider Duparc's songs the most rewarding in the French language you'll rejoice at this issue. Without hesitation, we would say Le Roux's are the most successful performances of these masterpieces in miniature since the war. In his foreword to this issue the veteran composer Henri Sauguet comments: 'The interpretations of François Le Roux and Danielle Borst are remarkable, not just for their vocal qualities and their emotional commitment but also for their exemplary use of words, which illustrates perfectly the profound unity of poetry and music.'

That almost says all that needs to be said, at any rate about Le Roux who has the lion's share of the burden. His voice can sometimes take on a rough edge but his understanding of the Duparc idiom is second to none, rivalling that of Panzéra and Bernac in the distant past, precisely because he realises what French can convey when sung with scrupulous care over diction.

Added to that he and his admirable pianist, Jeff Cohen, seem almost always to find exactly the right tempo for each *mélodie*. Le Roux is partnered in *La fuite* by Borst, another dedicated Duparcian who catches some of its trance-like beauty. The recorded sound is ideal. A 'must' for anyone interested in great performances of *mélodies*.

Marcel Dupré   French 1886-1971

Dupré studied with Guilmant, Vierne and Widor at the Paris Conservatoire (1902-14), returning as professor of organ (1926-54) while also serving as organist of St Sulpice (1934-71) and appearing internationally as a recitalist. His works introduced a Lisztian virtuosity and a contemplative modality into organ music; he also wrote religious symphonic poems. Alain and Messiaen were among his pupils.   **GROVE**music

Organ Works

Complete Organ Works, Volume 9
Entrée, méditation, sortie, Op 62. Les nymphéas, Op 54. Suite bretonne, Op 21. Poème héroïque, Op 33 (arr cpsr)
Jeremy Filsell org
Guild GMCD7188 (63' · DDD) Recorded on the organ of St Boniface Episcopal Church, Florida, USA   ⒫Ⓞ

It's sometimes the case that the reputation of great composers rests on a handful of works. With Dupré it's the two symphonies, the Op 7 Preludes and Fugues and the *Noël* Variations for which he's best known, but these compositions form a tiny proportion of his entire output. One of the many benefits of Guild's series is the discovery of hidden treasures, and much of the music on Volume 9 deserves to be heard more frequently.

The revelation here is *Les nymphéas*. This is a beautiful work, even as original as Debussy's *Images*, *Nocturnes* or the quieter moments of *Jeux*. It would make a marvellous orchestral suite; indeed, much of Dupré's organ writing has a quasi-orchestral character, and reflects his love and knowledge of the vast tonal palette of 20th-century instruments. You can also tell that, like Messiaen, he was an experienced writer of piano and chamber music.

We're indebted to Filsell for his special arrangement of *Les nymphéas* for this CD, and for his excellent performances throughout this volume. The choice of the organ at St Boniface, Florida, was a good one as it provides sensuous colours for the softer movements, plus glockenspiel effects for the *Suite bretonne*. The playing is backed up by fine recorded sound and comprehensive programme notes. There's no doubt that this series is setting the standard for Dupré interpreters of the future and will be a landmark in the history of organ recordings.

Complete Organ Works, Volume 10
Le chemin de la croix, Op 29
Jeremy Filsell *org*
Guild GMCD7193 (56' · DDD)   Ⓕ ○○

Complete Organ Works, Volume 11
Vêpres du commun des fêtes de la Sainte-Vierge, Op 18. Choral et Fugue, Op 57. Regina coeli, Op 64
Vocal Quartet; Jeremy Filsell *org*
Guild GMCD7198 (55' · DDD)   Ⓕ ○○

Complete Organ Works, Volume 12
79 Chorales, Op 28
Jeremy Filsell *org*
Guild GMCD7203 (72' · DDD)   Ⓕ ○○

All recorded on the organ of St Boniface Episcopal Church, Sarasota, Florida, USA

Thinking about 20th-century French music after Debussy and Ravel, the names of Messiaen and the members of Les Six would probably spring to mind. However, at the same time organists like Vierne, Tournemire, Alain, Langlais and Dupré himself were writing music every bit as original and as intense as the afore-mentioned composers. One of the many benefits of Guild's series (which concludes with these three volumes) is the opportunity to discover just how fine a composer Dupré was. Perhaps more than any of his contemporaries he managed to embrace both the sacred and the secular with utter conviction. *Le chemin de la croix* is one of his major works, and is a landmark piece of musical drama. One can hear links with the *Symphonie-Passion* of six years earlier, and David Gammie in his comprehensive accompanying notes points out the influence of these works on Duruflé's *Requiem* and Messiaen's *Les corps glorieux*. Filsell gives a suitably dramatic performance with some telling *rallentandos* at climactic moments.

All three compositions on Volume 11 were inspired by Gregorian chant, and each movement is preceded on this CD by the singing of the verse on which it's based. The vocal quartet includes the CD's producer Adrian Peacock and Filsell himself – an inspired and appropriate piece of programming. Listening to Filsell's flowing, atmospheric playing it's easy to imagine oneself sitting in a vast, incense-laden Parisian church, with glorious improvised music coming from the west-end grand orgue.

Dupré is remembered for writing music of extreme technical complexity, but Volume 12 shows that he was well capable of composing pieces for organs and organists of modest resources. The 79 Chorales take hymn tunes

which were all used by Bach as the basis for cho-rale-preludes. Many of Dupré's chorales are effective Bachian pastiches, but a handful have the unmistakable 20th-century French idiom. Again, Filsell's performances are beyond reproach, and he shows that Dupré was able to match JSB for solemnity and piety.

As is so often the case Naxos provides healthy competition, and Volume 11 of its Dupré series has a very fine performance of *Le chemin de la croix* from Mary Preston. She brings a greater clarity to the music, helped by the drier acoustic of the Meyerson Symphony Center at Dallas. However, Filsell in the more resonant acoustic of St Boniface Church, Sarasota, Florida brings more warmth, passion and drama to his inter-pretations, and this, coupled with Gammie's excellent insert-notes sways the balance in favour of the Guild series.

In all 12 volumes Filsell's playing has been consistently superb, and what has been most impressive is that his virtuosity has always been the servant of the music. The St Boniface organ may not have the éclat of a Cavaillé-Coll, but its clarity and attack enhance Dupré's complex textures, and the recordings are suitably warm and atmospheric. We must salute Filsell for what must surely rank as one of the greatest achievements in organ recordings.

Le chemin de la croix, Op 29
Ben van Oosten *org*
Dabringhaus und Grimm MDG316 0953-2
(62' · DDD) Played on the Cavaillé-Coll Organ, Saint-Ouen, Rouen   Ⓕ

Many collectors will instinctively be drawn to Ben van Oosten's choice of a genuine French organ. And not just any old French organ, but one of the finest extant Cavaillé-Colls captured in a record-ing of exemplary clarity, depth and presence. Against Jeremy Filsell's incisive precision and intensity (see above) van Oosten seems somewhat flabby and cumbersome. But his is a performance which exposes the very heart of Dupré's creation.

The work was originally conceived as an improvisation to accompany spoken verses from Paul Claudel's *Le chemin de la croix*. Van Oosten re-creates a tangible feeling of a 'living improvi-sation' and portrays a compelling sense of emo-tional reflection and musical response to the drama of these 14 scenes. Despite rare opportu-nities for open exhibitions of virtuosity or bra-vura display, *Le chemin de la croix* places as daunt-ing and formidable technical demands on the player as any of Dupré's works. But here those technical demands are overshadowed by van Oosten's powerful visionary zeal, hauntingly revealed in the portrait of the disconsolate Mary (Station IV), the nervous energy of Simon the Cyrenean as he attempts to bear the burden of the cross (Station V), and the compassion of Jesus as he comforts the tormented women of Jerusalem (Station VIII).

A release to be wholeheartedly recommended whatever the competition.

Choral Works

Dupré La France au Calvaire, Op 49ᵃ **Alain**
O Salutaris Langlais Festival Alleluia **Messiaen**
O sacrum convivium!
ᵃ**Helen Neeves** sop ᵃ**Catherine Denley** mez ᵃ**Matthew Beale** ten ᵃ**Colin Campbell** bar **Jeremy Filsell** org **Vasari Singers / Jeremy Backhouse**
Guild GMCD7239 (78' · DDD · T/t)   Ⓕ**OO**

La France au Calvaire is an astonishing work, setting, to quote the booklet note, 'a curious libretto' by René Herval who, like Dupré, was a native of Rouen. Appalled by the devastation wrought on his native city during the Second World War, Dupré vents all his anger and passion into this 65-minute oratorio, its movements dedicated to six French saints and framed by a Prologue and Final. Principally known for his organ music, it might seem strange to question Dupré's use of the organ here as the sole means of instrumental accompaniment. But despite Jeremy Filsell's stunning virtuosity and brilliant handling of the not always perfectly in tune Douai Abbey organ, the score seems to cry out for an orchestra.

No such reservations about the performance: in a word, stunning. The bleak ugliness of Christ nailed to the cross is compellingly portrayed by Matthew Beale, Catherine Denley makes an arresting France appealing for forgiveness for her misguided people, Colin Campbell fulfils the dual roles of St Denis and the voice of Christ with suitable gravitas and authority, and Helen Neeves is a beautifully innocent St Clotilde (magically set against a decidedly Messiaenic organ backdrop).

As for Jeremy Backhouse and his superb Vasari Singers, they excel even by their own high standards. The three motets which share the disc seem in comparison a trifle disappointing. But that disappointment is only because the motets precede a work of extraordinary emotional impact and a performance of exceptional power.

Quatre motets, Op 9ᵃ. De profundis, Op 18. Ave verum, Op 34 No 1. La france au Calvaire, Op 49 – Final. Deux motets, Op 53
Vasari Singers / Jeremy Backhouse
with **Jeremy Filsell**, ᵃ**Ian Curror** orgs
Guild GMCD7220 (80' · DDD · T/t)   Ⓕ

For all but a handful of devotees Marcel Dupré is inseparably associated with the organ. Dupré himself conceded this: 'I do not think of myself as a composer. I have specialised in the organ, and I do not have the reputation that composers have.' However, any thoughts that Dupré's choral music might merely be organ music with words are immediately quashed by even the briefest snatch of the extended *De profundis* (particularly the thrilling 'Et ipse redimet Israel' with the organ's great pillars of sound underpinning the richly textured and rhythmically exhilarating chorus). Here is truly impressive choral music.

True, the organ does figure prominently, occasionally assuming a decidedly virtuoso role, but it's clearly always the servant of the choir, and for the most part it's the choral lines rather than the organ accompaniments which require the greatest virtuosity. To that end it's hard to imagine a choral group more ideally suited to the task. The Vasari Singers are one of the most accomplished small choral groups of our time and for this compelling, passionate, often deeply moving and always technically demanding music, every ounce of their artistry is called into play. Guild's recording is wonderfully spacious yet crystal-clear, and Jeremy Filsell's organ support immaculate.

Maurice Duruflé   French 1902-1986

Duruflé studied with Tournemire, whose deputy at Ste Clotilde he became, and then at the Paris Conservatoire (1920-28) with Gigout and Dukas. In 1930 he was appointed organist of St Etienne-du-Mont and he toured internationally as a recitalist. His works are few, in a vivid modal style, and include the popular Requiem (1947).   **GROVE**music

---

Organ Works

'Veni Creator: The Complete Organ Music' Scherzo, Op 2. Prélude, Adagio et Choral varié sur le thème de 'Veni Creator', Op 4. Suite, Op 5. Prélude et Fugue sur le nom d'Alain, Op 7. Fugue sur le thème du Carillon des Heures de la Cathédrale de Soissons, Op 12. Prélude sur l'Introït de l'Epiphanie, Op 13. Meditation, Op posth
Hans Fagius org
BIS BIS-CD1304 (71' · DDD) Played on the 1928 Frobenius organ at Århus Cathedral, Denmark   Ⓕ

Listeners to his *Requiem* will recognise Duruflé's conservative and intensely personal musical language as heard in his organ music. The influence of Debussy, Dukas, Ravel, Tournemire and Vierne is evident, and like these composers Duruflé provides detailed performance indications. Hans Fagius, a former student of Duruflé's, scrupulously observes all the scores' markings, and this is one reason why he's now the top recommendation for this repertoire.

His performances have a flexible, seamless flow, and the playing has a slight understated quality which gives more clarity and impact than Eric Lebrun's flamboyant accounts. Fagius's interpretations are close in spirit to the recordings by the composer and his wife Marie-Madeleine Duruflé-Chevalier, and it's a shame that their authoritative performances are marred by poor sound quality. By contrast, BIS's recording of the 89-stop four-manual organ in Århus Cathedral is superbly realistic. The choice of this instrument was inspired; it has all the appropriate colours and it's set in a warm, generous acoustic.

Another bonus is the inclusion of the sensuous and recently discovered *Meditation*. Although the recordings by Lebrun and the Duruflés are very good, they must now stand aside and let this BIS disc take the place of honour, for this is a truly distinguished release of one of the finest corpus of organ music you'll ever hear.

Requiem

Requiem. Prélude et Fugue sur le nom d'Alain, Op 7. Quatre Motets sur des thèmes grégoriens, Op 10 **Fauré** Requiem, Op 48. Cantique de Jean Racine, Op 11. Messe basse **Poulenc** Mass in G. Salve Regina. Exultate Deo. Litanies à la vierge noire **Jonathon Bond, Andrew Brunt, Robert King** trebs **Benjamin Luxon** bar **Christopher Keyte** bass **St John's College Choir, Cambridge; Academy of St Martin in the Fields / George Guest** with **Stephen Cleobury** org
Double Decca ② 436 486-2DF2(149' · ADD)
Recorded 1969-76   Ⓜ️🅳➔

Here's almost two and a half hours of bliss. These are recordings to set aside for the time when, as the prayer says, 'the busy world is hushed'. Asked to characterise Fauré's and Duruflé's Requiems as compared with others, we might suggest words such as 'delicate', 'meditative', 'undramatic'; but that last would be a mistake. These performances certainly do not go out of their way to 'be' dramatic or anything else other than faithful to the music, but one is struck by the power exercised by those rare moments that rise to a *forte* and above. The choir is surely at its best, the trebles with their fine clear-cut, distinctive tone, the tenors (so important in the Fauré) graceful and refined without being precious, the altos exceptionally good, and only the basses just occasionally and briefly plummy or obtrusive in some way.

The Poulenc works further test a choir's virtuosity yet in the extremely difficult Mass, the choir seems secure, and in the *Salve Regina* they catch the necessary tenderness. The treble soloists sing beautifully, Christopher Keyte dramatises almost too convincingly in Duruflé's 'tremens factus', and Benjamin Luxon, his production less even, builds finely in Fauré's *Libera me*. These recordings have a vividness, certainly in the choral sound, that modern recordings generally lack.

Duruflé Requiem[a] **Fauré** Requiem, Op 48[b]. Pavane[c]
[b]**Robert Chilcott** treb [a]**Janet Baker** mez [b]**John Carol Case,** [a]**Stephen Roberts** bars[ab]**Choir of King's College Cambridge;** [a]**John Butt** org [bc]**New Philharmonia Orchestra /** [bc]**Sir David Willcocks,** [a]**Sir Philip Ledger**
EMI Great Recordings of the Century 37999-2
(65' · ADD) Recorded [bc]1968 & [a]1982   Ⓜ️🅾️➔

The first decision to be made is between the orchestral and the organ-accompanied versions of this most serene and other-worldly of Requiems. Duruflé expresses profundities with the most restrained and subtle of musical means – a momentary densening of texture, a minute

inflection of vocal line, a heightening from *piano* to *pianissimo* – and in a performance as scrupulously responsive as this, those subtleties need no orchestra to intensify them.

It is a very rare experience indeed to be able to describe a recording as near as can be to absolute perfection from start to finish, but this Faure's Requiem truly provides this experience. For the happy result the highest praise must go first and foremost to David Willcocks's inspiring and most sensitive direction of the exquisite work.

Additional recommendation

Requiem
Coupled with: **Fauré** Requiem
Murray; Allen; Corydon Singers; ECO / Best
Hyperion CDA67070 (75' · DDD)   🅵🅾️
  Beautifully judged performance of these two favourite (and similar) French Requiems. The glory of both performances is the choral work.

Henri Dutilleux   French b1916

Dutilleux studied with the Gallons, Büsser and Emmanuel at the Paris Conservatoire (1933-8), where he was appointed professor in 1970 after periods with French radio (1943-63) and at the Ecole Normale de Musique (from 1961). His first works suggest influences from Debussy, Ravel, Roussel and Honegger, but he developed as an isolated and independent figure, producing a relatively small output of great breadth and originality, predominantly of instrumental works; they include two symphonies (1950, 1959) and other orchestral pieces, piano music and the string quartet Ainsi la nuit (1976).
                                        GROVEmusic

Concertos

Cello Concerto, 'Tout un monde lointain'. Métaboles. Mystère de l'instant
Boris Pergamenschikov vc **BBC Philharmonic Orchestra / Yan Pascal Tortelier**
Chandos CHAN9565 (60' · DDD)   🅵🅳➔

This is the third issue in Chandos's Dutilleux series with the BBC Phil and Yan Pascal Tortelier. The virtues of those earlier issues remain evident here, with meticulously prepared, well-played performances, and recordings carefully adapted to the coloristic subtlety and textural delicacy of the music. *Métaboles* is particularly tricky to bring off, but this version is admirable in the way it builds through some dangerously episodic writing to underline the power of the principal climaxes, though a more sharply delineated sound picture could have reinforced these contrasts even more appropriately. Boris Pergamenschikov is an eloquent soloist in the Cello Concerto. Tortelier's account of *Mystère de l'instant* – using a full orchestral complement of strings – is excellently done. As with *Métaboles*, the structure is shaped with great flexibility and feeling for its ebb and flow, and this emerges as a highly dramatic score, despite the inherent reticence of Dutilleux's style.

Violin Concerto, 'L'arbre des songes'. Timbres, espace, mouvement. Deux Sonnets de Jean Cassou (orch cpsr) **Alain** (orch Dutilleux) Prière pour nous autres charnels
Olivier Charlier vn **Martyn Hill** ten **Neal Davies** bar
BBC Philharmonic Orchestra / Yan Pascal Tortelier
Chandos CHAN9504 (58' · DDD · T/t)　　　　ⒻⓄ

Timbres, espace, mouvement (1978, revised 1991) can be counted as Dutilleux's best orchestral composition, at once rooted in tradition yet persistently sceptical about conventional 'symphonic' values. It's a tricky score to bring off, and Tortelier is successful in negotiating its twists and turns of form. In the Violin Concerto (1985) Tortelier again favours a symphonic approach, and very effective it is too, with a soloist who's authoritative without being overly self-assertive. The disc also includes Dutilleux's orchestral arrangement of his Cassou settings, and also his orchestration, made in 1944, of Jehan Alain's touching prayer. Well-characterised contributions from Martyn Hill and Neal Davies complete this valuable release.

Symphony No 1

Symphony No 1. Cello Concerto, 'Tout un monde lointain'ᵃ. Timbres, espace, mouvement
ᵃ**Jean-Guihen Queyras** vc **Bordeaux-Aquitaine National Orchestra / Hans Graf**
Arte Nova 74321 92813-2 (80' · DDD)　　　　Ⓢ

The traditional French virtues of lightness, elegance, wit and so on are all very well, but they don't take us far with Dutilleux's music on their own. It's wonderfully inspiriting to hear, albeit under an Austrian conductor, an orchestra from the long underfunded French provinces finding this music's power, passion and eloquence.

Hans Graf enjoys Dutilleux's confidence, and from this recording it's easy to see why. The detail is all here, but so is the control of long paragraphs – few recordings of the slow movement of the First Symphony are as moving as this. The sound may not have quite the brilliance of the Chandos set, but do we always have to have brilliance?

Similarly, Jean-Guihen Queyras may not produce Rostropovich's matchless tone high up on the A string; but he has his own things to say and says them with authority. In *Timbres, espace, mouvement*, Graf impresses on us the sheer curiousness of many of the textures, just as van Gogh's 1889 picture *La nuit étoilée*, which inspired the work, stands far apart from so much contemporary painting.

The First Symphony is especially welcome. Amid all the congratulations after its first public performance in 1952, Pierre Boulez pointedly

turned his back on the composer. The usual explanation is that Dutilleux, eschewing the 12-note system, was clearly one of those who were, in Boulez's words, 'inadequate to the times'. Or was the younger man all too aware of this music's quality? Happily, these fences have been mended since. But the work is undoubtedly a masterpiece and the final resolution on to D flat major one of the great moments of 20th-century music.

Pascal Dusapin　　　　French b1955

Pascal Dusapin studied arts and aesthetics at the Sorbonne before attending seminars by Yannis Xenakis. He was composer-'in-residence' at the Lyon National Orchestra from 1993-4. His compositions cover most genres including four operas. His music is characterised by high levels of intensity achieved through very economiic means.

Perelà

Perelà
John Graham-Hall ten Perelà **Isabelle Philippe** sop
La Reine **Chantal Perraud** sop La Fille d'Alloro
Martine Mahé contr Une Pauvre Vieille **Nora Gubisch** mez La Marquise Olivia di Bellonda **Daniel Gundlach** counterten L'Archevêque **Gilles Yanetti** spkr Le Perroquet **Isabelle Pierre** spkr La Jeune Fille à la Flûte **Montpellier Opera Chorus; Montpellier National Orchestra / Alain Altinoglu**
Naïve Montaigne ② MO782168 (122' · DDD · S/T/t/N) Recorded live 2003　　　　Ⓜ

Pascal Dusapin is among the most significant composers at work today and it is good to see Naïve releasing this live account of his fourth stage work. *Perelà* is derived from Aldo Palazzeschi's 1911 futurist novel *Perelà uomo di fumo*. It concerns the eponymous hero's metamorphosis into existence, his arrival in a corrupt and decadent city – where he is first fêted as its saviour, then, after the accidental suicide of an admirer, condemned for his subversive influence – and his trial and incarceration, from where he returns to the ether.

It's a story which resonates in the past or present, from which Dusapin has fashioned not a narrow polemic or a moralistic opera, but one rich in incident of a necessarily symbolic yet never abstruse nature – an opera, moreover, whose complex textural and rhythmic interplay are derived from relatively simple harmonic means, ensuring musical cohesion over the course of 10 'chapters' which are widely contrasted in content and impact.

The opening chapter presents Perelà – created from the mothers Pena, Rete and Lama, the first two letters of each forming his name, and themselves reiterated as a kind of mantric trinity – on his way to the city, where he is accorded 'celebrity status', only to be knocked off a pedestal he never sought to occupy. Later chapters include a garish ball, with its on-stage orchestra and massed choir, a strange meeting with the Queen where the main conversation is provided by her parrot's repetition of 'Dieu', and the magical scene in which the solitary Perelà encounters a girl with a flute – the disembodied sonorities an understated pointer to his final evanescence.

The recording is an assured one. John Graham-Hall is superb in the title-role, its high tessitura accommodated with little strain. Nora Gubisch is commanding as the Marchesa whose hypochondria is not unempathetic, as witness her impassioned defence of Perelà in the trial scene. Isabelle Philippe's neutral tone is ideal for the Queen, as is Daniel Gundlach's hectoring falsetto for the Archbishop; the remaining roles are all characterfully delivered.

Alain Altinoglu directs with evident concern for the bigger picture, in sound which, for all its stage intrusions, has a realistic placement of voices and orchestra.

Antonin Dvořák   Bohemian 1841-1904

Dvořák studied with Antonín Liehmann and at the Prague Organ School (1857-9). A capable viola player, he joined the band that became the nucleus of the new Provisional Theatre orchestra, conducted from 1866 by Smetana. Private teaching and mainly composing occupied him from 1873. He won the Austrian State Stipendium three times (1874, 1876-7), gaining the attention of Brahms, who secured the publisher Simrock for some of his works in 1878. Foreign performances multiplied, notably of the Slavonic Dances, the Sixth Symphony and the Stabat mater, and with them further commissions. Particularly well received in England, Dvořák wrote The Spectre's Bride (1884) and the Requiem Mass (1890) for Birmingham, the Seventh Symphony for the Philharmonic Society (1885) and St Ludmilla for Leeds (1886), besides receiving an honorary doctorate from Cambridge. He visited Russia in 1890, continued to launch new works in Prague and London and began teaching at the Prague Conservatory in 1891 (where Joseph Suk was among his most gifted pupils). Before leaving for the USA he toured Bohemia playing the new Dumky Trio. As director of the National Conservatory in New York (1892-5) he taught composition, meanwhile producing the well-known Ninth Symphony ('From the New World'), the String Quartet in F, the String Quintet in E flat and the Cello Concerto. Financial strain and family ties took him back to Prague, where he began to write symphonic poems and finally had his efforts at dramatic music rewarded with the success of the fairytale opera Rusalka (1901). The recipient of honours and awards from all sides, he remained a modest man of simple tastes, loyal to his nationality.

In matters of style Dvořák was neither conservative nor radical. His works display the influences of folk music, mainly Czech (furiant and dumky dance traits, polka rhythms, immediate repetition of an initial bar) but also ones that might equally be seen as American (pentatonic themes, flattened 7ths); Classical composers whom he admired, including Mozart, Haydn, Beethoven and Schubert; Wagner, whose harmony and use of leitmotifs attracted him; and his close friend Brahms (notably his piano writing and mastery of symphonic form). Despite his fascination with opera, he lacked a natural instinct for drama for all their admirable wit and lyricism, his last five stage works rank lower than his finest instrumental music. Here his predilection for classical procedures reached its highest level of achievement, notably in the epic Seventh Symphony, the most closely argued of his orchestral works, and the Cello Concerto, the crowning item in that instrument's repertory, with its characteristic richness and eloquence, as well as in the popular and appealing Ninth Symphony and the colourful Slavonic Dances and Slavonic Rhapsodies. Among his chamber works, landmarks are the String Sextet in A Op 48, a work in his national style which attracted particular attention abroad; the F minor Piano Trio Op 65, one of the climaxes of the more serious, classically 'Brahmsian' side of his output – unlike the E minor Op 90, a highly original series of dumka movements alternately brooding and spirited; the exuberant Op-81 Piano Quintet; and several of the string quartets, notably the popular 'American' Op 96, with its pentatonic leanings, and the two late works, the deeply felt op.106 in G and the warm and satisfying Op 105 in A flat. GROVEmusic

Cello Concerto in B minor, B191

Cello Concerto[a]. Symphonic Variations
[a]**Pieter Wispelwey** vc
Budapest Festival Orchestra / Iván Fischer
Channel Classics ⌖ CCSSA25807 (63' · DDD)
Recorded live at the Budapest National Concert Hall, Palace of Arts in 2006   Ⓕ❶❷❸

Here we have an outstanding version of Dvořák's Cello Concerto, one to rival any version in the catalogue and imaginatively coupled with the much earlier *Symphonic Variations*. Pieter Wispelwey crowns his previous releases in this electrifying live recording, brilliantly accompanied by the Budapest Festival Orchestra under Iván Fischer.

It includes applause at the end of each performance, suggesting there is far less editing here than in many other live recordings. That ties in with the high-voltage performances, well recorded in atmospheric and finely detailed sound, with the soloist well balanced in the concerto. Wispelwey's playing is marked by crisp attack and exceptionally clean articulation, and though he allows an easing for the transition into the great second-subject melody, as well as in the mysterious G sharp minor reference to it in the central development section, he keeps romantic freedom well in check.

The Wispelwey first movement climax is triumphant with the orchestra weighty in tuttis, while the slow movement finds the soloist flexible, with magical shading of *pianissimi* leading to the hushed close. The finale is crisp and clean, with some wonderfully ripe-sounding horns suggesting Viennese influence. The hushed epilogue is refined, leading to a powerful final cadence.

In the *Symphonic Variations* Fischer holds the

structure cleanly together, crisply defining each of the 27 brief variations and the fugal finale. One marvels anew at Dvořák's inventive elaborations on a simple theme, on a par with the *Slavonic Dances*. An outstanding disc.

Cello Concerto
Tchaikovsky Variations on a Rococo Theme, Op 33
Mstislav Rostropovich vc **Berlin Philharmonic Orchestra / Herbert von Karajan**
DG The Originals 447 413-2GOR (60' · ADD) Recorded 1968 ⓜⷮ❶❶❶➻

There have been a number of outstanding recordings of the Dvořák Concerto since this DG record was made, but none to match it for the warmth of lyrical feeling, the sheer strength of personality of the cello playing and the distinction of the partnership between Karajan and Rostropovich. Any moments of romantic licence from the latter, who's obviously deeply in love with the music, are set against Karajan's overall grip on the proceedings. The orchestral playing is superb. You've only to listen to the beautiful introduction of the secondary theme of the first movement by the principal horn to realise that the BPO is going to match its illustrious soloist in eloquence, while Rostropovich's many moments of poetic introspection never for a moment interfere with the sense of a spontaneous forward flow. The recording is as near perfect as any made by DG in that vintage analogue era. It gives the cello a highly realistic presence, and if the passionate *fortissimo* violins lose just a fraction in fullness, and there seems to be, comparably, just a slight loss of resonance in the bass, the sound picture has an impressively clear and vivid focus.

In the coupled Tchaikovsky *Rococo* Variations, Rostropovich uses the published score rather than the original version. However, he plays with such masterly Russian fervour and elegance that any criticism is disarmed. The music itself continually demonstrates Tchaikovsky's astonishing lyrical fecundity, as one tune leads to another, all growing organically from the charming 'rococo' theme. The recording is marvellously refined. The description 'legendary' isn't a whit too strong for a disc of this calibre.

Dvořák Cello Concerto, B191
Herbert Cello Concerto No 2, Op 30
Gautier Capuçon vc
Frankfurt Radio Symphony Orchestra / Paavo Järvi
Virgin Classics 519035-2 (61' · DDD) ⒡❶➻

Though the name of Victor Herbert is nowadays associated above all with Broadway musicals like *Naughty Marietta*, Herbert was in fact a multi-talented musician, one of the world's leading cello virtuosos of the time and the composer of two cello concertos which greatly influenced Dvořák in the United States to write his supreme masterpiece. That makes this coupling of Dvořák's Cello Concerto with the second and finer of Herbert's an apt one, and Gautier Capuçon gives distinc-

---

DVOŘÁK CELLO CONCERTO – IN BRIEF

Mstislav Rostropovich; Berlin PO / Herbert von Karajan
DG 447 413-2GOR ⓜ❶❶❶➻
Ⓖ A longtime favourite, with sympathetic accompaniment from Karajan and his Berlin orchestra and pliant, flexible playing from Rostropovich at his most charismatic.

Mstislav Rostropovich; USSR SO / Yevgeni Svetlanov
BBC Legends BBCL4110-2 ⒡❶
Recorded at London's Royal Albert Hall the very day in 1968 when Soviet tanks rolled in Prague, this is a performance of extremes: orchestra and conductor sound like they want to dispatch it as quickly as possible, while the soloist uses the piece to project his pain and guilt. It is hugely powerful, though the mono sound is somewhat constricted.

Pieter Wispelwey; Budapest Fest Orch / Iván Fischer
Channel Classics CCSSA25807 ⒡❶❶❶
Straight to the top of the pile: a magnificent achievement from everyone concerned.

Yo-Yo Ma; New York PO / Kurt Masur
Sony Classical 07464 67173-2 ⒡
A very fine modern version of this popular work: Yo-Yo Ma betters his already fine first version, offering playing of both powerful discipline and apparent free-flying spontaneity. This is not Ma in sophisticated mode but rather offering a direct, simplicity that plays huge dividends in this ebulliently melodious music.

Pablo Casals; Czech PO / George Szell
Dutton mono CDEA5002 ⓜ
Casals's 1937 recording with the Czech Philharmonic is a classic with wonderfully idiomatic playing by the orchestra, gloriously directed by George Szell. This is a performance of incandescent beauty, the cellist's bow seemingly striking sparks off the string as he launches into the work's richly Romantic melodies.

Gautier Capuçon vc
Frankfurt RSO / Paavo Järvi
Virgin Classics 519035-2 ⒡❶➻
A strong and characterful version of the Dvořák coupled with the work that inspired it composition. Sensitively accompanied.

Pierre Fournier; Philharmonia / Rafael Kubelík
Testament SBT1016 ⒡
The first of Fournier's three recordings dates from 1948 and displays his customary ease and grace as a soloist. Kubelík conducts idiomatically drawing excellent playing from the young Philharmonia.

tive, characterful and intense performances of both works, well supported by Paavo Järvi and the Frankfurt orchestra, especially strong in its brass section.

In the Dvořák the fruity-toned Frankfurt horn gives a beautiful account of the great second-subject melody even though it is dangerously slow. In the exposition with soloist, Capuçon takes that section a fraction faster and the result is magical. As in the Herbert the slow movement is deeply elegiac, while the incisive finale leads to a dedicated account of the beautiful epilogue. Altogether a version of this much-recorded work which stands comparison with any in the catalogue, made the more attractive by the coupling.

Dvořák Cello Concerto
Herbert Cello Concerto No 2 in E minor, Op 30
Yo-Yo Ma vc
New York Philharmonic Orchestra / Kurt Masur
Sony Classical 07464 67173-2 (61' · DDD)   Ⓕ

Ma's and Masur's version of the Dvořák is among the very finest, matched by few and outshining most, including Ma's own previous version with Maazel and the Berlin Philharmonic (also available on Sony Classical). It's fascinating to compare Ma's two versions, the newer one more readily conveying weight of expression despite the less spotlit placing of the soloist, more disciplined yet more spontaneous-sounding. This time Ma's expressiveness is simpler and more noble, and the recording (made in Avery Fisher Hall, New York), once a trouble-spot for engineers, is fuller and more open than the Berlin one, cleaner in *tuttis*, with only a touch of unwanted dryness on high violins. Ma and Masur together encompass the work's astonishingly full expressive range, making it the more bitingly dramatic with high dynamic contrasts.

Herbert's concerto, first given in 1894, was almost certainly what prompted Dvořák to write his own concerto later that same year. Here it receives a high-powered performance, but one which doesn't overload the romantic element with sentiment, whether in the brilliant and vigorous outer movements or in the warmly lyrical slow movement. Ma's use of rubato is perfectly judged, with the slow movement made the more tender at a flowing speed. The finale is then given a quicksilver performance, both brilliant and urgent.

Dvořák Cello Concerto[a]
Schumann Cello Concerto in A minor, Op 129[b]
Tchaikovsky Pezzo capriccioso in B minor, Op 62[c]
Mstislav Rostropovich vc [a]**USSR State Symphony Orchestra / Evgeni Svetlanov;** [b]**London Symphony Orchestra;** [c]**English Chamber Orchestra / [bc]Benjamin Britten**
BBC Legends/IMG Artists [ab]mono BBCL4110-2
(71' · ADD) Recorded live [a]1968, [b]1961, [c]1968   Ⓕ ●

Truly legendary performances are rare, but this heroic account of the Dvořák Concerto deserves its place on collectors' shelves alongside such classics as Mravinsky's Shostakovich Eighth or Horenstein's Mahler *Symphony of a Thousand*. This concert offers us a piece of history in sound that raises questions about music and politics, music and personality, music and identity.

In the Cold War era, no Western tour by Russian artists was entirely without political resonance, and this London Prom took place on the very day that Soviet tanks rolled into Prague. With demonstrators outside the Royal Albert Hall, there was also dissent within. The performers might not have been directly to blame, yet had they not been dispatched knowingly, as cultural ambassadors? Svetlanov, at least, was something of an apparatchik. Moreover, the programme featured the Dvořák Concerto – an intensely nostalgic and nationalistic score, a natural focus for strong emotions.

On this privately sourced, somewhat compressed-sounding mono tape, you can hear the unease as Svetlanov and his raw-toned band tear into the work as if determined to get it over with as quickly as possible. It's the cellist, already in tears, whose transparently honest playing wins the audience over, as his sense of guilt and fury is transmuted into a potent requiem for the Czech Spring. The restated second subject is forcefully projected, suitably gutsy and passionate at the start, but it's the development which strikes deepest. Never has the first theme's metamorphosis from resolute, relatively short-breathed march to elegy struck home so movingly. The finale is almost too rushed until the tender, unmistakably tragic, coda arrives, presenting an extreme and all the more moving contrast.

The Schumann, though scarcely epoch-making in the same way, was recorded on the occasion of the cellist's first visit to the Aldeburgh Festival. It receives a glorious interpretation. The sound, considerably more refined and open, is still mono only with the orchestra rather backwardly placed. Strongly recommended.

Piano / Violin Concertos

Dvořák Piano Concerto
Schumann Piano Concerto in A minor, Op 54
Paolo Giacometti pf Arnhem Philharmonic **Orchestra / Michel Tilkin**
Channel Classics CCS17898 (71' · DDD)   Ⓕ

To say that Paolo Giacometti measures up well to the classic versions is to say a great deal. His playing has all the energy, sparkle, poetry and technical finish you could wish. He approaches the Dvořák with an admirable mixture of respect and enjoyment. And his Schumann is as urgent as the composer's markings suggest it should be, yet without sacrificing natural characterisation for the sake of making that point. Nor do the Dutch orchestra and conductor sound in any way out of their depth; on the contrary, they're clearly as engaged as their soloist in warm, lively music-making. The Channel Classics recording is also rich and well balanced. If the Schumann/

Dvořák coupling is just what you're looking for, there's no need to hesitate.

Piano Concerto[a]. The Golden Spinning-Wheel, B197
[a]**Pierre-Laurent Aimard** pf **Royal Concertgebouw Orchestra, Amsterdam / Nikolaus Harnoncourt**
Teldec 8573 87630-2 (68' · DDD) ⓕⓄ➔

Straight to the top of the list for this one! Even on its best showings – Richter and Carlos Kleiber, Firkušný under Somogyi – Dvořák's Piano Concerto has never quite managed to cast off its Cinderella rags. With this recording, the ball beckons, and there's no time limit. Granted, Brahms is still securely in the background and the concerto is hardly as pianistic as the best of its concerto-peers but the beauty of this performance is its utter naturalness, Pierre-Laurent Aimard easing around the solo part as if he's been playing it all his life, and Nikolaus Harnoncourt's sympathy for the work is obvious from the start. Together they make the most of the score's drama, giving the lie to Dvořák's supposedly ineffective piano writing. Albrecht Gaud's excellent booklet note credits the long-prevalent revision by Vilém Kurz as giving the part 'not only a more effective form' but also the virtue of extra clarity. Yet it appears that the original is used here and redeemed. Richter's clarity and Firkušný's knowing accent remain attractive, but Aimard's combination of intelligence and informality win the day. A magnificent CD.

Violin Concerto[a]. Piano Concerto[b]
[a]**James Ehnes** vn [b]**Rustem Hayroudinoff** pf
BBC Philharmonic Orchestra / Gianandrea Noseda
Chandos CHAN10309 (71' · DDD) ⓕ➔

The Russian pianist Rustem Hayroudinoff gives a commanding performance of the Dvořák Piano Concerto, always a tricky work to play thanks to unpianistic piano writing. Hayroudinoff basically follows the composer's original piano text but modifies it in places where he feels the original is ineffective in favour of Vilém Kurz's 'performing version'. Yet where he feels that Kurz's changes 'seem to push the piano part too far in the direction of a typical romantic concerto', he has 'found his own solutions for staying true to Dvořák's intentions'. Controversial or not, the result is a performance in which Hayroudinoff brings out the joyful, carefree quality of Dvořák's inspiration, demonstrating what a wonderful fund of good melodies it contains. The clarity of his articulation in the trickiest passagework is phenomenal, and his phrasing in the central *Andante sostenuto* is limpidly beautiful. Helped by full, rich sound which yet allows fine detail, Noseda and the BBC Philharmonic match the subtlety and point of the soloist's playing, establishing this as an outstanding modern version.

Having Dvořák's Violin and Piano Concertos on a single disc makes an apt and generous coupling. The Canadian violinist James Ehnes gives a strong, incisive performance with speeds on the fast side in the first two movements and with the *furiant* finale bitingly fresh. His rapid vibrato gives a distinctive timbre to his playing, making the slow movement less warmly romantic than it is in some rival versions, yet Ehnes offers real magnetism in his performance.

The recording, generally well-balanced, is yet less full and warm than in the Piano Concerto: strangely so, as both recordings were made by the same conductor and orchestra in the same venue.

Violin Concerto[a]. Piano Quintet in A B155[b]
Sarah Chang, [b]**Alexander Kerr** vns [b]**Wolfram Christ** va [b]**Georg Faust** vc [b]**Leif Ove Andsnes** pf [a]**London Symphony Orchestra / Sir Colin Davis**
EMI 557521-2 (72' · DDD) ⓕ➔

What an excellent idea for the brilliant young violinist Sarah Chang to couple her warm and powerful reading of the Dvořák Violin Concerto not with another concerto but with one of Dvořák's most popular chamber works. She shows again what a warmly sympathetic chamber-player she is. This time she shares the leadership with pianist Leif Ove Andsnes, an equally imaginative artist who similarly conveys a sense of spontaneity in almost every phrase.

As a group they give the impression of making music for fun, great artists enjoying themselves in the interplay of free expression, each challenging the others. So the first movement brings rapt playing from Chang, with Andsnes wonderfully clean in his articulation of fast triplets, and the viola player Wolfram Christ satisfyingly rich-toned in the second subject theme. The *Dumka* slow movement again sounds almost improvisatory, a fantasy movement, totally idiomatic, while the *Scherzo* is exceptionally light, taken at a challengingly fast tempo; the jauntiness of the finale is also lightly presented. Though the recording, made in the Mozartsaal of the Konzerthaus in Vienna, has less presence than some, it's clean and well balanced.

The performance of the Concerto with Sir Colin Davis, a powerful and understanding Dvořákian, similarly draws expressive playing from Chang in a performance which treats the unconventional structure of the first movement as rhapsodic without letting tensions slip. The sense of fantasy is again irresistible, with Chang exploiting dynamic extremes, as she does in the wistfully tender slow movement, while the slavonic dance of the finale is given a winning spring. The recording made at the Watford Colosseum enhances the feeling of a big-scale performance with full-bodied sound set in a lively acoustic.

Additional recommendations

Violin Concerto
Coupled with: **Suk** Fantasy
Suk vn **Czech Philharmonic Orchestra / Ančerl**

Supraphon SU1928-2 (69' · ADD)   Ⓜ
  A distinguished performance from this all-Czech
  line-up.

Symphonies

No 1 in C minor, B9, 'The Bells of Zlonice'; **No 2** in B
flat, B12; **No 3** in E flat, B34; **No 4** in D minor, B41; **No
5** in F, B54; **No 6** in D, B112; **No 7** in D minor, B141;
No 8 in G, B163; **No 9** in E minor, B178, 'From the
New World'

Complete Symphonies

Symphonies Nos 1-9. Scherzo capriccioso, B131.
Overtures – In Nature's Realm, B168; Carnival, B169;
My Home, B125a
London Symphony Orchestra / István Kertész
Decca Ⓑ 430 046-2LC6 (431' · ADD)
Recorded 1963-66   ⒷⓄⓄ↬

István Kertész recorded the Dvořák symphonies
in the mid-1960s, and his integral cycle quickly
achieved classic status; his exhilarating and vital
account of the Eighth Symphony rapidly
became a special landmark in the catalogue. The
original LPs are now collectors' items. These
magnificent interpretations became available
again in 1992, in glitteringly refined digitally
remastered sound, and it's a tribute to the
memory of this tragically short-lived conductor
that this cycle continues to set the standard by
which others are judged. He was the first conductor to attract serious collectors to the early
Dvořák symphonies, and his jubilant advocacy
of the unfamiliar First Symphony has never
been superseded. This work offers surprising
insights into the development of Dvořák's
mature style, as does the Second Symphony.
Kertész shows that Symphonies Nos 3 and 4
have much more earthy resilience than many
commentators might have us believe, insisting
that Dvořák's preoccupation with the music of
Wagner and Liszt had reached its zenith during
this period. The challenging rhetoric of the
Fourth has never found a more glorious resolution than here, with Kertész drawing playing of
quite gripping intensity from the LSO. The
Fifth Symphony and, to a still greater extent, the
Sixth reveal Dvořák's clear affinity with the
music of Brahms. Kertész's superb reading of
the Sixth, however, shows just how individual
and naturally expressive this underrated work
actually is, while the playing in the great climax
of the opening movement and the vigorous final
peroration remains tremendously exciting. In
the great final trilogy, he triumphs nobly with
the craggy resilience of the Seventh Symphony,
and he brings a dynamic thrust and momentum
to the Eighth. His *New World* is by turns indomitable and searchingly lyrical.
  The six-disc set also offers assertive and brilliant readings of the Overtures *Carnival*, *In
nature's realm* and the rarely heard *My home*,
together with a lucid and heroic account of the

Scherzo capriccioso. These definitive performances have been skilfully reprocessed, the sound
is astonishingly good, even by modern standards, and the playing of the London Symphony
Orchestra is often daringly brilliant.

Symphonies – selected

Symphonies Nos 5, 7-9.
Oslo Philharmonic Orchestra / Mariss Jansons
Brilliant Classics 92779 (131' · DDD)   ⓈⓄⓄ

With such lovable music, affectionate treatment
pays even greater dividends, and Jansons's Fifth is
pure joy. The pastoral opening with its theme for
two clarinets over shimmering strings is wonderfully subtle and relaxed, and the EMI engineers
have produced sound in the difficult acoustic of
the Oslo Konserthus that gives just the bloom
needed, combined with warmth and clarity. Jansons's Dvořák now fully matches the achievement
of his Oslo Tchaikovsky series for Chandos. As in
his Tchaikovsky, Jansons has a way of drawing
out expressive phrasing to make it sound totally
natural, without self-consciousness.
  The slow movement is warmly lyrical, but also
refined, and the playing of the Oslo orchestra
polished, with cleaner textures enhanced by the
recording. The scherzo is done with a playful
lilt, and with the horn whoops more exuberant
than in any of the rival versions. Jansons crowns
his reading with an account of the finale which at
the start dramatically hammers home the surprise of Dvořák's use of the minor mode and his
deliberate avoidance of establishing the home
key of F major. The arrival of that key at last is
then all the more warmly satisfying, leading
almost at once to the lusciousness of D flat major
and the soaring second subject, where the Oslo
violins play with a passion to make others seem
uncommitted.
  In every way except one this is a model performance. Maybe influenced by Dvořák's disown-
ing of the exposition repeat marks in No 6,
Jansons – as in his *New World* – fails to observe
that first movement repeat here too. His
accounts of the last three symphonies make this
a super-budget collection to treasure.

Symphony No 6. The Wild Dove
Czech Philharmonic Orchestra / Jiří Bělohlávek
Chandos CHAN9170 (63' · DDD)   Ⓕ↬

Bělohlávek has referred to his Czech orchestra's
'singing art of playing' and its 'mellow sound'
and indeed it's Bohemia's woods, fields and
wildlife, rather than energetic village green festivities, that linger in the memory here. Perhaps
you shouldn't expect a Czech Philharmonic
performance to 'go' or leap about excitedly in
the manner of Kertész's with the LSO; in these
days of high adrenalin, high contrast and high
definition, there's a lot to be said for a less assertive and vigorous approach, always artlessly
sung, and for this orchestra's Old World tim-

bres a Brahmsian fireside glow, for example, to the Symphony's first movement second subject on cellos and horns (beautifully eased in by Bělohlávek). These horns, always more rounded in tone than their rasping counterparts in London (Kertész), bear an obvious family resemblance to the woodwind, not only in timbre, but also in the use of vibrato (again, that 'singing art of playing'). And the 'silver moon' flute is one of this disc's principal joys. Bělohlávek also projects the drama of *The wild dove* with relish. Chandos guarantees a sepia-toned warmth throughout.

Symphony No 6. The Golden Spinning-Wheel, B197
Czech Philharmonic Orchestra / Sir Charles Mackerras
Supraphon SU3771-2 (71' · DDD) Ⓕ

Sir Charles Mackerras's vibrant interpretation easily holds its own in the most venerable company. Not only are the Czech Philharmonic, recorded live in October 2002, at their articulate and spirited best, but Mackerras directs the outer movements with a pliancy and keen sense of long-term proportion reminiscent of his mentor Talich, as well as Rowicki's magnificent (and sadly deleted) 1965 LSO account. He also extracts every ounce of songful poetry from the sublime slow movement, while the *Furiant* cross-rhythms of the *scherzo* skip to the manner born. The performance as a whole has a spine-tingling thrust, meriting a place alongside any of its distinguished rivals.

The Golden Spinning-Wheel is a studio recording from June 2001. A splendidly opulent and atmospheric reading, observant and affectionate, if without quite the narrative flair and expressive scope of Harnoncourt's riveting Concertgebouw account.

Symphony No 7. Nocturne in B, B47. The Water Goblin
Czech Philharmonic Orchestra / Jiří Bělohlávek
Chandos CHAN9391 (69' · DDD) ⒻⒹ➔

Bělohlávek is a lucid, sure-footed guide through Dvořák's mightiest symphonic utterance, and his sympathetic direction combines both warm-hearted naturalness as well as total fidelity to the score (dynamics are scrupulously attended to throughout). If it sounds just a little under-energised next to other vividly dramatic accounts, the sheer unforced eloquence and lyrical fervour of the playing always give enormous pleasure. Certainly, the first movement's secondary material glows with affectionate warmth, while the sublime *Poco adagio* emerges seamlessly, its songful rapture and nostalgic vein captured as to the manner born by this great orchestra (listen out for some gorgeous work from the principal flute, clarinet and horn).

The *Scherzo* trips along with an infectious, rhythmic spring, as well as an engaging poise and clarity; moreover, the dark-hued unsettling Trio (a casualty in so many rival performances) is han-

dled with equal perception. The finale, too, is immensely pleasing, marrying symphonic thrust with weighty rhetoric rather in the manner of Colin Davis's distinguished Amsterdam account. The closing bars are very broad and imposing indeed. A performance of considerable dignity and no mean stature, benefiting from vibrant Chandos engineering. The symphony is followed by a long-breathed, slumbering account of the *Nocturne* (gloriously played by the Czech PO strings) and the disc concludes with a fine *Water goblin*. Again, the orchestral response is as disciplined and poised as you could hope to hear.

Symphonies Nos 8 & 9
Berlin Philharmonic Orchestra / Rafael Kubelík
DG The Originals 447 412-2GOR (73' · ADD)
Recorded 1972 ⓂⒹ➔

These accounts are quite magnificent, and their claims on the allegiance of collectors remain strong. Their freshness and vigour remind one of what it was like to hear these symphonies for the first time. The atmosphere is authentic in feeling and the sense of nature seems uncommonly acute. Kubelík has captured the enthusiasm of his players and generates a sense of excitement and poetry. The playing of the Berlin Philharmonic is marvellously eloquent and, as is often the case, a joy in itself. The woodwinds phrase with great poetic feeling and imagination, and all the departments of this great orchestra respond with sensitivity and virtuosity.

The recording has great dynamic range and encompasses the most featherweight string *pianissimos* to the fullest orchestral *tutti* without discomfort. The listener is placed well back in the hall so that the woodwind, though they blend beautifully, may seem a little too recessed for some tastes, though it should be said that there's no lack of vividness, power or impact. The balance and the timbre of each instrument is natural and truthful; nothing is made larger than life and Kubelík has a natural warmth and flexibility. This will remain high on any list of recommendations for it has a vernal freshness that's wholly reviving.

Symphonies Nos 8 & 9
Budapest Festival Orchestra / Iván Fischer
Philips 464 640-2PH (78' · DDD) ⒻⓄⓄ➔

Ten years earlier Fischer recorded the Eighth Symphony with the same orchestra at the same venue. In terms of timings, the two readings are remarkably similar, and yet the later performance is warmer, more malleable and significantly more spontaneous. Both employ expressive string slides (a Fischer characteristic in Slavic music), most noticeably at the end of the *Scherzo*, where a snappy portamento on fiddles is echoed by the brass. Philips' recording has an extended dynamic range and a fuller, closer string sound.

While the Eighth, then, is given a bouncy, lyrical performance, 'localised' with the odd gypsy inflection, the *New World*, on the other hand, is intense and energetic. Indeed, it's some tribute to Fischer's musical perception that he views the two works in entirely different terms. Small dynamic details invariably tell with a new-found freshness. Just try sampling the difference between *forte* and *sforzando* among the basses in the first movement and the softness of the second subject, for once a genuine *ppp*. These and similar markings register even if you're not following the music with a score. Accents, too, are keenly observed, articulation is carefully judged and the string choirs have real bite. Indeed, there isn't a more enjoyable digital *New World* on the current market. Fischer's CD is a consistent joy, and is thoroughly recommended.

Symphony No 9, 'From the New World'.
Symphonic Variations, B70
Baltimore Symphony Orchestra / Marin Alsop
Naxos 8 570714 (65' · DDD) ⓈⓄ▷

Dvořák's *New World* has already been recorded by almost everyone who matters! But Marin Alsop makes it very much her own, with her fine Baltimore orchestra responding with an account full of warmth, moments of high drama, and, above all, finely paced with a flowing, spontaneous feeling. One notes the delightful flute-playing, the bold, strong trombones in tuttis, and the luminous grace of the strings, immediately apparent at the affectionate opening of both first and second movements. The delicate close of the *Largo*, after the songful repeat of the beautifully simple and very lovely cor anglais melody, is memorable. The movement's central episodes are equally poetic, particularly the gentle clarinet theme over the murmuring bass pizzicati.

The *Scherzo* bursts in, and the finale has all the impetus one could want. Yet overall, Alsop's is not a histrionic reading but one full of affectionate touches, the appealing little nudge at the end of the second subject of the first movement for instance, while the closing retrospective section of the finale is particularly satisfying.

What makes this disc doubly recommendable is the superb account of the *Symphonic Variations*, inspired but surprisingly neglected. It is a work which after the mysterious opening *Lento e molto tranquillo*, which is perfectly captured here, needs to move on flexibly but with plenty of impetus, capturing the continual changes of mood and colour. The extraordinary variety of invention and scoring captivates the ear, sometimes perky, sometimes gentle (like the enchanting little repeated-note flute solo, followed immediately by gruff trombones), until it reaches its genial fugal apotheosis and the performance sweeps to its folksy, grandiloquent close. The recording is outstanding in every way, well balanced and vivid in detail.

Symphony No 9. The Water Goblin, Op 107
Royal Concertgebouw Orchestra /
Nikolaus Harnoncourt

Teldec 3984-25254-2 (64' · DDD) ⒻⓄ▷

Harnoncourt has some distinguished Concertgebouw forebears, not least structure-conscious Sir Colin Davis and combustible Antál Dorati (both Philips). This, though, beats them all. Auspicious happenings register within the first few pages: carefully drawn woodwind lines; basses that calm meticulously from fierce *fortissimo* to tense *pianissimo*; provocative bassoons and an effortless passage into the lovely flute melody at 2'58". At the start of the development section *piano* violins really are played *leggiero* (lightly), a significant detail that most rivals gloss over. Middle and lower voices are granted their full flavour and the violin desks are divided. Harnoncourt's *Largo* is something of a minor miracle. Undulating clarinets register against shimmering string *tremolandos* and, beyond the beautifully judged approach to the *Meno* passage (bar 78), you suddenly hear quiet second-violin *pizzicato* chords (7'00") that you almost never notice in concert. The finale itself never sags, and for the home strait Harnoncourt treads a course somewhere between the printed *Allegro con fuoco* and the expressive broadening that Dvořák later sanctioned. Most admirable about Harnoncourt's Dvořák is its close proximity to nature: barely a minute passes that isn't somewhere touched by verdure or sunshine.

For the couplings, Harnoncourt gives us *The Water Goblin*, the most folk-like of Dvořák's Erben tone-poems where, as in the Symphony, middle voices rise to the fore and the stamping outer sections are played with great rhythmic bite. If you think that you know the *New World* back-to-front then Harnoncourt will have you thinking again.

Symphony No 9 **Martinů** Symphony No 2
Cincinnati Symphony Orchestra / Paavo Järvi
Telarc CD80616 (68' · DDD) Ⓕ

Having the most popular of Dvořák's symphonies coupled with one of the most approachable by a 20th-century Czech composer is a neat and original idea, particularly apt as both works were written in the United States. Paavo Järvi reveals his keen imagination and sharp concentration in both performances and under his guidance the Cincinnati SO is consistently excellent: ensemble more than matches that of rival versions.

The quality of the playing is highlighted by the refinement and clarity of the brilliant Telarc recording. In the Martinů Paavo Järvi brings out the Czech flavours in the writing: the first movement is open and fresh, with rhythms that echo Dvořák's *Slavonic Dances*.

In the *New World* Symphony, too, Paavo Järvi allows flexibility in tempo and phrasing but never sounds self-conscious or unspontaneous. Though there are many highly recommendable versions of this much-recorded work, this one is a strong candidate in every way; and, quite apart from the outstanding recording quality, has its unique coupling to commend it.

Additional recommendations

Symphony No 6
Coupled with: **Janáček** Sinfonietta
Bavarian Radio Symphony Orchestra / Kubelík
Orfeo C552011B (70' · ADD) Recorded live 1981   Ⓕ
A cherishable document captured in wholly
acceptable sound and a must-buy for all devotees
of this conductor. Live performance lends the
Sixth an easy, free-wheeling spontaneity and a
songful poetry that his studio version lacks. The
slow movement is an especial delight.

Symphony No 7
London Symphony Orchestra / C Davis
LSO Live LSO0014 (40' · DDD)   Ⓢ⊞➤
Davis masterminds a performance of authority. His
approach is more flexible and generously expressive
than his outstanding 1975 account,
but there's no want of symphonic thrust. That set
still reigns supreme but at the price this is one to
snap up.

Symphonies Nos 7, 8 and 9
Coupled with: Romance in F minor[a]. Symphonic
Variations
[a]**Gonley** *vn* [a]**English Chamber Orchestra, London
Philharmonic Orchestra / Mackerras**
Classics for Pleasure ② 575761-2 (150' · DDD)   Ⓑ
These are winning performances – rhythms
delightfully sprung, detail closely observed and
completely without point scoring. The Seventh
and Eighth are the gems here, but the rest in no
way disappoints.

Symphony No 8
Coupled with: The Noon Witch
Concertgebouw / Harnoncourt
Teldec 3984 24487-2 (51' · DDD)   Ⓕ⊞➤
A typical Harnoncourt interpretation with a
freshness of approach and attention to colour
and detail that spell winner.

Symphony No 9
Coupled with: Slavonic Dances, B83: Nos 6, 8; B147:
No 2
New York Philharmonic Orchestra / Masur
Apex 8573-89085-2 (60' · DDD) No 9 recorded live
1991   Ⓢ●
The slow movement is particularly outstanding,
with straight, simple phrasing conveying a deeply
emotional intensity. Though recorded live, Masur
achieves a precision of ensemble to rival that of a
studio performance.

Symphony No 9
Coupled with: Othello. In Nature's Realm.
Czech Philharmonic Orchestra / Ançerl
Supraphon SU3662-2 (70' · ADD)   Ⓜ
A truly great, remarkably unforced interpretation,
consistently illuminating and displaying an iron
grip unmatched on disc.

Symphony No 9
Coupled with: **Beethoven** Leonore Overture No 3.
Prokofiev The Love for Three Oranges – Suite
BBC Symphony Orchestra / Kempe

BBC Legends/IMG Artists BBCL4056-2 (71' · ADD)
Recorded live 1975   Ⓜ
A visionary reading, deeply meditative in the slow
movement.. The BBC SO, on exceptional form,
have *pianissimos* of breathtaking delicacy. The
extreme dynamic contrasts are beautifully caught
and the sound is vivid and fresh.

American Suite, B190

Dvořák American Suite, B190 **Suk** Scherzo
fantastique, Op 25. Serenade, Op 6
Prague Philharmonia / Jakub Hrůša
Supraphon SU3882-2 (66' · DDD)   Ⓕ

Still in his mid-twenties, Jakub Hrůša is a conductor to look out for. A pupil of Jiří Bělohlávek,
he has built up a formidable career in Europe
and America. Here he draws superb playing
from the orchestra which Bělohlávek founded.
    Dvořák's *American Suite* can easily seem square
and uninspired but Hrůša directs a magical performance. The descending opening phrase
immediately brings echoes of a spiritual. It is
fresh and rustic-sounding, growing more magnetic as it is repeated in melodic ostinato. The
Trio brings a brisk idea like a *Slavonic Dance*, and
the lively second-movement *Allegro* offers a lyrical Trio. The *Moderato* third movement echoes a
polonaise or polacca in its light and jaunty dotted
rhythms. The fourth movement is a warmly lyrical Nocturne opening with a lovely oboe theme,
while the vigorous finale brings folk-like accented
repeated chords again with oboe prominent,
slowing down before a final brisk pay-off.
    The two items by Josef Suk are given similarly
fresh and inspired performances. Suk was still in
his teens and a pupil of Dvořák when in 1892 he
completed his Serenade for Strings, and it
remains one of his most delightful works. There
are many echoes of Dvořák, not least in the long
third-movement *Adagio*; but already Suk was
beginning to reveal a distinctive voice, and the
writing for strings throughout is astonishingly
assured for a teenager.
    The *Scherzo fantastique* is darker and more dis-
tinctive, inventive in its contrasted sections, with
a swinging episode in triple-time lightening the
mood with a waltz-like episode. Again Hrůša's
performance could not be more winning, and the
Supraphon recording is full and vivid.

Czech Suite, B93

Czech Suite. Festival March, B88. The Hero's Song,
B199. Hussite, B132
Polish National RSO / Antoni Wit
Naxos 8 553005 (65' · DDD)   Ⓢ⊞➤

The Hero's Song, a colourful, rather sprawling
tone-poem, was Dvořák's last orchestral work
and isn't an easy piece to bring off. Wit finds
genuine nobility in it, while his gentle, mellow
way with the lovely *Czech Suite* also gives much
pleasure. The opening 'Praeludium' is just a

touch sleepy, but there's no want of lyrical affection or rhythmic bounce elsewhere and the whole performance radiates an idiomatic, old-world charm that really is most appealing.

As for the *Hussite* overture, Wit's clear-headed reading impressively combines dignity and excitement. Given such finely disciplined orchestral playing, the results are again both eloquent and characterful. This just leaves the rousing *Festival March* of 1879, splendidly done here, with the excellent Katowice brass sounding resplendent in their introductory call to arms. Recordings throughout possess a most agreeable bloom and transparency.

Slavonic Dances, B83 & B147

Slavonic Dances
Chamber Orchestra of Europe /
Nikolaus Harnoncourt
Teldec 8573-81038-2 (73' · DDD)   Ⓕ ⭕🅾️⭕▷

Each dance on this exciting disc is granted its rightful, rustic character. The *furiants* really move (Harnoncourt's readings of Op 46 Nos 1 and 8 are among the fastest on disc) and the Dumka of No 2 oscillates between tender reflection and feverish high spirits.

Harnoncourt's high energy levels never preclude delicacy, or transparency or even the occasional suggestion of sentiment. Tempo relations have been thought through to the last semiquaver though in general they're more dramatic than rival Iván Fischer's (Philips). That Harnoncourt loves this music is beyond doubt, and that he understands it beyond question. He delves among Dvořák's inner voices, pulling them to the fore like a magician freeing a rabbit, while others seem happier to let the music speak for itself. The Chamber Orchestra of Europe play superbly, all swelling curves and attenuated lines, with their pooled individuality shedding fresh light on virtually every piece. If you don't know the music, Harnoncourt will make you love it. And if you do know it, he'll make you love it even more.

Slavonic Dances
Cleveland Orchestra / George Szell
Sony Classical 69699 89845-2
(74' · ADD) Recorded 1963-5   Ⓑ

This reissue is something of a revelation. Both discs have been lovingly remastered and the quality is an amazing improvement over the old LPs. The remastering engineers seem to have discovered a whole bottom octave in the sound, which before had appeared to lack richness and weight to support the brilliant upper range. The *Slavonic Dances* are offered as Szell recorded them, with no repeats cut, so the phenomenal orchestral virtuosity is revealed in all its glory. There's much evidence of the conductor's many captivatingly affectionate touches of rubato and, throughout, this large orchestra follows Szell's every whim, with playing full of lyrical fervour

and subtlety of nuance, wonderful precision and a lilting rhythmic pulse. The recordings were made within the acoustics of Cleveland's Severance Hall, usually a pair of dances at a time. The result is infectiously spontaneous and this disc can't be recommended too highly; even if the close balance prevents any real *pianissimos* to register, the dynamic range of the music-making is still conveyed.

Additional recommendations

Slavonic Dances
Czech Philharmonic Orchestra / Sejna
Supraphon SU1916-2 (72' · ADD)   Ⓜ
  Sejna secures some wonderfully lithe and vivacious playing from his superb Czech band – an exhilarating treat.

Piano Quintet in A, B155

Piano Quintet in A. String Quintet in G, B49
Gaudier Ensemble (Marieke Blankestijn, Lesley Hatfield *vns* Iris Juda *va* Christoph Marks *vc* Stephen William *db* Susan Tomes *pf*)
Hyperion CDA66796 (66' · DDD)   Ⓕ

The pianist here is Susan Tomes, who encourages a performance full of mercurial contrasts that seem entirely apt. For example, in the second movement *Dumka* there's more light and shade, and the *Scherzo* sparkles even more, leading to a jaunty, exuberant finale. The G major String Quintet, the earliest of the two which Dvořák wrote, the one with extra double bass, is similarly lighter than the Chilingirian Quartet on Chandos. The Chilingirian is just as strongly characterised as the Gaudier, with a firmer, fuller tone. Marieke Blankestijn's violin is thinner than Levon Chilingirian's, but it can be just as beautiful, as in the lovely high-floating second subject of the slow movement. A fine disc.

Piano Quintet, Op 81 B155[a]. Bagatelles, Op 47 B79[b]
Frank Braley [a]pf/[b]harm [a]**Ensemble Explorations**
([b]Christine Busch, [b]Hyunjong Kang *vns*
Anna Lewis-Deeva *va* [b]Roel Dieltiens *vc*)
Harmonia Mundi HMC90 1880 (54' · DDD)   Ⓕ

Recorded in warm, full sound, pianist Frank Braley leads an often fiery and impulsive account of Dvořák's masterly Piano Quintet (1887), using a vintage Steinway of 1874. The clarity of his articulation adds sparkle to his freely romantic reading, matched by the players of Ensemble Explorations.

In the slow movement, marked *Dumka*, Braley leads a reading poised in the slower sections, making an effective contrast with the faster sections, which are not as sharply different as in most dumka movements. The contrasts of tone and dynamic are most persuasive. In the third-movement *Furiant*, all three readings are fast and light, while the finale inspires Braley and his partners to spring the rhythms infectiously, with thrust and swagger.

The coupling brings a welcome rarity, written in 1878, the year of the first set of *Slavonic Dances*, for two violins, cello and harmonium, an instrument popular at the time, particularly in America. The sequence is delightful in its exploiting of fresh ideas, and Braley readily adapts to the demands of the harmonium. It is not a generous coupling but a very attractive one, completing a first-rate disc, well recorded.

Piano Quartets

Piano Quartets – No 1 in D, B53; No 2 in E flat, B162
Domus (Krysia Osostowicz *vn* Timothy Boulton *va* Richard Lester *vc* Susan Tomes *pf*)
Hyperion CDA66287 (70' · DDD)   Ⓕ

These are two very enjoyable works. Hans Keller's description of the opening pages of the E flat Quartet as 'childish' is staggering – this from the leading campaigner against 'posthumous critical torture'! Childlike would be much more suitable, and this appealing characteristic is well brought out by the members of Domus: Susan Tomes's descent from incisive *fortissimo* clarity to *pianissimo* mystery in the opening bars is a delight, and fully prophetic of the kind of musicianship we're to hear. Two other unforgettable moments from this performance: the lovely return of the first movement second subject, with its heart-easing B major/E flat major modulation – very sensitive use of rubato here – and cellist Richard Lester's richly expressive solos at the beginning of the *Lento*.

The D major Quartet is a delightful, if not fully mature piece – it does tend to rely rather heavily on sequence and repetition. Domus makes sure we don't miss any of its virtues, but it doesn't force anything: the timing in the magical opening shift from D major to B major is finely judged, and Dvořák's wonderfully effortless melodies are affectionately shaped and shaded; admirable too the way Susan Tomes finds so much beauty in what often looks like conventionally decorative piano writing. In general the sound is very pleasing, intimate enough to draw one right into the performances without being intimidating, even in the somewhat histrionic second theme of the E flat Quartet's *Lento*. A richly rewarding disc.

String Quartets

No 1 in A, B8; **No 2** in B flat, B17; **No 3** in D, B18; **No 4** in E minor, B19; **No 5** in F minor, B37; **No 6** in A minor, B40; **No 7** in A minor, B45; **No 8** in E, B57; **No 9** in D minor, B75; **No 10** in E flat, B92; **No 11** in C, B121; **No 12** in F, B179, 'American'; **No 13** in G, B192; **No 14** in A flat, B193

String Quartets Nos 1-14; F, B120 (Fragment). Cypresses, B152. Quartettsatz. Two Waltzes, B105
Prague Quartet (Břetislav Novotny, Karel Přibyl *vns* Lubomír Malý *va* Jan Sírc *vc*)

DG ⑨ 463 165-2GB9 (589' · ADD) Recorded 1975-7
                                                      ⒷＯＯ

Like Schubert, Dvořák turned to the string quartet early in his career. The three complete quartets included in Vol 1 (Nos 1-3) show considerable facility in writing for strings (after all, Dvořák was a violinist), but it took him some time to arrive at a fully idiomatic quartet style. He also had to learn to rein in his natural expansiveness: the Third Quartet spins out its modest material to an astonishing 70 minutes – the first movement alone is longer than the whole *American* Quartet! The outer movements of the No 4 in E minor (Vol 2) show him concentrating admirably, though the later shortened version of the central *Andante religioso* is a considerable improvement.

So the interest of Vol 1 (three discs) is largely musicological. Despite this, with playing so fresh and authoritative even the impossibly long-winded Third Quartet has rewards to offer. Each performance has a strong sense of purpose, but that doesn't mean an inability to enjoy all those charming Dvořákian byways. Technically the playing is admirable.

The enjoyment increases through Vol 2. The violin cavatina in the *Andante* of the Fifth Quartet has just the right gentle lilt. Listening to the Prague in the first movement of No 7 you realise how what looks on the page like very simple music can come glowingly to life in the right hands – and the way they handle the slightly tricky *poco più mosso* at the second subject is very impressive.

The finest work in Vol 2 (discs 4-6) is undoubtedly the D minor Quartet, No 9. Volume 3 contains three gems: the E flat Quartet (No 10), the *American* and No 13 in G major – the outstanding work of the collection. The Prague are very sensitive to dynamic contrast (Dvořák's markings are often surprisingly detailed). There's plenty of fine music on these nine well-filled discs, all of it well performed, and the recordings are generally creditable.

String Quartets Nos 12 & 13
Vlach Quartet, Prague (Jana Vlachová, Ondřej Kukal *vns* Petr Verner *va* Mikael Ericsson *vc*)
Naxos 8 553371 (69' · DDD)   Ⓢ⊕

On the face of it, the Vlach Quartet's credentials would seem to be impeccable – the group's leader, Jana Vlachová, is the daughter of the great Josef Vlach – and, indeed, the players make a most pleasing impression on this vividly recorded Naxos coupling. They certainly produce a beguilingly rich, beautifully blended sound and bring to this music a big-hearted, songful fervour as well as textural mastery. What's more, Dvořák's characteristic, chugging cross-rhythms are handled with particular felicity. Interpretatively, their approach contrasts strongly with other readings in that the Vlach team adopt a coaxing, lyrically expressive stance (with the gorgeous slow movement of the *American* a highlight). In the case of the masterly

G major Quartet, these gifted newcomers show fresh insights (they're especially perceptive in those wistful reminiscences at the heart of the finale).

Additional recommendation

String Quartet Nos 12, 'American', and 13
Lindsay Quartet
ASV CDDCA797 (66' · DDD)   Ⓕ
 Sedicated, typically probing accounts from the Lindsays; the great G major Quartet comes off especially well here.

Piano Trios

Piano Trios – No 3 in F minor, B130; No 4 in E minor, B166, 'Dumky'
Florestan Trio (Anthony Marwood vn Richard Lester vc Susan Tomes pf)
Hyperion CDA66895 (68' · DDD)   Ⓕ

A favourite and appropriate pairing – Dvořák's most passionate chamber work in harness with one of his most genial. The F minor Piano Trio (1883) was contemporaneous with the death of Dvořák's mother; it anticipates something of the storm and stress that characterises the great D minor Seventh Symphony (1884-5) and the Florestan Trio serves it well. All three players allow themselves plenty of expressive leeway and yet the musical line is neither distorted nor stretched too far. The second movement *Allegretto* is truly *grazioso* and the qualifying *meno mosso* perfectly judged. The finale is buoyant rather than especially rustic, whereas the more overtly colourful *Dumky* Trio inspires a sense of play and a vivid suggestion of local colour. Throughout the performance, the manifest 'song and dance' elements of the score (heartfelt melodies alternating with folk-style faster music) are keenly projected. The recordings are first rate, as are the insert-notes. If you're after a subtle, musically perceptive coupling of these two works, then you could hardly do better.

Piano Trios – No 3 in F minor, B130; No 4 in E minor, B166, 'Dumky'
Smetana Trio (Jitka Cechová pf Jana Vonášková-Nováková vn Jan Páleníček vc)
Supraphon SU3872-2 (67' · DDD)   Ⓕ

Not surprisingly, the performance by the Smetana Trio is thoroughly idiomatic, with the many *dumka* speed-changes sounding totally natural and spontaneous. What instantly strikes the ear is the delicacy, the piano relatively light to bring out the filigree textures of much of the writing.

They also play with a hushed concentration, keeping the different sections tautly woven together. In the fifth of the six movements, there is a delightful pay-off at the end, and the finale is taken at a thrillingly fast tempo, though light textures bring complete clarity.

In No 3 there is an apt if subtle shift in the recording balance, with the piano weightier, reflecting the Brahmsian quality of much of the writing. Though in the conventional four movements instead of the six of No 4, it is a work on a bigger scale. Not surprisingly, the Czech flavours are brought out strikingly. The Supraphon sound is excellent.

Works for cello and piano

Dvořák Romantic Pieces, B150. Rondo, B171. Sonatina, B183 **R Strauss** Romanze, AV75. Cello Sonata, Op 6. Morgen, Op 27 No 4
Mischa Maisky vc **Pavel Gililov** pf
DG 477 7465GH (75' · DDD)   ⒻⒹ►

Richard Strauss's youthful Cello Sonata is often described as influenced by Mendelssohn. There are also touches of Brahms – and of Strauss himself. With hindsight, which is at least insight, the music shows not a few signs of the mature composer's harmonic colouring, and there is certainly plenty of his energy, sometimes doing duty for real invention. To this, Mischa Maisky and Pavel Gililov wholeheartedly respond, going at the powerful first movement with a panache that makes the most of the best in the music and sails airily through the odd clumsiness. Not even Maisky can do much for the rather flat *Andante* but he is well at ease with the separately composed *Romanze*, and with his own arrangement of the song *Morgen*, which does more than simply reiterate the vocal line.

Dvořák's Sonatina was originally a violin-and-piano piece for two of his children, and though Maisky takes it with a light touch, and despite clear and sympathetic piano accompaniment from Gililov, it does not really go as well on the cello. The last of the *Four Romantic Pieces*, which began life as a Trio and which Dvořák said he had hugely enjoyed writing, fares better in this arrangement; and the Rondo, in which it sounds as if Dvořák enjoyed himself more and more as it goes on, is charmingly played. An excellent recording deals admirably with the notorious balance problems of cello and piano.

Requiem Mass, B165

Requiem Mass. Mass in D, B153
Pilar Lorengar sop **Neil Ritchie** treb **Erzsébet Komlóssy** contr **Andrew Giles** counterten **Robert Ilosfalvy, Alan Byers** tens **Tom Krause** bar **Robert Morton** bass **Nicholas Cleobury** org **Ambrosian Singers; Christ Church Cathedral Choir, Oxford / Simon Preston; London Symphony Orchestra / István Kertész**
Double Decca ② 448 089-2DF2 (138' · ADD · T/t)
Recorded 1968   Ⓜ

Kertész's Requiem dates from 1968 and on all counts but one, it surpasses Karel Ančerl's classic 1959 set, reissued on DG in 1995 and coupled with Fischer-Dieskau's 1960 set of Dvořák's *Bibli-*

cal Songs with Jörg Demus. The exception is the rather too soft-grained singing of Pilar Lorengar as compared with the clear, more vibrant soprano of Maria Stader. But Lorengar's singing is particularly sensitive and appealing in the quieter passages. The lovely quality of Robert Ilosfalvy's voice tells beautifully in 'Liber scriptus proferetur' and in the opening section of the quartet, 'Recordare, Jesu pie'. Dvořák distributes short passages among the soloists impartially. They combine beautifully in the quartet, and the chorus with them in 'Pie Jesu Domine'. The hero of the occasion is Kertész. He gets choral singing and orchestral playing of the finest quality. It's abundantly evident that he cherishes a great love for this work. The Mass in D (sung in the original version with organ) sits well with the Requiem; Simon Preston produces a fine, well-balanced performance, with the Christ Church choristers on excellent form.

Mass in D

Dvořák Mass in D, Op 86
Eben Prague Te Deum 1989 **Janáček** Our Father
Dagmar Masková sop **Marta Benacková** mez
Walter Coppola ten **Peter Mikuláš** bass Lydie
Härtelová hp Josef Ksica org Prague Chamber
Choir / Josef Pancík
ECM New Series 449 508-2 (59' · DDD · T/t)   Ⓕ🅳➔

This imaginative coupling brings together three fine pieces of Czech church music in skilled and sympathetic interpretations. Dvořák's Mass has received a number of good recorded performances; this one, in the original 1887 version with organ, has a very well-matched quartet of soloists who blend smoothly with each other and with the chamber choir. It's a work of particular intimacy and charm, and these qualities mark this performance.

Janáček's setting of the Lord's Prayer dates from 1906, and is in turn a meditative piece, not without vivid illustrative touches appropriate to a work originally designed to accompany a sequence of devotional pictures; and Petr Eben's *Prague Te Deum* coincided, in 1969, with a moment of apparent release from political oppression. It has something of Janáček's suddenness in the invention, and a graceful melodic manner. Each of these works is in its way inward, personal and reflective, but they all share a Czech character.

Stabat mater

Stabat mater. Psalm 149
Lívia Aghová sop **Marga Schiml** contr **Aldo Baldin**
ten **Luděk Vele** bass Prague Children's Choir;
Prague Philharmonic Choir; Czech Philharmonic
Orchestra / Jiří Bělohlávek
Chandos ② CHAN8985/6 (96' · DDD)   Ⓕ⭕

The 10 sections of the *Stabat mater* are well laid out for the different vocal and instrumental forces and so avoid the monotony which might seem inherent in this contemplative and deeply sombre text. This performance was recorded in Prague Castle, and in it we feel the full dignity and drama of the work, an oratorio in all but name. The four solo singers convey genuine fervour and one feels that their sound, which is quite unlike that of British singers, must be akin to what the composer originally imagined. If they're a touch operatic, that doesn't sound misplaced and they perform well together, as in the second verse quartet 'Quis est homo'. The choral singing is no less impressive, and indeed the whole performance under Bělohlávek gets the balance right between reverent simplicity and intensity of feeling. Psalm 149 is a setting of 'Sing unto the Lord a new song' for chorus and orchestra and its celebratory mood provides a fine complement to the other work.

Additional recommendations

Coupled with: Legends
Mathis sop **Reynolds** mez **Ochman** ten **Shirley-Quirk**
bar Bavarian Radio Chorus and Symphony
Orchestra; English Chamber Orchestra / **Kubelík**
DG ② 453 025-2GTA2 (129' · ADD)   Ⓜ
    This warm-hearted work well deserves all the care
    and attention lavished upon it by the performers,
    who respond with evident enthusiasm to Kubelík's
    inspiring direction.

Cypresses

Cypresses, B11[a]. Cypresses, B152[b]
[a]**Timothy Robinson** ten [a]**Graham Johnson** pf
[b]**Delmé Quartet** (Galina Solodchin, John Trusler vns
John Underwood va Jonathan Williams vc)
Somm SOMMCD236 (80' · DDD · T/t)   Ⓕ

The charming sequence of 12 pieces for string quartet that Dvořák called *Cypresses* has been recorded fairly often, but the set of 18 folk-like songs on which they're based has been neglected. So this disc setting the two cycles side by side makes an illuminating coupling. His first essays in song-writing were inspired by his unrequited love for the elder of two sisters (he later married the younger one), and were not published in his lifetime. The cycle had to wait until 1983 for a first complete public performance. In their reflection of youthful love they provide a touching portrait of the young composer. Predictably, the quartet versions are subtler. The vocal line is generally transferred to violin or viola, with masterly transcription of the piano accompaniments, disguising their origin. A number were radically expanded.

The recording sets Timothy Robinson at a slight distance, and there's an occasional roughness to the top of his range. Still, he responds with warmth, and in idiomatic Czech, aided by responsive accompaniment from Graham Johnson. In the instrumental versions the Delmés phrase expressively within relatively broad speeds.

Songs

Gypsy Melodies, B104. In Folk Tone, B146.
Love Songs, B160. Biblical Songs, B185
Dagmar Pecková *mez* **Irwin Gage** *pf*
Supraphon SU3437-2 (69' · DDD · T/t)   Ⓕ

These four cycles make an excellent and generous coupling, with Dagmar Pecková, brilliantly
supported by Irwin Gage, a most persuasive
advocate. Hers is an ideal voice, unmistakably
Slavonic in timbre, yet firm and pure as well as
rich. She retains a freshness specially apt for the
songs inviting a girlish manner, including
Dvořák's most famous song, the fourth of the
seven *Gypsy Melodies*, 'Songs my mother taught
me', sounding fresh and new.
The four cycles represent the full span of
Dvořák's career. The eight *Love Songs*, B160
may officially date from 1888, but Dvořák in fact
reworked a selection from 18 songs he'd written
passionately at high speed over 20 years earlier
– charming pieces which already reveal his
unquenchable lyrical gift. Next chronologically
are the *Gypsy Songs* of 1800, bold and colourful,
here nicely contrasted by Pecková and Gage
with four simpler, less exotic songs, *In Folk Tone*,
of six years later. Last and longest is the cycle of
ten *Biblical Songs*, written in the United States in
1894, when he was feeling homesick. They are
more often sung by male singers, gaining from
weight and gravity, but here with the mezzo,
Pecková, they prove just as moving and intense.
The sound is clear and well balanced.

Seven Gypsy Melodies, B104. In Folk Tone, B146.
Eight Love Songs, B160. Four Songs, B124 – Oh what
a perfect golden dream; Downcast am I, so often.
Four Songs, B157 – Over her embroidery; Springtide;
At the brook. Four Songs, B23 – Obstacles; Medita-
tion; Lime trees. Songs from the Dvur Králové
Manuscript, B30
Bernarda Fink *mez* **Roger Vignoles** *pf*
Harmonia Mundi HMC90 1824 (69' · DDD)   Ⓕ

An all-Dvořák song recital may still seem a luxury.
The *Gypsy Songs*, and not just their famous fourth
('Songs my mother taught me'), have found a
secure place in the repertoire, but not much else is
heard at all regularly either in recital or on disc.
They may lack the variety of mood to constitute a
fully satisfying programme on their own, but they
never fail to give pleasure. One cause of the continued unfamiliarity of the B160 set is that Czech
is an alien language to most recitalists. Not, however, to the Argentinian mezzo Bernarda Fink,
who comes from a Slovenian family, lived in
Prague for a while and has made a special study of
Czech music. Her diction is very clear. Her tone is
rich and deep, and the manner has warmth and
dignity, though these seem to be its limits. If you
come to the *Gypsy Songs* with Anne Sofie von
Otter's recording in mind, you'll miss, in Fink's
singing, a lot of colour, imagination and temperament. But there may be some relief, too. Her

recording with Bengt Forsberg is exciting but
assertive. Fink and Vignoles may prove more
companionable. But this new issue is most welcome: tasteful and often lovely performances and
a generously comprehensive selection.

Additional recommendation

Dvořák Four Songs, B124 . In Folk Tone, B146. Eight
Love Songs, B160
Coupled with: **Janáček** Moravian Folk Poetry in
Songs **Martinů** New Miniatures. Mélodies pour une
amie de mon pays. Lullaby. Seven Songs on One
Page. New Slovak Songs
Magdalena Kožená *mez* **Graham Johnson**-*pf*
DG download 463 472-2GH (68' · DDD · T/t) Ⓕ ⓄⓄ🅑→

Though not currently listed on CD, this is a recital
well worth hunting down. The great gift of
Kožená's singing is the exceptional beauty of her
voice, rich, firmly placed, ample in power and
range, and now in its freshest bloom. For many,
these songs will be a most welcome discovery.

The Jacobin

The Jacobin
Václav Zítek *bar* Bohuš **Vilém Přibyl** *ten* Jiří **Daniela
Sounová** *sop* Terinka **Karel Průša** *bass* Count Vilém
René Tuček *bar* Adolf **Marcela Machotková** *sop*
Julie **Karel Berman** *bass* Filip **Beno Blachut** *ten*
Benda **Ivana Mixová** *mez* Lotinka **Kantilena Chil-
dren's Chorus; Kühn Chorus; Brno State Philhar-
monic Orchestra / Jiří Pinkas**
Supraphon ② 11 2190-2 (155' · ADD · T/t) Recorded
1977   Ⓕ

This was the first (and, so far, only) recording of
Dvořák's charming village comedy – for the
Jacobin of the title isn't a political activist but a
young man, Bohuš, returning from exile in Paris
to his stuffy old father, Count Vilém. The subplots include all manner of misunderstandings,
and set in the middle of them is the touching
figure of Benda, the fussy, rather pedantic but
wholly moving music-master. Dvořák is known
to have had in mind his own boyhood teacher,
Antonín Liehmann, whose daughter gives her
name, Terinka, to Benda's daughter. Beno Blachut celebrated his 64th birthday during the
making of this set. His was a long career, as well
as one of great distinction; he's still well able to
get round the lines of this part, and gives an
affecting picture of the old musician, never more
so than in the rehearsing of the welcome ode.
This is an idea that's cropped up in opera before,
but it's charmingly handled here.
Václav Zítek sings Bohuš pleasantly and Marcela Machotková trips away lightly as Julie.
Vilém Přibyl sounds less than his most energetic, though his voice is in good fettle; and
there's some lack of drive from Jiří Pinkas, who
might have done more to bring out the often
witty touches in Dvořák's scoring. Never mind:

this revived version of a delightful piece can be safely recommended.

Kate and the Devil

Kate and the Devil
Anna Barová *contr* Kate **Richard Novák** *bass* Devil Marbuel **Miloš Ježil** *ten* Shepherd Jirka **Daniela Suryová** *contr* Kate's mother **Jaroslav Horáček** *bass* Lucifer **Jan Hladík** *bass* Devil the Gate-keeper **Aleš Stáva** *bass* Devil the Guard **Brigita Sulcová** *sop* Princess **Natália Romanová** *sop* Chambermaid **Pavel Kamas** *bass* Marshall **Oldřich Polášek** *ten* Musician **Brno Janáček Opera Chorus and Orchestra / Jiří Pinkas**
Supraphon ② 11 1800-2 (119' · AAD · T/t) Recorded 1979 Ⓕ

Though this was never one of the best Supraphon recordings, it's perfectly serviceable. The plot is complicated, and broadly speaking concerns the bossy Kate who, finding herself a wallflower at the village hop, angrily declares that she would dance with the Devil himself. Up there duly pops a junior devil, Marbuel, who carries her off to hell, where her ceaseless chatter wearies Lucifer himself. The diabolical company is only too happy to allow the shepherd Jirka to remove her again. Jirka, attractively sung by Miloš Ježil, also manages to help the wicked but later repentant Princess to escape the Devil's clutches, and all ends well. The work has a proper coherence, and much good humour besides. Anna Barová's Kate is strong and full of character, but manages not to exclude the charm that should underlie her rantings at Marbuel, who's handsomely sung by Richard Novák. Brigita Sulcová similarly makes much of the unsympathetic Princess. Jaroslav Horáček enjoys himself hugely as Lucifer and Jiří Pinkas accompanies them well.

The King and the Charcoal Burner

The King and the Charcoal Burner
Dalibor Jenis *bar* King Matyás **Peter Mikuláš** *bar* Matěj **Michelle Breedt** *contr* Anna **Lívia Ághová** *sop* Liduška **Michal Lehotsky** *ten* Jeník **Markus Schäfer** *ten* Jindřich **Prague Chamber Choir; Cologne Radio Chorus and Symphony Orchestra / Gerd Albrecht**
Orfeo ② C678 062H (114' · DDD · S/T/t/N) Ⓕ Recorded live 2005

Dvořák's delightful *The King and the Charcoal Burner* was the second opera that he wrote and the first to be staged. In its first form it was abandoned during rehearsal as being too complex and Wagnerian, which led the composer to rewrite the piece completely, simplifying its textures and material. There followed two more versions which together form the basis of this version, recorded at concert performances in Cologne with an excellent cast of young Czech singers under Albrecht, an ever-sympathetic advocate.

The piece vies with Smetana's *The Bartered Bride* in the freshness of its Czech flavours. This marked the emergence of Dvořák's mature style, benefiting in this instance from his experience as a player in the opera orchestra in Prague. Very attractive it is, if without the sharp memorability of the Smetana's most striking numbers. Well balanced sound with voices exceptionally clear, each of them well defined with clear diction.

Lívia Ághová in the soprano role of Liduška, the charcoal burner's daughter, sings with beautiful, pure tone. She is first heard at her spinning-wheel, before the arrival of her lover, Jeník, sung with comparable purity by tenor Michal Lehotsky. The King, strongly sung by baritone Dalibor Jenis, lost in the forest in Act 1, is given shelter by the charcoal burner, Matěj – Peter Mikuláš in splendid voice. Though the King is attracted to the lovely Liduska, he recognises her genuine love for Jeník, and, after a test he devises for her, gives his blessing to their union amid general rejoicing. The chorus is a key element in the work, reflecting Dvořák's original inspiration prompted by hearing Meistersinger, with the Prague Chamber Choir and the Radio Choir singing with crisp, fresh ensemble.

Rusalka

Rusalka
Renée Fleming *sop* Rusalka **Ben Heppner** *ten* Prince **Franz Hawlata** *bass* Watergnome **Dolora Zajick** *mez* Witch **Eva Urbanová** *sop* Foreign Princess **Iván Kusnjer** *bar* Hunter, Gamekeeper **Zdena Kloubová** *sop* Turnspit **Lívia Ághová** *sop* First Woodsprite **Dana Burešová** *mez* Second Woodsprite **Hana Minutillo** *contr* Third Woodsprite **Kühn Mixed Choir; Czech Philharmonic Orchestra / Sir Charles Mackerras**
Decca ③ 460 568-2DHO3 (163' · DDD · T/t)
Ⓕ❶❷❸➤

Ⓖ Renée Fleming's tender and heartwarming account of Rusalka's Invocation to the Moon reflects the fact that the role of the lovelorn water nymph, taken by her in a highly successful production at the Met in New York, has become one of her favourites. Ben Heppner also has a special relationship with the opera, for the role of the Prince was the first he studied in depth as a student. He has sung it repeatedly since then, often opposite Renée Fleming, and both he and Mackerras have long harboured the ambition to make a complete recording.

The joy of this magnificent set, which won *Gramophone*'s Record of the Year 1999, is that in almost every way it fulfils every expectation and more, offering a recording with glowing sound that more than ever before reveals the richness and subtlety of Dvořák's score. As interpreted by Fleming and Mackerras, Rusalka's big aria at the start of Act 3, when having been rejected by the Prince, she seeks consolation in returning to the water, is as poignantly beautiful as the more celebrated Invocation to the Moon in Act 1, when she laments over loving a human. In addition, the climactic moments bring glorious top notes, firm and true up to B flat and B. Heppner, like Fleming, conveys his special affection for this music, unstrained up to top C, combining heroic power with lyric beauty.

Dolora Zajick as the Witch, Jezibaba, is characterful and fruity. Franz Hawlata as the Watergnome, Rusalka's father, is firm and dark, bringing a Wagnerian weight to the role. The engineers also thrillingly capture the off-stage effects so important in this opera, with the Watergnome balefully calling from the lake. Even the smaller roles have been cast from strength, all of them fresh, true and idiomatic. Strikingly, there isn't a hint of a Slavonic wobble from any of the singers. In the orchestra, too, the Czech horns are consistently rich and firm. And if anyone is worried about having four non-Czech principals, they're as idiomatic as any rivals.

The final glory of the set lies in the warmly understanding conducting of Charles Mackerras. In every way this matches and even outshines his supreme achievement in the Decca series of Janáček operas. In those you had the Vienna Philharmonic, but here the Czech Philharmonic is both a degree more idiomatic and just as opulent in tone, with superb solo work. The balance between voices and orchestra is well managed, with voices never drowned.

Rusalka
Cheryl Barker sop Rusalka **Rosario La Spina** ten Prince **Bruce Martin** bar Water Goblin **Elizabeth Whitehouse** sop Foreign Princess **Anne-Marie Owens** mez Ježibaba **Sarah Crane, Taryn Fiebig** sops **Dominica Matthews** mez Wood Nymphs **Barry Ryan** bar Gamekeeper/Huntsman **Sian Pendry** sop Kitchen Boy
Australian Opera Chorus and Orchestra / Richard Hickox
Chandos ③ CHAN10449 (153' · DDD · S/T/t/N)
Recorded live at the Opera House, Sydney in March 2007
Ⓕ**ⒶⒶⒶ**

Richard Hickox has made a bold choice in Dvořák's last and greatest opera, *Rusalka*, when there is a near-definitive version available on Decca with a mainly Czech cast and the Czech Philharmonic conducted by Sir Charles Mackerras (see above). Yet even in face of such competition there is a strong case for his new version from Chandos.

Cheryl Barker may not have so creamily beautiful a voice as Renée Fleming but she sounds more aptly girlish and fresh. Her big Act 1 solo, the Invocation to the Moon, flows far more easily than in Fleming's very beautiful but very expansive version, an obvious advantage. Tenor Rosario La Spina as the Prince is younger-sounding, more virile and more expressive than the Heldentenor Ben Heppner on Decca. As for Hickox, he conducts this magical score with a bite that brings out the elements so closely related to the *Slavonic Dances*, and the recording, made live in the

Sydney Opera House (a difficult venue), is clean and fresh.

The Australian cast, singing in Czech, sounds totally in tune with the Dvořák idiom, with each singer matching up to his or her Decca counterpart. Bruce Martin as the Water Goblin may not have so rich or well focused a voice as Franz Hawlata on Decca, but his is a strong and characterful performance, and as the witch Ježibaba, Anne-Marie Owens is satisfyingly rich and fruity, where her Decca counterpart is relatively thin-toned.

There is also a gain in that this has been recorded live from a stage production, notably in the thrilling conclusion of the Second Act. Surprisingly, Renée Fleming in Act 2 is less assured than in the other acts, while Cheryl Barker is consistent throughout, and her performance culminates in a deeply moving account of Rusalka's final solo, with a thrilling build-up.

A final choice must remain marginal, but anyone who wants a new-minted version of one of the most magical of all operas – with the harp signalling the other-worldly magic of Rusalka as Water Nymph, more atmospherically recorded than on Decca – this new Chandos version makes an excellent choice.

Rusalka
Milada Subrtová sop Rusalka **Eduard Haken** bass Watergnome **Marie Ovčačíková** contr Witch **Ivo Zídek** ten Prince **Alena Míková** mez Foreign Princess **Jadwiga Wysoczanská** sop First Woodsprite **Eva Hlobilová** sop Second Woodsprite **Věra Krilová** contr Third Woodsprite **Ivana Mixová** sop Turnspit **Václav Bednář** bar Hunter, Gamekeeper **Prague National Theatre Chorus and Orchestra / Zdeněk Chalabala**
Supraphon ② SU0013-2 (149' · ADD · T/t) Recorded 1961
Ⓕ**Ⓐ**

This excellent set boasts Eduard Haken, one of the great interpreters of the Watergnome, in robust voice, infusing the character with a rueful gentleness as well as a firmness of utterance. Ivo Zídek as the Prince was in his mid-thirties and in his prime at the time of this recording, singing ardently and tenderly and with a grace of phrasing that matches him well to Milada Subrtová's Rusalka. Hers is a beautiful performance, sensitive to the character's charm as well as to her fragility and pathos. The Slavonic tradition of the old watersprite legend places her in the line of the suffering heroine and it's a measure of Dvořák's success that her delicate appeal holds throughout quite a long opera, and her sinuous but never oversensual lines and the piercing harmony associated with her give her a unique appeal. Subrtová sings the part with unfaltering sensitivity. Zdeněk Chalabala, who died only a couple of months after completing this recording, handles the score with great tenderness and an affection that shines through every bar. This is a beautiful performance. The recording comes up remarkably well, too.

Rusalka (sung in English)
Eilene Hannan sop Rusalka **Rodney Macann** bass
Watergnome **Ann Howard** mez Witch **John
Treleaven** ten Prince **Phyllis Cannan** sop Foreign
Princess **Cathryn Pope** sop Woodsprite I **Eileen
Hulse** sop Woodsprite II **Linda McLeod** mez
Woodsprite III **Fiona Kimm** sop Kitchen Boy **Edward
Byles** ten Gamekeeper **Christopher Booth-Jones**
bar Hunter **English National Opera Orchestra /
Mark Elder**
Stage director **David Pountney**
Video director **Derek Bailey**
ArtHaus Musik 🟥DVD🟥 102 019 (159' · NTSC ·
4:3 · PCM stereo · 0). Recorded live in 1986   Ⓕ**OO**

The power-house regime of music director
Mark Elder and stage director David Pountney at ENO created many imaginative productions, of which this *Rusalka* was among the
finest. They set the fairytale opera in an
Edwardian nursery full of toys, with the
Watergnome as Rusalka's grandfather in a
wheelchair and the watersprite first seen on a
swing with her feet bound together, very
much an Alice in Wonderland figure. The
Witch is a wicked aunt, sinister in black as she
pronounces her curses: when Rusalka chooses
human form, she snarls: 'You'll be dumb for
evermore!'

The concept works well, with suggestions that
it is all just a dream. Motivations, characterisation and storyline are clarified and the fantasy is
intensified. In the title-role Eilene Hannan,
with her clear, bright soprano, sings powerfully,
and John Treleaven as the Prince shows no sign
of strain, even if he does not cut a very romantic
figure. Rodney Macann as the Watergnome
tends to steal the show, his dark, incisive bass
very characterful. Ann Howard is wonderfully
menacing as the Witch, while the fluttering
vibrato of Phyllis Cannan as the Foreign Princess adds to the exotic image (in Act 2, when
most of the characters are dressed in white, she
stands out in a crimson gown). The three
Woodsprites are lively, and incidental characters are well taken.

Mark Elder draws warm incisive playing
from the orchestra, adding to the dramatic
impact and underpinning the moving final
scene, when the Prince kisses Rusalka, knowing
it will mean his death.

Film

**'Deo Gratias – A documentary on the life of
Antonín Dvořák'**
Written and directed by Martin Suchánek
Includes movements from Symphony No 9, Piano
Concerto, Cello Concerto, Slavonic Dances, String
Serenade, 'American' Quartet, Biblical Songs, Te
Deum
Artists include **Gustav Rivinius** vc **Martin Kasik** pf
**Skampa Qt; Czech PO / Kout, Košler, Neumann;
Prague Philharmonic / Bělohlávek; Prague SO /
Delogu**
Video directors **Jan Bonaventura, Adam Rezek**

Supraphon 🟥DVD🟥 SU7007-9 (142' · NTSC · 16:9 · PCM
stereo & 2.0 · 0)   Ⓕ

'Deo Gratias' ('Thanks be to God'), Dvořák's
final comment on his life, is an admirably direct
and informative documentary, with plenty of
illustrations of people and places, complemented by historic film.

The opening, shots of the 1969 moon landing,
are a surprise, though we learn that, aptly, the
New World Symphony was playing on Neil
Armstrong's headphones as he stepped onto the
lunar surface. Other points are less surprising
but more revealing: reports from Dvořák's first
music school were unflattering, for example, and
his New York salary as director of the Conservatoire was 30 times higher than what he was getting at home.

The film contrasts the rapturous reception he
received in England, and later in the United
States, with the relative indifference and even
hostility that greeted him in Germany, and covers the composition of key works, giving us an
engaging portrait.

It's a pity that the musical items are single
movements rather than complete works, but the
selection is fair. The New World finale and the
first movement of the Cello Concerto, with
soloist Gustav Rivinius, are vintage recordings,
but the brilliantly played Piano Concerto finale
is recent.

Sir George Dyson   British 1883-1964

*Dyson studied at the Royal College of Music (1900-
1904) and later taught there (director from 1938),
and at several schools. His works include choral and
orchestral pieces (notably The Canterbury Pilgrims,
1931) and books.*   **GROVE**music

Symphony

Symphony. Concerto da chiesa. At the Tabard Inn
**Bournemouth Symphony Orchestra /
David Lloyd-Jones**
Naxos 8 557720 (73' · DDD)   Ⓢ**▷**

Acclaimed at its first performance in 1937,
Dyson's ambitious Symphony subsequently fell
into neglect as it followed on from a striking
sequence of symphonies written by British
composers in the 1930s such as Vaughan
Williams, Walton, Bax and Moeran. In the first
two movements, Dyson's determination to
strike a contemporary pose in an era symphonically dedicated to Sibelius seems to inhibit his
natural melodic gift, with often fragmentary
thematic material rarely developing into a
tune.

Yet in the third-movement variations – taking
the place of a scherzo – and most of all in the colourful finale, any inhibitions evaporate in warm,
free and colourful writing, echoing that in Dyson's Chaucerian choral work *The Canterbury*

Pilgrims. Helped by a clear, well-balanced recording, David Lloyd-Jones conducts a brilliant performance that clarifies textures noticeably.

Each of the three movements of the *Concerto da chiesa* for strings of 1949 is based on a medieval hymn melody, with *Veni Emmanuel* inspiring a darkly dedicated slow first movement. It is among Dyson's finest inspirations, a lament no doubt reflecting his mood after the Second World War. That melody returns transformed at the end of the joyful finale, which is based on the vigorous psalm tune *Laetatus sum*. The central *Allegretto* uses the carol-like *Corde natus* for lightly scored and fanciful variations. As in Elgar's *Introduction and Allegro* and Vaughan Williams's *Tallis* Fantasia, solo strings are beautifully and atmospherically set against the full string band, enhanced here by fine separation in the Naxos recording.

Originally designed to introduce *The Canterbury Pilgrims*, the overture *At the Tabard Inn* makes an attractive addition to a well-filled disc. All three works are superbly played and vividly recorded.

Quo Vadis

Quo Vadis
Cheryl Barker *sop* **Jean Rigby** *mez* **Philip Langridge** *ten* **Roderick Williams** *bar* **Royal Welsh College of Music and Drama Chamber Choir; BBC National Chorus and Orchestra of Wales / Richard Hickox**
Chandos ② CHAN10061 (102' · DDD · T/t) Ⓕ

Like so many British composers Dyson, even before he died in 1962, suffered neglect through writing in a conservative idiom that critics were all too ready to label 'out of date'. Originally written for the Three Choirs Festival in Hereford in 1939, its first performance was-cancelled because of the outbreak of war, and it was only given its premiere in Hereford a decade later. Dyson draws on the widest array of sources, boldly picking out passages from such poets as Campion, Vaughan, Herrick, Shelley, Newman and Bridges in an elaborate kaleidoscope, mixing them together in all but one of the nine substantial movements, even rearranging individual lines from Wordsworth's *Intimations of Immortality*. He also includes such well-known hymns as *God be in my head* and *New every morning* without hinting at the respective hymn tunes. Such a scheme might be expected to sound disjointed or bitty, but Dyson's response to each section of his text gives a seamless quality to each movement, with ecstatic choral climaxes designed to exploit the all-embracing acoustics of a great cathedral. The warm but well-defined recording helps to heighten the impact of the singing of the Welsh choristers. All four soloists are in superb voice, each of them strong, firm and characterful; and both choruses sing with fresh, incandescent tone. Dyson's idiom may not be as distinctive as that of those other 'agnostics at prayer', but with its lyrical warmth and fine control of texture, the result will delight all devotees of the English choral tradition.

The Canterbury Pilgrims

The Canterbury Pilgrims. In Honour of the City. At the Tabard Inn
Yvonne Kenny *sop* **Robert Tear** *ten* **Stephen Roberts** *bar* **London Symphony Chorus and Orchestra / Richard Hickox**
Chandos ② CHAN9531 (118' · DDD ·T) Ⓕ

 This superb offering of a full-length cantata based on the Prologue to Chaucer's *Canterbury Tales* bears out its reputation as Dyson's masterpiece. It's a fresh, tuneful work, aptly exuberant in its celebration of Chaucer. Following the scheme of Chaucer's Prologue, the 12 movements, plus Envoi, present a sequence of portraits, deftly varying the forces used, with the three soloists well contrasted in their characterisations and with the chorus acting as both narrator and commentator, providing an emotional focus for the whole work in two heightened sequences, the sixth and twelfth movements, moving and noble portraits of the two characters who aroused Dyson's deepest sympathy, the Clerk of Oxenford and the Poor Parson of a Town. If the idiom is undemanding, with occasional echoes of Vaughan Williams's *A Sea Symphony* and with passages reminiscent of Rachmaninov's *The Bells*, the cantata sustains its length well.

Outstanding among the soloists is Robert Tear who not only characterises brilliantly but sings with admirable fullness and warmth. The beautiful, fading close, when Tear as the Knight begins the first tale, moving slowly off-stage, is most atmospherically done. Yvonne Kenny and Stephen Roberts sing well too, but are less distinctive both in timbre and expression. The London Symphony Chorus sings with incandescent tone, superbly recorded, and the orchestra brings out the clarity and colourfulness of Dyson's instrumentation.

John Eccles   English 1668-1735

Eccles's greatest talent is revealed in his many songs. Remarkable for their beautifully contoured melodies and impeccable prosody, they quickly capture the mood and subtleties of the poetry and are eminently singable. Eccles brought the Restoration tradition to its close. After Purcell's death in 1695 he was undoubtedly the greatest of the Restoration theatre composers. Continuing in Purcell's footsteps, The Judgment of Paris was the last of the masques.
GROVEmusic

The Judgement of Paris

The Judgement of Paris[a]. Three Mad Songs[b]
Roderick Williams *bar* Mercury **Benjamin Hulett** *ten* aris [b]**Susan Bickley** *mez* Juno [b]**Claire Booth** *sop* Pallas [b]**Lucy Crowe** *sop* Venus [a]**Chorus of Early Opera Company; Early Opera Company / Christian Curnyn**
Chandos Chaconne CHAN0759 (62' · DDD) Ⓕ

Eccles's one-act 'semi-opera' (1701) calls for five solo singers, a choir and relatively modest instrumental resources – four-part strings, four trumpets, two recorders, kettledrums and continuo. Absent are castrati and countertenors. The music is tuneful, the boundaries between recitatives and airs often blurred. To address the lack of anguish or whiff of treachery in the masque, three 'mad' arias by the composer, each sung by a different soprano, are included at the end. The Early Opera Company band delivers delicately balanced homophonic accompaniments to the airs, varied by ground basses that remind us of Henry Purcell, and occasional solos, duos and quartets. As charming as it is, it doesn't bear comparison with opera seria of the day and, in particular, Handel's *Rinaldo*, presented to London audiences a decade later.

Christian Curnyn offers an unaffected, faithful reading of the printed score. If anything, it is understated, the instrumental forces reduced (the premiere employed 85 musicians in addition to the 'verse singers') and the recording acoustic intimate. Lucy Crowe's Venus may win the prize, but all of the soloists contribute beautifully judged portrayals.

Sir Edward Elgar   British 1857-1934

Elgar had violin lessons in Worcester and London but was essentially self-taught, learning much in his father's music shop. From the age of 16 he worked locally as a violinist, organist, bassoonist, conductor and teacher, also composing abundantly though not yet very individually: the accepted corpus of his works belongs almost entirely to the period after his 40th birthday.

His first attempt to establish himself in London was premature. He moved there with his wife Alice in 1889, but in 1891 they returned to Malvern, and he began to make a reputation more steadily with choral works: The Black Knight, The Light of Life, King Olaf and Caractacus. These were written within a specifically English tradition, but they were influenced also by German music from Weber, Schumann and Mendelssohn to Brahms and Wagner. The orchestral Enigma Variations (1899), in which each variation portrays a different friend of Elgar's, then proclaimed the belated arrival of a fully formed original style, taken further in the oratorio The Dream of Gerontius (1900), where the anxious chromaticism of a post-Parsifal manner is answered by the assurances of the Newman text: Elgar was himself a Roman Catholic, which may have been one cause of his personal insecurity. **GROVE**music

Cello Concerto

Cello Concerto. Sea Pictures
Jacqueline du Pré vc **Janet Baker** mez **London Symphony Orchestra / Sir John Barbirolli**
EMI 556219-2 (54' · ADD) Recorded 1965 Ⓕ❌❌❌Ⓓ

 Though both Jacqueline du Pré and Janet Baker were already well established and widely appreciated in 1965, this disc marked a turning point for both of them in their recording careers. With Barbirolli so warm-hearted and understanding an accompanist to each, these are both in every sense classic performances that can never be replaced.

Jacqueline du Pré's Elgar has been all the more appreciated, since her tragic illness has taken her away as a performer. In principle her espressivo may be too freely romantic, but the slow movement and epilogue remain supreme in their intensity, conveying in whispered *pianissimos* of daring delicacy an inner communion, while the bravura of the brilliant passages remains astonishing from an artist still only 20.

Until this recording, *Sea Pictures* had tended to be underprized even among Elgarians; but the passion, intensity and sheer beauty of this performance with each of the five songs sharply distinct rebutted any idea that – in reflection of verse of varying quality – it had anything of substandard Elgar in it. It's a work you'll probably never be able to listen to again without hearing in your mind Janet Baker's deeply individual phrasing on this disc. What strikes you most is the central relevance to Baker's whole career of the last stanza in 'Sabbath morning at sea', a radiant climax. 'He shall assist me to look higher' says the Barrett Browning poem, and the thrust of meaning as she sings it invariably conveys a *frisson* such as you rarely get on record.

Cello Concerto[a]
Bach Cello Suites[b] – No 1, BWV1007; No 2, BWV1008
Jacqueline du Pré vc [a]**BBC Symphony Orchestra / Sir John Barbirolli**
Testament [b]mono SBT1388 (72' · ADD)
[a]Recorded live 1967   Ⓟ❌❌

Jacqueline du Pré was 20 when she recorded Elgar's Cello Concerto with Barbirolli and the LSO August 1965 – an interpretation universally acclaimed for its profound expressiveness (see above). A second recording, taped live in 1970 with Daniel Barenboim and the Philadelphia Orchestra, has proved more controversial; du Pré's radiant intensity remains undimmed but instead of the nobility found in the EMI account one hears desperation, or something close to it.

This new Testament disc makes public another live document, recorded in Prague with Barbirolli and the BBC Symphony Orchestra. The general shape of this performance resembles the EMI recording, not surprisingly given that the studio session had taken place a little more than a year before. But while du Pré was always an electric player, the voltage clearly increased before an audience. One hears the difference immediately as she digs into the opening solo with startling urgency. Tempi, in general, are noticeably faster; and although Barbirolli and the orchestra occasionally fall behind, the phrasing is longer-breathed and the sections flow more smoothly one into the other.

Du Pré (onstage and a year on from the EMI version) finds a greater variety of mood in the score. The *dolcissimo* Elgar asks for at fig 8 (starting at 3'58" in the first movement) evokes an audible smile in the cellist's sound, for example. Or try her magical way with the swooping phrase at 3'10" in the *Adagio*: the high note is floated beautifully in the studio but in concert her tone and timing take one's breath away. Best of all, perhaps, is the finale's *Poco più lento* (beginning at 6'42"), where du Pré's playing has an emotive force and eloquence akin to the greatest Shakespearian oratory – Barbirolli and the orchestra provide splendid support here.

Youthful (and previously released) interpretations of Bach's first two cello suites round out the disc, but the Elgar here is valuable enough to merit the highest possible recommendation.

Elgar Cello Concerto[a] **Bloch** Schelomo[a] **Kabalevsky** Cello Concerto No 2 in G, Op 77[b] **Tchaikovsky** Variations on a Rococo Theme, Op 33[c]. Nocturne, Op-19 No 4[c]. Pezzo capriccioso, Op 62[c]. Andante cantabile, Op 11[c] **R Strauss** Don Quixote[d]
Steven Isserlis vc [a]**London Symphony Orchestra / Richard Hickox;** [b]**London Philharmonic Orchestra / Andrew Litton;** [c]**Chamber Orchestra of Europe / Sir John Eliot Gardiner;** [d]**Minnesota Orchestra / Edo de Waart**
Virgin Classics 561490-2 (51' · DDD)　　Ⓜ︎🅾️↦

Cellists are apt to 'come of age' in recordings of the Elgar. Isserlis was no exception. This is a wonderful account of the Concerto – brave, imaginative, individual – indeed, quite the most personal in its perception of the piece since the treasurable du Pré on EMI. And that, you'll appreciate, is saying something though not, we hasten to add, that the two readings are in any outward sense similar. Far from it. With Isserlis, the emotional tug is considerably less overt, the emphasis more on shadow and subtext than open heartache. Yet the inner light is no less intense, the phrasing no less rhapsodic in manner than du Pré. On the contrary. This is free-range Elgar all right, and like du Pré it comes totally without affectation. Both Isserlis and du Pré take an appropriately generous line on the first movement's sorrowful song, with Isserlis the more reposeful, the more inclined to open out and savour key cadences. The Scherzo itself is quite simply better played than on any previous recording; the articulation and definition of the semiquaver 'fours' would, we're sure, have astonished even the composer himself. From a technical point of view Isserlis is easily the equal, and more, of any player currently before us. And if you still feel that du Pré really did have the last word where the epilogue is concerned, then listen to Isserlis sinking with heavy heart into those pages preceding the return of the opening declamation. He achieves a mesmerising fragility in the bars marked *lento* – one last backward glance, as it were – and the inwardness of the final *diminuendo* is something to be heard and remembered. Hickox and the LSO prove model

collaborators. Don't on any account miss these performances.

Elgar Cello Concerto
Dvořák Cello Concerto in B minor, B191
Maria Kliegel vc
Royal Philharmonic Orchestra / Michael Halász
Naxos 8 550503 (73' · DDD)　　　　Ⓢ↦

The technical accomplishment of Kliegel's playing is balanced by a richness of musical insight that won't disappoint. The boldness of the opening soliloquy recalls du Pré at her finest, and yet Kliegel shares a yet deeper cup of grief in the world-weariness of the main first subject, carried with noble conviction. She takes a more improvisatory view in the lilting second group than du Pré.

The *Scherzo* is brilliantly done, and at a very fast tempo, but the conductor Michael Halász overlooks Elgar's precisely noted *A tempo* indication in response to the soloist's cantabile *largamente* statements at the end of each main section. The effect isn't only tedious, but is quite the reverse of the composer's intention, clearly stated in the score. The *Adagio* is thoughtfully played, avoiding unwelcome posturing or empty affectation, though Kliegel is, if anything, a little too cool and dispassionate here.

The finale is superbly paced, with the rumbustious militarism of the orchestration never allowed to dominate. The recording was made at Henry Wood Hall, and is full bodied and emphatic in major *tutti*s, yet one might have wished the overall balance to favour the soloist more than it does.

Cello Concerto **Walton** Cello Concerto
Daniel Müller-Schott vc
Oslo Philharmonic Orchestra / André Previn
Orfeo C621061A (60' · DDD)　　　　　Ⓕ

The Elgar and Walton cello concertos make a perfect coupling and this is the second time André Previn has conducted the pairing on disc. The first, some 20 years ago, had Yo-Yo Ma, still near the beginning of his career, and the LSO. Here he's with the young German cellist Daniel Müller-Schott and his own Oslo Philharmonic in an equally idiomatic reading.

Significantly, Müller-Schott writes his own booklet-notes, demonstrating his warm affection and understanding of both works. It is the passion of his playing that strikes home immediately – he uses a wider vibrato than Ma, and rather freer, less inhibited phrasing. That passion comes over not only in the slower music of the Elgar but also in the seemingly hesitating introduction to the second-movement *Scherzo*; and where Ma's reading of the slow movement is marked by refinement and nobility, Müller-Schott's is weightier. Similarly, in the central *Scherzo* of the Walton, where Ma is very fast and volatile, Müller-Schott is heavier-handed, though without losing the piece's sparkle.

The solo cello is balanced very far forward so that at the start of the Walton its sound obscures the subtle detail in the orchestration. That said, there is everything to enjoy in performances that are uninhibited, bringing out the warmth of both pieces. Many will forgive the odd balance when the performances are so convincing, even if Müller-Schott is not quite so imaginative or individual in his phrasing as Ma.

Cello Concerto, Op 85ᵃ. Falstaff, Op 68ᵇ.
Nursery Suiteᶜ   Ⓗ
ᵃBeatrice Harrison vc
ᵇᶜLondon Symphony Orchestra;
ᵃNew Symphony Orchestra / Sir Edward Elgar
Dutton mono CDBP9776 (76' · ADD)
From HMV originals   Ⓢ⊙

It was Mike Dutton, when he was at EMI, who supervised the transfer of all of Elgar's electrical recordings. That set has been available only intermittently, which makes Dutton's revised transfers of these three works specially valuable, particularly the 1928 recording of the Cello Concerto with Beatrice Harrison. It now has a satisfying weight and body, though Harrison's wiry tone is not to everyone's taste and the intonation is occasionally suspect.

The *Falstaff*, made at the opening of EMI's Abbey Road Studios in 1931, has always been impressive in transfers, and the recording of the *Nursery Suite* made in the same year with the dedicatees, the Duke and Duchess of York and Princesses Elizabeth and Margaret present, comes out brightly and clearly. The Royals were particularly delighted with 'The Wagon Passes', with the whistling of the carter charmingly portrayed. The septuagenarian Elgar put love into his performance, as he did also in *Falstaff* with its swaggering Prince Hal theme and tragic epilogue which so echoes the epilogue of Strauss's *Don Quixote*.

Additional recommendation

Coupled with: **Lutosławski** Cello Concerto
Wispelwey vc Netherlands Radio Philharmonic
Orchestra / Van Steen
Channel Classics CCS12998 (54' · DDD)   Ⓕ
   The utterly sympathetic performance of the Elgar displays both elasticity and plentiful re-creative fantasy. A notable achievement in every way.

Violin Concerto in B minor

Violin Concerto
Vaughan Williams The Lark Ascending
Nigel Kennedy vn City of Birmingham Symphony
Orchestra / Sir Simon Rattle
EMI 556413-2 (72' · ADD)   Ⓕ⊙

Astonishingly, in the case of the first two movements at least, this release, recorded during the week following a live concert at Birmingham's

ELGAR'S CELLO CONCERTO – IN BRIEF

Daniel Müller-Schott vc
Oslo Philharmonic Orchestra / André Previn
Orfeo C621061A (60' · DDD)   Ⓕ
A German-Norwegian-American version that proves splendidly that Elgar's very British voice can travel the world.

Pablo Casals; BBC SO / Sir Adrian Boult
Biddulph LAB144 (79' · ADD) or   Ⓜ
Backed by Boult at his authoritative best, Casals brings an irresistible physicality and capricious temperament to Elgar's nostalgic inspiration. An account to hear.

**Jacqueline du Pré; BBC Symphony Orchestra /
Sir John Barbirolli**
Testament SBT1388 (72' · ADD)   Ⓕ⊙⊙
Made a year after the classic EMI recording, here's another invaluable memento of du Pré's musical genius. The extra adrenalin pumping at a public performance is obvious in every bar. A fantastic document…

**Jacqueline du Pré; London SO /
Sir John Barbirolli**
EMI 556219-2 (54' · ADD)   Ⓕ⊙⊙⊙▷
Ⓖ For countless collectors the world over, du Pré's immortal 1965 recording with Barbirolli and the LSO tugs at the heartstrings like no other version before or since.

Steven Isserlis; London SO / Richard Hickox
Virgin Classics ③ 561490 2 (156' · DDD)   Ⓜ⊙▷
Unusually self-effacing, Isserlis eschews any vestige of overheated, heart-on-sleeve exaggeration. Intimacy and wistfulness are the keynotes.

Natalie Clein; RLPO / Vernon Handley
EMI 501409-2 (52' · DDD)   Ⓕ▷
A fine modern version from one of the UK's most accomplished young cellists. It combines imagination and poetry with a wonderfully expansive view of the work.

Truls Mørk; CBSO / Sir Simon Rattle
Virgin Classics 545356-2 (65' · DDD)   Ⓢ▷
Mørk and Rattle form an intelligent, dignified and irreproachably stylish partnership. Top-notch production-values. Comes with an equally compelling Britten Cello Symphony.

**Pieter Wispelwey; Netherlands RPO /
Jac van Steen**
Channel Classics CCS12998 (54' · DDD)   Ⓕ
Wispelwey is acutely alive to the strong strain of classicism that runs through Elgar's autumnal masterpiece. An unforced, deeply satisfying reading, with splendidly bright-eyed orchestral playing.

Symphony Hall in July 1997, fully re-creates the heady excitement of that memorable event. From every conceivable point of view – authority, panache, intelligence, intuitive poetry, tonal beauty and emotional maturity – Kennedy surpasses his 1985 *Gramophone* Award-winning EMI Eminence recording (now on Classics for Pleasure). The first movement is a magnificent achievement all round, with tension levels extraordinarily high for a studio project. Rattle launches the proceedings in exemplary fashion, his direction passionate, ideally flexible and texturally lucid (the antiphonally divided violins help). The CBSO, too, is on top form. But it's Kennedy who rivets the attention from his commanding initial entry onwards. There's no hiding in this of all scores and Kennedy penetrates to the very essence of 'the soul enshrined within' in his melting presentation of the 'Windflower' theme – Elgar's *dolce semplice* realised to tear-spilling perfection. The slow movement is almost as fine. Only the finale oddly dissatisfies. Not in terms of technical address or co-ordination (both of which are stunning); rather, for all the supreme accomplishment on show, the results aren't terribly moving. Despite any lingering doubts about this last movement we're still left with an enormously stimulating and well-engineered display.

The fill-up is a provocative account of *The Lark Ascending*, which Kennedy (whose tone is ravishing) and Rattle spin out to 17 and a half minutes.

Violin Concerto, Op 61
Gil Shaham vn **Chicago Symphony Orchestra / David Zinman**
Canary Classics CC06 (48' · DDD)
Recorded live at Orchestra Hall, Symphony Center, Chicago, in February 2007 Ⓕ ⃝

It is good to welcome an all-American performance of this most British of concertos that is so thrillingly passionate. David Zinman has said that of all concertos this is his favourite, something confirmed in the playing he draws from the Chicago Symphony, its richness as well as its characteristic polish. The detail revealed in the long *tuttis* also demonstrates the care with which Zinman has prepared this performance. The recording on the Canary Classics label (Gil Shaham's own) is taken from live performances, and that adds to the impact, with the opulent sound matching the playing.

The playing of the orchestra finds a perfect counterpart in the performance of Gil Shaham, always one of the most sensitive and responsive of the high-powered violin virtuosos. Amazingly, he has performed this work some 20 times in the last 10 years. His range of tone and of dynamic is extreme, some might feel too much so, when some of his *pianissimos*, as in the second subject of the first movement, are so gentle that they can barely be heard against the orchestra. Though in that key passage he slows

from the basic speed – something adopted by virtually every soloist in this work – there is nothing self-indulgent or sentimental in it, rather less so than in Kennedy's fine version with Vernon Handley conducting. Equally, Shaham's pronounced vibrato is always perfectly controlled.

The slow movement brings refinement and purity, while the main *Allegro* in the finale is fast and light, leading to a deeply dedicated account of the long accompanied cadenza. This now stands as one of the very finest versions of this concerto, and even though the disc, unlike most, offers no coupling, it is well worth the price. Under Solti as music director, the Chicago Orchestra produced one or two fine Elgar recordings, but the playing here is even warmer under Zinman.

Violin Concerto, Op 61[a]. Serenade, Op 20.
[a]**James Ehnes** vn
Philharmonia Orchestra / Sir Andrew Davis
Onyx ONYX4025 (61' · DDD) Ⓕ⃝⃝

Not since Nigel Kennedy's 1997 EMI remake with Sir Simon Rattle and the CBSO has the Elgar received a recording as thrillingly combustible, imaginative and involving as this. James Ehnes brings to this great concerto a rapt identification, tingling temperament and glowing ardour. Not only is Ehnes's technical address impeccable and intonation miraculously true, his contribution is remarkable for its intrepid emotional scope, athletic agility and (perhaps above all) jaw-dropping delicacy (nowhere more heart-tuggingly potent than in the finale's accompanied cadenza).

Ehnes is also fortunate in enjoying the support of Sir Andrew Davis, a proven Elgarian whose wonderfully perceptive conducting has authoritative sweep, elasticity and fiery passion to spare as well as a very special understanding of those moments of aching intimacy in which this of all scores abounds: what a ravishing backcloth he provides for the ineffable appearance of the 'Windflower' theme in the same movement; and how affecting are the strings' songful sighs in the ensuing *Andante*. One or two unruly timpani thwacks aside, the Philharmonia's response exhibits polish, grace and dedication.

Some might take issue with the sound which is a little shrouded and lacking something in alluring bloom (the actual balance is otherwise very much as you would hear from a seat in the stalls). No matter, this remains a performance of conspicuous pedigree and insight guaranteed to make you fall in love all over again with this sublime music and which can only boost Ehnes's standing as one of the most gifted and charismatic fiddlers around. Davis's utterly unforced and ravishingly moving account of the entrancing Serenade makes a cherishable pendant.

Violin Concerto[a]. Cello Concerto[b] Ⓗ
[a]**Yehudi Menuhin** vn [b]**Beatrice Harrison** vc

[a]**London Symphony Orchestra,** [b]**New Symphony Orchestra / Sir Edward Elgar**
EMI Great Recordings of the Century mono
566979-2 (75' · AAD) Recorded 1932, 1928   Ⓜ ○○○

Elgar's conducting for Menuhin in the Violin Concerto's opening orchestral *tutti* is magnificent, as is his solicitous, attentive accompaniment throughout the work. Menuhin's youthful, wonderfully intuitive musicianship in fact needed little 'instruction', and the success of the recording may be judged from the fact that there have been few periods in the years since it was first issued when it hasn't been available in some shape or form. Beatrice Harrison first studied the Cello Concerto for an abridged, pre-electric recording with Elgar conducting. So impressed was the composer then that he insisted that she should be the soloist whenever he conducted the work again. Their authoritative performance is deeply felt and highly expressive, but it has a quality of nobility and stoicism which comes as a refreshing change from some overindulgent modern performances.

Since the original matrices were destroyed, EMI's engineers had to return to the 1957 tape for this transfer; although the 1957 engineers did not quite capture all the body of the originals there's an impressive clarity in the transfer, now brightened a little more for CD. The 1970s transfer of the Harrison/Elgar Cello Concerto was impressively managed, and this reissue has given still more presence to the sound without any sense of falsification.

Violin Concerto[b] **Delius** Violin Concerto[a]   Ⓗ
Albert Sammons vn [a]**Liverpool Philharmonic Orchestra / Malcolm Sargent;** [b]**New Queen's Hall Orchestra / Henry Wood**
Naxos Historical mono 8 110951 (67' · ADD)
Recorded [b]1929, [a]1944   Ⓢ ○○○

 Albert Sammons' 1929 account of Elgar's Violin Concerto with Sir Henry Wood and the New Queen's Hall Orchestra remains the finest version ever made, outstripping even the legendary Menuhin/Elgar collaboration from three years later in terms of authoritative grip, intuitive poetry and emotional candour. Previous transfers to CD have varied from satisfactory to merely tolerable and unacceptably botched. So it's a pleasure to encounter Mark Obert-Thorn's judicious restoration for Naxos.

Delius heard Sammons perform the Elgar in May 1915, and was so bowled over that he set about writing a concerto for the formidable virtuoso. Sammons premiered the work with Boult in January 1919 but had to wait a full quarter of a century before committing it to disc. Here is another irreplaceable document: Sammons was an assiduous champion of this glorious music, and although the solo playing hasn't quite the effortless technical mastery of its companion here, his wise and unforced interpretation penetrates to the very core of

ELGAR'S SYMPHONIES – IN BRIEF

London PO / Sir Georg Solti
Decca ② 443 856-2DF2 (135' · ADD)   Ⓜ
Solti drives hard in any faster music but both slow movements have a tingling concentration and rapt hush that are deeply affecting. The LPO respond brilliantly throughout; lustrous Decca sound, too.

London Philharmonic Orchestra / Sir Adrian Boult
EMI ② 382151-2 (137' · ADD)   Ⓜ
A glorious memento of a great Elgarian. Not only does the set include the two symphonies but also *In the South*, the *Intoduction and Allegro* and *Grania and Diarmid*.

SYMPHONY NO 1

Hallé Orchestra / Sir John Barbirolli
BBC Legends BBCL4106-2 (67' · DDD)   Ⓢ ○○▷
The other great Elgarian knight: Barbirolli shares with Boult a profound feeling for this music and draws from the Hallé Orchestra playing of tremendous warmth and sweep. Just one of his six recordings, and a thing of joy none the less.

London SO / Sir Colin Davis
LSO Live LSO0017 (55' · DDD)   Ⓢ▷
Sir Colin's unhurried conception is crowned by a superbly exciting reading of the finale that sweeps all before it. The Barbican acoustic is not ideally opulent, but don't let that minor caveat put you off.

SYMPHONY NO 2

Hallé Orchestra / Sir John Barbirolli
EMI 764724-2 (66' · ADD)   Ⓜ○
A richly expansive performance, delivered by the Hallé *con amore*, with the slow movement in particular rising to an indescribable peak of emotion. One to snap up.

BBC SO / Sir Andrew Davis
Apex 0927-49586-2 (78' · DDD)   Ⓢ○○
Few rivals come close to equalling the all-round perception displayed by Sir Andrew Davis in his 1991 account of Elgar's multi-faceted masterpiece. With its meaty coupling of *In the South*, this is an exceptional bargain.

SYMPHONY NO 3

Bournemouth SO / Paul Daniel
Naxos 8 554719 (55' · DDD)   Ⓢ○○▷
One in the fast-growing discography for this newly created work, Daniel nails his Elgarian credentials to the mast with a reading that makes you believe wholeheartedly in every bar of this powerful work. The Bournemouth orchestra plays with burning conviction and the Naxos price makes it irresistible.

Delius's lovely vision. An admirable introduction to a truly great fiddler, irresistible at the price.

Additional recommendation

Violin Concerto
Kennedy vn **London Philharmonic Orchestra / Handley**
Classics for Pleasure 575139-2 (54' · DDD) Ⓑ
Kennedy's superb first recording of the Elgar Violin Concerto won the *Gramophone* Record of the Year in 1985 and is now at bargain price.

Symphonies

No 1 in A flat, Op 55; **No 2** in E flat, Op 63;
No 3 in C minor, Op 88

Symphonies – No 1; No 2. Cello Concerto.
Violin Concerto. 'Enigma' Variations.
Cockaigne, 'In London Town'. In the South,
'Alassio'. Froissart. Falstaff. Sea Pictures.
Chanson de matin. Chanson de nuit.
Elegy. Serenade. Introduction and Allegro.
Coronation March. Imperial March.
The Sanguine Fan. Contrasts
Featuring performances by **Janet Baker** *mez* **Alfredo Campoli**, **Rodney Friend**, **John Willison** vns **John Chambers** va **Paul Tortelier**, **Alexander Cameron** vcs **David Bell** org **London Philharmonic Orchestra / Sir Adrian Boult**, **Sir Edward Elgar**, **Vernon Handley**, **Sir Charles Mackerras**, **Sir Landon Ronald**, **Sir Georg Solti**
LPO ⑤ LPO0016/20 (6h 25' · ADD/DDD) Ⓜ

What a brilliant idea of the LPO to gather together Elgar recordings from many different sources, some rare and unexpected. They range from the composer's recordings with the newly founded LPO to Sir Charles Mackerras and Vernon Handley in the 1980s. Most Elgarians will know the great majority, but it is many years since the Campoli recording of the Violin Concerto, fresh and urgent, was freely available.

Most cherishable of all is a *Sea Pictures* with Janet Baker and Vernon Handley, a live recording from 1984 that was rescued from the Capital Radio archives; it's a wonderful alternative to the much-loved LSO/Barbirolli version. Baker's voice is still gloriously rich, and the live occasion inspires a performance of great urgency and intensity. The nobility in 'Sabbath Morning at Sea' is heart-stopping, from full-throated richness down to a hushed *pianissimo* on 'brooded soft on waters deep', and the attack in 'The Swimmer' is thrilling. Handley beautifully conjures up the surge of the sea in the brilliant orchestration.

Sir Adrian Boult is the principal contributor to the set in recordings from a number of labels. The excellent transfer gives wonderful body to the mono recording of the Violin Concerto while *Falstaff*, Boult's 1956 Nixa recording, has a restricted frequency range but still reveals plenty of detail, the close chilling. It is good, too, to have Paul Tortelier's warm and steadily paced reading of the Cello Concerto, and Handley's noble CfP version of the Second Symphony is valuable for the use of organ to reinforce the bass at a key point in the finale. Mackerras's *Imperial March*, made for Reader's Digest, is a rarity, and his other contribution, a 1985 *Enigma* Variations (EMI Eminence), brings an unusually slow 'Nimrod'.

It is good to have Elgar's own beautiful account of the Serenade for Strings, spacious in the slow movement, and his *Froissart*. From the 1930s, too, an excellent Coronation March by Sir Landon Ronald sounds wonderfully rich for the period. Solti's Decca recordings have tingling clarity and brilliance, warmth and panache.

A wonderfully rich collection that all Elgarians should try to hear. Praise must go to the transfer engineers.

Symphony No 1. Introduction and Allegro, Op 47
Hallé Orchestra / Sir John Barbirolli
BBC Legends/IMG Artists BBCL4106-2 (67' · ADD)
Recorded live 1970 Ⓕ Ⓞ

On July 24, 1970 Sir John Barbirolli conducted (and recorded) this inspired Hallé performance of Elgar's First Symphony in St Nicholas's Chapel, as his major contribution to the King's Lynn Festival. Four days later he suffered a fatal heart attack. There could be no finer memorial, for the acoustic of the chapel provides a wonderfully warm glow and the richest amplitude for the Hallé brass and strings, without blunting the *fortissimo*s. The depth of feeling and power in the performance has the genuine thrill of live music-making. For instance, there's an extraordinary central climax in the first movement, with the brass outbursts given a terrifying intensity; the apotheosis of the finale has similar emotional strength. Barbirolli invests the symphony's slow sad motto theme with a poignant nostalgia each time it appears; but most memorable of all is the richness of the opening of the *Adagio*, sustained throughout with Barbirolli's characteristic warmth of feeling, while the impassioned Hallé string playing is as rich in tone as it's heartfelt.

Fascinatingly, the interpretation looks back to his first 1956 Pye recording with his own orchestra (available on Dutton Laboratories). Both performances play for a little over 52 minutes, and the timings of each movement and the flexible inner relationships of tempo are very close. But this final version matches and even surpasses that first venture in its surging forward momentum, and the sound is far richer, obviously more modern. Everyone has their favourite version among the six, but no Elgarian will be disappointed with this account.

Symphony No 1
London Symphony Orchestra / Sir Colin Davis
LSO Live LSO0017 (55' · DDD) Ⓢ Ⓞ Ⓞ ▷

This thrillingly combustible account easily holds its own in the most exalted company. Davis's is a patient, noble conception, yet lacking absolutely nothing in thrusting drama, fresh-faced character and tender poetry. Certainly, Sir Colin steers a marvellously confident course through the epic first movement, the music-making always comprehensive in its emotional scope and hitting genuine heights in the development. The *Scherzo* is another great success, the glinting, defiant swagger of the outer portions counterbalanced by the delectable grace and point these eloquent players lavish on the Trio. Just one small interpretative quibble: Davis's inorganic slackening of tempo during the sublime transition into the slow movement (listen to Barbirolli's unforgettable 1956 Hallé account to hear how it should be done). As for the great *Adagio* itself, Davis's intensely devotional approach works beautifully. The finale positively surges with purposeful bite, fire and sinew, while the glorious closing pages really do raise the roof. The expertly balanced sound doesn't have quite the bloom that EMI and Decca achieved for Boult and Solti on their classic analogue versions, but it amply conveys the tingling electricity and physical impact of a special event. At this price, this is one to snap up.

Symphonies – No 1, Op 55; No 2, Op 63
London Philharmonic Orchestra / Sir Adrian Boult
Lyrita ② SRCD221 (100' · ADD) ⒻOO

In 1968, when Sir Adrian Boult recorded the two Elgar Symphonies for Lyrita, he wrote an open letter to *Gramophone*, couched diplomatically but reflecting his fury that at the sessions his recording manager had forced him on technical grounds to have all the violins on the left instead of his usual habit of dividing them between the two sections. That said, and 40 years on, the comparisons with Boult's other recordings of the Elgar symphonies demonstrate very clearly how fine they are, arguably the finest versions he ever recorded.

Compared with the EMI versions recorded less than five years later, they are tauter, the ensemble noticeably crisper. The recording is brighter and clearer in this transfer. The difference is particularly marked in No 2 which, as Elgar said, was a work which Boult was the first conductor to make a success after the disappointing reception given at its premiere. The comparison is closer with the mono recording of No 2, which Boult recorded with the BBC SO in 1945, a superb performance but which is still marginally outshone by the Lyrita version.

Symphony No 1, Op 55.
Organ Sonata No 1, Op 28 (orch Jacob)
BBC National Orchestra of Wales / Richard Hickox
Chandos ⊛ CHSA5049 (78' · DDD) ⒻOOⒹ

The SACD recording for this impressive Elgar First is spectacular; you really appreciate the sharpness of articulation of the Cardiff players. Hickox's interpretation is comparably impressive, particularly so in the first movement where he has a cunning way of presenting the great Elgarian melodies simply. In the tricky transition from two in a bar to three Hickox broadens the tempo where others follow the composer's example in keeping the minim beat steady; nonetheless he makes that moment a magnificent climax.

Hickox's control of such climaxes is masterly. In the *Scherzo* the articulation of the violins and the sharpness of attack is thrilling. In the great melodies of the slow movement Hickox tenderly brings out a songlike quality, making others seem a little studied. The delicate *pianissimo* as the third theme enters is breathtaking. The two great 'gulp' moments in the finale come at the climax of the passage where the theme of the slow introduction comes in augmentation; there Hickox comes near to matching Elgar himself in impact. Finally, he secures a superbly satisfying *crescendo* on the brass on the final chord.

The generous coupling adds to the attractions of the disc, an orchestration of a work which should be far better known. The qualities which make Hickox's reading of the Symphony so impressive come out here too.

Symphony No 1ᵃ. In the South, 'Alassio', Op 50ᵇ Ⓗ
London Philharmonic Orchestra / Sir Adrian Boult
Testament mono SBT1229 (69' · DDD) Recorded
ᵃ1949, ᵇ1955 ⒻOOO

 The first wonder of this very welcome transfer is the astonishing quality of the sound, mono only but full-bodied and finely detailed to give a keener sense of presence than the rather disappointing CD transfer of the 1976 stereo version, with a surprisingly wide dynamic range for a 1949 recording. When Boult recorded that final stereo version, he was already 87, and though as ever the reading is a noble one, beautifully paced, it has nothing like the same thrust and tension as this recording of nearly three decades earlier. In particular the heavenly *Adagio* has an extra meditative intensity in the way that Boult presents each of the great lyrical themes. The finale in particular has a bite and thrust far beyond that of the later account.

Boult's recording of *In the South*, made in 1955, brings out his thrustful side even more strikingly, with urgent speeds giving way in the lovely *Canto popolare* section to a honeyed beauty before an urgent yet finely controlled account of the coda. Sadly, the 1955 sound is shallower than that of six years earlier for the symphony, though there's ample weight for the brass theme of the second section.

Symphony No 2. In the South
BBC Symphony Orchestra / Sir Andrew Davis
Warner Apex 0927-49586-2 (78' · DDD) ⑤ⓈOO

In his finest achievement on record, Andrew Davis penetrates to the dark inner core of this great symphony. In the opening *Allegro vivace e nobilmente*, for example, how well he and his acutely responsive players gauge the varying moods of Elgar's glorious inspiration: be it in the exhilarating surge of that leaping introductory paragraph or the spectral, twilight world at the heart of this wonderful movement, no one is found wanting.

Davis's unerring structural sense never once deserts him, and the BBC Symphony Orchestra plays its heart out. Above all, it's in the many more reflective moments that Davis proves himself an outstandingly perceptive Elgarian, uncovering a vein of intimate anguish that touches to the very marrow; in this respect, his account of the slow movement is quite heart-rendingly poignant – undoubtedly the finest since Boult's incomparable 1944 performance with this very same orchestra – while the radiant sunset of the symphony's coda glows with luminous beauty.

Prefaced by an equally idiomatic, stirring *In the South*, this is an Elgar Second to set beside the very greatest. In every way a treasurable release.

Symphony No 2
BBC Philharmonic Orchestra / Sir Edward Downes
Naxos 8 550635 (56' · DDD)   Ⓢ ❶ ❷

Here's further proof that Edward Downes is an Elgarian to be reckoned with. This account of the Second Symphony is up there with the very best. In the first movement, Downes steers a clear-sighted course: here's the same unexaggerated, splendidly authoritative conception heard from this conductor in the concert hall. Unlike some rivals on record, Downes resists the temptation to give too much too soon, and this feeling of power in reserve lends an extra cumulative intensity to the proceedings; indeed, the coda here is absolutely thrilling. The ensuing *Larghetto* sees Downes striking a near-perfect balance between introspection and heart-warming passion. Both the *Rondo* and finale are ideally paced – the former not too hectic, the latter flowing to perfection, culminating in an epilogue of rare delicacy. Throughout, the BBC Philharmonic plays outstandingly for its former chief: the orchestra's golden-toned cello section must be singled out for special praise. Just a touch more clarity in *tuttis*, and the recording would have been ideal. A deeply sympathetic reading, possessing qualities to match any rival.

Symphony No 3
Bournemouth Symphony Orchestra / Paul Daniel
Naxos 8 554719 (55' · DDD)   Ⓢ ❶ ❷ ❸

How thrillingly urgent Elgar's unforgettably gaunt introductory bars sound here – a magnificent launch-pad for an interpretation of unswerving dedication, plentiful character and intelligence. Audibly galvanised by Paul Daniel's direction, the Bournemouth orchestra responds with infectious eagerness, polish and, most important, all the freshness of new discovery. In these newcomers' hands there's a rhythmic snap and athletic drive about the mighty opening movement that exhilarate. Where Davis perhaps scores over Daniel is in the spiritual, 'inner' dimension he brings to those ineffably beautiful bars at the start of the development section. Come the succeeding *Allegretto*, and Daniel's approach is more urgent, less evocative. The anguished slow movement welds a penetrating textural and harmonic clarity to a noble strength that's very moving. Best of all is the finale, which now emerges in a rather less piecemeal fashion than it does under Davis. Particularly good is the dark swagger that Daniel locates in both the *nobilmente* paragraphs, while the closing bars are magical, the final soft tam-tam stroke disappearing into the ether like some vast unanswered question. The sound is excellent in every respect. Another jewel in the Naxos crown, not to be missed.

Additional recommendation

Symphony No 3
BBC Symphony Orchestra / A Davis
NMC NMCD053 (56' · DDD)   Ⓕ
  An eloquent, profoundly involving performance with demonstration-worthy sound.

Enigma Variations

Variations on an Original Theme, 'Enigma', Op 36.
Cockaigne Overture, Op 40. Introduction and
Allegro, Op 47. Serenade for Strings
BBC Symphony Orchestra / Sir Andrew Davis
Warner Apex 0927-41371-2 (74' · DDD)   Ⓢ ❷

These are four of the best Elgar performances on disc available. First, the recording is superb, with near-perfect balance and a really natural sound. Second, the playing of the BBC Symphony Orchestra is first rate. Andrew Davis's conducting of all four works is inspired, as if he had forgotten all preconceived notions and other interpretations, gone back to the scores and given us what he found there. In *Cockaigne*, for example, the subtle use of *ritardando*, sanctioned in the score, gives the music that elasticity which Elgar considered to be an ideal requisite for interpreting his works. The poetry and wit of this masterpiece emerge with renewed freshness. As for the *Enigma* Variations, instead of wondering why another recording was thought necessary, you'll find yourself rejoicing that such a fine performance has been preserved to be set alongside other treasured versions. Each of the 'friends pictured within' is strongly characterised by Davis, but without exaggeration or interpretative quirks. Tempos are just right and the orchestral playing captures the authentic Elgarian sound in a manner Boult would have recognised. Similarly, in the *Introduction and Allegro*, how beautifully the string quartet is recorded, how magical are the gentle and so eloquent pizzicatos which punctuate the flow of the great melody. The fugue is played with real zest and enjoyment. This is music on a large scale and is played and conducted in that way, whereas the early *Serenade* is intimate and dewy-eyed and that's how it sounds here.

'Enigma' Variations[e] Three Bavarian Dances, Op 27 – Lullaby[d]. **Barbirolli** An Elizabethan Suite[e] **Bax** The Garden of Fand[b] **Butterworth** A Shropshire Lad[c] **Ireland** The Forgotten Rite[f]. Mai-Dun[g]. These Things Shall Be[h] **Purcell** Suite for Strings[i] **Vaughan Williams** Fantasia on 'Greensleeves'[j]. Fantasia on a Theme by Thomas Tallis[k]
[h]**Parry Jones** ten **Hallé** [h]**Choir and Orchestra / Sir John Barbirolli**
Dutton Laboratories mono ② CDSJB1022 (140' · ADD) Recorded at Houldsworth Hall, Manchester [k]1946, [e]1947, [ih]1948; [d]Kingsway Hall, London 1947; [fg]Abbey Road Studio, London 1949; Free Trade Hall, Manchester [a]1954, [bci]1956   Ⓑ Ⓞ

The long-buried treasure here is Barbirolli's very first recording of Elgar's *Enigma* Variations, never previously issued. It was recorded in Manchester in May 1947, only months before Barbirolli made his first published recording at EMI's St John's Wood studio. This newly unearthed version narrowly becomes the favourite rather than the later one. Both versions are perfectly satisfying in terms of sound, but interpretatively this unpublished version brings added advantages. The opening statement of the theme is lighter, more flowing and less emphatic, while even more important, 'Nimrod' is more warmly emotional, more spontaneous in expression, and the 'EDU' finale, taken at a marginally slower tempo, has no hint of the breathlessness which slightly mars the October performance at the end, again more warmly spontaneous sounding. Significantly Barbirolli's later stereo version of *Enigma* also adopts the slightly broader, less hectic speed.

The two Vaughan Williams items have never appeared before on CD, and both are very welcome. They may be less weighty than Barbirolli's stereo remakes, but the *Tallis* Fantasia, featuring a vintage quartet of Hallé principals, separates the quartet more clearly from the main body than the version with the Sinfonia of London, and again is more warmly expressive. The extra lightness of *Greensleeves*, too, sounds more spontaneous. Disc one contains the shorter works of Bax, Butterworth and Ireland. The performances all have a passionate thrust typical of Barbirolli, with the tenor, Parry Jones, and the Hallé Chorus matching the orchestra in their commitment.

'Enigma' Variations[a]. Pomp and Circumstance Marches, Op 39[b]
[a]**London Symphony Orchestra,** [b]**London Philharmonic Orchestra / Sir Adrian Boult**
EMI 764015-2 (55' · ADD) Recorded 1970, 1976 Ⓜ Ⓞ Ⓞ

Boult's 1970 recording of the *Enigma* Variations offers similar riches to those of Barbirolli with

ELGAR ENIGMA VARIATIONS – IN BRIEF

Royal Albert Hall Orchestra / Sir Edward Elgar
EMI 566979-2 (67' · ADD)   Ⓜ
Elgar's own 1926 recording positively oozes spontaneity and fantasy. Harnessed to the 14-year-old Menuhin's legendary 1932 version (with the composer) of the Violin Concerto.

Hallé Orchestra / Sir John Barbirolli
Dutton ② CDSJB1022 (140' · ADD)   Ⓑ Ⓞ
The first of Sir John's four recordings. Never previously issued, it features irrepressible playing and conducting of rare perception. Other Hallé/Barbirolli highlights on this Dutton double-pack include Bax's *Garden of Fand* and Ireland's *Mai-Dun* and *The Forgotten Rite*.

Hallé Orchestra / Sir John Barbirolli
EMI/IMG Artists ② 575100-2 (150' · ADD)   Ⓜ
Barbirolli's first stereo *Enigma*, originally engineered by a Mercury production-team for Pye, is a gloriously uninhibited conception. A heartwarming, indeed life-enhancing experience.

London SO / Pierre Monteux
Decca 452 303-2DCS (78' · ADD)   Ⓜ
Another vernally fresh interpretation from a great conductor. Monteux brings plenty of revealing insights to bear, the LSO are on top form and Decca's 1958 Kingsway Hall sound is astonishingly undated.

London SO / Sir Adrian Boult
EMI 567748-2 (55' · ADD)   Ⓜ Ⓞ Ⓞ ⇨
Sir Adrian's noble 1970 *Enigma* (the last of his four versions) dates from towards the start of his Indian summer in the recording studio, and remains a central recommendation.

Royal PO / Norman Del Mar
DG 429 713-2GGA (58' · ADD)   Ⓜ
The voluble expressive freedom of this interpretation owes much to the composer's own. Similarly, Del Mar invests the *Pomp and Circumstance Marches* with terrific élan.

Czech PO / Leopold Stokowski
Cala CACD0524 (76' · ADD)   Ⓜ
Stokowski's only Elgar recording enshrines an intepretation of abundant charisma and glowing affection. The sheer energy of it all is astounding, especially when you remember that the Old Magician had just turned 90!

Baltimore SO / David Zinman
Telarc CD80192 (62' · DDD)   Ⓜ
Now reissued at mid-price, Zinman's eagle-eyed, exceptionally poised account is a real tonic, and receives top-drawer Telarc sound to boot.

the additional bonus of a slightly superior recorded sound. Boult's account has authority, freshness and a beautiful sense of spontaneity: each variation emerges from the preceding one with a natural feeling of flow and progression. There's warmth and affection, coupled with an air of nobility and poise, and the listener is always acutely aware that this is a performance by a great conductor who's lived a lifetime with the music. You need only sample the passionate stirrings of Variation 1 (the composer's wife), the athletic and boisterous 'Troyte' variation, or the autumnal, elegiac glow of the famous 'Nimrod' variation to realise that this is a very special document indeed. The LSO, on top form, plays with superlative skill and poetry and the excellent recording has been exceptionally well transferred to CD. The *Pomp and Circumstance* Marches, recorded six years later with the London Philharmonic Orchestra, are invigoratingly fresh and direct – indeed the performances are so full of energy and good humour that it's hard to believe that Boult was in his late eighties at the time of recording! A classic.

Enigma Variations
BBC Symphony Orchestra / Sir Andrew Davis
Video director **Diana Hill**
Opus Arte *DVD* OA0917D (85' · 16:9 · PCM stereo & DTS 5.1 · 0) Includes documentary, 'A Hidden Portrait'   Ⓕ

Sir Andrew Davis's warmly committed performance of the *Enigma* Variations, atmospherically recorded in Worcester Cathedral, introduces a highly enjoyable documentary about the work and the 'friends pictured within'. Davis suggests that each variation, as well as reflecting the character of a particular friend, reveals much about Elgar himself, 'like an actor playing many roles'. Each section is illustrated with archive material and period reconstructions, happily with no dialogue, only Davis's narration. He describes and analyses nine of the 14 variations with orchestral clips and illustrations played on the piano.

So the first variation, 'CAE', depicting Elgar's wife Alice, concentrating on the central major-key section of the theme, includes a brief, passionate climax, 'showing his depth of feeling'. 'RBT', subject of the third variation, was the treasurer of the local golf club, who got Elgar accepted as a member even though his social class was against him. We're shown what used to be the clubhouse, now set in waste land. 'Nimrod' depicts the publisher August Jaeger and Elgar walking together, and Davis points to echoes of the slow movement from Beethoven's *Pathétique* Sonata. The intermezzo, 'Dorabella', brings a good portrait of the young Dora Penny, but after a reference to her cycling, ends absurdly on shots of a modern couple roller-blading – an example of fussy and intrusive visual illustration. Fairly enough, Davis favours the idea that the 13th variation, 'Romanza', represents not Lady Mary Lygon, as has generally been thought, but his first love, Helen Weaver,

who emigrated to New Zealand. Irritating are the accompanying shots of a soulful modern teenager on Lambeth Bridge looking at a launch bearing his girlfriend away.

The performance itself has no unwanted intrusions – just a sepia photo of the subject as each variation begins – and is a fine one.

Additional recommendations

'Enigma' Variations
Coupled with: Cockaigne. Serenade. Salut d'amor
Baltimore Symphony Orchestra / Zinman
Telarc CD80192 (62' · DDD)   Ⓕ
   An impressive performance. Zinman has the feel for the ebb and flow, the elasticity of the music, and he obtains idiomatic playing from the excellent Baltimore SO.

Falstaff

Falstaff. Froissart. Romance, Op 62[a]. Grania and Diarmid – Incidental Music and Funeral March
[a]**Graham Sheen** *bn* **BBC Symphony Orchestra / Sir Andrew Davis**
Warner Apex 2564 62200-2 (66' · DDD)   ⓈⓄⓄ

As digital *Falstaff*s go, Sir Andrew Davis's 1995 account with the BBC SO remains arguably the front-runner. If both Elgar himself and Barbirolli impart the greater vulnerability and compassion to the illimitably moving closing pages, the irresistible symphonic current coursing through Davis's meticulously observant conception provides ample compensation. The figure. Rodney Macann as the Watergnome tends to steal the show, his dark, incisive bass very characterful. Ann Howard is wonderfully menacing as the Witch, while the fluttering vibrato of Phyllis Cannan as the Foreign Princess adds to the exotic image (in Act 2, when most of the characters are dressed in white, she stands out in a crimson gown). The three Woodsprites are lively, and incidental characters are well taken.

Mark Elder draws warm incisive playing from the orchestra, adding to the dramatic impact and underpinning the moving final scene, when the Prince kisses Rusalka, knowing it will mean his death.

Pomp and Circumstance Marches

Pomp and Circumstance, Op 39 – No 1 in D; No 2 in A minor; No 3 in C minor; No 4 in G; No 5 in C.

Pomp and Circumstance Marches Nos 1-5[b]
Overtures – Froissart; Cockaigne[a]
[a]**Philharmonia Orchestra,** [b]**New Philharmonia Orchestra / Sir John Barbirolli**
EMI British Composers 566323-2 (62' · ADD)   Ⓜ Ⓑ➔

A splendid programme that finds Sir John celebrating London courtesy of Edward Elgar. The two overtures are beautifully done with ample shade to counterbalance the swagger. And it's a real treat to hear all five of the *Pomp and Circumstance* Marches, especially when played as sensitively as here. The rarely encountered Second and Fifth marches are superbly conducted, the Philharmonia are on top form.

Piano Quintet

Piano Quintet[a]. Violin Sonata[b]
The Nash Ensemble ([b]Marcia Crayford, [a]Elizabeth Layton vns [a]Roger Chase va [a]Christopher van Kampen vc Ian Brown pf)
Helios CDH55301-2 (65' · DDD)   Ⓑ**O**

Nash Ensemble members Marcia Crayford and Ian Brown give a most perceptive rendering of the Elgar Violin Sonata, one of the finest on disc. Crayford's admirably disciplined, exquisitely shaded contribution is a constant source of pleasure; Brown is an exemplary partner, acutely responsive and passionate, yet never forcing the tone. In the Quintet the playing of the Nash Ensemble evinces consummate refinement and total dedication; their heartwarmingly eloquent reading communicates strongly.

Violin Sonata

Elgar Violin Sonata in E minor, Op 82
Finzi Elegy in F, Op 22 **Walton** Violin Sonata
Daniel Hope vn **Simon Mulligan** pf
Nimbus NI5666 (62' · DDD)   Ⓕ**OO**

Ⓖ The coupling of the violin sonatas by Elgar and Walton is a most satisfying one, not unique on disc, and one which provides fascinating parallels. The Finzi *Elegy* is a very apt makeweight, the only surviving movement from a projected Violin Sonata written in a hectic period for the composer at the beginning of the Second World War.

The Elgar elicits a performance of high contrasts both in dynamic range – Hope uses daringly extreme *pianissimos* – and in flexibility of tempo. So in the first movement the opening at an urgent speed gives way to a very broad reading of the second subject, hushed and musingly introspective. Yet such freedom of expression goes with deep concentration, so that the structure is still firmly held together. In the finale, Hope conveys an improvisational quality, again using the widest dynamic range, finely matched by Mulligan.

With Hope's sweet, finely focused violin tone beautifully caught in the Nimbus recording – full and warm but less reverberant than some – and well balanced against the piano, this set makes an outstanding recommendation.

Organ Sonatas

Organ Sonatas – No 1, Op 28; No 2, Op 87a (trans I Atkins). Cantique, Op 3 No 1. Vesper

Voluntaries, Op 14. Chanson de Matin (arr AH Brewer). 'Enigma' Variations, Op 36 – Nimrod (arr WH Harris). Pomp and Circumstance No 4, Op 39 (arr GR Sinclair)
Thomas Trotter org
Regent REGCD256 (75' · DDD). Played on the Father Willis organ of Salisbury Cathedral   Ⓕ

It is extraordinary that no major label has got Thomas Trotter, the greatest British organist of his generation, cuffed hands and feet for life. It has been left to the small Wolverhampton-based Regent label to do the honours – and it does him proud.

There are few organs better suited to Elgar than Salisbury Cathedral's Willis. It speaks with a mellifluous, unforced authority in a clear acoustic that avoids the generalised rumblings of many English cathedrals. The G major Sonata unfolds with impressive breadth and command of structure, a dramatic contrast to the intimate *Cantique*, a short work derived from an early (1879) piece for wind quintet, and the attractive eight *Vesper Voluntaries* of 1889.

Three of the final four works are transcriptions by a Three Choirs triumvirate of Elgar's organist friends: the Organ Sonata No 2 arranged from the *Severn Suite* by Ivor Atkins (Worcester), *Chanson de matin* (Herbert Brewer of Gloucester) and *Pomp and Circumstance* No 4 by the work's dedicatee George Sinclair of Hereford – GRS and his bulldog Dan from the *Enigma* Variations. From the latter, 'Nimrod' is heard in the transcription by WH Harris (St George's, Windsor) and it is only here that one might have wished Trotter had opted for a more measured pace and emotional response. But throughout this superbly engineered recording his mastery of tonal gradation, innate stylistic sense and imaginative colouring make for a recording as rewarding as it is timely.

The Black Knight, Op 25

The Black Knight. Scenes from the Bavarian Highlands, Op 27
London Symphony Chorus and Orchestra / Richard Hickox
Chandos CHAN9436 (61' · DDD · T)   Ⓕ**Ⓟ➔**

Elgar completed *The Black Knight* in 1893 and it provided him with his first big success. The text tells of a sinister, unnamed 'Prince of mighty sway', whose appearance at the King's court during the feast of Pentecost has disastrous consequences. Elgar's score boasts much attractive invention, some of it strikingly eloquent and prescient of greater offerings to come. The choral writing is always effective, the orchestration already vivid and assured. Richard Hickox and his forces are dab hands at this kind of fare and their performance has great bloom and spaciousness. Similarly, in the tuneful, vernally fresh *Scenes from the Bavarian Highlands*, Hickox and his colleagues respond with commendable spirit and pleasing polish. Typical of Chandos,

ELGAR DREAM OF GERONTIUS – IN BRIEF

Nash, Ripley, Noble, Walker; Huddersfield Ⓗ
Choral Society, Liverpool PO / Sir Malcolm
Sargent
Testament ② SBT2025 (120' · ADD)   Ⓜ Ⓞ
Recorded as long ago as 1945, and still the
interpretative and artistic touchstone. Sargent
secures a searingly eloquent response from his
massed forces, Heddle Nash is unforgettable
and Gladys Ripley's 'Softly and gently' never
fails to activate the tearducts.

Lewis; Baker; Borg; Hallé Choir; Sheffield
Philharmonic Chorus; Ambrosian Singers;
Hallé Orchestra / Sir John Barbirolli
EMI ② 5735792 (98' · ADD)   Ⓜ Ⓞ Ⓞ
Last available at budget price, Barbirolli's
1964 set, though not currently listed, is worth
tracking down. Richard Lewis is not quite as
fresh-voiced as he was for Sargent a decade
earlier, and Kim Borg's a bit woolly, but
otherwise it's a performance to cherish.

Coote; Groves; Terfel; bHallé Youth Choir;
Hallé Choir and Orchestra / Sir Mark Elder
Hallé ② CDHLD7520 (94' · DDD · T/t) Ⓜ Ⓞ Ⓞ Ⓞ ➔
A wonderful resumption of the Hallé/Elgar
tradition. Very strongly cast, Elder delivers a
performance of wonderful sweep and style;
this is a modern interpretation to stand
alongside the greatest. -

Irwin; Lavender; Rose; City of Birmingham
Symphony Chorus and Orchestra / Sakari
Oramo
CBSO ② CD003 (122' · DDD)   Ⓜ Ⓞ
A superb modern version that makes a won-
derful memento of Sakari Oramo's reign at
the helm of the CBSO. An accomplished
Elgarian he draws fine performances from his
assembled forces. Jane Irwin is superb. And
the set includes a performance of the Enigma
Variations well worth hearing.

Gedda, Watts, Lloyd, John Alldis Choir, London
Philharmonic Choir, New Philharmonia
Orchestra / Sir Adrian Boult
EMI ② 566540-2 (135' · ADD)   Ⓜ
Opulently engineered, Boult's 1975 set
features the distinctive, Italianate timbre of
Nicolai Gedda in the title-role. Boult directs
with commendable energy and typical
humanity. A document to be treasured.

Davies, Palmer, Howell, London Symphony
Chorus & Orchestra / Richard Hickox
Chandos ② CHAN8641/2 (114' · DDD)   Ⓜ ➔
Now retailing at mid-price, Hickox's début
disc for Chandos brought this finely sung and
played *Gerontius*, with Arthur Davies engagingly ardent in the title-role. Parry's *Blest
Pair of Sirens* and *I was glad* make welcome
bonuses.

the recording is bright and clear, tonally beyond
reproach and with just the right balance between
choir and orchestra.

The Light of Life, Op 29

The Light of Life
Judith Howarth sop **Linda Finnie** mez **Arthur**
Davies ten **John Shirley-Quirk** bar **London**
Symphony Chorus and Orchestra / Richard Hickox
Chandos CHAN9208 (63' · DDD · T)   Ⓕ

In the glorious orchestral 'Meditation' Hickox's
conducting demonstrates a noble flexibility,
sensitivity to dynamic nuance and feeling for
climax. Equally the engineering, sumptuous yet
detailed, comes close to the ideal. The LSO and
Chorus contribute to proceedings in exemplary,
disciplined fashion. As The Blind Man, Arthur
Davies could hardly be more ardent, but his
slightly tremulous timbre won't be to all tastes.
John Shirley-Quirk, so eloquent and firm-toned
a Jesus for Groves (on EMI) back in 1980, now
shows signs of unsteadiness in the same part. On
the other hand, Linda Finnie and Judith
Howarth make a creditable showing. Hickox's
reading excels in precisely the areas where the
Groves was deficient, and *vice versa*. If you
already have the Groves reissue, hang on to it,
for it's by no means outclassed by the Hickox.
However, for anyone coming to this underrated
score for the first time, Hickox's must now be
the preferred version.

The Dream of Gerontius, Op 38

The Dream of Gerontius, Op 38
Alice Coote mez **Paul Groves** ten **Bryn Terfel** bass-
bar **Hallé Youth Choir; Hallé Choir and Orchestra /**
Sir Mark Elder
Hallé ② CDHLD7520 (94' · DDD · T/t)   Ⓜ Ⓞ Ⓞ Ⓞ ➔

For all sorts of reasons Barbirolli's famous Hallé
account has lived in everyone's hearts for
decades. It still will, because there is something
about the immediacy and wholeheartedness of
its vision that speaks as directly as ever. Mark
Elder's approach is more elusive. He draws us
patiently, unerringly, into the profound mystery
of the piece, judiciously weighing its theatricality against its inwardness. It is reverent in the
best sense, with breathless *pianissimi* and a
potency of atmosphere that takes hold from the
moment we enter the dying man's room. Just
listen to the Hallé strings in the Prelude, or the
introduction to Part 2. The stylistic finesse of
the playing, the very particular articulation, the
inbred *portamento* – all these qualities are testament to the fantastic work Elder has done with
the orchestra.
    It is, by a mile, the best-sounding *Gerontius* we
have had, handsome in its depth and breadth
with great spatial perspectives and a wonderful
sense of how the score is layered. Onto this
impressive sound stage comes Paul Groves's

Gerontius with a near-perfect blend of poetic restraint and high emotionalism – though some may feel that the 'operatic' hot-spots, 'Take me away!' being, of course, the hottest of them – are wanting in that last degree of heft. Elder and his sound team might have given us something more startling with that chord of 'utmost force' in the moment Gerontius finally glimpses his creator.

No lack of force or presence in Bryn Terfel's proclamation to 'Go forth!' – the portals of heaven open to that, as indeed they do with the arrival of the heavenly host for the great 'Praise to the Holiest' chorus. The Hallé choir bravely gather momentum in that, thanks to Elder's insistence on clear rhythmic articulation, and he achieves a simply stonking *crescendo* on the final chord, leaving the organ to plumb infinite depths.

Of course, Janet Baker's timbre still haunts every measure of the Angel's music, but the wonderful Alice Coote conveys great confidentiality in her highly personalised reading. 'Softly and gently' is gloriously enveloping – and maybe that's the word which ultimately best describes this fine and most satisfying recording.

The Dream of Gerontius[a]. Cello Concerto[b]   **H**
Gladys Ripley contr **Heddle Nash** ten **Dennis Noble** bar **Norman Walker** bass **Paul Tortelier** vc
Huddersfield Choral Society; [b]**BBC Symphony Orchestra;** [a]**Liverpool Philharmonic Orchestra / Sir Malcolm Sargent**
Testament mono ② SBT2025 (120' · ADD · T)
Recorded 1945-53.   Ⓕ**O**➟
Also available as a download or custom-made CD from www.pristineaudio.com

This pioneering set of *Gerontius* has come up newly minted in these superbly engineered transfers taken from 78rpm masters. That only enhances the incandescence and fervour of the reading itself, in virtually all respects the most convincing the work has received. Sargent's conducting, influenced by Elgar's, is direct, vital and urgently crafted with an inborn feeling for the work's ebb and flow and an overall picture that comprehends the piece's spiritual meaning while realising its dramatic leanness and force. Heddle Nash's Gerontius is unrivalled in its conviction and inwardness. He'd been singing the part since 1930, and by 1945 the work was in his being; he sang it from memory and had mastered every facet. 'Take me away' is like a searing cry of pain from the depth of the singer's soul. Gladys Ripley is a natural and communicative Angel, her flexible and appealing tone always a pleasure. The Liverpool Philharmonic lives up to its reputation at the time as the country's leading orchestra (in particular the sonorous string section), and the members of the Huddersfield Choral Society sing as if their lives depended on it.

Tortelier's Cello Concerto presents the Classical approach as compared with the Romantic one of du Pré, and is the best of Tortelier's readings of the work on disc, with his tone and phrasing at their firmest and most telling. A considered and unaffected reading among the best ever committed to disc.

Elgar The Dream of Gerontius **Parry** Ode at a Solemn Music, 'Blest Pair of Sirens'. I was glad
Felicity Palmer sop **Arthur Davies** ten **Gwynne Howell** bass **London Symphony Orchestra and Chorus / Richard Hickox**
Chandos CHAN8641/2 (114' · DDD · T)   Ⓜ

Hickox gives us a peculiarly immediate and urgent interpretation – not dissimilar from Rattle's on EMI – that has us thinking more than ever that *Gerontius* is an opera in everything but name, or at least a dramatic cantata, not an oratorio. His speeds tend to be quick, but only once, in 'Sanctus fortis', does the tempo feel hurried. Being a choral trainer of many years' standing, he naturally enough persuades them to sing with an impressive unanimity of purpose and with perhaps a wider range of dynamics than any other conductor. Perhaps an element of dignity and grandeur such as you find in Boult's and Barbirolli's EMI readings, both appreciably more measured, is missing, but little else. The sound of the chorus and excellent orchestra surpasses that on the Rattle version, Watford Town Hall proving as ever a good venue for the recording of large forces.

Arthur Davies has a stronger, more secure voice than any other tenor who has recorded Gerontius and, unlike several of them, he's in his prime as a singer. 'Mary, pray for me' and 'Novissima hora est' are sung with the appropriate sweet sadness, the duet with the Angel tenderly, and he enters with terrified power at 'Take me away'. He doesn't have the individuality of utterance or special affinity with the text, as for instance at 'How still it is!' that you get with Heddle Nash (for Sargent) and Sir Peter Pears (for Britten), or even quite the agony of the soul projected by Mitchinson (for Rattle), but it's an appreciable performance, firmly projected. Felicity Palmer's Angel is less successful. The intentions are right, the understanding is there, but the means to carry them forward are faulty: her singing, once she puts pressure on the tone, is uncomfortable to hear. Gwynne Howell is just about the best Priest and Angel of the Agony in any version. His warm, firm bass-baritone easily encompasses the different tessituras of the two 'parts'. This is a fine modern version.

The Kingdom, Op 51

The Kingdom[a]. Coronation Ode, Op 44[b]
[a]**Margaret Price,** [b]**Felicity Lott** sops [a]**Yvonne Minton** mez [b]**Alfreda Hodgson** contr [a]**Alexander Young,** [b]**Richard Morton** tens [a]**John Shirley-Quirk,** [b]**Stephen Roberts** bars [a]**London Philharmonic Choir and Orchestra / Sir Adrian Boult;**

^b**Cambridge University Musical Society Chorus;**
^b**Choir of King's College Cambridge;** ^b**New**
Philharmonia Orchestra / Philip Ledger
EMI British Composers ② 764209-2 (130' · ADD) Ⓜ◉

Boult was a passionate admirer of *The Kingdom* and, as ever, the unaffected devotion and authority of his advocacy is hard to resist. The two formidable contenders in the work are Leonard Slatkin and Richard Hickox. All three performers have much going for them. In short, Boult enjoys the strongest team of soloists, Hickox obtains the most disciplined and full-bodied choral work, and Slatkin secures the finest orchestral playing – indeed, the LPO are on inspired form, responding with an exemplary sensitivity, commitment and concentration which also marked out Slatkin's magnificent account of the Symphony No 2 set down with this same group some 17 months later. Slatkin also benefits from perhaps the best engineering, with Boult's Kingsway Hall production now sounding just a little pale and hard-edged in comparison. Where the EMI release really comes up trumps, though, is in the shape of its generous fill-up, Philip Ledger's superb, swaggering reading of the *Coronation Ode*. Ultimately, then, the Boult, must take the palm, especially at mid-price, though no devoted Elgarian should miss hearing Slatkin's gloriously lucid conception either.

Sea Pictures, Op 37

Sea Pictures. The Music Makers
Sarah Connolly *mez* **Bournemouth Symphony Chorus and Orchestra / Simon Wright**
Naxos 8 557710 (62' · DDD · T/t)   Ⓜ▶

The Music Makers is one of Elgar's most poignant and troubled utterances which movingly incorporates material from some of his greatest compositions, and it can hold its head high. Simon Wright steers a commendably clear-sighted course and coaxes an idiomatic response from his Bournemouth forces. Sarah Connolly proves scarcely less raptly responsive than Baker (for Boult), singing with glorious radiance, security and richness of tone; her delivery of the final line ('And a singer who sings no more') is deeply affecting.

Connolly also steps up to the mark in the *Sea Pictures* (which follows after too short a gap). Hers is a gripping, intelligent display, combining keen poetic and dramatic instinct with clarity of diction, all technical challenges effortlessly surmounted. A performance to hear alongside the classic Baker recording – reviewed on page 413.

Miscellaneous choral works

There is sweet music, Op 53 No 1. Deep in my soul. O Wild West Wind. Owls (An Epitaph). As torrents in summer. The Prince of Sleep. The Shower. The Fountain. My love dwelt in a northern land, Op 18 No 3. Death on the hills, Op 72. Love's Tempest, Op 73 No 1. Serenade. Evening Scene. Go, song of mine, Op 57. Scenes from the Bavarian Highlands, Op 27

Cambridge University Chamber Choir /
Christopher Robinson with **Iain Farrington** *pf*
Naxos 8 570541 (75' · DDD)   Ⓢ◉▶

Plaudits to Christopher Robinson and the Cambridge University Chamber Choir for their keenly prepared and fervent exploration of this still under-appreciated repertoire. And what an absorbing creative portrait of the composer they give us, stretching from 1889 and 'My love dwelt in a northern land' to 1925 and the delectably assured setting of Walter de la Mare's 'The Prince of Sleep'. Other bewitching gems along the journey include 'As torrents in summer'(from the epilogue of the 1896 cantata *King Olaf*), 'Evening Scene' (1905) and 'Go, song of mine' (1909). In the five items (Opp 71-73) from 1914 Elgar's treatment of the *a cappella* medium acquires an extra confidence (the writing at once dark, rich and penetrating), though perhaps the most sheerly gripping and diverse inspiration on this well filled anthology is to be found within the four Op 53 songs of 1907: sample the ear-tickling bitonality of 'There is sweet music' or ghostly gloom of 'Owls' (Elgar at his most daring and inscrutable).

One might hope for a fractionally tighter focus to what is an otherwise tonally true sound-picture (the words are not always ideally clear – Naxos does, thankfully, supply full texts). Otherwise, these commendably disciplined and infectiously spirited performances are sure to give pleasure. A tempting price, too!

Excerpts from Caractacus^a; The Dream of Gerontius^{c/d}; The Saga of King Olaf^e; Sea Pictures^f; The Spirit of England^h. Carillon, Op 75^b. Shepherd's Song, Op 16 No 1^g. With Proud Thanksgiving^j.   H
^h**Elsie Suddaby**, ^a**Isobel Baillie** sops ^c**Astra Desmond**, ^d**Muriel Brunskill**, ^f**Mary Jarred** contrs ^{cde}**Heddle Nash**, ^g**Walter Widdop**, ^a**Edward Reach** tens ^a**Arthur Cranmer**, ^a**Edward Brown** bars ^d**Horace Stevens**, ^c**Keith Falkner** basses ^g**Helen Perkin** pf ^a**Hereford Choral Society;** ^f**Preston Cecilian Choir;** ^{dh}**BBC Choral Society;** ^b**BBC Northern Orchestra / Crawford McNair;** ^e**BBC Opera Orchestra / Stanford Robinson;** ^{fh}**BBC Orchestra / Clarence Raybould;** ^d**BBC Symphony Orchestra /** ^{dh}**Adrian Boult;** ^a**City of Birmingham Orchestra / Percy Hull;** ^c**Hallé Choir and Orchestra / Malcolm Sargent**
Elgar Editions mono ③ EECD003/5 (3h 38' · ADD) BBC broadcast performances, recorded 1935-50   Ⓜ

This is one of the most exciting archival releases in recent years. The source is a collection of privately made recordings of BBC broadcasts between 1935 and 1950. Kenneth Leech was a remarkable man, an engineer employed originally on the railways, designing a searchlight for the Navy in wartime, composing and conducting works for orchestra, and living to be over 100. Putting his technical skills to the task of recording from the radio, he used aluminium discs running at 64rpm and applying 3-in-1 oil to reduce surface noise. The collection, which is now in the British Library, is particularly rich in Elgar, and it was on *Gramophone* critic Alan Blyth's urging that this compilation was issued to mark the 150th anniversary of Elgar's birth.

Everything here has its interest and value, but at the centre are two performances of *The Dream of Gerontius*: from 1935 under Sargent and 1936 under Boult. Both have Heddle Nash as Gerontius. Of the first, just over 70 minutes is preserved, with slightly over half an hour of the second, in separate excerpts but allowing all three soloists to be heard. Andrew Neill, in his introductory notes, does well to warn listeners about the fragmentary nature of the recordings, though much comes through with startling brightness; in particular, Nash's singing is heard throughout with perfect clarity. And it is glorious! Sargent conducts admirably but (and this is the other dazzling glory of what we hear) Boult brings such a charge to his performance we see how his orchestra at just this time became one fit for Toscanini.

There are several performers who in these broadcasts come to life as they never did in the studio; or rather, we come much nearer to the experience of hearing them in reality. Elsie Suddaby emerges as a valiant soprano, strong in spirit and sure in the thrust of her voice. Mary Jarred takes to the *Sea Pictures* like a Valkyrie. Astra Desmond has something of her heroine Clara Butt about her. Keith Falkner brings an unexpected operatic thrill to his 'Proficiscere'. And there is a new Widdop, from 1935, when they had stopped recording him; and what a mistake that was! These are precious retrievals: blessings on Kenneth Leech and all concerned.

Film

Elgar – A film by Ken Russell
Peter Brett Mr Elgar **Rowena Gregory** Mrs Elgar **George McGrath** Sir Edward Elgar **Ken Russell** Himself
British Film Institute **DVD** BFIVD524 (71' · 4:3 Black & White · 1.0 · 2) Includes commentary by Ken Russell and Michael Kennedy, historical footage and photo gallery ⓕ**OOO**

Originally screened in November 1962 as the 100th programme within the BBC's ground-breaking *Monitor* series, Ken Russell's 'Elgar' has lost none of its power to entrance, stimulate and provoke. If you never caught the film on television, prepare to be bowled over by the perfect marriage of music and pictures, especially during the scenes shot on and around Elgar's beloved Malvern Hills (against which the purposeful stride of the *Introduction and Allegro* for strings acts as a marvellously apt backdrop). Any minor factual anomalies along the way pale into insignificance when set against film-making of such poetry, wit and imagination. Pioneering, too, in as much as it was made at a time when Elgar's reputation was at a comparatively low ebb. Indelible images come thick and fast: Elgar's burgeoning love for Alice is exquisitely conveyed by the delicate interplay of four hands on the keyboard performing the piano-duet arrangement of *Salut d'amour*; the jaw-dropping transformation of Worcestershire Beacon into the cross-topped hill at Calvary (to the strains of 'Sanctus fortis' from *Gerontius*); or the composer on his bicycle rushing through the dappled woodland and heather. The result is an undisputed classic of British television.

Extras include rare home-film footage of the Three Choirs Festivals of 1929, 1930 and 1932 (during which we also see Elgar relaxing at home), as well as a November 1931 Pathétone movie-reel of the 74-year-old composer conducting the LSO in *Land of Hope and Glory*. Not to be missed.

George Enescu   Romanian 1881-1955

Enescu studied at the Vienna Conservatory (1888-94) and at the Paris Conservatoire (1895-9). Paris remained the centre of his professional life, though he spent much time in Romania as a teacher and conductor. He is regarded as the greatest and most versatile Romanian musician and was widely admired as a violinist. Apart from the two Lisztian Rhapsodies roumains for orchestra (1901) his music has been neglected, perhaps partly because of the complexity and diversity of his stylistic allegiances: Romanian folk music is a recurrent influence, but so too are Wagner and Reger and early Schoenberg. His output includes the opera Oedipe (1936), five symphonies (1905, 1914, 1921, 1934, 1941) and much chamber music. **GROVE**music

Romanian Rhapsodies

Poème roumain[a]. Romanian Rhapsodies – Nos 1 & 2. Suites for Orchestra – No 1; No 2; No 3, 'Villageoise'. Symphonie concertante for Cello and Orchestra[b].
[b]**Franco Maggio-Ormezowski** vc
[b]**Jean-Paul Barrellon** ob [a]Male voices
of the **Chorus of the Colonne Orchestra and the Audite Nova Vocal Ensemble; Monte Carlo Philharmonic Orchestra / Lawrence Foster**
Apex ② 2564 62032-2 (158' · DDD) ⑧➔

Enescu's three suites stand in relation to the symphonies rather as Tchaikovsky's suites relate to his symphonic works. The First opens with a striking prelude for strings in unison which in turn gives way to a gorgeous *Menuet lent*. The more formal Second Suite (which falls between the First and Second Symphonies) is based on Baroque models, while the relatively 'late' Third Suite, named *Villageoise* (it dates from 1938), overflows with invention, whether imitations of birdsong and children at play, or exquisite tone-painting of nature by day and night. Foster also offers us the early, 23-minute *Symphonie concertante* for cello and orchestra, his soloist Franco Maggio-Ormezowski unfolding its generous stream of melody with a warm, fluid tone.

Lawrence Foster's performances of these fascinating if occasionally over-effusive works provided a fitting tribute for the 50th anniversary of Enescu's death (1955). Do give this music a try. It combines the freshness of Dvořák with the earth-and-spirit daring of Bartók; and while not quite on a level with either, it comes pretty damned close.

String Quartets, Op 22

String Quartets, Op 22 – No 1 in E flat; No 2 in G
Ad Libitum Quartet (Adrian Berescu, Serban
Mereuta vns Bogdan Bisoc va Filip Papa vc)
Naxos 8 554721 (74' · DDD)   ⑤**O**▸

Enescu's 1920 First Quartet crams so much into 45-odd minutes that even two or three hearings barely scratch its surface. It's a veritable forest of invention, fairly Brahmsian in texture, organic in its thinking and frequently dramatic. The second movement incorporates sundry embellishments and effects (including the use of *sul ponticello*), and the finale features variations on a march-like theme. It will make wonderful if challenging listening for anyone who values quality ideas above economical structuring.

Although the two quartets share the single opus number, they're years apart chronologically, aeons if you consider their contrasting styles. The Second Quartet was Enescu's penultimate work, and breathes the heady aroma of Romanian folk music, especially in the slow movement and finale, which recall the world of the far better-known Third Violin Sonata. Shorter than the First Quartet by almost half, the Second feels tighter and more agile.

The Ad Libitum Quartet do a fabulous job. They attend to Enescu's endless technical demands with a devotion that translates to apparent effortlessness. Naxos's superior production secures a top recommendation and unbeatable value too.

Violin Sonatas

'Complete Works for Violin and Piano, Vol 1'
Violin Sonatas – 'Torso' Sonata; No 2, Op 6.
Impressions d'enfance, Op 28
Remus Azoitei vn **Eduard Stan** pf
Hänssler Classic CD98 239 (61' · DDD)   ⑤

'Complete Works for Violin and Piano, Vol 2'
Violin Sonatas – No 1, Op 2; No 3, 'dans le caractère
populaire roumain', Op 25. Ballade, Op 4a. Hora
Unirei. Impromptu concertant. Andante malinconico.
Tarantelle
Remus Azoitei vn **Eduard Stan** pf
Hänssler Classic CD98 240 (70' · DDD)   ⑤

Like Béla Bartók, Romanian composer-violinist-pianist George Enescu wrote violin music from a fairly early age, even earlier in fact: both the *Ballade* and *Tarantella* that feature on the second disc of this admirable survey are the products of a prodigiously gifted 14-year-old.

Both are world premiere recordings, forming part of a sequence of unusual short pieces that includes a racy *Hora Unirei* from 1917 (like an offbeat waltz), a playful *Impromptu concertant* (1903) and a brief but harmonically pungent *Andante malinconico* that Enescu wrote for a sight-reading competition just four years before he died. All five miniatures showcase the refined but vibrant performing style of Remus Azoitei, a distinctive player whose sound world echoes Enescu's own.

Azoitei's pianist Eduard Stan is memorably supple in terms of both rhythm and touch, vital attributes in the last and greatest of the violin works, the Third Sonata, with its tricky transitions, complex but spirited dance sequences and fiery climaxes, especially in the finale. Azoitei and Stan combine temperament, mastery of idiom and executive elegance in a very special way. They shape the music beautifully, so that what in some hands sounds like mere extended improvisation (a desirable attribute admittedly) also parades discernable form.

The five larger works all come off exceptionally well. Regarding the folky and atmospheric Impressions d'enfance Azoitei gives the impression of controlled rhapsodising, and so does his pianist. The earliest larger-scale work here is the First Sonata, another teenage essay, confident and fitfully memorable though predictably derivative, with Schumann coming most often to mind. Carl Flesch described the Second Sonata (1899) as 'one of the most important works of all sonata literature, whose neglect is totally unjustifiable'.

If the repertoire appeals, no need to look any further: this is a first-rate collection, although Lupu is also worth searching out, maybe as a supplementary purchase, especially for that orchestral *Caprice roumain*.

Enescu Violin Sonata No 3, 'dans le caractère populaire roumain', Op 25. Impressions d'enfance, Op 28
Ravel Sonata for Violin and Piano in G. Tzigane
Leonidas Kavakos vn **Péter Nagy** pf
ECM New Series 476 053-2 (78' · DDD)   ⑤**OO**

A compelling programme based principally around the figure of Georges Enescu, both as composer and as a performing phenomenon, the latter probably inspiring Ravel's Violin Sonata of 1897, a lavish essay redolent of early Debussy. Both Ravel pieces respond handsomely to Leonidas Kavakos's agile and refined approach, *Tzigane* in particular being meticulously prepared, the partnership with Péter Nagy ensuring clarity in matters of articulation and the 'pickup' of motives between violin and piano; you're unlikely to hear a more supportive or better gauged account of the piano part.

These aren't 'showy' performances. Though Kavakos is audibly appreciative of the folk flavouring in Enescu's Third Sonata, he treats the abstract element as paramount, suggesting keen parallels with the violin sonatas of Bartók. Again Nagy takes the greatest care over such issues as rhythm, texture and the shape of individual phrases: his precise musical thinking could serve as an object lesson in such matters. The high-spot of the performance is the cantorial closing section of the *Andante* second movement, so exquisitely turned and sustained. The graphic *Impressions d'enfance*, with its lullaby, caged bird and cuckoo-clock, chirping cricket and ecstatic dawn, is endlessly fascinating, again rich in folk references, the sort that Enescu worked in to his *Romanian Rhapsodies*.

These performances justify consideration for their warmth, intelligence and superb sound.

Einar Englund   Finnish 1916-1999

Englund studied with Palmgren and Carlsson at the Helsinki Academy (1933-41), with Copland at Tanglewood, and in Russia, where he was impressed by Prokofiev and Shostakovich. His works include five symphonies (1946-77), concertos and piano pieces.
GROVEmusic

Symphonies

Symphonies – No 2, 'Blackbird'; No 4, 'Nostalgic'.
Piano Concerto No 1[a]
[a]**Niklas Sivelöv** pf **Turku Philharmonic Orchestra / Jorma Panula**
Naxos 8 553758 (76' · DDD)   Ⓢ Ⓞ ▷

Einar Englund was the finest Finnish symphonist between Sibelius and Kokkonen, and the *Blackbird* Symphony is one of his best. You can hear why he so named it from the woodwind writing, particularly the solos for flute, although he grew wary of emphasising the title in later life. One of the most attractive features of all his music is its orchestration. Panula's account is superbly played, with excellent sound. The Fourth (1976), written in memory of Shostakovich, is less epic, though no less inventive. A chamber symphony for strings and percussion, its most effective movement is the sparkling but macabre *Scherzo*, 'Tempus fugit', haunted by the chiming of bells and the manic ticking of some outlandish clock. Here, as well as in the darkly poetic third span, 'Nostalgia', and concluding 'Epilogue', Panula finds great poetry. Naxos's centrepiece, though, is the first of Englund's two piano concertos. Englund's own recording disappeared from the catalogue long ago, but Niklas Sivelöv proves a fine advocate.

Symphonies – No 4, 'Dedicated to the Memory of a Great Artist'; No 5, 'To the Memory of JK Paasikivi'.
The Great Wall of China
Tampere Philharmonic Orchestra / Eri Klas
Ondine ODE961-2 (65' · DDD)   Ⓕ

The Fifth Symphony (1977) was recorded on LP by Jukka-Pekka Saraste; Englund once said this was too fast, so he would probably have approved

of Klas's better-judged version. Although titled *Sinfonia Fennica* ('Finnish' Symphony), the composer claimed it contained more of his wartime experiences than his famous *War* Symphony (No 1, 1946). In a bold, riveting single span, its full orchestration pairs very effectively with the strings and percussion of No 4. The suite from the incidental music to Max Frisch's *The Great Wall of China* (1949) is great fun. 'The Green Table Tango' and 'Rumba' reveal what an adept light/jazz composer he also was (under the pseudonym, Marcus Eje). The Tampere band are really put through their paces here and come through very well. If Panula's Naxos disc is still perhaps the best introduction to Englund's music, this disc should certainly be the next stop.

Manuel de Falla   Spanish 1876-1946

Falla studied in Cádiz. and from the late 1890s in Madrid, where he was a pupil of Tragó for the piano and Pedrell for composition. In 1901-3 he composed five zarzuelas in the hope of making money; then in 1905 came his first important work, the one-act opera La vida breve, which he revised before its first performance, in Paris in 1913. He had moved to Paris in 1907 and become acquainted with Dukas, Debussy, Ravel, Stravinsky and Albéniz, all of whom influenced his development of a style using the primitive song of Andalusia, the cante jondo, and a modern richness of harmony and colour. This was not an immediate achievement: he wrote little before returning to Madrid in 1914, but then came the piano concerto Noches en los jardines de España (1915) and the ballets El amor brujo (1915) and El sombrero de tres picos (1919), the latter presented by Diaghilev and designed by Picasso.

Like Stravinsky a few years before, he turned to a much sparer style and to the format of touring theatre in El retablo de maese Pedro (1923). He also began to concern himself with the medieval, Renaissance and Baroque musical traditions of Spain, reflected in his Concerto for harpsichord and quintet (1926). Most of the rest of his life he devoted to a vast oratorio, Atlántida, on which he worked in Granada (where he had settled in 1919) and after 1939 in Argentina. With Albéniz and Granados he was one of the first Spanish composers to win international renown and the most gifted of the three.
GROVEmusic

Nights in the gardens of Spain

Falla El amor brujo – ballet (complete)[a].
Noches en los jardines de España[b] La vida breve – Interlude and Dance
[a]**Sarah Walker** mez [b]**Margaret Fingerhut** pf
London Symphony Orchestra / Geoffrey Simon
Chandos CHAN10232X (57' · DDD)   Ⓜ Ⓞ ▷

The coupling of the complete *El amor brujo* and *Nights in the gardens of Spain* is sensible as the works are broadly contemporary (although the latter had a longer gestation period). This recording has to compete with much-praised earlier issues, but Geoffrey Simon and the Chandos sound engineers have something new and fresh to offer. The brighter lighting of the Chandos disc, while bringing great vividness to the ballet, is particularly striking in the *concertante* work. At the end of the *Nights* Simon's broadening brings a powerful feeling of apotheosis. Margaret Fingerhut's playing responds splendidly to the changes of mood and has plenty of personality.

In *El amor brujo* the singing of Sarah Walker with its vibrant, earthy vitality brings an added dimension of Flamenco drama at the outset and she is especially fine in the passionate closing 'Bells of the morning'. But in the set pieces like the 'Ritual Fire Dance', Simon's vigour and brilliance are very telling. The 'Interlude and Dance' from *La vida breve* makes a suitable encore.

JF & CFC Fasch
German 1688-1758 & 1736-1800

Johann Friedrich was descended from a line of Lutheran Kantors and theologians. His earliest musical studies were as a boy soprano in Suhl and Weissenfels, and at 13 he was enlisted by JP Kuhnau for the Leipzig Thomasschule; his first compositions followed the style of his friend Telemann. His son Carl Friedrich Christian is probably most important for stimulating the revival of choral singing in Germany. His Sing-Akademie led to the establishment of many similar organizations throughout Europe during the 19th century. **GROVE**music

CFC Fasch Concerto for Trumpet, Oboe d'amore and Violin **JF Fasch** Oboe Concerto. Concerto for Bassoon and Two Oboes. Concerto for Trumpet and Two Oboes. Overture, FWV K:d4   **P**
Paolo Grazzi ob **Alberto Grazzi** bn
Gabriele Cassone tpt **Massimo Spadano** vn
Ensemble Zefiro / Alfredo Bernardini ob
Deutsche Harmonia Mundi ② 88697 36792-2
(64' · DDD)   Ⓕ

Ensemble Zefiro alight here, with a languid and strumming (a very present theorbo throughout) southern European breeziness, on the bravura and warmth of Fasch's melodic landscape. The Trumpet Concerto is such an elegant example of the genre, the Bassoon Concerto one of the most virtuoso of its kind and the Oboe Concerto full of memorably poignant conceits – and both woodwind pieces also contain delectable slow movements. The brothers Grazzi hit the bull's eye in these demanding and unfailingly agreeable works.

Wheeling out top 'period' wind-players in music which exploited the plethora of early-18th-century talent in Germany (especially those in the court orchestra in Dresden) allows the listener to appreciate Fasch's rare idiomatic accomplishment in this field. If Telemann's Darmstadt Suites reveal the colorific imagination of Germany's leading composer, Fasch's Overture draws on a similar aesthetic of worldly gesture and a nonchalant command of orchestral dance-palates.

Save the occasional rushing, Zefiro celebrates the imagination and flair of Johann Friedrich with total authority. The final work is the triple concerto by his son, Carl Friedrich Christian. As expected, it's full of *galanterie*, Gabriele Cassone asserting – brilliantly – his established 'clarino' credentials in the stratospheric trumpet part, joined by the delicate, soft-grained dialogues of a violin and oboe d'amore. Impressive and delightful in equal measure.

Gabriel Fauré
French 1845-1924

Fauré was trained at the Ecole Niedermeyer (1854-65) as organist and choirmaster, coming under the influence of Saint-Saëns and his circle while working as a church musician (at Rennes, 1866-70; St Sulpice, 1871-3; the Madeleine, from 1874) and giving lessons. Though he met Liszt and was fascinated by Wagner, he sought a distinctive style in his piano pieces and numerous songs, which had to be composed during summer holidays. Recognition came slowly owing to the modernity of his music. In 1892 he became national inspector of the provincial conservatories, and in 1896 chief organist at the Madeleine and composition teacher at the Conservatoire, where his pupils included Ravel, Koechlin, Roger-Ducasse, Enescu and Nadia Boulanger; from 1905 to 1920 he was the Conservatoire's resolute and influential director, becoming celebrated for the vocal and chamber masterpieces he produced until his death.

Fauré's stylistic development can be traced from the sprightly or melancholy song settings of his youth to the bold, forceful late instrumental works, traits including a delicate combination of expanded tonality and modality, rapid modulations to remote keys and continuously unfolding melody. Widely regarded as the greatest master of French song, he produced six important cycles (notably the novel La bonne chanson Op 61) and three collections each of 20 pieces (1879, 1897, 1908). In chamber music he enriched all the genres he attempted, while his works for piano (chiefly nocturnes, barcarolles and impromptus) embody the full scope of his stylistic evolution. Among his few large-scale works, the popular and delicately written Requiem op.48 and the 'song opera' Pénélope (1913) are noteworthy. **GROVE**music

Ballade, Op 19

Fauré Ballade **Franck** Symphonic Variations, Op 46 **d'Indy** Symphonie sur un chant montagnard français in G, Op 25
François-Joël Thiollier pf **National Symphony Orchestra of Ireland / Antonio de Almeida**
Naxos 8 550754 (55' · DDD)   ⓈⒷ→

François-Joël Thiollier's playing is individual, often impulsive but always idiomatic, helped by the sensitive, guiding hand of a conductor well acquainted with the music. A more high-profile production would probably have retaken those passages where piano and orchestra co-ordination is occasionally fractionally awry, such as in the last variation of the Franck, but it might also have seemed less spontaneous. Thiollier's rubato is always distinctive and attractive; the style, particularly and crucially in the Fauré, properly fluid. Both the piano and the orchestra's woodwind are discreetly prominent, but internal balances are generally excellent.

Fauré Ballade[a] **Leigh** Concertino for Piano and Strings[b] **Mozart** Piano Concertos – No 15 in B flat, K450[c]; No 24 in C minor, K491[d]
Kathleen Long pf [a-c]**National Symphony Orchestra;** [b]**Boyd Neel String Orchestra / Boyd Neel;** [d]**Concertgebouw Orch / Eduard van Beinum**
Dutton Laboratories CDBP9714 (75' · ADD) Recorded 1940s Ⓢ Ⓢ **OO**

A richly experienced chamber musician, Kathleen Long (1896-1968) was partnered and praised by Casals, played Ravel's 'Ondine' to the composer and gave over 60 National Gallery concerts during the Second World War. Though her playing may initially seem too restrained, you find yourself wondering why you've never enjoyed music so much or been made so aware, however unobtrusively, of its innermost spirit. It's in Fauré's *Ballade* that she makes her finest impression. Indeed, it's difficult to imagine this magical work played more serenely or inwardly. Even French critics wary of foreign interpreters marvelled over this recording. Her affection is evident in every caressing bar and makes for a perfect conclusion to a delectable disc. Long was a born aristocrat of the keyboard and you'll look in vain for any overt or disfiguring drama in her lucid and stylish performance of Mozart's C minor Concerto. The recordings have come up well and the inclusion in the booklet of a 1950 *Gramophone* interview is an illuminating bonus.

Orchestral Works

Masques et bergamasques, Op 112. Ballade, Op 19. Pavane, Op 50. Fantaisie, Op 79. Pénélope – Overture. Elégie, Op 24. Dolly Suite (orch Rabaud)
Richard Davis fl **Peter Dixon** vc **Kathryn Stott** pf **BBC Philharmonic Orchestra / Yan Pascal Tortelier**
Chandos CHAN9416 (72' · DDD) Ⓕ

Masques et bergamasques, which takes its title from Verlaine's sad, mysterious poem *Clair de lune*, is a late stage work that the composer himself described as melancholy and nostalgic, but it's hardly romantic, being instead pointedly neo-classical in character and shape. The playing here under Yan Pascal Tortelier is very satisfying, as are the elegant flute solos of the exquisitely delicate *Pavane*, performed here without the optional chorus, and in *Dolly*. The rarely heard Overture to the opera *Pénélope* is also effectively presented here.

The biggest *concertante* work here, the *Ballade* of 1881, is Fauré's orchestration of his piano piece of the same name; it's gentle music that persuades and cajoles in a very Gallic way. Though not an overtly virtuoso utterance, it makes its own exacting technical demands on the soloist, among them being complete control of touch and pedalling. The highly regarded Fauréan Kathryn Stott meets these with consistent success.

There's little rhetoric and no bombast in Fauré's art, but how civilised he was, and what sympathetic interpreters serve him here! The recording is warm yet also delicate.

Piano Quintets

Piano Quintets – No 1 in D minor, Op 89; No 2 in C minor, Op 115
Domus (Krysia Osostowicz vn Timothy Boulton va Richard Lester vc Susan Tomes pf) **Anthony Marwood** vn
Hyperion CDA66766 (60' · DDD) Ⓕ**OOO**

 This isn't music that yields its secrets easily. Despite pages pulsing with all Fauré's sustained radiance and energy, the abiding impression is of music of such profound introspection that you often feel like an interloper who's stumbled into a private conversation. But perseverance reaps the richest rewards, and moments like the opening of the D minor Quintet, where Fauré achieves what's referred to in the insert-notes as a 'rapt weightlessness', or the closing pages of the C minor Quintet's *Andante moderato* send out resonances that finally embrace the entire work.

The otherworldly dance beginning the finale of the First Quintet, the wild catch-as-catch-can opening and elfin close of the C minor Quintet's *Allegro vivo*, or the grave serenity of the following *Andante moderato* – all these are at the heart of Fauré's simultaneously conservative and radical genius. Simply as a person he remained conscious of an elusiveness that baffled and tantalised even his closest friends, companions who felt themselves gently but firmly excluded from his complex interior world. Domus fully suggests this enigma, yet plays with an ardour and élan that would surely have delighted the composer ('people play me as if the blinds were down'). The recordings are superb.

Piano Quartets

Piano Quartets – No 1 in C minor, Op 15; No 2 in G minor, Op 45
Domus (Krysia Osostowicz vn Robin Ireland va Timothy Hugh vc Susan Tomes pf)

Hyperion CDA66166 (62' · DDD) Ⓕ**OOO**

The First Piano Quartet reveals Fauré's debt to an earlier generation of composers, particularly Mendelssohn. Yet already it has the refined sensuality, the elegance and the craftsmanship which were always to be hallmarks of his style and it's a thoroughly assured, highly enjoyable work which could come from no other composer's pen.

The Second Quartet is a more complex, darker work, but much less ready to yield its secrets. The comparatively agitated, quicksilver *Scherzo* impresses at once, however, and the complete work possesses considerable poetry and stature. Occasionally one might wish that Domus had a slightly more aristocratic, commanding approach to these scores, but the overall achievement is impressive, for their playing is both idiomatic and technically impeccable. The recording is faithful and well balanced.

Cello Works

Romance in A, Op 69[b]. Elégie, Op 24[b]. Cello Sonatas[b] – No 1 in D minor, Op 109; No 2 in G minor, Op 117. Allegretto moderato[a]. Sérénade, Op 98[b]. Sicilienne, Op 78[b]. Papillon, Op 77[b]. Andante[c]
Steven Isserlis, [a]**David Waterman** vcs
[b]**Pascal Devoyon** pf [c]**Francis Grier** org
RCA Victor Red Seal 09026 68049-2 (62' · DDD) Ⓕ

This, surely, is the most 'complete' of Fauré's complete works for cello yet to appear. Isserlis has unearthed the original version of the *Romance*, Op 69 (entitled *Andante*), with a sustained, chordal accompaniment for organ in place of the piano's broken chordal semiquavers, and a gracious flourish from the cello by way of adieu. Mystically accompanied by Francis Grier at the organ of Eton College Chapel, the cello's song, restored to the church, seems to acquire more depth.

In the more familiar version of this work, as throughout the disc, Pascal Devoyon is a partner in a thousand, keenly aware of Isserlis's respect for the 'discretion, reticence and restraint' once hailed as the hallmarks of Fauré's style. In fact only in the noble *Elégie* do we discover the full breadth and richness of this cello's (a 1745 Guadagnini) tonal range.

A world war, plus the private trauma of incipient deafness, helps to explain the yawning gulf between the miniatures and the two sonatas of 1918 and 1922. Skipping through the score of the First you notice that only once does Fauré use a dynamic marking above *forte*, relying on the word *espressivo* to elicit just that little extra intensity at moments of climax. This is appreciated by both artists, most movingly in the central *Andante*. In the first movement, however, it's Devoyon's piquant accentuation that brings home the music's menace. The urgency and *Elégie*-evoking heart-throb of the G minor work again benefit from the immediacy of keyboard

characterisation, and the variety of keyboard colour, underpinning this poetically introspective cellist's fine-spun line.

Cello Sonatas No 1 & 2. Berceuse, Op 16. Elégie, Op 24. Romance, Op 69. Trois Romances sans paroles, Op 17. Après un rêve, Op 7 No 1 (arr Casals). Vocalise-étude. Morceau de lecture. Serenade, Op 98. Papillon, Op 77. Sicilienne, Op 78
Xavier Gagnepain vc **Jean-Michel Dayez** pf
Zig Zag Territoires ZZT070602 (73' · DDD) Ⓕ**O**

Fauré's cello sonatas are not nearly so well known as his violin sonatas, but these two late works are well coupled with other cello works and some arrangements from songs (the ever-popular *Après un rêve* among them). The big exception is the *Elégie*, the first work Fauré specially wrote for the cello, here played with the reprise of the opening theme magically hushed. The Op 16 *Berceuse* is not to be confused with the *Berceuse* from the *Dolly Suite*, and comes here in a version designed either for violin or cello. As an exception, *Papillon* is a light and brilliant virtuoso showpiece.

The centrepiece of the recital comes in the two sonatas, both late works, very compact in their structure, the first dating from 1917, the year when Debussy too devoted himself to chamber music, and the second from 1921, when the style is even more purified. Each is in three movements, lively outer ones framing hushed and intense slow ones. The *Andante* of No 2 brings a simple, dedicated melody accompanied by plain chords on the piano.

The unusual aspect of this issue is the use of period instruments, a 1902 Erard piano accompanying an 1878 cello made in France, not notably different in timbre from a traditional cello and a modern Steinway, but adding point to a fine issue, well recorded, and issued in celebration of the label's 10th anniversary.

Cello Sonatas Nos 1 & 2. Elégie, Op 24. Papillon, Op 77. Sérénade, Op 98. Après un rêve, Op 7 No 1
Maria Kliegel vc **Nina Tichman** pf
Naxos 8 557889 (63' · DDD) Ⓢ▷

Maria Kliegel has made some formidable recordings for Naxos. Here she offers a collection of Fauré's cello music, centring on the two cello sonatas, both late works. To these she adds a varied collection of pieces not all originally written for the cello, such as the song *Après un rêve*.

The sonatas are nicely contrasted but Kliegel's performances with her regular accompanist Nina Tichman (her partner in the Xyrion Trio) cannot help bringing out the fact that though both works are satisfyingly compact, the musical material of No 2 is far more compelling, where the lyricism in No 1 rarely adds up to a recognisable tune. No 2 brings a crisply compact sonata-form first movement, a warmly lyrical slow movement building up to a powerful climax and a dashing finale with a spiky second subject. In both sonatas and in the shorter pieces Kliegel plays with an impressively wide dynamic range down to a mere whisper of *pianissimo*, perfectly articulated.

The *Elégie*, Fauré's most famous cello piece, comes in a moving performance, and the fluttering *Papillon*, written some years later, is a brilliant companion piece. The most famous of the other pieces on the disc is the haunting *Sicilienne*. The *Berceuse*, originally for violin, has been transcribed for a number of other instruments and *Après un rêve* comes in a clever cello transcription. Kliegel is on top form throughout; long may her recordings for Naxos continue.

Piano Works

Five Impromptus. Impromptu, Op 86. Thème et Variations in C sharp minor, Op 73. Romances sans paroles, Op 17. Quatre valses-caprices. 13-Barcarolles. Ballade in F sharp, Op 19. 13 Nocturnes. Souvenirs de Bayreuth[a]. Pièces brèves, Op 84. Dolly, Op 56[a]. Nine Préludes, Op 103. Mazurka in B flat, Op 32
Kathryn Stott, [a]**Martin Roscoe** *pfs*
Hyperion ④ CDA66911/4 (297' · DDD) Ⓜ**OO**

Fauré's piano works are among the most subtly daunting in all keyboard literature. Encompassing Fauré's entire creative life, they range through an early, finely wrought eroticism via sporting with an aerial virtuosity as teasing and light as the elements themselves (the *Valses-caprices*) to the final desolation of his last years. There, in his most powerful works (*Barcarolles* Nos 7-11, *Nocturnes* Nos 11-13), he faithfully mirrors a pain that 'scintillates in full consciousness', a romantic agony prompted by increasing deafness and a lack of recognition that often seemed close to oblivion. Few compositions have reflected a darker night of the soul, and Fauré's anguish, expressed in both numbing resignation and unbridled anger, could surely only be exorcised by the articulation of such profound and disturbing emotional complexity. The task for the pianist, then, is immense, but in Kathryn Stott Fauré has a subtle and fearless champion. How thrilled Fauré would have been by the sheer immediacy of Stott's responses. Time and again she throws convention to the winds, and although it would be surprising if all her performances were consistent successes, disappointments are rare. Sometimes her *rubato* and luxuriant pedalling soften the outlines of Fauré's starkest, most austere utterances. But such quibbles remain quibbles. The Fourth *Nocturne* is gloriously supple, and the 13 *Barcarolles* show Stott acutely responsive to passion and finesse alike. The *Pièces brèves*, too, are played with rare affection. Stott proves herself a stylish and intriguing pianist.

---

13 Barcarolles Ⓗ
Germaine Thyssens-Valentin *pf*
Testament mono SBT1215 (72' · ADD)

13 Nocturnes
Germaine Thyssens-Valentin *pf*
Testament mono SBT1262 (80' · ADD)

4 Valses caprices.
6 Impromptus Pièces brèves, Op 84
Germaine Thyssens-Valentin *pf*
Testament mono SBT1263 (73' · ADD)
All recorded 1956-9 Ⓕ**OOO**

Ⓖ Germaine Thyssens-Valentin (1902-87) was a great and inspired pianist; occasionally one hears Fauré playing that approaches, or even occasionally equals hers, but none that surpasses it. This review could be filled with a catalogue of her qualities, but her intimacy of expression demands first place. Fauré's music has a confiding quality to it, as though it were a message intended for an audience of one, and Thyssens-Valentin is in perfect accord with this. Those messages, however, especially in the later *Nocturnes* and *Barcarolles*, are often of great profundity, and she has both the heart and the technique to convey them.

Her sound, first of all, is wonderfully beautiful, a combination of the subtlest colour and great delicacy of touch ensuring that contrapuntal voices are in perfect balance. She's a mistress of the most refined *rubato*, extreme finesse of articulation and smooth, singing line. Although she excels in quiet delicacy, her strength when required is formidable but even in the strongest *fortissimo* she never makes an ugly sound.

She is, blessedly, aware that Fauré had a sense of humour, and not only in the frank exuberance of the *Valses caprices*. Nor is she one of those artists that it takes a while to get used to. On each of these discs the first track is immediately characteristic of her. The first Nocturne has immaculate voice-leading and the lightest-fingered *leggierissimo* playing imaginable; the first Barcarolle is wonderfully tender, its second idea poised and liquid; the first *Valse caprice* has rich fantasy, dazzling brilliance and adorable wit.

The exploration of Fauré's emotional and technical range through the *Barcarolles* and especially the *Nocturnes* has never seemed so absorbing, the companion on that voyage never so prodigal with insight. Truly, a great pianist.

Requiem

Requiem (original version – ed Rutter). Motets – Ave verum corpus; Tantum ergo; Ave Maria; Maria, Mater gratiae. Cantique de Jean Racine, Op 11 (orch. Rutter). Messe basse
Caroline Ashton, Ruth Holton *sops* **Stephen Varcoe** *bar* **Simon Standage** *vn* **John Scott** *org*
Cambridge Singers; City of London Sinfonia / John Rutter
Collegium COLCD109 (63' · ADD/DDD · T/t)
Recorded 1984. Ⓕ**OOO**▶

FAURÉ REQUIEM – IN BRIEF

Yan Pascal Tortelier
Chandos CHAN10113 (70' · DDD)   Ⓕ ⦿🅑▶
A warm and spacious mainstream perform-
ance that comes as part of an all-Fauré collec-
tion taking in the rarely heard *La naissance de
Vénus*.

John Rutter
Collegium COLCD109 (63' · ADD)   Ⓕ ⦿⦿⦿🅑▶
Rutter's recording of his own edition of
the original 1893 score retains its fascination. The sound is more closely balanced
than is usually the case with the larger-scale
traditional readings.

Sir David Willcocks
EMI 764715-2 (42' · ADD)   Ⓜ⦿⦿
A much-loved LP version, documenting the
excellence of the King's College Choir at its
mid-1960s peak, and still sounding well.

Philippe Herreweghe
Harmonia Mundi HMC90 1771 (76' · DDD)   Ⓕ⦿🅑▶
Herreweghe, the first to tape Jean-Michel
Nectoux's reconstruction of the composer's
lightly scored original (Harmonia Mundi
HMC90 1292), here gives new life to the
1901 version, again favouring surprisingly
broad tempos. The coupling is unique: a
period instrument performance of the Franck
Symphony.

Sir George Guest
Decca ② 436 486-2DF2 (149' · ADD)   Ⓜ
Fresh, vivid and relatively small-scale, the
Choir of St John's College, Cambridge, as
taped in 1975, shines in a twofer of French
choral classics.

Laurence Equilbey
Naïve V5137 (41' · ADD)   Ⓕ⦿⦿⦿
A quite ravishing version of the Requiem
from Accentus offering choral singing of
exquisite purity and control.

Sir Neville Marriner
Philips 446 084-2PH (54' · DDD)   Ⓕ
With Sylvia McNair and Thomas Allen the
outstanding soloists, Sir Neville Marriner's
1993 version uses the fuller orchestration but
never lets the music drag. His unusual makeweight is a select group of French orchestral
miniatures, exquisitely played.

Nadia Boulanger
BBC Legends BBCL4026-2 (75' · ADD)   Ⓕ
A blast from the past, Nadia Boulanger's
performance has dignity and gravitas, while
the rest of the programme, featuring music
by Nadia's short-lived sister Lili, has even
greater authority. She draws from her BBC
forces a performance on a grand scale but also
alive to the work's detail.

 Fauré began his Requiem in 1885, under
the impact of the death of his father, but
the work didn't take on the form in which
we now know it until 15 years later. The familiar
1900 score, therefore, can't really be regarded as
'definitive'; it's a compromise, rather, between
Fauré's original conception and what his publisher
no doubt saw as the practicalities of concert performance. It's Fauré uncompromised that John
Rutter has sought to restore in his edition of the
seven-movement 1892 version, and his performance of it, using a chamber orchestra, a small choir
and, in the 'Pie Jesu', a soprano who could easily be
mistaken for a treble (Fauré's own early performances used a boy soloist) is a most convincing argument for accepting this score as more 'authentic'
than the customary 1900 version.

The differences are audibly obvious, and most
are no less obviously improvements. The almost
omnipresent organ now sounds more like a continuo instrument than (as can easily happen with
the 1900 score) an unwelcome thickening of an
already dark orchestra. Above all, one is more
aware than in any other recording that the sound
in Fauré's head when he conceived the work
wasn't that of a conventional orchestra but the
rich, dark graininess of divided violas and cellos,
the radiant luminosity of the work provided not
by violins or woodwind but by the voices. It's
thus more unified than the later revision as well
as being more intimate. Rutter's chorus is a fine
one, immaculate of diction and pure of line;
Stephen Varcoe's light and unforced baritone
could well be just what Fauré had in mind and
Caroline Ashton's absolute purity in her brief
solo is most moving. The recording is excellent.

Requiem, Op 48. Cantique de Jean Racine, Op 11
Sandrine Piau sop **Stéphane Degout** bar **Accentus
Chamber Choir; French National Orchestra /
Laurence Equilbey**
Naïve V5137 (41' · DDD)   Ⓕ⦿⦿⦿

Can there may be a more profoundly beautiful
recording of Fauré's Requiem out there?
We defy any sensitive soul not to be transported
into a state of near rapture by the unspeakably
delicious *Sanctus*, the solo violin of Luc Héry
floating ethereally above the choral and orchestral textures like a skylark in full song.

What is it that makes this such a sublimely
beautiful recording of a work which, let's face it,
is more than generously represented in the catalogues? (For the record, this is the original scoring of the work – organ with chamber orchestra
minus violins – which was finally published in
1969.) It's not just the lovely sound produced by
the three dozen voices of Accentus, unquestionably one of the really top-notch choirs around at
the moment, or the angelic voices of the Maîtrise de Paris which point us heavenwards in the
closing *In Paradisum*. Nor can the credit for such
unremitting loveliness be laid wholly at the feet
of the members of the Orchestre National de
France, handling this famous score with rare
sensitivity and delicacy, or the wonderful pair of

soloists. Stéphane Degout brings immeasurable poise to the *Hostias*, while Sandrine Piau's *Pie Jesu* has a wholly unaffected aura of purity and innocence – and has the string response to each line ever before been captured on disc with such utter gentleness?

These are all exceptional elements, but the two things which transform this are the recording's location and Laurence Equilbey's inspired direction. The famous Parisian church of St Clotilde imbues the whole thing with an atmosphere of warmth and great tranquillity, the organ pedals perfectly proportioned (and superbly captured by the Naïve engineers), while Equilbey shapes and caresses every single phrase, every line, every note with the kind of loving care few conductors ever lavish on such a well known and technically undemanding score. The result is a genuinely revelatory reading.

Fauré Requiem (1901 version)[a] Ⓟ
Franck Symphony in D minor
[a]**Collegium Vocale**; [a]**La Chapelle Royale**; **Champs Elysées Orchestra, Paris / Philippe Herreweghe**
Harmonia Mundi HMC90 1771 (76' · DDD · T/t) Ⓕ Ⓞ ➔

Philippe Herreweghe's earlier recording of the Fauré *Requiem* (also Harmonia Mundi) used Jean-Michel Nectoux's edition of the original 1891 'chamber' score. This is the familiar 1901 version, with its full if curious orchestration, but in other respects this is a more 'authentic' reading than the earlier one. Period instruments are used, gut strings giving the sound a gentle luminescence, and instead of an organ Fauré's permitted alternative, a large harmonium, adds a reedy quality to the wind scoring. A shade more controversially, the work is sung in 'Gallican' Latin – 'Pié Zhesü' instead of 'Pie Yesou', 'Lüx perpétüa', and so on. Together with the other period details it makes the work sound distinctly Gallic: an admirable antidote to the Anglicised or even Anglicanised Fauré presented by the archetypally English cathedral and college choirs that have so often recorded it. Both soloists are excellent, Herreweghe's tempos are a little more alert than before and the recording is splendidly ample. Alongside gut strings the big advantage of a period orchestra in Franck is the beautifully smooth sound of the horns. The overall sound is more transparent than usual, and Franck's reputation for dense over-scoring seems more than ever unjustified. It's a fine and idiomatic performance and hugely enjoyable. A fascinating coupling, strongly recommended.

Requiem[a]. Pavane. Cantique de Jean Racine, Op 11. La Naissance de Vénus, Op 29[b]
[a]**Libby Crabtree**, [b]**Mary Plazas** sops [b]**Pamela Helen Stephen** mez [b]**Timothy Robinson** ten [ab]**James Rutherford** bass-bar
City of Birmingham Symphony Chorus; BBC Philharmonic Orchestra / Yan Pascal Tortelier
Chandos CHAN10113 (70' · DDD · T/t) Ⓕ Ⓞ ➔

It was the French music publisher Hamelle who suggested that Fauré expand his 'petit Requiem' (1893 version – as restored by John Rutter) into a 'version symphonique' (1900). However, if you like Fauré's evergreen sung by a large chorus supported by symphonic-strength strings and brass then this new recording will suit nicely.

The disc's sound is consistently warm, reverberant and engaging. The chorus are in committed form: unanimous, well blended and balanced. Aside from one ugly glitch from the sopranos in the Requiem's *Sanctus* ('hosanna-RIN-excelsis'), they should be congratulated on their clear diction. Unlike Philippe Herreweghe's 'authentic' recording, no attempt has been made to sing the Latin text with a French accent. Yan Pascal Tortelier's tempos are perfectly sensible, though the opening *Kyrie* is well below the metronome marking. Both soloists control their fervour admirably, and the organist Jonathan Scott conjures up a wide variety of (presumably) electronic organ tone, including a delicious hamonium-type combination in the 'Pie Jesu'.

The enjoyable makeweights *Pavane* and *Cantique de Jean Racine* both breathe the calm air of the Requiem. But the disc's revelation is a wonderful performance of the rarely heard *La Naissance de Vénus*, a 23-minute 'mythological scene' completed in 1895. It's a little gem.

Songs

The Complete Songs – 1, Au bord de l'eau
Les Matelots. Seule! La chanson du pêcheur. Barcarolle, Op 7 No 3. Au bord de l'eau. Tarentelle, Op 10 No 2. Les berceaux. Larmes. Au cimetière. Cinq Mélodies de Venise. Pleurs d'or. La fleur qui va l'eau. Accompagnement. Mirages. C'est la paix!. L'horizon chimérique
Felicity Lott, Geraldine McGreevy, Jennifer Smith sops **Stella Doufexis** mez **John Mark Ainsley** ten **Stephen Varcoe, Christopher Maltman** bars **Graham Johnson** pf
Hyperion CDA67333 (69' · DDD · T/t) Ⓕ Ⓞ Ⓞ

Few singers would give over a whole evening to Fauré's songs on the concert platform, and choosing a way of presenting them on disc obviously poses problems. Previous sets had all the songs in chronological order; others chose poets or moods: Graham Johnson and company have begun with songs about water. This means a lot of dreaming and melancholy, whether in Gautier's *Chanson du pêcheur* ('Ma belle amie est morte', also set by Berlioz), or Richepin's *Au cimitière*. The latter is given a most beautiful rendition by John Mark Ainsley, who otherwise only sings on two tracks, with Jennifer Smith in the sentimental *Pleurs d'or*, and the homage to Venice and its lovers in Marc Monnier's *Barcarolle*.

Three cycles are the main items here. Felicity Lott sings the *Cinq Mélodies de Venise*, which includes some of Fauré's best-known songs, 'Mandoline', 'En sourdine' and 'Green'. She brings to bear on them a lifetime's devotion to

French song. Her other contribution is *Au bord de l'eau*, to a poem by Sully-Prudhomme. This is made to sound very sad; taken faster it can be quite merry; it's a celebration of love, as well as a meditation on the passing of time.

Stephen Varcoe sings *Mirages*, Fauré's penultimate cycle (1919). As Graham Johnson writes in his fascinating notes, these poems by Brimont permitted Fauré 'uneventful passion'. Christopher Maltman is the other featured singer, in five separate songs and *L'horizon chimérique*. All the performances are elegant and well-balanced, but one misses the extra slight note of acid that native French singers bring to Fauré's songs.

Hyperion's sound is impeccable and in both his playing and accompanying essay, Graham Johnson penetrates to the heart of one of music's most subtle and enigmatic geniuses.

The Complete Songs – 2, Un paysage choisi
Mai, Op 1 No 2[f]. Dans les ruines d'une abbaye, Op 2 No 1[g]. Sérénade toscane, Op 3 No 2[e]. Lydia, Op 4 No 2[f]. Three Songs, Op 5[g] – No 1, Chant d'automne; No 3, L'Absent. Tristesse, Op 6 No 2[b]. Après un rêve, Op 7 No 1[e]. Puisqu'ici-bas, Op 10 No 1[bd]. Three Songs, Op 18 – No 2, Le voyageur[h]; No 3, Automne[b]. La fée aux chansons, Op 27 No 2[b]. Noël, Op 43 No 1[e]. Clair de lune, Op 46 No 2[a]. Spleen, Op 51 No 3[g]. Prison, Op 83 No 1[h]. Dans la forêt de septembre, Op 85 No 1[g]. Chanson, Op 94[g]. Les jardins clos, Op 106[c]. Il est né, le divin Enfant[b]. En prière[b]
[a]Felicity Lott, [b]Geraldine McGreevy, [c]Jennifer Smith *sops* [e]Stella Doufexis *mez* [e]John Mark Ainsley, [f]Jean-Paul Fouchécourt *tens* [g]Stephen Varcoe, [h]Christopher Maltman *bars* Graham Johnson *pf*
Hyperion CDA67334 (68' · DDD · T/t)   Ⓕ

Volume 2 of Hyperion's superb Fauré song series takes its theme from *Clair de lune* and an idealised landscape peopled with dreaming birds and sobbing fountains. It follows the composer from youth to old age, from the young charmer to the mature master to the inscrutable sage, imaginatively side-stepping all possible monotony. Fauré's dream world is a mirror of an occasionally innocent nature that received too many cruel knocks, reflected in music of light and darkness, courage and despair. All the singers involved in this ideally presented and recorded offering perform with a special ardour and commitment; Graham Johnson is, as always, a matchless partner and commentator.

Robert Fayrfax   British 1464-1521

Fayrfax was a Gentleman of the Chapel Royal by 1497, graduated MusB (1501) and MusD (1504) at Cambridge and was incorporated DMus at Oxford (1511). From 1509 until his death he was senior lay clerk there, and received many payments from Henry VIII for music MSS. 29 compositions by him survive (more than by any other English composer of his

generation), including two Magnificats, ten votive antiphons and secular pieces. He is important for his cultivation of the cyclic mass, of which six of his are known, all except one are based on a plainsong cantus firmus in the tenor of the full sections. His music is less elaborate than that of Cornysh and Taverner and uses restrained, carefully wrought melodic lines.
GROVEmusic

Missa Regali ex Progenie

(ed Skinner). Antiphona Regali ex Progenie. Missa Regali ex Progenie. Lauda Vivi Alpha et O. Magnificat Regali. Alas, for lak of her presens. That was my woe
The Cardinall's Musick / Andrew Carwood
ASV Gaudeamus CDGAU185 (78' · DDD · T/t)   Ⓕ

Fayrfax's *Missa Regali ex Progenie* and *Magnificat Regali* are both early works, written before 1504, perhaps to impress his royal patron, and both, particularly the Mass, show signs that the composer had yet to settle into his stride. The longer, wordy movements of the Mass (the *Gloria* and *Credo*) seem elusive, as though he were note-spinning rather than weaving the contrapuntal texture, even if the hallmarks of greatness are all there. The Cardinall's Musick, with its by now almost instinctive understanding of his music, gives as convincing a performance as anyone.

The votive antiphon *Lauda Vivi Alpha et O*, with its coda in praise of Henry VIII, probably dates from the time of or shortly after his coronation in 1509. This extended homage to the Virgin is rich in textural resonances, and a double meaning of 'O rosa gratie redolentissima' ('Most sweetly scented rose') was surely intended. Here the long-drawn-out vocal lines, shifts in scoring, intellectual transitions of harmony of Fayrfax's mature style are much in evidence and the work's richness is given its full due here. There's a striking contrast between this full-blown rose of a piece and the closed, but equally perfectly formed rosebud that is the duo 'That was my woe': it was a long way from ceremonial homage to semi-private entertainment in Tudor London. It's sung perfectly by Robin Blaze and Steven Harrold.

Magnificat, 'O Bone Ihesu'

Magnificat, 'O Bone Ihesu'. Missa, O Bone Ihesu. Salve regina. Most clere of colour. I love, loved and loved wolde I be. Benedicite! What dreamed I?
(all ed Skinner)
The Cardinall's Musick / Andrew Carwood
ASV Gaudeamus CDGAU184 (76' · DDD · T/t)   ⒻⓄ

The Cardinall's Musick put the focus here on Fayrfax's Mass *O bone Ihesu*. Tragically, only a single voice survives of the antiphon that was probably its model, so in that respect their recording can't be complete, unless David Skinner is prepared to indulge in the massive and quixotic task of reconstruction for this and other fragmentary survivals. But we do have a glorious *Magnificat* built on the same materials, one of the most widely distributed of all early Tudor works. By far the most commanding performance here is of that *Magnificat*: wonderfully controlled and perfectly tuned. The group is slightly rougher in the mass and the *Salve regina*, a work that stands rather apart from the style we otherwise know from Fayrfax, and which may be one of his earliest surviving works. Intriguingly, this is the piece that seems to show the strongest debts to composers from the Continent (especially Brumel), giving important insights into the evolution of his music. Similarly, the three songs presented here, in performances that are skilled but slightly wooden, show a remarkable affinity with other mainland music, particularly that of Alexander Agricola. These little three-voice works, with their beautifully evocative texts, can without any doubt be counted among the glories of early Tudor music.

turally in the absence of precise pitch patterns. The booklet-notes, tied as they are to certain timed events in the performance, are useful here, even if they risk suggesting that the music contains more obvious and extreme contrasts than this recording conveys.

With *Unsichtbare Farben* (1999) we are in the instrumental sound world that Ferneyhough has made his own, the paradoxical title – invisible colours – hinting at a music that aspires to transcend sound itself. It's not exactly that 'unheard melodies are sweeter' but that a music that constantly reaches towards silence can, under the right conditions, have a particularly poignant intensity. These performances are in safe, experienced hands, and the recordings are well conceived to convey the music's special refinements.

Brian Ferneyhough   British b1943

Ferneyhough studied at the Birmingham School of Music and then with Lennox Berkeley at the Royal Academy in London; he later worked with Ton Leeuw and Klaus Huber. He has followed a career as an academic at universities are varied as the University of California at San Diego, the Hague and Stanford. He has been associated with the New Complexity school, and while rejecting serialism has prusued a method of composition that embraces a formalist focus. His music is extremely complex and makes colossal demands on its performers. His work spans all genres and he was the recipient of the Ernst von Siemens Music Prize in 2007.

Funérailles I & II[a]. Bone Alphabet[b]. Unsichtbare Farben[c]
[b]**Christian Dierstein** perc
[a]Members of the **Arditti Quartet** ([c]Irvine Arditti vn Ralf Ehlers va Rohan da Saram vc); [a]**Recherche Ensemble** (Melise Mellinger vn Barbara Maurer va Lucas Fels vc Uli Fussengger db Virginie Tarrête hp) / **Lucas Vis**
Stradivarius STR33739 (50' · DDD)   Ⓕ

One of the particular attractions of this disc is its delineation of contrasts and continuities between Brian Ferneyhough's earlier and later compositions. The two *Funérailles*, which he worked on between 1969 and 1980, show the composer emerging from a turbulent expressionism which has affinities with the style of his principal teacher, Klaus Huber, into the kind of hyperfractured yet remarkably coherent manner of his full maturity. Ferneyhough doesn't approve of the two pieces being heard without other music in between, but even if his wishes are disregarded the second piece emerges as an extraordinarily radical analysis of its predecessor, bringing out the kind of aggressive eloquence that confirms Ferneyhough's position as one of the most resourceful expressionists of our time.

Bone Alphabet (1991) is a study of how register, colour and rhythm manifest themselves struc-

John Field   Irish 1782-1837

Field's early musical training came from his father and from Tommaso Giordani in Dublin, after which he was apprenticed to Muzio Clementi in London. He probably studied with Salomon. By 1801 he had established a reputation as a concert pianist and published his first important works, the piano sonatas Op 1. As a result of a successful continental tour with Clementi (1802-3) he remained in St Petersburg, becoming an idol of fashionable society there and in Moscow, teaching, giving concerts and composing until 1823, when illness overwhelmed him; he died in Moscow, having made one return visit to London and to other European cities.

During his lifetime Field was known chiefly for the sensitivity of his playing, especially his expressive touch, singing phrases and extreme delicacy, a striking contrast to the fashion for virtuoso display. This legendary playing style was supported by the publication of his 17 nocturnes, each a self-sufficient piece evoking a dreamy mood of sadness consoled; song-like in manner and texture, they anticipated Chopin's pieces of the same type by nearly 20 years and influenced Liszt and Mendelssohn. Among Field's other, more numerous works, the most important are the rondos and fantaisies for piano, the Kamarinskaya variations (1809) and the Air russe varié for piano duet (1808), and the seven piano concertos. At his best, he was the equal of any of the Romantic pianist-composers.   **GROVE**music

Piano Concertos

No 1 in E flat, H27; No 3 in E flat, H32
Benjamin Frith pf **Northern Sinfonia** / **David Haslam**
Naxos 8 553770 (52' · DDD)

Benjamin Frith presents a very formidable challenge to rival versions, at super-budget price. Both works are played with effortless fluency, plus all the immediacy and freshness of new discovery. In No 1 Frith is acutely responsive to the delicate charm of the Scottish-inspired

('*Twas within a mile of Edinboro' Town*) slow movement. He makes one aware of Field's teasing delight in the unexpected in the smiling outer movements, to which he brings a wide range of tone, and piquant accentuation in the last. There's warm, sympathetic support from the Northern Sinfonia under David Haslam. The performers revel in the composer's surprises of modulation, rhythm and orchestral colouring, while from the soloist there isn't a trace of the perfunctory in passagework. The recording (in a resonant venue) might be thought overforward and full, but it remains a true bargain.

Piano Concertos – No 2 in A flat, H31;   **P**
No 3 in E flat, H32
Andreas Staier fp **Concerto Köln / David Stern**
Warner Elatus 0927-49610-2 (62' · DDD)   Ⓜ**O**▶

For those who love the sound and capabilities of the modern piano, the fortepiano's thinner tone, distinctive timbre and more intimate dynamic scope (or, put another way, the lack of power) take some adjusting to. But once one is attuned to its tonal and colouristic possibilities, the daring nature of the piano writing emerges with striking force. Take the soloist's first entry in the Second Concerto, where the virtuosic power and originality delivers its full intended *frisson* and physicality when heard on an instrument being pushed to its limit. Andreas Staier is a brilliant pianist who allies dazzling technical élan to his acute musical insight and imagination. In the outer movements, his fingerwork is as precise and crystalline as his musical intelligence, with passagework assuming a quasi-melodic purpose, elevated to the level of what Gerald Abraham called 'significant line'.

The slow movement of the A flat Concerto, a brief contrasting *molto espressivo* song without words, is played with unaffected simplicity and clarity of line, while in the E flat major Concerto, Staier follows Field's own practice of interpolating one of his nocturnes as a slow movement by playing the well-known work in C minor. Staier is a most poetic and inspiring advocate, yet the success of these performances is as much due to the extraordinary clarity and impact of the Concerto Köln's orchestral playing. There's such an infectious generosity of spirit, such vivid character and crispness, with beautifully poised wind playing and a real bite from the brass and timpani. Try the opening of the finale of the Second Concerto, where, after the lilting melody is presented by the soloist, the full orchestra respond with invigorating gusto and rusticity, never losing their tonal blend or refinement. The recorded sound, too, is wonderfully clear and detailed.

Piano Concertos – No 5 in C, 'L'incendie par l'orage';
No 6 in C
Benjamin Frith pf **Northern Sinfonia /
David Haslam**
Naxos 8 554221 (57' · DDD)   Ⓢ**SO**▶

Benjamin Frith proves an ideal soloist in these attractive, decorative pieces. Like his close contemporary, Hummel, Field is much more adept at embroidering the themes which bubble from him than at developing them in a conventional way. The passagework which can seem just trivial needs both the virtuosity and the artistry of a pianist of charm such as Frith if it's to come fully alive and compel attention, as it does here.

Frith's articulation is sparklingly clear throughout with rapid scales and decorations pearly and wonderfully even, helped by the relatively intimate acoustic of the theatre in Gosforth where the recordings were made.

The title of the Fifth Concerto, *L'incendie par l'orage* ('Fire from the Storm'), is inspired by the passage of storm music towards the end of the central development section in the first movement. Surprisingly Field, the inventor of the nocturne and inspirer of Chopin, here avoids a full slow movement, contenting himself instead with a slow introduction to the jaunty finale. At least he makes amends in the Sixth Concerto, where the central *Larghetto* slow movement is a nocturne in everything but name, with soaring cantilena for the piano which might well have inspired Bellini. The finale is a sparkling polka-like movement, with passagework breathtakingly elaborate, which Frith rightly treats as fun music, a fine pay-off. Haslam and the Northern Sinfonia are well recorded, too, in the relatively small-scale acoustic.

Morton Feldman   American 1926-1987

One of American music' great originals, Morton Feldman received early musical instuction from Wallingford Riegger; he later worked with Stefan Wolpe but the truly significant encounter came in 1949 when he met John Cage. Heavily influenced the art scene in post-war New York, Feldman started experimenting with allowing his performers to determine the durations within a guiven tempo while at the same time adhering to strictly noted pitches. One of Feldman's most celebrated – and approachable – works is Rothko Chapel named after the place created by the painter for silent contemplation.

String Quartet

String Quartet (1979)
Group For Contemporary Music (Benjamin Hudson, Carol Zeavin vns Lois Martin va Joshua Gordan vc)
Naxos American Classics 8 559190 (79' · DDD)   Ⓢ▶

Morton Feldman has made it to Naxos American Classics! But not with some of his more accessible pieces such as *Rothko Chapel* or *The Viola in my Life* but with the challenging late String Quartet (1979) – a single span lasting nearly 80 minutes. When the original incarnation of this fine performance appeared, it was easy to imagine Feldman at his piano fastidiously conceiving his sounds through some kind of psychic transmission that somehow penetrated the fog of his uniquely personal conceptual confusions.

The String Quartet is long but never boring. Within the gamut of slow and mostly soft sounds there's intriguing variety and the players often ride a high wire of demanding harmonics. The occasional loud clusters – only nine of these – are like volcanic eruptions. By the time we reach the end Feldman has taught us to listen microscopically and the stop-start of the final section seems almost agonisingly moving.

The viola in my life

The Viola in my Life I–IV
Marek Konstantynowicz va **Cikada Ensemble;**
Norwegian Radio Orchestra / Christian Eggen
ECM New Series 476 5777 (40' · DDD)   Ⓕ

Anyone wanting an introduction to Morton Feldman's ravishing sound world could do worse than sample this ECM album before gingerly proceeding to tougher fare.

The Viola in my Life, Feldman's nostalgic cycle portraying the intimate web of associations he had with the instrument, is far from hardcore. The four parts of the cycle add up to a 40-minute listen and Feldman doesn't reach for such alienated extremes. The Cikada Ensemble and the Norwegian Radio Orchestra are expert, but it's a shame violist Marek Konstantynowicz tends towards the expressive hard-sell, overplaying gestures that Karen Phillips on Feldman's own recording (recently reissued on New World Records) keeps at an objective distance.

Paying full price for a 40-minute CD might make some smart. If so, the irony of a too-short Feldman CD won't be lost on others.

Gerald Finzi   British 1901-1956

Finzi studied privately with Farrar (1914-16) and Bairstow (1917-22) and lived most of his life in the country. Influenced by Elgar and Vaughan Williams as well as his teachers, he developed an intimate style and concentrated on songs, particularly settings of Hardy. Other works include a clarinet concerto (1949) and Dies natalis for high voice and strings (1939).   GROVEmusic

Cello Concerto, Op 40

Finzi Cello Concerto[a]
Leighton Cello Concerto, Op 31[b]
Raphael Wallfisch vc [a]**Royal Liverpool Philharmonic Orchestra / Vernon Handley;** [b]**Royal Scottish National Orchestra / Bryden Thomson**
Chandos CHAN9949 (72' · DDD)   ⒻⒷ→

The Cello Concerto is arguably Finzi's finest work, written at the very end of his life under the stress of knowing he was terminally ill. At just under 40 minutes it's planned on a massive scale. The first movement brings the darkest music, an extended *tutti* establishing a brooding tone of voice. The slow movement is in more characteristically tender pastoral vein, with a poignant tinge of melancholy, music originally conceived many years before its actual completion in 1951. Leighton's Cello Concerto is almost equally ambitious. Helped by full, warm Chandos sound, the Finzi receives a big, bold performance. With a good balance for the soloist, the panache of Wallfisch's playing comes over more forcefully, and the tenderness of the slow movement is reinforced at a more spacious speed.

Clarinet Concerto in C minor, Op 31

Clarinet Concerto in C minor. Five Bagatelles, Op 23 (orch Ashmore). Love's Labour's Lost—Soliloquies Nos 1-3. A Severn Rhapsody in D minor, Op 3. Romance in E flat, Op 11. Introit in F, Op 6
Robert Plane cl **Lesley Hatfield** vn
Northern Sinfonia / Howard Griffiths
Naxos 8 553566 (71' · DDD)   ⒮Ⓞ→

This is a highly commanding performance of Finzi's gorgeous Clarinet Concerto from Northern Sinfonia principal, Robert Plane. With his bright, singing tone and effortless technical mastery, there's no shortage of intuitive poetry from Plane in the sublime central *Adagio*. Howard Griffiths's conducting is exemplary. We also get an atmospheric account of Lawrence Ashmore's idiomatic orchestration of the *Five Bagatelles* (with the poignant 'Romance' a highlight), as well as exquisitely drawn renderings of both the *Romance* for strings and 'Three Soliloquies' from Finzi's incidental music for a 1946 BBC production of *Love's Labour's Lost*. The fragrant, very early *Severn Rhapsody* (1923) makes a welcome return to the catalogue under Griffiths's deeply felt advocacy, and Lesley Hatfield makes a touching soloist in the radiant *Introit* (the slow movement of a withdrawn Violin Concerto). The sound and balance are extremely truthful, though the acoustic may be a little over-resonant for some tastes.

Clarinet Concerto. Love's Labour's Lost – Suite, Op 28. Prelude in F minor, Op 25. Romance in E flat, Op 11. Eclogue for piano and orchestra, Op 10
Alan Hacker cl **Martin Jones** pf
English String Orchestra / William Boughton
Nimbus NI5665 (65' · DDD)   Ⓕ

Several other Finzi issues available include the Clarinet Concerto. Alan Hacker, however, encompasses all his colleagues' virtues, providing special insights and revelling in the brilliant writing. He also adds something extra – an almost mystical realisation of the music's poetic vision which is deeply moving. This is in spite of the fact that the string playing sometimes lacks polish and precision. Finzi wrote incidental music for a BBC production of *Love's Labour's Lost* and expanded it for a later open-air production. It's tuneful, graceful music, but one can't feel that the stage was Finzi's world. The disc is completed by two interesting early pieces for strings, the *Prelude* and *Romance*, both wholly characteristic of the composer and very well played.

Additional recommendation

Clarinet Concerto
Coupled with: Cello Concerto
Denman *cl* **RPO / Handley**
Lyrita SRCD236 (DDD)　　　　　　　Ⓕ⯈

　A gloriously mellow reading coupled with Yo-Yo Ma's first commercial recording of the Cello Concerto. Handley is on top form.

Violin Concerto

Violin Concerto[b]. Romance in E flat, Op 11[b]. Prelude in F minor, Op 25[b]. In Years Defaced[a] – To a Poet a Thousand Years Hence (orch C Matthews); When I Set Out for Lyonnesse (orch cpsr); In Years Defaced (orch Roberts); Tall Nettles (orch Alexander); At a Lunar Eclipse (orch Weir); Proud Songsters (orch Payne)
[a]**John Mark Ainsley** *ten* [b]**Tasmin Little** *vn* **City of London Sinfonia / Richard Hickox**
Chandos CHAN9888 (55' · DDD · T)　　Ⓕ**OO**⯈

Finzi began work on his Concerto for small orchestra and solo violin in 1925, dedicating it to Sybil Eaton, a talented young violinist and the object of the 24-year-old composer's unrequited love. He harboured considerable doubts about the opening movement, however, and when Eaton eventually gave the premiere in 1927 under Sargent, the Queen's Hall audience heard only the second and third movements. When Vaughan Williams programmed the concerto the following year, Finzi penned another first movement. Neither he nor the critics found much to please them, though, and the work wasn't heard again in its entirety until the present artists revived it in 1999. The highlight is the central, characteristically rapt *Molto sereno* that Finzi later recast as his Op 6 *Introit*. Of the two vigorous flanking movements, the finale leaves the stronger impression, but the concerto thoroughly deserves its new lease of life, and Little and Hickox's sparkling and stylish advocacy will win it many new friends.

　There's another first recording in the guise of the song cycle, *In Years Defaced*. Only one number, the 1928-32 setting of Hardy's 'When I set out for Lyonnesse', was actually orchestrated by Finzi, and, in an effort to place it in a more programme-friendly context, the Finzi Trust commissioned five contemporary composers to choose a song that might benefit from the extra colour an orchestral palette can provide. The resulting sequence is a joy from start to finish. Ainsley is a potent, irreproach-

ably sensitive presence throughout this imaginative and rewarding creation. Again, Hickox and the City of London Sinfonia accompany to the manner born. Lovely, airy sound further enhances the appeal of this disc.

Dies natalis

Dies natalis, Op 8. Intimations of Immortality, Op 29
John Mark Ainsley *ten* **Corydon Singers and Orchestra / Matthew Best**
Hyperion CDA66876 (67' · DDD · T)　　Ⓕ**OO**

What's central, and essential, is the capacity of Finzi's music to grow in the listener's mind over long years, deepening in appeal, strengthening in the conviction of its purpose. Moreover, these performances are marvellously good at clarifying the strengths. Rather more than their predecessors, they clarify structure and texture. The soloist is more distinctly focused in the recording balance, and this makes an important difference when the poet's words are such a vital element. Ainsley sings with grace and clarity. The small choir conveys a restrained presence in the *Intimations*; but for much of the time this kind of halo over the sound is appropriate, and in certain important passages the fewer numbers help to compensate with clearer definition. Highly recommended.

Finzi Dies natalis, Op 8[a]. Romance, Op 11
Walton Sonata for Strings
[a]**Toby Spence** *ten*
Scottish Ensemble / Jonathan Morton
Wigmore Hall Live WHLIVE0021 (64' · DDD)
Recorded live on October 13, 2007　　Ⓕ⯈

Tenor Toby Spence is the featured artist in this recital but the biggest work, taking up the second half of the programme, is Walton's Sonata for Strings, a fine work that has not been recorded nearly as often as it deserves. This is the piece, commissioned by Neville Marriner and the Academy of St Martin, that Walton brilliantly adapted from his String Quartet of 1947, making a work for strings in the great tradition of Elgar's *Introduction and Allegro* and Vaughan Williams's *Tallis* Fantasia.

　Misleadingly, the Sonata opens with a passage for the string quartet alone, before developing into a full string piece when the opening theme is repeated. What comes out very clearly is not just how memorable Walton's thematic material is, but how clear the sonata-form structure is. In some ways this is the last of what one might regard as the pre-war Walton works, written when his partner, Alice, Lady Wimborne, was dying painfully of cancer.

　The development section brings a strongly argued fugato, with the second-movement *Scherzo*, marked *presto*, bringing a dazzling arrangement of the quartet original. The slow movement is one of Walton's most beautiful, here given a deeply expressive performance by the Scottish Ensemble. Exceptionally for Walton, the reprise of the main material is extended, with the violas leading. The *Allegro molto* finale is vigorous with its cross rhythms and a more lyrical countersubject.

Toby Spence sings sensitively in Finzi's *Dies natalis*, setting words by the mystic poet Thomas Traherne, starting with a prose poem entitled 'Rhapsody'. That leads to three more poems, with a vigorous, exhilarating movement, 'Wonder', separating the two more reflective movements. It is among Finzi's finest works. The *Romance* for strings makes an attractive introduction to the programme. A first-rate issue.

Finzi Intimations of Immortality, Op 29[a]
Hadley The Trees so High[b]
[a]**Ian Partridge** ten [b]**Thomas Allen** bar [a]**Guildford Philharmonic** [b]**Choir and Orchestra; [b]New Philharmonia Orchestra / Vernon Handley**
Lyrita SRCD238 (77' · ADD · T)   Ⓕ Ⓑ

The works pair uncommonly well, especially in the way Finzi's opening follows Hadley's conclusion so naturally that the one might almost be a commentary on the other. And 'both of them speak of something that has gone': *The Trees* tells of wasted youth, the *Immortality* Ode of lost vision. There's a contrast in that Finzi's chosen text does not impose its form as Hadley's folksong does. The young man's life falls, very conveniently for the 'symphonic ballad', into four phases, or movements: youth, marriage, fatherhood, death. Wordsworth, on the other hand, alternately cheers himself up and relapses into sad acknowledgement of an unwelcome fact; he also speculates or, some would say, philosophises. In form, it doesn't help the musician and it leads Finzi, in its 'cheering up' vein, to be musically untrue to himself: he keeps thinking he's Walton, and can't get *Belshazzar's Feast* (of all surely alien works) out of his mind. It's a deeply moving composition nevertheless.

The recordings date from 1978 (Hadley) and 1975 (Finzi) and continue to impress as fine performances. They provide timely reminders that in Vernon Handley we had one of the best conductors of British music in this period. The orchestral playing gives pleasure throughout, while the Guildford choir is heard to better advantage in the Finzi. Both soloists are ideally suited, and if we make special mention of Ian Partridge it is because his is the major undertaking.

appointments as organist and choirmaster. At the same time he was an active and influential teacher at the organ school. His harmony manual, Nauka o harmonii, retained its usefulness for several decades. At St Vojtech (where the organist at that time was Dvořák) he trained the choir to its leading position in Prague and performed large-scale masses with soloists from the Provisional Theatre. In 1873, however, he began performing a cappella Renaissance works. This change is reflected in his own compositions.   GROVEmusic

---

Violin Concertos

Violin Concertos – No 1, Op 88[a]; No 2, Op 104
Ivan Zenatý vn
BBC Symphony Orchestra / Jiří Bělohlávek
Supraphon SU3691-2 (65' · DDD)
Recorded [a]live   Ⓕ Ⓑ

Little of Foerster's large output is widely known, yet, as this finely played, splendidly recorded disc demonstrates, he's an enthralling composer. His chromatic, highly expressive harmonic style and sophisticated orchestral writing place him firmly in the company of late Romantics such as Strauss, Elgar and his friend Mahler, but his music, with its clearly defined phrases and lyrical tone, retains a distinctively Czech character. Sometimes the resemblance to his nationalist forebears is clear – the opening of the First Concerto recalls Smetana in passionate mood, and the *Andante* middle movement of No 2 evokes a Dvořák-like pastoral atmosphere. Foerster differs, however, in the way he indulges his lyrical gift; in place of the positive rhythmic drive characteristic of both Dvořák and Smetana his tendency is to allow energy to subside into dreamy reverie – often extremely beautiful but, especially in the long first movement of the First Concerto, weakening the overall impact.

However, Foerster shows real originality. The First Concerto's third movement, a graceful, sensuous waltz with playful, decorative writing for the soloist, is unlike any other violin concerto finale I can think of. Op 104 is a more introspective work, with an unusual but satisfying form. After three or four minutes of what promises to be a mercurial finale, we're suddenly recalled to the sombre surroundings of the first movement, to hear a complete recapitulation, which Foerster had earlier omitted.

Ivan Zenatý plays with lovely tone and wide expressive range, contributing his own idiomatic cadenza to Op 88. The BBC SO under Bělohlávek matches his warmth and conviction.

Josef Bohuslav Foerster
Czech 1859-1951

Czech teacher, organist and composer, Foerster was born into an old Bohemian cantor family and continued the tradition by studying in Prague as a teacher (1849-51) and at the organ school. After being employed as an organist in Vyssí Brod, he returned to Prague and held

John Foulds
English 1880-1939

Largely self-taught and the son of a Hallé Orchestra bassoonist, Foulds composed copiously from childhood. During the 1890s he acquired performing experience as a cellist in theatre and promenade orchestras in England and Wales; he also travelled on the Continent. In

1900 he joined the ranks of the Hallé's cello section under Richter, who encouraged Foulds as a conductor, taking him to the 1906 festival of the Allgemeiner Deutscher Musikverein in Essen, where he met Delius, Humperdinck and Mahler. He also studied conducting with Lamoureux, Mahler and Nikisch.

A World Requiem (1919–21), composed in memory of the war dead of all nations, was recommended for national performance by the committee of the newly formed British Music Society and adopted by the British Legion as the musical component of the Armistice Night commemorations; its annual performances at the Royal Albert Hall during 1923–6, by a chorus and orchestra numbering over 1200 conducted by Foulds, constituted the first Festivals of Remembrance. GROVEmusic

Orchestral works

Three Mantras, Op 61b[a]. Mirage, Op 20. Lyra Celtica, Op 50[c]. Apotheosis (Elegy), Op 18[c]
[b]**Susan Bickley** *mez* [c]**Daniel Hope** *vn*
City of Birmingham [a]**Youth Chorus and Symphony Orchestra / Sakari Oramo**
Warner Classics 2564 61525-2 (78' · DDD) Ⓕ○○○⯈

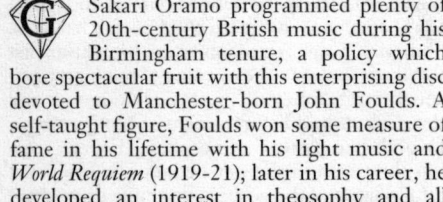

Sakari Oramo programmed plenty of 20th-century British music during his Birmingham tenure, a policy which bore spectacular fruit with this enterprising disc devoted to Manchester-born John Foulds. A self-taught figure, Foulds won some measure of fame in his lifetime with his light music and *World Requiem* (1919-21); later in his career, he developed an interest in theosophy and all things Eastern, and had spells in Paris and India (where he died of cholera).

The extraordinary *Three Mantras* (1919-30) originally served as the preludes to the three acts of Foulds's abandoned Sanskrit opera, *Avatara*. In the opening 'Mantra of Activity' Oramo daringly sets an even more propulsive tempo than does Barry Wordsworth on his pioneering Lyrita recording, yet with no loss of composure. A wordless female chorus intensifes the atmosphere of mystic awe that permeates the succeeding 'Mantra of Bliss'. The concluding 'Mantra of Will' strictly employs the seven-note modal scale of a South Indian raga. A daring, extended pause ushers in a flamboyantly savage pay-off (here rather more transparent and tidier in execution than under Wordsworth).

Next comes *Lyra Celtica*, a concerto for wordless voice and orchestra written between 1917 and the mid-1920s for his wife, the soprano Maud McCarthy. In the event Foulds completed only two of the three movements (the finale remains a 150-bar fragment). It's an alluring discovery, which deploys both microtones and quarter-tones (a Foulds trademark). Mezzo Susan Bickley rises valiantly to the challenge.

By comparison, *Apotheosis* (1909) and *Mirage* (1910) strike a rather more conventional note, though Daniel Hope's contribution in the former locates the lyrical beauty in this heartfelt elegy in memory of Joachim. Richard Strauss looms large in *Mirage*, an opulent 23-minute tone-poem with much arresting incident, which Oramo and the CBSO do proud.

The sound is hugely vivid and Calum Mac-Donald's annotation a model of its kind. Don't miss this gem of a release.

April – England,Op 48 No 1. Dynamic Triptych, Op 88. Keltic Suite – Keltic Lament Music Pictures: Group III, Op 33. The Song of Ram Dass.
Peter Donohoe *pf*
City of Birmingham Orchestra / Sakari Oramo
Warner Classics 2564 62999-2 (61' · DDD)   Ⓕ○⯈

Extraordinary how Fould's *Dynamic Triptych* opens, like an unstoppable current swirling around its seven-note mode, a tightly-woven study that goes to show how, given the right composer, confined harmony can work miracles. The slow second movement is cold but gripping, with strings that slide every now and then on a queasy bed of quarter-tones, the use of piano and timps fitfully anticipating Bartók's Second Concerto. The finale anticipates Martinů in the way that rhythmic patterns meet or converge, occasionally even Prokofiev with some brilliant running passagework from Peter Donohoe, who gives a superb performance.

April – England is an earlier piece that was later revised, spontaneous and wide-eyed *à la* Copland to start with then quietening for a noble, slower section in the manner of a passacaglia. The *Music-Pictures Group III* is earlier still (1912), the first of them prophesying the Sibelius of *Tapiola* with a huge climax, the mostly playful 'Columbine' featuring yet more destabilising quarter-tones. The 'Old Greek Legend' has something of an Elgarian tread about it and the lively 'Tocsin' finale ends just like the 'March to the Scaffold' from the *Symphonie fantastique*. In fact Berlioz is probably Foulds's nearest forebear; both men relished new sounds while holding fast to key aspects of tradition, and Foulds, like Berlioz, was a pretty stunning orchestrator.

As for the gorgeous 'Keltic Lament', how Stokowski would have basked in this amazing music! But, not having Mickey's magic wand to hand, Oramo and his Birmingham players will do very nicely. This is a really first-rate programme, a worthy follow-up to Oramo's first Foulds CD (see above) and a revealing window onto an unusual and innovative area of English music.

A World Requiem

A World Requiem
Jeanne-Michèle Charbonnet *sop* **Catherine Wyn-Rogers** *mez* **Stuart Skelton** *ten* **Gerald Finley** *bar*
Trinity Boys' Choir; Crouch End Festival Chorus; Philharmonia Chorus; BBC Symphony Chorus and Orchestra / Leon Botstein
Chandos ② 🎙 CHSA5058 (84' · DDD · T/t)
Recorded live at the Royal Albert Hall, London, on November 11, 2007   Ⓕ○⯈

Foulds conducted *A World Requiem*'s 1923 premiere at the Festival of Remembrance, using 1250 performers. This present performance, the first in more than 70 years, was given on Remembrance Day 2007, and, aside from a rather unwieldy soprano, is a triumph, with special praise due to baritone Gerald Finley and conductor Leon Botstein.

A World Requiem is the kind of piece that could only have grown from wholehearted sincerity, in this case a very personal and inspired response to the devastating losses and suffering in the First World War. Cast in 20 interlinking sections, much of the work's musical style emerges off the backs of Requiems by Verdi and Berlioz but what we actually hear is more reminiscent of Busoni, the sombre tread of the opening Requiem, the ethereal, half-lit solos and duets, and the searing climaxes, not to mention the spooky use of quarter-tones. The fifth movement 'Audite' includes a stirring summons to 'you men of all the continents', an impressive roll call of nations (individually named) and a plea for universal peace.

The contrast between the sombre-hued close of the first part and the day-bright opening of the second – a celebration of deliverance – could hardly be more telling. From here on, the mood and language become more esoteric and the scoring is often extremely delicate. Sections based on texts from Revelation and the Gospel of St John lead to an affirmation of Christ's spirit and the work ends in ecstatic joy.

Foulds's work is as ambitiously all-embracing as Mahler's Third or Eighth symphonies, and in its way almost as moving as Britten's *War Requiem* – though these are spontaneous reactions forged in the light of a first encounter. Posterity's work starts here but her ultimate verdict could well be pretty favourable. Calum MacDonald's booklet-notes serve as an invaluable listening aid.

César Franck   Belgian/French 1822-1890

Franck, French composer, teacher and organist of Belgian birth, was intended by his ambitious father for a career as a piano virtuoso. He studied at the Liège (1830-35) and Paris (1837-42) conservatories but found his true vocation only later through organist's appointments in Paris, chiefly that of Ste Clotilde (from 1858) and part-time teaching. His improvisatory skill attracted notice and led to his first major work, the remarkable Six pièces (1862), though another decade passed before he was appointed organ professor at the Conservatoire. From the mid-1870s until his death his creative powers lasted unabated. He wrote large-scale sacred works, notably the oratorio Les béatitudes (1879), and several symphonic poems such as Le chausseur maudit (1882) and Psyché (1888). But his achievements are evident especially in the symphonic, chamber and keyboard works in which he made one of the most distinguished contributions to the field by any French musician.

Here, in the Piano Quintet (1879), the Prélude, choral et fugue for piano (1884), the Violin Sonata (1886), the Symphony in D minor (1888) and the String Quartet (1889), his inherent emotionalism and a preoccupation with counterpoint and traditional forms found a balance, in turn decisively impressing his band of disciples, from Duparc, d'Indy and Chausson to Lekeu, Vierne, Dukas and Guilmant. Features of his mature style, indebted alike to Beethoven, Liszt and Wagner, are his complex, mosaic-like phrase structures, variants of one or two motifs; his rich chromaticism, often put to structural use in the 'chord pair'; and his fondness for cyclic, tripartite forms.   GROVEmusic

___

Symphony in D minor

Symphony in D minor. Symphonic Variations[a].
Les Eolides
[a]**Louis Lortie** pf **BBC Philharmonic Orchestra / Yan Pascal Tortelier**
Chandos CHAN9875 (62' · DDD)

With so many versions of the Symphony and the *Symphonic Variations* available, it's surprising that these two favourite orchestral works aren't coupled more often. Here Tortelier adds an attractive bonus in the evocative tone-poem *Les Eolides*.

His reading of the Symphony is no less than five minutes shorter than both the Karajan and Chailly versions. The reading isn't in any way perfunctory, rushed or trivial, but one made fresher, eliminating any suspicion of the glutinous or sentimental, helped by a cleanly defined yet atmospheric recording. The slow introduction, promptly repeated, is all the more effective for being taken at a flowing speed, with no feeling of haste, and the main *Allegro* is fresh and alert, less smooth than with either Karajan or Chailly. Tortelier is far closer to Monteux in his feeling for the idiom than either Karajan or Chailly, both taking a weighty view. In tempo Tortelier is very similar to Karajan and Monteux in the central *Allegretto*, with fine gradations of dynamic and a slightly raw-sounding cor anglais adding to the freshness. It's in the finale that Tortelier is most distinctive, his fast, urgent speed for the *Allegro non troppo* challenging the players of the BBC Philharmonic to produce exciting rather than genial results.

Louis Lortie is the excellent soloist in the *Symphonic Variations*, spontaneously poetic in the slow sections, sparkling and light in the *scherzando* finale. Tortelier is again at his most warmly understanding in *Les Eolides*, a work that can seem wayward, but which here is made light and fanciful in its luminously scored evocation of the breezes of heaven.

___

Additional recommendation

Symphony in D minor
Coupled with: **Fauré** Requiem
Champs Elysées Orchestra, Paris / Philippe Herreweghe

Harmonia Mundi HMC90 1771 (76' · DDD · T/t) ⒻO▸
A striking period-instrument version – reviewed in
detail on page 435

Symphonic Variations

Franck Symphonic Variations **Saint-Saëns** Piano
Concerto – No 2, Op 22; No 5, 'Egyptian', Op 103
Jean-Yves Thibaudet pf
Suisse Romande Orchestra / Charles Dutoit
Decca 475 8764DH (66' · DDD)   ⒻB▸

This scintillating disc finds Jean-Yves Thibaudet on notably effervescent form, revelling in
Saint-Saëns's pianistic brio and intricacy. He
makes a special case for the enchanting but still
neglected *Egyptian* Concerto, commenced in
Luxor, completed in Cairo and, according to
the composer, reflecting 'the joy of a sea voyage'. He brings a recognisably French clarity
and verve to the music's foaming figuration and
captures all of its audacity (an imitation of
croaking Nile frogs in the central *Andante* and
pumping boat engines in the riotous finale).
Hear his pin-point brilliance in the opening
Allegro animato where the pianist weaves a sparkling thread round the orchestral outline, his
fast-paced avoidance of sententiousness in the
long-winded *Andante* and his rush of adrenalin
in the split octave upsurge at the end of the
concluding *Molto allegro*, and you are made
conscious of a pianist whose virtuosity takes
wing in exactly the way prescribed by the composer.

Much the same could be said of Thibaudet's
performance of the Second Concerto, music
which as one writer put it journeys from Bach
to Offenbach. His *ad libitum* opening cadenza is
complemented by flashing fingers elsewhere,
and since there is inwardness as well as an irresistible élan and impetus in the Franck Variations, you could say that Thibaudet and France
(or in Franck's case, Belgium) go together like
a horse and carriage. Dutoit and the Suisse
Romande are all of a piece with their high-flying soloist and Decca's balance and sound are
exemplary.

String Quartet

Franck String Quartet **Fauré** String Quartet, Op 121
Dante Quartet (Krysia Osostowicz, Giles Francis vns
Judith Busbridge va Bernard Gregor-Smith vc)
Hyperion CDA67664 (67' · DDD)   ⒻO

Two swansongs, and in each case it's the composer's only string quartet. But how different
these works are – the Franck overflowing with
invention, drama and passion, while Fauré's
sparer textures and unchanging motion leave an
impression of reflective melancholy. Roger
Nichols's excellent notes point out, though, how
the music of both composers has the quality of
intériorité, of intimacy and self-examination.

This is a notably well-recorded disc; we're

placed, it seems, right in the middle of the
music-making, and from the opening bars of the
Franck we feel the intensity of the Dante's commitment. You may consider that their intense
approach, with powerful vibrato and bow pressure applied even to the voices filling out the
harmony, tends to become rather wearing. The
Dante performance is still a fine one, by turns
vigorous and tender, and with impressive variety
of expression.

In the Fauré there's a nice ebb and flow of
feeling as the music progresses – in a leisurely
way in the *Andante*, more purposeful in the
outer movements. Others may have come
closer to the heart of this elusive music, but you
may prefer the Dante's more earthy approach.
It's certainly playing of great accomplishment.

Piano Quintet in F minor

Franck Piano Quintet[a]
Mozart Clarinet Quintet in A, K581[b]
R Strauss Capriccio – Prelude[c]
Amadeus Quartet (Norbert Brainin, Siegmund
Nissel vns Peter Schidlof va Martin Lovett vc)
[b]**Gervase de Peyer** cl [a]**Clifford Curzon** pf [c]**Cecil
Aronowitz** va [c]**William Pleeth** vc
BBC Legends [a]mono BBCL4061-2 (77' · ADD)
Recorded live [a]1960, [b]1966, [c]1971   ⓜOOO

Rarely can a case for live rather than studio
performances have been made more persuasively than by the present disc, a study in contrasts if ever there was one. The Amadeus
Quartet was celebrated for its homogeneity
(accusations from critics of a plush or *de luxe*
style were rare), yet this superb ensemble
could easily accommodate other radically different players, and here Curzon's legendary
nervous intensity is accentuated by the Amadeus, who join him in a performance of the
Franck Quintet so supercharged it virtually
tears itself apart. Taken from a 1960 Aldeburgh Festival concert, it eclipses all others
(even Curzon's revelatory Decca disc). Curzon
and his colleagues hurl themselves at music
which clearly they see as hardly needing a
cooling agent. How free and rhapsodic is Curzon's reply to the Amadeus's opening *dramatico*, and what a savage explosion of pent-up
energy from all the players at 7'02"! Intonation may suffer in the finale's equestrian nightmare, but the concluding pages are overwhelming, and Curzon's darting *crescendo*s at
3'56" and 58" are like snarls of defiance.

At the opposite end of the spectrum is
Mozart's Clarinet Quintet, that assuaging and
elusive glory of the repertoire, played with all
Gervase de Peyer's serenity and elegance. Yet
again, the performance is essentially live, and
has the sort of vitality and imaginative subtlety
less easy to achieve or even countenance in the
studio. And the same could be said of Cecil
Aronowitz and William Pleeth, who join the
Amadeus for Strauss's Prelude to *Capriccio*,
aptly described in the notes as 'a sumptuous

effusion of very late romanticism'. The recordings (1960-71) are vivid and immediate, and odd noises off only add to the sense of occasion. Finally, a word of warning; this performance of the Franck isn't for late-night listening: you'll sleep more peacefully after the Mozart.

Piano Quintet[a]. String Quartet[b]. Violin Sonata[c]
[ab]**Ysaÿe Quartet** ([c]Guillaume Sutre, Luc-Marie Aguera vns Miguel da Silva va [b]Yovan Markovitch, [a]François Salque vcs) with [ac]**Pascal Rogé** pf
Ysaÿe Records ② YR03 (153' · DDD)   Ⓕ

Here's an enticing assemblage of Franck's three greatest chamber works, all splendidly recorded and offering stylish, powerfully communicative performances. The Ysaÿe version of the Quartet is superb – warm and friendly, with a greater range of tone colour and, in the less strenuous passages, more relaxed, a performance that fully realises the music's grandeur and intensity, and clearly articulating its complex forms.

In the Sonata, Guillaume Sutre plays many of the quieter passages with extreme delicacy; in a work that's often very strongly projected, he reminds us that at many points it's an intimately reflective work. And the passionate music, too, is given full measure. Rogé is a master at developing the grand sonority of Franck's piano writing, with beautifully balanced chords and arpeggios. Sutre, however, sometimes sounds a little colourless, the varied tonal palette he commands as a quartet leader momentarily deserting him.

The Quintet performance is magnificent. For this richly scored, darkly coloured work, players and engineers have combined to do full justice to the weight and depth of the textures while completely avoiding the drab sound that sometimes comes with the combination of piano and string quartet. And in all three works, the musicians command all the flexibility this highly expressive music needs, alongside the subtlety and discipline that leaves us feeling we're hearing the music rather than just one interpretation of it.

Piano Quintet[a]. Violin Sonata[b]
[a]**Schubert Ensemble of London** ([b]Simon Blendis, Jan Peter Schmolk vns Douglas Paterson va Jane Salmon vc [b]William Howard pf)
ASV Gold GLD4019 (65' · DDD)   Ⓕ

These works make the perfect Franck pairing; the dark, sinister mood of the Quintet offering a vivid contrast to the radiance of the Sonata. Both are imbued with Franck's passionate spirit and thrive under the Schubert Ensemble's full-blooded approach. By the time William Howard has finished the extravagant flourish leading from the slow introduction to the Quintet's first *Allegro* we're aware that this is to be an account that maximises its intense drama.

There's a care for accuracy, too – the way the rhythm at the start of the Quintet's finale is held in such firm control increases the sense of mounting tension. And in the Violin Sonata, Blendis and Howard make use of all Franck's numerous markings – for dynamics, speed modification and character – to get right inside the music.

You might feel that in the greatest performances of this music there's an expansiveness, a range of tone and expression, which we don't experience here. In the Sonata's first movement, as the violin melody reaches its climax and the piano takes the stage with the second theme, Howard's playing is quite dispassionate.

For truthful interpretations, powerfully projecting the character of each movement, the Schubert Ensemble can be enthusiastically recommended.

Cello Sonata

Franck Cello Sonata in A
Lekeu Cello Sonata in G **Ysaÿe** Solo Cello Sonata, Op 28. Rêve d'enfant, Op 14
Raphael Wallfisch vc **John York** pf
Cello Classics CC1009 (78' · DDD)   ⒻOO

Raphael Wallfisch's and John York's playing in the Franck has an air of spontaneity and enjoyment which exudes a very natural ebb and flow, while the ample ambience allows them to make the most of the 'big' moments, such as the central climax in the finale.

The disc also scores through its imaginative programming, placing the two Franco-Belgian sonatas alongside music by the great violinist who inspired them. Ysaÿe's unaccompanie Cello Sonata is an impressive, sombre work; as in the more familiar violin sonatas, echoes of the Baroque are placed within an impressionistic context. Wallfisch's account is magnificent – full-blooded, yet very clear and precise.

The Lekeu, with its opulent, passionate piano part and predominately lyrical string writing, transcribes just as effectively for the cello as does the Franck. And its grand emotions inspire a very wholehearted response. Thoroughly recommended.

Violin Sonata

Debussy Violin Sonata. Sonata for Flute, Viola and Harp **Franck** Violin Sonata in A **Ravel** Introduction and Allegro
Kyung-Wha Chung vn **Osian Ellis** hp **Radu Lupu** pf
Melos Ensemble
Decca 421 154-2DM (67' · ADD) Recorded 1962-77   ⓂOOOⒹ▸

 Here we have masterpieces from the French tradition in excellent performances that have won the status of recording classics. Kyung-Wha Chung and Radu Lupu are a fine duo who capture and convey the delicacy and poetry of the Franck Sonata as well as its rapturous grandeur, and never can the strict canonic treatment of the great tune in the finale have sounded more spontaneous and joyful. They are no less successful in the different world of the elusive Sonata which was Debussy's last work, with its smiles through tears and, in the finale, its echoes of a Neapolitan tarantella. The 1977 recording is beautifully balanced, with a natural sound given to both the violin and piano.

The Melos Ensemble recorded the Ravel *Introduction and Allegro* 15 years before, but here too the recording is a fine one for which no allowances have to be made even by ears accustomed to good digital sound; as for the work itself, this has an ethereal beauty that's nothing short of magical and Osian Ellis and his colleagues give it the most skilful and loving performance. A wonderful disc and a must-buy.

Franck Violin Sonata
Shostakovich Violin Sonata, Op 134
Sergey Khachatryan vn **Lusine Khachatryan** pf
Naïve V5122 (60' · DDD)   Ⓕ

The Khachatryans, brother and sister, make a formidable team. The recording is exceptional, too: finely balanced and with a wide dynamic range. The sound is so beautiful that one wondered, at moments during the Shostakovich, whether a harsher, more direct sonority might paint this dark work's bleak sound-picture more accurately, though it must be admitted that this duo is able to give the maximum intensity and force (as they clearly do in the ferocious second movement) while maintaining top tonal quality. At all events, this Shostakovich performance is extremely impressive, the technical difficulties seemingly of no account, and the vast design of the final passacaglia compellingly sustained with playing that ranges from precise and delicate, through mysterious and poetic, to the highest degree of force and energy (in the two solo variations).

There's outstanding playing, too, in the Franck, especially in the first movement, where the tonal range of Sergey Khachatryan's lyrical phrases gives them a powerful emotional pull. However, the performance as a whole doesn't quite fulfil this initial promise. The second movement lacks the passionate drive that some bring to it: it's a mistake, too, to allow the dynamic level to drop at the appearance of the soaring second theme – Franck only marks a diminuendo some bars later. In the following *Recitativo-Fantasia*, the composer again provides many clues; by virtually ignoring his *poco accels* and *molto lentos* the Khachatryans miss a crucial improvisatory element. It remains an enjoyable performance, however – very accomplished sonata-playing.

Piano Works

Prélude, choral et fugue. Prélude, aria et final. Grand caprice. Les plaintes d'une poupée. Danse lente. Choral No 3 in A minor (arr Hough)

Stephen Hough pf
Hyperion CDA66918 (68' · DDD)   ⒻO

Hough has a dream-ticket combination of virtues – astonishing agility, a faultless ear for texture, fine-tuned stylistic sensibility and an exceptional understanding of harmonic and structural tensions. He acknowledges all Franck's nuances, notated and implied, without ever disturbing the broader flow; he gives full rein to the heroic Lisztian cascades, without ever tipping over into melodrama. The only hint of a nit to be picked would be that the *fortissimo* arpeggiations in the 'Choral' don't ring as resonantly as they might. One can't imagine the calm at the end of the 'Aria' being better judged.

In their very different ways the almost comical bravura of the *Grand caprice* and the salon charm of the *Danse lente* and *Les plaintes d'une poupée* are extremely difficult to bring off with success. Yet anyone who has followed Hough's recording career will know that this sort of thing is meat and drink to him. As for his own transcription of the A minor *Chorale*, the unavoidable adjective is 'awesome'.

Organ Works

Pièce héroïque in B minor. Cantabile in B. Fantaisie in A. Grande pièce symphonique in F sharp minor, Op 17. Pastorale in E, Op 19. Fantaisie in C, Op 16. Prélude, fugue et variation in B minor, Op 18. Trois chorales – No 1 in E; No 2 in B minor; No 3 in A minor. Prière in C sharp minor, Op 20. Final in B flat, Op 21
Marie-Claire Alain org
Erato ② 2564-61428-2 (152' · DDD) Recorded on the Cavaillé-Coll organ, Saint-Etienne, Caen, France ⓈO

Alain is a completely involved communicator. More than anyone else she delves into the very soul of these works. Thus we have an intensely prayerful *Prière*, a majestically statuesque *Grande pièce symphonique* while the *Chorales* are delivered with an unexpected degree of fervour; perhaps the Third is a shade overfervent since some of the semiquaver figurations lack absolute clarity – something which after one or two hearings serves to heighten the excitement but which might, after repeated listening, become irritating. This is a highly authoritative release not just in terms of playing but also in Alain's accompanying notes. The Caen organ is a particularly fine specimen of a Cavaillé-Coll, dating from 1884 – 25 years after the St Clotilde organ for which Franck wrote much of this music. The recording captures it, and the church's atmosphere, effectively.

Girolamo Frescobaldi
Italian 1583-1643

Frescobaldi studied with Luzzaschi at Ferrara, where he also came under Gesualdo's influence. Soon after 1600 he went to Rome where in 1607 he became organist of S Maria in Trastevere. The same year he travelled with his patron, Guido Bentivoglio, to Brussels, but his experience of this centre of keyboard music left little imprint on him, except perhaps in the fantasias of 1608. In July 1608 Frescobaldi was elected organist of St Peter's, Rome.

In 1615 Frescobaldi secured a position with Duke Ferdinando Gonzaga at Mantua, but after three months he returned to Rome, remaining there until 1628 when he became organist at the Medici court in Florence. By the time he returned once more to Rome, in 1634, his fame was international and he was moving in the highest circles of patronage. In 1637 Froberger came from Vienna to study with him. Little is known of his other pupils, but his influence on keyboard playing and composition remained important for a century or more.

Frescobaldi is remembered chiefly for his keyboard music, much of which was published in 12 volumes (1608-14) with toccatas, canzonas, ricercares, dances and variations. His vocal music is of relatively small importance. His sacred works, including c40 motets, mostly for one to three voices and continuo, show none of the complexity and expressive intensity of the keyboard works. Perhaps his most characteristic vocal music is in an early volume of madrigals (1608), but two volumes of Arie musicali published during his years in Florence (1630) are also of interest.

GROVEmusic

Canzonas

Il Primo libro delle canzoni – La Bernadina; La Donatina; L'Altera; La Tucchina o La Superba; L'Ambitiosa; La Plettenberger; La Lievoratta; La Samminiata; La Diodata; La Nobile; Canzona Prima a due bassi; Canzona Quinta a due canti; Canzona Seconda a due canti e basso; Canzona Quinta a 4; Canzona Quarta a due canti e basso; Tre Canzona a canto e basso; Canzona Prima a 4; Canzona Seconda a 4; Canzona trigesima quinta
Les Basses Réunies / Bruno Cocset *vion*
Alpha ALPHA053 (65' · DDD)   Ⓕ

As this ensemble's name implies, viols are the start here, and part of the disc's attraction lies in the novelty of hearing these pieces, which are played often enough, in an instrumentation that largely dispenses with the more usual winds. The only touch of non-string colour is provided by the cornetto.

The role of the continuo is immeasurably enhanced, becoming not so much a backdrop to the solo lines as their foundation. And the continuo section is rich indeed: harp, claviorganum, theorbo and harpsichord. When everything comes together the result is as colourful and ear-tickling as anything to be heard on other recordings of this repertoire.

The performances rise to the music's challenges with elegance and barely any technical strain. This is a disc that grows on you with repeated listening, and demonstrates that Frescobaldi's canzonas are no less inventive than his keyboard music.

Keyboard Works

Il Primo libro di Ricercari et Canzoni francese   Ⓟ
Il Primo libro delle fantasie
Sergio Vartolo *hpd/org*
Naxos ② 8 553547/8 (132' · DDD)   ⓈⓄ▷

The *Fantasie* (1608) and *Ricercari* (1615) are the earliest of Frescobaldi's keyboard publications, and as neither has been issued complete before; to get both together, and at super-budget price, is treasure-trove indeed. Frescobaldi fanatics need read no further.

Vartolo's tendency to spin out the music at twice the length of most other interpreters can be rather off-putting, and doesn't always help the listener to grasp the overall design of formally complex pieces like the Toccatas. But these Fantasias and Ricercars are imitative, fugal pieces, more abstract in conception than the exuberant toccatas; recognising this, Vartolo avoids extreme tempi, and instead gives measured performances that gain in clarity what they have lost in eccentricity. These are (and this isn't intended to damn with faint praise) sensible performances, that give both composer and audience their due. Vartolo loosens up a bit in the playful *Canzoni Francesi* that conclude the book of Ricercars, but in this he follows the composer's lead, and demonstrates his own sensitivity to style.

Vartolo mostly performs on a modern copy of an Italian harpsichord, and on the organ of the Chiesa del Spirito Santo, Pistoia (built a few years after Frescobaldi's death). Suffice it to say that this recording would be a must-have at full price; as it is, you won't find better value anywhere.

Kenneth Fuchs   American b1956

Fuchs received his Bachelor of Music in composition from the University of Miami and his Master of Music and Doctor of Musical Arts degrees from the Juilliard School in New York City. His teachers included Milton Babbitt, David Diamond, Vincent Persichetti, David Del Tredici, Alfred Reed and Stanley Wolfe. He has worked in the music education system at various colleges: University of Oklahoma, the Manhattan School of Music, North Carolina School of the Arts and at Juilliard School. He is currently Professor of Composition at the University of Connecticut. He has written for orchestra, band, chorus, jazz ensemble, and chamber ensembles.

Orchestral works

Canticle to the Sun[a]. United Artists. Quiet in the Land[b]. Fire, Ice and Summer Bronze[b]. Autumn Rhythm[b]
[a]**Timothy Jones** *hn*
London Symphony Orchestra / JoAnn Falletta
[b]**members of the orchestra**
Naxos American Classics 8 559335 (64' · DDD)   Ⓢ▷

Kenneth Fuchs is an energetic American composer now in his early fifties who is based at the University of Connecticut. He has a wide range of compositions and is also involved in music education and administration. At Juilliard he was a contemporary of JoAnn Falletta, who very much wanted to make an orchestral CD of his music. The opportunity came in 2003 when she recorded a group of works with the LSO, which came out on Naxos in 2005. Fuchs was so stunned by the legendary expertise of the LSO in playing at sight for a recording that he wrote *United Artists* as a short tribute. It opens this second Naxos CD; a series of chamber works follows, and the disc closes with *Canticle to the Sun*, a horn concerto in which the British connection continues with the soloist Timothy Jones from the LSO.

United Artists is a kind of fanfare to this orchestra, who obviously enjoyed it – the idiom stems from Copland and early Carter. *Quiet in the Land* for mixed string and wind quintet is contemplative in mood, generally music of low density suitable for illustration. This aspect comes to the fore in *Autumn Rhythm*, inspired by the paintings of Jackson Pollock: it would make an apt soundtrack for a series of his pictures.

Canticle to the Sun is based on the familiar hymn-tune 'All Creatures of our God and King'. This is an imaginative idea where the soloist emerges from a tinkling backdrop and retains clear contact with the melody throughout, although it is never stated in full. The concerto adds up to a pastoral idyll with occasional spots for the timpani and lyrical cadenzas – all neatly played.

Andrea Gabrieli   Italian 1533-1585

Possibly a pupil of Willaert, in 1557-8 Andrea Gabrieli was organist of S Geremia, Cannaregio, and in 1562 was working in Munich, where he met Lassus. In 1566 he became organist of St Mark's, Venice, where he remained all his life. A prolific and exceptionally versatile composer, he was a leading figure in Venice, respected as a performer and teacher, 1576) and psalms (1583), as well as secular and instrumental works (1566-80); many pieces were published posthumously by his nephew Giovanni. He is chiefly famous for his sacred ceremonial music (notably Concerti, 1587), in which he brilliantly exploited the architecture of St Mark's, separating voices and instruments into cori spezzati to create imposing stereophonic effects, a style that greatly influenced other Venetian and German composers. His madrigals are more lightweight and homophonic than others of the time, some showing Lassus's influence. **GROVE**music

Madrigals

A Gabrieli 21 Madrigals – Caro dolce ben mio, perchè fuggire; Sento, sent'un rumor ch'al ciel si estolle; Mentr'io vi miro, vorrei pur sapere. Del gran Tuonante. Sassi, palae. Felici d'Adria. I'vo piangendo.

Asia felice. O beltà rara. Laura soave. O-passi sparsi. Amami, vita mia. Lasso, Amor mi transporta. Hor ch'a noi torna. Voi non volete, donna. Io mi sento morire. Mirami, vita mia. Chi'nde darà la bose. Ancor che col partire. Fuor fuori a sì bel canto. Dunque il commun poter **G Gabrieli** Canzoni – Canzon la spiritata
I Fagiolini; The English Cornett and Sackbut Ensemble / Robert Hollingworth
Chandos Chaconne CHAN0697 (77' · DDD · T/t) ⓅⒹ→

Andrea Gabrieli has always been something of a textbook composer, whose reputation falls under the shadow of his more famous nephew, Giovanni, the composer *par excellence* of the grand Venetian polychoral manner. Though Andrea's music may not plumb the depths of Giovanni's best pieces, his compositional range displays a versatility that the writing of his more considered relation surely lacks. Whereas Giovanni concentrated on liturgical composition, Andrea explored the gamut of contemporary styles and forms, from madrigals and lighter secular writing to dialect texts, church music, instrumental works, experimental theatre-pieces and music for Venetian festivities.

This imaginatively constructed disc, punctuated by instrumental items, presents as a main course a selection of Andrea's settings of Italian texts. These reveal an unexpected emotional complexity, robust and lively works being contrasted with more reflective ones. The former are characterised by an energetic rhythmic drive and bright sonorities in the upper registers, the latter by a mellifluous and sensitive approach.

There are also a few oddities, notably 'Asia felice', composed for an outdoor celebration of the Battle of Lepanto in 1571 – suitably enlivened here with unscripted interventions of organ, sackbuts and cornets – and the boisterous rendition of the dialect text 'Chi'nde darà la bose al solfizar', which evocatively breathes the air of the streets and squares of Renaissance Venice. Anyone smitten with the musical traditions of this most fascinating of all cities, shouldn't hesitate to buy this record.

Giovanni Gabrieli   Italian c1553/6-1612

Giovanni Gabrieli, like his uncle Andrea Gabrieli, with whom he studied, worked briefly at the Munich court (c1575-8) and in 1585 he became organist of St Mark's, Venice, and of the confraternity of S Rocco, posts he held for the rest of his life. After Andrea's death, he edited many of his works for publication. His own fame and influence were widespread and crucial, notably in northern Europe – Schütz was among his many pupils – and he represents the highest point of the High Renaissance Venetian school. He composed motets and mass movements and much of his sacred ceremonial music exploits the architecture of St Mark's, using contrasting groups of singers and players to create cori spezzati effects, but often in a more intense and dissonant style than his uncle's. His music for wind ensemble is lively and colourful and includes up-to-date concertato writing; the organ ricercares are in a well-developed and specific keyboard style. **GROVE**music

Sacrae Symphoniae

The 16 Sonatas and Canzonas from Sacrae P
symphoniae. Toccata quinti toni. Three Toccatas.
Intonatione-del noni toni
His Majesties Sagbutts and Cornetts /
Timothy Roberts org
Hyperion CDA66908 (75' · DDD)   Ⓕ

Giovanni Gabrieli is arguably the earliest composer to write a significant body of instrumental music to a formula which can be said to be truly idiomatic and timelessly palatable. The *Sacrae symphoniae* publication of 1597 is a mixed set of vocal and instrumental pieces and, in its grand design, preserves a glorious heyday of textural opulence, intimate and playful dialogue between galleries and unashamedly ostentatious virtuosity. His Majesties Sagbutts and Cornetts have augmented their chamber consort to form, as cornettist David Staff proudly proclaims, 'the largest group of cornett and sagbutt players to have been assembled from one city since the 17th century'. These wonderful 16 canzonas and sonatas make up the complete instrumental music of the 1597 collection. In essence it's the extensive juxtaposition between sombre blocks and glittering small-scale exchanges which gives the music its seminal quality of moving both inevitably and eventfully towards a self-assured resolution, befitting its aristocratic gait. Having a 'moderator' (in this case the fine keyboardist, Timothy Roberts), as opposed to an artistic director, is pragmatic and democratic but there's the odd moment where a strong artistic presence at the helm would have, ironically perhaps, empowered the musicians towards a more flexible and varied approach to articulation and colour. That said, there are some glorious and majestic sounds: you can fly to the buzzing *Canzon duodecimi toni a 10*, bathe in the fragrant harmonic mosaic of the three-choir *Canzon quarti toni a 15* and relish elsewhere the peculiarly delicate and sweet sounds of this ensemble. Overall, a notable and distinctive achievement.

Niels Gade   Danish 1817-1890

Danish composer, the most important figure in 19th-century Danish music. He trained as a violinist and played in the Royal Orchestra, Copenhagen, producing his official Op 1, the prize-winning concert overture Efterklange af Ossian in 1840. Encouraged by Mendelssohn, who was enthusiastic about his First Symphony (1841-2), he went to Leipzig as an assistant conductor of the Gewandhaus Orchestra, also meeting Schumann and composing the Mendelssohnian Third Symphony (1847) and String Octet (1848). In Copenhagen he reorganised the Musical

Society, establishing a permanent orchestra and choir which gave the premieres of his Symphonies nos. 4–8 and his large choral works ('Koncertstykke'), notably Comala (1846), and serving as co-director of the Copenhagen Academy of Music. Although the personal, Scandinavian colouring of his early works gave way to the German Romantic influence in his music after c 1850, he had an immense influence on the next generation of Danish composers. **GROVE**music

Symphonies

Symphonies – No 1 in C minor, 'On Zealand's fair plains', Op 5; No 5 in D minor, Op 25ᵃ
ᵃ**Ronald Brautigam** pf **Danish National Symphony Orchestra / Christopher Hogwood**
Chandos CHAN10026 (58' · DDD)   Ⓕ

Symphonies – No 3 in A minor, Op 15; No 6 in G minor, Op 32. Andante (Discarded First Movement from Symphony No 3). Echoes from Ossian, Op 1
Danish National Radio Symphony Orchestra / Christopher Hogwood
Chandos CHAN9795 (77' · DDD)   Ⓕ

If not the most adventurous of composers, and in his later years over-conservative, Gade in his youth certainly had his moments. his inventiveness is evident in all four symphonies presented here, albeit in very different ways. The Sixth (1856-7) is perhaps the most perfect, Classical in design although with a minatory feel suggestive at times of middle-period Haydn. If it stays within its own clearly defined harmonic and stylistic limits, the First, Third and Fifth do not. No 1 (1842), based on an old ballad and incorporating his own earlier setting of it, is bright and full of life: no wonder Mendelssohn and the Leipzig audience were enchanted.

The Third (1846-7) is a different proposition, more Romantic in tone, its first movement too much so causing the composer to replace it with a less radical opening span (the *Presto* tempo marking of which must still have raised a few eyebrows). The original *Andante – Allegro energico* is included here in its first recording, proving a fine if turbulent sonata *Allegro*.

The Fifth (1852) has a Mendelssohnian poise and grace plus one startling – if ultimately stillborn – innovation: the piano as an orchestral instrument. The Fifth is definitely not a concerto, but a true symphony with an extended keyboard part, sometimes as soloist, sometimes as colouristic device. The performances are all very nicely drawn, the First and Fifth particularly so.

Hans Gál   Austrian 1890-1987

Gál studied with Eusebius Mandyczewski and Guido Adler – formative influences that informed his later dual life as a composer and an academic. His precocious talent quickly assured a named for him and his works were widely performed. His second opera Die

heilige Ente was performed in 20 opera houses. With the rise of the Nazis he lost his job at the Mainz Conservatoiry where he was director and his music was no longer performed. At the suggestion of Donald Tovey he emigrated to the UK and from 1945 until his reirement he was a lecturer in music at Edinburgh University. He was also a co-founder of the Edinburgh Festival. His music, which numbers 110 published works, is tonal in nature but never bland or reactionary. He edited many of Brahms's major works and wrote books on Brahms, Schubert, Wagner and Verdi.

String quartets

String Quartets – No 1, Op 16; No 4, Op 99.
Improvisations, Variations & Finale on a Theme of Mozart
Edinburgh Quartet (Charles Mutter, Philip Burrin vns Michael Beeston va Mark Bailey vc)
Meridian CDE84530 (72' · DDD)   Ⓕ

String Quartets – No 2, Op 35; No 3, Op 95.
Five Intermezzi, Op 10
Edinburgh Quartet
Meridian CDE84531 (72' · DDD)   Ⓕ

Hans Gál's sophisticated but accessible musical language pushes the boundaries of formal design just about as far as they will go without fracturing, his slow movements poignant and tightly woven, his scherzi and finales invariably touched by understated humour.

Although stylistically distinctive, the First Quartet seems to take a good many of its cues from Brahms, Mendelssohn and, in the finale, Reger, a high-point being a slow movement that opens to ethereal harmonics and generates considerable intensity. Gál had a gift for eloquent melodic invention and the opening of the Second Quartet wafts in among weeping cadences, lightening just a little for a wistful second idea. An underplayed strain of melancholy permeates the canzone, placed third in a novel five-movement structure, and where gently arpeggiated cello chords suggest parallels with Dvořák.

The Third Quartet ferries us forwards by 40 more years. The playful *Scherzo* and finale frame another of Gál's memorably meditative slow movements, this one opening to an unaccompanied violin solo before the other strings gather round in what sounds like a consolatory embrace.

Gál published the last in 1972 when he was in his early eighties (though he still had some 15 years left to him), the introductory *Adagio* perhaps the most magical episode in the whole cycle, music that twice recurs later in a movement that subsequently gives way to another of Gál's wry scherzi. Like its predecessors it betrays the hand of someone steeped in the classical quartet tradition while at the same time having something uniquely his own to say. A set of five pleasantly diverting *Intermezzi* predates the cycle, and the *Improvisation, Variations & Finale on a Theme of Mozart* take us on a light-hearted excursion via the kind of writing Gál put to more 'serious' use for the masterly quartets. They provide the sort of music that seems to grow richer with each hearing, especially in such sympathetic performances. Very strongly recommended.

Piano Music

Complete Piano Works
Leon McCawley pf
Avie ③ AV2064 (3h 9' · DDD)   ⒻⓄⓄ→

To say that Hans Gál was unique is not to suggest that his work is quirky or inaccessible. Hardly a single track on this admirable and musically worthwhile collection lacks interest, colour or instant appeal. And yet Gál was no mindless lightweight: a strain of deeper meaning invariably lingers somewhere beneath his compact and attractive surfaces.

The first thing to say about this set is that Leon McCawley's playing could hardly be bettered: virtually every bar betrays a level of perception that would surely have warmed the composer's heart. Take the very first track on the first CD, the opening movement of Gál's Op 28 Piano Sonata of 1927, the numerous decorative harmonic digressions even within the first 30 seconds, the way McCawley ever so slightly stresses them but without disrupting the flow. Then try the *Quasi menuetto* second movement, a playful charmer stylistically placed somewhere between Prokofiev and Finzi. The early Suite, Op 22, is a genial sequence slightly reminiscent of Korngold (the Menuet) whereas the two post-war Sonatinas display more of a neo-classical leaning. All this, plus the three early Sketches, three Pieces and three Preludes (the middle piece achingly beautiful), fill just the first disc.

But the best is yet to come: two CDs of Preludes and Fugues, the 24 preludes written mostly in hospital in 1960, one a day while recovering from illness; the fugues, serene and clear-headed, the work of an unusually lucid 90-year-old. Both sets progress from their initial key (B for the Preludes, C for the Fugues) and ascend chromatically, with the last piece cast a semitone lower than the first. The Preludes are more akin to, say, Prokofiev's *Visions fugitives* than to Shostakovich's Preludes. The fugues, on the other hand, are rather more ascetic, pared to essentials but often intensely expressive.

So, a surprise journey that should encourage many a return visit, especially in performances as consistently sympathetic as these. Excellent sound.

Baldassare Galuppi   Italian 1706-85

Nicknamed 'Il Buranello' after his birthplace in the Venetian lagoon, Baldassare Galuppi is remembered today for inspiring a sonnet by Robert Browning rather than for his music. He was none the less a prolific composer leaving a large number of operas, particularly of opera buffa. He worked as maestro di capella at St Mark's in Venice as well as in London and St Petersburg (for Catherine the Great).

Opera arias

'Forgotten Arias of a Venetian Master'

L'Olimpiade – Superbo di me stesso. Scipione in Cartagine – Di madre ai cari amplessi. Il sagrifizio di Jephte – Ah, di Lete dall'onda profonda. Il trionfo della continenza – Cedo alla sorte. Antigono – È pena troppo barbara; Benché giusto a vendicarmi. Voi che languite. Concerti a quattro – G minor; B flat.
Catherine King *mez* **Il Canto di Orfeo / Gianluca Capuano** *hpd*
Avie AV2116 (72' · DDD · T/t) Ⓟ🔊➔

Avie here marks his 300th anniversary – largely forgotten amid the Mozart and Shostakovich junketings – with a clutch of *opera seria* arias from the 1730s and '40s, before he teamed up with the playwright Carlo Goldoni to become the most successful *opera buffa* composer of the day.

Metastasio, doyen of *opera seria* librettists, once complained that Galuppi's music failed to express fully the emotions of the poetry. He may have thought again if he had heard the gravely eloquent E minor aria from *Antigono*, where soft trumpets add their mournful gloss to the strings. If Galuppi's fiery bravura arias, *à la* Vivaldi, are less distinctive, his pathetic or soulful *arie d'affetto* reveal his feeling for graceful, shapely melody and delicate orchestral textures: say, in a touching aria from *Scipione in Cartagine* (again, subtly coloured by trumpets), or a number ('Voi che languite') from an unknown opera.

Though caught in an uncomfortably swimmy church acoustic, Catherine King sings these attractive arias with firm, clear tone (her predominantly 'straight' sound selectively warmed with vibrato), elegant phrasing and agile, precise coloratura. She is splendidly vehement in the virtuoso castrato aria 'Benché giusto a vendicarmi' from *Antigono*, tenderly musing in 'Voi che languite', and smoothly negotiates the wide leaps between registers in the *Scipione* aria.

Il Canto di Orfeo accompany with verve and imagination, and on their own give vivid performances of two of Galuppi's Concerti a quattro for solo strings: the sober, Corellian G minor, and the more galant concerto in B flat, whose racy finale the players deck out with all sorts of jokey effects, right up to their zany, Stravinskified ending. Outrageous, but fun.

(1946-52); tutor (1952-76) and director of music (1965-9) at Morley College; visiting director of music at St Paul's Girls' School (1962-75); and professor of harmony and counterpoint, RAM (1956-86). His compositional career effectively recommenced with the premiere of the Symphony No 1 at the 1951 Cheltenham Festival under Barbirolli. Its success led to several major commissions including Cantiones sacrae (1951–2) for the Three Choirs Festival, and the opera The Moon and Sixpence (1954-7) for Sadler's Wells Opera. Gardner's music is characterized by skilful craftsmanship and an eclecticism often arising from the nature of a particular work.

Orchestral works

Piano Concerto No 1, Op 34[a]. Symphony No 1, Op 2. Midsummer Ale, Op 73
[a]**Peter Donohoe** *pf* **Royal Scottish National Orchestra / David Lloyd-Jones**
Naxos 8 570406 (72' · DDD) Ⓢ➔

This coupling of two of John Gardner's major works, plus a sparkling comedy overture, could not be more welcome. He celebrated his 90th birthday in 2007, and has always been astonishingly prolific; maybe one reason for his neglect when there is so much to choose from.

The First Symphony (1946-47), the most extended work on the new disc, is in four movements spanning more than 40 minutes. The idiom is more abrasive than in Gardner's later works, with a grinding slow introduction leading to an *Allegro* with echoes of Walton in its jazzy syncopations, though with sharper harmonies. A chattering *Scherzo* in triple time leads to a *Lento* slow movement with whole-tone passages and orchestration echoing Debussy and Ravel. The finale is strongly rhythmic. As always in Gardner's music the orchestration is brilliantly clear, and after an interlude of stillness, the work ends with a ripe and optimistic D major chord.

The First Piano Concerto (1957) offers a contrasted idiom in its percussive echoes of the Bartók concertos, suiting Peter Donohoe's strong style admirably in a performance brilliantly backed by the RSNO. The clangorous opening movement leads to a still slow movement with echoes of Bartók but also of John Ireland. The finale brings more echoes of Walton and Arnold in music that is invariably attractive and distinctive.

The disc is dazzlingly rounded off with a rumbustious comedy overture *Midsummer Ale*, which should bring renewed attention to the composer's most attractive music.

John Gardner   English b1917

Gardner was organ scholar at Exeter College, Oxford (1935-9), where his teachers included Armstrong, Walker and Morris. After war service he was a répétiteur at the Covent Garden Opera Company

Gautier de Coincy   French 1177/8-1236

Gautier may have studied at Paris University; in 1214 he became prior at Vic-sur-Aisne and in 1233 abbot at Soissons. He wrote a massive verse narrative, Miracles de Nostre-Dame, in 1214-33, includ-

ing songs, and composed religious chansons. His work represents the earliest substantial collection of sacred, Marian songs in the vernacular, and drew on secular melodies, which are set to sacred or devotional words.

GROVEmusic

Miracles of Notre-Dame

Anonymous Benedicamus Domino. Hyer matin a l'enjournee. S'amours dont sui espris **Gautier de Coincy** Miracles de Nostre-Dame – Amours dont sui espris; Entendez tuit ensemble; Ma viele; D'un amour coie et serie; Quant ces floretes florir; Hui matin a l'ajournee; Roine celestre; Esforcier m'estuet ma vois; Amours qui set bein enchanter; Puisque voi la flour novele; Cui donrai je mes amours; Douce dame; De la sainte Leocade; Talens m'est pris orendroit; Pour Dieu traiez vous en la; Je pour yver
Harp Consort / Andrew Lawrence-King *hp*
Harmonia Mundi HMU90 7317 (70' · DDD · T/t) Ⓕ

There are so many difficulties for performers of Gautier de Coincy. Quite aside from the problems of all monophonic song from the 13th century (whether to use instruments or not, how literally to take the written notes, how much can be improvised and so on), most of the music is demonstrably not by him, but adaptations of well-loved pieces of his time. His main contribution is therefore the poetry. So an important feature of this issue is that the texts are treated with the utmost seriousness: the seven songs that form the core are all sung complete, all treated as coherent poems without gratuitous repetition of sections, all with the words taking absolute primacy in the performance, and all done in ways that makes it quite clear that the performers know exactly what they are singing about. There's something marvellously refreshing in the way they relish the sound of their texts, enunciated with a deliciously hard-edged approach to medieval French.

Around these seven songs, Andrew Lawrence-King has created a frame designed from shorter fragments. Many are instrumental renditions of the melodies, with some particularly remarkable and fascinating performances by Ian Harrison on cornett and shawm, alongside some astonishingly attractive examples of group improvisation.

Giuseppe Gazzaniga Italian 1743-1818

Study in Venice and Naples (with Niccola Piccinini), led to unltimately to the post of maestro di capella at Crema Cathedral. He was a prolific composer of opera buffa though posterity has relegated him well below Paisiello and Cimarosa.

Don Giovanni

Don Giovanni
Roberto Iuliano *ten* Don Giovanni **Linda Campanella** *sop* Donna Elvira **Cristina Mantese** *sop*
Donna Anna **Valentina Molinari** *sop* Maturina
Maurizio Leoni *bass* Pasquariello **Giorgio Trucco** *ten*
Duca Ottavio **Alberto Rota** *bass* Commendatore
Dario Giorgelè *ten* Biagio **Claudia Grimaz** *sop*
Donna Ximena **Luca Tamani** *ten* Lanterna
Teatro Donizetti Chorus, Bergamo; Fondazione Orchestra Stabile di Bergamo 'Gaetano Donizetti' / Pierangelo Pelucchi
Bongiovanni 🆅 AB20002
(130' · NTSC · 4:3 · PCM stereo and 5.1 · 0)
Recorded live 2005   Ⓕ

The booklet flags the 'impressive similarity' between Giuseppe Gazzaniga's *Don Giovanni*, premiered in February 1787, and Mozart's masterpiece first heard in Prague later the same year. True, there are occasional superficial musical resemblances; and while Da Ponte despised the librettist Giovanni Bertati as a 'dramatic cobbler', he was happy to appropriate many of his ideas for his own *Don Giovanni* libretto. What strikes you time and again, though, is the fathomless gulf between Gazzaniga's casually structured one-act romp, designed as a play-within-a-play for the Venice Carnival, and Mozart's tragi-comic masterpiece.

The atmosphere of Carnival frivolity is epitomised by the bitchy duet for Donna Elvira and the peasant girl Maturina (Mozart's Zerlina), and the all-singing, all-dancing frolic after the Don's distinctly un-terrifying descent to hell. There are several pleasantly spirited *buffo* numbers, including a duet for Pasquariello (the Leporello character) and Elvira, at the point where in Mozart Leporello sings his Catalogue aria, and the jolly Spanish-flavoured music that introduces the peasant couple. Elvira's second aria, with cello obbligato, has a touching dignity. Au fond, though, Gazzaniga's characterisation is stereotyped, his instrumental textures thin (just what the Venetians expected in 1787), his harmonies limited and predictable. But for the story, no one would think of reviving this *Don Giovanni* today.

Still, anyone curious about the subsoil from which the Mozart-Da Ponte opera grew should find this Bergamo performance more than acceptable. Alessio Pizzech's production, drawing on the imagery of the commedia dell'arte and the Venice Carnival, is visually inventive, with the 'realistic' action – usually watched by one or more of Don Giovanni's victims – counterpointed by dreamlike pantomime and surreal montages, sometimes arresting, sometimes flitting by too rapidly as filmed for the small screen. Though there are no specially distinguished voices among the cast, all have lively stage personalities and (being Italian helps) really relish their words. Tenor Roberto Iuliano, a distinctly louche, fleshy Don, sings his recitatives with devil-may-care bravado and brings a measure of seductive grace to his one aria. As his sidekick, Maurizio Leoni reveals a robust baritone and deft comic timing, while the Elvira – by far the biggest female role – compensates for some shrillnesss above the stave with the ardour of her phrasing. Orchestral playing is adequate, no more. There are subtitles for the opera, though, frustratingly for non-Italian speakers, not for Alessio Pizzech's half-hour spoken prologue, centring, Ariadne-like, on rehearsal squabbles and clashes.

Francesco Geminiani   Italian 1687-1762

Geminiani studied in Rome with Corelli and A Scarlatti, and in 1711 became leader of the opera orchestra in Naples. Settling in London in 1714, he earned instant success as a violin virtuoso and became one of the most influential teachers (of the violin and composition). He published a series of instrumental works, starting with the highly acclaimed violin sonatas Op 1 (1716). In the 1730s he made two lengthy visits to Ireland, and later spent time in the Netherlands and Paris. He settled in Dublin in 1759, giving his last known concert in 1760.

Geminiani's principal works are solo sonatas and concerti grossi. His model was Corelli, but he composed with originality, writing for a wider range of solo instruments and using a more sonorous and chromatic idiom; his music is more expressive and dramatic than Corelli's (though still contrapuntal). Most works have the traditional four-movement plan still popular in England. The violin sonatas Op 1 and Op 4 (1739) are especially difficult to play, and include cadenzas. Geminiani revised the former set as trio sonatas (c1757), and also made arrangements of others of his works. His 45 concerti grossi have a concertino of two violins, viola and cello; they include arrangements of sonatas by Corelli.   GROVEmusic

Concerti grossi

Geminiani Concerti grossi (after Corelli, Op 5)[a].   P
Cello Sonata in D minor, Op 5 No 2[b] **Corelli/**
Geminiani Sonata for Violin and Cello in A, Op 5 No 9[c]
[bc]**David Watkin** vc [b]**Alison McGillivray** vc [b]**Richard Egarr** hpd [a]**Academy of Ancient Music / Andrew Manze** [c]vn
Harmonia Mundi ② HMU907261/2 (144' · DDD)
                                                      F OO

Eighteenth-century English music lovers, it seems, were obsessed with the music of Corelli, in particular his *concerti grossi*; Manze's notes quote a lovely account of how, when the Op 6 concertos were first published in 1714, one London orchestra of gentlemen amateurs, led by a Mr Needler, couldn't stop themselves from playing through all 12 at one sitting. They were Corelli's only published concertos, however, so it isn't hard to see what a welcome sight the works presented on this disc must have been when they first appeared in the mid-1720s; immensely skilful arrangements by Corelli's London-based pupil Francesco Geminiani of the master's 12 violin sonatas, Op 5, they were to all intents a new set of Corelli concertos.

What held for Londoners back then should hold equally well for Baroque enthusiasts today;

these ingeniously crafted *concerti grossi* are a delight, their musical effectiveness in no way compromised by their origins. Listeners familiar with Corelli's Op 5 will doubtless have fun spotting what Geminiani has done with them (which goes well beyond straightforward orchestration); those who do not know the originals can just enjoy the music for what it is, which is to say bright, tuneful and invigorating.

Where Manze's particular success lies is in conjuring the atmosphere of the past and in the sheer joyousness and freshness which these performances convey. It's as if Mr Needler and his friends were before us, revelling in an unexpected Corellian bonus. Listen to the Academy of Ancient Music lustily laying into the thick chords in the final movement of Concerto No 4, dragging back the tempo and then charging off again, and you can almost see the complicit grins on their faces.

Manze is free with his embellishments, throwing in double-stops, blue notes and all manner of flourishes with an abandon that won't be to everyone's taste, but which contributes hugely to the enthusiastic tenor of the music-making as a whole. The orchestra is in fine form, offering a full sound whose occasional slight rawness is no bad thing in performances of such strength, directness and honesty.

Roberto Gerhard
                                Spanish/British 1896-1970

Gerhard studied in Barcelona with Granados and Pedrell and in Vienna and Berlin with Schoenberg (1923-8), returning to Barcelona to take an active part in musical life. His compositions from this period are few: they include the Schoenbergian Wind Quintet (1928), the cantata L'alta naixença del rei en jaume (1932) and the ballet Ariel (1934). In 1939 he left Spain and eventually settled in England, where he became much more productive, in a distinctly Spanish style. There were three more ballets (Don Quixote, 1941; Alegrias, 1942; Pandora, 1944), an opera (The Duenna, 1947), the symphony Homenaje a Pedrell (1941) and songs, besides the Violin Concerto (1943), which looks back to the early atonal works and forward to the dynamic, boldly colourful, serial compositions of his last two decades. This late development was rapid, from the Schoenbergian style of the First Quartet (1955) to the athematic, block-form, effect-filled Second (1962). It can be seen too in the cycle of four symphonies (1953, 1959, 1960, 1967) and the Concerto for Orchestra (1965), which move towards a Varèsian sound-drama (the Third Symphony has the sub-title 'Collages' and includes tape). Other late works include electronic pieces, much incidental music and pieces for ensemble (Concert for Eight, 1962; Hymnody, 1963; Libra, 1968; Leo, 1969).   GROVEmusic

Symphonies

Symphony No 2. Concerto for Orchestra

BBC Symphony Orchestra / Matthias Bamert
Chandos CHAN9694 (55' · DDD) Ⓕ Ⓓ➤

Although the avowed purpose of Gerhard's *Concerto for Orchestra* (1965) was to highlight the orchestra as an entity rather than its constituent sections or instruments, and while it may not have the immediate universal appeal of, say, Kodály's or Bartók's works with the same title, it has never been surpassed for its imaginative handling of instrumental sonorities or for its virtuoso demands on the players. It has to be said right away that this is a stunning performance: not merely does the BBC SO rise spectacularly to the work's demands, but Bamert shows himself exceptionally skilful at securing internal balances. It's worth quoting Gerhard's own words: 'My favourite listener is one who does not read explanatory programme notes ... I stand by the *sound* of my music, and it is the sound that must make the sense...a work of music takes shape only in the mind of the listener.'

Gerhard's Second Symphony has been represented on disc only by the revised version (*Metamorphosis*) which had had to be completed by Alan Boustead (available on Auvidis Montaigne); although Gerhard may have felt the original too cerebral, it was at least all his, and tough going as it undoubtedly is, it's very welcome to all interested in the mental processes of this quite exceptional musician. The opening of the work's second section, with its clicking percussion, is hauntingly mysterious, and the final nightmare palindrome *Scherzo* (of which only a fraction exists in the Boustead version) is one of his most astonishing creations. With first-class recording throughout, this must be regarded as an essential disc for all admirers of Gerhard.

Edward German   British 1862-1936

After study at the RAM with Ebenezer Prout, German joined the teaching staff of the Academy and during that period composed a number of works for RAM orchestra. Visits to Germany, and particularly Bayreuth, in the late 1880s, aroused an interest in opera. In 1888 he became music director of the Globe Theatre, composing incidental music for a number of Shakespeare productions. His two symphonies were admired by George Bernard Shaw. His most popular work, Merrie England (1902), is aligned more to the Savoy operas of Gilbert and Sullivan than to Grand German opera. He is widely credited as founding the light music school, inherited by composers such as Eric Coates and Haydn Wood.

Symphony No 1. Romeo and Juliet – Prelude.
The Tempter – Overture. Hamlet. The Willow Song
BBC Concert Orchestra / John Wilson
Dutton Digital Epoch CDLX7156 (77' · DDD)   Ⓕ

This collection of Edward German's orchestral music – none of it duplicated from earlier sets –

is perhaps generally less striking but all is warmly romantic and beautifully crafted music of real grace and refinement.

Two items derive from German's theatre commissions of the 1890s – the Overture to *The Tempter* and the *Romeo and Juliet* Prelude, which contains an especially beautiful love theme for strings. The longest single movement is the *Hamlet* symphonic poem, written for the 1897 Birmingham Festival and further demonstrating German's command of orchestral resources, if inviting questionable comparisons with Tchaikovsky's tone-poem of a few years earlier. *The Willow Song* was German's last work of any significance – a heartfelt outpouring for the Royal Academy of Music's centenary in 1922 but one that, at less than eight minutes, suggests a composer by then somewhat worked out. There are echoes of Tchaikovsky, too, as well as Dvořák and Parry in perhaps the major attraction here – the First Symphony, performed at the Crystal Palace in 1890 and never published for orchestra. Again it is full of arresting ideas and eminently tuneful, if never quite becoming an arresting entity.

John Wilson demonstrates an impressive feel for constructing larger forms. The result is a beautifully played and recorded CD that further fills out our knowledge of Britain's symphonic output before Elgar.

George Gershwin   American 1898-1937

Gershwin was essentially self-taught. He was first a song plugger in Tin Pan Alley and an accompanist. In his teens he began to compose popular songs and produced a succession of musicals from 1919 to 1933 (Lady, be Good!, 1924; Oh, Kay!, 1926; Strike up the Band, 1927; Funny Face, 1927; Girl Crazy, 1930); the lyrics were generally by his brother Ira (1896-1983). In 1924 he became famous: he wrote Rhapsody in Blue as a concerto for piano and Paul Whiteman's jazz band. Its success led him to devote increasing energy to 'serious' composition. His more ambitious works include the Piano Concerto in F (1925) and the tone poem An American in Paris (1928). But he continued composing for the musical theatre, and some of his most successful musicals (Strike up the Band, Girl Crazy, Of Thee I Sing) date from this period. In 1934-5 he wrote his 'American folk opera' Porgy and Bess, which draws on African-American idioms; given on Broadway, it was only a limited success. Gershwin went to Hollywood in 1936 and wrote songs for films. He was a sensitive songwriter of great melodic gifts and did much to create syntheses between jazz and classical traditions in his concert music and black folk music and opera in Porgy and Bess. GROVEmusic

Rhapsody in Blue

Gershwin Rhapsody in Blue. An American in Paris   Ⓗ
Grofé Grande Canyon Suite
New York Philharmonic Orchestra /

Leonard Bernstein pf
Sony Classical 07464 63086-2 (64' · ADD)
Recorded 1958-59   Ⓜ️Ⓞ🅑➔

Bernstein conducted and played the music of Gershwin with the same naturalness he brought to his own music. Here, *An American in Paris* swings by with an instinctive sense of its origins in popular and film music; no stilted rhythms or four-squareness delay the work's progress, and where ripe schmaltz is wanted, ripe schmaltz is what we get, devoid of all embarrassment. *Rhapsody in Blue* is playful and teasing, constantly daring us to try to categorise its style, and then confounding our conclusions. Although the solo passages from individual players are beautifully taken, the orchestra captures the authentic flavour of Gershwin's and Bernstein's idiom, and Bernstein pushes them to transcend the printed scores. His own playing in the *Rhapsody* is tantalisingly unpredictable. The recording is clear and bright, perhaps a touch hard-edged, and a little of the richness of the original LP issue might have been preferred by some, especially as the editing is now made more obvious.

Complete Music for Piano and Orchestra:
Rhapsody in Blue. Second Rhapsody. 'I Got Rhythm' Variations. Concerto in F
Anne-Marie McDermott pf
Dallas Symphony Orchestra / Justin Brown
Bridge BRIDGE9252 (73' · DDD)   Ⓕ🅞🅞

It's rare enough to have all four Gershwin works for piano and orchestra on a single disc but rarer still for each one to come near or top of the class. First, and unusually enough, McDermott and her (British) conductor do Gershwin the courtesy of playing all the scores uncut and observing his dynamics and performance instructions to the letter. Typical of their meticulous attention to detail is the first bar of the coda (*allegro con brio*) in the Concerto's first movement, almost always played *forte* but marked (and rendered here) *piano* by the orchestra, mp by the soloist, allowing a *crescendo* over the following eight bars. A small point, maybe, but it is what the composer asked for and is all the more effective.

Such preparation would mean little, though, if the performances did not fly off the page with verve and confidence, rhythmic precision and real style. The slow movement of the Concerto in particular is wonderfully characterised, all smokey blues with decadent solos from the muted first trumpet. The Dallas strings lend a Hollywood swoon to the big tunes in the famous *Rhapsody* and the Concerto while the remaining two pieces are more coherent and convincing than in the hands of some far more famous names. Strongly recommended.

Additional recommendation

Rhapsody in Blue   Ⓗ
Coupled with: An American in Paris. Piano Concerto

GERSHWIN RHAPSODY IN BLUE – IN BRIEF

Columbia SO / Bernstein pf   Ⓗ
Sony Classical 07464 63086-2 (64' · ADD)   Ⓜ️Ⓞ🅑➔
The free-wheeling zip and chutzpah of this famous 1958 recording are irresistible. Coupled with Lenny's abundantly charismatic renderings of Gershwin's *An American in Paris* and Grofé's *Grand Canyon* Suite.

McDermott; Dallas SO / Brown
Bridge BRIDGE9252 (73' · DDD)   Ⓜ️🅞🅞
A strongly recommendable anthology devoted to all of Gershwin's piano *concertante* works played with a terrific feel for the idiom.

London SO / Previn pf
EMI 566891-2 (65' · ADD)   Ⓜ️🅞
Previn's endearingly laid-back 1971 account sounds more glowing than ever in EMI's latest remastering. These artists' *An American in Paris* and Piano Concerto complete a fondly regarded Gershwin triptych.

Grimaud; Baltimore SO / Zinman
Erato 0630-19571-2 (55' · DDD)   Ⓕ🅞🅑➔
A beautifully shaped performance with an almosr classical feel but Zinman and his Baltimore orchestra bring a nice touch of pizzazz. Cool, but rather elegant!

Gershwin pf roll **Columbia Jazz Band / Tilson Thomas**
Sony Classical 07464 39699-2 (71' · ADD)   Ⓕ
Tilson Thomas's earliest recording cleverly fuses the composer's 1925 piano roll with Grofé's original jazz-band instrumentation. Coupled with *An American in Paris* and six of Gershwin's Broadway overtures.

San Franciscso SO / Tilson Thomas pf
Sony Classical 82876 60862-2 (77' · DDD) Ⓜ️🅞🅞🅑➔
Tilson Thomas's second version (and his first directing from the piano) has heaps of temperament, and again employs the original 1924 scoring. Brightly recorded, this could well be a first choice for many.

Los Angeles PO / Bernstein
DG 477 6352 (56' · DDD)   Ⓕ🅞🅑➔
Charismatic, outrageous but with buckets of personality, Bernstein brings his inimitable flair to Gershwin's *Rhapsody* as part of an all-American programme. (This performance is available in various couplings depending on your territory.)

Donohoe; London Sinfonietta / Rattle
EMI 508996-2 (56' · DDD)   Ⓑ🅑➔
The punchy jazz-band version given a terrific performance by Peter Donohoe (also available in a four-CD 'American Music' set from Rattle – 215014-2).

in F. Variations on 'I got rhythm'
Wild pf **Boston Pops Orchestra / Fiedler**
RCA Red Seal 74321 68019-2 (70' · ADD) Recorded
1959-61 　Ⓢ

Wild's pianism is often scintillating, and he
generates an infectiously sparky rapport with Fiedler and the Bostonians, whose exuberant, gently
affectionate *American in Paris* is a treat. RCA's
sound is astonishingly undated.

Piano Concerto

Gershwin Piano Concerto
Ravel Piano Concerto in G major
Hélène Grimaud pf
Baltimore Symphony Orchestra / David Zinman
Erato 0630-19571-2 (55 minutes : DDD) 　ⒻⓄ☞

Also available in a four-CD Apex set featuring
Grimaud in major piano concertos 　Ⓢ

This is a logical and satisfying coupling, and it
is surprising that it hasn't been recorded more
often. Both the Gershwin and Ravel concertos
are heavily influenced by jazz. Gershwin's,
written in 1925, is a strange mix of creative
spontaneity and formal constraint. The fusion
of popular and traditional elements clearly
influenced Ravel, whose G major Concerto
(completed in 1931) contains a seemingly
incongruous, yet superbly constructed, juxtaposition of American blues and jazz, Iberian
exoticism and neo-classicism.

Hélène Grimaud offers a straightforwardly
romantic view of these works, especially of the
Gershwin. She seems happiest with broad
melodic lines, such as in Gershwin's first movement, which she shapes with a wholly natural and
unforced beauty. Other pianists may go for a
more rhythmically buoyant and propulsive
approach, further playing up the jazz impulse, but
Grimaud's sincerity succeeds on its own terms.
There are times – most notably the slow movement of the Ravel – where her playing seems just
a little too straitlaced, or emotionally restricted.
In this movement, her left-hand-before-right
mannerism may irritate some listeners. But she
can never be accused of 'milking' the music, and
Ravel, who believed that a concerto should be
'light-hearted and brilliant, and not aim at profundity or at dramatic effects' would surely have
approved.

Piano Works

Of Thee I Sing – Prelude[a]; Jilted. Second Rhapsody[a].
The Shocking Miss Pilgrim – For you, for me, for
evermore. Cuban Overture[a]. Pardon My English –
Isn't it a pity? Variations on 'I got rhythm'[a]. Catfish
Row[a]. Shall we dance? – Let's call the whole thing
off[a]; They can't take that away from me[a]. Goldwyn
Follies – Our love is here to stay
Jack Gibbons pf
ASV White Line CDWHL2082 (77' · DDD) Items
marked [a] arr Gibbons. 　Ⓜ

This disc is mostly comprised of Gibbons's own
arrangements, based on Gershwin's film music,
two-piano pieces, and in the case of the 'Catfish
Row' *Porgy and Bess* suite, his orchestrations. The
longest work is the *Second Rhapsody*, composed
for a scene in the Gershwins' first Hollywood
movie, *Delicious*. The film starred Janet Gaynor
and Charles Farrell, and in this sequence the
heroine wanders frightened through Manhattan
– it might be rechristened *A Scotswoman in New
York*. George Gershwin referred to the main
tune as his 'Brahmsian theme' but today no one
would mistake it for anything but Gershwin.

The solo version of the *Cuban Overture* is Gibbons's own adaptation of Gershwin's four-hand
arrangement; like the 'Catfish Row' suite it
makes formidable demands on the pianist and
Gibbons gives them both virtuoso performances. The recital ends with three of the standards Gershwin wrote in Hollywood during the
last months of his life. 'They can't take that away
from me' must be a strong contender for the
greatest songs of the 20th century, and no one
hearing 'Our love is here to stay' can doubt that
a premonition of death lingered somewhere in
the composer's heart in the autumn of 1936.

Porgy and Bess

Porgy and Bess
Willard White bass Porgy **Cynthia Haymon** sop Bess
Harolyn Blackwell sop Clara **Cynthia Clarey** sop
Serena **Damon Evans** ten Sportin' Life **Marietta
Simpson** mez Maria **Gregg Baker** bar Crown
**Glyndebourne Chorus; London Philharmonic
Orchestra / Sir Simon Rattle**
EMI ③ 234430-2 (189' · DDD · T/t) 　ⓂⓄⓄⓄ☞

Ⓖ The company, orchestra and conductor from the outstanding 1986 Glyndebourne production re-create a very real
sense of Gershwin's 'Catfish Row' community
on this complete recording. Such is its atmosphere and theatricality, we might easily be back
on the Glyndebourne stage. From the very first
bar it's clear just how instinctively attuned Rattle and this orchestra are to every aspect of a
multi-faceted score. The cast, too, are so *right*,
so much a part of their roles, and so well integrated into the whole, that one almost takes the
excellence of their contributions for granted.
Here is one beautiful voice after another, beginning in style with Harolyn Blackwell's radiant
'Summertime', which at Rattle's gorgeously lazy
tempo, is just about as beguiling as one could
wish. Willard White conveys both the simple
honesty and inner strength of Porgy without
milking the sentiment and Haymon's passionately sung Bess will go wherever a little flattery
and encouragement take her. As Sportin'
Life, Damon Evans not only relishes the burlesque
elements of the role but he really *sings* what's
written a lot more than is customary. But the
entire cast delivers throughout with all the
unstinting fervour of a Sunday revivalist meeting. Sample the final moments of the piece – 'Oh

Lawd, I'm on my way' – if that doesn't stir you, nothing will.

Porgy and Bess   Ⓗ
William Warfield bass-bar Porgy **Leontyne Price** sop
Bess **Cab Calloway** ten Sportin' Life **John McCurry**
bar Crown **Joseph James** bar Jake **Helen Colbert**
sop Clara **Howard Roberts** ten Robbins **Helen
Thigpen** sop Serena **Leslie Scott** bar Jim **Moses
Lamar** bar Frazier **William Weasey** bar Undertaker
Walter Riemann spkr Detective **Helen Dowdy** mez
Strawberry Woman **Ray Yates** ten Crab Man **Eva
Jessye Choir; RIAS Light Orchestra, Berlin /
Alexander Smallens**
Guild mono ② GHCD2313/4 (139' · ADD)
Recorded live at Titania Palast, Berlin, on September
21, 1952   Ⓕ

In 1952 the US State Department funded a world tour of *Porgy and Bess*. The production by Everyman Opera eventually visited cities across the American continent, north and south, and gave the British, French, Italian, German, Czech and Russian premieres of Gershwin's opera. The tour inspired two famous memoirs, Truman Capote's *The Muses are Heard* and Maya Angelou's *Singin' and Swingin' and Getting Merry Like Christmas*. Both writers pay tribute to the array of talent the company possessed, from the veteran Cab Calloway as Sportin' Life to the then-unknown Leontyne Price as Bess.

Several years later Price and William Warfield recorded a disc of highlights for RCA, in which Price sings not only Bess but also Clara and Serena. Fine though that selection is, it has none of the immediacy and energy of this broadcast from Berlin in September 1952. By then the company had lived with the work for a year. There is a degree of improvisation from the chorus, the famous Eva Jessye Choir, as they enter into the spirit of the drama. Although it is a fairly complete version of the score, there are some cuts (for instance the Buzzard song), but where authentic performance practice is concerned this wins over every other recording.

William Warfield's Porgy is a noble achievement: as Angelou described him, 'he dragged the audience into his despair… his resonant voice straddled the music as he rode it'. Price's voice is at its youthful best – this is one of the earliest examples of her art on disc. In 'What you want wid Bess?' and 'I wants to stay here' she proves her star quality as well as her emotional commitment. Helen Colbert as Clara opens the proceedings with a lush 'Summertime' and Helen Thigpen rings the Berlin rafters with 'My man's gone now'. John McCurry is a fierce Crown, as Capote noted, 'high and heavy and somewhat forbidding'.

In those crucial cameos, Helen Dowdy hollers the Strawberry Woman's cry, and Ray Yates is the irresistible Crab Man (both created the roles). Cab Calloway's insinuating manner is just as effective in 'It ain't necessarily so' as it had been decades earlier in 'Kicking the Gong Around'. Some of the soloists are uncredited – who is the feisty Maria?

The sound is clear, well defined; the recording favours the voices, but Alexander Smallens, who conducted the first performance in 1935, somehow persuades some really hot playing from the RIAS Light Orchestra. No one who admires Gershwin's work should ignore this unique document.

Carlo Gesualdo   Italian c1561-1613

A nobleman and amateur musician, Gesualdo is notorious for having his first wife and her lover murdered in 1590; he married Leonora d'Este of Ferrara three years later. While at the Ferrarese court (1594-6) he played the lute and showed a passion for music and came to be accepted as a serious composer. He eventually retired to his castle at Gesualdo, sunk into a deep melancholy from which music alone could provide relief. His music was strongly influenced by Luzzaschi and Nenna, particularly the former in his use of serious, expressive, richly worked music even for quite light texts. He took great pains over word setting, allowing texts to be clearly heard and strongly expressed. Much of the music in his six madrigal books (1594-1611) and three sacred books (1603-11) uses unexpected harmonies and changes of key, dissonances and striking chromaticism in a highly original way, usually prompted by the emotions of the texts. GROVE*music*

Madrigals

Madrigals Books 1-3
**Gesualdo Consort, Amsterdam /
Harry van der Kamp**
CPO ② CPO777 138-2 (143' · DDD · T/t)   Ⓕ

This must rank among the most important recent additions to the madrigal discography, and a landmark in that of Gesualdo. The composer's reputation rests largely on his last three books of madrigals, which have been admirably served; but the first three had so far been less lucky. Their musical language is less strikingly 'original' than in the later books, and for that reason the interpretative challenge they represent is quite different.

This anthology succeeds brilliantly in dispelling the notion that Gesualdo was 'still finding his voice' in his earlier work. One's almost tempted to turn the traditional view on its head and regard the later music as a self-indulgently hyperbolised departure from the style of, say, the Third Book. Not quite believable, perhaps needless to say, but Harry van der Kamp and his singers have achieved something rather special here.

The Gesualdo Consort is a multinational ensemble, and though it includes no Italians, for sonic seduction they certainly rival their Italian counterparts while never losing sight of the music's rhetorical sense. The pleasure here consists in following Gesualdo's gradual widening of his technical and expressive resources: by the Third Book, the pieces are longer, the argument correspondingly more ambitious, the chromaticism more assertive. His 'Ancidetemi pur' (a re-reading of a set text in one of Arcadelt's most famous madrigals), for example, is very fine indeed. The singing is superb, with few slips to speak of, and none that detracts from the singers' expressive purpose. The continuo is unobtrusive but tastefully and sensitively deployed, and is given its head with a few keyboard intabulations that provide a welcome contrast.

Ahi, disperata vita. Sospirava il mio cor. O malnati messaggi. Non t'amo, o voce ingrata. Luci serene e chiare. Sparge la morte al mio Signor nel viso. Arde il mio cor. Occhi del mio cor vita. Mercè grido piangendo. Asciugate i begli ochi. Se la mia morte brami. Io parto. Ardita Zanzaretta. Ardo per te, mio bene. Instrumental items – Canzon francese. Io tacerò. Corrente, amanti
Les Arts Florissants / William Christie
Harmonia Mundi HMC90 1268 (55' · DDD · T/t)   Ⓕ

To many, Gesualdo is known above all for the *crime passionnel* that left his wife and her lover impaled on the same sword, but the notion that his highly charged music is the product of a tortured and unstable mind is, no doubt, over-romanticised. For this foray into the schizophrenic world of Gesualdo's five-voice madrigals, Les Arts Florissants have selected their programme from the last three books, pieces in which the highly mannered and exaggerated aspects of the composer's style reach their most extreme expression. Nevertheless, we should not think of all these works being undifferentiated in style, and one of the fascinations of this disc, which has been very carefully planned, is the insight it offers into the gradual emergence and sharpening of the features which characterise Gesualdo's late madrigalian manner.

Some of those elements can already be heard in *Sospirava il mio cor* from the Third Book, and by the last tracks they're present, with all their compositional distortions in full dress. William Christie and Les Arts Florissants are no strangers to the aesthetic of the Italian madrigal in its last decades. This recording, like so many of their productions, is full of surprises on both the large and small scales. The first, of a general kind, is the decision to add continuo accompaniments *avant la lettre*. This is justifiable on historical grounds, though less certain is the precise way it has been done with some passages within a piece still left *a cappella*. Less justifiable, if only on artistic grounds, is the performance of two madrigals on instruments alone (*Io tacerò* and *Corrente, amanti*); it makes little sense to attempt such highly charged word-driven music in this way. What may also surprise is the rather understated, almost classically pure character of the interpretations, though it is a relief that the calculatedly neurotic and deliberately out-of-tune manner so often turned out for Gesualdo has here been eschewed. These are technically very

fine and dramatically convincing and coherent readings which are certainly preferable to any other recordings of Gesualdo's madrigals currently available.

Tenebrae Responses

Tenebrae Responsories for Maundy Thursday
King's Singers (David Hurley, Robin Tyson *countertens* Paul Phoenix *ten* Philip Lawson, Gabriel Crouch *bar* Stephen Connolly *bass*)
Signum Records SIGCD048 (66' · DDD)   ⒻⒹ▸

It's perhaps in his music for Holy Week that Gesualdo's claim as a composer of real substance lies. By transferring his madrigal idiom to the sacred sphere so consummately, he shows he can work effectively within formal constraints that the secular works rarely impose. The formal severity of these Responses places in sharp relief his striking melodic turns and startling contrapuntal progressions. It's no wonder that vocal ensembles have been so attracted to them.

This recording joins a select and distinguished group, starting with the Hilliard Ensemble's complete set for ECM, and continuing with the Taverner Consort's set for Good Friday. The King's Singers have a brighter tone than the Hilliards, which makes for a more extrovert reading. In qualitative terms there's little to choose: perhaps in matters of intonation the Hilliards and the Taverners retain a slight edge. But this newcomer naturally takes its place alongside them in the front row, which speaks volumes for its quality.

Orlando Gibbons   British 1583-1625

Gibbons came from a musical family and was a chorister (1596-8) and student (1599-1603) at King's College, Cambridge. He joined the Chapel Royal in c 1603 and was one of its organists by 1615 (senior organist, 1625). In 1619 he became a virginal player at court and in 1623 organist at Westminster Abbey. He took the MusB at Cambridge (1606) and the DMus at Oxford (1622). One of the most important English composers of sacred music in the early 17th century, he wrote several Anglican services, popular in their day, and over 30 anthems, some imposing and dramatic (e.g. O clap your hands), others colourful and most expressive (See, the word is incarnate; This is the record of John). His instrumental music, also important, includes over 30 elaborate contrapuntal viol fantasias and over 40 masterly keyboard pieces. His madrigals (1612) are generally serious in tone (eg The Silver Swanne). GROVEmusic

Viol Works

Fantasias – a 3: Nos 1-4; a 6: Nos 1-6. Pavan and Galliard a 6. Three In Nomines a 5 – No 1; No 2. Pavan and Galliard in A minor, 'Lord Salisbury',

MBXX/18-19. Hosanna to the Son of David. O Lord, in thy wrath rebuke me not. Go from my window. Peascod time. The Silver swan ⓅΡ
Phantasm (Wendy Gillespie, Jonathan Manson, Markku Luolajan-Mikkola *viols*) / **Laurence Dreyfus** *viol* with **Asako Morikawa, Susanna Pell** *viols*
Avie AV0032 (72' · DDD) Ⓕ❶❷❸❹↦

Phantasm is a superb ensemble. They now turn their attention to the viol music of Orlando Gibbons, with a focus on the central works that are definitely for viols and definitely by Gibbons: the six great fantasies for six viols, the four marvellous fantasies for three viols and a selection of what is otherwise best of his viol music in five and six parts. They play with vast assurance and verve, always attractive, always with fresh and varied textures, always beautifully balanced. This is often playing of a breathtaking virtuosity that communicates the music with irresistible vitality. Some listeners may feel that they hit poor Gibbons a little hard, occasionally losing track of the poetry that's his own special contribution; others could feel that some tempos are chosen simply for bravado, especially in the dazzling performance of *Go from my window* that ends the disc. But this is classy playing and a major contribution to the catalogue.

As a slightly eccentric *bonne bouche* they steer away from the music with a violone, preferring to offer arrangements of keyboard pieces and vocal anthems. This is presumably to stress the unquestionable truth that music in those days wasn't often genre-specific; but in the event it emphasises that the greatest of Gibbons' viol pieces are perfectly suited to that particular ensemble.

Keyboard Works

The Woods So Wild ⓅΡ
Fantasias – in D minor, MBXX/5; in G, MBXX/6; in D minor, MBXX/7 (for double organ); in D minor, MBXX/8; in G minor, MBXX/9; in A minor, MBXX/10; in A minor, MBXX/11; in A minor, MBXX/12; in C, MBXX/13; in C, MBXX/14; Ground, MBXX/26. Italian Ground, MBXX/27. Pavan and Galliard in A minor, 'Lord Salisbury', MBXX/18-19. The Fairest Nymph, MBXX/43. Preludes – in A minor, MBXX/1; G, MBXX/2; in D minor, MBXX/3; in A minor, MBXX/4; The Woods So Wild, MBXX/29. Galliard, MBXX/23. Pavans – MBXX/16; MBXX/17. Coranto, MBXX/39
John Toll *org/hpd*
Linn Records CKD125 (73' · DDD) Ⓕ↦

John Toll succumbed to cancer in his early fifties, thus depriving the world of a supreme continuo player, in many ways unchallenged in his generation. This disc's quality deepens the sense of loss. The choice of Gibbons is itself intriguing for a man whose main career was in Baroque music. But it's clear from every note that this was a composer very close to Toll's heart, that he acknowledged the quiet poet who has perhaps the most distinctive voice of all composers from the age of Shakespeare.

Toll has focused on the most substantial works. All the Fantasias are here, as well as most of the Pavans; but most of the smaller dances are omitted. So we have a Gibbons of considerable seriousness, which Toll underlines by controlled playing that has not the slightest trace of self-indulgence. What we hear in Toll is the composer who was not just the 'best finger of that age' but also one of the finest contrapuntists and a man of marvellous musical imagination. The music is divided between two instruments. The late 17th-century organ at Adlington Hall sounds absolutely glorious, beautifully caught by the engineers, and played with sympathetic mastery; it's used not just for Fantasias but also for some of the music that one would more instinctively have thought intended for a harpsichord – with fascinating results. A modern Flemish-style harpsichord by Michael Johnson serves for the rest, but again not just for the dances. This is top-quality playing.

Sacred Vocal Works

O clap your hands. Great Lord of Lords. Hosanna to the Son of David. Prelude in Gᵃ. Out of the deep. See, see, the Word is incarnate. Preludes – No 3 in D minor, MBXX/3ᵃ. Lift up your heads. Almighty and everlasting God. First (Short) Service – No 6, Magnificat; No 7, Nunc dimittis. Second Service – No 3, Magnificat; No 4, Nunc dimittis. Fantazia of four partsᵃ. O God, the king of glory. O Lord, in Thy wrath rebuke me not
Oxford Camerata / Jeremy Summerly with ᵃ**Laurence Cummings** *org*
Naxos 8 553130 (65' · DDD · T) Ⓢ↦

The Oxford Camerata provides a representative selection of choral works by Gibbons, together with three of his organ pieces. The programme is introduced by a bright and busy performance of the eight-part *O clap your hands*, followed by the noble verse anthem *Great Lord of Lords* – and it's pleasing to hear in this piece, and in the other verse-anthems, the rich timbre of the countertenor Robin Blaze, a welcome acquisition for the Camerata, which has a great deal of vocal talent in its make-up. They tackle the gently moving *See, see, the Word is incarnate* with great confidence, together with the First and Second Services and the quiet collects with all the knowledge and aplomb of cathedral lay clerks or choral scholars from Oxford and Cambridge. Laurence Cummings plays two short preludes, the one in G major – a real test of agility – from *Parthenia* and that in D minor from Benjamin Cosyn's *Virginal Book*. The *Fantazia of four parts* is a most extraordinary work, quite hard to steady and control. A welcome addition to the programme.

Secular Vocal Works

Pavan and Galliard a 6. Fantasia a 2 No 1. Go from my window. Fantasias a 6 – Nos 3 & 5. Fantasia a 4 No 1 'for the great double bass'. Galliard a 3. In Nomine a 4. Pavan and Galliard in A minor, 'Lord

Salisbury'. Prelude in G. Masks – Lincoln's Inn mask;
The Fairest Nymph. Alman in G. Behold, thou hast
made my days. Glorious and powerful God. The First
Set of Madrigals and Mottets – Daintie fine bird;
Faire is the rose; I weigh not fortune's frown; I see
ambition never pleased; I feign not friendship where I
hate; The silver swanne
Tessa Bonner sop **Timothy Roberts** keybds **Red
Byrd; Rose Consort of Viols**
Naxos 8 550603 (68' · DDD · T)   ⑤⮑

Beautifully performed and finely recorded, this
selection of Gibbons's music is especially
attractive for its variety. At its richest it presents
writing for voice and viols combined, five parts
to each, or for viols alone, sometimes in six
parts. In lightest, most transparent texture
there's a charming piece for two viols. Three
keyboard instruments are used for solos:
virginals, harpsichord and organ. A soprano
also sings solos to viol accompaniment. Moods
and styles vary correspondingly. The *Masks*
and *Alman* for virginals have a high-spirited,
almost popular manner; the Fifth *Fantasia*
includes some unusual chromaticism and harmonic developments that for a while almost
anticipate Purcell.

Tessa Bonner sings with unvibrant purity;
but most striking here is the pronunciation.
It's one of the distinguishing marks of this
curiously named group, Red Byrd, that they
sing such music with vowel sounds modified to
fit theories about the English in which it would
originally have been sung. Thus the 'daintie
fine bird' tells 'oi sing and doy', and the 'u'
acquires a sort of umlaut in *I weigh not fortune's
frown*, 'weigh' and 'frown' also having a measure of rusticity. Perhaps it's a good idea, but it
does increase the desirability of printed texts in
the booklet.

The instrumental music is finely played, the
viols avoiding any imputation of belonging to
the squeeze-and-scrape school, and Timothy
Roberts's keyboard solos are particularly skilful,
in *legato* and fluency.

Eugène Gigout   French 1844-1925

*Gigout studied with Saint-Saëns at the Ecole Nieder-
meyer and associated with Fauré and Franck. In
1863 he became organist of St Augustin, Paris, and
in 1911 began teaching at the Conservatoire. Most of
his music is for organ.*   GROVEmusic

Organ Works

The Complete Organ Works, Volume 1
Rhapsodie sur des airs catalans. Suite de six pièces.
Trois pièces
Gerard Brooks org
Priory PRCD761 (77' · DDD) Played on the organ of
Perpignan Cathedral, France   Ⓕ
For lovers of organ sound this disc is an abso-

lute treasure. Perpignan's sumptuous Cavaillé-
Coll isn't an organ of memorable solo stops
but of deliciously blended, exquisitely balanced choruses. Full organ is warm and robust
while its plentiful soft-stops have a subtlety
and charm which, even in the face of the
omnipresent action clatter, this recording
captures with almost magical delicacy. The
fourth of the *Suite de six pièces*, an *Andantino* in
E minor, is lent distinction by the utter charm
of the contrasting soft flute and string choruses, while the first of the *Trois pièces* dances
across the manuals revealing tantalising
glimpses of colour richly enhanced by the
atmospheric acoustic of Perpignan's cathedral. All this is superbly captured in Priory's
rich, mellow recording.

In his deft handling of the instrument and his
keen sense of colour, Brooks proves that there's
much more to organ playing than big virtuoso
gestures. Which may be as well since there's little
scope for such things here. Not only do all 10
pieces on this disc completely avoid the virtuoso
and emotional excesses of Liszt, Widor and
Vierne, but none stretches much over 10 minutes
in duration. With the exception of the captivating
Rhapsodie sur des airs catalans, all are relatively
youthful works revealing a composer with a keen
sense of structure and a penchant for contrapuntal argument. A most attractive release.

The Complete Organ Works, Volume 2
Suite de six pièces (pub 1881). Deux pièces.
Interludium. Méditation
Gerard Brooks org
Priory PRCD762 (72' · DDD) Played on the Cavaillé-
Coll organ of St Ouen, Rouen   Ⓕ

The Complete Organ Works, Volume 3
Dix Pièces. Pièce Jubilaire. Poèmes Mystiques
Gerard Brooks org
Priory PRCD763 (75' · DDD) Played on the Cavaillé-
Coll organ of St Etienne, Caen   Ⓕ

Before Gerard Brooks embarked on his complete cycle, only two of Gigout's solo organ
pieces figured consistently on the *Gramophone*
database. One of those, the 'Grand choeur dialogué' (the sixth of the 1881 *Suite de six pièces*),
appears on the second disc of the series in a performance that makes it a highly treasurable
release. Brooks imbues it with great majesty and
splendour, letting it unfold with all the opulence
of a regal procession. Such spacious playing
allows us ample opportunity to savour the glorious sonic spectacle of the wonderful St Ouen
organ in Rouen, an instrument frequently
recorded, though never before with such stunning sound.

The third disc includes the most familiar of
Gigout's organ works; the *Dix Pièces* published
in Paris in 1892. There can be few organists
who don't possess this tome, if only for the
scintillating B minor Toccata, and it's been
recorded frequently. Brooks's may not be the
most impressive of these but he's impeccably

faithful to the score and, playing on what's described as 'one of the finest surviving examples of Cavaillé-Coll's work', we have here an unquestionably authoritative version, not just of the Toccata but all ten pieces. Even those that pass most organists by are revealed as musical gems ideally suited to a resourceful organ. Organ recordings of this calibre are few and far between.

Alberto Ginastera

Argentinian 1916-1983

Ginastera studied at the National Conservatory in Buenos Aires (1936-8) and made an early reputation with his ballet Panambí; (1940). Another nationalist ballet, Estancia, followed in 1941, when he was also appointed to the staff of the National Conservatory. During an extended visit to the USA (1945-7) he attended Copland's courses at Tanglewood; thereafter his life was divided between Argentina and abroad, his travels sometimes necessitated by changes of government. In 1971 he settled in Geneva.

Until the mid-1950s his music was essentially nationalist in a manner comparable with Bartók, Falla and Stravinsky, but he moved towards an atonal expressionism that has links with Berg and Penderecki: this made possible his late emergence as a composer of highly charged opera in which magic and fantastic elements are prominent (Don Rodrigo, 1964; Bomarzo, 1967; Beatrix Cenci, 1971). Other works include two piano concertos (1961, 1972), the Cantata para América mágica for soprano and percussion (1960) and three string quartets (1948, 1958, 1973). GROVEmusic

Orchestral Works

Panambí, Op 1. Estancia, Op 8ª
ªLuis Gaeta *bass/narr*
London Symphony Orchestra / Gisèle Ben-Dor
Naxos 8 557582 (73' · DDD) Ⓢ🄳➤

It was a characteristically bold step by the 21-year-old Ginastera to make his Op 1 an ambitiously scored orchestral ballet rather than a modest suite or chamber piece. Of course, he had written such works – mostly withdrawn and destroyed – but the one-act choreographic legend *Panambí* (1935-37) was several strides forward and as impressive a compositional debut as any.

Drawn from an Amerindian tribal legend, the plot concerns the love of Guirahu for the chief's daughter, Panambí, and the machinations of the local sorcerer, who also desires her. A battle between good and evil plays out across a single night, opening with wonderful, impressionistic moonlight and ending with a radiant hymn to the dawn. In between, the expertly scored music is largely restrained, though with some electrifying episodes along the way.

Panambí betrays Ginastera's formative influences clearly, *The Rite of Spring* and Ravel in particular. The vividly achieved, primitivist atmosphere (not unlike the music of Revueltas) necessary for the story is absent from his follow-up ballet, *Estancia* (1941). Some of the latter's music is so well known, thanks to the popular Suite, that it may surprise that this recording of the whole was a premiere. Absent, too, is the self-consciousness of *Panambí* as a public statement; in *Estancia* one can hear Ginastera relax as he whips up a greater storm.

Gisèle Ben-Dor and the LSO are splendid throughout. Luis Gaeta makes a splendid soloist in Estancia. Recommended.

Overture to the Creole 'Faust', Op 9. Pampeana No 3, Op 24. Estancia, Op 8a. Glosses on Themes of Pablo Casals, Op 48
Berlin Symphony Orchestra / Gabriel Castagna
Chandos CHAN10152 (66' · DDD) Ⓕ

Overture to the Creole 'Faust', Op 9. Pampeana No 3, Op 24. Estancia, Op 8a. Ollantay, Op 17
Odense Symphony Orchestra / Jan Wagner
Bridge 9130 (57' · DDD) Ⓕ

Either of these two well-produced discs would make a near-ideal introduction to this versatile composer's output, featuring three of his finest orchestral inspirations. If the suite from his ballet *Estancia* (1942) remains his best-known work, and its malambo finale one of the most famous pieces in Latin American music, the *Overture to the Creole Faust* (1943) can't be far behind. Both are outgoing, 'popular' items, whereas the 'symphonic pastoral' *Pampeana* No 3 (1954) is more obviously serious.

All three works receive committed performances on both discs. Castagna and the Berliners find a touch more magic in the *Pampeana*'s slower outer movements aided by Chandos's sumptuous sound, but the Danish players, led by their Venezuelan-born conductor, often have the edge in the swifter sections. In *Estancia*, the resonance of Chandos's recording works against the music: Bridge's drier, cleaner sound in the Carl Nielsen Hall in Odense is more successful. And while some of Jan Wagner's tempos seem a shade deliberate compared to Castagna's, he mostly justifies them by the pacing of each work *in toto*.

If there's little overall to choose between the newcomers, the fourth item on each may decide the matter. On Chandos comes a scintillating account of the second, full-orchestral version of the more harmonically advanced *Glosses on Themes of Pablo Casals*, originally written for strings to celebrate the Catalan cellist's centenary in 1976 and rescored a year later. In contrast, Bridge restores to the CD catalogue Ginastera's *Ollantay* (1947), a darkly colourful and dramatic folk-triptych that could be thought of as an Argentinian *Taras Bulba*.

If you want only one version of these pieces the Bridge is recommended.

Umberto Giordano   Italian 1867-1948

Giordano studied with Serrao at the Naples Conservatory between 1880 and 1890 and was commissioned, after showing promise in a competition, to write an opera: this was Mala vita, a verismo opera of some violence and crudity, given at Rome in 1892. After another failure (an old-fashioned romantic melodrama), he moved to Milan, where his Andrea Chénier was given, at La Scala, in 1896; with its French Revolutionary subject and its fervent, assertive style, it was an immediate success and has remained popular in Italy and beyond. Comparable success, at least in Italy, was met by Fedora (1898, Milan), but of his seven later operas only the comic Il re (1929, Milan), which was taken up by coloratura sopranos, enjoyed any real success although he remained a master of the intense, vehement, Massenet-influenced, theatrically effective style that gives Andrea Chénier its appeal. GROVEmusic

Andrea Chénier

Andrea Chénier
Plácido Domingo *ten* Andrea Chénier **Renata Scotto** *sop* Maddalena **Sherrill Milnes** *bar* Carlo Gérard **Michael Sénéchal** *ten* Incredible **Maria Ewing** *mez* Bersi **Gwendolyn Killebrew** *mez* Madelon **Jean Kraft** *mez* Countess **Allan Monk** *bar* Roucher **Terence Sharpe** *bar* Fléville **Stuart Harling** *bass* Fouquier-Tinville **Isser Bushkin** *bass* Schmidt **Malcolm King** *bass* Dumas **Piero De Palma** *ten* Abate **Nigel Beavan** *bass-bar* Maestro di casa **Enzo Dara** *bar* Mathieu **John Alldis Choir; National Philharmonic Orchestra / James Levine**
RCA ② 74321 39499-2 (114' · ADD · T/t)   Ⓜ

Choosing between this recording and the Decca Chailly (currently available only as a download), it might seem sensible to start with the tenor in the title-role, and here a strong inclination would be to plump for RCA and Domingo: he's in splendid voice, with a touch of nobility to his manner that makes for a convincing portrayal of a poet. Pavarotti (Chailly) begins with a rather leather-lunged Improvviso, but he later finds poetry in the role as well, especially when responding to his soprano, Caballé, who's rather stretched by the more exhausting reaches of her role and sounds audibly grateful for the occasional opportunities he gives her to float rather than belt a high-lying phrase. However, Pavarotti is an *Italian* tenor, and his Italianate sense of line adds one per cent or so of elegance to some phrases that even Domingo can't match. Caballé does many things beautifully, and her fine-spun *pianissimos* and subtle shadings only occasionally sound mannered, but the role is undeniably half a size too big for her. So it's for Scotto, you might say, and a hint of strain is audible once or twice, in her timbre rather than her phrasing. It's her phrasing that tips the balance back to RCA: Scotto is as subtle a vocalist as Caballé, but she gives meaning and eloquence to every phrase without ever breaking the long line,

which one can't always say of the Spanish soprano. Matters are about even as far as the baritones are concerned: Milnes acts admirably, but refrains from over-acting, and the voice is rich and characterful. In the supporting cast, but RCA's striking Bersi, vividly characterised Incredible, and their Roucher, too, aren't out-matched (only their Madelon, both fruity and acid – a grapefruit of a voice – is disappointing).

A lot of people will enjoy the huge energy and bustle of Levine's direction. It's vividly characterful, but a shade exhausting and overassertive. The flow of the music seems more natural in Chailly's hands, and orchestral detail is clearer. The Decca recording, too, is warmer.

Additional recommendation

Pavarotti Chénier **Nucci** Gerald **Caballé** Maddalena **Kuhlmann** Bersi **Varnay** Countess di Coigny **NPO / Chailly**
Decca download *410 117-2DH2* (107' · DDD)
Swings and roudabouts when compared with the RCA set; Chailly tends to over-conduct and Pavarotti takes some time to warm up. Both Nucci and Caballé are on good form, Caballé displaying her customary great artistry on nearly every page.

Andrea Chénier
Franco Corelli *ten* Andrea Chénier **Celestina Casapietra** *sop* Maddalena **Piero Cappuccilli** *bar* Carlo Gérard **Ermanno Lorenzi** *ten* Incredibile **Gabriella Carturan** *mez* Contessa de Coigny **Giovanna di Rocco** *mez* Bersi **Luigi Roni** *bass* Roucher **Leonardo Monreale** *bass* Pietro Fléville **Mario Chiappi** *bass* Fouquier Tinville **Renzo Gonzales** *bass* Schmidt **Florindo Andreolli** *ten* Abate **Cristina Anghelakova** *mez* Madelon **Giorgio Giorgetti** *bar* Mathieu **Milan RAI Chorus and Orchestra / Bruno Bartoletti**
Stage director **Vaclav Kaslik**
Hardy Classic Video 📀 HCD4008 (110' · NTSC · 4:3 · 1.0 · 0) Recorded at RAI-TV Studios, Milan 1973   Ⓕ

This is something of a find – a production produced in Milan's television studios in 1973 that does more than justice to Giordano's verismo work about personal conflicts at the time of the French Revolution. It's directed, with considerable imagination, by the Czech Vaclav Kaslik, at the top of his profession in the 70s. In realistic period sets he unerringly creates the milieu of a degenerate aristocracy in Act 1 and of the raw mob-rule of the Revolution in the succeeding acts. The only drawback is the poor lip-synch.

Conductor Bruno Bartoletti makes certain we're unaware of the score's weaker moments and releases all the romantic passion in Giordano's highly charged writing for his principals. Chénier was one of Corelli's most notable roles so it's good that his splendid portrayal has been preserved for posterity. He doesn't disappoint with his excitingly trumpet-like tones and finely moulded phrasing of the composer's grateful writing for his tenor hero, and – although already 52 – he still looks the part of the glamorous, challenging poet.

Cappuccilli was famous for his Gérard and here – at the height of his powers – he projects all the man's conflicting feelings with enormous conviction on a stream of burnished tone. Celestina Casapietra, a generally underrated soprano from Genoa, is just what Maddalena should be, and sings with a nice combination of tenderness and intense feeling. She and Corelli do full justice to their duets. The RAI orchestra plays well, but unfortunately it's too backwardly placed as regards the singers.

Madame Sans-Gêne

Madame Sans-Gêne
Mirella Freni sop Caterina **Giorgio Merighi** ten
Lefebvre **Mauro Buda** bar Napoleone **Andrea Zese**
bar Fouche **Valter Borin** ten Neipperg **Antonio
Feltracco** ten Vinaigre, Despreaux **Marzia Giaccaia**
sop Toniotta, Carolina **Muriel Tomeo** sop Giulia
Federica Bragaglia sop Principessa Elisa, La Rossa
Valerio Marletta bar De Brigole **Riccardo Ristori** bar
Gelsomino, Roustan **Alfio Grasso** bar Leroy **Muriel
Tomao** sop Madame Bulow **Modena Teatro
Comunale Chorus; Emilia Romagna 'Toscanini'
Symphony Orchestra / Stefano Ranzani**
Dynamic CDS247 (123' · DDD · T/t)   Ⓕ

In the not-so-distant past most 'serious' musicians thought Giordano beneath notice while opera-goers of a certain kind felt he was everything they stood for. These opinions were usually based on *Andrea Chenier* and (with slightly less conviction) *Fedora*. Otherwise a few excerpts from one or two lesser-known operas were gratefully heard but didn't allay suspicions that a wider acquaintance might prove disheartening. This set from the Italian-based company Dynamic invites us all to think again. The plot of *Madame Sans-Gene* is a rather charming variant on the theme of the Emperor's clothes; it's also about a star-struck girl who learns sense and returns to home and boyfriend. The premiere at La Scala in 1929 failed to impress, though Toscanini conducted and Toti Dal Monte sang the leading role. The score is elegantly lyrical and lively, modern in relation to Chenier as (say) *Gianni Schicchi* is in relation to *Manon Lescaut*.

Madame Sans-Gene is a comedy whose story takes a serious turn in Act 3, which for a while seems about to topple over into tragedy. Napoleon, previously a figure in the background, appears in person and in a bad mood, but is charmed and shamed into a talk about old times with the genial heroine and all ends well. At first Madame Sans-Gene, so-called, seems to be one of those tireless life-and-soul-of-the-party people who can be so wearing, but she develops into less of a turn and more of a character, while her chirpy vocal line eventually settles for a more rewarding warmth and lyricism. It's understandable that the role should be attractive to a star soprano who late in her career looks for something out of the way in which much is accom-

plished by personality. Mirella Freni's voice is still full bodied and to a large extent pure in quality, but for many years now has forfeited the firm evenness of its prime. She gives a genuine performance – and (not far off her 64th birthday) a remarkable one. The best singing, however, is that of the tenor, Giorgio Merighi. Mauro Buda as Napoleon shows an almost tenorial baritone which it would be good to hear in a part with more opportunities. Ranzani conducts with spirit. As a recording this is a great deal more satisfactory than the currently available alternative, taken from an Italian radio transmission in 1957.

Mauro Giuliani   Italian 1781-1829

In Vienna from 1806, Giuliani became famous as the greatest living guitarist, teaching, performing and composing a rich repertory for the guitar. He was also a cellist, playing in the premiere of Beethoven's Symphony No 7 (1813). In 1814 he became honorary chamber musician to Napoleon's second wife. He returned to Italy in 1819 and was patronised by the nobility. His works include three guitar concertos, sonatas, studies and variations for solo guitar, quartets and many duos (with flute or violin) for guitar and songs. GROVEmusic

Guitar Concerto No 1

Giuliani Guitar Concerto No 1 in A, Op 30
Schubert Sonata for Arpeggione and Piano in
A minor, D821 (arr Williams)
John Williams gtr **Australian Chamber Orchestra**
Sony Classical SK63385 (52' · DDD)   Ⓕ🅑➔

The guitar has played a part in several adaptations of the Schubert A minor Sonata, substituting for either the arpeggione or the piano, but never before with a string orchestra in the supporting role, reversing the bowed/percussive relationship. Good arranging doesn't consist of literal adherence to the original score but, as here, in making small changes to take advantage of the new instrumentation. Rarely has such a transmutation been accomplished with greater conviction. Put any doubts or prejudices you may have on the back burner and enjoy familiar beauty in new clothing. The Giuliani is familiar in every respect – except that of interpretation. What we have in this recording is the recognition of the relationship between instrumental and vocal music in Giuliani's work; it's apparent in his (and others') frequent adaptation of operatic music for the guitar, but has more or less escaped the attention of guitarists on record. The vocal quality of the writing is fully realised here, producing what might even be regarded as the first stylistically faithful recording of the First Concerto. The performances from both John Williams and the Australian Chamber Orchestra are exemplary and praise should also extend to the engineers who recorded them with such clarity and ideal balance. If you already have these works, don't let it deter you from adding this revelatory one to your collection.

Philip Glass American b1937

Glass studied at the Juilliard School and with Boulanger in Paris (1964-6) and worked with the Indian musicians Ravi Shankar and Alla Rakha. His minimalist works of 1965-8 (eg Two Pages) are 'experimental and exploratory' but later ones, for his own amplified ensemble, are more complicated (eg Music in Fifths). Since 1975 his works have nearly all been for the theatre. When Einstein on the Beach was given at the Met (1976) he became famous; further full-scale operas, Satyagraha (1980), Akhnaten (1984), The Making of the Representative for Planet 8 (1988) and The Voyage (1992), chamber operas and music theatre works followed. One of the most popular serious composers in the USA, he has also performed in rock and jazz. GROVEmusic

Cello Concerto

The Concerto Project, Volume 1
Cello Concerto[a]. Concerto Fantasy for Two Timpanists and Orchestra[b]
[a]**Julian Lloyd Webber** vc [b]**Evelyn Glennie,**
[b]**Jonathan Haas** perc **Royal Liverpool Philharmonic Orchestra / Gerard Schwarz**
Orange Mountain Music OMM0013 (45' · DDD) Ⓕ🅑➔

The Cello Concerto was conceived when Julian Lloyd Webber asked Glass to compose a work for the cellist's 50th birthday. Lloyd Webber says the piece, premiered in October 2001, contains technical hurdles he had not seen before, particularly in the opening cadenza, but for the listener it's not a difficult work. That cadenza, underpinned by muffled, percussive figures from the orchestra, is dramatic, with an undercurrent of ambiguous emotion, but it's also lithe and attractive, evocative of the classics of cello literature, not least Bach and Elgar. There are passages where the debate between orchestra and soloist seems to contrast those often-copied, easily parodied Glass mannerisms with his more melodically and harmonically expansive work of recent years. The result is one of the most engaging, impressive and beautiful things Glass has done. The slow movement, lyrical and graceful, sets us up perfectly for the shock of the opening of the finale, which bursts in with one of those 'accelerating train' episodes he does so effectively.

The gestation of the timpani concerto was more problematic. Despite their tuneful capabilities, timpani are associated primarily with melodrama and bombast and aren't an ideal choice for a concerto solo instrument. There are 14 of them here, presumably due to the need to negotiate fairly rapid movement through different keys. It all works remarkably well in the event. The fast first movement has exciting, ritualistic solo parts, perhaps influenced by South-East Asian and Japanese traditions. The slow movement manages to make the drums sound lyrical, embedded in settings of regal brass and pastoral woodwind. The cadenza preceding the third movement, highly athletic as it is, proves to be a warm-up for Evelyn Glennie and Jonathan Haas before the technical *tour de force* of the finale.

Piano Concerto No 2

Piano Concerto No 2, 'After Lewis and Clark'[a].
Harpsichord Concerto[b]
[a]**Paul Barnes** pf [b]**Jillon Stoppels Dupree** hpd
[a]**R Carlos Nakai** fl **Northwest Chamber Orchestra / Ralf Gothóni**
Orange Mountain Music OMM0030 (59' · DDD) Ⓕ🅑➔

This is certainly one of the most enjoyable recent releases of Glass's music. There is something fresh about both works, though the Glass fingerprints naturally also abound. The Piano Concerto No 2 takes its cue from the exploits of Lewis and Clark, who made the first overland expedition in the US in 1804-6, and the first movement is suitably epic in its feeling (something at which Glass is very good), with much expansive, dark-hued writing. The second has a hauntingly beautiful contribution from a Native American flute, something so riveting (especially in the hands of R Carlos Nakai) that one wishes Glass would write an entire work for the instrument. Only in the third movement does there seem to be too much archetypal Glassian triumphalism; but even here, when the 'slipped' variation technique of the second section begins, one's attention is held very firmly by the strangeness of the result. Paul Barnes is a shining soloist.

The harpsichord offers different challenges, but Glass seems to relish those, too; this concerto, with its more transparent orchestration, occasionally exotically Eastern flourishes, baroquisms and frequently unexpected harmonic moves, works an almost alchemical magic with the composer's familiar simple arpeggiated material. The third movement blasts off like a rocket. Soloist Jillon Stoppels Dupree notes that she rarely steps outside the world of the Baroque but that she was 'entranced' by the work when she came to work on it. Entrancing is a pretty good description of her performance, too. Both concertos are splendidly accompanied by the Northwest Chamber Orchestra under Ralf Gothóni, and recorded sound is full without being over-resonant.

Symphonies

Symphony No 2. Orphée ^= Interlude. Concerto for Saxophone Quartet and Orchestra
Raschèr Saxophone Quartet (Carina Raschèr *sop sax* Harry Kinross White *alto sax* Bruce Weinberger *ten sax* Kenneth Coon *bass sax*) **Vienna Radio**

Symphony Orchestra, Stuttgart Chamber Orchestra / Dennis Russell Davies
Nonesuch 7559-79496-2 (69' · DDD) Ⓕ🅑➔

Glass isn't a symphonist in the conventional sense, but neither was Messiaen. Glass himself has indicated that his large-scale orchestral works are conceived with their probable role in the conventions of concert programming in mind. This sounds outrageously manipulative when stated explicitly, but in fact it's nothing more than a description of the context of the symphonic form since its inception. He's also said that he devoted his earlier career to subtracting elements from his music and is now deciding what to put back in. In the case of this symphony, the specified element is polytonality, the presence of which in much 20th-century music is perhaps taken for granted. However, when it's added into this stripped-down and austere idiom, the results are certainly striking. The opening movement recalls the prelude to *Akhnaten*, the third and final movement reprises the chattering arpeggios of the composer's earlier works, closing with an exciting – and, indeed, viscera-loosening – *crescendo*. After recovering during the snippet from *Orphée*, we come to the marvellous Concerto. Conceived for performance either as a quartet or in this quartet-plus-orchestra version, this is a gloriously animated work, almost Coplandesque in many respects, yet remaining true to Glass's own vision. Despite being presented as the secondary work on this disc, its presence makes the whole recommendable.

Symphony No 3ª. The CIVIL WarS – Interludes Nos 1 & 2ª. The Voyage – Mechanical Balletᵇ. The Lightᵇ
ªStuttgart Radio Symphony Orchestra, ᵇVienna Radio Symphony Orchestra / Dennis Russell Davies
Nonesuch 7559-79581-2 (61' · DDD) Ⓕ🅑➔

Comparing Glass's Third Symphony with his Second finds the forces reduced from full orchestra to strings, the overall timing reduced by virtually half and the number of movements increased from three to four. Glass No 2 is long breathed, atmospheric and occasionally suggestive of Brucknerian vistas, whereas Glass No 3 is texturally lean and harmonically more adventurous than much of his previous work. It also seems to have taken in influences from some fairly unexpected sources.

The first movement is sombre and march-like while the second, which is built on compound meters, kicks out in all directions, switching to a gutsy *staccato* at 2'59". The pulse is constant, but the tone has altered, sometimes sidling nearer to Sibelius, sometimes a stone's throw from Shostakovich. At the start of the brief finale, there's even a hint of Kurt Weill, but one thing is for sure: if you play the Symphony blind, you might never guess that it's by Glass. The stylistic shift from mellow, arpeggiated dreamscape (a familiar Glassian aura that holds sway for most of *The Light*) to a sort of ecstatic acerbity, follows

through to the rest of the work. But there's another presence – less of a surprise, perhaps – later in the long third movement when the Arvo Pärt of *Cantus* seems to join the fray.

The idea of external influence extends to the interludes from *The CIVIL WarS*, where, as annotator David Wright tells us, Tchaikovsky's *Nutcracker* gets a look in, particularly in the Second Interlude with its *pas-de-deux*-like downward scales. 'Mechanical Ballet' (from *The Voyage*) and the expansive *The Light* are rather more what you'd expect from Glass: haunting narratives, always on the move yet tinged with melancholy. Even if you don't care for Glass's more familiar 'arpeggiated' style, do try the Third Symphony. It's different, and the performance is excellent.

In the Upper Room

In the Upper Room
Philip Glass Ensemble / Michael Riesman
Orange Mountain Music OMM0056 (45' · DDD) Ⓕ

Slightly over half the dances which Glass wrote for choreographer Twyla Tharp's *In the Upper Room* in 1986 were issued by CBS a year later under the title *Dance Pieces*, but this disc presents the complete cycle for the first time.

Comparing the two recordings makes for an interesting exercise in minimalist performance practice. When *Dance Pieces* was released, the trend was towards layering electronically manipulated and treated sounds over acoustic instruments to impart a more polished sheen to Glass's music. The result was clinical and, one suspects, driven at the time by corporate pressures to make the music as commercial as possible. Twenty years later, and Glass has decided to revisit the original masters in order to try to recapture the live sound which accompanied the original ballet production.

There is certainly more warmth and depth here, with the ebullient, processional Dance IX benefiting in particular from a more three-dimensional sonic facelift. At the same time the reinstated dances do little to supplement any perceived deficit in the abridged version, or the need to restore some kind of cyclic unity to the work. The disc's highlight, Dance VIII, with its haunting, fragile piano figure is already present in the original version, as are most of the weightier, more extended movements. The 'missing' dances are on the whole short and somewhat transitional in nature. All this adds further weight to the fact that there were sound reasons for leaving them out in the first place, although Glass aficionados will no doubt be glad to receive the complete set.

String quartets

Complete String Quartets (Nos 1-5)
The Smith Quartet (Ian Humphries,
Darragh Morgan vns Nic Pendlebury va
Deidre Cooper vc)
Signum Classics ② SIGCD117 (89' · DDD) Ⓜ🅑➔

If success was measured according to output and sales units alone, Glass would be head and shoulders above his contemporaries. His compositions for conventional combinations, including the five string quartets included on this disc, have already appeared on recordings by the Kronos and Duke quartets, but the Smith Quartet have been the first to release the complete cycle.

Quartets Nos 2 to 5, written between 1983 and 1991, form a neat and consistent set, from the enigmatic, introspective Second, via the expressive Third and quirkily bitonal Fourth, to the neo-romantic, almost Tchaikovskian opening gesture of the Fifth. The Smith Quartet's thoughtful and measured performance allows subtle metric, linear and textural features to rise unassumingly to the surface, enhanced on this recording by a clear, balanced stereo image, and played with characteristic precision and projection by the ensemble.

The First Quartet is something of an anomaly, however. Written soon after Glass's studies with Nadia Boulanger in Paris during the mid-1960s, it has been viewed either as a transitional work of marginal interest or a potent symbol of Glass's emerging minimalist style. What connects this work with later Glass – at least more than the Cageian silence – is the work's obsessive preoccupation with cyclical repetition, although the accompanying atonally charged atmosphere seems light years away from the lush harmonies of the Fifth Quartet.

The Hours

The Hours – original soundtrack
Michael Riesman pf **Lyric Quartet** (Rolf Wilson, Edmund Coxon vns Nicholas Barr va David Daniels vc) **Chris Laurence** db **orchestra / Nick Ingham**
Nonesuch 7559-79693-2 (58' · DDD) Ⓕ❍➼

'I love Glass's music,' writes Michael Cunningham in the note included with this recording, 'almost as much as I love [Virginia] Woolf's *Mrs Dalloway*, and for some of the same reasons. Glass, like Woolf, is more interested in that which continues than he is in that which begins, climaxes and ends; he insists, as did Woolf, that beauty often resides more squarely in the present than it does in the present's relationship to past or future.' Seldom has there been such a concisely eloquent description of Glass's work. And the analogy with Woolf is in this case quintessentially correct, for *The Hours* is a film with deals with Mrs Woolf, her creation Mrs Dalloway and, as we eventually learn, a Los Angeles housewife, Mrs Brown. The *present-ness* of their situations is what connects these three women, eternally containing the potential to leap into the future or regress into the past… Was there ever a more perfect film for Glass's current lyrical manner? He himself refers to his own past, quoting from his 'Glassworks' and 'Solo Piano' collections, and from as far back as his opera *Satyagraha*, but the way in which the material is treated here, clothed in nostalgic colours by piano, string quartet and orchestra, transforms it

inevitably into that eternal present. This album of music has a fragile beauty that never lapses into mere sentimentality.

Naqoyqatsi

Naqoyqatsi – Original Film Soundtrack
Yo-Yo Ma vc Members of the **Philip Glass Ensemble** (Lisa Bielawa sop Jon Gibson, Richard Peck saxs Andrew Sterman fl, picc, cl Michael Riesman kbd) **orchestra / Michael Riesman**
Sony Classical 509970 87709-2 (77' · DDD) Ⓜ❍➼

This is another colourful, barnstorming film score from Glass, and one that contains enough material of substance that it can stand quite successfully on its own. There are the expected Glass fingerprints – the powerful, pulsing, dark-hued 'heartbeat' opening, the rippling arpeggios of 'Religion', the clangorous vocal and orchestral writing in 'Intensive Time' and 'Point Blank', both of which recall parts of his opera *Akhnaten* – but there are also moments when he creates something quite new. In 'Massman' he explores the higher regions of the solo cello in some hauntingly lyrical music; and lyricism, of a non-Western kind, also characterises two remarkable sections for solo cello and percussion, 'New World' and 'Old World'. A more purely romantic sensibility is at work in 'Media Weather', as in other sections in passing, but it seems all of a piece with this interesting mixture of the familiar pulsing, glowing Glass and the less familiar, introspective lyrical composer. The performance is superb, and beautifully recorded.

Itaipú

The Canyon. Itaipú[a]
Atlanta Symphony [a]**Chorus and Orchestra / Robert Shaw**
Sony Classical 07464 46352-2 (56' · DDD) Ⓕ❍➼

The idea of spacious natural vistas has always been central to Glass's work. *Itaipú* and *The Canyon* are the second and third of his 'portraits of nature'. Itaipú is located on the Paraná River, which in turn forms the border between Brazil and Paraguay. It's the location of a massive hydro-electric dam with individual generators large enough to house a full symphony orchestra. So it's little wonder that Itaipú provided Glass with instant inspiration. The score itself is divided into four separate sections and calls on substantial orchestral and choral forces. Although consistent with his other work, *Itaipú* has an especially dark, rugged tonal profile. The hub of the work – 'The Dam' itself – is in the third movement, where brass and winds abet a pounding ostinato and a series of modulations redolent of such scenically aware late-Romantics as Sibelius, Bruckner and Roy Harris. It's one of the most arresting passages in Glass's output, and gives a vivid impression of the dam's overwhelming physical presence.

The Canyon is purely orchestral; it's built around two basic ideas, with a jagged middle section that heats up for a powerful climax. Less heavily scored than *Itaipú*, *The Canyon* utilises a large array of percussion, which Glass exploits with his usual ear for nuance. But *Itaipú* is the disc's main 'event' – a patient, cumulatively powerful essay, easily assimilated and well enough crafted to repay repeated listening. The recordings are cleanly balanced, the performances neat.

Alexander Glazunov
Russian/USSR 1865-1936

Glazunov studied privately with Rimsky-Korsakov (1879-81) and had his First Symphony performed when he was 16. He became a member of the circle around the patron Belyayev, who took him to meet Liszt in Weimar, and in 1899 was appointed to the St Petersburg Conservatory, which he directed from 1905 until leaving the Soviet Union in 1928. During these later years he composed relatively little: the bulk of his output, which includes nine symphonies, much else for orchestra, the ballet Raymonda (1897) and seven quartets, dates from before World War I. He has a significant place in Russian music in that he reconciled Russianism and Europeanism. He absorbed Balakirev's nationalism, Rimsky-Korsakov's orchestral virtuosity, Tchaikovsky's lyricism, Borodin's epic grandeur and Taneyev's contrapuntal skill. GROVEmusic

Violin Concerto in A minor, Op 82

Violin Concerto. Meditation, Op 32[a]
The Seasons, Op 67
[a]Aaron Rosand vn **Malaysian Philharmonic Orchestra / Kees Bakels**
Vox Classics VXP7907 (61' · DDD)　　　　Ⓕ❍

Aaron Rosand began recording for Vox in the late 1950s. Now in his seventies, his timbre and technique are as sure as ever. Moreover Rosand's very stylish playing of the delightful Glazunov Concerto brings a sense of having lived with this music over the decades, yet returning to it as to an old friend, with no possible hint of staleness. The beguiling opening theme floats off the bow with the most engaging warmth and an easy, natural *rubato*, which the conductor follows admirably. The richly shaped melody of the *Andante*, too, goes straight to the heart of the music: again Rosand's timbre is warm, his phrasing ravishingly lyrical. The finale dances away jauntily, its spirited rhythmic charisma echoed by the orchestra.

In short, this performance is very good indeed, worthy of comparison with the finest on disc (including Vengerov, Shaham, Mutter) and, in its security of the solo line, even approaches Heifetz. The gentle, rhapsodic *Meditation* makes a splendid encore while the recording is admirable, with a completely natural balance.

Glazunov Violin Concerto[a]
Prokofiev Violin Concertos Nos 1 & 2[b]
Maxim Vengerov vn [a]**Berlin Philharmonic Orchestra / Claudio Abbado;** [b]**London Symphony Orchestra / Mstislav Rostropovich**
Warner Elatus 0927-49567-2 (DDD)　　Ⓜ❍▣

Vengerov turns Glazunov's war-horse concerto from a display piece into a work of far wider-ranging emotions. It's a remarkable account, with Vengerov making you appreciate afresh what a wonderful and varied sequence of melodies Glazunov offers. It's characteristic of Vengerov how he shades and contrasts his tone colours. He reserves his big, Romantic tone for the third theme, where most rivals let loose sooner with less subtle results. His *rubato* is free but always spontaneous sounding, and the lolloping fourth section brings some delicious *portamento*. Predictably the dashing final section is spectacular in its brilliance, with orchestral textures fresh and clean.

Vengerov and Rostropovich take an unashamedly epic, wide-open-steppes view of Prokofiev's First Concerto rather than the pseudo-Ravelian one posited by Chung/Previn and Mintz/Abbado, but it works at least as well. His tone is gloriously rich, every note hit dead centre. No 2 is slightly less successful. The balance is partly to blame – the soloist rather too closely scrutinised – but there's also a lack of intimacy in the interpretation itself. Nevertheless, this is an extremely fine disc and comes thoroughly recommended.

Symphonies

Symphony No 6, Op 58. The Sea, Op 28.
Salomé, Op 90 – Introduction; Dance
Royal Scottish National Orchestra / José Serebrier
Warner Classics 2564 69627-0 (67' · DDD)　Ⓕ❍❍▣

From the formidable list of rival versions of the Sixth, arguably Glazunov's most powerfully dramatic symphony, dating from 1896, this one from José Serebrier and the Royal Scottish National Orchestra is among the very finest. Warm and approachable with Serebrier drawing beautifully moulded playing from the Scottish orchestra, with *rubato* perfectly judged and with the orchestra fine and resonant in vividly recorded, rich, unexaggerated sound.

Glazunov's lyrical second subjects were always striking, and the one in the first movement here is no exception. The structure is clearly defined with fine thrust from the performers, and with that theme coming thrillingly back *fortissimo* at the climax of the movement. The theme and seven variations which make up the second movement go with an easy flow, with the brassy climax of the seventh variation well controlled in its dynamic contrasts. The third movement is a charming allegretto with neo-classical overtones, while the finale is the most powerful movement of all with its Borodin echoes at the start and a most ingenious combination of sonata and double-variation form, all of which Serebrier brings out most persuasively.

The fill-ups, though much less powerful, are well worth hearing, two works that vie with the masterpieces of Debussy and Strauss. *La mer* of 1889 (antedating Debussy) is a richly evocative seascape with the harp very prominent, hardly equalling Debussy's masterpiece but very attractive, while the *Introduction and Dance from Salomé*, more conventional than the rest, were from incidental music that Glazunov wrote for a production of the Oscar Wilde play in 1908. There is a powerful gesture at the start of the Introduction with Salomé's Dance predictably getting faster and faster and with the horn-writing adding to the exotic orientalism. Altogether a splendid issue.

Symphony No 8 in E flat, Op 83. Cantata in Memory of Pushkin's 100th Birthday, Op 65[a]. Lyric Poem in D flat, Op 12
[a]**Ludmila Kuznetsova** *mez* [a]**Vsevolod Grivnov** *ten*
Russian State Symphony [a]**Cappella and Orchestra /**
Valéry Polyansky
Chandos CHAN9961 (67' · DDD · T/t)　　　Ⓕ🅑➔

Glazunov's Symphony No 8 opens confidently and lyrically, conductor Valéry Polyansky maintaining an easy-going momentum, later pressing forward, yet always holding the argument together. There's some lovely woodwind playing in the *Mesto* slow movement and the strings create a genuinely passionate climax. The *Scherzo* is given a purposeful thrust, and the finale doesn't outstay its welcome, with the chorale theme splendidly sonorous at the opening, the drive and tension of the playing well maintained to the end.

Also well captured here is the lovely *Poème lyrique* was admired by Tchaikovsky for its rich flow of Russian melancholy. But what makes this Chandos disc so very attractive is the *Cantata in Memory of Pushkin's 100th Birthday*, which is full of warmly lyrical ideas. Glazunov's flow of invention more than compensates for the doggerel poetry he was forced to set by the Grand Duke Constantine Romanov. The work is framed and interlaced by splendid, powerfully sung and very Russian choruses of gratitude. There's a lovely 'Berceuse' for the mezzo, here radiantly sung by Ludmila Kuznetsova, who redeems its sentimentality; a later aria of praise for the tenor is relished by Vsevolod Grivnov; finally comes a hymn in which the two soloists join, exultantly taken up by the chorus, with a burst of joy at the close. This one of those happy works, full of melody, that makes you feel glad to be alive. A truly memorable performance then, and the Chandos recording is well up to house standards.

Suite caractéristique

Suite caractéristique in D, Op 9. Le chant du destin, Op 84. Deux Préludes, Op 85
Moscow Symphony Orchestra / Igor Golovschin

Naxos 8 553857 (75' · DDD)　　　Ⓢ🅞➔

The eight-movement *Suite caractéristique* is vintage Glazunov, an orchestral transcription of piano pieces. Slavic melancholy characterises the 'Introduction', which serves to usher in an engaging 'Danse rustique'. The central, delicately scored 'Pastorale' is particularly charming and the following 'Danse orientale' is at first piquant, in the best Russian pseudo-oriental manner, but reaches an expansive climax, and the gentle beginning of the 'Elégie' is followed by a passionate interjection (in a surprisingly Tchaikovskian manner). The grand closing 'Cortège' makes a resplendent, very Russian ending. The two Préludes date from 1906 and 1908 respectively. One remembers, in a grave, valedictory mood, Vladimir Stassoff; the second (much more extended) opens surprisingly like Tchaikovsky's *Francesca da Rimini* and this curious leitmotif dominates the early part of the piece, which later produces a gentle, disconsolate chorale and a sonorously Wagnerian coda. It's played most impressively, as indeed is the Suite. The recording is good too.

Reinhold Glière
Ukraine/USSR 1875-1956

Glière studied at the Moscow Conservatory, where he became professor of composition (1920-41). His works, in the Russian epic tradition of Borodin and Glazunov, include three symphonies (the third subtitled 'Il'ya Muromets', 1911), concertos (one for coloratura soprano, 1943) and ballets (notably The Red Flower), as well as operas on central Asian themes using indigenous musical traditions, and chamber and piano music. GROVEmusic

---

Symphonies

Symphony No 3, 'Il'ya Mouromets', Op 42
London Symphony Orchestra / Leon Botstein
Telarc CD80609 (72' · DDD)　　　Ⓕ🅞➔

Recognisably breathing the same air as Stravinsky's *Firebird*, Scriabin's *Poem of Ecstasy* and Suk's *Asrael* Symphony, Glière's *Il'ya Mouromets* makes up in lusciousness and sweep what it slightly lacks in individuality, offering a superb vehicle for the modern orchestra and, indeed, for state-of-the-art hi-fi systems. The LSO and Leon Botstein have the edge in almost every respect over rival performances. Comparable to Downes in his tempos, albeit with a rather fleeter-footed finale, Botstein is less insistent in his accentuation and more emotionally generous with his phrasing, so the overall effect is less strenuous, more sensuously appealing, with the climaxes standing in higher relief. The LSO, on terrific form, command a slighter wider range of nuance, and Telarc's recording is a degree or two more spacious, without ever feeling overblown. Altogether, a very collectable disc.

Mikhail Glinka
Russian 1804-1857

Having come to know rural folk music in its purer forms, and receiving an unsystematic musical education in St Petersburg and on his sojourn in Italy (1830-33), Glinka neither inherited a tradition of sophisticated composition nor developed a distinctive and consistent personal style. But he exerted a profound and freely acknowledged influence on Balakirev, Rimsky-Korsakov, Mussorgsky, Borodin and Tchaikovsky, as well as on Prokofiev and Stravinsky. His first important compositions were a Capriccio for piano duet and an unfinished symphony, both applying variation technique to Russian themes.

It was his opera A Life for the Tsar (1836; originally Ivan Susanin) that established him overnight as Russia's leading composer. Though its national character derives from melodic content alone (mostly merely quasi-Russian), it is nevertheless significant for its novel, expressive Russian recitative and for its use of the leitmotif. His next opera, Ruslan and Lyudmila (1842), based on Pushkin's fantastic, ironic fairy-tale, was less well received, being structurally unsuited to the stage and musically haphazard, yet it contains elements of striking originality. In Paris (1844-5) Glinka enjoyed Berlioz's music and in Spain (1845-7) folk music and fresh visual impressions; two Spanish Overtures resulted, exceeded in inventiveness however by the kaleidoscopic orchestral variations Kamarinskaya (1848).

GROVEmusic

Orchestral Works

Capriccio brillante on the 'Jota aragonesa'. Souvenir d'une nuit d'été à Madrid. Symphony on Two Russian Themes. Overture in D. Kamarinskaya. Valse-fantaisie. Ruslan and Lyudmila – Overture; Dance; Chernomor's March
BBC Philharmonic Orchestra / Vassily Sinaisky
Chandos CHAN9861 (71' · DDD)   Ⓕ

This is a more comprehensive survey than that available on ASV with the Armenian Philharmonic under Loris Tjeknavorian. Both conductors include the two 'Spanish Overtures', the *Valse-fantaisie* and *Kamarinskaya* in closely matched performances. Sinaisky is rather faster and brighter in the first 'Spanish Overture', *Capriccio on the jota aragonesa*, and in the second, *Souvenir d'une nuit d'été*, he reflects more subtly the French grace that also lies within the music. Both conductors give good, vivid performances of the *Valse-fantaisie* and *Kamarinskaya*, with recordings that do justice to Glinka's brilliant orchestration. Thereafter the repertoire parts company. While Tjeknavorian gives the rest of his record up to a suite of six pieces from *A Life for the Tsar*, Sinaisky prefers *Ruslan and Lyudmila*, with a lively performance of the overture and then the Act 3 dances and the dwarf Chernomor's grotesque little march. This gives him room for the early Overture in D minor, which doesn't often feature on records, and for the *Symphony on Two Russian Themes*. The work

survives in only a single movement, but fascinatingly anticipates *Kamarinskaya*. For a highly enjoyable introduction to Glinka's orchestral music, indeed to his whole original way of thinking, this Chandos disc is the one to go for.

Christoph Gluck
Bohemian 1714-1787

Gluck's father was a forester in the Upper Palatinate (now the western extreme of Czechoslovakia); Czech was his native tongue. At about 14 he left home to study in Prague, where he worked as an organist. He soon moved to Vienna and then to Milan, where his first opera was given in 1741. Others followed, elsewhere in Italy and during 1745-6 in London, where he met Handel's music. After further travel (Dresden, Copenhagen, Naples, Prague) he settled in Vienna in 1752 as Konzertmeister of the Prince of Saxe-Hildburghausen's orchestra, then as Kapellmeister. He also became involved in performances at the court theatre of French opéras comiques, as arranger and composer, and he wrote Italian dramatic works for court entertainments. His friends tried, at first unsuccessfully, to procure a court post for him; but by 1759 he had a salaried position at the court theatre and soon after was granted a royal pension.

He met the poet Calzabigi and the choreographer Angiolini, and with them wrote a ballet-pantomime Don Juan (1761) embodying a new degree of artistic unity. The next year they wrote the opera Orfeo ed Euridice, the first of Gluck's so-called 'reform operas'. In 1764 he composed an opéra comique, La rencontre imprévue, and the next year two ballets; he followed up the artistic success of Orfeo with a further collaboration with Calzabigi, Alceste (1767), this time choreographed by Noverre; a third, Paride ed Elena (1770), was less well received.

Gluck now decided to apply his new ideals to French opera, and in 1774 gave Iphigénie en Aulide (as well as Orphée, a French revision of Orfeo) in Paris; it was a triumph, but also set the ground for a controversy between Gluck and Italian music (as represented by Piccinni) which flared up in 1777 when his Armide was given, following a French version of Alceste (1776). Iphigénie en Tauride followed in 1779 – his greatest success, along with his greatest failure, Echo et Narcisse. He now acknowledged that his career was over; he revised Iphigénie en Tauride for German performance, and composed some songs, but abandoned plans for a journey to London to give his operas and died in autumn 1787, widely recognised as the doyen of Viennese composers and the man who had carried through important reforms to the art of opera.

Gluck's opera reforms – they are not exclusively his own, for several other composers (notably Jommelli and Traetta) had been working along similar lines – are outlined in the preface he wrote, probably with Calzabigi's help, to the published score of Alceste. He aimed to make the music serve the poetry through its expression of the situations of the story, without interrupting it for conventional orchestral ritornellos or, particularly, florid and ornamental singing; to make the overture relevant to the drama and the orchestration apt to the words; to break down the sharp contrast between recitative and aria: 'in short to abolish all the abuses against which good sense and reason have long cried out in vain'. Orfeo exemplifies most of these principles, with its abandonment of simple recitative in favour of a more continuous texture (with orchestral recitative, arioso and aria running into one another) and its broad musical-dramatic spans in which different types of solo singing, dance and choral music are fully integrated. It also has a simple, direct plot, based on straightforward human emotions, which could appeal to an audience as the complicated stories used in opera seria, with their intrigues, disguises and subplots, could not.

He had a limited compositional technique, but one that was sufficient for the aims he set himself. His music can have driving energy, but also a serenity reaching to the sublime. His historical importance rests on his establishment of a new equilibrium between music and drama, and his greatness on the power and clarity with which he projected that vision; he dissolved the drama in music instead of merely illustrating it.   GROVEmusic

---

Opera Arias

Italian Arias   P
Antigono – Berenice, che fai?. **La clemenza di Tito** – Tremo fra' dubbi miei; Ah, taci, barbaro…Come potesti, oh Dio!; Se mai senti spirarti sul volto. **La corona** – Quel chiaro rio. **Ezio** – Misera, dove son!…Ah! non son io che parlo. **Il Parnaso confuso** – Di questa cetra in seno. **La Semiramide riconosciuta** – Ciascun siegua il suo stile…Maggior follia
Cecilia Bartoli mez
Akademie für Alte Musik Berlin / Bernhard Forck
Decca 467 248-2DH (68' · DDD · T/t)   ⑤ 🅾🅾🅾➔

This is something very much out of the ordinary. These eight arias, taken variously from Gluck's early operas (those preceding his 'reforms' that began with Orfeo in 1762) or his non-reform later ones, are almost wholly unfamiliar, but they have great power and character; and they're sung with an extraordinary emotional force and technical skill, not to say a sheer beauty of tone, that can't be matched by any other singer today. Cecilia Bartoli's range is formidable. In the first aria, from La clemenza di Tito, she sings with trumpet-like tone and brilliance of attack, throwing off wide-spanning arpeggios with evident abandon and dispatching coloratura with fluency and precision, each note articulated and perfectly tuned. The second, an elegantly pathetic little piece from the later Il Parnaso confuso, is a tour de force of delicate, tender pianissimo singing. The third, from Ezio, begins with an orchestral recitative of thrilling dramatic urgency and goes on to an aria of great passion. Bartoli is described as a mezzo-soprano here, and her voice does indeed chiefly lie in that range; but most of these are soprano arias, and she happily goes well above the stave – there's one slightly squally high C sharp in the first aria but she's usually pretty comfortable in her top

register. The accompaniments are splendidly sensitive and alert. A quite outstanding disc that no one who loves fine singing can miss.

Gluck Paride ed Elena – O del mio dolce ardor.   P
Orfeo ed Euridice – Che puro ciel!; Che farò senza Euridice. Alceste – Non vi turbate **Haydn** Il mondo della luna – Una donna come me. Orlando Paladino – Ad un sguardo, a un cenno solo. La fedeltà premiata – Deh soccorri un'infelice **Mozart** Le nozze di Figaro – Voi che sapete. Don Giovanni – Batti, batti; Vedrai, carino; In quali eccessi…Mi tradì quell'alma ingrata. Lucio Silla – Dunque sperar…Il tenero momento. La finta giardiniera – Dolce d'amor compagna. La clemenza di Tito – Ecco il punto, oh Vitellia…Non più di fiori
Anne Sofie von Otter mez
The English Concert / Trevor Pinnock hpd
Archiv Produktion 449 206-2AH (71' · DDD · T/t)
                                        ⑤ 🅾➔

For the sake of both vocal and family well-being, Anne Sofie von Otter has always followed the wise course of self-rationing in opera. This disc, an entirely personal selection of arias from the Viennese Classical period, means all the more to her including, as it does, arias sung by dramatic and passionate women 'most of whom', she admits in the accompanying notes, 'I have never performed on stage and, alas, probably never will'. They include La clemenza di Tito's Vitellia, whom she has irresistibly observed in her own role as Sesto: here she at last voices her guilt at implicating Sesto in her crime of passion, and expresses that unique fusion of sadness and desperation of 'Non più di fiori' in the eloquent company of Colin Lawson's basset horn, followed by Gluck's Alceste, again keenly observed by von Otter in a comprimario role. Gluck's Orfeo is familiar to her at first hand, and here The English Concert's introduction to the recitative preceding 'Che farò' creates exquisitely the 'nuova serena luce' of the Elysian fields against which her grief is the darker, the more plangent. The Mozart arias evoke memorable stage and concert performances by von Otter: a Cherubino whose phrasing combines with that of the wind soloists to create the warm breath of burgeoning sensuality in 'Voi che sapete'; a Cecilio (Lucio Silla) whose coloratura captures the thrilled anticipation of that 'tenero momento'; and a moustachioed Ramiro (La finta giardiniera) who pays ecstatic cantabile tribute to the power of love.

Alceste

Alceste   P
Teresa Ringholz sop Alcestis **Justin Lavender** ten Admetus **Jonas Degerfelt** ten Evander **Miriam Treichl** sop Ismene **Lars Martinsson** bar Herald Voice of Apollo **Adam Giertz** treb Eumelo **Emilie Clausen** treb Aspasia **Johan Lilja** bass High Priest Hercules, God of the Underworld **Mattias Nilsson** bar Bandit
Drottningholm Court Theatre Chorus and Orchestra / Arnold Östman

Naxos ③ 8 660066/8 (147' · DDD · T/t)   Ⓢ▷

Almost all critics of Gluck's two versions of *Alceste* – the Italian original, first given in Vienna in 1767, and the French revision or recomposition given in Paris in 1776 – regard the latter as superior: musically richer, more flexible, dramatically more persuasive, deeper in its treatment of the emotions and the humanity of the two central characters. But this performance of the Italian version treats the 1767 text on its own terms. Like the original *Orfeo*, the original *Alceste* is an opera pared down, in accordance with Gluck's and his librettist Calzabigi's reform principles, to deal with just a single issue: it's concerned exclusively with Alceste's sacrifice of her life to save that of her husband, Admeto, King of Thessaly, and the emotions that each of them and those around them feel. The performance is deftly paced and transparent in its textures. There's no portentousness about Östman's direction, and the Drottningholm orchestra ensures that the detail of accompanying textures is clearly heard, playing gently and lightly in the dances.

Teresa Ringholz has a voice of modest dimensions, which she uses in a natural way, with little vibrato, firm, surely tuned, clear and well focused. She catches Alceste's increasingly passionate determination, at the close of Act 1, as her resolution to die to save her husband hardens, with its magnificent climax in 'Ombre, larve'. Her controlled manner – there's no outburst of grief when she bids her children farewell at the end of the act, for example – catches well the stylised nature of Gluck's expression. Justin Lavender, as Admeto, is slightly less successful. He has a generous tenor – fuller and weightier than that of the other tenor, Jonas Degerfelt, who sings gracefully and also with vitality – and he brings to the music a good deal of passion that occasionally threatens to go beyond the scale of the performance as a whole. The smaller roles are very adequately done. This recording conveys effectively the intensity and the integrity of Gluck's vision.

Alceste

Janet Baker *mez* Alceste **Robert Tear** *ten* Admète **John Shirley-Quirk** *bar* Le Grand Prêtre; Un Dieu Infernal **Maldwyn Davies** *ten* Evandre **Philip Gelling** *bar* Le Héraut; Le Dieu Apollon **Jonathan Summers** *bar* Le Dieu Hercule **Matthew Best** *bass* L'Oracle **Chorus and Orchestra of the Royal Opera House, Covent Garden / Charles Mackerras**
Royal Opera House Records ② ROHS010 (146' · ADD · N/T/t) Recorded live on December 12, 1981 Ⓜ**OO**

It is wonderful to have her deeply moving portrayal (Janet Baker's farewell to Covent Garden) made available after all these years – if only it were on DVD! The sombre overture sets the scene: the orchestra under Charles Mackerras is admirable, trombones well to the fore, the unnecessary harpsichord a minor irritatant. In the opening number some wobbly sopranos

obtrude from time to time, but in general the choral contribution is excellent, albeit in rather occluded sound. However, the grand sweep of Gluck's design, the chorus's 'Ô Dieux! Qu'allons nous devenir?' and 'Ô malheureuse Admète!' framing Alcestis' solos, is weakened by the omission of a whole section. Other regrettable cuts include the powerful restatement of the chorus at the end of Act 2 and chunks of the final Chaconne.

Even more unsettling is the frequency with which, by Mackerras's sleight of hand, Alcestis' music abruptly shifts down a tone or a semitone. The booklet article praises Dame Janet for her singing of 'the repeated ascents from sustained A flat to A natural', but that is not what we hear. This is a pity, because it vitiates Gluck's tonal scheme, and it's when she is straining at the top of her range that Baker is at her most thrilling. The air in question is certainly gripping; but 'Divinités du Styx', sung at pitch, is stupendous.

In the scene where Admetus learns that Alcestis is sacrificing herself for him, the dramatic force that Baker and Tear bring to the accompanied recitative is exemplary. Make no mistake: gripes notwithstanding, this recording should be in every opera lover's collection.

Armide

Armide   ℙ

Mireille Delunsch *sop* Armide **Charles Workman** *ten* Renaud **Laurent Naouri** *bar* Hidraot **Ewa Podleś** *mez* Hate **Françoise Masset** *sop* Phénice, Mélisse **Nicole Heaston** *sop* Sidonie, Shepherdess, Lucinde **Yann Beuron** *ten* Artémidore, Danish Knight **Brett Polegato** *bar* Ubalde **Vincent le Texier** *bar* Aronte **Magdalena Kožená** *mez* Pleasure **Valérie Gabail** *sop* Naiad **Choeur des Musiciens du Louvre; Les Musiciens du Louvre / Marc Minkowski**
Archiv Produktion ② 459 616-2AH2 (139' · DDD · T/t)
Ⓟ**O▷**

'Perhaps the best of all my works', said Gluck of his *Armide*. But this, the fifth of his seven 'reform operas', has never captured the public interest as have *Orfeo*, *Alceste*, the two *Iphigénies* and even *Paride ed Elena*. Its plot is thinnish, concerned only with the love of the pagan sorceress Armide, princess of Damascus, for the Christian knight and hero Renaud, and his enchantment, disenchantment and finally his abandonment of her. But *Armide* has two features that set it apart. One is the extraordinary soft, sensuous tone of the music; Gluck said that it was meant 'to produce a voluptuous sensation', and that if he were to suffer damnation it would be for the passionate love duet in Act 5. Certainly his orchestral writing here has a warmth, a colour and a richness going far beyond anything in his other reform operas (apart from parts of *Paride ed Elena*). Second, there are several great solo dramatic scenes, two of them for Armide.

The success of *Armide*, then, depends critically on the Armide herself. Here it goes to Mireille Delunsch, who brings to it a good deal of intensity but doesn't have command of a wide range of tone, and doesn't seem to make much use of her words. There's some graceful singing in the softer music and the scene where she can't bring herself to kill Renaud is finely done, though ultimately perhaps her singing lacks real emotional tension. Renaud is sung by Charles Workman, in a strong tenor, sounding almost baritonal at times, but then singing the sleep song, 'Plus j'observe ces lieux', with soft, sweet tone and much delicacy. The lovers' duet in Act 5 is sung gently and with much charm. Among the other singers, Ewa Podles makes a strong impression as Hate with her large and steady voice. And Laurent Naouri shows a pleasant, firm baritone as Hidraot.

Minkowski makes much of the score's colour and flow. He uses a substantial orchestra, which plays lightly and flexibly and with rhythmic spring. He has a tendency towards quickish tempos here and there but is always attentive to the characterisation of individual numbers.

Le Feste d'Apollo

Le Feste d'Apollo
Aristeo
Ann Hallenberg *mez* Aristeo **Magnus Staveland** *ten*
Ati **Ditte Andersen** *sop* Cirene **Marie Lenormand**
mez Cidippe; Silvia

Bauci e Filemone
Ditte Andersen *sop* Bauci **Marie Lenormand** *mez*
Filemone **Magnus Staveland** *ten* Giove **Ann**
Hallenberg *mez* Una pastorella
Namur Chamber Choir;
Les Talens Lyriques / Christophe Rousset
Ambroisie ② AMB9995 (98' · DDD · S/T/t/N)   Ⓕ

This set, correctly described above, is confusingly entitled 'Philémon & Baucis', leading the unsuspecting browser to think that here perhaps is one of the obscure *opéras comiques* that Gluck composed for the court in Vienna around 1760. What is presented here though is part of *Le Feste d'Apollo*, an entertainment that Gluck assembled for the festivities marking the wedding of Maria Amalia, one of Maria Theresa's many daughters, to the Duke of Parma in 1769. The complete work began with a prologue and ended with a revised version of *Orfeo ed Euridice*.

In *Aristeo*, the bee-keeper Aristaeus is advised by his mother Cyrene to placate the wood nymphs and the gods, who are angry over his part in the deaths of Eurydice and Orpheus. He offers a sacrifice, his bees are restored to him, and he secures the love of Cydippe. In the second opera, Philemon and Baucis are, so to speak, given demigod vouchers for being the only people to show kindness to Jove as he wanders through Phrygia in disguise.

This is not exactly the stuff of high drama, but the music is never less than pleasant, and sometimes more. The music of Cyrene's aria, already used by Gluck – though the authorship is disputed – was to turn up as 'L'espoir renaît' in *Orphée et Euridice*. 'Di due bell'anime' in *Bauci e Filemone*

became the opening chorus of *Paride ed Elena*, and there are other self-borrowings and anticipations.

The more striking numbers include Aristaeus's 'Cessate, fuggite', brightly performed by Ann Hallenberg with violin and cello obbligato, and a ravishing duet, full of suspensions, for Philemon and Baucis. The real knockout is the coloratura aria for Baucis, which goes up to G in alt (a tone higher than the Queen of Night). Ditte Andersen will have you on the edge of your seat.

So, for different reasons, unfortunately, will the uningratiating tenor of Magnus Staveland, which makes the curtailing of Jove's first aria easier to bear. Much *secco* recitative is also cut, although there is no indication of this in the booklet. Christophe Rousset and the chorus and orchestra are all in fine fettle.

Iphigénie en Aulide

Iphigénie en Aulide
Lynne Dawson *sop* Iphigénie **José van Dam** *bass*
Agamemnon **Anne Sofie von Otter** *mez*
Clytemnestre **John Aler** *ten* Achille **Bernard Deletré**
bass Patrocle **Gilles Cachemaille** *bass* Calchas **René**
Schirrer *bass* Arcas **Guillemette Laurens** *mez* Diane
Ann Monoyios *sop* First Greek woman, Slave
Isabelle Eschenbrenner *sop* Second Greek woman
Monteverdi Choir; Lyon Opéra Orchestra /
Sir John Eliot Gardiner
Erato ② 2292-45003-2 (132' · DDD · T/t)   ⒻOO

Gluck's first reform opera for Paris has tended to be overshadowed by his other *Iphigénie*, the *Tauride* one. But it does contain some superb things, of which perhaps the finest are the great monologues for Agamemnon. On this recording, José van Dam sings a little coolly; but this only adds force to his big moment at the end of the Second Act where he tussles with himself over the sacrifice of his daughter and – contemplating her death and the screams of the vengeful Eumenides – decides to flout the gods and face the consequences. The cast in general is strong. Lynne Dawson brings depth of expressive feeling to all she does and her Iphigénie, marked by a slightly grainy sound and much intensity, is very moving. John Aler's Achille too is very fine and sings both with ardour and vitality. There's great force too in the singing of Anne Sofie von Otter as Clytemnestre. Gardiner's Monteverdi Choir sings with polish, perhaps seeming a little genteel for a crowd of angry Greek soldiers baying for Iphigénie's blood. But he gives a duly urgent account of the score, pressing it forward eagerly and keeping the tension at a high level even in the dance music. A period-instrument orchestra might have added a certain edge and vitality but this performance wants nothing in authority. Securely recommended.

Iphigénie en Tauride

Iphigénie en Tauride   Ⓟ
Christine Goerke *sop* Iphigénie; **Vinson Cole** *ten*

Pylade; **Rodney Gilfry** bar Oreste; **Sharon Baker**
sop 1st Priestess, Greek woman; **Jayne West** sop
2nd Priestess, Diana; **Stephen Salters** bar Thoas;
Mark Andrew Cleveland sngr Scythian; **Mark
Risinger** sngr Minister of the Sanctuary; **Boston
Baroque / Martin Pearlman**
Telarc Classics ② CD80546 (134' · DDD · T/t) Ⓕ🔴🔴

'With Gluck, there's a long sweep to the drama,'
says Martin Pearlman towards the end of his
introductory talk about *Iphigénie*, included here
at the end of the second CD. It's obvious from
his performance that this is how he sees the
work; and it's his capacity to sustain that 'long
sweep' that makes this version so compelling.

Pearlman, using period instruments, draws
vivid and dramatic playing from his admirable
group. He's particularly successful in the various
dances in the course of the opera, which, beautifully alive and springy in rhythm, never permit
the drama to flag, but emerge as an integral part
of it, not as decorative interludes. With these
clear textures, Gluck's orchestral colouring
comes across sharply as, too, does the lofty, hieratic quality of the work. There's tenderness as
well, and it's thanks partly to Pearlman's sensitive timing that the opera's climactic moment –
the sacrifice scene, where brother and sister at
last recognise each other – is so intense and
poignant.

Although it lies quite high, the role of Iphigenia
is often assigned to a mezzo, as if to heighten the
intensity. Christine Goerke is a true soprano,
which allows softer tones and more femininity
than one generally hears, but there's metal in
her voice, too (she doesn't altogether forgo
vibrato), and the weight of the tragedy is by no
means underplayed: listen to 'O malheureuse
Iphigénie' – enhanced by the fine line of the
oboe obbligato – or to her impassioned singing
of the noble aria at the beginning of Act 4. Rodney Gilfry provides a strong, manly Orestes and
is successful in conveying the tortures he's suffering. Vinson Cole gives a sympathetic reading
of Pylades – lyrical, shapely and expressively
phrased. There's excellent choral singing.

The principal rival recordings both have
rather starrier casts. Muti's is a big, modern
opera-house performance, powerful and exciting, Gardiner's more stylish, more concentrated
dramatically. But this set is just about first
choice.

Orfeo ed Euridice

Orfeo ed Euridice Ⓟ
Bernarda Fink contr Orfeo **Veronica Cangemi** sop
Euridice **Maria Cristina Kiehr** sop Amore **Berlin
RIAS Chamber Choir; Freiburg Baroque Orchestra
/ René Jacobs**
Harmonia Mundi ② HMC90 1742/3 (91' · DDD · T/t) Ⓕ

Orfeo comes in many guises. There's Gluck's
original Italian version, composed for Vienna in
1762, his adjusted version for Parma in 1769, his
French revision of 1774 for Paris, and then the

numerous, posthumous compromise texts that
seek the best of both worlds by incorporating
sections of the French version within the framework of the Italian. This version is 'pure' Italian,
and although this means forgoing such famous
and affecting music as the Dance of the Blessed
Spirits, 'Cet asile' and the enhanced ending to
'Che farò', as well as the big D minor Dance of
the Furies, it does offer a much more concentrated experience.

The tone of the performance is set by the
highly energetic overture, with its forceful
accents and its sharply defined textures and
dynamics. Jacobs takes pains throughout to give
a clear yet also rich quality to Gluck's highly
original orchestral textures and to shape his
phrases with style and awareness of the omni-
presence of dance. However, it's the singer of
Orpheus, even more than the conductor, who
gives character to a performance of this work.
Often nowadays it's sung by a countertenor in
preference to the contralto long favoured in the
role, which was composed for a castrato anyway.
So which voice better suits the semi-divine
Orpheus? Ultimately it depends on the artistry
of the singer. Bernarda Fink sings the role here
very beautifully and quite unaffectedly. Her
great strength lies in her smooth, natural and
very even tone and her command of line.

This is probably the best version of the Italian
original with a woman as Orpheus, and can be
recommended without hesitation to anyone
who prefers to avoid the male alto voice. If you
prefer to stick with the male voice the choice lies
between Michael Chance's beautifully sung version under Frieder Bernius (Sony) and Derek
Lee Ragin's ardent impersonation in Gardiner's
account; both are revealing, in quite different
ways, of this very special work.

Orphée et Eurydice
Magdalena Kožená ten Orphée **Madeline Bender**
sop Eurydice **Patricia Petibon** sop Amour
**Monteverdi Choir; Orchestre Révolutionnaire et
Romantique / Sir John Eliot Gardiner**
Stage director **Robert Wilson**
Video director **Brian Large**
EMI 📀 216577-9 (100' · NTSC · 16:9 · PCM Stereo
and DTS 5.0 · 0) Ⓕ

Alceste
Anne Sofie von Otter mez Alceste **Paul Groves** ten
Admète **Dietrich Henschel** bar High Priest; Hercules
Yann Beuron ten Evandre **Ludovic Tézier** bar Herald;
Apollo **Frédéric Caton** bass Oracle; Infernal God
Hjördis Thébault mez Coryphée
**Monteverdi Choir; English Baroque Soloists /
Sir John Eliot Gardiner**
Stage director **Robert Wilson**
Video director **Brian Large**
EMI 📀 216570-9 (134' · NTSC · 16:9 · PCM stereo
and DTS 5.0 · 0) Ⓕ

Orphée et Eurydice is performed in the arrangement that Berlioz made in 1859 for the French
mezzo-soprano Pauline Viardot. He based it on

the later, Paris, version of the opera, but restored the part of Orpheus to the alto tessitura of the original. His influence can also be detected in this recording of *Alceste*, an opera which likewise exists in two versions: incensed at the way the brass interjections in 'Ombre, larve' were obscured by the extra notes required for 'Divinités du Styx', Berlioz proposed a simple change to 'Ombres, larves'; and his suggestion is adopted here by John Eliot Gardiner. You won't find it in the documentation accompanying the DVDs, because there isn't any. No synopsis, no background articles, no timings; not even a list of 'chapters', except on-screen. And some detailed help is necessary, because the purchaser, in the case of *Orphée et Eurydice*, is getting neither pure Gluck nor pure Gluck/Berlioz.

Robert Wilson's production of *Orphée et Eurydice* is spare, bordering on minimalist. A blue background; cypresses in Act 1; a rock in the bleak Elysian Fields. There are some striking stage pictures, such as Orpheus silhouetted during the Dance of the Furies (another Gardiner restoration, not in fact danced), and the couple positioned on different levels in Act 3. The acting is more movement and gesture than facial expression: effective as far as it goes, but the Blessed Spirits look pretty miserable. One miscalculation is the failure to show Orpheus disobeying the gods' commands by turning to look at Eurydice, thereby bringing about her second death. Magdalena Kožená, then virtually unknown, sings Orpheus superbly, including the bravura air in Act 1 (orchestrated, incidentally, by Saint-Saëns). The latter is remarkable for the cadenza, a joint effort by Berlioz, Saint-Saëns and Viardot herself. Madeline Bender and Patricia Petibon have much less to do; they do it well, but Petibon is not helped by the variable sound quality.

The two operas are connected by a suspended cube which, seen at the end of *Orphée et Eurydice*, reappears in the overture to *Alceste* and many times thereafter. The chorus is heard but not seen: a cop-out, surely, but the dancers replacing the singers on stage provide an unforgettable image when they appear, arms upraised, between the columns of the temple. Silhouette again, and gesture, too. Anne Sofie von Otter, severe, hair scraped back, is the picture of regal dignity at her first appearance. Later, unable to look at the husband for whom she is sacrificing her life, her pain is palpable; at the end, after Apollo has descended with the reprieve, the camera focuses on the gentle smile that she permits herself.

The sharp-eyed will have noticed that two orchestras are employed: same players, different pitch. Even at the lower pitch, some of Alceste's music is transposed down. If von Otter is almost unbearably moving in the duets with Admetus, perhaps her finest moment is her scene, alone and terrified, at the entrance to Hades. Paul Groves as Admetus is almost as eloquent, and Dietrich Henschel, swinging an imaginary club, makes a hearty, no-nonsense Hercules. Both discs are well worth investigating.

Additional recommendations

Orfeo ed Euridice (abridged recording)　　　　　Ⓗ
Ferrier Orfeo **Ayars** Euridice **Vlachopoulos** Amor
**Glyndebourne Festival Chorus; Southern
Philharmonic Orchestra / Stiedry**　　　　　　Ⓢ**O**
Dutton mono CDBP9730 (63' · ADD) Recorded 1947

Though the sound may initially prove a little distracting, Dutton have done their best to clean it up, and Ferrier's singing more than makes up for it. Its beauty goes straight to the heart: a noble and intensely human Orfeo which deserves its place on every collector's shelves.

Orfeo ed Euridice
Baker Orfeo **Speiser** Euridice **Gale** Amor LPO /
Leppard
Erato 2292-45864-2　　　　　　　　　　　Ⓜ**O**

A wonderful memento of Baker's Orfeo, a glorious characterisation with its ardent, heatfelt emotional response. Strong, sinuous accompaniment from Leppard.

Vladimir Godár　　　　　Slovak b1956

A musician of extraordinarily broad musical sympathies, Godár is one of Slovakia's most respected. A scholar as well as a composer, he works in film as well as in 'classical' repertoire. He is a great admirer of the music of Bela Bartók and has a comparable fascination with folk music - something that has emerged through his musical collaborations with the singer Iva Bittová.

Choral works

'Mater'
Stálá matka (Stabat mater). Magnificat. Maykomashmalon. Uspávanky (Lullabies). Ecce puer. Regina coeli
Iva Bittová voc **Bratislava Conservatory Choir;
Solamente Naturali / Marek Štryncl**
ECM New Series 476 5689 (57' · DDD · T/t)　　Ⓕ**D▸**

To say that Vladímir Godár is a typical ECM discovery is certainly not to diminish either him or ECM. This Slovak composer uses a vocabulary in the works recorded here that will inevitably recall Górecki, and also at times Pärt and Tavener, though the music's emotional intensity, the particular way in which repetition is used and the use of certain sonorities and chords, relate much more to the Polish composer than the other two, very noticeably in the *Stabat mater*; aficionados of these composers will certainly enjoy what is recorded here. But though the music may recall them, it does not sound like any of them for any length of time: Godár has his own way of saying what he wants to say, which is, for him, intimately connected with what he calls 'musical archaeology', specifically Slovak culture, musical, literary and religious.

Thus there are works that draw upon Slovak translations of the *Magnificat* and *Stabat mater*, traditional lullabies, a Latin Regina coeli and, rather oddly, a single poem by James Joyce. The *Magnificat* is based very simply on the immediately recognisable first tone, for solo voice and dark string underpinning, but is interrupted by massive choral interjections of the word 'Magnificat' at its climax – a simple but effective device. There are conscious references to the Baroque at various points but folk monody – the archetypal lullaby of the mother – is what really holds all this material together.

Godár's transparent but strong style is greatly helped in this by the powerfully raw voice of the amazing Iva Bittová, but also by the precision of Solamente Naturali and the Bratislava choir.

Benjamin Godard   French 1849-1895

At the age of ten he was enrolled at the Paris Conservatoire and although he was considered a child prodigy as a violinist, he did not win any prizes at the Conservatoire, and his submissions in 1863 and 1864 for the Prix de Rome were unsuccessful. A prodigious worker, he soon began to establish a reputation as a composer in Germany and Spain as well as in France. Godard composed works in most genres with the exception of church music, but ultimately made his reputation as a composer of salon pieces for piano and of songs, albums of which were translated into English. His early promise did not really develop in his later works, although his early death from consumption meant that he had no chance to mature fully as a composer.

Concertante violin works

Concerto romantique, Op 35ᵃ. Violin Concerto No 2, Op 131ᵃ. Scènes poétiques, Op 46
ᵃ**Chloë Hanslip** vn **Slovak State Philharmonic Orchestra, Košice / Kirk Trevor**
Naxos 8 570554 (66' · DDD)   ⓈⒹ▶

Benjamin Godard (1849-95) was a prolific, fluent composer in many genres, but little of his output is familiar today. A string-player (he'd been a pupil of Henri Vieuxtemps), he writes for the violin with great panache, and Chloë Hanslip is in her element, making the most of the showy passagework, enjoying finding the right tone of voice for the different styles of melody – elegiac, sensuous or graceful – and attacking with passion the dramatic recitatives that join the movements of the *Concerto romantique*. The orchestral writing in both concertos is full of colour, if occasionally rather brash, and is performed here with considerable dash and spirit. There are some delightful solo contributions from oboe, clarinet and viola, in dialogue with the violin, during the little *Canzonetta* that separates the slow movement and finale of the *Concerto romantique*. Neither concerto comes near to rivalling Bruch or Tchaikovsky, but Godard is a skilful composer; it's music that's formally satisfying, consistently entertaining and sometimes memorable and touching. Hanslip, who's to be congratulated for taking on such unfamiliar repertoire, seizes on these high-spots – the second theme in Op 131's first movement, the moment in Op 35's sombre *Adagio* when the first turn to the major is made – and finds just the right colour to emphasise Godard's happy thought.

The *Scènes poétiques* are really salon music transposed to the concert hall. Kirk Trevor and the orchestra relish the imaginative instrumental colouring, though the performance sounds a little like music learnt in the studio, rather than familiar from many concert outings.

Leopold Godowsky
Polish/American 1870-1938

An American pianist and composer of Polish birth, Godowsky toured widely from the age of nine, making his American début in Boston in 1884. Tours of the USA and Canada followed and until 1900 he taught in Philadelphia and Chicago. Until World War II he continued to appear in Europe; his reputation as a Chopin interpreter was not enhanced by a series of elaborate Studies on the Etudes. His concert career ended in 1930. GROVEmusic

Studies

53 Studies on Chopin's Etudes
Marc-André Hamelin pf
Hyperion ② CDA67411/2 (158' · DDD)   ⒻⓄⓄⓄ

Godowsky's 53 studies on Chopin's 27 studies are the *ne plus ultra* of Romantic intricacy. Godowsky's wily disclaimer that, far from wanting to 'improve' on Chopin's matchless originals, he merely wished to extend the parameters of technique, hardly convinces purists, who dismiss his *magnum opus* as an outrageous gilding of the lily, an unforgivable powdering and rouging of Chopin's genius. For others, Godowsky's ingenuity, his ear-tickling wit and elegance, create edifices, indeed 'miracles of rare device'. But if heated debate still rages around the music, the quality of Hamelin's recording is entirely uncontroversial. Rarely can such a gargantuan task have been accomplished with such strength, grace and agility, with an ease bordering on nonchalance. His virtuosity is pre-eminent because it's so musical, and it's impossible to think of another living pianist who could have carried off this enterprise with comparable success. In lesser hands these *Etudes* can seem overweight; with Hamelin, even the densest, seemingly impenetrable textures are kept as light as air and everything is mobile, fluent and adroit. And so, to evoke Schumann, it's 'hats off, gentlemen' to this handsomely presented and finely recorded set. A truly phenomenal achievement.

Godowsky 53 Studies on Chopin Etudes, Op 10 –
No 1; No 2 (2nd version); No 4; No 5 (2 versions); No
6; No 11; No 12; Op 25 – No 1 (3rd version); No 3; No
5 (2nd version); No 9. Triakontameron – No 11, Alt
Wien. Waltz, Op 64 No 1 **Chopin** Etudes, Op 10 – No
1; No 2; No 4; No 5; No 6; No 12; Op 25 – No 1; No 5
Boris Berezovsky pf
Warner Classics 2564 62258-2 (55' · DDD)
Recorded live 2005   Ⓕ❶❷❸❹▷

Here, uniquely, you can hear Chopin and
Chopin-Godowsky side by side, marvelling or
shuddering at the way Chopin's original is
turned topsy-turvy and transformed into 'something rich and strange'. Recorded live, Boris
Berezovsky's performances of eight of Chopin's
Studies and 11 of Godowsky's arrangements
beggar description.

No more formidable young pianist exists and
his stunning recital balances prodigies of virtuosity with an unfaltering musical integrity. His
Op 10 No 1 study is *maestoso* indeed, and never
more so than when Godowsky's massive carillon
of sound is embellished with a counterpoint as
imperious as the last trump. Chopin's originals
are always musically rather than sensationally
characterised, the reverse of, say, Cziffra's dazzling if infamous distortions, yet Berezovsky's
way with Op 10 No 5 is of a rollicking bravura
that few could equal.

In the left-hand-only studies his tone conjures
up Neuhaus's description of Gilels, 'rich in
noble metal, a 24-carat gold that we find in the
voices of the great singers' and, throughout, you
are also reminded of Shakespeare's words: 'O, it
is excellent / To have a giant's strength, but it is
tyrannous / To use it like a giant.' Here, caught
'on the wing', there is none of that diffidence
that occasionally affects Berezovsky when at his
least concentrated but rather playing in the
grandest of grand Russian traditions.

For encores there are *Alt Wien*, as warm and
affectionate as Cherkassky though without a
trace of whimsy, and Godowsky's teasing elaboration of the *Minute* Waltz. Heard on this
form Berezovsky is the pianist of your dreams;
and it only remains to add that he plays the
third rather than the second version of Op 25
No 1 and that Warner's sound is superb.
Prolonged applause celebrates Berezovsky's
phenomenal achievement.

J Strauss II/Godowsky Symphonic Metamorphis on
Künstlerleben. Symphonic Metamorphosis on Wein,
Weib und Gesang. Symphonic Metamorphosis on
Die Fledermaus **Godowsky** Walzermasken – Pastell;
Französisch; Wienerisch; Portrait: Joh Str.
Triakontameron – Rendezvous; Alt Wien;
Terpsichorean Vindobona; The Salon; Memories.
O Strauss/Godowsky The Last Waltz
Marc-André Hamelin pf
Hyperion CDA67626 (69' · DDD)   Ⓕ❶❷

Here's another release that testifies to Marc-
André Hamelin's cultured musicianship,
extraordinary keyboard proficiency and unflap-

pable tonal control. His key assets include the
most together, impeccably voiced chords in the
business, plus octaves, trills and rapid leaps that
remain effortlessly even and focused, regardless
of tempo.

All of this comes into delightful play over the
course of the three big Strauss *Symphonic Metamorphoses*. Countless inner voices and contrapuntal rejoinders abound in these works, and
Hamelin makes them audible and clear without
resorting to the pianistic equivalent of red-ink
underlining or pop-up windows. Furthermore,
Hamelin is a seasoned and subtle orchestrator at
the piano; notice how he achieves such eloquent
shading of simultaneous *legato* and detached
phrases with no more help from the sustain
pedal than is necessary.

One could argue that Godowsky's pinpoint
tempo modifications throughout *Wein, Weib
und Gesang* might benefit from stronger characterisation, in the manner of Shura Cherkassky's
admittedly more capricious Decca recording,
although Hamelin eschews the older pianist's
cuts; in fact, Hamelin plays all three *Metamorphoses* complete, as written. As it happens, the
less demanding shorter selections from *Walzermasken*, *Triakontameron* and *The Last Waltz*
inspire some of Hamelin's most poetic, lyrically
inspired playing on disc.

All told, a stellar achievement, graced by
Hyperion's close-up yet ample engineering, plus
Godowsky biographer Jeremy Nicholas's thor-
oughly informative and penetrating annotations.

Heiner Goebbels   German b1952

*Goebbels's compositions reflect his interests in theatre,
noise, jazz, rock and critical views of the concert hall.
His works have been much influenced by film, montage being a favourite technique; in Surrogate Cities,
for example, a recording of Jewish chant is superimposed on the symphony orchestra. The ballet Red Run,
which includes sections of improvised material and
choreography for the musicians, was the first of several compositions on which Goebbels collaborated with
the Ensemble Modern. He has also directed his own
theatre and radio plays, frequently setting texts by
Heiner Müller. He won the Prix Italia for the third
time in 1996 for his radio play Roman Dogs.*

Landschaft mit entfernten Verwandten

Landschaft mit entfernten Verwandten
Georg Nigl bar **David Bennet** voc **German
Chamber Choir; Ensemble Modern / Franck Ollu**
ECM New Series 476 5383 (80' · DDD)   Ⓕ❶❷

Heiner Goebbels has gone a considerable way to
redefining what is possible in the theatrical
sphere. First seen at Geneva in 2002, this work
(its title translates as 'Landscape with Distant
Relatives') is the first that he has called an
'opera', though his use of the term characteristi-

cally fights shy of overt historical associations. A diverse range of sources is utilised, the main ones being Gertrude Stein's 1945 *Wars I Have Seen* and poems by Henri Michaux – largely from the late 1940s – which provide a specific temporal and cultural framework.

Within this framework, Goebbels arranges his texts so they become 'objects' to be encountered over a two-part journey – and with an emphasis on parallels between concepts of war from the Renaissance and modern eras. Predictably, the composer casts his stylistic net wide – but apart from a couple of misfires, inclusion of such as Moroccan dance and Bollywood film musics with spirituals and 'down-home' Americana is as thought-provoking as it is engaging.

The performance is as involving as one would expect, but while it is no hardship that the texts are included only in their original language, the visual dimension is absent. This is a pity, as stills reproduced in the booklet make one hanker after a DVD presentation. As a soundtrack, however, this disc makes for an engrossing experience.

Osvaldo Golijov

Argentinian/Israeli b1960

Golijov grew up in an Eastern European Jewish household in La Plata, Argentina. After studying piano at the local conservatory and composition with Gerardo Gandini he moved to Israel in 1983, where he studied with Mark Kopytman at the Jerusalem Rubin Academy. Upon moving to the United States in 1986, Golijov earned his PhD at the University of Pennsylvania, where he studied with George Crumb, and was a fellow at Tanglewood, studying with Oliver Knussen. Golijov was one of the composers commissioned by the Internationale Bachakademie Stuttgart to write pieces for the Passion 2000 project in commemoration of JS Bach. Golijov's contribution was La Pasión según San Marcos (The Passion according to St. Mark).

He has also composed for the Kronos Quartet and the St Lawrence Quartet, classical and Klezmer clarinetist David Krakauer and soprano Dawn Upshaw, who performed premieres of his new opera, Ainadamar. He composed for Francis Ford Coppola's movies Youth Without Youth and Tetro.

Oceana

Oceana[a]. Tenebrae[b]. Three Songs[c]
[a]**Luciana Souza** voc [c]**Dawn Upshaw** sop [a]**Elizabeth Remy Johnson** hp [a]**Jamie Haddad** perc [a]**Jay Anderson** db [a]**Scott Tennant**, [a]**John Dearman** gtrs [b]**Kronos Quartet**; [c]**Gwinnet Young Singers**; [ac]**Atlanta Symphony** [a]**Chorus and Orchestra / Robert Spano**
DG 477 6426GH (61' · DDD)　　Ⓕ Ⓑ→

With its boldly flavoured mix of styles, Golijov's *Oceana* (1996) looks forward to the *St Mark Passion* (2000) – the work that put him on the musical map. The solo part was written for renowned

Brazilian jazz singer Luciana Souza whose solos range from impassioned invocation to angular yet elegant breeziness. The choral part is of equal prominence, however, and some of it sounds surprisingly reminiscent of Philip Glass. The final section, 'Chorale of the Reef', makes the most powerful effect, with mesmeric, overlapping phrases, chant-like rhythms and darkly radiant harmonies. The Atlanta Chorus sing it with rapt conviction.

Oceana ebbs away to haunting silence, providing a natural segue to *Tenebrae* (2002), a lament for string quartet that somehow smiles through its tears. Generous arcs of slow-moving melody – often with trembling accompaniment – evoke the great Renaissance masters. Golijov introduces earthier elements – exotic scales, anxious heartbeats, flickering firelight – and the work comes full circle, concluding with a consoling meditation on a hopeful cadential gesture. Kronos, the dedicatees, give a heartfelt performance.

The Three Songs are drawn from diverse sources. 'Night of the Flying Horses' is adapted from Golijov's music for Sally Potter's film *The Man Who Cried*. The drop-dead gorgeous lullaby Dawn Upshaw intones at the beginning echoes Bizet's 'Je crois entendre encore' (an aria featured in the film), while the rhapsodic instrumental conclusion is inspired by Balkan gypsy band music. 'Lua descolorida' is yet another demonstration of Golijov's gift for melody – and for establishing an other-worldly atmosphere through the simplest means. Upshaw rightly describes it as the saddest C major song she knows. 'How Slow the Wind' (Emily Dickinson) taps into a vein of Mahlerian sorrow while ravishing the ear. Upshaw's love for this music is palpable in every bar, and Spano and the Atlanta Symphony provide firm yet supple emotional support. Absolutely not to be missed.

Ainadamar
Dawn Upshaw sop Margarita Xirgu **Jessica Rivera** mez Nuria **Jesús Montoya** voc Ruiz Alonso (Arresting officer) **Eduardo Chama** voc José Tripaldi (Guard) **Sean Mayer** voc Maestro **Robb Asklof** voc Torero **Kelley O'Connor** voc Federico García Lorca **Atlanta Symphony Chorus and Orchestra / Robert Spano**
DG 477 6165 (80' · DDD · N/T/t)　　Ⓕ Ⓞ Ⓑ→

Osvaldo Golijov has based this dramatic work around the life and death (at the hands of a Franco-ist Civil War firing squad) of the Spanish poet Federico García Lorca. *Ainadamar* (the 'fountain of tears', the Moorish name for the site near Grenada where Lorca died in 1936) is neither history nor fiction, rather a symbolic account of reactions to key moments in the poet's life.

The text, translated back into Spanish by the composer, suits Golijov's eclectic and anarchic mix of musics. At the start you hear low pedal notes similar to those that launch *Das Rheingold* or *Also sprach Zarathustra*. Within minutes we are closer to 'prog-rock' tracks of the 1970s like Led Zeppelin's *Kashmir* – a meeting of classical strings

and heavy-metal beat – or the soundscapes, featuring combinations of riffs and sound effects
(here horses' hooves or, chillingly in context,
echoing gunshots), of Roger Waters. From a
vocal point of view the score is deeply stained by
alternations of the Jewish chants of Golijov's
mother religion, the *cante jondo* of the flamenco of
Lorca's homeland, or the Argentinian tangos
worked up to symphonic proportions by Piazzolla
and his contemporaries. American minimalism (of
the John Adams variety) has left its mark too in the
obsessive use of repetitive cells or phrases.

The effect is compelling: these words and
scenes cry out for music, and Golijov delivers in
full measure. While the whole is anchored to a
subject of emotional power – Lorca, freakishly
like Pushkin, almost seemed to anticipate and
prepare his own fate – the lack of a conventional
narrative is a great plus. Like the controversial
Mass of Leonard Bernstein, *Ainadamar* is part
lament and part celebration, an action of the
mind rather than of dramatic events. The com-
fortable-sounding recording originates in performances by the characteristically adventurous
Roberto Spano and the Atlanta SO; not all the
cast are as famous as Golijov's champion Dawn
Upshaw but they partner her well in few-holds-
barred commitment.

Nicolas Gombert   Flemish c1495-c1560

Probably a native of Flanders and possibly a pupil of
Josquin (he composed a déploration on Josquin's
death, 1545), Gombert was a singer (from 1526)
and maître des enfants (from 1529) in Emperor
Charles V's court chapel, with which he travelled in
Europe and for which he also served unofficially as
composer. He was canon of Notre Dame, Tournai, by
1534. By 1540 he had been dismissed from the impe-
rial chapel but was probably pardoned (and granted a
benefice) c1552. Highly regarded by his contempo-
raries as a great innovator, he favoured dense tex-
tures and often used dark, rich timbres. He used
pervading imitation more consistently than anyone of
his own or an earlier generation, creating textures in
which the voices tend to be equally important. All but
two of his ten extant masses elaborate existing motets
or chansons. His motets (over 160 survive) (from
books, 1539, 1541, many in collections), are his most
representative works, each phrase of text having its
own expressive motif worked through the texture.
Other sacred works include eight fine Magnificats
and multi-voice works. His chansons (over 70) are
like the Netherlands motet only more animated and
often conceived on a broad scale. His music continued
to be printed until long after his death.

Motets

Ave Maria. Virgo sancta Catherina. Inviolata, integra,
et casta es, Maria. Tribulatio et angustia. Hortus
conclusus es. Aspice Domine quia facta est. Ne
reminiscaris, Domine. Pater noster. Ave sanctissima

Maria a 5. Ergone vitae
Brabant Ensemble / Stephen Rice
Hyperion CDA67614 (66' · DDD · T/t)   Ⓕ**OO**

This is the first disc to focus on the core of
Gombert, his motets. What we know of his
troubled life and extant music suggests that he
was not a '*Laetentur coeli*' sort of composer, and
so the opening *Tribulatio et angustia* is well chosen, being both one of the finest of them and
setting the mood for the rest. Barely a minute
has passed before the first of many dark spots of
extreme and focused dissonance, yet such harmonic knots never tie up the line. Indeed it's one
of very few discs of this repertoire you can happily play in its entirety.

This is in part a tribute to Gombert, who went
to the well so often and never returned empty-
handed; but also to the Brabant Ensemble and
Stephen Rice, who researched Gombert's
motets for a doctorate. Rice believes in a largely
steady tactus, which certainly suits the reflective
nature of these works, but by encouraging an
unusually individual and carefully balanced
vocal response, he avoids the pitfalls of relentless
consistency (The Tallis Scholars) and arrided
elision (one-per-part groups like Henry's Eight
and the Hilliard Ensemble). There is a welcome
and (in this music) novel belief in the power of
voices as voices rather than instrumental simula-
cra: try the sopranos halfway through *Hortus*
conclusus est for erotic Mariolatry at its most disconcertingly sensual. Arise, make haste, as they
sing, and hear this music.

Eugene Goossens   English 1893-1962

He started his musical education at the age of 10,
spending a year at the Bruges Conservatory. After his
return to England he gained a Liverpool Scholarship
to the RCM (1907), where his professors included
Rivarde for violin and Stanford for composition. His
contemporaries Benjamin, Bliss and Howells became
his lifelong friends. He made his conducting début
(April 1912) at an RCM public concert with his first
composition, Variations on a Chinese Theme. Goos-
sens's success as a conductor, and especially his role in
bringing modern and difficult works before a wide
public, proved detrimental to his own later career as
a composer.   GROVEmusic

Orchestral works

Symphony No 1, Op 58. Phantasy Concerto, Op 60ª
ª**Howard Shelley** pf **Melbourne Symphony**
Orchestra / Richard Hickox
Chandos Ⓢ CHSA5068 (65' · DDD/DSD)   Ⓕ**Oᗺ**

As swansongs go, this striking coupling of two of
Sir Eugene Goossens's meatiest large-scale offerings under the baton of the late Richard Hickox
really is something to cherish. The epic First
Symphony of 1938-40 has not lacked passionate

advocacy on disc but Hickox is more realistically recorded than any and draws arguably the most finely groomed orchestral playing. No one coming to this ambitious canvas for the first time could fail to be struck by Hickox's excitingly committed and typically red-blooded handling of what is a most imposing and rewarding creation.

The *Phantasy Concerto* dates from 1942 and this would appear to be its first commercial recording. Inspired in part by 'the fantastic and sinister character' of Edgar Allan Poe's *The Devil in the Belfry* and written for the Spanish pianist José Iturbi, it's an attractively spicy, densely plotted score in four linked movements lasting just over 25 minutes, in which the piano largely eschews ostentatious display in favour of a more *concertante* role ('conversational' was how Goossens described it). Howard Shelley is the fearless soloist and he receives alert support from Hickox and the Melbourne SO. Eminently truthful sound, too, with an astutely judged balance throughout.

Henryk Górecki   Polish b1933

Górecki studied with Szabelski at the Katowice Conservatory (1955-60) and with Messiaen in Paris. His music has connections with Penderecki, but its deepest affinities are with ancient Polish religious music, and it often shows a saintly simplicity. Most of his works are for orchestra or chamber ensemble; they include the chamber trilogy Genesis (1963) and three symphonies, the third of which achieved striking public success in the early 1990s.   GROVEmusic

Symphonies

Symphony No 2, 'Copernican', Op 31ª. Beatus vir, Op 38
ªZofia Kilanowicz sop Andrezej Dobber bar
Silesian Philharmonic Choir; Polish Radio Choir;
Polish National Radio Symphony Orchestra /
Antoni Wit
Naxos 8 555375 (67' · DDD)   Ⓢ▷

Górecki composed his Second Symphony in 1972 in response to a commission to mark the 500th anniversary of the birth of the Polish astronomer Nicolas Copernicus. It possesses a certain Janus-like quality in that it forms a bridge between his earlier 'modernist' works and his later 'reductionist' style, into which the ubiquitous Third Symphony falls. The Second Symphony comprises two movements, the first glancing back to the dissonance of earlier works, the second looking forward to more tonal pastures in which the seeds of the Third Symphony are in abundant evidence. Górecki's Copernican Symphony is an unsung masterpiece, and a greater and more impressively constructed work than the Third.

Beatus vir was composed in 1977 in response to a commission to mark the 900th anniversary of

the martyrdom of the Bishop of Cracow, Stanisław of Szczepanów. The opening pages are particularly striking and there are some marvellously scored moments in the remaining 24 minutes or so, though it doesn't attain the stature of the Second Symphony. That said, this disc is thoroughly recommended to anyone wanting to expand their appreciation of Górecki beyond the Third. The Copernican Symphony more than justifies the price of the disc alone and the performances and recorded sound throughout are exceptionally fine.

Symphony No 3, 'Symphony of Sorrowful Songs', Op 36
Dawn Upshaw sop **London Sinfonietta /
David Zinman**
Nonesuch 7559-79282-2 (54' · DDD)   Ⓕ❍❍❍▷

Górecki's Third Symphony has become legend. Composed in 1976, it's always had its champions and admirers within the contemporary music world, but in 1993 it found a new audience of undreamt-of proportions. A few weeks after its release, this Elektra Nonesuch release not only entered the top 10 in the classical charts, but was also riding high in the UK Pop Album charts. It became the biggest selling disc of music by a contemporary classical composer.

The Symphony, subtitled *Symphony of Sorrowful, Songs* was composed during a period when Górecki's musical style was undergoing a radical change from avant-garde serialism to a more accessible style firmly anchored to tonal traditions. The Symphony's three elegiac movements (or 'songs') form a triptych of laments for all the innocent victims of World War II and are a reflection upon man's inhumanity to man in general. The songs are beautifully and ethereally sung by Dawn Upshaw, and David Zinman and the London Sinfonietta provide an intense and committed performance of the shimmering orchestral writing. The recording quality is excellent.

Symphony No 3, 'Symphony of Sorrowful Songs', Op 36ª. Three Pieces in Old Style
ªZofia Kilanowicz sop **Katowice Radio Symphony Orchestra / Antoni Wit**
Naxos 8 550822 (66' · DDD · T/t)   Ⓢ❍❍▷

This recording is virtually as good as the better-known Zinman version. The performance is exceptionally fine, although the acoustic is more resonant, the orchestral choirs less closely balanced and Antoni Wit isn't as meticulous as Zinman in his observance of minor details. Interpretatively, Wit leaves the more austere impression. His relative inwardness squares convincingly with the symphony's harrowing texts and 'Sorrowful Songs' sub-title. If spectacular singing is your main priority, then Upshaw's is the vocal tour de force. Zofia Kilanowicz displays stronger lower registers and a brilliant, bleached-white soprano that reflects the score's innate pathos, its sense of shock. Her enunciation is more idiomatic, while her partial suspension of vibrato is a powerful interpretative ploy. What's most impressive about this performance is its spirituality; and given the overall excellence of the recording, the conducting and the singing, it's strongly recommended, particularly to those who have yet to discover the Symphony's hypnotic sound-world. It's also commended to those who do know the work but who find Upshaw and Zinman too 'plush'.

Kleines Requiem für eine Polka

Kleines Requiem für eine Polka, Op 66[a]. Harpsichord Concerto, Op 40[b]. Good Night, 'In memoriam Michael Vyner', Op 63
Dawn Upshaw sop **Sebastian Bell** fl **John Constable** pf **Elisabeth Chojnacka** hpd **David Hockings** perc **London Sinfonietta / [a]David Zinman, [b]Markus Stenz**
Nonesuch 7559-79362-2 (59' · DDD)　　Ⓕ Ⓞ ◐

Like a small café huddled within the shadow of some ancient church, Górecki's *Kleines Requiem für eine Polka* (1993) evokes feelings of paradox. The opening movement suggests distracted tranquillity. This is followed by a grating *Allegro* which approximates the sort of vicious 'knees-up' that Shostakovich penned whenever he bared his teeth at empty celebration. Later, we're back within the tranquil interior of Górecki's imagination – and it's there that we stay until the work ends.

The *Kleines Requiem für eine Polka* displays a profundity expressed via the simplest means. It's a pity, then, that the Harpsichord Concerto breaks the mood so quickly: one's initial impression is of a further violent 'episode' from the first work, although the stylistic contrast breaks the illusion soon enough. This is probably the most famous 20th-century harpsichord concerto after Falla's. Bach served as its creative prime mover, while Elisabeth Chojnacka is its dedicatee and most celebrated interpreter. Here she revels in the piece's playful aggression. It's an unrelenting display and in total contrast to *Good Night*, Górecki's deeply felt memorial to one of his staunchest supporters, Michael Vyner. The language is sombre, but never merely mournful. Mostly quiet and contemplative, *Good Night* is scored for alto flute, piano and tam-tam with Dawn Upshaw intoning Hamlet's 'flights of angels' in the closing movement. The work ends in a spirit of veiled ritual with a sequence of quiet gong strokes. The performance and recording are consistently fine.

Choral Works

Miserere, Op 44[a]. Amen, Op 35[e]. Euntes ibant et flebant, Op 32[e]. My Vistula, grey Vistula, Op 46[b]. Broad waters, Op 39[b]
[a]Chicago Symphony Chorus; [a]Chicago Lyric Opera Chorus / John Nelson; [b]Lira Chamber Chorus /

Lucy Ding
Nonesuch 7559-79348-2 (67' · DDD · T/t)　Ⓕ Ⓞ ◐

Miserere is an intensely spiritual, prayerful work in which Górecki responds with heartfelt passion to the political events of 1981 (a sit-in by members of Rural Solidarity which ultimately led to the democratisation of Poland). It's as intellectually demanding and emotionally compelling as anything by Górecki released on disc. Lovers of the Third Symphony will fall under its spell straight away, but it should gain respect from those less easily swayed by the opulent orchestral textures of that work, for here Górecki is using what's probably his favourite medium, the unaccompanied choir. The voices enter in a series of layered thirds until all ten parts begin an electrifying ascent through the word 'Domine' to the work's climax which, with the first statement of 'Miserere', suddenly bathes us in a quiet chord of A minor – a moment as devastatingly effective as an orchestra full of banging drums and crashing cymbals. John Nelson directs a hypnotic performance full of impact, his choral forces emotionally committed and technically excellent. The recording itself isn't technically excellent – there are a number of persistent background rattles and bangs; the church acoustic is a little cloudy and there's a haze of surface noise. But in the end, it only serves to reinforce this grainy aural picture of those dark times in Poland's recent history.

François-Joseph Gossec
French 1734-1829

At Paris Gossec was a violinist in La Pouplinière's orchestra, c 1751-1762, as well as a composer. In 1762-70 he directed the Prince of Condé's theatre at Chantilly, from c 1766 also serving the Prince of Conti; meanwhile he composed opéras comiques, notably Les pêcheurs (1766, Paris). He founded the Concert des Amateurs in 1769 and directed it until 1773; the orchestra was one of Europe's finest. In 1773-7 he was a director of the Concert Spirituel. From 1775 he held posts at the Opéra and presented various stage works there; the ballets were the most successful. From 1784 he directed the new Ecole Royale de Chant. At the Revolution he directed the band of the Garde Nationale and wrote numerous Revolutionary works for large forces. After 1799 his output declined, and he concentrated on teaching at the Conservatoire. **GROVE**music

Missa pro defunctis

Salomé Haller, Ingrid Perruche sops **Cyril Auvity** ten **Alain Buet, Benoît Haller** bars **Namur Chamber Choir; La Grande Ecurie et La Chambre du Roy / Jean-Claude Malgoire**
K617 ② K617152-2 (91' · DDD · T/t)　　　Ⓕ

Gossec is a name more often found in history books than on record collectors' shelves. During his long life he contributed to opera reform in Paris before the arrival of Gluck, was one of the directors of the Concert Spirituel, and wrote 50 symphonies. In old age he became the foremost composer of French revolutionary themes, and the first anniversary of the fall of the Bastille was commemorated with a performance of his *Te Deum* that featured over a thousand performers. The *Missa pro defunctis* had more modest origins. It was first performed in 1760, and aroused notable reaction due to the use of trombones, a novelty. The *Dies Irae* – featuring horns, clarinets and drums – became a popular concert item. The composer revised and revived it several times over the next two decades, and parts of the Mass were used for large-scale patriotic commemorations during the revolutionary period.

This recording, made in the chapel at Versailles in 2002, efficiently captures a special event. Occasionally the most intricate details in the accompaniment of soloists seem slapdash, but the rich and imposing grandeur of Le Grande Ecurie et La Chambre du Roy's woodwind and brass remind us that Gossec's fiery dramatic work was a clear influence on Berlioz's colossal choral works. The music sounds astonishingly Mozartian, despite its earlier origin. Jean-Claude Malgoire's strongest asset has always been to give performances with immediacy and character, albeit sometimes sacrificing technical perfection. But when his forces are on form, as they are here, the results are emotionally natural, musically dramatic and neatly direct.

Le Triomphe de la République

Le Triomphe de la République
Salomé Haller sop Laurette **Antonella Balducci** sop Goddess of Liberty **Guillemette Laurens** mez Aide-de-camp **Makato Sakurada** ten Thomas **Claudio Danuser** bar General **Philippe Huttenlocher** bass Old Man **Arnaud Marzorati** bass Mayor **Swiss Radio Choir; Calicantus Choir;**
I Barocchisti / Diego Fasolis
Chandos Chaconne ② CHAN0727 (73' · DDD)   Ⓕ

After the events of 1789, François-Joseph Gossec (1734-1829) became an ardent musical icon of the revolution: *Le Triomphe de la République* (1793) is a single-act lyric *divertissement*, written to glorify the victory of the Republic's army over anti-French troops led by the Duke of Brunswick at the battle of Valmy on September 20, 1792. In his informative essay, Carlo Piccardi explains that 'emerging from the houses of the aristocracy and the theatres into the wide-open public spaces, music was undergoing a radical change that was itself revolutionary'.

Diego Fasolis, the Swiss Radio Choir and the excellent I Barocchisti here provide a good account of Gossec's fervent piece of propaganda. The militant overture has sharp attack, bold brass and booming drums. The choruses 'Dieu du peuple' and 'Malheur au despotisme' bring to mind the kind of French revolutionary songs that

Beethoven reflected in his symphonies. Salomé Haller and Makato Sakurada sing their solos with conviction and pleasing timbres (the latter's 'Les habitans' is an elegantly orchestrated folk dance that seems like a curious compound between Gluck and Offenbach). There is little profound beauty or drama but Gossec's music can be spectacularly vivid: the warlike 'Dans le temps' has cannon-fire drums and military trumpets woven into its fabric. The best moment is the concluding masque of internationally flavoured dances representing the English, Swiss, Poles, Spanish and Africans lining up to acknowledge how marvellous the French are. Playing with different orchestral styles and colours seems to free Gossec from the yoke of politics enough for him to show what he is really capable of.

Louis Moreau Gottschalk
American 1829-1869

At 13 Gottschalk went to Paris for piano and composition lessons, and by 19, through the success of his 'Creole' piano pieces Bamboula, La savane and La bananier (the so-called Louisiana trilogy), his name was a household word throughout Europe. He was hailed as the New World's first authentic musical spokesman and his keyboard virtuosity was compared with Chopin's. After another charming genre piece, Le mancenillier (1851), and tours of Switzerland, France and Spain, 1850-52, he made his New York début. In touring the USA to increase his income, 1853-6, he catered ever more to the public taste for sensational effects (eg in Tournament Galop and The Last Hope). His most fruitful period, 1857-61, was spent in the Caribbean, where in relative seclusion he wrote some of his finest works, including Souvenir de Porto Rico, Ojos criollos (four hands), the Symphony no.1 ('La nuit des tropiques') and the one-act opera Escenas campestres. A second extended tour of the USA, 1862-5, produced little but the well-known Dying Poet and the duet La gallina. From his last years in South America, feverishly devoted to concert-giving, the most notable works are Pasquinade, the Grand scherzo and the Grande tarantelle for piano and orchestra. Although not an 'advanced' composer, Gottschalk was sensitive to local colour and often used quotation as both a musical and psychological device, as well as syncopated rhythms and jagged melodic lines – all traits associated with later music. **GROVE**music

Piano Works

Sospiro, RO214 Op 24. Marguerite, RO158 Op 92. Bataille, RO25 Op 64. Réponds-moi RO225 Op 50 (arr Wachtmann). Solitude, RO239 Op 65. Ballade No 8, RO16 Op 90. Tremolo, RO265 Op 58. Orfa, RO186 Op 71. El cocoyé, RO57 Op 80. Polka de salon, RO207 Op 1. Rayons d'azur, RO220 Op 77. La chasse du jeune Henri, RO54 Op 10
Philip Martin pf
Hyperion CDA67248 (68' · DDD)   Ⓕ

There's very little of Gottschalk's piano music on CD that hasn't been recorded by Philip Martin, the ideal exponent, but here's another whole collection of surprises – again a real enchantment from start to finish. It's interesting to hear Gottschalk's Op 1, the *Polka de salon*, published in Paris, which he wrote in his mid-teens. No particular character yet but genuine charm. More typical of the pianist-composer as pop star is *El cocoyé*, which gives a local carnival tune a flashy setting and brought the house down for Gottschalk's first recital in Havana in 1854. *Solitude* is a pretty nocturne inspired by Lamartine, Chopinesque but simpler. The middle section is a fine example of Martin's totally natural, relaxed melodic playing which perfectly fits the serenity of Gottschalk's lyricism. Martin knows how to pace Gottschalk's Caribbean syncopations, too, and is up to all the pyrotechnics.

O ma charmante, épargnez-moi, RO182. Grande fantaisie triomphale sur l'hymne national brésilien, RO108. Melody in D flat. Bamboula, RO20. The Dying Poet, RO75. Grande étude de concert, RO116, 'Hercule'. The last hope, RO133. Murmures éoliens, RO176. Symphony No 1, RO5, 'La nuit des tropiques' – Andante (arr Napoleão). La chute des feuilles, RO55. Tournament Galop, RO264
Philip Martin pf
Hyperion CDA66915 (73' · DDD)　　　　　　Ⓕ〇

It isn't only the playing here which gives such satisfaction, but the whole package is stylishly produced – Rousseau on the booklet cover and fine notes from Jeremy Nicholas. The piano sound from the fastidious Hyperion team is flawless. Martin, operating in a context where some pianists can hardly play softly at all, has a ravishing *pianissimo*. This makes *O ma charmante* and the perennial – but highly original – *The last hope* simply enchanting. Gottschalk is a real melodist. Martin understands the intimacies of the salon but he also lacks nothing in his transcendental virtuosity. The more flamboyant numbers, such as *Tournament Galop* prove this. About 10 years after Gottschalk's death, his pianist colleague, Artur Napoleão, made a piano arrangement of the first movement of Symphony No 1 (*Night in the tropics*) which Martin includes here. It's slightly drab compared with the orchestral version and soon feels repetitive. But don't let that put you off this outstanding continuation of Martin's Gottschalk series.

Charles François Gounod

French 1818-1893

Gounod studied privately with Reicha and at the Paris Conservatoire with Halévy (counterpoint) and Le Sueur (composition), winning the Prix de Rome in 1839. At Rome (1840-42) he was deeply impressed by the 16th-century polyphonic music (particularly Palestrina's) he heard in the Sistine Chapel and wrote some rather austere masses; for a time a church organist in Paris, he considered joining the priesthood. The climax of his liturgical work came in 1855 with the florid Messe solennelle de Ste Cécile, a favourite setting scarcely superseded by his 12 later ones (1870-92). Meanwhile he wrote a Gluckian, then a Meyerbeerian opera, both failures; the succeeding five, all first performed at the Théâtre-Lyrique, are the works by which he is remembered, namely the small-scale Le médecin malgré lui (1858) and Philémon et Baucis (1860), the triumphant Faust (1859), in which sensitive musical characterisation and a refreshing naturalness set new standards on the French operatic stage, and the major successes Mireille (1864) and Roméo et Juliette (1867).

In 1870 Gounod took refuge in England from the Franco-Prussian War, staying some four years to exploit the English demand for choral music. The first conductor of the Royal Albert Hall Choral Society (1871), he produced dozens of choruses and songs. But he experienced considerable intrigue in his private life, effectively marking the end of his fruitfulness as a composer. His oratorios for Birmingham, La rédemption and Mors et vita, if banal and facilely emotional, were nonetheless successful. Gounod's influence on the next generation of French composers, including Bizet, Fauré and especially Massenet, was enormous. Tchaikovsky and later Poulenc, Auric and Ravel admired his clean workmanship, delicate sentiment, gift for orchestral colour and, in his best songs, unpretentious lyrical charm. GROVEmusic

---

Symphonies

Symphonies No 1 & 2
Orchestra of St John's, Smith Square / John Lubbock
ASV CDDCA981 (65' · DDD)　　　　　　　Ⓕ

Gounod's symphonies aren't brow-furrowing and don't represent any advance in symphonic thought beyond Schumann and Mendelssohn, but they reveal Gounod in the Gallic tradition of elegantly crafted works with a light touch. The melodious, classically built and witty First Symphony, with its delicate second-movement fugue and vivacious finale, isn't to be peremptorily brushed aside. The longer Second Symphony makes an attempt to sound more serious, especially in the first movement and the dramatic *Scherzo* – the cantilena of the *Larghetto* is beautifully shaped here – but high spirits return in the finale. John Lubbock and his St John's orchestra are adept at the crisply neat treatment that this music demands. His wind section is outstanding, but in the finale of No 1 the violins too show real virtuosity. A warm but clean recorded sound adds to our pleasure.

Mélodies

Où voulez-vous aller?ᵃ. Le soirᵃ. Veniseᵉ. Ave Mariaᵇ. Sérénadeᵇ. Chanson de printempsᵃ. Au rossignolᵇ. Ce que je suis sans toiᵃ. Envoi de fleursᵃ. La pâqueretteᵇ. Boléroᵇ. Mignonᵃ. Rêverieᵇ. Ma belle amie est morte[b]. Loin du pays[b]. Clos ta paupière[a]. Prière[b]. L'absent[a]. Le temps des roses[a]. Biondina[c]. The Worker[c]. A lay of the early spring[c]. My true love hath my heart[b]. Oh happy home! Oh blessed flower![c]. The fountain mingles with the river[a]. Maid of Athens[c]. Beware! The Arrow and the Song[a]. Ilala: stances à la mémoire de Livingstone[c]. If thou art sleeping, maiden[c]

[a]**Dame Felicity Lott** sop [b]**Ann Murray** mez
[c]**Anthony Rolfe Johnson** ten **Graham Johnson** pf
Hyperion ② CDA66801/2 (136' · DDD · T/t)   Ⓕ

This well-filled two-CD set is surely the most wide-ranging single issue of Gounod's *mélodies*. The first of the discs confirms the commonly held view of Gounod. Almost without exception the songs are pleasing and sentimental, a sweetly scented posy of hymns to flowers, of rêveries and serenades. The selection includes two settings of poems that Berlioz had used in *Les nuits d'été*, plumbing the depths of the poetry, where Gounod is content to skim across the surface. In chronological order, the songs show how little Gounod's music deepened, but also how evergreen was his inspiration in melody and harmony.

To turn to the second disc is to have all your prejudices overturned. This comprises non-French settings, for which Gounod dons first Italian garb for the song cycle *Biondina*, and then English for a group of ten songs written during his stay in London in the 1870s. The Italian cycle is a delight. It would be impossible to guess the composer, as Gounod exchanges his customary flowing themes and rippling arpeggios for an ardent, Tosti-like vocal line over dry *staccato* chords. Anthony Rolfe Johnson catches its mix of sunny lyricism and Gallic sensitivity to perfection.

All three singers are on their best form, Rolfe Johnson bringing an air of intimate seductiveness to Byron's *Maid of Athens*.

Gounod L'Arithmétique. Au printemps. D'un coeur qui t'aime. O ma belle rebelle. Mignon. Par une belle nuit. Sérénade. La siesta. Fleur des bois. Les vacances. Le banc de pierre. Donne-moi cette fleur Lalo Puisqu'ici bas. Aubade. Dansons! **Saint-Saëns** Clair de lune. Dans les coins bleus. El desdichado. Pastorale. Rêverie. Le rossignol. Le soir descend sur la colline. Viens!
Les Demoiselles de ... (Sophie Marin-Degor sop Claire Brua mez Serge Cyferstein pf)
Alpha Productions ALPHA033 (70' · DDD · T/t)   ⒻⓄⓄ

Every now and then a disc comes along that paralyses the critical faculties: you know you should be trying to be objective, but somehow cold analysis seems almost obscene. So it is here. Though just one word of warning: for some tastes, Sophie Marin-Degor's soprano may seem a little shrill at *forte* in the higher reaches. But then French sopranos have been taxed with this since forever, and we probably have to accept that it goes with the territory.

In all other respects that territory, as explored here, is the land where the oranges bloom; or, if you prefer, 'l'île heureuse'. Both Marin-Degor and Claire Brua come to this repertory from the world of Baroque music, and they bring with them a cleanness of articulation and phrasing that's wholly delightful, sensitively and tactfully supported by Serge Cyferstein. Apart from the sheer sonorous pleasure of the disc, the balance all three artists maintain between expressive moment and formal shaping is almost perfection itself: key words come over with just a little emphasis, but not so much that we're aware of some vocal coach in the background saying 'Bring out the verb here!' Similarly, rhythms are accurately observed, and delicate *rubato* generally reserved for cadences.

This disc is stylish, responsive, impeccable in ensemble and tuning, sensuous, witty, moving… (that's enough epithets): utterly unmissable.

Faust

Faust
Richard Leech ten Faust **Cheryl Studer** sop
Marguerite **José van Dam** bar Méphistophélès
Thomas Hampson bass Valentin **Martine Mahé** mez
Siébel **Nadine Denize** sop Marthe **Marc Barrard** bar
Wagner **French Army Chorus; Toulouse Capitole Choir and Orchestra / Michel Plasson**
EMI ② 556224-2 (204' · DDD · T/t)   ⒻⓄ

Richard Leech as the hero sings his part with the fresh, eager tone, the easy *legato*, the sense of French style that it has so badly been wanting all these years, certainly since Nicolai Gedda essayed the role on the now rather aged Cluytens/EMI sets from 1953 and 1958. Gedda's voice may be more lyrical in the role, but Leech encompasses it with less effort, and creates a real character. It's extremely distinguished singing. Beside him he has an equally impressive loved one in Studer and antagonist van Dam. Studer finds herself another amenable *métier* in Gounod; her Marguerite isn't only sung with innate musicality, firm tone and expressive phrasing but also with a deep understanding of this style of French music in terms of nuance and the lighter touch. The Jewel song is a treasure, and to add to one's satisfaction Studer's French seems faultless.

Van Dam is a resolute, implacable Devil with a firm, even tone to second the insinuating characterisation. His voice may have dried out a little, but he remains a paragon of a stylist in all he attempts. The three French-speaking singers excel in subsidiary roles. Thomas Hampson is in places overextended as Valentin, a role that needs experience and perfect French.

Plasson almost but not quite kills the score with kindness. He so loves the piece that his tempos, especially in the more reflective moments, such as the start of the Garden scene, become much slower than the score predicates and demands. Against that must be set his respect for the minutiae of Gounod's often inspired writing for orchestra and a general warmth that lights the score from within. It was an inspired stroke to invite the French Army Chorus to sing the Soldiers' Chorus, delivered with such verve as to make it seem unhackneyed.

Faust (sung in English)
Paul Charles Clarke *ten* Faust **Mary Plazas** *sop* Marguerite **Alastair Miles** *bass* Méphistophélès **Gary Magee** *bar* Valentin **Diana Montague** *mez* Siébel **Sarah Walker** *mez* Marthe **Matthew Hargreaves** *bass* Wagner **Geoffrey Mitchell Choir; Philharmonia Orchestra / David Parry**
Chandos Opera in English Series ② CHAN3014 (208' · DDD · N/t) ⒻⒹ➔

After listening to this *Faust*, one can feel something very like awe. The structure is massive, the workmanship infinitely thorough, the boldness of stroke (dramatic and musical) almost breathtaking. No doubt the performance contributes to the awe. That's because in many ways it's a very good one, and partly because it underlines seriousness and grandeur. But it appears that David Parry has joined the swelling ranks of the slowcoaches. The Church scene and Faust's solo in the garden, for instance, are probably the slowest on record. Happily, there's nothing boring about it. This recording and its production keep the stage in view, and it's particularly good to have the chorus in such clear focus.

The principals, too, form a strongly gifted team. Paul Charles Clarke, the Faust, is an interesting tenor, thrustful both in tone and manner yet capable of gentleness and delicacy. He never lets us forget that this is *his* story; when he sings everything counts. By comparison, Alastair Miles's Méphistophélès seems a mild-mannered type with reserves of authority and a magnificent voice. The absence of overt devilry may pass as a virtue, but the absence of character is surely taking the disguise too far. Gounod's Mephisto is a joker, a man of the world and an exhibitionist; this one, rarely in the spotlight, loses it entirely when Marthe enters the garden in the person of Sarah Walker.

The Valentin, Gary Magee, has a fine, vibrant baritone and rises well to his high notes and big moments. Diana Montague is an excellent Siébel (and how she rises to hers). The Marguerite, Mary Plazas, is totally likeable, ingenuous but not winsomely so, touchingly sincere in her love and her loss, clean in the scale-work of her Jewel song, a little underpowered in the grand melody of the Church scene, but having a powerful high C in reserve. The English version by Christopher Cowell reads well.

Additional recommendation

Faust Ⓗ
Nash Faust **Licette** Marguerite **Easton** Mephistopheles **BBC Choir; orchestra / Beecham; Raybould**
Dutton Laboratories mono ② 2CDAX2001 (138' · ADD) Ⓜ

Recorded in 1929-30, Beecham's English version enshrines two wonderful performances by Heddle Nash and Miriam Licette. They are object lessons in style and diction. Beecham conducts with the lightest of touches.

Faust
Hadley Faust **Gasdia** Marguerite **Ramey** Méphistophélès **Welsh National Opera Chorus and Orchestra / Carlo Rizzi**
Teldec ② 4509-90872-2 (211' · DDD) Ⓕ
A wonderfully idiomatic and touching recording headed by Cecilia Gasdia and Jerry Hadley on top form. Rizzi can occasionally sound a little lax but this is still a set to consider.

Roméo et Juliette

Roméo et Juliette
Roberto Alagna *ten* Roméo **Angela Gheorghiu** *sop* Juliette **José Van Dam** *bass-bar* Frère Laurent **Simon Keenlyside** *bar* Mercutio **Marie-Ange Todorovitch** *sop* Stéphano **Alain Fondary** *bar* Capulet **Claire Larcher** *mez* Gertrude **Daniel Galvez Vallejo** *ten* Tybalt **Didier Henry** *bar* Paris **Till Fechner** *bar* Grégorio **Guy Flechter** *ten* Benvolio **Alain Vernhes** *bar* Duc **Christophe Fel** *bass* Frère Jean **Toulouse Capitole Chorus and Orchestra / Michel Plasson**
EMI ③ 556123-2 (180' · DDD · T/t) Ⓕ●

Michel Plasson is no stranger to this opera. He's recorded it once before for EMI in 1983, but compared with his earlier self Plasson is more assuredly his own man here, taking a broader view of the turbulent, dramatic opening. Then comes the chorus's introductory narration; the earlier Plasson recording puts great emphasis on story-telling, and isn't nearly as imaginative as the quieter, more intimate style he favours here, the chorus having more light and shade, better rhythmic pointing, more 'face'.

As Juliette Gheorghiu immediately makes her listeners echo the chorus's 'Ah! qu'elle est belle!', for the sound matches the imagined sight. Its beauty is more mature than Catherine Malfitano's (Plasson's earlier Juliette), but as the part develops towards tragedy so her warmer, richer tone is better able to embody the depth of feeling, and she brings a fine conviction to the despairing scene with Friar Laurence and to the scene of the potion.

Alagna's Romeo has youth on his side, and though he doesn't always sound too happy with the B flats of 'Ah, lève-toi, soleil', there are many, many things to enjoy. The opera also abounds in rewarding secondary roles – José Van Dam as the Friar is gravely firm and as fine as ever, while Simon Keenlyside is also excellent.

Gounod

Roméo et Juliette
Roberto Alagna *ten* Roméo **Angela Gheorghiu** *sop* Juliette **Frantisek Zahradnicek** *bass* Frère Laurent

Vratislav Kríz *bar* Mercutio **Ales Hendrych** *bass*
Capulet **Zdenek Harvánek** *bar* Paris **Kühn Mixed
Choir; Czech Philharmonic Chamber Orchestra /
Anton Guadagno** *Film director* **Barbara Willis
Sweete**
ArtHaus Musik 🆅🆅🆅 100 706 (90' · 16:9 · 2.0, 5.1 & DTS
5.1 · 0) Filmed on location in Zvikov Castle, Czech
Republic 2002   Ⓕ

Gounod's opera has been described as a love
duet with interruptions; here the interruptions
are much reduced. Other characters do indeed
appear and sing a phrase or two from time to
time, but Mercutio has no Queen Mab, Capulet
no 'jeunes gens', the Friar none of those solos
one calls less easily to mind, and Stephano the
page is eliminated altogether.

Events are similarly compressed. Important
news items such as Romeo's banishment and
Juliet's impending marriage are relegated.
Adjustments are made to such of the interruptions as remain (for instance, Romeo doesn't
take part in the mourning, 'O jour de deuil', for
Mercutio, but is seen walking away with Juliet
who has watched the unfortunate events from
her balcony and quite understands).

Indeed, there's a great deal of walking in this
production. Juliet walks home after her first love
duet and Romeo sings an abbreviated aria while
walking towards the second. He walks up a staircase to the balcony, in fact a nice long gallery
good for a gentle stroll. 'Ah, ne fuis pas encore' is
also sung on the move and when we meet Romeo
again, at dawn, he's still walking. The motif persists right up to the ambulatory death scene.

On the other hand, the countryside, the river,
the castle and the weather are all so beautiful that
it would be a sin to stay indoors, and as long as one
takes this film for what it is (which isn't Gounod's
five-act opera) there's much pleasure to be gained.
Gheorghiu sings feelingly and with tone to match
the natural beauties of earth and sky around her.
Alagna, but for his habit of 'lifting' to notes, gives
a stylish, sensitive performance and is in good
voice. The love duets can rarely have been better
sung, and that's what it's really all about.

Percy Grainger

American/Australian 1882-1961

*Grainger studied with Knorr and Kwast at the Hoch
Conservatory in Frankfurt (1895-9), where he
became linked with Balfour Gardiner, Quilter and C
Scott, and settled in London in 1901. Another close
friend was Grieg. During the next decade he
appeared widely as a concert pianist; he also took part
in the folksong movement, collecting and arranging
numerous songs. He was an unconventional man, in
his attitudes, his lifestyle and his music where he
experimented with a variety of techniques, including
rhythm freed from regular metre, polytonality,
improvisation and highly unusual instrumentation.
In 1914 he moved to the USA, where he taught in
Chicago and New York; he visited Australia several*

*times, helping the establishment of the Grainger
Museum at Melbourne. His large output, complicated by the fact that he often made several versions of
a piece, includes both original works and folksong
arrangements. He has suffered the fate of being
remembered more for what he called his 'fripperies'
than his larger works.*   **GROVE**music

Orchestral Works

Green Bushes, BFMS12. Lord Maxwell's Goodnight,
BFMS14 (both ed Barry Peter Ould). Hill Song No 2.
The Merry King, BFMS39[a]. Eastern Intermezzo.
Colonial Song, S1. Spoon river, AFMS2. The Power of
Rome and the Christian Heart. The Immovable Do.
County Derry Air, BFMS29. Ye Banks and Braes
O' Bonnie Doon, BFMS31. English Dance No 1
[a]**Paul Janes** *pf* **BBC Philharmonic Orchestra /
Richard Hickox**
Chandos CHAN9839 (70' · DDD)   ⒻⓄⓄ▶

Here's a recipe guaranteed to delight Grainger
acolytes and inquisitive newcomers alike: a liberal sprinkling of old friends, three of the composer's most ambitious creations and no less
than four world premiere recordings. Falling
into the last two categories comes the giddily
inventive *English Dance* No 1. Bearing the
inscription 'For Cyril Scott with long love', this
is the work of which Gabriel Fauré exclaimed:
'It's as if the total population were a-dancing.'
Hickox and company have already set down this
remarkable piece in its final scoring from 1924-
9; the present orchestration dates from 1906-9
and wears an even more exuberantly colourful
demeanour than its successor.

Originally conceived in 1907 for 24 winds (in
which guise it can be heard on Chandos), the
bracing, somewhat Delian *Hill Song* No 2 is
played in its final incarnation from 1948 for
symphony orchestra. That same year, Grainger
accepted a commission for an even more ambitious wind-band creation, *The Power of Rome and
the Christian Heart*, based on ideas from as far
back as 1918 and given here with the optional
string parts. It's an imposing, oddly moreish
affair, whose second half borrows material from
the 1943 orchestral essay *Dreamery* (Chandos) as
well as the first movement ('The Power of Love')
of the marvellous *Danish Folksong Suite*. From a
clutch of indelible favourites, to be singled out
are the well-upholstered 1919 orchestration of
the supremely touching *Colonial Song*, *Green
Bushes* and that memorably tangy 1920 harmonisation of the *Irish Tune from County Derry*.

Hickox secures a set of performances that are
simply past praise in their combination of stylish
swagger and heartwarming commitment to the
cause. Wonderful Chandos sound, too, irrepressibly vivid. Terrific stuff!

Youthful Suite. Molly on the Shore, BFMS1. Irish Tune
from County Derry, BFMS15. Shepherd's Hey,
BFMS16. Country Gardens. Early one Morning, BFMS
unnum. Handel in the Strand, RMTB2. Mock Morris,

RMTB1. Dreamery (ed Ould). The Warriors
(ed Servadei)
BBC Philharmonic Orchestra / Richard Hickox
Chandos Grainger Edition CHAN9584 (75' · DDD)

Featuring some ripe, beautifully clean-cut sonics, this collection is a great success for all
involved. As the opening, chest-swelling
'Northern March' of the *Youthful Suite* immediately shows, Hickox draws playing of infectious swagger from the ever-excellent BBC
Philharmonic (marvellous brass sounds especially). The suite boasts some striking invention, not least in the central 'Nordic Dirge' (a
hauntingly eloquent processional, incorporating plenty of 'tuneful percussion') and a winsome, at times almost Ivesian 'English Waltz'.
There follow seven of Grainger's most popular
miniatures in the orchestrations Gershwin
made for Leopold Stokowski. Hickox gives us
Grainger's original thoughts and a delectable
sequence they comprise, full of truly kaleidoscopic textural and harmonic variety. Hickox's
Country Gardens is perhaps marginally lacking
in twinkling good humour and entrancing
lightness of touch, but his infectious energy
and evident affection more than compensate.
Dreamery, described by Grainger as 'Slow
Tween-Play' (an epithet which, annotator
Barry Peter Ould suggests, 'could be construed
as his particular term for an intermezzo'),
appears here in the extended orchestral version.

For *The Warriors*, Hickox uses a new critical
edition prepared by the Australian Grainger
authority, Alessandro Servadei. Grainger's
orchestral palette has never sounded more gloriously extravagant. Then again, this impression is
just as much a tribute to Hickox's performance,
which is breathtaking in its virtuosic brilliance
and stunning co-ordination.

Music for Wind Band

The Power of Rome and the Christian Heart.
Children's March: Over the Hills and Far Away,
RMTB4. Bell Piece[a]. Blithe Bells. The Immovable Do.
Hill Songs – No 1; No 2. County Derry Air, BFMS29.
Marching Song of Democracy
[a]**James Gilchrist** ten **Royal Northern College of
Music Wind Orchestra / Timothy Reynish, Clark
Rundell**
Chandos Grainger Edition CHAN9630 (65' · DDD)

Rundell's compelling realisation of the extraordinary *Hill Song* No 1 – regarded by Grainger
as one of his finest achievements and performed here in its original guise for two piccolos, six oboes, six cors anglais, six bassoons
and double bassoon – was actually made by
BBC Manchester back in 1992; the remaining
items date from 1997 and benefit from the
splendid sound and balance achieved by
Chandos.

Another of Grainger's most striking wind-band
compositions opens the disc, namely the 12-
minute *The Power of Rome and the Christian Heart*.
Both the *Children's March* and *Bell Piece* feature
some unexpected vocal contributions. In the latter – a charming 'ramble' on John Dowland's
Now, O now I needs must part – Grainger incorporates a bell part specially written for his wife, Ella.
The delightfully piquant arrangements of *Blithe
Bells* and *The Immovable Do* date from March 1931
and November/December 1939 respectively.
These fine players equally revel in the 'scrunchy'
harmonies of the eventful version of *Irish Tune
from County Derry* (made in 1920 for military
band and pipe-organ). That just leaves the boisterous *Marching Song of Democracy*, which Rundell again directs as to the manner born.

Piano Works

Piano Music for four hands, Volume 3
Rondo. Crew of the Long Dragon. Fantasy on
George Gershwin's 'Porgy and Bess'. Ye Banks and
Braes, BFMS32. Tiger-Tiger, KS4/JBC9. Walking
Tune, RMTB3. **C Scott** Three Symphonic Dances.
Delius A Dance Rhapsody No 1, RTVI/18.
Grieg Knut Lurasens Halling II. **Addinsell** Festival.
Le Jeune La Bel'aronde. **Gershwin** Girl Crazy –
Embraceable you (all trans Grainger)
Penelope Thwaites, John Lavender pfs
Pearl SHECD9631 (78' · DDD)   Ⓕ

Volume 3 of Grainger's music for four hands
(Volume 2 is no longer available) contains
short original compositions and a number of
his transcriptions. These latter are fascinating
in their admirable combination of scrupulous
fidelity and creative rethinking for an entirely
different medium. You wouldn't necessarily
think that a transcription, even for two pianos,
of Delius's First *Dance Rhapsody* could possibly
work with any real degree of success. However,
the reality is that it works so well that some may
even prefer Grainger's version to the original.
In the *Porgy and Bess Fantasy* he treats the tunes
with loving respect, but as a pianist he can't
help seeing different ways of presenting them:
the very big gestures in 'My man's gone now'; a
searching little prelude to 'It ain't necessarily
so' implying all sorts of interesting things that
Grainger could have done with that slithery
little tune if he weren't obliged to play it
straight – which he then does, and with
sparkling enjoyment.

Grainger Jutish Medley, DFMS8. Colonial Song, S1.
Molly on the Shore, BFMS1. Harvest Hymn. Spoon
River, AFMS1. Country Gardens, BFMS22. Walking
Tune, RMTB3. Mock Morris, RMTB1. Ramble on
Themes from Richard Strauss's 'Der Rosenkavalier'.
Shepherd's Hey, BFMS4. Irish Tune from County
Derry, BFMS6. Handel in the Strand, RMTB2. The
Hunter in his career, OEPM4. Scotch Strathspey and
Reel, BFMS37. In a Nutshell Suite – No 4, The Gum-
suckers March. The Merry King, BFMS38. In Dahomey

Stanford (arr Grainger) Four Irish Dances, Op 89 –
No 1, A March-Jig; No 4, A Reel
Marc-André Hamelin pf
Hyperion CDA66884 (73' · DDD)   Ⓕ

This is perhaps one of the most riveting and satisfying anthologies of Grainger's music. Hamelin's
superb control and artistry just about sweep the
board if you're looking for a disc that not only
brings you all the old favourites but also explores
some of the less familiar music, such as Grainger's
arrangements of two of Stanford's *Irish Dances*,
the Cakewalk Smasher, *In Dahomey* or some of
the rather less familiar folk-music settings such as
The Merry King – the latter a delightful discovery.
The deceptive ease with which Hamelin presents
these pieces is quite breathtaking. The *Irish Tune
from County Derry*, for instance, contains some
exacting problems which call on the pianist to
play *ppp* in the outer fingers and *mf* with the middle in order to bring out the melody which
Grainger places almost entirely within the middle
register of the piano, and yet Hamelin makes it
sound incredibly natural.

Piano Transcriptions

Grainger Beautiful fresh flower. Lullaby. Paraphrase
on the Waltz of the Flowers from Tchaikovsky's Flower
Waltz. Free Settings of Favourite Melodies – Brahms:
Wiegenlied, Op 49 No 4; Handel: Hornpipe from the
Water Music; Fauré: Nell, Op 18 No 1; Fauré: Après
un Rêve, Op 7 No 1; R Strauss: Rosenkavalier Ramble;
Dowland: Now, O Now, I Needs Must Part. Gershwin
Transcriptions – The Man I Love; Love Walked In Scott
Handelian Rhapsody Stanford Irish Dances, Op 89
Byrd The Carman's Whistle **Delius** Air and Dance,
RTVI/21
Piers Lane pf
Hyperion CDA67279 (75' · DDD)   Ⓕ ⦿⦿

These short pieces range from simplicity to
elaboration, from innocence to experience;
most of them are homages to many of
Grainger's friends and honour his trenchant
belief in the sort of folk-melody that crosses all
barriers. Wherever you turn you'll hear music
'like a breath of spring air' (to quote Barry
Peter Ould's excellent note) and, more paradoxically, transcriptions that show Grainger's
originality.

Cyril Scott's *Handelian Rhapsody*, receiving
its first recording, may suggest Scott and
Grainger more than Handel but it's an intriguing oddity and one which rises to an impressive
grandeur. Stanford's Leprechaun is gentle and
confiding rather than mischievous and the
'Ramble on Love' from *Der Rosenkavalier* is a
sophisticated 'dish-up' of introspection and
open-hearted virtuosity. All this music makes a
wide variety of subtle and fierce demands, but
Piers Lane, weaving his expertise with the
lightest of touches, meets them with warmth
and brio. Heartache, heart-ease or a tantalising
mix of both all come within his style and everything is played with unfaltering command.

Grainger's 'woggles' (his idiosyncratic term for
tremolandi) can rarely have sounded more convincing and the Tchaikovsky Waltz is taken by
storm in a magnificent display of red-blooded
virtuosity.

The recording and presentation are immaculate. This is a dazzling, affectionate tribute to
the composer and pianist who once said: 'To
know a world of beauty and not to be able to
spread the knowledge of it is agonising.'

Songs

David of the White Rock[a]. Died for Love, BFMS10[a].
The Sprig of Thyme, BFMS24[a]. Willow, Willow,
OEPM1[a]. Near Woodstock Town[a]. Early one
morning[a]. In Bristol Town (arr Gibbs)[d]. Songs of the
North[a] – No 2, This is no my plaid; No 3, Turn ye to
me; No 4, Skye Boat Song; No 5, Weaving Song. The
Bridegroom Grat[a]. The Land O' the Leal[a] (both arr
Ould). Proud Vessel[a] (ed Thwaites). Under a bridge[ac].
Hubby and Wifey, DFMS5[ac]. The Lonely Desert-Man
sees the Tents of the Happy Tribes, RMTB9[abc].
Colonial Song[ab]. The Only Son, KS21[ab]. The Love
Song of Har Dyal, KS11[ac]. A Song of Autumn[a]. Five
Settings of Ella Grainger[a]. O Glorious, Golden Era[a].
Little Ole with his Umbrella[a]. Variations on Handel's
'The Harmonious Blacksmith'[a] (ed Ould). Harvest
Hymn[ae]. After-word[a]
Della Jones mez [a]**Penelope Thwaites** pf with
[b]**Mark Padmore** ten [c]**Stephen Varcoe** bar
[d]**George Black** gtr [e]**John Lavender** pf
Chandos Grainger Edition CHAN9730 (74' · DDD · T)
                                    Ⓕ⦿❚➤

Again Grainger amazes, amuses, arouses,
intrigues. These 'Songs for mezzo' originate in
Britain (with an excellent sequence of Scottish
songs), Jutland and Australia. Some are folksongs collected in the early years of the century; two have words by Kipling, five by Ella,
Grainger's wife, and some have no words at all.
The latter are fortifying antidotes to those text-
merchants who think that song is essentially
'about' the communication of words, whereas
everybody knows that you sing (la-la, dee-dee,
as in these of Grainger) because a tune has
taken your fancy and singing it makes you feel
better.

It's really Della Jones's record, or hers and that
of the admirable Penelope Thwaites. But the
menfolk appear occasionally and always to
effect. Mark Padmore is a resourceful tenor with
hints here that he has in reserve a vibrant, rather
Italianate body of tone. Jones herself is a natural for Grainger: she has the spirit to match, and,
like him, a certain ambiguity in her forthrightness, so that at times we're not quite sure what's
serious and what's a bit of fun. The *Colonial Song*
('Sentimental No 1') is unashamedly nostalgic,
but with an element of send-up too: in the piano
solos especially a joyful passage of inspired
improvisation that's both a joke and 'for real'.
Also for real is the prime quality of this disc, with
15 tracks 'premiere recordings' and 14 'premiere
recordings in this version'.

Enrique Granados   Spanish 1867-1916

Granados studied in Barcelona with Pedrell and in Paris (1887-9), then returned to Barcelona to work as a teacher, pianist and composer. His greatest success came with the piano suite Goyescas (1911), a sequence of highly virtuoso studies after paintings by Goya he expanded them to form an opera of the same title, produced in New York in 1916. His other works include songs, orchestral pieces and more piano music.
GROVEmusic

Danzas españolas

Granados 12 Danzas españolas, Op 37. 7 Valses poéticos. Allegro di concierto. El pelele. Danza lenta. Goyescas **Montsalvatge** Divagación. Sonatine for Yvette
Alicia de Larrocha pf
RCA Victor Red Seal ② 74321 84610-2 (147' · DDD)
Ⓑ🌓

Alicia de Larrocha, that incomparable interpreter of the Spanish repertoire, is here revisiting many of her favourite musical haunts. And if some of her former edge and fire, her tonal and stylistic luxuriance are now replaced by more 'contained' and reflective qualities, her warmth and affection remain undimmed. Her *rubato*, while less lavishly deployed than before, is potent and alluring, and each and every dance is played with rare naturalness and authority. But if a touch of sobriety occasionally blunts the fullest impact of these fascinating, most aristocratic idealisations of local Spanish life and colour, the actual playing is never less than masterly. The *Valses poéticos* are offered as an engaging encore. The recordings have much less range and reverberance than her previous ones on Decca; however, all lovers of this repertoire will want to add this to their collection.

Goyescas

Granados Goyescas **Albéniz** Iberia. Navarra
Alicia de Larrocha pf
Double Decca ② 448 191-2DF2 (141' · ADD)
Recorded 1972-6
Ⓜ🌑🌓➪

Alicia de Larrocha has been playing these works, the greatest in the repertoire of Spanish piano music, all her life. Complete technical assurance in these extremely demanding works has now become taken for granted, and Larrocha isn't unique in mastering their terrors; but though there have been other distinguished interpreters, her readings have consistently remained a touchstone. She employs plenty of subtle *rubato* but possesses the ability to make it sound as natural as breathing. In the true sense of that much misused word, this is classical playing, free from any superimposed striving for effect but responding fully to the music's sense of colour; and even in the densest of textures she's able to control con-

flicting tonal levels. *Goyescas*, which can tempt the unwary into exaggerated 'expressiveness', brings forth a wealth of poetic nuance, without losing shape. The recorded quality throughout always was good and here emerges as fresh as ever. Anyone who doesn't already possess these recordings should not hesitate to acquire them now – all the more since the two discs together cost the same as one full-price one.

Alexandr Grechaninov
Russian/American 1864-1956

Grechaninov studied at the Moscow Conservatory (1881-90) and with Rimsky-Korsakov at the St Petersburg Conservatory (1890-93) and worked as a piano teacher and folksong arranger; in 1910 he received a pension for his liturgical music. But that ceased with the Revolution, and in 1925 he settled in Paris, moving to the USA in 1929. His large output (nearly 200 opus numbers) includes operas, five symphonies, masses, songs and piano music.
GROVEmusic

All-Night Vigil

All-Night Vigil, Op 59. Nunc dimittis, Op 34 No 1.   Ⓟ
The Seven Days of the Passion, Op 58 – No 3, In Thy Kingdom[a]; No 6, Now the Powers of Heaven
[a]**James Bowman** *counterten* **Holst Singers / Stephen Layton**
Hyperion CDA67080 (63' · DDD · T/t)   Ⓕ🌑🌑

The *All-Night Vigil* is an outstanding achievement. Like Rachmaninov's famous setting, it's a selection of texts from the services of Vespers and Matins celebrated as a Vigil, though in current parish practice this lasts rather less than an entire night. Grechaninov sets fewer texts: the duration of the work is just over 47 minutes. Here we find the sustained chordal writing and slow-moving melodies oscillating around a few notes familiar from Rachmaninov, but Grechaninov has his own distinctive harmonic vocabulary, and his writing is less text-driven. Chant is an inspiration, but is also used in a different way from Rachmaninov: none is quoted in its entirety, the composer preferring instead to use fragments of various chants which are combined and juxtaposed with considerable freedom. He's a master of texture: listen to the astonishing darkness of sound produced by the scoring for lower voices in *Ot yunosti moyeya*, for example. Overall there's a feeling of luminosity in the writing, however, as well as an undeniable grandeur.

To round off the disc we're given three other liturgical works, including a dramatic setting of the Beatitudes (sung at the Divine Liturgy) with James Bowman as soloist. The Holst Singers under Stephen Layton are superb: they have a complete mastery of the style and the fine, rich choral timbre which the music demands. Very highly recommended.

Edvard Grieg   Norwegian 1843-1907

Grieg studied with EF Wenzel at the Leipzig Conservatory (1858-62), where he became intimately familiar with early Romantic music (especially Schumann's), gaining further experience in Copenhagen and encouragement from Niels Gade. Not until 1864-5 and his meeting with the Norwegian nationalist Rikard Nordraak did his stylistic breakthrough occur, notably in the folk-inspired Humoresker for piano Op 6. Apart from promoting Norwegian music through concerts of his own works, he obtained pupils, became conductor of the Harmoniske Selskab and helped found the Christiania Musikforening (1871), meanwhile composing his Piano Concerto (1868) and the important piano arrangements of 25 of Lindeman's folksongs (Op 17, 1869). An operatic collaboration with Bjornson came to nothing, but his incidental music to Ibsen's Peer Gynt (1875), the best known of his large compositions, produced some of his finest work. Despite chronic ill-health he continued to tour as a conductor and pianist and to execute commissions from his base at Troldhaugen (from 1885); he received numerous international honours. Among his later works, The Mountain Thrall Op 32 for baritone, two horns and strings, the String Quartet in G minor Op 27, the popular neo-Baroque Holberg Suite (1884) and the Haugtussa song cycle Op 67 (1895) are the most distinguished.

Grieg was first and foremost a lyrical composer; his Op 33 Vinje settings, for example, encompass a wide range of emotional expression and atmospheric colour, and the ten opus numbers of Lyric Pieces for piano hold a wealth of characteristic mood-sketches. But he also was a pioneer, in the impressionistic uses of harmony and piano sonority in his late songs and in the dissonance treatment in the Slåtter Op 72, peasant fiddle-tunes arranged for piano. GROVEmusic

---

Piano Concerto in A minor, Op 16

Grieg Piano Concerto **Schumann** Piano Concerto
Leif Ove Andsnes pf
Berlin Philharmonic Orchestra / Mariss Jansons
EMI 503419-2 (59' · DDD)   Ⓕ❍❍❍▶

It was the Grieg Concerto that first made the name of Leif Ove Andsnes on disc in 1990. The interpretation remains broadly the same, except that speeds are now rather brisker. However many times he's performed the Grieg, Andsnes retains a freshness and expressiveness that always sounds spontaneous. That inspirational quality is more markedly perceptible with the new version's faster tempos, but the expressive flights remain just as broad. In that contrast, he's firmly supported by Jansons and the Berlin Philharmonic, with playing not just refined but dramatic too in fiercely exciting *tutti*s. Schumann's cello melodies are gloriously warm, with textures in both works admirably clear, and Andsnes fully responds to Schumann's *espressivo* and *ritardando* requests.

Though both Stephen Kovacevich and Murray Perahia are equally spontaneous, they tend not to be quite so free in their expressive flights; EMI's finely balanced digital sound and the playing of the Berlin Philharmonic are also in this version's favour. Andsnes also offers slightly faster basic speeds than his rivals; particularly enjoyable is the free-flowing tempo for the central *Andantino grazioso* of the Schumann, which you'd never mistake for a simple *Andante*.

Grieg Piano Concerto, Op 16 **Saint-Saëns** Piano Concerto No 2, Op 22 **Schumann** Piano Concerto, Op 54
Orchestra of Opera North / Howard Shelley pf
Chandos CHAN10509 (79' · DDD)   Ⓕ❍❍▶

What a good idea to add to that favourite among LP couplings Saint-Saëns's most Bachian concerto, No 2. And the pleasure doesn't stop there. Howard Shelley is one of those musicians who quietly goes about his pianistic (and now conductorly) business without grabbing the limelight except for the odd award, but who is consistently impressive, unfailingly musical and only goes into the studio when he has something to say about a work. That is certainly the case here.

It's a particular delight to hear a reading odf the Schumann as fleet and joyous as this one. These are intimate performances, an effect no doubt enhanced by the fact that Shelley directs from the piano. Intimate but also sharply characterised. And when virtuosity is required, Shelley provides it in spades. Take the finale of the Schumann: textures are wonderfully transparent, the dotted rhythms are perky and precise, and there are plenty of striking colours from the orchestra (which throughout the disc proves itself a fine ensemble, with some particularly outstanding wind-players).

Shelley is just as persuasive in the Grieg, coaxing from the orchestra a real sense of narrative, some lovely oboe-playing and allowing the big tunes due space but never over-indulging them. The concerto's irresistible yearning quality is well caught too, particularly in the central movement, where he is almost a match for Lipatti. Again, tempi are generally fleet, and Shelley pays attention both to the marcato marking of the finale and its folk tinges without overstatement. These are certainly performances to put alongside the classics.

Technically, the Saint-Saëns is an ideal vehicle for Shelley's fingery kind of pianism and he is exceptional in the *Allegro scherzando*, the movement that out-Mendelssohns Mendelssohn. Again, the orchestra is utterly focused. The recorded quality here, as elsewhere, is exemplary.

Grieg Piano Concerto[b] **Debussy** Préludes – Book 1[a]
Arturo Benedetti Michelangeli pf
[b]**New Philharmonia Orchestra /**
Rafael Frühbeck de Burgos
BBC Legends/IMG Artists [b]mono/[a]stereo BBCL4043-2 (69' · DDD/ADD) Recorded live [b]1965, [a]1982
Ⓜ❍❍❍

GRIEG PIANO CONCERTO – IN BRIEF

Leif Ove Andsnes; Berlin PO / Mariss Jansons
EMI 557562 2 (59' · DDD) (F)OOOO⟶
A commanding, intrepidly imaginative
account from one of the supreme pianists of
our times, its pleasures enhanced by Jansons's
immaculate, powerfully responsive backing
with the Berliners.

Dinu Lipatti; Philharmonia Orchestra / (H)
Alceo Galliera
EMI 767163-2 (71' · ADD) (M)
Very special playing from Dinu Lipatti; the
poetry and rapt beauty of this famous 1947
performance linger long in the memory.
Currently only available in a five-disc Lipatti
retrospective - pure gold all of it!

Murray Perahia; Bavarian RSO / Sir Colin Davis
Sony Classical 82796 92736-2 (60' · DDD) (F)OO⟶
A performance to delight all admirers of this
aristocrat of the keyboard. Sir Colin Davis
and the Bavarian RSO also distinguish themselves, as do the Sony engineers.

Benno Moiseiwitsch; Philharmonia Orchestra / (H)
Otto Ackermann
Testament SBT1187 (70' · ADD) (F)O
Moiseiwitsch's vintage 1953 recording was
one of the mainstays of HMV's early LP cata-
logue.

Leif Ove Andsnes; Bergen PO / Dmitri
Kitaenko
Virgin The Classics 561996-2 (78' · DDD) (M)
Andsnes's earlier recording continues to
holds its own at mid-price. A softer-spoken
affair than his EMI remake, with poetry and
delicacy in perfect equilibrium.

Stephen Kovacevich; BBC SO / Sir Colin Davis
Philips 464 702-2PM (61' · ADD) (M)OO⟶
Kovacevich's indelibly fresh performance has
enchanted for over three decades now.
Felicities abound, not least the agile bravura
of the first-movement cadenza and captivating skip of the finale.

Arturo Benedetti Michelangeli; New Phil-
harmonia Orch / Rafael Frühbeck de Burgos
BBC Legends BBCL4043-2 (69' · ADD) (M)OOO
(G) Simply breathtaking artistry from the
great Italian pianist. This June 1965
performance generates a joyous, edge-of-seat
ardour that grips from the first bar to the
last.

Solomon; Philharmonia / Menges (H)
Testament SBT1231 (75' · ADD) (F)OO
Recorded late in his career, this performance
still captures Solomon's power and incandescence. This is a wonderful memento of a
great pianist.

(G) Somehow you feel it must be possible
to deliver the hackneyed opening flourishes of the Grieg Concerto with real
abandon and impetuosity, to get the orchestra
respond to them with genuine ardour, then for
the soloist to combine flow, virtuoso dash, fantasy and noble eloquence and to crown the
structural highpoints in a way that lifts you out
of your seat. Yet until you hear a performance
like this one you may never quite believe it can
be done. A sense of joyous rhapsody buoys up
Michelangeli's playing from first note to last, yet
everything is founded on a bedrock of high
intelligence, taste and natural authority. Witness too the fabulous tone-colours he draws
from the instrument. His slow movement is by
turns balmy and ecstatic, and the finale has terrific drive. And the virtuosity…! If your hair isn't
standing on end in the finale's coda you need an
urgent medical check-up. Forget the boxy
recording and the hissy background. This is a
performance that entirely merits the hysterical
cheers that greet it.

Seventeen years on, Michelangeli's Debussy
also provokes rapturous applause, but in this
instance it was probably partly a tribute to his by
this time legendary status – he was 63 and rapidly
becoming as famous for his cancellations as for his
performances. There are marvels of pianism here,
but an air of calculation hangs over much of the
playing. Those who have Michelangeli's 1978
DG studio version will find little to prefer here,
apart from the slightly warmer acoustic.

Grieg Piano Concerto **Schumann** Piano Concerto
Murray Perahia pf **Bavarian Radio Symphony**
Orchestra / Sir Colin Davis
Sony Classical 82796 92736-2 (60' · DDD)
Recorded live 1987, 1988 (F)OO⟶

Despite the hazards, Murray Perahia delights in
the inspirational heat-of-the-moment of a live
recording. Though there are no claps, coughs or
shuffles betraying the presence of an audience,
we're told both concertos were recorded live at
Munich's Philharmonie Gasteig. Of the two
works, the Grieg is better served by the immediacy and warmth of Perahia's response, whether
through rhythmic bite in livelier dance tempo or
total surrender to lyrical nostalgia elsewhere.
Never is there the slightest sacrifice of artistic
sensitivity or keyboard finesse.

His Schumann is no less ardent. In the spirited finale, as throughout the Grieg, any collector would be as happy with this performance as
that of Kovacevich for Philips. But in the first
two movements, it's Kovacevich who finds a
simpler, more confiding note – as well as more
artfully weaving the piano into the comparatively light texture as if it were part of the
orchestra instead of a spot-lit outsider. Davis
goes all the way in both works to uphold Perahia in his open-hearted point-making, and the
Bavarian Radio Symphony Orchestra gives him
all he asks. The sound is more clear-cut than
the old Philips.

Grieg Piano Concerto[a] **Schumann** Piano Concerto ⊞
in A minor, Op 54[a]. Romance in F sharp, Op 28 No 2.
Vogel als Prophet, Op 82 No 7 **Palmgren** West-
Finnish Dance, Op 31 No 5. Refrain de berceau
Benno Moiseiwitsch pf [a]**Philharmonia Orchestra /**
Otto Ackermann
Testament mono SBT1187 (70' · ADD) Recorded
1941, [a]1953 　　　　　　　　　　　　　　　　Ⓕ🔿

Few pianists have played the silken aristocrat
more engagingly than Benno Moiseiwitsch. His
outward impassivity hid an imaginative delicacy
and stylish nonchalance often mistaken for diffidence. Playful, individual, debonair, occasionally mischievous (why not expand on the last
pages of the Grieg Concerto's cadenza if you
feel like it?), he invariably had one more surprise
up his sleeve than you expected.

The Grieg Concerto sounds newly minted,
with markings such as *tranquillo e cantabile*
observed with special affection. The catalogue
may be filled with more openly confrontational
performances but Moiseiwitsch, who took music
more by stealth than storm, elegantly eclipses
the readings of so many more assertive keyboard
tigers. For encores there are classic performances of Palmgren and Schumann.

Both the Grieg and Schumann Concertos were
central to Moiseiwitsch's immense repertoire but,
as with so many other Russian pianists, Schumann
remained his greatest love. His opening to the
Schumann Concerto is under-stated (like a great
actor throwing away his lines), but his projection
of the principal theme has a matchless tonal
bloom and subtlety. How many other pianists
have eased their way through the central A flat
dreams with such unaffected charm? In the opening of the Intermezzo he's delightfully *grazioso*,
emphasising the *staccatos* as much as the manifold
feelings and colours, and in the finale his play of
light and shade are, again, inimitable Moiseiwitsch. Ackermann's partnership is arguably more
able than inspiring, but Testament's transfers of
recordings dating from 1941 to 1953 are superb.

Peer Gynt Suites

Grieg Peer Gynt – Suites Nos 1 & 2, Opp 46 & 55.
Holberg Suite, Op 40 **Sibelius** Legends, Op 22 –
No 2, The Swan of Tuonela. Kuolema – Valse triste,
Op 44. Finlandia, Op 26
Berlin Philharmonic Orchestra /
Herbert von Karajan
DG Karajan Gold 439 010-2GHS (78' · DDD) Ⓜ🔿🔿🔿➤

Very impressive indeed. Somehow one feels that
one could stretch out and touch the players, so
vivid is the sound here. In the *Peer Gynt* movements, there's much greater range and separation. *Peer Gynt* is most beautifully done. At times
you might think the wind could have been a
shade more distant, particularly in the 'By the
seashore' movement but there's no want of
atmosphere here – quite the contrary! Not to
put too fine a point on it, this is a marvellous
recording. In the *Holberg Suite*, the sound has

marvellous clarity and definition as well as
exemplary range. For some tastes it may be a
little too sophisticated but one's admiration for
it remains undimmed. The playing throughout
is beautifully cultured and there's wonderful
lightness and delicacy.

The present issue is Karajan's third account of
'The Swan of Tuonela' and it's regrettable that
he never committed to disc the four *Legends* in
their entirety. It's as powerful and atmospheric
an account as ever recorded, and the remaining
two pieces, 'Valse triste' and *Finlandia*, reinforce
the feeling that this partnership has never been
equalled. The stirring account of *Finlandia* is
incredibly wide-ranging – the orchestral playing
is really in a class of its own.

Peer Gynt – Suites: Nos 1 & 2, Opp 46 & 55.
In Autumn, Op 11. Symphonic Dances, Op 64
City of Birmingham Symphony Orchestra /
Sakari Oramo
Erato 8573-82917-2 (74' · DDD) 　　　　Ⓕ🔿🔿➤

As soon as the strings respond to the flute near
the beginning of *Peer Gynt*'s 'Morning' – longingly leaning on an expressive *ritardando* – you
sense this is a quality production. Done to death
it may be, but Grieg's vernal score still holds the
potential to seduce, enthral and entertain. Here,
charm and drama form a seductive alliance.
Sakari Oramo has an architect's sense of proportion and an athlete's sense of pacing. He also
knows how to shape and colour musical textures.
Ase's death ends with a full-bodied *pianissimo*
while the bassoon counter-subject that follows
Peer through 'The Hall of the Mountain King'
can rarely have sounded more mischievous.
Rather than push an unworkable *accellerando*,
Oramo moves with stealth, tightening the rhythm
as he goes, letting in an element of swagger
before speeding for the final chase. 'Ingrid's
Lament' enjoys powerfully drawn basses and an
unusually dramatic climax and 'Peer Gynt's Journey Home' allows ample space for the elements
to rage. Note how, at around 1'14", woodwinds
goad lower strings into action and the ensuing
tumult gradually gains momentum. As for 'Anitra' and the 'Arabian Dance', both benefit from
the CBSO's vivid but unforced characterisations.

The Concert Overture *In Autumn* takes its
point of departure from a song called *Autumn
Storms*. And if there's one aspect of Oramo's
performance that pips Beecham's stereo version
to the post, it's a feeling of what one might call
'weatheredness'. True, the superb recording
helps, but so do Oramo's rock-steady control of
rhythm and sense of atmosphere.

The *Symphonic Dances* are by turns lyrical or
exuberant, the last of them – the partially pensive A minor – being faster than Järvi's thinner-
sounding Gothenburg version by a good two
minutes. The Birmingham orchestra are consistently responsive to Oramo's very specific
demands. Credible rivals are headed by piquant
Sir Thomas in *Peer Gynt* and *In Autumn*, and by
Järvi in the *Symphonic Dances*. Oramo's Grieg

matches both, being less fussy than keen-eared and with a sense of play that does credit both to Ibsen's dramatic prompt and the folk-music roots of the concert works.

String Quartets

Grieg String Quartets – No 1 in G minor, Op 27; No 2 in F, CW146 **Schumann** String Quartet No 1 in A minor, Op 41 No 1
Petersen Quartet (Conrad Muck, Gernot Süssmuth *vns* Friedemann Weigle *va* Hans-Jakob Eschenburg *vc*)
Capriccio 10 476 (75' · DDD)   Ⓕ

Grieg String Quartet No 1 in G minor, Op 27
Mendelssohn String Quartet No 2 in A minor, Op 13
Shanghai Quartet (WeiGang Li, HongGang Li *vns* Zheng Wang *va* James Wilson *vc*)
Delos DE3153 (64' · DDD)   ⒻⓄ

Since Grieg owed much to Schumann, coupling their quartets seems a good idea. These G minor and A minor Quartets are written when the composers were in their thirties, although Grieg was a few years older. Yet it's his work that sounds more youthfully passionate, while the Schumann is a rather self-conscious homage to his friend Mendelssohn and classical models. The Petersens invest the Grieg G minor Quartet with *gravitas* and are skilful in linking the disparate sections of its structure. Their recording has a natural balance and an impressively wide dynamic rang; it also copes well with Grieg's forceful, semi-orchestral string writing. The whole performance has vigour and tenderness in good proportion, and a truly Scandinavian feeling. The unfinished F major Quartet is another sensitive performance and the work sounds no more incomplete than Schubert's *Unfinished* Symphony.

The Schumann is no less enjoyable; the artists are fully inside his idiom and make a consistently beautiful and meaningful sound. The Shanghai Quartet's brightly lit account of the Mendelssohn suggests a rich store of interpretative potential. Theirs is a sizzling, multi-coloured performance. The Grieg coupling is, if anything, even finer, with an *Allegro molto* first movement that truly is *ed agitato*, a warming *Romanze* and a superbly characterised *Intermezzo*. It's richly recorded.

Violin Sonatas

No 1 in F, Op 8; **No 2** in G, Op 13; **No 3** in C minor, Op 45

Violin Sonatas Nos 1-3
Henning Kraggerud *vn* **Helge Kjekshus** *pf*
Naxos 8 553904 (67' · DDD)   Ⓢ☻

This disc gives us consistently enjoyable performances. The two young Norwegians play with idiomatic style, and give the impression of expressing every aspect of the music. Their

eagerness at the start of Op 8's first *Allegro* sets the tone; the *doloroso* opening of Op 13, the delicacy and serenity of the E-major section of that sonata's middle movement, and the exciting 'Hall of the Mountain King' atmosphere they generate in the finale of Op 45 – these are just a few of the places where the pair convince us they've found exactly the right sound and manner of expression. Kraggerud's account of the 'big tune' in the last movement of Op 45, respecting all Grieg's marks of expression and phrasing, has real nobility. Highly recommendable.

Piano Works

Volume 1: Piano Sonata in E minor, Op 7. Funeral March for Rikard Nordraak, CW117. Melodies of Norway – The sirens' enticement. Stimmungen, Op 73. Transcriptions of Original Songs I, Op 41 – No 3, I love thee. Four Humoresques, Op 6. Four Piano Pieces, Op 1
Einar Steen-Nøkleberg *pf*
Naxos 8 550881 (72' · DDD)   Ⓢ☻

Volume 2: Two Improvisations on Norwegian Folksongs, Op 29. Melodies of Norway – A Ballad to Saint Olaf. 25 Norwegian Folksongs and Dances, Op 17. Transcriptions of Original Songs II, Op 52 – No 2, The first meeting. 19 Norwegian Folksongs, Op 66
Einar Steen-Nøkleberg *pf*
Naxos 8 550882 (70' · DDD)   Ⓢ☻

Volume 3: Four Album Leaves, Op 28. Six Poetic Tone-pictures, Op 3. Melodies of Norway – Iceland. Three Pictures from life in the country, Op 19. Three Pieces from 'Sigurd Jorsalfar', Op 56 – Prelude. Ballade in G minor, Op 24, 'in the form of variations on a Norwegian melody'
Einar Steen-Nøkleberg *pf*
Naxos 8 550883 (64' · DDD)   Ⓢ☻

Volume 4: Holberg Suite, Op 40. Melodies of Norway – I went to bed so late. Six Norwegian Mountain Melodies, CW134. Peer Gynt Suite No 1, Op 46 – Morning. 17 Norwegian Peasant Dances, Op 72
Einar Steen-Nøkleberg *pf*
Naxos 8 550884 (71' · DDD)   Ⓢ☻

These are the first four volumes of a complete Grieg cycle which stretches to no fewer than 14 discs. Since they are all at super-budget price they make a very competitive alternative to other complete or near-complete surveys. Einar Steen-Nøkleberg came into prominence during the 1970s and won numerous Norwegian and other prizes. He was professor of the piano at the Hanover Musikhochschule for a number of years and is the author of a monograph on Grieg's piano music and its interpretation.

8 550881: The first disc juxtaposes early pieces, the Sonata, Op 7, the Op 6 *Humoresques* and the *Funeral March for Rikard Nordraak*, all written in the mid-1890s with his very last piano work, *Stimmungen* (or 'Moods'), Op 73. He plays these bold and original pieces with great flair and understanding. Whatever its limitations there's much greater range in Grieg's piano music than is commonly realised and Steen-Nøkleberg is attuned to the whole spectrum it covers, whether in the Bartókian 'Mountaineer's Song' from the Op 73 to the charm and innocence of the *Allegretto con grazia*, the third of the *Humoresques*, Op 6. **8 550882**: The *19 Norwegian Folksongs* (1896) are remarkable pieces as Grieg himself knew. He wrote to the Dutch composer, Julius Röntgen, of having 'put some hair-raising chromatic chords on paper. The excuse is that they originated not on the piano but in my mind.' Readers will recognise No 14 as the source of the theme for Delius's *On hearing the first cuckoo in spring*. Steen-Nøkleberg plays them with great tonal finesse and consummate artistry.

8 550883: The most substantial work on this disc is the *Ballade* which Grieg wrote on his parents' death. This recording can hold its own with the best in this healthy area of the catalogue – even if there are moments when Steen-Nøkleberg seems too discursive. Yet what an imaginative colour he produces in the *Adagio* variation when the music suddenly melts *pianissimo*.

8 550884: The *Norwegian Peasant Dances* are amazing pieces for their period, and though their audacity and dissonance were later overtaken by Bartók, they still retain their capacity to surprise. The playing conveys the extraordinary character and originality of these pieces as do few others. The smaller pieces contained on this disc – as well as on its companions – are full of rewards.

Lyric Pieces, Book 1, Op 12 – No 1, Arietta; No 2, Waltz; No 5, Folksong; No 6, Norwegian; Book 2, Op 38 – No 6, Elegy; No 7, Waltz; No 8, Canon; Book 4 Op 47 – No 2, Album Leaf; No 3, Melody; No 4, Norwegian Dance; Book 5, Op 54 – No 3, March of the Trolls; No 4, Nocturne; Book 6, Op 57 – No 2, Gade; No 3, Illusion; No 6, Homesickness; Book 7, Op 62 – No 1, Sylph; No 4, Brooklet; No 5, Phantom; No 6, Homeward; Book 8, Op 65 – No 6, Wedding Day at Troldhaugen; Book 9, Op 68 – No 3, At your Feet; No 4, Evening in the Mountains; No 5, Cradle Song; Book 10, Op 71 – No 6, Gone; No 7, Remembrances
Leif Ove Andsnes pf
EMI 557296-2 (68' · DDD) Played on Grieg's piano at the Grieg Troldhaugen Museum, Bergen Ⓕ**OOO**🅑➔

Once again on home ground, Andsnes reminds you of his capacity to go directly to the heart of the matter. Taking you on a journey of increasing subtlety and introspection, he makes you aware that so much of this music is for those long winter nights. At the same time the music is so richly varied: 'Melody's insistent dactylic rhythm creates a strange unsettling poetic ambience, while the central oasis of calm in 'Wedding Day at Troldhaugen' would surely melt a heart of stone.

All Andsnes's performances have that deceptive simplicity which is his touchstone. His playing is always sensitive, never sentimental and with a bracing and essential 'touch of the codfish' (Grieg) when required. And while one would never want to be without Gilels' rapt DG performances (see below), praise could hardly be too high for a pianist who so enviably captures the poignant nature of a composer who Tchaikovsky once claimed had 'a glance like a charming and candid child'. Grieg's piano, with its distinctive timbre, provides an added touch of nostalgia.

Lyric Pieces – Arietta, Op 12 No 1. Berceuse, Op 38 No 1. Butterfly, Op 43 No 1. Solitary Traveller, Op 43 No 2. Album Leaf, Op 47 No 2. Melody, Op 47 No 3. Norwegian Dance, 'Halling', Op 47 No 4. Nocturne, Op 54 No 4. Scherzo, Op 54 No 5. Homesickness, Op 57 No 6. Brooklet, Op 62 No 4. Homeward, Op 62 No 6. In ballad vein, Op 65 No 5. Grandmother's Minuet, Op 68 No 2. At your feet, Op 68 No 3. Cradle Song, Op 68 No 5. Once upon a time, Op 71 No 1. Puck, Op 71 No 3. Gone, Op 71 No 6. Remembrances, Op 71 No 7
Emil Gilels pf
DG The Originals 449 721-2GOR (56' · ADD) Recorded 1974 Ⓜ**OOO**🅑➔

 Here, surely, is a classic recording, one of calibre and status for all time. Rarely can a great artist have declared his love with such touching candour. By his own admission Gilels discovered in Grieg's *Lyric Pieces* a 'whole world of intimate feeling' and at the sessions where these were recorded fought tirelessly to capture their intricate mix of innocence and experience. The results are of an unblemished purity, grace and contained eloquence. He brings the same insight and concentration to these apparent trifles as he did to towering masterpieces of the classic repertoire. The programme proceeds chronologically and one can appreciate the gradual but marked development in Grieg's harmonic and expressive language – from the folk song inspired early works to the more progressive and adventurous later ones. Gilels's fingerwork is exquisite and the sense of total involvement with the music almost religious in feeling. Never can Debussy's sniping estimate of Grieg', 'a pink bonbon filled with snow' (or DG's dreary accompanying notes), have seemed wider of the mark. The recordings remain as impeccable as the playing. This is a disc for everyone's desert island.

Lyric Pieces – selection. Holberg Suite, Op 40. Poetic Tone Pictures, Op 3
Katya Apekisheva pf
Quartz QTZ2061 (79' · DDD) Ⓕ**OOO**🅑➔

Cards on the table: Katya Apekisheva is a young pianist who has already achieved artistic greatness. Not even Emil Gilels, in his legendary DG Grieg recital, played more magically or, astonishingly, with greater finesse. How thrilled Irina Zaritskaya,

Apekisheva's teacher, would have been if she had lived to hear the fruit of her work with this profoundly gifted artist. A sonority of beguiling warmth and refinement and a rare poetic empathy quickly make you listen mesmerised as Apekisheva captures the very essence of Grieg's genius.

Here, in her mixed programme, she tells you with an often painfully beautiful and unforced eloquence of how Grieg's romantic temperament was easily clouded by depression and unease, of the way, for example in 'Homesickness' and 'Vanished Days', a heartbreaking state of mind is only temporarily modified by memories of happier times. The sense of the *Lyric Pieces* as Grieg's confessional diary is everywhere in Apekisheva's recital. In the Aria from the *Holberg Suite* she is deeply sensitive to the way Grieg's love and respect for the 18th century is coloured by a near-Franckian chromaticism and dark introspection. These works and everything else on this beautifully recorded album suggest an artistic fervour and commitment given to very few in any generation.

Peer Gynt

Peer Gynt – The Bridal March passes by; Prelude; 　
In the Hall of the Mountain King; Solveig's Song;
Prelude; Arab Dance; Anitra's Dance; Prelude;
Solveig's Cradle Song. Symphonic Dance, Op 64 –
Allegretto grazioso. In Autumn, Op 11. Old
Norwegian Romance with Variations, Op 51
Ilse Hollweg sop **Beecham Choral Society; Royal Philharmonic Orchestra / Sir Thomas Beecham**
EMI Great Recordings of the Century 566914-2
(77' · ADD) Recorded 1957　　　　　Ⓜ❶❷❸▷

Grieg's incidental music was an integral part of Ibsen's *Peer Gynt* and from this score Grieg later extracted the two familiar suites. This recording of excerpts from *Peer Gynt* goes back to 1957 but still sounds well and is most stylishly played. Included is the best known ('Anitra's Dance' is a delicate gem here) together with 'Solveig's Song' and 'Solveig's Cradle Song'. Beecham uses Ilse Hollweg to advantage, her voice suggesting the innocence of the virtuous peasant heroine. There's also an effective use of the choral voices which are almost inevitably omitted in ordinary performances of the two well-known suites: the male chorus of trolls in the 'Hall of the Mountain King' are thrilling, and the women in the 'Arab Dance' are charming. The other two pieces are well worth having too; *Symphonic Dances* is a later, freshly pastoral work, while the overture *In Autumn* is an orchestral second version of an early piece for piano duet. This reissue is further enhanced by the first release in stereo of the *Old Norwegian Romance*.

Songs

Haugtussa, Op 67. Two brown eyes, Op 5 No 1. I love but thee, Op 5 No 3. A swan, Op 25 No 2. With a

waterlily, Op 25 No 4. Hope, Op 26 No 1. Spring, Op 33 No 2. Beside the stream, Op 33 No 5. From Monte Pincio, Op 39 No 1. Six Songs, Op 48. Spring showers, Op 49 No 6. While I wait, Op 60 No 3. Farmyard Song, Op 61 No 3
Anne Sofie von Otter *mez* **Bengt Forsberg** pf
DG 477 6326 (68' · DDD · T/t)　　　Ⓜ❶❷❸▷

Ⓖ Von Otter is at the peak of her powers here, glorying in this repertoire. In the *Haugtussa* cycle she projects her imagination of the visionary herd-girl with absolute conviction. She's no less successful in the German settings that follow. The sad depths of *One day, my thought* from Six Songs, Op 48, the hopelessness of Goethe's *The time of roses* (Op 48 No 5), a setting of great beauty, are encompassed with unfettered ease, but so are the lighter pleasures of *Lauf der Welt*. Even the familiar *A dream* (Op 48 No 6) emerges as new in her daringly big-boned reading. Her readings are immeasurably enhanced throughout by the imaginative playing of Bengt Forsberg. They breathe fresh life into *A swan* and in the almost as familiar *With a waterlily*, another superb Ibsen setting, the questing spirit expressed in the music is marvellously captured by the performers. This should be regarded as a 'must' for any collector.

Six Ibsen Songs, Op 25. Six Songs, Op 48.
Melodies of the Heart, Op 5. Haugtussa, Op 67.
The Princess, EG133
Katarina Karnéus *mez* **Julius Drake** pf
Hyperion CDA67670 (68' · DDD)　　　Ⓕ❶❷

Anne Sofie von Otter's Grieg recital for DG (see above) did much to encourage singers outside Scandinavia to bring back to the concert platform – and the public again to listen to – songs which their great-grandparents knew well but their parents had almost forgotten. Now another front-ranking Swedish mezzo-soprano has recorded core components of the Grieg song repertoire. Like her compatriot, Katarina Karnéus includes the Op 67 'Mountain Maid' cycle, the Ibsen settings, the six German lyrics of Op 48 and the early Hans Christian Andersen 'Melodies of the Heart', adding, suitably, the less well known 'The Princess' to words by Bjørnstjerne Bjørnson.

Compare Karnéus, von Otter and Kirsten Flagstad (one of at least three recordings) in *Haugtussa*. Karnéus and Julius Drake are all over the imagery, scenery and sexuality of Garborg's verse novel in thrilling and well worked detail. Flagstad may appear at first hearing to be limiting herself to heroic declamation and her pianist (regular collaborator Edwin McArthur) just mapping out the written notes, but her sheer joy in singing her own language, and the subtlety of her pointing of the text (a half-smile, a raised eyebrow) and cunning use of her large voice make their own points. Von Otter has something of both sides – a weightier tone and more reserve than Karnéus but a much wider colour range than Flagstad chooses to deploy – and Bengt Forsberg is a magician in these accompaniments.

Elsewhere the Karnéus performances are good and lively in the Scandinavian lyrics (a passionate 'Jeg elsker dig', a good range of moods in the Ibsen settings), more formal in the German settings. All Saints Church in Finchley, north London, sounds especially resonant here, not everywhere an advantage in such text-oriented settings. Lots to enjoy and celebrate then, but don't ignore the competition.

Twelve Songs, Op 33. Five Songs, Op 26. For LM Lindemans's Silver Wedding. My little bird. She walked to the church. The Odalisque. To Christian Tønsberg. The Blueberry. The girl Gjenta. On Hamar's Ruins. The White and Red Roses.
Monica Groop *mez* **Roger Vignoles** *pf*
BIS BIS-CD1257 (68' · DDD · T/t)   Ⓕ

The important item here is the complete set of the Op 33 songs. Only the second song of the Op 33 set, *Våren* ('Last Spring'), has had many takers – Schwarzkopf and Tauber among them. The rest are lucky to have a single recording in the catalogue, if that.

Grieg had been recovering from the deaths of his parents and was going through a bad patch in his marriage when he set 12 poems by AO Vinje for his Op 33 set, hence their preoccupation with darker themes of mortality and mankind. Groop does well by them, making full use of her deep mezzo colouring. Her singing is beautiful, sympathetic, typically bringing a sense of calm and understanding to 'The Spring' ('Våren') and stretching to the weightier seriousness needed for a song such as 'First Things' ('Det fyrste').

Groop and accompanist Roger Vignoles are well paired, as both like to let the music flow naturally. This puts them in the opposite corner to Anne Sofie von Otter and Bengt Forsberg, whose award-winning Grieg recital (DG) comes with their personalities stamped on every bar. Where they're in competition (only three songs here), Von Otter and Forsberg are instantly memorable, achieving lift-off with a tremendous sense of elation in 'Hope' ('Et Håb') from the Op 26 set, albeit at the expense of some pulling-around of the tempo from the pianist. There are people who are resistant to the Swedish couple's bold way with Grieg and for them the more traditional approach of Groop and Vignoles will be preferable. The recording quality is first rate.

and songs (Tone-images, 1912-14; Four Impressions, 1912-16). He became closely concerned with oriental culture (Five Poems of Ancient China and Japan, 1916-17; ballet Sho-jo, 1917), while his last works, including the Piano Sonata (1918), show a free handling of dissonance paralleling Scriabin.
                                          GROVEmusic

Orchestral Works

Bacchanale. Clouds. Poem for Flute and Orchestra. The Pleasure-Dome of Kubla Khan. The White Peacock. Three Poems of Fiona McLeod. Three Tone-Pictures
Barbara Quintiliani *sop* **Carol Wincenc** *fl*
Buffalo Philharmonic Orchestra / JoAnn Falletta
Naxos 8 559164 (56' · DDD)   ⓈⓄ➐

Griffes represents the high point of American post-Romanticism. From his European training he inherited both the German and French traditions of Strauss and Debussy, fused them into something rich and strange, and in his later years became involved with Scriabin and oriental music. Much of his music has been regularly available on record, but this all-Griffes CD now makes the best showing for his hyper-sensitive responses to both literature and landscape.

Many of the works here are piano pieces fastidiously scored, with significant additions. *The White Peacock*, just possibly a cousin of Stravinsky's firebird, is the first of the *Roman Sketches* for piano, all prefaced with stanzas by Fiona McLeod (a *nom-de-plume* for William Sharp): the impressionistic *Clouds* is the last of these. The orchestral opulence of the *Three Poems of Fiona McLeod*, steeped in baleful Celtic twilights, makes the piano version seem anaemic; they're compellingly sung here by Barbara Quintiliani.

In the *Three Tone-Pictures* every picturesque detail of harmonically qualified melody is subtly imagined. The same applies to the *Poem* for flute and orchestra, where the continuity has the instinctive flow of Delius, beautifully realised by Carol Wincenc. *The Pleasure-Dome of Kubla Khan*, the most extended work in this anthology, is an ecstatic response to Coleridge's opium-saturated masterpiece.

Conductor JoAnn Falletta is completely sympathetic throughout, and there are neatly delivered solos from many of the Buffalo players. This is a revelatory Griffes release, decently recorded with a wide dynamic range: strongly recommended.

Charles Griffes   American 1884-1920

Griffes studied with Mary Selena Broughton in Elmira and with Humperdinck in Berlin, where he lived, 1903-7. He returned to teach in Tarrytown, NY. Up to c1911 his music was within the German Romantic tradition but he then developed a more Debussian style in piano pieces (The Pleasure-Dome of Kubla Khan, 1912; Roman Sketches, 1915-16)

Sofia Gubaidulina   Russian b1931

Gubaidulina studied with Peyko and Shebalin at the Moscow Conservatory (1954-62). During the 1960s and 70s she wrote primarily chamber music, which is characterised by a radical expansion of the range of musical sound and by use of serial techniques, as in Noch'v Memfise ('Night in Memphis', 1968). She then explored the potential of orchestral and vocal genres, paying particular attention to the role of rhythm and time; her experiments in the role of rests culminated in the solo for conductor in the symphony Stimmen Verstummen *(1986). In* Alleluja *(1990) she gives coloured light a rhythmic function and this determines the structure of the work. Her music has a strong religious basis.* GROVEmusic

Orchestral Works

Seven Last Words[a]. Flute Concerto, 'The Deceitful Face of Hope and of Despair'[b]
[b]**Sharon Bezaly** fl [a]**Torleif Thedéen** vc [a]**Mie Miki** accor **Gothenburg Symphony Orchestra / Mario Venzago**
BIS ⊛ BIS-SACD1449 (61' · DDD/DSD) Ⓕ◉Ⓓ▸

'Every interval,' Gubaidulina explains, 'creates a summation tone and a difference tone: an interval in the lowest register creates a difference tone which we recognise not as a tone but a pulsation.' At higher registers we 'hear the pulsation of the difference tone simultaneously with the original interval'. Gubaidulina sees this transition from pulse to tone and back (and, eventually, the loss of even the pulse) as a metaphor for hope and despair. *The Deceitful Face* Concerto exploits and explores this acoustical phenomenon and the emotional process of struggling against despair. As the piece unfolds, quiet passages inhabited by the flute soloist and other individual instruments are brutally invaded by outbursts from larger groupings. The flute part, impressively realised by Sharon Bezaly, finally gives way to the terrifying pulsing of the bass drum from which the piece first welled up.

Seven Last Words (1982) is a kind of companion piece to *In Croce* (1979), in which cello and bajan (Russian accordion) moved towards an explosive meeting from their extreme registers. Again, the crossing of lines is among the structural devices used to symbolise crucifixion. As is her custom, Gubaidulina asks her soloists to venture beyond the standard techniques of their instruments but, as ever, she does so in the service of expressiveness, not novelty. Her thorough command of instrumental colour (and, indeed, temperature) is put to brilliant use in evoking the contradictory emotions associated with Good Friday, from the pain and despair of the participants to the implicit hope of believers.

Gubaidulina Violin Concerto, 'In tempus praesens'[b]
Bach Violin Concertos[a] – BWV1041; BWV1042
Anne-Sophie Mutter vn [a]**Trondheim Soloists;**
[b]**London Symphony Orchestra / Valery Gergiev**
DG 477 7450GH (62' · DDD) Ⓕ◉Ⓓ▸

Anne-Sophie Mutter lost no time in recording the violin concerto written for her by Sofia Gubaidulina in 2006-7. In a single movement running for about 32 minutes, it shows the composer's concern to make a direct and immediate impact, avoiding complicated materials but using very expansive forms. It's possible to

sense the kind of allusions to Mahlerian archetypes that are no less prominent in Shostakovich or Schnittke. Yet Gubaidulina has her own very personal musical identity, and the concerto's strategies for playing off heights against depths, lament against affirmation, are very powerfully realised. The risks of rambling, improvisatory musing are triumphantly avoided, and the work's final stages appear to bring starkly opposed images of extinction and rebirth into a strongly ambivalent conclusion that both affirms and questions resolution.

This darkly inviting music is splendidly performed. You'd expect the Mutter/Gergiev combination to be combustible, and there is certainly no reticence or half-measures in the way the music's expressive core, its play with visions of hell and heaven, is exposed. Gestures towards traditional consonant harmony stand out strangely, and dancelike patterns are clearly not going to survive for very long in a context where brooding and turbulence are the principal qualities. The resplendent recording celebrates the score's rich colouring while never allowing the solo line, played with all this performer's natural theatricality and poise, to lose its prominence. Maybe, at one particularly stark climax, the hammered rhythmic repetitions in the orchestra seem over-emphatic. But urgency rather than reticence drives Gubaidulina's thought, and this performance never lets you forget it.

It would have been good to hear these performers in Gubaidulina's other major work for violin and orchestra, *Offertorium*. Instead, the pair of Bach concertos speak of a distant musical world in which stability and spontaneity achieved an extraordinary conjunction. The performances are neat, tidy, dispatched with elegance and vigour. Yet they reinforce the gulf that musically separates then from now, and all-Gubaidulina discs are not as common as they should be.

De profundis[a]. Seven Words[b]. Ten Preludes[c]
[ab]**Elsbeth Moser** bayan [c]**Boris Pergamenschikov** vc
[b]**Munich Chamber Orchestra / Christoph Poppen**
ECM New Series 461 897-2 (72' · DDD) ⒻⒹ▸

Recordings of Sofia Gubaidulina's music differ markedly as to presentation. Elsbeth Moser and Boris Pergamenschikov interpret *Seven Last Words*, meditations rather than commentaries on the biblical texts, with chamber-like inwardness. Their fervent confrontation in movement IV has a transparency of texture, incisive strings kept to the rear, which offsets the gestural immediacy of the experience. The final movement isn't so much valedictory as implosive, draining away in a haze of sound and emotion. The premiere recording by Friedrich Lips and Vladimir Tonkha, briefly available on Melodiya, has an impact like no other, but this new recording has a distinct and searching identity of its own. It's enhanced by the companion pieces. The *Ten Preludes* have become staples of the modern repertoire, harnessing technique to a range of moods which work perfectly as a sequence. *De profundis* is a classic of its medium, and while Gerd Draugsvoll on BIS draws visceral emotion from this quirky mix of dissonance and incantation, Moser's lucid unfolding probes deeper. Sound, here and in the *Preludes*, is a model of solo balance.

Chamber Works

In croce[a]. 10 Preludes. Quaternion[b]
Alexander Ivashkin, [b]Natalia Pavlutskaya, [b]Rachel Johnston, [b]Miranda Wilson vcs [a]**Malcolm Hicks** org
Chandos CHAN9958 (56' · DDD)   Ⓕ

A quaternion may be a mathematical operation, but there's nothing calculated or contrived about *Quaternion* for four cellos (1996), which here receives its first recording. At its best – as it certainly is here – Gubaidulina's music manages to combine a fiercely improvisatory freedom with a satisfying sense of balance and coherence. On one level *Quaternion* concerns the contrast between the mundane and the transcendent. Yet although the music contains strikingly immediate evocations of both the earthy and the uncanny, it never suggests the withdrawn serenity of a spirituality that regards the real world as 'lost'. Ivashkin and his colleagues achieve marvels of co-ordination, as well as an astonishingly wide range of colour, qualities enhanced by a truthful and well-balanced recording.

Two earlier works complete the programme. The *Ten Preludes* for solo cello (1974) encapsulate energy and expressiveness to highly charged poetic effect. *In Croce* for cello and organ (1979) transforms what could have been a simplistic exercise in the crossing over of two very different sound sources into a grippingly unpredictable drama of convergence and divergence. Both pieces have been recorded before, and you might welcome the chance to acquire the bargain-price version of *In Croce* in its alternative arrangement for cello and accordion (Naxos). But Alexander Ivashkin is a fine player, unsurpassed in Gubaidulina's music.

Francisco Guerrero   Spanish 1528-99

Guerrero was a pupil of Morales. He also taught himself the vihuela, harp, cornett and organ. He was maestro de capilla of Jaén Cathedral (1546-9) and then vice-maestro (1551) and maestro (1574-99) of Seville Cathedral. He visited Rome (1581-2), Venice and the Holy Land (1588-9). The most important 16th-century Spanish composer of sacred music after Victoria, he published 18 masses and c150 motets; because of their singable, diatonic lines, they remained in use in Spanish and Spanish-American cathedrals for more than two centuries after his death. He also published secular songs; many other works survive in anthologies and MSS.

Missa de la Batalla Escoutez

Missa de la Batalla Escoutez[ab]. Pange lingua[a].   Ⓟ
In exitu Israel[ab]. Duo Seraphim[a]. Regina coeli[b]
Magnificat[a]. Conditor alme siderum[a]
[a]**Westminster Cathedral Choir; [b]His Majestys Sagbutts and Cornetts / James O'Donnell**
Helios CDH55340 (72' · DDD · T/t)   ⒷⓄⓄ

Despite his suggestive name, Guerrero's parody of Janequin's *La Bataille de Marignan* isn't the work of a fighting man: fanfares and alarums are definitely off the agenda while he develops, in an often rather sober manner, the smooth counterpoint of his model. Only in the 'Osanna' does Guerrero let rip, a moment seized on with gusto by the choir and His Majestys Sagbutts and Cornetts. Guerrero spent his career at Seville Cathedral, where the chapter was one of the first in Spain to agree to the establishment of a permanent, salaried wind band to participate in processions and at other points in divine worship. It appears to have been one of Guerrero's duties to sort out what and when, and even how (scoring and ornamentation were part of his brief) the minstrels played.

The instruments (shawms, cornetts, sackbuts, dulcian and organ) subtly double the voices, adding depth to the sound, and strengthening major cadence points. Particularly striking is the earthy tone of the *bajón* (dulcian) reinforcing the bass line in proto-continuo fashion. In fact, it's in the other items on this CD that the combination of voices and instruments really comes into its own. The setting of the psalm *In exitu Israel* experiments with Guerrero's forces (including cornetts and recorders), resulting in an opulence of sound more readily associated with Venetian music of the period. But this isn't just an exercise in applied musicology. These are well-paced, intelligent performances that get inside the skin of Guerrero's marvellous music. Don't be surprised to find yourself humming the Spanish chant for the hymn *Conditor alme siderum* after this compelling rendition. The musicianship is superb, the technical element entirely satisfactory and satisfying.

Guerrero Missa de la Batalla Escoutez. Lauda mater ecclesia. Tota pulchra es, Maria. Hymn: Vexilla Regis. Song of Songs: Ego flos campi. Pange lingua
Janequin La guerre (La bataille de Marignan)
The Sixteen / Harry Christophers
Coro COR16067 (69' · DDD · T/t)   ⒻⓄⒺ

Westminster Cathedral Choir recorded Guerrero's 'Battle' Mass (based on Janequin's famous descriptive chanson) for Hyperion (see above), drawing on instrumental support from His Majestys Sagbutts and Cornetts. To this historically documented approach to performance The Sixteen now provide an *a cappella* alternative. But a more profound difference between the two interpretations is summed up in the question: to what extent ought the performance of a parody Mass (that is, a Mass based on earlier work) adopt not just the letter, but also the spirit of its model? The winds in the earlier recording helped James O'Donnell to evoke the martial atmosphere of the original Janequin song. The Sixteen take an altogether more placid approach throughout, with only the *Credo* rather more vigorous than the other movements. Whatever one's view of the matter, they defend their own with conviction: the *Agnus Dei* contains moments of great beauty, for which Guerrero too deserves some of the credit. It's a fine piece, and to have two contrasted interpretations of similar quality can only deepen one's appreciation of it.

The rest of the programme is on a similar level: particularly worth mentioning are Guerrero's two settings from the Song of Songs, *Tota pulchra es* and *Ego flos campi*. Helpfully, the model for Guerrero's Mass opens the programme. Some listeners may find it incongruous for a heartfelt Mass to have been based on such worldly sentiments; stranger still for Spanish composers to borrow from a work written to celebrate a victory against their own side! But it is good to hear The Sixteen tackle something secular and less than reverent for a change. The singers certainly seem to enjoy it.

Barry Guy
British b1947

A double-bass player as well as a composer, Guy's musical interests cross many genres. He is founder and artistic director of the London Jazz Comppsers Orchestra for whom he has written a number of works. Indeed nearly all his music derives from a personal relationship with the musicians he composes for – which also enables the improvisatory nature of music to connect at a remarkable keen level.

Folio
Muriel Cantoreggi, Maya Homburger vns
Barry Guy db **Munich Chamber Orchestra /**
Christoph Poppen
ECM New Series 476 3053 (58' · DDD)   ⓕⒹ▸

Barry Guy's *Folio* is a multi-movement cycle for string orchestra, inspired by a stage work by Nikolai Evreinov, *The Theatre of the Soul*, written in 1912. It is, in part, a reflection on the parallels between the historical situation of that time and place, and our own. Perhaps this dialogue of time and place explains the use of a Baroque and a modern violin among the work's soloists. The cycle brings together free-standing movements of varying length for string orchestra (which can be performed independently of the cycle), connected by a number of 'improvised commentaries' by a combination of the soloists and Barry Guy himself on the double bass. The bringing together of both improvised and through-composed music is another of the cycle's themes, and in several movements the two may occur simultaneously, with the soloist

being given a choice of materials from which to draw upon.

The longest work is the 20-minute 'Postlude – Ortiz I – Postlude'. It alternates between quasi-spectral harmonic fields and chaotic episodes, all of which exploit the string orchestra's potential for timbral cohesion and sheer power. Guy's experience as a string-player comes into its own here, and his own improvisations have real flair and a slightly understated virtuosity: one would have liked to hear more of them. The shorter movements are less contrasted within themselves, more concerned with a single idea. The intended overall structure is not easy to grasp at first hearing but the performance matches the composer's liking for striking, bold gestures and highly imaged detail. The work's 'quirkiness quotient' is consonant with a certain ECM house-style, with which its devotees will be instantly at home.

Pavel Haas
Czech 1899-1944

Haas studied composition at the Brno Conservatory in Janáček's masterclass (1920–22). He worked first in his father's business, then from 1935 as a private teacher of music theory, and finally taught music at the Jewish secondary in Brno. Haas took the style of Janáček as his starting point, and came closer to Janáček's compositional method than any of his other pupils. However, he developed this in his own way and soon achieved a mature individuality in the Wind Quintet Op 10, the Piano Suite Op 13 and the opera Sarlatán ('The Charlatan'). During the German Occupation he suffered persecution on account of his Jewish origin, performances of his compositions were banned, and neither he nor his wife were allowed to work. He was imprisoned in Terezín concentration camp (1941–4), where he continued to compose, including two of his best-known works, the Study for Strings (1943) and the Four Songs on Chinese Poetry (1944), which are linked to the Oboe Suite (1939) and the unfinished Symphony (1940–41) in expressing through music the struggle against Nazism. Haas died in a gas chamber at Auschwitz.

String quartets

Haas String Quartets – No 1, Op 3; No 3, Op 15
Janáček String Quartet No 1, 'The Kreutzer Sonata'.
Pavel Haas Quartet (Veronika Jarúšková, Marie
Fuxová vns Pavel Nikl va Peter Jarúšek vc)
Supraphon SU3922-2 (55' · DDD)   ⓕ**OO**

This disc's *Gramophone* Award-winning predecessor coupled the second string quartets of Haas and Janáček (see below), superbly played and including optional percussion in Haas's finale. Haas's Second (subtitled *From the Monkey Mountains*) is an amazing piece, but the Third is surely his masterpiece. It is both more concise and more tautly argued than the Second, less a journey into fantastical realms than an urgent, astringent drama, rhythmically driven and intensely heart-felt. And no wonder, given that the Quartet was composed in 1938 when Haas and his family were already marked for tragedy as part of a racially mixed community where an active Nazi faction was ready to pounce. Haas was destined for Aus-chwitz (where he was killed in 1944) and although it would be fanciful to read prophecy into the pages of this marvellous and varied work, the candour and emotional unrest that it expresses have inevitable associations. The longest move-ment is the last, a theme with variations which closes with a brief but pungent fugue and at times seems prophetic of Prokofiev's folk-derived Second Quartet of 1941.

The First Quartet (1921) plays for a continu-ous, action-packed 14 minutes and so impressed Haas's mentor Janáček that he had it performed. Although less striking than the Third, the First inhabits a similar climate, where temperature and colour shift with a degree of rapidity that suggests Janáček's influence, though Haas's musical language has a softer edge. In the hands of the Pavel Haas Quartet Janáček's own power-fully emotive First Quartet positively glows; one cannot but help ponder what Haas himself might have achieved had he too lived to com-pose at the ripe old age of 69! The Haas Quartet negotiate Janáček's fervid narrative without over-playing the drama, and they obviously rel-ish its novel and occasionally abrasive sound world. This is a superb release that deserves not merely to bask in the reflected glory of its prede-cessor, but to share in it. The sound is first-rate.

P **Haas** String Quartet No 2, 'From the Monkey Mountains', Op 7[a]
Janáček String Quartet No 2, 'Intimate Letters'.
[a]**Colin Currie** perc **Pavel Haas Quartet** (Veronika Jerůšková, Kateřina Gemrotová vns Pavel Nikl va Peter Jarůšek vc)
Supraphon SU3877-2 (58 minutes : DDD) Ⓕ❍❍❍

The catalogue is not short of recom-mendable versions of Janáček's *Intimate Letters* Quartet. But there are any num-ber of ways of bringing its hyper-passionate declarations off the page, and this young Czech quartet have plenty of ideas of their own about that. Once or twice that leads them into an over-calculated delivery. But try the third movement at 2'58" where, having fined the texture down to a whisper, Janáček gives the first violin an elec-trifying outburst: it's hard to imagine if that contrast has been made more emotionally real on record.

But then there is the 1925 Second Quartet by the composer whose name the players have adopted. This is the kind of piece that may make you wonder why you haven't heard it before. After a first movement that tellingly redeploys a number of patent Janáčekisms, Haas slips into the grotesque humour of Stravinsky's *Three Pieces for String Quartet* and once again fashions

a structure that transcends reliance on its model. In the finale whackiness goes a step further, with a rollicking jazz-folk fusion, brilliantly caught here together with the original drum-kit accom-paniment that Haas suppressed following adverse criticism at the premiere. The PHQ's streamlined but full-blooded playing is more than welcome, and if they are lining up the first Janáček and the first and third Haas for a follow-up CD, bravo! Superb recording quality too.

Reynaldo Hahn
Venezuelan/French 1875-1947

Hahn studied with Massenet at the Paris Conserva-toire. While in his teens he gained a reputation as a composer of songs, which he sang to his own accompa-niment in fashionable salons, gaining admittance to Proust's circle. But after 1900 he concentrated on the theatre, as conductor (at the Opéra from 1945) and as a composer of ballets, operas and operettas (Ciboul-lette, 1923; Mozart, 1925). GROVE music

---

Violin Concerto

Violin Concerto[ch]. Piano Concerto[dh]. Suite Hongroise[cdh]. Violin Sonata in C[ce]. Romance in A[ce]. Nocturne[ce]. Piano Quintet[eg]. Les feuilles blessées[bf]. Amour sans ailes[af]. Cinq petites chanson-s[af]. Neuf mélodies retrouvées[bf]. Méduse[af] – Chanson au bord de la fontaine; Danse, petite sirène. La dame aux camélias[af] – Mon rêve était d'avoir; C'est à Paris!; Au fil de l'eau
[a]**Catherine Dune** sop [b]**Didier Henry** bar [c]**Denis Cla-vier** vn [d]**Angeline Pondepeyre**, [e]**Dimitris Saroglou**, [f]**Stéphane Petitjean** pfs [g]**Quatuor Clavier** (Denis Clavier, Marie-France Razafimbadà vns Florian Wallez va Claire Breteau vc); [h]**Lorraine Philharmonic Orchestra / Fernand Quattrocchi**
Maguelone ③ MAG111 111 (203' · DDD · T/t) Ⓜ

Both the Violin Concerto and the Piano Con-certo belong to a period in Hahn's life when he knew that strange mixture of happiness and regret that comes to us all in our fifties. The great figures he had known in his youth were nearly all dead, the First World War had claimed many of his contemporaries, and the glamour that had once surrounded his name had faded. Yet in the Paris of the 1920s he had his biggest stage successes (*Ciboulette* and *Mozart*) and entered on the longest and happiest rela-tionship of his life with the tenor Guy Ferrant; all this seems to be expressed in the slow move-ment of the Violin Concerto. Here we have Hahn spinning a slow, languorous tune that hovers between dance and delirium. It's marked throughout *Tranquillo*, *Très calme*, *Amoroso* and *Sans rigueur*. Denis Clavier plays it with just the right air of restraint: as Jean Gallois writes in the notes, it's 'a song from the soul without pathos'.

The better-known Piano Concerto from 1930 is a slighter work. Perhaps its curious structure

– the second movement lasts less than three minutes – makes it seem a little jokey. Those who already have a recording should not be deterred from hearing this excellent performance: Angeline Pondepeyre takes the opening somewhat slower than Magda Tagliaferro in the historic recording conducted by the composer, but she brings out the jazzy element more.

The second CD starts with the Violin Sonata, composed in 1926. Denis Clavier and Dimitris Saroglou give a first-rate performance, the opening movement a beautiful questioning theme which gives way to a second, more romantic melody. The *Romance* and *Nocturne* are both real salon pieces, and the *Romance* in particular has a haunting tune. As for the Piano Quintet, this has some of Hahn's most passionate music in the slow movement. It's impossible not to believe that this piece – composed in 1920-21 – isn't a commentary on the tragic events of 1914-18.

The Quintet may be Hahn's personal reaction to the war, but while actually in the trenches, he composed music which was as far removed from the horrors as possible. His *Five Little Songs* were dedicated to Jan Bathori; it's very difficult for modern singers to hit off the mood of deliberate naivety in these songs, but it's good to have at least this performance.

Most of the other songs on the third CD in this set have not been recorded before: it's not difficult to see why; the heavy sentiment is so hard to take. *Feuilles blessées*, a cycle of 11 songs, is one of Hahn's most ambitious works. Didier Henry sings them with the right mixture of robust tone and detailed articulation.

The *Neuf mélodies retrouvées* were published a few years after Hahn's death. The final song, 'Sous l'oranger', is the most fun, a 'tango-haban-era' that seems to hark back to the Second Empire, that frivolous, dangerous period for which Hahn felt such nostalgia.

This set can't be recommended too highly. Three CDs might seem too much to the uninitiated, but if you only know his songs or operettas, these is a lot to surprise here.

Chamber Works

Premières valses[a]. Venezia (arr Pidoux)[b]. Piano Quartet[c]. Soliloque et forlane[d]. Cello Concerto (unfinished, ed Pollain)[e]
[be]**Roland Pidoux,** [b]**Pierre Cordier,** [b]**Renaud Guieu,** [b]**Antoine Lederlin,** [b]**Matthieu Lejeune,** [b]**Christophe Morin** vcs [c]**Quatuor Gabriel** ([ade]Yoko Kaneko pf Guillaume Plays vn [d]Vincent Aucante va Jérôme Pinget vc)
Maguelone MAG111 117 (72' · DDD)   Ⓕ

According to Jean Gallois's notes for this invaluable disc, the Quartet in G for violin, viola, cello and piano, was completed just a month before Hahn died in January 1947. If that's so, it can be listened to as a farewell, something that inevitably invokes Hahn's friendship with Marcel Proust. And even if

one were told that he'd composed the quartet when he was young and happy, it would still evoke a mood of regret and yearning. It's the beautiful *Andante*, the third movement, that's the heart of the piece. A song without words that seems to speak of the pain of long parting, of thoughts unspoken, it ends on a reflective note of acceptance. Even the dance-like final movement, which contains a perhaps unconscious quote from some of the music for Hahn's musical comedy *Mozart*, also has a bittersweet quality. The Quatuor Gabriel play it eloquently, without undue sentimentality.

The suite *Premières valses* for piano was composed in 1898, when Hahn was at the height of his youthful celebrity in Parisian society. The fifth waltz is subtitled 'A l'ombre rêveuse de Chopin', and the whole sequence seems to be a tribute to the style of the 1840s. Yoko Kaneko plays it with more emphasis on the Polish mood than Catherine Joly in her 1988 recording on Accord. This performance reveals more of the rhythmic inventiveness in these miniatures.

The romantic *Soliloque et forlane* was composed in 1937 as a test piece for the Conservatoire. Vincent Aucante and Kaneko bring out the playful Spanish quality in the *allegro scherzando* finale. Finally, Roland Pidoux's arrangement of Hahn's song cycle *Venezia* for cello sextet must be such an expensive proposition that you're unlikely to encounter it in the concert hall. The tunes are adorable.

Songs

A Chloris. Le rossignol des lilas. L'enamourée. Trois jours de vendange. Etudes latines—Lydé; Tyndaris; Phyllis. Les fontaines. Automne. Infidélité. Dans la nuit. D'une prison. Quand la nuit n'est pas étoilée. Fumée. Le printemps. Je me souviens. Quand je fus pris au pavillon. Paysage. Fêtes galantes. Nocturne. Mai. L'heure exquise. Offrande. Si mes vers avaient des ailes
Susan Graham sop **Roger Vignoles** pf
Sony Classical 07464 60168-2 (62' · DDD · T/t)   ⒻOO

Susan Graham brings to these songs a voice of lovely quality, excellent French and – in keeping with Hahn's own insistence – gives overriding importance to clarity of enunciation, the verbal meaning governing the vocal colour. It's certainly better to savour these songs a few at a time, but the programme has been well put together to show Hahn's range, from the Bachian pastiche of *A Chloris* or the antique simplicity of *Lydé* to the adventurous harmonic progressions of *Fumée*, *Le printemps* or *Je me souviens*, from the despairing pathos of *D'une prison* to the light-heartedness of *Quand je fus pris au pavillon*, from the quiet rapture of *Nocturne* to the passion of *Dans la nuit* (a splendid miniature). His outstanding gift for lyricism is evident throughout; *Le rossignol des lilas*, for example, is enchanting. Susan Graham perfectly captures these songs' elegant intimacy with a wealth of nuance, from the gentle tone of *L'enamourée* to the fullness of *L'automne*; and the way she floats the words 'l'heure exquise' is haunting. Roger Vignoles provides most sensitive partnership throughout: he has more scope in songs like *Les fontaines* or *Dans la nuit*, but equally noteworthy is his subtle treatment of the repeated pattern of *Infidélité*.

Douze rondels. Etudes latines. Si mes vers avaient des ailes. Paysage. Rêverie. Offrande. Mai. Infidélité. Seule. Les cygnes. Nocturne. Trois jours de vendange. D'une prison. Séraphine. L'heure exquise. Fêtes galantes. Quand la nuit n'est pas étoilée. Le plus beau présent. Sur l'eau. Le rossignol des lilas. A Chloris. Ma jeunesse. Puisque j'ai mis ma lèvre. La nymphe de la source. Au rossignol. Je me souviens. Mozart – Air de la lettre. O mon bel inconnu – C'est très vilain d'être infidèle. Ciboulette – C'est sa banlieue; Nous avons fait un beau voyage. Une revue – La dernière valse

Dame Felicity Lott *sop* **Susan Bickley** *mez* **Ian Bostridge** *ten* **Stephen Varcoe** *bar* **Graham Johnson, Chris Gould** *pfs* **London Schubert Chorale / Stephen Layton**
Hyperion ② CDA67141/2 (134' · DDD · T/t)   Ⓕ◉

The two cycles, *Douze rondels* and *Etudes latines*, are linked by a common fascination with the past. The *Douze rondels* were composed to poems in a medieval metre, which allowed Hahn to try his hand at pastiche madrigals and courtly ballads. The *Etudes latines* cast their gaze back still further in time to Classical antiquity. For Hahn, that era seemed to represent the ultimate in purity and sensuality rolled into one. This collection of 10 songs is a real discovery and rivals late Fauré, both in its refinement and mesmerising simplicity of utterance. Apart from a few moments when one would like a more substantial tone, Stephen Varcoe's light baritone suits Hahn very well and he's a refreshingly unaffected interpreter, who sings with grace and feeling. Susan Bickley is better at the larger canvas of a piece like *Quand la nuit n'est pas étoilée* than the more intimate songs but the most celebrated pair of all Hahn's *mélodies* goes to Dame Felicity Lott, whose sympathy for the French style could have no happier outlet. Both *Si mes vers avaient des ailes* and *L'heure exquise* are included here, the latter if not an hour, then at least two and a half minutes that are truly exquisite. They are both beautifully sung and are undisturbed by the discomfort around the top of the stave that sometimes mars Lott's singing elsewhere. At the end, she offers four operetta solos as an encore. Graham Johnson's accompaniments are as sensitive as ever. The piano could have been placed a little closer, but the voices have been well captured.

George Frideric Handel
German/British 1685-1759

Handel was the son of a barber-surgeon who intended him for the law. At first he practised music clandestinely, but his father was encouraged to allow him to study and he became a pupil of Zachow, the principal organist in Halle. When he was 17 he was appointed organist of the Calvinist Cathedral, but a year later he left for Hamburg. There he played the violin and harpsichord in the opera house, where his Almira was given at the beginning of 1705, soon followed by his Nero. The next year he accepted an invitation to Italy, where he spent more than three years, in Florence, Rome, Naples and Venice. He had operas or other dramatic works given in all these cities (oratorios in Rome, including La resurrezione) and, writing many Italian cantatas, perfected his technique in setting Italian words for the human voice. In Rome he also composed some Latin church music.

He left Italy early in 1710 and went to Hanover, where he was appointed Kapellmeister to the elector. But he at once took leave to take up an invitation to London, where his opera Rinaldo was produced early in 1711. Back in Hanover, he applied for a second leave and returned to London in autumn 1712. Four more operas followed in 1712-15, with mixed success; he also wrote music for the church and for court and was awarded a royal pension. In 1716 he may have visited Germany (where possibly he set Brockes's Passion text); it was probably the next year that he wrote the Water Music to serenade George I at a riverparty on the Thames. In 1717 he entered the service of the Earl of Carnarvon (soon to be Duke of Chandos) at Edgware, near London, where he wrote 11 anthems and two dramatic works, the evergreen Acis and Galatea and Esther, for the modest band of singers and players retained there.

In 1718-19 a group of noblemen tried to put Italian opera in London on a firmer footing, and launched a company with royal patronage, the Royal Academy of Music; Handel, appointed musical director, went to Germany, visiting Dresden and poaching several singers for the Academy, which opened in April 1720. Handel's Radamisto was the second opera and it inaugurated a noble series over the ensuing years including Ottone, Giulio Cesare, Rodelinda, Tamerlano and Admeto. Works by Bononcini (seen by some as a rival to Handel) and others were given too, with success at least equal to Handel's, by a company with some of the finest singers in Europe, notably the castrato Senesino and the soprano Cuzzoni. But public support was variable and the financial basis insecure, and in 1728 the venture collapsed. The previous year Handel, who had been appointed a composer to the Chapel Royal in 1723, had composed four anthems for the coronation of George II and had taken British naturalisation.

Opera remained his central interest, and with the Academy impresario, Heidegger, he hired the King's Theatre and (after a journey to Italy and Germany to engage fresh singers) embarked on a five-year series of seasons starting in late 1729. Success was mixed. In 1732 Esther was given at a London musical society by friends of Handel's, then by a rival group in public; Handel prepared to put it on at the King's Theatre, but the Bishop of London banned a stage version of a biblical work. He then put on Acis, also in response to a rival venture. The next summer he was invited to Oxford and wrote an oratorio, Athalia, for performance at the Sheldonian Theatre. Meanwhile, a second opera company ('Opera of the Nobility', including Senesino) had been set up in competition with Handel's and the two competed for audiences over the next four seasons before both failed. This period drew from Handel, however, such operas as Orlando and two with ballet, Ariodante and Alcina, among his finest scores.

During the rest of the 1730s Handel moved between Italian opera and the English forms, oratorio, ode and the like, unsure of his future commercially and artistically. After a journey to Dublin in 1741-2, where Messiah had its premiere (in aid of charities), he put opera behind him and for most of the remainder of his life gave oratorio performances, mostly at the new Covent Garden theatre, usually at or close to the Lent season. The Old Testament provided the basis for most of them (Samson, Belshazzar, Joseph, Joshua, Solomon, for example), but he sometimes experimented, turning to classical mythology (Semele, Hercules) or Christian history (Theodora), with little public success. All these works, along with such earlier ones as Acis and his two Cecilian odes (to Dryden words), were performed in concert form in English. At these performances he usually played in the interval a concerto on the organ (a newly invented musical genre) or directed a concerto grosso (his Op 6, a set of 12, published in 1740, represents his finest achievement in the form).

During his last decade he gave regular performances of Messiah, usually with about 16 singers and an orchestra of about 40, in aid of the Foundling Hospital. In 1749 he wrote a suite for wind instruments (with optional strings) for performance in Green Park to accompany the Royal Fireworks celebrating the Peace of Aix-la-Chapelle. His last oratorio, composed as he grew blind, was Jephtha (1752); The Triumph of Time and Truth (1757) is largely composed of earlier material. Handel was very economical in the re-use of his ideas; at many times in his life he also drew heavily on the music of others (though generally avoiding detection) – such 'borrowings' may be of anything from a brief motif to entire movements, sometimes as they stood but more often accommodated to his own style.

Handel died in 1759 and was buried in Westminster Abbey, recognised in England and by many in Germany as the greatest composer of his day. The wide range of expression at his command is shown not only in the operas, with their rich and varied arias, but also in the form he created, the English oratorio, where it is applied to the fates of nations as well as individuals. He had a vivid sense of drama. But above all he had a resource and originality of invention, to be seen in the extraordinary variety of music in the Op 6 concertos, for example, in which melodic beauty, boldness and humour all play a part, that place him and JS Bach as the supreme masters of the Baroque era in music.

GROVEmusic

Organ Concertos, Opp 4 & 7

Op 4 – No 1 in G minor; No 2 in B flat; No 3 in G minor; No 4 in F; No 5 in F   **P**
Op 7 – No 1 in B flat; No 2 in A; No 3 in B flat; No 4 in D minor; No 5 in G minor; No 6 in B flat. Harp Concerto in B flat, Op 4 No 6
Paul Nicholson org **Frances Kelly** hp
The Brandenburg Consort / Roy Goodman hpd
Hyperion ③ CDD22052 (154' · DDD)   Ⓜ

This recording was made at St-Lawrence Whitchurch on an organ Handel must certainly have played. It sounds well under Paul Nicholson's hands. There's plenty of brightly glittering passagework and rich diapason sound in such movements as the passacaglia-like first of Op 7 No 1; while the softer side of the instrument is particularly appealing in Op 4 No 5, where Nicholson, doubtless conscious that this is a transcription of a recorder sonata, draws from it some very sweet sounds. It has a mechanical action, and here and there the incidental noise may be disconcerting. Still, it's authentic, so possibly we should be grateful to have it reproduced. There's some very lively and at times virtuoso playing from Nicholson in the quick movements, with sturdy rhythms, and some of the dance movements go with a good swing too.

Nicholson gives good, precise accounts of the various solo fugues and the transcriptions and improvisatory movements used here when Handel offered merely an ad lib. He's a thoughtful player; his added ornamentation is always musical, intelligent and stylish. However, in several movements overdeliberate orchestral phrasing or accentuation can be damaging; this happens quite often and sometimes affects Nicholson's playing. Op 4 No 6 is played on the harp, with some very delicate timing from Frances Kelly. The bright, clear recording captures happily the acoustic of this moderate-sized church.

Six Organ Concertos, Op 4   **P**
Matthew Halls org **Sonnerie / Monica Huggett** vn
Avie AV2055 (73' · DDD)   ⒻⒹ►

Sonnerie elect to open this delectable recording with the bright, extrovert Concerto No 4, which Handel based on music he had rejected from his autograph of Alcina. Matthew Halls begins this with a fabulous flourish on the organ before Sonnerie launch in, setting the pace for the rest of this lively and engaging disc. Halls, using a fascinating Dutch chamber organ which is perfect for the intimately balanced ensemble, plays the solos in Concerto No 6 (the 'harp' concerto) with admirable delicacy and affection. Firmer music such as the Allegro from Concerto No 3 lacks nothing in intensity or drama. The bouncy finale of Concerto No 5 is a model of zesty vivaciousness.

These chamber performances are smaller than those Handel would have directed but one never feels that Sonnerie are weak or underpowered. Although Halls is sometimes accompanied by only six musicians, the slow movements are surprisingly lush and evocative. Inspiring interpretations that are a joy from beginning to end.

Concerti grossi

Op 3, HWV312-17; **Op 6**, HWV319-30
Concerti grossi, Opp 3 and 6 ℗
Handel & Haydn Society / Christopher Hogwood
Avie ③ (3 CDs for the price of 2) AV2065
(3h 36' · DDD) ℗⊟→

The London music publisher John Walsh threw Handel's Op 3 together in 1734 by organising various single orchestral movements into concertos without the composer's creative involvement or permission; the result was a hotchpotch. But Op 6 features 12 new concertos that Handel had deliberately composed as a coherent set during September and October 1739. While Op 6 is undeniably Handel's monumental masterpiece for the orchestra, there are a lot of excellent recordings that do much to promote the variety and charm of Op 3.

For this recording Christopher Hogwood uses a performance edition that takes into account manuscript sources that pre-date Walsh's compilation. It is good to have the Handel & Haydn Society's disciplined and lean performances available again thanks to this newly compiled and remastered reissue. The opening of Op 3 No 2 has deliciously sprung rhythms and fine solo concertino playing; the sublime cello duet in the following *Largo* is sinewy yet tender, its melancholic mood enhanced by the restrained oboe solo. Handel later added oboes and bassoons to some of the Op 6 concertos when they were performed in the theatre but Hogwood prefers Handel's original scoring for string orchestra throughout.

The Handel & Haydn Society's alert enthusiasm is tangible throughout these polished and stylish readings, originally recorded by Decca's much lamented early-music division L'Oiseau-Lyre. Hogwood directs with natural sensitivity and his tastefully emphasised suspensions and relaxed shaping of cadences are consistently perfect. The finest Op 6 on disc? Maybe not, but there is ample here to satisfy the fussiest Handelians.

Concerti grossi, Op 3 (HWV312-17). Sonata a cinque, HWV288 ℗
Academy of Ancient Music / Richard Egarr
Harmonia Mundi HMU90 7415;
🎵 HMU80 7415 (68' · DDD) ℗●⊟→

Handel's Op 3 *Concerti grossi* was his first published set of concertos, although scholars have regarded the level of his personal involvement in John Walsh's 1734 edition with suspicion. Richard Egarr suggests that Handel might have had more of a hand in the compilation of Op 3 than hitherto identified. Fresh speculation is a healthy opportunity to reconsider matters but the truly significant aspect of this recording is the new attention brought to Handel's charming music. It is hard to think of a lovelier

moment in all of Handel's orchestral works than the spellbinding cellos interweaving under a plaintive solo oboe in the *Largo* of No 2. Likewise, the immense personality of the solo organ runs during the finale of No 6 is a potently precocious display of Handel's genius at the keyboard. All such moments come across with vitality and passion.

The AAM has never committed Op 3 to disc before: under Egarr they sound as good as ever, perhaps even reinvigorated and a few degrees sparkier. These are for the most part lively performances full of fizzy finesse. There are several fine recordings that find a little more warmth, sentimentality and intimacy in the music, although the energetic brilliance so prominent in the AAM's crisply athletic playing has its own rewards. The musicians are unanimously immersed in the intricacies of the music, but special mention must be made of violinist Pavlo Beznosiuk's dazzling contribution to the dynamic finale of the 'Sonata a cinque' (a sort of violin concerto that Handel presumably composed for Corelli in Rome in about 1707).

Additional recommendation

Concerti grossi, Opp 3 & 6 ℗
Vienna Concentus Musicus / Harnoncourt
Teldec ④ 4509-95500-2 (237' · ADD/DDD) Recorded 1982-85 ⑧●
The fact is that there's ferocious creativity in every bar. Every opening slow movement is the prelude to a drama, every fugue a precisely related episode. The Vienna Concentus Musicus plays for the most part with a virtuosity and precision that's well highlighted by the slightly dry but transparent acoustic in which they're recorded.

---

12 Concerti grossi, Op 6 HWV319-30 ℗
Il Giardino Armonico / Giovanni Antonini
L'Oiseau-Lyre ③ 478 0319DX3 (168' · DDD) ⑧●⊟→

One can overlook a few of Il Giardino Armonico's eccentricities to listen to some generally intoxicating performances of Handel's most masterful instrumental compositions. Much of the credit for the intricate passagework and dynamic excitement must be given to fiddler Enrico Onofri, whose playing sparkles with articulate energy. The plunging interplay between *concertino* and *ripieno* groups is exhilarating. The Polonaise in No 3 is astonishingly robust, with its droning bass thrashed out; it certainly brings out the daring brilliance of Handel's musical imagination, though it seems rather short on the pastoral charm that the composer surely intended. The opening *Largo* and *Allegro* of No 5 possess panache and the opening of No 10 is tautly dramatic, but one misses the airy wit that such music may also convey.

Il Giardino Armonico's playing is never clumsy but incisive muscular approaches in contrapuntal movements seem overly severe. It is possible to find a more measured elegance and shapely sentimentality in Handel's music, but there is plenty of highly spiced food for thought served by Il Giardino Armonico.

---

12 Concerti grossi, Op 6　　　　　　　　　　P
Academy of Ancient Music / Andrew Manze vn
Harmonia Mundi ② HMU90 7228/9 (157' · DDD)　Ⓕ●

With one stride, Harmonia Mundi has stolen a march on Chandos Chaconne's rival set of Handel's Op 6 with Simon Standage's Collegium Musicum 90; by juggling with the order, the 12 concertos have been accommodated on only two CDs. The AAM is on sparkling form, clearly enjoying itself under Andrew Manze's leadership. Performances are invigoratingly alert, splendidly neat (all those semiquaver figurations absolutely precise) and strongly rhythmical but not inflexible, with much dynamic gradation which ensures that phrases are always tonally alive and sound completely natural (even if more subtly nuanced than Handel's players ever dreamt of). Manze's basically light-footed approach is particularly appealing, and he sees to it that inner-part imitations are given their due weight.

Speeds are nearly all fast, occasionally questionably so (though exhilarating), as in the first *Allegro* of No 1, the big *Allegro* of No 6 and the *Allegro* in No 9. But Manze successfully brings out the character of all the movements, and the listener can't fail to love the vigorous kick of his No 7 hornpipe. He's mostly sparing in embellishing solo lines except in Nos-6 and 11. Altogether this is an issue of joyous vitality.

Concerti grossi, Op 6 Nos 1-5　　　　　　　P
Collegium Musicum 90 / Simon Standage vn
Chandos Chaconne CHAN0600 (62' · DDD)　　Ⓕ●

Concerti grossi, Op 6 Nos 6-9　　　　　　　P
Collegium Musicum 90 / Simon Standage vn
Chandos Chaconne CHAN0616 (58' · DDD)　　Ⓕ●

Concerti grossi – Op 6 Nos 10-12; C, HWV318,　P
'Alexander's Feast'
Collegium Musicum 90 / Simon Standage vn
Chandos Chaconne CHAN0622 (56' · DDD)　　Ⓕ●

The first disc of the ever-fresh Op 6 *Concerti grossi* includes the oboe parts that Handel later added to Nos 1, 2, 5 and 6. The performances are brimful of vitality, and the clean articulation and light, predominantly detached style give the music buoyancy and help to bring out Handel's often mischievous twinkle in the eye. Speeds are generally brisk, with boldly vigorous playing, but Standage's team can also spin a tranquil broad line. Dynamics throughout are subtly graded, and except in one final cadence ornamentation is confined to small cadential trills.

On the second disc, except, in the sombre colours in the splendid G minor Concerto (No 6) – here with oboe and the agreeable addition of a theorbo to the continuo – there's a general air of cheerfulness that's most engaging. The fugue in

No 7 is wittily buoyant, the *Allegro* in No 9, borrowed from the *Cuckoo and the nightingale* Organ Concerto, could scarcely be more high-spirited, the final Passepied of No 6 and the Hornpipe of No 7 are spring-toed; and Standage's feeling for convincing tempos is nowhere better shown than in the long Musette of No 6, which in other hands can drag. Phrasing everywhere is shapely, and the surprise chords that interrupt the flow of No 8's Allemande are admirably 'placed'.

On the final disc the playing is always on its toes – positively twinkling in dance movements such as the concluding fugal gigue of No 12. The last two concertos, No 11 in particular, give Simon Standage an opportunity to shine as a soloist; his *ad lib* sections are tastefully done, without excesses; his semiquavers in the variants of the A major *Andante* are feather-light. All dynamics are well contrasted in a natural way, and the tempos nicely judged; a slightly faster repeat of the first half of No 10's fifth movement suggests the splicing of a different take. As a fill-up, we're presented with the *Alexander's Feast* concerto grosso, for which the string group is joined by oboes and bassoon. The excellent concertino of two violins and cello is thrown into high relief and the *Allegro* movements are performed with a delightful spring.

Water Music, HWV348-50

Water Music　　　　　　　　　　　　　　　P
Simon Standage, Elizabeth Wilcock vns
The English Concert / Trevor Pinnock hpd
Archiv Produktion 477 756-2 (54' · DDD)　　Ⓜ●●Ⓑ→

It's unlikely that George I ever witnessed performances that live up to this one. They are sparkling; tempos are well judged and there's a truly majestic sweep to the opening F major French overture; that gets things off to a fine start but what follows is no less compelling with some notably fine woodwind playing, so often the disappointing element in performances on period instruments.

In the D major music it's the brass department that steals the show and here, horns and trumpets acquit themselves with distinction. Archiv Produktion has achieved a particularly satisfying sound in which all strands of the orchestral texture can be heard with clarity. In this suite the ceremonial atmosphere comes over particularly well, with resonant brass playing complemented by crisply articulated oboes.

The G major pieces are quite different from those in the previous groups, being lighter in texture and more closely dance-orientated. They are among the most engaging in the *Water Music* and especially, perhaps, the two little 'country dances', the boisterous character of which Pinnock captures nicely.

Water Music. Music for the Royal Fireworks　P
L'Arte dell'Arco / Federico Guglielmo vn
CPO CPO777 312-2 (66' · DDD)　　　　　Ⓕ●●●

The tradition of dividing the *Water Music* into three separate suites dates back to the 1950s. The suspicion that Handel envisaged it as one long sequence of movements has informed a couple of fine recordings but this disc by L'Arte dell'Arco is the first such recording to be made since the earliest surviving manuscript copy of the music (dating from 1718) was rediscovered in 2004.

The strings play with polish and alertness. Federico Guglielmo leads proceedings expertly from the violin; his few solo flourishes are direct yet courtly. The famous Hornpipe is splendidly done, with a radiant balance between the pairs of trumpets and horns (who relish some tasteful ornaments in the *da capo*), and lovely solo fiddle-playing during the middle section.

Generally these performances are pleasantly contoured, though the continuo team occasionally become intrusive in faster music. However, it is good to hear musicians confident enough to play the *Lentement* more slowly than has become common. The Bourrée is thrillingly quick. The Country Dance sparkles with conviviality, although the recorder is a little uneven.

The Ouverture from the *Music for the Royal Fireworks* is given a vibrant and engaging performance. Guglielmo and his forces achieve the rare feat of ensuring that 'La Réjouissance' is coherently shaped. CPO's translator of the booklet has done a poor job of what seems to have been an interesting note by Guglielmo ('cembalo' is consistently mistranslated as 'cymbals'!) but the disc is warmly recommended.

Water Music. Music for the Royal Fireworks
Aradia Ensemble / Kevin Mallon
Naxos 8 557764 (71' · DDD)　　　Ⓢ➛

The *Water Music* has traditionally been divided into three suites, as it is here, but a recently rediscovered early manuscript copy confirms that Handel originally created one long sequence of movements. A more regretful aspect of this recording is a superfluous percussionist rattling away on a tambourine in several movements (for example, the hornpipe in Suite No 1). Kevin Mallon claims that this 'was often the practice in the 18th century' but there is not a single piece of evidence that Handel would have agreed.

Mallon's performance is otherwise, exemplary. Handel's melodies are nicely shaped, with colourful accompaniments that range between assertive energy and understated pathos. Resonant horns and elegant trumpets synthesise stylish wit and regal pomp in the famous 'Alla hornpipe' (Suite No 2). Brightness and subtlety co-exist with a charismatic swagger.

Mallon's sense of an attractive flowing pulse in the music carries through to the *Music for the Royal Fireworks*. The Ouverture has crisp, articulate phrasing, in which important details are stressed and then shade away to allow the next musical detail to come to the fore. The zesty Aradia Ensemble never succumb to monotonous tub-thumping. There is no shortage of excellent recordings that pair these beloved

---

HANDEL FIREWORKS AND WATER MUSIC – IN BRIEF

Le Concert Spirituel / Hervé Niquet
Glossa GCD921606 (62' · DDD)　　　Ⓕ
This comes closest of all 'authentic' recordings to gathering the forces Handel originally wrote for in both *Water* and *Fireworks*, with massed winds – horns using the natural intonation of their instruments to piquant effect – and some splendid drumming sessions! The sound is rather recessed to cope with the wide dynamic range, but the overall effect is stunning.

Le Concert des Nations / Jordi Savall
Astrée Naive ES9920 (74' · DDD)　　　ⒻⓄ
Using smaller though still substantial forces, Savall's performances are more refined than Niquet's but still very characterful, with a delightful sense of rhythmic swing, caught in less recessed sound.

London Classical Players / Roger Norrington
Virgin 545265-2 (69' · DDD)　　　Ⓕ
Neatly articulated, 'cleaner' playing than either Niquet or Savall, though perhaps lacking something of the character they find. Nonetheless the grandeur of the brass in the *Fireworks* is stirring.

Aradia Ensemble / Kevin Mallon
Naxos 8 557764 (71' · DDD)　　　Ⓕ➛
Nicely conceived performances, full of detail and with an attractive sense of theatre. You may regret the added percussion but there's no denying the sense of occasion that Mallon creates with his Canadian ensemble.

L'Arte dell'Arco / Federico Guglielmo
CPO CPO777 312-2 (66' · DDD)　　　ⓂⓄⓄⓄⓄ
A terrific new disc for Handel Year that dismantles the traditional suites and presents the music in one long and, here, thrilling sequence. This alert sprightly playing with plenty of excitement and genuine sense of occasion.

Berlin Philharmonic / Riccardo Muti
(Water Music only)
EMI 5864092 (60' · DDD)　　　Ⓑ
A highly unlikely line-up and a throw-back to an earlier time! This is none the less a spirited performance of the *Water Music* at an appealingly low price.

LSO / Charles Mackerras (Fireworks only)
Testament SBT1253 (76' · ADD)　　　ⒻⓄ
An historic first attempt to gather the forces Handel originally scored the *Fireworks* for, but using modern instruments. Some of the speeds are a touch ponderous by today's standards, but the sound is excellent and the overall effect breathtaking.

works together, but Mallon's interpretation is an attractive contender at budget price.

'WaterMusic. Music for the Royal Fireworks, HWV351
Le Concert Spirituel / Hervé Niquet
Glossa GCD921606 (62' · DDD) Ⓕ

Hervé Niquet celebrated the 15th anniversary of his group Le Concert Spirituel by assembling a hundred musicians at the Arsenal de Metz to produce what is claimed as 'the first historical recording' of the *Fireworks Music* and *Water Music*. We've had many versions on period instruments but till now only one recording of the *Fireworks Music* has attempted to assemble period instruments in the numbers that Handel is known to have had originally. That's the 1989 version for Hyperion by Robert King with the King's Consort, but he was content with 62 wind, brass and percussion players; Niquet, as in the *Water Music*, adds massed strings too. Sir Charles Mackerras's flamboyant recording of the *Fireworks Music* using vast wind forces has reappeared on Testament with great success, but that dates from the days of Handel on modern instruments.

Niquet goes further than most of his rivals, not only in assembling these numbers, but in applying early performance techniques. When he reports that the nine horn players 'performed their parts without "correcting" the natural intonation of their instruments', with mean-tone temperament imposed on the whole orchestra, it makes one apprehensive that the results would be painful to the modern ear. Happily this isn't so. The rawness of brass tone is so well controlled that it tickles the ear delightfully.

The massed woodwind players (24 oboes, 15 flutes and recorders, and 14 bassoons) add to the weight and tang of the sound, and though only two percussionists are listed, they're balanced to give maximum impact, with a spectacular timpani cadenza in the Overture to the Fireworks Music. The bass drum and timpani in the 'Gigue' which ends the G major *Water Music* Suite have similar panache.

The string sections are comparably large, but inevitably on gut strings their playing is less prominent, counterbalanced by such elaborations as the sparkling little cadenza for solo violin that links the 'Prelude' and 'Hornpipe' of the D major *Water Music* Suite.

As you'd expect, fast speeds predominate, sometimes so fast that they sound breathless: one marvels at the articulation of the wind and brass players in coping. Helped by atmospheric recording, one has a vivid impression of a grand ceremonial celebration. Niquet's is a fine achievement.

'Water Music – Recreating a Royal Spectacular'
The English Concert / Andrew Manze
Video director **Fergus O'Brien**
BBC/Opus Arte 📀 OA0930D
(78' · NTSC · 16:9 · PCM stereo and DTS 5.1 · 0) Ⓕ
This documentary's hypothesis for where, how

and why Handel performed his famous orchestral suites on the Thames makes for enjoyable viewing. Social historian Philippa Glanville presents two documents that describe the original event in 1717 (although both have been familiar to Handelians since they were reprinted in 1955). Political historian Jeremy Black takes us around Greenwich and Venice looking for clues to a possible political agenda for the barge party, comparing it to the spectacular ceremonies of La Serenissima that might have captured the imaginations of impressionable young Englishmen on the Grand Tour. A barge is given a make-over so that it resembles what Handel's musicians might have floated on. The soundtrack of the orchestra's trip down the Thames is obviously a studio recording with superimposed sound effects of river noises, although an acoustician tests some of The English Concert's players on the river to prove scientifically that Handel knew what he was doing when orchestrating the music.

The only missing ingredient in this reconstruction project is the involvement of a music historian. There is no discussion of the *Water Music*'s context within Handel's fascinating career. Andrew Manze's presence gives musical muscle; but it is a welcome corrective that the booklet features an essay by Donald Burrows which manages to cover all the missing elements while gently amending a few of the documentary's less convincing conjectures.

Music for the Royal Fireworks, HWV351

Music for the Royal Fireworks[d] Ⓗ
Berenice, HWV38 – Overture (arr Whittaker)[a].
Concerti a due cori in F, HWV333 (arr Mackerras)[b].
Concertos[c] – in D, HWV335a; F, HWV331. Water Music, HWV38-50 (arr Harty)[e] – Allegro; Bourrée; Hornpipe; Allegro decisio
[d]**Wind Ensemble;** [ce]**London Symphony Orchestra; Pro Arte Orchestra**[b] **/ Charles Mackerras**
Testament SBT1253 (76' · ADD) Recorded [ae]1956,
[bd]1959, [c]1977 Ⓕ ⊙

Over the night of 13-14 April 1959 in St Gabriel's Church, Cricklewood, a recording session took place, historic in every way, when the young Charles Mackerras conducted a band of 62 wind players plus nine percussionists in Handel's *Music for the Royal Fireworks*. With no fewer than 26 oboists topping the ensemble, it was only possible to assemble such a band after all concerts and operas had finished for the day.

They began at 11pm and finished at 2.30 in the morning, yet so far from sounding tired or jaded, the players responded to the unique occasion with a fizzing account of Handel's six movements. The success of this extraordinary project fully justified Mackerras's determination to restore the astonishing array of instruments that Handel himself had assembled for the original performance in Green Park in April 1749.

It's thrilling to hear that 1959 recording, at last transferred to CD, with sound that's still of demonstration quality, full and spacious, with a wide stereo spread. It's true that Mackerras takes the introduction to the overture and the 'Siciliana' at speeds far slower than he would choose today, but this was a recording which marked a breakthrough in what later developed as the period performance movement.

As a coupling for the *Fireworks Music*, Mackerras devised a composite *Concerto a due cori* which draws on two works written with that title around 1747. It makes a splendid piece, in which the massed horns bray gloriously.

Whatever the degree of authenticity, this is an electrifying collection, superbly transferred.

Music for the Royal Fireworks, HWV351. Concerti per due cori, HWV332-334
Ensemble Zefiro / Alfredo Bernardini
Deutsche Harmonia Mundi 88697 36791-2
(69' · DDD) Ⓕ🔴🔵🔴➔

The Italian ensemble Zefiro, directed by oboist Alfredo Bernardini, specialise in 18th-century music that gives prominence towards wind instruments. This lends itself to Handel's *Music for the Royal Fireworks*, written for the public celebrations of the Peace of Aix-la-Chapelle in London's Green Park (1749). Zefiro play the grand Ouverture with the perfect synthesis of splendour and dance-like charisma (too many versions possess too little of the latter). 'La réjouissance' trips along lightly without a hint of clumsiness, but still has ample juicy magnificence. There are several other good recordings available, but this zesty and fluid performance is a welcome change from stodgy readings in which everything is hammered home mercilessly. Zefiro bring a marvellous sense of light and shade to this music. Maybe Bernardini's sparkling and communicative approach would have been too subtle for the great British outdoors in 1749, but it is curious that this beautifully engineered recording was made outside in the cloisters of a former Jesuit college in Sicily.

Zefiro also perform all three of the *Concerti per due cori* (1747-48) that Handel arranged for orchestra and two 'choirs' of woodwind and brass. These were intended as entr'actes in oratorio concerts, and it is fun to play 'name that tune'. These shapely performances are phrased and paced to perfection, and exploit an enjoyable range of instrumental colours (whether oboe trios or bucolic horns, almost everything here feels right). This is one of the most enjoyable discs of Handel's orchestral music in a long time.

Orchestral and Ballet Music

Orchestral and Ballet Music from Alcina, Ⓟ
Ariodante, Arminio. Berenice, Rinaldo, Rodelinda and Serse
Collegium Musicum 90 / Simon Standage vn
Chandos Chaconne CHAN0650 (67' · DDD) Ⓕ🔵➔

Handel's music is never more winsome than when it's written for special occasions, not least operas. Several of the items in this programme are arias, but they aren't sung. Like today's musicals, though not for calculated commercial reasons, some became what we would now term pops, and Handel reworked them as instrumental pieces, so no liberty has been taken here in presenting them in that form. The charm of this music hasn't escaped the notice of others in recording studios, but it has never been more persuasively captured than it is by Collegium Musicum 90. Other recordings exist of the complete operas and some of the individual instrumental items, but *Arminio* is represented by only one aria; there's nothing run-of-the-mill about the fugal subject of the Overture, or its treatment, and the Minuet is winsome and light of step. Collegium Musicum 90 fields a team of 32 players but their sound is marvellously light and transparent even when in full flood, and their use of period instruments (or copies thereof) leads also to a natural, revelatory balance. Flawless recording and excellent notes by Standage complete an outstanding issue.

Trio Sonatas

Trio Sonatas, Op 2, HWV386-391
Sonnerie (Wilbert Hazelzet *fl* Monica Huggett, Emilia Benjamin *vns* Joseph Crouch *vc* Matthew Halls *hpd*)
Avie AV0033 (66' · DDD) Ⓕ➔

With their boldness of invention, their expressive range and their extraordinary variety of three-part textures, Handel's six Op 2 sonatas represent a peak of the trio sonata as a genre. Yet for some time there's been no complete recording of the set in the catalogue.

These are polished and sophisticated performances fill the gap admirably. There's much exquisitely turned detail, subtle timing, graceful shaping, and a happy sense of the musical logic. The two violinists play as if they were identical twins. Some listeners may feel these finely modulated performances lack the energy and freshness that ideally belong to the music, but there's a great deal to compensate for that, and you won't often hear this music more attentively, more lovingly played.

Trio Sonatas – Op 2 No 5 in G minor, HWV390;- Ⓟ
Op 5 Nos 4 & 7. Tra le fiamme, HWV170.
Notte placida e cheta, HWV142
Catherine Bott *sop* **Caroline Kershaw, Jane Downer** *recs/obs* **Nigel Amherst** *violone* **Jonathan Manson** *vc* **Purcell Quartet** (Catherine Mackintosh, Catherine Weiss *vns* Richard Boothby *va da gamba/vc* Robert Woolley *hpd*)
Chandos Chaconne CHAN0620 (70' · DDD · T/t) Ⓕ🔴

The idea of alternating trio sonatas with cantatas is a happy one, based perhaps on the idea that people play CDs for pleasure and not simply for reference. The two cantatas are rarities on record. *Tra le fiamme* is a spectacularly scored piece, its textures enriched by a viola da gamba obbligato and wind instruments (recorders in some numbers, oboes in another) as well as strings.

Notte placida e cheta is a delightful evocation of night, sleep and amorous reflection, with its opening aria full of sinuous, voluptuous interweaving violin lines and its soft, gently accompanied recitatives; it ends – a slightly rude awakening, perhaps, to chime with the words – with a fugal aria in which the singer takes one of the four contrapuntal parts along with the violins and the bass. Catherine Bott sings them very responsively, both to the words and to the sense of Handel's lines, with neatly placed detail and some attractively floated phrases. The viol obbligato is done in accomplished style by Richard Boothby, who supplies much of the continuo harmony with multiple stops.

In the Trio Sonatas there's some splendidly athletic playing from the violins of the Purcell Quartet, which plays with its usual spruce rhythms and conversational give and take. These are probably the most appealing performances currently available of these works.

Violin Sonatas

Violin Sonatas. Andante in A minor, HWV412. 📄
Allegro in C minor, HWV408
Andrew Manze *vn* **Richard Egarr** *hpd*
Harmonia Mundi HMU90 7259
(77' · DDD)   Ⓕ🅱▸

Uncertainty over the authenticity of the violin sonatas, coupled with the fact that Handel and his publisher were notoriously imprecise about which instruments his various solo sonatas were even intended for, has no doubt prevented many violinists from embracing them as they might in these scholarly times. But there's certainly a good CD's worth of material to be had, even if only five sonatas are thought to be definitely by Handel. Andrew Manze and Richard Egarr offer these, plus three questionable works originally published in one or other of two versions of Handel's Op 1 set of mixed solo sonatas and two authentic one-movement fragments. There isn't an unenjoyable note.

The recording was made immediately after this pair's *Gramophone* Award-winning set of sonatas by Pandolfi (Harmonia Mundi), and it shows them in the same world-beating form. These are performances brimming with vitality and imagination, transforming these sonatas from the polite, even rather staid music you might expect, into grand dramas full of incident, excitement and many little moments that make you sit up and listen. Manze's violin sings with wonderful, glowing tone (he's not afraid to use vibrato to achieve it), to which he adds a joyous assortment of flowery ornaments and emphatic double-stoppings. Egarr's contribution is no less crucial; surely the most inspired continuo improviser around at present, he draws an astounding and mercurial array of colours and textures from his harp-

chord. Whatever he does, though, it's never routine. This is a great chamber-music recording, made by a duo who complement each other to perfection.

Flute Sonatas

Flute Sonatas – in E minor, HWV359b; in G, 📄
HWV363b; in B minor, HWV367b; in A minor,
HWV374; in E minor, HWV375; in B minor, HWV376; in
D, HWV378; in E minor, HWV379
Barthold Kuijken *fl* **Wieland Kuijken** *va da gamba*
Robert Kohnen *hpd*
Accent ACC9180 (73' · DDD)   ⒻⓄ

In this recording of solo flute sonatas Barthold Kuijken plays pieces unquestionably by Handel as well as others over which doubt concerning his authorship has been cast in varying degrees. Certainly not all the pieces here were conceived for transverse flute – there are earlier versions of HWV363b and 367b, for example, for oboe and treble recorder, respectively; but we can well imagine that in Handel's day most, if not all, of these delightful sonatas were regarded among instrumentalists as more-or-less common property. Barthold Kuijken, with his eldest brother Wieland and Robert Kohnen, gives graceful and stylish performances. Kuijken is skilful in matters of ornamentation and is often adventurous, though invariably within the bounds of good taste. Dance movements are brisk and sprightly though he's careful to preserve their poise, and phrases are crisply articulated. This is of especial benefit to movements such as the lively *Vivace* of the B minor Sonata (HWV367b) which can proceed rather aimlessly when too *legato* an approach is favoured; and the virtuosity of these players pays off in the *Presto (Furioso)* movement that follows. In short, this is a delightful disc which should please both Handelians and most lovers of Baroque chamber music.

Recorder Sonatas

Sonatas for Recorder and Continuo – G minor, 📄
HWV360; A minor, HWV362; in C, HWV365; in F,
HWV369; in B flat, HWV377. Sonata for Flute and
Continuo in B minor, HWV367b
Marion Verbruggen *rec/fl* **Jaap ter Linden** *vc*
Ton Koopman *hpd/org*
Harmonia Mundi HMU90 7151 (58' · DDD)   ⒻⓄ

These are lively, intelligent performances. The recorder playing is outstandingly fine, sweet in tone, pointed in articulation, perfectly tuned, technically very fluent, and informed by a good understanding of the art of ornamentation. Marion Verbruggen's real command of Handel's language makes this CD is out of the ordinary. Some of Ton Koopman's accompaniments are a little busy (half are on the organ, half on the harpsichord), but it's all part of the sense of lively music-making that runs through this attractive disc.

Recorder Sonatas – in G minor, HWV360;   Ⓟ
in A minor, HWV362; in C, HWV365; in D minor,
HMW367a; in F, HWV369; in B flat, HWV377.
Keyboard Suite in E, HWV430
Pamela Thorby *rec* **Richard Egarr** *hpd/org*
Linn Records CD/SACD 🅢 CKD223 (74' · DDD)
        Ⓕ❶↦

Pamela Thorby, a regular member of the Palladian Ensemble, demonstrates versatility and virtuosity beyond question and is imaginatively accompanied by Richard Egarr, who also contributes a sparkling account of the Harpsichord Suite in E major. The recording was made from facsimiles of the autograph manuscripts, and the performances are commensurately vivid and immediate. One feels constantly gripped by the music, as if every single note matters.

There's no compulsive need for a cello on the basso continuo part, and on this occasion Thorby and Egarr manage perfectly well without one. Egarr uses a chamber organ on some of the sonatas, and although it's not historically likely in Handel's chamber sonatas, its musical effect is pleasing, and increases textural variety while removing the threat of monotony across 74 minutes of intense brilliance.

Keyboard Works

Handel Keyboard Suites – in F, HWV427; in D minor,
HWV428; in E, HWV430. Chaconne in G, HWV435 **D**
Scarlatti Keyboard Sonatas – in B minor, Kk27; in D,
Kk29; in E, Kk206; in A, Kk212; in C sharp minor,
Kk247; in D, Kk491; in A, Kk537
Murray Perahia *pf*
Sony Classical 07464 62785-2 (69' · DDD) Ⓕ❶❶❶↦

 In his projection of line, mass and colour Perahia makes intelligent acknowledgement of the fact that none of this is piano music, but when it comes to communicating the forceful effects and the brilliance and readiness of finger for which these two great player-composers were renowned, inhibitions are thrown to the wind. Good! Nothing a pianist does in the *Harmonious Blacksmith* Variations in Handel's E major Suite, or the Air and Variations of the D minor Suite could surpass in vivacity and cumulative excitement what the expert harpsichordist commands, and you could say the same of Scarlatti's D major Sonata, Kk29; but Perahia is extraordinarily successful in translating these with the daredevil 'edge' they must have. Faster and yet faster! In the Handel (more than in the Scarlatti) his velocity may strike you as overdone; but one can see the sense of it. It's quite big playing throughout, yet not inflated. Admirable is the way the piano is addressed, with the keys touched rather than struck, and a sense conveyed that the music is coming to us through the tips of the fingers rather than the hammers of the instrument. While producing streams of beautifully moulded and inflected sound Perahia is a wizard at making you forget the percussive nature of the apparatus. There are movements in

the Handel where the musical qualities are dependent on instrumental sound, or contrasts of sound, which the piano just can't convincingly imitate. And in some of the Scarlatti one might have reservations about Perahia's tendency to idealise, to soften outlines and to make the bite less incisive.

If you can't bear to hear it on anything other than the harpsichord, this record won't be for you. But Perahia is an artist, not just a pianist, and has an experience to offer that's vivid and musically considered at the highest level – not at all second best. The virtuosity is special indeed, and there isn't a note that hasn't been savoured.

Keyboard Suites – in F sharp minor, HWV431;   Ⓟ
in G minor, HWV432; in F minor, HWV433; in B flat,
HWV440; in G, HWV441; in G, HWV442 – Preludio
Sophie Yates *hpd*
Chandos CHAN0688 (71' · DDD)   Ⓕ❶↦

Sophie Yates brings formidable technique and strong dramatic feeling to these suites. The works of the first collection (1720, HWV426-33) are the more demanding, each of them opening with a prelude (or overture) – complex, pensive, often sombre – with a large-scale, fully worked fugue. Yates plays these in an appropriately rhetorical manner, rhythmically taut yet with enough flexibility and attentiveness to the music's caesuras to shape and characterise it, at the same time giving it some sense of the improvisatory. Then she takes the fugues at a lively pace, just a touch too fast for the music to sound comfortable: this is brilliant, edge-of-your seat playing.

Her playing, with its thoughtful details of timing, clearly conveys the structure of the music. She finds the same grandeur of manner in the *Passacaille* that ends the G minor Suite. For the rest, it's mainly dance music: some lively *courantes* and exuberant gigues, sober and deliberate allemandes, spacious and noble sarabandes – the crisp and precise fingerwork in that of the B flat Suite in the Second Set (1733), with its intensely detailed line, is a delight.

These are the most appealing versions of Handel's suites: fresh, alive, with a real command of style and technique but also just a hint of risk about the playing. Handel's harpsichord music has sometimes been called dull, but there isn't a moment here when you'd believe that.

'The Secret Handel'

Handel Water Music, HWV348-50 – Air in F; Bourée and Hornpipe in F. Chaconne, HWV435. Concerto, HWV487 – Allegro; Andante. Six Fugues or Voluntaries, HWV605-10 – Fugue, HWV610. Eight Keyboard Suites, Set I – Suite No 3, HWV428; Suite No 5, HWV430. Air, HWV464. Air, HWV467. Suite, HWV446a. Minuet, HWV545. Minuet, HWV547. Minuet, HWV546. Air, HWV469. Allemande, HWV479. Courante, HWV489. Prelude on 'Jesu meine Freude', HWV480 **Krieger** Aria and 24 Variations **Zachow** Suite – Sarabande; Gigue

Christopher Hogwood, ªDerek Adlam *clavs*
Metronome ② METCD1060 (99' · DDD)   Ⓕ

Alas, 'The Secret Handel' does not unveil any salacious facts about the composer's sexual orientation or hitherto unsuspected illegitimate offspring. However, Christopher Hogwood's illuminating booklet essay hints that the inclusion of a few short pieces by the Hallé organist Zachow and an aria and 24 variations by Krieger illustrate the kind of music that the young Handel might have copied in his long-lost manuscript keyboard book. Also, Hogwood's use of clavichord reflects the famous story that the boy Handel, forbidden to learn music by his disapproving father, smuggled a clavichord into his attic in order to practice secretly during the night.

On the first disc, which includes a version of Handel's third keyboard suite ornamented by Gottlieb Muffat, Hogwood plays an instrument built by the Hamburg keyboard builder Johann Albrecht Hass in 1761. Its plangent yet warm textures produce a fascinating sound, utterly different from the familiar hard brilliance of harpsichords. A fastidiously stylish performance of Aria and Variations in G ('The Harmonious Blacksmith') is a fine advocacy for the clavichord's virtues. On disc two, Hogwood plays two other keyboards, including a magical-sounding Gräbner instrument (Dresden, 1761) that is similar to a small Italian clavichord now in Maidstone Museum that reputedly belonged to Handel. A few movements from the *Water Music* show how Handel's music might have been conceived before the compositional skeleton was garbed in orchestral flesh. Hogwood's thoughtfully prepared programme and articulate playing is a laudable fusion of scholarly detail and artistic insight.

Dixit Dominus, HWV232

Dixit Dominus. Laudate pueri Dominum, HWV237
Saeviat tellus, HWV240. Salve regina, HWV241
Annick Massis *sop* **Magdalena Kožená** *mez*
Chœur des Musiciens du Louvre;
Les Musiciens du Louvre / Marc Minkowski
Archiv Produktion 459 627-2AH (78' · DDD · T/t)
                                    ⒻⒺⒺ▸

These pieces, written in Handel's early twenties, embody a kind of excitement and freedom, and a richness of ideas, that come from his contact with a different tradition and a sudden realisation that the musical world was larger and less constricted than he had imagined, tucked away in provincial middle and north Germany. You can hear him stretching his musical wings in this music. And it certainly doesn't fail to take off in these very lively performances. The quickish tempos habitually favoured by Marc Minkowski are by no means out of place here. The *Saeviat tellus*, although little recorded, is pretty familiar music, as Handel recycled most of it, notably the brilliant opening number in *Apollo e Dafne* and the lovely 'O nox dulcis' in *Agrippina*. This is a solo motet, as too is the *Salve regina*, notable for

the expressive vocal leaps and chromatic writing in the 'Ad te clamamus' and the solo organ and string writing in the 'Eia ergo' that follows. *Laudate pueri*, which uses a choir, is another fresh and energetic piece: the choir of the Musiciens du Louvre do their pieces in rousing fashion, and there's some happy oboe playing, as well as fine singing from Kožená, earlier on, in particular in the hugely spirited 'Excelsus super omnes'. The biggest item is the *Dixit Dominus*, where the choir sings very crisply. The illustrative settings of 'ruinas' tumbling down through the registers, and the 'conquassabit' that follows, are truly exciting; and the long closing chorus is done with due weight at quite a measured pace. These splendid performances truly capture the spirit of these marvellous pieces.

Handel Dixit Dominus **Caldara** Crucifixus. Missa Dolorosa
Balthasar-Neumann Choir and Ensemble /
Thomas Hengelbrock
Deutsche Harmonia Mundi CD/SACD
82876 58792-2 (63' · DDD · T/t)   ⒻⒺⒺ▸

Handel's *Dixit Dominus*, the magnificent psalm setting composed in Rome in 1707, seems to have an eternal power to startle and delight in equal measure. This performance captures the flamboyant tension and precocious genius that must have struck the 22-year-old's Roman patrons like a thunderbolt. The superb Balthasar-Neumann Choir possess laudable clarity and precision, although the in-house male soloists are less impressive than their rivals for John Eliot Gardiner and Andrew Parrott.

The soprano duet 'De torrente' is ideally hushed and plaintive, but apocalyptic moments such as 'Juravit Dominus' make Thomas Hengelbrock's version comparable with the most striking in the catalogue. The *staccato* chords on 'conquassabit' are delivered with impeccably controlled aggression. The orchestra is magnificent, with the contrast between first and second violins presented in thrilling SACD sound. Two theorbo players drive the music along with firm determination and make the opening of the 'Gloria' snap with an energetic bite.

Some of Hengelbrock's most important work has been the championing of Italian Baroque sacred music (especially Lotti). This time it's the turn of Antonio Caldara, a Venetian active in Rome at about the same time as Handel and was subsequently the most popular and prolific composer at the Viennese court of Emperor Charles VI. The *Kyrie* of the *Missa dolorosa*, composed in 1735, instantly establishes that Caldara was infinitely more than a mediocre talent blessed by good fortune, although the feeling persists that the Mass was made to fit circumstances rather than to endure for posterity. Its splendid moments range from the graceful bassoon solo in 'Domine Fili' to an abrasively dramatic 'Et resurrexit'. Caldara's reputation is further restored by the gorgeous 16-part *Crucifixus* which rounds off this exceptional disc. Highly recommended.

Coronation Anthems

Zadok the Priest, HWV258. **Let thy hand be strengthened**, HWV259. **The King shall rejoice**, HWV260. **My heart is inditing**, HWV261.

Coronation Anthems, HWV258-61. Ode for the Birthday of Queen Anne, 'Eternal Source of Light Divine', HWV74
Susan Gritton sop **Robin Blaze** counterten **Michael George** bass **King's College Choir, Cambridge; Academy of Ancient Music / Stephen Cleobury**
EMI 557140-2 (61' · DDD) Ⓕ❶➛

Recordings of the Coronation Anthems are usually winners – the old Willcocks one from King's, and the Preston one from Westminster Abbey certainly were in their day – and this one certainly hits the mark. It's a traditional enough reading, without eccentricities, with plenty of energy and duly grand in scale: listen to the noble opening of *Zadok the Priest*, the introduction beautifully sustained and shaped, and then overwhelmingly grand at the choral entry, whose weight and power may surprise you, bearing in mind the quite modest size of the King's choir. They know just how to manage this kind of music in the chapel acoustic, which is naturally appropriate to the music.

The other three are no less enjoyable. The clear young voices, free of the fuzziness and soft edges of most choirs, help in such movements as the first of 'Let thy hand be strengthened', or the lightly sprung first of 'My heart is inditing' and its vigorous finale too. The *Ode for the Birthday of Queen Anne*, one of Handel's earliest settings of English words is more of a rarity. This is a lively performance, with clear and light solo singing, notably from Robin Blaze. There are also admirable contributions from Susan Gritton and Michael George. Excellent choral singing, and the Academy of Ancient Music are on their toes throughout.

Coronation Anthems, HWV258-61. Messiah – Worthy is the Lamb; Amen. Jephtha – Overture. Organ Concerto, Op 4 No 4. Solomon – Arrival of the Queen of Sheba
The Sixteen / Harry Christophers
Coro COR16066 (70' · DDD · T) Ⓕ❶❶❶➛

There are plenty of very good recordings of the four anthems that Handel composed for the coronation of King George II and Queen Caroline, but this new one by The Sixteen leaps straight towards the top of the heap (those preferring to hear boy trebles might already admire the excellent version by King's College, Cambridge, under Cleobury, above).

We have come selfishly to expect reliability, stylishness and honest fine musicianship from Harry Christophers, his singers and instrumentalists. Yet these fresh, spontaneous and vivacious performances are revelatory. Not only is

the choral singing wonderfully clear, perfectly enunciated, beautifully phrased and impeccably tuned, but also the orchestral playing – an aspect too often relegated to auto-pilot in this repertoire – is brilliantly alert, bold and lyrical. *Zadok the Priest* never fails to make a strong impression even in average performances (and The Sixteen's expertly judged reading is anything but average), but the special quality of this disc is that the other three lesser-known anthems also receive performances that allow them to shine just as brightly as the most famous (and shortest) anthem. *My heart is inditing* is radiantly performed ('The King shall have pleasure in her beauty' is gorgeously shaped), *The King shall rejoice* is splendidly poised and paced, and the first part of *Let thy hand be strengthened* conveys the perfect juxtaposition of forthrightness and elegance. Christophers's sure direction locks onto the musical interest and richness of each section in the longer anthems (some other good versions rely on good openings and grand conclusions, but the bits in between sometimes get a bit lost). Coupled with a sparkling account of the Organ Concerto Op 4 No 4 (superbly played by Alastair Ross, and with a magnificent choral 'Alleluia' finale created for the 1735 revival of *Athalia*), a couple of orchestral interludes and the last chorus of *Messiah*, the judicious programme avoids the overkill factor one sometimes encounters when all four anthems are heard consecutively.

Donald Burrows's booklet-note is ideally detailed and accessible, and overall this disc ranks as The Sixteen's most exciting achievement in its impressive Handel discography.

Chandos Anthems

O praise the Lord with one consent, HWV254. Let God arise, HWV256a. My song shall be alway, HWV252
Dame Emma Kirkby sop **Iestyn Davies** counterten **James Gilchrist** ten **Neal Davies** bass **Choir of Trinity College, Cambridge; Academy of Ancient Music / Stephen Layton**
Hyperion CDA67737 (66' · DDD · T) Ⓕ❶

Here are three of the 11 so-called *Chandos Anthems* composed for James Brydges, the Earl of Carnarvon (from 1719 the First Duke of Chandos). Handel's music was tailor-made for fewer performers than those featured here. Nevertheless, the 40 members of the Choir of Trinity College, Cambridge, sing with flexibility and lightness. The opening chorus of *O praise the Lord with one consent* is crisply articulate and lightly shaped, and consonants are attacked with voracity. Most of the choral contributions have sweetness and delicacy. Stephen Layton lets the performers off the leash a little in the final pealing 'Alleluia' sections of each anthem, and in some dynamic passages of *Let God arise*, based on *Dixit Dominus*. The Academy of Ancient Music's playing is often understated, and the introductory sonatas of *Let God arise* and *My song shall be alway* feature convivial oboe solos played by Katharina Spreckelsen. The four illustrious soloists excel in numerous short movements. Iestyn Davies navigates some difficult low passages in 'Praise him, all ye that in his house' (HWV254) without traces of strain. Neal Davies is authoritative, James Gilchrist is on fine dramatic form in 'Like as the smoke vanisheth' (HWV256*a*), and Emma Kirkby shows her stylistic intelligence and masterful communication of text in the radiant opening of HWV252. It is enjoyable to hear some of Handel's lesser-known and more intimate English church music performed with such elegant restraint and skill.

Ode for St Cecilia's Day

Ode for St Cecilia's Day, HWV76. Cecilia, volgi un sguardo, HWV89. **P**
Carolyn Sampson sop **James Gilchrist** ten
Choir of The King's Consort;
The King's Consort / Robert King
Hyperion CDA67463 (78' · DDD · T/t) Ⓕ**OOO**

 This completes the series of recordings exploring the smaller works Handel inserted into his glorious setting of Dryden's *Alexander's Feast*. Robert King has previously recorded *The Choice of Hercules*, which was created for the 1751 revival. The tenor cantata *Look down, harmonious Saint* was intended as the interlude for the original run in 1736, but was rejected in favour of *Cecilia, volgi un sguardo*. It's a splendid idea to pair this seldom-heard Italian cantata with Dryden's sublime *Ode for St Cecilia's Day* that Handel created to fulfil the same function three years later.

This is a mouth-watering performance of Handel's colourfully gorgeous ode. 'The trumpets' loud clangour' features Crispian Steele-Perkins on fine form, flautist Rachel Brown enchants in 'The soft complaining flute', and Jonathan Cohen's cello solo in 'What passion cannot Music raise and quell!' is sweetly inspired. The King's Consort and Choir perform with perfect juxtaposition of flamboyance and taste. James Gilchrist sings with authority: he's a Handel tenor of the highest order.

This recording is in a class of its own when it comes to the seemingly effortless, beautiful singing of Carolyn Sampson, now the best British early music soprano by quite some distance. She's sensitively partnered by organist Matthew Halls in the sublime 'But oh! what art can teach', which has a breathtaking poignancy. Notwithstanding many agreeable past achievements, King has seldom produced a disc of such outstanding conviction.

L'Allegro, il Penseroso.... HWV55

L'Allegro, il Penseroso, ed il Moderato **P**
Patrizia Kwella, Marie McLaughlin, Jennifer Smith
sops **Michael Ginn** treb **Maldwyn Davies, Martyn**

Hill tens **Stephen Varcoe** bar **Monteverdi Choir;**
English Baroque Soloists / Sir John Eliot Gardiner
Erato ② 2292-45377-2 (116' · ADD · T/t) Recorded 1980
Ⓜ**OOO**

The score of *L'Allegro, il Penseroso ed il Moderato* is presented here virtually complete. The soprano aria 'But O, sad virgin' is omitted, which if you look at the marvellous opening for two cellos, seems savage indeed, but the music does rather lose its way in the long decorative passages for both voice and instruments, and its absence need not be regretted. The band is small and so is the superbly alert chorus. Playing and singing constantly delight by their delicacy. The three soprano soloists sound poised and clean cut. Jennifer Smith's high notes are an especial joy. Handel wanted a boy treble for two arias and presumably knew that their words were never very clear; this one produces some pretty sounds. The succession of charming miniatures is interrupted in the middle of Part 2 by more substantial items and a blaze of brilliant coloratura from several soloists. Martyn Hill's 'These delights' is triumphantly good, and the choral singing is excitingly precise. The final chorus in Part 2, a fugue with four subjects, is sublime, but he did not bother himself unduly with the final chorus in Part 3. But in general this is very likeable music, its charm, conciseness and emphasis on word-painting unlike anything else in Handel. The sound quality is very good.

L'Allegro, il penseroso ed il moderato **P**
Lorna Anderson, Susan Gritton, Claron McFadden
sops **Paul Agnew** ten **Neal Davies** bass **The King's Consort Choir; The King's Consort / Robert King**
Hyperion ② CDA67283/4 (138' · DDD · T/t) Ⓕ

This is the first truly complete recording of Handel's delectable pastoral ode. The early numbers of *L'Allegro* – literally 'the cheerful man' – have a spontaneous exuberance barely matched in Handel's output, while much of the music of *Il penseroso* ('The melancholy man') attains a contemplative ecstasy found elsewhere only in parts of *Theodora*. The whole work is suffused with an almost pantheistic sense of wonder and delight in the natural world. While alive to the *al fresco* gaiety of numbers such as 'Mirth, admit me of thy crew' and 'O let the merry bells', Robert King gives full value to the tranquil reflectiveness that lies at the core of the work, favouring broad tempos and gravely expressive phrasing. Occasionally, as in the soprano aria 'Straight mine eye hath caught new pleasures', his approach seems a shade too reverential. But for the most part he directs this glorious music with affection and relish, abetted by vivid orchestral playing and a typically responsive contribution from the chorus.

Susan Gritton is a soprano of rare accomplishment, with a warm, pure, yet highly individual timbre and a wonderful feeling for the broad Handelian line. Both the *scena* 'Come pensive nun' and the romantic nocturne 'Oft on a plat of rising ground', with its haunting evocation of 'the far-off curfew', are intensely moving; and, with the cellist Jane Coe, she makes an eloquent case for the long florid aria 'But O! sad virgin', omitted in the Gardiner recording. Lorna Anderson, if a mite less secure above the stave, brings an appealing plangent tone to the nightingale aria 'Sweet bird' (done complete here, whereas Gardiner makes drastic cuts) and a trancelike absorption to the sublime 'Hide me from Day's garish eye'. Some slightly odd vowel sounds apart, Claron McFadden's bright, eager tones and nimble coloratura serve the more extrovert arias well; Neal Davies is sturdy in his bucolic hunting number and mellifluous in his minuet aria in *Il moderato*; and Paul Agnew is personable and stylish, though his *legato* is rather shown up by Susan Gritton's in 'As steals the morn'.

Acis and Galatea, HWV49b

Acis and Galatea ⓟ
Sophie Daneman sop Galatea **Paul Agnew** ten Acis
Patricia Petibon sop Damon **Alan Ewing** bass
Polyphemus **Joseph Cornwell** ten Coridon **François
Piolino, David Le Monnier, Andrew Sinclair** tens
Les Arts Florissants / William Christie
Erato ② 3984-25505-2 (93' · DDD · T)　　ⓕⓞⓞⓞ

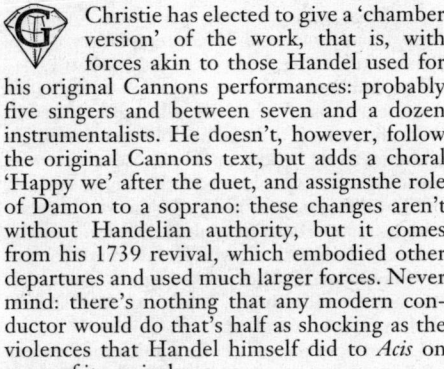

Christie has elected to give a 'chamber version' of the work, that is, with forces akin to those Handel used for his original Cannons performances: probably five singers and between seven and a dozen instrumentalists. He doesn't, however, follow the original Cannons text, but adds a choral 'Happy we' after the duet, and assigns the role of Damon to a soprano: these changes aren't without Handelian authority, but it comes from his 1739 revival, which embodied other departures and used much larger forces. Never mind: there's nothing that any modern conductor would do that's half as shocking as the violences that Handel himself did to *Acis* on some of its revivals.

Christie strongly emphasises the work's central division. He adopts rather speedy tempos throughout Act 1 (that is, up to 'Happy we'), which is concerned with pastoral love: Acis's 'Where shall I seek' and Damon's 'Shepherd, what art thou pursuing?' don't seem, respectively, like Larghetto and Andante, but the urgency and the joy of the lovers' mutual desire is strongly caught. In Act 2, where Polyphemus's shadow falls over their love, the sparkle and vitality give way to the pathetic and the elegiac. Christie's tempos here are steady, and his shaping of the act seems something of a departure: its climaxes here come not in 'The flocks shall leave the mountains' (when Acis is killed) and 'Heart, the seat of soft delight' (when he's immortalised as a river) – arguably the most powerful musical numbers – but in the ensembles, 'Mourn, all ye Muses!' and 'Must I my Acis still bemoan', where the sustained, gen-

tle singing of Christie's ensemble lends the music an emotional weight that it does not usually achieve. There are other, mostly smaller, points where Christie does new and different things, and some will not like them all. Christie's orchestra is one-to-a-part, as Handel's may have been: this seems to produce a slightly oboe-heavy balance in some items, and in the lightly scored pieces the continuo line seems over-weighted.

The opening scenes, then, are done more lustily, in two senses, than usual. The choral opening is remarkably hearty and robust. Sophie Daneman sings Galatea with something more than stylised pastoral sensuality: there's real intensity in her airs, with a pretty warbling recorder, very chirrupy, and sharply moulded phrasing, and particular sensuality in 'As when the dove'. If her 'Heart, the seat', at the end, seems to carry rather less emotional weight, that's part of the overall reading of the work. Paul Agnew makes an elegant Acis in Act 1, with an eager 'Where shall I seek' and 'Love in her eyes sits playing' done with quiet passion. 'Love sounds th'alarm', later, is lively but not quite stirring. Patricia Petibon's Damon is prettily sung, with a nice ring to the voice, and Alan Ewing's Polyphemus, done with spirit and humour in a well-focused, firm-edged voice and articulated with precision, is excellent.

Christie's version may not be everyone's answer, but it's a polished and strongly characterised performance, and well worth trying.

Acis and Galatea (original Cannons 1718 version) ⓟ
Susan Hamilton sop Galatea **Nicholas Mulroy** ten
Acis **Matthew Brook** bass Polyphemus **Thomas
Hobbs** ten Damon **Nicholas Hurndall Smith** ten
Coridon
The Dunedin Consort & Players / John Butt
Linn ② 💿 CKD319 (95' · DDD)　　ⓕⓞⓞⓑ➔

Handel's *Acis and Galatea* has been recorded often, but the original version written for small-scale performance by only five singers (soprano, three tenors and bass) and a small band at Cannons in 1718 has almost never been properly revived. This beggars belief because the Cannons version text makes more dramatic sense and the musical scale of it is charming. It is certainly among Handel's most perfect creations. Thankfully, John Butt has researched the performing conditions and text of the Cannons *Acis*. The philological aspects of the Dunedin Consort & Players' new recording are impeccable, and, better still, the performance is utterly magical.

The Sinfonia brims with unforced personality, after which the pastoral chorus 'O the pleasure of the plains' is relaxed, with the oboes given enough space to weave their imitative lines clearly. The five singers and the band are beautifully in proportion with each other, and Linn's sound recording is stunningly good. Susan Hamilton's light, articulate soprano is preferable to an operatic voice in the role of Galatea. Nicholas Mulroy's Acis is resonant and suave, combining muscularity with elegance. The madrigal-like beauty of 'Wretched lovers' is breathtaking: the blend and understanding between the five singers is deeply satisfying, and the menacing music to convey the arrival of Polyphemus is astutely integrated. Matthew Brook's Polyphemus is extrovert, powerful and amusing, but also arouses pity and tenderness from the listener in 'I rage, I melt, I burn'. The dialogue between the hapless would-be seducer and the disgusted Galatea is superbly enacted by Brook and Hamilton. The roles of Damon and Coridon are admirably sung by Nicholas Hurndall Smith and Thomas Hobbs.

Butt's direction from the harpsichord is a role model of taste and style, and he insightfully conveys the elusive changing tone of the story from pastoral romp into personal tragedy. Previous versions of merit still possess enduring appeal, but it seems to me that the Dunedins have transformed the way in which we can understand and enjoy Handel's lovely early English masterpiece.

Acis and Galatea (arr Mendelssohn)
Julia Kleiter sop Galatea **Christoph Prégardien** ten
Acis **Wolf Matthias Friedrich** bass Polyphemus
Michael Slattery ten Damon
**North German Radio Choir; Göttingen Festival
Orchestra / Nicholas McGegan**
Carus CARUS83 420 (73' · DDD)   (F)

The virtues of *Acis and Galatea* were clear enough more than a century later for the 19-year-old Mendelssohn to arrange the work for the Berlin Sing-Akademie in 1828-29 (with a German version of the libretto prepared by his sister Fanny). One might uncharitably (but accurately) criticise that the teenage Mendelssohn's feverish excitement at discovering Handel led to him throwing everything he could (almost including the kitchen sink, so it seems) at the music. Unlike Mozart's more discreet and softer reorchestration of *Acis* (1788), there is an intense amount of intervention in Mendelssohn's orchestral score, which is tailored for a full-scale symphony orchestra and large chorus.

Nicholas McGegan and his Göttingen Festival Orchestra gave the modern premiere of Mendelssohn's score at the 2008 Göttingen Handel Festival, and the ensuing recording is crisply detailed. The most amusing effects are huge bursts of brass and timpani explosions associated with Polyphemus, who is sung with gusto by Wolf Matthias Friedrich. Acis is sung with a hint of strain by Christoph Prégardien, and Julia Kleiter's Galatea is efficient.

The NDR Choir are jovial or doleful as the music requires. McGegan directs with liveliness, and it's hard to imagine this arrangement receiving a better advocate. It's bombastic and clumsy in comparison to Handel's delightful original, but the young Mendelssohn's perspective is entertaining.

Alexander's Feast, HWV75

Alexander's Feast[a]. Organ Concerto, Op 4 No 1 HWV289[b]. Harp Concerto, Op 4 No 6 HWV294[c]
[a]**Nancy Argenta** sop **Alan Partridge** ten [a]**Michael George** bass [b]**Paul Nicholson** org [c]**Andrew Lawrence-King** hp **The Sixteen; Symphony of Harmony and Invention / Harry Christophers**
Coro ② COR16028 (116' · DDD · T)   Ⓜ▷

Alexander's Feast, an ode to St Cecilia by the long-dead John Dryden, was set by Handel in 1736 and revised many times. Subtitled 'The Power of Musick', it describes a banquet held by Alexander the Great after his victory over the Persians. The singing and playing of Timotheus inspire Alexander to drunkenness, pity, love and revenge, one after the other. What has this to do with the patron saint of music, you might well ask? The answer comes in a commentary towards the end, when Dryden contrasts Timotheus's pagan skills with the invention of the organ and the celestial connections of 'Divine Cecilia', who 'enlarg'd the former narrow bounds'.

The music is superb, and it's given a superb performance here. The Sixteen (actually 18, with two extra sopranos and an all-male alto line) are a little lightweight in the grander choruses but they sing with precision and unforced tone. Over a swiftly moving ground bass, 'The many rend the skies' goes with a swing; their finest moment, though, is their hushed contemplation of the Persian king lying dead on the field of battle.

The lion's share of the solos goes to Nancy Argenta, whose fresh tones, admirably suited to 'War, he sung, is toil and trouble', are cunningly and effectively veiled for 'He chose a mournful muse', an accompanied recitative in the manner of 'Thy rebuke hath broken his heart'. Ian Partridge is superb in his subtle handling of the words, as he is with his wonderful breath control in 'Happy pair'. Michael George is perfect in 'Revenge, Timotheus cries': hissing snakes, flashing sparkles and all.

The orchestration is a constant delight. In some of the solo numbers Handel uses only violins and continuo; elsewhere he introduces a solo cello, a trumpet obbligato, recorders and horns. Best of all is the creepy middle section of 'Revenge, Timotheus cries', where he conjures up the 'ghastly band' of the Grecian dead with Neapolitan sixth cadences played by the violas and bassoons in octaves. All these opportunities are seized with relish by the Symphony of Harmony and Invention. In an unsuitable church acoustic, Harry Christophers sets unfailingly suitable tempi. And to add to our delight he includes the concerti detailed above that are integral to the piece.

Alexander Balus, HWV65

Alexander Balus   ℗
Lynne Dawson, Claron McFadden sops **Catherine Denley** mez **Charles Daniels** ten **Michael George** bass **New College Choir, Oxford; The King's**

Consort and Choir / Robert King
Hyperion ② CDA67241/2 (156' · DDD · N/T)   Ⓕ

Alexander Balus has never been one of Handel's more popular oratorios. That's mainly because its plot is by modern standards lacking in drama and motivation, and accordingly doesn't call forth the vein of his music that nowadays has the strongest appeal. It's essentially a sentimental drama, in which the interest centres on the characters' emotional reactions to their situations, amatory, political and religious, and these are rather static in the first two acts but much more powerful in the more eventful third with the deaths of both Alexander and Ptolomee.

Here we have a very capable, idiomatic, sensibly cast performance under Robert King. The choruses are especially accomplished. The New College Choir, supported by men from The King's Consort Choir, is confident, bright-toned and vigorous, clean in line and well balanced. Lynne Dawson sings beautifully in her firm and resonant soprano and her usual poised and unaffected style. Her singing of the lamenting music in the final act is particularly moving. Cleopatra has a couple of duets, one with some attractive interplay with the secondary character Aspasia, sung with much assurance by Claron McFadden. As Alexander, Catherine Denley sings with much confidence and directness in music that isn't all of special individuality. Jonathan is sung fluently and warmly, but very plainly, by Charles Daniels. Lastly there's Michael George, who's ideally suited to the villainous Ptolomee, with his forceful (but always musical) manner and the touch of blackness in his tone. The orchestral playing is accomplished, and often rather carefully shaped. The recitative moves at a steady but natural pace; ornamentation is generally modest. All Handelians will want to acquire this set, and others should not be put off by the indifferent press *Alexander Balus* has received from time to time.

Athalia, HWV52

Athalia   Ⓟ
Joan Sutherland *sop* Athalia **Emma Kirkby** *sop*
Josabeth **Aled Jones** *treb* Joas **James Bowman**
counterten Joad **Anthony Rolfe Johnson** *ten*
Mathan **David Thomas** *bass* Abner **New College
Choir, Oxford; Academy of Ancient Music /
Christopher Hogwood**
Decca Gramophone Awards Collection ② 475 201-2
(122' · DDD · N/T)   Ⓜ❶❷❸↦

Ⓖ *Athalia*, composed for Oxford in 1733 to a libretto that draws on Racine's play, tells of the usurping, apostate Jewish queen Athalia, and her overthrow when the prophet Joad and his wife Josabeth bring the true heir, the boy Joas, to the throne. The action is feebly handled by the librettist, Samuel Humphreys; but several of the characters are quite strong and Handel grasps the opportunities offered him for striking music.

Athalia fares best of all, musically, as one would expect; and it was a brilliant stroke of imagination to ask Joan Sutherland to take the role here. She's a great Handelian, but not a figure you expect to see in early-music circles. In the event, the slight disparity of approach between her and the other members of the cast serves ideally to symbolise the separation of Athalia from her fellow-Israelites. She uses more vibrato than the rest of the cast, but the singing is magnificent in its grandeur and its clear, bell-like, perfectly focused tone. Among the rest, Emma Kirkby is on her very best form, singing coolly, with poised musicianship, and with quite astonishing technical command at times. James Bowman, as Joad, has his moments, and always sounds well. David Thomas is dependable in the often very vigorous music for Abner; and as Athalia's priest, Mathan, Anthony Rolfe Johnson sings in shapely fashion. The boy Joas is sung, as it should be, by a boy, in this case Aled Jones, who gives a very controlled, exact performance, perhaps rather careful but of intense tonal beauty. At its best, the choral singing is first-rate, spirited, forthright and accurate, but it can have an air of the routine. There's much good, crisp orchestral playing, though some of the AAM's less positive characteristics are evident: an occasional moment of unsure ensemble, and a lack of broad shaping. These are however perfectionist quibbles: these discs, excellently recorded, give an admirable and often striking realisation of a choice work.

Esther, HWV50*b*

Esther (1732 version)   Ⓟ
**Rosemary Joshua, Rebecca Outram, Cecilia
Osmond** *sops* **Susan Bickley** *mez* **James Bowman**
counterten **Angus Smith, Andrew Kennedy,
Christopher Watson** *tens* **Christopher Purves** *bar*
**London Handel Choir and Orchestra / Laurence
Cummings**
Somm ② SOMMCD238/9 (137' · DDD)
Recorded live in March 2002   Ⓕ

This is a particularly welcome and important world-premiere recording. Handel composed Esther in about 1718-20 for James Brydges, the Earl of Carnarvon (and later Duke of Chandos), using a libretto that was anonymously adapted from Thomas Brereton's English translation of a play by Racine. This slender work, containing only six scenes, lays a strong claim to being the first English oratorio, but Handel seems not to have considered performing it for a public audience until 1732, when the entrepreneurial composer thoroughly revised the score to fit his company of Italian opera singers (including Senesino, Strada and Montagnana, who all sang in English), and enlisted the aid of the writer Samuel Humphreys to expand the drama with additional scenes. This is the historic version of Esther that launched Handel's oratorio career in London, but it has remained inexplicably neglected in modern times.

Laurence Cummings is one of our finest and most natural Handelian conductors. The Israelite Woman's sensuous opening number 'Breathe soft, ye gales' (featuring recorders, oboes, bassoons, harp, theorbo, five-part strings and organ) is neatly judged by the impressive London Handel Orchestra. The superb choir is enthusiastic and masterful, and the two inserted Coronation Anthems *My heart is inditing* and *Zadok the Priest* (the latter given a parody text) are both performed magnificently. James Bowman sounds a little fragile in the most extensive coloratura passages written for Senesino in 'Endless fame', and the part of Mordecai seems uncomfortably low for Susan Bickley (which is not helped by the dragging speed of 'Dread not, righteous Queen, the danger'), but in general the soloists form a consistently solid team. Christopher Purves is marvellous as the scheming and bullying evil minister Haman, and is equally good at singing the pitiful and lyrical 'Turn not, O Queen, thy face away' when the villain fears his deserved doom.

The all-round excellence of this live concert performance from Handel's parish church, St George's, Hanover Square, makes it an essential treat for Handelians.

Israel in Egypt, HWV54

Israel in Egypt   **P**
Nancy Argenta, Emily Van Evera sops **Timothy Wilson** counterten **Anthony Rolfe Johnson** ten **David Thomas, Jeremy White** basses **Taverner Choir and Players / Andrew Parrott**
Virgin Classics Veritas ② 562155-2 (135' · DDD · T)
ⒷⒹ➔

Israel in Egypt, of all Handel's works, is the choral one *par excellence* – so much so, in fact, that it was something of a failure in Handel's own time because solo singing was much preferred to choral by the audiences. Andrew Parrott gives a complete performance of the work, in its original form: that's to say, prefaced by the noble funeral anthem for Queen Caroline, as adapted by Handel to serve as a song of mourning by the captive Israelites. This first part is predominantly slow, grave music, powerfully elegiac; the Taverner Choir shows itself to be firm and clean of line, well focused and strongly sustained. The chorus has its chance to be more energetic in the second part, with the famous and vivid Plague choruses – in which the orchestra too plays its part in the pictorial effects, with the fiddles illustrating in turn frogs, flies and hailstones. And last, in the third part, there's a generous supply of the stirring C major music in which Handel has the Israelites give their thanks to God, in some degree symbolising the English giving thanks for the Hanoverian monarchy and the Protestant succession. Be that as it may, the effect is splendid. The solo work is first-rate, too, with Nancy Argenta radiant in Miriam's music in the final scene and distinguished contributions from David Thomas and Anthony Rolfe Johnson.

Jephtha, HWV70

Jephtha   **P**
Lynne Dawson, Ruth Holton sops **Anne Sofie von Otter** mez **Michael Chance** counterten **Nigel Robson** ten **Stephen Varcoe** bar **Alastair Ross** hpd **Paul Nicholson** org **Monteverdi Choir; English Baroque Soloists / Sir John Eliot Gardiner**
Philips ③ 422 351-2PH3 (158' · DDD · T)   ⒻⓄⓄⓄ➔

Jephtha has the same basic story as several eastern Mediterranean myths familiar to the opera-goer (in *Idomeneo* and *Iphigénie en Aulide*, for example), of the father compelled to sacrifice his child. In the event Jephtha's daughter Iphis isn't sacrificed: when, Abraham-like, her father has shown himself willing to perform God's will, and she has shown herself ready to accept it, an angel happily intervenes and commutes her sentence to perpetual virginity. But not before the tragic situation has provoked some of the noblest music Handel wrote. From the moment that Jephtha sees that it's his daughter who has to fall victim to his improvident oath, the music, hitherto on a good but not outstanding level, acquires a new depth, above all in the sequence at the end of Act 2. This recording does the work full justice. It could scarcely have been better cast. Nigel Robson seems ideal as Jephtha. He has due weight as well as vigour, style as well as expressive force. Lynne Dawson's Iphis is also a real success. Sometimes this role is done in a girlishly 'innocent' vein; she does more than that, establishing the character in the appealing love duet in Part 1. Her firm, well-focused, unaffected singing is just right for this role.

The other outstanding contribution comes from Michael Chance as Hamor, her unfortunate betrothed. Stephen Varcoe sings Zebul's music with due resonance and spirit, and Anne Sofie von Otter makes a distinguished contribution in Storgè's music: 'Scenes of horror' has a splendid attack and depth of tone, and 'Let other creatures die!' is spat out with rare power. Ruth Holton makes a pleasantly warm and mellifluous angel. The Monteverdi Choir is in fine voice, responsive to all that Gardiner asks of them. Here and there one might cavil at some of the dynamic shaping in the choruses, for example in 'Doubtful fear' in Act 3; and the Overture can be a trifle fussy in detail. But the broad vision of the work, the rhythmic energy that runs through it and the sheer excellence of the choral and orchestral contributions speak for themselves. Cuts are very few, and amply justified by authentic precedent. This recording is firmly recommended as the standard version of this great work.

Joseph and his Brethren, HWV59

Joseph and his Brethren   **P**
Yvonne Kenny sop **Catherine Denley** mez **Connor Burrowes** treb **James Bowman** counterten **John Mark Ainsley** ten **Michael George** bass

**New College Choir, Oxford; The King's Consort
Choir; The King's Consort / Robert King**
Hyperion ③ CDA67171/3 (164' · DDD · T/t)   Ⓕ

There's never been a complete, professional
recording of *Joseph and his Brethren*, a neglect
out of proportion to the merits of its music.
It's full of good and characteristic things, and
there are several scenes, including the extended
denouement in the last act, that are very moving. The work begins splendidly, with an
unusual overture heralding a deeply felt opening scene for Joseph, languishing in an Egyptian prison. The setting of his prophecy is
effective, with seven bars of darting arpeggios
for the years of plenty and seven of sparse
harmonic writing, *adagio*, for the famine years.
The rest of Act 1 celebrates Joseph's foresight,
preferment and marriage to Asenath, Phar-
aoh's daughter. The highlights of Act 2
include a prison scene for Simeon, an agonised G minor accompanied recitative and
aria, a beautiful, nostalgic idyll for Joseph, and
scenes for Joseph with his brothers which
incorporate a splendid outburst from Simeon,
an aria from Benjamin and a moving chorus
from the brothers, a sustained prayer and a
richly worked fugue.

The soloists dispatch all this music with spirit
and accuracy. James Bowman is in excellent
voice in the title-role, full, rich and duly agile in
the rapid music. *Joseph* is well suited to Robert
King's way of conducting Handel. This isn't a
specially dramatic performance, but carefully
moulded and intelligently paced. The choir
produces a sound that's bright and firm and the
singing is resolute. King is particularly good at
shaping the dynamics in a natural and unanimous way.

Messiah, HWV56

Messiah   Ⓟ
Arleen Auger *sop* **Anne Sofie von Otter** *mez*
Michael Chance *counterten* **Howard Crook** *ten*
John Tomlinson *bass* **The Choir of the English
Concert; The English Concert / Trevor Pinnock**
Archiv Produktion ② 4775904 (150' · DDD · T)
                                    ⓂⓄⓄ▷

How authentic is authentic? Trevor Pinnock
and The English Concert, while using period
instruments, are guaranteed to appeal very
widely to traditional lovers of Handel's masterpiece, who might as a rule opt for a performance with modern instruments. Pinnock gets
the best of both worlds. A distinctive point is
that, even more than his rivals, he brings out
the impact of timpani and trumpets, above all
in the 'Hallelujah' and 'Amen' choruses. There
he stirs the blood in a way that even Sargent
would have envied. Another point is that a
genuine, dark, firm, bass soloist has been chosen, John Tomlinson, who's ripely resonant
here. Traditionalists who lament the lack of
dark bass tone and the predominance of bari-

tonal shades in Handel today will doubtless
raise a cheer, and if it comes to authenticity,
Handel must surely have been thinking of just
such a voice, rather than anything thinner or
more discreet. Not only Tomlinson but Arleen
Auger too will delight listeners of all Handelian
persuasions. She has one of the sweetest, most
ravishing soprano sounds on any of the current
versions, and the warmth of expressiveness,
whether strictly authentic or not, brings many
of the most memorable moments in the whole
performance. Try the close of 'I know that my
Redeemer liveth', where the dramatic contrasts
of dynamic are extreme and masterfully controlled, without a hint of sentimentality. The
male alto, Michael Chance, also outshines his
direct rivals in artistry and beauty of tone, but
he's given only a proportion of the alto numbers. The majority are given to Anne Sofie von
Otter. Hers is another beautiful voice, finely
controlled. The recording is one of the finest
available, with plenty of bloom and with inner
clarity never making textures sound thin or
overanalytical.

Messiah
Carolyn Sampson *sop* **Catherine Wyn-Rogers** *contr*
Mark Padmore *ten* **Christopher Purves** *bass*
**The Sixteen; Orchestra of The Sixteen /
Harry Christophers**
Coro ② COR16062 (145' · DDD)
Includes bonus excerpts disc of previous Handel
recordings by The Sixteen   ⓂⓄⓄ▷

Over the past few decades Harry Christophers
and The Sixteen have performed *Messiah* about
150 times. This new Coro recording presents
them to better advantage than their uneven
1987 version for Hyperion: the choir remains
excellent 21 years later but the orchestra and
soloists are a vast improvement. Only one member of the choir and two orchestral players
repeat their roles in the 2008 performance, and
the violin section has swelled from seven to 12,
which helps to produce a stronger theatrical
sound. Christophers's interpretation nowadays
is just over four minutes longer than it was in
1987, so there are no radical changes in his overall pacing, but taking a few things a notch slower
suggests an increased confidence and maturity.

The contribution from the oboes is more telling and to the fore than one usually hears,
although the prominence of the organ as a continuo instrument is seldom convincing (nor is
the use of theorbo accompaniment in recitatives). The Sixteen's choral singing has clarity,
balance, shapely moulding of contrapuntal lines
and plenty of unforced power. When necessary,
resonant homophonic grandeur is achieved
without pomposity. The contrast between the
playful and solemn parts of 'All we like sheep' is
wondrously realised, and the soft sections of
'Since by man came death' are breathtaking.

Three of the soloists earned their spurs as members of The Sixteen. Mark Padmore, a choir
member in 1987 and here making his third (and

HANDEL'S MESSIAH – IN BRIEF

English Concert and Choir / Trevor Pinnock ℗
Archiv ② 423 630-2AH2 (150' · DDD) Ⓕ**OO**🅑➤
Grace and liveliness are the characteristics of Pinnock's fine performance that uses instruments Handel would have recognised, though, arguably, a smaller choir than he would have ideally wanted. Arleen Auger is outstanding in the aria 'I know that my redeemer liveth'.

Gabrieli Consort & Players / Paul McCreesh ℗
Archiv ② 453 464-2AH2 (130' · DDD) Ⓕ**OO**🅑➤
McCreesh favours drama above gracefulness, often to striking effect, though his chorus often sound slick rather than engaged with their text. However, he has a number of fine soloists, with Susan Gritton memorably touching in her two big arias.

London Sym Chorus & Orch / Sir Colin Davis
Philips ② 438 356-2PM2 (144' · ADD) Ⓜ
This 1966 *Messiah*, once thought to be a fresh reinterpretation of a very British institution, ironically became the 'traditional' *Messiah* many of us knew before the rise of such conductors as Pinnock and Norrington. Colin Davis's intelligent direction, using modern orchestral forces, has moments of high drama, and he has a sterling line up of soloists.

Collegium Musicum 90 / Richard Hickox ℗
Chandos ② CHAN0522/3 (141' · DDD) Ⓕ
Although using authentic instruments, this is another fine performance in the post-Colin Davis tradition, with an excellent line-up of soloists (including the young Bryn Terfel) and excellent choral singing.

Academy of Ancient Music; New College Choir, Oxford / Edward Higginbottom ℗
Naxos ② 8 570131/2 (142' · DDD) Ⓢ🅑➤
A performance to show of the magnificent treble voices of the New College Choir. A well-thought-out, nicely scaled reading – and competitively price too.

Dunedin Consort / John Butt ℗
Linn Records CKD285 (138' · DDD· T) Ⓕ**OOO**🅑➤
A wonderfully fresh and uplifting attempt to take us back to the work's first performance. Butt draws on a small 'company' of a dozen singers and wonderfully balances intimacy and drama. The sound is first rate, too. A worthy *Gramophone* Award winner in 2007

Huddersfield Choral Society; Liverpool PO / Malcolm Sargent Ⓗ
Dutton mono ② 2CDEA5010 (146' · ADD) Ⓑ**O**
For a generation of British listeners Sir Malcolm Sargent owned *Messiah*; here his 1946 recording has been lovingly cleaned up for the digital age.

best) *Messiah* recording as a soloist, could be a little lighter in 'Comfort ye', but his evangelical communication of words is highly effective in 'Thy rebuke hath broken his heart'. Carolyn Sampson and the orchestra's violins relish an equal dialogue in 'Rejoice greatly', and her coloratura sparkles with clarity and assurance. Christopher Purves sings 'For behold, darkness shall cover the earth' more softly than one usually hears, and 'The trumpet shall sound' is lyrical and suave (with splendid obbligato from Robert Farley). Christophers conducts with finesse and integrity. This fine team performance is a safe recommendation for anyone wanting to acquire an all-purpose 'period' *Messiah*.

Messiah ℗
Henry Jenkinson , Otta Jones , Robert Brooks *trebs* **Iestyn Davies** *counterten* **Toby Spence** *ten* **Eamonn Dougan** *bass* **Academy of Ancient Music; New College Choir, Oxford / Edward Higginbottom**
Naxos ② 8 570131/2 (142' · DDD) Ⓢ🅑➤

Taking his cue from Handel's 1751 performances, Edward Higginbottom assigns all the soprano solos to some talented boy trebles from the Choir of New College, Oxford. Otta Jones's contribution to 'He shall feed his flock' and Henry Jenkinson's 'I know that my redeemer liveth' are lovely testaments to Higginbottom's crusading 30 years with his choir. At best, Higginbottom's choir produces some marvelous moments ('All we like sheep', and one of the finest 'Amen' fugues on disc). Higginbottom's direction does not boil with dramatic intensity but instead simmers along with patience, elegant judgement and articulate tastefulness.

Some familiar music bears ripe fruit when taken a shade slower than has become common in recent times ('Glory to God' is splendid rather than hurried, and all the better for it). Ex-scholar Toby Spence is on fine form in 'Rejoice greatly', and Iestyn Davies's poetic singing is another enjoyable feature, although one might hanker for a more dramatic treatment of 'shame and spitting' ('He was despised'). 'The trumpet shall sound' resounds with David Blackadder's magnificent playing, and the Academy of Ancient Music play Handel's orchestral parts immaculately. This Naxos release will appeal to those who want an affordable *Messiah* that is beautifully played, brightly sung, sweetly satisfying and unashamedly English in its sentimental roots.

Messiah (Dublin version, 1742) ℗
Susan Hamilton *sop* **Clare Wilkinson, Annie Gill, Heather Cairncross** *mez* **Nicholas Mulroy** *ten* **Matthew Brook** *bar* **Edward Caswell** *bass* **Dunedin Consort / John Butt**
Linn Records CKD285 (138' · DDD· T) Ⓕ**OOO**🅑➤

For an infinitely rewarding fresh look at Handel's most familiar music, look no further than the

Dunedin Consort's performance of Handel's first version, premiered at Dublin in 1742. Bizarrely under-represented in concert and on disc, the Dublin score contains some fascinating music that Handel never reused, such as the substantial chorus 'Break forth into joy'. The exuberant direction by harpsichordist John Butt is meticulously stylish and utterly devoid of crassly pretentious egotism. The playing is unerringly spontaneous and dramatically integrated with singers who illustrate profound appreciation of text. Clare Wilkinson's 'He was despised' is most moving, Susan Hamilton effortlessly skips through a delicious 'Rejoice greatly', and bass Matthew Brook sings as if his life depends on it.

Butt bravely resolves to use the same forces Handel had at his disposal in Dublin, which means that the entire oratorio is sung by a dozen singers (with all soloists required to participate in the choruses, as Handel would have expected). Where this approach might risk worthy dull solos churned out by stalwart choir members, the Dunedin Consort's exemplary singers produce virtuoso choruses that are theatrically charged, splendidly poised and exquisitely blended. Old warhorses 'For unto us a child is born' and 'Surely he hath borne our griefs' are delightfully inspiring. Butt and the Dunedin Consort marry astute scholarship to sincere artistic expression and the result is comfortably the freshest, most natural, revelatory and transparently joyful *Messiah* to have appeared for a very long time. (It's also available as a download at numerous different bit-rates.)

Messiah   H
Dame Isobel Baillie sop **Gladys Ripley** contr **James Johnston** ten **Norman Walker** bass **Huddersfield Choral Society; Royal Liverpool Philharmonic Orchestra / Sir Malcolm Sargent**
Dutton Laboratories Essential Archive mono
② 2CDEA5010 (146' · ADD) Recorded 1946   Ⓑ●

From the 1940s until the early 1960s one of the greatest of regular British musical events (every bit as important as the Proms) was Malcolm Sargent's *Messiah*. He conducted it up and down the country, always to packed houses; indeed, to be able to attend the performance at Huddersfield Town Hall, you needed very special connections, for tickets were scarcer than an invitation to Buckingham Palace! Sargent usually omitted – as he does here – three numbers from Part 2 and four from Part 4. Even then, the performance time was two and a half hours without the interval. Apart from spacious tempos, He had his own ideas about Handelian style. Today we usually listen to a quite different kind of *Messiah*: brisker, often exchanging grandeur for exhilaration; so it's heart-warming to have the opportunity to return to a great tradition that Sargent kept alive for so many years.

This is made possible by one of Dutton Laboratories' most miraculous 78rpm transfers – the finest ever heard taken from 78s of any music – of Sargent's extraordinarily vivid and expansive

recording (the most spontaneous of the three he made). The four splendid soloists – that queen of oratorio sopranos, Dame Isobel Baillie; the rich-voiced Gladys Ripley; the warmly lyrical James Johnson; and the vibrant Norman Walker are right inside their parts. But the star of the performance is undoubtedly Isobel Baillie. Her first entry in 'There were shepherds' is a truly ravishing moment, while her gloriously beautiful 'I know that my Redeemer liveth' has never been surpassed on record. Sargent opens the work with a sumptuous presentation of the Overture, while his tempos for the choruses now sound very slow to ears used to 'authenticity'. He believed deeply in this music and he carried the listener with him. The hushed close of 'All we like sheep' almost brings tears to the eyes. The sound itself is truly astounding. At bargain price it's an ideal investment for anyone who relishes an old-fashioned, large-scale approach to Handel's *Messiah*.

The Occasional Oratorio, HWV62

The Occasional Oratorio
Susan Gritton, Lisa Milne sops **James Bowman**   Ⓟ
counterten **John Mark Ainsley** ten **Michael George** bass **New College Choir, Oxford; The King's Consort / Robert King**
Hyperion ② CDA66961/2 (144' · DDD · T)   Ⓕ

The occasion that called forth this work was the Jacobite rising of 1745 and its impending defeat. The Duke of Cumberland's victory at Culloden was yet to come. Handel, anticipating it, hit off the mood of the moment with a rousing piece full of appeals to patriotic feeling, partly through the traditional identification between the English Protestant culture of Hanoverian times with that of the biblical Hebrews. Much of the music comes from existing works, notably *Israel in Egypt*. The 'plot' pursues the familiar route of Anxiety-Prayer-Victory-Jubilation, but the work lacks the unity of theme and purpose of the great dramatic oratorios; if, however, you value Handel primarily because the music is so splendid you'll find a lot to relish here. King rises to the challenge of this sturdier side of Handel's muse and produces playing and singing full of punch and energy, and with that command of the broad Handelian paragraph without which the music lacks its proper stature.

The grand eight-part choruses, with the choir properly spaced, antiphonally, over the stereo span, make their due effect. King has a distinguished solo team. John Mark Ainsley's singing is particularly touching in the highly original 'Jehovah is my shield', where the rocking figures in the orchestra eventually turn out to symbolise sleep. Also very enjoyable is Susan Gritton's soprano, a sharply focused voice with a fine ring and due agility in the lively music and handled with taste and a keen feeling for the shape of phrases in the contemplative airs. A fine set.

Parnasso in Festa

Parnasso in Festa
Diana Moore *mez* Apollo; Euterpe **Carolyn
Sampson** *sop* Clio **Lucy Crowe** *sop* Orfeo **Rebecca
Outram** *sop* Calliope **Ruth Clegg** *mez* Clori **Peter
Harvey** *bass* Marte **Choir of the King's Consort;
The King's Consort / Matthew Halls**
Hyperion ② CDA67701/2 (132' · DDD · T/t)   Ⓕ

Parnasso in Festa was composed to mark the wedding in 1734 of Handel's favourite pupil, Princess Anne, to Prince William of Orange. A preview in the *Daily Journal* announced that the music was a mixture of 'single Songs, Duetto's, &c. intermix'd with Chorus's, some what in the Style of Oratorio's'. This was spot-on, as most of the numbers were recycled from *Athalia*, performed in Oxford the previous year but not yet heard in London. The setting is Mount Parnassus, where gods, Muses and assorted hangers-on are gathered to celebrate the marriage of Peleus and Thetis, the future parents of Achilles.

Much of the music is perfectly well suited to its new context. The Muse Clio's 'Verginelle dotte', for instance, is a perfect analogue to Josabeth's deathless 'Blooming virgins' in *Athalia*. And even when the sentiments are different – Clio's aria commending the happy pair to the care of the Graces is far removed from Athalia's 'My vengeance awakes me' – the result is not incongruous.

The cast is led by the superb Apollo of Diana Moore, a name new to me, who combines the range of a mezzo with the tone quality of a contralto. Her semiquaver runs in 'Torni pure', one of the few original numbers, are thrilling. With admirable support from Carolyn Sampson and the rest of the cast, and crisp choral and orchestral contributions under Matthew Halls, this recording should ensure that *Parnasso in Festa* will at last come into its own.

Saul, HWV53

Saul
**Nancy Argenta, Susan Gritton, Susan Hemington
Jones** *sops* **Andreas Scholl** *counterten* **Paul Agnew,
Mark Padmore, Tom Phillips, Angus Smith** *tens*
Julian Clarkson, Neal Davies, Jonathan Lemalu
basses
Gabrieli Consort and Players / Paul McCreesh
Archiv Produktion ③ 474 510-2AH3 (166' · DDD · T/t)
                                               ⒻⒶ⇒

The special strengths of Paul McCreesh's performance lie in the drama and the urgency he brings to the work, the keen sense of character he imparts to the music, the vigorous pacing that carries the action forward with the inevitability of a Greek tragedy. But *Saul* is a tragic work, and there's sometimes a want of the necessary gravitas. Nevertheless, this is a gripping and very inspiriting performance. The precision and flexibility of the Gabrieli Consort is a

constant delight; the voices are fresh and bright, the words well articulated. The Gabrieli Players, too, produce a fine and distinctive period orchestral timbre. Andreas Scholl makes an ideal David, with sweetness and unusual depth of tone, exceptional precision of rhythm and perfectly clear words: if you try 'O Lord, whose mercies' you will buy this set. Enjoyable, too, is Nancy Argenta's natural, delicately phrased singing of Micah's music, and Susan Gritton's telling portrayal of Saul's elder daughter, Merab. Saul himself, sometimes fiery, nearly always agonised, is effectively drawn by Neal Davies; and Mark Padmore's warm and gently graceful tenor is ideal for Jonathan's music.

There's no shortage of good recordings of this work. Gardiner's weighty version holds the field, but this version presents a serious challenge; the lightness and clarity, the livelier drama and the solo singing of Scholl in particular tell in favour of McCreesh.

Saul

Emma Bell, Rosemary Joshua *sops* **Lawrence
Zazzo** *counterten* **Finnur Bjarnason, Jeremy
Ovenden, Michael Slattery** *tens* **Gidon Saks, Henry
Waddington** *basses* **RIAS Chamber Choir, Berlin;
Concerto Köln / René Jacobs**
Harmonia Mundi ② HMC90 1877/8
(150' · DDD · T/t/N)   Ⓕ

Saul, Handel's first great oratorio, has over the last 15 years or so become one of his most popular on disc, a consequence no doubt of its textural and musical variety, dramatic urgency and sheer entertainment value. There is something for everyone here: rollicking choral celebrations of Israelite victories at the start, balanced at the end by outpourings of national grief, with the stern moral pronouncement of 'Envy, eldest born of hell!' in between; superb arias for a vivid cast of characters, one of whom is a compelling tragic hero of Shakespearian stature; and a good helping of instrumental interest, with Handel ingeniously using orchestral movements to signal the passing of time.

René Jacobs's recording followed only a little over a year after Paul McCreesh's well-regarded, high-production-value account for DG and readers familiar with both conductors' styles will know what kinds of contrast to expect. Jacobs's understanding of the dramatic workings of Baroque opera and oratorio is second to none and, as usual, his performance is outstandingly successful in linking Handel's sequences of numbers into a coherent whole, with recitatives flowing in and out of arias, and choruses arriving and departing with real purpose. The performance also gains theatrical presence by its punchy sound: the orchestra is well represented in the balance – undoubtedly a good thing in view of Concerto Köln's vibrant playing – while the RIAS Chamber Choir are encouraged to let dramatic concerns take precedence over the more smoothly produced 'English anthem' sound of McCreesh's Gabrieli Consort. Indeed, there is a distinctly continental whiff to Jacobs's choruses which he heightens (some might say distractingly) through the use of 'French'-style final-note trills.

Jacobs's customary attention to detail in recitatives, backed up by some imaginative instrumentation, also draws vital responses from his soloists; certainly Gidon Saks's manly Saul sounds more dangerously volatile in these than he does in his arias, though this may be more Handel's fault than his. The other singers strike a better balance and, while not as starry a line-up as McCreesh's (where the presence of Andreas Scholl as David will be recommendation enough for many), are nevertheless well chosen to achieve a 'company' result. Sopranos Rosemary Joshua and Emma Bell are effectively contrasted as Saul's daughters, while Jeremy Ovenden cuts a humane but incisively heroic figure as Jonathan. Lawrence Zazzo's David cannot match the sheer vocal allure of Scholl but comes across as more rounded figure – this, after all, is a character who has to be both a sensitive musician and a warrior-leader.

If it is dramatic involvement you want from *Saul*, then Jacobs's is the one to have, though it certainly should not turn you against McCreesh's classy product. If money is no object (and note that Jacobs gets his performance onto two discs to everyone else's three), you could do worse than treat yourself to more than one.

Semele, HWV58

Semele
Rosemary Joshua, **Gail Pearson** sops
Hilary Summers contr **Stephen Wallace** counterten
Richard Croft ten **Brindley Sharratt** bass
**Chorus and Orchestra of the Early Opera
Company / Christian Curnyn**
Chandos ③ CHAN0745 (170' · DDD)　Ⓕ❶❶❶Ⓑ

Of a handful of previous recordings of *Semele*, none was entirely satisfying. Which makes this new version – complete save for an aria for Cupid that Handel later pilfered for *Hercules* – all the more welcome. Christian Curnyn understands the unique *tinta* of this gorgeous score, and directs his spruce period band with a nice blend of nonchalant elegance and dramatic energy. Tempi are shrewdly judged, rhythms light and supple, and recitatives tumble inevitably into arias. The tragic dénouement in Act 3 has due weight and intensity, whether in the tenderly inflected accompanied recitatives for Jupiter and Semele, or the awed chorus of Thebans after the heroine's incineration.

As at the English National Opera, Rosemary Joshua, radiant of tone, dazzling in coloratura, makes Semele far more than an over-sexed airhead. She is trills ethereally in 'The morning lark', distils a drowsy, erotic languour in 'O sleep, why dost thou leave me?', and ornaments her 'mirror' aria, 'Myself I shall adore', with dizzy

glee. She is imploring and fiery by turns in her exchanges with Jupiter, and brings real pathos to the haunting siciliano 'Thus let my thanks be paid' and her sublime death scene. As Jupiter, Richard Croft fields a honeyed, sensuous tone (heard to advantage in a seductive 'Where're you walk') and formidable agility, though he could learn a thing or two about diction from Anthony Rolfe-Johnson (on Gardiner's Erato set).

Like Handel himself, Curnyn assigns the virago Juno and Semele's gentle sister Ino to the same singer. Hilary Summers, a true, deep contralto, characterises both roles well. Brindley Sherratt, with his oaky bass, offers vivid, witty cameos as Cadmus and Somnus, while Stephen Wallace sings Athamas's arias with smooth tone and a nimble florid technique, though a suspicion remains that the role lies a bit low for him. With excellent recorded sound and balance, and an informative essay from David Vickers, this becomes a clear first choice for an ever-enticing work.

Solomon, HWV67

Solomon　　　　　　　　　　　　　　　　Ⓟ
Andreas Scholl counterten **Inger Dam-Jensen,
Susan Gritton, Alison Hagley** sops **Susan Bickley**
mez **Paul Agnew** ten **Peter Harvey** bass **Gabrieli
Consort and Players / Paul McCreesh**
Archiv Produktion ③ 459 688-2AH3
(161' · DDD · T)　　　　　　　　　Ⓕ❶❶Ⓑ

Solomon is universally recognised as one of Handel's finest masterpieces, not only with magnificent choruses, but more importantly containing rapturous love music, nature imagery, affecting emotion and the vividly portrayed dramatic scene of Solomon's famous judgement over the disputed infant. This is in fact the only dramatic part of the oratorio; and each of the female characters appears in only one of the work's three parts. Paul McCreesh, responsive to the work's stature, employs an orchestra of about 60 (including a serpent as the bass of the wind group) and presents the oratorio in the original 1749 version, full and uncut.

It's been argued that even in so splendid a work Handel was fallible enough to include some dead wood. McCreesh, however, stoutly defends the original structural balance. In one respect, though, he does depart from Handel's intentions. By the time *Solomon* was written, he was using no castratos in his oratorios, and the title-role was deliberately designed for a mezzo-soprano; but here the chance to secure the pre-eminent countertenor Andreas Scholl was irresistible. The colour of Handel's predominantly female vocal casting (only Zadok and the smaller-part Levite being exceptions) is thus slightly modified. This historical infidelity is one of the few possible reservations about the set, which is a notable achievement. McCreesh is fortunate in his cast, too. Predictably, Scholl becomes the central focus by his beauty of voice, calm authority, charm and intelligent musicianship. Inger Dam-Jensen, as Solomon's queen, sounds suitably ecstatic in the florid 'Blessed the day' and amorous in 'With thee th'unsheltered moor', and her duet with Solomon flows with easy grace. To Susan Gritton falls the sublime 'Will the sun forget to streak', with its wonderful unison oboe-and-flute obbligato. As the high priest Zadok, Paul Agnew shines in the ornate 'See the tall palm'. A more positive and audible keyboard continuo would have been welcome, but this is a minor shortcoming, and the effect of the performance as a whole is deeply impressive, with such things as 'Will the sun', the grave interlude to 'With pious heart' and the elegiac chorus 'Draw the tear from hopeless love' haunting the listener's mind.

Solomon   P

Carolyn Sampson, Susan Gritton sops **Sarah Connolly** mez **Mark Padmore** ten **David Wilson-Johnson** bass **RIAS Chamber Choir, Berlin; Akademie für Alte Musik Berlin / Daniel Reuss**

Harmonia Mundi ② HMC90 1949/50
(155' · DDD · T/t)   F

In his pioneering *Handel's Dramatic Oratorios and Masques* (OUP: 1959), Winton Dean advocated the excision of several arias (mainly for the priestly figures of Zadok and the Levite) and the replacement of the closing chorus by the monumental 'Praise the Lord' – a policy followed by John Eliot Gardiner (Philips), though not by the completist Paul McCreesh (Archiv – see above). In his new recording, Daniel Reuss ditches the final chorus, though he omits just two arias, neither lamented. He also makes puzzling internal cuts in the duet for Solomon and the first harlot, and, more damagingly, the gorgeous opening number of the masque.

That said, the Harmonia Mundi recording is almost unreservedly enjoyable. Abetted by his crack period orchestra and 40-strong chorus, Reuss is responsive alike to the oratorio's ceremonial splendour and its fragrant pastoral tinta. The versions by Gardiner and McCreesh, balanced rather more in favour of the voices, generate an extra weight and sonorous magnificence in the great double choruses. But the vitality and refinement of the Berlin choir is always compelling. With terrific controlled raucousness from antiphonal wind and brass, the opening chorus of Act 2 is as elementally thrilling as it should be. At the other extreme, the Nightingale chorus, taken slowly and secretively, is at least the equal of McCreesh's in drowsy amorous enchantment.

Where the earlier recordings each have at least one unsatisfactory soloist, Reuss's solo line-up could hardly be bettered. Handel cast the role of Solomon with a mezzo-soprano. Reuss does likewise with Sarah Connolly, who sings with glowing, even tone, ardour (in the love scene), and rapt inwardness in Solomon's two 'nature' arias. Susan Gritton makes a gently sensuous queen (her musing 'With thee th'unshelter'd moor I'd tread' a highlight) and

probes the full poignancy and anguish of the first harlot's music. While yielding to Della Jones (Gardiner) and Susan Bickley (McCreesh) in sheer venom, Carolyn Sampson characterises with gusto as the second harlot, and beautifully softens her bright, vernal tone in 'Will the sun forget to streak?' The priests are in the expert hands of Mark Padmore (exemplary in his bouts of coloratura) and the gravely sonorous David Wilson-Johnson.

If you want this magnificent work complete, McCreesh's is the version to go for, while for consistently glorious Handel singing the new Harmonia Mundi recording, impressively directed by Reuss, takes the palm.

Theodora, HWV68

Theodora   P

Susan Gritton sop **Susan Bickley** mez **Robin Blaze** counterten **Paul Agnew, Angus Smith** tens **Neal Davies** bass **Gabrieli Consort and Players / Paul McCreesh**

Archiv Produktion ③ 469 061-2AH3 (184' · DDD · T/t)
   F **OOO**

Theodora, Handel's penultimate oratorio, was a failure in his own time. Until relatively recently it remained a rarity, but lately has come to be recognised as a masterpiece, although quite different in mood and treatment from most of his more familiar oratorios. This recording encourages attentive listening to its subtleties, because it's done with such affection, care and refinement. There's nothing sensational about it, no singer who overwhelms you with brilliance or virtuosity. But all the solo music is finely sung. Theodora herself is taken by Susan Gritton, who's won golden opinions recently, and will win more here for a great deal of lovely, clear and musicianly singing, with a quiet seriousness and unaffected intensity that are ideally suited to the role. Her presence at the centre of the tragic drama elevates it as a whole.

Irene, her fellow Christian, is sung with scarcely less distinction by Susan Bickley, coolly expressive in most of her music, more passionate in 'Defend her Heaven' in Act 2, a shapely performance with subtleties of timing. Didymus, originally a castrato role (very rare in oratorios), is sung by Robin Blaze, whose focused, even-toned countertenor – not a hint of the traditional hoot – serves well: this is fluent singing, with no great depth of tone, but very steady and controlled, with the detail precisely placed. As Septimius, Paul Agnew is in good voice, firm and full in tone, phrasing the music elegantly (although the Act 3 air is unconvincing, too bouncy and cheerful for the situation). Lastly, there's Neal Davies as the Roman ruler, Valens, whose excellent singing makes as persuasive a case as can be imagined for torturing Christians – his is a pleasantly grainy voice, with considerable warmth and fullness of tone, well suited to a figure representing authority, and he despatches the divisions with assurance.

Ornamentation is appropriate and tasteful, and McCreesh takes the recitative at a natural and relaxed pace. His main contribution, however, is in the well-sprung rhythms he draws from his Gabrieli singers and players, in the way he allows the lines to breathe, and in the sense of purpose and direction he imparts to the bass line. Add to this a keen sense of the right pace for each number, and you've the recipe for an outstanding reading of this noble work.

Theodora
Dawn Upshaw, Lorraine Hunt sops **David Daniels** counterten **Richard Croft** ten **Frode Olsen** bass **Orchestra of the Age of Enlightenment / William Christie** Stage and video director **Peter Sellars**
Warner Music Vision/NVC Arts 📀 0630 15481-2 (207' · NTSC · 4:3 · 2.0 · 2-6) Recorded live at Glyndebourne Opera House 1996   Ⓕ**OOO**

What a paradox it is that one of the great opera productions of our time should be of a work not intended for the stage. If you're repelled by the thought of Roman soldiers in US army uniforms and a Roman governor glad-handing like a US president, then think again. The score is of a matchless beauty, the production riveting, the individual performances flawless. Unmissable.

Cantatas

Aci, Galatea e Polifemo, HWV72   🅟
Sandrine Piau sop **Sara Mingardo** contr
Laurent Naouri bar **Le Concert d'Astrée / Emmanuelle Haïm** hpd
Virgin Classics ② 545557-2 (99' · DDD · T/t) Ⓕ**OO**▷

The cantata or serenata *a 3* (for three), *Aci, Galatea e Polifemo*, dates from Handel's visit to Naples in 1708, and it has almost nothing in common, except for its subject matter, with his exquisite English pastoral, *Acis and Galatea* for the Duke of Chandos's house at Cannons of 1718. As with so many of his Italian compositions, Handel used this enchanting creation of his youth as a sort of melody bank, lifting whole arias for insertion into his subsequent operas, so even if there are Handelians new to this work some of the music won't be entirely unfamiliar.

Aci, cast originally, one presumes, with a high soprano castrato, has two sublime arias, 'Qui l'augel da pianta in pianta' and his dying lament, 'Verso già l'alma col sangue' ('My soul pours out with my blood'). Both belong to Handel's most ravishing early inspirations, the first a simile aria in which the soprano voice 'competes' with birdsong supplied by oboe and violin solos, the second a wonderfully evocative representation of the dying hero's throbbing heart and intense anguish. This is topflight stuff, and Aci's music is superbly sung by

Sandrine Piau with her brilliant, steely yet still sweet soprano, used with quasi-instrumental technical accomplishment. Even though Galatea's music, written for a contralto, is less interesting, the Arcadian nymph is cast with the best singer here, the wonderful Sara Mingardo, one of the truly sublime Handelians of our time, who brings a dark sensuality to her love music and a heartbreaking outpouring of grief in the recative following Aci's death. Haïm's spirited and imaginative direction, her singers and a pristine modern recording weigh the balance in favour of this set.

'Delirio'   🅟
Aci, Galatea e Polifemo – Qui l'augel da pianta in pianta. Il delirio amoroso, HWV99. Mi, palpita il cor, HWV132
Natalie Dessay sop **Le Concert d'Astrée / Emmanuelle Haïm** hpd
Virgin Classics 332624-2 (62' · DDD · T/t)   Ⓕ**D**▷

Handel created his cantata *Il delirio amoroso* while in Rome in early 1707. Its text was written by Cardinal Benedetto Pamphili. The unusual inclusion of some dance movements suggests that it might have been presented in a simple sort of staging. Emmanuelle Haïm directs a performance that is relaxed and breezy, although Le Concert d'Astrée – featuring two harpsichords and two lutes – is bigger than some orchestras used on recent Baroque opera recordings. There are lovely contributions from oboist Patrick Beaugiraud, and the violinist Stéphanie-Marie Degand provides finely executed solos during the first aria, 'Un pensiero voli in ciel'. Natalie Dessay's coloratura is honey-toned and sweet.

While amiable and technically impressive, proceedings are curiously superficial. There is emotional depth in this cantata that the resolutely frothy approach fails to reach. Dessay does not convey the ramblings of 'delirious love', unlike Ann Murray's poetic interpretation with Harry Christophers (Coro).

The lush beauty of Dessay's impressive tuning, clear timbre and fine technique is beyond doubt in the aria 'Qui l'augel da pianta' from the Naples serenata *Aci, Galatea e Polifemo*. Haïm chooses a bizarrely slow tempo whereby Handel's 6/8 becomes a very lethargic 3/4. Not much of Handel's vocal part is left intact during repeats, when Dessay and Haïm carry out some brutally overelaborate re-composition. Dessay plucks out stratospheric notes at every opportunity, but there is more that could and should have been said in accordance to the parameters of Handel's notation. Nice though this disc is, it brings little depth or substance to Handel's music.

'Italian Cantatas, Vol 1: Le cantate per   🅟
il Cardinal Pamphili'
Il delirio amoroso, 'Da quel giorno fatale', HWV99. Pensieri notturni di Filli, 'Nel dolce dell'oblio', HWV134. Tra le fiamme il consiglio, HWV170. Figlio d'alte speranze, HWV113

Roberta Invernizzi sop
La Risonanza / Fabio Bonizzoni hpd
Glossa GCD921521 (66' · DDD · T/t)   Ⓕ●

Although titled 'Le cantate per il Cardinal Pamphili', only two of the four works on this disc were composed for Pamphili. But let's not be too pedantic: it launches La Risonanza's ambitious project to record all of Handel's Italian cantatas that feature a band of instruments. Fabio Bonizzoni's lightly articulated yet rapid whirl through the opening of *Tra le fiamme* is utterly unlike any of the existing pastoral-tinged performances but it perfectly conveys the imagery of a moth fatally attracted to the flame.

Roberta Invernizzi is an impassioned (and, of course, resolutely Italianate) interpreter who brings the dramatic sentiments of the poetry fully to life, while also delivering inch-perfect coloratura and stylish phrasing. Her blend of spectacular singing and emotional substance in 'Un pensiero voli in ciel' (*Delirio amoroso*) is possibly the most satisfying interpretation on disc.

The programme's coherence, Invernizzi's authoritative singing and La Risonanza's theatrically coloured playing have raised the performance standard for Handel's Italian cantatas. Bonizzoni's refreshing direction is entirely devoid of the coolly dispatched detachment or mannered feyness often found in this repertoire. This lovingly prepared series promises to be of the utmost importance to Handel lovers.

'Italian Cantatas, Vol 2: Le cantate per il   🅿
Marchese Ruspoli'
Armida abbandonata, HWV105[a]. Notte placida e cheta, HWV142[a]. Tu fedel? tu costante?, HWV171[a]. Alla caccia Diana cacciatrice, HWV79[ab]. Un'alma innamorata, HWV173[a]
[a]**Emanuela Galli,** [b]**Roberta Invernizzi** sops
La Risonanza / Fabio Bonizzoni hpd
Glossa GCD921522 (74' · DDD · T/t)   Ⓕ●●●

Once again La Risonanza deliver delectable performances at an unmatched level of thoughtful preparation, penetrating programming and artistic interpretation. This instalment contains five cantatas, four of which were composed in 1707 for Handel's principal Roman patron the Marquis Ruspoli (the origins of *Notte placida e cheta* are less clear). All of these pieces have been recorded before but never quite like this. Roberta Invernizzi is on sparkling form in the hunting cantata *Diana cacciatrice* and La Risonanza play with spirited elegance. The lion's share of the programme is sung by Emanuela Galli: *Armida abbandonata* receives a performance that surpasses all previous versions (no mean feat – the discography includes good performances by Ann Murray, Emma Kirkby and Véronique Gens). Galli sings with intensely dramatic conviction yet never at the expense of poetic style or good taste, and is equally convincing whether revealing the eloquence of Armida's broken heart or conveying the viciousness of her anger at Rinaldo. Fabio Bonizzoni nurtures performances that illustrate

the rhetorical power in Handel's music without ever over-egging the pudding: for instance, Galli's expression of the core question in *Tu fedel? tu costante?* is wonderfully convincing, and the softly duelling violins in 'Zeffiretti, deh! venite' are nothing short of perfection.

'Italian Cantatas, Vol 3: Le cantate per   🅿
il Cardinal Ottoboni'
Ah! crudel nel pianto mio, HWV78. No se emenderá jamás, HWV140. Qual ti riveggio, oh Dio, HWV150. Spande ancor a mio dispetto, HWV165
Raffaella Milanesi sop **Salvo Vitale** bass
La Risonanza / Fabio Bonizzoni hpd
Glossa ② GCD921523 (67' · DDD)   Ⓕ●●

It was once believed that the Venetian-born Cardinal Pietro Ottoboni was Handel's principal patron during the composer's exciting youthful years in Rome. Scholars now shy away from that verdict but he was a famous patron of the most respected Italian composers and his orchestra was led by Corelli. The cold truth is that not one of these four cantatas – which all date from about summer 1707 – has a verifiable connection with Ottoboni. There is flimsy evidence that the dramatic masterpiece *Qual ti riveggio* was written for him, and it is not difficult to imagine the astonishing solo violin passages were created specifically for Corelli to play. La Risonanza's Nick Robinson does a marvellous job with them; his playing is sweet, astute and sensitively contoured. Raffaella Milanesi's singing is as emotionally raw as possible while remaining impeccably stylish and melodically suave as she describes the anguished Hero's discovery of her drowned lover Leander's body. Fabio Bonizzoni ensures that the performances crackle with dramatic tension or plumb the depths of desolate melodic melancholy according to what Handel's music demands, but the most impressive aspect of these performances is the conductor's awareness of story-telling and judicious moulding of the musical flow. The short cantata *No se emenderá jamás* – Handel's only composition with Spanish words – has been recorded before but never with the rapturous effect achieved here. The bass cantata *Spande ancor a mio dispetto* also receives a benchmark performance. The concluding work, *Ah! crudel nel pianto mio*, presents conflicting emotions between elation and misery in love: the long introductory sonata is joyously played, with each musical gesture superbly executed, and Milanesi's singing is by turns chilling, sensitive, spirited or tender. This disc is further testament to the marvellous subtlety and richness of Handel's Roman music and contains Handel-singing, playing and direction of the absolute highest order.

'Italian Cantatas, Vol 4'   🅿
Aminta e Fillide, 'Arresta il passo', HWV83. Clori, mia bella Clori, HWV92
Nuria Rial, Maria Grazia Schiavo sops
La Risonanza / Fabio Bonizzoni hpd

Glossa GCD921 524 (67' · DDD)   Ⓕ**OO**

The fourth instalment of La Risonanza's survey of Handel's youthful Italian cantatas is devoted to two works probably composed for the Marquis Francesco Maria Ruspoli in Rome. There is no doubt that *Arresta il passo* (nicknamed 'Aminta e Fillide') is one of the young Handel's most likeable compositions. The Arcadian story of Aminta imploring Fillide to requite his love, and of her gradual melting towards his seduction, is told by La Risonanza in an affectionate and conversational way, with recitatives unhurried and performed with clarity, precision and elegance.

Bonizzoni resists the temptation to ham things up too much, and directs the music with a judicious ear for striking yet tasteful sonority. Sopranos Maria Grazia Schiavo (Aminta) and Nuria Rial (Fillide) achieve the elusive synthesis between stylised poetry, musical refinement and dramatic character. The radiant violin-playing in Fillide's 'Fu scherzo, fu gioco' is a delicately playful illustration of the text's reference to love being a joke and a game, and Rial sings the difficult vocal part effortlessly and with delicious sagacity. Schiavo is equally impressive in Aminta's 'Se vago rio', which has a spellbinding *pizzicato* string accompaniment and strange harmonic twists. Fillide's surprise at her emerging feelings of love for Aminta, and his increasing elation, are delightfully conveyed by all of the vocal and instrumental performers.

Clori, mia bella Clori (sung by Schiavo) also benefits from meticulous attention to detail, such as the exquisitely shaded duetting violins in 'Mie pupille'. La Risonanza once again show that Handel's youthful Italian compositions are breathtaking masterpieces of considerable refinement, subtlety and quality.

'Italian Cantatas, Vol 5'   Ⓟ
Clori, Tirsi e Fileno, 'Cor fedele', HWV96
Roberta Invernizzi, Yetzabel Arias Fernández sops
Romina Basso mez **La Risonanza /**
Fabio Bonizzoni hpd
Glossa GCD921 525 (75' · DDD)   Ⓕ**OO**

Probably composed for his principal Roman patron Marquis Francesco Maria Ruspoli in autumn 1707, Handel's pastoral drama, *Cor fedele, in vano speri* (usually called by its nickname 'Clori, Tirsi e Fileno') tells the story of the fickle serial seductress Clori and her two rival shepherd lovers Tirsi and Fileno. Despite taking oaths of fidelity to each, her intrigue is eventually exposed, and the three members of the love triangle agree to coexist peacefully as long as all concerned get some satisfaction from the arrangement.

Fabio Bonizzoni seems keen to emphasise the operatic atmosphere of this music, and the three singers are ideally cast. Roberta Invernizzi's virtuoso coloratura in Tirsi's furious denouncing of Clori in 'Tra le fere' is magnificent (the oboe solo passagework by Andrea Mion is also impressive). Yetzabel Arias Fernández is a fruit-

ier and deeper soprano than Invernizzi but still perfectly in proportion with the articulate music-making. Leila Schayegh's solo fiddling in 'Barbaro, tu non credi' is by turns brilliant and beguiling, as the minx Clori uses contrasting passionate fast music and mock-sorrowful slower passages to wangle her way back into Tirsi's favour. Fileno's "Sai perchè l'onda" is plaintively sung by Romina Basso.

Recitatives are performed with perfect poetic clarity and dramatic timing. Bonizzoni's Italian ensemble astutely diagnoses and communicates the affect of each movement in some of the youthful Handel's most freely imaginative music. The balance between instruments is consistently fine, warm and lyrical. In particular, Bonizzoni has the admirable knack of conveying the strong rhetorical elements in Handel's vivacious music, and the entire performance is beautifully executed with subtlety and charm. This is another essential disc from La Risonanza, whose project is shaping up to become the most rewarding Handelian discographic undertaking of the decade.

Notte placida e cheta, HWV142. Un' alma   Ⓟ
innamorata, HWV173. Figlio d'alte speranze,
HWV113. Agrippina condotta a morire, HWV110.
Concerto a quattro
Emma Kirkby sop **London Baroque**
BIS ⓈⒶⒸⒹ BIS-SACD1695 (67' · DDD/DSD)   Ⓕ**O▶**

The largest single legacy of Handel's years in Italy (in his early twenties) were around 100 chamber cantatas, from which Emma Kirkby and London Baroque have picked out four excellent examples from the 30 or so featuring one or two violins alongside the solo voice and continuo. In this they face strong competition from La Risonanza's series with Italian singers on Glossa, but the clash does no damage to either group as both have distinct virtues. For some, of course, the presence of Emma Kirkby will be enough to seal the deal, and indeed she is on superb form. Early on there are a few signs of a lack of her usual instrumental precision; but by the time she is showing off her artless virtuosity in the final aria of *Figlio d'alte speranze* and striding easily through 'Orrida, oscura', the first aria of the compellingly dramatic *Agrippina condotta a morire*, all worries have long been banished. Her interpretative intelligence and attention to words are a given but she can also catch a subtle mood, as in 'Quel povero core' from *Un' alma innamorata*, whose sense of resigned torment is enhanced by a sensitive contribution from the solo violin. Emanuela Galli captures this kind of intimate emotion even more affectingly in La Risonanza's performances, mind, but with a touch less vocal security.

The recorded sound, as often in London Baroque's recordings for BIS, is strangely resonant and steely. The 'Concerto a quattro' included here is claimed as a Handel work in its German 18th-century source but sounds like nothing of the kind.

Apollo e Dafne, 'La terra e liberata', HWV122. **P**
Crudel tiranno amor, HWV97
Nancy Argenta sop **Michael George** bass
Collegium Musicum 90 / Simon Standage
Chandos Chaconne CHAN0583 (58' · DDD · T/t) Ⓕ℗➔

Handel's *Apollo e Dafne* is a difficult work to put in context. Completed in Hanover in 1710 but possibly begun in Italy, its purpose isn't clear, while, as secular cantatas go, it's long (40 minutes) and ambitiously scored for two soloists and an orchestra of strings, oboes, flute, bassoon and continuo. But this isn't just a chunk of operatic experimentation: it sets its own, faster pace than the leisurely unfolding of a full-length Baroque stage-work, yet its simple Ovidian episode, in which Apollo's pursuit of the nymph Dafne results in her transformation into a tree, is drawn with all the subtlety and skill of the instinctive dramatic genius that Handel was.

This recording features the expert Handelian voices of Nancy Argenta and Michael George, and both convey their roles convincingly. Argenta's hard, clear tone seems just the thing for the nymph, who isn't required to be especially alluring but who does have to sound quick to anger and (literally) untouchable; and George strikes the right note as Apollo, bragging loudly at the opening of his superior skill in archery to Cupid before succumbing more gently, and in the end extremely touchingly, to Cupid's arts. The orchestra is bright and efficient, and the pacing of the work seems just right. This is superb Handel then, and, as if that were not enough, there's a bonus in the form of a shorter cantata for soprano and strings, *Crudel tiranno amor*. It's a beautiful piece indeed, and Argenta performs it perfectly.

German Arias, HWV202-10

Handel German Arias[a] **P**
Telemann Musique de table – 'Paris' Quartets:
G, E minor
[a]**Dorothea Röschmann** sop **Academy for Ancient Music, Berlin**
Harmonia Mundi HMC90 1689 (79' · DDD · T/t) Ⓕ⊙⊙

Handel's nine *German Arias* aren't as well known nor as often recorded as they deserve, perhaps because, being devotional music, they're generally rather solemnly, even earnestly performed. Dorothea Röschmann sings them delightfully. There's no lack of seriousness, or intensity, where it's called for. The instrumental support is highly polished, but arguably too varied in colour: what's the justification for switching bass instruments for an aria's middle section? The obbligato part is shared between violin, flute and oboe: the oboe seems to be a mistake in the high part of 'Meine Seele', with a rather squeaky effect – although Röschmann's exuberance at 'Alles jauchzet, alles lacht' ('all rejoice, all laugh') is happy. The Telemann 'Paris' quartets set off the arias well. Some of the playing in the E minor work is a

little sober, but the lively G major is done in lively and elegant fashion, with spruce rhythms. But Röschmann's Handel is the real joy: listen to 'Die ihr aus dunklen Grüften' and you won't be able to resist it.

Oratorio & Opera Arias

Belshazzar – Destructive War; Oh sacred oracles of truth. **Jephtha** – Dull delay, in piercing anguish; Up the dreadful steep ascending. **Messiah** – He was despised. **Saul** – O Lord, whose mercies; Brave Jonathan. **Semele** – Despair no more shall wound me; Your tuneful voice. **Theodora** – The raptur'd soul; Deeds of kindness; Kind Heav'n; Sweet Rose and Lilly
David Daniels counterten **Paris Orchestral Ensemble / John Nelson**
Virgin Classics 545497-2 (67' · DDD · N/T) Ⓕ⊙➔

The world's leading 'operatic' countertenor has sung on precious few of the abundant complete Handel recordings of the last decade so this selection of oratorio arias fills some of the gaps in the Daniels discography.

The American was to have sung Didymus in Paul McCreesh's Archiv recording of *Theodora* – the role of his Glyndebourne début in Peter Sellars's controversial 1995 staging – but he was unable to fit the preceding concerts into his burgeoning international schedule and was replaced by Robin Blaze. Not surprisingly, he includes four of Didymus's arias in his oratorio album, and rejoices in the wonderful music Handel composed for the young Italian castrato, Gaetano Guadagni. The sensuous colours of Daniels' falsetto are ideal in this music, which he sings with beguiling erotic ambiguity.

The same goes for David's ravishing 'O Lord, whose mercies numberless' – a prayer whose yearning melismata suggest passions more earthly than godly – from *Saul*. There's little cause for complaint, except perhaps about the use of the modern instrument Ensemble Orchestral de Paris rather than a period band, but at least John Nelson's conducting – particularly in the fast-moving numbers – is livelier than on his complete *L'allegro*. In excellent sound, this glorious disc comes highly recommended.

Hercules – Where shall I fly? **Joshua** – O had I **P** Jubal's lyre. **Theodora** – With darkness deep as is my woe. **Agrippina** – Pensieri, voi mi tormentate. **Alcina** – Ah! mio cor! Schernito sei! Amadigi di Gaula – Desterò dall'empia Dite. **Ariodante** – Dopo notte, atra e funesta; Scherza infida in grembo al drudo. **Giulio Cesare** – Cara speme, questo core. **Orlando** – Ah! stigie larve!...Già latra Cerbero...Vaghe pupille, no, non piangete, no. **Rinaldo** – Lascia ch'io pianga mia cruda sorte
Magdalena Kožená mez
Venice Baroque Orchestra / Andrea Marcon
Archiv Produktion 477 6547AH (76' · DDD) Ⓕ℗➔

With most items familiar from previous Handel aria anthologies, on paper this looks full of tired clichés. Thankfully, the stirring and passionate execution of Handel's music is anything but dull routine. Kožená and her Venetian accomplices might not be giving us anything deeply perceptive but everybody involved sounds as if they are engaged with the music. In particular, the Venice Baroque Orchestra sound admirably absorbed in the dramatic world of each aria.

Kožená has a good stab at this, too, but does not quite capture the personality and situation of each character. Alcina's heartbroken first encounter of a man being beyond her seductive power in 'Ah! mio cor!' is ravishing but its slowly creeping pathos is not a natural opener for a disc like this, and Kožená – albeit passionate – does not capture the depth of Alcina's complex psychological condition. An extrovert 'Cara speme' does not quite fit Sesto's emotional self-inquiry.

Kožená is much better at conveying the scheming Agrippina's anxious plea to the gods and 'Scherza infida' is finely judged, its best passages not too far off the benchmark set by Janet Baker, Sarah Connolly and Lorraine Hunt Lieberson (alas, it is let down by the staccato B section). The most convincing synthesis of musical outpouring and dramatic mood is Melissa's 'Desterò dall'empia dite' (from *Amadigi*).

In Dejanira's mad scene from *Hercules*, Kožená's affected vowels and hammed-up insanity rob it of the poignancy that understatement achieves much better; Dejanira is a distraught heroine, not a lunatic shrieking that the Martians have landed. A similar approach makes for an over-egged mad scene from *Orlando*. But despite the frequent limitation of one-dimensional characterisation, these appealing performances have strength and colour.

Ariodante – E vivo ancora … Scherza infida in grembo al drudo. **Giulio Cesare** – Cara speme, questo core; Va tacito e nascosto; L'angue offeso mai riposa; Al lampo dell'armi; Dall' ondoso periglio… Aure, deh, per pietà. **Rinaldo** – Cara sposa; Venti, turbini, prestate. **Rodelinda** – Pompe vane di morte!…Dove sei?; Vivi tiranno!. **Serse** – Fronde tenere…Ombra mai fù. **Tamerlano** – A dispetto
David Daniels counterten **Orchestra of the Age of Enlightenment / Sir Roger Norrington**
Virgin Classics Veritas 545326-2 (69' · DDD · T/t)

The ever-increasing popularity of Handel and his contemporaries, and their employment of alto castratos, has encouraged the development of countertenors capable of similar vocal feats to the original interpreters of the heroic roles in these works. Among these David Daniels can certainly be counted as a leading contender. He displays and deploys his talent here in a wide range of arias reflective and dramatic. His amazing technique runs through Tamerlano's virtuoso 'A dispetto' and Bertarido's 'Vivi tiranno!' without a blemish in the sound and with every division in its place yet part of a confidently

delivered whole: by and large Daniels's runs and embellishments are smoothly accomplished. In more reflective pieces such as Giulio Cesare's 'Aure, deh, per pietà' (he also tackles Sesto's 'Cara speme' from *Giulio Cesare*, a particularly liquid, subtle piece of singing), Bertarido's 'Dove sei?' and Ariodante's sad lament, 'Scherza infida', written for the great Senesino, he uses his impeccable Italian to express wide-ranging emotions. Throughout, Roger Norrington and the Orchestra of the Age of Enlightenment give excellent support. The recording is blameless so there's every reason for readers to sample this fine exposition of the countertenor's art.

'Great Oratorio Duets'
Jephtha – These labours past. **Joshua** – Oh peerless maid; Our limpid streams. **Belshazzar** – Great victor, at your feet I bow. **Susanna** – When thou art nigh; To my chaste Susanna's praise. **Theodora** – To see, thou glorious son of worth; Streams of pleasure ever flowing. **Solomon** – Welcome as the dawn of day; Ev'ry joy that wisdom knows. **Eternal Source of Light Divine** – Kind health descends. **Saul** – O fairest of ten thousand fair; At persecution I can laugh. **Deborah** – Where do thy armours raise me!; Smiling freedom, lovely guest. **Alexander Balus** – Hail wedded love. **Alexander's Feast** – Let imitate her notes above. **Esther** – Who calls my parting soul
Carolyn Sampson sop **Robin Blaze** counterten
Orchestra of the Age of Enlightenment / Nicholas Kraemer
BIS BIS-SACD1436 (71' · DDD/DSD · T)

'Great Oratorio Duets'? It seems a strange concept at first – not many of these pieces have made an individual name for themselves just yet. But then the point of this disc is evidently to bring together in mouthwatering partnership two of the most dulcet-voiced young Baroque singers Britain has to offer, and it does not take long to discover that that is a very good idea indeed. Carolyn Sampson's voice is bright and clear yet warmed by judiciously selected and moderated vibrato, while Robin Blaze has a more distinctively tangy sound, but they fit each other well and in their faultless display of Handelian style, lyricism and warmth they are in total mental and spiritual accord.

The music, meanwhile, does indeed have greatness. The vocal style of Handel's English oratorios does not recreate the virtuoso flashiness of the Italian operas but speaks in a more direct, lyrical manner, expressing with unimpeachable honesty all the sympathy and human understanding for which their composer is so revered. The majority here are love duets, but with what variety, from carefree (examples from *Jephtha* and *Susanna*) to chaste (*Deborah*) to ambiguously melancholy (*Joshua* and *Saul*). The forgiveness duet from *Esther* is indescribably tender (especially in this performance), the duet from *Saul* in which a love-drunk David is reluctant to leave when warned by his fiancée of approaching danger is effortlessly theatrical, and the two duets for the doomed lovers from *Theo-*

dora are works of pure and noble genius. If the performances in these last do not quite reach the heartbreaking intensity of which Peter Sellars's Glyndebourne production proved them capable, it is hard to see how that could ever be achieved in a recital; Sampson and Blaze surely manage as well as anyone ever could. With intelligent, kind-hearted accompaniments from Nicholas Kraemer and the OAE, this is a truly beautiful Handel recording, a disc to give pleasure for years to come.

Acis and Galatea – I rage, I melt, I burn!…O ruddier than the cherry. **Alcina** – Verdi prati, selve amene. **Alexander's Feast** – Revenge, revenge, Timotheus cries…Behold a ghastly band. **Berenice** – Si, tra i ceppi e le ritorte. **Giulio Cesare** – Va tacito e nascosto. **Judas Maccabaeus** – I feel the Deity within … Arm, arm, ye brave! **Messiah** – Thus saith the Lord…But who may abide?; Why do the nations?; Behold I tell you a mystery…The trumpet shall sound. **Orlando** – O voi del mio poter…Sorge infausta una procella. **Samson** – Honour and arms scorn such a foe. **Semele** – Where'er you walk. **Serse** – Fronde tenere…Ombra mai fù. **Te Deum in D, 'Dettingen'** – Vouchsafe, O Lord
Bryn Terfel *bass-bar* **Scottish Chamber Orchestra / Sir Charles Mackerras**
DG 453 480-2GH (73' · DDD · T/t) Ⓕ🅑➔

'I feel', sings Terfel with assurance in his voice matching the solemnly, expectantly, ceremonious opening bars; and then, the second time, 'I feel', but now with the awed conviction of one who has experienced 'the Deity within'. The adjustment, the change of expression, is small, and no doubt when described sounds obvious enough; but it's typical of the imaginative intelligence Terfel brings. And what of his singing, his voice production, his care for *legato*? As to the latter, conflict always lurks as expressive emphasis, shading and verbal naturalism assert their rights in the face of pure beauty and the evenness of the singing line. Terfel is one in whom the rival claims work their way to a compromise, though if one side has to win it will generally be the expressive element. A good example of the compromise is the second track, the 'Vouchsafe, O Lord', quietly and simply sung, preserving the movement's unity and yet with a power of feeling that, at 'let thy mercy lighten upon us', is as overtly emotional as an operatic aria.

The adapted arias, 'Where'er you walk', 'Verdi prati' and 'Ombra mai fù', justify their inclusion readily enough, and it's good to hear Terfel in the solos from *Messiah*. The singing here incorporates a good deal of embellishment, some of it of Mackerras's devising. He's excellent, sharing with Terfel an appreciation of the zest in Handel. The recording is vivid and clean.

Alessandro – Brilla nell' alma un non inteso ancor 🅟
Amadigi di Gaula – Ah spietato **Arianna in Creta** – Son qual stanco **Deidamia** – M'hai resa infelice **Faramondo** – Combattuta da due venti **Giulio**

Cesare – Che sento? oh Dio!; Se pietà di me non senti **Orlando** – Verdi piante, erbette liete **Partenope** – L'amor ed il destin **Rodelinda** – Ombre, piante **Scipione** – Scoglio d'immota fronte **Tamerlano** – Cor di padre
Sandrine Piau *sop* **Les Talens Lyriques / Christophe Rousset**
Naïve E8894 (67' · DDD · T/t) Ⓕ🅞🅞🅞

 Sandrine Piau and Christophe Rousset have been consistently stylish and perceptive Handelians together. Their musical flair and dramatic intelligence is marvellously captured here, and they have chosen arias that explore the full range of Handel's genius.

The experience starts with the spectacular 'Scoglio d'immota fronte', and the subsequent sequence weaves through wonderful contrasts. It's hard to capture the full dramatic sense and vivid personality of Handel's opera characters in a studio recital, yet they hit the bullseye every time, bringing out Cleopatra's despair, Rodelinda's eloquent grief for her apparently deceased husband, the heartbroken sorceress Melissa in *Amadigi di Gaula*, Deidamia's distress at losing Achilles to the Trojan war, and Partenope's gorgeous charisma.

Although some *da capo* sections stray a little too far from Handel's notation for the comfort of scholars, they all enhance the drama of the text, and each cadenza, showing panache and taste, is a breath of fresh air. The playing of Les Talens Lyriques is a model of clarity, vitality and theatrical wit. It was an inspired decision to close the recital with the sublime understatement of 'Son qual stanco', featuring a heartbreaking cello solo by Atsushi Sakaï. Rousset and Piau achieve the perfect synthesis of elegance, extravagance and emotion. This is may be the finest recital of Handel arias ever recorded.

'As steals the morn…' 🅟
L'Allegro, il Penseroso ed il Moderato – As steals the morn[a]. **Esther** – Tune your harps to cheerful strains. **Jephtha** – His mighty arm, with sudden blow; Waft her, angels, through the skies. **Samson** – Total eclipse; Did love constrain thee; Your charms to ruin led the way; Thus when the sun from's wat'ry bed; Let but that spirit. **Il trionfo del Tempo e del Disinganno** – Urne voi. **Alceste** – Enjoy the sweet Elysian grove. **Rodelinda** – Fatto inferno; Pastorello d'un povero armento. **Semele** – Where'er you walk. **Tamerlano** – Forte e lieto; Oh per me lieto, avventuroso giorno![ab]; Figlia mia
Mark Padmore *ten*
with [a]**Lucy Crowe** *sop* [b]**Robin Blaze** *counterten*
The English Concert / Andrew Manze
Harmonia Mundi HMU90 7422 (77' · DDD) Ⓕ🅞🅞➔

Underpinned by Andrew Manze's unobtrusive and warm-hearted English Concert, Mark Padmore uses his extraordinary diction and whispering chamber-like intimacy to remind us that the most exalted tenor arias from Handel's operas and oratorios can achieve true potency out of context.

Favourites like 'Where'er you walk' and 'Waft her, angels' appear to grow out of this varied programme without the sense of being lifted for a compilation; Padmore is a master of taste, restraint and unassuming gesture. 'Pastorello d'un povero' is a touching vignette and the soft singing elsewhere contributes to a concentrated and affecting juxtaposition of human vice and virtue in the *Tamerlano* scenas. As throughout, Padmore saves the greatest emotional impact for the *da capos* where coloration reaches new heights.

Indeed, it is the joy in conveying the emotional core of each situation which marks out this disc. Graphic dramatic effects abound (not least the Sultan's gradual giving up the ghost in 'Figlia mia' with a croaking realism) but this is a disc which celebrates Handel's capacity for incisive human observation, achieved more through reflective means than showpiece coloratura. It's a persuasive and thoughtful approach.

Padmore's lowest register can seem a touch insubstantial but this is a small gripe in a disc boasting – as its parting shot – the duet 'As steals the morn', a performance with the fine Lucy Crowe at her most alluring.

Arianna in Creta – Sdegnata sei; Oh patria! Sol ristoro; Salda quercia; Qual leon; Ove son: Qui ti sfido. **Ariodante** – Qui d'amor; T'amero dunque; Con l'ali di costanza; Scherza infida; Dopo notte, atra e funesta. **Giulio Cesare** – Svegliatevi nel core; Cara speme, questo core; L'angue offeso mai riposa
Angelika Kirchschlager *mez*
Basle Chamber Orchestra / Laurence Cummings
Sony Classical 82876 88952-2 (68' · DDD)   Ⓕ

One of the satisfying approaches to programming Handel arias is to get under the skin of a few chosen characters or singers. All the arias here were composed for the mezzo-soprano Durastanti or the castrato Carestini. Two less familiar arias from *Ariodante* put the popular 'Scherza infida' and 'Dopo notte' into a finer sort of context than usual for such programmes. Kirchschlager's singing is ardent and intelligent, but it is a pity that she did not wait to record Ariodante's arias until after she has sung the role on stage: 'Scherza infida' is perhaps too feminine and lovely here, without the brooding streak of bitter reproach.

Considering Kirchschlager's success in Glyndebourne's *Giulio Cesare*, it is inevitable that she gives dynamic renditions of Sesto's best three arias. The fullest source of delight here is Laurence Cummings's marvellous direction of the excellent period-instrument incarnation of the Basle CO; zesty in extrovert music and deeply eloquent in slow music. If nothing else, this is worth having for the tremendous performances of five arias from *Arianna in Creta*: Tauride's 'Qual leon' (featuring two horns) is one of Handel's finest baddie arias. Here, at long last, it gets the sort of recording it deserves.

'Duetti amorosi'
Admeto – Ah, si, morro; Alma mia, dolce ristoro. **Arminio** – Overture; Il fuggir, cara mia vita; Ritorna nel core vezzosa; Menuetto. **Muzio Scevola** – Ma come amar?. **Poro** – Caro amico amplesso!. **Rodelinda** – Ritorna, o caro e dolce mio. **Serse** – Troppo altraggi la mia fede. **Teseo** – Ti credo, si, ben' mio; Ah! Cruda gelosia!; Addio! Mio caro bene
Nuria Rial *sop* **Lawrence Zazzo** *counterten*
Basle Chamber Orchestra / Laurence Cummings
Deutsche Harmonia Mundi 88697 21472-2
(64' · DDD)   ⒻⓄ▶

'Duetti amorosi' is an imaginative and thoughtfully chosen programme of operatic duets (although the singers also get two arias each). Nothing predictable is included here, except perhaps the two items from *Rodelinda*, but the lovely performance of 'Ritorna, o cara' and the pathos-laden 'Io t'abbraccio' more than justify their presence. Picking a diverse selection of repertoire that skilfully conveys the expressive and stylistic breath of Handel's writing is certainly one of the often-ignored secrets of planning a successful Handel recital programme, and the performers' enthusiasm for reviving numbers from *Arminio* (including its fine overture), *Teseo*, *Muzio Scevola*, *Poro* (the gorgeous 'Caro amico amplesso') and *Admeto* deserves high praise.

Rial and Zazzo sing well, both individually and together: in the duets they are obviously listening sympathetically to each other; they seem to know when to emphasise vocal contrasts or blend closely. Laurence Cummings provides expert musical direction from the harpsichord, ensuring that everything is paced to perfection, and that the musico-dramatic characteristics presented in each piece speak with transparency to the listener; none of these performances would feel out of place in context of their parent works. The policy to dump the texts and translations onto a PDF is detestable.

'Heroes and Heroines'
Alcina – Act 3, Sinfonia; Sta nell'Ircana; Mi lusingha il dolce affetto; Entrée des songes agréables; Verdi prati **Ariodante** – Act 2, Sinfonia; Scherza infida; Dopo notte **Hercules** – Act 2, Sinfonia; Cease, ruler of the day; Where shall I fly **Solomon** – Arrival of the Queen of Sheba; Will the sun forget to streak
Sarah Connolly *mez* **The Symphony of Harmony and Invention / Harry Christophers**
Coro COR16025 (65' · DDD)   Ⓕ▶

Sarah Connolly is an exemplary Handel singer. Her recital is dominated by two roles she's performed at ENO, with arias from *Alcina* and *Ariodante*. 'Scherza infida' is an addictive mixture of vocal elegance and poignant desolation, and 'Mi lusingha' is sung with a beautiful simplicity that lacks for nothing in drama or passion. In contrast, the extravagant coloratura in 'Dopo notte' and the robust 'Sta nell'Ircana' capture the virtuoso thrills of heroic joy. In Dejanira's 'Where shall I fly?', she reminds us that taste and subtlety have an important place even in Handel's tormented and emotionally unstable creation. She avoids contrived intensity and allows the quality of the vocal writing to speak for itself.

Harry Christophers' direction is judicious, supportive yet never intrusive. It's pleasant to hear performances that are musically sensible, dramatically sensitive, and brave enough to apply understatement.

Ariodante – Dopo notte, atra e funesta. **Rodelinda** – Fatto inferno è il mio petto; Pastorello d'un povero armento. **Serse** – Fronde tenere e belle; Ombra mai fù; Più che penso alle fiamme del core; Crude furie degl'orrido abissi. **Tamerlano** – Oh per me lieto, avventuroso giorno![a]; Figlia mia; Ciel e terra armi di sdegno; Tu spietato, il vedrai. **La Resurrezione di Nostro Signor Gesù Cristo** – Così la tortorella; Caro figlio
Rolando Villazón ten with
[a]**Rebecca Bottone** mez [a]**Jean Gadoullet** counterten
Gabrieli Players / Paul McCreesh
DG 477 8056GH (59' · DDD) Also available in a deluxe limited edition with DVD, 477 8057GH2
Ⓕ**O**➔

Until making this recording Rolando Villazón had sung 'barely a note of Handel in public'. There will be some who will question whether his superstar status justifies yet another Handel aria disc, but much of this is invigoratingly performed, and has a smacking impact that some half-hearted anthologies desperately lack. It may be more difficult for some to overlook the inclusion of castrato arias with the vocal part knocked down an octave, which spoils the way the music is balanced, and is unnecessary to what is otherwise a decent programme, no matter how pleasantly the booklet-note attempts to justify it. But it's fair to acknowledge that Villazón's choice to record 'Ombra mai fù' follows in the footsteps of Caruso and Tito Schipa.

It is splendid to hear a singer of abundant personality leaping into the suicide scene from *Tamerlano* with such dramatic authority. Listening to Villazón's lively rendition of Bajazet's 'Ciel e terra armi di sdegno', one's eager to see him sing the role on stage. He certainly sings extrovert arias very well, albeit in a slightly idiosyncratic way. Moreover, the enthusiasm seems infectious: McCreesh's Gabrieli Players have rarely sounded better and more dramatically attuned in this repertoire. Grimoaldo's anguished soliloquy from *Rodelinda*, which resolves into a gorgeous pastoral aria, is excellently accompanied by the orchestra, although Villazón's soft lyrical singing occasionally feels a bit closed in, as if a champion racehorse is being kept in a paddock that is too small; in this regard 'Caro figlio' from *La Resurrezione* is much better sung. This disc is zany in some ways, but offers fine rewards.

Alessandro – Overture; Sinfonia; Che vidi?; No, più soffrir; Placa l'alma; Solitudine amate … ⓅP

Aure, fonti; Pur troppo veggio…Che tirannia d'Amor; Svanisci, oh reo timore…Dica il falso. **Admeto** – Il ritratto d'Admeto; La sorte mia vacilla; Quest'è dunque la fede…Vedrò fra poco. **Riccardo Primo** – Morte vieni…A me nel mio rossere … Quando non vede. **Siroe** – A costei, che dirò?; L'aura non sempre; Si diversi sembianti…Non vi piacque, ingiusti dei. **Tolomeo** – E dove, e dove mai … Fonti amiche; Ti pentirai, crudel
Catherine Bott, Emma Kirkby sops
Brandenburg Consort / Roy Goodman
Hyperion CDA66950 (76' · DDD · T/t)   Ⓕ**OO**

It was a happy idea to assemble a selection of Handel's arias written for the two sopranos whose famous rivalry coloured the last years of the first Royal Academy. Francesca Cuzzoni – impersonated here by Catherine Bott – was Handel's principal soprano from 1723, creating among other roles Cleopatra and Rodelinda. Faustina Bordoni – her roles here go to Emma Kirkby – arrived in 1726 and the two sang together in several operas including five new ones by Handel, all represented on this recording. Both were superlative singers and each had a characteristic style.

In his music composed for them, Handel clearly differentiated between their capacities, as this disc illustrates. The 'rival queens' first sang together in *Alessandro*, which is the opera most fully represented here. There are two of Cuzzoni's arias, one brilliant piece with rapid divisions, which Bott throws off in splendidly free fashion, and a pathetic one, a typical F-minor *siciliano*, taken very slowly here, allowing plenty of time for some expressive elaboration in the *da capo*. Of Faustina's music we have the exquisite *scena* that opens Act 2, including the aria, 'Aure, fonti', and the lively one with which the act closes. The aria typifies, in the way it demands and rewards precisely detailed singing, Handel's writing for her, and Kirkby's refinement of detail is remarkable. There's beautifully managed interplay between the singers in the *Alessandro* duet; they seem to feed one another with opportunities.

The programme is imaginatively put together and Goodman is a prompt and stylish accompanist. A thoroughly enjoyable disc.

'Amor e gelosia'
Admeto – Alma mia, dolce ristoro **Atalanta** – Amarilli?; Amarilli? Oh Dei! che vuoi? **Faramondo** – Del destin non mi lagno; Caro, tu m'accendi **Flavio** – Ricordati, mio ben **Muzio Scevola** – Vivo senz'alma, o bella **Orlando** – Finché prendi **Poro** – Caro amico amplesso!; Perfidi! Ite di Poro a ricercar nel campo; Se mai più sarò geloso; Se mai turbo il tuo riposo; Act 3, Sinfonia; Lode agli Dei!; Se mai turbo il tuo riposo **Rinaldo** – Scherzano sul tuo volto **Rodelinda** – Non ti bastò, consorte; Io t'abbraccio **Serse** – Gran pena e gelosia! **Sosarme** – Per le porte del tormento **Teseo** – Addio, mio caro bene **Silla** – Mio diletto, che pensi?; Sol per te, bell'idol mio
Patrizia Ciofi sop **Joyce Di Donato** mez Il
Complesso Barocco / Alan Curtis hpd

Virgin Classics 545628-2 (74' · DDD · T/t) Ⓕ❶❷❸❹➔

Ⓖ The duets in his operas are the special treats, coming at climactic points – most often, two lovers' supposedly final parting, or their ultimate reunion. Try 'Io t'abbraccio', from *Rodelinda*, or the wonderful 'Per la porte del tormento' from *Sosarme*. We have several pieces from *Poro*, first the intense little love duet in Act 2, and later the two arias in which Poro and Cleofide swear eternal fidelity – which they fling back at each other when, in a duet we also hear, both believe themselves betrayed. Then there's the delightful little minor-key duet from *Faramondo*, the quarrel duet from *Atalanta*, the charmingly playful piece from *Muzio Scevola*, and the extraordinary one for the pleading Angelica and the furious, maddened Orlando. Handel's understanding of the shades and accents of love are something to marvel at.

All are most beautifully sung by Patrizia Ciofi and Joyce DiDonato, who has just the right firmness and focus for a castrato role (as the mezzo voices almost always are here); both phrase beautifully, articulate and express the words clearly and tellingly, and ornament the *da capo* sections in a natural and tasteful fashion. The accompaniments, done by a chamber group under Alan Curtis with much refined timing of detail, add to the pleasures of this truly delectable CD.

'Furore'
Arias from Admeto, Amadigi di Gaula, Ariodante, Giulio Cesare, Hercules, Imeneo, Semele, Serse and Teseo
Joyce DiDonato *mez*
Les Talens Lyriques / Christophe Rousset
Virgin Classics 519038-2 (75' · DDD) Ⓕ❷❸➔

One of the most enjoyable 'gems from' Handel discs in recent years was 'Amor e gelosia', a recital of duets sung by Patrizia Ciofi and Joyce DiDonato (see above). DiDonato now presents a selection of arias, entitled 'Furore', that is just as fine; indeed, it's superior in that the accompaniment is provided by a chamber orchestra rather than the spare tones of the one-to-a-part Il Complesso Barocco.

The pieces are by no means all 'furious'. But most are passionate, and passion is something that DiDonato does well. A good example is the accompanied recitative 'Orride larve' from *Admeto*, where the king rages at his fate. The following aria is quite different, a calm acceptance of death that DiDonato sings with affecting simplicity.

Would that the same could be said of her cadenzas and embellishments. As with many other singers, the decorations hover on the borders of good taste; and starting the *da capo* of 'Sorge all'alma' a third higher was not a good idea.

The selection is refreshingly unhackneyed, 'Scherza infida' from *Ariodante* and 'Where shall I fly?' from *Hercules* being among the few predictable arias; and although there is an excerpt

from *Serse*, it isn't 'Ombra mai fu'. Full marks for including some *secco* recitatives.

Admeto, HWV22

Admeto, Re di Tessaglia Ⓟ
René Jacobs *counterten* Admeto **Rachel Yakar** *sop* Alceste **Ulrik Cold** *bass* Ercole, Apollo **Rita Dams** *mez* Orindo **James Bowman** *counterten* Trasimede **Jill Gomez** *sop* Antigona **Max van Egmond** *bar* Meraspe, A Voice **Il Complesso Barocco / Alan Curtis**
Virgin Classics Veritas ② 561369-2 (217' · ADD · N/T/t) Recorded 1979. Ⓕ

Admeto is full of fine things, particularly in its music for the two women – Alceste, the nobly self-sacrificing wife of King Admetus, and Antigona, the princess he'd once wooed but then rejected, who now returns after the supposed death of Alceste. The plot, then, is akin to Gluck's *Alceste*, but with an extra subplot that allows for touches of wit and irony and insights into human character.

When it was first released, the recording was something of a pioneer in the use of period instruments and performing conventions. Things have moved on, of course: it seems a bit dated now, heavier in manner than most Handel opera recordings of recent years. And some of the cast aren't wholly at home in a Baroque style where little vibrato is wanted. One thinks in particular of Rachel Yakar, but although her articulation and attack aren't always ideally clean she does bring a good deal of spirit to some of the arias. Jill Gomez's lighter, bell-like voice is more convincingly Handelian: she sings Antigona's music charmingly and with due agility, and expressively too in the beautiful Act 2 *siciliana*. James Bowman is in his best voice as Trasimede, Admetus's brother who loves Antigona. René Jacobs, however, lacks the heroic tones and the incisiveness that the role demands. Ulrik Cold makes a strong Ercole, with appropriately sturdy, masculine tone, and Meraspe is neatly and very stylishly sung by Max van Egmond.

Alan Curtis's direction is attentive to matters of style, but he sometimes lets the bass-line plod. Even so, Handelians needn't hesitate.

Agrippina, HWV6

Agrippina
Véronique Gens *sop* Agrippina **Philippe Jaroussky** *counterten* Nero **Ingrid Perruche** *sop* Poppea **Nigel Smith** *bar* Claudius **Thierry Grégoire** *counterten* Otho **Bernard Deletré** *bass* Pallas **Fabrice Di Falco** *counterten* Narcissus **Alain Buet** *bass* Lesbo
La Grande Ecurie et La Chambre du Roy / Jean-Claude Malgoire
Stage director **Frédéric Fisbach**
Video director **Tiziano Mancini**
Dynamic 📀 DV33431 (172' · NTSC · 4:3 · PCM stereo, 5.1 & DTS 5.1 · 0). Recorded live at the

Fisbach's production gives an amusing account, respectful yet inventive, of librettist Vincenzo Grimani's look at the shenanigans of ancient Rome. *Agrippina* shares three characters with *L'incoronazione di Poppea*, but at an earlier stage of the story, Poppea here being pursued by Otho, Nero and the emperor Claudius. Agrippina, Claudius's wife, spends the opera scheming to discredit Otho and to get Nero, her son by a previous marriage, designated as the next emperor.

The mood is light and ironic, but with a darker side as well. Against a minimalist set, above which French surtitles are, disconcertingly, sometimes visible, the costumes are exaggeratedly 18th-century. Poppea's yards of chiffon conceal two suitors simultaneously in a scene that anticipates *L'heure espagnole*. Nero, with rouged cheeks, sports an aubergine wig; the wigs of the other characters include various degrees of red, with a striking raspberry shade for Poppea. Otho wears no wig, perhaps to distinguish his genuine emotions from the buffoonery of Nero, Pallas and Narcissus.

In the accompanied recitative 'Otton, Otton' and the aria 'Voi che udite il mio lamento', with its aching suspensions in the strings, Thierry Grégoire gives moving expression to Otho's melancholy. As Claudius, Nigel Smith looks comically put out as Poppea fails to notice his preening, but strikes the right lyrical note with 'Vieni o cara'. To decorate the opening of 'Cade il mondo' and leave the *da capo* penny plain is surely to get things the wrong way round.

In the castrato role of Nero, Philippe Jaroussky shows an astonishing agility at soprano pitch. The penultimate aria, 'Come nube', is a *tour de force*. Ingrid Perruche has a nice lightness of touch for Poppea, as do Bernard Deletré as Pallas and Fabrice Di Falco as a mincing Narcissus. To Véronique Gens fall two of this delightful opera's best numbers: the heartfelt 'Pensieri' and the jaunty 'Ogni vento'. If she doesn't quite plumb the depths of the first, her performance overall is sharp and amusing.

mal instrumental resources Curtis employs and his keen sense of the architecture and pacing of Handel's music.

Handel knew his singers' individual strengths and played to them. Curtis, too, knows how to coax the best from his singers. Joyce DiDonato, Maite Beaumont and Karina Gauvin have worked with him before and contribute vividly informed portrayals of the principal characters that stand comparison with the best performances on previous recordings. Technically, DiDonato is superb: her Alcina is a complex, feminine creature, vain and vindictive – listen to her spine-tingling performance of 'Ombre pallide' and the recitative that precedes it in Act 2. Beaumont is at ease in Carestini's role as Ruggiero – heroic when required (as in 'Bramo di trionfar', the discarded aria, originally in Act 1 scene 7, that Curtis reinstated) – and more than equal to the demands of the much-loved 'Verdi prati' (Act 2). Gauvin, her silk-clad Morgana fully as manipulative as Alcina, and Prina, the ever faithful Bradamante, each bring tremendous spirit and sensuousness to their roles. If Van Rensburg's Oronte wavers momentarily in Act 3, Priante's steadfast Melisso and Cherici's courageous Oberto show the way. This could well be the *Alcina* we've been waiting for.

Additional recommendation

Fleming Alcina **Dessay** Morgana **Kuhlmann** Bradamante **Graham** Ruggiero **Les Arts Florissants / Christie** (coupled with Orlando, see page 539)
Erato ⑥ 2564-69653-2 (359' · DDD · N/T/t)   ⒻO

Fleming sings with great intensity. Her performance of this marvellous role is of a very high order. There are others to match. Susan Graham brings a firm, full mezzo, clear and agile. The famous 'Verdi prati' is very simply and beautifully sung, with no ornamentation at all, and the result amply justifies it. Kathleen Kuhlmann sings Bradamante with great vigour and resource and Natalie Dessay brings her full and warm soprano to Morgana's music. The orchestra is less aggressively 'period' in tone than some.

Alcina, HWV34

Alcina
Joyce DiDonato sop Alcina **Karina Gauvin** sop Morgana **Maite Beaumont** mez Ruggiero **Sonia Prina** contr Bradamante **Kobie Van Rensburg** ten Oronte **Vito Priante** bass Melisso **Laura Cherici** sop Oberto **Il Complesso Barocco / Alan Curtis**
Archiv Produktion ③ 477 7374AH3
(3h 23' · DDD)   ⒻOOOℬ

Alan Curtis clearly welcomed the chance to add this masterpiece to the gradually expanding list of Handel operas he has recorded with Il Complesso Barocco. This *Alcina* is polished and passionate, the standard of *da capo* ornamentation unsurpassed. The acoustical environment of this recording is near-perfect. Every detail can be clearly heard, in part because of the mini-

---

Ariodante, HWV33

Ariodante   ℗
Anne Sofie von Otter mez Ariodante **Lynne Dawson** sop Ginevra **Veronica Cangemi** sop Dalinda **Ewa Podles** mez Polinesso **Richard Croft** ten Lurcanio **Denis Sedov** bass King of Scotland **Luc Coadou** ten Odoardo **Choeur des Musiciens du Louvre; Les Musiciens du Louvre / Marc Minkowski**
Archiv Produktion ③ 457 271-2AH3 (178' · DDD · T/t)   ⒻOℬ

Lynne Dawson is the star of this show. In Act 2, where Ginevra finds herself inexplicably rejected and condemned by everyone, Dawson brings real depth of tone and feeling to her E minor lament, 'Il mio crudel martoro'; in the final act she shines in the desolate miniature 'Io ti bacio' and brings much fire to the outburst 'Sì, morro'. But she never transgresses the canons of Baroque style. Von Otter, too, has much marvellous music – the aria 'Scherza infida' is one of Handel's greatest expressions of grief – and she sings it beautifully, but she isn't really at one with his idiom and seems to lack a natural feeling for the amplitude of Handel's lines.

Yet there's much to enjoy here too, the beauty of the actual sound, the immaculate control, the many telling and musicianly touches of phrasing. But the noble, climactic triumphant aria, 'Dopo notte' doesn't have quite the effect it should. For that, however, Minkowski is partly to blame. Carried away, it almost seems, by the passion of the music, he's often inclined to go at it baldheaded, too fast and with a ferocity of accent that seems foreign to the style and dangerously close to ugly.

Veronica Cangemi makes a charming Dalinda, light, spirited and duly agile, with some gently pathetic expression in the delightful *siciliana* song early in Act 2. Ewa Podles brings her large, resonant voice to Polinesso's music; and the King of Scotland's fatherly music is done with due fullness and warmth by Denis Sedov, who covers the two-octave range with comfort and resonance.

Despite the driven quality of Minkowski's performance, especially in the high dramatic music of the latter part of the opera, the sheer passion of this set does give it claims to be considered first choice. The admirable McGegan performance is possibly a safer buy, and in some respects it's a more stylish performance, but the singing here, Lynne Dawson's above all, is on balance superior.

Ariodante
Ann Murray *mez* Ariodante **Joan Rodgers** *sop* Ginevra **Lesley Garrett** *sop* Dalinda **Christopher Robson** *counterten* Polinesso **Paul Nilon** *ten* Lurcanio **Gwynne Howell** *bass* King of Scotland **Mark Le Brocq** *ten* Odoardo **English National Opera Chorus and Orchestra / Ivor Bolton**
Stage director **David Alden**
Video director **Kriss Rusmanis**
Arthaus Musik 📀 100 064 (178' · Regions 2, 3, 5)
Ⓕ⚫

David Alden's staging of *Ariodante* was generally praised when it was first staged by WNO, a joint venture with ENO. This DVD is a recording of the much-admired revival at the ENO in 1996. Its appearance confirms the extraordinary perspicacity of Alden's production, which explains, from an almost Freudian viewpoint, the loves, hates, fears and fantasies of the principal characters so unerringly and deeply delineated in Handel's masterly score, in which aria after aria exposes new layers of emotional thrust and instability. Ann Murray gives a committed performance as the unhinged Ariodante and displays a physical and vocal virtuosity only occasionally vitiated by a harsh tone. The great arias, 'Scherza infida' and 'Dopo notte' are just the

climactic moments they should be. Joan Rodgers as Ginevra is hardly less impressive in her portrayal of the myriad feelings suggested by Handel and Alden.

Christopher Robson, as the villain Polinesso, is the very incarnation of evil lasciviousness, for which his edgy countertenor isn't inappropriate. Lesley Garrett gives Dalinda just the right touch of vulnerability as she submits to Polinesso's wiles while being sexually captivated by him. Gwynne Howell is the upright King to the life. Ivor Bolton conducts a vital, well-played account of the score with modern strings sounding very much like their period counterparts. Almost three hours of gripping music-drama pass in a trice, helped by the unbroken sequence of DVD. The sound is commendable, the picture superb.

Arminio, HWV36

Arminio   Ⓟ
Vivica Genaux *sop* Arminio **Geraldine McGreevy** *sop* Tusnelda **Dominique Labelle** *sop* Sigismondo **Manuela Custer** *mez* Ramise **Luigi Petroni** *ten* Varo **Syste Buwalda** *counterten* Tullio **Riccardo Ristori** *bass* Segeste **Il Complesso Barocco / Alan Curtis**
Virgin Veritas ② 545461-2 (147' · DDD · T/t)   Ⓕ

On the evidence of this very fine recording, *Arminio* can stand among the best of Handel's operas, full of beautiful and imagination. The first number, a minor-key duet largely in dialogue for Arminio and his wife Tusnelda, is done with an intensity and vitality that immediately involves you in the action. In Act 2 a series of more expansive arias unfolds: a pair for Arminio, one noble and the other furious, a striking one, austerely scored for Tusnelda, a more playful piece for Arminio's sister Ramise, and a spacious one – also almost an oboe concerto movement – for Sigismondo. This sequence is crowned by a sombre aria for Arminio, with hints of a music that foreshadows 'He was despised', and a soft-textured, sensuous *siciliana* aria for Tusnelda. This is musically one of Handel's finest acts.

The performance is excellently directed by Alan Curtis, who paces the opera well, keeping the recitative moving and characterising the arias clearly. Dominique Labelle is of star quality, delicate, precise, rhythmic, powerful where she needs to be. The lower castrato part, the title-role, is sung by Vivica Genaux, whose focused, slightly grainy voice serves ideally – there's singing of real brilliance here. Geraldine McGreevy gives a lot of pleasure too with her commanding singing in the *prima donna* role. *Arminio* isn't of the stamp of, say, *Giulio Cesare* or *Alcina*, but it has a lot of splendid music in it and is hugely enjoyable. Recommended.

Arianna in Creta, HWV32

Arianna in Creta
Mata Katsuli *sop* Arianna **Mary-Ellen Nesi** *mez* Teseo **Irini Karaianni** *mez* Carilda **Marita Paparizou**

mez Tauride **Theodora Baka** *mez* Alceste **Petros Magoulas** *bass* Minos **Orchestra of Patras / George Petrou**
Dabringhaus und Grimm ② MDG603 1375-2
(131' · DDD · T/t/N)   Ⓕ

This is the first commercial recording of *Arianna in Creta* but, just as importantly, it is also the last of Handel's surviving operas to be issued on CD. Handel, according to his usual practice for the London stage, chose to set an old Italian libretto: *Arianna e Teseo* set by Leonardo Leo for Rome in 1729, although a few of Handel's aria texts were instead taken from a pasticcio that his new London rival Porpora had organised at Naples in 1721.

Handel's opera portrays Theseus' love affair with the Cretan King Minos' daughter Ariadne, the hero's victory over the Minotaur, and his escape from the labyrinth. It ends happily, with the sentiment that love overcomes cruelty. None of the later dejection when Ariadne is forsaken on Naxos is portrayed.

Curiously, Porpora and the 'Opera of the Nobility' organised *Arianna in Nasso* at Lincoln's Inn Fields on December 29, 1733, just under a month before Handel's treatment of the Theseus and Ariadne story could make it to the King's Theatre stage. However, Handel's opera was a much greater success, notching up 16 performances and earning a prompt revival at the beginning of the following season. Produced between *Orlando* and *Ariodante*, *Arianna in Creta* does not quite match the pinnacles that surround it in the chronology of Handel's works but this new recording illustrates that it is high time Arianna's reputation was restored.

The cocky villain Tauride, who spends the opera spouting off at Teseo, opens proceedings with 'Mirami' (a marvellous portrayal of swaggering arrogance, not quite captured by the Orchestra of Patras's elegant phrasing but sung resolutely by Marita Paparizou) and the spectacular 'Qual leon' (featuring two magnificent horns, although it is rushed a fraction here). The secondary lovers Carilda and Alceste get a few impressive scenes too, especially Alceste's sublime 'Son qual stanco pellegrino' with a mellifluous cello solo (the soprano castrato Carlo Scalzi might have stolen the show with this in 1734). Soprano Mata Katsuli delivers Arianna's taxing arias with sensitivity.

However, the towering figure of the opera is Mary-Ellen Nesi's heroic Teseo. This was the first role Handel composed for the star castrato Carestini and every aria is a gem: 'Nel pugnar' is an extensive florid showpiece; sentimental reconciliation is tenderly expressed in 'Sdegnata sei con me'; and Handel rises to the challenge of the Minotaur scene with a stirring accompanied recitative and a dashing heroic aria ('Qùi ti sfido').

George Petrou has a firm grasp on Handelian style and presents a persuasive case for the opera's merits. The predominantly Greek cast and period-instrument orchestra will not be familiar to many but, despite some approximate orchestral intonation, they reveal that *Arianna in Creta* is well worth investigation.

Ezio, HWV29

Ezio   Ⓟ
Sonia Prina *sop* Valentiniano **Ann Hallenberg** *mez* Ezio **Anicio Zorzi Giustiniani** *ten* Massimo **Karina Gauvin** *sop* Fulvia **Marianne Andersen** *mez* Onoria **Vito Priante** *bass* Varo **Il Complesso Barocco / Alan Curtis**
Archiv Produktion ③ 477 8073AH3 (3h 6' · DDD· T/t)
                                                    ⒻⓄⓄ▣

Ezio is like a Roman thriller. Those wanting superficial thrills and glamorous wit from their Baroque operas might not know what to make of it, and the original audience in 1732 certainly didn't (it was one of Handel's worst commercial flops). However, it frequently shows the composer at his most masterful.

Alan Curtis sagely allows Handel's music to speak for itself unhindered by artificial gimmicks: ritornellos are subtle, continuo accompaniment of recitatives is exemplary for its pacing and judgement, and singers declaim their texts with utmost clarity. The sole disadvantage is that more passionate music is underplayed and lightweight, which means that sometimes it lacks dramatic punch and expressiveness. For instance, the dance-like courtliness in the overture is elegantly moulded but could do with some fiery intensity, and the final chorus is curiously underdone. So much of the performance is musically meticulous, but it would have flourished with a few more degrees of dramatic heat.

'Ecco alle mie catene', an emotional prison-scene aria at the end of Act 2, is sensitively sung by Ann Hallenberg but Il Complesso Barocco sound underpowered; a better synergy between instruments and voice is achieved in 'Se la mia vita'. Fulvia's dazzling *aria di bravura* 'La mia costanza' is impressive for Karina Gauvin's articulate stylishness and a fantastic cadenza. Sonia Prina's singing is admirable. Anicio Zorzi Giustiniani's fast runs are a bit dry in the superbly played 'Và! dal furor portata'. The unusual instrumentation for flutes and violette in Onoria's 'Quanto mai felice' is excellently played. Vito Priante sings Varo's splendid trumpet aria 'Già risonar d'intorno' with robust precision (Curtis adds a timpani part). Overall, this is an excellent and much-needed first complete recording, and confirms that *Ezio* is a fascinating serious drama.

Faramondo

Faramondo   Ⓟ
Max Emanuel Cencic *counterten* Faramondo **Sophie Karthäuser** *sop* Clotilde **Marina de Liso** *mez* Rosimonda **In-Sung Sim** *bass* Gustavo **Philippe Jaroussky** *counterten* Adolfo **Xavier Sabata** *counterten* Gernando **Fulvio Bettini** *bar* Teobaldo

Terry Wey *counterten* Childerico
Swiss Radio Chorus; I Barocchisti / Diego Fasolis
Virgin Classics ③ 216611-2 (166' · DDD)　　Ⓟ**O**Ⓑ➤

Faramondo (1738) was written after the remnants of the Opera of the Nobility and Handel's opera company merged together for one peculiar and unsuccessful season at the King's Theatre. Virgin Classics has made much of the fact that this is the first Handel opera recording in which all the male characters are sung at the correct pitch by male singers, but several of the illustrious countertenors involved occasionally drop a few notes down an octave in order to conserve their larynxes.

I Barocchisti's playing of the fine *concerto grosso*-style Overture is zesty. Handel's scoring of the chorus 'Pera, pera' doesn't include the drums and trumpets employed here, and a few more euros could have been saved by not using unhistorical organ and guitar in the continuo group. Sophie Karthäuser's light navigation of Clotilde's arias provides some nice moments ('Combattuta da due venti' is eloquent rather than tempestuous, but none the worse for a bit of measured clarity and detail in its oscillating orchestral figures). Philippe Jaroussky and Max Emanuel Cencic each give attractive performances of virtuoso arias. Adolfo's slow aria 'Se a' piedi tuoi morrò' is delightful for its polished orchestral playing and Jaroussky's pleasant singing. Cencic's high-lying tessitura and brilliant coloratura are almost flawless (the tender cavatina 'Sì, tornerò a morir' is beautifully judged by singer, orchestra and conductor; the heroic 'Se ben mi lusinga' is dazzling, but the duet 'Vado e vivo' has a few hints of strain). Xavier Sabata demonstrates his muskier voice in the enraged 'Voglio che mora, sì', but hams up his *da capo* too much. Marina de Liso gives a stunning performance of Rosimonda's turbulent 'Sì, l'intendesti, sì' (in which Diego Fasolis brings out exciting details in the accompaniment), and the bass villain Gustavo is resonantly sung by In-Sung Sim. Fasolis's direction is exemplary for its warmly authoritative expressiveness and fluent mastery over detail. *Faramondo* is revealed as a much better score than previously thought.

Fernando, re di Castiglia, HWV30

Fernando, re di Castiglia　　Ⓟ
Lawrence Zazzo *counterten* Fernando **Veronica Cangemi** *sop* Elvida **Marianna Pizzolato** *sop* Isabella **Max Emanuel Cencic** *counterten* Sancio **Filippo Adami** *ten* Dioniso **Antonio Abete** *bass-bar* Altomaro **Neal Banerjee** *ten* Alfonso
Il Complesso Barocco / Alan Curtis
Virgin Classics ② 365483-2 (149' · DDD)　　Ⓕ

Fernando is the abandoned first draft of Handel's opera *Sosarme* (1732). We do not know why Handel changed almost all the character names, the location of the action and the title during the composition process, but in either

guise the opera is full of top-drawer music. Alan Curtis has decided to reconstruct Fernando for philological reasons, although maybe the desire to bring us another 'premiere' had something to do with it.

Curtis's pacing and shaping of Handel's music is consistently subtle, astutely rhetorical and firmly connected to the libretto text. Although it might be possible to explore firmer muscularity and create a more vivid sense of surprise in the quicker music, there is something to be said for Curtis's shrewd reservation of such effects for when it is truly vital for the drama. For instance, Marianna Pizzolato's powerful arias 'Vado al campo' and 'Cuor di madre e cuor di moglie' are potently delivered moments of severe agitated passion that are all the more effective for the sweeter elegance that pervades much of this lovely score. The sublime duet 'Per le porte' is sung with poetic intimacy by Lawrence Zazzo and Veronica Cangemi. Zazzo sings his elegantly heroic aria 'Alle sfere della gloria' with supple clarity. Max Emanuel Cencic is impressive as the reticent Sancio, unwilling to be used as a pawn in his ruthless grandfather Altomaro's Machiavellian plans to tear the royal family apart. Antonio Abete gives an ideal account of the villain's arias.

The only weak link is Filippo Adami's vocally deficient Dionisio: natural Italian declamation in his extrovert recitatives is not enough to carry him through under-achieving blustery accounts of magnificent arias that deserve better. Il Complesso Barocco are excellent: *ritornelli* are intelligently weighted and phrased and instrumental contributions are patiently integrated with the singing. There are a few cuts to recitatives, but overall *Fernando* is one of Curtis's most consistent and pleasing Handel opera recordings.

Giulio Cesare, HWV17

Giulio Cesare　　Ⓟ
Jennifer Larmore *mez* Giulio Cesare **Barbara Schlick** *sop* Cleopatra **Bernarda Fink** *mez* Cornelia **Marianne Rørholm** *mez* Sextus **Derek Lee Ragin** *counterten* Ptolemy **Furio Zanasi** *bass* Achillas **Olivier Lallouette** *bar* Curio **Dominique Visse** *counterten* Nirenus **Concerto Köln / René Jacobs**
Harmonia Mundi ③ HMC90 1385/7 (243' · DDD · T/t)
　　Ⓕ**OOO**

Ⓖ　Handel's greatest heroic opera sports no fewer than eight principal characters and one of the largest orchestras he ever used. Undoubtedly this, and the singing of Francesca Cuzzoni (Cleopatra) and Senesino (Caesar), helped to launch *Giulio Cesare* into the enduring popularity that it enjoys to this day. But it's primarily the quality of the music, with barely a weak number in four hours of entertainment, that's made it such a favourite with audiences. Here the period instruments are an immediate advantage in giving extra 'bite' to the many moments of high drama without threatening to drown the singers in *forte* passages.

This performance is a particularly fine one with an excellent cast; Caesar, originally sung by a castrato, is here taken by the young mezzo, Jennifer Larmore. She brings weight and integrity to the role, seemingly untroubled by the demands of the final triumphant aria, 'Qual torrente'. Occasionally her vibrato becomes intrusive, but that's a minor quibble in a performance of this stature. Handel could just as well have called his opera 'Cleopatra' as she's the pivotal element in the drama, a role taken here by Barbara Schlick and sung with acuity and imagination. If Cleopatra represents strength in a woman, then Cornelia is surely the tragic figure, at the mercy of events. Her first aria, 'Priva son', here taken very slowly, shows Bernarda Fink to be more than equal to the role, admirable in her steady tone and dignity of character. Derek Lee Ragin's treacherous Ptolemy is also memorable, venom and fire injected into his agile voice.

A first-rate cast is supported by René Jacobs and Concerto Köln on fine form, though the continuo line is sometimes less than ideally clear. The recording is excellent.

Giulio Cesare (sung in English)
Dame Janet Baker *mez* Giulio Cesare **Valerie Masterson** *sop* Cleopatra **Sarah Walker** *mez* Cornelia **Della Jones** *mez* Sextus **James Bowman** *counterten* Ptolemy **John Tomlinson** *bass* Achilles **Christopher Booth-Jones** *bar* Curio **David James** *counterten* Nirenus **English National Opera Chorus and Orchestra / Sir Charles Mackerras**
Chandos Opera in English Series ③ CHAN3019
(244' · DDD · N)   Ⓜ Ⓞ ➤

This opera was a personal triumph for Dame Janet. As Caesar, she arms the voice with an impregnable firmness, outgoing and adventurous. Valerie Masterson shares the honours with Dame Janet, a Cleopatra whose bright voice gains humanity through ordeal. The tinkle of surface-wear clears delightfully in her later arias, sung with a pure tone and high accomplishment. As a total production, *Julius Caesar* was an outstanding achievement in ENO's history. Strongly cast, it had a noble Cornelia in Sarah Walker, a high-spirited Sesto in Della Jones, and in James Bowman a Ptolemy whose only fault was that his voice lacked meanness of timbre appropriate to the odious character. John Tomlinson's massive bass also commands attention. Mackerras's conducting is impeccable and the opera is given in clear, creditable English. (See next review for the video equivalent.)

Giulio Cesare (sung in English)
Janet Baker *mez* Giulio Cesare **Valerie Masterson** *sop* Cleopatra **Sarah Walker** *mez* Cornelia **Della Jones** *mez* Sextus **James Bowman** *counterten* Ptolemy **John Tomlinson** *bass* Achilles **Brian Casey** *sngr* Pothinus **John Kitchiner** *bar* Curio **Tom Emlyn**

Williams *counterten* Nirenus **English National Opera Chorus and Orchestra / Sir Charles Mackerras**
Stage director **John Copley**
Video director **John Michael Phillips**
ArtHaus Musik 🅳🆅🅳 100 308 (180' · 4:3 · 2.0 · 2 & 5 · N)
Recorded 1984   Ⓕ Ⓞ

This is a 1984 studio re-creation, with the original cast, of John Copley's ENO production. Mackerras's performing edition is by no means literally 'authentic'; arias are removed, including much of Sextus's role, recitatives are trimmed, and much of Caesar's role is transposed – inevitably, since it was written for the exceptionally low contralto castrato Senesino. The result is no travesty, however: it's fast-moving and dramatically satisfying, and conducted by Mackerras in the same spirit.

Copley also strives to avoid tedium, for instance backing *da capo* passages with stage activity – sometimes rather obviously. However, his staging, combining John Pascoe's warm-hued, vaguely 18th-century designs with more naturalistic acting, translates quite well to the screen – not least because the singers are so committed. Janet Baker displays great Handelian affinity. She not only delivers these difficult, florid arias with fiery élan and appropriate ornament, but infuses them with a real emotional intensity that sweeps one over the credibility gap.

Sarah Walker makes the lachrymose Cornelia almost as intense, and Valerie Masterson carries off Cleopatra's gorgeous music with admirable if slightly self-conscious virtuosity and a kittenish seductiveness reminiscent of Vivien Leigh. Della Jones is a splendid Sextus, and John Tomlinson a thunderously melodramatic Achilles. Though James Bowman's hooting tone is rather obtrusive, he plays Ptolemy as a petulantly Farouk-ish villain to fine comic effect.

Giulio Cesare
Sarah Connolly *mez* Giulio Cesare **Danielle de Niese** *sop* Cleopatra **Patricia Bardon** *mez* Cornelia **Angelika Kirchschlager** *mez* Sesto **Christophe Dumaux** *counterten* Tolomeo **Christopher Maltman** *bar* Achilles **Alexander Ashworth** *bass* Curio **Rachid Ben Abdeslam** *counterten* Nireno **Glyndebourne Chorus; Orchestra of the Age of Enlightenment / William Christie**
Stage director **David McVicar**
Video director **Robin Lough**
Opus Arte ③ 🅳🆅🅳 OA0950D (3h 46' · NTSC · 16:9 · PCM stereo and DTS 5.1 surround · 0) Recorded live during the Opera Festival, Glyndebourne, in 2005
Ⓕ Ⓞ Ⓞ Ⓞ

Ⓖ David McVicar's 2005 staging, revived the following summer, provoked a deal of contrasting views among the critical fraternity but was adored by the Glyndebourne public. Chief cause of their delight was the overtly sexual, high-hoofing performance of Cleopatra by the irrepressible Danielle de Niese (who is accorded a delightful 22-minute narrative on her Glyndebourne experience among the extras here). Her vocal command and stage presence are spectacular in every sense, and from her first aria she utterly seduces her audience. McVicar took advantage of her attractive skills to build the opera around her personality.

We are here in the high noon of British imperialism and the Ottoman Empire, with Caesar more like a late-19th-century English general than a Roman emperor, and with the Egyptian milieu heavily underlined by milling extras, now always a not-altogether welcome feature of a McVicar production. They clutter the stage and draw attention away from the principals, although one has to admit that the highly disciplined and often captivating choreography is brilliantly executed within Robert Jones's exotic sets. McVicar does at least allow the moments of serious drama to be played out without undue interference – such as the deeply moving duet that closes Act 1 and Cleopatra's 'Piangerò'. Finally it has to be said that only Glyndebourne allows for the rehearsal time to prepare such a complex and ingenious staging.

The musical side of things is equally well prepared and thought-through under William Christie's knowledgeable and commanding direction. He manages to balance with the same finesse and care the light and serious parts of the score, even if his love for Handel leads him to a few self-indulgently slow tempi. The OAE play lovingly and with period skills for him. By the time of this DVD recording, near the end of the run, the whole thing moves with eloquence matched by elegance.

De Niese sings her airy numbers as to the manner born, seconded by expertly erotic dancing. She manages most of the emotional substance of her sadder arias, but they sometimes seem wanting in the tonal weight ideally required. Sarah Connolly's thoroughly believable Caesar is sung with her firm tone and well schooled mastery of Handelian style, including subtle embellishments. This wilful and imperial Caesar manages to change moods as his music demands.

Some of the most accomplished and tender Handelian singing comes from Patricia Bardon's moving Cornelia and Angelika Kirchschlager's concerned Sesto, although the latter does slightly overplay the character's seemingly neurotic state of mind following his father's brutal death. The young countertenor Christophe Dumaux playing Tolomeo is suitably brat-like and spoilt. He, like most of the cast, fulfils all the stringent demands of this very physical staging. Christopher Maltman makes Achilles as nasty as he should be. The sense of teamwork all round is confirmed in the interviews included in the extras. Robin Lough's DVD direction is faultless.

Giulio Cesare

Graham Pushee *counterten* Giulio Cesare **Yvonne Kenny** *sop* Cleopatra **Rosemary Gunn** *mez* Cornelia **Elizabeth Campbell** *mez* Sesto **Andrew Dalton** *counterten* Tolomeo **Stephen Bennett** *bass* Achillas **Richard Alexander** *bass* Curio **Rodney Gilchrist**

HANDEL GIULIO CESARE – IN BRIEF

Jennifer Larmore *Giulio Cesare* **Barbara Schlick** *Cleopatra* **Concerto Köln / René Jacobs**
Harmonia Mundi HMC90 1385/7　　Ⓜ❍❍❍
Ⓖ A superb performance that took a *Gramophone* Award back in 1991. Jennifer Larmore is a powerful and technically magnificent Caesar, Barbara Schlick an imaginative and sweet-voiced Cleopatra, and Derek Lee Ragin a suitably poisonous Ptolemy. Jacobs demonstrates his mastery of 18th-century theatre with the superb Concerto Köln.

Dame Janet Baker *Giulio Cesare* **Valerie Masterson** *Cleopatra* **ENO / Sir Charles Mackerras**
Chandos CHAN3019　　Ⓜ❍
An outstanding performance from 1984 that enshrines Janet Baker's extraordinarily complete portrayal of Caesar. Valerie Masterson is a superb Cleopatra, bright toned and coquettish. James Bowman sings well as Ptolemy, though he could perhaps be nastier! Mackerras's command of the score is magnificent.

Dame Janet Baker *Giulio Cesare* **Valerie Masterson** *Cleopatra* **ENO / Sir Charles Mackerras**
ArtHaus Musik ⬛ 100 308　　Ⓜ❍
John Copley's English National Opera production is here taken into the studio and reveals the magnificent cast on top form, all revolving around Baker's emotionally powerful Caesar. Mackerras drives the score forward with his customary élan ensuring a performance of real dramatic intensity.

Marijana Mijanovic *Giulio Cesare* **Magdalena Kožená** *Cleopatra* **Les Musiciens du Louvre / Marc Minkowski**
Archiv 474 210-2AH3　　Ⓕ❍⊙➔
A strong challenger to the Jacobs set, with Majanovic a strong Caesar and Kožená a fine Cleopatra (though perhaps lacking the *n*th degree of voluptuousness). Anne Sofie von Otter is a superb Sesto and Charlotte Hellekrant a noble Cornelia. Minkowski's direction is generally pretty swift, though he can linger at particularly lovely moments.

Andreas Scholl *Giulio Cesare* **Inger Dam-Jensen** *Cleopatra* **Concerto Copenhagen / Lars Ulrik Larsen**
Harmonia Mundi ⬛ HMD990 9008/9　　Ⓕ❍
The same production as on the Euroarts version (see right) conducted by Hickox, but here with Andreas Scholl lifting it to even greater heights. He has developed as an actor and his singing, it almost goes without saying, is superlative. But the rest of the cast is very fine too, and Larsen directs with an exquisite feeling for Handelian style.

counterten Nireno **Australian Opera and Ballet
Orchestra / Richard Hickox**
Stage director **Francisco Negrin**
Video director **Peter Butler**
Euroarts **DVD** 205 3599 (208' · 4:3 · PCM stereo, 5.1 &
DTS 5.1 · 0). Recorded live at the Opera House,
Sydney, June 1994   (F)

Francisco Negrin's production of *Giulio Cesare*
is remarkably satisfying. Richard Hickox's musical direction is exemplary, with timing, tempi
and phrasing that never go awry. The modern-
instrument orchestra plays without a trace of
soggy over-indulgence. The singing is less uniformly ideal: Yvonne Kenny's gutsy coloratura
is undone by wobbly intonation, and Elizabeth
Campbell's Sesto inclines towards shrillness.
Rosemary Gunn's Cornelia isn't a convincing
drop-dead gorgeous icon who could initiate the
doom of lusting Egyptians, and her heavy vibrato
obscures the melodic beauty of 'Priva son d'ogni
conforto'. Stephen Bennett delivers a wonderful
'Tu sei il cor' which suggests that Achillas is
capable of greater eloquence and sincerity than
we'd suspected. Graham Pushee's lyrical Cesare
is consistently marvellous: his superbly acted role
as an enlightened ruler perfectly fits Negrin's
concept of him as representing ideal kingship,
which is how such figures were supposed to be
interpreted by Handel's Haymarket audience.

This is by no means a historical Baroque staging, but Negrin ensures that each strand of the
plot is faithful to both libretto and Handel's
music. He takes some daring risks with staging
while doing nothing to subvert the musical rhetoric or the purity of the narrative. He intelligently
allows the soliloquy convention to be respected.
Unlike so many directors who do not understand
Handel's dramatic power, he ensures that Cleopatra sings 'Piangerò' alone; the lack of distractions magnifies an intensely emotional moment.
The production nevertheless features plenty of
clever stagecraft. The most significant liberty
reaps handsome dividends: the role of Nireno is
incidental in the score, yet the director imagines
that he pulls all the strings behind the scenes to
ensure that all the plot-strands resolve happily.
It's common to admire a Handel opera performance for its singing while deploring the staging;
here, though, is a precious rare example of a production that's a joy.

Giulio Cesare
Andreas Scholl *counterten* Giulio Cesare **Inger
Dam-Jensen** *sop* Cleopatra **Randi Stene** *contr*
Cornelia **Tuva Semmingsen** *sop* Sesto **Christopher
Robson** *counterten* Tolomeo **John Lundgren** *bass*
Curio **Palle Knudsen** *bass* Achilla **Michael Maniaci**
counterten Nireno
Concerto Copenhagen / Lars Ulrik Mortensen
Stage director **Francisco Negrin**
Video director **Thomas Grimm**
Harmonia Mundi ② **DVD** HMD990 9008/9
(3h 36' · NTSC · 16:9 · PCM stereo and DTS 5.1 · 0)
Recorded live at the Royal Danish Theatre,
Copenhagen, in March 2005   (F)●

Francisco Negrin's production, though not
without judiciously applied humour in a few
places, is essentially of a serious nature (and
more so than his lighter and brighter Sydney
production, reviewed above). Unsurprisingly,
this sympathetic approach suits Handel's *opera
seria* to a tee. There are neither damaging large
cuts nor ill-advised reordering of movements,
and Negrin's ideas fully support the musico-dramatic nature of the characters as presented in
the libretto and score. The modernistic setting
laced with elements of ancient Egypt provides
the platform for a dark and brooding drama.
Where some directors use tricks to amuse the
audience, Negrin uses visual playfulness to illustrate a serious point about the characters (such
as the contest between elevating thrones in 'Va
tacito'). It is refreshing that at the end there is
little doubt that the good guys have triumphed:
Sesto is caked in Tolomeo's blood, which seems
to mark his coming of age in a brutal world, but
there is no attempt made to ridicule the victorious leading characters, who fully deserve their
happy ending.

Andreas Scholl's singing is consistently astute,
and his acting has advanced considerably in
subtlety since his operatic debut in Glyndebourne's *Rodelinda* nearly a decade ago. However, this is an excellent team performance.
Inger Dam-Jensen performs with the ideal sincerity and emotiveness that Cleopatra's character too often lacks in superficial productions.
Tuva Semmingsen's Sesto sings with crystal-
clear phrasing ('Cara speme' is heart-stopping).
Christopher Robson's singing is weak but his
acting as the nasty Tolomeo is superb in its timing of gestures (there is plenty of comedy in his
scenes, but he is brutal and menacing rather than
the simply camp idiot too often portrayed
onstage). Lars Ulrik Mortensen's direction of
the music from his harpsichord is well nigh perfect. This is not the most flamboyant or fancy
Giulio Cesare on DVD, but it is certainly the
most insightful and intelligent for drama, and
probably also the best for all-round musical
consistency.

Hercules, HWV60

Hercules
Gidon Saks *bass-bar* Hercules **Anne Sofie von**   P
Otter *mez* Dejanira **Richard Croft** *ten* Hyllus **Lynne
Dawson** *sop* Iole **David Daniels** *counterten* Lichas
Marcos Pujol *bar* Priest of Jupiter **Chœur des
Musiciens du Louvre; Les Musiciens du Louvre /
Marc Minkowski**
Archiv Produktion ③ 469 532-2AH3 (176' · DDD · T/t)
                                                   (F)●(D)▸

Hercules has never quite occupied the place it
merits in the Handel canon, even though it
includes some of his most powerfully dramatic
music. This is understood by Marc Minkowski,
whose intentions towards the work are made
clear frm the start of the Overture. But he's also
intent on maintaining its dramatic pace and

emphasising its range of feeling. His cast is well able to share his dramatic vision. Von Otter excels as Dejanira. This, rather than Hercules himself, is the central role, carrying the work's chief expressive weight. There's some beautifully shaped singing as in her opening air she mourns Hercules' absence, and she copes well with Minkowski's demanding tempo in 'Begone, my fears'. Lynne Dawson makes a delightful Iole, crystalline, airy, rhythmic, but able to call on more intensity where needed. 'My breast with tender pity swells' is truly lovely. Lichas' music is done with refinement but also vigour by David Daniels. Richard Croft, though often hurried by Minkowski, sings much of Hyllus' music with elegance, and his delicate sustained *pianissimo* in the *da capo* of 'From celestial seats descending', one of the most inspired pieces in the score, is remarkable. The choral singing is strong, secure, responsive, though the French choir is rather less euphonious than the best English ones. The orchestral playing is duly alert. This account benefits from fewer cuts than his rival Gardiner and superior solo singing.

Orlando, HWV31

Orlando (coupled with Alcina – see page 532) **P**
Patricia **Bardon** *mez* Orlando Rosemary **Joshua** *sop*
Angelica **Hilary Summers** *contr* Medoro **Rosa**
Mannion *sop* Dorinda **Harry van der Kamp** *bass*
Zoroastro **Les Arts Florissants / William Christie**
Erato ⑥ 2564-69653-2 (168' · DDD · T/t)   Ⓕ

Christie is very much concerned with a smooth and generally rich texture and with delicacy of rhythmic shaping. His management of the recitative could hardly be bettered and moments of urgency or of other kinds of emotional stress are tellingly handled. Sometimes he favours a rather sustained style in the arias, making the textures seem airless and heavy, and the lines within them too smooth. However, to set against it there's his exceptional delicacy of timing, his careful but always natural-sounding moulding of cadences and other critical moments in the score. Not many Handel interpreters show this kind of regard for such matters and it's a delight to hear Handel's music so lovingly nurtured; it also helps the singers to convey meaning. The cast is very strong. The title-role is taken by a mezzo, Patricia Bardon, who draws a firm and often slender line, with that gleam in her tone that can so enliven the impact of a lowish mezzo – the famous Mad Scene is magnificent. The Sleep Scene, with very sweet, soft-toned playing of the *violette marine*, is lovely.

Hilary Summers offers a very sensitively sung Medoro, pure and shapely in line. Harry van der Kamp makes a finely weighty Zoroastro, with plenty of resonance in his lower register; the last aria in particular is done in rousing fashion. As Angelica, Rosemary Joshua's musicianship comes through in her attractive phrasing and timing. Rosa Mannion's Dorinda is no less full

of delights, catching the character to perfection. Hogwood's lighter orchestral textures are appealing but the refinement of detail in the newer set is equally admirable.

Partenope, HWV27

Partenope
Rosemary **Joshua** *sop* Partenope **Kurt Streit** *ten*
Emilio **Stephen Wallace** *counterten* Armindo
Andrew Foster-Williams *bass-bar* Ormonte **Hilary**
Summers *contr* Rosmira **Lawrence Zazzo** *counterten*
Arsace Early Opera Company / Christian Curnyn
Chandos Chaconne ③ CHAN0719
(3h 10' · DDD · T/t)   Ⓕ ▶

Handel composed *Partenope* for the 1730 London season, less than a year into the so-called 'Second Academy' period in which he enjoyed increased artistic control over his productions. *Partenope* was a subject he had long coveted and with a new troupe of singers, less starry than before, he seems to have relished the chance to tone down the rattling virtuosity in favour of a more 'company' feel, and with it a more genuine and subtle mode of expression. He was helped by a strong libretto which is well set-out, humane with a touch of gentle humour, and features characters who are lifelike and credible.

Partenope, Queen of Naples, is wooed by three suitors – the overly proud enemy general Emilio, the mopy but deserving Armindo, and her own favourite, Arsace. Arsace, however, is tormented by the woman he left behind, Rosmira, who is hanging around and making mischief disguised as a man. Eventually, and after much soul-searching, Arsace forces her to reveal her identity by challenging her to a bare-chest duel (which she declines). The couple are reunited, Partenope settles for Armindo, and Emilio accepts his rejection philosophically.

Christian Curnyn conducts a highly competent performance thoroughly in the groove of modern Handelian style, with a cast that has no vocal weaknesses and many dramatic virtues: Rosemary Joshua as Partenope and Hilary Summers as Rosmira have the most technically demanding music, but Joshua's brightly confident singing also effortlessly suggests a woman both regal and desirable, while the dark-voiced Summers sounds like someone not to be messed with. Lawrence Zazzo conveys well the deepening suffering of Arsace, Stephen Wallace shows us the emerging nobility of Armindo, and if Kurt Streit sounds rather like a tenor stepping out of his usual Mozartian realm, then as the pompous Emilio he does need to be a little out of step with the others and his voice and Italian diction are both irresistibly splendid. In general the singing has a warmth to it, and although there are times when the recitatives could make room for more dramatic flexibility and conviction, this is nevertheless a thoroughly recommendable release for Baroque opera fans.

Rinaldo, HWV7

Rinaldo   P
David Daniels counterten Rinaldo **Cecilia Bartoli**
mez Almirena **Gerald Finley** bar Argante **Luba**
Orgonasova sop Armida **Bejun Mehta** counterten
Christian Sorcerer **Mark Padmore** ten Herald **Daniel**
Taylor counterten Eustazio **Bernarda Fink** contr
Goffredo **Catherine Bott** sop Siren I **Ana-Maria**
Rincón sop Donna, Siren II **Academy of Ancient**
Music / Christopher Hogwood
Decca L'Oiseau-Lyre ③ 467 087-2OHO3
(179' · DDD · T/t)   Ⓕ ΟΟΟ☞

In a sense, *Rinaldo* is at once Handel's most familiar and unfamiliar opera: familiar because, as his lavish first stage work for London, it has been much written about both by modern historians and by the composer's contemporaries; unfamiliar because the Handel opera revival of recent years has largely passed it by. Although there are numerous recordings of its two hit slow arias – 'Lascia ch'io pianga' and 'Cara sposa' – this is its first complete studio recording for over 20 years. It may not be Handel's most dramatically effective work (Act 3 marks time rather), and its magic effects and transformation scenes no doubt make it a tricky prospect for opera companies, but in many ways its rich orchestration and impressive set-piece arias make it ideal for recording. That much makes this release a welcome sight already; add the de luxe cast Decca has assembled for the purpose and it begins to look irresistible.

Top of the bill come David Daniels as the eponymous crusader knight and Cecilia Bartoli as his love Almirena. Daniels' heart-stopping countertenor voice is one of the marvels of our age. It isn't big, and though he's technically untroubled by the virtuoso runs of the quicker arias, some may feel it lacks some of the heroic power expected of a warrior; but there's an inner strength to it, and in the love music he's utterly convincing. Bartoli is equally impressive, though her singing is less well suited to Handel. She can deliver the most demanding music with almost frightening ease and force, and, as ever, she throws herself into her role, but one can't help thinking that a more natural and unaffected style would have been more appropriate for arias such as 'Lascia ch'io pianga' and 'Augeletti che cantate'. The rest of the cast is almost unwaveringly strong. Daniel Taylor is slightly less technically secure or forceful than the others (which is hardly a criticism), but he does well enough with the opera's least effective role as Goffredo's brother Eustazio.

Christopher Hogwood's direction is typically neat and well-mannered. He isn't a natural opera conductor – others may have found more magic in the enchanted gardens and more sensuality in the sirens who lure Rinaldo, and you sometimes get the feeling that he's rushing the singers at important moments – but he has an unerring sense of tempo, and the opera as a whole is well paced. The Academy of Ancient Music plays to a high standard, backed up by a startlingly virtuoso performance on the Drottningholm thunder machine and by some genuine birdsong at the beginning of Act 2.

This version may not be the last word on the opera, but for all-round standard of performance and production it currently wins hands down and it will take some beating.

Rodelinda, HWV19

Rodelinda, regina de' Langobardi   P
Simone Kermes sop Rodelinda **Marijana Mijanovic**
contr Bertarido **Steve Davislim** ten Grimoaldo **Sonia**
Prina contr Eduige **Marie-Nicole Lemieux** contr
Unulfo **Vito Priante** bar Garibaldo **Il Complesso**
Barocco / Alan Curtis
Archiv Produktion ③ 477 5391AH3 (3h 12' · DDD · T/t)
                        Ⓕ ΟΟ☞

Alan Curtis has done more than most to prove that many of Handel's 42 operas are first-rate music dramas – his *Admeto*, from 1979 (see page 465), was one of the first complete recordings of a Handel opera to feature period instruments and all voices at correct pitch without transpositions – but it is surprising to note that this is his first recording of an undisputed popular masterpiece.

Rodelinda, first performed in February 1725, is a stunning work dominated by a title-heroine who remains devoted to her supposedly dead husband Bertarido and scorns the advances of his usurper Grimoaldo. The potency of Handel's score was enhanced by the complexity of the villain, whose lust-driven cruelty gradually crumbles into a desire to abdicate in order to find spiritual peace. The scene in which the penitent tyrant's life is saved from assassination by the fugitive Bertarido is among Handel's greatest dramatic moments.

Simone Kermes is full of feisty courage, an assertive woman for whom Bertarido would credibly risk death to be reunited with. She takes no prisoners in some extravagant cadenzas, and sings 'Morrai, si' with thrillingly viscous venom. At the other extreme, 'Ritorna o cara' is simply gorgeous. There are some weaknesses. Marijana Mijanovic's Bertarido often slips under pitch on long notes and uses indiscriminate vibrato instead of singing through phrases. Her deficiencies with tuning and idiomatic expression are highlighted in two duets with Kermes (one not recorded before), particularly when Handel demands that they sing sustained notes in unison. There is a good case for using a fruity female contralto in castrato roles instead of an angelic countertenor but why Archiv seems keen to record Mijanovic's inadequate performances of Handel roles for his star castrato, Senesino is incomprehensible. A cursory comparison of Mijanovic's bizarrely unattractive 'Dove sei' with any of the impressive contributions from fellow contraltos Marie-Nicole Lemieux or Sonia Prina indicates that either would have better suited the role.

Otherwise, this has an abundance of good things. Il Complesso Barocco have sounded undernourished on some previous recordings but here play with admirable vitality and dramatic subtlety. Curtis has obviously worked hard to encourage his string players to understand what the singers are communicating: each aria is impeccably interpreted and intelligently paced. On the whole, Curtis's passion and experience ensure another typically persuasive and theatrical vindication of Handel's genius.

Rodrigo, HWV5

Rodrigo   P
Gloria Banditelli *mez* Rodrigo **Sandrine Piau** *sop*
Esilena **Elena Cecchi Fedi** *sop* Florinda **Rufus Müller**
ten Giuliano **Roberta Invernizzi** *sop* Evanco
Caterina Calvi *mez* Fernando **Il Complesso Barocco**
/ Alan Curtis *hpd*
Virgin Classics Veritas ② 545897-2 (155' · DDD · T/t)
  F

The music of Handel's Italian years has a unique freshness, a boldness of invention, a novelty in textures and lines – characteristics which distinguish his first Italian opera, *Rodrigo*, written in 1707 for the Medici court at Florence. This recording restores all that survives of the lyrical music, with one item composed in a more-or-less Handelian manner by Curtis and other Handel music imported to fit the original text. Curiously, the dances aren't included here, and – presumably in the interest of keeping the set to two CDs – there are many large cuts in the recitative. As a result some quite important sections are omitted and the often very close succession of lyrical numbers gives a slightly misleading impression of the opera. Even so the recording of this fine, often very moving and mostly inspiriting piece is warmly welcome.

Like most Italian operas of its time, it's essentially a succession of arias, mostly shorter ones than those of Handel's mature operas. As so often with Handel, much of the finest music comes in Act 2, with a pair of arias for Esilena (the second a furious outburst), and at the beginning of the next act, with Rodrigo and Esilena apparently facing death, Handel finds that marvellous vein of pathos familiar in his later operas. Alan Curtis, a man of the theatre, keeps the score moving along at a good pace. He conducts, as it were, from a 17th-century standpoint, with a flexibility over accent and metre that allows the music to move unusually freely. Yet he's rather predictable in his use of cadential *rallentandos*, and there are points where the orchestral discipline is a shade loose.

Sandrine Piau sings Esilena's part beautifully, with much attention to detail, to timing and

to phrasing, as well as with fluency and with a richness of tone unusual for her. Gloria Banditelli makes a sturdy Rodrigo, direct and accurate, and very controlled in the fast semiquaver passages. Elena Cecchi Fedi perhaps overdoes the characterisation of Florinda as a shrew, singing shrilly at times and with rather more shouting and pouting than is consistent with musical enjoyment. But the singing is powerful and brilliant in its way. There's competent and spirited playing from Il Complesso Barocco, and excellent notes from Anthony Hicks and Curtis.

Tamerlano, HWV18

Tamerlano   P
Nicholas Spanos *counterten* Tamerlano **Mary-Ellen**
Nesi *mez* Andronico **Tassis Christoyannis** *bar*
Bajazet **Mata Katsuli** *sop* Asteria **Irini Karaianni** *mez*
Irene **Petros Magoulas** *bass* Leone
Orchestra of Patras / George Petrou
Dabringhaus und Grimm ③ MDG609 1457-2
(3h 12' · DDD · T/t/N)   M

Tamerlano has done quite well on disc but this is the first recording to adopt the version that Handel decided on for the premiere. The story is grim. Tamerlano – Marlowe's Tamburlaine, now generally called Timur – has captured the Ottoman sultan, Bajazet, whose daughter Asteria he proposes to marry. In the end he marries Irene, to whom he was betrothed, and restores Asteria to her lover Andronico, but only after Bajazet has killed himself.

The audience's sympathies lie with the proud father. The part of Bajazet is usually taken by a tenor; but it lies very low, and it is here sensibly given to a baritone. Whereas Marlowe's Bajazeth spectacularly brains himself onstage, in this version the sultan takes poison and is carried off to die. The music moves from defiance to tenderness and back in recitative and arioso, which Tassis Christoyannis handles with consummate skill. He also expresses the character's dignity and resolve in his Act 1 arias with firm, focused tone.

Mata Katsuli is equally impressive as his daughter. Asteria is a strong character who accepts Tamerlano as her husband in order to murder him in bed, but she is desolate when she thinks Andronico has betrayed her. Katsuli sings with a most affecting passion, combined with tenderness.

Mary-Ellen Nesi makes a strong Andronico, the part written for Senesino. She is rich-toned, as at home in powerful accompanied recitative as in the semiquaver runs of 'Più d'una tigre'. Irini Karaianni is attractively smoky in her siciliano; lovely clarinets but here, as elsewhere, the continuo is inaudible in places. Nicholas Spanos as Tamerlano, 'Scythian Shepherde' though he be, is properly imperial, and he dispatches the coloratura of his last aria with an appropriately wild brilliance. Petros Magoulas has the right bluffness for Leone.

Apart from the problem of balance, there is nothing but praise for George Petrou and his period-instrument orchestra. Just to hear the swelling on a sustained bass note (in the Overture and in Tamerlano's second aria) is to be reassured that all will be well. All is indeed well, and this recording is a most rewarding surprise.

Tamerlano   **P**

Monica Bacelli *mez* Tamerlano **Thomas Randle** *ten*
Bajazet **Elizabeth Norberg-Schulz** *sop* Asteria
Graham Pushee *counterten* Andronicus **Anna
Bonitatibus** *sop* Irene **Antonio Abete** *bass* Leone
The English Concert / Trevor Pinnock
Stage director **Jonathan Miller**
Video director **Helga Dubnyicsek**
ArtHaus Musik *DVD* 100 702 (323' · 16:9 · 2.0 &
5.1 · 0 · N) Includes documentaries and interviews   Ⓕ

This is an uncommonly interesting examination of how a great Handel opera may be performed without insisting that only Baroque specialists need apply. Some of the singers here aren't obvious Handelians: Elizabeth Norberg-Schulz has something of the attack and occasionally the cutting edge of a lyric-dramatic soprano, while Thomas Randle quite often puts his voice under pressure in response to the extreme demands of Handel's first and most intensely dramatic major tenor role. And yet one hardly ever wishes for more 'authentic' voices. Both singers are very musical, well aware of the requirements of Handel's style; both, especially Randle, are highly accomplished actors – it's a minor but significant point that when either of them was on screen I neither watched nor needed the subtitles. Both, not wholly irrelevantly, are strikingly handsome.

That they can be so effective is largely due to Jonathan Miller's very plain but highly intelligent production, to Trevor Pinnock's alert and sympathetic direction and to the wonderfully intimate theatre at Bad Lauchstadt where the opera was filmed as part of the 50th Halle Handel Festival in 2001. The set is basic – a few mottled gold panels – the costumes are sumptuous, but in a theatre this size everyone in the audience can see facial expressions and the slightest gestures, and Miller has concentrated his direction on this. The result, at such a moment as when Bajazet and his daughter Asteria resolve on suicide rather than further humiliation by Tamerlano is intensely moving, as is the exquisite duet in which Asteria and her lover Andronico vow that their love will even survive her death.

Handelian voices or no, it is in short an utterly Handelian performance. The orchestra is splendid and Pinnock's pacing of the drama ideal.

Teseo, HWV9

Teseo   **P**
Eirian James *mez* Teseo **Julia Gooding** *sop* Agilea
Della Jones *mez* Medea **Derek Lee Ragin**

counterten Egeo **Catherine Napoli** *sop* Clizia
Jeffrey Gall *counterten* Arcane **François Bazola** *bar*
Sacerdote di Minerva **Les Musiciens du Louvre /
Marc Minkowski**
Erato ② 2292-45806-2 (148' · DDD · T/t)   Ⓜ

Teseo was Handel's third opera for London, given at the beginning of 1713. Exceptionally, its libretto was based on a French original, written by Quinault for Lully; it's a spectacular piece, in five acts, with Medea (after the events of *Médée*) and Theseus (before the events of *Hippolyte* or the Ariadne operas) as its central characters. It's Medea who, as slighted lover and jealous sorceress, provides the principal musical thrills; but the score is, in any case, an unusually rich and inventive one, with much colourful orchestral writing even before she turns up at the beginning of Act 2. When she does, she introduces herself with a *Largo* aria, 'Dolce riposo', of a kind unique to Handel in its depth of poetic feeling, with a vocal line full of bold leaps above throbbing strings and an oboe obbligato; but, lest we should think her docile, Medea hints at her true colours in the ensuing C minor aria, and by the end of the act she's singing furious recitative and fiery, incisive lines – real sorceress music. Her biggest scene comes at the start of the final act, a *Presto* vengeance aria, packed with raging rapid semiquavers. Handel scored the opera for a more varied orchestra than usual; there are recorders, flutes, oboes, bassoons and trumpets called for. The arias themselves tend to be rather shorter than usual for Handel. The work needs first-rate singing, and by and large receives it here. The role of Medea falls to Della Jones, a singer with a superb technique and a remarkable ability to identify with the role; she truly lives Medea's part and brings to it great resources of spirit and technique. Except when allowed to play too fast, too loudly or too coarsely, the Musiciens du Louvre are impressive. Several numbers are accompanied with only a continuo instrument, to good effect. The recitative always moves well, and appoggiaturas are duly observed.

Tolomeo re di Egitto, HWV25

Tolomeo re di Egitto
Ann Hallenberg *sop* Tolomeo **Karina Gauvin** *sop*
Seleuce **Pietro Spagnoli** *bar* Araspe **Anna
Bonitatibus** *mez* Elisa **Romina Basso** *mez* Alessandro
Il Complesso Barocco / Alan Curtis *hpd*
Archiv Produktion ③ 477 7106AH3
(148' · DDD · S/T/t/N)   ⒻⓄⓄ⇥

Tolomeo was the last opera Handel wrote for the Royal Academy of Music before the opera company dissolved in 1728. It is a fine work that combines pastoral charm with some powerfully melodramatic scenes. The best known aria is 'Non lo dirò col labbro' (famous in Somervell's arrangement 'Silent Worship'), here sung sweetly by Romina Basso.

There is not a weak link in this superb cast, with all the singers perfect for the vocal and dramatic properties of their roles. Ann Hallenberg's supple coloratura is perfectly aligned with dramatic awareness and melodic sensibility in numerous accompanied recitatives and arias: the sleep scene in Act 1 is beautifully judged and the hedonistic accompagnato that precedes 'Stile amare' is gripping. Anna Bonitatibus's singing is magnificent, and her ornamentation and cadenza are fabulous. Pietro Spagnoli sings the tyrant Araspe firmly but one also feels a degree of sympathy for his hopeless infatuation with Tolomeo's wife Seleuce. Karina Gauvin's singing is dramatic and colourful: her interplay with two recorders in 'Fonti amiche' is simple yet ravishing and the hushed 'Dite, che fa' (with muted strings and offstage echoes from *Tolomeo*) is utterly gorgeous.

Alan Curtis's recent Handel opera recordings have been admirable in patches but flawed by inconsistent casts and occasionally weedy instrumental playing. It is a delight to hear the Italian-based American harpsichordist and Il Complesso Barocco back on top-notch form in this delectable performance. The overture oozes with charisma and the orchestral playing is beautifully paced and articulated. Each ritornello shows finesse and a deep-rooted fondness for the subtleties in Handel's writing. Recitatives are never sluggish but Curtis does not force proceedings unnaturally, allowing the language and rhetoric enough space to work their magic. He has all the energy and dynamism necessary but also realises that courtliness and elegance are vital elements of Handel's music. All in all, this is a perfect Handel opera recording.

Howard Hanson   American 1896-1981

Hanson studied with Goetschius in New York and became director of the Eastman School (1924-64), where he was an influential teacher and founded the Institute of American music; he also promoted modern American music through his work as a conductor. His own music shows the influence of Sibelius, Grieg and Respighi (his teacher in Rome in the early 1920s). Among his works are seven symphonies, symphonic poems, choral pieces, chamber and piano music and songs. **GROVE**music

Symphonies

Symphony No 1 in E minor, 'Nordic', Op 21. Merry Mount Suite. Pan and the Priest, Op 26. Rhythmic Variations on Two Ancient Hymns
Nashville Symphony Orchestra / Kenneth Schermerhorn
Naxos 8 559072 (61' · DDD)   ⑤▷

The *Nordic* Symphony was completed when Hanson was in Rome studying with Respighi – stylistically it brings Sibelius south to Italy. The Nashville performance can be compared with the

Seattle orchestra under that fine Hanson interpreter, Gerard Schwarz. Schermerhorn is more spacious, taking a good two minutes longer overall – no bad thing in such hyperactive music, as it constantly strives towards the next climax. Schwarz is faster in the final *Allegro* but both performances are exciting and well recorded: the issue is settled by coupling and price.

There are many attractive features in the *Merry Mount Suite* – Charleston syncopation in the 'Children's Dance' and characteristic Hanson harmony oscillating between two chords at the start of the ecstatic 'Love Duet'. All supremely operatic, but the stage work still remains in limbo. The least-known piece here is the *Rhythmic Variations*, considered lost until recently, and cited as such in the *New American Grove*. This seems distinctly careless of someone, since Hanson recorded this late work himself in 1977. It's serenely spacious, utterly diatonic but no great rediscovery. *Pan and the Priest*, a vivid symphonic poem reaching pagan intensity, completes a bargain Hanson package that's well recorded, too.

Symphonies – Nos 2, 4 & 6; No 7, 'A Sea Symphony'. Fantasy Variations on a Theme of Youth. Elegy in memory of Serge Koussevitzky. Serenade, Op 36. Mosaics
Carol Rosenberger pf **New York Chamber Symphony Orchestra; Seattle Symphony Chorale and Orchestra / Gerard Schwarz**
Delos ② DE3705 (136' · DDD)   Ⓜ❶

Gerard Schwarz's red-blooded 1988 account of the Second Symphony (*Romantic*) remains a match for any rival. Schwarz and his excellent Seattle band do full justice to its dark opulence, concision and organic power. Similarly, there's no missing the communicative ardour and clean-limbed security of Schwarz's lucid reading of the Sixth. Commissioned in 1967 by the New York Philharmonic for their 185th anniversary season, it boasts a formidable thematic economy and intriguing formal scheme of which Hanson himself was justifiably proud. Its successor, *A Sea Symphony* from 1977, sets texts from Walt Whitman's *Leaves of Grass*. In the unashamedly jubilant finale Hanson fleetingly quotes from his *Romantic* Symphony of more than four decades earlier: it's a spine-tingling moment in a score of consummate assurance and stirring aspiration. Schwarz's traversal finds the Seattle Symphony Chorale on rousing form.

We also get exemplary renderings of the pretty 1945 Serenade for flute, harp and strings (a gift for Hanson's wife-to-be, Margaret Elizabeth Nelson) and characteristically inventive *Fantasy Variations on a Theme of Youth* from 1951 (with Carol Rosenberger a deft soloist), both these featuring Schwarz directing the New York Chamber Symphony. The present warm-hearted accounts of both the *Elegy in memory of Serge Koussevitzky* and *Mosaics* (which is a highly appealing set of variations written in 1957 for

Szell and the Cleveland Orchestra) need not fear comparison with the composer's own Mercury recordings. The engineering is wonderfully ripe.

Symphony No 2, 'Romantic'. Merry Mount – Suite.
Bold Island Suite. Fanfare for the Signal Corps
Cincinnati Pops Orchestra / Erich Kunzel
Telarc CD80649 (66' · DDD)   ⒻD→

Hanson was a skilled conductor and his recordings for Mercury are indispensable documents, though one's listening pleasure is hampered somewhat by the Eastman-Rochester Orchestra's lack of tonal weight and refinement. Hanson's lush, neo-romantic style demands richer, sweeter sounds. Luckily, that's just what the Cincinnati Pops Orchestra offer.

Interpretatively speaking, it seems that Kunzel has made a close study of Hanson's performances, for his approach is similarly incisive. Indeed, Kunzel's *Romantic* Symphony may be tauter and more propulsive than Hanson's own. Even the lyrical pages unfold with a sense of resolve and the conductor's refusal to draw out the rhetorical, brassy outbursts of the Symphony's outer movements mitigates the music's occasional tendency towards pomposity.

Another reason to favour the Telarc disc is that it includes the premiere recording of the *Bold Island* Suite (1961), an atmospheric, tuneful and typically clear-headed tone-poem. Warmly recommended to devotees of orchestral Americana.

Additional recommendation

Symphony No 2
Coupled with: **Barber** Violin Concerto
St Louis SO / Slatkin
EMI 747850-2 (68 · DDD)   ⓂD→
    A beautifully shaped performance, played with
    restrained passion, and coupled with an elegant
    reading of the Barber (with Elmar Oliveira).

Solo Piano Works

Sonata in A minor, Op 11. Two Yuletide Pieces, Op 19. Poèmes érotiques, Op 9. Three Miniatures, Op 12. Three Etudes, Op 18. Enchantment. For the First Time. Slumber Song
Thomas Labé pf
Naxos 8 559047 (76' · DDD)   ⓈD→

Much of this CD is an orgy of romantic piano music. Admirers of Hanson's *Romantic* Symphony or his one-time smash-hit opera *Merry Mount* (available on Naxos) will surely devour this collection, which includes unknown and unpublished music. A first impression is that the earliest works here, written around 1920, have the sort of ecstatic luxuriance that might be expected of a pupil of Respighi. But this influence came later since Hanson didn't start his three-year residence

in Rome until 1921. His background was Swedish and there's a Nordic, Sibelian intensity about his whole approach, although the fulsome piano style clearly stems from Liszt.

The earliest piece is probably the *Slumber Song*, a pure salon morsel, and the latest is the suite *For the First Time*. The three *Poèmes érotiques* (the fourth has disappeared) are what Hanson called his 'first studied attempt at psychological writing'. They are powerful in a surging melodic style where in several pieces the climaxes stem from an almost Tchaikovskian cathartic need to unburden tensions.

The striking three-movement Sonata (1918) has had to be completed from the composer's shorthand by Thomas Labé since it was never published, although Hanson performed it in 1919. The vivid improvisatory keyboard writing, at times extravagantly rhetorical, causes Labé to hit the piano rather hard in the last two movements. One can understand his enthusiasm, but there are times when a little more *cantabile* might have helped. However, nothing must detract from the real service that this CD does in bringing this music to public attention for the first time.

Karl Amadeus Hartmann
German 1905-1963

Hartmann studied with Haas at the Munich Academy (1924-7), with Scherchen and with Webern (1941-2). After the war he started the Musica Viva festival in Munich to present music that had been banned during the Nazi years, and most of his published works date from after this period. They include most importantly a cycle of eight symphonies (1936, 1946, 1947, 1949, 1950, 1953, 1958, 1962), which have a Brucknerian breadth while suggesting the influences of Reger, Berg, Stravinsky, Bartók and Blacher. He also wrote several concertos and vocal music including a chamber opera Simplicius Simplicissimus (1949), a strongly expressive work combining popular song, chorale and psalm-like recitation with symphonic method. GROVEmusic

Concerto funebre

Concerto funebreᵃ. Two Solo Violin Suites.
Two Solo Violin Sonatas
Alina Ibragimova vn ᵃ**Britten Sinfonia**
Hyperion CDA67547 (81' · DDD)   Ⓕ❍❍

It is such an obvious idea to combine Hartmann's *Concerto funebre* (1939, rev 1959) with the four unaccompanied works from 1927 that it's surprising that no company has thought of it before now. The Suites and Sonatas are not well known, not even being performed until the mid-1980s. Hartmann composed them while still a student with his mature style some years away, yet their muscularity, contrapuntal and harmonic élan and the sense of self-belief they exude show them to be products of a formidable, free-thinking creator. Ibragimova proves an ideal exponent, her tempi free and elastic (and mostly quite quick). Her fluency and flexibility pay great dividends time and again, as in the First Suite's central Rondo or concluding Ciaconna or the Second Suite's second span, *Fliessend*. Hyperion's sound-picture is natural.

Ibragimova's fiercely clear-eyed account of the *Concerto funebre*– alive to the music's expressive demands as well as its dynamic markings – faces stiff competition but need not fear comparison with any of the dozen or so rival accounts. Her technique is formidable to say the least and if marginal preferance is for Isabelle Faust (Harmonia Mundi), Ibragimova is on her shoulder, although Hyperion's couplings and recording quality, to say nothing of the excellent Britten Sinfonia, deserve a share in the plaudits. Recommended.

Orchestral works

Symphony No 4. Concerto funèbre[a]. Chamber Concerto[b]
[a]**Isabelle Faust** *vn* [b]**Paul Meyer** *cl* [b]**Petersen Quartet**
(Conrad Muck, Gernot Sussmuth *vns* Friedemann Weigle *va* Hans-Jakob Eschenburg *vc*) **Munich Chamber Orchestra / Christoph Poppen**
ECM New Series 465 779-2 (78' · DDD)   Ⓕ

When Hartmann opted for internal exile during the Nazi era, he took with him some key influences from the free musical world. Beam up around 0'33" into the third movement of the 1939 *Concerto funèbre* and you have a virtual quote from the first movement of Bartók's 1934 Fifth String Quartet. Hartmann completed his Chamber Concerto for Clarinet, String Quartet and String Orchestra in 1935, seven years after Bartók wrote his Fourth Quartet – which in turn barges headlong into Hartmann's second movement (an unmistakable reference to the Quartet's finale).

In the Chamber Concerto the melodic and structural profile of the first movement follows the profile of Kodály's 1933 *Dances of Galánta*. The language of the work is Magyar-inspired (even aside from the *Galánta* references) and the scoring lively and luminous.

The *Concerto funèbre* opens with a quotation (fully acknowledged this time) of the Hussite chorale 'Ye Who are God's Warriors', best known to Brits for its use in Smetana's *Má vlast*. The reference commemorates the Nazi betrayal of Czechoslovakia, though Hartmann's anger finds controlled expression in the *Allegro di molto* third movement.

The Fourth Symphony is scored for strings, and frames a lively *Allegro di molto* with two profound *Adagios* that, again, draw you in by virtue of their intense arguments. All three performances do Hartmann proud. Isabelle Faust's eloquent playing of the *Concerto funèbre* draws maximum effect from extremes in mood and temperature and outplays her rivals. With fine sound and programming, this is the ideal Hartmann primer.

Hamilton Harty   Irish 1879-1941

Best known today for his 'big-band' versions of Handel's music, Hamilton Harty was a prolific composer as well as a conductor of renown (he was conductor of the Hallé Orchestra from 1920). His large output, written in a lush, late-Romantic style, embraces symphonies, tone-poems (including his most popular work, With the wild geese), a violin concerto (first performed by Szigeti), a piano concerto, songs and a cantata. Much of his music is available for download from www.chandos.net

Orchestral works

Piano Concerto[a]. A Comedy Overture. Fantasy Scenes (from an Eastern Romance)
[a]**Peter Donohoe** *pf*
Ulster Orchestra / Takuo Yuasa
Naxos 8 557731 (55' · DDD)   Ⓢ➤

Harty wrote his Piano Concerto in 1922 and gave the first performance the following year with Beecham at the helm of the Hallé Orchestra. Unashamedly indebted to Tchaikovsky and Rachmaninov (the finale even boasts a near-crib from the latter's Second Concerto), it's a thoroughly endearing, red-blooded affair, but not without its occasional longueurs.

Or at least that's how it seemed up until now. Peter Donohoe and Takuo Yuasa drive a truly propulsive (and, it must be said, purposeful) course through both outer movements. The piano sometimes sounds a little tired but Donohoe's bravura is frequently jaw-dropping and there's no lack of enthusiasm or sensitivity about the orchestral support. A refreshing and instructive display.

The Concerto is preceded by a similarly mobile, mostly spick-and-span account of Harty's delightful *A Comedy Overture* of 1906 and what is the first commercial recording of the *Fantasy Scenes (from an Eastern Romance)*. These appeared in 1919 and comprise four fetching vignettes which nod appreciatively towards the likes of Rimsky-Korsakov, Borodin and Balakirev; Yuasa and company do them proud. Nor can there be any major grumbles about the recording, which is commendably truthful. Altogether a most enjoyable release and well worth its modest asking price.

Jonathan Harvey   British b1939

Harvey studied at Cambridge, privately with Erwin Stein and Hans Keller, and with Babbitt at Princeton (1969-70). He has taught at the universities of Southampton (1964-77) and Sussex. His early music shows enthusiasms ranging from Britten and Messiaen to Stockhausen and Davies, but since the early 1970s he has developed a more integrated style and has emerged as an outstanding composer of elec-

tronic music (*Mortuos plango, vivos voco, 1980*). Later pieces include *Madonna of Winter and Spring* (1986). **GROVE**music

Death of Light / Light of Death

Death of Light/Light of Death. Advaya. Ricercare una melodia (performed on oboe). Ricercare una melodia (performed on trumpet). Tombeau de Messiaen. Wheel of Emptiness
Ictus / Georges-Elie Octors
Cyprès CYP5604 (77' · DDD)   Ⓕ

Three of the compositions on this disc offer ideal introductions to Jonathan Harvey's work, showing how music centering on a single line, or instrument, can evolve into a potently imaginative discourse when that line or instrument is manipulated electronically. In *Ricerare una melodia* the moment of revelation comes when the electronic material opens out a much wider registral spectrum than that 'naturally' available on the trumpet or oboe. Something similar happens both in the brief *Tombeau de Messiaen*, where the interaction of piano and electronics unleashes a torrential, joyously uninhibited commemoration of the French master, and also in *Advaya*. All three of these works have been recorded before, but Harvey enthusiasts should still find it difficult to resist this new release, not only for its outstanding recording quality, but for the interest and substance of the programme as a whole. The disc ends with the most striking evidence of Harvey's versatility. *Death of Light/Light of Death* is scored for five performers, without electronics, but with the harpist doubling on tam-tam. It offers music of an intensity and, in the end, ceremonial solemnity which few composers today can match. With performances of supreme technical assurance and magnificently lucid sound, this is an outstanding disc in every respect.

Madonna of Winter and Spring

Madonna of Winter and Spring[a]. Percussion Concerto[b]. Song Offerings[c]
[c]**Penelope Walmsley-Clark** sop [b]**Peter Prommel** perc [ab]**Netherlands Radio Philharmonic Orchestra / Peter Eötvös;** [c]**London Sinfonietta / George Benjamin**
Nimbus NI5649 (78' · DDD · T/t)   Ⓕ ⊙⊙

This is an impressive disc indeed: a strong cast, a varied programme, and music of great integrity and beauty. In relation to many British scores that have garnered recent critical praise, Harvey more than holds his own. The three pieces – two of them recorded here for the first time – date from the 1980s and 90s. Each introduces a 'foreign' element to the orchestra in a slightly different way. There are elements of the competitive streak between soloist and orchestra in the Percussion Concerto; in *Song Offerings* relations between the two elements are more symbiotic, as one might expect; but in *Madonna of Winter*

and Spring, the most extended piece here, the 'foreign' element is assumed by synthesisers and electronics. This piece, in particular, sums up Harvey's preoccupations: the interaction of the different media, and the programmatic elements derived from the composer's faith.

At intervals the orchestra recedes, creating electro-acoustic 'windows' reminiscent of similarly mixed-media scores (Birtwistle and Boulez come to mind); at others, individual instruments appear in a quasi-soloistic context, adding an extra dimension to the texture. Moreover, the quality of these interpretations gives this recording a special appeal. The electro-acoustic element is well captured, and conveys something of the spatial imaging mentioned in the composer's insert-notes.

All three pieces receive committed, dynamic interpretations: if only contemporary music could always enjoy such advocacy.

Body Mandala / Timepieces

Tranquil Abiding[b]. Body Mandala[b]. Timepieces[bc]. White as Jasmine[ab]. ...towards a Pure Land[b]
[a]**Anu Komsi** sop **BBC Scottish Symphony Orchestra / [b]Ilan Volkov, [c]Stefan Solymon**
NMC NMCD141 (80' · DDD)   Ⓕ ⊙⊙⊙⊡

There is so much to praise about the works on this CD that it's hard to know where to begin. Jonathan Harvey's music juxtaposes moments of disarming simplicity, of naivety almost, with others of considerable sophistication and intricacy. Often these are held in fine balance, the former giving the listener an accessible entry-point or anchor, and allowing the latter considerable scope for development within an audibly logical discourse. The opening premise of both *Tranquil Abiding* and *Body Mandala* are cases in point: in the first, an alternation of two sonorities carries the piece forwards inexorably to its conclusion. By contrast, the arc structure of ... *towards a Pure Land* engenders considerable discontinuity. Each piece inhabits its own space. The virtuosity of Harvey's orchestration is breathtaking at times (try the conclusion of the second of the three *Timepieces*, for example), but it is virtuosity in the service of deeply intelligent musical argument; there's nothing merely flashy or self-serving.

Not surprisingly to those familiar with Harvey's concerns, all but one of these pieces explore different facets of spirituality, particularly those drawn from Eastern religions. Perhaps the most immediately involving is *White as Jasmine*, based on texts by a 12th-century Hindu saint. Here, soprano Anu Komsi delivers a superbly controlled performance of great vocal beauty. In her first entry, she is virtually indistinguishable from the surrounding instruments (and it's satisfying, by the way, to hear singing in which each pitch can be clearly discerned, vibrato notwithstanding). But the musicianship here transcends questions of technique: all the participants deserve equal credit for their involvement in a richly rewarding project. A worthy winner of a *Gramophone* Award for Contemporary music.

Passion and Resurrection

Passion and Resurrection
Carolyn Foulkes, Alison Smart sops **Kim Porter** contr **Andrew Mackenzie-Wicks** ten **Stuart Macintyre** bar **BBC Singers; Sinfonia 21 / Martin Neary**
Sargasso ② SCD28052 (85' · DDD · T)
Recorded live 1999   Ⓕ

Were the audience warned that they'd be called on to lend their voices to this performance, recorded by the BBC in 1999? This score is as much a 'liturgical action' as an oratorio (or 'church opera', as it's described in the booklet). It was written for a community celebration at Winchester Cathedral, and most of the text is a translation of extant Passion Plays.

Harvey's ability to combine chant-like idioms (and actual plainchant hymnody) within a predominantly atonal context is quite uncanny. The work opens with a familiar passage from the Book of Common Prayer which gradually morphs into more angular cadences, but there's nothing wilful in the transformation.

The libretto faithfully follows Christ's Passion and Resurrection. In the Passion men's voices and low brass predominate, and the writing is harsher, more angular, the treatment of pacing more earth-bound. The Resurrection sequence points out the greater involvement of women (through their voices); the register is consistently higher, the sense of time more suspended. There's little abstraction in the score – in fact, Harvey allows himself a surprising degree of literal-mindedness: you can even hear the nails being driven in at the Crucifixion.

The action is set in a most direct way, yet never 'talks down' to the congregation or the listener, and the performance is dramatic and well shaped. The BBC Singers and Sinfonia 21 have plenty of body; the strings have much to do; and the brass interventions are most striking. The postlude is quite literally 'recessional', as very low instruments gradually disperse throughout the church of St John's, Smith Square: this spatial element stands in for many of Harvey's preoccupations, and the effect is nicely rendered by the engineers.

Joseph Haydn   Austrian 1732-1809

Haydn, the son of a wheelwright, was trained as a choirboy and taken into the choir at St Stephen's Cathedral, Vienna, where he sang from c1740 to c1750. He then worked as a freelance musician, playing the violin and keyboard instruments, accompanying for singing lessons given by the composer Porpora, who helped and encouraged him. At this time he wrote some sacred works, music for theatre comedies and chamber music. In c1759 he was appointed music director to Count Morzin; but he soon moved, into service as Vice-Kapellmeister with one of the leading Hungarian families, the Esterházys, becoming full Kapellmeister on Werner's death in 1766. He was director of an ensemble of generally some 15-20 musicians, with responsibility for the music and the instruments, and was required to compose as his employer – from 1762, Prince Nikolaus Esterházy – might command. At first he lived at Eisenstadt, c30 miles south-east of Vienna by 1767 the family's chief residence, and Haydn's chief place of work, was at the new palace at Eszterháza. In his early years Haydn chiefly wrote instrumental music, including symphonies and other pieces for the twice-weekly concerts and the prince's Tafelmusik, and works for the instrument played by the prince, the baryton (a kind of viol), for which he composed c125 trios in 10 years. There were also cantatas and a little church music. After Werner's death church music became more central, and so, after the opening of a new opera house at Eszterháza in 1768, did opera. Some of the symphonies from c1770 show Haydn expanding his musical horizons from occasional, entertainment music towards larger and more original pieces, for example Nos 26, 39, 49, 44 and 52 (many of them in minor keys, and serious in mood, in line with trends in the contemporary symphony in Germany and Austria). Also from 1768-72 come three sets of string quartets, probably not written for the Esterházy establishment but for another patron or perhaps for publication (Haydn was allowed to write other than for the Esterházys only with permission); Op 20 clearly shows the beginnings of a more adventurous and integrated quartet style.

Among the operas from this period are Lo speziale (for the opening of the new house), L'infedeltà delusa (1773) and Il mondo della luna (1777). Operatic activity became increasingly central from the mid-1770s as regular performances came to be given at the new house. It was part of Haydn's job to prepare the music, adapting or arranging it for the voices of the resident singers. In 1779 the opera house burnt down; Haydn composed La fedeltà premiata for its reopening in 1781. Until then his operas had largely been in a comic genre; his last two for Eszterháza, Orlando paladino (1782) and Armida (1783), are in mixed or serious genres. Although his operas never attained wider exposure, Haydn's reputation had now grown and was international. Much of his music had been published in all the main European centres; under a revised contract with the Esterháza his employers no longer had exclusive rights to his music.

His works of the 1780s that carried his name further afield include piano sonatas, piano trios, symphonies (Nos 76-81 were published in 1784-5, and Nos 82-7 were written on commission for a concert organisation in Paris in 1785-6) and string quartets. His influential Op 33 quartets, issued in 1782, were said to be 'in a quite new, special manner': this is sometimes thought to refer to the use of instruments or the style of thematic development, but could refer to the introduction of scherzos or might simply be an advertising device. More quartets appeared at the end of the decade, Op 50 (dedicated to

Haydn

the King of Prussia and often said to be influenced by the quartets Mozart had dedicated to Haydn) and two sets (Opp 54-5 and 64) written for a former Esterházy violinist who became a Viennese businessman. All these show an increasing enterprise, originality and freedom of style as well as melodic fluency, command of form, and humour. Other works that carried Haydn's reputation beyond central Europe include concertos and notturnos for a type of hurdy-gurdy, written on commission for the King of Naples, and The Seven Last Words, commissioned for Holy Week from Cadíz Cathedral and existing not only in its original orchestral form but also for string quartet, for piano and (later) for chorus and orchestra.

In 1790, Nikolaus Esterházy died; Haydn (unlike most of his musicians) was retained by his son but was free to live in Vienna (which he had many times visited) and to travel. He was invited by the impresario and violinist JP Salomon to go to London to write an opera, symphonies and other works. In the event he went to London twice, in 1791-2 and 1794-5. He composed his last 12 symphonies for performance there, where they enjoyed great success; he also wrote a symphonie concertante, choral pieces, piano trios, piano sonatas and songs (some to English words) as well as arranging British folksongs for publishers in London and Edinburgh. But because of intrigues his opera, L'anima del filosofo, on the Orpheus story, remained unperformed. He was honoured (with an Oxford DMus) and fêted generously, and played, sang and conducted before the royal family. He also heard performances of Handel's music by large choirs in Westminster Abbey.

Back in Vienna, he resumed work for Nikolaus Esterházy's grandson (whose father had now died); his main duty was to produce masses for the princess's nameday. He wrote six works, firmly in the Austrian mass tradition but strengthened and invigorated by his command of symphonic technique. Other works of these late years include further string quartets (Opp 71 and 74 between the London visits, op. 76 and the Op 77 pair after them), showing great diversity of style and seriousness of content yet retaining his vitality and fluency of utterance; some have a more public manner, acknowledging the new use of string quartets at concerts as well as in the home. The most important work, however, is his oratorio The Creation in which his essentially simple-hearted joy in Man, Beast and Nature, and his gratitude to God for his creation of these things to our benefit, are made a part of universal experience by his treatment of them in an oratorio modelled on Handel's, with massive choral writing of a kind he had not essayed before. He followed this with The Seasons, in a similar vein but more a series of attractive episodes than a whole.

Haydn died in 1809, after twice dictating his recollections and preparing a catalogue of his works. He was widely revered, even though by then his music was old-fashioned compared with Beethoven's. He was immensely prolific: some of his music remains unpublished and little known. His operas have never succeeded in holding the stage. But he is regarded, with some justice, as father of the symphony and the string quartet: he saw both genres from their beginnings to a high level of sophistication and artistic expression, even if he did not originate them. He brought to them new intellectual weight, and his closely argued style of development laid the foundations for the larger structures of Beethoven and later composers. **GROVE**music

Cello Concertos

No 1 in C, HobVIIb/1; No 2 in D, HobVIIb/2

Cello Concertos Nos 1 & 2
**Academy of St Martin in the Fields /
Mstislav Rostropovich** vc
EMI 5672342 (49' · ADD) Recorded 1975　　Ⓕ**ⓄⓄ**

This deserves a place on any collector's shelf. With Rostropovich directing from the bow the ASMF sounds a little less sturdy than usual, a little more lithe in the First Concerto. The scale of its first movement is little short of perfection: everything a *Moderato* should be, with Rostropovich humming along non-chalantly in its second theme. He's leisurely in the *Adagio*, playing it as an extended meditation which exists almost outside time. Without ever losing the life of the melodic line, Rostropovich progresses as slowly as it's humanly possible to do without total stasis; and, to wonderfully joyful effect, breaks all records for speed in the finale. Every note, every sequential phrase is there in its place, secured by glintingly true intonation and needle-sharp dramatic timing. The almost complete absence of physical stick and finger sound which Rostropovich and his engineers manage between them makes the latter two movements of the Second Concerto a most pleasing experience. Rostropovich takes deep, long breaths: the surface of his slow movement is glassy, every fragment of bowing and phrasing given the microscopic hair-pin treatment. For his deep, instinctive understanding of scale, and for Britten's cadenzas, many collectors' preferences in these concertos will remain with Rostropovich.

Cello Concertos – Nos 1 & 2; No 4 in D, HobVIIb/4
(formerly attributed to Haydn)
Gautier Capuçon vc
Mahler Chamber Orchestra / Daniel Harding
Virgin Classics 545560-2 (66' · DDD)　　Ⓕ**ⓄⓄ**Ⓑ-

Still in his early twenties, Gautier Capuçon plays the cello with the control and wisdom of a much older musician. The lightness of his touch and the consistent clarity of his bow strokes are quite admirable in themselves, but when combined with an uncanny sweetness of tone in the higher registers they're breathtaking. These qualities suit the two Haydn concertos very well indeed and bestow upon the modest little anonymous D major Concerto unexpected dignity and charm.

Daniel Harding, conducting the Mahler Chamber Orchestra, opts for *galant* rather than driven tempi. The scale of his orchestral forces enables him to establish a relationship with the soloist more akin to chamber music than is usually heard in these works. There's lightness of articulation throughout, conveying both intimacy and vitality.

Their reading of the C major Concerto, while not strongly imprinted, is truly Classical in its delicacy and refinement. It's shapely and spirited but never forced. It's the second item, the D major Haydn, which proves the highlight. In the opening movement Capuçon conjures the darting image of a water sprite, who can nevertheless steal time in all the right moments. The doublestops are dizzying and the chords in the poetic cadenza are exquisitely rolled. The *Adagio* takes on the aura of a meditation; Capuçon seems detached while gently supported by the orchestra, in a reverie of his own. When it comes, the elaboration that serves in the place of a cadenza is perfectly attuned to the moment. The final *Allegro* is never allowed to go 'peasant', remaining instead in the aristocrat's drawing room where it sparkles and glows.

Keyboard Concertos

Piano Concertos – in G, HobXVIII/4; in F, HobXVIII/3; in D, HobXVIII/11
**Norwegian Chamber Orchestra /
Leif Ove Andsnes** pf
EMI 556960-2 (54' · DDD) Ⓕ**ⓄⓄⓄ**ⓑ

Like Emanuel Ax on Sony, Leif Ove Andsnes confines himself to the three concertos that have been fully authenticated. Had the works generally known as 'the Haydn piano concertos' been these three and not a rag-bag of juvenilia and pieces attributed to Haydn, the canon might have been more highly thought. But even the slightest work can dazzle and delight if it's performed as well as these are here. Where Ax's performances have a slightly monochrome feel, everything tapped out (there's much audible fingerwork) with the same well-adjusted mix of energy and sensibility, Andsnes's playing is altogether more various, while perfectly at one with itself stylistically. Ax's Franz Liszt Chamber Orchestra is the more idiomatic of the two ensembles in the D major Concerto's *Rondo all'Ungarese*, but that's about the only occasion on which it has the edge over Andsnes's stylish and highly articulate Norwegian Chamber Orchestra; and even here Andsnes himself scores points for a less noisy plunge into the interlude in D minor and a more sunlit and finely flighted way with the episode which follows. The Norwegian players are never afraid to play full out, a strategy which the explicit but carefully balanced recording is happy to underwrite. Thus the players make much of the 'look here, young man' chromaticisms in the first movement of the D major Concerto as the piano chatters irrepressibly on; and they contribute decisively to the superbly articulated – nay, revelatory – performance of the G major Concerto with which the disc begins. After a splendidly jaunty account of the first movement, Andsnes pushes this G major Concerto to its limits with a decidedly skilfully shaped account of the glooming C major slow movement and a dashing account of the concluding *Presto*. His playing of the *Largo cantabile* of the F major Concerto – the concerto's centrepiece and its *raison d'être* – is the very embodiment of sweetness and light. This is a simply marvellous disc.

Keyboard Concertos – in G, HobXVIII/4; in F, HobXVIII/6[a]; in D, HobXVIII/11 Ⓟ
Andreas Staier fp **Freiburg Baroque Orchestra /
Gottfried von der Goltz** [a]vn
Harmonia Mundi HMC90 1854 (64' · DDD) Ⓕ**ⓄⓄ**

Many concertos are attributed to Haydn but these three are undisputedly authentic. The keyboard part in No 4 falls in a narrow compass; Andreas Staier introduces variety by ornamenting the slow movement and decorating fermatas in all movements. His embellishments are very good indeed, even if he is ornate in places. (If you dislike ornament, you should choose the Andsnes, who sticks to the letter and does so most artistically.)

A rarity is No 6 for violin and keyboard, its outer movements the least interesting with sequential passages. The emotive slow movement (mostly a conversation between the two soloists) redeems matters and gives Gottfried von der Goltz a chance to show his mettle as a sensitive violinist.

In the finest work, No 11, the orchestral exposition is an ideal *Vivace*, the first theme lilting over repeated quavers generating the right degree of forward tension, and the bass line given its full due, oboes and horns colouring the texture tellingly. A similar degree of perception, with Staier's contribution equally telling, is heard throughout. The recording is expertly balanced and tonally truthful. An outstanding disc.

Trumpet Concerto

Haydn Trumpet Concerto, HobVIIe/1
Hummel Trumpet Concerto **Neruda** Trumpet Concerto **Torelli** Trumpet Concerto, 'Estienne Roger'
**Deutsche Kammerphilharmonie, Bremen /
Alison Balsom** tpt
EMI 216213-0 (53' · DDD) Ⓕ**ⓄⓄ**ⓑ

Haydn and Hummel composed their concertos for Anton Weidinger's newfangled keyed trumpet, whose timbre was appreciably softer than the natural trumpet (contemporaries likened it to an oboe or clarinet). More than any performance, Alison Balsom brings out the mellow, even veiled, colouring of so much of the writing. Where clarion brilliance is in order she can peal out with the best of them. But what lingers in the memory is the lyrical grace of her phrasing, and her delicacy of shading.

In the entertaining Hummel Concerto, with its palpable Mozart cribs, she mingles tonal subtlety and swagger in the opening movement, spins a refined, beautifully modulated line in the slow movement, and makes the finale's pyro-technics properly dazzling. The spruce Deutsche Kammerphilharmonie match her all the way in sensitivity and rhythmic verve.

Moving back in time, Balsom savours the bold, bugling fanfares of Torelli's miniature concerto and makes a persuasive case for a pleasant, if hardly distinctive, mid-18th-century concerto by the Czech Johann Baptist Neruda, written for the corno da caccia but forgivably pilfered by trumpeters hard-up for solo concertos. In sum, a stunning recital from a poet of this traditionally martial instrument.

Additional recommendation

Haydn Trumpet Concerto
Coupled with: trumpet concertos by **Albinoni, Corelli, Hertel, Hummel, JM Molter, Mozart, FX Richter, J Stamitz** plus works by JS Bach, Clarke and Gounod
Hardenberger tpt **Preston** org
ASMF / Marriner; LPO / Howarth; ^b**I Musici**
Philips Duo ② 464 028-2PM2 (148' · DDD)   Ⓜ**O**

This is probably the finest single collection of trumpet concertos in the catalogue. The trumpet-ing on this disc is truly splendid and Hardenberger (or the record's producers) have ensured that the accompaniments are distinguished and full of characterful detail.

Symphonies

No 1 in D; **No 2** in C; **No 3** in G; **No 4** in D; **No 5** in A; **No 6** in D, 'Le matin'; **No 7** in C, 'Le midi'; **No 8** in G, 'Le soir'; **No 9** in C; **No 10** in D; **No 11** in E flat; **No 12** in E; **No 13** in D; **No 14** in A; **No 15** in D; **No-16** in B flat; **No 17** in F; **No 18** in G; **No 19** in D; **No 20** in C; **No 21** in A; **No 22** in E flat, 'Philosopher'; **No 23** in G; **No 24** in D; **No 25** in C; **No 26** in D minor, 'Lamentatione'; **No 27** in G; **No-28** in A; **No 29** in E; **No 30** in C, 'Alleluja';

No 31 in D, 'Hornsignal'; **No 32** in C; **No 33** in C; **No 34** in D minor; **No 35** in B flat; **No 36** in E flat; **No 37** in C; **No 38** in C; **No 39** in G minor; **No 40** in F; **No 41** in C; **No 42** in D; **No 43** in E flat, 'Mercury'; **No 44** in E minor, 'Trauersinfonie'; **No 45** in F sharp minor, 'Farewell'; **No 46** in B; **No 47** in G, 'Palindrome'; **No 48** in C, 'Maria Theresia'; **No 49** in F minor, 'La passione'; **No 50** in C; **No 51** in B flat; **No 52** in C minor; **No 53** in D, 'Imperial';

No 54 in G; **No 55** in E flat, 'Schoolmaster'; **No 56** in C; **No 57** in D; **No 58** in F; **No 59** in A, 'Fire'; **No 60** in C, 'Il distratto'; **No 61** in D; **No 62** in D; **No 63** in C, 'La Roxelane'; **No 64** in A, 'Tempora mutantur'; **No 65** in A; **No 66** in B flat; **No 67** in F; **No 68** in B flat; **No 69** in C, 'Loudon'; **No 70** in D; **No 71** in B flat; **No 72** in D; **No 73** in D, 'La chasse'; **No 74** in E flat; **No 75** in D; **No 76** in E flat; **No 77** in B flat; **No 78** in C minor; **No 79** in F; **No 80** in D minor;

No 81 in G; **No 82** in C, 'L'ours'; **No 83** in G minor, 'La poule'; **No 84** in E flat; **No 85** in B flat, 'La reine'; **No 86** in D; **No 87** in A; **No 88** in G, 'Letter V'; **No 89** in F; **No 90** in C; **No-91** in E flat; **No 92** in G, 'Oxford'; **No 93** in D; **No-94** in B flat, 'Surprise'; **No 95** in C minor; **No 96** in D, 'Miracle'; **No 97** in C; **No 98** in B flat; **No 99** in E flat; **No 100** in G, 'Military'; **No 101** in D, 'Clock'; **No 102** in B flat; **No 103** in E flat, 'Drumroll'; **No 104** in D, 'London'.

Symphonies – boxed sets

Symphonies – Nos 1-104; 'A' in B flat; 'B' in B flat.
Sinfonia concertante in B flat, HobI/105, 'No 105'
Philharmonia Hungarica / Antál Dorati
Decca 448531-2 LC33 (33 discs: ADD) Recorded 1969-73   Ⓑ**O**

Dorati's famous integral recording of all 104 of the published Symphonies now returns in a Decca bargain box containing 33 CDs. It still holds its place in the catalogue as the only com-plete set to contain everything Haydn wrote in this medium, including the Symphonies 'A' and 'B', omitted from the original numbering scheme because at one time they were not thought to be symphonies at all. The survey also encompasses additional alternative movements for certain works (notably Nos 53 and 103) and alternative complete versions of the *Philosopher* Symphony and No 63, which are fascinating. The remastering confirms the excellence of the vintage Decca sound. No more needs to be said, except that the one minus point in these very convincing modern-instrument performances is Dorati's insistence on measured, often rustic tempos for the minuets. For those who can run to the complete series this is self-recommending – a source of inexhaustible pleasure.

Symphonies, Nos 1-104
Austro-Hungarian Haydn Orchestra / Adám Fischer
Brilliant Classics 99925 (33 discs: DDD)
From Nimbus originals recorded 1987-2001   Ⓢ Ⓢ**OO**

Also available on eight discs of MP3 files (192 kbps) to download

It was little short of tragic that the very last box of symphonies in Adám Fischer's Haydn series for Nimbus, Nos 21 to 39 plus the Symphonies A and B, appeared just as the demise of that label was announced in January 2002. The final box was the finest of the series, but all too few copies reached the shops, making this 33-disc box cov-ering all the symphonies very welcome indeed, even if over the 14 years that it took to complete the project, the quality and style varied.

That final box of 20 symphonies was a superb culmination to the project. Not only are they a fascinating sequence of works written in the 1760s when the young Haydn was busy experi-menting, the performances are outstanding. They were recorded as recently as 2000 and

2001, and far more than the earliest recordings in the series, they take full note of period practice while staying faithful to modern instruments. More than ever one registers the individual virtuosity of the various soloists in the orchestra, often challenged to the limit by fast speeds. So a movement like the variation finale of No 31, the *Hornsignal*, features a sequence of brilliant soloists such as Haydn might have been writing for in his Esterházy orchestra – violin, cello, horn and so on, even double bass. It's a performance full of panache, with the four horns braying out superbly.

Other striking symphonies in the group include No 22 in E flat, *The Philosopher*, with its extraordinary parts for two cors anglais. Also the *Alleluia* Symphony, No 30 in C, with trumpets and drums dramatically added to the usual published scoring – brought in later, according to HC Robbins Landon, by Haydn as an option. The minor-key works in this last batch, such as the *Lamentatione*, No 26 in D minor, and best of all, No 39 in G minor, are fine examples of Haydn's *Sturm und Drang* manner, with Fischer heightening dynamic contrasts to good effect. No 39 brings an example of Fischer's mastery when he enhances the tension of the nervy opening and exaggerates the pauses; he's far more effective in that movement than Dorati .

While with those symphonies recorded at the beginning of the project, from 1987 to 1990, comparisons with the Dorati series have the merits of each balanced fairly evenly, the advantage certainly tips in favour of Fischer as the project developed. For the *London* Symphonies, Nos 93 to 104, the first to be recorded, the Nimbus engineers – working in the very hall at the Esterházy Palace which Haydn used – produce rather washy sound, whereas the works recorded later benefit from a sharper focus. In those early recordings, too, the slow movements tend to be taken at the sort of broad speeds of tradition, with warmly expressive phrasing.

At that point, no doubt, Fischer was just beginning to woo his select band of Austrian and Hungarian musicians away from their usual Romantic manners. In his notes Fischer makes a point of describing the unfolding development of the project over 14 years. He becomes increasingly aware of historically informed style, notably in faster speeds for both slow movements and *minuet*s (which increasingly acquire a *scherzo*-like flavour), giving him a clear advantage over Dorati. Also the string playing comes closer to that found in period orchestras, with lighter phrasing and less marked use of vibrato.

That development is noticeable as early as the recordings made in 1994-5, when most of the *Sturm und Drang* symphonies were covered – broadly those in the late 40s and early 50s in the regular Breitkopf numbering. Finales in particular, taken fast, have all the bite and wildness one could want, with pinpoint attack. The very earliest symphonies in numerical order, Nos 1 to 20, were recorded early in the project between 1989 and 1991, with results that are more variable. The

---

HAYDN'S 'LONDON' SYMPHONIES (NOS 93-104) – IN BRIEF

Orchestra of the 18th Century / Frans Brüggen   Ⓟ
Philips ② 468 546-2PM2 (Nos 93, 94, 97, 99, 102, 103) & ② 468 927-2PM2 (Nos 95, 96, 98, 100, 101, 104)   Ⓜ

Not Brüggen at his best, but he always has good ideas, and if at times he makes this beautifully proportioned works feel somewhat Beethovenian, his rhythmic snap invariably charms.

Concertgebouw Orchestra / Sir Colin Davis
Philips 442 614-2PM2 (Nos 93, 94, 97, 99, 100, 101) & 442 611-2PM2 (Nos 95, 96, 98, 102, 103, 104)   ⓂⓄ🅑▸

A magnificent achievement from Sir Colin Davis: urbane, witty and stylish with superb playing by the Concertgebouw Orchestra. Tempi and are beautifully judged and inter-related, and the whole cycle has an effortless ease. A real treasure trove. The recordings, made in Amsterdam's Concertgebouw, are excellently done.

London PO / Eugen Jochum
DG ④ 474 364-2GC5   Ⓜ▸

With extra performances of Nos 88, 91 and 98 (from the Berlin PO and Bavarian RSO), this is a real bargain. The LPO play superbly and Jochum gives a series of gloriously cultivated, fresh and often quite enchanting performances. He lavishes great affection on this music, and since it's Haydn, that affection is returned in plenty. The LPO recordings from 1970-71 are excellent, the 'extras' are from the 1950s and early 60s. Packaged in a little slimline box, this set is as economical of your shelving as your wallet.

London Festival Orchestra / Ross Pople
Arte Nova ④ 74321 72109-2   Ⓢ

A sympathetic rather than earth-shattering set of the 'London' Symphonies from Pople and his London-based band. The string section is relatively small, and the recording acoustic is quite tight and dry. Pople's direction is straightforward, sprightly and sensitive to Haydn's many opportunities for solo display (invariably stylishly done).

Royal PO / Sir Thomas Beecham
EMI ② 585770-2 (Nos 93-98) & 585513-2 (Nos 99-104)   Ⓗ   ⒷⓄ

Spread over two two-CD sets, here's Haydn interpretation of wit, urbanity and lashings of style. Beecham was a magnificent Haydn conductor, allowing the music to fizz and sparkle but also bringing out its more songful moments. His RPO at the time was on magnificent form, matching its conductor's unique style with playing of terrific warmth and panache. Classics of their kind.

---

finale of No 12, for example, marked *Presto*, is taken surprisingly slowly, almost like a *minuet*. No 13, very adventurously for that early period, uses four horns, yet because of the reverberant acoustic they don't ring out as prominently as those used in works like the *Hornsignal*, recorded later.

Even in these early symphonies, recorded near the beginning of the project, the trios in *Minuets* have solo strings, and regularly the vigour and thrust of *Allegros* is exhilarating, with rhythms lifted and admirably crisp ensemble.

This is a set guaranteed to encourage collectors to delve into works which from first to last convey the joy in creation that's the unfailing mark of this ever-welcoming master. If you have an MP3 player or listen via your computer Nimbus offer the entire cycle on eight discs of MP3 files, easily downloaded for use with your iPod.

Symphonies – smaller sets

'The Paris Symphonies'
Symphonies – No 82, 'L'ours'; No 83, 'La poule'; No 84; No 85, 'La reine'; No 86; No 87
Concentus Musicus, Vienna / Nikolaus Harnoncourt
Deutsche Harmonia Mundi ③ 82876 60602-2 (3h 6' · DDD)　　　Ⓜ**OO**

When the members of a Parisian concert society commissioned a set of symphonies from Haydn in the mid-1780s they would have looked forward to receiving works of the most up-to-date and sophisticated kind by the genre's acknowledged master. The arrival of a recording of the 'Paris' Symphonies by Nikolaus Harnoncourt and the Vienna Concentus Musicus will have aroused a similar sense of anticipation in some and, just as Haydn must have surpassed expectations with his six superb creations, so the wonders of this three-disc set are surely more than even Harnoncourt fans can have hoped for.

(Three discs? Yes, Harnoncourt takes every repeat going, which means sonata-movement second halves, full sets of repeats for minuets and trios and even a repeat for No 85's slow introduction, with the result that most of the performances come in at just over half an hour.) But if this makes for one more disc than the norm, there is certainly no danger of the music outstaying its welcome. For the pre-Revolution Parisians these were grand works of powerful and unrelenting invention, and Harnoncourt's achievement is to remind us of the fact, revealing in these underrated masterpieces a brilliance and muscle that can almost make us forget 200 years of symphonic history.

For that alone we should be thankful, but these are also just about the most enjoyable and involving Paris performances you are likely to come across. The Concentus Musicus are on superb form, serving up a sound both clear and substantial, with horns a more than usually dark flavouring. And Harnoncourt is typically alert to every message the music has for us, drawing

drama, humour, tenderness and colour at all turns, leaving the listener nothing to do but gasp, smile or glow in his wake.

There is barely room here to list this set's distinguishing delights, but among the most memorable are the fooling with the placing of the final chords of No 82, the leisured unrolling of the main theme of No 84's first movement, the fiercely stabbing wind chords of No 83's finale, and the gloriously unleashed pedal notes at the climax of No 85. Furthermore, Harnoncourt treats each symphony – indeed each movement, each bar – on its own terms. Harnoncourt has shown here that there is more to the 'Paris' Symphonies than the bluff, rolling bonhomie of some interpreters – so much more, in fact, that you have to wonder if they can ever be the same again.

Symphonies Nos 93-4, 97, 99 & 100-101
Concertgebouw Orchestra / Sir Colin Davis
Philips Duo ② 442 614-2PM2 (ADD/DDD) Recorded 1975-81　　　Ⓜ**OO**Ⓑ

Symphonies Nos 95-6, 98 & 102-104
Concertgebouw Orchestra / Sir Colin Davis
Philips Duo ② 442 611-2PM2 (ADD/DDD) Recorded 1975-81　　　Ⓜ**OO**Ⓑ

A superb achievement. It's nigh-on impossible to imagine better 'big-band' Haydn than you encounter here on Colin Davis's four well-filled CDs. His direction has exemplary sparkle and sensitivity. Minuets are never allowed to plod, outer movements have an ideal combination of infectious zip and real poise, and the humour is always conveyed with a genial twinkle in the eye. Quite marvellous, wonderfully unanimous playing from the Amsterdam orchestra, too (the woodwind contributions are particularly distinguished), with never a trace of routine to betray the six-year recording span of this acclaimed project. The Philips engineering, whether analogue or digital, is of the very highest quality, offering a natural perspective, gloriously full-bodied tone and sparkling textures within the sumptuous Concertgebouw acoustic. Invest in this set: it will yield enormous rewards for years to come.

Additional recommendations

Symphonies Nos 6-8
Northern Chamber Orchestra / Ward
Naxos 8 550722 (59' · DDD)　　　ⓈⒷ
A lot to enjoy in the popular Times of Day trilogy, with their colourful and entertaining *concertante* writing. The Northern Chamber Orchestra is a lively, responsive group, and fields a personable bunch of soloists No one staking a fiver on this disc could possibly be disappointed.

Symphonies Nos 22, 29 & 60
Northern Chamber Orchestra / Ward
Naxos 8 550724 (60' · DDD)　　　ⓈⒷ

A winning performance that fully captures the composer's infectious wit.

Symphonies Nos 43, 46 & 47
Cologne Chamber Orchestra / Müller-Brühl
Naxos 8 554767 (64' · DDD)   Ⓢ🅓➔

A beefier sound than from many chamber orchestras but with ample detail. Müller-Brühl's speeds can't be faulted, with *Allegros* crisp and alert and slow movements kept flowing. A worthy rival for existing versions, whether on period or modern instruments.

Symphonies Nos 55-69
Austro-Hungarian Haydn Orchestra / Fischer
Nimbus ④ NI5590/4 (317' · DDD)   Ⓢ

A most attractive collection, on modern instruments in the helpful acoustic of the Haydnsaal of the Esterházy Palace at Eisenstadt. Fischer's fine control of dynamics is illustrated in the subtlety of echo phrases, clear but unexaggerated.

Symphonies Nos 49, 52 & 58
Heidelberg SO / Fey
Hänssler Classic 98.236 (77' · DDD)   Ⓕ🅓➔

Symphonies Nos 57, 59 & 65
Heidelberg SO / Fey
Hänssler Classic 98.526 (74' · DDD)   Ⓕ🅞🅞🅓➔

Symphonies Nos 69, 86 & 87
Heidelberg SO / Fey
Hänssler Classic 98.268 (76' · DDD)   Ⓕ🅞🅓➔

Thomas Fey's series with his Heidelberg SO was one of the musical discoveries of Haydn Year. A pupil of both Bernstein and Harnoncourt, he brings excitment and flair to a sound that owes much to period-instrument practice. Bracing!

Symphonies Nos 41-47, 50-52, 64 & 65, 82-87 (Paris) & 88-90   🅟
Tafelmusik / Weil
Sony Classical ⑦ 88697 48044-2 (452' · DDD)   Ⓢ🅞🅞

A very appealing collection of Haydn symphonies performed on period instruments. As well as the 'Paris' Symphonies (Nos 82-87), Bruno Weill includes many of the lesser-known middle-period works. Everything is done with great style, lively attention to rhythm and a generous openness to Haydn's wit and humour. The *Farewell* Symphony (No 45) receives one of the best performances on disc. Competitively priced this is an excellent single set Haydn symphony collection.

Symphonies Nos 82-87 (Paris), 88, 93-104. The Creation. Harmoniemesse. Paukenmesse. Nelsonmesse. Theresienmesse.
New York Philharmonic Orchestra / Bernstein
Sony Classical ⑫ 88697480452 (DDD)   Ⓢ

Leonard Bernstein was an enthusiastic and passionate Haydn conductor. Everything was done on a grand scale, but it is never overblown or inflated. Bernstein's innate sense of rhythm ensures dance movements genuinely dance, and he responds to Haydn's jokes well. The four Masses make an attracive make-weight with some beautiful singing, both solo and choral.

Symphonies arr Chamber Ensemble

London Symphonies arr Salomon, Volume 1   🅟
Symphonies (arr Salomon) Nos 93[a], No 94[b], 101[a]
Florilegium Ensemble (Ashley Solomon *fl* James Johnstone *fp* [a]Kati Debretzeni, [b]Rodolfo Richter *vns* Jane Rogers *va* Jennifer Morsches *vc*)
Channel Classics SACD hybrid CCSSA19603 (72' · DDD)   Ⓕ

Johann Peter Salomon, violinist, composer and impresario, was a shrewd businessman. Not only did he organise Haydn's two triumphant visits to London in the 1790s, visits which directly prompted the composition of the 12 *London* Symphonies, but he bought the rights to those masterpieces on Haydn's final return to Vienna in August 1795. Instead of issuing them in full score, in 1798 he published versions for domestic music-making. The basic ensemble is a string quartet and flute, plus a full keyboard part. This music is readily available in its original garb, but these arrangements are worth hearing. Some effects that must have sounded so original to early listeners stand out even more with this chamber ensemble than they do with a full orchestra. The extra transparency generally benefits fast movements. First-movement development sections strike the listener more sharply in their chamber guise, particularly the minor-key darkness of the *Surprise*, which recalls Haydn's *Sturm und Drang* style. The famous 'surprise' itself is intensified by Florilegium's dynamic response. These arrangements, well recorded with stylish if occasionally abrasive period performances and the advantage of an SACD alternative, can be warmly recommended to anyone who's intrigued.

Flute Quartets

Cassation in F, HobII/20. Divertissement in B flat, HobII/B4. Flute Quartet in A, HobII/A4. Notturno No-1 in C, HobII/25
Linos Ensemble
Capriccio 10 719 (68' · DDD). Recorded 1994   Ⓕ

These highly polished, enthusiastic performances have a compelling immediacy. The diverse choice of pieces amply shows the excellent soloistic skills of Linos's members and its deftly balanced ensemble. Close recording presents the group's eloquence and vitality in fine, clear detail. The delightful, open-air qualities of this repertoire are exemplified by the F major *Cassation*, whose good humour is captured with buoyant vigour in the opening *Allegro*; with stately elegance in the two minuets, affecting melodiousness in the *Adagio*, and an engaging swing in the final rondo. The extrovert B flat *Divertissement* offers a charming display of fluent, conversational playing, a style the Linos exploits to particular effect in the lively alternation of different instrumental groupings in the elegant A major Quartet for flute and strings. The infectiously high-spirited, effervescent exchanges between flute and oboe in the witty C major *Notturno* sum up the allure of this entertaining issue.

String Quartets

Op 0 in E flat
Op 1: No 1 in B flat, 'La chasse' **No 2**
in E flat **No 3** in D **No 4** in G **No 5** in E flat **No 6** in C
Op 2: No 1 in A **No 2** in E **No 3** (spurious) **No 4** in F
No 5 (spurious) **No 6** in B flat
Op 3 Nos 1-6 (spurious)
Op 9: No-1 in C **No 2** in E flat **No 3** in G
No 4 in D minor **No 5** in B-flat **No 6** in A
Op 17: No 1 in E **No 2** in F **No 3** in E flat
No 4 in C minor **No 5** in G **No 6** in D
Op 20, 'Sun': No 1 in E flat **No 2** in C **No 3** in G
minor **No 4** in D **No 5** in F minor **No 6** in A
Op 33 'Gli Scherzi': No 1 in B minor
No 2 in E flat, 'Joke' **No 3** in C, 'Bird'
No 4 in B flat **No 5** in G **No 6** in D
Op 42 in D
Op 50 'Prussian': No 1 in B flat **No 2** in C
No 3 in E flat **No 4** in F sharp minor **No 5** in F, 'Dream'
No 6 in D, 'Frog'
Op 54 'Tost': No 1 in G **No 2** in C **No 3** in E
Op 55 'Tost': No 1 in A **No 2** in F minor, 'Razor'
No 3 in B flat
Op 64 'Tost': No 1 in C **No 2** in B minor **No 3** in B flat
No 4 in G **No 5** in D, 'The Lark' **No 6** in E flat
Op 71 'Apponyi': No 1 in B flat **No 2** in D
No 3 in E flat
Op 74 'Apponyi': No 1 in C **No 2** in F **No 3** in G
minor, 'Rider'
Op 76 'Erdödy': No 1 in G **No 2** in D minor, 'Fifths'
No 3 in C, 'Emperor' **No 4** in B flat, 'Sunrise'
No 5 in D **No 6** in E flat
Op 77 'Lobkowitz': No 1 in G **No 2** in F
Op 103 in D minor (unfinished)

Complete String Quartets

Op 0; Op 1 – Nos 1ᵃ, 2, 3, 4ᵃ & 6 in Cᵃ; Op 2 –
Nos 1, 2ᵃ, 4ᵃ & 6; Opp 9, 17, 20, 33, 42ᵃ, 50ᵃ,
54, 55, 64, 71, 74, 76, 77 & 103
Angeles Quartet (Kathleen Lenski, Steven Miller,
ᵃSara Parkins *vns* Brian Dembow *va* Stephen
Erdody *vc*)
Philips (21 discs) 464 650-2PX21(140' · DDD) Ⓜ🅾🅾

The most relevant comparisons for this collection are the Aeolian Quartet on Decca and the Kodály Quartet on Naxos. The all-digital Naxos series features performances that are, in the main, musically reliable and technically proficient. But turn back to the 1973-6 Aeolian series, and every work becomes an event, every quirk of harmony, rhythm or timing is etched with maximum relish.

Comparative disc layouts begin to differ from CD 3, and the Angeles omit *The Seven Last Words*, a work which, beautiful as it is, wasn't originally written for string quartet. Recording-wise, Philips favours a warm, open sound, balanced much as you would hear it from the centre

stalls in a smallish-size concert hall. Decca's analogue recordings are closer, dryer, more sensitive to extraneous noise and commonly balanced in favour of Emanuel Hurwitz's first violin. It's a clear and intimate sound frame and the leader bias actually suits the divertimento-style early quartets, but Philips's more refined engineering makes for less strenuous listening in concert-length sessions. A handful of edits are the only blots on Philips's otherwise immaculate aural landscape.

The svelte texture of the Angeles' pooled sound, their consistent evenness in full chords and the musical like-mindedness of individual players, whether in excited *prestos* or in shared *rubato* is admirable. As to contrasts in playing styles, think of the relatively smooth-toned Juilliard or Emerson Quartets (Angeles) as compared with the internally differentiated Amadeus Quartet (Aeolian). The Angeles are generally lighter, faster and subtler in their use of tone colouring whereas the Aeolians' roster of virtues includes strong (even emphatic) characterisation, consistently flexible phrasing and a more pungent approach to rhythm.

Surfing the set for good sampling points brings us, initially, to the early quartets, where both groups sport some superb first-violin solo work, tastefully inflected with Lenski, more candidly expressive with Hurwitz. A particularly telling comparison is provided by the quietly contrapuntal Minuet of Op 17 No 1, where the Angeles' seamless *legato* contrasts against the Aeolians' near *staccato*. The exquisite *Adagio* of Op 20 No 6 is another good place to compare, the Angeles with their perfectly timed pauses, warm cello line and overall restraint set against the more romantic, even rhapsodic, Aeolian. Listening to the first bars of Op 33 No 1 is like eavesdropping on a small gathering mid-conversation, where the cello line gradually gains in urgency. The Angeles' *sotto voce* handling of the *scherzo* to Op 33 No 3 is wonderful: it's rather more pensive than the Aeolians and marks much more of a contrast with the chirping trio.

Op 50 No 4's *Andante* anticipates the dramatic interjections that trouble various late Schubert slow movements. Both groups are effective here, though when the cello marks an expected change of key two minutes or so into the movement, it's the Aeolian's Derek Simpson who makes the biggest impact: you can almost see the rosin erupt from his strings. In Op 50 No 5 late Beethoven springs more readily to mind, but there the Angeles' extra speed and restraint is more effective. Note how beautifully they negotiate the quiet alternation between upper and lower voices towards the end of Op 50 No 6's *Poco adagio* and the sudden blossoming that follows. Then again, Op 54 No 1's mobile *Allegretto* second movement harbours the potential to switch from tenseness to lyrical effusiveness, which the Angeles exploit to the full, as they do for the rhapsodising *Adagio* of Op 54 No 2. Late Beethoven is evoked once more, this time the Cavatina from Op 130.

Beam up around three minutes into the *Adagio* of the *Lark* Quartet (Op 64 No 5) and you'll note how skilfully the Angeles cue a *ritardando*, while the bracing finale to Op 74 No 3 has just the right bounce to offset all the breathless excitement. The *Sunrise* Quartet (Op 76 No 4) opens like a spring flower (never more so than in the Angeles' ecstatically controlled performance) and Op 77 No 1's cheeky *Allegro moderato* bounds in with perfectly modulated high spirits.

Turning to other competition, the Lindsays, Amadeus, Vienna Konzerthaus, Quatuor Mosaïques, Pro Arte and Takács, all have added substantiallyto the Haydn quartet discography, and all have their value. However, in this particular context it really is a head-to-head contest between two 'complete' sets similarly presented.

Richard Wigmore contributes detailed annotation, quite different from Lindsay Kemp's overview for Decca, but just as useful and equally well written. The Angeles appeal perhaps primarily for their restrained expressiveness and consistent attention to detail. Philips's superior recording is another bonus. The Aeolians generate more immediate heat but, ultimately, the Angeles' intelligence and cooler blending pay the higher musical dividends.

String Quartets Op 1

String Quartets: Op 1 No 1. Op 20 Nos 2 & 5.   Ⓗ
Op 50 No 3. Op 54 Nos 1-3. Op 64 Nos 3 & 4.
Op 74 No 3. Op 76 Nos 3 & 4. Op 77 No 2
Pro Arte Quartet (Alphonse Onnou, Laurent Halleux
vns Germain Prévost *va* Robert Maas *vc*)
Testament mono ③ SBT3055 (229' · ADD) Recorded
1931-8   Ⓕ�O

Haydn String Quartets: Op 1 No 6. Op-20   Ⓗ
Nos 1 & 4. Op 33 Nos 2, 3 & 6. Op 50 No 6. Op 55
Nos 1 & 3. Op 64 No 6. Op 71 No 1. Op 74 Nos 1 &
2. Op 77 No 1 **Hoffstetter** String Quartets, Op 3 –
No 4 in B flat; No 5 in F
Pro Arte Quartet (Alphonse Onnou, Laurent Halleux
vns Germain Prévost *va* Robert Maas *vc*)
Testament mono ③ SBT4056 (243' · ADD) Recorded
1931-8   ⒻO

The Pro Arte Quartet's first London appearance in 1925 prompted *The Times* to declare, 'One has never heard it surpassed, and rarely equalled, in volume and beauty of tone, in accuracy of intonation and in perfection of balance between the parts' – and that could well be the verdict on these sets. The musicians' tempos invariably seem just right and their phrasing has an inner life that's extraordinarily potent. Alphonse Onnou and Laurent Halleux were superbly matched, and Halleux often led in their early days. Such virtuosity as the quartet exhibits is effortless and totally lacking in ostentation. Though the actual sound is dated – the string tone is wanting in bloom and freshness – the ear soon adjusts; but these transfers might have made a little more space between movements.

String Quartets, Op 1 Nos 1-6
Petersen Quartet (Conrad Muck, Gernot Sussmuth
vns Friedemann Weigle *va* Hans-Jakob Eschenburg *vc*)
Capriccio ② 10 786/7 (99' · DDD)   ⒻO

The history of the string quartet in effect began with these cheerful, compact *Divertimenti a quattro*, as the composer titled them; and though they contain only spasmodic hints of future glories, their freshness and exuberance make for highly pleasurable listening.

The Petersen Quartet responds vividly to the music's youthful verve, with polished ensemble, keen attack and a wide spectrum of colour and dynamics. Purists may raise an eyebrow at the special effects the players deploy in repeats, especially in minuets – added touches of imitation, pizzicato and even *col legno*. But the young Haydn, famed for his mischievous humour, may have enjoyed these liberties. The recording combines clarity with an attractive church resonance.

String Quartets, Op 9

String Quartets, Op 9 Nos 1, 3 & 4
Kodály Quartet (Attila Falváy, Tamás Szabó *vns*
Gábor Fias *va* János Devich *vc*)
Naxos 8 550786 (52' · DDD)   ⓈⒹ⯈

String Quartets, Op 9 Nos 2, 5 & 6
Kodály Quartet (Attila Falváy, Tamás Szabó *vns*
Gábor Fias *va* János Devich *vc*)
Naxos 8 550787 (58' · DDD)   ⓈⒹ⯈

Overshadowed by four dozen later masterpieces, Haydn's Op 9 has usually received short shrift from players and commentators. The most familiar is the D minor, No 4, described by Hans Keller as 'the first great string quartet in the history of music'. The minor mode at this period (1769-70) invariably drew something special from Haydn, and this work stands apart from the others for its intensity of expression, its mastery of texture and development and the sheer character of its ideas. The opening *Allegro moderato* could well have been at the back of Mozart's mind when he came to write his own great D minor Quartet, K421. The Kodály Quartet is, as ever, a sympathetic Haydn exponent, impressing with its slightly old-fashioned warmth of sonority, the natural musicality of its phrasing and care for blend, balance and intonation, though the boomy church acoustic hardly helps.

String Quartets, Op 20

String Quartets, Op 20 Nos 1-6   Ⓟ
Quatuor Mosaïques (Erich Höbarth, Andrea Bischof
vns Anita Mitterer *va* Christophe Coin *vc*)
Astrée Naïve ② E8802 (147' · DDD)   ⒻOOO

The Op 20 String Quartets date from the composer's so-called *Sturm und Drang* period, though Haydn's increasingly frequent use of the more dramatic and 'serious' minor mode in these pieces can perhaps be attributed just as much to the fruitful influence of the three operatic projects he had been working on just a few years previously. Moreover, these quartets reveal a greater preoccupation with counterpoint than any of his music to that date, and the great fugal finales of Nos 2, 5 and 6 clearly herald the consummate craftsman so overwhelmingly displayed in the mature quartets to come. These wonderfully flexible performances display an altogether breath-taking refinement, sensitivity and illumination. Indeed, in terms of expressive subtlety, imaginative intensity and sheer depth of feeling, the Mosaïques' achievement in these marvellous works is unmatched.

String Quartets, Op 20 – Nos 1, 3 & 4
The Lindsays (Peter Cropper, Ronald Birks vns
Robin Ireland va Bernard Gregor-Smith vc)
ASV CDDCA1027 (79' · DDD)   Ⓕ〇

String Quartets, Op 20 – Nos 2, 5 & 6
The Lindsays
ASV CDDCA1057 (66' · DDD)   Ⓕ〇

The Lindsays are Haydn interpreters of rare understanding and communicative flair. Their characterisation is bold and decisive, enhanced by a scrupulous observation of the composer's expression and dynamic markings. Faster movements tend to be more urgent, less ruminative, than those from the Quatuor Mosaïques. The *zingarese* cross-rhythms of No 4's Minuet have an abrasive edge, and the *Presto e scherzando* finale is no mere frolic in The Lindsays' hands – its wit can scathe and sting, and the closing theme, with its gypsy *acciaccaturas*, has an almost manic insistence. Elsewhere they bring an ideal warmth and lyricism to the opening movement of No 1, characteristically phrasing in long, eloquent spans, and a quixotic energy to the outer movements of the G minor, No 3, where the Quatuor Mosaïques is broader and tougher. In the Minuet The Lindsays' singing line and flexibility of pulse realise to the full Haydn's searching harmonic progressions; and the lulling E flat Trio is exquisitely floated. Each of the slow movements reveals dedication and profound identification. The players vindicate their dangerously slow tempo in the sublime *Affettuoso e sostenuto* of No 1 with the breadth and intensity of their phrasing, subtlety of colour and feeling for harmonic flux. As ever, the occasional moment of impure intonation is a small price to pay for performances of such colour, character and spontaneity.

The Lindsays observe all the important marked repeats and the recording is vivid and truthful. Characterisation of the sharply contrasted Nos 2, 5 and 6 is invariably vivid, phrasing is alive and inventive, and the players combine a scrupulous care for Haydn's dynamic and expression markings with a strong feeling for the music's larger contours.

String Quartets, Op 33

String Quartets, Op 33 Nos 1-6   Ⓟ
Quatuor Mosaïques (Erich Höbarth, Andrea Bischof
vns Anita Mitterer va Christophe Coin vc)
Auvidis Naïve ② E8801 (121' · DDD)   Ⓕ〇〇〇

Ⓖ The Mosaïques, at a rather slower tempo than usual, find in the theme-and-variation finale of the G major Quartet, No 5, an unsuspected reflective tenderness. The theme itself is played with a characteristic touch of flexibility and a gentle lift to the dotted rhythms; in the first variation Erich Höbarth shapes his decorative semiquavers *fioriture* with apparently spontaneous fantasy; the luminous, high-lying textures of the second are exquisitely realised; and even the *Presto* send-off has a delicacy and whimsy in keeping with what has gone before. The Mosaïques' readings of the slow movements in the so-called *Joke* (No 2) and *Bird* (No 3) Quartets are again outstanding in their grave tenderness, their sensitivity to harmonic flux and the improvisatory freedom Erich Höbarth brings to his ornamental figuration. The *Bird*, in particular, receives as searching a performance as ever heard: in the first movement the players steal in almost imperceptibly, respond vividly to the music's richness and wit, and bring a spectral *pianissimo* to the mysterious lull in the development. The Slavonic finale, one of several movements to benefit from the lighter, more flexible period bows, goes with terrific fire and panache.

From the teasingly timed initial upbeat of the D major Quartet, No 6, the Mosaïques' performances have all the familiar hallmarks: inventive phrasing, subtly varied colour, a sure sense of organic growth and a spontaneous-sounding delight in Haydn's inspired unpredictability. Tempo and manner in the opening *Vivace assai* of No 6 are, typically, gentler than that of the equally imaginative Lindsays, the articulation lighter and more delicate, as you would expect from period strings. They catch ideally the music's glancing *scherzando* spirit, with a delightfully eager, quick-witted give-and-take between the instruments. Like The Lindsays, the Mosaïques vividly play up the contrast between the perky, high-stepping D major theme and alternating D minor melody. But the Mosaïques flex the tempo more freely and play with the length of Haydn's upbeats, to witty or pathetic effect.

In the *Andante* of the B minor Quartet (No 1) the Mosaïques arguably overdo the whimsical hesitations. However, their unusally reflective way with this movement, and the sense of remoteness they bring to the strange, spare second theme is very appealing. The undervalued B flat Quartet (No 4) is a delight throughout, from the puckish opening movement, with its quasi-improvisatory freedom to the comic exuberance of the finale; the vitality and point of the inner voices' semiquavers in the finale's G minor episode are typical of the character brought to seemingly routine accompanying figuration.

This set has playing that marries uncommon style, technical finesse and re-creative flair. The recording has an attractive ambient warmth.

String Quartets – Op 33; Op 42
Festetics Quartet (István Kertész, Erika Petöfi vns Péter Ligeti va Rezsö Pertorini vc)
Arcana ② A414 (145' · DDD)   Ⓕ

The veteran Festetics Quartet are uneasy with *presto* finales. But they aren't slack; instead they are tautly metrical so the notes do not flow freely across the bar-lines. It may be an aspect of their style that is direct, sharp in attack and stricter than usual in rhythm, yet far from indifferent. In all the works these musicians meticulously observe phrase indications, choose dynamics where there are none, repeat both parts of a Minuet after its Trio and differentiate between the various accents. Equally meticulously they probe the slow movements of Op 33. Haydn is said to have been in love at the time he wrote this set; and, austerity of approach notwithstanding, it is easy to discern in, say, the *Largo* of No 4 an ardent lyric for the lady, Luigia Polzelli. Not unexpectedly, the *Largo e cantabile* of No 5 is seen in an even more ascetic light, G minor starkly affirmed, the violins (antiphonally separated, as always with this group) contributing to a bare-boned interpretation of the text. Not comfortable. But the Festetics don't buy comfort and the close, 'rosiny' sound brings the results right into the room. No mistaking the message. No mistaking the gauntlets either. Unsettling – but required listening.

String Quartets, Op 33 Nos 1, 2 & 4
The Lindsays (Peter Cropper, Ronald Birks vns Robin Ireland va Bernard Gregor-Smith vc)
ASV CDDCA937 (62' · DDD)   ⒻO

The Lindsays' is chamber-music-making of unusual flair, untouched by the faintest hint of routine. In their uncommonly grave, inward readings of the slow movements of the E flat and B flat Quartets they sustain a daringly slow tempo magnificently, phrasing in long, arching spans, always acutely sensitive to harmonic movement, as in their subtle colouring of Haydn's breathtaking tonal excursions in No 4. Beethoven is evoked in The Lindsays' swift, mordant reading of No 1's epigrammatic *Scherzo*: rarely have the waspish part-writing and the abrupt, disconcerting contrasts in dynamics and articulation been so vividly realised. Typically, it makes the most of the complete change of mood and texture in the major-key Trio, finding an almost Viennese sweetness of tone and phrase, complete with touches of *portamento*. The finale, fast, fierce, utterly uncomical, has a distinct whiff of the Hungarian *puszta* here, both in the wild gypsy figuration and the mounting passion of the sequence

in the development. The Lindsays bring an ideal spaciousness and flexibility to the urbane, quietly spoken first movement of the E flat Quartet, No 2, taking due note of Haydn's *cantabile* marking. In the finales of this Quartet and No 4 they bring vital, inventively varied phrasing, palpably relishing Haydn's exuberance and comic sleight of hand.

String Quartets, Op 33 Nos 3, 5 & 6
The Lindsays (Peter Cropper, Ronald Birks vns Robin Ireland va Bernard Gregor-Smith vc)
ASV CDDCA938 (61' · DDD)   ⒻOO

The Lindsays eclipse all comers in range of colour, vital, creative phrasing and emotional penetration. They respond gleefully to the subversive comedy that pervades each of the three works – most overtly in the Slavonic-influenced finale of *The Bird* (No 3), and in the outrageous *Scherzo* of No 5, where with explosive *sforzandos* and sly touches of timing they relish to the full Haydn's rhythmic and dynamic mayhem. But time and again in this music wit is suddenly suffused with poetry; and they bring a glancing delicacy and grace of interplay to, say, the startling tonal deflexions in the opening *Vivace assai* of No 6. With their slower-than-usual tempo and wonderfully tender, contained *sotto voce*, the second movement of No 3, where Haydn transmutes the Minuet-scherzo into a hymn, becomes the expressive core of the quartet. The Lindsays constantly provoke you to respond afresh to Haydn; to his wit, comic exuberance and his often unsuspected profundity.

String Quartet, Op 42

Haydn String Quartet, Op 42 **Schumann** String Quartet No 3 in A, Op 41 No 3
Shostakovich String Quartet No 3 in F, Op 73
Allegri Quartet (Peter Carter, David Roth vns Jonathan Barritt va Bruno Schrecker vc)
Naim Audio NAIMCD016 (73' · DDD)   Ⓕ

Haydn's exquisite Op 42 is given an especially winning rendition, the *Andante ed innocentemente* first movement donning a degree of understatement that reflects its equivocal personality.

Following it with Shostakovich's Op 73 was an inspired idea: the former ends quietly and the latter opens with a sort of distracted innocence, marking time before the real drama starts. The argument suddenly intensifies, playfully, provocatively, though characterisation is cleverly differentiated. In the second movement, Prokofiev is an obvious point of reference and there has rarely been a more delicately pointed account of the weird, tiptoe *staccato* passage that emerges out of the first idea. The third movement is a striking precursor of the 10th Symphony's violent 'Stalin' *Scherzo*, the slow movement redolent of the 12th Symphony's noble opening and the long finale ending in a mood of veiled mystery.

Above all, this is profoundly natural playing and the recordings maintain a realistic 'small concert-hall' ambience throughout.

The disc ends with an affectionate, flexible performance of Schumann's loveliest string quartet. The opening *Andante espressivo* sets the mood while the ensuing second set (1'19") is limpid and rapturous, and the finale – which in some hands can seem repetitive – is given precisely the right degree of rhythmic emphasis. Again one senses wholehearted identification between the repertoire and its interpreters – and while one may question the wisdom of mixed-repertory CD programmes, this one is so well planned and well played, that it can be recommended even to those who already own recordings within cycles.

String Quartets, Op 54

String Quartets, Op 54 Nos 1-3
The Lindsays (Peter Cropper, Ronald Birks *vns*
Robin Ireland *va* Bernard Gregor-Smith *vc*)
ASV CDDCA582 (66' · DDD)   Ⓕ**OO**

All three quartets are in the usual four-movement form but they contain many surprises: in No 1, the false recapitulation in the first movement, the dark modulations in the following sonata-form *Allegretto* and the Hungarian gipsy flavour (anticipated in the Minuet) and mischievousness of the final rondo. No 2 has a rhapsodic fiddler in its second movement, a nostalgic minuet with an extraordinarily anguished trio, and an *Adagio* finale in which a *Presto* section turns out to be no more than an episode.

A notable feature of No 3 is its ternary-form *Largo cantabile*, the centre of which is more like a mini-concerto for the first violin; 'Scotch snaps' pervade the Minuet, and pedal points the finale. The performances and the recording are superb, marked by unanimity, fine tone, suppleness of phrasing, and acute dynamic shaping; in the second movement of No 1 there are hushed passages whose homogeneity and quality of sound are both quite remarkable. Overall, this recording is irresistible.

String Quartets, Op 55

String Quartets, Op 55 Nos 1-3
The Lindsays (Peter Cropper, Ronald Birks *vns*
Robin Ireland *va* Bernard Gregor-Smith *vc*)
ASV CDDCA906 (64' · DDD)   Ⓕ**O**

Most immediately striking of the trilogy is the F minor work, No 2, with its searching double variations on related minor and major themes (a favourite form in Haydn's later music), spiky, rebarbative second movement *Allegro* and strangely spare contrapuntal Minuet. The A major, No 1, has much of this key's traditional brilliance, with ample scope for the leader's creative virtuosity in the outer movements and

the stratospheric trio of the minuet; in contrast the noble, wonderfully scored *Adagio cantabile* prefigures the profound slow movements of Haydn's final years. The more inward-looking No 3 in B flat is specially remarkable for the varied recapitulations in the flanking movements, astonishingly free and inventive even for Haydn, and the subtle chromatic colouring in all four movements which may just owe something to the quartets Mozart had dedicated to Haydn three years earlier. Here and there The Lindsays' intonation is less than true, but as so often with this group, this is a small price to pay for performances of such colour and penetration. The balance, as with many recent quartet recordings, is a shade closer than ideal but the overall sound picture is very acceptable.

String Quartets, Op 64

String Quartets, Op 64 Nos 1-3
Kodály Quartet (Attila Falvay, Tamás Szabo *vns*
Gábor Fias *va* János Devich *vc*)
Naxos 8 550673 (64' · DDD)   Ⓢ▷

String Quartets, Op 64 Nos 4-6
Kodály Quartet
Naxos 8 550674 (65' · DDD)   Ⓢ▷

The so-called *Lark* (No 5), with its soaring opening melody and *moto perpetuo* finale, is perhaps the most immediately fetching of all Haydn's quartets. But No 6 is at least as fine, with its intimate and intensely argued opening movement, its poignant, exquisitely textured *Andante* and a finale full of instrumental fooling and insouciant contrapuntal virtuosity. Of the other works, No 2 is one of Haydn's most astringent pieces, from its tonally deceptive opening to the mordant, unsettling humour of the finale. Quartets Nos 3 and 4 return to a more familiar vein of sociable wit. Both are endlessly subtle and surprising in their arguments, with *cantabile* slow movements of peculiar candour and eloquence. Quartet No 1, the least favoured of the six is certainly the plainest in its thematic ideas. But it's an absorbing, immensely sophisticated piece, exploring an astonishing range of textures; the recapitulation of the leisurely first movement opens up marvellous new harmonic vistas, while the central development of the finale is a canonic *tour de force*. The Kodály Quartet has rightly won plaudits for its wonderfully civilised playing; mellow and lyrical, far removed from the highly strung brilliance cultivated by many modern quartets. Ensemble and intonation are first class, tempos generally spacious, with broad, natural and beautifully matched phrasing. It's at its very finest where Haydn is at his most searching; and the Quartets Nos 2, 5 and 6 each receive outstanding, deeply considered performances. In one or two movements the Kodály's penchant for slowish tempos leads to a slight dourness. Against that, it brings a deliciously lazy *Ländler* lilt, enhanced by the first violin's *portamentos*, to the Trio of No 6, and a grave, inward intensity to each of Haydn's slow movements. The recording, made in a Budapest church, is resonant and less intimate than is ideal in this music.

String Quartets, Opp 71 and 74

String Quartets, Op 71 Nos 1-3
Kodály Quartet
Naxos 8 550394 (62' · DDD)   ⑤🅑➤

String Quartets, Op-74 Nos 1-3
Kodály Quartet
Naxos 8 550396 (63' · DDD)   ⑤🅑➤

The Kodály Quartet plays with evident joy and an easy neatness of ensemble. There's never a hint of routine and the inter-communication is matched by enormous care for detail. Just sample the elegant *Andante* with variations which form the slow movement of Op 71 No 3, or the witty Minuet which follows, or any of the consistently inspired Op 74 set. The hushed intensity of playing in the *Largo assai* of Op 74 No 3 is unforgettable. The recordings are wholly natural and balanced within a well-judged acoustic; the sound is of the highest quality and documentation is excellent. At their modest price this pair of CDs is irresistible.

String Quartets, Op 71
The Lindsays
ASV Gold GLD4012 (68' · DDD)   Ⓕ

These must be the least well known of Haydn's later quartets, poorly represented over the years in recital programmes and on disc, yet they show Haydn at the height of his powers. When he first came to London in 1791 his string quartets proved popular items in his public concerts; back in Vienna preparing for his second London visit, he designed these new works especially for public performance, with attention-grabbing opening gestures and brilliant concertante writing for all four instruments.

As we've come to expect from The Lindsays' Haydn, these are deeply considered performances, bringing out the full individuality of each movement – the sensuous, romantic atmosphere of No 1's *Adagio*, the zany, high-spirited character of No 2's opening *Allegro*, with its leaping octave motif shared out between the instruments. The Lindsays' lively tone quality and robust manner powerfully convey the rhythmic verve that's a mirror of Haydn's extraordinary creative energy; sometimes the playing sounds a bit too forceful. Whether you already know Op 71 or not, you're bound to enjoy this splendid issue.

String Quartets, Op 76

String Quartets, Op 76 Nos 1-3
The Lindsays (Peter Cropper, Ronald Birks *vns*

Robin Ireland *va* Bernard Gregor-Smith *vc*)
ASV CDDCA1076 (75' · DDD)   Ⓕ🅞

These are among the finest Haydn quartet recordings heard in years, performances which will quickly establish themselves as classics. They are consistently a degree more refined in texture and control of dynamic than the Lindsays' earlier live recordings, and the ensemble is more polished. Yet the feeling of spontaneity is just as intense, with Haydn's witty moments pointed even more infectiously, as in the finale of Op 76 No 2, where in the main theme the little upward *portamentos* at the end of the eighth bar are delectably timed on each occurrence. The studio sound is fuller, too, and far better balanced, so that one can register far more clearly than before the first violin's rapid triplets in the finale of the *Emperor*; it's ideally crisp articulation. Matching the new performances of the *Fifths* and the *Emperor*, The Lindsays' account of Op 76 No 1 is just as strongly characterised. The sense of fun in the opening *Allegro con spirito* is deliciously brought out, leading on to an account of the sublime *Adagio*, both dedicated and refined, which conveys a Beethovenian depth of expression, making most rivals sound superficial.

String Quartets, Op 76 – Nos 4-6
Lindsay Quartet
ASV CDDCA1077 (78' · DDD)   Ⓕ🅞🅞

Here, in the last three Op 76 quartets, you've Haydn interpretations that bring forth the full range of expression in these inspired works of his official retirement. They aren't just polished and refined but communicate with an intensity that simulates live performance. No 5 in D was one of the works which The Lindsays recorded earlier live at the Wigmore Hall, but the extra subtlety this time means that rhythms are a degree more liltingly seductive, in which humour is more delightfully pointed, as in the repeated cadence-figure at the start of the finale, with comic pauses beautifully timed.

The quiet opening of No 4, which gave rise to the nickname 'Sunrise', gently insinuates itself before the full thrust of the *Allegro* takes over; with its heightened contrasts, it could not be more captivating. Most strikingly, too, the slow movements in each of these three quartets are given a visionary intensity, matching The Lindsays' treatment of the slow movement of No 1 in the companion disc.

Here is music from the last years of Haydn's career which in these performances has you thinking forward to middle or late Beethoven and the new world of the 19th century. So the *Adagio* of No 4 brings a hymn-like dedication, not least in the dark E flat minor episode, and the astonishing modulations in the *Fantasia* slow movement of No 6 convey the tingle of new discovery, with magical *pianissimos* for contrast. This was a work which for Donald Tovey marked a tailing-off of inspiration, but one registers the opposite with The Lindsays, when the *adagio* Fantasia gives way to such witty treatment both in the *presto* Minuet (in fact a *scherzo*), with its weird leaps, and the *Allegro spirituoso* finale.

With refined sound that draws out the subtleties of balance between these players, here's another disc of Haydn from The Lindsays that sets the highest standards.

String Quartets, Op 77

String Quartets – Op 77 Nos 1 & 2; Op 103 in   **P**
D minor (unfinished)
Quatuor Mosaïques (Erich Höbarth, Andrea Bischof vns Anita Mitterer va Christophe Coin vc)
Astrée Naïve E8800 (62' · DDD)   Ⓕ

Anyone who thinks that period-instrument performance means austerity and coolness should listen to this disc. Here's playing full of expressive warmth and vigour. The opening of Op 77 No 1 is done duly gracefully, but with a sturdy underlying rhythm and the *Scherzo* is crisp and alive. Then the first movement of the F major work is beautifully done, with many sensitive details; and the lovely second movement is ideally leisurely, so that the players have ample room for manoeuvre and the leader makes much of his opportunities for delicate playing in the filigree-like high music. The players show a real grasp of structure and illuminate the key moments with a touch more deliberation or a little additional weight of tone. These performances, clearly recorded, are competitive not merely within the protected world of 'early music' but in the bigger, 'real' world too!

Seven Last Words, Op 51

The Seven Last Words, Op 51, HobIII Nos 50-56
Rosamunde Quartet
ECM New Series 461 780-2 (66' · DDD)   ⒻⓄⓄ▷

This reading is alert not only to musical texture, but to the modulating phrase and the dramaturgy of key changes between movements. The playing is limpid and subtly coloured, sparing of vibrato (in that respect the Rosamunde are heedful of various period-instrument models) and, at the beginning of the third movement, suspended in a sense of rapture. Another imaginative aspect of this performance is the way it reflects the sense of the text, just as Haydn does in those movements that seem to follow the pattern of the words he set. This feeling of narrative is especially keen in the fourth movement, 'Woman, behold thy son!' and the closing 'Earthquake'.

The list of virtues is fairly simple to enumerate: variety and refinement of tone, internal clarity, historical awareness, imagination and a certain poise that not all its rivals can claim in equal measure. It serves well as a compromise between period-instrument clarity and modern-instrument warmth. Against strong competition its fuller instrumental sonority is marginally to be preferred. A first-rate CD of a wonderful score.

Seven Last Words, Op 51ᵃ (interspersed with Seven Gregorian Responsories for Holy Weekᵇ)
ᵃ**Carmina Quartet** (Matthias Enderle, Susanne Frank vns Wendy Champney va Stephan Goerner vc)
ᵇ**Schola Romana Lucernensis / Father Roman Bannwart**
Claves 50-2002 (74' · DDD · T/t)   ⒻⓄ

Haydn's *Seven Last Words* was designed for performance in Holy Week, in the Santa Cueva grotto in Cádiz, with discourses from the bishop on each of the seven utterances followed by Haydn's musical meditation. Originally these were orchestral pieces, not the string quartet versions (arranged by Haydn to widen access to the music) which are more often given today. Haydn was concerned that 'seven *Adagios*' would be exhausting to the listener, and probably wouldn't have favoured performing them without a break. The idea of interspersing them with Holy Week Gregorian responsories is certainly an appropriate solution.

The group singing them here is a mixed choir, although we hear either the men or the women, never the two together. They sing in a carefully moulded style, cadences softly rounded off; ensemble is precise, from the women especially. The Carmina Quartet plays with a remarkably wide range of expression. The Introduction is quite fiercely done, and the 'Terremoto' at the end has a violence and is taken at a pace that almost obscures the pulse of the music.

In between, they play the 'seven *Adagios*' (as Haydn called them – actually three *Largos*, two *Graves*, a *Lento* and an *Adagio*) as they would any other Haydn slow movement. The first is quite relaxed and lyrical, although its accents are well marked, and it has touches of added ornamentation. Refinement and delicacy of line characterise the second, and the third, the E major meditation on 'Mother, behold thy son', is done with much tenderness.

In the fourth their realisation of Haydn's notated ornaments – the appoggiaturas in bars 2 and 4, and at several points later – are oddly perverse and disturbing: one played short, the other long, although the second phrase is a clear echo of the first. No 5 ('I thirst') again draws some very telling soft playing from the quartet, but also pained *forzato* accents, and there's forceful expression of 'Consummatum est', along with moments of tenderness. They play the E flat No 7 with the sense of calm and fulfilment that Haydn surely sought. Their tempos, generally, are well chosen, perhaps faster at times than many quartets take these pieces, but this helps bridge the gulf between Haydn's normal mode of expression and the special significance of this remarkable music.

Additional recommendation

Fitzwilliam Quartet   **P**
Linn Records CKD153 (62' · DDD)   Ⓕ
A chaste, inward reading on period instruments, deeply musical, swifter than some but always thoughtfully articulated. A compelling recording.

Piano Trios

HobXV – No 1 in G minor; **No 2** in F; **No 5** in G;
No 6 in F; **No 7** in D; **No 8** in B flat; **No 9** in A;
No 10 in E flat; **No 11** in F minor; **No 12** in E minor;
No 13 in C minor; **No 14** in A flat; **No 15** in G;
No 16 in D; **No 17** in F; **No 18** in A; **No 19** in G
minor; **No 20** in B flat; **No 21** in C; **No 22** in E flat;
No 23 in D minor; **No 24** in D; **No 25** in G, 'Gypsy
Trio'; **No 26** in F sharp minor; **No 27** in C; **No 28** in
E; **No 29** in E flat; **No 30** in E flat; **No 31** in E flat
minor; **No 32** in G; **No 34** in E; **No 35** in A; **No 36** in
E flat; **No 37** in F; **No 38** in B flat; **No 39** in F; **No 40**
in F; **No 41** in G; **No C1** in C; **No f1** in E flat

Complete Piano Trios
Beaux Arts Trio (Menahem Pressler *pf* Isidore Cohen
vn Bernard Greenhouse *vc*)
Philips ⑨ 454 0982 (453' · DDD)   ⑧ⓄⓄⓄ⮕

This is a remarkable and, indeed,
invaluable box, which is unlikely to be
challenged, let alone surpassed. Nowadays, it is not often possible to hail one set of
records as a 'classic' of the gramophone in quite
the same sense as, say, Schnabel's Beethoven
sonatas or the Busch late Beethoven quartets.
Yet this set can surely be said to enjoy this status.
The playing of the Beaux Arts Trio is of the
highest musical distinction, Menahem Pressler's
contribution is little short of inspired; the set
offers astonishingly lifelike recorded sound, and
the repertoire is unfailingly fresh and inventive.
The performances follow the Critical Edition
prepared by HC Robbins Landon, whose tireless researches have increased the number of
trios that we know in the standard edition from
31 to 43. These are records to which one returns
with pleasure and profit, for this music is sane
and intelligent, balm to the soul in a troubled
world. Indeed, it is a set that will last a lifetime.

Piano Trios – Nos 18, 24, 25 & 29
Vienna Piano Trio (Wolfgang Redik *vn*
Marcus Trefny *vc* Stefan Mendl *pf*)
Nimbus NI5535 (60' · DDD)   ⒻⓄ

The *Gypsy* Trio, No 25, may have been written
in and for London, but this ensemble's short,
snappy bowing, stomping piano accents and
instinctive fluctuations of tempo and pulse in the
finale, locate the work in the grape-treading,
Romany heart of the Burgenland. The steps of
the dance shape and pervade the E-flat Trio,
too, in the jaunty rhythms of the opening *Allegretto*, and the boisterous and cross-accented
Allemande of its finale. Among countless
delights in these bold performances is the sensitivity to the power of silence, and the short,
hushed half-tones within the long-breathed
lines of the *Andante* of the A-major Trio. And,
not least, the perceptive understanding and
judgement of the shifting qualities of an *Allegro*
which so well supports the structure of the outer

movements of the D-major, as well as enabling
many a clearly articulated yet fanciful variation
in the *Gipsy* Trio. These recordings are close,
sometimes breathy, always thrillingly true.

Piano Trios – Nos 24, 25, 26 & 27
Florestan Trio (Anthony Marwood *vn* Richard Lester
vc Susan Tomes *pf*)
Hyperion CDA67719 (64' · DDD)   ⒻⓄⓄ⮕

Tomes and her partners identify themselves
fully with the emotional scale of these works,
ostensibly meant for domestic use on small pianos. But their scope suggests that Haydn structured them for the powerful English Broadwood
instruments suited to the concert hall. The
noise-quelling opening chord of No 24 would
have stopped rowdy audiences of the day in their
tracks.

There is so much from the Florestan to stop us
in our tracks too, not least in their feel for
expressing the content of these sparsely marked
scores, as in the finale of No 24 when *Allegro ma
dolce* in D major changes to a stabbing D minor
before returning to the original key. The musicians intuitively recreate the return even more
sweetly. Their interpretative acumen is unimpeachable. The continuous triplets in the Adagio of No 26, tiresome if badly played, are
instead profoundly yielding. And the *Presto*
finale of No 27 isn't driven on cruise control.

A very special disc, recorded in detailed, front-
row sound.

Keyboard Sonatas

HobXVI: No 1 in C **No 2** in B flat **No 3** in C **No 4** in
D **No 5** in A (doubtful) **No-6** in G **No 7** in C **No 8** in
G **No 9** in F **No 10** in C **No 11** in G **No 12** in A
(doubtful) **No 13** in E (doubtful) **No 14** in D **No 15**
(spurious) **No 16** in E flat (doubtful) **No 17** (spurious)
No 18 in B flat **No 19** in D **No 20** in C minor **No 21**
in D **No 22** in E **No 23** in F **No 24** in D **No 25** in E
flat **No 26** in A **No 27** in G **No 28** in E flat **No 29** in F
No 30 in A **No 31** in E **No 32** in B minor **No 33** in D
No 34 in E minor **No 35** in C **No 36** in C sharp minor
No 37 in D **No 38** in E flat **No 39** in G **No 40** in G
No 41 in B flat **No 42** in D **No 43** in A flat **No 44** in
G minor **No 45** E flat **No 46** in A flat **No 47** in F **No
48** in C **No 49** in E flat **No 50** in C **No 51** in D **No 52**
in E flat **Deest** E flat (doubtful)

Piano Sonatas: HobXVI —Nos 20, 32, 34, 37, 40, 42,
48-52. HobXVII – No 4, Fantasia in C; No 6, Variations
in F minor; No 9, Adagio in F
Alfred Brendel *pf*
Philips ④ 478 1369 (205' · ADD/DDD)   ⒻⓄⓄⓄ⮕

These sonatas are magnificent creations, wonderfully well played by
Alfred Brendel. Within the order and
scale of these works Haydn explores a rich diversity of musical languages, a wit and broadness of

expression that quickly repays attentive listening. It's the capriciousness as much as the poetry that Brendel so perfectly attends to; his playing, ever alive to the vitality and subtleties, makes these discs a delight. The sophistication innate in the simple dance rhythms, the rusticity that emerges, but above all, the sheer *joie de vivre* are gladly embraced. Brendel's continual illumination of the musical ideas through intense study pays huge dividends. The recording quality varies enormously between the different works and though the close acoustic on some of the later discs could be faulted for allowing one to hear too much of the keyboard action, it certainly brings one into vivid contact with the music.

Piano Sonatas: HobXVI – Nos 23, 24, 32, 37, 40, 41, 43, 46, 50 & 52
Marc-André Hamelin pf
Hyperion ② CDA67554 (145' · DDD)　　Ⓕ**OOO**

For long confined to the by-ways of the repertoire, the ever-phenomenal Marc-André Hamelin now breaks out into the light with a two-disc set of Haydn sonatas. And unlike Haydn who considered himself less than a wizard of the keyboard, Hamelin is a prodigious virtuoso. Here, he remains one, in a full if not entirely inclusive sense, often susceptible to Haydn's wit, to vertiginous music which can veer to the right just when you expect it to turn left, and vice versa.

He is brilliantly alert to the first Menuetto from No 43, to a dance at once perky and serious, almost as if the composer with his toy fanfares was trying unsuccessfully to keep a straight face. And he can be hauntingly limpid and serene, as in the alternately calm and troubled *Adagio* from No 46. However, in No 23 one longs for Hamelin to relax his virtuoso prowess. Here, there is an unmistakable sense of hurry, of Haydn's riches glimpsed rather than savoured, of a composer's piquancy nearly bustled out of existence. Others, too, have achieved greater grandeur in the final E flat Sonata or made the storm clouds scud more menacingly across the B minor Sonata's finale (Andsnes, Ax and, most of all, Brendel). None the less, these are astonishing performances. Hyperion's sound and presentation are, as always, immaculate.

Piano Sonatas: HobXVI – Nos 26, 32, 36-7, 49
Leif Ove Andsnes pf
EMI 556756-2 (58' · DDD)　　Ⓕ**O**B→

This disc offers delectable performances of five shrewdly contrasted works: two troubled, trenchant minor-key sonatas from the 1770s juxtaposed with a pair of lightweight pieces from the same period and culminating in the great E flat Sonata. Andsnes is responsive to the individual character of these sonatas, to their richness and variety of incident, and their sheer unpredictablility. With his wide spectrum of colour and dynamics he makes no apologies for using a modern Steinway. But his playing, founded on a pellucid *cantabile*

touch and diamantine passagework, marries classical refinement and clarity with a spontaneous exuberance, a sense that the next phrase is yet to be created. Andsnes is always ready to add stylish and witty touches of embellishment to the repeats. The opening movements of both minor-key sonatas have a lithe, sinewy urgency, above all in the vehement sequences of their developments, together with a rare delicacy of nuance: and here, as elsewhere, you notice how alive and concentrated is his *piano* and *pianissimo* playing. Andsnes brings a bright, buoyant yet lyrical approach to the E flat Sonata's outer movements, to the wonderful *Adagio* a limpid line, a subtly flexed pulse and, in the B flat minor central episode, a true sense of passion. This is just the sort of playing – joyous, imaginative, involving – to win Haydn's sonatas a wider following. The recording of the E flat, made in a church in Oslo, has slightly more ambient warmth than that of the remaining sonatas, recorded at EMI's Abbey Road studios. But throughout, the piano sound is natural and present without being too closely miked.

Piano Sonatas: HobXVI Nos 35-9
Jenö Jandó pf
Naxos 8 553128 (62' · DDD)　　Ⓢ**O**B→

The exquisite, classical balance evident in these six sonatas makes them rewarding examples of Haydn's exploitation of the piano's broad expressive range and rich textural variety. This volume in Jenö Jandó's complete edition presents these pieces in a compelling, modern-instrument version. For example, there's brilliance and sparkle in the opening movements of the D major and E flat Sonatas; warmth and dramatic intensity in the slow movements (most notably in the Baroque echoes of the Sonatas in C major and D major), and an appealing blend of wit and elegance in finales such as the third movement of the D major Sonata. Most remarkable, though, is the G major, where Jandó's precision and sensitive balance of linear and harmonic dimensions convey its concerto character and Haydn's imaginative approach to form. Try Jandó's engaging account of the opening *Allegro*, his deft balance of the slow movement's effective blend of major and minor, and his exuberant virtuosity in the finale.

Haydn Keyboard Sonata HobXVI – No 44
Prokofiev Piano Sonatas – No 2, Op 14; No 6, Op 82. Visions fugitives, Op 22. Legend, Op 12 No 6
Sviatoslav Richter pf
BBC Legends mono BBCL4245-2 (76' · ADD)
Recorded live in 1961　　Ⓕ**O**

Sviatoslav Richter is at the top of virtually everybody's short list of great pianists, and the reasons are not hard to find. His range was engulfing, even when he took a personal and surprising dislike to the most exalted repertoire, weeding out, for example, those Beethoven sonatas he considered less than convincing. This added spice to his early status, further enlivened by his first, belated appearances in the West.

On his arrival in New York and London in the '60s, anticipation pulsed at fever pitch and in the first of three London recitals, now blessedly released by BBC Legends, his unique quality was unmistakable. It is no exaggeration to say that his Haydn and Prokofiev recital was among the greatest ever heard on the South Bank. Here, Haydn's mischief is captured with a silken magic and dexterity peculiarly Richter's own, and who else could characterise so acutely the stylised oddity of Prokofiev's *Visions fugitives*? No one has touched Richter's way with the Second Sonata, its self-consciously prickly utterance resolved in a near-classical transparency. Everything is taken by stealth rather than storm with an unforgettably lyrical second subject, though with an unflagging impetus reserved for the *Scherzo* and for the finale's Tom and Jerry-cartoon caperings. The underlying menace of the composer's *inquieto* direction in the Eighth Sonata is frighteningly caught, a dark and introspective journey that leads through the *Andante*'s faux naïf charm to a finale of blistering strength and propulsion.

Piano Sonatas: HobXVI Nos 49-52
Jenö Jandó *pf*
Naxos 8 550657 (62' · DDD)   ⑤🅑➔

The keyboard sonatas which Haydn originally intended for piano, such as the four considered here, show hi's exploration of the instrument's capacity for greater dynamic variation. Jandó is sensitive to the relationship between motif and dynamics which is particularly evident in the E flat and D major Sonatas respectively. Aided by clear recorded sound, Jandó's warmth in the lyrical passages provides a dramatic contrast to his crisp, positive approach in the livelier music. Jandó's glittering technique has a high profile in the other two sonatas in the programme. His well-turned readings are uncontroversial, but they lack nothing in excitement. Sample the finale of the E flat Sonata, where the wealth of expressive detail at an extremely fast tempo is breathtaking.

Piano Sonatas HobXVI No 33, 36, 43, 45 & 46
Emanuel Ax *pf*
Sony Classical 509970 89363-2 (78' · DDD)   Ⓕ🅑➔

Harpsichord sonorities are never far away here; indeed, they're clearly suggested in the outer movements of No 45. Since it's an early work, Haydn is likely to have written it for this instrument. Not that Emanuel Ax is concerned; he takes the modern piano on its own terms and shuns imitation without alienating these sonatas from their period. Perhaps the sharp transients of a harpsichord or fortepiano might have sharpened the rhetoric of Haydn's musical language. But if some of the force has been blunted by the nature of the piano, then grace, melancholy or lyricism are enhanced. The *Adagio* of No 46

shows how much feeling he can bring to the music through tonal inflexions, and broadening or telescoping the line without breaking stylistic boundaries. In the last movement he's adroit and incisive. Witty, too, in his timing of the demisemiquaver flourishes in the first movement of No 33; but inexplicably straitlaced in the finale because he doesn't decorate any of the repeats in the variations. The contrasts in the last movement of No 36 don't escape his notice. He's sombrely circumspect in the C sharp minor Menuet, brightly expressive in the Trio, perceptive in the Menuet's *da capo* return, as if as a shadow of its former self. The recording is a bit close and bass-shy, but offers no impediment to concentrated listening.

Masses

Masses – in C, Missa in tempore belli (Paukenmesse), HobXXII/9; in B flat, Missa Sancti Bernardi von Offida (Heiligmesse), HobXXII/10. Insanae et vanae curae 🅟
Joanne Lunn *sop* **Sara Mingardo** *contr*
Topi Lehtipuu *ten* **Brindley Sherratt** *bass*
**Monteverdi Choir; English Baroque Soloists /
Sir John Eliot Gardiner**
Philips 470 819-2PH (79' · DDD · T/t)   Ⓕ🅞➔

This rounds off Gardiner's excellent series of the six late Masses, all supreme masterpieces, which Haydn wrote for the nameday each year of the Princess Esterhazy. There's also room for a valuable extra in the motet *Insanae et vanae curae*. Haydn salvaged it from his Italian oratorio *Il ritorno di Tobia*, after he had pruned it, saying that it was 'too good to waste'. With a Latin text replacing the original Italian, it inspires Gardiner and his brilliant team to a searing performance, very different from those you'd get from a cathedral choir.

The Masses also find Gardiner on incisive form. The contrast with Hickox's Chandos cycle is most striking in the *Gloria* of the *Heiligmesse*. Where Hickox makes the music swagger happily, Gardiner directs a biting, crisp reading, with spotlit drums and trumpets and marginally less spring in the rhythm. Contrasts elsewhere are similar, if less marked; Hickox is warmer and more joyful where Gardiner, with some extreme speeds is consistently crisp and fresh.

Both Masses were written in 1796 and the *Heiligmesse* first performed on the Princess's nameday that year. The *Paukenmesse* was held over until 1797, though it had been heard in Vienna the previous December. Not only are both Masses smaller in scale than the succeeding four, the *Paukenmesse* at least is more lyrical, less grandly symphonic that those masterpieces. Haydn is still intent on springing surprises; he characteristically ends each with vigorous, even military settings of the 'Dona nobis pacem' which foreshadow Beethoven' illustration of war in the *Missa solemnis*.

The recording is clear and well balanced, highlighting the pinpoint ensemble of Gardiner's choir and his excellent team of soloists.

Masses – in G, Missa 'Rorate coeli desuper',   ℗
HobXXII/3; in B flat (Schöpfungsmesse), HobXXII/13
(with alternative setting of the Gloria)
Susan Gritton sop **Pamela Helen Stephen** mez
Mark Padmore ten **Stephen Varcoe** bar **Collegium
Musicum 90 Chorus; Collegium Musicum 90 /
Richard Hickox**
Chandos Chaconne CHAN0599 (62' · DDD · T/t)
Ⓕ**O**▶

The *Creation* Mass is no less resplendent or
searching than, say, the *Nelson* Mass or the *Harmoniemesse*, a glorious affirmation of Haydn's
reverent, optimistic yet by no means naive faith.
Even by Haydn's standards, the work is startling
in its exploitation of colourful and dramatic key
contrasts, as in the sudden swerve from F major
to an apocalyptic *fortissimo* D flat at 'Judicare
vivos'; the *Benedictus*, characteristically, moves
from serene pastoral innocence (shades of 'With
verdure clad' from *The Creation*) to urgent intensity in its central development; and the sublime
G major *Agnus Dei* has a profound supplicatory
fervour extraordinary even among the composer's many memorable settings of this text.

This reading eclipses previous recordings in
the quality of its choir and soloists, the subtlety
of Hickox's direction and the vividness and
transparency of the recorded sound. In faster
movements like the *Kyrie* and the openings of
the *Gloria* and *Credo* Hickox strikes just the right
balance between dignity and happy, pulsing
energy, relishing each of Haydn's dramatic
coups; and he brings a marvellous clarity and
verve, and a sure sense of climax, to the chromatically inflected fugues in the *Gloria* and at
'Dona nobis pacem'. Abetted by his first-rate
orchestra, Hickox is always alive to the felicities
of Haydn's scoring, while the 24-strong professional choir is superbly responsive throughout.

We also get the alternative version of the
Gloria, and the ultra-compressed (6'49") and
instantly forgettable *Missa rorate coeli desuper*,
which David Wyn Jones, in his excellent note,
wryly describes as 'a reminder of how perfunctory church music in 18th-century Austria could
be'. It's neatly dispatched by Hickox and his
forces, but inevitably comes as an anticlimax.

Masses – in E flat (Great Organ Mass), HobXXII/4a; ℗
in C, Missa Celensis (Mariazeller), HobXXII/8
Susan Gritton sop **Louise Winter** mez **Mark Pad-
more** ten **Stephen Varcoe** bar **Alan Watson** org
Collegium Musicum 90 / Richard Hickox
Chandos Chaconne CHAN0674 (71' · DDD)   Ⓕ**OO**▶

This concluding issue in Richard Hickox's
prize-winning Haydn Mass series follows a similar pattern to earlier discs, offering exhilarating
performances which wear their period style
lightly. Gardiner for Philips is by a fraction the
more crisply incisive, with pinpoint attack and
clean textures: Hickox generally prefers slightly
broader speeds, with full, immediate sound,
more clearly bringing out the joy of Haydn's
inspiration as well as the drama.

Both of these Masses are relatively neglected,
even on disc. The *Great Organ* Mass, dating
from 1768-9, seems not to have been composed for a special occasion, but, exceptionally, because Haydn wanted to write it. It's a
distinctive work, both in its choice of key,
E flat, rare for a Mass of the time, and for
replacing oboes in the orchestra with two cor
anglais.

The role of the organ is far more important,
though; its Baroque figuration attractively decorative, while the *Benedictus* includes a concertante organ part, accompanying the quartet of
soloists. Choosing light registration, Ian Watson
produces delightful sounds throughout, with
delicate organ decorations set in contrast with
the relatively plain choral writing. As in the rest
of the Hickox series, the singing and playing of
Collegium Musicum 90 is most stylish.

Hickox has a special relish for Haydn's rhythmic exuberance, as in the syncopated Amens in
the *Sanctus* and the robust 6/8 rhythms of the
'Dona nobis pacem' at the very end.

The *Mariazeller* Mass, written much later in
1782, was the last Mass setting that Haydn composed before the final six masterpieces, and
already points forward. As in those late Masses,
the *Kyrie* is in a compressed sonata form: a slow
introduction leads to a vigorous *Allegro*, with the
'Christe eleison' as the development section.
Clearly, Haydn was already thinking of his Mass
settings in symphonic terms, with striking key-
changes also relating to Haydn's symphonic writing. Even more than in the *Great Organ* Mass,
Hickox brings out the vitality of the writing, as in
the extraordinary 'Dona nobis pacem' at the end,
so wildly syncopated it's almost jazzy. A splendid
culmination to an outstanding series.

Masses – in D minor, Missa 'Sunt bona mixta', ℗
HobXXII/2; in C, Missa Cellensis (Cäcilienmesse),
HobXXII/5.
Susan Gritton sop **Pamela Helen Stephen** mez
Mark Padmore ten **Stephen Varcoe** bass
Collegium Musicum 90 / Richard Hickox
Chandos CHAN0667 (70' · DDD · T/t)   Ⓕ**OO**▶

This is the only current recording of the fragmentary *Missa sunt bona mixta malis*, consisting only of
a brief setting of the *Kyrie* followed by a more
expansive setting of the *Gloria*, which is cut off
after the 'Gratias agimus tibi'. Improbably, the
score was discovered as recently as 1983 in a farm-
house in the north of Ireland. Dating from 1768,
it's tantalising having only a fragment when the
contrapuntal writing presents Haydn at his most
striking in this period. It makes a fascinating supplement to Hickox's superb account of the longest
setting of the liturgy that Haydn ever composed.
The title of the *Missa cellensis* – referring to the
small Austrian town of Mariazell – is misleading in
two ways. It's obviously so when there's another,
later Mass also entitled *Cellensis*, but equally
because it seems highly unlikely that so ambitious
a work as this was ever designed for such a place as
Mariazell: it was more probably written for a

grand occasion in Vienna. So it would surely be less confusing to return to the usual title for this work, 'St Cecilia Mass'.

This is a 'cantata-mass' very different from Haydn's usual settings which involve a single movement for each of the six sections of the liturgy. Here instead, the liturgy is divided into 18 separate movements. Hickox's new version gains over the fine Preston issue from the late 1970s in weight and warmth of expression, helped by the Chandos recording which, while warm, allows ample detail in the many splendid contrapuntal passages. The choir's sopranos are amply bright and boyish and achieve a crisp ensemble. The soloists make an outstanding, responsive team.

Masses – in G, Missa Sancti Nicolai (Nikolaimesse), **P**
HobXXII/6; in B flat, Missa Sancti Bernardi von Offida
(Heiligmesse), HobXXII/10
Lorna Anderson sop **Pamela Helen Stephen** mez
Mark Padmore ten **Stephen Varcoe** bar
Collegium Musicum 90 / Richard Hickox
Chandos Chaconne CHAN0645 (62' · DDD · T/t) ⓕⒹ▸

With fresh, inspiriting work from soloists, chorus and orchestra, the performance of the so-called *Heiligmesse* captures the symphonic impetus and the spiritual and physical exhilaration of this gloriously life-affirming music. Hickox opts for Haydn's original scoring, minus the horn parts and the enhanced parts for clarinets that he later added for a performance in Vienna's Court Chapel. Hickox is ever responsive to the drama and colour of Haydn's orchestral writing, while the 24-strong chorus sings with firm, well-nourished tone over a wide dynamic range and a real care for the meaning of the text. The many high-lying entries are always true, never strained or overblown, and the sopranos rise unflinchingly to their frequent high B flats. The soloists have less to do here than in Haydn's other late Masses: but, led by the plangent, beseeching soprano of Lorna Anderson, they sing with a chamber-music grace and intimacy.

The appealing *Missa brevis* is cast in the 'pastoral' key of G major. Again, the soloists make their mark both individually and in ensemble, with Anderson floating a beautiful line in the 'Gratias' and Mark Padmore launching the expressive G minor 'Et incarnatus est' with gently rounded tone and graceful phrasing. The recorded sound is clear, spacious and carefully balanced, combining vivid orchestral detail with plenty of impact from the chorus.

Masses – in B flat, HobXXII/7, Missa brevis **P**
Sancti Johannis de Deo ('Little Organ Mass');
in B flat (Theresienmesse), HobXXII/12
Janice Watson sop **Pamela Helen Stephen** mez
Mark Padmore ten **Stephen Varcoe** bar
Collegium Musicum 90 Chorus; Collegium
Musicum 90 / Richard Hickox
Chandos CHAN0592 (60' · DDD · T/t) ⓕⒹ▸

Hickox generates the physical and spiritual elation essential to this music, calling to mind Haydn's own much-quoted remark that whenever he praised God his heart leapt with joy. In the glorious *Theresienmesse* of 1799 Hickox's manner is particularly fine in the exultant, springing *Gloria* and the rough-hewn vigour of the *Credo*. He understands, too, the Mass's dramatic and symphonic impetus, bringing a powerful cumulative momentum to the sonata-form 'Dona nobis pacem' and thrillingly tightening the screws in the closing pages. The choir is placed forward, though never at the expense of orchestral detail, keenly observed by Hickox. His uncommonly well-integrated solo quartet framed by the sweet-toned Janice Watson and the gentle, mellifluous Stephen Varcoe, sings with a chamber-musical grace and refinement in the 'Et incarnatus est' and the *Benedictus*. And their supplicatory tenderness in the 'Dona nobis pacem' contrasts arrestingly with the choir's urgent demands for peace.

Hickox also captures the peculiar serenity and innocence of the much earlier *Missa brevis Sancti Johannis de Deo*, or *Little Organ Mass*, its intimacy enhanced here by the use of solo strings. A disc guaranteed to refresh the spirit.

Mass in C, Missa in tempore belli (Paukenmesse), **P**
HobXXII/9. Te Deum in C, HobXXIII/1. Te Deum in
C, HobXXIIIc/2. Alfred, König der Angelsachsen,
HobXXX/5 – Aria des Schutzgeistes; Chor der
Dänen
Nancy Argenta sop **Catherine Denley** mez **Mark**
Padmore ten **Stephen Varcoe** bar **Jacqueline Fox**
spkr **Collegium Musicum 90 Chorus and**
Orchestra / Richard Hickox
Chandos Chaconne CHAN0633 (64' · DDD · T/t)
ⓕⓄ▸

Few other conductors on disc convey so happily the drama, symphonic power and spiritual exhilaration of these glorious works than Richard Hickox. He's fully alive to the ominous unease that permeates the great *Mass in Time of War*, but while others strive for maximum dramatic and rhetorical effect, he directs the Mass with a natural, unforced sense of phrase and pace. The playing of Collegium Musicum 90, led by Simon Standage, is polished and athletic, with detail sharply etched, while the chorus sings with fresh tone and incisive attack. The four soloists are well matched in the anxious C minor *Benedictus*; elsewhere Nancy Argenta brings a pure, slender tone, and a graceful sense of phrase to the *Kyrie*, while in the 'Qui tollis' Stephen Varcoe deploys his mellow baritone with real sensitivity.

The fill-ups are imaginatively chosen. The two *Te Deum* settings epitomise the immense distance Haydn travelled during his career, the rococo exuberance and strict species counterpoint of the little-known early work contrasting with the grandeur and massive, rough-hewn energy of the 1799 setting.

HAYDN NELSON MASS – IN BRIEF

Soloists; The English Concert and Choir / Trevor Pinnock
Archiv Produktion 423 097-2AH   ⒻⓄⓄⓄ▷
A thrilling performance from 1989 of Haydn's 'Mass in times of fear'. Pinnock directs with a winning buoyancy that doesn't neglect the work's charged mood. His soloists are superb and The English Concert Choir sing with tremendous power.

Soloists; Monteverdi Choir; English Baroque Soloists / John Eliot Gardiner
Philips 470 286-2PH   ⒻⓄⓄ▷
Another superb performance characterised by magnificent choral work and thrilling orchestral playing. Gardiner brings his characteristic feel for a work's drama thrillingly to bear on this great work.

Soloists; Collegium Musicum 90 and Choir / Richard Hickox
Chandos CHAN0640   ⒻⓄ▷
Part of Hickox's fine Haydn Mass series, this is well worth hearing, but it's outclassed by the Pinnock and Gardiner for the sheer precision and intensity of their approach. Splendidly recorded, though.

Soloists; London Symphony Chorus; City of London Sinfonia / Richard Hickox
Decca 448 983-2   Ⓑ
If you like Hickox's way with this music but prefer modern instruments, this is well worth acquiring. Excellent solo singing with Barbara Bonney the radiant soprano, and firm, focused choral work from the London Symphony Chorus.

Soloists; Choir of King's College, Cambridge; London SO / Sir David Willcocks
Decca 458 623-2   Ⓑ
Sir David Willcocks's 1962 King's College performance of the *Nelson* Mass takes its place alongside the excellent series of Haydn Masses recorded by George Guest at St John's College, Cambridge.

The two numbers of incidental music Haydn completed for the play *King Alfred* in 1796, shortly before embarking on the Mass, are a real collectors' item. Argenta sings the first hymn-like E flat aria with chaste elegance, while choir and orchestra palpably enjoy themselves in the following number, a rollicking, brassy celebration of the Danes' victory over the Anglo-Saxons. Invigorating performances and first-class recorded sound, with an ideally judged balance between chorus and orchestra.

Mass in D minor (Nelsonmesse), HobXXII/11. Ⓟ
Te Deum in C, HobXXIIIc/2
Dame Felicity Lott *sop* **Carolyn Watkinson** *contr*
Maldwyn Davies *ten* **David Wilson-Johnson** *bar*

The English Concert and Choir / Trevor Pinnock
Archiv Produktion 423 097-2AH (50' · ADD · T/t)
  ⒻⓄⓄⓄ▷

 The British Admiral had ousted the Napoleonic fleet at the Battle of the Nile just as Haydn was in the middle of writing his *Nelson* Mass. Although the news could not have reached him until after its completion, Haydn's awareness of the international situation was expressed in the work's subtitle, 'Missa in Augustiis', or 'Mass in times of fear'. With its rattle of timpani, pungent trumpet calls, and highly strung harmonic structure, there's no work of Haydn's which cries out so loudly for recording on period instruments; and it's the distinctive sonority and highly charged tempos of this performance which set it apart. The dry, hard timpani and long trumpets bite into the dissonance of the opening *Kyrie*, and the near vibrato-less string playing is mordant and urgent. The fast-slow-fast triptych of the *Gloria* is set out in nervously contrasted speeds, and the *Credo* bounces with affirmation. Just as the choral singing is meticulously balanced with instrumental inflexion, so the soloists have been chosen to highlight the colours in Pinnock's palette.

Masses – in D minor (Nelsonmesse), HobXXII/11; Ⓟ
in B flat (Theresienmesse), HobXXII/12. Te Deum in C, HobXXIIIc/2
Donna Brown *sop* **Sally Bruce-Payne** *mez* **Peter Butterfield** *ten* **Gerald Finley** *bass* **Monteverdi Choir; English Baroque Soloists / Sir John Eliot Gardiner**
Philips ② 470 286-2PH (89' · DDD · T/t)   ⓂⓄⓄⓄ

Dating respectively from 1798 and 1799, the *Nelsonmesse* and the *Theresienmesse* are the third and fourth of the six Masses written for the nameday of the Princess Esterházy. That was a period during the Napoleonic wars when Prince Esterházy, Nikolaus II had economised by dismissing his Harmonie or windband. Even so, in 1798 for the *Nelsonmesse*, Haydn, seeking to reflect the mood of the times (hence the official title, *Missa in angustiis* – 'Mass in straitened times'), brought in three trumpets and timpani, and their impact is all the greater when set against strings and organ alone.

That heightened contrast is a point which comes out with thrilling attack in Gardiner's performance at the very opening of the *Kyrie*. This vigorous *Allegro*, typical of Haydn but totally untypical of Mass-settings, introduces martial fanfares, which recur through the whole work. Though Haydn composed the Mass in a mere 53 days in the summer of 1798, just when Nelson was winning the Battle of Aboukir, Haydn knew nothing of that victory till later, and the Nelson association dates from two years later when the admiral visited Eisenstadt, and the Mass was given in his honour.

Gardiner's treatment of the fanfares offers only the first of dozens of examples where his crisp, incisive manner highlights the extraordinary originality of this work. The *Theresienmesse* brings similar revelations. Here, in addition to trumpets and timpani, Haydn scored for two clarinets, and though this is a less sharply dramatic, more lyrical work, a martial flavour is again introduced. There are surprises aplenty, as in the sudden silence of the orchestra in the setting of the word 'miserere' at the end of the 'Gratias agimus tibi', or the setting of 'Et incarnatus' in the *Credo* in the rare key (in this context) of B flat minor, and 'Et vitam venturi' set in a galloping 6/8 time or the bold, square opening of *Agnus Dei* in bare octaves at an unapologetic *forte*. Such points must have startled early listeners, and Gardiner's treatment makes one appreciate that with new ears.

In this respect he even outshines Richard Hickox, whose prize-winning Mass series for Chandos brings equally enjoyable performances of both these works, just as energetic and a degree warmer, thanks in part to the recording acoustic. Gardiner's team, on the other hand, has markedly cleaner separation of textures, with soloists and chorus more sharply defined. Gardiner's Monteverdi Choir as ever sings with passion, brilliance and fine precision, and his soloists are all outstanding, fresh and youthful-sounding with firm clear voices.

As a splendid, very apt bonus there's a superb account of the magnificent ceremonial C major *Te Deum*.

Mass in B flat (Harmoniemesse), HobXXII/14.　**P**
Salve regina in E, HobXXIIIb/1
Nancy Argenta sop **Pamela Helen Stephen** mez
Mark Padmore ten **Stephen Varcoe** bar **Collegium**
Musicum 90 Chorus; Collegium Musicum 90 /
Richard Hickox
Chandos Chaconne CHAN0612 (59' · DDD · T/t)
ⒻⓄ🅑➔

Haydn's first major work, the *Salve regina* of 1756, is here juxtaposed with his last, the *Harmoniemesse* of 1802, so-called because of its exceptionally full scoring for woodwind. The gulf between the two works, in sophistication, mastery and emotional range, is predictably vast. Yet, in their very different ways, both reconcile the formal liturgical conventions of their era with the expression of Haydn's own life-affirming religious faith. Hickox and his forces ideally capture this sense of celebratory spiritual energy. Tempos are lively, rhythms alert and vital. In the Mass Hickox generates an exhilarating symphonic momentum in, say, the opening sections of the *Gloria* and *Credo*, and, aided by an outstandingly clear, well-balanced recording, realises to the full such dramatic *coups* as the sudden swerve into A flat in the recapitulation of the 'Benedictus' and the martial fanfares that slew the music from D major to B flat at the start of the 'Dona nobis pacem'. The steely edged valveless trumpets are thrilling here; and elsewhere the wind players do rich justice to Haydn's glorious writing, nicely balancing rusticity and refinement.

Nancy Argenta's innocent, bell-like tones and graceful sense of line are heard to touching effect in the 'Et incarnatus est' of the Mass. In the *Salve regina*, she also reveals her deft, fluent coloratura technique. No great depths in this youthful work, but Haydn's setting of the Marian antiphon is elegant and affecting, with a command of shapely, Italianate melody and a feeling for dramatic contrast. This is certainly the most memorable work of Haydn's from the 1750s and aptly complements Hickox's fervent, inspiring reading of the *Harmoniemesse*.

Il ritorno di Tobio

Il ritorno di Tobia, HobXXl/1
Roberta Invernizzi, Sophie Karthäuser sops
Ann Hallenberg mez **Anders Dahlin** ten
Nikolay Borchev bass **Cologne Vocal Ensemble;**
Capella Augustina / Andreas Spering
Naxos ③ 8 570300/2 (169' · DDD · T)　　Ⓢ🅑➔

Probably no major Haydn work is harder to 'sell' today than his Italian oratorio *Il ritorno di Tobia*, composed for a Viennese benevolent society during the winter of 1774-75. Far from being a prototype Creation and Seasons, *Tobia* is in effect a sacred *opera seria*, powered by a succession of gargantuan arias, with, in its original version, just three choruses for contrast. For a 1784 revival Haydn spruced it up with two extra choral numbers, including a cataclysmic 'storm' chorus that has become well known as the motet *Insanae et vanae curae*.

The prime stumbling-block is the libretto by Giovanni Gastone Boccherini, brother of the more famous Luigi. With its murders, monsters and miracles, the story of Tobias from the Apocrypha could have been a composer's gift. Instead, Boccherini laboriously observes Classical convention and sets Tobias's adventures entirely in the past tense. When Tobias and his new wife, the serially widowed Sara (husbands one to seven have all been murdered by the demon Asmodeus), eventually appear, the action grinds forward with stultifying slowness, weighed down by reams of sententious moralising. 'Delay could prove fatal', says Tobias to his mother Anna as he prepares to cure his father Tobit's cataract with the gall of a sea monster. He then launches into an eight-minute 'parable' aria, to which his mother rejoinders, 'A just sense of urgency spurs him on'.

Yet while *Tobia* is a virtual non-starter dramatically, Haydn's music is carefully and elaborately composed and, provided you can adjust to the leisurely time-frame, often inspired. The choruses are all superb, the arias inventive and vastly challenging. They include spectacular vocal concertos, enlivened by Haydn's genius for tone-painting, a dulcet E major love song for Tobias, and a terrific F minor 'nightmare' scene for Anna. The oratorio's jewel, though, is Sara's radiant 'Non parmi essere', with its luxurious concertante writing for flutes, oboes, cors anglais, bassoons and horns.

HAYDN'S CREATION – IN BRIEF

Janowitz; Ludwig; Wunderlich; Krenn; Fischer-Dieskau; Berry; Vienna Singerverein; Berlin PO / Herbert von Karajan
DG ② 449 761-2GOR2   Ⓜ **OOOO**▷

A *de luxe* line-up for Karajan's *Creation* (Wunderlich's death halfway through the recording meant that Werner Krenn recorded the recitatives). Karajan's feeling for the music is considerable, and he brings drama as well as intimacy to it.

McNair; Brown; Schade; Finley; Gilfry; Monteverdi Choir; English Baroque Soloists / Sir John Eliot Gardiner   Ⓟ
Archiv Produktion ② 449 217-2AH2   Ⓕ **OOOO**▷

A very fine period-instrument version full of drama and imaginative response to the text. Gardiner's wonderful choir sings superbly and his EBS play thrillingly.

Karthäuser; Kühmeier; Spence; Werba; Henschel; Les Arts Florissants / William Christie   Ⓟ
Virgin Classics ② 395235-2   Ⓑ

A wonderful entry into the Haydn discography by Christie and his French forces. He characterises vividly and lets the music speak for itself. A fine modern period version.

Kermes; Mields; Davislim; Mannoc; Chung; Balthazar-Neumann Choir and Ensemble / Thomas Hengelbrock   Ⓟ
Deutsche Harmonia Mundi ② 05472 77537-2   Ⓕ

A swift, exciting period-instrument recording that has a freshy, appealing youthful feel to it. The soloists are delightful and Hengelbrock's chorus is excellent.

Röschmann; Schade; Gerhaher; Arnold Schoenberg Choir; Concentus Musicus Wien / Nikolaus Harnoncourt   Ⓟ
Deutsche Harmonia Mundi ② 82876 58340-2   Ⓕ **OO**

Harnoncourt returns to *The Creation* after 18 years, this time on period insturments, and gives a wise, spiritually satisfying performance. The soloists are superb and the chorus sing magnificently. A period version to rival the Gardiner.

Im; Kobow; Müller-Brachmann; Cologne Vocal Ensemble; Capella Augustina / Andreas Spering
Naxos ② 8 557380/1   Ⓢ **OO**▷

A splendid bargain-price version which combines power and freshness. Youthful voices and a fine chorus add to its attractions.

Piau; Persson; Massey; Padmore; Harvey; Davies; Gabrieli Consort and Players / Paul McCreesh   Ⓟ
Archiv ② 477 7361AH2   Ⓕ **OOOO**▷

A superb English language *Creation* done on a grand scale. Magnificent!

This new recording is even better than that the old (and long-deleted) Dorati version. The pacing is generally sharper (crucial in the many accompanied recitatives), while the period instruments of the Capella Augustina make for altogether tangier, more transparent sonorities than Dorati's smoothly upholstered RPO. Valveless brass lour and exult in the choral numbers, while the faintly breathy, bucolic period woodwind carol enchantingly in "Non parmi essere". This aria is exquisitely sung by the pellucid-toned Sophie Karthäuser, a true classical stylist, who negotiates the coloratura in her opening aria with grace and panache. The other female singers match her in virtuosity and vocal allure. The bell-toned Roberta Invernizzi is properly dazzling in the flamboyant arias for the (disguised) Archangel Raphael, while mezzo Ann Hallenberg uses the text imaginatively and brings a ferocious intensity to her nightmare aria, abetted by Spering's dangerous energy and the baleful colouring of brass and cors anglais. In the predominantly lyrical role of Tobit, Nikolay Borchev impresses with his warm, soft-grained bass and sympathetic phrasing. Only the pleasant but protein-deficient tenor of Anders Dahlin, as Tobias, leaves one wanting more. The choral singing is fresh and eager, though, as so often, the recorded balance rather favours the orchestra. There is also too much pingy harpsichord continuo for some tastes. But these are minor drawbacks in a stunning performance of some glorious, under-valued music. Haydn lovers should snap it up as a matter of urgency.

The Creation (Die Schöpfung)

Die Schöpfung   Ⓟ
Sylvia McNair, Donna Brown *sops* **Michael Schade** *ten* **Rodney Gilfry, Gerald Finley** *bars*
Monteverdi Choir; English Baroque Soloists / Sir John Eliot Gardiner
Archiv Produktion ② 4776327 (101' · DDD · T)
     Ⓜ **OOOO**▷

With Gardiner's first down-beat it's obvious that Chaos's days are numbered. Not that 'days' (strictly speaking) are in question till the mighty words have been spoken, and then, in this performance, what an instantaneous blaze! No premonitory intimation (of pre-echo in the old days whereas now even the faintest stirring in the ranks of the choir will do it), but a single-handed switching-on of the cosmic power-grid and a magnificently sustained C major chord to flood the universe with light. This is one of the great characteristics here: the superbly confident, precise attack of choir and orchestra. Enthusiasm, then, in plenty; but how about the mystery of Creation? It's certainly part of the aim to capture this, for the bass soloist's 'Im Anfange' ('In the beginning') with *pianissimo* chorus has rarely been so softly and so spaciously taken: the Spirit that moved upon the face of the waters is a veiled, flesh-creeping presence, felt again in the first sunrise and the 'softer beams with milder light' of the first moon. Even so, others have incorporated this element more naturally.

Gardiner has an excellent Raphael in Gerald Finley, and gains from having extra singers for Adam and Eve, especially as the Eve, Donna Brown, brings a forthright style doubly welcome after the somewhat shrinking-violet manner and breathy tone of Sylvia McNair's Gabriel. On the whole, Gardiner is sound: yet his is a fun Creation and a real enrichment of the library. Against others of comparable kind, Gardiner stands firm as an easy first choice: a re-creator of vision, a great invigorator and life-enhancer.

Die Schöpfung   P
Sunhae Im sop **Jan Kobow** ten **Hanno Müller-Brachmann** bass **Cologne Vocal Ensemble; Capella Augustina / Andreas Spering**
Naxos ② 8 557380/1 (105' · DDD)   ⑤◐◐▷

Recorded in Cologne in July 2003 by German Radio, this issue offers a first-rate period performance of Haydn's masterpiece, lively and well sung. Since other issues of *Die Schöpfung* in the super-budget category use modern instruments it fills an important gap, particularly as the digital sound is so clear and transparent. Andreas Spering successfully brings out the composer's eternal freshness.

The prelude representing Chaos is taken slowly, markedly more so than by Gardiner or Brüggen, but that brings out all the more the abrasiveness of Haydn's daring dissonances. After the extreme hush of that opening the choral cry of 'Licht' is shattering in its impact; in the following tenor aria Spering shows his true colours in a crisp, faster-than-usual *Andante* that's exhilaratingly carefree, not least at the felicitous passage, marked *sotto voce*, when the chorus sings of 'eine neue Welt'. His speeds are generally on the fast side, but when, as in the prelude, the marking is *Largo* as opposed to *Andante* or *Adagio*, he takes a measured view.

The Cologne Vocal Ensemble is a relatively compact body, incisive in its attack, and set in a helpful but not over-large acoustic. The three soloists are all excellent and youthful-sounding.

An outstanding bargain.

The Creation (sung in English)
Sandrine Piau, Miah Persson sops **Ruth Massey** contr **Mark Padmore** ten **Peter Harvey** bar **Neal Davies** bass **Gabrieli Consort and Players / Paul McCreesh**
Archiv Produktion ② 477 7361AH2 (110' · DDD)   Ⓕ◐◐▷

Haydn and his librettist Baron van Swieten conceived *The Creation* as the first bilingual oratorio and would surely have been perplexed that Anglophone record-buyers seem to prefer the work in German. The main problem, of course, is that the Baron's command of English failed to match his self-confidence, prompting many attempts to improve on the original.

On this new recording, Paul McCreesh's emendations are less radical than those on the two other available versions in English (from Simon Rattle and Robert Shaw), but on the whole more successful, retaining all the Milton-inspired quaintness of van Swieten's text while rectifying his mistranslations and clumsy Germanic word order.

Language apart, McCreesh's recording differs from its period competitors in scale: where they typically use a smallish professional choir and an orchestra of around 50, McCreesh pits a 113-strong band against a chorus of similar numbers. Abetted by the glowing, spacious acoustics of Watford Town Hall, the big celebratory choruses make a more powerful impact than in any of the rival period versions. Occasionally – say in the rollicking fugue in 'Awake the harp', here done at a constant *fortissimo* – one would have welcomed more nuanced dynamics. But there is no denying the incandescence of the climaxes to 'The heavens are telling' and the final 'Praise the Lord, uplift your voices'.

In all the choruses McCreesh's pacing – eager but never hectic – and rhythmic energy are wonderfully inspiriting. He is acutely responsive, too, to the work's mystery and awe, daring, and vindicating, slower-than-usual tempi for 'Chaos' (launched by the most apocalyptic of timpani rolls), the Sunrise and the first morning in Paradise, celestially evoked by the Gabrieli's trio of flutes. A pity, though, that he allows the cannon-fire timpani to pre-empt Haydn's cosmic blaze at 'light'.

McCreesh's trump card is his solo team, superb both individually and as an exceptionally sensitive ensemble. Has the trio near the close of Part 2, 'On thee each living soul awaits', ever been sung with such radiant inwardness? Other highlights include Sandrine Piau's graceful, smiling 'With verdure clad', here a truly happy song to the spring, Mark Padmore's tender *legato* in Haydn's portrayal of the first woman, and Neal Davies's deep, velvet softness in 'the limpid brook' and his hieratic reverence in the sublime arioso 'Be fruitful all, and multiply'. Peter Harvey, supple and lyrical, and Miah Persson, with a touch of sensuousness in her vernal tone, are beautifully paired as Adam and Eve. For a *Creation* in English, this new version – exhilarating, poetic and marvellously sung – becomes the prime recommendation.

Die Schöpfung
Edith Mathis sop **Christoph Prégardien** ten **René Pape** bass **Lucerne Festival Chorus; Scottish Chamber Orchestra / Peter Schreier**
Video Director **Elisabeth Birke-Malzer**
ArtHaus Musik DVD 100 040 (109' · Region 0)   Ⓕ

This enjoyable performance of Haydn's supreme choral masterpiece was recorded at the Lucerne

Festival of 1992. It takes place in the appropriate setting of an evocative baroque church, which isn't identified either on screen or in the (inadequate) supporting booklet. The small choir sings with attentive enthusiasm, and is weak only in the tenor department. The Scottish Chamber Orchestra players cover themselves in glory both as an ensemble and individually, and they're adept at imposing period practice on modern instruments. Schreier's direction is relaxed and benevolent, yet his keen ear for rhythmic precision and flexibility in phrasing is constantly felt.

The soloists are all Swiss. The veteran Mathis remains a paragon of classical style, phrasing her arias and contributions to the ensembles with firm tone and finely honed phrasing. Prégardien's liquid, silvery tenor and sensitive way with words is just what the tenor part calls for. The young Pape's sonorous bass and confident delivery are ideal; he and Mathis make an appealing Adam and Eve in Part 3.

The video direction is discreet, and prompt in homing in on the right performer at the right time. The sound picture is as spacious and well defined.

The Seasons (Die Jahreszeiten)

Die Jahreszeiten   P
Barbara Bonney sop **Anthony Rolfe Johnson** ten
Andreas Schmidt bar **Monteverdi Choir; English Baroque Soloists / Sir John Eliot Gardiner**
Archiv Produktion ② 431 818-2AH2 (127' · DDD · T/t)
Ⓕ❍❍↦

The comparative unpopularity of Haydn's *The Seasons* when considered against *The Creation* is understandable perhaps, but it isn't all that well deserved. Less exalted its subject and libretto may be, but its depiction of the progress of the year amid the scenes and occupations of the Austrian countryside drew from its composer music of unfailing invention, benign warmth and constant musical-pictoral delights. As usual, Gardiner and his forces turn in disciplined, meticulously professional performances, though the orchestra is slightly larger – and consequently a tiny bit less lucid – than the sort you might nowadays find playing a classical symphony. The choir, however, performs with great clarity and accuracy, and brings, too, an enjoyable sense of characterisation to their various corporate roles.

The soloists all perform with notable poise and intelligence: Barbara Bonney's voice is pure and even, Anthony Rolfe Johnson sounds entirely at ease with the music, and Andreas Schmidt is gentle-voiced but certainly not lacking in substance. A first-class recommendation.

Die Jahreszeiten
Marlis Petersen sop **Werner Güra** ten **Dietrich Henschel** bar **RIAS Chamber Choir, Berlin; Freiburg Baroque Orchestra / René Jacobs**

Harmonia Mundi CD/SACD ② HMC80 1829/30 (125' · DDD · T/t)
Ⓕ❍❍❍

It would be hard to imagine a more joyful account of Haydn's culminating masterpiece. Jacobs and his outstanding team perfectly capture the exuberance with which the composer seemed to be defying the years. Infectious rhythms bring out the fun of *The Seasons* from the start, and when in Simon's first aria Haydn quotes from the slow movement of the *Surprise* Symphony, Jacobs nudges the music persuasively. And in the final chorus of 'Summer', the lowing cattle and quail's cry, and chirping crickets and croaking frogs, sound witty, not naive.

In all this Jacobs is helped by a clear and immediate recording. The RIAS Chamber Choir is a fair match for Gardiner's Monteverdi Choir, and the soloists are first-rate, fresh and youthful-sounding. A final choice is a matter of taste but this newer account's greater sense of relaxation and feeling for the fun in the writing make its claims second to none.

Additional recommendation

The Seasons (highlights)
Janowitz sop **Hollweg** ten **Berry** bar **Chor der Deutschen Oper, Berlin; Berlin Philharmonic Orchestra / Karajan**
EMI Encore 574977-2 (DDD)   Ⓑ
A fine, polished reading, well recorded.

Folksong arrangements

Scottish Songs for William Whyte
Lorna Anderson sop **Jamie MacDougall** ten
Haydn Trio Eisenstadt
Brilliant Classics ③ 93453 (3h 32' · DDD · T/t)   Ⓢ

'Up in the morning early' is the title of one of these songs, and we gather from the singer that it's not for her. But if the music of one composer could be guaranteed to cheer the process it would be Haydn's. In whatever mood he writes he carries a wholesome conviction that life is good.

His folksong arrangements are the unexpected, joyous and fairly lucrative work of old age. He came to them through the advances of George Thomson of Edinburgh, and previous volumes in this admirable edition have included the 200-odd written for that enterprising collector and publisher. His contributions were so successful that competitors became interested, and Haydn, on to a good thing, did not turn them down.

His immense output was maintained at an amazingly consistent standard of freshness and apparently effortless invention. Equally consistent is the standard of performance, the singers ideally suited to their task, the instrumentalists unfailingly lively and stylish in their playing.

The distinctive feature of this fourth volume is that these songs were written for one of the rival publishers, William Whyte, and include some of the best-known such as 'John

Anderson, my Jo' and 'Auld lang syne', set to a jaunty, light-footed rhythm with no hint of Hogmanay mawkishness. Tales of laddies sent to the wars and lasses left forlorn at home are familiar subject-matter. Some, like 'The braes of Bellenden', come close to the condition of what we call art-song, and several of the melodies require of the singer nimble fluency over a wide range. For ourselves, we are never in danger of forgetting that all are in the Scottish folk tradition, for the texts require frequent recourse to the thoughtfully provided glossary – alas in microscopic type!

Opera arias

'L'infedeltà costante'   🅟
La fedeltà premiata – Sinfonia; Barbaro conte… È questa la mercè; Dell' amor mio fedele; Placidi ruscelletti. **Orlando paladino** – Sinfonia; Ad un guardo. **La vera costanza** – Sinfonia; Misera, chi m'aiuta…; Dove fuggo. **L'infedeltà delusa** – Ho un tumore in un ginocchio; Trinche vaine allegramente. **L'isola disabitata** – Overtura; Se non piange un infelice. Arianna a Naxos. Sono Alcina, e sono ancora, HobXXIVb/9 (insertion aria for Gazzaniga's L'isola di Alcina). D'una sposa meschinella, HobXXIVb/2 (insertion aria for Paisiello's La frascatana)
Anna Bonitatibus *mez*
Il Complesso Barocco / Alan Curtis
Deutsche Harmonia Mundi 🔊 88697 32632-2 (78' · DDD/DSD)   🅕🅞🅓➔

A captivating, show-stealing Cherubino at Covent Garden, Italian mezzo Anna Bonitatibus quarries arias from Haydn's still rarely aired Eszterháza operas, ranging from a brace of *buffo* songs for the disguised Vespina in *L'infedeltà delusa*, via numbers for the gentle shepherdess Celia and the upwardly mobile Amaranta from *La fedeltà premiata*, to the fisher-girl Rosina's magnificent, despairing outburst from *La vera costanza*.

She also throws in two modestly charming 'insertion' arias Haydn composed for Eszterháza revivals of operas by Paisiello and Gazzaniga, and ends with the great keyboard-accompanied cantata *Arianna a Naxos* that quickly became a favourite in the salons of Vienna and London.

On disc Bonitatibus's quick vibrato, characteristic of singers south of the Alps, may initially faze those accustomed to 'straighter' voices in 18th-century music. Sometimes – as in the opening of Arianna's final aria – she sacrifices a pure *legato* to intensity of expression. That said, Bonitatibus brings to each of these portraits a rich, flavoursome voice and a flair for characterisation, relishing the sound and sense of the words (an Italian always has a head start in this repertoire). She is splendidly imperious in Alcina's fiery entrance aria (*Orlando paladino*), amusingly over-the-top in Vespina's consumptive old woman act, and catches every shade of the distraught Rosina's fluctuating emotions.

Alan Curtis is not the most poetic of fortepianists in *Arianna*, and as conductor sometimes lets rhythms plod in slower numbers. But in the main he encourages lively, characterful playing from his period band, whether in a rip-roaring account of the 'hunting' overture to *La fedeltà premiata* (which Haydn recycled as the finale to Symphony No 73) or as eager colluders in Vespina's comic play-acting.

L'anima del filosofo, ossia Orfeo ed Euridice –   🅟
Chi spira e non sprea; Il pensier sta negli aggetti; Mai non sia inulto. **Armida** – Se dal suo braccio; Teco lo guida al campo. **La fedeltà premiata** – Sappi, che la bellezza; Mi dica, il mio signore; Di questo audace ferro. **L'incontro improvviso** – Noi pariamo santarelli. **L'infedeltà delusa** – Non v'e rimedio. **L'isola disabitata** – Chi nel cammin d'onore. **Il mondo della luna** – Non aver di me sospetto[a]; Che mondo amabile. **Orlando Paladino** – Mille lampi d'accese; Ombre insepolte. **La vera costanza** – Non sparate… mi disdico. Dice benissimo, HobXXIVb/5. Un cor sì tenero, HobXXIVb/11
Thomas Quasthoff *bass-bar* [a]**Genia Kühmeier** *sop*
Freiburg Baroque Orchestra / Gottfried von der Goltz
DG 477 7469GH (63' · DDD · T/t)   🅕🅞🅞🅓➔

'These arias are glorious music that give me more pleasure each time I sing them,' enthuses Thomas Quasthoff of his Haydn anniversary recital encompassing 11 roles from nine operas. Judging the arias by Mozartian standards (unfair, but hard to avoid when the idiom is so similar), we might feel that Haydn's response to character and dramatic situation can occasionally seem too amiably non-committal. Far more often, though, Quasthoff's encomium is well justified, whether in the sharp comic portrayals of assorted dolts, lechers and buffoons, the sepulchral solo for the Stygian ferryman Caronte (*Orlando Paladino*), or the graceful *cantabile* arias for Creonte from the London opera *L'anima del filosofo*. If Haydn's operas are alien territory for you, the range and inventiveness of these arias (plus one duet) may come as a surprise.

Quasthoff's performances are vividly imagined and splendidly sung. He characterises each role with relish. As ever, he savours the sound and sense of the words, greedily gobbling up his consonants in the song of the gluttonous monk Calandro (*L'incontro improvviso*). In serious mode, he brings a gravely eloquent *legato* to the numbers for Caronte and Creonte, and commands both the height and the depth for the fine, dignified arias from *Armida* and *L'isola disabitata*.

Once or twice Quasthoff's softer singing sounds unsupported, starved of natural resonance. Nit-pickers might also point to moments where he coarsens his tone in the name of dramatic intensity. But these are minor provisos. Quasthoff has done a still-neglected corner of Haydn's output proud, and the rhythmically lively Freiburg period band match him all the way in colour and gusto.

L'anima del filosofo

L'anima del filosofo, ossia Orfeo et Euridice   Ⓟ
Uwe Heilmann ten Orfeo **Cecilia Bartoli** mez
Euridice, Genio **Ildebrando d'Arcangelo** bass
Creonte **Andrea Silvestrelli** bass Pluto **Angela
Kazimierczuk** sop Baccante **Roberto Scaltriti** bar
First Chorus **Jose Fardilha** bass Second Chorus
Colin Campbell bar Third Chorus **James Oxley** ten
Fourth Chorus **Chorus and Orchestra of the
Academy of Ancient Music /
Christopher Hogwood**
L'Oiseau-Lyre ② 452 668-2OHO2 (124' · DDD · T/t)
Ⓕ Ⓞ ◗

Christopher Hogwood builds his band on the
model of those prevalent in late 18th-century
London theatres. Not only does his phrasing
and articulation discover no end of witty and
poignant nuances, but the grave austerity of the
string playing, and the plangency of the early
woodwind instruments are eloquent advocates
of an opera whose uncompromisingly tragic
ending owes more to Ovid and Milton than to
operatic tradition. Hogwood also remembers
that Haydn was writing for a Handelian London
choral tradition: his chorus, be they cast as
Cupids, Shades or Furies, have robust presence,
and sculpt their lines with firm muscle.

Cecilia Bartoli takes the role of Euridice. In
her very first aria, 'Filomena abbandonata', she
understands and eagerly re-creates the type of
coloratura writing which simultaneously fleshes
out the central nightingale simile and incarnates
the single word 'crudeltà'. Her unmistakable,
melting half-voice comes into its own as emotion first clouds reason, only to create the fatal
emotional extremes to which she gives voice so
thrillingly. Uwe Heilmann is just the tenor of
rare agility and wide vocal range vital for this
particular Orfeo. The minor parts are strongly
profiled: d'Arcangelo is a stern, noble Creonte,
Silvestrelli a fearsome, stentorian Pluto – and
there's even a convincing *strepito ostile* off-stage
as Euridice's abduction is attempted in Act 2.
Beyond the detail, it's the poignancy of the
musical drama at the heart of this strange, grave
Orfeo which Hogwood reveals with such sympathetic and imaginative insight.

Orlando Paladino

Orlando Paladino   Ⓟ
Patricia Petibon sop Angelica **Christian Gerhaher**
bar Rodomonte **Michael Schade** ten Orlando
Werner Güra ten Medoro **Johannes Kalpers** ten
Licone **Malin Hartelius** sop Eurilla **Markus Schäfer**
ten Pasquale **Elisabeth von Magnus** mez Alcina
Florian Boesch bass Caronte
Concentus Musicus Wien / Nikolaus Harnoncourt
Deutsche Harmonia Mundi ② 82876 73370-2
(141' · DDD · S/T/t/N). Recorded live   Ⓕ

Nikolaus Harnoncourt boldly proclaims that
Orlando Paladino 'is one of the best works in

18th-century music theatre'. Written to commemorate a visit by Russian royalty to Eszterháza that never materialised, *Orlando Paladino*
was first performed in 1782, in celebration of
Prince Nikolaus's name-day.

Sabine Gruber's conversational essay explains
how Haydn's musical portraits show an astute
affection for Ariosto's epic poem. Although
Haydn's *Orlando Paladino* seems part-pantomime,
part-fantasy, these characters are never conscious
that they are not what they protest to be. Like
Ariosto, Haydn lets the audience in on the joke
but the characters remain blissfully oblivious to
the hypocrisy or naivety of their richly ironic
statements to themselves and each other.

Harnoncourt's exemplary team of singers
deliver deadpan comedy. For instance, Werner
Güra takes on an *opera seria* posture as the romantic 'hero' Medoro in 'Parto, Ma, oh Dio': the
glorious musical language suggests he suffers
from sincere passion, but his real motivation is
cowardice. One imagines that Patricia Petibon's
Angelica is merely emulating the heroic fidelity
and courage of women like Mozart's Konstanze
but during 'Non partir, mia bella face' one suspects that there is sincerity in her after all:
Angelica is facing possible abandonment and her
vulnerability shows through. Michael Schade's
voice is smokier than it used to be but his powerful resonant high notes, expressive weight and
authority suggest that Orlando is more victim
than villain. Only the comic secondary roles sung
by Markus Schäfer and Malin Hartelius get
hammed up, but they each sing with élan.

There is a vivid sense of dramatic intensity in
this live concert recording. It is historically absurd
to employ a lute as part of the continuo team in a
late-18th-century opera but Harnoncourt leads
Concentus Musicus Wien through a fizzing theatrical performance. This is comfortably among
the finest Haydn opera recordings, although the
stingy omission of scene numbers and stage directions from the libretto is unhelpful.

Michael Haydn   Austrian 1737–1806

*Michael Haydn, younger brother of Joseph Haydn,
sang with his brother at St Stephen's Cathedral,
Vienna, and in 1757-63 was Kapellmeister to the
Bishop of Grosswardein. From 1763 he was court
musician and Konzertmeister to the Prince-Archbishop of Salzburg, also writing music for the court.
He had much contact with the Mozart family, and
he, Mozart and Adlgasser wrote an act each of the
oratorio Die Schuldigkeit des ersten Gebots (1767).
He became organist at the Holy Trinity Church in
1777, and cathedral organist (succeeding Mozart) in
1781. Under the church reforms of the 1780s he
wrote simpler sacred music; meanwhile his reputation grew, and he later composed several works for the
Empress Maria Theresia. Among his pupils was the
young Carl Maria von Weber.*

Haydn contributed most in the field of sacred music, writing 38 masses and over 300 other church works; most are for four solo voices, four-part choir and orchestra (sometimes with wind instruments). Fugues often appear, and some masses are in a strict contrapuntal style; there is less florid solo writing than in many sacred works of the day. His Requiem in C minor (1771) probably influenced Mozart's later setting. His instrumental works include c40 symphonies, many of them vigorous and inventive and some having fugal finales, concertos, minuets etc, and chamber music including many divertimentos, 12 string quartets and four duets for violin and viola (which Mozart made into a set of six). He also composed Singspiels, incidental music to Voltaire's Zaire (1777), an opera seria (1787), oratorios, cantatas and other secular vocal works. His partsongs for unaccompanied male voices were among the earliest written. **GROVE**music

Masses

Requiem (Missa pro defuncto Archiepiscopo Sigismundo), MH155 KI I/8. Missa in honorem Sanctae Ursulae, MH546 KI I/18
Carolyn Sampson sop **Hilary Summers** contr **James Gilchrist** ten **Peter Harvey** bass **The King's Consort Choir; The King's Consort / Robert King**
Hyperion ② CDA67510 (84' · DDD · T/t) Ⓜ ❍❍❍

Robert King suggests that Michael Haydn's Requiem of 1771 for the Archbishop-Prince of Salzburg reflects a personal outpouring of grief for the loss of Haydn's beloved patron and the recent death of his infant daughter. The fervent expressions of grief, consolation and hope must have made some impression on the 15-year-old Mozart. A comparison with Mozart's Requiem setting of 20 years later is inevitable: Haydn didn't give his solo quartet anything that compares with the immediacy of Mozart's 'Tuba mirum', but the older man's masterful choral writing, brilliant orchestral scoring and sensitive use of solo voices created plenty of musical riches and dramatic moods, such as the brooding *Kyrie* and the bursting energy of the 'Dies irae'.

The quartet of soloists is impeccable; the choir and orchestra of The King's Consort prove to be increasingly assured and dynamic with each recording released. Robert King's measured and emphatic direction makes it easy to appreciate why the Requiem was performed at his brother Joseph's funeral in 1809.

His interpretation of the sunnier, extrovert *Missa in honorem Sanctae Ursulae* (1793) helps the music to sound natural and spontaneous. In some respects the Mass is an even finer composition, full of charismatic and inventive musical charms (it's worth buying for Carolyn Sampson's ravishing 'Benedictus' alone).

Anybody who enjoys the choral works of Mozart and Joseph Haydn will be delighted by this double-disc set, and will probably concur that Michael Haydn's neglect in the shadow of his younger friend and older brother is substantially corrected by these exquisite performances.

Johann Heinichen   German 1683-1729

Initially an advocate, German composer and theorist Heinichen composed music for the Weissenfels court, then moved to Leipzig (1709), where he presented operas and directed a collegium musicum. He also worked at Zeitz and Naumburg. In 1710-16 he lived in Italy and had two operas staged in Venice in 1713. From 1717 he was Kapellmeister (with JC Schmidt) at the Dresden court. **GROVE**music

Concertos

Concertos – C, S211; G, S213; G, S214,'Darmstadt'; Ⓟ S214, Venezia'; G, S215; G, S217; F, S226; F, S231; F, S232; F, S233; F, S234; F, S235. Serenata di Moritzburg in F, S204. Sonata in A, S208. Movement in C minor, S240
Musica Antiqua Köln / Reinhard Goebel
Archiv Produktion ② 4776330 (137' · DDD)
Ⓕ ❍❍❍▷

Ⓖ   Johann David Heinichen was a contemporary of Bach and one of an important group of musicians employed by the Dresden court during the 1720s and 1730s. As well as being an inventive composer, Heinichen was also a noted theorist and his treatise on the continuo bass was widely admired. All the music collected here was probably written for the excellent Dresden court orchestra and most of it falls into that rewarding category in which north and central German composers were pre-eminent. Vivaldi had provided effective models but the predilection for drawing upon other influences, too, gives the concertos of the Germans greater diversity. Heinichen admittedly doesn't so readily venture into the Polish regions whose folk-music gives such a piquancy to Telemann's concertos and suites, but the wonderful variety of instrumental colour and deployment of alternating 'choirs' is every bit as skilful. Your attention will be held from start to finish. Much of the credit for this must go to Reinhard Goebel and his impeccably drilled Musica Antiqua Köln. Some of these pieces might well seem less entertaining in the hands of less imaginative musicians and it would be untruthful to claim that everything is of uniform interest. Each concerto fields its own distinctive wind group drawing variously upon recorders, flutes, oboes, bassoons and horns, the latter always in pairs, in addition to *concertante* parts in many of them for one or more violins and cellos. There's little need to say more. The recorded sound is first-rate, and Goebel's painstaking essay is fascinating to read.

Te Deum

'Christmas at the Court of Dresden'
Heinichen Pastorale in A, 'Per la notte della Nativitate Christi'. Te Deum **Ristori** Messa per il Santissimo Natale di Nostro Signore. Motetto

pastorale **Schürer** Christus natus est nobis. Jesu redemptor omnium **Seger** Praeludium
Christine Wolff sop **Britta Schwarz** contr **Martin Petzold** ten **Sebastian Knebel** org **Dresden Körnerscher Singverein; Dresden Instrumental-Concert / Peter Kopp**
Carus 83 169 (78' · DDD · T/t)   Ⓕ

This charming disc has been lovingly researched and produced: the liturgical model is the Christmas Eve service said at the Dresden Court during the mid-18th century. All the composers were closely associated with Dresden, and the choir, orchestra and conductor are all from that city too.

Peter Kopp is a stylish director, and his youthful choir and orchestra are magnificent. The soloists are capable, although the soprano and alto don't always blend convincingly in Schürer's *Christus natus est*. Heinichen's *Te Deum* is replete with brilliant horns, exhilarating choruses and moments of pastoral tenderness. Giovanni Alberto Ristori, a Bolognese musician who settled in Dresden, composed his *Messa per il Santissimo Natale* in 1744. It's full of glorious and lyrical moments evoking shepherds and the Nativity. The elegant performance of Ristori's *O admirabile mysterium* goes to show what we lost when most of his church music was destroyed during World War II. Almost all the works here are receiving their first recordings; Carus deserves credit for its illuminating exploration of the rich Dresden school of Baroque sacred music.

Hans Werner Henze   German 1926

Henze studied at a music school in Brunswick and, after war service, with Fortner at the Institute for Church Music in Heidelberg (1946-8). At first he composed in a Stravinskian neo-classical style (First Symphony, 1947), but lessons with Leibowitz in 1947-8 encouraged his adoption of 12-note serialism. Unlike such contemporaries as Stockhausen, however, he held his music open to a wide range of materials. Occasionally he made his obeisance to Darmstadt (Second Quartet, 1952), but his large, varied output of this period also shows the continuing importance to him of neo-classicism, Schoenbergian or Bergian expressionism and jazz. Nor was he dismissive of old forms or, in particular, the theatre: he conducted the Wiesbaden ballet (1950-53) and composed ballets (Jack Pudding, 1951; Labyrinth, 1951) and operas (Boulevard Solitude, 1952).

In 1953 he moved to Italy, where his music became more expansive, sensuous and lyrical and he concentrated on a sequence of operas (König Hirsch, 1956; Elegy for Young Lovers, 1961) and cantatas (Kammermusik, 1958; Cantata della fiaba estrema, 1963). The climax to this period came with a rich and elaborate but also dynamic treatment of The Bacchae in the opera The Bassarids (1966), followed by a period of self-searching; that was externalised in the Second Piano Concerto (1967) and eventually gave rise to an

outspoken commitment to revolutionary socialism. Henze visited Cuba (1969-70), where he conducted the first performance of his Sixth Symphony, incorporating the tunes of revolutionary songs. He also developed a bold, poster style in music-theatre works (El Cimarrón, 1970), leading to his dramatisation of class conflict in the opera We Come to the River (1976).

But he was also continuing his exploration of an expressionist orchestral sumptuousness in such works as Heliogabalus imperator (1972) and Tristan (1974), and an enjoyment in reinterpreting old musical models (Aria de la folía española for chamber orchestra, 1977). Recent works continue his highly personal synthesis of past and present, lyricism and rigour.   GROVEmusic

Concertos

Violin Concertos – No 1; No 2ª; No 3
Torsten Janicke vn ªUlf Dirk Mädler bar
Magdeburg Philharmonic Orchestra / Christian Ehwald
Dabringhaus und Grimm 🔊 MDG601 1242-2
(86' · DDD)   Ⓕ

The concerto has been central to Henze's output throughout his career, even if many works do not bear the title 'concerto' or, as with the Requiem, exist in fusion with other genres. This formal freedom is evident in the three violin concertos. The vibrant First (1948), begun while he was still studying with Fortner, shows his initial, halting attempts at 12-note composition, an ambitious endeavour embarked on with no formal guidance (though the stylistic bedrock is still Hindemith). While a little learning may be a dangerous thing, here it goes a long way indeed. The Concerto teems with magical sounds pointing the way to the operas of the 1950s and '60s.

Concerto and theatre collide in the Second (1971), written at the height of Henze's early period of political engagement. Scored for solo violin (at one point amplified, and whose player is instructed to wear a flowing black tailcoat and plumed tricorn hat), solo baritone, tape and an ensemble of 33 instruments, this expressionist score is dominated by Hans Magnus Enzensberger's poem *Homage to Gödel* with its central image of the 'liar' Münchhausen extricating himself from a quagmire by pulling at his own pigtail. From it Henze conjures a fascinating sonic tapestry, a most original rethink of the whole notion of the role of the individual that is the Concerto's core concern.

There is a literary connection in No 3 (1997, given here in its 2002 revision), consisting of three character portraits drawn from Thomas Mann's *Doktor Faustus*: Esmeralda, the child 'Echo' and Rudi Schwerdtfeger. The Concerto has common traits with Henze's enchanting Shakespearian Eighth Symphony and is similarly rich in ideas and imagery. The performances by Torsten Janicke are strongly characterised and virtuosic, and Christian Ehwald draws sympathetic accompaniments from the well drilled Magdeburg Philharmonic, recorded somewhat distantly but clearly.

Symphonies

Symphonies Nos 7 & 8
**Berlin Radio Symphony Orchestra / Marek
Janowski**
Wergo WER6721-2 (60' · DDD)   Ⓕ◐

Inspired by three speeches in *A Midsummer
Night's Dream*, Henze's Eighth (1992-93) is the
most beguiling and immediately appealing of
them, beautifully written for the orchestra and
luminous in tone. Janowski and his Berlin players audibly relish Puck's putting a girdle round
the earth (though in under eight minutes, not
Shakespeare's 40!), traversing from middle C to
the polar extremes of the orchestra's register.
There's fun in the *Ballabille scherzo* where
Janowski catches the Stravinskian rhythmic
undertow.

This is the third outing for the Seventh (1984),
making it Henze's most recorded. Sadly, the
strongest account – Rattle's, made for EMI
while still at Birmingham – is currently unavailable. Despite differences in approach, not least
in duration with Rattle three and a half minutes
slower (mostly in the sonata-form second movement and finale), Janowski's will do very nicely.
True, Janowski does not match Rattle's impulsion in the opening *Tanz* (also in sonata form)
but his performance catches fire in the central
movements, especially in the *Scherzo*'s macabre
depiction of the instruments of torture used on
the poet Hölderlin. Janowski's finale – much
swifter than Rattle's – is wholly convincing. If
the symphonies alone are your priority, Janowski's disc is the best option.

Symphony No 8. Adagio, Fuge und Mänadentanz
(Suite from the opera 'The Bassarids'). Nachtstücke
und Arien[a]
[a]**Claudia Barainsky** *sop* **Gürzenich Orchestra,
Cologne / Markus Stenz**
Phoenix Edition 113 (74' · DDD)   Ⓕ

The three pieces on this disc range across the
majority of Henze's mature career, from 1957 to
2005. Earliest is *Nachtstücke und Arien*, a vocal-
and-orchestral diptych setting poems by Ingeborg Bachmann, perhaps the dearest of Henze's
early collaborators, framed and separated by
three orchestral 'night pieces'. Henze had written to Bachmann two years before about how he
wished 'to write the most beautiful contemporary music' and in this rapt score he took a huge
step towards that aim. So much so, indeed, that
it prompted Boulez, Nono and Stockhausen to
stage a petulant walk-out at the premiere. Claudia Barainsky sings beautifully and Markus
Stenz directs a taut account.

The *Adagio, Fuge und Mänadentanz* is the most
recent item, premiered in 2005 but extracted
from Henze's finest opera, *The Bassarids* (1966).
The opera was premiered under Christoph von
Dohnányi who, 39 years later, requested this 25-
minute suite and conducted its first perfor-

mance. Drawn from the third of the opera's four
acts (or movements: it is constructed as a two-
hour symphony in four movements), it forms a
compellingly satisfying whole.

So too, though, does the major item here, the
Eighth Symphony, commissioned by the Boston
Symphony Orchestra and premiered by them in
1993. Inspired by three scenes in *A Midsummer
Night's Dream*, the Eighth is – like Beethoven's
and Vaughan Williams's – something of a relaxation between the mightier edifices of the Seventh and Ninth but an utter delight from first
bar to last. The Gürzenich Orchestra play with
real inspiration under Stenz's intelligent direction. Recommended.

Symphony No 10. La selva incantata. Quattro poemi
**Montpellier National Orchestra /
Friedemann Layer**
Accord 476 7156 (60' · DDD) Recorded live 2004   Ⓕ

After the monumental Ninth, Henze's Tenth
(1997-2000) resumes an engagement with some
of the concerns of its immediate predecessors.
The Seventh and Eighth had literary roots, in
Hölderlin and Shakespeare respectively. There
is no programme as such here, but as the titles of
the four movements – 'A Storm', 'A Hymn', 'A
Dance', 'A Dream' – suggest, there is a large
illustrative element in the music. The result is a
fascinating orchestral panoply that, when one
listens deeper, is a true symphony. Henze's harmonic language in his symphonies may not
always please purists, but there is always a clear
(if occasionally halting) flow and, whatever their
diverse inspirations, the four movements have a
logical and unified progression.

It is enormously encouraging to see a French
label tackling such a project. And almost as surprising is having a French orchestra tackle so
German a set of pieces. The Montpellier players
emerge with flying colours, giving well drilled,
exciting performances with a real sense of occasion. In the *Quattro poemi* (1955) they catch at
least as well as their Wergo rivals the 'turbulent
emotionalism and spacious, questing lyricism'
that lies at the heart of the music, while *La selva
incantata* (1991) really buzzes along – as does the
Scherzo of the symphony. Accord's sound is
nicely lucid without being spectacular.

Nachtstücke und Arien

Drei sinfonische Etüden. Quattro poemi. Nachtstücke
und Arien[a]. La selva incantata[a]
[a]**Michaela Kaune** *sop* **North German Radio
Symphony Orchestra / Peter Ruzicka**
Wergo WER6637-2 (61' · DDD)   Ⓕ

This attractive compilation fills significant gaps in
the current discography of Henze's earlier compositions. The main work, *Nachtstücke und Arien*,
dates from 1957, and mortally offended avant-
garde puritans at its premiere by its revival of full-
blooded lyricism, less than 10 years after Strauss's

Four Last Songs was supposed to have said a final farewell to such self-indulgence. This sumptuous, at times explosively dramatic music, comes across well in this performance. Michaela Kaune sings with poise and, where necessary, an apt operatic flair. The recorded sound throughout is adequate, though not especially well defined.

Like the other works on the disc, *Nachtstücke und Arien* owes far more to the post-Romantic *espressivo* of Berg and Schoenberg than it does to Strauss. It's most directly indebted to Henze's own opera *König Hirsch*, the major work of the 1950s in which he gave his new-found love of melody the fullest rein. With *La selva incantata* (The enchanted forest, 1991) we find Henze revisiting *König Hirsch* and recasting some of its most characterful music in purely orchestral form. *Three Symphonic Studies* and *Four Poems* for orchestra were both written in the 1950s, and although less fully rounded than *Nachtstücke und Arien*, they all have Henze's typical blend of turbulent emotionalism and spacious, questing lyricism. In the relatively extended first *Study* the risk of aimless drifting isn't altogether avoided. But this lapse is corrected with interest in the shorter, more tightly controlled *Poems*. The romantic resonances confirm how fruitful the experience of composing for the theatre, and engaging with earlier German traditions, had become for Henze. Those resonances continue in most of his finest later works, but the idiomatic performances on this disc let you hear some of their earliest manifestations.

Operas

Boulevard Solitude
Laura Aikin sop Manon Lescaut **Pär Lindskog** ten
Armand des Grieux **Tom Fox** bass Lescaut **Hubert Delamboye** ten Lilaque père **Pauls Putnins** bass
Lilaque fils **Marc Canturri** bar Francis
Cor Vivaldi; Palau de la Música Catalana Chamber Choir; Liceu Grand Theatre Symphony Orchestra, Barcelona / Zoltán Peskó
Stage director **Nikolaus Lehnhoff**
Video director **Xavi Bové**
Euroarts ◪**DVD** 205 6358 (102' · NTSC · 16:9 · PCM stereo, 5.1 and DTS 5.1 · 0). Recorded live at the Liceu Theatre, Barcelona, in March 2007   Ⓕ**○**

The sceptical voices were disappointingly persistent when the Royal Opera's reopening season in 2000 staged the UK premiere of Henze's first opera. Could a 90-minute one-acter by a 26-year-old hold attention, and fill seats? That it did so, and eventually did so triumphantly, was a measure not only of the composer's precocious theatrical gifts but of Nikolaus Lehnhoff's production, which held faith with the decision of Henze and his librettist Grete Weil to update Prévost's story to the period of its premiere in 1952. The action centres around a grand central railway station, full of the impersonal grandeur and busy movement of human flotsam and jetsam that are the natural property of such places.

Billy Wilder and Henri-Georges Clouzot make their mark on the continual cutting between scenes; Xavi Bové's direction for video is unusually subtle, taking full advantage of Henze's extended intermezzi to watch clocks and art-deco pillars.

Bernhard Kontarsky's pacing was tighter in London, catching more of the clickety-clack of Henze's percussion writing but Peskó and the Liceu band are up to the mark, letting the sly allusions to jazz and Weill in the intermezzi live on borrowed time. Henze's Manon is knowingly self-condemned from the outset, one feels, with greater self-possession than her literary and operatic ancestors from Prévost to Puccini. Not that that makes for static loss of drama or fulfilment, when her story gradually cedes to the hopeless infatuation of des Grieux. Laura Aikin is a strong, sluttish Manon, fuller of voice and more voluptuous of figure than the devastating femme fatale of Alexandra von der Weth at Covent Garden. Both steal the show in their own way, as Lulus deserve to.

Pär Lindskog reprises his central role, at least as much Rodolfo as Alwa. Tom Fox as Lescaut could afford to bluster and shout a little less, but the smaller roles always bear the composer's *legato* lines in mind. Henze takes a bow at the end, and it must have been moving for him to see how his forgotten child has grown up and stood on his own feet.

Der Prinz von Homburg
William Cochran ten Elector of Brandenburg **Helga Dernesch** sop Electress of Brandenburg **MariAnne Häggander** sop Princess Natalie **François Le Roux** bar Prince Friedrich von Homburg **Claes-Håkan Ahnsjö** ten Count Hohenzollern **Hans Günter Nöcker** bass-bar Field Marshal Dörfling **Bavarian State Orchestra / Wolfgang Sawallisch**
Stage director **Nikolaus Lehnhoff**
Video director **Eckhart Schmidt**
ArtHaus Musik ◪**DVD** 100 164 (105' · 16:9 · 2.0 · 2 & 5)
Recorded live 1994   Ⓕ**○○**

Der Prinz von Homburg (1958-60) was composed at a time of burgeoning acclaim for Henze. The librettist, Ingeborg Bachmann, fashioned a splendid reduction of Kleist's famous drama of the dreamy aristocrat who, distracted by love into disobeying orders in battle, is given the choice of escaping condemnation if he feels the verdict unjust. Only when he accepts the inevitability of his sentence, and walks out to face execution, is he pardoned.

Henze's crisp and vital music is a remarkable, natural-sounding fusion (controversially for the time) of the influences of Schoenberg and Stravinsky. And Eckhart Schmidt's film is a most faithful record of Lehnhoff's 1994 production. Le Roux is almost ideal as the lovestruck dreamer Prince, alternately distracted and impetuous. His chemistry with MariAnne Häggander – who sings beautifully – is tangible, essential for a successful production, though it's William Cochran, rich-voiced and expressively stern as the severe but not unbending Elector, who steals the show. Sawallisch directs the Bavarian State Orchestra impeccably, the sound spacious and clear. *Der Prinz von Homburg* may not be as spectacular as *König Hirsch* or *The Bassarids*, or as directly popular as *Der junge Lord*, but it remains one of Henze's most completely achieved and important operas. Its appearance on DVD (there's no CD equivalent) is unequivocal cause for celebration.

L'Upupa und der Triumph der Sohnesliebe
Laura Aikin sop Badi'at **Matthias Goerne** bar al Kasim **John Mark Ainsley** ten Demon **Alfred Muff** bar Old Man **Hanna Schwarz** mez Malik **Günther Missenhardt** bar Dijab **Axel Köhler** counterten Adschib **Anton Scharinger** bass-bar Gharib
Vienna State Opera Concert Choir; Vienna Philharmonic Orchestra / Markus Stenz
Stage director **Dieter Dorn**
Video director **Brian Large**
Euroarts **DVD** 2053929 (143' · NTSC · 16:9 · PCM stereo, 5.1 & DTS 5.1 · 0). Recorded live at the Salzburg Festival, August 2003   Ⓕ**OO**

The title of Henze's 'German comedy in 11 tableaux based on the Arabic' translates as 'The Hoopoe and the Triumph of Filial Love'. Setting his own libretto, and regarding the work as his farewell to the lyric stage, the composer casts a wryly retrospective eye on the magic and absurdity of the medium. This parable of the good son, al Kasim, who embarks on a dangerous quest for the beautiful, exotic hoopoe bird lost and longed for by his father, follows many time-honoured operatic precedents as the hero undergoes various trials and tribulations before finding true love and returning home safely, to be greeted by his grateful and loving father.

During al Kasim's quest for the hoopoe, his main companion and helper is a gently comic 'demon' who's more a fallen guardian angel than a Mephistopheles. The composer's affection seems centred on this character, portrayed by John Mark Ainsley with a restraint that makes the element of pathos the more effective. During this final 10 minutes the music is purely orchestral, its poetic blend of eloquence and regret as touching in its distinctive way as Strauss's valedictory epilogue for *Capriccio*.

This recording from the Salzburg premiere is in most respects a delight for both eye and ear. It's no great weakness that the young lovers, well sung and acted by Matthias Goerne and Laura Aikin, seem relatively one-dimensional alongside Ainsley's helpful, bewildered demon, and the stage production fits the work's knowingly light-hearted tone without overdoing the comic exoticism. With strong support from such seasoned character-singers as Hanna Schwarz and Alfred Muff, the only weak link is the rather pallid countertenor of Axel Köhler.

Technically, Brian Large is well practised in the art of avoiding excessive nudging of the viewer with obtrusively prolonged close-ups,

and Markus Stenz is the ideal conductor to bring out the essential threads of Henze's richly diffuse musical weave.

Louis Hérold   French 1791-1833

Hérold studied at the Paris Conservatoire with Louis Adam, Kreutzer, Catel and Méhul (who became the dominant influence on his style), composing his first opera in Italy in 1814. For several years he had difficulty finding adequate texts and his works frequently failed. Not until the delightful Marie (1826) did he score a triumphant success, meanwhile working as an accompanist at the Théâtre-Italien in Paris and later as singing coach at the Opéra, where he composed music for five ballets, including La somnambule and La fille mal gardée. The two operas for which he is remembered – Zampa, ou La fiancée de marbre (1831; originally Le corsaire) and the finer Le pré aux clercs (1832) – were both popular successes, the first full of effective theatrical situations and showing the brilliant tenor Chollet to advantage, the second treating thoughtfully a controversial subject. Such accomplished scores suggest that had Hérold lived longer, he might have fulfilled his ambitions to compose grand opera.   **GROVE**music

La fille mal gardée

La fille mal gardée – excerpts (arr Lanchbery)
Orchestra of the Royal Opera House, Covent Garden / John Lanchbery
Decca Ovation 430 196-2DM (51' · ADD) Recorded 1962   Ⓜ**O**

The Royal Ballet's *La fille mal gardée* remains a source of perpetual delight, not least for the music that John Lanchbery arranged largely from Hérold's patchwork score for the 1828 version. The Clog dance is the obvious highlight; but there are felicitous moments throughout, with snatches of Rossini, Donizetti *et al* cropping up all over the place.

This recording is the original one that Lanchbery conducted when the ballet proved such a success in the Royal Ballet's repertoire in 1960. He later recorded the score complete; and ballet lovers will consider this fuller version essential. However, others will find that the complete score rather outstays its welcome by comparison with this constantly uplifting selection. A most compelling recommendation.

Hildegard of Bingen   German 1098-1179

German composer, abbess and mystic Hildegard of Bingen's writings include much lyrical and dramatic poetry which has survived with monophonic music.

Hildegard of Bingen

The *Symphonia armonie celestium revelationum* contains musical settings of 77 poems arranged according to the liturgical calendar. The poetry is laden with imagery and the music, based on a few formulaic melodic patterns, is in some respects highly individual. Her morality play *Ordo virtutum* contains 82 melodies in a more syllabic style. She also wrote medical and scientific treatises, hagiography and letters and recorded her many visions.

GROVEmusic

Vocal Works

'A Feather on the Breath of God'
Columba aspexit. Ave, generosa. O ignis spiritus Paracliti. O Jerusalem. O Euchari, in leta vita. O viridissima virga. O presul vere civitatis. O Ecclesia
Gothic Voices / Christopher Page with **Doreen Muskett** *symphony* **Robert White** *reed drones*
Hyperion CDA66039 (44' · DDD) Ⓕ❶❶❶⭢

Here's a collection of choice gems from one of the greatest creative personalities of the Middle Ages. We've limited means of assessing how these inspired pieces were performed in Hildegard's time; but the refreshingly unsophisticated timbre of the four sopranos and the reedy, almost boyish, vocal quality of the contralto are convincing enough to transport the listener right back to the unpolluted atmosphere of her cloister. Most to be savoured are the unaccompanied items, amounting to 50 per cent of the total. Indeed, since the notes make a point of telling us us that 'distractions such as the intrusion of instrumental decorations' were to be avoided, why did the producer go out of his way to introduce symphony and reed drones in the performance of the other 50 per cent? However, this is a delightful recording. When it was first released it sparked new interest in the music of the Middle Ages, and it remains a jewel in Hyperion's crown.

Favus distillans. Et ideo puelle. O tu illustrata. O vos angeli. Studium divinitatis. O ignee Spiritus. O rubor sanguinis. O orzchis Ecclesia. O gloriosissimi lux vivens angeli. Rex noster promptus est. Deus enim in prima muliere. De patria. Sed diabolus in invidia. Nunc gaudeant materna viscera Ecclesia
Sinfonye (Jocelyn West, Vivien Ellis, Stevie Wishart, Emily Levy, Vickie Couper, Julie Murphy)
Members of the Oxford Girls' Choir
Celestial Harmonies 13127-2 (62' · DDD· T/t) Ⓕ❶

Stevie Wishart succeeds in putting Hildegard's music across chiefly by her imaginative choice of singers, which includes quite young girls. The tuneful, unsophisticated timbre of the youngest voices acts as a foil to the sturdy chest voices of the older women – which have a quality of their own, somewhat akin to that of Hungarian folk singers. Such contrasts seem typical of the whole Hildegardian picture. Hildegard herself was made up of contrasts: she's both ecstatic and quietly tender; she can be passionate while maintaining a sense of decorum; she's erotic but also chaste.

We could do without the hurdy-gurdy and dispense with the drones and improvised organum. What's left is a penetration of Hildegard's music that rarely comes through in other interpretations. One thinks particularly of the composer's portrayal of the mystery of the Incarnation in *O tu illustrata* and also, particularly, of the remarkably sustained lines of ecstasy in *O vos angeli* – this extraordinary outpouring ranging over two octaves, but which yet has shape and structure for all Hildegard's protestations that she'd never studied her art formally.

Ferdinand Hiller   German 1811-1885

When he was ten Hiller played a concerto by Mozart at a public concert. Several important artists showed an interest in him, among them Spohr, Speyer, Moscheles and Mendelssohn who became Hiller's closest friend and on whose recommendation he went to Weimar to become one of Hummel's pupils (1825–7). As a productive, versatile and cultured composer, Hiller occupied a prominent position among his contemporaries; however, Schumann recognized that 'despite mastery of formal techniques' (and occasional originality) his music on the whole 'lacked that triumphant power which we are unable to resist'. His best work is represented by the Piano Concerto op.69, the songs and some of the piano pieces, in particular the Sonata op.47 and the Ghazèles. His opera Die Katakomben also contains many inspired passages.

Piano Concertos

Piano Concertos – No 1, Op 5; No 2, Op 69; No 3, 'Concerto espressivo', Op 170
Tasmanian Symphony Orchestra / Howard Shelley pf
Hyperion CDA67655 (76' · DDD) Ⓕ❶❶❶

History can be a cruel judge, for it is hard to dismiss such a confident, superbly crafted piece as the F sharp minor (Second) Concerto of 1843. It is one of the gems of the genre, the first to be written in that key and with many surprising features such as the soloist kicking off proceedings fiercely and without any introduction, the written-out cadenza opening with a subsidiary rather than principal theme, and the birdsong figuration and unusual left-hand rhythmic accompaniment in the andante espressivo.

Piano Conerto No 1 (1831) is a brilliant display vehicle in the Parisian manner of the day which, however, owes more to Chopin and Moscheles (its dedicatee) than Herz or Kalkbrenner. In No 3 (1874), presumed lost until recently, Hiller again strives to be innovative in terms of structure and handling of material, keeping his soloist fully occupied despite the work's subtitle and dominant character. Inferior they may be to No 2 but, especially in performances like these, well worth hearing.

Once more, one has to take off one's hat to Howard Shelley for leading such exuberant performances while simultaneously tackling demanding keyboard writing with amazing agility, innate elegance and complete stylistic empathy.

Paul Hindemith German 1895-1963

Hindemith studied as a violinist and composer (with Mendelssohn and Sekles) at the Hoch Conservatory in Frankfurt (1908-17) and made an early reputation through his chamber music and expressionist operas. But then he turned to neo-classicism in his Kammermusik No 1, the first of seven such works imitating the Baroque concerto while using an expanded tonal harmony and distinctively modern elements, notably jazz. Each uses a different mixed chamber orchestra, suited to music of linear counterpoint and, in the fast movements, strongly pulsed rhythm.

During this early period Hindemith lived as a performer: he was leader of the Frankfurt Opera orchestra, and he played the viola in the Amar-Hindemith Quartet (1921-9) as well as in the first performance of Walton's Viola Concerto (1929). Much of his chamber music was written in 1917-24, including four of his six quartets and numerous sonatas, and he was also involved in promoting chamber music through his administrative work for the Donaueschingen Festival (1923-30). However, he also found time to compose abundantly in other genres; including lieder (Das Marienleben, to Rilke poems), music for newly invented mechanical instruments, music for schoolchildren and amateurs, and opera (Cardillac). In addition, from 1927 he taught at the Berlin Musikhochschule.

His concern with so many branches of music sprang from a sense of ethical responsibility that inevitably became more acute with the rise of the Nazis. With the beginning of the 1930s he moved from chamber ensembles to the more public domain of the symphony orchestra, and at the same time his music became harmonically smoother and less intensively contrapuntal. Then in the opera Mathis der Maler (preceded by a symphony of orchestral excerpts) he dramatised the dilemma of the artist in society, eventually opposing Brechtian engagement and insisting on a greater responsibility to art. Nevertheless, his music fell under official disapproval, and in 1938 he left for Switzerland, where Mathis had its first performance. He moved on to the USA and taught at Yale (1940-53), but spent his last decade back in Switzerland.

His later music is in the style that he had established in the early 1930s and that he had theoretically expounded in his Craft of Musical Composition (1937-9), where he ranks scale degrees and harmonic intervals in order from most consonant (tonic, octave) to most dissonant (augmented 4th, tritone), providing a justification for the primacy of the triad. His large output of the later 1930s and 1940s includes concertos and other orchestral works, as well as sonatas for most of the standard instruments. His

search for an all-encompassing, all-explaining harmony also found expression in his Kepler opera Die Harmonie der Welt.

Orchestral works

Mathis der Maler Symphony[a]. Symphonia serena[b]. Concert Music[c]. Der Schwanendreher[d]. Symphonic Metamorphoses on Themes of Carl Maria von Weber[d]. Nobilissima visione[d].
[d]**Tabea Zimmermann** va [a]**Berlin Philharmonic Orchestra / Herbert von Karajan,** [b]**Philharmonia Orchestra / Paul Hindemith,** [d]**Bavarian Radio Symphony Orchestra / David Shallon,** [cd]**Philadelphia Orchestra /** [c]**Eugene Ormandy,** [d]**Wolfgang Sawallisch**
EMI 20th Century Classics ② 2068632 (145' · ADD)

Ⓜ Ⓞ ➔

An excellent two-disc mid-price Hindemith collection containing some pretty impressive performances. The Philadelphia recordings are very fine: both Ormandy and Sawallisch demonstrating a real feel for this colourful (and much underrated) music. The glorious Philadelphia Sound pays huge rewards in these scores. The Karajan Mathis also shows off a great orchestra, and the conductor's skill at bringing out the atmosphere of a work is a real plus here.

Tabea Zimmermann isn't as forceful a soloist as the composer in *Der Schwanendreher* but she and David Shallon emphasise the work's lyrical qualities, and find an appealing delicacy in the piece. Hindemith himself directs the Philharmonia (then on top form) in the rarely heard *Symphonia serena* and draws some magnificent playing from this outstanding ensemble.

Mathis der Maler. Symphonic Metamorphosis on Themes of Carl Maria von Weber. Nobilissima Visione
Philadelphia Orchestra / Wolfgang Sawallisch
EMI 555230-2 (71' · DDD)

Ⓕ ➔

The Philadelphia players for Sawallisch give taut performances that simply outclass the competition. Another plus point is the unusual running order that achieves a better musical balance, starting with the most brilliant piece, the *Symphonic Metamorphosis*, and increasing in weight to the resounding brass Alleluias at the climax of the *Mathis* Symphony. EMI's sound is relatively recessed. Given the spacious acoustic of Memorial Hall and the conductor's largeness of vision this is entirely apposite, with no loss of detail.

Violin Concerto

Konzertmusik for Brass and Strings, Op 50. Violin Concerto[a]. Symphonic Metamorphosis on Themes of Carl Maria von Weber
[a]**Leonidas Kavakos** vn **BBC Philharmonic Orchestra / Yan Pascal Tortelier**
Chandos CHAN9903 (66' · DDD)

Ⓕ Ⓞ ➔

Here are top-notch performances and recordings of one of Hindemith's best-loved works and one of his more unaccountably neglected pieces. The benchmark recordings of the *Symphonic Metamotphosis* are those by Blomstedt and Sawallisch. The BBC Philharmonic are not quite in the same league as the San Francisco (at least under Blomstedt) or Philadelphia bands, but provide an invigoratingly energetic performance.

Leonidas Kavakos is the sweet-toned soloist in the unaccountably neglected Violin Concerto, which thankfully is coming into fashion in the studio. Even Oistrakh is worsted in some passages by the fleet-fingered Kavakos, but the Russian's account, directed by the composer, remains essential (though sadly not currently available). Where his cannot compete now with the newcomer is in recording quality. For our money, Kavakos and Tortelier are now the market leader.

Kammermusiken

Kammermusiken – No 1, Op 24 No 1;-No 2; No 3, Op 36 No 2; No 4, Op 36 No 3; No 5, Op 36 No 4; No 6, Op 46 No 1; No 7, Op 46 No 2. Kleine Kammermusik No 1 for Wind Quintet, Op 24 No 2
Konstanty Kulka *vn* **Kim Kashkashian** *va* **Norbert Blume** *va d'amore* **Lynn Harrell** *vc* **Ronald Brautigam** *pf* **Leo van Doeselaar** *org* **Royal Concertgebouw Orchestra / Riccardo Chailly**
Double Decca download ② 473 722-2DF2 (138' · DDD) Ⓜ️ＯＯＯ🅳➔

Ⓖ Hindemith's series of *Kammermusik* ('Chamber Music') began in 1921 as an iconoclastic response to the hyper-intense emotionalism of German Expressionist music over the previous 15 years. It continued until 1927, at which point he began to rationalise the harmonic and expressive foundations of his style. This, then, is neo-classicism with a German accent; as such it was to be a vital force in sweeping away the cobwebs of late romanticism; Walton, Prokofiev, Shostakovich and Britten were among those who, however indirectly, would feel the benefit.

The music is also immensely enjoyable in its own right. Hindemith cheekily throws together disparate idioms and sheer force of personality is all that guards against anarchy. All this is done with more than half an eye on the performers' enjoyment of recreation, and the fine array of artists assembled by Chailly savour every detail. Recording quality is exemplary.

Additional recommendation

Coupld with Der Schwanendreher
BPO / Abbado
EMI 397711-2
As the Chailly set appears to have limited distribution, do consider the Abbado discs. While lacking a little of the gem-like incisiveness of his

compatriot's Concertgebouw version, it is needless to say magnificently played.

String Quartets

Hindemith String Quartet No 3, Op 22   Ⓗ
Prokofiev String Quartet No 2 in F, Op 92
Walton String Quartet in A minor
Hollywood Quartet (Felix Slatkin, Paul Shure *vns* Paul Robyn *va* Eleanor Aller *vc*)
Testament mono SBT1052 (74' · ADD) Recorded 1951
                                                    Ⓕ

Although many accounts of the Prokofiev have appeared over the years, none has approached, let alone surpassed, the Hollywood version of the Second Quartet. The same would no doubt apply to the Hindemith but for the fact that there have been fewer challengers. What a wonderful feeling for line these players had, what an incredible, perfectly matched and blended ensemble – and how well these transfers sound! That goes for the Walton, too: there's no other account of it that makes so positive a case for it.

Viola Sonatas

Viola Sonatas – Op 11 No 4; Op 25 No 4; Viola Sonata (1939). Nobilissima visione – Meditation
Lawrence Power *va* **Simon Crawford-Phillips** *pf*
Hyperion CDA67721 (58' · DDD)   ⒻＯ

Paul Hindemith isn't exactly the first composer you think of when the term 'hit tune' is mentioned but the opening Fantasie of his F major Viola Sonata (Op 11 No 4) of 1919 comes pretty close to providing one, especially as 'sung' by viola-player Lawrence Power. 'Might almost be by Brahms...' says Malcolm MacDonald in a typically persuasive and informative booklet-note, which is surely true. The finale is a fairly assertive mood-breaker, pianist Simon Crawford-Phillips marking a dramatic contrast in tempo and colour (now this really does sound like 'updated' Brahms). The grittier Sonata of 1939 also includes a Phantasie, placed third in the structure rather than first. This is the Hindemith of the *Mathis der Maler* Symphony, purposeful music, square-jawed, angular, confident and assertive, though with more fanciful elements too – especially in the finale, which at times is both playful and delicate.

Macdonald notes the possible influence of Bartók on the Sonata Op 25 No 4 (1922), which seems a justified claim. This is another strong piece, more percussive than the 1939 Sonata, with a desolate but heart-rending slow movement that is savagely interrupted by the finale's aggressive arrival. The CD (Vol 1 of 'The Complete Hindemith Viola Music' is what it's called), which is superbly recorded, is completed with a sensitive performance of the serene Meditation from *Nobilissima visione* in Hindemith's own arrangement for viola and piano. As to the performances, not since the days of William Primrose has Hindemith's viola music been played with such warmth and conviction. A 100 per cent success story.

Violin Sonatas

Violin Sonatas – E flat, Op 11 No 1; D, Op 11 No 2; E (1935); C (1939)
Ulf Wallin *vn* **Roland Pöntinen** *pf*
BIS CD761 (56' · DDD) Ⓕ**O**

The E major Sonata of 1935 is brief (under 10 minutes long) and uncomplicated, yet it's familiar Hindemith from first note to last. The C major work (1939) is more complex and grave, and probably the finest of them. The longest sonata, and most conservative in idiom, is the D major. Both Op 11 works were written in 1918 while Hindemith was on active service, and are remarkable for bearing few traces of either the grimness of the Great War or the composer's personal voice. Both deserve wider currency. This issue is also welcome in including the fragmentary abandoned finale of Op 11 No 1, a rustic dance not in keeping with the symmetry of the whole. The sweet-toned Ulf Wallin is fully attuned to Hindemith's wavelength, and Pöntinen provides exemplary support. The recording is typical BIS (ie excellent). A splendid disc.

Ludus tonalis

Ludus tonalis. Suite '1922'
Boris Berezovsky *pf*
Warner Classics 2564 63412-2 (75' · DDD) Ⓕ**B→**

It's a long way from music like Chopin/Godowsky (which Berezovsky has recorded so superbly) to Hindemith's large-scale cycle of 12 fugues alternating with 11 interludes, the whole topped and tailed by a Prelude which returns, in retrograde inversion, as a Postlude. So how does he fare in *Ludus tonalis* (1942)?

In a word, impressively. There's no attempt to beef up Hindemith's contrapuntal sobriety with spurious expressiveness, but a searching sense of line and a feeling for polyphonic give-and-take make the quieter fugues absorbing, while the extrovert ones positively sizzle with attitude. As for the more freely composed Interludes, dexterity and fantasy combine to project maximum energy and atmosphere, especially in the cheeky cross-rhythms of Interlude 4. While Berezovsky doesn't quite convince that *Ludus tonalis* embodies the white heat of inspiration from beginning to end, he comes as close as any pianist could, or should.

Hindemith's early *Suite '1922'* offers the player more conventional digital rewards, which Berezovsky clearly relishes, with even the rather pallid central 'Nachtstück' revealing unexpected depths. In its riotous 'Shimmy' and 'Ragtime' movements, 'prodigies of virtuosity' are there in abundance, helped along by an exceptionally vivid recording.

Requiem for those we love

When Lilacs Last in the Door-yard Bloom'd (Requiem for those we love)
Jan DeGaetani *mez* **William Stone** *bar* **Atlanta Symphony Chorus and Orchestra / Robert Shaw**
Telarc CD80132 (62' · DDD · T) **OO**

Hindemith's *Requiem* is a setting of Whitman's poem – the lilacs piled on President Lincoln's coffin as it was taken across the country after his assassination just as the Civil War was over, the thrush symbolising his own mourning, and the then fallen Western star (hailed at Lincoln's inauguration as a good omen) – further layers of association were added when, 80 years later almost to the day, President Roosevelt died as the Second World War was coming to an end. It includes a tragedy-laden sinfonia, arias, recitatives, marches, a massive double fugue and a passacaglia. It isn't, however, the great technical virtuosity – in places as close-packed as Whitman's verse – which leaves the most lasting impression, but the haunting beauty of much of the setting.

Robert Shaw gives a superlative and moving performance and receives an outstandingly vivid recording. He knows the work perhaps more intimately than anyone (having commissioned it from Hindemith in 1945 for his Collegiate Chorale in New York), and he makes the most of every expressive nuance, every shade of dynamics, though without losing the overall shape. There's greater subtlety in the playing of the prelude than ever before; the big brass chords have weight and fullness without stridency, and the orchestral playing generally is first-rate; it would scarcely be possible to find a more sympathetic baritone than William Stone, an unforced lyrical singer with clean technique and exemplary enunciation, or a sweeter or purer-voiced mezzo than Jan DeGaetani.

Das Unaufhörliche

Das Unaufhörliche
Ulrike Sonntag *sop* **Robert Wörle** *ten* **Siegfried Lorenz** *bar* **Berlin Radio Children's Choir; Berlin Radio Chorus and Symphony Orchestra / Lothar Zagrosek**
Wergo ② WER6603-2 (95' · DDD · T/t) Ⓕ

The oratorio *Das Unaufhörliche* ('The One Perpetual') was Hindemith's longest concert work. It never established itself in the repertoire (although Boult conducted the UK premiere as early as 1933). It's cast in three parts, the first describing the 'one perpetual' itself, the second its effect on diverse areas of activity (including art, science and love), the third Humankind's reaction away from it and final acquiescence. How closely Hindemith accorded with the poet Gottfried Benn's viewpoint is a matter for conjecture, but his evanescent score matched the poem's expansiveness of theme and nobility of utterance. In this alone it pointed the way to *Mathis der Maler*, for there's nothing here akin to the *Kammermusiken* or *Neues vom Tage* (a smash-hit in Berlin at the time).

This is the work's first recording and the performance is a fine one with good sound. Flies in the ointment? Soprano Ulrike Sonntag, who seems too often to be straining for her notes and whose intonation isn't always secure, and Wergo's failure to provide a translation of Benn's spoken introduction, recorded in 1932 and included as the final track. These are quibbles, however, and should not deter anyone from investing in this important release.

Die Harmonie der Welt

Die Harmonie der Welt
Arutiun Kotchinian *bass* Kaiser Rudolf II, Kaiser Ferdinand II, Sun **François Le Roux** *bar* Kepler, Imperial Mathematician, Earth **Robert Wörle** *ten* General Wallenstein, Jupiter **Christian Elsner** *ten* Ulrich, Kepler's assistant, Late soldier, Mars **Michael Burt** *bass* Pastor in Linz, Mercury **Reinhard Hagen** *bass* Tansur, Saturn **Michael Kraus** *bar* Baron Starhemberg **Daniel Kirch** *ten* Kepler's brother **Tatiana Korovina** *sop* Susanna, Venus **Michelle Breedt** *contr* Kepler's mother, Luna **Sophia Larson** *sop* Little Susanna **Berlin Radio Symphony Chorus and Orchestra / Marek Janowski**
Wergo ③ WER6652-2 (161' · DDD · T/t)   Ⓕ

Die Harmonie der Welt is one of Hindemith's major works, perhaps his major post-war work. He first seems to have contemplated an opera on the polymath Johannes Kepler in the late 1930s, in the wake of *Mathis der Maler*. But it wasn't until 1955 that serious work was started on the libretto, although, as with *Mathis* two decades before, he had already written a symphony using themes reserved for the opera.

There are also superficial similarities in subject treatment between the two stage works. *Die Harmonie* is an opera about an astronomer-cum-philosopher rather than science, just as *Mathis* had been about an artist, not painting. Kepler's career is set in the context of his time, culminating in the tumultuous Thirty Years' War, just as Grünewald's had been set against the 16th-century Peasants' Revolt. Yet Kepler isn't as involved in the whirl of events as Mathis; he stands apart from them, concerned increasingly just to resolve his theories about the harmony of the world. In the end his search is vain and he dies with the word 'Futile' on his lips.

By the time of the premiere, Hindemith's star had waned and some critics regarded the opera also as futile, especially when compared to *Cardillac* and *Mathis*. But in several respects it's just as successful musically, its symphonic coherence and integration more consistently achieved than in earlier stage works and the composer had grown as an artist. If some of the characterisation is two-dimensional, this is made to serve the symbolic

aspects of the whole, most clearly in the final scene as the main characters assume celestial roles in a cosmic passacaglia, the incandescent culmination of which truly raises the roof.

Marek Janowski directs a splendidly paced and committed performance, with some fine singing and playing from the forces of Berlin Radio. François Le Roux turns in a thoughtful and multi-faceted account of Kepler, with Robert Wörle's conniving but ultimately doomed Wallenstein and Christian Elsner's Ulrich the pick of the rest. Recorded in the Jesus-Christus-Kirche, Berlin, the sound is clear and spacious, the acoustic and balance serving the music better than in most theatres. A marvellous achievement, strongly recommended.

Das lange Weihnachtsmahl

Das lange Weihnachtsmahl
Ruth Ziesak *sop* Lucia; Lucia II **Ursula Hesse von den Steinen** *contr* Mutter Bayard; Ermengarde **Herman Wallén** *bar* Sam; Roderick **Arutiun Kotchinian** *bass* Brandon **Christian Elsner** *ten* Charles **Rebecca Martin** *mez* Genevieve **Michaela Kaune** *sop* Leonora **Corby Welch** *ten* Roderick II **Berlin Radio Symphony Orchestra / Marek Janowski**
Wergo WER6676-2 (48' · DDD · T/t/N)   Ⓕ

Hindemith's final and least-known opera, based on a 1931 play by Thornton Wilder, *Das lange Weihnachtsmahl* ('The Long Christmas Dinner') is – like his earliest essays in the genre – cast in a single act. Unlike them, however, it is a subtle and luminous conception, with none of the provocative and lurid (although undeniably exciting) Expressionism of his twenties. What catches the ear from the start are the limpid scoring and vocal lines, developing the beauty of tone found in the orchestral *Marienleben* songs and more intimate passages in *Die Harmonie der Welt*.

The opera depicts in 50 minutes a remarkable domestic panoply set across 90 years, encapsulated during the Christmas dinners of the Bayard family. Wilder conflates these (culminating in the Great War) into a freely evolving single event, with characters emerging from one side of the stage (denoting birth) and leaving by the other (denoting death).

Hindemith and Wilder blurred the distinctions between several characters and their descendants to underline familial continuity, appearing, being developed and reprised like musical themes. Chief among them is Lucia, sung radiantly by Ruth Ziesak, who dominates the first six scenes until departing, only to reappear briefly as her granddaughter in Scene 9. Lucia's husband Roderick – sung solidly by Herman Wallén – eventually returns as his grandson Sam. Ursula Hesse von den Steinen brings great dignity to her portrayals of ageing matriarch Mother Bayard (who recalls when native Americans lived hard by) and Cousin Ermengarde, whose last exit through the dark door leaves the old house finally empty.

Janowski directs a fluent, superbly paced account, sung well throughout, accompanied by some splendid orchestral playing. Wergo's sound is rich.

Mathis der Maler

Mathis der Maler
Roland Hermann bar Mathis **Josef Protschka** ten Albrecht **Gabriele Rossmanith** sop Regina **Sabine Hass** sop Ursula **Harald Stamm** bass Riedinger **Heinz Kruse** ten Hans Schwalb **Victor von Halem** bass Lorenz von Pommersfelden **Hermann Winkler** ten Wolfgang Capito **Ulrich Hielscher** bass Truchsess von Waldberg **Ulrich Ress** ten Sylvester von Schaumberg **John Cogram** ten Der Pfeiffer des Grafen von Helfenstein **Marilyn Schmiege** mez Helfenstein **North German Radio Chorus; Cologne Radio Chorus and Symphony Orchestra / Gerd Albrecht**
Wergo ③ WER6255-2 (166' · DDD · T/t)   Ⓕ

Mathis der Maler is one of the pinnacles of 20th-century German opera. It's become axiomatic to see in it a parable of the times, with Hindemith using the turbulent world of 16th-century Germany to mirror the Nazi Reich and his place in it. But in reality *Mathis* is a spiritual and historical opera, not a political one. Rudolf Stephan in his note plays down the political angle; if Hitler hadn't risen to power until, say, 1936, one doubts that *Mathis* would have turned out much different. Gerd Albrecht's acquaintance with Hindemith's music goes back to the early 1960s, before the composer's death. Hindemith even sanctioned some retouching of the orchestration in *Mathis* made by Albrecht for a festival performance, though it isn't made clear whether Albrecht has applied it here. Rarely have Hindemith's often heavy textures sounded so clear.

As to the music, isn't the brief concluding 'Alleluia' duet that crowns the sixth tableau one of *the* great moments in 20th-century opera? You'll be convinced from your first hearing of it. There are fine moments aplenty in Albrecht's reading, not least where familiar passages from the *Mathis* Symphony surface and precipitate some of the most intense music of the opera.

Roland Hermann is, perhaps, a shade stolid in places as the painter (though his world-weariness in the final scene is just right); Josef Protschka makes a most authoritative Cardinal, acting as a perfect foil to Hermann's Mathis. They head a fine cast, supported by some lusty singing and playing from German radio forces.

Sancta Susanna

Sancta Susanna
Susan Bullock sop Susanna **Della Jones** mez Clementia **Ameral Gunson** mez Old Nun **Mark Rowlinson** spkr Farmhand **Maria Treedaway** spkr Maid **Leeds Festival Chorus**
Drei Gesänge, Op 9. Das Nusch-Nuschi, Op 20 – Dances. Tuttifäntchen – Suite

Susan Bullock sop **BBC Philharmonic Orchestra / Yan Pascal Tortelier**
Chandos CHAN9620 (70' · DDD · T/t)   Ⓕ▷►

Sancta Susanna is one of three early stage works Hindemith composed in the wake of the First World War, its companions being *Mörder, Hoffnung der Frauen* and *Das Nusch-Nuschi*, based on a play for Burmese marionettes and represented here by its dances. He earned a living at the Frankfurt Opera during this period, so it's natural that he nurtured operatic ambitions. *Sancta Susanna* enjoyed a certain notoriety in its day. Fritz Busch refused to conduct the premiere on account of its blasphemous plot. It tells briefly of a young nun, Susanna, inflamed by the legend she hears from Sister Clementia, of a girl coming naked to the altar to embrace the life-size figure of Christ on the Cross. For this blasphemy she's buried alive. Aroused and undeterred, Susanna strips off and rips the covering from Christ's torso. She's terrified when a huge spider falls on to her head from the crucifix and, horrified by her deed, begs the nuns to wall her up. A drastic cure for arachnophobia or blasphemy! The opera is short, concentrated, highly imaginative and resourceful in its use of sonority; and its expressionist musical language is so powerful that at the end of its barely 23 minutes you feel you've heard a much longer piece. It's superbly done here. No praise can be too high for the singers and for the delicacy, eloquence and power of the playing Tortelier draws from his orchestra. The recorded sound is of demonstration quality in its unforced naturalness.

The gorgeous Straussian *Drei Gesänge*, Op 9, are very vehement and passionate, and at times wildly over the top, but their assured craft and confident ambition is breathtaking. Susan Bullock performs them with thrilling panache. The dances from *Nusch-Nuschi* are just as expertly done.

Joseph Holbrooke   British 1878-1958

A pupil of Corder at the Royal Academy of Music, Holbrooke was influenced by Wagner and early Strauss. His large output, dating mostly from the beginning of the century, includes operas (among them the huge trilogy The Cauldron of Anwyn), symphonies, symphonic poems, chamber music and much for piano. **GROVE**music

Piano Concerto No 1

Holbrooke Piano Concerto No 1, Op 52, 'The Song of Gwyn ap Nudd' **Wood** Piano Concerto in D minor
Hamish Milne pf **BBC Scottish Symphony Orchestra / Martyn Brabbins**
Hyperion CDA67127 (69' · DDD · T)   Ⓕ OO

Holbrooke's ambitious First Piano Concerto is by some margin the most impressive orchestral piece of his to appear on disc. Dubbed a symphonic poem by its creator, it follows the narrative of a poem based on a Welsh legend by his patron Lord Howard de Walden entitled *The Song of Gwyn ap Nudd*. Yet the work can also be appreciated perfectly well as a red-blooded Romantic concerto in the grand tradition. Holbrooke handles proceedings with deft resourcefulness and a vaulting sweep. It receives outstandingly eloquent and tirelessly committed treatment in this performance.

An altogether more straightforward confection is the D minor Piano Concerto by Haydn Wood (1882-1959), who, before he made his name in the field of light music, was a gifted violinist and composition pupil of Stanford. Indeed, Stanford conducted the Queen's Hall premiere of Wood's big-boned D minor Concerto in July 1909. Grieg's Concerto is the obvious template, and there are stylistic echoes of Tchaikovsky, Rachmaninov and MacDowell. The opening movement is full of effective display, and boasts a ravishing secondary idea. By far the best music comes in the central *Andante* – a haunting, deeply felt essay, boasting some wistfully fragrant orchestral sonorities. Not a great work, by any means, but incurable romantics will devour it.

Heinz Holliger   Swiss b1939

Holliger studied with Veress, in Paris, and with Boulez in Basle. Since the mid-1960s he has appeared internationally in a repertory ranging from Baroque oboe concertos to works written for him by Berio, Henze and Lutosławski. He has a bright tone and extraordinary phrasing technique and has introduced new effects (eg. harmonics, double trills, chords). His compositions were initially Boulezian but have drawn nearer to Berio and Kagel in making the actual performance the main point (String Quartet, 1973). **GROVE**music

Violin Concerto

Holliger Violin Concerto, 'Hommage à Louis Soutter'ᵃ **Ysaÿe** Solo Violin Sonata in D minor, 'Ballade', Op 27 No 3
Thomas Zehetmair vn ᵃ**South West German Radio Symphony Orchestra, Baden-Baden and Freiburg / Heinz Holliger**
ECM New Series 476 1941 (54' · DDD)   Ⓕ**❍❍❶**

During 1993-5 Heinz Holliger composed a three-movement Violin Concerto of about half an hour. Shortly before this recording of 2002 he added a 17-minute Epilogue: 'I want to show that music can age, be sapped of vital energy and end in agony.' The concerto is inscribed as homage to Louis Soutter, a Swiss-born violinist and painter (1871-1942) whose troubled images of violence and despair haunted Holliger for many years. The Epilogue is called 'Before the massacre', after one of Soutter's macabre paintings from 1939.

The concerto clearly isn't a lighthearted piece, but neither is it emptily depressing or dishearten-

ening. Soutter studied with Ysaÿe, so Holliger starts from Ysaÿe's short Third Sonata, played here as a prelude. The first three movements offer a dazzling portrait of virtuosity under strain. The Epilogue is much tougher, but Holliger does not totally renounce all suggestions of compassion for human victims of violence and fanaticism. This may be ageing, agonised music, but its effect is less of futility than of hushed awe in the face of a creative impulse that refuses to lie down and die.

These positive impressions owe much to the artistry of Thomas Zehetmair, who has been associated with the concerto from the beginning. The recording gives a needle-sharp aural image of the progress from bright colours and brittle textures to dark evanescence.

Robin Holloway   British b1943

Holloway studied with Goehr (from 1960) and at Cambridge, where in 1974 he was appointed lecturer. His large output covers many genres (including numerous songs) and shows a remarkable command of diverse styles: some pieces lovingly reinterpret Romanticism (Scenes from Schumann for orchestra, 1970); others are strikingly positive in their modernism (The Rivers of Hell for chamber ensemble, 1977). His first opera, Clarissa, a study of rape, was given by the English National Opera in London in 1990. **GROVE**music

Concertos for Orchestra

Second Concerto for Orchestra, Op 40
BBC Symphony Orchestra / Oliver Knussen
NMC NMCD015M (34' · DDD)   Ⓜ**❍❍❍❶**

 A North African holiday was the stimulus for Robin Holloway's Second Concerto for Orchestra. The extremes of contrast, he tells us ('opulence and austerity, richness and drabness, brilliant light and dense shadow … And above all, the noises … the polyphony of hammering, tapping, thudding, tinkling, bashing …'), haunted him and were soon demanding to be turned into music. The experience seems also to have set him off on a more enigmatic, private voyage through his musical past. We hear a few particularly aching bars from Act 2 of *Tristan*, and rather more of Chopin's F sharp major Barcarolle; while a strange, broken tune on muted trombone metamorphoses neatly into Parry's *Jerusalem*. It's bewildering, but gripping. Holloway can swerve from lush, late Romanticism to strident modernism and back again with the alarming speed of an opium dream; but as with any really revelatory dream, the more you probe it, the more lucid it seems. When you reach the end, you feel you want to go back and soak in the experience all over again, and then go away somewhere and ponder its riddles.

The members of the BBC Symphony Orchestra play as though each one of them were engaged on his or her own voyage of discovery. Oliver Knussen's triumph in pulling it all together, and then shaping and shading it so lovingly, is just one of the technically miraculous aspects of this disc; another is that the production team have somehow turned BBC Maida Vale Studio No 1 into a fine, spacious acoustic, with details beautifully focused. It all adds up to a quite fascinating disc.

 GROVEmusic

Third Concerto for Orchestra, Op 76
London Symphony Orchestra / Michael Tilson Thomas
NMC NMCD039 (45' · DDD) Recorded live 1996
Ⓕ**O**☛

The first ideas for the Third Concerto for Orchestra came during a trip through South America: there are sound pictures of Lake Titicaca, riotous New Year's Day celebrations in the Bay of Bahia, the slow train-crossing of the Great Brazilian Swamp and the huge, satanic slag heap at the Potosì Silver Mine. Holloway jotted them all down on the spot: then his notebook was stolen, and it took another 13 years to recall them and finish the piece. By then, the alchemical processes of memory had transformed the original musical impressions into something quite different. What might have been simply a descriptive tone-poem finally emerged as a powerful and unusual musical argument – a huge slow movement, with a moderately fast dance-like finale, which evolves from tiny scraps of motifs (there's hardly a 'theme' in sight). And yet much of the original 'illustrative' character of the piece remains.

String and woodwind textures recall dense, overripe rain forest foliage; the dark, 'sluggish' first movement suggests the movement of a vast, slow, muddy river; extravagant sensuousness contrasts with clangorous bells or craggy brass. This recording, based on its 1996 premiere, is quite an achievement. It's rare for a conductor and an orchestra to show such a compelling grasp of the shape and atmosphere of a work at its first performance. Technically the sound has none of the usual problems associated with a live recording – virtually no intrusive noise, good balance, warm tone.

Gilded Goldbergs

Gilded Goldbergs (for two pianos after JS Bach), Op 86
Micallef-Inanga Piano Duo (Jennifer Micallef, Glen Inanga *pfs*)
Hyperion ② CDA67360 (98' · DDD)   Ⓜ**OO**

Holloway's initial prompt for these stunning two-piano transcriptions of Bach's *Goldbergs*, was his frustration as a single pianist at his 'inability to clarify the close-weave canons or manage the more fiendish hand-crossing numbers so

idiomatic on a two-manual harpsichord'. So far, so pleasurable – but then inevitably the full artistic implication of what he was doing struck home. It was only later, after much agonised self-questioning, that he decided to 'go for the gilding and lose the guilt!' Bach's original is thrown in at the deep centre of a swelling harmonic sea, sometimes as a moment of ineffable calm (Variation 18, a 'canon in sixths'), at other times more like an oncoming tidal wave (Variation 29, 'Toccata with clusters'). The use of modulation is often alarming but always musically effective and never more so than in an ingenious re-working of the closing 'Quodlibet' (Variation 30), which traverses 'all 12 keys', ending in D. Holloway's ear for nuance, and the ingenuity of his invention, will leave you open-mouthed with admiration. Whatever your CD priorities to date, this one surely has to fly straight to the top of your wants list.

Fantasy-Pieces on...'Liederkreis'

Holloway Fantasy-Pieces on the Heine 'Liederkreis' of Schumann, Op 16. Serenade in C, Op 41*b*
Schumann Liederkreis, Op 24
Toby Spence *ten* **Ian Brown** *pf*
Nash Ensemble / Martyn Brabbins
Hyperion CDA66930 (75' · DDD · T/t)   Ⓕ**O**

A contemporary composer takes a 19th-century classic, Schumann's song cycle *Liederkreis*, and sets it in a musical frame of his own devising: a short, astringent 'Praeludium' and four extended movements, the style hovering between pure homage and what the composer calls 'phantasmagorical collage'. Certainly sufficient to cause hackles to rise! But the result, entitled *Fantasy-Pieces on the Heine 'Liederkreis' of Schumann* is uniquely fascinating, haunting and increasingly rewarding the more one goes back to it.

Brief though it is, the 'Praeludium' is just enough to tell the ear that the performance of *Liederkreis* that follows isn't going to be the whole story. Holloway picks up magically on Schumann's ending, in a short movement, 'Half asleep' (what follows is, at times, intensely dream-like). Then come an *Adagio*, a *Scherzo* and a finale – on one level, symphonic, on another, an intricate series of references and cross-references based on Schumann's songs (not all from *Liederkreis*). The manner drifts between masterful irony and fleeting moments of intense self-revelation. *Liederkreis* remains *Liederkreis*, and yet something profound and (in the wider sense) modern is added.

The Serenade in C is a kind of post-modern *divertimento*. Scored for the same forces as Schubert's Octet, it alternates, charmingly and teasingly, between sensuous Viennese cosiness, something closer to the salon Elgar, and delightful, end-of-the-pier vulgarity – though with a more acerbic harmonic colouring from time to time. Play a short extract to a musical friend and he/she might well date it before the First World War. But nothing is ever what it seems for very long; the disruptive subtlety of *Fantasy-Pieces* is here too, despite the seeming holiday feeling.

Splendid performances from the Nash Ensemble – colourful, precise and sensitive to Holloway's kaleidoscopic shifts in mood. The recordings are quite excellent: the change in perspective for the Schumann songs makes perfect aural sense.

Vagn Holmboe   Danish 1909-1996

Holmboe studied with Høffding and Jeppesen in Copenhagen, and with Toch in Berlin, then returned to Copenhagen to work as a teacher (at the conservatory), critic and composer. He is the leading Danish symphonist after Nielsen (he has composed 11, 1935-82) and composer of a series of 14 string quartets (1949-75), regarded as the most important Scandinavian contributions to the genre since World War Two. He has also written operas, vocal and chamber music. His style is unproblematic if not immediately accessible, influenced by Nielsen, Hindemith and Stravinsky.   GROVEmusic

---

Chamber Concertos

Chamber Concertos – No 8, 'Sinfonia Concertante', Op 38; No 10, 'Wood, Brass and Gut', Op 40. Concerto giocondo e severo, Op 132. The Ill-Tempered Turk, Op 32b
Aalborg Symphony Orchestra / Owain Arwel Hughes
BIS BIS-CD917 (68' · DDD)   ⓕ🅑▶

Holmboe the concerto writer had a very different agenda from Holmboe the symphonist, and nowhere does that become more apparent than in *Chamber Concerto* No 8 (1945), subtitled *Sinfonia concertante*, a splendid work that's a direct precursor of the magnificent *First Chamber Symphony* (1953). Owain Arwel Hughes underscores the music's internal cohesion and plays down the Hindemithian overtones. No 10 (1945-6) is a bracing early example of Holmboe's metamorphosis technique, its nine sections acting like variations within a traditional concerto format: the sections in pairs respectively form an introduction and three 'movements', with the last acting as coda.

Holmboe devotees will be particularly keen on the other two works, both novelties. The *Cheerful and Severe* Concerto is a single (12-minute) movement, though like the Tenth, divided into sections; here, though, they are compressed to form a compellingly fluent design in the composer's late, luminous style. More fascinating still is the suite, made (with some recomposition) in 1969 from the music of the still-unperformed ballet *Den Galsindede Tyrk* (1942-4). The opening 'Dance of the Executioner' has echoes of the contemporaneous Fifth Symphony, while later movements – for instance, the central 'Dance of the Trees' – point towards the Sixth and Seventh (1947-50).

But the music also seems eminently danceable, making its neglect all the more astonishing. Heartily recommended.

Chamber Concertos – No 11 for Trumpet and Orchestra, Op 44; No 12 for Trombone and Orchestra, Op 52; Tuba and Orchestra, Op 127. Intermezzo concertante, Op 171
Håkan Hardenberger *tpt* **Christian Lindberg** *tbn* **Jens Bjørn-Larsen** *tuba* **Aalborg Symphony Orchestra / Owain Arwel Hughes**
BIS CD802 (55' · DDD)   ⓕ🅑▶

The Trumpet Concerto has a leanness of texture and neo-classical air that will surprise those familiar with Holmboe's symphonies. Hardenberger's first entry creates an electricity that's maintained throughout the work – indeed, the disc as a whole. No 11's tripartite design recurs, condensed into a single movement, in No 12: a brief, expressively crucial slow section framed by a large-boned *Allegro* (rather grave in character in the trombone work), and a good-humoured, rollicking finale. The Tuba Concerto (1976), by contrast, requires a full orchestral complement, its one integrated span bearing little semblance of traditional three-movement form. It's the most dramatic and exploratory work here, both in mood and sonority, the demands of which on tuba virtuosos over the years have occasioned it to be played in slightly differing versions, especially with regard to the taxing cadenza. The short *Intermezzo concertante* reaffirms that the tuba really can sing. Wonderful music, wonderfully performed and recorded.

Chamber Concertos – No 1, Op 17[a]; No 3, Op 21[b]; No 7, Op 37[c]. Beatus parvo, Op 117[d]
[c]**Gordon Hunt** *ob* [b]**Martin Fröst** *cl* [a]**Noriko Ogawa** *pf* [d]**Danish National Opera Chorus; Aalborg Symphony Orchestra / Owain Arwel Hughes**
BIS BIS-CD1176 (78' · DDD · T/t)   ⓕⓞ▶

A word about nomenclature. Holmboe composed 13 chamber concertos between 1939 and 1956 as a series with small-orchestral accompaniment, similar but not so homogeneous a set as Hindemith's *Kammermusiken*. Much later he renamed them just concerti, which is how BIS in its continuing series (coupled with other concertante works; this is the third issue) refers to them. Dacapo's integral set of the 13 curiously retained the chamber tag.

Irrespective of titles, they make a fine set. The concertos are extremely diverse and may surprise those who know only the symphonies and quartets. Hannu Koivula's nicely paced and well-thought-through interpretations for Dacapo, although a touch studio-bound, set a formidable standard to follow. As with the Brass and Orchestral Concertos, Owain Arwel Hughes more than rises to that challenge with tempi usually a touch swifter and more urgent, and the recorded sound more resonant, giving a warmer sound picture of each work.

This is particularly true in the First Concerto for piano, strings and timpani, where Ogawa is more sympathetically placed and not recessed as was Anne Øland. Ogawa's technique is also the stronger and she shapes Holmboe's neo-romantic lines even more splendidly than her rival.

In the Clarinet and Oboe Concertos honours are a little more even, though Martin Fröst and Gordon Hunt just shade the decision. There's a 'bigness' to Fröst's tone that Niels Thomsen cannot quite match and Hunt's incisive playing that's just about perfect. There's nothing inadequate about the Dacapo issues, but if you're in two minds about buying this newcomer consider the bonus of Holmboe's charming cantata *Beatus parvo*, a kind of concerto for amateur forces full of that marvellous luminosity that characterised so much of his music in his last decades. Strongly recommended.

Symphonies

Symphonies – No 11, Op 144; No 12, Op 175; No 13, Op 192
Aarhus Symphony Orchestra / Owain Arwel Hughes
BIS CD728 (63' · DDD)

Few who have invested in this series so far can doubt that these are among the most commanding symphonies to have emerged in post-war Europe. Some might even argue that they're *the* finest since Sibelius and Nielsen. All credit to Owain Arwel Hughes and the Aarhus orchestra for their committed advocacy and to BIS for recording them in such vivid, naturally balanced sound. The 11th, composed in 1980, is quintessential Holmboe, and its atmosphere resonates in the mind long after you've heard it. To quote Knud Ketting's notes, 'the symphony's climax in dynamic and emotional terms comes in the second movement and it then slowly retreats within itself…[it] is cast as a strong arch, which impresses at first hearing, and commands increasing admiration on closer acquaintance'. The arabesque that opens the symphony seems to come from another world and the transparent, luminous textures communicate the sense of a spiritual quest that one rarely encounters in modern music. The 12th is a taut, well-argued piece, and is, like its two companions on this disc, in three movements. No one listening to the 13th, written at the instigation of Owain Arwel Hughes, would think that it was the work of an 85-year-old. There have been other octogenarian symphonies, but none that sounds quite so youthful or highly charged as this.

Symphonic Metamorphoses

Symphonic Metamorphoses – No 1, Op 68, 'Epitaph'; No 2, Op 76, 'Monolith'; No 3, Op 80, 'Epilog'; No 4, Op 108, 'Tempo variabile'

Aalborg Symphony Orchestra / Owain Arwel Hughes
BIS CD852 (75' · DDD)

In form the symphonic metamorphosis is an off-shoot of the symphonic fantasia (but of a kind radically different from Sibelius's *Pohjola's Daughter*), each of these four very different from its companions. The vigour and luminous orchestration of the symphonies are present, as are many of the internal developmental processes, but not the level of integration. Holmboe's priorities here are unlike those of many others of his pieces, yet the music coheres perfectly on its own terms. Hughes is fully inside Holmboe's idiom, whether in the single-minded determination of *Monolith* or in the visionary *Epilog*, one of the composer's most searching utterances, prefiguring both the Ninth Symphony (1969) and *Requiem for Nietzsche*. This is extraordinary music.

Sinfonias

Symphonias I-IV, Op 73. Chairos
Danish Radio Sinfonietta / Hannu Koivula
Dacapo ② (two-for-the-price-of-one) 8 226017/8 (114' · DDD)

These four sinfonias for strings (1957-62) can be played either as independent pieces or – in a very particular sequence – as a large meta-symphony, *Chairos*, in which the four movements of Sinfonia IV frame and interlock with the single spans of I-III. Dacapo present, intelligently, both versions, each on its own disc.

Holmboe explained that 'Chairos means "time" in the psychological sense, that is the passage of time as we sense it', in contrast to measured time (Chronos). Sinfonias I-III all embrace the main elements of traditional symphonism in their unbroken designs, the first two adopting broadly a slow-fast ground plan, III the reverse. If IV's sequence of prelude, interludes and postludes suggests something lightweight, this is misleading, for it's a highly impressive structure; the movement titles are relevant mostly for the larger composition. It's unclear when Holmboe conceived this unusual double-form. The expressive characters and relative brevity of I and III suggest that he may have had a larger design in mind at first, though II, at 19 minutes, the longest by far of the four, hints at a totally separate genesis.

However the music started out, the achievement of *Chairos* is splendid testament to Holmboe's near-unique skill as a composer in the 20th century. In its larger form, it evinces a freedom of line and spontaneity of incident that suggests the tyranny of beat and bar-line had been cast off, yet in reality all is closely argued and achieved by total precision of means. Koivula and the Danish Radio Sinfonietta embrace this dichotomy in the music's soaring lines (which in the highest registers can sound just a touch thin) and multi-faceted fantasy. Dacapo's sound is of demonstration quality. Strongly recommended.

Gustav Holst

British 1874-1934

Holst studied at the Royal College of Music with Stanford, and in 1895 met Vaughan Williams, to whom he was close for the rest of his life. From 1905 he taught at St Paul's Girls' School in Hammersmith. Like Vaughan Williams, he was impressed by English folksong, but also important was his reading in Sanskrit literature (chamber opera Savitri, composed1908; Choral Hymns from the Rig Veda, 1912) and his experience of the orchestral music of Stravinsky and Strauss (he had played the trombone professionally). In The Planets (1916) he produced a suite of seven highly characterful movements to represent human dispositions associated with the planets in astrology, and his interest in esoteric wisdom is expressed too in his cantata The Hymn of Jesus (1917). But his very varied output also includes essays in a fluent neo-classicism (A Fugal Concerto for flute, oboe and strings, 1923; Double Violin Concerto, 1929), a bare Hardy impression (Egdon Heath, 1927) and operas. GROVEmusic

Egdon Heath

A Somerset Rhapsody, H87. Beni Mora, H107. Invocation, H75. A Fugal Overture, H151. Egdon Heath, H172. Hammersmith, H178
Tim Hugh vc **Royal Scottish National Orchestra / David Lloyd-Jones**
Naxos 8 553696 (69' · DDD)   ⓈⒹ

This superb recording was made in the Henry Wood Hall, Glasgow. Lloyd-Jones has as his two weightiest items the Hardy-inspired *Egdon Heath*, arguably Holst's finest work, as well as the prelude and fugue *Hammersmith*, comparably dark and intense. In the latter he chooses the wind-band version, achieving a subtlety of shading in phrasing and dynamic amply to justify that striking choice. The Naxos sound is vividly atmospheric while letting one hear inner detail. Lloyd-Jones generally adopts flowing speeds and is objective in his interpretation while bringing out to the full the tenderness and refinement of the writing. Particularly beautiful is the performance of *A Somerset Rhapsody* which opens the disc, with the cor anglais solo ravishingly played. The six works are neatly balanced, three dating from before the climactic period of *The Planets* and *The Hymn of Jesus*, and three after. Particularly valuable is the atmospheric *Invocation* for cello and orchestra of 1911, rather dismissed by Imogen Holst, but here given a yearningly intense, deeply thoughtful performance with Tim Hugh as soloist. This is a highly recommendable offering, whether for the dedicated Holstian or the newcomer wanting to investigate work outside *The Planets*.

The Perfect Fool

The Perfect Fool, Op 39. The Golden Goose, Op 45 No 1ª. The Morning of the Year, Op 45 No 2ª. The Lure

ªThe Joyful Company of Singers;
BBC National Orchestra of Wales / Richard Hickox
Chandos ⓇⓈ CHSA5069 (68' · DDD)   ⒻⓄⒹ

Though our modern age continues to extol *The Planets* as most archetypal of its composer, this recording of music written and completed during the 1920s serves only to reiterate that Holst's musical purview was much broader, and while he never enjoyed recognition for his ballet music (with the exception perhaps of *The Perfect Fool* as an orchestral suite), his originality rarely faltered. All the works featured here – a 'must' for all Holst fans – reveal how he built steadily on the experimental paradigms of *The Planets* with an orchestral technique second-to-none, 'naked' (as Vaughan Williams once described) in its exposed, gossamer textures.

Holst's distinctive sound is carefully manicured in this recording; the rapid 'mercurial' passages of string- and wind-writing of *The Perfect Fool* are delivered with exemplary crispness and vitality; the superimposed fourth harmonies of the unfamiliar *The Lure*, which develop mysterious bitonal 'saturnine' textures, look forward to the composer's unaccompanied choral masterpiece *The Evening Watch* as well as the desolate landscape of *Egdon Heath*, while the two choral ballets, *The Golden Goose* and *The Morning of the Year* (the former being weaker in quality) ebb and flow between Jovian elation and the more bizarre neo-classicism hinted at in 'Uranus' and the strange modernist textures of the later *Choral Fantasia*. Hickox certainly brings an electric appeal to these little-known, pointillistic scores as does the more finely tuned sense of ensemble between mystical voices and orchestra.

Perhaps the most compelling item on this disc, however, is *The Lure* which gives us a 'reworking' of *The Perfect Fool* but with a different climactic outcome derived from the warmer timbres and harmonies of the *Ode to Death*.

The Planets

The Planets
Women's voices of the Montreal Symphony Chorus and Orchestra / Charles Dutoit
Decca Gramophone Awards Collection 476 1724 (53' · DDD)   ⓂⓄⓄⓄⒹ

Ⓖ   *The Planets* is Holst's most famous work, and its success is surely deserved. The musical characterisation is as striking as its originality of conception: the association of 'Saturn' with old age, for instance, is as unexpected as it's perceptive. Bax introduced Holst to astrology, and while he wrote the music he became fascinated with horoscopes, so it's the astrological associations that are paramount, although the linking of 'Mars' (with its enormously powerful 5/4 rhythms) and war also reflects the time of composition. Throughout, the work's invention is as memorable as its vivid orchestration is full of infinite detail. No recording can reveal it all but this one comes the closest to doing so. Dutoit's individual performance is in a long line of outstanding recordings.

Holst The Planets[a]
(with **C Matthews** Pluto, The Renewer[a]) **Komarov**
Fall Pintscher Towards Osiris **Saariaho** Asteroid 4179 'Toutatis' **Turnage** Ceres
[a]**Berlin Radio Choir; Berlin Philharmonic Orchestra / Sir Simon Rattle**
EMI ② (two discs for the price of one) 359382-2 (84' · DDD)   Ⓜ❶❶Ⓓ

Near the beginning of his EMI career Simon Rattle recorded his first *The Planets*. It is excellent, but next to this spectacular new account it rather pales away. That 1982 recording cannot compare with the blazing brilliance, warmth and weight of the new one, which fully brings out the glory of the Berlin sound. Some may find the wide dynamic hard to cope with domestically – too loud at climaxes if the soft passages are to be clearly heard – but the body of sound is most impressive, with string *pianissimi* in 'Venus', 'Saturn' and 'Neptune' of breathtaking beauty.

Rattle's interpretation has intensified over the years. 'Mars' is more menacing and the dance rhythms of 'Jupiter' and 'Uranus' have an extra lift. Clearly the Berlin players have taken to this British work in the way they did for Karajan. Colin Matthews's 'Pluto' is given an exceptionally bold performance which exploits the extremes.

The second disc has four works commissioned by Rattle, dubbed 'Asteroids'. Kaija Saariaho, celebrating the asteroid Toutatis and its complex orbit, uses evocative textures and woodwind repetitions in ostinato patterns, much in line with Holst's technique. Matthias Pintscher's *Osiris* is more individual, featuring a spectacular trumpet solo in celebration of the Egyptian deity who became ruler of the underworld. Again, the piece is reflective rather than dramatic.

Mark-Anthony Turnage's *Ceres* is energetic with jazzy syncopations typical of the composer, while *Komarov's Fall* by Brett Dean, formerly a viola player in the orchestra, builds up to an impressive climax before fading away on evocative trills. Rattle's boldness in offering such unusual couplings is amply justified, even if most purchasers will concentrate on the superb version of a favourite piece.

Holst The Planets[a] **Elgar** Variations on an Original Theme, Op 36, 'Enigma'[b]
[a]**Geoffrey Mitchell Choir;** [a]**London Philharmonic Orchestra,** [b]**London Symphony Orchestra / Sir Adrian Boult**
EMI Great Recordings of the Century 567748-2 (78' · ADD) Recorded [a]1978, [b]1970   ❶❶

From the famous first run-through – for it can scarcely have been more – at the Queen's Hall in 1919, Boult had a long association with *The*

Planets. This splendid set from 1978 has been admirably remastered. Boult, in the composer's words, 'first made the *Planets* shine' and he always had something special to say about the music on all his recordings. Apart from public performances, he made five recordings of the work, and this is considered by many to have been the finest. His interpretation varied very little throughout his long association with the suite, only being temporarily shaken when he heard the reissue of Holst's own very different 1926 performance. However, he stuck to his own view, which Holst thoroughly approved of.

The actual performance has an indefinable 'rightness' about it, a supreme authority that makes it difficult to imagine the score being interpreted in any other way. Has 'Mars' ever resounded with more terrifying ferocity? In 'Venus' the playing has a translucent beauty, while the impish 'Mercury' really sparkles. 'Jupiter' has marvellous exuberance and sparkle, its big tune lent enormous dignity and humanity. 'Saturn', too, is paced to perfection (the central climax has a massive inevitability about it), and 'Uranus' goes about his mischievous antics with terrific swagger.

If you've never heard Boult's *Planets*, you should investigate this set immediately. Plenty of *Enigma* recordings have been added to the catalogue since 1970, but none has surpassed it in authority and fidelity. There's also a slightly elegiac feel to the phrasing, as if Boult, no sentimentalist, was nevertheless aware that his *Enigma* days must be numbered. Yet the faster variations have the vitality and brio you might expect from a younger conductor. The LSO's performance is excellent, and the recording too.

Holst The Planets[a] (includes extra version of Neptune with original ending). Lyric Movement **C Matthews** Pluto
Tim Pooley va **Hallé Orchestra and** [a]**Choir** (women's voices) / **Mark Elder**
Hyperion CDA67270 (75' · DDD)   Ⓕ

Unusually popular repertoire for Hyperion; but the special interest here is *Pluto*, commissioned by the Hallé's outgoing director Kent Nagano to illustrate the eighth planet, discovered only in 1930. For proper effect, though, it obviously demands a decent *Planets*, which happily it receives. If the Hallé lack the glitz and sheen of Dutoit's and Karajan's orchestras, then they offer a warmly idiomatic sound which suits the generally expansive yet detailed approach of their new director Mark Elder, as well as the full-blooded, rather forward recording.

Mars, with balefully clear percussion, steers a middle way between the machine-gun tempo favoured by the composer and Haitink's leaden grimness. *Venus* and *Mercury* are sensuous, even lingering, but *Jupiter* is refreshingly vibrant and dancing. Tension slackens somewhat in *Saturn*, but spaciousness and detail make more sense of *Uranus* than usual, although the transcendent organ *glissando* is somewhat underwhelming.

HOLST'S THE PLANETS – IN BRIEF

BBC SO / Sir Adrian Boult   Ⓗ
Beulah 2PD12 (70' · ADD)   Ⓜ
Set down in January 1945, this is the earliest and most exciting of the five recordings under the maestro, who, in the words of the composer, 'first caused *The Planets* to shine'.

London PO / Sir Adrian Boult
EMI 567748-2 (79' · ADD)   ⓂⓄ
Dedicatee Boult's final, unerringly paced account of a work with which, perhaps more than any other in his vast repertoire, he was most closely associated.

Montreal SO / Charles Dutoit
Decca 476 1724 (53' · DDD)   ⓂⓄⓄⓄ▷
Holst's colourful canvas has rarely been captured with such lustre or transparency by a recording team. Dutoit conducts with infectious bounce and plenty of twinkling affection.

London SO / André Previn
EMI 𝗗𝗩𝗗 492399-9 (75' · ADD)   Ⓕ
Originally made in quadraphony, Previn's memorable version leaps out of the speakers with startling impact, and is stunningly well played by the LSO at its early-70s peak. At present only available in DVD-Audio format.

Berlin PO / Sir Simon Rattle
EMI 359382-2 (84' · ADD)   ⓂⓄⓄ▷
Rattle's second recording finds the BPO on incandescent form – and with a series of miniature 'asteroids' as a bonus this is a highly recommendable version.

Hallé Orchestra / Mark Elder
Hyperion CDA67270 (75' · DDD)   Ⓕ
Like the Rattle recording, this one adds Colin Matthews's 'Pluto' (a Hallé commission) and Elder and his orchestra respond with a performance of idiomatic warmth and enthusiasm. The recording is vivid and surprisingly immediate.

BBC SO / Sir Andrew Davis
Warner Apex 8573 89087-2 (64' · DDD)   Ⓢ▷
Davis's admirably prepared account won't break the bank and enjoys sumptuous, stunningly well-defined recording – try 'Saturn' with its devastating climax and floorboard-throbbing organ pedals.

Royal Liverpool Philharmonic Orchestra / Sir Charles Mackerras
Virgin ② 561510-2 (121' · DDD)   Ⓢ
Mackerras invariably achieves spontaneous, communicative results on disc and this highly enjoyable 1990 *Planets* is no exception. This is a very satisfying, highly musical performance.

Neptune is suprisingly lush, with a chorus as alluring as ethereal. Which, in the main version here, fades out to *Pluto* – a flashing *scherzo*, inspired by the rushing particles of the so-called 'solar wind'. Matthews wisely avoids Holstian pastiche, linking it to the original by tempo – Holst's favoured 5/4 – and sound; celesta, glockenspiel and jittery percussion create fleeting reminiscences of the other planets. The result is appealing, postmodern but lyrical, yet ultimately unsatisfying. Like a spectacularly modern wing grafted onto a classic building, it stimulates by contrast, yet the uneasy lack of unity diminishes both.

A separate piece, linked companionably rather than umbilically, might have been more effective. As the composer disarmingly admits, Pluto's planetary status is pretty dubious, anyway. The *Lyric Movement*, with a fine soloist, raises hopes for some more rare Holst from this particular team.

The Planets. Egdon Heath, H172
BBC Symphony Chorus and Orchestra / Sir Andrew Davis
Warner Apex 8573-89087-2 (64' · DDD)   Ⓢ▷

This is a mightily impressive account of *The Planets*. The high is undoubtedly 'Saturn', whose remorseless tread has rarely seemed more implacable. Aided by orchestral playing that's both memorably concentrated and rapt, Holst's textures in the closing section acquire a breathtaking translucency, and how memorably the BBC SO brass thrusts home the terrifying central climax. 'Neptune', too, is exceptionally successful: ethereally delicate *tremolando* harps set the scene for a tone picture of exquisite beauty, graced by choral work of notable purity from the women of the BBC Symphony Chorus. Elsewhere, 'Mercury' darts hither and thither in suitably impish fashion. 'Venus' is cool and chaste: if the BBC violins can't quite command the bloom and sheen of the very finest groups, the liquidity and poise of the woodwind are most striking. And the burst of energy at the close of 'Jupiter' is genuinely exhilarating. The spectacularly ample sound certainly makes the mischievous antics of 'Uranus' a feast for the ears, and Davis handles the coda superbly, plunging the listener into a world which is unnerving in its bleakness. He shows comparable perception in the similarly remote terrain of *Egdon Heath*, and succeeds in conveying much of the sombre intensity of Holst's cloud-hung evocation.

Additional recommendations

A Somerset Rhapsody

Coupled with: Beni Mora. A Fugal Overture. Hammersmith. Japanese Suite. Scherzo
London Philharmonic Orchestra; LSO / Boult
Lyrita SRCD222 (62' · ADD)   Ⓕ
Conducted by one of the composer's greatest friends and staunchest advocate, this release is still in the front rank.

Choral works

The Cloud Messenger, H111[aef]. The Hymn of Jesus,
H140[ef]. A Choral Fantasia, H177[bdg]. A Dirge for Two
Veterans, H121[dg]. Ode to Death, H144[eg]. Ave Maria,
H49[c]. Motets, H159-60[c] – The Evening-Watch. This
have I done for my true love, H128[c]. Seven Partsongs,
H162[bdg]. O lady, leave that silken thread, H4[c]. Short
Partsongs, H13[c] – Soft and gently through my soul. The
autumn is old, H1[c]. Winter and the birds,
H App I/40[c]
[a]Della Jones *mez* [b]Patricia Rozario *sop* [c]Finzi
Singers / Paul Spicer; [d]Joyful Company of Singers;
London Symphony [e]Chorus and [f]Orchestra, [g]City
of London Sinfonia / Richard Hickox
Chandos Two for One ② CHAN241-6 (147' · DDD)
Ⓜ Ⓞ➔

The Cloud Messenger is a 43-minute work of considerable imaginative power. Before its previous
single-issue release it had been virtually forgotten since its disastrous premiere under Holst's
baton in 1913. It shows the composer already
working on an epic scale---something that casts
light on the subsequent eruption of *The Planets*.
It's marvellous to have the work on disc, though,
as you might expect, it's uneven. Those who
admire the ascetic rigour of his later music may
share Imogen Holst's reservations, and find the
score disappointingly 'backward'. There are
certainly echoes of Vaughan Williams's *A Sea
Symphony* and several older models. On the
other hand, the glittering approach to the sacred
city on Mount Kailasa and the stylised orientalism of the climactic dance are new to British
music; another world, that of 'Venus', is fore-
shadowed in the closing pages.

One of the few incontrovertible masterpieces
in Holst's output, the familiar *Hymn of Jesus* has
seldom received a better performance on disc.
The choral singing itself is splendidly crisp, but
the lively acoustic can blunt the impact of
Holst's acerbic harmonies.

Songs

Hymns from the Rig Veda, H90[c]. Six Songs, H69[a]. Four
Songs, H132[ad]. 12 Songs, H174[b]. Margrete's cradle
song, H14 No 2[a]. The Heart Worships, H95[a]
[a]Susan Gritton *sop* [b]Philip Langridge *ten*
[c]Christopher Maltman *bar* [d]Louisa Fuller *vn* Steuart
Bedford *pf*
Naxos 8 557117 (76' · DDD · T) Ⓢ➔

The Four Songs for voice and violin, settings of
medieval texts, were inspired by the composer
hearing one of his pupils singing to herself and
playing her violin in Thaxted Church.They're
singularly moving, especially in this plangently
toned performance by Susan Gritton. She is no
less remarkable in the Six Songs, early pieces in
which Holst perfectly responds to an eclectic
choice of poetry, nowhere more so than in the
opening piece from Tennyson's 'In Memoriam'.

Philip Langridge is equally well suited to the 12
Humbert Wolfe settings, to which he brings his
customary gift of an immediate response to the
texts in hand. His empathy with poet and composer here couldn't be closer. The *Vedic* Hymns
are more rarified, mystical territory and not so
easy for singer or listener to encompass. Christopher Maltman does well by them, except where an
incipient beat sometimes spoils pleasure in his
singing.

Pianist Steuart Bedford is responsive to all the
varying moods of these groups, and in the opening group Louisa Fuller is the sensitive violinist.

Bo Holten   Danish 1948

*Holten is equally well known as a choral conductor as
he is as a composer. He founded the vocal ensembles
Ars Nova and Musica Ficta both of which he honed
into outstanding groups, and with whom he performed and recorded extensively. As a composer he
has written over 100 works, including three operas,
numerous pieces for unaccompanied choir and scores
for film.*

First Snow[d]. Tallis Variations[de]. Visdom og Galskabad.
Psalm 104 'Hvor er dine værker mange'[c]. Egos flos
campi[c]. Ebbe Skammelsøn[bd]. Triumf att finnas till[d]
[a]Klaudia Kidon *sop* [b]Jesper Juul Sørensen *tbn*
Danish National [c]Girls' Choir, [d]Choir and [e]Strings
of the Symphony Orchestra / Bo Holten
Chandos CHAN10320 (60' · DDD · T/t) Ⓕ➔

Bo Holten has written a substantial corpus of
choral music but, as he observes in his notes to the
recording, 'the tonal style of my writing has not
really seemed politically correct to the bodies
commissioning music in Denmark'. While many
composers who have written large amounts of
choral music in many countries would say substantially the same thing, it should not be forgotten that Holten is also an accomplished orchestral
composer. Indeed, the two worlds come together
in the *Tallis Variations* (1976). At least, they are
intended to come together though it's hard to
explain the feeling of incompleteness that remains
after such a promising clash of sound worlds of
strings and choir.

Many of the other works recorded here also
draw on Holten's extensive knowledge of early
music (particularly Renaissance polyphony) but
perhaps the most successful work on the disc is
one of the oddest, defying easy categorisation:
Ebbe Skammelsøn (2001) is based on an old Danish
ballad and is a kind of mini-opera featuring choir,
12 soloists and solo trombone. The trombone's
psychological commentary lends an extraordinary strangeness to the piece, interacting and at
the same time somehow defining the ritualistic
anger of the work as conveyed by the singers. The
grandiose (and technically challenging) setting of
Edith Södergran's *Triumf att finnas till* provides a
fitting conclusion to this accomplished, varied
and magnificently sung collection.

Arthur Honegger
French/Swiss 1892-1955

Honegger studied from 1911 at the Paris Conservatoire, then returned to Switzerland for military service (1914-15), though Paris remained his home. He was a member of Les Six, and set Cocteau's libretto in his stylised opera Antigone (1927), but he had no time for Satie or for the group's flippancy: he was acutely aware of artistic responsibility and took his guidelines from Bach and Beethoven.

His harmony, though fundamentally tonal, is often dense and wide-ranging, set in motion by a vigorous rhythmic propulsion that suggests Baroque formality wielding modern means: that is the manner of his oratorio-style stage works, including Le roi David (1921) and Jeanne d'Arc au bûcher (1938). His other works include five symphonies (1930, 1941, 1946, 1946, 1951), three 'symphonic movements' (Pacific 231, 1923; Rugby, 1928; No 3, 1933), chamber pieces, songs and much incidental music.

GROVEmusic

Cello Concerto

Cello Concerto, H72ª. Une cantate de Noël, H212ᵇ. Prélude, fugue et postlude, H71ª. Horace victorieux, H38
ᵇ**James Rutherford** bar ª**Alban Gerhardt** vc
BBC National Chorus and Orchestra of Wales / Thierry Fischer
Hyperion CDA67688 (76' · DDD · T/t)   Ⓕ●

The works collected here cover the full range of Honegger's mature career, from the volatile 'mimed symphony' *Horace victorieux*, his first major orchestral utterance (1920-21), to his final completed work, *Une cantate de Noël* (1952-53). In expressive range, the music alternates from Yuletide light and shade to the Stravinskian high jinks of the Cello Concerto's finale (1929), to the high drama of *Horace victorieux*, not otherwise available.

Horace victorieux was the first real indication of Honegger's natural genius for large-scale orchestral composition. Based on Livy's bloodthirsty tale of Publius Horatius, the score combines vigorous, martial allegros depicting the combat and evocative lyrical episodes for the uneasy love of Horatius's sister for her enemy, Curiatius. Heard in abstract, it proves a compelling symphonic poem of elemental power. There is a hint of the same quality in the less intense *Prelude, Fugue and Postlude* Honegger extracted in 1948 from his 1929 score for *Amphion*, although its atmosphere – based on Greek myth – is quite peaceable. There is a real touch of Christmas to the Cantata, one of Honegger's most popular works despite its gloomy, tonally ambiguous opening quarter. It is excellently sung.

Fischer directs controlled but expressive accounts of all four works which would grace any collector's shelves. Gerhardt is excellent in the Concerto, although its delicate, plaintive opening is eclipsed by proximity to *Horace*'s

close. Hyperion's superb recording has much to commend it, dealing superbly with some huge dynamic ranges.

Symphonies

No 1 in C; **No 2** for Strings and Trumpet obbligato in D, H153; **No 3**, H186, 'Liturgique'; **No 4** in A, H191, 'Deliciae basiliensis' **No 5** in D, H202, 'Di tre re'

Symphonies Nos 1-5. Three Symphonic Movements – Pacific 231, H53; Rugby, H67; No 3, H83. Pastorale d'été, H31
Suisse Romande Orchestra / Fabio Luisi
Cascavelle ③ RSR6132 (174' · DDD)   Ⓕ●

In most respects this recording is excellent. The textures are clear and sharp, and passages like the contrapuntal *tour de force* in the last movement of the Fourth Symphony are all the more impressive for it. The Suisse Romande's solo woodwind are fresh and seductive, with a particularly fine first oboe while, on the other hand, the clarity of the recording can bring with it a certain bleakness, entirely appropriate at the beginning of the Fifth Symphony, which here comes over rather like Sibelius.

In first two symphonies, Luisi's tempos sound just a little heavy. But his penchant for slower speeds brings notable rewards both in the central movement of the Third Symphony and in the final *Adagio* of the third *Symphonic Movement*. Luisi is alive to the strong element of melancholy and disillusion in this music – strong also in Honegger himself. In the opening of the Second Symphony, Luisi recognises the call of fate, that changeth not. A large measure of Honegger's disillusion came from what he saw as the triumph of the forces of collectivism over the individual human spirit, and in the Third Symphony Luisi brings out the solo cello line in the third movement as the voice of the composer crying out against the waste of war.

Honegger Symphonies Nos 2 & 3
Stravinsky Concerto in D
Berlin Philharmonic Orchestra / Herbert von Karajan
DG The Originals 447 435-2GOR (72' · ADD)
Recorded 1969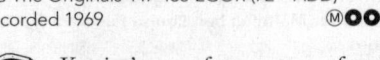

Ⓖ Karajan's performances of these Honegger symphonies enjoy legendary status – and rightly so. This recording remains in a class of its own for sheer beauty of sound and flawless ensemble. The French critic, Bernard Gavoty, once spoke rather flightily of Karajan 'transcending emotions and imparting to them that furnace heat that makes a work of genius give off light if brought to the desired temperature' – but it's true! There's a luminous quality and an incandescence about these performances.

The Stravinsky Concerto in D major was written within a year of the *Symphonie liturgique* and may perhaps be a little too 'cultured' and not spiky enough for some tastes. The lightness of touch, sprightliness of rhythm and flawless ensemble of the Berlin Philharmonic Orchestra are an absolute joy in themselves.

Alan Hovhaness   American 1911-2000

Hovhaness studied with Converse at the New England Conservatory. His earliest music, though Romantic in harmony, reflects his interest in Renaissance style; from 1943 he began to incorporate elements of his Armenian heritage, and in the 1950s, when he travelled widely, he embraced non-Western and experimental procedures. From c1960 he took a keen interest in Japanese and Korean music, which affected his style; only in the 1970s did he return to a more Western style, richer and more spacious. An individual feature is his way of treating elements (harmony, tone colour etc) as either predominant or else neutral; any note may be exclusively linear, vertical, textural or rhythmic. Most of his work is broadly religious in inspiration; he is enormously prolific, having reached his first 60 symphonies in the mid-1980s, with corresponding production in other orchestral music, choral and solo vocal works, piano and chamber music. GROVEmusic

Concertos

Cello Concerto, Op 17[b] Symphony No 22, 'City of Light', Op 236[b].
[a]**János Starker** *vc* **Seattle Symphony Orchestra /** [b]**Alan Hovhaness,** [a]**Dennis Russell Davies**
Naxos 8 559158 (61' · DDD)   Ⓢ🅑➤

City of Light (1970) has some lovely ideas, like the surprisingly sweet and simple string melody in the middle of the 'Angel of Light' movement, and the third movement, *Allegretto grazioso*, which sounds like a minuet in oriental garb. The outer movements, however, outstay their welcome.

On the other hand, the Cello Concerto (1936) is required listening for Hovhaness admirers. The composer destroyed several hundred of his compositions during a period of self-reflection in the early 1940s, but the concerto survived the cull, finally receiving its premiere in 1999. The music's modal tinge is pure Hovhaness, but there is a spareness to the writing that sets it apart from its successors. Indeed, the tone is unrelievedly elegiac, making the Elgar Concerto seem positively jovial by comparison. János Starker brings sad nobility to the ruminative solo part, and Dennis Russell Davies makes the most of the *Das Lied von der Erde*-like orchestral texture in a warmly recommended disc.

Concerto for Two Pianos and Orchestra[abd]. Piano Concerto, 'Lousadzak'[ade]. Mihr[ab]. Ko-Ola-U[ac]. Vijag[ac]
[a]**Martin Berkofsky,** [b]**Atakan Sari,** [c]**Sergei**

Podobedov *pfs* [d]**Nikolai Zherenkov** *vn* [e]**Globalis Symphony Orchestra / Konstantin Krimets**
Black Box BBM1103 (55' · DDD)   Ⓕ🅑➤

Alan Hovhaness bucked most of the late 20th century's modernist trends, which may explain why his music doesn't sound all that dated. The Concerto for Two Pianos (1954) could have been written yesterday, in fact; with its intermingling of raga and fugue, it's the kind of east-meets-west venture that still seems to be the rage. Yet it's also thornier music than those familiar with, say, the composer's *Mysterious Mountain* Symphony (his best-known work) might expect, and it could surprise those who think of him as bland.

There's quite a bit of stark dissonance, particularly in the second movement, in which the pianists climb volatile symphonic terrain in jagged, quasi-atonal arpeggios. The solo parts are the opposite of flashy, though, and often seem to blend into the orchestra's percussion section. When they do get a chance to step forward, however, pianists Martin Berkofsky and Atakan Sari make an impressive showing; the gamelan-like passagework in the finale, for example, chimes exquisitely.

Berkofsky gets more of a chance to flex his muscles in the *Lousadzak* Concerto (1944). Marco Shirodkar points out in the booklet-note that Hovhaness, who is so often thought of as a musical conservative, actually anticipated many soon-to-be-hip aleatory techniques. Note the nervous, chattering *pizzicato* that accompanies the piano's stark cadenza: it's actually 'improvised' by the strings. Less dramatically incisive than the Double Concerto, the music has a spare sensuality that's equally, if not more, delectable.

In both concertos the Globalis Symphony Orchestra play expertly under Konstantin Krimets. Three exotically tinged pieces for two pianos fill out the disc and they, too, are sensitively rendered. An important and attractive addition to Hovhaness's discography.

Symphonies

Symphonies – No 2, 'Mysterious Mountain', Op 132; No 50, 'Mount St Helens', Op 360; Symphony No 66, 'Hymn to Glacier Peak', Op 428. Storm on Mount Wildcat, Op 2 No 2
Royal Liverpool Philharmonic Orchestra / Gerard Schwarz
Telarc CD80604 (72' · DDD)   Ⓕ

It's easy to dismiss the music of Hovhaness, who was was suspiciously prolific, with opus numbers nearing 500. But despite such sustained productivity over more than seven decades, his work is stylistically consistent – so much so, in fact, that some only half-jokingly claim he wrote the same symphony 67 times. Certainly, the profusion of sing-song fugues and modal, hymn-like tunes throughout his output can give a feeling of predictability.

And yet listening to the opening movement of the *Mount St Helens* Symphony (1982), it's difficult not to be entranced, even awed, by the music's sensuous beauty – those luminous clouds of strings, that majestic rising theme in the horns, then, a little later, the delicate spinning of the harp and a procession of ecstatic, exotic woodwind solos. Perhaps the depiction of the volcano's eruption is a bit primitive, though it's fascinating that Hovhaness seems to view the explosion not only as an elemental event but also as a ritualistic one.

Hymn to Glacier Peak (1992), the composer's penultimate symphony, is also appealing. As the title suggests, it has a preponderance of hymn-like melody, yet there's a touching valedictory quality to the music. The finale is particularly effective, moving from hymn to one of Hovhaness's most tuneful fugues via a darkly atmospheric interlude.

Warmly recommended: this would make an excellent introduction to Hovhaness's music.

Symphony No 63, 'Loon Lake'. Guitar Concerto No 2[a]. Fanfare for the New Atlantis
[a]**Javier Calderón** gtr **Royal Scottish National Orchestra / Stewart Robertson**
Naxos American Classics 8 559336 (59' · DDD) ⓢ🅑

Alan Hovhaness's Second Concerto was commissioned by the great Narciso Yepes in 1985 but wasn't premiered until 1990, shortly before Yepes's death. It's classic Hovhaness, with numerous hymn-like passages for the strings contrasted with lively *pizzicato* sections and fugal textures; the guitar meanwhile rejoices in puckish, modally rich dances enlivened by frequent changes of time signature and broad cantorial utterances. Bolivian-born Javier Calderón's playing is tonally refined and rhythmically supple, qualities which are best savoured in his own third-movement cadenza.

The disc opens with Hovhaness's *Fanfare for the New Atlantis*, in which a slumbering orchestra gradually awakens to the call of a solo trumpet before rushing strings, rumbling timpani and bold brass chords bring the work to a thrilling, Wagnerian climax as the lost city of Atlantis rises anew from the waves. The Symphony No 63, *Loon Lake*, was commissioned by the New Hampshire Music Festival and the Loon Preservation Society in 1987. Here, songs both avian and pastoral punctuate a luminous, if occasionally overcast, orchestral skyscape.

The RSNO under Stewart Robertson is excellent throughout; good recorded sound and notes by Hovhaness's widow Hinako Fugihara Hovhaness further enhance what is another excellent release.

Khaldis, Op 91

Khaldis, Op 91[a]. Mount Katahdin, Op 405[b].
Fantasy, Op 16[c]

[ab]**Martin Berkofsky**, [c]**Alan Hovhaness** pfs [a]**William Rohdin**, [a]**Dan Cahn**, [a]**Francis Bonny**, [a]**Patrick Dougherty** tpts [a]**Neal Boyar** perc
Crystal CD814 (52' · ADD) Recorded [c]1970, [a]1972, [b]1999   Ⓕ

Khaldis (1951) has a connection with the late Hovhaness's well-known *St Vartan* symphony (1950) in their common use of a quartet of trumpets: the composer wanted a piece he could play with them and a percussionist alone. It's a striking work – named from the god of the universe of the pre-Armenian Urarduan people – full of apocalyptic visions. The even-movement structure has the feel of a set of studies rather than an integrated concerto, the brass tending to play en bloc and one movement scored as if for some primordial trio of giants.

The sonata *Mount Katahdin* (1986-7) doesn't sound almost a career later than *Khaldis*. The four movements resemble the sequence of a Bach orchestral suite, with the imposing opening 'Solenne', succeeded by three tiny movements, lighter in character and acting as foils for the first. The central 'Jhala of Larch Trees' is particularly lovely. Berkofsky plays with evident love and conviction, and these are persuasive performances, whether from 1972 or 1999 (*Mount Katahdin*).

Most fascinating of all is Hovhaness's own account of the *Fantasy*, written *c*1936 and also once available on a Poseidon LP. A mesmeric performance of a mesmeric piece, the 10 sections or 'steps' built from Indian ragas utilise Cowellesque devices such as playing the strings inside the instrument with fingers, plectrum, marimba mallet or timpani stick. The sound overall is acceptable but the remastered *Khaldis* and *Fantasy* are a touch lacking in depth.

Herbert Howells   British 1892-1983

Howells studied with Stanford and Wood at the Royal College of Music, where he taught from 1920 almost to his death. He also succeeded Holst at St Paul's Girls' School (1932-62) and was professor of music at London University. His music is within an English diatonic tradition embracing Elgar, Walton and Vaughan Williams. The earlier works include two piano concertos and chamber pieces, but most of his music is choral, including c15 anthems, a concert Requiem (Hymnus Paradisi, 1938, first performed 1950), Masses, anthems and motets and some fine songs. Deeply tinged by the English choral tradition, Howells's music reflects a subtle and fastidious craftsman who was capable of a restrained, individual eloquence.   GROVEmusic

---

Piano Concertos

Piano Concertos[a] – No 1 in C minor, Op 4; No 2 in C, Op 39. Penguinski
[a]**Howard Shelley** pf **BBC Symphony Orchestra / Richard Hickox**

Chandos CHAN9874 (71' · DDD) Ⓟ Ⓞ ▷

An astonishing revelation, especially to anyone who still thinks of Herbert Howells as a nostalgic English rhapsodist, more at home in an organ loft than a concert hall. The First Piano Concerto is very early (1914 – Howells was 22) and hasn't been performed for many years because its last few bars are missing (John Rutter has provided them). It reveals the young Howells as more Russian than English – the dazzlingly flamboyant keyboard writing is strongly reminiscent of Rachmaninov – and with hardly a trace of English reserve as he brandishes theme after theme, intensifying many of them to heights of impassioned eloquence.

One or two lyrical paragraphs suggest the 'real' Herbert Howells. But who, the Second Piano Concerto demands, was he? This work was abused at its premiere (one critic shouted 'Thank God that's over!') and Howells, deeply wounded, withdrew it immediately. Indeed, although it's a lot closer to 'real' Howells in its rhapsodic lyricism, there's another quality which is angular, sometimes dissonant, tough and determined.

Surely we shall get closer to the real Howells, lifelong admirer of the arch-conservative Stanford, in *Penguinski*, from its title an obvious satire on Stravinsky? But in fact the sidelong glances at him are admiring and affectionate, and the robust humour is Howells' own. There's more to him than we had imagined, and his stature is increased, not diminished, by the realisation that he was once an exuberant Romantic, that his ears were sharp and that he had a sense of humour.

Enthusiastic, virtuoso, very slightly rough-cornered performances and a sumptuously rich recording.

Chamber Works

Howells String Quartet No 3, 'In Gloucestershire'
Dyson Three Rhapsodies
Divertimenti (Paul Barritt, Rachel Isserlis *vns* Gustav Clarkson *va* Sebastian Comberti *vc*)
Hyperion Helios CDH55045 (64' · DDD) Ⓑ

If you don't yet know Howells's masterly *In Gloucestershire* (the last of his three works for string quartet), an exquisitely wrought, hauntingly atmospheric creation, then immediate investigation is recommended.

The coupling, too, is a delight. Completed between 1905 and 1912, Dyson's youthful *Three Rhapsodies* form a most appealing triptych, uncommonly fluent, tightly knit and always evincing an engaging, at times positively Straussian lyrical grace. Divertimenti give another first-rate display brimful of commitment and communicative warmth. The airy, natural sound complements its budget-price.

Further listening

Howells Rhapsodic Quintet

Coupled with: **Frankel, Holbrooke, Arnold Cooke** and **Maconchy** Clarinet Quintets
King *cl* **Britten Quartet**
Hyperion Helios CDH55105 (66' · DDD) Ⓑ

Howells' *Rhapsodic Quintet* is a jewel, while no one could fail to be touched by the elegiac last movement of Frankel's eloquent Quintet. Thea King forms a stylish and sensitive partnership with the much-missed Britten Quartet. At budget price, don't miss it.

Organ Sonata No 2

Organ Sonata No 2. Six Pieces (1940-45)
Graham Barber *org*
Priory PRCD524 (67' · DDD) Recorded on Hereford Cathedral organ Ⓕ

These are powerful, authoritative performances which ooze the spirit of Howells – that odd mixture of emotional detachment with a hint of deep personal passion, an undercurrent of tragedy and an almost improvisatory fluidity of structure. The Sonata has a formal structure which makes it easy to follow while the *Six Pieces* give such a kaleidoscopic array of organ colours that the ear is continually enchanted. The Hereford organ is a lovely instrument. Priory has, in focusing the microphones on the organ, expunged much of the building's aural ambience, but the sound is an utter delight to the ear.

Evening Services

Evening Services – G; Collegium Sancti Johannis Cantabrigiense; New College, Oxford; Collegium Regale; Sarum; York. Magnificat and Nunc Dimittis
The Collegiate Singers / Andrew Millinger with **Richard Moorhouse** *org*
Priory PRCD745 (65' · DDD) Ⓕ Ⓞ

Howells wrote 20 settings of the evening canticles. His first setting (1918), the freshly vigorous work of the Stanford pupil, sets out on the long life's musical journey with bone and muscle. The gentler passages have a light-footed grace, and in exultation the spirit flares; this is the music of purposeful movement, where the more 'Howells' he becomes the more the firm lines of the Stanford pupil dissolve, and the nearer he draws to a music of mystical stasis. The opening of the Collegium Regale *Magnificat* has something of this, the great thing being that he can still pull out of it (with the strong-boned 'He hath shown strength with his arm', for instance). It's a pity that the series hasn't been arranged chronologically; it would have been good to follow the order of composition, seeing which parts of his musical system he developed and which he left unexercised.

The other slightly faltering element in this welcome release concerns the choice of a choir of mixed voices. The women scrupulously adhere to the tonal ideal, but boy trebles and male altos have a distinctive quality, and Howells's own sound is less distinctive without them. It's an extremely good choir, and they're under careful, intelligent direction, yet making a chance comparison with the choir of Bristol Cathedral in the G major setting one can't help rejoicing in a character (individual as a face) which those trebles possessed and for which the Collegiate sopranos substitute a collective identity somewhat depersonalised.

The recorded sound is fine, balance between choir and the excellent organist is well judged, and the acoustic resonance is sufficient to form an appropriate setting while preserving the clear articulation. The selection here also includes two premiere recordings (the York Service and the 1941 setting for men's voices, performed, as the score suggests, by women).

Requiem

Requiem[a]. Choral and Organ Works. Collegium Regale – Communion Service[ab]. St Paul's Service[ab]. Like as the hart[a]. Long, long ago[a]. Take Him, Earth, for Cherishing[a]. Organ Rhapsody No 3[b]. Paean[b]
[b]**Ian Farrington** org [e]**St John's College Choir, Cambridge / Christopher Robinson**
Naxos 8 554659 (76' · DDD · T)   ⓈⒹ▸

Howells, probably more than any other composer, extended the cathedral repertoire in the 20th century. Here his music is performed by one of the best choirs. Under Christopher Robinson, St John's has preserved its distinctive character (the bright tone of its trebles a famous part of it) and, as this record demonstrates, has gained in vigour and clarity of purpose. Immediately notable is the choice of relatively quick speeds. Howells sometimes appears to invite a relaxed style of performance which isn't to his advantage.

St John's tempo suits the acoustic. This applies to a similar comparison with the Choir of King's College in its more reverberant chapel, singing the Communion Service dedicated to it: the more opulent sound matches the broader tempo, St John's achieving (as in the *Sanctus*) clearer effects within a narrower spectrum. Their discs also have in common the *Rhapsody No 3* for organ, and whereas the expansive performance at King's includes a murmurous *pianissimo* next-thing-to-silence, the quicker, more sharply defined one at St John's has a dramatic urgency.

The choice of programme is particularly happy, with one of the lesser-known Evening Services (the 'St Paul's') and one of the best known of Howells's anthems (*Like as the hart*).

Additional recommendation

Requiem
Coupled with: Take him, earth, for cherishing.
Vaughan Williams Mass in G minor. Te Deum
Coxwell, Seers sops **Chance** counterten **Salmon** ten
J Best bass **Corydon Singers / M Best**
Hyperion Helios CDH55220 (67 · DDD)   Ⓑ

A fine performance of the *Requiem* and attractive couplings.

Hymnus Paradisi

An English Mass – Hymnus Paradisi
Julie Kennard sop **John Mark Ainsley** ten
Liverpool Philharmonic Choir; Royal Liverpool Philharmonic Orchestra / Vernon Handley
Hyperion CDA66488 (80' · DDD · N/T)   Ⓕ

The *Hymnus Paradisi* is music awash with ecstasy, and the listener may resist becoming part of this swimmingly coloured dream. But further listening proves this is not so: that is, the better you know it, the more you see in it of form, energy and pain. The pain is real enough, as biographical facts attest. Howells wrote it as a method of escape from 'the crippling numbness of loss', as he described the effect upon him of his son's death from polio at the age of ten. The work was so full of the emotion of that time that for many years it had to remain private, and it was only with the approach of the 15th anniversary of the death that he showed it to Vaughan Williams and arrangements were made for its inclusion in the Three Choirs Festival of 1950.

A strong performance helps, and Vernon Handley brings real intensity: there is a feeling for the dramatic quality in the score, the crises and relaxations, without losing sight of the essential lyricism. The soloists on the recording sing with sensitivity and pleasing tone.

Jenö Hubay   Hungarian 1858-1937

Violinist and composer, Hubay studied violin with Joachim, and later gave concerts with Liszt. He was a close friend and later executor of Vieuxtemps who recommended Hubay to head violin studies at the Brussels Conservatory. His legacy is large inclusing operas and over 200 works for violin.

Violin Concertos – No 1; No 2. Suite, Op 5
Hagai Shaham vn **BBC Scottish Symphony Orchestra / Martyn Brabbins**
Hyperion CDA67498 (73' · DDD)   Ⓕ

Here's a disc to demonstrate what an outstanding lyricist Jenö Hubay was, particularly in the first of the concertos, the *Concerto dramatique*, in which one good tune follows another, each of them a candidate for the sort of virtuoso figuration designed to show off the brilliance of the soloist. Hubay himself was a formidable violinist who, to celebrate his 50th birthday in 1908, played this concerto in a concert when his other three violin concertos were played by his pupils Josef Szigeti, Franz von Vecsey and Stefi Geyer, dedicatee of Bartók's early Violin Concerto No 1.

Hubay composed that first concerto in 1884-85 for his former teacher, Joseph Joachim, and much of the writing tends to bring to mind

Bruch's concertos, which is no disadvantage. No 2 dates from around 1900 and though the first movement is less distinguished, with a rather rigid main theme like a patriotic song, it too is a tuneful piece. The second and third movements are even more attractive, a charming interlude leading to a sparkling Hungarian dance finale.

The Suite, Op 5 (1877-88), another *concertante* work for violin, starts rather unpromisingly with a gavotte which, with its square main theme and hammered double-stopping, sounds more like a march. The other three movements are freer-running in their lyricism: genre pieces, an 'Idylle' marked *Andantino*, an Intermezzo and a dazzling finale full of virtuoso writing, which misleadingly opens with a brief reminiscence of the opening movement.

Hagai Shaham plays not just with brilliance but with great imagination, avoiding any idea that this is just superficial display music. As in so many of Hyperion's concerto recordings, Martyn Brabbins and the BBC Scottish SO demonstrate what sympathetic accompanists they are, consistently giving an impression of live music-making. The full and vivid recording made in Caird Hall, Dundee, equally lives up to the high standard expected in Hyperion's enterprising concerto series.

Tobias Hume   English c1570-1645

An officer in the Swedish and Russian armies, Hume played the viol and entered Charterhouse almshouse in London in 1629. His two published lyra viol tablatures (1605, 1607) contain all his known works – dances, descriptive and programmatic pieces and songs.   GROVEmusic

Musicall Humors

Captaine Humes Pavan. A Souldiers Resolution. Deth. Life. Captaine Humes Galliard. Touch me lightly. A Pavane. My hope is decayed. A Souldiers Galliard. Beccus an Hungarian Lord. The Second part. A Question. An Answere. The new Cut Good againe. The Duke of Holstones Almaine. Hark! Hark!. The Spirit of Gambo: The Lord Dewys favoret Humorous Pavin. Love's Farewell
Jordi Savall *va da gamba*
Alia Vox AV9837 (70' · DDD)   Ⓕ**O**

Tobias Hume was a professional soldier and a 'gentleman' (read amateur) composer, and virtuoso of the bass viol. His *Musicall Humors* (1605), a large collection of solo pieces, is the first publication devoted to the lyra viol, a style of playing that treated the instrument polyphonically, like a lute. Hume reveals himself as a distinct, even eccentric, personality, and an inventive composer, expanding the viol's normal range with such unusual devices as *col legno* ('Drum this with the backe of your Bow').

Jordi Savall's cultivated, elegant style is very appropriate for much of the music; occasionally he adopts a more earthy manner to great effect – for example in *A Souldiers Resolution*, with its trumpet and drum imitations. When Captain Hume's *Humors* become more reflective, in a piece like *Beccus an Hungarian Lord*, Savall uses varied bow strokes and dynamic shadings with great artistry, to bring out the music's dignified, sombre character.

In characterising the music so strongly, Savall's rhythms are often very free; the rushing scalic divisions and lingering approaches to cadences balance one another, and prevent the music ever seeming stiff or mechanical. It's a finely produced disc, too, with a fascinating essay about the composer by David Pinto.

Johann Hummel   Austrian 1778-1837

A child prodigy and a pupil of Mozart (Vienna, 1786-8), Hummel undertook an extended tour (1789-92) throughout northern Europe with his father, arousing particular interest in England, where he met Haydn. Back in Vienna he studied with Albrechtsberger, Salieri and Haydn, giving lessons to support himself. He held a position as Konzertmeister to Prince Nikolaus Esterházy (1804-11) and, after a period of writing piano and chamber music for Vienna, returned to the concert platform. He was Kapellmeister in Stuttgart (1816-18) and Weimar (from 1819), where he conducted the court theatre and many concerts, knew Goethe and other luminaries and still had time to teach and compose; he toured regularly as a pianist and worked tirelessly on his important piano method (1828). The climax of his career came in 1830 with a trip to Paris and London. Despite his public and financial success – he had an excellent business sense and systematised multinational music publishing – he remained a warm and simple person. His playing was praised for its clarity, neatness, evenness, superb tone and delicacy, products of his preference for the light-toned Viennese piano; he excelled at improvisation. Ferdinand Hiller was among his pupils. Hummel wrote some of the finest music of the last years of Classicism, with ornate Italianate melodies and virtuoso embroidery; his later music shows more expression and variety, including imaginative harmony and long flights of lyricism.   GROVEmusic

Piano Concertos

Piano Concerto No 4 in E, Op 110.
Double Concerto in G, Op 17
Hagai Shaham *vn* **London Mozart Players / Howard Shelley** *pf*
Chandos CHAN9687 (63' · DDD)   Ⓕ**O**

Shelley is outstanding in this music, blending classical and Romantic elements perfectly. These two concertos are wonderfully infectious. The E major occupies a kind of bridge between Mozart and Chopin, although Mozart's depth and subtlety are in a different vein. Hummel is more of a show-off, and his music almost smiles at you, its charm and sparkle eschewing any pretentiousness. Throughout, Shelley conveys the music's *joie de vivre*, revelling in the figurative passagework. The Double Concerto may have been inspired by Mozart's *Sinfonia concertante*, K365; it doesn't have the same harmonic or lyrical variety as the E-major Concerto, but it's a charming work, especially when so persuasively played. Shelley's well-proportioned piano part is perfectly complemented by Hagai Shaham's sweet-toned violin. Shelley fulfils his dual role admirably, and the London Mozart Players respond well to his playing and conducting. The recorded sound is first-rate. A lovely disc.

Piano Concerto No 5 in A flat, Op 113. Concertino in G, Op 73. Gesellschafts Rondo in D, Op 117
London Mozart Players / Howard Shelley pf
Chandos CHAN9558 (59' · DDD)   ⒻⒹ➔

These are decorous rarities played with an assured brilliance and affection. Hummel's Mozartian rather than Chopinesque bias declares itself most obviously in his Op-73 *Concertino*, though even here the figuration has a recognisably Hummelian froth and sparkle. Too charming to be vacuous, such surface brio has little in common with Mozart's depth and subtlety, and for music of greater romantic range and ambition we turn to the A-flat major Concerto, with its fuller scoring and lavishly decorated solo part. Lovers of a fine-spun, operatic cantilena will warm to the central 'Romanze'. The *Gesellschafts Rondo* commences in solemn *Adagio* vein before turning to a bustling and ceremonious *Vivace*. It may be that Hummel 'puffed, blew and perspired' when he played but he won the admiration of Chopin (a hard master to please) and his style is infectious when projected with such unfailing expertise by Howard Shelley in his dual role as pianist and conductor. The Chandos recordings are exceptionally well balanced.

Trumpet Concerto

Hummel Trumpet Concerto in E flat **Haydn** Trumpet Concertos in E flat, HobVIIe/1; in Cᵃ
Concertos by **Albinoni, Corelli, Hertel, JM Molter, Mozart, FX Richter, J Stamitz**. Works by JS Bach, Clarke and Gounod
Håkan Hardenberger tpt **Simon Preston** org
Academy of St Martin in the Fields / Sir Neville Marriner; ᵃ**London Philharmonic Orchestra / Elgar Howarth;** ᵇ**I Musici**
Philips Duo ② 464 028 (148' · DDD)   ⓂⓄ

This is probably the finest single collection of trumpet concertos in the catalogue. When it first appeared in 1987 (the Hummel and Haydn have since been recoupled with a later set as listed here) it created overnight a new star in the firmament of trumpeters.

The two finest concertos for the trumpet are undoubtedly those of Haydn and Hummel, and Hardenberger plays them here with a combination of sparkling bravura and stylish elegance that are altogether irresistible. Hardenberger opens with the famous Hummel Concerto, played in E major rather than the usual E flat, which makes the work sound bolder and brighter than usual. The finale with its crisp articulation, fantastic tonguing and tight trills, displays a genial easy bravura, yet overflows with energy and high spirits. Marriner and his Academy accompany with characteristic finesse and warmth, with the lilting dotted rhythms of the first movement of the Hummel, seductively jaunty. The lovely *Andante* of the Haydn is no less beguiling, and both finales display a high-spirited exuberance and an easy bravura which make the listener smile with pleasure.

The recording gives him the most vivid realism and presence, but it's a pity that the orchestral backcloth is so reverberant; otherwise the sound is very natural. A superb disc.

Cello Sonata

Hummel Cello Sonata **Moscheles** Cello Sonata No 2. Melodic-Contrapuntal Studies (after Bach's Well-Tempered Clavier) – No 4 (after Book 2 No 7); No 8 (after Book II No 6); No 9 (after Book 1 No 4)
Jiří Bárta vc **Hamish Milne** pf
Hyperion CDA67521 (65' · DDD)   Ⓕ

Hummel and Moscheles make an apt pair: each was a keyboard virtuoso who wrote prolifically. Yet where Hummel has been well represented on disc lately, Moscheles is far more neglected. That makes the new issue specially valuable. Their careers overlapped, but Moscheles lived for 33 years more after Hummel died, actively composing till the last. The works here appeared some three decades apart – not that the stylistic contrast is at all marked, for both adopted an easily lyrical style celebrating the early 19th rather than the 18th century, with Mendelssohn more of an influence than Mozart.

This is particularly so in Moscheles's Cello Sonata of 1850-51, with one or two echoes of the Mendelssohn Octet and with a *Scherzo* marked *ballabile*, sparkling in the way one expects of Mendelssohn. The younger composer, a close friend, also influenced Moscheles in his devotion to Bach, represented here by the three *Melodic-Contrapuntal Studies*, involving flowing melodic writing for the cello neatly fitted to Bach's original keyboard Preludes.

Following tradition, Moscheles gives priority to the piano over the cello in describing the work, not surprising from a pianist-composer, and this recording rather brings that out; the sensitive cellist, Jiří Bárta, is regularly overshadowed. What is more unexpected is how the last two movements echo Czech music, not just in the rhythms and melodic shapes of some of the themes but in the alternation of speeds; that suggests that Moscheles was influenced by the

Czech dumka. The Sonata is rounded off with a dashing movement in which Moscheles encourages the pianist to show off in several passages.

Otherwise this is a work designed for intimate music-making, and that is even more clearly so in the Hummel Sonata, which opens with a triple-time *Allegro amabile*. 'Amiable' is an apt description of the piece, not just in that lyrical first movement but the central *Romanze* which is rather like early Beethoven. Here, too, there are echoes of the music of eastern Europe in the finale, maybe influenced by Hummel's tours of Russia and Poland.

Though it is a pity that Bárta is not presented as a full equal to Milne (who plays brilliantly), the recording balance is largely to blame. An attractive disc nonetheless.

Piano Trios

Piano Trios – No 2; No 5; No 6
Voces Intimae Trio (Richard Cecchetti *fp* Luigi de Filippi *vn* Sandro Meo *vc*)
Warner Classics 2564 62595-2 (61' · DDD)   Ⓕ Ⓓ➜

Piano Trios – No 1; No 3; No 4; No 7
Voces Intimae Trio
Warner Classics 2564 62596-2 (70' · DDD)   Ⓕ Ⓓ➜

Unlike most of Hummel's chamber works the piano trios are relatively well covered on disc – not surprising when they offer such a free flow of attractive ideas. The difference in this new cycle is that the players use period instruments and there is a positive advantage in a having a light and slightly twangy fortepiano in place of a modern concert grand. So in the second-movement *Andante* of the First Trio, the transition from the *pizzicato* arpeggios on the cello at the start to similar figuration from the fortepiano, a restored instrument of 1815, is much more winningly integrated in this lively performance. The interplay between the players is a delight.

Those who resist period instruments may find that the bright tone of the violin with little vibrato is a shade aggressive but the vigour of the performances is magnetic. The lightness of touch of this antique fortepiano allows Richard Cecchetti to play with phenomenal clarity of articulation even in the fastest movements, such as the *Presto* finale of No 1.

What makes the Voces Intimae performances even more sparkling than the excellent ones from the Beaux Arts Trio from the late 1990s (Philips) is that, playing at speeds generally a shade less extreme in fast movements, they have more room for expressive pointing and phrasing, giving shape to passages that might otherwise seem hectic. That is so in the witty finale of No 3 – in a sort of polka rhythm which sounds like an ancestor of a Gilbert and Sullivan patter song – and in the finale of No 7.

Anyone wanting to sample before investing in the complete cycle should plump for the second disc whose four compact works are likely to quickly charm. The forward recording is admirably clear and full.

Solo Piano Works

Piano Sonatas – No 3 in F minor, Op 20; No 5 in F sharp minor, Op 81; No 6 in D, Op 106
Stephen Hough pf
Hyperion CDA67390 (69' · DDD)   Ⓕ Ⓞ

Stephen Hough's splendid issue is in its way as revelatory as his *Gramophone* Award-winning recordings of the piano concertos. He revels in the element of display which Hummel, one of the leading pianists of his day, must have brought out in his own performances.

These three works are arguably the most interesting of Hummel's nine solo sonatas. The most radical is No 5, with the composer in 1819 enthusiastically throwing himself behind the new romantic movement. A strikingly angular opening motif leads to an argument which, in a very free rendering of sonata form, brings surges of energy set against moments of reflection; there are many unexpected melodic and harmonic twists and few passages of conventional figuration, such as those that weaken the piano concertos.

The slow movement, too, opens surprisingly, with a heavyweight *fortissimo* gesture, before settling down to a yearning melody, anticipating Chopin's Nocturnes but more bare in texture, with cantilena echoing *bel canto* opera. The finale is a wild Slavonic dance, fierce and energetic in headlong flight, again dotted with unexpectedly angular ideas.

In the Sixth Sonata in 1824 Hummel was rowing back from the romantic stance of Op 81. The first movement establishes a much lighter tone and is more conventional in structure, exceptionally clear in its presentation of sonata form. The opening theme, for all its lightness of texture, has characteristically quirky twists, and leads to a warmly lyrical second subject, rather like Weber. The second movement *Scherzo*, the most striking of the four, is a fast mazurka, leading to a slow movement rather like a Mendelssohn *Song without Words* and a virtuoso finale, light in texture at the start and ending, after all the display, in an unexpected throwaway cadence.

Sonata No 3 in F minor, dating from 1807, again starts gently before developing quirks typical of Hummel. The slow movement then surprisingly has the marking *Maestoso*, majestic, strong and forthright rather than conventionally lyrical, leading to another virtuoso finale, relatively brief, with cross-hand, Scarlatti-like leaps for the left hand.

Masses

Mass in B flat, Op 77. Mass in D, Op 111.
Offertorium, 'Alma Virgo', Op 89a[a]
[a]**Susan Gritton** sop **Collegium Musicum 90 /
Richard Hickox**
Chandos Chaconne CHAN0681 (76' · DDD · T/t)
Ⓕ Ⓞ Ⓞ Ⓞ ➜

When the glories of Haydn's late Masses have been widely appreciated, it's sad that Hummel's have been so neglected. They are for chorus and orchestra alone, without soloists, which may have deterred potential performers. However, while they can't quite match late Haydn or Beethoven in originality, they're lively, beautifully written, and full of striking ideas, inspiring Hickox and his team to performances here just as electrifying as those they have given of Haydn, and just as vividly recorded.

Hummel follows Haydn in both Masses in his fondness for fugues. Similarly, he follows Haydn in offering joyfully energetic settings of 'Dona nobis pacem', only unlike Haydn he doesn't end either Mass on a *fortissimo* cadence, instead fading down the final phrases, maybe for liturgical reasons in the context of a church performance. Hummel, like Haydn and Beethoven before him, fully brings out the drama of the liturgy, though in both settings of 'Et resurrexit' he begins not with a sudden *fortissimo* but with a rising *crescendo*, as though a crowd of bystanders are gradually appreciating the wonder of it.

Another symbolic point is that the Mass in B flat, dating from 1810, the year before Hummel left the Esterházy court, includes a setting of the *Credo* with distinctive unison and octave passages for the chorus, as though to emphasise unity of belief. In both masses the settings of the *Sanctus* are surprisingly brief, even perfunctory, yet the musical ideas could not be more striking, with a gently flowing 6/8 setting in the D major work and a bold setting in the B flat Mass which crams into the shortest span surprisingly varied ideas.

Thanks to the imagination of Richard Hickox, we're finally able to discover the joys of Hummel's Masses. An extremely fine disc.

Mass in E flat, Op 80. Quod quod in orbe, Op 88. Te Deum in D
Susan Gritton sop **Ann Murray** mez **James Gilchrist** ten **Stephen Varcoe** bar **Collegium Musicum 90 / Richard Hickox**
Chandos Chaconne CHAN0712 (62' · DDD · T/t)
Ⓕ**ⓄⓄ**▶

The second in Richard Hickox's Hummel Mass edition concentrates on works written soon after Hummel was appointed *Konzertmeister* to Prince Esterházy in 1804. Hummel was keen – the Mass was completed four months before the September deadline. In his booklet-note David Wyn Jones suggests the composer may have been trying to pre-empt his potential rival, Johann Fuchs, who was nominally in charge of church music for the prince. The result has a winning freshness. As in the first disc, Hickox captures the joy of Hummel's inspiration, with clean attack and fine diction from chorus and soloists.

That clarity extends to the superb setting of the *Te Deum*, written at high speed to celebrate peace with Napoleon in 1805. Each section of the elaborate text is strikingly characterised without holding up the urgency established in

the opening fanfares. The graduale *Quod quod in urbe* is another fine, neglected work. The Blackheath Concert Hall recording is full and clear: this is shaping up to be an outstanding series.

Mass, S67/W13[a]. Salve regina, S79/W18[b]
[ab]**Susan Gritton,** [a]**Rachel Nicholls** sops [a]**Pamela Helen Stephen** mez [a]**Mark Padmore** ten [a]**Stephen Varcoe** bar **Collegium Musicum 90 Chorus; Collegium Musicum 90 / Richard Hickox**
Chandos CHAN0724 (57' · DDD · T/t)
Ⓕ**Ⓞ**▶

The D minor Mass of 1805 was the second of five that Hummel wrote for Prince Esterházy, carrying on from Haydn's late masterpieces. D minor was the key chosen by Haydn for his *Nelson* Mass seven years earlier but Hummel's opening could hardly be more different. If its persistent syncopations on repeated notes at the start suggest a curious hesitancy, one can look to Mozart's Piano Concerto No 20 as a direct inspiration; this *Kyrie* develops from hesitancy into blazing confidence.

Throughout, Hummel seems intent on taking the listener by surprise: the *Gloria* emerges in a positive D major on a bold unison motif using the notes of the common chord but develops quickly into elaborate counterpoint; the *Credo* starts lyrically, the opposite of a positive affirmation of belief, though that is developed as the movement progresses. Hummel intended to write a thoughtful rather than a sharply dramatic setting, with the soloists generally treated as a corporate team set against the full choir: the tenor solo for 'Et incarnatus est', sung with honeyed tone by Mark Padmore, is a striking exception. The brief *Sanctus* is positive with military overtones; the *Benedictus* in triple time starts with the soloists alone; while the *Agnus Dei* finally returns us to D minor before the triumphant setting of 'Dona nobis pacem'.

The *Salve regina* of 1809, the year Haydn died, may have been written for a memorial event to Hummel's great predecessor, but it is anything but elegiac in its operatic style with elaborate coloratura for the soprano soloist, here glowingly sung by Susan Gritton. Richard Hickox again proves an ideal interpreter, drawing superb playing and singing.

Missa solemnis in C, W12. Te Deum, W16
Patricia Wright sop **Zam McKendree-Wright** contr **Patrick Power** ten **David Griffiths** bar **Tower Voices New Zealand; New Zealand Symphony Orchestra / Uwe Grodd**
Naxos 8 557193 (57' · DDD)
Ⓢ▶

This, the longest of Hummel's five Masses, is another invigorating example, coupled with an electrifying setting of the *Te Deum*. Both were written in 1806 and feature martial reminders that this was the period of the Napoleonic Wars.

The *Te Deum* opens with a rousing march, and with one or two relaxed passages for contrast –

illustrating this long and varied prayer-text – continues in a single span. It ends with a brisk and triumphant *fugato*, quite different from the sombre close most often heard in Anglican settings. It's a delight. Uwe Grodd draws an exhilarating performance from his forces.

The performance of the Mass is equally successful. The grandeur of the writing is established in the slow introduction to the *Kyrie*, leading to a brisk main *Allegro* (following Haydn's lively practice in *Kyries*) in a rhythmic triple time. The martial flavour of the writing is evident from the *Gloria*'s opening fanfares and continues into the *Credo*, until a sharp change of key to a warm A major brings a relaxed and lyrical setting of 'Et incarnatus', followed by the clashing discords of the 'Crucifixus'. 'Et resurrexit' restores the military mood. One moment to relish comes after the last of the calls of 'Credo' on 'Et vitam venturi' (track 4, 9'09") with two rising scale passages clearly intended to send you up to Heaven in their exhilaration.

Brodd opts to use his admirable soloists throughout the *Benedictus*, even though the autograph suggests otherwise. It works very well, with imitative writing for the soloists set against the four-square tread of the orchestra. With the *Agnus Dei* Hummel at last writes a meditative movement, slow and hushed, which develops into chromatic writing in a minor key, before the 'Dona nobis pacem', as in Haydn's masses, brings a joyful close. Grodd inspires vigorous playing and singing from his forces, who are freshly and cleanly recorded.

Engelbert Humperdinck

German 1854-1921

Humperdinck studied at the Cologne Conservatory (1872-6) and at the Royal Music School in Munich (1877-9), meeting Wagner in Naples and assisting him with Parsifal at Bayreuth (1881-2). After interludes in Paris, Spain, Cologne and Mainz (working for B Schotts Sohne), he moved to Frankfurt as a teacher and opera critic, also writing his most famous work, Hänsel and Gretel (1890-93; given its début at Weimar under Richard Strauss); by 1900 he was in Berlin, teaching, composing operas and writing Shakespearean incidental music (among his most successful work). The operatic version of Königskinder, another characteristic piece in his naive, folklike style, was first performed in New York in 1910; like Hänsel und Gretel it started from simple song settings and went through an intermediate stage to a full opera, showing Wagnerian harmonic and textural influences. **GROVE**music

Hänsel und Gretel

Hänsel und Gretel 	[H]
Elisabeth Grümmer *sop* Hänsel **Elisabeth Schwarzkopf** *sop* Gretel **Maria von Ilosvay** *mez* Gertrud **Josef Metternich** *bar* Peter **Anny**

Felbermayer *sop* Sandman, Dew Fairy **Else Schürhoff** *mez* Witch **Choir of Loughton High School for Girls; Bancroft's School Choir; Philharmonia Orchestra / Herbert von Karajan**
EMI Great Recordings of the Century mono ②
567061-2 or Naxos 8110897/8 (108' · ADD · T/t)
Ⓜ❶❷➔

The EMI CD transfer has opened up the mono sound, putting air round the voices and instruments, giving presence. Where the earlier transfer of this set sounded disappointingly flat, this one is brighter, clearer, fuller, with textures clarified. The voices better defined and separated.

A full stereo recording would have been better still, but it was this recording which Walter Legge would often cite in conversation, when he mounted his curious hobby-horse, questioning the value of stereo over mono. The scene he picked on was where children hear the cuckoo in the forest: there the distancing of the cuckoo-call does indeed simulate stereo atmosphere, but that's far clearer this time than last.

The performance remains a classic, with Karajan plainly in love with the music, and the two principals singing immaculately. This isn't for those who resist the child-voice inflexion of Schwarzkopf and Grümmer, but everyone else will register the mastery in singing and acting. The thinness of Anny Felbermayer's voice as the Sandman is an unwelcome contrast, but this is otherwise a satisfyingly Germanic team.

Hansel and Gretel (in English)
Jennifer Larmore *mez* Hansel **Rebecca Evans** *sop* Gretel **Robert Hayward** *bar* Peter **Rosalind Plowright** *mez* Gertrude **Diana Montague** *mez* Sandman **Sarah Tynan** *sop* Dew Fairy **Jane Henschel** *mez* Witch **New London Children's Choir; Philharmonia Orchestra / Sir Charles Mackerras**
Chandos/Peter Moores Foundation Opera in English ② CHAN3143 (91' · DDD · S/T/N) Ⓜ❶❷➔

When a perfectly serviceable version of *Hansel and Gretel* in English already exists on CfP, it is generous as well as bold for the Peter Moores Foundation to sponsor this new one. In every way it replaces the old. That was an EMI effort in 1964 using multichannels – the result: unnecessarily close voices and a dim orchestra. On Chandos the recording is clear and beautifully separated yet with an agreeable bloom on voices and instruments.

The Canadian Mario Bernadi, then briefly the Sadler's Wells company's music director, conducts a lively performance but Sir Charles Mackerras is altogether more inspired and imaginative, with pointing and phrasing that readily match Karajan's masterly conducting on the classic mono EMI set.

Though the CfP singers, from the old Sadler's Wells company, are good with clear, firm voices, their 'prunes and prisms' enunciation of words harks back to a pre-war tradition, dating the performance. This time, following the practice at English National Opera, the David Pountney translation is used, fresher and more idiomatic, helping the starry cast of soloists, led by Jennifer Larmore and Rebecca Evans, both superb in the title-roles, nicely contrasted while blending well together.

There is strong casting, too, for the Witch, with Jane Henschel refusing to caricature the role in 'funny-voice' singing; Rosalind Plowright, gravitating down to mature mezzo, as the Mother, and Robert Hayward as the Father, don't guy their characterisations, either; while there are good contrasts between the bright Dew Fairy of Sarah Tynan and the warm Sandman of Diana Montague.

All told, this set will clearly stand the test of time as an English version, rivalling even the best of versions in the original German. The exhilaration of the final scene in particular is irresistible, with Mackerras drawing a genuinely Viennese-sounding lilt in the waltz rhythms of the 'Witch is dead' duet, the destruction of the Witch's House powerfully conveyed and the revival of the gingerbread children movingly done. The fresh young voices of the New London Children's Choir are beautifully caught.

Hänsel und Gretel
Antigone Papoulkas *mez* Hansel **Anna Gabler** *sop*
Gretel **Hans-Joachim Ketelsen** *bar* Peter (Father)
Irmgard Vilsmaier *mez* Gertrud (Mother) **Iris
Vermillion** *mez* Witch **Lydia Teuscher** *sop* Sandman;
Dew Fairy **Dresden State Opera Women and
Children's Chorus; Staatskapelle Dresden /
Michael Hofstetter**
Stage director **Katharina Thalbach**
Video director **Paul Smaczny**
Euroarts 205 5888 (108' · NTSC · 16:9 · PCM stereo,
5.1 and DTS 5.1 · 0)
Recorded live at the Semperoper, Dresden, in
December 2006   Ⓕ

This DVD version of *Hänsel und Gretel* starts well with the glorious horns of the Dresden Staatskapelle in the overture, and Michael Hofstetter draws warmly expressive playing in a work very much central to their repertory. The recording, live in the helpful acoustic of the Semperoper, adds to expectation, with eager children in the large audience.

That said, Katharina Thalbach's production will not please everyone. Grotesquerie rather than charm is the keynote. Hansel and Gretel are portrayed as dolls with crude make-up on spotty faces. Even their movements mimic those of puppets. Costumes are those of German peasants, with the drunken father still more of a caricature, both in costume and acting. The sets and designs by Ezio Toffolutti, minimal and stylised, are undistracting.

Other characters, too, match the grotesque illustrations in traditional German fairy-tale books, which seem strangely old-fashioned to us. The exception is the Witch, characterfully sung by Iris Vermillion, initially glamorous in a form-fitting scarlet gown with shiny high boots but transformed into an old crone when she

takes off her wig, revealing a bald head, huge false ears and a hump on her back. Small wonder the children push her into the oven.

The cuckoo is another sort of doll, shooting out from the wings on a spring, with the gigantic sweets of the Witch's house let down from the flies, and with the little house itself made up of gigantic biscuits. The Sandman is another doll, and the Dew Fairy appears wearing ice skates around her neck. The captured children are revealed as sweets, until Hansel with a broom frees them all, and they form a long line to shake hands with Hansel and Gretel in a very Germanic way.

The staging tells the story clearly and believably but the trendy ideas come too thick and fast for comfort. Singing is generally good if not outstanding. Hansel (Antigone Papoulkas) and Gretel (Anna Gabler) are diminutive figures with clear, bright voices, and Hans-Joachim Ketelsen as the Father and Irmgard Vilsmaier as the Mother sing strongly; Lydia Teuscher is jewel-bright as the Sandman and the Dew Fairy. Excellent singing, too, from the chorus of children and women.

Königskinder

Königskinder
Jonas Kaufmann *ten* King's Son **Ofelia Sala** *sop*
Goose Girl **Detlef Roth** *bar* Fiddler **Nora Gubisch**
mez Witch **Jaco Huijpen** *bass* Woodcutter **Henk
Neven** *bass* Landlord **Fabrice Mantegna** *ten* Broom-
maker **Nelly Lawson** *sngr* Broom-maker's Daughter
Hans-Otto Weiss *bar* Senior Councillor **Mareen
Knoth** *mez* Landlord's Daughter **Marc Dostert** *ten*
Tailor **Diana Schmid** *contr* Stable Maid
**Opera Junior Children's Chorus; Latvian Radio
Choir; Montpellier National Orchestra /
Armin Jordan**
Accord ③ 476 9151 (165' · DDD · S/T/t/N)   Ⓕ

While it can never match the mastery of the fairy-tale *Hänsel und Gretel*, this seriously neglected opera offers much fine music. The plot is over-complicated and the piece rather long but musically there is much to enjoy, not least the duets and ensembles.

This new version has the advantage of being recorded live, giving it dramatic tautness under the sympathetic direction of Armin Jordan. He draws incisive singing from the multiple choruses, not least the children's, and the excellent cast is superbly led by Jonas Kaufmann, who sings the strenuous role of the King's son with beauty and freedom.

Ofelia Sala as the Princess-Goose Girl has an attractively warm soprano with her vibrato well controlled, well contrasted with the mature-sounding Witch of Nora Gubisch. As the Fiddler, Detlef Roth sings one of the most freely lyrical passages in the opera near the beginning of Act 3 – a memorably simple folklike melody – in a finely controlled *pianissimo*; but his more outgoing solo leading up to that finds his voice so strained and uneven one would not recognise him as the same singer. Other characters strongly taken include Mareen Knoth as the Landlord's Daughter, and the delightfully fresh-toned child soloist Nelly Lawson as the Broom-maker's Daughter.

The set offers a complete libretto and English translation. Against that there is the minor drawback that the number of tracks in each act – five only for Acts 1 and 3, four for Act 2 – is far too few for so complex a score. Recommended nonetheless.

Sigismondo d'India   Italian c1582-1629

As a young man d'India travelled in Italy, notably to Florence, and in 1611 he became chamber music director at the Turin court; he left in 1623, working in Modena and Rome. His five books Le musiche (1609-23) contain chamber monodies, varied in style but often of great emotional intensity, and duets; he also published eight volumes of madrigals (1606-24), some highly chromatic and expressive, villanellas and motets.   **GROVE**music

Madrigals

Il primo libro de madrigali
La Venexiana (Valentina Coladonato, Nadia Ragni *sops* Lucia Sciannimanico *mez* Giuseppe Maletto, Sandro Naglia *tens* Daniele Carnovich *bass*) / **Claudio Cavina** *counterten*
Glossa GCD920908 (49' · DDD · T/t)   Ⓕ

The northern and southern Italian madrigal traditions meet in the person of Sigismondo d'India. The date of publication of this, his *First Book of Madrigals* (1606) reveals him to be one of the last of the genre's most significant figures. By this time the majority of Monteverdi's publications were already in existence, and Gesualdo's too. The influence of both is clearly audible, and not just in the music.

One of the most memorable tracks is *Felice chi ti miro*, although much of the tripartite *Interdette speranze* is equally impressive. Sometimes you feel that a phrase or sentiment might have been more dramatically and elastically projected, or lingered over and savoured. As to tuning, it's generally very accurate, and the slightest slip stands out. But that's the problem with tuning: standards are so high nowadays that critics risk expecting something inhuman, or at least superhuman. This will do just fine. A movingly dramatic account.

Vincent d'Indy   French 1851-1931

French composer, teacher, conductor and editor of early music. His famed veneration for Beethoven and Franck has unfortunately obscured the individual character of his own compositions, particularly his fine orchestral pieces descriptive of southern France. As a teacher his influence was enormous and wide-ranging, with benefits for French music far outweighing the charges of dogmatism and political intolerance. D'Indy's somewhat academic corpus of chamber music (including three completed string quartets) is generally less interesting than his orchestral works which, while always manifesting his concern for the utmost structural coherence, invariably contain important programmatic or symbolic elements; above all, nature painting brought out his full imaginative mastery of orchestral texture.

Orchestral works

Jour d'été à la montagne, Op 61. La forêt enchantée, Op 8. Souvenirs, Op 62
Iceland Symphony Orchestra / Rumon Gamba
Chandos CHAN10464 (63' · DDD)   ⒻⒹ▸

Three of d'Indy's most colourful works show him not only as an impressionist in a Debussian mould but also influenced by Wagner and folk music from his own culture. *La forêt enchantée* (1878) is described as a 'légende-symphonique' and is inspired by an epic ballad by Ludwig Uhland. D'Indy creates a mysteriously expectant opening atmosphere, then Knight Harald and his followers ride out vigorously. Female elves seduce his followers, but Harald loftily resists their enticements and gallops off to reach an enchanted spring, where the elves are waiting for him. This time he yields to their alluring invitation before slipping into a 'centuries-lasting' sleep.

By the time the masterly *Jour d'été à la montagne* was written some 30 years later, d'Indy's style had matured. While the Wagnerian sensuality remains, here the influences from Debussy and even Ravel are very potent: there's a daybreak with an orchestral chorus of birds. The sultry central movement, 'Après-midi sous les pins', includes lively folk dancing before the clouds arrive, with thunder in the distance. Twilight transforms the mood for 'Soir' and the work closes in nocturnal bliss.

D'Indy wrote *Souvenirs* almost immediately afterwards (in 1906) in memory of his wife (represented by a leitmotif, Bien-Aimée), recalling the couple's idyllic summers together and again evoking the countryside. This *idée fixe* is continually transformed before the music darkens and 12 harp harmonics set the time of Isabelle's death at midnight; the evocation ends in sad serene acceptance.

The rich orchestration in all three works is superbly realised by the excellent Iceland Symphony Orchestra under Rumon Gamba and the state-of-the-art Chandos recording; definitely a key record of d'Indy's orchestral output.

Wallenstein, Op 12. Saugefleurie, Op 21. Choral varié, Op 55[a]. Lied, Op 19[a]
[a]**Lawrence Power** *va* **BBC National Orchestra of Wales / Thierry Fischer**

Hyperion CDA67690 (74' · DDD)　　　Ⓕ❂

Here's another rewarding d'Indy anthology courtesy of Hyperion, which finds Thierry Fischer obtaining commendably spruce and bright-eyed results from his BBC Welsh forces. The lengthiest (and earliest) offering here is *Wallenstein*. Begun in 1870 but not completed until 1881, it's a highly ambitious 37-minute trilogy based on Schiller's eponymous drama and reveals the budding composer as an unabashed acolyte of Liszt and Wagner. Fortunately the melodic invention (and its cyclical deployment) is as striking as it is satisfying (even on a first hearing the tunes stick in the memory), as is the ripe, unclotted orchestration – d'Indy clearly knew his *Tristan*, *Siegfried* and *Götterdämmerung* inside out.

The 1884 tone-poem *Saugefleurie* distils a most touching, fairy-tale charm (the music depicting the royal hunt readily calls to mind Franck's *Le chasseur maudit* of two years earlier), and once again d'Indy handles his outsize orchestral forces with conspicuous skill. Both the Op 19 Lied (written in the same year as Saugefleurie) and 1903 *Choral varié* prove very fetching discoveries, especially when Lawrence Power plays with selfless dedication, sense of poetry and lustrous tone.

A toothsome and notably enterprising collection, this, with splendidly ample and atmospheric sound to match.

John Ireland　　　British 1879-1962

Ireland studied at the Royal College of Music, first as a pianist, then as a composer under Stanford (1897-1901), under whom he gained command of a solid Brahmsian style radically altered during the next two decades by the impressions of Debussy, Ravel and Stravinsky. The result was a sequence of lyrical piano pieces, but also substantial chamber works, including two piano trios (1906, 1917) and two violin sonatas (1909, 1917). Meanwhile he served as organist and choirmaster at St Luke's, Chelsea (1904-26), later returning to the RCM to teach (1923-39). Postwar works include the symphonic rhapsody Mai-Dun (1921, one of many works suggestive of English landscape), the Piano Concerto (1930), a classic of 20th-century English music, and Legend for piano and orchestra (1933).　　　GROVEmusic

Orchestral works

Epic March. The Forgotten Rite. A London Overture. Mai-Dun. The Overlanders. Scherzo and Cortège on Themes from Julius Caesar. Tritons
London Philharmonic Orchestra / Sir Adrian Boult
Lyrita SRCD240 (76' · ADD)　　　Ⓕ❂➔

Assembled from three of Boult's four Lyrita LPs devoted to Ireland, this generous programme launches with the red-blooded symphonic prelude *Tritons* (a student offering from 1899). Boult and the LPO do not shirk the melodrama and go on to lend equally dedicated advocacy to the magical 1913 prelude *The Forgotten Rite* and glowering 1921 symphonic rhapsody *Mai-Dun*.

The stand-out track remains Boult's wonderfully spry and observant account of *A London Overture* (1936), which is easily a match for Barbirolli's almost exactly contemporaneous LSO version for EMI. The 1942 *Epic March*, too, glints with memorable defiance. The *Julius Caesar* diptych is less immediately gripping, but the five-movement suite compiled by Charles Mackerras from Ireland's 1946 score for Ealing Studios' *The Overlanders* certainly has its moments, not least the touching 'Romance' (which plunders material from *A Downland Suite* of 1932) and infectiously jaunty outer portions of the central 'Intermezzo'.

Considering some of these sessions took place as long ago as December 1965, the judiciously refurbished sound still packs quite a punch. Altogether a very welcome reissue.

A Downland Suite (arr Ireland and Bush). Orchestral Poem in A minor. Concertino pastorale. Two Symphonic Studies (arr Bush)
City of London Sinfonia / Richard Hickox
Chandos CHAN9376 (64' · DDD)　　　Ⓕ❂

Hickox gives a sensitive account of the *Downland Suite* and extracts great expressive intensity from the glorious second movement 'Elegy'. The *Concertino pastorale* is another fine work, boasting a most eloquent opening 'Eclogue' and tenderly poignant 'Threnody', towards the end of which Ireland seems to allow himself a momentary recollection of the haunting opening phrase of his earlier orchestral prelude, *The Forgotten Rite*. In 1969 Ireland's pupil, Geoffrey Bush, arranged two sections of the score for the 1946 film *The Overlanders* which were not incorporated into the 1971 concert suite compiled by Sir Charles Mackerras. The resulting, finely wrought *Two Symphonic Studies* were recorded many years ago by Sir Adrian Boult for Lyrita and Hickox proves just as sympathetic an interpreter, whereas the *Orchestral Poem* in A minor is here receiving its recorded début. This is a youthful essay, completed in 1904, some three years after Ireland's studies with Stanford.

It's a worthy rather than especially inspiring effort, with hardly a glimpse of the mature manner to come, save for some particularly beautiful string writing.

Violin Sonatas

Violin Sonatas – No 1 in D minor[a]; No 2 in　　Ⓗ
A minor[b]. Phantasie Trio in A minor[c]. The Holy Boyd
[ac]**Frederick Grinke,** [b]**Albert Sammons** vns
[cd]**Florence Hooton** vc [ab]**John Ireland,** [c]**Kendall Taylor,** [d]**Lawrence Pratt** pfs

Dutton Laboratories Historic Epoch mono CDLX7103
(73' · ADD) Recorded 1930-45?　　　　　　Ⓜ️**OO**

Such was the critical acclaim that greeted the
March 1917 premiere of Ireland's Second Violin
Sonata that the 37-year-old composer's reputation
was cemented virtually overnight. The performers
on that momentous occasion were the legendary
Albert Sammons and pianist William Murdoch.
Some 13 years later Sammons finally set down his
thoughts on this glorious music with Ireland himself at the piano. Quite why this valuable document
never saw the light of day until now is a mystery, so
all gratitude to Dutton for granting a long overdue
lease of life to a nobly spacious rendering of such
palpable feeling and insight.

As for the First Violin Sonata, Frederick
Grinke's 1945 Decca recording (again with the
composer) continues to strike as, quite simply,
the most perceptive interpretation of this early
offering ever encountered, possessing a compelling sweep and tingling concentration that grip
from first measure to last. The November 1938
recording of the *Phantasie Trio* is yet another
cherishable display, the playing wonderfully
alive and always radiating a most winning
understanding and spontaneity.

Good, if not exceptional transfers. Urgently
recommended all the same.

Chamber works

Fantasy Sonata[a]. The Holy Boy[a]. Sextet[b]. Trio[c]
Robert Plane *cl* [b]**David Pyatt** *hn* [c]**Alice Neary** *vc*
[ac]**Sophia Rahman** *pf*
[b]**Maggini Quartet** (Lorraine McAslan, David Angel
vns Martin Outram *va* Michal Kaznowski *vc*)
Naxos 8 570550 (66' · DDD)　　　　　　Ⓢ**O**▶

This disc is a most welcome addition to the catalogue of recordings of John Ireland's chamber
music in that its principal focus is the range of
pieces that the composer wrote for clarinet,
played here with ravishing lyricism and conviction by Robert Plane, who has surely now fully
occupied the shoes of the late Thea King in his
championship of British clarinet music. Plane's
kinship with this music is clear from the more
Brahmsian hues of the Sextet (1898), the limpid
lyricism of *The Holy Boy* arrangement (1913), to
the extrovert passion of the *Fantasy Sonata* for
Clarinet (1943) where he is arguably at his most
impressive.

Though the Sextet, a student work, betrays a
deference to Brahms, there is a freshness and
fluency about the material as well as a flair for
the idiom, which compares favourably with
those prodigious chamber works of Hurlstone,
Coleridge-Taylor (both RCM fellow students)
and, later, Frank Bridge. An attractive novelty
on this CD is the Clarinet Trio which Ireland
completed in 1913 but withdrew after two performances. Left incomplete and in manuscript
at Ireland's death, it has been reconstructed skilfully by Stephen Fox. Plane, Alice Neary and
Sophia Rahman give a sensitive reading of a style

that is much more distinctly 'Irelandesque' in its
assimilation of French sonorities and sound-
moments, Plane's hushed playing being especially enthralling.

Piano works

Piano Works, Volume 1
Sarnia. London Pieces. In Those Days. Prelude in
E flat. Ballade. Columbine. Month's Mind
John Lenehan *pf*
Naxos 8 553700 (60' · DDD)　　　　　　Ⓢ**O**▶

Piano Works, Volume 2
Merry Andrew. The towing-path. Rhapsody. Two
Pieces (1924-5). Decorations. Leaves from a Child's
Sketchbook. The darkened valley. Sonatina. Three
Pastels. Two Pieces (1921). Summer evening
John Lenehan *pf*
Naxos 8 553889 (71' · DDD)　　　　　　Ⓢ**O**▶

The pleasures here are many. John Lenehan is a
very accomplished performer: not only is his
technical address impeccable, but he also has a
strikingly wide dynamic range and sophisticated
variety of tone colour, both of which he uses to
poetic effect throughout. That Lenehan has a
real affinity for Ireland's muse is immediately
evident from his raptly intimate delivery of the
gentle opening diptych, *In Those Days*. Similarly,
in the extraordinarily imaginative, harmonically
questing *Ballade* of 1929 he rises superbly to the
elemental fury of the remarkable central
portion, with its brooding echoes of the 'Northern' Bax from the same period. Elsewhere,
Columbine is a treat, as is the ravishing *Month's
Mind* and the haunting Prelude in E flat. Lenehan's supremely affectionate and articulate
advocacy will surely win Ireland many friends.

On Volume 2 there's a strong feeling of how
purely local influences (Pangbourne and the
Thames Valley in *The towing-path*, Le Fauvic
beach, Jersey in 'The Island Spell', to take two
examples) are transcended to become statements of wider poetic import.

The large-scale *Rhapsody*, with its powerful Fauréan overtones, is relished by Lenehan, a strong,
sympathetic interpreter, and time and again he
makes you wonder at works aptly described as
'some of the most appealing English piano music
written this century, too long neglected.'

Complete Piano Works
Alan Rowlands *pf*
Lyrita mono ③ REAM3112 (3h 45' · ADD)
Recorded 1959-63　　　　　　　　　　Ⓜ️

Piano Works, Volume 3
Piano Sonata. The Almond Tree. Ballade of London
Nights. Equinox. Greenways. On a Birthday Morning.
Two Pieces. Preludes. Soliloquy. Spring will not wait
John Lenehan *pf*
Naxos 8 570461 (73' · DDD) Ⓢ

Piano Music by John Ireland, Volume 1

Piano Sonata. Decorations. London Pieces. Ballade.
Sonatina
Mark Bebbington pf
Somm SOMMCD074 (69' · DDD)   Ⓕ

Comparative listening to the meaty Sonata that
Ireland wrote between 1918 and 1920 (the one
work common to all three releases) finds both
Rowlands and Bebbington allowing themselves
rather greater breathing space than the more
urgently propulsive Lenehan (who whips up
quite a gale in the first movement's development). Each is a mightily convincing proponent,
though Rowlands's interpretation carries particular authority: during the late 1950s he studied intensively with Ireland (the booklet contains a most engaging and fascinating personal
reminiscence) and it was Rowlands whom the
composer recommended to Richard Itter of
Lyrita for its complete recorded edition.

With no editing facilities available, single takes
were a necessity in sessions spanning January
1959 to March 1963 which took place in the
music room of Itter's Buckinghamshire home.
Captured in perfectly acceptable mono sound,
Rowlands's memorably intimate performances
betoken a very special empathy for this repertoire. Indeed, his playing throughout these three
well filled CDs evinces a selfless dedication,
recreative wonder and abundant poetic instinct.

As for the two new collections, Lenehan
effortlessly maintains the favourable impression
left by the first two instalments in his series
(reviewed above). With his pellucid, exquisitely
variegated tonal palette, he makes a gorgeous
thing of *The Almond Trees*, plumbs real depths in
Spring will not wait and the central "Cypress"
from *Green Ways*, and masterminds superbly
involving accounts of the gale-tossed *Equinox*
and mercurial *Ballade of London Nights*. What's
more, he has been accorded crystal-clear yet
nicely atmospheric engineering.

For first-timers, however, Bebbington's programme provides a pretty much ideal introduction, containing two of Ireland's most popular
and durable achievements, namely *Decorations*
and *London Pieces* – both given with such winning aplomb, scrupulous care and heartwarming
sense of new discovery that it's hard not to fall in
love with them all over again (the vernally fresh
'Chelsea Reach' positively beams with joy).
Elsewhere, Bebbington displays wonderful control in the leaner-textured and economically
argued *Sonatina*, just as he is acutely responsive
to the fearful undertow of the *Ballade* (close
cousin to the riveting *Legend* for piano and
orchestra). Somm's sound is clean and true.

Songs

The Bells of San Marie. During Music. Five Poems by
Thomas Hardy. Three Songs to Poems by Thomas
Hardy. I have twelve oxen. If there were dreams to
sell. Marigold – Youth's Spring (Tribute); Penumbra;
Spleen. Santa Chiara, 'Palm Sunday, Naples'. Sea
Fever. Songs Sacred and Profane – The Salley

Gardens. Tryst in Fountain Court. The Vagabond.
We'll to the woods no more. When I am dead, my
dearest. Tutto è sciulto. Great Things. Two Songs –
The Cost
Roderick Williams bar **Iain Burnside** pf
Naxos 8 570467 (66' · DDD)   Ⓢ Ⓞ ➔

Despite the popularity of 'Sea Fever' and (literally) two or three others, the songs of John Ireland are often found oddly inaccessible. Of all
the acknowledged masters of English songs in
the 20th century Ireland is the hardest to pin
down, to identify even. It has something to do
with an elusiveness about his writing for the
voice. When you look at the piano parts you feel
contact with a pair of hands (his) touching the
keyboard; but (with few exceptions) it's hard to
believe that he 'sang' the songs as he wrote. The
point here is that Roderick Williams is such a
good singer he can make the voice part sound
vocal and natural in a way not many have succeeded in doing. The songs are high for baritone, low for tenor, and they are written in a way
that seems not to know of the difficulties of passing from one area of the voice to another or
returning to a particular region with uncomfortable persistency. For Roderick Williams such
difficulties seem hardly to exist. The listener's
task eases proportionally.

Before going further, it should be said that the
pianist, Iain Burnside, plays with a sureness of
touch to match the highly skilled naturalness of
Williams's singing. And it has to be added that
Williams still does not seem to be a communicator in song in the sense that we can see the
images flash before him (Terfel-like) as he sings
the words. Sometimes, as in *The Vagabond*
(Masefield, not Stevenson) and *If there were
dreams to sell*, he catches the mood extraordinarily well even so. Williams and Burnside find
a clearer feeling for Ireland's anxious tenderness
and uneasy joy than in any previous recital of his
songs.

Charles Ives   American 1874-1954

*Ives was influenced first by his father, a bandmaster
who had libertarian ideas about what music might
be. When he was perhaps 19 (the dating of his music
is nearly always problematic) he produced psalm settings that exploit polytonality and other unusual
procedures. He then studied with Parker at Yale
(1894-8) and showed some sign of becoming a relatively conventional composer in his First Symphony
(1898) and songs of this period. He worked, however,
not in music but in the insurance business, and composition became a weekend activity – but one practised
assiduously: during the two decades after his graduation he produced three more symphonies and numerous other works.*

*The only consistent characteristic of this music is
liberation from rule. There are entirely atonal pieces,
while others are in the simple harmonic style of a
hymn or folksong. Some are systematic and abstract*

in construction; others are filled with quotations from the music of Ives's youth: hymns, popular songs, marches etc. Some, like the Three Places in New England, are nostalgic; others, like the Fourth Symphony, are fuelled by the vision of an idealist democracy. He published his 'Concord' Sonata in 1920 and a volume of 114 songs in 1922, but composed little thereafter. Most of his music had been written without prospect of performance, and it was only towards the end of his life that it began to be played frequently and appreciated. **GROVE**music

Symphonies

Symphonies – No 1; No 4. Central Park in the Dark
Dallas Symphony Orchestra / Andrew Litton
Hyperion 🎵 SACDA67540 (78' · DDD/DSD)
Recorded live   Ⓕ**O**

Symphonies – No 2; No 3, 'The Camp Meeting'.
General William Booth Enters into Heaven[c]
[c]**Donnie Ray Albert** *bar* **Dallas Symphony**
Orchestra / Andrew Litton
Hyperion 🎵 SACDA67525 (69' · DDD/DSD)
Recorded live   Ⓕ**O**

Ives's symphonies were premiered almost 50 years after they were written – practically nothing was performed when he wrote it – but against all the odds they have achieved classic status. The composer was dismissive about the First Symphony, a student work, but this is now its eighth available recording. Litton has strong climaxes in the first movement, although there's a tendency for the woodwind to get swamped by the strings and brass, and sustains an almost Mahlerian passion in the *Adagio*. There's a magical *pianissimo* at the start of *Central Park in the Dark* with no evidence of the audience at all – apparently they were warned that the performance was being recorded!

Each recording of the Fourth is defined by the inevitably different balance of the dense textures in the second and fourth movements. For example Litton, supported by one associate conductor, rightly has the orchestral piano prominent in the shattering second movement and in the mystical finale the voices enter with unique effect. It's good to hear a little more than usual of the offstage players both here and in the first movement.

The spacious Second Symphony takes its pervasive popular melodies and makes them symphonic – again a completely convincing performance. The only shock is the dissonant raspberry blown as the final chord – that's what folk fiddlers did to show the evening was over. The Third Symphony is saturated in hymn tunes and anyone familiar with earlier recordings will notice the few extra bits in the latest edition of the score. The bonus is a gutsy delivery of Becker's orchestral arrangement of the song *General William Booth Enters into Heaven*.

Overall these two CDs are a winning representation of the Ives symphonies with the fine Dallas Symphony consistently impressive throughout.

One might want to look back at certain historic versions of individual symphonies, but as a package this is well recorded, fastidiously presented and deservedly pre-eminent.

Symphony No 2. Robert Browning Overture
Nashville Symphony Orch / Kenneth Schermerhorn
Naxos 8 559076 (67' · DDD)   Ⓢ➤

Ives's Second Symphony isn't as well served on CD as might be expected. Bernstein gave the premiere in 1951 some 40 years after the work's composition. What's new about this Nashville release is that it uses Jonathan Elkus's edition made for the Charles Ives Society for both works. The main difference for the listener is that the exposition of the second movement of the Symphony is repeated. That this helps the overall balance in this extended, somewhat repetitive movement is debatable. When it comes to Bernstein, he quite unnecessarily cut 16 measures from the last movement. His tempos may be considered slow in the third and fourth movements, but in both his recordings the work luxuriates in a way that nobody else achieves.

The *Robert Browning Overture* is one of Ives' most visionary pieces, with declamatory trumpet parts that make Scriabin's *Poème de l'extase* seem reticent. The mystical calm of the opening is memorably caught in the Nashville performance; the energetic passages are vivid, although some textures inevitably get submerged. It's a great relief to have the obvious errors in the score corrected. This puts earlier recordings such as Stokowski's beyond the pale and it's well worth buying this CD for the *Browning Overture* alone, although both works in these carefully considered editions make a bargain pair.

Additional recommendation

Symphony No 2.
Coupled with: The Gong on the Hook and Ladder.
Tone Roads – No 1. A Set of Three Short Pieces –
Largo cantabile, Hymn. Hallowe'en. Central Park in
the Dark. The Unanswered Question
NYPO / Bernstein
DG download *429 220-2GH* (68' · DDD)   Ⓕ**OO**➤
  Although Bernstein thought of Ives as a primitive
  composer, these recordings reveal that he had a
  deep understanding of his music. The standard of
  playing rom the NYPO, both here and in the disc's
  series of technically demanding shorter pieces, is
  remarkably high. Essential for any collection.

Symphony No 3, 'The Camp Meeting'. The
Unanswered Question. Central Park in the Dark.
Overture and March, '1776'. Holidays – Washington's
Birthday. Country Band March
Northern Sinfonia / James Sinclair
Naxos 8 559087 (52' · DDD)   Ⓢ➤

James Sinclair has been a dedicated Ives scholar and performer for more than 30 years, which means this CD has to be something special. First on this issue comes the hymn-saturated Third Symphony, where Sinclair uses some of the thinly sketched options in the manuscripts. This means there's a bit extra in the distance at the end of the first two movements and slighty more of the barely audible bells, ingeniously made to sound like an outdoor carillon, at the end of the last movement, compared with Slatkin and the St Louis orchestra. There are more distant effects if you listen carefully.

In *The Unanswered Question* Sinclair uses the version with two flutes and two clarinets rather than four flutes for the attempted answers to the questioning trumpet. Then, in *Central Park in the Dark*, he uses a battered upright piano for the bits taken from the 1899 hit-song 'Hello! ma Baby' which suggests the tavern scene in Berg's *Wozzeck*. It works, but unfortunately the piano, marked *fff*, almost fades out at the climax.

There are two little-known early pieces which Ives drew on for 'Putnam's Camp', the second of *Three Places in New England*. The *Country Band March* has hilarious junketings as an affectionate reflection of the mistakes of amateur players – Sinclair takes an option without the final chord which leaves the dilatory saxophonist exposed after the end. Then the *Overture and March*, '*1776*' goes to town with a brass player using the wrong instrument so that quite a lengthy passage comes out in parallel semitones! Vintage Ives, all played with completely idiomatic feeling and adequately recorded.

Symphony No 4 – Fugue[c]. Orchestral Set No 1, 'Three Places in New England'. Charlie Rutlage[a][d]. The Circus Band[b][c]. From the Steeples and the Mountains[c]. General William Booth Enters into Heaven[b][c]. In Flanders Fields[a][d]. Memories[a][d]. The Pond[a][b][c]. Psalm 100[b][c]. Serenity[a][c]. They are There![a][b][c]. The Things our Fathers Loved[a][d]. Tom Sails Away[a][d]. The Unanswered Question[c]
[a]**Thomas Hampson** *bar* [b]**San Francisco Girl's Chorus; San Francisco Symphony Chorus and** [c]**Orchestra / Michael Tilson Thomas** [d]*pf*
RCA Red Seal 09026 63703-2 (65' · DDD) Recorded live 1999 Ⓕ**O**Ⓑ▸

If anyone has a hot-line to the cortex of Ives's imagination, it's Michael Tilson Thomas. The programme he's devised here isn't so much a journey, more a stream of consciousness through the hinterlands of Ives Americana. It's about the things that mattered to Ives: the times, places, events that fashioned the nation and enabled it to find its own way. It's a landscape of ballad songs and snatches, of hymns, marches, tall tales and short orders, assembled exactly as the man remembered them and entirely in keeping with the chaotic comedy of life. But above all, it's about the spirit within us all – great and small.

From the Steeples and the Mountains is classic Ives: a visionary statement fashioned from bare essentials, bells and brass dissonances always just a whisper away from a recognisable hymn tune. Then from the mountains to the back yard – rec-

ollections of a very American childhood. Picket fences and parlour songs. Like *The Things Our Fathers Loved* written 16 years after the craggy bell and brass piece. You can be sure the Ives chronology will constantly wrong-foot you. Thomas Hampson is the man entrusted with these rich pickings from the Ives songbook. He lustily makes a drama out of a crisis in *Charlie Rutlage*, a cowboy song turned operatic *gran scena*. Later he's the Salvation Army's General William Booth banging the drum for all his pimps, floosies, and drunks – his 'saved souls' – as he leads them towards that great courthouse in the sky. Then one of the most heartfelt of all Ives songs, *Tom Sails Away* – a life in a song from cradle to grave.

Such juxtapositions make this all-live compilation especially affecting. Hard to believe that this is a live recording, so astonishingly lucid and transparent is the multi-layered orchestral sound. Tremendous impact, too.

Finally, a beautiful performance of that little masterpiece *The Unanswered Question*, as close as we get to an understanding of what spirituality actually meant to Ives. A superb disc.

Orchestral sets

Three Orchestral Sets
Malmö Chamber Chorus; Malmö Symphony Orchestra / James Sinclair
Naxos 8 559353 (63' · DDD) Ⓢ▸

This is a fascinating release that offers Ives's three Orchestral Sets for the first time. The curtain is raised with the first of them, *Three Places in New England*, in its original version – this stands somewhere between the *Country Band March* and the later, more familiar *Three Places*. At this stage there's no piano part and the conflicting march rhythm in 'Putnam's Camp' is missing as well as its dissonant opening. Both the First and Second Sets are vintage Ives, with his unforgettable reaction to the sinking of the Lusitania that brought the US into the First World War at the end of the Second Set.

But the novelty here is the Third Set. The first two movements come from sketches edited by David Gray Porter. The opening *Andante* has a structure similar to *Central Park in the Dark* with typical Ives chords and a texture building to a crisis with something left hanging softly at the end. The second movement is called 'During Camp Meetin' Week: One Secular Afternoon'. This again is Ives's idiosyncratic territory with lots of quotations including 'Columbia the Gem of the Ocean' twice and a four-part hymn about the Day of Judgement – not so secular after all?

Completing works by Ives has become an industry that the composer would have welcomed. The perhaps over-extended last movement of this Third Set, realised by Nors Josephson, at times sounds like Varèse, although it begins and ends softly. Well recorded, idiomatic performances all round – a real Ives discovery.

Violin Sonatas

Violin Sonatas – No 1; No 2; No 3; No 4, 'Children's Day at the Camp Meeting'
Curt Thompson *vn* **Rodney Waters** *pf*
Naxos 8 559119 (77' · DDD)　　　　　Ⓢ⯈

The four violin and piano sonatas are at the core of Ives's chamber music output. The style oscillates because Ives was uncertain about his more radical visions and admitted he'd tried to compromise. But this gives all four of them an enlarged frame of reference, saturated with quotations as usual, but relating to European sonata traditions as well. There's everything to savour from these performances on Naxos: lovely soft textures in the transcendental meditations, well recorded, and everything hectic is under control. Warning: the distant violin in the second movement of No 1 isn't a balance fault – Ives specified that the pianist should overwhelm the defenceless muted violin! This is now the version to choose.

Piano Sonata No 2, 'Concord'

Piano Sonata No 2, 'Concord, Mass.: 1840-60'ᵃ. Ann Streetᵇ. The Cageᵇ. The Circus Bandᵇ. A farewell to landᵇ. The Housatonic at Stockbridgeᵇ. The Indiansᵇ. Like a sick eagleᵇ. Memoriesᵇ. Septemberᵇ. Serenityᵇ. Soliloquyᵇ. Songs my mother taught meᵇ. Swimmersᵇ. The things our fathers lovedᵇ. Thoreauᵇ. 1, 2, 3ᵇ. A sound of distant hornᵇ
ᵇ**Susan Graham** *sop* ᵃ**Emmanuel Pahud** *fl* ᵃ**Tabea Zimmermann** *va* **Pierre-Laurent Aimard** *pf*
Warner Classics 2564 60297-2 (79' · DDD)　Ⓕ**OO**⯈

Charles Ives to complaining pianist: 'Is it the composer's fault that man has only ten fingers?' Listening to Pierre-Laurent Aimard play the *Concord* Sonata it isn't Ives's dry wit but the assertion that man has only ten fingers that you begin to question. Nothing he wrote was 'reasonable' as in playable, singable. Everything was a stretch, a note or chord or counterpoint too far. Technically optimistic, spiritually aspirational. In a sense Aimard is almost too good, the realisation of everything Ives was striving for in this piece. You can almost hear Ives thinking: 'OK, if that's possible, let's go somewhere else…'

Actually, the *Concord* Sonata goes wherever you want it to go. Its starting point is American literature but its substance is in ideas. Ives the transcendentalist: beyond the American dream. An amazing stream of consciousness. Concord is a town in Massachusetts, it's where American Independence was bloodily born; but it's also a word for harmony, and for Ives there's harmony in extreme diversity. The big moments in the sonata are all born out of flux. Ideas and notes boil over in the second movement, 'Hawthorne', but at its heart is the basic conflict between the earthly body and its free spirit. The body resists, the spirit meditates. There are moments here where you'd swear two pianists were involved. You'd also swear that the sorrowful song so

fleetingly alluded to by solo viola (Tabea Zimmerman) in the first movement or the remnant of solo flute (Emmanuel Pahud) in the last are figments of your imagination.

Ives's imagination – his rampant theatricality – should have made for great operas. Instead he wrote songs: capsule dramas laid out not in scenes or acts but moments in time. Susan Graham inhabits 17 such moments – nostalgic ('Songs my mother taught me'), visionary ('A sound of distant horn'), cryptic ('Soliloquy'), brutal ('1, 2, 3'), expectant ('Thoreau') – and the feminine and masculine qualities of her voice, to say nothing of her musical sensibility, easily encompass the 'expectancy and ecstasy' promised by the song 'Memories' – which appropriately enough recalls her (and others like her) as a little girl 'sitting in the opera house'. Aimard is again a one-man band. Almost literally so in 'The Circus Band'. When Graham shouts 'hear the trombones', you really do.

Additional recommendation

Piano Sonata No 2
Coupled with: **Barber** Piano Sonata
Hamelin *pf*
Hyperion CDA67469 (62' · DDD)　　　　　Ⓕ
　A superb recital of two sharply opposed American sonatas. Hamelin subdues his awe-inspiring command to a purely musical end.

Songs

'A Song – For Anything'

A Song – For Anything. Du alte Mutter. Ann Street. Berceuse. The Cage. Charlie Rutlage. Elégie. Feldeinsamkeit. General William Booth Enters into Heaven. The Greatest Man. The Housatonic at Stockbridge. Ich grolle nicht. Like a Sick Eagle. Memories. The New River. Remembrance. Serenity. The Side Show. Slugging a Vampire. Swimmers. 1, 2, 3. The Things Our Fathers Loved. Thoreau. Tom Sails Away. Walking. Weil' auf mir. West London. Where the Eagle. Yellow Leaves. Tolerance. When Stars are in the Quiet Skies
Gerald Finley *bar* **Julius Drake** *pf*
Hyperion CDA67516 (71' · DDD · T/t)　　　Ⓕ**OO**

These songs, drawn from Ives's 200, can encourage at one extreme a rough declamatory style and at the other an almost voiceless intimacy. Without in any way underplaying, Finlay is always essentially a singer – his tone and command of the singing line are a pleasure in themselves. But he also has the absolute mastery of the composer's idioms and, with Julius Drake, his fearless and totally committed pianist, the technical, virtuosic skills to realise his intentions with (amid all the quirks) complete conviction of naturalness.

This is a selection that very satisfactorily balances early and late, rumbustious and contemplative. Several of the early German settings are included, always beautiful and always developing with some touch that is entirely personal. Of a quite distinctive beauty are those like *Remembrance*, *Berceuse*, and *The Housatonic at Stockbridge* where voice and piano work a dreamy, misty spell. And still more characteristic are the settings of his own verses evoking memories of childhood. The 'character' songs (such as *Charlie Rutlage*) and the 'big' numbers (*General William Booth Enters into Heaven*) become less prominent than they commonly seem in a recital group where they are programmed as an effective tour de force. The total impression is of an astonishing individuality and, more importantly, of a completely honest, dauntless and increasingly to be valued musical identity.

'Romanzo (di Central Park)'

At the river. The Children's Hour. The Circus Band. Down East. Evening. Evidence. Ilmenau. In Flanders Fields. In the Alley. The Last Reader. Mists. My Native Land. A Night Song. On the Counter. Premonitions. Romanzo (di Central Park)ᵃ. The See'r. Slow march. Songs My Mother Taught Me. They Are There!ᵃ To Edith. Two Little Flowers. Watchman. Omens and Oracles. A Christmas Carol. The South Wind. The World's Wanderers. Those Evening Bells. Allegro. The Light that is Felt

Gerald Finley *bar* **Julius Drake** *pf* with
ᵃ**Magnus Johnston** *vn*
Hyperion CDA67644 (62' · DDD · T/t) Ⓕ⚫

This is the second volume of Ives songs from this accomplished team; their first Ives volume (reviewed above) contained some of the blockbusters like *Charlie Rutlage* and *General William Booth* but the mood of this volume is fairly sedate. In particular some of the early songs in a conventional style are treated with the same seriousness that Finley would apply to Lieder.

An unusual but effective feature here is the provision of violin obbligato both for the jingoistic wartime song *They Are There!* and the mawkish take-off *Romanzo (di Central Park)*. Sentimentality is a Victorian characteristic but in *Songs My Mother Taught Me*, as elsewhere in Ives, the emotion is genuine so it invariably convinces.

Many of the songs are transposed down – hard work for the pianist and it makes some of the textures rather dense. The contemplative ones are delivered with an impressive serenity and Finley has his own way of attacking the razzle-dazzle of something like *The Circus Band* or *They Are There!* He's close-miked, which works best in the intimacy of the quieter songs.

Psalms

Psalm 14, The fool hath said. Psalm 24, The Earth is the Lord's. Psalm 25, Unto Thee O Godᶜ. Psalm 42, As pants the hartᵇᶜ. Psalm 54, Save me, O God, by Thy name. Psalm 67, God be merciful unto us. Psalm 90, Lord, thou hast been our dwelling placeᵃᵇᶜᵉ. Psalm 100, Make a joyful noise unto the Lordᵉ. Psalm 135, Praise ye the Lordᶜᵉ. Psalm 150, Praise ye the Lordᵈᵈ

ᵃ**Aleksandra Lustig** *sop* ᵇ**Julius Pfeiffer** *ten*
ᶜ**Kay Johannsen** *org* ᵈ**Collegium Iuvenum**;
South West German Radio Vokalensemble;
ᵉMembers of the **Stuttgart Radio Symphony Orchestra / Marcus Creed**
Hänssler Classic CD93 224 (45' · DDD) Ⓕ⚫⚫⚫D►

Ives worked with choirs as a young organist; his father's choir tried out versions of some of these pieces but they wouldn't have got very far. Most of these psalms began life in the 1890s but Ives went on revising them into the 1920s.

The most familiar is Psalm 67, *God be merciful unto us*, with its superimposed gentle bitonal chords – expertly balanced in this performance. Psalm 90 sets a pattern followed in some of the others – there's a low C held in the organ pedal throughout, consonant chords or unison passages erupt into clusters and back, and a generally mystical atmosphere prevails. This is emphasised by three sets of bells and a low gong 'as church bells in distance' that characterise the serene final section. There are more prominent bells in the jubilant Psalm 100. Nobody but Ives could have dreamt up textures like these.

Psalm 135 adds trumpet, trombone, timpani and tenor and bass drums. The percussion creates a subdued march effect against the choir singing in five-time, and there's word-painting for the vapours, lightning and winds. Psalm 25 has extended canons between male and female voices, the whole thing underpinned again by long held pedal notes in the organ. Ives's early Victorian style is represented by Psalm 42, with a lovely solo from Julius Pfeiffer.

These 10 psalms are not first recordings but most of them have dropped out of the catalogue, so this is largely unknown Ives. This fine collection is a revelation in performances like these from the outstanding Stuttgart choir.

Gordon Jacob   English 1895-1984

English composer, teacher and writer. He was educated at Dulwich College and, after active service in World War I, studied with Stanford, Howells, Boult and Vaughan Williams at the RCM. He was on the teaching staff there from 1924 until his retirement in 1966, and his pupils included Malcolm Arnold, Imogen Holst, Horovitz and Maconchy. Jacob's active career as composer spanned 60 years, during which time the character of his output faithfully reflected the changes in opportunity open to composers of a conservative idiom. In common with other more traditional composers of the time his music went into eclipse with the rise of the avant garde in the 1960s.

Symphonies

Symphonies – No 1; No 2
London Philharmonic Orchestra / Barry Wordsworth

Lyrita SRCD315 (66' · DDD)　　　Ⓟ◗

Gordon Jacob's First Symphony (1929) employs sizeable forces (including triple woodwind and two harps) and has five movements: two feisty and purposeful *Allegros* frame the whole edifice, while its dashing central *Scherzo* is flanked by two slow movements, the first of which in particular possesses an elegiac demeanour that accords with the work's inscription to the memory of the composer's favourite brother, Anstey (a victim of the First World War – Jacob, too, served in the trenches). It would make a terrific 'Guess who?' item: on a first encounter the names of Vaughan Williams, Holst, Elgar, Walton, Bliss, Poulenc and Stravinsky might appear. The more you return to it, however, the more individual the voice that emerges. Barry Wordsworth lends this powerful, criminally neglected discovery clearheaded, fervent advocacy, and the LPO are on their toes throughout. Completed in 1945, the Second Symphony was premiered under Boult in a May 1946 broadcast; Rudolf Schwarz gave the first public performance two years later. Cast in the traditional four movements and described by Jacob as 'a meditation on war, suffering and victory', it's tautly argued, full of healthy contrapuntal vigour (at times it calls to mind Nielsen) and concludes with a cleverly crafted passacaglia or 'Ground' – perhaps subconsciously influenced by, and yet fascinatingly different from, the finale of Vaughan Williams's roughly contemporaneous Fifth Symphony. These performers bring great tonal heft and intensity (especially in the plangent slow movement), admirably serving this bracing music.

With its agreeably tangible and airy sound in the best Lyrita tradition, this stimulating pairing of two impressive British symphonies merits immediate investigation.

Jacquet of Mantua　　French 1483-1559

Jacquet was a singer to the Modenese house of Rangoni and in 1525, with Willaert, served at the Este court at Ferrara. The following year he settled in Mantua, where for 30 years he dominated musical life. He was also titular maestro di cappella of the Cathedral of SS Peter and Paul there (1534-59). Jacquet was the leading master of sacred polyphony between Josquin and Palestrina and a prolific composer. In his sacred music (which includes over 20 masses and numerous motets) he appears a skilled craftsman alert to new ideas: smoothly arched lines, symmetry of phrase and fluency. His later motets show clearly his stylistic change to pervading imitation as the generating principle.　　GROVEmusic
GROVEmusic

Lamentations of Jeremiah

Lamentations of Jeremiah
Michel Lonsdale spkr **Ensemble Jachet de**

Mantoue (Raoul de Chenadec *counterten* Thierry Bréhu, Eric Raffard *tens* James Gowings *bar* Philippe Roche *bass*)
Calliope CAL9340 (64' · DDD · T/t)　　　Ⓕ

Both Jews and Christians use these texts liturgically, the Jews to commemorate the destruction of Jerusalem in 586BC, the Western Christian Church during the Office of Tenebrae on the last three days of Holy Week. Jacquet of Mantua's set of *Lamentations* for Holy Week was published posthumously in 1567, but probably dates from several decades earlier, when he was employed by Ercole Gonzaga, Cardinal Bishop of Mantua.

The singers, a recently formed ensemble based in Brittany, are joined for the recording by the Parisian actor Michel Lonsdale. The recital is planned so that the different sections fall into place in a natural sequence of three days, each divided into three lessons and each lesson into a series of verses, introduced by Hebrew letters.

Before each of the lessons Lonsdale reads, quietly and most beautifully, an early 16th-century French translation of what's to follow. The singers continue with the same spirit of deep and utter sorrow, expressed with totally controlled emotion throughout the performance. It's never overdone. The vocal blend is excellent, and the spoken voice adds just enough relief.

The booklet notes are of interest and importance, the illustrations discreet and sober. The whole CD is a model of beauty and perfection.

Leos Janáček　　Moravian 1854-1928

Janáček was a chorister at the Augustinian 'Queen's' Monastery in Old Brno, where the choirmaster Pavel Křižkovský took a keen interest in his musical education. After completing his basic schooling he trained as a teacher and, except for a period at the Prague Organ School, he spent 1872-9 largely as a schoolteacher and choral conductor in Brno. In 1879 he enrolled at the Leipzig Conservatory, where he developed his interest in composition under the strict and systematic supervision of Leo Grill. After a month in Vienna he returned to Brno in May 1880; there he became engaged to one of his pupils, Zdenka Schulzová, whom he married in July 1881.

In Brno, Janáček took up his former activities, and also founded and directed an organ school and edited a new musical journal, Hudební listy. After composing his first opera, S'árka, he immersed himself in collecting Moravian folk music, which bore fruit in a series of orchestral suites and dances and in a one-act opera, The Beginning of a Romance. This was favourably received in 1894, but Janáček withdrew it after six performances and set to work on Jenůfa.

During the long period of composition of Jenůfa (1894-1903), Janáček rethought his approach to opera and to composition in general. He largely abandoned the number opera, integrated folksong firmly into his music and formulated a theory of 'speechmelody', based on the natural rhythms and the rise and fall of the Czech language, which was to influence all his ensuing works and give them a particular colour through their jagged rhythms and lines. Jenůfa was soon followed by other operatic ventures, but his reputation in Brno was as a composer of instrumental and choral music and as director of the Organ School. Outside Moravia he was almost unknown until the Prague premiere of Jenůfa in 1916. The creative upsurge of a man well into his 60s is explained partly by the success of Jenůfa in Prague and abroad, partly by his patriotic pride in the newly acquired independence of his country, and perhaps most of all by his passionate, though generally distant, attachment to Kamila Stösslová, the young wife of an antique dealer in Pisek, Bohemia.

Between 1919 and 1925 Janáček composed three of his finest operas, all on subjects with special resonances for him: Kát'a Kabanová with its neglected wife who takes a lover, The Cunning Little Vixen with its sympathetic portrayal of animals (and particularly the female fox), and The Makropoulos Affair with the 'ageless' woman who fascinates all men. Each was given first in Brno and soon after in Prague. His 70th birthday was marked by a doctorate from the Masaryk University in Brno. Early in 1926 he wrote the Sinfonietta for orchestra, characteristic in its blocks of sound and its forceful repetitions, and later that year his most important choral work, the Glagolitic Mass. While performance of his music carried his fame abroad, he started work on his last opera, From the House of the Dead, which he did not live to see performed. It received its premiere in April 1930 in a version prepared by his pupils Bretislav Bakala and Osvald Chlubna.

Janáček's reputation outside Czechoslovakia and German-speaking countries was first made as an instrumental composer. He has since come to be regarded not only as a Czech composer worthy to be ranked with Smetana and Dvořák, but also as one of the most substantial and original opera composers of the 20th century. GROVEmusic

Orchestral Works

Sinfonietta. The Cunning Little Vixen – Suite. Taras Bulba. Jealousy. Sárka – Overture. Kát'a Kabanová – Prelude. Schluk und Jau
Czech Philharmonic Orchestra /
Sir Charles Mackerras
Supraphon ② SU3739-2 (92' · DDD)   Ⓕ🔵🔵

Issued to celebrate the 150th anniversary of the composer's birth, this two-disc set of orchestral works may be the last Janáček recording from our greatest advocate of his work, Sir Charles Mackerras. Where his pioneering Pro Arte recording of the Sinfonietta has an earthy quality and Decca's Vienna version is ripe and resonant, the new one is generally lighter and more flexible. The live performance brings dividends in its flow and the build-up of excitement, thrillingly caught when the fanfare theme returns to cap the finale.

Where most versions of the Cunning Little Vixen Suite use Václav Talich's reorchestration, Mackerras has gone back to the original. As he says, the orchestral writing may seem unusual, but it certainly isn't amateurish, where Talich's version, for all its beauty, 'rather emasculates the acid sounds produced for the insects'. but it certainly isn't amateurish, where Talich's version, for all its beauty, 'rather emasculates the acid sounds produced for the insects'.

Mackerras includes two tiny interludes for Kát'a Kabanová which he discovered in Prague, written when the German Theatre needed more time for scene changes. Rightly, he regards them as little jewels, well worth preserving.

The rarity is the incidental music for Gerhardt Hauptmann's play, Schluck und Jau, which Janáček was writing at the time of his death. The first of the two completed movements brings intriguing echoes of the fanfares in the Sinfonietta and the second in 5/8 time is equally original in its instrumentation, with deep trombones and stratospheric violins.

The helpful acoustic of the Rudolfinum gives a mellow quality to the refined playing of the Czech Philharmonic, with ample space round the sound, without underplaying the contrasts of wind and strings which are so typical of the composer.

Sinfonietta. Taras Bulba. The Cunning Little Vixen – Suite
Bamberg Symphony Orchestra / Jonathan Nott
Tudor 🔊 TUDOR7135 (62' · DDD)   Ⓕ🔵

Released to mark the Bamberg Symphony Orchestra's 60th anniversary, this powerful Janáček triptych reinforces the favourable impression made by these artists both on disc and in concert. Jonathan Nott's Sinfonietta is something of a 'grower', a thoughtful, defiantly unsensational reading which takes a number of hearings to reveal its lasting qualities. Aside from a hint of fluster at the più mosso marking in the finale, the Bambergers respond with striking accomplishment to their British chief, who directs with intelligence, thrusting purpose and a keen eye for detail. Admittedly, there's greater tenderness in the initial Moderato of the central tableau than Nott chooses to find (Kubelík and his wonderfully pliable and expressive Bavarian RSO really do melt the heart every time) but how judiciously he controls his massed forces in the jubilant panoply towards the close – the cumulative effect is properly rousing, noble and unflashy. A shame the sound doesn't quite 'open out' ideally here, though otherwise there can be nothing but praise for a vividly truthful co-production between Tudor and Bavarian Radio.

The suite from The Cunning Little Vixen – not Talich's much-loved overview but an earlier, 16-minute selection by Brno-born František Jílek (1913-93) – also offers much to enjoy. Only Taras Bulba slightly disappoints: articulate, painstakingly prepared and observant, yes, but it never truly catches fire.

String Quartets

Janáček String Quartets – No 1, 'The Kreutzer

Sonata'; No 2, 'Intimate Letters' **Schulhoff** String
Quartet No 1
Talich Quartet (Jan Talich, Petr Macecek vns Vladimir
Bukac va Petr Prause vc)
Calliope CAL9333 (57' · DDD) Ⓕ ⚫⚫

This recording announces itself with a richness
and directness of expression as remarkable as the
previous Talich Quartet's restraint (which, it
has to be said, occasionally registers as mere
circumspection). Sample the last two minutes or
so of the *Kreutzer Sonata* for an abandon that's
almost guaranteed to set the pulse racing. Or,
especially if you have somehow been immune to
Janáček in the past, see if you can resist the eruptive passion in the third movement of *Intimate
Letters*. Given the extraordinary problems with
establishing authoritative texts for these pieces,
there is no question whatsoever of a single recommendation. Perhaps the rather unremitting
sweetness of Jan Talich's tone would be the
nearest thing to a potential drawback. Even so,
this new issue surely has to figure on the shortest
of future short lists.

Schulhoff doesn't even get a billing on the
cover. But his succinct, Bartókian First Quartet
– dazzlingly inventive and light on its feet – significantly enhances the disc's appeal. Thanks to
the Talichs' range of colour and expression, the
Presto first movement fairly leaps off the page,
and the skittish twists and turns of the succeeding *Allegretto* and the upfront peasant pungency
of the *Alla slovacca* third movement are delivered
with equal relish. After which the rhapsodic and,
ultimately, anxiously withdrawn final movement
makes for an unexpected but logical, even
haunting, conclusion. There have been several
highly praised CD recordings of the piece but
these are now variously difficult to acquire; all
the more reason to welcome this new, trenchant
account. The vivid Czech recordings place the
instruments rather further forward than usual
but not inappropriately so in this passionately
communicative repertoire.

String Quartets[a] – No 1, 'The Kreutzer Sonata'; No 2,
'Intimate Letters'. Violin Sonata[a]. Pohádka (Fairy
Tale)[b]
Brodsky Quartet ([a]Andrew Haveron, Ian Belton vns
Paul Cassidy va [b]Jacqueline Thomas vc)
with [ab]**Martin Cousin** pf
Brodsky Records BRD3503 (74' · DDD) Ⓕ

The Brodskys use the standard scores of 1945
and 1949, and almost without exception keep
precisely to the very intricate markings. They
have also absorbed the detail of the scores with
great understanding, so that the often abrupt
time changes or sudden, even violent alternations of dynamics make complete expressive
sense. Further, there is a perceptive response to
the sense of dance rhythms that lies within much
of the invention and from time to time rises to
the surface – frantically in the Second Quartet's
Presto, with a charming if slightly wry lilt in its
third movement before the passionate outbursts

JANÁČEK STRING QUARTETS – IN BRIEF

Talich Quartet
Calliope CAL9333 Ⓕ ⚫⚫
Full of imagination and idiomatic touches,
the Talich must top the list of superb interpretations. These are superb performances
that really drill to the core of the works.

The Lindsays
ASV CDDCA749 Ⓕ
Another pair of superb performances, The
Lindsays play with febrile intensity and
minute attention to the numerous shifts of
mood and emotional temperature.

New Helsinki Quartet
Warner Apex 0927 40603-2 Ⓢ
A super-budget coupling worth considering:
stylish playing and a real sense of the music's
variety. Generously coupled with Dvořák's
delightful *Cypresses*.

Vlach Quartet
Naxos 8 553895 Ⓢ
Played with passion and imagination, here's
another well-filled and competitively priced
coupling well worth considering.

Skampa Quartet
Supraphon SU3486-2 Ⓕ ⚫
Tremendous performances that are not
afraid to explore some of Janáček's more
extreme sonic demands: they almost revel in
making sounds that are simply ugly, but they
justify it by the intelligence of their overall
approach.

Smetana Quartet
Testament SBT1074/5 Ⓕ ⚫
Slightly awkwardly spread over two
individual full-price discs, each coupled with
Dvořák, the Smetana Quartet really convey
the passion and intensity of these two great
works. The 1960s sound is outstanding.

Pavel Haas Quartet
Supraphon SU3922-2 (No 1) Ⓕ ⚫⚫
Supraphon SU3877-2 (No 2) Ⓕ ⚫⚫⚫
Coupled with Pavel Haas's two string quartets (and reviewed on page 496), the Pavel
Haas Quartet give searing, intense performances of Janáček's two quartets. There is a
glow to the playing here than it revealed by
very few groups. These young musicians
from the Czech Republic have rightly won
awards for their playing.

Quatuor Diotima
Alpha ALPHA133 (68' · DDD) Ⓕ ⚫⚫
A fascinating first recording of the new
Bärenreiter edition of the quartets, which
also employs the viola da gamba in the Sec-
ond. A major new Janáček recording.

of the theme. These are fine, thoughtful performances, well able to bear comparison with the best of the others available.

This disc includes two members of the Brodsky Quartet in earlier Janáček pieces, the engaging *Pohádka* ('Fairy Tale') of 1910 and the rather more conventional Violin Sonata of 1914 which Janáček revised in 1921. Both are attractively and sensitively played.

String Quartets – No 1, 'The Kreutzer Sonata'[a];
No 2, 'Intimate Letters' (two versions)[a/b]
Quatuor Diotima ([ab]Naaman Sluchin, [ab]Yun-Peng
Zhao vns [a]Franck Chevalier va [ab]Pierre Morlet vc)
[b]**Garth Knox** va da gamba
Alpha ALPHA133 (68' · DDD)   ⒡**OO**

The Diotima Quartet claim the first recording of the new Bärenreiter edition of Janáček's *Intimate Letters* Quartet. And this is no small matter of the odd slur, dot and accidental. Whole phrases come out with startlingly unfamiliar textures and tempo relationships; the floaty five-note downward scale motif in the second movement is no longer in regular whole tones and only has four notes; sundry bowed notes are now plucked, and so on. Performers have always had tough choices to make in this piece; from now on they'll be even tougher.

There's apparently even an option for the end to be played stratospherically on the viola rather than merely high on the violin, which is what the Diotimas do in their reconstruction of how the piece might have sounded with Janáček's programmatically inspired notion of using viola d'amore instead of viola. That conclusion defeats even an exponent as fine as Garth Knox (and curiously the end of the 'straight viola' recording is also unhappy, with unwanted open-string resonance jarring against the D flat major tonic). But elsewhere Knox wields his instrument to wonderfully expressive effect, its sympathetic strings creating their own magic halo and drawing the ear even when the instrument isn't carrying the main line.

The Kreutzer Sonata is just as carefully prepared and as full-bloodedly executed; however, issues of text and instruments apart, it would be hard to part with the superbly passionate Pavel Haas Quartet's Janáček recordings (see pages 498 and 499), because by a small but definite margin the young Czechs are more liberated and give a feeling of being more inside the music. That said, the Diotimas' double initiative, on top of their always classy execution, makes this new disc indispensable to the Janáček aficionado.

String Quartets – No 1, 'Kreutzer Sonata'; No 2,
'Intimate Letters'
Skampa Quartet (Pavel Fischer, Jana Lukášová vns
Radim Sedmidubský va Peter Jarůšek vc)
Supraphon SU3486-2 (41' · DDD)   ⒡**OO**

Janáček changed his mind a great deal, especially about the Second Quartet, on the way

from composition to performance and even after that. Most records use the scores published in Prague respectively in 1945 and 1949 as 'revised editions'. However, Milan Skampa published further revisions in 1975 and 1979, and these are what are used here by the quartet which studied under him at the time of its formation in 1989.

The differences depend mostly upon dynamic markings and emphases. To these the present players give great attention, stressing the sudden changes of tempo or dynamics and the consequent abrupt changes of mood which mark the music. They also pay particular attention to coloration of tone. In the First Quartet, for instance, where the seducer of the Tolstoy-inspired 'plot' makes his mincing entrance, the sound is deceptively warm within the delicacy; other quartets play the theme with almost disdainful thinness, but the Skampa allow him his dangerous charm.
In the final movement of the Second Quartet, there's a searing discord marked to be played *fortississimo* but right up near the bridge where string tone is weakest: the outcome is a horrible sound, and the Skampa believe that that's what's meant. In short, these are sharp, well-considered performances, vivid in detail and excellently judged in structure. They take their place in the catalogue beside the marvellous Talich Quartet (reviewed above) and the Pavel Haas Quartet's discs reviewed on pages 498 and 499.

Piano Sonata 1.X.1905

Piano Sonata 1. X. 1905, 'From the street'.
On an Overgrown Path. In the mists. Reminiscence
Charles Owen pf
Somm SOMMCD028 (73' · DDD)   ⒡**O**

It says much for Charles Owen and his understanding of this composer that a young British pianist should present this music with such a distinctive voice. As is evident from the first of the two movements of the Sonata, he's even more strikingly successful than Rudolf Firkušný (reviewed below), doyen of Czech pianists, at bringing out the quirky side of Janáček's writing. So the jagged little flurries of notes that bite away in contrast to the poetic lyricism of the opening are presented in sharper focus than with either Firkušný or Mikhail Rudy, an effect which directly echoes Janáček's orchestral writing. Here and throughout the disc Owen is helped by the clarity of the recording.

The qualities which distinguish Owen's performance of the sonata recur in the other works. Where Firkušný is regularly faster in a freely expressive style, and Rudy (on EMI) markedly slower, with *rubato* not always so idiomatic, Owen's middle way offers sharper focus and more refined dynamics. So his performances of the two series of miniatures which make up *On an Overgrown Path* reflect the composer's folk influences in their lyrical freshness, both in the songful pieces and the dances. In the four movements of *In the Mists*, Owen matches Firkušný in spontaneity; indeed, he gives an almost improvisatory feel to the suite. The tiny *Reminiscence*, a product from the year Janáček died, makes a moving supplement.

Glagolitic Mass

Glagolitic Mass (original version, ed Wingfield)[a].
Kodály Psalmus Hungaricus, Op. 13[b]. [a]**Tina Kiberg** *sop* [a]**Randi Stene** *contr* **Peter Svensson** *ten* [a]**Ulrik Cold** *bass* [a]**Per Salo** *org* [b]**Copenhagen Boys' Choir; Danish National Radio Choir and Symphony Orchestra / Sir Charles Mackerras**
Chandos CHAN9310 (63' · DDD · T/t)　　　　Ⓕ➔

Mackerras's version is of particular interest as it embodies another of the reconstructions that have been painstakingly made of Janáček's original intentions in different works as his stature has drawn greater scholarly interest. This one has been made by Paul Wingfield. He has gone into the nature of his restorations in great detail in his excellent monograph on the work in the Cambridge Music Handbooks series (CUP: 1992), and summarizes them in his note to this recording. Briefly, they involve the playing of the Intrada at the beginning and the end, in the Introduction a very complex rhythmic pattern and in the 'Gospodi pomiluj' ('Kyrie') use of quintuple metre instead of the familiar four-in-a-bar (both far more effectively), and fierce timpani interjections in the wild organ solo. There are other points; but in any case, most interested listeners will care less for them in detail than for the heightened force and impact of the music. This it certainly now (or once again) has.

These matters make it regrettable that, despite marvellous handling of the work by Mackerras, there are problems with a quartet of soloists that is less than exciting, and a recording that even with the most modern techniques can obscure the detail of the music and the clarity of the words. This should not detract from the interest of the disc, which every lover of the work must want to hear. Those who acquire it will have the additional benefit of a fine performance of Kodály's *Psalmus Hungaricus*, though the restored Mass is naturally the occasion for recommendation and choice.

Glagolitic Mass[a]. Sinfonietta, Op 60[b]
Felicity Palmer *sop* **Ameral Gunson** *mez* **John Mitchinson** *ten* **Malcolm King** *bass* **Jane Parker-Smith** *org* [a]**City of Birmingham Chorus and Orchestra;** [b]**Philharmonia Orchestra / Sir Simon Rattle**
EMI Great Recordings of the Century 566980-2 (62' · DDD · T/t)　　　　ⓂⒽ➔

'I am not an old man, and I am not a believer – until I see for myself.' Thus Janáček replied angrily to a critic after the premiere of his *Glagolitic Mass*. This is a gritty, masterful performance of a jagged, uncomfortable masterpiece. Its unusual title stems from the script of the ancient Slavonic text (*Glagol*) which Janáček set to music. Rattle's is a full-blooded, urgent view of the work, with particularly fine solo contributions from Felicity Palmer and John Mitchinson. That the language is an unfamiliar one is occasionally evident in the chorus, though they, like the orchestra, give totally committed performances under Rattle's inspired leadership.

Also included on this disc is the *Sinfonietta*, which is as much a study in orchestration as form, with the melody of the fourth movement appearing unaltered no fewer than 14 times, changed only in orchestral colour. It's brilliantly played here, with the 12 trumpets coming up gleaming in the final climax.

The Eternal Gospel

The Eternal Gospel[a]. The Excursions of Mr Brouček – Orchestral Suite. The Ballad of Blaník. The Fiddler's Child[b]
[a]**Gweneth-Ann Jeffers** *sop* [a]**Adrian Thompson** *ten* [b]**Elizabeth Layton** *vn* **Edinburgh Festival Chorus; BBC Scottish Symphony Orchestra / Ilan Volkov**
Hyperion CDA67517; SACDA67517 (60' · DDD · T/t)　　　　Ⓕ●●

Fans of the *Glagolitic Mass* should definitely make a beeline for Janáček's 1913 cantata *The Eternal Gospel*. Radiating a comparable spiritual and theatrical fervour, it's a setting of a text by Jaroslav Vrchlický inspired by the commentary on the Book of Revelation by the 12th-century mystic Joachim of Fiore, that serves up a seductive brew of rapt lyricism and tingling drama. Much of the solo vocal writing possesses a truly operatic scope and there are some memorably ardent choral interjections. The gifted young Israeli conductor Ilan Volkov masterminds a laudably disciplined and full-throated account of this bracing rarity, and the sound has commendable spread and amplitude (especially in its SACD format).

The rest of the programme is no less enticing. *The Fiddler's Child* (1913) and *The Ballad of Blaník* (1919) are compact and often bewitchingly lovely tone-poems with patriotic leanings; and the disc concludes with an orchestral suite from the satirical two-part opera *The Excursions of Mr Brouček* (1908-17). A thoroughly diverting 21-minute sequence it makes, too: just try the fairground sway of the 'Moon Waltz' or the young lovers' ineffably tender tryst ('Before Dawn') that brings the curtain down on the first half. If it's festive spectacle you're after, the last two movements ('Song of the Hussites' and 'Procession of the Victors') have it by the spadeful.

Performance-wise, there are no real grumbles. Although the music-making has not quite the irresistible tang you get from native interpreters in this repertoire, Volkov (not yet 30 and with talent to spare) directs with considerable flair and sensitivity. If their string section inevitably can't match up to, say, the Czech PO's for sheer heft or tonal lustre, the BBC Scottish SO play with admirable precision and infectious enthusiasm; leader Elizabeth Layton is a warm-hearted, songful presence in *The Fiddler's Child*. Hyperion's glowing natural sound-frame sets the seal on a first-rate anthology.

The Cunning Little Vixen

The Cunning Little Vixen.
The Cunning Little Vixen – orchestral suite (arr Talich)
Lucia Popp *sop* Vixen, Young vixen **Dalibor Jedlička** *bass* Forester **Eva Randová** *mez* Fox **Eva Zikmundová** *mez* Forester's wife, Owl **Vladimir Krejčik** *ten* Schoolmaster, Gnat **Richard Novák** *ten* Priest, Badger **Václav Zítek** *bar* Harašta **Beno Blachut** *ten* Pásek **Ivana Mixová** *mez* Pásek's wife, Woodpecker, Hen **Libuše Marová** *contr* Dog **Gertrude Jahn** *mez* Cock, Jay **Eva Hříbiková** *sop* Frantik **Zuzana Hudecová** *sop* Pepik **Peter Saray** *treb* Frog, Grasshopper **Miriam Ondrášková** *sop* Cricket **Vienna State Opera Chorus; Bratislava Children's Choir; Vienna Philharmonic Orchestra / Sir Charles Mackerras**
Decca ② 417 129-2DH2 (109' · DDD · T/t) Ⓕ**ⓄⓄⓄ**▷
Also available in a nine-CD set containing From the House of the Dead. Jenůfa. Kát'a Kabanová. The Makropulos Affair. Sinfonietta. Taras Bulba and the suite from The Cunning Little Vixen. Decca 475 6872DC9

Janáček used the most unlikely material for his operas. For *The Cunning Little Vixen* his source was a series of newspaper drawings, with accompanying text, about the adventures of a vixen cub and her escape from the gamekeeper who raised her. The music is a fascinating blend of vocal and orchestral sound – at times ludicrously romantic, at others raw and violent. Mackerras's Czech training has given him a rare insight into Janáček's music, and he presents a version faithful to the composer's individual requirements. In the title-role, Lucia Popp gives full weight to the text while displaying all the richness and beauty of her voice.

There's a well-chosen supporting cast of largely Czech singers, with the Vienna Philharmonic to add the ultimate touch of orchestral refinement. Decca's sound is of demonstration quality.

The Cunning Little Vixen
Eva Jenis *sop* Vixen **Thomas Allen** *bar* Forester **Hana Minutillo** *contr* Fox **Libuše Márová** *mez* Forester's Wife, Owl **Josef Hajna** *ten* Schoolmaster, Mosquito **Richard Novák** *bass* Parson, Badger **Ivan Kusnjer** *bar* Harašta **Jean-Philippe Marlière** *bass* Innkeeper, Dog **Sarah Connolly** *mez* Innkeeper's Wife, Cock, Jay **Florence Bonnafous** *sop* Hen **François Martinaud** *sop* Woodpecker **Châtelet Choir; Hautes-de-Seine Maîtrise; Orchestre de Paris / Sir Charles Mackerras**
Stage director **Nicholas Hytner**
Video director **Brian Large**
ArtHaus Musik 📀 100 240 (98' · 16:9 · 2.0 · 2 & 5)
Ⓕ**Ⓞ**

Mackerras conducts with all the vibrancy of his landmark CD recording, plus the immediacy of live performance, and if the Orchestre de Paris has leaner strings and less secure brass than the VPO, it still responds well. Hytner's production was an instant hit at the time, with good reason. The forest scenes rely heavily on dance, as Janáček's notes suggest, so the set is a ballet-style level stage with hanging flats; but within those constraints it comes alive with clever imagery and gaudy colour.

Eva Jenis is a vivacious, characterful Vixen, though not as creamy as Popp on the CD. Janáček's vocal casting isn't observed consistently; Hana Minutillo makes a fine contralto Fox, but there's a case for giving the role to a male voice, as the Dog is here. Richard Novák and Josef Hajna, in the important animal/human roles, and Ivan Kusnjer's roughneck Poacher provide firmly idiomatic support, but Allen's grizzled Forester remains the lynchpin. His final paean to the renewing force of Nature, with Mackerras in full lyrical flow, is magical. A strong recommendation.

The Excursions of Mr Brouček

The Excursions of Mr Brouček
Jan Vacík *ten* Brouček **Peter Straka** *ten* Mazal; Blankytný; Petřík **Roman Janál** *bar* Sacristan; unigrove; Domšík **Maria Haan** *sop* Málinka; Etherea; Kunka **Zdeněk Plech** *bass* Würfl; Wonderglitter; Councillor **Martina Bauerová** *mez* Young Waiter; Student **Lenka mídová** *mez* Housewife; Kedruta **Ivan Kusnjer** *bar* Apparition
BBC Singers; BBC Symphony Orchestra / Jiří Bělohlávek
DG ② 477 7387GH2 (123' · DDD · S/T/t/N)
Ⓕ**ⓄⓄⓄ**▷

Mr Brouček's excursions may have carried him to the moon and the 15th century, but it took him longer to travel beyond his native land into the opera houses and recording studios of the world. But what a lovable work it is. The first excursion in particular is packed with vivid invention; the second dips deeper into wells of Czech history. It all needs the sharp hand and light touch with the agile rhythms which Bělohlávek brings to it. He is not helped by a recording that sets the singers too far back and obscures a good deal of the words, especially in the chorus, though matters improve once the moon is reached. Jan Vacík gives a lively account of poor Brouček, first stranded among the moon aesthetes and then mired in religious controversy, preserving the little man's dignity and allowing him a touching quality that sees him through it all. If he lacks the warmth and the rounded character of Vilém Přibyl, this is still a fresh and attractive portrayal.

There is, as always, much doubling in the cast. Peter Straka is an elegant Mazal and Petřík, lightly caricaturing his own elegance to send up the posturing Azurean poet. Maria Haan is a lively Málinka, putting on airs and graces for Ethcrea and returning to a fresh simplicity for

Peter's lover Kunka. The many other parts include sturdy contributions from Roman Janál and Zdeněk Plech, though the sense of atmosphere and the depth of feeling which lies under all the satire are richer with Jílek's handling of both singers and orchestra.

House of the Dead / Makropulos Affair

From the House of the Dead[a]. Mládi[b]. Nursery rhymes[c]
Dalibor Jedlička bar Goryanchikov **Jaroslava Janská** sop Alyeya **Jiří Zahradníček** ten Luka (Morosov) **Vladimir Krejčík** ten Tall Prisoner **Richard Novák** bass Short Prisoner **Antonín Svorc** bass-bar Commandant **Beno Blachut** ten Old Prisoner **Ivo Zídek** ten Skuratov **Jaroslav Souček** bar Chekunov, Prisoner acting Don Juan **Eva Zigmundová** mez Whore **Zdeněk Soušek** ten Shapkin, Kedril **Václav Zítek** bar Shishkov **Zdeněk Svehla** ten Cherevin, A Voice **Vienna State Opera Chorus; Vienna Philharmonic Orchestra / Sir Charles Mackerras;** [c]**London Sinfonietta Chorus;** [bc]**London Sinfonietta / David Atherton**
Decca ② 430 375-2DH2 (123' · DDD/ADD · T/t)
Ⓕ❍❍❍▷

The Makropulos Affair. Lachian Dances[a]
Elisabeth Söderström sop Emilia Marty **Peter Dvorský** ten Albert Gregor **Vladimir Krejšík** ten Vítek **Anna Czaková** mez Kristina **Václav Zítek** bar Jaroslav Prus **Zdeněk Svehla** ten Janek **Dalibor Jedlička** bass Kolenatý **Jiří Joran** bass Stage technician **Ivana Mixová** contr Cleaning woman **Beno Blachut** ten Hauk-Sendorf **Blanka Vitková** contr Chambermaid **Vienna State Opera Chorus; Vienna Philharmonic Orchestra / Sir Charles Mackerras;** [a]**London Philharmonic Orchestra / François Huybrechts**
Decca ② 478 1711 (118' · ADD · T/t) Recorded 1978
Ⓕ❍❍❍▷

Also available in a nine-CD set containing The Cunning Little Vixen. Jenůfa. Kát'a Kabanová. Sinfonietta. Taras Bulba and the suite from The Cunning Little Vixen. Decca 475 6872DC9

From the House of the Dead (the 1980 *Gramophone* Record of the Year) was here recorded for the first time in its proper, original version; and this revealed it as even more of a masterpiece – a work, indeed, to count among the handful of masterpieces of 20th-century opera. The loss of the final chorus, a sentimental addition, is but the most striking of the clarifications: throughout, the sound is sharper, the textures are sparer, and this serves to sharpen the effect and to give the singers more clearly differentiated support. The cast is led, nominally, by Goryanchikov, but the character isn't really the hero of an opera that has no heroes, and in which all are heroes, though Dalibor Jedlička sings him warmly and well. The prisoners are skilfully contrasted in Janáček's writing so as to make an apparently random yet actually well-structured group; there isn't a weak performance among them.

The Makropulos Affair does have a heroine, in the tragic figure of Emilia Marty; and here Elisabeth Söderström gives one of her greatest recorded performances. She succeeds amazingly in conveying the complexity of the character, the elegance yet flinty cynicism, the aloofness yet vulnerability, the latent warmth that can flower into such rich expressive phrases and then be reined in with a sense of nervy panic. She's only really alarmed by Prus, the most formidable of the men around her, powerfully sung by Václav Zítek. Mackerras is again masterly. This is a recording to set among great performances of it.

As with *From the House of the Dead*, there's an essay by John Tyrrell that not only gives the listener the best possible introduction to the opera but is also a contribution to scholarship. The fill-ups, *Mládi* and the *Nursery rhyme*, come from David Atherton's splendid 1981 set of five LPs devoted to Janáček; the *Lachian Dances* set is a rather less successful companion to *Makropulos*.

From the House of the Dead
Olaf Bär bar Gorjančikov **Eric Stoklossa** ten Aljeja **Stefan Margita** ten Luka **Peter Straka** ten Tall Prisoner **Vladimir Chmelo** bar Short Prisoner **Jiří Sulženko** bass Commandant **Heinz Zednik** ten Old Prisoner **John Mark Ainsley** ten Skuratov **Jan Galla** bass Cekunov **Arnold Schoenberg Choir; Mahler Chamber Orchestra / Pierre Boulez**
Stage director **Patrice Chéreau**
Video director **Stéphane Metge**
DG **DVD** 073 4426GH
(148' · NTSC · 16:9 · PCM stereo and DTS 5.1 • 0)
Includes documentary, 'The Making of The House of the Dead'. Recorded live at the Vienna Festival in 2007
Ⓕ❍❍

Nearly 30 years have elapsed since Boulez and Chéreau last created a new production together – the Paris premiere of the Cerha completion of *Lulu*. In the interim the conductor has taken on repertoire he might have blanched at in those days (Bruckner, Janáček, even Richard Strauss) while the director became more involved in the cinema and the plays of his late partner Bernard-Marie Koltès. Their return, in a staging shared by four houses, shows the old fires undiminished, although the heightened realism and visual beauty still practised by Chéreau's team (his designer Richard Peduzzi has worked with him since their schooldays) have changed little over the years and, inevitably, lack the radical edge they had in the 1970s.

Janáček's (and Dostoyevsky's) prisoners are modernised painlessly to a non-specific 20th-century gulag surrounded (except in the river bank scene, here a huge rubbish dump, that opens Act 2) by Peduzzi's trademark steep Italianate high walls. As in all his productions and films, Chéreau's directing turns everyone into such complete and natural actors that the descriptive term 'acting' seems almost redundant. Even in Act 3, where Janáček's dramaturgy calls for perhaps one prisoner story too many, the staging's pulse never falters. Only the plays in Act 2 feel a little too carefully stylised (and

Eastern-influenced) for these prisoners to have put on themselves, although they're unfailingly reflective of the characters in the main story.

Boulez once said that he began conducting in order to achieve really good performances of modern works. Now in his 80s, he is still operating at that level in this tricky score (he uses the Mackerras/Tyrrell critical edition), treading the finest balance, as did Janáček, between reported emotion and outright passion. It really is invidious in this ensemble piece to pick out individuals, but Ainsley creates a compellingly dangerous near-ballet out of Skuratov's insanity, and Bär and Stoklossa limn beautifully the growing closeness of the nobleman Gorjančikov and the young Aljeja. The sound picture does justice to Boulez's balances, while the camera-work and editing are a lot happier than the bumpy film of the 2005 Chéreau/Aix *Così*.

The Makropulos Affair (sung in English)
Cheryl Barker sop Emilia Marty **Robert Brubaker** ten Albert Gregor **John Graham-Hall** ten Vítek **Elena Xanthoudakis** sop Kristina **John Wegner** bar Baron Jaroslav Prus **Thomas Walker** ten Janek **Neal Davies** bass-bar Dr Kolenat **Graeme Danby** bass Stage Technician **Kathleen Wilkinson** contr Cleaning Woman **Graham Clark** ten Hauk-Sendorf **Susanna Tudor-Thomas** contr Chambermaid **English National Opera Chorus and Orchestra / Sir Charles Mackerras**
Chandos/Peter Moores Foundation Opera in English ② CHAN3138 (126' · DDD · S/N/T) Ⓕ

This is Mackerras's second recording. The first, in 1979, in his series of groundbreaking Janáček recordings for Decca (above), had the Vienna Philharmonic in radiant form accompanied a fine cast singing in Czech. It says much for the quality of the ENO Orchestra that for this new version in English the playing is equally polished, and often outshines that of the Viennese in its extra dramatic bite.

The recording brings an advantage, too – not as plushy as the Viennese version and with extra separation and clarity in a clearly focused acoustic. Those qualities suit the work better, which, as Sir Charles points out, is 'a different kind of music': Janáček emphatically did not want to sound like Strauss or Puccini. That extra clarity and separation means the words are astonishingly clear.

Cheryl Barker rivals Elisabeth Söderström on Decca in dramatic bite and when in Act 3 Emilia is at last given a sustained solo, Barker is even more powerful, aptly abrasive and less moulded. Though the American Robert Brubaker cannot quite match Peter Dvorsky on Decca, it is a focused, compelling performance. In some of the smaller roles the Czech singers had an advantage but their counterparts here run them close. On any count both versions have one marvelling at the score's emotional thrust and dramatic compulsion, original in every way and one of Janáček's supreme masterpieces.

Jenůfa

Jenůfa
Elisabeth Söderström sop Jenůfa **Wieslaw Ochman** ten Laca **Eva Randová** mez Kostelnička **Petr Dvorskü** ten Steva **Lucia Popp** sop Karolka **Marie Mrazová** contr Stařenka **Václav Zitek** bar Stárek **Dalibor Jedlička** bass Rychtar **Ivana Mixová** mez Rychtarka **Vera Soukopová** mez Pastuchyňa, Tetka **Jindra Pokorná** mez Barena **Jana Janasová** sop Jano **Vienna State Opera Chorus; Vienna Philharmonic Orchestra / Sir Charles Mackerras**
Decca ② 414 483-2DH2 (130' · DDD) Ⓕ🅜OOOⒹ➔
Also available in a nine-CD set containing From the House of the Dead. The Cunning Little Vixen. Kát'a Kabanová. The Makropulos Affair. Sinfonietta. Taras Bulba and the suite from The Cunning Little Vixen. Decca 475 6872DC9

 Janáček's first operatic masterpiece is a towering work, blending searing intensity with heart-stopping lyricism. It tells of Jenůfa and the appalling treatment she receives as she's caught between the man she loves and another who finally comes to love her. But dominating the story is the Kostelnička, a figure of enormous strength, pride and inner resource who rules Jenůfa's life and ultimately kills her baby. Randová's characterisation of the role of the Kostelnička is frightening in its intensity yet has a very human core. The two men are well cast and act as fine foils to Söderström's deeply impressive Jenůfa. The Vienna Philharmonic plays beautifully and Mackerras directs magnificently. The recording is all one could wish for and the booklet is a mine of informed scholarship.

Jenůfa
Roberta Alexander sop Jenůfa **Anja Silja** sop Kostelnička **Philip Langridge** ten Laca **Mark Baker** ten Števa **Menai Davies** contr Grandmother Buryja **Robert Poulton** bar Foreman of the Mill **Gordon Sandison** bar Mayor **Linda Ormiston** mez Mayor's Wife **Alison Hagley** sop Karolka **Sarah Pring** sop Barena **Lynne Davies** sop Jano **Glyndebourne Festival Chorus; London Philharmonic Orchestra / Sir Andrew Davis** Stage director **Nikolaus Lehnhoff** Video director **Derek Bailey**
ArtHaus Musik 🅓🅥🅓 100 208 (118' · 4:3 · 2.0 · 2 & 5)
Recorded live in 1989 Ⓕ🅞

Nikolaus Lehnhoff's acclaimed 1989 Glyndebourne production makes a welcome appearance on DVD, the picture a touch grainy but still a dramatic improvement over the videotape, the sound still more so. Andrew Davis's conducting emphasises the score's lyricism without diminishing its rhythmic vigour and folk resonances. The staging, in Czech despite its Anglophone cast, is just as idiomatic. If Act 1's mill looks somewhat cramped on the old Glyndebourne stage, the indoor scenes gain a natural, sometimes claustrophobic, intimacy, well captured in Derek Bailey's direction.

The performers display the same naturalness. Roberta Alexander's heroine is sung with a warmth and fervour that exactly captures Jenůfa's open and loving nature. Langridge is a rather mature Laca, but his sinewy tenor and twisted, hungry demeanour render the character's distorting jealousy and inner decency equally credible and sympathetic. Lehnhoff and Silja play the Kostelnička as the traditional black-clad puritan rather than the less sophisticated old peddler woman, pious and desperate, whom Janáček drew from the original play. But her steely tones and incisive diction movingly illuminate the fiercely proud and loving nature, warped (as a restored solo reveals) by marital abuse, which makes her so fanatically protective of Jenůfa; her murderous Act 2 soliloquy and conscience-stricken terror are harrowing.

Additional recommendations

Jenůfa

Mattila Jenůfa **Silvasti** Laca **Silja** Kostelnička **Hadley** Steva **Royal Opera House Orchestra / Haitink**
Erato ② 0927-45330-2 (139' · DDD · T/t) Recorded live 2001   Ⓕ

Haitink may not topple the Mackerras version from its pedestal but it makes a deeply rewarding and valid alternative, especially collectable for Mattila's heroine and Silvasti's superlatively sung Laca.

Jenůfa (sung in English)

Watson Jenůfa **Robson** Laca **Barstow** Kostelnička **Wedd** Števa **Welsh National Opera Chorus and Orchestra / Sir Charles Mackerras**
Chandos/Peter Moores Foundation Opera in English
② CHAN3106 (120' · DDD · T/t)   Ⓜ▶

A superb issue rivalling Mackerras's Award-winning Decca recording. If anything, the intense emotion comes over even more powerfully. For those who prefer opera in translation, this is the one to choose.

Kát'a Kabanová

Kát'a Kabanová. House of the Dead. The Cunning Little Vixen. Jenůfa. The Makropulos Affair. Sinfonietta. Taras Bulba and the suite from The Cunning Little Vixen
Elisabeth Söderström sop Kát'á Kabanová **Petr Dvorsky** ten Boris **Naděžda Kniplová** contr Kabanicha **Vladimír Krejčík** ten Tichon **Libuše Márová** mez Varvara **Dalibor Jedlička** bass Dikoj **Zdeněk Svehla** ten Kudrjáš **Jaroslav Souček** bar Kuligin **Jitka Pavlová** sop Glaša **Gertrude Jahn** mez Fekluša
Vienna State Opera Chorus; Vienna Philharmonic Orchestra / Sir Charles Mackerras
Decca ⑨ 475 6872DC9 (ADD · N/T/t)   Ⓕ●●●▶

Ⓖ Kát'á, a free spirit, is imprisoned by marriage into, and domicile with, a family in a provincial Russian town on the Volga. The family is manipulated by her widowed mother-in-law. The only son (Kát'á's husband) is spineless, and Kát'á looks for escape in love. She finds the love, but true escape only in suicide. Janáček focuses on his heroine, giving her at least two of the most moving scenes in opera: the first where, to music of shimmering, seraphic beauty she describes her childhood imagination given free rein by sunlight streaming through the dome in church; and the second in the last scene where, after confessing her adultery, she concludes that 'not even God's own sunlight' gives her pleasure any more. Söderström has the intelligence and a voice which guarantees total credibility; and of the superb all-Czech supporting cast one might only have wished for a slightly younger-sounding sister-in-law. Mackerras obtains the finest playing from the VPO; and Decca reproduces the whole with clarity, atmosphere, ideal perspectives and discernible stage movement – only a detectable levelling of the score's few extreme *fortissimos* points to the recording's vintage.

At the moment *Kát'á* is only available in a nine-CD box set of all of Mackerras's Janáček recordings, but you might be able to find copies of the original set, or download just the opera you require.

Katya Kabanova (in English)
Cheryl Barker sop Katerina **Jane Henschel** mez Marfa Kabanova **Peter Hoare** ten Tichon Kabanov **Gwynne Howell** bass Dikoi **Robert Brubaker** ten Boris Grigoryevich **Victoria Simmonds** mez Varvara **Peter Wedd** ten Vanya Kudryash **Kathleen Wilkinson** mez Glasha **Owen Webb** bar Kuligin **Chorus and Orchestra of the Welsh National Opera / Carlo Rizzi**
Chandos/Peter Moores Foundation Opera in English
② CHAN3145 (92' · DDD · S/N/T)   Ⓜ●▶

This is the fifth Janáček opera in Chandos's Opera in English series, and with vivid, well separated sound, balancing the voices in front of the orchestra, the first impression is how clear the words are from the singers of the Welsh National Opera production on which the recording is based.

Carlo Rizzi, who conducted the live performances for WNO, is a persuasive Janáček interpreter. It is fascinating to compare this version with Mackerras's Decca recording with the Vienna Philharmonic and an excellent, mainly Czech cast, Elisabeth Söderström taking the title-role. If that recording is marginally richer and weightier than the new Chandos, the strings of WNO play with comparable refinement. Rizzi's interpretation in all three acts is a degree more urgent, with speeds consistently faster, no doubt reflecting his experience of conducting it live.

As in the English *Makropulos Case*, the principal singer is Cheryl Barker, fresh, clear and powerful, more girlish-sounding than Söderström. Jane Henschel is outstanding as Marfa Kabanova, the rich widow who persecutes her daughter-in-law, wonderfully rich and firm throughout her range. The three tenor roles are exceptionally well taken, even if the contrasts between Robert Brubaker as Boris, Peter Wedd as Kudryash and Peter Hoare as Tichon, husband of Katya and son of Marfa, are not ideally marked. Gwynne Howell as the merchant Dikoi, uncle of Boris, is also excellent.

The old Norman Tucker translation is used with some minor amendments by Rodney Blumer, *nom de plume* of critic Rodney Milnes, with words admirably clear throughout, adding to the dramatic impact of the piece. Another outstanding issue in the Opera in English series.

Kát'á Kabanová

Nancy Gustafson *sop* Kát'á Kabanová **Barry McCauley** *ten* Boris **Felicity Palmer** *mez* Kabanicha **Donald Adams** *bass* Dikoj **Ryland Davies** *ten* Tichon **John Graham-Hall** *ten* Kudrjáš **Louise Winter** *mez* Varvara **Robert Poulton** *bar* Kuligin **Christine Bunning** *mez* Glaša **Linda Ormiston** *mez* Fekluša **Rachael Hallawell** *mez* Woman **Christopher Ventris** *ten* Bystander **Festival Chorus and Orchestra / Sir Andrew Davis**
Stage director **Nikolaus Lehnhoff**
Video director **Derek Bailey**
ArtHaus Musik ② 100 158 (99' · Regions 2 & 5)
Recorded live in 1988   (F)

This transfer to DVD of a 1988 Virgin VHS houses an entirely recommendable staging by Lehnhoff for Glyndebourne. He directs his excellent cast with an astonishing ability to delineate their inner feelings, receiving the most positive response from Nancy Gustafson in the title-role. She presents, from her initial entry, an overwrought, highly impressionable girl frustrated beyond endurance by the casual attentions of her husband Tichon, and longing for the erotic charge offered by the attractive Boris. When she finally capitulates to his advances, she mirrors the sense of release tinged with guilt evinced in the music. Her singing is firm, soaring, vibrant. Palmer is the very picture of buttoned-up severity as Kabanicha. Her command over Kát'á and Tichon is terrible to behold. Davies suggests Tichon's lack of backbone. McCauley's Boris conveys the man's ability to infatuate the repressed Kát'á. His tenor is keen, though under strain in the upper register. Andrew Davis brings out all the passion and anguish in the wonderful score. Tobias Hoheisel's sets derive from Russian art of the period of the story's genesis.

John Jenkins   English 1592-1678

A lutenist and lyra viol player, Jenkins was in London in 1634 and was appointed a court theorbo player in 1660. He lived with several East Anglian families, including Roger North's at Kirtling, Cambs. (1660-66), but was never officially attached to any. He was important for his consort music, notably for viols, which were widely popular among amateur

players; his c 800 surviving pieces are pre-eminent in lyrical invention, structural organization and sonority. He had a command of the English virtuoso 'division' style. He composed both in the traditional many-voice consort style and in the new Italian three-part manner, often writing for treble, two basses and organ or two trebles and bass, moving towards a new violin-influenced phrase structure.   GROVEmusic

---

Consort music

19 Divisions on a Ground – Division in A. 12 Fantasias in six parts – No 3; No 8; No 5. Two Fantasia-Suites in two parts fantasia-air-corant – A minor. Eight Fantasia-Suites in four parts – No 3. Two In Nomines in six parts. Pavan and Galliard, 'Newarke Seidge'. Two Pavans in six parts – No 2. Galliard
Ensemble Jérôme Hantaï
(François Fernandez, Simon Heyerick *vns* Jérôme Hantaï, Kaori Uemura, Catherine Arnoux, Alix Verzier *viols* Brian Feehan *lte* Maude Gratton, Pierre Hantaï *orgs*)
Naïve Astrée E8895 (60' · DDD)   (F)

It's common enough to find recordings of Purcell or Byrd from Continental ensembles, but to have a distinguished group such as this playing a more insular figure like John Jenkins comes as something of a pleasant surprise. English composers of his generation have something very distinctive to offer, even though they may not score as highly as some of their Continental contemporaries in terms of historical eminence.

Jenkins's idiom isn't as angular as that of his contemporary William Lawes, though he can trade in 'those sourest sharps and uncouth flats' along with the best of them, and match Lawes' energy (as in the *Newark Siege*, one of the gems of this collection). The generous tone of Hantaï's ensemble (in which the continuo is an audibly well-nourished presence) lends the gentler pieces a warm glow. And when required, they certainly can play their socks off: the *Newark Siege* sees them switch from swashbuckling truculence to more melancholy repose at the end with barely a hint of changing gear.

This is chamber-music, and chamber music-making, of real distinction.

---

12 Fantasias in six parts. Two In nomines in six parts. Two Pavans in six parts
Phantasm (Wendy Gillespie, Jonathan Manson, Markku Luolajan-Mikkola *viols* with Emilia Benjamin, Mikko Perkola *viols*) / **Laurence Dreyfus** *viols*
Avie AV2099 (66' · DDD)   (F)⯈

His discography may not be extensive, perhaps, but in terms of quality John Jenkins has been remarkably well served on disc. His music makes enough demands on players to be more than a match for all but the most intrepid consorts. On that count Phantasm have few worries, though as with the previous recordings, there is the odd moment to remind one that these superlative musicians, too, may find themselves taxed (here, it is especially the top Cs on the treble viol. Never mind; the real interest in this recording lies in the different approach Phantasm bring to this music. The slightly languid, Carolinian reserve one so associates with the repertory is replaced by a more incisive, top-down approach, with sharper attacks and more forthright articulation.

This brings the viol consort nearer to the sound and feel of the string quartet than it has ever been on disc. Whether that reflects what a viol consort is 'about' is a moot point, but to hear music of this refinement and subtlety in a new light is exciting. Of the three available anthologies, Phantasm's is most focused on the six-part consorts and they do their formidable reputation no harm here; if they coax listeners into snapping up more of his music, they will have done right by Jenkins, too.

17 Fantasias in five parts. Pavans – in G; in G minor; in F
Phantasm (Laurence Dreyfus, Wendy Gillespie, Jonathan Manson, Markku Luolajan-Mikkola viols) with Mikko Perkola viol
Avie AV2120 (73' · DDD)

Lawrence Dreyfus's devotion to John Jenkins's cause is little short of messianic. If his booklet-notes don't make the point eloquently enough, consider that the composer is the first to receive not one but two anthologies from Phantasm. The previous disc, devoted to his six-part consorts (see above), departed from previous Jenkins anthologies in forgoing any continuo, and this companion volume follows suit. It's hard not to share Dreyfus's enthusiasm: the playfulness and spontaneity of Jenkins's invention is infectious, and on at least one occasion (the close of Fantasy 15, in which a potentially clichéd downward sequence proliferates almost to the point of absurdity) he had me laughing aloud.

Musically, this new recording is a worthy successor to the six-part disc. Technically speaking, the ensemble is as zestful as ever, and practically flawless in execution. The only possible reservation one might have concerns the programming, which consists almost entirely of Fantasies, with only three Pavans to counterbalance them. As the durations are roughly consistent (three to four minutes for the Fantasias and around five for the Pavans), the effect is less varied than on the previous recording, which included a couple of In nomines as well. The decision to exclude continuo further limits the possibilities for variation. But the whole point of this recording is that a single disc is insufficient to do him justice. On that count, it recommends itself.

Josquin Desprez   French c1440-1521

Josquin was a singer at Milan Cathedral in 1459, remaining there until December 1472. By July 1474 he was one of the 'cantori di capella' in the chapel of Galeazzo Maria Sforza. Between 1476 and 1504 he passed into the service of Cardinal Ascanio Sforza, whom he probably accompanied in Rome in 1484. His name first appears among the papal chapel choir in 1486 and recurs sporadically; he had left the choir by 1501. In this Italian period Josquin reached artistic maturity.

He then went to France (he may also have done so while at the papal chapel) and probably served Louis XII's court. Although he may have had connections with the Ferrara court (through the Sforzas) in the 1480s and 1490s, no formal relationship with the court is known before 1503 when, for a year, he was maestro di cappella there and the highest-paid singer in the chapel's history. There he probably wrote primarily masses and motets. An outbreak of plague in 1503 forced the court to leave Ferrara (Josquin's place was taken by Obrecht, who fell victim in 1505). He was in the north again, at Notre Dame at Condé, in 1504; he may have been connected with Margaret of Austria's court, 1508-11. He died in 1521. Several portraits survive, one attributed to Leonardo da Vinci.

Josquin's works gradually became known throughout western Europe and were regarded as models by many composers and theorists. Petrucci's three books of his masses (1502-14) reflect contemporary esteem, as does Attaingnant's collection of his chansons (1550). Several laments were written on his death (including Gombert's elegy Musae Jovis), and as late as 1554 Jacquet of Mantua paid him tribute in a motet. He was praised by 16th-century literary figures (including Castiglione and Rabelais) and was Luther's favourite composer.

Josquin was the greatest composer of the high Renaissance, the most varied in invention and the most profound in expression. Much of his music cannot be dated. Generally, however, his first period (up to c1485) is characterised by abstract, melismatic counterpoint in the manner of Ockeghem and by tenuous relationships between words and music. The middle period (to c1505) saw the development and perfection of the technique of pervasive imitation based on word-generated motifs. This style has been seen as a synthesis of two traditions: the northern polyphony of Dufay, Busnois and Ockeghem, in which he presumably had his earliest training, and the more chordal, harmonically orientated practice of Italy. In the final period the relationship between word and note becomes even closer and there is increasing emphasis on declamation and rhetorical expression within a style of the utmost economy. **GROVE**music

Masses

Missa L'homme armé sexti toni. Missa L'homme armé super voces musicales
A Sei Voci / Bernard Fabre-Garrus; Maîtrise des Pays de Loire / Bertrand Lemaire
Astrée Naïve E8809 (74' · DDD · T/t)

Josquin's Masses on *L'homme armé* have one of the most impressive recording pedigrees of the early Renaissance, but A Sei Voci's is probably the finest so far. There's superlative singing, a compelling, enveloping acoustic presence, and above all an interpretative logic, a sure-footedness of tempo and of phrasing that makes sense of some of Josquin's most prolix and demanding music. First comes *Sexti toni*, which is sung for the first time in the range that the sources' low clefs seem to imply. Where all the previous recordings have women on the top line (in a correspondingly higher tessitura), here it's taken by countertenors, supplemented on occasion by the children of the Maîtrise des Pays de Loire. The sunny, almost genial tone of previous recordings gives way to a quite unsuspected, darker and more interiorised but still luminous sound world.

The contrapuntal intensity of the final *Agnus Dei* is wonderful to hear, especially after the restrained scoring of much of what precedes it. Still more impressive, perhaps, is the performance of *Super voces musicales*, Josquin's most extended work, and certainly one of his most abstract and intellectually challenging. In the past, its very abstraction bred a suspicion that here was a work easier to admire than to love. Fabre-Garrus and his singers change all that: the intellectual toughness is still there, but in addition they make clear the Mass's rhetorical logic in a way that previous recordings never quite managed. Rarely has Josquin's achievement appeared so compelling. In short, this recording is a revelation.

Missa 'Malheur me bat'. Virgo prudentissima. Liber generationis Jesu Christi. Ave Maria…virgo serena. Baiséz moy. Que vous ma dame/In pace in idipsum. Victimae paschali laudes. Comment peult avoir joye
The Clerks' Group / Edward Wickham
ASV Gaudeamus CDGAU306 (71' · DDD · T/t)　　Ⓕ

The Clerks' Group once again earn our gratitude by heading straight for the top-class works that lack modern, top-class recordings. The Mass *Malheur me bat* is one of Josquin's most resourceful treatments of received material, taking all three voices of a secular piece and treating each separately, each in different ways; and in the magnificent final movement he follows an almost comical two-voice canon at the second with a broad treatment in six voices with two canons running simultaneously. As a display of contrapuntal techniques, this may well be his most stunning composition.

The Clerks' Group can seem less polished than previously. Intonation isn't always out of the top drawer. And the speeds chosen often seem perplexing, but on further listening, it seems that they're trying to tackle different musical problems; they're going for the music, and that has to be good.

This is particularly the case in the most welcome novelty here, the *Liber generationis*, Josquin's setting of the genealogy from St Matthew's gospel. How wonderful to have this and the other works here in seriously skilled performances.

Missa Pange lingua. Missa La sol fa re mi
The Tallis Scholars / Peter Phillips

Gimell CDGIM009 (62' · DDD · T/t)　　ⒻⓄⓄⓄⒹ➔

This is absolutely superb. We must accept that Josquin is unlikely to have heard this music with two women on the top line, but they do it so well that only a fundamentalist would mark the disc down for that. It should also be said that the least successful performance on the entire disc is in the opening *Kyrie* of this Mass where there's a certain brutality in the approach; and although The Tallis Scholars make much of the 'Benedictus' and the last *Agnus Dei*, there may still be better ways of doing it. On the other hand, as just one example among many, these were the first musicians to make the 'Osanna' truly successful and understand why Josquin should have chosen to compose it that way. But they sing even better in the Mass, *La sol fa re mi*. Again and again in the singing one has the feeling that Josquin's lines are projected with an understanding and clarity that have rarely been heard before. The *La sol fa re mi* of the title denotes (among other things) the melodic passage which appears over 200 times in the course of the work with its intervals unchanged – which may not seem a recipe for the kind of music one would want to hear. But Josquin treats his material with such astonishing sophistication that you're rarely aware of the melodic fragment as such; and Phillips is scrupulously careful never to emphasise the melody except in places – such as the end of the second 'Osanna' – where it's clearly intended to work as an ostinato. This performance shows that the *La sol fa re mi* belongs with the greatest works of its era.

Missa 'D'ung aultre amer'. Adieu mes amours. Ave Maria, virgo serena. Cela sans plus. De tous biens playne. Fortuna d'un gran tempo. Mille regretz. Planxit autem David. Tu solus qui facis mirabilia. La Bernardina. Qui belles amours. Sanctus 'D'ung aultre amer'. Tu lumen, tu splendor Patris. Victimae paschali laudes/D'ung aultre amer. Ile fantazies de Joskin
Claire Wilkinson sop **Andrew Lawrence-King** hp
Alamire / David Skinner
Obsidian CD701 (68' · DDD)　　ⒻⓄⓄ

This is a most ingeniously devised Josquin recitals. Laying emphasis on works of his early maturity, it records the composer's apparent obsession with Ockeghem's rondeau *D'ung aultre amer*. Josquin reworked it several times, including a Mass that generated several minor 'spin-offs', which are also presented here. The Mass is reckoned to be one of his earliest. It is certainly his shortest, and arguably the least well-known (and some scholars in fact dispute Josquin's authorship). But it has an immediate appeal that links it (in attitude, at least) to the songs that make up the rest of the disc. These are engagingly sung by Claire Wilkinson, accompanied on the harp by Andrew Lawrence-King, who gets a few solo spots of his own. The combination of harp and voice works very well and offers a new way of hearing some old favourites: that said, the sound recording seems to make the harp a touch louder than it might be.

The recital is ingenious because alongside this relatively neglected Mass it seamlessly works in a few sacred works that count among Josquin's most popular: the ubiquitous *Ave Maria, virgo serena*, and above all *Planxit autem David*, which receives a particularly moving account. This is the first recording by Alamire, a new ensemble boasting familiar English singers under the guidance of David Skinner. Their approach is direct and unaffected, and to judge by the results they appear to have enjoyed these recording sessions.

Missa, 'Hercules Dux Ferrarie'. Salve regina. Miserere mei, Deus. Virgo salutiferi
De Labyrintho / Walter Testolin
Stradivarius STR33674 (60' · DDD · T)   Ⓕ

Josquin's Mass for Ercole, Duke of Ferrara, is one of his finest, and has received several good recordings. De Labyrintho's performance has a rhythmic fluidity that relieves the Mass's inflexibly four-square construction. This ensemble is one to watch out for: its blend is full and focused, yet softly rounded; and the individual voices (heard in the sections with reduced scoring) are of similar quality. Walter Testolin uses countertenors on the top line in the Mass, and women in the motets. Such decisions seem sensible in principle, and prove just as effective in practice. There is a pleasing variety of atmosphere: compare to the twilit first *Agnus dei* with the *Credo*'s robust conclusion.

The motets are anything but fillers; sufficiently contrasted to confirm the first impression of De Labyrintho's versatility. It's heartening to hear an Italian ensemble tackling Josquin so felicitously: after all, most of the music on this disc was composed in Ferrara.

Additional recommendation

Josquin Hercules Missa Dux Ferrariae. **Josquin, Gombert, Compère** Motets & chansons
Hilliard Ensemble
Virgin Veritas 562346-2 (118' · DDD)   Ⓑ
  The Hilliards take a different approach to the Mass from Labyrintho, and maintain a rugged emphasis on the tactus. A fine bargain.

Missa Gaudeamus. Recordare virgo Mater. Regina caeli. Missa Ave maris stella. Virgo salutiferi/Ave Maria
A Sei Voci; Maîtrise des Pays de Loire / Bernard Fabre-Garrus bass
Auvidis Astrée E8612 (68' · DDD · T/t)   Ⓕ

Bernard Fabre-Garrus has long been experimenting with different ways of performing renaissance polyphony. It seems that each of his recordings offers a new sound; and in this particular case his novelty is to use the children of the Maîtrise des Pays de Loire – both boys and

girls – to sing the top line of Josquin's Mass *Gaudeamus*. This is one of Josquin's most rhythmically intricate works, so there's a major challenge here; just occasionally the rhythms slip a little. But to compensate for that there's a stirring energy to their singing; and part of the elegance of Fabre-Garrus performances has always been in his fluid, linear approach to polyphony, which works splendidly here. Moreover, with just six singers on the three lower lines, he always manages to produce a beautifully clear and balanced texture. This is a very successful and exciting performance of one of Josquin's most stunning masterpieces. His astonishingly varied treatment of the *Gaudeamus* melody ranges from straight imitation through unusually long-held tenor notes (that have a stunning effect on the work's harmonic rhythm), via bravura exercises in ostinato, to the heart-stopping modulations of the final *Agnus Dei*.

The plainchants are sung with an unusual lucidity and energy. The motets include the rarely heard *Recordare virgo Mater*, which gives a special opportunity for the children to sing in three parts; and they end with a superlatively eloquent and clear performance of one of Josquin's most famous five-voice motets, *Virgo salutiferi*.

Songs and Instrumental Music

Master of Musicians – Songs and instrumental music by Josquin des Prez, and his pupils and contemporaries
Includes **Josquin** Adieu mes amours[b]. Bergerotte savoysienne[c]. Comment peult avoir joye. De tous biens pleine – à 3; à 4. Dido – Fama malum à 4[abcd]; Dulces exuviae à 4. El grillo[abcd]. Faulte d'argent[ab]. Je me complains[bc]. Mille regretz[abcd]. Pauper sum ego[d]. Petite camusette[ab]. Pleine de dueil[bc]. Se congié prens[ab] – Recordans de mia segnora; à 6. Si j'avoys Marion. Si j'ay perdu mon amy – à 3; à 4. Le villain. Also includes works by **Agricola, Alonso, Anon, Févin, Gerle, Isaac, Japart, Orto, Le Roy** and **Spinacino**
[a]**Belinda Sykes** contr [b]**John Potter** ten [c]**Jennie Cassidy** mez [d]**Robert Evans** bar London Musica Antiqua (John Bryan rec/crumhn/viol Alison Crum rec/crumhn/viol/hp Jacob Heringman viol/lte/gtr Roy Marks crumhn/viol Rebecca Miles rec) / **Philip Thorby**
Signum SIGCD025 (68' · DDD · T/t)   ⒻⒹ▷

The secular music of Josquin has not always been very successful in recordings. Many of the pieces are very short – some can seem like exercises for something else, and others make little sense unless they're understood in the wider context of other settings based on the same material. The last problem is solved here by the inclusion of a lot of the related settings alongside those of Josquin. And the recording solves the first problem by unapologetically offering no fewer than 37 tracks, with the pieces grouped together so they flow cleanly from one to the next; it also resists some of the more outgoing pieces, so that the whole disc occupies a consistent sound world.

That sound world is mostly a gentle one, with the lines flowing quite fast in an easy playing style that can occasionally lose a few details but compensates with clarity of design. The musicians also cultivate a sound that favours vivacity and flair over constant attention to all the details of intonation; but that, too, is good, because everything is lively and full of variety. The instruments used range from viols and lutes to an ensemble of recorders and even one of crumhorns (played with an admirable restraint). And the singers offer all the variety of tone-colour one might expect from a group spearheaded by John Potter.

Many pieces here have never been recorded before; and the disc has the twin benefits of being remarkably accessible for easy listening as well as providing a marvellous basis for closer understanding. Most enjoyable.

André Jolivet   French 1905-1974

Profoundly impressed at an early age by the music of Debussy, Dukas and Ravel, Jolivet determined on a musical career. He studied with Paul Le Flem who introduced him to Edgard Varèse who agreed to take him on as a student. A later encounter with Messiane led to the foundation of 'La spirale', an avant-garde chamber music society. From 1945 to 1959, Jolivet was musical director of the Comédie Française writing 14 scores for plays performed there; he later taught compsition at the Paris Conservatoire.

Violin Concerto

Jolivet Violin Concerto **Chausson** Poème
Isabelle Faust vn **Deutsches Symphony
Orchestra, Berlin / Marko Letonja**
Harmonia Mundi HMC90 1925 (48' · DDD)   Ⓕ

A new issue of Jolivet's Violin Concerto (1972), the 12th and last of his *concertante* works and held by some to be his musical testament, is long overdue so this splendid account from Isabelle Faust is cause for real celebration.

The Concerto is not immediately easy listening, being a tough late example of Jolivet's primitivist idiom. While outwardly conforming to conventional classical design, internally each movement is a freewheeling, evolving structure. The opening *Appassionato* retains a few traces of sonata form and is volatile and lyrical by turns. Its ethereal coda is a fine example of the acuity of Jolivet's inner ear as well as Faust's feather-light touch, much in evidence throughout the complex, central *Largo*. Here the steel in Faust's playing is much in evidence in its faster, eruptive episodes. The finale is the most straightforward in manner, centred on the virtuoso cadenza.

It is fascinating to return to Chausson's intensely romantic *Poème* (1894) – with which the disc starts – after Jolivet's richly coloured, piled-up textures. Although stylistically worlds apart, both works share a heady, exotic expres-

sion. Faust is equally convincing in both, ably supported by the Deutsches Symphony Orchestra conducted by Marko Letonja and bright, close sound. The playing-time is not generous but the pairing is very effective as it stands and in performances like these self-recommending.

Niccolò Jommelli   Italian 1714-1774

Born and educated in Naples, Jommelli established a major reputation as an opera composer and an opera theorist. He lived and worked in Rome and Venice before, in 1753, taking the post of Kapellmeister to the Duke Karl-Eugen at Württemberg, near Stuttgart. It was here, in 1763, that he met the young Mozart who was passing through the city with his father. He wrote over 60 operas, many to libretti by Metastasio

Armida abbandonata

Armida abbandonata
Ewa Malas-Godlewska sop Armida **Claire Brua** mez
Rinaldo **Gilles Ragon** ten Tancredi **Véronique Gens**
sop Erminia **Laura Polverelli** mez Rambaldo **Patricia
Petibon** sop Ubaldo **Cécile Perrin** sop Dano
Les Talens Lyriques / Christophe Rousset
Ambroisie ③ AMB9983 (181' · DDD · T/t)   ⒻOO

The first performance of *Armida abbandonata* was attended by the 14-year-old Mozart, who wrote to his sister that it was 'beautiful, but too serious and old-fashioned for the theatre'. That tells us something about the taste of the Neapolitan audience, which didn't care for the richness and subtlety of the music. And the music is superb.

Jommelli was born in 1714 and, like Gluck, an exact contemporary, he moved away from the conventions of Metastasian *opera seria* to a more flexible style that included choruses and ballets in accordance with the French taste of his ducal employer at the Württemburg court. His accompanied recitatives are particularly fine. One example comes in Act 2: the recitative begins with a descending chromatic phrase in the second violins and includes a weeping figure that is incorporated into the following aria.

Ewa Malas-Godlewska, so touching there, rages impressively in 'Odo, furor, dispetto' ('Hatred, fury, spite'): its *staccato* scales anticipate Elettra's outburst in *Idomeneo*. That Mozart owed a debt to Jommelli is also suggested by a florid metaphor aria for Tancredi that looks ahead to Idomeneo's 'Fuor del mar'; and although Erminia is no servant, her second aria might well put the listener in mind of Despina in *Così fan tutte*. Gilles Ragon and Véronique Gens are but two in a matchless cast from the rest of which there is space to single out only the gloriously rich-toned Laura Polverelli. Christophe Rousset conducts his fine musicians in a gripping, well-paced performance. A wonderful recording.

Dmitry Kabalevsky
Russian/USSR 1904-1987

Kabalevsky had a liberal education, wrote poetry and painted and showed promise as a pianist. The family moved to Moscow in 1918, where he studied the piano with Selyanov and from 1925 at the Moscow Conservatory with Catoire and Myaskovsky, the latter a formative influence; in 1932 he returned to teach at the conservatory (full professor from 1939). He was also involved in organisational and union activities, and worked in the music publishing house. The period 1932-41 was prolific, with much dramatic music (including the first version of his opera Colas Breugnon) and the first three symphonies. In the war years he turned to topical works on heroic patriotism. After the party decree of 1948 he worked towards a more lyrical idiom, as seen in his concertos of the ensuing years; later he worked in operetta and topical cantatas. Kabalevsky occupied an important role in Soviet music, as writer, spokesman on cultural policy, teacher and administrator as well as composer.
GROVEmusic

Cello Concerto No 2

Kabalevsky Cello Concerto No 2 in G, Op 77
Khachaturian Cello Concerto **Rachmaninov** (trans Rose) Vocalise, Op 34 No 14
Mats Lidström vc **Gothenburg Symphony Orchestra / Vladimir Ashkenazy** pf
BIS CD719 (65' · DDD) Recorded live 1995   Ⓕ

This coupling offers performances of two works which, if not masterpieces, are still sufficiently rewarding to be in the regular concert repertory. Ashkenazy creates an evocative opening atmosphere for the first movement of the Kabalevsky, when after mysterious string pizzicatos the soloist steals in with a gentle, singing tone. The soliloquy continues, for the work's unusual structure, with its three unbroken sections linked by cadenzas, invites an improvisational approach well understood by Mats Lidström.

The Khachaturian Concerto opens with a flamboyantly coloured orchestral declamation before the cello sails off with vigorous animation. This is followed by a sinuous Armenian theme from the wind which the cello takes up ruminatively, with well-judged *espressivo*. Yet it's the energetic main theme that dominates and the soloist is carried along on its impetus, while ardently recalling the secondary material, finally leading to an exciting sequential coda. The finale offers the busy, rumbustious Khachaturian we know so well from the Violin Concerto. This composer's major works (with the exception of the Violin Concerto) can seem rather inflated, but here the combined concentration of Lidström and Ashkenazy minimises this impression. As an encore we're given a beautiful, restrained account of Rachmaninov's *Vocalise*. The recording is of high quality and well balanced, but a shade over-resonant, though the ear adjusts.

Piano Concertos

Piano Concertos – No 1; No 4, 'Prague'.
Symphony No 2
Kathryn Stott pf
BBC Philharmonic Orchestra / Neeme Järvi
Chandos CHAN10384 (68' · DDD)   ⒻⒹ

As the work of a 24-year-old seeking to make his mark, Kabalevsky's First Piano Concerto is unsurprisingly replete with references to the Russian concerto tradition. Yet just as one notes the seemingly blatant echoes of Rachmaninov's *Paganini* Rhapsody in the slow movement, one realises that the Rhapsody post-dates the Concerto by six years: evidently Rachmaninov was doing the echoing. Moreover, along with the stylistic affinities comes a less predictable tone of wistful introspection and an urge for symphonic consistency, qualities readily attributable to the influence of Kabalevsky's teacher, Myaskovsky. All this is superbly delineated by Kathryn Stott, completing her outstanding survey of the four Kabalevsky piano concertos with these superbly considered accounts.

Kabalevsky's Second Symphony is again clearly indebted to Myaskovsky. Its relatively conventional layout is capped by a *Scherzo* that mutates rather neatly into a finale and puts the earnestness of the first two movements firmly behind it. Järvi knocks several minutes off the normal timing of the second and third movements by virtue of a robust, no-nonsense approach.

Stott and Järvi steer the Fourth Concerto home in just under 12 minutes, mainly by taking a less drawn-out approach to the slow movement than in the composer's own recording. In most respects they surpass that unsubtle if disciplined version. Beautifully recorded and executed, the new Chandos disc is self-recommending for collectors of Soviet music and/or 20th-century piano concertos.

Mauricio Kagel
German b1931

Composer, film maker and playwright of Argentine birth, Kagel is increasingly regarded as among the most important of late 20th-century European composers, his elaborate imagination, bizarre humour and ability to play with almost any idea or system has brought powerful and unexpected drama to the stage and concert hall. GROVEmusic

'The Mauricio Kagel Edition'
Pandorasbox, bandoneonpiece.
Tango Alemán. Bestiarium: Music for Bird Calls. (Hörspiel) Ein Aufnahmezustand
Mauricio Kagel band/voc **Alejandro Barletta** band **Jorge Risi** vn **Carlos Roqué Alsina** pf **Beth Griffith, Mesías Maiguashca** whistles **Peter Brötzmann** reeds/voc **Heinz-Georg Thor** bass **Michael Vetter** rec/voc **Alfred Feussner** voc **Deborah Kagel** voc

William Pearson voc **Christoph Caskel** perc/voc
Film: 'Ludwig van'
Winter & Winter ③ (2 CDs + 1 DVD 📀) 910 128-2
(3hr 15' · ADD)   Ⓕⓞ

Beethoven shows up at Bonn Station in 1970 to survey how the culture industry is marking his bicentenary. That delicious conceit is the basis for *Ludwig van*, Mauricio Kagel's miraculous film now available for the first time on DVD. Beethoven himself holds the wobbly camera during the first section of the film, and we only ever get to see his buckled shoes as he minces through the streets.

There are road works outside the Beethoven-haus as Our Hero visits his erstwhile lodgings and has to hotfoot it over barriers to reach his front door, where he's met by a jobsworth doorman who insists he buy a ticket. Kagel is the composer who made Bach the narrator of his own story in the *St Bach Passion* and he's relishing this histori-cal gibberish. Incongruous historical overlays provoke high comedy while creating weird Philip K Dickian reality-busting narratives. But most importantly this technique licenses Kagel to unravel the trajectory of evolving traditions; and the slapstick over, he gets dark.

Inside the house, Beethoven is confronted by rotting busts of his own form everywhere while sheet music tumbles out of a cavernous cupboard – in his bicentenary year is his music being cele-brated or exploited? Ludwig van's most famous scene is next as the camera zooms into Beethoven's music room where every surface is pasted with fragments of his scores. Until now Kagel's music has consisted of jokey arrange-ments of LvB lollipops for a wheezing wind ensemble, but now musicians follow the direction of the camera as it pans around these haphazardly arranged scores. Musical syntax breaks down and familiar phrases are mulched into a chaotic soundscape that curiously re-energises them as empiric sources of sound.

Another narrative jump and Kagel is featured in an earnest television show discussing Beethoven; one guest puts the boot into Karajan (a particular hate figure for the post-Darmstadt avant-garde) for conducting the orchestra rather than the score. Kagel looks on with gleeful mis-chief beaming from both eyes.

Alongside the DVD are two CDs of remas-tered near-contemporaneous material – the first documents Kagel's own performances of three intriguing works climaxing in *Bestiarium: Music for Bird Calls*, while the second is his seminal, hyperactive radio piece *(Hörspiel) Ein Aufnahm-ezustand*. Of course, it's a paradox worthy of Kagel himself that this set is released to celebrate his own 75th birthday – geddit?

Imre Kálmán   Hungarian 1882-1953

Kálmán studied with Koessler at the Budapest Acad-emy. The success of his first operetta, The Gay Hus-
sars (1908), led him to settle in Vienna, where he produced more such works in Viennese-Hungarian style (Die Csárdásfürstin, 1915; Gräfin Mariza, 1924). In 1939 he moved to Paris, and from there in 1940 to the USA.   GROVEmusic*

Die Csárdásfürstin

The Gypsy Princess **Yvonne Kenny** sop Sylva Varescu **Michael Roider** ten Edwin Ronald **Mojca Erdmann** sop Countess Stasi **Marko Kathol** ten Count Boni **Karl-Michael Ebner** ten Feri von Kerekes, Notary **Hellmuth Klumpp** spkr Rohnsdorff **Heinz Holecek** bar Prince **Yvonne Kálmán** spkr Princess
Plus orchestral excerpts from Der Zigeunerprimás, Die Faschingsfee, Das Hollandweibchen and Der Teufelsreiter
Slovak Philharmonic Chorus; Slovak Radio Symphony Orchestra / Richard Bonynge
Naxos ② 8 660105/6 ⑨ 6 110075-76
(114' · DDD · S/N)   Ⓢⓞⓞ

The English title of Kálmán's most celebrated operetta is a misnomer. The heroine is a princess not of gypsies but (as the German title, *Die Csárdásfürstin*, indicates) of the *csárdás*; she's a Budapest cabaret-singer in love with a young aristocrat. Its score shows Kálmán at his most flu-ent, with a succession of gloriously tuneful hit numbers that mix spicy Hungarian rhythms with the more graceful strains of the Viennese waltz. Individual numbers have often been committed to disc, but complete recordings have been much less frequent. Yet to appreciate the overall struc-ture of Kálmán's operetta scores you really need to hear his elaborately constructed act finales, in which musical reprises are interspersed with pas-sages of dialogue and melodrama.

Apart from sensibly reducing the opening orchestral flourishes from three to one, Bonynge typically gives us total fidelity to what Kálmán actually wrote. He brings out to the full Kálmán's highly charged rhythms, every detail of the exotic orchestration, and the contrasts of mood between the fiery big numbers and the moments of melancholy and sadness in the Acts 1 and 2 finales. Among a wholly admirable cast, Yvonne Kenny provides the vocal strength, fire and beauty required by the title role. A wonder-ful bargain.

Jouni Kaipainen   Finnish b1956

An enthusiastic writer on music as well as composer, Kaipainen determined on a career in music after an encounter, aged 13, with Beethoven's Eroica. He studied at the Sibelius Academy with Sallinen and Heininen, developing an eclectic approach to composi-tion. Despite harmony anchored in free dodecaphony, melody is among the basic elements of Kaipainen's music. His style has continually moved towards greater melodiousness and accessibility.
GROVEmusic

Orchestral works

Horn Concerto[a]. Cello Concerto No 1[b]
[a]**Esa Tapani** hn [b]**Marko Ylönen** vc
Finnish Radio Symphony Orchestra / Hannu Lintu
Ondine ODE1062-2 (65' · DDD)   Ⓕ

Jouni Kaipainen first came to notice in the early
1990s with the premieres of his First Symphony,
two-piano concerto *Ladders to Fire* and the
clarinet concerto *Carpe diem!*. His musical style,
while recognisably built on late-20th-century
aesthetics, is advanced but not aggressive, post-
modern tonal with much that is jovial and pleasingly lyrical. This new disc makes a good introduction to his sound world.

The Horn Concerto (2000-01) is cast in the
usual three movements, a cadenza climaxing the
opening *Allegro maestoso*, in which there is a delicious tension between Kaipainen's 21st-century
harmonic language and the decidedly 19th-cen-
tury expressive manner of the solo part. The
serene *Larghetto* was still being written when its
course, like that of Sallinen's Eighth Symphony,
was irrevocably changed by the events of 9/11.
Kaipainen's jocular side comes to the fore in the
ebullient, virtuosic final *Vivace*.

In the First Cello Concerto (2002) the orchestral colours are more autumnal, like Dvořák or
Elgar, but the vigour of the outer movements is
more Hindemithian. The 17-minute opening
movement is really a conflation of two spans, a
long *Andante febbrile* introduction which is
recalled at the close of the succeeding *Allegro con
brio*. As if to balance this, the central *Largo* connects via a cadenza to the brilliant final *Allegretto*.

Esa Tapani and Marko Ylönen are exemplary
soloists, playing with plenty of verve. Hannu
Lintu and the Finnish Radio Symphony Orchestra accompany expertly and everyone sounds as
if they enjoyed themselves.

Symphony No 3. Bassoon Concerto
Otto Virtanen bn
Tampere Philharmonic Orchestra / Hannu Lintu
Ondine ODE1089-2 (74' · DDD)   Ⓕ Ⓞ ➤

Jouni Kaipainen's first two symphonies were in
one and two movements respectively but Kaipainen suggests no conclusions should be drawn
from the fact that the Third (2004) is in three.
The latest symphony is half as long again as No
2 and twice as epic, roaring away from the very
first bar. While there are moments of reflection
and calm, once it has you in its grip it does not
let go. Vividly scored with many solos and
ensembles interspersed between passages of
invigorating orchestral power, there is a clear
thread from start to end. Devotees of Peter
Mennin's or Karl Amadeus Hartmann's music
will find much to enjoy here.

The symphony boasts several prominent bassoon solos in its first half and his concerto for the
instrument (2005), dedicated to Finland's bassoonists, followed almost immediately. Deli-

ciously unconventional in format and treatment,
it is cast in four movements. The delightful
Scherzo is based on music for a children's play
(where a piccolo dances with a bassoon); placed
between two serious but multi-layered spans, it
is as surreal a discontinuity as anything in early
Shostakovich. A rip-roaring *presto* finale completes a disarmingly subtle creation.

The Tampere Philharmonic's playing is electrifying, superbly marshalled by Hannu Lintu,
with Otto Virtanen the exemplary soloist.
Sound of demonstration quality. Splendid.

Giya Kancheli   Georgian 1935

*Kancheli studied at the Tbilisi Conservatory (1958-
63), where he has taught since 1972. He is recognised
as one of the most radical thinkers in Georgian music.
His works, using folk music, include six symphonies
(1967-81), jazz pieces and musicals.*

GROVEmusic

Liturgy for Viola and Orchestra

Liturgy for Viola and Orchestra, 'Mourned by the
Wind'. Bright Sorrow
Ian Ford, Oliver Hayes trebs **France Springuel** vc
**Cantate Domino Chorus; I Fiamminghi /
Rudolf Werthen**
Telarc CD80455 (72' · DDD)   Ⓕ Ⓞ

Givi Ordzhonikidze, the editor of a well-known
book on Shostakovich, was one of Kancheli's
closest friends and staunchest supporters, and it
was the sense of loss after his death in 1984 that
prompted the composition of the heart-rendingly beautiful *Liturgy* (subtitled *Mourned by the
Wind*). The other inspiration was Yuri Bashmet,
for this four-movement lament was originally a
Viola Concerto. It goes superbly on the cello
too, thanks to France Springuel's passionate
advocacy, and in this form it inevitably invites
comparisons with Tavener's *The Protecting Veil*.

A common feature of these two pieces is that
they can seem almost unbearably moving if they
catch you in the right mood and yet almost
unbearably protracted if they don't. Yet for all the
obvious gestures of lamentation and assuaging,
Liturgy isn't a tear-jerking piece. In fact the texture is for the most part quite transparent, and
Kancheli constantly steers away from potentially
manipulative clichés on to stonier paths.

The Flemish orchestra gives a wonderfully
controlled performance and Telarc's recording
quality is superb. *Bright Sorrow* again draws from
the bottomless well of lamentation which is the
ex-USSR composer's special curse and privilege. It bears the dedication, 'To children, the
victims of war', hence the choice of two boy
soloists, symbolising the innocent victims of the
last world war addressing themselves to the
present-day generation. The soloists sing only
·slow, fragmented lines, conveying the fragility

of innocence. The second half of the work seems to be gaining strength and optimism, but these are soon obliterated, leaving behind only a heart-broken crippled waltz.

Highly recommended, whether or not you already have the Kancheli 'bug'.

Styx

Kancheli Styx[a] **Tavener** The Myrrh-Bearer[b]
[ab]**Maxim Rysanov** va [b]**Rihards Zalupe** perc
[a]'Kamer...' Choir; [b]Latvia State Choir;
[a]Liepaja Symphony Orchestra / Maris Sirmais
Onyx Classics ONYX4023 (78' · DDD) Ⓕ🅞➔

Maxim Rysanov's viola has an inward, lamenting quality. And it feels as though the chorus and orchestra (from Latvia's third city) are living and breathing every note. Crucially, the acoustic of Riga's Dome Cathedral has a rich resonance, wonderfully captured. The sound stage is as wide and deep as the music demands. Expressive extremes register as more abrupt, more startling and more challenging – harder-edged in their ecstasy. The music first transfixes, then scalds, and when consolation intervenes it feels multi-faceted and somehow palpably wise. The texts of *Styx* consist of a succession of names and words, all of profound and intimate significance to the composer. This performance makes one really feel that significance.

The extraordinary qualities of Latvian choral singing – fullness of tone, *legato* and intense stillness – have been often extolled. In *The Myrrh-Bearer* there is the added advantage of the kind of *basso profundo* richness that one would imagine Tavener can only rarely have found in the UK. Whether his piece is perhaps a little too reliant on those subterranean tones, and whether the pairing with Kancheli reveals a slight thinness of invention, are suspicions that may either firm or fade with further acquaintance. In the meantime, all that seems important is to surrender to the urgency and fervour of another extraordinary performance.

In short, here is a disc to blow the mind of anyone already in tune with these composers, and possibly one that may even lead a few sceptics towards a Damascene conversion.

...à la Duduki

...à la Duduki. Trauerfarbenes Land
Vienna Radio Symphony Orchestra / Dennis Russell Davies
ECM New Series 457 850-2 (57' · DDD) Ⓕ🅞➔

...*à la Duduki* (a 'duduki' is a Georgian folk-reed instrument) should prove the ideal introduction to Kancheli's current style. And while a momentary encounter might suggest familiar territories revisited (vast terrains sparsely but dramatically populated), the musical material is more immediately striking, the scoring more texturally variegated, and the time sequences – even the rhetori-

cal uses of silence – quite different from those in Kancheli's other recent work. Furthermore, echoes of modern jazz frequently fall within earshot. *Trauerfarbenes Land* ('Country the Colour of Mourning') employs a large orchestra and is different again, being nearly twice as long as ...*à la Duduki* and darker in tone.

The opening has solo piano and *fortissimo* trombones hammer what sounds like a recollection of Carl Ruggles before six significant quavers (which turn up again later, in different hues and keys) mark a dramatic dynamic contrast. Time and again Kancheli's penchant for 'cliff-hanger' climaxes bring us to the edge of a towering aural precipice. This is the music of personal displacement: desolate, spacious, occasionally cryptic, and with sudden pangs of sweetened nostalgia that flutter across the canvas like torn diary jottings tossed by the wind. Dennis Russell Davies and producer Manfred Eicher conjure between them a precision-tooled sound picture where every grade of nuance is meticulously reported. Performance standards are unusually high throughout, so much so that it's hard to imagine either work being better played. An exceptional release of some extraordinarily powerful music.

Lament

Lament (Music of mourning in memory of Luigi Nono)
Maacha Deubner sop **Gidon Kremer** vn
Tbilisi Symphony Orchestra / Jansug Kakhidze
ECM New Series 465 138-2 (42' · DDD · T/t) Ⓕ

Music of lamentation has long been Kancheli's preoccupation, and this *Lament*, inscribed to the memory of Luigi Nono, has all the familiar Kanchelian moods: damaged soulfulness, peremptory outbursts and transfigured sadness, invoked aphoristically yet stretched to a hypnotic unbroken 42-minute span. Initial dots of sound on the solo violin grow into painfully sweet bursts of melody, suggesting a context only the composer himself knows and which the listener has to grope towards. Meanwhile a non-vibrato singer intones prayerful fragments. Kremer's violin becomes an eloquent voice; Maacha Deubner's soprano becomes a celestial instrument. Just as you sense the need for new ideas, the orchestra's sculpted orchestral chords gain a pulverising force, and before long all hell breaks loose. The slight residual rawness of the Tbilisi brass is a treasurable authentic feature here, and the entire score is conducted faithfully by the man who knows Kancheli's music better than any musician alive. Eventually the text of Hans Sahl's poem, *Strophen*, reveals the under-lying substance. The recording is first-rate.

Nikolai Kapustin   Russian b1937

Kapustin, born in the Ukraine, graduated from the Moscow Conservatoire in 1961 and for some years made a living as a jazz pianist and arranger. His music is nearly all instrumental or orchestral, and is characterised by its use of jazz and rock idioms.

Piano Sonata No 6

Suite in the Old Style, Op 28. Eight Concert Etudes, Op 40. Variations, Op 41. Bagatelle, Op 59 No 9. Piano Sonata No 6, Op 62. Five Etudes in Different Intervals, Op 68. Sonatina, Op 100
Marc-André Hamelin pf
Hyperion CDA67433 (78' · DDD)   ⓕ **O**

'Crossover' is an old rather than recent tradition, whether the jazz elements are peripheral as in Ravel or central as in Kapustin. Jed Distler, writing for Hamelin's disc in a style as witty and engaging as the music itself, speaks of a Chick Corea-based language that lifts a romantic virtuoso tradition into a beguiling quasi-improvisational style and holds it up to a fun-house mirror. Such high-pitched claims arguably fail to account for too many family likenesses (be they variations, studies or sonatas) or a style that too often suggests composition as a facile rather than arduous process (like Saint-Saëns, Kapustin 'produces music as an apple-tree produces apples'). Nonetheless, there are many scintillating surprises. The Variations' gawky theme blossoms into the sort of elaboration that would have made Bill Evans envious, while the second of the Op 40 Etudes ends with a passing memory of Liszt's *Au bord d'une source*, reminding you of Kapustin's work as a virtuoso pianist with Alexander Goldenweiser. No 6, *Pastoral*, a dream encore, sends a tiny cell-like motif spinning through a variety of guises. The Bagatelle's perky tune would not be out of place 'in a Brazilian Chorino' (Distler) and everything on this remarkable disc is played with a nonchalant aplomb and magical dexterity hard to imagine from any other pianist. Hamelin is in his element, and he's been immaculately recorded.

Mieczysław Karłowicz

Polish 1876-1909

Trained as a violinist, he was active in the Warsaw Music Society and a strong supporter of the 'Young Poland' artistic movement, advocating the newest techniques in Polish orchestral music. Among his works are symphonic poems using thematic transformation and reflecting pantheism, sorrow and Wagnerian ideas of love and death, including Eternal Songs (1908) and Stanisław i Anna Oswiecimowie (1912). GROVEmusic

Orchestral works

Eternal Songs, Op 10. Lithuanian Rhapsody, Op 11. Stanisław and Anna of Oświecim, Op 12
BBC Philharmonic Orchestra / Yan Pascal Tortelier

Chandos CHAN9986 (67' · DDD)   ⓕ **OOO**▸

 What a fine composer Mieczysław Karłowicz might have become, had he not died at the age of 32 in an avalanche in the Tatra mountains. He had already produced a clutch of symphonic poems in a post-Wagnerian style, strongly pantheistic in outlook and, in the case of *Stanisław and Anna of Oświecim*, with a dash of illicit love thrown in. These luxuriant works set him broadly beside such near-contemporaries as Rachmaninov, Zemlinsky or Suk, and there are even signs in the 'Song of Eternal Being' (third and last of the *Eternal Songs*) of an individuality that might one day have become as powerful as Janáček's. This is, for the most part, sultrily ecstatic music, that hangs fragrantly or ominously in the air and seems to be constantly about to break through to some visionary realm. Even the relatively jaunty *Lithuanian Rhapsody* eventually turns wistful in a rather moving way.

If you've a taste for lush late-Romanticism but haven't yet encountered Karłowicz, you've a treat in store, not least because these are fine performances. His music has never been more than fleetingly represented in the catalogue. Back in 1990 there was a two-disc Chant du Monde compilation of the symphonic poems from the Silesian Philharmonic; but their courageous efforts are easily outclassed by the BBC Philharmonic and Yan Pascal Tortelier, as is the recording by Chandos's customary rich sound-stage.

Symphony in E minor, 'Rebirth', Op 7. Serenade in C, Op 2. Bianca da Molena, Op 6
BBC Philharmonic Orchestra / Gianandrea Noseda
Chandos CHAN10171 (73' · DDD)   ⓕ **O**▸

This second BBC Philharmonic Karłowicz disc complements the first with three earlier works. Composed in the first two years of the 20th century, Karłowicz's 40-minute *Rebirth* Symphony is very much of its time – not just in its ambitious programmatic span from existential despair to world-saving apotheosis, but in its opulent post-Tchaikovskian idiom. Though he clearly overreached himself, this is a need-to-know piece for anyone interested in the aspirational *Zeitgeist* prevalent before the First World War. Most immediately appealing, perhaps, is the slow movement, which features a tender song-like theme that British listeners may connect with the hymn 'My song is love unknown'.

The symphonic prologue *Bianca da Molena* is extracted from music for a now forgotten Polish play; not surprisingly it contains many echoes of Wagner. The Serenade for String Orchestra is an apprentice piece with a certain charm, notably in the vaguely *Parsifal*ian slow movement, which helps to compensate for the disappointment of the cursory finale.

The BBC Philharmonic's playing and Chandos's recording uphold their customary high standards.

Episode at a Masquerade. Returning Waves.
The Sorrowful Tale
BBC Philharmonic Orchestra / Gianandrea Noseda
Chandos CHAN10298 (60' · DDD) ⓕ Ⓓ➤

With this third disc the BBC Philharmonic complete a fine survey of Karłowicz's orchestral music. Now we can finally enjoy this music in all its rich, velvet-draped luxury.

This instalment is, admittedly, something of a mopping-up exercise, the best of Karłowicz's output being found on the first of the BBC Philharmonic's discs (see above). The Nietzschean pessimism of *Returning Waves* and *A Sorrowful Tale* relates strongly to the Richard Strauss of *Tod und Verklärung* pretensions, albeit without the transfiguration. Here the music sounds as though it has overdosed on Wagner and turned to César Franck for the antidote, compounding rather than solving its problems in finding an individual voice.

In *Episode at a Masquerade* – completed by Grzegorz Fitelberg following the composer's tragically early death in a skiing accident – there are attractive, though passing and presumably coincidental, affinities with the Elgar of *Cockaigne*. Here, too, the overall atmosphere is far removed from the frivolity that the title (and indeed the opening pages of the score) might suggest.

The BBC Philharmonic's dynamic principal conductor, Gianandrea Noseda, took the reins from Yan Pascal Tortelier after their first Karłowicz disc. He has a sure instinct for the music's indulgent textures and melodramatic effusiveness, and orchestral playing and recording are both of the highest class. Self-recommending, then, to explorers of late-Romantic byways.

Reinhard Keiser   German 1674-1739

Keiser wrote operas for Brunswick from c1693 and in 1694 became court chamber composer. From 1696-7 he was Kapellmeister at Hamburg, and from 1700-1701 also Kapellmeister to the Schwerin court. As joint director of the Hamburg Theater-am-Gänsemarkt, 1702-7, he presented 17 of his own operas. Der Carneval von Venedig (1707), which included local dialect, was especially successful. He remained active in Hamburg until 1718. After a period as a guest Kapellmeister at Stuttgart he served intermittently at Copenhagen. He was back in Hamburg by 1723 and in 1728 became Kantor of the cathedral. The Singspiel Der hochmüthige, gestürzte und wieder erhabene Croesus (1730), a version of a 1710 opera, was among his last stage works.

Keiser was the central and most original figure in German Baroque opera, and wrote over 80 stage works. Most have serious German texts, which cover a wide range of subjects and often include allegorical or comic elements. They are notable for their dramatic flavour and skilful characterisation. Italian

and French musical elements appear (including Italian arias from 1703), with dramatic recitatives and ariosos, varied aria forms and inventive instrumentation. His several Passions, oratorios and cantatas show similar features. Among his other works are sacred music and trio sonatas. Handel drew heavily on his works in his own. GROVEmusic

---

Croesus

Croesus
Roman Trekel *bar* Croesus **Werner Güra** *ten* Atis **Salomé Haller** *sop* Clerida **Brigitte Eisenfeld** *sop* Trigesta **Johannes Mannov** *bass* Cyrus **Markus Schäfer** *ten* Eliates **Dorothea Röschmann** *sop* Elmira **Graham Pushee** *counterten* Halimacus **Johanna Stojković** *sop* Nerillus **Klaus Häger** *bass* Orsanes **Kwangchul Youn** *bass* Solon **Kurt Azesberger** *ten* Elcius **Hanover Boys' Choir; Berlin RIAS Chamber Choir; Akademie für Alte Musik Berlin / René Jacobs**
Harmonia Mundi ③ HMC90 1714/6 (188' · DDD)
ⓕ ○○○

Reinhard Keiser was principal opera composer at Hamburg's celebrated Theatre on the Goosemarket from 1697 to 1704 and from 1707 to 1718, returning intermittently, under Telemann's direction, between 1722 and 1735 when he retired after the death of his wife. During the first of these periods, a young man called Georg Friedrich Händel joined his theatre's orchestra and during his temporary absence composed three operas for the Goosemarket opera house, including *Almira* (1705) to a libretto set by Keiser.

Keiser's opera, given the catchy title *Die Unbeständigkeit weltlicher Ehre und Reichthums der hochmüthige/gestürzte/und wieder erhabene Croesus* ('The inconstancy of earthly glory and riches of the proud, deposed and rehabilitated Croesus') at its first performance in 1711, is called by the *New Grove* one of 'a handful of masterpieces' and René Jacobs concurs in his evangelising essay, 'Why Produce *Croesus* today?' printed in Harmonia Mundi's lavish booklet. The answer to Jacobs's question lies in the quality of the music, which will come as a delightful surprise to Baroque lovers.

The music itself is sheer bliss from first to last, and has a succession of variously characterised arias – the most exquisite are alloted to the heroine Elmira, ravishingly sung by Dorothea Röschmann, the most moving to the deposed Croesus (Roman Trekel) in his prison or facing his death in the flames of a sacrificial fire. The beauties of the work are manifold – the beginning of Act 2 is a pastoral scene in which peasants sing folksongs, and there's a delicious chorus for the peasant children extolling the joys of kissing lips as sweet as nuts. Suffice it so say that anyone who has enjoyed Handel's operas will be delighted by Keiser's.

The solo singing is uniformly first class, with eloquent performances from Trekel as Croesus, and from Werner Güra as his dumb son

Atis, whose speech is restored by the shock of an assassination attempt on his father. Klaus Häger as Elmira's villainous, unwanted admirer is first-class, too. There are also vivid contributions from Graham Pushee, Salomé Haller and the performers of the two comic servants, Brigitte Eisenfeld and Kurt Azesberger. This is another outstanding Jacobs resurrection and a great Baroque operatic discovery too.

Albert Ketèlbey   British 1875-1959

Ketèlbey appeared as a solo pianist and conducted internationally. He was a popular composer of light orchestral pieces (In a Monastery Garden, 1915; In a Persian Market, 1920). GROVEmusic

In a Persian Market

In a Persian Marketª. In a Monastery Gardenª The Adventurers. Chal Romano Suite romantique. Caprice pianistique. The Clock and the Dresden Figures. Cockney Suite – No 3, At the Palais de Danse; No 5, Bank Holiday. In the Moonlight. Wedgwood Blue. Bells across the Meadows. Phantom melody.
ªSlovak Philharmonic Male Chorus; Bratislava Radio Symphony Orchestra / Adrian Leaper
Marco Polo 8 223442 (74' · DDD)   Ⓕ❍

The obvious Ketèlbey favourites (*In a Monastery Garden, In a Persian Market, Bells across the Meadows*) are played with a grace and sensitivity that never invites unfavourable comparison with earlier recordings of the same pieces. If others in the same somewhat maudlin vein (*In the Mystic Land of Egypt, In a Chinese Temple Garden, Sanctuary of the Heart*) are missing, it's to give us the opportunity to hear some of his unjustly overshadowed compositions. And what delights there are! Overexposure to Ketèlbey's more stereotyped, highly perfumed compositions has disguised what varied and inventive music he composed. Once you acquaint yourself with the charms of *The Clock and the Dresden Figures, In the Moonlight* and the invigorating open-air spirit of *Chal Romano*, you'll want to hear them again and again.

Aram Khachaturian
Russian/USSR 1903-1978

Khachaturian, a bookbinder's son, at first studied medicine; he received his musical education comparatively late, studying the cello and composition under Myaskovsky at the Moscow Conservatory (1929-37). He came to wider notice in 1936 with his Piano Concerto and his Violin Concerto (1940), and was active from 1937 in the Union of Soviet Composers. Most of his best-known works, including the ballet Gayaney, date from the 1940s. In common with

other Soviet composers, he was subject to official criticism in 1948; but his colourful, nationally tinged idiom was far removed from modernistic excess. He concentrated on film music in the ensuing years, and took up conducting and teaching.

His later works include 'concert rhapsodies' which re-interpret concerto form. His career represents the Soviet model of the linking of regional folklorism with the central Russian tradition; his Armenian heritage is clear in his melodies and his vitality, but in disciplined form. His greatest strengths lie in colourful orchestration and effective pictorialism.
GROVEmusic

Piano Concerto

Piano Concerto. Dance Suite. Five Pieces for Wind Band – Waltz; Polka
Dora Serviarian-Kuhn pf **Armenian Philharmonic Orchestra / Loris Tjeknavorian**
ASV Platinum PLT8510 (59' · DDD)   Ⓜ❍

In the Piano Concerto Dora Serviarian-Kuhn and her Armenian compatriot, Loris Tjeknavorian, are in every way first-class: both identify naturally with the sinuous oriental flavour of the melodic lines and understand that the outer movements need above all to convey thrusting vitality; here there's plenty of drive and rhythmic lift. But what primarily makes this performance memorable is Serviarian-Kuhn's sense of fantasy, so that her various cadential passages, for all their brilliance, are charismatically quixotic rather than merely bravura displays.

The other works on the disc are small beer. The 'Waltz' for wind band has an engaging carousel flavour; the somewhat vulgar 'Polka' which follows roisterously suggests the circus. The *Dance Suite* goes through the usual Khachaturian routines with which he likes to clothe his agreeable but at times rather insubstantial Armenian folk ideas. Easily the most memorable movement is the first and much the longer of the two Uzbek dances, which opens gently and touchingly.

The performances here are excellent and vividly recorded.

Flute Concerto

Khachaturian Flute Concerto (transcribed from the Violin Concerto by J-P Rampal)ª
Ibert Flute Concertoª. Pièce
Emmanuel Pahud fl
ªTonhalle Orchestra, Zurich / David Zinman
EMI 557563-2 (64' · DDD)   Ⓕ🅑➤

Most flute concertos are lightweight, so it isn't surprising that flautists are keen to expand the repertory, adapting more ambitious works. That's how, on the suggestion of the composer himself, Jean-Pierre Rampal in 1968 came to prepare a brilliant transcription of Khachaturian's Violin Concerto. In the concert-hall a soft-grained flute can't cut through orchestral textures in the way a violin can, but on disc careful balancing has produced a successful result.

The flute naturally lacks the required incisiveness for the first subject, but there are obvious gains in the lyrical second subject: Emmanuel Pahud's gentle tone and fine shading bring out echoes of Dvořák in *New World* vein, where the violin had more of a gypsy flavour. Rampal and Pahud effectively replace the cadenza's double-stops with little arpeggiated flourishes, and surprisingly little seems changed. Better still is the slow movement, where Pahud's exquisitely hushed playing finds a mystery and tenderness in the hypnotic, Satie-like melody. In place of the finale's brilliant extroversion on the violin, Pahud's flute offers a cheeky lightness.

Ibert's unaccompanied *Pièce* makes an interlude between the concertos: a work which owes its easily improvisatory flow to Debussy's *Syrinx*. The Flute Concerto was written for Marcel Moyse in 1934; the finale's mix of 6/8 and 3/4 metres brings a sharp, jazzy flavour. What sets Pahud's performance apart is the depth of feeling he conveys in the slow movement: poignantly mysterious, with breathtaking *pianissimo*s matched by the strings of the Tonhalle Orchestra under David Zinman. The long, slow middle section in the finale, too, has a slinky quality, as in a *valse grise*. The recording is full and clear.

Violin Concerto in D minor

Khachaturian Violin Concerto
Sibelius Violin Concerto
Sergey Khachatryan *vn* **Sinfonia Varsovia /**
Emmanuel Krivine
Naïve V4959 (70' · DDD)   Ⓕ**O**

Sergey Khachatryan is among the most compelling players of his generation. Being the youngest-ever winner of the Sibelius Competition (2000) he was bound to record the Sibelius Concerto. Interestingly, his conductor, Emmanuel Krivine, had already recorded the work with a star player of a slightly older generation, Vadim Repin. Common to both is a mellow, fairly soft-core approach to the orchestral score, the new Sinfonia Varsovia recording, probably using a smaller band, warmer overall and with superior sound quality. Khachatryan's approach is smoother and more flexible, especially in the first movement's first cadenza, which he accelerates by stages, and the great leap that launches the second cadenza, which he edges into on a finely calculated *crescendo*. He moves around the score with comparative ease, always intense though with a mode of attack that stops short of roughness. His sound in the lower registers is rich and fulsome, yet even at *piano* or thereabouts, he still manages to sustain a full-bodied tone.

Similar qualities inform the Khachaturian Concerto with a crisp, lightly articulated opening and seductive handling of the first movement's second set. In the finale Khachatryan knows how to coax a workable ebb and flow, ease his tone, lighten tension to facilitate a change in

musical current. Again, Krivine and his team are sympathetic collaborators for a highly commendable performance.

Khachaturian Violin Concerto
Glazunov Violin Concerto
Prokofiev Violin Concerto No 1
Julia Fischer *vn* **Russian National Orchestra /**
Yakov Kreizberg
Pentatone ⏾ PTC5186 059 (80' · DDD/DSD) Ⓕ**OO**

As Julia Fischer explains in the booklet-notes to this, her first CD, she has an abiding love of the Khachaturian Concerto, a work she found impossible to sell to concert-promoters. The freshness of her way with the Khachaturian is immediately striking in the chattering figuration of the opening, and she brings a rare tenderness to the lyrical second subject. The orchestral sound is impressive, too. Though Itzhak Perlman and Lydia Mordkovitch produce a beefier sound, the refinement of Fischer's performance makes it equally compelling. This concerto has claims to be the composer's finest work, claims which the yearning tenderness of the slow movement support. The clarity of Fischer's performance in the finale brings lightness and sparkle.

In the Glazunov, too, it's the clarity and subtlety of Fischer's playing that marks out her reading. She finds the tenderness of the slow middle section of this one-movement work, and gives an easy swing to the bouncy rhythms of the final section. In the Prokofiev she takes a meditative view of the wistful melodies, the element, she says, that most attracts her, even if she does not quite reach the depths of Kyung-Wha Chung's version.

A unique coupling, superbly recorded, that could hardly be more recommendable.

Gayaneh – Suite No 2

Khachaturian The Widow of Valencia – Suite.
Gayaneh – Suite No 2 **Tjeknavorian** Danses
fantastiques
Armenian Philharmonic Orchestra /
Loris Tjeknavorian
ASV CDDCA884 (65' · DDD)   Ⓕ**O**

The Widow of Valencia is an early work (1940), yet already reveals the composer's fund of good tunes. He admitted its lack of authentic Spanishness, and though the 'Introduction' opens with flashing southern Mediterranean gusto, it soon makes way for a sultry Armenian melody of best local vintage. But why worry? Altogether this is a most winning suite, without a dull bar, piquantly scored and brilliantly presented by an orchestra that's completely at home and clearly enjoying themselves. They also give us another suite, comprising six indelible numbers – for the most part little known – from Khachaturian's masterpiece, *Gayaneh*. Tjeknavorian's own *Danses fantastiques* frequently burst with energy and the gentler dances have that Armenian flavour so familiar in *Gayaneh*. Brilliant playing in glittering yet spacious sound.

Spartacus

Khachaturian Spartacus: Ballet Suite No 1 – Variations of Aegina and Bacchanalia; Scene and Dance with Crotalums; Dance of the Gaditanian Maidens and Victory of Spa Spartacus: Ballet Suite No 2 – Adagio of Spartacus and Phrygia Gayaneh – Sabre Dance; Dance of the Rose Maidens; Dance of the Kurds; Lullaby; Lezghinka. Masquerade – Waltz; Nocturne; Mazurka; Romance; Galop. **Ippolitov-Ivanov** Caucasian Sketches, Suite 1, Op 10
Armenian Philharmonic Orchestra /
Loris Tjeknavorian
ASV CDDCA773 (76' · DDD)   Ⓕ

On this recording the 'Sabre Dance' from *Gayaneh* bursts into the room with explosive impetus and bite. The Sabre dancers are closely followed by the young maidens who come in as if the sabres were being flourished directly behind them, and hard on their heels come the Mountaineers who obviously have the Abominable Snowman in hot pursuit. With the brilliant recording projecting everything in burnished primary colours the effect is exhilarating, yet a shade wearing, so that the haunting 'Lullaby' provides a welcome respite. But not for long, as the 'Lezghinka' immediately develops a similar, almost frenetic thrust (rather more here than in the composer's own recording).

The *Masquerade* Suite has comparable spirit and gusto but some of its charm evaporates in consequence – notably in the 'Waltz', with the ebullient closing 'Galop' suggesting a circus band in an agreeably vulgar manner. The music from *Spartacus* is comparably vibrant and energetic, and although the famous 'Adagio of Spartacus and Phrygia' opens with a beguiling aura of romantic anticipation, the climax develops great Slavonic ardour.

Ippolitov's *Caucasian Sketches* are little more than picture postcards with sinuous sub-Rimsky-Korsakov eastern melodies. Tjeknavorian makes the most of the oriental atmosphere thus generated, but cannot disguise the fact that the hit number, the spectacular closing 'Procession of the Sardar' is head and shoulders above the rest in memorability. It is played with great elan and here Brian Culverhouse's brightly lit recording comes fully into its own.

Zoltán Kodály   Hungarian 1882-1967

Kodály was brought up in the country; he knew folk music from childhood and also learnt to play the piano and string instruments, and to compose, all with little tuition. In 1900 he went to Budapest to study with Koessler at the Academy of Music, and in 1905 he began his collaboration with Bartók, collecting and transcribing folksongs. They also worked side by side

as composers, and Kodály's visit in 1907 to Paris, bringing back Debussy's music, was important to them both: their first quartets were played in companion concerts in 1910, marking the emergence of 20th-century Hungarian music.

Kodály, however, preferred to accept rather than analyse folk material in his music, and his style is much less contrapuntal and smoother harmonically. His major works, notably the comic opera Háry János, the Psalmus hungaricus, the 'Peacock' Variations for orchestra and the Dances of Marosszék and Galánta draw on Magyar folk music (unlike Bartók, he confined himself to Hungarian material). His collecting activity also stimulated his work on musical education, convincing him of the value of choral singing as a way to musical literacy. He taught at the Budapest Academy from 1907, and after World War Two his ideas became the basis of state policy, backed in part by his own large output of choral music, much of it for children, as well as other exercise pieces, and was widely used as a model abroad.
GROVEmusic

Symphony in C

Symphony in C. Summer Evening. Magyar Rondo
Christopher Warren-Green *vn*
Philharmonia Orchestra / Yondani Butt
ASV CDDCA924 (54' · DDD)   Ⓕ

Kodály's only Symphony has an engagingly pastoral quality, with mild but memorable thematic material, lively – even somewhat overwrought – musical arguments and notably scenic orchestration. Yondani Butt presents a volatile view of the piece, with weighty textures and a fairly intense delivery, especially in the first movement's emphatic development section. The slow movement, an elegiac *Andante* based on folk-style motives, is appealingly atmospheric, while the fresh-faced finale generates plenty of rustic excitement. *Summer Evening* underlines the music's alternation of dance and reverie, whereas Butt's invigorating performance of the rarely heard but strangely more-ish *Magyar Rondo* (shades of Bartók's *Romanian Folk Dances*) has the Philharmonia playing like a generously augmented gipsy band, with stylish solo work from Christopher Warren-Green. Enthusiasm and sincerity are much in evidence throughout this well-recorded concert, while the odd spot of executive ruggedness is fairly appropriate to the music's outdoor character.

Dances from Galánta

Dances from Galánta[a]. Dances of Marosszék[a]. Háry János[a] – concert suite; The Flute-Playing Hussar; The Old Woman; The Jewish family; Háry riding Lucifer; The two gipsies. Dancing Song[b]. St Gregory's Day[c]. See the gipsies[b]
[b]**Budapest Children's Choir Magnificat;**
[c]**Kecskemét Children's Choir Miraculum;**
[a]**Budapest Festival Orchestra / Iván Fischer**

Kodály Orchestral

Philips 462 824-2PH (66' · DDD · T/t)　Ⓕ🔘🔘🠖

Iván Fischer and his Hungarian band join the most august company in this wonderful repertoire. As both sets of dances amply demonstrate, Fischer's Budapest Festival Orchestra is no less virtuosic than Ormandy's dazzling Philadelphians or Ferenc Fricsay's exemplary Berlin RSO, and its impassioned playing melds an earthy physicality, tangy exuberance and improvisatory flair to consistently telling effect. Add to the mix Fischer's wittily observant direction (an abundance of affectionate *rubato* in the opening section of the *Marosszék Dances* especially, allied to a generous quotient of 'gypsy' slides from the strings elsewhere), and the results are irresistible. Similarly, their *Háry János* Suite is immensely engaging. After a spectacularly good introductory 'sneeze', Fischer sees to it that Kodály's great arcs of melody are truly *espressivo cantabile* as marked. Napoleon's battlefield antics are hilariously depicted (splendidly bolshy trombones), while Fischer's thrusting 'Intermezzo' has joyous swagger. Moreover, for all the giddy festivities of the brassy 'Entrance of the Emperor and his Court', Fischer still manages to extract plenty of ear-burning detail. Five miniatures from the original *Singspiel* are also included, programmed separately from the suite; in 'The two gypsies' Fischer shares fiddling duties with Gábor Takács-Nagy. Last but not least we get three choral offerings from 1925-9, which are delivered with captivating freshness and charm by the two admirable children's choirs here.

A peach of an issue, complemented by an irrepressibly vivid recording.

Cello Sonatas

Solo Cello Sonata, Op 8. Cello Sonata, Op 4. Three
Chorale Preludes (after Bach)
Maria Kliegel vc **Jenö Jandó** pf
Naxos 8 553160 (64' · DDD)　Ⓢ🔘🠖

Maria Kliegel rises to the challenge of Kodály's Solo Sonata with considerable gusto: harmonics, *glissandos*, *sul ponticello*, fiery arpeggios – all are expertly employed and delivered via a nicely rounded tone. Kliegel's lustrous account of the *Adagio* underlines harmonic similarities with late Liszt and the folky, one-man-band finale has ample panache. The appreciative booklet-note relates Bartók's enthusiasm for the Solo Sonata's 'unusual and original style…[and] surprising vocal effects'. In fact, no other work by Kodály is so profoundly Bartókian in spirit. The Sonata, Op 4, is a far milder piece, though forthright expressive declamation sits at the centre of the first movement and the second is infused with the spirit of folk music. Kliegel and Jenö Jandó are in musical accord, and the recording is very good – although if you listen to the 'Bach-Kodály' tracks and wait for the Solo Sonata to start, you'll note a huge expansion in the cello's recorded profile. The three *Chorale Preludes* that open the pro-

gramme are 'attributed Bach' and enjoy the rich trimmings of a thunderous piano part (Busonicum-Liszt, with a snatch of Bartók for good measure) and a warm flood of tone from Kliegel.

Kodály Solo Cello Sonata, Op 8. Cello Sonata, Op-4[a]
Novák Cello Sonata, Op 68[a]
Jiří Bárta vc [a]**Jan Cech** pf
Supraphon SU3515-2 (73' · DDD)　Ⓕ

Kodály's Solo Cello Sonata is among the strongest, most searching of all his works, arguably the finest of all works for unaccompanied cello since Bach's suites, and here it receives a performance of exceptional power, precision and clarity from Jiří Bárta. His command in tackling the most formidable of technical problems means that he's able to keep a steady tempo and clarify textures with clean attack on double stopping, all seemingly without strain. Yet the intensity of his performance never flags, with a rare depth of concentration in the dark central *Adagio*. In the folk-dance rhythms of the *Allegro* finale he's volatile and thrusting, again using a formidable dynamic range that's well caught by the recording.

The same goes for the accompanied Cello Sonata. Bárta is well-matched by his pianist, Jan Cech: they make light of the problems presented by the many tempo changes in both movements, an opening Fantasia and a weighty finale, by giving an improvisatory feel. The folk element is heightened by an element of rawness, with the players striking sparks off each other.

The Supraphon disc has a substantial supplement in one of Vitezslav Novák's late works, a Cello Sonata. Written in 1941 during the Nazi occupation of Czechoslovakia, it represented an eruption of hatred against the invaders. Though it may not quite match the two Kodály works in emotional power, the passionate character of this closely argued single movement – bringing together elements of a multi-movement sonata structure – is most impressive, particularly in a performance as commanding as this.

Kodály Cello Sonata, Op 4 **Janáček** Pohádka
Liszt Elégies – No 1, S130; No 2, S131. La lugubre
gondola, S134
Anne Gastinel vc **Pierre-Laurent Aimard** pf
Astrée Naïve V4748 (50' · DDD)　Ⓕ

This is an imaginative piece of programme planning, with arrangements of Liszt's *Elégies* and *La lugubre gondola* separated by Kodály's Sonata and Janáček's *Pohádka*. Liszt, writing in the 1870s and early 1880s, sounds as modern as either of the composers writing in 1910; indeed, there's much in his augmented-chord harmony and his fondness for unusual scales that influenced Kodály, while Janáček also admired him and used his religious music for teaching. This is Romantic music outside the mainstream of European musical romanticism. Gastinel and Aimard give performances as intelligent as these juxtapositions suggest, oblique and dark in the linking figure of Liszt, especially with *La lugubre gondola*, one of the most extraordinary late piano pieces. Kodály's sonata is played with a quiet intensity, rhapsodic in manner but strongly held together by the clarity of emphasis on the motto theme and its musical implications. Janáček's pieces can sound sharper and quirkier than here, and in such performances make their point more strongly; but this playing is of a piece with the whole approach. Gastinel has a clean, resinous tone, and a strong sense of line; she's well partnered by Aimard, and the recording is balanced.

Missa brevis

Kodály Laudes organi. Missa brevis
Janáček (ed Wingfield) Mass in E flat
Andrew Reid *org* **Westminster Cathedral Choir /
James O'Donnell**
Hyperion CDA67147 (73' · DDD · T/t)　　Ⓕ**OO**

Janáček began his Mass around 1908, left it to gather dust for 20 years, then turned it into the first draft of the *Glagolitic Mass*. Paul Wingfield's reconstruction draws substantially on the original draft of the *Glagolitic Mass* to the extent of including a complete movement (the *Sanctus*) from it. Clearly Janáček knew best, and the only distinguishing moments are those bits recognisably from the *Glagolitic Mass*. Unquestionably, though, both the *Missa brevis* and *Laudes organi* are among Kodály's most inspired creations. Yet new recordings of favourite works are prone to disappoint. Not this one. If anything, this stunning performance, crowned by Andrew Reid's masterly organ playing, raises this setting of dog-Latin verses in praise of the organ and commissioned by the American Guild of Organists even higher. About 20 years before *Laudes organi*, the *Missa brevis* was first performed in this version for organ and chorus (it was originally an organ solo) in a bomb shelter during the 1944-5 Siege of Budapest. From such an inauspicious start, the work has fared remarkably well on record and this release represents an undoubted climax. It's a simply glorious performance and, in short, should not be missed.

Charles Koechlin　　French 1867-1950

Koechlin studied with Massenet, Gédalge and Fauré at the Paris Conservatoire from 1890 and was associated with such contemporaries as Ravel, Schmitt and Debussy (whose Khamma he largely orchestrated in 1913). As a public figure he soon became noted more for his writings on music and for his teaching (Milhaud and Poulenc were pupils) than for his composing, which at all periods was prolific. His output is enormous: there are over 200 works with opus numbers, many of them big symphonic, choral or chamber pieces. His symphonic poem Les bandar-log (1939), one of seven works based on the Jungle Book stories, *shows his knowledgeable and sometimes satirical view of a wide range of contemporary musical languages, as does his Seven Stars' Symphony (1933), a portrait gallery of the contemporary cinema. Other works include symphonic poems, choral works, songs and instrumental sonatas, as well as numerous small pieces for diverse combinations. Some reflect his communist sympathies, some are polytonal, some influenced by his love of Bach. His uncompromising and unworldly nature contributed to his unjust neglect.*
GROVEmusic

Orchestral Works

La course de printemps, Op 95ª. Le buisson ardent,
Opp 171 & 203ᵇ
Stuttgart Radio Symphony Orch / Heinz Holliger
Hänssler Classic Faszination Musik 93 045
(73' · DDD) Recorded live ª2000, ᵇ2001　　Ⓕ**OO**

The influence of Rudyard Kipling's *Jungle Book* on Koechlin was profound and *La course de printemps*, which gestated over a very long period, was the finest of the tone poems he gathered together under the composite title *Le livre de la jungle*. Although the events depicted are certainly connected with the character and life of Mowgli, the music itself is above all evocative of the jungle itself, its exotically humid atmosphere and unpredictable bursts of violence and animal energy. The underlying sinister ambience is balanced by a Ravelian sensuality (there's even is a hint of *Daphnis* in the dawn evocation of the opening), while the mysteriously gentle but lustrous string monody which closes the work is other-worldly in its vision of a voluptuous moonlit spring night. Koechlin's scoring is headily brilliant and one is engulfed in its rich panoply, so that for all the music's ecclecticism, it has a life and individuality of its own.

Le buisson ardent makes an ideal coupling. An evocation of rebirth – at times passionately intense in the strings, but with the ondes martenot later used to represent the ethereal voice of the reborn spirit. The work climaxes with a lusciously positive affirmation, but closes gently and rapturously. A superb introduction to Koechlin's exotic sound-world.

Vers la voûte étoilée. Le Docteur Fabricius
Christine Simonin *onde* **Stuttgart Radio Symphony
Orchestra / Heinz Holliger**
Hänssler Classic 93 106 (64' · DDD)　　Ⓕ

Much of Koechlin's highly individual orchestral music remains unexplored: indeed, both works here are premiere recordings. Before he became a composer, Koechlin wanted to be an astronomer and his fascination with the 'starry firmament', and the dream-world it evoked, is sensuously created in the arch-like structure of *Vers la voûte étoilée* ('Towards the vault of stars'). Written in the early 1920s and revised in 1939, this demonstrates the composer's exotic sound-world in a nocturnal piece that doesn't outstay its welcome.

The stars in the heavens return in *Le Docteur Fabricius*, written 1941-4, a more ambitious, large-scale symphonic poem with a philosophical underlay, based on a short story by the composer's uncle. The narrative describes a visit to the mysterious house in which the nihilistic Doctor Fabricius has cut himself off from the world. After an austere opening, dolorous chorales symbolise the philosophical disillusion, interrupted by a strident, fugal revolt and interwoven with moments of sadness. A powerfully scored chorale suggests that human hope always re-emerges. The visitor looks out to the starry firmament (the ondes martenot-rich scoring suggests Messiaen) and then, in a passage of radiant exultation, the spirit of Ravel hovers over the music to evoke the consolation of Nature. After an explosion of joy the music returns to the serene, withdrawn evocation of the opening.

Koechlin's powers as an orchestrator ensure his vision is powerfully communicated. Heinz Holliger is very much at home here, and the Stuttgart Radio orchestra play most responsively. The recording is full and atmospheric, though one ideally needs a more voluptuous ambience. But this is well worth trying.

Erich Wolfgang Korngold
Austro/Hungarian 1897-1957

Korngold, an American composer of Austro-Hungarian origin, was the son of the music critic Julius Korngold (1860-1945). He studied with Zemlinsky and had spectacular early successes with his ballet Der Schneemann (1910, Vienna) and operas Violanta (1916) and Die tote Stadt (1920). In 1934 he went to Hollywood and wrote some fine film scores. After World War II he wrote orchestral and chamber pieces, including a Violin Concerto and Symphony in F sharp, in a lush, Romantic style.
GROVEmusic

Violin Concerto

Korngold Violin Concerto[a]. Rózsa Violin   Ⓗ
Concerto, Op 24[b]. Tema con variazioni, Op-29a[b].
Waxman Fantasy on Bizet's 'Carmen'[c]. **Jascha Heifetz** *vn* **Gregor Piatigorsky** *vc*
[b]**Chamber Orchestra;** [a]**Los Angeles Philharmonic Orchestra / Alfred Wallenstein;** [b]**Dallas Symphony Orchestra / Walter Hendl;** [c]**RCA Victor Symphony Orchestra / Donald Voorhees**
RCA Victor Gold Seal [ac]mono/[b]stereo
09026 61752-2 (70' · ADD) Recorded 1946-63   ⓄⓄ➔

Heifetz's legendary recording of the Korngold Concerto serves a double purpose: as an effective introduction to Korngold's seductive musical style, and as the best possible example of Heifetz's violin artistry. The work itself was written at the suggestion of Bronislaw Huberman, but it was Heifetz who gave the premiere in 1947. It calls on material that Korngold had

also used in three of his film scores, although the way he welds the themes into a three-movement structure is masterly enough to suggest that the concerto came to him 'of a piece'. The very opening would be enough to seduce most listeners. Miklós Rózsa's Concerto has its roots in the composer's Hungarian soil, and echoes of Bartók are rarely absent. But whereas Korngold's score is taken from movie music, Rózsa's (or parts of it) became a film score – namely, *The Private Life of Sherlock Holmes*.

Rózsa's self-possessed, skilfully written *Tema con variazoni* was taken, in 1962, from a much larger work then in progress, but Heifetz and Piatigorsky play it in a reduced orchestration. As to the *Carmen Fantasy* by Franz Waxman (another notable film composer), its luscious tunes and frightening technical challenges were written with the great violinist in mind. It's a stunning piece of playing, and wears its years lightly. The other recordings sound far better, and the Rózsa items are in stereo.

Violin Concerto[a]. Gesang der Heliane[b]. Much Ado About Nothing[b]. Suite, Op 23[c]
[ac]**Benjamin Schmid,** [b]**David Frühwirth** [c]**Hanna Weinmeister** *vns* [c]**Quirine Viersen** *vc* [c]**Silke Avenhaus,** [b]**Henri Sigfridson** *pfs* [a]**Vienna Philharmonic Orchestra / Seiji Ozawa**
Oehms Classics OC537 (79' · DDD)
Recorded live 2004   ⒻⓄ

Austrian virtuoso Benjamin Schmid has been winning golden plaudits, especially on the continent, and this terrific live Salzburg Festival performance of Korngold's Violin Concerto demonstrates why. Not only does he generate a spine-tingling rapport with Seiji Ozawa and the Vienna Philharmonic but his playing, brimful of elegance, affectionate warmth and temperament, betokens a very real empathy with this gorgeous score.

One readily forgives any tiny slips along the way, given the big-hearted dedication, spontaneity and palpable sense of occasion that leap out of the speakers. The audience were understandably enthralled, too – so much so that their enthusiastic applause at the end of the first movement seems to take Schmid by surprise (he takes a few bars to settle at the start of the slow movement). Otherwise, it's a genuine 'tingle fest' from start to finish: the opening *Moderato nobile* is ideally glowing and heartfelt, the slow movement has exactly the right blend of innocence, intimacy and tenderness, while the boisterous finale is imbued with a wicked sense of fun. In all of this Ozawa and the VPO play their full part.

Towards the end of the festival Schmid teamed up with his chamber ensemble in the Mozarteum for the marvellous five-movement Suite for two violins, cello and piano (left hand) that Korngold wrote in 1930 for Paul Wittgenstein. It's been a lucky work in the recording studio, with excellent versions listed above. These splendidly accomplished and watchful newcomers convey the greatest sense of teamwork and joy of new discovery but all three groups impressively surmount the technical challenges of Korngold's urgently communicative inspiration and wisely eschew any temptation to wallow in the heaven-sent 'Lied'.

The main offerings frame perhaps rather less distinctive performances of music from *Much Ado About Nothing* and *Das Wunder der Heliane*. However, the rewards elsewhere are copious. No major grumbles, either, with the sound on these Austrian Radio tapes – and the price is right, too.

Korngold Violin Concerto **Brahms** Violin Concerto
Nikolaj Znaider vn
Vienna Philharmonic Orchestra / Valery Gergiev
RCA Red Seal 88697 10336-2 (66' · DDD)   ⓕⒷ﹢

There are readings of the Brahms that take their time, but the plush grandeur of Znaider and the VPO seems almost too opulent. The finale, too, misses an element of dance, of impishness even, so well caught by Julia Fischer (see page ??). Instead, we get a wall of sound both terrifying and awe-inspiring. But tempi apart, there is also much to celebrate here. Znaider is one of the greatest artists of his generation, and his consummate musicianship and glorious depth and range of tone are everywhere apparent, to particular effect in the *Adagio* of the Brahms, where Znaider's discreet portamenti make the most of the floating lines.

So, unquestionably top-notch playing from all concerned, even if the interpretation is less convincing. The Korngold is a different matter. This should have seemed a mere bon-bon after the Brahms, but such is the commitment from Znaider, Gergiev and the orchestra that it's a wonder from start to finish. They relish the composer's extraordinary ear for orchestral colour, especially the shattering climax of the first movement and the work's zany brass-fuelled ending.

Throughout, there's an ideal marriage of brilliance and warmth. The sound picture places the soloist very firmly centre-stage, but with playing this scintillating that's not a complaint.

Additional recommendation

Coupled with: **Korngold** Much Ado about Nothing – Maiden in the Bridal Chamber; Dogberry and Verges; Intermezzo; Hornpipe **Barber** Violin Concerto, Op 14
Shaham vn **LSO / Previn** pf
DG 439 886-2GH (71' · DDD)   ⓕⒷ﹢
  Shaham is yearningly warm without being sentimental, and clean and precise in attack and Previn is a superb accompanist. The suite from *Much Ado About Nothing* provides a delightful makeweight.

Film Music

The Sea Hawk (excerpts). The Prince and the Pauper (excs). The Private Lives of Elizabeth and Essex (excs). Captain Blood (excs). (Scores reconstructed and

assembled by Patrick Russ)
London Symphony Orchestra / André Previn
DG 471 347-2GH (68' · DDD)   ⓕⓄ﹢

Erich Korngold was the pioneer composer of the Hollywood film score during the 1930s and 40s. Errol Flynn starred in the films whose scores are featured on this CD, playing assorted dashing heroes swashbuckling their way through four slices of English history.

The line-up assembled here could not be bettered. Previn knows just how this music should go while the LSO bring the prerequisite pizzazz and élan that the music needs to take wing. The dexterity with which they negotiate the heavily scored cue 'Duel Continued' from *The Sea Hawk* (track 8) would prompt anyone to give a spontaneous round of applause.

The brilliant panoply of brass and strings that opens *The Sea Hawk* at once denotes these as 'action' films, but Previn's way with the music isn't to let the mood be dictated by the 'separate card' by which each moment in the credits was given a specific number of seconds on the screen. So the broad string theme of *The Sea Hawk* unfolds with a symphonic breadth akin to that majestic opening of Vaughan Williams's *A Sea Symphony*. In *The Prince and the Pauper* the LSO respond in true Romantic style to Korngold's luxuriant expansion of his material, and it comes across in this most affectionate performance as Korngold's finest cinematic achievement. A marvellous recording sets the seal on a definitive account of this splendid music.

The Sea Hawk – Suite (ed Gamba)
Manchester Chamber Choir;
BBC Philharmonic / Rumon Gamba
Chandos CHAN10438 (77' · DDD)   ⓕⓄ﹢

Rumon Gamba's 77-minute suite in six parts from Korngold's towering score for *The Sea Hawk* (1940) sensibly follows the action and will leave no listener in any doubt as to the giddy fecundity of top-flight invention and awesome architectural sweep of Korngold's exhilarating canvas. All the big set pieces are here, not least the unforgettable choral recapitulation of the main title ('Strike for the shores of Dover!'), while the gorgeous love music for Thorpe and Dona Maria is always most touchingly attended to (for a taster try track 14, 'Rose Garden').

Suffice to say, the orchestral playing under Gamba's judiciously paced lead has a sophisticated sheen, appropriate sense of spectacle (stellar brass contribution, as ever from this source) and whole-hearted commitment that testify to the BBC Philharmonic's unimpeachable credentials in this repertoire.

Apart from one jarringly audible page-turn, Chandos's production values leave nothing to be desired; indeed, the sound is gloriously wide-ranging, sumptuous and detailed. Throw in a particularly handsome booklet and it will by now be clear that every true Korngold fan should make haste to this terrific release.

The Sea Wolf. The Sea Wolf – trailer. The Adventures of Robin Hood – Suite
BBC Philharmonic Orchestra / Rumon Gamba
Chandos CHAN10336 (76' · DDD)　　　　Ⓕ⮕

For Michael Curtiz's 1941 big-screen adaptation of Jack London's *The Sea Wolf* (starring Edward G Robinson as Wolf Larsen, the sadistic captain of the sealer Ghost), Korngold produced one of his most searching scores. As Brendan G Carroll observes in his absorbing booklet-notes, anyone coming to this music after the playful, swash-buckling fireworks of, say, *The Sea Hawk*, *Captain Blood* or *The Adventures of Robin Hood* may well be caught unawares by its comparatively uncompromising demeanour.

The ominous 'Main Title' immediately sets the tone and demonstrates Korngold's masterly handling of an extremely large orchestra, which originally included the now defunct Novachord (patented by Hammond as the world's first synthesizer). Perhaps the most striking piece of scoring occurs in the 'Love Music', where a solo harmonica intones one of Korngold's most sweetly poignant melodies against a backcloth of strings. It's a rare moment of tenderness in an otherwise predominantly moody 55-minute sequence.

There's a bonus in the shape of the music for the trailer (the opening measures of which recycle material from Korngold's own score for *The Prince and the Pauper*) and the collection concludes with an irresistible four-movement concert suite from *The Adventures of Robin Hood*. Korngold slimmed down the orchestration and conducted performances in Oakland and San Francisco in 1938.

Needless to say, Rumon Gamba and the BBC Philharmonic are completely at home in this colourful repertoire (the superb brass section has a field day) and the sound is as spectacularly rich and detailed as one could possibly wish. Recommended with enthusiasm.

Suite, Op 23

Suite, Op 23. Piano Quintet in E, Op 15
Claire McFarlane, Jan Peter Schmolck vns **Schubert Ensemble of London** (Simon Blendis vn Douglas Paterson va Jane Salmon vc William Howard pf)
ASV CDDCA1047 (69' · DDD)　　　　Ⓕ

This supremely stylish interpretation of the Op 23 Suite (1930) has much to commend it, occupying a satisfying middle ground between the Czech Trio's endearingly homely view and the far more grandly virtuoso approach espoused by Sony's starry team. Not for the first time on disc, William Howard's superior brand of pianism is a real boon, and the whole performance radiates an affection and gentle purposefulness that are genuinely appealing.

Korngoldians will surely want to acquire this ASV coupling for the marvellous Piano Quintet, which here receives a reading that marries refreshing spontaneity to notable architectural elegance. Dating from 1921 and composed just after *Die tote Stadt*, it's an exuberantly confident offering cast in three movements. These artists audibly revel in Korngold's taxing, yet sumptuously rewarding writing, and the recording is handsome and true.

Violin Sonata, Op 6

Violin Sonata in D, Op 6. Sonett für Wien, Op 41. Much Ado About Nothing – Dogberry and Verges; Intermezzo; Hornpipe; Bridal Morning. Das Wunder der Heliane – Gesang der Heliane. Der Schneemann – Serenade. Die tote Stadt – Glück, das mir verblieb; Mein Sehnen, mein Wähnen (all arr cpsr). Märchenbilder, Op 3 – The Gnomes (arr Révay)
Detlef Hahn vn **Andrew Ball** pf
ASV CDDCA1080 (70' · DDD)　　　　Ⓕ○○

This is an indispensable disc gathering together the complete works for violin and piano – all superbly performed – including no fewer than three world-premiere recordings.

The disc opens with the remarkably early, but emotionally mature, Violin Sonata in D – a ravishing work that ranks among Korngold's major compositions. The Sonata is lyrical and expansive and has all the characteristics of Korngold's melodic and harmonic idiom – there's certainly nothing apprentice about this piece. Hahn and Ball give a beautifully crafted performance indeed and have truly absorbed the essence of this masterly score.

Korngold's suite of incidental music for *Much Ado About Nothing* has enjoyed a certain amount of currency in its original orchestral version, but less so in Korngold's own arrangement for violin and piano heard here. The transition works marvellously, being ideally suited to the intimacy of chamber music. The second movement, 'Dogberry and Verges', a grotesque march depicting the two drunken night-watchmen, pays passing homage to Korngold's childhood idol Gustav Mahler, and elsewhere in the suite there are constant intimations of the film scores of later years.

The remainder of the disc is devoted to smaller arrangements of works, including two extracts from the opera *Die tote Stadt* and one from *Das Wunder der Heliane* as well as the gorgeous song setting *Sonett für Wien* (In Memoriam), Op 41, the theme of which Korngold also used in the 1946 film *Escape Me Never*. The sound recording is excellent.

Complete Piano Music

Sonatas – Nos 1-3. Don Quixote. Der Schneemann. Märchenbilder. Four Waltzes for Piano. Four little caricatures for children. What the woods tell me. Zwischenspiel – Act 3 Intermezzo. Piano Trio. Potpourri from 'Der Ring des Polykrates' (arr Ruffin)ª. Much Ado

About Nothing. Geschichten von Strauss. Der
Schneemann – Four easy pieces. Schauspiel Overture.
Grand Fantasy on 'Die tote Stadt' (arr Rebay)[a]
Martin Jones, [a]**Richard McMahon** *pfs*
Nimbus ④ NI5705/8 (5h · DDD)   Ⓢ

A hearty three cheers to this complete Korngold cycle from the indefatigable and inexplicably underrated Martin Jones. The first two
discs have those extraordinary works composed
between 1908 and 1910 that put the infant
Korngold into the Mozart-Mendelssohn prodigy class – the first two piano sonatas, *Don
Quixote*, the ballet-pantomime *Der Schneemann*, *Was der Wald erzählt*, and seven *Märchenbilder*. The final 'Epilog' contains one of his
most beautiful melodies, and here Jones captures the *Weltschmerz* of the composer's own
treasurable 1951 recording.

The Piano Trio in D major, completed just
before Korngold's 13th birthday, is played in the
previously unrecorded four-hand version. In
this and the 1911 *Schauspiel* Overture (arranged
by Korngold's friend Ferdinand Rebay), Jones is
joined by Richard McMahon. Written in language of pre-nascent maturity that was to
develop little over the composer's lifetime, these
pieces constitute one of Western music's more
noteworthy miracles.

These four well-filled discs are completed by
Rebay's substantial (18'31") Grand Fantasy on
themes from *Die tote Stadt*, and Korngold's fantasy
on Johann Strauss themes. Stylish, lovingly prepared, classily played and with an excellent 10-
page booklet from Korngold's biographer Brendan
G Carroll, this valuable addition to the catalogue cannot be praised too highly.

Vocal Works

Abschiedslieder, Op 14[a]. Tomorrow, Op 33[ac]. Einfache
Lieder, Op 9[a]. Much Ado About Nothing, Op 11 –
Overture; Maiden in the Bridal Chamber; Dogberry
and Verges; Intermezzo; Hornpipe; Garden Music.
Prayer, Op 32[bc]
[a]**Gigi Mitchell-Velasco** *mez* [b]**Stephen Gould** *ten* [a]**Jo-
chem Hochstenbach** *pf* [c]**Ladies of the Mozart Choir,
Linz; Bruckner Orchestra, Linz / Caspar Richter**
ASV CDDCA1131 (66' · DDD)   Ⓕ**Ⓞ**

Caspar Richter and his fresh-faced band give a
polished and affectionate performance of the
delightful suite Korngold drew from his 1918
incidental score to a Vienna Burgtheater production of *Much Ado about Nothing*. They include the
fragrant (and previously unrecorded) 'Garden
Music' that opens Act 3, the haunting main
theme of which Korngold subsequently incorporated into the third movement of his violin and
piano arrangement (beloved of such legendary
fiddlers as Heifetz, Kreisler, Elman and Seidel).
Other rarities include the first recording of the
Op 32 *Prayer* for tenor, female choir and organ, as
well as a long-overdue digital successor to Charles
Gerhardt's pioneering RCA performance of
Tomorrow, a six-minute work for mezzo-soprano,

female choir and orchestra, originally written for
the 1943 film *The Constant Nymph*.

Another first recording is the orchestral version
of 'Nachtwanderer' from the six *Einfache Lieder*.
Korngold orchestrated these songs in 1917, and
in this guise most of the rest of the set has been
recorded by Barbara Hendricks on EMI. Six
years later, in 1923, Korngold orchestrated his
masterly *Abschiedslieder* of 1920, whose demand-
ingly wide-ranging melodic lines occasionally
strain the otherwise appealing mezzo here, Gigi
Mitchell-Velasco. That apart, these consistently
communicative performances – captured in
decent, truthfully balanced sound – arouse nothing but praise. A must for all Korngold fans.

Sonett für Wien, Op 41. Abschiedslieder, Op 14. Drei
Lieder, Op 18. Drei Lieder, Op 22. Fünf Lieder, Op 38.
Songs of the Clown, Op 29. Four Shakespeare Songs,
Op 31. Unvergänglichkeit, Op 27
Sarah Connolly *mez* **William Dazeley** *bar*
Iain Burnside *pf*
Signum Classics SIGCD160 (74' · DDD · T/t) Ⓕ**ⓄⓄ**▷

Those for whom Korngold's music is an
acquired taste may not feel the need for another
CD, but this new collection is exceptionally well
performed and recorded. The mixture of songs
in German and English works very well, and
having two voices sharing them in some groups
means that any sense of monotony is avoided.

As in his operas and film scores, one can hear
Korngold drawing on different influences – there
are a couple of songs that seem like affectionate
parodies of Mahler, others in which he is moving
away from his Viennese roots and assimilating
American and English styles. The *Four Shakespeare Songs*, Op 31, are particularly engaging,
William Dazeley really letting go in 'When birds
do sing', and Sarah Connolly bringing all her
artistry to bear on Desdemona's Willow Song.
Both singers are sometimes stretched to the limits
of their resources, especially in Korngold's songs
composed after the disappointing reception
accorded to his 'gargantuan' opera *Das Wunder
der Heliane*. The first of the *Drei Lieder*, Op 18, is
a setting of a poem by Hans Kaltneker (author of
Heliane), 'In meine innige Nacht', which Dazeley
sings with great intensity. Korngold's last song,
'Sonnett für Wien' (which gives the disc its title)
is another, posthumously published, poem by
Kaltneker. In this song, one feels that Korngold
was bidding farewell not only to Vienna, the city
of his youthful success, but to music and life itself.
Iain Burnside plays Korngold's often fiercely difficult accompaniments with obvious affection and
relish. This is a very beautiful disc, recommended
even to those who think they don't care for
Korngold's style.

Sursum corda

Sursum corda, Op 13. Die kleine Serenade ('Baby
Serenade'), Op 24. Der Schneemann – Prelude;
Serenade. Die tote Stadt – Prelude to Act II[a]. Das

Wunder der Heliane – Interlude
[a]**Karen Robertson** sop [a]**Tibor Pazmany** org
Linz Bruckner Orchestra / Caspar Richter
ASV CDDCA1074 (62' · DDD)   (F)

This disc is a must for newcomers to Korngold.
Richter presents a beautifully rounded and balanced programme, headed by a virtuoso, highly
charged account of the Prelude to Act 2 from the
opera *Die tote Stadt*, with a finely sung, if brief
contribution from soprano Karen Robertson.
Although there's no film music by Korngold on
this disc, the symphonic overture *Sursum corda*,
with its uplifting, heroic themes, did eventually
provide material for the film score to *The Adventures of Robin Hood* some 18 years later. Richter
and his players deliver a wonderfully impassioned
and incident-packed performance. The *Baby Serenade* was composed shortly after the birth of
Korngold's second son Georg, and is a delightful
five-movement suite describing a day in the life of
his baby son. Korngold's perceptive and often
humorous sketches are brilliantly matched in a
performance that simply exudes affection and fun
– check out the wonderfully characterised performances in the jazzy 'Baby tells a story', track 6.
The disc is nicely rounded off with the orchestral
Interlude from *Das Wunder der Heliane* – more
voluptuous playing in what must be some of
Korngold's most voluptuous music.

Die Kathrin

Die Kathrin
Melanie Diener sop Kathrin **David Rendall** ten
François **Robert Hayward** bass-bar Malignac **Lilian
Watson** sop Chou-Chou **Della Jones** mez Monique
**BBC Singers; BBC Concert Orchestra /
Martyn Brabbins**
CPO ③ CPO999 602-2 (162' · DDD · T/t)   (F) ●

This is the first modern performance and recording of Korngold's last stage work. *Die Kathrin* is
separated by 10 years from its predecessor, *Das
Wunder der Heliane*. Between *Heliane* and *Die
Kathrin*, Korngold's career had changed. From
being the wunderkind of the 1910s, he had developed into the film composer and arranger of
large-scale operettas. If *Heliane* is the most grandiose of his operas, *Die Kathrin* is the most unpretentious; Korngold had thought of labelling it a
folk-opera. The story is simple. The hero,
François, is a singer who has been conscripted into
the army. He falls in love with Kathrin, leaving
her pregnant. She loses her job, follows him to
Marseilles, where in a vaguely *Tosca*-like plot-twist
François is implicated in the murder of the villain,
who has actually been shot by one of the cabaret
girls. Five years pass, François returns to find
Kathrin and his child. The opera ends with a rapturous love duet. The music is full of typically lush
Korngold scoring. In the night-club scene, obligatory in any 1930s opera, there are two catchy
numbers, and Korngold brings in such fashiona-
bly jazzy instruments as a trio of saxophones and a
banjo. The cast is exceptionally strong. Diener has

just the right weight of voice for Kathrin, and
Rendall makes François into a very positive hero.
Brabbins brings out the essentially Puccinian side
of the score; in its structure the opera resembles
La rondine more than a little: *verismo* didn't die
with *Turandot*. Devotees of Korngold's music
won't need any encouragement. Those with a
taste for tuneful, Romantic opera, sometimes
bordering on operetta, should give it a chance.

Die tote Stadt

Die tote Stadt
Torsten Kerl ten Paul **Angela Denoke** sop Marietta
Bo Skovhus bar Frank; Fritz **Daniela Denschlag** mez
Brigitta **Simina Ivan** mez Juliette **Stella Grigorian**
sop Lucienne **Lukas Gaudernak** ten Gaston
Eberhard Lorenz ten Victorin **Michael Roider** ten
Count Albert **Salzburg Boys' and Girls' Choir;
Vienna State Opera Chorus; Mozarteum Orchestra
Salzburg; Vienna Philharmonic Orchestra /
Donald Runnicles**
Orfeo d'Or ② C634 042I (121' · DDD)
Recorded live 2004   (F) ●

The production by Willy Decker of Korngold's
most famous opera at the 2004 Salzburg Festival
created something of a sensation, and now
makes its welcome arrival on CD. Georges
Rodenbach's 1892 novel *Bruges la morte*, on
which the 22-year-old Korngold and his father
based the libretto, deals with a man's obsession
with his dead lover. In 1920 this struck an immediate spark with audiences recovering from the
aftermath of the First World War and, with
Korngold's mixture of big, soupy tunes and a
sort of post-Wagnerian gloom, it was an
immediate hit.
  Although there is a good deal of noise from
movements on stage, the sound quality here is
exceptionally vivid for a live event. Though
Denoke is no Jeritza, she has an attractive voice
and joins Kerl sweetly in the famous duet 'Glück,
das mir verblieb'. They both hurl themselves into
the increasingly violent scenes as the fantasy affair
progresses. Bo Skovhus is his usual glamorous
self, doubling the roles of Fritz and Frank, the
faithful guardian of his friend's sanity.
  Runnicles and the Vienna Philharmonic play
the piece with some fire, bringing out every one
of Korngold's ragbag of Puccini, Strauss and
Wagner allusions. You have to be in the mood
for an overdose of kitsch but when it works, as it
does here, *Die tote Stadt* still packs a punch.

Fritz Kreisler   Austrian 1875-1962

*After study at the Vienna Conservatory and the
Paris Conservatoire Kreisler toured the USA (1888-
9). Real recognition came in 1899, after a concert
with the Berlin PO under Nikisch. His London début
was in 1902 and in 1910 he gave the premiere of
Elgar's Concerto. He lived in Berlin, 1924-34, and*

in 1939 settled in the USA, becoming an American citizen in 1943. His last concert was in 1947. Kreisler played with grace, elegance and a sweet, golden tone with a pronounced vibrato. His repertory included brief pieces of his own, some of them semi-pastiche pieces which he initially ascribed to composers such as Tartini and Pugnani, some of them sugary Viennese morsels, all beautifully written to display brilliant, subtle and expressive violin playing.

GROVEmusic

Compositions and Arrangements-

Original Compositions and Arrangements –   **H**
works by Kreisler and arrangements of works by
Bach, Brandl, Dvořák, Falla, Glazunov, Heuberger,
Poldini, Rimsky-Korsakov, Schubert, Scott,
Tchaikovsky and Weber
Fritz Kreisler vn with various artists
EMI Références mono 764701-2 (78' · ADD) Recorded
1930-38   **OOO**

Kreisler Praeludium and Allegro in the style of
Pugnani. Schön Rosmarin. Tambourin chinois, Op 3.
Caprice viennois, Op 2. Précieuse in the style of
Couperin. Liebesfreud. Liebesleid. La Gitana.
Berceuse romantique, Op 9. Polichinelle. Rondino on
a theme by Beethoven. Tempo di Menuetto in the
style of Pugnani. Toy Soldier's March. Allegretto in
the style of Boccherini. Marche miniature viennoise.
Aucassin and Nicolette, 'Canzonetta medievale'.
Menuet in the style of Porpora. Siciliano and
Rigaudon in the style of Francoeur. Syncopation
Joshua Bell vn **Paul Coker** pf
Decca 444 409-2DH (63' · DDD)   **ⒻⒹ➜**

Years of encores have guaranteed the cult longevity of Kreisler's music – certainly among violinists. Kreisler's disc consists of his own pieces and a large number of arrangements. Some of the latter are pretty feeble musically, yet the great violinist's unique artistry and magical tone-quality shine through. Sometimes he doesn't land right in the middle of a note, but always plays with the timing and phrasing of a great singer. Nothing is routine or set in his playing, which has a continual feeling of discovery and freshness. The transfers are excellent.

Joshua Bell learned Kreisler from his teacher, the late Josef Gingold, yet his approach is anything but 'old school'. He habitually avoids the pitfalls of imitation, flashiness and patronising overkill, preferring instead to revisit the music with modern ears. His *Caprice viennois* is light-years removed from the composer's own, a fresh-faced, strongly characterised reading that trades sentimentality for just a hint of jazz. And there's that inseparable twosome, *Liebesfreud* and *Liebesleid*, the latter displaying Bell's tone at its most alluring. The longest piece here is the *Praeludium and Allegro in the style of Pugnani* which he gives the full treatment, deftly pointing the *Allegro*, relishing passagework and double-stopping with impressive accuracy. Some pieces seem indivisible from Kreisler's own very individual tone and phrasing, *Polichinelle*, for

example, and *Marche miniature viennoise*, both of which paraded the sort of personalised *rubato*, timing and tone-production that have for so long seemed part of the music's very essence.

Bell's smooth, witty and keenly inflected readings make for elevated entertainment: they may not replace the composer's own, but they do provide a youthful and in many ways illuminating alternative. The recordings are excellent, but Coker's fine accompaniments occasionally seem overprominent.

Viennese Rhapsody
Albéniz/Kreisler Tango, Op 165 No 2 **Dvořák/Kreisler** Slavonic Dances – B78: No 2 in E minor; B145: No 2 in E minor **Falla/Kreisler** La vida breve – Danse espagnole **Granados/Kreisler** Andaluza, Op 37 No 5 **Kreisler** Caprice viennois, Op 2. Tambourin chinois, Op 3. Berceuse romantique, Op 9. Viennese Rhapsodic Fantasietta. Zigeuner-capriccio. La gitana. Polichinelle. Aucassin and Nicolette. Liebesleid. Liebesfreud. Slavonic Fantasie **Scott/Kreisler** Lotus Land, Op 47 No 1 **Wieniawski/Kreisler** Etude-Caprice in A minor, Op 18 No 4
Leonidas Kavakos vn **Péter Nagy** pf
BIS CD1196 (71' · DDD)   **ⒻOO**

Leonidas Kavakos's Kreisler is authentic in the best meaning of that term, namely a keen approximation both of the music's spirit and of the composer's inimitable playing style. Few Kreisler recitals have recalled, in so much minute detail, the warmth, elegance and gentlemanly musical manners of the master himself. It was an inspired idea to open the programme with that nostalgic evocation of Old Vienna, the eight-minute *Viennese Rhapsodic Fantasietta*, a Korngold sound-alike that can't waltz without smiling wistfully or even shedding the odd tear. Kavakos has mastered that lilting 3/4 to a T. His tone is uncannily familiar – cooler and less vibrant perhaps than Kreisler's own during the earlier part of his recording career but with a similarly consistent (though never overbearing) vibrato. But don't imagine that these performances are mere imitations: an individual personality does come through, it's just that a Kreislerian accent has become part of the mix – at least for the purposes of this recital. The programme has been very well chosen, ending with what are surely Kreisler's three most famous miniatures – *Liebesleid*, *Liebesfreud* and *Caprice viennois*. The *Slavonic Fantasie* after Dvořák is among the most interesting, incorporating as it does the first of the four *Romantic Pieces*. Cyril Scott's *Lotus Land* is haunting and exotic, while Kreisler's own *Zigeuner-capriccio* provides a fine example of Kavakos's slightly melancholy puckishness. Péter Nagy's stylish accompaniments add yet more flavour to the menu.

György Kurtág   Romanian 1926

Kurtág studied with Veress and Farkas at the Budapest Academy (1946-55) and with Milhaud and Mes-

Kurtág

siaen in Paris (1957); in 1967 he began teaching at the Budapest Academy. His works are few and mostly short, suggesting a combination of the most abstract Bartók and late Webern, though with a strong lyrical, expressive force (and sometimes ingenious wit). Most of his compositions are for chamber forces, sometimes with solo voice. Among the best known are The Sayings of Péter Bornemisza (1968), a 'concerto' for soprano and piano in 24 short movements, and Messages of the Late RV Troussova (1980) for soprano and orchestra. Some of his pieces (eg 15 songs, 1982) use the cimbalom. GROVEmusic

String Quartets

Aus der Ferne III. Officium breve, Op 28. Ligatura, Op 31b. String Quartet, Op 1. Hommage à Mihály András (12 Microludes), Op 13
Keller Quartet (András Keller, János Pilz *vns* Zoltán Gál *va* Ottó Kertész *vc*) **Miklós Perényi** *vc* **György Kurtág** *celesta*
ECM New Series 453 258-2 (49' · DDD)   Ⓕ

This disc, devoted exclusively to Kurtág's music for string quartet, is of great significance, and both performance and recording are equal to the enterprise. The Keller Quartet have secure technique as well as emotional commitment, while ECM has provided a warm yet spacious acoustic for this expressive music. The journey begins with Kurtág's Op 1 of 1959, in a world, dominated by expressionistic fragmentation, of which he's clearly the master. Eighteen years later, in the Op 13 *Microludes*, Kurtág has perfected his own personal style, in which small, separate forms are linked together, and the music's allusions – to Bartók and Webern, in particular – are subsumed into a lyrical, dramatic discourse. The fruits of Kurtág's long apprenticeship are most evident here in the superb *Officium breve* of 1988-9, a miracle of textural imagination and musical thought whose richly varied language is distilled further into the two miniatures – *Ligatura* (also 1989) and *Aus der Ferne* (1991). By now Kurtág's music is characterised by a concentrated homogeneity, and by a harmony whose tensions, and stability, are the result of bringing convergence and divergence into confrontation. The result is memorable, and these fine recordings provide immensely rewarding listening.

Játékok

Játékok – excerpts from Books 1-5 & 8. Transcriptions from Machaut to Bach – No 46, Gottes Zeit ist die allerbeste Zeit (Bach: BWV106); No 48, Aus tiefer Not (Bach: BWV687); No 50, Trio Sonata in E flat (Bach: BWV525/1); No 52, O Lamm Gottes unschuldig (Bach: BWV*deest*)
György Kurtág, Márta Kurtág *pf duet*
ECM New Series 453 511-2 (50' · DDD)   Ⓕ

If any contemporary composer can persuade the musical world that compositions of between 30 seconds and four minutes in length are the natural vehicle for progressive post-tonal music, that composer is Kurtág. This sequence of pieces, the longest of which lasts just over five minutes, offers a very special experience. The disc contains a selection from his ongoing sequence of 'games' (*Játékok*) for solo piano and piano duet. They're a mixture of studies and tributes, not explicitly pedagogic in *Mikrokosmos* mode, but ranging widely in technical demands and style, from fugitive fragments, in which even the smallest element tells, to the extraordinary flamboyance of a *Perpetuum mobile* containing nothing but *glissandos*. Most are sombre in tone, and even the more humorous items have a bitter side. For access to another musical world, Kurtág has included four Bach transcriptions, music whose serenity and confidence speaks immediately of utter remoteness from the real present. The performances risk overprojection but they're supremely characterful, and the close-up recording reinforces the impression of music that's mesmerically persuasive in its imagination and expressiveness.

Játékok (Games) – selection. Transcriptions from Machaut to Bach – Gottes Zeit ist die allerbeste Zeit (BWV106)
Gábor Csalog *pf* with contributions from **Aliz Asztalos, Ha Neul-Bit, András Kemenes** *pfs* **György Kurtág, Márta Kurtág** *pianino*
Budapest Music Center BMCCD123 (65' · DDD)   Ⓕ

Recording a complete edition of György Kurtág's *Játékok* is no small undertaking: the combined eight volumes comprise myriad pieces of often extreme brevity, with the range of expression traversed similarly all-encompassing. This is music which is poised between the discipline of an exercise and spontaneity of a whim: 'Games' played out as a fruitful interchange between technique and inspiration. A previous recording covered the first four volumes, and the most pleasurable way to encounter this music has hitherto been through the miscellany from György and Márta Kurtág (ECM). Both make brief appearances here, along with other Kurtág protegés, but the bulk of the enterprise is entrusted to Gábor Csalog, his dexterous pianism and scrupulous attention to dynamic nuance being vital components in the success of the disc. The 58 individual pieces are arranged into two parts – 34 and 31 minutes each – that together offer a conspectus of the conceptual and emotional territory explored by this music: a diary in sound with no obvious parallels in its stark directness and vehement honesty.

Newcomers could profitably sample an insouciant 'Prelude and Fugue in C' (No 5), the contemplative 'Hommage à Ferenc Berényi' (29), the rediscovery of sound in 'Fundamentals' (44), or a serene rendering of the BWV106 Sinfonia – one of numerous Bach transcriptions that can be integrated into the selection. Vividly realistic sound and pertinent notes, as always from BMC. Further discs are planned, and the complete edition should soon be available for download: iPod-friendly Kurtág could prove a whole new listening experience.

Kafka Fragments

Kafka Fragments
Juliane Banse sop **András Keller** vn
ECM New Series 476 3099 (59' · DDD) Ⓕ🅑➤

Over nearly 50 years, György Kurtág has composed several major song-cycles – *Kafka Fragments* being the biggest in size and scope. Written over an intensive spell in 1985-86, the selection and editing of texts had actually been taking place since Kurtág came across Kafka's writings during his studies in Paris three decades earlier, and this release of creative energy permeates the music to a degree typical of this most inscrutable yet fiercely communicative of composers.

The combination of voice and violin should not be taken to imply emotional restraint, any more than the brevity of the texts imposes arbitrariness on the formal trajectory of this hour-long cycle. The 19 fragments of Part 1 present facets of a skewed but all-encompassing 'worldview' – set in relief by the lengthy single setting of Part 2, 'The true path', that is the becalmed centre of Kafka's (hence Kurtág's) expressive universe. The 12 numbers that comprise Part 3 build in intensity to the authentically Kafkaesque vision of 'Scene on a tram', with its sense of the surreal in the everyday, then Part 4 reconfigures previous gestures in a further eight numbers, culminating in 'The moonlit night dazzled us…', with its aura of bleak transcendence.

In its vast extremes of elation and despair, *Kafka Fragments* is both unnerving and inspiring. Juliane Banse is fully at ease with its myriad emotional shades and techniques of realising them. András Keller offers playing of real insight. Recorded with spacious immediacy and extensively annotated, this is a fitting commemoration of Kurtág's 80th birthday: no one thus encountering his music for the first time will be left unmoved.

Works for chorus

Omaggio a Luigi Nono, Op 16. Songs of Despair and Sorrow, Op 18ª. Eight Choruses, Op 23
Stuttgart Vocal Ensemble; ªEnsemble Modern /
Marcus Creed
Hänssler Classic CD93 174 (41' · DDD) Ⓕ

In its concision and intensity, György Kurtág's choral music pursues a similar approach to his instrumental work. All three cycles were begun during 1979-81, though the process of completion was very different. *Omaggio a Luigi Nono* (1981) evolved quickly, perhaps because expressive consistency overrides technical diversity – the cycle centring on texts by Rimma Dalos that paraphrase earlier sources so as to reinforce their sentiments by seeming to contradict them. In their relative purity as choral music, they differ markedly from *Eight Choruses*, to poems by Dezsö Tandori (1984) – aphorisms posing as riddles, embodied in writing that evokes a near-orchestral range of sonority, an 'instrumentation' that is made graphic in *Songs of Despair and Sorrow* (1994). These settings of mainly short-lived Russian poets embody some of Kurtág's most plangent writing, aided by an ensemble – two harmoniums and four bayans (Russian accordions) alongside brass, strings and percussion – remarkable for the way it is subsumed into the chorus as if an extension of that being communicated.

The interplay between chorus and ensemble could have been more tangibly conveyed; otherwise the performances are as responsive to the music's emotional extremes as one would expect from the Stuttgart singers, abetted by the natural sound-balance and penetrating notes. Those deterred by the short playing-time should bear in mind not only the impact of these works but also that they form a sequence complete in itself – beyond which nothing remains to be added.

Helmut Lachenmann   German b1935

Lachenmann studied with David at the Stuttgart Musikhochschule (1955-8) and with Nono in Venice (1958-60). In 1966 he began teaching. In later works he simplified his forms and lessened the extent of aesthetic intervention in his material.
GROVEmusic

Das Mädchen mit den Schwefelhölzern

Das Mädchen mit den Schwefelhölzern (Tokyo version, 2000)
Nicole Tibbels, Eiko Morikawa sops **Helmut Lachenmann** spkr **Mayumi Miyata** shô **Yukiko Sugawara, Tomoko Hemmi** pfs **Stuttgart Vocal Ensemble; South West German Radio Symphony Orchestra, Baden-Baden and Freiburg / Sylvain Cambreling**
ECM New Series ② 476 1283 (113' · DDD) Ⓕ

Das Mädchen mit den Schwefelhölzern, the composer's first piece of music theatre, is based on Hans Christian Andersen's The *Little Match Girl*, which he interprets as an attack on a cold and indifferent society. The piece has appeared previously on the Kairos label. There isn't much to choose between the two recordings in terms of performance, but the new ECM version has a pleasing precision that suits Lachenmann's vision well. The chief difference between the two versions lies in a substantial revision under-

taken by the composer. The oft-recorded '...
zwei Gefühle...' scene is here abridged, subtly
altering the work's balance while not quite
diminishing the sequence's importance to the
whole. Though the work has been shortened
only barely, it's possible that a greater concision
results, aided perhaps by the slightly tauter
sound. Lachenmann's music demands the listener's active engagement, a determined effort
at understanding, but here are rewards to be
reaped from perseverance.

Edouard Lalo   French 1823-1892

*Lalo studied at the Lille Conservatory and in Habe-
neck's class at the Paris Conservatoire. As a violinist
and teacher in Paris in the 1850s he showed an
unfashionable inclination towards chamber music,
playing Classical string quartets and composing
string trios and a noteworthy quartet. During the
1870s he attracted attention for his instrumental
works, especially for the Symphonie espagnole
(1874), a five-movement violin concerto, and the
powerful Cello Concerto (1877). After disappointment at the poor reception of his opera Fiesque
(1866-7), he took up stage music again in 1875,
winning success with Le roi d'Ys (1888), on which his
operatic fame has rested; his ballet score Namouna
(1881-2) became popular as a series of orchestral
suites. Among the hallmarks of Lalo's music, the
vigour of which stands in contrast to the style of
Franck's pupils and the impressionists, are his
strongly diatonic melody, piquant harmony and
ingenious orchestration.*   GROVEmusic

Cello Concerto

Lalo Cello Concerto **Massenet** Fantaisie **Saint-Saëns**
Cello Concerto No 1 in A minor, Op 33
Sophie Rolland vc BBC Philharmonic Orchestra /
Gilbert Varga
ASV CDDCA867 (65' · DDD)   Ⓕ Ⓞ

Sophie Rolland's performance of the Lalo
Concerto is surely as fine as any recorded. It
opens with great character, thanks to Gilbert
Varga's strong accompaniment, and the solo
playing is joyously songful. But Rolland is at
her finest as she plays her introduction to the
finale with commanding improvisatory spontaneity. The orchestra bursts in splendidly and
she shows her technical mettle with some
bouncing bowing in the attractive closing
Rondo. The Saint-Saëns Concerto brings
similar felicities. Massenet's *Fantaisie* opens
dramatically and is rhythmically vital, flowing
onwards boldly to produce a winningly sentimental yearning melody which the soloist
clearly relishes. A cadenza then leads to a
charming, very French Gavotte, and the piece
ends jubilantly. It really is a find, and it could
hardly be presented more persuasively. The
recording is near perfect.

Cello Concerto in D minorᵃ. Cello Sonataᵇ.
Chants russes, Op 29ᵇ
Maria Kliegel vc ᵇ**Bernd Glemser** pf
ᵃ**Nicolaus Esterházy Sinfonia / Michael Halász**
Naxos 8 554469 (60' · DDD)   Ⓢ Ⓓ→

Maria Kliegel views the Concerto as a strong,
dramatic work, and she has just the qualities –
impressive, powerful tone and brilliant technique – to bring it off. The early exchanges with
the orchestra establish her heroic presence,
which she then relaxes to give a soft, delicate
account of the second theme. The orchestral
interruptions sound suitably stern and implacable – although the many loud, *staccato* chords
for full orchestra become somewhat wearisome.
The finale is excellent; a robust, serious
approach allied to energetic, bouncy rhythms.
Throughout, the orchestra sounds warmly
Romantic, the important solo wind parts full of
character.

The Sonata, too, is well worth hearing. Written 20 years before the Concerto, it's still a fully
mature work, mixing grand Lisztian gestures
with classical formal outlines and ingenious,
colourful harmony. Kliegel and Glemser play
with fine style and intense commitment, encompassing the high Romanticism and, in the outer
movement, Lalo's characteristically forceful
rhythmic manner. *Chants russes* is an arrangement of the middle movement of the *Concerto
russe* for violin – it's very effective as a cello
piece. Kliegel's soft, refined sound near the end
is especially memorable.

Violin Concerto

Violin Concerto in F, Op 20ᵃ. Concerto russe, Op 29ᵃ.
Scherzo. Le roi d'Ys – Overture
ᵃ**Olivier Charlier** vn BBC Philharmonic Orchestra /
Yan Pascal Tortelier
Chandos CHAN9758 (72' · DDD)   Ⓕ

This collection opens splendidly with a spank-
ingly good performance of the Overture to *Le
roi d'Ys*, with its melodrama, brassy splashes and
a rather memorable swooning cello solo. It has
all the gusto and panache of a Beecham performance and is certainly the finest account on
disc since Paray's old Mercury version. Then
come the two *concertante* violin works, both written with Sarasate in mind (separated by the
comparatively familiar *Scherzo*, given here with
rumbustious zest). Why are they not better
known? The Violin Concerto has plenty going
for it, a nicely coloured palette, a disarmingly
nostalgic lyrical melody to haunt the first movement, followed by a delightful, songful *Andante*,
which Olivier Charlier plays with engaging delicacy. But the real surprise is the *Concerto russe*,
virtually another *Symphonie espagnole*, but with
Slavic rather than Spanish ideas, and very good
ones too. Its lovely slow movement, the 'Chant
russe', opens with a chorale and the violin steals
in with a genuine Russian folk tune, which (with
its rhythmic snaps) is astonishingly reminiscent

of the Bruch *Scottish Fantasy*. Charlier plays it most tenderly and the result is gently ravishing. The 'Intermezzo', with its off-beat timpani interjections and catchy main theme, is delicious, rhythmically sparkling in Charlier's hands, and there's another luscious secondary theme to come in the middle. The finale opens with a burst of sombre Slavonic passion from the strings, and another folk melody arrives. Soon the music quickens, culminating in a vivacious conclusion, with Charlier's contribution always lightly sparkling. Highly recommended.

Symphonie espagnole

Lalo Symphonie espagnole, Op 21ª **Vieuxtemps**
Violin Concerto No 5 in A minor, Op 37[b]
Sarah Chang vn ªRoyal Concertgebouw Orchestra,
[b]Philharmonia Orchestra / Charles Dutoit
EMI 555292-2 (52' · DDD) Recorded ªlive 1995, [b]1994
Ⓕ➡

The *Symphonie espagnole* is a more ambitious piece than the Vieuxtemps, and Lalo's inventive Spanishry holds up well throughout the five movements. Dutoit's approach has impetus, so when the *malagueña* secondary theme arrives, it makes a shimmering contrast. The delicious piping woodwind *crescendo* and *decrescendo* which begins the finale sets the scene for scintillating *salterello* fireworks from the soloist. The dash to the home straight brings vociferous applause, which makes one realise that the concentration and spontaneity of the performance has been helped by the presence of an audience, who aren't apparent until this point. Certainly the splendidly resonant Concertgebouw sound and perfect balance would never give the game away.

Vieuxtemps's Fifth Concerto opens disarmingly, but the *tutti* gathers strength in Dutoit's hands before Chang steals in silkily and proceeds to dominate the performance with her warm lyricism and natural, flowing *rubato*. In a performance like this it remains a small-scale work to cherish, for it hasn't a dull bar in it. The recording is warm and full, the balance treating the relationship between the violin and the Philharmonia Orchestra as an equal partnership.

Constant Lambert British 1905-1951

Lambert entered the Royal College of Music when he was 17, and was becoming well known by the time he was 20. He was the first English composer commissioned by Dhiagilev (Romeo and Juliet, 1926), initiating a lifelong association with ballet as a conductor and composer: he wrote Pomona (1927) for Nizhinska and Horoscope (1938) for the Vic-Wells Ballet, of which he was founder musical director (from 1931). But he also wrote concert pieces, preferring unconventional genres and anti-traditional tastes for jazz and Stravinsky: such works include The Rio Grande for piano, chorus and orchestra (1927), the Concerto

for piano and nonet (1930-31) and the choral orchestral 'masque' Summer's Last Will and Testament (1932-5). He stood in sharp relief against the background of English musical life and had wide-ranging interests. A lively critic, he wrote the stimulating Music Ho! a Study of Music in Decline (1934).
GROVEmusic

Piano Concerto

Concerto for Piano and Chamber Orchestraª.
Merchant Seamen Suite. Pomona. Prize-Fight
ªDavid Owen Norris pf BBC Concert Orchestra /
Barry Wordsworth
ASV White Line CDWHL2122 (66' · DDD) ⓂⓄⓄ

More gaps in the Lambert discography are enterprisingly plugged by these sensitive and shapely performances, which display most agreeable dash and commitment. The Piano Concerto recorded here isn't that unnervingly bleak 1930-31 creation for soloist and nine players but one from 1924 that remained in short score, never to be heard in the composer's lifetime. Now, thanks to the editorial skills of Giles Easter brook and the late Edward Shipley, we can at last savour another astonishingly mature and skilful product of Lambert's youth. Not only is the concerto tightly organised and brimful of striking invention, it also plumbs expressive depths, not least in the *Andante* slow movement which contains music as achingly poignant as any he penned. David Owen Norris does full justice to the glittering solo part, and he receives splendid support from Barry Wordsworth and the BBC Concert Orchestra.

Prize-Fight (Lambert's first ballet score) is earlier still, begun in 1923, completed the following year and overhauled one last time in 1927. It's a veritable romp, pungently scored in the manner of Satie and Milhaud, and with something of the anarchic spirit of Georges Auric's deliciously daft contributions to those glorious Ealing Comedies. In point of fact, Lambert had long been a connoisseur of the silver screen before he finally embarked on his first film score in 1940, for a flag-waving documentary entitled *Merchant Seamen*. Two years later, he compiled the present five-movement suite, and a superior specimen it is. *Pomona* we've had before. Wordsworth's spacious realisation occasionally lacks something in sheer effervescence and dry wit. But this is a most enjoyable and valuable compilation and the recording is vivid and truthfully balanced.

Tiresias

Tiresias. Pomona
English Northern Philharmonia / David Lloyd-Jones
with ªMichael Cleaver pf
Hyperion CDA67049 (72' · DDD) ⒻⓄ

Constant Lambert's *Tiresias* was commissioned for the Festival of Britain in 1951 and the subject had been preoccupying the composer for over 20 years. In the event, the ailing Lambert struggled to meet his July deadline and called upon colleagues like Robert Irving, Alan Rawsthorne, Elisabeth Lutyens, Gordon Jacob, Denis Apivor, Humphrey Searle and Christian Darnton to help him finish the orchestration. Lambert directed eight performances in all, but the work was coolly received and he died the following month, just two days before his 46th birthday.

The instrumentation of *Tiresias* calls for neither violins nor violas and features a notably varied battery of percussion as well as an important role for piano obbligato (brilliantly played here by Michael Cleaver). The music has a dark-hued intimacy and at times starkly ritualistic demeanour which probably baffled that glitzy first-night audience. However, Lambert's achievement is ripe for reassessment, and David Lloyd-Jones's meticulously prepared realisation allows us to revel anew in the score's many effective set-pieces. Stravinsky and Ravel are prime influences, but the work is suffused with that distinctive mix of keen brilliance and bleak melancholy so characteristic of its creator. The present account is all one could wish for.

Pomona (1927) is much earlier and altogether lighter in tone. Deftly scored for a chamber orchestra of 34 instrumentalists, *Pomona* comprises eight delightfully inventive numbers whose neo-classical spirit breathes very much the same air as that of Stravinsky and Les Six from the same period. Again, the performance is first-rate and the sound quite admirable.

Romeo and Juliet

The Bird Actors. Pomona. Romeo and Juliet
Victoria State Orchestra / John Lanchbery
Chandos CHAN9865 (56' · DDD)   Ⓕ Ⓞ

The really good news here is the CD début of *Romeo and Juliet*, one of only two ballet scores that Diaghilev commissioned from British composers for his Ballets Russes. It's a frothy romp firmly in the Stravinsky/Poulenc/ Milhaud mould – and a brilliantly confident achievement for a 20-year-old student – but, strange to relate, there's barely a glimpse of the sheer expressive scope of either *Pomona* or *The Rio Grande* (not to mention the remarkable Piano Concerto). We've long needed a worthy successor to Norman Del Mar's affectionate Lyrita version with the ECO; happily, Lanchbery and company have plugged the gap with notable success. Not only does the orchestral playing evince infectious zest and unswerving dedication to the cause, Lanchbery directs with palpable relish throughout.

He also gives us an enjoyably lithe account of *Pomona* and a sparkling curtain-raiser in the guise of *The Bird Actors*, a three-minute overture which originally began life as the finale of an even earlier ballet entitled *Adam and Eve*. The sound throughout is lively and full-bodied, without perhaps being in the very top flight.

Romeo and Juliet[a]. Pomona[a]. Music for Orchestra[b]. Summer's Last Will and Testament – King Pest: Rondo Burlesca[c]
[a]**English Chamber Orchestra / Norman Del Mar**;
[b]**London Philharmonic Orchestra / Barry Wordsworth**; [c]**Royal Philharmonic Orchestra / Simon Joly**
Lyrita SRCD215 (73' · [a]ADD/DDD)   Ⓕ Ⓑ→

Norman Del Mar's effervescent pairing of *Romeo and Juliet* (1924-25) and *Pomona* (1926) ranked high on many an enthusiast's Lyrita wish-list and the first thing to say is that the 30-year-old Kingsway Hall production leaps out of the speakers with startling bite and tangibility in its silver-disc reincarnation. Although the intervening years have brought other rewarding versions of these two delicious ballets, Del Mar's vintage performances project with a tangy zest, charisma and infectious rhythmic spring all their own. The ECO's distinguished woodwind roster leave an especially personable impression and both scores.

The fill-ups (recorded in 1989 and 1993 but previously unreleased) are worth having too. *King Pest* (a scary helter-skelter ride fairly grinning with malice) comes from Lambert's towering 1932-35 'masque' *Summer's Last Will and Testament* and Simon Joly's spirited realisation with the RPO makes an enjoyable pendant to the complete work. More valuable still is the long-overdue revival of *Music for Orchestra* (completed in 1927, when Lambert was still only 22). Barry Wordsworth and the LPO strain every sinew in what, amazingly, appears to be this little masterpiece's first stereo recording.

Rued Langgaard   Danish 1893-1952

Aged 11, Langgaard made his début in Copenhagen as organist and improviser. A series of trips to Berlin led to the performance of his hour-long Symphony No 1 (1908-11) by the Berlin PO in 1913. The musical community in Denmark, however, regarded the highly productive but reserved and solitary composer with scepticism. After his opera Antikrist was turned down by Copenhagen's Royal Theatre in 1925, he turned his back on modernism and openly criticised Danish musical life and Nielsen's influence on it. His Straussian music, coloured by religion and symbolism, did not concur with the anti-Romantic and sober attitude dominant in Denmark around 1930. Interest in his work was reawakened in the 1960s, Music of the Spheres in particular being seen as anticipating the avant-garde music of the 60s. GROVEmusic

Music of the Spheres

Music of the Spheres. Four Tone Pictures
Gitta-Maria Sjöberg sop **Danish National Radio Choir and Symphony Orchestra / Gennadi Rozhdestvensky**
Chandos CHAN9517 (53' · DDD)   Ⓕ Ⓞ→

Music of the Spheres (1916-18) is probably Langgaard's most important – certainly most original – work. So radical did its sonic experiments seem even in the late 1960s that Ligeti no less, when inspecting the score, quipped that he had merely been a 'Langgaard imitator' all along. The manipulation of blocks of sound rather than conventional thematic development does have much in common with trends in post-Second World War avant-garde composition (though stemming from impressionism), but other contemporaries of Langgaard's, such as Schoenberg and Scriabin, had traversed similar terrain at least in part. The main difference between Langgaard and Ligeti lies in the former's reliance on a fundamentally tonal language, however eccentrically deployed, and *Music of the Spheres* seems in hindsight to be a bridge between two other highly virtuosic scores with celestial connotations: Holst's *The Planets* and Ligeti's *Atmosphères*. The *Tone Pictures* (1917) were written alongside this extraordinary work, yet possess none of its stature: four charming songs, they seem effusive and outmoded by comparison. Chandos's sound is superb.

Orlande de Lassus

Franco/Flemish 1532-1594

Lassus served Ferrante Gonzaga of Mantua from c1544, accompanying him to Sicily and Milan (1546-9). He worked for Constantino Castrioto in Naples, where he probably began to compose, then moved to Rome to join the Archbishop of Florence's household, becoming maestro di cappella of St John Lateran in 1553. After returning north, to Mons and Antwerp, where early works were published (1555-6), he joined the court chapel of Duke Albrecht V of Bavaria in Munich as a singer (1556). He married in 1558. Although a Catholic, he took over the court chapel in 1563 and served the duke and his heir, Wilhelm V, for over 30 years, until his death. In this post he consolidated his position by having many works published and travelling frequently (notably to Vienna and Italy, 1574-9), establishing an international reputation. The pope made him a Knight of the Golden Spur in 1574.

One of the most prolific and versatile of 16th-century composers, Lassus wrote over 2000 works in almost every current genre, including masses, motets, psalms, hymns, responsorial Passions and secular pieces in Italian, French and German. Most of his masses are parody masses based on motets, chansons or madrigals by himself or others; the large number of Magnificats is unusual. His motets include didactic pieces, ceremonial works for special occasions, settings of classical texts (some secular, e.g. Prophetiae Sibyllarum, 1600), liturgical items (offertories, antiphons, psalms, eg Psalmipoenitentiales, 1584) and private devotional pieces. He issued five large volumes of sacred music as Patrocinium musices (1573-6), and after his death in 1594 his sons assembled another (Magnum opus musicum, 1604).

Admired in their day for their beauty, technical perfection and rhetorical power, the motets combine the features of several national styles – expressive Italian melody, elegant French text-setting and solid northern polyphony – enhanced by Lassus's imaginative responses to the texts. His secular works reveal a cosmopolitan with varied tastes. The madrigals range from lightweight villanellas (Matona mia cara) to intensely expressive sonnets (Occhi, piangete); the chansons include 'patter' songs and reflective, motet-like works; and among the German lieder are sacred hymns and psalms, delicate love-songs and raucous drinking-songs. This versatility and this wide expressive range place Lassus among the most significant figures of the Renaissance period.

GROVEmusic

Masses

Missa Entre vous filles. Missa Susanne un jour. Infelix ego[a]
Oxford Camerata / Jeremy Summerly
Naxos 8 550842 (68' · DDD · [a]T/t)

The Masses *Entre vous filles* and *Susanne un jour* show Lassus at his best, full of variety and invention, music of an immediate impact; in fact, they display exactly the same qualities as the better-known motets. The Oxford Camerata has understood this well, taking considerable care with the nuances of the text and really enjoying the music's rich sonorities. Sometimes a slight imprecision in the playing of chords is detectable, but this is more than outweighed by the sense of melodic contour and the powerful, somewhat dark and austere sound which conveys so well the spirit of the music. With over 68 minutes of some of the finest 16th-century polyphony available at such a low price, no one should hesitate.

William Lawes

British 1602-1645

William Lawes, the younger brother of Henry Lawes, was probably a chorister at Salisbury Cathedral until the Earl of Hertford placed him under the tutelage of his own music master, John Coprario. In 1635 Lawes was appointed 'musician in ordinary for the lute and voices' to Charles I, though he was probably in Charles's service before then. In 1642 he enlisted in the royalist army and accompanied the king on campaigns; he was killed during the battle to relieve the garrison at Chester.

Lawes was a gifted, versatile and prolific composer. The stylised dance suite is the basic vehicle for his chamber music, often with a preceding fantasia or pavan. In his viol consorts he exhibited late Renaissance traits, but the larger part of his chamber music uses violins in the concertante style of early Baroque violin music with continuo. It includes the 'Harpe' consorts, a unique collection of variation suites for violin, bass viol, theorbo and harp. Of Lawes's vocal music, over 200 songs are extant, many of them composed for court masques and other theatrical entertainments. He is considered the leading English dramatic composer before Purcell. Much of his church music – c50 anthems and ten sacred canons or rounds – is also of high quality, The Lord is my Light being one of the finest verse anthems of its period.

GROVEmusic

Consort Setts

Consort Setts a 6 – in G; in C; in F; in B; in C.
Fantazy a 6 in F
Phantasm (Wendy Gillespie *viol* Jonathan Manson, Varpu Haavisto *tvios* Susanne Braumann, Markku Luolajan-Mikkola *bvios*) / **Laurence Dreyfus** *viol*
Channel Classics CCS17498 (60' · DDD)   Ⓕ OO

Dreyfus writes passionately about the music, referring to 'a Dionysian frenzy hell-bent on breaking civilised taboos' and 'jubilant incantations'. So what do we hear? A subtly resonant, particularised landscape: in effect an Elysian soundscape. Gone is the corporate consort sound we learned to relish in former decades, replaced with rather more democratic textures. With seeming ease, the voice of each viol emerges and withdraws on cue as the music unfolds with sublime logic and unquestionable momentum.

The best setts are perhaps the two in minor keys, which offered Lawes a richer harmonic palette and the players greater expressive possibilities. The harmonically bizarre first Fantazy of the C minor Sett must have excited 17th-century ears, which, if they were lucky, were treated as we are here to an excitingly paced second Fantazy, then an 'Inomine' ('sinewy' and sustained at first, then quicker in the second section, the plainchant exquisitely interwoven and at the same time plain for all to hear), and finally a vibrant Aire, resplendent in its swaggering repeated notes and syncopated dash. Whether it would make so vivid an impression from another ensemble is doubtful. Dreyfus's unselfconscious hyperbolic enthusiasm aside, these are beautifully thought-out, sympathetic performances, worthy of a cultivated monarch and the composer's quatercentenary. A superb disc.

Jean-Marie Leclair   French 1697-1764

French composer and violinist Leclair was initially a dancer. He lived from 1723 in Paris, where he became a prominent soloist and began producing violin sonatas (from 1723). He also appeared abroad, and in 1733 became ordinaire de la musique du roi at the French court. In 1738-43 he served the court of Orange in the Netherlands and (in 1740-43) François du Liz at The Hague. He then lived mainly in Paris, where he was murdered (probably by his nephew). Foremost in Leclair's output are over 60 solo, duet and trio sonatas for violin. In these he imbued the Italian style with French elements more successfully than most of his contemporaries, using short ornamented phrases and colourful harmonies;

the idiom reflects his own virtuoso technique. He also composed concertos, minuets, suites etc, ballet music, an opera (Scylla et Glaucus, 1746) with many striking features and other vocal music. He was an influential teacher and is considered the founder of the French violin school.

GROVEmusic

Violin Concertos

Violin Concertos – Op 7: No 1 in D minor;   Ⓟ
Op 10: No 3 in D; No 4 in F; No 6 in G minor
Collegium Musicum 90 / Simon Standage vn
Chandos Chaconne CHAN0589 (59' · DDD)   Ⓕ Ⓞ ➔

This disc contains Leclair's most vivacious and attractive works, played with great élan, sensitivity and neatness, and recorded with exemplary clarity and balance. The concertos represent a high-water mark in 18th-century violin technique, with extensive double-stopping, an extended range that soars up to heights scarcely ventured previously, rapid scales and flying arpeggios, and elaborate figurations of all kinds. To all of this Standage brings a seasoned virtuosity which he places totally at the service of the music's grace: his bowing in particular commands admiration. From the stylistic viewpoint these concertos are interesting for their mingling of French and Italian elements. There are Vivaldian unisons, but French dance forms for the middle movements – a pair of minuets in the D minor, minuets *en rondeau* in the G minor, a pair of gavottes with unusual interplay between solo and *tutti* in the F major, and an ornate solo line over supporting reiterated chords in the D major. Standage adds spontaneous embellishments of his own on repeats.

Violin Sonatas

Violin Sonatas, Op 1 – No 1 in A minor;   Ⓟ
No 3 in B flat; No 8 in G; No 9 in A
François Fernandez vn **Pierre Hantaï** hpd
Philippe Pierlot va da gamba
Astrée Naïve E8662 (64' · DDD)   Ⓕ

Leclair's Op 1 set was so successful when it was first published in 1723 that it had to be reprinted four times. Though it makes considerable technical demands on the violinist, the composer himself was at pains not to employ virtuosity as an end in itself and to condemn the 'trivialisation' of players who exaggerated the speed of quick movements. Leclair also, like Couperin, was insistent that performers should not add ornamentation of their own – though in the four sonatas here only the initial *Adagio* of No 3 is much decorated. Rather did he place emphasis on 'le beau chant' – expressive *cantabile*, which is well exemplified in the first movements of Nos 1, 8 and 9. The crisp *Allegro*, with its rapid dipping across strings, and the *Largo* of No 3 make play with multiple stopping, including double trills, and there's vigorous cross-string work too in the ebullient Giga of No 1. Leclair shows himself fond of the rondeau form with long episodes, and the Sarabande of No 9 is a set of variations. This last has an athletic gamba line, as does the whole of the G major Sonata; and the alert and positive continuo playing here (from both gamba and harpsichord) is a special pleasure. But naturally the main spotlight falls on François Fernandez, whose lively, pointed bowing, delicate fast movements and graceful slow ones (like the gentle G major Musette) do full justice to Leclair's attractive invention.

Ernesto Lecuona   Cuban 1895-1963

Born into a musical family, he played the piano from an early age and wrote his first song when he was 11. He graduated from the National Conservatory in Havana in 1913 and soon made his first appearance as a composer-pianist. Then, after further studies with Joaquín Nin, he made several tours of Latin America, Europe and the USA as the leader of a dance band, Lecuona's Cuban Boys, which became quite well known. For some years he lived in New York, where he wrote for musicals, films and the radio. In his concerts he usually performed his songs and dances for piano, as well as light pieces by other late 19th-century and early 20th-century Cuban composers. His salon piano pieces, using 'white' peasant and Afro-Cuban rhythms, found wide favour, and many of his songs, too, achieved great popularity. GROVEmusic

Songs

'On a Night Like This'
Siempre en mi corazón. Como presiento. Allá en la sierra. Tu no tienes corazón. Mi corazón se fué. Dame de tus rosas. ¡No es por ti! La habanera – ¡Mira! Dame el amor. Que risa me da. La comparsa. Al fin. Se abrieron las flores. Conga Cuba. Amor tardio. En una noche así. Devuélveme el corazón. Primavera de ilusión. Un amor vendrá. Me has dejado. No me engañarás. Rumba mejoral. No me mires ni me hables. Mi amor fue una flor. Canción del amor triste.
Carole Farley sop **John Constable** pf
BIS BIS-CD1374 (70' · DDD · T/t)   Ⓕⓞ

It's curious to think that Paul Hindemith and Ernesto Lecuona were almost exact contemporaries, born a couple of months apart in 1895 and dying within five weeks of each other at the end of 1963. Yet, despite this closeness in time, their music had no real common ground. Hindemith was no mean song-writer, though not especially prolific, unlike the Cuban Lecuona for whom song was a paramount form of expression: he wrote around 400 of them.

For this recording Carole Farley undertook a protracted detective hunt through libraries, publishers, basements and packing cases to arrive at her selection of 25 love songs. Hers is a fine and varied choice, highlighting Lecuona's undeniable gifts as a melodist and word-setter,

ranging between the overtly romantic – as in the opening *Siempre en mi corazón* ('Always in my heart') and *Primavera de ilusión* ('Spring of Illusion') – to fast and lively songs such as *Que risa me da* ('Oh, what a laugh') and *Conga Cuba*. In between these are more lilting songs such as *Como presiento* ('The feeling I have') and *Amor tardio* ('Belated love'), directly Latin numbers such as *Allá en la sierra* ('High in the Sierra') and the dramatic, scena-like *Canción del amor triste*.

Farley sings all the songs with great finesse and warmth of feeling. Very occasionally, as in *Se abrieron las flores* ('The flowers opened'), her vibrato doesn't suit Lecuona's clean lines. She's accompanied sympathetically by the excellent John Constable, whose playing is a model of precision yet catches that feeling of improvisation that is an essential part of these songs. The recording is wonderfully pure and clear.

Franz Lehár   Austro/Hungarian 1870-1948

The son of a military bandmaster and composer, Lehár studied in Prague with Foerster and Fibich and followed his father in an army career. In 1902 he resigned to work in Vienna as a conductor and composer, notably of operettas, achieving spectacular international success with Die lustige Witwe (1905), Der Graf von Luxemburg (1909) and Zigeunerliebe (1910). These and others restored the fortunes of the Viennese operetta and opened the genre to a greater musical and dramatic sophistication. After World War One his time seemed to have passed, but then came new successes, many written for Richard Tauber: Paganini (1925), Der Zarewitsch (1927), Friederike (1928), Das Land des Lächelns (1929) and Giuditta (1934). His other works include waltzes, marches and songs. GROVEmusic

Concertino for Violin and Orchestra

Tatjana – Prelude, Act 1; Prelude, Act 2; Prelude, Act 3; Russian Dances. Fieber. Il guado. Concertino for Violin and Orchestra in B flat minor. Eine Vision: meine Jugendzeit. Donaulegenden, 'An der grauen Donau'
Robert Gambill ten **Latica Honda-Rosenberg** vn **Volker Banfield** pf **North German Radio Philharmonic Orchestra / Klauspeter Seibel**
CPO CPO999 423-2 (70' · DDD · T/t)   Ⓜ

Lehár's mastery of the orchestra has never been in doubt; and here's further evidence of his technical accomplishment. Such touches of the operetta composer as are here are of the more ambitious operetta scores such as *Zigeunerliebe*. More often it's Wagner, Richard Strauss and Korngold who come to mind. Throughout, the music is tastefully and evocatively written, and with a supreme confidence in the handling of a large orchestra. *Tatjana* was an early operatic attempt of which Lehár was especially fond, and its preludes and dances capture the starkness of its Siberian setting. *Il guado* ('The Ford') and the concert overture *Eine Vision* are works from the *Lustige Witwe* years, when Lehár was still seeking to determine in which direction his future lay. The former is a symphonic poem with some attractively rippling writing for the piano, the latter a recollection of the Bohemian countryside of his youth. The elegant *Concertino* for violin and orchestra, which has been recorded previously, is a student work that demonstrates his affection for his own instrument. *Fieber* is the starkest piece in the collection – a bitter First World War portrayal of a soldier in the throes of a deadly fever. *Donaulegenden* gives glimpses of the familiar waltz-time Lehár, but a Lehár looking back sadly at a bygone age. What other operetta or waltz composer could have written music as powerful, gripping and spine-tingling as this? Do try it!

Waltzes / Overtures

Gold und Silber, Op 79. Wiener Frauen – overture. **H**
Der Graf von Luxemburg – Waltz; Waltz Intermezzo.
Zigeunerliebe – overture. Eva – Wär' es auch nichts
als ein Traum von Glück; Waltz Scene. Das Land des
Lächelns – overture. Die lustige Witwe – concert
overture
Zurich Tonhalle Orchestra / Franz Lehár
Dutton mono CDBP9721 (66' · ADD) Recorded 1947
Ⓢ**O**

These were the 77-year-old composer's last recordings. Most were reissued on LP (latterly on the Eclipse label), but here they're complete for the first time. Mostly the selections represent obvious items from Lehár's melodic output. However, the inclusion of the *Wiener Frauen* overture is an especial joy, representing Lehár at his less familiar but most melodic and inventive. The operetta's principal character was a piano tuner, and the overture includes an ingenious passage where one hears the piano being tuned up before launching into one of Lehár's most luxuriant and beautiful waltzes.

In his excellent notes Malcolm Walker aptly describes these recordings as, in a sense, Lehár's last will and testament. Slower and more indulgent than his earlier recordings they may be; but never for a moment the slightest bit ponderous. Rather they're full of nostalgia, wonder and joyful pride – lovingly caressed performances by a master melodist, master orchestrator and master conductor. The transfers have been excellently done from original shellac discs. Filtering may be required to minimise hiss; but it's more than worth while for uniquely beautiful recordings of some of the most heavenly melodies ever created.

Frühling

Frühling. Elfentanz. Hungarian Fantasy, Op 45ᵃ
Stefanie Krahnenfeld sop Hedwig **Alison Browner**
sop Toni **Robert Wörle** ten Lorenz **Markus Köhler**
bar Ewald ᵃ**Mark Gothoni** vn **Deutsche Kammer-**

akademie Neuss / Johannes Goritzki
CPO CPO 999 727-2 (78' · DDD · T/t)   Ⓕ

A completely unfamiliar Lehár operetta is a surprise indeed, and an utterly delightful treat it turns out to be. Set against the background of a Viennese housing shortage, it's a 'show-within-a-show' piece, featuring amorous goings-on between a composer, his librettist and two office typists. And it's the composer who gets the girl!

It's cast on an altogether smaller scale than usual for Lehár: just four soloists, without chorus, and for smaller orchestra. Though the style is unmistakable, the music is geared to a more intimate environment – no big, cloying waltzes, everything altogether more airy and light.

Actually the recording appears to be not so much of *Frühling* but its later manifestation *Frühlingsmädel*, produced in Berlin in 1928. For this the composer added brass instruments, composed one new number, inserted orchestral arrangements of three earlier piano compositions, and most importantly added a couple of popular dance numbers. The last two numbers – the syncopated 'Wenn eine schöne Frau befiehlt' and 'Komm, die Nacht gehört der Sünde' – show Lehár at his most seductive. The score also has a wonderful duet for the two male characters discussing the delights of a lady's wardrobe, as well as a typical Lehár march duet for the two lovers.

CPO has given the piece a winning performance, admirably capturing its lightheartedness and in splendidly clear sound. This CD is altogether a sheer delight.

Giuditta

Giuditta (sung in English)
Deborah Riedel sop Giuditta **Jerry Hadley** ten
Octavio **Jeffrey Carl** bar Manuele Biffi, Antonio
Andrew Busher spkr Duke **Naomi Itami** sop Anita
Lynton Atkinson ten Pierrino **William Dieghan** ten
Sebastiano **English Chamber Orchestra / Richard
Bonynge**
Telarc CD80436 (78' · DDD · T)   Ⓕ

Giuditta was Lehár's last stage work and the peak of his compositional development. Written for the Vienna State Opera, it's a highly ambitious score, containing some fiendishly difficult vocal writing and using a large orchestra featuring mandolin and other exotic instruments. For this recording some two hours of music have been compressed into 78 minutes by means of snips here and there and the omission of a couple of subsidiary numbers. The piece has a *Carmen*-like story, about the disenchanted wife of an innkeeper who persuaded a soldier to desert, before eventually abandoning and ruining him as she goes from lover to lover. The best-known number is Giuditta's 'On my lips every kiss is like wine', here gloriously sung by Deborah Riedel; the leading male role was written for Tauber, and there are some marvellous and demanding tenor solos, equally superbly sung by the impressive Jerry Hadley. Despite writing for the opera house, Lehár remained faithful to his formula of interspersing the music for the principal couple with sprightly dance numbers for a comedy pair, here in the hands of Naomi Itami and Lynton Atkinson. Assisted by Richard Bonynge's lilting conducting, these contribute richly to the appeal of the recording.

Die lustige Witwe (The Merry Widow)

Die lustige Witwe   H
Elisabeth Schwarzkopf sop Hanna **Erich Kunz** bar Danilo **Anton Niessner** bar Zeta **Nicolai Gedda** ten Camille **Emmy Loose** sop Valencienne **Josef Schmidinger** bass Raoul **Ottakar Kraus** bar Cascada
**Philharmonia Orchestra and Chorus /
Otto Ackermann**
EMI mono 5858222 (72' · ADD) Recorded 1953
Ⓕ ❶❶❶❶➓

Ⓖ This is a star-studded performance. Emmy Loose has exactly the right appealing kind of voice for the 'dutiful wife' who plays with fire, and Nicolai Gedda is a superb Camille, sounding extraordinarily like Tito Schipa at his best. His high notes ring out finely and his caressing lyrical tones would upset a far better-balanced woman than the susceptible Valencienne. These two sing their duets beautifully, both excelling in the second act duet, in which Gedda has the lion's share. Nothing in this recording, except Schwarzkopf's 'Vilja', is so ravishing as his soft tone in the second half of the duet ('Love in my heart is waking'), which begins 'Sieh' dort den kleinen Pavillon' ('See over there the little pavilion') which is perhaps the loveliest in the score. Erich Kunz has not the charm but more voice and a perfect command of the style the music requires; and he's very taking in the celebrated Maxim's song. He speaks the middle section of the little song about the Königskinder possibly because the vocal part lies uncomfortably high for him; and perhaps his rich laughter would not be considered quite the thing in the diplomatic service. But his is, in most ways, a very attractive and lively performance. The Baron's part was probably much written up for George Graves but here what little he has to do is done well by Anton Niessner.

Elisabeth Schwarzkopf sings Hanna radiantly and exquisitely. She commands the ensembles in no uncertain manner and makes it clear that the 20-million-francs widow would be a personage even if she had only 20 centimes. It's a grand performance, crowned with the sensuous, tender singing of the celebrated waltz in Act 3. The chorus singing is first-rate and its Viennese abandon sounds absolutely authentic, whatever its address. Otto Ackermann conducts with total understanding, and notable sympathy for the singers, and the members of the Philharmonia Orchestra play like angels for him. The recording is as good as one can reasonably expect and, very important in such a score, the string tone is lovely throughout.

Die lustige Witwe
Cheryl Studer sop Hanna **Boje Skovhus** bar Danilo **Bryn Terfel** bass-bar Zeta **Rainer Trost** ten Camille **Barbara Bonney** sop Valencienne **Uwe Peper** ten Raoul **Karl-Magnus Fredriksson** bar Cascada **Heinz Zednik** ten Njegus **Richard Savage** bar Bogdanowitsch **Lynette Alcantara** sop Sylviane **Philip Salmon** ten Kromow **Constanze Backes** mez Olga **Julian Clarkson** bass Pritschitsch **Angela Kazimierczuk** sop Praškowia **Wiener Tschuschenkapelle; Vienna Philharmonic Orchestra / Sir John Eliot Gardiner**
DG 439 911-2GH (80' · DDD · T/t)   Ⓕ ❶❶➓

This is a truly great operetta interpretation. Gardiner's approach is on an altogether more inspired plane than his rivals. In the Viennese rhythms, he shows himself utterly at home – as in the Act 2 Dance scene, where he eases the orchestra irresistibly into the famous waltz. But there are also countless instances where Gardiner provides a deliciously fresh inflexion to the score. The cast of singers is uniformly impressive. If Cheryl Studer's 'Vilja' isn't quite as assured as some others, her captivatingly playful 'Dummer, dummer Reitersmann' is typical of a well-characterised performance. As Danilo, Boje Skovhus acquits himself well with a polished performance and he offers a natural, more human characterisation than his rivals, while Barbara Bonney is superb. Not the least inspired piece of casting comes with Bryn Terfel, who transforms himself outstandingly well into the bluff Pontevedran ambassador. As for Gardiner's personally selected chorus, they make Monteverdi to Montenegro and Pontevedra seem the most natural transition in the world. DG's recorded sound has an astonishing clarity and immediacy, as in the way the piccolos shriek out at the Widow's Act 1 entrance or in the beautiful *pianissimo* accompaniment to the 'Vilja-Lied'.

Schön ist die Welt

Schön ist die Welt
Elena Mosuc sop Princess Elisabeth; Mercedes **Zoran Todorovich** ten Prince Georg; Count Sascha **Roland Kandlbinder** ten Director **Isabella Stettner** sop First lady **Masako Goda** sop Second lady **Andreas Hirtreiter** ten First man **Wolfgang Klose** bass Second man **Bavarian Radio Chorus; Munich Radio Symphony Orchestra / Ulf Schirmer**
CPO CPO777 055-2 (77' · DDD · S/N)   Ⓕ

Through-composed operetta? An apparent contradiction in terms, but that was exactly what Lehár succeeded in doing with Act 2 of his 1914 *Endlich allein*, the score which, revised (but not much in its key central act) as a vehicle for Richard Tauber in 1930, became *Schön ist die Welt*. Two royal intendeds, reluctant to commit to an arranged marriage, come together as strangers. Princess Elisabeth (in 1914 she was an American adventuress called Dolly, but we'll let that pass) and Crown Prince Georg (incognito as an Alpine guide) walk in the peaks, pick flowers, hear over the radio that there are fears for Her Highness's safety, are stranded overnight by an avalanche – and fall in love. At this Lehár throws all the range of his nonpareil orchestral skills, paralleling and anticipating Strauss's *Alpine Symphony* (written 1914-15) and, in the first of the three sections which comprise Act 2, encompassing an extraordinary rolling road of tone-poem, accompanied recitative and duet, an 'operettic' symphony of singing. The last section of the act delivers both a full evocation of the avalanche and a few-holds-barred love duet. Acts 1 and 3 – as was Lehár's later model in, for example, Paganini – are pure social comedy, picking up the 'lower' couple of the royal equerry and a tango dancer (taken here by the same singers) and unveiling a Butterfly-influenced duet for Georg and Elisabeth.

As Lehár's career – and his blood-brotherhood relationship with Tauber – progressed, he demanded increasing virtuosity of his principal singers. Elena Mosuc and Zoran Todorovich, names well known in European opera houses, are absolutely assured in style, language and technique. Their accomplishment is matched by the affectionate, well-scaled conducting of Ulf Schirmer.

Good radio studio sound, too, but once again CPO's booklet lets things down – no libretto; scanty, inaccurate plot summary; incomprehensible English-as-foreign language translation. Nonetheless, despite the omission of all the witty dialogue (including that radio broadcast) don't hesitate.

Tatjana

Tatjana
Roland Schubert bass Sergej; **Dagmar Schellenberger** sop Tatjana **Herbert Lippert** ten Alexis **Karsten Mewes** bar Sasha **Carsten Sabrowski** bass-bar Djerid, Nikolajev **Sebastian Bluth** bar Pimen **Olaf Lemme** bar Punin **Hanne Fischer** mez Raisa **Dieter Scholz** bass Starost von Uslon **Berlin Radio Chorus and Symphony Orchestra / Michail Jurowski**
CPO ② CPO999 762-2 (122' · DDD · T/t)　　Ⓕ

Franz Lehár was a reluctant operetta composer. His ambitions lay in serious music. When his three-act *Kukuška* was produced in Leipzig in 1896 he promptly resigned his job as military bandmaster, only to resume the drudgery of military service when it failed. Not until 1902, when he was 32, did conducting and composition enable him to give up the uniform for good. He didn't abandon *Kukuška* but later revised the work as *Tatjana*, achieving productions in 1905 at Brno, and in 1906 at the Vienna Volksoper. By then *Die lustige Witwe* had begun its triumphant progress around the globe. Lehár conducted a Leipzig radio performance of *Tatjana* in 1937; but that was it until the Berlin Radio concert performance in April 2001 that's preserved on these two CDs.

The opera opens on the banks of the Volga in the 1840s, moves on to the mines of Siberia, and ends on the Russian steppes. There, in the snow, the lovers Alexis, a soldier, and Tatjana, the daughter of a Volga fisherman, die together.

Lehár's musical language is very much of its time. There are hints of Wagner, perhaps rather more of Tchaikovsky's own Tatyana in *Eugene Onegin*, and something of the ill-fated love-match of Puccini's *Manon Lescaut*. The setting reminds us specifically of Giordano's *Siberia*. Yet the composer the music most obviously evokes is Lehár himself – the orchestral master who so expertly captured local colour and who could weave instrumental strands into a ravishing orchestral whole. The performance is very capably done, if with the atmosphere of a concert performance rather than a full staging. Herbert Lippert's Alexis is sung with clarity and brilliance, if a touch short on true passion. Dagmar Schellenberger's Tatjana is a shade too mature, lacking purity in her upper ranges, and yet overall agreeably done. It remains a piece of beautiful lyrical writing, brilliant orchestral colouring and impassioned melody.

Peter Lieberson　　American b1946

Informal study with Milton Babbitt led to further work at Columbia University with Wuorinen and Sollberger. He worked as an assistant to Leonard Bernstein in 1972 and was an assistant producer of the Young Person's Concerts for CBS. He also founded and conducted two contemporary music ensembles. His interest in Buddhism started to emerge through his music, intially in his Piano Concerto (1980-83), written for Peter Serkin. In 1997 he wrote his first opera, Ashoka's Dream. He has written concertos for horn (for William Purvis) and cello (for Yo-Yo Ma). His marriage, in 1999, to the mezzo-soprano Lorraine Hunt, led to a number of fine vocal works.

GROVEmusic

Neruda Songs

The Neruda Songs
Lorraine Hunt Lieberson mez
Boston Symphony Orchestra / James Levine
Nonesuch 7559 79954-2 (32' · DDD)　　Ⓜ ⊙⊙

Not so long ago, 'lush' and 'romantic' were words that would never figure in a description of Peter Lieberson's music. 'Rigorous', perhaps; 'intellectually stimulating', definitely. Of its integrity there was never any question. But deep down, the works were spun with the kind of cool brilliance that commands respect but rarely invites love. Then Lieberson met Lorraine Hunt, and for the next nine years – until her death from breast cancer in July 2006 – the Ice Man of music slowly melted.

Tributes to the mezzo-soprano have come in from all corners of the musical globe but none is more touching than *The Neruda Songs*, jointly commissioned by the Boston Symphony Orchestra and the Los Angeles Philharmonic, and premiered only a year or so before her death. What makes this collaboration particularly poignant is that, like any offspring, one can find traits of both parents: Lieberson's cerebral qualities are warmly humanised, Hunt Lieberson's shimmering vocal sensuality restrained from over-indulgence. These brilliantly crafted songs deserve all the attention they can get; after a respectful period of mourning, other singers need to pick up the mantle.

Clearly this piece is a big advancement for Lieberson. The famously complex Lieberson now has the gift to be simple, and his future works bear watching. That spiritual connection comes around all too rarely and would that it could be repeated. Unfortunately, at slightly more than 30 minutes, this recording is all we've got.

Jón Leifs · Icelandic 1899-1968

Leifs studied in Leipzig (1916-22) and conducted various German orchestras. He wrote orchestral, vocal and piano music based on Icelandic folk music, which he championed. GROVEmusic

Organ Concerto

Concerto for Organ and Orchestra, Op 7ᵃ. Dettifoss, Op 57ᵇ. Fine II, 'Farewell to Earthly Life', Op 56ᶜ. Variazioni pastorale, Op 8
ᵃ**Björn Steinar Sólbergsson** org ᵇ**Loftur Erlingsson** bar ᶜ**Reynir Sigurdsson** vib ᵇ**Hallgrím's Church Motet Choir; Iceland Symphony Orchestra / En-Shao**
BIS CD930 (56' · DDD)　　　　ⒻⓄ

Well received at its 1935 premiere in a Nazi-arranged Nordic music festival, Leifs' Organ Concerto was execrated later once the Jewish connections of Leifs's wife had become known. A piece long heard-of but unheard, this performance reveals the concerto to be a truly original utterance. Björn Steinar Sólbergsson gives a consummate rendition of what sounds like a monstrously difficult solo part.

The orchestra is given music of unusual delicacy (for this composer) in the *Variazioni pastorale* (on a theme from Beethoven's *Serenade*, also Op 8), though the pastoralism is more redolent of Roy Harris than Beethoven. In this work, also completed in 1930, Leifs's real voice again emerges gradually, and the return of Beethoven's theme at the close is wonderfully surreal – though the tonal framework remains more conventional than in the later works. *Fine II* (1963) is one of two orchestral endings Leifs penned for his unfinished Edda oratorio, *Twilight of the Gods*. *Dettifoss* (1964) is the third of Leifs's tone paintings (the others are *Geysir* and *Hekla*) of Icelandic natural wonders, though here he conceived of a dialogue between poet Einar Benediktsson and the huge waterfall rather than straight depiction. Thumpingly good perform-

ances from all concerned, captured in spectacular sound to match the landscape.

Edda, Part 1: The Creation of the World
Gunnar Gudbjörnsson ten Bjarni Thor Kristinsson bass-bar **Schola Cantorum; Iceland Symphony Orchestra / Hermann Bäumer**
BIS ☐ BIS-SACD1350 (76' · DDD · T/t)　　ⒻⓄⓄ

Jón Leifs was a true original and his *Edda* oratorio cycle was one of his most original inspirations. Planned in the 1920s as a single oratorio on the Völuspá, it grew into an epic tetralogy – though without a hint of Wagnerian romanticism – covering the world's creation, its gods, 'Twilight' and 'Resurrection' setting a patchwork text which reads like a compendium on each subject. Sadly, Leifs only lived to complete the first two parts.

The 13 movements of 'The Creation of the World' (1932-39) tell of the giant Mir and his death at the hands of Odin and his brothers and their fashioning of the Earth, Sea and Heavens – and the first men – from the corpse; the remaining sections then describe its nature.

To relate this epic narrative Leifs deployed a huge orchestra with a large percussion section (including rocks struck with hammers), organ, ocarina, bagpipes and a quartet of lurs, reconstructions of ancient Viking horns. Yet the orchestration – occasionally unleashed to sensational effect – is mostly used with restraint, nowhere more so than in the huge eighth movement, 'Night, Morning', where the dynamics rarely rise above piano.

This performance, recorded in the wake of the work's long overdue complete premiere in 2006, sounds thrilling, the BIS engineering catching the huge dynamic range, weight and delicacy of sound. Bäumer holds everything together with finesse and the orchestra play the atmospheric accompaniment marvellously. The main plaudits go, however, to the chorus who sing their extremely difficult parts with compelling conviction. Leifs's slightly ungainly style may not be to everyone's taste but his score is far more varied than first impressions suggest. Like it or loathe it, this is one of the recording events of the year.

Kenneth Leighton · British 1929-1988

Leighton studied at Oxford and with Petrassi in Rome, and in 1970 was appointed professor at Edinburgh University. His music is in a 12-note but fundamentally diatonic style; its romanticism is expressed in lyrical melody, instrumental colour and virtuoso solo writing. It includes Catholic church music, concertos, chamber and instrumental pieces. GROVEmusic

Symphony No 2

Symphony No 2, 'Sinfonia mistica'. Te Deum laudamus

Sarah Fox sop **BBC National Chorus and Orchestra of Wales / Richard Hickox**
Chandos CHAN10495 (57' · DDD · T)   Ⓕ**O**▶

Composed during 1973-74 in direct response to the death of his mother, Leighton's *Sinfonia mistica* is scored for soprano, chorus and orchestra. Described by its creator as 'a requiem or a meditation on the subject of death which usually becomes so more real to us in the second half of life', the symphony has six movements and sets texts by such great metaphysical poets as John Donne, Thomas Traherne and George Herbert, while also making telling use of the 1865 American hymn tune *The Shining River*. The linked 'Meditation' and 'Elegy' at the work's heart manifest an especially potent beauty, serenity and compassion, but, truth to tell, inspiration soars consistently high in this cogently wrought and (above all) profoundly humane utterance. This is music which will amply repay repeated listening. The orchestral version of the glorious 1964 *Te Deum laudamus* makes a rewarding postscript.

Both performances are beyond reproach. Sarah Fox sings with refulgent tone, commendable accuracy and shining intelligence; and Richard Hickox rallies the BBC Welsh forces to same dizzy heights. Outstandingly vivid sound, too, with a perfectly judged balance throughout. Miss at your peril.

Chamber works

Piano Trio, Op 46[abc]. Partita, Op 35[ac]. Metamorphoses, Op 48[ab]. Elegy, Op 5[ac]
[a]**Michael Dussek** pf [b]**Lorraine McAslan** vn
[c]**Andrew Fuller** vc
Dutton Epoch CDLX7118 (77' · DDD)   **O**

Although a fair amount of his music for voices has been recorded, Kenneth Leighton's orchestral and instrumental music is seriously under-represented in the catalogue. This most impressive disc gives a good idea of what we're missing: superbly crafted music of at times overwhelming intensity. The craft and the intensity are inseparable: there's as little here of mere technical cleverness as there is of self-indulgent emotional display; the emotion both needs and is concentrated by tight control.

The Piano Trio is a characteristic example, its first movement building from close working of a broad, sweeping theme and a more subdued and shadowy one to a bitter eloquence slightly reminiscent of Shostakovich before a shadowy, drained conclusion. Calm is eventually achieved, but not serenity. The Partita has similar energy but a less fraught quality; there's even a sort of bony wit, again recalling Shostakovich, to some of the variations of the finale.

Metamorphoses, although ostensibly a single 21-minute movement, could be read as a monothematic sonata, with a quite violent *scherzo* and a slow finale, by turns poignant and ghostly. The very early *Elegy* reveals some of Leighton's English roots: descendants of its sustained lyrical theme can be heard in the later pieces, but there are some harmonic shifts that John Ireland would have approved.

The programme, in short, is an ideal introduction to this important but still underrated composer. He's not underrated by these artists, however, who play with passionate conviction and splendid risk-taking attack; they're admirably recorded.

A Sequence for All Saints, Op 75. O God, enfold me in the sun. Morning Canticles. The World's Desire. A Sequence for Epiphany, Op 91. Rockingham
Wells Cathedral Choir; Wells Cathedral School Chapel Choir / Matthew Owens with
David Bednall org
Hyperion CDA67641 (76' · DDD)   Ⓕ**O**

Written in 1978 for the West Riding Cathedrals Festival, *A Sequence for All Saints* is a major score for large choir and organ, its five sections running continuously and containing some of Leighton's more sumptuous passages alongside those characteristic hallmarks: driving, repetitive rhythms, extended sequences and the piling on of harmonic tension. Larger still – weighing in at around half an hour – is *The World's Desire*, a BBC commission for a work reflecting facets of both Western and Eastern liturgy relating to the Feast of the Epiphany. It was premiered by the BBC Northern Singers in 1984. Between these come a typically celebratory anthem with a suitably dazzling organ part, *O God, enfold me in the sun*, a set of three Morning Canticles and an organ piece based on the hymn tune *Rockingham*.

Matthew Owens has certainly brought the Wells Cathedral Choir to the very peak of excellence; it ranks as probably the finest English cathedral choir at the moment. Supplemented by singers from the Wells Cathedral School Chapel Choir, the two large-scale works are delivered with great power and breadth, David Bednall's organ accompaniments as full of colour and pizzazz as one could want. It all adds up to stunning performances of outstanding music, a composer fully in sympathy with the practicalities of performance and musicians who are utterly at home with this distinctive musical idiom. Leighton's memory is well served in this superb release.

Additional recommendation

Sacred Choral Music
Crucifixus pro nobis, Op 38. An Easter Sequence, Op 55. Evening Service, 'Collegium Magdalenae Oxoniense'. Evening Service, Op 62. Give me the wings of faith. Rockingham. Veni creator spiritus. What love of this is thine?
Oxley ten **Whitton** org **Steele-Perkins** tpt **St John's College Choir, Cambridge / Robinson**
Naxos 8 555795 (67' · DDD)   Ⓢ▶

Our reviewer summed up: 'In this business of record-reviewing I find, on the positive side, music and performances I like, more that I admire, some that I love, but not much that evokes affirmation from the soul. This does.'

Ruggiero Leoncavallo
Italian 1858-1919

Italian composer and librettist Leoncavallo studied literature at Bologna University. The failure of an early opera, I Medici (1893), conceived as the first of a Renaissance trilogy (unrealised) and written for Giulio Ricordi who rejected it, prompted him, in a defiant quest for fame, to write the poem and music of Pagliacci (Milan, 1892), the single work for which he is widely known. In its economy and consistent impetus, notably with the commedia dell'arte playlet and the Zola-inspired prologue invoking naturalism, the opera represents a skilful exploitation of the 1890s verismo trend; it made Leoncavallo a celebrity overnight. That success was never repeated. However, he set La bohème (1897) in opposition to Puccini and the sentimental Zazà (1900) was favourably received. One of the first composers to become involved with gramophone records, he wrote the popular song Mattinata (recorded by Caruso, 1904) and conducted Pagliacci (1907), both for the G and T Company.
GROVEmusic

Pagliacci

Pagliacci
Carlo Bergonzi ten Canio **Joan Carlyle** sop Nedda
Giuseppe Taddei bar Tonio **Rolando Panerai** bar
Silvio **Ugo Benelli** ten Beppe **Chorus and Orchestra
of La Scala, Milan / Herbert von Karajan**
DG The Originals 449 727-2GOR (78' · ADD · T/t)
Recorded 1965   ❶❶❶➼

Conviction and insight instil this *Pagliacci* with excitement and real drama. A troupe of actors arrives to give a performance of a *commedia dell'arte* play. The illustration of real love, life and hatred is portrayed in the interplay of Tonio, Silvio, Nedda and her husband Canio. As the two rivals, Caro Bergonzi and Giuseppe Taddei are superb.

Taddei's sinister, hunch-backed clown, gently forcing the play-within-the-play closer to reality until it finally bursts out violently is a masterly assumption, and Karajan controls the slow build-up of tension with a grasp that few conductors could equal. The forces of La Scala, Milan respond wholeheartedly and the 1965 recording sounds well.

Leoncavallo Pagliacci   Ⓗ
Giuseppe di Stefano ten Canio **Maria Callas** sop
Nedda **Tito Gobbi** bar Tonio **Rolando Panerai** bar
Silvio **Nicola Monti** ten Beppe

Mascagni Cavalleria rusticana
Maria Callas sop Santuzza **Giuseppe di Stefano** ten
Turiddu **Rolando Panerai** bar Alfio **Anna Maria
Canali** mez Lola **Ebe Ticozzi** contr Lucia

**Chorus and Orchestra of La Scala, Milan /
Tullio Serafin**
EMI mono ② 586830-2 (141' · ADD · T/t) Recorded
1954   Ⓑ❶❶➼

The sound here is much more confined than on the Karajan set, though more immediate. Serafin conducts swifter-moving performances, yet ones quite as notable as Karajan's for pointing up relevant detail. All four interpretations carry with them a real sense of the theatre and are quite free from studio routine. It's difficult to choose between the casts on these two sets. Callas lives the characters more vividly than anyone. The sadness and anguish she brings to Santuzza's unhappy plight are at their most compelling at 'io piango' in 'Voi lo sapete' and at 'Turiddu mi tolse' in her encounter with Alfio, where the pain in Santuzza's heart is expressed in almost unbearable terms. As Nedda, she differentiates marvellously between the pensiveness of her aria, the passion of her duet with Silvio, and the playfulness of her *commedia dell'arte* acting.

Her partner in both operas is di Stefano They work up a huge lather of passion in the big *Cavalleria* duet, and the tenor is wholly believable as the caddish Turiddu. In the immediacy of emotion of his Canio, it's the tenor's turn to evoke pity. Di Stefano does it as well as any Canio on record without quite having the heroic tone for the latter part of the opera. Panerai is a strong Alfio on the Sèrafin set, but Guelfi, with his huge voice, is possibly better suited to this macho part. It's impossible to choose between the two Tonios, both pertinently cast. Taddei plays the part a little more comically, Gobbi more menacingly. Callas or Karajan enthusiasts will have no difficulty making their choice. Others may be guided by quality of sound. With either you'll be ensured hours of memorable listening.

Pagliacci
Giovanni Martinelli ten Canio **Queena Mario** sop
Nedda **Lawrence Tibbett** bar Tonio **Alfio Tedesco**
ten Beppe **George Cehanovsky** bass Silvio
**Metropolitan Opera Chorus and Orchestra,
New York / Vincenzo Bellezza**
Walhall mono WLCD0226 (70' · ADD)
Recorded live on March 10, 1934   Ⓖ❶❶➼

People talk dismissively about 'those crackly old records'. Here it is the stage that crackles – with energy. The charge runs through orchestra and chorus. And never mind about the recording being old: it is uncommonly vivid. The feeling of the house, keyed up for its matinee double-bill (*Salome* to follow) is itself part of the show: another layer to the play-within-the-play. At the centre are two towering individual performances – Martinelli's Canio and Lawrence Tibbett's Tonio.

Tibbett combines the gusto of old-time theatre with some rare refinements of the vocal art, and he is in magnificent voice. Martinelli sings as in a slowly consuming fire, his arioso a nobly sustained utterance in which Leoncavallo's music realises most completely its capacity for tragic intensity. Nor should Queena Mario's Nedda pass as over-shadowed: she too makes the part live dramatically, and her light, pure voice is skilfully used, in a way worthy of her teacher, the great Marcella Sembrich.

György Ligeti   Hungarian 1923-2006

Ligeti studied with Farkas, Veress and Járdányi at the Budapest Academy, where he began teaching in 1950. During this period he followed the prevailing Kodály-Bartók style in his works while also writing more adventurous pieces (First Quartet, 1954) that had to remain unpublished. In 1956 he left Hungary for Vienna. He worked at the electronic music studio in Cologne (1957-8) and came to international prominence with his Atmosphères (1961), which works with slowly changing orchestral clusters. This led to teaching appointments in Stockholm (from 1961), Stanford (1972) and Hamburg (from 1973).

Meanwhile he developed the 'cloud' style in his Requiem (1965) and Lontano for orchestra (1967), while writing an absurdist diptych for vocal soloists and ensemble: Aventures (1966) and Nouvelles aventures (1966). His interests in immobile drifts and mechanical processes are seen together in his Second Quartet (1968) and Chamber Concerto (1970), while the orchestral Melodien (1971) introduced a tangle of melody. The combination of these elements, in music of highly controlled fantasy and excess, came in his surreal opera Le grand macabre (1978). His subsequent output has been diminished by ill-health, although it includes a Horn Trio (1982) in which perverse calculation is carried into Romanticism. Other later works include Monument, Selbstporträt, Bewegung, for two pianos (1976), two pieces for harpsichord (1978), two Hungarian studies for chorus (1983) and a book of piano studies (1985).   GROVEmusic

Concertos

'Clear or Cloudy – Complete Recordings on Deutsche Grammophon'
Atmosphères. Cello Concerto. Chamber Concerto. Concerto for Flute, Oboe and Strings. Lontano. Melodien. Piano Concerto. Violin Concerto. Six Bagatelles. Mysteries of the Macabre. Three Pieces. Ten Pieces. Ramifications. String Quartets – No 1, 'Métamorphoses nocturnes'; No 2. Cello Sonata. Etudes, Book 1 Nos 2 & 4. Organ Study No 1, 'Harmonies'. Volumina. Lux aeterna. Die grosse Schildkröten-Fanfare vom Südchinesischen Meer. Aventures. Nouvelles Aventures
Various artists
DG ④ 477 6443GH4 (5h 9' · DDD/ADD)   Ⓑ

Anyone still wondering why all the fuss about Ligeti could do no better than start here. The chronological ordering of each disc reveals not differing preoccupations but growing mastery

in realising their potential: from the internalised dialogue of the Cello Sonata (1948-53) to the self-defining, dramatic genius of the Second Quartet (1968); from everyone's big discovery of the Ligeti Sound in *Atmosphères* (1961) to its self-assured apex in *Melodien* (1971).

Most of the DG recordings were made in the 1980s and early 1990s, and represent a Second Wave of Ligeti recordings. They lack on one hand the buzz (acoustic and musical) of Wergo's pioneering work, and on the other the composer's imprimatur on the complete edition shared between Sony and Warner. Clear or cloudy? Definitely clear. What else would you expect with Pierre Boulez in charge? He leaves extroversion to the singers in *Aventures/Nouvelles Aventures*, but you hear more of the notes than on any of the other four versions. Ligeti didn't shun old-fashioned virtuosity, he revelled in it, and so do Pierre-Laurent Aimard and Saschko Gawriloff in the late concertos for piano and violin.

Gems from this set date from when the music was wet on the page. The LaSalle Quartet don't treat the Second Quartet as a monolith of 20th-century quartet-writing; listening to them there is no sense of the compilation aesthetic that others have found in the piece. The frankly scary sounds that Gerd Zacher gets from an organ in *Volumina* surpass even his own Vox recording from the same period (1968). And the Kontarsky piano duo are irresistible in the Three Pieces, the triptych Ligeti wrote with them in mind. The second panel is a 'Self portrait with Reich and Riley (and Chopin's there somewhere)'. Hardly since Beethoven has music been able to laugh at itself and be worthy of the joke…

Violin Concerto[a]. Cello Concerto[b]. Piano Concerto[c]
[a]**Saschko Gawriloff** vn [b]**Jean-Guihen Queyras** vc
[c]**Pierre-Laurent Aimard** pf **Ensemble InterContemporain / Pierre Boulez**
DG 439 808-2GH (67' · DDD)   Ⓕ❍❍❍▷

The Violin Concerto (1992) is music by a composer fascinated with Shakespeare's *The Tempest*: indeed, it might even prove to be a substitute for Ligeti's long-mooted operatic version of the play. There are plenty of 'strange noises', the result not just of Ligeti's latter-day predilection for ocarinas, but of his remarkable ability to play off natural and artificial tunings against each other. This work is superior to the Piano Concerto because the solo violin is so much more volatile and poetic as a protagonist, an animator who 'fires up' the orchestra, functioning as a leader at odds with the led. Saschko Gawriloff is a brilliantly effective soloist, and well served by a sharply defined yet expressive accompaniment – Boulez at his most incisive – and a totally convincing recording. The other works are played and recorded with similar success. The Cello Concerto (1966) is a particularly powerful reminder of the strengths of the earlier Ligeti, where simple, basic elements generate anything but minimal consequences.

Cello Concerto[b]. Violin Concerto[c]. Clocks and
Clouds[a]. Sippal, dobbal, nádihegedüvel, 'With pipes,
drums, fiddles'[d]
[d]**Katalin Károlyi** mez [c]**Frank Peter Zimmermann** vn
[b]**Siegfried Palm** vc [d]**Amadinda Percussion Group;**
[a]**Cappella Amsterdam;** [abc]**Asko Ensemble;**
[abc]**Schönberg Ensemble / [abc]Reinbert de Leeuw**
Teldec 8573 87631-2 (67' · DDD)   Ⓕ**Ⓞ**➔

This CD forms an ideal overview of Ligeti's work
and a great introduction to his music. The Cello
Concerto (1966) juxtaposes the primary Ligetian
musical 'types' of this period – frozen, imperceptibly changing planes of sound, and surreal gestures which collide in manic and unpredictable
ways. Good that Siegfried Palm was able to
record a work he himself premiered, in an
account less perfectly realised but more characterful than that by Jean-Guihen Queyras
(reviewed above). As the title implies, *Clocks and
Clouds* (1973) superimposes rigour and freedom
– with a nod towards Minimalist thinking of the
period – to create the archetypal Ligeti composition. In what is surprisingly its first commercial
recording, balance between voices and ensemble
could have had greater spatial depth, but the
ethereal nature of the soundscape comes through
unimpeded.

In just a decade, the Violin Concerto has
established itself as a modern classic, combining
Ligeti's love of polyrhythmic interplay and varied tunings and a heady recall of his Bartókian
heritage. Frank Peter Zimmermann yields to
Saschko Gawriloff in the finely judged poise of
the opening *Vivacissimo* and Intermezzo. Elsewhere, however, his greater immediacy pays off,
with a visceral edge to the closing cadenza that's
truly hair-raising. If marginally less accurate
than Boulez in his handling of the orchestra,
Reinbert de Leeuw is more alive to its extremes
of emotional anguish and deadpan humour,
bringing the music vividly to life.

With personable notes from the composer,
this is certainly the Ligeti disc that should be in
everyone's collection.

Lontano

Lontano[a]. Atmosphères[a]. Apparitions.
San Francisco Polyphony[a]. Concert Românesc
Berlin Philharmonic Orchestra / Jonathan Nott
Teldec 8573-88261-2 (55' · DDD) [a]Recorded live 2001
          Ⓕ**Ⓞ**

Here at last are the scores with which the composer first made his name in the early 1960s
(*Apparitions* and *Atmosphères*); here also is *Lontano*
(1967), one of the finest orchestral scores of the
20th century, and *San Francisco Polyphony* of 1974,
which inaugurates the more self-consciously virtuosic and referential approach that characterises
Ligeti's subsequent works for large forces (*Le
Grand Macabre*, and the concertos for piano, violin
and horn); and, as a postscript of sorts, an early
score from the composer's pre-Western period.
The latter has its first recording here; rather more

incredibly (given its position in Ligeti's output), so
does *Apparitions*. On the last count alone, this
recording is simply a must for anyone interested
in 'new music'.

The two premieres here are studio recordings,
whereas *Atmosphères*, *Lontano* and *San Francisco
Polyphony* were recorded live. A previous recording of *Atmosphères* and *Lontano* with the Vienna
Philharmonic under Claudio Abbado was also
live, and unsatisfactory on a number of counts
(not least unwanted audience 'participation').
Thankfully there are very few such problems
here: the general accuracy is commendable,
considering the difficulty of co-ordinating dozens of individual lines (for example, getting 80-
odd instruments to attack *pianissimo* together at
the beginning of *Atmosphères*: the Berliners just
about manage it; at any rate, they're nearer the
mark than any of the other recordings). The
sound-quality has all the requisite impact and
delicacy, and the orchestra's shaping of line and
continuity (and, when required, their opposites)
is equally persuasive.

String Quartets

String Quartets – No 1, 'Métamorphoses
nocturnes'; No 2
Artemis Quartet (Heime Müller, Natalia Prischepenko
vns Volker Jacobsen va Eckart Runge vc)
Virgin Classics 336934-2 (43' · DDD)   Ⓕ**Ⓞ**

Few string quartets of the late 20th century are as
often performed as these, and it was only a matter of time before one of the up-and-coming
younger ensembles took up the challenge thrown
down by the Arditti Quartet in their recent re-
recording of both pieces for Sony (their earlier
reading on Wergo dates from the late 1970s).
The First Quartet, *Métamorphoses nocturnes*,
dates from Ligeti's Hungarian period, and the
evident debt to Bartók notwithstanding, his
approach to mass and textural transformation is
recognisable to anyone familiar with his later
music. To their credit, the Artemis let the music
breathe, and make much of Ligeti's impish
humour: both works are theatrical and benefit
from being 'played up', which the Artemis do
perhaps more freely than the Ardittis.

The Artemis are miked closely, but the sound
still allows for some beautifully differentiated,
'atmospheric' timbres (like the 'organ-stops' of
bar 71, first movement). There's also a more
palpable sense of immediacy, and a more riotous
climax in the most abrupt passages (the *ferocis-
simo* fourth movement, most obviously). The
Artemis offer a sufficiently different view from
the Ardittis to make for an unmissable alternative. First-time buyers need not hesitate.

Etudes

Etudes Books 1-3. Musica ricercata
Pierre-Laurent Aimard pf
Sony Classical 07464 62308-2 (65' · DDD) Ⓕ**ⓄⓄⓄ**➔

Pierre-Laurent Aimard is not just a modern-music specialist but an artist of phenomenal gifts, and excellently recorded here. First impressions of the music are likely to be of its immediacy. The complexities are a problem only for the pianist – whatever the sources of Ligeti's inspiration, his ideas serve only a musical/poetic purpose. Central to these dazzling pieces is his longstanding interest in composing with layers of material in different metres or different tempos and in producing what he calls 'an illusion of rhythm'; evident, too, are his more recent preoccupations with modern mathematics, in particular the young science of dynamical systems which seeks to explain the precarious balance between pattern and chaos, order and disorder. Ligeti's powerful imagination is fuelled by many things, but there's no question of needing a special key to enter his world. The music is enough. There can be no doubt that Ligeti's *Etudes* belong with the greatest piano music of this or any other century. They are amazing.

Le grand macabre

Le grand macabre
Sibylle Ehlert sop Venus, Gepopo **Laura Claycomb** sop Amanda **Charlotte Hellekant** mez Amando **Derek Lee Ragin** counterten Prince Go-Go **Jard van Nes** contr Mescalina **Graham Clark** ten Piet the Pot **Willard White** bass Nekrotzar **Frode Olsen** bass Astradamors **Martin Winkler** bar Ruffiak **Marc Campbell-Griffiths** bar Schobiak **Michael Lessiter** bar Schabernack **Steven Cole** ten White Minister **Richard Suart** bass Black Minister **London Sinfonietta Voices; Philharmonia Orchestra / Esa-Pekka Salonen**
Sony Classical Ligeti Edition ② S2K62312 (102' · DDD · T/t) Recorded live 1998　　　　　Ⓕⓞ

Le grand macabre, a comedy about the end of the world, an elaborate game of musical time-travel, an ambiguous dance on the brink of an abyss, looks more and more like the key opera of the end of the 20th century. Direct comparison between this version and Elgar Howarth's splendid 1987 Wergo performance is difficult, because Ligeti extensively revised the score in 1996, and it's that 'final version', as he calls it, that's recorded here. He's made a number of cuts, a great deal of what was originally spoken dialogue is now sung and there have been many changes to the scoring, making it more practical but also thinning it out. The reduction of spoken dialogue and the lightening of the orchestral texture make life a little easier for the singers (though not for the soprano singing Gepopo, which Ligeti has described as an attempt to out-Zerbinetta Zerbinetta) and for the players. The whole performance is rather more assured than Howarth's and the score's beauties are more lovingly polished. It now sounds rather closer to a 'normal' opera and, perhaps inevitably, lacks a degree of Howarth's alarming impact.

Interestingly enough, it's Salonen's performance, sung in English to a French audience, that draws more laughs at the jokes. Sibylle Ehlert is spectacularly virtuoso and Willard White's gravity is effective in the role of Nekrotzar. Graham Clark is hugely exuberant as Piet the Pot, and Steven Cole and Richard Suart make a splendid double-act of the two Ministers. Jard van Nes and Frode Olsen are perhaps inhibited by the English language from making Mescalina and Astradamors as grotesque as they can be, though both sing well, as does every other member of the cast. The recording, like the performance, is a little more comfortable, rather less in-your-face, than Howarth's. This version is the one to have – Ligeti's revisions are all improvements, and the performance is a fine one – but the older one has a shade more of the quality that Ligeti says he has hoped for in stage productions of the opera, that of 'demoniacal farce'.

Douglas Lilburn　　New Zealand b1958

In 1936 Percy Grainger awarded Lilburn the Grainger Prize for Forest, which committed him to music rather than literature, for which he had decided gifts. He studied with Vaughan Williams at the Royal College of Music, returning to his native New Zealand in 1940 to discover he'd won four prizes as part of the centennial celebrations. He later taught at Victoria University in Wellington.

Orchestral works

Aotearoa Overture. A Birthday Offering. Drysdale Overture. A Song of Islands. Festival Overture. Forest. Processional Fanfare
New Zealand Symphony Orchestra / James Judd
Naxos ② 8 557697 (75' · DDD)　　　　　Ⓢ

The ardour and sheen displayed by the NZSO, to say nothing of James Judd's elegant and purposeful direction, is deeply impressive. The engineering is beguilingly warm, rich and truthful. Certainly, readers with a fondness for, say, Sibelius, Barber or Vaughan Williams should find plenty to savour.

Both the captivating 1940 overture *Aotearoa* (the Maori name for New Zealand) and 1946 tone-poem *A Song of Islands* pave the way for the first two symphonies (if you like what you hear, make haste to the gloriously lyrical and big-hearted Second). The other stand-out item is *A Birthday Offering*. Written in 1956 for the 10th anniversary of the NZSO, this score explores more astringent expression and affords each section of the orchestra ample opportunity for display. The music combines a whiff of Tippett with the open-air manner of Copland – and there are even intriguing pre-echoes of James MacMillan's 'keening' string writing.

Sibelius's kindly presence looms over the tone-poem *Forest* (an apprentice effort from 1936) and the following year's infinitely more assured

Drysdale Overture, whose idyllic beauty reflects the unspoilt North Island landscape in and around the hill farm where Lilburn was raised. This well-filled disc concludes with the bracing 1939 *Festival Overture* and *Processional Fanfare*, a 1961 arrangement for three trumpets and organ of the student song *Gaudeamus igitur*, which the composer reworked 24 years later for small orchestra. Lovely stuff – and a bargain of the first order.

Magnus Lindberg Finnish b1958

Following piano studies, Lindberg entered the Sibelius Academy where his composition teachers included Rautavaara and Heininen. Heininen encouraged his pupils to explore the works of the European avant-garde, and this led c1980 to the founding of the informal grouping known as the Ears Open Society, through which Lindberg and his contemporaries aimed to encourage a greater awareness of mainstream modernism. Lindberg's compositional breakthrough came with two large-scale works, Action-Situation-Signification (1982) and Kraft (1983-5). Action, the work in which Lindberg first turned to musique concrète, led to his founding with Esa-Pekka Salonen the experimental Toimii Ensemble. This group, in which he plays piano and percussion, has provided him with a laboratory for his sonic development. During the late 1980s Lindberg's music approached a new modernist classicism, in which many of the communicative ingredients of a vibrant musical language (harmony, rhythm, counterpoint, melody) were reinterpreted. Key scores in this period were the orchestral/ensemble triptych Kinetics (1988), Marea (1989-90) and Joy (1989-90), reaching fulfilment in Aura (1993-4) and Arena (1994-5). Major works including Feria (1997), Cantigas (1999), the Cello Concerto (1999), the Clarinet Concerto (2003) and most recently Sculpture (2005) have established Lindberg's international reputation as one of today's leading orchestral composers. **GROVE**music

Clarinet Concerto

Clarinet Concerto[a]. Gran Duo. Chorale
[a]**Kari Kriikku** *cl*
Finnish Radio Symphony Orchestra / Sakari Oramo
Ondine ODE1038-2 (51' · DDD)　　　Ⓕ**ⓄⓄⓄ**➔

The clarinet has featured prominently as a solo instrument in Magnus Lindberg's output throughout his career, though it was only in 2002 that he set about writing a concerto for his longtime colleague Kari Kriikku. The finished article, however, is really very different from 1980s pieces such as *Ablauf* and *Linea d'ombra*.

Running for 25 minutes, the work's four sections play continuously, if not seamlessly. Beautifully written for the instrument, there are hints of Debussy in the opening pages and – in the orchestration – of Barber and Copland later on, but the Concerto is in no way derivative. It proceeds with ineluctable momentum through a varied tonal landscape (including some decidedly jazz-like passages) to an ecstatic peroration that is deeply moving and uplifting, before closing out serenely: Rautavaara meeting Gershwin, perhaps.

There is something of Rautavaara's manner in the modest *Chorale* (2001-2), written to precede Berg's Violin Concerto (both use the chorale *Es ist genug*). The larger *Gran Duo* for winds and brass (1999), with its suggestions of Stravinsky's *Symphonies of Wind Instruments*, is utterly different though no less impressive. The duo is between the woodwinds and brass *en masse*, the work a bracing dialogue across some 20 minutes with fascinating incidents along the way, not least where the textures pare down to chamber proportions, though the dark-hued coda has considerable cumulative power. Very strongly recommended.

Lindberg Violin Concerto **Sibelius** Violin Concerto
Lisa Batiashvili vn **Finnish Radio**
Symphony Orchestra / Sakari Oramo
Sony Classical 88697 12936-2 (57' · DDD)　Ⓟ**ⓄⓄ**➔

It's been said that Magnus Lindberg forges his works more from harmony and rhythm than from unfolding melodic lines, and the celestial acrobatics of this neatly constructed Violin Concerto, a real star-burst of a piece, tend to bear out that theory. It was premiered last year in New York, the soloist, as here, Lisa Batiashvili, whose agility and tonal sweetness serve as an ideal foil for the blinding colours on Lindberg's constantly shifting canvas. The work opens like a bright light descending, the soloist a first among equals who, beyond her brief cadenza, witnesses a gradual darkening of orchestral texture. The harmonic complexion can be either ravishing or dissonant, and the range of musical gesture, from ethereal reverie to Bartókian dance is consistently gripping. The breathless stream of invention recalls Lindberg's similarly hyperactive Clarinet Concerto – anyone who enjoyed that work should relish this one too.

Sibelius's Concerto provides a comforting disc companion, especially as the performance so memorably focuses on the dreamier elements of the first movement. Batiashvili bows a seamless, sensual line, her tone smooth as silk. Sakari Oramo conducts a cleanly detailed and warmly articulated accompaniment, stronger on pulse than on drama, and at times sounding almost like chamber music. Those who like their Sibelius flinty or rough-hewn might find this reading just a little too civilised, though for me the joy of hearing everything so considerately thought through and 'joined up' more than compensates for a lack of elemental drive. In any case it's the Lindberg that makes this disc unmissable.

Orchestral works

Concerto for Orchestra. Sculpture. Campana in aria[a]
[a]**Esa Tapani** hn
Finnish Radio Symphony Orchestra /

Sakari Oramo
Ondine ODE1124-2 (64' · DDD)   ⓕ❶❷➤

Magnus Lindberg has been dedicated in exploring the potential of the modern orchestra, as this disc confirms. Odd that *Campana in aria* (1998) was unrecorded until now, as its lively investigation of horn sonority makes for the composer's most entertaining *concertante* piece, especially when Esa Tapani is so in control of its virtuosity.

Each decade in his maturity has seen Lindberg pen an orchestral work as a statement of intent: thus the modernist outpouring of *Kraft* (1985), then the reconciliation of innovation and tradition in *Aura* (1994). Fine that the Concerto for Orchestra (2003) is a further step along this path, but quality is simply lacking – whether in the actual ideas or, especially, the interplay of textures such that the harmonies sound derivative of earlier works, while melodic lines are insufficiently defined. Ensemble writing in the latter half fails to sustain momentum, and the apotheosis is perfunctory by Lindberg's standards. Fortunately, *Sculpture* (2005) seems intent on righting its predecessor's wrongs – not least in its skilful mediating between extremes of motion without sacrificing either harmonic or textural intricacy, with a final section that fairly saturates the sound-space.

Quite a piece with which to have opened the Walt Disney Concert Hall in Los Angeles. Sakari Oramo and the Finnish RSO fully appreciate its opportunities for meaningful orchestral display and are accorded spacious sound that lacks nothing in impact. Sculpture makes this a mandatory purchase for Lindberg's admirers, many of whom may well find in the Concerto more than incidental pleasures.

Franz Liszt   Hungarian 1811-1886

Liszt was taught the piano by his father and then Czerny, establishing himself as a remarkable concert artist by the age of 12. In Paris he studied theory and composition with Reicha and Paer; he wrote an opera and bravura piano pieces and toured France, Switzerland and England before ill-health and religious doubt made him reassess his career. Intellectual growth came through literature, and the urge to create through hearing opera and especially Paganini, whose spectacular effects Liszt transferred to the piano in original works and operatic fantasias. Meanwhile he gave lessons and began his stormy relationship (1833-44) with the (married) Countess Marie d'Agoult. They lived in Switzerland and Italy and had three children.

The greatest pianist of his time, Liszt composed some of the most difficult piano music ever written and had an extraordinarily broad repertory, from Scarlatti onwards; he invented the modern piano recital. To help raise funds for the Bonn Beethoven monument, he resumed the life of a travelling virtuoso from 1839-47; he was adulated everywhere he went. In 1848 he took up a full-time conducting post at the Weimar court,

where, living with the Princess Carolyne Sayn-Wittgenstein, he wrote or revised most of the major works for which he is known, conducted new operas by Wagner, Berlioz and Verdi and, as the teacher of Hans von Bülow and others in the German avant-garde, became the figurehead of the 'New German school'. In 1861-9 he lived mainly in Rome, writing religious works (he took minor orders in 1865); from 1870 he journeyed regularly between Rome, Weimar and Budapest. He remained active as a teacher and performer to the end of his life.

Two formal traits give Liszt's compositions a personal stamp: experiment with large-scale structures (extending traditional sonata form, unifying multi-movement works), and thematic transformation, or subjecting a single short idea to changes of mode, rhythm, metre, tempo or accompaniment to form the thematic basis of an entire work (as in Les préludes, the Faust-Symphonie). His 'transcendental' piano technique was similarly imaginative, springing from a desire to make the piano sound like an orchestra or as rich in scope as one. In harmony he ventured well beyond the use of augmented and diminished chords and the whole-tone scale; the late piano and choral works especially include a strikingly advanced chromaticism.

Piano works make up the greater part of Liszt's output; they range from the brilliant early studies and lyric nature pieces of the first set of Années de pèlerinage to the finely dramatic and logical B minor Sonata, a masterpiece of 19th-century piano literature. The piano works from the 1870s onwards are more austere and withdrawn, some of them impressionistic, even gloomy (Années, third set). Not all the piano music is free of bombast but among the arrangements, the symphonic transcriptions (notably of Berlioz, Beethoven and Schubert) are often faithful and ingenious, the operatic fantasias more than mere salon pieces.

Liszt invented the term 'sinfonische Dichtung' (symphonic poem) for orchestral works that did not obey traditional forms strictly and were based generally on a literary or pictorial idea. Whether first conceived as overtures (Les préludes) or as works for other media (Mazeppa), these pieces emphasise musical construction much more than story-telling. The three-movement Faust Symphony too, with its vivid character studies of Faust, Gretchen and Mephistopheles, relies on technical artifice (especially thematic transformation) more than musical narrative to convey its message; it is often considered Liszt's supreme masterpiece. Although he failed in his aim to revolutionise liturgical music, he did create in his psalm settings, Missa solemnis and the oratorio Christus some intensely dramatic choral music.   GROVEmusic

Piano Concertos

No 1 in E flat, S124; **No 2** in A, S125; **No 3** in E flat, S125a, Op Posth (ed Rosenblatt)

Liszt Piano Concertos Nos 1ᵃ & 2ᵃ.
Beethoven Piano Sonatas Nos 10, 19 & 20
Sviatoslav Richter pf **London Symphony Orchestra / Kyrill Kondrashin**
Philips 50 Great Recordings 464 710-2PM (70' · ADD)

Recorded ᵃ1961, 1963 Ⓜ❍❍❍▷

These were recognised as classic performances virtually from their first appearance. They're characterised not only by the intense expressiveness·of Richter's playing, but also by very careful balances of orchestral texture which hitherto hadn't been much apparent in recordings of these works. Throughout, the emphasis is on poetic insight, dramatic impact; these interpretations have in these and other regards exerted a considerable influence. Yet even if sensitive readings of Liszt's concertos are now less rare, this in no way weakens the impression made by Richter's and Kondrashin's. In short, these are among the great Liszt recordings.

Piano Concertos Nos 1 & 2. Totentanz, S126
Krystian Zimerman pf
Boston Symphony Orchestra / Seiji Ozawa
DG 423 571-2GH (56' · DDD) Ⓕ❍▷

This is playing in the grand manner. From the start of First Concerto you're aware of a consciously leonine approach. Zimerman even deliberately takes risks in a few technically perilous places where some of his colleagues, at least in the studio, play safe; and indeed his octaves in the opening cadenza are an example. The result sounds spontaneous and, yes, even brave. Ozawa and the orchestra are behind the soloist in all this. Not only do lyrical sections sing with subtlety, the big passages also are shapely. There's plenty of drive in this Concerto.

In the Second Concerto Zimerman adopts a different approach; he evidently considers it a more poetic piece and the playing style, strong though it is, is to match. Finely though he handles the gentler music, there are odd sniffs and hums in the *molto espressivo* passage following the D flat major cello solo, and also in the last of the work's quiet sections. In the gorgeously grisly *Totentanz*, both the music and the playing should make your hair stand on end. The sound has a depth that suits the music and the piano is especially impressive. Zimerman's freshness (he reminds us that this is a young man's music), and the coupling, makes this disc a most desirable one.

Piano Concertos Nos 1 & 2. Totentanz, S126
Eldar Nebolsin pf **Royal Liverpool Philharmonic Orchestra / Vasily Petrenko**
Naxos 8 570517 (54' · DDD) Ⓢ❍❍❍▷

Not only can the performances hold their own with the very best of the same three works but the individual concertos compare with those by the likes of Katchen and Richter. They are that good. And if the opening of *Totentanz* doesn't quite make you jump out of your skin quite like Raymond Lewenthal's, Nebolsin and Petrenko are almost as chillingly shocking. The fugato (Var 5) is attacked with thrilling pace and precision on a par with the very best.

Nebolsin, winner of the first Sviatoslav Richter International Piano Competition in 2005, is a virtuoso of power and poetry. While allowing the music to breathe, he plays in long paragraphs without, as it were, having to come up for air. Try the scintillating final pages of the FirstConcerto in which Petrenko, always an alert partner, catches the ball and runs with it. Recorded sound is exemplary. At super-budget price, the disc is a real bargain.

Liszt Piano Concerto No 1
Chopin Piano Concerto No 1 in E minor, Op 11
Martha Argerich pf **London Symphony Orchestra / Claudio Abbado**
DG The Originals 449 719-2GOR (56' · ADD)
Recorded 1968 ❍❍▷

These performances, in DG's beautifully refurbished sound, remain as fanciful and coruscating as the day they were made. Argerich's fluency and re-creative spark dazzle and dumbfound to a unique degree but, given her reputation for fire-eating virtuosity, it's perhaps necessary to say that both performances quiver with rare sensitivity as well as drama. Time and again she gives a telling and haunting poetic counterpoint to her, arguably, more familiar way of trailing clouds of virtuoso glory. Abbado partners his mercurial soloist as to the manner born, finding (in the Chopin in particular) a burgeoning sense of wonder where others sound dry and foursquare.

Liszt Piano Concerto No 1, S124 **Prokofiev** Piano Concerto No 1, Op 10 **Shostakovich** Concerto for Piano, Trumpet and Strings, Op 35
Lise de la Salle pf **Gábor Boldoczki** tpt **Gulbenkian Foundation Orchestra, Lisbon / Lawrence Foster**
Naïve V5053 (60' · DDD) Ⓕ❍❍

With this scintillating and eagerly awaited recording, 19-year-old Lise de la Salle makes her concerto debut on disc. Once again her performances are of the highest quality, her rushes of adrenalin balanced by her precise calibration and control. Even with front-runners such as Argerich and Hamelin in the Shostakovich she holds her own, combining her freshness and ebullience with many personal and enchanting touches.

In the Liszt she is fearless in the face of every treacherous obstacle, but is also romantic and free-wheeling in the *Quasi adagio*. The *Allegro vivace* is acutely focused rather than given with a weaker if more familiar balletic grace, and in the finale de la Salle's ultra-brilliance and vivacity are very much her own. Indeed, she makes you imagine Liszt's delight if he had been able to hear such youthful aplomb.

Again, de la Salle is off like the proverbial greyhound at Prokofiev's first *poco più mosso* yet she also captures all of the central *Andante assai*'s bittersweet, faux romanticism. She is admirably recorded and partnered by Lawrence Foster, while trumpeter Gábor Boldoczki joins in her sense of fun and mischief in the Shostakovich.

Additional recommendations

Piano Concertos
Coupled with: Fantasia on Hungarian Folk Themes, S123 **Chopin** Andante spianato and Grande polonaise in E flat, Op 22
Richter pf LSO / Kondrashin
BBC Legends/IMG Artists mono BBCL4031-2 (69' · ADD) Live recording   Ⓜ

> Richter's London debut concerts in July 1961 were the sensation of the season, and the Liszt piano concertos at the Royal Albert Hall were the climax. Solos are miked very close by today's standards but only in this respect do the concertos yield to the famous Philips studio versions, made a little later during the same London visit.

Piano Concertos[ab]
Coupled with: Mephisto Waltz. Transcendental Study, S139 No 1[c]. Grand Fantaisie de bravoure sur La Clochette de Paganini
Ogdon pf [a]**Bournemouth Symphony Orchestra / Silvestri;** [b]**BBC Symphony Orchestra / C Davis**
BBC Legends/IMG Artists [c]mono BBCL4089-2 (73' · ADD) Recorded live, 1967-71   Ⓕ

> Ogdon plays here with all those characteristics inseparable from his genius: his improvisatory daring, his thrills, spills and poetry. An invaluable issue with excellent sound, he plays as if his life depended upon it.

A Dante Symphony, S109

A Dante Symphony[a]. Années de pèlerinage – deuxième année, S161, 'Italie' – No 7, Après une lecture du Dante (fantasia quasi sonata)[b]
[a]**Berlin Radio Women's Chorus;** [a]**Berlin Philharmonic Orchestra / Daniel Barenboim** [b]pf
Warner Elatus 2564-61780-2 (67' · DDD) [a] recorded live 1992   Ⓜ Ⓞ

This disc proves conclusively that the *Dante Symphony*, a contemporary of the *Faust Symphony*, no longer needs its apologists. Tone, full and rounded, firm and true, and rock-steady pacing elevate the opening beyond its all-too familiar resemblance to a third-rate horror-film soundtrack. As the work progresses, together with the countless examples of Berlin tone and artistry filling out, refining or shaping gestures in often revelatory ways, one becomes aware of Barenboim's skill in maintaining the large-scale tension he's created. As for the final choral Magnificat, if Liszt owed Wagner a debt of gratitude for persuading him to conclude the symphony with the 'noble and softly soaring' bars that precede a more noisily affirmative appended coda, in Barenboim's Magnificat (and much else in the symphony), it's Wagner's debt to Liszt that's more readily apparent; the *Parsifal*ian radiance of these final pages is unmistakable. More

importantly, for once they sound convincingly conclusive. The live recording is spacious, focused and expertly balanced.

The *Dante* Sonata was recorded with the kind of risk-taking abandon and occasionally less than perfect execution that you might expect from a live event. Improvisatory, impulsive and full of extreme contrasts, Barenboim's *Dante* Sonata is vividly pictorial. The instrument itself (closely miked and widely spaced) sounds larger than life. This recording is riveting.

A Faust Symphony, S108

A Faust Symphony
Kenneth Riegel ten **Tanglewood Festival Chorus; Boston Symphony Orchestra / Leonard Bernstein**
DG The Originals 447 449-2GOR (77' · ADD) Recorded 1976   Ⓜ Ⓞ Ⓞ ➔

David Gutman's absorbing booklet-note for the Leonard Bernstein release tells how at a Tanglewood concert in 1941 Bernstein scored a triumph in modern American repertoire and Serge Koussevitzky conducted the first two movements of *A Faust Symphony*. Some 20 years later Bernstein himself made a distinguished recording of the work, faster than this superb 1976 Boston remake by almost five minutes yet ultimately less involving. The passage of time witnessed not only an easing of tempo but a heightened response to individual characters, be it Faust's swings in mood and attitude, Gretchen's tender entreaties or the unpredictable shadow-play of 'Mephistopheles'. Orchestral execution is first-rate, the strings in particular really showing their mettle (such biting incisiveness), while Bernstein's pacing, although often slower than average, invariably fits the mood. The sound too is far warmer and more life-like than its rather opaque New York predecessor, although when it comes to the tenor soloist in the closing chorus, Kenneth Riegel is rather strident.

A Faust Symphony
András Molnár ten **Hungarian State Choir; Orchestra of the Franz Liszt Academy / András Ligeti**
Naxos 8 553304 (73' · DDD)   Ⓢ ➔

There's a lot right with this performance, not least being its outspoken acknowledgement of Faust's stormy character. Liszt's first-movement portrait receives zestful advocacy, less polished than some, perhaps, but fired by immense gusto. The recording, too, is endowed with plenty of body, while András Ligeti's vocal promptings vie with Toscanini's in *La bohème*! Gretchen is quite comely and Ligeti effectively traces both her darker moods and those passages associated with Faust's yearning. Mephistopheles is more angry than 'ironico' and if you want confirmation of Ligeti's Lisztian mettle, then try from 5'49" through the following minute or so: it's quite thrilling. True, woodwind pointing isn't as vivid as under, say, Leonard Bernstein, but there's certainly no lack of enthusiasm. The Orchestra of the Franz Liszt Academy gives its all and the Hungarian State Choir makes noble music of the final chorus, even though András Molnár's wobbly tenor proves to be something of a distraction. It's a compelling if flawed production, less carefully prepared than its best rivals but more spontaneous than most.

'Symphonic Poems, Vol 2'
A Faust Symphony. Von der Wiege bis zum Grabe
BBC Philharmonic Orchestra / Gianandrea Noseda
Chandos CHAN10375 (80' · DDD)   ℗**O**▷

Volume 2 in Chandos's series of Liszt's orchestral works includes the *Faust Symphony*, his crowning masterpiece, in a performance of supreme clarity and assurance. To achieve such stylistic empathy and lucidity in an hour-long force-of-nature work (the conductor has dropped the choral ending), showing Liszt's transformation of themes and characters at its height, is a daunting achievement. Time and again you are made to realise that accusations (still made in some quarters) of theatricality, of fustian and bombast, are largely the result of inadequate performances that put superficial display before true musicianship. Gianandrea Noseda immediately engages you in Faust's opening and troubled questioning with the promise of epic variations to come. Gretchen's radiance emerges truly *andante soave, dolcissimo e tranquillo e molto*, allowing the music's gently sighing lines and phrases to contrast to maximum effect with Mephistopheles's snapping accentuation and glittering diablerie. Indeed, so precise and articulate is the playing that you are left to wonder if Liszt, like Milton in *Paradise Lost*, was of the Devil's party without realising his ironic bias or inclination. Such a possibility is, however, erased in Liszt's final symphonic poem, *Von der Wiege bis zum Grabe*, where the opening 'Cradle' and closing fade-out suggest the composer's vision at its most ethereal and elevated. Chandos's sound is superb; you could hardly wish for more eloquent advocacy.

Hungarian Rhapsodies, S359

(Orch cpsr/Doppler) – **No 1** in F minor (piano No-14); **No 2** in D minor (piano No 2 in C sharp minor); **No 3** in D (piano No 6 in D flat); **No 4** in D minor (piano No 12 in C sharp minor). **No 5** in E minor (piano No 5); **No 6** in D, 'Carnival in Pest' (piano No 9 in E flat)

Hungarian Rhapsodies Nos 1-6
Budapest Festival Orchestra / Iván Fischer
Philips 456 570-2PH (60' · DDD)   ℗**OO**▷

Fischer's idiomatic foray into this well-worn repertoire is distinguished by tonal lustre and high spirits, with the authentic gipsy violin of József 'Csócsi' Lendvay lending a touch of added spice to No 3 (i.e. the piano No 6) and a tangy cimbalom much in evidence throughout. *Rubato* is legion, though more improvisatory than schmaltzy. Liszt's orchestrations are used for Nos 4-6, with Liszt and Doppler in No 3, and Doppler alone in No 2. Even if you've never particularly liked Doppler's version of the Second, Fischer's performance is so vivid, so imaginative of phrasing, that you may well be won over. Charm abounds. There's plenty of power, too, with meaty brass and growling *crescendos* at the start of No 4, and a riot of colour to close No 6. Fischer's *Hungarian Rhapsodies* are as frisky as foals and as flavoursome as goulash, as dashing and as dancing as anyone might want. They are further aided by excellent, full-bodied sound (especially impressive at high playback levels).

Symphonic Poems

'Symphonic Poems, Vol 1'
Ce qu'on entend sur la montagne. Orpheus.
Les préludes. Tasso
BBC Philharmonic Orchestra / Gianandrea Noseda
Chandos CHAN10341 (79' · DDD)   ℗**O**▷

Volume 1 of Liszt's complete symphonic poems augurs well for the releases. Gianandrea Noseda and the BBC Philharmonic remind you at every turn that the days of a lofty critical dismissal of this uneven but pioneering and romantically audacious music are surely over. Coldly objective complaints about Liszt's lack of craftsmanship or melodic distinction have been echoed in other more stylishly phrased complaints: for Clara Schumann there was 'too much of the tinsel and the drum' while Edward Sackville-West could see little beyond 'the expensive glare and theatricality'. But Liszt was nothing if not ambitious and if there are elements of truth in such accusations, they fail to convey the wider picture. Better an attempt to scale the heights than a safe repose on the lower slopes.

Ce qu'on entend sur la montagne is, indeed, epic in design and intention, seizing on Victor Hugo's obsession with the eternal battle between the forces of good and evil, of light and dark. But if Hugo's poem leaves us with an uneasy resolution, Liszt, a devout Catholic, ends with a radiant state of holiness. *Tasso*, too, celebrates final acclaim after the artist's trials and tribulations, and *Les préludes* attempts to unite four disparate ideas. *Orpheus* also conveys the victory of civilising art over baser forces.

Such music makes huge demands and these are met by Noseda with unfaltering command and lucidity. What could so easily topple into bombast is presented with an enviable clarity and acuteness. Excellent sound and presentation.

'Symphonic Poems, Vol 3'
Festklänge, S101. Héroïde funèbre, S102.
Mazeppa, S100. Prometheus, S99
BBC Philharmonic Orchestra / Gianandrea Noseda
Chandos CHAN10417 (71' · DDD)   ℗**O**▷

No one could accuse Liszt of a lack of largesse. Here, once more, is one dramatic gesture after another to startle and provoke Liszt's contemporaries who, indifferent to such generosity, quibbled over the length of the massive *Héroïde funèbre* and dismissed *Mazeppa* as vulgar and meretricious. Again, it is possible to see in all these works Liszt's lifelong preoccupation with the triumph of good over evil and, more personally, the recognition due to him long after his death. True, there are times when his reliance on sequence and chromaticism to intensify his themes can seem like so much padding and it says much for the BBC Philharmonic under Gianandrea Noseda that they once more temper drama with discretion.

They achieve a special sense of exultance rather than bombast in *Festklänge*, written to celebrate Liszt's planned marriage to the Princess Carolyne Sayn-Wittgenstein. And they are no less successful in the vast spans of the *Héroïde funèbre*, a still desolating tribute to those who suffered 'throughout the whole spectrum of human carnage' (Liszt). Fluent and eloquent as ever, Noseda and his orchestra have once more been superbly recorded.

'Symphonic Poems, Vol 4'
Hamlet, S104. Hungaria, S103. Hunnenschlacht, S105. Die Ideale, S106
BBC Philharmonic Orchestra / Gianandrea Noseda
Chandos CHAN10490 (80' · DDD) ⓕ❍❍➍

Volume 4 of Chandos's superb cycle of Liszt's symphonic poems takes us through *Hungaria*, *Hamlet* and *Hunnenschlacht* ('The Battle of the Huns') to *Die Ideale*. Liszt's orchestral resources and easy sense of the picturesque still provoke endless debate among avid Lisztians and equally avid detractors. And it is true that his ever-ready susceptibility can involve stock-in-trade gestures and responses, and a wholly 19th-century rhetoric. Yet when performed with such superfine brilliance as here, everything is made irresistibly vital and graphic.

Here you sense how Liszt's first audiences were fired to a renewed sense of nationalism as they listened to *Hungaria*, a glorified Hungarian rhapsody where muted fanfares and foreboding lead to ultimate triumph and freedom from repression. *Hamlet* to an even greater extent achieves its stature through extreme contrasts of violence and introspection, while *Hunnenschlacht* is alive with a whirling chromaticism and insistent rhythm making terms such as marziale, eroico and trionfante as central to its theme as in *Hungaria*. Again, *Die Ideale* may commence with a gloomy quote from Schiller but all possible pessimism is resolved by Liszt's preoccupation with duality; with triumph and defeat, good and evil, etc. All these qualities are conveyed by orchestra and conductor in a way that tells you that true virtuosity is achieved through discipline rather than a more generalised and garish drama. This finely recorded disc is a glorious addition to the series.

Via crucis

Liszt Via Crucis **Satie/Cage** Socrate
Dezsö Ránki, Edit Klukon pfs
Budapest Music Center BMCCD100 (61' · DDD) ⓕ

The way John Cage arranged Erik Satie's *Socrate* for two pianos is simple and quite ingenious. He dovetails Satie's original piano accompaniment between both instruments and generally replicates the vocal line in unison octaves deployed in different registers. As a result, together with the loss of text, we get no sense of the original's dry, declamatory drama. But we do get Satie's ambling gait, pretty harmonies and, especially in the final pages, stark simplicity.

Without choral forces and the organ's sustaining power, Liszt's *Via Crucis* (based on the 14 Stations of the Cross) emerges as a rather severe exercise where bare-bone single lines shuttle between bleak block chords and *tremolos*. Sometimes it sounds static, yet certain moments prove quite effective, such as Station 11's pounded-out opening chords that mirror Christ being nailed to the Cross. The Ránki/Klukon duo make the best case for these arrangements and play with sustained, long-lined concentration and intelligent dynamic scaling that is far more difficult to achieve than it appears to the casual ear. In any event, if you're interested in these works without singers, this excellently engineered release recommends itself.

Piano Sonata in B minor, S178

Liszt Piano Sonata. Hungarian Rhapsody No 6
Brahms Two Rhapsodies, Op 79 **Schumann** Piano Sonata No 2 in G minor, Op 22
Martha Argerich pf
DG Galleria 437 252-2GGA (64' · ADD) Recorded 1963-72 ⓜ❍❍❍➍

 No one could accuse Martha Argerich of unstructured rêverie or dalliance and her legendary DG performance of the Liszt Sonata from 1972 suggests a unique level of both technical and musical achievement. Her prodigious fluency unites with a trail-blazing temperament, and Valhalla itself never ignited to such effect as at the central *Andante*'s climax. Both here and in the final *Prestissimo* there are reminders that Argerich has always played octaves like single notes, displaying a technique that few if any could equal. There are times when she becomes virtually engulfed in her own virtuosity yet this is a performance to make other pianists turn pale and ask, how is it possible to play like this?

Argerich's Schumann, too, is among her most meteoric, headlong flights. In terms of sheer brilliance she leaves all others standing yet, amazingly, still allows us fleeting glimpses of Eusebius (the poetic dreamer in Schumann, and one of his most dearly cherished fictions). The Brahms and Liszt *Rhapsodies*, taken from Argerich's very first 1963 DG disc, are among the most incandescent yet refined on record. The sound, when you bother to notice it, is excellent. (The Liszt and Brahms works, are also included in a compilation disc reviewed in the Collections section; refer to the Index.)

Piano Sonata. Fünf Kleine Klavierstücke, S192 – in E; in A flat; in F sharp; in F sharp. Nuages gris, S199. La lugubre gondole, S200 (2nd version). RW Venezia, S201. Schlaflos, Frage und Antwort, S203. En rêve, S207. Unstern: sinistre, disastro, S208
Paul Lewis pf
Harmonia Mundi HMC90 1845 (60' · DDD)   Ⓕ**O**

Once considered musically incomprehensible and technically unplayable, the Liszt Sonata is now part of the repertoire of virtually every pianist of note. Yet even in a crowded marketplace (where Horowitz, Gilels, Richter, Argerich, Brendel, Pollini and others jostle for attention) Paul Lewis's recording stands out for its breadth, mastery and shining musicianship.

Eschewing all obvious display, he concentrates on the Sonata's monumental weight, grandeur and ever-elusive inner poetry. His sense of drama is dark and intense, and his reading of the central *Andante sostenuto* alone puts his performance in the highest league. Lewis's octaves in the final *Prestissimo* blaze before the retrospective coda are of a pulverising strength; with him the Sonata regains its stature among music's most formidable milestones.

Moving to the music of Liszt's final years, Lewis ranges from *Nuages gris*, much admired by Stravinsky, its language anticipating Debussy, Bartók and even Schoenberg, to *Unstern* (literally, and in Shakespearean terms, 'unstarred'), music of a sinister violence. If there's solace in the relatively benign world of the four *Little Pieces* and *En rêve* it's quickly shattered by *La lugubre gondole II*, a desolate elegy anticipating Wagner's funeral.

This isn't music for late-night listening, more an invitation to 'sleepless question and answer'. But these pieces are played with a rapt and haunting sense of their attenuated beauty, making this one of the finest, most intelligently planned Liszt recitals for many years. Harmonia Mundi's sound is of demonstration quality.

Piano Sonata. Vallée d'Obermann. Funérailles. Rapsodie espagnole
Arnaldo Cohen pf
BIS BIS-CD1253 (73' · DDD)   Ⓕ**OO**

Arnaldo Cohen's playing blazes with the risk-taking, spontaneity and urgency of a live concert. His *Funérailles* is a truly great performance, perfectly structured, a real sense of angry desolation, and the central 'cavalry charge' emerging more logically from its context than in any other account. In the Rhapsody, he provides the requisite bravura thrills but also does Liszt the honour of eschewing the vapidity which so many bring to

LISZT PIANO SONATA – IN BRIEF

Martha Argerich
DG 437 252-2GGA   Ⓜ**OOO**▷
A performance of torrential passion and technical mastery, Argerich's Sonata is a work of huge emotional range. Dating from 1972, this is a roller-coaster ride that still thrills and moves.

Mikhail Pletnev
DG 476 7237   Ⓜ▷
A real demonstration of Pletnev's pianist mastery: he demonstrates a staggering range of colour and texture, all couched with spectacular technical ease.

Nikolai Demidenko
Hyperion Helios CDH55184   Ⓜ
An imperious and beautifully conceived performance that veers between playing of terrific weight and fingerwork of a filigree lightness. There's phenomenal authority in Demidenko's approach that some might find dauting, but it's most impressive pianism.

Claudio Arrau
Philips 464 713-2PM   Ⓜ▷
Few pianists coveyed the opulence of Liszt's work as did Claudio Arrau, a master of the Olympian stance. This is a towering achievement and a great memento of a major artist.

Paul Lewis
Harmonia Mundi HMC90 1845   Ⓕ**O**
A deeply impressive recording by a pianist of the younger generation demonstrating aristocratic playing and a real sense of poetry.

Arnaldo Cohen
BIS BIS-CD1253   Ⓕ
A powerful and technically hugely impressive performance from Cohen which sets this mighty work in an interesting context. Fine recorded sound.

Yundi Li
DG 471 585-2   Ⓕ▷
A splendid second disc from this impressive young Chinese pianist (a Chopin Piano Concerto winner). He is clearly a Lisztian of serious credentials and draws a host of fabulous colours from his instrument which have been sensitively captured by DG.

'Wild About Liszt'
Earl Wild pf
Ivory Classics ② 📀 IC77777   Ⓕ**OO**
No survey of the Liszt sonata would be complete without representation of one of the US's most virtuoso virtusosos. Earl Wild's sonata wasn't commercially recorded for this video but the sound is acceptable. But what playing!

it. *Vallée d'Obermann* emerges as an inspired dramatic tone poem, to which Cohen adds the element of white-hot improvisation; in colour and temperament he yields little to Horowitz's famous RCA recording (nla). The Liszt Sonata, Cohen's second recording, mingles narrative and textual clarity with a musical maturity and heady virtuosity in the Richter class.

Piano Sonata. Two Légendes, S175. Scherzo and March, S177
Nikolai Demidenko pf
Helios CDH55184 (67' · DDD)   Ⓕ

Even in an impossibly competitive field Demidenko's Liszt Sonata stands out among the most imperious and articulate. His opening is precisely judged and once the Sonata is under its inflammatory way his virtuosity is of a kind to which few other pianists could pretend. The combination of punishing weight and a skittering, light-fingered agility makes for a compulsive vividness yet his economy in the first *cantando espressivo*, sung without a trace of luxuriance or indulgence, is no less typical. There are admittedly times when he holds affection at arm's length, but just as you're wondering why he commences the central *Andante* so loudly he at once withdraws into a wholly apposite remoteness or reticence. The final climax, too, is snapped off not only with a stunning sense of Lisztian drama but also with an even truer sense and understanding of Liszt's score and instructions. Demidenko's couplings are no less autocratic, with a capacity to make seemingly arbitrary ideas sound unarguable. His *Légendes* are far from benign, yet his tautness and graphic sense of their poetic power carry their own authority. He's in his element in the *Scherzo* and March's diablerie, music which, coming after the two *Légendes*, affects one like an upside-down crucifix, or some dark necromancy. The recording is outstanding.

'Wild About Liszt'
Includes American, British and Dutch TV broadcast performances; documentary and performances from Wynyard in 1986 and a selection of audio-only interviews
Earl Wild pf
Ivory Classics ② 📀 IC77777
(6h 1' · NTSC · 4:3 · PCM stereo · 0)   ⒻOO

Earl Wild (born 1915) is the last great representative of those pianists directly influenced by the playing of Rachmaninov and Hoffman: he has an all-encompassing repertoire; he composes; he transcribes; he has one of the finest mechanisms in history; he produces some of the most beautiful sounds you will ever hear from the piano (as he says himself, he was brought up to play as though every member of the audience were blind).

Among history's very greatest Liszt pianists, he is heard here in no fewer than three full-length Liszt recitals. They were recorded before an audience over three evenings in July 1986 at

Wynyard, the ancestral home of the Ninth Marquess of Londonderry, to commemorate the 100th anniversary of the death of Liszt.

'Liszt the Poet' includes the Ballade No 2, a wonderfully proportioned *Dante* Sonata, *Funérailles* and *Mephisto* Waltz No 1 with Wild's own and (in my opinion) much improved ending; 'Liszt the Transcriber' has 'hyphenated' Bach, Verdi, Schumann, Chopin, Paganini (stunning) and the Beethoven-Liszt Symphony No 1; 'Liszt the Virtuoso' is dominated by the B minor Sonata. Though not professionally filmed, the sound recording is quite acceptable while the picture quality is second generation video. There is also an enjoyable, homespun documentary of Wild's visit to Wynyard, the tour of the jaw-dropping estate and its immense house (boasting its own organ and played briefly by the pianist) conducted by the piano-loving Marquess himself.

On the second DVD is a 1974 BBC recital/interview with the much-missed Robin Ray who elicits the memorable quote that 'the difference between playing a piece like the d'Albert Scherzo and, say, Beethoven Op 111 is that in the d'Albert you are a decorator; in the Beethoven you are an architect. A pianist should be able to be both.' There's an interview on the occasion of Wild's 90th birthday concert at the Concertgebouw and an additional 124 minutes of audio features: Wild lecturing (with some wickedly funny anecdotes) in 2003, interviewed by John Amis for the BBC in 1986 and Sharon Eisenhour for Philadelphia's WUHY station in 1982. What a cornucopia!

Années de pèlerinage

Années de pèlerinage – Première année. Venezia e Napoli, S162
Sergio Fiorentino pf
APR APR5583 (72' · ADD) Recorded 1962-3   OO

The third volume of Sergio Fiorentino's early Liszt recordings made during the 60s unites the contemplative (volume 1) and the virtuoso (volume 2). These performances are of a rare virtuosity and imaginative delicacy, and it's doubtful whether the sense of bells ringing gently and exultantly through the crystalline Swiss air in 'Les cloches de Genève' has often been caught more evocatively. He rightly makes the gloomy and Byronic 'Vallée d'Obermann' the nodal and expressive centre of the cycle, fully justifying and sustaining his audaciously slow tempo (after all, it's marked *lento*) and, throughout, his performances are alive with the sort of fantasy and freedom that eluded Jorge Bolet in his more cautious *Gramophone* Award-winning Decca recording.

Sadly Fiorentino recorded only one work from the official Italian *Année* ('Sposalizio') so this disc ends with its supplement, *Venezia e Napoli*, a garland of encores that show off his poetic resource and, in the 'Tarantella', quicksilver brilliance. His early Saga recordings often suggested an enviable, if occasionally flippant facility, but here he's at his finest; even when he playfully tampers with the score (in 'Les cloches de Genève) it's usually to Liszt's advantage. The transfers have come up trumps.

Années de pèlerinage, année 2: Italie, S161 – Sposalizio; Il penseroso; Canzonetta del Salvatore Rosa; Sonetto 47 del Petrarca; Sonetto 104 del Petrarca; Sonetto 123 del Petrarca; Après une lecture du Dante (Fantasia quasi sonata). Mephisto Waltz No 1, 'Der Tanz in der Dorfschenke', S514
Libor Novacek pf
Landor Records LAN278 (73' · DDD)   Ⓕ

Libor Novacek's command of the keyboard is very impressive and he aspires to the highest interpretative ideals in this Second Book of *Années de pèlerinage* which, like the First, contains some of Liszt's finest music.

This artist takes time to express his views about these masterpieces. He is not in a hurry, not even in overtly virtuoso pieces such as the *Dante* Sonata and the First *Mephisto Waltz*. There is an expansive dignity to Novacek's playing that spares them from falling into a trough of banality, as often happens. How a similar approach works at a slow tempo (basically *lento*) may be heard in the Petrarch Sonnet No 123 where Liszt tries to convey its spirit through numerous marks of expression. Novacek doesn't balk at observing them. Nor does he balk at emotional involvement with the music; and both virtues are duplicated everywhere. An unobtrusively excellent recording.

Années de pèlerinage – Année 1: Suisse, S160; Année 2: Italie, S161; Année 3, S163
Daniel Grimwood pf
SFZ Music ② SFZM0208 (129' · DDD)   Ⓕ**OO**

Listening to Liszt's musical description of his travels through Switzerland and Italy affords the same kind of pleasure as reading a prose journal. Daniel Grimwood, fast making a name for himself as an original and discriminating musician, has chosen to play the cycle on an Erard piano of 1851, an instrument by Liszt's favourite maker built at around the same time as he was radically revising the 16 earlier works that would make up the first two volumes of *Années de pèlerinage*. Tuned to the (unequal) Bach-Lehman temperament (a'=440), the Erard produces the sound Liszt would have heard when composing and playing these works.

This would be just another interesting period-instrument recording were it not for the performances. These are out of the top drawer, for Grimwood is not merely a keyboard colourist (*Au bord d'une source*, for instance, and the two *Thrénodies* from Book 3 emerge as early examples of Impressionism, enhanced by the Érard's harp-like treble register in quieter passages); he throws himself with abandon into the bravura writing of *Vallée d'Obermann* and the *Dante Sonata*, and turns in a delightfully perky *Canzo-*

netta del Salvator Rosa. It's an enthralling journey that throws new light on these poetic ideals of the Romantic era and, with hardly a pause between each item, leaves the listener, as it would any traveller on the Grand Tour, awed by the wonders of nature, the spectacular scenery and the glories of Italian culture.

Additional recommendation

Années de pèlerinage – Deuxième année: Après une lecture du Dante
Coupled with: Valse oubliée No 4,. Mephisto Waltzes Nos 1, 2 and 4. Die Zelle in Nonnenwerth. Ballade No 2. Harmonies poétiques et réligieuses No 9
Andsnes pf
EMI 570022-2 (74' · DDD)   Ⓕ
   Leif Ove Andsnes's *Dante* Sonata is outstandingly well paced and his Ballade excitingly coloured and powerfully projected.

---

12 Grandes Etudes, S137

Complete Solo Piano Music, Volume 34
Douze Grandes Etudes, S137. Morceau de salon, S142
Leslie Howard pf
Hyperion CDA66973 (76' · DDD)   Ⓕ

In this first recording of the concert version of the *Douze Grandes Etudes* (1837), Leslie Howard brings his customary technical wizardry to bear on this outrageously difficult music in an arresting virtuoso display that demonstrates Liszt's consummate skill at transforming musical material. Moreover, despite Liszt's exhortation that only the later revisions of the studies should be played, there's a great deal to recommend the 1837 set, as these performances attest. The extreme technical demands of these pieces have led to critical scorn, but the challenges they contain aren't designed merely for display, but are the result of the composer's comprehensive exploitation of the piano's expressive capabilities. Saint-Saëns said that 'in Art a difficulty overcome is a thing of beauty' and, in the present instance, Howard's own triumph over the monumental difficulties posed by these pieces reveals the astonishing beauty of Liszt's 'orchestral' use of tone colour and sparkling virtuosity.

---

19 Hungarian Rhapsodies, S244

No 1 in C sharp minor; **No 2** in C sharp minor; **No 3** in B flat; **No 4** in E flat; **No 5** in E minor, 'Héroïde-Elégiaque'; **No 6** in D flat; **No 7** in D minor; **No 8** in F sharp minor, 'Capriccio'; **No 9** in E flat, 'Carnival in Pest'; **No 10** in E; **No 11** in A minor; **No-12** in C sharp minor; **No 13** in A minor; **No 14** in F minor; **No 15** in A minor 'Rákóczy'; **No 16** in A minor, 'For the Munkascy festivities in Budapest'; **No-17** in D minor; **No 18** in F sharp minor, 'On the occasion of the Hungarian Exposition in Budapest'; **No 19** in D minor

Hungarian Rhapsodies Nos 1-19. Rhapsodie
espagnole, S254
Roberto Szidon pf
DG ② 453 034-2GTA2 (156' · ADD) Recorded 1972
⊙⊙⤵

This well-known set has been in and out of the
catalogue a number of times, always to considerable acclaim. And the performances are every bit
as good as everybody has always said. Although
individual readings of isolated *Rhapsodies* may
surpass Szidon's, taken as a whole this is certainly the most pleasurable set available. Szidon's technique is especially geared towards
clarity of passagework and rhythmic precision
and he also possesses a convincingly dreamy
temperament that enables the slow passages to
emerge with a rare distinction. His technical
mastery is in no doubt and this is playing of great
flair, with a natural feeling for rubato. The *Rapsodie espagnole* is a welcome bonus. The sound is
sympathetic and vivid.

Harmonies poétiques..., S173

Harmonies poétiques et religieuses, S173
Steven Osborne pf
Hyperion ② two-for-the-price-of-one CDA67445
(84' · DDD) Ⓜ⊙⊙

Steven Osborne follows his superlative Hyperion
recording of Messiaen's *Vingt Regards sur
l'Enfant-Jésus* with Liszt's *Harmonies poétiques et
religieuses*, surely a precursor of Messiaen's masterpiece. Attuned to the mystic heart at the centre
of Liszt's Catholicism, Osborne once more shows
the sort of stylistic ease and tonal magic that come
to very few young pianists. Sacred and profane
love blend with a wholly Lisztian alchemy.
In 'Invocation', the magnificent gateway to the
cycle, Osborne offers up its quasi-orchestral rhetoric with immense power but without bombast.
The 'Bénédiction' is daringly understated in pages
that can all too easily topple into lavish, tear-laden
emotionalism. 'Pensées des morts' is a triumph of
alternating anguish and exultation. If all conventional pomp and circumstance are erased by the
brisk tempo in the opening of 'Funérailles',
Osborne's performance is still a marvel of concentrated musicianship and indiv- iduality. In the
Andante lagrimoso he conjures an uncanny stillness
in music whose painful climbing looks ahead to
the dark, attenuated utterances of Fauré's final
years, while the final 'Cantique d'Amour' resolves
all past torment in a paean of praise for the union
of two traditionally opposed ideas of love.
Few more radiant or deeply considered Liszt
recordings have ever been made. Hyperion's
sound is immaculate.

Hungarian Themes..., S242

Complete Solo Piano Music, Volume 29. Hungarian
Themes and Rhapsodies, S242
Leslie Howard pf

Hyperion ② CDA66851/2 (159' · DDD) Ⓕ

When listening to these 22 pieces, officially entitled *Magyar Dalok* and *Magyar Rapszódiák*, you at
once realise you've heard many a snatch of them
before. And not surprisingly, for in fact they're
the source of most of what eventually emerged as
Liszt's world-wide best-sellers, the *Hungarian
Rhapsodies*. The composer revels in the lavishly
decorative, cimbalom-coloured, improvisational
style of the gypsies, in the process making
demands on the pianist variously described by
Leslie Howard in his insert-notes as 'devil-may-
care, frighteningly difficult, frenetic, hand-split-
ting' and so on. Whether because of Liszt's own
waning interest in platform pyrotechnics, or the
fact that only he could really bring them off, simplification seems to have been the primary aim
when recasting these first flings as *Hungarian
Rhapsodies*. But as Howard reveals, there are losses
as well as gains in the maturer Liszt. Despite
moments of protracted rodomontade there's a
vast amount of enjoyment to be had.

Petrarch Sonnets

Complete Solo Piano Music, Volume 21
Soirées musicales, S424. Soirées italiennes, S411.
Nuits d'été à Pausilippe, S399. Tre sonetti del
Petrarca, S158. Venezia e Napoli, S159. La serenata e
L'orgia (Grande fantaisie sur des motifs des Soirées
musicales), S422. La pastorella dell'Alpi e Li marinari
(Deuxième fantaisie sur des motifs des Soirées
musicales), S423
Leslie Howard pf
Hyperion ② CDA66661/2 (157' · DDD) Ⓕ

The two discs comprising Vol 21 of Howard's
enormous cycle remind us of the young Liszt's
love affair with Italy, the spotlight now falling
primarily-on frolics with Rossini, Mercadante
and Donizetti in lighter, lyrical vein. The special
interest of the two original sets of pieces included,
i.e. the three *Sonetti del Petrarca* and the four *Venezia e Napoli*, is that Howard introduces them as
first written (*c*1839 and 1840 respectively) before
Liszt's characteristically painstaking later revisions. There's much to enjoy in the playing itself,
especially in simpler contexts when gondolas
glide through calm waters, or lovers dream, or
shepherds dance. Melody, so important throughout, is nicely sung.

Totentanz

Impromptu in F sharp, S191. Nuages gris, S199. La
lugubre gondola, S200 Nos 1 & 2. Unstern: sinistre,
disastro, S208. Totentanz, S525. Danse macabre
(Saint-Saëns), S555. Réminiscences des Huguenots
(Meyerbeer), S412
Arnaldo Cohen pf
Naxos 8 553852 (71' · DDD) Ⓢ⤵

Arnaldo Cohen is as poetically and imaginatively intrepid as he's technically coruscating,

and all these performances offer refinement and ferocity in equal proportion. Few pianists could identify or engage so closely with music that hovers on the edge of silence or extinction (*Nuages gris*, *La lugubre gondola* Nos-1 and 2), or that sparks and sports with a truly devilish intent (*Danse macabre*, *Totentanz* and so on). In the *Danse macabre* the music emerges from Cohen's fingers supercharged with malevolence. On the other hand he can send the F sharp *Impromptu* spiralling into a true sense of its ecstasy, or momentarily inflect *Nuages gris* in a manner that accentuates rather than detracts from its abstraction and economy. He makes something frighteningly bleak out of *Unstern* (or 'Evil Star'), with its savagely dissonant climax and its unresolved hymnal solace, yet is no less at home in *Réminiscences des Huguenots*, dismissing ambuscades of treacherous skips, octaves and every other technical terror with a telling mix of verve and nonchalance. These, then, are performances of rare lucidity, virtuoso voltage and trenchancy, and all quite excellently recorded.

Transcendental Etudes

12 Etudes d'exécution transcendante, S139
Jenö Jandó *pf*
Naxos 8 553119 (64' · DDD) ⓈⒹ➤

The 12 *Transcendental Etudes* are the ultimate test of quasi-orchestral virtuosity and of the capacity to achieve nobility and true eloquence. Jandó perhaps lacks diabolic *frisson* in the more ferocious numbers but his performances, overall, aren't disfigured by wilful, sensational attributes or hysteria. No-1 is an impressive, dramatically pointed, curtain-raiser, and he can hell-raise with assurance in 'Mazeppa'. His 'Feux follets' hardly sparks with the brilliance of, say, some of the full-blooded accounts of certain Russian artists, but even when it hardly modulates from study to tone-poem it's still more than capable (higher praise than you might think where such intricacy is concerned). He flashes an impressive rapier at the start of 'Eroica' and there's plenty of swagger and facility in the so-called 'Appassionata' *étude*. 'Chasse-neige', too, proceeds with a fine sense of its menacing start to a howling, elemental uproar before returning to distant thunder. Jandó is less assured in introspection, yet it has to be said that all-encompassing versions of the *Transcendental Etudes* are hard to come by. Jandó is impressively recorded.

Transcriptions

Oberon – Overture, S574 (Weber). Fantasia on themes from Le nozze di Figaro and Don Giovanni, S697 (Mozart). Ernani Paraphrase, S432. Miserere du Trovatore, S433. Rigoletto Paraphrase, S434. Réminiscences de Boccanegra, S438 (Verdi). Valse de concert sur deux motifs du Lucia et Parisina, S214/3 (Donizetti). Réminiscences de Robert le diable (Meyerbeer) – Cavatine; Valse infernale, S413. Les

Adieux – Rêverie sur un motif de Roméo et Juliette, S409 (Gounod). Schwanengesang and Marsch from Hunyadi László, S405 (Erkel). Lohengrin – Elsa's Bridal Procession, S445/2; Two Pieces, S446. Fantasy on themes from Rienzi, S439 (Wagner)
Leslie Howard *pf*
Hyperion ② CDA66861/2 (153' · DDD) Ⓕ

Liszt's operatic outings range from literal transcriptions, such as the opening *Oberon* Overture, to the most free fantasias, like that on motives from *Rienzi* at the end of the disc. The sequence is artfully planned to provide the maximum contrast between Liszt as lion and dove, with four of the 16 items earmarked as 'first recordings'. Of these, the Gounod *Roméo et Juliette* Rêverie is a tender, nocturne-like idyll that not for a second outstays its welcome. Liszt scholars may nevertheless be still more grateful for Howard's rescue of the other three, and first and foremost the nearly 22-minute long Fantasia on themes from *Le nozze di Figaro and Don Giovanni*. Though self-indulgently protracted, its thematic interweavings *en route* still take your breath away. With Verdi and Wagner we're on more familiar ground, where it goes without saying that Howard has formidable CD rivals. But throughout the disc there's a spaciousness in his characterisation that far more often than not compensates for momentary technical strain or loss of finesse. His tonal range is certainly wide, ranging from the deep, dark, brooding intensity he finds for the *Ernani* and *Il trovatore* excerpts to his translucent delicacy in the upper reaches of Gounod's Rêverie. Apart from a slightly metallic touch above a certain dynamic level in the treble, the recorded sound quality can best be described in a nutshell as ripe.

Adelaïde, S466. Sechs geistliche Lieder, S467. An die ferne Geliebte, S469. Lieder von Goethe, S468 (Beethoven). Lieder, S547 (Mendelssohn). Lieder, S485 (Dessauer). Er ist gekommen in Sturm und Regen, S488. Lieder, S489 (Franz). Two songs, S554 (Rubinstein). Lieder von Robert und Clara Schumann, S569. Provenzalisches Lied, S570. Two songs, S567. Frühlingsnacht, S568. Widmung, S566 (Schumann)
Leslie Howard *pf*
Hyperion ② CDA66481/2 (147' · DDD) Ⓕ

Few composers have ever shown a more insatiable interest in the music of others than Liszt, or devoted more time to transcribing it for the piano. Here Howard plays 60 of Liszt's 100 or so song transcriptions, including several by the lesser-known Dessauer, Franz and (as composers) Anton Rubinstein and Clara Schumann, alongside Beethoven, Mendelssohn and Robert Schumann. The selection at once reveals Liszt's variety of approach as a transcriber no less than his unpredictability of choice. Sometimes, as most notably in Beethoven's concert aria, *Adelaïde*, the keyboard virtuoso takes over: he links its two sections with a concerto-like cadenza as well as carrying bravura into an amplified coda. But after the dazzling pyrotechnics of many of his operatic arrangements, the surprise is the self-effacing simplicity of so much included here.

The five songs from Schumann's *Liederalbum für die Jugend* are literal enough to be played by young children. Even his later (1880) fantasy-type transcriptions of Rubinstein's exotic *The Asra* has the same potent economy of means. Howard responds keenly to mood and atmosphere, and never fails, pianistically, to emphasise the 'singer' in each song – in response to the actual verbal text that Liszt was nearly always conscientious enough to write into his scores. The recording is clean and true.

Christus, S3

Christus
Henriette Bonde-Hansen *sop* **Iris Vermillion** *mez*
Michael Schade *ten* **Andreas Schmidt** *bar* **Cracow Chamber Choir; Stuttgart Gächinger Kantorei Stuttgart Radio Symphony Orchestra / Helmuth Rilling**
Hänssler Classic Exclusive Series ③ CD98 121
(162' · DDD · T/t) Recorded live 1997   Ⓕ

Christus is essentially a contemplative work and so could really be said to exist in a different time-scale to most music. Much of the opening part, the 'Christmas Oratorio', uses very simple melody and harmony, and is studiously undramatic. Helmuth Rilling does well not to charge it with too much colour, and, if listened to as meditation rather than drama, what can seem static takes on a positive atmosphere as a group of long reflections on the Christmas events. This is a far cry from the sensational Liszt of the early virtuoso years, not yet reaching the terse, inward pieces of the last years. There's greater drama in the middle part, 'After Epiphany', especially in the superb scene of Christ walking on the water. Although there's still the suggestion that a wonder is being contemplated, Liszt stirs up a terrific storm. This part also includes the beautiful setting of the Beatitudes, sung by Andreas Schmidt with a degree of uncertainty which he entirely sheds when he comes to pronounce the sentences in Part 3 ('Passion and Resurrection') for the scene of the Agony in the Garden. The long *Stabat mater* is beautifully controlled by Rilling. His soloists support him well. The recording does excellent justice to Liszt's wide-ranging orchestration.

Henry Litolff   French 1818-1891

French composer and pianist. He was a concert artist, conductor, music publisher, festival organiser, piano teacher and salon composer but is remembered chiefly for his four piano concertos entitled concertos symphoniques (c1844-67); their conception as symphonies with piano obbligato greatly impressed Liszt (who dedicated his Concerto No 1 to Litolff), and their scherzos contain some of his most brilliant writing.
GROVEmusic

Concertos symphoniques

Concertos symphoniques – No 3 in E flat, Op 45;
No 5 in C minor, Op 123
Peter Donohoe *pf* **BBC Scottish Symphony Orchestra / Andrew Litton**
Hyperion CDA67210 (66' · DDD)   Ⓕ●

Litolff's dauntingly ambitious structures accommodate every possible style, looking forwards and backwards Janus-style, yet reaching out in the strange almost Alkanesque oddity of the Fifth Concerto's last two movements towards a more personal and distinctive style. Admired by Tchaikovsky, Liszt and Berlioz (though with some telling reservations), Litolff enjoyed a hectic career which is mirrored in writing of a formidable intricacy. So even if claims that he was 'the English Liszt' and that his development sections are similar to late Beethoven seem far-fetched, the sheer energy and resource of Litolff's writing are absorbing. Few pianists could approach, let alone top, Peter Donohoe's blistering virtuosity in these works. His performances throughout are as rock-steady as they're dazzling, sweeping aside torrents of notes with both affection and authority. Hear him in the exultant whirl which opens the Third Concerto's finale, and you can only marvel at such unfaltering command, ideally complemented by Andrew Litton and the BBC Scottish orchestra.

Miguel Llobet   Catalan 1878-1938

Llobet is given credit for bringing the classical guitar into the modern musical world of international concert tours. He also contributed new works and transcriptions to the repertory and introduced the public to works by Falla, Villa-Lobos, Ponce and others. (Falla wrote Homenaje pour le tombeau de Claude Debussy in response to Llobet's persistent requests for a new work for guitar.) In 1925 he made the first electric recordings on the classical guitar. Llobet's tally of approximately 75 publications includes 13 known original compositions, among them his guitar arrangement of Catalan folk songs, Diez canciones populares catalanas (1899-1918); of these the best known, El mestre (c1900), is harmonically one of the most advanced guitar works of its time and was much admired by Segovia.

Guitar works

'Respuesta'
Llobet Catalan Folksongs. Seven Original Compositions. Five Preludes. Four Historical Arrangements **Quijano** Three estilos argentinos (arr Llobet)
Stefano Grondona *gtr*
Stradivarius ② STR33770 (87' · DDD)   Ⓕ

Miguel Llobet was a supremely gifted performer whose playing impressed not only fellow guitarists Segovia and Tárrega but also Albéniz, Fauré, Debussy and Ravel. This set brings together all of Llobet's compositions for solo guitar. Grondona plays an 1887 Torres and, for the *Canciones catalanas*, adopts gut treble strings and silver-wound silk basses.

The playing is exceptional. Apart from employing generous *rubato* and *portamenti* – integral to the correct interpretation of this repertoire – Grondona gently emphasises Llobet's adopting a certain fingering or register in order to exploit every resource of the guitar. This is as obvious in 'Respuesta', the virtuoso title-track from the *Seven Original Compositions*, with its rapid *tremolo* and arpeggio effects, as it is in the veiled world of pianissimo harmonics found in many of the Catalan folksong arrangements (the introduction to 'La Preço de Lleida' being a perfect example). An outstanding release in every way.

Alonso Lobo

Spanish c1555-1617

A choirboy at Seville Cathedral, Lobo studied at Osuna University and was a canon there by 1591. He assisted Guerrero at Seville Cathedral from 1591, becoming maestro de capilla of Toledo Cathedral in 1593 and of Seville in 1604. He published masses and motets, some for double choir (1602); many other sacred works are in MSS. Victoria esteemed him as an equal and he was long regarded as one of the finest Spanish composers.

GROVEmusic

Masses

Lobo Missa Maria Magdalene. O quam suavis est, Domine. Quam pulchri sunt. Ave regina caelorum. Versa est in luctum. Credo quod Redemptor. Vivo ego, dicit Dominus. Ave Maria **Guerrero** Maria Magdalene
The Tallis Scholars / Peter Phillips
Gimell CDGIM031 (63' · DDD · T/t) Ⓕ🅑➔

Alonso Lobo is best known for one work, his setting of the funerary *Versa est in luctum*. This is undoubtedly a masterpiece of its kind but to have it placed alongside other pieces from his 1602 collection affords a welcome chance to assess his composition skills more fully. Lobo's music is sonorous in a manner that's direct and unfussy in effect, though often highly expressive, and always structured with the utmost technical control. Take, for example, the *Ave Maria*, an 8-in-4 canon (in other words, four more voices are generated from the original quartet) which emanates a sense of absolute serenity. In fact, each of the motets explores a different aspect of the compositional techniques brought to the genre, and the Mass is equally fine, Lobo making the spacious textures of the motet, *Maria Magdalene* by his teacher Guerrero a distinguishing feature of his own setting of the

Ordinary. The Tallis Scholars are on superb form, the overall sound vibrant and immediate with solo sections providing contrast through a more introspective approach. Even if you've never bought a CD of late-Renaissance polyphony, try this one. You'll be bowled over.

Ego flos campi. Lamentations. Missa O rex gloriae. Missa Simile est regnum caelorum
Choir of King's College London / David Trendell
ASV Gaudeamus CDGAU311 (75' · DDD · T/t) Ⓕ

This CD confirms the high calibre of Lobo's sacred polyphony: the excellent mixed choir present two masses (*O rex gloriae* and *Simile est regnum caelorum*, based on motets by Palestrina and Guerrero respectively, and printed in Madrid in 1602), together with a magnificent setting of the *Lamentations* and the motet *Ego flos campi*.

The masses have carefully honed vocal lines and that sense of vertical spaciousness that characterises the sacred polyphony of 16th-century Iberian composers. The choir sing with absolute conviction and total security, as if they really know the music rather than as if it were a very competent read-through. Trendell paces it all well, the tempo never seeming forced or plodding. The motet is deservedly popular, but the recently discovered six-voice setting of the *Lamentations* is an absolute winner, with meltingly beautiful suspensions, often in the upper voices, in the Hebrew letter sections; the choir again captures just the right degree of intensity without slipping into over-indulgence.

The fresh sound of this student choir combines energy and clarity in a most appealing way. This fine recording will enrich anyone's collection of Renaissance polyphony.

Pietro Locatelli

Italian 1695-1764

Locatelli studied the violin in Rome and in 1717-23 played in the basilica of S Lorenzo in Damaso. He was appointed to the Mantuan court in 1725 but gave concerts elsewhere (especially Germany), gaining a high reputation; his playing was noted for its virtuosity and sweetness. From 1729 he worked mostly as a teacher and orchestral director in Amsterdam. Locatelli wrote almost exclusively sonatas and concertos. The first of his four concerto grosso sets (1721) is the most Corellian (particularly its Christmas Concerto); his later music is more progressive. His influential L'arte del violino (1733) contains 12 solo violin concertos in a Venetian idiom like Vivaldi's and 24 caprices for solo violin. Among Locatelli's other works are solo and trio sonatas.

GROVEmusic

Concerti grossi

12 Concerti grossi, Op 1 – No 2; No 4; No 7; No 8, 'Christmas'; No 9; No 11

Freiburg Baroque Orchestra /
Gottfried von der Goltz vn
Harmonia Mundi HMC90 1889 (61' · DDD)   Ⓕ

By offering us a single CD of just six of these Op 1 Concerti grossi, published in 1721 when Locatelli was in his mid-twenties, Freiburg Baroque Orchestra allow us to imagine that they have selected the ones they really believe in. It also enables them to start the disc with its most enchanting music, the first movement of Concerto No 11, in which a glorious solo violin cantilena soars soulfully and searchingly over a gently chugging orchestral accompaniment. It is a gripping, haunting opening and the promise it offers is duly realised in the superb music-making that follows. Such quality is only what we have come to expect from the Freiburgers, of course. Here they present us with a hearteningly full, satisfyingly fibrous string sound, together with all their usual hallmarks of fine ensemble and naturally lively and intelligent musicianship. First-rate Baroque concertos in first-class performances.

into overemphasis and that's beautifully attuned to Loewe's illustrative manner. Fischer-Dieskau and Demus are ideal partners, Demus responding quickly and with an ear for the sinister that often marks the piano writing and its subtle use of motive. Not just a composer of ballads, Loewe was also a Lieder writer in the great German tradition, and this is too often overlooked, but not by Fischer-Dieskau.

Two songs alone, from this magisterial collection, are witness to Loewe's stature. They are settings of the wonderful poems from the second part of *Faust* in which Lynceus, the lynx-eyed watcher on the tower, sees the magical appearance, of Helen of Troy herself. He, incarnating the gift of the perception of visual beauty, after a life of watching from his tower can conceive of nothing that could surpass this wonder; and, in the second song, hymns his gratitude to the gift of sight. Loewe's two settings are beautiful responses to the poetry of a great artist with the gift of an ideal simplicity. These two songs alone should persuade the responsive listener to make the exploration.

Carl Loewe   German 1796-1869

Loewe, a pupil of Türk at Halle, began composing songs and instrumental pieces at an early age, also singing his own ballads to great acclaim. Among his finest early solo vocal works are settings of Goethe's Erlkönig *(1818) and Byron's* Hebrew Melodies *(Opp 4, 5, 13 and 14). He was a prolific composer in many media, but his other works, including the operas (notably* Emmy, *1842) and oratorios, string quartets and piano works (in particular some programmatic sonatas and the tone poem* Mazeppa, *Op 27), were not as acclaimed as his narrative songs. Their accompaniments and modified strophic style, incorporating dramatic and lyrical passages, make a vivid impression (eg* Archibald Douglas, *Op 128); the fairy element in many of his folklore settings (eg* Herr Oluf *and* Tom der Reimer*) creates colour and melodic interest. From 1820 to 1865 Loewe worked in Stettin as a conductor, organist and teacher, yet it was through his recital tours that he won international fame; the Viennese called him 'the north German Schubert'.*   **GROVE**music

Antonio Lotti   Italian c1667-1740

Lotti, a pupil of Legrenzi in Venice, became an organist at St Mark's in 1690, eventually becoming maestro di cappella (1736). He also taught at the Ospedale degli Incurabili (Galuppi was one of his pupils); he wrote sacred music for both institutions. From 1692 he composed operas, mostly serious: he presented c30, the last four (1717-19) in Dresden. His large output includes oratorios, secular cantatas, duets, madrigals, instrumental pieces and numerous masses, motets and psalms. Most of his sacred choral works have no orchestral accompaniment; many, such as a Miserere of 1733, remained in use long after his death. His output bridges the late Baroque and early Classical styles and his late works are notable for their elegance and skilful counterpoint.   **GROVE**music

Missa Sapientiae

Lotti Missa Sapientiae
Bach Magnificat in E flat, BWV243a
Balthasar-Neumann Choir and Ensemble /
Thomas Hengelbrock
Deutsche Harmonia Mundi 05472 77534-2
(62' · DDD · T/t)   Ⓕ

Lieder

Ballada and Lieder
Dietrich Fischer-Dieskau bar **Jörg Demus** pf
DG ② 449 516-2GX2 (156' · ADD · T/t)
Recorded 1968-79   Ⓜ🅾🅾

All the best-known ballads are included here, magnificently sung by a great artist at the height of his powers. *Edward, Herr Oluf, Heinrich der Vogler, Prince Eugen, Der Zauberlehrling*: these and others are sung with a wonderful sense of the graphic, conveyed through an appreciation of the colour of the words that never descends

Thanks to his only well-known piece, the eight-part *Crucifixus*, Antonio Lotti has a reputation as a Baroque conservative, fuddy-duddily turning out nothing but church music in old-fashioned, Palestrina-inspired counterpoint. Yet, if there were such men in 18th-century Italy, Lotti – singer, organist and later *maestro* at St Mark's in Venice, but also composer of around 20 operas – wasn't one of them. For proof one need only sample this impeccably 18th-century short Mass for soloists, choir and orchestra, a work that Bach and Handel made copies of, and which evidently left its mark on both of them.

Handel actually 'borrowed' two bits of it for oratorios, but further stylistic resemblances are plain to hear. As for Bach, it's hard to believe that the meandering choral chromaticisms and coaxing accompaniment of the 'Qui tollis' weren't in his mind when he fashioned the 'Crucifixus' of the B minor Mass. Furthermore, Lotti must have known Vivaldi personally; we don't who wrote first, but anyone familiar with the Vivaldi *Gloria* will spot similarities of approach in several movements. This is a fascinating find, and well performed by the pleasingly cohesive Balthasar-Neumann Ensemble, who convey its mood of bright confidence.

The coupling is Bach's *Magnificat* in its original E flat version, which differs from its better-known D major revision in several respects: the most significant are four irresistible extra movements for Christmas. Recordings are rare, though there is recent competition from Philippe Herreweghe. Of the two, Herreweghe's is the more 'traditional' performance, with a polished chorus, fine soloists and brassy trumpets. Hengelbrock achieves greater intimacy, and he's also more urgent.

Requiem

Requiem in F. Credo. Miserere
Balthasar-Neumann Choir and Ensemble / Thomas Hengelbrock
Deutsche Harmonia Mundi 05472 77507-2
(68' · DDD · T/t)   Ⓕ

Lotti's Requiem Mass in F major is considered by Thomas Hengelbrock the most important Requiem before Mozart's. It's full of expressive contrast: Lotti has an affection for a quasi-Palestrina style on the one hand and the skill to deploy more up-to-date techniques on the other. This Requiem is essentially in the late Baroque idiom, occasionally recalling certain of Vivaldi's larger sacred vocal pieces. The sections differ from the sequence usually encountered in later 18th-century Requiem Masses. There's neither *Sanctus*, 'Benedictus' nor *Agnus Dei*, but instead a very extended 'Dies irae' as well as a much shorter 'Requiem aeternam', *Kyrie* and Offertory. Full of theatrical gestures, supple polyphony, warmly seductive harmony and some beautiful melodies, the Requiem holds attention from start to finish. The contrasts are often striking, as between the hushed opening section and the awesome introduction to the 'Dies irae'. The *a cappella Miserere* is sung with clarity and finesse. The five-movement *Credo* is a supple piece for choir and strings with some affecting, shimmering harmonies in the 'Crucifixus'. As well as full mass settings, Lotti seems also to have favoured separate autonomous sections such as this, themselves subdivided into short units. The splendid performances bring this highly charged music to life.

Nicholas Ludford   English c1490-1557

He is considered to be one of the most important and innovative composers in early Tudor England. The majority of Ludford's festal settings of the Mass and his Magnificat are copied in the so-called Caius and Lambeth Choirbooks. Both books are enormous productions, copied by the same hand, and were probably commissioned by Edward Higgins, a prominent royal lawyer who held a canonry at St Stephen's from 1517, and who was Master of Arundel College, Sussex, from 1520. The two six-part masses (Missa 'Videte miraculum' and Missa 'Benedicta et venerabilis') best exemplify Ludford's command of full, rich and sonorous writing.

Missa Benedicta

Missa Benedicta. Ave cuius conceptio. Domine Jesu Christe
New College Choir, Oxford / Edward Higginbottom
K617 K617 206 (63' · DDD)   ⒻⓄⓄⓄ

 Though not as showy as Taverner, Ludford's more understated idiom is every bit as persuasive. Repeated listening reveals great subtlety in the handling of texture, an exhilarating sense of confidence in formal planning, and real melodic inspiration. The opening of each movement is identical, and excludes the trebles, whose subsequent appearance in a different context is nicely managed. From the point of view of repertoire this is a major issue.

Here, New College's trebles show how much young singers can achieve in the way of cohesiveness, coherence and sheer persuasiveness of melodic shape. That speaks volumes, considering that, of all the English choral repertory written for trebles, this is perhaps the most difficult for today's youngsters to master. It's difficult to argue that adult female singers are demonstrably better equipped than boys: the advantage of bigger lungs is offset by the careful choice and placement of breaths. For the rest, the tone of these particular trebles is expressive in itself.

Paweł Łukaszewski   Polish b1968

Born in the southern Polish city of Czestochowa, a major destination of pilgrimage for the celebrated Black Madonna icon of the Virgin Mary housed in the Paulist monastery of Jasna Góra, Lukaszewski has an understandable affinity with religious music. Musically he may perhaps be aligned with Górecki, Pärt and Tavener but he feels more drawn to traditional harmonies which he supplements by vocal effects.

Ave Maria. Beatus vir, Sanctus Paulus.
Beatus vir, Sanctus Antonius. Beatus vir, Sanctus

Martinus. Two Lenten Motets. O Antiphons.
Psalm 102. Nunc dimittis
Trinity College Choir, Cambridge / Stephen Layton
Hyperion CDA67639 (66' · DDD · T/t)   Ⓕ**⒪⒟**

This is a lovely disc of enchanting choral music. Possibly the Trinity College Choir does not always provide the warmth of tone such unashamedly expressive music demands, but that is more than compensated for by the sheer intensity of Stephen Layton's direction: only the hardest of musical hearts will remain unmelted by such committed interpretations.

It was for Layton that Paweł Łukaszewski produced his setting of the *Nunc dimittis*. In its beautifully measured phrases, immaculately tailored textures and ingenious use of light and shade to invoke light shining out of darkness, it is a gem which receives here a beautifully poised account. Effusive reference in the booklet to Łukaszewski's masterful handling of the concluding fade-out – 'a hackneyed effect in the hands of lesser composers' – did get the juices of critical scepticism running for a bit until heard, along with all the other potentially hackneyed choral effects (polytonal clusters in *Memento mei, Domine*, frequently reiterated dynamic contrasts in *Beatus vir, Sanctus Martinus*, continually repeated melodic and rhythmic motifs in *O Sapientia*), and realised that here is a composer who really is a true master of the art of *a cappella* writing and for whom other people's experiments and gimmicks are an essential tool in conveying a profound emotional message.

Once or twice – notably in a saccharine setting of the *Ave Maria* (although the purity of Rebecca Lancelot's voice manages to divert any cloying character) and an over-clichéd *Crucem tuam adoramus* – the musical quality is compromised by emotional effect, but all in all this is a lovely disc. It has been difficult to draw this CD out of the player, so frequently has it been played. There's no higher praise.

Jean-Baptiste Lully
Italian/French 1632-1687

A French composer of Italian birth, Lully was taken from Florence to Paris in 1646 by Roger de Lorraine, Chevalier de Guise, who placed him in the service of his niece, Mlle de Montpensier. At her court in the Tuileries Lully got to know the best in French music and, despite his patroness's dislike of Mazarin and her involvement in the Fronde, he was no stranger to Italian music either. After the defeat of the Frondists, Mlle de Montpensier was exiled to St Fargeau. Lully obtained release from her service and on the death of his friend Lazzarini, in 1653, was appointed Louis XIV's compositeur de la musique instrumentale. From 1655 his fame as dancer, comedian and composer grew rapidly, and his disciplined training of the king's 'petite bande' earned him further recognition. In 1661 he was made surintendant de la musique et compositeur de la musique de la chambre and in 1662

maître de la musique de la famille royale. By then he was a naturalised Frenchman, and in July 1662 he married Madeleine Lambert.

Lully then collaborated with Molière on a series of comédies-ballets which culminated in Le bourgeois gentilhomme (1670). After that he turned to opera, securing the privilege previously granted to Perrin and forestalling potential rivals with oppressive patents granted by the king. He chose as librettist Philippe Quinault, with whom he established a new and essentially French type of opera known as tragédie lyrique. Between 1673 and 1686 Lully composed 13 such works, 11 of them with Quinault.

During this time Lully continued to enjoy the king's support. His greatest personal triumph came in 1681 when he was received as secrétaire du Roi. After the king's marriage to Mme de Maintenon in 1683 life at court took on a new sobriety; it was perhaps in response to this that Lully composed much of his religious music. During a performance of his Te Deum in January 1687 he injured his foot with the point of a cane he was using to beat time. Gangrene set in, and within three months he died, leaving a tragédie lyrique, Achille et Polyxène, unfinished.

At his death Lully was widely regarded as the most representative of French composers. Practically all his music was designed to satisfy the tastes and interests of Louis XIV. The ballets de cour (1653-63) and the comédies-ballets (1663-72) were performed as royal entertainments, the king himself often taking part in the dancing.

The tragédies lyriques (1673-86) were kingly operas par excellence, expressing a classical conflict between la gloire and l'amour; Louis himself supplied the subject matter for at least four of them and certainly approved the political sentiments of the prologues. Lully's music was correspondingly elevated, in the stately overtures, the carefully moulded 'récitatif simple' and the statuesque choruses; many of the airs, too, draw as much attention to the galant mores of the court as to the stage action. Finally, the Versailles grand motet, of which the Miserere is an outstanding example, was designed to glorify the King of France as much as the King of Heaven.

GROVEmusic

Suites

L'Orchestre du Roi Soleil   Ⓟ
Première Suite: Le bourgeois gentilhomme.
Deuxième Suite: Le divertissement royal. Troisième Suite: Alceste
Le Concert des Nations / Jordi Savall
Alia Vox AV9807 (64' · DDD)   Ⓕⓞ

Le Concert des Nations offers here a compendium of Lully's music from the heyday of the court of Louis XIV (widely assumed to have been at Versailles, but in fact from before the move from Paris). The pieces, drawn from a variety of Lullian sources to make up three entertainments (or *divertissements*), provide Savall with opportunities to present his musicians in Lully's spectrum of ensemble textures. The players respond to the rhythmic vitality of the music, adding ornamentation with tremendous precision and flair, but the secret of the obvious success of this recording is the rightness of the tempos, whether for a dance, a battle, a gust of wind or a funeral. Those who saw the film *Tous les matins du monde* will be familiar with Lully's 'March pour la Cérémonie turque' and will immediately hear the difference even a few years has made to Savall: the playing on this new recording more effectively captures the military character without caricaturing the janissary element. The real stars of the recording, however, are the percussion players, Michèle Claude and Pedro Estevan, whose command of the possibilities for accompanying this repertory would have impressed even Lully. Whole evenings of Lully are still an acquired taste, but a recording of highlights as good as this is something anyone who enjoys Baroque music would wish to own.

Grands Motets

Miserere. Quare fremuerunt. Domine salvum fac regem. Jubilate Deo
Amel Brahim-Djelloul *sop* **Howard Crook, Damien Guillon** *countertens* **Hervé Lamy** *ten* **Arnaud Marzorati** *bass* **Les pages et les chantres de la Chapelle; Musica Florea / Olivier Schneebeli**
K617 K617157 (53' · DDD · T/t)   Ⓕ

Grands motets, requiring lavish vocal and instrumental resources, always signalled important occasions at the French court. Until the advent of public concerts in Paris in the 1720s they were performed exclusively by the king's musicians for the court. Olivier Schneebeli has assembled an admirable survey of these large-scale settings of psalm texts, which were excerpted and arranged to convey *doubles entendres* flattering to Louis XIV and his policies. The music employs an orchestra with a full continuo complement, a choir and a *petit chœur* of soloists that relies on high male voices. The only concession to modern times is the use of sopranos instead of castrati in the top part and the inclusion of girls among the pages.

The survey begins with Lully's first *grand motet*, the *Jubilate Deo* (1660), celebrating both the marriage of the king and a peace treaty. The *Miserere* (1663), frequently performed during Lully's lifetime, has remained his best-known work. *Quare fremuerunt* (1685) was composed at a difficult time, when he most needed to please the king. From first to last, one can easily hear the ways in which Lully experimented with his forces, refining the role of the orchestra, the ways in which the soloists relate to the choir, and how he was influenced by his experience of opera.

The singers are attentive to Schneebeli's direction; the five soloists contribute singly, in dialogue with one another and in concert with the choir. Musica Florea's sweet sound suggests a refreshing departure from current ideas of Lullian style.

Acis et Galatée

Acis et Galatée   Ⓟ
Jean-Paul Fouchécourt *ten* Acis **Véronique Gens** *sop* Galatée **Monique Simon** *sop* Diane, Second Naiad **Jean-Louis Meunier** *ten* Comus **Howard Crook** *ten* Apollon, Télème, Priest of Juno **Françoise Masset** *sop* Scylla, Dryad **Rodrigo del Pozo** *counterten* Tircis **Mireille Delunsch** *sop* Aminte, Abundance, First Naiad **Laurent Naouri** *bar* Polyphème **Thierry Félix** *bar* Neptune, Sylvan **Chœur des Musiciens du Louvre; Les Musiciens du Louvre / Marc Minkowski**
Archiv Produktion ② 453 497-2AH2 (107' · DDD · T/t)
                                                    ⒻOOↃ

Acis et Galatée was Lully's last completed opera, and one of his greatest. A *pastoral héroïque* performed in 1686 to entertain the Dauphin during a hunting party at the Duc de Vendôme's château, it employs many features of his *tragédies en musique* – vocal ensembles, instrumental movements and an enhanced use of the orchestra in general; and each act contains a *divertissement* with choruses and dances. One of the glories of the score is the concluding *passacaille*, which with instrumental sections builds up from single voices to chorus. There's also a small but affecting chaconne for Galatea in Act 2; but another glorious moment is the lengthy scene in which she discovers the body of her lover and calls on her father, Neptune, who guarantees Acis immortality by transforming him into a river. Marc Minkowski brings out all the drama of the work by thoughtful treatment of the verbal text, intelligent pacing and varied instrumental articulation and weight: especially striking are the rough sonorities of the march in which Polyphemus first appears, and the intensity of the lovers' angry confrontation in Act 2. Jean-Paul Fouchécourt projecting the image of an ardent youthful lover, and Véronique Gens that of a passionate goddess, are both excellently cast, but Laurent Naouri almost steals the scene from them with his fearsomely powerful Polyphemus: Howard Crook contributes valuably in various roles, though he's ill at ease in the very highest register. There's considerable finesse in the chorus singing, and the theorbo continuo is admirable. An altogether splendid performance of a masterpiece.

Cadmus et Hermione

Cadmus et Hermione
André Morsch *bar* Cadmus **Claire Lefilliâtre** *sop* Hermione **Arnaud Marzorati** *bass* Arbas; Pan **Jean-François Lombard** *ten* La Nourrice; Dieu champêtre **Isabelle Druet** *mez* Charite; Melisse **Arnaud Richard** *bass* Draco; Mars **Camille Poul** *sop* L'Amour; Palès **Le Poème Harmonique / Vincent Dumestre**
Stage director **Benjamin Lazar**
Video director **Martin Fraudreau**
Alpha 📀 ALPHA701 (123' · NTSC · 16:9 · PCM stereo and 5.1 · 0)   Ⓕ

Lully's *Cadmus et Hermione* (1673) inaugurated the era of *tragédie lyrique* that held sway until the Revolution. The performances by both singers and dancers are first-rate, thanks in no small part to Vincent Dumestre's clear and zestful conducting and the responsiveness of the orchestra. André Morsch as Cadmus, Claire Lefilliâtre as Hermione and Arnaud Marzorati as the cowardly confidant Arbas deserve particular praise. All are at ease with the theatrical gestures of the time, and the choreography by Gudrun Skamletz and Anne Tournié is stylish and entertaining.

The costumes are exquisitely crafted and so, too, the masks and the maquillage, bringing to life the images Berain left us. The giant Draco's dinosaur coat is a triumph, although some of the women's costumes seem a trifle short for the time. Other pleasures include the carefully researched scene sets with marvellous machinery (transporting gods and operating monsters) and the striking quality and quantity of light, originally generated by candles and oil lamps.

Among the musical high-points are the chaconne that ends Act 1; Cadmus's and Hermione's farewell in Act 2; the divertissement that ends Act 3; the moment when Cadmus and Hermione are reunited in Act 4, tellingly in a minor key; and the divertissement that concludes Act 5. Important, too, are the comic scenes with servants in Acts 2 and 3 – a holdover from the *comédies-ballet* of the previous decade, which Lully avoided in later operas.

Persée

Persée
Cyril Auvity *ten* Persée **Marie Lenormand** *sop*
Andromède **Stephanie Novacek** *mez* Cassiope
Monica Whicher *sop* Mérope **Olivier Laquerre** *bass-bar* Céphée; Méduse **Alain Coulombe** *bass* Phinée
Colin Ainsworth *ten* Mercure **Vilma Vitols** *sop*
Vénus **Tafelmusik Chamber Choir and Baroque Orchestra / Hervé Niquet**
Stage director **Marshall Pynkoski**
Video director **Marc Stone**
Euroarts 𝗗𝗩𝗗 205 4178 (127' · NTSC · 16:9 · PCM stereo, 5.1 and DTS 5.1 · 0)
Recorded live at the Elgin Theatre, Toronto, on April 28, 2004   Ⓕ

A warm welcome to the first opera by Lully to appear on DVD. Staged performances of his *tragédies lyriques* being rare, at least in the UK, it's good to be able at last to assess one of them as a drama. *Persée*, to a libretto by Philippe Quinault, Lully's usual collaborator, was first performed in 1682, a year before *Phaëton*. As with all such works the purpose was to flatter, none too subtly, the person and the reign of Louis XIV; indeed, the subject was chosen by the Sun King himself, and the sycophantic composer made an explicit comparison between Louis and Perseus in the dedication.

The story, taken from Ovid's *Metamorphoses*, is a conflation of two legends: Perseus' slaying of Medusa and his rescue of Andromeda. Cassio-peia has incurred the wrath of Juno, who sends Medusa to terrorise the country. With Medusa dead, Juno causes Cassiopeia's daughter, the princess Andromeda, to be chained to a rock at the mercy of a monster. Perseus swoops from the sky to kill the monster, Venus descends as a *dea ex machina* to take the hero, his beloved and her parents up to heaven, and everybody lives happily ever after. Everybody, that is, except for Merope, fruitlessly in love with Perseus, who dies accidentally; and Phineus, Andromeda's betrothed, whom Perseus turns to stone with Medusa's head.

As a drama, then, there's not much going for *Persée*, especially as Perseus benefits from divine assistance: a sword from Vulcan, a shield from Athena, a helmet from Pluto, not to mention the presence of Mercury, who sends Medusa to sleep. But there's much pleasure to be had from the choral and balletic contributions to the divertissements and from individual scenes.

This production from Toronto is dressed and choreographed in traditional style and the direction is both lively and respectful, the characters encouraged to gesture expressively. Monica Whicher and Alain Coulombe are good as the disappointed lovers; Olivier Laquerre, stentorian as Andromeda's father, has a fine old time camping up the transvestite role of Medusa. Cyril Auvity's Perseus, rather pinched in tone, is outsung by Colin Ainsworth's Mercury, who is nonsensically given a solo belonging to one of the mortals.

Hervé Niquet is a sympathetic conductor, moving seamlessly through recitative, air and ensemble; the orchestra suffers from a recorded balance that favours the theorbo.

A short scene for Medusa's fellow Gorgons is pointlessly cut. The entire allegorical Prologue is omitted, too; no great loss, perhaps, but it should have been mentioned in the booklet. But let's not end on a carping note: this enterprising issue is cause for celebration.

Proserpine

Proserpine
Salomé Haller *sop* Proserpine **Bénédicte Tauran** *sop*
La Paix **Stéphanie d'Oustrac** *sop* Cérès **Hjördis Thébault** *mez* La Victoire **Blandine Staskiewicz** *mez*
Aréthuse; Cyané **Cyril Auvity** *ten* Alphée **François-Nicolas Geslot** *counterten* Mercure **Benoît Arnould** *bass* Ascalaphe **Marc Labonnette** *ten* Jupiter;
Crinise **Pierre-Yves Pruvot** *bar* La Discorde **João Fernandes** *bar* Pluton **Le Concert Spirituel / Hervé Niquet**
Glossa ② GCD921 615 (152' · DDD)   Ⓕ

Lully's *tragédie lyrique* for 1680 tells the familiar tale of Proserpine's abduction by the underworld king Pluton, the upset it causes her mother Cérès, and of the compromise solution reached in which Proserpine must each year alternate six months above and below ground. It is not much action on which to base a five-act opera, and indeed Lully's librettist, the ever-excellent Quinault, adds to it by building up

Cérès and her love affair with Jupiter and adding a parallel pair of lovers, Aréthuse and Alphée, with a rival for the latter in Ascalaphe. There is also liberal use of stage effects (including an impulsive role for Mount Etna) which we CD listeners will have to imagine for ourselves. Surprisingly, what it is not padded out with are the kind of extended decorative set-piece sung-and-danced divertissements that form such a large part of Lully's earlier operas.

The opera is a flexible mixture of arioso, dance and chorus, and Niquet clearly enjoys the task of joining its separate elements into a coherent whole. Perhaps in doing so he can be a little hasty with its conversational element, but the way he steers the music around its corners with no bumps and awkward corners betokens considerable musical and dramatic involvement. And as ever he is capable of generating an almost visceral excitement and urgency, not just in Lully's glorious and imaginative choral writing but in the sensual urgency of his orchestral textures. The all-French-speaking cast does not contain stars but makes strong and convincing contributions throughout, with Salomé Haller, Stéphanie d'Oustrac, Blandine Staskiewicz and Cyril Auvity giving special pleasure. Indeed, this is a model 'company' reading, one in which everyone performs as if it really matters.

Roland

Roland
Nicolas Testé bass Roland **Anna Maria Panzarella**
sop Angélique **Olivier Dumait** counterten Médor
Monique Zanetti sop Témire, Bélise **Robert
Getchell** counterten Astolfe **Salomé Haller** sop
Logistille **Evgueniy Alexiev** bass Ziliante,
Demogorgon **Emiliano Gonzalez-Toro** ten Tersandre
Anders J Dahlin counterten Coridon **Marie-Hélène**
Essade sop Une pastourelle **Delphine Gillot** sop La
Gloire **Lausanne Opera Chorus; Les Talens Lyriques
/ Christophe Rousset**
Ambroisie ③ AMB9949 (161' · DDD · T/t)　　Ⓕ❍

Coming from a composer who relied so much on spectacle, it's astonishing how vividly this opera's drama comes to life on disc. *Roland* is about the power of love to persuade the knight Roland to put aside his pursuit of glory and, when thwarted in love, to drive him to a short-lived madness, from which he recovers sufficiently to return to the battlefield. There are no mythological gods within earshot, although Glory, Fame and Terror put in cameo appearances at the end. The agile chorus members of the Opéra de Lausanne adapt their tone to evoke fairies, oriental islanders, shepherds and shepherdesses and the ghosts of dead heroes.

Lully's music displays emotion and wit, and is often ravishing, and in Christophe Rousset's experienced hands, beautifully paced. Five acts slip by quickly, abetted by a succession of musical triumphs. There's exquisite chamber music and moments of extreme drama. (Not even Lully's orchestra could have performed the mad

scene with the speed and clarity of Les Talens Lyriques.) But Lully's trademark masterstroke is the series of monologues and dialogues over ground basses delivered by Angélique and Médor which culminates in the great chaconne with orchestra and chorus that ends Act 3.

The role of Roland is sung with dignity and touching vulnerability by Nicolas Testé. Angélique is sympathetically characterised by Anna Maria Panzarella, as is gentle, steadfast Médor, by Olivier Dumait. Emiliano Gonzalez-Toro delights us with fluent ornamentation, and Salomé Haller with the beauty of her tone.

This recording is destined to win accolades. Recommended highly.

Witold Lutosławski　　Polish 1913-1994

Lutosławski studied with Maliszewski at the Warsaw Conservatory (1932-7) and soon made his mark as a pianist and composer, though few works from before 1945 have been published. He then developed a clear, fresh tonality related to late Bartók displayed in the Little Suite for orchestra (1951), the Concerto for Orchestra (1954) and the Dance Preludes for clarinet and piano (1954). But that style was short-lived: in the late 1950s he was able to essay a kind of serialism (Funeral Music for strings, 1958) and to learn from Cage the possibility of aleatory textures, where synchronisation between instrumental lines is not exact (Venetian Games for chamber orchestra, 1961). Most of his subsequent works were orchestral, fully chromatic, finely orchestrated in a manner suggesting Debussy and Ravel, and developed from an opposition between aleatory and metrical textures. These include his Second (1967), Third (1983) and Fourth (1993) symphonies, concertos for cello (1970) and for oboe and harp (1980), and settings of French verse with chorus (Three Poems of Henri Michaux, 1963), tenor (Paroles tissées, 1965) and baritone (Les espaces du sommeil, 1975). During this period he was also internationally active as a teacher and conductor of his own music. GROVEmusic

Cello Concerto

Cello Concerto. Livre pour orchestre. Novelette.
Chain 3
Andrzej Bauer vc **Polish National Radio Symphony
Orchestra / Antoni Wit**
Naxos 8 553625 (73' · DDD)　　Ⓢ⤷

This is an excellent disc; fine music, well played and recorded, and all at the special Naxos price. The earliest composition, *Livre* (1968), was the first work completed by Lutosławski after the Second Symphony, and it shows him at his freshest and boldest, as if relieved to be free (if only temporarily) from the burden of one of music's weightiest traditions. With its well-nigh surreal juxtapositions of strongly contrasted materials, and the unusual ferocity of its tone – the 'book' in question must have been of the blood and thunder variety – *Livre* reveals a Lutosławski quite different from the relatively benign, ironic master of the later works. Coming immediately after *Livre*, the Cello Concerto has an even wider expressive range: indeed, in the balance it achieves between lamenting melodic lines and mercurial scherzo-like writing, coupled with a tendency to home in on crucial pitch-centres, it sets out the basic elements of the composer's later style.

This performance owes a great deal to Antoni Wit's skilful shaping of the music's alternations between relatively free and precise notation, and this skill is even more evident in the remaining orchestral scores. *Novelette*, completed in 1979, is Lutosławski's response to his first American commission; it's far more cogent and concentrated than its title might lead you to expect. *Chain-3* (1986) is one of the best later works, let down only by some rather perfunctory quasi-tonal harmony near the end. But this doesn't undermine the impression the disc as a whole conveys of some of the most characterful and individual music of the last 30 years.

Concerto for Orchestra

Concerto for Orchestra. Funeral Music. Mi-parti
BBC Philharmonic Orchestra / Yan Pascal Tortelier
Chandos CHAN9421 (55' · DDD)   Ⓕ**OO**➼

Tortelier's virtues as a conductor – expressive warmth allied to a special rhythmic buoyancy – are apparent in a sizzling account of the *Concerto for Orchestra*. The musical flow is firmly controlled, yet the effect is never inflexible, and the technical precision and the alertness of the playing is something for the listener to revel in. The sound is bright, well differentiated dynamically, and even if the BBC's Manchester studio lacks some of the depth and atmosphere of Chicago's Orchestra Hall, as caught in Barenboim's version, this recording is generally more vivid, in keeping with a performance which has precisely the kind of bite and energy that the score demands. It's good that Chandos and Tortelier chose *Mi-parti* to complete the disc, since of all Lutosławski's later instrumental works this one makes out the best possible case for his radical change of technique around 1960.

Symphonies

Symphony No 1. Chantefleurs et Chantefables[a]. Jeux vénetiens. Postlude No 1. Silesian Triptych[a]
[a]**Olga Pasiecznik** sop **Polish National Radio Symphony Orchestra / Antoni Wit**
Naxos 8 554283 (73' · DDD)   Ⓢ

Juxtaposing Lutosławski's early Symphony No 1 with the late *Chantefleurs et Chantefables* reinforces the fundamentally French associations of this composer's very personal musical voice; to

contemplate how the symphony's exuberant embrace of a Roussel-like idiom was complemented, more than 40 years later, by the subtle Ravellian overtones of *Chantefleurs et Chantefables* is to recognise that the radical gestures of *Jeux vénetiens* (1961) have worn less well than Lutosławski's more 'conservative' qualities. Indeed, the wild piano cadenza in *Jeux vénetiens* now evokes the high jinks of Ibert's *Divertissement* rather than the liberated avant-garde ethos of more determinedly progressive musical minds. The downbeat ending is far more memorable.

Olga Pasiecznik's singing is outstanding, especially in *Chantefleurs*, where she easily surpasses Dawn Upshaw in subtlety and Antoni Wit turns in strongly characterised, well-shaped accounts of all the scores. The playing is eloquent as well as energetic, and although, as with earlier Naxos volumes, the recordings are rather glassy and generalised, the music's range of colour and variety of texture is never in doubt. With such a well-filled disc, why did Naxos decide to include the first of the Three Postludes? The composer himself was clearly happy for the piece to appear on its own, but in a series with pretensions to completeness the full set is surely a must.

Symphony No 3. Concerto for Orchestra
Chicago Symphony Orchestra / Daniel Barenboim
Warner Elatus 0927-49015-2 (58' · DDD) Recorded live 1992   ●

Lutosławski's Third Symphony was commissioned by the Chicago SO and first performed by them under Sir Georg Solti in 1983, but only nine years later did the orchestra record the work. None of the versions made in the interim can equal Barenboim's blend of refined detail and cumulative power, and the Warner recording is also more faithful to the dynamics marked in the score. The *Concerto for Orchestra*, completed almost 30 years before the symphony, is comparatively conservative in style, but it possesses ample substance to match its panache. It also remains a formidable challenge to an orchestra. As with the symphony, Barenboim's strength is the large-scale creation and sustaining of tension, and the recording contains the heavy climaxes without draining them of clarity or impact.

Piano Sonata

Lutosławski Piano Sonata **Salonen** Yta II. Three Preludes. Dichotomie **Stucky** Four Album Leaves. Three Little Variations for David
Gloria Cheng pf
Telarc CD80712 (72' · DDD)   Ⓕ**O**➼

All three composers have so far written relatively little for solo piano: indeed, Steven Stucky's two brief sets of pieces, attractive if stylistically anonymous, are distinctly minor works. The Salonen pieces cover the greater part of his composing – from the Boulezian clarity of *Yta II* (1985) to the Dutilleux-like poise of *Three Preludes* (2005); though it is only the Ligetian duality of *Dichotomie* (2000), the stark discontinuity of 'Mécanisme' vividly complemented by the gradual accumulation of 'Organisme', that stands out as a notable addition to the contemporary repertoire.

Much the most important item here is Lutosławski's Piano Sonata (1934). His earliest surviving major work, it remained unpublished until after his death and is only now receiving its first recording. Perhaps Lutosławski's rapidly evolving idiom led him to doubt the authenticity of a piece influenced by Ravel and, to a lesser degree, Debussy and Fauré; yet the control of momentum in the opening *Allegro* and the understated eloquence of the *Andante* unfold with no mean formal mastery, and if the finale's attempt at apotheosis is at all self-conscious, the winding-down of its coda is effortlessly achieved. Cheng dispatches it with sensitivity and insight (as she does this collection as a whole), and one can only echo Stucky as to the timeliness of this recording. Clear, well balanced sound and a disc that no one interested in modern piano music should pass over.

Sergey Lyapunov   Russian 1859-1924

Lyapunov studied at the Moscow Conservatory but, attracted by the nationalism of the new Russian school, became a pupil of Balakirev, a dominating influence. He taught and conducted in St Petersburg, also appearing as a pianist and composing prolifically, often in the style of other composers (Schumann, Chopin, Mendelssohn, Balakirev and above all Liszt); his brilliant technical studies op.12 recall Liszt's Transcendental Studies. Besides piano showpieces (still in the repertory), he wrote distinctive, lyrical piano miniatures, orchestral works, notably the Solemn Overture on Russian Themes (1896), and many songs.   GROVEmusic

Piano Concertos

Piano Concertos – No 1 in E flat minor, Op 4; No 2 in E, Op 38. Rhapsody on Ukrainian Themes, Op 28
Hamish Milne *pf* **BBC Scottish Symphony Orchestra / Martyn Brabbins**
Hyperion CDA67326 (59' · DDD)   (F)⊙⊙

Hyperion celebrates the 30th release in its invaluable The Romantic Piano Concerto series with a disc of Lyapunov's works for piano and orchestra as beautiful as it's comprehensive. Whether in Opp 4, 28 or 38, you could never fail to guess the composer's nationality, and even when you sense Balakirev's eagle-eyed scrutiny of the First Concerto or Liszt's influence in the Second, Lyapunov's style invariably transcends the sources of his inspiration. Indeed, it's no exaggeration to say, as Edward Garden does in his excellent accompa-

nying essay, that the hushed nocturnal opening to the Second Concerto is among the loveliest in the repertoire, setting the stage for every starry-eyed wonder.

The writing is as lavish and ornate as even the most ardent lover of Russian Romantic music could wish – at 3'35" it's like some richly embroidered cloth winking and glinting with a thousand different lights and colours. More generally, everything is seen through such a personal and committed perspective that all sense of derivation or of a tale twice told is erased.

Such an overall impression wouldn't occur if the performances were less skilful or meticulously prepared. Hamish Milne holds his head high, lucidly and affectionately throughout, commanding cascades of notes; he's stylishly partnered by Martyn Brabbins. There's competition in the Second Concerto from the urbane and scintillating Howard Shelley who is rather more immediately recorded on Chandos. But to have all three works on a single disc is an irresistible bonus.

Symphony No 1

Symphony No 1, Op 12. Polonaise, Op 16 Piano Concerto No 2, Op 38[a]
[a]**Howard Shelley** *pf*
BBC Philharmonic Orchestra / Vassily Sinaisky
Chandos CHAN9808 (65' · DDD)   (F)

Sergei Lyapunov has always been a shadowy figure, his derivative yet distinctive voice drowned by his more celebrated compatriots and even by his contemporaries Taneyev, Liadov and Arensky. Yet hearing the First Symphony in a performance of this calibre you're reminded of the way Lyapunov's melodic appeal is complemented by brilliant craftsmanship.

The opening motif is sufficiently brief to invite elaboration and to play a key role in music as coherent as it's heartfelt. The chromatic undertow as the music eases into the *poco più tranquillo*, its mix of sweetness and unrest looks ahead to Rachmaninov's Second Symphony, and if the themes are less memorable than in that towering Romantic masterpiece they're marshalled and directed with great compositional skill. Vassily Sinaisky and the BBC Philharmonic Orchestra allow the long sinuous lines of the *Andante sostenuto* to unfold with an unfaltering tact and commitment, and in the balletic *Scherzo*, with its memories of Tchaikovsky, he realises all of the music's captivating grace and charm.

If Borodin is a key influence in the symphony then Liszt is central to the thinking behind the Second Piano Concerto. Lyapunov, after all, paid an eloquent tribute to Liszt in his 12 *Transcendental Etudes* for solo piano, a magnificent if uneven creation, and not surprisingly the lavish and intricate pianism in the Second Concerto is a Romantically inclined pianist's dream. Certainly its succulent themes and star-dust decoration could hardly be spun off more beguilingly than by Howard Shelley. His relaxed mastery and enviably elegant style inform every bar of this most seductive work.

The recordings are magnificent; no lover of Russian Romantic by-ways can afford to be without this.

Edward MacDowell

American 1860-1908

MacDowell studied the piano in Paris (with Marmontel), Wiesbaden and Frankfurt (Carl Heymann), as well as composition (with Raff, at the Hoch Conservatory in Frankfurt), taking his first post at the Darmstadt Conservatory. Liszt heard his First Modern Suite and First Piano Concerto and strongly encouraged him; by 1884 German firms had published 10 of his works. After several years in Wiesbaden he moved to Boston in 1888 to pursue a performing career. His Second Piano Concerto and First and Second Orchestral Suites won success there and in New York, and he was increasingly accepted as a leading figure in American musical life. Compositions of the Boston years included his popular Woodland Sketches, Sonata tragica and Sonata eroica and the Six love Songs. In 1896 he became the first professor of music at Columbia University; besides organising the new department, he conducted a New York men's glee club and composed some of his best piano music – Sea Pieces, the Third and Fourth Sonatas, New England Idyls – and many male choruses. He left Columbia in 1904 but continued to teach privately; after his death his summer home at Peterborough, New Hampshire, was converted into an artists' colony (still active).

MacDowell was a Romantic by temperament, with a musical imagination shaped by nature and literature (notably poetry and Celtic and Nordic legends). His style derives largely from Schumann, Liszt, Wagner, Raff and especially Grieg and, though not innovatory, influential or distinctively American, retains a certain melodic freshness and attractive orchestral colouring. GROVEmusic

Piano Concertos

Piano Concertos – No 1 in A minor, Op 15[a];
No 2 in D minor, Op 23[a]. Hexentanz, Op 17 No 2[a].
Romance for Cello and Orchestra, Op 35[b]
[a]**Stephen Prutsman** pf [b]**Aisling Drury Byrne** vc
**National Symphony Orchestra of Ireland /
Arthur Fagen**
Naxos 8 559049 (56' · DDD)   ⓈⒹ→

Music of another time, another age, the MacDowell piano concertos can, in the right hands, seem more endearing than quaint or overblown. Both may satisfy conventional notions of dark and light, of tragedy and skittishness, but their heart-easing, lavishly decorated themes understandably attracted Liszt. Stephen Prutsman, a brilliant and versatile pianist, plays with ease and fluency, tossing aside the *Presto* movements from both concertos with an enviable sheen, though arguably without a necessarily commit-

ted or potent romanticism. Suave and engaging in the Grieg-haunted *Andante tranquillo* from the A minor Concerto, he loses his poise in the deeply welling *più mosso, con passione* from the D minor Concerto's first movement, and it's here, in particular, that one misses Van Cliburn's unforgettable warmth and virtuosity. No pianist has played this concerto with such magisterial command or emotional generosity; indeed, it sounds as if it was written for him. Eugene List, too, shows a higher degree of involvement than Prutsman, though it must be admitted that the latter's occasional reticence results from Naxos's recessed sound, which irons out much sense of dynamic perspective or variety. Too often Prutsman is confined to the shadows when he should be centre-stage. The National Symphony Orchestra of Ireland has its uneasy moments, but world-premiere recordings of the *Hexentanz*, in an arrangement for piano and orchestra, and the *Romance* for cello and orchestra make this a tempting issue.

Guillaume de Machaut

French c1300-1377

Machaut entered the service of John of Luxembourg, King of Bohemia, as a royal secretary, c1323. The king helped him to procure a canonry in Reims, which was confirmed in 1335; Machaut settled there c1340, although he continued in royal service until the king's death (1346). He then served various members of the French high nobility, including John, Duke of Berry, his later years being dedicated to the manuscript compilation of his works.

With his prolific output of motets and songs, Machaut was the single most important figure of the French Ars Nova. He followed and developed the guidelines of Philippe de Vitry's treatise Ars nova and, in particular, observed Vitry's unprecedented advocation of duple time in many of his works, even in his setting of the Ordinary of the Mass. Only in some of his lais and virelais and the Hoquetus David did he consistently adhere to 13th-century rhythmic patterns and genres. His own rhythmic style is novel in its use of variety and motivic interest, particularly through syncopation, and in his development of isorhythmic techniques: all but three of his 23 motets, and four of the movements of the Messe de Nostre Dame –one of the earliest polyphonic settings of the Mass Ordinary – are isorhythmic. In secular music, Machaut set a wide range of poetic forms, all of which are illustrated in his long narrative poem, the Remede de Fortune (probably an early work). While the relationship between text and music is most closely observed in the monophonic lais and virelais, a highly flexible approach is adopted in the three-voice motets so that the subtle treatment of the text avoids the symmetricality of complete isorhythm. More progressive features of Machaut's style – an increased awareness of tonality, the use of unifying rhythmic motifs – are found in his polyphonic settings of rondeaux and ballades, while melodic considerations are to the fore in his virelais. GROVEmusic

Messe de Nostre Dame

Messe de Nostre Dame. Je ne cesse de prier (Lai 'de la fonteinne'). Ma fin est mon commencement
The Hilliard Ensemble / Paul Hillier
Hyperion CDA66358 (54' · DDD · T/t)   Ⓕ Ⓞ

Machaut's *Messe de Nostre Dame* is the earliest known setting of the Ordinary Mass by a single composer. Paul Hillier avoids a full reconstruction on this release: his deference to 'authenticity' restricts itself to the usage of 14th century French pronunciation of the Latin. His ensemble sings two to a part, with prominent countertenors. It's arguable whether the musicians sing the chant at too fast a tempo but they're smooth and flexible, and the performance as a whole is both fluid and light in texture. Also included on this release are two French compositions. The wonderful *Lai 'de la fonteinne'* is admirably sung by three tenors and is pure delight – providing food for the heart as well as for the intellect. The rather more familiar *Ma fin est mon commencement*, with its retrograde canon, completes this admirable disc.

Messe de Nostre Dame. Felix virgo/Inviolata/Ad te suspiramus
Schola Gregoriana, Cambridge / Mary Berry
Herald HAVPCD312 (76' · DDD · T/t)   Ⓕ

This is neither the first recording of Machaut's most famous work to have been made in Rheims Cathedral, where the composer worked, nor the first to present the Mass as part of a 'liturgical reconstruction'. (The first distinction belongs to the Oxford Camerata's recording for Naxos, the second to the Taverner Consort's for EMI.) As a liturgical reconstruction, this is more nearly complete than the Taverner's, to the extent of including the celebrant's *sotto voce* recitation during the Secret.

The plainchant is especially well managed: the beginnings of the longer chant items are sung by a soloist in a rapt, florid style described fairly precisely by contemporary theorists. And as ever in this type of programme, it is most instructive to experience sacred polyphony unfolding in its natural environment (that is, as a literal outgrowth of chant), rather than as the 'bleeding chunks' in which we so often consume it. The Schola Gregoriana recording is currently alone in offering this opportunity.

That said, the polyphony itself doesn't quite have the polish of other recordings. This is felt particularly in the *Gloria* and *Credo*, whose fast-moving 'close harmony' demands a degree of unanimity (both rhythmic and intonational) that these singers do not quite achieve (it's high tenors – as on the Tavener recording – not countertenors who best impart the slightly astringent 'bite' that brings Machaut's dissonances most vividly to life). Whether or not you agree, this stimulating recording is unlikely to be the first choice for the polyphony itself.

Motets

De souspirant cuer, M2. Fine Amour, qui me vint navrer, M3. Puis que la douce rousée, M4. Qui plus aimme, M5. Lasse! Je suis en aventure, M7. Ha! Fortune, M8. O livoris feritas, M9. Helas! Où sera pris confors, M10. Fins cuers dous. Eins que ma dame d'onnur, M13. Faus Samblant m'a deceü, M14. Se j'aim mon loyal ami, M16. Bone pastor, M18. Diligenter inquiramus, M19. Biauté parée de valour, M20. Veni creator spiritus, M21. Plange, regni respublica, M22. Inviolata genitrix, M23
The Hilliard Ensemble (David Gould, David James *countertens* Rogers Covey-Crump, Steven Harrold *tens* Gordon Jones *bar*)
ECM New Series 472 402-2 (63' · DDD · T/t)   Ⓕ Ⓞ Ⓞ ➔

This is a landmark recording and a courageous venture. It's probably the first devoted to Machaut's motets, containing no fewer than 18 of the 23 that survive. It's certainly the first to present them in the order in which Machaut himself presented them in his own manuscripts. And the performances are of a truly mandarin refinement. Here are The Hilliard Ensemble with goodness knows how many combined years of experience performing this kind of music in public; they aren't just on the top of their form but also constantly showing the fruits of that experience.

The results of that refinement may surprise some listeners. Tempos tend to be rather slower than on earlier recordings: it's as though they feel no need for lily-gilding, no need to apologise for the music, where earlier performances injected possibly gratuitous energy into Machaut's lines. Dissonances are often made to disappear almost without trace, which will disappoint those who thought the clashes to be the very lifeblood of Machaut's music. (It must be absolutely clear that this was an informed decision by The Hilliards, many of whom have performed this music with other groups over the years.) Diction tends to be clearer than in some recent recordings, and – perhaps most surprising of all – they refrain from adopting current views on the early French pronunciation of Latin. These are all features that could make some listeners find it a touch dull; they might even find that they scarcely recognise old favourites. But they're superbly done, and the performances give the best avenue yet to gaining access to Machaut's still perplexing but always irresistible art.

Sir Alexander Mackenzie
British 1847-1935

Mackenzie studied in Germany and at the Royal Academy of Music, by 1865 becoming known in Edinburgh as a violinist and conductor. In the 1880s he won a reputation as one of England's leading composers, chiefly with the oratorio The Rose of Sharon (1884). From 1885 he lived in London, conducting the Novello Oratorio Concerts and, from 1888, serving as an influential principal of the RAM he also conducted for the Philharmonic Society (1892-9) and occasionally for the Royal Choral Society, making a tour of Canada in 1903. He received a knighthood (1895) and created KCVO (1922). A workmanlike composer, Mackenzie produced successful choral works, vocal settings (many of Scottish poets) and descriptive orchestral pieces, often imaginative and satisfying if also somewhat derivative. GROVEmusic

Scottish Concerto

Mackenzie Scottish Concerto, Op 55 **Tovey**
Piano Concerto in A, Op 15
Steven Osborne pf **BBC Scottish Symphony Orchestra / Martyn Brabbins**
Hyperion CDA67023 (62' · DDD)   Ⓕ

From the horns' call to arms at the outset of the piece to the irrepressible merrymaking of the closing pages, Edinburgh-born Sir Alexander Mackenzie's *Scottish Concerto* (1897) spells firm enjoyment, and it's astonishing that this is its first recording. Cast in three movements, each of which employs a traditional Scottish melody, it's a thoroughly endearing and beautifully crafted work which wears its native colours without any hint of stale cliché or cloying sentimentality; indeed, the canny wit, genuine freshness and fertile imagination with which Mackenzie treats his material are in evidence throughout the work.

By contrast, Edinburgh-based Sir Donald Tovey's Piano Concerto (1903) exhibits a rather more formal demeanour, its three movements brimful of youthful ambition and possessing a very Brahmsian solidity and dignity. Tovey's idiomatically assured writing isn't always entirely untouched by a certain academic earnestness, but on the whole any unwanted stuffiness is deftly kept at bay. In fact, repeated hearings only strengthen one's admiration for this work.

No praise can be too high for Steven Osborne's contribution, while the excellent Martyn Brabbins draws a splendidly stylish and alert response from his fine BBC group. Sound and balance are excellent too.

James MacMillan   British b1959

MacMillan studied at Edinburgh University and then with Casken at Durham University. In 1990 he became affiliate composer of the Scottish Chamber Orchestra he has since become visiting composer for the Philharmonia (London) and artistic director of its Contemporary Music Series. His music is noted for its energy and emotional power, its religious and political content and its references to Scottish folk music. Major works include The Beserking (1990), a piano concerto for Peter Donohoe; Sinfonietta (1991); and Veni, Veni, Emmanuel (1992), Sym-

phony No 2 (1991) and Symphony No 3 (2002). His 50th birthday saw concerts at the BBC Proms and the Edinburgh Festival, and 2010 sees the US premiere of his St Passion Passion (2008) under Sir Colin Davis. MacMillan is also working on a Violin Concerto (for Vadim Repin) and a Piano Concerto.
                                            GROVEmusic

Piano Concerto No 2

A Scotch Bestiary[a]. Piano Concerto No 2[b]
Wayne Marshall [a]org/ [b]pf
BBC Philharmonic Orchestra / James MacMillan
Chandos CHAN10377 (64' · DDD)   Ⓕ🅓➔

James MacMillan's *A Scotch Bestiary* is 'motivated by the great American cartoon makers who represented human characters in animal form,' says the composer, and is 'inspired by human archetypes and personalities encountered in Scottish life over the years'. The work's playful subtitle of 'Enigmatic variations on a zoological carnival at a Caledonian exhibition' acknowledges debts to Elgar, Saint-Saëns and Mussorgsky; indeed, the striding opening theme imitates the metre of (and linking role taken by) 'Promenade' in *Pictures at an Exhibition*. It's a caustic, loopy and exhilarating showpiece for organ and orchestra.

The Second Piano Concerto is scored for piano and strings, and is in three movements, the first of which, 'Cumnock Fair', initially appeared in 1999. This fretful dance fantasy's original title, 'Hoodicraw Peden', refers to a 17th-century Taliban-esque zealot, the subject of an Edwin Muir poem which witheringly refers to 'Burns and Scott, sham bards of a sham nation', thereby providing the titles for the concerto's remaining movements. 'Shambards' mockingly quotes the waltz from the Mad Scene in *Lucia di Lammermoor* while the lusty violin reel that launches 'Shamnation' acquires an increasingly desperate energy as it hurtles giddily towards the piano's unhinged, unnerving final flourish.

In both works Wayne Marshall covers himself in glory, as, for that matter, does the BBC Philharmonic under the composer's direction. The sound is superlative to match.

Tryst

Tryst[a]. Adam's Rib[b]. They Saw the Stone had been Rolled Away[a]. Í (A Meditation on Iona)[a]
[b]**Scottish Chamber Orchestra Brass**; [a]**Scottish Chamber Orchestra / Joseph Swensen**
BIS CD1019 (59' · DDD)   Ⓕ

This is the third recording of *Tryst* – extraordinary for a contemporary orchestral work. But its individuality is still as striking now as when it first appeared: especially so in this taut, gripping version. MacMillan touches, as warmly and directly as Mahler. The sounds can be violent, acerbic or prickly (as indeed they can in

Mahler!); the keening string lament at the heart of the work isn't always easy on the ear, and yet it all speaks – it's plainly the work of someone who urgently wants to tell us something. So too are the performances. Joseph Swensen brings the passionate enthusiasm to *Tryst*, and to *Í*, that has made his concerts with the Scottish Chamber Orchestra such events in Scotland. *Í* (pronounced 'ee') is a quite astonishing work. The subtitle, 'A Meditation on Iona', might suggest something romantically atmospheric, with soft, lilting Celtic accents. In fact this is hard, intense, sometimes eerie music: a tribute to St Columba, the muscular, fiercely contentious monk who brought Christianity to Scotland and founded the monastic college of Iona – perhaps also a reminder of St Paul's words about working out one's salvation with 'fear and trembling'.

Along with this come two short, brooding pieces, which are dominated by the sound of brass: *Adam's Rib* and *They saw the Stone had been Rolled Away*, the latter giving more than a foretaste of MacMillan's Symphony, *Vigil* – the concluding part of the trilogy *Triduum*. As with *Triduum*, the success is total: powerful, concise works, powerfully and understandingly performed, in crisp, clear recordings.

Veni, veni, Emmanuel

Veni, veni, Emmanuel[a]. After the tryst[b]. '... as others see us ...'[c]. Three Dawn Rituals[c]. Untold[c]
[a]**Evelyn Glennie** *perc* [b]**Ruth Crouch** *vn* [b]**Peter Evans** *pf* [ac]**Scottish Chamber Orchestra / **[a]**Jukka-Pekka Saraste**, [c]**James MacMillan**
Catalyst 09026 61916-2 (68' · DDD)　Ⓕ**OO**

Taking the Advent plainsong of the title as his basis, MacMillan reflects in his continuous 26-minute sequence the theological implications behind the period between Advent and Easter. The five contrasted sections are in a sort of arch form, with the longest and slowest in the middle. That section, 'Gaude, Gaude', expresses not direct joy as the Latin words might suggest but a meditative calm, using the four relevant chords from the plainsong's refrain as a hushed ostinato. Over that the soloist on the marimba plays an elaborate but gentle and intensely poetic cadenza. The main sections on either side are related dances based on hocketing repeated notes and full of jazzy syncopations, with powerful sections for Advent and Easter respectively framing the work as a whole. The plainsong emerges dramatically as a chorale at the climax of the second dance section, a telling moment.

The composer's notes are most helpful, but they deliberately keep quiet about the coda, where MacMillan brings off another dramatic coup. After the soloist has worked through the widest range of percussion in the different sections, there's a gap when players in the orchestra pick up and start playing little jingling bells, and the soloist progresses up to the big chimes set on a platform above the rest of the orchestra. The very close of the work brings a *crescendo* of chimes intended to reflect the joy of Easter in the Catholic service and the celebration of the Resurrection. Disappointingly though, the preparatory jingles are gentle and discreet, and even the final chimes are devotional rather than exuberant. Even so, this is a magnificent representation of one of the most striking and powerful works written by any British composer of the younger generation.

String Quartets

String Quartets – No 1, 'Visions of a November Spring'; No 2, 'Why is this night different?'. Memento. Tuireadh[a]
[a]**Robert Plane** *cl* **Emperor Quartet** (Martin Burgess, Clare Hayes *vns* Fiona Bonds *va* William Schofield *vc*)
BIS BIS-CD1269 (74' · DDD)　Ⓕ**O**

Visions of a November Spring, James MacMillan's First String Quartet, was completed in 1988 and already bears many a stylistic trait of the composer who was to create such a stir two years later with *The Confession of Isobel Gowdie*, not least a mastery of the singing line and the distinctive, 'keening' quality of the string writing itself. The work is cast in two movements, the much lengthier second of which perhaps doesn't quite add up to the sum of its impressive parts.

No such reservations, however, apply to the Second Quartet from 1998, whose title, *Why is this night different?*, comes from the question posed by the youngest member of the family during the Jewish rite of Seder on the first night of Passover. The father answers by telling of the flight of the children of Israel from Egypt. The result is an arrestingly powerful and sure-footed masterwork, ideally proportioned, economically argued and always evincing a riveting narrative and emotional scope. Similarly, *Tuireadh* (Gaelic for 'lament') for clarinet and string quartet packs a wealth of pungent and varied expression into its single-movement frame. MacMillan wrote it in 1991 as a 'musical complement' to Sue Jane Taylor's sculpture in memory of the victims of the Piper Alpha oil rig disaster, having also been greatly moved by a letter from a grieving mother who recalled how, during the memorial service, 'a spontaneous keening sound rose gently from the mourners assembled on the boat'. *Tuireadh* is a deeply compassionate threnody, as is the much briefer, sparer and no less haunting *Memento* for string quartet (1994), which (as so often with this composer) shows the influence of the ancient oral tradition of Gaelic psalmody still practised in the Western Isles today. Performances throughout are as superlatively disciplined as they're tirelessly eloquent; sound, balance and presentation are all beyond reproach. Another MacMillan/BIS triumph.

The Birds of Rhiannon

The Birds of Rhiannon. Magnificat. Exsultet. Nunc dimittis. Mairi. The Gallant Weaver

**BBC Singers; BBC Philharmonic Orchestra /
James MacMillan**
Chandos CHAN9997 (71' · DDD)   Ⓕ**O**Ⓓ▸

MacMillan's colours can be garish, his gestures histrionic, but his is an art of passion and commitment: these are the effects of a composer seeking to make you feel and react strongly as well as think deeply. His admixture of Celtic cultural nationalism, leftist politics and Catholicism may be too rich for the blood of some 21st century connoisseurs, but it provides affecting and memorable listening experiences. This CD resolutely demonstrates the point.

The setting of Burns's *Gallant Weaver* (1997) is MacMillan at his gentlest and most intimate, but this only softens you up for *Rhiannon* (2001), inspired by a tale from the Mabinogion, an ancient Welsh collection. *The Times* described its Proms premiere as unwieldy and florid with overworked and impoverished motifs. Maybe the performance has since been refined: here it sounds polymorphous and full of incident. More importantly, there's a cogent musical argument, even if not of the most sophisticated or subtle kind.

The *Magnificat*, a BBC Millennium commission heard here in the version for choir and orchestra, still includes an organ part which powers the violent ensemble interjections in the closing minutes.

He's already handsomely represented on disc, but this is as good an introduction as you'll get.

St John Passion
Christopher Maltman bar
**London Symphony Chorus and Orchestra /
Sir Colin Davis**
LSO Live ② · Ⓢ LSO0671 (90' · DDD · T/t)
Recorded live   Ⓑ

An 80th-birthday gift for Sir Colin Davis, James MacMillan's 90-minute setting of the *St John Passion* divides into two parts and is cast in 10 movements, the last of which comprises a deeply affecting and cathartic orchestral elegy (described by the composer as 'a song without words'). A baritone is allotted the sole principal part of Christus, a chamber choir acts as the Narrator/Evangelist and a large chorus is assigned all other duties. In the booklet MacMillan relates how some ideas from his 2007 opera *The Sacrifice* have found their way into the score. "I was also aware," he continues, "of the paradoxical tension created between the two highly contrasted musical contexts – liturgical chant and music drama."

In the central role Christopher Maltman gives one of his finest performances to date, sonorous, assured and reassuringly firm of tone. The choral and orchestral contributions are likewise beyond reproach, with the superb LSO brass in particular totally unfazed by MacMillan's at times scarily vertiginous demands. The microphones convey it all with startling immediacy, although, as is customary from this source, there's precious little in the way of ingratiating glow.

Even after a number of hearings, nagging doubts remain as to whether the work as a whole measures up to the exalted level of inspiration or possesses quite the communicative force of *Quickening* but it's valuable to have such an imperious realisation of what is a hugely sincere and often gripping narrative. MacMillan's many admirers will deem it an essential acquisition.

Mass

Mass[ab]. A New Song[ab]. Christus vincit[a]. Gaudeamus in loci pace[b]. Seinte Mari moder milde[ab]. A Child's Prayer[a]. Changed[ab]
[a]**Westminster Cathedral Choir / Martin Baker** with
[b]**Andrew Reid** org
Hyperion CDA67219 (66' · DDD · T/t)   Ⓕ**OO**

MacMillan's choral music is more often than not a direct response to his own Christian faith. The Mass recorded here was commissioned by Westminster Cathedral for the 'Glory of God in the Millennium Year of the Jubilee' and unlike MacMillan's two previous Masses, which were composed for congregational use, was specifically written for performance by a professional choir. It's through-composed and this provides a sense of structure, continuity and flow that greatly enhances its accessibility when heard out of context – on disc rather than celebrated. That MacMillan intended the Mass for practical use is apparent by his choice of vernacular rather than the Latin text. His often eclectic style is very much in evidence; the score glimmers with echoes of Howells and Duruflé, especially in the Kyrie and in his often quasi-orchestral organ writing, but in general it's MacMillan's individual voice that shapes this impressive and deeply felt setting. The Gloria contains some particularly effective music, not least some marvellously atmospheric organ writing, and the crepuscular Agnus Dei lingers in the mind long after the final notes die away. Of the remaining works on the disc, A New Song and A Child's Prayer (dedicated to the victims of the Dunblane tragedy) stand out as particularly fine examples of MacMillan's choral writing. As a bonus we're treated to the wonderfully translucent organ solo Gaudeamus in loci pace, beautifully performed by Andrew Reid. Performances throughout are exceptionally fine, the recorded sound radiantly atmospheric. A must.

Quickening[a]. The Sacrifice – Three Orchestral Interludes
[a]**Hilliard Ensemble** (Robin Blaze *counterten* Rogers Covey-Crump, Steven Harrold *tens* Gordon Jones bar) [a]**City of Birmingham Symphony Orchestra Chorus and Youth Chorus; BBC Philharmonic Orchestra / James MacMillan**
Chandos · Ⓢ CHSA5072 (60' · DDD/DSD · T/t)
     Ⓕ**OO**Ⓓ▸

Quickening is a 45-minute cantata to a text by Michael Symmons Roberts that both celebrates and explores the themes of birth, new life and parenthood. 'The title,' explains MacMillan, 'refers explicitly to the instant of conception – "the quickening of seed that will become ripe grain" – or the moment that a woman first feels her baby kick.' It's a hugely ambitious but never intimidating canvas, the sizeable forces required (four solo voices, children's chorus and chamber organ, mixed chorus and a large orchestra including triple woodwind and a battery of percussion) and MacMillan's deployment of them inviting parallels with Britten's *War Requiem*. After the expectant wonder and awe-struck mystery of the opening movement ('Incarnadine'), darker images of violence, menace, war and fragility occupy the two central tableaux ('Midwife' and 'Poppies'), before the ecstatic apex and magical fade-out of 'Living Water'. There's absolutely no missing this music's visceral impact, spiritual fervour and strength of conviction, attributes that should hopefully ensure it a place in the repertoire.

A powerful experience, in sum, and a work well worth getting to know. It's preceded by the Three Interludes that MacMillan has drawn from his second opera, *The Sacrifice*, based upon an ancient Welsh tale (from *The Mabinogion*) of love, warring clans and self-sacrifice. Inspiration runs high in this communicative orchestral triptych, the second and third movements of which owe a not inconsiderable debt to the Passacaglia and Storm from *Peter Grimes*. It certainly whets the appetite for a complete recording of the opera.

Suffice it to say, the composer secures admirably disciplined and committed results from all involved. What's more, Stephen Rinker's sound boasts spectacular amplitude, definition and range.

Seven Last Words from the Cross

Seven Last Words from the Cross[a].
Te Deum[b]. On the Annunciation of the Blessed Virgin[b]
Polyphony; [b]Britten Sinfonia /
Stephen Layton with [b]**James Vivian** org
Hyperion CDA67460 (69' · DDD)　　　Ⓕ

Seven Last Words was commissioned by the BBC in 1993 for Holy Week 1994, when it was broadcast in seven short programmes, a 'word' per day. It remains a highly compelling work. Under Stephen Layton, it certainly receives an impressive performance; an intense, deeply felt interpretation, full of beautiful and affecting singing, with all the elements – string orchestra, featured violin, choir and soloists – nicely balanced.

The other two works, *On the Annunciation of the Blessed Virgin* (1997) and *Te Deum* (2001), receive their premiere recordings. *On the Annunciation* is an intricate but approachable setting for five-part choir and organ of a poem by the 17th-century poet Jeremy Taylor. The luminous lines for voices finally give way to a gradually fading dance for organ. The echoes of Messiaen in this device are matched by some

of the organ chords and figures in the dramatic *Te Deum*, written to mark the Queen's Golden Jubilee. From the contemplative opening phrases for male voices, somewhat reminiscent of Mahler's *Urlicht*, a dazzling part emerges for solo soprano, sung in characteristically stunning fashion by Elin Manahan Thomas. As ever, MacMillan incorporates all his allusions, including those to Scottish traditional music, into an utterly individual style. The performance confirms Polyphony's place in the front rank of choirs.

Raising Sparks

Raising Sparks[a]. Piano Sonata. Barncleupédie. Birthday Present. For Ian.
[a]**Jean Rigby** *mez* **John York** *pf* [a]**Nash Ensemble** (Ian Brown *pf* Philippa Davies *fl* Richard Hosford *cl* Marianne Thorsen, Elizabeth Wexler *vns* James Boyd *va* Paul Watkins *va* Skaila Kanga *hp*) /
Martyn Brabbins
Black Box BBM1067 (57' · DDD)　　　Ⓕ

Martyn Brabbins and the Nash Ensemble here offer a superb recording premiere of a major work by James MacMillan. Like much of his music, it has a religious base. The big difference this time is that whereas his source of inspiration generally lies at the heart of his Roman Catholicism, this time is it the Jewish tradition. *Raising Sparks*, a 35-minute cantata on the theme of creation and redemption, is inspired by a poem by Michael Symmons Roberts and by the writing of the Jewish author, Menahem Nahum; the work takes one inexorably through a kaleidoscopic sequence of symbolic images, with one vivid simile piled on another in Roberts's striking language. MacMillan, for whom the poems were written, responds to the poet's verbal colour with musical ideas, often onomatopoeic but always striking and dramatic, within a taut musical structure. The vocal line, though taxing, is more lyrical than in many new works, superbly sung by Jane Rigby, while the instrumental accompaniment is endlessly inventive, with the piano (the masterly Ian Brown) generally the central instrument in the ensemble, with the fifth of the songs accompanied simply by the occasional note sounded on the piano and no more. Otherwise Brown leads the Nash players in a totally committed performance, very well recorded.

The four piano works which come as coupling find the pianist John York just as dedicated. The Piano Sonata of 1985 in three movements is much the most demanding, far grittier than the rest, inspired by the extreme winter of that year. It remains so potent in MacMillan's mind that he used it as the basis for his Second Symphony of 1999. The first of the piano pieces, *For Ian*, then brings release into pure tonality and lyricism, a strathspey full of Scottish-snap rhythms. After that *Birthday Present* seems a sombre gift, musically striking nonetheless, and the final *Barncleupédie* (1990) rounds things off lightheartedly. Backing up a masterly major work, these are occasional pieces which readily earn their place.

Miscellaneous choral works

'Bright Orb of Harmony'
MacMillan O bone Jesu. Mitte manum tuam.
A Child's Prayer. Sedebit Dominus Rex
Purcell Jehova quam multi sunt hostes mei.
Miserere mei. Remember not, Lord, our offences.
Beati omnes qui timent Dominum. Let mine eyes
run down with tears. O dive custos. Funeral
Sentences for Queen Mary – First Set. Thou knowest,
Lord, the secrets of our hearts (1695)
The Sixteen / Harry Christophers
Coro COR16069 (66' · DDD · T/t)
Recorded live   (F)◯↦

These performances were recorded live during the opening concert of The Sixteen's 2009 Choral Pilgrimage to celebrate both Purcell's 350th birthday and Scottish composer James MacMillan's 50th. Thus, while the anthems, motets and the first set of *Funeral Sentences* by Purcell presented here definitely tends towards the sombre, and MacMillan's musical language often has recourse to a stark muscularity, the darkness invariably gives way to light in the form of ecstatic melismas and lucent major-mode harmonies.

Throughout, the choral sound is rich yet unfailingly transparent – as obvious in the opening *Jehova quam multi sunt hostes mei* of Purcell as in MacMillan's masterly *O bone Jesu*. But the solo work is equally impressive – listen, for example, to tenors Simon Berridge and Mark Dobell and bass Eamonn Dougan in Purcell's *Let mine eyes run down with tears* or sopranos Grace Davidson and Charlotte Mobbs in the same composer's splendid *O dive custos*.

Christophers's direction is, as always, forever alert to the relationship between words and music – especially close with these two composers – while ensuring the careful delineation of the overall musical structure and each phrase, period and paragraph within it. Some minor blemishes aside, 'Bright Orb of Harmony' deserves to be set among that constellation of previous dazzling recordings by an ensemble that is less a choir, more an institution.

Stuart MacRae   British b1976

After reading Music at Durham University with Philip Cashian, Sohrab Uduman and Michael Zev Gordon, MacRae studied composition at the Guildhall School of Music and Drama with Simon Bainbridge and Robert Saxton. He was a finalist in the 1996 Lloyd's Bank Young Composer's Workshop when the BBC Philharmonic gave the first professional performance of Boreraig. From 1999 to 2003, MacRae was Composer in Association with the BBC Scottish Symphony Orchestra. Echo and Narcissus –

MacRae's first work for dance – was premiered at the Linbury Studio of the Royal Opera House in May 2007.

Orchestral works

Violin Concerto[a]. Three Scenes from the Death of Count Ugolino[b]. Motus[c]. Stirling Choruses[d]
[a]**Christian Tetzlaff** vn [b]**Loré Lixenberg** mez
[ad]**BBC Scottish Symphony Orchestra / Ilan Volkov;**
[bc]**Birmingham Contemporary Music Group /**
Susanna Mälkki
NMC NMCD115 (68' · DDD)   Ⓜ◯↦

A disc devoted to Stuart MacRae is timely, as the 30-year-old composer has built a considerable reputation. As the composer remarks in his booklet-note, all four pieces (written between 1999 and 2004) outline a journey. Abstractly, in the Birtwistle-like division of brass in the hieratic *Stirling Choruses* and the vividly soloistic sextet of *Motus*, whose progress from the fractured and discursive to the sustained and cumulative recalls that of the fine trumpet concerto *Interact*; graphically, as in the Dante texts relating the Infernal afterlife of Count Ugolino, even if the vocal line seems overwrought – at least when delivered with the vehemence of Loré Lixenberg – in the context of instrumental writing itself rich in expressive detail. The Violin Concerto is the most impressive work here: a successful formal recasting of the genre with the emotional emphasis on its finale, a striking amalgam of cadenza and apotheosis that handles the orchestra with considerable finesse. Dedicated playing from Christian Tetzlaff, along with the BCMG and BBC Scottish SO. An important release.

Leevi Madetoja   Finnish 1887-1947

Madetoja studied with Sibelius in Helsinki (1906-10), with d'Indy in Paris (1910-11), and in Vienna and Berlin (1911-12), then worked in Helsinki as a teacher, critic and composer. His works, often using Ostrobothnian folk music and French techniques, are skilfully orchestrated; they include the operas The Ostrobothnians (1923) and Juha (1934), three symphonies (1916, 1918, 1926) and much choral music.
GROVEmusic

Piano works

Complete Piano Works
Mika Rännäli pf
Alba ② ABCD206 (81' · DDD)   Ⓜ
Recorded live 2004

With Madetoja's operas, symphonies and songs now decently represented in the catalogue, the time is ripe for his even more rarely heard piano music. It consists almost entirely of miniatures (there are 33 tracks on the two CDs) and most of it dates from the 1910s – the first half of his career. Not conspicuously individual and often somewhat four-square in phrasing, the style feels like an organic continuation of Grieg and Tchaikovsky, enlivened by mildly diverting harmonic and melodic turns. Part of its attraction is an underlying melancholy. One readily agrees, too, with Mika Rännäli's identification of its 'childlike charm, a touch of mischief, wild boisterousness'. The minority of more extrovert pieces can be quite pianistically demanding without ever qualifying as virtuosic.

By far the most ambitious work is the three-movement cycle *Garden of Death*. 'One of the best and most poignant works in all Finnish piano literature,' Rännäli calls it, and that proves no overstatement. The austere, elegiac first movement, composed in memory of the composer's brother who was shot by the Red Guard in 1918 during the Finnish Civil War, brings strong echoes of Rachmaninov. It is followed by a volatile and disturbing waltz with an impressive, sombre conclusion, and by a wistful, restless berceuse.

Rännäli has an interesting mixed portfolio. He is not only a composer but also three-times Finnish champion in Latin American and ballroom dancing – a not irrelevant attribute, perhaps, given Madetoja's penchant for minuets, waltzes and gavottes. Live performances these may be but they are scrupulously clean in execution and engaging in temperament. Everything is flexible and nicely to scale. Beautifully judged recording quality too.

Songs

The Land in our song. Lieder, Op 2 – Since thou didst leave; Alone; Winter morning; Starry night. Dark-hued leaves, Op 19 No 1. Serenade, Op 16 No 1. Folk Songs from Northern Ostrobothnia, Op 18. Songs of Youth, Op 20*b*. Take up that fair kantele again. A flower is purest when opening. Lieder, Op 25 – From afar I hear them singing; Wintry road; Birth-place; Sometimes weeping in the evening. I would build a hut, Op 26 No 3. Song at the plough, Op 44 No 1. Lieder, Op 49 – Hail, O daylight in the North; Finland's Tree. Lieder, Op 60 – My longing; Evening. Lieder, Op 71 – I want to go home; The word of the Master. Song of the winter wind
Gabriel Suovanen *bar* **Gustav Djupsjöbacka** *pf*
Ondine ODE996–2 (79' · DDD · T/t)   Ⓕ**O**

The 32 songs are chronologically laid out. After the late-Romantic elegiac *lingua franca* of the Op 2 set, the first of Op 9, 'Dark-hued leaves', startles with its affinities with Rachmaninov; this gem of a piece is on the short list for all Finnish song recitals. Composed in 1913, the first of the *Songs of Youth*, Op 20*b*, couldn't be published until Finland's independence from Russia after the First World War, which is no surprise, given that its text is demonstratively nationalistic ('Arise, O young sons of Finland…Saved and cherished shall our homeland soon be!') and its melody strong and catchy. This is an altogether

impressive opus, whose concluding 'Christmas song' has become one of Finland's best-loved carols. With Op 25 we're back to the ecstatic tone of the earlier songs. Perhaps most impressive of this set is No 2, 'Wintry Road', with its tolling Brittenish ostinato and air of painful asceticism. Swedish-born baritone Gabriel Suovanen is well attuned both to the late-Romantic manner of Madetoja's early songs and to the ardent national-patriotic tone of his later ones. And his pianist, Gustav Djupsjöbacka, supplies stylish accompaniments. Recording quality is fine, and collectors of Nordic and/or song repertoire should not hesitate.

Albéric Magnard   French 1865-1914

Magnard, of a serious disposition, produced severe, formalistic works – mainly orchestral and chamber music and operas – taking Wagner, Beethoven, Gluck and his teacher d'Indy as models. Canon and fugue pervade much of his output, though the Third Symphony (1896) and the opera Bérénice (1909), his masterpiece, show a refreshing clarity of scoring and a lyric simplicity. GROVEmusic

Symphonies

Symphonies Nos 1-4
BBC Scottish Symphony Orchestra / Jean-Yves Ossonce
Helios ② CDD20068 (140' · DDD)   Ⓑ**O**

The name of Albéric Magnard began to impinge on us only 30 years ago, and there have been recordings of three of his symphonies, the opera *Guercoeur*, and a five-disc set of his chamber music and songs; but he seems doomed to be a composer whose music survives only via recordings: his impact on the concert life of this country has been virtually nil; nor has he been much better served in his native France. Not that he would have cared overmuch: during his life (brought to an abrupt end at the start of the First World War by German invaders who set fire to his country house) he made little attempt to get his music performed, being paranoically sensitive to any suspicion of nepotistic influence, as his father was a powerful newspaper proprietor. By all accounts he was withdrawn and austere; perhaps in keeping with that image his music isn't for the casual listener who looks for facile attractiveness, but is in a somewhat Teutonic way rewarding for the serious-minded in its skilfully crafted and thoughtfully lyrical character.

The First Symphony (1890) shows the unmistakable influence of Wagner in the *religioso* slow movement. Despite the adoption of the cyclic principle championed by his teacher Vincent d'Indy, under whose watchful eye the work was written and who must have smiled approvingly at his pupil's fluent contrapuntal technique, Magnard's proliferation of ideas threatens structural continuity, especially in the first movement. In contrast to that movement's initial brooding atmosphere, the Second Symphony begins more sunnily and spiritedly, and the following *Scherzo* (which replaced an earlier fugue) is a bucolic 'Danses' tinged with introspection. The emotional core of the symphony is the luxuriant *Chant varié*, and the work ends in an almost light-hearted mood. The Third Symphony's striking organum-like opening leads to an *Allegro* by turns vigorous and contemplative. Next comes a *Scherzo* headed 'Danses' (as in the previous symphony), a mocking soufflé with a wistful central section – an altogether captivating movement that's anything but austere. The movingly tense slow movement's long lines are subverted by menacing outbursts that build to a stormy climax before subsiding; and there's a finale which combines exuberance and lyricism with a return to the symphony's very first theme. This is certainly the work to recommend to newcomers to Magnard.

Several years elapsed before the appearance of his last symphony in 1913, and by then his overall mood had darkened. The turbulent passion that characterises the first movement, presented in dramatically colourful orchestration, is also mirrored in the finale: between them come a highly individual *Scherzo* with strange oriental-type passages and a lengthy, anguished slow movement. The BBC Scottish Symphony Orchestra is on splendid form throughout; their efforts have been recorded in exemplary fashion.

Gustav Mahler   Austrian 1860-1911

From 1875 to 1878 Mahler was at the Vienna Conservatory, where he studied the piano, harmony and composition. After that he attended university lectures, worked as a music teacher and composed Das klagende Lied, a cantata indebted to the operas of Weber and Wagner but also showing many conspicuously Mahlerian features.

In 1880 he accepted a conducting post at a summer theatre at Bad Hall, and was engaged in a similar capacity in 1881 and 1883 at the theatres in Ljubljana and Olomouc. In autumn 1883, he became music director at Kassel. He found conditions uncongenial, but an unhappy love affair with one of the singers led to his first masterpiece, the song cycle Lieder eines fahrenden Gesellen, and the inception of the closely related First Symphony.

Early in 1885 Mahler secured the post of second conductor at the Neues Stadttheater in Leipzig, to begin in July 1886. The intervening year he spent at the Landestheater in Prague, where he had the opportunity of conducting operas by Gluck, Mozart, Beethoven and Wagner. At Leipzig, in January 1887, he took over the Ring cycle from Arthur Nikisch, who fell ill, and convincingly established among critics and public his genius as an interpretative artist. The following year he completed Weber's unfinished comic opera Die drei Pintos (its successful performances in 1888 made Mahler famous and provided a useful source of income) and fell in love

with the wife of Weber's grandson. It was through the Webers that he discovered in 1887 the musical potential of Des Knaben Wunderhorn, a collection of folklike texts by Arnim and Brentano which provided Mahler with words for all but one of his songs for the next 14 years.

Disagreements with colleagues led to Mahler's resignation at Leipzig in May 1888 and to his dismissal a few months later from Prague, but within a few weeks he secured a far more important appointment at the Royal Opera in Budapest. His first year there was overshadowed by the illness and deaths of his parents and his sister. Though he was successful in bringing the opera house into profit and improving standards and repertory, the imminent appointment of an Intendant with artistic control made his situation untenable; he resigned and became first conductor at the Stadttheater, Hamburg. Despite a stifling artistic atmosphere and a heavy workload, Mahler returned to composition and at his summer retreat in the Salzkammergut completed the Second and Third Symphonies. 1895 brought both tragedy, when his youngest brother committed suicide, and success, with the premiere of the Second Symphony in Berlin in December. Now a conductor of international stature and a composer of growing reputation, he turned his attention to the Vienna Hofoper. The main obstacle was his Jewish origins; so he accepted Catholic baptism in February 1897 and was appointed Kapellmeister at two months later.

At Vienna Mahler brought a stagnating opera house to a position of unrivalled brilliance. In 1901 he had a villa built at Maiernigg on the Wörthersee in Carinthia, where he spent the summers composing. In 1902 he married Alma, daughter of the artist Emil Jakob Schindler, and though their life together was not untroubled the security benefited his creative life. At Maiernigg he completed Symphonies Nos 5-8 and in 1904 the Kindertotenlieder, settings of five poems by Rückert on the death of children. The death of Mahler's own elder daughter, Maria, from scarlet fever three years later left him distraught. In Vienna Mahler was surrounded by radical young composers, including Schoenberg, Berg, Webern and Zemlinsky, whose work he supported and encouraged. His propagation of his own music, however, aroused opposition from a section of the Viennese musical establishment, and when the campaign against him, led by an anti-semitic press, gained momentum he turned to New York, where he spent his last winters as conductor, first of the Metropolitan Opera and, from 1910, of the New York PO. He continued to spend the summers in Europe, where he undertook further conducting and completed the valedictory Ninth Symphony and Das Lied von der Erde. This last, a setting of six Chinese poems in German translation, took the shape of a large-scale symphony for two voices and orchestra but Mahler, whose fear of death and sense of fate had been intensified by the diagnosis of a heart condition in 1907, refused to number the work 10, citing Beethoven, Schubert and Bruckner. He did, however, start work on a 10th symphony, but died before he could complete it.

Although as a conductor Mahler achieved fame primarily in opera, his creative energies were directed almost wholly towards symphony and song. Even in the early Das klagende Lied, there are stylistic features to be found in his mature music, for example the combining of onstage and offstage orchestras, the association of high tragedy and the mundane, the drawing on folksong ideas and the dramatic-symbolic use of tonality. This last reappeared in his early masterpiece, the Lieder eines fahrenden Gesellen, which has an evolutionary tonal scheme paralleling the changing fortunes of the travelling hero. In the 1890s Mahler was much influenced by the Wunderhorn poems, in his symphonies as well as his songs, for he often used song to clarify an important moment in the structure of a symphony, for example 'Urlicht' in No 2, which he found himself unable to continue after writing the imposing first movement. No 3 is more idiosyncratic; again, its dramatic scheme evolved with recourse to song and chorus. No 4 returns to tradition, in a first movement of rare wit and subtlety; here the poetic idea is the progress from experience to innocence (with a Wunderhorn song finale). While No 2, 'The Resurrection', moves from C minor to E flat, No 4 goes from G major to the 'heavenly' E major. Parody, irony and satire are important in Mahler's thinking during these years, with popular invention (like the children's round in no.1 and the march tunes of No 3) and elements of distortion.

Nos 5, 6 and 7 are sometimes regarded as a trilogy, although No 5 is a heroic work, with a narrative running from its opening funeral march through the agitated Allegro to a Scherzo and a triumphant conclusion. The symphony moves from C sharp minor to D major. No 6, a tragic work – and in many musicians' view, his greatest symphony for its equilibrium between form and drama – begins and ends in A minor; the finale makes it clear that there is no escape for the implied hero and indeed his death is symbolically enacted in the movement's shattering climax. The shape of No 7, which moves from E minor to C major, is less satisfying; possibly, with its dark, nocturnal middle movement, it is consciously built round the poetic concept of darkness moving towards the light of the finale. The largest-scale of Mahler's symphonies is No 8, the so-called 'Symphony of a Thousand', in which the second part is a vast synthesis of forms and media embodying the setting of the final scene of Goethe's Faust as an amalgam of dramatic cantata, oratorio, song cycle, Lisztian choral symphony and instrumental symphony. This public pronouncement was followed by one of his most personal, Das Lied von der Erde, influenced in its vocal writing and woodwind obbligatos by Mahler's new interest in Bach. His last two symphonies return to the four-movement scheme of the middle-period ones, incorporating extensions of the character movements of his earlier works with the new type of slow first movement (followed up in the unfinished 10th) and ending with an Adagio in a mood of profound resignation. Mahler's extension of symphonic form, of the symphony's expressive scope and the use of the orchestra (especially the agonised timbres he obtained by using instruments, particularly wind, at the top of their compass) represent a pained farewell to Romanticism; different aspects were followed up by the Second Viennese School, Shostakovich and Britten. **GROVE**music

Symphonies

No 1 in D; No 2 in C minor, 'Resurrection'; No 3 in D minor; No 4 in G; No 5 in C sharp minor; No 6 in A minor; No 7 in E minor; No 8 in E flat, 'Symphony of a Thousand'; No 9 in D; No 10 in F sharp minor

Complete Symphonies

Symphonies – No 1[a]; No 2[b] (with **Cheryl Studer** sop **Waltraud Meier** mez **Arnold Schoenberg Choir**); No 3[b] (**Jessye Norman** sop **Vienna Boys' Choir; Vienna State Opera Chorus**); No 4[b] (**Frederica von Stade** mez); No 5[a]; Nos 6[c] & 7[c]; No 8[a] (**Studer, Sylvia McNair, Andrea Rost** sops **Anne Sofie von Otter** mez **Rosemarie Lang** contr **Peter Seiffert** ten **Bryn Terfel** bass-bar **Jan-Hendrik Rootering** bass **Tölz Boys' Choir; Berlin Radio Chorus; Prague Philharmonic Chorus**) Nos 9[b] & 10[b] – Adagio [a]**Berlin Philharmonic Orchestra;** [b]**Vienna Philharmonic Orchestra;** [c]**Chicago Symphony Orchestra / Claudio Abbado**
DG ⑫ 447 023-2GX12 (718' · ADD/DDD · T/t) Recorded 1977-94

The current pre-eminence of Gustav Mahler in the concert hall and on disc isn't something that could have been anticipated – other than by the composer himself. Hard now to believe that his revival had to wait until the centenary celebrations of his birth in 1960. And yet by 1980 he was more widely esteemed than his longer-lived contemporaries Sibelius and Strauss and could suddenly be seen to tower over 20th-century music much as Beethoven must have done in a previous age. By this time too, a new generation of conductors had come to the fore, further transforming our perceptions of the composer. Claudio Abbado is arguably the most distinguished of this group and, while his interpretations will not satisfy every listener on every occasion, they make an excellent choice for the library shelves, when the price is reasonably competitive and the performances so emblematic (and arguably central to our understanding) of Mahler's place in contemporary musical life.

Of the alternatives, Haitink's package has the fewest expressive distortions while Bernstein's is the most ceaselessly emotive of them all; neither has Abbado's particular combination of qualities. It's probably no accident that Donald Mitchell's notes for this set are focused on the nature of Mahler's 'modernity'. For it's that ironic, inquisitive, preternaturally aware young composer who haunts this conductor's performances. Not for Abbado the heavy, saturated textures of 19th-century Romanticism, nor the chilly rigidity of some of his own 'modernist' peers. Instead an unaffected warmth and elegance of sound allows everything to come through naturally – in so far as the different venues and DG's somewhat variable technology will permit – even in the most searingly intense of climaxes.

Abbado presents Mahler as a fluent classicist, and is less concerned to characterise the surface

MAHLER'S SYMPHONIES – IN BRIEF

Various orchs / Claudio Abbado
DG ⑫ 447 023-2GX12 (11 hr 58' · DDD) Ⓜ◉◐▷
The Italian conductor's dramatic, carefully moulded way with Mahler is best experienced live, but there's no lack of polish or refinement from his *de luxe* performers.

New York Philharmonic / various
NYP9801/12 ⑫ (15 hr 3' · ADD) Ⓕ◉◉
A valuable box for connoisseurs, documenting the orchestra's long Mahler tradition (dating back to when the composer was its music director). Boulez in No 3, Mitropoulos in No 6 and Kubelík in No 7 are highlights.

Concertgebouw Orchestra / Bernard Haitink
Philips ⑩ 442 050-2PB10 (11 hr 32' · DDD) Ⓜ◐▷
Haitink's grasp of the music's many contrasts has sharpened since he made these recordings, but their unaffected clarity stands the test of time.

Frankfurt RSO / Inbal
Brilliant ⑮ 92005 (14 hr 40' DDD) Ⓢ
Denon's fine engineering, the Alte Oper's welcoming acoustic and Inbal's headstrong interpretations are an even more tempting proposition at super-budget price.

NYPO, Israel PO / Bernstein
Sony ⑫ 88697 45369-2 (11 hr 53 ' · ADD) Ⓑ◉◉
The heartfelt passion of possibly the composer's most famous interpreter is well known; his unerring composer's ear for the traffic of Mahler's vast forces and structures is often overlooked. Adds *Das Lied* and a fascinating documentary 'Gustav Mahler Remembered: Reminiscences by Mahler's Associates and by Musicians Who Played Under His Baton'.

SWR Orchestra Baden-Baden / Gielen
Hänssler ⑬ 931330 (12 hr 31' ADD) Ⓑ◉
Age has mellowed and deepened the Mahler interpretations of this one-time colleague of the avant-gardistes. Fine sound shows off Gielen's forensic ear for detail; Mahler's stature as pivotal figure between centuries is clearer than ever.

Bavarian Radio SO / Kubelík
DG ⑩ 463 738-2 (10 hr 51' · ADD) Ⓑ◐▷
The Czech conductor brings an unfussy clarity to Mahler's dance rhythms that can be even more moving than the breast-beating approach. Ideal for those new to Mahler.

West German Radio Symphony Orchestra, Cologne / Gary Bertini
EMI ⑪ 340238-2 (12h 54' · DDD) Ⓑ◉◉◉▷
Bertini scores on nearly every count. His lovingly molded, wonderfully idiomatic performances are enormously satisfying. This is real class at a very affordable price.

battle of conflicting emotions than to elucidate the underlying symphonic structure. The lack of Solti's brand of forthright theatricality can bring a feeling of disappointment. But even where he underplays the drama of the moment, sufficient sense of urgency is sustained by a combination of well-judged tempos, marvellously graduated dynamics and precisely balanced, ceaselessly changing textures. The propulsion comes from within.

It was in November 1907 that Mahler famously told Sibelius that 'the symphony must be like the world. It must embrace everything.' And perhaps it's only today that we see this as a strength rather than a weakness in his music. He wrote music that's 'about' its own past while at the same time probing into all our futures, music that's so all-embracing and communicates with such directness that we can make it 'mean' whatever we want it to, confident that we alone have really understood the code. Abbado lacks Bernstein's desire to explore these limitless possibilities, but some will count that as a blessing. These are committed and authoritative performances.

The Mahler Broadcasts 1948-82 Ⓗ
Symphonies – No 1 (recorded live 1959)[ac]; No 2 (**Kathleen Battle** *sop* **Maureen Forrester** *contr* **Westminster Choir**; rec 1982)[afm]; No 3 (**Yvonne Minton** *mez* **Camerata Singers; Little Church around the Corner Boys' Choir; Trinity Church Boys' Choir; Brooklyn Boys' Choir** rec 1976)[adm]; No 4 (**Irmgard Seefried** *sop* rec 1962)[ah]; No 5 (rec 1980)[akm]; No 6 (rec 1955)[ag]; No 7 (rec 1981)[ae]; No 8 (**Frances Yeend, Uta Graf, Camilla Williams** *sops* **Martha Lipton, Louise Bernhardt** *contrs* **Eugene Conley** *ten* **Carlos Alexander** *bar* **George London** *bass-bar* **Schola Cantorum; Public School No 12 Boys' Choir, Manhattan**; rec 1950)[bj]; No 9 (rec 1962)[ac]; No 10 – Adagio; Purgatorio (rec 1960 & 1958)[ag]. Lieder eines fahrenden Gesellen (**Dietrich Fischer-Dieskau** *bar* rec 1964)[ai]. Das Lied von der Erde (**Kathleen Ferrier** *contr* **Set Svanholm** *ten* rec 1948)[bl]
[a]**New York Philharmonic Orchestra**, [b]**Philharmonic Symphony Orchestra of New York** / [c]**Sir John Barbirolli**, [d]**Pierre Boulez**, [e]**Rafael Kubelík**, [f]**Zubin Mehta**, [g]**Dimitri Mitropoulos**, [h]**Sir Georg Solti**, [i]**William Steinberg**, [j]**Leopold Stokowski**, [k]**Klaus Tennstedt**, [l]**Bruno Walter**
New York Philharmonic mono/[m]stereo
⑫ NYP9801/12 (903' · ADD) Also contains interviews and reminiscences about Mahler Ⓕ◉◉

Available from www.newyorkphilharmonic.org

Not your average collection of Mahler symphonies, but one which, with pride, charts in words and music, the impact of the composer's final two years (1909-11) in and on New York and the important part the city's orchestra subsequently played in spreading the Mahler message. Consideration was given, when choosing what to include, to the New York players' own views and memories of the concerts or conductors; and to featuring symphonies from conductors who never took them into the studio. Bernstein is conspicuous by his absence, but it would seem that rights aren't currently available for the release of his Mahler broadcast tapes. We hear, though, from the man whose Mahler was Bernstein's model; and Mitropoulos's 1960 Sixth Symphony must have been a hard act for Bernstein to follow. Mitropoulos delivers the symphony's integrity and unpalatable truths with a grim and arguably more compelling single-mindedness. Apart from the slow movement (placed second, and gloriously played), there's little relief from the symphony's battering march to tragedy.

Latterly interpreters have also been more protean in the Eighth's expansive Faust fantasy, and it would be idle to pretend that other conductors don't make more than Stokowski of the contrasts explicitly indicated in Mahler's score. Stokowski in 1950 opted for an unusually moderate range of tempos (starting with a swift *Andante*), and it's impossible to say whether he was playing safe, attempting to dignify the folksy inspiration, or bringing us something of the manner in which Mahler himself conducted the work (Stokowski was present at the Eighth's Munich world premiere in 1910). Whatever the case, along the way there are as many attractions as there are inevitable insecurities, and it's worth hearing, not least for the First Part of the symphony, which bears the unmistakable stamp of greatness, and the sound is a marvel for its years.

The earliest recording here is a vital, controlled and incisive 1948 *Das Lied von der Erde* from Walter, with Kathleen Ferrier making her American début. Set Svanholm tends to press ahead of the beat, but it's a rare pleasure to hear the tenor songs as resolutely conquered and characterised. As for Ferrier's contribution, there's little to choose between this and her famous 1952 Decca Vienna account made with a more relaxed Walter. The later recording perhaps presents the richer portrait of a unique vocal phenomenon, and a cathartic release of emotion in the final pages not matched in New York. Aptly enough for this enterprise, applause has been retained at the end of the works, even if, in the case of *Das Lied*, one wishes that the audience had waited a few seconds longer. But audience noise during the music can be frustrating. Time may well be standing still at the start of Barbirolli's 1959 First Symphony, but the audience is still finding its way to the seats.

Matters improve, possibly because, as one of the concert's critical notices informs us, only part of the audience stayed to the end. And the part that did was witness to some engaging features, such as the pronounced, and for the time, deeply unfashionable string *portamentos*, and a *Scherzo* with big boots and rustic charm laid on by the barrow-load. The *Scherzo* of Barbirolli's 1962 New York Ninth Symphony is of a consistently coarser cut than his 1964 Berlin studio recording for EMI, and arguably benefits from it, though there's little evidence for the booklet's general assessment of the Berlin Ninth as 'rather disengaged from the work's churning emotions'.

And the brightly analytical (and stereo) Berlin recording does allow clearer perception of the details of – future archival revelations apart – Barbirolli's finest taped Mahler symphony interpretation. Solti's Fourth Symphony (also 1962), as we know from his two Decca studio recordings, was unexpectedly graceful, with a long-breathed slow movement, and admirable discipline and refinement, even if that refinement streamlines the work's bolder colours and sardonic edge.

All the New York recordings enjoy good balances; those already mentioned are all in very decent, if occasionally pale, mono sound. The stereo tapings aren't ideally flattering to New York's violins, but benefit from a wider dynamic range. The deployment of the various on- and off-stage forces in Mehta's 1982 Second is a major achievement for a live recording. This was a special occasion for all involved (the orchestra's 10,000th concert), and although Mehta's view of the work is neither particularly lofty nor radical, the excitement in the hall has transferred to disc admirably. The pleasures of Boulez's 1976 performance of the Third Symphony include a typical (and often very sensuous) cultivation of inner workings, concern for outer structure, very precisely graded dynamics, and a strikingly individual *rubato*. Rarely has the sudden tumult and its immediate aftermath at the end of the third movement – proclamatory brass receding over shimmering strings – cast such a spell.

Tennstedt had the ability, at the moment of performance, to persuade listeners that the music could and should sound no other way, and his 1980 New York Fifth Symphony runs the full gamut of 'no tomorrow' intensity, intervention, riotous colour and perfectly formed details.

In contrast, the years between Kubelík's Bavarian Radio Seventh (recorded for DG in 1970) and this 1981 New York account appear to have prompted a radical rethink. Or maybe Kubelík is responding to the extra heft of the New York orchestra and ephemeral concert conditions to push out the boundaries. Still recognisable, if moderated, are the sharp features and deliberately soured tone lending menace to both the second and third movements, and an *Andante amoroso* cajoled into a diversion of wonderfully graceful, fresh-voiced charm. But the much broader manner maximises the far-flung sonorities, in the first movement, at the expense of line and general decorum.

Naturally there are fluffs, early entries and an occasional *rubato* prompting untidiness, but the vast majority demonstrates a level of professionalism and innate ability to produce the right sort of sound at the right time that have made and maintained the orchestra as one of the world's ideal Mahler instruments.

Symphonies – Nos 1 & 2 (**Elly Ameling** sop **Aafje Heynis** contr **Netherlands Radio Chorus**); No 3 (**Maureen Forrester** contr **St Willibrord Church Boys' Choir; Netherlands Radio Chorus**); No 4

(Ameling); Nos 5-8 (**Ileana Cotrubas, Heather Harper, Hanneke van Bork** sops **Birgit Finnila** mez **Marianne Dieleman** contr **William Cochran** ten **Hermann Prey** bar **Hans Sotin** bass **St Willibrord and Pius X Children's Choir; Collegium Musicum Amstelodamense; Amsterdam Toonkunst Choir; Amsterdam Stem des Volks Choir**); No 10 – Adagio **Concertgebouw Orchestra / Bernard Haitink**
Philips Bernard Haitink Symphony Edition
442 050-2PB10 (692' · ADD) Recorded 1962-71　Ⓜ Ⓞ

If space is at a premium, this set is undeniably attractive, though the multilingual illustrated booklet dispenses with texts and translations, and several symphonies are awkwardly spread between discs. For a generation of record buyers it was these sane, lucid, sometimes insufficiently demonstrative Concertgebouw readings that represented a way into music previously considered unacceptable in polite society. Haitink's phrasing has an appealing natural simplicity, his rhythmic almost-squareness providing welcome reassurance. The preoccupation with conventional symphonic verities of form and structure doesn't preclude striking beauty of sound and the recordings have come up well in the remastering. There's some residual hiss.

Haitink's early No 1 (1962), his first taping of a Mahler symphony, is usually reckoned the least satisfactory of his career. True, the third movement doesn't quite work: Haitink's attempts at 'Jewishness' are so self-conscious that the results sound rhythmically suspect, not quite together rather than convincingly ethnic. The real problem is the boxed-in sound, uncharacteristically rough and ready, with none of the cool tonal lustre which characterised subsequent LPs from this source.

The Fourth receives a similarly straightforward account with a wonderfully hushed *Poco adagio* and few if any of the aggressive mannerisms which have marred more recent versions. The restraint can border on inflexibility at times. The first movement lacks a certain element of fantasy with everything so very accurate and together, and, while Elly Ameling makes a lovely sound in the finale, the orchestra's animal caricatures aren't really vulgar enough, the sense of wonder and awe in the face of heaven rather muted at the close. Though inevitably lacking the gut-wrenching theatricality and hallucinatory colour of Bernstein, the Seventh has none of the staidness and rigidity that occasionally prompts doubts about Haitink's Mahlerian credentials. It emerges here as a high point of the series, second only to the celebrated Ninth. The opening is deceptively cool and brooding; thereafter the interpretation is unexpectedly driven and intense, even if Mahler's fantastical sonorities are left to fend for themselves. Only those who feel the nth degree of nightmarish 'exaggeration' to be vital to the expression of the whole need have any doubts. The finale is effectively held together but should perhaps sound more hollow than this.

If you must have the Mahler symphonies under a single conductor, Haitink could arguably be the man to go for. His objectivity won't spoil you for alternative readings. Nevertheless you wouldn't want to miss out on Bernstein, unrelenting in his desire to communicate the essentials of these scores, taking his cue from Mahler's remark that 'the symphony must be like the world. It must be all-embracing'. Haitink is more circumspect, the music's vaunting ambition knowingly undersold.

Symphonies Nos 1-9; No 10 – Adagio.
Das Lied von der Erde
Marianne Haggander, Krisztina Laki, Lucia Popp, Julia Varady, Maria Venuti sops **Marjana Lipovšek, Florence Quivar** mezs **Anne Howells, Gwendolyn Killebrew** contrs **Ben Heppner, Paul Frey** tens **Alan Titus** bar **Siegfried Vogel** bass **West German Radio Symphony Orchestra, Cologne / Gary Bertini**
EMI ⑪ 340238-2 (12h 54' · DDD)　Ⓢ Ⓞ Ⓞ Ⓞ Ⓞ ➤

Gary Bertini's 1984-91 Cologne Radio Mahler cycle is the most consistently satisfying on disc, in terms of its lovingly idiomatic and world-class performances, plus robust, realistic engineering that truly replicates the dynamic impact and spatial depth that these scores convey in the best concert halls.

A colleague aptly and accurately likened Bertini's emphasis on the proverbial big picture to Rafael Kubelík's DG Mahler cycle, although Bertini's Cologne musicians operate on an altogether higher level of first-desk refinement and chamber-like sensitivity to the composer's extraordinary palette of orchestral colour. The strands of the Tenth's *Adagio*'s pulverising climactic chords are powerfully yet clearly delineated to the point where you can take dictation from what you hear.

The brass sail through the Fifth's difficult writing with equal aplomb to stare their he-man Solti/Chicago colleagues in the eye, while the soft woodwinds and exposed strings create a haunting atmosphere in the Eighth's second movement to gently joust with Tennstedt or Nagano for top position. At the same time, Bertini's fervency sometimes gives Leonard Bernstein's magnetism a run for its money, as one readily hears in the First's klezmer tinges, the Seventh's rollicking coda and the most rabble-rousing moments of the Ninth's inner movements. By contrast, Bertini turns in one of the few very slow readings of the finale that rivets your attention in every bar.

Bertini also benefits from terrific singing, highlighted by a tightly knit ensemble in the Eighth (baritone Alan Titus especially stands out as Pater Ecstaticus), plus Ben Heppner and Marjana Lipovšek on ringing, communicative form throughout *Das Lied* (both this and the Eighth stem from live Tokyo performances). And in the Fourth's finale, the late Lucia Popp surpasses her EMI recording under Tennstedt. To be certain, earlier reviews pinpoint weak spots, such as the Sixth's relatively clunky first movement or the Second's finale's fleeting inaccuracies, but these are nitpicks in face of so much excellence elsewhere.

For cost, convenience and quality, there's no better Mahler deal on the planet.

Symphonies Nos 1-9; No 10 – Adagio.
Das Lied von der Erde
Israel Philharmonic Orchestra; London Symphony Orchestra; Vienna Philharmonic Orchestra / Leonard Bernstein
Video directors **Humphrey Burton & Tony Palmer**
DG ⑨ 📀 073 4088GH9 (13h 24' · NTSC · 4:3 · PCM stereo and DTS 5.1 · 0). Includes a bonus disc of rehearsals. Recorded 1971-76   Ⓕ⚫⚫

Between 1971 and 1976 Humphrey Burton directed filmed concerts of Bernstein conducting the nine Mahler symphonies, along with *Das Lied von der Erde* and the *Adagio* from the unfinished Tenth. Previous VHS and laserdisc incarnations suffered from uneven sound and occasional discrepancies of synchronisation between screen image and audio. Happily, DG's new DVD edition not only corrects these problems but also refurbishes the soundtracks in vibrant 5.1 surround sound.

Little can be added to the many words written about Bernstein's intense affinity for and ardent advocacy of Mahler. Indeed, the musicality and specificity of Bernstein's body language often seems to create parallel universes to each score's emotional peaks and dynamic valleys. One doesn't have to turn up the volume to sense the exultation and drive with which Bernstein inspires the huge forces in the Eighth's first part or the Second's final pages, gauging the protracted climaxes as he clenches his baton with both hands in long, agonising downward strokes. Watch, too, how Bernstein's eagle eyes and decisive hands anticipate tricky entries and tempo changes in the Fifth's second movement and the Seventh's first with unshakeable authority, or how he instantaneously adjusts dynamics and aligns rhythmic vagaries (the Fourth's opening bars, the Third's percussion).

Yet for all of Bernstein's podium choreography, he also knows when to stand back and simply let the musicians play, casually passing the baton back and forth between his hands, as in stretches of the Third's and Ninth's final movements and the Tenth's *Adagio*. And, like a benign sovereign, he frequently shoots his players and singers encouraging glances, with plenty of smiles to reward the Vienna Philharmonic's first-desk soloists, as well as their counterparts in the LSO (No 2) and the Israel Philharmonic (*Das Lied*). Burton's visual style works hand-in-glove with Mahler's orchestration and dynamic game plans, saving close-ups for quiet passages and quick inserts that underline instrumental entrances.

In general, Bernstein's filmed Mahler interpretations represent a centre-point between the raw excitement characterising much of his pioneering 1960s CBS/Sony cycle and his riper, often more expansive late-1980s remakes. On balance, the video Fourth, Fifth and Ninth are Bernstein's finest performances of these works. The Fifth is faster and more incisively shaped than his 1987 traversal and the Vienna players get better as the performance progresses. Edith Mathis looks as radiant as she sings in the Fourth's finale. The Vienna Ninth is notable for the other-worldly stillness and delicacy of the final pages while the central movements bring the sort of abandon he shows in his 1960s Ninth.

A bonus disc provides additional and valuable context. 'Four Ways to Say Farewell' combines rehearsal and performance footage of the Ninth as a backdrop to Bernstein's narration, where he fancifully if plausibly likens the first movement's long-short rhythmic motive to Mahler's irregular heartbeat. Rehearsals of the Fifth reveal an even more balletic, gesticulative conductor than the public usually saw, along with important insights into the music's character (at one point Bernstein cajoles the brass to play 'like in Italian opera', pinpointing the influence of Verdi on Mahler that most critics gloss over).

A *Das Lied* rehearsal shows Christa Ludwig haggling over the breakneck tempo Bernstein sets in the 'Von der Schönheit' central section. Then there is Bernstein at the piano, chain-smoking, giving an informal discourse on the work's symbolism and chamber-like orchestration ('You have to prepare an entire orchestra as if it was a string quartet').

In an age when Mahler's symphonies are ubiquitous, it's fascinating to witness the missionary zeal of Bernstein more than three decades ago, claiming how his 'acting out' the music rather than merely beating time helps him to convince his orchestras of the its greatness. With Bernstein at the helm, one doesn't take Mahler's greatness for granted.

Symphonies – No 1; No 2, 'Resurrection'[a]
[a]**Sylvia McNair** *sop* [a]**Jard van Nes** *contr*
[a]**Ernst Senff Chorus; Berlin Philharmonic Orchestra / Bernard Haitink**
Video director **Barrie Gavin**
Philips Ⓕ 📀 074 3131PH
(152' · NTSC · 4:3 · PCM stereo and DTS 5.1 · 0)   Ⓕ

Symphony No 3
Florence Quivar *contr* **Tölzer Knabenchor; Ernst Senff Women's Chorus; Berlin Philharmonic Orchestra / Bernard Haitink**
Video director **Barrie Gavin**
Philips Ⓕ 📀 074 3132PH
(106' · NTSC · 4:3 · PCM stereo and DTS 5.1 · 0)   Ⓕ

Symphonies – No 4; No 7
Sylvia McNair *sop* **Berlin Philharmonic Orchestra / Bernard Haitink**
Video director **Barrie Gavin**
Philips Ⓕ 📀 074 3133PH
(140' · NTSC · 4:3 · PCM stereo and DTS 5.1 · 0)
All from Philips VHS originals   Ⓕ

Perhaps it's unfair to scrutinise Philips's visual record of Haitink's early-1990s Mahler performances with the BPO so soon after Universal brought out their Bernstein Mahler DVD set (see above). You could scarcely imagine two more disparate Mahler conductors. While Bernstein's charismatic body language often seems to mirror the music, Haitink avoids all flamboyance. The casual viewer might even infer a sense of detachment in his frequently half-shut eyes and all-too-rare smiles. Indeed, there seem to be more close-ups of separate orchestral sections and their first-desk representatives than of the conductor. Still, it looks and sounds as if the Berlin musicians are drawn into the Dutch conductor's fluid stick technique, clear beat, economy of gesture and seasoned awareness of when not to interfere.

Furthermore, the inconsistent sound quality of Bernstein's early-1970s films yields to the present edition's robust, full-bodied digital sonics. Indeed, the Second Symphony finale's offstage brass and the transparent scoring of No 7's two 'night music' movements emerge more atmospherically when experienced via surround sound's multichannel ambience.

Although Haitink's studio Concertgebouw Mahler cycle pretty much outclasses the aborted Berlin studio cycle he began in the late 1980s, the presence of an audience (and camera crew) sometimes elicits more animated, urgent and emotionally three-dimensional music-making on the part of both conductor and orchestra. The Third Symphony is a striking case in point. In contrast to the square and flaccid 1990 Berlin studio version, this live account from a year later features greater tension in the outer movements and a wider degree of colour and inflection within the second and third movements. Florence Quivar's more opulent contralto timbre also contrasts to Jard van Nes's lighter-toned agility.

By contrast, the First and Fourth differ little from their generally excellent studio twins. Both Firsts feature an opening movement whose blended sonorities unfold in a leisurely and organic way, plus an overly languid third movement where the dotted rhythms are stilted and unswinging. However, in the finale, the brass and percussion truly give their all live. The Fourth's bucolic nature absorbs Haitink's relaxed, poetic leadership and astute attention to the composer's specific gradations of soft dynamics. In the finale, Sylvia McNair vividly describes the kingdom of heaven without once dropping her rounded tone's effortless composure.

The Seventh hits and misses; there's little sense of surprise in the first movement's tempo transitions, while the *Scherzo*'s angular, mysterious qualities and chamber-like delicacy only turn up in flashes. Once the adrenalin kicks in for the finale, it stays there, and you're actually happy when Haitink doesn't ease up for the *grazioso* episodes. Similarly, in the *Resurrection*, Haitink saves his most energetic and inspired capabilities for the sprawling finale, where the chorus, organ and myriad percussion make uplifting, joyful noise. If you happened to have cranked up the volume during the soft passages, the subsequent climaxes will pin you to the wall in time for the neighbours to complain. Nothing sexy about the bonus features: a Mahler timeline, a slideshow of photos of the composer, and promos for other Universal Classics DVD releases.

Symphony No 1

Symphony No 1. Lieder eines fahrenden Gesellen
Dietrich Fischer-Dieskau bar **Bavarian Radio Symphony Orchestra / Rafael Kubelík**
DG The Originals 449 735-2GOR (67' · ADD · T/t)
Recorded 1967 Ⓜ**O**🔗➔

Rafael Kubelík is essentially a poetic conductor and he gets more poetry out of this symphony than almost any other conductor who has recorded it. Although he takes the repeat of the first movement's short exposition, it's strange that he should ignore the single repeat sign in the *Ländler* when he seems so at ease with the music. Notwithstanding a fondness for generally brisk tempos in Mahler, Kubelík is never afraid of rubato here, above all in his very personally inflected account of the slow movement. This remains a delight. The finale now seems sonically a little thin, with the trumpets made to sound rather hard-pressed and the final climax failing to open out as it can in more modern recordings. The orchestral contribution is very good even if absolute precision isn't guaranteed.

Dietrich Fischer-Dieskau's second recording of the *Lieder eines fahrenden Gesellen* has worn rather less well, the spontaneous ardour of his earlier performance (with Furtwängler and the Philharmonia) here tending to stiffen into melodrama and mannerism. There's much beautiful singing, and he's most attentively accompanied, but the third song, 'Ich hab' ein glühend Messer', is implausibly overwrought, bordering on self-parody. By contrast, Kubelík's unpretentious, Bohemian approach to the symphony remains perfectly valid. A corrective to the grander visions of those who conduct the music with the benefit of hindsight and the advantages of digital technology? Perhaps.

Symphony No 2, 'Resurrection'

Symphony No 2
Arleen Auger sop **Dame Janet Baker** mez
City of Birmingham Symphony Chorus and Orchestra / Sir Simon Rattle
EMI Great Recordings of the Century
② 345794-2 (86' · DDD) Ⓜ**OOO**🔗➔

 Where Simon Rattle's interpretation is concerned, we must go into the realm of a giant Mahlerian like Klemperer. For we're dealing here with conducting akin to genius, with insights and instincts that can't be measured with any old yardstick. Rattle's sense of drama, of apocalyptic events, is so strong that at the final chords one is awed. None of this could have been achieved without the CBSO, which here emerges as an orchestra of world class. Such supple and rich string playing, such expressive woodwind and infallibly accurate and mellow-toned brass, could be mistaken as belonging to Vienna, Berlin or Chicago. Attention to dynamics is meticulous, and contributes immeasurably to the splendour of the performance. A double *pianissimo* is really that, so when triple *forte* comes along its impact is tremendous. Some outstanding features can be pinpointed: the haunting beauty of the *portamento* horn playing and the strings' sensitive and perfectly graded glissandos at fig 23; the magical entry of flute and harps just after fig 3 in the second movement; and the frightening eruption of the two *fortissimo* drum notes just after fig 51 in the same movement. Dame Janet Baker is at her most tender in 'Urlicht', with Arleen Auger as the soul of purity in the finale. The CBSO Chorus is magnificent. Indeed the whole finale is an acoustic triumph. This in a spiritual class of its own and the recording is superb.

Symphony No 2
Elisabeth Schwarzkopf *sop* **Hilde Rössl-Majdan** *mez* **Philharmonia Chorus and Orchestra / Otto Klemperer**
EMI Great Recordings of the Century 567235-2
(72' · ADD · T/t) Ⓜ️Ⓞ▷

You emerge from Klemperer's first movement unharrassed, unsettled in the knowledge that this extraordinary music has something much more to yield. You miss those elements of high risk, the brave rhetorical gestures, the uncompromising extremes, in Klemperer's comparatively comfortable down-the-line response. He knocks minutes off most of the competition (yes, it's a fallacy that Klemperer was always slower), paying little or no heed to Mahler's innumerable expressive markings in passages which have so much to gain from them. Take, for example, the magical shift to remote E major with the *ppp* emergence of the second subject where Klemperer allows himself no lassitude whatsoever in the *rubato* despite Mahler's explicit requests to the contrary. Likewise the grisly procession of cellos and basses which begins the approach to the awesome climax of the development. How little Klemperer makes of their cadaverous first entry or Mahler's long backward glance just prior to the coda. But then, come the deceptive second movement minuet, something happens, the performance really begins to find its space. Klemperer's scherzo is ideally big-boned with fine rollicking horns and a lazy trio with lovely old-world close-harmony trumpets. And the finale, growing more and more momentous with every bar, possesses a unique aura. Not everyone is convinced by Klemperer's very measured treatment of the Judgement Day march. The grim reaper takes his time but the inevitability of what's to come is somehow the more shocking as a result. Klemperer's trumpets peak thrillingly in the bars immediately prior to the climax itself – and what a seismic upheaval he and his orchestra pull off at this point. The rest is sublime: marvellous spacial effects, off-stage brass and so on, an inspirational sense of the music burgeoning from the moment the chorus breathe life into the Resurrection Ode. It's a pity that in those days so many technical blemishes were allowed to make it to the final master, though EMI's digital remastering of this almost legendary reading is superb.

Symphony No 2
Lisa Milne *sop* **Birgit Remmert** *contr* **Hungarian Radio Choir; Budapest Festival Orchestra / Iván Fischer**
Channel Classics ② 💿 CCSSA23506
(82' · DDD · T/t) ⒻⓄⓄ▷

Stylistically, Fischer is right on the money. He has a keen nose for Mahler's particular brand of the ebb and flow of the music, the way it speaks, or rather sings; the bucolic and melodramatic elements of the score are vividly conflicted; and best of all Fischer really breathes in the atmosphere of Mahler's precipitous flight to eternity. The second theme of the first movement, which Mahler requests enter tentatively, shyly, does exactly that – Fischer's violins are barely audible, a rosy horizon briefly glimpsed through this bleak and forbidding landscape.

Few take this first movement to the edge of possibility that Mahler so clearly envisaged. Fischer does not shirk the often reckless extremes of tempo and dynamics but nor does he throw caution to the four winds in the terrifying stampede to its cliff-hanging climax. Leonard Bernstein is probably still alone in doing just that. But there are many other compensations here: a great sense of logic and line, a second movement whose homespun accenting belongs to a bygone era, likewise the close-harmony trumpets in the trio of the third movement so touchingly redolent of another time, another place.

But the crowning glory is, as it should be, the finale – and it is here that Fischer, his performers and his engineers, really excel. The 'special effects' of Mahler's elaborate Judgement Day fresco have rarely been so magically realised. The offstage horns are so breathtakingly remote as to suggest the world of the living left far behind. Moments of quite extraordinary stasis precede the sounding of the Dies irae and the hushed entry of the chorus. And come the peroration (resplendent with fabulous horns), Fischer knows that it is with that final *crescendo* of the chorus and only then that the heavens really open. Impressive.

Symphony No 3

Symphony No 3. Four Rückert Lieder. Kindertotenlieder
Martha Lipton *mez* **Dietrich Fischer-Dieskau** *bar* **Women's chorus of the Schola Cantorum; Boys' Choir of the Transfiguration; New York Philharmonic Orchestra / Leonard Bernstein**
Sony Classical ② SM2K61831 (142' · ADD) Recorded 1962 Ⓜ️▷

Few who experienced Bernstein's passionate advocacy of Mahler's musical cause in the 1960s were left untouched by it. These recordings date from those years and the flame of inspiration still burns brightly about them almost 40 years later. The CBS recordings were clearly manipulated, but the sound – at best, big and open but trenchant and analytically clear – suited Mahler's sound world especially well. Bernstein's account of the Third Symphony is as compelling an experience and as desirable a general recommendation now as when it first appeared. The New Yorkers are on scintillating form under the conductor they have most obviously revered in the post-war period. This is a classic account, by any standards. Bernstein himself is a subtle and self-effacing pianist. Fischer-Dieskau scales the musical heights in several of the *Rückert* Lieder.

Symphony No 3[a]. Kindertotenlieder[b]
Kathleen Ferrier contr
[a]**BBC Symphony Orchesta / Sir Adrian Boult**;
[b]**Concertgebouw Orchestra, Amsterdam /**
Otto Klemperer
Testament mono ② SBT2 1422 (131' · ADD)
Includes interview with Kathleen Ferrier
Recorded [a]November 29, 1947, [b]July 12, 1951   🅟🔘

It is difficult, even now, not to be awestruck by the professionalism and unassuming good sense of Sir Adrian Boult. In the winter of 1947-48, the BBC Third Programme took the daring and controversial decision to broadcast the complete Mahler symphonies and Nos 1, 3, 5, 7 and 8 were prepared and conducted by Boult.

His performance of the Third Symphony, a UK premiere, is lucid and unaffected. It is also exceptionally well shaped orchestrally, no mean achievement with a work the players had never seen before. The playing isn't flawless. Post-war raids on London's pool of orchestral players by Beecham and Legge had robbed the BBC SO of some of its former lustre. Passengers are clearly being carried in the horn and trombone sections yet such is Boult's professionalism the wider picture is largely unaffected.

The BBC saved none of the performances. This off-air recording was preserved on a set of acetate discs which Jon Tolansky discovered in a shop in Manchester in 1981. Kathleen Ferrier's presence made the find doubly important. She gives an exceptionally beautiful performance of 'O Mensch!', lovingly accompanied by Boult. What's more, transfer engineer Paul Bailey has done a remarkable job tidying up a patch of badly disintegrating sound near the end of 'O Mensch!'.

Added to the Mahler Third are a noisily recorded live 1951 Amsterdam Kindertotenlieder dryly conducted by Klemperer whom Ferrier disliked, and an interview she gave to CBC in 1950. Hearing Ferrier speak is interesting. Dark-voiced, careful of accent, and not afraid to correct her less than adequate interviewer, she sounds not unlike Margaret Thatcher after her voice had been lowered.

Symphony No 4

Symphony No 4
Kathleen Battle sop
Vienna Philharmonic Orchestra / Lorin Maazel
Sony Classical Digital Masters 07464449082
(75' · DDD)   🅑🔘🔘➟

On this 1985 recording, Kathleen Battle sings the symphony's rapt coda in a consciously intimate manner which might roughly be dubbed the 'Listen with Mother' style. By that, no offence is meant either to 'Listen with Mother', one of the many things which the BBC radio used to do so well, or to Kathleen Battle. Maazel's version is throughout a very inward-looking one, and in saying that one merely points to the fact that it is a very, very Viennese performance; in Vienna, Mahler's Vienna or Maazel's, introspection is an unavoidable condition of being. What's more, only in Vienna will you hear string and, in its special way, wind playing such as is provided here for Maazel in the long-drawn slow movement. In Maazel's 1970 performance, now on Pearl, the conducting and the Berlin RSO playing of the slow movement are a considerable disappointment; here it is simply 22 and a half minutes of unadulterated pleasure.

Maazel has always conducted the symphony's first movement in a relaxed, springy, Bruno Walter-ish way. Away from the score, the ear that is innocent of Mahler's many abstruse changes of tempo may think them rather artificial; but the playing of the VPO is such that one listens, hypnotized.

Symphony No 4
Juliane Banse sop
Staatskapelle Dresden / Giuseppe Sinopoli
Profil PH07047 (60' · DDD)   🅟🔘

'Glorious' and 'sublime' were among the epithets applied to the playing of Dresden's 'Royal Chapel' ensemble when Mahler's Fourth Symphony was first performed in the city in 1908. Both epithets could be applied to the playing on this latter-day realisation under Giuseppe Sinopoli. People obsess about the Berlin and Vienna Philharmonics but under the right leadership the Dresden orchestra, which Sinopoli led from 1992 until his death at the age of 54 nine years later, can surpass either with its flawless ensemble and understated eloquence. There isn't an ugly note or gratuitously unpleasant sound in the *Scherzo* yet no jot of the music's wit, grace and sinister humour is lost. After which, the playing of the slow movement really is a glimpse of musical heaven on earth, the string playing glowing like old gold.

Sinopoli made a studio recording of the Fourth with the Philharmonia Orchestra in the early 1990s. The Dresden reading is essentially unchanged but its realisation is in a different league. The start may seem unduly brisk but a series of exquisitely shaped transitions take us into calmer waters and a succession of ever more enchanted landscapes where the performance reveals its essentially introspective side. Some might think it too introspective in those espressivo interludes where the pulse marginally hangs fire.

In the finale's calm opening and meditative close Sinopoli takes a very slow tempo indeed, way below the one Mahler himself adopts on his 1905 piano roll. Lorin Maazel takes a similar tempo in his celebrated 1984 recording with the Vienna Philharmonic. He, though, has Kathleen Battle, a brighter-voiced, less lustrous-sounding soloist than Sinopoli's excellent Juliane Banse. He also guards against somnolence by sharper pointing of the music's barcarolle-like rhythm. Not that straight comparisons are really in order here. Orchestrally, this is archive gold. It is also a happy reminder of a conductor whose prodigious intellect and idiosyncratic ways could never entirely mask the fact that he was a good man and a wonderful musician.

Symphony No 4
Miah Persson sop **Budapest Festival Orchestra Conductor / Iván Fischer**
Channel Classics CCSSA26109 (57' · DDD/DSD)

What no one will deny is the amazing unanimity and precision of the playing here and the superlative quality of the sound engineering. But how to read a work that can feel brittle as well as heart-warming and graceful? Despite Iván Fischer's eminently sane and central pacing overall, he courts controversy with inconsistencies of tone between (and individualised inflexions within) the four movements.

Some maestros choose between neo-classical modernity and old-world *Gemütlichkeit*. Fischer gives us both and more: he gives us instability. Rather than taking his cue from the opening bars in which the jingling sleigh bells might be construed to lose their way, Fischer mixes them down, introducing his own eccentric nuance a fraction later. He permits an oasis of exquisite repose just before the movement's final flourish yet much of the rest is unsettling. While details unearthed are revelatory – often linear, maybe functional, certainly more than merely illustrative – the quest can seem obsessive, at odds with the sense of ease indicated by the composer. Make no mistake however, the playing has character and conviction, the divided violins enhancing transparency albeit at some expense of weight and blend. Less self-regarding or at least less wilful since the idiosyncrasies are intrinsic, the *Scherzo* goes wonderfully well, with solo violin and clarinets in particular excelling themselves. The slow movement is just a little pale, as if Fischer were deliberately avoiding the calculated sublimity and cushioned string tone associated with big-band performances of late Beethoven. The gates of Heaven are flung open with a great blare, possibly a bit much for home listening but replicating the immediacy of the

concert hall. In the finale, Fischer achieves novelty chiefly through understatement, mindful of the need to avoid coyness at all costs. Miah Persson is ideally cast and as she invokes Saint Martha it's as if we're transported to a small village church, the organ made tangible in the exquisite treatment of the accompanying instrumental texture. This is just one of countless imaginative touches on an exceptional hybrid SACD.

Symphony No 4 (arr Stein)
Kate Royal sop **Manchester Camerata / Douglas Boyd**
Avie AV2069 (57' · DDD) Recorded live 2004

Erwin Stein's reduction, for solo string quintet (including double bass), flute doubling piccolo, oboe doubling cor anglais, clarinet doubling bass clarinet, piano, harmonium and percussion, was prepared at a time when even the members of Arnold Schoenberg's immediate circle had limited access to the real thing. Even today, some find the transcription focuses the mind wonderfully on the music's contrapuntal essence, others that it is intrinsically a period piece, more redolent of the palm court. Suffice to say that Douglas Boyd and his group offer a performance that is unfailingly fresh and alert.

Andrew Keener's production is the crispest, most immediate the score has received on disc. Out goes evocative distancing. In comes the tangible wheeze of the harmonium, the respiration of sundry woodwind players and the low-level vocalising of Boyd himself.

Douglas Boyd's Mahler may feel overly straightforward but he knows the territory, having directed Schoenberg's reduction of *Das Lied* as well as Mahler's own string quartet arrangements in Manchester. He has further aces up his sleeve: the helpful booklet-notes by Philip Borg Wheeler, the participation of Kate Royal, fresh-voiced soprano winner of the 2004 Kathleen Ferrier competition and, on CD, the highly competitive price.

Symphony No 5

Symphony No 5
Berlin Philharmonic Orchestra / Sir Simon Rattle
EMI 557385-2 (69' · DDD) Recorded live 2002

Mahler's Fifth is a terror to bring off but, brought off, is a joy beyond measure. It made a fine nuptial offering for Rattle and the Berliners on 7 September 2002 – festive yet challenging, a tragi-comic revel and a high-wire act to boot. 'The individual parts are so difficult,' wrote Mahler, 'they call for the most accomplished soloists.' Rattle brought the prodigious first horn to the apron of the stage for his obbligato contribution in the *Scherzo*. Mengelberg's conducting score, which Mahler used for the work's Amsterdam premiere in 1906, has an annotation to this effect, and the practice was followed at the work's English premiere in 1945, but we're left wondering what would have happened if Rattle hadn't brought the player forward. EMI's recording is splendidly explicit, but the horn section, which plays a crucial role at key moments, seems oddly distant on CD.

The *tutti* sound Rattle draws from the orchestra is clean and sharply profiled, not unlike the Mahler sound Rafael Kubelík tended to favour. Rattle's tempo for the *Adagietto* is a good one by modern standards (not too slow) and the string playing has a lovely diaphanous quality, but you may find the playing over-nuanced.

Nowadays it isn't unusual to hear rhythm and line sacrificed to detail and nuance as old-established symphony orchestras are made to rethink their readings by conductors schooled in the arcana of ancient performance practice. Rattle has done his fair share of this. What's interesting about this live Mahler Fifth is the degree to which the detail is absorbed and the line maintained.

Like most latter-day conductors, Rattle tends to underplay the march element in the first movement. Mahler in his 1905 piano roll, Walter, and Haitink in his superb 1969 Concertgebouw recording all preserve this. Some may find the approach too dry-eyed in the long-drawn string threnody at figure 2. But an excess of feeling can damage both opening movements (the second is a mirror of the first) if the larger rhythm is obscured. Rattle, like Barbirolli and Bernstein in his superb Vienna Philharmonic recording, treats the threnody more as a meditation than a march, but the pulse isn't lost and the attendant tempos are good. The frenzied B flat minor Trio is particularly well judged. The second movement is superb (the diminished horn contribution notwithstanding) and none but the most determined sceptic could fail to thrill to the sense of adventure and well-being Rattle and his players bring to the *Scherzo* and finale, even if Barbirolli (studio) and Bernstein (live) both reach the finishing line in rather more eloquent and orderly fashion that this talented but still occasionally fragile-sounding Berlin ensemble.

As a memento, the CD is a triumph of organisation and despatch. As a performance and as a recording, it has rather more character and bite than Abbado's much admired 1993 Berlin version. Indeed, it can safely be ranked among the half dozen or so finest performances on record. It isn't perfect, but do you know of one that is?

Mahler Symphony No 5 **Adès** Asyla
Berlin Philharmonic Orchestra / Simon Rattle
Video director Bob Coles
EMI 🅓 490325-9 (125' · 16:9, · 2.0, 5.1 &
DTS 5.1 · 0) Includes feature 'Simon Rattle in conversation with Bob Coles'   Ⓕ🅞🅞

Rattle's performance of the Mahler is discussed above. In the *Scherzo* the DVD format makes it easier to accept the front-stage placement of the obbligato horn – not a whim of Rattle's but a decision based on precedent and scholarship. As sceptics like Klemperer and Scherchen might have observed, it doesn't make the movement any shorter, yet Rattle feels he's cracked it after the initial doubts candidly discussed in the accompanying talk.

Nor is there any doubting the energetic brilliance of Adès's *Asyla* (the plural of 'asylum' used in both its meanings, as a place of refuge and of madness). For the uninitiated/unconvinced, it should help that the zany percussion effects can be seen as well as heard. The Berliners are encouraged to loosen up for its vernacular element, without perhaps plunging in quite as wholeheartedly as the audio-only CBSO.

If you don't instinctively recoil from the prospect of additional noises off and some rather insistent close-ups of the participants, a great occasion is well represented here. Surprisingly perhaps, the director doesn't zero in on the brass for their climactic chorale, giving us the orchestra in long-shot before the precipitate dash to the finishing line. The sound, not quite as clear as it might be in such densely scored passages, is still eminently acceptable; the images are wonderfully crisp.

Symphony No 5
New Philharmonia Orchestra / Sir John Barbirolli
EMI Great Recordings of the Century 566910-2-
(74' · ADD) Recorded 1969   🅜🅞🅞🅟

Sir John Barbirolli's Fifth occupies a special place in everybody's affections: a performance so big in spirit and warm of heart as to silence any rational discussion of its shortcomings. Some readers may have problems with one or two of his sturdier tempos. He doesn't make life easy for his orchestra in the treacherous second movement, while the exultant finale, though suitably bracing, arguably needs more of a spring in its heels. But against all this, one must weigh a unity and strength of purpose, an entirely idiomatic response to instrumental colour and texture (the dark, craggy hues of the first two movements are especially striking); and most important of all that very special Barbirollian radiance, humanity – call it what you will. One point of interest for collectors – on the original LP, among minor orchestral mishaps in the *Scherzo*, were four bars of missing horn obbligato (at nine bars before fig 20). Not any more! The original solo horn player, Nicholas Busch, has returned to the scene of this momentary aberration (Watford Town Hall) and the absent bars have been ingeniously reinstated. There's even a timely grunt from Sir John, as if in approval. Something of a classic, then; EMI's remastering is splendid.

Symphony No 5
Vienna Philharmonic Orchestra / Leonard Bernstein
DG 4776334 (75' · DDD) Recorded live 1987   🅜🅞🅞🅟

Bernstein's tempo for the Funeral march in the first movement of the Fifth Symphony became slower in the 23 years that separated his New York CBS recording from this one, made during a performance in Frankfurt. The strings-only passage at fig 15 in the first movement is exquisitely played, as is the long horn solo in the *Scherzo*. And there's one marvellously exciting moment – the right gleam of trumpet tone at one bar before fig 29 in the second movement. Best of all is Bernstein himself, here at his exciting best, giving demonic edge to the music where it's appropriate and building the symphony inexorably to its final triumph.

Thanks to a very clear and well-balanced recording, every subtlety of scoring, especially some of the lower strings' counterpoint, comes through as the conductor intended. One is made aware of the daring novelty of much of the orchestration, of how advanced it must have sounded in the early years of this century. Here we get the structure, the sound and the emotion. The *Adagietto* isn't dragged out, and the scrupulous attention to Mahler's dynamics allows the delightfully silken sound of the Vienna strings to be heard to captivating advantage, with the harp well recorded too. Bernstein is strongest in Mahler when the work itself is one of the more optimistic symphonies with less temptation for him to add a few degrees more of *Angst*.

Symphony No 5
Lucerne Festival Orchestra / Claudio Abbado
Video director Michael Beyer
Euroarts 𝔻𝔙𝔻 205 4079 (74' · 16:9 · PCM stereo, 5.1 and DTS 5.1 · 0)
Recorded live in Lucerne 2004. Includes multiple viewing angles ⒻⓄⓄⓄ

Claudio Abbado's Mahler Fifth is magnificent. It helps that the band is the Lucerne Festival Orchestra, that most exalted of all *ad hoc* ensembles, rather than the Gustav Mahler Jugendorchester. It does make a difference in Lucerne to have a raft of seasoned players joining the core contingent from the Mahler Chamber Orchestra. The visual dimension is stronger, too, with the option to switch to the so-called 'Conductor Camera' and experience Abbado from a player's perspective. If this strikes some readers as a gimmick I can only say that I welcome it as a natural use of the new medium.

Listen without the images, though, and it quickly becomes apparent that Abbado's previous, audio-only account (DG, subsequently revamped for SACD) is sonically superior, with greater hall ambience and less tendency for wind, brass and percussion to lose themselves in the mix. It's not as if the conductor's conception has changed a great deal. His Fifth has always displayed a tad less inner intensity than some of the great readings of the past but with compensating elegance and grace. Once again the famous *Adagietto* steals in with a magic inevitability that few have matched. Those with limited budgets might do well to consider Leonard

Bernstein's Unitel Mahler cycle (though it represents quite a substantial single outlay – see below). That said, Abbado's music-making is as fine as you will find anywhere today and his admirers should be well satisfied.

Symphony No 6

Symphony No 6
San Francisco Symphony Orchestra / Michael Tilson Thomas
SFS Media/Avie ② 821936-0001-2 (87' · DDD) SACD/CD player compatible ⓂⓄ🕩

This recording of Mahler's Sixth Symphony was made from performances planned long before the events of September 11 gave the San Francisco Symphony's choice of repertory extraordinary resonance. And it's a credit to both Michael Tilson Thomas and the orchestra that this ferocious performance is carried out without hysteria or self-indulgence. Tempos are judiciously chosen. In the first movement, for example, Tilson Thomas's *Allegro energico, ma non troppo* is only a hair's breadth slower than Bernstein's in his Vienna Philharmonic recording, yet the difference is enough to give proper weight to the march. Indeed, the SFS strings dig very deep to produce a dark, throaty tone of startling vehemence. Ardently played and generously phrased, the 'Alma' theme provides welcome consolation – and how longingly Tilson Thomas clings to the final peaks of its melody.

Gunshot-like *sforzando*s from the timpani introduce the *scherzo*, sharply etched here with stinging dotted rhythms. The trios are similarly pointed – though affectionately *grazioso*, as Mahler requests – and rather deliberately paced, like a long-forgotten dance now remembered in slow motion. The *Andante moderato* is also treated expansively, but the tension never sags. Tilson Thomas mis-steps only once in the sprawling finale, pressing too hard at the end of the introduction so that the orchestra arrives prematurely at the main tempo – a minor flaw and quickly forgiven.

A more impressive start to Tilson Thomas and the SFS's Mahler cycle is difficult to imagine. Less mannered than Bernstein, and more emotionally engaged than Karajan, this is an exceptionally intense and, under the circumstances, remarkably coherent performance that isn't to be missed. Very good sound quality, too, from the orchestra's new in-house label.

Symphony No 6
London Symphony Orchestra / Valery Gergiev
LSO Live 💿 LSO0661 (77' · DDD/DSD)
Recorded live at the Barbican Hall, London in November 2007 ⒷⓄⓄ🕩

Valery Gergiev is one of the most charismatic maestros on the circuit and his Mahler series in London has aroused passionately divergent responses. If you prize the textural elucidation that Claudio Abbado brings to these scores you probably won't care for Gergiev's broader, coarser brush. The raw excitement he engenders may seem beside the point.

This Sixth is dark, sometimes impenetrable, an impression offset only by a raft of sublime *pianissimi*. The silken shimmer of the first movement's central pastoral reverie with cowbells carefully distanced offers surprising relief. Elsewhere Gergiev drives the argument forward with the kind of sullen, monolithic power he applies to Shostakovich at his most barren. While his main tempo is only fractionally faster than Bernstein's, it seems rushed even for this most neurotic of symphonic openers. The exposition repeat is taken. The serene *Andante moderato*, placed second as is now the fashion, is soon being harried towards a climax that blares unmercifully. There's more variety of tone in the *Scherzo*, though it's the finale which really hits home, the orchestra whipped into a frenzy that may or may not be idiomatic but certainly strikes sparks.

If you're looking for a quick-fire, single-disc Sixth with a difference, Gergiev has more gravitas than previous Soviet-trained conductors, even when he's racing. LSO Live backs him up with an impactful, immediate, rather airless sound encoded as a hybrid SACD. The bright-edged, multi-linear treatment favoured by exponents as ostensibly dissimilar as Bernstein and Boulez simply isn't on Gergiev's agenda. Instead, a trail is blazed for a visceral, even thuggish brand of music-making. Yes, these sounds thrilled many in the hall but would you want to revisit them at home? At bargain price you can afford to find out. The enthusiastic applause has been removed.

with the full weight of sonority long thought uniquely theirs – yet reservations soon fall away. For all its fine detailing, Abbado's finale lacks nothing in intensity, with a devastating corporate thrust that may or may not have you ruing DG's decision to include an applause track.

A more serious stumbling block is the maestro's decision to place the *Scherzo* third, following the lead of Del Mar, Barbirolli, Rattle and others. Purchasers of a single disc CD version available in some parts of the world, or indeed the download, can re-programme, of course, but technical constraints for the hybrid SACD disc, available in the UK, have led DG to opt for a pair of discs containing two movements apiece. It must, however, be pointed out that the extra cost is borne by the manufacturer, not the consumer. And, apart from two curious pockets of resonance in the finale (on either side of the 10-minute mark), Christopher Alder's team achieves a much more realistic balance than you'll find in the conductor's previous live Mahler issues. If a little cavernous, the effect is blessedly consistent, allowing us to appreciate that Abbado's sweetly attenuated string sound is just as beautiful as Karajan's more saturated sonority, a testament to the chamber-like imperatives of his latter-day music-making, not to mention the advantage of adequate rehearsal time!

The finale's hammer-blows are clearer and cleaner than ever. Abbado does not include the third of these before the final coda but the hard, dry brutality of his clinching *fortissimo* is guaranteed to take you by surprise. Donald Mitchell provides excellent booklet-notes to cap a remarkable release.

Symphony No 6
Berlin Philharmonic Orchestra / Claudio Abbado
DG 477 5573 (80' · DDD/DSD)
Recorded live 2004   Ⓕ**ⓄⓄⓄ**▷

 Whatever the revolution in playing standards since January 1966, when Barbirolli conducted Mahler's Sixth in Berlin, you'd be hard-pressed to encounter a tauter, more refined performance than this, or one that dispenses so completely with the heavy drapes of old-style Mahler interpretation. The work concluded Abbado's first Philharmonie programme since passing the reins to Sir Simon Rattle, an occasion bound to provoke standing ovations and a little myth-making, too. Now, with the music repositioned on the sunny side of the Alps and seen through the prism of the Second Viennese School, an effortless, sometimes breathtaking transparency prevails.

In the first movement, Abbado's sparing use of *rubato* precludes the full (de-)flowering of the 'Alma theme' in the Bernstein manner, and there are some curiously stiff moments in the *Andante moderato*, here an iridescent intermezzo quite unlike Karajan's Brucknerian slow movement. This may not be a Sixth for all seasons and all moods – the Berliners rarely play

---

Symphony No 6. Kindertotenlieder Rückert-Lieder
Christa Ludwig *mez* **Berlin Philharmonic Orchestra / Herbert von Karajan**
DG The Originals ② 457 716-2GOR2 (129' · ADD)
Recorded 1974-5   Ⓜ**ⓄⓄ**▷

Karajan's classic Sixth confirmed his belated arrival as a major Mahler interpreter. Only Bernstein, in his more emotive, less consciously beautifying way, left recorded performances of comparable strength and conviction. Karajan's understanding of Mahler's sound world – its links forward to Berg, Schoenberg and Webern as opposed to retrospective links with Wagner – is very acute. Combining this with a notable long-term control of rhythm, Karajan is sustains not only the composer's lucidly stated tragic case but also Mahler's exploration of materials drawn from different sound worlds and even, in the Scherzo, from different areas of the inherited musical tradition. This Scherzo is a masterly achievement by composer, conductor, and orchestra alike. Also, the engineers have tidied up the very end of the symphony, where the bass tuba's entry over drum and *ff pizzicato* basses no longer betrays quite so obviously its origin as part of a separate take.

The *Rückert Lieder* are memorably sung by Christa Ludwig who is eloquently supported by the Berlin wind players who are recorded with gratifying immediacy.

Symphony No 6
London Philharmonic Orchestra / Klaus Tennstedt
LPO ② LPO0038 (84' · ADD)
Recorded live at the Royal Albert Hall, London on August 22, 1983   Ⓑ**OO**

Tennstedt exposes every nerve-ending of the piece from start to finish. Trenchancy is there with a vengeance from the word go – big-boned and punchy with snappy trombone accents. Alma's theme burgeons, the Albert Hall acoustic accentuating the bigness with strident clarinets and the ripest horns. Big sounds, big rubatos, big everything. In the rapt cow-bell-festooned middle section Tennstedt feels personal, 'connected', to the ache in the recollection of Alma's theme and as the movement propels to its major-key (and short-lived) resolution.

But it is the parodistic grotesqueries of the off-kilter *Scherzo* that really show up the real Mahlerian. Here's why Mahler's first (and one believes last) instinct was to place the *Scherzo* second. With Tennstedt the shock of that hellish descent back into A minor – with the march rhythm now dislocated to suggest an army of undead amputees – is seriously unsettling. And lest anyone suggest (as they so often do in criticism of Bernstein) that Tennstedt is guilty of over-egging the trios of this movement, let them consider the objective: the very essence of caricature (be it a Viennese ländler or some other awkward country dance) is exaggeration.

So it's a corker, this performance. It sounds pretty good for 1983, though the BBC fashion then for a more 'open' sound slightly compromises the unflinching immediacy of the reading. And what a shame, after all the fantastical trials and tribulations of the finale, writ so thrillingly large here, that some idiot cannot resist yelling 'Bravo' to effectively destroy the fade to black at the close.

Additional recommendations

Symphony No 6
London Symphony Orchestra / Jansons
LSO Live ② LSO0038 (82' · DDD)   Ⓢ**➜**

Symphony No 6
Coupled with: **Henze** Sebastian im Traum
Royal Concertgebouw Orchestra, Amsterdam / Mariss Jansons
RCO Live ② 🔊 RCO06001 (99' · DDD/DSD)   Ⓕ
Quite a dilemma: two virtually identical performances from Jansons. The acoustic of the Concertgebouw provides better sound and the RCO give a slightly more spacious reading. Otherwise, it's swings and roundabouts: maybe the lush Henze coupling is the clincher.

Symphony No 7

Symphony No 7
Chicago Symphony Orchestra / Claudio Abbado
DG Masters 445 513-2GMA (79' · DDD)   Ⓕ**OO➜**

Abbado's account of Mahler's Seventh was always a highlight of his cycle and remains the ideal choice for collectors requiring a central interpretation in modern sound. Steering a middle course between clear-sightedness and hysteria, and avoiding both the heavy, saturated textures of 19th-century romanticism and the chilly rigidity of some of his own 'modernist' peers, he is, as the original review reported, 'almost too respectable'. That said, it's all to the good if the forthright theatricality and competitive instincts of the Chicago orchestra are held in check just a little. Even where Abbado underplays the drama of the moment, a sufficient sense of urgency is sustained by a combination of well-judged tempos, marvellously graduated dynamics and precisely balanced, ceaselessly changing textures. For those put off by Mahler's supposed vulgarity, the unhurried classicism of Abbado's reading may well be the most convincing demonstration of the music's integrity. This is a piece Abbado continues to champion in concert with performances at the very highest level.

Symphony No 7
London Symphony Orchestra / Valery Gergiev
LSO Live 🔊 LSO0665 (72' · DDD)
Recorded live 2008   Ⓑ**OO➜**

For some Valery Gergiev's dark, pumped-up Seventh might prove to be the high-point of his Mahler cycle. True, the over-the-barricades manner precludes much in the way of subtlety but it does hold in tight unity a score that can sprawl into incoherence. Much is paced a notch faster than usual, though not the introduction which is spacious and strong. The playing is consistently assured; the sound powerfully immediate. The reading has a monolithic drive that is nothing if not distinctive.

What Gergiev doesn't deliver is a sense of this music's teeming inner life. No point looking here for either Claudio Abbado's delicate attention to line and colour or Leonard Bernstein's emotive, micro-managed *rubato*. Gergiev's inner movements come across as diligent but brusque. While his idiosyncratic seating arrangements (including antiphonal violins) make for some interesting effects, it's the resilience of the LSO brass at high decibels you're likely to remember, not the meaningful interplay of independent and interdependent strands.

The applause which greeted this performance at London's Barbican Hall has been surgically removed for this hybrid SACD incarnation. The critics will be as divided over its merits as they were following the live performance. Happily, LSO Live's competitive pricing means you can decide for yourself.

Symphony No 7
New York Philharmonic Orchestra /
Leonard Bernstein
Sony Classical Bernstein Century Edition SMK60564
(80' · ADD) Recorded 1965   Ⓜ️▷

We are often assured that great conductors of an
earlier generation interpreted Mahler from
within the Austrian tradition, encoding a sense
of nostalgia, decay and incipient tragedy as distinct from the in-your-face calamities and neuroses proposed by Leonard Bernstein. Well, this
is one Bernstein recording that should convince
all but the most determined sceptics. It deserves
a place in anyone's collection now that it has
been transferred to a single disc at mid-price.
The white-hot communicative power is most
obvious in the finale which has never sounded
more convincing than it does here; the only
mildly questionable aspect of the reading is the
second *Nachtmusik*, too languid for some. The
transfer is satisfactory, albeit dimmer than one
might have hoped. It sounds historic, but historic in more ways than one.

Mahler Symphony No 7[a]
Mozart Symphony No 41, 'Jupiter', K551[b]
London Philharmonic Orchestra /
Klaus Tennstedt
BBC Legends ② BBCL4224-2 (111' · ADD)
Recorded live in [a]1980 and [b]1985   Ⓕ⚫⚫

The Seventh was not an especial high-point of
Tennstedt's Mahler symphony cycle with the
London Philharmonic – not that it's a bad performance, per se, it just never really catches fire. A
live performance from 1993 (EMI), made at one
of the conductor's last public appearances, is considerably more compelling, though the first
movement is encumbered by some dangerously
slow tempi. This BBC Legends release comes
from a 1980 concert given at the Edinburgh Festival just a few months before Tennstedt and the
LPO took the work into EMI's Abbey Road studios. It's a revelation. Yes, the interpretative outline is similar in both accounts – and the live version is not without its technical stumbles, of
course – but how fervent the playing is here, and
how much more sense Tennstedt's tempo manipulations make. Listen, for example, beginning at
9'05" in the first movement where a vast landscape of breathtaking purity is conjured, or to the
movement's end, which is driven with just the
right amount of brute force, it seems, to set one's
heart pounding. The *Scherzo* is appropriately
eerie, full of shadows and shrieks, yet it sings, too
– a weird and powerful effect. Most impressive of
all, perhaps, is the treacherous finale, where
Tennstedt and the orchestra make the most of the
music's manic mood swings. This is, without a
doubt, a great Mahler Seventh.

Mozart's *Jupiter* Symphony would have benefited from an acoustic less cavernous than the
Albert Hall, but it's still a stylish performance.
The slow movement is given an operatic sense of
dramatic purpose, the Minuet has a surprisingly

songful grandeur, and the joyousness of the
finale is not merely exuberant but heartfelt.
Treasurable.

Symphony No 8, 'Symphony of a Thousand'

Symphony No 8
Heather Harper, Lucia Popp, Arleen Auger *sops*
Yvonne Minton *mez* **Helen Watts** *contr* **René Kollo**
ten **John Shirley-Quirk** *bar* **Martti Talvela** *bass*
Vienna Boys' Choir; Vienna State Opera Chorus;
Vienna Singverein; Chicago Symphony Orchestra /
Sir Georg Solti
Decca 475 7521 (80' · ADD · T/t) Recorded 1971.
                    Ⓜ️⚫⚫▷

Of the so-called classic accounts of the Eighth
Symphony, it's Solti's which most conscien-
tiously sets out to convey an impression of large
forces in a big performance space, this despite
the obvious resort to compression and other
forms of gerrymandering. Whatever the inconsistencies of Decca's multi-miking and overdub-
bing, the overall effect remains powerful even
today. The remastering has not eradicated all
trace of distortion at the very end and, given the
impressive flood of choral tone at the start of the
'Veni creator spiritus', it still seems a shame that
the soloists and the Chicago brass are quite so
prominent in its closing stages. As for the performance itself, Solti's extrovert way with Part 1
works tremendously without quite erasing
memories of Bernstein's ecstatic fervour. In Part
2, it may be the patient Wagnerian mysticism of
Tennstedt that sticks in the mind. Less inclined
to delay, Solti makes the material sound more
operatic. Yet for its gut-wrenching theatricality
and great solo singing, Solti's version makes a
plausible first choice – now more than ever.
Also, it has been squeezed onto a single CD,
albeit at full price.

Symphony No 8
Viktoria Yastrebova, Ailish Tynan, Liudmilla
Dudinova *sops* **Lilli Paasikivi, Zlata Bulycheva** *mezs*
Sergey Semishkur *ten* **Alexey Markov** *bar* **Evgeny**
Nikitin *bass* **Choir of Eltham College; Choral Arts**
Society of Washington; London Symphony Chorus
and Orchestra / Valery Gergiev
LSO Live ⚙️ LSO0669 (77' · DDD · T/t)
Recorded live at St Paul's Cathedral, London in 2008.
                    Ⓑ▷

As a concert venue St Paul's Cathedral's problems remain acute: chief culprit is the building's
notorious nine-second reverberation period
which gives climaxes earth-shattering power but
reduces inner detail to mush.

In these circumstances the conductor's role is
mainly one of damage limitation. Not that Gergiev chooses sluggish tempi to palliate the
acoustics. Indeed he tends to plough on as precipitately as ever at section ends. Not for him the
grand but apocryphal slowing into the first
movement recapitulation as favoured by Bern-

stein *et al*. Some exaggerated enunciation by the far-flung choral groups is presumably designed to maximise audibility. Meanwhile most of the soloists proffer Mariinsky German in vaguely Verdian style and the ladies aren't always in tune. James Mallinson and his sound team do their best with the microphones, ensuring that unique moments such as the stratospheric apparition of the Mater Gloriosa are captured for posterity. There's a more than usually sweet-toned sentimentality about much of Part 2.

Belying the thrills and spills of an event in which many of the performers will have been unable to hear each other or catch much more than a glimpse of their maestro, the final Chorus Mysticus brings a real sense of gravitas and uplift. The massed voices are wonderfully hushed at the start even if the offstage trumpets register less impressively at the close (everyone sounds offstage at St Paul's). Whether this is a tribute to Gergiev's sense of the dramatic, the professionalism of his assembled artistes or sheer good luck is difficult to tell.

Shorn of applause, the reading is neatly accommodated on a single hybrid SACD and makes an appropriately idiosyncratic climax to a controversial cycle. The packaging, quite sumptuous for a bargain issue, has full texts and translations.

Additional recommendations

Symphony No 8
Juliane Banse, Christine Brewer, Soile Isokoski
sops **Jane Henschel, Birgit Remmert** *contrs* **Jon Villars** *ten* **David Wilson-Johnson** *bar* **John Relyea** *bass* **Toronto Children's Choir; London Symphony Chorus; City of Birmingham Symphony Youth Chorus, Chorus and Orchestra / Sir Simon Rattle**
EMI 557945-2 (74' · DDD · T/t) Ⓕ**O**▷
Recorded live 2004
   Thrilling, euphoric, hair-raising – Rattle holds the
   score in a perpetual state of wonder.

Symphony No 8
Coupled with: Symphony No 4[a]
[a]**Popp, Connell, Wiens, Lott, Schmidt, Denize, Versalle, Hynninen, Sotin Tiffin Boys' School Choir; LPO & Choir / Tennstedt**
EMI download ② 361572-2 (128' · DDD)
Recorded 1986. Ⓜ**OOO**▷
   Tennstedt's performance leaves no doubt that he
   believes totally in Mahler's creation. It has a rapt,
   almost intimate, quality that makes his reading all
   the more moving. The soloists are on excellent
   form and the choruses sing with conviction. The
   reading of the Fourth Symphony too is outstandingly idiomatic and well played (worth tracking
   down on CD, but a download is available).

Symphony No 9

Symphony No 9. Kindertotenlieder. Five Rückert-Lieder
Christa Ludwig *mez* **Berlin Philharmonic Orchestra**

/ Herbert von Karajan
DG Double ② 453 040-2GTA2 (132' · ADD) Recorded 1979-80 Ⓜ**OOO**▷

 Mahler's Ninth is a death-haunted work, but is filled, as Bruno Walter remarked, 'with a sanctified feeling of departure'. Rarely has this symphony been shaped with such understanding and played with such selfless virtuosity as it was by Karajan and the BPO.

For this reissue the tapes have been picked over to open up the sound and do something about the early digital edginess of the strings. There's still some occlusion at climaxes; and if those strings now seem more plasticky than fierce, it's impossible to say whether the conductor would have approved. Karajan came late to Mahler and yet, until the release of his rather more fiercely recorded 1982 concert relay (below), he seemed content to regard this earlier studio performance as perhaps his finest achievement on disc.

The attraction is greatly enhanced by Christa Ludwig's carefully considered Mahler performances of the mid-1970s. The voice may not be as fresh as it was when she recorded the songs in the late 1950s, but there are few readings of comparable nobility. She articulates the text with unrivalled clarity, and 'In diesem Wetter' at least is positively operatic. How much of the grand scale should be attributed to Karajan? It's difficult to say; the voice is sometimes strained by the tempos. This collection isn't to be missed.

Symphony No 9
Berlin Philharmonic Orchestra / Herbert von Karajan
DG ② 4390242 (85' · DDD)
Recorded live 1982 Ⓜ**OOO**▷

 Choice between the 1982 Karajan classic and the analogue studio recording is by no means easy. Both versions won *Gramophone* Awards in their day. This live performance remains a remarkable one, with a commitment to lucidity of sound and certainty of line. There's nothing dispassionate about the way the Berlin Philharmonic tears into the Rondo-Burleske, the agogic touches of the analogue version ironed out without loss of intensity. True, Karajan doesn't seek to emulate the passionate immediacy of a Barbirolli or a Bernstein, but in his broadly conceived, gloriously played *Adagio* the sepulchral hush is as memorable as the eruptive climax. The finesse of the playing is unmatched.

Symphony No 9
Berlin Philharmonic Orchestra / Claudio Abbado
DG 471 624-2GH (81' · DDD) Recorded live 1999
  Ⓕ**OO**▷

Claudio Abbado began his career with Mahler and has been conducting the composer for his entire professional life. The Ninth and, above all, the Seventh, have consistently brought out the best in him.

Abbado's previous recording of No 9, taped live in Vienna, is now only available in his boxed set of the complete symphonies (DG, reviewed on page 625). Much acclaimed as an interpretation, its airless sound wasn't to all tastes. This account is another multi-miked extravaganza with sonic shortcomings that are immediately apparent. The opening bars establish a wide open sound stage (complete with hiss) that implodes with the appearance of the harp. That harp is always on the loud side, trumpets are almost always too reticent, the bass feels synthetic and there are troublesome changes of perspective. None of which is enough to nullify the obvious sincerity and conviction of a performance that simply gets better and better as it proceeds. This really is live music-making (the last big first movement climax at 16'54" isn't together), but the inner movements are beyond reproach, ideally paced and characterised and superbly realised. The finale is content to plumb the depths in its own way – as sensitive as any of its celebrated rivals if without the point-scoring you may be used to.

Where some interpreters feel bound to choose between structural imperatives and subjective emotions, proffering either proto-Schoenbergian edginess or late Romantic excess, Abbado has the confidence to eschew both the heavily saturated textures of his predecessors and the chilly rigidity of some of his own 'modernist' peers. Instead, his unaffected warmth allows everything to come through naturally. There remains something self-effacing about his musical personality. And yet there's sunlight – and a certain tenderness – in this account of the Ninth that you won't find anywhere else, a fluency and ease that's something to marvel at. For those put off even now by the composer's supposed vulgarity, Abbado's readings constitute a convincing demonstration of the music's integrity.

The awed silence that greets the expiration of the Ninth may or may not be stage-managed, but it seems genuine.

Symphony No 9
Berlin Philharmonic Orchestra / Sir Simon Rattle
EMI ② 501228-2 (84' · DDD)   Ⓕ**OO**Ⓓ➔

In his previous recording of Mahler's Ninth Symphony, made live with the Vienna Philharmonic in 1993, Simon Rattle tapped into the music's emotional extremes to produce a surprisingly volatile reading full of precipitous *accelerandi* and wrenching *ritardandi*. There's some of that volatility in this new account from Berlin, too, though it's certainly less pronounced. There are places, too, where more tenderness wouldn't come amiss: the entrance of the solo violin in the first movement's recapitulation is so much sweeter in Vienna. But Rattle and the Berliners are also capable of taking one's breath away. Listen later in the same movement, as they gather the seemingly chaotic tangle of

melodic filaments together, creating a single, gigantic, darkly radiant chord.

The rustic dances in the second movement have a strong, rough-hewn quality, even if they sound slightly dour when compared with the more *gemütlich* charm of, say, Abbado's Berlin recording. Rattle doesn't push hard in the *Rondo-Burleske* until the end; instead, he aims for clarity and articulateness, and scrupulously observes all the dynamic twists and turns. It's an effective approach, though less adrenalin-pumping than Karajan.

It's in the final *Adagio*, however, that Rattle and his orchestra make the most powerful impact. The strings sound gorgeous, of course, yet there's grit as well as radiance in their tone. And it's only in the final pages that the earthy impurities are leeched, leaving a breath-like purity that ebbs into rapt silence.

Symphony No 9
San Francisco Symphony Orchestra / Michael Tilson Thomas
Avie/SFSO ② 821936 00072 (90' · DDD/DSD)
Recorded live 2004   Ⓕ Ⓓ➔

Tilson Thomas immediately establishes a profoundly rapt atmosphere, and the orchestra take what can best be described as a *bel canto* approach, singing their lines with warmth and poised intensity. In keeping with this, the conductor allows the players considerable rhythmic freedom. Yet one always senses a firm hand on the tiller, and the music is never pulled out of shape, as sometimes seems the case in, say, Bernstein's later recording for DG.

Some may feel that there's insufficient grit or angst here, and certainly the second movement ländler is hearty rather than coarse and the *Rondo-Burleske* could sneer more viciously – though the thrilling *accelerando* in the latter movement's coda is likely to get one's adrenalin pumping. But, to be fair, Tilson Thomas doesn't entirely neglect the music's darker qualities, and these often creep into one's consciousness rather subtly.

The interpretation's lasting impression, however, is one of lyrical radiance. In the symphony's final pages, Tilson Thomas tenderly holds the melodic shards together so one hears the song continue, even through the silences. And the evanescent glow of the strings at the end – like the last glimmer of light immediately after sunset – is not so much wistful as consolatory. An unusually moving experience, then, and one that marks yet another high point in this continuing cycle.

Additional recommendation

Symphony No 9   Ⓗ
Vienna Philharmonic Orchestra / Walter
Dutton Laboratories mono CDBP9708 (71' · ADD)
Recorded 1938   Ⓢ**OO**
This is a historic document – the Ninth's first commercial recording conducted by its dedicatee. Few modern performances offer more intensity in the

first movement (Rattle and Bernstein perhaps excepted). Don't be taken aback by the technical lapses of the VPO; this is music-making in which scrappiness and fervour are indissolubly linked. The original surface noise is filtered to near inaudibility – Dutton's restoration is a must-have.

Symphony No 10

Symphony No 10 (ed Cooke)
Berlin Philharmonic Orchestra / Sir Simon Rattle
EMI 556972-2 (77' · DDD) Ⓕ ❶❶❶↦

Ⓖ Rattle previously recorded Deryck Cooke's performing version of Mahler's incomplete 10th in June 1980 and the passionate sensitivity of his reading helped win over a sceptical public at a time when we were much less keen to tamper with the unfinished works of dead or dying artists. These days, it's almost as if we see in their unresolved tensions some prophetic vision of the life to come. Over the years, Rattle has performed the work nearly 100 times, far more often than anyone else. Wooed by Berlin, he repeatedly offered them 'Mahler ed Cooke' and was repulsed. He made his Berlin conducting début with the Sixth. But, after the announcement in June 1999 that he had won the orchestra's vote in a head-to-head with Daniel Barenboim, he celebrated with two concert performances of the 10th. A composite version is presented here. As always, Rattle obtains some devastatingly quiet string playing, and technical standards are unprecedentedly high in so far as the revised performing version is concerned. Indeed, the danger that clinical precision will result in expressive coolness isn't immediately dispelled by the self-confident meatiness of the violas at the start. We aren't used to hearing the line immaculately tuned with every accent clearly defined. The tempo is broader than before and, despite Rattle's characteristic determination to articulate every detail, the mood is, at first, comparatively serene, even Olympian. Could Rattle be succumbing to the Karajan effect? But no – somehow he squares the circle. The neurotic trills, jabbing dissonances and tortuous counterpoint are relished as never before, within the context of a schizoid *Adagio* in which the Brucknerian string writing is never undersold.

The conductor has not radically changed his approach to the rest of the work. As you might expect, the scherzos have greater security and verve. Their strange hallucinatory choppiness is better served, although parts of the fourth movement remain perplexing despite the superb crispness and clarity of inner parts. More than ever, everything leads inexorably to the cathartic finale, brought off with a searing intensity that has you forgetting the relative baldness of the invention. Berlin's Philharmonie isn't the easiest venue: with everything miked close, climaxes can turn oppressive but the results here are very credible and offer no grounds for hesitation. In short, this new version sweeps the board even more

convincingly than the old. According to reports of the first night, Rattle was called back and accorded two Karajan-style standing ovations after the orchestra had left the stage. There's no applause here, but it isn't difficult to imagine such a scene. Rattle makes the strongest case for an astonishing piece of revivification that only the most die-hard purists will resist. Strongly recommended.

Symphony No 10 (ed Cooke)
South West German Radio Symphony Orchestra / Michael Gielen
Hänssler Classic 93 124 (77' · DDD) Ⓕ

It has become harder for interpreters to make their mark in what has become standard fare, yet Michael Gielen pulls it off. He has reversed his attitude to the nascent Tenth to present here an intriguing realisation of Deryck Cooke's performing version.

Gielen's narrative is not invested with Rattle's passion (see above). He prefers to lay bare its gaunt, unfinished state, exposing even parts of the *Adagio* as the harmonic frame over which Mahler would have stretched more complex contrapuntal detail. No longer an inexorable meditation, the movement becomes rather an unfinished dialogue between arrest and movement. The orchestral sound is lean and light with some exceptionally hushed playing from the strings and no lack of exquisite detail. The transparency means that contested ingredients like the deployment of glockenspiel in the second movement and Cooke's discarded side-drum and xylophone parts in the fourth really register. And has there ever been a more perfectly judged *Purgatorio*?

The finale can be achingly tender but only where necessary. That great flute melody is almost plain as well as pure, but what care is lavished on the strings' delicately nuanced response! Rattle goes for the opposite effect, the Berlin flautist floating his tone more poignantly, the strings avoiding the hint of sentimentality. Under Gielen the upward thrust of the heart-wrenching sigh concluding the work takes you by surprise: he has a way of foregrounding emotive detail before retreating to a more expository Klemperer-like stoicism.

Orchestral songs

Kindertotenlieder[a]. Rückert-Lieder[b] Lieder eines fahrenden Gesellen[a]
Dame Janet Baker *mez* [a]**Hallé Orchestra**, [b]**New Philharmonia Orchestra / Sir John Barbirolli**
EMI 566981-2 (65' · ADD ·T/t) Ⓕ❶↦

The songs of the *Lieder eines fahrenden Gesellen* ('Songs of a Wayfarer') are quoted from Mahler's First Symphony and the fresh, springtime atmosphere is shared by both works. The orchestration has great textural clarity and lightness of touch. The *Kindertotenlieder*, more chromatically expressive than the earlier work, tap into a darker, more complex vein in Mahler's spiritual and emotional make-up. The *Rückert-Lieder* aren't a song cycle as such but gather in their romantic awareness and response to the beauties of the poetry a unity and shape that binds them. Baker and Barbirolli reach a transcendental awareness of Mahler's inner musings. Barbirolli draws from the Hallé playing of delicacy and precision, establishing a clear case for having this CD in your collection.

Mahler Fünf Rückert-Lieder **Wagner** Wesendonck Lieder. Tristan und Isolde – Prelude; Mild und leise (Liebestod)
Felicity Lott sop **Schumann Quartet**
(Tedi Papavrami vn Christoph Schiller va
François Guye vc Christian Favre pf)
Aeon AECD0858 (53' · DDD)   (F)O

The Schumann Quartet's pianist, Christian Favre, has made these clear, practical transcriptions (rather than arrangements, the booklet-note stresses) inspired by Chausson's *Chanson perpetuelle*, and with a view to adding to the chamber music literature from the Romantic world of song. So expect a scaled-down report on the works concerned rather than Schoenberg's interventionist way with Johann Strauss or Brahms, or the risk-taking panache of Liszt's operatic adaptations.

Not the least virtue of the exercise is that we get Dame Felicity Lott in repertoire she might otherwise not have attempted. Her performance of the Liebestod – or 'Verklärung' as we should call it – is such an object lesson in engagement with the text, sensuality and controlled power that one might imagine the late Carlos Kleiber (whose favourite Marschallin she was) contemplating a further recording of the opera with her. The *Wesendonck*s have a similar sensual (and lean) intelligence, devoid of the stuffy Victorian abstractions that Mathilde's dreadful poetry can often produce in performance. And, if this is not the ideal-est voice for the darker corners of the *Rückert-Lieder*, you'll need to hear what Lott makes of the poems. The *Tristan* Prelude is fine too; it's just that it doesn't have a voice part. Good recordings, and 100 per cent worth it for the singing.

Kindertotenlieder. Lieder eines fahrenden Gesellen. Fünf Rückert-Lieder. Lieder und Gesänge – No 1, Frühlingsmorgen; No 3, Hans und Grethe; No 5, Phantasie aus Don Juan; No 10, Zu Strassburg auf der Schanz; No 11, Ablösung im Sommer; No 12, Scheiden und Meiden; No 13, Nicht wiedersehen!
Stephan Genz bar **Roger Vignoles** pf
Hyperion CDA67392 (73' · DDD · T/t)   (F)

Stephan Genz's voice and style place him above his many noted contemporaries. His mellifluous baritone recalls that of a young Thomas Hampson, but his understanding of the Lieder genre is even more penetrating, as this Mahler recital reveals. Each song is shaped as a whole yet with subtleties of phrase and word-painting that seem inevitable in every respect, especially as the chosen tempi always seem the right ones.

Performing and listening to these songs with piano is inevitably a more intimate experience than when they are heard in their orchestral garb. The pair's rapport is evident throughout. Memorable are the the poise and stillness of 'Ich atmet' einen Linden duft' from the *Rückert-Lieder*, the eloquent sadness of 'Nicht Wiedersehen' and the restrained sorrow of the whole of *Kindertoten-lieder*. Not a hint of sentimentality, such a danger in Mahler, spoils the experience of the composer's deeply felt emotions.

Hyperion's recording, beautifully balanced, catches the true quality of Genz's voice and the refinement of Vignoles's playing. This disc is an experience not to be missed by any lover of Mahler and/or of Lieder.

Das klagende Lied

Das Klagende Lied
Marina Shaguch sop **Michelle DeYoung** mez
Thomas Moser ten **Sergei Leiferkus** bar
**San Francisco Symphony Chorus and Orchestra /
Michael Tilson Thomas**
Avie 821936 0017-2 (67' · DDD/DSD · T/t)
Recorded live in 1996   (F)OOO

What a glorious prospect Mahler's first major work opens up for us – and how beautifully it is realised here. The original three-part version of this ambitious folkloric cantata is like a musical manifesto of pretty well all Mahler to come. Horn calls in the prelude to 'Wald-märchen' ('Forest Tale') awaken his unique nature-world; elfin woodwind fanfares intimate martial music as far as the Seventh and Eighth symphonies; the First Symphony (third movement) is germinating at the close of part 1, the opening of the Second is already in place with the first bars of 'Der Spielmann' ('The Wandering Musician'); and with 'Hochzeitsstück' ('Wedding Feast') Mahler seems to find himself in Act 2 of Wagner's *Göt-terdämmerung* contemplating the opera he never wrote. But more startling than anything in *Das Klagende Lied* is Mahler's feeling for, and command of, the orchestra – and this from a composer who'd never heard a note of his own orchestration.

Recorded in 1996 (and originally released by RCA), the subtle detailing and nuancing of this performance indicates painstaking preparation but arrives in our living rooms sounding as if the ink is still wet on the page. Each repetition of that madrigal-like choral *ritornello* intensifies the lamentation of the title until release is found in the anguish of the wronged queen and soprano Marina Shaguch hurls out her leaping vocal line to bring down the walls of the castle. That's Mahler's innate theatricality for you. Quite a piece, and quite a performance.

Des Knaben Wunderhorn

Des Knaben Wunderhorn – Revelge[b]. Das irdische Leben[a]. Verlor'ne Müh[ab]. Rheinlegendchen[a]. Der Tamboursg'sell[b]. Der Schildwache Nachtlied[ab]. Wer hat dies Liedlein erdacht?[a]. Lob des hohen Verstandes[b]. Des Antonius von Padua Fischpredigt[b]. Lied des Verfolgten im Turm[ab]. Trost im Unglück[ab]. Wo die schönen Trompeten blasen[a]
[a]**Elisabeth Schwarzkopf** sop [b]**Dietrich Fischer-Dieskau** bar **London Symphony Orchestra / George Szell**
EMI Great Recordings of the Century 567236-2
(50' · ADD · T/t) Recorded 1968　　Ⓜ❶❶❶▷

EMI's classic recording made in 1968 more or less puts all rivals out of court. Even those who find Schwarzkopf's singing mannered will be hard pressed to find more persuasive versions of the female songs than she gives, while Fischer-Dieskau and Szell are in a class of their own most of the time. Bernstein's CBS version, also from the late 1960s but with less spectacularly improved sound than EMI now provide, is also very fine, but for repeated listening Szell, conducting here with the kind of insight he showed on his famous Cleveland version of the Fourth Symphony, is the more controlled and keen-eared interpreter. Also, few command the musical stage as Fischer-Dieskau does in a song like 'Revelge' where every drop of irony and revulsion from the spectre of war is fiercely, grimly caught. Strongly recommended.

Das Lied von der Erde

Das Lied von der Erde
Christa Ludwig mez **Fritz Wunderlich** ten
Philharmonia Orchestra, New Philharmonia Orchestra / Otto Klemperer
EMI 566892-2 (64' · ADD) Recorded 1964-6　Ⓜ❶❶▷

In a famous BBC TV interview Klemperer declared that he was the objective one, Walter the romantic, and he knew what he was talking about. Klemperer lays this music before you, even lays bare its soul by his simple method of steady tempos (too slow in the third song) and absolute textural clarity, but he doesn't quite demand your emotional capitulation as does Walter. Ludwig does that. In the tenor songs, Wunderlich can't match Patzak, simply because of the older singer's way with the text; 'fest steh'n' in the opening song, 'Mir ist als wie im Traum', the line plaintive and the tone poignant, are simply unsurpassable.

By any other yardstick, Wunderlich is a prized paragon, musical and vocally free. The sound on the revived EMI is very fresh: with voice and orchestra in perfect relationship and everything sharply defined, the old methods of the 1960s have nothing to fear here from today's competition. These two old recordings will never be thrust aside; the Walter for its authority and intensity, the feeling of being present on an his-

---

MAHLER'S DAS LIED VON DER ERDE – IN BRIEF

Urmana; Schade; Vienna PO / Pierre Boulez
DG 💿 471 635-2 (61' · DDD)　　　Ⓕ❶❷▷
A real ensemble effort whose guiding light is Boulez. With the help of DG's sound, textures glint with unprecendented clarity; the very end is possibly the most evocative on record.

Ferrier; Patzak; Vienna PO / Bruno Walter　Ⓗ
Decca 466 576-2DM (89' · ADD)　　Ⓜ❶❶▷
This classic meeting of minds in mono now has a better depth of sound than ever before in Decca's latest remastering. The human appeal of Ferrier's 'Farewell' is still magnetic.

Ludwig; Wunderlich; Philharmonia / Otto Klemperer
EMI 566892-2 (64' · ADD)　　　Ⓜ❶❶▷
Another conductor who knew Mahler and worked with him: both singers are in gloriously full voice.

Hodgson; Mitchinson; BBC Northern SO / Jascha Horenstein
BBC Legends BBCL4042-2 (61' · ADD)　Ⓜ❶❶
Horenstein's live legacy of long-breathed Mahler is at last gaining deserved recognition. This is a meditative, deeply felt *Das Lied*. Hodgson eclipses many greater names.

Ferrier; Lewis; Hallé / Sir John Barbirolli　Ⓗ
APR mono APR5579 (77' · ADD)　　Ⓕ❶❶
Ferrier is in even fuller, finer voice here than for Walter, with a richer, more expansive canvas painted by the Hallé and that most passionate of Mahlerians, Barbirolli. Restricted sound.

Baker; Kmentt; Bavarian RSO / Rafael Kubelík
Audite 95491 (62' · ADD)　　　　Ⓑ❶
No survey could be without Janet Baker's sensitive, heartfelt response to the long final 'Farewell': in Kmentt she finally has a partner who is almost her equal, and, in concert, Kubelík finds new expressive heights and depths.

Fischer-Dieskau; King; Vienna PO / Leonard Bernstein
Decca 466 381-2DM (67' · ADD)　　　Ⓜ▷
If you want Mahler's sanctioned alternative, with a baritone singing the mezzo songs, this is a first choice: Fischer-Dieskau's vast experience in Lieder is telling here, and so are King's credentials as a Wagnerian.

Rigby; Tear; Première Ensemble / Mark Wigglesworth
RCA 09026 68043-2 (69' · ADD)　　　Ⓕ
Schoenberg's arrangement reduces the orchestra to a chamber ensemble, and allows the singers to project with more subtlety while exerting an authentic Mahlerian pull.

toric occasion, the Klemperer for its insistent strength and beautiful singing.

Das Lied von der Erde[a]. Three Rückert-Lieder   H
Kathleen Ferrier contr [a]**Julius Patzak** ten
Vienna Philharmonic Orchestra / Bruno Walter
Decca 4665762 (75' · ADD) Recorded 1952
or Naxos 8.110871 (75' · ADD)   M●●●●▷

The 1952 Walter will never lose its place at the heart of any review of *Das Lied* recordings. Walter obtains even richer, more impassioned, more pointed playing from the Vienna Philharmonic than in 1936 in, of course, improved sound. With his disciple Ferrier as alto soloist, her songs are richly, warmly voiced, and taken, particularly in the finale, to the limits of emotional involvement. Few have attempted to identify so completely with the work's ethos of farewell and its thoughts of eternity. Ferrier envelops one to the core of one's being. The wholly idiomatic and wonderfully expressive Patzak is the near-ideal tenor.

Additional recommendations

Hodgson contr **Mitchinson** ten **BBC Northern Symphony Orchestra / Horenstein**
BBC Legends/IMG Artists BBCL4042-2 (73' · ADD) Recorded live   M
Horenstein gives us a deeply eloquent, valedictory reading. Its sustained intensity, revelatory attention to orchestral detail and wonderful overview of the work make it a classic worthy to be set alongside readings by Walter, Klemperer and Reiner.

Pierre de Manchicourt
Franco-Flemish c1510-1564

A choirboy at Arras Cathedral, Manchicourt was director of the choir at Tours Cathedral in 1539, master of the choirboys at Tournai Cathedral in 1545 and maître de chapelle there later year. By 1556 he was a canon at Arras Cathedral. Manchicourt succeeded Nicolas Payen as master of Philip II's Flemish chapel in Madrid; it is possible that was also master of Philip's Spanish chapel. His output inludes numerous Masses and motets. GROVEmusic

Regina caeli. Cuidez vous que Dieu nous faille. Peccantem me quotidie. Missa Cuidez vous que Dieu nous faille. Magnificat secundi toni. Osculetur me. Ne reminiscaris, Domine
Brabant Ensemble / Stephen Rice
Hyperion CDA67604 (67' · DDD · T/t)   F●

Even in his lifetime, Manchicourt's fame was not what it might have been. There were so many fine composers in the mid-16th-century that it's no easy matter to explain what it is that makes certain composers' music stand out. Manchicourt's has something of Gombert's

concentration of materials, with textures that are just as full but rather brighter; and his considerable contrapuntal ingenuity is often laced with wit (as in the canonic *Regina caeli*). From the song by Richafort on which he bases his Mass *Cuidez vous que Dieu nous faille*, Manchicourt has a knack of selecting those moments that can be expanded and developed into large-scale passages of considerable rhetorical power. The small-scale as well as the medium-length motets are also worth hearing.

The sound recording is very fine, though the dominance of the trebles slightly obscures the contrapuntal working of the lower voices. All the same, this is a must-have for anybody interested in Renaissance music, marginal or not.

Tigran Mansurian
Lebanese b1939

Since settling in Armenia in 1947 at the age of eight (he was born in Lebanon), Tigran Mansurian has been a leading voice in his adoptive country's contemporary music scene. He found his way towards a fusion of indigenous folk traditions (their spirit more than their letter) and a musical language rooted in East European modernism. More than most, however, he has steered clear of the easy options of minimalism, neo-tonalism and heart-on-sleeve spirituality.

String Quartets – No 1; No 2. Testament
Rosamunde Quartet (Andreas Reiner, Simon Fordham vns Helmut Nicolai va Anja Lechner vc)
ECM New Series 476 3052 (50' · DDD)   F▷

In the first two string quartets – composed in 1983-84 (there is a third from 1993) – and the short *Testament* of 2004 dedicated to ECM's Manfred Eicher, the influence of Bartók looms large, though Shostakovich is also there in the background. These works join a long and honourable tradition in Russian chamber music as an arena for private memorialisation, for confessions shared between artistic souls. In fact both are in the best sense musicians' music, in that they trace long lines of expressive thought, the ideas ebbing and flowing naturally. In every movement there are memorable ideas that connect and reveal new prespectives on repeated hearings.

In an unsensational way, therefore, this is one of the most satisfying discs of unfamiliar music for a long time. Credit for that impression must go in large part to the sensitivity and musicianly insight of the Rosamunde Quartet and to another beautifully judged recording from ECM.

Marin Marais
French 1656-1728

Marais, the central figure in the French bass viol school, spent his life in Paris, much of it in royal serv-

ice. *A pupil of Sainte-Colombe and protégé of Lully, he composed four operas (1693-1709 – notably Alcione, 1706, famous for its storm scene) that form an important link between Lully and Campra. But his greatest significance lies in his five collections of music for one to three bass viols (1686-1725), comprising over 550 pieces. As well as the usual dances, they include character pieces that are among his finest works, and they possess an eloquence and refinement of line and richness of ornamental detail that perfectly display the qualities of his instrument. The Pieces en trio (1692) are recognised as the first appearance of the trio sonata in France.*

GROVEmusic

Pièces de viol

Pièces de viole, Livre 2 – Part 1: Ballet en rondeau; Ⓟ
Couplets de folies; Prélude; Cloches ou carillon. Part 2: Prélude lentement; Chaconne en rondeau; Tombeau pour M de Ste Colombe; Prélude; Allemande; Courante; Pavan selon de goût des anciens compositeurs de luth; Gavotte; Rondeau en vaudeville; Gigue; Chaconne; Fantaisie
Markku Luolajan-Mikkola, Varpu Haavisto *vas da gamba* **Eero Palviainen** *lte* **Elina Mustonen** *hpd*
BIS CD909 (73' · DDD)   Ⓕ

The most substantial pieces here are the set of variations of *La folia*, and the *Tombeau pour M-de Ste Colombe* in memory of Marais's mentor. His idiom embodies a paradox that's peculiarly French, in that it demands a very high technical standard, yet its proper expression requires the utmost restraint. The young Finnish viol-player, Markku Luolajan-Mikkola, is a founder-member of Phantasm. Here he holds his own with elegance and reserve, although in the slower pieces one might have wished for more rhythmic flexibility. The continuo section consists of another viol-player, and a theorbo or harpsichord (though in the variations on *La folia*, the two are combined). This works well for the most part, though the high partials of the harpsichord tend to drown the viols: the lute is far less obtrusive. The problem of balance also intrudes when the soloist is in the lower range. But as an introduction to Marais's art this is hard to fault – try his Pavan 'in the style of the bygone lute composers': a real treat.

Further listening

Tous les matins du monde (soundtrack)   Ⓟ
Music by **Couperin, Lully, Marais** and **Sainte-Colombe**
Le Concert des Nations / Savall *va da gamba*
Alia Vox AV9821 (76' · DDD)   Ⓕ
This magical disc occupies the more inward world of the solo gamba repertoire, taking in moving and thoughtful compositions such as Marais' *La rêveuse* and Sainte-Colombe's deeply moving *Les pleurs*. Savall shows himself throughout to be a master worthy of these great viol-playing composers.

Luca Marenzio   Italian 1553/4-1599

Possibly a pupil of Contino in Brescia, Marenzio moved to Rome in c1574 and served cardinals and other wealthy patrons (including Luigi d'Este) until 1586. During these years he published copiously and gained an international reputation. He travelled in 1587, visiting Verona, and briefly served Ferdinando de' Medici in Florence, where in 1589 he composed intermedi for the ducal wedding festivities. He returned to Rome later that year, residing with the Duke of Bracciano untilc 1593, when he entered Cardinal Cinzio Aldobrandini's service; he held a Vatican apartment in 1594. In 1595-6 he visited the Polish court, returning to Rome in 1598.

One of the most prolific madrigalists of the period, Marenzio published over 400 madrigals and villanellas in at least 23 books (1580-99). They range widely, from light pastorals to serious sonnets (these mostly from later years), and are notable for their striking mood- and word-painting. They long remained popular in Italy and elsewhere, especially England. His motets, though less well known, also feature much verbal imagery and religious symbolism.   GROVEmusic

Madrigals

Madrigals – Book 1: Così moriro i fortunati amanti; Ⓟ
Deh rinforzate il vostro pianto; Dolorosi martir, fieri tormenti; Frenò Tirsi il desio; Liquide perle Amor da gl'occhi sparse; Per duo coralli ardenti; Tirsi morir volea; Book 2: Là dove sono i pargoletti Amori; E s'io doglio, Amor; Fuggi speme mia, fuggi; Vaghi e lieti fanciulli; Book 4: Caro Aminta pur voi; Donne il celeste lume; Nè fero sdegno mai donna mi mosse; Non può Filli più; Book 5: Basciami mille volte; Consumando mi vo di piaggia in piaggia; Book 6: O-verdi selv'o dolci fonti o rivi; Udite, lagrimosi; Book 7: Cruda Amarilli; Ma grideran per me le piagge; Book-9: Così nel mio parlar; Et ella ancide, e-non val c'huom si chiuda **Philips** Tirsi morir volea **Terzi** Intavolatura di liuto, libro primo – Liquide perle Amor, da gl'occhi sparse
Il Concerto Italiano / Rinaldo Alessandrini *hpd*
Opus111 OP30245 (74' · DDD)   Ⓕ⦿⦿⦿

 Marenzio's music was known throughout Europe during his lifetime; its success was based on what one contemporary identified as its 'new, fresh style, pleasing to the ear, with some simple counterpoint and without excessive artifice', a characterisation that applies more to the earlier books than to the late ones. It's this style which lies at the heart of Rinaldo Alessandrini's selection (though there are plenty of pieces from the later books as well), and the performances nicely capture its essential spirit, its communicability and transparent craftmanship occasionally disturbed (as in 'Dolorosi martir') by more serious intent. These beautifully paced and architecturally controlled performances, many of which make intelligent and appropriate use of added continuo instruments, present the most persuasive argument for understanding the reasons for Marenzio's enormous reputation, throughout Italy and beyond, at the start of the 1580s. Highly recommended.

John Marsh
English 1752-1828

The most important of Marsh's extant compositions, the Eight Favorite Symphonies published between 1784 and 1800, reveal a composer well-versed in the requirements of the mixed professional and amateur provincial orchestras he encountered. Concertante parts for more able players are judiciously juxtaposed with easier tutti writing, and in a work like the Conversation Sinfonie, for two orchestras, composed in 1778, Marsh also shows a keen awareness of orchestral colour, disposing his two groups so as to pit high instruments against low.

Symphonies

Symphonies – No 2; No 6; No 7, 'La Chasse'; No 8. A Conversation Symphony
London Mozart Players / Matthias Bamert
Chandos CHAN10458 (64' · DDD)   Ⓕ🅑▶

Limited invention, but this English gentleman's music is certainly agreeable. Though Marsh's invention can be banal and short-breathed, there is an indefinable quality of robust Englishness to many of his melodies. Several movements have a distinct whiff of Handel, especially the catchy country-dance finale of No 8, with its piquant changes of instrumental colouring (shades here of the *Water Music*). There are rollicking Handelian fanfares, too, in the first movement and minuet of the most ambitious and massively scored symphony, No 6, though Marsh's acknowledged inspiration here was Haydn's late symphonies. The 'London Bach', Johann Christian, is another unmissable influence, above all in the *Conversation Symphony*, an original take on Bach's symphonies for double orchestra.

As ever in their 'Contemporaries of Mozart' series, Matthias Bamert and the LMP give carefully prepared, well-paced performances, rhythmically lively without falling into autopilot, and balancing polish with a down-to-earth directness crucial to Marsh's music. Among a clutch of expert soloists, the horns deserve a tip of the hat for their brave braying in the brief 'hunting' symphony, No 7. The recording has an attractive bloom. A modestly pleasing curio, recommended to anyone who likes to venture down 18th-century symphonic byways.

Frank Martin
Swiss 1890-1974

Martin, the son of a Calvinist minister, was deeply impressed by a performance of the St Matthew Passion he heard at the age of 10. He studied with Joseph Lauber and worked from 1926 with Jaques-Dalcroze, then in his Piano Concerto no.1 (1934) and Symphony (1937) adopted Schoenbergian serialism while retaining an extended tonal harmony that looked to Debussy: the mature fusion of these elements into a style marked by dissonant chords, smooth part-writing and 'gliding tonality' did not come until the dramatic chamber oratorio Le vin herbé (1941), soon followed by two larger oratorios, In terra pax (1944) and Golgotha (1948), as well as by the Petite symphonie concertante for harp, harpsichord, piano and strings (1945) and the Sechs Monologe aus 'Jedermann' (1943, orchestrated 1949). In 1946 he moved to the Netherlands; he also taught at the Cologne Musikhochschule (1950-57). His later works include the operas Der Sturm (1956, Vienna Staatsoper) and Monsieur de Pourceaugnac (1963, Geneva), a large-scale Requiem (1972) and many concertante pieces, among them concertos for violin and harpsichord (both 1952) and a second for piano (1969).
GROVEmusic

Piano Concertos

Piano Concertos – No 1[a]; No 2[b]. Ballade[a]
Danse de la peur[ab]
[a]**Sebastian Benda**, [a]**Paul Badura-Skoda** pfs **Svizzera Italiana Orchestra / Christian Benda**
ASV CDDCA1082 (74' · DDD)   Ⓕ

What Martin's music needs is performances of understanding but also affection, and ASV deserves congratulation for the shrewd casting of this disc. Sebastian Benda was a composition pupil of Martin's, and once recorded the *Ballade* with him conducting. The Second Piano Concerto was written for Paul Badura-Skoda, and he too recorded it with the composer. The conductor here is too young to share the two pianists' warm memories of Martin, but he's Sebastian Benda's son, and the sense of all three collaborating in a tribute is strong.

Martin is often described as a serialist, but this isn't true. He used 12-note rows, but only to discipline his melodic language, which is tonal, strong and lyrical. The First Concerto might just as well have been subtitled 'The Dramatic' and Benda plays it with flair and great enjoyment, as he does the gentler but no less varied *Ballade*. The Second Concerto, a late work, is one of Martin's finest, with a profusion of bold, striking ideas and opportunities for grand rhetoric. Badura-Skoda plays it as though he were delighted to make its acquaintance again.

Perhaps the orchestra could have done with two or three extra desks of strings, but the recording is excellent and the performances all that could be desired.

Cello Concerto

Cello Concerto[a]. Ballade[b]. Eight Preludes[c]
[ab]**Christian Poltéra** vc [bc]**Kathryn Stott** pf
[a]**Malmö Symphony Orchestra /
Tuomas Ollila-Hannikainen**

BIS BIS-CD1637 (66' · DDD)　　　　　　Ⓕ

Frank Martin's Cello Concerto, so eloquently and sensitively played here, is a real discovery. It is no exaggeration to state that this rapt performance presents this noble concerto with an inspirational intensity to compare with the celebrated Du Pré/Barbirolli recording of the Elgar Concerto. The works share a similar deep, poignant, meditative feeling, although Martin's concerto also has a distinct valedictory character, expressive melancholy which suggests personal loss.

The soloist opens with a gloriously lyrical theme which is to dominate the movement (commentators have likened it to Vaughan Williams). A skittish development is in tarantella rhythm with bolder clashes of angry dissonance but at the close comes the balm of the return of the ravishing opening material. Unexpectedly, the touching central *Adagietto* is in the form of a passacaglia. This sadness is all but dispelled in the brilliantly rhythmic finale, yet the lyricism creeps back and even the tarantella returns briefly before the close.

The (much earlier) *Ballade* is a free fantasia-like dialogue between cello and piano, Kathryn Stott and Christian Poltéra enjoying a perfect partnership. Martin dallied with Schoenberg's 12-note system and he uses it in the Eight Preludes. But he had no intention of giving up tonality, and the result is a stunning set of great variety and resource, thrillingly played by Stott.

This disc, given state-of-the-art recording makes an ideal introduction to Martin's music.

Mass for Double Choir

Martin Mass for Double Choir. Passaille[a] **Pizzetti**
Messa di requiem. De profundis
Westminster Cathedral Choir / James O'Donnell
[a]*org*
Hyperion CDA67017 (71' · DDD · T/t)　　ⒻⓄⓄⓄ

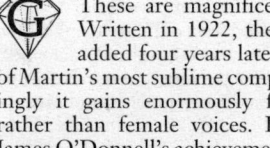 These are magnificent performances. Written in 1922, the *Agnus Dei* being added four years later, the Mass is one of Martin's most sublime compositions. Surprisingly it gains enormously from using boys' rather than female voices. It's a measure of James O'Donnell's achievement with Westminster Cathedral Choir that the gain in purity and beauty is never at the expense of depth and fervour. This is an altogether moving and eloquent performance, often quite thrilling and always satisfying.

This disc brings us a fine performance by O'Donnell of the *Passacaille* and the Pizzetti *Messa di Requiem*, also composed in 1922. The received wisdom is that it is in his *a cappella* music that Pizzetti is at his finest; in his 1951 monograph Guido Gatti spoke of his setting as 'the most serene and lyrical of all... from Mozart's to Gabriel Faure's'. Serene and lyrical it most certainly is, and it will come as a revelation to those encountering it for the first time. There is a fervour and a conviction about

the Westminster performances of both the Requiem and the 1937 *De profundis*. The luminous tone this choir produce in both these inspired and masterly works will ring in your ears long after you have finished playing this splendidly recorded disc.

Maria-Triptychon

Passacaglia[ab]. Polyptyque[b]. Maria-Triptychon.
[a]**Juliane Banse** *sop* [b]**Muriel Cantoreggi** *vn*
German Radio Philharmonic Orchestra / Christoph Poppen
ECM New Series 173 3930 (58' · DDD)　　　Ⓕ

Polyptyque is one of Martin's most impressive scores, with its impassioned lyricism held, as if in liquid suspension, by the cooler instrumental textures of solo violin and double string orchestra and the inner drama of its sequence of depictions from the Passion story. The alternating fast and slow movements cover by turns Christ's entry into Jerusalem (listen to the seething string textures representing the palm-waving crowd), the Last Supper, Judas, Gethsemane, Christ's scourging and – rather than Calvary – his glorification.

There is a link to the *Maria-Triptychon* (1967-68) through the latter's finale, a setting of the 'Stabat mater dolorosa'. This triptych for soprano, violin and orchestra was written for the husband-and-wife duo of Wolfgang Schneiderhan and Irmgard Seefried, and opens with dovetailed settings of the Ave Maria and Magnificat, the latter forming an impressive, intense climax (ECM does not provide the texts in the booklet). Unlike *Polyptyque*, however, *Maria-Triptychon* is a work that needs concentrated listening to secure its full impression.

The *Passacaglia* Martin wrote in 1944 for organ and orchestrated richly 18 years later has become one of his better-known works. Here, his devotion to Bach's music is made manifest in sound with organ-like sonorities surviving the transcription and a gripping Busonian power. Poppen directs hugely impressive performances from his excellent soloists and orchestra. ECM's sound is, as usual, crystal clear and superb. A winner.

Le vin herbé

Le vin herbé
Sandrine Piau *sop* **Steve Davislim** *ten* **Jutta Böhnert** *sop* **Berlin RIAS Chamber Choir;**
Scharoun Ensemble / Daniel Reuss
Harmonia Mundi Ⓕ ② HMC90 1935/6
(112' · DDD · T/t)　　　　　　　　ⒻⓄⓄ

Scored for 12 voices, piano and string septet, Frank Martin's setting of the legend of Tristan and Isolde, with its very understated emotions, sparse texture and deliberately limited harmonic vocabulary, has enjoyed a somewhat chequered history on record.

The RIAS Chamber Choir bring rather more than 12 voices to this recording – including the eight principal solo roles, there are a total of 29 singers listed – but, unquestionably, they preserve the intimacy and directness of expression which is so essential in any performance of *Le vin herbé*. It is clearly not to enrich the overall body of sound that Daniel Reuss has brought in so many voices, but he has clearly selected them, both in ensemble and solo, with painstaking care to underline the essential character of each of the individual tableaux, and even at the most climactic moments, there are never more than a handful singing together.

Such an approach pays remarkable dividends in that it allows the three main sections of the work to focus more clearly on their very different specific human characteristics. In the first, 'The Love Potion', while their love may have been chemically induced, there is no doubting the sense of mutual affection and respect with which the calm stateliness of Steve Davislim and the unaffected poise of Sandrine Piau portray Tristan and Isolde. The second, 'The Forest of Morois', deals with compassion and forgiveness and Jonathan de la Paz Zaens' portrayal of King Mark exudes profound goodness in a way which sheds a totally new light on the word 'kingly'. The third, 'Death', covers jealousy and reconciliation and Hildegard Wiedemann is utterly convincing in the somewhat difficult role of the vaguely treacherous Isolde of the White Hands.

Alongside all this runs a beautifully crafted instrumental accompaniment, far more involved in the drama than the booklet notes imply by suggesting that it is 'like the scenery in a play'. There is immense sensitivity in the way the individual members of the Scharoun Ensemble handle the amazingly fluid instrumental textures, the very understatedness of which drives the fundamental message home far more powerfully than a whole plethora of dramatic orchestral gestures. Driven along with a powerful sense of urgency by Reuss, this is an intense and deeply moving performance which, complete with lavish packaging and a superlative recorded sound, brings to the catalogue something which it has never had before; a really first-rate and compelling performance of this most important of Martin scores.

Vicente Martín y Soler
Spanish 1754-1806

Martín y Soler was in the service of the Spanish Infante by 1780 and composed operas and ballets for Italian cities in 1779-85; he also wrote zarzuelas. He then began a famous collaboration with the librettist Da Ponte in Vienna, presenting three Italian opera buffe. In 1788-94 he was at the Russian court as a composer and teacher, returning there in 1796 after a period in London, and becoming inspector of the Italian court theatre. He composed some 20 stage works in all; his ten opere buffe, among the finest of the period, contain expressive and dance-like melodies. GROVEmusic

La capricciosa corretta

La capricciosa corretta
Josep Miquel Ramon *bar* Fiuta **Marguerite** Ⓟ
Krull *sop* Donna Ciprigna **Yves Saelens** *ten* Lelio
Enrique Baquerizo *bar* Bonario **Katia Velletaz** *sop*
Isabella **Carlos Marin** *bar* Don Giglio **Raffaella**
Milanesi *sop* Cilia **Emiliano Gonzalez-Toro** *ten*
Valerio **Les Talens Lyriques / Christophe Rousset**
Naïve ② E8887 (135' · DDD · T/t)   Ⓕ

Mozart's affectionate quotation from Martín y Soler's *Una cosa rara* in the *Don Giovanni* dinner music suggests he admired his Spanish contemporary, whose music was praised by others as 'sweet' and 'graceful'. Such descriptions remain apt for a charming and brilliantly executed performance that's essential for anybody curious about late 18th-century opera beyond Mozart.

The best operas of his later years were produced in London. *La capricciosa corretta* was first performed at the King's Theatre in 1795 under the title *La scuola dei maritati*; Its plot concerns the marriage of an older man to a young second wife whose excessive vanity and capriciousness makes life miserable for everybody else.

The libretto was by Lorenzo da Ponte. There are illuminating musical and dramatic parallels with, most notably, *Così fan tutte* and *Le nozze di Figaro*. 'Se figli vi siamo' is a gorgeous lyrical quintet, graced with sensitive woodwind colour, that wouldn't be out of place in *Così*. 'Qui vive, e respira' is a tender tenor aria in which Lelio softly enthuses about the woman he loves: it's a striking counterpart of Ferrando's 'Un' aura amorosa'. Valerio's mock-martial aria 'Un fucil, un spadon' is an intriguing close descendant of Figaro's 'Non più andrai', with a lightly scored military accompaniment illustrating a text about taking up a post in the army.

Individual personalities aren't portrayed to quite such memorable effect as in Mozart, of course, but there's plenty of distinctive music to overcome the inevitable comparisons.

Christophe Rousset's cast of relative unknowns deliver a competent and committed team performance. Les Talens Lyriques savour the music with their customary zest and astute musical intelligence.

Bohuslav Martinů
Bohemian 1890-1959

Martinů studied at the Prague Conservatory (1906-10), then worked as a teacher and orchestral violinist before going to Paris in 1923. There he studied with Roussel and developed a neo-classical style, sometimes using jazz (La bagarre, 1926; Le jazz, 1928, both for orchestra). He began to apply himself to Czech subjects (ballet Špalíček, 1933; operas The Miracles of Mary, 1935, Comedy on the Bridge, 1937; Field Mass for male voices, wind and percussion, 1939), but not exclusively: this was also the period of his fantasy opera Julietta (1938) and of numerous concertos. In

1940 he left Paris, and the next year arrived in New York, where he concentrated on orchestral and chamber works, including his first five symphonies. From 1948 his life was divided between Europe and the USA: this was the period of his Sixth Symphony (1953), Frescoes of Piero della Francesca for orchestra (1955) and opera The Greek Passion (1961). He was one of the most prolific composers of the 20th century, imaginative in style, with energetic rhythms and powerful, often dissonant harmony, but uneven in quality. GROVEmusic

Concertos

Duo concertante for Two Violins and Orchestra, H264ª. Concerto for Two Violins, H329ᵇ. Concerto for Flute, Violin and Orchestra, H252ᶜ
ᶜ**Janne Thomsen** *fl* ᵃᵇᶜ**Bohuslav Matoušek,** ᵃ**Régis Pasquier,** ᵇ**Jennifer Koh** *vns* **Czech Philharmonic Orchestra / Christopher Hogwood**
Hyperion CDA67671 (55' · DDD)   Ⓕ

Written in Martinů's best 1930s concerto grosso style, the *Duo concertante*'s three movements (fast-slow-fast) are limpidly scored, allowing the flowing, interweaving lines of the soloists to sound to best advantage; as the excellent booklet-notes say, 'an extraordinary musical experience'.

For this equally vibrant recording, Régis Pasquier partners Bohuslav Matoušek while Jennifer Koh appears with Matoušek in the Concerto in D major (1950). Unlike its predecessor, the later work is in the standard 19th-century concerto format – one reason why Martinů did not number the works – and structurally quite different. For one thing, there is no real slow movement, the central span (dovetailed into the finale) being moderate in pace with a *più vivo* central section. In atmosphere it is one of those fleet-footed yet serene works in which Martinů's inspiration seems just to beam from ear to ear.

This first volume, in what will be a series of four devoted to Martinů's *concertante* works for violin, is completed by another enchanting early double concerto, for flute and violin, penned in just 10 days in 1936. There is no hint of rush in its fresh and lively invention, the solo roles played with beguiling ease by Janne Thomsen and Matoušek. Accompanied by the Czech Philharmonic – in whose second violin section the composer played in the 1920s – this disc is an utter delight from start to finish.

Concerto for Violin, Piano and Orchestra, H342. Concerto da camera, H285ª. Czech Rhapsody, H307 (arr Teml)
Bohuslav Matoušek *vn* ª**Karel Košárek** *pf* **Czech Philharmonic Orchestra / Christopher Hogwood**
Hyperion CDA67672 (65' · DDD)   Ⓕ

Hogwood and Hyperion here focus on the concertos for violin with piano. In the *Concerto da camera* (1941), the keyboard is part – albeit a prominent one – of the strings-and-percussion accompaniment. Commissioned by Paul Sacher

for the leader of his Basle Chamber Orchestra, it was premiered to great success in Switzerland (Martinů having just started his American exile at the time). With its fresh invention and lively demeanour, this remains one of his more popular concertos although it has never received its due on disc. This newcomer sets that omission straight, however, crisply performed and immaculately recorded.

The same applies to its companion pieces. H342 (1952-53) is a true duo concerto, outwardly conventional in format but expressively complex, as Aleš Březina notes in the booklet: 'Enigmatic and highly personal…structurally driven by its emotional nature, [and] probably echoes the crisis in the composer's personal life.' Musically, the work feels like an accompanied sonata for piano and violin with each soloist supporting and occupying the forefront by turns and the orchestra – which enjoys its own 'solo' passages – providing an additional dimension to the discourse.

The disc concludes with Jiří Teml's idiomatic orchestration of the *Czech Rhapsody* (1945), written for Kreisler and intended to be accompanied orchestrally; for various reasons the final version was never completed. Premiered by Régis Pasquier in 2001, it is a splendid piece, warm and lyrical and beautifully played. Strongly recommended.

Violin Concertos – No 1, H226a; No 2, H293
Bohuslav Matoušek *vn* **Czech Philharmonic Orchestra / Christopher Hogwood**
Hyperion CDA67674 (54' · DDD)   ⒻⓄⓄ

Martinů's two violin concertos have very different histories. The First was created for Dushkin in 1931, much tinkered with over the next few years and then 'lost' until unearthed in 1968. The Second (1943) was written in just two months for Mischa Elman, premiered before the year was out and taken up by several violinists soon afterwards, often being programmed unnumbered until its predecessor came to light.

Josef Suk set the benchmark for both but his recordings, still in the Supraphon catalogue, have been overtaken by this newcomer and, in No 2, by Isabelle Faust's superb recent account (see below). Matoušek and Hogwood certainly have the measure of both scores and in the Second run Faust and Bělohlávek close. Couplings may prove decisive; one recommendation is for the Hyperion set as a whole. Strongly recommended.

Violin Concerto No 2, H293a. Toccata e due canzoni, H311b. Serenade No 2, H216
ª**Isabelle Faust** *vn* ᵇ**Cédric Tiberghien** *pf* **Prague Philharmonia / Jiří Bělohlávek**
Harmonia Mundi HMC90 1951 (63' · DDD)   Ⓕ

Hot on the heels of Hyperion's series of Martinů's works for violin and orchestra (see above) comes this brilliant new account of the

Second Concerto (1943), played with verve and a real feeling for the idiom by Isabelle Faust. What a fine player of the modern repertoire she is and her sweet, precise tone allows Martinů's angular lyricism – or is that lyrical angularity? – to open out for maximum appeal. Superbly supported by the Prague Philharmonia under Bělohlávek, this is as brilliantly played an account as has appeared on disc.

Orchestra and conductor are heard to excellent effect in the other major work, the *Toccata e due canzoni* (1946). Written for Paul Sacher, this invigorating cross between chamber symphony and concerto grosso (though with an extensive piano part, played with nicely suggestive power by Cédric Tiberghien) is both a product of its time – catching the relief, horror and war-weariness in equal measure – and a timeless classic. Yet through its many dramatic moments Martinů's radiant humanism, overtly displayed in the Concerto, shines through. Despite some slight scratchiness of ensemble and tuning in the upper strings in the opening pages, this is a strong performance, taut and purposeful.

Sandwiched between the two is the delightful Second Serenade (1932), scored for string orchestra and inhabiting the joyful folk world of the ballet palíček. Thrown off with élan, music and performance spotlight the splendid engineering that is an unobtrusive delight of this excellent disc. Recommended.

Symphonies

Symphonies Nos 1 & 2
Bamberg Symphony Orchestra / Neeme Järvi
BIS CD362 (61' · DDD)   Ⓕ

Symphonies Nos 3 & 4
Bamberg Symphony Orchestra / Neeme Järvi
BIS CD363 (63' · DDD)   Ⓕ

Symphonies Nos 5 & 6
Bamberg Symphony Orchestra / Neeme Järvi
BIS CD402 (59' · DDD)   ⒻⓄ

Despite his travels throughout his formative years as a composer, Martinů remained a quintessentially Czech composer and his music is imbued with the melodic shapes and rhythms of the folk-music of his homeland. The six symphonies were written during Martinů's America years and in all of them he uses a large orchestra with distinctive groupings of instruments which give them a very personal and unmistakable timbre. The rhythmic verve of his highly syncopated fast movements is very infectious, indeed unforgettable, and his slow movements are often deeply expressive, most potently, perhaps, in that of the Third Symphony which is imbued with the tragedy of war. The Bamberg orchestra plays marvellously and with great verve for Järvi, whose excellently judged tempos help propel the music forward most effectively. His understanding of the thrust of Martinů's structures is impressive and he projects the music with clarity. The recordings are beauti-

fully clear, with plenty of ambience surrounding the orchestra, a fine sense of scale and effortless handling of the wide dynamic range Martinů calls for. It's enthusiastically recommended.

Symphonies Nos 3 & 4
Czech Philharmonic Orchestra / Jiří Bělohlávek
Supraphon SU3631-2 (63' · DDD)   ⒻⓄⓄ

This is Jiří Bělohlávek's third recording of Martinů's life-enhancing Fourth Symphony (1945) and his second with the Czech Philharmonic. Both those predecessors possess considerable merits but must now yield to this newcomer. Not only is the orchestral playing in the luxury class, but Bělohlávek's reading is as shapely as it's involving. He masterminds a selfless and unforced ccount of the Third (1944), an altogether more troubled work than its successor, and whose homesick undertow is potently realised here (the heartrending closing pages are precisely that). Bělohlávek's, too, is a meticulously prepared performance of compassion and insight that does justice to a riveting work. Throughout, the inimitable, silvery sonority of this great orchestra has been admirably captured by the Supraphon engineers.

Symphony No 4. Memorial to Lidice. Field Mass[a]
[a]**Ivan Kusnjer** bar **Czech Philharmonic** [a]**Chorus and Orchestra / Jirí Bělohlávek**
Chandos CHAN9138 (65' · DDD · T/t)   ⒻⓄ

The luscious, intricately scored pages of the big-hearted Fourth Symphony sound opulent in this recording. For the most part, the playing is glorious, intoxicating in its richness and sure-footed poise. But there's some lack of intensity and temperament, so, for a more considered Bělohlávek account, look to his more recent Supraphon disc, reviewed above.

His performance of the *Field* Mass, on the other hand, is an undoubted success. It's wonderfully fervent, boasting a noble-toned, impassioned contribution from the baritone, Ivan Kusnjer, and disciplined, sonorous work from the men of the Czech Philharmonic Chorus. Chandos's recording captures it all to perfection: blend and focus impeccably combined. The moving *Memorial to Lidice* completes this ideally chosen triptych. Bearing a dedication 'To the Memory of the Innocent Victims of Lidice', Martinů's score was written in response to the destruction of that village by the Nazis in June 1942. One of the composer's most deeply felt creations, this is an eight-minute orchestral essay of slumbering power, incorporating at its climax a spine-chilling quotation from Beethoven's Fifth. It, too, receives sensitive advocacy here.

Chamber Works

Piano Quartet. Quartet for Oboe, Violin, Cello and Piano. Viola Sonata. String Quintet

Joel Marangella *ob* Isabelle van Keulen, Charmian Gadd, Solomia Soroka *vns* Rainer Moog, Theodore Kuchar *vas* Young-Chang Cho, Alexander Ivashkin *vcs* Daniel Adni, Kathryn Selby *pfs*
Naxos 8 553916 (73' · DDD)　　　　　　 Ⓢ⊕

The Quartet for oboe, violin, cello and piano is a highly attractive piece in the busy yet unfussy neo-classical style that Martinů made so much his own. Its opening theme is quite captivating, but all three movements have charm. The other music is hardly less delightful. The Viola Sonata is an eloquent work from the mid-1950s, composed three years after the *Rhapsody-Concerto* for the same instrument and orchestra. These were vintage years in Martinů's creativity. The String Quintet is the earliest work, dating from his Paris years, and shows the influence of Roussel. Although the first movement is perhaps not top-drawer Martinů, the slow movement is most imaginative. The performances are often touched with distinction and are never less than eminently serviceable. Adni could perhaps be a little more supple in the Piano Quartet of 1942 though in general he plays with spirit. There's plenty of air round the players and the recording is lifelike and well balanced.

Duo for Violin and Viola, H331. Duos for Violin and Cello – No 1, H157; No 2, H371. Three Madrigals. Piece for Two Cellos, H377. String Trio No 2, H238
Pavel Hula *vn* Josef Kluson *va* Michal Kanka *vc*
Praga Digitals PRD250 155 (68' · DDD)　　　 Ⓕ

It doesn't look promising: a whole disc of string duos and trios by a composer that even his warmest admirers admit was both over-prolific and uneven. Maybe it has something to do with the fact that Martinů was a string player himself, but the level of invention here is very high, and it often emerges in the forms of nervous, energetic *toccata* and folk-rooted lyricism that those admirers will recognise as 'real Martinů'. The *Three Madrigals*, for the apparently austere combination of violin and viola, in fact combine both those veins with such a sheer enjoyment of virtuoso string technique that you'll be convinced that at least four players are involved. In the central movement an archetypal Martinů melody blissfully emerges from clouds of trills and double stopping, while in the third he delightedly manages to suggest that Domenico Scarlatti was very probably born in Moravia.

There are pleasures like those in most of the movements here. Martinů quite often, notably in his only surviving String Trio, rewards his players for negotiating his energetic toccatas with brilliant but never merely showy cadenzas, and these fine players respond with ample tone and real sympathy for his idiom and for the touching nostalgia that often underlies it. The recording is satisfyingly full. Warmly recommended.

Works for Violin and Piano, Volume 1
Violin Sonatas – C, H120; D minor, H152; No 1, H182.

Concerto, H13. Elegy, H3. Impromptu, H166. Five Short Pieces, H184.
Bohuslav Matoušek *vn* Petr Adamec *pf*
Supraphon ② SU3412-2 (121' · DDD)　　　 Ⓕ⊙

Supraphon's decision to present the music in more or less chronological order makes it all the easier to chart a fascinating stylistic journey spanning some 36 years. The 19-year-old Martinů wrote his impassioned *Elegy* in 1909, and the comparatively straightforward violin writing contrasts dramatically with the piano's big-boned, unashamedly dramatic contribution. Strangely, the following year's Concerto proves to be anything but. Indeed, one wonders whether its title was a leg-pull on the young composer's part, for its 27-minute progress totally eschews any ostentatious display in favour of a sunny simplicity and open-hearted playfulness. With the ambitious Sonata in C from 1919, we encounter an increasing confidence and fluency, though there's still little sign of the composer's mature voice. Matoušek and Adamec form a consistently stylish partnership, and the recordings are rich and airy to match. A truly notable achievement.

Orchestral songs

Nipponari, H68[a]. Magic Nights, H119[b]. Czech Rhapsody, H118[c]
[a]Dagmar Pecková, [b]Ľubica Rybárska *sops* [c]Iván Kusnjer *bar* Kühn Mixed Choir; Prague Symphony Orchestra / Jiří Bělohlávek
Supraphon SU3956-2 (73' · DDD · T/t)　　 Ⓜ⊕

With Martinů's mature and middle-period works staples of the repertoire, one forgets that he did not spring, fully formed, into the compositional world as a neoclassicist. *Nipponari* is a set of seven songs to Japanese poems for soprano and small orchestra written in 1912 when he was in his early twenties. Delightfully scored, there is nothing in its sound world of the later master who here provides a shimmering accompaniment to the wistful texts. In places there are resonances of Rimsky's *Kitezh*, too, and British ears may detect stylistic parallels with early Bax, or the Brian of *In memoriam*. Dagmar Pecková is a radiant soloist.

Magic Nights dates from six years later and uses Chinese texts from the same source as *Das Lied von der Erde* to enchanting if less exalted effect. There is a touch of Debussy in the orchestral sound, which requires a larger ensemble than *Nipponari*. Ľubica Rybárska yields nothing to Pecková in beauty of tone.

The major item here, however, is the cantata *Czech Rhapsody* from 1918 (not the violin and orchestra work of 1945), written just a few months before *Magic Nights*. It is a rare example of politically motivated music in Martinů's canon, imbued with patriotic feelings at impending independence, and was his first nationwide success. The grandiloquence of the opening section and close are beautifully caught by Bělohlávek and the Pavel Kühn Chorale sings the polyglot text (including Psalm 23) with fervour. The Prague Symphony Orchestra accompanies splendidly throughout and the superb acoustic of the Dvořák Hall is captured superbly. The recordings may be 20 years old but they sound wonderful. Highly recommended.

The Greek Passion

The Greek Passion
John Mitchinson ten Manolios **Helen Field** sop
Katerina **John Tomlinson** bass Grigoris **Jeffrey Lawton** ten Panait; Andonis **Arthur Davies** ten
Yannakos **Geoffrey Moses** bass Fotis **Rita Cullis** sop
Lenio **Phillip Joll** ten Kostandis **Catherine Savory** sop Nikolio **John Harris** ten Michelis **Michael Geliot** spkr Ladas **Jana Jonášová** sop Despinio **David Gwynne** bass Patriarcheas Archon **Kühn Children's Chorus; Prague Philharmonic Choir; Brno Philharmonic Orchestra / Sir Charles Mackerras**
Film director **Tomáš Simerda**
Supraphon 🅼🆅🅳 SU7014-9
(93' · NTSC · 16:9 · PCM stereo and 5.1 · 0)   Ⓕ

The story of Martinů's penultimate opera begins with a priest allotting roles in the local Passion play to various congregation members. When a group of refugees arrive begging land (their village having been sacked by the Turks) the would-be actors begin to assume the roles of their characters. Thus, after the priest rejects the refugees on the pretext that they carry cholera, Manolios, assigned to play Christ, directs them towards Mount Sarakina where there is room to spare, while the pedlar Yannakos, playing Peter, repents of a scheme to deprive the refugees of their valuables in exchange for essentials. Panait, allotted the role of Judas, is incensed by the change of heart of Katerina, playing Mary Magdalene, who is drawn into a close spiritual bond with Manolios, who rejects his fiancée, Lenio, who in turn becomes engaged to another. In the end, Manolios's identification with Christ and sympathy for the plight of the refugees becomes too much for the priest, who excommunicates him. In a confrontation outside the church, Manolios is killed by Panait and the Passion play ended.

Supraphon's film is not of a stage or even studio performance, but was made for Czech Television in 1999 as a kind of outside broadcast, set around a real stone-built village and church. The recording is that made in 1981 in Brno using the local orchestra and Czech choruses by Sir Charles Mackerras with soloists from Welsh National Opera. The live actors, for the most part Czechs, mouth the English text very well, though differences in mime technique are at times striking.

The outdoor setting works remarkably well, centred on the village square, the church, various cottages and the hillside where the refugees attempt to eke out a new home. The recording still sounds sumptuous, the elision of certain segments has been done expertly and for those

unfamiliar with Martinů's radiant score, this film – ending with the iconic image of the dead Manolios on the church steps, should prove a compelling and moving experience.

Julietta

Three Fragments from 'Julietta', H253a[a].
Suite from the opera 'Julietta', H253b
[a]**Michele Lagrange** sop [a]**Magdalena Kožená** mez
[a]**Steve Davislim** ten [a]**Alain Vernhes** bar
[a]**Frédéric Goncalves** bass-bar **Czech Philharmonic Orchestra / Sir Charles Mackerras**
Supraphon SU3994-2 (53' · DDD)   Ⓕ🅞🅞🅳➤

Extracted by the composer in 1939 (two years after completing the opera), these three substantial excerpts were designed as a cantata or *Singspiel* for five singers with orchestra. Martinů hoped to use the cantata to secure a production of the opera in France to which end he set the text in French (unlike the Czech of the opera), thereby returning to the language of Neveux's original play. As it turned out, he was not successful.

At almost 21 and 12 minutes apiece, Martinů's first and last movements seem very substantial for fragments. While showcasing the marvellously lyrical writing for the operatic principals, the extract none the less remains true to the spirit of the original. Thus the surreal fifth scene from Act 2 opens out the expressive landscape after the long patchwork taken from the previous two scenes, while the final extract is essentially the Act 3 finale. Mackerras directs a wonderful performance and while Kožená sings the title-role beautifully she is in excellent company.

The Czech Philharmonic Orchestra play superbly throughout, not least in the sensible coupling of Zbyněk Vostřák's expert arrangement of three of *Julietta*'s orchestral episodes. Given Supraphon's top-notch sound and in the absence of a complete recording from these performers, this scintillating disc cannot be recommended highly enough.

Joseph Marx   Austrian 1863-1945

He began composing in earnest at the age of 26 and within four years (1908–12) wrote around 120 songs. His name became known in Vienna, where in 1914 he was offered the post of professor of theory at the music academy. In 1922 he became director of the academy. From 1931 to 1938 he was music critic for the Neues Wiener Journal and after World War II worked in the same capacity for the Wiener Zeitung. Later he brought out the valuable Weltsprache Musik (Vienna, 1964), which deals with acoustics, tonality, aesthetics and musical philosophy. It was typical of his extreme conservatism that the index contained no mention of Schoenberg, Berg or Hindemith. **GROVE**music

Six Pieces for Piano. Herbst-Legende (Adagio).
Carneval (Nachstück). Canzone. Die Flur der Engel
Tonya Lemoh pf
Chandos CHAN10479 (55' · DDD)　　　　ⒻⓄ➔

This intriguing recital shows Marx as a defiantly throwback composer often struggling to find his individual voice in a particularly turbulent musical period. Brahms's B minor and E flat Rhapsodies are surely the seeds allowed to germinate in the opening Rhapsody, the first of the Six Pieces (though it is more complex and demanding than either), and the fugue from the Prelude and Fugue is Reger-like, massive, daunting and strenuous. On the other hand, there is something oddly English about the love of fourths in the *Albumblatt* – almost as if John Ireland had strayed into Vienna – and the Ballade, too, suggests a refugee from English pastoralism. There is something of York Bowen here (the Second Ballade?) though with a sprawling and improvisatory argument and an attempt to accommodate many (too many?) ideas. The *Humoreske* presents a gnomic though grandly expansive dance.

Just when your ear is longing for less cloyingly rich textures, for greater simplicity and transparency, it is rewarded with four world-premiere recordings where Marx becomes less ambitious and more persuasive and confiding. Sample the 1916 Rhapsody and 'The Angel's Meadow', music lost in its own archaic world and sidestepping any easy or predictable resolutions. The performances of this very demanding programme by Tonya Lemoh are as powerful and eloquent as you could wish and she has been admirably recorded.

Orchestral songs

Herbstchor an Pan[bc]. Barkarole[a]. Zigeuner[a]. Der bescheidene Schäfer[a]. Selige Nacht[a]. Sommerlied[a]. Marienlied[a]. Maienblüten[a]. Waldseligkeit[a]. Und gestern hat er mir Rosen gebracht[a]. Piemontesisches Volkslied[a]. Ständchen[a]. Hat dich die Liebe berührt[a]. Morgengesang[c]. Berghymne[c]. Ein Neujahrshymnus[c]
[a]**Christine Brewer** sop [b]**Trinity Boys' Choir**;
[c]**Apollo Voices**; BBC Symphony [c]**Chorus
and Orchestra / Jiří Bělohlávek**
Chandos CHAN10505 (72' · DDD · T/t)　　　Ⓕ➔

The most substantial work in this selection of Joseph Marx's orchestral songs and choral pieces is the *Herbstchor an Pan* ('Autumn Hymn to Pan'), his first orchestral work (1911) but one in which his easy mastery of a rich instrumental palette is already evident. His idiom was formed early and changed little: indeed, he had little sympathy with change, and notoriously failed to mention Schoenberg, Berg or even Hindemith when he brought out *Weltsprache Musik*, a book of aesthetics and philosophy, in the last year of his life, 1964.

It should be no surprise, then, to find that here is a rich, post-Wagnerian manner, luscious in harmony and sensuous in orchestration. Chris-

tine Brewer has the floating purity of voice to soar easily over Marx's beautifully judged textures in, for instance *Selige Nacht* and *Maienblüten*, both rapt in manner and unashamedly reflective, the latter suggesting the atmosphere of Strauss's *Four Last Songs*. Some similarity betwen Marx and Delius suggests that they had both moved away from Wagnerian harmony in comparable directions, influenced by a pantheistic response to nature: lovers of Delius's *Sea Drift* may appreciate the harmonic flavour and modulatory side-slips of the *Herbstchor an Pan*. It is in this vein that Marx seems at his most effective; the more exuberant songs sound rather laboured and their jollity contrived. Bělohlávek draws a suitably rich manner from the orchestra and gives Brewer loyal support with textures that are full but always lucid, and served well by the recording.

Pietro Mascagni　　　Italian 1863-1945

Mascagni studied with Ponchielli and Saladino at the Milan Conservatory (1882-4), then worked as a touring conductor and wrote Guglielmo Ratcliff (c1855). His next opera was the one-act Cavalleria rusticana, which was staged in Rome in 1890 and won him immediate international acclaim: it effectively established the vogue for verismo. None of his later operas was anything like so successful, though some numbers from L'amico Fritz (1891) and the oriental Iris (1898) have survived in the repertory. Later works include the comedy Le maschere (1901), the unexpectedly powerful Il piccolo Marat (1921) and Nerone (1935), this last testifying to his identification with fascism. 　GROVEmusic

Cavalleria rusticana

Cavalleria rusticana
Renata Scotta sop Santuzza **Plácido Domingo** ten
Turiddu **Pablo Elvira** bar Alfio **Isola Jones** mez Lola
Jean Kraft mez Lucia **Ambrosian Opera Chorus;
National Philharmonic Orchestra / James Levine**
RCA Red Seal 74321 39500-2 (71' · ADD · T/t)
Recorded 1978　　　　　　　　　　　ⒻⓄ➔

This was a strong contender in an overcrowded field when it was first released. You'd be hard pressed to find either a more positive or a more intelligent Turiddu or Santuzza than Domingo or Scotto. Scotto manages to steer a precise course between being too ladylike or too melodramatic. She suggests all the remorse and sorrow of Santuzza's situation without resorting to self-pity. Her appeals to Turiddu to reform could hardly be more sincere and heartfelt, her throbbing delivery to Alfio, 'Turiddi mi tolse l'honore', expresses all her desperation when forced to betray her erstwhile lover, and her curse on Turiddu, 'A te la mala pasqua', while not resorting to the lowdown vigour of some of her rivals, is filled

MASCAGNI & LEONCAVALLO: 'CAV & PAG' – IN BRIEF

La Scala Chorus and Orchestra / Herbert von Karajan
DG 457 764-2GOR (Cav) Ⓜ︎Ⓞ
DG 449 727-2GOR (Pag) Ⓜ︎Ⓞ
Karajan and his La Scala forces bring a real feel of the theatre to these two much-loved works. Bergonzi, Panerai, Carlyle and Cossotto are on top form. And the Scala chorus are thrilling in the great choral numbers.

Philharmonia / Riccardo Muti
EMI 763650-2 Ⓜ︎
With Carreras at his most intense and Renata Scotto are her most moving Muti's 'Pag' is very fine. Caballé is a fabulous Santuzza in 'Cav' - and the set has the luxury casting of Astrid Varnay as Mama Lucia.

La Scala Chorus and Orchestra / Tullio Serafin Ⓗ
EMI 556287-2 Ⓜ︎Ⓞ
This is Callas's show though with Di Stefano and Gobbi on stage with her, you can be sure of some high-class drama. Serafin conducts with authority and passion.

National PO / Giuseppe Patanè
Decca 414 590-2DH2 Ⓕ⊞➔
Pavarotti and Freni, Varady and Cappuccilli - here's another dream-team. Actually it is Varady who steals the show with her passionate idiomatic singing - enough to make one lament her scarcity on record in Italian repertoire.

La Scala Chorus and Orchestra / Georges Prêtre
Philips 411 484-2PH (Pag) Ⓕ
Teresa Stratas sings opposite Domingo in a recording made as the soundtrack of a filmed version. But she really has to be seen for maximum effect. Domingo, as always, gives a totally committed performance, but is on better form for Levine.

National PO / James Levine
RCA 74321 39500-2 (Cav) Ⓕ⊙⊞➔
Real sparks fly between Domingo's Turiddu and Scotto's Santuzza as they clash and her sense of remorse is palpable. Levine conducts with great sweep and subtlety.

La Scala Chorus and Orchestra / Franco Ghione
Nimbus NI7843/4 (Pag) Ⓗ
Pearl GEMMVD9288
Naxos 8 110258 Ⓜ︎/Ⓢ
Here are three of the numerous incarnations of Benjamino Gigli's 1935 interpretation of Canio. Even if this is not going to be your first choice, it deserves to be heard for the passion and beauty of his singing. The cast has a wonderfully idiomatic approach to this oh-so-Italian opera!

with venom. Domingo proved how committed he was to his role when the part was first given to him at Covent Garden in the mid-1970s. He gives an almost Caruso-like bite and attack to Turiddu's defiance and (later) remorse, and finds a more appropriate timbre than Bergonzi (for Karajan, reviewed under Leoncavallo). He also delivers the Brindisi with an appropriately carefree manner, oblivious of the challenge awaiting him. Pablo Elvira's Alfio is no more than adequate, and the other American support is indifferent.

Levine's direction, as positive as Karajan's, is yet quite different. He goes much faster, and time and again catches the passion if not always the delicacy of Mascagni's score. He's well supported by the superb NPO. With a bright and forward recording, this reading of the work is wholly arresting.

Cavalleria rusticana (sung in English) Ⓗ
May Blyth sop Santuzza **Heddle Nash** ten Turiddu
Marjorie Parry mez Lola **Justine Griffiths** contr Lucia
Harold Williams bar Alfio **Chorus and Orchestra of the British National Opera Company / Aylmer Buesst**
Leoncavallo Pagliacci (sung in English)
Miriam Licette sop Nedda **Frank Mullings** ten Canio
Harold Williams bar Tonio **Heddle Nash** ten Peppe
Dennis Noble bar Silvio **Chorus and Orchestra of the British National Opera Company / Eugene Goossens**
Divine Art mono ② 27805 (112' · ADD · T)
Both recorded in 1927 Ⓜ︎

As Andrew Rose, the man responsible for this transfer, points out, there was a period when Columbia records were known for their 'silent surfaces', and happily he has had access to early copies of the originals from this period. The clarity and immediacy of sound reveal performances which at best give pleasure by any standards and, at less than that, are fascinating as period documents.

In *Cav* the violin-playing does credit to nobody, yet this loose, slithery style must then have been acceptable, even 'authentic'. In *Pag* the male chorus sings with unabashed gusto in tones that (inaccurately no doubt) we tend to call 'beery'. Then the pronunciation is very much of its period, every 'r' rolled (as in 'charrm') and the 'I' sounds (Nash was a great one for this) shaded to 'Ae'. The translations represent the kind of thing the current 'Opera in English' series on Chandos is keen to avoid: a favourite is Nedda's beautifully enunciated 'For such a passion / The whip is the fashion'. But there's fine singing, and not only from Nash. Harold Williams, a little shy of the high notes, is splendidly firm and resonant in both operas. Miriam Licette is a very un-Italian Nedda but her 'take' of the high notes is distinctly that of a Marchesi pupil. Similarly, May Blyth is a lightweight Santuzza but still provides much to admire. Of Mullings's Canio, the throatiness and discomfort in the upper range are to some extent offset by a warmly personal timbre and intense dramatic commitment.

The *Pagliacci* also suffers from moments of distortion due to overloading on the originals. The *Cav* suffers from a somewhat hectic rush to get everything on to the 10-inch disc. And it is notable that the orchestra pulls up its metaphorical socks for Eugene Goossens.

Mascagni
Cavalleria rusticana
Violeta Urmana *sop* Santuzza **Vincenzo La Scola** *ten* Turiddu **Dragana Jugovich** *mez* Lola **Viorica Cortez** *contr* Mamma Lucia **Marco Di Felice** *bar* Alfio
Leoncavallo
Pagliacci
Vladimir Galouzine *ten* Canio **María Bayo** *sop* Nedda **Carlo Guelfi** *bar* Tonio **Antonio Gandia** *ten* Beppe **Ángel Ódena** *bar* Silvio
Chorus and Orchestra of the Teatro Real, Madrid / Jesús López-Cobos
Stage director **Giancarlo del Monaco**
Video director **Angel Luis Ramírez**
Opus Arte ② 📀 OA0983D
(3h 21' · NTSC · 2.0 and DTS 5.1 · 0)
Recorded live in February and March 2007   Ⓕ

It is a genuine pleasure to welcome a new production of *Cav and Pag* that presents the contrasting tales of jealousy and infidelity with sincerity and dramatic flair. Giancarlo del Monaco and his designer, Johannes Leiacker, set *Cavalleria* in a stark townscape of white painted buildings and masonry, the black-clad Sicilian women silhouetted under the fierce sunlight. The Easter Hymn is made all the more tense by a parade of penitents dragging a cross. Violeta Urmana and Vincenzo La Scola are well paired as Santuzza and Turridu, their confrontation interrupted by the unusually attractive Lola of Dragana Jugovich. Marco di Felice conveys the terrible pain that Alfio feels on learning of his wife's affair – the fight between him and Turridu is played out onstage, the challenge taken up when a glass of wine is emptied on to the floor. The great Viorica Cortez is a dignified Mamma Lucia. As Turridu's body is carried away at the end, the scene changes seamlessly into the opening of *Pagliacci* (the Prologue to which is sung from the stalls right at the start of the evening by Carlo Guelfi).

From the 1890s setting of *Cav* we have moved forward 50 years, and the travelling players arrive in a lorry, with posters for the show on the outside – the mood is a bit like Fellini's *La Strada*. From the outset, this *Pagliacci* becomes a really painful story to watch. María Bayo is superb as Nedda, tough and wilful, but trapped by the overbearing Canio of Vladimir Galouzine. His voice is very baritonal in quality, the high notes not always easily achieved, but what tremendous authority and passion he brings to the part; he really has it in him to become the leading dramatic tenor of our time. All the other parts are well cast and the crowd scenes are beautifully handled. Jesús López-Cobos leads the Madrid forces in a performance that could not easily be surpassed anywhere nowadays. Angel Luis Ramírez, deserves high praise for capturing Del Monaco's intense staging so well.

Additional recommendation

Cavalleria rusticana
Cossotto *sop* Santuzza **Bergonzi** *ten* Turiddu **Guelfi** *bar* Alfio **Martino** *mez* Lola **Ellegri** *mez* Lucia **Chorus and Orchestra of La Scala, Milan / Karajan**
DG The Originals 457 764-2GOR   Ⓜ▶
A truly red-blooded performance, masterfully controlled by Karajan who draws some fabulous playing from his Milan orchestra.

Jules Massenet   French 1842-1912

Massenet entered the Conservatoire at the age of 11 as a piano pupil of Adolphe Laurent. He later studied harmony with Reber and composition with Ambroise Thomas, winning the Prix de Rome in 1863. In Rome he got to know Liszt and, through him, Constance de Sainte Marie, who became his pupil and, in 1866, his wife. The following year his opera La grand'tante was given at the Opéra-Comique, and in1873 Marie-Magdeleine at the Théâtre de l'Odéon initiated a series of drames sacrés based on female biblical characters. Many of his secular operas, too, are in effect portraits of women.

In 1878 Massenet was made a teacher of composition at the Conservatoire, where he remained all his life, influencing many younger French composers, including Charpentier, Koechlin, Pierné and Hahn. In his own music he began to move away from the suave, sentimental melodic style derived from Gounod and to adopt a more Wagnerian type of lyrical declamation. The change is apparent in Manon (1884), which placed Massenet in the forefront of French opera composers, and still more in Werther (1892). But as early as 1877, in Hérodiade, Massenet had begun to modify the symmetry and loosen the syntax of his melodies to give them a more speaking, intimate, conversational character. Repetitions are usually masked or transferred to the orchestra while the voice takes a lyrical recitative line in the Wagnerian manner; literal repetitions are carefully calculated to provide an insistent, emotional quality. Often his melodies have a swaying, hesitant character. By Werther, the relationship of voice and orchestra is more sophisticated, and that opera contains clear examples of Massenet's dissolution of formal melody into rhapsodic recitative-like writing as evolved by Wagner. Massenet's music is harmonically conservative, rarely venturing beyond modest chromaticisms; rhythmically, it is original in the variations he uses to give the melody a more caressing, intimate character. He had a characteristically French ear for orchestral nuance. Though primarily a lyrical composer, he was also a master of scenes of action, as for example at the opening of Manon.

After Sapho (1897) Massenet scored few major successes. His conception of opera became outdated long before his death and his position as France's lead-

ing opera composer was finally challenged when Debussy's Pelléas et Mélisande was given at the Opéra-Comique in 1902. GROVEmusic

Ballet music

Massenet Le Cid. Scènes pittoresques. La vierge – le dernier sommeil de la vierge. **Saint-Saëns** Wedding Cake
City of Birmingham Symphony Orchestra / Louis Frémaux
EMI Encore 575871-2 (72' · ADD) Recorded c1971
Ⓑ**O**

Frémaux's Massenet collection provides most enjoyable listening. This is highly tuneful music, and it's directed with appropriate vigour and refinement as the individual numbers require. The ballet music from *Le Cid* is full of the authentic rhythms of Spain, and there's real excitement in such numbers as the 'Aragonaise', where the members of the CBSO respond most admirably to Frémaux's demands for dynamic variation and instrumental shading. At the quieter end of the spectrum, the delightful 'Madrilène', with its solos for cor anglais and flute, is most charmingly done. Similar sensitivity is shown throughout the contrasted *Scènes pittoresques*. The further inclusion of the 'Last Sleep of the Virgin' – once a Beecham lollipop – was an inspired idea. The recorded sound throughout is spacious and well balanced.

Arias

'Amoureuse: Sacred and Profane Arias'
La Grand' Tante – Je vais bientôt quitter. **Marie Magdeleine** – O mes soeurs. **Eve** – O nuit.
La Vierge – O mon fils; Rêve infini. **Hérodiade** – Il est doux, il est bon. **Le Cid** – Plus de tourments; Pleurez mes yeux. **Sapho** – Ce que j'appelle beau; Solitude-demain, je partirai; Vais-je rester ici? **Grisélidis** – Loÿs! Loÿs! **Chérubin** – Vous parlez de péril. **Ariane** – Avec tes compagnes guerrières; Je comprends un héros! Un roi; Ils mentaient! A quoi bon. **Songs** – Sainte Thérèse prie; Amoureuse
Rosamund Illing sop **Australian Opera and Ballet Orchestra / Richard Bonynge**
Melba Recordings 301080 (75' · DDD · T/t)   Ⓕ

Most of the items here are rarities, some unpublished, all attractive. The performances are excellent: Rosamund Illing is a soprano well-known over here, but never heard on records to better advantage, and Richard Bonynge's convinced advocacy and feeling for style constitute another guarantee of value. To this should be added a proviso. Everything is tuneful in the grand, late 19th-century understanding of the word; but everything is also rather sweet on the palate. Still, for anyone in the least interested it's not a record to miss.

Among the operas, *Sapho* will still be unfamiliar to most, and *Ariane* to practically all. The three excerpts here are arias for Ariadne herself,

and include the final pages with the call of the Sirens and a hauntingly plaintive B minor melody for the dying heroine, who descends into the sea holding a high A natural of heavenly softness, firm to the end.

These roles were written for a diverse range of singers, but the Australian soprano adapts easily and, except on a few slightly worn *fortissimo* high notes, sings most beautifully. The orchestra is recorded with vivid immediacy and makes the most of Massenet's imaginative scoring. One for the shopping list.

Massenet: Le Cid – Ah! tout est bien fini… O souverain. **Grisélidis** – Je suis l'oiseau. **Le Mage** – Ah! Parais ! Parais, astre de mon ciel[b]. **Manon** – Enfin, Manon… En fermant les yeux[a]; Je suis seul!… Ah! fuyez, douce image. **Le Roi de Lahore** – Voix qui me remplissez d'une innefable ivresse. **Roma** – Je vais la voir! Tout mon être frémit[b]. **Werther** – Lorsque l'enfant revient d'un voyage; Ah! bien souvent mon rêve s'envole… Pourquoi me réveiller
Gounod: Faust – Quel trouble inconnu me pénètre!; Salut, demeure chaste et pure. **Mireille** – Mon cœur est plein d'un noir souci!; Anges du paradis.
Polyeucte – Stances: Source délicieuse. **La Reine de Saba** – Inspirez-moi, race divine. **Roméo et Juliette** – L'amour! l'amour; Salut! tombeau sombre
Rolando Villazón ten with [a]**Natalie Dessay** sop French Radio [b]**Chorus and Philharmonic Orchestra / Evelino Pidò**
Virgin Classics 545719-2 (67' · DDD · T/t) Ⓕ**OOO**▷

 This is mostly well-planned and executed recital mixes favourites with extracts from operas that have remained rarities, even with the increased interest in late 19th-century repertory. It begins with Rodrigue's great prayer, 'O souverain' from Act 3 of *Le Cid*. Rolando Villazón sings this with an attractive quiet introspection to start with, but then there is metal and passion in his voice for the climax. Of the other well-known Massenet items, it's good to hear Werther's 'Lorsque l'enfant' as well as the show-stopping 'Pourquoi me réveiller?'. In 'En fermant les yeux' from *Manon*, Natalie Dessay provides Manon's brief phrases, and Villazón makes a really sensitive dreamer. 'Ah, fuyez' goes well too, but it will be the arias from *Roma*, *Grisélidis* and *Le Mage* that will attract most listeners. In all Massenet's output is there a more seductive tune than the one that forms the centre of the *Roma* scene, 'Soir admirable'? This is done very well by Warren Mok in the complete recording, but Villazón outshines him.

Of the Gounod arias, Faust's 'Salut demeure' fares the best, but again it will be the extracts from *Polyeucte* and *La Reine de Saba* that will please immediately.

Villazón has established himself as one of the most promising among the new generation of tenors. His French has improved recently, but there is the odd difficulty still with certain vowels. Accompaniment, recording and presentation are first-rate.

Manon

Massenet Manon[a] **Berlioz** Les nuits d'été, Op 7[b] H
Debussy La damoiselle élue[c]
Victoria de los Angeles sop Manon [c]**Carol Smith**
mez [a]**Henri Legay** ten Des Grieux [a]**Michel Dens** bar
Lescaut [a]**Jean Borthayre** bass Comte des Grieux
[a]**Jean Vieuille** bar De Brétigny [a]**René Hérent** ten
Guillot [a]**Liliane Berton** sop Poussette [a]**Raymonde
Notti** sop Javotte [a]**Marthe Serres** sop Rosette
[c]**Radcliffe Choral Society; Boston Symphony
Orchestra / Charles Munch**; [a]**Opéra-Comique Choir
and Orchestra / Pierre Monteux**
Testament mono ③ SBT3203 (213' · ADD · T/t)
Recorded in 1955   Ⓕ OO

Recorded in mono in 1955, the set fell at a unique
point in the opera's history on disc.
Previous recordings from the 78rpm era had
captured the special Opéra-Comique spirit for
posterity, but they hold limited sonic appeal to
present-day collectors; later recordings have up-
to-date sound, but their international casts generally can't claim the same sense of style. Only with
this 1955 set do we get the best of both worlds.

Already at the time a practised exponent of
Manon on stage, de los Angeles makes a vivid
heroine, allowing us to *see* every expression passing across her face, almost as if we were watching
a video. Maybe the role lies a little high for her,
but de los Angeles surprised herself on the day of
recording by hitting the high D in the Cours-la-
Reine scene. Monteux's skill in his native French
repertoire is second to none, and he brings exemplary sparkle to the music. 1It would be possible
to find fault with various members of the supporting cast, but that's to miss the point. They
sing with a grace and wit that nobody from outside the Opéra-Comique tradition can replicate
easily. Henri Legay did not have a great tenor
voice, but the poetry and the passion of Des
Grieux come as second nature to him. Michel
Dens's lively Lescaut and Jean Borthayre's serious Comte des Grieux are no less idiomatic; and
the delectably perfumed Guillot of René Hérent
is a collector's item in the best sense of the term,
as he had been singing this role with the company since his début in 1918.

There's now a clear choice between this reissue and EMI's fine new Pappano set. Opera
collectors will probably want both.

Manon
Angela Gheorghiu sop Manon; **Roberto Alagna** ten
Des Grieux; **Earle Patriarco** bar Lescaut; **José van
Dam** bass-bar Comte des-Grieux; **Nicolas Rivenq**
bar De Brétigny; **Gilles Ragon** ten Guillot; **Anna
Maria Panzarella** sop Poussette; **Sophie Koch** mez
Javotte; **Susanne Schimmack** mez Rosette; **Nicolas
Cavallier** bar Innkeeper; **Chorus and Symphony
Orchestra of La Monnaie / Antonio Pappano**
EMI ③ 557005-2 (163' · DDD · T/t)   Ⓕ OOOↃ

EMI has had the good sense to build this set
around Pappano's own company at La Monnaie,

a Francophone group of singers who give an
authentic flavour that non-French-speakers
can't hope to match. The piece is given
absolutely complete, including the splendidly
played ballet.

Nothing of the myriad character of Massenet's
popular work escapes Pappano's eye and ear. He
has a near-perfect idea of how to pace the score
and he persuades his orchestra and chorus to
play and sing with the utmost respect for pertinent detail, so important in Massenet, and to
follow, as do the soloists, the many expressive
markings demanded by the composer.

Gheorghiu's is a Manon to savour in practically
every respect. Suitably coquettish in her first solo,
she turns ruminative, plangent for her second,
'Voyons, Manon'. The farewell to her little table
is inward and pensive, tone subtly shaded with the
'larmes dans la voix' so admired in native French
singers. To the Gavotte and the recitative preceding it, Gheorghiu brings the outward aplomb
and, in the second verse, the hint of sadness
required. The prayer at St Sulpice has all the
urgency and the sense of apprehension as to how
Des Grieux, now a servant of the church, will
respond to her. Throughout these solos, Gheorghiu prudently follows Massenet's scrupulous
instructions as to dynamics and phrasing with
unforgettable results, not to mention the sheer
glory of her singing, outclassing her compatriot,
the sensitive Ileana Cotrubas, who recorded the
role for Plasson too late in her career.

If Alagna doesn't quite equal his wife's example, he's an ardent, French-sounding Des
Grieux, always suggesting the Chevalier's
obsessive love for his 'Sphinx étonnant'. The
Dream, finely phrased as it is, hasn't quite the
individuality that Ansseau, Heddle Nash (in the
famous pre-war broadcast now on Dutton) or
Gedda and others, brought to it, mainly
because his tone has become a shade occluded. At
At St Sulpice, it rings out more truly. 'Ah fuyez,
douce image' begins in nicely reflective fashion
and the B flat climaxes are suitably impassioned. In most respects he surpasses the
ageing Kraus for Plasson, even when he isn't
quite as elegant.

Earle Patriarco, a young American baritone,
proves an excellent Lescaut, keen with the text
and properly cynical in manner. Still better is
José van Dam as Le Comte (he sang the part for
Plasson), words shaped so meaningfully onto
tone, his spoken contribution faultlessly timed.
All the smaller parts are enthusiastically taken,
small decorations on a masterly interpretation.
Given an exemplary recording for balance and
presence, this set is about as good as you'll get
today (or maybe any day) of this adorable piece.

Many will have an affection for the 1956 EMI
set with Victoria de los Angeles's *nonpareil* of a
Manon and Monteux as her elegant conductor,
but the work is cut, the recording is dated. This
new version is the one to introduce a new generation to a work of which Beecham declared: 'I
would give up all the *Brandenburgs* for *Manon*
and would think that I had profited by the
exchange.'

Manon
Natalie Dessay sop Manon **Rolando Villazón** ten
Des Grieux **Manuel Lanza** bar Lescaut **Samuel
Ramey** bass Comte des Grieux **Francisco Vas** ten
Guillot **Didier Henry** bar De Brétigny **Cristina
Obregón** mez Poussette
**Chorus and Orchestra of the Gran Teatre del
Liceu, Barcelona / Victor Pablo Pérez**
Stage director **David McVicar**
Video director **François Roussillon**
Virgin Classics ② DVD 505068-9 (175' · NTSC · 16:9 ·
PCM stereo, 5.0 and DTS 5.0 · 0)   Ⓕ

David McVicar's production of *Manon* takes a
more than usually harsh view of the story, too
often softened by Rococo prettiness. Here,
everything and everybody is for sale, and behind
the façade of 18th-century Paris lurks a world of
corruption, disease and perversion. It is thrilling, sometimes even slightly shocking, and
throughout the direction of the cast is faultless:
every scene bears re-viewing for the amount of
detail and dramatic energy that is released.

It is unlikely that Natalie Dessay will ever give a
greater performance than this. First glimpsed as a
gawky schoolgirl, wearing a travelling-coat two
sizes too large, she grows into a coquettish lover,
then a manipulative, avaricious courtesan before
our eyes. Her singing of each of the great arias is
equally fascinating, with delicate embellishments
at such moments as 'Profitons de la jeunesse', and
a really touching 'Adieu, notre petite table', ending up lying in a foetal position on top of the
table. The scene in which she and Rolando Villazón size each other up before speaking is exquisitely managed.

Villazón makes a passionate hero. His interpretation is much more extrovert than Dessay's, and
there are several moments when one would have
wished him to sing yet more softly. This is considerably more subtle, though, than his reading of
the same part in the modern-dress production in
Berlin last year. Manuel Lanza makes a seductive,
sleazy Lescaut, and Francisco Vas is sinister
rather than just amusing as the vengeful Guillot.
Although his demeanour is suitably dignified as
Des Grieux père, Samuel Ramey's voice now has
such a perilous wobble that 'Epouse quelque
brave fille' is rather painful, in the wrong way.

Tanya McCallin's set – a steep amphitheatre
from which extras watch the action played out
centre-stage – complements her costumes,
inspired by the paintings of Chardin rather than
the usual sugary Fragonard. The choreography
of Michael Keegan-Dolan reaches its height in
the elaborate hunting ballet in the Cours-La-
Reine scene, one of Massenet's happiest bits of
Baroque pastiche. It is hard to imagine that we
will see another *Manon* to equal this for a long
time: highly recommended.

Thaïs

Thaïs
Renée Fleming sop Thaïs; **Thomas Hampson** bar
Athanaël; **Giuseppe Sabbatini** ten Nicias; **Estefano**

Palatchi bass Palémon; **Marie Devellereau** sop
Crobyle; **Isabelle Cals** mez Myrtale; **Enkelejda
Shkosa** mez Albine; **Elisabeth Vidal** sop La
Charmeuse; **David Grousset** bass Servant;
**Bordeaux Opera Chorus; Bordeaux-Aquitaine
National Orchestra / Yves Abel**
Decca ② 466 766-2DHO2 (147' · DDD · T/t) Ⓕ**OO**⬗

At last – a modern recording of *Thaïs* with a
soprano who can sing the title-role. All we need is
a soprano with a fabulously beautiful voice, idiomatic French, a sensuous *legato*, pure high notes
up to a stratospheric top D, and the ability to leave
every listener weak at the knees. Where was the
problem? Renée Fleming makes it all sound so
easy. Her success a couple of years ago at the
Opéra Bastille in Paris with Massenet's *Manon*
showed that she has an affinity for this composer.
As Thaïs, a role with a similar vocal profile, she
proves equally well cast. Within minutes of her
entrance it's clear that neither of the other sets
from the last 25 years will be able to touch her.
Fleming simply has a vocal class that puts her in a
different league and there's just enough individuality in her singing to give Fleming's Thaïs a personality of her own, and vocal loveliness brings a
bloom to her every scene.

The Athanaël she leaves behind is Thomas
Hampson, who is her match in sensitivity and
roundness of tone. Their duet at the oasis in the
desert is beautifully sung, every word clear, every
phrase shaped with feeling. If only Hampson were
equally good at getting beneath the skin of the
operatic characters he plays. In the case of
Athanaël there's plenty of psychological complexity down there to uncover, but Hampson seems
unwilling to engage the character's dark side.

Occasionally, one regrets that Abel doesn't
have the New Philharmonia at his disposal, as
Maazel does, but the subtlety of colour and
accent that he draws from the Orchestre
National Bordeaux-Aquitaine are a world apart
from Maazel's constant up-front aggression.
The famous 'Méditation', elegantly played by
the young French violinist Renaud Capuçon,
and featuring swoony background chorus is a
dream. Add in a first-class Decca recording and
it will be clear that this new *Thaïs* has pretty well
everything going for it.

Werther

Werther
Patricia Petibon sop Sophie **Angela Gheorghiu** mez
Charlotte **Roberto Alagna** ten Werther **Jean-Paul
Fouchécourt** ten Schmidt **Thomas Hampson** bar
Albert **Jean-Philippe Courtis** bass Magistrate **Jean-
Marie Frémeau** bass Johann **London Symphony
Orchestra / Antonio Pappano**
EMI ② 556820-2 (128' · DDD · T/t)   Ⓕ**O**

Alagna is the first French-speaking tenor to
record the role for a long time and his diction
throughout is clear and full of emotion. At the
climax of his big aria, 'Pourquoi me reveiller?' in
Act 3, he sings 'O souffle du printemps?' with a

beautiful head tone. And he can't resist singing it full out the second time around – just as Alfredo Kraus and many others often did.

Whether or not Angela Gheorghiu would be suitably cast as Charlotte on stage, she makes a vivid impression on disc. The obvious comparisons with Gheorghiu are two other sopranos who have recorded the part, Ninon Vallin in the historic set under Cohen (see below), and Victoria de los Angeles in the Prêtre version, itself now sounding close to historic. But both Vallin and de los Angeles were also Carmens – on disc at least – and both sound more mature as characters than Gheorghiu does.

The sound on this new recording is fine, the conducting of Pappano taut and passionate. But, oh dear, what a lot of recordings of *Werther* there are now to choose from. The historic Cohen is probably the most completely satisfying version. Not everyone, however, wants to listen to historic mono. Amongst the new *Werthers* the Pappano scores mostly because of Alagna's heroic assumption of the title-role.

Additional recommendation

Werther   H
Vallin *sop* Charlotte **Till** *ten* Werther **Paris Orch /**
Cohen
Naxos mono 8 110061/2   Ⓜ️Ⓓ▶
Recorded in 1931, this is still the most moving and idiomatic version around. A classic set.

William Mathias   Welsh 1934-1992

Mathias is regarded as one of the most significant Welsh composers of the 20th century and one of the few to establish an international reputation. He enjoyed early success with instrumental and orchestral music, but eventually composed in virtually all musical genres. His later popularity in the fields of choral and particularly church music gave him a high profile. He often stressed that he did not regard his church music as peripheral in any way to his main output, observing no distinction between the sacred and the secular and viewing his vocation very much in line with the medieval Welsh 'praise' poets.

                          GROVEmusic

Complete Organ Works
Richard Lea *org*
Priory ② PRCD870 (151' · DDD)
Played on the organ of the Metropolitan Cathedral, Liverpool   Ⓕ🅞

Here, at last, we have the first truly comprehensive survey of Mathias's organ music, including pieces very few organists ever knew existed (notably the *Prelude, Elegy and Toccata* of 1955, his earliest known foray into writing for the instrument). It is also useful to have the particularly complex *Antiphonies* prefaced by the two ancient hymns on which it is based – even if tre-

ble James Orrell is placed so far distant that you have to strain your ears to hear him intone the *Vexilla regis* – and to hear that remarkably confusing Welsh hymn tune *Braint* given out by the Liverpool Welsh Choral before Mathias's ingenious but, if you don't know the tune, not always coherent, Variations.

On top of all this comes really first-rate playing from Richard Lea, organist and assistant director of music at Liverpool Metropolitan Cathedral, and a magnificent, demonstration-quality recording of what is one of the greatest English organs of the 20th century. Lea has real fire in his spirit and Mathias's characteristically angular rhythms and jocular dancing melodies leap out of the pages with almost hypnotic persuasiveness. Everything here is a performance to be reckoned with and while it might be said that, in places, Mathias was inclined to resort to stock devices giving some of these pieces a certain sameness, Lea's masterly handling of the instrument and his understanding of the music ensures that every single note stands out proudly as never a wasted note.

Colin Matthews   British b1946

Matthews collaborated with Deryck Cooke on the performing version of Mahler's Tenth Symphony. He was also assistant at Aldeburgh to Britten (1971–6), with particular involvement in Death in Venice and the Third String Quartet, and he worked with Imogen Holst (1972–84). After Britten's death he edited for publication various works left in manuscript. Matthews's orchestral works demonstrate the archetypal weight and expressive seriousness of a major symphonic composer, an impression reinforced by his ability to generate and sustain musical argument across large structures. Throughout his career Matthews has also maintained a steady output of chamber music including three string quartets, two oboe quartets, songs, piano music (notably the Eleven Studies in Velocity, 1987) and arrangements or adaptions of music by other composers including Britten, Mahler, Dowland, Berlioz, Purcell and Schubert.

                          GROVEmusic

Orchestral works

Alphabicycle Order[a]. Horn Concerto[b]
[a]**Henry Goodman** *narr* [b]**Richard Watkins** *hn*
[a]**children's choir; Hallé Orchestra /** [b]**Sir Mark Elder,**
[a]**Edward Gardner**
Hallé CDHLL7515 (54' · DDD)   Ⓕ🅞▶

Elemental musical images of sorrow and farewell can be as prominent in contemporary composers as they were in Purcell, Beethoven or Mahler. Ligeti's Horn Trio is a particularly memorable instance, and Colin Matthews's Horn Concerto has a set of comparable associations, including the *Les adieux* Sonata and the 'Abschied' from *Das Lied von der Erde*.

Cast as a sequence of elegies, predominantly lyrical but with occasional outbursts of rage, Matthews's music sustains its dark, questing spirit under the confident control of Sir Mark Elder in this first recording, and soloist Richard Watkins is an unfailingly eloquent presence, even when heard in the distance, offstage. The spatial aspects of the piece benefit from being seen as well as heard, but the drawbacks of a sound-only encounter are minimal, so strong is the character of the music.

In one sense the contrast provided by the companion piece could hardly be more extreme. *Alphabicycle Order*, for children's choir, narrator and orchestra, is a joyously witty musical response to Christopher Reid's brilliantly surreal traversal of the alphabet, and the evident relish with which it is tackled by the Hallé's young singers, backed to the hilt by narrator Henry Goodman and the orchestra under Edward Gardner, shows just how enjoyable it must have been for everyone involved. But Matthews brings an edge and panache to the music – echoing but never merely imitating Britten – which turns what could have been simply a fun piece into something stronger and more durable. These are two excellent recordings of notably substantial 21st-century compositions.

Chamber works

Divertimento[a]. String Quartet No 2[b]. Oboe Quartet No 1[c]. Triptych[d]. Five Concertinos[e]
[c]**Melinda Maxwell** ob [b]**Brindisi Quartet**;
[d]**Schubert Ensemble**; [e]**Haffner Wind Ensemble**;
[ac]**Divertimenti Ensemble** / [a]**Oliver Knussen**
NMC NMCD149 (64' · DDD)　　　Ⓕ◗

Contemporary composers sink or swim in a sea of perplexingly diverse memories and stimuli – a condition that has been particularly acute since the 1970s. These chamber works from the 1980s show Colin Matthews at his most buoyant, cresting the waves with exuberance and flair. Whether he's reacting to a powerful emblem of late romanticism, as with the Divertimento's initial quote of chords from Strauss's *Metamorphosen*, or confronting turbulent, Ligeti-like avant-gardisms – the String Quartet No 2 – he is never in danger of being submerged by mighty models. His own voice is unmistakable and, in these pieces, all the more appealing for the compactness and directness of the way the music speaks.

One strategy for ensuring stylistic independence is to lead a source, such as the opening gambit of Strauss's ambivalent, fervent lament, into uncharted waters which are more capricious than grief-stricken, fulfilling the Divertimento's promise to entertain with no hint of triviality. The first Oboe Quartet is another instance of purposeful impetuosity, cast in a form which owes as much to the English Fantasy tradition as to Germanic sonata schemes. While compactness reaches its apogee in the *Triptych* for piano quintet, a study in the very different

capacities of piano and strings to sustain as well as to indulge in glittering display, the Five Concertinos for Wind Quintet make witty play with the ensemble's need to resist tendencies to converge into homogenous uniformity. Most powerful of all is the Second Quartet, in a revised version that keeps the balance between fast and slow impulses on a knife-edge throughout. These recordings may be on the dry side acoustically, but the performances fizz and brood to the manner born.

David Matthews　　　British b1943

Elder brother of Colin Matthews, he studied classics at Nottingham University, took lessons in composition with Milner, and received further advice and encouragement from Maw. He also collaborated with Deryck Cooke on the performing version of Mahler's Tenth Symphony, and during 1966–9 he was music assistant to Britten. Although Matthews began composing at 16, his first acknowledged work dates from the age of 25. He soon found that his affinities led in an alternative direction to the post-Darmstadt trends of the 1960s. Drawing inspiration from the rhythmic vitality and spirited individual approach of Tippett, he has evolved his own deeply expressive sound world – Romantic in character, vibrant in melody and rooted in an expanded tonal harmony – while preserving a classical lucidity and poise, and striving to re-evaluate and breathe fresh life into the traditional 'objective' forms of symphony and string quartet.

GROVEmusic

The Music of Dawn. Concerto in Azzurro[a]. A Vision and a Journey
[a]**Guy Johnston** vc
BBC Philharmonic Orchestra / Rumon Gamba
Chandos CHAN10487 (71' · DDD)　　　Ⓕ◗

Of these three orchestral works, only one – *A Vision and a Journey* – is termed a 'symphonic fantasy'. Yet *The Music of Dawn* and *Concerto in Azzurro* could also be similarly described. They too rely on flexibly organised single-movement structures that display strong and positive links with the great 19th-century tradition of the programme symphony and tone-poem.

The earliest of the three, *The Music of Dawn*, is a richly scored response to a painting by Cecil Collins that makes no bones about sharing its musical imagery with other representations of sunrise and the sense of new beginnings – by Wagner, Strauss, Ravel, Schoenberg – but in a spirit of homage rather than dependency, creating something distinctive out of the contrasts between dance-like exuberance and soulful lyricism, and always with a personal angle on what in other contexts might be heard as explicit allusions to earlier models.

A Vision and a Journey reinforces the aspirational theme, suggesting a kind of pilgrim's progress, or hero's life, as it travels through well defined stages of fervent, at times rhapsodic questing. There are brief hints of Tippett in the string writing, but the heritage represented by such ultra-Romantic composers as Bax and Bantock is not spurned either, in a dramatic and engaging fantasia which is all the more effective for its imaginative way with some very simple basic ideas.

Concerto in Azzurro – 'concerto in blue' – is another evocation of light, sky, and an underlying sense of the transcendent. Although its insistent rhythmic and melodic patterns risk earnestness now and again, the concerto builds persuasively to a marvellously understated, touchingly poetic ending. Guy Johnston is a technically immaculate soloist, while Rumon Gamba with the BBC Philharmonic are excellent throughout in first-rate recordings.

Nicholas Maw   British 1935-2009

Maw studied with Berkeley at the Royal Academy of Music (1955-8) and Boulanger and Deutsch in Paris (1958-9). He taught in England and the USA. His music represents the extension of a solid tonal tradition, traceable back through Britten, Tippett, Bartók and Strauss, all influences on a style of fresh vigour. Among his works are the operas, One Man Show (1964), The Rising of the Moon (1970) and Sophie's Choice (2002), orchestral pieces and chamber music. His monumental orchestral work Odyssey was given in 1987.   GROVEmusic

Violin Concerto

Violin Concerto
Joshua Bell vn **London Philharmonic Orchestra / Sir Roger Norrington**
Sony Classical SK62856 (42' · DDD)   ⓕ**O➔**

For over a quarter of a century Maw has been investigating lines of musical development that were left dangling when modernism cut them. He's not so much writing 'neo-Brahms' or 'neo-Strauss' as exploring the enticing paths that they opened up, but which post-Schoenbergians have not pursued. The enormous orchestral *Odyssey* that he began in the early 1970s has had many satellites and successors, but the roots of his mature style have never been clearer than in this concerto, written for a virtuoso of the most archetypally romantic instrument of them all. It's a concerto that Joseph Joachim would have loved as much as Joshua Bell so evidently does. Full of warmly eloquent melody, the concerto is fundamentally lyrical in all four of its movements, but there's vital energy too, plentiful opportunity for sparkling virtuosity, many beautifully expressive orchestral solos and, in the *Scherzo* and finale especially, magnificently rich multi-layered climaxes. The performance is remarkably fine, the recording clean but not

clinical. A violin concerto for all who love the violin and its music.

String Quartet No 3

Maw String Quartet No 3 **Britten** String Quartet No 3. Three Divertimentos
Coull Quartet (Roger Coull, Philip Gallaway vns Gustav Clarkson va Nicholas Roberts vc)
Somm Céleste Series SOMMCD065 (60' · DDD)   ⓕ

The Coull Quartet have often played Nicholas Maw's Third Quartet since giving its premiere in 1995, and this recording – in exceptionally lucid sound – testifies to their mastery of its tricky technical details and their sensitivity to its expressive character.

It begins in a spirit of restless lyricism which builds compellingly, eloquence and drama intensifying in ways which place the music firmly in the tradition of Berg and Bartók without any hint of abject dependency. The work is crowned by a concluding passacaglia which creates tension from the superimposition of contrasting layers of texture before reaching a climax with a unison line for all four players, a moment of revelation which subsides into a regretful resolution.

The chordal material at the end hints at the opening of Maw's later opera *Sophie's Choice*, and this is one reason why the ideal coupling for the quartet would have been the recent string sextet in which Maw uses material from the opera. The sextet probably wasn't complete when this recording was planned, however, and the Coull have chosen a quartet, Britten's Third, which has certain stylistic and formal features in common with Maw's.

Despite some lack of necessary rawness in the second and fourth movements, this is an admirable account, and particularly successful in projecting the chaconne finale as music constantly on the verge of breakdown. The Britten has been much recorded, and several other performances are as impressive as this one. Even so, its presence does nothing to reduce the feeling that this is an outstanding release.

Hymnus

Hymnus[a]. Little Concert[b]. Shahnama[b]
[a]**Oxford Bach Choir;** [a]**BBC Concert Orchestra,** [b]**Britten Sinfonia / Nicholas Cleobury**
ASV CDDCA1070 (74' · DDD)   ⓕ

Hymnus is firmly rooted in the tradition of large-scale English choral works, full of luminous harmonies, rich choral textures and fine, eminently singable lines. The music is compelling, accessible and distinctive and the choral writing clearly designed to be demanding yet well within the scope of a large amateur choral society. Maw wrote it in 1996 to mark the centenary of the 200-voice Oxford Bach Choir and, as it was intended primarily to display a large chorus, there are no solo parts and the orchestral accompaniment is relatively discreet. The net result of this is that the choir has virtually no respite throughout the work's 33-minute duration, which probably accounts for the sense of tiredness and strain that permeates this recording. Climaxes (and there are a great many of those in the work) appear to overstretch the choir while the gentler passages fail to exhibit the kind of precision and polish which characterises the choir's live performances. The BBC Concert Orchestra also seems to lack that final polish, but much of this may well be attributed to a strangely boxy and claustrophobic recording. It's a splendid work and there are some worthy performers, all of which deserve rather better than this.

The other two works on the disc more than compensate for any shortcomings to be found in *Hymnus*. Nicholas Daniel produces an amazing range of moods and colours – from the exquisitely lyrical to the robustly athletic – in the *Little Concert* for oboe, two horns and strings, while the atmospheric and evocative *Shahnama*, nine brief movements inspired by an 11th-century Persian epic, is beautifully captured in Nicholas Cleobury's nicely spaced and tautly directed performance.

Billy Mayerl

British 1902-1959

Mayerl studied in the junior department of Trinity College of Music (1914-19) and worked as a pianist for silent films and in hotel bands playing American popular music. His first composition Egyptian Suite was published in 1919. In 1921 he joined Bert Ralton's band (later called the Savoy Havana Band) which regularly broadcast in the early years of the BBC. In 1926 he left that band for the music hall and founded his own school of music which pioneered teaching by post, using records. With Nippy (1930) his career moved to music theatre and he composed and directed several musical comedies which were successful at the time. He was a regular broadcaster before World War Two but the War marked the end of his celebrity. He continued as a performer despite ill health and was editor of The Light Music Magazine (1957-8). **GROVE**music

---

Piano Works

Mayerl Crystal Clear. Orange Blossom. Piano Exaggerations. Pastorale Exotique. Wistaria. Canaries' Serenade. Shy Ballerina. Puppets Suite, Op 77. Piano Transcriptions – Body and Soul; Deep Henderson; Tormented; Sing, you sinners; Cheer up; Have you forgotten?; The object of my affection; Is it true what they say about Dixie?; I need you; Love was born; I'm at your service **Parkin** Mayerl Shots, Sets 1 & 2. A Tribute to Billy Mayerl
Eric Parkin pf
Priory PRCD544 (80' · DDD)   Ⓕ

Nobody since the master himself has come anywhere near Parkin's easy technical mastery and fastidious musicianship in this delightful

music. Some pianists hit the more demanding pieces quite hard: Parkin, like Mayerl, knows better and his playing is consistently light and subtle. This has always been his approach, allied to a faultless sense of pace and rhythm. However, Mayerl, apart from perfecting the piano novelty, also contributed to the English pastoral tradition, which Parkin knows equally well. *Shy Ballerina* is charmingly done with *rubato* which would be quite out of place in Mayerl's numbers. The three-movement *Puppets Suite* is a *tour de force*.

As a bonus Parkin adds two sets of his own pieces called *Mayerl Shots*. He explains that, as a result of practising lots of Mayerl, further ideas surfaced spontaneously in a similar idiom. These are all fluent tributes and there are even quotations for the specialists. Essential listening.

Mayerl Scallywag. Jasmine. Oriental. Minuet for Pamela. Fascinating Ditty. Funny Peculiar. Chopsticks. Carminetta. Mignonette. Penny Whistle. Piano Transcriptions – Me and my girl; Blue velvet; Sittin' on the edge of my chair; The pompous gremlin; My heaven in the pines; Alabamy bound; Stardust; Please handle with care; Two lovely people; Two hearts on a tree; You're the reason why. Studies in Syncopation, Op 55 – Nos 7, 10, 14, 15 & 18
Parkin Mayerl Shots, Set 3
Eric Parkin pf
Priory PRCD565 (76' · DDD)   Ⓕ

This release, 'Scallywag', has its own discoveries, notably the *Studies in Syncopation*, which parallel Bartók's *Mikrokosmos* in this field. There are three books of six pieces each, dating from 1930-31, and Parkin plays five of them, proving that they aren't just exercises but real music. There are gems in the transcriptions – Carmichael's *Stardust*, Mayerl's own 'You're the reason why' from his 1934 show *Sporting Love*, and a forgotten but lovely tune by Peter York called *Two hearts on a tree*. The Spanish *Carminetta* is Mayerl's equivalent of Joplin's *Solace*. And there's real comedy – totally appreciated and effectively realised by Parkin – in *Chopsticks* and *Penny Whistle*.

In addition, Eric Parkin gives us his own response to Mayerl in a similar idiom – a third set of his *Mayerl Shots*. The recording is adequate.

Mayerl April's Fool. Beguine Impromptu. The Big Top – Clowning; Entrance; Trapeze. Three Contrasts, Op 24 – Pastoral. The Forgotten Forest. From a Spanish Lattice. In my Garden: Autumntime – Amber Leaves. In my Garden: Summertime – Alpine Bluebell; Meadowsweet. Four Insect Oddities – Praying Mantis; Ladybird Lullaby. Three Japanese Pictures, Op 25 – The Cherry Dance. Jill All Alone. Leprechaun's Leap. Piano Exaggerations – Antiquary. Postman's Knock. Siberian Lament. Song of the Fir-Tree. Three Syncopated Rambles – 6am: The Milkman (Scherzo). Weeping Willow. Minuet for Pamela **French/Mayerl** Phil the Fluter's Ball
Leslie De'Ath pf
Dutton Epoch CDLX7211 (77' · DDD)   Ⓜ

Leslie De'Ath's selection focuses less on the early virtuoso pieces that made Mayerl's name as 'lightning fingers' than on some of the more relaxed lyrical works in the central English tradition of Bridge, Ireland and Scott. This CD offers such gems as the *In my Garden* set from the late 1940s, which would make ideal teaching pieces, although most of Mayerl's music has been out of print for years. Why?

De'Ath has obviously chosen the pieces he likes best rather than representing the sets in which Mayerl chose to publish them. There are now plenty of contenders on CD; De'Ath sees Mayerl, especially in the later pieces, as belonging to the classical tradition. This is a personal anthology, well recorded with good notes from De'Ath, and it reminds us that Mayerl's music is an essential part of the British piano repertoire and that it's the responsibility of classical pianists to put it across, although few will do it with this kind of infectious enjoyment.

John McCabe
British b1939

McCabe studied at the Royal Manchester College and with Genzmer in Munich, then returned to England to work as a pianist, critic and composer; in 1983 he became director of the London College of Music. His works, in an extended tonal style relating to Hartmann and Nielsen, include three symphonies (1965, 1971, 1978), much other orchestral music, chamber and keyboard pieces. **GROVE**music

Piano Concertos

Arthur Pendragon – Ballet Suite No 1. Piano Concerto No 1[a]. Pilgrim
[a]**John McCabe** *pf* **BBC Scottish Symphony Orchestra / Christopher Austin**
Dutton Digital Epoch CDLX7179 (73' · DDD) (F)

It's long been a source of amazement why McCabe's splendid First Piano Concerto, written for the 1967 Southport Centenary Festival, has not been recorded before so Dutton's committed advocacy is unequivocally to be welcomed.

The concerto's rhythmic élan is a feature prominent in most of his output, including *Pilgrim* for double string orchestra (1998, arranged from a string sextet original). Although Bunyan's book was the inspiration, the single-span Pilgrim is not illustrative, rather a slow fantasia with two quicker sections, like a scherzo and trio in negative. As with the concerto's finale, Pilgrim shows how danceable McCabe's concert music is (several works have been successfully choreographed).

The largest item is a suite from his recent ballet diptych, *Arthur* (1998-2001), the four movements deriving from the first part, *Arthur Pendragon*, all but the finale from its first act. The vigour and drive of 'Uther and the Tribes' and 'The Tourney' (in which Arthur draws Excalibur from the Stone) contrast with the poignant beauty of 'Igraine and Uther'. The finale, 'The Lovers', is a complex conflation of two pas de deux for Lancelot and Guinevere and the ballet's climax, Arthur's vain and misguided massacre of the innocents (attempting to destroy the infant Mordred). Powerful stuff, the BBC Scottish SO's performance under Christopher Austin is inspired. With excellent sound, this issue is very strongly recommended.

Piano Concerto No 2 (Sinfonia Concertante)[a].
Concertante Variations on a Theme of Nicholas Maw.
Six-minute Symphony. Sonata on a Motet
[a]**Tamami Honma** *pf* **St Christopher Chamber Orchestra / Donatas Katkus**
Dutton Laboratories Epoch CDLX7133 (64' · DDD) (F)

This is an intriguing orchestral programme of pieces dating mostly from the 1970s. Despite the disparity in dates there's remarkable stylistic consistency, even to the extent of the occasional twang of Tippett in the string writing, as in the delightful *Six-minute Symphony* (1997) – invigoratingly rattled off in 5'18" – as in the *Concertante Variations* of 1970.

Why this latter work should be better known: it may lack the exuberance and virtuosity of Britten's *Frank Bridge* Variations but is subtler and more integrated. So, too, is the wonderful *Sonata on a Motet* (1976), McCabe's atmospheric, closely argued fantasia on Tallis's *Spem in alium*. Curiously, it's in the *Sonata*, rather than the *Concertante Variations*, that he allows his source to be distinctly heard, as for example in the climactic, rip-roaring fugue on the Elizabethan's ground bass. By contrast, the *Six-minute Symphony* eschews variation form for a real symphonic plan in miniature.

The largest piece, by virtue of its internal cohesion and gravitas rather than mere duration, is the Second Piano Concerto (1970). Subtitled *Sinfonia Concertante*, the music plays out on three levels: solo piano, a concertino group of nine instruments and the orchestra. Listen past the dissonance of the opening minute: what emerges, like order from chaos, is one of the finest post-war piano concertos.

Tamami Honma, something of a McCabe expert, plays brilliantly, as do the splendid St Christopher Chamber Orchestra of Vilnius under Donatas Kalkus's smart direction. Excellent sound, too. Very strongly recommended.

Symphony No 4

Symphony No 4, 'Of Time and the River'. Flute Concerto[a]
[a]**Emily Beynon** *fl*
BBC Symphony Orchestra / Vernon Handley
Hyperion CDA67089 (56' · DDD) (F)(O)

John McCabe's Fourth Symphony, some half an hour in duration, has something Sibelian about its utterly inevitable, ever-evolving progress. Behind the frequently prodigal surface activity, one is acutely aware of the inexorable tread of a grander scheme – a preoccupation with time mirrored in Thomas Wolfe's novel *Of Time and the River*, from which the work derives its subtitle. The very opening idea is momentarily reminiscent of Britten, and there's a magnificent passage in the second movement that recalls Vaughan Williams at his visionary best. Yet McCabe's score possesses a strong individuality, formal elegance and abundant integrity too. With dedication and scrupulous perception, Handley secures a disciplined and alert response from the BBC SO. The engaging Flute Concerto composed for James Galway in 1989-90 proves both resourceful and communicative. There's much that genuinely haunts here, not least the gently lapping opening idea (inspired by watching the play of waves on a Cornish beach), the ravishing dialogue between the soloist and orchestral flutes and the delightful emergence soon afterwards of an entrancingly naive, folk-like theme. Emily Beynon gives a flawless account of the demanding solo part, and is immaculately partnered by Handley and his BBC forces.

Edward II

Edward II
Royal Ballet Sinfonia / Barry Wordsworth
Hyperion ② CDA67135 (114' · DDD)   ⒻⓄ

Commissioned by the Stuttgart Ballet, choreographed by David Bintley, *Edward II* is McCabe's third ballet score, and draws its story-line from Christopher Marlowe's eponymous drama and the medieval courtly satire, *Le roman de Fauvel*. Quite apart from the meaty intrigue, complex character relationships and psychological pathos of the plot, McCabe's music communicates a captivating expressive fervour. It isn't just the superbly judged orchestration (colourful extras include triple woodwind and electric guitar) and wealth of memorable invention that impress. Above all, it's his ability to forge his tightly knit material into a dramatically convincing and organically coherent whole that marks him out as a composer of exceptional gifts. No praise can be too high for Barry Wordsworth's fluent, pungently theatrical direction, not to mention the unstinting application of the excellent Royal Ballet Sinfonia. The excitingly truthful sound allies razor-sharp focus to a most pleasing bloom, too.

Virgilio Mazzocchi   Italian 1880-1646

Mazzocchi studied at the seminary in Civita Castellana and took lower orders in 1614. He moved to Rome, where, according to Pitoni, he studied music with his brother Domenico, who from 1621 was in the service of Cardinal Ippolito Aldobrandini. In 1629 he was briefly maestro at S Giovanni in Laterano and in the same year he was appointed to the Cappella Giulia at S Pietro, where he served until his death. From about 1630 Mazzocchi's duties as maes-

tro and court musician increased rapidly, and he sometimes delegated to Domenico the composition of music for religious feasts. GROVEmusic

Mazzocchi Vespro della Beata Vergine
Carissimi O dulcissimum Mariae nomen. Exsurge cor meum. Salve Regina **Frescobaldi** Canzona a due cori
Palestrina Ave maris stella
Cantus Cölln; Concerto Palatino / Konrad Junghänel
Harmonia Mundi HMC90 2001 (69' · DDD · T/t)   Ⓕ

This disc includes settings of the five Vesper psalms and the Magnificat, all published posthumously. Interspersed with these are motets by Mazzocchi and his contemporary, Giacomo Carissimi (on the back of the packaging they are confusingly called antiphons). Together with a *Salve regina* by Carissimi (which is indeed an antiphon), a canzona by Frescobaldi and an Ave maris stella by the much earlier Palestrina, they make up a reconstructed 'Vespers for the Virgin'.

The psalms are scored for double choir, which means that – as the singers of Cantus Cölln number eight – they are sung one to a part. They are doubled, though, by a small string group and the cornett and trombones of Concerto Palatino, and the sound is surprisingly rich. The homophonic passages are leavened with concertato sections, when the brass is silent. This provides a welcome variety, as a little quasi-Venetian splendour goes quite a long way.

Mazzocchi shows himself to be a very competent practitioner, well worth hearing. Surge amica mea, for two sopranos, is a setting of two of the less erotic verses from the *Song of Solomon*, ending with a melismatic 'Alleluia'. Even more ear-tickling is Carissimi's *Exsurge cor meum*, sung here by a tenor, with the excellent cornett of Bruce Dickey taking one of the two obbligato parts. Konrad Junghänel conducts with plenty of verve; a raised eyebrow for the reference to 'Rome in the 18th century' on the back cover.

Nikolay Medtner   Russian 1880-1951

Medtner studied the piano under Safonov at the Moscow Conservatory (1897-1900) and had composition lessons with Arensky and Taneyev, though was mostly self-taught. In 1921 he left Russia. He settled in Paris (1925-35), but was out of sympathy with musical developments there and found a more receptive audience in London, where he spent his last 16 years. He belonged in the line of Russian composer-pianists, though his music is close too to the Schumann-Brahms tradition. His works include three piano concertos (1918, 1927, 1943), much solo piano music, three violin sonatas and songs. GROVEmusic

---

Piano Concertos

No 1 in C minor, Op 33; **No 2** in C minor, Op 50;
No 3 in E minor, Op 60

Piano Concerto No 1. Piano Quintet in C, Op posth
Dmitri Alexeev pf **New Budapest Quartet; BBC
Symphony Orchestra / Alexander Lazarev**
Hyperion CDA66744 (59' · DDD)   Ⓕ

For Dmitri Alexeev the First Concerto is Medtner's masterpiece, an argument he sustains in a
performance of superb eloquence and discretion.
Even the sort of gestures later vulgarised and
traduced by Tinseltown are given with an aristocratic quality, a feel for a love of musical intricacy
that takes on an almost symbolic force, but also
for Medtner's dislike of display. Time and again
Alexeev makes you pause to reconsider Medtner's
quality, and his reserve brings distinctive reward.
The early *Abbandonamente ma non troppo* has a
haunting improvisatory inwardness and later, as
the storm clouds gather ominously at 11'55", his
playing generates all the necessary electricity.
How thankful one is, too, for Alexeev's advocacy
of the Piano Quintet where, together with his
fully committed colleagues, the New Budapest
Quartet, he recreates music of the strangest, most
unworldly exultance and introspection. Instructions such as *poco tranquillo (sereno)* and *Quasi
Hymn* take us far away from the turbulence of the
First Concerto (composed in the shadow of the
First World War) and the finale's conclusion is
wonderfully uplifting. The recordings are judiciously balanced in both works, and the BBC
Symphony Orchestra under Lazarev are fully
sympathetic.

Medtner Piano Concerto No 1. Aus 'Claudine von
Villa-Bella', Op 6 No 5 (arr Sudbin)
Tchaikovsky Piano Concerto No 1, Op 23
Yevgeny Sudbin pf
São Paulo Symphony Orchestra / John Neschling
BIS 🔊 BIS-SACD1588 (71' · DDD/DSD)   ⒻⓄⓄⓄⒹ▸

To describe 26-year-old Yevgeny Sudbin as
music's brightest young star pianist is in a sense to
do him a disservice. For he is above all an artist,
and here in his eagerly awaited concerto debut on
disc he gives us a Tchaikovsky First of spine-tingling brilliance, poetry and vivacity. This is never
the Tchaikovsky you have always known, but an
arrestingly novel rethink with the concentration
on mercurial changes of mood and direction.
Here, amazingly, is one of the most familiar of all
concertos rekindled in all its first glory, brimming
over with zest and shorn of all the clichés that
have adhered to it over the years.

In the first movement Sudbin's octaves ring
out like a giant carillon, while the *Andantino*'s
central *prestissimo* becomes in such extraordinary
hands a true firefly scherzo. Not even Cherkassky at his finest possesed a more elfin sense of
difference or caprice. And to think that all this
and more is accomplished without the lift, or
hindrance, of a major competition success.

Medtner's massive First Concerto, too, could
hardly be played with a more burning clarity and
commitment. Medtner's music remains formidably inaccessible, despite displaying the outward trappings of Romantic rhetoric yet Sudbin

clearly believes in every note and his playing
evinces, as on live occasions, a rare sense of
affection. Such poetry is confirmed in his
encore, his own transcription of Medtner's song
Liebliches Kind! It only remains to add that BIS's
balance and sound are of demonstration quality
and that the São Paulo SO under John Neschling sound as if influenced by neighbouring
Rio's carnival spirit, so infectiously do they
respond to their radiant soloist.

Piano Concertos Nos 2 and 3
Nikolai Demidenko pf **BBC Scottish Symphony
Orchestra / Jerzy Maksymiuk**
Hyperion CDA66580 (74' · DDD)   ⒻⓄⓄⓄ

 This splendid disc is given a fine
recording, good orchestral playing
from a Scottish orchestra under a
Polish conductor and, above all, truly coruscating and poetic playing from the brilliant young
Russian pianist Nikolai Demidenko. Medtner
was a contemporary and friend of Rachmaninov;
he settled in Britain in the 1930s, and like Rachmaninov he was an excellent pianist. But while
the other composer became immensely popular,
Medtner languished in obscurity, regarded as an
inferior imitation of Rachmaninov who wrote
gushing music that was strong on gestures but
weak on substance. The fact is that he can be
diffuse (not to say long-winded) and grandiose,
and memorable tunes are in short supply, so that
his music needs to be played well to come off.
When it is, there's much to enjoy, as here in
Demidenko's hypnotically fiery and articulate
accounts.

Piano Concertos Nos 2 and 3. Arabesque in   Ⓗ
A minor, Op 7 No 2. Fairy Tale in F minor, Op 26 No 3
Nikolay Medtner pf
Philharmonia Orchestra / Issay Dobrowen
Testament mono SBT1027 (77' · ADD) Recorded 1947
Ⓕ

The strong Russian flavour of the ornate writing
is evident, as is the composer's masterly understanding of the piano. Listening to the composer
himself in the Second's first *molto cantabile a
tempo, ma expressivo* or the Third's *dolce cantabile*
is to be made doubly aware of his haunting and
bittersweet lyricism. The streaming figuration
in the Second Concerto's *Romanza* is spun off
with deceptive ease, a reminder that while
Medtner despised obvious pyrotechnics he was a
superb pianist. Two exquisitely played encores
are included (the ambiguous poetry of the
A minor *Arabesque* could be by no other
composer), and the 1947 recordings have been
superbly remastered.

Piano Concertos Nos 1 & 3
Konstantin Scherbakov pf
Moscow Symphony Orchestra / Vladimir Ziva
Naxos 8 553359 (70' · DDD)   ⓈⓄⒹ▸

Naxos completes its Medtner concerto cycle with Scherbakov. To have such Romantic richness – once the province of specialists – offered on a bargain label is cause for celebration in itself; to have it performed and recorded with such tireless commitment is a double blessing. That said, the performances on the first disc suffered from the soloist's poetic parsimony and an oppressive ill balance from Naxos. But this second disc is successful on all counts. Scherbakov, praised by Richter and recently hailed as a 'modern Rachmaninov', is now more attuned to Medtner's widely fluctuating idiom, complementing his virtuosity with inwardness and conviction. Sample the passage beginning at 6'30" in the Third Concerto's finale and you'll hear the sort of eloquence that warms the hearts of all true Russians.

Commissioned by Moiseiwitsch, an early and courageous champion of Medtner, the Third Concerto, subtitled 'Ballade', flows like some primeval river of the imagination, its burgeoning course inspired by Lermontov's *Water Spirit*, while the First Concerto's often epic gestures blend a bittersweet Russian Romanticism with themes of an almost Elgarian cut. Scherbakov's agility at, say, the *con moto* (8'38") is never at the expense of a composer whose bravura is always poetically motivated. Lovers of Romantic piano concertos need look no further.

Piano works

Sonata in F minor, Op 5. Two Fairy Tales, Op 8. Sonata Triad, Op 11. Sonata in G minor, Op 22. Sonatas, Op 25 – No 1 in C minor, 'Sonata-Skazka'; No 2 in E minor, 'The Night Wind'. Sonata-Ballade in F sharp, Op 27. Sonata in A minor, Op 30. Forgotten Melodies – Set I, Op 38; Set II, Op 39. Sonata romantica in B flat minor, Op 53 No 1. Sonata minacciosa in F minor, Op 53 No 2. Sonate-Idylle in G, Op 56
Marc-André Hamelin pf
Hyperion ④ CDA67221/4 (279' · DDD)　　　Ⓜ❍

With this classic recording of the 14 piano sonatas, Medtner's star soared into the ascendant. Superlatively played and presented, it effects a radical and triumphant transition from years of indifference to heady acclaim. True, Medtner was celebrated by Rachmaninov as 'the greatest composer of our time' and championed by pianists such as Moiseiwitsch, Horowitz and Gilels, yet his music fell largely on deaf ears. Such irony and enigma lie in the music itself, in its distinctive character, colour and fragrance. Listeners were understandably suspicious of music that yields up its secrets so unreadily, almost as if Medtner wished it to remain in a private rather than public domain. Moments of a ravishing, heart-stopping allure, and heroics on the grandest of scales are apt to occur within an indigestible, prolix and recondite context. On paper everything is comprehensible, yet the results are never quite what you expect. Much of the writing, too, is formidably complex, with rhythmic intricacies deriving from Brahms and whimsicalities from Schumann supporting a recognisably Slavic yet wholly personal idiom.

Such writing demands a transcendental technique and a burning poetic commitment, a magical amalgam achieved with delicacy, drama and finesse by Marc-André Hamelin. Interspersing the sonatas with miniatures containing some of Medtner's most felicitous ideas, he plays with an authority suggesting that such music is truly his language. Hamelin achieves an unfaltering sense of continuity, a balance of sense and sensibility in music that threatens to become submerged in its own passion. Readers uncertain of Medtner's elusive art should try the *Forgotten Melodies* (and most of all 'Alla reminiscenza'). Such heaven-sent performances will set you journeying far and wide, their eloquence accentuated by Hyperion's sound.

Songs

The Angel, Op 1a. Winter Evening, Op 13 No-1. Songs, Op 28 – No 2, I cannot hear that bird; No 3, Butterfly; No 4, In the Churchyard; No 5, Spring Calm. The Rose, Op 29 No 6. I loved thee well, Op 32 No 4. Night, Op 36 No 5. Sleepless, Op 37 No 1. Songs, Op-52 – No 2, The Raven; No 3, Elegy; No 5, Spanish Romance; No 6, Serenade. Noon, Op 59 No 1. Eight Songs, Op 24
Ludmilla Andrew sop **Geoffrey Tozer** pf
Chandos CHAN9327 (60' · DDD) Recorded 1993.
Texts and translations included　　　　　　Ⓕ

Musical Opinion, reviewing the newly published Op 52 in 1931, concluded that, Medtner could hardly be considered 'a born song writer'. It says something for the achievement of Ludmilla Andrew that the 'unvocal' character of Medtner's writing is hardly evident at all, though, to be fair, the first three songs from Op 52 are perhaps the very ones in which the voice is most hard-pressed and in which it's even possible to feel that they might do very well as piano solos. In the 'Serenade' (No 6), the piano part *is* an accompaniment, and the singer brings to it a charm and delicacy worthy of its dedicatee, Nina Koshetz. Geoffrey Tozer is an excellent accompanist. His playing of 'Winter Evening', with its evocative rustling start, is superb; but always, along with the sheer virtuosity, there's a responsive feeling for mood and coloration. There are songs in which the piano takes over. Yet in many the interest is evenly distributed, and these are among the most delightful in the repertoire.

Felix Mendelssohn　German 1809-1847

Mendelssohn came from a distinguished intellectual, artistic and banking family in Berlin (the family converted from Judaism to Christianity in 1816, taking the additional name 'Bartholdy'). He studied the piano with Ludwig Berger and theory and composition with Zelter, producing his first piece in 1820; thereafter, a profusion of sonatas, concertos, string symphonies, piano quartets and Singspiels revealed his increasing mastery of counterpoint and form. Besides family travels and eminent visitors to his parents' salon, early influences included the poetry of Goethe (whom he knew from 1821) and the Schlegel translations of Shakespeare; these are traceable in his best music of the period. His gifts as a conductor also showed themselves early: in 1829 he directed a pioneering performance of Bach's St Matthew Passion at the Berlin Singakademie, promoting the modern cultivation of Bach's music.

A period of travel and concert-giving introduced Mendelssohn to England, Scotland (1829) and Italy (1830-31). In 1833 he took up a conducting post at Düsseldorf, concentrating on Handel's oratorios. Among the chief products of this time were The Hebrides, the G minor Piano Concerto, Die erste Walpurgisnacht, the Italian Symphony and St Paul. But as a conductor and music organiser his most significant achievement was in Leipzig (1835-47), where to great acclaim he conducted the Gewandhaus Orchestra, championing both historical and modern works, and founded and directed the Leipzig Conservatory (1843).

Composing mostly in the summer holidays, he produced Ruy Blas Overture, a revised version of the Hymn of Praise, the Scottish Symphony, the Violin Concerto Op 64 and the fine Piano Trio in C minor (1845). Meanwhile, he was intermittently (and less happily) employed by the king as a composer and choirmaster in Berlin, where he wrote highly successful incidental music, notably for A Midsummer Night's Dream (1843). Much sought after as a festival organiser, he was associated especially with the Lower Rhine and Birmingham music festivals. His death at the age of 38, after a series of strokes, was mourned internationally.

With its emphasis on clarity and adherence to classical ideals, Mendelssohn's music shows alike the influences of Bach (fugal technique), Handel (rhythms, harmonic progressions), Mozart (dramatic characterisation, forms, textures) and Beethoven (instrumental technique), though from 1825 he developed a characteristic style of his own, often underpinned by a literary, artistic, historical, geographical or emotional connection; indeed it was chiefly in his skilful use of extra-musical stimuli that he was a Romantic. His early and prodigious operatic gifts, clearly reliant on Mozart, failed to develop, but his penchant for the dramatic found expression in the oratorios as well as in Ruy Blas Overture, his Antigone incidental music and above all the enduring Midsummer Night's Dream music, in which themes from the overture are cleverly adapted as motifs in the incidental music. The oratorios, among the most popular works of their kind, draw inspiration from Bach and Handel and content from the composer's personal experience, St Paul being an allegory of Mendelssohn's own family history and Elijah of his years of dissension in Berlin. Among his other vocal works, the highly dramatic Die erste Walpurgisnacht, Op 60 (on Goethe's poem greeting springtime) and the Leipzig psalm settings deserve special mention; the choral songs and lieder are uneven, reflecting their wide variety of social functions.

After an apprenticeship of string symphony writing in a classical mould, Mendelssohn found inspiration in art, nature and history for his orchestral music. The energy, clarity and tunefulness of the Italian have made it his most popular symphony, although the elegiac Scottish represents a newer, more purposeful achievement. In his best overtures, essentially one-movement symphonic poems, the sea appears as a recurring image, from Calm Sea and Prosperous Voyage and The Hebrides to The Lovely Melusine. Less dependent on programmatic elements and at the same time formally innovatory, the concertos, notably that for violin, and the chamber music, especially some of the string quartets, the Octet and the two late piano trios, beautifully reconcile classical principles with personal feeling; these are among his most striking compositions. Of the solo instrumental works, the partly lyric, partly virtuoso Lieder ohne Worte for piano (from 1829) are elegantly written and often touching.　　　　　　　GROVEmusic

Piano Concertos

No 1 in G minor, Op 25; No 2 in D minor, Op 40; A minor (piano and strings); E; A flat (both two pianos)

Piano Concertos – Nos 1 and 2. Capriccio brillant in B minor, Op 22. Rondo brillant in E flat, Op 29. Serenade and Allegro giocoso, Op 43
Stephen Hough pf **City of Birmingham Symphony Orchestra / Lawrence Foster**
Hyperion CDA66969 (75' · DDD)　　　Ⓕ**OO**

With Stephen Hough's Mendelssohn we enter a new dimension. The soft, stylish arpeggios that open the first work here, the Capriccio brillant, announce something special. But this is just a preparation for the First Concerto. Here again, 'stylish' is the word. One can sense the background – especially the operatic background against which these works were composed. The first solo doesn't simply storm away, fortissimo; one hears distinct emotional traits: the imperious, thundering octaves, the agitated semiquavers, the pleading appoggiaturas. The revelation is the First Concerto's slow movement: not a trace of stale sentimentality here, rather elegance balanced by depth of feeling. Some of the praise must go to the CBSO and Foster; after all it's the CBSO violas and cellos that lead the singing in that slow movement. Foster and the orchestra are also effective in the opening of the Second Concerto – too often dismissed as the less inspired sequel to No 1. The first bars are hushed, sombre, a little below the main tempo, so that it's left to Hough to energise the argument and set the pace – all very effective.

Double Piano Concertos – E; A flat
Benjamin Frith, Hugh Tinney pfs
RTE Sinfonietta / Prionnsías O'Duinn
Naxos 8 553416 (74' · DDD)　　　Ⓢ➔

Mendelssohn was 14 when he completed his first two-piano Concerto in E major, and still

MENDELSSOHN'S VIOLIN CONCERTO – IN BRIEF

Yehudi Menuhin; Colonne Concerts Orchestra / George Enescu Ⓗ
Naxos 8 110967 (75' · ADD) Ⓢ
The youthful Menuhin at his most mercurial and dauntingly accurate. A captivating display, as are its bedfellows, the 17-year-old prodigy's legendary 1933 Lalo *Symphonie espagnole* and Chausson *Poème*.

Josef Suk; Czech PO / Karel Ančerl
Supraphon SU3663-2 (79' · ADD) Ⓢ
Suk at his incomparably eloquent, unaffected best. Ančerl and the Czech PO provide luminous support, and Supraphon's mid-60s sound has come up very freshly.

Alfredo Campoli; London PO / Sir Adrian Boult Ⓗ
Beulah 1PD10 (74' · ADD) Ⓜ
This lovely performance dates from May 1958; the slow movement in particular has a homely, fireside glow that's irresistible. Pleasing early stereo. Paired with these artists' underrated account of the Elgar Concerto.

Anne-Sophie Mutter / Leipzig Gewandhaus Orchestra / Kurt Masur
DG 4778001 (73' · DDD + DVD) Ⓕ▷
It's impossible not to be impressed by Mutter's playing. Every last detail has been dissected and considered, every phrase is minutely shaded; the subtleties of her bowing could in themselves fill a review.

Nigel Kennedy; English Chamber Orchestra / Jeffrey Tate
EMI 749663-2 (71' · DDD) Ⓕ Ⓞ▷
One of Kennedy's first forays into mainstream repertory, this 1987 account of the Mendelssohn has not a hint of routine about it. As well as the ubiquitous Bruch G minor, the disc also contains Schubert's little-known Rondo.

Kyung Wha Chung; Montreal SO / Charles Dutoit
Decca 460 976-2DM (79' · DDD/ADD) Ⓕ▷
A personable and polished alliance from Chung and Dutoit, glowingly engineered. Now generously coupled with Chung's classic 1971 pairing of Bruch's First Concerto and *Scottish Fantasia* with Kempe.

Joshua Bell; Camerata Academica Salzburg / Sir Roger Norrington
Sony Classical SK89505 (70' · DDD) Ⓕ▷
Not everyone will go a bundle on Bell's own first-movement cadenza, but this remains a likeable, stimulating account. Perky, clean-limbed playing from the Salzburg chamber orchestra under Norrington, and very realistic sound.

only 15 when he followed it with a considerably longer (rather too long) and more ambitious second in A flat. And it's to the great credit of Benjamin Frith and Hugh Tinney that without a score at hand, you would be hard-pressed to guess who was playing what.

You'll be as impressed by their attunement of phrasing in lyrical contexts as by their synchronisation in all the brilliant semiquaver passage-work in which both works abound. Their uninhibited enjoyment of the imitative audacities of the later work's finale is a real tour de force.

Under Prionnsías O'Duinn the RTE Sinfonietta plays with sufficient relish to allow you to forget that the recording is perhaps just a little too close. In short, a not-to-be-missed opportunity to explore the young Mendelssohn at bargain price.

Violin Concerto in E minor

Mendelssohn Violin Concerto
Bruch Violin Concerto No 1 in G minor, Op 26
Schubert Rondo in A, D438
Nigel Kennedy vn
English Chamber Orchestra / Jeffrey Tate
EMI 749663-2 (71' · DDD) Ⓕ Ⓞ▷

These are exceptionally strong and positive performances, vividly recorded. When it comes to the two main works, Kennedy readily holds his own against all comers. His view of the Mendelssohn has a positive, masculine quality established at the very start. He may at first seem a little fierce, but fantasy goes with firm control, and the transition into the second subject on a descending arpeggio (marked *tranquillo*) is radiantly beautiful, the more affecting by contrast with the power of what has gone before.

Kennedy is unerringly helped by Jeffrey Tate's refreshing and sympathetic support. Though it's the English Chamber Orchestra accompanying, there's no diminution of scale. With full and well-balanced sound, the piece even seems bigger, more symphonic than usual. In the slow movement Kennedy avoids sentimentality in his simple, songful view. The coda is always a big test in this work, and Kennedy's and Tate's reading is among the most powerful and exciting on record.

The Bruch brings another warm and positive performance, consistently sympathetic, with the orchestra once more adding to the power. Kennedy's more than a match for rival versions, again bringing a masculine strength which goes with a richly expressive yet unsentimental view of Bruch's exuberant lyricism as in the central slow movement. Thoroughly recommended.

Additional recommendation

Coupled with: **Berg** Violin Concerto **Bruch** Violin Concerto No 1 in G minor, Op 26
Suk vn **Czech Philharmonic Orchestra / Ančerl**
Supraphon SU3663-2 (79' · ADD) Recorded 1966-8 Ⓕ
Josef Suk gives an outstanding performance of the Mendelssohn – his playing combines his usual

technical polish and fine tone with unaffected expression. The orchestra has exemplary internal balance and rhythmic poise. The Bruch has similar virtues, and there's more great music-making in the Berg. The sound has been remastered and is uncommonly clear: highly recommended.

Symphonies

Symphonies – **No 1** in C minor, Op 11; **No 2** in B flat, Op 52, 'Hymn of Praise'; **No 3** in A minor, Op 56, 'Scottish'; **No 4** in A, Op 90, 'Italian'; **No 5** in D, Op 107, 'Reformation'.

Symphonies Nos 1-5. Overtures – A Midsummer Night's Dream; Die schöne Melusine; The Hebrides, 'Fingal's Cave'; Ruy Blas; Meerestille und Gückliche Fahrt; Trumpet Overure.
Elisabeth Connell, Karita Mattila sops **Hans-Peter Blochwitz** ten **London Symphony Chorus and Orchestra / Claudio Abbado**
DG ④ 471 467-2GB4 (4h 15' · DDD)   ⑧❶❶❶❶❿

It is in the choral Second Symphony that the advantage of the wide-ranging digital sound comes out most strikingly, in clarifying the big tuttis with choir, at the same time providing extra weight of sound, notably in the way that pedal notes on the organ come over in a rich and realistic way. As to interpretation, Abbado in the first instrumental movement conveys a keener sense of joy with a wide expressive range. The yearning 6/8 movement is the more haunting too at Abbado's much slower speed, and though Abbado's slower speed for the *Andante religioso* brings obvious dangers of sweetness and sentimentality, he manages to avoid them completely with his warm but unmannered phrasing. Again, in the choral finale Abbado's speeds tend to be a degree more relaxed and the sense of joyful release is all the keener. His three soloists are very fine and their tonal beauty and natural feeling for words and phrasing are a delight. So too is the singing of the London Symphony Chorus, particularly beautiful in the chorale, 'Nun danket alle Gott'. Abbado's expansiveness and his more luminous choral sound has one forgetting the obvious shortcomings of the work with its unavoidable element of Victorian blandness.

It is that avoidance of Victorian blandness which is striking in Abbado's accounts of Nos 1 and 5. In No 1 he is tough and biting, slower and simpler in the second movement, returning to a tough, dark manner for the Minuet and finale. This is a performance which has one marvelling that Mendelssohn could have ever have countenanced the idea of the Octet *Scherzo* as substitute, a piece so different in mood. The first movement of the *Reformation* finds Abbado in dramatic mood, and crisper and again quicker in the second movement *Allegro vivace*. (For individual comments on the *Scottish* and *Italian* symphonies see following review.)

As for the overtures they too bring fresh and attractive performances, very fast and fleet in

the fairy music of *A Midsummer Nights Dream* and with the contrast between first and second subjects of *The Hebrides* underlined. This was one of Abbado's biggest recording projects with the orchestra of which he was music director, and remains a richly rewarding legacy.

Symphony No 3 in A minor, 'Scottish', Op 56. Violin Concerto in E minor, Op 64ª. A Midsummer Night's Dream – Overture; Wedding March
ª**Frank-Michael Erben** vn
Leipzig Gewandhaus Orchestra / Kurt Masur
Video director **Bob Coles**
Arthaus Musik 🆅 100 030 (82' · Region 0)   Ⓕ

This concert's visual interest rests squarely on the players and conductor; its setting is the anodyne modern Gewandhaus auditorium. Fortunately the director doesn't resort to Karajanesque gimmickry to compensate. Masur is a pleasure to watch as he shapes his interpretations, underpinned by the orchestra's clear, airy textures, which come over with proper clarity in the Dolby Digital Stereo soundtrack. His *Dream* Overture has plenty of fleet-footed magic, and needs only more of a smile. Erben, the orchestra's leader, is a fluent, committed but unspectacular soloist in the concerto, and is none the worse for that; it's refreshing to hear Mendelssohn speaking for himself. The *Scottish* Symphony is a fine performance, capturing the first movement's melancholy with great grace, and there's plenty of energy in the *Scherzo* and final movement. Only the Wedding March seems rather short of vitality. Visually natural if not especially exciting, it's an engaging programme, and represents a decent body of music for the money.

String Symphonies

String Symphonies Nos 1, 6, 7 and 12
Nieuw Sinfonietta Amsterdam / Lev Markiz
BIS CD683 (70' · DDD)   Ⓕ

Amazing stuff, brilliantly performed. The first of the symphonies fair bursts from the staves, with a chuckling finale that would surely have delighted Rossini. And although the Sixth Symphony's finale harbours hints of miracles to come, Mendelssohn's mature personality is more comprehensively anticipated in the Seventh. Again, the finale suggests the ebullient, life-affirming manner of the orchestral symphonies, albeit sobered by a spot of fugally formal writing later on. The 12th Symphony opens with a Handelian sense of ceremony, goes on to incorporate a characteristically tender *Andante* and ends with a finale that, to quote Stig Jacobsson's enthusiastic notes, 'dies away to *pizzicato* and a subsequent *accelerando* which recalls Rossini'. This is truly delightful music, the playing both sensitive and exciting, while BIS's sound is impressively full-bodied.

MENDELSSOHN'S SYMPHONIES NOS 3, 4 & 5 – IN BRIEF

London SO / Claudio Abbado (Nos 3 & 4)
DG 427 810-2GDC (71' · ADD) ⓜ️🅞🅞▷
Abbado imparts a winning sense of structural direction and emotional abandon to these works. The myth of Mendelssohn the simple prodigy is satisfyingly exploded.

LCP / Roger Norrington (Nos 3 & 4) 🅟
EMI 561735-2 (65' · ADD) ⓜ️🅞▷
Right from the start of No 4, this offers something different: period instruments and good engineering give a radically altered view of balances and textures without stopping one from revelling in the joy Norrington himself clearly takes in these works.

Berlin PO / James Levine (Nos 3 & 4)
DG 427670-2GH (71' · DDD) 🅕🅞▷
Levine whips up the Berliners in performances of fizzing energy and airborne grace: the edgy dance of the *Italian*'s finale is as exhilarating as any on disc.

Madrid SO / Peter Maag (Nos 3 & 4)
Arts 47506-2 (70' · ADD) 🅑🅞🅞
The orchestra may not be top-rank but Peter Maag has trained it to give wonderfully wise, humane performances of Mendelssohn and Mozart. A clear budget choice.

Orchestra of the 18th Century / Frans Brüggen (Nos 3, 4 & 5) 🅟
Philips 456 267-2PH2 (120' · DDD) ⓜ️▷
Another period set, with a more reflective approach: Nos 3 & 5 are especially intriguing.

Vienna PO / John Eliot Gardiner (Nos 4 & 5)
459 156-2GH (77' · DDD) 🅑🅞▷
DG's engineering, the VPO at their most twinkle-toed and Gardiner's zeal for contrapuntal clarity combine to offer amazing levels of clarity and rhythmic buoyancy. The revised version of the Fourth is an illuminating bonus.

Leipzig Gewandhaus / Kurt Masur (Nos 3 & 4)
Warner Apex 0927 49817-2 (67' · DDD) Ⓢ
Masur has always been renowned for his joyful, straightforward performances of a composer for whom he has a special affection. Mendelssohn was director of the Leipzig orchestra and they play with an authenticity all their own.

COE / Nikolaus Harnoncourt (Nos 3 & 4) 🅟
Warner Classics 9031 72308-2 (69' · DDD) 🅕▷
No speed-merchant, ultra-authentic versions these: the young virtuosos of the Chamber Orchestra of Europe respond zestfully to Harnoncourt's cultured direction, which does much to reveal Mendelssohn's sophisticated sense of symphonic direction.

Octet

Octet, Op 20[a]. Song Without Words, Op 109[b].
Variations concertantes, Op 17[b]. Assai tranquillo[b]
[a]**Ensemble Explorations** (Christine Busch, Lydia Forbes, Zhang Zhang, Francis Reusens *vns* Guus Jeukendrup, Marten Boeken *vas* Geert Debiève *vc*)
with **Roel Dieltiens** *vc* [b]**Frank Braley** *pf*
Harmonia Mundi HMC90 1868 (50' · DDD) 🅕🅞🅞

It's easy to love the Mendelssohn Octet, and the account from Ensemble Explorations is irresistible. True, the recorded sound is rather too resonant, but the playing has real fire and vitality, and the more soulful solo passages, violinist Christine Busch's especially, are truly eloquent; at the first movement's climactic moments her tone rings out effortlessly above the texture. The recent Emerson version is more sharply recorded, with much finely polished detail, yet their earnestly projected tone doesn't give the sense of joyful flight that characterises this new recording. The *Scherzo* may seem a little tame after the brilliant, high-speed Emersons, but it catches the nocturnal atmosphere and leaves room for an exciting increase in speed for the *Presto* finale. The cello and piano items are played with beautiful expression; Frank Braley clearly enjoys his 1874 Steinway.

Mendelssohn Octet[b] **Beethoven** Piano Trio No 4, Op 11[a]
Nash Ensemble (Ian Brown *pf* [a]Richard Hosford *cl* [b]Marianne Thorsen, [b]Laura Samuel, [b]David Adams, [b]Malin Broman *vns* [b]Lawrence Power, [b]Philip Dukes *vas* Paul Watkins, [b]Timothy Hugh *vcs*)
Wigmore Hall Live WHLIVE0001 (55' · DDD)
Recorded live 2005 ⓜ️

This is a recording from a concert given in March 2005; a very good recording, too, combining intimacy with the warm ambience familiar to Wigmore Hall concertgoers. And the performances are splendid: there's no doubting the genuine enthusiasm of the applause at the end of each work.

The outer movements of the Mendelssohn have plenty of fire and spirit. The climax of the first movement's development section is grand and intense, with the following *pianissimo* full of romantic mystery and suspense. This performance isn't quite on a level with the account by Ensemble Explorations (see above), whose leaner tone and clearer textures (despite a less attractive, over-resonant acoustic) bring the work's rhythmic and expressive character into sharper focus.

The Nash *Scherzo* is beautifully precise and delicate, but its very fast tempo pre-empts, to some extent, the effect of the finale. (Ensemble Explorations, with a gentler but still fantastical *Scherzo*, leave room for the *Presto* of the last movement to increase the level of excitement.) The Nash's interpretation scores, however, through the immediacy of the recorded sound, and a live-performance sense of occasion, of joy in playing together. The Beethoven is just as impressive, the players seeming to inspire one another to make the most of this lively, colourful music. Particularly appealing is the way they bring out the character of each of the finale's variations without compromising the music's overall impetus.

String Quartets

No 1 in E flat, Op 12 **No 2** in A, Op 13 **No 3** in D, Op 44 No 1 **No 4** in E minor, Op 44 No 2 **No 5** in E flat, Op 44 No 3 **No 6** in F minor, Op 80

String Quartets Nos 1-6. String Quartet (1823).
Four Pieces for String Quartet,Op 81. Octet.
Emerson Quartet (Eugene Drucker, Philip Setzer vns
Lawrence Dutton va David Finckel vc)
DG ④ 477 5370GH4 (242' · DDD)   Ⓕ**⒪Ⓞ**Ⓓ➡

Cycles of Mendelssohn's string quartets are no longer a rarity and now the Emersons issue a full cycle that includes not only the early E flat work of 1823 and the Op 81 miscellaneous pieces but the Octet, which as a recording *tour de force* they play with themselves, as it were.

The Emersons have much to offer. One of their outstanding qualities is a sympathy for the tensions that so often lie within Mendelssohn's most apparently open music. They are also sensitive to the subtleties in his forms, above all in the first movements where there can lie a greater degree of emotional turbulence than is immediately evident. The *Scherzo* of the Fifth Quartet has a vehemence as well as a vigour, which the Emersons discover in the fierce figuration, and which is to some degree realised with the music's unexpected outcome in a fugue. If the Emersons' response to the finale seems overemphatic, this may be heard as the product of a movement that Mendelssohn marks emphatically, perhaps because the animation in the music does not seem to come from as deep as it does elsewhere in the quartets. There is, on the other hand, a delightful freshness of response to the whole of the Third Quartet (actually the last of the Op 44 set of three to have been written). The final tarantella whirls along brilliantly.

In Quartet No 2, with its questioning motto 'Ist es wahr?' ('Is it true?'), the Emersons handle the opening movement lightly but again with that underlying touch of anxiety; they play the *Adagio* gravely and sense well the disturbance that informs the complexity of the finale. Their flexibility of response suits the opening movement of the First Quartet (they are more direct with the more straightforward opening movement of No 4), and they play the pretty *Canzonetta* quite lightly and briskly.

The last quartet, Op 80, Mendelssohn's masterpiece in the form, at once sums up his preoccupations in the previous quartets and sets them in a more profound context. The modulations within a sonata form movement, which with Mendelssohn are so often colourful or elegant, here take on a darker tinge which the Emersons understand, and they play the closing dozen bars of the *Adagio* with a touching sadness: the composer had recently learnt of the death of his beloved sister Fanny.

String Quartets Nos 1 & 6
Henschel Quartet (Christoph Henschel, Markus Henschel vns Monika Henschel va Mathias D Beyer-Karlshøj vc)
Arte Nova 74321 96521-2 (49' · DDD)   Ⓢ**Ⓞ**

The Henschel Quartet is a strong, well-unified group (three of the four are siblings); its ardent, robust approach suits Mendelssohn, and they sustain the lyrical expansiveness of Op 12's first movement and *Andante* in fine style. Christoph Henschel uses fingerings that involve many audible changes of position, as early 19th-century violinists are known to have done. By the mid-20th century, violin slides had become a no-go area, but, performed as stylishly as they are here, they contribute powerfully to the music's emotional effect.

Refinement clearly isn't a priority for the Op 80 Quartet, Mendelssohn's last major work, which he composed in Switzerland in the wake of the sudden death of his sister Fanny. It's uninhibited confessional music, like the two Smetana quartets. Only the *Adagio* offers some tentative relief from the prevailing bleak, almost desperate mood: this is the least satisfactory part of the Henschels' interpretation – the many slurred moving parts need a stronger sense of direction. In the other three movements they demonstrate in memorable fashion just how stark and uncompromising the music is.

Piano Trios

Piano Trios Nos 1 & 2
Florestan Trio (Anthony Marwood vn Richard Lester vc Susan Tomes pf)
Hyperion CDA67485 (54' · DDD)   Ⓕ

With its unforgettable opening cello theme, the D minor First has always been the more favoured of the two. But in a performance as subtle and impassioned as the Florestan's, the C minor Second seems at least as fine. The powerful, almost Brahmsian first movement alone should give the lie to the cliché that Mendelssohn's genius declined irredeemably after the brilliance of youth. While always keeping the potentially dense textures lucid (Susan Tomes's refined, singing tone and articulation a constant pleasure), the Florestan play this with a mingled fire and lyrical tenderness that it's hard to imagine bettered.

The flowing barcarolle slow movement has a crucial quality of innocence, and the flickering nocturnal *Scherzo* is as delicate and pointed as you could wish, at a tempo close to Mendelssohn's optimistically fast marking, while the finale drives impulsively towards its triumphant chorale apotheosis, grandly inevitable rather than bombastic.

From the yearning opening, the great cello melody surging across the barlines, the Florestan are equally vivid in the D minor Trio. Scrupulously observant, as ever, of Mendelssohn's detailed dynamic markings, they make you more than usually aware of how much of the music is held down to *piano* and *pianissimo*; and the moment at the start of the recapitulation, where Richard Lester's warm cello is counterpoised with violinist Anthony Marwood's fragile, floated descant, is as magical as you will hear.

Again the Florestan favour an easily flowing tempo for the song-without-words slow movement, phrasing in long spans (uncommonly pure, luminous duetting from Marwood and Lester) and finding a touch of playfulness when the main theme returns. Just as fine are the irresistible airborne *Scherzo* and the finale, where the Florestan, taking note of the qualifying *un poco tranquillo*, make the opening march unusually pensive before sweeping forward with an authentically Mendelssohnian mix of restless agitation, grace and lyrical fervour. Pleasure in these superb performances is enhanced by a beautifully natural recording and Robert Philip's detailed, illuminating notes.

Piano Trios Nos 1 & 2
Julia Fischer vn **Daniel Müller-Schott** vc
Jonathan Gilad pf
Pentatone ⏺. PTC5186 085 (59' · DDD/DSD)   Ⓕ

Chamber music with star players doesn't always work: lack of rehearsal time or oversized egos can often lead to performances high on surface glitz but low on understanding. Not here though: these young artists, already making waves in their individual careers, give us a recording of Mendelssohn's delectable piano trios that sparkles and fizzes from the outset.

The opening of the D minor Trio No 1 is a touch simpler than the Florestan's recent acclaimed reading but its urgency sweeps you along. They are particularly fine in the scherzi of both trios, with delightful portamenti in the D minor which seem to say 'look how easy this is'. In the finale, the new trio set off at a dancing pace; the Florestan are a touch steadier, which makes for an even more explosive contrast as the movement hots up.

The C minor Trio has long lived in the shadow of the D minor. It's darker, slower to reveal its secrets. The new version fully captures its ruggedness, the way that melodies are hewn from the musical material, rather than simply emerging complete as in No 1. The only real quibble is their spacious tempo for the second movement, a Venetian gondola song in all but name. It's played with great tenderness but does seem rather over-extended.

All in all, this new recording is irresistible, with the three players caught in a wholly natural ambience. It's always a good sign when you don't want to stop playing a disc long enough to write about it.

Cello Sonatas

Cello Sonatas – No 1 in B flat, Op 45; No 2 in D,   Ⓟ
Op 58. Variations concertantes, Op 17. Assai
tranquillo. Song without words, Op 109
Steven Isserlis vc **Melvyn Tan** fp
RCA Red Seal 09026 62553-2 (62' · DDD)   ⒻⓄ

Isserlis and Tan offer idiomatic, well-turned performances full of freshness and vigour. Try the First Sonata in B flat major (which Mendelssohn wrote for his brother, Paul, in 1838), where the second movement's dual function as scherzo and slow movement is convincingly characterised, and the music's passionate outbursts sound arrestingly potent. Isserlis's and Tan's fine blend of subtlety and panache affectingly conveys the nostalgic mood of the *Variations concertantes*, and culminates powerfully in the work's conclusion. In the D major Second Sonata, Isserlis's and Tan's spontaneity and energy in the outer movements, skilfully controlled variety of timbre and touch in the *Scherzo*, and dramatic opposition of chorale (piano) and recitative (cello) in the third movement sound immensely compelling. In the *Assai tranquillo*, as in the charming *Song without words*, Op 109, sympathetic tonal balance between cello and fortepiano in the softly lit recording brings out the music's sentiment. Isserlis and Tan effectively draw out the work's inconclusive ending to create a telling analogy of the eternal nature of friendship. Excellent balance and crisp, restrained recording helps vividly to evoke this music's Romantic atmosphere.

Variations sérieuses, Op 54

Variations sérieuses in D minor, Op 54. Piano Sonata
in E, Op 6. Three Preludes, Op 104a. Three Studies,
Op 104b. Kinderstücke, Op 72, 'Christmas Pieces'.
Gondellied in A. Scherzo in B minor
Benjamin Frith pf
Naxos 8 550940 (65' · DDD)   ⓈⒹ

The multiplicity of notes in Mendelssohn's piano music sometimes lays him open to the charge of 'note-spinning'. So what higher praise for Benjamin Frith than to say that thanks to his fluency, not a single work outstays its welcome here. The unchallengeable masterpiece is the *Variations sérieuses*, so enthusiastically taken up by Clara Schumann, and still a repertory work today. Frith characterises each variation with telling contrasts of tempo and touch without sacrificing the continuity and unity of the whole. Equally importantly, he never lets us forget the *sérieuses* of the title.

No less impressive is his sensitively varied palette in the early E-major Sonata (unmistakable homage to Beethoven's Op-101) so often helped by subtle pedalling. But surely the recitative of the *Adagio* at times needs just a little more intensity and underlying urgency. Of the miniatures the six *Kinderstücke* ('Christmas Pieces' – written for the children of a friend) emerge with an unforced charm. As music they lack the romance of Schumann's ventures into a child's world, just as the *Three Studies* do of Chopin's magical revelations in this sphere. However, Frith's fingers never let him down. In the first B-flat Study he even seems to acquire a third hand to sustain its middle melody. For sheer seductive grace, the independent *Gondellied* haunts the memory most of all.

With pleasantly natural sound, too, this disc is quite a bargain.

Songs without words

Songs Without Words – Op 19 Nos 1 & 3; Op 30 No 6, 'Venetianisches Gondellied No 2'; Op 38 No 2; Op 53 Nos 2 & 3; Op 67 Nos 3, 4 & 5; Op 85 No 4; Op 102 No 2; in F sharp minor; in F; in E flat. Albumblatt, Op 117. Rondo capriccioso, Op 14. Gondellied in A. Klavierstück in G minor
Sebastian Knauer pf
Berlin Classics 0016372BC (71' · DDD)   Ⓕ**OO**

One of the main reasons for the success of this disc is that instead of doggedly ploughing his way through a chronologically ordered selection of *Songs Without Words*, Sebastian Knauer has chosen only those which appeal to him and about which he has something individual to say. At least, that is the impression one gets from his playing.

For Mendelssohn specialists there are the added bonuses of four world premiere recordings: the Songs in F sharp minor and F major (sans opus numbers) are heard here in the first edition of the 2001 Viennese Urtext; the Song in E flat is a completion by Mendelssohn's biographer Larry Todd (who also contributes the booklet here); Op 102 No 2 in D major is a 'recording of the dedicated original score' (no further information is given).

Realistically captured, with strong, sweeping accounts of the *Variations sérieuses* as the programme's centrepiece and the *Andante and Rondo capriccioso* with which Knauer rounds off proceedings, this is a distinguished contribution to the 200th anniversary celebrations.

Mendelssohn Three Caprices, Op 33 – No 2; No 3. Prelude, Op 104a No 2. Rondo capriccioso, Op 14. Songs Without Words – selection. Three Studies, Op 104b. Variations sérieuses, Op 54. Suleika, Op 34 No 4. A Midsummer Night's Dream – Scherzo (arr Rachmaninov). Scherzo, Op 16 No 2 **Liszt** Mendelssohn Lieder, S547 – Suleika; Auf Flügeln des Gesanges
Bertrand Chamayou pf
Naïve V5131 (65' · DDD)   Ⓕ**O**

There was a time in the 19th century when Mendelssohn's *Songs Without Words* were regularly regarded as the third great collection of piano music after Beethoven's 32 sonatas and Bach's 48 Preludes and Fugues. While Chopin's piano music is still dominant, Mendelssohn's star as a pianist-composer has faded. It is a splendid idea of the young Toulouse-born French pianist Bertrand Chamayou to choose five of the most striking *Songs Without Words* and make them a centrepiece for what he describes as a 'Liederabend without words'.

The *Songs Without Words* are among the least difficult of the pieces here technically, but the other pieces are much more demanding, not just the two bigger pieces, the *Variations sérieuses* and the *Rondo capriccioso*, but such pieces as the *Three Studies*. It says much for Chamayou's virtuosity and artistry that he makes the results so magnetic. He opens with a brief and powerful Prelude in B minor, leading to a sparkling account of the *Rondo capriccioso* bringing out echoes of the *Scherzo* from *A Midsummer Night's Dream*, which right at the end of the recital comes as a tailpiece in Rachmaninov's arrangement.

The articulation in the *Three Studies* is phenomenally clear and light, as it is too in Chamayou's dazzling account of the *Caprices*. There are similar qualities in the longest and most ambitious of the pieces, the *Variations sérieuses*. Along with the *Songs Without Words* it is good too to have Liszt's surprisingly unshowy arrangements of Mendelssohn's most famous Lied, 'On Wings of Song'. Clean, clear sound to match the playing.

Organ works

'Complete Organ Works, Volume 1'
Allegro assai (ed Bate)[b]. Fughetta in A[c]. Two Fugues – in E minor[d]; in D[a]e. Organ Sonata No 1, Op 65[f]. Prelude and Fugue, Op 37 No 1[g]. Six Little Pieces – Prelude in D minor[g]. Four Studies[c]e. Andante and Variations[b]. Chorale Prelude, 'Nim von uns, Herr'[g]
Jennifer Bate with [a]**Martin Stacey** orgs
Somm Céleste Series SOMMCD050 (73' · DDD)
Played on the organs of [b]All Saints Church, Margaret St, London; [c]St Stephen's Church, Bournemouth; [d]Temple Church, Fleet St, London; [e]St John's Church, Upper Norwood, London; [f]St Matthew's Church, Bayswater, London; [g]Wimborne Minster, Wimborne, Dorset   Ⓕ

In Jennifer Bate's impressive discography of British organ music she has taken pains to match each individual piece with an appropriate organ. Technically speaking, Mendelssohn may not have been British, but his magnificent Sonatas and Preludes and Fugues were all composed for the British market, so it is entirely fitting that Bate pays the same attention to detail over his music as she does over the genuine, home-grown article.

In this series, which will eventually stretch to five discs, Bate has recorded all 68 pieces contained in a newly published edition of Mendelssohn's complete organ works. It goes without saying that her playing is hugely impressive and impeccably stylish, the virtuoso passagework delivered with almost flawless precision.

The surprise at finding, among the six English

organs chosen for this repertoire, Wimborne Minster, with its neo-Baroque organ, is quickly assuaged by Bate's intelligent use of stops included in the 1867 rebuild. Appropriately this instrument is used for the more contrapuntal pieces. For the First Sonata she uses the more opulent-sounding Walker instrument of St Matthew's, Bayswater, while the sumptuous Hill organ of St Stephen's, Bournemouth (here relocated from Dorset to Hampshire, where it was located when the organ was built in 1898), is ideal in the first three of the Four Studies.

Beyond the First Sonata and the Prelude and Fugue, the only piece here to have established itself in the repertory is the lovely *Andante and Variations* which here, played with disarming fluidity on the organ of All Saints, Margaret Street, provides a real highlight on a disc which is infinitely more rewarding than an initial glance at the track-listing might imply.

Choruses

Six Choruses, Op 88. Four Choruses, Op 100.
Der Erste Frühlingstag, Op 48. Im Freien zu
singen, Op 41. Im Grünen, Op 59
**RIAS Chamber Choir, Berlin / Hans-Christoph
Rademann**
Harmonia Mundi HMC90 1992 (66' · DDD) Ⓕ Ⓞ ▶

But how delightful! Here come Herr Mendelssohn and his choir, walking across the fields making directly for our neck of the woods where we are about to enjoy our own déjeuner sur l'herbe. Certainly Mendelssohn liked to take his singers out into the country and particularly to the woods, the 'temple of harmony' as one of his part-songs has it. And if they sang Mendelssohn's pleasant compositions as beautifully as the RIAS choir sing them here, how welcome they would be. Even Wordsworth, listening to the 'still, sad music of humanity', might not have been too put out; for these, on the whole, are Wordsworthian poems, and the settings, however trim and cultivated, are closer to Wordsworth's Nature than to the world of business and 'greetings where no kindness is'.

They are, in fact, kindly works, kindly on the ear and on the voices. Essentially homophonic in their writing for unaccompanied choir, they never leave the individual parts without interest, whether a point of harmony, an imitative phrase or a solo lead. Within the equable sameness of the manner there are many variations and shades of expression. The RIAS Chamber Choir, with their irreproachable homogeneity of tone and flawless intonation, are alive to all the finer points of phrasing and coloration.

Elijah (sung in English)
Renée Fleming, Libby Crabtree *sops* **Patricia** Ⓟ
Bardon, Sara Fulgoni *mezzos* **Matthew Munro** *treb*
John Mark Ainsley, John Bowen *tens* **Neal Davies**
bar **Bryn Terfel** *bass-bar* **Geoffrey Moses** *bass*
Edinburgh Festival Chorus; Orchestra of the Age

of Enlightenment / Paul Daniel
Decca ② 455 688-2DH2 (131' · DDD· T) Ⓕ ▶

Paul Daniel and Bryn Terfel ensure that this is one of the most dramatic performances of the oratorio on disc. The young conductor, with the advantage of an excellent period instrument orchestra, has looked anew at the score and as a reveals much of the rhythmic and dynamic detail not always present in other performances, at least those available in English. His accomplishment in terms of pacing and balance is also praiseworthy, and he earns further marks for using the trio, quartet and double quartet of soloists Mendelssohn asks for in specific pieces, so as to vary the texture of the music.

Bryn Terfel simply gives the most exciting and vivid account of the prophet's part yet heard. His range, in terms of vocal register and dynamics, is huge; his expression, mighty and immediate, befits a man of Elijah's temperament. As the score demands, anguish, anger and sympathy are there in full measure, displayed in exceptional definition of words, and when this Elijah calls on the Lord for the saving rain, the Almighty could hardly resist such a commanding utterance. Yet there's always the inwardness part of the role demands. As far as the other soloists are concerned, for the concerted numbers Daniel has chosen voices that nicely match each other in timbre. The chorus is alert and unanimous in both attack and well thought-through phrasing, but its actual sound can be a little soft-centred, partly because all-important consonants are ignored. The orchestral playing is exemplary.

Elijah (sung in German)
Christine Schäfer *sop* **Cornelia Kallisch** *contr*
Michael Schade *ten* **Wolfgang Schöne** *bass-bar*
**Stuttgart Gächinger Kantorei; Stuttgart Bach
Collegium / Helmuth Rilling**
Hänssler Classic ② 98 928 (128' · DDD · T/t) Ⓕ

Rilling brings out arrestingly the drama of the piece, turning it into a well-varied, exciting quasi-opera, a far from traditional view of the oratorio. The vicissitudes of the prophet's eventful life, his reaction to events, the challenge to Baal, the encounter with Jezebel, have never sounded so electrifying. For that we have to thank Rilling's disciplined chorus biting in diction, precise and convincing in attack. Yet they can also provide the most sensitive, ethereal tone, as in Nos 28 and 29, trio and chorus, 'Siehe, der Hüter Israels'.

The orchestral playing is no less arresting. Furthermore, as Elijah, Schöne unerringly or authoritatively captures his many moods. Here is the courageous man of action as he confronts Baal's followers and ironically taunts them, the sense of fiery conviction in 'Ist's nichts des Herrn Wort', of doubt in 'Es ist genug', and finally the wonderful Bachian serenity in 'Ja, es sollen wohl Berge weichen', all evoked in the most positive and imaginative delivery of the text. The voice itself, a firm, expressive bass-baritone, is ideal for the role, one on which the singer has obviously lavished much time and consideration – to excellent effect. The same can be said for Schäfer, who brings a Silja-like conviction to all her work. Anyone hearing her declaim 'Weiche nicht' would never be afraid again. The voice itself is interesting, gleaming and yet not without a fair degree of warmth in the tone.

Kallisch is almost as convincing in the mezzo solos and gives us a wonderfully malign portrayal of Jezebel. Schade is a fresh-voiced, communicative Obadiah, and he's another who's vivid with his words. The recording, however, is slightly too reverberant, but the added space around the voices doesn't preclude immediacy of impact.

Gian-Carlo Menotti American 1911-2007

An American composer of Italian origin, Menotti studied at the Milan Conservatory and the Curtis Institute (with Scalero, 1928-33), where a co-student was Samuel Barber, his close friend for whom he later wrote librettos. He won success with his comic one-act opera Amelia al ballo (1937), which was taken up by the Met in 1938 and led to an NBC commission for a radio opera, The Old Maid and the Thief (1939). A grand opera, The Island God (1942, Met), was a failure; but it was followed after the war by the chamber opera The Medium (1946), a supernatural tragedy notable for its sinister atmosphere; it was paired with his short comedy The Telephone (1947) for a Broadway run of 211 performances, 1947-8. The full-scale political melodrama The Consul (1950), in a post-Puccini verismo style, and The Saint of Bleecker Street (1954), an effective drama in the same serious style, enjoyed much success, as had the television Christmas opera Amahl and the Night Visitors (1951). His later works include more operas and orchestral pieces, including several works for children written in a direct and appealing style. More ambitious works (such as Goya, 1986), have been criticised as musically thin and too derivative. In 1958 he founded the Spoleto Festival of Two Worlds, which he directed until 1967. GROVE*music*

Violin Concerto

Violin Concerto[a]. The Death of Orpheus[b]. Muero porque no muero[c]. Oh llama de amor viva[d]
[c]**Julia Melinek** sop [b]**Jamie MacDougall** ten
[d]**Stephen Roberts** bar [a]**Jennifer Koh** vn
[bcd]**Spoleto Festival Choir and Orchestra /
Richard Hickox**
Chandos CHAN9979 (61' · DDD)   Ⓟ▣➡

Gian-Carlo Menotti's lyrical Violin Concerto, one of his most popular instrumental works, is here neatly coupled with premiere recordings of three cantatas written in the last 20 years, products of his active old age in his seventies and eighties. Hickox draws from the Festival

Orchestra warmly persuasive readings of works which may be unashamedly eclectic, but are powerfully convincing in such committed performances. The young American violinist, Jennifer Koh, is the excellent soloist. The first movement with its sequence of flowing melodies could easily seem to meander, but Koh and Hickox give it a clear shape, with each new idea emerging seductively. The slow movement, played with hushed dedication, has a tender poignancy here; an intrusive brass motif leads to the central cadenza, technically demanding but not showy. The vigorous finale features a jaunty main theme and ends with virtuoso fireworks, rounding off a piece that deserves resurrecting in the concert-hall too.

The two Spanish language cantatas were written respectively in 1982 and 1991 for the Catholic University in Washington. Menotti confesses to having lost his religious faith, and perhaps understandably here writes sensuous music closer to Puccini's opera, *Suor Angelica*, than to any religious model. Julia Melinek is the vibrant soloist in the St Teresa setting, with her marked vibrato well-controlled. Stephen Roberts, the responsive soloist in the St John of the Cross setting, is caught less happily, his voice ill focused.

The Death of Orpheus, to an English text by Menotti himself, is even more dramatic, based on the legend of Orpheus being killed by Thracian women in a bacchanalian frenzy. Orpheus's song emerges as a broad diatonic melody, with choral writing of Delian sensuousness and the tenor's part with Britten-like echoes. Jamie MacDougall is the expressive soloist, with the chorus fresh and incisive in all three cantatas.

Operas

Help, Help, the Globolinks!
Edith Mathis sop Emily **Arlene Saunders** sop
Madame Euterpova **Raymond Wolansky** bar Dr
Stone **William Workman** bar Tony **Kurt Marschner**
ten Timothy
**North German Radio Children's Choir; Hamburg
Philharmonic State Orchestra / Matthias Kuntzsch**
Stage director **Gian Carlo Menotti**
Video director **Joachim Hess**
ArtHaus Musik 🔲 101 281 (71' · NTSC · 4:3 · PCM
mono · 0) Recorded 1969   Ⓕ

Directed by the composer with all the colourful melodrama of an American B-movie, the soloists of Hamburg's late-1960s house ensemble get a real chance to shine in what is virtually the world premiere of Menotti's children's sci-fi opera. In the libretto – a jolly collision between *The War of the Worlds*, the Munchkins from the land of Oz and *Hansel and Gretel* – only (tonal) music and musicians can save the earth from the invading Globolinks and their electronic (ie, non-musical) voices. Nikolas Schöffler (lighting) and Alwin Nikolais (costumes and Globolink choreography) make essential contributions to the visual realisation of the aliens as sinister, flexible lampshades, and the creation of a spooky atmosphere a cut above most contemporary TV series.

The score is an eclectic mix of Menotti's trademark second-generation *verismo* – handy for the tantrums of the principal role, Madame Euterpova, a wacky mid-European music teacher – and Kurt Weill-like recitative and marching rhythms for the children and their driver whose school trip goes astray in the forest. This musical storytelling has a compelling narrative simplicity which, like Benjamin Britten's, never becomes saccharine or patronising. The characters, especially the three supporting teachers, have a pleasing Roald Dahl wackiness, making them natural stage roles.

It's not everyday you get to see Edith Mathis as a violin-playing schoolgirl, or Arlene Saunders (the company's Agathe and Eva) as the eccentric music teacher with a *Bewitched*-style nose. Wolansky too is genuinely funny as the confused, and unmusical, head of the school who becomes the one human sacrifice to the Globolinks. Sterling digital restoration seconds the fine balance of the production between comic and serious, making for an unintended but most effective tribute to Menotti's wide-ranging theatrical creativity.

The Telephone **Poulenc** La voix humaine
Carole Farley sop **Russell Smythe** bar
Scottish Chamber Orchestra / José Serebrier
Video Artists International **DVD** VAIDVD4374
(65' · 4:3 · PCM stereo · 0)   Ⓕ

Menotti's 1947 curtain-raiser about the girl who can't be torn away from the telephone makes an ideal opera for television. While Carole Farley as Lucy receives three incoming calls – each presented as an aria – Russell Smythe as Ben tries to propose marriage. In the end, the only way he can get her attention is to go downstairs to the local diner and call her on a pay-phone. His look of bewildered exasperation as she gabbles on with her friends now seems very up-to-date. Who has not witnessed similar scenes, one half of a duo twiddling their thumbs as their partner natters on a mobile?

Poulenc's monodrama presents more of a challenge. The setting, too, is very well detailed, suggesting the emptiness of the woman's life, the bottle of pills on the bedside table, the bathroom door ajar. The emotions on display in Cocteau's text, though, are too big to be easily contained in the intimate medium of video. Inevitably, the camera is mostly focused on Farley's face, and though her acting is very fine, all the facial gestures and eye-rolling seem too much and her voice too loud for the small bedroom.

Sound and picture are excellent; José Serebrier and the SCO enter into all the light-heartedness of the Menotti, and hold back until the big orchestral climaxes in the Poulenc. It's hard to imagine a a better version of *The Telephone* coming along, but for *La voix humaine* we must wait for the release of the 1970 film with Poulenc's original interpreter, Denise Duval.

Aarre Merikanto   Finnish 1893-1958

Aarre Merikanto, son of the composer Oskar Merikanto (1868-1924), studied with Reger in Leipzig (1912-14) and Vasilenko in Moscow (1915-16), and taught at the Helsinki Academy (1936-58). His opera Juha (1922) invites comparison with Janáček; other works, in a highly coloured, chromatic style, include three symphonies (1916, 1918, 1953), three piano concertos (1913, 1937, 1955) and chamber music. GROVEmusic

---

Piano Concertos

Piano Concertos Nos 2 & 3. Two Studies. Two Pieces
Matti Raekallio pf
Tampere Philharmonic Orchestra / Tuomas Ollila
Ondine ODE915-2 (55' · DDD)   Ⓕ

Merikanto's Second and Third Piano Concertos (from 1937-8 and 1955 respectively) are typical of his later output – contrapuntally inventive and impressionistic in scoring. Both have an engaging Prokofievan brio in the brisk outer movements and a Rachmaninovesque Romanticism in the lyrical central *adagios*. Yet Merikanto never entirely forsook his adventurous harmonic writing, and especially in the Second the result – allied to considerable formal lassitude – is suggestive of (of all people) Villa-Lobos. Granted it's with a Nordic not a Brazilian accent, but think here of works such as *Momoprecoce* and *Bachiana* No 3 as much as the piano concertos; those who know both will appreciate the similarity.

Matti Raekallio is a pianist of real technical ability and musical sensibility. He has the measure of both concertos, and the Second in particular could well become popular as an alternative to Prokofiev's Third or the *Paganini* Rhapsody. The purely orchestral *Two Studies* and *Two Pieces* (1941), though much slighter affairs, are by no means insignificant trifles. Tuomas Ollila secures more than competent performances from the Tampere orchestra, matched by excellent sound. A real delight.

Pan, Op 28

Lemminkäinen, Op 10. Pan, Op 28. Four Compositions. Andante religioso. Scherzo
Tampere Philharmonic Orchestra / Tuomas Ollila
Ondine ODE905-2 (54' · DDD)   Ⓕ

Aarre Merikanto's career divided broadly into three phases, those of apprentice, radical and conservative, and there are works from each present on this valuable issue. Critical hindsight accords (quite rightly) that the brief radical phase, roughly corresponding to the 1920s, was the most valuable, though at the time Merikanto's modernistic approach – and that of his like-minded contemporaries, Ernest Pingoud and Väinö Raito – was derided. Only one piece here represents this period, the highly accomplished tone-poem, *Pan* (1924), a wonderful, evocative, yet robust score, possessed of a very Nordic brand of impressionism. *Lemminkäinen* (1916), by contrast, seems immature, and rather parochial. A Sibelian shadow lies heavily across its quarter-hour duration, yet without a trace of the older composer's own *Lemminkäinen* tone-poems. There's little of the latter's emotional and psychological depth – or musical range – but instead a prevailing rollicking good humour broken occasionally by more serious moments. The remaining works all date from the early stages of Merikanto's post-modern period, when he reverted to a simpler, more accessible idiom. The *Four Compositions* (1932) make a very effective and satisfying set, and whereas the *Andante religioso* (1933) seems like a piece out of context, the *Scherzo* (1937) is entirely convincing on its own. The performances are sympathetic and well recorded.

Olivier Messiaen French 1908-1992

Messiaen studied at the Paris Conservatoire (1919-30) with Dukas, Emmanuel and Dupré, and taught there (1941-78) while also serving as organist of La Trinité in Paris. Right from his first published work, the eight Preludes for piano (1929), he was using his own modal system, with its strong flavouring of tritones, diminished 7ths and augmented triads. During the 1930s he added a taste for rhythmic irregularity and for the rapid changing of intense colours, in both orchestral and organ works. Most of his compositions were explicitly religious and divided between characteristic styles of extremely slow meditation, bounding dance and the objective unfolding of arithmetical systems. They include the orchestral L'ascension (1933), the organ cycles La nativité du Seigneur (1935) and Les corps glorieux (1939), the song cycles Poèmes pour Mi (1936) and Chants de terre et de ciel (1938), and the culminating work of this period, the Quatuor pour la fin du temps for clarinet, violin, cello and piano (1941).

During the war he found himself surrounded by an eager group of students, including Boulez and Yvonne Loriod, who eventually became his second wife. For her pianistic brilliance he conceived the Visions de l'amen (1943, with a second piano part for himself) and the Vingt regards sur l'enfant Jésus (1944), followed by an exuberant triptych on the theme of erotic love: the song cycle Harawi (1945), the Turangalîla-symphonie with solo piano and ondes martenot (1948) and the Cinq rechants for small chorus (1949). Meanwhile the serial adventures of Boulez and others were also making a mark, and Messiaen produced his most abstract, atonal and irregular music in the Quatre études de rythme for piano (1949) and the Livre d'orgue (1951).

His next works were based largely on his own adaptations of birdsongs: they include Réveil des oiseaux for piano and orchestra (1953), Oiseaux exotiques for piano, wind and percussion (1956), the immense Catalogue d'oiseaux for solo piano (1958) and the orchestral Chronochromie (1960). In these, and in

his Japanese postcards, Sept haïkaï for piano and small orchestra (1962), he continued to follow his junior contemporaries, but then returned to religious subjects in works that bring together all aspects of his music. These include another small-scale piano concerto, Couleurs de la cité céleste (1963), and monumental Et exspecto resurrectionem mortuorum for wind and percussion (1964). Thereafter he devoted himself to a sequence of works on the largest scale: the choral-orchestral La Transfiguration (1969), the organ volumes Méditations sur le mystère de la Sainte Trinité (1969), the 12-movement piano concerto Des canyons aux étoiles (1974) and the opera Saint François d'Assise (1983). GROVEmusic

Collections

'1908-1992 – 100th Anniversary Box Set'
Artists include **Michèle Command, Ann Murray** sops **Philip Langridge** ten **Emmanuel Pahud** fl **Wolfgang Meyer** cl **Christoph Poppen, Andrew Watkinson** vn **Manuel Fischer-Dieskau** vc **Jeanne Loriod, Cynthia Millar** ondes **Martha Argerich, Michel Béroff, Rolf Hind, Yvonne Loriod, John Ogdon, Marie-Madeleine Petit, Alexandre Rabinovitch, Roger Vignoles** pfs **Olivier Messiaen, Naji Hakim** orgs **BBC SO / Dorati; BPO / Rattle; London Sinfonietta / Edwards; LSO / Previn; Orch de Paris / Baudo**
EMI ⑭ 217466-2 (15h 40' · ADD/DDD) ⓈⒺ

'Les premiers enregistrements, 1956-1963'
Oiseaux exotiques. Turangalîla-Symphonie. Quatuor pour la fin du temps. Visions de l'Amen. Catalogue d'oiseaux. Cantéyodjayâ. Vingt regards sur l'Enfant-Jésus. Sept Haïkaï
Artists include **André Vacellier** cl **Jean Pasquier** vn **Etienne Pasquier** vc **Olivier Messiaen, Yvonne Loriod** pfs **Jeanne Loriod** onde **Percussion de Strasbourg; Domaine Musicale Orchestra / Pierre Boulez; ORTF National Orchestra / Maurice Le Roux**
Accord ⑦ 480 1045 (8h 4' · ADD) Ⓢ

The 14-CD EMI set is one of those incredibly useful, disarmingly cheap, completist pull-togethers, this one boasting classic Messiaen moments like Previn's 1977 *Turangalîla-Symphonie*, Dorati's penetrating 1964 *Chronochromie*, Rattle's *Eclairs sur l'Au-delà*, Martha Argerich's and Alexandre Rabinovitch's *Visions de l'Amen* and Messiaen's own performances of his organ works.

For those wanting to look deeper into Messiaen's evolution and history, the Accord set of early recordings featuring Messiaen, Loriod and contemporary acolytes is essential. The set begins with Messiaen's and Loriod's 1962 recording of *Visions de l'Amen* (their second version; an original 1949 account is lost to hopeless sound) and it's a cunningly paced, keenly nuanced performance where articulation and timbre have been carefully considered. Loriod's 1956 account of the *Vingt regards* has a thrilling atmosphere of discovery, and the *Catalogue d'oiseaux* she cut in '59 has bravura attack,

MESSIAEN TURANGALÎLA-SYMPHONIE – IN BRIEF

Donohoe; Murail; CBSO / Rattle
EMI 586525-2   ⓂⓄ➔
Rattle's innate feeling for orchestral colour combined with his skill in negotiating huge and complex scores pays off richly with a fine modern recording. Coupled with the *Quartet for the End of Time* and *La merle*.

Crossley; Murail; Philharmonia / Salonen
Sony Classical SBK89900   Ⓑ➔
Recorded at almost exactly the same time as the Rattle, his contemporary Esa-Pekka Salonen takes a similarly probing approach. Beautiful, silky playing by the Philharmonia and, again, superb soloists.

Aimard; Kim; BPO / Nagano
Teldec 2564 62162-2   ⒻＯＯＯ
Nagano draws playing of quite thrilling excitement from the great Berlin orchestra: maybe they'd never played it before, but they give it 150 per cent. Pierre-Laurent Aimard throws off the piano part with typical aplomb. The top recommendation.

Thibaudet; Harada;
Royal Concertgebouw / Chailly
Decca 436 626-2DH   ⒻＯ➔
If you want to hear this amazing score as never before, try this SACD remix: the Concertgebouw Orchestra relish the contrasts and the beautiful acoustic of their hall adds its own magic.

Weigl; Bloch; Polish Nat RSO / Wit
Naxos 8 554478/9   ⓈＯ➔
A boldy recorded and played performance that makes the most of the work's dynamic and emotional extremes. Wit couples it, more logically, with *L'ascension*. A fine bargain alternative to the single-CD Salonen.

Shelley; Hartmann-Claverie; BBC PO /
Y P Tortelier
Chandos CHAN9678   Ⓕ
Often overlooked by more seemingly glamorous line-ups, this is a fine modern version in typically glorious sound. The BBC Philharmonic sounds really world-class.

Y Loriod; J Loriod; Bastille Opera Orch /
M-W Chung
DG 431 781-2GH   Ⓕ➔
An 'authentic' performance, perhaps, with Messiaen's widow playing the piano. Chung shows himself a natural Messiaen interpreter and draws from his Bastille orchestra some wonderfully idomatic playing.

although her later Erato set is more seasoned.

In the mid-1950s Pierre Boulez's Domain Musical society gave many Messiaen premieres, and Boulez's account of the insanely exacting *Sept Haïkaï* and a joyous performance of *Oiseaux exotiques* from Rudolf Albert, recorded at Domaine Musical events, enjoy a marvellous sense of time and place. Messiaen's own recording of the *Quartet for the End of Time*, featuring cellist Etienne Pasquier (with whom he was interred in Stalag VIII-A), is technically wobbly and shrill by modern standards, but has a rooted emotional authenticity that never tries too hard to make its point. The only low-point is Maurice Le Roux's *Turangalîla*: an apparently fine performance, but the recording is so lamely transferred it's impossible to tell either way.

Turangalîla-symphonie

Turangalîla Symphonie (1990 revised version)
Pierre-Laurent Aimard *pf* **Dominique Kim** *ondes*
Berlin Philharmonic Orchestra / Kent Nagano
Teldec 8573 82043-2 (73' · DDD)   ⒻＯＯＯ

Turangalîla is a difficult score, and to record it live is risky. Even when the orchestra is the Berlin Philharmonic? Yes, since the work is very far from the centre of their repertoire. Whether despite or because of that risk this is a splendidly exciting performance; more surprisingly it's also for the most part a very accurate and detailed one. The textures and colours of the third movement are finely balanced, as they are even in the headlong exuberance of its successor. Although the precision of the seventh seems to understate its balefulness the complex textures and superimposed rhythms of the ninth are outstandingly clear and fascinating. The soloists are admirable; the extremes of the piano part, in particular, are just what Aimard is good at. There are one or two imprecisions of balance, but this is among the two or three best accounts of *Turangalîla* available.

Et exspecto resurrectionem...

Et exspecto resurrectionem mortuorum.
Chronochromie. La ville d'en-haut
Cleveland Orchestra / Pierre Boulez
DG 445 827-2GH (58' · DDD)   ⒻＯ➔

Boulez has spoken of his pleasure at performing Messiaen with an orchestra relatively unfamiliar with his music. It sounds as though the Cleveland Orchestra must have enjoyed it too. You would expect them to, perhaps, in such a passage as that in the fourth movement of *Et exspecto*, where the two superimposed plainchant melodies return together with the noble 'theme of the depths' – it has great splendour, as does the chorale melody of the finale, rising at the end to a satisfyingly palpable *fffff*. And in this performance of *Chronochromie* you can hear why Messiaen said that certain pages of it were a double homage to Berlioz and Pierre Schaeffer, the

French pioneer of electronic music. In the work's penultimate section, the famous 'Epode' in which 18 string players impersonate different birds, the obvious problems of clarity and precision are expertly negotiated: the players really seem to enjoy their dawn chorus.

Absolute rhythmic precision and the clarity of colour that comes from meticulous balance are among the other pleasures of these performances. They make a most satisfying coupling, too. The recordings are excellent: clean but not clinical and ample in range.

Visions de l'Amen

Visions de l'Amen[a]. Fantaisie burlesque. Pièce pour le tombeau de Paul Dukas. Rondeau
Steven Osborne, [a]**Martin Roscoe** pfs
Hyperion CDA67366 (61' · DDD) ⒻⓄ

It's axiomatic (to use a favourite word of the French) that the Messiaens' own 1962 disc of *Visions* is irreplaceable. At the same time it raises the common interpretative problem when composers play their own music: should we follow what they say in musical and verbal notes, or what they do?

Such problems don't arise with the three early pieces, which hardly show Messiaen at his best, but the metronome mark for the very slow first movement of *Visions*, which literally sets the groundwork for the cycle, dictates a duration of 6'15". He and his wife, Yvonne Loriod, dispatch it in 4'30". Steven Osborne and Martin Roscoe (like the old Regis recording by Peter Hill and Benjamin Frith) prefer to believe the score, and the result is an impressively relentless sweep from the faintest *pppp* to a searing *fff*.

Messiaen's library was full of astonomical picture-books, and his interpretation of the whole work brings out the violence and local disorder involved in the act of creation, even if the ultimate goal (here, a resplendent A major chord) is always in view. This superbly engineered Hyperion disc is true to his Technicolor vision.

Indeed, it's in the rich and immediate piano sound that this version scores most notably over Hill and Frith's, where the playing is no less accurate or intense. Particularly beautiful is a sudden *pianissimo* early in the fourth movement, and there are some decidedly upfront birds from Osborne in the next. (Messiaen always insisted that townspeople, who knew only the sparrow, had no idea how deafening birds in a forest could be.) In the final movement Osborne and Roscoe throw authenticity aside; their *Modéré, joyeux* goes uninhibitedly for the second epithet. And wonderfully exciting it is.

Catalogue d'oiseaux

Catalogue d'oiseaux
Roger Muraro pf
Accord ② 465 768-2 (DDD) ⒻⓄ

Muraro demonstrates both formidable pianism and an outstandingly imaginative response to Messiaen's imaginative world. The dynamic range is wide, the colouring often subtly beautiful, the virtuosity quite breathtaking at times. The virtuoso and the poet are in ideal balance here – magnificent rocky landscapes, vivid greens and blues! This is an outstanding reading throughout, and one can only echo the audience's applause after 'The Wood Lark' and their cheers at 'Cetti's Warbler'. Recommended.

Huit préludes

Huit préludes. Etudes de rythme – No 1, Île de feu I; No 4, Île de feu II. Vingt regards sur l'Enfant-Jésus – No 4, Regard de la Vierge; No 10, Regard de l'esprit de joie; No 15, Le baiser de l'Enfant-Jésus
Angela Hewitt pf
Hyperion CDA67054 (76' · DDD) Ⓕ

Hewitt has few equals in Messiaen. The very early *Préludes* (Messiaen was studying with Dukas when he wrote them) mightn't seem the ideal repertory in which to demonstrate this, but she plays them with exquisitely controlled colour, clarity and eager love for the music. In this performance they're full of luminous shot and shaded colours that are typical of the mature Messiaen, and in the final virtuoso number she seems even to have discovered an early draft for a theme in the *Turangalîla* Symphony. Her melodic lines are strong, her sonorities rich, but her loud playing is never noisy or forced. She has that crucial quality needed of a Messiaen pianist: patience. Patience to let a chord register and fade, patience never to pre-empt a climax. In the two *Île de feu* pieces she shows that she can produce hard-edged sonorities as well as subtle ones. And all her gifts as a Messiaen pianist are evident in 'Le baiser de l'Enfant-Jésus': the tempo is patient, the contemplation rapt, the embellishments delicately precise, with a magical change of colour as the sunlit *hortus conclusus* at the centre of the movement is reached. The recording is finely sensitive to the exceptional beauty of Hewitt's sound.

Préludes. Catalogue d'oiseaux – Book 3 No 6, L'Alouette Lulu; Book 5 No 9, La Bouscarle. Quatre études de rythme – Ile de feu 1; Ile de feu 2
Pierre-Laurent Aimard pf
DG 477 7452GH (60' · DDD) ⒻⓄ▸

Pierre-Laurent Aimard knew Messiaen and studied with Yvonne Loriod, yet these personal associations result in playing of intense sobriety. Indeed, the initial impression, in the first of the early *Préludes*, is of unusual restraint. While pianists anxious to underline the links with Debussy often opt for impressionistic washes of sound, Aimard achieves insight through clarity, a quality aided by superb sound-recording, with a rich range of meticulously graded dynamic levels, and just the right amount of space and resonance around the instrument.

Aimard's technical virtuosity comes through in the evenness of his voicing and the pearly delicacy with which Messiaen's intricate ornamental writing is projected. Nevertheless, when turbulence and incisiveness are required, as in the *Ile de feu* studies, they emerge naturally and inevitably. Aimard never polishes away the rough edges of this music, and one only wishes that the other pair of studies in rhythm had also been included.

Messiaen was at his most ambitious in the grand perspectives of the 13-movement *Catalogue d'oiseaux*, and the two items included here offer a particularly strong contrast. With 'La Bouscarle' – so much more mellifluous a title in French than 'Cetti's Warbler' – diversity is paramount, and although Aimard is characteristically lucid and uncompromising, not least in his timing of the silences near the end, this piece never seems one of the composer's more cogent inspirations. On the other hand, the ravishing alternation of chorales and cadenzas in 'L'Alouette Lulu' ('The Woodlark') is marvellously sustained in this mesmerising account, a miracle of tonal refinement and digital fluency. It caps a disc that promises to give ever more subtle rewards on repeated hearing.

Vingt regards sur l'enfant Jésus

Vingt regards sur l'enfant Jésus
Pierre-Laurent Aimard pf
Teldec ② 3984-26868-2 (116' · DDD)   Ⓕ**OO**

Any review of the *Vingt regards* should begin by discussing how well the pianist conveys the cycle's visionary awe and builds its disparate sections into a true cycle. But here the virtuosity is so remarkable that even listeners with a profound distaste for Messiaen – for whom the 15th *Regard* ('The kiss of the infant Jesus') is a by-word for sentimental religiosity – may listen open-mouthed. Sheer virtuosity is an important part of the cycle's language: one of the functions of *Regard* No 6 ('By Him all was made') is to astonish, and the power and excitement of Aimard's playing are indeed astonishing. Virtuosity is also desirable if Messiaen's demands for a huge palette of colour and orchestral or super-orchestral sonorities are to be met. In No 14 ('The gaze of the angels') his notes evoke 'powerful blasts of immense trombones'; Aimard's prodigious range of timbre and dynamic provide just the sound that Messiaen must have imagined. The penultimate *Regard* makes a more extreme demand: that in the hushed coda the player should recall a passage from the *Fioretti* of St Francis where 'the angel drew his bow across the string and produced a note so sweet that if he had continued I should have died of joy'. Here the effect is suggested not by virtuosity but intense concentration, stillness and purity of colour. Could it have been a little slower? Possibly; Aimard's timing is faster than most and a few of his silences could have been held longer but his dazzling technique and fabulous range of colour make this the most spectacular reading of the *Vingt regards* yet.

Vingt regards sur l'enfant Jésus
Steven Osborne pf
Hyperion ② CDA67351/2 (127' · DDD)   Ⓕ**OOO**

 There are a number of recordings of *Vingt Regards* available, most of them very good indeed. Even the finest, though, provoke very slight reservations: an occasional suspicion of hurry in Pierre-Laurent Aimard's outstanding account, a few misjudgments in Roger Muraro's, and so on. There are no such reservations about the reading by Steven Osborne, who's revealed as a pianist of exceptional gifts.

Messiaen's widow, Yvonne Loriod, invited Osborne to study the work with her after she heard him playing other music by her late husband. One can hear throughout not only her influence but, even more, the qualities in his playing that led her to make the offer. His command of sonority is prodigious: if you've never been able to take Messiaen's talk about the 'colour' of particular chords seriously, then Osborne's playing may change your mind. He also has a remarkable dynamic range. These two qualities combine to provide both clarity and a tremendous climax in the virtuoso quasi-fugal textures of No 6 ('By Him was everything made') and, at the other end of the spectrum, to make perfect sense of Messiaen's description of the opening bars of No 17 ('The Gaze of Silence'): 'The music seems to emerge from silence as colours emerge from the night.' Nor is he insensible to the fact that some of the *Regards* are frankly showy. No 10 ('Gaze of the Spirit of Joy') is dazzling; No 16 ('Gaze of the Prophets, the Shepherds and the Magi') is barbarously colourful. Perhaps most significant of all, he finds in No 15 ('The kiss of the child Jesus') not only the sweet quietness of its opening but the spectacular Lisztian display of its later pages. The recording is ideally responsive to the wide range of sound he draws from the instrument.

Additional recommendation

Complete Keyboard Works
Hill pf
Regis ⑦ RRC7001 (8 hours 5' · DDD) Recorded mid-1980s (also available separately)   Ⓑ
Peter Hill delivers immaculate readings of some of the most technically and philosophically challenging works in the repertoire. The series enjoyed the close support of Messiaen, and you can hear why. The sound in the early volumes occasionally suffers from too close a recording.

Complete Organ Works

Complete Organ Works
Jennifer Bate org
Regis ⑥ RRC6001 (454' · DDD) Recorded on the organs of L'Eglise de la Sainte-Trinité, Paris, and St Pierre de Beauvais Cathedral, 1981, 1983, 1987   Ⓑ**O**

Messiaen was of towering importance to the world of 20th-century music, yet the seven-and a-half hours of his compositions for organ are a salutary reminder of how little time he had for that century's secular and humanistic aspirations. It's therefore only proper that recordings of the organ works should be made in church, not concert hall or studio. Jennifer Bate made the first recording of Messiaen's last and longest cycle, *Livre du Saint Sacrement*, switching from Beauvais to the composer's own Parisian church, Sainte-Trinité. Though hailed as 'a monumental achievement' when new, later judgements have been more critical.

Bate's set stands up well, especially in the *Livre du Saint Sacrement*, where she relishes the extraordinary diversity of material and mood even more intensely than the cooler though never-less-than commanding Olivier Latry (DG). The other large-scale later cycle, *Méditations sur le mystère de la Sainte Trinité*, reinforces this basic distinction between the two interpreters, and although Latry has the more refined instrument and the more sophisticated recording, his slow tempos (Messiaen never gives metronome marks) can seem too slow, as in the eighth *Méditation*, 'Dieu est simple – les Trois sont Un'. Bate's set makes an excellent bargain-price recommendation.

Livre du Saint Sacrement

Livre du Saint Sacrement
Michael Bonaventure *org*
Delphian ② DCD34076 (117' · DDD)
Played on the Rieger organ of St Giles's Cathedral,
Edinburgh   Ⓕ

Michael Bonaventure's complete Messiaen project (this is Volume 3) returns to St Giles's Cathedral in Edinburgh and its stunning Rieger organ, which dates from 1992.

Messiaen's farewell to the organ, the *Livre du Saint Sacrement*, was composed in 1984-85 and first performed by Almut Rössler in Detroit in 1986. Messiaen spoke of this *Book of the Blessed Sacrament* as a summation of the experience gained from improvising each Sunday at the Église de la Saint-Trinité in Paris, where he was organist for over 60 years. There is no shortage of familiar Messiaenic thumbprints: dislocated ideas, meandering dribbles of plainsong, chirpy birdsong, slow, development-less sudden and spectacular bolts of anger; and those endlessly messy chords that desperately need to resolve.

Playing from memory, Bonaventure takes just under two hours, slightly longer than Olivier Latry at Notre-Dame (DG). Movements 1-4 serve as a prelude or ante-Communion. Movements 5-11 follow events in the life of Jesus, and 12-18 contemplate the mysteries of the Sacrament.

This uneven, over-long piece poses considerable challenges to both player and listener, there being few moments of comfortable repose. The more athletic passages (for example in the Alleluia final – originally entitled 'La Visitation') bounce along with a redeeming joy.

Despite the generous acoustic the Rieger organ is recorded cleanly. It is especially effective in the echo effects in the short fourth movement, 'Acte de Foi'.

La nativité du Seigneur

La Nativité du Seigneur. Apparition de l'église
éternelle. Le banquet céleste.
Gillian Weir *org*
Priory PRCD921 (75' · DDD) Recorded on the 1928
Frobenius organ of Århus Cathedral 1994   ⓂⓄ

Remastered, these outstanding recordings made in Århus Cathedral are a model of how to combine atmosphere and clarity in this music, and no other player seems quite to equal Weir's remarkable identification with the reflective and dramatically explosive extremes of Messiaen's idiom. At the risk of being accused of heresy, it's possible to doubt whether *La Nativité du Seigneur* really works as a compositional whole, given the surely undeniable imbalance between mediative and more dynamic music. But Weir evidently has no such doubts, sustaining the long, quiet episodes with particular sensitivity and irresistible conviction: if you're to perform the work complete, this is how it has to be. So, despite the achievements of both Olivier Latry and Jennifer Bate across the full range of Messiaen's organ works, Gillian Weir's performances again claim the definitive status which they were accorded when they were first released.

La nativité du Seigneur. Le banquet céleste
Jennifer Bate *org*
Unicorn-Kanchana DKPCD9005 (62' · DDD)
Recorded on the organ of Beauvais Cathedral 1980
     ⒻⓄ

La nativité du Seigneur comprises nine meditations on themes associated with the birth of the Lord. Messiaen's unique use of registration gives these pieces an extraordinarily wide range of colour and emotional potency and in Bate's hands (and feet) it finds one of its most persuasive advocates. She was much admired by the composer and is so far the only organist to have recorded his complete works for the instrument. *Le banquet céleste* was Messiaen's first published work for the organ and is a magical, very slow-moving meditation on a verse from St John's Gospel (VI, 56). The faithful recording captures both the organ and the large acoustic of Beauvais Cathedral to marvellous effect.

Le banquet céleste

Apparition de l'église éternelle. Le banquet céleste.
Les corps glorieux
Timothy Byram-Wigfield *org*
Delphian DCD34024 (65' · DDD). Played on the organ

of St George's Chapel, Windsor Castle   Ⓕ

Timothy Byram-Wigfield's programme highlights Messiaen's earlier works, the main emphasis falling on the seven-movement sequence from 1939, *Les corps glorieux*. It's clear from the outset that this will be a strongly delineated reading, with well managed contrasts of registration given added clarity by the superb quality of the recording. It's a very physical sound but the vibrating beats of sustained notes are never oppressive, and the reading has a sense of direction and purpose which even manages to make a compelling experience out of the 15-minute central movement, 'Combat de la Mort et de la Vie'.

The two shorter pieces are well contrasted, with *Le banquet céleste* given a satisfying build-up, and *Apparition de l'église éternelle* magnificently forthright and implacable. This is a highly successful disc and augurs well for Byram-Wigfield's projected survey of Messiaen's early organ music.

Saint François d'Assise

Saint François d'Assise
Dawn Upshaw *sop* L'Ange **José Van Dam** *bass-bar*
Saint François **Chris Merritt** *ten* Le Lépreux **Urban Malmberg** *bar* Frère Léon **John Aler** *ten* Frère Massée **Guy Renard** *ten* Frère Elie **Tom Krause** *bar* Frère Bernard **Akos Banlaky** *ten* Frère Sylvestre **Dirk d'Ase** *bass* Frère Rufin **Jeanne Loriod, Valerie Hartmann-Claverie, Dominique Kim** *ondes martenots* Arnold Schoenberg Choir; Hallé Orchestra / Kent Nagano
DG 20/21 ④ 445 176-2GH4 (236' · DDD· N/T/t) Ⓕ**OO**

The breakthrough for Messiaen's only opera came with the Salzburg Festival production unveiled in August 1992, Esa-Pekka Salonen conducting. Van Dam and his monks still wore habits, but Peter Sellars's production concept broke with the composer's 'realistic' Umbrian spectacle to put Dawn Upshaw's Angel in a grey business suit, while his trademark video monitors relayed associated imagery. He even invented a second Angel, one that doesn't exist in the score, who dances and mimes.

Nagano took up the reins for the 1998 Salzburg revival as captured here in DG's live recording, and there's no mistaking the remarkable authority and technical self-confidence of the results. Van Dam's definitive Saint François is a remarkable achievement for an artist on the cusp of his sixth decade and his identification with the role is profound. Upshaw too is well cast, with just enough tonal weight to underpin her fresh, ardent, mobile singing. It's mostly plain sailing in the subsidiary roles, although Malmberg's French is still as dodgy as the choir's. The musicians of the Hallé have been drilled to the peak of perfection, closely scrutinised by vivid, upfront sound that doesn't always give their glittering sonorities a natural perspective in which to expand.

All Messiaen's trademarks are here: the birdsong, the modal rigour (especially for the word setting which is crystal clear), the basic triads given new harmonic context and heft, the post-Stravinskian dances. There are also distant echoes of *Boris Godunov* and *Pelléas et Mélisande*. Uninitiated listeners should perhaps try Act 1 scene 3 (the curing of the leper) where the mosaic construction permits a breathtaking conjunction of ideas from timeless chant through 1960s modernism, to childlike eruptions of joy and premonitions of holy minimalism. *Saint François d'Assise* can make *Parsifal* seem like an intermezzo, but it exerts a uniquely hypnotic spell. Strongly recommended.

Giacomo Meyerbeer
German 1791-1864

Meyerbeer was born into a wealthy Jewish merchant family in Berlin and studied composition with Zelter (1805), B. A. Weber (1808) and Abbé Vogler in Darmstadt (1810-11), winning success more as a pianist than a composer. After a study tour in Italy (1816-25), where he met artists, librettists and impresarios and wrote six notable operas (especially the impressive Il crociato in Egitto, 1824), he gained a reputation equal to Rossini's. From 1825 he worked chiefly in Paris but was always on the move, taking cures, producing his operas in major European cities and auditioning new singers; in 1842, indisputably the world's leading active opera composer, he became Prussian Generalmusikdirektor – he was dismissed in 1848 but directed the Berlin royal court music until his death. Having first conquered the Paris Opéra with the five-act Robert le diable (1831), he and his most important collaborator Eugène Scribe created the famous Les Huguenots (1836), then began work on Le prophète and L'africaine, both of which suffered long delays from casting difficulties; Le prophète was eventually received enthusiastically with Pauline Viardot as Fidès (1849), while the premiere of L'africaine (1865) became a brilliant posthumous tribute to its composer.

Cultivating a consistently realistic style, 'expressive monumentalism', Meyerbeer conceived of grand opera as a whole, blending social content, historical material and local colour; exploitation of the horrific was an essential ingredient, along with massive crowd scenes building up a grandiose volume of sound and long passages of demanding solo singing. But these were allied to innovations, notably in the orchestra and in the deliberate creation of 'unbeautiful' sound. He was widely admired for his care over historical details, his melodic invention in ballet scenes and his grasp of the capabilities of individual singers.
GROVEmusic

Opera arias

Il crociato in Egitto – Queste destre l'acciaro di morte[a]; Ah! Non ti son piú cara[b]; Cara mano dell'amore[c]; Sogni, e ridenti[d]. **Emma di Resburgo** – Di gioia, di pace[e]. **L'esule di Granata** – Sí, mel credi[f].

Margherita d'Anjou[g] – Pensa e guarda; Amico, all
erta! **Romilda e Costanza** – Che barbaro tormento[h].
Semiramide riconosciuta – Il piacer, la gioja scenda[i]
[eh]**Bronwen Mills**, [d]**Linda Kitchen**, [e]**Maria Bovino**, [bdi-]
[bde]**Yvonne Kenny** sops [h]**Anne Mason**, [bde]**Diana Mon-**
tague, [f]**Patricia Spence**, [cd]**Della Jones** mezs [ad]**Bruce**
Ford, [h]**Chris Merritt**, [e]**Harry Nicoll**, [e]**Paul Nilon**,
[d]**Ugo Benelli** tens [eg]**Geoffrey Dolton**, [d]**Ian Platt**,
[g]**Russell Smythe** bars [fg]**Alastair Miles** bass **Geoffrey**
Mitchell Choir; [abcd]**Royal Philharmonic Orchestra**;
[efghi]**Philharmonia Orchestra / David Parry**
Opera Rara ORR222 (69' · DDD · N)   Ⓕ

Meyerbeer, born 1791, was in Italy from 1816 to
1824. On this showing, you're tempted to think
he should have stayed there. He's remembered
for the big Paris operas, such as *Les Huguenots*, *Le*
prophète and *L'Africaine*, hugely successful in their
time but latterly somewhat buried in their own
grandeur. The Italian period was nearer to the
18th century and Mozart. There was also the
presence of Rossini (almost exactly Meyerbeer's
age); and the music is that of a young man, gifted,
energetic, confident and wealthy. The operas
were admired and, remarkably, he was accepted
by the public, despite being a German and having
an unfashionable interest in orchestration.

These excellent selections include something
of all six operas from the eight years in Italy,
with *Il crociato in Egitto* returning regularly like
the theme in a rondo. All the recordings are
drawn from previous issues in the Opera Rara
catalogue. One of the most attractive numbers is
the semi-comic trio from *Margherita d'Anjou* in
which Margaret's protectors pit their wits
against those of Richard, Duke of Gloucester. In
fact, it seems fairly typical of Meyerbeer at this
stage: his genius seems to lie in the light touch,
the graceful phrase, the felicitous orchestral
scoring; if there's a weakness, it's revealed in the
grandly dramatic moments, for which his music
remains incorrigibly jolly.

The other great delight of the disc is the singing. Meyerbeer's vocal line, like Rossini's, is
written for virtuosos, and that, almost without
exception, is a description to which the soloists
can lay claim. Each has to negotiate passagework
of a kind that half a century ago would have
made everybody shake their head and say it
couldn't be done by 'today's' singers. Bruce
Ford, particularly, performs wonders in the
revised (Trieste) version of *Crociato*; Alistair
Miles is on top form in *L'esule di Granata*; but all
do well, carrying off their respective prizes with
easy competence and no fuss.

L'Africaine

L'Africaine
Shirley Verrett mez Sélika **Plácido Domingo** ten
Vasco da Gama **Ruth Ann Swenson** sop Inès **Justino**
Diaz bass Nélusko **Michael Devlin** bass-bar Don
Pédro **Philip Skinner** bass Don Diégo **Joseph**
Rouleau bass Grand Inquisitor **Kevin Anderson** ten
Don Alvar **Patricia Spence** mez Anna **Mark Delavan**
bar High Priest of Brahma **San Francisco Opera**

Ballet, Chorus and Orch / **Maurizio Arena**
Stage director **Lotfi Mansouri**
Video director **Brian Large**
ArtHaus Musik 🎥 100 216 (194' · 4:3 · 2.0 · 2 & 5)
Recorded live 1988   Ⓕ

Handsomely staged and sumptuously costumed,
this famous 1972 production makes good viewing; and the DVD sound is a distinct improvement on the original video. The singers benefit
as much as the orchestra; Shirley Verrett in particular is heard to advantage, her high notes
shining out with ease and purity, while Justino
Diaz has body and warmth of tone as well as the
command and panache for his exhilarating role.
Domingo's voice is caught with the metal
revealed rather at the expense of its characteristic richness, but there's a glorious thrust and
passion in his singing and acting. A voice that
sounds equally well in video and DVD is that of
the young Ruth Ann Swenson, whose freshness
and refinement are memorable and touching.
Meyerbeer's last opera exhibits the mastery of a
lifetime in high places. It has the required ingredients in due proportion, with a moving individuality in its quiet ending, where Verrett's
imaginative portrayal makes a strong contribution. Maurizio Arena, treats the score appreciatively, with care and precision.

Margherita d'Anjou

Margherita d'Anjou
Annick Massis sop Margherita d'Anjou **Bruce Ford**
ten Duke of Lavarenne **Daniela Barcellona** mez
Isaura **Alastair Miles** bass Carlo Belmonte **Fabio**
Previati bar Michele Gamautte **Pauls Putninš** ten
Riccardo **Colin Lee** ten Bellapunta **Roland Wood** bar
Orner **Geoffrey Mitchell Choir; London**
Philharmonic Orchestra / David Parry
Opera Rara ③ ORC25 (172' · DDD · T/t)   Ⓕ

Margaret of Anjou, the widow of Henry VI, is
more familiar to us as the embittered old crone
in Shakespeare's *Richard III*. In the opera she's
relatively young and beautiful, and loved by the
tenor, a married man. The action takes place in
Scotland where Margaret's forces are being pursued by Richard's. The tenor's dilemma is
whether to follow his strong inclination to
remain the Queen's lover or to return to his loving wife, Isaura, who, unknown to him, has followed him to Scotland in disguise.

The opera is called a *melodramma semiseria*,
which is appropriate partly because from the
very first bars of the Overture it's clear that we
can't be expected to take it seriously, and partly
because another principal role is that of the
comical army surgeon, Michele, who in the nick
of time summons a doughty troop of Highland-
ers to thwart Richard, who at that point has the
rest of the cast at his mercy.

The first notes – 'diddly-diddly um-pom-pom'
– may well deter the listener from going further,
especially as the fatuous motif is heard six times
more, plus twice in the minor and several times

referentially in *crescendo*. But that would be a pity. The singing and orchestration are good, and the *semiseria* element stimulates invention and interest: Isaura's plaintive aria and hopeful cabaletta are combined with a *buffo* subtext for Michele, and in the cottage scene of Act 2 the tension of Richard's unsocial visit is partly diffused, partly increased, by Michele's prevarications, a surreal situation along the lines of Richard III-meets-Benny Hill. Margherita has a gentle and rather beautiful solo. Particularly charming are the choruses that come just before, slightly suggestive of the villagers in *Cavalleria rusticana*.

Daniela Barcellona as Isaura has a rich contralto that takes flight in the final solo, surprisingly snatched from the eponymous soprano. She, Annick Massis, is a great find, pure and warm in tone, and accomplished in technique. Bruce Ford gives special pleasure in his *cantabile* aria 'Tu, che le vie segrete'. Fabio Previati plays Michele effectively, singing well and keeping the patter on its toes without too much clowning. Alastair Miles's Carlo, potentially the most interesting character, is admirably fluent in passagework but rather lacking in colour and bite. Chorus and orchestra are in good form, David Parry helping to bring out the best in them, as in Meyerbeer, too.

Robin Milford   English 1903-1959

He studied at the RCM with Holst, Vaughan Williams and R.O. Morris. Able to devote himself almost entirely to composition, Milford soon developed into a prolific composer in all genres. He made his first impact with a Double Fugue for Orchestra, published in 1927, and the oratorio A Prophet in the Land, performed at the 1931 Three Choirs Festival. Despite successful first performances, many of his more ambitious orchestral works remained in manuscript; other works, including a full-scale opera, The Scarlet Letter (1958–9), adapted from the novel by Hawthorne, has remained unpublished and unperformed. Milford reached his widest audience through his choral works, chamber music and songs.

GROVEmusic

My Lady's Pleasure. Four Hardy Songs[a] – The Colour; Tolerance. Cradle Song[a]. Daybreak[a]. Reputation Square. Four Songs[a] – So Sweet Love Seemed; Elegy; Love on my Heart[a]. Four Seasonable Songs[a] – Pleasure it is; This Endris Night. Prelude, Air & Finale. Swan Songs[a]. Jenifer's Jingle. Days and Moments – An Epitaph[a].
[a]**Phillida Bannister** *contr* **Raphael Terroni** pf
Toccata Classics TOCC0009 (78' · DDD)　　　Ⓕ

The piano works so deftly essayed by Raphael Terroni on this useful issue date from the 1920s and '30s – a happy period in Milford's life, which was soon to be blighted by the death (in a road accident) of his beloved five-year-old son Barnaby, followed by poor health, crippling self-doubt and three suicide attempts.

Reputation Square is a deliciously poised arrangement of a set of six hornpipes. Finer still are the bright-eyed *Jenifer's Jingle* (sic), ruminative and pastoral *My Lady's Pleasure* and the *Prelude, Air and Finale*, the latter a highly inventive, rewardingly serene and (above all) subtly integrated triptych which suggests that exploration of some of Milford's as yet unrecorded large-scale compositions might prove beneficial.

Although the influence of Finzi and Warlock is inescapable, the strongest of Milford's song-settings – notably 'The Colour' (the second of the *Four Hardy Songs* from 1939) and the unpublished set of nine *Swan Songs* (1948-51) – possess a frequently captivating melodic charm and directness of expression to which many will rightly respond, especially when contralto Phillida Bannister sings with such infectious commitment and tangible projection. Terroni, too, accompanies with watchful sensitivity, and there can be no complaints about either Michael Ponder's truthful production or Peter Hunter's assiduously detailed notes. This generously filled anthology deserves every success.

Darius Milhaud   French 1892-1974

Milhaud studied with Widor, Gédalge and Dukas at the Paris Conservatoire and became associated with Claudel, who took him to Rio de Janeiro as his secretary (1916-18): he wrote incidental music for Claudel's translation of the Oresteia (1922), making innovatory use of chanting chorus and percussion; he also drew on Brazilian music in his ballet L'homme et son désir (1918). But Claudel's influence was briefly succeeded by Cocteau's, and he became a member of Les Six; works of this period include the ballet Le boeuf sur le toit (1919). In 1922 he sought out jazz in Harlem and used the experience in another ballet, Le création du monde (1923). Thereafter he travelled widely, taught on both sides of the Atlantic and produced a colossal output in all genres, normally in a style of fluent bitonality. There are 12 symphonies and much other orchestral music, sacred and secular choral music, 18 quartets and songs, and a large number of operas.

GROVEmusic

Le boeuf sur le toit / La création du monde

Milhaud Le boeuf sur le toit. La création du monde
Ibert Divertissement **Poulenc** Les biches – Suite
Ulster Orchestra / Yan Pascal Tortelier
Chandos CHAN9023 (68' · DDD)　　　ⒻⒹ➔

Here is 1920s French music directed by a conductor who's completely in the spirit of it, and plenty of spirit there is, too. Except for Ibert's *Divertissement*, this is ballet music. Poulenc's suite from *Les biches*, written for Diaghilev's ballet company and first heard in Monte Carlo, is fresh and bouncy and stylishly played here, although Chandos's warm recording, good though it's, takes some edge off the trumpet tone; the genial nature of it all makes us forget that it's a unique mix of 18th-century *galanterie*, Tchaikovskian lilt and Poulenc's own inimitable street-Parisian sophistication and charm. As for Ibert's piece, this is uproariously funny in an unbuttoned way, and the gorgeously vulgar trombone in the Waltz and frantic police whistle in the finale are calculated to make you laugh out loud. Milhaud's *Le boeuf sur le toit* also has Parisian chic and was originally a kind of music-hall piece, composed to a scenario by Cocteau. It was while attending a performance of it in London in 1920 that the composer first heard the American jazz orchestra that, together with a later experience of New Orleans jazzmen playing 'from the darkest corners of the Negro soul' (as he later expressed it), prompted him to compose his masterly ballet *La création du monde*. Tortelier and his orchestra understand this strangely powerful music no less than the other pieces. This is a most desirable disc.

Violin Sonatas

Saudades do Brasil, Op 67 – Leme; Ipanema (arr Lévy). Suite for Violin, Viola and Piano, Op 157*b*. Quatre Visages, Op 238. Sonatine for Violin and Viola, Op 226. Sonatas for Viola and Piano – No 1, Op 240; No 2, Op 244. Sonatine for Viola and Cello, Op 378
Paul Cortese *va* **Michel Wagemans** *pf*
with **Joaquín Palomares** *vn* **Frank Schaffer** *vc*
ASV CDDCA1039 (78' · DDD)⁣ Ⓕ

Paul Cortese here brings his rich, warm tone and flawless technique to Milhaud's viola music. Of the seven works presented here, four were written in the 1940s while Milhaud was teaching at Mills College in the USA. Exceptions are the two arrangements from the early *Saudades do Brasil*; the Suite (which includes a jaunty Provençal-flavoured overture, and an engagingly cheery finale); and the much later *Sonatine* for violin and cello, which contains an unexpectedly emotional slow movement. Of the four other works, the *Sonatine* is easy-flowing small-talk, unmemorable save for the energetic final fugue; *Quatre Visages*, however, reveals Milhaud's sly wit in its characterisations of four women – a sunnily contented Californian, a chatterbox from Wisconsin, an earnest creature from Brussels and a vivacious Parisienne. The First Viola Sonata is one of his most endearing works, indulging to the full his penchant for canonic writing. The Second Sonata is less overtly bracing; its central *Modéré* is charged with expressive drama, while the finale is a rough-and-tumble which tempts Michel Wagemans, alert as he is, into being too loud for his partner – as he sometimes is elsewhere, notably in the early Suite.

Scaramouche (arr two pianos)

Le boeuf sur le toit, Op 58*a* (arr cpsr). Scaramouche, Op 165*b*. La libertadora, Op 236*a*. Les songes, Op 237. Le bal martiniquais, Op 249. Carnaval à la nouvelle-orléans, Op 275. Kentuckiana, Op 287
Stephen Coombs, Artur Pizarro *pfs*
Hyperion CDA67014 (62' · DDD)⁣ Ⓕ

Milhaud was an inveterate traveller who absorbed influences from many national styles. The music here exudes infectious dance impulses, languid geniality, knockabout humour and *joie de vivre*. It may inhabit a limited expressive sphere, but providing you don't expect introspection or searching profundity you won't be disappointed. There's enjoyment at every turn, whether in the foot-tapping 'Brazileira', the Satie-esque simplicity of the 'Valse' from *Les songes*, or the breezy music-hall atmosphere of *Le boeuf sur le toit*, with its wonderfully imaginative piano writing. The performances are exemplary. Stephen Coombs and Artur Pizarro both enjoy the byways of the piano repertory, and, even if Pizarro is the more starry soloist, they're well matched as a duo. Coombs's top part is suitably bright and sharply lit, and is offset by Pizarro's more subtle colouring. They revel in the protracted playfulness of *Le boeuf sur le toit*, where their feeling for Hispanic exoticism is matched by their virtuosity. The recorded sound is excellent.

Ernest Moeran⁣ British 1894-1950

Moeran studied at the Royal College of Music (1913-14) then, after war service, with Ireland (until 1923) who, with Delius, was a dominant influence on his early music. In the early 1930s he retired to the Cotswolds, where he wrote his Symphony in G minor (1937), a work of Nature lyricism drawing on Sibelian thematic methods. His other works, all marked by meticulous craftsmanship, include the Sinfonietta (1944) and orchestral Serenade (1948), concertos for violin (1942) and cello (1945), chamber music and songs.⁣ GROVEmusic

Symphony

Symphony in G minor[a]. Sinfonietta. Overture for a Masque.
London Philharmonic Orchestra;
[a]**New Philharmonia / Sir Adrian Boult**
Lyrita SRCD247 (78' · ADD) Recorded 1968-75
Ⓕ❍❍❍

G⁣Boult's affection for the G minor Symphony is in every phrase of this rapt and gloriously warm-hearted performance. The New Philharmonia are on blistering form and, thankfully for us, captured in a sumptuous recording of stupendous definition, depth and enticing warmth. In *Gramophone*'s original review in 1975, Edward Greenfield was unequivocal in his praise: 'Anyone who loves English music, and who has never heard this heart-warming music, should go at once to this record.'

String Quartets

String Quartets – No 1 in A minor; No 2 in E flat.
String Trio in G
Maggini Quartet (Laurence Jackson, David Angel
vns Martin Outram va Michal Kaznowski vc)
Naxos 8 554079 (59' · DDD)   ⓈⓄ⇨

The A minor Quartet dates from 1921, when
Moeran was a pupil of John Ireland at the Royal
College of Music. It's an enormously fluent, folk-
song-inspired creation, full of Ravelian poise;
indeed the last movement of the three (an exhilarating rondo) owes much to the finale of the
French master's F major Quartet. The
Maggini Quartet accords the piece wonderfully
assured, flexible advocacy. The E flat Quartet,
discovered among Moeran's papers after his
death, appears to be another early effort. It's cast
in just two movements, the second of which is an
ambitious linked slow movement and finale, full
of ambition and tender fantasy, and containing
some truly magical inspiration along the way.
Perhaps this movement's intrepid thematic and
emotional diversity engendered sufficient niggling doubts in Moeran's mind for him to sup-
press the whole work. Certainly, in a performance as convinced and convincing as this, its
melodic fecundity and unpretentious, out-of-
doors charm will endear it to many.
  That leaves the masterly String Trio of 1931,
which, in its impeccable craft, rhythmic pungency (the opening *Allegretto giovale* is in 7/8),
gentle sense of purpose and unerring concentration (above all in the deeply felt slow movement), represents one of Moeran's finest
achievements. The Magginis reveal a relish for
Moeran's exquisitely judged part-writing and
give an admirably polished, affectionate rendering. Sound and balance are excellent throughout
this enterprising, hugely enjoyable collection.

Johann Melchior Molter

German 1696-1765

*After attending the Gymnasium in Eisenach, where
JS Bach had earlier been a pupil, Molter entered the
service of the Margrave Carl Wilhelm of Baden-
Durlach who sent him to Italy to study Italian style.
His musical duties were broad, allowing him to write
music for the church as well as secular works, possibly
including operas. Molter was tasked with reorganising of the court's musical establishment, a role he
carried out with skill.*

Clarinet concertos

Molter Clarinet Concertos – No 1, MWV6:36; No 3,
MWV6:38; No 4, MWV6:39 **Mozart** Clarinet
Concerto, K622
Kari Kriikku cl **Tapiola Sinfonietta / John Storgårds**
Ondine ODE1056-2 (62' · DDD)   Ⓕ

Kari Kriikku's basic tone is light and fluid, his
articulation and dynamics inventively varied.
In the first movement of the Mozart he finds a
hint of playfulness amid the music's familiar
autumnal lyricism, enhanced by witty, spontaneous-sounding touches of ornamentation. But
with his acute sensitivity to harmonic flux, he
never underestimates the moments where the
music seems to turn in on itself: say, in the shift
to A minor in the first-movement recapitulation (for which he finds a haunting, withdrawn
new colour), or in the melancholy shadows that
flit across the bubbling surface of the finale.
Under John Storgårds, the Tapiola Sinfonietta
(with violins properly divided left and right)
provide typically polished, stylish support, and
shape even apparently routine accompanying
figures like the oscillating quavers in the *Adagio*
with finesse.
  Kriikku swaps basset-clarinet for a stratospheric D clarinet in three concertos by Johann
Melchior Molter, written in the late 1740s
when the clarinet was still in its infancy. The
music, often sounding like a cross between
Vivaldi and CPE Bach at his most complaisant,
is agreeable, if hardly distinctive. But Kriikku
draws miracles of delicate shading from his
piercing, trumpet-like instrument, whether in
the bouncy *Allegros* (though you may be fazed
by his jokily over-the-top cadenza in the finale
of No 4); or in the soulful minor-key slow
movements of Nos 1 and 4.
  In both Mozart and Molter, Ondine's recorded
sound has an attractive transparency and glow,
with an ideally judged balance between clarinet
and orchestra.

Federico Mompou   Spanish 1893-1987

*Mompou studied in Barcelona and with Motte-Lac-
roix and Samuel-Rousseau in Paris, where he
remained until 1941 except for a return to Barcelona
in 1914-21; he then settled in his native city. His
output consists almost entirely of small-scale piano
pieces and songs in a fresh, naive style indebted to
Satie and Debussy; he aimed for maximum expressiveness through minimum means, often achieving a
melancholy elegance.*   GROVEmusic

Música callada

Música callada
Herbert Henck pf
ECM New Series 445 699-2 (63' · DDD)   Ⓕ

Listening to this disc is rather like entering a
retreat. There's a rapt, contemplative atmosphere
around these 28 miniatures written between 1959
and 1967 as an attempt to express St John of the
Cross's mystic ideal of 'the music of silence'.
Practically all slow-moving, using repetition as a
structural device but avoiding keyboard virtuosity, and rarely rising even to a *forte*, they seem to

acknowledge descent from Erik Satie via the impressionists, though harmonically much freer and sometimes harsher – even, occasionally, stepping inside the area of atonality. No 3 has a child-like innocence in its folkloric theme: Mompou's fascination with bell-sounds finds echoes in Nos 5, 17 and 22. Overall there's a sense of tranquil self-communion which, paradoxically, exerts a strange spell on the listener. Herbert Henck, a specialist in 20th-century music, plays this collection with tender sensitivity and an ideally suited luminosity of tone, and he's finely recorded. An exceptional and haunting issue.

Preludes

Cançons i danses – Nos 1, 3, 5, 7, 8 & 9. Preludes – Nos 1, 5, 6, 7, 9 & 10. Cants mágics. Charmes. Variations. Dialogues. Paisajes
Stephen Hough pf
Hyperion CDA66963 (77' · DDD)   Ⓕ**OOO**

The music of Federico Mompou may appear at first to consist of little more than charming, delicately scented but dilettantish salon near-improvisations with marked overtones of Erik Satie; but it's significant that his earliest works (in the 1920s) are imbued with a sense of mystery and wonder. Later he was to progress from an ingenuous lyricism (in the *Songs and dances*) to a profounder contemplation and mysticism, to greater harmonic and keyboard complexity (*Dialogues*) and finally, in the 1946-60 *Paisajes* ('Landscapes'), to a more experimental, less tonal idiom. In the hands of an imaginative pianist like Stephen Hough this other-worldly quality becomes revelatory. Hough's command of tonal nuance throughout is ultra-sensitive, he catches Mompou's wistful moods to perfection, and on the rare occasions when the music lashes out, as in *Prelude* No 7, he's scintillating. In the more familiar *Songs and dances* he's tender in the songs and crisp rhythmically in the dances. He treats the 'Testament d'Amelia' in No 8 with a good deal of flexibility, and because Mompou declared (and demonstrated in his own recordings) that 'it's all so free', he takes the fullest advantage of the marking *senza rigore* in No 5, which reflects Mompou's lifelong fascination with bell sounds.

12 Préludes. Suburbis. Dialogues. Cants magics. Chanson de berceau. Fêtes lointaines
Jordi Masó pf
Naxos 8 554448 (79' · DDD)   Ⓢ🢂

Vol 1 of Jordi Masó's Mompou cycle was given the warmest of welcomes and Vol 2 is no disappointment, either. Everything is presented with crystalline clarity, and if the manner is unusually robust it's never less than musicianly. Directions such as *énergiquement* and *très clair* (Prélude No 2), the *forte* climax of Prélude No 6 or the sudden blaze of anger that erupts in Prélude No 7 are arguably more sympatheti-

cally conveyed than Mompou's gentler, more characteristic instructions (*con lirica espressione* in Prélude No 8 or *un peu plus calme* in the second 'Gitanes' from *Suburbis*). It's almost as if Masó, a vibrant and articulate pianist, wished to draw attention away from sentimental and salon associations, and direct us towards Mompou's underlying fervour and what Wilfrid Mellors calls (in his invaluable book *Le jardin retrouvé*) the 'pre-melodic' nature of Mompou's vocal lines (in *Cants magics*) or the evocation of a remote, prehistoric world. Masó's boldness is potent and arresting and his comprehensive undertaking makes comparison with Hough and Martin Jones a marginal issue. So although he's less tonally subtle than Jones, his playing is vital and idiomatic, qualities highlighted by the bright, immediate sound.

Songs

'Combat del Somni'
Cançó de la fira. Cantar del alma. Combat del Somni – Damunt de tu, només les flors; Aquesta nit un mateix vent; Jo et pressentia com la mar; Fes-me la vida transparent; Ara no sé si et veig encar. Comptines – Margot la pie; Petite fille de Paris; Rossinyol joli; Aserrín, aserrán; J'ai vu dans la lune; Pito, pito, colorito; Fréderic tic, tic; D'alt d'un cotxe. Sant Marti. L'hora grisa. Cançoneta incerta. Cuatro melodías
Marisa Martins mez **Mac McClure** pf
Columna Música 1CM0136 (54' · DDD)   Ⓕ

Wilfred Mellors may have called him 'a minor muse' but Mompou's sense of 'truth', whether expressed in memories of a paradisal childhood or in a mystical catholicism, results in a unique and instantly recognisable voice. Few composers have achieved so much so economically; and at his greatest, in, for example, *Cantar del alma*, the final song on this disc, Mompou creates a form of divine monotony, his religious fervour captured with a simplicity that is in a special sense transcendental.

Inspired by the poetry of St John of the Cross, such music, where singer and pianist commune separately rather than together, is vitally related to *Musica callada*, his similarly inspired piano cycle. Indeed, there are many family likenesses between the songs and the piano music where the composer's distinctive world, whether playful or ecstatic, is expressed with a tantalising brevity.

Marisa Martins and Mac McClure make an ardent case for a special corner of the repertoire and they have been well recorded. Unfortunately they have been less well presented. Tomas Marco's note is both assertive and uninformative, only one of the 22 songs on offer is translated into English (inconsiderate for those whose Catalan is, shall we say, a little rusty), the texts do not tally with the index and the last four lines of *Cantar del alma* are missing. Sadly, gratitude for Columna Música's enterprise is qualified by such lapses in presentation.

Jean-Joseph de Mondonville

French 1711-1772

In the 1730s violinist and composer Mondonville was in Lille; then he settled in Paris, where he won fame as soloist and composer. He became sous-maître to the royal chapel in 1740 and intendant in 1744. His music is notable for its imaginative textures. Best known were his sonatas for harpsichord and violin (1734), among the earliest accompanied keyboard music, and those for harpsichord, violin and voice (1748); his 17 grands motets (among the finest since Lalande's and like his, much performed at the Concert Spirituel) and 10 stage works (1742-71) were also popular. GROVEmusic

Grands motets

Grands motets – Dominus regnavit; In exitu Israel; **P**
De profundis
Sophie Daneman, Maryseult Wieczorek *sops* **Paul Agnew, François Piolino** *tens* **Maarten Koningsberger** *bar* **François Bazola** *bass*
Les Arts Florissants / William Christie
Erato 0630-17791-2 (72' · DDD · T/t)　　　Ⓕ❍

Mondonville's *grands motets* were enormously popular for many years at the Concert Spirituel in Paris. They follow the pattern laid down by Lalande and continued by Rameau, but with more independent instrumental parts and incorporating Italian influences (e.g. *da capo* arias) and operatic elements. These three on psalm texts are deeply impressive. *Dominus regnavit* (1734) was perhaps the earliest of Mondonville's *grands motets* and, besides its polyphonic opening chorus, is notable for two verses entirely for high-register voices and instruments, an operatic *tempête*, and a stunning complex 'Gloria patri'. *De profundis* (1748), written for the funeral of a Chapel Royal colleague, is by its nature sombre, and ends not with the usual 'Gloria patri' but with 'Requiem aeternam' and a fugue. The initial chorus was praised to the sky by contemporaries: other highlights are a baritone aria over a free chaconne bass, and a chorus illustrating 'morning' and 'night' by high and low voices respectively. There's even more illustrative music in the 1755 *In exitu Israel*: what amounts to a dramatic scena, with agitated strings and rushing voices for the 'fleeing sea', dotted figures for the mountains 'skipping like rams', and tremolos and vocal melismas for the 'trembling earth'. The performances are vivid, with very good soloists, an alertly responsive chorus and a neat orchestra.

Stanisław Moniusko   Polish 1819-1872

The leading Polish composer of the 19th century, Moniusko studied in Berlin, encountering works by Weber, Marschner and Lortzing. His opera Halka

(1848) was to establish his European reputation. His large output is focused mainly on the voice - operas (of which The Haunted Manor is of importance), songs and choral works – though he did leave some orchestral and chamber works.

Halka

Halka
Tatiana Borodina *sop* Halka **Oleh Lykhach** *ten* Jontek **Aleksandra Buczek** *mez* Zofia **Mariusz Godlewski** *bar* Janusz **Radosław Żukowski** *bass* Stolnik **Zbigniew Kryczka** *bass* Dziemba **Jacek Ryś** *bar* Piper **Rafał Majzner** *ten* Mountaineer
Orchestra, Chorus and Ballet of the Wrocław Opera / Ewa Michnik
Stage and video director **Laco Adamik**
Dux Recordings 🎬 DUX9538
(136' · PAL · 16:9 · 2.0 and 5.0 · 0)
Recorded live at the Wrocław Opera in September 2005　　　　　　　Ⓕ

Even in its final form from 1858 (the original dates from 10 years earlier), *Halka* is uneven and derivative, but it is precisely its variable quality that makes the work so fascinating. For all the reliance on early-19th-century German and Italian models, one can hear a national operatic language begin to take shape.

The plot is straightforward. The engagement party of the noble Janusz is disturbed by Halka, a peasant girl with whom he had fathered a child, now dead. Halka refuses to accept that Janusz has deserted her despite the promptings of Jontek, whose love for Halka is utterly unrequited. As Halka's despair deepens into madness, she contemplates burning down the church in which the wedding takes place but relents; on forgiving Janusz, she drowns herself. Wrocław Opera's account, given to mark the 60th anniversary of the company's stage, is full-blooded and vivid. Laco Adamik's sensitive video direction of his own production is a model of clarity, capturing the sweep of the grander passages as well as the more intimate moments. Despite the predominantly monochrome costumes – the aristocrats are mostly in white, the commoners in black – the use of colour throughout is telling, especially in the vivid dance numbers in Acts 1 and 3. The light of the first-act party gradually darkens as Halka's anguish deepens and the action moves back to Janusz's estate. Yet it is in Acts 3 and 4 that Moniuszko's music becomes its most affecting and emotional, in contrast to the superficiality of Stolnik's house.

Tatiana Borodina catches the heroine's fluctuating mental states, from radiant joy to dark desperation, with equal force, her voice rich and powerful although showing some strain in the highest passages. Oleh Lykhach and Mariusz Godlewski are excellent as Jontek and Janusz, the latter especially catching the character's vacillation between cowardice and guilt. The company as a whole is excellent and the orchestra is strongly directed by Ewa Michnik. Recommended.

Stephen Montague   American b1943

Born in New York and educated in Florida, Montague also studied conducting in Salzburg. He is equally active as a performer as a composer and has won numerous prizes for his music. He is interested in electronics and has frequently written for a combination of acoustic and electornic instruments.

Southern Lament

Haiku. Southern Lament[a]. Midnight Sun. Chorale for a Millennium Sunset[c]. Headless Horseman. Thanksgiving Hymn. A Crippled Ghost at Halloween. Beyond the Milky Way[c]. Dagger Dance[d]. Paramell Va. Night Frost Settles on a Pumpkin. Something's in Grandma's Attic[d]. For Merce C at the Barbican[d]. After Ives…: Four Studies[b]
Philip Mead *pf* with [a]**Monica Acosta** *voc* [b]**Nancy Ruffer** *fl* [c]**Elysian Quartet**; [b]**Sousa Band /** [bd]**Stephen Montague** *pf/elec*
NMC NMCD118 (79' · DDD)   Ⓕ

Stephen Montague is an American composer-performer who has lived in the UK for more than 30 years, during which time he has developed an enterprising international career. He honestly admits his sources in Ives, Cowell, Cage and minimalism, and the CD ends with four of his *Studies* 'after Ives'. That wonderful hymn tune 'What a friend we have in Jesus' (compare Montague's treatment with the third movement of Ives's Piano Sonata No 1) shows the unabated power of diatonic harmony, although there are surprises, and 'Forever JPS' is a spectacular which brings in the voice of Sousa himself as well as the London Sousa Band in *Stars and Stripes*.

Montague points out that when he borrows melodies, unlike Ives he usually quotes them complete. There's plenty of that with the varied settings of the tunes in *Southern Lament*. Then there are several short occasional pieces showing variety and ingenuity, but *Haiku* with live electronics and computer tape is more substantial. This is a subtle, oriental-influenced piece with the live piano gracefully repetitive and the electronics sustaining this mood. When Montague uses electronics the sound is always beguiling; if he's minimalist he gets somewhere rather than being stuck in a groove; and he even manages to use tone-clusters with a light touch.

This is a consistently enjoyable portrait of a composer who knows how to focus his appeal. Terrific performances from Philip Mead, all well recorded.

Philippe de Monte   Flemish 1521-1603

Flemish composer. He was a choirboy at Mechlin and then served the Pinelli family in Naples (1542-51). In 1554 he was in Antwerp and then England (where he met Byrd), serving in the private chapel of Philip II of Spain (Mary Tudor's husband). He was next in Rome, probably with Cardinal Orsini, and from 1568 until his death he was Kapellmeister at the Habsburg court in Vienna (later Prague). Prolific, successful and progressive in outlook, he composed over 1100 madrigals in 34 books (1554-1600, often reprinted), spiritual madrigals (5 bks, 1581-93) and chansons (1585), as well as some 40 masses (mostly MS) and over 250 motets (10 bks, 1572-1600).*   GROVEmusic

Missa Aspice Domine

Monte Missa Aspice Domine. Factum est silentium. Miserere mei, Domine. Pie Jesu, virtus mea. Clamavi de tribulatione mea. O suavitas et dulcedo **Jacquet of Mantua** Aspice Domine
Christ Church Cathedral Choir, Oxford / Stephen Darlington
Metronome METCD1037 (58' · DDD)   Ⓕ

What a feast for lovers of Renaissance polyphony, and the only available recording of Philippe de Monte's parody mass *Missa Aspice Domine*, based on a motet by an earlier composer, Jacquet of Mantua, also included here. In general Stephen Darlington adopts a faster tempo for the mass than for the slow-moving motet, but the mood is still quietly pleading. One of the loveliest forward-looking movements is the Angus Dei: the trebles lead with the finely structured melody, the lower voices being more of an accompaniment than a clearly defined part of the polyphonic texture. Two of de Monte's original motets that follow are again settings of texts of earnest supplication. The most moving is the *Miserere*, with its opening phrases marked by an imaginative chord progression. Of the other three, we hear the composer's surprisingly loud-sounding 'silence in heaven' as Michael does the dragon in (*Factum est silentium*).

Claudio Monteverdi   Italian 1567-1643

Monteverdi studied with Ingegneri, maestro di cappella at Cremona Cathedral, and published several books of motets and madrigals before going to Mantua in about 1591 to serve as a string player at the court of Duke Vincenzo Gonzaga. There he came under the influence of Giaches de Wert, whom he failed to succeed as maestro di cappella in 1596. In 1599 he married Claudia de Cattaneis, a court singer, who bore him three children, and two years later he was appointed maestro di cappella on Pallavicino's death. Largely as the result of a prolonged controversy with the theorist GM Artusi, Monteverdi became known as a leading exponent of the modern approach to harmony and text expression. In 1607 his first opera, Orfeo, was produced in Mantua, followed in 1608 by Arianna. The dedication to Pope Paul V of a grand collection of church music known as the Vespers (1610) indicated an outward looking ambition, and in 1613 Monteverdi was appointed maestro di cappella at St Mark's, Venice.

Monteverdi

There Monteverdi was active in reorganising and improving the cappella as well as writing music for it, but he was also able to accept commissions from elsewhere, including some from Mantua, for example the ballet Tirsi e Clori (1616) and an opera, La finta pazza Licori (1627, not performed, now lost). He seems to have been less active after c1629, but he was again in demand as an opera composer on the opening of public opera houses in Venice from 1637. In 1640 Arianna was revived, and in the following two years Il ritorno d'Ulisse in patria, Le nozze d'Enea con Lavinia (lost) and L'incoronazione di Poppea were given first performances. In 1643 he visited Cremona and died shortly after his return to Venice.

Monteverdi can be justly considered one of the most powerful figures in the history of music. Much of his development as a composer may be observed in the eight books of secular madrigals published between 1587 and 1638. The early books show his indebtedness to Marenzio in particular; the final one, Madrigali guerrieri et amorosi, includes some pieces 'in genere rappresentativo' – Il ballo delle ingrate, the Combattimento di Tancredi e Clorinda and the Lamento della ninfa – which draw on Monteverdi's experience as an opera composer. A ninth book was issued posthumously in 1651.

Orfeo was the first opera to reveal the potential of this then novel genre; Arianna (of which only the famous lament survives) may well have been responsible for its survival. Monteverdi's last opera L'incoronazione di Poppea, though transmitted in not wholly reliable sources and including music by other men, is his greatest masterpiece and arguably the finest opera of the century. In the 1610 collection of sacred music Monteverdi displayed the multiplicity of styles that characterise this part of his output. The mass is a monument of the prima prattica or old style. At the other extreme the motets, written for virtuoso singers, are the most thorough-going exhibition of the modern style and the seconda prattica. **GROVE**music

---

Selva morale

Selva morale e spirituale   **P**
Cantus Cölln; Concerto Palatino / Konrad Junghänel
Harmonia Mundi ③ HMC901718/20
(230' · DDD · T/t)   Ⓕ**OOO**

Monteverdi's last publication has always been something of a stepchild in his output, perhaps partly because of its sheer size and variety: there's lots of music in it that's hard to pigeon-hole. It's a massive assembly of some 40 pieces, some apparently very early, many from those mysterious years after the 1610 *Vespers*, and a few perhaps very late. In style they range from the purest academic polyphony of the *stile antico* to the most elaborate concerted music with intricate and showy instrumental parts, from the simplest melodic writing to virtuoso floridity with extreme vocal ranges. In this complete recording Konrad Junghänel has effectively made the first and third CDs into approximate vespers collections, with the second CD containing most of the music that can't be fitted into the others.

This works extremely well, not least because those who aren't ready to sit through it all at one sitting can get a satisfying musical unit from any one of the discs.

The 12 singers of Cantus Cölln have among them enough variety of colour to keep the sound lively and interesting. They are always clear, disciplined and balanced; and Junghänel directs the often episodic works with a firm control of their shape. The peerless Johanna Koslowsky leads much of the time in the larger pieces and contributes marvellous solo numbers. For the large-range bass solos Stephan MacLeod makes the impossible lines sound almost effortless. This set is a remarkable achievement.

1610 Vespers

Vespro della Beata Vergine (with alternative six-voice Magnificat). Missa In illo tempore   **P**
Rebecca Outram, Carolyn Sampson *sops* **Daniel Auchincloss, Charles Daniels, James Gilchrist, Nicholas Mulroy** *tens* **Robert Evans, Peter Harvey, Robert MacDonald** *basses* **The King's Consort Choir; The King's Consort / Robert King**
Hyperion ② CDA67531/2 (137' · DDD · T/t);
Ⓢ ② SACDA67531/2
        Ⓕ**OO**

Despite four wonderful volumes of Monteverdi's sacred music from The King's Consort, nothing will prepare you for the ecstatic consequences of taking seriously at least one aspect of Monteverdi's so-called *seconda pratica* – using much freer counterpoint, with an increasing hierarchy of voices: that the word is mistress of the music. And what ecstasy!

Never mind the majestic opening psalm: just listen to the eloquent gestures in the 'Dixit Dominus', which range from the declamatory to the reticent with astonishing flexibility. Or the freedom and delicacy of tenor James Gilchrist in the 'Nigra sum', equally matched by the fragile spaciousness of Caroline Sampson's and Rebecca Outram's 'Pulchra es'.

Spaciousness soon loses its fragility in the propulsive 'Nisi Dominus' and the 'Lauda Jerusalem' with its luxuriant finale. And although the 'Sonata sopra Sancta Maria' is still preferable with a solo soprano line, its instrumental variations are here dispatched with such fluency it's hard not to be won over; the 'Ave maris stella' is similarly eloquent. The second disc includes equally superb performances of the alternative six-voice Magnificat and the *Missa In illo tempore*.

The cumulative effect here is of a dazzling chiaroscuro that Monteverdi surely would have recognised. With its use of full choir, King's recording has room to manoeuvre – which gives the imagination more room to take flight.

Vespro della Beata Virgine (ed Parrott/Keyte)   **P**
Taverner Consort; Taverner Choir; Taverner Players / Andrew Parrott
Virgin Classics ② 212685-2 (106' · DDD)   Ⓑ**O**⇨

The technical and interpretative problems of the Monteverdi *Vespers* of 1610 are legion. Should the entire volume be performed as an entity, or just the psalms, or perhaps a mixture of psalms and motets? Since the vocal lines in the original are heavily ornamented, does this preclude the addition of further embellishment after the manner of contemporary instruction books? Which portions should be sung chorally (and how large should such a 'choir' be?), and which by the soloists? How should the continuo be realised?

The central controversy concerns five non-liturgical compositions inserted among the Marian psalms, hymn and 'Magnificat'. These, the sacred *concerti* described on the title-page as 'suitable for the chapels or private chambers of princes', don't conform textually to any known Marian office but occur in Monteverdi's collection in positions normally occupied by psalm antiphons. Here the *concerti* are performed as substitutes for the antiphons missing from Monteverdi's collections. One effect is to make this version feel more unified and monumental.

Both physically and emotionally the *concerti* are presented here as the focal points of the *Vespers*. Certainly they're the occasion for some of the most spectacular singing. The essential ingredient is the performance of Nigel Rogers, surely the most accomplished and convincing singer of the early 17th-century Italian virtuoso repertory. He gives persuasive and seemingly effortless performances in three of the *concerti* in his mellifluous, dramatic yet perfectly controlled manner. In two cases, 'Audi coelum' and 'Duo Seraphim', he's well matched with Andrew King and Joseph Cornwell. 'Pulchra es', sung by Tessa Bonner and Emma Kirkby, seems comparatively rather understated.

One important feature of Andrew Parrott's interpretation is its fundamental conception, historically accurate, of the *Vespers* as chamber work rather than a 'choral' one. Thus only one instrument is used per part, the harpsichord is employed very sparingly, and the basic continuo group is restricted to organ and chitarrone. Following the same principle, one voice per part is taken as the norm. The result is a clarity of texture, evident from the opening bars, which allows correct tempos to be used without stifling often intricate rhythmic features. Another fundamental choice represents something of a novelty. Both 'Lauda Jerusalem' and the 'Magnificat' are transposed down a fourth here, as they should be according to the convention relating to the clef combinations in which they were originally notated. This brings all the vocal parts into the tessitura of the rest of the work, and restores the instruments to their normal ranges. Whether or not the result is less 'exciting' than the version we're used to hearing has only partly to do with questions of musicality. For the rest, one of the lasting virtues of this well-balanced, unobtrusive recording is that it allows us to hear the *Vespers* sounding something along the lines that Monteverdi intended.

MONTEVERDI'S VESPERS – IN BRIEF

Taverner Consort / Andrew Parrott 🅿
Virgin Veritas ② 561662-2 (148' · DDD) Ⓑ🅾➔
The first recording to engage fully with the scholarly debates regarding the form, purpose and pitch of the work, this 1984 version is a comprehensive and radical attempt to reconstruct a festal Vespers service, the music reordered so that it no longer seems to work towards a proto-Wagnerian climax.

Les Arts Florissants / William Christie 🅿
Erato ② 3984 23139-2 (100' · DDD) Ⓕ🅾
Christie's version, made with relatively large choral and instrumental forces in a resonant venue, conveys the flair, spontaneity and warmth of his live music-making.

Concentus Musicus / Nikolaus Harnoncourt 🅿
Teldec ② 2564-69464-8 (105' · DDD) Ⓜ
Harnoncourt in 1986 prefers more rugged sonorities and bigger scoring than those modern rivals who look above all for clarity and simplicity.

Monteverdi Choir / John Eliot Gardiner 🅿
Archiv ② 429 565-2AH2 (106' · DDD) Ⓕ
This large-scale live recording (Gardiner's second) was made in Venice's St Mark's Basilica. It captures the drama as well as the ceremonial aspect of the work, despite sometimes cloudy recorded sound (See Archiv 073 035-9 for the spectacular DVD).

Concerto Itaiano / Rinaldo Alessandrini 🅿
Naive ② OP30403 (105' · DDD) Ⓕ🅾🅾
A striking and thought-provoking performance from Alessandrini that uses a 'soloistic' approach to impressive effect. Try and hear a little before you buy: it will either repel or entrance. We think the latter...

Concentus Musicus / Réné Jacobs 🅿
Harmonia Mundi ② HMC90 1566/7 (104' · DDD)Ⓕ
More intimate than most, with a dramatic flair that eludes most English versions. Jacobs relates the work to its madrigal inspirations.

Monteverdi Choir etc / John Eliot Gardiner 🅿
Decca ② 443 482-2 (106' · ADD) Ⓜ🅱➔
Gardiner's first version was made with some of the finest English singers of the day and the legendary Philip Jones Brass Ensemble. It may not be as polished, but its vitality stands up well to the later version.

The King's Consort Choir; The King's Consort / Robert King 🅿
Hyperion ② CDA67531/2 (137' · DDD) Ⓕ🅾🅾
A performance of almost rhapsodic power that finds these assembled musicians on incandescent form. King conducts with glorious flexibility and clearly inspires his colleagues to give of their considerable best.

Monteverdi Vespro della Beata Vergine
Cima Concerti ecclesiastici – Sonata per il violino, ▣
cornetto e violone; Sonata per il violino e violone
Sophie Marin-Degor, Maryseult Wieczorek sops
Artur Stefanowicz, Fabián Schofrin countertens
Paul Agnew, Joseph Cornwell, François Piolino
tens **Thierry Félix, Clive Bayley** basses
**Les Sacqueboutiers de Toulouse; Les Arts
Florissants / William Christie** hpd/org
Erato ② 3984-23139-2 (100' · DDD · T/t)   Ⓕ❍

This is in some ways an oddly old-fashioned
approach to the 1610 *Vespers*. With a substantial choir and sometimes highly varying orchestration, William Christie creates a warm and
glowing sound. Part of his emphasis is on texture and flow, so Monteverdi's often sharp dissonances tend to have a soft edge; and there are
some occasionally irrelevant pitches buried in
the polyphonic web. He faces the challenge of
putting the 'Lauda Jerusalem' and the 'Magnificat' at a pitch standard a fourth lower than
the rest (which he has at a modern concert
pitch). And that's where the rich orchestration
pays its dividends; the resulting almost impossibly low bass lines, particularly in the 'Et misericordia' section of the 'Magnificat', sound
clear and lucid with their instrumental doubling. He also benefits from the splendid low
range of the tenors he uses: they manage to
make the 'Gloria Patri' section a true climax to
the work, and they give the 'Duo Seraphim'
perhaps the most convincing performance
available anywhere because they're so beautifully matched. Christie prefaces each of the
psalms with a chant introit; and he follows the
order of the print except in putting 'Duo Seraphim' before the 'Sonata sopra Sancta Maria'.
To fill the gap where Monteverdi put 'Duo
Seraphim' he introduces a sonata by Cima,
superbly played by a team led by the violinist,
François Fernandez; another sonata
by Cima separates the 'Lauda Jerusalem' from
'Duo Seraphim'. There's a warmth and generosity here that are undeniably attractive; the
movements mentioned go better than anything
else available; and everything is done at the
level of skill and musicality that we've come to
expect from Christie and his group.

Vespro della Beata Vergine   ▣
Roberta Invernizzi sop **Monica Piccinini, Anna
Simboli** mezs **Sara Mingardo** contr **Francesco
Ghelardini** counterten **Luca Dordolo, Vincenzo Di
Donato, Gianluca Ferrarini** tens **Pietro Spagnoli,
Furio Zanasi** bars **Daniele Carnovich, Antonio
Abete** basses **Concerto Italiano /
Rinaldo Alessandrini**
Naïve ② OP30403 (105' · DDD · T/t)   Ⓕ❍❍

Rinaldo Alessandrini has waited long before
committing to disc his thoughts on Monteverdi's most famous sacred publication. On the
issues that have divided modern performers
he's unflappably pragmatic. In keeping with
Concerto Italiano's general approach, the vocal

lines in 'choral' pieces are taken by soloists who
step out of the ensemble, on the grounds, he
says in the notes, that 'We possess no sources
attesting choral performance of this music.' He
sticks to the published order, observing that no
single liturgical event can account for the presence of every piece in the collection. Finally, he
transposes the *Lauda Jerusalem* and the *Magnificat* on the grounds that failure to do so
would entail enlarging the overall ensemble.
These are decisions that continue to divide
scholars. Suffice it to say that a clear vision
results which has the virtue of coherence,
though it comes at the cost of dramatic effects
that many continue to hold dear. But the
notion that this work wasn't conceived on the
grand scale in which some performers dress it
up in no way diminishes the greatness of the
music.

Other details of execution aren't quite so persuasive. In some of the later psalms, rhythmic
detail tends to get lost in the overall sound, less-
ening one's appreciation of Monteverdi's contrapuntal virtuosity, and giving a certain 'floaty'
quality that can be distracting. Not for Alessandrini the pinpoint precision and analytical clarity of, say, the Monteverdi Choir. However, the
instruments give wonderfully punchy accounts
of the Sonata, and at times the sackbuts and
continuo come wonderfully close to impersonating a percussion section.

Those with a fixed conception of the work may
fail to be convinced. Put mischievously, there's
something here to displease nearly everyone.
But there are many moments that will return
you to the music more violently; and you have to
take seriously what so distinguished a Mon-
teverdian has to say.

Madrigals

'La Venexiana – Live in Corsica'
Madrigals from Books 2, 4, 5, 6, 7, 8 and 9.
Lamento d'Arianna
La Venexiana / Claudio Cavina counterten
Glossa GCD920015 (64' · DDD) Recorded live 2002   Ⓕ

This live anthology is a clever way of offering a
'sampler' of La Venexiana's survey of Monteverdi's madrigals without resorting to the mere
duplication of their existing catalogue. It gives
an idea of the ensemble's qualities as performers
and of the 'buzz' that a live rendition of these
pieces can generate.

The interpretations are not markedly different
from their studio counterparts, and since
excerpts are included of only those books that
have already been issued complete, there are
perhaps fewer surprises than one might have
liked. An exception is the *Lamento d'Arianna*,
published in Monteverdi's lifetime in a collective anthology. Rossana Bertini's rendition is
unselfconsciously involving, though its conclusion might have been better paced (it appears to
end rather abruptly). The other soloistic pieces
(such as 'Bel pastor' or 'Gira il nemico') do not

quite have the same impact, largely because some of the stage effects get lost in translation. In 'Bel pastor', the shepherd's protestations of love (in response to his lover's repeated demands) seem increasingly forced and tetchy. The comic effect must have been considerable but on the recording it doesn't really 'click'.

The best performances are of the earlier books, particularly Book 2, where La Venexiana's qualities of ensemble are allowed to come to the fore. By Latin standards the audience's response is polite but it stops short of rapture: a verdict with which it's tempting to agree.

Madrigals – Book 2, Il secondo libro de' madrigali
La Venexiana / Claudio Cavina counterten
Glossa GCD920922 (70' · DDD · T/t)   Ⓕ

La Venexiana's cast for Book 2 is virtually identical to Concerto Italiano's a decade earlier. Here La Venexiana has the edge. Concerto Italiano zipped through the whole book in just under an hour; given that the same singers take more than 10 minutes longer in the new version it's perhaps surprising that the two approaches don't sound more different. Claudio Cavina doesn't fragment the text in the manner of his rival, but his more leisurely readings generate a more effective charge by lingering over Monteverdi's climactic build-ups (as in the last line of *Mentr'io mirava fiso*, to mention just one instance), and he has the edge on intonation.

Madrigals – Book 3, Il terzo libro de madrigali
La Venexiana (Rossana Bertini, Valentina Coladonato, Nadia Ragni sops Paola Reggiani mez Giuseppe Maletto, Sandro Naglia tens Daniele Carnovich bass) /
Claudio Cavina counterten
Glossa GCD920910 (63' · DDD · T/t)   ⒻⓄⓄⓄ

The masterly anthology of styles in Book 3 presents very specific challenges in performance precisely because of its variety. La Venexiana have an excellent understanding of the essentially polyphonic nature of such works as *La giovinetta pianta* and are therefore quite superb in the more difficult mixed style of *O dolce anima mia*, *Stracciami pur il core* or *Se per estremo ardore*, whose complicated rhetorical devices are brought off with perfection. Such brief transcendent moments as 'non può morir d'amor alma fedele' in *Stracciami pur il core*, or 'ingiustamente brami' in *O dolce anima mia*, far from seeming isolated jewels, arise here naturally from their context, which is no mean achievement for the uncharted waters that Monteverdi was navigating in these experimental but masterly works. The singers also have the full measure of the Tasso cycles of Book 3 entering fully into the polychrome, storm-lit intensity of the emotional and musical landscape. La Venexiana's dark hues and dramatic but not histrionic approach sound unbeatable. A very fine disc indeed.

Madrigals, Book 6 Il sesto libro de madrigali
Concerto Italiano / Rinaldo Alessandrini hpd
Naïve OP30423 (64' · DDD · T/t)   Ⓕ

Monteverdi's Sixth Book of Madrigals (1614) is significant for including both traditional polyphonic and *stile nuove* concerted madrigals. In his booklet-notes, Rinaldo Alessandrini points out that this is also a 'book of partings': many of the madrigals seem to have been written much earlier than the published date, at a time when Monteverdi suffered the loss of his wife Claudia and his live-in pupil, the singer Caterina Martinelli. All the texts deal with loss both temporary or permanent – although it's touching to note that the final madrigal, *Presso un fiume tranquillo*, paints a lovers' reconciliation possibly emblematic of a Heavenly reunion.

When discussing this repertoire it's almost a cliché to say that Concerto Italiano's approach is analytical, La Venexiana's more broadly coalescent (on Glossa). However, this new recording really goes far beyond the supple elegance of line for which La Venexiana are famous, with Alessandrini and his crew employing a tense, edgy rhetoric to reveal an inner psychology while sacrificing neither precision of ensemble nor beauty of sound. Concerto Italiano are now such a sensitive instrument that they respond to the emotional exigencies of the texts like silk to the breeze. Listen to the passionate *terza parte* of the *Lamento d'Arianna*; or the final line of *Zefiro torna*, where the drawn-out dissonances are almost physically painful; or the incredible dynamic and rhythmic control in the Sestina; or the fluid, frighteningly accurate ornamentation in *Qui rise, o Tirsi*. You could find 100 such examples without ever conveying the many excellences of this recording.

Madrigals – Book 7, Il settimo libro de' madrigali
La Venexiana / Claudio Cavina counterten
Glossa ② GCD920927 (137' · DDD · T/t)   Ⓕ

Book 7 (1619) gathers together works that must have been written many years apart. The common denominator is its consistent use of instruments in conjunction with the voices. Recording the complete book is a considerable undertaking, only previously achieved by the Consort of Musicke (Virgin Veritas, nla).

La Venexiana's free approach to rhythm is alive to the spirit of the music. *Ohimé, dov'è il mio ben* manages to be a set of variations on the Romanesca theme, and something else entirely: they convince you that this double-reading is precisely what Monteverdi intended. Though not everything reflects the multi-faceted Monteverdi aesthetic, the pieces that are recorded less often still shed a useful light on his working process. As the first *intégrale* by a modern Italian ensemble, this is a significant addition to the catalogue.

Madrigals – Book 8, Il ottavo libro di madrigali;
'Madrigali guerrieri et amorosi'

Maria Cristina Kiehr, Salomé Haller *sops* Marisa
Martins *mez* Bernarda Fink *contr* Christophe
Laporte *counterten* John Bowen, Jeremy Ovenden,
Mario Zeffiri, Kobie van Rensburg *tens* Victor
Torres *bar* Antonio Abete, Renaud Delaigue *basses*
Concerto Vocale / René Jacobs
Harmonia Mundi ③ HMC90 1736/7 (156' · DDD · T/t)
Ⓕ**OO**

The blurb on the jacket says, 'Indispensable',
and this is hardly an exaggeration. A complete
Book 8 would be enough to whet any Mon-
teverdian's appetite; but fortunately, completeness isn't the only reason to hail the new arrival.
Jacobs's well-rounded team of singers is perhaps
most effective in the large ensembles, which
have a festive opulence about them, while allowing the necessary shadings to come into play:
such things as the opening of 'Hor che'l ciel' and
'Ardo, avvampo' are admirably done, the one
suitably mysterious and opaque, the other happily (but convincingly) chaotic. And with one or
two exceptions the soloists acquit themselves
handsomely, too: Bernarda Fink's title-role in
the *Lamento della ninfa* is very affecting – one of
the high-points of the set.

Jacobs's deployment of instruments, even on
the continuo, is measured – even sparing, by his
standards – but rich enough to evoke the splendid courtly entertainments for which these
pieces were conceived. The instrumentalists are
perhaps too easily overlooked in this repertoire:
they don't draw attention to themselves here,
but sound very solid and grounded.

Jacobs's feeling for the music's dramatic qualities is keen, and unsurprisingly encompasses the
largest pieces, the 'one-act' operas *Il-ballo delle
ingrate* and *Combattimento di Tancredi e Clorinda*.
For these, some may prefer Concerto Italiano's
recording, which includes both pieces on a single disc, but Jacobs's less wilful readings are still
most involving. By any objective criteria, Jacobs
has pulled it off. So if you're looking for a single
recording, this is a natural first choice.

'Banquet of the Senses'
Longe, mi Jesu. Madrigals, Book 4 (Il quarto libro de
madrigali) – Ah dolente partita; Io mi son giovinetta;
Ohimè, se tanto amate; Piange e sospira; Quel
augellin che canta; Sfogava con le stelle; Si ch'io
vorrei morire. Madrigals, Book 7 (Concerto: settimo
libro de madrigali) – Parlo, miser'o taccio?
Consort of Musicke (Emma Kirkby, Evelyn Tubb *sops*
Mary Nichols *contr* Andrew King, Joseph Cornwell
tens Simon Grant *bass* Gabriele Micheli *org*) /
Anthony Rooley *lte*
Brilliant Classics 🅳🆅🅳 99784 (48' · 16:9 · 5.1 · 0)   Ⓜ

This programme, released on VHS by the
Consort's own label Musica Oscura in 1993, has
now reappeared on DVD, and deserves attention both for its fine music-making and adventurous conception.

The performances are recorded in the banquet-
ing apartments of the Gonzaga dukes of Mantua,
for whose entertainment many of these madrigals

were created. In this intriguing setting, beneath
the famously sensuous Mantuan frescoes, the
Consort make a brave stab at recreating those
original performances, mini-masques almost,
with costume and dance. Rooley links them with
an amiably informative commentary. The result
is a welcome reminder of just how much of this
music's magic we lose in the customary stuffed-
shirt recital. Nevertheless, it isn't a total success.
There's still something ineffably polite about it
all, the wholesome 'G&S' jollity that tends to
creep in when the English middle-classes aspire
to the orgiastic. In the languishing *Parlo, miser'o*,
the appearance of Mesdames Kirkby, Tubb and
Nichols in diaphanous *deshabillé* could not be less
than stirring, but can't quite shed the aura of a
merry Roedean dorm party.

All the same, this is an engaging and original
programme, and founded on first-rate performances. It isn't long, but it isn't expensive either,
and well worth investigating.

'The Sacred Music – 4'
Adoramus te, Christe. Domine, ne in furore.
Exulta, filia Sion. Salve, o regina. Salve regina.
Laetatus sum I. Salve regina I. Beatus vir III.
Dixit Dominus II. Sanctorum meritis II. Magnificat II.
Laudate Dominum III
**The King's Consort Choir; The King's Consort /
Robert King**
Hyperion CDA67519 (70' · DDD · T/t)   Ⓕ

The fourth volume of Robert King's exploration
of Monteverdi's sacred music continues to mix
pieces from different sources: the composer's
authorised collection *Selva morale e spirituale*,
the posthumous Venetian collection *Messa a
quattro voci e salmi*, and various Italian anthologies. The beginning of *Laetatus sum I* instantly
establishes the impeccable technical credentials
of these stunning performances. The organ and
chitarrone continuo is steady and sure-footed,
joined a few bars later by a flamboyant violin
duel stunningly dispatched by Simon Jones and
Andrea Morris, and then crowned with a glorious duet by Carolyn Sampson and Rebecca
Outram. The Choir of The King's Consort
reinforce tutti passages with some splendid contributions and meet the florid, extrovert eight-
part writing in *Dixit Dominus II* with colourful
commitment. In the motet *Adoramus te*, Christe
– not to be confused with the comparably beautiful but better known *Christe adoramus, te* – the
choir shows its skill at gentler music, although I
wonder if the use of solo voices might have been
equally attractive and closer to what Monteverdi
would have expected.

Charles Daniels and James Gilchrist beautifully judge several intimate tenor solos; Gilchrist's glorious and heartfelt singing in *Salve
regina I* features some wonderful echo contributions from Daniels. Their tender communication of the text and sweet high registers consolidate their status as the finest English tenors of
their type. Robert King never rushes the music
but cannily treads the fine line between dizzying

excitement and authoritative splendour. Even if you already admire seminal recordings of Monteverdi sacred music by the likes of Andrew Parrott, Konrad Junghänel and Rinaldo Alessandrini, there are plenty of less familiar gems included that make this series essential.

L'incoronazione di Poppea

L'incoronazione di Poppea   **P**
Sylvia McNair sop Poppea **Dana Hanchard** sop Nerone **Anne Sofie von Otter** mez Ottavia, Fortune, Venus **Michael Chance** counterten Ottone **Francesco Ellero d'Artegna** bass Seneca **Catherine Bott** sop Drusilla, Virtue, Pallas, Athene **Roberto Balcone** counterten Nurse **Bernarda Fink** contr Arnalta **Mark Tucker** ten Lucano, First Soldier **Julian Clarkson** bass Lictor, Mercury **Marinella Pennicchi** sop Love **Constanze Backes** sop Valleto **Nigel Robson** ten Liberto, Second Soldier **English Baroque Soloists / Sir John Eliot Gardiner**
Archiv Produktion ③ 447 088-2AH3 (191' · DDD · T/t) Recorded live 1993   Ⓕ

The central question was always about how much needs to be added to the surviving notes in order to make *Poppea* viable on stage. Gardiner and his advisers believe that nothing needs adding and that the 'orchestra' played only when explicitly notated in the score and was a very small group. To some ears this will have a fairly ascetic effect, but it's firmly in line with current scholarly thinking. To compensate, there's a rich group of continuo players who play with wonderful flexibility. And Gardiner's spacious reading of the score bursts with the variety of pace you might expect from a seasoned conductor of early opera. Sylvia McNair is a gloriously sensuous Poppea: from her sleepy first words to the final duet she's always a thoroughly devious character, with her breathy, come-hither tones. Complementing this is Dana Hanchard's angry-brat Nerone, less even in voice than one might hope, but dramatically powerful nevertheless. Whether they quite challenge Helen Donath and Elisabeth Söderström for Harnoncourt is a matter of opinion, but they certainly offer a viable alternative.

The strongest performances here, though, come from Michael Chance and Anne Sofie von Otter as Ottone and Ottavia, both of them offering superbly rounded portrayals. Again they face severe challenges from Harnoncourt's unforgettable Paul Esswood and Cathy Berberian, but here the challenge is more equal. Francesco Ellero d'Artegna is perhaps the most vocally skilled Seneca to date.

The fact that this was recorded at a public concert is noticeable only occasionally.

L'Incoronazione di Poppea
Maria Ewing sop Poppea **Dennis Bailey** ten Nerone **Cynthia Clarey** sop Ottavia **Dale Duesing** bar Ottone **Robert Lloyd** bass Seneca **Elizabeth Gale** sop Drusilla **Glyndebourne Chorus; London Philharmonic Orchestra / Raymond Leppard**

Stage director **Peter Hall**
Video directors **Peter Hall, Robin Lough**
Warner Music Vision/NVC Arts 📀 0630 16914-2 (155' · NTSC · 4:3 · PCM stereo · 2-6) Recorded live at the Glyndebourne Festival, 1984   Ⓕ◐

Raymond Leppard's edition of *Poppea*, first staged at Glyndebourne in 1962, opened many people's eyes and ears to Monteverdi for the first time. By 1984, though, when Glyndebourne mounted this new production, his Respighi-isation of Monteverdi's sparse original was distinctly old hat. The allegorical prologue was restored; but as well as the lush string textures there remained the downward transposition of castrato roles and the squeezing of three acts into two. Yet only the most fanatical devotee of historically informed performance could fail to respond to this wonderful production with sumptuous designs by John Bury.

Peter Hall's production is, quite properly, dominated by Poppea. Maria Ewing is the personification of sensuousness, singing with rich tone throughout. She brilliantly conveys Poppea's ruthless ambition, her steely determination to become empress at all costs. By the end you feel that Poppea and Nero richly deserve each other, and the empress Ottavia is well shot of her husband. Hall frequently has his singers addressing the camera: a bold move, but one that forces the viewer to become involved in the fate of these mainly rather unappealing characters.

The drawbacks of Leppard's edition notwithstanding, this is a great theatrical experience.

L'Orfeo

L'Orfeo   **P**
Ian Bostridge ten Orfeo **Patrizia Ciofi** ten Euridice **Natalie Dessay** sop La Musica **Alice Coote** ten Messenger **Sonia Prina** ten Speranza **Mario Luperi** ten Caronte **Véronique Gens** ten Prosperina **Carolyn Sampson** ten Nymph **Lorenzo Regazzo** ten Plutone **Christopher Maltman** ten Apollo Shepherd III **Paul Agnew** ten Eco Shepherd II **Pascal Bertin** ten Shepherd I **Richard Burkhard** ten Shepherd IV **European Voices; Le Concert d'Astrée / Emmanuelle Haïm**
Virgin Classics Veritas ② 545642-2 (96' · DDD)   Ⓕ◐◐

Instead of attempting an intellectual reconstruction of *L'Orfeo*, Emmanuelle Haïm presents a full-blooded reinvention of the opera that's firmly modernistic. The cast is primarily composed of world-class opera and recital singers: the overall result is even, cohesive and without vocal blemishes. Some sopranos represent the legacy of 'authenticity' better than others. Natalie Dessay's forthright declamation as La Musica in the exquisite prologue is emotive, but can't eclipse Gardiner's astute Lynne Dawson. In contrast, Carolyn Sampson's fleeting contribution as a Nymph is gorgeously refined and elegantly poised, suggesting that she might make a fine La Musica if given the chance. Véronique Gens is a creamy Prosperina whose tangible pity for Orfeo makes her a very human goddess. Alice Coote's Messenger provides the most compelling moment with a haunted voice full of eloquent pain. The title-role suits Ian Bostridge, and his thoughtfully considered singing effortlessly ranges between smouldering gestures in 'Vi ricorda ò bosch' ombrosi' and shivering disbelief when the messenger tells him Euridice is dead.

European Voices incline towards a full-blooded operatic sound rather than a cool choral blend. Le Concert d'Astrée serve as a linchpin that propels the drama forward with obsessive momentum. The pumping sackbuts during the introductory toccata indicate that the ensuing drama isn't going to be dull, and Les Sacqueboutiers also provide a splendid regal entrance to a vision of Dante's Inferno in Act 3. The strings produce *ritornellos* of magnificent sensitivity and resonating eroticism. Haïm does, though, excessively pepper Monteverdi's score with prominent and improvisational percussion.

Haïm's performance has a much stronger Italianate sense than the comparatively English school that's hitherto dominated the discography, and her compelling perspective possesses a lively spirit that makes the listening hours fly by. Purists will be divided over the liberties she takes, but her performance is a stimulating alternative to the fine pedigree of recordings that has preceded it.

L'Orfeo

John Mark Ainsley ten Orfeo **Juanita Lascarro** sop Euridice **Brigitte Balleys** sop Messenger **Russell Smythe** ten Apollo, Shepherd II **David Cordier** alto La Musica **Michael Chance** counterten Speranza **Mario Luperi** bass Caronte **Bernarda Fink** mez Proserpina **Dean Robinson** bass-bar Plutone; Shepherd IV **Jean-Paul Fouchécourt** ten Shepherd I, Eco **Douglas Nasrawi** ten Shepherd III **Suzie Le Blanc** sop Nymph **Tragicomedia; Concerto Palatino / Stephen Stubbs**
Stage director **Pierre Audi**
Video director **Hans Hulscher**
Opus Arte ② 🆅🆅 OA0928D (140' · 16:9 · PCM stereo and DTS 5.1 · 0)
Recorded live at Het Muziektheater, Amsterdam, in July 1997. Extra features include Illustrated Synopsis, Cast Gallery, Introduction to the Opera and Interviews   Ⓕ

In a perceptive documentary made during rehearsals, director Pierre Audi comments that *L'Orfeo* is 'an opera about the crisis of an artist: whether art and life are really compatible; what the personal intimate experience of an artist in confronting love and death has to do with his own artistic expression'. Audi's production is starkly conceptual in some ways but the performance has a simplicity and fidelity to the drama. Carefully timed effects, controlled gestures and economical directness have a powerful impact. The action is focused around a circular pool of water set towards the back of the stage, behind a dilapidated wall that is used for different purposes – such as sinking to become the passage-

way to Hades. The Arcadian frolics of the shepherds and nymphs allow dancing, skipping and splashing in the pool; but later, flames emerge to transform it into the Styx.

Audi weds his own ideas about characters to a faithful reproduction of the libretto. Audi's action shows that the Messenger who brings news of Euridice's death is shunned by the Arcadians, whose society is evidently only superficially pleasant (this reinforces the idea that all earthly pleasure is fleeting, as Orfeo is told by his father Apollo in the opera's conclusion). Plutone's bargain with Orfeo is a vindictive mind game with his wife Proserpina, who desires Orfeo. Likewise, Orfeo seems to yearn for Proserpina despite his quest for Euridice, thus making his moral character tarnished. Audi's skill is to make these ambiguities subtle and paradoxical, for Orfeo's grief and confusion at his permanent loss of Euridice lack nothing in sincerity.

John Mark Ainsley's blend of head and chest voices has beauty and depth, and his acting is equally impressive. Bernarda Fink provides outstanding singing and acting as Proserpina, and Michael Chance delivers a compelling cameo as La Speranza. But it was a bizarre decision to cast David Cordier as an androgynous La Musica who struggles to sing poetically, especially when Suzie Le Blanc – the ideal soprano for this part – steps forward for only a few solo lines.

There are assured contributions from Jean-Paul Fouchécourt, Russell Smythe, Dean Robinson, Brigitte Balleys and Juanita Lascarro. Mario Luperi looks the part as a giant-like Caronte, although his fast vibrato will not please everybody. The trump card is the superb accompaniment from Concerto Palatino and Tragicomedia, expertly directed by Stephen Stubbs.

Il Ritorno d'Ulisse in Patria

Il Ritorno d'Ulisse in Patria   🅿
Christoph Prégardien ten Ulisse **Bernarda Fink** contr Penelope **Christina Högmann** sop Telemaco, Siren **Martyn Hill** ten Eumete **Jocelyne Taillon** mez Ericlea **Dominique Visse** counterten Pisandro, Human Fragility **Mark Tucker** ten Anfinomo **David Thomas** bass Antinoo **Guy de Mey** ten Iro **Faridah Subrata** mez Melanto **Jörg Dürmüller** ten Eurimaco **Lorraine Hunt** sop Minerva, Fortune **Michael Schopper** bass Nettuno, Time **Olivier Lallouette** bass Giove **Claron McFadden** sop Giunone **Martina Bovet** sop Siren, Love **Concerto Vocale / René Jacobs**
Harmonia Mundi ③ HMC90 1427/9 (179' · DDD · T/t)   Ⓕ🔵🔵

The only surviving manuscript score of this major musical drama, preserved in Vienna, presents an incomplete version of three acts. For this recording, René Jacobs has, within the spirit of 17th-century music-making, added more music by Monteverdi and others to expand the work to a satisfying five-act structure suggested by some surviving librettos. He has also considerably expanded the scoring, very much enlivening the instrumental palette that Monteverdi would have had available to him for his original production in Vienna in 1641, and the result is powerful and effective.

The extensive cast, led by Christoph Prégardien in the title-role, is excellently chosen, not only for vocal quality but also for a convincing awareness of Monteverdi's idiom. Without that, the performance could have seemed tame, and that's nowhere better exemplified than in Act 1, Scene 7 where Ulysses awakes, wondering where he is and what's to happen to him. Prégardien here manages to convey as much depth of feeling as a Pagliaccio yet stays clearly within the bounds of Monteverdi's expressive style. The result is a *tour de force*, one of the many within this production. The adept instrumental contribution certainly helps to maintain variety throughout the work, and an accompaniment suited to the sentiments expressed by the vocalists is always possible with these resources. Ultimately, this production is very much one for our time. It's a practical solution to the problems of performing music of another age, and one that turns out to be inspired, moving and totally compelling.

with such an extraordinary range of vocal beauty and immediacy of expression? This extends to all the characters.

Of the two caveats here, the durability of Harnoncourt's big-band score with its bold instrumental canvas is likely to be a source of debate. Monteverdi left only a shell of his musical genius and, as convention dictated, the performers filled in the rest. The logic of using the greatest array of coloration to suit the context of characterisation and emotional states is highly plausible for all those who value music drama – and Monteverdi, more to the point – in pastels rather than charcoal. Yet there are moments when the spirit of realisation enters the realm of transcription, especially in the richly endowed brass ensembles used for divine intervention. A later baroque soundworld occasionally prevails, and the luminosity of the moment is lost. However, the warm glow of assured fidelity in 'Hor di parlar e tempo' – where Ulysses's *accompagnato* recitative lends authenticity to the composer's primal communicative instincts – is ravishing and persuasive. The DVD production is flawed only by some poor dubbing in Act 2.

Il Ritorno d'Ulisse in Patria
Dietrich Henschel *bar* Ulisse, Humana fragilità
Vesselina Kasarova *sop* Penelope **Jonas Kaufmann**
ten Telemaco **Boguslaw Bidzinski** *ten* Eurimaco
Anton Scharinger *ten* Giove **Reinhard Mayr** *bass*
Antinoo **Martin Zysset** *ten* Pisandro **Martin Oro**
counterten Anfinomo **Isabel Rey** *sop* Minerva,
Amore **Thomas Mohr** *ten* Eumete **Pavel Daniluk**
bass Nettuno **Giuseppe Scorsin** *bass* Time **Martina**
Janková *sop* Fortune **Giunone Cornelia Kallisch**
mez Ericlea **Malin Hartelius** *sop* Melanto **Rudolf**
Schasching *ten* Iro La Scintilla Orchestra, Zurich /
Nikolaus Harnoncourt
Stage director **Klaus-Michael Grüber**
Video director **Felix Breisach**
ArtHaus Musik **DVD** 100 352 (155' · 16:9 · 2.0 & 5.1 · 0)
Notes included   Ⓕ

The renowned collaborations between Zurich Opera and Nikolaus Harnoncourt in the 1970s and early 80s were crucial milestones in projecting historically aware performance away from historicism-for-its-own-sake, towards vitally conceived productions for contemporary audiences. *Il Ritorno* enjoyed great success in 1977 in Jean-Pierre Ponnelle's imaginative staging: Harnoncourt's opulent instrumental palette lifted the hearts of many, though only the eyebrows of the purists. In this musical 'revival' to celebrate 25 years of the swashbuckling original, Harnoncourt allows the nobility of the score to roll unimpeded by the driven intensity of the older recorded account on Teldec from 1971.

The vocal contributions are more eloquent than ever, with outstanding contributions from Vesselina Kasarova and Dietrich Henschel. Can Monteverdi have ever heard this opera sung

Cristóbal de Morales
Spanish c1500-1553

Morale is recognised as the most important figure in early 16th-century Spanish sacred music. He received his early musical education in Seville and in 1526 was appointed maestro de capilla of Avila Cathedral. In 1531 he resigned and by September 1535 was a singer in the papal chapel in Rome. He left in 1545 and was appointed maestro de capilla at Toledo Cathedral. He then fell ill and in 1547 renounced the position. On returning to Andalusia he became maestro de capilla to the Duke of Arcos at Marchena (1548-51). In 1551 he became maestro de capilla at Málaga Cathedral.

His works, almost all liturgical, include over 20 masses, 16 Magnificats, two Lamentations and over 100 motets. The Magnificats, perhaps the best known of his works, are permeated by Gregorian cantus firmi ; his Lamentations are characterised by a sober homophonic style. In his motets he often used chant associated with the text, as a melodic point of departure (eg Puer natus est) or as an ostinato figure (eg the five-voice Tu es Petrus), but he seldom borrowed entire melodies. Their texture is characterised by free imitation with exceptional use of homophonic sections to stress important words or portions of text. The two masses for the dead and the Officium defunctorum are the most extreme examples of Morales's sober style. He had thorough command of early 16th-century continental techniques and his style is better compared to Josquin, Gombert and Clemens than to his Spanish contemporaries. He favoured cross-rhythms, conflicting rhythms, melodic (but not harmonic) sequence and repetition, harmonic cross-relations, systematic use of consecutives and occasional daring use of harmony. **GROVE**music

Masses

Missa 'Si bona suscepimus' **Crecquillon** Andreas
Christi famulus **Verdelot** Si bona suscepimus
The Tallis Scholars / Peter Phillips
Gimell CDGIM033 (56' · DDD · T/t)   Ⓕ**OO**

The Tallis Scholars move into new territory for
them: Cristóbal de Morales is perhaps the most
admired Spanish composer of all time, to judge
from the distribution and longevity of his works.
But not nearly enough of his music has appeared
on disc. In particular, the six-voice Mass *Si bona
suscepimus* appears not to have been recorded
before. It was printed in his first book of Masses
(1544) and undoubtedly comes from his years in
the papal chapel. At first listening, there may be
something almost too serene about its flawless
counterpoint that flows with effortless invention. But there's an abundance of arresting detail
in here, and he uses the six voices with an astonishing variety of textures.

The Tallis Scholars are up to their usual
standards of magnificent sound colour, nicely
judged balance and extremely pure intonation.
There's nothing overtly Spanish in the performance: they simply sing what's in the music,
without imposing too much externally. They
hardly ever rush or slow down severely, preferring to allow the music to unfold at its own
flexible pace. That could seem bland until you
compare the sound with the introductory five-
voice motet of Verdelot on which the Mass is
based, or indeed the marvellous Crecquillon
motet that ends the disc; these immediately
sound quite different.

Sancta Maria, succerre miseris. Beati omnes qui
timent Dominum. Lamentations of Jeremiah – Coph:
Vocavi; Zai: Candidiores; Nun: Vigilavit. Gaude et
laetare, Ferrariensis civitas. Salve regina a 4. Regina
caeli a 6. Spem in alium. Magnificat primi toni
Brabant Ensemble / Stephen Rice
Hyperion CDA67694 (73' · DDD · T/t)   Ⓕ**O**

This recording suggests how central is
Morales's position within the High Repertoire. Often spoken of as a precursor of Palestrina, here (as in the Lamentations settings
that open the programme) he seems just as
clearly to prefigure Lassus's own penitential
mode (especially at 'Nun: Vigilavit'). Stephen
Rice leaves aside the Mass repertory in favour
of the motet. Following the Lamentations set,
this selection is mostly of Marian pieces. The
single exception is an impressive celebratory
piece commemorating the elevation of
Ippolito d'Este, brother of the Duke of Ferrara, to the cardinalate. Unlike some of the
Marian motets this has not been recorded
before, and it shows off a more public side of
the composer.

The motets range in scoring from four to six
voices, but whatever the number of voices, the
counterpoint is always perfectly intelligible.

Obviously that's due to the clarity of the composer's textures, but it also reflects well on the
Brabant Ensemble, who turn in very solid readings, subdued or serene, as text and music
demand. In the Magnificat, the intensity steps
up a notch, reaching an impressive climax.
Indeed, the ensemble quality here belies the fact
that only four voices are involved (except at the
very end); this is the Brabant Ensemble at their
most vigorous and confident. For this reading,
Rice opts for the polyphonic setting of all the
verses, rather than alternate half of them with
plainchant, a common practice of the time. In a
fast-growing discography, this is a valuable addition.

Assumption Mass – Toledo Cathedral, c1580   Ⓟ
Morales Ave regina caelorum. Exaltata est sancta
Dei genitrix. Missa Benedicta est regina caelorum
Cabezón Beata viscera Mariae Virginis. Tiento sobre
el hymno, 'Ave Maris stella' **Ceballos** O pretiosum et
admirabile sacrementum **F Guerrero** Ave Maria.
Dulcissima Maria **Ribera** Beata mater **Torrentes**
Asperges Mej **Plainchants** – Introitus; Oratio;
Graduale and Alleluia; Offertorium; Prefacio; Pater
noster; Communio; Postcommunio
**Orchestra of the Renaissance / Richard Cheetham
and Michael Noone**
Glossa GCD921404 (76' · DDD · T/t)   Ⓕ

This is a reconstruction of a Mass for the
Assumption as it might have been heard in
Toledo Cathedral in about 1580. It follows very
much the pattern established by the group's
previous discs, with a mixture of musical items
that can be pegged, however loosely, to a particular occasion or type of occasion. Here the
research into the rich musical repertory and the
musico-liturgical practice of Toledo Cathedral
by guest conductor Michael Noone makes for a
particularly compelling example of the reconstruction genre.

The ways in which instruments and voices are
used is well thought out, and the music, including those pieces by the less well-known
Toledan *maestros* Ribera and Torrentes, is of
the highest quality. Similar care has been taken
over the sources for the plainchant which, as on
earlier recordings by the Orchestra of the Renaissance, is performed with just the right inflections and sense of pace by the bass Josep
Cabré.

It's clear that Morales's music continued to be
performed in Spanish cathedrals throughout the
16th century and beyond, and the superb Mass
Benedicta est regina caelorum makes it easy to see
why. It's performed well by singers and instrumentalists alike, the harp and dulcian adding a
distinctive shimmer and depth to the overall
soundpool of voices, shawms and sackbuts.
Overall, the performances are restrained with a
good sense of natural flow, if perhaps occasionally lacking in intensity. An impressive and very
attractive CD that grows with repeated listening
into one of the most convincing 'occasional'
recordings in the catalogue.

Ignaz Moscheles   German 1794-1870

*A pupil of BD Weber in Prague and of Albrechts-
berger and Salieri in Vienna, Moscheles became a
piano recitalist, travelling throughout Europe
(1815-25). Settling in London (1825-46), he
taught at the RAM established a series of 'historical
soirées' (in which he performed Bach and Scarlatti on
the harpsichord), wrote fashionable salon music and
conducted the Philharmonic Society; he was a friend
of Mendelssohn, conducted the London premiere of
Beethoven's Missa solemnis (1832) and translated
Schindler's biography as The Life of Beethoven
(1841). From 1846 he was professor at the Leipzig
Conservatory. His best compositions are his piano
sonatas (some for duet), in which a classical balance is
tempered with an early Romantic dynamism, and his
studies (still used).* GROVEmusic

Piano Concertos

Piano Concertos – No 2 in E flat, Op 56; No 3 in G
minor, Op 58. Anticipations of Scotland: A Grand
Fantasia, Op 75
**Tasmanian Symphony Orchestra /
Howard Shelley** pf
Hyperion CDA67276 (76' · DDD)   Ⓕ❍❍

Both the Second and Third Concertos bristle
with enough savage jumps and hurdles to throw
a less than first class performer; woe betide the
pianist without flawless scales and arpeggios
(often twisting into awkward and unpredictable
patterns). Moscheles' contemporaries, hungry
for heart-stopping acrobatics, surely left the
concert hall thrilled and gratified. But there are
also many fascinating purely musical surprises.

Most engagingly, Moscheles was highly
responsive to local colour, paying tribute to his
adopted city of London in his Fourth Concerto
by quoting the 'March of the Grenadiers' and, in
his *Anticipations of Scotland: A Grand Fantasia*, to
folk songs and dances north of the border. Who
can resist the assurance of 'Auld Robin Grey'
(though even he breaks out into a flash of virtuosity) or a strathspey sufficiently perky to set all
true Scotsmen's blood tingling.

The recordings, made in Tasmania, are excellent, and the Tasmanian Symphony Orchestra
enter into the spirit of things with verve and
affection. In short, a disc of aristocratic brilliance and distinction.

Wolfgang Amadeus Mozart
Austrian 1756-1791

*Mozart, son of Leopold Mozart, showed musical gifts
at a very early age, composing when he was five and
when he was six playing before the Bavarian elector
and the Austrian empress. Leopold felt that it was
proper, and might also be profitable, to exhibit his
children's God-given genius (Mozart's sister was a
gifted keyboard player), so from mid-1763-6 the
family set out on a European tour. Mozart astonished
his audiences with his precocious skills; he played to
the French and English royal families, had his first
music published and wrote his earliest symphonies. In
1767 they were off again, to Vienna, where hopes of
having an opera by Mozart performed were frustrated by intrigues. 1770-73 saw three visits to Italy,
where Mozart wrote two operas (Mitridate, Lucio
Silla) and a serenata for performance in Milan, and
acquainted himself with Italian styles. Summer
1773 saw a further visit to Vienna where he wrote a
set of string quartets and, on his return, a group of
symphonies including Nos 25 in G minor and 29 in
A. Apart from a journey to Munich for the premiere
of his opera La finta giardiniera early in 1775, the
period from 1774 to mid-1777 was spent in Salzburg, where Mozart worked as Konzertmeister at
the Prince Archbishop's court; his works of these years
include masses, symphonies, all his violin concertos,
six piano sonatas, several serenades and divertimentos and his first great piano concerto, K271.*

*In 1777 he was sent, with his mother, to Munich
and to Mannheim, but was offered no position
(though he stayed over four months at Mannheim,
falling in love with Aloysia Weber). His father then
dispatched him to Paris: there he had minor successes,
notably with his Paris Symphony, no.31, deftly
designed for the local taste. But prospects there were
poor and Leopold ordered him home, where a superior
post had been arranged at the court. He returned
slowly and alone; his mother had died in Paris. The
years 1779-80 were spent in Salzburg, playing in
the cathedral and at court, composing sacred works,
symphonies, concertos, serenades and dramatic music.
But opera remained at the centre of his ambitions,
and an opportunity came with a commission for a
serious opera for Munich. He went there to compose it
late in 1780; his correspondence with Leopold is
richly informative about his approach to musical
drama. The work, Idomeneo, was a success. In it
Mozart depicted serious, heroic emotion with a richness unparalleled elsewhere in his works, with vivid
orchestral writing and an abundance of profoundly
expressive orchestral recitative.*

*Mozart was then summoned to Vienna, where the
Salzburg court was in residence on the accession of a
new emperor. Fresh from his success, he found himself
placed between the valets and the cooks; his resentment towards his employer, exacerbated by the
Prince-Archbishop's refusal to let him perform at
events the emperor was attending, soon led to conflict,
and in May 1781 he resigned, or was kicked out of,
his job. He made his living over the ensuing years by
teaching, by publishing his music, by playing at
patrons' houses or in public, by composing to commission; in 1787 he obtained a minor court post as Kam-
mermusicus, which gave him a reasonable salary and
required nothing beyond the writing of dance music
for court balls. He earned, by musicians standards, a
good income, but lavish spending and poor management caused him financial difficulties. In 1782 he
married Constanze Weber, Aloysia's sister.*

*In his early years in Vienna, Mozart built up his
reputation by publishing, playing the piano and, in
1782, having an opera performed: Die Entführung aus dem Serail, a German Singspiel
which went far beyond the usual limits of the tra-*

dition with its long, elaborately written songs. The work was successful and was taken into the repertories of many provincial companies (for which Mozart was not however paid). In these years, too, he wrote six string quartets which he dedicated to the master of the form, Haydn: they are marked not only by their variety of expression but by their complex textures, conceived as four-part discourse, with the musical ideas linked to this freshly integrated treatment of the medium.

In 1782 Mozart embarked on the composition of piano concertos, so that he could appear both as composer and soloist. He wrote 15 before the end of 1786, with early 1784 as the peak of activity. They represent one of his greatest achievements, with their formal mastery, their subtle relationships between piano and orchestra (the wind instruments especially) and their combination of brilliance, lyricism and symphonic growth. In 1786 he wrote the first of his three comic operas with Lorenzo da Ponte as librettist, Le nozze di Figaro: here and in Don Giovanni (given in Prague, 1787) Mozart treats the interplay of social and sexual tensions with keen insight into human character that – as again in the more artificial sexual comedy of Così fan tutte (1790) – transcends the comic framework, just as Die Zauberflöte (1790) transcends, with its elements of ritual and allegory about human harmony and enlightenment, the world of the Viennese popular theatre from which it springs.

Mozart lived in Vienna for the rest of his life, though he undertook a number of journeys to Salzburg, Prague, Berlin and Frankfurt. The last Prague journey was for the premiere of La clemenza di Tito (1791), a traditional serious opera written for coronation celebrations, but composed with a finesse and economy characteristic of Mozart's late music. Instrumental works of these years include some piano sonatas, three string quartets written for the King of Prussia, some string quintets, which include one of his most deeply felt works (K516 in G minor) and one of his most nobly spacious (Kn C), and his last four symphonies – one (No 38 in D) composed for Prague in 1786, the others written in 1788 and forming, with the lyricism of No 39 in E flat, the tragic suggestiveness of No 40 in G minor and the grandeur of No 41 in C, a climax to his orchestral music. His final works include the Clarinet Concerto and some pieces for masonic lodges (he had been a freemason since 1784). At his death from a feverish illness whose precise nature has given rise to much speculation (he was not poisoned), he left unfinished the Requiem, his first large-scale work for the church since the C minor Mass of 1783, also unfinished. Mozart was buried in a Vienna suburb, with little ceremony and in an unmarked grave, in accordance with prevailing custom.

This Concertgebouw survey of four wind concertos dates across a fair span of Mozart's adulthood. The First Horn Concerto was composed for Mozart's friend Joseph Leutgeb at Vienna in 1791; modern-day counterpart Jacob Slagter employs a warmly refulgent tone in his lively performance. Next, we have the First Flute Concerto (Paris, 1778). Emily Beynon's neatly executed, charming playing is well suited to the celebratory, sunny first movement. The Concertgebouw strings contribute hushed accompaniment in the *Andante ma non troppo*.

Mozart's Salzburg years are represented by his Bassoon Concerto (1774) and Oboe Concerto (written in 1777 for the Italian oboist Giuseppe Ferlendis, who had joined the Salzburg court only a few months before). Bassoonist Gustavo Nuñez plays with fruity directness, displaying stunning agility in the *Allegro* and poignant playing in the *Andante ma adagio*. Alexei Ogrintchouk's oboe provides a melancholic *Adagio non troppo* and a fluent impression of Mozart's felicitous inventiveness in the gleeful Rondo. All four soloists are principals of the Royal Concertgebouw Orchestra. The chamber incarnation sounds playful yet at ease. Phrases are shaded off and chords often shortened, but there is no self-consciousness or evident struggle in the pervading cheerful spirit.

Clarinet Concerto in A, K622

Clarinet Concerto. Clarinet Quintet in A, K581
Thea King *basset cl* [b]**Gabrieli String Quartet**
(Kenneth Sillito, Brendan O'Reilly *vns* Ian Jewel *va*
Keith Harvey *vc*) [a]**English Chamber Orchestra /
Jeffrey Tate**
Hyperion CDA66199 (64' · DDD)   ⒻⓄ

The two works on this disc represent Mozart's clarinet writing at its most inspired; however, the instrument for which they were written differed in several respects from the modern clarinet, the most important being its extended bass range. Modern editions of both the Clarinet Concerto and the Quintet have adjusted the solo part to suit today's clarinets, but Thea King reverts as far as possible to the original texts, and her playing is both sensitive and intelligent. Jeffrey Tate and the ECO accompany with subtlety and discretion in the concerto, and the Gabrieli Quartet achieves a fine rapport with King in the Quintet. Both recordings are clear and naturally balanced, with just enough distance between soloist and listener.

Bassoon Concerto, K191

Bassoon Concerto. Flute Concerto No 1.
Horn Concerto No 1. Oboe Concerto
Emily Beynon *fl* **Alexei Ogrintchouk** *ob*
Gustavo Nuñez *bn* **Jacob Slagter** *hn*
Concertgebouw Chamber Orchestra
Pentatone ⏺ PTC5186 079 (71' · DDD/DSD)   ⒻⒹ⏴

Clarinet Concerto. Clarinet Quintet
Jack Brymer *cl* **London Symp[hony Orchestra / Sir
Colin Davis; Allegri Quartet**
Philips 442 390-2PM (50' · ADD) Recorded 1973
                                       ⒻⓄⓄⒹ⏴

From the many recordings of the concerto Jack Brymer made, this mid-price coupling is well worth looking for. With Davis a master-Mozartian coaxing elegant playing from the LSO, Brymer delivers a performance of poetry and charm. The Clarinet Quintet is no less delightful.

Flute Concertos

No 1 in G, K313; **No 2** in C, K314. **Andante in C major**, K315. **Flute and Harp Concerto** in D, K299 Flute Concertos Nos 1 & 2 (cadenzas by Aho). Andante, K315. Rondo, KAnh184
Sharon Bezaly fl **Ostrobothnian Chamber Orchestra / Juha Kangas**
BIS ⊕ BIS-SACD1539 (56' · DDD)   Ⓕ**OO**

Israeli flautist Sharon Bezaly offers delectable performances of the familiar Mozart concertos. The composer famously protested that he loathed the flute, though he was far too much of a pro to slip from his customary fastidious standards. In the fast movements he is at his most puckish and insouciant, while the slow ones, especially the *Adagio ma non troppo* of the G major, infuse graceful galanterie with exquisite poetry.

To both concertos, plus the two separate movements (of which the D major Rondo is a transcription of the dapper C major Rondo for violin, K373), Bezaly brings pure, delicately coloured tone – beautiful throughout its range – phenomenal agility and breath control, and an impish sense of fun. The *Allegros* have an elegant bounce, with soloist and the ever-alert Ostro-bothnian Chamber Orchestra relishing their quickfire interplay. Repeats are always a cue for imaginative new phrasings; and time and again Bezaly provokes a smile with her playfully varied bravura passagework.

Bezaly opts for a lighter tonal palette than usual and favours a cooler, simpler (and argu-ably more Mozartian) approach in slow move-ments. Where she steps right out of period is in the cadenzas. Specially written by Kalevi Aho, these refract and fragment Mozart through a 21st-century prism, exploiting the whole compass of the flute and giving Bezaly scope to explore intriguing new colours. Pur-ists may throw up their hands. But if you can adjust to the time-travelling you may find Aho's cadenzas ingenious, entertaining and strangely touching.

Flute and Harp Concerto. Horn Concerto No 3, K447. Concerto for Two Pianos and Orchestra, K365
Frank Theuns fl **Ulrich Hübner** hn
Marjan de Haer hp **Yoko Kaneko** fp
Anima Eterna Orchestra / Jos van Immerseel fp
Zig Zag Territoires ZZT060201 (67' · DDD)   Ⓕ**OOO**

Director and fortepianist Jos van Immerseel is a veritable pioneer of period Mozart. Belgian period-instrument orchestra Anima Eterna's exuberant performances reveal a natural union

of pioneering spirit and refreshing musical fla-vours. The performers show commendable integrity in their approach to using historical instruments: the characteristics and origins of the solo instruments are each enthusiastically described in the booklet-note but the loving care given to detail in this joyful music means this is never in danger of seeming merely a dour academic exercise.

The invigorating Concerto for two pianos (Salzburg, 1779-80) opens proceedings with a revitalising fix of blazing horns, vibrant wood-wind and articulate strings. Anima Eterna's stunning playing in the tuttis is perfectly bal-anced with the fluent playing of Immerseel and Yoko Kaneko. After such *joie de vivre*, the Flute and Harp Concerto (Paris, 1778) features sensi-tively judged playing from Frank Theuns and Marjan de Haer. Seldom thas there been such an affectionate and warmly stylish performance of the *Allegro*, and the *Andantino* is ravishing.

Ulrich Hübner plays with attractive immedi-acy in the Third Horn Concerto, composed around 1787: the poetic *Romance* has a lyrical elegance one seldom hears from even the best natural horn players, and an infectiously sunny performance of the dance-like *Allegro* concludes this magnificent recording with a charismatic flourish. These performances are radiant: if you buy only one Mozart CD this anniversary year, let it be this one.

Horn Concertos

No 1 in D, K412; **No 2** in E flat, K417; **No 3** in E flat, K447; **No 4** in E flat, K495

Horn Concertos Nos 1-4. Piano Quintet in E flat,  K452
Dennis Brain hn **Philharmonia Orchestra / Herbert von Karajan**
EMI mono 566898-2 (55' · ADD) Recorded 1953
Ⓕ**OOOⒷ**

Dennis Brain was the finest Mozartian soloist of his generation. Again and again Karajan matches the graceful line of his solo phrasing (the *Romance* of No 3 is just one ravishing example), while in the *Allegros* the crisply articulated, often witty comments from the Philharmonia violins are a joy. The glorious tone and the richly lyrical phrasing of every note from Brain himself is life-enhancing in its radi-ant warmth. The *Rondos* aren't just spirited, buoyant, infectious and smiling, although they're all these things, but they have the kind of natural flow that Beecham gave to Mozart. There's also much dynamic subtlety – Brain doesn't just repeat the main theme the same as the first time, but alters its level and colour. His legacy to future generations of horn players has been to show them that the horn – a notoriously difficult instrument – can be tamed absolutely and that it can yield a lyrical line and a range of

MOZART'S HORN CONCERTOS – IN BRIEF

**Dennis Brain; Philharmonia Orchestra /
Herbert von Karajan**   H
EMI mono 566898-2 (77' · ADD)   ⓂⓄⓄⓄ⟐

Ⓖ Timelessly neat and elegant orchestral playing under Herbert von Karajan accompanies Dennis Brain's flawless and characterful playing – truly an all-time classic which transcends the mono sound.

Michael Thompson; Bournemouth Sinfonietta
Naxos 8 553592 (76' · DDD)   Ⓢ⟐
Sparkling performances on modern instruments by the Bournemouth Sinfonietta under the direction of the soloist, Michael Thompson, who performs scholarly editions prepared by John Humphries. A top bargain choice.

English Chamber Orchestra / Barry Tuckwell *hn*
Decca 458 607-2DM (69' · DDD)   Ⓜ
Fluent and charming performances by Barry Tuckwell, who also directs the English Chamber Orchestra's idiomatic accompaniment, in his third studio recording of these concertos

David Pyatt; ASMF / Neville Marriner
Warner Classics 2564-69719-9 (69' · DDD)   ⓂⓄ
Though recorded in 1996, the slightly plush string tone and close-focus miking of David Pyatt's mellow-toned horn makes these accounts sound a tad old-fashioned even next to Karajan and Brain. Nonetheless, these are affectionate performances which will please those wanting modern instrumentation in stereo sound.

Eric Ruske; Scottish CO / Charles Mackerras
Telarc CD-80367 (64' · DDD)   Ⓕ
Attractive performances with golden horn tone complemented by idiomatic orchestral playing in spacious sound. Richard Suart singing Flanders and Swann's *Ill wind* makes an unusual encore.

Alan Civil; Philharmonia / Otto Klemperer   H
Testament SBT1102 (72' · ADD)   Ⓕ
Another historic performance. Alan Civil's tone is more full bodied and his humour more earthy than Brain's. The orchestral accompaniment, however, is not always ideally co-ordinated with the soloist.

Teunis Van der Zwart *hn* **Freiburg Baroque**   Ⓟ
Orchestra / Gottfried von der Goltz
Harmonia Mundi HMC90 1946 (66' · DDD)   Ⓕ
Though only recorded in Concertos Nos 1 and 4, Teunis Van der Swart gives irresistable performances full of the full-throated joy that natural horns can convey so freely. Gottfried von der Goltz and the Freiburgers provide thrilling support.

colour to match any other solo instrument. He was tragically killed, in his prime, in a car accident while travelling home overnight from the Edinburgh Festival. He left us this supreme Mozartian testament which may be approached by others but rarely, if ever, equalled, for his was uniquely inspirational music-making, with an innocent-like quality to make it the more endearing. It's a pity to be unable to be equally enthusiastic about the recorded sound. The remastering leaves the horn timbre, with full Kingsway Hall resonance, unimpaired, but has dried out the strings. This, though, remains a classic recording.

Horn Concertos Nos 1-4. Horn Quintet in E flat, K407
David Pyatt *hn* **Kenneth Sillito** *vn* **Robert Smissen,
Stephen Tees** *va* **Stephen Orton** *vc* **Academy of St
Martin in the Fields / Sir Neville Marriner**
Warner Classics 2564-69719-9 (70' · DDD)   ⓂⓄ

David Pyatt, *Gramophone*'s Young Artist of the Year in 1996, provides performances in which calm authority and high imagination fuse; and this disc comlements the nobility and urbanity of Dennis Brain. Although there can be no direct comparison with Anthony Halstead, Pyatt's is very much in that mode of supple, understated and often witty playing, accompanied by truly discriminating orchestral forces. Soloist and orchestra create a constantly shifting and lively pattern of dynamic relationships. Pyatt makes the music's song and meditation his own. Compared with the dark, dream-like *cantabile* of Brain, he offers in the Second Concerto an *Andante* of cultivated conversation and, in the Third, a *Romanza* of barely moving breath and light. His finales trip the light fantastic. The Second Concerto's springing rhythms reveal wonderfully clear high notes; the Third is nimble and debonair without being quite as patrician as Brain's; and the Fourth creates real mischief in its effervescent articulation. The cadenzas by Terry Wooding (to the first movements of the Third and Fourth Concertos) epitomise Pyatt's performances as a whole: longer and more daringly imaginative than those of Brain, while remaining sensitively scaled and fancifully idiomatic. The concertos are imaginatively and unusually coupled with a fine performance of the Horn Quintet in E flat.

Horn Concertos Nos 1-4; E, K494a. Rondos for Horn and Orchestra – D, K514 (cptd Süssmayr); E flat, K371. Fragment for Horn and Orchestra in E flat, K370b (both reconstr Humphries)
Bournemouth Sinfonietta / Michael Thompson *hn*
Naxos 8 553592 (76' · DDD)   Ⓢ⟐

This isn't just an excellent bargain version of the horn concertos, superbly played and recorded, but a valuable example of Mozartian scholarship on disc. Michael Thompson, directing the Bournemouth Sinfonietta with point and flair, plays the four regular concertos in revised texts prepared by John Humphries, as well as offering reconstructions by Humphries of two movements, designed as the outer movements, an *Allegro*, K370b and a *Rondo*, K371, for an earlier horn concerto written soon after Mozart arrived in Vienna. The Rondo played here as the second-movement finale of K412 is Humphries' reconstruction from recently discovered sources, and is much more imaginative than the Süssmayr version. It's a revelation too in the most popular of the concertos, No-4, to have extra passages, again adding Mozartian inventiveness. For example, the *tutti* in the first movement before the development section is extended in a charming few extra bars. Thompson, for 10 years the Philharmonia's first horn, isn't only technically brilliant, but plays with delectable lightness and point, bringing out the wit in finales, and the tenderness in slow movements. As conductor and director, he also draws sparkling and refined playing from the Sinfonietta, very well recorded in clear, atmospheric sound. An outstanding issue for both specialist and newcomer alike.

Oboe Concerto in C, K314

Mozart Oboe Concerto **R Strauss** Oboe Concerto
Douglas Boyd ob
Chamber Orchestra of Europe / Paavo Berglund
ASV CDCOE808 (44' · DDD) Ⓕ

This coupling links two of the most delightful oboe concertos ever written. Mozart's sprightly and buoyant work invests the instrument with a chirpy, bird-like fleetness encouraging the interplay of lively rhythm and elegant poise. Boyd's reading captures this work's freshness and spontaneity beautifully.

If the Mozart portrays the sprightly side of the instrument's make-up the Strauss illustrates its languorous ease and tonal voluptuousness. Again Boyd allows himself the freedom and breadth he needs for his glowing interpretation; he handles the arching melodies of the opening movement and the witty *staccato* of the last with equal skill. Nicely recorded.

Piano Concertos

No 1 in F, K37; **No 2** in B flat, K39; **No 3** in D, K40;
No 4 in G, K41; **No 5** in D, K175; **No 6** in B flat, K238;
No 8 in C, K246; **No 9** in E flat, K271, 'Jeunehomme';
No 11 in F, K413/K387a; **No 12** in A, K414/K385p;
No 13 in C, K415/K387b; **No-14** in E flat, K449;
No 15 in B flat, K450; **No-16** in D, K451; **No 17** in G, K453; **No 18** in B flat, K456; **No 19** in F, K459; **No 20** in D minor, K466; **No 21** in C, K467; **No 22** in E flat, K482; **No 23** in A, K488; **No 24** in C minor, K491; **No 25** in C, K503; **No 26** in D, K537, 'Coronation'; **No 27** in B flat, K595

Piano Concertos Nos 1-27
English Chamber Orchestra / Murray Perahia pf

Sony Classical ⑫ 82876 87230-2 (608' · ADD/DDD)
Recorded 1975-84 Ⓜ ⦿ ⦿➤

Mozart concertos from the keyboard are unbeatable. There's a rightness, an effortlessness, about doing them this way that makes for heightened enjoyment. So many of them seem to gain in vividness when the interplay of pianist and orchestra is realised by musicians listening to each other in the manner of chamber music. Provided the musicians are of the finest quality, of course. We now just take for granted that the members of the English Chamber Orchestra will match the sensibility of the soloist. They are on top form here, as is Perahia, and the finesse of detail is breathtaking.

Just occasionally Perahia communicates an 'applied' quality – a refinement which makes some of his statements sound a little too good to be true. But the line of his playing, appropriately vocal in style, is exquisitely moulded; and the only reservations one can have are that a hushed, 'withdrawn' tone of voice, which he's little too ready to use, can bring an air of self-consciousness to phrases where ordinary, radiant daylight would have been more illuminating; and that here and there a more robust treatment of brilliant passages would have been in place. However, the set is entirely successful on its own terms – whether or not you want to make comparisons with other favourite recordings. Indeed, we now know that records of Mozart piano concertos don't come any better played than here.

Piano Concertos – Nos 6, 15 & 27
Chamber Orchestra of Europe /
Pierre-Laurent Aimard pf
Warner Classics 2564 62259-2 (77' · DDD) Ⓕ ⦿➤

There are not many composers for whom one could programme three concertos in the same key. Nevertheless, Mozart allegedly associated B flat major with happiness and with his fecund genius there is little risk of boredom.

A modern grand piano can sound heavy in Mozart's earlier concertos but Pierre-Laurent Aimard handles the solo writing in Concerto No 6 (K238), composed in Salzburg in 1776, with graceful agility. No 15 (K450), composed in Vienna in 1784, shows Mozart's increased emotional complexity and sophisticated use of the orchestra. Aimard encourages orchestral interjections to extend organically from the piano solos; the *Andante* expresses profound yearning in the most civilised manner possible; the last movement bubbles with affection.

In Mozart's last piano concerto, K595, the sunny optimism evident in the other B flat concertos is mingled with melancholic moods in the substantial opening movement (it lasts nearly a quarter of an hour, compared to the seven-minute *Allegro aperto* which opens K238).

The Chamber Orchestra of Europe produce soft-grained performances in which glossy elegance is favoured over dramatic colour. Woodwind contributions are gently massaged into the texture and the horns seem a little distant and subdued but the orchestra produce lean textures and tight rhythms. Aimard directs from the keyboard, an authentic approach that has been avoided by some of the finest period-instrument Mozartians. In true Glenn Gould style, you can occasionally hear him humming along, this immersion in the music nurturing an admirable sensation of unity and harmony.

Piano Concertos Nos 9 & 21
English Chamber Orchestra / Murray Perahia pf
Sony Classical 07464 34562-2 (59' · DDD)　Ⓜ️Ⓞ

Perahia's fine Mozart playing is a feature of the musical scene that has been with us for decades. There's a delightful freshness and crispness as well as the kind of authority that convinces us that this is the only way to perform the music – that is, until another masterly account comes along. Perahia's choice of tempos is a case in point, yet he seems natural rather than merely predictable and one recalls how even fine musicians can often go astray on this matter which Wagner and Stravinsky alike regarded as crucial. Are there any reservations? Well, perhaps the CD sound is just that little bit close and bright, but with music-making of this quality that doesn't seem to matter.

The grave *Andantino* of No 9 is given weight without exaggeration. In No 21 Perahia doesn't give the first movement the *maestoso* element suggested in some editions: instead there's a delightful flexibility and Leporello-like charm. However, it might be that the G minor passage before the second subject and the E minor one in the development are too soft and yielding, charming though they're in themselves. Perahia's own cadenza is effective and in keeping with his chosen approach. In the famous *Andante* also, Perahia plays with great feeling and poise.

Piano Concertos – No 9, K271; No 23, K488.
Northern Sinfonia / Imogen Cooper pf
Avie AV2100 (62' · DDD)　　　　　　Ⓕ

Imogen Cooper's strongly projected, stylistically sensitive performance stands up even alongside such distinguished modern versions as Uchida, Brendel and Schiff. With crystalline articulation and an exhilarating range of colour and dynamics, Cooper never lets you forget that the so-called *Jeunehomme* (K271) is a concerto of radical extremes, both within and between movements.

In the opening *Allegro* especially admirable is her vocal lyricism in the 'second subject', her powerfully directed passagework and the impassioned sweep of the wonderful modulating sequences near the start of the recapitulation. Some may feel she lingers overly in the C minor *Andantino*, though she always balances expressive *rubato* with an eloquent feeling for the long line. She conjures a new forlorn bleakness in the

quasi-operatic recitatives towards the end, and rightly makes the cadenza the emotional climax of the movement. Despite odd moments of slack ensemble, the Northern Sinfonia play with style and verve.

Cooper is equally responsive to the radiant, wistful and (in the *Adagio*) elegiac lyricism of K488. Again she illuminates, vividly, affectionately, yet with no hint of sentimentality, the music's shifting moods and colours while maintaining a strong melodic flow. When the main theme of the *Adagio* returns, after the serenading grace of the brief A major episode (beautifully realised here), she enhances its pathos with delicately expressive embellishments. After this, the airborne finale keeps elegance and animal spirits in ideal balance. Anyone who wants this particular coupling will find Cooper and the Northern Sinfonia (wonderfully tangy clarinets, incidentally, in K488) among the subtlest, liveliest and most probing of Mozartians.

Piano Concertos Nos 11, 12 & 14
English Chamber Orchestra / Murray Perahia pf
Sony Classical 07464 42243-2 (70' · ADD/DDD)Ⓜ️Ⓞ↪

Piano Concertos Nos 20 & 27
English Chamber Orchestra / Murray Perahia pf
Sony Classical 07464 42241-2 (63' · ADD/DDD)Ⓜ️Ⓞ↪

These discs happily epitomise some of the best qualities of the complete Perahia/ECO set. Always intelligent, always sensitive to both the overt and less obvious nuances of this music, Perahia is firstly a true pianist, never forcing the instrument beyond its limits in order to express the ideas, always maintaining a well-projected singing touch. The superb ECO reflects his integrity and empathy without having to follow slavishly every detail of his articulation or phrasing. K414 and K413 are charming and typically novel for their time, but do not break new ground in quite the way that K449 does. Here, Mozart's success in the theatre may have suggested a more dramatic presentation and working of ideas for this instrumental genre. K595 is a work pervaded by a serenity of acceptance that underlies its wistfulness. Mozart had less than a year to live, and the mounting depression of his life had already worn him down, yet there's still a sort of quiet joy in this music. The vast range of styles, emotions, and forms that these few works encompass are evocatively celebrated in these performances, and admirably captured in civilised recordings.

Piano Concertos Nos 12 & 19
London Mozart Players / Howard Shelley pf
Chandos CHAN9256 (52' · DDD)　　　　Ⓕ

These are clear and stylish readings. The playing of Shelley and the London Mozart Players is assured, relaxed and enjoyable, allowing the music to unfold naturally. Shelley demonstrates his fine judgement of tempo, and textures are well served; the recording gives quite a bold sound to his modern piano, but its overall immediacy and warmth aren't excessive and the balance is just right. Phrasing also deserves praise: Shelley and his expert team shape the music gracefully without falling into the slightly mannered delivery which can affect other artists in this repertory. Finally, cadenzas have the right balance of freedom and formality. Perhaps the two 'slow' movements here—the quotes are because that of K414 is an *Andante* and K459's is an *Allegretto* – are richer in style than will suit some tastes: they do not sound authentic in period-performance terms, but then this is another kind of performance and perfectly convincing. The recordings are of high quality.

Piano Concertos Nos 15[a], 23[b] & 24[b]   Ⓗ
Solomon pf **Philharmonia Orchestra /** [a]**Otto**
Ackermann, [b]**Herbert Menges**
Testament mono SBT1222 (80' · ADD)
Recorded 1953-55   Ⓕ

It was Abram Chasins, the American pianist and critic, who noted in Solomon a 'proportionate grandeur that instead of seeming to lack power appeared not to desire it.' Others have spoken of his 'matchless austerity', and listening once more to his Mozart is to be reminded of the essential truth of such comments. Mozart may have felt that K450 (No 15) is a concerto 'to make the pianist sweat', but it's difficult to imagine even a single bead of perspiration on Solomon's brow as he tosses off cascades of notes with superlative ease and elegance. In his hands the *Andante*'s set of variations comes as close to Elysium as you could wish, while the finale has a delectable lightness that makes it a true dance of the gods.

In K488 (No 23), Solomon's lucidity, in the canonic interplay, for example, is of a sort granted to very few pianists, and his refinement in the closing pages of the ineffable F sharp minor *Adagio* suggests all his inimitable but lightly worn authority. In K491 (No 24) he shares with Clara Haskil, another supremely prized Mozartian, a characteristic way of taking one of Mozart's two minor-key concertos by stealth rather than by storm, though he compensates for what some may see as undue restraint by giving us Saint-Saëns' storming cadenza. The 1953-5 recordings have been superbly remastered, and his musical partners, Otto Ackermann and Herbert Menges, are as inspired as their soloist.

Piano Concertos Nos 15 & 16
English Chamber Orchestra / Murray Perahia pf
Sony Classical 07464 37824-2 (50' · DDD) ⓂⓄⓄⓄ➤

Ⓖ This is an interpretation of the highest calibre: Perahia's delicious shaping of even the longest and most elaborate phrases, his unfailingly clear and arresting articulation, and his delicacy and refinement of

tone are without parallel. Perahia's attention is, moreover, by no means restricted to the solo parts: even the tiniest details of the orchestral writing are subtly characterised, and the piano and orchestra take on the character of a dialogue – sometimes poignant, often witty or sparklingly humorous. The two works are admirably contrasted: the 15th is largely light and high spirited, while the first movement of the 16th is almost Beethovenian in its grandeur and purposefulness, and both concertos have typically beautiful slow movements. The recordings are superb.

Piano Concertos – Nos 17 & 20
Scottish Chamber Orchestra /
Piotr Anderszewski pf
Virgin Classics 344696-2 (63' · DDD)   ⒻⒹ➤

Mozart performed the K466 Concerto at the Mehlgrube Casino on February 11, 1785. It is hard to imagine what the Viennese made of its dark, brooding D minor opening. Piotr Anderszewski superbly captures the uneasy mingling of melancholic passion and revolutionary fervour. This dynamic and impressively balanced performance is full of powerful arguments and emotional pressure.

Anderszewski's well-proportioned playing is in equal partnership with the SCO (perhaps the cohesive blend is a benefit of Anderszewski's directing from the keyboard). The central *Romanze* flows unhindered by saccharine sweetness, and the finale is lean and muscular, though lacking nothing in gracefulness.

In Concerto No 17 Anderszewski's navigation of the piano is articulate, bold and beautiful. His direction is admirably paced, although one imagines that these transparent textures have benefited from the orchestra's lessons in period style from Sir Charles Mackerras: clean-toned strings, precise timpani and brass, and eloquent woodwind flourishes contribute plenty to this attractive disc.

Piano Concertos Nos 18 & 20
Richard Goode pf **Orpheus Chamber Orchestra**
Nonesuch 7559-79439-2 (58' · DDD)   ⒻⓄⓄ

With a first-rate balance and quality of sound, here's a Mozart concerto record to transcend considerations of style and stance. The excellence of Richard Goode's playing isn't surprising, but the quality of his collaboration with the Orpheus Chamber Orchestra is special: and the beautiful thing about Mozart performance of this calibre is that the two seem inseparable. The freshness and placing of the detail are to be savoured, but it's the long view which holds and persuades. In the D minor Concerto's first movement the brilliant piano writing is so thrilling here because it's projected as being essential to the expression, not just a decoration of it. Goode is particularly impressive in the way he handles the three successive solo statements at the start of the development without slackening pace. They are subtly different in feeling, one from the other, and although he isn't the first player to have noticed this, it's characteristic of his distinction to have kept the detail and the overview in balance. He plays his own cadenza in the finale, in place of Beethoven's. He has some good ideas about dynamics in this last movement, and Mozart's lightening of mood at the turn to the major key towards the end has rarely sounded such an inspiration. The B flat Concerto, K456, is equally enjoyable. The outer movements are brisk and light on their feet, even balletic, but all the colours – and the shadows which pass over the face of the music – are there, just as one wants. At the end, you feel you've had glorious entertainment, and a discourse that has touched on the deepest things. You may well be puzzled as to how Goode achieves so much while appearing to do so little. In this the orchestra matches him, as it also matches his spontaneity.

Piano Concertos Nos 19 & 27
Orpheus Chamber Orchestra / Richard Goode pf
Nonesuch 7559-79608-2 (55' · DDD)　　Ⓕ🔘

The opening *tutti* of K595 (No 27, which comes first on the disc) makes a striking impact, not only thanks to the crisp, alert playing but to the full, bright, immediate recording. The piano enters with similarly full and immediate sound – very different from the more transparent piano sound on a rival Decca release with András Schiff – but then the orchestra seems to move further off. It's an inconsistency of balance that's disconcerting for no more than a moment or two, but might well make a hypercritical artist or producer have reservations.

·What matters is the liveness of the experience that Goode and his partners provide. His approach is more purposeful, more direct than that of Schiff, who favours speeds consistently a shade broader than Goode's. The natural weight and gravity of Goode's playing, reflecting his equivalent mastery as a Beethovenian, emerges clearly in such moments as the hushed B minor opening or the development in the first movement of K595, an extraordinary modulation for a movement in B flat major, or in the opening solo of the *Larghetto* which follows. Not that Goode's Mozart has anything remotely heavy about it in the wrong way. His lightness and wit in the finales of both concertos is a delight.

In the finale of K459, Goode, like Schiff, opts for a very fast *Allegro assai*, drawing on his phenomenal agility. Some may prefer a slightly more relaxed tempo, such as Murray Perahia, for example, adopts, with more swagger and fun in it, but Goode's playing is thrilling from first to last.

Piano Concertos Nos 20 & 24
Alfred Brendel pf **Scottish Chamber Orchestra /**
Sir Charles Mackerras

Philips 462 622-2PH (60' · DDD)　　Ⓕ🔘➔

Brendel's conception of Mozart's two minor-key concertos has altered in countless nuances and emphases but little in fundamentals since his 1973 Philips recordings with Marriner. His sensibility, pianistic refinement and sheer questing intelligence remain as compelling as ever. Neither performance will entirely please those who favour a barnstorming approach.

More than in 1973, Brendel is at times concerned to draw out the music's elegiac resignation than to highlight its more obvious passion and turbulence. But more than most pianists he constantly illuminates the smaller and larger shapes of the music with his range of colour and dynamics. In both opening movements, for instance, he brings a speaking eloquence to the piano's initial solo theme and then in the development finds a subtly altered tone of voice, in response to the gradually darkening musical landscape, for each of its reappearances.

Another Brendel hallmark is his variety of tone and articulation in rapid passagework, which is purposefully directed in accordance with its place in the overall scheme. Again he provides apt and spontaneous-sounding embellishments and 'in-filling' at fermatas, this time allowing himself greater freedom in decorating the spare lines of the slow movements; again, he uses his own cadenzas in both concertos, more adventurous in their thematic development than any of Mozart's own surviving examples.

In the opening *tutti* of K491 one can hear the extra character Mackerras brings to the music compared to Marriner – the impact of raw, louring brass (tamed by Marriner) at strategic moments, for instance, or his attentive shaping of inner strands to enhance the tension. The recording has an attractive spaciousness and ambient warmth, though in K491 the keyboard occasionally obscures important thematic ideas on oboes, clarinets and bassoons.

Piano Concertos Nos 23 & 24
Orpheus Chamber Orchestra / Richard Goode pf
Nonesuch 7559-79489-2 (56' · DDD)　　Ⓕ🔘

This is the third Mozart CD Richard Goode and the Orpheus Chamber Orchestra have made, and collaborations of this kind must necessarily be rare. The demands this sort of music-making imposes on the players are considerable. But so are the potential rewards. They are evident here in the exceptional focus and concentration of the playing. Polished you might expect it to be, but the allure and spontaneity are a joy. First impressions are likely to be of details of scoring in the orchestral expositions of the first movements, details that may not go unnoticed in other performances but which rarely receive such voicing and definition. The pianist doesn't disappoint either. Judge him by his first entry in this concerto, in the solo theme: there's none more difficult to get right. Goode has the range, the control and the rhetoric. He passes another difficult test in this first movement by supplying an impressive cadenza. It's an outstanding account of this movement, to be returned to again and again. There's no falling off in the other two either.

The A major, K488, equally well illuminated, has light and air from a different world. Indeed, there's an airborne quality to the finale, done here with the utmost vivacity, and a hint of that too in the open textures and the easy, glorious buoyancy of the first movement. The recorded sound is exemplary.

Piano Concertos Nos 23 & 24 (plus Nos 20, 26, 27)
Sir Clifford Curzon pf **London Symphony Orchestra / István Kertész**
Decca Legends ② 468 491-2DL2 (ADD) Recorded 1967   Ⓜ🔘🔘

In a list of all-time best recordings of Mozart piano concertos these should have a place. The balances of piano with orchestra are just right, and the sound has come up freshly on CD, with clarity and a nicely truthful character. In the No 24 the wind isn't as forward as recordings favour these days, but from the LSO as distinguished soloists and as a wind chorus their contributions tell. Kertész gives Curzon nicely judged support: it sets him off, in a frame, even if it does appear a mite neutral at times and strangely limp in the presentation of the variation theme at the start of the finale of the C minor Concerto. These days, some people might consider the interpretations dated, or unreconstructed. Curzon doesn't decorate the bare, leaping intervals at the close of the slow movement of K488, and he's restrained too in the C minor. But the performances seem to be beyond fashion.

The slow movements are especially fine. In the *Larghetto* of No 24, unfolding at an ideal tempo, Curzon gives the impression of walking while he speaks to us. The gravity of the F sharp minor Adagio of No 23 is a different thing; but there, again, he's unaffected and completely unsentimental, direct in manner even while projecting the deepest feeling. He reminds us that the best interpreters do not impose but find a way of letting the music speak through them.

Piano Concertos Nos 9 & 25
Orpheus Chamber Orchestra / Richard Goode pf
Nonesuch 7559-79454-2 (63' · DDD)   Ⓕ🔘🔘

The opening of No 25 sounds tremendous, with a leathery thwack to the kettledrums and the orchestra suitably weighty. Although the acoustic is a bit dry, there's a satisfying depth to the sonority, and the balance and placing of the instruments is absolutely perfect. All the colours are vivid. In contrast to many players of the modern instrument, Goode doesn't pull his punches and makes this first movement a most glorious procession, imposing but never ponderous. His tempo has a propulsive energy and an underlying fitness that makes possible some

relaxation of it in the broader paragraphs of the solo part. Wonderful slow movement too, flowing admirably, and it's a tricky one to get right.

This concerto has rarely been recorded so successfully, but the Ninth has been done better. Many of the virtues enjoyed by No 25 apply here also. It needs a different rhetoric, and Goode supplies it, but he waxes and wanes, and there's something a shade impersonal about him. The reservations concern the first movement principally, where it's as if he were saying: 'I do not need to attract your attention, this beautiful thing Mozart has made we are going to lay out before you'. However, this is still a Mozart concerto disc to give exceptional pleasure. And what teamwork! The musical focus sustained here isn't something often encountered outside chamber music.

Piano Concerto No 26. Rondos – D, K382; A, K386
English Chamber Orchestra / Murray Perahia pf
Sony Classical 07464 39224-2 (DDD)   Ⓕ🔘➔

This is one of the most distinguished of Perahia's Mozart concerto recordings. The D major Concerto, No 26, isn't, perhaps, a work of such individuality as the 12 concertos which preceded it, or the only one which succeeded it (No 27), yet it used to be one of the most popular, probably because it has a convenient nickname (*Coronation*). Now, curiously enough, it isn't played all that often and of the available recordings, Perahia leads the field: dignified yet never aloof in the first movement, eloquent in the central *Larghetto*, and marvellously agile and dexterous in the florid concluding *Rondo*. He plays his own characteristically stylish cadenza in the first movement (Mozart's own has not survived). As a coupling Perahia gives us the two concert *Rondos*: K382 in D, a Viennese alternative finale for the Salzburg D major Concerto, K175; and K386 in A, presumably the original, rejected finale of K414. The A major *Rondo* has had an eventful history, having been cut into pieces in the 19th century for use as greeting cards (!), and patched together subsequently by numerous editors, including Alfred Einstein, Paul Badura-Skoda, Sir Charles Mackerras, and Erik Smith. The version performed here has a different ending which was discovered by Peter Tyson. It was completed by Paul Badura-Skoda and this is its first recording. The performances are sheer delight and, as in the concerto, the ECO plays, quite literally, *con amore* – a spirit evidently shared by the Sony recording team.

Mozart Piano Concerto No 27. Concerto for Two Pianos and Orchestra in E flat, K365/K316a
Schubert Fantasia, D940
Emil Gilels, Elena Gilels pfs **Vienna Philharmonic Orchestra / Karl Böhm**
DG The Originals 463 652-2GOR (59' · ADD) 🔘🔘🔘➔

This is the most beautiful of Mozart playing, his last piano concerto given here by Emil Gilels with total clarity. This is a classic performance, memorably accompanied by the VPO and

Böhm. Suffice it to say that Gilels sees every-thing and exaggerates nothing, that the per-formance has an Olympian authority and seren-ity, and that the *Larghetto* is one of the glories of the gramophone. He's joined by his daughter Elena in the Double Piano Concerto in E flat, and their physical relationship is mirrored in the quality, and the mutual understanding of the playing: both works receive marvellous inter-pretations. We *think* Emil plays first, Elena sec-ond, but could be quite wrong. The VPO under Karl Böhm is at its best; and so is the quality of recording, with a good stereo separation of the two solo parts, highly desirable in this work.

Additional recommendation

Piano Concertos Nos 9, 14, 15, 17, 18
Coupled with: Rondo in D, K382
Uchida *pf*; **English Chamber Orchestra / Tate**
Philips Duo ② 473 313-2PM2 (107' · DDD) **O** ☙

Wonderfully imaginative interpretations that show soloist, orchestra and conductor in perfect rapport.

Violin Concertos

No 1 in B flat, K207; **No 2** in D, K211; **No 3** in G, K216; **No 4** in D, K218; **No 5** in A, K219; **D**, K271a

---

Violin Concertos Nos 1-5[a]. Adagio in E, K261[c]. Rondo in C, K373[a]. Sinfonia concertante in E flat, K364[b]
[a]**Arthur Grumiaux** *vn* [b]**Arrigo Pelliccia** *va*
[ab]**London Symphony Orchestra / Sir Colin Davis;**
[c]**New Philharmonia Orchestra / Raymond Leppard**
Philips Duo ② 438 323-2PM2 (153' · ADD)
Recorded 1961-4 **O**

These performances of the five standard violin concertos, the *Sinfonia concertante* and a couple of other pieces were much admired when they came out on LP, and they continue to earn praise for their crispness, lightness and elo-quence. Grumiaux was also fortunate in his partner in the *Sinfonia concertante*, for Pelliccia is also an expert Mozartian and they give a per-formance of this beautiful piece that's expressive but still avoids self-indulgent romanticism. In the solo concertos, too, Grumiaux plays caden-zas that suit the music in length and style. Both Sir Colin Davis and Raymond Leppard are sym-pathetic partners in this repertory, and since the playing of the two London orchestras is no less satisfying, this issue scores all round artistically. The 1960s recordings do not sound their age, and are pleasing save for a little tape hiss and an excess of bass that hardly suits the style of this translucent music. However, that's a small price to pay when so much else is admirable, and Grumiaux's fine tonal palette is well caught.

Violin Concertos Nos 1-5. Sinfonia concertante, K364[a]
Giuliano Carmignola *vn* [a]**Danusha Waskiewicz** *va*
Orchestra Mozart / Claudio Abbado

Arkiv Production ② 477 7371AH2 (129' · DDD)
Ⓕ**OOO**☙

Virtuoso 'violinism' and energising direction notwithstanding, neither Giuliano Carmignola nor Claudio Abbado seems inspired by the B flat Concerto, K207. Nor does slick dispatch do much for the first movement of the D major, K211; but this is not the shape of things to come. Carmignola steps away from neutrality in the succeeding *Andante*. The music breathes a life of its own as he ardently inflects its phrases to shape the tension and relaxation of his line which – as elsewhere – he also embellishes. And pauses are decorated with lead-ins. Here is personal involve-ment that from now on is present in full flower.

It's a flowering for Abbado too, as he summons a passionate advocacy that takes in the implica-tions of key and time signatures on atmosphere and pacing, uses dynamic markings and intuitive accents to keep rhythm aloft, adjusts the timbres of the wind instruments (oboes are vivid or sub-dued, horns play *in alto* or *basso*) to suit the colouration he requires, and aerates the orches-tral fabric for maximum clarity. Conducting and interpretation are in the realms of greatness – and no mistake.

In the solo concertos, Carmignola is recorded with varying but small changes of volume. His positioning is steadier in the *Sinfonia concertante*; and so is his placement with the artistic, if slightly reticent, Danusha Waskiewicz. Never-theless, their skilled dovetailing and intelligent use of tone colour speak of symbiosis. Abbado remains *primus inter pares*, watchful, supportive and fortifying. Pity the sound isn't always clear and detailed. Superlative music making deserves consistently superlative recording.

Violin Concertos Nos 1-5. Serenade No 7 in D, 'Haffner', K250 – Andante; Menuetto; Rondo
Pamela Frank *vn* **Zurich Tonhalle Orchestra / David Zinman**
Arte Nova Classics ② 74321 72104-2 (139' · DDD) Ⓢ

What a good idea to include the violin concerto movements from the *Haffner* Serenade as a filler, rather than the more usual group of extra movements for violin and orchestra. The Sere-nade shows the 20-year-old Mozart with his imagination at full stretch; Frank, Zinman and the Zurich orchestra revel in the wit, the sensu-ous expressiveness and the melodic fecundity of this still neglected music. Throughout the two discs Pamela Frank gives us violin playing of great technical purity. The music speaks to us without any affectation, yet respecting Mozart's indications and such 18th-century conventions as tailing off the weak beats of the bar. She's given a splendidly positive, well-considered accompaniment. The bouncy rhythms and per-fect orchestral balance of the opening *tutti* to K216 establish a sense of *joie de vivre* that carries over into the violin playing.

Zinman's care for detail ensures that nothing of importance is overlooked: on the many occasions where the bass is carried by the second violin or viola these lines are given a bit of extra emphasis to highlight the harmonic movement. The horns deserve special mention; their purity of tone and rhythmic poise give a real sparkle to the outer movements of K207 and to the middle section of the *Haffner* Minuet, spectacularly scored for violin and wind. Zinman also wrote the cadenzas (except in K219, where Frank plays the famous Joachim ones) – they're imaginative and stylish, but don't always sound improvisatory enough and occasionally seem too long. Frank is supported by an unusually characterful orchestra and very crisp, clear recording. A fantastic bargain.

Violin Concertos Nos 1-5. Adagio, K261. Rondos – K269; K373
Mozart Anniversary Orchestra / James Ehnes *vn*
CBC Records ② SMCD5238 (143' · DDD)   Ⓕ

'It flowed like oil,' wrote Mozart to his father apropos of his own performance of one of his violin concertos. The composer's delighted verdict is equally applicable to James Ehnes's vital, elegant, beautifully proportioned playing of all five concertos. Still barely 30, the Canadian violinist here reinforces his credentials as one of the most brilliant and discerning players of his generation, with a sweet, gleaming tone and a purity of intonation that are second to none. Among classic recordings, Ehnes is closest to the poised, patrician Arthur Grumiaux (see above), though his touch, like the excellent orchestra's (hand-picked from the cream of North American players) is that much lighter.

In the *Allegros*, Ehnes's gracefully finished phrasing and glistening, strongly directed passagework are a constant pleasure, while his intense singing line and delicate variations of colour make each of the slow movements memorable. From what we know of 18th-century practice, his tempi for the *Adagios* of K207 and K216 are improbably broad, but he vindicates them with playing of rapt eloquence.

If there's a reservation it is that Ehnes can underplay the teenage composer's irreverence and sense of fun. Other violinists, including Pamela Frank (Arte Nova), Pekka Kuusisto (Ondine) and, using gut strings and a classical bow, Andrew Manze (Harmonia Mundi – see below), have found more playfulness in a movement like the opening *Allegro* of K216; and all three bring more earthy gusto to the Hungarian folk tune in K216's finale and the Janissary music in K219. Their cadenzas are also crisper and wittier than Ehnes's, which are aptly in scale but tend to over-indulge in double-stopping.

These gracious, subtly expressive performances, glowingly recorded, can take their place with the finest modern-instrument versions. For a single recording of the complete concertos, though, the palm stays with Frank, who may not quite match Ehnes's tonal lustre but catches that much more of the music's coltish zest.

Violin Concertos – Nos 2 & 4, K218.
Sinfonia concertante, K364[a]
[a]**Lawrence Power** *va* **UBS Verbier Festival Chamber Orchestra / Maxim Vengerov** *vn*
EMI 378374-2 (79' · DDD)   ⒻⓄ▶

How do you decide the tempo for *Allegro maestoso* without a metronome marking? Mozart's instruction in the first movement of the *Sinfonia concertante* is ambiguous, yet most musicians unequivocally lean towards *Allegro*. Maxim Vengerov does not; he firmly fixes on *maestoso*. The result is stately, but not easy-going. You'll glean that from the two opening chords nicely gauged to convey *sfp*, and in the unusually flaring forte on the following dotted crotchet/quaver figure which is double-dotted for extra emphasis. This is but one of many touches to suggest that Vengerov is not simply directing the ensemble; he conducts. And what he discerns as tension and release in the music make their mark through a chosen tempo that also allows the partnership time to observe dynamic minutiae, to nuance phrases and shape paragraphs. Viola player Lawrence Power is Vengerov's equal. The unified pliancy of their playing intensifies the melancholy of the slow movement, its cadenza offering a particularly good example of their rapport. Microphone balance, in relation to themselves and to the orchestra, is good.

Both soloists lavish attention on this masterpiece. To his credit, Vengerov lavishes as much attention on the other works, too. A proviso though: throughout, artistry is expressed within a style that in today's meaning would not be considered 'authentic'. Its antithesis, warm romanticism, may not suit all tastes. Neither may the sound, which lacks the ultimate in airy spaciousness. But don't let such factors put you off; these performances ought not to be ignored.

Violin Concertos Nos 3-5
The English Concert / Andrew Manze *vn*
Harmonia Mundi HMU90 7385 (76' · DDD)   Ⓕ

Andrew Manze's vivid notes stress the 19-year-old composer's delight in the novel, the unexpected. He points out that 'these concertos verge on the operatic' and, true to his word, gives performances that for inventiveness, impish fun and close, conspiratorial rapport between soloist and orchestra have never been bettered.

First movements combine swagger, elegance and exceptional delicacy of touch, with the semiquaver passagework imaginatively, often playfully, inflected. Hair-shirt authenticists may object to Manze's fondness for stretching a phrase here, teasing out a cadence there. To me, his *rubato* always sounds natural and spontaneous. In the slow movements he strikes a fine balance between vernal innocence and sensuous yearning, drawing a wonderfully eloquent cantabile line and warming his pure, silvery tone with a discreet and subtle use of vibrato.

Monica Huggett on her fine Virgin Classics set is coolly gracious in the *Adagios* of K216 and 219. But Manze, with his broader tempi, wider palette of colour and more supple phrasing, finds more expressive depth. Typically he can make you think afresh about the music. In the recapitulation of K219's *Adagio*, for instance, the music momentarily dips from E major to E minor (6'35"). Most performers either fail to register this, or introduce a more veiled, withdrawn colour. Manze, strikingly and effectively, does the opposite, making the turn to the minor a cue for a sudden passionate intensification of tone, briefly disturbing the rapt, Arcadian idyll. And has the soloist's wistful envoi in K218 – a simple rising and falling scale that Mozart added as an afterthought – ever been as magically hushed as here?

Manze has plenty of fun with the finales, relishing the contrasts between courtly decorum and the more rustic episodes. His harsh, earthy tones in the 'Strassburger' folk tune in K216 (at 4'01") create a strong whiff of the Hungarian puszta; and he tears with manic glee into the wild 'Turkish' episodes of K219, all the more startling after the guileless grace of the minuet. Other delights include Manze's witty, sometimes slightly zany 'lead-ins', which always sound joyously improvised (and probably were), and his brief, stylistically apt cadenzas. Huggett's fresh, buoyant performances have long been the prime period-instrument recommendation. But the palm now goes to Manze, in symbiotic partnership with the superb English Concert and beautifully recorded by Harmonia Mundi.

Serenades

No 6 in D, K239, 'Serenata notturna'; **No 7** in D, K250/K248b, 'Haffner'; **No 9** in D, K320, 'Posthorn'; **No 10** in B flat for 13 wind instruments, K361/K370a, 'Gran Partita'; **No 11** in E flat, K375; **No 12** in C minor, K388/K384a; **No 13** in G, K525, 'Eine kleine Nachtmusik'

Serenades Nos 6 & 13. Divertimento in D, K136.
Adagio and Fugue in C minor, K546
Ferenc Liszt Chamber Orchestra / János Rolla
Hungaroton HCD12471 (50' · ADD/DDD)   Ⓕ

The *Eine kleine Nachtmusik Serenade* is a favourite which will never be in any danger of oblivion. The Hungarian Ferenc Liszt Chamber Orchestra plays splendidly with an exceptionally alert style, but with a slightly heavier sound, a slightly solider style, than the Orpheus Chamber Orchestra. Nevertheless, this is to point to minor differences in the two perfectly sensible approaches, not to suggest that either of the performances is in any way materially superior to the other. Another common factor of the two discs is their inclusion, along with the *Nachtmusik*, of Serenade No 6.

The Divertimento here offers a degree of instrumental contrast, adding a few wind players

to the basic orchestra of strings. Perhaps rather more of the built-in different sounds of these two groups could have been made in the present recording; but the *Serenade* remains an enchanting one. The Divertimento, also in D, lacks corresponding colour, but is nevertheless, quite a strong work; and the C minor *Adagio and Fugue* (an arrangement by Mozart himself from a piano duo) offers a very noticeably strong *Adagio*, and a fugue in which Mozart makes one of his few explorations – a successful one – of an earlier contrapuntal idiom.

March, K249. Serenade No 7, 'Haffner', K250
**Netherlands Chamber Orchestra /
Gordan Nikolitch** vn
Pentatone ⓈⒶ PTC5186 097 (57' · DDD)   ⒻⓄ▸

The *Haffner*, a wedding serenade for the marriage of Elizabeth Haffner in July 1776, was an outdoor summer piece, which was not good for the band, whose members were expected to move around. Thus there are no timpani; and certainly no cellos, because there were aristocratic guests (the bride's father had been burgomaster of Salzburg), so lowly musicians couldn't sit while they stood. When Mozart later shortened this eight-movement work to a five-movement 'symphony', he enhanced the orchestration with cellos and drums.

Gordan Nikolitch goes further. He incorporates these instruments into the original format, thus turning the Serenade into a fuller work. It has a stately expansiveness that only switches to a militaristic snap in the first movement of the Serenade, percussion now lending point both to a regal *Allegro maestoso* and, leading from it, a fiery *alla breve Allegro molto*. In the following *Andante*, the first of three 'violin concerto' movements, Nikolitch shows that he is as superlative a violin soloist as he is a conductor, as unerring in his understanding of lyrical eloquence as he is of dramatic timing. He never puts a foot wrong. Neither does Pentatone's production, which keeps the perspectives steady (for example, the violin is properly balanced with the ensemble and not pulled forward for the cadenzas).

The range, transparency and tonal veracity of the recording offer a total vindication of SACD. This is a tremendous disc.

Serenades – No 10, 'Gran partita', K361; No 11, K375
Berlin Philharmonic Wind Ensemble
EMI 343424-2 (71' · DDD)   ⒻⒹ▸

A challenge for any group performing Mozart's great wind serenades is finding a happy balance between a euphonious ensemble blend and pungent individual characterisation. In both works here – the so-called *Gran partita* for 12 wind instruments plus double bass, and the E flat Serenade K375 – the princely Berlin Philharmonic Wind Ensemble achieve this beautifully.

The players respond exuberantly to the rustic elements of K375 – the two jaunty minuets and the bubbly finale, with its gleeful exchanges between the instruments. But their immaculately tuned performance is even more remarkable for its subtlety and poetic shaping, whether in the first movement (done quite spaciously, in keeping with its *maestoso* marking), the melancholy C minor Trio of the first Minuet (magical soft horn playing here) or the rapt *Adagio*.

The Berliners are truly athletic and ebullient in the first movement of the *Gran partita*, yet never underestimate its symphonic import. As in K375, the instrumental interplay is managed with delightful elegance and ease. There's a crucial sense of fun, too, in the rollicking finale, with the players adding cheeky touches of ornamentation and tellingly varying the dynamics on repeats.

Characterisation is just as apt and imaginative in the other movements. The two minuets are sharply contrasted in tempo, the first quite stately (yet with an underlying urgency in the haunting G minor trio), the second briskly bucolic, with a relaxed swing to its Ländler second Trio. The dulcet outer sections of the *Romanze* are offset by an unusually mysterious, disquieting C minor central *Allegretto*, held down to *piano*, as Mozart asks; and the variations in the sixth movement are full of felicities, from the frolicking first variation to the ravishing fifth, where the first oboe sings with vocal eloquence against softly lulling basset-horns and clarinets. Here and elsewhere the players get the often tricky instrumental balances exactly right; and thanks, too, to EMI's beautifully judged recording inner details of part writing – especially from the bassoons – that usually go for little or nothing register perfectly.

Serenades – No 10, 'Gran Partita', K361; No 12, K388
London Winds / Michael Collins *cl*
Onyx Classics ONYX4012 (73' · DDD) ⓕⓞ⊞➔

Led with flair and imagination by Michael Collins, London Winds give a vital, refined performanceof the *Gran Partita*, exceptionally transparent in texture and full of felicitous detail: the wonderfully veiled *pianissimo* coda of the Romanze fifth movement, for instance; or the eloquently phrased oboe cantilena against the dulcet murmurings of clarinets and basset horns in the *adagio* variation.

Outer movements are crisp and athletic, with an easy, quick-witted sense of instrumental interplay; and the two minuets are sharply contrasted, the first done as a stately menuetto galante, its G minor Trio more elegiac than agitated, the second as a perky Ländler. Some may raise an eyebrow at the use of contrabassoon instead of Mozart's prescribed double bass (contrabassoons had notoriously unreliable plumbing in the 1780s). But there are gains in overall blend, even if you might miss the double bass's *pizzicato* twangs in the second minuet's beery Trio. The only reservation comes with the *Adagio* third movement, the work's emotional core, where the pulsing accompaniment

impinges too prominently on the soaring exchanges of oboe, clarinet and basset horn.

As a fill-up London Winds offer that most undiverting of serenades, K388, in a fine performance, amply powerful and urgent but notable for its poetry and inwardness, whether in the sorrowful, syncopated variant of the 'second subject' in the opening *Allegro*'s recapitulation, or the Trio's exquisite 'mirror canon', celestially floated here by oboes and bassoons.

Mozart Serenade No 13, 'Eine kleine Nachtmusik'. Adagio and Fugue in C minor, K546 **Anonymous** (arr L Mozart) Cassation in G, 'Toy Symphony' **Pachelbel** Canon and Gigue
Academy of St Martin in the Fields / Sir Neville Marriner
Philips 416 386-2PH (52' · DDD) ⓕ⊞➔

Sir Neville Marriner here collects a miscellaneous group of popular classical and Baroque pieces in characteristically polished and elegant performances. The only roughness – and that deliberate – is in the extra toy percussion of Leopold Mozart's *Cassation*, with its long-misattributed *Toy* Symphony. The anonymous extra soloists enjoy themselves as amateurs might, not least on a wind machine, but what's very hard to take is the grotesquely mismatched cuckoo-whistle, an instrument which should readily be tunable.

Eine kleine Nachtmusik brings a performance plainly designed to caress the ear of traditional listeners wearied with period performance. The second-movement *Romanze* is even more honeyed than usual on muted strings. The oddity of the Pachelbel item is that the celebrated Canon – taken unsentimentally if sweetly at a flowing speed – is given a reprise after the fugue. The recording is warm and well balanced.

Divertimentos

Divertimentos – B flat, K287; D, K205
Salzburg Mozarteum Camerata Academica / Sándor Végh
Capriccio 10-271 (59' · DDD) ⓕⓞ

Mozart's Divertimento, K287 is a six-movement work cast on quite a large scale, and is scored for two violins, viola, two horns and bass, a combination that presents some difficulties of balance. Toscanini and Karajan solved the problem in a way by recording the work with a full orchestral string section, but this brings its own problems, for Mozart's score demands playing of virtuoso standard, and anything less is ruthlessly exposed. Sandor Végh's smallish string band is of high quality, and has a pleasantly rounded tone quality. The engineers have managed to contrive a satisfactory balance that doesn't sound at all unnatural, and the sound quality is very good. Végh directs an attractive, neatly pointed performance that steers a middle course between objective classicism and expressive warmth. The

Divertimento, K205, has five movements, but none lasts longer than five minutes, so the work is much shorter and more modest than K287. Scoring is for violin, viola, two horns, bassoon and double bass, to provide another difficult but well resolved problem for the engineers. Végh directs another charcterful, delightful performance, to round off a very desirable disc.

Divertimentos – F, K247; D, K334
Gaudier Ensemble (Jonathan Williams, Christiaan Boers hns Marieke Blankestijn, Lesley Hatfield vns Iris Juda va Stephen Williams db)
Hyperion CDA67386 (76' · DDD)   Ⓕ

How lucky the burghers of Salzburg, in Mozart's day, who had such music as this to accompany their family celebrations! Mozart wrote a small group of divertimentos for strings and horns for the local aristocracy during his later years there, to augment his salary and prestige, and he did it with a mastery of technique that enabled him to find exactly the right blend of high spirits, warmth of expression and wit.

When they've been recorded, it's nearly always been with an orchestra rather than a solo group. In Austria in Mozart's time, the word 'divertimento' signified solo performance, and there's a world of difference between what a sensitive solo fiddler and what a galumphing orchestra can do with that top line, in terms of technique, expressiveness and flexibility. And in these performances the bass part is played not by a cello, but, as was preferred in Salzburg, a double bass, which provides a different relationship to the upper voices, and the one that Mozart clearly intended.

The Gaudier Ensemble catch the mood of the music perfectly. The elegant sentiment of the slow movements (there are two in each work) is happily conveyed – listen to the sweetness of violinist Marieke Blankestijn's phrasing in the *Adagio* of K247 and her gentle, unassuming eloquence in that of K334. In the latter work the second violin is called on, too, for some degree of virtuosity, but it's to Blankestijn that most of the rapid and stratospheric music goes, and she copes in style. She also phrases the famous first minuet here gracefully. Mozart's second minuets (each divertimento has six movements) are usually more rumbustious, with the horns prominent, and these too are heartily done. Altogether this is a delectable record.

Mozart Divertimento in D, K334[a]   Ⓗ
Schubert Quintet for Piano and Strings in A, 'The Trout', D667[b]
Members of the Vienna Octet (Willi Boskovsky, [a]Philipp Matheis vns Günther Breitenbach va Nikolaus Hubner vc Johann Krump db [a]Joseph Velba, [a]Otto Nitsch hns [b]Walter Panhoffer pf)
Pearl mono GEM0129 (72' · ADD) Recorded 1950   Ⓕ

Mozart's Divertimento for two horns and strings, K334, is one of his ripest and most engaging *pièces d'occasion* and this is a marvellous performance of it. Indeed, some skimping of repeats and a couple of cuts in the finale notwithstanding, this classic, out of the catalogues now for more than 30 years, is still the version to have.

Like the still too little regarded Vienna Konzerthaus Quartet, the Vienna Octet was one of the glories of post-war Viennese musical life. Willi Boskovsky, one of its founders, was a particular inspiration. Boskovsky may not have been every recording producer's dream. A wonderfully inspirational player, he would not necessarily play a take the same way twice. The results, though, are a joy; his playing, and the playing of the ensemble as a whole, is always burnished, idiomatic, intensely alive. The same could be said of this famous 1950 recording of Schubert's *Trout* Quintet, though the Vienna Octet's remake, recorded with Sir Clifford Curzon in 1957 when Boskovsky was still leading, is one of those gramophone classics difficult to knock off its perch. The original Decca LPs of the present performances (Pearl hasn't had access to the original tapes) were often said to be wiry in sound and difficult to reproduce, though this isn't true of the Mozart. Here, it sounds a million dollars. Tracking the latter movements of the *Trout* LP, though, has clearly not been easy. A barely audible amount of surface noise and a tiny amount of incipient distortion persists. That said, the new disc is indispensable.

Symphonies

No **1** in E flat, K16; No **2** in B flat, K17 (attrib L Mozart); No **4** in D, K19; No **5** in B flat, K22; No **6** in F, K43; No **7** in D, K45; No **7***a* in G, K45a, 'Alte Lambach'; No **8** in D, K48; No **9** in C, K73; No **10** in G, K74; No **11** in D, K84; No **12** in G, K110; No **13** in F, K112; No **14** in A, K114; No **15** in G, K124; No **16** in C, K128; No **17** in G, K129; No **18** in F, K130; No **19** in E flat, K132; No **20** in D, K133; No **21** in A, K134; No **22** in C, K162; No **23** in D, K181; No **24** in B flat, K182; No **25** in G minor, K183; No **26** in E flat, K184; No **27** in G, K199; No **28** in C, K200; No **29** in A, K201; No **30** in D, K202; No **31** in D, K297, 'Paris'; No **32** in G, K318; No **33** in B flat, K319; No **34** in C, K338; No **35** in D, K385, 'Haffner'; No **36** in C, K425, 'Linz'; No **38** in D, K504, 'Prague'; No **39** in E flat, K543; No **40** in G minor, K550; No **41** in C, K551, 'Jupiter'; (**No 42**) in F, K75; (**No 43**) in F, K76; (**No 44**) in D, K81; (**No 45**) in D, K95; (**No 46**) in C, K96; (**No 47**) in D, K97; (**No 55**) in B flat, KApp214; **F**, KAnh223; **B flat**, K74g

---

Complete Symphonies   Ⓟ
The English Concert / Trevor Pinnock
Archiv Produktion ⑪ 471 666-2AB11
(13 hours, 36' · DDD)   ⒷⓄ▷

This set is pure joy. These are period performances, but there's nothing hair-shirt about them. Pinnock caresses the slow movements with great affection, and throughout there's a sense of fun and enjoyment. What's exciting is the sweetness of the period-instrument sound and the suppleness and flexibility The English Concert brings to the music. They play, much of the time, as if it were chamber music, particularly in second subjects – the lyrical passages, that is, where they shape the phrases with a warmth and refinement you hardly expect in orchestral music. Timing is quietly witty, yet not at all contrived or artificial: it's the sort of expressive refinement that depends on listening to one another, not on the presence of a conductor. There's large-scale playing, too.

The middle symphonies are especially good. The opening of the brilliant K133 (No 20) has a splendid swing, with its prominent trumpets, and a real sense of a big, symphonic piece. K184 (No 26) is duly fiery and its accents are neatly judged. K201 and K202 (Nos 29 and 30) are both very impressively done: an eloquent rather than a fiery account (though something of that too) of the opening movement of K201, with a particularly euphonious and shapely *Andante*. The finales of both are done with exceptional vitality and the rhythmic resilience that's characteristic of these performances.

Pinnock's *Jupiter* (No 41) is truly outstanding. The first movement is duly weighty, but energetically paced, and its critical junctures timed with a keen sense of their role in the shape of the whole. In the *Andante* he draws an extraordinarily beautiful, almost sensuous sound from The English Concert, and the lines are moulded with tenderness. This, above all, is the quality that distinguishes Pinnock's recordings from all others, this natural and musical sound, deriving from the way the players are intently listening to one another; and it's fitting that it reaches its high point in the *Jupiter*. As for the finale: well, it's decidedly quick, giving the impression of a performance in which the orchestra is pressed to an extent that its ensemble playing is under stress, though it holds together. It's a very bold, outspoken reading, which leaves one gasping afresh at the music's originality.

In short, quite outstanding performances, unfailingly musical, wholly natural and unaffected, often warmly expressive in the slow music and always falling very happily on the ear, with no trace of the harshness that some think is inevitable with period instruments. They are excellently recorded, with the properly prominent wind balance helping to characterise the sound world of each work.

Symphonies Nos 1, 2, 4 & 5
Abel (formerly attrib Mozart) Symphony, Op-7 No-3
Northern Chamber Orchestra / Nicholas Ward
Naxos 8 550871 (59' · DDD)　　　　　Ⓢ➡

Symphonies Nos 6-10
Northern Chamber Orchestra / Nicholas Ward
Naxos 8 550872 (56' · DDD)　　　　　Ⓢ➡

These two discs of Mozart's first 10 symphonies offer a unique view of the composer's earliest years of apprenticeship as a symphonist.

Ward and his orchestra show a sensitive response to the wealth of stylistic influences apparent in these works. Purists may question the inclusion of two of the symphonies, Nos 2 and 3, since neither work is actually by Mozart. The former is attributed to the composer's father, Leopold, while the latter is Mozart's orchestration of C F Abel's E flat Symphony, Op 7 No 3. However, when they're played with such engaging style and elegance as here, these two works add a further important dimension to Mozart's early symphonic output. Where J C Bach's influence is most powerful (Symphonies Nos 1, 4, 5 and 6), the NCO presents the music's contrasting thematic characters with fine clarity, balancing the music's beautifully transparent textures with appropriate lightness of touch. The inclusion of trumpets and drums in the next three symphonies (Nos 7, 8 and 9) announces the young composer's growing brilliance and stature. In these pieces, the NCO moves into a higher gear, revealing Mozart's potent originality, with powerfully dramatic *tutti*s and expressively sung *andantes*. Mozart made his first trip to Italy in 1770, and the symphony he wrote in Milan that year (No 10) shows his enthusiastic incorporation of Italian stylistic models. Here the NCO's deliciously spacious orchestral playing shows Mozart's ravishing originality, with dramatic opposition of gesture and instrumentation in the exuberant *allegros* and a beguilingly graceful slow movement that winningly displays a keen awareness of the composer's innovative touches. These are indeed splendid performances, admirably complemented by vivid recordings.

Symphonies Nos 15-18
Northern Chamber Orchestra / Nicholas Ward
Naxos 8 550874 (58' · DDD)　　　　　Ⓢ➡

After Mozart returned from his first extended tour of Italy in 1771 he embarked on a number of symphonic projects that show his astonishing assimilation and transformation of the Italian overture, with crisp, transparent orchestration and suppleness of expression. The influence of Sammartini and J C Bach – whose music could be heard at concerts in Salzburg during 1772 when these pieces were written – is especially apparent in the bold thematic gestures and civilised discourse between wind and strings. Nicholas Ward and the NCO bring their customary style and eloquence to this music in performances that evocatively portray its blend of formal unity, radiant vitality and occasionally – as in the rhythmically imaginative finale of the C major Symphony – rustic charm. Opening *allegros* are suitably vivacious, *andantes* are graceful and poignant and the vigorous finales bristle with energy. The first movement of the C major Symphony offers a more potent dramatic formula, with subtly poetic triplets and tense tremolos; however, the highlight of the programme is the F major Symphony (No 18), which Saint-Foix described as 'the first of [Mozart's] great symphonies'. Here, Ward's and the NCO's dramatically compelling account, beautifully presented in a natural, spacious recording, brilliantly highlights the music's operatic qualities.

Symphonies Nos 21-24 & 26
Northern Chamber Orchestra / Nicholas Ward
Naxos 8 550876 (53' · DDD)   ⑤▶

This is a chance to enjoy Mozart's inexhaustibly imaginative assimilation and transformation of Italian operatic models. Ward's balanced orchestral textures reveal Mozart's fragrant orchestration with great clarity in the A major Symphony. Sample the second movement's deftly handled interplay of strings, woodwind and horns, and buoyantly stately Menuetto that culminates effectively in the finale's restless drive. The complete musical satisfaction provided by the four Italian-overture symphonies that comprise the remainder of the programme is due to the fullness and vigour of the orchestration itself, and to the Northern Chamber Orchestra's lively performances. The opening *allegros* and cheerfully effervescent finales bubble with infectious vitality, while the slow movements give the opportunity for more intimate instrumental ensembles. Most impressive, however, is the E flat major work, which originated as the overture to the play *Lanassa*. Here, Ward and the NCO compellingly portray the dramatic violence of the opening *Presto*, the despair of its minor-key *Andante* and the exuberant rhythms of its finale. The recording is atmospheric.

Symphonies Nos 25, 28 & 29
Prague Chamber Orchestra / Sir Charles Mackerras
Telarc CD80165 (78' · DDD)   ●

Here are three symphonies from Mozart's late teens, written in Salzburg, in crisply articulated performances. The first of them is a *Sturm und Drang* piece in G minor, a key that the composer reserved for moods of agitation. Mackerras takes the orchestra through the big opening *Allegro con brio* of No 25 with drive and passion, although it's unlikely that Mozart would have expected a Salzburg orchestra in the 1770s to play as fast as this skilful body of Czech players. The gentle *Andante* comes therefore as a relief, though here too Mackerras keeps a firm rhythmic grasp on the music, and indeed a taut metrical aspect is a feature of all three symphonies as played here, so that minuets dance briskly and purposefully and finales bustle. However, the sunlit warmth of the beautiful A major Symphony, No 29, comes through and the bracing view of the other two symphonies is a legitimate one, though giving little or nothing in the direction of expressive lingering, much less towards sentimental indulgence. The Prague Chamber Orchestra is an expert ensemble, not overlarge for this style of

music, and the recording is without doubt admirably clear although a little reverberant.

Symphony No 33. Serenade No 9
Academy of St Martin in the Fields / Iona Brown
Hänssler Classic CD98 129 (59' · DDD)   Ⓕ

Symphony No 35. Serenade No 7
Academy of St Martin in the Fields / Iona Brown *vn*
Hänssler Classic CD98 173 (72' · DDD)   Ⓕ

Each disc brings together a middle-period symphony and a contemporaneous Serenade. The sound recording has a sharpness of focus and sense of presence more often associated with the finest analogue recordings of the 1960s and 1970s. It's surprising to find that the venue was Henry Wood Hall, for this sounds rather more intimate than most recordings made there, with plenty of bloom but no excessive reverberation. This is Mozart sound, using modern instruments but with some concern for the crisper manners encouraged by period performance, that in its freshness and beauty makes one want to go on listening. The finale of the Symphony No 33, for example, brings a hectic speed which doesn't sound at all breathless, with featherlight triplets, and similarly in the finale of the *Posthorn* Serenade with which it's coupled. Exceptionally, in that Serenade, Iona Brown opts for a more relaxed speed and more moulded style in the lovely minor-key *Andantino* of the fifth movement. The posthorn in the Trio of the second Minuet is this time much more brazen and more forwardly balanced than before.

The coupling of the *Haffner* Symphony and *Haffner* Serenade is specially apt. Iona Brown herself is the virtuoso soloist in the Serenade, lighter than ever in the *moto perpetuo* scurryings of the fourth-movement Rondo. For those who continue to resist period performances in this repertory these are very refreshing discs.

Symphonies Nos 35-6 & 38-41   🄷
Berlin Philharmonic Orchestra / Karl Böhm
DG The Originals ② 447 416-2GOR2 (146' · ADD)
Recorded 1959-66   Ⓜ

These performances come from the first ever complete set of Mozart symphonies (reviewed above), and they still represent 'big orchestra' Mozart at its most congenial. The contrast between Böhm's sparkling Mozart, both elegant and vigorous, and the much smoother view taken by Karajan on his countless recordings with the same orchestra, works almost entirely in Böhm's favour here. Interpretatively, these are performances very much of their time, with exposition repeats (as in the first movement of No 40) and with minuets taken at what now seem like lumbering speeds. However, the slow movements certainly flow easily enough, and finales bounce along infectiously.

Consistently they convey the happy ease of Böhm in Mozart, even if the recording is beefy by today's standards, not as transparent as one now expects in this repertory, whether on modern or period instruments.

There's some inconsistency between the different recordings, all made in the Jesus-Christus Kirche in Berlin. The best sound comes from the sessions in 1966 for the *Linz* and No 39 – satisfyingly full without any perceptible edginess on violins – and the least good from 1959 for the *Prague*, where high violins sound rather fizzy. Yet the very precision of the CD transfers encourages one to highlight such points. In practice most collectors will find the sound more than acceptable enough in all six symphonies to convey the warmth of Böhm in Mozart without distraction.

Symphonies Nos 36 & 38
Prague Chamber Orchestra / Sir Charles Mackerras
Telarc CD80148 (66' · DDD)　　　　　Ⓕ◐

Mozart wrote his *Linz* Symphony in great haste (five days to be precise), but needless to say there's little evidence of haste in the music itself, except perhaps that the first movement has all the exuberance of a composer writing on the wing of inspiration. The slow movement with its siciliano rhythm certainly has no lack of serenity, although it has drama too. The *Prague* Symphony was written only three years later, yet Mozart's symphonic style had matured and the work is more ambitious and substantial.

A glorious spaciousness surrounds Sir Charles's performances. The fullness of the sound helps to add weight to climaxes without going beyond the bounds of volume that Mozart might have expected. Sir Charles captures the joy and high spirits that these symphonies embody without in any way undermining their greatness. This vivacity is emphasised by the East European sound of the Prague Chamber Orchestra. Mackerras adopts some aspects of the modern approach to Mozart performance: he includes harpsichord continuo, his minuets are taken trippingly, one-to-a-bar, and he prefers bowing that's crisper, more detached, and pointed. The very rightness of the result is recommendation enough.

Symphony No 38. Piano Concerto No 25 in C, K503ᵃ.
Ch'io mi scordi di te … Non temer, amato bene, K505ᵇ
ᵇ**Bernarda Fink** sop **Lausanne Chamber Orchestra / Christian Zacharias** ᵃᵇpf
Dabringhaus und Grimm MDG340 0967-2
(73' · DDD)　　　　　Ⓕ◐

Here Christian Zacharias successfully experiments with a nicely balanced Mozart group of symphony, aria and concerto. He himself takes multiple roles, conducting a fresh and lively account of the *Prague* Symphony, and acting as piano soloist not only in the Concerto, directing the weighty K503 from the keyboard, but also providing a crisply pointed obbligato in the most taxing of Mozart's concert arias, *Ch'io mi*

scordi di te. The sense of freedom and spontaneous enjoyment is enhanced by the clarity of the recording, made in the Metropole, Lausanne. Though *tuttis* are big and weighty, Zacharias finds rare transparency in lighter passages, and a vivid sense of presence throughout. One of Zacharias's great merits as a Mozart pianist is the crispness of his articulation; he defines each note with jewelled clarity.

The Symphony, too, is given a refreshing performance, with due weight in the first movement and light, crisp articulation in the finale. Some may feel that Zacharias underplays the gravity of the central *Andante*, but nowadays few will object to a flowing tempo such as one expects in a period performance.

Most striking of all, though, is the concert aria. Bernarda Fink, officially a mezzo, isn't just untroubled by the soprano tessitura but gives a characterful interpretation, pointing words and phrases with delightful individuality. Using her lovely creamy tone-colours, Fink offers one of the most impressive of all readings since Schwarzkopf's. Her contribution crowns a consistently enjoyable programme.

Symphonies – Nos 38 & 41
Freiburg Baroque Orchestra / René Jacobs
Harmonia Mundi HMC90 1958 (69' · DDD)　　Ⓕ◐

Such has been the admiration (if not always affection) for René Jacobs's Mozart operas, and so striking have been the contributions of the period orchestras involved, that it seems only natural that he should try his hand at a couple of the great man's symphonies. The results fascinate in places and infuriate in others, but never lack for talking-points.

The *Jupiter* is the more successful, showing the kind of 'inside-out' rethink with which Roger Norrington used to enrage and delight. The first movement is playful, with Jacobs toning down the Olympian grandeur and mischievously emphasising the *buffo* elements – the chuckling third theme is given the special treatment of a slower tempo and subsequent *accelerando*, with one statement even adorned with an exuberant upward violin slide. The slow movement, luminous and taken at a perfectly judged brisk walking pace, will be less contentious, but not so the Minuet, which races by at an initially disturbing yet ultimately exhilaratingly satisfying one-in-a-bar. After all this creative energy, the surprisingly steady finale seems to lack ideas by comparison, though its contrapuntal panache gains much from the clarity Jacobs draws from the excellent Freiburg band.

Crisp and boisterous orchestral playing likewise characterises the *Prague*, though here Jacobs seems to find it more difficult to find a way into the heart of the music. The first movement has a stricter pulse than in the *Jupiter*, and, while the development emerges as a thrilling battleground, the second subject's beautifully consoling woodwind lines are shown none of the loving tenderness they deserve. The *Andante*

MOZART'S SYMPHONIES NOS 40 & 41 – IN BRIEF

Cleveland Orchestra / George Szell   Ⓗ
Sony Classical 69699 89834-2 (73' · ADD)   ⒷO
With No 35, the *Haffner*, thrown in, this is great value. Szell's approach is stylish and, obviously, 'big band', but he presents this music with appropriate scale. The late-1950s sound is pretty good.

English Baroque Soloists /   Ⓟ
Sir John Eliot Gardiner
Philips 426 315-2PH (75' · DDD)   ⓂOO
Vivid, dramatic period-instrument accounts that in no way diminish the reach and ambition of these two masterpieces.

The English Concert / Trevor Pinnock   Ⓟ
DG 474 229-2 (73' · DDD)   Ⓜ
Smaller in scale than Gardiner's readings, Pinnock invests these works with great spring and vitality – at times they almost dance along.

Berlin PO / Karl Böhm
DG 439 472-2GCL (73' · ADD)   Ⓑ
Urbane, autumnal Mozart from one of his greatest interpreters. The BPO are very stylish, and a charming *Eine kleine Nachtmusik* from the VPO adds to the CD's allure.

Vienna PO / Leonard Bernstein
DG 445 548-2GM (69' · DDD)   ⓂOOᐅ
Recorded in 1984, Bernstein's Mozart is beautifully conceived: full of light and shade with no sense of overweight or over-dramatising. A charmer of a disc.

Scottish CO / Sir Charles Mackerras
Linn ② 🎧 CKD308 (139' · DDD   ⒻOOᐅ
As part of a set of Mozart's last four symphonies, Mackerras gives the sort of unforced, imaginative and beautifully balanced performance you would except of such a master Mozartian. The SCO plays with a perfect balance of modern-instrumental style and period-infused manners.

Concertgebouw Orchestra /
Nikolaus Harnoncourt
Warner Elatus 0927 49622-2 (74' · DDD)   Ⓜ
Harnoncourt always has someting fascinating to say in Mozart, but these are somewhat eccentric readings: the *Jupiter* is epic and certainly more succesful than No 40, which never quite settles down.

Anima Eterna / Jos van Immerseel   Ⓟ
Zig Zag Territoires ② ZZT030501 (104' · DDD)   Ⓕ
A delightful, poetic set that seems illuminated by a genuine love for the music. Symphonies Nos 39-41 are supplemented by the Bassoon Concerto: and everything comes up as if newly minted.

seems uncertain of its tempo (Jacobs is not the first conductor to struggle here), and the finale does not quite convince at its supersonic speed. Nevertheless, this is an intriguing and invigorating disc; Jacobs's *Jupiter*, at least, qualifies as among the most thought-provoking of recent years.

Symphonies Nos 38-41
Scottish Chamber Orchestra / Sir Charles Mackerras
Linn ② 🎧 CKD308 (139' · DDD)   ⒻOOᐅ

There is no need to argue the credentials of Sir Charles Mackerras as a Mozart interpreter, so let us just say that this double CD of the composer's last four symphonies contains no surprises – it is every bit as good as you would expect. Like many modern-instrument performances these days it shows the period-orchestra influence in its lean sound, agile dynamic contrasts, sparing string vibrato, rasping brass, sharp-edged timpani and prominent woodwind, though given Mackerras's long revisionist track-record it seems an insult to suggest that he would not have arrived at such a sound of his own accord. And in any case his handling of it – joyously supported by the playing of the Scottish Chamber Orchestra – is supremely skilled; rarely will you hear such well judged orchestral balance, such effective marrying of textural transparency and substance. The *Jupiter* in particular has a wonderful bright grandeur, yet reveals details in the brilliant contrapuntal kaleidoscope of the finale that too often go unheard.

Seldom, either, will you hear such expertly chosen tempi; generally these performances are on the quick side, but rather than seeming hard-driven they exude forward momentum effortlessly worn. Nowhere is this better shown in the slow movements (even with all their repeats they never flag, yet their shifting expressive moods are still tenderly drawn), but also conspicuously successful are the slow introductions to Symphonies Nos 38 and 39 and the Minuet movements of Nos 40 and 39.

These are not Mozart performances for the romantics out there, but neither are they in the least lacking in humanity. No, this is thoroughly modern-day Mozart, full of wisdom and leaving the listener in no doubt of the music's ineffable greatness.

Symphonies Nos 39-41. Bassoon Concerto   Ⓟ
Jane Gower bn
Anima Eterna / Jos van Immerseel
Zig Zag Territoires ② ZZT030501 (104' · DDD)   Ⓕ

Jos van Immerseel, better known as fortepianist than conductor, sets quickish tempos in almost all the movements of Symphonies Nos 39 and 40. The overall effect is of vitality, brightness and clarity, with contrapuntal interplay much more apparent than usual. There are few of the usual tragic overtones in the gracefully played

Andante; of No 39, or the usual darkness and foreboding in No 40. All this comes partly from the period instruments, and the perceptive way they're handled. Van Immerseel balances them carefully, has little or no string vibrato and clearly requires precise articulation. That's why we hear more of the inner lines.

In the *Jupiter*, however, the approach is less chamber-music-like. This is a trumpets-and-drums symphony, so the manner is more forceful, sometimes rather abrupt; but the first movement is powerfully shaped. Again a quickish *Andante* with Mozart's textures illuminated to fine effect. The dense writing in the minuet profits from a finely balanced texture, and so above all does the finale, where you're constantly aware of all that's going on below the surface. It's passionate, too: listen to those timpani thwacks in the development and the power of the extraordinary recapitulation. The amazing five-part counterpoint of the coda is heard with unprecedented clarity.

These may not be everyone's performances. But they should be treasured: if you think you know these symphonies back to front, these versions will enable you to listen to the music afresh and hear new things in it.

The Bassoon Concerto filler is enjoyably played by Jane Bower on a period bassoon, delightfully uneven in tone but always beautifully tuned and with many neatly imaginative touches.

Clarinet Quintet in A, K581

Mozart Clarinet Quintet
Brahms Clarinet Quintet in B minor, Op 115
Karl Leister *cl* **Berlin Soloists** (Bernd Gellermann, Bernhard Hartog *vns* Wolfram Christ *va* Jörg Baumann *vc*)
Warner Apex 0927-44350-2 (71' · DDD) Ⓑ

This is a familiar and successful coupling of two of the most beautiful works written for clarinet and strings. Karl Leister gives most beautifully easy, charming, relaxed performances of both works, and the recordings are pleasantly fresh and immediate. There's no lack of sparkle in Mozart's final variations, and the Hungarian tinges are beautifully touched upon in the Brahms; the slow music in both works is reflective and tender without any loss of poise. Here are two beautiful performances that can be warmly recommended.

Clarinet Quintet[b]. Adagio, KAnh94/K580*a*[a].
Flute Quartet, K285[c]. Quintet, K452[d]
Ensemble 360 ([c]Guy Eshed *fl* Adrian Wilson *acor*[a]/[d]*ob* [bd]Matthew Hunt *cl* [d]Benjamin Hudson *bn* [d]Tim Jackson *hn* [a]Sara Bitlloch, [bc]Donald Grant *vns* [abc]Martin Saving *va* [abc]Marie Bitlloch *vc* [d]Tim Horton *pf*)
ASV Gold GLD4022 (76' · DDD) ❍Ⓕ

The Sheffield-based Ensemble 360 – a flexible group of up to 11 players – have been drawing enthusiastic audiences with their informal and inventive concerts, often in offbeat venues. As this attractively planned debut CD confirms, their playing is fresh and lively, free from any whiff of bland routine. The Flute Quartet, offered as an aperitif, is blithe and impish in its outer movements, delicately, coolly wistful in the Watteau-esque *Adagio*.

In the miraculous Piano and Wind Quintet, Ensemble 360 phrase imaginatively, delight in their quick-witted repartee, and handle the ever-shifting balances with care and finesse. Ensemble 360 are marvellously vivid in the finale, here less gracious, more playful than usual, with the main theme's contrasts of *forte* and *piano* piquantly realised.

The unfinished *Adagio*, K580*a*, opening uncannily like the motet Ave verum corpus, was probably intended for clarinet and three basset-horns, though it sounds well enough in this (anonymous) completed version for cor anglais and strings. Best of all here is the Clarinet Quintet, performed by Matthew Hunt on the basset clarinet, with its treacly extra low notes displayed to pungent effect in, say, the Ländler-like second Trio of the Minuet. With its briskish speeds, this won't necessarily please those who like to have the Quintet's autumnal associations underlined. But the performance has a natural flow and grace allied to many sensitive touches of colour and timing. Especially appealing are the fire and tension of the first-movement development, the easy lilt of the Minuet (wittily embellished on its final repeat) and the finale's gleeful sense of fun, stilled in the haunting A minor variation, where the solo viola makes delicately expressive use of portamento. The rollicking send-off sets the seal on a touching and thoroughly delightful performance.

String Quintets

No **1** in B flat, K174 No **2** in C minor, K406
No **3** in C, K515 No **4** in G minor, K516 No **5** in D, K593 No **6** in E flat, K614

String Quintets Nos 1-6
Arthur Grumiaux, Arpad Gérecz *vns* **Georges Janzer, Max Lesueur** *vas* **Eva Czako** *vc*
Philips Trio ③ 470 950-2PTR3 (170' · ADD) Recorded 1973 Ⓜ❍❍❍

Of the six works Mozart wrote for string quintet, that in B flat major, K174, is an early composition, written at the age of 17. It's a well-made, enjoyable work, but not a great deal more than that. The C minor work, K406, is an arrangement by Mozart of his Serenade for six wind instruments, K398. It's difficult not to feel that the original is more effective, since the music seems to sit a little uncomfortably on string instruments. But the remaining four works, written in the last four years of Mozart's life, are a different matter. The last string quintets from Mozart's pen were extraordinary works, and the addition of the second viola seems to have pulled him to still greater heights. It has been suggested that Mozart wrote K515 and K516 to show King Friedrich Wilhelm II of Prussia that he was a better composer of string quintets than Boccherini, whom the King had retained as chamber music composer to his court. There was no response, so he offered these two quintets for sale with the K406 arrangement to make up the usual set of three. K593 and K614 were written in the last year of his life. Refinement is perhaps the word that first comes to mind in discussing these performances, which are affectionate yet controlled by a cool, intelligent sensitivity. The recordings have been well transferred, and Grumiaux's tone, in particular, is a delight to the ear.

String Quintet No 3. String Quartet No 16 in E flat, K428
Louise Williams va The Lindsays (Peter Cropper, Ronald Birks vn Robin Ireland va Bernard Gregor-Smith vc)
ASV CDDCA992 (67' · DDD)   (F)

Here's a fine performance of the great C major Quintet. The Lindsays take the first movement at a true *Allegro*, so that it bowls along in top gear, the details vivid and sharply etched. Much of this grandest and most spacious movement in Mozart's chamber output is marked to be played softly: in the Lindsays' hands the wonderful counterpoint in the development section can be heard with exceptional clarity as the tension builds up, but not the dynamic. The *Andante* sounds the more touching for never being overplayed, and it's a special pleasure to hear how the most florid passages for first violin and first viola fit effortlessly into the rhythmic scheme. In the finale, Peter Cropper introduces some beautifully played portamentos in the main theme, and the whole movement sounds delightfully witty and happy. The E flat Quartet, K428, is cool and stylish, which suits this enigmatic work rather well. The Lindsays' way of using Mozart's marks of expression and articulation to make the music speak feels absolutely right, especially in their delicate, refined *Andante*, and it's good to hear the quartet played with all its repeats. The recording has a nice intimate quality.

Flute Quartets

Flute Quartets – D, K285; G, K285a; C, K285b; A, K298
Emmanuel Pahud fl Christoph Poppen vn Hariolf Schlichtig va Jean-Guihen Queyras vc
EMI 556829-2 (59' · DDD)   (F)▷

There may be only one movement of any emotional weight, the B minor *Adagio* of the First Quartet, K285, but in that brief cantilena Pahud finds a mystery and subtlety of dynamic shading that outshine almost any rival. For the rest he consistently conveys the fun in the writing here.

The A major work may run the dangerous course of parodying the banalities of the contemporaries whom Mozart despised, but Pahud still finds charm in the invention, helped by the warm, imaginative playing of his string partners. Pahud's lighter, more sparkling playing, with his fresh, clear tone is preferable to Galway's more Romantic approach at generally broader speeds, and with phrasing more heavily underlined in characteristically full flute tone. Pahud also observes second-half repeats as well as first in the sonata-form first movements of the first three quartets. Recommended.

Piano Quartets

No 1 in G minor, K478; **No 2** in E flat, K493

Piano Quartets – Nos 1 & 2; E flat, K452 (arr)   **P**
Sonnerie (Monica Huggett vn Emilia Benjamin va Alison McGillivray vc Gary Cooper fp)
ASV Gaudeamus CDGAU212 (76' · DDD)   (F)

Sonnerie go one – rather a large one – better than their recorded rivals in the Mozart piano quartets by including an extra work: the piano quartet arrangement (not generally thought to be Mozart's own) of the Quintet for piano and wind. The work, so artfully composed around the sound and capacities of the oboe, clarinet, bassoon and horn, loses the motivation for its particular thematic structure in transcription but is nevertheless a worthwhile bonus.

Not that these performances need any bonus. They have exceptional musical vitality, as though the music is being freshly thought through as it unfolds and the players are newly fired by its ideas. The G minor Quartet in particular is given a large-scale, outspoken performance, vigorous, dark-toned in the first movement, with an almost alarmingly vivid and strongly shaped account of the development section. There's drama in the *Andante*, too, which is expansively done, and the finale of the E flat work, too, is done with great spirit – here the pianist is very much in the driving seat – and there are many happy details of timing and dynamic gradation.

Mozart's wit is beautifully captured in K493, yet this is a deeply serious performance, strongly argued, with the mystery and logic of his unusual modulations fully grasped. The first movement here, taken at a rather steady tempo, is particularly successful, with Cooper taking his time over the expression of its ideas and Monica Huggett and her colleagues playing the lyrical secondary material with much warmth.

Piano Quartets Nos 1 & 2
Isaac Stern vn **Jaime Laredo** va **Yo-Yo Ma** vc
Emanuel Ax pf
Sony Classical Theta SMK89794 (56' · DDD)   (M)

This grouping of star names offers performances of imagination and insight. In the E flat Quartet, K493, it isn't just Isaac Stern and Yo-Yo Ma whose solo entries have one sitting up, but also Jaime Laredo in the rare moments when Mozart gives a solo to the viola. Speeds are beautifully chosen, and in both works the performances convey a happy spontaneity. Emanuel Ax shows what a natural, individual Mozartian he is. The G minor work is in many ways parallel to the great piano concertos of the period, with the piano regularly set against the strings in ensemble, and Ax readily establishes the sort of primacy plainly required. He's a shade robust at the start of the central *Andante* but in fast music as in slow his gift of pointing rhythms and moulding phrases is consistently persuasive and imaginative.

The recording, made in the Manhattan Center, New York, is a degree drier than in many of the current rival versions, but there's ample bloom on the sound, fitting very well in a domestic listening room.

Piano Quartets Nos 1 & 2
Paul Lewis *pf* **Leopold String Trio** (Marianne Thorsen *vn* Scott Dickinson *va* Kate Gould *vc*)
Hyperion CDA67373 (63' · DDD)　　　Ⓕ**OO**

These are unusually expansive works, their first movements each close on 15 minutes' music, prolific in their thematic matter and richly developed. They demand playing that shows a grasp of their scale, playing that makes plain to the listener the shape, the functional character of the large spans of the music.

Paul Lewis and the Leopold String Trio, playing on modern instruments, excel in this, with their feeling for its structure and its tension, particularly in the first movement of the G minor, and especially at its great climax at the end of the development section, which is delivered with a compelling power and a sense of its logic. This performance is exemplified by its carefully measured tempo, its poise and its subtle handling of the balance between strings and piano. The *Andante* is unhurried, allowing plenty of time for expressive detail; and the darker colours within the finale, for all its G major good cheer, are there too.

The spacious and outgoing E flat work is no less sympathetically done, with plenty of feeling for its special kind of broad lyricism; particularly attractive are the gently springy rhythms and the tenderness of the string phrasing in the first movement, and Lewis's beautifully shaped phrasing in the *Larghetto*. A real winner, this disc: warmly recommended.

String Quartets

No 1 in G, K80 **No 2** in D, K155 **No 3** in G, K156 **No 4** in C, K157 **No 5** in F, K158 **No 6** in B flat, K159 **No 7** in E flat, K160 **No 8** in F, K168 **No 9** in A, K169 **No 10** in C, K170 **No 11** in E flat, K171 **No 12** in B flat, K172

No 13 in D minor, K173 **No 14** in G, K387 **No 15** in D minor, K421 **No 16** in E flat, K428 **No 17** in B flat, K458, 'Hunt' **No 18** in A, K464 **No 19** in C, K465, 'Dissonance' **No 20** in D, K499, 'Hoffmeister' **No 21** in D, K575 **No 22** in B flat, K589 **No 23** in F, K590

String Quartet No 17. Oboe Quartet. Horn Quintet
Nicholas Daniel *ob* **Stephen Bell** *hn* **The Lindsays**
(Peter Cropper *vn* Ronald Birks *vn/va* Robin Ireland *va* Bernard Gregor-Smith *vc*)
ASV CDDCA968 (68' · DDD)　　　　　Ⓕ

The Lindsays really make the *Hunt* Quartet sparkle. One could describe their approach as middle-of-the-road; they're as meticulous as many period-instrument groups about details of phrasing, and avoid excessive accents and vibrato, yet their sound is modern, and the care over detail doesn't preclude a very spontaneous approach in which the music's feeling is compellingly communicated. In the Oboe Quartet Nicholas Daniel matches the string players' care over articulation and detailed expression, and plays with exceptional technical polish and brilliance. His gleaming tone is capable of great expressive range. The Horn Quintet is perhaps not quite such an individual or remarkable work as the two quartets. And you may find yourself longing for the extra character and beauty that a fine performance with the natural horn would have had. Yet this is a highly recommendable reading, too. The recording is very lifelike.

String Quartets Nos 20 & 22　　　　　Ⓟ
Quatuor Mosaïques
Astrée Naïve E8834 (63' · DDD)　　　Ⓕ**OO**

This release completes the Mosaïques' recording of the 10 mature Mozart Quartets: an outstanding achievement. Apart from the clear, rich sound of the period instruments and the precise, beautiful tuning, what impresses about this Mozart playing is the care for detail, the way each phrase is shaped so as to fit perfectly into context while having its own expressive nuances brought out clearly. This often leads the quartet to use more *rubato*, to make more noticeable breathing spaces between sentences than many other groups do.

In the first movements of both these quartets, for instance, the Mosaïques adopt a very similar tempo and tone to the Quartetto Italiano, but the Italians aren't so rhythmically flexible. The Mosaïques make us listen to and appreciate the significance of each detail as it unfolds. With this approach there might be a danger of sounding contrived, but even when adopting a mannered style, as in the *Minuet* of K499, the Mosaïques retain a strong physical connection with the music's natural pulse – by comparison the Italiano here seem a trifle heavy and humourless.

The slow movements of both quartets are taken at a flowing pace, making possible an unusual degree of expressive flexibility. All repeats are made, including those on the Minuet's *da capo* in K499. The longer the better when the playing is as exceptional as this.

Piano Trios

No 1, K496; No 5, K548. Divertimento, K254
Florestan Trio (Susan Tomes *pf* Anthony Marwood *vn* Richard Lester *vc*)
Hyperion CDA67609 (60' · DDD)　　　Ⓕ

So much of Mozart's instrumental music is opera by other means. The Florestan understand this as well as any group, and better than most. At the start of K548's airy finale, Susan Tomes's gracefully demure piano is swiftly countered by Anthony Marwood's raffish *forte* riposte: and this sense of delighted, quick-witted dialogue between quasi-operatic protagonists runs through the whole movement, abetted by touches of sly, subtle timing, from Marwood especially. No performance of this piece brings such a smile to the face.

The Florestan have the knack of bringing alive even apparently neutral figuration, of sensing the possibilities of interplay in what may look like a simple theme-plus-accompaniment texture. Piano and violin dominate in these works, especially in the breezy early Divertimento, K254. But Richard Lester's warm, nutty timbre contributes crucially to the music's colour, here and elsewhere, while he takes his chances when Mozart gives the cello an equal voice in the texture: say, in the first-movement development of K496, where the Florestan typically conjure a vivid operatic imbroglio.

As usual, the Florestan choose flowing speeds in the slow movements, which may initially faze those who know the music from the revered Beaux Arts versions. In in the 6/8 *Andante* of K496 the Florestan show that a graceful dance lilt, even a hint of skittishness, need not preclude an eloquent response to Mozart's extraordinary remote modulations.

Talk of an outright winner is always dangerous, butthe Florestan's sparkling, inventive performances make them a top recommendation for the complete Mozart trios, their claims enhanced by the warm, ideally balanced recording.

Piano Trios – No 3, K502; No 4, K542; No 6, K564
Florestan Trio (Susan Tomes *pf* Anthony Marwood *vn* Richard Lester *vc*)
Hyperion CDA67556 (59' · DDD)　　　Ⓕ

The prolific Florestan here offer three trios, including the two finest, K502 and K542. These are beautifully judged performances, generally fleeter of foot, airier of texture and more intimate in tone than those from Barenboim and colleagues on EMI (see below), with an ideal balance between the instruments (Richard Lester's cello always a telling presence, even when his role is apparently incidental). In K542 the Florestan catch the peculiar Mozartian mix of radiance and passion in the outer movements without any of the excessive

lingerings of the EMI performance.

The fast movements of the other two trios – the brilliant, concerto-like K502 and the ingenuous K564 – are just as delightful in their verve, their gleeful, quick-witted repartee and the vitality with which the players invest even routine-looking accompanying figuration. Occasionally, as in the finale of K564, Barenboim and Co are just that much more vivid. But far preferable is the Florestan's flowing tempo and naturally expressive phrasing in K502's *Larghetto*.

For those wanting K502 and K542 on a single disc, the Florestan enchant with their ebullience and spontaneous delight, and find a winning tenderness in the first movement of K542 and choose a sprightly, lilting tempo in same trio's *Andante grazioso*.

Piano Trios – No 1, K496[a]; No 2, 'Kegelstatt', K498[b]; No 3, K502[a]; No 4, K542[a]; No 5, K548[a]; No 6, K564[a]
Daniel Barenboim *pf* [b]**Matthias Glander** *cl* [a]**Nikolaj Znaider** *vn* [b]**Felix Schwartz** *va* [a]**Kyril Zlotnikov** *vc*
EMI ② 344643-2 (125' · DDD)　　　ⒻⒷ►

The record companies fell over each other to bring out single discs or sets of piano trios during Mozart year. EMI offers a near-complete cycle, omitting the early Divertimento, K254, but including the wonderful *Kegelstatt* Trio for the (in 1786) unprecedented combination of clarinet, viola and piano.

With Barenboim at the keyboard no Mozart performance is ever dull. And despite a recording that balances the violin too closely, sometimes giving a bright glare to Nikolaj Znaider's normally sweet tone, there is plenty to enjoy in these performances: the bold sweep of K496's opening *Allegro*, for instance, with Barenboim and Kyril Zlotnikov relishing Mozart's spirited dialogues between keyboard and the newly emancipated cello; the mingled grace and swagger of the outer movements in the underestimated K548, full of typically deft touches of shading and timing; or the popular-style finale of the final trio, K564, where Barenboim and his accomplices choose an ideal, relaxed allegretto and give a lusty kick to the rhythms in the rustic waltz.

Appealing, too, is the mobile tempo and gentle flexibility of phrase in the not-so-slow movement of K542, perfectly poised between an *ancien régime* gavotte and a Schubertian 'walking' *andante*. In contrast, the central movements of K502 and K548 are taken broadly, with *molto espressivo* phrasing that some will find ideally soulful, others, including me, over-romanticised. The *Andante* first movement of the Kegelstatt is also dangerously slow and 'backward-leaning' but this proviso apart, the performance is warmly sung, with a notably rich, throaty viola.

Violin Sonatas

Violin Sonatas – No 1, K6; No 26, K378/K317d;　Ⓟ
No 27, K379/K373a; No 36, K547
Rachel Podger *vn* **Gary Cooper** *fp*

Channel Classics ⟨SACD⟩ CCSSA21804 (77' · DDD/DSD)
Ⓕ**OO**

This is Volume 1 of a complete set, and the series certainly gets off to a cracking start. The recording gives the fortepiano (an Adlam copy of a 1795 Anton Walther instrument) a full, rich, sound; the balance with the violin is excellent – it's as though we're listening in a small but resonant room.

The noble introductory *Adagio* of K379 sounds wonderfully colourful, and is followed by an unusually passionate, intense performance of the Sonata's G minor *Allegro*. It's taken at a faster tempo than usual, and we're persuaded to think of it as a worthy forerunner of the great G minor works to come. It's the CD's high point, perhaps, but the first two movements of K378 run it close; the opening *Allegro moderato* is spacious, flexible and expressive, and the second movement warm and sensuous.

Gary Cooper plays with considerable freedom, often spreading chords to soften their impact or for extra expressiveness, and ornamenting repeated passages most imaginatively. Rachel Podger doesn't generally ornament her part; her accompaniments are unforced and flow easily, and she enjoys taking the lead, playing boldly yet with sensitivity.

Mozart's first sonata, K6, begun when he was six, is a lively piece, but you'd never guess the composer. And K547, intended as an educational piece, has nothing of the expressive depth of the other late sonatas. But Cooper and Podger's playing remains suited to the music's character, unaffectedly bringing out its charm and vitality.

Violin Sonatas – No 2, K7; No 15, K30; No 18, Ⓟ
K301; No 20, K303; No 33, K481
Rachel Podger vn **Gary Cooper** fp
Channel Classics ⟨SACD⟩ CCSSA22805 (67' · DDD/DSD)
Ⓕ

Gary Cooper and Rachel Podger's projected set of the Mozart duo sonatas (of which this is the second volume) will be more complete than most, including the works he wrote for keyboard with accompanying violin between the ages of seven and 10. Of course these can't be compared to the later sonatas but they're certainly not without interest; and on the present disc the progress between No 2 and No 15 is striking – the latter's *Adagio* shows an enormous increase in expressive range (further extended by Gary Cooper's extravagant decoration of the repeats) with the violin complementing the melody most effectively. The decision to use the same fortepiano for all the sonatas may not be the most accurate historical way of presenting them but, as Cooper points out, it does help the listener to hear them as belonging to a single line of development.

Both artists show an impressive command of the rhetorical 18th-century approach to phrasing and expression, giving a very lively air to the music-making – there are no flat, routine

moments. The theatrical manner of No 18's first movement inspires a wonderfully bright, colourful performance, and the contrasts inherent in the two-speed opening movement of No 20 are brilliantly realised.

Some may find the continually active style of playing a step too far, and there were places, in the first movement of No 33, for example, where a calmer, less eventful approach might have been welcome. But the great *Adagio* of this sonata has a beautiful sense of line and, throughout, the marriage of expertise and stylistic awareness results in truly treasurable performances.

Violin Sonatas – No 3, K8; No 13, K28; No 28, Ⓟ
K380; No 32, K454. Andante and Fugue, K402.
Andante and Allegretto, K404
Rachel Podger vn **Gary Cooper** fp
Channel Classics ⟨SACD⟩ CCSSA23606
(78' · DDD/DSD)
Ⓕ

The brief K8 Sonata is one of three that the eight-year-old Mozart played for Louis XV with his father on the harpsichord. No great statement in comparison with one of the masterpieces here, say K454, but amazingly original given Mozart's tender age, with a bright, strutting minuet-finale that Gary Cooper and Rachel Podger throw off with winning mock-insouciance. All the accolades heaped upon these two are fully justified: the playfulness, the teamwork, the unanimity of gesture and appreciation of musical line, especially from Podger. Cooper's poetic responses are nicely displayed at the start of K380's *Andante con moto*: the way he manipulates the instrument's potential for shifting colours, bold and resonant to start, then at the theme's return with a more muted sound. Podger sails an expressively curved top line, largely (though not exclusively) without vibrato. There's real sparkle to the opening *Allegro* of K28, composed in The Hague by the quickly developing 10-year-old, JC Bach by now a discernible influence.

The first movement of K402 recalls *Don Giovanni*'s Minuet (it was written during roughly the same period) while K404, though thematically memorable, barely makes the four-minute mark. K454 is the masterpiece, the most substantial work and the most Romantic in style. Podger and Cooper employ their period-performance manners to pleasing effect, especially in the serene *Andante* and the keenly accented *Allegretto*. Full marks for these fresh, thoroughly accomplished and well-recorded performances.

Violin Sonatas – No 4, K9; No 14, K29; Ⓟ
No 19, K302; No 21, K304; No 35, K526
Rachel Podger vn **Gary Cooper** pf
Channel Classics ⟨SACD⟩ CCSSA24607 (76' · DDD/DSD)
Ⓕ

The most poignant music here is the two-movement E minor Sonata (K304) that Mozart wrote in Paris not long after his mother died, a piece much beloved of Arthur Grumiaux and Clara Haskil, who recorded and played the work in recital. Rachel Podger and Gary Cooper also make a fine job of it, a more expansive one than we usually hear. Not that their tempi are anything less than well chosen: the extra length originates in their choice to repeat both halves of the first movement. Cooper's playing at the start of the Minuet second movement is both delicate and elegant whereas the muted, ethereal sound both players conjure for the centre of K9's finale is remarkable. The galant early D major Sonata (K29) shows JC Bach's influence and the vividly orchestrated colouring of this Podger-Cooper rendition seems to underline that influence. Cooper's tendency to expressively desynchronise chords, in parts of K302's Rondeau, for example, is very appealing.

The really big event musically speaking is the magnificent A major work (K526), the last but one of Mozart's violin sonatas; the first movement is as extrovert as it is inventive (especially in terms of its varied rhythmic emphases), the slow movement one of Mozart's finest – a justified prompt for both players to favour an almost operatic approach. Podger in particular adjusts and alters her tone projection more effectively and expressively than most period players do. Most attractive is the duo's relative freedom, their refusal to be bound by bar-lines: there's an appealing fluidity about their playing. Add excellent sound, and the recommendation is clinched.

'Duo Sonatas, Vol 1'   **P**
Violin Sonatas – No 18, K301; No 19, K302; No 20, K303. Variations on an Andantino, 'Hélas, j'ai perdu mon amant', K360. Variations on, 'La bergère Célimène', K359
Duo Amadè (Catherine Mackintosh vn Geoffrey Govier fp)
Chandos Chaconne CHAN0755 (66' · DDD)   ⒻⒹ➔

For Catherine Mackintosh and Geoffrey Govier the 'rules' of historically informed performance have become second nature; we get the impression they're playing for sheer enjoyment of the music. All the distinctive moments are appreciated and given due emphasis but in a spontaneous way, the interpretative points never going beyond what musicians with good rapport might do on the spur of the moment. Yet it's obvious that Govier and Mackintosh are careful, as well as spirited, interpreters. The recorded sound and balance are excellent, and they artfully control their dynamics so that principal and subsidiary lines are clearly distinguished.

The concluding Rondo of K302 contains many octave passages shared by piano and violin; here, with precise matching of tone colour, articulation and volume, Govier and Mackintosh turn what might seem like a rare lapse of Mozartian imagination into a delightful colouristic device. In the first movement of this sonata they make the most of the quasi-orchestral writing, with its pulsating *crescendi*, horn imitations

and *tremolando* effects. Colourful in a different way is the minor section in K301's finale, where the con sordino piano's soft quality perfectly supports the poised violin melody.

You may wonder whether to favour Duo Amadè or the impressive Podger/Cooper team (see aobe). The latter mix into their programmes the juvenile works from the 1760s, but if you are most interested in the great series of works starting with K301, Duo Amadè may suit you better.

Piano Duets

Sonatas for Keyboard Duet – K358; K497. Andante and Variations, K501. Orgelstück Fantasia für eine Uhr, K608. Fugue, K401
Andreas Groethuysen, Yaara Tal pf
Sony Classical SK93868 (62' · DDD)   ⒻⓄ

Sonatas – for Keyboard Duet, K19d; for Two Pianos, K448. Sonata Movements for Keyboard Duet – K357; K500. Adagio and Fugue, K546. Larghetto and Allegro, Kdeest
Andreas Groethuysen, Yaara Tal pf
Sony Classical 82876 78363-2 (65' · DDD)   ⒻⓄ

Yaara Tal and Andreas Groethuysen live and breathe as one on these two wonderful discs in which every performance emerges not merely as 'the best' (if we're talking critical comparisons) but life-affirming. Technically, each fiddly ornament, every phrase shape and every degree of pedalling is miraculously co-ordinated – not that one is ever made aware of such prosaic elements for the music simply flows, newly minted, in joyous, stylish effusion. Here are Wolfgang and Nannerl having a thoroughly enjoyable afternoon, smiling and winking at each other as they negotiate some of the more mischievous twists and turns.

The final movement of the B flat Sonata, K358, has rarely bubbled along like this, while the F major Sonata, K497, confirms its place as a masterpiece with its passages of eerie Schubertian prescience. The playing of this duo marks a clear if subtle distinction between one that comes together occasionally for festivals and recordings, and one that does it every day as a vocation.

Mozart Sonata for Two Keyboards, K448 **Schubert** Divertissement, D823 – Andantino varié. Fantasie, D940.
Katia Labèque, Marielle Labèque pfs
KML Recordings KML1117 (53' · DDD)   Ⓕ

The Labèque sisters offer a truly superlative account of the great F minor Fantasy in rich, warm-blooded sound. Rarely has the weft and warp of the score been so clearly yet spontaneously realised, its question-and-answer dialogue played with such perfect (and natural) even-handedness. As Malcolm Bilson and Robert D Levin observe in their booklet, with the fugato in the final section and the work's climax that leads to the final restatement of the opening, 'agony and resignation make no concession to the listener's longing for release'. The *Andantino varié* in B minor is the delectable second movement of Schubert's *Divertissment sur des motifs origineaux [sic] français* (no one seems to have identified these 'original French motifs').

The disc concludes with another masterpiece of the piano duo repertoire. Once more the interplay in Mozart's D major Sonata is superbly handled, merrily witty in the outer movements and yielding an unusually elegiac *Andante*. One oddity: the opening phrase of the Rondo's theme (in 2/4) consists of two groups of four semiquavers and one quaver; the Labèques play the first semiquaver as an appoggiatura and turn the second into a (accented) dotted quaver – unsettling.

Piano Sonatas

No 1 in C, K279 **No 2** in F, K280 **No 3** in B flat, K281 **No 4** in E flat, K282 **No 5** in G, K283 **No 6** in D, K284 **No 7** in C, K309 **No 8** in A minor, K310 **No 9** in D, K311 **No 10** in C, K330 **No 11** in A, K331 **No 12** in F, K332 **No 13** in B flat, K333 **No 14** in C minor, K457 **No 15** in F, K533 **No 16** in C, K545 **No 17** in B flat, K570 **No 18** in D, K576

Piano Sonatas Nos 1-18. Fantasia, K475
Mitsuko Uchida pf
Philips Complete Mozart Edition ⑤ 468 356-2PB5
(325' · DDD)   ⑧❍❍❍

 By common consent, Mitsuko Uchida is among the leading Mozart pianists of today, and her recorded series of the piano sonatas won critical acclaim as it appeared and finally *Gramophone* Awards in 1989 and 1991. Here are all the sonatas, plus the *Fantasia* in C minor, K475, which is in some ways a companion piece to the sonata in the same key, K457. This is unfailingly clean, crisp and elegant playing, that avoids anything like a romanticised view of the early sonatas such as the delightfully fresh G major, K283. On the other hand, Uchida responds with the necessary passion to the forceful, not to say *Angst*-ridden, A minor Sonata, K310. Indeed, her complete series is a remarkably fine achievement, comparable with her account of the piano concertos. The recordings were produced in the Henry Wood Hall in London and offer excellent piano sound; thus an unqualified recommendation is in order for one of the most valuable volumes in Philips's Complete Mozart Edition. Don't be put off by critics who suggest that these sonatas are less interesting than some other Mozart compositions, for they're fine pieces written for an instrument that he himself played and loved.

Mozart Piano Sonata No 6, K284. Rondo, K511. Variations on 'Ah, vous dirai-je, maman', K265

Prokofiev Piano Sonata No 3. Toccata, Op 11. Ten Pieces from Romeo and Juliet, Op 75 – excerpts
Lise de la Salle pf
Naïve ② V5080 (91' · DDD). Includes bonus 26-minute DVD documentary, 'Lise de la Salle, majeure!', directed by Jean-Philippe Perrot   Ⓕ

Young talent does not come more brilliantly or ardently alive than this. Clearly designed to demonstrate this 19-year-old pianist's versatility, Naïve's album showcases her in radically different composers and finds her equally persuasive in both. De la Salle is tremulously expressive in Mozart's A minor Rondo, making every bar pulse and breathe with a special life and prophecy of romantic things to come. She revels in the bustle and ceremony of the D major Sonata, K284. Hear her enviable perle in the last-movement Vars 1 and 3, her change to minor-key contemplation in Var 7, in the florid musings of Var 11 – and in her pinpoint definition and character in the K265 Variations – and here you surely have a young pianist born for Mozart.

But then she is no less successful in Prokofiev's diablerie, finding time, despite her headlong tempo, for piquant asides in the Toccata, for a loving romantic dalliance in parts of the Third Sonata and for a reminder in her selection from *Romeo and Juliet* of delicacy and affection beneath Prokofiev's outwardly prickly and intractable nature. This superb album concludes with a short DVD showing De la Salle exclaiming over what she clearly sees as her enchanted life (while acknowledging the hard work involved). All things being equal, she is clearly on the threshold of a major career. Her freshness and vitality are already something very special.

Piano Sonatas Nos 8 & 15. Courante, K399. Gigue, K574. Rondo, K511. March, K408/1
Richard Goode pf
Nonesuch 7559 79831-2 (60' · DDD)   Ⓕ❍❍❍

 A Mozart programme such as this, which includes two of the greatest sonatas and the A minor Rondo, leaves absolutely no margin for error or insufficiency, nor indeed for anything at all approximate or generalised. It's given to very few to play Mozart as well as Richard Goode, who seems to pitch the rhetoric just right and sustain an ideal balance of strength and refinement.

It's quite big playing, and the range of sonority is appropriate to the A minor Sonata, K310, in particular; no other recent recording realises so well the sharp contrasts, the cross-cut abutments of dynamics, which are such a striking feature in all three movements. Goode has a characteristic touch of urgency that has nothing to do with impetuosity or agitation of the surface, but rather with carrying the discourse forward and making us curious about what will happen next. In the *presto* finale, where Brendel is choppy and rather slow, Goode is exciting and articulate, wonderfully adept at getting from one thing to another.

There's little to choose between these players in the composite F major Sonata, K533. Brendel is at his finest in the dark, far-reaching middle movement; both of them relish the challenge of characterising the multifariousness of the first; Goode is especially convincing in the last movement.

He gives you the overview, too, often powerfully. While admiring the flux of intensities, dynamics, shapes and colours he sets before you in the Rondo, you might wonder three-quarters of the way through whether the totality was going to achieve enough weight. But the coda is to come – passionate and desolate, a close without parallel in Mozart's instrumental music – and at moments such as this you can be assured that Goode will surprise and certainly not disappoint. The shorter pieces, enterprisingly chosen, set off the great works admirably. Exceptional sound throughout – like the playing, quite out of the ordinary run.

The Mozart Tapes
Piano Sonatas – No 1, K279; No 2, K280; No 3, K281; No 4, K282; No 5, K283; No 9, K311; No 10, K330; No 12, K332; No 13, K333; No 16, K545. Fantasia, K475
Friedrich Gulda pf
DG ③ 477 6130GM3 (3h 33' · ADD)
Recorded live in 1980   Ⓜ

Friedrich Gulda made a series of Mozart sonata recordings shortly before playing all the sonatas in three cycles of concerts during February 1981. They remained unissued during the pianist's lifetime and survived only on cassette dubs from the presumably lost mastertapes. Their first CD appearance adds up to an absorbing listening experience, once you get past the inevitable hiss plus patches of flutter and signal overload.

The close microphone placement shrouds Gulda's Bösendorfer with a harpsichord-like patina that also evokes the fuzzy ping of a vintage Wurlitzer electric piano, yet the pianist's wide dynamic range and hard-hitting accents are anything but emasculating. Indeed, Gulda's Mozart positively rocks, because it's mostly about rhythm. It's not about Gieseking's rippled symmetry, Schiff's ornaments (although Gulda's no slouch in this department), Krauss's angular harmonic stresses or Arrau's operas in miniature. Gulda's unswerving, atomically steady tempi and occasionally downbeat-oriented phrasing never sound mechanical, for two reasons. One, his inner rhythm always conveys a sense of swing in that it's firmly grounded yet forward moving. Two, Gulda's left hand is his trump card. Listen anywhere, really, and notice how much variety the pianist gleans from the composer's endless Alberti basses, how he brings out important melodic elements within the figurations, or how he gets the most dramatic (as opposed to merely theatrical) mileage out of signpost bass octaves without a trace of contrivance or Gouldian exaggeration.

At long last, we have Mozart piano sonata slow movements that you can slow-dance to, if that's your desire. More and more details rise to the surface with each rehearing, although it's best to absorb Gulda's Mozart in small doses – just one or two sonatas at a time. A stimulating release.

Fantasias

Adagio in B minor, K540. Fantasias – C minor, K396; D minor, K397; C minor, K475. Gigue in G, K574. Kleiner Trauermarsch in C minor, K453a. Minuet in D, K355. Rondos – D, K485; F, K494; A minor, K511
Christian Zacharias pf
Dabringhaus und Grimm MDG340 0961-2
(67' · DDD)   Ⓕ

Most of Mozart's single piano pieces are the product of some special stimulus: they aren't the daily bread of music-making, like the sonatas, but something rather more piquant. Christian Zacharias groups the pieces interestingly, starting with a D major-based section: the D minor *Fantasia*, the D major *Rondo*, the B minor *Adagio* and the D major *Minuet*, as if making a kind of free sonata of them. He omits the *Allegretto* portion of the *Fantasia* (on the grounds, it seems, that Mozart left it unfinished), and leads directly from the *Fantasia* into the *Rondo*. The B minor *Adagio* is one of Mozart's darkest, most inward pieces: written at a difficult moment in his life, it invites autobiographical interpretation with its sense of defeat and protest. Zacharias's sombre, subdued performance underlines such thoughts, and in the very chromatic K355 *Minuet*, too, his playing is dark and impassioned.

The C minor *Fantasia*, K396, is a rarity: a completion by Maximilian Stadler of a fragment that Mozart wrote for keyboard and violin. One can't imagine a performance much more persuasive than this; and in the authentic C minor *Fantasia* Zacharias plays beautifully, again with fire in the turbulent sections and with exquisite gentleness in the coolly reflective music such as the B flat episode. The K494 *Rondo* – more familiar in its revised version as finale of the K533 Sonata – is played in a more relaxed manner; in the A minor *Rondo*, K511, Zacharias beautifully captures the 'sentimental' tone and provides a performance of great delicacy and refinement, again drawing the full depth of expression from Mozart's harmonic subtleties.

Masses

Missae breves – G, K49/K47d[a]; D minor, K65/K61a[b];   ℗
D, K194/K186ha; C (Spatzenmesse), K220/K196bb
[a]**Christine Schäfer**, [b]**Angela Maria Blasi** sops
[a]**Ingeborg Danz**, [b]**Elisabeth von Magnus** mezzos
[a]**Kurt Azesberger**, [b]**Uwe Heilmann** tens [a]**Oliver
Widmer** bar [b]**Franz-Josef Selig** bass **Arnold
Schoenberg Choir; Vienna Concentus Musicus /
Nikolaus Harnoncourt**
Teldec Das Alte Werk 3984-21818-2 (69' · DDD · T/t) Ⓕ

These youthful Masses, composed between 1768 and 1775, are among Mozart's most concise – K65, in particular, is a *Missa brevis* with a vengeance. Brevity was *de rigueur* in the Salzburg liturgy and we can hardly blame Mozart for rattling unceremoniously through the long texts of the *Gloria* and *Credo*. With minimal scope for musical development, much of the writing in the two earlier works, especially, is perfunctory – the 12-year-old composer dutifully going through the motions. As so often in late 18th-century Masses, the central mystery of the 'Et incarnatus est – Crucifixus' prompts a more individual musical response; and the *Benedictus* of K65 is a touching little duet for soprano and alto soloists based, surprisingly, on a descending chromatic motif, a traditional trope of lamentation. For all the conventional bustle of their faster movements, the two later Masses are more varied in their textures and more memorable in their ideas. Both the settings of the *Benedictus* have the grace and airiness of 18th-century Austrian churches. But the high point in each work is the *Agnus Dei*, especially that of K194, with its harmonic poignancy and dramatic alternations of solo and chorus. Occasionally Nikolaus Harnoncourt's direction can sound over-insistent – in, say, the *Kyrie* of K49, with its almost aggressive *marcato* articulation. But for the most part he chooses apt, mobile tempos, keeps the rhythms buoyant and characterises vividly without betraying the music's blitheness and innocence.

Both individually and in consort the soloists make the most of their limited opportunities, with delectable tone and phrasing from the two sopranos, Christine Schäfer and Angela Maria Blasi. The recorded balance is excellent, catching Harnoncourt's sharply etched orchestral detail while giving ample presence to the polished and responsive choir.

Mass in C, 'Coronation', K317. Vesperae solennes de confessore in C, K339. Epistle Sonata in C, K278/K271e ⊞
Emma Kirkby *sop* **Catherine Robbin** *mez* **John Mark Ainsley** *ten* **Michael George** *bass* **Winchester Cathedral Choir; Winchester Quiristers Academy of Ancient Music / Christopher Hogwood** with **Alastair Ross** *org*
L'Oiseau-Lyre 436 585-2OH (54' · DDD · T/t) Ⓕ⤷

It's difficult to think of many recordings of Mozart's church music that so happily captures its character – the particular mixture of confidence, jubilation and contemplation – as Hogwood's. His unfussy direction, broad phrasing, lively but generally unhurried tempos and happy details of timing serve splendidly in the Coronation Mass, the finest of Mozart's completed mass settings; the solemnity of the *Kyrie*, the fine swing of the *Gloria* and the energy of the *Credo*, with due pause for its rapt moment at the 'Et incarnatus', all these come over with due effect. Arguably the 'Osanna' is rather quick, but its jubilation is splendid. And the sweetness of the *Benedictus* is ravishing.

Not more so, however, than the *Agnus*, for

there, at a decidedly slow tempo, Hogwood allows Emma Kirkby to make the most of this very sensuous music, which she duly most beautifully does. The soloists are altogether an excellent team, with two refined voices in the middle and Michael George a firm and sturdy bass. The inclusion of the K278 Epistle Sonata is a happy notion. The *Vesperae solennes de confessore* is a setting of the five vesper psalms and the Magnificat, made in 1780, a year after the Mass, for some church feast in Salzburg. With admirable singing from the choir and a spacious recording with exceptionally good stereo separation that properly conveys the ecclesiastical ambience, this is a disc to treasure.

Mass in C minor, K427(ed Maunder) ⊞
Arleen Auger, Lynne Dawson *sops* **John Mark Ainsley** *ten* **David Thomas** *bass* **Winchester Cathedral Choir; Winchester Quiristers; Academy of Ancient Music / Christopher Hogwood**
L'Oiseau-Lyre Florilegium 425 528-2OH (51' · DDD · T/t) Ⓕ⤷

Mozart left unfinished the work that ought to have been the choral masterpiece of his early Viennese years but there's enough of it to make up nearly an hour's music – music that's sometimes sombre, sometimes florid, sometimes jubilant. Hogwood avoids any charge of emotional detachment in his steady and powerful opening *Kyrie*, monumental in feeling, dark in tone; and he brings ample energy to the big, bustling choruses of the *Gloria* – and its long closing fugue is finely sustained. The clarity and ring of the boys' voices serve him well in these numbers. There's a strong solo team, headed by the late Arleen Auger in radiant, glowing voice and, as usual, singing with refined taste; Lynne Dawson joins her in the duets, John Mark Ainsley too in the trio. But this is essentially a 'soprano mass' – Mozart wrote it, after all, with the voice of his new wife (and perhaps thoughts of the much superior one of her sister Aloysia) in his mind – and Auger, her voice happily stealing in for the first time in the lovely 'Christe', excels in the florid and expressive music of the 'Et incarnatus' (where Richard Maunder has supplied fuller string parts than usual, perhaps fuller than Mozart would have done had he finished the work). Hogwood directs with his usual spirit and clarity.

Mozart Mass in C minor, 'Great'[a]
Beethoven Ah! perfido, Op 65[b]
Haydn Berenice che fai, HobXXIVa/10[c]
[ac]**Sarah Connolly,** [ab]**Camilla Tilling** *sops* [a]**Timothy Robinson** *ten* [a]**Neal Davies** *bass* **Gabrieli Consort and Players / Paul McCreesh**
Archiv Produktion 477 5744AH (74' · DDD · T/t) Ⓕ❍❍⤷

Discussing the C minor Mass in a booklet interview, Paul McCreesh remarks that 'any attempt to complete it runs the risk of negating the qual-

Schäfer; Fink; Streit; Finley; Arnold Schoenberg Choir; Concentus Musicus Wien / Nikolaus Harnoncourt   🅟

DHM 82876 58705-2 (50' · DDD)   Ⓕ🅞🅞

Strong, sombre and punchy by turns, Harnoncourt's second recording is as idiosyncratic as one expects from him, while benefiting from a stellar line-up of soloists.

McNair; Watkinson; Ataiza; Lloyd; ASMF and Chorus / Sir Neville Marriner

Philips 432 087-2PH (50' · DDD)   Ⓕ🅞🅑➔

Consistent and considered, Marriner offers the conventional text with both dignity and polish. Exceptionally fine choral singing.

Panzarella; Stutzmann; Prégardien; Berg; Les Arts Florissants / William Christie   🅟

Erato 0630 10697-2 (54' · DDD)   Ⓜ🅞

Using period instruments, Christie goes none the less for a big-scale, surprisingly emotive rendering. He employs a nicely balanced team of soloists.

Gritton; Rogers; Robinson; Rose; Scottish CO and Chorus / Sir Charles Mackerras

Linn CKD211 (55' · DDD)   Ⓕ

Susan Gritton leads the soloists in Sir Charles Mackerras' recent rethink. He uses the Robert Levin edition in which the traditional text is retained only in so far as it agrees with 'idiomatic Mozartian practice'.

della Casa; Malaniuk; Dermota; Siepi; Vienna Philharmonic Orchestra / Bruno Walter   🅗

Orfeo C430961B (76' · ADD)   Ⓕ

A taut and powerful account from Walter's final Salzburg Festival concert (1956) with soprano Lisa della Casa in glorious voice and the VPO playing with fierce commitment.

M Price; Schimdt; Schreier; Adam; Staatskapelle Dresden / Peter Schreier

Philips 475 205-2PGR (53' · DDD)   Ⓜ🅞🅑➔

Peter Schreier won the *Gramophone* Choral Award in 1984 with this dedicated reading, a little heavy by contemporary standards, yet still compelling thanks to Margaret Price's ravishing singing and the magnificence of the Leipzig Radio Choir.

Rubens; Braun; Davislim; Zeppenfeld; Munich Philharmonic Orchestra / Christian Thielemann

DG 477 5797GH (54' · DDD)   Ⓕ🅑➔

A rather old-fashioned approach maybe, with broad tempi and rich tone, but there's no denying the power of Thielemann's conception. He traverses the work with the inexorable build-up that you might expect from a Bruckner symphony interpretation.

ity of what survives'. Most editors and performers agree, confining themselves to the sections Mozart actually composed, and filling out the missing parts in the *Credo*, 'Et incarnatus est' and *Sanctus-Osanna*.

Paul McCreesh gives us the familiar torso in a reading that combines a smallish chorus numbering around 30 with a period-instrument band. At a fairly urgent tempo, McCreesh's soloists, the radiant Camilla Tilling and the rich-toned Sarah Connolly, are excellent, with Connolly unfazed by her flights into high soprano territory. Elsewhere, Tilling perfectly catches the wondering pastoral innocence of the 'Et incarnatus est', taken at a gently lilting two-in-a-bar. In the choral numbers McCreesh is on top form.

There have been excellent period-instrument recordings from Hogwood and Gardiner (see below), but McCreesh, sharply responsive both to the Mass's neo-Baroque monumentality and its Italianate sensuousness, is at least their match in drama and colour; and DG's recording is exemplary. The Gabrieli Consort sing with precision, fresh, firm tone and marvellous dynamic control, while the strings play with notable grace and refinement in the solo numbers. The *Kyrie* unfolds with an inexorable tread (McCreesh is specially good at creating and maintaining rhythmic tension), and the 'Cum Sancto Spiritu' fugue, taken at the swiftest possible tempo, combines dancing agility with a thrilling cumulative sweep.

McCreesh's claims as a top recommendation are enhanced by the additional items, two magnificent, quasi-operatic scenas by Haydn and Beethoven. Connolly, in the Haydn (again taking the high tessitura, complete with top Cs, in her stride), and Tilling are both superb, marrying a classical nobility of line with a profound identification with the plights of these suffering heroines in extremis.

Mass in C minor, 'Great' (ed Schmitt/Gardiner)
Sylvia McNair *sop* **Diana Montague** *mez* **Anthony Rolfe Johnson** *ten* **Cornelius Hauptmann** *bass*
Monteverdi Choir; English Baroque Soloists / John Eliot Gardiner
Philips 420 210-2PH (54' · DDD · T/t)   Ⓕ🅞🅑➔

Writers on Mozart sometimes take him to task for the alleged mixture of style in the C minor Mass, in particular the use of florid, 'operatic' solo writing amidst all the severe ecclesiastical counterpoint. To object is to misunderstand the nature of Mozart's religion, but it takes a performance as stylistically accomplished as this one to make the point in practice. The usual stumbling-block is the 'Et incarnatus', with its richly embellished solo line and its wind obbligatos. Sung as it is here, by Sylvia McNair, beautifully refined in detail, it's indeed passionate, but passionately devout. McNair is deeply affecting in the 'Christe', taken quite spaciously and set in a measured Kyrie of great cumulative power which also has some fine, clean singing from the Monteverdi Choir.

As with Gardiner's version of the Requiem you might wish for the sound of a boys' choir (why go to the trouble of having authentic instruments if you then use unauthentic voices?) but the bright, forward tone of his sopranos is very persuasive. The music is all strongly characterised: the 'Gloria' jubilant, the 'Qui tollis' grandly elegiac with its solemn, inexorable march rhythm and its dying phrases echoed between the choirs, the 'Credo' full of vitality. Some of the 'Cum sancto spiritu' fugue is too heavily accented, though. Nevertheless, a confident recommendation.

Requiem, K626

Requiem. Ave verum corpus in D, K618   P

Anna Maria Panzarella sop **Nathalie Stutzmann** contr **Christoph Prégardien** ten **Nathan Berg** bass **Les Arts Florissants / William Christie** Erato 0630-10697-2 (54' · DDD · T/t)   (M)O

Les Arts Florissants provides a substantial, dramatic reading: the tempo for the 'Requiem aeternam' is slow but malleable, and Christie is ready to make the most of the changes in orchestral colour or choral texture and, indeed, to dramatise the music to the utmost. He has little truck with any notion that this is an austere piece: he sees it as operatic, almost romantic – and the result is very compelling. There are surprising things: 'Quantus tremor', in a very weighty account of the 'Dies irae', for example, is hushed rather than terrifying; the 'Recordare' is slow to the point of stickiness; there are rather mannered *crescendos* in the *Sanctus*; and often cadences are drawn out. The powerful choruses of the Sequence are imposingly done, and the grave 'Lacrimosa' wonderfully catches the special significance not only of the music itself but also of the fact that this is the moment where Mozart's last autograph trails off. The choral singing is sharply etched and generally distinguished. Although the solo singing isn't uniformly outstanding the soprano's melting tone can be very appealing, and Prégardien is an excellent stylist; the *Benedictus* is particularly impressive: shapely and refined. This is a reading full of character and imaginative ideas, very much a conscious modern interpretation of the work and very finely executed. The disc is completed by perhaps the only piece which can reasonably follow the Requiem, the *Ave verum corpus*, in a slow, hushed, rather romantic reading that's undeniably moving.

Requiem

Christine Schäfer, Bernarda Fink sops **Kurt Streit** ten **Gerald Finley** bar **Arnold Schoenberg Choir; Concentus Musicus Wien / Nikolaus Harnoncourt** Deutsche Harmonia Mundi CD/SACD ⏺ 82876 58705-2 (50' · DDD · T/t)   (F)OO

Nikolaus Harnoncourt's recent choral projects seem consciously to be reconciling some of the treasured values of his upbringing, alongside deeply held beliefs as to how a famous score can be illuminated through a 'period' lens. This recording integrates past and present in a way

his previous reading from over 20 years ago simply couldn't. The main difference between the two is the interpretative assurance of his latest version; it's far clearer in its message, and articulated with greater rhetorical awareness.

While the *Dies Irae* is a set-piece of graphic, biting and eerie terror, the previous *Kyrie* is treated as a quasi-liturgical introit, unfolding gradually with an understated elegance. The *Tuba Mirum* is also unusual, less statuesque than normal, with a highly charged trombone solo both triumphant and imploring. The solo singers, individually and collectively, are tinged with a glow of deep regret; they sing with a palpable sense of interdependent ensemble and sustained poignancy.

As you'd expect from Harnoncourt, there's a studied punchiness, and the *Confutatis* leaves us with a series of striking contrasts, with 'salva me' as a gesture of impending loneliness for the *Recordare*: the strings shadow the soloists with questing and characterful figures, belying the restless and unsentimental approach to the *Lacrimosa*. The Arnold Schoenberg Choir is highly responsive in the modern way, yet unmodish in their soft-edged attack and heterogeneous timbre. Harnoncourt conceives of an almost jocular majesty in the *Domine Jesu* and *Benedictus*. Of course, there has to be a moment for the iconoclast in him: here it's the *Hostias*, taken at almost twice the usual speed.

This isn't a Requiem that comforts and stirs in the expected ways; instead, a curious and enigmatic undertow of human vulnerability emerges, presenting Mozart's valedictory essay in a striking new light.

Litaniae…, K243

Litaniae de venerabili altaris sacramento, K243   P Mass in C, K257, 'Credo'

Angela Maria Blasi sop **Elisabeth von Magnus** contr **Deon van der Walt** ten **Alistair Miles** bass **Arnold Schoenberg Choir; Vienna Concentus Musicus / Nikolaus Harnoncourt** Teldec Das Alte Werk 9031-72304-2 (61 minutes: DDD · T/t)   (F)

The *Litaniae de venerabili altaris sacramento* of 1775 has powerful claims to be reckoned the finest of Mozart's church works before the C minor Mass and Requiem; but it's never quite had the recognition it deserves. Or the performance until now. It's a deeply felt work, from the grave, warm opening of the *Kyrie*, through the imposing 'Verbum caro factum' and the graceful 'Hostia' that succeeds it, the 'Tremendum' with its almost Verdian menace and the appealing 'Dulcissum convivium' (a soprano aria with soft textures supplied by flutes and bassoons), the highly original 'Viaticum' and the resourcefully and lengthily developed 'Pignus' to the *Agnus*, a beautiful soprano aria with solo writing for flute, oboe and cello. The performance here under Nikolaus Harnoncourt rightly sees no need to apologise for the stylistic diversity of the work.

The issue is made still more attractive by the inclusion of a Mass setting of the same year, one of Mozart's most inventive and original in its textures and its treatment of words. Altogether a very attractive record.

Exsultate, jubilate, K165

Exsultate, jubilate. 'Coronation' Mass, K317 – Agnus Dei. Regina coeli, K108. Regina coeli, K127. Sancta Maria, mater Dei, K273. Sub tuum praesidium, K198. Vesperae de Domenica, K321 – Laudate Dominum. Vesperae solennes de confessore, K339 – Laudate Dominum
Carolyn Sampson sop **Choir of The King's Consort; The King's Consort / Robert King**
Hyperion CDA67560 (66' · DDD · T)   Ⓕ

Though clearly designed as a showcase for a young British singer who seems to be getting better by the minute – the presence of a number of excerpts and a double-tracked duet are evidence of that – it is nevertheless strongly focused on Mozart's Salzburg church music, offering in addition to some of the usual suspects a few relative rarities. It is also a reminder of how, even in works which make no attempts at great depth, the young composer was a marvel of fluency, grace and freshness. There are times in his teenage music when you can really feel the enjoyment he took in his own ability; on this disc you can sense it being transferred to the performances.

Emma Kirkby recording some of these pieces a few years back (likewise doing *Exsultate, jubilate* in the alternative 'flute' version), and while Carolyn Sampson's singing does not sound like Kirkby's, her rounder voice gives the listener much the same kind of pleasure. What more could you want in these works than a soloist who places every note with joyous precision, moves from one to another so cleanly, and demonstrates at every turn such intelligent but unfussy musicianship? She also has wonderful control of dynamics, beautifully demonstrated in the restrained cadenza of *Exsultate*'s slow middle section, or the hushed reprise of the *Agnus Dei* from the *Coronation* Mass.

The orchestral accompaniments are ably conducted by Robert King, and if the choral singing is not the most polished you will hear, its lusty commitment certainly adds to the honest pleasure of the performances. This is a sunny and unpretentious disc which deserves to be among the successes of the Mozart year.

Concert Arias

Un bacio di mano, K541[b]. Davidde penitente, K469 – A te, fra tanti affanni[a]. Mentre ti lascio, K513[b]. Misero! o sogno ... Aura, che intorno spiri, K431/K425b[a]. Per pietà, non ricercate, K420[a]. Si mostra la sorte, K209[a]. **Così fan tutte** – Al fato dan legge[ab]; Rivolgete a lui lo sguardo[b]; Secondate, aurette amiche[ab]; Un' aura amorosa[a]; Donne mie, la fate a tanti[b]. **Don Giovanni** – Deh! vieni alla finestra[b]. **La finta giardiniera** – Con

un vezzo all'italiana[b]
[a]**Christoph Genz** ten [b]**Stephan Genz** bar
La Petite Bande / Sigiswald Kuijken
Deutsche Harmonia Mundi 82876 55782-2
(59' · DDD · T/t)   Ⓕ

The Genz brothers are among the most promising of young singers. Regrettably, Mozart wrote only two duets for tenor and baritone (from *Così fan tutte*), both rather brief: both are sung here. Their programme gives us other music from from *Così*, including the testing tenor aria, 'Un' aura amorosa', which Christoph sings smoothly and sweetly in the traditional manner of German lyric tenors, with a faint hint of nasality and very little vibrato, although a touch more softness in the voice would have been welcome. He does find some of that in the superb concert aria *Misero! o sogno*, and gives a strong, large-scale reading of *Per pietà, non ricercate*.

Stephan sings 'Donne mie', a delightfully light and shapely performance, with the refinement of a Lied singer, and he also does the Guglielmo aria that Mozart (sensibly) rejected, 'Rivolgete a lui', where he catches delightfully the jocular swagger, the sexual braggadocio. He gives a duly impassioned account of *Mentre ti lascio*, even if the bottom of his voice in this rather low-lying aria isn't as powerful as the top. Don Giovanni's Serenade is admirable, but a touch more of soft sensuality, of covered tone, might have served. Here the voice is well forward, but for most of the disc the orchestra is unusually prominent, and the rich detail of Mozart's scoring comes through clearly, aided by the period instruments and Sigiswald Kuijken's sensitive and alert direction.

Al desio di chi t'adora, K577. Alma grande e nobil core, K578. Ch'io mi scordi di te?, K505[a]. Vado, ma dove? oh Dei!, K583 **La clemenza di Tito** – Non più di fiori. **Così fan tutte** – In uomini, in soldati; Per pietà; È amore un ladroncello. **Idomeneo** – Padre, germani, addio! **Le nozze di Figaro** – Non so più; Voi che sapete; Deh vieni non tardar.
Magdalena Kožená mez [a]**Jos van Immerseel** fp
Orchestra of the Age of Enlightenment / Sir Simon Rattle
Archiv Produktion 477 6272AH (64' · DDD · T/t)   Ⓕ

'Singing Mozart is second nature to her,' enthuses Rattle of Magdalena Kožená. 'Each woman on each track is a completely distinct personality.' Promotional hype? Well, in hyper-Beckmesserish mode you could say her *legato* in 'Per pietà' is not quite seamless, the tempo for 'Deh vieni' a touch too jaunty. But this is barrel-scraping. If anyone has recorded a lovelier Mozart recital in recent years, we've yet to hear it. In her early thirties, Kožená is now consummate mistress of her art. Her liquid high mezzo, with its easy upward extension, combines warmth with the bloom and freshness of youth, while her coloratura, on display in 'Al desio di chi t'adora', is as brilliant and expressive as Bartoli's, yet without the Italian diva's intrusive aspirates.

Beyond this, Rattle's claim is hard to refute. Cherubino (whose 'Voi che sapete' is sung in an embellished version published in 1810) and Dorabella (a blithe, flighty 'È amore un ladroncino') are the only roles here in Kožená's stage repertoire. But she 'lives' each of these wide-ranging characters intensely, from the remorseful Vitellia in *La clemenza di Tito* (sorrow etched into the texture of her voice) via the tenderness and anguish of Ilia in *Idomeneo* to a delightfully sly, knowing Despina. The vivid, tangy accompaniments from Rattle and the OAE go well beyond mere good style, with a classy basset-horn obbligato from Anthony Pay in the Vitellia aria. Fortepianist Jos van Immerseel is an equally sympathetic partner in an impassioned yet intimate performance of *Ch'io mi scordi di te*.

Al desio di chi t'adora, K577[a]. Bella mia fiamma... Resta, o cara, K528[a]. Vado, ma dove? oh Dei!, K583[a]. Voi avete un cor fedele, K217[a]. **Le nozze di Figaro** – Un moto di gioia, K579[a]

[a]**Cecilia Bartoli** *mez* **Vienna Concentus Musicus / Nikolaus Harnoncourt**
Video director **Brian Large**
BBC/Opus Arte 🄳🅥🄳 OA0820D (112' · 16:9 · 2.0, 5.1 & DTS 5.1 · 0)   Ⓕ

No doubt this concert, recorded at Graz's elegant Stefaniensaal, is aimed primarily at Bartoli-philes, who will not be disappointed; it's predictably impressive, if a shade short. Mozart's so-called concert arias are formidable pieces, some actually alternatives for his own and other operas, but others, in particular *Bella mia fiamma*, created to challenge ambitious singers such as Josepha Duschek. Bartoli copes with characteristic aplomb, tossing off bravura trills and alarming roulades just effortlessly enough not to be infuriating. The advantage of video, though, is that we can actually see the feeling with which she infuses even the most conventional sentiments, as vivid as her stage interpretations – though with her characteristically earthy twinkle never far off.

What's more, though, this is one of the best-recorded concerts, not just in its excellent picture and first-rate surround-sound, but in its video direction. Shooting in a lower, mellower light than usual, Brian Large captures the platform drama in vividly immediate close-up, without Karajan-style excesses. Thoroughly recommended.

Additional recommendation

Lieder and Concert Arias
Schwarzkopf *sop* **Brendel, Gieseking** *pfs* **LSO / Szell**
EMI Références 574803-2 (ADD) Recorded 1955, 1968
A classic disc – the fruitful collaboration Ⓜ🅞🅞🅓➔ of great artists. Schwarzkopf was 39 when she recorded the Lieder, mature in resources but still amazingly capable of the clarity of youth.

Opera arias

La clemenza di Tito – Parto, parto; Deh, per questo; Ecco il punto, o Vitellia... Non piu di fiori. **Così fan tutte** – E'amore un ladroncello. **Don Giovanni** – Vedrai, carino **Le nozze di Figaro** – Non so più; Voi che sapete; Giunse alfin il momento ... Deh vieni. **Concert Arias** – Chi sa, chi sa, qual sia, K582; Alma grande e nobil core, K578; Ch'io mi scordi di te?, K505
Cecilia Bartoli *mez* **András Schiff** *pf* **Peter Schmidtl** *basset cl/basset hn* **Vienna Chamber Orchestra / György Fischer**
Decca 430 513-2DH (58' · DDD · T/t) Ⓕ🅞🅓➔

Mozart wrote some of his most appealing music for the mezzo-soprano voice with the roles of Cherubino and Susanna in *Le nozze di Figaro*, Dorabella in *Così fan tutte* and Zerlina in *Don Giovanni* each boasting at least one memorable aria. Alongside these this disc includes a handful of concert arias including *Ch'io mi scordi di te?* which was written for the farewell performance of the great mezzo Nancy Storace with Mozart playing the *concertante* piano role. Here with as innate an interpreter of Mozart's piano writing as András Schiff and a voice so remarkably self-assured as Cecilia Bartoli's the electricity of that first, historic performance seems almost to be recreated. And, here as elsewhere, György Fischer directs the splendid Vienna Chamber Orchestra with disarming sensitivity while the recording is wonderfully warm and vibrant.

Cecilia Bartoli boasts a voice of extraordinary charm and unassuming virtuosity: her vocal characterisations would be the envy of the finest actresses and her intuitive singing is in itself a sheer delight. But she also brings to these arias a conviction and understanding of the subtleties of the language which only a native Italian could. Listen to the subtle nuances of 'Voi che sapete', the depth of understanding behind Dorabella's seemingly frivolous 'E'amore un ladroncello'; these aren't mere performances, but interpretations which cut to the very soul of the music. No Mozart lover should be without this CD.

La clemenza di Tito – Deh per questo istante; Ecco il punto ... Non più di fiori vaghe catene. **Così fan tutte** – Temerari ... Come scoglio; Ei parte ... Per pietà, ben mio. **Don Giovanni** – Batti, batti; In quali eccessi ... Mi tradì. **Le nozze di Figaro** – Non so più cosa son; Porgi, amor. **Concert arias** – Oh, temerario Arbace! ... Per quel paterno amplesso, K79. Ch'io mi scordi di te ... Non temer, amato bene, K505
Véronique Gens *sop* **Orchestra of the Age of Enlightenment / Ivor Bolton** *with* **Melvyn Tan** *fp*
Virgin Classics Veritas 545319-2 (59' · DDD · T/t) Ⓕ🅞🅓➔

Véronique Gens is one of the most engaging and stylish Mozart sopranos around, as this sampler of her art confirms. Under the exacting baton of Ivor Bolton, the OAE show sharp and eager teeth to match her own highly strung recitative in 'In quali eccessi'. And this Donna Anna demonstrates more than one-dimensional *Angst* as the orchestra's wind soloists breathe in sympathy with every moment of *palpitando* in Gens's own supple phrasing. There's a similar focus on the emotional potential of breath in a 'Non so più' whose fierce frustration flies out of eloquent consonants. Steady control of breath and tone bring a moving poise to 'Non più di fiori', where Vitellia's horrified introspection finds empathy in the basset horn obbligato. And as Sesto, Gens moulds the moist clay of some of Mozart's most beautiful melodic contours in 'Deh, per questo istante'. There's her Countess and Zerlina to enjoy as well, with the two exquisitely sculpted and sparingly but powerfully ornamented arias from *Così fan tutte*.

La clemenza di Tito – Deh, se piacer mi vuoi.
Così fan tutte – Ah, scostati!...Smanie implacabili; Temerari...Come scoglio. **La finta giardiniera** – Se l'augellin sen fugge; Và pure ad altri in braccio
Concert arias – Alma grande e nobil core, K578. Basta, vincesti...Ah, non lasciarmi, K486a. Chi sà, chi sà, qual sia, K582. Ch'io mi scordi di te...Non temer, amato bene, K505[a]. Misero me!...Misero pergoletto, K77.
Elina Garanča *mez* [a]**Frank Braley** *pf*
Salzburg Camerata / Louis Langrée
Virgin Classics 332631-2 (62' · DDD · T/t)　　Ⓕ➔

Elina Garanča's voice is warm and ample, its quality enriched in the lower register but still full-bodied, pure and resonant on the top B flats. Her *legato* and fluency are alike well schooled, her intervals exceptionally clean and her feeling for light-and-shade at any rate aware that it exists. Room for developments lies principally in this area: she is not inexpressive but there is more to be made of the emotions and the part words play in their communication.

The selection of arias, concert and operatic, makes for a satisfying programme. Much is on the grand scale: injured women cry out against malign fate and determine to confront it. This includes, we note, both the mezzo and soprano leads in *Così fan tutte*: essentially sung in the same voice (she does not audibly 'turn soprano' for 'Come scoglio') and, one might well conclude, by the same character. The lighter, more intimate tone used in *Ch'io mi scordi di te* is welcome, and welcome too are some lesser known concert arias, most of all *Ah, non lasciarmi*, which has a melody almost as lovely as the now-famous 'Ruhe sanft' from *Zaide*. The longest is the profoundly set *Misero me!*, where the intricacies of the implied dramatic situation form something of a barrier, but where the sustained powers of the music and the singer impress deeply.

Thinking of comparisons, she is richer and warmer than Teresa Berganza, less imaginative and personally involved than Cecilia Bartoli, but also free of mannerisms. With lively accompaniment by the Salzburg Camerata, this is an exceptionally successful debut recital.

'Tutto Mozart'
Bastien und Bastienne – Diggi, daggi. **Così fan tutte** – Soave sia il vento[ab]; Il core vi dono[b]. **Don Giovanni** – Madamina, il catalogo è questo; Là ci darem la mano[a]; Deh! vieni alla finestra. **Le nozze di Figaro** – Non più andrai; Crudel! perchè finora[a]; Aprite un po' quegli occhi. **Die Zauberflöte** – Der Vogelfänger bin ich ja; Bei Männern[a]; Ein Mädchen oder Weibchen; Pa-Pa-Pa-Papagena[a]. Un bacio di mano, K541. Così dunque tradisci...Aspri rimorsi atroci, K432. Io ti lascio, o cara, addio, KAnh245/K621a. Nun liebes Weibchen, ziehst mit mir, K625/592a[a]. Männer suchen stets zu naschen, K433/K416c
Bryn Terfel *bass-bar* with [a]**Miah Persson** *sop* [b]**Christine Rice** *mez* **Scottish Chamber Orchestra / Sir Charles Mackerras**
DG 477 5886GH (63' · DDD · T/t)　　Ⓕ🅞🅞➔

Unlike many showcase CDs for famous singers, this one has been carefully planned to demonstrate Terfel's many-faceted gifts as a Mozartian, boxing the compass of roles and pieces for bass-baritone. Familiar items are interspersed with unfamiliar ones, and the singer, who writes how well Mozart wrote for his kind of voice, is heard in all the roles he has sung on stage (the exceptions include Papageno, for which his figure is unsuited, although in purely vocal terms he proves a lively and sympathetic bird-catcher). His Figaro, which begins and ends the programme, is nicely distinguished from his Count Almaviva, both brought before us by his pointed use of the Italian text. Similarly his suave, insinuating Giovanni is very different from his earthy Leporello, the timbre for each part cleverly differentiated. From *Così fan tutte*, he briefly undertakes Alfonso, another role he hasn't assumed on stage, in the Farewell trio, then switches to Guglielmo for 'Il core vi dono' where he woos the attractive Dorabella of Christine Rice.

Of the rarer operatic items and separate arias he gives a particularly dramatic account of 'Così dunque tradisci' and finds the gentle *Entführung*-like humour of the incomplete 'Männer suchen stets zu naschen' to his liking, with Miah Persson (unfairly not credited on the CD front) as partner to the inauthentic nonsense of 'Nun liebest Weibchen'.

The quality of the disc is confirmed by Sir Charles Mackerras's authoritatively Mozartian direction and fine playing from the SCO. The recording has both space and presence.

La clemenza di Tito, K621

La clemenza di Tito　　　　　　　　　　Ⓟ
Uwe Heilmann *ten* Tito **Della Jones** *mez* Vitellia **Cecilia Bartoli** *mez* Sesto **Diana Montague** *mez* Annio **Barbara Bonney** *sop* Servillia **Gilles Cachemaille** *bar* Publio **Academy of Ancient Music Chorus; Academy of Ancient Music / Christopher Hogwood**
L'Oiseau-Lyre Ⓕ 444 131-2OHO2 (137' · DDD · T/t) Ⓕ

Hogwood has assembled a remarkable cast, with certainly two, perhaps three, outstanding interpretations. First among them must be Cecilia Bartoli, who rightly establishes Sextus as the central character, the one whose actions and whose feelings are the focal point of the drama. The opening number is the duet 'Come ti piace, imponi', where the firm and pure sound of Bartoli's voice, in contrast with the contained hysteria of Vitellia's, at once defines the opera's basis. It's clear from her singing that she reads Sextus, for all his weakness in giving way to Vitellia, as a man of integrity, one of the noblest Romans of them all.

Then there's Della Jones's remarkable Vitellia. There are lots of interesting and emotionally suggestive touches in her singing; her rich bottom register is magnificent and the top Bs have no fears for her. Uwe Heilmann's Titus is marked by much subtle and finely shaped singing and a keen awareness of how phrasing conveys sense. Occasionally the tone is inclined to be nasal, but that doesn't interfere with a very sympathetic and often moving reading. Hogwood's keen awareness of what, expressively speaking, is going on in the music, and his refusal to be tied to a rigid rhythmic pulse in order to make it manifest, is one of the strengths of this recording. The recitatives are sung with a great deal of life and awareness of meaning, not simply gabbled at maximum speed. These aren't Mozart's own work, and are usually heavily cut. While some may feel that the inclusion of every note is an advantage to the opera, others may not unreasonably take the opposite view. At any rate, the discs' tracking is arranged so that a new track begins for each aria, which enables listeners to make their own cuts without difficulty.

La clemenza di Tito
Mark Padmore ten Tito **Bernarda Fink** mez Sesto
Alexandrina Pendatchanska sop Vitellia **Sunhae Im**
sop Servilia **Marie-Claude Chappuis** mez Annio
Sergio Foresti bass Publio **RIAS Chamber Choir;**
Freiburg Baroque Orchestra / René Jacobs
Harmonia Mundi ② HMC90 1923/24;
HMC80 1923/24 (134' · DDD · T/t)　　　　Ⓕ

La clemenza di Tito
Rainer Trost ten Tito **Magdalena Kožená** mez
Sesto **Hillevi Martinpelto** sop Vitellia **Lisa Milne** sop
Servilia **Christine Rice** mez Annio **John Relyea** bass
Publio **Scottish Chamber Orchestra and Chorus /**
Sir Charles Mackerras
DG ② 477 5972GH2 (128' · DDD · S/T/t/N)　　Ⓕ🅑➔

Critics, scholars and biographers once damned Mozart's last serious opera (composed almost simultaneously with *Die Zauberflöte* but performed at Prague three weeks earlier). Few of these estimable commentators had the opportunity or inclination to appreciate the virtues of *opera seria*. Nowadays it seems that anybody who respects the musico-dramatic merit of operas composed before 1780 will suffer no problems admiring Mozart's finely crafted enlightenment opera. Metastasio's libretto (adapted by Caterino Mazzolà) focuses on the poignant dilemmas of three formidable protagonists: the benevolent and well intentioned Emperor Tito, maligned by the hateful Vitellia, whose insatiable thirst for vengeance finds a gullible instrument in her youthful lover Sesto.

It is good to read René Jacobs's passionate advocacy for Metastasio's dramaturgy; he openly acknowledges where he has taken some liberties with Mozart's score but it does not guarantee that all of his solutions are convincing, attractive or necessary. Most noteworthy elements in Jacobs's direction could split opinion: the liberal application of pulling back the orchestra in the Overture's opening bars is contrasted with sudden over-accelerations (contrived or revitalising?); elaborately ornamented piano solos or seemingly 'improvised' flourishes from the cello are inserted before some recitatives (intrusive absurdities or imaginative colour?); Mozart's notation of rhythms is frequently interpreted in unpredictable and unconventional ways (reappraisals or mannerisms?); Mozart's magnificent quintet at the end of Act 1 is far too rapid to be a sensible interpretation of the tempo marking Allegro assai (fully charged theatricality or losing the music's potential impact?).

There are unequivocally good things on offer: Mark Padmore's smooth-toned Tito has unforced purity, his arias are eminently civilised and his two accompanied recitatives make the Emperor's anguish and inner conflict regarding his treasonous friend's fate transparent. He brings agile coloratura and a sweet top A flat to 'Se all'impero, amici Dei'. Alexandrina Pendatchanska's dark timbre, dramatic conviction and ambitious ornaments in 'Deh se piacer mi vuoi' make her villainous Vitellia formidable (although the stilted shaping of the line 'alletta ad ingannar' seems unnatural). Bernarda Fink's plangent contributions capture Sesto's desperate struggle between honour and love.

There are few Mozartians of Mackerras's standard: every aria, ensemble, march, chorus and recitative is steeped in absorbing Mozartian rhetoric, colour, personality and style. There are no traces of artificiality or idiosyncrasy. Period brass and timpani lend precision and idiomatic colour, and the modern strings and woodwind are stirring, balanced and lyrical. From the first few minutes of the stirring yet immaculately judged overture, he delivers something special.

Rainer Trost's voice has lost its youthful purity since his memorable Ferrando in John Eliot Gardiner's *Così fan tutte* a little over a decade ago, but the acquisition of darkness and striking authority suits the dignity of his compassionate 'Del più sublime soglio'. His richly textured coloratura and Mackerras's flowing grandeur are marvellous companions in the opera's jubilant final chorus ('Tu, è ver, m'assolvi, Augusto').

Hillevi Martinpelto's seductive Vitellia makes Sesto's obsession thoroughly convincing: 'Deh, se piacer mi vuoi' has the perfect synthesis of power, passion and purity (her ornamentation is every bit as courageous as any of Jacobs's singers, but also fits smoothly with the harmony). She magnificently conveys Vitellia's voyage from vulnerability to penitent heroism in 'Ecco il punto', and follows it with a radiant 'Non più di fiori' (few sopranos manage to get the audience to end up sympathising with Vitellia to this extent).

However, Magdalena Kožená's Sesto steals the show. She is an outstanding Mozart singer; she sings her heart out in the dynamic accompanied recitative 'Oh Dei, che smania è questa' that leads into the quintet at the end of Act 1 (Mackerras and the SCO strings respond with stunning energy), and her arias are consistently marvellous.

Mackerras and Jacobs both provide fresh impetus to the least-regarded opera of Mozart's maturity. If one must choose between them, the veteran pays richer dividends than the maverick.

La clemenza di Tito
Philip Langridge ten Tito **Ashley Putnam** sop Vitellia **Diana Montague** mez Sesto **Martine Mahé** mez Annio **Elzbieta Szmytka** sop Servilia **Peter Rose** bass Publio **Glyndebourne Festival Chorus; London Philharmonic Orchestra / Sir Andrew Davis**
Stage director **Nicholas Hytner**
Video director **Robin Lough**
ArtHaus Musik 🖭 100 406 (143' · 4:3 · 2.0 · 2 & 5)
Recorded live at Glyndebourne 1991   Ⓕ**O**

This performance shows Glyndebourne at its peak in terms of preparatory work and ensemble playing. Add Andrew Davis's superbly taut and perceptive conducting and it's no wonder that here you feel *Tito* to be very near the top of the Mozartian operatic canon, a very different opinion from that which was current for so many years.

At the heart of the performance on stage are Philip Langridge as the clement yet tormented emperor of the title, acting – especially with his eyes – and singing with extreme eloquence, and Diana Montague's equally committed account of Sesto's part, a character so obviously torn, almost fatally, between his erotic love for Vitellia and his deep friendship for Tito. Montague also acts movingly with her eyes, and her singing is noble, warm and technically flawless. As the scheming Vitellia, Ashley Putnam somehow manages to enact both the character's classical origins while suggesting a soap-opera villainess. Vocally she's always willing, but sometimes the flesh is weak, particularly in the higher reaches.

Martine Mahé keeps up the high standard with her urgently sung and acted Annio. So does Peter Rose as the upright and concerned Publio. Only Elzbieta Szmytka, as Servilia, seems to be operating on a more conventional level of operatic expression. The LPO is on its best form. Robin Lough's video direction is spot on. The sound balance is faultless. Even so, main credit for this arresting event goes to Hytner.

Così fan tutte, K588

Così fan tutte
Elisabeth Schwarzkopf sop Fiordiligi **Christa Ludwig** mez Dorabella **Hanny Steffek** sop Despina **Alfredo Kraus** ten Ferrando **Giuseppe Taddei** bar Guglielmo **Walter Berry** bass Don Alfonso **Philharmonia**

Chorus and Orchestra / Karl Böhm
EMI Great Recordings of the Century ② 567379-2
(165' · ADD · T/t) Recorded 1962   Ⓜ**OOO**Ⓑ→

 Così fan tutte is the most balanced and probing of all Mozart's operas, formally faultless, musically inspired from start to finish, emotionally a matter of endless fascination and, in the second act, profoundly moving. It has been very lucky on disc, and besides this delightful set there have been several other memorable recordings. However, Karl Böhm's cast could hardly be bettered, even in one's dreams. The two sisters are gloriously sung – Schwarzkopf and Ludwig bring their immeasurable talents as Lieder singers to this sparkling score and overlay them with a rare comic touch. Add to that the stylish singing of Alfredo Kraus and Giuseppe Taddei and the central quartet is unimpeachable. Walter Berry's Don Alfonso is characterful and Hanny Steffek is quite superb as Despina.

The pacing of this endlessly intriguing work is measured with immaculate judgement. The emotional control of the characterisation is masterly and Böhm's totally idiomatic response to the music is arguably without peer. However, two modern recordings, using period instruments, do offer stimulating alternative views.

Così fan tutte (sung in English)
Janice Watson sop Fiordiligi **Diana Montague** mez Dorabella **Toby Spence** ten Ferrando **Christopher Maltman** bar Guglielmo **Lesley Garrett** sop Despina **Sir Thomas Allen** bar Don Alfonso **Geoffrey Mitchell Choir; Orchestra of the Age of Enlightenment / Sir Charles Mackerras**
Chandos/Peter Moores Foundation Opera in English
③ CHAN3152 (161' · DDD · T)   Ⓜ Ⓑ→

Sir Peter Moores comments that the phrase 'Così fan tutte' is 'almost impossible to translate' into English. Thus it is that the delivery of Ferrando and Guglielmo's pronouncement, under the cynical tutorship of Don Alfonso, is one of the few lines that have not been translated in this volume of the Opera in English series (Alfonso's exclamation 'Misericordia!' is the other one left intact, and rightly so). Sometimes opera in English sounds too close to Gilbert and Sullivan at their cheesiest, but in a sparkling comedy such as *Così fan tutte* that is not necessarily a bad thing: in fact this is tremendously enjoyable because it allows Anglophones to concentrate on exactly what the characters are saying. So if Opera in English brings a wider audience closer to the heart of Mozart's and da Ponte's masterpiece, then it can only be a wonderful thing.

Of course, it helps that the music has seldom sounded as glorious as it does in the hands of Sir Charles Mackerras and the Orchestra of the Age of Enlightenment. Both are consummate Mozartians, and the pacing, ebb and flow of the music is near-perfect. In particular, the OAE's woodwind are on ravishing form. In terms of stylishness, orchestral sound and the sentimental strength of the playing, this *Così* is on a par with the finest period-instrument versions (Öst-man and Gardiner), and arguably has more heart than the OAE's previous recording under Sir Simon Rattle (EMI). The three ladies are animated (but not consistently pleasing on the ear), so the three men steal the show vocally: Sir Thomas Allen is, of course, a renowned Don Alfonso of authority and warmth, Christopher Maltman is a suave Guglielmo, and Toby Spence delivers some of the best Mozart tenor-singing in a long time. Although he falls short in softer music, he brings ringing clarity and declamatory emotion to "Tradito! Schernito!" (here "Her ter-reason is poison").

Così fan tutte

Miah Persson *sop* Fiordiligi **Anke Vondung** *mez* Dorabella **Ainhoa Garmendia** *sop* Despina **Topi Lehtipuu** *ten* Ferrando **Luca Pisaroni** *bar* Guglielmo **Nicolas Rivenq** *bass* Don Alfonso

Glyndebourne Chorus; Orchestra of the Age of Enlightenment / Iván Fischer

Stage director **Nicholas Hytner**

Video director **Francesca Kemp**

Opus Arte ② *DVD* OA0970D (3h 30' · NTSC · 16:9 · PCM stereo & DTS 5.1 · 0)

Recorded live at the Opera House, Glyndebourne, on June 26 and July 1, 2006. Extra features include Insights with Iván Fischer, Nicholas Hytner and members of the cast　　　　　　　　Ⓕ**❍❍❍**

Ⓖ Since 1934 when Glyndebourne revived this then-neglected work and began its run of success it has presented a succession of exemplary stagings all within the parameters of da Ponte's libretto. When this, the latest, was produced it was universally hailed: as faithful a representation of the equivocal comedy as one could wish. That's confirmed by this DVD.

Both Despina and Alfonso are played tradition-ally and with notable brio by Garmendia and Rivenq. The delightful Persson and Vondung make a wholly believable and vocally attractive Fiordiligi and Dorabella, and deliver their music in ideal Mozartian tone and style. Similarly Lehtipuu is a charming and wide-eyed Ferrando and Pisaroni a warm-voiced and personal Gug-lielmo. They both woo with seductive charm.

As reviews at the time reported, Fischer con-ducts with an unassumingly correct sense of timing and has the inestimable advantage of the OAE's period instruments.

Così fan tutte

Erin Wall *sop* Fiordiligi **Elina Garanča** *mez* Dorabella **Barbara Bonney** *sop* Despina **Shawn Mathey** *ten* Ferrando **Stéphane Degout** *bar* Guglielmo **Ruggero Raimondi** *bass* Don Alfonso

Mahler Chamber Orchestra / Daniel Harding

Stage director **Patrice Chéreau**

Video director **Stéphane Metge**

Virgin Classics ② *DVD* 344716-9 (179' · NTSC · 16:9 · PCM stereo, 5.0 and DTS 5.0 · 0).

Recorded live at the Aix-en-Provence Festival in July 2005　　　　　　　　　　　　　　　　Ⓕ

Patrice Chéreau's production is full of strokes of near-genius from old (Chéreau, his regular set designer Richard Peduzzi, his photogenic Don Alfonso, Ruggero Raimondi), not so old (Bar-bara Bonney's unhackneyed Despina) and new (Daniel Harding – a thrilling Mozart conductor on the wing – Elina Garanča's Dorabella, and the men) but, at least as filmed here, is often less than the sum of its parts.

In Act 1 Chéreau and Peduzzi rely too often on clichés. The fact that they're their own cli-chés – an aesthetic that they invented – may only worry those who know their stagings well. They design an empty theatrical space with 18th-century Noh theatre actors as providers of props and furniture and a huge (and distract-ing) 'No Smoking' instruction on the back wall, perhaps a reference to their first Mozart suc-cess in early-1970s Spoleto. Blocking tics from the Bayreuth *Ring* and other shows abound – the chain of people going nowhere just before the boys leave for supposed military service, the painters' scaffold that takes them there, the endless running around and singing in the 'wrong' directions. All the while, there's a very serious intent here and a studiedly conscious recreation of 18th-century patterns in both costumes (Caroline de Vivaise) and movement that compels admiration.

After the interval Chereau, always a compel-ling observer of sexual love, comes into his ele-ment. The comic/erotic balance of the boys' success with the others' girls is brilliantly detailed. The 18th-century quotes seem more integrated. The last scene – helped by Bonney's well-acted shock and breakdown when Despina realises she's been duped too – is dark but, sig-nificantly, not twisted out of shape to fit an intel-lectual conceit. All end up in a kind of exhausted, nervous embrace.

Musically, things are also mixed. The best of Harding's *Così* is as earthily thrilling (and pun-gent) as his *Giovanni* and recent *Zauberflöte*; elsewhere this is work-in-progress, but his Klemperer-on-original-instruments approach is appealing. Erin Wall is stretched by both Fiordiligi's big set-pieces but acts them with conviction. Raimondi compensates for an inevi-table lack of pure voice by charismatic phrasing and acting. The men are good – a nice combina-tion of character and virtuosity; Garanča and Bonney are exceptional.

Mixed down by Arte TV channel from four live performances (and filmed rather bumpily), the soundtrack does not always sync with what you see, but it's a distraction you soon forget.

Così fan tutte

Amanda Roocroft *sop* Fiordiligi **Rosa Mannion** *sop* Dorabella **Eirian James** *mez* Despina **Rainer Trost** *ten* Ferrando **Rodney Gilfry** *ten* Guglielmo **Claudio Nicolai** *bass* Don Alfonso **Monteverdi Choir; English Baroque Soloists / Sir John Eliot Gardiner**

Stage director **Sir John Eliot Gardiner**
Video director **Peter Mumford**
Archiv 📀 073 026-9AH2 (193' · 16:9 · 5.1 · 0)
Recorded live at the Théâtre du Châtelet, Paris 1992
Ⓕ⚫

When this staging was presented in 1992, in various theatres, Gardiner decided to be his own director because he didn't trust any available alternative to be faithful to Da Ponte's and Mozart's original. In the circumstances his was a sensible decision because his deeply discerning stage interpretation perfectly seconds his own musically perceptive reading. His keen understanding of what this endlessly fascinating work is about is made plain in his absorbing essay in the booklet.

The first advantage of this film of the opera is Carlo Tommasi's ravishing décor that accords with what the libretto predicates, conjuring before our eyes 18th-century Naples overlooked by Vesuvius. Then Gardiner's direction makes all-too-clear the emotional turmoil engineered by Don Alfonso's cynical plans to test the ladies' constancy. At all times it's responsive to the music, except when members of the cast march through the stalls and when certain scenes are more sexually explicit than would have been contemplated in Mozart's age.

Amanda Roocroft's Fiordiligi is intrepidly sung, her tone always firm and gleaming, and she acts expressively. She's partnered, as originally intended, by a soprano Dorabella. Rosa Mannion proves an apt foil for her sister, and is deliciously flighty when falling for her 'Albanian' lover. Rainer Trost is the young, fluent, eager Ferrando who makes the most of his taxing music, although his second aria, 'Ah! lo veggio', is here excluded. His vulnerable portrayal is a nice contrast to Rodney Gilfry's macho Guglielmo. The four voices blend well in the many ensembles.

In the pit, Gardiner's direct, big-scale yet sensitive conducting is the engine-room of the performance, superbly sustained by his period-instrument band. Peter Mumford's video direction is faultless; so is the sound picture. All in all, it would be amazing if any successor surpasses this DVD's achievements on all sides. Recommended without reservation.

Don Giovanni, K527

Don Giovanni   Ⓗ
Eberhard Waechter *bar* Don Giovanni **Joan Sutherland** *sop* Donna Anna **Elisabeth Schwarzkopf** *sop* Donna Elvira **Graziella Sciutti** *sop* Zerlina **Luigi Alva** *ten* Don Ottavio **Giuseppe Taddei** *bar* Leporello **Piero Cappuccilli** *bar* Masetto **Gottlob Frick** *bass* Commendatore **Philharmonia Chorus and Orchestra / Carlo Maria Giulini**
EMI Great Recordings of the Century ③ 567869-2
(162' · ADD · T/t) Recorded 1959   Ⓜ⚫⚫↦

Although this set is over 40 years old, none of its successors is as skilled in capturing the piece's drama so unerringly. It has always been most recommendable and Giulini captures all the work's most dramatic characteristics, faithfully supported by the superb Philharmonia forces of that time. At this stage of Giulini's career, he was a direct, lithe conductor, alert to every turn in the story and he projects the nervous tension of the piece ideally while never forcing the pace, as can so easily happen. Then he had one of the most apt casts ever assembled for the piece. Waechter's Giovanni combines the demonic with the seductive in just the right proportions, Taddei is a high-profile Leporello, who relishes the text and sings with lots of 'face'. Elvira was always one of Schwarzkopf's most successful roles: here she delivers the role with tremendous intensity. Sutherland's Anna isn't quite so full of character but is magnificently sung. Alva is a graceful Ottavio. Sciutti's charming Zerlina, Cappuccilli's strong and Italianate Masetto and Frick's granite Commendatore are all very much in the picture. The sound is so good, the set might have been recorded yesterday.

Don Giovanni   Ⓟ
Rodney Gilfry *bar* Don Giovanni **Luba Orgonasova** *sop* Donna Anna **Charlotte Margiono** *sop* Donna Elvira **Eirian James** *mez* Zerlina **Christoph Prégardien** *ten* Don Ottavio **Ildebrando d'Arcangelo** *bass* Leporello **Julian Clarkson** *bass* Masetto **Andrea Silvestrelli** *bass* Commendatore **Monteverdi Choir; English Baroque Soloists / Sir John Eliot Gardiner**
Archiv Produktion ③ 445 870-2AH3 (176' · DDD · T/t)
Recorded 1994   Ⓕ↦

Gardiner's set has a great deal to commend it. The recitative is sung with exemplary care over pacing so that it sounds as it should, like heightened and vivid conversation, often to electrifying effect. Ensembles, the Act 1 quartet particularly, are also treated conversationally, as if one were overhearing four people giving their opinions on a situation in the street. The orchestra, perfectly balanced with the singers in a very immediate acoustic, supports them, as it were 'sings' with them. That contrasts with, and complements, Gardiner's expected ability to empathise with the demonic aspects of the score, as in Giovanni's drinking song and the final moments of Act 1, which fairly bristle with rhythmic energy without ever becoming rushed. The arrival of the statue at Giovanni's dinner-table is tremendous, the period trombones and timpani achieving an appropriately brusque, fearsome attack. Throughout this scene, Gardiner's penchant for sharp accents is wholly appropriate; elsewhere he's sometimes rather too insistent. As a whole, tempos not only seem right on their own account but also, all-importantly, carry conviction in relation to each other. Where so many conductors today are given to rushing 'Mi tradì', Gardiner prefers a more meditative approach, which allows his soft-grained Elvira to make the most of the aria's expressive possibilities.

Rodney Gilfry's Giovanni is lithe, ebullient, keen to exert his sexual prowess; an obvious charmer, at times surprisingly tender yet with the iron will only just below the surface. Suave and appealing, delivered in a real baritone timbre, his Giovanni is as accomplished as any on disc. Ildebrando d'Arcangelo was the discovery of these performances: this young bass is a lively foil to his master and on his own a real showman, as 'Madamina' indicates, a number all the better for a brisk speed. Orgonasova once more reveals herself a paragon as regards steady tone and deft technique – there's no need here to slow down for the coloratura at the end of 'Non mi dir' – and she brings to her recounting of the attempted seduction a real feeling of immediacy. As Anna, Margiono sometimes sounds a shade stretched technically, but consoles us with the luminous, inward quality of her voice and her reading of the role, something innate that can't be learnt.

Nobody in their right senses is ever going to suggest that there's one, ideal version of *Don Giovanni*; the work has far too many facets for that, but for sheer theatrical *élan* complemented by the live recording, Gardiner is among the best, particularly given a recording that's wonderfully truthful and lifelike.

Don Giovanni   **P**
Johannes Weisser *bar* Don Giovanni **Olga Pasichnyk** *sop* Donna Anna **Alexandrina Pendatchanska** *sop* Donna Elvira **Sunhae Im** *sop* Zerlina **Kenneth Tarver** *ten* Don Ottavio **Lorenzo Regazzo** *bass* Leporello **Nikolay Borchev** *bass* Masetto **Alessandro Guerzoni** *bass* Commendatore **Berlin RIAS Chamber Choir; Freiburg Baroque Orchestra / René Jacobs**
Harmonia Mundi ③ HMC90 1964/6 (170' · DDD · S/T/ t/N)   Ⓕ●

If Jacobs is hardly the first modern conductor to present the opera in its 'original colours', his *Don Giovanni* is among the liveliest and most enjoyable on offer. It is certainly one of the most brilliantly played. The Freiburg band, forwardly balanced, are eager, involved participants in the drama. Mozart's wonderful woodwind commentaries are as pungent as you will hear, while rasping, minatory valveless brass and gunfire period timpani create a properly terrifying frisson in the Commendatore's retribution scene.

Jacobs being Jacobs, there are controversial things here. Tempi can suddenly spurt forward or slow down, usually – as in the opening scene – with dramatically exciting results. Both finales hurtle forward with thrilling impetus. Elsewhere speeds can sound a shade frenetic: in the Act 1 Quartet, for instance, or in Zerlina's two arias. As in Jacobs's *Figaro*, the recitatives are done in a natural, conversational style, with fortepiano and cello adding their creative 'commentaries', like the instruments in the arias.

For Jacobs, Donna Elvira is the opera's central female character. Accordingly, he casts Anna with the relatively light-toned Olga Pasichnyk, who sings 'Non mi dir' tenderly and gracefully, and sounds more sorrowful than vengeful in 'Or sai chi l'onore' – a more vulnerable and more like-

able figure than usual. Conversely, Alexandrina Pendatchanska's Elvira is as hysterically obsessive as any on disc, with a mingled desperation and tragic grandeur in her big Act 2 recitative: it's an exciting performance, certainly, though her phrasing can be disconcertingly gusty.

Smooth *legato* is hardly a priority for Johannes Weisser either. His Giovanni is less the sinister, demonic anti-hero, more an over-sexed, heedless young bounder with a taste for danger and a penchant for cruelty. He is casually seductive with Sunhae Im's coquettish, sweet-toned Zerlina, rapier-sharp in his exchanges with Leporello, where his youthful, tenorish timbre contrasts strongly with Lorenzo Regazzo's bass-baritone. Regazzo's is a charismatic performance, never descending to caricature; his lubricious relish in the Catalogue aria does not preclude a hint of elegance. The mellifluous-toned Kenneth Tarver makes a sympathetic, concerned Ottavio, the Masetto is aptly sullen, the Commendatore amply imposing. But few could deny the zest, sweep and sheer theatrical charge of this recording.

Don Giovanni   **H**
Cesare Siepi *bar* Don Giovanni **Elisabeth Grümmer** *sop* Donna Anna **Elisabeth Schwarzkopf** *sop* Donna Elvira **Erna Berger** *sop* Zerlina **Anton Dermota** *ten* Don Ottavio **Otto Edelmann** *bass* Leporello **Walter Berry** *bass* Masetto **Raffaele Arié** *bass* Commendatore **Vienna State Opera Chorus; Vienna Philharmonic Orchestra / Wilhelm Furtwängler**
Orfeo d'Or mono ③ C624 043D (3h' · ADD · S/N) Recorded live at the Felsenreitschule, Salzburg on July 27, 1953   Ⓕ

This 1953 version is probably the most satisfying we have of Furtwängler's *Giovanni*s in the Salzburg series. 1950 brought together a more exciting cast (Gobbi in the title-role, Welitsch as Anna, Seefried as Zerlina and Kunz as Leporello) but is not so well recorded; 1954 has the same cast as '53, with the exception of Deszö Ernster who sings a disastrously wobbly Commendatore, but it doesn't lift as this does. The 'constants' in all three casts are Elisabeth Schwarzkopf and Anton Dermota, both of them unequivocal assets and consistent in their excellence over all three years. Cesare Siepi was a Giovanni to see as well as hear: his opulent, sonorous tone is welcome, less so its bass-weighted character and his graceless way with the Serenade. Otto Edelmann's Leporello flashes vividly into existence as a character every so often and is always well sung. Walter Berry is festival-casting as Masetto, and Raffaële Arié, if not ideally empyrean, is more steady than Greindl (1950) who is firmness itself compared with Ernster (1954).

Elisabeth Grümmer's 'Non mi dir' is a comparable high spot, the slow speed probably working for her in the second half but posing a fearsome challenge in the first. This, however, is much her best singing; elsewhere she is often tremulous and even shrill. Of Erna Berger's 52-year-old Zerlina

MOZART DON GIOVANNI – IN BRIEF

Eberhard Waechter Don Giovanni **Joan** Ⓗ
Sutherland Donna Anna **Elisabeth Schwarzkopf**
Donna Elvira **Philharmonia Chorus & Orchestra /**
Carlo Maria Giulini
EMI ③ 567869-2 (163′ · ADD)   Ⓜ**OO**⮫
Among an increasingly vast choice this
remains a prime recommendation, both for
its rich-voiced, characterful singers and
Giulini's mercurial conducting.

Rodney Gilfry Don Giovanni **Luba Orgonasova**
Donna Anna **Charlotte Margiono** Donna Elvira
Monteverdi Choir; English Baroque Soloists /
Sir John Eliot Gardiner   Ⓟ
Archiv ③ 445 870-2AH3 (176′ · DDD)   Ⓕ⮫
An immensely dynamic, theatrical perfor-
mance recorded live, with a magnetic young
Don heading a splendidly fresh cast. Original
instruments, but this is a field leader by any
standards.

Bo Skovhus Don Giovanni **Christine Brewer**
Donna Anna **Felicity Lott** Donna Elvira **Scottish**
Chamber Chorus & Orchestra / Sir Charles
Mackerras
Telarc ③ CD80420 (183′ · DDD)   Ⓕ
Mackerras conducts the excellent Scottish
players with characteristically theatrical
energy, uniting a fine cast in an unusual
sense of ensemble.

Johannes Weisser Don Giovanni **Olga Pasichnyk**
Donna Anna **Alexandrina Pendatchanska** Donna
Elvira **Freiburg Baroque Orchestra / René**
Jacobs   Ⓟ
Harmonia Mundi ③ HMC90 1964/6 (170′ · DDD)
   Ⓕ**O**
A younger Giovanni than we're used to is at
the centre of Jacobs's thrillingly dramatic
reading. Love it or hate it you're unlikely to
remain unmoved by this great score.

Thomas Allen Don Giovanni **Carol Vaness** Donna
Anna **Maria Ewing** Donna Elvira **Glyndebourne**
Festival Chorus, London PO / Bernard Haitink
EMI ③ 747037-8 (172′ · DDD)   Ⓕ**O**
Derived from Glyndebourne's legendary
Peter Hall production, this has a fine dra-
matic atmosphere, with Thomas Allen's
silken, sinister Giovanni confronting Carol
Vaness under Haitink's urbane direction.

Thomas Allen Don Giovanni **Carol Vaness** Donna
Elvira **Andrea Rost** Zerlina **Cologne Opera**
Chorus; Cologne Gürzenich Orchestra / James
Conlon
ArtHaus Musik 🖭 100 020 (173′)   Ⓕ
A straightforward staging, visually accept-
able, if not thrilling, but with a fine cast, even
if Thomas Allen's Don has aged a little since
Glyndebourne. Ferruccio Furlanetto is a live-
wire Leporello, Conlon conducts with brio.

a listener might well suppose her a talented
ingénue, and 'Vedrai, carino' goes particularly
well at Furtwängler's comfortable *andante*.

And in the end it all comes back to Furtwängler. Certainly this is Mozart viewed with
fore-knowledge of Beethoven, whereas the
modern approach prefers to look as from the
18th-century inheritance. Those who love the
opera more than a particular conception of it
will love this performance.

Don Giovanni   Ⓗ
Cesare Siepi bar Don Giovanni **Sena Jurinac** sop
Donna Elvira **Leyla Gencer** sop Donna Anna **Richard**
Lewis ten Don Ottavio **Geraint Evans** bass Leporello
Mirella Freni sop Zerlina **Robert Savoie** bass
Masetto **David Ward** bass Commendatore **Chorus**
and Orchestra of the Royal Opera House, Covent
Garden / Georg Solti
Royal Opera House Heritage Series mono ③
ROHS007 (173′ · ADD). Recorded live in 1962   Ⓜ

There was always a sense of tightened standards
in the house when Solti conducted, and a Zeffirelli production usually meant a move into the
first class onstage. If the opera was Don
Giovanni, there was a likely prospect of, if not a
night of the seven stars, at least an ensemble with
some starry elements. So on February 19, 1962,
all was set fair for a good evening.

And that's what it surely was, the audience making its presence, receptivity and enjoyment felt
even at this remove. If a commensurate joy is not
experienced at home, that may have to do with
the rather dry acoustic caught in this clear but not
ingratiating recorded sound. And it may be that
we're spoilt for choice in the *Giovanni* market.
But then, if we buy these archive recordings it's
usually not so much for the opera itself as for
something specific about the performance.

Here, what we might call the connoisseur-
interest centres on the Donna Anna of Leyla
Gencer. She was a singer sufficiently undervalued by the record companies to attain cult status. She proves an excellent Mozartian stylist,
singing both arias with exemplary cleanness and
precision, and characterising with warmth and
nobility. Her Ottavio is Richard Lewis. No con-
noisseur-interest there, I imagine, yet his was
the performance which gave me most pleasure.
Again the two arias are exemplary, 'Dalla sua
pace' in its grace and sweetness, 'Il mio tesoro' in
its clear articulation within the long sustained
phrases. The recording demonstrates how incisive his voice could sound in a large house.

The others do more or less as expected, Jurinac
with sturdy tone and ever-dependable technique, Freni with crystalline purity, Siepi with
generous sonority, Evans with broad humour
and a degree of vocal opulence in reserve. The
Solti touch is specially evident at certain points,
such as the start of the finale, springing to life
like a soul new risen. Shortly after that appears
another resurrected soul – Sir David Webster
paying tribute to Bruno Walter, who had died
two days previously.

Don Giovanni
Simon Keenlyside bar Don Giovanni **Joyce DiDonato** mz Donna Elvira **Marina Poplavskaya** sop Donna Anna **Ramón Vargas** ten Don Ottavio **Kyle Ketelsen** bass Leporello **Miah Persson** sop Zerlina **Robert Gleadow** bar Masetto **Eric Halfvarson** bass Commendatore
Chorus and Orchestra of the Royal Opera House, Covent Garden / Sir Charles Mackerras
Stage director **Francesca Zambello**
Video director **Robin Lough**
Opus Arte ② 🅳🆅🅳 OA1009D (3h 22' · NTSC · 16:9 · PCM stereo and DTS 5.1 · 0) Recorded live   Ⓕ**OO**

This is eminently listenable and surprisingly viewable – 'surprisingly' because complaints were commonly heard concerning the production. It's not particularly edifying to see so much of Simon Keenlyside's torso or to have Giovanni taking his last supper in shorts, but by modern standards it's almost tasteful. And the singing is almost uniformly fine. If one of the cast is to be named above the rest, that should be Joyce DiDonato, an outstandingly accomplished Elvira, brilliantly projected, interestingly conceived, her singing concentrated in tone. Marina Poplavskaya's Anna is both dignified and sympathetic, and she too has remarkable command of the necessary technique. Yet the voice itself doesn't serve quite as well as one might have hoped, wanting more heft in 'Or sai chi l'onore' and more ease of passage in 'Non mi dir'. Miah Persson is an adorable Zerlina, and one liked what she and others were encouraged to do by way of vocal ornamentation.

Of the men, Giovanni is the least tested vocally though it's all to the good if he can turn a serenade as ingratiatingly as Keenlyside does. Ramón Vargas hardly looks a suitable lover for this Donna Anna but he sings both arias like the admirably reliable and gifted artist he is and has been for a good many years now. The Masetto looks rather too like the Leporello but that hardly matters and both deserve their applause. The Commendatore's uneven voice production does matter in spite of his sonorous bass notes and imposing stage presence. Mackerras at the helm is such a reassuringly familiar and well loved figure that we may be tempted to take him for granted. Happily the Covent Garden audience shows every sign of appreciation and the final curtain-call is deservedly his.

Don Giovanni
Sir Thomas Allen bar Don Giovanni **Carolyn James** sop Donna Anna **Carol Vaness** sop Donna Elvira **Kjell Magnus Sandve** ten Don Ottavio **Ferruccio Furlanetto** bass Leporello **Andrea Rost** sop Zerlina **Reinhard Dorn** bass Masetto **Matthias Hölle** bass Commendatore **Cologne Opera Chorus; Cologne Gürzenich Orchestra / James Conlon**
Stage director **Michael Hampe**
Video director **José Montes-Bequer**
ArtHaus Musik 🅳🆅🅳 100 020 (173' · Region 0) Recorded live 1991   Ⓕ**O**

If you're tired of and/or irritated by modern, psychological stagings of Don Giovanni, this traditional yet highly intelligent Cologne production will come as a blessed relief. In Michael Hampe's own dark-hued, spare and consistent sets, the drama moves swiftly to its appointed end, and the only disappointment is his failure to make Giovanni's descent into Hell at all threatening. Hampe is adept at giving his characters just enough to do without taking them beyond the bounds of the feasible in terms of acting while singing. In the title-role Allen probably needed no coaching at all, as by 1991 he was acknowledged as the leading Giovanni of his day, perhaps any day. He confirms that reputation here in an interpretation that blends in about equal measures magnetism, single-minded seductive purpose and cruelty. His murderous intents towards the Commendatore and Masetto, and his beating and threatening of Leporello all exhibit the idea of the Don as near-psychopath. Allen sings the role with total command of every nuance in aria, ensemble and recitative. It's a riveting performance, finely seconded by Furlanetto's Leporello, also alive to every aspect of his part's text and movement.

Nobody else in the cast achieves quite that level of distinction, although Carol Vaness, hitherto an Anna, sings Elvira with spirit and acts convincingly within a given convention. Her warm, firm soprano is equal to all the demands Mozart places on it. Carolyn James is a properly distraught Anna and sings with some flair, but her largish voice hardens uncomfortably under pressure. The Ottavio is adequate, no more, as is true of the Masetto and Commendatore, but Rost's youthful, appealing Zerlina is worth watching and hearing, especially in her encounter with Giovanni, where she exactly evinces the girl's uncertain, vulnerable reactions.

Conlon conducts a direct, unfussy reading at sensible speeds, very much in agreement with the action taking place above him, and his orchestra plays with grace and drive as required. The picture and sound are exemplary.

Don Giovanni
Wojciech Drabowicz bar Don Giovanni **Regina Schorg** sop Donna Anna **Véronique Gens** sop Donna Elvira **Marisa Martins** sop Zerlina **Marcel Reijans** ten Don Ottavio **Kwangchul Youn** bass Leporello **Felipe Bou** bass Masetto **Anatoly Kocherga** bass Commendatore **Palau de la Música Catalana Chamber Choir; Orchestra Academy of the Gran Teatre del Liceu, Barcelona / Bertrand de Billy**
Stage director **Calixto Bieito**
Video director **Toni Bargalló**
Opus Arte Ⓕ ② 🅳🆅🅳 OA0921D (156' · NTSC · PCM stereo and DTS 5.1 · 0) Recorded live at the Gran Teatre del Liceu, Barcelona in December 2002   Ⓕ

Calixto Bieito's staging of Mozart's opera buffa caused something close to apoplexy among the more conservative daily newspapers when it appeared at the London Coliseum in the early 2000s. Was this because, like Da Ponte's libretto, the Catalan director's vision of the last hours in the life of the 'extremely licentious', not-very-noble man is set in a contemporary world of sex, violence, remorse and social and psychological breakdown?

The crises that bind these characters' lives together are explored with unflinching directness. Regina Schorg's virtuoso Donna Anna, happily bonking Wojtek Drabowicz's charismatic, sleazy Giovanni in the back seat of her father's car (Kwangchul Youn's infectiously energetic Leporello is the chauffeur), has to call out her boring, safe boyfriend Don Ottavio (Marcel Reijans, superb playing Mr Nobody) when Giovanni slashes out too hard at interfering daddy (Anatoly Kocherga, a busman's holiday from his noted Boris). Mozart hints at all kind of hidden dangers as Anna makes Ottavio swear to avenge her; Bieito suggests that she's trading sex for a cover-up of the fatal accident that her actions provoked. The always tricky Ottavio/Anna relationship continues in this vein (her invention of what happened with Giovanni before 'Non mi dir' is another tease), via Anna's bitchy frustration when she realises (Act 1 Quartet) that Elvira (Véronique Gens) was an event in Giovanni's life, up to the point when Ottavio gains some small satisfaction (but almost by force) in her second aria.

That is all to concentrate on one relationship to give a flavour of Bieito's approach. There are any number of other illuminations – the Giovanni/Leporello hierarchy of control/exploitation/need; the tabloid, Ibiza clubworld of Masetto and Zerlina; Gens's terrifyingly complete portrait of a woman who loves too much; the convincing resituating in today's clothes of a world where indulgent caprice and exploitation can literally destroy people's lives. This, then, is no concert in costume but, even if you think you prefer your Don Giovanni as a clone of Errol Flynn's 1930s Elizabethan movies, do try this serious, black and often wickedly funny piece of theatre.

The musical performance has its own distinction, as well as complete integration with the staging concept.

Don Giovanni

Carlos Álvarez bar Don Giovanni **María Bayo** sop Donna Anna **Sonia Ganassi** sop Donna Elvira **Maria José Moreno** sop Zerlina **José Bros** ten Don Ottavio **Lorenzo Regazzo** bass Leporello **José Antonio Lopez** bass Masetto **Alfred Reiter** bass Commendatore
Madrid Symphony Chorus and Orchestra / Victor Pablo Pérez
Stage director **Lluis Pasquel**
Video director **Robin Lough**
Opus Arte ② OA0958D (3h 28' · NTSC · 16:9 · PCM stereo and DTS 5.1 · 0). Recorded live at the Teatro Real, Madrid, in October 2005 Ⓕ

Updating is more or less de rigueur in today's operatic circles and Madrid once again comes up

with the goods in a wholly plausible re-siting of *Giovanni* to 1940s Spain. The transfer of the various scenes is by and large convincing and Lluis Pasquel's perceptive ideas about the characters illuminate afresh the familiar story, with the opera's saturnine side very much to the fore.

Carlos Álvarez, a Giovanni recalling in voice George London in the part, wholly dominates this opera with a nasty, driven reading of the lecher and bully. Like London, he sings with dark-hued intensity throughout. His must be the best Don about today. By his side is Lorenzo Regazzo as Leporello: he proves a wonderfully resourceful actor and singer, and a proper alter ego to his master. Their enactment of the cemetery scene is masterly in all respects.

José Bros is a concerned Ottavio, whose long-breathed 'Il mio tesoro' is a wonder. Much the most exciting of the female singers is Sonia Ganassi's deeply felt, urgently sung Elvira, her 'Mi tradì' a bravura performance. María Bayo seems over-parted and uninteresting as Anna, and the Zerlina is ordinary, as is her Masetto.

Underlining the whole venture is the keenly shaped, fast-moving musical direction of Victor Pablo Pérez, a conductor obviously worth watching. Speeds are on the fast side, welcome in this long work and well tailored to the cast. The Madrid Symphony is its customary alert self. The same can be said for Robin Lough's video direction.

Die Entführung aus dem Serail, K384

Die Entführung aus dem Serail
Christine Schäfer sop Konstanze **Patricia Petibon** sop Blonde **Ian Bostridge** ten Belmonte **Iain Paton** ten Pedrillo **Alan Ewing** bass Osmin **Jürg Löw** spkr Pasha Selim **Les Arts Florissants / William Christie**
Erato ② 3984 25490-2 (127 minutes · DDD · T/t) Ⓕ

Reviewing the Strasbourg production of which this recording is based, *Opera*'s Andrew Clark commented that Christie sets 'brisk but flexible tempos, and builds the ensembles into a fever of musical jubilation'. That is all amply confirmed in this finely balanced, intimate recording. In the Overture and some of the early numbers, Christie is inclined to clip his rhythms with accents almost brusque, but once the Pasha and Konstanze appear on the scene, he settles into an interpretation that evinces the elevated sensibility that informs his Rameau, Handel on disc, strong on detail but never at the expense of the whole picture.

But then he has by his side a Konstanze to stop all hearts. Having delivered herself of a fleet, easy 'Ach, ich liebte', Schäfer (who wasn't in the original cast) pierces further than does any other interpreter into the soul of the woman who is both physically and emotionally imprisoned. From the deeply felt, vulnerable recitative leading into 'Traurigkeit' she pours out Konstanze's woes in that pure, plaintive, highly individual tone of hers and, above all, offers a wonderfully fresh and inward execution of the text. With

Christie going all the way with her, musically speaking, 'Traurigkeit' itself is heart-rending in its G minor sorrowing, 'Martern aller Arten' the epitome of determined defiance and resolution. Try the final section from 'Doch du bist entschlossen' – have you ever heard it sound so resolute, so detailed?

In the great Act 2 Quartet and the last-act duet, where Mozart peers into his musical future, she is just as moving and inspires Bostridge to equal heights of tender inflexion. At first you may find Bostridge lightweight for Belmonte, but in the context of this period-instrument performance, with a small band, his silvery voice and Mozartian know-how carry the day, though his voice sometimes sounds disconcertingly similar to the nimble, ingratiating tenor of the Pedrillo, Iain Paton.

Like her mistress in her role, Petibon gives us a Blonde to make us forget just about every other soprano in the part on disc. She plays with and smiles through her opening aria with a delightful freedom of technique and expression, nothing daunted by its tessitura, even adding decorations to the already-demanding vocal line (the whole recording is literally adorned by small embellishments, naturally delivered). She maintains this high standard throughout in a winning performance.

As Osmin, Ewing's vibrant, individual bass-baritone is attractive on its own account but, as on the other period-instrument performances, one does rather miss a true bass voice in such a low-lying part, and Ewing proves a benevolent, homely Osmin rather than a threatening one. But, like all the other singers and the keenly spoken Pasha of Low, he fits easily into the performance's overall and likeable concept, so I am not inclined to labour this slight drawback.

Christie includes all the recently rediscovered music, but opts for a shorter amount of dialogue than many. Its delivery is easy and idiomatic. And the recording is excellent.

man who, we sense, has awakened her sexually. Far from resisting his advances, she and the youthful, half-westernised Pasha, subtly and believably portrayed by Steven van Watermeulen, can hardly keep their hands off each other during her opening aria; and the longing she sings of in 'Traurigkeit' here takes on a very different meaning. Yet even in the final vaudeville, exchanged glances with the Pasha suggest an undertow of regret for romantic passion and exotic adventure sacrificed in the cause of duty.

While there are irritating details in Simons's modern-dress production, it is psychologically credible, often compelling. Laura Aikin vividly portrays Konstanze's fluctuating emotions in dialogue and aria. If 'Traurigkeit' ideally needs a softer, more plangent colour, she makes 'Martern aller Arten' a graphic embodiment of her conflicting feelings of desire and guilt, charging the stratospheric coloratura with a sense of neurotic desperation.

In Simons's conception Belmonte is an anxious, self-absorbed ditherer, understandably fazed by Konstanze's initial coolness towards him. Wearing a more-or-less permanently bemused air, Edgaras Montvidas sings his four arias with firm, sappy tone, if no special grace of phrasing. Michael Smallwood makes a likeable, resourceful Pedrillo, cheerfully enduring Osmin's sadistic hair-pulling and nose-tweaking; and Mojca Erdmann, clad in mini-skirt and high-heeled patent leather boots, is a delightful, thoroughly self-assured Blonde, impatient with Konstanze's soul-searching, and using her sexual power to reduce Kurt Rydl's formidable, orotund Osmin to a doe-eyed baby. In keeping with the whole production, comic gags are largely eschewed. Constantinos Carydis conducts the excellent Netherlands CO with zest and a fair sense of period style. While many will prefer a more comically straightforward staging, Simons's production certainly makes you think afresh about Mozart's ostensibly innocent, happily-ever-after harem *Singspiel*.

Die Entführung aus dem Serail
Laura Aikin *sop* Konstanze **Edgaras Montvidas** *ten* Belmonte **Kurt Rydl** *bass* Osmin **Mojca Erdmann** *sop* Blonde **Michael Smallwood** *ten* Pedrillo **Steven van Watermeulen** *spkr* Bassa Selim
Netherlands Opera Chorus; Netherlands Chamber Orchestra / Constantinos Carydis
Stage director **Johan Simons**
Video director **Misjel Vermeiren**
Opus Arte ② **DVD** OA1003D (3h 34' · NTSC · 16:9 · PCM stereo and DTS 5.1 · 0)　　　　　　Ⓕ

Director Johan Simons's take on *Die Entführung* is summed up by a remark in one of the accompanying interviews: 'At the end people see that the Pasha is a much better match for Konstanze than Belmonte is.' Other productions have suggested a mutual attraction between the heroine and her oriental captor. Simons carries this to extremes. His staging is dominated by Konstanze's inner struggle between her loyalty to her betrothed and her disturbing feelings for the

Die Entführung aus dem Serail
Malin Hartelius *sop* Konstanze **Magali Léger** *sop* Blonde **Matthias Klink** *ten* Belmonte **Loïc Felix** *ten* Pedrillo **Wojtek Smilek** *bass* Osmin **Shahrokh Moshkin-Ghalam** *spkr* Pasha Selim **Europa Academy Chorus; Les Musiciens du Louvre / Marc Minkowski**
Stage directors **Jerome Deschamps** and **Macha Makeïeff**
Video director **Don Kent**
Bel Air Classiques **DVD** BAC028 (128' · NTSC · 16:9 · PCM stereo, 5.0 and DTS 5.1 · 0)　　　　　Ⓕ

This lively production originated at Baden Baden in 2003 and moved to the Aix-en-Provence Festival the following year where it was filmed. Marc Minkowski is the moving spirit of the performance and 'moving' is the right epithet, as most of his speeds are on the fast side. No harm in that when the work is so lengthy. He assembled a fine young cast, all of whom are up to their taxing parts, headed by Malin Hartelius as Konstanze, who is at once a visually attractive performer, absolutely tireless in her three arias, and at the same time projects a very moving portrayal. She is partnered by a promising young tenor in Matthias Klink as Belmonte. He is deprived of one of his arias but sings the rest with fluency and makes an eager young lover. Magali Léger is a bright-buttoned Blonde with voice to match, and her Pedrillo, Loïc Felix, is a suitable partner.

Wojtek Smilek is, unusual for the part, more friendly than awesome as Osmin. But in a way the star of the cast is Shahrokh Moshkin-Ghalam, who makes the Pasha Selim both sympathetic and believable. The stage direction and sets are simple and quite effective, but in no way match those on the recently reissued Covent Garden production under Solti, which is also admirably cast. Take your pick.

Die Entführung aus dem Serail
Eva Mei sop Konstanze **Patrizia Ciofi** sop Blonde **Rainer Trost** ten Belmonte **Mehrzad Montazeri** ten Pedrillo **Kurt Rydl** bass Osmin **Markus John** spkr Pasha Selim **Chorus and Orchestra of Maggio Musicale Fiorentino / Zubin Mehta** Stage director **Eike Gramss** Video director **George Blume**
TDK Mediactive ⓓ DVD DV-OPEADS (136' · 16:9 · 2.0, 5.1 & DTS 5.1 · 0)　　　　　Ⓕ Ⓞ

What a pleasure it is to come upon this *Seraglio*, freshly recorded in Florence's beautiful Teatro della Pergola. It's straightforward without being staid, a crisp, witty, fast-moving production – and in Christoph Wagenknecht's colourful set, a seascape fronted with swiftly sliding panels in Turkish patterns, visually delightful as well.

Musically, too, it holds its end up. Zubin Mehta isn't an ideal Mozartian, but he conducts with affectionate warmth and theatrical verve, and he has a first-rate cast. Eva Mei, a passionate (if disconcertingly Turkish-looking) Konstanze, sings with a fiery virtuosity that makes 'Marten aller Arten' genuinely expressive and no mere showpiece. Rainer Trost, technically adept if occasionally reedy, copes elegantly even with the fiendish 'Ich baue ganz', but plays Belmonte as rather a ninny, leaving the real heroism to Mehrzad Montazeri's livewire, fresh-voiced Pedrillo. Patrizia Ciofi's Blonde is a truly terrifying little spitfire with a penetrating, glassy voice that unfortunately splinters around high E, but she strikes comic sparks off Kurt Rydl's magnificent Osmin. He sings with irresistible gusto, lacking only that last ounce of *buffo* richness, and thankfully plays not some proto-Ayatollah, but the baffled, vulnerable bully the music depicts. Young viewers may appreciate his pet watch-crocodile.

This performance is very satisfying – and entirely recommendable.

Idomeneo, re di Creta, K366

Idomeneo　　　　　　　　　　　　　　Ⓟ
Anthony Rolfe Johnson ten Idomeneo **Anne Sofie von Otter** mez Idamante **Sylvia McNair** sop Ilia

Hillevi Martinpelto sop Elettra **Nigel Robson** ten Arbace **Glenn Winslade** ten High Priest **Cornelius Hauptmann** bass Oracle **Monteverdi Choir; English Baroque Soloists / Sir John Eliot Gardiner**
Archiv Produktion ③ 431 674-2AH3 (211' · DDD · T/t)
　　　　　　　　　　Ⓕ Ⓞ Ⓞ Ⓞ ➤

Ⓖ　This is unquestionably the most vital and authentic account of *Idomeneo* to date on disc (though see the more recent review of the Mackerras set below). We have here what was given at the work's first performance in Munich plus, in appendices, what Mozart wanted, or was forced, to cut before that premiere and the alternative versions of certain passages, so that various combinations of the piece can be programmed by the listener. Gardiner's direct, dramatic conducting catches ideally the agony of Idomeneo's terrible predicament—forced to sacrifice his son because of an unwise row. This torment of the soul is also entirely conveyed by Anthony Rolfe Johnson in the title role to which Anne Sofie von Otter's moving Idamante is an apt foil. Sylvia McNair is a diaphanous, pure-voiced Ilia, Hillevi Martinpelto a properly fiery, sharp-edged Elettra. With dedicated support from his own choir and orchestra, who obviously benefited from a long period of preparation, Gardiner matches the stature of this noble *opera seria*. The recording catches the excitement which all who heard the live performances will recall.

Idomeneo
Ian Bostridge ten Idomeneo **Lorraine Hunt Lieberson** mez Idamante **Lisa Milne** sop Ilia **Barbara Frittoli** sop Elettra **Anthony Rolfe Johnson** ten Arbace **Paul Charles Clarke** ten High Priest **John Relyea** bass Oracle **Dunedin Consort; Edinburgh Festival Chorus; Scottish Chamber Orchestra / Sir Charles Mackerras**
EMI ③ 557260-2 (203' · DDD · T/t)　　Ⓕ Ⓞ Ⓞ

There were golden opinions for the *Idomeneo* given at 2001's Edinburgh Festival by these performers, and here it is on CD. The work is given complete, at the marvellously extravagant length at which Mozart initially planned it, bar some small (and authentic) cuts in the *secco* recitative. And it works. It works triumphantly, in fact. That's partly due to Mackerras's truly inspired reading of the score, and his insights into the meaning of its musical gestures. This is a score full of gestures, heavy with emotional significance, not only in the arias and the ensembles but perhaps above all in the orchestral recitative that abounds in this score as in no other of Mozart's. It's partly the expressiveness of Mackerras's handling of what's, in effect, Mozart's emotional commentary on the unfolding of the plot that makes this performance so powerful. He has a clear vision of the expressive messages that Mozart transmits through texture or harmony or dynamic or rhythmic refinement.

The performance is also full of dramatic energy. During the Overture you experience that tingle in your spine that comes of the expectation of a curtain about to rise. Never mind that this isn't a 'period instrument' performance: the textures are as lucid as one could wish, the articulation as light and precise, the balance as just. Tempos are unhurried.

Ian Bostridge makes a strong Idomeneo. His opening aria, 'Vedrommi intorno', is exquisitely done, smoothly and lovingly phrased. Mozart wrote it in a traditional style to flatter the voice of his original singer, Anton Raaff. Just here and there, and especially in the closing aria, one might perhaps have liked more variety of tone and in particular more soft and lyrical colouring. Idamante, originally a castrato part, is sung by a mezzo, and one can't imagine one much better than Lorraine Hunt Lieberson: it's a lovely, focused sound, with the firm centre that a male part needs, and there are many happy details of phrasing. Lisa Milne provides a sympathetic yet not frail Ilia, with a clear and warm ring to the voice. The singing of Barbara Frittoli as Elettra has properly a bit more edge to it and there's plenty of tension and power to her first aria and especially her stormy final one, 'D'Oreste, d'Ajace'. With Anthony Rolfe Johnson to sing Arbace, both of that character's arias (as well as his important accompanied recitatives) are given, understandably, although the second in particular isn't on the level of most of the score – Mozart probably excluded both of them in his own performances. It's a joy to hear them so beautifully sung; the *legato* line and the smooth large leaps in the first are a delight.

The chorus is first-rate, and there's excellent orchestral playing. This set, enshrining Mackerras's profound and mature understanding of the music, is deeply moving; readers are urged to buy it.

Idomeneo
Philip Langridge ten Idomeneo **Jerry Hadley** ten Idamante **Yvonne Kenny** sop Ilia **Carol Vaness** sop Elettra **Thomas Hemsley** bar Arbace **Anthony Roden** ten High Priest **Roderick Kennedy** bass Voice of Neptune **Glyndebourne Chorus; London Philharmonic Orchestra / Bernard Haitink**
Stage director **Trevor Nunn**
Video director **Christopher Swann**
Warner Music Vision/NVC Arts 5050467 3922-2-9 (181' · NTSC · 4:3 · 2.0 · 2-6) Recorded live Ⓢ

Trevor Nunn produced his first opera, *Idomeneo*, Glyndebourne in 1983, with felicitous results. John Napier's designs imaginatively evoke the Cretan milieu, supported by restrained, dignified costumes and lighting. The spare setting now seems a model beside what usually passes for decor today. Within it Nunn directs his principals and chorus with economic yet pointed care.

Philip Langridge is a compellingly distraught and haunted Idomeneo, singing with his customary feeling for word-painting. He easily encompasses the longer version of 'Fuor del mar'. Carol Vaness offers a fiery, richly contoured Elettra. Yvonne Kenny's beautifully sung Ilia is more conventional and Jerry Hadley is a fresh, pleasing Idamante. Bernard Haitink conducts a lithe, forward-moving account of the score, though you'll need a high volume setting to get the best out of the sound.

Lucio Silla
Lothar Odinius ten Lucio Silla **Simone Nold** sop Giunia **Kristina Hammarström** mez Cecilio **Henriette Bonde-Hansen** sop Cinna **Susanne Elmark** sop Celia **Jakob Naeslund Madsen** ten Aufidio **Ars Nova Copenhagen; Danish Radio Sinfonietta / Adám Fischer**
Dacapo ③ 8 226069/71 (170' · DDD) Ⓕ

The Milan premiere of *Lucio Silla*, on Boxing Day 1772, was a near-fiasco: ham acting from the last-minute tenor and the prima donna in a sulk. But from the second performance Mozart's second *opera seria* was an unalloyed triumph. The libretto is lumbering, sententious and dubiously motivated, culminating in an astonishing volte-face in which the sadistically ruthless Emperor suddenly morphs into a paragon of Enlightenment clemency. Not that this would have bothered 16-year-old Mozart's audiences one iota. What they came for – and got in spades – were varied and inventive arias that showcased the star singers.

The central roles of Giunia and her betrothed, the banished senator Cecilio (written for the castrato Rauzzini), inspired Mozart to his most powerful operatic music to date: darkly coloured accompanied recitatives that look forward to *Idomeneo*, Cecilio's anguished aria of parting, 'Ah, se a morir', a Gluckian *ombra* aria for Giunia as she prepares for death, and a dramatic trio that pits the two lovers against the raging Emperor.

This 2001-02 recording from Danish Radio archives is well sung and excitingly conducted. Adám Fischer encourages playing of quivering energy from the trim, lean-toned Danish orchestra. In the accompanied recitatives the players grieve and rage as vividly as the singers. Only Fischer's jerky tempo fluctuations, *à la* Harnoncourt, in the trio fail to convince.

While there are no big names among the soloists, they have fresh, youthful-sounding voices, and cope elegantly with Mozart's coloratura demands. As the put-upon heroine Giunia, Simone Nold sings with grace and agility, and fiery intensity, too – try the agitated Act 2 aria 'Parto, m'affretto'. Kristina Hammarström impresses especially in Cecilio's sombre memento mori scene in Act 1 and the spectacular vengeance aria 'Quest' improvviso tremito'. The secondary pair of lovers, Cecilio's friend Cinna and the Emperor's blithely innocent sister Celia, are equally well cast, Susanne Elmark dispatching high *staccato* passages with delightful insouciance.

The recording gives the orchestra plenty of presence without short-changing the singers. This is now the version to have of an ambitious, over-long but often richly expressive opera.

Le nozze di Figaro, K492

Le nozze di Figaro   P
Lorenzo Regazzo bass Figaro **Patrizia Ciofi** sop
Susanna **Simon Keenlyside** bar Count Almaviva
Véronique Gens sop Countess Almaviva **Angelika
Kirchschlager** mez Cherubino **Marie McLaughlin** sop
Marcellina **Antonio Abete** bass Bartolo Antonio
Kobie van Rensburg ten Don Basilio, Don Curzio
Nuria Rial sop Barbarina **Ghent Collegium Vocale;
Concerto Köln / René Jacobs**
Harmonia Mundi ③ HMC90 1818/20 (172′ · DDD · T/t)
Ⓕ🅞🅞🅞🅞

René Jacobs always brings new ideas to
the operas he conducts, and even to a
work as familiar as *Figaro* he adds
something of his own. First of all he offers an
orchestral balance quite unlike what we are used
to. Those who specially relish a Karajan or a
Solti will hardly recognise the work, with its
strongly wind-biased orchestral balance: you
simply don't hear the violins as the 'main line' of
the music. An excellent corrective to a tradition
that was untrue to Mozart, to be sure, but possibly the pendulum has swung a little too far.

Jacobs is freer over tempo than most conductors. The Count's authoritarian pronounce-
ments are given further weight by a faster
tempo: it gives them extra decisiveness, though
the music then has to slow down. There are
other examples of such flexibility, sometimes a
shade disconcerting, but always with good dramatic point. The Count's Act 3 duet with
Susanna is one example: the little hesitancies
enhanced and pointed up, if perhaps with some
loss in energy and momentum. Tempos are
generally on the quick side of normal, notably in
the earlier parts of the Act 2 finale; but Jacobs is
willing to hold back, too, for example in the
Susanna-Marcellina duet, in the fandango, and
in the G major music at the dénouement where
the Count begs forgiveness.

The cast is excellent. Véronique Gens offers a
beautifully natural, shapely 'Porgi amor' and a
passionate and spirited 'Dove sono'. The laughter in Patrizia Ciofi's voice is delightful when
she's dressing up Cherubino, and she has space
in 'Deh vieni' for a touchingly expressive performance. Then there's Angelika Kirschlager's
Cherubino, alive and urgent in 'Non so più',
every little phrase neatly moulded. Lorenzo
Regazzo offers a strong Figaro, with a wide
range of voice – angry and determined in 'Se
vuol ballare', nicely rhythmic with some softer
colours in 'Non più andrai', and pain and bitterness in 'Aprite'. The Count of Simon Keenlyside is powerful, menacing, lean and dark in
tone. Marie McLaughlin sings Marcellina with
unusual distinction.

Strongly cast, imaginatively directed: it's a
Figaro well worth hearing.

Le nozze di Figaro   P
Bryn Terfel bass-bar Figaro **Alison Hagley** sop
Susanna **Rodney Gilfry** bar Count Almaviva **Hillevi
Martinpelto** sop Countess Almaviva **Pamela Helen
Stephen** mez Cherubino **Susan McCulloch** sop
Marcellina **Carlos Feller** bass Bartolo Francis
Egerton ten Don Basilio, Don Curzio **Julian Clarkson**
bass Antonio **Constanze Backes** sop Barbarina
**Monteverdi Choir; English Baroque Soloists /
Sir John Eliot Gardiner**
Archiv Produktion ③ 439 871-2AH3 (179′ · DDD · T/t)
Recorded live 1993   Ⓕ🅞🅞

The catalogue of *Figaro* recordings is long, and
the cast lists are full of famous names. In this
version only one principal had more than half a
dozen recordings behind him, and some had
none at all. Yet this version can stand comparison with any, not only for its grasp of the drama
but also for the quality of its singing. It's more
evidently a period-instrument recording than
many under Gardiner. The string tone is pared
down and makes modest use of vibrato, the
woodwind is soft-toned. The voices are generally lighter and fresher-sounding than those on
most recordings. and the balance permits more
than usual to be heard of Mozart's instrumental
commentary on the action and the characters.
The recitative is done with exceptional life and
feeling for its meaning and dramatic import,
with a real sense of lively, urgent conversation.

Bryn Terfel and Alison Hagley make an outstanding Figaro and Susanna. Terfel has enough
darkness in his voice to sound menacing in 'Se
vuol ballare' as well as bitter in 'Aprite un po'
quegli occhi'; it's an alert, mettlesome performance – and he also brings off a superlative 'Non più
andrai'. Hagley offers a reading of spirit and
allure. The interplay between her and the woodwind in 'Venite inginocchiatevi' is a delight, and
her cool but heartfelt 'Deh vieni' is very beautiful.
Once or twice her intonation seems marginally
under stress but that's the small price you pay for
singing with so little vibrato. Hillevi Martinpelto's
unaffected, youthful-sounding Countess is enjoyable; both arias are quite lightly done, with a very
lovely, warm, natural sound in 'Dove sono' especially. Some may prefer a more polished, sophisticated reading, of the traditional kind, but this is
closer to what Mozart would have wanted and
expected.

Rodney Gilfry provides a Count with plenty of
fire and authority, firmly focused in tone; the
outburst at the *Allegro assai* in 'Vedrò mentr'io
sospiro' is formidable. Pamela Helen Stephen's
Cherubino sounds charmingly youthful and
impetuous. There's no want of dramatic life in
Gardiner's direction. His tempos are marginally
quicker than most, and the orchestra often
speaks eloquently of the drama.

Le nozze di Figaro   H
Cesare Siepi bass Figaro **Hilde Gueden** sop
Susanna **Alfred Poell** bar Count Almaviva
Lisa della Casa sop Countess Almaviva **Suzanne
Danco** sop Cherubino **Hilde Rössl-Majdan** contr
Marcellina **Fernando Corena** bass Bartolo **Murray
Dickie** ten Don Basilio **Hugo Meyer-Welfing** ten

Don Curzio **Harald Pröglhöf** bass Antonio **Anny Felbermayer** sop Barbarina **Vienna State Opera Chorus; Vienna Philharmonic Orchestra / Erich Kleiber**
Decca Legends ③ 478 1720 (172' · ADD) Recorded 1955 ⓂOO

Kleiber's *Figaro* is a classic of the classics of the gramophone: beautifully played by the Vienna Phil, conducted with poise and vitality and a real sense of the drama unfolding through the music. It's very much a Viennese performance, not perhaps as graceful or as effervescent as some but warm, sensuous and alive to the interplay of character. At the centre is Hilde Gueden, whose Susanna has echoes of operetta, although she remains a true Mozartian stylist. Lisa della Casa's Countess may not be one of the most dramatic but the voice is full yet focused. Suzanne Danco's Cherubino isn't exactly impassioned, and is really as much girlish as boyish, but it's still neat and musical singing. The balance among the men is affected by the casting of Figaro with a weightier singer than the Count. But Alfred Poell's Count makes up in natural authority and aristocratic manner what he lacks in sheer power, and he shows himself capable of truly sensual singing in the Act 3 duet with Susanna.

There are excellent performances, too, from Corena's verbally athletic Bartolo and Dickie's alert, ironic Basilio. However, the true star is Erich Kleiber. The beginning of the opera sets your spine tingling with theatrical expectation. Act 1 goes at pretty smart tempos, but all through he insists on full musical value. There's no rushing in the confrontations at the end of Act 2 – all is measured and properly argued through. The sound is satisfactory, for a set of this vintage, and no lover of this opera should be without it.

Le nozze di Figaro Ⓗ
Heinz Blankenburg bar Figaro **Mirella Freni** sop Susanna **Gabriel Bacquier** bar Count Almaviva **Leyla Gencer** sop Countess **Edith Mathis** sop Cherubino **Carlo Cava** bass Bartolo **Johanna Peters** sop Marcellina **Hugues Cuénod** ten Don Basilio **John Kentish** ten Don Curzio **Derick Davies** bass Antonio **Maria Zeri** sop Barbarina **Patricia McCarry** sop Bridesmaid **Glyndebourne Chorus; Royal Philharmonic Orchestra / Silvio Varviso**
Glyndebourne ③ GFOCD001-62 (162' · ADD) Recorded live on June 9, 1962 Ⓕ

Glyndebourne and *Figaro*: they go together like Christmas and mistletoe. Except, of course, that at Glyndebourne you hope for a lovely summer evening. That vintage year of '62 was the one which saw the return of Carl Ebert to produce not only this Figaro but also Glyndebourne's first *Pelléas*.

The young Silvio Varviso also made his Glyndebourne debut as conductor of Figaro. Count (Gabriel Bacquier) and Countess (Leyla Gencer) were other newcomers and Mirella Freni was singing Susanna for the first time anywhere. As heard here, everything takes its place with a

MOZART LE NOZZE DI FIGARO – IN BRIEF

Lorenzo Regazzo Figaro **Simon Keenlyside** 🄿 Count Almaviva **Véronique Gens** Countess Almaviva **Collegium Vocale; Concerto Köln / René Jacobs** ⓂOOO
Harmonia Mundi ③ HMC90 1818/20 (172' · DDD)
A new contender in a crowded field, Jacobs's performance is idiosyncratic but both finely detailed and entertaining, with a particularly strong cast.

Bryn Terfel Figaro **Rodney Gilfry** Count Almaviva **Hillevi Martinpelto** Countess Almaviva **Monteverdi Choir; English Baroque Soloists / Sir John Eliot Gardiner**
Archiv ③ 439 871-2AH3 (179' · DDD) ⒻO
A brilliant period-instrument set recorded live. Brisker and lighter-hued than the old school, with a superior cast but a rather obtrusive audience.

Cesare Siepi Figaro **Alfred Poell** Count Almaviva **Lisa della Casa** Countess Almaviva **Vienna State Opera Chorus; Vienna PO / Erich Kleiber** Ⓗ
Decca ③ 478 1720 (172' · ADD) ⓂOO
In the great Viennese tradition, conducted with fleet-footed dramatic energy, with a cast of rather heavyweight but exceptionally beautiful voices, albeit on a recording that is showing its age.

Samuel Ramey Figaro **Thomas Allen** Count Almaviva **Kiri Te Kanawa** Countess Almaviva **London Opera Chorus, London PO / Sir Georg Solti**
Decca ③ 410 150-2DH3 (169' · DDD) ⒻO⇥
Large-scale Mozart, but conducted with irresistible verve and wit, and an outstanding ensemble, all in a brilliant modern recording.

Hermann Prey Figaro **Dietrich Fischer-Dieskau** Count Almaviva **Gundula Janowitz** Countess Almaviva **Deutsche Oper Chor & Orch / Karl Böhm**
DG ③ 449 728-2GOR3 (173' · ADD) Ⓜ
Strongly cast with Janowitz a fiery Countess; Troyanos is a sparky Cherubino and Mathis enchanting as Susanna. Fischer-Dieskau and Prey spar splendidly. And over everything, Böhm presides magnificently. The sound is still immediate and impressive.

Heinz Blankenburg Figaro **Gabriel Bacquier** Count Almaviva **Leyla Gencer** Countess **Royal Philharmonic Orchestra / Silvio Varviso**
Glyndebourne ③ GFOCD001-62 (162' · ADD) Ⓕ
A 1962 night at Glyndebourne that enshrines the best Mozartian style of the old house. The young Silvio Varviso conducts with wonderful panache and the cast includes Mirella Freni's enchanting Susanna and Gencer's world-weary Countess. Blankenburg and Bacquier spar splendidly.

delightful combination of freshness and assurance, and the audience clearly (and more audibly after the interval) responds appreciatively.

The recording seems to catch the stage action almost as well as if it were a DVD, though the women's voices are apt to acquire that bright hard edge which is the accursed associate of digital remastering: still, not as badly as some. Even dear old Hugues Cuénod is endowed with a more prickly *forte* than he surely ever had in his voice live. At least the two baritones are unaffected, and their performances, both as pure singing and as 'expression', are delightful. Gencer's vibrant, almost tragic tone distinguishes her Countess, and as (nearly) always at Glyndebourne the ensemble work is a model of stylish efficiency.

Le nozze di Figaro
Knut Skram bass Figaro **Ileana Cotrubas** sop
Susanna **Benjamin Luxon** bar Count Almaviva **Kiri Te
Kanawa** sop Countess Almaviva **Frederica von
Stade** mez Cherubino **Nucci Condò** sop Marcellina
Marius Rintzler bass Bartolo **Glyndebourne Chorus;
London Philharmonic Orchestra / John Pritchard**
Stage director **Peter Hall** Video director **Dave
Heather**
ArtHaus Musik **DVD** 101 089 (185' · NTSC · 4:3 · PCM
stereo · 0) Recorded live   Ⓕ

Peter Hall's Glyndebourne *Figaro* of 1973 was his memorable first effort at staging Mozart, and was much praised at the time. His unfussy production is set in John Bury's lived-in, warmly coloured decor and combines well with John Pritchard's unassumingly stylish conducting. Dave Heather's TV direction is worthy of the original, and the picture looks as if it might have been filmed yesterday. The sound, however, lacks a little in clarity and range.

The cast that season was choice. Kiri Te Kanawa, youthful of mien, glowing of voice, sings the Countess. It is a wonderful memento of her great promise and appreciable achievement at the time. Her admirably priapic Count is Benjamin Luxon, singing with firm, velvet tone and a fine line. The participants below stairs are of equal stature. Ileana Cotrubas is an alert, cool-headed and warm-hearted Susanna, and she sings faultlessly. Knut Skram, her Figaro, isn't such a definite character, but is unobtrusively right. The young Frederica von Stade's Cherubino is sparky and wide-eyed if vocally a little thin. It's a cast welded into a true and rewarding ensemble.

Die Zauberflöte, K620

Die Zauberflöte   Ⓟ
Rosa Mannion sop Pamina **Natalie Dessay** sop
Queen of Night **Hans-Peter Blochwitz** ten Tamino
Anton Scharinger bass Papageno **Reinhard Hagen**
bass Sarastro **Willard White** bass Speaker **Steven
Cole** ten Monostatos **Linda Kitchen** sop Papagena
Anna Maria Panzarella sop Doris Lamprecht mez

Delphine Haidan contr First, Second and Third
Ladies **Damien Colin, Patrick Olivier Croset,
Stéphane Dutournier** trebs First, Second and Third
Boys **Christopher Josey** ten First Armed Man, First
Priest **Laurent Naouri** bass Second Armed Man,
Second Priest **Les Arts Florissants / William Christie**
Erato ③ 0630-12705-2 (150' · DDD · T/t)   Ⓜ

With a background primarily in the French Baroque, William Christie comes to *Die Zauberflöte* from an angle quite unlike anyone else's; yet this is as idiomatic and as deeply Mozartian a reading as any. In the booklet-note Christie remarks on the unforced singing that's one of his objectives, much more manageable with the gentler sound of period instruments. All this is borne out by the performance itself, which falls sweetly and lovingly on the ear.

Overall the performance is quick and light-textured – and often quite dramatic. Some may find Christie less responsive than many more traditional interpreters to the quicksilver changes in mood, yet this is a part of his essentially broad and gentle view of *Die Zauberflöte*. His cast has few famous names, though there's Hans-Peter Blochwitz, probably the finest Tamino around these days. As Pamina, Rosa Mannion has much charm and a hint of girlish vivacity, but blossoms into maturity and passion in 'Ach, ich fühl's', whose final phrases, as the wind instruments fall away, leaving her alone and desolate, are very moving. Natalie Dessay's Queen of Night is forthright, clean and well tuned, with ample weight and tonal glitter.

The orchestral playing from Les Arts Florissants is polished, and the translucent sound is a joy. In short, Christie offers a very satisfying, acutely musical view of the work.

Die Zauberflöte
Dorothea Röschmann sop Pamina **Erika Miklósa**
sop Queen of Night **Christoph Strehl** ten Tamino
Hanno Müller-Brachmann bass-bar Papageno **René
Pape** bass Sarastro **Kurt Azesberger** ten Monostatos
Julia Kleiter sop Papagena **George Zeppenfeld**
bass Speaker **Arnold Schoenberg Choir; Mahler
Chamber Orchestra / Claudio Abbado**
DG ② 477 5789GH2 (149' · DDD · T/t) Recorded live
2005   Ⓕ↪

This is certainly the most desirable version using modern instruments to appear since Solti's second recording in 1990. That said, its characteristics are rather nearer William Christie's 1995 period-performance (reviewed above). Abbado undertook the opera for the first time in performances in Italy in 2005, directed by his son (the production was seen at the 2006 Edinburgh Festival). On this occasion, he conducts a direct, keenly articulated, inspiriting account of the score, obviously aware of what has been achieved in recent times by the authenticists, yet when he reaches the work at its most Masonic – the Act 2 trio and the scene with the Armed Men, Tamino and Pamina – Abbado, directing his beloved Mahler Chamber Orchestra, gives the music its true and wondrous import. The playing throughout is alert and scrupulously articulated.

Casts varied between performances; here Abbado assembled one predominantly chosen from a youngish generation of German-speaking singers, each of whom approaches his or her role with fresh sound and interprets it in impeccably Mozartian style. The Tamino and Pamina are well nigh faultless. Tamino has been taken by many outstanding tenors on disc but Christoph Strehl sings with a Wunderlich-like strength and beauty, and rather more light and shade than his famous predecessor brought to the role. His is a wonderfully virile, vital reading that gives pleasure to the ear, as much in ensemble as in aria. He is partnered by Dorothea Röschmann, who has already appeared as Pamina at Covent Garden, and in many other houses. Her full-throated, positive singing, finely shaped, cleanly articulated, is a true match for Strehl's.

Hanno Müller-Brachmann is a properly lively and amusing Papageno, and delivers the role in a richer bass-baritone than many interpreters provide. He doesn't attempt a Viennese accent in the dialogue (a fairly full version), but brings plenty of simple humour to the part. The high and low roles are well catered for. The Hungarian coloratura Erika Miklósa has been making a speciality of Queen of Night over the past few years and shows just why in a technically secure and fiery account of her two arias. René Pape sings Sarastro: now at the peak of his career, he conveys all the role's gravity and dignity in a gloriously sung performance. Kurt Azesberger is a suitably nasty Monostatos.

Abbado allows a few neatly executed decorations. The extensive dialogue, spoken in a manner suitable for the theatre, sometimes sounds over-emphatic in the home, with the Papagena as an old woman the worst culprit. The recording is reasonably well balanced. As a whole the performance conveys a welcome immediacy and spontaneity and the daring of Abbado's way with the score is very alluring.

The Magic Flute (sung in English)
Rebecca Evans sop Pamina **Elizabeth Vidal** sop Queen of Night **Barry Banks** ten Tamino **Simon Keenlyside** bar Papageno **John Tomlinson** bass Sarastro **Christopher Purves** bass Speaker **John Graham-Hall** ten Monostatos **Lesley Garrett** sop Papagena **Majella Cullagh** sop First Lady **Sarah Fox** sop Second Lady **Diana Montague** mez Third Lady **Geoffrey Mitchell Choir; London Philharmonic Orchestra / Sir Charles Mackerras**
Chandos/Peter Moores Foundation Opera in English
② CHAN3121 (137' · DDD · S/T/N)　　　Ⓕ**ⓄⒶⒷ**

No work makes better sense in the vernacular than Mozart's concluding masterpiece. The composer and, assuredly, Schikaneder would have approved of giving the work in the language of the listeners, and when you have to hand such a witty, well-worded translation as that of Jeremy Sams, it makes even better sense. Sir Charles Mackerras has always been an advocate of opera in English when the circumstances are right.

As ever, he proves himself a loving and perceptive Mozartian. Throughout he wonderfully contrasts the warmth and sensuousness of the music for the good characters with the fire and fury of the baddies, and he persuades the LPO to play with a lightness and promptness that's wholly enchanting, quite the equal of most bands on the other available versions.

In no way is his interpretation here inferior to his German one on Telarc; indeed, in the central roles of Tamino and Pamina the casting for Chandos is an improvement, and Keenlyside is fully the equal of Thomas Allen on the Telarc set. Keenlyside's loveable, slightly sad, very human and perfectly sung Papageno is at the centre of things. Rebecca Evans's voice has taken on a new richness without losing any of its focus or delicacy of utterance. Everything she does has sincerity and poise, although her diction might, with advantage, be clearer.

The recording is fine apart from an over-use of thunder and lightning as sound effects. Anyone wanting the work in English needn't hesitate to acquire this set, the first-ever on CD.

Die Zauberflöte
Ulrike Sonntag sop Pamina **Deon van der Walt** ten Tamino **Cornelius Hauptmann** bass Sarastro **Andrea Frei** sop Queen of Night **Thomas Mohr** bar Papageno **Patricia Rozario** sop Papagena **Sebastian Holecek** bass-bar Speaker **Kevin Connors** ten Monostatos **Elizabeth Whitehouse** sop First Lady **Helene Schneiderman** mez Second Lady **Renée Morloc** mez Third Lady **Ludwigsburg Festival Choir and Orchestra / Wolfgang Gönnenwein** Stage director **Axel Manthey** Video director **Ruth Kärch**
ArtHaus Musik 🄳🅅🄳 100 188 (147' · 4:3 · 2:0 · 0)　Ⓕ**Ⓞ**

This is one of the most wondrous and simple stagings of Mozart's elevated *Singspiel* yet. As its musical attributes are almost as excellent, it's an experience no one with DVD should miss. The action is choreographed in a manner precisely fitting the mood of the moment, serious or comic. Details, such as the dragon, animals responding to Tamino's flute, the arrival of the three Boys, the evocation of fire and water and several others, often invitations to director's *bêtises*, all march here with the thought-through and pleasing-to-look-at concept. How happy that it should be preserved on video, though a pity it's in 4:3 rather than in widescreen format.

Gönnenwein conducts a reading that fits perfectly with what's happening on stage in terms of unaffected, rhythmically firm and keenly articulated playing from his fine orchestra. Deon van der Walt's Tamino is a well-known quantity but he surpasses himself here in strong tone and finely moulded phrasing. He has a fit partner in Ulrike Sonntag's pure-voiced, moving Pamina. Thomas Mohr, though unflatteringly attired, is a nicely unfussy and gently amusing Papageno. Good and

MOZART DIE ZAUBERFLÖTE – IN BRIEF

Ruth Ziesak Pamina **Uwe Heilmann** Tamino
Kurt Moll Sarastro **Vienna State Opera Choir;**
Vienna PO / Sir Georg Solti
Decca ② 433 210-2DH2 (152′ · DDD)   Ⓕ⊙○▷
Crisply brilliant yet warm and well-paced
conducting, with a superlative cast, clear-
voiced and refreshingly youthful – except for
Kurt Moll's appropriately grave Sarastro –
drawn from a stage production, and vividly
recorded. Solti's Mozart at its freshest.

Rosa Mannion Pamina **Hans-Peter Blochwitz** Ⓟ
Tamino **Reinhard Hagen** Sarastro **Les Arts**
Florissants / William Christie
Erato ③ 0630 12705-2 (150′ · DDD)   Ⓜ
The best original-instrument version and
among the best ever, a graceful, well-paced
reading with plenty of magic and a memora-
ble cast including Rosa Mannion's passionate
Pamina, Natalie Dessay's cut-glass Queen
and Willard White the Speaker.

Tiana Lemnitz Pamina **Helge Rosvaenge** Ⓗ
Tamino **Wilhelm Strienz** Sarastro **Favres Solisten**
Vereinigung; Berlin PO / Sir Thomas Beecham
Naxos mono ② 8.110127/8 (130′ · AAD)   Ⓜ⊙○
A pre-war classic in very reasonable sound,
albeit dialogue-free, vibrantly conducted by
Beecham with a memorable cast including
Tiana Lemnitz and the great Gerhard Hüsch
as Papageno.

Gundula Janowitz Pamina **Nicolai Gedda**
Tamino **Gottlob Frick** Sarastro **Philharmonia**
Chorus and Orchestra / Otto Klemperer
EMI ② 567388-2 (134′ · ADD)   Ⓜ▷
Old-fashioned, grave and monumental, omit-
ting dialogue, but enshrines some glorious
singing from Nicolai Gedda, the young
Lucia Popp and Gundula Janowitz, and
Elisabeth Schwarzkopf and Christa Ludwig
among the Ladies.

Rebecca Evans Pamina **Barry Banks** Tamino
John Tomlinson Sarastro **London Philharmonic**
Orchestra / Sir Charles Mackerras
Chandos/Peter Moores Foundation Opera in
English ② CHAN3121 (137′ · DDD)   Ⓜ⊙○▷
A superb English-language version that is not
only beautifully cast (Keenlyside, Garrett and
Tomlinson all ideal), but majesterially con-
ducted by a great Mozartian.

Elizabeth Norberg-Schulz Pamina **Herbert**
Lippert Tamino **Georg Tichy** Papageno **Failoni**
Orchestra, Budapest / Michael Halász
Naxos ② 8 660030/1 (149′ · DDD)   Ⓢ▷
A fine bargain-priced introduction, a satisfyingly theatrical performance with a cast
including rising stars such as Herbert Lippert
and Hellen Kwon, and Halász's lively conducting, very well recorded.

evil, at bottom and top of the range, aren't so happily done. Hauptmann's visually impressive
Sarastro lacks vocal presence and tends to
unsteadiness. Similarly Frei's formidable figure as
Queen of Night produces an edgy, uncontrolled
sound. Ladies and Boys are all admirable.

The video direction is sensitive; the sound, for
the most part clear and well balanced, suffers
from occasional moments of distortion. But that
shouldn't detract from your enjoyment of this
life-enhancing experience.

Modest Mussorgsky
Russian 1839-1881

*Mussorgsky's mother gave him piano lessons, and at
nine he played a Field concerto before an audience in
his parents' house. In 1852 he entered the Guards'
cadet school in St Petersburg. Although he had not
studied harmony or composition, in 1856 he tried to
write an opera the same year he entered the Guards.
In 1857 he met Dargomïzhsky and Cui, and
through them Balakirev and Stasov. He persuaded
Balakirev to give him lessons and composed songs and
piano sonatas.*

*In 1858 Mussorgsky passed through a nervous or
spiritual crisis and resigned his army commission. A
visit to Moscow in 1859 fired his patriotic imagination
and his compositional energies, but although his music
began to enjoy public performances his nervous irrita-
bility was not entirely calmed. The emancipation of the
serfs in March 1861 obliged him to spend most of the
next two years helping manage the family estate; a
symphony came to nothing and Stasov and Balakirev
agreed that 'Mussorgsky is almost an idiot'. But he
continued to compose and in 1863-6 worked on the
libretto and music of an opera, Salammbô, which he
never completed. At this time he served at the Ministry
of Communications and lived in a commune with five
other young men who ardently cultivated and
exchanged advanced ideas about art, religion, philosophy and politics. Mussorgsky's private and public lives
eventually came into conflict. In 1865 he underwent
his first serious bout of dipsomania (probably as a reaction to his mother's death that year) and in 1867 he
was dismissed from his post.*

*He spent summer 1867 at his brother's country
house at Minkino, where he wrote, among other
things, his first important orchestral work, St John's
Night on the Bare Mountain. On his return to St
Petersburg in the autumn Musorgsky, like the other
members of the Balakirev-Stasov circle (ironically
dubbed the 'Mighty Handful'), became interested in
Dargomïzhsky's experiments in operatic naturalism.
Early in 1869 Musorgsky re-entered government
service and, in more settled conditions, was able to
complete the original version of the opera Boris
Godunov. This was rejected by the Mariinsky Theatre and Mussorgsky set about revising it. In 1872 the
opera was again rejected, but excerpts were performed
elsewhere and a vocal score published. The opera committee finally accepted the work and a successful production was given in February 1874.*

*Meanwhile Mussorgsky had begun work on
another historical opera, Khovanshchina, at the same*

time gaining promotion at the ministry. Progress on the new opera was interrupted partly because of unsettled domestic circumstances, but mainly because heavy drinking which left him incapable of sustained creative effort. But several other compositions belong to this period, including the song cycles Sunless and Songs and Dances of Death and the Pictures at an Exhibition, for piano, a brilliant and bold series inspired by a memorial exhibition of drawings by his friend Victor Hartmann. Ideas for a comic opera based on Gogol's Sorochintsy Fair also began to compete with work on Khovanshchina; both operas remained unfinished at Musorgsky's death. During the earlier part of 1878 he seems to have led a more respectable life and his director at the ministry even allowed him leave for a three-month concert tour with the contralto Darya Leonova. After he was obliged to leave the government service in January 1880, Leonova helped provide him with employment and a home. It was to her that he turned on February 23, 1881 in a state of nervous excitement, saying that there was nothing left for him but to beg in the streets; he was suffering from alcoholic epilepsy. He was removed to hospital, where he died a month later.

Many of Mussorgsky's works were unfinished, and their editing and posthumous publication were mainly carried out by Rimsky-Korsakov, who to a greater or lesser degree 'corrected' what Mussorgsky had composed. It was only many years later that, with a return to the composer's original drafts, the true nature of his rough art could be properly understood.
GROVEmusic

Pictures at an Exhibition (orch Ravel)

Mussorgsky (orch Ravel) Pictures at an Exhibition
Tchaikovsky Symphony No 4
Orchestre National du Capitole de Toulouse / Tugan Sokhiev
Naïve V5068 (76' · DDD)　　　　Ⓕ**OO**

Every so often a disc comes along that really makes you sit up. This is such a disc. Tugan Sokhiev is back in his element dispensing star quality with almost every bar of this coupling. If the ability to create atmosphere, to transport, to excite, to provoke reassessment of a piece, are the first signs of greatness then Sokhiev's beautifully heard and richly imagined account of Mussorgsky's *Pictures* is very much the promise of things to come. It is the case throughout that the subtlety, the piquancy, the Frenchness of Ravel's colourations appear disarmingly pristine – as in 'why have I never noticed that before?' One quibble amid everything that is so well judged (and so well played) is the increasing of tempo as 'The Great Gate of Kiev' is finally flung wide. Why?

No quibbles at all about the Tchaikovsky, though. Seriously, this is one of the most impressive accounts since the days of Markevitch and Mravinsky. Sokhiev makes real musical and emotional sense of the notoriously hazardous first movement. The listless, febrile nature of it reaches great heights in the development and coda where the hair-raising *tremolando* restatement of the first subject achieves real catharsis. Indeed, Sokhiev's songful Toulouse

woodwinds – so poetic in the *Andantino* – cannot for long disguise an air of desperation. The whizz-bang finale delivers that in spades.

Pictures at an Exhibition[a] (orch Ravel).
Night on the Bare Mountain (arr Rimsky-Korsakov).
Khovanshchina – Prelude (orch Shostakovich).
Sorochintsï Fair – Gopak (orch Liadov)
Vienna Philharmonic Orchestra / Valery Gergiev
Philips 468 526-2PH (52' · DDD) [a]Recorded live 2000
Ⓟ**O**▸

This is a larger-than-life reading of *Pictures*, which underplays the subtleties of colouring introduced by Ravel in favour of more earthly Russian flavours. The coupling is an all-Mussorgsky one, surprisingly rare in the many versions of this work.

This live account brings some superb playing, with fast, brilliant movements dazzlingly well played, and with the speed bringing an edge-of-seat feeling from perils just avoided, something not usually conveyed in a studio performance. The opening 'Promenade', taken squarely, establishes the monumental Russian quality, enhanced by the immediacy of the sound. Even the 'Hut on Fowl's Legs' seems larger than life, and the performance culminates in an account of the 'Great Gate of Kiev' shattering in its weight and thrust.

That and the all-Mussorgsky coupling establish a clear place for this new issue in an over-stocked market, even though the coupling isn't generous. The regular Rimsky version of *Night on the Bare Mountain*, though not recorded live, brings a performance to compare in power with *Pictures*, with very weighty brass, while Shostakovich's orchestration of the *Khovanshchina* Prelude, though less evocative than it can be, is warm and refined, with the Gopak added as a lively encore.

Pictures at an Exhibition (orch Ravel). A Night on the Bare Mountain – 2 versions: orch Mussorgsky; orch Rimsky-Korsakov. The Fair at Sorochintsï – Gopak. Khovanshchina – The departure of Prince Golitsïn
Ukraine National Symphony Orchestra / Theodore Kuchar
Naxos 8 555924 (63' · DDD)　　　　Ⓢ**▸**

Ravel's orchestration of *Pictures at an Exhibition* was commissioned by Koussevitzky as a showpiece for his superb Boston orchestra, and it proves just as impressive here to demonstrate the excellence of the National Symphony Orchestra of the Ukraine. The colour palette of the woodwind is a joy, as we discover in both 'Tuileries' and the deliciously cheeping 'Unhatched Chickens'; and how beautifully the solo saxophone sings his sad serenade outside 'The Old Castle'. In representing the bold profile of 'Samuel Goldenberg', the massed lower strings show their splendid body of tone, and the punch of the brass entry in 'Catacombae' has the richest underlying resonance in a performance full of eerie menace. The percussion come fully into their own in 'The Hut on Fowl's Legs', where the bass drummer adds dramatic weight and point. The 'Great Gate of Kiev' is given with the full, rich orchestral sonority now thrillingly expansive, and Kuchar broadening the final statement of the great chorale to give the listener a tingling *frisson* of satisfaction.

It was an original and fascinating idea to record both the original Mussorgsky score of *Night on the Bare Mountain* alongside the Rimsky arrangement, for in many ways they're entirely different works, something Theodore Kuchar underlines by his contrasting interpretations. It may be unfashionable to say so, but however inspired and original Mussorgsky's draft score is in conception, the all-but-recomposed Rimsky-Korsakov piece is the finer work overall. With a superbly rasping opening from the heavy brass, and thrusting forward momentum, Kuchar readily captures its intitial and recurring malignant force, deftly amalgamating the jollity of Rimsky's interpolated brass fanfares, then producing a magically peaceful close, with radiant playing from the Russian woodwind.

To sum up, this is a quite remarkable CD on all counts – outstandingly fine orchestral playing, vividly exciting and very Russian musicmaking, and a very tangible sound picture, consistently in the demonstration bracket.

Pictures at an Exhibition (orch Ravel). A Night on the Bare Mountain (arr Rimsky-Korsakov). Khovanshchina – Prelude, Act 1, 'Dawn over the Moscow River'
Atlanta Symphony Orchestra / Yoel Levi
Telarc CD80296 (50' · DDD) Recorded 1991   Ⓕ

When this was released, Telarc established a position for it as sonically the most spectacular set of *Pictures* among the many in the current catalogue. And it's a very fine performance too. The programme opens with *A Night on the Bare Mountain* – the brass sound is special, with great richness and natural bite with no exaggeration. The performance overall is both well paced and exciting. Perhaps Levi's evil spirits aren't as satanic as some, but they make an impact and the contrasting melancholy of the closing section is very touching, with the tolling bell nicely balanced and the clarinet solo poignantly taking over from the gently elegiac strings.

The characterisation of *Pictures at an Exhibition* is no less successful, although it's an essentially mellower view than, for example, Sinopoli's highly praised DG version with the New York Philharmonic Orchestra. Levi's is a performance where the conductor makes the most of the colour, and brilliant orchestral effects of Ravel's inspired score, revealing much that often goes unheard – the grotesquerie of 'Gnomus' isn't accentuated, but one greatly enjoys the attack of the lower strings which are very tangible indeed; a doleful bassoon introduces 'The Old Castle' and the saxophone solo has a satin-like finish on the timbre to produce an elegant melancholy; the woodwind in 'Tuileries' is gentle in its virtuosity. Levi holds back a little for the delicate

string entry and the whole piece has a captivating lightness of touch. The final climax is unerringly built and at the very close the brass and strings produce an electrifying richness and weight of sound, to bring a *frisson* of excitement, with the tam-tam resounding clearly. Then there's silence, and out of it steals the exquisite opening of the *Khovanschchina* Prelude, with its poetic evocation of dawn over the Kremlin. Levi goes for atmosphere above all else and doesn't make too much of the climax, but the coda with its fragile woodwind halos is most delicately managed. This disc is a first choice if state-of-the-art recording is your prime consideration.

Pictures at an Exhibition (orch Stokowski)

Mussorgsky Pictures at an Exhibition (orch Stokowski). A Night on the Bare Mountain. Boris Godunov – Symphonic Synthesis (arr/orch Stokowski) Khovanshchina - Entr'acte (Act IV) **Stokowski** Traditional Slavic Christmas Music. **Tchaikovsky** 2 Morceaux, Op 10 – Humoresque. Six Songs, Op 73 – No 6, Again, as before, alone
Bournemouth Symphony Orchestra / José Serebrier
Naxos 8 557645 (77 minutes : DDD)   ⓈⓄ▷

Stokowski's orchestrations, as flamboyant and full of flair as his interpretations as a conductor, have increasingly been accepted and welcomed on disc, a good sign that rigidly purist attitudes have nowadays softened. This Naxos collection of Stokowski's arrangements offers outstanding performances by the Bournemouth Symphony Orchestra, brilliantly recorded.

Few would claim that Stokowski's arrangement of *Pictures at an Exhibition* matches, let alone outshines, that of Ravel. But with its weighty brass it is certainly more Russian. In fact – one of the most serious shortcomings – Stokowski omits two of the movements, 'Tuileries' and the 'Market Place at Limoges' on the grounds that they are too French. Yet Serebrier's new performance makes it very convincing with speeds well chosen and the brass wonderfully incisive.

The atmospheric qualities of the *Boris Godunov* Symphonic Synthesis come over superbly too, starting with a hauntingly rarefied bassoon solo, even if the recording catches the clicking of the keys. The mystery of the chimes in the Coronation scene as well as the Death scene are more evocatively handled. If *A Night on the Bare Mountain* finds the Naxos recording rather less immediate than in the other items, the weight of the arrangement comes over well, and the *Khovanshchina* Entr'acte has impressive weight and clarity.

The extra items also weigh in Serebrier's favour: an arrangement of a Tchaikovsky song that explores an astonishingly wide emotional range within a tiny span and the jolly *Humoresque*, a piano piece that Stravinsky memorably used in his ballet *The Fairy's Kiss*. Finally, a baldly effective piece, attributed to Stokowski himself, based not just on a Christmas hymn but on Ippolitov-Ivanov's *In a Manger*.

Pictures at an Exhibition (piano)

Mussorgsky Pictures at an Exhibition **Balakirev**
Islamey **Ravel** Gaspard de la nuit
Freddy Kempf pf
BIS ⊚ BIS-SACD1580 (65' · DDD)   Ⓕ

After a perhaps necessary break Freddy Kempf
returns to the studio armed with a formidable
programme formidably played. In the Mussorgsky his immense energy and facility allows him
an unusual degree of freedom with a brisk opening Promenade followed by an unleashing of his
virtuoso credentials in 'Gnomus'. He takes a
uniformly forte view of 'Bydlo' (though his final
fading of the vision is masterly). And so, too, is
his enviable verve in both 'Ballet of the
Unhatched Chicks' and 'Limoges'. 'Baba Yaga'
is boldly characterised, and there is a dramatic
splash of colour, a sudden pedal haze at 1'12" in
'The Great Gate of Kiev'.

In Ravel's *Gaspard* every teeming complexity is
resolved with the coolest of mind and hands.
You may query a lack of rhetoric or broadening
at the climax of 'Ondine' (it is marked *un peu plus
lent*) and a less than fully sympathetic way with
the many *piano* and *pianissimo* markings in
'Scarbo'. Yet this is among the finer recordings
of this much-recorded masterpiece. In Balakirev's *Islamey* Kempf relishes everything the
composer throws at him. This is 'live' virtuosity
with a vengeance, with absolutely no hint of a
safety net, of playing within studio confines.

A superb, brilliant-toned Steinway has been
captured in admirable sound, and this recital is
among the finest of Freddy Kempf's offerings to
date.

Boris Godunov

Boris Godunov (first version)
Nikolai Putilin bar Boris Godunov **Viktor Lutsiuk** ten
Grigory **Nikolai Okhotnikov** bass Pimen
Fyodor Kuznetsov bass Varlaam **Konstantin
Pluzhnikov** ten Shuisky **Nikolai Gassiev** ten Missail
Zlata Bulycheva mez Fyodor **Olga Trifonova** sop
Xenia **Yevgenia Gorokhovskaya** mez Nurse **Liubov
Sokolova** mez Hostess **Evgeny Akimov** ten
Simpleton **Vassily Gerello** bar Shchelkalov **Grigory
Karassev** bass Nikitich **Evgeny Nikitin** bass Mityukha
Yuri Schikalov ten Krushchov

Boris Godunov (second version)
Vladimir Vaneyev bass Boris Godunov **Vladimir
Galusin** ten Grigory **Olga Borodina** mez Marina
Nikolai Okhotnikov bass Pimen **Fyodor Kuznetsov**
bass Varlaam **Konstantin Pluzhnikov** ten Shuisky
Nikolai Gassiev ten Missail **Evgeny Nikitin** bass
Rangoni, Mityukha **Zlata Bulycheva** mez Fyodor
Olga Trifonova sop Xenia **Yevgenia Gorokhovskaya**
mez Nurse **Liubov Sokolova** mez Hostess **Evgeny
Akimov** ten Simpleton **Vassily Gerello** bar
Shchelkalov **Grigory Karassev** bass Nikitich **Yuri
Schikalov** ten Krushchov **Andrei Karabanov** bar
Lavitsky **Yuri Laptev** ten Chernikovsky **Chorus and**

Orchestra of the Kirov Opera / Valery Gergiev
Philips ⑤ 462 230-2PH5 (306' · DDD · T/t)   ⓂⓄⓄ↦

What we have here is, literally, two operas for
the price of one. That's to say, the two discs
containing Mussorgsky's first *Boris Godunov* and
the three containing his second are available at
five discs for the normal cost of three. And, in a
real sense, what we're dealing with is two operas.
First, a brief resumé of the facts. In 1868-9
Mussorgsky composed seven scenes: outside the
Novedevichy Monastery, Coronation outside
the Kremlin, Pimen's Cell, the Inn, the Tsar's
rooms in the Kremlin, outside St Basil's Cathedral, Boris's Death in the Kremlin. When these
were rejected by the Imperial Theatres in 1872,
he made various revisions. To meet objections
about the lack of female roles, Mussorgsky
added the two scenes with the Polish princess
Marina Mniszek; he also substituted the final
Kromy Forest scene for the St Basil's scene. He
made a large number of adjustments, some of a
minor nature, some rather more significant
(such as dropping Pimen's narration of the murder of the young Tsarevich), and one huge, the
complete rewriting of the original fifth scene, in
the Kremlin, sometimes known as the Terem
scene. This was the work that he resubmitted,
and which was first performed in St Petersburg
in 1874. Rimsky-Korsakov's famous version
(which does much more than reorchestrate) was
first heard in 1896, and for many years superseded its predecessors.

However, it has increasingly been recognised
that *Boris* II isn't a revision of *Boris* I but a different
work, both as regards the view of the central character and his place in the historical narrative, and
also as regards the rethought musical technique
and sometimes change of idiom which this has
brought about. Therefore the present set makes a
real contribution to our understanding and enjoyment of Russia's greatest opera. It follows that
there have to be two singers of the central role.
Putilin (*Boris* I) is in general more capacious in
tone, more brooding and lofty, in the Terem
scene more embittered and harsh, willing to act
with the voice. Vaneyev is a decidedly more
immediate and human Boris, tender with his son
Fyodor (a touching, engaging performance from
Zlata Bulycheva) both in the Terem and at the
end, not always as dominating as this Tsar should
be but sympathetic, allowing his voice to blanch as
death approaches, and especially responsive to the
melodic essence of Mussorgsky's speech-deliv-
ered lines. This enables him to be rather freer with
the actual note values. It doesn't necessarily matter that much: Mussorgsky changed his mind over
various details, and the important thing is to use
his notes to create character rather than be too
literal with what the different versions propose.
Pimen, strongly sung with a hint of the youthful
passions that he claims to have abjured, is sung by
Nikolai Okhotnikov more or less identically in
both performances.

The only character, apart from Boris, to be
accorded two singers is Grigory, the False
Dmitri. Viktor Lutsiuk (*Boris* I) is strenuous,

MUSSORGSKY/RAVEL PICTURES AT AN EXHIBITION – IN BRIEF

Chicago SO / Fritz Reiner
RCA 09026 61958 2 (71' · ADD)   Ⓜ◐➔
An all-time classic from Reiner's legendary days at the helm of the Chicago Symphony. Bold characterisation and orchestral playing of tremendous conviction. The astonishingly vivid stereo dates from 1957.

Boston SO / Serge Koussevitzky
RCA mono 09026 61392 2 (75' · ADD)   Ⓜ
It was Koussevitzky who commissioned and premiered Ravel's orchestration in 1922. This electrifying first recording from eight years later shows off the phenomenal articulation and tonal breadth of his fabulous Boston orchestra.

Cleveland Orchestra / George Szell
Sony SBK48162 (74' · ADD)   Ⓑ◐◐
Dazzling stuff from Szell and his immaculate Clevelanders. This partnership's irresistibly swaggering suites from Kodály's *Hary János* and Prokofiev's *Lieutenant Kijé* make up an unbeatable bargain triptych.

Berlin PO / Claudio Abbado
DG 445 238-2GH (65' · DDD)   Ⓕ◐➔
Abbado has long been a doughty Mussorgsky conductor. These live *Pictures* from 1993 are studded with newly minted detail, outstandingly well played by the Berliners.

Atlanta SO / Yoel Levi
Telarc CD80296 (50' · DDD)   Ⓕ
Levi's is a thoughtful interpretation, but by no means lacking in sheer personality or heady excitement. The Telarc engineering astonishes in its sheer weight of sonority and X-ray-like transparency.

Oslo Philharmonic / Mariss Jansons
EMI Encore 350824-2 (127' · ADD)   Ⓢ◐
Sitting alongside Rimsky-Korsakov favourites, Jansons's *Pictures* are typically full of colour and imagination. And the fine Oslo orchestra plays with tremendous flair.

National SO of Ukraine / Theodore Kuchar
Naxos 8 555924 (63' · DDD)   Ⓢ➔
Kuchar conducts with palpable relish and secures an enthusiastic response from his hard-working band. A super bargain all round from Naxos.

Vienna PO / Valery Gergiev
Philips 468 526-2PH (52' ·DDD)   Ⓕ◐➔
Assembled from a series of live concerts in Vienna's Musikverein during April 2000. Gergiev takes the listener on an illuminating journey, culminating in a simply majestic evocation of 'The Great Gate of Kiev'.

obsessed, vital; Vladimir Galusin (*Boris* II) can sound more frenzied, and has the opportunity with the addition of the Polish acts to give a convincing portrayal of a weak man assuming strength but being undermined by the wiles of a determined woman. Here, she's none other than Olga Borodina, moodily toying with her polonaise rhythms and then in full sensuous call. Yevgenia Gorokhovskaya is a jolly old Nurse in the *Boris* II Terem scene. The rest of the cast do not really change their interpretations from one *Boris* to another, and indeed scarcely need to do so: it isn't really upon that which the differences depend. Liubov Sokolova sings a fruity Hostess, welcoming in Fyodor Kuznetsov a Varlaam who can really sing his Kazan song rather than merely bawling it. Konstantin Pluzhnikov makes Shuisky move from the rather sinister force confronting Boris in the Terem to a more oily complacency in the Death scene: many Shuiskys make less of the part. Evgeny Nikitin is a creepy, fanatical Rangoni, Vassily Gerello a Shchelkalov of hypocritical elegance, Evgeny Akimov a sad-toned Simpleton. Gergiev directs strong, incisive performances, accompanying sympathetically and controlling the marvellous crowd scenes well.

However, it's a pity that he allows fierce whistles to drown the speeding violins opening the Kromy Forest scene (the music can be heard only when it returns), and he hasn't been given sufficient clarity of recording with the chorus. The words are often obscure, even with the boyars in the Death scene, and far too much is lost in the crowd exchanges. This is regrettable for a work that, in either incarnation, draws so much on realistic detail of articulation. Nevertheless, these five discs form a fascinating set, one no admirer of this extraordinary creative achievement can afford to ignore.

Boris Godunov (1874 version)
Anatoly Kotcherga *bass* Boris **Sergei Larin** *ten* Grigory **Marjana Lipovšek** *mez* Marina **Samuel Ramey** *bass* Pimen **Gleb Nikolsky** *bass* Varlaam **Philip Langridge** *ten* Shuisky **Helmut Wildhaber** *ten* Missail **Sergei Leiferkus** *bar* Rangoni **Liliana Nichiteanu** *mez* Feodor **Valentina Valente** *sop* Xenia **Yevgenia Gorokhovskaya** *mez* Nurse **Eléna Zaremba** *mez* Hostess **Alexander Fedin** *ten* Simpleton **Albert Shagidullin** *bar* Shchelkolov **Wojciech Drabowicz** *ten* Mitukha, Krushchov **Slovak Philharmonic Chorus; Berlin Radio Chorus; Tölz Boys' Choir; Berlin Philharmonic Orchestra / Claudio Abbado**
Sony Classical ③ 07464 58977-2 (200' · DDD · T/t)   Ⓕ◐

Few conductors have been more diligent than Claudio Abbado in seeking the truth about this vast canvas. He chooses the definitive 1872-4 version, adding scenes, including the complete one in Pimen's cell and the St Basil's scene from 1869. His is a taut, tense reading – grand, virtuosic, at times hard-driven, favouring extremes of speed and dynamics. The orchestra is very much in the foreground, sounding more emphatic than would ever be the case in the opera house.

Kotcherga has a superb voice, firmly produced throughout an extensive register. His is a Boris avoiding conventional melodrama and concerned to show the loving father.

The ambitious lovers are well represented. Indeed, Larin is quite the best Grigory yet recorded on disc, sounding at once youthful, heroic and ardent, and quite free of any tenor mannerisms. Lipovšek characterises Marina forcefully: we're well aware of the scheming Princess's powers of wheeler-dealing and erotic persuasion. The recording is of demonstration standard: it's most potent in the way that it captures the incisive and pointed singing of the combined choruses in their various guises. Here all is vividly brought before us by conductor and producer in the wide panorama predicated by Mussorgsky's all-enveloping vision.

Boris Godunov (complete version, 1872)
Robert Lloyd bass Boris Godunov **Alexei Steblianko** ten Grigory **Olga Borodina** mez Marina **Alexander Morosov** bass Pimen **Vladimir Ognovenko** bass Varlaam **Yevgeny Boitsov** ten Shuisky **Igor Yan** ten Missail **Sergei Leiferkus** bass Rangoni **Larissa Dyadkova** mez Feodor **Olga Kondina** sop Xenia **Yevgenia Perlassova** mez Nurse **Ludmila Filatova** mez Hostess **Vladimir Solodovnikov** ten Simpleton **Mikhail Kit** bar Shchelkalov **Yevgeny Fedotov** bass Nikitich **Grigory Karasyov** bass Mityukha **Kirov Opera Chorus and Orchestra / Valery Gergiev** Stage directors **Andrei Tarkovsky, Stephen Lawless** Video director **Humphrey Burton** Philips DVD 075 089-9PH2 (221' · NTSC · 4:3 · 2.0, DTS 5.1 · 0) Recorded live at the Mariinsky Theatre, St Petersburg 1990   Ⓕ

Film director Andrei Tarkovsky, famous for science-fiction classics *Solaris* and *Stalker* and the historical epic *Andrei Rublev*, was a master of symbolic effect – the gigantic pendulum, the grotesquely faceless Idiot, living statuary, the angelic murdered child amid falling snow. But against such stylisation the action, vividly captured by video director Humphrey Burton, comes correspondingly alive, no stiff Bolshoi pageant; chorus and soloists act their hearts out.

Borodina is an ideal Marina, beautiful and burnished of tone but chillingly self-absorbed; perhaps rightly, she strikes more sparks with Leiferkus's vampiric, honey-toned Rangoni than with Steblianko's stolid but lyrical Pretender. Ognovenko's Varlaam is somewhat young and baritonal, but foreshadows stardom, as does Dyadkova's superbly touching, plangent Feodor. Boitsov's Shuisky, Morosov's noble Pimen and Solodovnikov's Idiot are less outstanding but still excellent. The only outsider is at the centre. Robert Lloyd's Boris first appears (reflecting contemporary portraits) moustached but beardless; the customary hedge appears in later acts, neatly marking the passing years. His finely shaded *basso cantante* has been criticised for being too light, but such doubts fade before his idiomatic-sounding Russian and magnificent characterisation, culminating in a truly harrowing death scene.

MUSSORGSKY BORIS GODUNOV – IN BRIEF

Vladimir Vaneyev Boris **Vladimir Galusin** Grigory **Olga Borodina** Marina **Nikolai Okhotnikov** Pimen **Kirov Opera / Valery Gergiev** Philips 462 230-2PH5   ⓂⓄⒹ⟩
This is a mandatory purchase for *Boris* fans: a five-CD set which contains both the original 1869 version and the 1872 revision complete with its Polish scene. Gergiev's sympathy for this music is total, and he draws staggering performances from his excellent Kirov musicians.

Anatoly Kotcherga Boris **Sergei Larin** Grigory **Marjana Lipovžek** Marina **Samuel Ramey** Pimen **Berlin PO / Claudio Abbado** Sony Classical 07464 58977-2   ⓂⓄ
A spectacular recording of the 1872-4 version (with some extra scenes). Anatoly Kotcherga is superb in the title-role, and the remainder of the cast is on splendid form. The ambience of the Berlin Philharmonie adds to the recording's magnificence.

Robert Lloyd Boris **Alexei Steblianko** Grigory **Olga Borodina** Marina **Igor Morosov** Pimen **Kirov Opera / Valery Gergiev** Philips DVD 075 089-9PH2   ⓂⓄ
The superb 1990 Andrei Tarkovsky production seen here in an adaptation for the Kirov Opera comes up splendidly on DVD. Robert Lloyd is masterly in the title-role, and the remainder of the cast has been assembled from strength. Gergiev's direction is first-rate.

Evgeni Nesterenko Boris **Vladimir Atlantov** Grigory **Elena Obratsova** Marina **Alexander Ognivtsiev** Pimen **Kirov Opera / Mark Ermler** Regis RRC3006   Ⓢ
With the excellent Evgeni Nesterenko in the title-role, this 1982 Bolshoi recording under the ever-dependable Mark Ermler makes a fantastic bargain. Obtratsova and Atlantov offer strong support.

Boris Christoff Boris, Pimen, Varlaam **Dimitr Ouzounov** Grigory **Evelyn Lear** Marina **Paris Conservatoire Orchestra / André Clutyens** EMI mono 567881-2   ⓂⓄ
This 1962 recording enshrines Boris Christoff's *tour de force* in the three central roles (Boris, Pimen and Varlaam) – a feat he'd done 10 years earlier before on disc for Dobrowen. Cluytens is an idiomatic conductor with a good feel for the scale of this extraordinary work.

Gergiev's reading is less brilliant than his dual recording, often rather soft-centred; but he still brings out the sheer anguished beauty of the score. The excellent stereo soundtrack has also been remastered into DTS surround-sound, and very airy and ambient this sounds, from the opening wave of applause sweeping across the auditorium.

Additional recommendation

Nesterenko Boris **Atlantov** Grigory **Obraztsova**
Marina **Ognivtsiev** Pimen **Eizen** Varlaam **Lissovski**
Shuisky **Baskov** Missail **Mazurok** Rangoni **Bolshoi**
Theatre Chorus and Orchestra / Mark Ermler
Regis ③ RRC3006 (190' · ADD · S/N) Recorded 1982
ⓢ

A performance in the old Bolshoi style using the
Rimsky-Korsakov edition. At its super-budget
price, this magnificent 1982 set is an easy recommendation.

Khovanshchina

Khovanshchina
Aage Haugland bass Ivan Khovansky **Vladimir**
Atlantov ten Andrey Khovansky **Vladimir Popov** ten
Golitsin **Anatolij Kotscherga** bar Shaklovity **Paata**
Burchuladze bass Dosifey **Marjana Lipovšek** contr
Marfa **Brigitte Poschner-Klebel** sop Susanna **Heinz**
Zednik ten Scribe **Joanna Borowska** sop Emma
Wilfried Gahmlich ten Kouzka **Vienna Boys' Choir;**
Slovak Philharmonic Choir; Vienna State Opera
Chorus and Orchestra / Claudio Abbado
DG ③ 429 758-2GH3 (171' · DDD · T/t)
Recorded live 1989
ⒻⓄⓄ▷

The booklet-essay suggests that Mussorgsky's
music constantly poses a question to his Russian
compatriots: 'What are the causes of our country's continuing calamities, and why does the
state crush all that is good?'. Anyone who follows
today's news from Russia and then experiences
this opera will understand what's meant, and
while we observe with sympathy we seem no
nearer than the citizens of that great, tormented
country to finding solutions for its endemic problems. However, Mussorgsky was not the least of
those Russian musicians who found lasting
beauty in her history and he expressed it in a powerfully dramatic idiom that drew on folk-music
and had both epic qualities and deep humanity as
well as an occasional gentleness. There's also an
element here of Russian church music, since
Khovanshchina has a political and religious theme
and is set in the 1680s at the time of Peter the
Great's accession. Since the work was unfinished
when Mussorgsky died, performances always
involve conjectural work, and the version here –
which works convincingly – is mostly that of
Shostakovich with the choral ending that Stravinsky devised using Mussorgsky's music.

The cast in this live recording isn't one of star
opera singers, but they're fully immersed in the
drama and the music, as is the chorus and the
orchestra under Abbado, and the result is deeply
atmospheric.

Nikolay Myaskovsky
Russian 1881-1950

Myaskovsky studied for a military career but entered
the St Petersburg Conservatory (1906-11), where

his teachers included Lyadov and Rimsky-Korsakov.
He served in the war, and from 1921 taught at the
Moscow Conservatory. He was not an innovator but
was an influential, individual figure working within
the Russian tradition. His large output is dominated
by the cycle of 27 symphonies (1908-50), highly
regarded in and outside Russia in his lifetime. He also
wrote 13 string quartets (1913-49), choral and
chamber music.

Violin Concerto in D minor, Op 44

Myaskovsky Violin Concerto
Tchaikovsky Violin Concerto in D, Op 35
Vadim Repin vn
Kirov Orchestra / Valery Gergiev
Philips 473 343-2PH (72' · DDD)
ⒻⓄⓄⓄ▷

It's the Myaskovsky that really makes
this disc a 'must-have'. His Violin Concerto was premiered by David Oistrakh
in Leningrad in 1939. As with Tchaikovsky's
Concerto, the opening *tutti* plays for less than a
minute and the slow movement is touchingly
lyrical. The rather melancholy first movement is
built on a grand scale and includes an expansive
cadenza where Repin's mastery is virtually the
equal of Oistrakh's. It's forceful music, epic in
scale and earnestly argued, the sort of piece that
Gergiev thrives on.

Listening to Repin's Tchaikovsky Concerto
(his second recording of the work) confirms
just how far he's journeyed in a few years.
Tone projection is stronger, attack more
aggressive and his solo demeanour seems better focused than before, far more confident
and spontaneous. Mixed in with these improvements are one or two affectations, but it's a
cracking performance, one of the best from the
younger generation. The recording sounds
like a digital update of the sort of blowsy in-
your-face sonics typical of the first stereo
recordings of the late 1950s. Nevertheless, a
fabulous disc.

Symphonies

Symphonies – No 17, Op 41; No 21, Op 51.
Salutatory Overture, Op 48
Russian Federation Academic Symphony
Orchestra / Evgeni Svetlanov
Alto ALC1023 (77' · DDD)
ⓢ

Complete Symphonies. Orchestral Works
USSR State Symphony Orchestra; Russian
Federation Academic Symphony Orchestra /
Evgeni Svetlanov
Warner Classics ⑯ 2564 69689-8 (20h 38' · DDD)
ⓈⓄⓄⓄ

Though presumably similarly sourced,
the transfers on these two issues are not
always identical in matters of balance
and equalisation. The main drawback of the
Warner set is the skimpiness of its annotations.

Alto remains committed to giving us the contextual material such unfamiliar scores can scarcely do without. Its makeweight here is a case in point. A seemingly innocuous overture, it turns out to have been the composer's contribution to Stalin's 60th birthday celebrations in 1939. In which case its avoidance of vulgarity may even be considered quietly heroic.

Of the two symphonies in the Alto instalment, the 17th (1936-37) is indubitably a large statement. Composed at the height of the Great Terror, its idiom seems a little more extroverted than usual, Rachmaninov crossed with Khachaturian perhaps. The epic slow movement will be a must for listeners with a sweet tooth even if things could, with advantage, move on a little faster! Liadov meets Korngold in the Trio of the third. You may well have come across this performance in an earlier Melodiya incarnation.

The 21st (1940) was long Myaskovsky's calling-card. It was commissioned by the Chicago SO and there are vintage recordings originating from both sides of the Iron Curtain. None is as long-breathed as this one. Perhaps one can forgive the blaring confusion of Svetlanov's climaxes for the nobility of his take on the elevated, Roy Harris-style opening section. The score's most memorable idea, referencing Rimsky's *Antar* Symphony, has that authentic Myaskovsky lyricism in spades and of course Svetlanov milks it for all it's worth. Glorious heartfelt stuff although those brought up on more tautly controlled readings may cry self-indulgence. As usual the playing ranges from the inspired to the sketchy, the results compellingly 'noble' even where manifestly flawed.

For anyone coming fresh to the composer and his world, the Warner set provides an extraordinarily economical, if potentially mystifying, entrée.

Conlon Nancarrow   Mexican 1912-1997

Nancarrow was born in the United States, and studied with Slonimsky, Piston and Sessions in Boston (1933-6), but lived in Mexico from 1940. From the late 1940s he composed exclusively for player piano. His studies exploit the instrument's potential for rhythmic complexity and textural variety, creating showpieces of virtuosity far beyond a human performer's capabilities, with arpeggios, trills, glissandos, leaps, widely spaced chords and complex counterpoint. He was concerned with tempo, especially the 'temporal dissonance' of several rates occurring simultaneously, and with formal structure. His music first received serious attention only in the 1970s.

GROVEmusic

Instrumental works

Studies and Solos
Studies for Player Piano[a] – Nos 3b[h], 3c[e], 3[d], 4[f], 6[f], 9[d], 14[d], 15[g], 18[f], 19[d], 26[d]. Prelude[a]. Sonatina[ag]. Three Canons for Ursula[b]. Blues[b]. Three Two-Part Studies[c]. Tango?[c]

(trans [d]Helena Bugallo; [e]Bugallo-Williams; [f]Erik Ona; [g]Yvar Mikhashoff; [h]Amy Williams)
[a]**Bugallo-Williams Piano Duo** ([b]Helena Bugallo, [c]Amy Williams pfs)
Wergo WER6670-2 (63' · DDD)   Ⓕ

Conlon Nancarrow moved from the US to Mexico City in 1940 largely because of his communist affiliations. He spent the rest of his life there in almost total isolation, composing for player-pianos because he knew performers would never cope with his complex rhythms. Times have changed, and pianists and ensembles have been taking up the challenge by using transcriptions of some of his studies. Those used here are by composers Yvar Mikhashoff and Erik Ona and the Bugallo-Williams duo themselves. The results are simply stunning.

Nancarrow's experience as a jazz trumpeter and knowledge of *The Rite of Spring* were catalysts for a distinctive contrapuntal idiom, in which separate voices are superimposed at different speeds leading to acoustic overcrowding and apparent chaos. But it's all finely controlled: several pieces stop dead on a unison or a major chord.

By the late 1970s Nancarrow was beginning to be rediscovered and, in a more appreciative context, wrote for live performers again, including *Tango?* and *Three Canons for Ursula* (Oppens). The studies work just as well with live pianists as with the twangy sound of Nancarrow's own player-pianos. Obviously some of the very fast studies will never be playable, but, since he allowed some transcription, there's no harm when performers of this calibre can rise to the occasion so brilliantly. This wonderfully affirmative music not only questions conventional notions about rhythm but provides a uniquely exhilarating experience for the listener – well recorded and really attractive in every way.

Studies for Player Piano, Vol 2
Dabringhaus und Grimm MDG645 1403-2
(68' · DDD)   Ⓕ

Why release yet another set of Nancarrow studies, given that these mechanical masterpieces merely replicate themselves every time a roll is activated inside the player piano? First, the well-known Wergo recording made in Nancarrow's Mexico City home in 1988 was flawed in certain respects. Of the two pianos equipped to play these studies, Nancarrow's preferred instrument – possessing a softer, warmer tone – was in need of reconditioning. It was decided to record the whole set on a piano normally reserved for more dense rhythmic studies. Its tinny honky-tonk timbre thus created a skewed impression of Nancarrow's studies. They sounded even more strange and eccentric than intended.

Second, after the Wergo release other player piano pieces have come to light, including *For Yoko* and the Study No 51 (aka *#3750*). Jürgen

Hocker's new recording for MDG therefore plugs some gaps and restores the studies to their original state. And what a difference it makes to hear these works afresh, but also in sequential (though not necessarily chronological) order. Like a well-oiled machine, the Bösendorfer grand plays out Nancarrow's highly inventive studies with surprising ease and dexterity, almost as if it had been designed to do nothing else.

This second volume in a projected five-part series, consisting of Nos 13-32, contains arguably some of Nancarrow's best music. The first seven or so studies explore a number of related canonic conundrums and proportional puzzles, playfully resolving onto a tonic chord or octave unison with Escher-like logic. Study No 20 sees Nancarrow relax mathematical processes for a more controlled improvisatory approach, but No 21 – the famous Canon X – is surely one of the disc's highlights. An extraordinary example of controlled chaos, two parts are made to pound out obsessively the same cyclical 54-note row while simultaneously speeding up and slowing down, their rhythmic trajectories momentarily coinciding.

José de Nebra   Spanish 1702-1768

José de Nebra was principal organist of the Spanish royal chapel and the Descalzas Reales convent at Madrid from 1724; in 1751 he became deputy director of the chapel and head of the choir school. A highly successful theatre composer, he had 57 stage works performed in Madrid and Lisbon in 1723-30 and 1737-51 (none in 1731-6). Whether secular or sacred, they combine comic, folklike and tragic elements, and all include spoken dialogue. He also wrote (especially from the 1740s) music for the royal chapel.
GROVEmusic

Tempestad grande amigo

'Napoli/Madrid'
Nebra Tempestad grande amigo[acd] **Petrini** Graziello e Nella[ac] **Vinci** Erighetta e Don Chilone[ad]. Sinfonia per archi. Adónde fugitivo[b].
Triste, ausente, en esta selva[a]. Cuando infeliz destino[b]
[a]**Roberta Invernizzi**, [b]**Cristina Calzolari** sops
[c]**Giuseppe de Vittorio** ten [d]**Giuseppe Naviglio** bar
Capella della Pietà de'Turchini / Antonio Florio
Naïve OP30274 (72' · DDD · T/t)   Ⓕ

For more than two centuries Naples was a province of Spain, and after this ended in 1707 the remarkable cross-fertilisation of culture between them did not stop. Much of the Italian music featured here has been edited from sources in Spanish collections. The vast bulk of it is devoted to Leonardo Vinci (one of the most celebrated Italian opera composers of the 1720s). Only one short piece tacked onto the end is actually Spanish: a colourful fandango

from José de Nebra's zarzuela *Vendado es amor, no es ciego* (1744) in which three singers mockingly compare the squabbling goddesses of classical antiquity to bickering mothers-in-law.

Antonio Florio and Cappella della Pietà de'Turchini have already given unstinting service to the cause of music from Naples, but this is one of their best recordings so far. The playing and singing are theatrically charged without ever becoming crass or forced, and there is a lean articulacy evident throughout. This is no mean feat in two cliché-ridden intermezzi in which the comedy relies largely on long recitatives, but the programme has been intelligently chosen: Vinci's *Erighetta e Don Chilone* (in which a young widow hoodwinks a wealthy old hypochondriac into marrying her by posing as a doctor) is entirely different in tone and style to Giuseppe Petrini's *Graziello e Nella* (in which a young man – sung by a woman – heaps ridicule upon an old woman – sung by a man – who thinks she is still young and gorgeous). If these are fascinating and mildly amusing rather than magnificent, three *cantate con strumenti* by Vinci (sung in contemporary Spanish versions) offer ample musical rewards. *Triste, ausente, en esta selva* is superbly sung by Roberta Invernizzi – the central accompanied recitative is spectacular and highly dramatic. Cristina Calzolari is equally impressive in the other two cantatas. These cantatas give us a precious insight into why Vinci was reputedly one of Handel's favourite composers.

Carl Nielsen   Danish 1865-1931

Nielsen had a poor, rural upbringing, though his father was a musician and he learnt to play the violin, brass instruments and the piano. He studied at the Copenhagen Conservatory (1884-6), then continued having lessons with Orla Rosenhoff. In 1890-91 he travelled to Germany, France and Italy, and began his Brahmsian First Symphony (1892); from 1889 to 1905 he played the violin in the Danish court orchestra.

During the decade from the First Symphony to the Second ('The Four Temperaments', 1902) he developed an extended tonal style, but compacted and classical in its logic: the relatively few works of this period include the string quartets in G minor and E flat, the cantata Hymnus amoris and the opera Saul and David. Here he showed a gift for sharp musical characterisation, pursued in his second opera, the comedy Maskarade (1906) and other works, while his parallel command of large-scale, dynamic forms was affirmed by the Third Symphony (Sinfonia espansiva, 1911) and the Violin Concerto (1911).

From this period he was an international figure and went abroad often to conduct his own music, while working in Copenhagen as a conductor and teacher. At the same time his music became still more individual in its progressive tonality (movements or works ending in a key different from the initial one), 'group polyphony' (the orchestra being treated as an assembly of ensembles in counterpoint), vigorous rhythmic drive and dependence on a harmony not so much of chords as of focal pitches. His chief works were still symphonies (no. 4 'The Inextinguishable', 1916; No.5, 1922) and chamber pieces (F major quartet, 1919; Serenata in vano for quintet, 1914), but he also produced numerous songs and hymn tunes, in addition to incidental scores. **GROVE**music

Clarinet Concerto

Nielsen Clarinet Concerto **Lutosławski** Dance Preludes **Prokofiev** Flute Sonata in D, Op 94 (arr Kennan)
Richard Stoltzman cl **Warsaw Philharmonic Orchestra / Lawrence Leighton Smith**
RCA Red Seal 09026 63836-2 (66' · DDD)   Ⓕ

Richard Stoltzman's Nielsen, Prokofiev and Lutosławski compilation is a fine achievement. He brings to the Nielsen Concerto both virtuosity and depth of characterisation. There may be other ways of presenting this complex musical character-study but hid fluency and broad expressive range are as impressive as any modern recorded account. The Warsaw Philharmonic under Lawrence Leighton Smith sound exceptionally well prepared. They lend a natural idiomatic pliancy to the Lutosławski *Dance Preludes*, where Stoltzman is perkiness personified, and make a fine foil for him in the Concerto.

Kent Kennan's orchestration of the Prokofiev Flute Sonata is also well worth hearing – indeed, well worth taking up by other clarinettists. This is a tactful and adroit arrangement for chamber orchestra. Stoltzman lavishes care on the solo part, making a persuasive case for the *Scherzo* as an *allegretto scherzando* rather than Prokofiev's suggested *presto*. His romanticised approach to the slow movement is less convincing, but his earthy characterisation of the finale is admirable. RCA's recording quality is outstanding.

Violin Concerto

Nielsen Violin Concerto[a]. **Sibelius** Violin Concerto in D minor, Op 47[b]
Cho-Liang Lin vn
[a]**Swedish Radio Symphony Orchestra**,
[b]**Philharmonia Orchestra / Esa-Pekka Salonen**
Sony Classical 07464 44548-2 (69' · DDD) Recorded 1987-8   Ⓜ❍❍❍

At the time it was first issued, this was the best recording of the Sibelius Concerto to have appeared for over a decade, and probably the best ever of the Nielsen. It remains one of the classic concerto recordings of the century. Cho-Liang Lin brings an apparently effortless virtuosity to both concertos. He produces a wonderfully clean and silvery sonority, and there's no lack of aristocratic finesse.

Only half a dozen years separate the two concertos, yet they breathe a totally different air. Lin's perfect intonation and tonal purity excite admiration and throughout them both there's

a strong sense of line from beginning to end. Esa-Pekka Salonen gets excellent playing from the Philharmonia Orchestra in the Sibelius and almost equally good results from the Swedish Radio Symphony Orchestra.

Flute Concerto

Clarinet Concerto. Flute Concerto. Violin Concerto.
Gareth Davies fl **Kevin Banks** cl **Jonathan Carney** vn **Bournemouth Symphony Orchestra / Kees Bakels**
Naxos 8 554189 (79 minutes : DDD)   ⓈⒹ➤

For those on a limited budget, this outstandingly generous Naxos anthology will prove a pretty irresistible purchase. In the glorious Violin Concerto, Jonathan Carney turns out to be a thoroughly musical soloist, his sweet-toned contribution at once unforced and affectionate. Tempos are unfailingly well-judged, and Kees Bakels and the Bournemouth orchestra accompany with admirable spirit. Deftly as Carney plays, however, he doesn't possess quite the noble poise and silk-spun purity of Cho-Liang Lin, whose irreproachably eloquent 1988 version (above) with Esa-Pekka Salonen and the Swedish RSO continues to dominate the digital stakes. The Clarinet Concerto brings another capable, committed display. Bournemouth SO principal Kevin Banks copes manfully with the taxingly virtuosic solo part. Gareth Davies is a shapely, nimble advocate of the delectable Flute Concerto. Memories of dedicatee Holger Gilbert-Jespersen are not banished, but this remains a likeable reading all the same. Reasonable value overall, then, and a pretty decent recording too.

Overtures

Helios. Pan and Syrinx. Rhapsody Overture: An imaginary trip to the Faroe Islands. Amor and the Poet – Overture. Maskarade – Overture; Dance of the Cockerels. Master Oluf Rides – Prelude. Saul and David – Prelude. Snefrid. Willemoes – Prelude, Act 3
Danish National Symphony Orchestra / Thomas Dausgaard
Dacapo 🔊 6 220518 (72' · DDD)   Ⓕ❍❍❍Ⓓ➤

This is outstanding, and unmissable for Nielsen collectors – and not only for the less familiar items, all of which have been recorded before (not badly, either). The Danish Radio Symphony must have played the *Saul and David* and *Maskarade* excerpts and the *Helios* Overture more times than they can count. But for Dausgaard they relish every detail, without ever sounding self-conscious. To call the balance in the 'Cockerels' Dance' felicitous would be an understatement; it is revelatory. Nor is affectionate an adequate word for Dausgaard's interpretations of all the music on this disc; there is love here, and a sense of crusading mission.

The praises of the *Rhapsody Overture* and *Pan and Syrinx* could be sung just as extravagantly. As could those over the theatre music excerpts, all of which lead to or from the world of Nielsen's symphonies. Given playing of such finesse and bite (one virtually takes idiomatic understanding for granted) they all feel like gems in their own right.

Here's a Nielsen disc that comes about as close to the ideal as one could hope to hear, and it eclipses almost all others in its field. Dacapo's recording quality is top-drawer, and there is an exemplary essay from Jørgen I Jensen.

Symphonies

No 1 in G minor, FS16; **No 2** FS29, 'The Four Temperaments'; **No 3**, FS60, 'Sinfonia espansiva'; **No 4**, FS76, 'The inextinguishable'; **No 5**, FS97; **No 6**, FS116, 'Sinfonia semplice'

Symphonies Nos 1, 2 & 3[a]. Maskarade – Overture. Aladdin – Suite, FS89
[a]**Nancy Wait Fromm** *sop* [a]**Kevin McMillan** *bar*
San Francisco Symphony Orchestra /
Herbert Blomstedt
Double Decca 460 985-2DF2 (134' · DDD) Ⓜ❶❶❶➔

Nielsen always nurtured a special affection for his First Symphony – and rightly so, for its language is natural and unaffected. It has great spontaneity of feeling and a Dvořákian warmth and freshness. Blomstedt's recording is vital, beautifully shaped and generally faithful to both the spirit and the letter of the score. The recording is very fine: the sound has plenty of room to expand, there's a very good relationship between the various sections of the orchestra and a realistic perspective. The Second and Third are two of Nielsen's most genial symphonies, both of which come from the earliest part of the century, in performances of the very first order.

The Second (1902), inspired by the portrayal of *The Four Temperaments* (Choleric, Phlegmatic, Melancholic, Sanguine) that he had seen in a country inn, has splendid concentration and fire and, as always, from the right pace stems the right character. Moreover the orchestra sounds inspired, for there's a genuine excitement about its playing. Indeed Blomstedt's accounts are by far the most satisfying available. The Third, *Espansiva*, is even more personal in utterance than *The Four Temperaments*, for during the intervening years Nielsen had come much further along the road of self-discovery. His melodic lines are bolder, the musical paragraphs longer and his handling of form more assured. It's a glorious and richly inventive score whose pastoral slow movement includes a part for two wordless voices. Blomstedt gives us an affirmative, powerful reading and in the slow movement, the soprano produces the required ethereal effect.

The sound is very detailed and full bodied, and in the best traditions of the company. Blomst-

edt's *Espansiva* has greater depth than most accounts; the actual sound has that glowing radiance that characterises Nielsen, and the tempo, the underlying current on which this music is borne, is expertly judged – and nowhere better than in the finale.

Symphony No 1. Flute Concerto. Rhapsody Overture: An imaginary trip to the Faroe Islands, FS123
Patrick Gallois *fl* **Gothenburg Symphony Orchestra / Myung-Whun Chung**
BIS CD454 (63' · DDD)   Ⓕ

This recording of the First Symphony is hardly less fine than that of Blomstedt. Tempos are generally well judged and there's a good feeling for the overall architecture of the piece. It gets off to a splendid start and Chung shapes the second group affectionately. He doesn't put a foot wrong in the slow movement, which has a splendid sense of line, and phrasing which is attentive but never overemphatic. The finale is exhilaratingly played. Throughout the work Chung knows how to build up to a climax and keep detail in the right perspective. As always, the Gothenburg Symphony plays with enthusiasm and spirit, as if it has always lived with this music and yet, paradoxically, is discovering it for the first time.

The Rhapsody Overture, *An imaginary trip to the Faroe Islands*, begins most imaginatively but inspiration undoubtedly flags. The performance of the Flute Concerto is rather special. It's most strongly characterised by Patrick Gallois who plays with effortless virtuosity and an expressive eloquence that's never over- or understated. His purity of line in the first movement is quite striking and he has the measure of the poignant coda. His dynamic range is wide, the tone free from excessive vibrato and his approach fresh.

Symphonies Nos 2 & 3
National Symphony Orchestra of Ireland / Adrian Leaper
Naxos 8 550825 (68' · DDD)   Ⓢ➔

The vital current on which every phrase must be borne in Nielsen needs to flow at higher voltage. This is music which needs to be played at white heat. Well, there's certainly no lack of electricity in Leaper's reading of the Second. He sets a cracking pace for the first movement, the choleric temperament, and hardly puts a foot wrong in its three companions. His tempos in the *Sinfonia espansiva* are well judged and sensible throughout all four of the movements. The finale, where many conductors get it wrong, seems to be just right. These are more than just serviceable performances: they're very good indeed and the Irish orchestra sounds well rehearsed and inside the idiom. You can pay more and do worse although some collectors will think the additional polish one gets from Blomstedt or Myung-Whun Chung is worth the extra outlay. These latter performances continue to grow in stature, and it's no mean compliment to the Naxos versions to say that they give them a very good run for their money. Naxos doesn't identify the singers in the slow movement of the *Espansiva*.

No one investing in this issue and then going on to either of the Blomstedt accounts is going to feel that they have been let down. The recording team secures a very decent balance: well laid-back wind and brass, with good front-to-back perspective and transparency of texture.

Nielsen Symphony No 4, 'The Inextinguishable'[a]
Sibelius Symphony No 3, Op 52[b]
Hallé Orchestra / Sir John Barbirolli
BBC Legends BBCL4223-2 (65' · ADD)
Recorded in [a]1965 and [b]1969   (F)

Each of these performances, recorded live in the Royal Albert Hall, makes a heavier entrance than in any modern recording. But not many bars have gone by before it is clear that the emphatic playing is a sign not of lethargy but of significant things being imparted. No one in the UK was making a more passionate case for Nielsen in 1965 (the composer's centenary year) than Barbirolli. And the Sibelius four years later also gets right to the heart of the matter, moving towards its blazing conclusion with a fantastic sense of inevitability – a classic single-breath performance.

True, there are slips, especially in *The Inextinguishable*: some rank trombone intonation in the big first-movement tune, then the string figuration in the purgatorial first phase of the development section so clipped that the upbeats are mostly inaudible, also some wheezy string solos in the third movement. But the rushing scales heralding the finale are real edge-of-the-seat, devil-take-the-hindmost stuff, and the finale itself, though on the steady side, feels as though it is working through life-and-death issues, with the timpanists all but bursting the skins in their cannonades.

In fact the atmosphere of both Prom occasions is almost tangible, and not only because the recording quality itself is remarkably successful in capturing depth of field. Barbirolli must have prepared his players to the hilt, then told them to let rip on the night. So for two half-hours it feels as though nothing on earth was more important for them than devoting themselves to these symphonic masterworks. The quietness of the audience and their ovations afterwards suggest that the message must have got across.

Symphonies Nos 4-6. Little Suite in A minor, FS6[a].
Hymnus Amoris[b]
[b]**Barbara Bonney** sop [b]**John Mark Ainsley,** [b]**Lars Pedersen** tens [b]**Michael W Hansen,** [b]**Bo Anker Hansen** bars **San Francisco Symphony Orchestra / Herbert Blomstedt;** [a]**Danish National Radio Symphony Orchestra /** [a]**Ulf Schirmer**
Double Decca 460 988-2DF2 (142' · DDD)   (M)(O)(B)

The Fourth and Fifth are two of Nielsen's most popular and deeply characteristic symphonies.

Blomstedt's are splendid performances. The Fourth occupied Nielsen between 1914 and early 1916 and reveals a level of violence new to his art. The landscape is harsher; the melodic lines soar in a more anguished and intense fashion (in the case of the remarkable slow movement, 'like the eagle riding on the wind', to use Nielsen's own simile). Blomstedt's opening has splendid fire and he isn't frightened of letting things rip. The finale with its exhilarating dialogue between the two timpanists comes off splendidly.

The Fifth Symphony of 1922 is impressive, too: it starts perfectly and has just the right glacial atmosphere. The climax and the desolate clarinet peroration into which it dissolves are well handled. The recording balance couldn't be improved upon: the woodwind are well recessed (though clarinet keys are audible at times), there's an almost ideal relationship between the various sections of the orchestra and a thoroughly realistic overall perspective.

Blomstedt's account of the Sixth Symphony is a powerful one, with plenty of intensity and an appreciation of its extraordinary vision. It's by far the most challenging of the cycle and inhabits a very different world from early Nielsen. The intervening years had seen the cataclysmic events of the First World War and Nielsen was suffering increasingly from ill health. Blomstedt and the fine San Fransisco orchestra convey the powerful nervous tension of the first movement and the depth of the third, the *Proposta seria*.

Complete Symphonies
Danish National Symphony Orchestra /
Michael Schønwandt
Video director **Pia Borgwardt**
'The Light and the Darkness' – A documentary written and directed by **Karl Aage Rasmussen**
Dacapo ③ *DVD* 2 110403/5 (5h 26' · NTSC · 16:9 · 2.0 and DTS 5.1 · 0)   (F)

The number of Nielsen symphony cycles has grown steadily, with more than a dozen available. For this new DVD cycle, Schønwandt took orchestra and works back into the concert hall in November 2004, coming out with leaner, fitter accounts than his CD versions, well prepared and played with undeniable enthusiasm. Timings overall are swifter compared with the CD set but while there is more fire in the collective belly the performances do not consistently raise the roof or possess the electricity that Bernstein, Blomstedt or Vänskä found in this repertoire.

There are some reservations about the orchestral sound, particularly in Nos 1 and 2 where it occasionally lacks weight – the climax of the Second's opening *Allegro collerico*, for instance. However, from the outset of the *Sinfonia espansiva* (No 3) the textures are fuller-bodied; perhaps the slightly cavernous acoustic of the Danish Radio Concert Hall was a factor, perhaps the orchestra were pacing themselves knowing the task ahead. The recorded balance is good throughout.

The video direction is of fairly standard concert broadcasting type, mixing orchestral panoramas with interesting details. The latter are overused and long before the Fifth one begins to wonder whether there were more than two pretty violinists in the first section, if the tuba was alone in having an engraving or only the trombonists could see their reflections in the bells of their instruments. The direction hits the spot, however, in the finale of No 4, *The Inextinguishable*, where the camera angles along both sets of rampaging timpani, with the brass caught between as if in crossfire.

The set is augmented by an extra disc with a useful documentary by composer Karl Aage Rasmussen setting the music in the context of Nielsen's turbulent personal life. The English translation is read in curiously stilted fashion by Paul Hillier. Make sure that your DVD player is NTSC-capable or everything in colour will appear a rather unhealthy shade of pink (the sound is unaffected). On Disc 1, when playing movements individually, the menu irritatingly reverts to the First Symphony, whereas on Disc 2 it remembers where you were. All in all, though, a very worthwhile issue.

Wind Quintet, FS100

Nielsen Wind Quintet, FS100 **Fernström** Wind Quintet, Op 59 **Kvandal** Wind Quintet, Op 34. Three Sacred Folktunes, Op 23b
Oslo Wind Quintet (Tom Ottar Andreasson *fl* Lars Peter Berg *ob* Arild Stav *cl* Hans Peter Aasen *bn* Jan Olav Marthinsen *hn*)
Naxos 8 553050 (70' · DDD)   Ⓢ➜

This thoroughly entertaining CD combines three very different and unfamiliar works with what's probably the finest wind quintet ever penned. The major item here is the Nielsen: a glorious work which achieves the rare combination of seriousness of expression as well as being utterly relaxed in tone. The Oslo ensemble is a little slower than usual, but its measured tempos are most convincing; indeed, in the finale they highlight musical connections with Nielsen's Fifth and Sixth Symphonies in ways rarely heard. The Swede John Axel Fernström was undeniably a minor composer. If his music doesn't possess many visionary qualities it's certainly well crafted and his 1943 Quintet is an engaging concert opener. Johan Kvandal from Norway is a weightier proposition and better-known outside of his native country than is Fernström. Kvandal's Quintet, Op 34 (1971), was written for the Oslo ensemble and is serious and high-minded in tone, contrasting effectively with both the Fernström and Kvandal's own *Sacred Folktunes* of 1963. In the Quintet's fast second movement Kvandal adopts a rather Shostakovichian manner, even alluding to the Soviet master's 12th Symphony, though to what purpose is unexplained. The idiomatic playing is reproduced in a slightly flat recording, although the Naxos sound has great immediacy.

String Quartets

No 1 in G minor, FS4; **No 2** in F minor, FS11; **No 3** in E flat, FS23; **No 4** in F, FS36

String Quartets Nos 1 & 2
Oslo Quartet (Geir Inge Lotsberg, Per Kristian Skalstad *vns* Are Sandbakken *va* Oystein Sonstad *vc*)
Naxos 8 553908 (62' · DDD)   Ⓢ➜

Nielsen wrote five quartets in all between 1882 and 1919, although two exist in different versions, and the opus numbering is contradictory. This may explain why Naxos gets itself into such a pickle over the numbering of the G minor and F minor Quartets here, the second and third he composed. (The early D minor of 1882-3 remains unnumbered.) The G minor, Op 13 (FS4; 1887-8 but thoroughly rewritten in 1898) is No 1 and the F minor, Op 5 (FS11; 1890) is No 2. The front cover cites the works correctly as 'Quartets No 1, Op 13. No 2, Op 5', but the back cover has 'Quartet No 1 in F minor, Op 5 (Rev 1898)' and 'No 2 in G minor, Op 13 (1890)', managing thus to confuse both dates and numbering. Although in his notes Keith Anderson lays out the composition history quite simply, he refers only to the opus numbers, which should be consigned to oblivion and replaced by the more accurate Fog-Schousboe numbers.

The performances are as clear-sighted as the labelling is a mess. As with the first volume, the Oslo are sympathetic exponents, and do not overlay any extraneous expression on the music as the disappointing Zapolski for Chandos did. Like the almost exactly contemporaneous early Sibelius quartets, there's barely a hint of the familiar, mature Nielsen in either work, but both are well crafted and beautifully written for the instruments. The Oslo seem completely at home in the style, more so than either the Kontra for BIS (who, like the Zapolski, have the benefit of top-quality sound) or Danish (Kontrapunkt) Quartets, making them come alive as none of their rivals manage. The recording is, like Volume 1, a touch confined but not constricted; that aside, this disc can be unreservedly recommended.

String Quartets Nos 3 & 4
Oslo Quartet (Geir Inge Lotsberg, Per Kristian Skalstad *vns* Are Sandbakken *va* Øystein Sonstad *vc*)
Naxos 8 553907 (57' · DDD)   Ⓢ

Why is it that quartets of international standing have not taken up the Nielsen quartets (or the Berwald or Stenhammar for that matter). They are marvellous pieces and their neglect outside Scandinavia seems quite unaccountable. This release by the Oslo Quartet is refreshingly straightforward, full of vitality and spirit. Both scores are played with evident feeling but without any intrusive expressive exaggeration. The recordings are a little closely balanced, and as a result *fortissimo* passages can sound a touch fierce and wiry, for example in the closing page or so of the first movement of the F major (seven minutes into track 5). A pity the Oslo doesn't have as well-balanced a recording as Chandos and the Danish engineers provide for the Zapolski. The quartet is scrupulous in observing dynamic markings and gives totally dedicated, idiomatic performances. Artistically it's the finest at any price point.

String Quartets Nos 1-4. Movements for String Quartet, FS3*c*

Danish Quartet (Tim Frederiksen, Arne Balk-Møller *vns* Claus Myrup *va* H Brendstrup *vc*)

Kontrapunkt ② 32150/1 (138' · DDD)   Ⓕ

Nielsen composed two quartets and a string quintet during his student years. There was a gap of eight years between the F minor Quartet and the Third, in E flat, Op 14 (FS23) during which Nielsen had written his First Symphony, and another eight before the F major, Op 44 (FS36) saw the light of day. By this time he had written his opera, *Saul and David* and the best part of *Maskarade* as well as the Second Symphony.

The Danish Quartet is very sensitive to dynamic nuance and phrases imaginatively. The F major Quartet goes deeper than the Third. There's a grace, an effortless fluency and a marvellous control of pace. Ideas come and go just when you feel they should; yet its learning and mastery is worn lightly. Though the earlier quartets aren't such perfect works of art, they're always endearing. The Danish Quartet is completely inside this music and is totally persuasive. In spite of the closely balanced recording this set gives real pleasure and can be recommended with enthusiasm.

Piano works

Complete Piano Works

Martin Roscoe *pf*

Hyperion ② CDA67591/2 (114' · DDD)   Ⓕⵔ

Nielsen's patchy output for the piano has not received the sustained attention the rest of his music has, yet Hyperion's is not the first complete recording. We've had sets from Arne Skjold Rasmussen, John McCabe and Mina Miller, of her own critical edition; here Roscoe plays David Fanning's 2006 revisiting of the music.

These new recordings are sonically the best yet. Roscoe is famed for his touch and his playing's delicacy and finesse is evident throughout, from the early Five Pieces (1887-90) to the *Piano Music for Young and Old* (1930). In the Op 45 Suite *Det Luciferiske* (1919-20), he emphasises the lighter side – Lucifer was the bringer of Fire and Light after all – while in the Three Pieces (1928) he gets the balance between expression and experimentation just right (as does Leif Ove Andsnes in his selection).

However, there is more to Nielsen in his keyboard works than subtlety: the bigger pieces need power and at times Roscoe seems reticent compared to his rivals. He is on record as finding *Det Luciferiske*'s finale expressively 'terrifying' yet that quality is absent from his playing.

This applies elsewhere, whether the trifling *Festival Prelude for the New Century* which Miller makes more substantial, or the *Humoresk-Bagatelles*' electrifying 'The Jumping Jack'. Miller is generally livelier (some may argue over-characterised) but is let down by a somewhat clattery instrument; hers remain an impressive achievement. Roscoe's need more time to make their full impression as he lets the music make its own mark. While it may be invidious to judge a set on a single work, perhaps it is the treatment of the wonderful *Chaconne* (1916) that provides the truest benchmark: Roscoe is at his best here, showing a clear grasp of its structure and momentum.   **GROVE**music

---

Luigi Nono   Italian 1924-1990

A leading figure in the postwar European avant garde, he asserted his independence from that circle in the late 1950s, exploring a passionate social and political commitment through the most advanced technical means, electronics especially. While political messages are less explicit in his works from the late 1970s onwards, he sought in his last decade, through an extreme concentration of musical material and a meticulous attention to sound itself, modes of listening and performing which would embody on a more intimate level the same ethical concerns with perception, communication and human interaction.

No hay caminos, hay que caminar...Andrei Tarkovsky[a]. 'Hay que caminar' sognando[b]. Caminates...Ayacucho[c]

[c]**Susanne Otto** *contr* [c]**Roberto Fabbriciani** *fl* [b]**Irvine Arditti**, [b]**Graeme Jennings** *vns* [c]**Freiburg Soloists Choir;** [c]**Freiburg (im Breisgau) Experimental Studio;** [c]**Cologne Radio Chorus and** [a]**Symphony Orchestra / Emilio Pomarico**

Kairos ② 0012512KAI (86' · DDD)   Ⓕ

Prometeo

Monika Bair-Ivenz, Petra Hoffmann *sops* **Susanne Otto** *contr* **Noa Frenkel** *counterten* **Sigrun Schell, Gregor Dalal** *spkrs* **Freiburg Soloists Choir; Recherche Ensemble; Members of the Freiburg Philharmonic Orchestra; Members of the South West German Radio Symphony Orchestra, Baden-Baden and Freiburg / Peter Hirsch, Kwamé Ryan**

Col Legno ② 🔊 WWE2SACD20605 (135' · DDD · T/N)   Ⓕ

These two splendid sets between them contain a substantial proportion of Luigi Nono's output in the last decade of his life: a complete studio recording of his stage work, *Prometeo* (subtitled 'a tragedy of listening'), and the first complete recording of his *Caminantes* trilogy. Common to all of late Nono is a concern with sound events stripped to bare essentials: usually built on held notes and localised clusters punctuated by more discrete gestures, the music moves slowly – sometimes very slowly. Occasionally, disconcerting, more consonant sonorities are sketched, especially in *Prometeo*, which incorporates materials from earlier music. Not infrequently, near-silence prevails over a span of minutes. The demands made of the listener are considerable, but so. arguably, are the rewards.

The music makes considerable demands of the performers as well, both practically and interpretatively: with the exception of the two-violin piece '*Hay que caminar' sognando*, all these pieces mobilise large forces, including voices, with or without live electronics. The role of the latter, incidentally, is underlined by the use of SACD technology: Nono, who was born and died in Venice, was fond of invoking the spatial, polychoral effects of the Gabrielis. Finally, the role of silence or near-silence is such that the risk involved in live recordings is very great, any extraneous noise the potential 'killer' of an otherwise great performance. So in both these recordings there is a real sense of achievement, and one comes away, apart from anything else, with a profound gratitude to all concerned!

Of the two sets, the more immediately accessible is the one from Kairos, due to the greater variety of media: apart from the two-violin piece, Nono's last completed work, it includes *No hay caminos, hay que caminar...Andrei Tarkovsky*, scored for seven instrumental groups, and the still longer *Caminates...Ayacucho*, for three orchestral groups, choir, soloists (both vocal and instrumental), organ, electronics and percussion. The sense of scale is not markedly different in these works from that of the opera, though the spans of stillness are necessarily shorter, as a rule. In *Prometeo*, the avoidance of narrative doesn't exclude some impressive build-ups: the first tre voci episode consists of single voices very gradually evolving into much louder, complex sounds. It's a particularly moving climax, its effectiveness inversely proportional to Nono's use of the strategy.

Both sets are essential listening and both are lovingly produced: *Prometeo* is accompanied by two booklets, including a 'listening score' in which the different text sources are colour-coded.

Vítezslav Novák   Bohemian 1870-1949

Novák studied with Jiránek and Dvořák at the Prague Conservatory (1889-92) and was powerfully influenced by the folk music of Moravia and Slovakia, which he began to collect and study in 1896. The result was an outpouring of symphonic poems and songs, culminating in the dramatic cantata The Storm (1910) and the large-scale tone poem Pan for piano (1910). A skilled melodist and contrapuntist, he retained an essentially late Romantic style, which was supported by a meticulous technique.

GROVEmusic

De profundis

Toman and the Wood Nymph, Op 40. Lady Godiva, Op 41. De profundis, Op 67
BBC Philharmonic Orchestra / Libor Pešek
Chandos CHAN9821 (66' · DDD)   Ⓕ**Ⓞ**⤷

Vítězslav Novák was a keen walker and each piece on this absorbing CD testifies to his vivid sense of outdoors. He was also fascinated by the female psyche and two of the works programmed bring rival viragos to mind: Smetana's 'Šárka' (in the opening pages of *Lady Godiva*) and Strauss's *Salome* (the close of *Toman and the Wood Nymph*).

Yet for all their lustre, excitement and charm, even *Godiva* and *Toman* can't rival the oppressive power of Novák's wartime masterpiece *De profundis*, a work that surely levels with Martinů's *Lidice* as being among the most poignant musical memorials of the period. Composed during the Nazi occupation of Czechoslovakia, *De profundis* finds Novák employing a significantly darkened palette, though the exultant closing section (track 7) bears little resemblance to the various politically motivated 'happy endings' that were surfacing elsewhere. Novák's use of the organ runs parallel with Scriabin's in *The Poem of Ecstasy* (albeit to very different effect).

Libor Pešek shows obvious sympathy for this repertoire and the playing of the BBC Philharmonic reaches formidable heights of passion, notably at the close of *De profundis*. Alternative discs of Novák's music are few and far between, and hard to come by.

Piano Quintet, Op 12

Piano Quintet in A minor, Op 12. 13 Slovak Folksongs. Songs of a Winter Night, Op 30
Magdalena Kožená *mez* **Radoslav Kvapil** *pf* **Kocian Quartet** (Pavel Hůla, Jan Odstrčil *vns* Zbynek Padourek *va* Václav Bernášek *vc*)
ASV CDDCA998 (67' · DDD · T/t)   Ⓕ

Novák's A minor Piano Quintet of 1896 was composed in the wake of his first fruitful study of the folk-song traditions of both Moravia and Slovakia. It's an accomplished creation, comprising a finely sustained *Allegro molto moderato*, an effective central theme and variations (based on a 15th-century Czech love-song) and a joyous finale. Seven years later, Novák produced his piano suite, *Songs of a Winter Night*. Its four movements make a charming set, ranging in mood from the wistful intimacy of 'Song of a moonlight night' to the gleeful merry-making of the last in the series ('Song of a carnival night'). Even during the ecstatic pealing that marks the climax of the memorable 'Song of a Christmas night', Novák's piano writing always remains wonderfully pellucid, a factor that also adds to the listener's enjoyment of his six volumes of Slovak songs, 13 of which are heard here.

Gems include the plaintive *Sedla mucha* ('A fly sat on a cornflower') with its bewitching piano traceries, the harmonically searching *Svic, mila*, *mas komu* ('Light the lamp, my love') and the tragic tale of *Chodzila Mariska* ('Mariska's walking along the bank').

Radoslav Kvapil and the Kocian Quartet form a thoroughly convincing alliance in the early Piano Quintet. The excellent Kvapil also shines in the solo suite, and in the song sequence he provides some tenderly idiomatic support to the characterful mezzo, Magdalena Kožená.

Jacob Obrecht Netherlands c1450-1505

Obrecht was zangmeester at Utrecht, c1476-8, then choirmaster for the Corporation of Notre Dame at St Gertrude, Bergen op Zoom, 1479-84. He then became singing master at Cambrai, and on 13 October 1486 was installed as succentor at St Donatien, Bruges. After a visit to Italy he was appointed maître de chapelle at Bruges in 1490. In 1494 his name appears in the records of Notre Dame, Antwerp, and from then until his retirement in 1500 he alternated between Antwerp and Bergen op Zoom. He died of the plague while on a visit to Ferrara. As early as 1475 Tinctoris had mentioned him with the best and most renowned musicians, and other evidence suggests that he commanded the greatest respect. He wrote mainly sacred music. **GROVE**music

Missa Sub tuum praesidium

Missa Sub tuum presidium. Salve regina. Ave Regina caelorum. Ave maris stella. Alma Redemptoris Mater. Magnificat. Beata es Maria
Ars Nova / Paul Hillier
Ars Nova VANCD02 (63' · DDD · T/t) Ⓕ

Missa Sub tuum praesidium. Factor orbis. Salve crux. Salve regina a 3. Beata es Maria. Benedicamus in Laude. Mille Quingentis
The Clerks' Group / Edward Wickham
ASV Gaudeamus CDGAU341 (70' · DDD · T/t) Ⓕ

Back in the days of LPs, *Sub tuum presidium* was one of the first of Obrecht's masses to appear, and a second recording followed soon after. But 30 years have elapsed since then, so these two CDs are long overdue.

The scholar Birgit Lodes recently suggested that *Sub tuum praesidium* may be one of Obrecht's last mass settings. It's concise, both in terms of length and economy of means; at the same time its rich scoring packs a real punch. Its premise is typical of Obrecht at his most rational, but also visionary. The *Kyrie* begins with three voices; each movement adds another, culminating in the seven-voice *Agnus dei*. The *cantus firmus* recurs virtually unchanged in each movement, a fixed point; but as new voices and new chants (all of them Marian) are progressively added, the identity of the original plainchant is increasingly obscured as the texture thickens.

The tension between these two complementary processes generates a peculiar magic, and

Ars Nova's performance captures this crucial feature. There's a certain lack of security in matters of detail, that may be put down to the recording venue: the church acoustic seems to dull the rhythmic angularity that characterises much of the mass: bursts of rapid runs often seem to lose crispness and direction, and Hillier's brisk tempos at the start of sections have a tendency to slacken.

Though Hillier sets more consistent tempos (and in this work consistency is surely a virtue: the contrasts in tempo in The Clerks' *Kyrie* are a bit forced), Wickham makes his decisions tell more meaningfully. Where Ars Nova occasionally sound rushed, The Clerks hold every rhythmic detail, every imitative flourish in place.

The role of the title *cantus firmus* is nicely contrasted in the two versions: with Hillier (who has more than one soprano on each line, even when the music divides into several top lines) the additional voices superimpose themselves on the main chant, as though actively obscuring it; Wickham splits his two sopranos once occasion demands it, so that the plainsong gives the impression of receding gradually, as though of its own accord, into the distance. In the *Sanctus* and *Agnus dei* Wickham takes his foot off the throttle: that's one solution to the score's increasing complexity, and though Hillier maintains the tension, it's Wickham and his singers who defend their conception more persuasively.

The accompanying Marian motets on the Ars Nova disc are generally well sung, even though in a few cases (such as the oft-recorded six-voice *Salve regina*) more characterful alternatives are available.

The Clerks' recording, a return to form for the group, is one of the strongest and well-rounded introductions to Obrecht in the catalogue. *Salve crux* and *Factor orbis* rank among his most impressive statements. The Clerks don't eclipse memories of the Orlando Consort in *Salve crux*, but their reading offers a most effective contrast. Even a slender-looking piece such as the three-voice *Salve regina* is handled with a sure-footedness that signals regained confidence; the astonishing conclusion has a delicacy one mightn't readily associate with its composer. Every piece contains similarly striking insights, where music and musicians are perfectly in sync. *Beata es, Maria* has been recorded many times but never more lucidly than here. This seems to be the first recording of *Mille quingentis*, Obrecht's memorial to his father, a work whose hieratic structure doesn't inhibit depth of feeling.

Johannes Ockeghem

Flanders c1410-1497

The earliest reference to Ockeghem as a singer shows that he was a vicaire-chanteur at Notre Dame, Antwerp, for a year from June 24, 1443. His déploration on Binchois' death (1460) suggests a connection with the Burgundian ducal chapel where Busnois and

Dufay worked. He entered the service of Charles I, Duke of Bourbon, in Moulins in the mid-1440s and was a member of the chapel in 1446-8. In the year ending September 30, 1453 he is cited in the French court archives 'nouveau en 1451'. This service continued during Louis XI's reign, though he held other offices, including a canonry at Notre Dame, Paris (1463-70). In 1470 he visited Spain, in 1484 Bruges and Dammes. After Louis death he remained premier chapelain and was still on the payroll in 1488. He enjoyed an enviable personal and professional reputation. His most imposing works are his Mass settings. Several are based on pre-existing material, sacred or secular. The level of contrapuntal skill and artistic excellence of his music laid a foundation for the achievements of Josquin's generation.

Masses

Ockeghem Missa Ecce ancilla Domini. Missa Dei mater. Ave Maria. **Josquin des Prez** Déploration sur la mort de Johannes Ockeghem **Obrecht** Salve regina
The Clerks' Group / Edward Wickham
ASV Gaudeamus CDGAU223 (64' · DDD)　Ⓕ

Ockeghem Missa travail suis. Mort tu as navré. S'elle m'amera/Petite Camusette. Permanent vierge/Pulchra es/Sancta Dei genetrix. Missa sine nomine a 5. Intemerata Dei mater **Barbigant** Au travail suis
The Clerks' Group / Edward Wickham
ASV Gaudeamus CDGAU215 (55' · DDD)　Ⓕ

The Clerks Group's recording of the Mass *Ecce ancilla Domini* remains one of their most satisfying achievements; how exciting it was to hear one of Ockeghem's most perfect Masses sung with such authority. Indeed, there are very few recordings of 15th-century polyphony to match this one. Their more recent disc is scarcely less impressive, and it, too, includes works that express Ockeghem's art in contrasted but typical ways. The five-voice Mass *Sine nomine* may seem slight on paper, but the Clerks' men make clear its effectiveness. And *Au travail suis* is one of the most strikingly distinctive of all 15th-century cycles, a study in contrasted, kaleidoscopic textures. Here, as elsewhere, the Clerks are mellifluous and slick: at times this is to the detriment of the music's delicious asperities (try the end of the *Credo*), but those who find the rival Pomerium Musices' account too mannered will welcome this more measured approach.

Lovers of vocal polyphony owe Edward Wickham and his singers a vote of thanks.

Missa Cuiusvis Toni (four versions: Dorian, Phrygian, Lydian and Mixolydian). Intemerata Dei mater
Ensemble Musica Nova / Lucien Kandel
Aeon ② AECD0753 (115' · DDD)　Ⓕ

This is a recording that was waiting to happen: to do full justice to Ockeghem's famous Mass designed for performance 'on whatever tone you choose', you really need to hear several complete versions side by side, and this is the first to present it that way. What's more, Ensemble Musica Nova's performances are technically superior to any that have been committed to disc so far.

The precise number of possible versions intended by Ockeghem has long been a matter of conjecture, but recently scholars have come back round to the idea that there may have been no more than three (starting on re, mi, and fa). Here, there are four, comprising the Dorian, Phrygian, Lydian and Mixolydian modes. For what it's worth, the last two are so close as to be virtually indistinguishable (which supports the view that the Mixolydian version is superfluous). Inevitably, given the uncertainties attending modal usage in medieval polyphony, one can take issue with certain decisions affecting the 'colour' of each mode. The decision, for instance, to interpret many Bs as flat in the Phrygian is slightly confusing.

In each version, the modal final (roughly equivalent to the home key in tonal music) is sung on the same absolute pitch. As well as being sound from a historical standpoint, this eliminates at a stroke any problems of range and tessitura: the singers deliver each version with the same ease. In addition, each version is sung at precisely the same tempo. Though this decision is less self-evident, it has at least the virtue of consistency.

Ensemble Musica Nova are a mixed choir singing two-to-a-part in a sympathetic acoustic that allows for contrapuntal clarity and a sound image at once warm and bright. Just occasionally one detects signs of tiredness, at the beginning of the Mixolydian *Sanctus* for instance, where there is also an inexplicable 'gain'. But these really are quibbles in the face of such an enterprising project: the music is glorious?

Ockeghem Missa L'homme armé. Ave Maria. Alma redemptoris mater **Josquin Desprez** Memor esto verbi tui **Plainchant** Alma redemptoris mater. Immittet angelus Domini **Anonymous** L'homme armé
Oxford Camerata / Jeremy Summerly
Naxos 8 554297 (57' · DDD · T/t)　ⓈⓄ▸

The centrepiece here is Ockeghem's *L'homme armé* Mass. It may be one of his earliest Masses, dating perhaps from the early 1450s. It's also one of his most curious. For the most part it lies in a relatively high register, belying his usual predilection for low bass ranges; but every now and again the basses descend in spectacular fashion. In the third *Agnus* they hold down the tune in very long notes, while the other voices seem to float above them. Seldom before in the history of music can the articulation of time have been so clear a feature of a piece's design: it seems almost to have been suspended altogether. It's an extraordinary moment, difficult to pull off in performance, but here the singers seem to have got it right. Elsewhere, Summerly's approach is nicely varied, but on the whole more meditative than emphatic. The performance grows in stature with each movement, as though keeping pace with the cycle's ambition. The reading isn't without the odd glitch, but taken as a whole it's a fine achievement. The accompanying motets work very well, but it's a shame that the choir's richness of sound isn't quite matched by the acoustic. But the overall impression is resoundingly positive: those new to Ockeghem should find this disc too good an opportunity to pass up.

Ockeghem Missa prolationum. **Obrecht** (attrib) Humilium decus. **Busnois** Gaude coelestis Domina. In hydraulis. **Pullois** Flos de spina. **Josquin Desprez** Illibata Dei Virgo nutrix
The Clerks' Group / Edward Wickham
ASV Gaudeamus CDGAU143 (65' · DDD)   Ⓕ

This recording focuses on one of the most astonishing compositional feats of the second half of the 15th century: Ockeghem's *Missa prolationum*. The successive movements of the Ordinary of the Mass are based on double canons that progress from the unison to the octave, while at the same time the composer also exploits the inherent ambiguity of the mensural system (and hence the work's title) of the later Middle Ages so that the rhythmic relationships between the voices are constantly being transformed. The astonishing thing is how effortlessly Ockeghem weaves his complex polyphonic web, and this is reinforced here by the unfettered, direct way in which The Clerks' Group approaches the music. Although there are only eight singers in the group, they bring a very satisfactory mix of the vocal agility one might expect from a small ensemble and the ability to sing through the long-breathed lines favoured by Ockeghem, without ever sounding strained or thin. The overall sound is closely recorded, but it never lacks richness or blend.

Although at first sight the five motets on the disc seem only loosely related to each other and to the Mass, there are potentially illuminating links: several of the composers appear to pay homage, whether directly or indirectly, to one another's pieces and in general they all opt for quite self-consciously complex structures yet create a musical idiom that's lucid and full of emotional responses to the texts they chose to set. No one could seriously doubt that this is the Franco-Netherlandish school at its best.

Ockeghem Requiem. Fors seulement. Missa Fors seulement **Brumel** Du tout plongiet/Fors seulement **La Rue** Fors seulement
The Clerks' Group / Edward Wickham
ASV Gaudeamus CDGAU168 (71' · DDD · T/t)   Ⓕ**OOO**

Ⓖ Top billing goes to the Requiem, Ockeghem's most widely recorded work, and perhaps his most enigmatic piece, stylistically very wide-ranging and diverse. Aesthetic judgement is hard to pass, since it may well be incomplete; but the surviving movements contain some of his most arresting inspirations. This is the first version of any quality to feature sopranos on the top lines. Incidentally, no recording of the Requiem is uniformly excellent; on the other hand, the words of the Mass for the dead conjure up many associations, and The Clerks deserve praise for the verve and imagination with which they respond to the work's interpretative challenges.

The fillers are the works built on Ockeghem's song *Fors seulement* (which includes Antoine Brumel's *Du tout plongiet*). It's difficult to decide which to praise more highly: the pieces themselves, which are incomparable, or the singing, which represents The Clerks' finest achievement to date. *Fors seulement* inspired a flowering of astonishing pieces scored for very low voices (initiated, it appears, by the composer himself): in both the Mass and in *Du tout plongiet*, the basses descendto written low Cs. In addition, these pieces are exceptionally richly scored (the Mass and the La Rue song are five-voice works), creating polyphony as dense and as dark as a strong Trappist ale. The Clerks achieve almost miraculous linear definition here, without losing an iota of the music's sensuous appeal: that's quite a feat, given the low pitch and awesome contrapuntal complexity involved. This must be counted as a major achievement.

Jacques Offenbach
German/French 1819-1880

Offenbach's career began with a year's study at the Paris Conservatoire and several years experience as a solo and orchestral cellist; he became a theatre conductor in 1850, finally getting his own stage works performed in 1855. Writing mainly for the Bouffes Parisiens, he reached the peak of his international success in the 1860s; revivals and tours, as well as the score of his serious opera Les contes d'Hoffmann (unfinished, completed by Guiraud), dominated the 1870s.

With Johann Strauss II, Offenbach was one of the two outstanding composers in popular music of the 19th century and writer of some of the most exhilaratingly gay, tuneful music ever written. Offenbach's comic subjects, usually satirical treatments of familiar stories with a sharp glance at contemporary society and politics, are enhanced by none-too-subtle musical devices. **GROVE**music

Gaîté parisienne

Gaîté Parisienne. Offenbachiana (both arr Rosenthal)
Monte Carlo Philharmonic Orchestra / Manuel Rosenthal
Naxos 8 554005 (68' · DDD)   Ⓢ▸

Manuel Rosenthal was 92 when he made this recording – his third – of *Gaîté Parisienne*, his ballet for Massine that had produced such a storm of applause in Monte Carlo back in 1938. He made very clear why he was anxious to do so: not only had there been poor recordings, cut versions and mauled arrangements of his score by others, but in his own previous recordings he had felt obliged to accommodate the dancers' wishes as regards tempos, and now he wanted to treat his work symphonically, with more spacious speeds that would enable details of the orchestration to emerge fully for the first time. So we can now accept this 45-minute version as authentic, and the more deliberate pace adopted in some places (beautifully and expressively so in the Barcarolle) in no way diminishes the brilliant impact of his treatment of Offenbach's heady tunes. The Monte Carlo orchestra, long familiar with the work, give their all to the aged maestro, with voluptuous string playing in lyrical sections; and the recording is exceptionally vivid. But the real joy of this disc is *Offenbachiana*, music drawn from a handful of the stage works arranged by Rosenthal while forced to kick his heels in Berlin for a fortnight owing to a recording equipment breakdown in 1953. This is a subtler, wittier and, if anything, even more scintillating score. Absolutely not to be missed!

Operetta and opera arias

'Entre Nous – Celebrating Offenbach'
Artists include **Cassandre Berthon, Mark le Brocq, Laura Claycomb, André Cognet, Loïc Félix, Yvonne Kenny, Jennifer Larmore, Colin Lee, Alastair Miles, Diana Montague, Alexandra Sherman, Mark Stone, Elizabeth Vidal, Mark Wilde; London Philharmonic Orchestra / David Parry**
Opera Rara ② ORR243 (154' · DDD · T/t)   Ⓕ**OO**

Offenbach composed over 100 works for the stage, only a few of which have been recorded complete. This groundbreaking set offers 41 extracts from two dozen comic operas from the master of irony and melody, ranging from the early *Une nuit blanche* – which was on the bill at the opening night of Les Bouffes Parisiens in 1855 – to elaborate spectacles such as *Les bergers*, an essay in time travel from ancient Greece to modern France, *Vert-Vert*, which features a dead parrot, and *Le voyage dans la lune*, in which the Moonfolk catch that dirty disease from Earth – love.

Offenbach tailored all his operas to particular performers, and it is a challenge to modern singers to find their own way of suggesting the outsize personalities of such stars as Hortense Schneider and Zulmar Bouffar. Colin Lee is splendid in an aria written for Etienne Pradeau in *La rose de Saint-Flour*, in which a stuttering coppersmith brings a cooking-pot as a gift to his beloved. Yvonne Kenny and Alexandra Sherman offer the contrasting personalities of the two heroines of *La créole*, while Jennifer Larmore takes on the shade of Schneider in *La diva*, with an outrageous parody of the Act 2 finale of *La traviata*. From *Geneviève de Brabant* comes a nifty little rondo about a pâté, sung by Cassandre Berthon, and Offenbach's first opera based

on a story by ETA Hoffmann, *Le roi carotte*, gives us a 'Ronde de chemins de fer', one of the earliest operatic train journeys. *Le fifre enchanté* has a giddy coloratura marching song which Laura Claycomb negotiates with panache. Even from the extracts it's easy to gauge the thin line Offenbach and his librettists were treading vis-à-vis the censors with works like *La jolie parfumeuse* (hear Mark Stone sing 'Pardieu!'), *Les Braconniers* – Diana Montague in a typical Bouffar moment celebrating her lover's 'grosse frimousse' – and *L'île de Tulipatan*, a satire on the folly of emperors, as Loïc Félix as King Cacatois sings about gossip columns. All but dedicated misanthropes will find this set entrancing; highly recommended.

La belle Hélène

La belle Hélène   Ⓟ
Felicity Lott sop Hélène **Yann Beuron** ten Pâris **Michel Sénéchal** ten Ménélas **Laurent Naouri** bar Agamemnon **François Le Roux** bar Calchas **Marie-Ange Todorovitch** mez Oreste **Eric Huchet** bar Achille **Alain Gabriel** ten Ajax I **Laurent Alvaro** bar Ajax II **Hjördis Thébault** sop Bacchis
Les Musiciens et Choeur des Musiciens du Louvre / Marc Minkowski
Virgin Classics ② 545477-2 (118' · DDD · T/t)   Ⓕ**OO**

From its very first bars, this recording strikes a chord of authenticity. Too often Offenbach's works are recorded with large orchestra, huge chorus and swimming-bath acoustics. Offenbach himself was perfectly happy to accept larger forces when available, but they do rather swamp the gossamer lightness and piquancy of what he actually composed. This newcomer derives from a stage production received enthusiastically at the Châtelet in Paris in September 2000.

The feeling of a stage production pervades the recording in its integration of dialogue and music, as also in the uninhibited singing and playing of Orestes' opening couplets. Marie-Ange Todorovitch performs with appropriately boyish high spirits throughout, and Michel Sénéchal as Ménélas, Laurent Naouri as Agamemnon and François Le Roux as Calchas ensure this recording is cast from strength. Although Felicity Lott's Hélène lacks that distinctive French way of wrapping the voice round the words in her great arias, she succeeded in capturing Paris (the city as well as the Trojan prince). What appeals especially is her lightness of voice compared with the mezzo tones of many other interpreters. Yet the voice and interpretation that captivate the ear most here are those of Yann Beuron as Pâris. His honeyed tones are heard to absolute perfection throughout, but his *pianissimo* singing of the final verse of the 'Judgement of Paris' makes it an especially model interpretation. Moreover, Beuron has music to sing that isn't in any previous recording – a lullaby, complete with dove cooing, preceding the Dream Duet. There's more, too. In the 1865 German version, the scene of the Game of Goose was longer than in the 1864 French original, and here it's longer still. But most importantly, this is a sparkling, beautifully paced recording and is now a clear first choice for what's surely Offenbach's most captivating operetta.

La belle Hélène 🅟
Dame Felicity Lott sop Hélène **Yann Beuron** ten p
Paris **Michel Sénéchal** ten Ménélas **Laurent Naouri**
bar Agamemnon **François Le Roux** bar Calchas
Marie-Ange Todorovitch mez Oreste **Eric Huchet**
bar Achille **Alain Gabriel** ten Ajax I **Laurent Alvaro**
bar Ajax II **Hjördis Thébault** sop Bacchis **Stéphanie**
d'Oustrac sop Leoena **Magali Léger** sop Parthoenis
Choeur et Musiciens du Louvre / Marc Minkowski
Stage director **Laurent Pelly**
Video director **Ross MacGibbon**
TDK 📀 DV-OPLBH (153' · 16:9 · 2.0, 5.0 & DTS
5.0 · 2) Includes documentary, 'Behind the Scenes'
🅕❍❍❍

Minkowski triumphs here – this is the most idiomatic Offenbach conducting since René Leibowitz. DVD reveals how deftly he propels Pelly's splendidly loopy production. The alarmingly tinny opening bars come from a bedside TV, before which a frustrated housewife dozes. As the music proper starts, her dreams become the production, full of glamorous magazine imagery – royalty, travel, sun-kissed Greek beaches – without ever quite leaving the bedroom. It's properly surreal, satirical and sexy.

Dame Felicity fits this perfectly, a soprano Helen as opposed to Harnoncourt's mezzo Vesselina Kasarova (on ArtHaus Musik, reviewed below), slightly more mature but no less alluring and displaying greater comic talent. She wafts dizzily through the action in a hilarious haze of newly liberated lubricity, her delightful Franglais enhancing the comedy. Beuron sings Paris with uncommonly melting tone, even in his fiendish yodelling song, and radiates fresh-faced toyboy charm. Menelaus is the veteran Sénéchal, beaming with complacent idiocy; with Le Roux's manic Calchas and Naouri's stiff-necked Agamemnon their Patriotic Trio is a gem. Todorovitch's Orestes is delightful, as are 'his' floozies Leoena and Parthoenis, and the lesser kings. There isn't a weak link, the fresh-voiced chorus and dancers mingling roles and costumes with manic energy. One of the best DVDs yet.

La belle Hélène
Vesselina Kasarova mez Hélène **Steve Davislim** ten
Achille **Deon van der Walt** ten Paris **Oliver Widmer**
bar Agamemnon **Ruben Amoretti** ten Ajax I **Cheyne**
Davidson bar Ajax II **Ruth Rohner** sop Bacchis
Carlos Chausson bar Calchas **Volker Vogel** ten
Ménélas **Liliana Nichiteanu** mez Oreste **Jakob**
Baumann bar Slave Zurich Opera House Chorus
and Orchestra / Nikolaus Harnoncourt
Stage director **Helmut Lohner**
Video director **Hartmut Schottler**
Arthaus Musik 📀 100 086 (124' · Region 0)
Recorded live 1997 🅕❍

This Zurich production from 1997 fully enters into the spirit of Offenbach's satirical romp, hardly ever stepping over into farce. Everything is at once disciplined, contained and at the same time appropriately zany under the observant stage direction of Helmut Lohner.

In the pit is Harnoncourt to ensure that the musical values are as exemplary as the visual ones. His Zurich band is of a suitably small enough size to allow for all the instrumental detail to be clearly delineated. Strings use little vibrato. The composer's innate wit is to the fore. In sum, the score sounds fresh-minted.

The polyglot cast, speaking and singing excellent French, enjoys its collective self, headed by Kasarova's languidly erotic Helen. She sings her music in a suitably suggestive manner, flaunting her vocal as much as her physical attributes. Deon van der Walt, a lively Paris, sings with the sweetness and sensitivity of the best French tenors of the past in this genre. The comic roles are all enthusiastically taken, but among the lesser parts Liliana Nichiteanu steals the honours with her cheeky Oreste, sung in a firmly projected, attractive mezzo and with a glint in her eye – surely a star in the making.

Add perceptive video direction by Hartmut Schottler and superb sound and you have what amounts to an outright winner.

Les contes d'Hoffmann

Les contes d'Hoffmann
Plácido Domingo ten Hoffmann **Dame Joan**
Sutherland sop Olympia, Giulietta, Antonia, Stella
Gabriel Bacquier bar Lindorf, Coppélius,
Dapertutto, Dr Miracle **Huguette Tourangeau** mez
La Muse, Nicklausse **Jacques Charon** ten Spalanzani
Hugues Cuénod ten Andrès, Cochenille,
Pitichinaccio, Frantz **André Neury** bar Schlemil **Paul**
Plishka bass Crespel **Margarita Lilowa** mez Voice of
Antonia's Mother **Roland Jacques** bar Luther
Lausanne Pro Arte Chorus; Du Brassus Chorus;
Suisse Romande Chorus and Orchestra /
Richard Bonynge
Decca② 417 363-2DH2 (143' · ADD · T/t)
Recorded 1968 🅕❍❍➔

This is a wonderfully refreshing set. The story emerges crystal-clear, even the black ending to the Giulietta scene in Venice, which in Bonynge's text restores the original idea of the heroine dying from a draught of poison, while the dwarf, Pitichinaccio shrieks in delight. One also has to applaud his rather more controversial decision to put the Giulietta scene in the middle and leave the dramatically weighty Antonia scene till last. That also makes the role of Stella the more significant, giving extra point to the decision to have the same singer take all four heroine roles. With Dame Joan available it was a natural decision, and though in spoken dialogue she's less comfortable in the Giulietta scene than the rest, the contrasting portraits in each scene are all very convincing, with the voice brilliant in the doll scene, warmly sensuous in the Giulietta scene and powerfully dramatic as well as tender in the Antonia scene. Gabriel Bacquier gives sharply intense performances, firm and dark vocally, in the four villain roles, Hugues Cuénod contributes delightful vignettes in the four *comprimario* tenor roles, while Domingo establishes at the very start the distinctive bite in his portrait of Hoffmann; a powerful and a perceptive interpretation. The recording is vivid, and the listener is treated to some first-class playing from the Suisse Romande Orchestra.

Les contes d'Hoffmann
Raoul Jobin ten Hoffmann **Renée Doria** sop Ⓗ
Olympia **Vina Bovy** sop Giulietta **Géori Boué** sop
Antonia **Fanély Revoil** mez Nicklausse **Louis Musy**
bar Lindorf **André Pernet** bass Coppélius **Charles
Soix** bass Dapertutto **Roger Bourdin** bar Dr Miracle
René Lapelletrie ten Spalanzani **Camille Maurane**
bar Hermann **Chorus and Orchestra of the Opéra-
Comique, Paris / André Cluytens**
Naxos Historical ② 8110214/15 (130' · ADD · T)
Recorded 1948   Ⓢ●

In the 1930s in Paris, Raoul Jobin and José Luccioni were the two great opera matinée-idols. Jobin, a French Canadian, made his début in 1930 and was soon singing at both the Opéra, as Faust, Lohengrin and Raoul in *Les Huguenots*, and at the Opéra-Comique, where he was a favourite Hoffmann and Don José. This recording may perhaps find him just a little late in his career. His years at the Metropolitan (throughout the German occupation) obviously took their toll, when he sang roles that were too heavy for him in such a huge theatre. However, the splendour of this set is the authenticity of the vocal style and the diction of such stalwarts of the Opéra-Comique ensemble as Louis Musy, Roger Bourdin, Fanély Revoil (better known as an operetta singer) and, luxurious casting, Camille Maurane in the small part of Hermann.

The three heroines are well inside their roles, but they're afflicted with a little strain in the higher-lying passages. Renée Doria sang all these parts later in her career – when this recording was made she was just at the outset, having made her début in Paris in 1944. Her Olympia is strong on the *staccato* notes but a bit fragile in the long phrases – this doll broke quite easily, one imagines. In the same act, André Pernet, a great figure from pre-war Paris is a superb Coppélius. In the Venice act, Vina Bovy is dramatically convincing as Giulietta, but hasn't much vocal sheen left (she made her début in 1919). Géori Boué, the Antonia, is one of the great figures from French post-war opera, but one feels that Giulietta would have been her role ideally. As for Jobin, despite some strain, he makes a convincing poet. Although there's such strong competition on CD where *Hoffmann* is concerned, this historic version is without doubt essential listening for a sense of style if the work absorbs you.

Orphée aux enfers

Orphée aux enfers
Yann Beuron ten Orphée **Natalie Dessay** sop
Eurydice **Jean-Paul Fouchécourt** ten Aristeus-Pluto
Laurent Naouri bar Jupiter **Lydie Pruvot** sop Juno
Ewa Podles mez Public Opinion **Steven Cole** ten John
Styx **Véronique Gens** sop Vénus **Patricia Petibon** sop
Cupid **Jennifer Smith** sop Diane **Etienne Lescroart**
ten Mercury **Virginie Pochon** sop Minerva **Grenoble
Chamber Orchestra; Chorus and Orchestra of the
Opéra National de Lyon / Marc Minkowski**
EMI ② 556725-2 (110' · DDD · T/t)   Ⓕ●▶

Orphée aux enfers may be Offenbach's best-known operetta, but it's had limited attention on disc. The lightly scored original 1858 version was in two acts and four scenes. The spectacular 1874 version had lots of extra songs and ballet numbers. Since this latter demands huge forces, it's scarcely viable on stage today. The usual solution in the theatre is thus to add selected numbers from the 1874 version to the 1858 text, and this is what was done for the performances at Geneva, Lyons and Grenoble that formed the basis of this recording. Home listeners may prefer to make their own selections of numbers, and musicologically questionable decisions such as the rescoring of 1874 pieces for 1858 orchestral resources become more exposed. What matters most, though, is the quality of performance, and the pleasures of this one are formidable.

Above all, Natalie Dessay's exchanges in the First Act with her despised violinist husband (the admirable Yann Beuron) are superbly done. So is her sighing over Jean-Paul Fouchécourt's Aristeus, whose two big solos show equal elegance. Later come Laurent Naouri's formidable Jupiter and cameos such as Etienne Lescroart's agile performance of Mercury's song and Patricia Petibon's deliciously winning account of Cupid's 'Couplets des baisers'. Ensemble numbers are extremely well done and throughout, Marc Minkowski provides thoughtful, lively direction.

What causes doubt is the tendency towards overstatement, from the opening monologue of Eva Podles's Public Opinion, where almost every word seems to be given exaggerated emphasis, through Aristeus's crude falsetto in his opening solo, to a curiously mechanical version of John Styx's 'Quand j'étais roi de Béotie' and some gratuitous vocal gymnastics in the 'Hymne à Bacchus'. Ultimately, however, those doubts are banished by the virtues.

Minkowski's is a consistently imaginative performance, and at its best a superbly musical version of Offenbach's sparkling creation.

Orphée aux enfers
Yann Beuron ten Orpheus **Natalie Dessay** sop
Eurydice **Jean-Paul Fouchécourt** ten Aristeus-Pluto
Laurent Naouri bar Jupiter **Lydie Pruvot** mez Juno
Martine Olmeda mez Public Opinion **Steven Cole**
ten John Styx **Maryline Fallot** sop Venus **Cassandre
Berthon** sop Cupid **Virginie Pochon** sop Diane

Etienne Lescroart *ten* Mercury **Alketa Cela** *sop*
Minerva **Grenoble Chamber Orchestra; Chorus and
Orchestra of the Opéra National de Lyon / Marc
Minkowski**
Stage director **Laurent Pelly**
Video director **Jean-Pierre Brossmann**
TDK Mediactive ② DV-OPOAE(123' · 16:9 · PCM
Stereo, 5.1 & DTS 5.1 · 0)   Ⓕ

Before their acclaimed *La belle Hélène*, Laurent
Pelly and Marc Minkowski staged Offenbach's
first great success for Lyon Opera in the same
pleasantly outrageous manner. Minkowski's
conducting again recalls Leibowitz's classic
recordings – bone-dry, sprightly and slightly
manic. Certain quirks in the CD version, in
particular the destructive speed of Eurydice's
sensuous 'Bacchus Hymn', are explained if not
excused by Pelly's production – as manic and as
refreshing, in his clever use of dancers, surreal
sight gags, and cheerfully unfettered sex. His
'backstage' settings make less sense than
Hélène's, but the Cloud-Cushion-Land Olympus is inspired.

The hard-worked cast respond superbly, notably Natalie Dessay's modern Parisienne
Eurydice, dressy, leggy, and neurotic, delivering
zinging coloratura while bouncing on a sofa or
perched high on a stage lift.

Minkowski occasionally forces the pace, and
Pelly's high camp sometimes tips over into shrill
vulgarity. The remastered surround-sound is
rather stagey, occasionally losing voices in
unfriendly perspectives. It's still treasurable, and
vastly superior to its only DVD rival, a dismal
Brussels staging. Avoid that; buy this; rejoice.

La vie parisienne

La vie parisienne
Laurent Naouri *bar* Baron de Gondremark **Marie
Devellereau** *sop* Gabrielle **Jean-Sébastien Bou** *bar*
Raoul de Gardefeu **Marc Callahan** *bar* Bobinet **Maria
Riccarda Wesseling** *mez* Métella **Michelle
anniccioni** *sop* La Baronne **Jean-Paul Fouchécourt**
ten Frick **Lyon National Opera Chorus and
Orchestra / Sébastien Rouland**
Stage director **Laurent Pelly**
Video director **François Roussillon**
Virgin Classics ⒹⓋⒹ 519301-9 (135' · NTSC · 16:9 ·
PCM stereo, 5.0 and DTS 5.1 · 0)
Recorded live in December 2007   Ⓕ●

La Belle Hélène
Felicity Lott *sop* Hélène **Yann Beuron** *ten* Paris
Michel Sénéchal *ten* Ménélas **Laurent Naouri** *bar*
Agamennon **François Le Roux** *bar* Calchas
Les Musiciens du Louvre / Marc Minkowski
Stage director **Laurent Pelly**
Video director **Ross MacGibbon**
ArtHaus Musik ⒹⓋⒹ 107 000 (153' · 16:9 · PCM stereo,
5.1 and DTS 5.1 · 2). Recorded live at the Théâtre du
Châtelet, Paris, in 2000   Ⓕ●●

Both these productions by Laurent Pelly of classic Offenbach *opéras-bouffes* are somewhat radical in their staging. Neither of them presents the
works in a way one would choose to see very
often, but they are performed with such vigour
and vaudevillian élan that it's hard to resist their
appeal.

La vie parisienne was conceived by Offenbach's
librettists, Henri Meilhac and Ludovic Halévy,
as an entertainment for and about the hordes of
tourists visiting Paris for the 1867 Exposition
Universelle. Pelly and his designer Chantal
Thomas update it to the present, so that instead
of waiting for the train in Act 1, the two heroes,
Bobinet and Raoul de Gardefeu, are in the arrivals section of an international airport. This
scene is punctuated by many irritating announce-
ments over the loudspeakers. To a large extent
this spoils the scene, so it's a relief when it
changes to Raoul's exquisitely minimalist apartment. Here the action perks up with the arrival
of Marie Devellereau as the glove-seller, Gabrielle, and Jean-Paul Fouchécourt as Frick, the
bootmaker. The riotous finale, as the table-
d'hôte guests are summoned to dinner, really
goes with a swing. Best of all is Act 3, when all
the girls, impersonating aristocrats, arrive in
haute-couture black gowns and march around
like catwalk mannequins. In particular, Brigitte
Hool as Pauline joins Laurent Naouri as the
duped Swedish baron in a splendid account of
'O, beau nuage'. The finale, culminating in the
ensemble 'Tout tourne, tout danse' really won
me over. The last act is in a somewhat sleazy
disco, but again the sheer energy of the dancing
and the whole spirit of irreverence is so well
caught that one feels like joining in the applause.
Sébastien Rouland leads the orchestra and chorus of the Lyon Opéra in a performance that is
true to the spirit, if not the letter, of the work.
Jean-Sébastien Bou and Marc Callahan as Raoul
and Bobinet make a terrific pair of womanising
socialites, Jesus Garcia a vigorous Brésilien, and
in her few moments Michelle Canniccioni is
suitably eager as the Baroness out to savour the
delights of Paris.

Musically, *La Belle Hélène* from the Châtelet is
a stronger proposition. The production is even
more extreme, everything happening as if in the
dream of a suburban housewife, played by Dame
Felicity Lott with her usual mixture of restraint
and comic irony. Everyone is consequently in
pyjamas and night attire a lot of the time. (The
same recording has been issued on CD from
Virgin). Yann Beuron is a salty Paris, and the
presence of Michel Sénéchal, François Le Roux
and again Laurent Naouri ensures that vocal
values triumph over some of the excesses of the
production.

Tarik O'Regan   British b1978

*After studying at both Oxford and Canbridge,
O'Regan between New York City and Trinity College, Cambridge, where he is Fellow Commoner in
the Creative Arts. He has held the Fulbright Chester*

ORFF CARMINA BURANA – IN BRIEF

Janowitz; Stolze; Fischer-Dieskau; Deutsche Opera Chorus and Orchestra / Eugen Jochum
DG 447 437-2GOR (56' · DDD) Ⓜ❍❍❍❶

Recorded in the presence of the composer back in 1968. The soloists are very vivid, with Janowitz quite ravishing in her restraint and purity of tone. The chorus is superb.

Armstrong; English; Allen; London Symphony Chorus and Orchestra / André Previn
EMI 566899-2 (63' · ADD) Ⓜ❍❍❶

Still one of the great recordings of the work full of excitement, event and above all good humour. Allen is magnificent, and the sound, from 1975, still sounds amazingly vivid.

Walmsley-Clark; Graham-Hall; Maxwell; London Symphony Chorus and Orchestra / Richard Hickox
Regis RRC1136 (64' · DDD) Ⓑ❍

Hickox the choral trainer is shown off here to great effect in an exciting and vivid performance reissued at budget price. The solo singing is good too, so definitely worth considering if you're on a budget.

Matthews; Brownlee; Gerhaher; Berlin Radio Chorus; Berlin PO / Sir Simon Rattle
EMI 557888-2 (60' · DDD) Ⓕ❍❶

An invigorating revisiting of an ever-popular score: Rattle has stripped it down and rebuilt in a way that will either entrance or annoy. Thrillingly alive and superbly recorded.

Rutter; Randle; Eiche; Bournemouth choruses and SO / Marin Alsop
Naxos 8 570033 (62' · DDD) Ⓢ❶

A performance that has divided the critics. On the positive side are Alsop's innate sense of rhthm and the male soloists sing with real character. But some have found it all a little underpowered. Try and sample before you purchase – but it is a bargain!

Hendricks; Aler; Hagegård; London Symphony Chorus and Orchestra / Eduardo Mata
RCA 74321 53657-2 (60' · DDD) Ⓑ❍❶

Another stunning LSO *Carmina Burana* that employs Mata's rhythmic virtusity to spectacular effect. Full of character and beautifully sung. A superb budget version.

Popp; Van Kesteren; Prey; Bavarian Radio Chorus; Munich Radio Orchestra / Kurt Eichhorn
RCA ⒹⓋⒹ 74321 85285-9 (78') Ⓕ

Jean-Pierre Ponnelle's racy video interpretation takes Eichhorn's fine 1975 performance as its soundtrack. It's all a lot of fun and gives the work a dramatic outlet that in concert it often so desperately seems to aspire too.

Schirmer Fellowship in Music Composition at Columbia University and a Radcliffe Institute Fellowship at Harvard. He has also served on the Visiting Faculty of Yale University's Institute of Sacred Music. His music has been performed by the BBC Symphony Orchestra, London Sinfonietta, Estonian Philharmonic Chamber Choir and Los Angeles Master Chorale. He is currently working on an opera based on Joseph Conrad's Heart of Darkness.

Threshold of Night. Care Charminge Sleepe. Had I not seen the sun. The Ecstasies Above. Tal vez tenemos tiempo. Triptych. I had no time to hate
Company of Voices; Conspirare / Craig Hella Johnson
Harmonia Mundi Ⓢ HMU80 7490
(60' · DDD/DSD) Ⓕ❍❶

Tarik O'Regan can justifiably stake a claim as one of the leading British choral composers of his generation. This is supported to an extent by the seven choral compositions contained on this recording.

At the basis of O'Regan's style lies a thoroughgoing understanding of both the English choral tradition and medieval music, a knowledge gained from studies at Oxford and Cambridge. But recent works suggest that he casts his creative net much wider these days. Post-minimal and pop features can be detected in the use of straightforward harmonic progressions and melodic repetitions in the final sections of both *The Ecstasies Above* and *Triptych*, where O'Regan dispenses with contrapuntal complexity for a direct and unadorned approach. If this suggests an American influence then it is also evident in his choice of text settings, with Edgar Allan Poe and Emily Dickinson's poetry framing the collection.

However, it is sometimes difficult not to draw comparisons between the often static, sometimes propulsive, polymodal layers incorporated throughout O'Regan's music (especially effective in *Care Charming Sleepe*) and similar processes at work in the choral writing of John Adams. In contrast, Adams has effected a fine timbral and textural balance between voices and instruments in his music – homogeneity rather than hierarchy – but one senses that the string instruments contained on this recording struggle to find their place in and among the dense choral web.

Carl Orff
German 1895-1982

Orff studied at the Munich Academy and later, in 1920, with Kaminski. In 1924, with Dorothee Günther, he founded a school for gymnastics, music and dance. His adult works seek to make contact with primitive kinds of musical behaviour, as represented by ostinato, pulsation and direct vocal expression of emotion; in this he was influenced by Stravinsky (Oedipus Rex, The Wedding), though the models are coarsened to produce music of a powerful pagan sen-

sual appeal and physical excitement. All his major works, including the phenomenally successful Carmina Burana (1937), were designed as pageants for the stage.

Carmina Burana

Carmina Burana
Gundula Janowitz sop **Gerhard Stolze** ten **Dietrich Fischer-Dieskau** bar **Schönberg Boys' Choir; Chorus and Orchestra of the Deutsche Oper, Berlin / Eugen Jochum**
DG The Originals 447 437-2GOR (56' · ADD · T/t)
Recorded 1967   Ⓜ 🅞🅞🅞🅞➛

Since its original release, Jochum's performance has consistently been a prime recommendation for this much-recorded piece. Listening to it again in the superbly remastered sound, one can easily hear why. He pays great attention to detail – particularly with regard to tempo and articulation – yet the performance as a whole has a tremendous cogent sweep and the choruses have terrific power. The more reflective sections aren't neglected, however, and movements such as 'Stetit Puella', with Janowitz sounding alluring and fey, have surely never been more sensitively handled. Stolze is ideal as the roasted swan and Fischer-Dieskau encompasses the very varied requirements of the baritone's music with ease. This distinguished performance, authorised by the composer and here sounding better than ever, retains its place at the head of the queue.

Johann Pachelbel   German 1653-1706

Pachelbel was taught by two local musicians, Heinrich Schwemmer and GC Wecker. In 1669 he entered the university at Altdorf and was organist of the Lorenz-kirche there, but left after less than a year for lack of money and in 1670 enrolled in the Gymnasium Poeti-cum at Regensburg, where he continued musical studies with Kaspar Prentz. After about five years as deputy organist at St Stephen's Cathedral, Vienna (1673-7), and a year as court organist at Eisenach, Pachelbel was appointed organist of the Predigerkirche at Erfurt in June 1678, where he remained for 12 years. During this time he was outstandingly successful as organist, composer and teacher (his pupils included Johann Christoph Bach). He left Erfurt in 1690 and, after short periods as organist in Stuttgart and Gotha, returned to Nuremberg, where he was organist at St Sebald until his death. Pachelbel was a prolific composer. His organ music includes c70 chorales (mostly written at Erfurt), 95 Magnificat fugues (for Vespers at St Sebald) and non-liturgical works such as toccatas, preludes, fugues and fantasias. His preference for a lucid, uncomplicated style found fullest expression in his vocal music, which includes two masses, some important Vespers music and arias and sacred concertos. His modest contributions to chamber music include a canon that is now his best-known work. **GROVE**music

Canon

Pachelbel Canon and Gigue **Mozart** Serenade No 13. Adagio and Fugue in C minor, K546
Anonymous (arr L Mozart) Cassation in G, 'Toy Symphony'
Academy of St Martin in the Fields / Sir Neville Marriner
Philips 416 386-2PH (52' · DDD)   🅕🄳➛

Sir Neville Marriner here collects a miscellaneous group of popular classical and Baroque pieces in characteristically polished and elegant performances. Pachelbel's celebrated Canon – taken unsentimentally if sweetly at a flowing speed – is given a reprise after the fugue; unusual but why not? Warm, well-balanced recording.

Keyboard Suites

Keyboard Suites – C, S25; D minor, S26; E minor, S28; E minor, S29; F, S32; G minor, S33; G minor, S33b; G, S34; A, S36
Joseph Payne hpd
BIS CD809 (74 minutes: DDD)   🅕

First-class recordings of fine organ music and motets by Pachelbel seem to have been unable to plant his name in the minds of the general musical public other than as the composer of that attractive but over-recorded canon. These suites (definitely for harpsichord, not organ) are all printed in the Denkmäler der Tonkunst in Bayern series, but except for Nos 29, 32 and 33b their authorship is very questionable. Whoever wrote them, however, they contain some very impressive movements, and Pachelbel displays some intriguing rhythmic quirks on occasion.

Each of the suites consists of an allemand, courant and saraband, plus a 'gyque' [sic] in all but two cases; No 33 includes a lively 'ballett', Nos. 25, 36 and 28 a gavotte (that in A major a very jolly one); there are doubles in Nos 29 and 36. Playing on a copy of a bright-toned early Flemish instrument, Joseph Payne offers clean and vital performances, with neat ornaments; now and then, in his desire for expressiveness or to draw attention to a point, he's a bit mannered, but in general his playing is most appealing and he's recorded with total fidelity.

Giovanni Pacini   Italian 1796-1867

Pacini studied singing with Marchesi in Bologna, then turned to composition. Between 1813 and 1867 he wrote nearly 90 operas, first modelling them on Rossini and later, after contact with Bellini's works, giving more attention to harmonic and instrumental colour. He was gifted with melodic invention, used to effect in a variety of cabaletta types; his accompaniments and ensemble writing are weak by comparison. In 1833 increased competition from Bellini and

Donizetti caused his five-year withdrawal from the stage and he established a music school at his home in Viareggio and composed sacred works for the ducal chapel in Lucca, of which he was director from 1837. But with the immensely successful Saffo (1840), considered his masterpiece, he entered a period of more mature opera composition. Though his success and reputation outside Italy were limited, his musical weaknesses can be attributed chiefly to the circumstances in which he worked. In the face of formidable competition within Italy, he satisfied a sophisticated public for half a century. GROVEmusic

Carlo di Borgogna

Carlo di Borgogna
Bruce Ford *ten* Carlo **Elizabeth Futral** *sop* Leonora di Jork **Roberto Frontali** *bar* Arnoldo **Jennifer Larmore** *mez* Estella **Helen Williams** *sop* Amelia **Dominic Natoli** *ten* Lord Athol **Gary Magee** *bar* Gugliemo d'Erlach **Geoffrey Mitchell Choir; Academy of St Martin in the Fields / David Parry**
Opera Rara ③ ORC21 (184' · DDD · T/t)   Ⓕ●

First, a word to enthusiasts, to those with a special interest in early 19th-century opera, who may, perhaps, have acquired and enjoyed other operas of Giovanni Pacini that have appeared on records in recent years for the first time and who may look with some eagerness at this review. Don't read it! To borrow a well-known slogan of our time: just do it!

The one point that's well known about Pacini's career is that it divides in two, with a four-year period of retirement for further thought and study. From this he emerged with his masterpiece *Saffo* (1840), and the general assumption has been that the operas from before the divide are inferior. In particular, it's understood that Pacini himself recognised this, his shortcomings being brought home to him by the relative failure of the last opera he wrote before 'resting'. That opera was *Carlo di Borgogna*. It's an opera well set-up with characters and situations; more importantly, one in which the forms themselves almost guarantee satisfaction if they're handled by such a master as Pacini was. We aren't necessarily looking here for originality but (in no debased sense) for entertainment. As a matter of fact, originality is to be found as well: it's a curious feature of Pacini's writing that, while he can at one moment follow his stated theme with a sequential phrase of disheartening banality, he may also at any moment provide a harmonic or rhythmic lift that delights as it surprises.

The dominant character is Estella, Charles's true love who turns savage on being dropped in favour of an arranged marriage but changes tack again as she tries to warn him that he's going to his death. Jennifer Larmore takes full advantage of her opportunities, sings the difficult role with some depth of vocal colour, is the assured mistress of technique and gives her words a vivid intensity of expression. The lower men's voices are strongly cast, with Gary Magee wasted in a role with little to sing. Bruce Ford takes the name-part, his tone virile, runs and *gruppetti*

delivered with fluency we used to be told had disappeared with singers of the golden age.

As ever, David Parry conducts with a conviction to which his players respond, and the Mitchell Choir sing with precision and fresh tone. As to recorded sound, slightly closer contact with the soloists might be preferable, but for many this will be just about the right balance.

Maria, Regina d'Inghilterra

Maria, Regina d'Inghilterra
Nelly Miricioiu *sop* Mary Tudor **Bruce Ford** *ten* Riccardo Fenimoore **José Fardilha** *bass* Ernesto Malcolm **Mary Plazas** *sop* Clotilde Talbot **Alastair Miles** *bass* Gualtiero Churchill **Susan Bickley** *mez* Page **Benjamin Bland** *bass* Raoul **Geoffrey Mitchell Choir; Philharmonia Orch / David Parry**
Opera Rara ③ ORC15 (172' · DDD · T/t)   Ⓕ

Pacini wrote happily within the formal conventions of Italian opera in his time. Opening chorus, aria and cabaletta, duet likewise in two 'movements', big ensemble as finale of the middle act, 'brilliant' solo for *prima donna* just before the final curtain. A great point about the plot is the scope it provides for duets, which are both plentiful and good. There are choruses of merrymakers, soldiers and Londoners out for blood. The ensemble, an excellent example of its kind, comes at the point when Fenimoore is cornered and feelings run high. So do the voices. We're lucky to have Bruce Ford: at a *fortissimo* he may sound underpowered, and he doesn't play imaginatively with *mezza voce* effects, but in florid passages he moves swiftly and gracefully, he appears to be comfortable with the tessitura, and in the prison scene, which provided Ivanov with his greatest success, he sings with feeling and style.

The women have suitably contrasting voices, Mary Plazas's fresh and high, Nelly Miricioiu's older in tone, more dramatic in timbre. Both are expressive singers, and though Miricioiu too habitually resorts to the imperious glottal emphasis associated with Callas and Caballé, she brings conviction to all she does. The baritone, José Fardilha, has a touch of the flicker-vibrato that can give distinctive character, and Alastair Miles confers nobility of utterance upon the vindictive Chancellor. The cast, in fact, is worthy of the opera, which in this recording has probably its most important performance since the première of 1843. There's fine work from the Philharmonia under Parry. Recorded sound is well balanced, and the production handles the drama well. You are likely to play it straight through from start to finish, chafing at any interruption; and that says something for both the music and the drama.

Juan Gutiérrez de Padilla
Spanish c1590-1664

Born in Málaga Padilla bcame maestro di capilla in

Cadiz, where he is also known to have been a ordained priest. In 1622 he was named cantor and assistant maestro at Puebla Cathedral in Mexico with an annual salary of 500 pesos. With Gaspar Fernandes as its director, the cathedral at that time boasted one of the finest musical establishments in Spanish America, on a par with the best in Europe. As well as Latin sacred music, Padilla wrote numerous vernacular villancicos. Written in, or based on, a popular style, they were intended for the large and enthusiastic crowds attracted to services at Puebla Cathedral partly by the special music composed for specific feast days. **GROVE**music

'Streams of Tears'

Missa Ave regina caelorum. Deus in adiutorium. Mirabilia testimonia tua. Stabat mater. Transfige, dulcissime Domine. Lamentations. Tristis est anima mea. Versa est in luctum. Pater peccavi. Salve regina. Ave regina caelorum
The Sixteen / Harry Christophers
Coro COR16059 (67' · DDD)   Ⓕ Ⓞ➔

Padilla's music has been awaiting a recording such as this for some time: the earliest of the transcriptions on this recording date from the mid-1980s, when, at the prompting of Bruno Turner, British choirs were persuaded to take an interest in the music of early Spanish America. A number of publications, concerts and recordings resulted from this initiative, and the music entered to some degree into the repertoire. It is good, therefore, to see it revisited by a choir of the calibre of The Sixteen at this distance in time.

The music, much of which is fully scored – Padilla, a Spaniard who emigrated to Mexico, was particularly deft at double-choir writing – and richly sonorous, is just the kind of fare that The Sixteen excel at – the two-choir *Mirabilia testimonia tua* and the most extensive work on the disc, the *Missa Ave regina*, are fine examples. But another aspect of Padilla's style, delicate and crystalline, is seen in smaller-scale motets such as *Pater peccavi, Versa est in luctum* (a significant contribution to the Iberian tradition of settings of that text) and the intense, dissonant *Stabat mater*, as well as the remarkable devotional motet *Transfige, dulcissime Domine*, for two sopranos, alto and bass; these more intimate works also receive fine readings. In many ways, the *Salve regina* reconciles both styles to perfection, just as it does the 'old' polyphony and the new Italianate style, alternating between them and building into a positively incandescent work. The odd rather heavy-handed entry from the men apart, these works bring out the very best in The Sixteen, supple, powerful and full of colour.

Nicolò Paganini   Italian 1782-1840

Through his technique and extreme personal magnetism Paganini was not only the most famous violin virtuoso but drew attention to the significance of virtuosity as an element in art. He studied with his *father, Antonio Cervetto and Giacomo Costa and composition with Ghiretti and Paer in Parma. From 1810 to 1828 he developed a career as a 'free artist' throughout Italy, mesmerising audiences and critics with his showmanship; notable compositions were the bravura variations Le streghe (1813), the imaginative 24 Caprices Op 1 and the second and third violin concertos, surpassing in brilliance any that had been written before. After conquering Vienna in 1828 he was equally successful in Germany (Goethe, Heine and Schumann admired him), Paris and London (1831-4). His hectic international career finally shattered his health in 1834, when he returned to Parma. Apart from his unparalleled technical wizardry on the instrument, including the use of left-hand pizzicato, double-stop harmonics, 'ricochet' bowings and a generally daredevil approach to performance – all of which influenced successive violinists – he is most important for his artistic impact on Liszt, Chopin, Schumann and Berlioz, who took up his technical challenge in the search for greater expression in their own works.* **GROVE**music

Violin Concertos

No 1 in E flat, Op 6; **No 2** in B minor, Op 7, 'La campanella'

Violin Concertos Nos 1 & 2
Ilya Kaler *vn* **Polish National Radio Symphony Orchestra / Stephen Gunzenhauser**
Naxos 8 550649 (67' · DDD)   Ⓢ➔

Ilya Kaler is a Russian virtuoso, a pupil of Leonid Kogan. He's a first-rate fiddler and an excellent musician. Paganini's once fiendish pyrotechnics hold no terrors for him, not even the whistling harmonics, and how nicely he can turn an Italianate lyrical phrase, as in the secondary theme of the first movement of the First Concerto. Then he can set off with panache into a flying *staccato*, bouncing his bow neatly on the strings when articulating the delicious *spiccato* finales of both works. Stephen Gunzenhauser launches into the opening movements with plenty of energy and aplomb and is a sympathetic accompanist throughout. How nicely the violins shape the lyrical ritornello introducing the first movement of the Second, and there's some sensitive horn playing in the *Adagio*. Kaler's intonation is above suspicion and he's naturally balanced: there's none of the scratchiness that can ruin your pleasure in Paganinian pyrotechnics. With excellent notes, this is a superior product at super-bargain price. The recordings were made in the Concert Hall of Polish Radio in Katowice. It has an ideal ambience for this music: nicely warm, not clouded. Great value on all counts.

Paganini Violin Concerto No 1 **Spohr** Violin Concerto No 8, 'In modo di scena cantante'
Hilary Hahn *vn* **Swedish Radio Symphony Orchestra / Eiji Oue**
DG 477 6232GH (58' · DDD)   Ⓕ➔

After nearly 200 years Paganini still poses considerable challenges but Hilary Hahn's superior technique surmounts them easily, the highest and fastest passages accomplished with clarity, excellent intonation and no compromise on tonal quality. The notorious double-harmonics episode in the finale sounds are wonderully secure and beautiful.

And Hahn's musicianship is of a high order; we hear the Concerto not as the patchwork of showy tricks and memorable tunes it often seems, but as a well crafted, unified work. Other violinists may have produced performances with more edge-of-the-seat excitement but few have excelled Hahn for finesse. Rather than striving to present the soloist as a heroic figure, she's content, with sympathetic orchestral support, to let us hear the concerto as a beautiful, enthralling piece.

In the Spohr, Hahn plays the recitative sections with splendid, bold expressiveness, and in the brilliant final movement shows a winning combination of strength, delicacy and lyricism. Her very slow speed in the first aria, though, doesn't work: the music appears to stand still, with a complete change of mood for the contrasting episode. It's an outstanding disc, however, and can only enhance Hahn's reputation.

Cantabile in D, Op 17[a]. Violin Concerto Nos 1[b] & 2 (arr vn/pf)[a]. Introduction and Variations on 'Nel cor più non mi sento' from Paisiello's 'La Molinara', Op 38. Moses-Fantasie[a]
Ilya Gringolts vn [a]**Irina Ryumina** pf
[b]**Lahti Symphony Orchestra / Osmo Vänskä**
BIS CD999 (72' · DDD)
                                                        (F)

Ilya Gringolts is an outstanding young Russian violinist; with this Paganini programme he began his recording career at the deep end. He's able to surmount the ferocious technical demands, and has, too, a notably rich, beautiful, unforced tone. In the unaccompanied *Nel cor più non mi sento* Variations, he seems rather careful – missing the passionate directness that some bring to this piece. But Gringolts's more expansive and delicate account is equally valid, the theme, with its freely expressive ornamentation, especially appealing. The other shorter items work well, too, in particular the elegant *Cantabile* – originally for violin and guitar. Only *La campanella* is a bit disappointing: one feels the need for a more vigorous approach, and despite the finesse of the playing it's difficult not to regret the absence of the orchestra.

The First Concerto benefits from a truly outstanding accompaniment, performed (and recorded) with a wonderful sense of space and balance. Even the bass drum and cymbal parts are played with sensitivity – what can sound like a crudely overloaded score emerges here full of colour and grandeur. With such fine orchestral sonority, one might wonder what the concerto would sound like in its original key. Paganini played it in E flat, by tuning his strings a semitone higher, and wrote the orchestral parts in the higher key; his aim was to produce a more

brilliant, penetrating sound. Present-day soloists, understandably, prefer the standard tuning for such a demanding work.

Gringolts plays with sweetness or brilliance as required, though perhaps the first movement didn't need so many extreme tempo changes and perhaps the *Adagio* should have had a more dramatic tone, to match the darkly romantic orchestration. But the finale is terrific, with all the verve and high spirits you could want.

Violin and Guitar Duos

Centone di sonate Nos 7-12
Moshe Hammer vn **Norbert Kraft** gtr
Naxos 8 553142 (72' · DDD)   (S)(B)→

The *Centone di sonate* (a 'hotchpotch of sonatas') consists of 18 'sonatas' which are really salon works with a variety of movements – none of them in sonata form. Whether Paganini, who wrote them sometime after 1828, intended these pieces for public performance or merely for the use of the then abundant amateur musicians isn't known. As usual in his works of this genre, it's the violin that hogs the limelight while the guitar remains a humble bag-carrier. The guitar parts are indeed so simple that they would have been within the reach of any amateur who was capable of keeping his end up with another musician; Segovia considered them beneath his dignity and refused many invitations to play them with famous partners! Nothing is harder than to be 'simple': Mozart managed it, while at the same time being deceptively complex; Paganini did it at a far less sublime level, with sentimental, cheerful and pert tunes. Truth to tell, they aren't the kind of works which impel one to listen to them at one sitting except for the most devoted *aficionado* of Paganini's violinistic voice or of hearing the guitar in an unremittingly subservient but genuinely complementary role.

These splendid performances on modern instruments make no claim to 'authentic' status, but they're no less appealing for that. They squeeze every last drop from the music with (inauthentically) full sound, and a Siamese-twin tightness of ensemble that was probably rare amongst those who played these works in Paganini's own time. In the end, these works have a charm that's hard for any but the most straitlaced to resist. It's unlikely that the *Centone* will ever be better played and/or recorded.

Six Sonatas for Guitar and Violin, Op 2. Cantabile e Valtz, Op 19. Variazioni di bravura on Caprice No 24. Duetto amoroso. Sonata per le gran viola e chitarra
Scott St John vn **Simon Wynberg** gtr
Naxos 8 550759 (59' · DDD)   (S)(B)→

Six Sonatas for Guitar and Violin, Op 3. Sonata concertata in A, Op 61. 60 Variations on 'Barucabà', Op 14. Cantabile in D, Op 17
Scott St John vn **Simon Wynberg** gtr

Naxos 8 550690 (54' · DDD) ⓢ↦

Several of the violin/guitar duos testify to Paganini's amorous inclinations: the sections of the *Duetto amoroso* spell out the course of an affair, from beginning to separation, and may have been aimed (unsuccessfully, one imagines) at the Princess Elisa Baciocchi in Lucca. His conservative harmonic vocabulary springs few surprises and his melodies sometimes verge on banality, but by dint of sheer charm and technical ingenuity he somehow gets away with it; only the po-faced could resist an admiring smile at his effrontery. Collectively, these works present the full range of Paganini's technical armoury – left-hand pizzicatos, high harmonics, double-stopping, 'sneaky' chromatic runs and the rest, and Scott St John betrays no difficulty in dealing with every googly that comes his way. More than that, in the daunting *Sonata per le gran viola e chitarra* (celebrating Paganini's acquisition of a Stradivarius instrument) cocks a snook at every viola joke that ever was. Wynberg proves as well matched a partner as St John could have wished for. Violinists, guitarists and lovers of winsomeness for its own sake should revel in these very well-recorded discs.

24 Caprices, Op 1

24 Caprices
Itzhak Perlman *vn*
EMI Great Recordings of the Century 567237-2
(72' · ADD) Ⓜ️Ⓞ↦

This electrifying music with its dare-devil virtuosity has long remained the pinnacle of violin technique, and the *Caprices* encapsulate the essence of the composer's style. For a long time it was considered virtually unthinkable that a violinist should be able to play the complete set; even in recent years only a handful have produced truly successful results. Itzhak Perlman has one strength in this music that's all-important, other than a sovereign technique – he's incapable of playing with an ugly tone. He has such variety in his bowing that the timbre of the instrument is never monotonous. The notes of the music are dispatched with a forthright confidence and fearless abandon. The frequent double-stopping passages hold no fear for him. Listen to the fire of No 5 in A minor and the way in which Perlman copes with the extremely difficult turns in No 14 in E flat; this is a master at work.

The set rounds off with the famous A minor Caprice, which inspired Liszt, Brahms and Rachmaninov, amongst others, to adapt it in various guises for the piano.

24 Caprices
Leonidas Kavakos *vn*
Dynamic CDS66 (77' · DDD) Ⓕ Ⓞ

The Greek Leonidas Kavakos, who won first prize at the 1988 Paganini Competition in Genoa, as well as taking the 1991 *Gramophone* Concerto

Award for the Sibelius Violin Concerto, is given a recorded sound that favours the lower strings of the violin, so much so that the sonority resembles a viola. He takes a truly intelligent view of the musical potential of Paganini's frequently tortuous-sounding Caprices. He also has a pretty formidable playing equipment and captures the mysterious and obsessive side of the music.

The acoustic is spacious and affords an objective and balanced view of the music. He doesn't treat the Caprices as if they were merely *études*, but follows the composer's tempo markings with fidelity, notably in the Sixth Caprice. Kavakos saves his best playing for last: the final, and best-known, Caprice is quite superb.

24 Caprices
Tanja Becker-Bender *vn*
Hyperion CDA67763 (80' · DDD) Ⓕ Ⓞ

After nearly 200 years, the Paganini *Caprices* still present a formidable challenge to violinists. The character of the music may persuade them to adopt a bold, theatrical approach (without minding too much about small imperfections of tuning or passages of rough tone); others may prefer a more careful, considered attitude, striving for accuracy and beauty. Tanja Becker-Bender belongs to the second camp. For a few minutes you might wonder if she is missing something of the virtuoso thrill transmitted, but soon you'll be won over.

Adopting generally slower speeds, she has time to turn the music gracefully, articulate cleanly, achieve remarkable purity of tuning, and use variations of tone-colour to open up the music's expressive potential. This results in a sparkling, cleaned-up version of Paganini, sounding the more amazing for its polish and clarity, and bringing into focus the poetic, romantic sensibility that enthralled the composer's contemporaries. Rarely have the flute and horn imitations in the Ninth Caprice been more persuasively performed, and in No 21, marked *amoroso*, Becker-Bender manages to retain a tender, intimate tone where many of her rivals equate amorousness with crude intensity. The more brilliant pieces are just as successful. Paganini himself would surely have been impressed and delighted.

Giovanni Palestrina Italian c1525/6-1594

Palestrina was a pupil of Mallapert and Firmin Lebel at S Maria Maggiore, Rome, where he was a choirboy from at least 1537. He became organist of S Agapito, Palestrina, in 1544 and in 1547 married Lucrezia Gori there; they had three children. After the Bishop of Palestrina's election as pope (Julius III) he was appointed maestro di cappella of the Cappella Giulia in Rome (1551), where he issued his first works (Masses, 1554); during 1555 he also sang in the Cappella Sistina. Two of Rome's greatest churches then procured him as maestro di cappella, St John Lateran (1555-60) and S Maria Maggiore (1561-6), and in 1564 Cardinal Ippolito d'Este engaged him to oversee the music at his Tivoli estate. From 1566 he also taught music at the Seminario Romano, before returning to the Cappella Giulia as maestro in 1571.

During the 1560s and 1570s Palestrina's fame and influence rapidly increased through the wide diffusion of his published works. So great was his reputation that in 1577 he was asked to rewrite the church's main plainchant books, following the Council of Trent's guidelines. His most famous Mass, Missa Papae Marcelli, may have been composed to satisfy the council's requirements for musical cogency and textual intelligibility. Palestrina ranks with Lassus and Byrd as one of the greatest Renaissance masters. The nobility and restraint of his most expressive works established the almost legendary reverence that has surrounded his name and helped set him up as the classic model of Renaissance polyphony.   **GROVE**music

For sheer beauty of sound, this recording is unsurpassed. The choice of a programme of music by Palestrina, the one composer ever to have been honoured by official ecclesiastical recognition, was inspired. This CD represents several high points of solemn liturgy; a six-part polyphonic Mass, *Ecce ego Johannes*, and two groups of motets, including a festal psalm, two penitential pieces, antiphons for the feasts of St Peter and St Cecilia and a solemn *alternatim Magnificat*. What's very admirable about the whole performance is the excellent integration of the choir. Ivan Moody underlines in his notes Palestrina's skill in the seamless interweaving of homophony and flowing counterpoint; the choir, in its turn, moves from one to the other with the utmost ease and art. In particular, the give-and-take of dovetailing produces a perfect balance. In this respect, top praise for the trebles, with a firm, mature tone and assured flexibility.

Masses

Missa Dum complerentur. Dum complerentur. Magnificat VI toni. Motets, Book 3 – Alleluia: Veni Sancte Spiritus. Veni sancte spiritus (plainchant). Spiritus sanctus replevit totam domum. Veni Creator Spiritus
Westminster Cathedral Choir / Martin Baker
Hyperion CDA67353 (71' · DDD · T/t)   Ⓕ◐

The opening six-part motet, *Dum complerentur*, a vivid description of the coming of the Holy Spirit as a 'mighty rushing wind', has a text calculated to stimulate any composer. Palestrina's stirring motet reappears completely transformed in his Mass, quiet and pleading in the *Kyrie*, exuberant in the *Gloria*. The choir catches the spirit of each movement with remarkable flexibility .

The choir's renowned, so-called Continental, vocal quality has persisted throughout its existence, even with a succession of very different choir directors. Due in part to the building's acoustic, this factor almost certainly affects their singing of the chant. The beautiful Carolingian *Alleluia: Veni Sancte Spiritus*, with its melisma on the word 'amoris', is an excellent illustration of the trebles in full flight, singing with enormous confidence in the vast cathedral. In alternation with the low voices in the sequence *Veni Sancte Spiritus*, they have the edge over the men who sound a trifle strained on their top notes.

Palestrina's double choir version of this text shows the whole choir in top form, revelling in the composer's exciting rhythmic acrobatics: while never departing from the noble majesty of his style, Palestrina describes with thrilling realism the many-voiced confusion when 'they all began to speak in a multitude of different tongues'. Highly recommended.

Missa ecce ego Johannes. Cantantibus organis. Laudate pueri. Magnificat IV toni. Peccantem me quotidie. Tribulationes civitatum. Tu es Petrus
Westminster Cathedral Choir / James O'Donnell
Hyperion CDA67099 (65' · DDD · T/t)   Ⓕ◐

Missa Assumpta est Maria. Missa Sicut lilium inter spinas. Motets – Assumpta est Maria a 6; Sicut lilium inter spinas I. Plainchant: Assumpta est Maria
The Tallis Scholars / Peter Phillips
Gimell CDGIM020 (72' · DDD · T/t)   Ⓕ▷

In this recording of *Missa Assumpta est Maria* Peter Phillips has included the motet on which this work is based, together with another parody mass, the *Sicut lilium* with its corresponding motet. It's illuminating to hear how the larger-scale compositions unfold with reference to the original motets: close study reveals much about the compositional processes of the High Renaissance, but any listener will be able to appreciate the organic relationship between motet and Mass.

In addition, Phillips has deliberately paired two sharply contrasted parody Masses: *Assumpta est Maria*, the better known, is thought to be one of Palestrina's last masses, while *Sicut lilium* dates from relatively early in his career. The former, with its major tonality and *divisi* high voices, is marvellously bright and open, and is given an outgoing performance; the latter, inflected with chromaticism and melodic intervals that constantly fall back on themselves, is darker-hued and more plaintive, a mood well captured here in the intensity of the singing. But what's perhaps most striking is the difference in compositional technique between the two works: *Sicut lilium* relies largely onimitative textures for the unfolding of its structure (though there are the customary block chords on phrases such as 'et homo factus est', performed here with magical effect), while *Assumpta est Maria* makes far greater use of vocal scoring as a formal device, and thus looks forward to the contrast principle of the Baroque. The Tallis Scholars make the most of the contrasted blocks of sound here, achieving an impressive vocal blend and balance. The phrasing, particularly in the *Kyrie*, is perhaps a little too mannered and the very beautiful *Agnus Dei* verges on the narcissistic and therefore becomes too static. The flow in the *Missa Sicut lilium*, though, is excellent throughout.

Music for Holy Week

Anonymous Hosanna filio David **Palestrina** Stabat
mater. Domine Jesus in qua nocte. Improperia. Terra
tremuit. Motets, Book 2 – Pueri Hebraeorum. Fratres
ego enim accepi. Victimae Paschali. Crux fidelis/
Pange lingua. O Domine, Jesu Christe. Populi Meus.
Ardens est cor meum. Congratulamini mihi omnes.
Haec Dies. Crucem Sanctam Subiit. Magnificat III
Toni a 6
The Cardinall's Musick / Andrew Carwood
ASV Gaudeamus CDGAU333 (79' · DDD · T/t) Ⓕ

This recording of Palestrina's music for Holy
Week opens with the strong rising fifth of the
Palm Sunday plainchant antiphon *Hosanna filio
David*. We go on to experience the solemn
moments of the liturgy through music of outstanding dignity and beauty. After the Procession,
the stern Palm Sunday Offertory *Improperium*, a
slow foreboding of what is to come, is viewed with
quiet calm. The same mood is captured in two
settings of the Institution of the Eucharist, the
first subdued and hushed, despite the massive
means – eight voices – the second even more so,
with five low voices. The Good Friday *Reproaches*
and *Crux fidelis* are expressed simply but effectively by choral homophony alternating with
chant. Carwood's restraint, blending of timbres
and careful phrasing can't be faulted.

In Palestrina's monumental *Stabat Mater* for
double choir is central to the recording. Carwood highlights every articulation of the architecture, guiding the listener from suffering to
hope. The subtle final entries of 'Paradisi gloria'
reflect the calm of the earlier pieces, but with a
glow foreshadowing the victory to come.

Christ's resurrection is marked in *Terra tremuit* by great leaping octaves and fifths and rapid
rising scales. Mary Magdalene's fruitless searching, followed by the gentlest possible singing of
the Alleluias in the antiphon *Ardens est*, finally
yields to total rejoicing in the double choir
responsory *Congratulamini*: the singers capture
her moment of ecstasy; she's seen the risen
Lord, and her joy is complete. The Easter gradual *Haec dies* is all lightness and flight, with cries
of 'exultemus' chasing each other. The final
sequence, *Victimae paschali laudes*, is a brilliantly
dramatic interpretation with vigorous and
imaginative rhythmic variety.

Music for Holy Saturday Ⓟ
Lamentations, Book III – I-III. Stabat mater.
Benedictus for Holy Week. Sicut cervus. Responsories
and Antiphons
Musica Contexta / Simon Ravens
Chandos Chaconne CHAN0679 (60' · DDD · T/t)
Ⓕ**O**➔

This outstanding recording of music for Holy
Saturday opens with two lessons from the third
of Palestrina's four settings of texts from *Lamentations*, passages chanted during the Office of
Tenebrae on the last three days of Holy Week.

The third lesson is Palestrina's superb setting of
the *Prayer of Jeremiah*.

The performance is objectively straightforward, allowing the music, in its utter poignancy
expressed with marked restraint, to speak for
itself. The clarity of the individual voices is
remarkable and the acoustic clear, yet warm:
even the six-part final cry, 'Jerusalem… conver-
tere ad Dominum Deum tuum', comes across
with perfect intelligibility. In the chanted liturgy
each lesson is followed by a florid reponsory,
and full marks should go to Musica Contexta for
transcribing these chants from Giovanni Guidetti's edition of 1587, which naturally comes
from the right place and is of the right date.

Though the responsories might have been better in a slower, more determinedly solemn style,
these singers are well on the way to achieving
perfection here. It's particularly interesting to
hear them sing Palestrina's wonderful *Sicut cervus*,
with its surging phrases, and also his famous *Stabat
mater* for double choir, displaying that dramatic
alternation between antiphonal choir and combined choral sections. For maximum effect, more
antiphonal distinction might have helped in the
choir – versus – choir sections; but overall this is
a well-thought-out and moving performance.

Giovanni Antonio Pandolfi
Italian fl1660-1669

*Italian composer and violinist Pandolfi is a shadowy
figure known only for handful of violin sonatas. He
was among the instrumentalists of Archduke Ferdin-
and of Austria at Innsbruck when his opp 3 and 4
violin sonatas were published in 1660 and there is
little doubt a 1669 volume of sonatas attributed to
'D. Gio. Antonio Pandolfi' is by the same composer.*
GROVEmusic

Violin Sonatas

Six Sonatas per chiesa e camera, Op 3. Ⓟ
Six Sonatas for Violin and Continuo, Op 4
Andrew Manze *vn* **Richard Egarr** *hpd*
Harmonia Mundi HMG507241 (80' · DDD) Ⓜ**OOO**

 These are virtuoso performances of
some quite extraordinary music. Each
sonata has its own descriptive subtitle
and a movement layout which seems reluctant to
conform to any set pattern. Presumably the sections have their own tempo indications, though
these aren't disclosed either in the booklet or in
the listing on the reverse side of the box. A pity,
since there are lots of interesting and unusual
juxtapositions of a strikingly nonconformist
nature. Much of the writing is characterised by
virtuoso figurations which, especially in faster
movements, might become a little wearisome in
the hands of a lesser player. But Manze seems to
sense this danger and averts it with panache and a
highly developed sense of fantasy. Slow movements, on balance, are more interesting. There's

an especially memorable one in *La Clemente*, the fifth sonata of Op 3, with a pathos-laden aria-like character. Manze plays it sensitively and the result is touching. Several movements have a strong ostinato element and, in *La Monella Romanesca*, the third piece from Op 4, we have a set of variations on a melody contained in the bass.

Harpsichordist Richard Egarr is a lively and an imaginative accompanist throughout. In short, an exhilarating recital of music whose exoticism, melancholy and wild, passionate outbursts resist categorisation and convenient definition. Strongly recommended.

Andrzej Panufnik   Polish/British 1914-1991

He began his formal musical training in 1932 at the Warsaw Conservatory, taking classes in percussion before transferring to theory and composition. His first acknowledged work, the Piano Trio, was composed in 1934. After graduating in 1936, he studied conducting with Weingartner in Vienna (1937–8) before following the well-trodden path of inter-war Polish composers to Paris. During World War II Panufnik stayed in Warsaw and participated in its severely restricted musical life, notably as a duo-pianist with Lutosławski in café concerts and underground events, but also conducting the premières of his Uwertura tragiczna (or Tragic Overture) and second wartime symphony. In 1944–5 all his manuscripts were inadvertently destroyed by an occupant of a friend's Warsaw apartment. After the war, Panufnik reconstructed several of these lost scores and in the process persuaded the publishers PWM to adopt clearer score layouts – since universally familiar – which left pages blank of all but the active playing parts. Between 1945 and 1947 he worked mainly as a conductor, firstly of the Kraków PO and then of the Warsaw PO. Panufnik was soon acknowledged as an innovatory composer thanks largely to Circle of 5ths and the orchestral Lullaby and Nocturne, all composed in 1947. In the same year he was awarded the Szymanowski Prize for the Nocturne, while in 1949 his Sinfonia rustica took the Chopin Prize.

Despite his almost hermetic compositional world, Panufnik's aesthetic remained firmly rooted in 18th- and 19th-century practices, drawing on tonal, rhythmic and gestural conventions as a counterweight to his deployment of pitch cells. If some of his more severe works appear over-formulated, others demonstrate a keen ability to harness geometric designs to progressive effect.

GROVEmusic

Symphonies

Symphonies – No 3, 'Sinfonia sacra'; No 5, 'Sinfonia di sfere'. Heroic Overture. Landscape
Tampere Philharmonic Orchestra / John Storgårds
Ondine ODE1101-5 (75' · DDD)   Ⓕ

Panufnik's music has always seemed more elusive than its demonstrable surface suggests. Even the

wartime *Heroic Overture* – a work that plays to the gallery and knows it – has a more sober subtext as the Polish patriotic song on which it's based is secreted in the background. Is its relegation a symbol of repression? Could be, but Panufnik's driving optimism simultaneously transforms his source into a beacon of hope, something to be aspired to at a time of uncertainty.

The Tampere Philharmonic deliver a rhythmically propulsive and dramatically epic performance. Throughout the disc, the Tampere brass sound has the swank and punch of a big band, while the string-playing is fastidiously nuanced – power-house sheets of sound rain down as required, and *pianissimi* are acutely hushed. This honed orchestral playing makes for a *Sinfonia sacra* that's a revelation. Probably Panufnik's most popular symphony, the work begins with brass fanfares embedded with tart harmonic ambiguities that Storgårds has primed with snarling clarity. His sense of pace, as Panufnik strips the orchestra down to strings alone and rebuilds again over a 30-minute duration, has the precision of sonar and supreme dramatic flair.

Panufnik's increasing interest in geometry governed much of the music he wrote in the 1970s, the *Sinfonia di sfere* included. The beauty of the music became highly objectified, just as his ear for piquant harmonies and idiosyncratic orchestration intensified. A potent combination, equally powerfully in the execution.

Roxanna Panufnik   British b1968

Roxanna Panufnik, the daughter of the composer Sir Andrzej Panufnik, studied composition at the Royal Academy of Music. She has written opera, ballet, music theatre, choral works, chamber music and music for film and television.

Westminster Mass

Westminster Mass[a]. Douai Missa Brevis[b]. Spring[c]. Prayer[d]. The Christmas Life[e]. Angels Sing![f]
[bd]**Bridget Corderoy,** [c]**Katherine Seaton,** [ce]**Helen Semple** sops [be]**David Rees-Jones bass** [cef]**Jeremy Filsell** org [bcdef]**Joyful Company of Singers / Peter Broadbent;** [a]**Westminster Cathedral Choir;** [a]**City of London Sinfonia / James O'Donnell**
Warner Classics 2564 60292-2 (65' · DDD · T/t)   Ⓕ▷▶

This recording of the *Westminster Mass* first appeared in 1999 alongside music by Howells, Pärt and Tavener – strange bedfellows for such a vibrant and positive composer. Now Warner Classics has had the good sense to devote an entire disc to Roxanna Panufnik's choral music, and so reveals what a superb composer for choir she is.

More than her deft handling of choral forces, what stands out is her instinctive feel for words; whether they are the Latin text of the Mass (the *Douai* Mass; the Westminster one uses English), the complex poetry of Gerard Manley Hopkins, or simple Christmas verses for Polish children, she treats them with equal respect, and while there's some delicious word-painting, particularly in the Hopkins setting, *Spring*, her real skill lies in an ability to find, in musical language, the essence of the texts.

The passionate *Douai* Mass was composed in 2001 for a mixed *a cappella* group, and stretches choral technique to the highest professional level. It provides a glorious showcase for Peter Broadbent and his outstanding Joyful Company of Singers; its highly effective quasi-Orthodox chanting and almost oriental decorative lines are magnificently sung by David Rees-Jones and a sumptuous-voiced Bridget Corderoy.

The disc takes its title from a setting of four Polish Christmas Carols composed for an Ealing Children's choir. *Angels Sing!* is full of youthful spirit and occasional naivety, but heard here performed by this exceptionally accomplished group, with Jeremy Filsell an astonishingly virtuoso accompanist, one wonders just how gifted those Ealing children must have been.

Sir Hubert Parry
British 1848-1918

Parry studied at Oxford and with Pierson and Dannreuther, publishing songs, church music and piano works from the 1860s. He taught at the Royal College of Music from 1883 (succeeding Grove as director in 1894), also becoming professor at Oxford (1900-1908) and president of the Musical Association (1901-8). Among his scholarly interests were Bach and the history of musical style, on which he wrote perceptively. His cantatas Scenes from Prometheus Unbound (1880), Blest Pair of Sirens (1887) and L'allegro ed il penseroso (1890) made a decisive impact for their poetic merit and advanced (Wagnerian) idiom. The anthem I was glad (1902), the choral Songs of Farewell (1916) and many of the unison songs including The Lover's Garland and Jerusalem show a similar regard for text and a fresh lyricism. GROVEmusic

Complete Organ Works

Fantasia and Fugue in G (1882 & 1913 vers)[a]. Three Chorale Fantasias[a]. Chorale Preludes, Sets 1[a] & 2[b]. Elegy in A flat[a]. Toccata and Fugue in G[a]. Elégie[b] **Various** A Little Organ Book in Memory of Sir Hubert Parry[b]
James Lancelot *org*
Priory ② PRCD682AB (135' · DDD) Ⓕ❍❍❍

 It's all too easy to dismiss Parry's music as being workmanlike and living in the shadow of Bach and Brahms. Yet there's real beauty and passion here, and at his best Parry can match the intensity of his contemporary Max Reger.

The appeal of this recording is enhanced by the inclusion of both the published and unpublished versions of the C major Fantasia and Fugue, and also by *A Little Organ Book*. This latter collection is an intensely moving tribute to Parry by 13 of his friends, colleagues and pupils (including Stanford, Bridge and Thalben-Ball).

This recording presents the best possible advocacy for Parry, and the combination of Lancelot and the Durham Willis/Harrison organ is, to coin a phrase, a 'dream ticket'. The greatness of Lancelot's playing lies in the perfect fusion of meticulously honed detail with an effortless flow to the whole performance. He fully exploits the beauty and grandeur of Durham's magical organ, and of all the available CDs, this one is the finest showcase for this most charismatic of cathedral instruments. The excellence of the playing is matched by the recording. Quite simply, this is a definitive, outstanding, glorious recording.

I was glad... / Jerusalem

I was glad when they said unto me. Evening Service in D, 'Great'. Songs of Farewell. Hear my words, ye people. Jerusalem
Timothy Woodford, Richard Murray-Bruce *trebs* **Andrew Wickens, Colin Cartwright** *countertens* **David Lowe, Martin Pickering** *tens* **Bruce Russell, Paul Rickard** *bars* **John Heighway** *bass* **Roger Judd** *org* **Choir of St George's Chapel, Windsor / Christopher Robinson**
Hyperion CDA66273 (58' · DDD · T) Ⓕ

The more of Parry's music one comes to know, the more apparent it becomes that the received opinion of him is askew. Take the 1882 settings of the *Magnificat* and *Nunc dimittis*, for instance. These, amazingly, were not published until 1982. This recording – another example of Hyperion's courageous policy – shows how un-Victorian in the accepted sense they're. In other words, they're bold, unconventional and unsanctimonious – like quite a lot of Victorian church music, one may add. Perhaps the big anthem, *Hear my words* (1894) shows more signs of conventionality, but it has an attractive part for solo soprano (treble here) and ends with the hymn 'O praise ye the Lord'. The St George's Chapel Choir, conducted by Christopher Robinson, sings these works with more ease than it can muster for the famous and magnificent Coronation anthem *I was glad*, ceremonial music that not even Elgar surpassed. A sense of strain among the trebles is always evident. Although a wholly adult choir in the *Songs of Farewell* might be preferable, these are assured and often beautiful performances – excellent diction – of these extraordinarily affecting motets. English music doesn't possess much that's more perfect in the matching of words and music than the settings of 'There is an old belief' and 'Lord, let me know mine end', invidious as it is to select only two for mention. A stirring *Jerusalem* completes this enterprising recording, which brings the sound of a great building into our homes with absolute fidelity.

Arvo Pärt

Estonian b1935

Pärt was a pupil of Eller at the Tallinn Conservatory until 1963 while working as a sound producer for Estonian radio (1957-67); in 1962 he won a prize for a children's cantata (Our Garden) and an oratorio (Stride of the World). Early works followed standard Soviet models, but later he turned to strict serial writing, in rhythm as well as pitch (Perpetuum mobile,1963) and then collage techniques (Symphony No 2, 1966; Pro et contra for cello and orchestra,1966). In the 1970s he came into contact with plainchant and the music of the Orthodox Church, which affected his music both technically and spiritually. This is seen in, for example, Symphony no.3 (1971) and the cantata Song for the Beloved (1973) as well as Tabula rasa for three violins, strings and prepared piano (1977). The music of other composers is evoked, drawing on minimalist techniques of repetition, in such works as Arbos for chamber ensemble (1977, Janácek), Summa for tenor, baritone and ensemble (1980, Stravinsky), Cantus in Memory of Benjamin Britten for bell and strings (1980, Britten). GROVEmusic

Symphony No 3

Estonian National Symphony Orchestra / Paavo Järvi
Virgin Classics 545501-2 (73' · DDD) Ⓕ ⦿ Ɗ→

With Arvo Pärt the terms of comparison normally used for focusing differences between this or that recording tend to fall redundant. Pärt's mature music responds most readily to luminous textures, carefully timed silences and mastery of line, and only rarely to the more subjective impulses of dramatic conducting.

Järvi's performance of the first movement suggests urgent parallels with the fraught confrontations in Nielsen's Fifth. And there's more than a hint of 'the spring water purity of Sibelius's Sixth Symphony' in the finale. Everywhere one senses the hovering spectre of early music, but this Third Symphony is the ideal stepping stone for first-timers who wish to journey from standard symphonic fare to Pärt's cloistered tintinnabulation.

The more familiar tintinnabulation pieces work very well, with Järvi opting in the *Cantus* and *Festina lente* for warmer textures than some rivals, which usefully underlines Pärt's quietly cascading harmonies. There are those who will still prefer a more chaste sonority, the sort favoured on virtually all the ECM productions. But Paavo Järvi's more central approach will appeal to those who until now have heard in Pärt's music ascetic denial rather than quiet affirmation. Recommended.

Additional recommendation

Coupled with: Tabula rasa[a]. Collage on B-A-C-H.

[a]**Hatfield,** [a]**Hirsch** *vns* **Ulster Orchestra / Yuasa**
Naxos 8 554591 (52' · DDD) Ⓢ Ɗ→

Yuasa's reading is somewhat akin to Järvi's first (BIS) recording – certainly for tempo. The Ulster brass are excellent and if the Orchestra's strings aren't quite on a par with those in Bamberg and Gothenburg, they're still pretty good. Quality samplings of Pärt don't come any cheaper.

Fratres / Summa

Fratres (seven versions). Summa. Festina Lente. Cantus in Memory of Benjamin Britten.
Peter Manning *vn* **France Springuel** *vc*
Mireille Gleizes *pf* **I Fiamminghi**
Telarc CD80387 (79' · DDD) Ⓕ

Telarc's Fratres-Fest proves beyond doubt that good basic material can be reworked almost *ad infinitum* if the manner of its arrangement is sufficiently colourful. This sequence is particularly imaginative in that it alternates two varied pairs of *Fratres* with atmospheric original string pieces, then separates the last two versions with the sombre pealing of *Festina Lente*. The first *Fratres* opens to a low bass drone and chaste, ethereal strings: the suggested image is of a slow oncoming processional – mourners, perhaps, or members of some ancient religious sect – with drum and xylophone gradually intensifying until the percussive element is so loud that it resembles Copland's *Fanfare for the Common Man*. One envisages aged figures who have been treading the same ground since time immemorial, whereas the frantically propelled, arpeggiated opening to the version for violin, strings and percussion leaves a quite different impression. Still, even here the music does eventually calm and Peter Manning provides an expressive solo commentary.

Next comes the gentle cascading of Pärt's *Cantus in Memory of Benjamin Britten*, with its weeping sequences and lone, tolling bell. The eight-cello *Fratres* uses eerie harmonics (as does the cello and piano version that ends the programme), whereas *Fratres* for wind octet and percussion is cold, baleful, notably Slavonic-sounding and occasionally reminiscent of Stravinsky. The alternation of *Summa* (for strings) and the quartet version of *Fratres* works nicely, the former more animated than anything else on the disc; the latter, more intimate. The performances are consistently sympathetic, and the recordings are excellent.

Lamentate

Lamentate[a]. Da pacem Domine[b]
[a]**Alexei Lubimov** *pf* [b]**Hilliard Ensemble;** [a]**Stuttgart Radio Symphony Orchestra / Andrey Boreyko**
ECM New Series 476 3048 (43' · DDD · T) Ⓕ Ɗ→

The main piece on this latest release has passages of visceral power unheard in Pärt's work for almost three decades. *Lamentate* was inspired by Anish Kapoor's gigantic sculpture *Marsyas*, which filled the Turbine Hall at Tate Modern in London. Confronted with this monumental work, Pärt felt he was standing before his own body after death. 'I had a strong sense of not being ready to die,' he says, 'and was moved to ask myself what I could still accomplish in the time left to me.' *Lamentate* is intended as a lament for the living, 'struggling with the pain and hopelessness of this world'. The solo piano part can be seen as the first person narrative of an individual, beset by challenges represented by the orchestra, which uses sharper textures, more dramatic gestures and a broader range of colours than we usually expect from this most controlled and ascetic of composers. It makes one eager to know what his next step will be.

In *Da pacem Domine* (2004), for which Sarah Leonard extends the Hilliard's range, Pärt takes a ninth-century antiphon as his starting-point, floating the serene, radiant lines of this prayer for peace with characteristic airy grace, slowly opening up the textures and exploring some tart harmonies before returning to a final consoling chord.

Berliner Messe

Berliner Messe. Magnificat. Seven Magnificat
Antiphons. The Beatitudes. Annum per Annum.
De profundis
Polyphony / Stephen Layton with **Andrew Lucas** org
CDA66960 (74' · DDD · T/t)   Ⓕ

Pärt's music is about equilibrium and balance – balance between consonance and dissonance, between converging voices and, in the context of a CD such as this, between the individual works programmed. Stephen Layton has chosen well, starting with the variegated *Berliner Messe* and closing with the starkly ritualistic *De profundis*, a memorable and ultimately dramatic setting of Psalm 130 for male voices, organ, bass drum and tam-tam, dedicated to Gottfried von Einem. The Mass features two of Pärt's most powerful individual movements, a gently rocking 'Veni Sancte Spiritus' and a *Credo* which, as Meurig Bowen's unusually perceptive notes remind us, is in essence a major-key transformation of the better-known – and more frequently recorded – *Summa*. Everything here chimes to Pärt's tintinnabulation style, even the brief but fetching organ suite *Annum per Annum*, where the opening movement thunders an alarm then tapers to a gradual *diminuendo*, while the closing coda shoulders an equally well-calculated *crescendo*. The five movements in between are mostly quiet, whereas *The Beatitudes* flies back to its opening tonality on 'a flurry of quintuplet broken chords'. It's also the one place that witnesses a momentary – and minor – blemish on the vocal line, but otherwise Layton directs a fine sequence of warmly blended performances. Polyphony employs what one might roughly term an 'early music' singing style, being remarkably even in tone, largely free of vibrato and alive to phrasal inflexions.

If you're new to Pärt's music, then this disc would provide an excellent starting-point. Maybe the individually shaded *Seven Magnificat Antiphons* first, then tackle the *Berliner Messe*, followed, perhaps, by the *Magnificat*.

Berliner Messe[a]. Bogoróditse Djévo. I am the True
Vine. Kanon pokajanen – Ode IX. The Woman with
the Alabaster Box. Tribute to Caesar.
Pro Arte Singers, [a]**Theatre of Voices / Paul Hillier**
bar with [a]**Christopher Bowers-Broadbent** org
Harmonia Mundi HMU90 7242 (58' · DDD · T/t)   Ⓕ Ⓞ

I am the True Vine was composed in 1996 for the 900th anniversary of Norwich Cathedral, whereas *Tribute to Caesar* and *The Woman with the Alabaster Box* were commissioned in 1997 for the 350th Anniversary of the Karlstad Diocese in Sweden. Both works bear witness to a widened expressive vocabulary and, like *I am the True Vine*, take their creative nourishment from the power of words.

The remaining items can also be heard, in one form or another, on alternative recordings. Hillier's reading of the beautiful Ninth Ode from *Kanon pokajanen* is slower by some two minutes than Toñu Kaljuste's première recording of the parent work on ECM (an absolute must for Pärt devotees), which is surprising given the less reverberant acoustic on the new CD. Both here and in the *Berliner Messe*, ECM's sound-frame suggests greater space and tonal weight, though this latest production is equally effective in its own quite different way. Pärt's 'revision' of the *Messe* is an update of his original score (which is warmly represented in its full-choir guise on Hyperion). In a second version (the one featured on ECM), the organ part was replaced by a string orchestra, whereas a third version (the one offered here) features an organ revision of the string score. Comparing Hillier's vocal quartet recording with Kaljuste's string version with choir inclines one towards the silvery organ registrations in the *Credo* and depth of organ tone in the *Agnus Dei*. As for the rest, there's sufficient contrast between the two to warrant owning – or at least hearing – both. With fine sound quality, first-rate singing and concisely worded annotation (by Paul Hillier) this should prove a popular, indeed an essential, addition to Pärt's ever-growing discography.

Como cierva sedienta

'Orient and Occident'
Como cierva sedienta[a]. Orient and Occident.
Ein-Wallfahrtslied[a]
Swedish Radio [a]**Choir and Symphony Orchestra /
Tonu Kaljuste**
ECM New Series 472 080-2 (47' · DDD)   Ⓕ Ⓞ Ⓞ Ⓞ ▷

This programme represents a retreat from the remote cloister where for so long Arvo Pärt invited us to join him, a definite shift from the aerated tintinabuli. The purity remains, so do the spare textures and, to a limited extent, earlier stylistic traits. Pärt's voice is always recognisable. And yet who, years ago, could have anticipated the tempered tumult that erupts in the third movement of *Como cierva sedienta*, a half-hour choral drama commissioned by the Festival de Música de Canarias?

This recording subscribes to ECM's well-tried aesthetic, in which clarity, fine-tipped detail and carefully gauged perspectives are familiar priorities. The texts come from Psalms 42 and 43, opening with 'As the hart panteth…' (Psalm 42). Even in the first few seconds, after chorus and bell have registered, vivid instrumental colour signals a fresh departure. It's almost as if Pärt is relishing textures previously denied him, like a penitent released from fasting. Take the second movement, 'Why art thou cast down, my soul?', which opens among lower strings then switches to tactile *pizzicati* and woodwinds that are almost Tchaikovskian in their post-Classical delicacy. The long closing section is pensive but conclusive: a dramatic opening, drum taps that recall Shostakovich 11, expressively varied instrumental commentary, quiet string chords later on and a closing episode filled with equivocal tranquillity.

The two shorter works are also significant. *Wallfahrtslied* (1984, 'Song of Pilgrimage'), a memorial to a friend, is presented in the revised version for strings and men's choir. Again Pärt engages a lyrical muse, particularly for the emotionally weighted prelude and postlude whereas the accompaniment to the main text (Psalm 121, 'I lift up mine eyes unto the hills…'), a combination of *pizzicato* and shudderingbowed phrases, suggests a lament tinged with anger.

The seven-minute string piece *Orient and Occident* has 'a monophonic line which runs resolutely through [it]', to quote Pärt's wife. Snake-like oriental gestures, coiled with prominent *portamenti* (the sort used by Indian orchestras) sound like an Eastern variant of Pärt's earlier string works. The choral pieces, though, are the prime reasons for investing in this exceptional and musically important release.

Da pacem

'Da pacem'
An den Wassern zu Babel. Magnificat. Nunc dimittis. Dopo la vittoria. Da pacem Domine. Two Slavic Psalms. Salve regina. Littlemore Tractus
Estonian Philharmonic Chamber Choir / Paul Hillier with **Christopher Bowers-Broadbent** *org*
Harmonia Mundi HMU90 7401 (65' · DDD · T/t)　Ⓕ

This collection showcases four compositions from this decade alongside some earlier works, most of which have been revised, as is Pärt's habit, within the past 15 years. While his methodology has remained much the same, Pärt admitted a greater harmonic and textural richness over that period, and this relative lushness is superbly realised by the EPC Choir without ever betraying the fundamental asceticism of Pärt's sound.

The album opens with the most recent piece, *Da pacem Domine* (2004), a typical work not least because of its slow harmonic speed coupled with increasingly intense light and colour. It contrasts with *Salve regina* (2001-2) which, as Hillier comments, could almost be 'a dream sequence from a film about a peasant community' in the early passages. Indeed, at first hearing one could almost confuse it with something Preisner might have written for Kieslowski, although there are enough characteristic chords and intervals to mark it out as Pärt. The Psalms (1984), with their unusually strong Slavonic tinge, again show the variety Pärt can achieve within restricted means. As always, Hillier and his colleagues have done Pärt proud. This beautiful release is another compelling illustration of the emotional and textural intensity central to the composer's art.

Mein Weg hat Gipfel und Wellentäler[c].
Da pacem Domine[ac]. In principio[ab]. La Sindone[ab].
Cecilia, vergine romana[ab]. Für Lennart in memoriam[c]
[a]**Estonian Philharmonic Chamber Choir;**
[b]**Estonian National Symphony Orchestra;**
[c]**Tallinn Chamber Orchestra / Tõnu Kaljuste**
ECM New Series 476 6990 (71' · DDD)　Ⓕ Ⓞ▶

These recent works demonstrate a certain expansion in Pärt's horizons. They still dwell in the niche of lapidary minimalism, but while they keep faith with their trademark 'tintinnabulatory' style, they now use it with flexibility and flow. The dramatic directness of *In principio*, at 20 minutes the longest work on this CD, has one thinking of Janáček or even the Icelander Jón Leifs, not to speak of its candidly neo-Bachian progressions; exhilaration emanates from this score, along with piety and lamentation. Of the other works for chorus and orchestra, *Cecilia, vergine romana* commemorates in more restrained terms the martyrdom of the third-century Roman noblewoman adopted 1200 years later as the patron saint of music, while the five-minute *Da pacem Domine* is a statuesque tribute to the victims of the 2004 Madrid terrorist bombings.

La Sindone ('The Shroud'), for trumpet, trombone, four percussionists and strings, leaves more room for listeners to find their own symbolic meaning in its frequent silences. *Mein Weg* ('My Path'), for 14 strings and percussion, is nothing to do with autobiography but a response to an extract from the French-Jewish poet Edmond Jabès's *Livre des questions* concerning the vissicitudes of life, and the disc ends with an austere memorial to Lennart Meri, president of Estonia from 1992 to 2001. Superbly performed and recorded
.

Passio

Passio Domini nostri Jesu Christi secundum Johannem
Mark Anderson *ten* **Robert Macdonald** *bass*

Tonus Peregrinus / Antony Pitts
Naxos 8 555860 (62' · DDD) ⓈⓄⓄ⇨

Arvo Pärt's *Passio* is a shining beacon among countless late 20th-century religious works that confronted the formidable prospect of a new millennium. Put briefly, *Passio* sets St John's gospel to a simple but powerful triadic musical language, its prescribed forces limited to a small chorus, a handful of solo voices and a chamber-size instrumental line-up consisting of organ, violin, oboe, cello and bassoon. Pärt treats the text as paramount and yet there's scarcely a hint of word painting in the accepted sense of the term. Spiritual underlining, yes, with telling support from the solo instruments. There are no written dynamics save for the opening, marked *Langsam* and *forte*, and the close, a *Largo* that blossoms from *pianissimo* to triple *forte*. Which doesn't mean that the singers are expected to deliver monotonously uninflected lines. Thankfully, none of them does.

Tonus Peregrinus shape phrases with a certain degree of freedom, just as choirs on rival versions have done before them. And Antony Pitts comes up trumps in his ability to keep lines lively and fluid, blending or clarifying as the text dictates. His is an excellent reading, always alert to Pärt's shifting harmonic plane and with consistently fresh voices, the women especially. Robert Macdonald's 'inward' portrayal of Jesus is nicely judged and Pitts's instrumental group is more than adequate.

Viewed overall, Tonus Peregrinus and Naxos have done Pärt proud. If this is your first *Passio*, rest assured that all the essentials are there. And if you want a top-grade specimen of quality music from the past 40 years, you won't find better. *Passio* truly is a wonderful work.

Nunc dimittis

'Triodion'

Dopo la vittoria. Nunc dimittis. ...which was the son of.... I am the true vine. Littlemore Tractus[a]. Triodion. My heart's in the Highlands[ab]. Salve regina
[b]**David Jones** *counterten* [a]**Christopher Bowers Broadbent** *org* **Polyphony / Stephen Layton**
Hyperion CDA67375 (77' · DDD · T/t) ⒻⓄⓄ

Meurig Bowen's notes observe that choral pieces composed in the 1990s suggested Pärt was moving into 'more complex, exotic harmonic territory'. Some of his music began to give a glimpse of what was described as 'an attractively post-Minimalist aspect' of the composer's recent work. All rather premature, perhaps, since, as Bowen acknowledges, Pärt subsequently returned to a more strictly diatonic, triadic approach.

Even so, the staccato, carol-like episodes bracketing *Dopo La Vittoria*, commissioned in 1991 and delivered in 1997, come as a shock, but the bulk of the piece is more recognisably by Pärt, and the *Nunc dimittis*, with its lovely, lambent solo part for soprano Elin Thomas, evoking Allegri's *Miserere*, assuages all doubts.

The idea of Pärt setting Burns might surprise, but *My heart's in the Highlands*, with its serene, Pachelbel-like organ line and pellucid vocal by countertenor David James, is a triumph. In the hymn-like *Littlemore Tractus* and *Salve Regina*, warm melodies and bursts of colourful chords mellow Pärt's sound without detracting from its sublime, ethereal beauty. Polyphony's performance is gorgeous.

Anthony Payne   British b1936

Best known as the man who gave us Elgar's 'Third Symphony', Anthony Payne came to professional composition quite late in life. His very distinct musical voice has blossomed through his numerous works for chamber forces, the medium in which he excels. Initially he developed a technique loosely derived from various numerical systems that were increasingly linked to the more musical concept of interval size. Many of his vocal works were written for his wife, Jane Manning. **GROVE**music

Empty Landscape – Heart's Ease. Scenes from The Woodlanders[a]. Of Knots and Skeins. Poems of Edward Thomas[a]. The Stones and Lonely Places Sing
[a]**Jane Manning** *sop* **Jane's Minstrels / Roger Montgomery**
NMC NMCD130 (79' · DDD) ⓂⒹ⇨

Anthony Payne's musical response to English pastoral is wide-ranging, welcoming challenges and shunning easy options. This programme, with two vocal and three instrumental works composed over a period of nearly a quarter of a century, gives a good sense of his scope, and also of his strengths.

The three *Poems of Edward Thomas* for soprano and piano quartet respond imaginatively to some fine poetry, as Payne matches the rhythmic economy and energy of 'Words' as effectively as the juxtaposition of images normally kept separate – steam trains and birdsong – in 'Adlestrop'. Thomas Hardy's prose in his novel *The Woodlanders* is no less evocative, but setting prose is always more difficult. Payne's solution is to invest particular poetic force in the instrumental representations of seasonal flux, underlining the obvious analogies between nature and humanity, and leading to a strong climax with the memorable final sentence 'the funereal trees rocked and chanted their dirges unceasingly'.

Of the three purely instrumental works, it's good to be reminded of the sustained expressive power and inventiveness of Payne's relatively early tone-poem for mixed sextet *The Stones and Lonely Places Sing*. The raw intensity which is so striking here is more muted in the later pieces, though comparable issues are at stake. *Empty Landscape – Heart's Ease* just manages to keep moves into bleakness at bay, while *Of Knots and Skeins* offers a more abstract interpretation of comparable concerns in its poised interactions of harmonic and melodic forces. With accomplished performances and spacious recording, this disc does Payne proud.

Krzysztof Penderecki   Polish b1933

Penderecki was a pupil of Malawski at the Kraków Conservatory (1955-8), where he has also taught. He gained international fame with such works as Threnody for the Victims of Hiroshima for 52 strings (1960), exploiting the fierce expressive effects of new sonorities, but in the mid-1970s there came a change to large symphonic forms based on rudimentary chromatic motifs. Central to his work is the St Luke Passion (1965), with its combination of intense expressive force with a severe style with archaic elements alluding to Bach, and its sequel Utrenia, in which Orthodox chant provides musical material and at the same time a sense of mystery. His operas have been admired for their dynamic expression even if their discrete vignettes offer more opportunity for characterisation than development. GROVEmusic

A Polish Requiem

A Polish Requiem
Izabella Kłosinska sop **Jadwiga Rappé** contr
Ryszard Minkiewicz ten **Piotr Nowacki** bass
Warsaw National Philharmonic Choir and Orchestra / Antoni Wit
Naxos ② 8 557386/7 (99' · DDD · T/t)   Ⓢ▶

The *Polish Requiem* had its origins in a setting of the *Lacrimosa* dedicated to Gdansk shipyard workers who died during clashes with the Communist authorities in 1970. Though the work's tendency to swing between bombast and sentimentality may make you long for the austerity of an Arvo Pärt, if you approach it as a valid attempt to continue the tradition of 19th-century concert Requiems – Verdi's, above all – then you may well feel it has much to offer.

This performance is well played and conducted, Antoni Wit ensuring that the big climaxes make their effect without labouring the less eventful episodes. The choral singing is robust, though the sustained high writing is demanding enough to give the Polish Philharmonic Choir some anxious moments. Of the vocal soloists, both Jadwiga Rappé and Piotr Nowacki are excellent, but the normally reliable Izabella Kłosinska was clearly under strain, and Ryszard Minkiewicz also sounds out of sorts in places. The sound is typical of Naxos's Polish recordings in being rather too bright and generalised for music that depends for its effect on such strong contrasts between the very quiet and the extremely loud.

Further listening:

St Luke Passion
Izabella Klosinska sop **Adam Kruszewski** bar
Romuald Tesarowicz bass **Krzysztof Kolberger** spkr

Jaroslaw Malanowicz org **Warsaw Boys' Choir; Warsaw Philharmonic Choir; Warsaw National Philharmonic Orchestra / Antoni Wit**
Naxos 8 557149 (76' · DDD)   Ⓢ▶

The relatively brief moments of almost expressionistic drama come off best, aided by a pungently immediate recording, complete with rasping organ and blazing brass. The soloists are all excellent. Given the importance of the spoken narration, the absence of text and translation is unfortunate, though Richard Whitehouse's track-cued synopsis is better than nothing.

Giovanni Pergolesi   Italian 1710-1736

While studying with Durante in Naples Pergolesi worked as a violinist, and in 1731 he presented his first stage work, a dramma sacro. He became maestro di cappella to the Prince of Stigliano in 1732 and to the Duke of Maddaloni in 1734. Several more stage works followed for Naples and an opera seria, L'Olimpiade (1735), for Rome.

Only moderately popular in his lifetime, Pergolesi posthumously attained international fame as a leading figure in the rise of Italian comic opera. He wrote two commedie musicali, with both buffo and seria elements, and three comic intermezzos, each staged with an opera seria by him. His other works include sacred music (notably a Stabat mater of 1736), chamber cantatas and duets, and a few instrumental pieces. GROVEmusic

Stabat mater

Stabat mater. Salve regina in C minor   Ⓟ
Emma Kirkby sop **James Bowman** counterten
Academy of Ancient Music / Christopher Hogwood
L'Oiseau-Lyre Florilegium 425 692-2OH
(52' · DDD · T/t)   Ⓕ▶

Pergolesi's *Stabat mater*, written in the last few months of his brief life, enjoyed a huge popularity throughout the 18th century. But modern performances often misrepresent its nature, either through over-romanticising it or by transforming it into a choral work. None of these are qualities overlooked in this affecting performance, for Emma Kirkby and James Bowman are well versed in the stylistic conventions of Baroque and early classical music—and their voices afford a pleasing partnership. Both revel in Pergolesi's sensuous vocal writing, phrasing the music effectively and executing the ornaments with an easy grace. Singers and instrumentalists alike attach importance to sonority, discovering a wealth of beguiling effects in Pergolesi's part writing. In the *Salve regina* in C minor Emma Kirkby gives a compelling performance, pure in tone, expressive and poignant, and she's sympathetically supported by the string ensemble. The recording is pleasantly resonant.

Messa di S Emidio

Pergolesi Messa di S Emidio [a] |P|
A Scarlatti Messa per il Santissimo Natale
Concerto Italiano / Rinaldo Alessandrini
Naïve OP30461 (58' · DDD) (F)(O)(→)

These two Masses were performed in Rome almost 30 years apart by composers both strongly associated with Naples. The *Messa di S Emidio* is one of only two works that are accepted as authentic Pergolesi Mass settings, although different versions survive. It was apparently composed for a service in the Neapolitan church of S Maria della Stella de' PP Minimi in 1732, but Pergolesi later revised it for several choirs and two orchestras (the version recorded here). Concerto Italiano's 10 singers and 19 instrumentalists (including two horns and two trumpets) make an extraordinary noise in the stacking chords that commence the volatile *Kyrie*. Some of Alessandrini's singers suffer from dodgy tuning at first, but things soon settle down, and reflective moments are particularly well performed.

The disc concludes with an impressive account of Alessandro Scarlatti's magnificent *Messa per il Santissimo Natale*. Written in 1707 for the Roman Basilica S Maria Maggiore, it shows Scarlatti's mastery at fusing Renaissance *stile antico* for two choirs (with very little doubling) with solo voice passages and imaginative instrumental parts for two violins. Concerto Italiano are on especially good form in Scarlatti's finely woven counterpoint (*Agnus Dei* is exquisite), though both neglected Masses benefit from Alessandrini's articulately shaped interpretations.

La serva padrona

La serva padrona[b]. Livietta e Tracollo[a] |P|
[a]**Nancy Argenta** *sop* Livietta [a]**Werner van Mechelen** *bass* Tracollo [b]**Patricia Biccire** *sop* Serpina [b]**Donato di Stefano** *bass* Uberto
La Petite Bande / Sigiswald Kuijken *vn*
Accent ACC96123D (80' · DDD · N/t) Recorded live 1996 (F)

La serva padrona is given here with a rare but comparable companion-piece. *Livietta e Tracollo* is also for two characters, light soprano and *buffo* bass, with two sections, originally to be played in the intervals of the evening's *opera seria*. Rather more complicated and improbable than *La serva padrona*, it tells of a girl disguised as a French peasant (male) seeking vengeance on a robber who in turn appears disguised as a pregnant Pole. She succeeds in the first half, but in the second the man, now disguised as an astrologer, has more luck and they agree to get married. Musically it isn't so very inferior to *La serva*. Both have more wit in the music than in the libretto, with deft parodies of *opera seria* and a popular appeal in the repeated phrases of their arias.

The performance is a lively one, with Nancy Argenta a resourceful and not too pertly soubrettish Livietta. Kuijken's Petite Bande plays with a distinctively 'period' tone; the speeds are sprightly and the rhythms light-footed. In both works, the women are better than the men, who lack the comic touch. Patricia Biccire sings attractively, especially in her 'sincere' aria, 'A Serpina penserate', and she paces her recitatives artfully. A lower Baroque pitch is used and the final number is the short duet, 'Per te io ho nel core', as in the original score.

Pérotin   French c1155/60-c1225

Pérotin was the most celebrated musician involved in the revision and re-notation of the Magnus liber (attributed to Léonin). Two decrees by the Bishop of Paris concerning the 'feast of the fools' and the performance of quadruple organum, from 1198 and 1199, have been associated with Pérotin since the theorist known as Anonymous IV stated that he composed four-voice settings of both the relevant texts. Attempts to identify him at Notre Dame have proved inconclusive. He may have been born c1155-60, revised the Magnus liber 1180-90 subsequently composed his three- and four-voice works and died in the first years of the 13th century; or he wrote the four-voice works early in his career, revised the Magnus liber in the first decade of the 13th century and died c1225. **GROVE**music

Viderunt omnes / Sederunt principes

Pérotin Viderunt omnes. Alleluia, Posui Adiutorium. Dum sigillum summi Patris. Alleluia, Nativitas. Beata viscera. Sederunt principes **Anonymous** Veni creator spiritus. O Maria virginei. Isias cecinit
Hilliard Ensemble (David James *counterten* John Potter, Rogers Covey-Crump, Mark Padmore, Charles Daniels *tens* Gordon Jones *bar*) / **Paul Hillier** *bar*
ECM New Series 837 751-2 (68' · DDD · T) (F)(O)(→)

This is a superb and original recording. It gives musical individuality to a group of works that have hitherto tended to sound much the same. Moreover, as a special attraction for those wanting to see artistic individuality in early composers, it includes all but one of the identifiable works of Pérotin. Inevitably his two grand four-voice organa take up much of the record. At nearly 12 minutes each they may have been the most ambitious polyphonic works composed up to the end of the 12th century. The Hilliard Ensemble adopts a suave and supple approach to both *Viderunt* and *Sederunt*, softening the pervasive rhythms that can make them a shade oppressive and showing a clear view of the entire architecture of each piece. They surge irrepressibly from one section to another, creating a musical momentum that belies the admirably slow speeds they generally adopt. They also beautifully underline the musical differences between the two works, producing a sound which seems a credible reflection of what one might have heard at Notre Dame in the late 12th century. Particularly exciting is the way in which the musicians grasp at the individual dynamic of each work: the huge open spaces they create to project the text of the magical *O Maria virginei*; the breakneck virtuosity in their swirling performance of *Dum sigillum*, the gently modulated rhythms in the strophic *Veni creator*; the harder edge in their tone for *Alleluia Nativitas*; and so on. This is a recording of the highest distinction.

Allan Pettersson   Swedish 1911-1980

Pettersson, a pupil of Olsson and Blomdahl at the Stockholm Conservatory (1930-39), played the viola in the Stockholm PO (1939-51), then went to Paris for further study with Honegger and Leibowitz. Back in Sweden he concentrated on composition, in particular on large-scale, single-movement symphonies in an impassioned diatonic style (there were eventually 15, c1950-78); he also wrote concertos, songs and chamber pieces.   GROVEmusic

Symphonies

Symphonies Nos 5 & 16
John-Edward Kelly sax **Saarbrücken Radio Symphony Orchestra / Alun Francis**
CPO CPO999 284-2 (65' · DDD)   Ⓜ

The orchestral playing is full of commitment, the account of the 40-minute Fifth (1960-62) sounding tremendously vivid; Francis has the edge over rival versions where it counts, in his overall view of this magnificent work. Yet the coupling – the last symphony the Swede completed – is better still. No 16 was written in 1979 for the American saxophonist Frederik Hemke. Here Kelly, who has made some minor modifications to the solo part for reasons explained in the booklet (the ailing composer appears to have been uncertain of the instrument's range), glides through the hair-raising virtuosity with breathtaking ease. This is the kind of advocacy Pettersson, who never heard the work, can only have dreamed of. An excellent disc.

Symphonies Nos 7 & 11
Norrköping Symphony Orchestra / Leif Segerstam
BIS CD580 (70' · DDD)   Ⓕ

Most of Pettersson's major works are constructed as large, unified movements (although he was an accomplished miniaturist) and Nos 7 and 11, respectively 46 and 24 minutes in length, are no exceptions. The former in some ways is unrepresentative of the composer; the obsessiveness of mood and hectoring tone are present, especially in the *Angst*-ridden first and third spans, but the range of expression is much wider than in most of his other works. Composed in 1967-8, it has a unique atmosphere, both haunting and haunted,

which will stay with you for a long time. His melodic genius is confirmed in the long and heartfelt central threnody, as well as by the beautiful quiet coda, truly music to 'soften the crying of a child'; its delivery by the Norrköping players has just the right amount of detachment. Segerstam's tempos permit the work to breathe and resonate not unlike Mahler. The 11th Symphony (1974) is less combative in tone, although it has its moments, and isn't on the same elevated plane as the Seventh. The recording quality is first-rate, allowing both the devastating power and delicate fine detail of these scores to emerge equally well.

Hans Pfitzner   German 1869-1949

Pfitzner, a pupil of Knorr and Kwast at the Hoch Conservatory, Frankfurt, was a teacher in Berlin, Strasbourg and Munich until 1934, when he was relieved of his post. His earlier works, including the operas Der arme Heinrich (1895) and Die Rose vom Liebesgarten (1901), are Wagnerian, but in Palestrina (1917) he produced a remarkable piece of operatic spiritual autobiography, contrasting the pressures of the everyday world with the inner certainties of artistic genius. One of his certainties was of the supremacy of the German Romantic tradition – he was a powerful patriot – which he supported in polemical exchanges with Berg and implicitly in the cantatas (Von deutscher Seele, 1921; Das dunkle Reich, 1929) which were his main works after Palestrina. He also wrote three symphonies (1932, 1939, 1940), concertos for the piano (1922), the violin (1923) and two for the cello (1935, 1944), chamber music (including three string quartets) and c100 songs.   GROVEmusic

Piano Trio

Violin Sonata in E minor, Op 27. Piano Trio in F, Op 8ᵃ
Benjamin Schmid vn ᵃ**Clemens Hagen** vc
Claudius Tanski pf
Dabringhaus und Grimm MDG312 0934-2 (70' · DDD)   ⒻⓄ

The Sonata is a fine piece from Pfitzner's maturity, while the much earlier Piano Trio is one of the most extraordinary works for the medium you're likely to have ever heard. To be sure, enterprising chamber players hunting for neglected repertory may well have come across early critical reactions to both these pieces, and references to (for example, in the case of the Trio) Pfitzner's 'sick imagination' and the work's 'monstrous length' might put anyone off. When he wrote it Pfitzner was in despair at his financial and other problems; he told a friend that after finishing it all he wanted was to die. It does at times suggest a man at the end of his tether, but also a composer chronicling such a state when at the height of his powers.

It's long, extremely tense, at times weirdly obsessive, even hysterical, but all this takes place within a cunningly plotted ground plan. After the strange and powerful contrasts of the first movement, with its wild coda, the noble but perilously assaulted main theme of the slow movement, the dance-like but fraught and nervous *Scherzo*, Pfitzner begins his finale with a choleric gesture which soon fades to pathos and pallor. After 10 minutes of desperate attempts to climb out of this pit, a positive coda seems possible, but when the music turns instead to utterly euphonious calm the listener is likely to be moved by what seems in context heroic as well as wonderfully beautiful.

The Sonata, from 1918, sounds like a demonstration – with various modernisms obvious – that Pfitzner's late Romantic style and prodigious craft still had abundant life in them. Its inexhaustible inventiveness and the beauty of its themes are accompanied by a considerable enjoyment of virtuosity: Pfitzner, you realise, is having a high old time. Both works are vastly welcome, in short, but that they should be so superbly played goes beyond all reasonable expectations.

Montague Phillips   English 1885-1969

Philips studied organ and composition at the Royal Academy of Music. He first made a name with popular ballads composed for his wife, the soprano Clara Butterworth, who also starred in the work to which his fame was due above all, the light opera The Rebel Maid (1921) was a popular success. For the centenary of the RAM in 1922 he composed The Song of Rosamund and he was for many years professor of harmony and composition there. He composed many works for orchestra, but only the lighter pieces, which showed off his talents to greater advantage, made any real mark.   GROVEmusic

Piano concertos

M Phillips Piano Concertos – No 1; No 2
Hely-Hutchinson The Young Idea
David Owen Norris pf
BBC Concert Orchestra / Gavin Sutherland
Dutton Epoch CDLX7206 (69' · DDD)   Ⓜ

Purely for sound quality, this disc is a winner. It is a sumptuous, full-blooded recording with a richly resonant bass matched by the soloist's powerful Fazioli. Both concertos are real finds. The F sharp minor First Concerto (1907) has not been played for more than 95 years; the E major (1919) especially, once a favourite of conductor Vilem Tausky, is tremendously effective. It would bring the house down were it played at the Proms again (it received its premiere there in 1920) if only for the last movement's big tune which simultaneously combines Celtic lament, Elgarian *nobilmente* and a (prescient) celluloid weepie. True, the orchestra has the best of this, but the soloist, by the time of its final full statement, has earned a few bars' rest. Talking of whom, Norris gives the performance of his life in

these two works, handling the bravura writing with aplomb and total conviction. He also has a marvellous repose at the keyboard – in the slow movement of the First Concerto, for example, before it builds to its shattering climax. Less, he knows, is more.

The final (eight-minute) work, aptly subtitled 'Cum Grano Salis' is, as the composer noted only three years after its publication in 1931, 'hopelessly out of date' and a somewhat bathetic appendage to the grand romance of Phillips's concertos.

Orchestral Works

A Surrey Suite, Op 59. Moorland Idyll, Op 61. Revelry Overture, Op 62. A Spring Rondo. A Summer Nocturne. A Shakespearean Scherzo: Titania and her Elvish Court. Sinfonietta in C, Op 70. Arabesque, Op 43 No 2. The Rebel Maid – Jig; Gavotte; Graceful Dance; Villagers' Dance
BBC Concert Orchestra / Gavin Sutherland
Dutton Laboratories Epoch CDLX7140 (76' · DDD)
Ⓜ Ⓞ

Phillips's music, like that of Sullivan, German and Coleridge-Taylor, was on the more serious side of 'light'. He had a thorough technical musical grounding at the Royal Academy of Music, where he was later professor of composition, and he was also a church organist and accompanist. These are emphatically not radio jingles but concert items of genuine symphonic status. If the sparkling *Revelry* Overture, with which the programme opens, evokes Eric Coates's *Merrymakers* Overture, much of the rest is Elgarian in its grandeur. The orchestration is bold and accomplished, with a use of brass that, as Lewis Foreman's expert notes indicate, sometimes suggests Phillips's Academy contemporary Bax.

The once widely popular dances from *The Rebel Maid* (a light opera whose entire score merits rediscovery) may recall German's dance sets in their concept, but they're made of sturdier stuff. The moving *Moorland Idyll*, the picturesque and varied Surrey Suite, the sparkling *Titania and her Elvish Court* and the charming *Arabesque* all constitute music to be treasured. Phillips's voice, so eloquently served here by fine performances and recording, deserves to be heard not just as light music but in a wider British music context.

Astor Piazzolla   Argentinian 1921-1992

A child prodigy on the bandoneón, Piazzolla emigrated with his family to New York in 1924. In 1954 he won a scholarship to study with Boulanger, who encouraged him in the composition of tangos. Piazzolla's unique version of the tango, which initially met with opposition, included dissonance, jazz elements and chromaticism. By the 1980s his work had finally become accepted in Argentina and had begun to be espoused by classical artists.

GROVEmusic

Tangos

Piazzolla Libertango (arr Calandrelli). Tango Suite (arr S Assad) – Andante; Allegro. Le Grand Tango (arr Calandrelli). Sur – Regreso al amor. Fugata. Mumuki. Tres minutos con la realidad. Milonga del ángel. Histoire du Tango – Café 1930 (all arr Calandrelli) **Calandrelli** Tango Remembrances
Yo-Yo Ma *vc* **Antonio Agri** *vn* **Nestor Marconi, Astor Piazzolla** *bandoneón* **Horacio Malvicino, Odair Assad, Sérgio Assad, Oscar Castro-Neves** *gtrs* **Edwin Barker, Héctor Console** *db* **Kathryn Stott, Gerardo Gandini, Leonardo Marconi, Frank Corliss** *pfs*
Sony Classical 07464 63122-2 (64' · DDD) Ⓕ B→

Yo-Yo Ma is the latest international artist to surrender to the spell of the Argentinian dance: he can also be heard on the soundtrack of the film, *The Tango Lesson*. Here, surrounded by a brilliant group of experts in the genre, he presents with wholehearted commitment a well-varied programme of Piazzolla pieces. They range from the melancholy or sultry to the energetic or fiery. Among the latter, *Fugata* is ingenious, *Mumuki* richly eloquent, and *Tres minutos con la realidad* nervily edgy: in this last, Kathryn Stott understandably earned the admiration of her Argentinian colleagues. She also shines with Yo-Yo Ma in an exciting performance of *Le Grand Tango*: his playing in the *Milonga del ángel* is outstandingly beautiful. Special mention must also be made of some spectacular virtuosity by the Assad brothers in the *Tango Suite*. The characteristic bandoneón is featured with the cellist in *Café 1930*; and by technological trickery Yo-Yo Ma partners Piazzolla himself (recorded in 1987) in a confection called *Tango Remembrances*. Those who are already fans of this genre will be in no need of encouragement to procure this disc.

Concerto for bandoneón

Concerto for Bandoneón, Strings and Percussion[a].
Las cuatro estaciones porteñas (arr Franzetti).
Mar del Plata 70 (arr Carli). Sinfonía Buenos Aires
[a]**Juan José Mosalini** *band*
**Württemberg Philharmonic Orchestra /
Gabriel Castagna**
Chandos CHAN10419 (71' · DDD) Ⓕ B→

Gabriel Castagna gives us the first recording of the *Sinfonía Buenos Aires*. Composed in 1951, it is far more ambitious in scope than the Sinfonietta – and more daring, as well. The music's tightly coiled rhythms are typical of the composer, certainly, but there's an edgy grandeur and harmonic pungency here that's like nothing else in his output. Indeed, with its onslaught of percussion and blazing brass, the wailing climax of the slow movement put me in mind of Shostakovich's Eighth Symphony. Castagna inspires some ferocious playing from his German orchestra, particularly in the frenetic and feral finale.

The Concerto for bandoneón, strings and percussion (1979) is played with verve, too. Juan José Mosalini puts a jaunty spring in the rhythms of the solo part, a delectable reminder of the score's dance-music roots. José, Carli's full-orchestra arrangement of *Mar del Plata 70* retains the tango's acerbic character. Less appealing is Carlos Franzetti's transcription of *Cuatro estaciones porteñas*: Franzetti is a marvellous composer himself, and this suite is expertly scored, but the results are overly lush.

Film

'Tango Maestro'

Documentary featuring archive performance footage with contributions from Daniel Barenboim, Gary Burton, Yo-Yo Ma, Kronos Quartet, Gotan Project, Joanna MacGregor, James Crabb
Written, narrated and directed by **Mike Dibb**

'Tango nuevo'

Piazzolla's last recorded studio concert
Video director **Tony Staveacre**
Astor Piazzolla bandoneón, with various artists
Opus Arte 🖸DVD OA0905D (3h 33' · 4:3 and 16:9 · 2.0 · 0) Extra features include 'Piazzolla: The Man and his Music' Ⓕ

'Piazzolla was a musical genius,' says film director Fernando Solanas (for whom Piazzolla composed in the 1980s) in Dibb's documentary, 'but his social and political views were not exactly advanced. In this he was a little like Borges. But despite his questionable opinions, he succeeded in expressing the anguish, melancholy, nostalgia and depression so typical of the man from Buenos Aires.' There was a good deal more to the man, as Dibb teases out from a host of colleagues and friends. Piazzolla was, and remains, a controversial figure in Argentina: his rejuvenation of the moribund tango genre offended a great number of his compatriots.

There is much telling testimony from fellow musicians. Jazz percussionist Gary Burton relished the chance of working with Piazzolla to become a tango performer; Nadia Boulanger called her student an 'idiot' for avoiding the 'true Piazzolla' – the tango composer. Those who played in his bands – including his son Daniel – speak of him with a mixture of reverence and remembered terror (of the demands man and music made). Although the music is fêted worldwide, the man was flawed. Driven and passionately obsessed, his relationships with both children were difficult in later life.

Tanguedia – 'a mixture of tango, tragedy and comedy' and one of Piazzolla's numbers for Solanas's *Tangos, el exilio de Gardel* – features in his last studio recording, preserved in Tony Staveacre's film 'Tango nuevo', along with *Milonga del Angel, Adios Nonino, Zero Hour* and the deliberately hyphenated *Sex-tet*. Piazzolla's physicality as a performer is manifest, the hub around which everything on the stage revolves. (A bonus track features a recent *Milonga del Angel* with Joanna MacGregor, James Crabb and members of Piazzolla's 1980s quintet.) Ultimately, his reputation will depend on whether such music survives and if his revivification of the tango ('vertical rape', Borges called it) is a springboard for future composers or another dead end. This unanswerable question aside, these two well-produced films (accompanied by additional unedited interviews) flesh out the hidden depths of a very human composer, who was much more than the music he wrote but whose music came to be so much more than the man.

John Pickard   British b1963

Pickard read for his BMus degree at the University of Wales, Bangor, where his composition teacher was William Mathias. Between 1984 and 1985 he studied with Louis Andriessen at the Royal Conservatory in The Hague, Netherlands on a Dutch Ministry of Culture Scholarship. He was awarded a PhD in composition in 1989 and, from 1993, has been Senior Lecturer in Music at the University of Bristol.

Pickard is best known for a series of powerful orchestral and instrumental works. He has written four symphonies and other orchestral works of symphonic dimensions: Sea-Change (1989), The Flight of Icarus (1990), Channel Firing (1992-93) and the Trombone Concerto: The Spindle of Necessity (1997-98). His music has been widely praised for its large-scale architectural sense and bold handling of an extended tonal idiom. His four string quartets (1991, 1993, 1994, 1998), have received particular acclaim.

The Flight of Icarus

The Flight of Icarus. The Spindle of Necessity[a].
Channel Firing
[a]**Christian Lindberg** *tbn* **Norrköping Symphony Orchestra / Martyn Brabbins**
BIS BIS-CD1578 (66' · DDD)   Ⓕ❍❍❍

In many respects, *The Flight of Icarus* (1990) was John Pickard's breakthrough work, at least into the wider national consciousness, partly thanks to its London premiere at the 1996 Proms but also due to its clear structure, accessible (though not unchallenging) musical language and the sheer élan of its orchestral writing. Playing continuously, its three compelling sections are indicative of the ascent of Icarus and Daedalus from their Minoan confinement, their exhilarating albeit turbulent flight and Icarus's catastrophic fall, prompting a wonderfully direct, emotive elegy (all the more remarkable for a composer then just 27).

Icarus remains Pickard's best-known orchestral work, unjustly since three years later he trumped it with *Channel Firing*, written in memory of his teacher, William Mathias.

Inspired by Thomas Hardy's dark pre-Great War poem where the dead in a churchyard are woken by naval gunnery practice and assume it is the Day of Judgement, Pickard constructs a gripping symphonic poem redolent of not-quite-apocalypse: it is not time for the dead to be judged, Europe is not yet in the grip of war; but both are coming.

Separating these full-orchestral conceptions is a concerto for trombone, strings and percussion showing a quite different side to his musical character. Like *Icarus*, *The Spindle of Necessity* (1998) derives from Greek myth via Plato's Republic. Here the textures are often gossamer-thin, with light percussion interweaving with natural string overtones and translucent harmonies. Lindberg plays the emotionally detached solo part with consummate skill while Brabbins draws sensational playing from the Norrköping orchestra in what must have been terra incognita. BIS's sound as always is first rate. Highly recommend.

Walter Piston   American 1894-1976

Piston trained as a draughtsman before studying composition at Harvard (1919-24) and with Dukas and Boulanger in Paris; he then returned to Harvard (1926-60), becoming a renowned theory teacher. His textbook Harmony (1941) has been widely used. His music is in a clear, tonal style suggesting the neo-classical Stravinsky, Fauré and Roussel: the main works include eight symphonies (1937-65), five string quartets (1933-62) and the ballet The Incredible Flutist (1938). **GROVE**music

Violin Concertos

Violin Concertos Nos 1 & 2. Fantasia for Violin and Orchestra
James Buswell *vn* **National Symphony Orchestra of Ukraine / Theodore Kuchar**
Naxos 8 559003 (61' · DDD)   Ⓢ❍▣

Piston's First Violin Concerto, written in 1939, has much in common with the Barber, including a similar abundance of individual melody. The heart of the work is in the moving, pensive central *Andantino molto tranquillo*. With just a hint of Gershwin in its bluesy opening, the movement is essentially searching and ruminative. This is a masterpiece, as will be confirmed when other violinists take it up.

The Second Concerto, written two decades later, is less obviously 'popular', its atmosphere more elusive. But its opening is similarly haunting and the more one hears it the more one is drawn by its depth of inner feeling. The extended, pensive *Adagio* introduces a serene and very beautiful theme, which later forms a canonic duet with the flute. The finale is another sparkling, jaunty rondo. The *Fantasia* is a late work, first performed in 1973. In five intricately related sections, its language more dissonant with almost feverish, bravura *allegros* framed by troubled, lonely *adagio* passages, dominated by the soloist, which have been described as 'painfully aware and transcendentally serene'. The closing section is profoundly gentle.

It may seem remarkable that these works should make their CD début played by a Russian orchestra, but it plays the music with splendid commitment, much subtlety of expression and fine ensemble too. The sure idiomatic feeling is explained by the fact its conductor, Theodore Kuchar, moved to the Ukraine from Cleveland, Ohio. James Buswell is a superbly accomplished and spontaneous soloist, and the recording is first class.

Symphony No 4

Symphony No 4. Capriccio. Three New England Sketches
Seattle Symphony Orchestra / Gerard Schwarz
Naxos American Classics 8 559162 (52' · DDD) ⑤**O**→

Those unfamiliar with Piston's work should investigate this Naxos disc that repackages performances originally issued on Delos. This one is arguably the best of the lot as it features the Fourth Symphony (1951) and the *Three New England Sketches* (1959), two of the composer's greatest and most attractive scores.

The Fourth's rollicking syncopations show that Piston had been listening closely to Copland's ballets. This is a symphony in the true sense, though, and its musical ideas are as lucidly argued, profoundly uttered and strongly structured as any in the classical repertoire. Perhaps the surface dissonance of 'Seaside', the first of the *Sketches*, might be off-putting to some, but how could anyone resist the exquisite colours Piston conjures up. 'Summer Evening', with its flitting, twittering evocation of insect activity, is as vivid as the best of Mendelssohn's *scherzos*, and the craggy majesty of 'Mountains' is truly awesome.

We also get the delightfully atmospheric *Capriccio for Harp and Strings*, and the quality of both the performances and recorded sound is as impressive as ever. At budget price, this disc should prove utterly irresistible.

Fantasy

The Incredible Flutist – Suite. Fantasy for English Horn, Harp and Strings. Suite for Orchestra. Concerto for String Quartet, Wind Instruments and Percussion. Psalm and Prayer of David
Scott Goff *fl* **Glen Danielson** *hn* **Theresa Elder Wunrow** *hp* **Juilliard Quartet** (Robert Mann, Joel Smirnoff *vns* Samuel Rhodes *va* Joel Krosnick *vc*)
Seattle Symphony Chorale and Orchestra / Gerard Schwarz
Delos DE3126 (68' · DDD)   Ⓕ

Gerard Schwarz's flutist fixes you with his limpid tone. However, it will always be known as the

score with the Tango. Schwarz goes with the flow, the sway of the melody, but it can never linger long enough. The *Fantasy* enters darkened Elysian fields – Piston's lyricism sits well with this distinctive voice of sorrow and regret. We can trace their kinship right back to the composer's first published work – the orchestral *Suite* of 1929. At its heart is a long and intense pastorale: the cor anglais is there at the inception. Framing it, motoric syncopations carry us first to a kind of drive-by the blues with bar-room piano and Grappelli violin. The finale is essentially a fugal work-out: high-tech Hindemith. Piston's very last work, the *Concerto*, is 10 eventful minutes where the imperative is once again pitted against the contemplative. The mixing of timbres is masterly, a fleck of woodwind or a brush of tambourine or antique cymbal speaking volumes. But at the centre of gravity is the Juilliard Quartet, moving in mysterious ways. In fact, the last words uttered here are those of the *Psalm and Prayer of David* – a rare vocal setting for Piston, and as such, refreshingly open, unhackneyed, unhieratical. Performance and recording are superb.

Amilcare Ponchielli   Italian 1834-1886

After studying at the Milan Conservatory Ponchielli settled in the provinces as an organist and municipal band conductor, repeatedly attempting to establish himself as an opera composer. He finally won success in 1872 with the much-revised I promessi sposi, in 1874 with the Ricordi commission I lituani and above all in 1876 with La Gioconda. As professor of composition at the Milan Conservatory (from 1880) he taught Puccini and, briefly, Mascagni. He also composed much sacred music for S Maria Maggiore, Bergamo. Of his works, only La Gioconda, on a text drawn by Boito from Hugo, is in the modern repertory. GROVEmusic

La Gioconda

La Gioconda[a]   Ⓗ
Bellini Norma – Casta diva[d]; Mira, o Norma[b]
Donizetti Lucrezia Borgia – Com'è bello!; M'odi, ah m'odi[d] **Rossini** Guglielmo Tell – Selva opaca[d] **Verdi** Ernani – Fa che a me venga[c]. La forza del destino[d] – Madre, pietosa Vergine; La Vergine degli angeli. I lombardi[d] – Te, Vergin santa; O madre dal cielo
Giannina Arangi-Lombardi *sop* La gioconda; [a]**Alessandro Granda** *ten* Enzo Grimaldi; [a]**Gaetano Viviani** *bar* Barnaba; [a]**Camilla Rota** *mez* La Cieca; [a]**Corrado Zambelli** *bass* Alvise Badoero; [ab]**Ebe Stignani** *mez* Laura Adorno; [a]**Aristide Baracchi** *bar* Zuàne; [a]**Giuseppe Nessi** *ten* Isèpo; [c]**Enrico Molinari** *bar*; [a]**Chorus and Orchestra of La Scala, Milan**; [bcd]**Orchestra / Lorenzo Molajoli**
Naxos Historical mono ③ 8 110112/4 (169' · ADD) Recorded 1926-33   ⑤**O**

Outstanding among Italian operatic sets of the interwar years, this was also the first complete recording of Ponchielli's masterpiece. Inevitably the sound quality of 1931 is at some disadvantage; the carefully orchestrated score, large-scale ensembles and off-stage effects need more space and clarity to do them full justice. Yet, to compensate, the voices have the vivid immediacy of their period and the transfers are excellent.

The work of chorus and orchestra is certainly among the strengths of the performance. That in turn reflects on the conductor, Lorenzo Molajoli. The three male principals were also Scala singers, though not in this opera. Alessandro Granda, a Peruvian who made his Italian début in 1927, was also Columbia's Pinkerton and Cavaradossi; as Enzo in *La Gioconda* he's perhaps a little too slender and lacking in heroic potential, yet the tone is incisive and the characterisation convincing. The baritone Gaetano Viviani is most exciting, a Ruffo-imitator perhaps and a bit throaty, but rich, vibrant, grandly sinister and not unsubtle. These aren't qualities shared by the Alvise, Corrado Zambelli, who sings with dull authority and unimpressive low notes: a pity they did not have Tancredi Pasero for the part. Mind, if they had, that would have meant the addition to the cast of one more singer with a fast vibrato (Camilla Rota's La Cieca being another), which might have proved all too much for listeners of more modern times. Stignani, whose young voice was ideal for the part of Laura, is free of it, and Arangi-Lombardi relatively so. But she, the heroine of the recording, is one of the main reasons for acquiring this set, which also includes a selection of her solo recordings, giving a fuller portrait of a highly distinguished artist.

Regarded by her contemporaries as a singer of the old school, she presents a Gioconda more appealing to modern tastes than the overcharged *verismo*-style of predecessors such as Eugenia Burzio. She brought to the role the refinements heard in her arias from *Lucrezia Borgia*, *I lombardi* and *La forza del destino*. There's also a thrilling intensity about her singing, so that, although Lauri-Volpi in his book *Voci parallele* (Garzanti: 1955) recalls that as an actress she was never quite able to liberate the impulses of her personality, one would be most unlikely to guess as much from these records.

La Gioconda   🅗
Maria Callas *sop* La Gioconda **Fiorenza Cossotto** *mez* Laura Adorno **Pier Miranda Ferraro** *ten* Enzo Grimaldo **Piero Cappuccilli** *bar* Barnaba **Ivo Vinco** *bass* Alvise Badoero **Irene Companeez** *contr* La Cieca **Leonardo Monreale** *bass* Zuane **Carlo Forte** *bass* A Singer, Pilot **Renato Ercolani** *ten* Isepo, First Distant Voice **Aldo Biffi** *bass* Second Distant Voice **Bonaldo Giaiotti** *bass* Barnabotto **Chorus and Orchestra of La Scala, Milan / Antonio Votto**
EMI mono ③ 556291-2 (167' · DDD) Recorded 1959
Ⓜ🅞

Ponchielli's old warhorse has had a bad press in recent times, which seems strange in view of its melodic profusion, his unerring adumbration of

Gioconda's unhappy predicament and of the sensual relationship between Enzo and Laura. But it does need large-scale and involved singing – just what it receives here on this now historic set. Nobody could fail to be caught up in its conviction. Callas was in good and fearless voice when it was made, with the role's emotions perhaps enhanced by the traumas of her own life at the time. Here her strengths in declaiming recitative, her moulding of line, her response to the text are all at their most arresting. Indeed she turns what can be a maudlin act into true tragedy. Ferraro's stentorian ebullience is most welcome. Cossotto is a vital, seductive Laura. Cappuccilli gives the odious spy and lecher Barnaba a threatening, sinister profile, while Vinco is a suitably implacable Alvise. Votto did nothing better than this set, bringing out the subtlety of the Verdi-inspired scoring and the charm of the 'Dance of the Hours' ballet. The recording sounds excellent for its age.

Francis Pott   British b1957

A chorister as a child, Pott latter sang with choirs at New College, Oxford, Temple Church London and Winchester Cathedral. An academic, Pott is currently working on a study of Nikolay Medtner. He has composed for various forces, but the main focus is on organ and choral music. His most ambitious work to date is an oratorio A Song on the End of the World, *composed for the 1999 Three Choirs Festival.*

'Meditations and Remembrances'
Jesu dulcis memoria – 'Jesu, the very thought of thee'. Mass in Five Parts. A Meditation.
A Remembrance. O Lord, support us all the day long. Introduction, Toccata and Fugue. Turn our Captivity (Psalm 126)
Christ Church Cathedral Choir, Dublin / Judy Martin with **Tristan Russcher** *org*
Signum Classics SIGCD080 (71' · DDD · T/t)   Ⓕ🅓➔

Some composers are difficult to pigeonhole. The unsuspecting listener really can't help it if other composers' stylistic thumbprints spring to mind. In the case of Francis Pott he readily acknowledges the abiding influence of Byrd, 'that venerable, artistically transcendent and yet vulnerably human face of enduring Englishness'. True, they share a sense of long-limbed phrases and eschew saccharinity. Couple this to the astringency of Kenneth Leighton and the contrapuntal rigour of Rubbra and you have part of the picture.

For poets Pott favours Traherne (*A Meditation* and *A Remembrance*), Newman (*O Lord, support us*), the Psalmists and St Bernard of Clairvaux. The unaccompanied Mass in Five Parts arches and glows, rolling along unhurriedly, the few lively passages being the climaxes in the *Gloria* and the bouncy 'Osanna' conclusion to the *Sanctus* and *Benedictus*. Wisely, the Mass sequence is interrupted by the motet *Jesu dulcis memoria* (with its beautiful alto solo sung by Áine Mulvey), and the *Introduction, Toccata and Fugue*, played with clarity and aplomb by the young Australian-born organist Tristan Russcher.

The disc's programme is perfectly balanced. The performances are authoritative, passionate and convincing. The two dozen mixed voices of the Christ Church Cathedral Choir are more than a match for their English counterparts. The organ accompaniments are unobtrusive (unlike an occasional whoosh from the Dublin traffic) and, under Judy Martin's expert direction, everything flows seamlessly. A beautiful disc in every sense.

Francis Poulenc   French 1899-1963

Poulenc's background gave him a musical and literary sophistication from boyhood, and he was already a publicly noted composer by the time he took lessons with Koechlin (1921-4): such works as his Apollinaire song cycle Le bestiaire (1919) and Sonata for two clarinets (1918) had shown the Stravinsky-Satie inclinations that assure him a place among Les Six. His ballet Les biches (1924), written for Dyagilev, established his mastery of the emotions and musical tastes of the smart set, opening a world of suavity and irony that he went on to explore in a sequence of concertante pieces: the Concert champêtre for harpsichord, the Aubade with solo piano and the Concerto for two pianos.

Around 1935 there came a change in his personal and spiritual life, reflected in a sizeable output of religious music, a much greater productivity and an important contribution to French song. Yet the basis of his style was unchanged: Stravinsky, Fauré and contemporary popular music continued to be his sources, even in the devotional music and the larger sacred works. The songs include four cycles. But his output of instrumental music, apart from the many piano pieces of a private character, continued to be modest: his most important later orchestral piece is the G minor Organ Concerto with strings and timpani (1938), which journeys between Bach and the fairground, while his main chamber works were the sonatas for flute, oboe and clarinet.

Music for the stage also continued to occupy him. There was another ballet, Les animaux modèles (1942), scores for plays and films, and a new departure into opera, begun with the absurd Apollinaire piece Les mamelles de Tirésias and pursued with more seriousness in his deeply felt tragedy of martyrdom, Dialogues des Carmélites (1957), as well as a setting of Cocteau's telephone monologue La voix humaine (1959).   GROVEmusic

---

Organ Concerto

Concerto for Organ, Strings and Timpani in G minor. Suite française, d'après Claude Gervaise. Concert champêtre
Elisabeth Chojnacka hpd **Philippe Lefebvre** org

Lille Symphony Orchestra / Jean-Claude Casadesus
Naxos 8 554241 (59' · DDD)   ⓈⒷ→

Elisabeth Chojnacka gets off to a head start against most others who have recorded the *Concert champêtre* by using the right kind of instrument: she understands that it's much sillier to play newish music on a period instrument than old music on a modern one. The effective proportions secured here between her deft playing and the orchestra also owe much to Jean-Claude Casadesus's nice sense of judgement and to the work of an excellent recording team.

It was particularly perverse of Poulenc to ask a harpsichord to contend with large brass and percussion sections and then, a decade later, employ only strings and timpani in his concerto for the intrinsically far more powerful organ; and that perversity is underlined here by using the massive organ of Notre Dame, Paris – though once again the recording technicians have skilfully succeeded in producing a string sonority that doesn't suffer beside the organ's awesome thunders. You can't help wondering whether Poulenc really had such a giant sound in mind, but it's undeniably thrilling; and the quieter moments are captured with commendable clarity and calm. From the interpretative point of view, it's quite a performance. The wind and percussion of the Lille orchestra get a chance to demonstrate their quality in accomplished playing of the spry dances of the *Suite française*. This is an eminently recommendable disc.

Poulenc Organ Concerto **Saint-Saëns** Symphony No 3, 'Organ' **Barber** Toccata festiva
Olivier Latry org
Philadelphia Orchestra / Christoph Eschenbach
Ondine ⓢ ODE1094-5 (79' · DDD/DSD)
Recorded live 2006   ⒻⓄⓄ

Eschenbach's Poulenc is heavily romanticised, squeezing every last drop of pathos from the score and finding many moments of ravishing beauty. Latry is, for the most part, a willing accomplice – only in the swaying rhythm of the *subito andante moderato* do conductor and soloist seem at odds with each other – and while it is left to him to root out the music's austere and acerbic sides, he clearly relishes Eschenbach's slow tempi in reaching the work's two powerful climaxes. This performance may miss many of Poulenc's subtleties in its single-minded striving for loveliness but the wildly enthusiastic cheering from the audience seems wholly justified given the unusual breadth of this reading.

The recording was made at the inaugural concerts of the new organ of Philadelphia's Verizon Hall, which included the almost obligatory Saint-Saëns Symphony. Properly, this is more a test of how well an organ integrates with an orchestra than a vehicle for the organ itself, and on those terms this proves to be a wholly successful performance. Eschenbach's intuitive reading casts the work in a rich perspective, the opening possessing a tangible atmosphere of menace while the second movement's *Presto* positively fizzes with energy.

The organ shows its stature (the booklet tells us that, with 6938 pipes, it is the largest concert-hall organ in the US) with palpable depth in the first movement and majestic presence in the finale; but the real star of the show here is the Philadelphia Orchestra itself. Mouth-watering wind solos, gorgeous string-playing and a wonderfully crisp and cohesive sound (as it must be in what sounds a dreadfully dry acoustic) combine to create rather more memorable moments than we have a right to expect; the string entry just before the close of the first section is, as they say, to die for.

Piano Concertos

Piano Concerto. Concerto for two pianos[a]. Aubade
François René Duchâble,
[a]**Jean-Philippe Collard** *pfs* **Rotterdam Philharmonic Orchestra / James Conlon**
Warner Apex 2564-62552-2 (55' · DDD)   Ⓑ

An appealing bargain collection of Poulenc's *concertante* piano music. Duchâble is a stylish player in the Piano Concerto and is joined by Collard for the sparkling Double Piano Concerto – and they find a glorious sense of poise in the languid slow movement. Conlon and his Rotterdam orchestra accompany with panache. The stylistic inconsistency of the various sections of the *Aubade* (appreciation of which really depends on a knowledge of the story of the ballet for which it was intended) is perhaps the reason for its comparative lack of popularity – it includes Poulenc's characteristic pianistic helter-skelter, ingenuous wistful lyricism, gamin pertness and Stravinskian angularity, ending with a typical Stravinskian repetition of a single phrase.

Concert champêtre

Les animaux modèles[b]. Concert champêtre[ab].
Improvisations[a] – No 13; No 15
[a]**Stefano Bollani** *pf*
[ab]**Filarmonia '900 del Teatro Regio di Torino / Jan Latham-Koenig**
Avie AV2135 (74' · DDD)   ⒻⓄ

Poulenc's third and final ballet, *Les animaux modèles*, was begun, he wrote, 'in the darkest days of the summer of 1940, and one way or another I wanted to find a reason for hope in the future of my country'. The fables of La Fontaine provided him with the plot and it was first performed on August 8, 1942, in occupied Paris (in the penultimate section, 'Les deux coqs', Poulenc mischievously quotes the song *Non, non, vous n'aurez pas notre Alsace-Lorraine* for an audience made up mainly of German officials).

Why we don't hear this delicious score more often is a mystery. Too many good tunes, probably. Its eight movements are quintessential Poulenc with the characteristic mélange of harmonic and stylistic influences that make their composer's voice so unmistakable. There is also a good deal of self-plagiarising (spot the quotes from the Organ Concerto and the contemporaneous *Babar the Elephant*). Only one other recording is currently available, apart from the abbreviated version recorded by Georges Prêtre from 1966. The Turin players match the Parisians every step of the way with their incision, sure-footedness and sheer panache.

Stefano Bollini, whose career has been mainly in jazz, makes a good fist of the *Concerto champêtre* (commissioned by the harpsichordist Wanda Landowska, of course, but sanctioned by the composer to be played on the piano as well), rounding off the disc with his own 'elaborations' of two of Poulenc's late Improvisations, No 13 from 1958 and No 15 ('Hommage à Edith Piaf'), from 1959, the last of the cycle.

Chamber works

Complete Chamber Works

Sextet for Piano and Wind Quintet[a]. Trio for Oboe, Bassoon and Piano[b]. Flute Sonata[c]. Oboe Sonata[d]. Clarinet Sonata[e]. Violin Sonata[f]. Cello Sonata[g]. Sonata for Two Clarinets[h]. Sonata for Clarinet and Bassoon[i]. Sonata for Horn, Trumpet and Trombone[j]. Villanelle[k]. Elégie[l]. Sarabande[m]
The Nash Ensemble (Philippa Davies [ac]*fl/kpicc* [abd]Gareth Hulse *ob* [aehi]Richard Hosford, [h]Michael Harris *cls* [abi]Ursula Leveaux *bn* [aij]Richard Watkins *hn* [j]John Wallace *tpt* [j]David Purser *tbn* [f]Leo Phillips *vn* [g]Paul Watkins *vc* [m]Craig Ogden *gtr*) [a·g/k]**Ian Brown** *pf*
Hyperion ② CDA672556 (146' · DDD)   Ⓕ

Invidious as it may seem to pick out just one of these excellent artists, special mention must be made of Ian Brown, who plays in nine of the 13 works included and confirms his standing as one of the most admired and musicianly chamber pianists of our day. He knows, for example, how to control Poulenc's boisterous piano writing in the Sextet without sacrificing the sparkle, and as a result the work coheres better than ever before. Like the Trio (whose opening reveals Stravinskian influence), it's a mixture of the composer's madcap *gamin* mood and his predominantly melancholy bittersweet lyricism. The latter characteristic is most in evidence in his most enduring chamber works: the solo wind sonatas with piano, all three of which were in the nature of *tombeaux*, the Flute Sonata for the American patron Mrs Sprague Coolidge, that for clarinet for Honegger, and that for oboe for Prokofiev. All are given idiomatic, sensitive and satisfying performances by the Nash artists.

The *Elégie* for Dennis Brain was a not altogether convincing experiment in dodecaphony: Poulenc had earlier dabbled in atonality and polytonality in the little sonatas (really sonatinas) for, respectively, two clarinets and for clarinet and bassoon. There's a touching reading of the little *Sarabande* for guitar. A hint of the guitar's tuning at the start of the second movement is almost the only Spanish reference in the Violin Sonata, which was composed *in memoriam* the poet Lorca, whose loss is bitterly suggested in the angry finale. In this work Poulenc allotted to the piano (his own instrument) rather more than equal status in the duo – a situation rather paralleled in the lighthearted Cello Sonata, over which the composer dallied longer than any other of his works – but balance in both is finely judged by the performers and the recording team.

The whole issue wins enthusiastic recommendation: it bids fair to become the undisputed yardstick for the future.

Gloria

Gloria. Stabat mater
Janice Watson *sop* **BBC Singers; BBC Philharmonic Orchestra / Yan Pascal Tortelier**
Chandos CHAN9341 (56' · DDD · T/t)   Ⓕ Ⓞ

We are immediately struck, at the start of the *Gloria*, by the radiantly warm but clean orchestral sonority: only later does an uneasy suspicion arise that, apparently seduced by the sound, the recording engineers may be favouring it at the expense of the chorus, especially at orchestral *fortes*. But it's committed and thoroughly secure choral singing, perhaps most easily appreciated in some of the unaccompanied passages – tender in the almost mystic 'O quam tristis' and firm-toned at 'Fac ut ardeat' (both in the *Stabat mater*); it gives real attack at 'Quis est homo' (just holding its own against the orchestra); the sopranos can produce a bright, ringing tone; and only the very first line of the *Stabat mater*, lying low in the basses, needed to be a bit stronger (as in most performances). Janice Watson is a sweet-voiced soloist with very pure intonation; but she could with advantage have strengthened her consonants throughout.

Tortelier gives intensely felt readings of both works – the murmurous ending of the *Stabat mater* and the thrilling *fortissimo* chords at 'Quoniam' in the *Gloria* spring to mind – and fortunately he keeps the vocal 'Domine Deus' entry moving at the same pace as at its introduction. He takes the Stravinskian 'Laudamus te' fast and lightly; the only questionable speed is of 'Quae moerebat', which sounds too cheerful for the words ('mourning and lamenting'). These are performances of undoubted quality.

Gloriaª. Exultate Deo. Quatre Motets pour le temps de Noël. Quatre Motets pour un temps de pénitence. Salve regina
ª**Susan Gritton** *sop* **Polyphony;** ª**Trinity College Choir, Cambridge;** ª**Britten Sinfonia / Stephen Layton**
Hyperion CDA67623 (56' · DDD)   Ⓕ Ⓞ Ⓞ Ⓞ

From the very outset of the *Gloria* it's clear that this is a performance of real distinction. The gloriously pompous opening orchestral fanfare

 has a swagger and a self-satisfied strut which is one of those rare moments on disc where you would wish it were tracked separately so that you could just play it over and over again. But to do that would miss the scintillating choral entry, the basses starting the ball rolling with the kind of pent-up energy which you just know is going to explode in the most spectacular way. Other recordings have a pleasant, smiley quality here; Stephen Layton's crew has an almost piratical swagger, buoyantly breasting Poulenc's turbulent waves of barely restrained exuberance.

The 38 voices of Polyphony are augmented by 31 from Trinity College, Cambridge, while an unusually hefty contingent of orchestral players makes up the Britten Sinfonia on the disc. What results is not only music-making of immense power and vibrancy – take the riveting declamation 'Qui sedes ad dexteram Patris', hardly subtle or even particularly refined (the men shout and the brass blares) but unbelievably spine-tingling – but also an ability, brilliantly directed by Layton, to capture Poulenc's 'half hooligan, half monk' musical persona (in Claude Rostand's oft-quoted aphorism). Thus, in the final chorus of the *Gloria*, after the boisterous start, we have a moment of profound sanctity and another, crowned with incredible delicacy by Susan Gritton, of mouth-watering enchantment.

Not everything is quite so enticing: Gritton wallows a little too much perhaps in the 'Domine Deus', mischievously abetted by Layton's almost kitsch romanticism. But it is the vivid sense of unfettered joy in the *Gloria* and the matchless intensity of feeling revealed in the motets that make this such a gloriously distinguished disc.

Unaccompanied choral works

Mass in G. Quatre motets pour un temps de pénitence. Quatre motets pour le temps de Noël. Exultate Deo. Salve regina
Berlin RIAS Chamber Choir / Marcus Creed
Harmonia Mundi HMC90 1588 (52' · DDD · T/t)   Ⓕ

There has never been a more beautiful performance of the *Salve regina*. And elsewhere this virtuoso choir displays, beyond impeccably pure intonation and chording (chorus-masters everywhere will note with envy the sopranos' clean, dead-sure attacks on high notes), a sensitivity to verbal meaning, dynamics and vocal colour that argues not only skilful direction but a complete ease and absorption into the music's often chromatic nature by all the singers. They bring a bright-eyed tone to the *Exultate Deo*, awe to 'O magnum mysterium' (in the Christmas motets), and a striking diversity of timbre to 'Tristis est anima mea' (in the penitential motets); in the Mass they interpret to perfection the *doucement joyeux* indication of the *Sanctus*. They appear to have been recorded in some large church, but without any problems of resonance and the words are extremely clear throughout. In all, this is a first-class disc.

Chanson à boire. Sept chansons. Figure humaine.
Quatre petites prières de Saint François d'Assise.
Un soir de neige
RIAS Chamber Choir, Berlin / Daniel Reuss
Harmonia Mundi HMC90 1872 (54' · DDD · T/t)　　Ⓕ

Poulenc's earliest work for unaccompanied chorus is the 1922 *Chanson à boire* that concludes this disc. It was a commission from the Harvard Glee Club, composed while Poulenc was in the middle of trying to finish *Les biches*. It has some of the same uninhibited joie de vivre that distinguishes the ballet (which also has choral movements, seldom heard now). The male voices of the RIAS Chamber Choir give it a good, robust performance. It is typically mischievous of Poulenc to have chosen this 17th-century drinking song (from the same collection as his later *Chanson gaillardes*), to be sung while America was in the early years of Prohibition.

There could be no greater contrast than the *Quatre petites prières*, to words by St Francis of Assisi. Poulenc composed this at the request of his nephew, Frère Jérome Poulenc, for the choir at the abbey of Carrières-sous-Poissy. The direct simplicity of St Francis's verse is reflected in the music, which does not try to add any extra emotion.

Pierre Bernac wrote that 'from their first meeting, Poulenc felt an immediate bond of sympathy' with the poet Paul Eluard. All but two of the *Sept chansons* of 1935 are settings of Eluard. This was one of Poulenc's first large-scale choral pieces and the poems, at turns surreal and erotic, inspired him to a work of glittering sophistication. *Figure humaine*, from 1943, is considered by many to be one of Poulenc's most perfect compositions. Eluard's poems were circulated anonymously during the Occupation and the climactic 'Liberté' is the single most affecting work to have come from Poulenc's reaction to the Second World War and its atrocities. *Un soir de neige*, composed in December 1944, during the first winter after the Liberation, while the war in Europe was still raging, is in contrast a quietly reflective chamber cantata. It is indicative of Poulenc's often-cited dual personality that he should have composed this while he was at work on *Les mamelles de Tirésias*.

Although there are no French names listed among the members of the RIAS Chamber Choir, the clarity of diction achieved here is first-rate. The balance and the acoustic of the Jesus Christus Kirche in Berlin are sympathetic. A beautiful disc, which is a fine introduction to Poulenc's choral music.

Figure humaine. Sept chansons. Un soir de neige
Accentus Chamber Choir / Laurence Equilbey
Naïve Classique V4883 (39' · DDD · T/t)　　ⒻⓄ

Poulenc's choral music is particularly treacherous territory. One moment you're singing what sounds like Janequin or Passereau, the next you're into jagged, almost atonal lines and harmonies that seem to tear at the ether. And the contrasts are often abrupt and have to be managed at speed with every syllable of the French in place. Incredibly, the Accentus Chamber Choir under Equilbey's direction meet all these challenges with flying colours. Not only that, but their phrasing is unfailingly sensitive to the verbal shifts of the poems and no less to the harmonic and textural shifts of Poulenc's music. It's unlikely that a non-French choir would be able to achieve these standards.

Tuning and ensemble are impeccable, tone quality excellent and the varied textures sharply characterised within a spacious acoustic and with slightly distant recording.

Mélodies

Banalités. Bleuet. Chansons gaillardes. Chansons villageoises. Dernier poème. Quatre poèmes. Métamorphoses – C'est ainsi que tu es. Montparnasse. Poèmes – C. Priez pour paix. Rosemonde. Tel jour, telle nuit – Bonne journée; Une ruine coquille vide; Une herbe pauvre; Je n'ai envie que de t'aimer;Nous avons fait la nuit
Michel Piquemal *bar* **Christine Lajarrige** *pf*
Naxos 8 553642 (67' · DDD)　　Ⓢ**ⓄⓄⒹ→**

The first time Michel Piquemal met Pierre Bernac, for whom most of these songs were written, Piquemal recalls that Bernac said: 'I am very moved, because what you're doing is exactly what Francis Poulenc was hoping for. He would have been happy.' Afterwards Piquemal studied both with Bernac and Denise Duval, the two singers who were closest to the composer, so this recital is part of a real, authentic tradition. The greatest challenge for a singer comes in the best-known songs, for instance *Montparnasse* and 'C'. Piquemal doesn't disappoint. He hasn't got the luxurious voice for the lyrical climax of the first, at the words 'Vous êtes en réalité un poète lyrique d'Allemagne / Qui voulez connaître Paris,' but he delivers all the complicated Apollinaire verse in this and the cycle *Banalités* with a complete understanding of the necessary balance between stressing the irony and maintaining the strict forward-moving musical line.

The one group that wasn't composed for a light baritone is *Chansons villageoises*, which, although sung and recorded by Bernac, was intended for a Verdi baritone; 'Un tour de chant symphonique' Poulenc called it. Like Bernac, Piquemal doesn't have the opulent vocal quality here that Poulenc was looking for, but instead he has an actor's way with the words that brings personality and humour to a text such as the opening 'Chanson du clair tamis' – *très gai et très vite* in Poulenc's marking. All the brilliance of Maurice Fombeure's poetry gains clarity from Piquemal's diction and sense of fun, while the ensuing sadness of 'C'est le joli printemps' and the macabre parable of 'Le mendiant' are sharply contrasted.

If you want to sample this disc, try *Bleuet*, and the 'sensitive lyricism' that Bernac wrote of. It's one of the saddest songs Poulenc composed, with its image of the young soldier, the blue referring to the uniform of the conscript who has seen such terrible things while he's still almost a child. It has to be sung 'intimately', wrote Poulenc; Bernac, however, thought that it should also be 'virile and serious'. The penultimate line in which the boy faces the reality – he knows death better than life – is sung by Piquemal with a natural feel for the simplicity of the poem, never overdoing the emphasis, and never becoming arch.

At Naxos's low price this is a first-rate introduction to Poulenc's songs, but more than that it's an example of the best kind of French singing. Christine Lajarrige is a sensitive accompanist, for Poulenc always acknowledged that his songs are duets, for voice and piano.

Dialogues des Carmélites

Dialogues des Carmélites   Ⓗ
Denise Duval *sop* Blanche de La Force **Régine Crespin** *sop* Madame Lidoine **Denise Scharley** *mez* Madame de Croissy **Liliane Berton** *sop* Soeur Constance **Rita Gorr** *mez* Mère Marie **Xavier Depraz** *bass* Marquis de La Force **Paul Finel** *ten* Chevalier de La Force **Janine Fourrier** *sop* Mère Jeanne **Gisèle Desmoutiers** *sop* Soeur Mathilde **Louis Rialland** *ten* L'Aumônier **René Bianco** *bar* Le Geôlier **Jacques Mars** *bar* L'Officier **Raphael Romagnoni** *ten* First Commissaire **Charles Paul** *bar* Second Commissaire **Michel Forel** *ten* Thierry **Max Conti** *bar* Javelinot **Chorus and Orchestra of the Opéra, Paris / Pierre Dervaux**
EMI Great Recordings of the Century mono ②
562751-2 (144' · ADD · T) Recorded 1958   Ⓜ**OO**

In the history of French opera *Dialogues des Carmélites* is a worthy successor to Debussy's *Pelléas* and indeed its touching heroine Blanche shares much of the troubling troubled, out-of-this-world, fey personality of her predecessor. As for the writing, Poulenc is as accomplished a master at setting the French language in a melodic yet at the same quasi-*parlando* style as Massenet, and his use of a large orchestra is at once fastidious and convincing conservative but never derivative, though inevitably there are influences, mostly beneficial ones.

It is evident from this recording that the singers were inspired by the piece to give of their considerable best. With the benefit of hindsight we can judge that this was a final flowering of the authentic school of French singing. Denise Duval is part of the long line of clear-voiced, incisive sopranos in the Heldy mould. She catches here all the conflicting facets of Blanche's personality, girlish, wilful, frightened, elated as the role requires. Crespin, even though at this early stage of her career was already not altogether happy above a high G is a moving, authoritative Madame Lidoine. Still better is Rita Gorr's commanding yet sympathetic Mother Marie and Denise Scharley's haunted and haunting Old Prioress, quite devastatingly desparate in her death scene. Liliane Berton is a

charming Sister Constance, and the smaller roles are finely taken, not least Louis Rialland as the hapless, helpless Chaplain.

Pierre Dervaux conducts an inspired, inspiriting account of the work, attentive to both its smaller detail and to its grander, elevated passages, raising the final scene of martyrdom to a proper degree of intensity as some inner strength and group-fervour grips the nuns. As compared with the vocal score, there are a few cuts and changes in the voice parts, both sanctioned by Poulenc. The mono recording is more than adequate. For anyone interested in 20th-century opera, this is a 'must': we are unlikely to have another recording and certainly not one so authentic as this.

Dialogues des Carmélites
Catherine Dubosc *sop* Blanche de la Force **Rachel Yakar** *sop* Madame Lidoine **Rita Gorr** *mez* Madame de Croissy **Brigitte Fournier** *sop* Soeur Constance **Martine Dupuy** *mez* Mère Marie **José van Dam** *bass-bar* Marquis de la Force **Jean-Luc Viala** *ten* Chevalier de la Force **Michel Sénéchal** *ten* L'Aumônier **François Le Roux** *bar* Le Geôlier **Lyon Opéra Chorus and Orchestra / Kent Nagano**
Virgin Classics ② 358657-2 (152' · DDD · T/t) Ⓕ**OOO**

Poulenc's *chef d'œuvre* is one of the few operas written since *Wozzeck* that has survived in the repertory – and deservedly so. It's written from, and goes to, the heart, not in any extrovert or openly histrionic way but by virtue of its ability to explore the world of a troubled band of Carmelite nuns at the height of the terrors caused by the French Revolution, and do so in an utterly individual manner. Poulenc unerringly enters into their psyches as they face their fatal destiny. Nagano responds with perceptible keenness to the sombre, elevated mood and intensity of the writing and unfailingly delineates the characters of the principals as they face their everyday martyrdom. The magisterial authority of Martine Dupuy's Mère Marie, the agony of Rita Gorr's Old Prioress, the inner torment of Catherine Dubosc's Sister Blanche, the restraint of Rachel Yakar's Madame Lidoine, the eager charm of Brigitte Fournier's Sister Constance are only the leading players in a distribution that's admirable in almost every respect. The score is for once given complete. The atmospheric recording suggests stage action without exaggeration.

The Carmelites (sung in English)
Catrin Wyn-Davies *sop* Blanche de la Force **Ashley Holland** *bar* Marquis de la Force **Peter Wedd** *ten* Chevalier de la Force **Ryland Davies** *ten* Chaplain **David Stephenson** *bar* Jailor **Felicity Palmer** *mez* Madame de Croissy **Orla Boylan** *sop* Madame Lidoine **Josephine Barstow** *sop* Mother Marie **Sarah Tynan** *sop* Sister Constance **Jane Powell** *mez* Mother Jeanne **Anne-Marie Gibbons** *mez* Sister Mathilde
English National Opera Chorus and Orchestra / Paul Daniel

Chandos ② CHAN3143 (144' · DDD · S/T/t/N)　Ⓕ

Poulenc's *Carmelites* had its definitive recording with the original cast in 1958 under Dervaux (EMI – see above) but a performance in the vernacular recorded in the studio following stage performances has its own relevance, especially when it is conducted with such conviction as by Paul Daniel, who restores the interludes not on the French set. He draws intense, beautiful playing from his orchestra, helped by one of Chandos's most immediate, well-aired recordings.

The first third of the performance is commanded by Felicity Palmer's lacerating performance as the Old Prioress. This is a gift of a role for a mezzo of a certain age and Palmer makes the most of it as she conveys the old woman's seeming loss of faith and fear of death. Every word is filled with meaning and delivered with amazing power. The rest of the cast creates a more mixed impression. Exceptional artist that she is, Josephine Barstow isn't wholly happy in voice as Mother Marie. But the most serious flaw concerns the central role of Blanche. Of all parts this one demands clear, clean high notes; whenever Catrin Wyn-Davies strays above the stave, her tone loses colour and *in extremis* the high notes are distinctly uncomfortable on the ear. In compensation she does catch most of Blanche's troubled character.

As Sister Constance, Sarah Tynan sings with charm and ease. As the new Prioress, Orla Boylan provides an admirable line; her final solo before the executions is most moving. Smaller parts are taken variably, but the veteran tenor Ryland Davies is a model of style and feeling as the Chaplain, and Peter Wedd makes his mark in the ungrateful role of the Chevalier de la Force. Nothing will ever replace the classic Dervaux recording but those who saw this production or want to have the work in the vernacular will welcome the new issue and Daniel's rewarding interpretation.

Les dialogues des Carmélites
Didier Henry *bar* Marquis de la Force **Anne Sophie Schmidt** *sop* Blanche de la Force **Laurence Dale** *ten* Chevalier de la Force **Léonard Pezzino** *ten* L'Aumônier **Christophe Fel** *bass* Le geôlier **Nadine Denize** *mez* Madame de Croissy **Valérie Millot** *sop* Madame Lidoine **Hedwig Fassbender** *mez* Mère Marie **Patricia Petibon** *sop* Soeur Constance **Michèle Besse** *contr* Mère Jeanne **Allison Elaine Cook** *mez* Soeur Mathilde **Ivan Ludlow** *ten* L'Officier **Vincent de Rooster** *ten* First Commissaire **Merih Kazbek** *bass* Second Commissaire **Yves Ernst** *bar* Thierry **Jenz Kiertzner** *bar* Javelinot **Rhine National Opera Chorus; Strasbourg Philharmonic Orchestra / Jan Latham-König**
Stage director **Marthe Keller**
Video director **Don Kent**
ArtHaus Musik 📀 100 004 (149' · Region 0)　Ⓕ 〇

Marthe Keller's staging of Poulenc's austere, deeply eloquent opera was produced at the Opéra du Rhin early in 1999. Keller's simple ideas march precisely with the intentions of the original, the plain sets and economy of movement mirroring the direct simplicity of Poulenc's beautiful score.

Every artist here performs in a wholly dedicated fashion as part of a well-tutored ensemble, no one more so than Anne Sophie Schmidt in depicting the psychological struggle and vulnerability of the central character, Blanche de la Force. With her greatly expressive features and her refined voice, Schmidt's portrayal is starkly moving. In complete contrast is Petibon's bright, radiant, perfectly sung Constance. Among the older members of the Convent community, Nadine Denize plays her two scenes as the Old Prioress with the authority and concentration they call for, going to her death as she loses her faith in an agonising bout of self-understanding. Hedwig Fassbender is all stern authority as Mother Marie, although one senses sympathy behind the harsh exterior, which is how this part should be. Valérie Millot is outwardly more sympathetic and warm as the new Prioress, Madame Lidoine, who instils courage in her charges when it comes to the crunch and, one by one, they go to the guillotine.

Video direction, sound and picture quality are admirable. This is one of the most worthwhile opera performances yet to appear on DVD.

La voix humaine

La voix humaine. La dame de Monte-Carlo
Felicity Lott *sop* **Suisse Romande Orchestra / Armin Jordan**
Harmonia Mundi HMC90 1759 (51' · DDD)　Ⓕ

Poulenc was certainly in close touch with his anima. His heroines, often suffering, as in these two works, readily take upon themselves his own depressive and even hysterical character. But not only is the rejected woman in *La voix humaine* Poulenc himself (he admitted as much), she's also Denise Duval, the first interpreter of the work, for whom it was written. Duval said that both she and the composer were in what the tabloids call 'love tangles' at the time and that the work spoke for both of them. So it's a brave act for any other soprano to compete with her 1959 recording, let alone someone who isn't French.

Felicity Lott is one of the few British sopranos who could hope to come close. And she does. The voice is in excellent shape, the French likewise. The recording doesn't place her so firmly in the limelight as Duval's, while Jordan draws fine playing from the orchestra – maybe not quite as explosive as Prêtre in the emotional outbursts, but if anything with more of the *sensualité orchestrale* that Poulenc asked for. And if she doesn't quite get the necessary hysteria and vulgarity, she very nearly does. She seems more at home in *La dame de Monte-Carlo*, also on a Cocteau text but this time in verse. The top of the voice is radiant where Mady Mesplé's is sometimes shrill and marred by heavy vibrato, and throughout she captures exactly the right tone of outraged dignity.

Michael Praetorius   German 1571-1621

The son of a strict Lutheran, Praetorius was educated at Torgau, Frankfurt an der Oder (1582) and Zerbst (1584). He was organist of St Marien, Frankfurt (1587-90), before moving to Wolfenbüttel, where he was court organist from 1595 and Kapellmeister from 1604. He temporarily served the Saxon court (1613-16), chiefly at Dresden, where he met Schütz and got to know the latest Italian music, and he worked in many other German cities. The most versatile German composer of his day, he was also one of the most prolific.   GROVEmusic

Christmas Music

'Mass for Christmas Morning'
Roskilde Cathedral Boys' Choir and   Ⓟ
Congregation; Gabrieli Consort; Gabrieli Players /
Paul McCreesh
Archiv Produktion 439 250-2AH (79' · DDD · T/t)ⒻⓄ➔

The aesthetic of contrast, so central to early Baroque spectacle (sacred or profane), is inspired here by the traditional part played by the congregation in Lutheran worship. Praetorius's music for the *figuraliter* (the vocal/ instrumental choirs) is greatly influenced by fashionable Venetian techniques. But what's striking is the way the old *alternatim* practices of the Protestant church blend so naturally with the intricate textures and scorings of a colourful Italian-style canvas, ranging from intimate dialogues to full grandiloquent sonority. What's more, the centrality of the chorale is never compromised. Despite all these ingredients, it's McCreesh's research and imagination that make this service such a powerful testament to the faith expressed by Lutherans of Praetorius's generation, and indeed by subsequent generations to which Bach was so indebted.

The service follows, to all intents and purposes, the Mass of the Roman rite (sung distinction by the Gabrieli Consort though the sopranos seem a little unsure in the *Kyrie*) interspersed with a versatile array of motets, hymns, prayers, intoned readings, a superbly conceived and suitably mysterious Pavan by Schein for the approach to Communion and several rhetorically positioned organ preludes. For a congregation, the Gabrieli Consort and players are joined by the boys of Roskilde Cathedral, Denmark and a some local amateur choirs. The effect is remarkable for its fervour in the hymns; now one can see why *Von Himmel hoch da komm ich her* inspired so many settings in the 17th century.

Other familiar tunes include *Quem pastores*, *Wie schön leuchtet der Morgenstern* in a shimmering prelude by Scheidt followed by a delicately nuanced motet on the same tune. *In dulci jubilo* is treated to a flamboyant setting by Praetorius featuring six trumpets. The spacious acoustic of the cathedral exhibits McCreesh's acute timbral sense; definition isn't ideally sharp but this is a small price to pay for a natural perspective which embraces the sense of community worship essential for this project.

André Previn   German/American b1929

American conductor, pianist and composer of German birth, Previn studied in Berlin and at the Paris Conservatoire and moved to Los Angeles in 1939. His early career was in the film industry and as a jazz pianist. He made his conducting début in 1963 and was conductor-in-chief of the Houston SO, 1967-70. From 1965 he has been heard with the LSO (principal conductor, 1969-79), notably in strongly coloured late Romantic or early 20th-century music. He conducted the Pittsburgh SO, 1976-86, and headed the RPO, Los Angeles and Oslo POs. He has composed operas and orchestral and chamber works.   GROVEmusic

A Streetcar Named Desire

A Streetcar Named Desire
Renée Fleming *sop* Blanche Dubois **Elizabeth
Futral** *sop* Stella Kowalski **Rodney Gilfry** *bar* Stanley
Kowalski **Anthony Dean Griffey** *ten* Mitch **Judith
Forst** *mez* Eunice Hubbell **San Francisco Opera
Orchestra / André Previn**
Stage director **Colin Graham**
Video director **Kirk Browning**
ArtHaus Musik 🆅 100 138 (167' · 16:9 · 2.0 · 2, 5)   Ⓕ

Perhaps the most convincing portrayal is that of Rodney Gilfrey as the rough worker Stanley, perpetually chewing, smoking or drinking, periodically exploding into violence, but with beefy baritone always beautifully produced. Anthony Dean Griffey is almost equally good as the naive, mother-loving Mitch, so cruelly deceived by Blanche; while Elizabeth Futral does quite wonderfully well as the tender Stella. For all the beauty of her arias and her high notes throughout, perhaps the least convincing is Renée Fleming herself. Partly, this is because Previn too often pushes the voice into its higher reaches irrespective of natural speech patterns. It's almost as though he was determined to emphasise that this is opera, not musical theatre. In addition, though, Fleming's starry presence requires some suspension of belief to accept the full extent of Blanche's mental deterioration. But overall the work makes gripping listening and viewing, and the DVD is a marvellous memento of what was surely a significant landmark in operatic history.

Sergey Prokofiev   Russian 1891-1953

Prokofiev showed precocious talent as a pianist and composer and had lessons from Glier from 1902. In 1904 he entered the St Petersburg Conservatory, where *Rimsky-Korsakov, Lyadov and Tcherepnin were among his teachers; Tcherepnin and Myaskovsky, who gave him valuable support, encouraged his interest in Scriabin, Debussy and Strauss. He had made his début as a pianist in 1908, quickly creating something of a sensation as an enfant terrible, unintelligible and ultra-modern – an image he was happy to cultivate. His intemperateness in his early piano pieces, and later in such works as the extravagantly Romantic Piano Concerto No 1 and the ominous No 2, attracted attention. Then in 1914 he left the conservatory and travelled to London, where he heard Stravinsky's works and gained a commission from Diaghilev: the resulting score was, however, rejected (the music was used to make the Scythian Suite); a second attempt, Chout, was not staged until 1921.*

Meanwhile his gifts had exploded in several different directions. In 1917 he finished an opera on Dostoyevsky's Gambler, a violently involved study of obsession far removed from the fantasy of his nearly contemporary Chicago opera The Love for Three Oranges, written in1919 and performed in 1921. Nor does either of these scores have much to do with his Classical Symphony, selfconsciously 18th-century in manner, and again quite distinct from his lyrical Violin Concerto No 1, written at the same period and in the same key. There were also piano sonatas based on old notebooks alongside the more adventurous Visions fugitives, all dating from 1915-19.

Towards the end of this rich period, in 1918, he left for the USA; then from 1920 France became his base. His productivity slowed while he worked at his opera The Fiery Angel, an intense, symbolist fable of good and evil (it had no complete performance until after his death, and he used much of its music in Symphony No 3). After this he brought the harsh, heavy and mechanistic elements in his music to a climax in Symphony No 2 and in the ballet Le pas d'acier, while his next ballet, L'enfant prodigue, is in a much gentler style: the barbaric and the lyrical were still alternatives in his music and not fused until the 1930s, when he began a process of reconciliation with the Soviet Union.

The renewed relationship was at first tentative on both sides. Romeo and Juliet, the full-length ballet commissioned for the Bolshoi, had its première at Brno in 1938, and only later became a staple of the Soviet repertory: its themes of aggression and romantic love provided, as also did the Eisenstein film Alexander Nevsky, a receptacle for Prokofiev's divergent impulses. Meanwhile his own impulse to remain a Westerner was gradually eroded and in 1936 he settled in Moscow, where initially his concern was with the relatively modest genres of song, incidental music, patriotic cantata and children's entertainment (Peter and the Wolf, 1936). He had, indeed, arrived at a peculiarly unfortunate time, when the drive towards socialist realism was at its most intense; and his first work of a more ambitious sort, the opera Semyon Kotko, was not liked.

With the outbreak of war, however, he perhaps found the motivation to respond to the required patriotism: implicitly in a cycle of three piano sonatas (Nos 6-8) and Symphony No 5, more openly in his operatic setting of scenes from Tolstoy's War and Peace, which again offered opportunities for the two extremes of his musical genius to be expressed. He also worked at a new full-length ballet, Cinderella.

In 1946 he retired to the country and though he went on composing, the works of his last years have been regarded as a quiet coda to his output. Even his death was overshadowed by that of Stalin on the same day. GROVEmusic

---

Piano Concertos

No 1 in D flat, Op 10; **No 2** in G minor, Op 16; **No 3** in C, Op 26; **No 4** in B flat, Op 53 (left-hand); **No 5** in G, Op 55

Piano Concertos Nos 1-5
Vladimir Ashkenazy pf
London Symphony Orchestra / André Previn
Decca ② 452 588-2DF2 (126' · ADD) Recorded 1974-5
Ⓜ**○○**⊕→

While it's true that the Prokofiev piano concertos are an uneven body of work, there's enough imaginative fire and pianistic brilliance to hold the attention even in the weakest of them; the best, by common consent Nos 1, 3 and 4, have stood the test of time very well. As indeed have these Decca recordings. The set first appeared in 1975, but the sound is fresher than many contemporary digital issues, and Ashkenazy has rarely played better. Other pianists have matched his brilliance and energy in, say, the Third Concerto, but very few have kept up such a sure balance of fire and poetry. The astonishingly inflated bravura of the Second Concerto's opening movement is kept shapely and purposeful and even the out-of-tune piano doesn't spoil the effect too much. And the youthful First has the insouciance and zest its 22-year-old composer plainly intended.

Newcomers to the concertos should start with No 3: so many facets of Prokofiev's genius are her, and Ashkenazy shows how they all take their place as part of a kind of fantastic story. But there are rewards everywhere, and the effort involved in finding them is small.

Prokofiev Piano Concertos Nos 1 & 3
Bartók Piano Concerto No 3, Sz119
Martha Argerich pf
Montreal Symphony Orchestra / Charles Dutoit
EMI 556654-2 (70' · DDD) Ⓕ**○○**

Martha Argerich's return to the studios in two concertos she has not previously recorded is an uplifting moment. As always with this most mercurial of virtuosos, her playing is generated very much by the mood of the moment, but you may well be surprised at her relative geniality with Dutoit here. Her entire reading is less hard-driven, her opening arguably more authentically *brioso* than ferocious, her overall view a refreshingly fanciful view of Prokofiev's youthful iconoclasm. The central *Andante assai* is inflected with an improvisatory freedom she would probably not have risked earlier in her career and in the *Allegro scherzando* she trips the light fantastic, reserving a suitably tigerish attack for the final octave bravura display.

Again, while her performance of the Third Concerto is less fleet or nimble-fingered than in her early legendary disc for DG with Abbado; it's more delectably alive to passing caprice. Part-writing and expressive detail interest her more than in the past and there's no lack of virtuoso *frisson* in the first movement's concluding quasi-fugal *più mosso* chase. Once more Argerich is unusually sensitive in the central *Andantino*, to the fourth variation's plunge into Slavic melancholy and introspection. Personal and vivacious throughout, she always allows the composer his own voice.

This is true to an even greater extent in Bartók's Third Concerto where her rich experience in chamber music makes her often *primus inter pares*, a virtuoso who listens to her partners with the greatest care. Dutoit and his orchestra achieve a fine unity throughout. The recordings are clear and naturally balanced and only those in search of metallic thrills and rushes of blood to the head will feel disappointed.

Prokofiev Piano Concerto No 2, Op 16
Ravel Piano Concerto
Yundi Li *pf* **Berlin Philharmonic Orchestra /
Seiji Ozawa**
DG 477 6593GH (51' · DDD)   Ⓕ Ⓞ➔

This unusual coupling contrasts two wildly different works. For some, Prokofiev's Second Piano Concerto is a work of genius, while for others it remains a monstrosity. Holding up a malevolent distorting mirror to Russian Romanticism, it carries the uneasy modernism of Rachmaninov's Fourth Concerto to its logical and devastating conclusion. Ravel's G major Concerto, on the other hand, recalls the spirits of Mozart and Saint-Saëns and contains a slow movement that is among the composer's most touching creations. Prokofiev's Concerto is daunting and massive, Ravel's an enchanting *jeu d'esprit*.

Certainly Yundi Li (superbly partnered by Seji Ozawa and the Berlin Philharmonic) has few doubts about either concerto. Indeed, his performance of the Prokofiev, in its prodigious, unflagging power and brilliance, far surpasses any other in the catalogue. His *moto perpetuo* scherzo is *vivace* with a vengeance and the colossal first movement's combined development and cadenza is played with an authority that will make lesser mortals pale with envy and admiration. He is no less attuned to Ravel's charm and vivacity, to music seen through a glass brightly rather than darkly, touching off the central *Adagio* with a moving simplicity and whirling us through the finale with a dazzling and engaging *joie de vivre*. It only remains to add that this superlative young Chinese pianist is heard in the full glory of DG's sound at its most opulent and crystalline.

Prokofiev Piano Concerto No 5 **Ravel** Piano Concerto in G **Schlimé** Three Improvisations

Francesco Tristano Schlimé *pf*
Russian National Orchestra / Mikhail Pletnev
Pentatone ⊕ PTC5186 080 (65' · DDD)   Ⓕ

Here is music-making to wonder at. Rarely in their history can the two concertos have been performed with such meticulous care and affection. The Luxembourg-born, 25-year-old pianist includes Pletnev – his more-than-distinguished partner on this disc – among his teachers and has won first prize in one of the less celebrated competitions (so often venues of true musical discovery).

What sadness and introspection he conveys beneath Ravel's clowning surface, shadowed, as it were, by the Left Hand Concerto, by an inwardness mirrored in his own haunting *Three Improvisations*. The central *Adagio* emerges as a timeless reverie, making it hard to recall a performance of greater magic or tonal translucency, a far cry indeed from a more superficial tradition emanating from Marguerite Long, the work's dedicatee. In the Prokofiev Schlimé and Pletnev take an almost chamber music-like view of the grotesquerie and acrobatics and the result is lyrical and musicianly in a wholly fresh and unsuspected way. Nothing sounds bleak or conventionally percussive and a mysterious, winter-fairytale aura hangs over the entire work (never more so than in the *Larghetto*).

Schlimé confesses that he has always felt impelled to play what he calls his 'other' music, in this case improvised reflections on the two concertos. Recorded late one night in the Moscow Conservatoire, they were added with Pletnev's blessing, and the concluding mournful, jazzman's chime is very much music that registers 'long after it was heard no more'. Pentatone's sound and balance are exemplary.

Violin Concertos

No 1 in D, Op 19; **No 2** in G minor, Op 63

Prokofiev Violin Concerto No 2
Glazunov Violin Concerto in A minor, Op 82
Tchaikovsky Souvenir d'un lieu cher, Op 42 – No 1, Méditation (orch Glazunov)
Nikolaj Znaider *vn* **Bavarian Radio Symphony Orchestra / Mariss Jansons**
RCA Red Seal 74321 87454-2 (57' · DDD)   Ⓕ Ⓞ➔

Znaider's confident, abundantly characterful account of the Prokofiev is probably the finest since Vadim Repin's similarly stimulating 1995 version with Nagano and the Hallé. Znaider brings an extra lyrical ardour and tender intimacy to Prokofiev's soaring melodies, not to mention a greater rhythmic swagger in the finale. But what really lifts this account to special heights is the chamber-like rapport and concentration Znaider generates with Mariss Jansons and the Bavarian Radio SO, whose playing is a model of scrupulous observation and profound musicality. Time and again, these intelligent artists will have you gasping anew at the giddy beauty and wondrous fantasy of Prokofiev's stunningly inventive inspiration, and theirs is a strongly communicative performance which grips from first measure to last.

The Glazunov receives a reading notable for its refreshing thoughtfulness and unforced, 'old world' charm. By the side of the dazzlingly slick Vengerov, Znaider emerges as an altogether more personable and imaginative story-teller, yet there's heaps of panache and twinkling affection when needed, and his playing has none of the slight technical shortcomings that take the shine off Shaham's less distinctive account.

A slight niggle concerns the slightly up-front solo balance, which imparts a certain nasal wiriness to Znaider's tone in the upper reaches.

Prokofiev Violin Concertos Nos 1 & 2[a]
Glazunov Violin Concerto[b]
Maxim Vengerov vn [a]**London Symphony Orchestra / Mstislav Rostropovich;** [b]**Berlin Philharmonic Orchestra / Claudio Abbado**
Warner Elatus 0927-49567-2 ((72' · DDD)   Ⓜ ⊙☰➔

Vengerov and Rostropovich take an unashamedly epic, wide-open-steppes view of Prokofiev's First Concerto rather than the pseudo-Ravelian one posited by Chung/Previn and Mintz/Abbado, but it works at least as well. His tone is gloriously rich, every note hit dead centre. Closely observed digital recording uncovers a wealth of detail, most of it welcome. Towards the end of the first movement, the approach to the reprise of the opening melody on solo flute with harp, muted strings and lightly running tracery from the soloist is very deliberately taken, and the long-breathed finale builds to a passionate, proto-Soviet climax. The central scherzo is predictably breathtaking in its virtuosity. However committed you are to alternative interpretations, this demands to be heard.

No 2 is slightly less successful. The balance is partly to blame – the orchestra a remote presence, the soloist rather too closely scrutinised – but there's also a lack of intimacy in the interpretation itself. Even if the finale has its impressive passages, there isn't quite enough light-hearted Spanishry in a piece written not to Soviet order but for Robert Soëtans to play in Madrid. Vengerov's sometimes overwrought manner, though, fits this music like a glove.

Symphony-Concerto (for cello)

Symphony-Concerto[a]. Cello Sonata in C, Op 119[b]
Han-Na Chang vc [a]**London Symphony Orchestra / Antonio Pappano** [b]pf
EMI 557438-2 (62' · DDD)   Ⓕ ☰❍❍❍

Ⓖ   Chang and Pappano offer a fiercely communicative Symphony-Concerto (nb: EMI has reverted to the outmoded nomenclature of *Sinfonia Concertante*) and an equally distinctive, though more conventionally ruminative account of the Sonata.

It's fair to assume that the Korean cellist is the youngest exponent of these pieces on disc, and it shows in the best possible way as her youthful vivacity meets Prokofiev's mature style. Although still in her teens, she's an experienced, even mature recording artist with several fine discs under her belt. Her taut, ardent conception of the main work here, music that can often come across as rambling and discursive, is the most radical thing she has done, knocking minutes off the timings of almost every previous recording. The first movement is perfectly pitched, never self-indulgent, and it's easy to forgive any momentary lack of unanimity when editing might have impaired the forward thrust of the music-making. Chang's authoritative style reaps huge rewards from 7'25", where the theme sings out in the very highest register.

The central *scherzo* is sensationally swift and articulate but deeply felt too, with more emotional as well as physical precision than in previous performances barring Rostropovich's own. Prokofiev's sometimes wan lyricism is revivified by Chang's refined sensibility; her phrasing truly breathes with the music and the vulnerable, confessional quality she reveals may well bring a tear to the eye. Autumnal half-lights are usually more potent for being strictly rationed, and Pappano is forthright as well as 'sensitive', giving us some minatory, Soviet-sounding brass interventions amid the hustle and bustle.

It's not only the refined direction that brings new colour, clarity and lustre to Prokofiev's orchestral fabric. EMI's sound is top-notch, and you may be taken aback to discover just how terrific this orchestra can sound in a sympathetic recording studio. The cellist is placed closer than would be the case in live concert, but such technically invulnerable playing can take it. Han-Na Chang's disc is quite superb.

Symphonies

No 1 in D, Op 25, 'Classical'; No 2 in D minor, Op 40; No 3 in C minor, Op 44; No 4 in C, Op 47 (original 1930 version); No 4 in C, Op 112 (revised 1947 version); No 5 in B flat, Op 100; No 6 in E flat minor, Op 111; No 7 in C sharp minor, Op 131

Symphonies Nos 1-7 (including two versions of No 4)
London Symphony Orchestra / Valery Gergiev
Philips ④ 475 7655PM4 (4h 20' · DDD)
Recorded live 2004   Ⓜ ❍❍❍☰➔

Ⓖ   In comparison with Shostakovich, Sergey Sergeyevich Prokofiev's less caring personality, lack of social and political engagement and frequent failure to consider what a symphony might be (beyond a mould to be filled with wonderful tunes and short-term effects) need not alter the fact that there is some tremendous music here which deserves to be on every collector's shelf. For all its protean variety it's an idiom that responds well, perhaps better

PROKOFIEV SYMPHONY NO 5 – IN BRIEF

Berlin PO / Herbert von Karajan
DG 463 613-2GOR (78' · ADD) Ⓜ❶❶❶▷
DG 437 253-2GGA (71' · ADD) Ⓜ❶❶❶▷

🏆 Recorded in 1968, Karajan's interpretation remains a classic. (The first listed CD couples it with his rather soft-grained Stravinsky *Rite of Spring*; the second, more appropriately, with the *Classical* Symphony, No 1.) Karajan's is a rich, long-breathed conception with full-blooded Berlin sonority.

Leningrad PO / Mariss Jansons
Chandos CHAN8576 (38' · DDD) Ⓕ❶▷
Short on playing time but heavy on temperament. Jansons gives a very fine performance and draws some superb playing from the St Petersburg orchestra, but he does force the work at times, over-pressuring lines that really don't need it.

City of Birmingham SO / Sir Simon Rattle
EMI 388694-2 (64' · DDD) Ⓑ❶❶▷
Coupled with Prokofiev's ear-shattering *Scythian* Suite, Rattle's Fifth is a tremendous performance, lighter on its toes than either Jansons or Karajan, and sounding magnificent. This Rattle at his most re-creatively imaginative.

Royal Scottish National Orchestra / Neeme Järvi
Chandos CHAN8450 (57' · DDD) Ⓕ▷
A wonderful natural, unfussy reading with the RSNO on fine form and Chandos's recording is nicely handled – but for a modern version Rattle does have the edge. The coupling is a delightful *Waltz Suite*.

Paris Conservatoire Orchestra / Jean Martinon Ⓗ
Testament SBT1296 (72' · ADD) Ⓜ
Coupled with the gorgeous No 7, Martinon's Fifth is a strong performance, muscular and imaginative. Obviously the 1959 sound leaves a little to be desired, but for those interested in fine conductors of yore this is well worth considering.

Slovak PO / Stephen Gunzenhauser
Naxos 8 550237 (61' · DDD) Ⓕ▷
Coupled with a rather lacklustre No 1, Gunzenhauser offers a very fine reading full of incident and nice detail. The Slovak band play superbly and the recording quality is very fine. An excellent budget price alternative.

London SO / Valery Gergiev
Philips ④ 475 7655PM4 (4h 20' · DDD) Ⓜ❶▷
Only available as part of Gergiev's complete Prokofiev symphony cycle, this is a fine, romantic Fifth with rich, dark playing from a clearly inspired LSO.

than Shostakovich's, to Valery Gergiev's extrovert, sometimes brusque approach.

The new performances of the Second, Sixth and Seventh are probably the finest on CD. While the Third packs a supercharged punch, it may be found too raw and driven for its subtleties to register. The familiar *Classical* No 1 gets the most destabilising treatment with a stodgy opening movement and a whirlwind finale.

The cycle was taped live during Gergiev's Barbican series in May 2004 and emerges now not on the orchestra's own label but in Philips livery. Given the venue's acoustic problems, sound-quality is better than one dared hope – bold, immediate and lacking only the last ounce of depth and allure. As those who attended will recall, the maestro directed with a toothpick and a gestural armoury all his own. Whatever the difficulties, the players deliver the goods with a hefty, if not overly refined, sonority we shall doubtless be hearing more of in the future. A pity that there was no space for the optimistic final flourish Prokofiev tacked onto his Seventh Symphony in pursuit of Stalin Prize winnings. Both alternatives were given in concert. That said, there's enough toughness and disquiet in what has gone before to make its omission feel right. We do get both editions of the Fourth, not always the case in previous recorded *intégrales*. Any sense of disappointment there may be associated with the music's relative poverty of invention, though there is more charm in the material than the conducting allows.

Swallowed whole as it must be, the set nonetheless confirms Gergiev as Prokofiev's most ardent contemporary advocate. The visceral thrust and passion of the LSO's playing knocks the likes of Ozawa's Berlin Philharmonic into a cocked hat. Strongly recommended.

Prokofiev Symphony No 5[a]
Stravinsky The Rite of Spring[b]
Berlin Philharmonic Orchestra / Herbert von Karajan
DG The Originals 463 613-2GOR (78' · ADD)
Recorded [a]1968, [b]1977 Ⓜ❶❶❶▷

Karajan's 1968 Prokofiev Fifth is a great performance. Whenever one compares it with later versions inevitably the DG account holds its place at the top of the list. The analogue recording was uncommonly good for its time. With the advantage of the Jesus-Christus Kirche acoustics, the sound is full and spacious, naturally defined and balanced; there's a slightly leonine quality to the strings and a natural bloom on woodwind and brass. Karajan lived with the work for a decade before he recorded it and this is immediately apparent in the way the first movement unfolds so inevitably. The ironic opening of the *Scherzo* with its flawless BPO articulation brings a splendid but unexaggerated bite, and in the more lyrical central section every subtle detail of colour comes over. The passionate string threnody of the *Adagio* (what playing, what intensity!) is superbly underpinned by darker wind murmurings; the tangibly hushed close leads naturally to the mellower opening of the essentially upbeat finale with its throbbing horns and instant echoes of *Romeo and Juliet*.

Karajan's *Rite of Spring* came a decade later and is more controversial. Stravinsky had been sarcastically scathing about the conductor's earlier 1964 account, even describing one section as 'tempo di hoochie-koochie'. So, Karajan let the work rest, and when he re-recorded it in January 1977 it was done in one single uninterrupted take. The result has less visceral excitement than some but it's still very rewarding, combining both the symphonic and balletic aspects of this extraordinary score, with the BPO providing much sheer beauty of sound, as in the ravishing melancholy of the opening of Part II and the haunting 'Evocation des ancêtres', although other versions find more pungent drama when the horns enter later. The Philharmonie sound is excellent and both CD transfers are expertly managed to retain the full character of the originals.

Romeo and Juliet, Op 64

Romeo and Juliet
Kirov Theatre Orchestra / Valery Gergiev
Philips 50 Great Recordings ② 464 726-2PM2
(144' · DDD)　　　　　　　　　　　　　⊕🅑➔

This great ballet score has been very lucky on records. Both Previn's EMI set and the Decca Maazel recording, are very distinguished and make a powerful impression on the listener. This Russian recording could not be more different. It was made in the Kirov Theatre in Leningrad and has the fullness and amplitude characteristic of the finest western recordings, not surprising, as the recording team was from Philips. The orchestral playing, too, is superb by any international standard and has none of the sharp edges or raucousness we used to associate with Soviet *fortissimos*. If there were a criticism of the playing it would be to suggest that at times it's almost over-cultivated. The Introduction has a striking grace and flexibility, a sophistication of light and shade that some listeners mightn't expect. The action of the opening street scene and the sequence of events which follows is delineated with much delicacy of effect, crisp clear rhythms, great energy when called for, in the 'Morning dance', for instance and the most stylish instrumental response from all departments of the orchestra.

Perhaps it's all a shade mellow (Maazel demonstrated how pungent Prokofiev's scoring could sound) and the mood of the 'Balcony scene' is pure romanticism, relaxed and without sexual ardour: the strings float ethereally, there's a beautifully played violin solo, and at the climax the listener is quite carried away. The great climax of 'Juliet's funeral' generates richly intense string playing and resoundingly powerful brass. But there's no sense of utter despair. So this is a performance to enjoy for the lyric feeling of Prokofiev's score and for the marvellous orches-

tral playing, but the starkness of the tragedy is more heartrendingly conveyed elsewhere.

Peter and the Wolf, Op 67

Peter and the Wolf[a]. Symphony No 1. March in B flat minor, Op 99. Overture on Hebrew Themes, Op 34*bis*[b]
[a]**Sting** narr [b]**Stefan Vladar** pf **Chamber Orchestra of Europe / Claudio Abbado**
DG 429 396-2GH (50' · DDD)　　　　　　　🅕🅞➔

Abbado and the multi-talented Sting offer a lively and beautifully crafted account of Prokofiev's ever popular *Peter and the Wolf*. Any fears that the original freshness of Prokofiev's creation may be lost in favour of a less formal approach are soon dispelled – Sting is an effective and intelligent storyteller capable of capturing the imagination of adults and children alike, and there's never a feeling of contrivance or mere gimmickry.

Cello Works

Cello Concertino in G minor, Op 132 – Andante. Cello Sonata in C, Op 119. Solo Cello Sonata in C sharp minor, Op 134 (ed Giovale). Adagio in C, Op 97*b* No 10. Ballade in C minor, Op 15. Chout, Op 21*a* (arr Sapozhnikov) – The Buffoon and his Wife; Dance of the Buffoons' Wives; Dance of the Buffoons' Daughters; In the Merchant's Bedroom; Quarrel of the Buffoon and the Merchant
Alexander Ivashkin vc **Tatyana Lazareva** pf
Chandos CHAN10045 (68' · DDD)　　　　　　　🅕

Captured in the Maly Hall of the Moscow Conservatory where much of Prokofiev's work was first heard, it's surprising to find so many aspects of the composer's style represented, from the Romanticism of the early *Ballade* through the spiky dissonances of *Chout* to the elegiac, unfinished Solo Sonata. Aided by characterful piano-playing by Tatyana Lazareva, Ivashkin's recital compares most favourably with his similar programme on Ode for which he was accompanied by a more reticent pianist; although the earlier disc includes the Concertino movement in the guise of Rostropovich's cello quintet arrangement, the absence of the *Chout* transmogrification makes the Chandos collection appear better value.

We start with the familiar Cello (and piano) Sonata, a highly polished and deeply felt account with Lazareva providing a weighty, authentically Russian accompaniment. The *Ballade* is surely the best version yet of this increasingly popular work. Good though Wallfisch's expansive reading is, Ivashkin surpasses him in his juxtaposition of the 19th-century style of the opening and the ghostly second idea, hushed to a real *pianissimo*. Instead of Wallfisch's 'March' from *The Love for Three Oranges*, we get a *Chout* selection arranged by the Russian cellist Roman Sapozhnikov; again the rendition is technically spotless. Finally comes the Sonata for cello alone, its nostalgic opening brought off perfectly. Ivashkin's playful treatment of the central gavotte-like section reminds us that he can do humour as well.

Violin Sonatas

Violin Sonatas – No 1, Op 80; No 2, Op 94a.
March, Op 12 No 1. Cinq Mélodies, Op 35b.
The Love for Three Oranges, Op 33 – Marche.
Romeo and Juliet, Op 64 – Masks
Gil Shaham vn **Orli Shaham** pf
Canary Classics CC02 (73' · DDD)   Ⓕ

The Shahams, brother and sister, make a formidable team. It's obvious throughout that they're entirely comfortable playing together, effortlessly accommodating any freedoms in timing and matching each other's tone and dynamics. Granted that the Shahams' insistence on clearly separating each phrase sometimes results in a loss of momentum (in the opening *Moderato* of the Op 94 Sonata, for instance), these still emerge as brilliant, highly expressive performances. The particularly wide dynamic range – of the recording as well as of the playing – here works decisively to the music's advantage. And, especially in the *Cinq Mélodies*, we hear some wonderfully subtle shades of expression: both players have clearly entered right into Prokofiev's distinctive idiom. They show the divergent natures of the two sonatas exceptionally vividly – Op 80 sombre and concentrated, Op 94 full of ebullient fantasy.

Prokofiev Violin Sonata No 2   Ⓗ
K Khachaturian Violin Sonata, Op 1
Szymanowski Violin Sonata in D minor, Op 9
David Oistrakh vn **Vladimir Yampolsky** pf
Testament mono SBT1113 (65' · ADD) Recorded 1955
                                                    Ⓕ

David Oistrakh's playing is, at its best, a calming force in an agitated world – intelligent, considered (just occasionally overcalculated), invariably poised, big-toned and confident. You know what to expect and are rarely disappointed, and these excellent refurbishments of key Oistrakh performances from the 1950s lend a characteristic narrative quality to a wide variety of repertoire.

Best perhaps is the Prokofiev sonata, which Oistrakh himself instigated in reaction to hearing the flute-and-piano original. The playing is quietly confidential in the first and third movements, pert in the *Scherzo* and exuberant in the closing *Allegro con brio*. Oistrakh's phrasing is incisive without sounding aggressive (most notes retain their full measure of tone, even at speed), while his handling of rhythm is both supple and muscular. Szymanowski's post-Romantic Op 9 is lusciously full-toned and expertly negotiated by Yampolsky, while the reading of Karen Khachaturian's Op 1 – a pleasant piece reminiscent of Kabalevsky, the lighter Shostak-

ovich and, occasionally, Gershwin – proves to be another masterly performance, especially in the delightful *Andante*.

This is a quite superb disc, expertly annotated and very well presented. The Prokofiev Second Sonata is as near definitive as anyone has a right to expect, while the remainder is typical of a violinist whose aristocratic playing and artistic diplomacy remain an inspiration to us all.

Piano Sonatas

No 1 in F minor, Op 1; **No 2** in D minor, Op 14;
No 3 in A minor, Op 28; **No 4** in C minor, Op 29;
No 5 in C, Opp 38/135; **No 6** in A, Op 82; **No 7** in
B flat, Op 83; **No 8** in B flat, Op 84; **No 9** in C,
Op 103; **No 10** in E minor, Op 137

Prokofiev Piano Sonata No 4 in C minor,
Op 29 **Rachmaninov** Etudes-tableaux, Op 39 – No 3
in F sharp minor; No 4 in B minor **Scriabin** Piano
Sonata No 9, 'Black Mass', Op 68 **Tchaikovsky** The
Seasons, Op 37a – January; May; June; November
Sviatoslav Richter pf
BBC Legends/IMG Artists BBCL4082-2 (67' · ADD)
Recorded live 1966   ⒻOO

Recorded live at Richter's beloved Aldeburgh in 1966, this issue shows an incomparable pianist at the height of his powers. Indeed, it would be difficult to imagine a more authentic yet personal voice in Prokofiev's Fourth and Scriabin's Ninth Sonatas. Richter carved out a special niche in Prokofiev's Fourth Sonata, the most cryptic and ambiguous of the series written in a language that can seem oddly exclusive and inaccessible to those born outside Russia. No other pianist has approached Richter in this work, in his capacity to clarify so much awkward writing while at the same time (in the central *Andante assai*) acknowledging a wholly individual utterance full of dark confidences and, in the finale, a forced gaiety alive with stiff virtuoso challenges resolved in a mock-triumphant coda.

Few performances of the Scriabin have been more stealthily mobile or breathed a more satanic menace. For once, directions such as *avec une douceur de plus en plus caressante et empoisonnée* are made meaningful rather than merely idiosyncratic or eccentric. Yet, in more amiable territory Richter is enviably poised, less remote or enigmatic in Mozart's G major Sonata, K283, than one might have expected. His opening *Allegro* is gently flowing and is memorably contrasted with his brilliantly vivacious finale.

The recordings have come up excellently, allowing us to appreciate Richter's range, unique empathy in Russian music and endlessly thought-provoking musicianship in all their glory.

Alexander Nevsky, Op 78

Alexander Nevsky. Scythian Suite, Op 20
Linda Finnie sop **Scottish National Chorus and**

Orchestra / Neeme Järvi
Chandos CHAN8584 (60' · DDD · T/t)   Ⓕ

At the chill opening of Järvi's fine version of *Alexander Nevsky* one can really feel the bitter wind of the Russian winter. The acoustics of the Caird Hall in Dundee where these Chandos recordings were made adds an extra atmospheric dimension to this splendidly recorded performance. The choral entry has an affecting poised melancholy, yet their geniality in the call to 'Arise ye Russian people' has a ring of peasantry. The 'Battle on the Ice' is the enormously spectacular climax, with the bizarre dissonance of the orchestral *scherzando* effects given tremendous pungency capped by the exhilarating shouts of fervour from the singers. Linda Finnie's contribution is most eloquent too and Järvi's apotheosis very moving. The *fortissimo* force of Chandos's recording is especially telling. As a coupling, Järvi chooses the ballet *Ala and Lolly*, originally written for Diaghilev which, when rejected by him, became the *Scythian Suite*. Its aggressive motoric rhythms are as powerful as anything Prokofiev wrote (indeed, their primitive force has an element of almost brutal ugliness to which you may not wholly respond) but the lyrical music is top-quality Prokofiev. 'It remains one of his most richly imaginative, harmonically sophisticated and wonderfully atmospheric scores', suggests Robert Layton in the notes. Certainly Järvi has its measure and so do the Chandos engineers, but it's not music for a small flat.

Ivan the Terrible, Op 116

Ivan the Terrible – complete film music
Irina Chistyakova contr **Dmitry Stepanovich** bass
**Vesna Children's Choir; Yurlov State Capella;
Tchaikovsky Symphony Orchestra / Vladimir
Fedoseyev**
Nimbus ② NI5662/3 (99' · DDD)   Ⓕ⊙

This is a must for completists, in that it's produced in association with a new edition of the score (1997), collating all that survives of the composer's contribution to the project. Indeed, Fedoseyev goes so far as to include music from the Russian Orthodox Liturgy that occurs in the completed films but isn't actually by Prokofiev.
 Confused? Let's recap. Part 1 of Eisenstein's masterpiece was released in 1946 to worldwide acclaim, though Stravinsky for one did not care for its mix of iconography and melodrama. In poor health, Prokofiev recommended that Gavriil Popov take over as composer for Part 2. Later he did after all resume work – only to find the film withheld from distribution. Soviet officials found its portrayal of Ivan's psychological decline too negative and, no doubt, too close to home. Which isn't to say that Prokofiev intended to encode any criticism of Stalin in the notes. The film was released in the USSR in 1958, by which time plans to complete the trilogy had been abandoned, its prime movers long dead.

We know Prokofiev thought highly enough of the score to re-use sections of it, but he left no guidelines for presenting it in the concert hall. The oratorio we always used to hear was fashioned in 1962 by Abram Stasevich; it provided the missing element of continuity by reshaping the cues to fit a chronological narrative. Muti recorded this to superb effect. Christopher Palmer's solution for Järvi was to dispense with Stasevich's interpolated speaker, whereas Rostropovich revived the melodramatic element in an edition by Michael Lankester with English-language narration (Sony Classical). Gergiev's forceful version left the music to fend for itself, but was still based on Stasevich.
 By cutting out the middleman, Fedoseyev now goes to the top of the heap as the most scholarly option. He produces a more convincing, well-prepared performance than many that have come out of Russia of late. Not all of what he presents is familiar even from the films, and there's a certain amount of crudely illustrative material. His orchestra, the present-day manifestation of the USSR broadcasting band with which Rozhdestvensky was associated in the 1960s and 1970s, acquits itself well: crude primary colours predominate, and the brass players avoid inauthentic finesse. Gergiev has only the mock-Soviets of the Rotterdam Philharmonic, though his Kirov chorus aren't outclassed by the Yurlov State Capella deployed here. Admittedly, Fedoseyev's contralto is extremely Russian, which you may find difficult in 'The song of the beaver'. Nor does he race in with quite Gergiev's irresistible flair. That said, Nimbus's Moscow-made recording is technically much better than you might expect.
 The two-disc package includes a helpful account of the working methods of Prokofiev and Eisenstein, while key episodes are discussed in more depth and cross-referenced to the relevant tracks. Eisenstein's fraught relationship with the authorities and the suppression of *Ivan* Part 3 are also discussed, an attempt being made to disentangle the score from its inescapably propagandist aspect. True, the project's public role as a glorification of Soviet tyranny need not be as dominant as it can seem to be in Stasevich's oratorio. Whether it's better served here may depend on your attitude to listening to music in short, sharp (albeit authenticated) bursts.

On Guard for Peace

The Queen of Spades – Symphonic Suite (arr and elaborated by M Berkeley). On Guard for Peace, Op 124[a]
[a]**Irina Tchistjakova** mez/narr **Niall Doherty** treb
Royal Scottish National Orchestra [a]**Junior Chorus**,
[a]**Chorus and Orchestra / Neeme Järvi**
Chandos CHAN10519 (66' · DDD)   Ⓕ➔

On Guard for Peace is a product of the darkest days of Stalinist repression and hence complicit with what David Fanning termed 'mass ideological brainwashing'. Under a cloud post-1948, his first wife interned and his income drastically cut, Prokofiev had no choice but to supply the sort of cantata the regime required, having gone out of his way to nail down an ideologically foolproof text. There are cute kids, emblematic doves and big tunes. Recurring references to the supervisory role of the Leader and Teacher are both explicit and chilling.

Neeme Järvi has a background in the old Soviet bloc and a long track record in conducting Prokofiev's music for Chandos. His approach is urgent and forthright. Bold sound makes his Scottish forces sound as if they too might hail from St Petersburg and the swimming-pool resonance swallows up the flaws. Soloist Irina Tchistjakova, a youngish mezzo of slightly alarming old-school vibrancy, also narrates.

The unexpected pairing is a Royal Ballet commission perpetrated by Michael Berkeley, chiefly from material Prokofiev had intended to underscore a projected Mikhail Romm film of *The Queen of Spades*. Berkeley's treatment seems diffuse, probably because the best bits had already been recycled by Prokofiev himself, notably in the slow movement of the Fifth Symphony. Prokofiev fanciers will wonder why an actual ballet score such as *On the Dnieper* (similarly plotted) or a finished orchestral piece like the *Russian Overture* could not have been pressed into service instead.

The Fiery Angel, Op 37

The Fiery Angel
Galina Gorchakova sop Renata **Sergei Leiferkus** bar Ruprecht **Vladimir Galusin** ten Agrippa **Konstantin Pluzhnikov** ten Mephistopheles **Sergei Alexashkin** bass Faust **Vladimir Ognovanko** bass Inquisitor **Evgeni Boitsov** ten Jakob Glock **Valery Lebed** bass Doctor **Yuri Laptev** ten Mathias **Mikhail Kit** bar Servant **Evgenia Perlasova** mez Landlady **Larissa Diadkova** mez Fortune teller **Olga Markova-Mikhailenko** contr Mother Superior **Yevgeny Fedotov** bass Innkeeper **Mikhail Chernozhukov** bass First Neighbour **Andrei Karabanov** bar Second Neighbour **Gennadi Bezzubenkov** bass Third Neighbour **Tatiana Kravtsova** sop First Nun **Tatiana Filimoniva** sop Second Nun **Chorus and Orchestra of the Kirov Opera / Valery Gergiev**
Philips Gramophone Awards Collection ② 476 1826 (119' · DDD · T/t) Recorded live 1993 Ⓜ❍❍❍

Ⓖ The opera is no blameless masterpiece – Prokofiev's indulgence in lurid sensationalism sometimes gets the better of his artistic judgement. But that sounds a pretty po-faced judgement in the face of the overwhelming power which so much of this score exudes. This Maryinsky performance comes live from what's clearly a highly charged occasion in one of the world's great opera houses. That brings with it the disadvantage of a constrained opera-pit acoustic, which makes some of Prokofiev's over-the-top scoring seem pretty congested. But the immediacy and clarity of the sound, plus the orchestra's rhythmic grasp, ensures that the effect

is still blood-curdling. If Leiferkus's distinctive rich baritone at first sounds a touch microphoney, the ear can soon adjust to that too, and Gorchakova brings intense beauty as well as intensity to Renata's hysterics, taking us right inside the psychological drama. The supporting roles are filled with distinction and this makes a huge difference to the sustaining of dramatic tension, the *crescendo* which Prokofiev aimed to build through his five acts. Considering the extent of the stage goings-on there's remarkably little audience distraction on the recording.

The Love for Three Oranges, Op 33

The Love for Three Oranges (sung in English)
Bruce Martin bass King of Clubs **John Mac Master** ten Prince **Deborah Humble** contr Princess Clarissa **Teddy Tahu Rhodes** bar Leandro **William Ferguson** ten Truffaldino **Warwick Fyfe** bar Pantaloon **Jed Arthur** bass Tchelio **Elizabeth Whitehouse** sop Fata Morgana **Wendy Dawn Thompson** contr Linetta **Sally-Anne Russell** mez Nicoletta **Alison MacGregor** sop Ninetta **Arend Baumann** bass Cook **Richard Alexander** bass Farfarello **Catherine Carby** mez Smeraldina **Opera Australia Chorus; Australian Opera and Ballet Orchestra / Richard Hickox**
Chandos ② CHAN10347 (99' · DDD · T/t) Ⓕ
Recorded live 2005

It has been noted that with Prokofiev's sole operatic success the original Russian is perhaps less vital than with most of his operas, and in many ways the very best way to experience the work is in the vernacular. Well, now here's the chance for English speakers to prove that pudding. Prokofiev's sense of humour (or rather Carlo Gozzi's, filtered through adapter-producer Vsevolod Meyerhold and colleagues to Prokofiev, who then wrote his own libretto) has kept something of its edge, thanks to its mixture of mild cruelty and pantomime sauciness – it is the sight of Fata Morgana accidentally showing her knickers that cures the Prince of his melancholic hypochondria and draws upon him the curse of loving three oranges. Tom Stoppard's translation comes nicely off the page and seems relatively congenial to the voices.

Hickox and his Australians have a ball throughout, and the recording somehow captures all the sparkiness of live performance without the usual excessive dryness of an opera-house acoustic. Crucially, the chorus and orchestra sound as fully engaged as the soloists themselves. All we lack is the additional fun of the curtain calls, which – authenticity or otherwise – extend an all but irresistible invitation to reuse the famous March. Without that the ending inevitably feels a bit of a let-down.

In a sense the serious collector has to have Gergiev for the original Russian text (Phlips, not currently listed) but also Nagano's (in French), because Prokofiev was involved in the French adaptation of the text which featured in the first performances. But for the most instant enjoyment, the new issue will surely score highest for native English speakers. The Chandos documentation is fine, though why it has bothered to print the French text alongside the English is a mystery.

The Love for Three Oranges (sung in French)
Gabriel Bacquier bar King of Clubs Jean-Luc Viala ten Prince Hélène Perraguin mez Princess Clarissa Vincent le Texier bass-bar Leandro Georges Gautier ten Truffaldino Didier Henry bar Pantaloon Farfarello Gregory Reinhart bass Tchelio Michèle Lagrange sop Fata Morgana Consuelo Caroli mez Linetta Brigitte Fournier sop Nicoletta Catherine Dubosc sop Ninetta Jules Bastin bass Cook Béatrice Uria-Monzon mez Smeraldina Lyon Opera Orchestra and Chorus / Kent Nagano
Stage director Louis Erlo
Video director Jean-François Jung
ArtHaus Musik [DVD] 100 404 (106' · 16:9 · 2.0 · 2 & 5)
Recorded live 1989   Ⓕ❶

Yet another classic opera video reappears refreshed. The DVD, though, metaphorically flicks a light-switch to reveal that the fresh, fluent conducting and singing are only elements in a splendidly lively, witty and thoroughly integrated production.

As the production's pace demands, the singers are mostly young, although old stagers Jules Bastin and Gabriel Bacquier provide resonant ballast. Jean-Luc Viala's chubby, light-toned Prince, Georges Gautier's amiable wide-boy Truffaldino, Vincent le Texier's reptilian Leandro, Michèle Lagrange's Wagnerian Fata Morgana, Catherine Dubosc's delicate Ninetta – they're all excellent, but the real star is the ensemble, with no weak links and the benefit of natural French. Whether or not this is the 'original' language, Prokofiev approved it; more viewers will understand it; and it fits the vocal line at least as well as the Russian. The DVD transfer refreshes the original recording but also reveals its limitations: slightly thin sound and some grain in the picture. But you'll enjoy yourself too much to care.

Semyon Kotko, Op 81

Semyon Kotko
Tatiana Pavlovskaya sop Sofya Ekaterina Solovieva sop Lyubka Lyudmila Filatova mez Semyon's mother Olga Markova-Mikhailenko mez Khivrya Olga Savova mez Frosya Evgeny Akimov ten Mikola Nikolai Gassiev ten Klembovsky, Workman Viktor Lutsiuk ten Semyon Kotko Vladimir Zhivopistev ten German interpreter Viktor Chernomortsev bar Tsaryov Yuri Laptev bar Von Wierhof Gennady Bezzubenkov bass Tkachenko Grigory Karasev bass Ivasenko Andrei Khramtsov bass German NCO, German sergeant Yevgeny Nikitin bass Remeniuk Kirov Opera Chorus and Orchestra / Valery Gergiev
Philips ② 464 605-2PH2 (137' · DDD · T/t)   Ⓕ

Valentin Katayev's tale of a local hero getting his girl despite strife with a prospective in-law is the kind of thing an opera-lover would normally take in their stride. What makes Semyon Kotko hard to live with isn't the fact that the soldier-boy returning to his village in the Ukraine at the end of the First World War is so unimpeachably virtuous, nor even that the Germans who break up the wedding preparations and lay waste to the village are so one-dimensionally villainous – it's rather that the reactionary-collaborator father-in-law-to-be, Tkachenko, is so obviously a token of Soviet propaganda. Prokofiev would probably never have considered such subject-matter at all had it not been for the political climate of the late 1930s and he did his best to make a working compromise between the order of the day and the kind of melodious simplicity he wanted to cultivate. He took Katayev's prose-draft as it stood and sought to minimise its schematic and propagandist elements. In Act 3 he came up with two of his most effective 'dramatic crescendos', first for the arrival of the reactionary Ukrainian cavalry, then for the burning of Semyon's cottage.

There are more fine moments in Act 4, where the oppositional writing for Soviets and Germans has something of the power of Alexander Nevsky, composed just before the opera. There's also some attractively pungent folk-imitation writing in the second tableau of Act 1. Some less distinguished scenes suggest a rummaging through Prokofiev's cast-off ideas for all-purpose filler material, but such passages aren't so extensive or so deadly as to destroy all enjoyment. This splendid recording plugs another major gap in the discography of opera. Gergiev's interpretation is ardent and well paced, his orchestra is in fine fettle, and his soloists are of high quality. Prokofiev gives little or no opportunity for star turns, but Viktor Lutsiuk's Semyon is passionate and youthful-sounding, and Tatiana Pavlovskaya as his beloved Sofya is radiant. The recording is free from the dryness and sudden shifts of perspective that have dogged some previous issues in this Mariinsky series.

Giacomo Puccini   Italian 1858-1924

While still a student at the Milan Conservatory, Puccini entered a competition for a one-act opera. He failed to win, but the opera Le villi came to the attention of the publisher Giulio Ricordi, who arranged a successful production at the Teatro del Verme in Milan and commissioned a second opera. The libretto, Edgar, was unsuited to Puccini's dramatic talent and the opera was coolly received at La Scala in April 1889. It did, however, set the seal on what was to be Puccini's lifelong association with the house of Ricordi.

Manon Lescaut. produced at Turin in 1893, achieved a success such as Puccini was never to repeat and made him known outside Italy. Among the writers who worked on its libretto were Luigi Illica and Giuseppe Giacosa, who provided the librettos for Puccini's next three operas. The first of these, La bohème, widely considered Puccini's masterpiece, but with its mixture of lighthearted and sentimental scenes and its largely conversational style was not a success when produced at Turin in 1896. Tosca, Puccini's first excursion into verismo, was more enthusiastically received by the Roman audience at the Teatro Costanzi in 1900.

Later that year Puccini visited London and saw David Belasco's one-act play Madam Butterfly. This he took as the basis for his next collaboration and he considered it the best and technically most advanced opera he had written. He was unprepared for the fiasco attending its first performance in February 1904, when the La Scala audience was urged into hostility, even pandemonium, by the composer's jealous rivals; in a revised version it was given to great acclaim at Brescia the following May. By then Puccini had married Elvira Gemignani, the widow of a Lucca merchant, who had borne him a son as long ago as 1896. The family lived until 1921 in the house at Torre del Lago which Puccini had acquired in 1891. Scandal was unleashed in 1909 when a servant girl of the Puccinis, whom Elvira had accused of an intimate relationship with her husband, committed suicide. A court case established the girl's innocence, but the publicity affected Puccini deeply and was the main reason for the long period before his next opera.

This was La fanciulla del West, based on another Belasco drama it was given its première at the Metropolitan Opera, New York, in December 1910. In all technical respects, notably its Debussian harmony and Straussian orchestration, it was a masterly reply to the criticism that Puccini repeated himself in every new opera.

Differences with Tito Ricordi, head of the firm since 1912, led Puccini to accept a commission for an operetta from the directors of the Vienna Karltheater. The result, La rondine, though warmly received at Monte Carlo in 1917, is among Puccini's weakest works, hovering between opera and operetta and devoid of striking lyrical melody. While working on it Puccini began the composition of Il tabarro, the first of three one-act operas (Il trittico) which follow the scheme of the Parisian Grand Guignol – a horrific episode, a sentimental tragedy (Suor Angelica) and a comedy or farce (Gianni Schicchi). This last has proved to be the most enduring part of the triptych and is often done without the others, usually in a double bill.

In his early 60s Puccini was determined to 'strike out on new paths' and started work on Turandot, based on a Gozzi play which satisfied his desire for a subject with a fantastic, fairy-tale atmosphere, but flesh-and-blood characters. During its composition he moved to Viareggio and in 1923 developed cancer of the throat. Treatment at a Brussels clinic seemed successful, but his heart could not stand the strain and he died, leaving Turandot unfinished. After his wife's death in 1930, his house at Torre del Lago was turned into a museum.

Puccini's choral, orchestral and instrumental works, dating mainly from his early years, are unimportant, though the Mass in A flat (1880) is still performed occasionally. His operas may not engage us on as many different levels as do those of Mozart, Wagner, Verdi or Strauss, but on his own most characteristic level, where erotic passion, sensuality, tenderness, pathos and despair meet and fuse, he was an unrivalled master. His melodic gift and harmonic

sensibility, his consummate skill in orchestration and unerring sense of theatre combined to create a style that was wholly original, homogeneous and compelling. He was fully aware of his limitations and rarely ventured beyond them. He represents Verdi's only true successor, and his greatest masterpiece and swansong, Turandot, belongs among the last 20th-century stage works to remain in the regular repertory of the world's opera houses. GROVEmusic

---

Messa di Gloria

Messa di Gloria². Preludio sinfonico. Crisantemi
²**Antonello Palombi** ten ²**Gunnar Lundberg** bar
Hungarian Radio Orchestra and ²**Choir /**
Pier Giorgio Morandi
Naxos 8 555304 (60' · DDD · T/t)   ⓈⓄ🄳

This recording is to be preferred to Antonio Pappano's very fine account on EMI – and it's not just a question of price. If the recorded sound isn't as opulent as EMI's, it's very clear and lets in the light. If the dynamic contrasts aren't so big, they're also rather more refined. Generally Giorgio Morandi prefers slightly faster speeds, though not so fast as Pappano when he really gets up some steam in the last sections of the *Gloria*. But in context Morandi brings out the inherent excitement very effectively and naturally whereas Pappano underlines it. With Pappano the majestic Verdian unisons of the 'Qui tollis' broaden like a great smile across a large face: it's grand fun but tends towards vulgarity. Of the work as a whole, Morandi and his forces give a more youthful performance. There's an easy lightness of step (the *Gloria* sets off with a dance). The chorus is particularly fresh in tone and response, and the tenor soloist, Antonello Palombi, is more gracefully lyrical and Italianate in timbre than either Alagna (with Pappano) or his predecessor Carreras (with Scimone). The baritone is less apt and certainly no match for Hampson (Pappano) or Prey (Scimone); musical nevertheless, and blending well with his colleague in the *Agnus Dei*. In the string piece, *Crisantemi*, Morandi's somewhat quicker tempo, still answering to the marking *andante mesto*, is welcome, keeping mawkishness at bay and limiting the over-exposure of rather thin material.

Opera Arias

La bohème – Sì, mi chiamano Mimì; Donde lieta uscì.
Gianni Schicchi – O mio babbino caro. **Madama Butterfly** – Un bel dì vedremo; Che tua madre; Tu, tu, piccolo iddio. **Manon Lescaut** – In quelle trine morbide; Sola, perduta, abbandonata. **La rondine** – Chi il bel sogno di Doretta. **Suor Angelica** – Senza mamma, O bimbo. **Tosca** – Vissi d'arte. **Turandot** – Signore, ascolta!; In questa reggia; Tu, che di gel sei cinta
Julia Varady sop
Berlin Radio Symphony Orchestra / Marcello Viotti
Orfeo C323941A (52' · DDD)   ⒻⓄⓄ

A lovely and somewhat surprising record by the most fascinating and patrician lyric soprano of the present age: 'surprising' because, though Varady is associated closely enough with Verdi, the Puccini connection is less readily made, 'lovely' because the voice is still so pure, the style so musical and the response so intelligent, immediate and full-hearted. She adjusts wonderfully well to the Italian idiom, lightening the vowels, freeing the upper range, allowing more *portamento* than she would probably do in other music, yet employing in its use the finest technical skill and artistic judgement.

Her singing of Magda's song in *La rondine* opens the record and introduces a singer who sounds (give or take a little) half her actual age: Varady's début dates back to 1962. In Mimì's narrative she sings with so fine a perception of the character – the hesitancies, the joy in 'mi piaccion quelle cose' – that Schwarzkopf's exquisite recording comes to mind, just as, from time to time, and especially in the *Madama Butterfly* excerpts, the finely concentrated, tragic restraint of Meta Seinemeyer is recalled. It's good to hear, too, how sensitively Varady differentiates between characters, Manon Lescaut having that essential degree of additional sophistication in tone and manner. What runs as a thread through all these characterisations is a feeling for their dignity. Mimì doesn't simper. Sister Angelica doesn't sob. Lauretta has resolution in her pleading. Butterfly, Liù and Tosca are what they should be: women whose pathos lies not in their weakness but in a passionate, single-minded fidelity. That leaves Turandot, which is a mistake. That is, she's outside the singer's scope and should remain so: it isn't merely a matter of vocal thrust, weight and stamina, but also of voice-character, although the performance of her aria has clear merits. None of which should deter purchase; overall this is singing to treasure.

Madama Butterfly – Un bel dì vedremo; Tu, tu piccolo iddio[a]. **La bohème** – Mi chiamano Mimì; Quando m'en vo; Donde lieta usci. **Edgar** – Addio, addio mio dolce amor?; Nel villaggio d'Edgar. **Gianni Schicchi** – O mio babbino caro. **La fanciulla del West** – Laggiù nel Soledad. **Manon Lescaut** – In quelle trine morbide; Sola, perduta, abbandonata. **La Rondine** – Chi il bel sogno di Doretta? **Suor Angelica** – Senza mamma. **Turandot** – Signore, ascolta!; Tu che di gel sei cinta; In questa reggia[a].
Le villi – Se come voi piccina
Angela Gheorghiu *sop* [a]Roberto Alagna *ten*
Giuseppe Verdi Symphony Chorus and Orchestra, Milan / Anton Coppola
EMI 557955-2 (70' · DDD)   Ⓕ❶❶▷

This is a considerable addition to this ever-enterprising artist's growing discography. Just when many of us were declaring there would never be anyone to take on Renata Tebaldi's mantle in *spinto* roles, here's Angela Gheorghiu doing just that. There is a similar strength of tone, breadth of phrasing and attention to musical and verbal detail. Everything she achieves

here is technically assured, thought through and emotionally rewarding.

Her Mimì in Decca's *La bohème* was an appealing, cleanly articulated reading, and it still is, even if the youthful bloom isn't quite so much in evidence. Musetta, though, is now very much her role, her Waltz Song sung with zest adding to the fullness only a few others have brought to the piece. One can hear why EMI wanted 'Un bel dì vedremo' at its top: Gheorghiu's account is overwhelming, as is the death scene. She's almost as moving in *Suor Angelica*'s 'Senza mamma'. Magda's solo and 'O mio babbino caro' are as smiling and therefore as winning as they should be. From *Turandot*, Liù's pains and sorrows are encompassed with ease and an apt *morbidezza*, with finely poised *pianissimo* high notes.

This is a deeply satisfying traversal of the Puccini canon, well supported by the Milan orchestra and Anton Coppola, artistic director of Florida's Opera Tampa.

La bohème

La bohème   Ⓗ
Victoria de los Angeles *sop* Mimì **Jussi Björling** *ten* Rodolfo **Lucine Amara** *sop* Musetta **Robert Merrill** *bar* Marcello **John Reardon** *bar* Schaunard **Giorgio Tozzi** *bass* Colline **Fernando Corena** *bass* Benoit, Alcindoro **William Nahr** *ten* Parpignol **Thomas Powell** *bar* Customs Official **George del Monte** *bar* Sergeant **Columbus Boychoir; RCA Victor Chorus and Orchestra / Sir Thomas Beecham**
EMI Great Recordings of the Century mono ②
567750-2 (108' · ADD · T/t)
or Naxos 8.111249/50
Recorded 1956   Ⓜ❶❶❶▷

The disadvantages of this famous Beecham *Bohème* are obvious. It's a mono recording and restricted in dynamic range. The sense of space for the complex crowd scene of Act 2 is to emerge with the maximum impact is inevitably lacking; the climaxes here and elsewhere are somewhat constricted; no less important, it's sometimes harder to focus on the subtleties of Puccini's orchestration. It was also made in a great hurry, and this shows in a number of patches of slightly insecure ensemble, even a couple of wrong entries. But there's no other important respect in which it doesn't stand at least half a head (often head and shoulders) above its more recent rivals. Nobody has ever been so predestinately right for the role of Mimì than Victoria de los Angeles: right both in vocal quality and in sheer involvement with every word and every musical phrase that Mimì utters. Beyond a certain point (usually a certain dynamic level) most sopranos stop being Mimì and simply produce the same sound that they would if they were singing Aida or Tosca. De los Angeles rarely does this; even under pressure (and Beecham's unhurried tempos do put her under pressure at times), the very difficulties themselves are used as an expressive and inter-pretative resource. Hers is the most moving and involving Mimì ever recorded. And Björling's is the most musical Rodolfo. He has the reputation of having been a bit of a dry stick, dramatically (on stage he looked like the other Bohemians' elderly, portly uncle), but on record he's the one exponent of the role to be credible both as a lover and as a poet. His voice is fine silver rather than brass, it can caress as well as weep, and his love for Mimì is more often confided than it is bellowed for all Paris to hear. This, indeed, is one of the most conspicuous differences between Beecham's account and most others: its simple belief that when Puccini wrote *pp* he meant it. Beecham (whose spell over his entire cast – in which there's no weak link – extends as far as teaching his Schaunard, John Reardon, an irre-sistibly funny, cut-glass English accent for the parrot-fancying milord) makes one realise what an intimate opera this is, how much of it is quiet, how many of its exchanges are *sotto voce*, and he thus enables his singers to use the full range of their voices and to employ subtleties of colour, phrasing and diction that are simply not avail-able to a voice at full stretch (and in the process he largely cancels out the disadvantage of his recording's restricted dynamic range). It's the same with his handling of the orchestra: one would expect Beecham to seem understated, but again and again one turns back to his reading and discovers nothing missing – he has achieved as much or more with less. This is as complete a distillation of Puccini's drama as you're likely to hear.

(The EMI set is not currently listed in the UK, and the Naxos is not available in the United States, Australia and Singapore due to possible copyright restrictions.)

La bohème
Mirella Freni *sop* Mimì **Luciano Pavarotti** *ten* Rodolfo **Elizabeth Harwood** *sop* Musetta **Rolando Panerai** *bar* Marcello **Gianni Maffeo** *bar* Schaunard **Nicolai Ghiaurov** *bass* Colline **Michel Sénéchal** *bass* Benoit, Alcindoro **Gernot Pietsch** *ten* Parpignol **Schoenberg Boys' Choir; Berlin German Opera Chorus; Berlin Philharmonic Orchestra / Herbert von Karajan**
Decca ② 421 049-2DH2 (110' · ADD · T/t)   Ⓕ**ⓞⒹ**

Pavarotti's Rodolfo is perhaps the best thing he has ever done: not only the finest recorded account of the role since Björling's on the Bee-cham set, but adding the honeyed Italianate warmth that even Björling lacked. He can't quite match Björling's poetic refinement, and he's less willing to sing really quietly, but Pavarotti's sincerity counts for a great deal: his pride as he declares his vocation as a poet, the desperate feigning of his 'Mimì è una civetta' are points that most tenors miss or treat as mere opportu-nities for a big sing. His latter-day image may tend to hide it, but this recording is a reminder that Pavarotti is an artist of intelligence and delicacy as well as splendour of voice.

His Mimì, Freni, sings beautifully and sensi-tively. Panerai is a strong, vividly acted Mar-cello. Harwood is an interesting Musetta: her tiny narration, in Act 4, of her meeting with the stricken Mimì is a gripping moment, and her waltz-song in Act 2 is a passionate (and irresisti-ble) avowal to Marcello. Karajan is a great Puc-cini conductor who can linger over the beauties of orchestration without losing his grip on the drama or relaxing his support of the singers. There aren't many operas of which a better case can be made for having more than one account in your collection. For a modern *La bohème* to supplement the Beecham this Karajan set must go to the top of the list.

La bohème
Anna Netrebko *sop* Mimì **Rolando Villazón** *ten* Rodolfo **Nicole Cabell** *sop* Musetta **Boaz Daniel** *bar* Marcello **Stéphane Degout** *bar* Schaunard **Vitalij Kowaljow** *bass* Colline **Tiziano Bracci** *bass* Alcindoro **Kevin Connors** *ten* Parpignol
Bavarian Radio Symphony Chorus and Orchestra / Bertrand de Billy
DG ② 477 6600GH2 (105' · DDD · S/T/t/N)
Recorded live at the Philharmonie am Gasteig, Munich in April 2007   Ⓕ**ⓞⒹ**

Vividly recorded, vigorously conducted and sung by a distinguished cast still in their rela-tively youthful prime, it presents the score with an appeal that will be readily felt by newcomers and with a freshness that will make those of riper years feel… well, feel young again.

Act 1 moves quickly up to Mimì's entry. The vigour is not brash or wearing; there are moments of respite, but it is conducted as a sym-phonic unit, a first-movement *allegro giocoso*. The love music takes its natural pace, though it adds a silent beat immediately following Mimì's solo and another before the start of 'O soave fanci-ulla'. The Second Act registers clearly as a sym-phonic scherzo, or, in this arrangement where you play the first CD without a break, as an extended Mozartian finale. The various elements – the main solo group, the Christmas Eve crowd, the children (in splendidly disciplined high spir-its), the stage band – are all well defined and the great ensemble runs its joyful course so that we can almost feel ourselves to be part of it.

Among the singers, it is important that Mar-cello has the presence and gaiety to be the life and soul and Boaz Daniel has all of that. Sté-phane Degout as Schaunard may be a little too like him for the purposes of the recording but is lively and stylish. The Colline, Vitalij Kowal-jow, is less effective. The lovers Anna Netrebko and Rolando Villazón are a famous pair and deservedly so. His voice is richly distinctive, his style genial and ardent. Netrebko is pure-toned and ample in climaxes. As Musetta, Nicole Cabell shows many of the qualities of a well cast Mimì – might Netrebko (a little solid and sturdy in vocal character for the Mimì of these acts) not have made a brilliant Musetta, as Welitsch did? In the remaining acts no such qualms arise.

Netrebko sings with feeling and imagination and Villazón is an inspired, golden-voiced Rodolfo. In fact, these are as finely performed as in any recording. The orchestra play almost as though reading a supplementary libretto, so vivid is their commentary. This is a recording which takes its place alongside the acknowledged 'classics'.

La bohème
Mirella Freni sop Mimì **Gianni Raimondi** ten Rodolfo **Adriana Martino** sop Musetta **Rolando Panerai** bar Marcello **Gianni Maffeo** bar Schaunard **Ivo Vinco** bass Colline **Carlo Badioli** bass Benoit **Carlo Badioli** bass Alcindoro **Franco Ricciardi** ten Parpignol **Giuseppe Morresi** bass Sergeant **Carlo Forti** bass Customs Official **Chorus and Orchestra of La Scala, Milan / Herbert von Karajan**
Stage director **Franco Zeffirelli**
Video director **Wilhelm Semmelroth**
DG 🔵 DVD 073 027-9GH (111' · 4:3 · 2.0 · 0) Recorded 1965   Ⓕ🔵🔵

Dating from 1965, this is a thoroughly old-fashioned opera film. As was often Karajan's practice, the singers mime to their own pre-recording, not always in perfect synchronisation, and to see an ample *fortissimo* phrase launched with apparently no effort at all is disconcerting. Zeffirelli's La Scala sets have been reproduced but amplified for the purpose of filming, and the joins between 'real' and painted fence in the Barrière d'Enfer scene, for example, are very obvious. The lighting is often most unconvincing when the action is so would-be naturalistic: a single candle can fill the stage with light, and the proverbial blind man with half an eye would have no difficulty in finding Mimì's dropped key.

And yet it's as near an ideal *Bohème* as you could hope to find. Firstly because there are no 'guest artists' – this is La Scala's *Bohème* cast of the period; all are at home in this production and with each other – and all are believably young or youngish Bohemians. Mirella Freni was near the beginning of her international career, her voice at its freshest, and her acting is all the more affecting for its restraint: a downcast glance, a shy smile. Gianni Raimondi partners her very well and sings with elegance and ardour. Rolando Panerai is an immensely likeable and finely sung Marcello, Gianni Maffeo hardly his inferior as Schaunard and Ivo Vinco is a tow-haired, cheroot-smoking young philosopher. Adriana Martino's Musetta is, if you like, conventionally tarty in her vivid scarlet décolleté gown, but she sings charmingly. Karajan sounds as though he's enjoying himself thoroughly, never pressing the music or his singers too hard, quite often indulging both with a *rubato* that encourages long and eloquent line. The recorded balance is at times peculiar: Rodolfo's friends are evidently in the street below when they urge him to hurry, but they must have climbed the fire escape to comment ironically that he has 'found his poetry' in Mimì. The lovers sound properly off-stage at the end of Act 1 but they're quite

visibly on it, in the doorway. But even these little flaws are oddly endearing; this is definitely a *Bohème* to live with.

La bohème
Mirella Freni sop Mimì **Luciano Pavarotti** ten Rodolfo **Sandra Pacetti** sop Musetta **Gino Quilico** bar Marcello **Nicolai Ghiaurov** bass Colline **Stephen Dickson** bar Schaunard **Italo Tajo** bass Benoit, Alcindoro **Chorus and Orchestra of the San Francisco Opera / Tiziano Severini**
Stage Director **Francesca Zambello.**
Video Director **Brian Large**
ArtHaus Musik 🔵 DVD 100 046 (116' · Region 0)
Recorded live 1988   Ⓕ🔵

This recording received a complimentary review from John Steane when it appeared in LaserDisc format back in May 1993. One can share his enthusiasm for the restraint and experience of Freni and Pavarotti, who (even in 1988, when the performance took place) didn't look like the young lovers predicated by the libretto, but who made up for it with the 'rich humanity' (JBS's words) of their portrayals, although both evinced the occasional moment of strain that confirms they were no longer in the full flush of vocal youth. Ghiaurov, at 59, remains a tower of strength as Colline, although his voice sounds a shade rusty. These veterans tend to show up the relatively casual, upfront performances of the remaining singers. The conductor is sympathetic to the needs of singers and score.

The staging is traditional in the best sense, even if it can't rival the great Zeffirelli/La Scala production, also with Freni (reviewed above). Brian Large has his cameras in the right place at the right time, with a fine balance of distant and close-up shots. The sound has plenty of atmosphere, but the voices aren't given enough prominence.

La bohème
Inva Mula sop Mimì **Aquiles Machado** ten Rodolfo **Laura Giordano** sop Musetta **Fabio Maria Capitanucci** bar Marcello **David Menéndez** bar Schaunard **Felipe Bou** bass Colline **Juan Tomás Martínez** bass Benoit **Alfredo Mariotti** bass Alcindoro **Gonzalo Fernández de Terán** ten Parpignol **Federico Gallar** bass Sergeant **Mario Villoria** bass Customs Official
Madrid Symphony Chorus and Orchestra / Jesús López-Cobos
Stage director **Giancarlo del Monaco**
Video director **Robin Lough**
Opus Arte ② DVD OA0961D (149' · NTSC · 16:9 · PCM stereo and DTS 5.1 · 0). Recorded live at the Teatro Real, Madrid, in March 2006. Also available on BluRay   Ⓕ🔵🔵

This *Bohème* is a glorious vindication of traditional staging at its imaginative, re-creative best. Giancarlo Del Monaco here turns his attention to the much more popular work and comes up with a humdinger of a production, beautifully

PUCCINI'S LA BOHÈME – IN BRIEF

Victoria de los Angeles Mimì **Jussi Björling**
Rodolfo **Lucine Amara** Musetta **Columbus**
Boychoir; RCA Victor Chorus & Orchestra /
Sir Thomas Beecham
EMI mono ② 567750-2 (107' · AAD)   Ⓜ❍❍❍
A classic, with extra electricity derived from
the hasty recording, with Beecham's living,
vivid conducting and a superb cast, both stel-
lar and supporting, even though the mono
sound is less kind to the orchestra.

Mirella Freni Mimì **Luciano Pavarotti** Rodolfo
Elizabeth Harwood Musetta **Schönberg Boys'**
Choir; Berlin Deutsche Oper Chorus; Berlin PO
/ Herbert von Karajan
Decca ② 421 049-2DH2 (110' · ADD)   Ⓕ❍▷
Karajan's lush but eloquent Puccini, with
top-notch voices, Pavarotti in particular, that
at least equal Beecham's. Magnificent orches-
tral playing in an equally fine recording.

(In English) **Cynthia Haymon** Mimì **Dennis**
O'Neill Rodolfo **Marie McLaughlin** Musetta
Peter Kay Children's Choir; Geoffrey Mitchell
Choir; Philharmonia Orchestra / David Parry
Chandos ② CHAN3008 (111' · DDD)   Ⓕ
Despite the stilted old translation a highly
enjoyable recording, warmly conducted and
sung by a cast of international standing, and
very directly communicative.

Anna Netrebko Mimì **Rolando Villazón** Rodolfo
Nicole Cabell Musetta **Bavarian RSO and**
Chorus / Bertrand de Billy
DG ② 477 6600GH2 (105' · DDD)   Ⓕ❍▷
A terrific new Bohème with the operatic duo
of the moment in the lead roles. And both
Netrebko and Villazón acquits themselves
with honours. The bohemians are a lively
bunch and the whole thing has the whiff of
the stage about it. De Billy conducts with
great verve and poetry. Worthy to stand
alongside the 'classics'.

Ileana Cotrubas Mimì **Neil Schicoff** Rodolfo
Marilyn Zschau Musetta **Royal Opera House**
Chorus and Orchestra / Lamberto Gardelli
NVC Arts 📀 4509 99222-2 (118')   Ⓕ
Of several DVD Bohèmes, this is the most
convincing: an immensely vital production in
richly atmospheric sets. Cotrubas, Allen and
a vivid supporting cast are affectionately
conducted by Gardelli.

Cheryl Barker Mimì **David Hobson** Rodolfo
Christine Douglas Musetta **Australian Opera**
Chorus and Orchestra / Julian Smith
Arthaus Musik 📀 100 954 (113')   Ⓕ❍
The famous stage production by Baz Luhr-
man in its original and genuinely operatic
approach. It's engaging, heartfelt and may
well captivate opera newcomers with its
1950s Paris setting and youngish cast.

set by Michael Scott in period, fast-moving and
full of pertinent detail. The director has obviously had the support of his charges: seldom is a
cast and chorus so responsive. In the pit López
Cobos's experienced hand is at all times in evidence, as he draws eloquent and lively playing
from the Madrid Symphony, which doubles as
the opera-house band.

Centre-stage is Inva Mula's appealing, vulnerable and intensely sung Mimì (justly given a
tremendous ovation at the close). She sings with
finely shaped and expressive phrasing, nowhere
more so than in her Act 3 Farewell, and she is
always believable as a consumptive. At first
glance, Aquiles Machado hardly fits one's idea of
a romantic poet but he lives Rodolfo with so
much feeling and identification with the role
that doubts are banished, and there is much
sensitivity and passion in his singing.

A notable 'find' is the Marcello of Fabio Maria
Capitanucci, a bold singer and natural actor.
The other Bohemians are youthfully engaging.
Laura Giordano is not quite at her best in
Musetta's Waltz Song but elsewhere is very
much inside her role: her exit on a bicycle in Act
3 is a nice touch. Robin Lough is the perceptive
video director.

La bohème
Cristina Gallardo-Domâs sop Mimì **Marcelo Álvarez**
ten Rodolfo **Hei-Kyung Hong** sop Musetta **Roberto**
Servile bar Marcello **Natale de Carolis** bar
Schaunard **Giovanni Battista Parodi** bass Colline
Matteo Peirone bass Benoit **Giuseppe Verdi**
Chorus, Milan; Children's Choir, Chorus and
Orchestra of La Scala, Milan / Bruno Bartoletti
Stage director **Franco Zeffirelli**
Video director **Carlo Battistoni**
TDK 📀 DV-OPBOH (134' · 16:9 · PCM stereo, 5.1 &
DTS 5.1 · 0) Recorded live February 2003   Ⓕ❍

This La Scala production is particularly good at
capturing the Christmas spirit in the Latin Quarter and the snows of a wintry dawn at the Barrière
d'Enfer. But that's Zeffirelli. In such operas, he
runs the theatre of the heart's desire. No doctri-
naire imposition of misery on the audience; on
the contrary, wherever you look on stage there's
something to gladden the eye. In the current
orthodoxy of operatic production, this is revolutionary. It's beautiful to look at, meticulous in
detail, and true to the score and the book.

Vocally we're, let's say, a little lower than
the angels. Marcelo Álvarez sings a thoroughly
competent Rodolfo: his voice has warmth, it's
evenly produced and is sensitively used. The
frailty of Cristina Gallardo-Domâs's Mimì
extends too much to the voice itself: often its
limitations can be overlooked, or accepted as
part of a very touching portrayal, but there are
times where a more substantial and firmly
placed tone is wanted. The Musetta, Hei-Kyung
Hong, is delightful in all respects; and a woman
with so much life in her deserves a more animated Marcello – Roberto Servile's voice being
no more varied or expressive than his face.

But nothing seriously spoils the joy of this. The sound is fine, team-working among the Bohemians has the combination of precision and apparent spontaneity which betokens inspired and thorough rehearsal. The orchestral playing under Bruno Bartoletti carries an assurance that never lapses into mere routine.

Additional recommendations

La bohème
Carreras Rodolfo **Ricciarelli** Mimì **Putnam** Musetta **Wixell** Marcello **Royal Opera House Chorus and Orchestra / C Davis**
Philips ② 442 260-2PM2 (106' · ADD)   ⓂⒷ

Carreras and Ricciarelli make a wonderful pair of lovers – totally credible, their fresh, supple voices totally suited to the roles – while Davis conducts somewhat coolly.

Edgar

Edgar
Adriana Damato sop Fidelia **Plácido Domingo** ten Edgar **Marianne Cornetti** mez Tigrana **Juan Pons** bar Frank **Rafal Siwek** bass Gualtiero
Santa Cecilia Academy Chorus, Rome; Santa Cecilia Academy Orchestra, Rome / Alberto Veronesi
DG 477 6102GH2 (85' · DDD · T/t)   ⓂⓄⒷ

Edgar, Puccini's second opera, composed in 1888 and first given the following year at La Scala, has never really caught on. The title-role is the only Puccini tenor lead role that Plácido Domingo has never sung until now. In his 65th year (the recording was made in 2005, just after his Covent Garden Siegmund) it is a tribute to his tenacity and vigour that he should have learned it, and gone on to give such a convincing performance. There is no hint of strain, and throughout an arduous three acts he uses his voice with all his accustomed commitment and fervour.

The music is full of pre-echoes of Puccini's later works and the orchestra is constantly employed in a remarkably confident and innovative way for a beginner in his late twenties. What no one can do is to rescue the opera from its libretto. Fernando Fontana based it on a story by Alfred de Musset, in which the hero burns down his own house to show his contempt for his fellow countrymen. He makes off with the hysterical and sacrilegious gypsy Tigrana, but then grows tired of their illicit liaison and yearns for Fidelia, the girl next door back in the Tyrol. After a victorious battle, he has his armour sent home, and in disguise as a monk, watches his own funeral. At the last moment, as he prepares to escape with Fidelia, the seductress Tigrana stabs her to death.

The finale of Act 1, in which Edgar defends Tigrana against the townspeople, builds up to a spectacular ensemble. The opening of Act 2, with a mournful woodwind solo which looks forward to the prelude to 'E luceven le stelle' in *Tosca*, has Edgar's big aria, 'L'orgia, chimera dall'occhio ardente'. There is a passionate duet, in which he rejects Tigrana. The final act, the most confusing dramatically, has a pair of beautiful arias for Fidelia.

Domingo is well partnered by Marianna Cornetti as Tigrana and Adriana Damato as Fidelia. Juan Pons takes the rather ungrateful role of Frank, Fidelia's brother, and a rival for Tigrana's affections. The emotional turmoil in which Edgar finds himself is not unlike that of Don José in Carmen – a man torn between the lure of raw sex and the ideal of virtuous simplicity. Edgar tries to take advantage of both, with tragic consequences.

Alberto Veronesi conducts an often exciting performance, the first studio-made set (the Sony and Naïve versions both derive from concerts). Carlo Bergonzi and Renata Scotto for Sony and Carl Tanner and Julia Varady for Naïve provide stiff competition – not many people would find it necessary to own two recordings, let alone three, of this early work. Nevertheless, the new set is an easy recommendation.

Puccini retained an affection for the score and made several revisions of it, the final one as late as 1905. However, he called it 'warmed-up soup', adding cruelly but accurately that the subject was 'unbelievable trash'.

La fanciulla del West

La fanciulla del West
Carol Neblett sop Minnie **Plácido Domingo** ten Dick Johnson **Sherrill Milnes** bar Jack Rance **Francis Egerton** ten Nick **Robert Lloyd** bass Ashby **Gwynne Howell** bass Jake Wallace **Paul Hudson** bass Billy Jackrabbit **Anne Wilkens** sop Wowkle **Chorus and Orchestra of the Royal Opera House, Covent Garden / Zubin Mehta**
DG ② 474 840-2GOR2 (130' · ADD · T/t) Recorded 1977   ⓂⓄⓄⓄⒷ

 This opera depicts the triangular relationship between Minnie, the saloon owner and 'mother' to the entire town of gold miners, Jack Rance, the sheriff and Dick Johnson (alias Ramerrez), a bandit leader. The music is highly developed in Puccini's seamless lyrical style, the arias for the main characters emerge from the texture and return to it effortlessly. The vocal colours are strongly polarised with the cast being all male except for one travesti role and Minnie herself. The score bristles with robust melody as well as delicate scoring, betraying a masterly hand at work. Carol Neblett is a strong Minnie, vocally distinctive and well characterised, while Plácido Domingo and Sherrill Milnes make a good pair of suitors for the spunky little lady. Zubin Mehta conducts with real sympathy for the idiom.

La fanciulla del West
Mara Zampieri sop Minnie **Plácido Domingo** ten Dick Johnson **Juan Pons** bar Jack Rance **Sergio**

Bertocchi *ten* Nick **Luigi Roni** *bass* Ashby **Mario Chingari** *bar* Jake Wallace **Aldo Bramante** *bass* Billy Jackrabbit **Nella Verri** *mez* Wowkle **Antonio Salvadori** *bar* Sonora **Ernesto Gavazzi** *ten* Trin **Giovanni Savoiardo** *bar* Sid **Orazio Mori** *bar* Bello **Francesco Memeo** *ten* Harry **Aldo Bottion** *ten* Joe **Ernesto Panariello** *bar* Happy **Pietro Spagnoli** *bass* Larkens **Claudio Giombi** *bass* José Castro **La Scala Chorus and Orchestra, Milan / Lorin Maazel**
Stage director **Jonathan Miller**
Video director **John Michael Phillips**
Opus Arte 🅓🅥🅓 OALS3004D (144' · 4:3 · 2.0 · 0 · N/T/t)
Recorded live at Teatro alla Scala, Milan, 1991.

This DVD of *La fanciulla del West* presents Jonathan Miller's atmospheric production for La Scala, with sets by Stefanos Lazaridis and costumes by Sue Blane. The cast is strong, and Lorin Maazel proves a warmer, more idiomatic Puccinian here than he generally was in his audio recordings for CBS/Sony. His direction makes one marvel afresh at the imagination and colour in this score, distinct from other Puccini operas in its obsession with the whole-tone scale.

Miller's production takes the melodrama seriously, with realistic sets and period costumes. It even manages to bring off the improbable scene in Act 2 when Sherriff Rance finds Dick Johnson's blood dripping down from the loft of Minnie's cabin, leading to the game of poker when Minnie blatantly cheats. Though at the end Dick and Minnie get no further than the back of the stage instead of riding off into the sunset, the authentic gulp of emotion is well caught in this rare Puccini happy ending.

Plácido Domingo is in superb voice, and wins ovations for each of his big solos. Juan Pons is wonderfully firm and dark of tone as Jack Rance. Though Mara Zampieri as Minnie sings with clear focus and no suspicion of a wobble, the result is often near to hooting – a strong performance, nonetheless.

Camerawork is a little fussy but not too distracting. Not only is the documentation fuller than usual in DVD booklets, with a facsimile of the opera-house's cast-list on the back, it also contains a complete (if minuscule) libretto and translation.

Madama Butterfly

Madama Butterfly
Renata Scotto *sop* Madama Butterfly **Carlo Bergonzi** *ten* Pinkerton **Rolando Panerai** *bar* Sharpless **Anna di Stasio** *mez* Suzuki **Piero De Palma** *ten* Goro **Giuseppe Morresi** *ten* Prince Yamadori **Silvana Padoan** *mez* Kate Pinkerton **Paolo Montarsolo** *bass* The Bonze **Mario Rinaudo** *bass* Commissioner **Rome Opera House Chorus and Orchestra / Sir John Barbirolli**
EMI Great Recordings of the Century ② 567885-2 (142' · ADD · T/t) Recorded 1966 Ⓜ🅞➔

This is Barbirolli's *Butterfly*; despite Scotto's expressiveness and Bergonzi's elegance it's the conductor's contribution that gives this set its

durability and its hold on the affections. The Rome Opera Orchestra isn't the equal of the Vienna Philharmonic for Karajan. However, the rapport between conductor and orchestra and their mutual affection for Puccini are evident throughout, and they make this the most Italianate of all readings. It's hugely enjoyable, not just in the big emotional outpourings (like the Act 2 interlude, where Barbirolli's passionate gasps and groans spur the orchestra to great eloquence) but in many tiny moments where you can almost see the conductor and his players lovingly and absorbedly concentrating on subtleties of phrasing and texture.

There's a lot of good singing, too. Scotto's voice won't always take the pressure she puts on it, but her portrayal is a touching and finely detailed one. The ever stylish Bergonzi sings with immaculate phrasing and perfect taste, Panerai is an outstanding Sharpless (beautifully sung, the embodiment of anxious, pitying concern) and di Stasio's Suzuki is attractively light-voiced and young-sounding.

The recording, however, is a bit narrow in perspective, rather close (really quiet singing and playing rarely register as such) and some of the voices are edged or slightly tarnished in loud passages. Barbirolli's set is perhaps for those who find the meticulously refined detail of Karajan studied (also ravishing and stunningly recorded); those, in short, for whom Latin warmth and impulsive open-heartedness are indispensable in this opera. They will find those qualities here, with singing to match, and won't mind the occasional strident patch.

Madama Butterfly
Mirella Freni *sop* Madama Butterfly **Luciano Pavarotti** *ten* Pinkerton **Robert Kerns** *bar* Sharpless **Christa Ludwig** *mez* Suzuki **Michel Sénéchal** *ten* Goro **Giorgio Stendoro** *bar* Prince Yamadori **Elke Schary** *mez* Kate Pinkerton **Marius Rintzler** *bass* The Bonze **Hans Helm** *bass* Commissioner **Vienna State Opera Chorus; Vienna Philharmonic Orchestra / Herbert von Karajan**
Decca ③ 417 577-2DH3 (145' · ADD · T/t) Recorded 1974 Ⓕ🅞➔

In every way except one the transfer of Karajan's radiant Vienna recording for Decca could hardly provide a firmer recommendation. The reservation is one of price – this Karajan is on three discs, not two, at full price. However it does allow each act to be self-contained on a single disc, and for such a performance as this no extravagance is too much. Movingly dramatic as Renata Scotto is on the Barbirolli set, Mirella Freni is even more compelling. The voice is fresher, firmer and more girlish, with more light and shade at such points as 'Un bel dì', and there's an element of vulnerability that intensifies the communication. In that, one imagines Karajan played a big part, just as he must have done in presenting Pavarotti – not quite the super-star he is today but already with a will of his own in the recording studio – as a Pinkerton of exceptional subtlety, not just a roistering cad but in his way an endearing figure in the First Act.

Significantly CD brings out the delicacy of the vocal balances in Act 1 with the voices deliberately distanced for much of the time, making such passages as 'Vienna la sera' and 'Bimba dagli occhi' the more magical in their delicacy. Karajan, in that duet and later in the Flower duet of Act 2, draws ravishing playing from the Vienna Philharmonic strings, getting them to imitate the *portamento* of the singers in an *echt-Viennes* manner, which is ravishing to the ear. Christa Ludwig is by far the richest and most compelling of Suzukis.

Madama Butterfly
Angela Gheorghiu *sop* Cio-Cio-San **Jonas Kaufmann** *ten* Pinkerton **Enkelejda Shkosa** *mez* Suzuki **Fabio Capitanucci** *bar* Sharpless **Gregory Bonfatti** *ten* Goro **Raymond Aceto** *bass* Bonze **Chorus and Orchestra of the Accademia Nazionale di Santa Cecilia / Antonio Pappano**
EMI ② 264187-2 (135' · DDD · T/t)　　Ⓕ❂❂➔

Approaching such a familiar work one waits for something individual, a clue to the artist's vision of the role. This came at the beginning of Act 2, in the scene between Suzuki and Butterfly when she describes Pinkerton's departing words, 'Quell'ultima mattina'. Gheorghiu somehow conveys not only the depth of Butterfly's love but also her inner knowledge that, in fact, her belief in Pinkerton's devotion is hopeless. This is a mature interpretation which suggests strength above all, so that the touches of vulnerability are added with subtlety; this performance could be her best Puccini role since Magda in *La Rondine* more than a decade ago. The rest of the cast live up to her standard: Jonas Kaufmann is an ardent Pinkerton although he cannot suggest a touch of youthful charm, the only possible redeeming feature for this anti-hero. Enkelejda Shkosa is a vivid Suzuki and Fabio Capitanucci the sympathetic Sharpless.

Conducting the orchestra and chorus of the Santa Cecilia Academy, Antonio Pappano takes a less driven and melodramatic way with the score than Karajan in his three recordings; it's nearer in mood to Barbirolli (a favourite), though there is no lack of passion at the great climaxes – just listen to the spine-tingling moment of the sighting of the ship. So, a fine new *Butterfly*, unlikely to topple some of the great recordings of the past but worthy to set beside them.

Madama Butterfly　　　　　　　　　Ⓗ
Victoria de los Angeles *sop* Madama Butterfly **John Lanigan** *ten* Pinkerton **Geraint Evans** *bar* Sharpless **Barbara Howitt** *mez* Suzuki **David Tree** *ten* Goro **David Allen** *bar* Prince Yamadori **Joyce Livingstone** *mez* Kate Pinkerton **Michael Langdon** *bass* The Bonze **Ronald Firmager** *bar* Imperial Commissioner **Harry Gawler** *bass* Registrar **Chorus and Orchestra of the Royal Opera House, Covent Garden / Rudolf Kempe**

PUCCINI MADAMA BUTTERFLY – IN BRIEF

Renata Scotto *Madama Butterfly* **Carlo Bergonzi** *Pinkerton* **Rolando Panerai** *Sharpless* **Rome Opera Chorus & Orch / Sir John Barbirolli**
EMI ② 567885-2 (142' · ADD)　　Ⓜ❂➔
In one of his rare operatic showings Barbirolli created a warmly idiomatic, Italianate performance, fluent, detailed and superlatively sung by a distinguished cast, even if the recorded sound is not up to the very best.

Mirella Freni *Madama Butterfly* **Luciano Pavarotti** *Pinkerton* **Robert Kerns** *Sharpless* **Rome Vienna State Opera Chorus, Vienna PO / Herbert von Karajan**
Decca ③ 417 577-2DH3 (145' · ADD)　　Ⓕ❂➔
A stunningly beautiful performance, in Karajan's conducting, measured and luxuriant yet still dramatic, with two thrilling central performances, sounding younger than Barbirolli's, a fine supporting cast and an outstanding recording.

Victoria de los Angeles *Madama Butterfly* **John Lanigan** *Pinkerton* **Covent Garden Chorus and Orchestra / Rudolf Kempe**　　　　Ⓗ
Royal Opera House Heritage Series ② ROHS006 (122' · ADD)　　Ⓢ❂❂
An astounding central performance that won't leave a dry eye in the house takes its place in a real company performance.

Maria Callas *Madama Butterfly* **Nicolai Gedda** *Pinkerton* **Chorus & Orchestra of La Scala, Milan / Herbert von Karajan**　　　　Ⓗ
EMI ② 556298-2 (139' · AAD)　　Ⓕ❂➔
Magnificently compelling despite the mono sound, with Maria Callas a heartbreaking Butterfly, Nicolai Gedda an intensely romantic Pinkerton and Karajan more vividly theatrical than in his much later recording.

Angela Gheorghiu *Madama Butterfly* **Jonas Kaufmann** *Pinkerton* **Santa Cecilia Chorus and Orchestra / Antonio Pappano**
EMI ② 264187-2 (135' · DDD)　　Ⓕ❂❂➔
Possibly Gheorghiu's finest Puccini role to date: a wonderfully rounded, considered performance. Kaufmann is an ardent Pinkerton and Pappano conducts with his customary style and passion. A very fine modern set.

Ying Huang *Madama Butterfly* **Richard Troxell** *Pinkerton* **Orchestre de Paris / James Conlon**
Columbia 🄳🅅🄳 CDR24673 (128')　　Ⓕ
A cinematic version, somewhat indulgently directed by Frédéric Mitterand, with reasonable lip-sync. The very young Ying Huang is a light-voiced but deeply touching Butterfly, and though Richard Troxell is only serviceable as Pinkerton, this is still unusual and enjoyable.

Royal Opera House Heritage Series mono ②
ROHS006 (122' · ADD). Recorded live in 1957 Ⓜ**OO**

This quite overwhelming performance has the advantage of Victoria de los Angeles's unique Cio-Cio-San, fulfilling every aspect of the taxing but rewarding title-role. She made two commercial recordings of the work, but here heard live she surpasses both with a reading that, as far as singing and acting with the voice are concerned, is shattering, every emotion, every phrase ideally presented. It comes across the years with such heartfelt feeling and at the close such tragedy that it goes to the top of *Butterflies* on disc.

As Alexandra Wilson points out in her well researched notes, de los Angeles was 33 at the time and at the apex of her career. She's never fazed either by the intimate solos of Act 2 or the strength needed for 'Un bel dì', and her final dying solo is as moving as I have ever heard it.

No less remarkable is Kempe's conducting – taut, immediate and, when needed, loving. His Covent Garden orchestra plays its heart out for him. Both in small and big things, the work could hardly sound more deeply felt than here. The large climaxes are shattering, the many moments of intimacy so touching.

Another reason why we are unlikely to hear the work so well done again is the overall sense of a company and ensemble, each member of it a dedicated singer. Today such a thing has ceased to exist. John Lanigan never had a truly Italianate tenor, but his keen voice and articulation and his commitment to the role of Pinkerton are satisfying enough on their own terms. The young Geraint Evans, singing Sharpless for the first time, is as warm and sympathetic as he should be in this tricky role. Barbara Hewitt is a natural, clear-voiced Suzuki. Michael Langdon roars loudly as the threatening Bonze. Only David Tree's dry-voiced Goro is a bit of a trial.

Of course, de los Angeles's studio-made sets have better sound, and the versions with Callas and Scotto, in a different vein, remain remarkable; but at this moment it is hard to imagine hearing a more soulful, dramatic traversal of the work than we have here.

Manon Lescaut

Manon Lescaut
Mirella Freni *sop* Manon Lescaut **Luciano Pavarotti** *ten* Des Grieux **Dwayne Croft** *bar* Lescaut **Giuseppe Taddei** *bar* Geronte **Ramon Vargas** *ten* Edmondo **Cecilia Bartoli** *mez* Singer **Federico Davia** *bass* Innkeeper, Captain **Anthony Laciura** *ten* Dancing Master **Paul Groves** *ten* Lamplighter **James Courtney** *bass* Sergeant **Chorus and Orchestra of the Metropolitan Opera / James Levine**
Decca ② 440 200-2DHO2 (120' · DDD · T/t) Ⓕ

With Luciano Pavarotti a powerful Des Grieux, James Levine conducts a comparably big-boned performance of *Manon Lescaut*, bringing out the red-blooded drama of Puccini's first big success, while not ignoring its

warmth and tender poetry in exceptionally full, vivid sound with the voices well in front of the orchestra. In the title-role Freni's performance culminates in an account of the big Act 4 aria, more involving and passionate than any of the others on rival versions, with the voice showing no signs of wear, and with her sudden change of face at the words 'terra di pace' ('a land of peace') bringing a magical lightening of tone. That aria makes a thrilling climax, when too often this act can seem a letdown. In this as in so much else, Levine conveys the tensions and atmosphere of a stage performance in a way that owes much to his experience at the Metropolitan.

More completely than other versions, it avoids the feeling of a studio performance. Reactions to Pavarotti as Des Grieux will differ widely. The closeness of balance means that in volume his singing rarely drops below *mezzo forte*, but there's little harm in having so passionate a portrait of Des Grieux as Pavarotti's. Needless to say, the hero's big emotional climaxes in each of the first three acts come over at full force. The rest of the cast is strong too, with Dwayne Croft a magnificent Lescaut. Many collectors will count this a clear first choice among current versions.

Manon Lescaut Ⓗ
Maria Callas *sop* Manon Lescaut **Giuseppe di Stefano** *ten* Des Grieux **Giulio Fioravanti** *bar* Lescaut **Franco Calabrese** *bass* Geronte **Dino Formichini** *ten* Edmondo **Fiorenza Cossotto** *mez* Singer **Carlo Forti** *bass* Innkeeper **Vito Tatone** *ten* Dancing master **Giuseppe Morresi** *bass* Sergeant **Franco Ricciardi** *ten* Lamplighter **Franco Ventrigilia** *bass* Captain **Chorus and Orchestra of La Scala, Milan / Tullio Serafin**
EMI ② 556301-2 (120' · ADD · T/t) Recorded 1957
Ⓟ**OO**ᗺ►

This performance is unique, with Act 4 for once a culmination in Callas's supreme account of the death scene. She may present a rather formidable portrait of a young girl in Act 1, but here the final act with its long duet and the big aria, 'Sola, perduta, abbandonata', is far more than an epilogue to the rest, rather a culmination, with Callas at her very peak. Di Stefano, too, is on superb form and Serafin's pacing of the score is masterly. Di Stefano wipes the floor with most of his rivals past and present: in Act 4 he has a concerned tenderness for Manon that others can only sketch, his debonair charm in 'Tra voi belle' is incomparable and (rarest of virtues among tenors) he never sings past the limits of his voice. Fioravanti as Lescaut and Calabrese as Geronte sing well if not very characterfully.

However, digital CD remastering in this instance loses out. A break has to be made in Act 2 – in a fairly innocuous place before the duet 'Tu, tu, amore tu'. The first two acts make up a total timing only a few seconds over the 75-minute limit, but evidently it was enough to prevent them going on to a single CD. That said, the CD brings the same advantages in refining the original boxy sound without glamorising it in false stereo, plus the usual advantages of absence of background and ease of finding places. For an account of *Manon Lescaut* which comes fully to terms with the opera's huge contrasts of colour and mood you'll also have to have a modern recording, for with all its improvements the sound here remains very dry.

La rondine

La rondine.
Le villi – Prelude; L'Abbandono; La Tregenda;
Ecco la casa … Torna ai felice dì. Morire!
Angela Gheorghiu *sop* Magda **Roberto Alagna** *ten*
Ruggero **Inva Mula-Tchako** *sop* Lisetta **William
Matteuzzi** *ten* Prunier **Alberto Rinaldi** *bar* Rambaldo
Patricia Biccire *sop* Yvette **Patrizia Ciofi** *sop* Bianca
Monica Bacelli *mez* Suzy **Riccardo Simonetti** *bar*
Périchaud **Toby Spence** *ten* Gobin **Enrico Fissore**
bar Crébillon **London Voices; LSO / Antonio
Pappano** *pf*
EMI ② 556338-2 (131' · DDD· T/t) Ⓕ ❍❍❍❻ᐅ

It couldn't be more welcome when a recording transforms a work, as this one does, setting it on a new plane. *La rondine* ('The Swallow'), Puccini's ill-timed attempt to emulate Lehár in the world of operetta, was completed during the First World War. It's long been counted his most serious failure. Puccini's cunning has never been in doubt either, for he and his librettists interweave elements not just of *La traviata* but of *The Merry Widow* and *Die Fledermaus*, not to mention earlier Puccini operas. His melodic style may be simpler than before, but one striking theme follows another with a profusion that any other composer might envy. What Pappano reveals far more than before is the subtlety with which Puccini interweaves his themes and motifs, with conversational passages made spontaneous-sounding in their flexibility. Above all, Pappano brings out the poetry, drawing on emotions far deeper than are suggested by this operetta-like subject, thanks also to Gheorghiu's superb performance, translating her mastery as Violetta to this comparable character. Magda's first big solo, 'Che il bel sogno di Doretta', finds Gheorghiu at her most ravishing, tenderly expressive in her soaring phrases, opening out only at the final climax. From first to last, often with a throb in the voice, her vocal acting convinces you that Magda's are genuine, deep emotions, painful at the end, intensified by the ravishing beauty of her voice.

As Ruggero, Alagna has a far less complex role, winningly characterising the ardent young student. What will specially delight Puccinians in this set is that he's given an entrance aria about Paris, 'Parigi è una città', which transforms his otherwise minimal contribution to Act 1. The partnership of Gheorghiu and Alagna highlights

the way that Puccini in the melodic lines for each of his central characters makes Ruggero's more forthright, Magda's more complex. Among much else, the role of the poet, Prunier, is transformed by the clear-toned William Matteuzzi in what's normally a *comprimario* role. Not only is his relationship with Magda beautifully drawn, his improbable affair with the skittish maid, Lisetta, is made totally convincing too, mirroring Magda's affair. For the fill-ups, the excerpts from *Le Villi*, warm and dramatic, make one wish that Pappano could go on to record that first of Puccini's operas, with Alagna giving a ringing account of Roberto's aria, as he does of the song, *Morire!* – with Pappano at the piano. Originally an album-piece written for a wartime charity, Puccini used it, transposed up a semitone, with different words, as the entrance aria for Ruggero. Altogether a set to treasure.

Tosca

Tosca
Maria Callas *sop* Tosca **Giuseppe di Stefano** *ten* Ⓗ
Cavaradossi **Tito Gobbi** *bar* Scarpia **Franco
Calabrese** *bass* Angelotti **Melchiorre Luise** *bass*
Sacristan **Angelo Mercuriali** *ten* Spoletta **Alvaro
Cordova** *treb* Shepherd Boy **Dario Caselli** *bass*
Sciarrone **Dario Caselli** *bass* Gaoler
**Chorus and Orchestra of La Scala, Milan /
Victor de Sabata**
EMI 562890-2 (108' · ADD · N/T/t) Ⓜ ❍❍❍❻ᐅ
EMI 585644-2 (108' · ADD · N/S) Ⓑ ❍❍❍❻ᐅ
Naxos 8 110256-2 (108' · ADD · N/S) Ⓢ ❍❍❍❻ᐅ
Regis RRC2065 (108' · ADD · N/S) Ⓕ ❍❍❍

In this remastering of one of the classic performances of the gramophone, one of Walter Legge's masterpieces as a creative recording producer, you barely miss stereo recording. With offstage effects for example – so important in Puccini – precisely placed, there is a sense of presence normally reserved for twin-channel reproduction. In the long duet between Tosca and Cavaradossi in Act 3 you can even detect a difference of placing between the two singers, Callas set at a slight distance, though whether or not to offset a microphone problem with so biting a voice one can only guess. The immediacy is astonishing, and the great moment of the execution with trombones rasping and the fusillade reproduced at a true *fortissimo* has never been represented on record with greater impact. The contrasts of timbre are beautifully brought out – amazingly wide with Gobbi as with Callas and with di Stefano producing his most honeyed tones. Though there is less space in the Milan acoustic than we have grown used to in the age of stereo, the separation of voices and orchestra is excellent, with the strands of the accompaniment to 'Vissi d'arte', for example, finely clarified. Only in the big Te Deum scene at the end of Act 1 is there a hint of overloading.

Wonderful as Gobbi's and di Stefano's performances are, and superbly dramatic as de Sabata's conducting is, it is the performance of the unique Callas in the title-role that provides the greatest marvel, and here more than ever one registers the facial changes implied in each phrase, with occasional hints of a chuckle (usually ironic) more apparent than on LP. A truly Great Recording of the last Century which is available in numerous guises. Naxos's transfer is particularly impressive, but if you want top-class supporting material, the mid-price EMI is the one to go for.

Tosca
Angela Gheorghiu sop Tosca **Roberto Alagna** ten Cavaradossi **Ruggero Raimondi** bar Scarpia **Maurizio Muraro** bass Angelotti **Enrico Fissore** bass Sacristan **David Cangelosi** ten Spoletta **Sorin Coliban** bass Sciarrone **Gwynne Howell** bass Gaoler **James Savage-Hanford** treb Un pastore **Tiffin Children's Choir; Royal Opera House Chorus and Orchestra / Antonio Pappano**
EMI ② 557173-2 (114' · DDD) Ⓕ●🡒

Antonio Pappano's conducting alone would make this a *Tosca* of distinction, whether in big matters (the voicing of those snarling opening chords) or tiny ones: the carefully measured pause after Tosca asks Cavaradossi whether he's happy at the prospect of stealing away to their villa: he's preoccupied and hasn't really been listening. The orchestral sound is splendidly full whenever it needs to be, but never at the expense of fine detail, and Pappano's pacing is admirable: the Act 2 dialogue between Tosca and Scarpia, for example, inexorably builds in tension instead of being feverish from the outset, as is too often the case.

Gheorghiu's Tosca responds to this. She's impetuous, nervously intense, but capable also of a lovely, quiet purity). She's a very complete Tosca, indeed, and intelligently capable of bringing her own perceptions to the role. After the killing of Scarpia, her 'And before him all Rome trembled!' is neither triumphant nor melodramatic but wondering and fearful: she's aghast at what she has done and already suspects that this isn't the end of the matter. Her 'Vissi d'arte' is most beautiful, her intimacy in the first scene with Cavaradossi tender and touching.

In that passage Alagna responds to her delicacy, and in Act 3 he receives her acting lesson with a touch of humour. Elsewhere he's in fine, mostly full voice, nowhere near as subtle as Gheorghiu. His tone hardens under pressure once or twice, and his *mezza voce* can sound thin, but he's never short of vocal glamour: a creditable but not especially interesting Cavaradossi.

Raimondi's Scarpia, on the other hand, is very interesting. The quieter shades of his voice now need careful management (and besides, it's darker and softer-grained than a true dramatic baritone), but although he may initially seem to lack authority his reading is full of finesse.

A very fine *Tosca*, in short, not quite in the same league as the celebrated Callas/di Stefano/Gobbi/de Sabata (see above), but giving all the others an exciting run for their money. The recording is all that could be wished.

Tosca
Montserrat Caballé sop Tosca **José Carreras** ten Cavaradossi **Ingvar Wixell** bar Scarpia **Samuel Ramey** bass Angelotti **Piero De Palma** ten Spoletta **Domenico Trimarchi** bar Sacristan **William Elvin** bar Sciarrone, Gaoler **Ann Murray** mez Shepherd Boy **Chorus and Orchestra of the Royal Opera House, Covent Garden / Sir Colin Davis**
Philips Duo ② 438 359-2PM2 (118' · ADD · S) Recorded 1976 Ⓜ

Caballé's Tosca is one of the most ravishingly on record, with scarcely a less than beautiful note throughout, save where an occasional phrase lies a touch low for her. She doesn't quite have the 'prima donna' (in quotes, mind) temperament for the part (the coquettish malice of 'but make her eyes black!', as Tosca forgives Cavaradossi for using a blonde stranger as model for his altarpiece of the Magdalen, isn't in Caballé's armoury; either that or she knows that her voice would sound arch attempting it), but her portrayal is much more than a display of lovely sounds. She's precise with words, takes minute care over phrasing, and she knows to a split second where dead-centre precise pitching becomes crucial. Carreras's Cavaradossi is one of his best recorded performances: the voice untarnished, the line ample, and if he's tempted at times to over-sing one forgives the fault for the sake of his poetic ardour. Wixell is the fly in the ointment: a capable actor and an intelligent artist, but his gritty timbre lacks centre and thus the necessary dangerous suavity.

Davis's direction is flexible but dramatic and finely detailed, and the secondary singers are all very good. The recording, despite some rather unconvincing sound effects, still sounds very well, with space around the voices and a natural balance between them and the orchestra. It's pity Philips should have saved space by omitting the libretto.

Tosca
Leontyne Price sop Tosca **Giuseppe di Stefano** ten Cavaradossi **Giuseppe Taddei** bar Scarpia **Carlo Cava** bass Angelotti **Piero De Palma** ten Spoletta **Fernando Corena** bass Sacristan **Leonardo Monreale** bass Sciarrone **Alfredo Mariotti** bass Gaoler **Herbert Weiss** treb Shepherd Boy **Vienna State Opera Chorus; Vienna Philharmonic Orchestra / Herbert von Karajan**
Decca Legends ② 475 7522 (114' · ADD · T/t) Recorded 1962 Ⓜ●●

Karajan's classic version of *Tosca* was originally issued on the RCA label, but produced by John Culshaw of Decca at a vintage period. The first surprise is to find the sound satisfying in almost every way, with a firm sense of presence and with each voice and each section of the orchestra cleanly focused within the stereo spectrum. Less surprising is the superiority of this version as an interpretation. Karajan was always a master Puccinian, and this set was a prime example. A typical instance comes at the end of Act 1, where

Scarpia's *Te Deum* is taken daringly slowly, and conveys a quiver of menace that no other version begins to match. An extra nicety is the way that in the instrumental introduction to Cavaradossi's first aria, 'Recondita armonia', he treats it as the musical equivalent of a painter mixing his colours, the very point Puccini no doubt had in mind. Karajan, though individual, and regularly challenging his singers is most solicitous in following the voices. It's fascinating to note what expressive freedom he allows his tenor, Giuseppe di Stefano, and he makes Leontyne Price relax, giving a superb assumption of the role, big and rich of tone; the voice is the more beautiful for not being recorded too closely.

Tosca
Catherine Malfitano sop Tosca **Richard Margison** ten Cavaradossi **Bryn Terfel** bar Scarpia **Mario Luperi** bass Angelotti **John Graham-Hall** ten Spoletta **Enrico Fissore** bass Sacristan **Jef van Wersch** bass Sciarrone **Ton Kemperman** bass Gaoler **Andreas Burkhart** treb Shepherd Boy
Royal Concertgebouw Orchestra, Amsterdam / Riccardo Chailly
Stage director **Nikolaus Lehnhoff**
Video director **Misjel Vermeiren**
Decca **DVD** 074 3201DH
(137' · NTSC · 16:9 · PCM stereo and DTS 5.1 · 0)
Recorded live at Het Muziektheater, Amsterdam
Includes bonus documentary, 'Tosca – Behind the Scenes'   Ⓕ

This is a 'strong' *Tosca*, using the adjective in the sense in which it is sometimes applied to language (meaning 'thoroughly disgusting'). But then, you might say, that's *Tosca* being true to itself: it tells of a thoroughly disgusting state of affairs, when a man can be arrested by party thugs, taken off to headquarters for torture and summary execution, and a woman is at the mercy of a dictator's lust. Its official description is 'a melodrama in three acts', and a melodrama this is, with jeering villain, manly hero and distraught heroine. And as though to drive the point home, Tosca acts and is costumed and made up to look like an old-time star of the silent screen. To that extent we know it's make-believe. There are also scenery and props to persuade us to take it for real. And the sets are heavy with symbols suggesting 'significance'. But yes, it's 'strong': a good *Tosca*, one might have to concede.

Certainly it has a good, no, a magnificent Scarpia. Terfel is in fine voice, and his acting and singing are as one. In both, his style is forceful without exaggeration or over-emphasis. Richard Margison is a likeable Cavaradossi, his well placed tenor reliably meeting the challenges of the role, and he himself, never a conventionally romantic figure, gaining sympathy notwithstanding. And Malfitano, a Tosca without any special vocal allure, exercises her personality and compels attention. A gaunt, sonorous Angelotti, a Sacristan who huffs and puffs effectively, and a Spoletta even nastier than his

---

PUCCINI TOSCA – IN BRIEF

Angela Gheorghiu *Tosca* **Roberto Alagna** *Cavaradossi* **Ruggero Raimondi** *Scarpia* **Tiffin Children's Choir, Chorus and Orchestra of the Royal Opera House / Antonio Pappano**
EMI ② 557173-2 (114' · ADD)   ⒻⓄ⯈
An excellent modern recording, distinguished by Gheorghiu's passionate, nervy Tosca and Pappano's dramatic conducting, with Alagna's lyrical Cavaradossi and Ruggero Raimondi's veteran Scarpia.

Monserrat Caballé *Tosca* **José Carreras** *Cavaradossi* **Ingvar Wixell** *Scarpia* **Chorus and Orchestra of the Royal Opera House / Sir Colin Davis**
Philips ② 438 359-2PM2 (118' · DDD)   Ⓜ
Richly theatrical conducting by Davis, with Montserrat Caballé a compelling heroine and José Carreras at his ardent best, although Ingmar Wixell is an uncompelling Scarpia.

Leontyne Price *Tosca* **Giuseppe di Stefano** *Cavaradossi* **Giuseppe Taddei** *Scarpia* **Vienna State Opera Chorus, Vienna PO / Herbert von Karajan**
Decca ② 466 384-2DM2 (114' · DDD)   ⓂⓄⓄ⯈
Much finer than Karajan's later recording. Leontyne Price and Giuseppe di Stefano are wonderfully rich-voiced and passionate, Taddei a hellishly charismatic Scarpia, with Karajan balancing detail and drama superbly.

Maria Callas *Tosca* **Giuseppe de Stefano** Ⓗ *Cavaradossi* **Tito Gobbi** *Scarpia* **Chorus and Orchestra of La Scala, Milan / Victor de Sabata**
EMI ② 562890-2 (110' · AAD)   ⓂⓄⓄⓄ⯈
EMI ② 585644 2 (110' · AAD)   ⒷⓄⓄⓄ
Naxos ② 8 110256/57 (110' · AAD)   ⓈⓄⓄⓄ
This could still be called a definitive *Tosca*, with Callas, Di Stefano and Gobbi striking sparks off the score and each other, supported by de Sabata's masterly conducting and a still impressive recording.

(In English) **Jane Eaglen** *Tosca* **Dennis O'Neill** *Cavaradossi* **Gregory Yurisitch** *Scarpia* **Geoffrey Mitchell Choir, Philharmonia Orchestra / David Parry**
Chandos ② CHAN3000 (118' · DDD)   ⒻⓄ
Exceptionally competitive English-language recording, with idiomatic performances from Jane Eaglen, Dennis O'Neill and Gregory Yurisitch, ripely conducted by David Parry.

Maria Callas *Tosca* **Renato Cioni** *Cavaradossi* **Tito Gobbi** *Scarpia* **Chorus and Orchestra of the Royal Opera House / Carlo Felice Cillario**
EMI ② 562675-2 (109' · AAD)   Ⓜ
A historic 1964 live broadcast from Covent Garden, with Callas and Gobbi splendidly fierce antagonists, Renato Cioni a fine Cavaradossi and well conducted by Cillario, although the mono sound is clear but rather lean.

master, help to fill in the background. The Concertgebouw, subordinated in balance to the singers, play well under Riccardo Chailly's enlightened direction.

Tosca

Maria Guleghina *sop* Tosca **Salvatore Licitra** *ten* Cavaradossi **Leo Nucci** *bar* Scarpia **Giovanni Battista Parodi** *bass* Angelotti **Ernesto Gavazzi** *ten* Spoletta **Alfredo Mariotti** *bass* Sacristan **Silvestro Sammaritano** *bass* Sciarrone **Ernesto Panariello** *bass* Gaoler **Virginia Barchi** *treb* Shepherd Boy **Chorus and Orchestra of La Scala, Milan / Riccardo Muti**
Stage director **Luca Ronconi**
Video director **Pierre Cavasillas**
TDK Mediactive *DVD* DV-OPTOS (121' · 16:9 · 2.0, 5.1 & DTS 5.1 · 0 · N)   Ⓕ

In March 2000 Muti conducted a staged performance of *Tosca* for the first time, only the second Puccini opera he'd conducted at La Scala. As this live-recorded DVD powerfully reveals, he emerged as the hero of a great occasion. The high-voltage electricity is unflagging, with the drama timed to perfection, the whole magnetically compelling from first to last. It makes one regret that he's so rarely turned to Puccini. But as the music director at La Scala since 1986, he knows unerringly how to pace his singers, letting them phrase expansively where needed, yet holding the structure firmly together.

Maria Guleghina makes a formidable Tosca, very believable in her jealousy, using a rich tonal range, with just a touch of vinegar at the top. She's at her finest in the great scene with Scarpia in Act 2, leading up to a radiant account of 'Vissi d'arte' and a chilling murder, even though the very ordinary dinner-knife she uses looks an unlikely weapon. The veteran Leo Nucci, tall, thin and mean, is most compelling as the police chief, at times a smiling villain, though the voice has its occasional roughness. As Cavaradossi, Salvatore Licitra may be an unromantic figure, and he's heavy-handed at the start in 'Recondita armonia', but he develops from there, and in Act 3 he sings superbly with fine shading of tone for 'E lucevan le stelle' and the duet with Tosca.

Luca Ronconi's production, well-directed for television by Pierre Cavasillas, consistently heightens the dramatic conflicts. The sets of Margherita Palli, as redesigned by Lorenza Cantini, bring a surreal contradiction between realism and fantasy, looking like conventional sets that have been hit by an earthquake, with uprights at all angles. Sections of scenery are retained from act to act, with an increasing pile of debris left behind. That makes the battlements of the Castel Sant'Angelo look like a bomb-site, which Tosca has to climb before flinging herself to her death. The idea, presumably, is to reflect the distorted mind of Scarpia, though in this *verismo* opera pure realism might be said to work best of all.

Tosca

Renata Tebaldi *sop* Tosca **Eugene Tobin** *ten* Cavaradossi **George London** *bar* Scarpia **Gustav Grefe** *bass* Angelotti **Hubert Buchta** *ten* Spoletta **Heinz Cramer** *bass* Sacristan **Siegfried Fischer-Sandt** *bass* Sciarrone **Wilhelm Baur** *bass* Gaoler **Claudia Hellmann** *treb* Shepherd Boy **Stuttgart State Opera Chorus and Orchestra / Franco Patanè** *Stage and Film directors* Uncredited
Video Artists International *DVD* VAIDVD4217 (126' · 4:3 Black & White · 1.0 · 0) Recorded live at the Stuttgart Staatsoper, 1961   Ⓕ

Coming to this historic video recording after Muti's La Scala version is to register a quite different operatic world. Recorded in black and white at a performance in the Stuttgart Staatsoper in June 1961, it offers a sound, conventional production with in-period costumes and realistic if symmetrical sets by Max Fritzsche. The film direction too is highly conventional.

This DVD is specially valuable for Renata Tebaldi's assumption of the title-role. So dominant in our memories has Maria Callas's characterisation become, that we tend to forget that the role of Tosca was just as central in the repertory of her great rival of the time, Tebaldi, whose firm, creamy tones, perfectly controlled, could hardly be more sharply contrasted with the thrillingly individual, if at times flawed, singing of Callas. Tebaldi seemed to represent the essence of the *prima donna*, grand in a traditional way, and who better to play the role of Tosca?

There's ample evidence here of that commanding security in the role, with Tebaldi in 1961 still at her peak. Yet as recorded in limited mono sound, with voices well forward of the orchestra, at times there's an untypical edge on the creamy tone at the top. True to form, Tebaldi rises magnificently to the challenge of 'Vissi d'arte' in Act 2, with fine shading of tone and flawless *legato* in that moment of repose. That said, one has to note that in her acting this Tosca isn't so much passionate as stately.

Eugene Tobin as Cavaradossi, like many tenors, starts lustily, and then gets more expressive as he goes along, never betraying signs of strain. George London makes a handsome Scarpia, imperious and vehement both in his acting and in his singing. Yet as so often in recordings, his pitching is often vague. Franco Patanè as conductor is at times over-emphatic, again presenting a conventional view, and rarely conveying the sort of magnetism that makes the Muti performance so gripping.

Worth buying to hear Tebaldi in her prime.

Tosca

Magda Olivero *sop* Tosca **Alvinio Misciano** *ten* Cavaradossi **Giulio Fioravanti** *bar* Scarpia **Giovanni Foiani** *bass* Angelotti **RAI Chorus and Orchestra, Turin / Fulvio Vernizzi**
Stage director **Mario Lanfranchini**
With documentary, 'A tu per tu con Magda Olivero, artista e donna', including arias by Alfano, Cilea,

Franck, Gounod, Handel, Mascagni, Puccini and Verdi
Hardy Classic Video **DVD** HCD4011
(208' · NTSC · 4:3 · 1.0 · 0)   Ⓕ

The production of *Tosca* dates from 1960. Ah, those naïve times when people believed it was set in Scarpia's Rome (not in Mussolini's, for example). The date is 1800 and the Battle of Marengo is news. And the scenery is for real. You could nose your way around Sant'Andrea della Valle, and feel quite at home in the Palazzo Farnese.

As for the *prima donna*, Magda Olivero (born 1910, debut 1932) has thought out every move, every expression, creating the conviction of living the whole role afresh here and now. She also sings with distinction. Try her in phrases like 'le voce delle cose' for delicacy and the great two-octave lunge of 'Io quella lama piantai nel cor' for power. Her Scarpia isn't so very far inferior to Gobbi: suave and brutal by turns, with fine resonance. Cavaradossi is likeable, both vocally and dramatically; Angelotti, for his brief operatic life, is outstanding.

The documentary of 2003 puts 1960 in perspective. It includes glimpses of Olivero singing in Milan the previous year, marking the 25th anniversary of Callas's death. It's a weirdly ethereal sound, sometimes very flat, but flat in a beautiful way. She sings *Panis angelicus*, and at a late stage is joined by her tenor pupil Danilo Formaggio. In interviews Olivero tells of the tenors in her career, from Schipa to Domingo, including a long story about appeasing Gigli. But the best things are three excerpts filmed in 1965: a delicately acted scene from *Iris*, authentic voice and style for Alfano's *Risurrezione*, and the great solo from Act 1 of *La traviata*. The last is astonishing in every way: the 'Ah, fors' è lui' muses privately; the 'Follies' are sudden, impetuous; the 'vortici' brilliant with nervous energy; top Cs that swell and diminish as you thought they did only in text-books; and a top E flat which you hadn't thought would be in her voice at all. And this is a youngster of 55.

It's a pity we don't get a taste of her pre-war recordings: that would have deepened the perspective. Seeing her at 92 leaves us with admiration and wonder for this extraordinary woman and her unquenchable devotion to her art.

Il trittico

Il tabarro
Carlo Guelfi *bar* Michele **Maria Guleghina** *sop* Giorgetta **Neil Shicoff** *ten* Luigi **Riccardo Cassinelli** *ten* Tinca **Enrico Fissore** *bass* Talpa **Elena Zilio** *mez* Frugola **Barry Banks** *ten* Ballad-seller **Angela Gheorghiu** *sop* Lover **Roberto Alagna** *ten* Lover
**London Voices; London Symphony Orchestra /
Antonio Pappano**

Suor Angelica
Cristina Gallardo-Domâs *sop* Suor Angelica
Bernadette Manca di Nissa *contr* Princess **Felicity**

Palmer *mez* Abbess **Elena Zilio** *mez* Monitoress
Sara Fulgoni *mez* Mistress of the Novices **Dorothea Röschmann** *sop* Sister Genovieffa **Judith Rees** *sop* Sister Osmina **Rachele Stanisci** *sop* Sister Dolcina **Francesca Pedaci** *sop* Nursing Sister **Anna Maria Panzarella** *sop* First Almoner Sister, First Lay Sister **Susan Mackenzie-Park** *sop* Second Almoner Sister **Deborah Miles-Johnson** *contr* Second Lay Sister **Rosalind Waters** *sop* Novice **London Voices; Tiffin Boys' School Choir; Philharmonia Orchestra /
Antonio Pappano**

Gianni Schicchi
José van Dam *bass-bar* Gianni Schicchi **Angela Gheorghiu** *sop* Lauretta **Roberto Alagna** *ten* Rinuccio **Felicity Palmer** *mez* Zita **Paolo Barbacini** *ten* Gherardo **Patrizia Ciofi** *sop* Nella **James Savage-Hanford** *treb* Gherardino **Carlos Chausson** *bass* Betto di Signa **Luigi Roni** *bass* Simone **Roberto Scaltriti** *bar* Marco **Elena Zilio** *mez* La Ciesca **Enrico Fissore** *bass* Spinelloccio **Simon Preece** *bar* Pinellino **Noel Mann** *bass* Guccio

London Symphony Orchestra / Antonio Pappano
EMI ③ 556587-2 (162' · DDD · T/t)   ⒻⒹ

No previous recordings bring such warmth or beauty or so powerful a drawing of the contrasts between each of the three one-acters in Puccini's triptych as these. It's Pappano above all, with his gift for pacing Puccini subtly, who draws the set together. In each opera he heightens emotions fearlessly to produce unerringly at key moments the authentic gulp-in-throat, whether for the cuckolded bargemaster, Michele, for Sister Angelica in her agonised suicide and heavenly absolution, or for the resolution of young love at the end of *Gianni Schicchi*. It will disappoint some that the starry couple of Angela Gheorghiu and Roberto Alagna don't take centre-stage, but quite apart from their radiant singing as Lauretta and Rinuccio in *Gianni Schicchi* – not least in that happy ending, most tenderly done – they make a tiny cameo appearance in *Il tabarro* as the off-stage departing lovers, a heady 45 seconds. It's the sort of luxury touch that Walter Legge would have relished. No doubt Gheorghiu would have been just as persuasive as Giorgetta in *Il tabarro* and as Sister Angelica, but having different sopranos in each opera sharpens the contrasts. Maria Guleghina makes a warm, vibrant Giorgetta, and the touch of acid at the top of the voice adds character, pointing to the frustration of the bargemaster's wife.

Even more remarkable is the singing of the young Chilean soprano, Cristina Gallardo-Domâs as Sister Angelica. Hers is a younger, more vulnerable Angelica than usual. Her vocal subtlety and commanding technique go with a fully mature portrayal of the nun's agony, her defiance of the implacable Princess as well as her grief over her dead son. As with Gheorghiu, the dynamic shading brings *pianissimos* of breathtaking delicacy. The Princess is powerfully sung by Bernadette Manca di Nissa, her tone firm and even throughout. Felicity Palmer, with her tangy mezzo tone, is well contrasted as the Abbess, and she's just as characterful as the crabby Zita in *Gianni Schicchi*. The casting in *Suor Angelica* is as near flawless as could be, with Elena Zilio and Dorothea Röschmann outstanding in smaller roles. Zilio is the only singer who appears in all three operas, just as effective as Frugola in *Il tabarro*, though there her full, clear voice isn't always distinguishable from Guleghina as Giorgetta. Among the men Carlo Guelfi makes a superb Michele, incisive, dark and virile. He brings out not just the anger but the poignancy of the bargemaster's emotions, as in the duet with Giorgetta, when they lament what might have been. Neil Shicoff makes a fine Luigi, the nerviness in his tenor tone aptly bringing out a hysterical quality in the character. The male *comprimarios* are vocally more variable, if always characterful, as they are too in *Gianni Schicchi*. As Schicchi himself José van Dam's voice perfectly conveys the sardonic side of the character, and the top Gs he has to negotiate are wonderfully strong and steady. Maybe the full voice he uses for the name 'Gianni Schicchi', when in impersonation of old Buoso he's dictating the new will, makes too obvious a contrast with the quavering old man imitation, but it's what Puccini asked for.

Also worthy of praise is the sumptuous and atmospheric sound. Off-stage effects are magical, and always thanks to Pappano and fine playing from both the LSO and Philharmonia, the beauty and originality of the carefully textured instrumentation can be appreciated with new vividness. This is a set to renew your appreciation of operas that represent Puccini still at his peak.

Il trittico
Il tabarro
Piero Cappuccilli *bar* Michele **Sylvia Sass** *sop* Giorgetta **Nicola Martinucci** *ten* Luigi **Sergio Bertocchi** *ten* Tinca **Aldo Bramante** *bass* Talpa **Eleonora Jankovic** *mez* Frugola **Ernesto Gavazzi** *ten* Ballad-seller **Anna Baldasserini** *sngr* Lover I **Bruno Brando** *sngr* Lover II

Suor Angelica
Rosalind Plowright *sop* Suor Angelica **Dunja Vejzovic** *contr* Princess **Maria Garcia Allegri** *mez* Abbess **Nella Verri** *mez* Mistress of the Novices **Giovanna Santelli** *sop* Sister Genovieffa **Maria Dalla Spezia** *sop* Sister Osmina **Midela d'Amico** *sop* Sister Dolcina

Gianni Schicchi
Juan Pons *bar* Gianni Schicchi **Cecilia Gasdia** *sop* Lauretta **Yuri Marusin** *ten* Rinuccio **Eleonora Jankovic** *contr* Zita **Ferrero Poggi** *ten* Gherardo **Anna Baldasserini** *sop* Nella **Alessandra Cesareo** *contr* Gherardino **Franco Boscolo** *bass* Betto di Signa **Mario Luperi** *bass* Simone **Giorgio Taddeo** *bar* Marco **Nella Verri** *mez* La Ciesca **Claudio Giombi** *bass* Spinelloccio **Virgilio Carbonari** *bar* Notary **Pio Bonfanti** *bass* Pinellino **Ruggero Altavilla** *bass* Guccio

Orchestra and Chorus of La Scala, Milan / Gianandrea Gavazzeni
Stage director **Sylvano Bussotti**
Video director **Brian Large**
Warner Music Vison/NVC Arts **DVD** 5050467-0943-2-1 (161' · NTSC · 4:3 · PCM stereo · 2-6) Recorded at La Scala, Milan, 1983   Ⓕ

This Warner DVD offers idiomatic performances from La Scala of Puccini's trilogy. The productions are broadly traditional, with an ultra-realistic set for the grand guignol of *Il tabarro* and rather more stylised settings for *Suor Angelica* and *Gianni Schicchi*.

Casting is strong in *Il tabarro*, with Piero Cappuccilli in his prime as Michele, the cuckolded bargemaster. His appeal to Giorgetta, his estranged wife, is so passionate and tender that his climactic solo has your total sympathy. Sylvia Sass as Giorgetta tends to overact; the steely edge in her voice helps keep your sympathies with Michele. As Luigi, Nicola Martinucci is powerful and unstrained. Outstanding among the others is Eleonora Jankovic as La Frugola, firm of voice and characterful without overacting. The staging of the murder and Michele's revealing of the body under his cloak, always tricky to bring off, is neatly managed.

The stylised set for *Suor Angelica* is unobjectionable. What dominates, as it should, is Rosalind Plowright's moving performance of the title role. Next to her, Dunja Vejzovic is disappointing, not so much vocally as in appearance and personality; she seems too young and lightweight; hardly the unforgiving Princess. The nuns are nicely touched in, and the chorus is impressive. Brian Large's direction sidesteps the final and sentimental vision of Angelica's dead child.

Gianni Schicchi is placed in an enormous apartment with a panoramic view over Florence. The claustrophobia that can add point to the comic story is entirely absent, but the set is undistracting. Eleonora Jankovic again stands out among the incidental characters as the old woman, Zita, and Yuri Marusin as Rinuccio copes well with his big aria. Lauretta, his lover, is strongly cast, with Cecilia Gasdia luxuriantly drawing out 'O mio babbino caro' in finely shaded phrases, to the delight of the Scala audience. Juan Pons is a firm and commanding Schicchi, taking centre-stage from his first entry.

Turandot

Turandot
Dame Joan Sutherland *sop* Princess Turandot **Luciano Pavarotti** *ten* Calaf **Montserrat Caballé** *sop* Liù **Tom Krause** *bar* Ping **Pier Francesco Poli** *ten* Pang, Prince of Persia **Piero De Palma** *ten* Pong **Nicolai Ghiaurov** *bass* Timur **Sir Peter Pears** *ten* Emperor Altoum **Sabin Markov** *bar* Mandarin **Wandsworth School Boys' Choir; John Alldis Choir; London Philharmonic Orchestra / Zubin Mehta**
Decca ② 414 274-2DH2 (117' · ADD · T/t) Recorded 1972   Ⓕ ⓞⓞ▶

Turandot is a psychologically complex work fusing appalling sadism with self-sacrificing devotion. The icy Princess of China has agreed to marry any man of royal blood who can solve three riddles she has posed. If he fails his head will roll. Calaf, the son of the exiled Tartar king Timur, answers all the questions easily and when Turandot hesitates to accept him, magnanimously offers her a riddle in return – 'What is his name?'. Liù, Calaf's faithful slave-girl, is tortured but rather than reveal his identity kills herself. Turandot finally capitulates, announcing that his name is Love. Dame Joan Sutherland's assumption of the title role is statuesque, combining regal poise with a more human warmth, while Montserrat Caballé is a touchingly sympathetic Liù, skilfully steering the character away from any hint of the mawkish. Pavarotti's Calaf is a heroic figure in splendid voice and the chorus is handled with great power, baying for blood at one minute, enraptured with Liù's nobility at the next. Mehta conducts with great passion and a natural feel for Puccini's wonderfully tempestuous drama. Well recorded.

Turandot   🄷

Maria Callas *sop* Princess Turandot **Eugenio Fernandi** *ten* Calaf **Dame Elisabeth Schwarzkopf** *sop* Liù **Mario Borriello** *bar* Ping **Renato Ercolani** *ten* Pang **Piero De Palma** *ten* Pong **Nicola Zaccaria** *bass* Timur **Giuseppe Nessi** *ten* Emperor Altoum **Giulio Mauri** *bass* Mandarin **Chorus and Orchestra of La Scala, Milan / Tullio Serafin**

EMI mono ② 556307-2 (118' · ADD · T/t)
Recorded 1957   Ⓜ️**OO**▷

To have Callas, the most flashing-eyed of all sopranos as Turandot, is – on record at least – the most natural piece of casting. Other sopranos may be comparably icy in their command, but Callas with her totally distinctive tonal range was able to give the fullest possible characterisation. With her, Turandot was not just an implacable man-hater but a highly provocative female. One quickly reads something of Callas's own underlying vulnerability into such a portrait, its tensions, the element of brittleness. With her the character seems so much more believably complex than with others. It was sad that, except at the very beginning of her career, she felt unable to sing the role in the opera house, but this recording is far more valuable than any memory of the past, one of the most thrillingly magnetic of all her recorded performances, the more so when Schwarzkopf as Liù provides a comparably characterful and distinctive portrait, far more than a Puccinian 'little woman', sweet and wilting.

Next to such supreme singers it was perhaps cruel of Walter Legge to choose so relatively uncharacterful a tenor as Eugenio Fernandi as Calaf, but at least his timbre is pleasingly distinctive. What fully matches the positive character of the singing of Callas and Schwarzkopf is Serafin's conducting, which is sometimes surprisingly free, but in its pacing invariably captures colour, atmosphere and mood, as well as

---

PUCCINI TURANDOT – IN BRIEF

Joan Sutherland *Turandot* **Luciano Pavarotti** *Calaf* **Montserrat Caballé** *Liù* **John Alldis Choir; London PO / Zubin Mehta**

Decca ② 414 274-2DH2 (117' · ADD)   Ⓕ**OO**▷

Slightly unexpected casting pays dividends in this exciting set, with Mehta luxuriating in the exotic textures, and all three principals bringing out the sheer beauty of the vocal writing.

Maria Callas *Turandot* **Eugenio Fernandi** 🄷 *Calaf* **Elisabeth Schwarzkopf** *Liù* **Chorus and Orchestra of La Scala, Milan / Tullio Serafin**

EMI ② 556307-2 (118' · AAD)   Ⓜ️**OO**▷

In this mono recording Callas is a less powerful ice-princess than many, but more compelling, despite an unexciting Calaf. With Serafin's vigorous support she and Schwarzkopf infuse the performance with memorable feeling.

Katia Ricciarelli *Turandot* **Plácido Domingo** *Calaf* **Barbara Hendricks** *Liù* **Vienna State Opera Chorus, Vienna PO / Herbert von Karajan**

DG ② 423 855-2GH2 (DDD)   Ⓕ

Flawed by the casting of Katia Ricciarelli, game but overparted, this is still a very exciting set, with Plácido Domingo's thrilling Calaf, Barbara Hendricks' appealing Liù, and Karajan's monumentally lustrous reading.

Birgit Nilsson *Turandot* **Jussi Björling** *Calaf* **Renata Tebaldi** *Liù* **Rome Opera Chorus and Orchestra / Erich Leinsdorf**

RCA ② RD85932 (115' · ADD)   Ⓕ

With Molinari-Pradelli's more likeable version unavailable, this is the only way to enjoy Birgit Nilsson's spectacular Turandot, here alongside Jussi Björling's ardent Calaf, with Renata Tebaldi's creamy Liù and a good supporting cast.

Eva Marton *Turandot* **Michael Sylvester** *Calaf* **Lucia Mazzaria** *Liù* **San Francisco Opera Chorus and Orchestra / Donald Runnicles**

ArtHaus Musik 📀 100 088 (123')   Ⓕ

Marton is unsteady, Michael Sylvester a strong but unphotogenic Calaf, but with Runnicles' theatrical conducting and David Hockney's glowingly original sets, this is an enjoyable production, well worth considering.

Giovanna Casolla *Turandot* **Sergei Larin** *Calaf* **Barbara Frittoli** *Liù* **Maggio Musicale Chorus and Orchestra, Florence / Zubin Mehta**

RCA 📀 74321 60917-2   Ⓕ

The famous staging in Beijing's Forbidden City is robustly conducted by Mehta and well worth a look, even if Sergei Larin's Calaf and Barbara Frittoli's Liù outshine Gianna Casolla's serviceable Turandot.

dramatic point. The Ping, Pang and Pong epi-sode has rarely sparkled so naturally, the work of a conductor who has known and loved the music in the theatre over a long career.

The conducting is so vivid that the limitations of the mono sound hardly seem to matter. As the very opening will reveal, the CD transfer makes it satisfyingly full-bodied. Though with its rich, atmospheric stereo the Mehta set remains the best general recommendation, it's thrilling to have this historic document so vividly restored.

Turandot
Birgit Nilsson sop Turandot **Giuseppe di Stefano** ten Calaf **Leontyne Price** sop Liù **Nicola Zaccaria** bass Timur **Kostas Paskalis** bass-bar Ping **Ermanno Lorenzi** ten Pang **Murray Dickie** ten Pong **Peter Klein** ten Altoum **Alois Pernerstorfer** bass-bar Un Mandarino **Vienna State Opera Chorus and Orchestra / Francesco Molinari-Pradelli**
Orfeo d'Or mono ② C757 082I (113' · ADD)
Recorded live on June 22, 1961   Ⓕ Ⓞ

It's not so hard to think oneself present, espe-cially when the recording is as vivid as this and the performance so compelling. It was a special night in Vienna. Karl Löbl wrote it up (and partly down) for his paper at the time, and now, contributing the notes for this issue, says of his generation that they didn't know how lucky they were. He is clearly convinced that, whatever the shortcomings then, they were great times com-pared with the pallid present.

And it's true we have no Birgit Nilsson now. She is in magnificent form here. Though she is singing much of the time from some way back on stage, the sound is still immensely powerful, and when she does come down front for the final duet we mentally take a step or two back. Much of the special interest, however, lies with the Calaf and the Liù. Di Stefano wins through by the conviction of all he sings: blazing, for instance, in the enigmas. Leontyne Price, too, brings unusual intensity to her role. Vibrant and warm in tone, she shades her phrases sensitively, disappointing only in that she does not resist the temptation to make an effect by investing the B flat of "Signore, ascolta" with a *crescendo*. The others – the aged Emperor, the deposed King and the three quaint Ministers – are strongly cast, and the chorus make a grand contribution. Molinari-Pradelli conducts with more character than in the famous studio set, and the recording picks out details of orchestration we may well have missed in other, technically better bal-anced, versions.

Additional recommendation

Turandot (sung in English)
Eaglen Turandot **O'Neill** Calaf **Plazas** Liù **Bayley** Timur **New London Children's Choir; Geoffrey Mitchell Choir; Philharmonia Orchestra / Parry**
Chandos/Peter Moores Foundation Opera in English
② CHAN3086 (135' · DDD · T)   Ⓜ

The great glory of this set is Jane Eaglen's Turan-dot. There's no strain even in the most taxing passages, a firmness and a clarity that hasn't always marked her recordings. O'Neill gives a strong, heroic reading, but with the occasional moment of strain. Thoroughly recommended.

Le villi

Le villi
Sylvie David Narrator **Melanie Diener** sop Anna **Aquiles Machado** ten Roberto **Ludovic Tezier** bar Guglielmo **Radio France Chorus; French Radio Philharmonic Orchestra / Marco Guidarini**
Naïve V4958 (71' · ADD · N/T/t)   Ⓕ Ⓞ

Puccini's first two operas may have been written before he came to full maturity, but they do not deserve the neglect that they have suffered on disc. If the complications of *Edgar* detract from its impact, *Le Villi* might almost suffer from the oppo-site problem, when the story – very similar to that of Adam's ballet, Giselle, with the Willies (*Le Villi*) destroying the faithless lover, Roberto – is so severely telescoped. After Act 1, when Roberto leaves swearing loyalty to Anna, a narrator has to be introduced, to explain first that Roberto has been led astray and then that Anna has died of a broken heart. Where the CBS/Sony set had Tito Gobbi as narrator, the new one has Sylvie David, lighter and more conversational. The telescoping of the story also involves two striking interludes, The Abandonment and The Witches' Sabbath, a superb showpiece, which Pappano also recorded as fill-ups for his set of *La Rondine*.

Marco Guidarini proves a convincing Puccini-an, bringing out the dramatic bite of such pas-sages as these, as well as moulding the big melo-dies affectionately. The Sony set had Lorin Maazel conducting, but he was not helped by the closeness of the Sony sound, which at times makes him sound too aggressive. Equally Renata Scotto is not flattered by the closeness, and though both she and Plácido Domingo as Roberto are more characterful than Melanie Diener and Aquiles Machado on the new disc, the refinement of sound helps to make the fresh, sensitive singing of the newcomers just as enjoyable. Equally Ludovic Tezier is clear and direct as Anna's father Gug-lielmo. Very welcome indeed.

Henry Purcell   British 1659-1695

Purcell was a chorister in the Chapel Royal until his voice broke in 1673. He was then made assistant to John Hingeston, whom he succeeded as organ maker and keeper of the king's instruments in 1683. In 1677 he was appointed composer-in-ordinary for the king's violins and in 1679 succeeded his teacher, Blow, as organist of Westminster Abbey. From 1680 he began writing music for the theatre. In 1682 he was appointed an organist of the Chapel Royal. His court appointments were renewed by

James II in 1685 and by William III in 1689, and on each occasion he had the duty of providing a second organ for the coronation. The last royal occasion for which he provided music was Queen Mary's funeral in 1695.

Purcell was one of the greatest composers of the Baroque period and one of the greatest of all English composers. His works include the fantasias for viols (masterpieces of contrapuntal writing in the old style) and some of the more modern sonatas for violins which reveal an acquaintance with Italian models. In time Purcell became increasingly in demand as a composer, and his theatre music in particular made his name familiar to many who knew nothing of his church music or the odes and welcome songs he wrote for the court. During the last five years of his life Purcell collaborated on five semi-operas in which the music has a large share, with divertissements, songs, choral numbers and dances. His only true opera (ie with music throughout) was Dido and Aeneas, written for a girls school at Chelsea; despite the limitations of Nahum Tate's libretto it is among the finest of 17th-century operas. GROVEmusic

Complete Ayres for the Theatre

The History of Dioclesian, or The Prophetess, Z627ᵇ. King Arthur, Z628ᵇ. The Fairy Queen, Z629ᵇ. The Indian Queen, Z630ᵇ. The Married Beau, Z603ᵃ. The Old Bachelor, Z607ᵇ. Amphitryon, Z572ᵃ. The Double Dealer, Z592ᵃ. Distressed Innocence, Z577ᵃ. The Gordian Knot Unty'd, Z597ᵃ. Abdelazer, Z570ᵃ. Bonduca, Z574ᵃ. The Virtuous Wife, Z611ᵃ. Sonata While the Sun Rises in 'The Indian Queen'ᵇ. Overture in G minorᵃ. Sir Anthony Love, Z588 – Overtureᵃ. Timon of Athens, Z632ᵃ. The Indian Queen, Z630 – Symphonyᵇ
ᵃThe Parley of Instruments; ᵇThe Parley of Instruments Baroque Orchestra / Roy Goodman
Helios ③ CDS44381/3 (209' · DDD) Ⓑ

All these works were published within 18 months of Purcell's death. The 13 suites of choice movements from plays and semi-operas, entitled *A Collection of Ayres, compos'd for the Theatre, and upon other occasions,* may well have been the editing work of Purcell's brother, Daniel. Whoever it was had a rare combination of musical integrity and commercial flair: the pieces lifted from Purcell's interpolations to plays are often reordered and arranged with a deftness and charm which conveys the spirit of the theatre as well as heightening the loss and poignancy of Purcell's passing. How moving the Rondeau Minuet from *The Gordian Knot Unty'd* must have seemed to those who knew and loved Purcell.

As a major retrospective of Purcell's life in the theatre, the *Ayres for the Theatre* mainly comprise instrumental dances from their original sources, though there are several movements readapted from sung airs, such as 'Fairest isle' from *King Arthur* and 'If love's a sweet passion' from *The Fairy Queen.* The tunes are wonderful and varied, the inner part-writing skilful and the rhythmic imagination knows no bounds.

Even so, this isn't music where more than a suite at a time can be recommended for ultimate satisfaction: stop while you still want more. And more you'll most certainly want with Roy Goodman's alert and distinctive direction. If a few of the movements sound a touch mundane and lack dynamism as one follows on from another, the positive side is that the performances are never forced and rarely mannered. For the semi-opera 'suites', Goodman employs a full orchestra. What The Parley of Instruments has in abundance is a cordiality of expression which seems so absolutely right, especially in the slower airs.

Fantasias

Fantasias – three part, Z732-4; four part, Ⓟ
Z735-43; five part, 'upon one note', Z745. In Nomines
– G minor, Z746; G minor, 'Dorian', Z747
Joanna Levine, Susanna Pell, Catherine Finnis *viols*
Phantasm (Laurence Dreyfus, Wendy Gillespie, Jonathan Manson, Markku Luolajan-Mikkola *viols*)
Simax PSC1124 (51' · DDD) ⒻⓄⓄⓄ

 Purcell's contrapuntal mastery is dazzling, with the points of imitation in the various sections of each fantasia treated in double or triple counterpoint, inversion, augmentation and all other technical devices – for instance, the initial subjects of fantasias Z739, 742 and 743 at once appear in mirror images of themselves – but the music's deep expressiveness and the dramatic tension created by its chromaticisms and unpredictable harmonies make it clear that he certainly had performance in mind (a matter of some dispute), even if, because of the king's dislike of such intellectual pursuits, only privately by conservative-minded music-lovers. It's this expressiveness which Phantasm emphasises in this recording, both in their varied dynamics and in their use of vibrato. Speeds here are in general fast and there's great variety of bowing and hence of articulation.

Keyboard works

Eight Keyboard Suites, Z660-669. Chaconne, ZT680. Ground, ZT681. A New Ground, ZT682. Ground in Gamut, Z645. Ground ZD221. Round O, ZT684. Ground, ZD222
Richard Egarr *hpd*
Harmonia Mundi HMU90 7428 (75' · DDD) ⒻⓄⓄⒺ▸

While the eight posthumously published suites (with judiciously selected miscellany to create some elbow-room between each) are woefully unknown, they are beautifully crafted. Purcell's keyboard style rarely reverts to French luxuriance, rather more questing in its unpredictable steers, deliberately wrong-footed harmonic inflections, often quite tough textures and extended lyrical journeys.

Richard Egarr's devotion to these pieces comes in the form of studied spaciousness which allows these rich strains to become gently infused into our listening habits. This is no background tafelmusik, which is why it requires our indulgence, to stop and follow the thread – especially in the sustained narrative of the minor-key suites.

If the Almand of the G major Suite offers homage to the exquisite character-piece Almans of Gibbons, the A minor work is prescient of 18th-century models in its directed figuration and the grandiloquence of its easy conflation of French and Italian styles. Indeed, one of Egarr's greatest achievements is to challenge the home-spun perception of this repertoire and present it as great keyboard music. The C major Suite is a wonderful demonstration of this, as is the gamey tuning of the D major work with its burly final hornpipe. The harpsichord by Joel Katzman (after Ruckers) covers all the bases with its disarming colour, clarity and resonance. An outstanding recital.

Anthems and Services

Complete Anthems and Services, Volume 7   Ⓟ
I was glad when they said unto meᵇ. I was glad when they said unto me, Z19ᵃ. O consider my adversity, Z32ᵇ. Beati omnes qui timent Dominum, Z131. In the black dismal dungeon of despair, Z190. Save me, O God, Z51ᵇ. Morning and Evening Service in B flat, Z230 – Te Deum; Jubilate. Thy Way, O God, is Holy, Z60. Funeral Sentences for the death of Queen Mary IIᵇ – Drum Processional; March and Canzona in C minor, Z860; Man that is born of Woman, Z27; In the midst of Life, Z17ᵇ; Thou know'st Lord, Z58b; Thou know'st Lord, Z58c
Mark Kennedy, Eamonn O'Dwyer, James Goodman trebs **Susan Gritton** sop **James Bowman, Nigel Short** countertens **Rogers Covey-Crump, Charles Daniels, Mark Milhofer** tens **Michael George, Robert Evans** basses ᵃ**New College Choir, Oxford;** ᵇ**The King's Consort Choir; The King's Consort / Robert King**
Hyperion CDA66677 (70' · DDD · T/t)   Ⓕ
Also available on Hyperion CDS44141/51 (11 discs) Ⓑ

This CD is made up predominantly of anthems, devotional songs and a morning service (a functional, though not perfunctory, setting of the *Te Deum* and *Jubilate*) most of which disclose the range and quality of the composer's sacred *oeuvre* near its best. Of the two settings of *I was glad*, the first was, until not long ago, thought to be the work of John Blow. This full anthem more than whets our appetite with its agreeable tonal and melodic twists; when the *Gloria* arrives, we're assured that this is vintage Purcell by the sensitive pacing as much as an exquisite contrapuntal denouement. The earlier setting is more poignant. Opening with a string symphony in the spirit of a Locke consort, the music blossoms into a deliciously Elysian melodic fabric. Good sense is made of the overall shape and the soloists are, as ever, excellent. *Beati omnes* is a positive gem; this may well have been written for the composer's wedding. Of the small-scale pieces,

In the black dismal dungeon is the real masterpiece; it's delivered astutely by the secure and musicianly voice of Susan Gritton.

Finally to the funeral pieces. Here we have an ominous procession from the Guild of Ancient Fifes and Drums and the first appearance of four 'flatt' trumpets – as opposed to two plus two sackbuts; the effect of this subtle timbral change makes extraordinary sense of the music, engendering a new grandeur and uncompromising clarity as would have befitted such an occasion. The vocal performances are earthy and impassioned.

Odes & Welcome Songs

Odes for St Cecilia's Day – 'Hail, bright Cecilia', Z328; 'Welcome to all the pleasures', Z339
Susan Hamilton, Siri Thornhill sops **Robin Blaze, Martin van der Zeijst** countertens **Mark Padmore** ten **Jonathan Arnold, Peter Harvey, Jonathan Brown** basses **Collegium Vocale / Philippe Herreweghe**
Harmonia Mundi HMC90 1643 (73' · DDD · T)   Ⓕ

The two famous St Cecilian Odes reflect a remarkable polarity in the composer's creative priorities: the shorter of the two, *Welcome to all the pleasures*, is a supreme amalgamation of Fishburn's words and Purcell's music, bursting with contained subtlety and enchantment. There's also a unique sense of conveying something novel, in this case an inaugural tribute on 22 November 1683, to the patron saint of music, henceforth annually celebrating 'this divine Science'. *Hail, bright Cecilia* from 1692 is three times longer and explores all the startling orchestral sounds which changed English music towards something approaching a Handelian palette. It's also truly *fin de siècle* (some might say Newtonian) in ambition and the imagery is as breathtakingly splendid now as it was when the Victorians first revered it for its boldness and scale. Such qualities clearly animate Herreweghe and he shapes this music with rapture and precision.

The whole is infectiously fresh and never rushed. Herreweghe is sensitive to the nuances which irradiate from Purcell's colouring of words. He largely uses English voices. 'Hark! hark! each tree' boasts the versatile and effortless alto of Robin Blaze who, with the assured Peter Harvey, achieves a delightfully naturalistic lilt. One blip here is the piping soprano in 'Thou tun'st this world' (Susan Hamilton) where the voice seems technically and expressively limited. But for beauty of sound Herreweghe is your man.

Songs

She loves, and she confesses, Z413. Amintas, to my   Ⓟ
grief I see, Z356. Corinna is divinely fair, Z365. Amintor, heedless of his flocks, Z357. He himself courts his own ruin, Z372. No, to what purpose, Z468. Sylvia, 'tis true you're fair, Z512. Lovely Albina's come

ashore, Z394. Spite of the godhead, pow'rful love, Z417. If music be the food of love, Z379/3. Phyllis, I can ne'er forgive it, Z408. Bacchus is a pow'r divine, Z360. Bess of Bedlam, Z370, 'From silent shades'. Let formal lovers still pursue, Z391. I came, I saw, and was undone, Z375. Who can behold Florella's charms?, Z441. Cupid, the slyest rogue alive, Z367. If prayers and tears, Z380. In Chloris all soft charms agree, Z384. Let us, kind Lesbia, give away, Z466. Love is now become a trade, Z393. Ask me to love no more, Z358. O Solitude! my sweetest choice, Z406. Olinda in the shades unseen, Z404. Pious Celinda goes to prayers, Z410. When Strephon found his passion vain, Z435. The fatal hour comes on apace, Z421. Sawney is a bonny lad, Z412. Young Thirsis' fate, ye hills and groves, deplore, Z473
Barbara Bonney, Susan Gritton sops **James Bowman** counterten **Rogers Covey-Crump, Charles Daniels** tens **Michael George** bass **Mark Caudle, Susanna Pell** vas da gamba **David Miller** lte/theorbo / **Robert King** org/hpd
Hyperion CDA66730 (76' · DDD · T)   Ⓕ

This third and last volume of Purcell's non-theatrical secular songs consummates a most rewarding survey of 87 songs with more of the same: a vocal palette of six singers who are by now so steeped in the nuances of Purcell's strains that even the slightest offering sparkles with something memorable. The treasure is shared between Barbara Bonney and Susan Gritton who complement each other superbly. Gritton, becoming more refined in characterisation and tonal colour by the day, is allotted the free-style and dramatic pieces while to Bonney's fluid and sensual melisma is designated the more strophic or *cantabile* settings. *Lovely Albina's come ashore* is one of the composer's most mature creations, tantalisingly hinting at a new, tautly designed and classically balanced type of song. This work, *If music be the food of love* (the best of the three versions) and *I came, I saw* are striking examples of how exceptionally Bonney negotiates Purcell's skipping and curling contours and makes these songs sound even finer creations than we previously thought. *From silent shades* ('Bess of Bedlam') is Purcell's quintessential mad-song and Gritton has the measure of it all the way; packed full of incident, imagery and musical detail, her narration is clear and finely judged, reporting the tale with irony and change of colour. The CD is beautifully documented.

'Music of Henry Purcell'
Includes performances by **John Whitworth** counterten **Granville Jones, Neville Marriner, Peter Gibbs** vns **George Malcolm** hpd **Oriana Concert Choir and Orchestra; Kalmar Chamber Orchestra of London / Michael Tippett; Concentus Musicus, Vienna / Nikolaus Harnoncourt; Leonhardt Baroque Ensemble / Gustav Leonhardt** hpd **Deller Consort / Alfred Deller** counterten
Musical Concepts ⑦ MC194 (6h 19' · ADD)   Ⓢ

This second volume of Vanguard's reissued recordings of Alfred Deller and his consort

comprises works by Purcell, the composer most closely associated with Deller, and consists of six CDs, well packaged and with a CD-Rom giving access to more detailed information. The first two present a mixed programme of songs, duets and instrumental pieces. The third has a complete performance of *Dido and Aeneas* conducted by Deller and recorded in 1965. The remaining discs include the *Odes to St Cecilia, Come, ye Sons of Art* and music for the Masque in *Dioclesian*, the whole collection ending with Blow's *Ode on the Death of Mr Henry Purcell*.

In his middle and later years Deller habitually lightened notes above the centre of his range, so that his style became somewhat predictable and the evenness of his production somewhat impaired. That accounts for main differences between these later performances of such 'signature' pieces as 'Music for a While' and 'Sweeter than Roses': the purity of tone, the extraordinary resonance of lower and middle notes, the technical skill and sensitivity of his singing all remain. As a conductor, he had difficulties, and it cannot be claimed that the *Dido* is a success. Some stodgy speeds and sluggish rhythms, a pantomime coven of witches, a Dido lacking nobility of tone and an Aeneas out of oratorio make it hard for other contributions (most notably Helen Watts's sorceress) to have their due effect. Still, no doubt the best way of avoiding disappointment is to be prepared for it.

That Deller could conduct well, holding his place along with the highly professional Harnoncourt in his *Dioclesian* and the very personally involved Tippett in *Hail, bright Cecilia*, is evident in the Odes. Stylish playing by George Malcolm and other instrumentalists (including the young violinist Neville Marriner) gives further pleasure. The album celebrated not only Deller himself but his generation who did so much to bring Purcell out of the text books, the full range of his genius revealed.

Dido and Aeneas

Dido and Aeneas   Ⓟ
Stephen Wallace counterten Second Witch **Gerald Finley** bar Áeneas **Rosemary Joshua** sop Belinda **Lynne Dawson** sop Dido **John Bowen** ten First Sailor **Dominique Visse** counterten First Witch **Maria Cristina Kiehr** sop Second Woman **Susan Bickley** mez Sorceress **Robin Blaze** counterten Spirit **Clare College Choir, Cambridge; Orchestra of the Age of Enlightenment / René Jacobs**
Harmonia Mundi HMX290 1683 (60' · DDD · T)   Ⓜ❶

Dido is a conveniently short piece, one whose concentrated musical language and quicksilver dramatic juxtapositions are well suited to the recorded medium, giving full rein to Purcell's imagination and raising it out of its habitually stilted stage conventions. This is where Charles Mackerras's 1967 Archiv recording succeeded, especially in Tatiana Troyanos's exquisite pacing of Dido's noble and tragic demise; also successful in bringing out the work's full imaginative impact were the recent smaller-scale but atmospheric accounts from Andrew Parrott (Emma Kirkby as Dido) and Ivor Bolton (Della Jones on Teldec) and – the pick of the crop until now – Christopher Hogwood, with the sensual immediacy of Catherine Bott as Dido.

René Jacobs was one of the very few luminaries of the current Baroque dramatic scene not to have tackled this singular masterpiece. He does so, like Hogwood, with a gaggle of top-class singers; when you can casually call on Maria Cristina Kiehr to sing her tuppenceworth of Second Woman, not to mention Robin Blaze as Spirit and Dominique Visse as First Witch, it augurs well for a new benchmark recording. Rosemary Joshua's Belinda is a straightforward, dramatically unobtrusive but essential presence, never manipulated to be more of an influence in Dido's life than Purcell clearly relates in the lady-in-waiting's offerings of advice, revealed in 'Pursue thy conquest love'. Act 2 is where things really get going, after the fairly perfunctory introduction to the solid hunk that is Aeneas. Whether you choose to cast your Sorceress as male or as a crooning hag, the part is crucial to the temperament of a performance, made neither to be too camp nor too earnest in delivery. Susan Bickley is a fine Sorceress of the old school, precise, yet retaining an authority through quality of tone rather than pantomime.

Jacobs' richly paletted, pacey and boldly theatrical reading will prove a breath of fresh air to those who feel that Purcell's music in general can withstand being 'un-Englished' for want of new approaches to colour, characterisation and the composer's inimitable lyrical undercurrent. The odd instrumental dance seems a touch lacking in native roughage, but the finely proportioned Orchestra of the Age of Enlightenment bound through the Grove's Dance are even more purposeful in the First Sailor's song that opens Act 3. Lynne Dawson will disappoint few in her devastated, long-breathed and honest 'Lament', elegantly turned (if not vocally peerless) and, crucially, consequential of so much that has passed before. The last chorus is more beautifully sung than you've ever heard: a true funeral rite. These are the elusive ingredients of a compelling and truly involved reading. Imaginative and invigorating, Jacobs has revitalised *Dido*.

Dido and Aeneas
Sarah Connolly *mez* Dido **Gerald Finley** *bar* Aeneas **Lucy Crowe** *sop* Belinda **Patricia Bardon** *mez* Sorcerer **William Purefoy** *counterten* Spirit **Sarah Tynan** *sop* Second Woman **John Mark Ainsley** *ten* Sailor **Carys Lane** *sop* First Witch; Chorus **Rebecca Outram** *sop* Second Witch; Chorus **Choir and Orchestra of the Age of Enlightenment / Elizabeth Kenny, Stephen Devine**
Chandos Chaconne CHAN0757 (70' · DDD · T/t) Ⓕ●▶

Here is England's first great opera presented with a truly cohesive sense of theatrical purpose, one which unusually allows the drama to unfold in a close identification with each of the cameo

characters. That said, Sarah Connolly is the driving force from the start; she's a singer who, on her own admission, is obsessed with Dido. Consequently we have a supremely wide-ranging, tragic and experienced queen from the start, inhabiting the shadows of 'Ah! Belinda' with early signs of deplorable fate, which are accentuated by an extended symphony luxuriating poignantly on this resonating conceit.

Lucy Crowe's Belinda is a splendid foil for Connolly's self-absorption, with her astute and increasingly desperate buoying up. The Sorceress of Patricia Bardon oozes class with an implacable display of vocal authority over cheap cliché, joined by two witches who gossip like a couple of housewives in the launderette. And then there's that single-tracked Aeneas, whom Purcell gives nothing of great moment. Gerald Finley parades the conventional Trojan Prince with generic regret and a smattering of hubris.

The textural lightness of the OAE, for whom a certain emotional reserve ultimately appears all the more powerful, is another feature of this excellent recording, as is the outstandingly deft co-direction of Elizabeth Kenny and Steven Devine.

Dido and Aeneas   Ⓟ
Véronique Gens *sop* Dido **Nathan Berg** *bass-bar* Aeneas **Sophie Marin-Degor** *sop* Belinda **Claire Brua** *sop* Sorceress **Sophie Daneman** *sop* Second Woman, First Witch **Gaëlle Mechaly** *sop* Second Witch **Jean-Paul Fouchécourt** *ten* Spirit, Sailor **Les Arts Florissants / William Christie**
Erato 4509-98477-2 (52' · DDD · N/T)   Ⓕ▶

William Christie's reading of *Dido* is very much in terms of the reputed French influence on Purcell. Overdotting, reverse dotting and *inégalité* are used throughout; the lines are often heavily embellished in the manner of Lully. This is a perfectly justifiable approach to the music, since there's little direct evidence to say exactly how much the French style dominated in England. This version, with single strings, an excellent small choir and a slightly obtrusive harpsichord, stands well alongside what's available. Apart from a few moments' inattention in Belinda's 'Haste, haste to town', you'd hardly notice that most of the cast are Francophone, except in that Nathan Berg's imposing bass-baritone finds it slightly easier to exploit the colour and the meaning of Aeneas's words. Véronique Gens is a lucid and sensible Dido, partnered by a sprightly Belinda from Sophie Marin-Degor and a good Second Woman from Sophie Daneman. Claire Brua's Sorceress is a splendidly insinuating conception, with a slithering melodic style.

Perhaps the main musical distinction of this version is the way Christie presents the final paragraphs. Up to this point he's taken generally quick speeds, and he runs the final confrontation of Dido and Aeneas at a headlong tempo, which works well. Then he comes almost to a standstill at the moment when Aeneas leaves the stage, choosing an unusually slow speed for the chorus

'Great minds against themselves conspire'. This makes way for a dangerously slow Lament, which is heart-stopping, and the final chorus, which is not.

Additional recommendation

Dido and Aeneas
Baker Dido **Herincx** Aeneas **Clark** Belinda
English Chamber Orchesta / A Lewis
Decca 466 387-2DM (53' · ADD) Recorded 1961 Ⓜ

A very early recording by Janet Baker in a role she was to make her own. Lewis directs a traditional but sensitive account of the score.

The Fairy Queen

The Fairy Queen Ⓟ
Gillian Fisher, Lorna Anderson sops **Ann Murray**
mez **Michael Chance** counterten **John Mark
Ainsley, Ian Partridge** tens **Richard Suart, Michael
George** basses **The Sixteen Choir and Orchestra /
Harry Christophers**
Coro ② COR16005 (133' · DDD · N/T) �Ⓜ Ⓞ ▷

The Fairy Queen is hardly an 'opera' in the conventional sense: its musical virtues lie in the composer's uncanny ability to summon a discrete, potent atmosphere whose capacity to move the listener lies outside a sustained dramatic context. The masques draw heavily on vernacular situations and a form of tragicomedy which requires a crafty hand in performance.

Harry Christophers allows the music to breathe with a warm spontaneity, encouraged by a strong and diverse vocal cast. Gillian Fisher is a touch disappointing, but the likes of Ann Murray (who's both radiant and a misfit in one), Michael Chance, John Mark Ainsley, Ian Partridge, Richard Suart and Michael George present a greater array of characterisation than any other extant reading. Just sample the wonderful slapstick between Mopsa and Coridon. Christophers strikes most imploringly at the heart of Purcell's native sensibilities (Partridge's Phoebus sums it up) for a satisfying performance capturing the indigenous humour, grandeur and poignancy of Purcell's exquisite score.

The Indian Queen

The Indian Queen Ⓟ
Emma Kirkby, Catherine Bott sops **John Mark
Ainsley** ten **Gerald Finley** bar **David Thomas** bass
Tommy Williams sngr **Chorus and Orchestra of the
Academy of Ancient Music / Christopher Hogwood**
Also includes additional Act by Daniel Purcell
Decca 475 052-2 (73' · DDD · N/T) Ⓜ

Christopher Hogwood makes us realise that for all the constraints, this score isn't inherently small-scale and warrants all the subtlety of colour that can be achieved using 12 soloists and a decent-sized choir and orchestra. Needless to

say, he conveys a consistent, logical and meticulous understanding of the score. The orchestral playing is crisp and transparent, the AAM's articulation allowing the integrity of the inner parts to be heard to the full without compromising blend. Among a distinguished line-up of singers, John Mark Ainsley gets the lion's share and is perhaps marginally more effective as the Indian Boy than as Fame, but such gloriously mellifluous and controlled singing can only enhance the reputation of this work.

Emma Kirkby is in fine fettle and she executes the justly celebrated 'I attempt from love's sickness' with her usual communicative panache. Then comes the pleasurably contrasted voice of Catherine Bott: 'They tell us that your mighty powers' could not be in better hands. David Thomas as Envy, with his two followers in the Act-2 masque, highlights this brilliant scene as the work of a true connoisseur of the theatre. Mature Purcell is most strongly felt in the deftly ironic invocation by the conjurer, Ismeron, whose 'Ye twice 10,000 deities' is delivered authoritatively by Gerald Finley, though the lulling to sleep, before the God of Dream's gloomy non-prediction, is unconvincing. The quality of music shines very brightly in this reading, though the performance is perhaps a touch calculated in places. Recommended.

The Indian Queen Ⓟ
Tessa Bonner, Catherine Bott sops **Rogers Covey-
Crump** ten **Peter Harvey** bass **Purcell Simfony
Voices; Purcell Simfony / Catherine Mackintosh** vn
Linn Records CKD035 (60' · DDD) Ⓕ

If *The Indian Queen* is less ambitious than the other three 'operas' there's the sure touch here of the composer at his most mature and adept. The Prologue, in which he had the rare opportunity to set an extended dialogue, is beautifully balanced, and the music in Act 3 – when Zempoalla's ill-fated love is prophesied by Ismeron the magician in 'Ye twice 10,000 deities' – ranks alongside the finest moments in Purcell's output. The small-scale character of the work, compared to its siblings, is taken a stage further by the Purcell Simfony, which employs a minute chamber-size group of four strings, doubling oboe and recorder, single trumpet and drums. The soloists sing with airy restraint but each responds to these Hilliard-esque proportions with a rhythmic buoyancy and direct intimacy which projects a finely gauged overall conception of the work.

If the expressive power of the music is at times rather glazed, there's a sure atmosphere which is captured by recorded sound that's both warm and yet never imposing. The ensemble isn't always first-rate but there's nothing too worrisome and the instrumental numbers are elegantly shaped. Tessa Bonner gets the lion's share of the solo soprano numbers, ahead of the more colourful Catherine Bott, though the former's comparatively brittle sound has a crystalline quality which suits Catherine Mackintosh's consistent, if austere strategy.

In short, this release is consistently touching, one which in a paradoxical way gets under the skin despite the recessed emotional climate it conveys.

King Arthur

King Arthur   🅟
Véronique Gens, Claron McFadden, Sandrine Piau, Susannah Waters sops **Mark Padmore, Iain Paton** tens **Jonathan Best, Petteri Salomaa, François Bazola-Minori** basses **Les Arts Florissants Chorus and Orchestra / William Christie**
Erato ② 4509-98535-2 (90' · DDD · N/T)   Ⓕ**OOO**

If the co-operation with John Dryden led to a unity of vision in terms of music's expressive role in the overall drama, Purcell was limited to a historical patriotic fantasy with little room for the magic and pathos of, say, the superior *Fairy Queen*. Yet in the context of a stage presentation, Purcell's music shines through strongly. On disc though, with just the music, not even the dramatic powers of William Christie can restore its place in the overall scheme. But never mind, this is a score with some magnificent creations and Christie is evidently enchanted by it. The choral singing is richly textured, sensual and long-breathed, yet always alert to a nuance which can irradiate a passage at a stroke, as Christie does in the bittersweet close of 'Honour prizing' – easily the best moment in Act 1. The instrumental movements are finely moulded so that sinewy counterpoint and rhythmic profile are always strongly relayed. The songs, too, have been acutely prepared and are keenly characterised without resorting to excess. All the basses deliver their fine music with aplomb.

If there's one drawback to extracting the musical numbers from the 'opera' when they've so clearly been delivered in a theatrical context, it's that the contextual characterisations lend themselves less well to the musical continuity of a CD. *King Arthur* without the play is dramatically a nonsense, so why try to pretend? Christie doesn't, but makes the strongest case yet for this music.

Additional recommendation

King Arthur
Gens, Bayodi, Jarrige, Auvity, Cornwell, Harvey Le Concert Spirituel / Hervé Niquet
Glossa GCD921608 (76' · DDD · N/T)   Ⓕ
The triumph of this reading is its joy and vigour. Unlike other non-British Purcellians, Niquet doesn't fall foul of projecting an excessive Frenchified view at the cost of the composer's indigenous and expressive language.

The Tempest

The Tempest[a]. Suite in G minor, Z770 –   🅟
Overture[b]. Chaconne for Strings in G minor, Z730[c].

Sonata for Trumpet and Strings No 2 in D, Z850[d]. If ever I more riches did desire, Z544[e]. The Indian Queen – Trumpet Overture[f]
[a]**Michael Colvin** ten Aeolus; [ae]**Meredith Hall** sop Amphitrite; [a]**Rosemarie van der Hooft** mez Ariel; [ae]**Gillian Keith** sop Dorinda; [a]**Brett Polegato** bar Neptune, First Devil; [ae]**Paul Grindlay** bass-bar Second Devil; [a]**Robert Stewart** voc Third Devil; [e]**Nils Brown** ten [df]**Norman Engel** tpt **Aradia Baroque Ensemble / Kevin Mallon** vn
Naxos 8 554262 (76' · DDD · T)   Ⓢ🅓➤

There's so much pleasure to be had from Purcell's semi-operas that it's easy to wish we had more of them. Much of *The Tempest* is thought to have been written by other hands, but that's no reason for refusing to give it shelf-room. The score is cast in the same mould as Purcell's fully accredited dramatic works and offers a similar range of music. Director Kevin Mallon doesn't fuss over shaping the slower music, and the fast numbers go with plenty of zest. The ensemble includes oboes, recorders and bassoons, quite sparingly used, and bells for the setting of Ariel's 'Full fathom five'. The line-up of solo singers has no weak links and a few real strengths. Brett Polegato may lack authority in the role of Neptune, but sings with a fine, warm, well-rounded tone. Meredith Hall brings a winning sensitivity to the long solo 'Halcyon days' and finds an ideal soprano partner in the young Gillian Keith. Purcell's setting of 'If ever I more riches did desire' and his Trumpet Sonata No 2 are substantial makeweights. The recording acoustic is more church than theatre, but lively enough. Recommended.

Miscellaneous

Bess of Bedlam, 'From silent shades', Z370. The Blessed Virgin's Expostulation, Z196. An Evening Hymn on a Ground, 'Now that the sun hath veil'd his light', Z193. The Fatal hour comes on apace, Z421. O! fair Cederia, hide those eyes, Z402. O Solitude! my sweetest choice, Z406. When first Amintas sued for a kiss, Z430. Yorkshire Feast Song, Z333 – The Bashful Thames. The Fairy Queen, Z629 – If love's a sweet passion; Now the night is chased away; Thrice happy lovers (Epithalamium); O let me weep (The Plaint). The Indian Queen, Z630 – I attempt from love's sickness; They tell us that your mighty powers. King Arthur, Z628 – Fairest isle. The Mock Marriage, Z605 – Man is for woman made. Oedipus, Z583 – Music for a while. Pausanias, Z585 – Sweeter than roses. If music be the food of love
Carolyn Sampson sop with
Andrea Morris, Sarah Sexton vns **Jane Rogers** va **Anne-Marie Lasla** va da gamba **Elizabeth Kenny** arch lute/theo **Laurence Cummings** hpd/spin
BIS   BIS-SACD1536 (72' · DDD/DSD · T)   Ⓕ**O**🅓➤

It is immediately obvious from the first few songs that this disc is truly special. Carolyn Sampson's singing is deliciously enjoyable for its sweet tuning, flawless intonation, impeccable stylishness, shapely phrasing of melodic lines and textual awareness. Each of these 19 songs, mostly taken from Purcell's operas and music for theatre plays, are given judicious performances. The programme admirably shows the variety of characteristics and styles in Purcell's writing, and Sampson achieves the perfect degree of joyful radiance, seductiveness, witty comment or bittersweet melancholy in each song. 'Sweeter than roses' is an old warhorse for early music singers, but the poetry has seldom seemed so personal as it does in Sampson's heart-rending rendition. The Plaint from *The Fairy Queen* is beautifully done and the line 'he's gone and I shall never see him more' is remarkable for its stylish precision and emotional truthfulness (the performance is also notable for Sarah Sexton's superb solo violin-playing).

The supporting players always sound as if they are fully interested in the subtle nuances of the music. Well known favourites such as 'Music for a while', 'Fairest isle' and 'I attempt from love's sickness to fly' are excellently done, but several of the relatively obscure songs ('The fatal hour' and 'From silent shades') are shown to be equally rewarding and engaging. First-class new recordings of Purcell's music are much too rare, and this one deserves to be an enormous success.

Sergey Rachmaninov
USSR/American 1873-1943

Rachmaninov studied at the Moscow Conservatory (1885-92) under Zverev (where Scriabin was a fellow pupil) and his cousin Ziloti for piano and Taneyev and Arensky for composition, graduating with distinction as both pianist and composer (the opera Aleko, given at the Bolshoi in 1893, was his diploma piece). During the ensuing years he composed piano pieces (including his famous C sharp minor Prelude), songs and orchestral works, but the disastrous premiere in 1897 of his Symphony No 1 brought about a creative despair that was not dispelled until he sought medical help in 1900: then he quickly composed his Second Piano Concerto. Meanwhile he had set out on a new career as a conductor, appearing in Moscow and London; he later was conductor at the Bolshoi, 1904-6.

By this stage, and most particularly in the Piano Concerto No 2, the essentials of his art had been assembled: the command of the emotional gesture conceived as lyrical melody extended from small motifs, the concealment behind this of subtleties in orchestration and structure, the broad sweep of his lines and forms and loyalty to the finer Russian Romanticism inherited from Tchaikovsky and his teachers. During the remaining years to the Revolution these provided him with the materials for a sizable output of operas, liturgical music, orchestral works, piano pieces and songs. In 1909 he made his first American tour as a pianist, for which he wrote the Piano Concerto No 3.

Soon after the October Revolution he left Russia with his family for Scandinavia; in 1918 they arrived in New York, where he mainly lived thereafter, though he spent time in Paris, Dresden and

Switzerland. There was a period of creative silence until 1926 when he wrote the Piano Concerto No 4, followed by only a handful of works over the next 15 years, even though all are on a large scale. During this period, he was active as a pianist on both sides of the Atlantic (though never again in Russia). As a pianist he was famous for his precision, rhythmic drive, legato and clarity of texture. GROVEmusic

Piano Concertos

No 1 in F sharp minor, Op 1; **No 2** in C minor, Op 18; No 3 in D minor, Op 30; **No 4** in G minor, Op 40. **Rhapsody on a Theme of Paganini**, Op 43

Piano Concertos Nos 1-4. Paganini Rhapsody
Earl Wild *pf* **Royal Philharmonic Orchestra / Jascha Horenstein**
Chandos ② CHAN10078 (134' · ADD) Recorded 1965
Ⓜ Ⓞ 🔂

Such is the luxuriance of sound revealed in these remasterings, it's difficult to believe the recording date; and such is the quality of the piano playing that it's easy to understand why Chandos should have wanted to go to such trouble. There aren't so many Rachmaninov pianists who dare to throw caution to the wind to the extent that Earl Wild does in the outer movements of the First Concerto, fewer still who can keep their technical poise in the process. The improvisatory feel to the lyricism of the slow movement is no less remarkable. Wild's panache is every bit as seductive in No 4, and the *Paganini* Rhapsody is a rare example of a performance faster than the composer's own – devilishly driven in the early variations and with tension maintained through the following slower ones so that the famous eighteenth can register as a release from a suffocating grip, rather than an overblown, out-of-context exercise in grandiosity. Because of his lightness and touch Wild's tempos never seem excessive. Undoubtedly he shifts the balance from languishing pathos and overwhelming grandeur towards straightforward exuberance; but that may be no bad thing for refreshing our view of the composer. It keeps us in touch with an earlier tradition. The RPO appears to be revelling in the whole affair, in a way one wouldn't have immediately associated with Horenstein. To pick on the very few weaknesses, the very relaxed clarinet tone in the slow movement of Concerto No 2 rather misses the character, and elsewhere in this work the balance engineers rather crudely stick a microphone under the cello section's nostrils. But then the solo playing in this concerto is generally a little disappointing too, as though Wild had actually played the piece rather too often. In No 3 there are the hateful cuts to contend with, and one senses that the performance has been rather thoughtlessly modelled on the composer's own, idiosyncrasies and all. None the less, for the sake of the outstanding performances of Nos 1 and 4 and the Rhapsody, and for the unique combination of old-style bravura and modern sound, this issue earns a strong recommendation.

Piano Concertos Nos 1-4
Vladimir Ashkenazy pf **London Symphony Orchestra / André Previn**
Double Decca ② 444 839-2DF2 (135' · ADD) Recorded 1970-72
🅜🅞🅞➡

Despite the recording dates, the sound and balance are superb, and there's nothing to cloud your sense of Ashkenazy's greatness in all these works. From him every page declares Rachmaninov's nationality, his indelibly Russian nature. What nobility of feeling and what dark regions of the imagination he relishes and explores in page after page of the Third Concerto. Significantly his opening is a very moderate *Allegro ma non tanto*, later allowing him an expansiveness and imaginative scope hard to find in other more 'driven' or hectic performances. His rubato is as natural as it's distinctive, and his way of easing from one idea to another shows him at his most intimately and romantically responsive. There are no cuts, and his choice of the bigger of the two cadenzas is entirely apt, given the breadth of his conception. Even the skittering figurations and volleys of repeated notes just before the close of the central *Intermezzo* can't tempt Ashkenazy into display and he's quicker than any other pianist to find a touch of wistfulness beneath Rachmaninov's occasional outer playfulness (the *scherzando* episode in the finale).

Such imaginative fervour and delicacy are just as central to Ashkenazy's other performances. His steep unmarked *decrescendo* at the close of the First Concerto's opening rhetorical gesture is symptomatic of his Romantic bias, his love of the music's interior glow. And despite his prodigious command in, say, the final pages of both the First and Fourth Concertos, there's never a hint of bombast or a more superficial brand of fire-and-brimstone virtuosity. Previn works hand in glove with his soloist. Clearly, this is no one-night partnership but the product of the greatest musical sympathy. The opening of the Third Concerto's *Intermezzo* could hardly be given with a more idiomatic, brooding melancholy, a perfect introduction for all that's to follow. If you want playing which captures Rachmaninov's always elusive, opalescent centre then Ashkenazy is hard to beat. (The Second Concerto is available on a single disc and is reviewed on page 885.)

Piano Concertos Nos 1-4. Rhapsody on a Theme of Paganini, Op 43
Stephen Hough pf **Dallas Symphony Orchestra / Andrew Litton**
Hyperion ③ CDA67501/2; SACDA67501/2
CD/SACD 🔊 (146' · DDD)
🅕🅞🅞🅞
Concertos recorded live at the Morton H Meyerson Symphony Center, Dallas, April-May 2004

Hough. Litton. Rachmaninov concertos. Hyperion. Already a mouth-watering prospect, isn't it? So, like the old Fry's Five Boys chocolate advert, does Anticipation match Realisation in these five much-recorded confections?

The answer is 'yes' on almost every level. Culled from one or more live performances the concertos may be, but they manifest a real sense of occasion. Hough has clearly been burning to record these pieces for years. Litton is one of the world's most adept accompanists. He and his Dallas players offer exemplary support, with bright precision, purring strings and a judiciously blended brass section. A handsomely voiced piano brings a near-perfect balance; only in the final pages of the studio-made *Paganini* Rhapsody does Hough struggle to make himself heard.

Unlike most of his peers, he takes the composer at his word (scores and recordings) in matters of tempo, dynamics and the performance practice of Rachmaninov's musical language, as he makes clear in a trenchant apologia in the superb booklet-note (by David Fanning).

Where Wild and Argerich seem glib in the cadenzas of the First and Third Concertos respectively, Hough imparts the right sense of heroic struggle; not even Rachmaninov caresses the second subject of the First Concerto's finale so beguilingly; the notoriously tricky opening pages of the Second Concerto's finale are dispatched with breathtaking élan, as is the last movement of the Third Concerto.

It's quite an achievement when each of Hough's five performances rivals the greatest versions recorded individually by other pianists (the younger Horowitz in the Third, for example, Michelangeli in the Fourth). As a competitive set, that from the much-lamented Rafael Orozco comes close to matching Hough's fleet-fingered ardour, but is less impressively recorded; Howard Shelley offers a convincing, slower alternative with powerful, weighty tone. Overall, though, only Earl Wild (1965) and, before that, Rachmaninov himself truly convey the composer's intentions with such miraculous fluency, passion and stylistic integrity.

Piano Concertos – Nos 1 & 2
Krystian Zimerman pf
Boston Symphony Orchestra / Seiji Ozawa
DG 459 643-2GH (62' · DDD)
🅕🅞🅞🅞➡

The catalogue may bulge with recordings of these two concertos, yet the verve and poetry of these performances somehow forbid comparison, even at the most exalted level. Zimerman claims that Rachmaninov says everything there is to say about the First Concerto in his own performance. But had Rachmaninov heard Zimerman he might have been envious. Zimerman opens in a blaze of rhetorical glory before skittering through the first *Vivace* with the sort of winged brilliance that will reduce lesser pianists to despair. The cadenza is overwhelming, and at 4'36" in the central *Andante*'s starry ascent his *rubato* tugs painfully at the heartstrings. In the finale, despite a dizzying tempo, every one of the teeming notes is pinpointed with shining clarity.

The Second Concerto also burns and coruscates in all its first heat. A romantic to his fingertips, Zimerman inflects one familiar theme after another with a yearning, bittersweet intensity that he equates in his interview with first love. Every page is alive with a sense of wonder at Rachmaninov's genius. Seiji Ozawa and the Boston orchestra are ideal partners, and DG's sound and balance are fully worthy of this memorable release.

Piano Concertos Nos 1 & 2 in Cᵃ
Leif Ove Andsnes pf
Berlin Philharmonic Orchestra / Antonio Pappano
EMI 474813-2 (59' · DDD) ᵃRecorded live 2005
Ⓕ❍❍❍🠖

 With no shortage of fine versions of this pairing from which to choose, EMI must rely on the undoubted selling power of its Norwegian star to make this release stand out from the rest. It is certainly a worthy contender for the Top Ten when aided by the world-class Berlin Phil, a conductor who is in the Barbirolli class of adroit accompanists, superb recorded sound and a beautifully voiced piano.

With judicious tempi (though, as is now customary, slightly slower than the composer's) and a well-nigh ideal balance between piano and orchestra, instrumental detail is tellingly observed, such as the bassoon and clarinet counterpoint at the beginning of the second movement of the First Concerto and the triangle in its finale, both well integrated into the sound picture, even if there is a hint of the engineer's hand.

Nor is there anything mannered about the soloist, though some may wish he was slightly less well mannered. Andsnes here gives the lie to those who find his playing on the cool side of emotional but he is always the reliable guest who never gets drunk, no matter how much alcohol he has consumed. The fiery section of the cadenza in the First Concerto, for example, runs out of steam in the final bars to which Byron Janis, for instance, brings a despairing vehemence.

The Second Concerto (live, as opposed to the studio First, but without any appreciable difference in acoustic and balance) is, similarly, given a Rolls-Royce reading with which only the pickiest could find fault. The last movement, though, is something special and the final appearance of its glorious second subject, greeted with a mighty timpani wallop and braying brass, is heart-stopping. The audience rightly roar their approval.

Piano Concerto No 2. Paganini Rhapsody
Vladimir Ashkenazy pf
London Symphony Orchestra / André Previn
Decca Ovation 417 702-2DM (58' · ADD) Recorded
1970-72   Ⓜ❍❍🠖

What emerges most obviously here is the keen poetic individuality of Ashkenazy as a

---

RACHMANINOV
PIANO CONCERTOS – IN BRIEF

Krystian Zimerman; Boston PO / Seiji Ozawa
DG 459 643-2GH (62' · DDD)   Ⓕ❍❍❍🠖
Ⓖ Zimerman's incendiary pianism trounces all-comers in the First Concerto, not excluding the composer himself. The Second, more ruminative in mood, comes over less well, thanks in part to a recording balance that attenuates the orchestral sound.

Stephen Hough; Dallas SO / Andrew Litton
Hyperion ② CDA67501/2; SACDA67501/2
(62' · ADD)   Ⓕ❍❍❍
A stunning new set of the four concertos and *Paganini* Rhapsody played with towering virtuosity by Hough. A real winner.

Leif Ove Andsnes; Berlin Philharmonic Orchestra / Antonio Pappano
EMI 474813-2 (59' · DDD)   Ⓕ❍❍❍🠖
Powerful yet poetic accounts of the first two concertos. Pappano matches Andsnes with accompaniments of uncommon sympathy and style.

Arturo Benedetti Michelangeli; Philharmonia Orchestra / Ettore Gracis
EMI 567238-2 (47' · ADD)   Ⓜ❍❍
Less surgingly romantic than some, Michelangeli's transcendental pianism and refined sensibility come together in this classic coupling of Rach 4 and the Ravel G major, available continuously since the late 1950s.

Sergey Rachmaninov; Philadelphia Orchestra / Leopold Stokowski, Eugene Ormandy   Ⓗ
Nos 2 & 3: Naxos 8 110601 (65' · ADD)   Ⓢ🠖
Nos 1 & 4: Naxos 8 110602 (71' · ADD)   Ⓢ🠖
Rachmaninov's own fastidious, never lugubrious 78 rpm performances remain indispensable, more than just historical documents despite their primitive recording technology.

Vladimir Ashkenazy; London SO / André Previn
Decca ② 444 839-2DF2 (135' · ADD)   Ⓜ❍
Vladimir Ashkenazy's fresh and involving analogue stereo set with André Previn and the LSO dates from the early 1970s. The pianist demonstrates great poetic imagination and lightning reflexes as well as his formidable bravura and characteristic weight of sonority.

Rachmaninov interpreter. The composer himself is far rougher with his music than Ashkenazy ever is. Those who like Rachmaninov concertos to sound forceful above all will no doubt have reservations, but rarely has this work sounded so magically poetic. That isn't just Ashkenazy's doing – his *rubato* is consistently natural – but the work of Previn and his players. Orchestral detail emerges more clearly than on other recordings, but thanks to finely balanced orchestral recording (no exaggeration of big violin tone) there are no gimmicks.

The playing of both Ashkenazy and the LSO continually conveys the impression not of a warhorse but of a completely new work; even such a favourite passage as the return of the slow-movement main theme just before fig 26 is pure and completely unhackneyed. But the performance which clinches the success of this delightful venture is that of the *Paganini* Rhapsody, magical from beginning to end in its concentrated sense of continuity, with the varying moods over the 24 variations leading inevitably from one to another. There's no great splurge of emotion on the great eighteenth variation, but instead there's a ripe sense of fulfilment, which is utterly tasteful. Although the final surprising quiet cadence could be pointed with more wit, the rest has so much delicacy that it's a marginal reservation.

Piano Concerto No 3ª. Cello Sonata in G minor, Op 19 – Andante (arr Volodos). Morceaux de fantaisie, Op 3 – No 5, Sérénade in B flat minor. Morceaux de salon, Op 10 – No 6, Romance in F minor. Preludes – F minor, Op 32

No 6. Prelude in D minor. Etudes-tableaux, Op 33 – No 9 in C sharp minor
Arcadi Volodos pf
ªBerlin Philharmonic Orchestra / James Levine
Sony Classical 50997 06438-4 (61' · DDD) ℗**OO**

Straight into the top flight of Rachmaninov Thirds goes Arcadi Volodos's recording, made live at the Berlin Philharmonie. So many things about it are distinguished and thrilling. Volodos's phrasing is consummately tasteful, all the way through to the cadenza. There his textures are superbly graded, his tone never glaring, even under the pressure of torrents of notes. All's well, in fact, until mid-way in the first-movement cadenza, where he inserts a hiatus before the *Allegro molto*. It sounds terribly calculated, as does the way he steers the cadenza towards its main climax. A couple of mannerisms in a performance are neither here nor there, but what's bothersome – and this is increasingly noticeable in the slow movement and the finale – is that such initiatives don't feel part of an organically conceived interpretation. Just a whiff of self-consciousness can be enough to cancel out a host of poetic or virtuoso touches. So, while a listener may be amazed, and a pianist envious, at the clarity and velocity Volodos can bring to the toccata in the finale, in context it feels like a gratuitous display.

Though this isn't a world-beater, it's certainly one to assess at the highest level. Nothing but praise can be showered upon the BPO for their wonderfully cushioned accompaniment, and upon Levine for his avoidance of all the usual pitfalls. The piano is quite forwardly balanced, so that every tiniest note emerges bright as a new pin; and, given how wonderfully Volodos shapes everything, it's fine, although you do occasionally feel that you aren't hearing the orchestra in its full glory.

As for the solo pieces, the Cello Sonata arrangement is a marvel. It floats ecstatically, with air seemingly blowing through the textures as if through a Chekhovian country house on a cool summer evening. It's heavenly, and the other solos are little short of that.

Piano Concerto No 3ª. Suite No 2 for Two Pianos, Op 17ᵇ
Martha Argerich, ᵇ**Nelson Freire** pfs ªBerlin Radio Symphony Orchestra / Riccardo Chailly
Philips 50 Great Recordings 464 732-2PM (62' · DDD) Recorded live 1982 Ⓜ**OOO**▷

 Rarely in her extraordinary career has Argerich sounded more exhaustingly restless and quixotic, her mind and fingers flashing with reflexes merely dreamt of by other less phenomenally endowed pianists. Yet her Rachmaninov is full of surprises, her opening *Allegro* almost convivial until she meets directions such as *più vivo* or *veloce*, where the tigress in her shows her claws and the music is made to seethe and boil. The cadenza (the finer and more transparent of the two) rises to the sort of climax that will make all pianists' hearts beat faster and her first entry in the 'Intermezzo' interrupts the orchestra's musing with the impatience of a hurricane. But throughout these pages it's almost as if she's searching for music that will allow her virtuosity its fullest scope. In the finale she finds it, accelerating out of the second movement with a sky-rocketing propulsion. Here the music races like wildfire, with a death-defying turn of speed at 7'21" and an explosive energy throughout that must have left audience, conductor and orchestra feeling as if hit by some seismic shock-wave.

Rachmaninov Piano Concerto No 3, Op 30 Ⓗ
Tchaikovsky Piano Concerto No 1, Op 23
Kabalevsky Rondo, Op 59
Van Cliburn pf
Moscow Philharmonic Orchestra / Kyrill Kondrashin
Testament mono SBT1440 (80' · ADD) ℗**OO**

Here, published for the first time, are the performances that sealed the Texan's first prize in the inaugural International Tchaikovsky Piano Competition, earning him a ticker-tape welcome back home and the Soviet bureaucrats red faces.

The strings are acidic, the solo cello sounds like an alto sax, the piano is frequently clunky-toned, the Moscow coughers are out in force and Cliburn has his fair share of fluffs and fudges – but none of this matters. There is a palpable sense of occasion, one in which all concerned sense they are witnessing history in the making as Cliburn gives the performances of his life. No wonder the audience erupts after the first movement of the Tchaikovsky. The *allegro vivace* assai section of the slow movement is taken at a daring pace, while the final pages are as thrilling as any on disc.

The second item on the programme was the *Rondo* by Kabalevsky, a *pièce imposé* written especially for the occasion. On this disc, Testament places it as the final work after the Rachmaninov. It's hardly a masterpiece but Cliburn dignifies it by treating it like one. And then Rach Three. Despite the sonic imperfections and some scarily uncoordinated moments, this one punches a hardly less emotional impact than Cliburn's astounding RCA recording. The first-movement cadenza (Cliburn plays the bigger of the two) will make the hairs stand up on the back of your neck; the finale's peroration will sweep you away. Whatever that magical, indefinable gift is, Cliburn had it in 1958, his annus mirabilis.

Rachmaninov Piano Concerto No 3 **Tchaikovsky** Ⓗ
Piano Concerto No 1 in B flat minor, Op-23
Vladimir Horowitz *pf* **New York Philharmonic Symphony Orchestra / Sir John Barbirolli**
APR mono APR5519 (66' · ADD)
Recorded live 1940-41   Ⓕ**OOO**

Ⓖ This is the Rachmaninov Third to end all Rachmaninov Thirds, a performance of such super-human pianistic aplomb, pace and virtuosity that it makes all comparisons, save with Horowitz himself, a study in irrelevance. Horowitz's 1930 recording with Albert Coates made Artur Rubinstein pale with envy; goodness knows how he'd have reacted had he heard Horowitz and Barbirolli! Taken from a 1941 New York broadcast (with apologies from the producer for snaps, crackles, pops and the like) Horowitz's tumultuous, near-apocalyptic brilliance includes all his unique and tirelessly debated attributes; his swooning rubato, thundering bass and splintering treble, his explosive attack, his super-erotic inflexions and turns of phrase. Try the skittering *scherzando* variation just before the close of the central *Intermezzo* and note how the pianist's velocity eclipses even his legendary recording with Fritz Reiner. This ultimate wizard of the keyboard is in expansive mood in the Tchaikovsky. There are ample rewards, too, for those who rejoice in Horowitz at his most clamorous, for the thunder and lightning of this 'Tornado from the Steppes'. The performance ends in what can only be described as a scream of octaves and an outburst by an audience driven near to hysteria. Barbirolli and the New York Philharmonic Symphony Orchestra are equal to just about every twist and turn of their volatile soloist's argument and so these performances

(and most notably the finale of the Rachmaninov) are simply beyond price.

Rachmaninov Piano Concerto No 4   Ⓗ
Ravel Piano Concerto in G
Arturo Benedetti Michelangeli *pf*
Philharmonia Orchestra / Ettore Gracis
EMI Great Recordings of the Century 567238-2
(47' · ADD) Recorded 1957   Ⓜ**OOO**▶

Ⓖ In crude and subjective terms Michelangeli makes the spine tingle in a way no others can approach. How does he do it? This is the secret every pianist would love to know, and which no writer can ever pin down. But it's possible to give some general indications. It isn't a question of technique, at least not directly, because Ashkenazy, for example (on Decca) can match their most virtuoso feats; indirectly, yes, it's relevant, in that there are dimensions in Michelangeli's pianism which allow musical conceptions to materialise which might not dawn on others. Nor is it a question of structure, in the narrow sense of the awareness of overall proportions, judicious shaping of paragraphs, continuity of thought; but the way structure is projected and the way it's transmuted into emotional drama; these things are critical.

In one way or another most of the recordings in this section respond vividly to the excitement of Rachmaninov's dramatic climaxes; but with Michelangeli these climaxes seem to burst through the music of their own volition, as though an irresistible force of nature has been released. It's this crowning of a structure by release, rather than by extra pressure, which gives the performance a sense of exaltation and which more than anything else sets it on a different level. It enables him to be freer in many details, yet seem more inevitable as a whole.

The impact of all this would be negligible without a sympathetically attuned conductor and orchestra. Fortunately that's exactly what Michelangeli has. Michelangeli's Ravel is open to criticism, partly because many listeners feel uncomfortable with his persistent left-before-right mannerism in the slow movement and with his unwarranted textual tinkerings (like changing the last note). But he's as finely attuned to this aloof idiom as to its temperamental opposite in the Rachmaninov.

And although the recording can't entirely belie its vintage, it does justice to one of the finest concerto records ever made.

Symphonies

No 1 in D minor, Op 13; **No 2** in E minor, Op 27; **No 3** in A minor, Op 44

Symphonies Nos 1, 2ᵃ & 3ᵇ. Symphonic Dances, Op 45. The isle of the dead, Op 29. Vocalise (arr cpsr). Aleko – Intermezzo; Gipsy Girls' Dance
London Symphony Orchestra / André Previn

RACHMANINOV SYMPHONY NO 2 – IN BRIEF

**Philadelphia Orchestra /
Eugene Ormandy**
Sony ② SB2K63257 (137' · ADD)   Ⓜ
Ormandy and the Philadelphians gave us the first stereo Rachmaninov symphony cycle, and their account of the Second generates a heady sweep that makes it easy to forgive some niggling cuts.

**Russian National Orchestra /
Mikhail Pletnev**
DG 439 888-2GH (64' · DDD)   Ⓕ❶❶➪
Pletnev's is a superbly controlled and enviably sure-footed performance, if a bit too cool and calculated for some tastes. Full bodied, though not ideally clear recording.

London SO / André Previn
EMI 566982-2 (74' · ADD)   Ⓜ❶❶➪
Many collectors maintain an unswerving allegiance to Previn's famous account from 1973, now sounding more refulgent than ever in its latest remastering.

**Concertgebouw Orchestra /
Vladimir Ashkenazy**
Decca ② 448 126-2DF2 (139' · DDD)   Ⓜ❶➪
An enjoyably red-blooded account with bags of temperament and athleticism. Ripe Decca engineering, albeit not quite as resplendent as on the two other instalments in Ashkenazy's Rachmaninov symphony cycle.

Berlin PO / Lorin Maazel
DG 457 913-2GGA (75' · DDD)   Ⓜ
Maazel's is an urgently intense conception, and accordingly he drives an unusually swift course through the first movments. High-powered orchestral playing, but the sound is just a tad fierce and unglowing.

**National SO of Ireland /
Alexander Anissimov**
Naxos 8 554230 (58' · DDD)   Ⓢ➪
The Dublin orchestra may not be world-beaters but there's absolutely nothing slip-shod about their contribution. Anissimov's deeply felt, keenly pondered conception enjoys realistic sound.

**Budapest Festival Orchestra /
Iván Fischer**
Channel Classics CCSSA21698 (65' · DDD)   Ⓕ❶
More musical alchemy from Iván Fischer and his Budapest orchestra. A real sense of dialogue permeates this malleable, joyous performance, whose textual revelations are legion. The sound, not surprisingly from this source, is superb.

EMI ③ 764530-2 (227' · ADD) Recorded 1974-6
Ⓜ❶❶➪

Rachmaninov's three symphonies reflect three very different phases in his creative development: the first (1895) is a stormy synthesis of contemporary trends in Russian symphonic music, the Second (1906-7), an epic study in Tchaikovskian opulence, and the third (1935-6) a seemingly unstoppable stream of original ideas and impressions. The Second was the first to gain wide acceptance, and with good reason. It shares both the key and general mood of Tchaikovsky's Fifth. Cast in E minor, its initial gloom ultimately turns to triumph, and the symphony includes enough glorious melodies to keep Hollywood happy for decades.

The First Symphony had a difficult birth, largely through the incompetent musical mid-wifery of Alexander Glazunov whose conducting of the work's premiere apparently left much to be desired. However, it's an immensely promising piece and although undeniably the product of its times, prophetic not only of the mature Rachmaninov, but of other Northern voices, including – occasionally – the mature Sibelius. Both the Third Symphony and its near-contemporary, the *Symphonic Dances* find Rachmaninov indulging a fruitful stream of musical consciousness, recalling motives and ideas from earlier compositions, yet allowing gusts of fresh air to enliven and rejuvenate his style. Both works have yet to receive their full due in the concert hall, although the strongly evocative *Isle of the dead* is more securely embedded in the repertory.

What with these and a trio of warming shorter pieces, André Previn's mid-1970s LSO package is an excellent bargain. The performances are entirely sympathetic, avoiding familiar interpretative extremes such as slickness, bombast and emotional indulgence. Previn shows particular understanding of the Third Symphony, the *Symphonic Dances* and *The isle of the dead*, works that represent Rachmaninov at his most innovative and assured. The Second Symphony is played without cuts (not invariably the case, even today) and the recordings are generous in tone and revealing of detail.

Symphonies Nos 1-3
Concertgebouw Orchestra / Vladimir Ashkenazy
Double Decca ② 448 116-2DF2 (140' · DDD) Ⓜ❶❶➪

Ashkenazy has made few more distinguished discs as conductor than his Rachmaninov symphony recordings of the early 1980s. The downside of the repackaging in this 2CD format is that you have to put up with a change of disc half-way through the Second Symphony and lose the shorter orchestral works included in the Previn set. Previn is the most natural but not always the most electrifying of Rachmaninov interpreters and many will find Ashkenazy preferable, particularly in No 1. Although some of Ashkenazy's speeds seem unnaturally pressed –

he fairly tips us into the first movement reprise having declined to cap the climax with unvalidated bells – the excitement is infectious. Previn's LSO isn't at its best in the *Larghetto*, but in the corresponding movement of the Second Symphony the boot is on the other foot. Not that Ashkenazy isn't convincing too – so long as you can forget the Previn. Ashkenazy's volatile approach is at its most extreme in the Third, the mood much less autumnal than it usually is, with the fruity Concertgebouw brass unconstrained. Such an unashamedly episodic rendering of the score has its drawbacks, but the virtuosic energy and Romantic gush are hard to resist. The recordings sound very well indeed.

Symphony No 2. Vocalise, Op 34 No 14.
Budapest Festival Orchestra / Iván Fischer
Channel Classics ⊚ CCSSA21698 (65' · DDD) ⓕⒹ➤

A new century brings a fresh start – at least, that's the feeling that Iván Fischer engenders here. He conducts the piece as Rachmaninov might have played it: with a free and malleable sense of spontaneity. It's the romantic more than the epic that Fischer emphasises. Words like ardent, fleet, airborne appear in my listening notes. In short, a narrative imperative.

The first movement quickly shakes off the lugubriousness of its introduction. It's a low-cholesterol sound that Fischer produces as layer upon layer of string texture and finally flutes carry us towards the first subject. Channel Classics has complemented his reading with a lovely, open and natural production. The blend is all Fischer's, though.

Nothing shy about the second subject of the scherzo, though. Rachmaninov's written *portamento* can sound horribly contrived here – pasted dutifully between notes rather than evolving effortlessly from the rise and fall of the phrase. But then Fischer's Budapest strings aren't about imitating the Rachmaninov style; they inhabit it.

Fischer's musical storytelling is exceptional. What do those sombre brass shadings tells us at the close of the scherzo? Rarely have they ever sounded quite so unsettling. Nor has the opening of the slow movement – arriving as it does mid-sentence – sounded more like Rachmaninov abruptly changing the subject. Anything but confront the demons. The eternal clarinet solo (ravishingly played here) may be sad but it's songful (in a way that the melancholic *Vocalise*, the filler here, is songful). You don't need words to feel the regret.

Fresh and engaging, then and well worth your attention – guaranteed to clear your head of preconceptions.

Symphony No 3. Morceaux de fantaisie, Op 3 – No 3, Mélodie in E; No 4, Polichinelle in F sharp minor (both orch anon)
National Symphony Orchestra of Ireland / Alexander Anissimov
Naxos 8 550808 (52' · DDD) ⓈⒹ➤

Barely represented on disc a generation ago, Rachmaninov's orchestral works are firm favourites these days, and it's no surprise Naxos has entered the lists. Can Anissimov hope to compete in a field that includes Ashkenazy's high-octane digital accounts in sundry bargain formats? Perhaps surprisingly the answer is yes, for the conductor produces a highly distinctive performance of the Third, inspiring his orchestra to playing of considerable warmth and flair. Sound quality is excellent, too. String tone is crucially important with this composer, and here again any worries prove unfounded. Not for Anissimov the 'neurotic' Russianness of Ashkenazy's Rachmaninov. Like Jansons, he disregards the first-movement exposition repeat, but he makes the orchestral voices speak with a gentler tone. There are shattering climaxes when the music calls for them, and the symphony ends in rousing style; elsewhere the sophisticated languor and careful phrasing recall Previn's famous recording. Although some will be disappointed with the generally slow tempos, there's an unusual wholeness of musical vision and pacing which never sacrifices the needs of the larger structure to the lure of momentary thrills. Despite the short measure, this is thoroughly recommendable at the price.

The Isle of the Dead/Symphonic Dances

The Isle of the Dead. Symphonic Dances
London Philharmonic Orchestra / Vladimir Jurowski
LPO LPO0004 (51' · DDD) Recorded live 2003-04
Ⓜ🔾🔾

The electricity Jurowski can generate is clearly established in the *Symphonic Dances*, leading up to a thrilling close, and if the hushed sequence of *The Isle of the Dead* is not a work to bring such a rush of adrenalin, the mystery of this piece inspired by Böcklin's great painting is perfectly caught. These are fine performances that gain in tension from being recorded live. Even if this involves some odd balances the definition of detail is good and one can readily rectify the rather low level of the CD transfer.

What for many might give pause is that, by the standards of rival versions (both Previn and Jansons pair Symphony No 1 with *The Isle of the Dead* and Symphony No 3 with the *Symphonic Dances*), this is an ungenerous coupling, even when you take into account the fact that Jurowski's speeds are broader. Yet these LPO performances are both recommendable and will delight anyone wanting a disc from this exciting conductor.

Trio élégiaque

Rachmaninov Trio élégiaque, Op 9
Shostakovich Piano Trio No 2
Dmitri Makhtin vn **Alexander Kniazev** vc
Boris Berezovsky pf

Warner Classics 2564 61937-2 (79' · DDD)   ⓕⒹ▶

Rachmaninov's only substantial piano trio remains a relative rarity in the catalogue. It's not hard to see why, for this is more of an Ugly Sister than a Cinderella. True, there are many passages of beauty and poignancy, but overall it's an oddly structured piece, with two substantial movements followed by an almost throwaway finale.

This new reading comes closer than most to concealing the work's flaws. The opening movement is wonderfully realised, a single sweep of grief mingled with love and regret (it was written on the death of Tchaikovsky). And the second couldn't be more musically played. It's a highly piano-centric work, but you never feel that Berezovsky is hogging the limelight, superbly matched as he is by his compatriots. By contrast, the finale, despite its portentous, Brahmsian opening, is over all too soon, as if Rachmaninov simply ran out of steam.

It's tantalising that Rachmaninov left no recording of his own. But in the case of Shostakovich's Second Trio, we've had the composer at the keyboard on two occasions (various labels). Comparison is salutary: most modern interpretations seem sluggish by comparison (though admittedly Shostakovich plays fast and loose with his own tempo indications), particularly in the finale. Berezovsky, Makhtin and Kniazev are even more satisfying than the very good performance from the Wanderer Trio; their take on the following Passacaglia ideally balances profundity with unaffectedness. Their restraint is much more potent than the tacky exaggerations of Argerich, Kremer and Maisky, in a live performance from 1998.

Only a couple of niggles: the string players apparently ignore the *con sordino* instruction in the finale, and at one point in the Passacaglia there's a very prominent exhalation from one of them – bothersome enough to make one wonder why it was left in. The recording is warm and convincingly balanced and complements the superb performances.

Complete Piano Music

Variations on a Theme of Chopin, Op 22. Variations on a Theme of Corelli, Op 42. Mélodie in E, Op 3 No 3. Piano Sonatas – No 1 in D minor, Op 28; No 2 in B flat minor, Op 36 (orig version); No 2 in B flat minor, Op 36 (rev version). 10 Preludes, Op 23. 13 Preludes, Op-32. Prelude in D minor. Prelude in F. Morceaux de fantaisie, Op 3. Morceau de fantaisie in G minor. Song without words in D minor. Pièce in D minor. Fughetta in F. Moments musicaux, Op 16. Fragments in A flat. Oriental Sketch in B flat. Three Nocturnes – No 1 in F sharp minor; No 2 in F; No 3 in C minor. Quatre Pièces – Romance in F sharp minor; Prélude in E-flat minor; Mélodie in E; Gavotte in D. 17 Etudes-tableaux, Opp 33 & 39.
Transcriptions – **Bach** Solo Violin Partita No 3 in E, BWV1006 – Preludio, Gavotte, Gigue **Behr** Lachtäubchen, Op 303 (pubd as Polka de VR) **Bizet** L'Arlésienne Suite No 1 – Menuet **Kreisler** Liebesleid. Liebesfreud **Mendelssohn** A Midsummer Night's

Dream, Op 61 – Scherzo **Mussorgsky** Sorochinsky Fair – Gopak **Rachmaninov** Daisies, Op 38 No 3. Lilacs, Op 21 No 5. Vocalise, Op 34 No 14 (arr Kocsis) **Rimsky-Korsakov** The Tale of Tsar Saltan – The Flight of the Bumble-bee **Schubert** Die schöne Müllerin, D957 – Wohin? **Tchaikovsky** Cradle Song, Op 16 No 1
Howard Shelley pf
Hyperion Ⓑ CDS44041/8 (449' · DDD)   ⓂⓄ

This Hyperion set is a significant testament to Howard Shelley's artistry. Pianistically impeccable, he understands what Rachmaninov was about. The original piano works span 45 years of the composer's life. The earliest pieces here, the *Nocturnes*, strangely owe allegiance neither to Field nor Chopin, but are very much in the mid- to late 19th-century Russian salon style. The Third, in C minor, has nothing whatever to do with its title. Nicely written too, but still uncharacteristic, are four pieces from 1888, which amply demonstrate that from his early teens the composer had something individual to say. The *Mélodie* in E major is memorable for its hypnotic use of piano tone. Hyperion's recording quality can be heard at its very best here; there's real bloom and colour. Written shortly after his First Piano Concerto in the early 1890s, the *Morceaux de fantaisie*, Op 3 bring us to familiar Rachmaninov. The ubiquitous Prelude in C sharp minor is the second number but Shelley tries to do too much with it; he's more effective in the *Sérénade* with its Spanish overtones. In the E flat minor *Moment musical*, Op-16 one feels that he's able to master Rachmaninov's swirling accompaniments idiomatically. In Variation No 15 of the *Variations on a Theme of Chopin* he succeeds in bringing the notes to life, getting his fingers around the fleet *scherzando* writing.

The first set of Preludes is mainstream repertoire. In the warmly expressive D-major Prelude he lends the piece a strong Brahmsian feel and it emerges as very well focused. He transforms the C minor into a restless mood picture. The First Sonata is often dismissed as being unwieldy but Shelley gives it a symphonic stature and allows it to be seen in conjunction more with the composer's orchestral writing. Shortly after the Third Concerto Rachmaninov wrote the Op 32 Preludes. Shelley conjures up an exquisite moonlit scene for the G major, but he's not as impressive in the B minor. However, with him it's always the music that dictates the course of the interpretation. In the two sets of *Etudes-tableaux* he excels, as he does too in the Second Sonata. He draws together the disparate elements of the finale with terrific mastery and is the equal of the 'Horowitz clones' for technique. In the *Corelli* Variations he's not quite in tune with the scope of the work but is outstanding in the transcriptions, if a little straight-faced. The recorded sound is never less than serviceable and is sometimes excellent.

Piano Sonata No 2

Piano Sonata No 2. Variations on a Theme of Corelli. Cinq Morceaux de fantaisie

Bernd Glemser pf
Oehms OC558 (75' · DDD)   Ⓕ

Bernd Glemser is described in the booklet as
having 'a particular affinity for the works of
Sergei Rachmaninov'. And judging by this CD,
that's not something to quibble with. This is a
recording which allows you to concentrate
purely on the music and the artist's interpretation, and not be distracted by any worrying
deficiencies in recorded sound, piano tone or
pianistic technique: it's all there. Glemser's
golden, burnished sound is a treat for the ears
in the *Corelli* Variations and, indeed, throughout.

The Piano Sonata No 2 is heard in its original
version with a few references to and additions
from the revised version. Glemser's impassioned reading is as tempestuous as it is heartfelt, among the most magnificent on disc. It is
also a pleasure to hear the complete *Morceaux*
– the famous C sharp minor Prelude is the second of the set (and a fine, fiery account it is,
too) – the highlight of which is the Mélodie,
No 3. A fleeting magical moment at 1'39"
makes you catch your breath. The revised version of this and the Sérénade, No 5, concludes
the disc, the former amounting to Rachmaninov's transcription of his own work. All in all,
then, a disc to relish.

Rachmaninov Piano Sonata No 2. Variations on a
Theme of Chopin. Daisies. Lilacs **Kreisler** (arr
Rachmaninov) Liebesfreud. Liebesleid
Yevgeny Sudbin pf
BIS 🔊 BIS-SACD1518 (64' · DDD/DSD)   Ⓕ

After the richly deserved acclaim that greeted his
debut disc of Scarlatti, Yevgeny Sudbin moves
onto home ground. And here, surely, is a young
virtuoso in the widest, most encompassing sense.
Sudbin makes an unforgettable case for the *Chopin*
Variations, a florid and uneven work, though at its
finest (in, say, Variation 21) as memorable as anything in Rachmaninov. Omitting the quickly
aborted fugue of Variation 12 and choosing the
quiet rather than rumbustious coda, he is breathtakingly fleet in Variations 7-8 and goes through
Variations 9-10 with all guns firing. Hear him in
the whirling measures of Variation 20 (complete
with sky-rocketing *ossia*) in page after page of dark,
lyrical introspection and you will be hard pressed
to recall a more talented or deeply engaged young
artist.

The Second Sonata, played here in Sudbin's
own Horowitz-based conflation, is equally
inspired, going out in a spine-tingling final blaze
of glory. In the two song transcriptions he sounds
warmly committed to their floral enchantment.
Again, whether in love's joys or sorrows, Sudbin
evinces a deft and super-sensitive virtuosity; and
even though competition in both the Variations
and the Sonata is intense he creates an entirely
individual aura. His own personal and informative notes provide a crowning touch to this well
recorded, deeply heartfelt recital.

'Unknown Rachmaninov'
Piano Sonata No 2, Op 36. Etudes-tableaux, Op 39 –
No 2; No 6; No 9. 24 Preludes – Op 23 No 5; Op 32
No 12. Fugue. Suite
Denis Matsuev pf
RCA Red Seal 88697 15591-2 (60' · DDD)   Ⓕ

Denis Matsuev is a virtuoso in the grandest of
grand Russian traditions who returns us to the
great days of Emil Gilels. He possesses the sort
of technique which begins where others end,
and here in Rachmaninov his playing is truly
'stewed in Russian juices'.

His recital, entitled 'Unknown Rachmaninov', is
in fact a mix of the familiar and newly discovered. And while the piano version of the D
minor orchestral Suite is hardly characteristic,
let alone vintage Rachmaninov, it is played up to
the hilt by Matsuev. The D minor Fugue is a
more convincing discovery with its prophecy of
the E minor *Moment musicaux* demanding and
receiving a red-hot virtuosity. Again, Matsuev
may have you longing for the fuller 1913 version
of the Second Sonata but his playing blazes with
such towering strength and conviction that he
leaves you with virtually no grounds for complaint. His pace in the 'Red Riding Hood' A
minor *Etude-tableau* is hair-raising and the earlier *Etude* in the same key is given with a scale
and romantic turbulence that declare the pianist's nationality in every bar. The G minor Prelude can scarcely have been played more stunningly in its entire history. This excellently
recorded disc presents the most trenchant and
commanding Rachmaninov recital in years.

Corelli Variations

Rachmaninov Variations on a Theme of Corelli,
Op 42 **Tchaikovsky** The Seasons, Op 37b
Hideyo Harada pf
Audite 🔊 AUDITE92 569 (68' · DDD)   Ⓕⵔ

What a compelling coupling this is, and how
good to hear Tchaikovsky's still-underrated
cycle given a reading which conveys its grit and
grandeur as well as its beauty. The cycle was
commissioned by the editor of a St Petersburg
journal, *Le Nouvelliste*, and the pieces were published as a kind of musical part-work. When the
set was published complete, each piece was
headed by lines of verse by a Russian poet, Tolstoy and Pushkin among them, though such is
the vividness of Tchaikovsky's writing that the
music needs no explanation.

Tchaikovsky's flitting lark (March) and his
irresistible walzes for April and December are a
particular delight in Hideyo Harada's hands.
She's not afraid of full-blooded climaxes either,
as witness the choppier waters of June's initially
lilting barcarolle. And her 'Autumn Song'
(October) is desolate enough to soften the hardest of hearts.

Harada is also up against some very fine
recordings of Rachmaninov's *Corelli* Variations,
that solo masterpiece just one opus number

apart from his unaccountably more popular *Paganini* Variations. The subtlety with which Harada approaches the theme itself sets the scene for a reading that thrills as much for its nuance as for its brilliance – especially the extrovert Vars 11, 16 and 18. The wonderfully warm recording sets the seal on a highly recommendable disc.

Etudes-tableaux, Opp 33 & 39

Etudes-tableaux – Opp 33 & 39
Rustem Hayroudinoff pf
Chandos CHAN10391 (62' · DDD)   Ⓕ

These are meticulously prepared and observed readings – if Rachmaninov asks for *ppp legatissimo* or sharply contrasted dynamics from one bar to the next, then Hayroudinoff takes the composer at his word, a courtesy to Rachmaninov not granted by every pianist.

But Hayroudinoff goes much further than mere accuracy. If he cannot quite equal the composer's breathtaking nonchalance in the three he recorded (Op 33 Nos 2 and 7 in 1940, and Op 39 No 6 in 1925), he comes close. His rich tone and beefy attack serve him well in such passages as the ecstatic climax to the Op 39 E flat minor study (superbly paced and structured) and the pealing bells of Op 39 No 9; he sings with a touching simplicity in the C major and first of the A minor Op 39 studies.

Temperamentally he is right inside the music. This is powerful Rachmaninov playing that transcends the artificial constraints of the recording studio.

Preludes

Preludes – Op 3 No 2; Op 23; Op 32
Steven Osborne pf
Hyperion CDA67700 (79' · DDD)   ⒻOOO

It's all too easy to coarsen Rachmaninov's melodic genius with an overtly applied emotionalism, its clearly drawn lines becoming smudged. But Osborne conveys both the monumentality of these pieces, even the most fleeting, and their very human qualities. It's rare to find the balance so acutely achieved. The composer himself, of course, knew how to achieve that equilibrium, but then he had a head start.

Yet this is only a starting-point – the detail is equally delectable: the way that Osborne shapes the tear-stained melody of Op 23 No 4, for instance, and picks out the line from the dark, bustling figuration of Op 23 No 7 or the left-hand countermelody of Op 23 No 8. Then, in the Op 32 set, there's the simplicity of the second, with its incessant tolling around the note C, through to the meditative quality of No 10, the line rising out of the depths as sonorously as Debussy's cathedral. Another fascination is the way Osborne's range of touch puts the Preludes into such a clear historical context.

Osborne throws down the gauntlet with a towering C sharp minor Prelude: it's arguably too slow but makes an apt curtain-raiser on a set that glories in the magnificence of this music. And while there's no empty barn-storming on display here, that's not to say the technical challenges are shirked or underplayed in any way. There are few pianists who offer such range and depth of palette.

Additional recommendation

Preludes, Op 23 – Nos 1, 2, 4, 5, 8; Op 32 – Nos 1, 2, 6, 7, 10, 12
Coupled with: **Beethoven** Piano Sonata No 11. Variations and Fugue on an Original Theme, 'Eroica' **Chopin** Nocturnes – Op 72 No 1; Op 15 No 1 **Haydn** Piano Sonata in E, HobXVI:22 **Schumann** Symphonic Etudes
Richter pf
BBC Legends/IMG Artists ② BBCL4090-2
(144' · ADD) Recorded live 1967-9   ⓂO
These performances took place when Richter was as his height, his early insecurity resolved in playing of imperious mastery. Richter's empathy for his great compatriot is overwhelming and the sound is excellent. This is phenomenal playing.

Liturgy of St John Chrystostom, Op 31

Liturgy of St John Chrysostom
King's College Choir, Cambridge / Stephen Cleobury
EMI 557677-2 (75' · DDD)   ⒻOO

This recording may well consolidate its place in the repertoire, for it's a triumph. Compared with the Vigil the writing is generally sober, though there are unforgettable moments such as the opening of the Second Antiphon, which allows the boys' crystalline tone to shine. In fact, the King's choir make a virtue of an apparent limitation, producing an astounding choral blend in the simple responses of the litanies that punctuate the Liturgy.

The most famous section of the work is the lovely Lord's Prayer, movingly sung with fine attention to detail. Other sections, such as the Beatitudes ought also to attract the attention of any discerning choir director. Only in the Creed do the choir slightly lose the spring in their step; perhaps inevitable with such a lengthy setting in an unfamiliar language.

The great majority of the priest's and deacon's intonations have been included. This makes sense of the whole, and proves, if it needed proving, that Rachmaninov knew all about liturgical pacing. This aspect of the recording benefits from the magnificent bass and fluent Slavonic of Protodeacon Peter Scorer, who has the lion's share. If Deacon Tobias Sims, singing the celebrant's parts, can't entirely disguise his English origins, the contrast between the two voices also helps convey the liturgical feeling. There are excellent booklet-notes by Archimandrite Kyril Jenner.

Liturgy of St John Chrysostom
Flemish Radio Choir / Kaspars Putnins
Glossa ⊛ GCDSA922203 (65' · DDD/DSD)　Ⓕ●

Rachmaninov's Liturgy is less well known than
his Vigil ('Vespers'), but has nevertheless gained
in popularity with western choirs as a concert
item in recent years, though the double-choir
setting of the Lord's Prayer has always enjoyed a
certain renown, often being sung in an English
paraphrase. It is far more than a mere sketch for
the more famous work, too, though the links are
clear – anyone hearing the opening psalm, 'Bla-
goslovi, dushe moya', for the first time will
immediately make the connection.

The Flemish Radio Choir's rendition is very fine
indeed, reverent, well paced and at the same time
electrically atmospheric (and also including sufficient of the celebrant's petitions that it comes
across neither as an artificial celebration nor a
concert suite) and the magnificent SACD sound is
just what such a riveting performance merits. The
only criticism is of their very light 'l' sound, which
truly gives them away as non-Russians.

There is strong competition but, curiously,
none is Russian; indeed, the King's College
recording is as unrepentantly and beautifully
English as you could wish for. In an ideal world
one would have to have all of them, and if you
have room on your shelves for one more, do add
this new recording to your collection. There is
one aspect in which the other three score, however – they include full texts and translations,
while for the new disc they must be downloaded.

Further listening

Vespers
**National Academic Choir of Ukraine 'Dumka' /
Savchuk**
Regis Records RRC1043 (62' · DDD)　Ⓢ
　A first-rate bargain issue to compete with the very
　best. The Ukrainian choir is a superb body of
　singers, producing a beautifully warm, dark-hued
　sound and with an extraordinary sense of pacing.
　Their *piano* singing is unrivalled on disc.

Songs

12 Songs, Op 21. 15 Songs, Op 26. Were you
hiccoughing?. Night
Joan Rodgers sop **Maria Popescu** mez **Alexandre
Naoumenko** ten **Sergei Leiferkus** bar **Howard
Shelley** pf
Chandos CHAN9451 (72' · DDD · T/t)　Ⓕ●

Two figures in particular haunt this second volume of Chandos's survey of Rachmaninov's
songs – Feodor Chaliapin and Rachmaninov
himself. They had become friends in the years
when they worked together in an opera company and when Rachmaninov was concentrating
on developing his piano virtuosity. As a result
the Op 21 songs are dominated by an almost
operatic declamatory manner coupled with

formidably difficult accompaniments. Leiferkus
rises splendidly to the occasion, above all in
'Fate' (Op 21 No 1), and so throughout the
songs does Howard Shelley. He's unbowed by
the technical problems and he understands the
novel proportions of songs in which the piano's
participation has an unprecedented role. He also
enjoys himself in the roisterous exchanges with
Leiferkus in what's really Rachmaninov's only
lighthearted song, *Were you hiccoughing?*

The songs for the other voices are less powerful, in general more lyrical and intimate.
Alexandre Naoumenko only has five songs, and
they aren't, on the whole, among the more
striking examples, but he responds elegantly to
'The fountain' (Op 26 No 11). Maria Popescu
gives a beautiful account of one of the most
deservedly popular of them all, 'To the children' (Op 26 No 7), and of the remarkable
Merezhkovsky setting, 'Christ is risen' (Op 26
No 6). Joan Rodgers is enchanting in 'The
Lilacs' (Op 21 No 5) and moving in the song
acknowledging that love is slipping away,
'Again I am alone' (Op 26 No 9). She has complete mastery of the style, and nothing here is
finer than her arching phrase ending 'How
peaceful' (Op 21 No 7) – 'da ty, mechta moya'
(and you, my dream) – with Shelley gently
articulating Rachmaninov's reflective piano
postlude from the world of Schumann.

14 Songs, Op-34. Letter to K S Stanislavsky. From the
Gospel of St John. Six Songs, Op 38. A prayer.
All wish to sing
Joan Rodgers sop **Maria Popescu** mez
Alexandre Naoumenko ten **Sergei Leiferkus** bar
Howard Shelley pf
Chandos CHAN9477 (68' · DDD · T/t)　Ⓕ●

This set opens with a powerful dramatic outpouring, *Letter to KS Stanislavsky*. In fact it's a
formal letter of apology, for unavoidable
absence from a gathering, which Rachmaninov
sent for Chaliapin to sing to Stanislavsky; and
one of the most touchingly elegant phrases is
simply the date on the letter, October 14, 1908.
Perhaps he was showing a rare touch of irony in
using his full lyrical powers in such a context; but
at any rate, the piece nicely prefaces the two collections of his last phase of song-writing, before
he left Russia for exile.

Some of his greatest songs are here, coloured
in their invention by the four great singers
whose hovering presence makes the disposition
of this recital between four similar voices a
highly successful idea. The Chaliapin songs go
to Sergei Leiferkus, occasionally a little overshadowed by this mighty example (as in 'The
raising of Lazarus', Op 34 No 6) but more often
his own man, responding to the subtly dramatic,
sometimes even laconic melodic lines with great
sympathy for how they interact with the words,
as with the Afanasy Fet poem 'The peasant' (Op
34 No 11). Alexandre Naoumenko inherits the
mantle of Leonid Sobinov, and though he sometimes resorts to a near-falsetto for soft high

notes, he appears to have listened to that fine tenor's elegance of line and no less subtle feeling for poetry. Pushkin's 'The muse' (Op 34 No 1) is most tenderly sung, and there's a sensitive response to line with 'I remember this day'.

Maria Popescu has only two songs, 'It cannot be' and 'Music' (Op 34 Nos 7 and 8), but she has a light tone and bright manner. Joan Rodgers is exquisite in the most rapturous and inward of the songs (the great Felia Litvinne was the original here). Of the Op 38 set, Rachmaninov was particularly fond of 'The rat-catcher' (No 4), and especially of 'Daisies' (No 3), which she sings charmingly, but it's hard to understand why he did not add 'Sleep'. He might have done had he heard Rodgers's rapt performance with Howard Shelley, the music delicately balanced in the exact way he must have intended between voice and piano as if between sleep and waking.

Jean-Philippe Rameau
French 1683-1764

Rameau's early training came from his father, a professional organist; he went to a Jesuit school, then had a short period of music study in Italy. In 1702 he was appointed maître de musique at Avignon Cathedral, and spent the next 20 years in various organist posts in France.

By 1722 he was in Paris, where he was to remain; he had left his organist post at Clermont Cathedral to supervise the publication of his Traité de l'harmonie, a substantial and controversial work about the relationship of bass to harmony. The Traité brought him to wide attention. As a composer, he was known only for his keyboard music and his cantatas, though he had written some church music.

His ambitions, however, lay in opera and at the age of 50 he had his first opera, Hippolyte et Aricie, given at the Opéra. It aroused great excitement, admiration, bewilderment and (among the conservative part of the audience) disgust. It was fairly successful, as were the operas that followed, including the opéra-ballet Les Indes galantes.

In 1745 Rameau was appointed a royal chamber music composer; thereafter several of his works had their premieres at court theatres. Nine new theatre works followed in the mid-late 1740s, beginning with La princesse de Navarre and the comedy Platée; but from 1750 onwards only two major works were written, for Rameau was increasingly involved with theory and a number of disputes, with Rousseau, Grimm and even former friends, pupils and collaborators such as Diderot and D'Alembert. When Rameau died he was widely respected and admired, though he was seen too as unsociable and avaricious.

Rameau's harpsichord music is notable for its variety of texture, originality of line and boldness of harmony. But his chief contribution lies in his operas, especially those in the tragédie lyrique genre. He anticipated Gluckian reform by relating the overture to the ensuing drama. He brought to the numerous dances a wide range of moods using a richly varied orchestral palette and bold melodic lines. He wrote

many fine pathetic monologues, usually at the beginnings of acts, with intense, slow-moving vocal lines and rich, sombre accompaniments. His recitative, while following the Lullian model, is more flexible in rhythms and more expressive in its declamation. Such tragédies as Hippolyte et Aricie and Castor et Pollux stand among the great creations of French musical drama. **GROVE**music

Suites

Naïs – Orchestral Suites. Zoroastre – Orchestral Suites
Orchestra of the Eighteenth Century /
Frans Brüggen
Glossa GCD921106 (64' · DDD)   Ⓕ

No corner of the operatic repertory offers a greater wealth of freestanding orchestral dances than the French Baroque, and no composer wrote such a rich and enjoyable array of them as Rameau, that master blender of melodic inspiration, rhythmic irresistibility and orchestral colour. While Rameau's dances tend to be integrated into the action more than most, you do not really need to study the plots of these operas too much to enjoy the music they deliver. In the end the music is just there to be enjoyed, and in any case Rameau himself was not always that particular; those familiar with his harpsichord pieces will recognise a few old friends wearing hastily chosen new clothes.

As for the performances, little needs to be said about them save that they meet the Orchestra of the Eighteenth Century's normal high standards – impressively weighted sound, tight ensemble and excellent style – and are all the more admirable for being recorded live in concert, as usual.

Pièces de clavecin en concerts

Pièces de clavecin en concerts
Trevor Pinnock hpd **Rachel Podger** vn
Jonathan Manson va da gamba
Channel Classics CCS19098 (67' · DDD)   Ⓕ**OO**

Rameau's 1741 collection represents a major and entirely logical departure from the trio sonata and suite traditions that had held sway in Western European chamber music since the beginning of the 17th century. Rameau's textures are uniquely complex, demanding of the players a heightened awareness of their role in the musical texture at hand.

These are balanced and refreshingly musical performances that will draw you back again and again to savour the gracefulness and the kaleidoscopic blending of instrumental colours they bring to the music. Pinnock's playing is lively and engaging, inspiring and inspired. His accuracy is breathtaking, his ornamentation jewel-like. Podger and Manson respond with clarity and shapely phrasing, even in the hair-raising 'Tambourins' (Troisième Concert).

A movement such as 'La Boucon' (Deuxième Concert) is made wonderfully languid, 'La Timide' (Troisième Concert) sinuous but never oppressively so; and 'La Pantomime' (Quatrième Concert) is altogether civilised. And 'La Marais' (Cinquième Concert), which concludes the CD, reminds us how well the tone of a violin and viol can blend when produced by players of this calibre.

Pièces de clavecin

Premier Livre de pièces de clavecin (1706) – Suite **P** in A minor. Pièces de clavecin (1724, rev 1731) – Suite in E minor, Suite in D
Sophie Yates hpd
Chandos Chaconne CHAN0659 (71' · DDD) ⒻⓄⓄⒹ⁺

The release of a CD devoted to Rameau's harpsichord music is relatively rare. But it's less Rameau, and much more French keyboard music in general, that suffers neglect from an over-cultivated image. However, if Rameau's music is highly allusive, it's also possessed of an immediacy that makes it approachable today. Sophie Yates's firmly grounded yet sensitive and spirited playing will quickly dispel any lingering reservations, and she writes with authority and charm in the accompanying booklet (and plays here a copy of a 1749 Goujon harpsichord made by Andrew Garlick).

Yates's astute selection from Rameau's output is bound to please. The first suite, in A minor, is from the book of Pièces de clavecin published shortly after Rameau arrived in Paris in 1706, and displays a youthful brilliance that relies heavily on ornamentation (as, for example, in the Allemande 1 and the Courante) and, delightfully, occasionally reveals a certain provincialism – although Rameau never travelled to Italy, he clearly made certain assumptions about life there: his 'La Vénitienne' makes particular allusion to the beggars' bagpipe and hurdy-gurdy.

The second and third suites, from his later book of 1724 (rev 1731), are altogether more stylish and sophisticated. The E minor Suite begins sedately and with the gravitas befitting an Allemande, but is otherwise shot through with fashionable, pastoral rondeaux, and includes two of Rameau's best-known party pieces, 'Le rappel des oiseaux' and 'Tambourin'. The D minor Suite amuses with pièces de caractère (the flirtatious 'La follette', the devious 'Le lardon' and the pathetic 'La boiteuse') and amazes with the virtuosity of 'Les tourbillons' and 'Les Cyclopes'. But only a player of Yates's calibre can address the musical subtleties of 'Les soupirs', the deceptive 'Les niais de Sologne' and the sensuous 'L'entretien des muses'. A tour de force in every sense.

'La Pantomime'

Pièces de clavecin – in G major-minor; in A major-minor; in D minor. Pièces de clavecin en concertᵃ – La Coulicam; La Livri; Air pour les esclaves africains; La Forqueray; La Cupis; La Pantomime
Skip Sempé with ᵃ**Olivier Fortin** hpds

Paradizo PA0005 (58' · DDD). Includes bonus DVD Ⓕ

Skip Sempé is known for a love of spontaneity, which informs his solo performances and enlivens the duos. Technically demanding if idiomatic, Rameau's music has the power to impress and amuse. Asked what he thought was most important to Rameau, Sempé replied 'nobility and humour'. Both can be found in abundance on this CD (the former in the Sarabande, the latter in Le Triomphe and Les Cyclopes, which together with La Dauphine epitomise extrovert virtuosity) – but further delights await in L'Inharmonique and L'entretien des Muses, where we hear – thanks to Sempé's formidable command of 'rhetorical syntax' – Rameau seemingly conducting an inner dialogue with himself.

In the tradition begun by Couperin, Sempé and Fortin perform five duo arrangements of single Pièces de clavecin en concert and one air from Les Indes galantes. The luxuriant textures that result are perfect for La Forqueray, evoking as it does a viol-player known for his excesses, but they're less successful in other pieces where details are blurred and subtlety compromised, if nevertheless their phrasing is beautifully judged.

Several of the duo tracks from the CD are duplicated on the accompanying DVD, allowing us to glimpse the recording process. Commenting on the challenge of performing with another harpsichordist, Sempé concedes that it is almost impossible to achieve 'razor-edged' vertical precision and that instead the guiding principle is 'touch-oriented horizontality'. He's too modest. With a minimum of eye contact, their timing is perfection.

Motets

Deus noster refugium. In convertendo. **P**
Quam dilecta
Sophie Daneman, Noémi Rime sops **Paul Agnew** ten **Nicolas Rivenq** bar **Nicolas Cavallier** bass
Les Arts Florissants / William Christie
Erato 4509-96967-2 (70' · DDD · T/t) ⒻⓄⓄⓄ

All three motets date from relatively early in Rameau's career, before he had really made a name for himself, yet all show to a certain extent some of the characteristics that 20 years or so later would so thrillingly illuminate his operas. Deus noster refugium, for instance, features impressive depictions of nature in turmoil that would not sound out of place in Hippolyte et Aricie, and all three begin with long, expressive solos not unlike the opening of an act from a tragédie-lyrique. Quam dilecta does sound a little more 'churchy' than the others, with its impressive, rather Handelian double fugue, but In convertendo – a work which Rameau heavily revised well into his operatic Indian summer in 1751 – absolutely reeks of the theatre.

Drop anyone familiar with the composer's operas into the middle of this piece, and surely only its Latin text would give away that this is church music. It comes as no surprise to find Christie going to town on this dramatic element. The slightly dry acoustic of the Radio France studio is a help, as are the forceful, penetrating qualities of the solo and choral singers. But it's Christie's command of gesture, pacing and contrast which really gives these performances such an invigorating character.

Castor et Pollux

Castor et Pollux   P
Howard Crook ten Castor **Jérôme Corréas** bass Pollux **Agnès Mellon** sop Télaïre **Véronique Gens** sop Phebe **René Schirrer** bar Mars, Jupiter **Sandrine Piau** sop Venus, Happy Spirit, Planet **Mark Padmore** ten Love, High Priest **Claire Brua** sop Minerve **Sophie Daneman** sop Follower of Hebe, Celestial Pleasure **Adrian Brand** ten First Athlete **Jean-Claude Sarragosse** bass Second Athlete
Les Arts Florissants / William Christie
Harmonia Mundi ③ HMC90 1435/7 (173' · DDD · T/t)
Ⓕ🅾

Castor et Pollux was Rameau's second *tragédie en musique*. Its first performance was in October 1737, but the opera was greeted with only moderate enthusiasm. It was only with the composer's thoroughly revised version of 1754 that it enjoyed the popularity that it deserved. The revision tautened a drama which had never been weak, but it dispensed with a very beautiful Prologue. Christie and Les Arts Florissants perform Rameau's first version, complete with Prologue. The librettist, Pierre-Joseph Bernard, was one of the ablest writers with whom Rameau collaborated and his text for *Castor et Pollux* has been regarded by some as the best of 18th-century French opera. Bernard focuses on the fraternal love of the 'heavenly twins' and specifically on the generosity with which Pollux renounces his immortality so that Castor may be restored to life. Christie's production was staged at Aix-en-Provence in the summer of 1991 and recorded by Harmonia Mundi a year later. This performance realises the element of tragedy, and Christie's singers sound very much at home with French declamation. A very beautiful score, affectionately and perceptively interpreted.

Les fêtes d'Hébé

Les fêtes d'Hébé   P
Sophie Daneman sop Hébé, Une Naïde, Eglé **Gaëlle Méchaly** sop L'amour **Paul Agnew** ten Momus, Le ruisseau, Lycurgue **Sarah Connolly** mez Sapho, Iphise **Jean-Paul Fouchécourt** ten Thélème, L'oracle, Mercure **Luc Coadou** bass Alcée **Laurent Slaars** bar Hymas **Matthieu Lécroart** bar Le fleuve **Maryseult Wieczorek** mez Une Lacédémonienne, Une bergère **Thierry Félix** bar Tirtée, Eurilas **Les-Arts Florissants / William Christie**
Erato ② 3984-21064-2 (148' · DDD · T/t)
Ⓕ🅾🅾🅾

Rameau produced one of his most engaging

 scores for *Les fêtes d'Hébé*. The entertainment comprises a prologue and three *entrées*. All is prefaced with a captivating two-movement Overture whose playful second section has much more in common with a Neapolitan *sinfonia* than a traditional opera overture in the French mould. The dances belong to one of the composer's fruitiest vintages and Christie has capitalised upon this with a sizeable band which includes, where appropriate, a section of musettes, pipes and drums. The singers are carefully chosen for their contrasting vocal timbres and the line-up, by and large, is strong.

The leading roles in each of the opera's four sections are fairly evenly distributed between Sophie Daneman, Sarah Connolly, Jean-Paul Fouchécourt, Paul Agnew and Thierry Félix. The first three of this group are consistently engaging; their feeling for theatre, and their intuitive ability to seek out those aspects of Rameau's vocal writing which enliven it, seldom fail, and they bring considerable charm to their performances. Agnew, too, is on strong form though in the lower end of his vocal tessitura, required for the role of Momus in the Prologue, he sounds less secure than in his more accustomed *haute-contre* range. That can be heard to wonderful effect elsewhere and, above all, in a duet for a Stream and a Naiad (first *Entrée*) in which he's joined by Daneman. This beguiling little love-song is proclaimed with innocent fervour and tenderness. Félix has a rounded warmth and resonance and his occasional weakness of poorly focused tone has here been largely overcome. *Les fêtes d'Hébé* contains a wealth of inventive, instrumentally colourful and evocative dances. Small wonder that audiences loved it so much in the 1720s: with music of such vital originality, how could it be otherwise? Christie and Les Arts Florissants have possibly never been on crisper, more disciplined form than here, revelling in Rameau's beguiling pastoral images, tender and high-spirited in turn. A ravishing entertainment, from start to finish.

Hippolyte et Aricie

Hippolyte et Aricie   P
Mark Padmore ten Hippolyte **Anne-Maria Panzarella** sop Aricie **Lorraine Hunt** sop Phèdre **Laurent Naouri** bass Thésée **Eirian James** mez Diane **Gaëlle Mechaly** sop L'Amour, Female Sailor **Nathan Berg** bass Jupiter, Pluton, Neptune **Katalin Károlyi** mez Oenone **Yann Beuron** ten Arcas Mercure **François Piolino** ten Tisiphone **Christopher Josey** ten Fate I **Matthieu Lécroart** bar Fate II **Bertrand Bontoux** bass Fate III **Mireille Delunsch** sop High Priestess **Patricia Petibon** sop Priestess, Shepherdess **Les Arts Florissants / William Christie**
Erato ③ 0630-15517-2 (182' · DDD · T/t)   Ⓕ🅾🅾🅾

 William Christie adheres throughout to the 1733 original (Rameau revised the start of Act 2 in 1757), in so doing opening up some passages previously omitted. He uses an orchestra with a good string weight and it plays with security both of ensemble and intonation, and with splendidly crisp rhythms. Despite the opera's title, the main characters are Theseus and his queen Phaedra, whose guilty passion for his son Hippolytus precipitates the tragedy. Phaedra is strongly cast with a passionate Lorraine Hunt who's particularly impressive in the superb aria, 'Cruelle mère des amours', which begins Act 3. Throughout the opera, one is also struck by the profusion of invention, the unobtrusive contrapuntal skill, the charm and colour of the instrumentation and the freedom allotted to the orchestra. The work's final scene, for example, set in a woodland, is filled with an enchanting atmosphere, ending, after the customary chaconne, with 'Rossignols amoureux' (delightfully sung by Patricia Petibon). Anna-Maria Panzarella makes an appealingly youthful Aricia, and Mark Padmore is easily the best Hippolytus on record. Pains have been taken with the whole cast over the expressive delivery of words and neatness of ornamentation; and production values such as the proper perspective for the entry of the crowd rejoicing at Theseus's return have been well considered.

Zoroastre

Zoroastre   Ⓟ
Mark Padmore ten Zoroastre **Nathan Berg** bar
Abramane **Gaëlle Méchaly** sop Amélite **Anna Maria Panzarella** mez Erinice **Matthieu Lécroart** bar
Zopire, God of Revenge **François Bazola** bass
Narbanor **Eric Martin-Bonnet** bass Oramasès
Ariman **Stéphanie Revidat** sop Céphie **Les Arts Florissants / William Christie**
Erato ② 0927-43182-2 (157' · DDD · T/t)   Ⓕ**OO**

To describe *Zoroastre* as one of Rameau's most uncompromising music-dramas may seem strange when you consider that when it was revived in 1756, seven years after its premiere had met a rather lukewarm reception, it was in a heavily revised version in which the love interest had been stepped up. The story is of the endless struggle between good and evil which dominates the religion Zoroastre himself has founded.

Rameau's prime concern isn't with Zoroastrianism, but the elemental magic scenes and the intensely human emotions of love, jealousy, vengeance and rage thrown up by the story. Even so, there's a concentrated seriousness of intent about this work which sets it apart from standard *tragédie lyrique*. The French practice of blurring the distinction between recitatives and arias is intensified, so that choruses and snatches of melody fly past in a breathless, flexible flow of incident. And Rameau's music conjures massive dramatic contrasts, ranging from ineffably tender love scenes for Zoroastre and Amélite in Acts 3 and 5 to the almost oppressive demonic power of the subterranean incantations of Act 4, led by the strongly drawn characters of Abramane and Erinice.

The cast is in the best Les Arts Florissants tradition of dramatic commitment and intelligent treatment of text. Mark Padmore has the perfect

high tenor for Zoroastre, able to charm in tender moments yet rage in the confrontational scenes without losing any of its essential sweetness, while Nathan Berg makes a strong and fearsome-sounding Abramane. Even more impressive, however, are the two principal sopranos: Anna Maria Panzarella gives her all as the tormented Erinice, while Gaëlle Méchaly is wonderfully bright and clear as Amélite. There are odd moments of vocal weakness among some of the other roles, but they cause no serious damage. The chorus and orchestra both perform for Christie with great vigour, the former contributing memorably to the underworld scenes, and the latter performing delightfully in the opera's many dances.

Einojuhani Rautavaara   Finnish b1928

Rautavaara studied with Merikanto at the Helsinki Academy (1948-52), where from 1966 he taught, and with Persichetti at the Julliard School (1955-6). His large output shows a variety of stylistic resource (Russian nationalists, Hindemith and advanced serialism) and he has written in many genres; notable is The True and False Unicorn (1971) for chorus, orchestra and tape.   GROVEmusic

Flute Concerto, Op 63

Flute Concerto, 'Dances with the Winds'[a].
Anadyomene. On the Last Frontier[b]
[a]**Patrick Gallois** fl [b]**Finnish Philharmonic Choir; Helsinki Philharmonic Orchestra / Leif Segerstam**
Ondine ODE921-2 (59' · DDD)   Ⓕ**O**

Anadyomene (1968) suggests a Turner canvas recast in sound. It opens restlessly among undulating pastels, the tone darkens further, there are brief comments from flute and bass clarinet, the brass prompts a swelling climax, then the mood gradually becomes more animated before we're ferried back whence we came. It's 'a homage to Aphrodite, born of the sea foam, the goddess of love', and a very appealing one at that. The colourful Flute Concerto *Dances with the Winds* is a more extrovert piece with Nielsen as a fairly certain forebear. It shares its material between ordinary flute, bass flute, alto flute and piccolo. The action-packed opening movement withstands some fairly aggressive interjections from the brass, the brief second movement recalls the shrill sound world of fifes and drums; the elegiac *Andante moderato* offers plenty of jam for the alto flute, and the finale's striking mood-swings have just a hint of Bernsteinian exuberance.

Rautavaara's prompt for *On the Last Frontier* (1997) was an early encounter with *The Narrative of Arthur Gordon Pym* by Edgar Allan Poe. He calls it 'a seafaring yarn in the typical boys' reading mould' and responds accordingly with a 24-minute slice of descriptive musical reportage, not of Poe's exact 'narrative', but of an imagined *Last Frontier* based on ideas from the story's closing section. It's an eventful, majestic, slow-burning tone-poem, nourished further by some distinctive instrumental solos and with telling use of a full-blown chorus.

No texts are provided, and yet the aura of unexplored maritime depths and a sense of mystery associated with them carry their own wordless narrative. All three works are expertly performed and exceptionally well recorded.

Piano Concerto No 3

Piano Concerto No 3, 'Gift of Dreams'[a]. Autumn Gardens
Helsinki Philharmonic Orchestra /
Vladimir Ashkenazy [a]pf
Ondine ODE950-2 (68' · DDD)   Ⓕ◐

Autumn Gardens extends the Rautavaarian experience at least one step beyond the Seventh Symphony. You sense it especially in the animated finale, which begins *giocoso e leggiero* before a Baroque-style, four-note figure slowly makes its presence felt. The figure is first heard on the bassoon, then shifts timbre and focus (timpani and bells play a crucial role later on), inspiring the strings to lyrical heights. The piquantly scored first movement conjures a gentle beating of wings, with glowing modulations that sometimes darken, though they never cloud the issue. The reflective central movement follows without a break.

The Third Piano Concerto (1998) is stronger meat. More meditative than its predecessors though visited by some cluster-like dissonances, it seems to take its principal stylistic cue from the middle movement of Bartók's Second Piano Concerto. The opening string chord motive is simple, austere, the piano writing bold or decorative rather than overtly pianistic. As a whole, it's cast vaguely in the manner of Delius or Debussy, more an orchestral tone-poem with piano than a display piece. The most striking movement is the second, which incorporates some fairly harsh brass writing and memorably beautiful closing pages. The *Energico* finale calls in the big guns and is well served by Ondine's recording team, but one could imagine a more forceful performance. Otherwise, things go well. The disc closes with an interview, a disarmingly natural slice of dialogue where the composer relates to Ashkenazy how he views his works as received phenomena. That, for the most part, is precisely how his music sounds – like audible episodes drawn from nature, messages that, in a world seduced by banal artifice, are all too easily ignored.

Cantus arcticus, Op 61

Cantus arcticus, Op 61 (Concerto for Birds and Orchestra) with taped birdsong. Piano Concerto No 1, Op 45[e]. Symphony No 3, Op 20

[a]**Laura Mikkola** pf **Royal Scottish National Orchestra / Hannu Lintu**
Naxos 8 554147 (74' · DDD)   Ⓢ◐

No other new music stands to benefit more from extensive exposure, not so much because of its quality (which is beyond question), as because of an almost tangible connection with nature, than that by Rautavaara. One constantly senses the joy of a man alone with the elements: awe-struck, contented, inspired. Bird-song comes from all directions, literally in the 'Concerto for birds and orchestra' or *Cantus arcticus*, which sets taped bird-song against a rustic orchestral backdrop. The tape blends well with the music and is very atmospheric. The young Finnish conductor Hannu Lintu directs a fine performance. The First Piano Concerto and Third Symphony (out of seven) receive good performances, most notably the Brucknerian Symphony, an impressive and often dramatic work that begins and ends in the key of D minor. The orchestration incorporates four Wagner tubas, though some of the finest material is also the quietest. The slow movement is sullen but haunting, the *Scherzo* occasionally suggestive of Nielsen or Martinů and the finale brings the parallels with Bruckner fully within earshot. The First Piano Concerto has a brilliance and immediacy that should please orchestral adventurers and piano *aficionados*. The solo writing employs clusters and much filigree fingerwork, but it's the noble, chorale-like second movement that leaves the strongest impression. Laura Mikkola gives a good performance. Naxos gives a full sound picture and overall, this is an excellent CD, concisely annotated by the composer.

Manhattan Trilogy

Manhattan Trilogy. Symphony No 3
Helsinki Philharmonic Orchestra / Leif Segerstam
Ondine 🔊 ODE1090-5 (54' · DDD/DSD)   Ⓕ

Manhattan Trilogy. Symphony No 8,
'The Journey'. Symphony No 6, 'Vincentiana' –
IV: Apotheosis (revised version)
New Zealand Symphony Orchestra / Pietari Inkinen
Naxos 8 570069 (56' · DDD)   Ⓢ

Rautavaara studied at the Juilliard School in 1955-56 and *Manhattan Trilogy* (2004) was commissioned to celebrate its centennial. In recalling his youthful sojourn in the Big Apple, the composer deployed the full panoply of his late orchestral manner in a hugely engaging triptych describing his 'hopeful Daydreams', 'sudden Nightmares of doubt' and 'slowly breaking Dawn of the personality'. Where Segerstam's vivid interpretation, allied to Ondine's sumptuous recording, glows through its 20 minutes, Inkinen provides a beautifully focused reading, nearly two minutes swifter, with every detail brought out to telling effect.

Not the most gripping of Rautavaara's recent orchestral essays *Manhattan Trilogy* is nonetheless accomplished. What connects it to the Third Symphony (1959-61) is the treatment of the past. The symphony – one of the finest of the post-war period, serially organised within a vibrant tonal framework – recreates the idiom of Bruckner from a late-1950s sensibility and, ironically, remains the more progressive.

Rautavaara's most recent symphony, the Eighth (1999), was memorably recorded by Segerstam (Ondine). Inkinen once again produces a refined interpretation with crystal-clear detail although Segerstam achieved more grandeur in the peroration. Choice here really will depend on couplings (the Harp Concerto on Ondine). The revision of the Sixth Symphony's finale as a – presumably – stand-alone concert piece shorn of its part for synthesiser works well enough, though it is no substitute for the whole work, for which turn to Max Pommer's bracing account (also with the Helsinki Philharmonic) for Ondine. In context, though, the Naxos programme works most effectively and is a near-perfect introduction to Rautavaara's late manner. Both discs are highly recommendable; at its price, the Naxos is hard to beat but Ondine has the Third. Buy both!

Symphonies

Symphony No 1. Book of Visions. Adagio celeste
National Orchestra of Belgium / Mikko Franck
Ondine ⊚ ODE1064-5 (76' · DDD)   Ⓕ

Rautavaara's First Symphony, written in 1955 in four movements, was recast in 1988 – not wholly convincingly – as a diptych. In 2003 Rautavaara added a new slow movement based on a song composed in the 1950s. The result is better balanced and Mikko Franck's account has considerable poise.

Rautavaara's euphonious late style is perfectly adapted for visionary slow movements, so it may surprise that *Adagio celeste* (1997, given here in its 2000 version) is based on a 12-note row. More relevantly, it is derived from a sensuous romantic poem by Lassi Nummi: it is broadly languorous in tone with a strong undertow.

Wonderfully subtle is an apt description for the four-movement *Book of Visions* (2003, rev 2005). Running to a full 40 minutes, the work superficially has a Henzian ground plan with its succession of four tales of 'Night', 'Fire', 'Love' and 'Fate'. However, its internal processes, while organic, have goals other than the symphonic and it calls to mind Lutosławski's *Livre pour orchestre* (however stylistically remote). Its emotional vision is the most intense of the works here, much of it autobiographical in essence. Franck proves a most sympathetic interpreter and draws fine playing from the National Orchestra of Belgium. Excellent sound.

Symphony No 7, 'Angel of Light'. Annunciations
Kari Jussila *org* **Helsinki Philharmonic Orchestra / Leif Segerstam**
Ondine ODE869-2 (65' · DDD)   Ⓕ**O**

The Seventh Symphony's opening *Tranquillo* evokes a calm though powerful atmosphere, with many Sibelian points of reference, especially in recognisable echoes of the *Largo* fourth movement from Sibelius's Fourth Symphony, whereas the closing *Pesante-cantabile* is more in line with the symphonic world of Hovhaness. The Angel idea originates in a series of works (*Angels and Visitations* and *Angel of Dusk*, for instance), the reference being to 'an archetype, one of mankind's oldest traditions and perennial companions'. This Jungian axis is reflected in monolithic chords, ethereal harmonic computations (invariably broad and high-reaching) and an unselfconscious mode of musical development. Readers schooled in the more contemplative works of Górecki, Pärt and Tavener will likely respond to this spatially generous essay, though Rautavaara's language is more a celebration of nature than any specific religious ritual.

Comparisons with the *Annunciations* (for organ, brass quintet, wind orchestra and percussion) find the earlier work far harsher in tone, much more demanding technically (it calls for a formidable organ virtuoso) and more radical in its musical language. The style ranges from the primeval drone that opens the work through canon, 'bird forest' activity and the novel effect of having the 'notes of a dense chord weirdly circulating in the room' when the organ motor is switched off. Kari Jussila rises to the various challenges with what sounds like genuine enthusiasm (his fast fingerwork is amazing) while Leif Segerstam and his orchestra exploit the tonal drama of both works. The recordings are warm and spacious.

String Quartets

String Quartets Nos 1 & 2. String Quintet, 'Unknown Heavens'
Jan-Erik Gustafsson *vc* **Jean Sibelius Quartet**
(Yoshiko Arai-Kimanen, Jukka Pohjola *vns* Matti Hirvikangas *va* Seppo Kimanen *vc*)
Ondine ODE909-2 (62' · DDD)   Ⓕ

Here we encounter not one Rautavaara, but three: the fledgling student captivated by folklore; the dodecaphonic zealot stretching the expressive potential of 'the system'; and the triumphant melodist basking in his own unique brand of harmonic complexity. The stylistic leap from the Second Quartet to the Quintet, or *Unknown Heavens* is more a matter of tone than temperament. All three works are ceaselessly active, the First (1952) being perhaps the leanest, and the last (1997) the richest in texture. *Unknown Heavens* takes its name from an earlier work for male chorus, which Rautavaara quotes, initially in the second bar of the first movement ('when the second violin answers the question opposed by the first,' as Rautavaara writes), many times thereafter, and then significantly revised at the start of the fourth movement. The third begins as a cello duet, sure justification of why five players are employed where the Kuhmo Music Festival originally commissioned a piece for four. 'The work seemed to acquire a will of its own,' writes Rautavaara. The equally well-performed string quartets are stylistically rather more challenging. The First Quartet plays for just over 11 minutes and inhabits a mildly rustic world roughly akin to Kodály. Best here is the *Andante*'s haunting coda, whereas the 1958 Second Quartet is at its most inventive for the faster second and fourth movements. The current Rautavaara is more relaxed, more contemplative, wiser and softer-grained than his former self. He seems happier reflecting nature than organising abstract patterns: you sense that the Quintet is authentically self-expressive, whereas the quartets speak interestingly about nothing in particular. The recordings are full-bodied and well balanced.

Piano Works

Etudes, Op 42. Icons, Op 6. Partita, Op 34. Piano Sonatas – No 1, 'Christus und die Fischer', Op 50; No 2, 'The Fire Sermon', Op 64. Seven Preludes, Op 7
Laura Mikkola pf
Naxos 8 554292 (61' · DDD)   Ⓕ➔

The most interesting aspect of hearing piano music by a composer known primarily for his orchestral work is in spotting those inimitable harmonic fingerprints that help define his musical personality. Rautavaara's piano music is full of tell-tale signs, even in an early work like the Op 7 *Preludes*, where he indulged a sort of clandestine protest against the 'neo-classical' confines he experienced in Helsinki and America. Rautavaara was studying with Copland at the time but chose to keep his *Preludes* to himself. And yet it's Copland's Piano Sonata that spontaneously comes to mind during the austere opening of his 'The Black Madonna of Blakernaya' from *Icons*, perhaps the most striking of all his solo piano works. The translucent colours in 'The Baptism of Christ' make a profound effect, as does the serenity of 'The Holy Women at the Sepulchre'. Aspects of 'angels' seem prophetically prevalent – whether consciously or not – in the *Etudes* of 1969. Each piece tackles a different interval: thirds in the first, sevenths in the second, then tritones, fourths, seconds and fifths. The third is reminiscent of Messiaen, and the fifth of Bartók, but Rautavaara's guiding hand is everywhere in evidence. Spirituality is an invariable presence, especially in the two piano sonatas, though the Second ends with an unexpected bout of contrapuntal brutality. Perhaps the most instantly appealing track is the brief but touching central movement of the three-and-a-half minute *Partita*, Op 34, with its gentle whiffs of Bartók. Laura Mikkola plays all 28 movements with obvious conviction. Naxos's recorded sound is excellent.

Choral works

'Complete Works for Male Choir'
Tuomas Katajala ten **Talla Vocal Ensemble / Pasi Hyökki; YL Male Voice Choir / Matti Hyökki**
Ondine ② ODE1125-2D (99' · DDD · T/t)   Ⓜ

YL divide up the works between the main body and their 10-man offshoot, the Talla Vocal Ensemble – the latter, incidentally, are superb in the two *TS Eliot Preludes* (1956, rev 1967). Ondine's recording is rich, with great presence, matched by singing of urgency and vividness. And YL and Talla's interpretations have impetus and power, as in the half-hour-long *A Book of Life* (1972), which is split between the two groups (as are the *Four Serenades*, 1978), setting 11 poems – including texts by Rilke, Rimbaud, Goethe, Emily Dickinson and Whitman – in five languages.

The greater textural palette attained through using two differently sized choirs is more akin to that found in some early-music recordings. Perhaps there's a loss of intimacy and a certain dreamy quality – for instance in the Psalms (1968-71) or some of the folksong arrangements. But this is a small price to pay for the gains which, for collectors of Rautavaara, will chiefly be the quartets of songs to poems by Aleksis Kivi (arr 2005) or from the opera *Rasputin* (arr 2006), not otherwise issued.

Aleksis Kivi

Aleksis Kivi
Jorma Hynninen bar Aleksis Kivi **Lasse Pöysti** spkr
August Ahlqvist; **Eeva-Liisa Saarinen** mez Charlotta
Helena Juntunen sop Hilda **Gabriel Suovanen** bar
Young Aleksis **Marcus Groth** buffo JL Runeberg **Lassi Virtanen** ten Mikko Vilkastus **Jaako Kietikko** bass
Uncle Sakeri **Jyväskylä Sinfonia / Markus Lehtinen**
Ondine ② ODE1000-2D (98' · DDD · T/t)   Ⓕ

Idyll turned to nightmare, optimism to disillusionment, creative fruitfulness to barren schizophrenia and premature death. The tragic fate of the founder of Finnish-language literature has haunted Rautavaara ever since his youth. The opera *Aleksis Kivi* (1995-6) was the melodious crystallisation of a lifetime's pondering. Kivi (1834-72) was active while Swedish words still predominated in Finnish literature, the Finnish poet Johan Ludvig Runeberg having been the best-known Swedish-language exponent of the genre. Kivi's descent from lyrical flights of pastoral fancy to mental derangement was caused in part by damning assessments of his work from the poet and aesthetician August Ahlqvist, the only speaking role in the opera. Ahlqvist is portrayed here by the actor Lasse Pöysti, whose rhythmically inflected recitation is utterly bewitching. Musically *Aleksis Kivi* calls on a varied array of styles. The Prologue depicts Kivi as despondent, despairing and deranged, the music dark and grainy, with a reptilian clarinet in the foreground and a skilfully deployed synthesiser. The scoring is economical throughout (strings, clarinets, percussion) but those who gravitate most readily to his 'angel' orchestral works will likely respond best to the First Act, music filled with mellow light which reflects, in its rich, constantly shifting hues, the protagonist's inspirational flights. The performance is consistently good, the mezzo Eeva-Liisa Saarinen excelling as Charlotta. Confidently conducted, keenly played and vividly recorded, *Aleksis Kivi* is a powerful narrative written with the kind of descriptive facility that Bartók employed for *Bluebeard's Castle*.

Maurice Ravel   French 1875-1937

Ravel's father's background was Swiss and his mother's Basque, but he was brought up in Paris, where he studied at the Conservatoire, 1889-95, returning in 1897 for further study with Fauré and Gédalge. In 1893 he met Chabrier and Satie, both of whom were influential. A decade later he was an established composer, at least of songs and piano pieces, working with luminous precision in a style that could imitate Lisztian bravura (Jeux d'eau) or Renaissance calm (Pavane pour une infante défunte); there was also the String Quartet, somewhat in the modal style of Debussy's but more ornately instrumented. However, he five times failed to win the Prix de Rome (1900-1905) and left the Conservatoire to continue as a freelance musician.

During the next decade he was at his most productive. There was a rivalry with Debussy but Ravel's taste for sharply defined ideas and closed formal units was entirely his own, as was the grand virtuosity of much of his piano music from this period, notably the cycles Miroirs and Gaspard de la nuit. Many works show his fascination with things temporally or geographically distant, with moods sufficiently alien to be objectively drawn: these might be historical musical styles, as in the post-Schubertian Valses nobles et sentimentales, or the imagination of childhood, as in Ma mère l'oye, the East (Shéhérazade) or on Spain (Rapsodie espagnole, the comic opera L'heure espagnole) or even ancient Greece in the languorous ballet Daphnis et Chloé, written for Diaghilev.

Diaghilev's Ballets Russes were also important in introducing him to Stravinsky, with whom he collaborated on a version of Mussorgsky's Khovanshchina, and whose musical development he somewhat paralleled during the decade or so after The Rite of Spring. The set of three Mallarmé songs with nonet accompaniment were written partly under the influence of Stravinsky's Japanese Lyrics and Schoenberg's Pierrot lunaire, and the two sonatas of the 1920s can be compared with Stravinsky's abstract works of the period in their harmonic astringency and selfconscious use of established forms.

However, Ravel's Le tombeau de Couperin predates Stravinsky's neo-classicism, and the pressure of musical history is perhaps felt most intensely in the ballet La valse where 3/4 rhythm develops into a dance macabre: both these works, like many others, exist in both orchestral and piano versions, testifying

to Ravel's superb technique in both media (in 1922 he applied his orchestral skills tellingly to Mussorgsky's Pictures at an Exhibition). Other postwar works return to some of the composer's obsessions: with the delights and dangers of the child's world (the sophisticated fantasy opera L'enfant et les sortilèges), Spanishness (Boléro and the songs for a projected Don Quixote film), and the exotic (Chansons madécasses). His last major effort was a pair of piano concertos, one exuberant and cosmopolitan (in G), the other (for left hand only) more darkly and sturdily single-minded. Ravel died after a long illness.

Piano Concertos

Piano Concerto in G[ab]. Piano Concerto for the Left Hand[ac]. Valses nobles et sentimentales (orch cpsr)[b]
[a]**Krystian Zimerman** pf [b]**Cleveland Orchestra,**
[c]**London Symphony Orchestra / Pierre Boulez**
DG 449 213-2GH (56' · DDD)   ⓕ**OOO**➔

Zimerman's pianism is self-recommending. His trills in the first movement of the G major Concerto are to die for, his passagework in the finale crystal-clear, never hectic, always stylish. For their part Boulez and the Clevelanders are immaculate and responsive; they relish Ravel's neon-lit artificiality and moments of deliberate gaudiness. That goes equally for the *Valses nobles*, which have just about every nuance you'd want, and none you wouldn't. The recording is generous with ambience, to the point where some orchestral entries after big climaxes are blurred. Otherwise detail is razor-sharp and one of the biggest selling-points of the disc. Zimerman's humming may be a slight distraction for some listeners, especially in the Left-Hand Concerto, where you may not be always convinced that the LSO knew quite what it was supposed to do with the long notes of the main theme, and where there's a slight lack of tension in exchanges between piano and orchestra. There again, had the G major Concerto not been so wonderful those points might not have registered at all, for this is playing of no mean distinction. In the Left-Hand Concerto, Zimerman's phenomenal pianism sets its own agenda and brings its own rich rewards.

Orchestral Works

Boléro. Pavane pour une infante défunte. Daphnis et Chloé – Suite No 2. Ma mère l'oye – Pavane de la Belle au bois dormant; Les entretiens de la belle et la bête; Petit Poucet; Laideronnette, Impératrice des Pagodes; Apothéose: Le Jardin féerique
Cincinnati Symphony Orchestra / Paavo Järvi
Telarc CD80601 (63' · DDD)   ⓕ**OOO**

Most of this disc is very enjoyable. Järvi is always in absolute control, and one or two moments of unscheduled *rubato* in *La valse* can be forgiven, such was the tact and intelligence with which they were

RAVEL PIANO CONCERTOS – IN BRIEF

Krystian Zimerman; London SO, Cleveland Orchestra / Pierre Boulez
DG 449 213-2GH (56' · DDD)   Ⓕ❍❍❍

Ⓖ A *Gramophone* Award winner in 1999, this truly magnificent achievement enshrines musicianship of the highest calibre. Zimerman is on top form, his pianism quite astonishingly clear and precise and Boulez is a superb accompanist.

Louis Lortie; London SO / Frühbeck de Burgos
Chandos CHAN8773 (57' · DDD)   Ⓕ❍➔

Fine playing and rich, idiomatic accompaniment makes this a fine CD (the coupling is Fauré's *Ballade*). Lortie is best in the Concerto – his Left-Hand Concerto is slightly eccentric – but the sound he makes, and as captured by Chandos is most appealing.

Jean-Philippe Collard; French National Orchestra / Lorin Maazel
EMI 574749-2 (64' · DDD)   Ⓑ❍➔

Another *Gramophone* Award winner – and the version to get if you're watching the pennies. Collard is on sparkling form, and Maazel is in his element in this music. There's real fizz here, and there are some generous solo piano works as coupling.

Anne Quéffelec;
Strasbourg PO / Alain Lombard
Apex 8573 89232-2 (66' · ADD)   Ⓢ❙➔

Coupled with Debussy's *Fantaisie*, Anne Quéffelec gives thoughtful, very delicate performances of the two Ravel concertos and demonstrates why she is so highly regarded. Lombard accompanies sympathetically so if you're looking for these works and you're on a budget this makes a fine alternative to the Collard, more inward-looking, perhaps.

PIANO CONCERTO IN G

Martha Argerich; Berlin PO / Claudio Abbado
DG 447 438-2GGA (71' · ADD)   Ⓕ❍➔

Coupled with a fiery Prokofiev Third Concerto, Argerch's G major Concerto is outstanding, with filligree-textured fingerwork, rhythmic vitality of crystal and a wonderful identification with the work's idiom. A magnificent performance.

Arturo Benedetti Michelangeli;   Ⓗ
Philharmonia / Ettore Gracis
EMI 567238-2 (47' · ADD)   Ⓜ❍❍➔

Simply the classic recording. Michelangeli demonstrates his total sympathy for the work. The Philharmonia on top form in this great disc from 1957. Coupled with Rachmaninov No 4, this is one of EMI's Great Recordings of the Century – and no one would surely question that accolade!

managed. Any conductor must balance the impulse to lilt *à la viennoise* against what appears to be Ravel's implicit instruction not to vary the tempo until around halfway. Järvi does it well and, notably, his speed for the return of the opening is spot on the original, not faster as so often happens.

His *Boléro* is on the quick side, but there's no feeling of scramble, and the only things to miss are the extra trombone slides from Ravel's disc, which unfortunately have never found their way into the score. The *Pavane* is lovely in all respects – steady but not stodgy – and the *Daphnis* suite has all the colour and warmth one could ask for. Just occasionally in *Ma mère l'oye* the balance isn't ideal: in the first movement the cor anglais momentarily obscures the clarinet, and in 'Laideronnette' the piccolo, too, is lost in its lower reaches. The only moment where Järvi's identification with the music seems to falter is with his handling of the 'Retenu/A tempo' marking leading into the final peroration of 'Le jardin féerique'. But these are small points to set against the quality of the whole.

Daphnis et Chloé

Daphnis et Chloé. La valse
Berlin Radio Chorus; Berlin Philharmonic Orchestra / Pierre Boulez
DG 447 057-2GH (71' · DDD)   Ⓕ❍➔

Increasingly, for considering modern recordings of *Daphnis*, it seems you must banish memories of 1959 Monteux; put behind you the most playful, mobile, texturally diaphanous, rhythmically supple account of the score ever recorded; one that's uniquely informed by history and selfless conductorial wisdom. For some, Monteux's view may remain a rather moderate one – certainly in terms of basic tempo and basic dynamic range; and Ravel's score suggests tempos and dynamics which modern performances, and especially recordings, have more faithfully reproduced.

Boulez has acquired a wealth of experience of conductorial wisdom since his first New York recording of *Daphnis*. Here he has the Berlin Philharmonic Orchestra on top form to sustain and shape melody within some of his strikingly slow tempos (such as the opening, and Part 3's famous 'Daybreak'), and who remain 'composed' in his daringly fast ones (the 'Dance of the young girls around Daphnis' and the 'Danse guerrière' – one of the most exciting on disc). Just occasionally, you feel that there are parts of the work that interest him less than others. But anyone who doubts Boulez's ability to achieve, first, a sense of ecstasy should hear this 'Daybreak'; secondly, a refined radiance, should try the first embrace (track 5, 2'49"; at this point, this is also one of the very few recordings where you can hear the chorus); or, thirdly, to characterise properly the supernatural, listen to the 'flickering' accents he gives the string *tremolo* chords in the 'Nocturne'.

The chorus work, not least in the so-called 'Interlude', is outstanding; the harmonic boldness of this passage was just as startling in New York, but the Berlin chorus, unlike the New York one, is here properly set back.

In general, DG's recording strikes exactly the right compromise between clarity and spaciousness, much as Decca's did for Dutoit. With the added lure of an expansive and often massively powerful *La valse* (spectacular timpani), this is now the most recommendable modern *Daphnis* available.

Daphnis et Chloé[a]. Shéhérazade – Ouverture
[a]**MDR Rundfunkchor, Leipzig; Lyon National Orchestra / Jun Märkl**
Naxos 8 570992 (71' · DDD)   ⓈOOB→

This Naxos disc, in dazzling sound, demonstrates that under its latest music director, Jun Märkl, the Lyon National Orchestra's standards remains high. This is one of the most spectacular of showpieces among ballet scores, and the Lyon orchestra gives a powerful and subtle performance, with the wind and brass soloists outstanding.

The Leipzig Radio Choir, which comes from where Märkl was last in charge, adds to the glow of the performance, which can match almost any version in the catalogue. Naxos has again demonstrated its rare ability to produce excellent discs at bargain price. The shimmering sounds of the Daybreak movement are perfectly caught, with the wind nicely defined, and the final Danse générale rounds the performance off thrillingly.

To add to the attractions a substantial fill-up is offered. The Ouverture *Shéhérazade* is a student work but already demonstrates Ravel's gift for creating magical orchestral textures, very reminiscent of Debussy but not entirely derivative with its climactic fanfares leading to a hushed close. It provides a delightful makeweight to an outstanding disc.

Additional recommendation

Daphnis et Chloé
Coupled with: Rapsodie espagnole. Pavane pour une Infante défunte. La valse
London Symphony Orchestra and Chorus / Abbado
DG Trio ③ 469 354-2GTR3 (200' · DDD)   ⓂOB→
A very desirable set, with the LSO putting on its best, totally convincing, French accent. Abbado's *Daphnis et Chloé* is reminiscent of that from Monteux. The sophistication and power of these performances is something to marvel at.

String Quartet in F

Ravel String Quartet **Debussy** String Quartet, Op 10 **Fauré** String Quartet, Op 121
Quatuor Ebène (Pierre Colombet, Gabriel Le

RAVEL'S STRING QUARTET – IN BRIEF

Quartetto Italiano
Philips 464 699-2PM (52' · ADD)   ⓂOB→
One of the cornerstones of the chamber catalogue. The Italians perform with a nimble grace and sense of wonder that never pall. The 1965 recording still sounds good to modern ears.

Vlach Quartet
Supraphon SU3461-2 (56' · ADD)   Ⓜ
An interpretation of uncommon re-creative eagerness and genuine staying power. This distinguished Czech ensemble respond with all the freshness of new discovery. Admirably remastered 1959 sound.

Melos Quartet
DG Galleria 463 082-2GGA (53' · ADD)   ⓂOB→
The Melos always put the music first and have both consumate artistic flair and impeccable technical address to commend them. DG's production-team strike a most natural balance.

Juilliard Quartet
Sony 8279 69262-2 (74' · DDD)   ⒻOO
The Juilliards bring a wealth of experience and enviable sense of purpose to Ravel's masterly quartet. A heartfelt, concentrated reading, beautifully recorded.

Ebène Quartet
Virgin Classics 519045-2 (80' DDD)   ⒻOOOB→
Ⓖ A stunning new recording that approaches perfection. These players are completely inside this miraculous score and play like four angels. Magnificent!

Ad Libitum Quartet
Naxos 8 554722 (57' · DDD)   ⓈB→
An arresting, sparkily individual rendering from this gifted young Romanian group, winners of the 1997 Evian String Quartet Competition. Coupled with a highly perceptive account of Fauré's elusive but alluring Quartet.

Petersen Quartet
Capriccio 10860 (68' · DDD)   Ⓕ
Exceptionally refreshing and articulate music-making. Part of a hugely rewarding programme including Milhaud's First Quartet and attractive works by Chausson and Lekeu.

Belcea Quartet
EMI 574020-2 (71' · DDD)   ⓈOOOB→
Ⓖ An auspicious start to what promises to be a stellar career. Uncommonly well-integrated quartet playing and winner of the Best Debut Recording Prize at the 2001 *Gramophone* Awards.

RAVEL GASPARD DE LA NUIT – IN BRIEF

Martha Argerich
EMI 557101-2 (52' · ADD)   ⒻOO
A wildly exciting concert performance from 1978, with Argerich live in Amsterdam shaving four minutes off the timing of her previous LP version (see below).

Martha Argerich
DG 447 438-2GOR (71' · ADD)   ⓂO➔
For those who prefer studio recordings, Argerich's highly regarded 1974 taping has been added to her famous pairing of the Ravel G major and Prokofiev Third Piano Concertos. This one has both raw passion and wonderfully controlled gradations of touch and tone.

Pierre-Laurent Aimard
Warner Classics ② 2564 62160-2 (59' · DDD)   ⒻOOO➔
Intriguingly coupled with music by Elliott Carter, this disc aligns Ravel with some of the most visionary of 20th composers.

Ivo Pogorelich
DG 463 678-2GOR (73' · ADD)   Ⓜ➔
The unpredictable Pogorelich at his very best, accomplishing miracles of tone colour, refinement and control, with a coruscating final 'Scarbo'. The couplings are both piano sonatas: Prokofiev No 6 and the Chopin B flat minor.

Arturo Benedetti Michelangeli
BBC Legends BBCL4064-2 (78' · ADD)   Ⓕ
A scintillating BBC studio performance of 1959 in which Michelangeli seeks to convey the details of the score with what some hear as inhuman exactitude.

Pascal Rogé
Decca ② 440 836-2DF2 (142' · DDD)   ⓂOO➔
Rogé eschews sensationalism in his elegantly achieved Ravel complete solo piano music. The set includes a *Gaspard* whose relative restraint and Gallic economy won't spoil you for other readings.

Angela Hewitt
Hyperion ② CDA67341/2 (138' · DDD)   Ⓕ
The pellucid qualities of Hewitt's Bach playing are applied to the French master with compelling results in this set. An initially cool, slow-burn *Gaspard* with very clear textures in luminous sound.

Jean-Yves Thibaudet
Decca ② 433 515-2DH2 (130' · DDD)   ⒻO➔
The complete Ravel piano music as pianistic *tour de force*. Thibaudet's high-flying *Gaspard* is given greater impact by the vigour and immediacy of Decca's recording.

Magadure *vns* Mathieu Herzog *va* Raphaël Merlin *vc*)
Virgin Classics 519045-2 (80' · DDD)   ⒻOOO➔

Among the many breathtaking moments on the Ebène Quartet's CD, there is one in particular that keeps calling one back. It occurs at around 1'14" into the Ravel's slow movement, the second set, which enters like a bittersweet memory before a literal recollection of the Quartet's opening motif. Other subtle details of interpretation include the chord at 2'03" that underpins a transformation of the first subject before the same chord leads directly into the second subject – and when it does, utterly changing in character, turning warmer, more openly inviting. The ebb and flow of the passage at 5'29" where the second subject rides above an arpeggiated accompaniment, music that looks both forwards to Debussy's own *La mer* and backwards to Rimsky's *Sheherazade* (or so it seems). There's a fluidity to the Ebène's playing of both works that suits the music's character, a mood of wistfulness too that the Ravel especially benefits from. This improvisatory approach is hardly surprising from an ensemble that is also celebrated for its jazz performances.

It was a brilliant idea to include Fauré's late Quartet which, in a sense, provides the linchpin for all three works, the Ravel having been composed in Fauré's class to mark the 10th anniversary of Debussy's quartet, and which is dedicated to Fauré. An extraordinary work by any standards, ethereal and other-worldly with themes that seem constantly to be drawn skywards, Fauré's Quartet responds well to the Ebène's sensitised approach.

Anyone requiring this particular trio of works won't be disappointed, which makes the various pairings of the Ravel and Debussy quartets on their own seem somewhat less enticing.

Complete Piano Works

Complete Solo Piano Works
Angela Hewitt *pf*
Hyperion ② CDA67341/2 (138' · DDD)   ⒻO

Angela Hewitt's set of Ravel's piano music is a remarkable feat of the most concentrated imaginative delicacy, wit and style. Fresh from her success in Bach she shows how such prowess – namely a scrupulous regard for the score, an acute ear for part-writing, for polyphony, and for meticulous clarity and refinement – can bring extensive rewards. Everything in her performances betokens the greatest care and a special empathy for Ravel's neo-Classicism, for his way of paying affectionate tribute to the past while spicing its conventions with a wholly modern sensibility. Everything in the *Pavane* is subtly graded and textured, the pedalling light and discreet, with a special sense of luminous poetry when the theme makes its final and magical reappearance. No distorting idiosyncrasy is allowed within distance of *Le tombeau de Cou-*

perin, yet nothing is taken for granted.

Her *Gaspard* is a marvel of evocation through precision. Gone are old-fashioned vagueness and approximation: her 'Le gibet' is surely among the most exquisitely controlled on record. Again, her opening to 'Scarbo' is alive with menace because all four of Ravel's directions are so precisely observed; and if she's too sensible to yearn for, say, Martha Argerich's chilling virtuoso *frisson* she makes no concessions to wildness, impetuosity or telescoped phrasing. Nothing is done in the heat of the moment; she keeps Ravel's nightmare under control rather than allowing it to engulf her.

Yet Hewitt can be as romantically yielding as she's exact. In the return of the principal idea from 'Oiseaux tristes' (*Miroirs*) she achieves an extraordinary sense of stillness, of 'birds lost in the sombre torpor of a tropical forest'.

Hyperion's sound is of demonstration quality. Hewitt joins Gieseking, Rogé, Thibaudet and Lortie among the most distinguished if entirely different Ravel cycles on record, and easily withstands comparison.

Gaspard de la nuit

Ravel Gaspard de la nuit **Carter** Night Fantasies. Two Diversions. 90+
Pierre-Laurent Aimard pf
Warner Classics ② 2564 62160-2 (59' · DDD)
Includes bonus CD with illustrated talk by Pierre-Laurent Aimard Ⓕ   Ⓕ**OOO**🅑

One could expect Pierre-Laurent Aimard's account of *Gaspard de la nuit* to have pleased the composer mightily: totally focused and attentive to the text, scrupulously controlled in sound and movement, the articulation of the continuity as Ravel insisted it should be, that's to say with the unity of time preserved, in all three pieces. No otiose slowings. Nothing imposed, only revealed. Be expressive, be dazzling, be magical, be a virtuoso story-teller, but get on with it (as Ravel might have said), and above all play in time.

With the composer looking over his shoulder, the pianist might murmur that there's also the little matter of taking care of every note, intellectually and technically, and of being able not only to play them but to conjure a range of sonority and a rhythmic context in which everything happens at the right time. Aimard might agree that *Gaspard de la nuit*, consisting as it does of three highly contrasted pieces, is not just hugely demanding but an encyclopedic work, in the sense that the performance of it is the measure of all the artistic and technical qualities of the mature player. Difficult to over-praise his achievement here for its freshness and authority and the impeccable pianistic address, and the only reservation, a very small one, has to do with the lack of a touch of fury, or frenzy, in his characterisation of 'Scarbo': the dwarf is a hideous little devil, not just a mischievous one…

The conjunction of Ravel and Elliott Carter may not be attractive to everyone but Aimard

sees a commitment to new music as part of his job; would that there were more artists like him. On a bonus disc Aimard talks well about how the Carter pieces are made, and for people unfamiliar with them this could be a way in. How Carter's pieces are made is very much their raison d'être: his is predominantly a music of lines, of contrapuntal voices highly differentiated in character and movement and in their stability one against another, and how these may be built into structures rich in polyrhythmic effects.

Night Fantasies is the major work for piano of Carter's maturity, and it has a lot going on. It's admirable but unmemorable, masterly music which offers much to the mind but not enough refreshment to the spirit, as if a dimension were missing. The three shorter pieces, in which the play of invention is delightful in itself, raise expectations less and satisfy them more. But in Carter, as in Ravel, Aimard's advocacy is wonderful. The excellent recording derives from the large hall of the Konzerthaus in Vienna; the acoustic has character and the sound is at an apt distance.

Gaspard de la nuit. Valses nobles et sentimentales. Jeux d'eau. Miroirs. Sonatine. Le tombeau de Couperin. Prélude. Menuet sur le nom de Haydn. A la manière de Borodine. Menuet antique. Pavane pour une infante défunte. A la manière de Chabrier. Ma mère l'oye[a]
Pascal Rogé, [a]**Denise-Françoise Rogé** pfs
Double Decca ② 440 836-2DF2 (142' · ADD)
Recorded 1973-94   Ⓜ**OO**🅑

Everything is expressed with a classic restraint, elegance and economy, an ideal absence of artifice or idiosyncrasy. Rogé knows precisely where to allow asperity to relax into lyricism and vice versa, and time and again he finds that elusive, cool centre at the heart of Ravel's teeming and luxuriant vision. True, those used to more Lisztian but less authentic Ravel may occasionally find Rogé diffident or *laissez-faire*. But lovers of subtlety will see him as illuminating and enchanting. How often do you hear *Ma mère l'oye* given without a trace of brittleness or archness, or find *Jeux d'eau* presented with such stylish ease and tonal radiance? Rogé may lack something of Thibaudet's menace and high-flying virtuosity in 'Scarbo' (also on Decca) but how memorably he re-creates Ravel's nocturnal mystery. Even if one misses a touch of cruelty behind Ondine's entreaty, few pianists can have evoked her watery realm with greater transparency. Arguably one of the finest Ravel recordings available.

Miroirs

Ravel Miroirs **Schumann** Kreisleriana
Herbert Schuch pf
Oehms OC541 (64' · DDD)   Ⓕ**OO**

Herbert Schuch is a 27-year-old Romanian whose recording debut is of an intimidating mas-

RAVEL SHEHERAZADE – IN BRIEF

Régine Crespin
Suisse Romande Orchestra / Ernest Ansermet
Decca 460 973-2   Ⓕ❍❍❍➔
Sultry, langourous yet sung with a richness of tone, this is a classic version this ravishing work. Ansermet accompanies exquisitely.

Susan Graham
BBC Symphony Orchestra / Yan Pascal Tortelier
Warner Classics 2564 61938-2   Ⓕ❍❍➔
Coupled with Chausson's delicious *Poème de la mer et de l'amour*, here's a *Shéhérazade* to cherish with a wonderful range of colours and emotions.

Anne Sofie von Otter
Cleveland Orchestra / Pierre Boulez
DG 471 614-2GH   Ⓕ❍➔
Von Otter is making quite reputation in French music and this glorious disc merely enhances that reknown. Her singing is magnificently controlled and coloured and Boulez is a superb partner

Felicity Lott
Suisse Romande Orchestra / Armin Jordan
Aeon AECD0314   Ⓕ
A lighter voiced *Shéhérazade* than usual, but the delicacy of Lott's approach is very attractive and Armin Jordan accompanies with typical style and the Geneva orchestra recalls the Crespin version with its full tone. The couplings are Chausson and Duparc

Elisabeth Söderström
BBC Symphony Orchestra / Pierre Boulez
BBC Legends BBCL4153-2   Ⓜ❍
Caught live in London's Royal Albert Hall, Söderström gives a performance to rival the best letting her voice soar from smokey mezzo to translucent soprano. Boulez makes the orchestral accompaniment shimmer with colour. A fascinating and mesmerising performance.

Kiri Te Kanawa
Brussels National Opera Orchestra / Jeffrey Tate
EMI 586652-2   Ⓑ
It's hard not to warm to Te Kanawa's rich, luxurious soprano and she rides the orchestral line with glorious ease. She doesn't dig as deep into the text as many other sopranos.

Victoria de Los Angeles
Orchestre de la Société des Concerts du Conservatoire / Georges Prêtre
EMI Great Recordings of the Century 3458242   Ⓜ❍➔
De Los Angeles brings all the langour, poetry and irony to this entrancing cycle: her Spanish passion bringing something special.

tery and stylistic assurance. Wherever you turn in the intricate mosaic of Schumann's *Kreisleriana* you will hear playing impossible to fault and easy to praise. The opening upsurge is truly *agitatissimo*, as boldly coloured and inflected as the magically chiming central section is spun off with a special inwardness and insight. The *sehr langsam* and its following, flowing *bewegter* could hardly be phrased more eloquently; and if the pace of No 7 is wild, the control is absolute. Schuch is no less immaculate in Ravel's *Miroirs*. Never for an instant do you hear the sort of diffidence or nonchalance that often passes for an authentic French style. 'Alborada del gracioso' is thrown off with the most concentrated verve and brilliance and the final ascent in 'Noctuelles' is a marvel of pianissimo delicacy and precision. Every chord in 'La vallée des cloches' is weighted and textured to perfection. Such playing has been faultlessly groomed for competition success (Schuch has won three international events in a year) and if there is an occasional suspicion that one is listening to an overly calculating if superlative pianist rather than a more spontaneous and acute artist, this is never less than a magnificent album. Oehms's sound is admirable.

Songs

Ravel Shéhérazade. Menuet antique. Pavane pour une infante défunte. Le Tombeau de Couperin. **Debussy** Danse sacrée et danse profane. Trois Ballades de François Villon. Cinq Poèmes de Charles Baudelaire – Le jet d'eau
Alison Hagley *sop* **Anne Sofie von Otter** *mez*
Cleveland Orchestra / Pierre Boulez
DG 471 614-2GH (76' · DDD · T/t)   Ⓕ❍❍➔

Anne Sofie von Otter is really exploiting the French repertory nowadays. After her Mélisande and Carmen, and Chaminade and Offenbach recitals, here she tackles Ravel's *Shéhérazade* with total success. From the first cry of 'Asie' in the opening song, von Otter beguiles using a hushed, yet expectant quality. Throughout her soft singing is exquisite. The balance between voice and orchestra has all the subtlety this extended prologue requires. At the sinister line, 'Je voudrais voir des assassins', she employs a harsh edge to the voice that's immediately echoed in the orchestral climax. As the poet describes the story-telling, Boulez brings the song to its end with a perfect *diminuendo*, leading into the mysterious 'Flute enchantée'. Here again von Otter's control of dynamics pays off with a gorgeous 'mysterieux baiser'.

The final song is also the most difficult. In its ambiguity, 'L'indifférent' mustn't be overstressed, and yet that ironic remark at the end, 'Ta démarche feminine et lasse' needs to be not so much regretful as a sigh of half-amused resignation.

Le Tombeau de Couperin, in its orchestral version, is an equally difficult challenge which Boulez and the Cleveland orchestra bring off with precision. With the other two orchestral arrangements of piano pieces, the *Pavane* and the *Menuet Antique*, again Boulez achieves such clarity that even these over-familiar works sound surprising and fresh.

The Debussy *Danses*, for harp and strings, serve as a sort of interlude, leading into the other three-song event, the *Trois Ballades de François Villon*. These are so often sung by a baritone; indeed, they were premiered by Jean Périer, the first Pelléas, so it's a slight jolt to hear them done by a soprano. Alison Hagley deals well enough with what Jane Bathori used to call the 'rough and quite choppy' vocal lines of the first song, 'Ballade de Villon à s'amye', but the fuller, darker tones of a baritone might be more appropriate in the central prayer. The account of the chattering wives of Paris brings the programme to a merry conclusion. The disc is a most enjoyable combination of orchestral music and song. The sound throughout is exceptionally vivid, and Boulez, the orchestra and his soloists provide exemplary performances at almost every turn: heartily recommended.

Chants populaires – Chanson française; Chanson italienne; Chanson hébraïque; Chanson écossaise. Don Quichotte à Dulcinée. Deux epigrammes de Clément Marot. Un Grand sommeil noir. Les Grands vents venus d'outre-mer. Histoires naturelles. Deux Mélodies hébraïques. Cinq mélodies populaires grecques. Noël des jouets. Ronsard à son âme. Sur l'herbe
Gerald Finley bar **Julius Drake** pf
Hyperion CDA67728 (71' · DDD · T/t) Ⓕ◐

There is a vast gulf between the bibulous bravado of the 'Chanson à boire' that Ravel included in his *Don Quichotte à Dulcinée* songs and the bleak, dark despair of his Verlaine setting *Un Grand sommeil noir*. Placing them next to one another in this fine selection of over two dozen songs emphasises the broad expressive range that Ravel was able to embrace. It also throws into focus the way that Gerald Finley and Julius Drake can so evocatively tap their emotional substance.

These exquisitely crafted miniatures, whether in the folk-inspired *Chants populaires* and *Cinq mélodies populaires grecques* or in the tender *Noëls des jouets* to a text of Ravel's own, show his creative fastidiousness in a consistently positive light: the mood might be robust or rarefied, but Ravel's sense of colour and atmosphere is infallible. The imagery of the *Histoires naturelles*, for example, testifies to Ravel's intuitive response to poetry and to his precise placing of the tonal brushstrokes. In this respect, the piano is an essential collaborator, etching in the background for the gliding grace of the swan or the chirping of the cricket.

Drake draws the ear ineluctably into Ravel's imaginative world, as he does elsewhere in the cool restraint of *Ronsard à son âme* or the turbulence and shifting currents of *Les Grands Vents venus d'outremer*. Finley's mellifluous, malleable baritone is similarly an ideal match for this rep-

ertoire, with lines eloquently floated, nuances subtly voiced and character sensitively defined. This is a beguiling programme, beautifully performed.

Operas

L'enfant et les sortilèges
Magdalena Kožená *mez* L'Enfant **Annick Massis** *sop* Le Feu; La Princesse; La Rossignol **Nathalie Stutzmann** *contr* Maman; La Tasse Chinoise; La Libellule **Sophie Koch** *mez* La Bergère; La Chatte; L'Ecurieul; Un Pâtre **José van Dam** *bar* La Fauteuil; Un Arbre **François Le Roux** *bar* L'Horloge Comtoise; Le Chat **Jean-Paul Fouchécourt** *ten* La Théière; Le Petit Viellard; La Rainette **Mojca Erdmann** *sop* Une Pastorelle; La Chauve-souris; La Chouette

Ma Mère l'Oye
Berlin Philharmonic Orchestra / Sir Simon Rattle
EMI 264197-2 (73' · DDD) ◗▷

L'enfant et les sortilèges[a]
L'Enfant **Geneviève Després** *mez* Maman; La Libellule; L'Ecureuil **Kirsten Gunlogson** *mez* La Tasse Chinoise; Un Pâtre; La Chatte **Philippe Castagner** *ten* La Théière; La Petit Viellard; La Rainette **Ian Greenlaw** *bar* L'Horloge Comtoise; Le Chat **Kevin Short** *bass-bar* Le Fauteuil; Un Arbre **Agathe Martel** *sop* La Princesse; La Chauve-souris **Cassandre Prévost** *sop* Le Feu; Le Rossignol **Julie Cox** *sop* La Bergère; Une Pastourelle; La Chouette

Shéhérazade
Julie Boulianne *mez* [a]**Chattanooga Boys Choir**; [a]**Chicago Symphony Chorus**; **Nashville Symphony** [a]**Chorus and Orchestra / Alastair Willis**
Naxos 8 660215 (64' · DDD) Ⓢ▷

In many ways *L'enfant et les sortilèges* is an ideal opera for recording. The imagination can create stage pictures of the fire, the shepherds, the trees and the animals, and a balance between orchestra and voice is possible that will do justice to Ravel's orchestral effects – what Ned Rorem once called 'lusciously carefree, with its daft blues and dizzy foxtrots'. These two new additions to the catalogue will not displace three classic recordings that have held the field for decades – those conducted by Ernest Bour (Testament), Ernest Ansermet (Decca) and Lorin Maazel (DG).

However, both have strong casts and are very well recorded. Simon Rattle has long held the work in affection. In the new recording his approach is somewhat more symphonic, especially compared with the Naxos CD, taken from a live performance in Nashville, which has a slightly earthier feel to it. The line-up of soloists in Berlin could hardly be starrier but the American group does not lose face in comparison. The roles are shared out differently. Ravel stipulated that the same singer ought to sing the Fire, the Princess and the Nightingale – as Annick Massis does for Rattle, whereas in Nashville these are shared between Cassandre Prévost and Agathe

Martel. As the child, Magdalena Kožená manages to seem suitably boyish and wilful, Julie Boulianne has a more mature sound. The fill-up items are well chosen: *Ma Mère l'Oye*, lusciously played by the Berlin Philharmonic for Rattle, *Shéhérazade* done with feeling by Boulianne for Alastair Willis and the Nashville Symphony.

Alan Rawsthorne   British 1905-1971

Rawsthorne studied as a pianist at the Royal College of Music and abroad with Petri; only at the end of the 1930s did he begin to make a name as a composer. Influenced by Hindemith, he developed a highly crafted and abstract style, chiefly in concertos and other orchestral works. His inclination towards motivic thinking and variation structures brought some approximation to 12-note techniques, but tonal centres remained important. He wrote three symphonies (1950, 1959, 1964), two piano concertos (1939, 1951), two violin concertos (1948, 1956), three string quartets (1939, 1954, 1964) and sonatas for viola, cello and violin. GROVEmusic

Piano Concertos

Piano Concertos – No 1; No 2. Improvisations on a theme by Constant Lambert
Peter Donohoe pf **Ulster Orchestra / Takuo Yuasa**
Naxos 8 555959 (57' · DDD)   Ⓢ⒪▷

Rawsthorne's First Piano Concerto, originally written with just strings and percussion accompaniment, was introduced in its later full orchestral form at a 1942 Promenade Concert by Louis Kentner. The Second was commissioned by the Arts Council for the 1951 Festival of Britain and premiered by Clifford Curzon in the then-new Royal Festival Hall. He later recorded it with Sargent and the LSO on a 10-inch LP for Decca. *The Record Guide*'s review commented on the 'open air tune in the finale with an instant appeal' and suggested the work would achieve the 'wide popularity it certainly deserves'. Alas that never came about. Peter Donohoe plays the First with an effervescent lightness of touch that emphasises the *scherzando* element of the first movement. Yuasa provides witty orchestral detail – there's an engaging contribution from the bassoon – and yet still finds the underlying lyrical melancholy. He opens the Chaconne hauntingly, and the following dialogue with the piano has a compelling delicacy. The Tarantella finale brings an infectious élan and splendid momentum. Donohoe's brilliant solo contribution has all the sparkle you could want, and the gentle pay-off of the brief coda is neatly managed.

In the Second Concerto the fluidity of Donohoe's playing is particularly appealing, and the overall balance – though the opening flute solo is perhaps a little recessive – is mostly admirable. Donohoe and Yuasa deftly manage the quixotic changes of mood of the initally 'rather violent'

Scherzo (the composer's description) and lead naturally into the wistful *Adagio semplice*, with its nostagic clarinet cantilena answered so exquisitely by the piano.

The *Improvisations* are based on a seven-note theme from Lambert's last ballet, *Tiresias*. They are widely varied in mood and style, and, even though Rawsthorne flirts with serialism, the variations are friendly and easy to follow, and the listener's attention is always fully engaged. Certainly this Naxos disc can be strongly recommended, especially to those who have not yet before encountered Rawsthorne's always rewarding music.

Cello Concerto

Symphonic Studies. Oboe Concerto[a]. Cello Concerto[b]
[a]**Stéphane Rancourt** ob [b]**Alexander Baillie** vc
Royal Scottish National Orchestra / David Lloyd-Jones
Naxos 8 554763 (72' · DDD)   ⓈⓄ○▷

David Lloyd-Jones directs a swaggering, affectionate and ideally clear-headed account of Rawsthorne's masterly *Symphonic Studies* (1939), one of the most stylish and exuberantly inventive products of British music from the first half of the last century. The work's formal elegance, impeccable craftsmanship and healthy concision are exhilarating. It's an impressively assured orchestral début, its tightly knit 20-minute span evincing a remarkable emotional scope. The present performance is a great success, a worthy successor, to both Lambert's classic 1946 Philharmonia version (now happily restored on Pearl) and Pritchard's admirable 1975 Lyrita recording with the LPO.

First heard at the 1947 Cheltenham Festival, the Concerto for Oboe and String Orchestra was composed for Evelyn Rothwell. Brimful of gentle melancholy, it's another delectably clean-cut creation, whose touchingly eloquent first movement is succeeded by a wistfully swaying, at times cryptic *Allegretto con morbidezza* and a spirited, though never entirely untroubled *Vivace* finale. Impeccable solo work from RSNO principal oboe Stéphane Rancourt and a spick-and-span accompaniment to match.

There's another first recording in the guise of the Cello Concerto (1965). This is a major achievement, a work to rank beside Rawsthorne's superb Third Symphony and Third String Quartet of the previous year in its unremitting concentration and nobility of expression. A strongly lyrical vein runs through the notably eventful, ever-evolving opening movement, whereas the central *Mesto* mixes dark introspection with outbursts of real anguish. The clouds lift for the rumbustious finale. A substantial, deeply felt utterance, in short, which will surely repay closer study. Soloist Alexander Baillie gives a stunningly idiomatic rendering; Lloyd-Jones and the RSNO offer big-hearted, confident support. Apart from a hint of harshness in the very loudest *tutti*s of the *Symphonic Studies*, Tim Handley's engineering is immensely vivid and always musically balanced. Overall, a wonderfully enterprising triptych.

Violin Concertos

Violin Concertos Nos 1 & 2. Cortèges – fantasy overture
Rebecca Hirsch *vn* **BBC Scottish Symphony Orchestra / Lionel Friend**
Naxos 8 554240 (64' · DDD)   Ⓢ Ⓞ ▶

Rawsthorne enthusiasts should waste no time in snapping up this disc, containing music-making of perceptive dedication and impressive polish. He completed his First Violin Concerto in 1947, dedicating the score to Walton (there's a quotation from *Belshazzar's Feast* just before the end). Cast in just two movements, it's a lyrically affecting creation that weaves a spell, especially in a performance as dignified and consistently purposeful as this. However, the revelation comes with the Second Concerto of 1956. Rebecca Hirsch and Lionel Friend locate a deceptive urgency and symphonic thrust in the opening *Allegretto* that genuinely compel. If anything, the succeeding *Poco lento* wears an even more anguished, nervy demeanour, the music's questing mood very well conveyed. By contrast, the finale proceeds in serene, almost carefree fashion, its witty coda forming a delightfully unbuttoned conclusion to a striking, much-underrated work. As a curtain-raiser Naxos gives us the fantasy overture *Cortèges*. Commissioned by the BBC and premiered at the 1945 Proms by the LSO under Basil Cameron, it's a well-wrought essay, pitting an eloquent *Adagio* processional as against an irrepressible *Allegro molto vivace* tarantella. The composer develops his material with customary skill, and Friend draws a committed and alert response from the BBC Scottish SO. Boasting a spacious, bright and admirably balanced sound picture (no attempt to spotlight the soloist), here's an enormously rewarding issue and a bargain of the first order.

Concerto for String Orchestra

Concertante pastorale[a]. Concerto for String Orchestra. Divertimento. Elegiac Rhapsody. Light Music. Suite for Recorder and String Orchestra[b] (orch McCabe)
[a]**Conrad Marshall** *fl* [a]**Rebecca Goldberg** *hn* [b]**John Turner** *rec* **Northern Chamber Orchestra / David Lloyd-Jones**
Naxos 8 553567 (64' · DDD)   Ⓢ Ⓞ ▶

The most substantial offering here, the resourceful and magnificently crafted *Concerto for String Orchestra*, dates from 1949. David Lloyd-Jones and his admirably prepared group give a performance which, in its emotional scope and keen vigour, outshines Boult's 1966

recording with the BBC Symphony Orchestra (nla). Not only does Lloyd-Jones achieve a more thrusting urgency in the outer movements, he also locates an extra sense of slumbering tragedy in the *Lento e mesto*. He gives a sparkling account of the immensely engaging *Divertimento*, written for Harry Blech and the London Mozart Players in 1962; the rumbustious concluding 'Jig' is as good a place as any to sample the spick-and-span response of the Northern Chamber Orchestra. The *Concertante pastorale*, written for the Hampton Court Orangery Concerts, is an atmospheric, beautifully wrought 10-minute essay for solo flute, horn and strings. It's succeeded by the perky *Light Music* for strings, composed in 1938 for the Workers' Music Association and based on Catalan folk-tunes. Then there's McCabe's expert orchestration of the miniature Suite for recorder and strings, the second of whose four linked movements is a reworking of a ballad from the *Fitzwilliam Virginal Book*. But the most exciting discovery has to be the 1963-4 *Elegiac Rhapsody*, a deeply felt threnody for string orchestra written in memory of Rawsthorne's friend, the poet Louis MacNeice. Not only does it pack a wealth of first-rate invention and incident into its 10-minute duration, it attains a pitch of anguished expression possibly unrivalled in this figure's entire output.

Symphonies

Symphonies – No 1; No 2, 'A Pastoral Symphony'[a]; No 3
[a]**Charlotte Ellett** *sop* **Bournemouth Symphony Orchestra / David Lloyd-Jones**
Naxos 8 557480 (75' · DDD · T)   Ⓢ Ⓓ ▶

David Lloyd-Jones directs Rawsthorne's three symphonies with evident conviction, and secures a consistently enthusiastic and spruce response from the Bournemouth SO. He improves on Sir John Pritchard's 1975 Lyrita account of the terse, immaculately scored First Symphony (1950), bringing elegant proportion and thrusting purpose. As for its luminous and poignant successor, *A Pastoral Symphony* (1959), honours are more equally divided. Lloyd-Jones distils rather more in the way of gentle melancholy, whereas Nicholas Braithwaite and the LPO on Lyrita achieve the greater poise.

Norman Del Mar's BBC SO version of the imposing Third (1964) has done sterling service down the years, but Lloyd-Jones fully matches its blazing commitment, tying up the symphonic threads to even more clinching effect in the finale (whose peaceful coda recalls material from the opening movement), while distilling every ounce of brooding atmosphere and forceful emotion from the stately tread of the second movement 'Alla Sarabanda'.

A touch of rawness aside, the recording is hugely vivid, offering a pretty much ideal combination of bite and amplitude. The disc represents irresistible value for money.

Film Music

The Captive Heart – Suite. Lease of Life – Main Titles and Emergency. Burma Victory – Suite. Saraband for Dead Lovers – Saraband and Carnival (all arr Schumann). West of Zanzibar – Main Titles. The Cruel Sea – Main Titles and Nocturne. Where No Vultures Fly – Suite. Uncle Silas – Suite. The Dancing Fleece – Three Dances (all arr and orch Lane)
BBC Philharmonic Orchestra / Rumon Gamba
Chandos CHAN9749 (73' · DDD)   Ⓕ**OⒹ**

Incapable of shoddy craftsmanship, and truly a 'composer's composer', Rawsthorne brought a professional integrity, great clarity of expression and unerring economy of thought to every field of music in which he worked, not least the 27 film scores he penned between 1937 and 1964. Here are selections from nine scores in all, the arranging and orchestrating duties being shared by the indefatigable Philip Lane and Gerard Schumann. *The Cruel Sea* (1953) is the best-known offering, its evocative, slumbering power and noble defiance as eloquent as ever. Bernard Herrmann, who knew a thing or two about the genre, rated *Uncle Silas* (1947) one of the greatest film scores he'd ever encountered: try the delightfully flirtatious 'Valse caprice'. The charming 'Three Dances' from *The Dancing Fleece* (a Crown Film Unit production promoting British wool) can almost be viewed as a 'trial run' for *Madame Chrysanthème*, the one-act ballet Rawsthorne wrote in 1955for Sadlers Wells. The first track is an extended (18-minute) suite from the 1946 POW drama, *The Captive Heart*, and there are also generous excerpts from *Where No Vultures Fly* and the documentary *Burma Victory* (full of decidedly superior, stirring invention). Keller was especially complimentary about *Lease of Life* (1954), a Robert Donat vehicle for which Rawsthorne supplied a 'rich miniature score' lasting about 13 and a half minutes, and the collection concludes with a flourish in the shape of the superbly swaggering 'Prelude and Carnival' from *Saraband for Dead Lovers* (1948). Gamba draws playing of panache and infectious enthusiasm from the BBC Philharmonic, with spectacularly wide-ranging Chandos sound. Not to be missed!

Chamber Works

Piano Quintet[a]. Concertante for Violin and Piano[b]. Piano Trio[c]. Viola Sonata[d]. Cello Sonata[e]
[abc]**Nadia Myerscough**, [e]**Mark Messenger** vns [a]**Helen Roberts**, [d]**Martin Outram** vas [ace]**Peter Adams** vc [a]**John McCabe**, [bce]**Yoshiko Endo**, [d]**Julian Rolton** pfs
Naxos 8 554352 (70' · DDD)   Ⓢ**OOⒹ**

Here's a disc brimming with high-quality music and superlative performances. The Piano Quintet, from 1968, is cast in a single continuous movement divided into four contrasting sections. Although only 15 minutes long, the quintet abounds with musical ideas and interest. Much of

the material is vigorous, powerful and concisely presented, but there's much poetry, too, particularly in the *Lento non troppo* section and the brief epilogue that closes the energetic opening section. The *Concertante* for violin and piano is a much earlier work dating from the mid-1930s and, although early influences such as Shostakovich and even Busoni in 'Faustian' mood can be detected, it's perhaps among the earliest of Rawsthorne's works in which his own voice begins to emerge. First performed by the distinguished Menuhin-Cassadó-Kentner Trio, the Piano Trio of 1963 contains much impressive and finely crafted material, as well as a good deal of colourful soloistic writing. The Viola Sonata dates from 1937, but the score was lost shortly after its premiere only to be rediscovered in a Hampstead bookshop and revised in 1954. The Sonata is something of a watershed in Rawsthorne's early output, and shows a considerable advance in style and technique from the *Concertante* of only a few years earlier, and both this and the equally fine Cello Sonata of 1948 are particularly valuable additions to the catalogue. Performances throughout are first class, although John McCabe's commanding reading of the Piano Quintet (he played for the work's premiere) stands out as exceptionally authoritative and compelling.

Jean-Fery Rebel French 1661-1747

After serving the Count of Ayen in Spain, 1700-1705, Rebel became a leading member of the French king's 24 Violons and the Académie Royale de Musique orchestra. He later held court posts including that of chamber composer (from 1726) and was active as a harpsichordist and conductor. An innovatory and esteemed composer, he wrote various vocal works, string sonatas, 'symphonies' for the Académie Royale dancers including Les caractères de la danse (1715), Terpsichore (1720) and the much admired Les elemens (1737), which begins with a famously alarming dissonance to represent chaos.
         GROVEmusic

Violin Sonatas

Violin Sonatas, Op 2 – B minor; D major Recueil de douze sonates à II et III parties – Le tombeau de Monsieur de Lully; La Pallas; L'Apollon; La Brillante
L'Assemblée des Honnestes Curieux (Alba Roca vn Baldomero Barciela bar vio Ronaldo Lopes theo Chiao-Pin Kuo hpd) / **Amandine Beyer** vn
Zig Zag Territoires ZZT051102 (56' · DDD) Ⓕ**O**

For many people, if Jean-Fery Rebel is known as anything more than a name, it is for one chord – the spectacular dissonance which conjures primeval chaos at the opening of his ballet suite *Les elemens*. Yet, as the members of L'Assemblée des Honnestes Curieux maintain here, he should perhaps be better remembered for his chamber works, which include some of the earliest duo and trio sonatas to be composed in France (they probably date from the 1690s), and which were noted in their day for successfully combining 'Italian genius and fire' with 'French wisdom and tenderness'.

It seems a reasonable claim, too: the sonatas on this disc – taken from sets Rebel published in 1712 and 1713 – intermingle *lentement* and *gracieusement* movements of great Gallic sweetness and melodic refinement with *vistes* and *gays* whose violinistic flair and vigour call to mind the ever-influential Corelli. And if that 'Chaos' crush-chord suggests that Rebel had a taste for harmonic adventure, then that is backed up by these pieces, which contain a number of bold moves.

All of the works on this disc are available elsewhere, but this new release scores a hit by mixing works, and therefore textures, from both publications. That is not the only thing that makes the disc worth your money, however, for the performances are first-rate, with impeccable and vigorous ensemble-playing put at the service of rich and intelligent expression – note how when the achingly sad opening movement of *Le tombeau de Monsieur de Lully* returns at the end the intensity is cranked up by leaving out the harpsichord. Well recorded, too, this disc is all pleasure.

Max Reger

German 1873-1916

Reger studied with Riemann (1890-95) in Munich and Wiesbaden (where his drinking habits began); in 1901 he settled in Munich and in 1907 moved to Leipzig to take a post as professor of composition at the university, though he was also active internationally as a conductor and pianist. He was appointed conductor of the court orchestra at Meiningen in 1911 and in 1915 moved to Jena.

During a composing life of little more than 20 years, he produced a large output in all genres, nearly always in abstract forms. He was a firm supporter of 'absolute' music and saw himself in a tradition going back to Bach, through Beethoven, Schumann and Brahms; his organ music, though also affected by Liszt, was provoked by that tradition. Of his orchestral pieces, his symphonic and richly elaborate Hiller Variations and Mozart Variations are justly remembered; of his chamber music the lighter-textured trios have retained a place in the repertory, along with some of the works for solo string instruments. His late piano and two-piano music places him as a successor to Brahms in the central German tradition. He pursued intensively, and to its limits, Brahms's continuous development and free modulation, often also invoking the aid of Bachian counterpoint. Many of his works are in variation and fugue forms; equally characteristic is a great energy and complexity of thematic growth. **GROVE**music

---

Four Symphonic Poems, Op 128

Four Symphonic Poems after Arnold Böcklin.
Variations and Fugue on a Theme of JA Hiller

Royal Concertgebouw Orchestra / Neeme Järvi
Chandos CHAN8794 (67' · DDD)   Ⓕ Ⓞ ⊕

Mention of Reger's name in 'informed' circles is likely to produce a conditioned reflex: 'Fugue!' In his day he was the central figure of the 'Back to Bach' movement, but he was also a romantic who relished all the expressive potential of the enormous post-Wagnerian orchestra. Chandos exploits the open spaces of the Concertgebouw, forsaking some healthy transparency for an extra spatial dimension; a more sumptuous glow.

With Järvi's instinct for pacing in late romantic music, and his great orchestra's evident delight in the copious riches of the discovery, for the *Hiller* Variations, this disc is very tempting. Anyone who warms to Vaughan Williams's *Tallis Fantasia* will immediately respond to the 'Hermit playing the violin', the first of the four *Böcklin* tone-poems; Debussy's 'Jeux de vagues' from *La mer* was obviously in Reger's mind for the second poem 'At play in the waves'; and the 'Isle of the dead' is Reger's no less doom- and gloom-laden response to the painting that so captured Rachmaninov's imagination. The final painting, 'Bacchanal', was described as a Munich beer festival in Roman costume – an entirely fitting description for Reger's setting of it!

Clarinet Quintet

Clarinet Quintet[a] . String Quartet in E flat, Op 109.
[a]**Karl Leister** *cl* **Vogler Quartet** (Tim Vogler, Frank Reinecke vns Stefan Fehlandt va Stephan Forck vc)
Nimbus NI5644 (72' · DDD)   Ⓕ

Who could fail to smile at the winding lyricism that opens both these works, or at the self-possessed fugue that potters gleefully at the end of the Op 109 String Quartet? This is music that simply had to be written, complex music maybe, but with so much to say at so many levels that once you enter its world, you're hooked. Previous recordings of the gorgeous Clarinet Quintet have included two with Karl Leister, though for sheer naturalness, musicality and team spirit, this new production will be hard to beat. Reger's frequent allusions to early musical modes inspire playing of rare sensitivity. Humour surfaces in the *scherzo*'s rough and tumble, a downward scale idea backed by lively *pizzicatos*, teasingly discursive and with a sunny, song-like *Trio*. The slow movement recalls Brahms's Quintet but without the gypsy element, while the theme-and-variation finale reminds us that Reger's homage to Mozart extends beyond the chosen key of A major. The String Quartet is more openly argumentative, especially in the first movement. Hints of Taranto inform the tarantella-like *scherzo*, whereas the slow movement combines hymn-like nobility with more echoes of Brahms. The closing fugue is the work of a joyful creator drunk on counterpoint, though there's plenty to engage the heart as well as the mind. The

Vogler commands a wide range of tonal colour and is ideal for all Doubting Thomases who'd have you believe that Reger is a bore.

Cello Sonatas

Cello Sonatas – No 1, Op 5; No 2, Op 28; No 3, Op 78; No 4, Op 116. Three Suites, Op 131c
Alban Gerhardt vc **Markus Becker** pf
Hyperion ② CDA67581/2 (138' · DDD) Ⓕ⬤

Max Reger is often blamed for thickness of musical texture, but although the piano-writing here is certainly prolix, the first two sonatas are imbued with a Brahmsian/classical romanticism and a virility which keeps the music thoroughly alive. The First Sonata surges passionately and heroically at the opening yet the touching second subject sighs very personally, the *Adagio 'con gran affetto'* is gently lyrical and the finale is skittish. The Second Sonata also sails off agitato and has a brilliant but more muted *Scherzo* and an engaging Trio. An Intermezzo replaces the slow movement and the finale is a graceful *grazioso*.

The last two sonatas are more mature, major works in which Reger has left Brahms behind and found his own voice. The highlight of No 3 is a substantial set of variations, Busoni's speciality, and the final sonata is even more impressive, with the cello introducing a kind of motto theme; the melodic writing in the secondary material is characteristically chromatic. There follows a whimsical, tarantella-like *Scherzo*, a warmly expressive slow movement and an engaging *Allegretto con grazia* finale.

The Cello Suites are in a direct line from Bach, although not collections of Baroque dances but three- or four-movement works. No 1 ends with a jolly fugue and No 2 includes both a Gavotte and a Gigue. Easily the finest is the Third with its richly sustained, intensely melodic Prelude, a brilliantly contrasted Scherzo and another appealing set of variations for its finale.

This is a stimulating package, very well played: both artists produce the passionate response demanded of them. Alban Gerhardt has a warm, resonant middle register and Markus Becker is well able to undertake the music's considerable virtuosity. The recording is vivid and clear.

Piano Trios

Piano Trios – B minor, Op 2; E minor, Op 102
Gunter Teuffel va **Parnassus Trio** (Wolfgang Schröder vn Michael Gross vc Chia Chou pf)
Dabringhaus und Grimm MDG303 0751-2
(67'· DDD) Ⓕ⬤

It was very wise to programme Reger's masterly Op 102 E-minor Trio before its B-minor predecessor. Unsuspecting listeners who jump straight in at Op 2 will discover a pleasing if discursive piece, forged in the shadow of Brahms, with an opening *Allegro appassionato* which, although half the length of its dis-

companion's first movement, seems twice as long. The *Scherzo* is frumpish, the closing *Adagio con variazioni* sombre and somewhat long-winded. And yet the use of viola in place of a cello has its attractions, and there are numerous telling glimpses of the mature Reger.

The E minor Trio is something else again, a rugged masterpiece, with a finely structured opening *Allegro moderato, ma con passione* (the three stages of its argument are divided equally within a 15-minute framework), a mysterious *Allegretto* that opens in the manner of later Brahms then suddenly lets in the sunlight, and a noble, hymn-like *Largo* that recalls 'The Hermit with the Violin' from the *Böcklin* Portraits. Reger's Second Trio is full of audacious modulations and striking dramatic gestures; it *is* long (something in excess of 40 minutes), but never outstays its welcome. No one could reasonably ask for more than the Parnassus Trio offers, either in terms of drama or of interpretative subtlety. If you love Brahms, and fancy diving in among a plethora of stimulating musical complexities, invest without delay. If you love melody, there's plenty of that, too.

Violin Works

Solo Violin Sonata No 7 in A minor, Op 91ᵃ.
Three Solo Viola Suites, Op 131dᵇ
Luigi Alberto Bianchi ᵃvn/ᵇva
Dynamic CDS383 (56' · ᵇADD/ᵃDDD)
Recorded ᵃ1992, ᵇ1977 Ⓕ

Violin Sonata in C, Op 72. Little Sonata in A, Op 103b No 2. Tarantella in G minor. Albumblatt in E flat
Ulf Wallin vn **Roland Pöntinen** pf
CPO CPO999 857-2 (60' · DDD) Ⓕ⬤⬤⬤

 The variety of Reger's music could hardly be better suggested than by this pair of discs. Reger the wild modernist (by the standards of 1903) is vividly before us in the headlong, turbulent, disconcertingly chromatic outer movements of the Op 72 Sonata, with their huge variety of moods and frequent abrupt changes of direction. But the *Little Sonata* of only six years later is almost classical by comparison; it's much more direct, economically worked and tightly argued. And in all the unaccompanied music in Luigi Alberto Bianchi's recital we meet Reger paying sincere and often touching homage to Bach.

Bianchi's disc is beautiful but poignant. The three Suites for viola were recorded in 1977 on a large and sumptuously rich-toned viola by the brothers Amati, the Medicea. It was stolen three years later; Bianchi began playing the violin instead and eventually acquired a fine Stradivari, the Colossus, upon which in 1992 he recorded the unaccompanied Violin Sonata. That too was stolen six years thereafter, and apart from the interest of the music and the eloquence of the playing this disc has the sad value of being perhaps the last that we shall hear of two exceptional instruments. Reger's love for the violin is as evident in the

Op 91 Sonata as is his reverence for Bach. All the movements are like Bach in late-Romantic dress, and the finale is a magnificent chaconne.

Ulf Wallin plays with a slightly narrower tone than Bianchi, which works well in the tumultuous gestures of Op 72. But he and Roland Pöntinen are just as alive to Reger's moments of withdrawn pensiveness and long lines, which need care if their chromatic shifts aren't to make them seem diffuse; they never do here. The recordings are excellent.

Organ Works

Chorale Fantasias, Op 52 – Wachet auf, ruft uns die Stimme. Pieces, Op 145 – Weihnachten. Organ Sonata No 2 in D minor, Op 60. Symphonic Fantasia and Fugue, Op 57
Franz Hauk org
Guild GMCD7192 (73' · DDD) Played on the Klais organ of Ingolstadt Minster   Ⓕ**o**

Opinions about Reger's music are polarised between admirers and detractors. The latter group would say of him, as Emperor Joseph II did of Mozart, that he wrote too many notes. Even in this new century the complexity of his scores still presents an awesome challenge to performers and listeners alike. Yet the rewards are immense; Reger is arguably even as great a composer as Liszt. His radical, eclectic approach took organ music to new dimensions, and he fully deserves a whole CD to himself. He's well served here by an inspired choice of player, instrument and venue. Hauk's performances are amazingly virtuoso; he brings clarity of rhythm and articulation to the faster passages and a serene poetry to the quieter moments. He plays the spectacular Klais organ of Ingolstadt Minster, which must be one of the best instruments in Europe. Its brilliant *tutti*, combined with a 12-second reverberation, does full justice to Reger's epic climaxes, and there are some ravishing colours in the softer sections. As resident organist, Hauk knows this instrument intimately, and exploits all the available colours and dynamics. Guild's fine recording stops the reverberation from becoming excessive, and captures the organ's full dynamic range. Whatever your views on Reger, this disc can be unreservedly recommended as an overwhelming and uplifting experience.

Choral Works

Drei geistliche Gesänge, Op 110. 3 Gesänge, Op 39
Danish National Radio Choir / Stefan Parkman
Chandos CHAN9298 (56' · DDD · T/t)   Ⓕ

Mere mentions of Reger's *a cappella* music will send sensitive souls scurrying to the nearest Karaoke lounge. Visions of myriad notes covering the page would frighten most choirs away, but these singers are made of sterner stuff. They're undaunted by complex contrapuntal structures, devious chromatic harmonies and textures so thick you need a forage knife to get through them. They not only weave their way through Reger's characteristically tangled scores without a moment's doubt, but illuminate the paths so clearly one hardly notices the dense musical undergrowth all around. Parkman has a clear-sighted view of what's wanted, and, aided by singers whose pure, perfectly blended tone is a joy to hear, he follows his vision unfalteringly: everything falls neatly into place, making real musical sense. The hefty Op 110 Motets (ostensibly in five, but often diverging into as many as nine independent parts) can sound oppressively heavy, but here offer some of the most sublimely beautiful moments yet captured on CD. A triumph of skill over adversity if ever there was one.

Johannes Regis   Franco-Flemish c1425-96

In contrast to the peripatetic careers of many of his contemporaries, there is no record of Regis ever having worked or travelled outside the diocese of Cambrai, and his ties both to Dufay and to Cambrai Cathedral apparently remained strong. Regis's most innovative and influential works are his cantus-firmus motets in five voices. These represent one of the earliest sustained attempts to compose in five parts and appear to have been models for younger musicians such as Obrecht, Compère, Weerbeke and Josquin.

Complete Works
The Clerks' Group / Edward Wickham
Musique en Wallonie ② MEW0848/9 (127' · DDD)   Ⓕ

Johannes Regis is certainly not a household name, mainly because very little of his music survives, far less than for the two figureheads of his generation, Ockeghem and Busnoys. Scholars have rated him for many years, but for lovers of early polyphony, the chance to hear his output in the round will be indeed be a treat, because this is a master of the first rank who sounds quite unlike either of his more famous colleagues. Listen to his marvellous *Puisque ma dame*, not only one of the most unusual songs of its time, but also an instantly seductive one.

The best-known part of his output, and the one that proved the most influential, is his motets. Most are on texts that were rarely set, or even specially written. The Christmas motet *O admirabile commercium* is at once boldly conceived and playful, intricately detailed but punctuated by well staged, memorable gestures; and his *Ave Maria...Virgo serena* probably inspired Josquin's earliest surviving masterpiece. Then there are the Masses: the one on *L'homme armé* is perhaps the more immediately outgoing, a worthy contribution to an illustrious tradition; but the more reflective *Ecce ancilla/Ne timeas* Mass grows in stature with repeated listening. However little music survives, one senses that with Regis, as with Ockeghem, each work explores, and resolves, its own set of challenges.

Much of this has been recorded once before in performances of real value, but the cumulative effect of hearing it all done by a single group yields a different level of insight. That the group in question is on top form is more than a bonus. Edward Wickham's choice of tempi is sure-footed, as a result of which most details simply fall into place. The close recording captures the energy and zest with which they tackle the music. Add the stylish presentation and an informative text, and the project makes the leap from self-recommending to essential listening: wonderful.

Steve Reich   American b1936

Reich studied drumming when he was 14 with the New York Philharmonic Orchestra timpanist; later he took a degree in philosophy at Cornell (1953-7) and studied composition at the Juilliard School (1958-61) and at Mills College (1962-3) with Milhaud and Berio, also becoming interested in Balinese and African music. In 1966 he began performing with his own ensemble, chiefly of percussionists, developing a music of gradually changing ostinato patterns that move out of phase, creating an effect of shimmering surfaces; this culminated in Drumming (1971), a 90-minute elaboration of a single rhythmic cell. From c1972 he added harmonic change to his music, and later (Tehillim, 1981) melody. He has also worked with larger orchestral and choral forces (The Desert Music, 1983). Different Trains (1988), for string quartet and tape, won a Grammy for best new composition. GROVEmusic

Different Trains

Different Trains. Triple Quartet. The Four Sections.
Lyon National Orchestra / David Robertson
Naïve Montaigne MO782167 (65' · DDD)   Ⓕⓞ

This version of *Different Trains*, a reworking of the original string quartet version, impresses immediately by the richness of its vastly expanded sound palette. It reveals that inside that frenetic chamber work was a much larger piece trying to get out, and here it is, fully realised, as it were, in glorious technicolor. Some of the writing has an almost Beethovenian quality. It's a hugely impressive performance of a work that has, quite literally, grown in stature. And, of course, if you're going to record Reich with 48 strings, you may as well include the largest version of *Triple Quartet* from 1999, scored for 36 of them.

If in going back to *The Four Sections* for orchestra from 1986 one has the feeling that much is inchoate, it's also true that all the elemental power of the more recent works is there, too, and the Lyon musicians react to it with fantastic energy and precision. A major addition to the Reich discography.

Drumming

Drumming
Synergy Vocals; Ictus / Georges-Elie Octors
Cyprès CYP5608 (55' · DDD)   Ⓕ

Drumming is from 1971, but it has lost none of its strength. The players of Ictus here put their hearts and souls into a work that demands ferocious concentration (though other approaches are possible – a composer friend once said that it was quite the best music for building bookcases), and which rewards accordingly. Now, we know that nobody likes the label 'minimalist' any more, but with music of this quality it's very hard to find that description insulting. This performance is quite the equal of, and possibly more colourful than, Reich's second version, on Nonesuch, and clearly outstrips the original, less trim DG version.

Daniel Variations

Daniel Variations[a]. Variations for Vibes, Pianos & Strings[b]
[a]**Los Angeles Master Chorale / Grant Gershon;**
[b]**London Sinfonietta / Alan Pierson**
Nonesuch 7559 79949-4 (52' · DDD)   Ⓕⓞ

Reich's interest in variation has not been confined to music alone; he also employs linguistic variation to examine the relationship between sound and sense, and even uses language to frame wider moral, philosophical and religious concerns. This is heard in the *Daniel Variations*. Composed in response to the futile killing of the American reporter Daniel Pearl in 2002, and premiered in October 2006 at the highly successful 'Phases' retrospective at London's Barbican Centre, the work combines short biblical excerpts with contemporary textual commentary to create a dark and often unsettling sound world. Much of this is derived from Reich's juxtaposition of block-like structures with a set of harmonic axes which emphasise the most traditionally unstable of all intervals – the augmented fourth (or tritone).

In contrast, the *Variations for Vibes, Piano & Strings* displays Reich's musical inventiveness at its ebullient and infectious best. Given a top-notch workout by Alan Pierson and members of the London Sinfonietta, the *Variations* alternately powers and glides throughout a tautly structured three-movement design – by way of a series of simultaneously unfolding canonic layers – which zigzag their way inexorably towards a quite thrilling close. Critics often lament Reich's shift away from the strict processes of his early minimalist style but all the techniques discovered along the way are still present here: rhythmic goal-orientation, harmonic clusters rich in overtones and upper partials, and a complex but audible polyphonic weave. And all underpinned by those variations, no less.

Music for 18 Musicians

Music for 18 Musicians
Anonymous Ensemble / Steve Reich pf
ECM New Series 821 417-2 (57' · ADD)
Recorded 1978   Ⓕ Ⓞ

Reich's first recording of *Music for 18 Musicians*
was a landmark release in the history of new
music on record and showed what a towering
masterpiece it is. The recording was produced by
Rudolf Werner for DG, following the release of a
three-LP set of *Drumming*, *Six Pianos* and *Music
for Mallet Instruments, Voice and Organ*. Legend
has it that Roland Kommerell, at that time head
of German PolyGram, foresaw the commercial
potential of Reich's piece but realised that DG
was not the best vehicle to market the recording.
Kommerell therefore offered the recording
instead to Manfred Eicher of ECM, a company
which had hitherto only released jazz and rock.
The ECM release sold well over 100,000 copies,
around 10 times higher than might be expected of
a new music disc.

The 1978 recording still sounds beguilingly
fresh. When Steve Reich and Musicians came to
re-record *Music for 18 Musicians* for Nonesuch's
10-CD box set in 1996, their performance was
amazingly 11 minutes longer than the ECM
version. Normally, you would expect such a big
difference to come from a slower tempo, but in
fact the underlying pulse of both recordings is
virtually identical. This is because of the unusual
structure of *Music for 18 Musicians*, where the
gradual fading-in and fading-out of different elements aren't given a fixed number of repetitions
but are played simply as long as it takes for this
process to happen. In the 1996 version these fade-
ins and fade-outs are more finely graded and
require more repetitions than in the 1978 version.

Electric Guitar Phase

Electric Guitar Phase (arr Frasca)[a]. Music for Large
Ensemble[b]. Tokyo/Vermont Counterpoint (arr
Yoshida)[c]. Triple Quartet[d]
[a]**Dominic Frasca** gtr [c]**Mika Yoshida** mari [d]**Kronos
Quartet** (David Harrington, John Sherba vns Hank
Dutt va Jennifer Culp vc) [b]**Alarm Will Sound;** [b]**Ossia /
Alan Pierson**
Nonesuch 7559-79546-2 (54' · DDD)   Ⓕ Ⓞ

Triple Quartet is Reich's first new work for the
Kronos Quartet since writing his masterpiece
Different Trains in 1988. It may disappoint –
there doesn't appear to be anything particularly
new or different happening here. *Electric Guitar
Phase*, on the other hand, shows precisely what's
missing in *Triple Quartet*. The American guitarist Dominic Frasca has arranged *Violin Phase*,
originally composed for four violins in the heady
days of 1967, for four overdubbed guitars, and
the result is sheer joy. Such is Frasca's sensitivity
to every nuance of phrasing between the four
lines that this recording is a classic for the mini-

malist genre, easily eclipsing the violin original
in terms of intensity and tonal variety.

Up to now performances of Reich's music have
been dominated by the composer's participative
presence, even in larger concert works such as
The Desert Music. His predilection for earthy,
well-grounded tempos set the norm for performances of his music throughout the 1970s
and 80s. Two recordings here are fascinating
because they were made without Reich's active
participation. In this recording of *Music For
Large Ensemble*, the melodic invention at this
jazzy, vibrant tempo sounds almost as if Reich
had been listening to Ghanaian and Scottish folk
music. Yet this is nothing compared
to *Tokyo/Vermont Counterpoint*, where Mika
Yoshida's articulation is so fast that at times you
feel helium had escaped in the studio. This is
compulsory listening for anyone who appreciates a little perversity now and again.

Piano Phase

Sextet. Piano Phase. Eight Lines
**The London Steve Reich Ensemble /
Kevin Griffiths**
CPO CPO777 337-2 (57' · DDD)   Ⓕ

Time was when Steve Reich's music was the
exclusive domain of his own ensemble: then he
was signed to Boosey & Hawkes and his scores
were eagerly picked up by a second generation of
interpreters. The result has done nothing but
good for Reich's music as 'outsider' groups inevitably bring fresh nuance to works designed for a
specific pool of musicians. The London Steve
Reich Ensemble – who trade under the great
man's name with his blessing – was formed by
students from the Royal Academy of Music in
2005 and they quickly demonstrate that Reich's
sleeve-note claim that 'these performances pulse
with life' is more than puffery. *Eight Lines* – a 1983
rewrite of the Octet – is less sour than the Reich
Ensemble's own recording, and sits comfortably
in a conversational slipstream that is highly
rewarding. *Piano Phase* is monumental and steely,
again a point of departure from the original.

But most intriguing is the Sextet from 1984, a
work that has been unfairly neglected on disc
since Reich's recording. Scored for a trademark
ensemble of keyboards and mallet percussion,
Reich focuses on how he might make the ensemble sound more instrument-heavy than it actually is. Curvaceous bowed vibraphone strokes
are a beautiful counterpoint to the inherently
brittle ensemble attack and are judiciously highlighted. The cleanness of the recording certainly
helps: low-register piano figurations have a
throbbing clarity that creates telling perspective
against the rest of the ensemble.

Violin Phase

Violin Phase[c]. Eight Lines[b]. New York Counterpoint[a].
City Life[d]

[a]**Roland Diry** cl [c]**Jagdish Mistry** vn [bd]**Ensemble Modern** / [b]**Bradley Lubman**, [d]**Peter Rundel**
RCA Red Seal 74321 66459-2 (66' · DDD)   (F)

The most focused work here, *Violin Phase* (1977), wears its purposefulness on its sleeve. Jagdish Mistry scintillates as the soloist, never letting go of the tension for a second, so when the end comes, you wait expectantly for that thread to be picked up again. *Eight Lines*, the reworked version of the *Octet* (1979/83) is also purposeful, moving gently from the early phase style to the melodic chanting-inspired style of the later *Tehillim*. While it's undeniably exciting, *New York Counterpoint* (1985) doesn't quite have that edge-of-the-seat adrenalin-powered quality that you can feel so clearly in *Violin Phase*. *City Life*, though beautifully written and, in many senses, a witty work (something that's caught wonderfully in the Ensemble Modern's sharp-edged performance), leaves one adrift, without any clear idea of its purpose. If you want unforgettable performances of *Violin Phase* and *Eight Lines*, Ensemble Modern's account is the one to go for.

You Are (Variations)

You Are (Variations)[a]. Cello Counterpoint[b]
[b]**Maya Beiser** vc [a]**Los Angeles Master Chorale**;
[a]**Ensemble Modern** / **Grant Gershon**
Nonesuch 7559 79891-2 (39' · DDD)   (F)

With *You Are (Variations)*, Reich has consciously moved sideways from recent works such as *The Cave* and *Three Tales* and returned to the earlier sound worlds of *Tehillim* and *The Desert Music*. Scored, like those works, for vocal ensemble and instruments, it also follows their lead in dealing in a more meditative fashion than the decidedly interrogative *Three Tales*, say, intended to do, with fundamental questions of existence (hence, of course the title's 'You Are'). The texts, all very short, in English and Hebrew, are drawn from an 18th-century Jewish mystic, the Psalms, Wittgenstein and the Talmud. While this bare list may sound highly improbable and even contradictory, Reich himself has said that he spent six months looking for the right texts, and they do indeed have a forceful logic and cohesion.

The shortness of the texts means that Reich has gone back to the techniques of *Tehillim*, in which very short ideas are also varied, rather than to the longer-breathed constructions of *The Desert Music*, and there is no doubt that it's the aphoristic nature of the texts and their accompanying musical ideas that gives the work its power. The performance positively glitters; it seems quite clear that the Los Angeles Master Chorale under Grant Gershon are responding to the work's intrinsic glow, the sense of spontaneity – the swing – in the music that Reich has rediscovered. And that swing is a fundamental element in *Cello Counterpoint*, which rounds off the disc. It is performed in this version by the remarkable Maya Beiser (formerly of the Bang

On A Can All Stars) with seven pre-recorded parts – it may also be performed by eight live cellists. Beiser manages to make the eight parts sound very often as though they were one gigantic humming, strumming instrument, and while at times Reich's contrapuntal chugging seems a little worthy, there's no doubt that this is a work of real substance.

City Life

Proverb. Nagoya marimbas. City Life
Bob Becker, **James Preiss** marimbas **Theatre of Voices** (Andrea Fullington, Sonja Rasmussen, Allison Zelles sops Alan Bennett, Paul Elliott tens) **Steve Reich Ensemble** / **Paul Hillier; Bradley Lubman**
Nonesuch 7559-79430-2 (42' ·DDD)   (F)(O)

The Wittgenstein quotation 'How small a thought it takes to fill a whole life' serves as the basis of *Proverb* for three sopranos, two tenors, vibraphones and two electric organs, a composition that was premiered as a partial work 'in progress' at a 1995 Prom. The complete piece (it plays for some 14 minutes) holds together very well. Three sopranos 'sing the original melody of the text in canons that gradually augment, or get longer', whereas Perotin's influence can be heard in the tenor parts.

Reich's skill at inverting, augmenting and transforming his material has rarely sounded with such immediacy. After a virtuoso, pleasantly up-beat *Nagoya marimbas* lasting four and a half minutes, comes *City life*, probably Reich's best piece since *Different Trains*. The sound-frame includes air brakes, pile drivers, car alarms, boat horns and police sirens, all of which are loaded into a pair of sampling keyboards and played alongside the instrumental parts. The first movement opens with what sounds like a distant relation of Stravinsky's *Symphonies of Wind Instruments* then kicks into action on the back of a Manhattan street vendor shouting 'Check it out'. The second and fourth movements witness gradual acceleration – the second to a pile driver, the fourth to a heartbeat – and the third has the two sampling keyboards engaging in top-speed crossfire based on speech samples. The last and most dissonant movement utilises material taped when the World Trade Centre was bombed in 1993.

City life is a tightly crafted montage, formed like an arch (A-B-C-B-A), lean, clever, catchy and consistently gripping. In fact the whole disc should thrill dyed-in-the-wool Reichians and preach convincingly to the as-yet unconverted. The sound is excellent.

Ottorino Respighi   Italian 1879-1936

Respighi studied with Torchi and Martucci at the Liceo Musicale in Bologna (1891-1901), then had lessons with Rimsky-Korsakov during visits to Russia (1900-1903). In 1913 he settled in Rome, teaching

and composing. He is best known as the composer of highly coloured orchestral pieces, capitalising on the most brilliant aspects of Rimsky-Korsakov, Ravel and Strauss: Fontane di Roma (1916), Pini di Roma (1924), Vetrate di chiesa (1925), Trittico botticelliano (1927), Gli uccelli (arrangements of pieces by earlier composers, 1927) and Feste romane (1928). His interest in the past is to be heard not only in his arrangements of Arie antiche for orchestra but in the use of plainchant and the church modes in such pieces as the Concerto gregoriano (for violin, 1921) and the Quartetto dorico (1924). He also wrote operas (La bella dormente nel bosco, 1921) and vocal works. He was greatly helped by his wife, Elsa (b 1894), herself a composer. GROVEmusic

Piano Concerto in A minor

Piano Concerto. Toccata. Fantasia slava
Konstantin Scherbakov pf **Slovak Radio Symphony Orchestra / Howard Griffiths**
Naxos 8 553207 (51' · DDD) ⓈD→

All these pieces are otherwise available in decent performances, but at this price how could anyone with the slightest weakness for Respighi hesitate? Scherbakov and Griffiths do a good deal more than dutifully go through the motions, the soloist in particular playing with delicacy and affection, grateful for the opportunities to demonstrate how well he would play Liszt or Rachmaninov, but in the *Toccata* he's interested as well in Respighi's more characteristic modal vein; as a Russian, he demonstrates that this too, like so much in Respighi, was influenced by the time he spent in Russia.

Russian soloist, English conductor and Slovak orchestra all enjoy the moment in the *Fantasia slava* where Respighi presents a morsel of Smetana in the evident belief that it's a Russian folk-dance, but the Concerto and the *Fantasia*, both very early works, aren't patronised in the slightest.

The *Toccata* isn't so much an exercise in the neo-Baroque, often though its dotted and florid figures promise it, more of an essay on how far one can be neo-Baroque without giving up a post-Lisztian keyboard style and comfortable orchestral upholstery. But in a slow and florid central section, a rather melancholy aria that passes from the soloist to the oboe, to the strings and back again, there's a real quality of Bachian utterance translated not unrecognisably into a late Romantic language. Scherbakov sounds touched by it, and obviously wants us to like it. The recordings are more than serviceable, but each work is given only a single track.

Roman Trilogy

Pines of Rome; Fountains of Rome; Roman Festivals

Fontane di Roma. Pini di Roma.
Feste romane. Il tramonto[a]

[a]**Christine Rice** mez **Santa Cecilia Academy Orchestra, Rome / Antonio Pappano**
EMI 394429-2 (81' · DDD) ⒻO→

What more appropriate orchestra to record the three Roman colour-scapes of Respighi than Rome's greatest orchestra under its music director, Antonio Pappano? In every way this new version is more than a match for the fine Dutoit version of the trilogy (Decca). As in Italian opera, Pappano has a natural feeling for flexible phrasing without exaggeration, and here he has even more resilience in his springing of rhythms than Dutoit, while the fine EMI recording offers clean separation and a wide dynamic range to match even the brilliant Decca.

It adds to the attractions of the disc that as a bonus Pappano offers the lovely setting of Shelley in translation for mezzo and strings, *Il tramonto* ('The Sunset'), beautifully sung with clear, firm tone by Christine Rice. Dutoit puts the trilogy pieces in his chosen order while Pappano presents them in chronological order, ending with the noisiest – and least inspired – *Roman Festivals*. Nonetheless, Pappano conducts that, as he does the earlier two pieces, with all the flamboyance needed for such boldly extrovert music.

These are unashamed picture-postcards in music, and the images they evoke are always exceptionally vivid. One slight reservation is that the recording of a nightingale that the adventurous Respighi includes towards the close of the 'The Pines of the Janiculum' is so faint you can barely hear it. Pappano's trilogy now stands as a model for a colourful and ideal coupling, particularly with such an apt fill-up as *Il tramonto*.

Roman Trilogy
Royal Philharmonic Orchestra / Enrique Bátiz
Naxos 8 550539 (61' · DDD) ⓈO→

This Naxos disc is an extraordinary bargain; it would be recommendable at full price; in the super-bargain area it's unbeatable. It has such excitement and verve that you can accept an extra degree of brazen extroversion, indeed revel in it. In *Roman Festivals* the opening 'Circuses' is immensely spectacular, its character in the unfettered gladiatorial tradition of the Coliseum: the trumpets and drums are quite thrilling. The gossamer opening of 'The Jubilee' leads to the most dramatic climax. In the 'October Festival' the strings play their Latin soliloquy very exotically for Bátiz. The closing section brings a gentle mandolin serenade. The great clamour of the Epiphany celebrations which follow unleashes a riotous *mêlée* from the RPO, which sounds as if it's enjoying itself hugely, and the obvious affinity with the final fairground scene of Petrushka is all the more striking when the strings have that bit more bite. The *Pines* and *Fountains* are also very fine. When the unison horns signal the turning on of the Triton Fountain, and the cascade splashes through the orchestra, the RPO unleashes a real flood. Yet the lovely, radiant evocation of the central movements of *The Pines*, and the sensuous Italian light of the sunset at the Villa Medici, are most sensitively realised by the RPO, and at the very beginning of the finale, 'The Pines of the Appian Way', the ever present sound, with its growling bass clarinet, gives a sinister implication of the advancing Roman might.

Brazilian Impressions

Impressioni brasiliane, 'Brazilian Impressions'. Vetrate di chiesa, 'Church Windows'. Rossiniana.
Buffalo Philharmonic Orchestra / JoAnn Falletta
Naxos 8 557711 (65' · DDD) ⓢ🄳►

Naxos offers another group of rich and exotic Respighi works which demonstrate his extraordinary gift for brilliant orchestrations. The longest and most ambitious is *Church Windows*, though curiously the idea of linking the four pieces with great paintings only came after the work was finished. He chose The Flight into Egypt for the gentle opening piece, St Michael the Archangel for the vigorous second, The Matins of St Clare for the third and St Gregory the Great for the grandest piece, described by Edward Johnson as like a papal coronation in sound.

Brazilian Impressions stemmed from a visit that the composer made to Brazil. He planned a sequence of five pieces, but by 1928 he had completed only three, and left it at that for the first performance in 1928 in Rio. The first is a nocturne, 'Tropical Night', with fragments of dance rhythms hinted at in the sensuous textures. The second piece is a sinister picture of a snake farm Respighi visited, with hints of birdsong, while the final movement is a vigorous and colourful dance.

Rossiniana of 1925 is Respighi's attempt to follow up the enormous success of *La boutique fantasque*. It's also based on pieces by Rossini, this time using some of his piano trifles, *Les riens*. The first is a sort of barcarolle, the second a lament and the third an intermezzo featuring the celesta. In the finale he comes nearest to the ebullience of *La boutique fantasque* in a tarantella, but colourful as these pieces are, they hardly rival those in the earlier suite. Well worth hearing, though. The Buffalo Philharmonic under music director JoAnn Falletta is treated to warm and spectacular recording, apt for such exotica.

Church Windows

Church Windows. Brazilian Impressions. Roman Festivals
Cincinnati Symphony Orchestra / Jesús López-Cobos
Telarc CD80356 (71' · DDD) ⓕ⦿

You might easily argue that neither *Church Windows* nor *Brazilian Impressions* is quite as successful as the 'essential' Respighi of the Roman Trilogy. The only answer to that, López-Cobos seems to suggest, is to take the music perfectly

seriously and pay scrupulous attention not just to its potential for sonorous spectacle but to its wealth of beautifully crafted detail. The gong at the end of the second movement of *Church Windows* is magnificently resonant, as is the organ in the finale, and the work is given an extra inch or two of stature by sensitive handling of those moments that need but don't always get delicacy. He pays such care to character and detail in 'Butantan', that creepy depiction of a snake-farm in *Brazilian Impressions*, that you can not only recapture the real, crawling horror that Respighi experienced there, but discover in the music also a queer sort of Debussian grace as well. And as for *Roman Festivals*, well, what's wrong with 20-odd minutes of wide-screen spectacular once in a while? But if every colour is precisely rendered, the quiet passages as affectionately turned as they are here, what skill is to be found in it, what a gift for immaculately precise instrumental detail. With that sort of handling all three pieces sound quite worthy of sharing shelf space with *Pines* and *Fountains*. The recording is spectacular.

La Boutique fantasque

Respighi La Boutique fantasque. La Pentola magica
Bach Prelude and Fugue in D, BWV532 (orch Respighi)
BBC Philharmonic Orchestra / Gianandrea Noseda
Chandos CHAN10081 (80' · DDD) ⓕ🄳►

Noseda's vigorous account of *La Boutique fantasque* makes a fine coupling with two rarities which similarly show off Respighi's brilliance as an orchestrator of others' music. *La Pentola magica* ('The magic pot') is a ballet score from 1920 whose scenario has been lost, though the titles of the ten brief movements give an idea of the Russian story behind it. Respighi drew on relatively neglected Russian composers such as Grechaninov, Arensky and Rubinstein, and Polish-born Pachulski, as well as including his arrangements of Russian folk themes. Slow music and a relaxed mood predominates in evocative orchestration. His joy in orchestral sound is even more striking in the exuberant account of his arrangement of Bach's D major Prelude and Fugue, with rich, weighty brass and dramatic contrasts of timbre and dynamic. The performance of *La Boutique fantasque* has similar zest. The playing of the BBC Philharmonic is expressive, with *rubato* that dancers wouldn't welcome on stage. The speeds tend to be a trifle extreme, bringing an apt and enjoyable sense of danger in the pointing of the tricky woodwind flurries dotted through the score. The Chandos sound, satisfyingly full and bright, matches the performance.

La sensitiva

La sensitiva[b]. Deità silvane[a]. Nebbie[b]. Aretusa[b]
[a]**Ingrid Attrot** sop [b]**Linda Finnie** mez

BBC Philharmonic Orchestra / Richard Hickox
Chandos CHAN9453 (60' · DDD · T/t)   Ⓕ**O**🅑➔

In some of Respighi's comparatively neglected pieces, his accustomed richness and subtlety of orchestral colour go with a certain lack of melodic individuality. Once or twice in *Deità silvane* ('Woodland gods'), one wishes that the poems' classical imagery would lead him towards an evocation or even a direct quotation from Italian music's 'classical' past of the kind that so often renders his better-known music so memorable. In *La sensitiva* ('The sensitive plant'), however, his care for the imagery and prosody of Shelley's poem (in Italian translation) was so responsive that striking melodic invention was the result. The orchestral colour of the piece is exquisite, the succession of ideas (the sensitive plant is image both of unhappy lover and spurned artist) a good deal more than merely picturesque. In a performance as expressive as this it seems one of Respighi's best works, and a good deal more sophisticated than he's generally given credit for. *Aretusa* is fine, too, with bigger dramatic gestures, even richer colour and some magnificent sea music.

The much better-known *Nebbie* is another example of Respighi finding a genuinely sustained melodic line in response to a text which obviously meant a great deal to him. Everything here is played with a real care for Respighi's line as well as his sumptuous but never muddy colours. First-class recording.

Silvestre Revueltas   Mexican 1899-1940

Revueltas studied in Mexico City, Austin and Chicago, his teachers including Tella and Borowski. From 1929 to 1935 he was assistant conductor of the Mexico SO, for which he composed rhythmically vigorous, boldly coloured pieces, most famously Sensemayá *(1938).*   GROVEmusic

Orchestral Works

Revueltas Homenaje a Lorca. Planos. Ocho x Radio. El Renacuajo Paseador. Pieza para doce instrumentos. Sensemayá. Caminando. Este era un Rey. Hora de Junio **J Pomar** Preludio y Fuga ritmicos
Juan Carlos Tajes *spkr* **Ebony Band, Amsterdam / Werner Herbers**
Channel Classics CD/SACD 🄯 CCSSA21104
(67' · DDD) Recorded live   Ⓕ

The sheer verve and power of his music leads one to think of Revueltas as primarily an orchestral composer, but many of his works are written for relatively modest forces (or started out that way, like *Sensemayá*, given a spirited performance here). Often, it's the ferocity of his sound – and liberal use of percussion – that gives the music a bigger texture than its actual layout might sug-

gest. Even so relatively modest a piece as the playful octet *Ocho x Radio* (1933) feels like a small orchestral score. Curiously, the early *Pieza para doce instrumentos* (1929; left untitled by Revueltas) seems much smaller in scale despite being longer. The four movements chart a gentle course in increasing tempi from *Lento* to *Allegro*. Here the burlesque and grotesque strains in his musical psyche were yet to be allowed full rein, but were unleashed in *El renacuajo paseador* ('The Wandering Tadpole', 1933), with its quotations and teasing allusions. The tiny suite describes how a tadpole meets an untimely end after going out for a drink with a mouse, the moral of which did not deter the composer from terminal alcoholism. *Caminando* (1937) is a real find.

One of the final projects Revueltas worked on was Luis Córdova's 'caustic satire on fascism', *Este era un Rey* ('Once there was a King', 1940). The *Preludio y Fuga ritmicos* by his close friend José Pomar completes a splendid disc – derived from concert performances – that deserves every success. Highly recommended.

Nicolay Rimsky-Korsakov
Russian 1844-1908

Apart from piano lessons, a love for the music of Glinka and a fascination with opera orchestras, Rimsky-Korsakov had little preparation for a musical career – he trained as a naval officer – until he met Balakirev (1861), who captivated him, encouraging his attempts at composition, performing his works and introducing him to Borodin, Dargomïzhsky, Cui and Mussorgsky. He wrote songs, orchestral works and an opera (The Maid of Pskov, 1873) before becoming professor at the St Petersburg Conservatory (1871) and inspector of naval bands (1873-84), teaching himself harmony and counterpoint, conducting at Balakirev's Free School and collecting folksongs. His next opera, May Night (1880), engaged his full creative powers with its blend of the fantastic and the comic (the realm in which he was to score most of his greatest successes), while Snow Maiden (1882) evoked a deeper world of nature-mysticism. Official duties at the imperial chapel (1883-91), work on the deceased Mussorgsky's and Borodin's manuscripts and advising for the publisher Belyayev interrupted composition, but he did produce the three colourful orchestral works by which he is best known, Sheherazade, the Spanish Capriccio and the Russian Easter Festival Overture, during 1887-8, after which he devoted himself to opera. Of the 12 dramatic works from Mlada (1892) to The Golden Cockerel (1909), Kitezh (1907) stands out for its mystical and psychological depths.   GROVEmusic

Fantasy on Russian Themes

Rimsky-Korsakov Fantasy on Russian Themes, Op 33
Taneyev Concert Suite, Op 28
Lydia Mordkovitch *vn*
Royal Scottish National Orchestra / Neeme Järvi

Chandos CHAN10491 (65' · DDD)　　Ⓕ Ⓞ Ⓓ+

There's Russian and there's Russian. The St Petersburg and Moscow schools of composition are typified with this coupling. Rimsky-Korsakov's *Fantasy on Russian Themes* is self-evidently home-grown with the real magic conjured through the composer's elegant sleight of hand. The first of Rimsky's pair of themes – the reflective one – is alluded to and even elaborated upon before emerging in its entirety. It's almost as if the sultana Sheherazade is spinning her tall tales once more. Lydia Mordkovitch does so alluringly, making much of the moment when all is finally revealed. The ensuing *Lento* is beautiful and evocative, achieving transfiguration in rapt harmonics over impressionistic *tremolandi*.

Mordkovitch has mellowed. She has refined her intonation, curbed her edgy dynamism. She is seeking and finding more tenderness. The heat of the moment, though, is still there and she dispatches Rimsky's not inconsiderable pyrotechnics, his double- and triple-stopped passagework, with fiery determination. On the threshold of Taneyev's splendid *Concert Suite* she flashes her pride in the opening declamation suggesting some kind of curious pact between Paganini and Wagner.

This substantial work represents an altogether more rigorous level of sophistication from the Rimsky. The Motherland feels remote; the tone is almost exclusively central European. Taneyev also pays his respects to classicism. The second movement 'Gavotte' starts as an 18th-century pastiche but its attitude is entirely late-Romantic. So, too, the almost Mahlerian *Wunderhorn*-esque atmosphere of the central 'Fairy-tale' whose shadowy chromatic theme might have been shaved off the opening of César Franck's D minor Symphony. It's like Taneyev has wilfully shrugged off his Russian ancestry.

Mordkovitch does give the piece its Russian accent, though, and Neeme Järvi's Royal Scottish National Orchestra fully exploit its visionary aspects – nowhere more so than in the 'finale e coda' of the *Theme with Variations* where the whole work achieves sublimation. Mordkovitch's intonation is truly tested here but there's no denying the intensity she culls from a chromaticism that is right on the edge of reason.

Scheherazade, Op 35

Rimsky-Korsakov Scheherazade **Balakirev** Islamey (arr Lyapunov) **Borodin** In the Steppes of Central Asia
Kirov Orchestra / Valery Gergiev
Philips 470 840-2PH (63' · DDD)　　Ⓕ Ⓞ Ⓞ Ⓓ+

Recorded under live conditions but without an audience in St Petersburg's Mariinsky Theatre, this *Scheherazade* is the most red-blooded, exciting account of Rimsky-Korsakov's orchestral warhorse currently available, helped by full, immediate sound of a richness rare in Russian recordings. The magnetism is established from the start, with Gergiev completely dispelling the

feeling that this is a work which keeps stopping and starting too often for its own good. Consistently you register that these are players who have the music in their blood, with *rubato* naturally inflected. In expressive freedom Gergiev is often less extreme than Reiner or Karajan, as in the *quasi recitando* bassoon solo near the start of the second movement or the *espressivo* oboe solo which follows, in which Gergiev notes also the *a tempo* marking, keeping it steady. The virtuosity of the St Petersburg soloists conveys an edge-of-seat tension, particularly when Gergiev opts for challengingly fast speeds in the climactic passages of the second and fourth movements.

This is a work written over only a few weeks, and far more than usual this is a performance that, defying the many changes of tempo, conveys that urgency of inspiration. Yet Gergiev brings out points of detail in the brilliant instrumentation normally bypassed, as in the upward *glissando* for the cellos in the opening section of the third movement, either ignored or merely hinted at by others.

Two points might be counted controversial. The tempo for that opening section of the third movement, 'The Young Prince and Princess', is markedly slower than with the others. Yet in context Gergiev conjures extra contrast with the other movements. The other point is that, though the recorded sound has spectacular weight and power over the widest range, it's clear that reverberation has been added to a recording made in a relatively dry theatre acoustic. Happily, it doesn't get in the way of orchestral detail. Both performance and recording, whatever the acoustic juggling, have a power that pins you back in your seat.

Scheherazade. The Tale of Tsar Saltan, Op 57 – Tsar's farewell and departure; Tsarina in a barrel at sea; The three wonders
Philharmonia Orchestra / Enrique Bátiz
Naxos 8 550726 (61' · DDD)　　Ⓢ Ⓞ Ⓓ+

Bátiz proves an impulsive, purposeful interpreter. In the second movement, his performance is more lilting Ozawa's, with rubato more persuasive, helped by superb Philharmonia wind-playing. The fanfares which interrupt in echelon (track 2) are brisk rather than weighty, confirming a more volatile approach than Ozawa's. In the third movement the Philharmonia strings may not be quite as rich as the Viennese, but with the excellent, well-balanced recording revealing more inner detail the result is more refined, with a delectably lilting clarinet entry on the *grazioso* dance-rhythm (track 3). David Nolan's violin solos are more individually rhapsodic, if not always as immaculate tonally as the Viennese. In short, this budget issue is at least as compelling and just as exciting as its full-priced rival, and rather better recorded. The fill-up can be warmly recommended too, three movements from the five which Rimsky included in the orchestral suite of musical pictures from *Tsar Saltan*, starting with the delectable march entitled the 'Tsar's farewell and departure'. The other movements are 'Tsarina in a barrel at sea' and 'The three wonders', with the over-played 'Flight of the Bumble-Bee' hardly missed.

Scheherazade. Capriccio espagnol
London Symphony Orchestra / Sir Charles Mackerras
Telarc CD80208 (60' · DDD) Recorded 1990   Ⓕ**O**

Sir Charles Mackerras, a vibrant interpreter of Russian music, throws himself into this music with expressive abandon, but allies it to control so that every effect is realised and the London Symphony Orchestra plays these familiar works as if it was discovering them afresh. Together they produce performances that are both vivid and thoughtful, while the solo violin in *Scheherazade* is seductively and elegantly played by Kees Hulsmann, not least at the wonderfully peaceful end to the whole work. The finale, featuring the storm and shipwreck is superbly done, the wind and brass bringing you to the edge of your seat. This sensuous and thrilling work needs spectacular yet detailed sound, and that's what it gets here, the 1990 recording in Walthamstow Town Hall giving us a CD that many collectors will choose to use as a demonstration disc to impress their friends. The performance and recording of the *Capriccio espagnol* is no less of a success.

Joaquin Rodrigo   Spanish 1901-1999

Rodrigo, blind from the age of three, studied with Antich in Valencia and Dukas in Paris (from 1927), also receiving encouragement from Falla. His Concierto de Aranjuez for guitar and orchestra (1939) made his name and established his style of tuneful and smoothly colourful Hispanicism: his later works include similar concertos for violin, piano, cello, harp and flute as well as songs and small instrumental pieces, several for guitar.   **GROVE**music

---

Concertos (including 'de Aranjuez')

Concierto de Aranjuez[a]. Concierto andaluz[a]. Fantasía para un gentilhombre[b]
[a]**Ricardo Gallén** gtr [b]**EntreQuatre Quitar Quartet** (Jesús Prieto, Roberto Martínez, Carlos Cuanda, Manuel Paz gtrs) **Asturias Symphony Orchestra / Maximiano Valdes**
Naxos 8 555841 (68' · DDD)   Ⓢ➔

Concierto en modo galante[b]. Canconeta[a]. Concierto como un Divertimento[b]. Concierto de estío[a]
[a]**Mikhail Ovrutsky** vn [b]**Asier Polo** vc **Castille and León Symphony Orchestra / Max Bragado-Darman**
Naxos 8 555840 (78' · DDD)   Ⓢ➔

Piano Concerto (Concierto heroico – ed Achúcarro)[a]. Juglares. Homenaje a la Tempranica. Música para un jardín

[a]**Daniel Ligorio Ferrándiz** pf **Castille and León Symphony Orchestra / Max Bragado-Darman**
Naxos 8 557101 (60' · DDD)   Ⓢ➔

The focus of these three volumes is on concertos, the most popular and arguably the best segment of Rodrigo's orchestral music. The best known are those for guitar and orchestra, of the very numerous recordings of which these are 'good enough to keep'. Lest anyone might think that the *Concierto para piano y orquesta* listed on Volume 4 is a previously overlooked work, it's in fact the *Concierto heroico* in modestly repackaged form. Achúcarro revised it with the composer's consent to make the work 'slightly more dynamic'. This is now the definitive form and performance of the concerto. The 'symphonic essay' *Juglares* (1923) was Rodrigo's first orchestral work, brief but characteristic of the music of Valencia, where he lived before going to Paris to study. It has no other current recording. All the remaining works on these three discs have alternative recordings but though one may prefer the warmer-sounding version of the *Concierto de estío* by Agustín León Ara, the composer's son-in-law, on the EMI set, these recordings are in every respect comparable with the 'opposition'.

Concierto de Aranjuez[a]. Three Piezas españolas[b]. Invocacíon y danza[c]. Fantasía para un gentilhombre[d]
Julian Bream gtr [a]**Chamber Orchestra of Europe / Sir John Eliot Gardiner;** [d]**RCA Victor Chamber Orchestra / Leo Brouwer**
RCA Victor 09026 61611-2 (69' · DDD) Recorded [abc]1982-83, [d]1987   Ⓜ**OOO**

 In the early 1980s Bream had entered a phase when his musical and technical powers were at their height, which he too recognised and celebrated in this remarkable album. With it he confirmed that he's Segovia's truest and best successor, though in no sense his imitator, and established a benchmark in the history of the guitar on record. Everything he touched turns to music, and is here recorded with the utmost reality. If anyone is wondering why he should here have taken his third bite at Aranjuez's cherry, it was in order to 'go digital' but in the event this proved a subsidiary *raison-d'être*. At the time the COE was no casual band assembled for a session, but a newly formed orchestra of young players from several countries, greeting the concerto as a fresh experience and playing it with splendid precision and vitality. John Eliot Gardiner's conducting is unfailingly idiomatic. Who catalysed whom is hard to say, but Bream certainly responded with the *Aranjuez* of his life, eloquently phrased and passionate; nothing is lost in the recording and the guitar is 'prestidigitalised' into unfailing audibility. This version of the concerto must remain the touchstone for a very long time, reaffirming the thoroughbred character of a warhorse that often sounds tired and overworked.

Leo Brouwer is a man of so many musical parts that the loss of one of them – his role as a virtuoso guitarist – has passed almost unnoticed; here he plays one of the others, that of conductor. What better than to provide the ammunition for others to fire, and to direct the campaign yourself? *Fantasía para un gentilhombre* has its own merits and demerits, with Bream stressing the musical rather than the virtuoso elements, adopting somewhat slower tempos than other interpreters in most of the movements – that of the final 'Canarios' is more in keeping with the character of the dance itself. Brouwer's splendid control of the orchestra reflects his experience of both sides of the concerto 'fence'. This disc is a must.

Rodrigo Concierto de Aranjuez **Castelnuovo-Tedesco** Guitar Concerto No 1 in D, Op 99
Villa-Lobos Guitar Concerto
Norbert Kraft *gtr* **Northern Chamber Orchestra / Nicholas Ward**
Naxos 8 550729 (60' · DDD)   Ⓢ**Ⓞ▶**

The time has long passed when it was possible to point to any one recording of any of these concertos (the Rodrigo in particular) as 'The Best'; as with players, one can only discern a 'top bracket' within which choice depends finally on personal preference – or allegiance to your favourite performer, or indeed with the other works on the disc. Norbert Kraft's accounts of these concertos takes its place therein. In this recording Kraft is placed forwardly enough for every detail to be heard, but not to create an impression of artificiality. The Northern Chamber Orchestra plays with freshness and is alert to every detail and the beautifully clear recording catches it faithfully. A bargain.

Concierto madrigal

Concierto madrigal. Danza de la Amapola[a]. Evocaciones – Mañana en Trianea[a]. Gran marcha de los subsecretarios[a]. Piezas – Fandango del ventorrillo[a]. Serenata española[a]. Sonada de adiós, 'Hommage à Paul Dukas'[a]. Tonadilla ([a]arr Peter Katona, Zoltán Katona)
Peter Katona, Zoltán Katona *gtrs* **Rotterdam Chamber Orchestra / Conrad van Alphen**
Channel Classics CCS16698 (62' · DDD)   Ⓕ**Ⓞ**

The best of the established guitar duos have consisted of players who are/were either married or blood-related – favourable conditions for in-built empathy. Presti-Lagoya set the pace in the 1960s, one which has still to be fully matched. Now we have the Hungarian duo of the Katona twins, possessed of a technique most others can only dream of. Their needlesharp unanimity of thought and attack is such that listening 'blind' you might wonder how a player could possibly have so many digits. Rodrigo wrote only two works for two guitars, the *Tonadilla* and (with orchestra) the *Concierto madrigal*. Neither has been better recorded than here. In the latter the recorded balance often tips slightly in favour of the orchestra,

but this is a minor quibble. In order to flesh out the aprogramme the Katonas have made admirable arrangements of six piano pieces written between 1931 and 1981, and these magnificently played versions for two guitars should keep Rodrigo aficionados happy enough. The Katonas have yet to parallel the emotional depth and warmth of Presti-Lagoya, but they have youth on their side and, being in total command of every other necessary 'tools', they may well become world-beaters. This is a stunning disc, to which the orchestra and recording engineers have made fitting contributions.

Concierto madrigal. Concierto para una fiesta
Ricardo Gallén, Joaquín Clerch *gtrs* **Asturias Symphony Orchestra / Maximiano Valdés**
Naxos 8 555842 (62' · DDD)   Ⓢ▶

The *Concierto madrigal* is, like the *Fantasía para un gentilhombre*, a tribute to times past though, since the first movement briefly tugs a forelock to Monteverdi, and the madrigal *O felici occhi miei* plays a key role, it isn't an exclusively Spanish one. It's a fascinating work, with ten movements full of diversity and maybe the one of the 'family' that deserves a place on that distant desert island. As with the *Concierto para una fiesta*, this is a recording that can hold its own with any of its rivals – finely played with good sound from all concerned, excellently balanced and faithfully recorded. The *Concierto para una fiesta* was commissioned by a wealthy Texan as a present for the coming-out party of his daughters, admirers of Pepe Romero. He and the composer were reported at the time to be chuckling at the thought of listening (in Heaven) to others struggling to play it. Time passes, however, and there are now several good recordings of the work by others, of whom Ricardo Gallén is now one. Technical skills have been steadily on a rising curve for decades and, whether or not the curve is asymptotic, its highest point has yet to be attained indefinitely by one single guitarist. Around every corner there may be an equally fast or even faster 'gun'. It isn't the most riveting of Rodrigo's concertos for solo guitar, but it's notable for its slow movement, a clear souvenir of that of the *Concierto de Aranjuez*, and Gallén's performance certainly does it justice.

Per la flor del lliri blau

Per la flor del lliri blau. A la busca del más allá. Palillos y Panderetas. Dos danzas españolas[a]. Tres viejos aires de danza
[a]**Lucero Tena** *castanets* **Castilla y León Symphony Orchestra / Max Bragado Darman**
Naxos 8 555962 (69' · DDD)   Ⓢ▶

At the heart of this volume are two of Rodrigo's finest orchestral works – *Per la flor del lliri blau* (1934) and *A la busca del más allá* (1976). The former is a symphonic poem based on a Valencian legend in which the three sons of a dying king go in search of a blue lily whose magic powers can save their father. The outcome is successful but tragic, as clearly depicted as that of the eponym of Elgar's *Falstaff*. *A la busca del más allá* was commissioned by the Houston Symphony for the bicentennial celebrations in the US. Their choice of composer may seem curious, but it proved a wise one. Its title ('In search of what lies beyond') reflected Houston's status as the centre of space exploration. How would Rodrigo, who had until then devoted his attention to all things Spanish and was then 75, deal with such an unfamiliar demand? The answer was that he did so with skill and imagination, leaving little or no trace of Spanishry. The curtain rises and falls with a long roll on an undamped cymbal, and the principal motif of what separates these events contains a 'questioning' tritone. The performances of all the 'fillers' are exemplary but it's the two large works that make this recording indispensable to Rodrigo lovers.

Solo Piano Works

Piano Music, Volume 1
Al'ombre de Torre Bermeja. Air de Ballet sur le nom d'une Jeune Fille. Bagatela. Berceuse de Otoño. Berceuse de primavera. Cuatro Estampas andaluzas. Pastorale. Cincos Piezas del siglo XVI. Cuatro Piezas. Preludio de Añoranza. Serenata española. Sonada de adiós, 'Hommage à Paul Dukas'. Zarabanda lejana. Fantasía que contrahace la harpa de Ludovico
Artur Pizarro pf
Naxos 8 557272 (70' · DDD)   ⓈⓄⒹ

Rodrigo's piano music appears infrequently in the recital room, though excellent two-CD surveys have appeared: Gregory Allen on Bridge and Sara Marianovich on Sony. Now comes a first-class collection from the perceptive and sympathetic Artur Pizarro, who opens brilliantly with Rodrigo's evocation of Albéniz, *A l'ombre de Torre Bermeja*, here, as elsewhere, bringing out its affinities with the guitar. *Cuatro Piezas* include a glittering 'Fandango' and a touchingly pensive 'Prayer of the Princess of Castille', while among the *Andalusian Pictures* (*Cuatro Estampas andaluzas*), 'Twilight over the Guadalquivir River' makes a reflective contrast with the quirky bravura of the devilish 'Seguidillas'. Among the simpler items, the nostalgic *Preludio*, and delicate *Pastorale*, the rippling *Serenata española* and charming *Air de Ballet* are all highly beguiling. Pizarro captures the varying moods of this music very well. This generous collection is vividly recorded and with excellent booklet-notes by Graham Wade.

Philippe Rogier   Flemish 1561-1596

Rogier was a chorister at Philip II of Spain's chapel from 1572; he was ordained, becoming vice-maestro

in 1584 and maestro de capilla in 1586. Of his large output (at least 250 works), only 16 motets (1595), five masses (1598) and a few chansons and other sacred works survive. GROVEmusic

Missa Ego sum qui sum

Rogier Missa Ego sum qui sum. Laboravi in gemitu meo. Heu mihi Domine. Vias tuas. Taedet animam meam. Peccavi quid faciam tibi. Dominus regit me
Gombert Ego sum qui sum
Magnificat / Philip Cave
Linn Records CKD109 (75' · DDD · T/t)   ⓅⓄⒹ

So much first-rate 16th-century music still remains unrecorded, but here's a welcome addition. Philippe Rogier's death at the age of 35 in 1596 cut short a prolific stream of music. Worse was to come. In 1734 a fire destroyed the library of the Spanish royal chapel, which must have held a large number of his compositions (at the time of his death he was chief court musician to Philip II). How large a number can be gauged from the terrible earthquake that struck Lisbon in 1755, swallowing up the royal library along with 243 works. Today we're left with only 51, of which the present recital represents a sizeable proportion.

Rogier's music has Palestrina's imposing solidity and classical feel, but is more florid and freer in its use of dissonance. In this sense it looks forward to later Iberian music of the 17th century, achieving a sustained intensity in the motets. The Mass is a consummate demonstration, the skilful working out of a motet by Gombert, whose influence is very audible. The booklet-note rightly points out how Rogier develops his model in very different directions: the sequences that conclude most movements are persuasively managed, but sound utterly unlike Gombert.

Rogier's Mass *Domine Dominus noster* appears in a fine recording on Ricercar. But Magnificat's interpretation is of a different order. This is singing in the English tradition, but with greater warmth and richness than we're used to from mixed choirs of this kind. Given Rogier's predilection for fully scored writing, that richness pays dividends, as does the relatively large cast of 18 singers. Interpretation and music are well matched in more ways than one. Neither are strikingly original, but both make a striking impression.

Guy Ropartz   French 1864-1955

Ropartz was born into an artistic family who encouraged his interest in music. He read law but on graduating moved to Paris to study at the Conservatoire. He took lessons with Franck and Massenet. He became director of the conservatoire in Nancy where he made a huge impact. His musical voice is conservative clearly betraying his years with Franck. GROVEmusic

Rhapsodie[a]. Pêcheur d'Islande. Oedipe à Colone
[a]**Henri Demarquette** vc **Orchestre de Bretagne /**
Kirill Karabits
Timpani 1C1095 (57' · DDD)   Ⓕ

Literature, the sea and Brittany were recurrent
sources of inspiration throughout the life of
Joseph-Guy Ropartz. Like Bax, he had been a
poet in his twenties but for *Pêcheur d'Islande*
('Iceland Fisherman', 1890-91) and *Oedipe à
Colone* (1914) he turned to Pierre Loti and
Sophocles respectively. Although never a seaman like Roussel, the marine influence is strong
in *Pêcheur d'Islande* and the *Rhapsodie* for cello
and orchestra (1928), both of which make use of
folksongs from Brittany, and in his best known
work, the huge Third Symphony.

For those unfamiliar with Ropartz's style – and
there are quite a few discs devoted to his music –
he was much influenced by Franck and Fauré.
There are Magnard resonances, too, though
Ropartz was the more intuitive, less rigorous
creator. In *Pêcheur d'Islande*, for example, the
opening 'La mer d'Islande' ('Iceland's Sea') is
subtitled 'Symphony' but there is little genuinely
symphonic in the music. Rather, as in the central
'Scène d'amour', the music is evocative in a fantasia-like way. The lively finale, 'Les danses', however, does illustrate the protagonists' wedding.
There is more of the descriptive in the suite from
his incidental music to *Oedipe à Colone*. In places
the music even hints that Brittany's shores are
lapped by the Aegean!

The Orchestre de Bretagne's performances are
full of verve and sound well prepared, and they
and Karabits accompany the lyrical and smooth-
toned Henri Demarquette nicely in the *Rhapsodie*.
Timpani's sound is spacious and warm.

etiam sperasti. Il secondo libro de madrigali – Mia
benigna fortuna; Schiet'arbuscel. Il quarto libro de
madrigali – Se ben il duol
Huelgas Ensemble / Paul van Nevel
Harmonia Mundi HMC90 1760 (65' · DDD · T/t)   Ⓕ

The Huelgas Ensemble have recorded a masterly
recital of works by Cipriano de Rore, subtitled
'Music, Mirror of the text'. That's an apt description of much of Rore's output, but the inspired
and truly brilliant way in which he achieves his
goal is what has left his mark upon future generations of composers. The major work of the collection is Rore's seven-part 'parody-cum-*cantus-
firmus*' *Missa Praeter rerum seriem*, with its flowing
melody and showers of taut little imitations. Based
on a motet by Josquin and dedicated to Duke
Ercole d'Este, in whose service Rore was enrolled
in 1547, the composer hails his master by name in
the tenor part of every movement. The remainder
of the programme includes such widely different
pieces as the charming little eight-part love-song
Mon petit cueur, with its full canonic imitation and
wonderful final cadence, and the slow-moving
five-part responsary for Holy Saturday *Plange
quasi virgo*. Another striking piece is the four-
part madrigal *Calami sonum ferentes*, which
exploits the lowest range of the basses in slowly
rising chromatic scales. But possibly the most
original and forward-looking of all are the last
two pieces, in which Rore promotes his own,
very personal, technique of chordal homophony.
The anguished experimental *Se ben il duol* is a
small masterpiece, and so is the fully developed
motet on a text from Virgil, *Dissimulare etiam
sperasti*. Huelgas rises to the challenge of interpreting, with colour and genius, this amazing
music describing Dido's despair.

Cipriano de Rore   Flemish 1515/16-1565

*Rore was in Italy by the 1540s; he was associated with
Willaert and others in Venice. He was established as
a composer by 1547, when he was maestro di cappella
at the Ferrarese court. In 1559 he moved to Brussels
to serve Margaret of Parma, governor of the Netherlands, in 1561 to Parma, to enter Ottavio Farnese's
service, and in 1563 to Venice, where he was briefly
maestro di cappella at St Mark's. He returned to
Parma in 1564. The most influential of the earlier
madrigalists, he produced over 120 Italian madrigals, as well as c80 sacred motets, masses, a Passion,
secular motets and chansons. His early madrigals,
mainly serious in tone, show a masterly fusion of
sophisticated Franco-Flemish polyphony and Italian
lyricism, with controlled use of imagery, while his
later ones include marked progressive elements; these
were much admired by Monteverdi.* GROVEmusic

Missa Praeter rerum seriem

Missa Praeter rerum seriem. Calami sonum ferentes.
Mon petit cueur. Plange quasi virgo. Dissimulare

Ned Rorem   American b1923

*Rorem studied with Sowerby in Chicago (1938-9)
and with Thomson (1944) and Diamond in New
York, also attending the Curtis Institute (1943) and
the Juilliard School. From 1949 to 1958 he was
based in Paris, though spent two of those years
in Morocco: his published diaries of this and later
periods are flamboyantly candid. His large output
includes symphonies, instrumental pieces and choral
music, though he has been most productive and
successful as a composer of songs.* GROVEmusic

Concertos

Piano Concerto No 2[a]. Cello Concerto[b]
[a]**Simon Mulligan** pf [b]**Wen-Sinn Yang** vc
Royal Scottish National Orchestra / José Serebrier
Naxos 8 559315 (59' · DDD)   Ⓢ➔

How remarkable that two such delectable concertos should be receiving their world premieres
on disc. Unapologetically romantic and accessible, those qualities may well have mitigated

against acceptance among the industry's fashion-mongers. The Second Piano Concerto (1951) was written for Julius Katchen and was given its first performance by that superb pianist in 1954. Since then it has lain dormant until its present revival by Simon Mulligan whose brilliance, ideally matched by José Serebrier, is worthy of Katchen himself. Here, the ghosts of Ravel, Françaix, Gershwin, Stravinsky and, most of all, Poulenc, jostle for attention. Yet Rorem's idiom is as personal as it is chic. The final pages of the central 'Quiet and Sad' movement, where the piano weaves intricate tracery round the orchestral theme, may owe much to the *Adagio assai* from Ravel's G major Concerto but it maintains its own character. The finale, 'Real Fast', is an irresistible *tour de force* played up to the hilt by Mulligan.

In the Cello Concerto Rorem happily eschews a conventional form, giving programmatic subtitles to each section. These range from 'Curtain Raise' to 'Adrift', offering Wen-Sinn Yang a rich opportunity, whether playing primus inter pares or revelling in Rorem's alternating nostalgia and effervescence. Finely recorded, it's a clear winner.

Chamber Works

Book of Hours[a]. Bright Music[b]. End of Summer[c]
The Fibonacci Sequence ([ab]Anna Noakes *fl* [c]Julian Farrell *cl* [a]Gillian Tingay *hp* [bc]Kathron Sturrock *pf* [bc]Jonathan Carney, [b]Ursula Gough *vns* [b]Michael Stirling *vc*)
Naxos American Classics 8 559128 (60' · DDD)

⑤OO▶

In Ned Rorem's *End of Summer* (1985) for clarinet, violin and piano, dramatic juxtapositions seem to be the work's organising principle. Without postmodern trickery, Rorem shows us that seemingly disparate elements can coexist quite happily. One hears a similar kind of musical détente going on in parts of *Bright Music* (1987) for flute, two violins, cello and piano – particularly in the opening Fandango, inspired by the image of a rat inside a rubbish bin. This is a substantial, delightful suite, centered on a brilliant *scherzo* movement ('Dance-Song-Dance') that enfolds one of Rorem's loveliest tunes. The slow movement (entitled 'Another Dance') is an expansive, aching song without words, and the whirlwind finale a clever and ultimately unsettling take on the last movement of Chopin's *Funeral March* Sonata.

Book of Hours (1975), for flute and harp, is structured on the timetable of monastic prayer, beginning with Matins and continuing through Lauds all the way to Vespers and Compline. There are few sweet melodies here, though Rorem's language is always expressive. 'Sext (Noon)' is especially touching, with the flute's shakuhachi-like *glissandi* sighing over the harp's exquisitely fragile song.

The performances by the Fibonacci Sequence are consistently polished and persuasive.

Clear recording, too, though the instruments are placed very close to the microphones. Very strongly recommended.

Songs

Santa Fé – No 2, Opus 101; No 4, Sonnet; No 8, The wintry mind; No 12, The sowers. Clouds. Early in the morning. The serpent. Now sleeps the crimson petal. I strolled across an open field. To a young girl. Jeanie with the light brown hair. Ode. For Poulenc. Little elegy. Alleluia. Look down, fair moon. O you whom I often and silently come. I will always love you. The tulip tree. I am rose. The Lordly Hudson. O do not love too long. Far far away. For Susan. A journey. Sometimes with one I love. Love. Orchids. Stopping by woods on a snowy evening. Do I love you more than a day? Ferry me across the water. That shadow, my likeness
Susan Graham *sop* **Malcolm Martineau** *pf* with **Ensemble Oriol** (Christiane Plath *vn* Sebastian Gottschick *va* Friedeman Ludwïg *vc*)
Erato 8573-80222-2 (61' · DDD · T)

⑤OO▶

If Rorem's songs aren't as well known as those of Copland or Cole Porter it's probably because they're more difficult to sing. The earliest here is from 1947 (*The Lordly Hudson*, on a poem by Paul Goodman), the latest from 1983 (*That shadow, my likeness*, one of several Walt Whitman settings). Most of the others, though, were composed in the 1950s when Rorem was living in France. One could look for obvious French influences – Rorem was a close friend of Auric and Poulenc – but strangely it's the later songs, from the cycle *Santa Fé* on poems by Witter Bynner, that have a more Gallic sound, the piano and string trio accompaniment having that aching, nostalgic mood which Rorem himself describes as 'a period removed from Time and, like the act of love, [it] has no limits, no beginning nor end.' The only song in French is a poem by Ronsard, an ode to peace, but two songs are about Paris. *Early in the morning*, a poem by Robert Hillyer, is an evocation of a young poet in love in and with Paris, its accompaniment a homage to all the sad waltzes that murmur their recollections of the city from Satie to Kosma. *For Poulenc*, written especially by Frank O'Hara for Rorem to set as part of an album of songs in memory of Poulenc, describes all the city in mourning.

Rorem called his autobiography *Knowing when to stop*, and it's a wonderful description of his own songs. The strength and beauty of his settings lies in their directness and candour. He doesn't linger, the poem and song are one, the melody growing from the accompaniment into the vocal line, but just as you seem able to grasp it, it's gone. Martineau plays with an unfailing sensitivity, giving the tiny shifts of mood from exuberance to elegiac melancholy their exact weight.

Alleluia. Are you the new person?. As Adam early in the morning. Ask me no more. Early in the morning. Far Far Away. Full of life now. I am Rose. I strolled

across an open field. Little Elegy. Love in a Life. Lullaby of the Woman of the Mountain. Memory. My Papa's Waltz. Nantucket. Night Crow. The Nightingale. Now sleeps the crimson petal. O you to whom I often and silently come. Orchids. Root Cellar. Sally's Smile. See how they love me. The Serpent. Snake. Spring. Stopping by Woods on a Snowy Evening. Such beauty as hurts to behold. Visits to St Elizabeth's. The Waking. What if some little pain... Youth, Day, Old Age and Night
Carole Farley sop **Ned Rorem** pf
Naxos 8 559084 (58' · DDD)   ⑤🅳

Seventeen of these 32 songs aren't otherwise available on disc, and they include some of Rorem's finest and most haunting. The utter simplicity that weaves a magic spell in *Nantucket*, the beautiful paralleling of Gerard Manley Hopkins's ecstatic imagery in *Spring*, the bare but deeply eloquent *Such beauty as hurts to behold*, the amiable contemplation of old age and possible immortality in *Full of life now* – all these are warmly welcome, and it's good to have for the first time a complete recording of Rorem's nine settings of Theodore Roethke. Carole Farley's diction is so immaculate that you'll hardly need the booklet of texts, and her acute response to words must be one reason why Rorem so willingly collaborated with her on this recording. About the voice itself some might have a reservation. Although Farley fines her tone down for the most part effectively her sound is basically operatic. But rejecting this disc on that account would mean foregoing the infectious lilt of *The Nightingale*, the amply lyrical, movingly expressive *Love in a life*, the beautiful long lines of *Ask me no more* and all the others mentioned. No, admirers of Rorem's unique talent will simply have to have this collection. His piano-playing is beautifully supportive.

Six Songs for High Voice. Ariel[a]. Ode. Last Poems of Wallace Stevens[b]. Alleluia. Jack l'éventreur
Laura Aikin sop [a]**Nicola Jürgensen** cl
[b]**Gerhard Zank** vc **Donald Sulzen** pf
Orfeo C620 041A (66' · DDD · T)   ⑤

Interest continues in Ned Rorem's vocal music – more than 300 solo songs and numerous song-cycles. There's little duplication between Laura Aikin's recital and those of Susan Graham and Carole Farley (above). Since Rorem often favours the mezzo voice, it's a surprise to find him in the high soprano stratosphere.

Jack l'éventreur ('Jack the Ripper') has lots of odd imagery: the murderer is dressed in tweed, with a rose between his teeth. The *Six Songs for High Voice*, to poems by Dryden and Browning, were scored originally for orchestra, but here arranged for piano. Aikin relishes the coloratura flourishes, but like all high sopranos isn't always able to get the words across. The Wallace Stevens settings, for voice, piano and cello, are linked by two instrumental solos, accentuating the sense of a journey through experience, a growth of feeling and understanding. In *Ariel*, on poems by Sylvia Plath, the clarinet takes over as a third voice;

Nicola Jürgensen provides a spectacular obbligato to the slightly jazzy settings and here Aikin's words are splendidly clear.

Donald Sulzen's accompaniments accentuate Rorem's sometimes severe, sometimes complex keyboard writing. Aikin is a singer to watch, and this is a major addition to the discography.

Johann Rosenmüller

German c1619-1684

Rosenmüller first worked as an organist and teacher in Leipzig, but was imprisoned (on suspicion of homosexuality) in 1655. From 1658 he was a trombonist at St Mark's, Venice, and in 1678-82 also composer at the Ospedale della Pietà. Finally he returned to Germany as court Kapellmeister at Wolfenbüttel. A prolific composer, he was important in transmitting Italian styles to Germany, where his music was especially popular. He published four instrumental collections, which move from simple dance suites to Italianate ensemble sonatas; the 12 sonatas of 1682 include much fugal writing.   GROVEmusic

Sacred Music

'Weihnachtshistorie'
Gloria in excelsis Deo. Lieber Herre Gott. Entsetze dich, Natur. Es waren Hirten auf dem Felde bei den Hürden. Nihil novum sub sole. Christus ist mein Leben. Ich freue mich in dir. O nomen Jesu
Cantus Cölln; Concerto Palatino / Konrad Junghänel lte
Harmonia Mundi HMC90 1861 (78' · DDD · T/t)   ⑤

Cantus Cölln has already championed Rosenmüller's Venetian music in a trail-blazing recording of his Vespers, and now explore his less familiar earlier period: almost all the featured music was created for Christmas at Leipzig. *Es waren Hirten auf dem Felde bei den Hürden* was composed 20 years before Schütz's celebrated *Weihnachtshistorie*; it swells in scope from a cluster of shepherds to a resplendent heavenly host. Further to the flamboyance of Rosenmüller's theatrical writing, there are moments of sweet simplicity. He performed *Entsetze dich, Natur* on Christmas Day 1649; it's the most impressive piece on a disc full of treasures.

Cantus Cölln and Concerto Palatino give a masterclass in sonorous contrasts between finely shaded intimacy and colourful grandeur. The singers and instrumentalists are technically impeccable, and Konrad Junghänel directs with his usual sensitivity and taste.

Gioachino Rossini

Italian 1792-1868

Rossini's parents were musicians, his father a horn player, his mother a singer. He learnt the horn and

singing, and as a boy sang in at least one opera in Bologna, where the family lived. He studied there and began his operatic career when, at 18, he wrote a one-act comedy for Venice. Further commissions followed, from Bologna, Ferrara, Venice again and Milan, where *La pietra del paragone* was a success at La Scala in 1812. This was one of seven operas written in 16 months, all but one being comic.

This level of activity continued in the ensuing years. His first operas to win international acclaim come from 1813, written for different Venetian theatres: the serious *Tancredi* and the farcically comic *L'italiana in Algeri*, the one showing a fusion of lyrical expression and dramatic needs, the other moving easily between the sentimental, the patriotic, the absurd and the sheer lunatic. Two operas for Milan were less successful. In 1815 Rossini went to Naples as musical and artistic director of the Teatro San Carlo, which led to a concentration on serious opera. But he was allowed to compose for other theatres, and from this time date two of his supreme comedies, written for Rome, *Il barbiere di Siviglia* and *La Cenerentola*. The former has claims to be considered the greatest of all Italian comic operas, eternally fresh in its wit and its inventiveness. It dates from 1816; initially it was a failure, but quickly became the most loved of his comic works. The next year saw *La Cenerentola*, a charmingly sentimental tale in which the heroine moves from a touching folksy ditty as the scullery maid to brilliant coloratura apt to a royal maiden.

Rossini's most important operas in the period that followed were for Naples. The third act of his *Otello* (1816), with its strong unitary structure, marks his maturity as a musical dramatist. The Neapolitan operas, even though much dependent on solo singing of a highly florid kind, show an enormous expansion of musical means, with more and longer ensembles and the chorus an active participant; the accompanied recitative is more dramatic and the orchestra is given greater prominence. Rossini abandoned traditional overtures as well. In 1822 he married Naples' leading soprano Isabella Colbran, but it proved an ill match.

Among the masterpieces from this period are *Maometto II* (1820) and *Semiramide* (1823). In 1823 Rossini left for London and Paris where he took on the directorship of the Théâtre-Italien, composing for that theatre and the Opéra. Some of his Paris works are adaptations (*Le siège de Corinthe* and *Moïse et Pharaon*); the opéra comique *Le Comte Ory* is part-new, *Guillaume Tell* wholly. This last, widely regarded as his chef d'oeuvre, is a rich tapestry of his most inspired music, with elaborate orchestration, many ensembles, spectacular ballets and processions in the French tradition, opulent orchestral writing and a new harmonic boldness.

At 37, he retired from opera composition. He left Paris in 1837 to live in Italy, but suffered prolonged and painful illness there. Isabella died in 1845 and the next year he married Olympe Pélissier, with whom he had lived for 15 years. He composed hardly at all during this period (the *Stabat mater* belongs to his Paris years); but he went back to Paris in 1855, and his health, humour and urge to compose returned. He wrote a quantity of pieces for piano and voices that he called *Péchés de vieillesse* ('Sins of Old Age'), including the graceful and economical *Petite messe solennelle* (1863). GROVEmusic

Overtures etc

'Discoveries'

Robert Bruce – Overture (arr Niedermeyer). Péchés de Vieillesse, Book 3, 'Morceaux réservés' – Le chant des Titans. Grande Fanfare (Le Rendez-vous de chasse). Guillaume Tell – Final du Divertissement; Pas-de deux. Ermione – Sinfonia. Moïse et Pharaon – Ouverture et Introduction[b]. La Siège de Corinthe – Ballabile-Galop. Inno alla pace, 'È foriera la Pace'[cd]. Hymne, 'De l'Italie et de la France'[ac]. Hymne à Napoléon III et à son vaillant peuple[b]

[a]**Laura Giordano** sop [b]**Ildar Abdrazakov,** [c]**Michele Pertusi** bars [d]**Nelson Calzi** fp **Giuseppe Verdi Chorus and Symphony Orchestra, Milan / Riccardo Chailly**

Decca 470 298-2DH (69' · DDD · T/t) Ⓕ**ⓄⓄ**▷

Philip Gossett calls this 'a Rossinian curio cabinet'. 'A banquet made with leftovers from the Rossini kitchen' would do as well. Whatever the analogy, the art is as much in the assembling of the materials as in the materials themselves. The most familiar music – gleanings from *Zelmira*, *Armida* and *La donna del lago* – is to be found in the very first item, the overture to the Rossinian pastiche *Robert Bruce*, assembled for the Paris Opéra in 1846 by the composer Louis Niedermeyer. The other orchestral items are all *echt*-Rossini. The splendid *Le Rendez-vous de chasse* for four hunting horns and orchestra dates from the time of the composition of *Guillaume Tell* and could almost be a pendant to it. But the pillars of the anthology are the splendid *Le Chant des Titans* and three of Rossini's grand but little-known occasional hymns. The earliest of these is *De l'Italie et de la France*, written in 1825 for Charles X's coronation; the latest, written in 1867 when Rossini was 75, is the grandiose *Hymne à Napoléon III à Son Vaillant Peuple*. It all goes with a tremendous swing and the cannon-and-church-bells end is spectacular. The voltage of Chailly's performances is unremitting high, as is the attention to shading and fine detail. This is conducting Toscanini or De Sabata would have been hard-pressed to better. The recordings, in Milan's new Auditorium di Milano, are also spectacularly good, vivid yet sensitive to the smallest detail.

Songs

'Soirées musicales'

Soirées musicales – La promessa[a]; Il rimprovero[b]; La partenza[c]; L'orgia[c]; L'invito[b]; La pastorella dell'Alpi[a]; La gita in gondola[c]; La danza[c]; La regata veneziana[ab]; La pesca[ab]; La serenata[ac]. Mi lagnerò tacendo II[b]. Péchés de vieillesse – Book 2, Album français: Les Adieux à la vie[a]; L'Orpheline du Tyrol[b]; Book 3, Morceaux réservés: L'esule[c]; Les amants de Séville[bc]; Book 11, Miscellanée de musique vocale: La chanson du bébé[a]. La regata veneziana[b]

[a]**Miah Persson** sop [b]**Stella Doufexis** mez [c]**Bruce Ford** ten **Roger Vignoles** pf

Hyperion CDA67647 (79' · DDD · T/t)　　　Ⓕ

This is a classic case of 'spoiling the ship for a ha'porth of tar', as well as further evidence of Hyperion's uncharacteristically uncertain touch with Rossini. Having taken the trouble to engage three distinguished singers to record the *Soirées musicales*, they have drawn the line at employing a fourth, the bass required for the final duet 'Li marinari'. The disc cannot therefore be the 'library' recording of *Les soirées* we currently need. After the 11 numbers from *Soirées musicales*, we are given a further nine songs plucked somewhat randomly from the later *Péchés de vieillesse*.

That said, there is much to enjoy on the record. The ordering and voice allocation of *Les soirées* is open to variation. The eight solo songs are generally sung by a soprano or a mezzo, 'La danza' by the tenor. Here the tenor has three of the songs. In 'La danza' memories of singers from Caruso to Pavarotti are perhaps a shade too insistent. Elsewhere in *Les soirées*, Bruce Ford shows every sign of shifting from opera to chanson with skill and imagination; the duet 'Les amants de Séville' from *Péchés* in which he partners mezzo Stella Doufexis is one of the disc's highlights. The two women barely put a foot wrong, though Miah Persson's Alpine shepherdess is preferable to her somewhat over-indulged *bébé*. The real star of the record is pianist Roger Vignoles. Rossini's writing for the piano is highly idiosyncratic. It requires a first-rate technique, a sure sense of style and an ability to bring off with insouciance all manner of hair's-breadth effects. Vignoles has the measure of all this and more.

Petite messe solennelle

Petite messe solennelle
Daniella Dessì *sop* **Gloria Scalchi** *mez* **Giuseppe Sabbatini** *ten* **Michele Pertusi** *bass* **Chorus and Orchestra of the Teatro Comunale, Bologna / Riccardo Chailly**
Decca ② 444 134-2DX2 (82' · DDD · T/t)　　Ⓜ⊙

A proper representative of the orchestrated version of the *Petite messe* has been long overdue. Chailly's performance is a glorious heart-warming affair. Not that you're likely to be convinced right away. To ears accustomed to the *Kyrie* in its original form, the texturing here is pure suet. Nor does the sound of the largish and here rather distantly placed choir seem especially well focused in the *Christe eleison*. Gradually, though, the ear adjusts, the musicians warm to their task, the performance gets into its stride. The Bologna Chorus sings the *Gloria* and *Credo* with passion, clarity and love. The tenor is adequate, the bass superb, the two girls absolutely fabulous. If the *Crucifixus* can never be as painful as it's in the sparer original version, this is amply offset by the sheer beauty of Daniella Dessì's singing and by the hair-raising force of the 'Et resurrexit'

(superbly recorded) as Chailly and his choir realise it.

By the end, after Gloria Scalchi's deeply affecting account of the *Agnus Dei*, you begin to wonder whether the orchestral version wasn't more than a match for the original. It isn't, but it's an indication of the cumulative eloquence of this utterly inspired performance that it comes to seem so.

Stabat mater

Stabat mater　　　　　　　　　　　　Ⓟ
Krassimira Stoyanova *sop* Petra Lang *mez* Bruce Fowler *ten* Daniel Borowski *bass* RIAS Chamber Choir, Berlin; Academy for Ancient Music, Berlin / Marcus Creed
Harmonia Mundi HMC90 1693 (57' · DDD · T/t)　Ⓕ⊙

One of the first, and best, recordings of this splendid but interpretatively elusive work was made in Berlin in 1954 under the direction of Ferenc Fricsay. Like the present recording, it featured the RIAS (Berlin Radio) Chamber Choir, though in those days the fledgling choir was supplemented in the full choruses by the famous St Hedwig's Cathedral Choir. Now on its own, it acquits itself superbly in all movements and dimensions with its own conductor, the English-born Marcus Creed. That this recording uses period instruments might seem in so obviously 'vocal' a piece to be of no particular moment. In practice, the work's prevailingly dark orchestral colours are memorably realised by the instrumentalists of Berlin's Academy for Ancient Music. In the grand opening movement, the four soloists are recorded uncomfortably far forward; but if you can establish an agreeable level for this movement, the rest of the performance sounds very well indeed. Choir and orchestra are themselves unfailingly well balanced.

Creed's reading is full of character: immensely strong but always sensitively paced. Rossini might have raised an eyebrow at Creed's fondness for romantically protracted codas; equally, he would have applauded his sensitive moulding of the accompaniments, matched shrewdly but never indulgently to the singers' (and the music's) needs. The soloists, highly talented, are excellent, more than a match for most rival teams.

Opera Arias

La donna del lago – Tanti affetti in tal momento. **Elisabetta, Regina d'Inghilterra** – Quant' è grato all'alma mia; Fellon, la penna avrai. **Maometto II** – Ah! che invan su questo ciglio; Giusto ciel, in tal periglio. **Le nozze di Teti e di Peleo** – Ah, non potrian reistere. **Semiramide** – Serenai vaghirai … Bel raggio lusinghier. **Zelmira** – Riedi al soglio
Cecilia Bartoli *mez* **Chorus and Orchestra of the Teatro La Fenice, Venice / Ion Marin**
Decca 436 075-2DH (59' · DDD · T/t)　　　Ⓕ⊙➜

This sparkling disc brings together a collection of arias Rossini composed for one of the great *prima donnas* of the 19th century, his wife, Isabella Colbran. It's tempting to wonder whether even she could match Cecilia Bartoli, one of the most luscious, most exciting voices in opera. All those dazzling chromatic runs, leaps, cadenzas and cascading coloraturas are handled with consummate ease. Throughout she sounds as if she's enjoying the music; there's always an engaging smile in the voice, although she's properly imperious in the extracts from *Elisabetta* and disarmingly simple in the prayerful 'Giusto ciel, in tal periglio' from *Maometto II*. The orchestral and choral forces provide a delightful intimacy, with some cheeky woodwind solos and fruity brass passages.

The recording, produced at the Teatro La Fenice by Decca veteran Christopher Raeburn, favours the voices but gives it just enough distance to accommodate high Cs and astounding A flats at the bottom of the range. The orchestral perspective is changeable but satisfactory. For Rossini and Bartoli fans, this disc is a must.

Aureliano in Palmira – Overture; Perché mai le luci apprimo. **Tancredi** – Overture; Oh patria! Dolce e ingrate patria. **Semiramide** – Overture; Eccomi…Ah, quel giorno; In si barbara sciagura. La donna del lago – Mura felici; Quelle spietate…Ah si pera
Max Emmanuel Cencic counterten Le Motet de Genève Vocal Ensemble; Geneva Chamber Orchestra / Michael Hofstetter
Virgin Classics 385788-2 (74' · DDD)   Ⓕ

If countertenors can sing Handel, why not Rossini? Among the many fine singers Rossini heard during his student days in Bologna, two were especially important: the castrato Giovan Battista Velluti and the young Spanish soprano Isabella Colbran. Hearing both on the same stage must have been an astonishing experience: the old order of the castrati, doomed to extinction, side by side with the new order of singing actresses whose brilliantly developed coloratura techniques were in some sense a bequest from the castrati. Purity of tone, flexibility of technique and a 'profoundly penetrating accent' were what most impressed Rossini about the castrati. It was a different sound from that of the modern countertenor but the stylistic principles are not a hundred miles removed.

The singing of Viennese countertenor Max Emmanuel Cencic is distinguished by good rhythm, crisp divisions and clear, expressive word use. The range these roles require sits comfortably on his voice. The G below the stave is rounded and full, the two octaves beyond are clear and bright, albeit with a marked vibrato in places. Cencic's musicianship is generally impeccable: a tribute to the values instilled in him during his time in the Vienna Boys' Choir which he left in 1992, nine years before his decision to 're-create' himself as a countertenor.

Rossini created one operatic role for Velluti, in *Aureliano in Palmira*. Having antagonised the company with his self-regarding antics, Velluti is said to have made next to no impact onstage. Cencic does not disappoint in the opera's celebrated pastoral plaint or in Tancredi's cabaletta 'Di tanti palpiti'. However, it is the scene from Act 2 of *Semiramide* which provides the recital's high-point. Hamlet-like, Arsace recognises his mother's guilt (in an expressive transition finely realised by Cencic) alongside his duty to avenge his father's death, as music familiar from the overture anticipates the crises to come.

With three overtures, Cencic's contributions add up to just 49 minutes. Short measure, you might think, but more than enough to give one a sense of what a talented countertenor can bring to Rossini.

Armida – Dove son io![9]. **Aureliano in Palmira** – Se tu m'ami, o mia regina[b]. **Bianca e Falliero** – Cielo, il mio labbro ispira[c]. **Elisabetta, Regina d'Inghilterra** – Qant'è grato all'alma mia[a]. **Mosè in Egitto** – Mi manca la voce[e]; Porgi la destra amata[h]. **Semiramide** – Se la vita[f]. **Vallace** – Viva Vallace! Vallace Viva[i]. **Zelmira** – Riedi al soglio[d]
Nelly Miricioiu with [ehi]**Patrizia Biccire** sops [bc]**Enkelejda Shkosa** mez [i]**Antonia Sotgiù** voc [ceg]**Bruce Ford,** [dehi]**Barry Banks,** [h]**Dominic Natoli** tens [cdhi]**Gary Magee,** [hi]**Dean Robinson** bars [f]**Alastair Miles** bass [i]**Simon Bailey** voc [acdhi]**Geoffrey Mitchell Choir; Academy of St Martin in the Fields / David Parry**
Opera Rara ORR211 (67' · DDD · T/t)   Ⓕ Ⓞ

Rossini is a difficult composer to anthologise. Callas and Walter Legge or Sutherland and Bonynge might have come up with something fascinating and fabulous had they been so minded. Caballé did: the eminently collectable *Rossini Rarities* disc she produced for the Rossini bicentenary in 1968. For the rest, successful recitals have been few and far between, indifferent singing or poor planning principally to blame. Not so Opera Rara's Rossini Gala. Patric Schmid's inventive programme focuses on Rossini's Naples period and the extraordinary array of roles he created for the great Spanish soprano Isabella Colbran. What distinguishes this recital is that it doesn't only anthologise set-piece arias. Rossini gave Colbran some grand entrances and some even grander exits, and there are examples of both here: Queen Elizabeth's arrival and Zelmira's final florid song of thanksgiving. But there are also two wonderful quartets, two exquisite duets, a famous *coup de théâtre* (the Act 2 finale of *Mosè in Egitto* with its terrific lightning-strike), and one of Rossini's finest pieces of music-theatre: the scene near the start of Act 2 of *Semiramide* where the Queen and her lover, the adulterous regicide Assur, have rows worthy of the Macbeths over events which are beginning to overshadow them.

Miricioiu isn't a *bel canto* specialist; Santuzza is as much her territory as Semiramide. In neither role is the technique perfectly honed, but the effect is rarely less than compelling. Every one of the heroines presented here is vividly depicted, with a distinguished supporting cast helping to etch each scene into the imagination.

The gala ends with an intriguing rarity which has nothing to do with Colbran or Miricioiu. *Vallace* is a shortened, revised and relocated version of *Guillaume Tell* prepared for La Scala, Milan, in 1836-7. Austrian tyranny being an uncongenial subject to Milan's Austrian rulers, the libretto was recast to show English tyranny instead: Edward I's bloody crusade against the Scots, with William Wallace as a Scottish Tell. Rossini wasn't much involved in the adaptation, though he did agree to recast the finale scene so that the opera could end with a reprise of the overture's famous *pas redoublé*. It's that revised finale we have here, a travesty of Schiller (and Rossini), but great fun.

Playing, choral work and conducting for this Rossini Gala are all of a high order of excellence. As is the engineering (the lightning strike in *Mosè in Egitto* isn't for the faint-hearted). As always with Opera Rara, the accompanying 116-page booklet is superlatively informative. At the price of a single full-price CD, the disc is a terrific bargain, not least for the splendid hawk's-eye view the programme provides of 'serious' Rossini.

Il barbiere di Siviglia

Il barbiere di Siviglia
Roberto Servile *bar* Figaro **Sonia Ganassi** *mez*
Rosina **Ramon Vargas** *ten* Count Almaviva **Angelo Romero** *bar* Bartolo **Franco de Grandis** *bass* Don
Basilio **Ingrid Kertesi** *sop* Berta **Kázmér Sarkany**
bass Fiorello **Hungarian Radio Chorus; Failoni Chamber Orchestra, Budapest / Will Humburg**
Naxos ③ 8 660027/9 (158' · DDD · N/T) Ⓢ**ⓄⓄ**▷

Not everyone will approve, but there are ways in which this super-budget set of *Il barbiere di Siviglia* puts to shame just about every other version of the opera there has been. Those it may not please are specialist vocal collectors for whom *Il barbiere* is primarily a repository of vocal test pieces. If, however, you regard *Il barbiere* (Rossini, ex-Beaumarchais) as a gloriously subversive music drama – vibrant, scurrilous, vital – then this recording is guaranteed to give a great deal of pleasure.

'Performance' is the key word here. Humburg is described in the Naxos booklet as 'Conductor and Recitative Director', and for once the recitatives really are part of the larger drama. The result is a meticulously produced, often very funny, brilliantly integrated performance that you'll almost certainly find yourself listening to as a stage play. With a virtually all-Italian cast, the results are a revelation. The erotic allure of the duet 'Dunque io son' is striking. Similarly, Don Basilio's Calumny aria, superbly sung by Franco de Grandis, a black-browed bass from Turin who was singing for Karajan, Muti and Abbado while still in his twenties. This takes on added character and colour from the massive sense of panic created by de Grandis and the

admirable Dr Bartolo of Angelo Romero when Basilio comes in with news of Almaviva's arrival in town.

The Overture is done with evident relish, the playing of the Failoni Chamber Orchestra is nothing if not articulate. Aided by a clear, forward recording, a *sine qua non* with musical comedy, the cast communicates the Rossini/Sterbini text with tremendous relish. They're never hustled by Humburg, nor are they spared: the *stretta* of the Act 1 finale is a model of hypertension and clarity. This *Il barbiere* jumps to the top of the pile.

Il barbiere di Siviglia
Sesto Bruscantini *bar* Figaro **Victoria de los Angeles** *sop* Rosina **Luigi Alva** *ten* Count Almaviva
Ian Wallace *bass* Dr Bartolo **Carlo Cava** *bass* Don
Basilio **Duncan Robertson** *ten* Fiorello **Laura Sarti**
mez Berta **Glyndebourne Festival Chorus; Royal Philharmonic Orchestra / Vittorio Gui**
EMI Great Recordings of the Century mono ②
567762-2 (141' · ADD · T/t) Recorded 1962
Ⓜ**ⓄⓄⓄ**▷

Perhaps it's a shade misleading to refer to this classic EMI recording as a 'Glyndebourne' set. It has all the ingredients of a Glyndebourne production: notably the cast, the orchestra and chorus, and that doyen of Rossini conductors, Vittorio Gui. But as far as can be ascertained, there was no actual stage production of *Il barbiere* in 1962. Nor was the recording, for all its dryness and sharp-edged immediacy, actually made at Glyndebourne. It's a well-honed, conservatively staged stereophonic studio recording made by EMI in its Abbey Road Studio No 1. Gui's performance is so astutely paced that, while the music bubbles and boils, every word is crystal-clear. This is a wonderfully declaimed reading of the score, but also a beautifully timed one. Gui's steady tempos allow the music to show its underlying toughness, and he secures characterful playing from the RPO, the wind players in particular. Where Victoria de los Angeles is so memorable is in the beauty of her singing and the originality of the reading. There has never been a Rosina who manages to be both as guileful and as charming as she. Team her up with the incomparable Sesto Bruscantini and, in something like the nodal Act 1 duet, 'Dunque io son', you have musical and dramatic perfection. Ian Wallace is a fine character actor, given plenty of space by Gui, allowing his portrait of Dr Bartolo to emerge as a classic compromise between the letter and the spirit of the part.

Il barbiere di Siviglia
Manuel Lanza *bar* Figaro **Vesselina Kasarova** *mez*
Rosina **Reinaldo Macias** *ten* Count Almaviva
Elizabeth Magnuson *mez* Berta **Carlos Chausson**
bar Doctor Bartolo **Valery Murga** *bar* Officer **Nicolai Ghiaurov** *bass* Don Basilio **Kenneth Roberson** *bass*
Ambrogio **Zurich Opera House Chorus and**

Orchestra / **Nello Santi** Stage director **Grischa Asagaroff** Video director **Felix Breisach**
TDK Euro Arts ② 📀 DV-OPBDS (161' · 16:9 · DTS 5.1 & 2.0 ·-0)   ⒡

This set offers a novel but never outlandish view of a familiar work. It's most distinguished by Luigi Perego's utterly delightful décor, which places the action in the art deco period. The gimmicky first scene has Almaviva arriving on a motor-cycle with sidecar and Figaro on a bicycle, but once indoors Asagaroff's direction proves witty, eschewing slapstick, making the characters larger than life, as perhaps they should be, but never to the point of exaggeration. He's helped by a youthful cast. Although rather young-looking, Carlos Chausson's fine observation of Bartolo's quirks are in the best tradition of the role, and his singing of his virtuoso aria is masterly. Manuel Lanza's slightly too laid-back and modern Figaro, and Reinaldo Macias's subtly acted, adequately sung Almaviva form part of a true ensemble. At its centre is Vesselina Kasarova's Rosina; she gives a typically individual performance, full in tone, clean in *fioriture*, but a bit too dramatically calculated. Nicolai Ghiaurov, though his voice is a shadow of its former self, makes a genial Basilio. Veteran conductor Nello Santi's reading of the score is clean-cut, never drawing attention to itself, always aware of Rossini's irresistible orchestration. A thoroughly enjoyable performance.

Il barbiere di Siviglia
Hermann Prey bar Figaro **Teresa Berganza** mez Rosina **Luigi Alva** ten Almaviva **Enzo Dara** bar Doctor Bartolo **Paolo Montarsolo** bass Don Basilio **Stefania Malagù** mez Berta **Renato Cesari** bass Fiorello **Luigi Roni** bar Officer **Hans Kraemmer** bass Ambrogio **Milan La Scala Orchestra and Chorus / Claudio Abbado** Stage director **Jean-Pierre Ponnelle** Video director **Ernst Wild**
DG 📀 073 021-9GH (142' · 4:3 ·2.0 · 0)   ⒡

Claudio Abbado's youthful Beatle-cut marks the age of this film, still one of the better screen *Barbiere*s if not absolutely the best. Jean-Pierre Ponnelle based it on his Scala stagings, but filmed it, as he always preferred, in studio with lip-sync, more successfully than most. As a result, it looks and sounds very much fresher on DVD than contemporary videotapes.

The very strong cast reproduces that of Abbado's 1972 CD recording, but with La Scala forces. Teresa Berganza, often rather unexciting in sound alone, reveals a charming presence here, only a shade mature for a role she'd sung since the 1950s. In the manner of that era her Rosina is coquette rather than minx, but her slightly resinous tone and sensuous delivery makes 'Contro il cor' irresistible. You'd never guess Luigi Alva had been singing Almaviva for just as long, still youthful-looking, honeyed and elegant, even if his heavily aspirated ornament – the 'ha-ha' effect – wouldn't be acceptable today. Hermann Prey has everything a good Figaro needs, but despite his warmly incisive baritone and cheerfully egocen-

ROSSINI IL BARBIERE DI SIVIGLIA – IN BRIEF

Roberto Servile Figaro **Sonia Ganassi** Rosina **Ramón Vargas** Almaviva **Hungarian Radio Chorus; Failoni Chamber Orchestra / Will Humburg**
Naxos ③ 8 660027/9 (158' · DDD)   Ⓢ🅞🅞🅳
Happily one of the best is also among the cheapest; fresh, full and brilliantly conducted, with a ripely Italianate cast including star-in-the-making Ramón Vargas.

Thomas Allen Figaro **Agnes Baltsa** Rosina **Francisco Araiza** Almaviva **Ambrosian Opera Chorus; ASMF / Sir Neville Marriner**
Decca ② 470 434-2DOC2 (148' · DDD)   Ⓜ🅞🅞🅳
None the worse for international star quality. Marriner conducts a superlative, characterful cast with infectious sparkle and warmth, and first-rate recording.

Sesto Bruscantini Figaro **Victoria de los Angeles** Rosina **Luigi Alva** Almaviva **Glyndebourne Festival Chorus; Royal PO / Vittorio Gui**
EMI 567762-2 (141' · ADD)   Ⓜ🅞🅞🅞🅳
⟐ A magical performance, not least because it derives from a much-loved Glyndebourne production. Gui's conducting is warm and affectionate, his stars more light-hearted and witty than brashly comic.

Nathan Gunn Figaro **Elina Garanča** Rosina **Lawrence Brownlee** Almaviva **Bavarian Radio Chorus; Munich Radio Orchestra / Miguel Angel Gómez-Martínez**
Sony Classical ② 82876 80429-2 (152' · DDD)
Recorded at a concert performances this is a *Barber* with a lot of spirit. Nathan Gunn is an energetic, bouncy Figaro and if Garanča could afford to smile a little more she sings with a lovely tone. And Gómez-Martínez keeps everything bubbling along elegantly.

Tito Gobbi Figaro **Maria Callas** Rosina **Luigi Alva** 🄷 Almaviva **Philharmonia Orchestra / Alceo Galliera**
EMI ② 556310-2 (132' · ADD)   ⒡🅳
An inauthentic soprano Rosina is still a gain when it's Callas, with Gobbi's warmly robust Figaro as foil; she makes an enchanting spitfire, with some showy ornamentation. The experienced cast are splendid and Galliera's conducting wonderfully theatrical. One of the most thoroughly comic sets.

Hermann Prey Figaro **Teresa Berganza** Rosina **Luigi Alva** Almaviva **Chorus and Orchestra of La Scala, Milan / Claudio Abbado**
DG 📀 073 021-9GH (142')   ⒡
A rather old-fashioned cinematic version in lip-sync, but still enjoyable and well worth considering for Abbado's rich but lively conducting and a very strong cast, even if Prey, though excellent, seems insufficiently Italianate, and Berganza is a shade mature.

tric, athletic characterisation he simply isn't idiomatic enough. Enzo Dara's pompous, foppish Bartolo is amusingly observed and richly sung, but he suffers unduly from the film's major drawback, the direction.

Ponnelle feels obliged to reinforce the comedy with a barrage of ingenious but spurious business, such as Basilio's alchemical explosions, and choppy editing. The effect is enjoyable but overdone.

Il barbiere di Siviglia
David Malis bar Figaro **Jennifer Larmore** mez Rosina **Richard Croft** ten Almaviva **Renato Capecchi** bar Doctor Bartolo **Simone Alaimo** bass Don Basilio **Leonie Schoon** mez Berta **Roger Smeets** bass Fiorello, Officer **Netherlands Opera Chorus; Netherlands Chamber Orchestra / Alberto Zedda**
Stage director **Dario Fo**
Video director **Hans Hulscher**
ArtHaus Musik 🅿 100 412 (154' · 4:3 · PCM stereo · 2 & 5) Recorded 1991 Ⓕ❶❶❶

We've cursed modern producers and their productions often enough, but here's a delight. The conductor, working with his own edition of the opera, is Alberto Zedda. But when the director and designer, Dario Fo, takes the last, climatic bow, he deserves every cheer he gets.

The performance was filmed at the Netherlands Opera in 1991, but the production dates back to 1987, and was Fo's first for the operatic stage. Employing a group of mime artists, he places the action in a *commedia dell'arte* setting and opens with a brilliant pantomime-accompaniment to the overture. The ideas match the music, and the visual style suits the elegance of Zedda's orchestral players. Throughout the opening solos, chorus and duet, a delightful ingenuity of movement plays along with the singers, who have the youth and elasticity of voice, limb and spirit to cope with the thousand-and-one tasks thrown at them. There's very little sense of distraction or overloading; just a feast of melody, wit and energy.

The tenor Robert Croft impresses most: his tone is clear; his scales are fluent and evenly articulated, and he can apply vocal decoration with panache and delicacy. The Figaro, another American, David Malis, has personality and bright high notes. Jennifer Larmore's Rosina, better when seen than merely heard, is strong-voiced and technically accomplished. Renato Capecchi is a memorable Bartolo, distinct from the potbellied bumbler of convention.

In the theatre the production might be found too restless, but, expertly filmed, it's just about the most enjoyable comic opera production available on DVD.

Il barbiere di Siviglia
Nathan Gunn bar Figaro **Elina Garanča** mez Rosina **Lawrence Brownlee** ten Almaviva **Bruno de Simone** bar Doctor Bartolo **Kristinn Sigmundsson** bass Don Basilio **Giovanna Donadini** mez Berta **Roberto Accurso** bass Fiorello

Bavarian Radio Chorus; Munich Radio Orchestra / Miguel Angel Gómez-Martínez
Sony Classical ② 82876 80429-2 (152' · DDD · S/N). Recorded live. Enhanced CD features libretto with translations in PDF format Ⓕ

Here's a *Barbiere* light of heart and light of touch, graceful in style, with fresh, young-sounding voices (where appropriate), well schooled so as to make those forbiddingly difficult vocal flights sound like flights of fancy, quick as thought and natural as intuition.

It's a concert performance and carries with it a real sense of enjoyment. The Overture moves with relish as from one good thing to another, and movement is the motto for most of the first act. Fiorello and the chorus are no clod-hoppers and the Count is no show-off. 'Ecco ridente' has the assurance of a young aristocrat who has practised his scales and scorns the use of aspirates. Figaro likewise wears his skills and his energy lightly, the brag and bounce of his introductory solo kept within civilised limits. Their duet is a ball-game of high velocity neatly played in time to an inexhaustible supply of rhythm and melody.

The Rosina is Elina Garanča who is not very liberal with her smiles. The possibility of fun is admitted with 'farò giocar' but the keynote is determination ('vincerò'). Later the characterisation warms, but right from the start we have been won by the beauty of her tone and the accomplishment of her florid work, never going hard or shrill at the top and keeping the voice whole and even throughout its range. Her guardian, Doctor Bartolo, in this version is a lightweight *buffo* baritone rather than the usual bumbling fatty, and it's left to the Basilio to play the traditional tricks.

At times during this First Act, one may wish for a moment here and there to linger over phrases or merely to savour the sound of a fine voice. In compensation, the conductor offers a clear view in which everything has its place. In Act 2 he makes room for more expansion. In both, the clarity of ensemble is a delight, as is the elegant playing of the Munich orchestra.

La Cenerentola

La Cenerentola
Teresa Berganza mez Angelina **Luigi Alva** ten Don Ramiro **Renato Capecchi** bar Dandini **Paolo Montarsolo** bar Don Magnifico **Margherita Guglielmi** sop Clorinda **Laura Zannini** contr Tisbe **Ugo Trama** bass Alidoro **Scottish Opera Chorus; London Symphony Orchestra / Claudio Abbado**
DG Double ② 459 448-2GTA2 (144' · ADD · T/t) Recorded 1971 Ⓜ❶❶▷

Rossini's Cinderella is a fairy-tale without a fairy, but no less bewitching for that. In fact the replacement of the winged godmother with the philanthropic Alidoro, a close friend and adviser of our prince, Don Ramiro, plus the lack of any glass slippers and the presence of a particularly unsympathetic father character, makes the whole story more plausible. La Cenerentola, Angelina, is more spunky than the average pantomime Cinders. She herself gives Don Ramiro one of her pair of bracelets, charging him to find the owner of the matching ornament, and thus taking control of her own destiny. Along the way, Don Ramiro and his valet Dandini change places, leading to plenty of satisfyingly operatic confusion and difficult situations.

This recording, when originally transferred to CD, was spread across three discs, but has now been comfortably fitted into two at mid-price. It gives a sparkling rendition of the score with a lovely light touch and well-judged tempos from Abbado and the LSO. Virtuoso vocal requirements are fully met by the cast. The chief delight is Teresa Berganza's Angelina, creamy in tone and as warm as she's precise. The supporting cast is full of character, with Luigi Alva a princely Don Ramiro, Margherita Guglielmi and Laura Zannini an affected and fussy pair of sisters, and Renato Capecchi, gleeful and mischievous as he takes on being prince for a day. The recording sounds more than usually well for its age.

Additional recommendation

Bartoli Angelina **Matteuzzi** Don Ramiro **Corbelli** Dandini **Bologna Teatro Comunale Chorus and Orchestra / Chailly**
Decca ② 436 902-2DH2 (148' · DDD) Ⓕ🄳➔

For Bartoli fans, a cherishable set that doesn't quite match the sparkle of the Abbado. Matteuzzi sings well and there are some nicely drawn characters. Chailly directs with spirit.

Le Comte Ory

Le Comte Ory
Juan Diego Flórez ten Comte Ory **Stefania Bonfadelli** sop Adèle **Alastair Miles** bar Gouverneur Marie-Ange **Todorovitch** mez Isolier **Bruno Praticò** bar Raimbaud **Marina De Liso** mez Ragonde **Rossella Bevacqua** sop Alice **Prague Chamber Choir; Teatro Comunale Orchestra, Bologna / Jesús López-Cobos**
DG ② 477 5020 (130' · DDD · T/t) Recorded live 2003
Ⓕ🅞🅞➔

Le Comte Ory is the first great French-language comic opera. A late work (Paris, 1828), sensuous, witty and exquisitely crafted, it's always been something of a connoisseur's piece.

The selling point here is the Ory, Juan Diego Flórez, and very striking he is, too. He has terrific presence, a well-nigh flawless technique, and a keen sense of the French vocal style. Jesús López-Cobos, an old Rossini hand, conducts robustly but with style. He overdrives the Act 1 ensemble in which the villagers come to Ory with their requests but paces to perfection the action within the celebrated nocturnal Trio in Act 2.

It would be nice to have a French Raimbaud, but Bruno Praticò, an old hand, knows how to

ring the changes in a strophic patter-song. The only problematic *comprimario* role is that of Ory's Tutor. His Act 1 aria, a bespoke commission for the great French *basse chantante* Nicolas Levasseur, is a devil of a piece to bring off; López-Cobos races through the aria in a vain attempt to disguise the fact that Alastair Miles isn't entirely at ease with it.

The recprding has colour, life, dash, brio, and a measure of wit. It also has Juan Diego Flórez. Enough to be going on with? Absolutely. An *Ory* for the connoisseur? Not entirely.

La donna del lago

La donna del lago
Carmen Giannattasio sop Elena **Kenneth Tarver** ten Uberto (Giacomo) **Patricia Bardon** mez Malcolm **Gregory Kunde** ten Rodrigo di Dhu **Robert Gleadow** bass Douglas d'Angus **Francesca Sassu** sop Albina **Mark Wilde** ten Bertram; Serano **Edinburgh Festival Chorus; Scottish Chamber Orchestra / Maurizio Benini**
Opera Rara ③ ORC34 (160' · DDD · S/T/t/N)
Recorded live in 2006 Ⓕ🅞

One of Rossini's most attractive scores, *La donna del lago* is both bold and delicate, at one moment looking ahead to Verdi, at several others suggesting a Mozartian affinity. The orchestral writing offers colour, adornment and a steady supply of additional interest. For the voice, opportunities for brilliance are matched by passages of sustained lyrical elegance. Dramatically, the construction is effective, the tension well contrived, with characters and situations that can touch the heart.

Live in Edinburgh's Usher Hall, Gregory Kunde, in the fearsome role of Rodrigo, sounded at times foggy, almost as though singing through a cold, his tone breaking free with startling clarity on the high notes. The recording is more evenly voiced, the low notes clearer, the top not quite so exciting. And whereas the memory of Carmen Giannattasio as Elena is of something very special, the recorded sound seems not quite to catch the distinctive beauty of her tone throughout the range. Also the recording is without applause: and there was much.

It was an evening of general rejoicing in the singers' art. Perhaps the greatest enthusiasm of all greeted Kenneth Tarver, especially after his solo at the beginning of Act 2: and that comes out on record exactly as remembered, a model of *legato* singing from the start and blissfully even and precise in florid work later on.

Though this was a concert performance, all was fully expressive and, if one couldn't claim a high degree of dramatic involvement, at least as a member of the audience one felt interest and sympathy. The orchestra is well to the fore, and its playing is certainly a main strength, Maurizio Benini conducting with spirit and finesse. Offstage band and chorus are also effectively recorded, and a well-chosen version of the text is presented. Opera Rara also bring its habitual generosity and scholarship to the accompanying booklet, with a handsome box and stylish packaging.

La donna del lago

Sonia Ganassi *mez* Elena **Maxim Mironov** *ten*
Uberto/Giacomo **Marianna Pizzolato** *mez* Malcolm
Ferdinand von Bothmer *ten* Rodrigo di Dhu **Wojtek
Gierlach** *bass* Douglas d'Angus **Olga Peretyatko**
sop Albina **Stefan Cifolelli** *ten* Serano
**Prague Chamber Choir; Tübingen Festival Band;
Kaiserslautern Radio Orchestra / Alberto Zedda**
Naxos ② 8 660235/6 (147' · DDD · S/N)   ⑤⤷

Like the excellent Opera Rara recording (reviewed above), this new Naxos set was also made live in 2006. An excess of mid-act applause notwithstanding, it offers yet another distinguished account of the score. Key to the set's success is the cast of rising young stars of the Rossini circuit which veteran conductor and Rossini editor Alberto Zedda has assembled. Maxim Mironov is memorable as the King and there are equally compelling performances by Sonia Ganassi, Marianna Pizzolato and Ferdinand von Bothmer. The set faces stiff competition from Philips's budget-price reissue of the Muti but it is a more than useful addition to the *La donna del lago* discography.

Elisabetta, regina d'Inghilterra

Elisabetta, regina d'Inghilterra
Jennifer Larmore *mez* Elisabetta **Bruce Ford** *ten*
Leicester **Majella Cullagh** *sop* Matilde **Manuela
Custer** *mez* Enrico **Colin Lee** *ten* Guglielmo **Antonio
Siragusa** *ten* Norfolk **Geoffrey Mitchell Choir;
London Philharmonic Orchestra / Giuliano Carella**
Opera Rara ② ORC22 (147' · DDD · T/t)   Ⓕ

Rossini wrote *Elizabeth, Queen of England* for the star-studded San Carlo Opera in Naples in 1815. The plot is a verse reduction of a half-remembered drama by an Italian advocate out of an entertaining but historically implausible English romance. Larmore makes a formidable Elizabeth; beautifully sung, her performance has presence, character, and a real sense of ingrained authority. The lovely *cantabile* duet for Elizabeth and Matilde at the start of Act 2 is sung to perfection by Caballé and Masterson on Philips' rival set but there's a greater depth of emotion, a grainier, gutsier feel to Larmore's performance with Majella Cullagh's equally characterful, if not at every point inch-perfect, Matilde. There's little to choose between Bruce Ford's Leicester and Carreras's for Philips – Carreras perhaps wins on points with a certain added youthful allure – but Opera Rara's Antonio Siragusa is a more compelling Norfolk than Ugo Benelli, who sings splendidly but without much menace. Siragusa is very fine. With such strong casting, it goes without saying that the great confrontations in the opera – Elizabeth and Norfolk, Leicester and Norfolk, and so on – all come

vividly to life. The Opera Rara performance has a lovely rich, dark feel to it. This is partly to do with Carella's conducting and the London Philharmonic's playing; partly to do with the fact that orchestration is clearly different in places. For first-time buyers, this is the set to go for.

La gazza ladra

La gazza ladra
Carlos Feller *bass* Fabrizio Vingradito **Nucci Condò**
mez Lucia **David Kuebler** *ten* Giannetto **Ileana
Cotrubas** *sop* Ninetta **Brent Ellis** *bar* Fernando
Villabella **Alberto Rinaldi** *bass-bar* Gottardo (Il
Podestà) **Elena Zilio** *mez* Pippo **Erlingur Vigfússon**
ten Isacco **Eberhard Katz** *ten* Antonio **Klaus Bruch**
bass Giorgio **Ulrich Hielscher** *bass* Ernesto **Cologne
Opera Chorus; Gürzenich Orchestra, Cologne /
Bruno Bartoletti**
Stage director **Michael Hampe**
Video director **José Montes Pagano**
ArtHaus Musik ▭DVD▭ 102 203 (3h 2' · NTSC · 4:3 · PCM
stereo · 0). Recorded live at the Cologne Opera in
1987   Ⓕ

In an odd way, *La gazza ladra* is as disorientating as Shakespeare's *Measure for Measure*, which answers the old definition of tragi-comedy as a form of drama bringing characters near to death 'which maketh it no comedy', yet ends happily so that it is no tragedy either. On first acquaintance Rossini's opera *semiseria* can have you seriously worried. The title, overture and opening scenes induce the sure expectation of a comedy of nothing more serious than errors. The Mayor's dastardly designs upon Ninetta give the framework for a plot and the father's return as a deserter from the wars thickens it; but it still comes as quite a profound shock when Ninetta is sent to prison.

When the court sentences her to death we rub our eyes. They strike up the funeral march and we say 'Oh no!'. But Rossini and his librettist risk a stage further towards tragedy as Ninetta sings her last prayer and is led off to execution out of our sight. Of course other developments are in hand and the musical conventions assure us that what seems now inevitable must take a turn for the better. But there is a distinct element of touch-and-go, which makes the opera a remarkable piece for its time, and for its composer. It also presents a challenge to the producer and the whole company, a challenge well met here, with the right balance struck, and no undermining of one half by the other.

Sets, costumes and acting are all under sensible direction and there are none of those silly diversionary indulgences that have become so habitual in recent years. There are four good vocal performances: by Elena Zilio and Nucci Condò, both sturdy mezzos; by David Kuebler, an accomplished lyric tenor; and by the grand veteran Carlos Feller, looking rather like Bertrand Russell but endowing the old croaker with a full-bodied and still resonant bass voice. The baritones are sonorous but uneven, while Ileana Cotrubas as the heroine sometimes touches the heart but at this stage in her career rarely delights the ear. Bartoletti and his players do justice to Rossini's score, as do the video director and his crew to the events onstage.

Guglielmo Tell

Guglielmo Tell
Sherrill Milnes bar Guglielmo Tell **Luciano Pavarotti** ten Arnoldo **Mirella Freni** sop Matilde **Della Jones** mez Jemmy **Elizabeth Connell** mez Edwige **Ferrucio Mazzoli** bass Gessler **Nicolai Ghiaurov** bass Gualtiero **John Tomlinson** bass Melchthal **Cesar Antonio Suarez** ten Un pescatore **Piero De Palma** ten Rodolfo **Richard Van Allan** bass Leutoldo
Ambrosian Opera Chorus; National Philharmonic Orchestra / Riccardo Chailly
Decca ④ 417 154-2DH4 (235' · ADD · T/t) Ⓕ Ⓞ➔

If ever there was a case for armchair opera it's Rossini's *Guglielmo Tell*. The very limitations which have made it, so far, a non-repertory work, give space for the imagination to redress the balance: the short, Rousseau-esque scenes of life by Lake Lucerne, the distant entrances and exits of shepherds and huntsmen, the leisurely but perfectly balanced side-vignettes of fisherman, hunter, child.

Thanks to the clarity and liveliness of the recording itself and, above all, the shrewd casting, this set creates a vivid charivari of fathers, sons, lovers and patriots, all played out against some of Rossini's most delicately painted pastoral cameos. Chailly keeps up the undercurrent of tension between private love and public loyalty, as well as working hard the rustic jollity of the score. Tell himself could hardly have a better advocate than Sherrill Milnes. Arnoldo and Matilde, too, are cleverly cast. Pavarotti contains the coarse, direct impulsiveness of Arnoldo's shepherd stock with the tenderness of love, in his characteristic charcoal *cantabile* and the numbness of his remorse.

Mirella Freni, singing opposite Pavarotti as the forbidden Princess Matilde, phrases with aristocratic poise, folding into every fragment of embryonic *bel canto* the fragile ardour of a young girl's love. The vocal chemistry between them in their Act 2 declaration of love is a lively incarnation of their roles. A similarly interesting patterning of vocal timbres is produced by the casting of Elizabeth Connell as Edwige, Tell's wife, and of Della Jones as Jemmy, their son. Their last-act Trio with Matilde is matched by the contrasting colours of the basses of Ghiaurov, Tomlinson and Van Allan: their roles may be small, but their characters are vividly stamped on an excellent ensemble performance.

L'inganno felice

L'inganno felice
Annick Massis sop Isabella **Raúl Giménez** ten Bertrando **Rodney Gilfry** bar Batone **Pietro**

Spagnoli bass Tarabotto **Lorenzo Regazzo** bar Ormondo **Le Concert des Tuileries / Marc Minkowski**
Erato 0630-17579-2 (78' · DDD · T/t) Recorded live 1996 Ⓕ Ⓞ

This is a fine and tremendously enjoyable recording of an exquisite early Rossini one-acter. The plot resembles that of a late Shakespearian comedy. Set in a seaside mining community, it's concerned with the discovery and rehabilitation of Isabella, Duke Bertrando's wronged and, so he thinks, long-dead wife. It's a work that's comic and serious, witty and sentimental; and there, perhaps, lies the rub. Rossini, especially early Rossini, is meant to be all teeth and smiles, yet *L'inganno felice* isn't quite like that. The very *mise-en-scène* is odd: 'seaside' and 'mining' being, in such a context, strangely contradictory concepts. This is a splendid performance, using a chamber ensemble of about 30 players. It's recorded with pleasing immediacy, which begins bullishly but settles to intimacy when the drama requires.

The score is full of vocal pitfalls, not least for the tenor and for the baritone Batone. But Giménez and Gilfry cope more than adequately, with enough in reserve to produce moments of genuine ease and beauty. Annick Massis is a charming Isabella, good in her first aria, ravishing in her second. The final scene the work's finest sequence, is set at night amid the mining galleys and is beautifully performed.

L'italiana in Algeri

L'italiana in Algeri
Jennifer Larmore mez Isabella **Raúl Giménez** ten Lindoro **Alessandro Corbelli** bar Taddeo **John del Carlo** bass Mustafà **Darina Takova** sop Elvira **Laura Polverelli** mez Zulma **Carlos Chausson** bass-bar Haly
Geneva Grand Theatre Chorus; Lausanne Chamber Orchestra / Jésus López-Cobos
Teldec ② 0630-17130-2 (147' · DDD · T/t) Ⓕ Ⓞ

This recording is hard to fault on any count. López-Cobos revels in all aspects of this dotty comedy, timing everything to perfection, enthusing his accomplished orchestra and cast to enjoy their collective self. First there's a magic moment as Isabella and Lindoro espy each other for the first time, and comment on the joy of reunion; then the main section gets under way to a perfectly sprung rhythm from the conductor, with all the passage's detail made manifest; finally the *stretta* is released with the kind of vitality that sets the feet tapping.

Larmore obviously thoroughly enjoys the role and conveys that enjoyment in singing that matches warm, smiling tone to bravura execution of her *fioriture*. She's a mettlesome Isabella, who knows how to tease, then defy her would-be lover, Mustafà, and charm her real amour, Lindoro, her 'Per lui che adoro' sung with an immaculate line and sensuous tone, its repetition deftly embellished. Finally 'Pensa alla patria' evinces a touch of true *élan*.

Lindoro is taken by that paragon among Rossini tenors, Raúl Giménez, who presents his credentials in 'Languir per una bella', honeyed tone succeeded by fleet runs. He's no less successful in his more heroic Cavatina in Act-2. Corbelli, another master-Rossinian, is witty as the put-upon Taddeo, his textual facility a marvel.

The American bass-baritone John del Carlo is a characterful Mustafà, managing to suggest, as Rossini surely intended, a paradox of lovesick tyrant and ludicrous posturing without ever overstepping the mark into farce, and rolling Italian and his rotund roulades off his tongue with idiomatic assurance. The recording is up to Teldec's impeccably high standard.

L'italiana in Algeri
Marilyn Horne *mez* Isabella **Ernesto Palacio** *ten* Lindoro **Domenico Trimarchi** *bar* Taddeo **Samuel Ramey** *bass* Mustafà **Kathleen Battle** *sop* Elvira **Clara Foti** *mez* Zulma **Nicola Zaccaria** *bass* Haly **Prague Philharmonic Chorus; I Solisti Veneti /
Claudio Scimone**
Erato Libretto ② 2292-45404-2 (140' · ADD · N/T)
Recorded 1980   Ⓜ

Written within the space of a month during the spring of 1813, and with help from another anonymous hand, Rossini's *L'italiana in Algeri* was an early success, and one which went on to receive many performances during the 19th century, with an increasingly corrupt text. A complete reconstruction was undertaken by Azio Corghi and published in 1981; this recording uses this edition which corresponds most closely to what was actually performed in Venice in 1813. *L'italiana* is one of Rossini's wittiest operas, featuring as did a number of his most successful works a bewitching central character, in this case Isabella, who makes fun of her various suitors, with the opera ending with a happy escape with her beloved, Lindoro, a typical *tenorino* role. This fine recording has plenty of vocal polish. Scimone's biggest asset is Marilyn Horne as Isabella: possibly the finest Rossini singer of her generation and a veteran in this role, she sings Rossini's demanding music with great virtuosity and polish. Her liquid tone and artful phrasing ensure that she's a continuous pleasure to listen to. She's strongly supported by the rest of the cast: Kathleen Battle is a beguiling Elvira, Domenico Trimarchi a most humorous Taddeo, and Samuel Ramey a sonorous Bey of Algiers. Ernesto Palacio's Lindoro, however, has patches of white tone and is correct rather than inspiring. Scimone's conducting is guaranteed to give considerable pleasure.

The Italian Girl in Algiers (highlights in English)
Jennifer Larmore *mez* Isabella **Barry Banks** *ten* Lindoro **Alan Opie** *bar* Taddeo **Alastair Miles** *bass* Mustafà **Sarah Tynan** *sop* Elvira **David Soar** *bass*

Haly **Anne Marie Gibbons** *mez* Zulma **Geoffrey Mitchell Choir; Philharmonia Orchestra / Brad Cohen**
Chandos Opera in English CHAN3160 (77' · DDD)
 Ⓜ Ⓞ

Rossini's *The Italian Girl* distils readily onto a single CD. The First Act is substantially there and the Second can survive without the Quintet. The only gripe concerns the decision to end with Isabella's Rondo. Rossini finished serious and mixed-mode operas this way but not the out-and-out comedies. The final vaudeville runs for around 2'20" and should have been included.

With opera in English, translation is key. Arthur Jacobs's translation in the vocal score of the Ricordi Critical Edition is a workmanlike affair but it isn't a patch on David Parry's brilliant new version. Lines from Isabella's cavatina are typically felicitous: "Through years of practising / I have perfected / The gesture languishing / The sigh affected".

Jennifer Larmore has recorded the opera in Italian (Teldec) but her English Isabella, superbly articulated and projected, is both formidable and funny. Her Act 2 cavatina, played with the original cello obbligato, is the lyric highlight. Happily, the three men in her life are equally vividly characterised: Alan Opie as her hang-dog admirer Taddeo, Barry Banks a most eloquent Lindoro, and Alastair Miles as the lascivious Mustafà. Fifty years ago there was barely a bass in Europe who could find his way around Mustafà's bumbling coloratura, let alone project the text as Miles does here.

Brad Cohen conducts superbly, bringing out the strength and expressive range of music that revels in the thrill of sexual confrontation and the speed and power of the vortex into which so-called civilised society can all too rapidly vanish.

L'italiana in Algeri
Christianne Stotijn *mez* Isabella **Maxim Mironov** *ten* Lindoro **Marco Vinco** *bass* Mustafà **Ruben Drole** *bar* Haly **Giorgio Caoduro** *bar* Taddeo **Elisaveta Martirosyan** *sop* Elvira **Sabina Willeit** *mez* Zulma **Arnold Schoenberg Choir; Mahler Chamber Orchestra / Riccardo Frizza**
Stage director **Toni Servillo**
Video director **Vincent Bataillon**
Bel Air Classiques 🆅 BAC025 (135' · NTSC · 16:9 · PCM stereo, 5.1 and DTS 5.1 · 0). Recorded live at the Aix-en-Provence Festival in June 2006   Ⓕ

Aix-en-Provence is generally a guarantor of musical excellence and this performance is no exception. Maxim Mironov may not be as well known as Flórez but he is rightly the *tenore di grazia* of choice for leading Rossini houses much as Nicolai Gedda and Luigi Alva were a generation or so ago. In those days, no bass was capable of singing Mustafà properly, without cuts and with all the notes in place. Marco Vinco, one of a new breed of Rossini basses, is exemplary.

Christianne Stotijn is not the most fetching or dynamic of Isabellas but she will 'do'.

Conductor Riccardo Frizza makes the most of his eight minutes on camera in the overture, play-acting like a fantasy conductor in front of his gramophone before bringing the orchestra to its feet for time-consuming bows and solo plaudits. What follows, however, is taut and well drilled. Space is given for the comedy to flower, though Frizza's tempo is too quick in the wonderful duet between Isabella and Taddeo 'Ai capricci' (the marking is *Allegro* not *Allegro molto*) where he appears oblivious to the fact that Rossini's use of musical form is a key contributor to the comedy (Isabella flattening Taddeo with a rejoinder which also happens to be a sonata-form recapitulation). The duet barely raises a smile from the audience.

A single set does service throughout: an empty stage dominated by a three-story ziggurat that can be transformed into the prow of a three-deck ocean liner at the drop of a painted cloth. For much of the evening there is movement in and around the ziggurat but no production to speak of – unless you count Haly being sent into the audience to sing his chirpy sorbet aria 'Le femmine d'Italia'. It is in effect a colourfully costumed concert. That said, director Toni Servillo's minimalist approach works well in the pivotal Act 2 quintet and climactic Act 2 trio. As stage comedy *L'italiana* must seem pretty thin stuff to modern audiences, yet the various elements in the Rossini cuisine come together most agreeably in the closing scenes of this Aix production.

Matilde di Shabran

Matilde di Shabran
Juan Diego Flórez ten Corradino **Annick Massis** sop
Matilde di Shabran **Hadar Halevy** mez Edoardo
Bruno de Simone bass Isidoro **Chiara Chialli** mez
Contessa d'Arco **Gregory Bonfatti** ten Egoldo
Lubomír Moravec ten Rodrigo **Bruno Taddia** bass
Raimondo Lopez
**Prague Chamber Choir; Galicia Symphony
Orchestra / Riccardo Frizza**
Decca ③ 475 7688DHO3 (3h 9' · DDD). Recorded at
the Teatro Rossini, Pesaro, in August 2004 Ⓕ❋❋❋

Here is treasure indeed: a memorable recording of Rossini's grand, exhilarating, yet down the years too-little-noticed *Matilde di Shabran*. A comic-heroic romp written for the 1821 Roman carnival but substantially revised for Naples later that same year, the opera is an important staging-post between Rossini's two earlier Roman entertainments, *Il barbiere di Siviglia* and *La Cenerentola*, and their Parisian successors *Il viaggio a Reims* and *Le Comte Ory*. The opera soon dropped from the repertory, dogged by travellers' tales of a bizarre plot (a raving misogynist, a mad poet, damsels being thrown off cliffs) and an impossible-to-sing leading role.

This 2004 Pesaro production, based on Jürgen Selk's new Critical Edition, catches Flórez at the peak of his powers. The plot is less complicated than its genesis might suggest. Corradino, a parody tyrant said to loathe women, poets, and all other affronts to his masculinity, resides in a Spanish castle whose welcome notices include such gems as 'He who enters here will have his neck broken'. In Act 1, he is trapped into loving. With the tyrant tyrannised, Act 2 finds him in a series of even bigger fixes, from which he is eventually rescued by the poet he once threatened to liquidate and the woman he has loathed, loved and tried to kill.

Spectacular as the role of Corradino is, there are no solo arias. This is ensemble opera *par excellence*. His spectacular entry – pure Errol Flynn – turns into a quartet. His first meeting with Matilde takes place in the latter half of the Act 1 Quintet. Later, despite Corradino's best efforts to silence young Edoardo, their Act 2 duet remains just that: a duet. The joke fails, of course, if the singer playing Corradino lacks the wherewithal to drive a coach and horses through Rossini's cunningly contrived maze. Flórez is terrific, literally so at times.

Matilde is sister to Isabella and Rosina, albeit a soprano brandishing high C sharps and the occasional top F. Unlike Corradino, she does have a solo aria, the opera's showpiece finale, vividly thrown off by Annick Massis, who is well matched to Flórez histrionically and vocally. The two other leading players are Isidoro, a down-at-heel poet who ends up running the show, and the androgynously charming Edoardo, captive son of Corradino's arch-enemy Don Raimondo. Rossini conceived the roles for the Neapolitan *buffo* Antonio Parlamagni and his daughter, Annetta, then refined them in the rewrite. In Naples, Isidoro was played (as here, in Neapolitan dialect) by the legendary *buffo* Carlo Casaccia. Decca's Bruno de Simone is the gamest of Isidoros, Hadar Halevy a mellifluous-sounding Edoardo.

Isidoro bears the brunt of the stretches of *secco* recitative: eight minutes before the Act 1 finale, a further stretch as the plot thickens midway through Act 2. None of this hangs heavy. This being a distillation of five live theatre performances, the entire cast and fortepiano player Rosetta Cucchi are fully engaged with the drama.

Riccardo Frizza's conducting is fierce and sharp-edged in the modern style. Occasionally one misses that Gui-like turn of the wrist which distinguishes the musician from the martinet but Frizza's marshalling of the all-important ensembles is rarely less than masterly. The recording has the voices well forward, the orchestra a little too much to the rear. If the stereo placings are to be believed, Flórez was always centre-stage: understandable but oddly wearisome.

La pietra del paragone

La pietra del paragone
Sonia Prina mez Clarice **Jennifer Holloway** sop
Aspasia **Laura Giordano** sop Fulvia **François Lis** bass

Asdrubale **José Manuel Zapata** ten Giocondo **Joan Martín-Royo** bass Macrobio **Christian Senn** bass-bar Pacuvio **Filippo Polinelli** bass Fabrizio
Ensemble Matheus / Jean-Christophe Spinosi
Stage directors **Giorgio Barbiero Corsetti** and **Pierrick Sorin**
Video director **Philippe Béziat**
Naïve ② **DVD** V5089 (3h 51' · NTSC · 16:9 · 2.0 · 0)
Ⓕ**OOO**

Ⓖ This is an utterly remarkable and fantastically enjoyable theatre-cum-video staging of Rossini's *La pietra del paragone*. Philippe Béziat, who has described the production as 'the most original I have seen for a long time on the operatic stage', created his own filmic realisation during live performances in Paris's Théâtre du Châtelet. His breathtakingly precise and witty filming adds a further dimension to the experience.

So how, precisely, does it work? Watched by three video cameras that stand centre-stage, the performers play out the action in a blue virtual reality space devoid of scenery. On the edge of the stage are a series of miniature sets, equipped with their own bespoke cameras. Behind and above the singers is a bank of six video screens onto which the images of the players and the set designs are mixed and superimposed. To take just one example (there are hundreds as the performance unfolds), a tennis ball placed by the lovelorn Giocondo on the miniaturised set appears on screen as large yellow garden seat on which he appears to perch to sing his aria.

This aspect of the production – Rossini meets Magritte – is the work of the celebrated video artist and specialist in comic burlesque, Pierrick Sorin. As in a Magritte painting, the interplay of image and reality blurs our perceptions sufficiently to make us wonder whether what we thought to be reality is merely a construction of the mind. This is itself pure Rossini. At some point in a Rossini commedia the characters will question their grasp of reality. In more abstract pieces such as *Il turco in Italia* or *La pietra* itself (its plot the equivalent of a feature-length version of Friends rewritten by a specialist in black comedy) the sense of the drama being played out in a world that is not entirely real is all the more marked.

Stage director Giorgio Barberio Corsetti directs a gem of production. The video set designs, which have a chic minimalist 1920s feel to them, are the work of Sorin and Corsetti in collaboration with Cristian Taraborrelli whose vivid modern-dress costuming works brilliantly both on the all-blue virtual reality set and in the vibrantly coloured video show above.

The singers, a richly talented ensemble of rising young stars, are superb, not only in their delivery of Rossini's text but in their mastery of the hugely difficult task of playing simultaneously to camera and to the audience. Film close-ups can be cruel to singers but they turn this to their advantage, building facial movements into a larger ensemble of gesture and mime. Jean-Christophe Spinosi's conducting of his period band Ensemble Matheus is a tour de force, funny in its own right. This is Rossini conducting of real point, colour, vibrancy and drive.

The DVD comes in a stylishly produced 100-page hardback rich in background information, including two superb essays by Rossini scholar Damien Colas. The show runs for two hours 40 minutes but since its ingenuity appears to know no bounds there are no longueurs. In the annals of Rossini performance, this is an important and entertaining landmark creation.

Semiramide

Semiramide
Dame Joan Sutherland sop Semiramide **Marilyn Horne** mez Arsace **Joseph Rouleau** bass Assur **John Serge** ten Idreno **Patricia Clark** sop Azema **Spiro Malas** bass Oroe **Michael Langdon** bass Ghost of Nino **Leslie Fryson** ten Mitrane **Ambrosian Opera Chorus; London Symphony Orchestra / Richard Bonynge**
Decca ③ 475 7918 (168' · ADD · T/t)
Recorded 1966
Ⓜ**OO**

Wagner thought it represented all that was bad about Italian opera, and Kobbe's *Complete Opera Book* proclaimed that it had had its day – but then added that 'were a soprano and contralto to appear in conjunction in the firmament the opera might be successfully revived'. That was exactly what happened in the 1960s, when both Sutherland and Horne were in superlative voice and, with Richard Bonynge, were prominent in the reintroduction of so many 19th-century operas that the world thought it had outgrown. This recording brought a good deal of enlightenment in its time. For one thing, here was vocal music of such 'impossible' difficulty being sung with brilliance by the two principal women and with considerable skill by the men. Then it brought to many listeners the discovery that, so far from being a mere show-piece, the opera contained ensembles of quite compelling dramatic intensity. People who had heard of the duet 'Giorno d'orroré' were surprised to find it remarkably unshowy and even expressive of the ambiguous feelings of mother and son in their extraordinary predicament. It will probably be a long time before this recording is superseded.

Tancredi

Tancredi
Ewa Podles contr Tancredi **Sumi Jo** sop Amenaide **Stanford Olsen** ten Argirio **Pietro Spagnoli** bar Orbazzano **Anna Maria di Micco** sop Isaura **Lucretia Lendi** mez Roggiero **Capella Brugensis; Collegium Instrumentale Brugense / Alberto Zedda**
Naxos ② 8 660037/8 (147' · DDD)
Ⓢ**O⯈**

Tancredi is a seminal work in the Rossini canon, mingling a new-found reach in the musical architecture with vocal and instrumental writing of rare wonderment and beauty. The singing is splendid throughout, with a cast that's unusually starry. Podles has sung the role of Tancredi to acclaim at La Scala, Milan; the Amenaide, Sumi Jo, is a touch cool at first, too much the pert coloratura but this isn't an impression that persists. Hers is a performance of wonderful vocal control and flowering sensibility.

Podles, a smoky-voiced Pole, likes to go her own way at times. In the event, though, she and Sumi Jo work well together, and they sound marvellous. Podles also manages, chameleon-like, to adjust to the purer, more obviously stylish Rossini manner of a singer who's very unlike herself, the American tenor Stanford Olsen. His portrait of the conscience-stricken father Argirio matches singing of grace and impetus with great fineness of dramatic sensibility. As a result, something like the scene of the signing of his daughter's death-warrant emerges here as the remarkable thing it is.

Alberto Zedda is lucky to have at his disposal another of those wonderfully stylish chamber orchestras and chamber choirs that Naxos seem able to conjure at will. The aqueously lovely preface to Tancredi's first entrance is a representative example of the players' ear for Rossini's delicately limned tone-painting. The recording itself is beautifully scaled.

Il turco in Italia

Il turco in Italia
Michele Pertusi bass Selim **Cecilia Bartoli** mez Fiorilla **Alessandro Corbelli** bar Don Geronio **Ramón Vargas** ten Don Narciso **Laura Polverelli** mez Zaida **Francesco Piccoli** ten Albazar **Roberto de Candia** bar Prosdocimo **Chorus and Orchestra of La Scala, Milan / Riccardo Chailly**
Decca ② 458 924-2DHO2 (142' · DDD · T/t)
Ⓕ ❶❶❶❷

Chailly has recorded the work before, but in the years since he's matured as a Rossini conductor, and the Scala orchestra has this music under its fingers; there's an energy and vitality to this playing that's infectious. For his earlier recording, Montserrat Caballé was an underpowered Fiorilla; but Cecilia Bartoli is full of fire and mettle here (her 'Sqallido veste bruna' is sensational). Michele Pertusi is a fine Selim whose performance seems to breathe stage experience – it's a characterisation that's as vocally fine as it's theatrically adept. Alessandro Corbelli, reinforcing his credentials as a Rossini singer of flair and panache, is a strongly characterised Geronio. This is a recording that smacks of the theatre, and unlike so many so-called comic operas, has lost nothing in its transfer to disc. Under Chailly's baton it fizzes and crackles like few other sets – recitatives are dispatched with the assurance of native Italian speakers, and with a genuine feeling for the meaning of the text. Decca's recording is beautifully judged and the set makes a fine modern alternative to the now classic (but cut) 1954 recording under Gavazzeni with Maria Callas.

Il viaggio a Reims

Il viaggio a Reims
Anastasia Belyaeva sop Madame Cortese **Larisa Youdina** sop Contessa di Folleville **Anna Kiknadze** mez Marchesa Melibea **Irma Guigolachvili** sop Corinna **Alexei Safiouline** bar Don Alvaro **Dmitri Voropaev** ten Cavalier Belfiore **Daniil Shtoda** ten Conte di Libenskof **Edouard Tsanga** bass Lord Sidney **Nikolaï Kamenski** bass Don Profondo **Vladislav Ouspenski** bass Barone di Trombonok **Alexeï Tannovistski** bass Don Prudenzio **Mariinsky Theatre Orchestra / Valery Gergiev**
Stage director **Alain Maratrat**
Video director **Vincent Bataillon**
Opus Arte 🎥 OA0967D (135' · NTSC · 16:9 · PCM stereo and DTS 5.1 · 0)
Recorded live at the Théâtre du Châtelet, Paris in 2005. Extra features include Illustrated Synopsis and Cast Gallery   Ⓕ

Il viaggio a Reims was the Théâtre Italien's offering to the celebrations surrounding the coronation of Charles X in the summer of 1825, a showcase for Italian music-making in Paris. Since the Russians later supplanted the Italians as purveyors of high-class art to the French, there is something apt about this Russian revival of *Il viaggio* in Paris's Théâtre du Châtelet.

A stylishly designed concert in costume, it is a latter-day showcase for the rising stars of the Mariinsky Theatre. The orchestral players are seated at the rear of the stage. Decked out in cream-coloured evening attire, they make an effective backdrop to the primary colours of Mireille Dessingy's haute couture costumes. Events, such as they are, are mainly played out along the front of the stage and on a T-shaped catwalk that extends into the auditorium. Since this is not a full-blown theatre staging, there is no grand visual display in the closing scene.

The opening sequence is unpromising. The staging is aimless and the words of the hotel housekeeper, delivered from a stage box, are inaudible because the sound engineer has omitted to provide her with a microphone. Things improve as the cast warms to its task and individual singers begin to catch the eye and the ear. The staging, however, continues to be variable. Don Profondo's catalogue aria manages to be both messy and dull, yet the duet between Count Libenskof and Belfiore is a delight. Corinna and her harp are awkwardly separated but the idea of having the solo flautist playing alongside the diffident Lord Sidney dressed as a silver-clad Rosenkavalier is an inspired one. Gergiev conducts in a brown racing trilby. The reading is exquisitely paced, the ensemble work often stunningly good, remarkably so given the fact that conductor and orchestra are behind the singers.

There is no attempt here to adapt the tributes to Charles X to latter-day political concerns, let alone rewrite the end as Dario Fo did – cruelly, wittily, timelessly – in his famous Helsinki production. The Russians play the score as written, a number of small cuts notwithstanding.

Nino Rota
Italian 1911-1979

Rota studied at the Milan Conservatory, privately with Pizzetti (1925-6), with Casella in Rome, and at the Curtis Institute (1931-2). In 1939 he joined the staff at the Bari Conservatory (director from 1950). He wrote fluently in a cool, direct style: his output includes operas (notably The Italian Straw Hat, 1955), three symphonies, concertos and instrumental pieces, besides numerous film scores (many for Fellini, Visconti and Zeffirelli). GROVEmusic

Piano Concertos

Piano Concertos – E minor; C
Massimo Palumbo pf **I Virtuosi Italiani / Marco Boni**
Chandos CHAN9681 (64' · DDD) Ⓕ Ⓞ ➔

Both these works are unashamedly Romantic and nostalgic in style. The E minor Piano Concerto was composed in 1960, at the same time as Rota's music for Fellini's film *La dolce vita*. As if in answer to the extreme cynicism of that and much of his other film music, the concerto seems to be a questioning exploration of the remaining possibilities in a modern, Romantic form. The opening *Allegro-tranquillo* movement begins with a dreamlike theme on the piano which is then taken up by the orchestra and developed as a sort of conversation – the orchestra insisting on a heroic, almost martial sound, while the piano and woodwind reiterate the original soft mood. The first movement is over 16 minutes: away from the rule of the film-editor's stop-watch Rota felt free to indulge himself. The same four-note figure that runs through the opening is taken up in the second movement, a quiet, slow section with a haunting intensity. The finale continues the awake-in-a-dream contrasts.

Rota composed four piano concertos, but the date of the one in C major seems to be in doubt. It's earlier than 1960, and is a sparer, jauntier work, in mood more reminiscent of the 1920s. It, too, presents a dialogue between the quest-like piano part and the orchestra asserting a darker mood.

Both concertos are played by Massimo Palumbo with brilliant technique; the recorded sound is excellent.

Symphonies

No 1 in G; No 2 in F, 'Tarantina – Anni di pellegrinaggio'
Norrköping Symphony Orchestra / Ole Kristian Ruud
BIS BIS-CD970 (63' · DDD) Ⓕ

It's fascinating to encounter these early works by Nino Rota, written when he was in his twenties, after a period of study in the USA. Rota's early career was as a church musician, something to which he returned late in life, after decades composing for the screen and the theatre. The influences in the First Symphony (1935-9) include Sibelius and Stravinsky but perhaps more significantly Copland and Hindemith. It's clearly a youthful work, a bit long-winded, but showing Rota's already firm grasp of complicated and sophisticated orchestration. The last, fourth, movement especially seems to have a maturity that points towards future greatness.

The Second Symphony, which he began in 1937, while still at work on the First, is even more Coplandesque. What would this have sounded like to an audience in the 1930s? (It wasn't performed until 1970.) In one way it would have seemed conservative in the extreme, showing no tendency towards atonality or any influence of jazz. The score carries a subtitle, 'Tarantina – Anni di pellegrinaggio', referring to the period Rota spent in the extreme south of Italy, teaching in Taranto. It could be dismissed as 'light music', and the style wouldn't have offended the most sensitive ears, yet each movement is full of beautiful instrumental detail and constructed in a pleasing way. Rota had yet to find his unmistakable voice, one infused with irony and humour, which would make him the perfect match for Fellini. Devotees of his film music may find these symphonies bland, but anyone who enjoys the contemporary style of Alwyn or Coates in England will find them worth while. The orchestra plays both symphonies with a good sense of period manner, never overdoing the lush sound.

Orchestral Works

Il Gattopardo – Dances. La Strada – Orchestral Suite. Concerto soirée[a]
[a]**Benedetto Lupo** pf **Granada City Orchestra / Josep Pons**
Harmonia Mundi HMC90 1846 (64' · DDD) Ⓕ

This lavishly packaged CD brings together two suites from Rota's most famous film scores plus a *concertante* piece for piano and orchestra which quotes from his film work.

There's a seven-movement suite from *La Strada* (1954) directed by Fellini, with whom Rota collaborated frequently. The brilliant opening sets the scene for the raffish charms of the film's circus folk, depicted in colourful orchestration and with vibrant, tuneful music that conveys the atmosphere of life under the big top. His themes, both romantic and rhythmically infectious, are skilfully interwoven between movements.

Rota wrote the music for Visconti's *Il Gattopardo* ('The Leopard', 1963), before the film was shot. He probably knew that the set piecewas to be a lavish ballroom sequence lasting over an hour in the original print. The sequence begins with a previously unpublished waltz by Verdi (in Visconti's private collection) and continues in a manner akin to Verdi's own ballet music. The intention was to give the impression of 'a modest ensemble hired for the occasion' and this is just the treatment it receives from the Granada orchestra under Josep

Pons. Nothing is inflated or allowed to disturb the seamless flow of this delightful dance music.

Proportion and balance are just right, too, for the modest and endearing *Concerto soirée* in which the fetching piano writing, very much the centre of attention, is brilliantly performed by Benedetto Lupo and wittily executed by the orchestra. A most attractive disc.

Alec Roth   British b1948

After eading music at Durham University, Roth studied at the Academy of Indonesian Performing Arts (ASKI) in Surakarta. he has held include Founder and Artistic Director of the Royal Festival Hall Gamelan Programme; Music Director of the Baylis Programme, English National Opera; Composer in Association, Opera North; Composer in Residence, Wellington College; and Lecturer in Music, University of Edinburgh. His collaborations with the Indian writer Vikram Seth include two song cycles.

Songs in Time of War. Chinese Gardens
Mark Padmore ten **Philippe Honoré** vn
Alison Nicholls hp **Morgan Szymanski** gtr
Signum Classics SIGCD124 (62' · DDD)   Ⓕⓞ▷

Alec Roth the composer and Vikram Seth the poet become so much of a unit during the course of these song-cycles that one feels it would be quite natural to ask Roth for a personal background to the poems and query Seth about the whistling-tune or some other feature of the music. The style (of both) is idiosyncratic – a carefully versified informality of talk, a structural development of musical motifs that sounds like free recitative. The *Chinese Garden* songs (Roth's is the Dr Sun Yat Sen Classical garden in Vancouver) are modern, while the *Songs in Time of War* derive from 8th-century China, but there is modernity in that too, just as the themes of the others might have found recognition and a response in ages of the past.

These are attractive works, the *Songs in Time of War* probably striking deepest though in an utterly non-ponderous, unpretentious way. The music takes interesting turns, as when a cynical blues passage emerges from the timeless observation that 'the great are always paid in disuse and neglect'. The resources of voice and instruments are imaginatively exploited. And the performances (by the 'creator' artists) are excellent. If the disc constitute an introduction to this composer, it is one you won't regret following up.

Albert Roussel   French 1869-1937

After embarking on a naval career, in 1894 Roussel began studies with Gigout, moving on to train with d'Indy and others at the Schola Cantorum (1898-

1908) where in 1902 he began teaching. In 1909 he made a tour of India and Indo-China, and he drew on that experience in writing his Hindu opera-ballet Padmâvatî; (1923), though other works, like the vocal-orchestral Evocations (1911) and ballet Le festin de l'araignée (1913), had already shown his ability to leaven d'Indyism with exotic material and Ravellian brilliance.

In the Symphony No 2 (1921), he moved on to an almost polytonal density, but in the 1920s his music (like Ravel's) became more spare and astringent, though still with a rhythmic vigour and motivic intensity that can be seen as a highly personal extension of Schola thinking. His later, neo-classical works, marked by wide-ranging regular themes and motoric rhythms, include the Symphonies Nos 3 and 4, the orchestral Suite in F, the Piano Concerto, the String Quartet and two ballets, Bacchus et Ariane and Aenéas.   **GROVE**music

Symphonies

Symphonies – No 1, 'Le poème de la forêt'; No 4
Orchestre de Paris / Christoph Eschenbach
Ondine ODE1092-2 (67' · DDD)   Ⓕ▷

For a work composed originally as independent items, Roussel's impressionist First Symphony (1904-06) works surprisingly well. True, its structure is unorthodox, each of the four movements – which form a seasonal cycle from winter to autumn – larger than its predecessor, but it all flows together remarkably well, adding up to rather more than a picturesque set of tone-poems or suite. Small wonder it so impressed early audiences.

Roussel refined his symphonic style considerably over time, so comparing the First with the Fourth of three decades later shows just how far he had travelled. The Fourth is an abstract masterpiece, typically mixing up compositional rigour, lyrical intensity and rhythmic élan. If the Fourth does not quite match the Apollonian drive of No 3, this is because it is a very different type of work to its celebrated forebear.

As with his recording of No 2, Eschenbach's accounts are highly evocative and beautifully phrased. Tempi are again broad, working well in *Le poème de la forêt* where he relishes the poetry of this quietly sumptuous score. In the Fourth, however, after finely shaped readings of the first two movements, the third and fourth are dispatched with a lightness bordering on the throwaway. What makes this newcomer recommendable is the superb playing and Ondine's first-rate sound.

Symphony No 2. Bacchus et Ariane – Suites Nos 1 and 2
Orchestre de Paris / Christoph Eschenbach
Ondine ODE1065-2 (78' · DDD)   Ⓕⓞ▷

The familiar exuberant Roussel style, a synthesis of Busoni-esque Young Classicality and impressionism heard here in the two suites from

Bacchus et Ariane, did not come easily. His move away from a successful early manner was accelerated by the Great War and was somewhat directionless when he began his Second Symphony in the summer of 1919. When completed two years later, the score showed both a leap in the dark and the crucial step towards the manner of his best known music.

Yet the Second Symphony remains deep in eclipse from its two magnificent successors, despite its shimmering, multi-textured instrumentation, its moments of rapt beauty and illustrative nature. Partly constructed in places from episodes from his abandoned opera *Le roi Tobol*, the symphony – Roussel's longest – is also the most complex and elusive. Here and there are tantalising foretastes of the sound world of the Third, yet its structure lacks the latter's clean lines, seeming more a hybrid with the symphonic fantasia: prophetic of post-Second World War symphonism.

Eschenbach's account is strong on both atmosphere and clarity of line. He takes broad tempi, adding almost four minutes to Charles Dutoit's duration (Teldec). Ondine's sound is superb. The juxtaposition with the two *Bacchus et Ariane* concert suites makes for a rich programme, all brilliantly played by the Orchestre de Paris. Roussel's symphony has lived far too long in the shadows; this disc should help bring it out into the light.

Symphony No 3. Bacchus et Ariane
Royal Scottish National Orchestra /
Stéphane Denève
Naxos 8 570245 (63' · DDD) Ⓢ🅑➔

The Third is the most sheerly exciting of Roussel's four symphonies. The pounding, soaring opening *Allegro vivo* has become iconic but there is far more to the symphony than that, with an *Adagio* of great emotional range, two scherzos (one embedded in the slow movement) and a whirlwind finale that fuses all the expressive elements together by its close.

The RSNO's performance is fully alive to the music's sweep and irrepressible *joie de vivre* as well as its more lyrical aspects. There is an edge-of-the-seat quality to the interpretation that is winning. In the third span, *Vivace*, Denève pushes on and here, as in the *Allegro con spirito* finale, he outpaces his rivals. But it is with its sound and orchestral balance that this newcomer scores, making audible a wealth of detail often submerged.

The woodwinds in particular benefit and their superb playing illuminates *Bacchus et Ariane*. The cover states that the complete ballet is being presented whereas the track listings show Suites Nos 1 and 2. There is little appreciable difference, the suites mirroring the two acts and published this way after the lacklustre premiere. Suite No 2 has become a warhorse for Francophile conductors but there is much to enjoy in the First. If you are coming new to Roussel, this is the perfect introduction. Highly recommended.

Bacchus et Ariane

Bacchus et Ariane, Op 43. Le festin de l'araignée, Op 17
BBC Philharmonic Orchestra / Yan Pascal Tortelier
Chandos CHAN9494 (68' · DDD) Ⓕ🅞🅞➔

Unlike his contemporary Dukas, Roussel has been somewhat sidelined as a 'connoisseur's composer'. That presumably means that he didn't write fat, lush tunes that could be exploited in television commercials, but produced works of vigorous ideas and more subtle quality. Record companies used to fight shy of his music – the Third and Fourth Symphonies have indeed maintained a foothold, but with the ballet *Bacchus et Ariane*, which is closely linked with the Third, we've mostly been given only its second half. Here are alert, rhythmically vital performances of Roussel's two most famous ballets, which even at the most exuberantly excited moments (like the 'Bacchanale' in *Bacchus*) preserve a truly Gallic lucidity, and which Tortelier marks by a captivating lightness of touch; and when it comes to quiet passages one could not ask for greater tenderness than in the beautiful end of Act 1 of *Bacchus*, when Bacchus puts Ariadne to sleep.

Le festin de l'araignée, written 18 years earlier, is in a quite different style. Where Bacchus's trenchant idiom at times makes one think of Stravinsky's *Apollon Musagète*, *Le festin* (which had the misfortune to be overshadowed by the *Rite of Spring*, produced only eight weeks later) is atmospheric and more impressionistic (in the same vein as Roussel's First Symphony). It's a score full of delicate invention, whose one weakness is that for its full appreciation a knowledge of its detailed programme is needed – and that's provided here in the booklet.

The BBC Philharmonic play it beautifully. If this is 'connoisseur's music', then be happy to be called a connoisseur: you'll find it delectable.

Pancrace Royer   French 1705-1755

French composer, harpsichordist, organist and administrator. His father was sent by Louis XIV to be the intendant of gardens and fountains at the court of Savoy. Royer acquired a great reputation for playing the harpsichord and organ (Laugier) and as a composer, was a brilliant and influential contemporary of Rameau through much of the latter's career.

Pièces de clavecin – La Majestueuse: Courante; La Zaïde: Rondeau; Les matelots: Modérément; L'Incertaine: Marqué; L'Aimable: Gracieux; La Bagatelle; Suitte de la Bagatelle; La Remouleuse: Rondeau; Les tendres sentiments: Rondeau; Le vertigo: Rondeau; Allemande; La Sensible: Rondeau; La marche des scythes: Fièrement
Christophe Rousset hpd
Naïve AM151 (59' · DDD) Ⓕ🅞

Pancrace Royer's one book of *Pièces de clavecin*, published in 1746, is full of spark and variety, ranging from the dulcet 'La Zaïde' to the robust jollity of 'Les matelots', and from the eloquence of 'La Sensible' to the dizzyingly quirky virtuosity of 'Le vertigo'. And while it is Rameau who rightly dominates our knowledge of the musical times in which Royer lived as harpsichord teacher to Louis XV's daughters, composer of operas and director of Paris's prestigious Concert Spirituel, as a keyboard composer in the imaginative, full-bodied mould of someone like Forqueray, Royer need not be considered as totally blotted out by the more famous composer's shadow.

Yet this disc is one of only a handful devoted to Royer's harpsichord music. Remarkably, it is also the second by Christophe Rousset, his first having been 15 years ago for L'Oiseau-Lyre. The first noticeable difference is in the harpsichords themselves; first time around Rousset had an easy-toned 1751 Hemsch, but this time he uses a composite 18th-century instrument, more aggressive in sound, more 'zingy' at the top end and with less of the Hemsch's mellow resonance. This is not without knock-on effect; whereas before there was a stylish elegance and easy grace of line in the way Rousset dispatched these demanding pieces, now there is a sense that, while his technique remains as enviable as ever, he has to work harder at the music, draw things out more, become more mannered. Harpsichord enthusiasts unfamiliar with Royer's generous musical personality should take this opportunity to make his acquaintance now.

Miklós Rózsa
Hungarian/American 1907-1995

Raised in Budapest and on his father's rural estate, Rósza was exposed to Hungarian folk music from an early age. He studied piano with his mother (who was at the Budapest Academy with Bartók) and violin and viola with his uncle, a musician with the Royal Hungrian Opera. By the age of seven he was composing. In 1926 he was a student at the Leipzig Conservatory; by 1929 his chamber works were being performed and promoted throughout Europe. In 1931 moved to Paris where he finished his Theme, Variations and Finale, a work that soon gained international recognition. He was introduced to the film music genre through Honegger and from 1935-9 composed for London Films under Hungarian-born producer Alexander Korda. In 1940 he travelled with Korda to Hollywood to complete the score of The Thief of Baghdad and was soon in great demand as a freelance film composer and conductor. As a staff member at MGM (1948-62), he became one of the most highly regarded composers in the industry, writing music for over 100 films. The essence of his musical style springs from his early experiences with Hungarian peasant music. His works are also infused with the sentimental lyricism of the gypsy tradition.
GROVEmusic

Concertos

Viola Concerto, Op 37a. Hungarian Serenade, Op 25
ªGilad Karni *va* **Budapest Concert Orchestra MÁV / Mariusz Smolij**
Naxos 8 570925 (61' · DDD)　　Ⓢ➤

The recording industry's sustained interest in Rózsa's concert music is heartening and this new disc from Naxos is its latest manifestation. Both works exhibit fully the strengths and appeal of the composer's output as a whole, from its impeccable craftsmanship to its lilting Hungarian accent. The personal voice – close stylistically at times to Kodály and Bartók – is recognisably that of the film composer whose music graced the silver screen for so long.

The *Hungarian Serenade* started life in the early 1930s as his Op 10 for strings but Ernö von Dohnányi persuaded the young composer to recast it for a larger orchestra with a punchier finale. The work underwent several further revisions before emerging as the work given here. It's is high-quality light music and is superbly played here.

Gilad Karni's ardent interpretation of the Viola Concerto is especially welcome. A fine player and former Lionel Tertis Competition prize-winner, Karni audibly relishes the work's dark colours and rich writing. The Concerto had a difficult genesis (for Rózsa), taking four years to complete with several interruptions by film work which the composer later claimed ruined the flow. Yet the finished result does not betray this, its four movements holding together as if written in a single burst of inspiration. Karni proves a fine advocate and the Budapest orchestra provide excellent support.

'Three Choral Suites'
Ben-Hur. King of Kings. Quo Vadis
Mormon Tabernacle Choir; Cincinnati Pops Orchestra / Erich Kunzel
Telarc CD80631 (62' · DDD)　　Ⓕ

At the time of his death in 1995, the Hungarian-born composer and Hollywood veteran Miklós Rózsa had been planning to turn three of his famous epic film scores – *Ben-Hur*, *Quo Vadis* and *King of Kings* – into concert works of equally biblical proportions. These completed choral suites owe their existence to Rózsa's associates and pupils (most notably Daniel Robbins), but there's no doubt that their essence is strictly that of Rózsa himself.

What's so striking about hearing these works in close proximity is the paradox of having essentially the same musical forces and a similarly focused musical language yield such diverse results. The Overture to *Ben-Hur* sets an imposing tone, historically speaking, yet this loosens up a bit in *Quo Vadis* with the choral text changing midway through from Latin to English (as well as including an English narration). Seeing how every great historical figure in Hollywood speaks English regardless of era or ethnicity, I suppose one shouldn't expect too much here in the way of linguistic consistency.

Once again, Erich Kunzel and the Cincinnati Pops display the very qualities, including attention to orchestral colour and full commitment to unabashedly emotional sentiment, that keep performances of this type from either pandering or slumming. The clarity of the orchestra is something of a strange fit with the 360-voice Mormon Tabernacle Choir, which relies less on musical precision than overwheming the listener through sheer force of sound, but one would have to think hard to conceive of a more memorable performance of these works.

Anton Rubinstein · Russian 1829-1894

Celebrated as one of the greatest pianists of the 19th century, Rubinstein was a hugely influential figure on the Russian music scene. He was a prolific composers achieving his greates successses from the 1860s onwards with his Fouth Piano Concerto and opera, The Demon (1871).

'Romantic Piano Concerto, Volume 38'
Rubinstein Piano Concerto No 4
Scharwenka Piano Concerto No 1
Marc-André Hamelin pf
BBC Scottish Symphony Orchestra / Michael Stern
Hyperion CDA67508 (60' · DDD)   Ⓕ

Described by one respected critic as the greatest living pianist, Marc-André Hamelin soars to ever new heights of virtuosity. His phenomenal if nonchalantly deployed dexterity is matched by a cool, lyrical insight, making these performances virtually unsurpassable. Earl Wild's account of the Scharwenka, aptly described in America as 'a wing-ding of a romp', is a hard act to follow but there are few pianists of world class more adept at trumping other people's aces than Hamelin. Here it is possible to see his Scharwenka as equally dashing and razor-sharp as Wild's but with a subtler, more inclusive sense of poetry. There is never a question of virtuosity for its own sake.

Writing of Rubinstein's Fourth – and best – Piano Concerto, the august authors of *The Record Guide* once claimed that if the swelling introduction promises great things, all that emerges is a rather large mouse. But such words were written long before the advent of Hamelin, whose brilliance sets every potentially tired page alive with a truly blazing conviction. His concentrated force in the finale sweeps all before it, and he pulls out all the stops in the gloriously over-the-top conclusion.

Hamelin is superbly partnered and recorded, and lovers of lush, romantic melody embellished with hundreds and thousands of winking sequins need look no further. This extraordinary pianist now needs to be heard in the widest repertoire – not just in music's byways, however tempting and scintillating.

Edmund Rubbra · British 1901-1986

Rubbra, a pupil of Scott and of Holst and Morris at the Royal College of Music (1921-5), worked as a pianist, teacher and critic before his appointment as lecturer at Oxford (1947-68). His music took some while to develop independence from Ireland, Bax and Holst, but his First Symphony (1937) begins to show a characteristic style of rhapsodic growth tautened by thematic working and almost incessant polyphonic activity. His later works include 10 more symphonies, of which No 9 is an oratorio-like work (Sinfonia sacra, 1972), besides concertos for viola, piano and violin, four string quartets (1933-77), masses and motets (he became a Roman Catholic in 1948).

GROVEmusic

Violin Concerto

Violin Concerto. Improvisations on Virginal Pieces by Giles Farnaby. Improvisation
Krysia Osostowicz vn
Ulster Orchestra / Takuo Yuasa
Naxos 8 557591 (57' · DDD)   ⓈⒹ+

Composed in 1959, the Violin Concerto is one of Rubbra's most compelling large-scale offerings, comprising a masterly opening *Allegro* that finds lyrical intensity and organic growth in blissful accord, a ravishing central 'Poema' (whose gentle rapture harks back to the 'Canto' slow movement of the Sixth Symphony from 1954) and a wonderfully earthy finale, full of bracing vigour and rhythmic élan. The 1956 *Improvisation* for violin and orchestra also repays close inspection, a 12-and-a-half-minute essay of notable economy of thought and expressive variety that salvages material from an earlier *Fantasia* for violin and orchestra from the mid-1930s.

Not only is Krysia Osostowicz thoroughly steeped in the idiom but she plays with great spirit and beauty of tone and is unfazed by any technical hurdles. No grumbles with the sensitive reading of the *Improvisation*, in which Osostowicz generates a stimulating rapport with Takuo Yuasa and the Ulster Orchestra. However, in the Concerto one might have preferred a touch less reserve and more in the way of songful joy from her collaborators – not to mention a greater sense of impetus in the first movement. Explicit, if slightly clinical sound.

Fortunately, the 1946 *Improvisations on Virginal Pieces by Giles Farnaby* show conductor and orchestra in more spontaneous, personable form. It's a most beguiling, concise score. In all a very likeable and useful disc.

Symphonies

Symphony No 3, Op 49. Symphony No 7 in C, Op 88
BBC National Orchestra of Wales / Richard Hickox
Chandos CHAN9634 (71' · DDD)   ⒻⓄⓄ

All 11 symphonies also available as a boxed set,

Chandos CHAN9944 (5 CDs for price of 4)

For some years the Third Symphony was a repertory piece, at least on BBC programmes, but it fell out of favour in the late 1950s. Commentators have noticed a certain Sibelian cut to its opening idea (with woodwind in thirds) but everything else strikes you as completely personal. There's a whiff of Elgarian fantasy in the fourth variation of the finale. It's been called the most genial and relaxed of Rubbra's symphonies but there's a pastoral feel to many of the ideas, bucolic even, in the same way that there is about the Brahms Second Symphony. Brahms springs to mind in the masterly variations and fugue of the finale, for not long before, Rubbra had orchestrated the Brahms *Handel* Variations.

Hickox and his players give a very persuasive and totally convincing account of the symphony. Anyone coming to the Seventh for the first time, particularly in this performance, will surely not fail to sense the elevated quality of its musical thought. Its opening paragraphs are among the most beautiful Rubbra ever penned, and it's evident throughout that this is music that speaks of deep and serious things. This performance speaks with great directness and power. The horn playing in the opening is eloquent and the orchestral playing throughout is of a uniformly high standard. These are magnificent and impressive accounts, and the recording is truthful and splendidly balanced.

Symphony No 5 in B flat, Op 63. Symphony No 8, 'Hommage à Teilhard de Chardin', Op 132. Ode to the Queen, Op 83[a]
[a]**Susan Bickley** *mez* **BBC National Orchestra of Wales / Richard Hickox**
Chandos CHAN9714 (64' · DDD · T)　　　　　Ⓕ

In the early 1950s Rubbra's Fifth Symphony was a repertory piece and broadcast frequently. Ten years later it had all but disappeared from programmes, and although a second recording was made by the late Hans-Hubert Schönzeler, this is its first digital recording, and the finest account of the Fifth ever. Part of the success of Hickox's series is his instinctive feeling for the tempo at which this music best comes to life and his scrupulous adherence to dynamic markings. Find the right tempo and everything falls into place; observe every dynamic nuance and the textures achieve the right degree of transparency. The quality of the recording also plays an important part: there's great detail, presence and warmth.

The Eighth Symphony (1966-8), subtitled *Hommage à Teilhard de Chardin*, was composed in a very different climate, for by the late 1960s Rubbra's music was out of fashion. The new symphony had to wait three years for its first performance in Liverpool. The thought of the Catholic philosopher Teilhard de Chardin had a great influence on Rubbra. The music's mystical feel and luminous texture are at times reminiscent of Holst. The Eighth speaks of deep and serious things and in this performance proves a powerful musical experience.

The Ode to the Queen is something of a discovery. Commissioned by the BBC to celebrate the Elizabeth II's Coronation, it's Rubbra's only song cycle with full orchestra. The songs are inspired and beautifully sung. A triumphant conclusion to Richard Hickox's Rubbra cycle.

Symphony No 9, 'Sinfonia sacra', Op 140.
The Morning Watch, Op 55
Lynne Dawson *sop* **Della Jones** *mez* **Stephen Roberts** *bar* **BBC National Chorus and Orchestra of Wales / Richard Hickox**
Chandos CHAN9441 (57' · DDD · T)　　　ⒻⓄ

The Ninth (1973) is Rubbra's most visionary utterance, and its stature has so far gone unrecognised. (This is its only recording.) Its subtitle, *Sinfonia sacra*, gives a good idea of its character. It tells the story of the Resurrection very much as do the Bach Passions. There are three soloists: the contralto narrates from the New Testament, while the soprano takes the part of Mary Magdalen and the baritone that of Jesus. Other parts, those of disciples and angels, are taken by the chorus, which also functions outside the action, in four settings of meditative Latin texts from the Roman liturgy or in Lutheran chorales to which Rubbra put verses by Bernard de Nevers. The symphonic dimension is reinforced by the opening motive, which pretty well dominates the work. Its argument unfolds with a seeming inevitability and naturalness that's the hallmark of a great symphony.

Its depth and beauty call to mind only the most exalted of comparisons and it should be heard as often as *Gerontius* or the *War Requiem*. This is music of an inspired breadth and serenity and everyone connected with this magnificent performance conveys a sense of profound conviction. *The Morning Watch* is one of Rubbra's most eloquent choral pieces. It dates from 1946, and so comes roughly half-way between the Fourth and Fifth Symphonies. A setting of the 17th-century metaphysical poet, Henry Vaughan, it too is music of substance and its long and moving orchestral introduction is of the highest order of inspiration.

Additional recommendations

Symphonies Nos 3 and 4
Couplings. A Tribute for Ralph Vaughan Williams on his 70th Birthday. Resurgam Overture
Philharmonia Orchestra / Del Mar
Lyrita SRCD202 (73' · DDD)　　　　　　　Ⓕ
　Dedicated performances of these superb symphonies under Norman Del Mar. The coupling, *Resurgam*, is a late work of great beauty.

Sinfonia concertante

Sinfonia concertante, Op 38[a]. A Tribute, Op 56[d]. The Morning Watch, Op 55[b]. Ode to the Queen, Op 83[c]

ᶜ**Susan Bickley** *mez* ᵃ**Howard Shelley** *pf*
BBC National ᵇ**Chorus and Orchestra of Wales /**
Richard Hickox
Chandos CHAN9966 (62' · DDD)   Ⓕ

A mouth-watering reissue comprising four outstandingly eloquent performances. The stand-out item here has to be Howard Shelley's imperious traversal of the big-boned *Sinfonia concertante* for piano and orchestra. Certainly, the opening 'Fantasia' exhibits an exhilarating thematic resource and craggy, almost Bartókian resilience. It's the finale, however, which contains the work's most rewarding, deeply felt inspiration: this is a prelude and fugue of grave nobility, economy and poise, whose elegiac countenance reflects Rubbra's sense of loss at the death of his teacher and good friend, Gustav Holst.

Next comes an affectionate account of *A Tribute* (Rubbra's 70th-birthday tribute to Vaughan Williams), followed by *The Morning Watch*, a noble choral setting of Henry Vaughan's mystic poem which possesses a power and radiance that can't fail to impress. Last, but not least, there's *Ode to the Queen* (1953); employing texts by three Tudor poets (Crashaw, D'Avenant and Campion), it's a charming, 13-minute creation, the two extrovert outer songs framing a *Poco adagio e tranquillo* setting of chaste beauty. Mezzo Susan Bickley is ideally cast, and Hickox tenders bright-eyed support. Superb sound throughout, enormously ripe and wide-ranging.

String Quartets

String Quartets – No 2, Op 73ᵃ; No 4, Op 150ᵇ. Lyric
Movement, Op 24ᶜ. Meditations on a Byzantine
Hymn, 'O Quando in Cruce', Op 117ᵃᵈ
ᶜ**Michael Dussek** *pf* ᵃᵇᶜ**Dante Quartet** (Krysia
Osostowicz *vn*/ᵈ*va* Declan Daly *vn* Judith Busbridge
ᵈ*va* Alastair Blayden *vc*)
Dutton Laboratories Epoch CDLX7114 (59' · DDD)   Ⓜ⒪

Completed in 1951, the Second Quartet is a marvellously inventive piece, beautifully scored for the medium, unfailingly purposeful and full of beguilingly subtle rhythmic and harmonic resource. Bearing a dedication to Robert Simpson, the two-movement Fourth Quartet of 1975-7 was one of Rubbra's last major works. Probing and intensely poignant, it's another hugely eloquent, seamlessly evolving affair which repays repeated hearings. The Dante Quartet prove outstandingly sympathetic proponents of Rubbra's noble inspiration, their playing urgently expressive and tonally ingratiating. Pianist Michael Dussek joins proceedings for a stylish and delectably unforced account of the *Lyric Movement* of 1929, an expertly wrought essay for piano quintet which itself grew out of an earlier, discarded string quartet. Tony Faulkner's Maltings sound is excellent on the whole, if just a fraction too closely balanced. No matter, a wonderful disc.

String Quartets – No 1 in F minor, Op 35; No 3, Op 112.
Cello Sonata, Op 60ᵃ. Improvisation for Unaccompanied Cello, Op 124.
ᵃ**Michael Dussek** *pf* **Dante Quartet**
Dutton Epoch CDLX7123 (72' · DDD)   ⓂⓄⓄ

Rubbra originally conceived the first of his four string quartets in 1933. Thirteen years later, he overhauled his thoughts and added a new finale. Dedicated to Vaughan Williams and beautifully laid out for the medium, it's an invigorating and purposeful work, boasting a particularly memorable slow movement. The Third Quartet of 1963 is even finer; its seamlessly evolving structure demonstrates Rubbra's subtle ear for harmony and counterpoint. The three movements play without a break, and once again the *Adagio* centrepiece plumbs great depths.

It's good that the Dante Quartet have lost no time in completing their Rubbra cycle for Dutton. The previous coupling of Quartets Nos 2 and 4 was shortlisted for a *Gramophone* Award, and if anything this disc attains an even greater level of accomplishment and perception. These are eloquent readings that strike a perfect equilibrium between communication and rigour. Bouquets, too, for the Dante's young French cellist, Pierre Doumenge, who teams up with pianist Michael Dussek for a cogent and impassioned account of the 1946 Cello Sonata (more convincing than either comparative rival). Doumenge also shines in the unaccompanied *Improvisation* from 1964. The production values are exemplary. This is a most rewarding release.

Violin Sonatas

Violin Sonatasᵃ – No 1, Op 11; No 2, Op 31; No 3, Op
133. Four Pieces, Op 29ᵃ. Variations on a Phrygian
Theme, Op 105
Krysia Osostowicz *vn* ᵃ**Michael Dussek** *pf*
Dutton Laboratories Epoch Series CDLX7101
(59' · DDD)   ⓂⓄ

Rubbra's First Violin Sonata is a notable achievement all round: its first two movements exhibit a bittersweet lyricism that will strike a chord with anyone who has ever responded to, say, John Ireland's glorious Second Violin Sonata or the chamber music of Howells. By contrast, the 'Fugal Rondo' finale intriguingly pursues an altogether more sturdy, determinedly neo-Classical mode of expression.

Written six years later in 1931, the Second Sonata already reveals a wider emotional scope, as well as a striking use of progressive tonality that at least one contemporary critic found 'disturbing and unnecessary'. Championed by the great Albert Sammons, it will come as a substantial discovery to many: comprising an eventful, ever-evolving first movement, a strong, but never sentimental 'Lament' centrepiece, and a quasi-Bartókian finale, its wild exuberance seems to look forward across the decades to the last movement of this same figure's Violin Concerto of 1959.

Framing that are the *Four Pieces* for beginners and the unaccompanied *Variations on a Phrygian Theme*, a work of compact resourcefulness. But even finer is the Third Sonata. It's a wondrous piece, its sense of purpose, rapt intuition and profound serenity irresistibly calling to mind Rubbra's Eighth Symphony, and it fully deserves the exalted advocacy it receives here. Indeed, Ososticowicz and Dussek form an outstandingly sympathetic partnership.

Piano Works

Prelude and Fugue on a Theme of Cyril Scott, Op 69. Sonatina, Op 19. Introduction, Aria and Fugue, Op 104. Preludes, Op 131. Nemo Fugue. Studies, Op 139. Invention on the Name of Haydn, Op 160. Fantasy Fugue, Op 161. Teaching Pieces, Op 74ᵃ
Traditional (arr Rubbra) Fukagawa
Michael Dussek, ᵃ**Rachel Dussek** pfs
Dutton Laboratories Epoch CDLX7112 (62' · DDD) Ⓕ

Rubbra was an excellent pianist, and his output for the instrument spans pretty much his entire career. It's the earliest work here, the Sonatina of 1928-9, that proves by far the most technically demanding. Whereas the raptly lyrical first two movements have something of the outdoor tang of Vaughan Williams and Howells, the finale seems to stand apart, its timeless, intuitive spirit and bracing contrapuntal mastery the hallmarks of Rubbra's mature voice.

Other stand-out items include the noble *Introduction, Aria and Fugue*, the pithy Four Studies of 1970-71 and the Eight Preludes, Rubbra's most substantial piano offering, completed in 1966. The latter comprise a hugely rewarding sequence, the organic wholeness of Rubbra's luminous inspiration often calling to mind his masterly Eighth Symphony. Suffice it to say, Michael Dussek acquits himself extremely well throughout, and he has been sympathetically recorded.

Vocal Works

Missa Cantuariensis, Op 59ᵃᵇ. Magnificat and Nunc dimittis in A flat, Op 65ᵃᵇ. Missa in honorem Sancti Dominici, Op 66ᵃ. Prelude and Fugue on a Theme of Cyril Scott, Op 69 (arr Rose)ᵇ. Tenebrae, Op 72ᵃ. Meditation, Op 79ᵇ
ᵃ**St John's College Choir, Cambridge /**
Christopher Robinson ᵇorg
Naxos 8 555255 (71' · DDD · T/t) ⓈⓄⓄ⊅

Christopher Robinson and his St John's College Choir prove especially eloquent, humane advocates of the eight-part *Missa Cantuariensis*. We've long needed a top-notch digital recording of this, the first of Rubbra's five Mass settings. Robinson and company rise to the challenge admirably, not least in the exuberant concluding *Gloria* with its lung-burstingly high tessitura. We also get a thoroughly idiomatic rendering of the taut and imposing *Magnificat* and *Nunc dimittis* in A flat that Rubbra wrote two years later.

In the glorious *Missa in honorem Sancti Dominici* from 1949 (inspired by Rubbra's own conversion to Roman Catholicism the previous year, on the feast day of St Dominic) our Cambridge group doesn't quite match the sumptuous blend, miraculous unanimity or spine-tingling fervour displayed by James O'Donnell's Westminster Cathedral Choir (to quote the composer: '…this is not austere music…red blood runs through its veins!'). On the other hand, these newcomers sound wholly captivated by the nine motets that make up the remarkable Op-72 *Tenebrae*. Boasting an infinitely subtle harmonic and contrapuntal resource, these timeless, wonderfully compassionate settings of the responsories used during Matins on Maundy Thursday show Rubbra very much at the height of his powers, encompassing an extraordinarily wide dramatic and expressive range. Robinson also gives us two instrumental bonuses in the rapt *Meditation* for organ, Op 79, and Bernard Rose's transcription of the more substantial *Prelude and Fugue on a Theme of Cyril Scott* (originally written for piano in 1950 to celebrate Scott's 70th birthday). Throw in Naxos's praiseworthy production, and you've a bargain of the first order.

Missa Cantuariensis, Op 59. Missa in honorem Sancti Dominici, Op 66. St Non's (That Virgin's Child Most Meek), Op 114 No 2. Dormi Jesu, 'The Virgin's Cradle Song', Op 3
St Margaret's Westminster Singers /
Richard Hickox
Chandos CHAN10423 (47' · ADD) Ⓜ⊅

How good it is to have these deeply sympathetic performances (which were recorded in the presence of the grateful composer at St Alban's Church, Holborn, over one December day in 1975) restored to the catalogue. Richard Hickox and the St Margaret's Westminster Singers bring to both these rapt and timeless Mass settings an unhurried, intuitive understanding and devotional glow. The two unaccompanied carols are special too, in particular the ravishing *Dormi Jesu* (Rubbra's first published work, written in 1924 when he was a student of Holst).

With the mastertape sadly damaged beyond repair, Chandos had no option but to turn to a pristine copy of the original 1976 RCA LP. In the circumstances, the transfer to CD is remarkably successful, for the sound remains rich, clear and atmospheric. Detailed notes by the composer and Timothy Storey enhance the appeal of a mid-price reissue that long-standing Rubbrarians will surely want to own.

Poul Ruders   Danish b1949

Ruders studied piano and organ at the Odense Conservatory and graduated from the Royal Danish Conservatory in 1975. He worked initially as a church organist and freelance keyboard player.

Although he had some lessons from Nørholm and orchestration from Kar Rasmussen, he describes himself as an essentially self-taught composer.

Ruders is widely recognised as the leading Danish composer of his generation. The large proportion of his works are for orchestra or large chamber ensemble; some of his scores use electronic keyboards and samplers. Ruders has developed a flexible musical language, organised only by his own 'homespun' systems; freely atonal but able to incorporate tonal references. His command of idiomatic instrumental and vocal writing, his strong sense of drama and his readiness to explore extremes of experience enable him to communicate directly and powerfully with audiences. **GROVE**music

Violin Concerto No 1

Violin Concerto No 1[a]. Etude and Ricercare[b]. The Bells[c]. The Christmas Gospel[d]
[c]**Lucy Shelton** *sop* [ab]**Rolf Schulte** *vn* [c]**Speculum Musicae / David Starobin** *gtr* [a]**Riverside Symphony Orchestra / George Rothman;** [d]**Malmö Symphony Orchestra / Ola Rudner**
Bridge BCD9057 (62' · DDD · T)   ⓕ🅞

Ruders' First Violin Concerto (1981) begins as routine minimalist auto-hypnosis. But it develops some wonderfully inventive ways of disrupting and reassembling itself. Admittedly the last movement, with its chaconne based on Vivaldi and Schubert, tiptoes on the border of sensationalism. Otherwise the work could join Schnittke's Fourth as one of the few contemporary violin concertos with a strong claim to standard-repertoire status. Schulte gives an intense account of the solo part; the Riverside orchestra is tight in discipline, the recording close. All these factors help to make the overall musical impression extremely vivid. Less persuasive is Ruders's vocal writing in *The Bells* (the same Edgar Allen Poe texts set by Rachmaninov), and there's something not quite convincing about the instrumental setting too – perhaps too uniform an intensity, too much frantic heterophony. *The Christmas Gospel*, tossed off in two weeks for a mixed animation and live-action film, is darkly impressive – necessarily simple and direct, but still rewarding, even when divorced from the visual images.

The Handmaid's Tale

The Handmaid's Tale
Marianne Rørholm *mez* Offred **Hanne Fischer** *mez* Double **Poul Elming** *ten* Luke **Ulla Kudsk Jensen** *mez* Offred's Mother **Anne Margrethe Dahl** *sop* Aunt Lydia **Dijna Mai-Mai** *sop* Moira **Lise-Lotte Nielsen** *sop* Janine **Annita Wadsholt** *contr* Moira's Aunt **Susanne Resmark** *contr* Serena Joy **Kari Hamnøy** *contr* Rita **Aage Haugland** *bass* Commander **Gert Henning-Jensen** *ten* Nick **Elsebeth Lund** *sop* Ofglen **Pia Hansen** *mez* New Ofglen **Bengl-Ola Morgny** *ten* Doctor **Elisabeth Halling** *mez* Warren's Wife **John Laursen** *ten* Commander X **Uffe Henriksen** *bass* First Eye and Guard **Morten Kramp** *bass* Second Eye and Guard Royal Danish Opera Chorus and Orchestra / Michael Schønwandt
DaCapo ② 8 224165/6 (144' · DDD · T/t) Recorded live 2000   ⓕ🅞🅞

Ruders says of his vividly imaginative opera, based on Margaret Atwood's novel, that he composed it as though he were directing a film. Precisely: it's divided into 44 scenes, some very short, several incorporating flashbacks in which present and past sometimes appear simultaneously. The opera's 'present' is the not-too-distant future, a hideous fundamentalist autocracy in which women have no rights, not even to read and write, and those of them convicted of 'gender-treachery' (adultery, second marriage, contraception, abortion) are compelled to become 'Handmaids', ritually impregnated by the husbands of childess women. The central character, Offred (Of Fred – the name of the man whose property she now is), is portrayed by two singers: her present, brainwashed and imperfectly remembering self, and Offred as she was in 'Time Before', happily married (though as her husband's second wife a 'gender traitor' to the new order) with a five-year-old daughter. The opera depicts the brutal totalitarianism of 'Time Now', Offred's relationship with the Commander (Fred) and his alarming wife, her longing for her dimly remembered husband and child and her enlistment in a sort of resistance group. But it's in the very nature of the plot that we never learn her ultimate fate.

It's also in the plot's nature that it needs a great variety of types of music, as we move from past to present, from the grim rituals of Time Now to Offred's memories of Time Before. Ambiguous music, too, since in this shadowy, threatening world things are often not what they seem. Ruder's great achievement is to provide that variety and ambiguity from within the resources of his own style; in particular, he balances on the tightrope from tonality to atonality with great skill. The rituals of the Handmaids are accompanied by simple, chorale-like chants with 'minimalist' accompaniment. The most striking passage to emerge from the score is a duet for the two Offreds in which both voices seem to be yearning for a tonal resolution, but can no more achieve it than two people 20 years apart in time can meet.

Ruders has been best known for his prodigiously resourceful orchestral writing, and he surpasses himself here: electronic keyboards, samplers and additional percussion are added to the large orchestra, but many of the strangest, most nightmarish or most radiant sounds are produced by normal instruments used with brilliant originality. Some of the more monstrous inhabitants of this nightmare world are portrayed in vocal lines that go to extremes, but far more often the writing for voices is idiomatically singable. The cast, among whom there isn't one single weak link, sing their hearts out, and Schønwandt conveys the kaleidoscopic colours of Ruder's score with a remarkable degree of clarity. The recording is first class.

Kafka's Trial

Kafka's Trial
Johnny Van Hal *ten* Josef K **Gisella Stille** *sop*
Miss Bürstner; Felice Bauer **Marianne Rørholm** *mez*
Miss Montag; Greta Bloch; Leni **Gert Henning-
Jensen** *ten* Inspector; Court Recorder; Titorelli
Michael Kristensen *ten* Deputy Manager;
Businessman Block **Johan Reuter** *bar* Interrogator;
Uncle Albert **Hans Lawaetz** *bass* Jailer Franz **Anders
Jakobsson** *bass* Jailer William **Bo Anker Hansen** *bar*
Manager of the Bank; Lawyer Huld **Hanne Fischer**
mez Washerwoman; Hunchback **Ole Hedegaard** *ten*
Flogger; Chaplain **Royal Danish Opera Chorus and
Orchestra / Thomas Søndergård**
DaCapo ② 8 226042/3 (125' · DDD · T/t)   Ⓕ

The enigmatic, nightmarish *The Trial* is, after
Metamorphosis, probably Franz Kafka's most
celebrated tale. Left in fragmentary form at his
death, it has fascinated playwrights (such as Steven Berkoff), film-makers (among them Georg
Pabst and Orson Welles) and opera composers
(Gottfried von Einem and Gunther Schuller not
least) for decades for both its state of incompletion – it has a beginning, an end but only part of
the middle – and its surreal, uncomfortable storyline. Is it moral fable, black satire, utter nonsense? Poul Ruders's opera to Paul Bentley's
intelligent libretto, premiered in March 2005, is
at least the seventh such treatment but where
theirs differs from previous versions is in the
attempt to link directly the creation of the story
to events in Kafka's life.

As Bentley explains in the booklet, the young
Czech writer may have been inspired to write *The
Trial* not through any political motive but rather
because he had himself been subject to a 'tribunal'
of sorts in Berlin, in which his fiancée – Felice
Bauer – tired of his puppyish but equivocal devotions and an act of infidelity put him on trial in the
lobby of his Berlin hotel. Alongside her in this
kangaroo court was her friend, Greta Bloch, with
whom he had been unfaithful but whom Felice
had sent on purpose to meet him. From his letters, extracts of which form the basis of the long
opening Prelude (featuring a troupe of mime-dancers who act as postmen and comment silently
on the action) and the series of 'counter-scenes'
that run like a skein through the setting of the
novel, it is clear Kafka was in love with both
women. Was he set up? Whether or not, the
episode clearly had a profound effect on him and
has been the subject of much scholarly debate and
at least one previous stage play, by Jan Hartman.

The two jailers aside, each character has a double
life (not an unusual theatrical device, for sure, but
rarely carried through in so thoroughgoing a fashion as here): Kafka alternates with his antihero, the
tetchy, vacillating, powerless Joseph K – energetically sung by Johnny Van Hal – while Gisella Stille
is superb as both the ambivalent fiancée Felice and
Joseph K's brittle amour Miss Bürstner. Felice's
accomplice Greta is sung with passion by Marianne Rørholm, doubling in two other roles from
the book, Miss Montag and Leni. Ruders's setting

is nervous and mostly fast-paced, the music incorporating tonal and modern expressionist elements,
splashes of klezmer colouring (particularly for
Kafka himself) but little that might be called
comic. Yet the score abounds in moments where
the orchestral accompaniment – deftly played by
the Royal Danish Orchestra – seems to be mocking the hapless K/Kafka. In the end, *Kafka's Trial* is
an unsettling rather than disturbing work, fascinating without being insightful, but undeniably entertaining.

John Rutter   British b1945

*One of the most popular and widely performed composers of his generation, Rutter studied at Clare College, Cambridge, then taught at Southampton University, returning to Clare College as director of
music in 1975. He left in 1979 to devote himself to
composition and founded the Cambridge Singers
with whom he has made many recordings of both his
own and others' music. His works are predominately
vocal; his musical style draws upon the British choral
tradition but also late 19th-/early 20th-century
European music, especially Fauré and Duruflé.*
     GROVEmusic

Mass of the Children

Mass of the Children[a]. Shadows[b]. Wedding Canticle[c]
[a]**Angharad Gruffydd Jones** *sop* [ab]**Jeremy Huw
Williams** *bar* [c]**Daniel Pailthorpe** *fl* [bc]**Stewart French**
gtr [a]**James McVinnie** *org* [a]**Farnham Youth Choir;
Clare College** [ac]**Choir and** [a]**Chamber Ensemble,
Cambridge / Timothy Brown**
Naxos 8 557922 (67' · DDD · T/t)   Ⓢ

Choirs love to sing Rutter's music, audiences
love to hear it and, if reviewers are lukewarm,
the record/ticket-buying public compensates
with effective demonstrations of its enthusiasm.

Rutter believes the seed of the Mass, premiered at Carnegie Hall in 2003, was planted
when, as a member of the Highgate School
choir, he performed on the original 1963
recording of Britten's *War Requiem*. This
inspiration is nowhere more clear than in the
introduction to the *Gloria*, which recalls Britten's use of brass, woodwind and percussion.

Rutter re-imagines Britten's brilliant juxtaposition of adult and children's voices in a joyful
context. Like his model, he mixes Latin liturgy
with poetry: here, the texts include poems by
Archbishop Ken and William Blake. The *Kyrie*
opens vividly with a sunny, breezy setting of
Ken's 'Awake my soul', the *Domine Deus* begins
effectively with a bassoon ostinato against mysterious long notes, but his openings often raise
expectations which, for me, are seldom fulfilled.
The *Sanctus* evokes Fauré at best, Lloyd Webber
at worst, and early in the *Agnus Dei* some phrases,
startlingly, recall Penderecki's *St Luke Passion*.
But fear not, this is mostly unmistakably Rutter.

The shades of Britten and Pears hover over *Shadows* (1979), a cycle of pleasant settings of 16th- and 17th-century poems, paying tribute to the lute-song tradition. The *Wedding Canticle* is sweet, airy and graceful. Rutter's many fans will not be disappointed.

Requiem

Requiem[a]. Hymn to the Creator of Light. God be in my head. A Gaelic Blessing. Psalmfest – No 5, Cantate Domino. Open thou mine eyes[b]. A Prayer of St Patrick. A Choral Fanfare. Birthday Madrigals – No 2, Draw on, sweet night; No 4, My true love hath my heart. The Lord bless you and keep you
[a]**Rosa Mannion,** [b]**Libby Crabtree** sops **Polyphony; Bournemouth Sinfonietta / Stephen Layton**
Hyperion CDA66947 (69' · DDD · T/t) Ⓕ⚫

Here is music finely crafted, written with love for the art and an especial care for choral sound. It's melodious without being commonplace, harmonically rich without being sticky, modern in the graceful way of a child who grows up responsive to newness but not wanting to kick his elders in the teeth. He gives us the heart's desire. But he's on too familiar terms with our heart's desires, he doesn't extend them, or surprise us into realising that they were deeper and subtler than we thought. This is by way of cautiously savouring a remembered taste, which could readily be indulged without perceived need for an interval: one item leads to another and before we know it the pleasurable hour is over. The Requiem is the longest work; the other pieces vary from two to just over six minutes. Most are unaccompanied and show the choir of 25 voices as another of those expert groups of assured and gifted professionals that are among the principal adornments of modern musical life. Their capacity as a virtuoso choir is tested in the *Cantate Domino* and *Choral Fanfare*, but Rutter writes for real singers (not just singer-musicians) and their tone is unfailingly beautiful. The two soloists are excellent.

Additional recommendation

Coupled with: Advent anthem, 'Arise, shine'. Go forth into the world in peace. Toccata in seven. Variations on an Easter theme for organ duet. A Clare Benediction. Musica Dei donum. Come down, O Love divine.
Thomas sop **Jones** fl **Hooker** ob **Nicholas Rimmer, Collon** org **Dorey** vc **Clare College Choir, Cambridge; Members of the City of London Sinfonia / Brown**
Naxos 8 557130 (69' · DDD· T/t) Ⓢ⚫⚫➼
A fine selection of Rutter's work, recorded with the choir of Rutter's own Cambridge college. They're fresh and natural, thoroughly musical in feeling and professional in care. The version of the *Requiem* is the scoring for solo instruments and organ, rather than the full orchestral score heard on Hyperion.

Gloria

Gloria[abc]. Come down, O Love divine. Lord, make me an instrument of thy peace[b]. To everything there is a season. I my Best-beloved's am. Praise the Lord, O my Soul[ac]. I will lift up mine eyes[b]. As the bridegroom to his chosen[b]. A Clare Benediction. The Lord is my light and my salvation. Go forth into the world in peace. Thy perfect love[b]. Te Deum[ac]
Polyphony, [a]**The Wallace Collection;** [b]**City of London Sinfonia / Stephen Layton** with [c]**Andrew Lumsden** org
Hyperion CDA67259 (79' · DDD · T/t) Ⓕ

This superb disc contains a balanced cross-section of Rutter's sacred choral music, spanning over a quarter century and featuring several first recordings. Rutter's stylistic hallmarks are all here: an unfailing knack to get to the root of the text, exquisitely balanced vocal writing, melting harmonies, intensely sweet turns of phrase, short ecstatic climaxes, but also a willingness to be astringent, and rhythmically powerful. There are nods to pageantry, for example in the conclusion of the *Gloria* with its Waltonian swagger, some decliously *echt* Sullivan at the end of the *Te Deum* and, in *I my Best-beloved's am*, an occasional vision of the neo-Byzantine soundworld of his fellow Highgate School pupil, John Tavener.

The artistry of the 25 full-bodied voices of Polyphony is beyond reproach, only suffering a deficit in sheer volume when pitted against the full fury of The Wallace Collection. Sumptuously recorded, all the forces involved play to perfection. Greatly enjoyable.

Five Traditional Songs

Rutter Five Traditional Songs **Vaughan Williams** Five English Folksongs **Traditional** (arr Rutter) I know where I'm going. Down by the sally gardens. The bold grenadier. The keel row. The cuckoo. She's like the swallow. Willow song. The willow tree. The miller of Dee. O can ye sew cushions? Afton water. The sprig of thyme. She moved through the fair (arr Runswick). The lark in the clear air (arr Carter)
Cambridge Singers; City of London Sinfonia / John Rutter
Collegium COLCD120 (66' · DDD · T) Ⓕ⚫

Pleasure in singing is almost the *raison d'être* of this disc. Rutter not only provides us with a healthy dollop of nostalgia, but gives these songs a whole new lease of life in some characteristically scrumptious arrangements. For some, though, there's always the danger that the superficial charms of Rutter's arrangements can smother the fundamental beauty of the original melody. But then one would argue that he doesn't attempt to follow in the footsteps of the great folksong arrangers (he pays tribute to this tradition by including Vaughan Williams's *Five English Folksongs*). His arrangements belong more to the light music tradition; what Messrs Binge, Coates and Tomlinson achieved with orchestral colours Rutter finds primarily through vocal ones – and it's significant that the very finest arrangements here (including a ravishing 'Golden Slumbers') are unaccompanied. The singers are outstanding.

Frederic Rzewski — American b1938

Rzewski was a pupil of Thompson and Spies at Harvard (1954-8) and of Wagner and Strunk at Princeton (1958-60). In 1962-4 he was associated with Stockhausen and in 1966-71 he was a member of Musica Elettronica Viva, based in Rome. During this period his music gained a socialist message (e.g. Coming Together, 1972) and he has explored folk and popular melodies; his works are characterized by drive and intensity. GROVEmusic

Main Drag

Rzewski Main Drag. Coming together[b]. Attica[a]. Les Moutons de Panurge **Ielasi** Untitled (September 02) (original reworking of Attica) **Passarani** Left mouse button doesn't know what the right mouse button is doing (original remix of Les Moutons de Panurge) **Rimbaud** Dawnfire Mix (remix of Main Drag) [a]**Frederic Rzewski,** [b]**Frankie HI NRG** spkrs **Alter Ego** (Manuel Zurria fl Poalo Ravaglia cl Francesco Peverini vn Francesco Dillon vc Oscar Pizzo pf) **Monica Lomero, Akane Makita** kybds **Gianluca Ruggeri** perc **Giuseppe Pistone** elec gtr **Massimo Ceccarelli** bgtr Stradivarius STR33631 (70' · DDD)   Ⓟ Ⓞ

Churning rhythm and seemingly minimalist, rigorously controlled melodic patterns characterise three of Frederic Rzewski's early works presented by the superbly accomplished Italian new-music ensemble Alter Ego.

Coming Together and *Attica* date from 1971-2, and were written in response to specific incidents in the wake of the 1971 prisoners' revolt at New York's Attica State Prison, an event that ended in violent, tragic consequences. Both works employ texts that are spoken with agonising deliberation, systematic repetition and long spaces between words. As a result, one senses, in *Coming Together*, the inner turmoil beneath the plain yet ambiguous language of a letter written by Sam Melville (one of the prisoners killed in the uprising). For *Attica*, Rzewski's intense, raspy delivery of the line 'Attica is in front of me' effectively contrasts to the musicians' suave, lyrical interplay, quite different from Group 180's faster, harder-edged recording of the piece.

Rzewski's 1969 *Les Moutons de Panurge* encompasses a steadily accelerating unison line whose sequence of notes gradually accumulates and diminishes. In this concert performance, an added live electronic component by Marco Passarani starts with scattered handclaps and gradually escalates into massed crowd noises that only the enthusiastic audience response can possibly top.

Main Drag finds Rzewski revisiting these compositional techniques as phrases from an eight-note scale deftly ricochet from one instrument to the next like restless pinballs. This is followed by Passarani's driving, propulsive remix of the original by Robin Rimbaud, aka Scanner.

The disc also offers remixed interpretations of *Attica* and *Les Moutons de Panurge*. Both reveal how well Rzewski's methodology lends itself to the sound world of contemporary dance and ambient music. Robin Rimbaud compresses *Main Drag*'s single notes into murky chords that fly over a background of fleeting static. Giuseppe Ielasi gently crushes *Attica*'s lyrical lines into a canvas of B flat major jelly, with soft, insect-like blips dancing over it. Rzewski was doing similar stuff more than 30 years ago with Musica Elettronica Viva on far less sophisticated sound and recording equipment, but that's another story.

Kaija Saariaho — Finnish b1952

After studying with Paavo Haininen at the Sibelius Academy, Helsinki, she worked for Brian Ferneyhough and Klaus Huber at the Musikhochschule in Freiburg (1981-2) and attended a computer music course at IRCAM in Paris in 1982. She is interested in enlarging the potential of traditional instruments and uses electronic instruments and computers to that end. For Lichtbogen (1985-6), for nine instruments and live electronics, a computer was used in the precompositional stage. She also makes use of extramusical stimuli, such as texts or natural phenomena: Nymphéa (Jardin secret III) (1987), for string quartet and live electronics, employs models from nature for abstract musical composition. GROVEmusic

Orchestral works

Orion. Notes on Light[a]. Mirage[ab] [b]**Karita Mattila** sop [a]**Anssi Karttunen** vc **Orchestre de Paris / Christoph Eschenbach** Ondine ODE1130-2 (63' · DDD) Recorded live in 2008   Ⓟ Ⓞ Ⓑ→

Light is the element that allies Kaija Saariaho to so many of her Nordic peers; that, plus related things such as fire, sky, eclipse and mirage, all of which feature as titles or subtitles in the three pieces recorded here. Musical textures that shimmer, scintillate, explode, darken and extinguish are her bridge between modernism and tradition, and potentially also the listener's path from familiar modes of listening into her fascinating, never vulgarly gratifying, realm of sonic imagination.

These performances from the '100% Finland' festival in Paris are just about ideal as introductions to Saariaho, and self-recommendable for anyone already initiated. Two out of three are world premieres, and it will surely not be long before other soloists take up the crusade begun so valiantly by Anssi Karttunen and Karita Mattila. The two combine to magical effect in *Mirage*, where they jointly interpret the transformations of the woman in Mexican shaman-healer María Sabina's ecstatic text (set in English). By comparison *Notes on Light* feels just a fraction long for its material; whereas *Orion* – inspired by the mortal and cosmic aspects of the mythological hunter – deserves to figure on any short list for orchestral masterpiece of the new millennium.

Kaleidoscopic orchestral colour, remote from human gesture and drama but rich in intellectual imagination, is a dimension in which Christoph Eschenbach excels, and demonstration recording quality of the kind Ondine supplies is the other notable ingredient in this compelling programme.

Camille Saint-Saëns

French 1835-1921

Saint-Saëns was a child prodigy and his dazzling gifts early won him the admiration of Gounod, Rossini, Berlioz and especially Liszt, who hailed him as the world's greatest organist. He was organist at the Madeleine, 1857-75, and a teacher at the Ecole Niedermeyer, 1861-5, where Fauré was among his devoted pupils. He also pursued a range of other activities, organising concerts of Liszt's symphonic poems (then a novelty), reviving interest in older music, writing on musical, scientific and historical topics, travelling often and widely and composing prolifically; on behalf of new French music he co-founded the Société Nationale de Musique (1871). A virtuoso pianist, he excelled in Mozart and was praised for the purity and grace of his playing. Similarly French characteristics of his conservative musical style – neat proportions, clarity, polished expression, elegant line – reside in his best compositions, the classically orientated sonatas (especially the first each for violin and cello), symphonies (No 3, the Organ) and concertos (No 4 for piano, No 3 for violin. He also wrote 'exotic', descriptive or dramatic works, including four symphonic poems, in a style influenced by Liszt, using thematic transformation, and 13 operas, of which only Samson et Dalila (1877), with its sound structures, clear declamation and strongly appealing scenes, has held the stage. Le carnaval des animaux (1886) is a witty frolic; he forbade performances in his lifetime, Le cygne apart. From the mid-1890s he adopted a more austere style, emphasising the classical aspect of his aesthetic which, perhaps more than the music itself, influenced Fauré and Ravel. GROVEmusic

Cello Concertos

No 1 in A minor, Op 33; **No 2** in D minor, Op 119

Cello Concerto No 1. Le carnaval des animaux – The swan[a]. Romance in F, Op 36[b]. Romance in D, Op-51[b]. Cello Sonata No 1 in C minor, Op 32[b]. Chant saphique in D, Op 91[b]. Gavotte in G minor, Op-posth[b]. Allegro appassionato in B minor, Op 43[b]. Prière, Op 158

Steven Isserlis *vc* [a]Dudley Moore, [b]Pascal Devoyon *pfs* [c]Francis Grier *org* London Symphony Orchestra / Michael Tilson Thomas
RCA Victor Red Seal 09026 61678-2 (67' · DDD)
Recorded 1992   Ⓕ

'Concerto!' was a Channel Four TV series that showed participating soloists in rehearsal, in conversation with Dudley Moore and Michael Tilson Thomas and, ultimately, in performance, which resulted in several recordings, of which this is one. This disc is recommendable not so much for Steven Isserlis's Cello Concerto – smooth and intelligent as that is – as for the fill-ups. *The swan* has Moore and Tilson Thomas as joint accompanists, elegantly executed, but the items with Pascal Devoyon are especially valuable, the First Cello Sonata full of elegantly tailored drama, the two *Romances*, *Chant saphique* and *Gavotte* palpable charmers, tastefully played; and the headstrong, thematically memorable *Allegro appassionato*, one of the finest shorter pieces in the cellist's repertory. The disc is enhanced by the opportunity of hearing the rather affecting but relatively unfamiliar *Prière*, composed for André Hekking just two years before Saint-Saëns's death.

Cello Concerto No 2 in D minor, Op 119[c]. La muse et le poète, Op 132[ac]. Romance in E flat, Op 67[c] (orch cpsr). Cello Sonata No 2 in F, Op 123[b]
Steven Isserlis *vc* [a]Joshua Bell *vn* [b]Pascal Devoyon *pf* [c]North German Radio Symphony Orchestra / Christoph Eschenbach
RCA Red Seal 09026 63518-2 (76' · DDD)   Ⓕ

Steven Isserlis follows up his earlier outstanding release of Saint-Saëns's cello music with another that's even more revelatory. This disc concentrates on the more neglected cello works that Saint-Saëns wrote towards the end of his long career. It's true that neither Concerto nor Sonata quite matches its predecessor in memorable melody, but Isserlis, in powerful, imaginative performances, brings out other qualities to show how unjust their neglect is. That's particularly true of the Sonata, which, vividly supported by Pascal Devoyon, rivals Brahms's magnificent Second Cello Sonata in heroic power and scale. At 33 minutes, this is easily the longest of Saint-Saëns's cello works, its ambitious tone of voice instantly established (as it is in the Brahms) and then masterfully sustained throughout the first movement. The second-movement *scherzo*, almost as long and far more than just an interlude, is a sharply original set of variations, leading to a songful slow movement which in turn leads up to a passionate climax. Then in the surgingly energetic finale, both Isserlis and Devoyon articulate the rapid passagework with thrilling clarity.

The cello writing in the Second Concerto is rather less grateful, with its thorny passages of double-stopping, but the two-movement structure characteristic of Saint-Saëns works well, with each divided clearly in two, *Allegro* into

Andante, *Scherzo* into cadenza and reprise of *Allegro*. Making light of technical problems, Isserlis is persuasive both in the bravura *Allegros* and in the hushed meditation of the slow section. Yet neither he nor Eschenbach can quite overcome the truncated feeling at the end, when the reprise of the opening material is so short.

The *Romance* is an adaptation of the slow fourth movement of the Cello Suite, Op 16, a charming piece which Saint-Saëns reworked several times. Yet best of all is the lyrical dialogue of *La muse et le poète*. Inspired by Alfred de Musset's poem, *La nuit de mai*, it opens with Saint-Saëns at his most luscious, reflecting de Musset's role as a hothouse romantic among French poets. It then moves seamlessly through contrasted episodes, with the violin (superbly played by Joshua Bell) representing the muse and the cello as the poet himself. A generous collection, warmly recorded.

Additional recommendation

Cello Concertos Nos 1 and 2
Coupled with: Suite, Op 16 (arr vc/orch). Allegro appassionato in B minor, Op 43. Le carnaval des animaux – The swan
Kliegel vc **Bournemouth Sinfonietta / Monnard**
Naxos 8 553039 (62' · DDD)   Ⓢ🔁

Maria Kliegel performs the Second Cello Concerto with impressive panache and precision. The First, too, is well played, though not a first choice for the work.

Piano Concertos

No 1 in D, Op 17; **No 2** in G minor, Op 22;
No 3 in E flat Op 29; **No 4** in C minor, Op 44;
No 5 in F, Op 103, 'Egyptian'

Piano Concertos Nos 1-5. Wedding Cake, Op 76. Rapsodie d'Auvergne, Op 73. Africa, Op 89. Allegro appassionato, Op 70
Stephen Hough pf **City of Birmingham Symphony Orchestra / Sakari Oramo**
Hyperion ② CDA67331/2 (155' · DDD)   ⒻⓄⓄⓄ

 If Saint-Saëns's idiom once answered – and maybe still does – to qualities fundamental to the French musical character, it must be said straight away that Hough sounds the complete insider. He commands the range of the big statements, whatever their character, as well as sparkle and panache, a sense of drama and seemingly inexhaustible stamina; and he can charm. Yet perhaps most delightful is the lightness and clarity of his decorative playing. It's a bonus for the virtuoso passages not to sound hectic or overblown – for Saint-Saëns, virtuosity always had an expressive potential. There's an air of manufacture about the writing sometimes, certainly, but as Hough knows, there must be nothing mechanical in its delivery. Sweeping across the keyboard, dipping and

soaring through the teaming notes, he flies like a bird. He manages to convey what makes these pieces tick: fine workmanship, fantasy, colour, and the various ways Saint-Saëns was so good at combining piano and orchestra. The orchestra has plenty to do. These scores are textbooks of lean but firm orchestration from which at least one major French composer learned (Ravel, another eclectic, who must have seen the 'old bear' as a kindred spirit). The days are past when the CBSO under Louis Frémaux was considered Britain's 'French' orchestra, but with Sakari Oramo it does splendidly here, playing alertly with its inspiring soloist as he does with it (another plus). The recording balances are fine, with lovely piano sound and plenty of orchestral detail in natural-sounding perspectives.

Saint-Saëns Piano Concerto No 2   Ⓗ
Rachmaninov Piano Concerto No 3 in D minor, Op 30
Shostakovich Prelude and Fugue in D, Op 87 No 5
Emil Gilels pf **Paris Conservatoire Orchestra / André Cluytens**
Testament mono SBT1029 (65' · ADD) Recorded 1954-6   ⒻⓄⓄ

Gilels was a true king of pianists, and these Paris- and New York-based recordings only confirm his legendary status. Here, again, is that superlative musicianship, that magisterial technique and, above all, that unforgettable sonority. What breadth and distinction he brings to the first movement of the Saint-Saëns, from his fulmination in the central octave uproar to his uncanny stillness in the final pages. High jinks are reserved for the second and third movements, the former tossed off with a teasing lightness, the latter's whirling measures with infinite brio. An approximate swipe at the *Scherzo*'s flashing double-note flourish, a false entry and a wrong turning five minutes into the finale offer amusing evidence of Gilels's high-wire act. No performance of this concerto is more 'live', and it's small wonder that Claudio Arrau included it among his desert island favourites.

Gilels's Rachmaninov is altogether more temperate yet, once more, this is among the few truly great performances of this work. His tempo is cool and rapid, and maintained with scintillating ease through even the most formidable intricacy. The cadenza – the finer and more transparent of the two – billows and recedes in superbly musical style and the climax is of awe-inspiring grandeur and the central *scherzando* in the finale is as luminous as it's vivacious. The finale's *meno mosso* variation is excluded and, it has to be said, Cluytens's partnership is distant and run of the mill. But the recordings hardly show their age in such admirably smooth transfers. Gilels's 'encore', Shostakovich's Prelude and Fugue No 5 is like a brilliant shaft of light after the Rachmaninov. The performance is perfection, entirely justifying Arthur Rubinstein's comment after hearing him play in Russia: 'If that boy comes to the West, I shall have to shut up shop'.

SAINT-SAËNS, SYMPHONY NO 3, 'ORGAN' – IN BRIEF

Peter Hurford; Montreal SO / Charles Dutoit
Decca 475 7728 (58' · DDD)   Ⓜ︎ⓄⓄ➔
A thrilling performance (and recording) of this highly coloured work. Dutoit draws some ravishing playing from his superb Canadian orchestra and Peter Hurford, who must have played it dozens of times, brings his characteristic imagination to the score. Coupled with Poulenc's Organ Concerto.

Olivier Latry; Philadelphia Orchestra / Christoph Eschenbach
Ondine 1094-5 (79' · DDD)   ⒻⓄⓄ➔
Another performance that matches top-notch musicianship with a first-rate recording. Eschenbach directs a vivid performance with Olivier Latry supplying some truly dazzling playing. The couplings are the Poulenc Organ Concerto and Samuel Barber's *Toccata Festiva*.

Simon Preston; Berlin Philharmonic / James Levine
DG 419 6172 (46' · DDD)   ⒻⓄ➔
The mighty Berlin Philharmonic are on top form here and combined with the miight of the organ virtually pins one to the seat. Levine relishes the score's variety and whips up averitable whirlwind of sound. The coupling is a witty and affectionate performance of Dukas's *Sorcerer's Apprentice*.

Gadston Litaize; Orchestre de Paris / Daniel Barenboim
DG 474 612-2GOR (56' · DDD)   Ⓕ➔
Another mid-price alternatve for this favourite score. Barenboim draws some thrilling playing from the Paris orchestra and the sound – slightly fierce – merely adds to the sense of drama. Generously coupled with three orchestral excerpts from *Samson et Dalila* and *Danse macabre*.

Gillian Weir; Ulster Orchestra / Yan Pascal Tortelier
Chandos CHAN8822 (53' · DDD)   ⒻⓄ➔
The beautifully judged Chandos recording makes this a joy for the ears: recorded with the organ *in situ* rather than grafted on, the balance os very skilfully managed. And Tortelier makes it sound more French than many other performances. The coupling is a lovely performance of the Second Symphony.

Noel Rawsthorne; RLPO / Loris Tjeknavorian
Regis RRC1262 (62' · ADD)   Ⓢ
Recorded in Liverpool Cathedral, with its vast acoustic, this performance takes a little getting used to, but it's full of spectacle and makes an excellent budget-price alternative. Coupled with *Carnival* and the *Danse macabre*.

Saint-Saëns Piano Concerto No 4 in C minor, Op 44ᶜ. Etude en forme de valse, Op 52 No 6ᵈ **Franck** Symphonic Variationsᵃ **Ravel** Piano Concertoin Dᵇ   Ⓗ
Alfred Cortot pf ᵃ**London Philharmonic Orchestra / Landon Ronald;** ᵇ**orchestra,** ᶜ**Paris Conservatoire Orchestra /** ᵇᶜ**Charles Munch**
Naxos Historical 8 110613 (60' · ADD)   ⓈⓄⓄ

Here are performances of a timeless vitality and validity. The exception is the Ravel Concerto, which is wildly approximate and confused. Elsewhere, though, there's a super-abundance of wit and charm – of Cortot at his most beguiling. His capacity to be free and ecstatic, yet bracingly unsentimental was one of his most exhilarating qualities, and his *rubato* at the start of the Saint-Saëns makes modern rivals such as Rogé (Decca), Collard (EMI) and Hough (Hyperion) pale in comparison. At 8'12" (*dolce tranquillo legato*) there's a classic instance of the *cantabile* for which he was celebrated, and in the final pages of the same movement an inimitably limpid and delicate poetry. Again, in the central *Allegro vivace*, his famous or infamous scrambles and skirmishes are never at the expense of the music's innate elegance and style, and who else has spun off the Concerto's closing cascades with such glitter and aplomb? Cortot's playing may not have been note-perfect but there's no doubt that he was every inch the virtuoso. As an encore, there's Saint-Saëns's *Etude en forme de valse*, and while the 1931 recording is by no means the equal of the legendary 1919 disc, a performance that prompted Horowitz's envy, it's gloriously alive with Cortot's verve and magic. Mark Obert-Thorn's transfers are exceptional and all lovers of past but ever-present greatness will want this second and final Naxos volume of Cortot's sadly few concerto recordings.

Violin Concertos

No 1 in A, Op 20; No 2 in C, Op 58; No 3 in B minor, Op 61
Philippe Graffin vn **BBC Scottish Symphony Orchestra / Martyn Brabbins**
Hyperion CDA67074 (76' · DDD)   ⒻⓄ

The first two violin concertos of Saint-Saëns were composed in reverse order. The Second is the longer and lesser-known of the two, but the First Concerto more resembles the thematic charm and concise design of the First Cello Concerto. Cast in a single short movement that falls into three distinct sections, it launches the soloist on his way right from the start, and features a delightful central section with some felicitous woodwind writing. Hyperion holds a trump card in Philippe Graffin, whose elegant, emotionally charged playing is strongly reminiscent of the young Menuhin, and whose understanding of the idiom is second to none – certainly among modern players.
Saint-Saëns's First Violin Concerto was composed in 1859, whereas his Second preceded it

by a year. Unexpectedly, the first movement's thematic material has an almost Weberian slant. The orchestration is heavier than in the First, and the musical arguments are both more formal and more forcefully stated. It's a more overtly virtuoso work than the First Concerto, and perhaps rather less memorable, but again Graffin weaves a winsome solo line and Martyn Brabbins directs a strong account of the orchestral score, with prominently projected woodwinds. The relatively well-known Third Concerto (1880) is roughly the same length as the Second (around half an hour), but is more consistently interesting. The basic material is of higher quality, the key relations more telling and orchestration infinitely more delicate. No other recording liberates so much of the score's instrumental detail, probably because most of Graffin's predecessors have been balanced way in front of the orchestra.

Symphony No 3, 'Organ'

Symphony No 3[a]. Le carnaval des animaux[b]
Peter Hurford org [a]**Montreal Symphony Orchestra;**
[b]**London Sinfonietta / Charles Dutoit**
Decca 475 7728 (58' · DDD)　　　Ⓜ︎Ⓞ︎Ⓞ︎↦

In 1886 Saint-Saëns poured his considerable experience as an unequalled virtuoso of the organ, piano and practitioner of Lisztian unifying techniques into his *Organ* Symphony; it instantly put the French Symphony on the map, and provided a model for Franck and others. With its capacity for grand spectacle (aside from the organ and a large orchestra, its scoring includes two pianos) it has suffered inflationary tendencies from both conductors and recording engineers. Dutoit's (and Decca's) achievement is the restoration of its energy and vitality. Poulenc's wonderful Gothic Organ Concerto receives a terrific performance, the drama and intensity unleashed with amazing power. As with the Saint-Saëns, the Decca recording is superbly handled.

The Carnival of the Animals

Le Carnaval des animaux[a]. Fantaisie, Op 124[b]. Prière, Op 158[c]. Romance, Op 36[d]. Septet, Op 65[e]. Samson et Dalîla – Mon cœur s'ouvre à ta voix[f]
[a]**Emmanuel Pahud** fl [a]**Paul Meyer** cl [e]**David Guerrier** tpt [a]**Florent Jodelet** perc [acdef]**Frank Braley,** [a]**Michel Dalberto** pfs [abe]**Renaud Capuçon,** [ae]**Béatrice Muthelet,** [ae]**Esther Hoppe** vns [acdef]**Gautier Capuçon** vc [ae]**Janne Saksala** db [b]**Marie-Pierre Langlamet** hp
Virgin Classics 545603-2 (63' · DDD)　　ⒻⓄ︎Ⓞ︎↦

'What hard things,' wrote Saint-Saëns, 'have been said against virtuosity!… The fact must be proclaimed from the house-tops – in art a difficulty overcome is a thing of beauty.' There are many such beauties in *Le Carnaval des animaux*, and their difficulties aren't for the faint-hearted or the technically challenged, especially where

the two pianists are concerned. On this disc not only are the difficulties overcome, but dispatched with tremendous verve and wit.

In the Septet the players rightly refuse to make more of the music than is really there. This light touch allows us to relish Saint-Saëns's professionalism: every part in the texture has its own shape and colour and, if there were compositional difficulties to be overcome, you'd never know. The four shorter pieces on this splendid disc include the delicious *Fantaisie* for violin and harp, and three arrangements for cello and piano taken from the horn, organ and operatic repertoires.

Orchestral Works

Danse macabre in G minor, Op 40. Phaéton in C, Op 39. Le rouet d'Omphale in A, Op 31. La Jeunesse d'Hercule in E flat, Op 50. Marche héroïque in E flat, Op 34. Introduction and Rondo capriccioso in A minor, Op 28[a]. Havanaise in E, Op 83[a]
[a]**Kyung-Wha Chung** vn [a]**Royal Philharmonic Orchestra; Philharmonia Orch / Charles Dutoit**
Decca 425 021-2DM (66' · ADD)　　　Ⓜ︎Ⓞ︎↦

It's enough to make you weep – Saint-Saëns wrote his first tune at the age of three, analysed Mozart's *Don Giovanni* from the full score when he was five, and at 10 claimed he could play all Beethoven's 32 piano sonatas from memory. There's some consolation that, according to a contemporary, physically 'he strangely resembled a parrot', and perhaps even his early brilliance was a curse rather than a blessing, as he regressed from being a bold innovator to a dusty reactionary. In his thirties (in the 1870s) he was at the forefront of the Lisztian avant-garde. He was the first Frenchman to attempt Liszt's new genre, the 'symphonic poem', bringing to it a typically French concision, elegance and grace. Charles Dutoit has few peers in this kind of music; here's playing of dramatic flair and classical refinement that exactly matches Saint-Saëns intention and invention. Decca's sound has depth, brilliance and richness.

Chamber Works

Bassoon Sonata, Op 168[a]. Caprice sur des airs danois et russes, Op 79[b]. Clarinet Sonata, Op 167[c]. Oboe Sonata, Op 166[d]. Piano Quartet, Op 41[e]. Piano Quintet, Op 14[f]. Septet, Op 65[g]. Tarantelle, Op 6[h]
Nash Ensemble ([bh]**Philippa Davies** fl [bd]**Gareth Hulse** ob [bch]**Richard Hosford** cl [a]**Ursula Leveaux** bn [g]**Mark David** tpt [efg]**Marianne Thorsen,** [g]**David Adams,** [f]**Benjamin Nabarro** vns [efg]**Lawrence Power** va [efg]**Paul Watkins** vc [g]**Duncan McTier** db **Ian Brown** pf)
Hyperion ② CDA67431/2 (134' · DDD)　　　ⒻⓄ︎

Saint-Saëns's chamber music fares better in the concert hall than the recording studio, perhaps because musicians tend to listen less to academic name-calling ('conservative', 'too prolific') than to the music itself. The three late wind sonatas in particular have received far fewer recordings than their status as repertoire staples deserves. Try the kinky-Baroque first movement of the Oboe Sonata, jauntily phrased by Gareth Hulse, or the *animato* second of the Clarinet Sonata, garbed in rich Mozartian cloth by Richard Hosford. The Bassoon Sonata is notable for its fresh and gentle wit and skirting of cliché: Ursula Leveaux does it proud, with especially luscious tone in the opening *Allegretto*.

Surprises are fewer in the earlier works, but none is less than,'finely put together' to echo Ravel's assessment. Hummability quotient is high in the Piano Quartet and Quintet, and off the scale in the Septet. The late Lionel Salter used to complain in *Gramophone* that recordings of the Septet tend to sound like a trumpet concerto; not this one. If you employ hit artists like Maurice André they will tend to hog the microphone but, happily, Mark David is a more sensitive soul who's fully imbibed the Nash's joyous spirit of corporate music-making, and Hyperion's engineers have placed him at a respectable distance. If anything it's Ian Brown's piano that takes centre-stage, and that's no bad thing, except in the extensive fugal finales to the Piano Quartet and Quintet where Saint-Saëns, most unusually, seems to over-run himself. The *Caprice* and *Tarantelle*, for all Philippa Davies's sparkling contributions, perhaps bear fewer repetitions, but the set is really sheer delight: let's hear it for imaginative conservatism.

Bassoon Sonata, Op 168[a]. Caprice sur des airs danois et russes, Op 79[b]. Clarinet Sonata, Op 167[c]. Oboe Sonata, Op 166[d]. Piano Quartet, Op 41[e]. Piano Quintet, Op 14[f]. Septet, Op 65[g]. Tarantelle, Op 6[h]
Nash Ensemble ([bh]Philippa Davies *fl* [bd]Gareth Hulse *ob* [bch]Richard Hosford *cl* [a]Ursula Leveaux *bn* [g]Mark David *tpt* [efg]Marianne Thorsen, [g]David Adams, [f]Benjamin Nabarro *vns* [efg]Lawrence Power *va* [efg]Paul Watkins *vc* [g]Duncan McTier *db* Ian Brown *pf*)
Hyperion ② CDA67431/2 (134' · DDD)　　Ⓕ**OO**

Saint-Saëns's chamber music fares better in the concert hall than the recording studio, perhaps because musicians tend to listen less to academic name-calling than to the music itself. The three late wind sonatas in particular have received far fewer recordings than their status as repertoire staples deserves. Try the kinky-Baroque first movement of the Oboe Sonata, jauntily phrased by Gareth Hulse, or the *animato* second of the Clarinet Sonata, garbed in rich Mozartian cloth by Richard Hosford. Or, particularly, the Bassoon Sonata, for its fresh and gentle wit and skirting of cliché: Ursula Leveaux does it proud, with especially luscious tone in the opening *Allegretto*.

Surprises are thinner on the ground in the earlier works but none is less than, to echo Ravel's assessment, 'finely put together'. Hummability quotient is high in the Piano Quartet and Quintet, and off the scale in the Septet. The late Lionel Salter used to complain that recordings of the Septet tend to sound like a

trumpet concerto; not this one. If you employ hit artists like Maurice André they will tend to hog the microphone but, happily, Mark David is a more sensitive soul who has fully imbibed the Nash's joyous spirit of corporate music-making, and Hyperion's engineers have placed him at a respectable distance.

If anything it is Ian Brown's piano that takes centre-stage, and that's no bad thing except in the extensive fugal finales to the Piano Quartet and Quintet where Saint-Saëns, most unusually, seems to over-run himself. Sheer delight.

Piano Trios

Piano Trios – Nos 1 & 2
Florestan Trio (Anthony Marwood *vn* Richard Lester *vc* Susan Tomes *pf*)
Hyperion CDA67538 (60' · DDD)　　Ⓕ**OOO**

Well, the Florestan Trio have done it again – a sure-fire *Gramophone* Award nominee. Indeed, such is the cumulative emotional impact of these performances that tears welled up during the wonderful *fortissimo* climax of the E minor Trio's first movement – that even before the astonishing intensity of the final, precipitous *Allegro*. 'Cumulative' because most of the time the Florestan prefer stealth and suggestion; they don't wear their hearts on their sleeves. Instead they offer, like Saint-Saëns's art, a filigree lightness and clarity that somehow twists itself into an ever-deepening pattern of turmoil.

Listen to the underlying wistfulness in the F major Trio: how the élan of the first movement's final chords provides a springboard into a cheerful bucolic landscape that is nevertheless crossed with clouds – this brought about by a web of delicate rhythmic and tonal shading in the string-playing stretched over Susan Tomes's dancing, pellucid framework.

Or the maturity and self-confidence in the E minor: nothing is forced, everything flows – from the stormy first movement through the lighter central movements (and here the languid descending phrases of the *Andante con moto* are beautifully sculpted by both Marwood and Lester) to the complex yet never turgid imitative writing of the last. Recorded sound and accompanying notes are, of course, impeccable. No argument: just buy it.

Organ works

Three Preludes et Fugues, Op 99. Cyprès, Op 156a. Fantaisie, Op 101. Fantaisie No 3, Op 157. Fantaisie (1857). Bénédiction nuptiale, Op 9. Marche religieuse, Op 107
Andrew-John Smith *org*
Hyperion CDA67713 (78' · DDD)
Played on the Cavaillé-Coll organ of La Madeleine, Paris　　Ⓕ

Andrew-John Smith's clever programming alternates the Three Preludes and Fugues,

Op 99, with the three Fantaisies and other works. Wisely, he begins and ends the CD with the loudest and most extrovert pieces, namely the E flat major Prelude and Fugue and the E flat Fantaisie. In between there are long stretches of quiet, introspective music, and listeners may long for the more dramatic compositions of Franck, Vierne or Widor. However, at his best Saint-Saëns has an originality and charm all his own; possibly no other French organist-composer could have produced the delicate beauty of the B major Prelude or the *Bénédiction nuptiale*.

It's clear from his highly detailed booklet-notes plus his polished and stylish performances that Smith is an enthusiastic advocate of Saint-Saëns. What prevents this CD achieving its fullest impact is a cautious approach by player and sound engineers to the cavernous acoustic of the church of La Madeleine. The potential loss of detail leads Smith to adopt tempi which are sometimes slower than the composer's moderato and *sans lenteur* markings. Meanwhile the 1846 four-manual 58-stop Cavaillé-Coll organ is recorded close-up, and although we gain clarity we lose the sense of grandeur with a large instrument ringing around a massive edifice.

On the plus side, Smith's warm and sympathetic *rubato* is a constant delight, and his inspired choice to make the recording on an instrument played regularly by Saint-Saëns means that listeners can relish the authentic Gallic tones of the splendid La Madeleine organ.

Mélodies

Chanson (Nouvelle chanson sur un vieil air). Guitare. Rêverie. L'attente. Le chant de ceux qui s'en vont sur la mer. Le pas d'armes du Roi Jean. La coccinelle. A quoi bon entendre. Si vous n'avez rien à me dire. Dans ton coeur. Danse macabre. Mélodies persanes, Op 26 – La brise; Sabre en main; Au cimetière; Tournoiement. Marquise, vous souvenez-vous?. La Cigale et la Fourmi. Chanson à boire du vieux temps. Nocturne. Violons dans le soir. Guitares et mandolines. Une flûte invisible. Suzette et Suzon. Aimons-nous. Temps nouveau. Le vent dans la plaine. Grasselette et Maigrelette
François Le Roux bar **Krysia Osostowicz** vn **Philippa Davies** fl **Graham Johnson** pf
Hyperion CDA66856 (78' · DDD · T/t)   Ⓕ❍

This is the most resounding blow yet to be struck for the *mélodies* of Saint-Saëns. François Le Roux, with his incisive diction and ability to characterise each song, is a real champion for the man, once so successful, who became, as Graham Johnson puts it in the booklet, 'a footnote' rather than a chapter in the history of French music.

Many of the poems that Saint-Saëns set were used by other composers, for instance *Dans ton coeur*, which became Duparc's *Chanson triste*, by 'Jean Lahor' (Henri Cazalis). The first song of the *Mélodies persanes*, 'La brise', is full of eastern

promise, the second, 'Sabre en main' a rollicking bit of toy-soldier galloping away, but just as you're beginning to think that Johnson is shooting himself in the foot by being so ironic about the music they're performing comes the hauntingly beautiful fifth song, 'Au cimetière', with its quietly rippling accompaniment and the languorous poem about the lovers sitting on a marble tomb and picking the flowers. Le Roux sings this with controlled, quiet intensity.

Johnson makes the point that it's of little importance from which part of the composer's life the songs come, he embodies that totally French 19th-century style, sometimes anticipating Hahn and Massenet, sometimes harking back to Boieldieu. If a setting of La Fontaine's fable about the cicada and the ant is pure salon charm, then the final 'Grasselette et Maigrelette' Ronsard *chanson*, composed when Saint-Saëns was 85 in 1920, is a vivacious *café-concert*-style evocation of old Paris.

Samson et Dalila

Samson et Dalila
Plácido Domingo ten Samson **Waltraud Meier** mez Dalila **Alain Fondary** bar Priest **Jean-Philippe Courtis** bass Abimelech **Samuel Ramey** bass Old Hebrew **Christian Papis** ten Messenger **Daniel Galvez-Vallejo** ten First Philistine **François Harismendy** bass Second Philistine **Chorus and Orchestra of the Bastille Opera, Paris / Myung-Whun Chung**
EMI ② 754470-2 (124' · DDD · T/t)   Ⓕ❍❍

This is the most subtly and expertly conducted performance of this work to appear on CD, excellent as others have been in this respect, and also the best played and sung. Chung's achievement is to have welded the elements of pagan ruthlessness, erotic stimulation and Wagnerian harmony that comprise Saint-Saëns's masterpiece into a convincing whole. His success is based on the essentials of a firm sense of rhythm and timing allied to a realisation of the sensuousness and delicacy of the scoring. Whether in the lamenting of the Hebrews, the forceful music written for the High Priest, the heroics of Samson, the sensual outpourings of Dalila, or the empty rejoicing of the Bacchanale, he and his orchestra strike to the heart of the matter – and that orchestra plays with Gallic finesse, augmented by a dedicated discipline.

The choral singing, though too distantly recorded, is no less alert and refined, with a full range of dynamic contrast. Meier's Dalila is a fascinating portrayal of this equivocal anti-heroine, seductive, wheedling, exerting her female wiles with the twin objects of sexual dominance and political command. All her sense of purpose comes out in her early greeting to the High Priest, 'Salut à mon père'; then she's meditative and expectant as Dalila ponders on her power at 'Se pourrait-il'. The set numbers are all sung with the vocal ease and long phrase of a singer at the zenith of her powers. She makes more of the text than Domingo who sings in his familiar, all-purpose style, admirable in itself, somewhat missing the particular accents brought to this music by the great French tenors of the past. They exist no more and one must salute the sterling and often eloquent tones of Domingo.

Alain Fondary is superb as the High Priest, firm and rich in tone, commanding and vengeful in delivery: the most compelling interpreter of the part on disc, *tout court*. Ramey is luxury casting as the Old Hebrew, but as this is a part once sung by Pinza, Ramey probably felt he wasn't slumming it. After an unsteady start, he sings the small but important role with breadth and dignity. As Abimelech, Jean-Philippe Courtis makes much of little. Apart from the two reservations already made, the recording is admirable, with a wide and spacious sound, and the soloists forward, but well integrated. This must now be the outright recommendation for this work.

Additional recommendation

Vickers Samson **Gorr** Dalila **Paris Opera Orchestra / Prêtre**
EMI Great Recordings of the Century ② 567598-2
(121' · ADD) Ⓜ**Ⓞ**▶

A classic recording with Rita Gorr's magnificent Dalila towering over the performance. Vickers, too, is superb. The sound isn't perfect but don't let that deter you.

King Samson **Ludwig** Dalila **Munich RSO / Patanè**
RCARed Seal 8869745118-2 (134' · ADD))Ⓑ

Not the most idiomatic of recordings but there's some classy singing here, though one would have liked Ludwig to take a few more risks. Patanè presides over everything with passion.

Antonio Salieri   Italian 1750-1825

Salieri studied with Gassmann and others in Vienna, and also knew Gluck (who became his patron) and Metastasio. In 1774 he succeeded Gassmann as court composer and conductor of the Italian opera from 1788 he was also court Kapellmeister. He made his reputation as a stage composer, writing operas for Vienna from 1768 and presenting several in Italy, 1778-80. Later he dominated Parisian opera with three works of 1784-7; Tarare (1787), his greatest success, established him as Gluck's heir. In 1790 he gave up his duties at the Italian opera. As his style became old-fashioned his works lost favour, and he composed relatively little after 1804, but he remained a central and influential figure in Viennese musical life. His many pupils included Beethoven, Schubert and Liszt. There is little evidence of any intrigues against Mozart, still less of the charge of poisoning.

Salieri's c40 Italian operas are traditional in their emphasis on melodic expression, but they also show Gluck's influence, with dramatic choral writing,

much accompanied recitative and careful declamation: some combine seria and buffa elements.
GROVEmusic

Opera Arias

Armida – E non degg'io seguirla…Vieni a me. **La grotta di Trofonio** – La ra la. **Il ricco d'un giorno** – Dopo pranzo addormentata; Eccomi piu che mai. **La scuola de' gelosi** – Che dunque! **La secchia rapita** – Questo guajo mancava. **Palmira, Regina di Persia** – Voi luingate invano; Lungi da me. **La fiera di Venezia** – Vi sono sposa e amante. **La Cifra** – E voi da buon marito; Alfin son sola. **La finta scema** – Se lo dovessi vendere
Cecilia Bartoli *mez* **Orchestra of the Age of Enlightenment / Adám Fischer**
Decca 475 100-2DH (68' · DDD) Ⓕ▶

As the leading figure in Viennese operatic life for some three decades, and successful too in Venice and Paris, Antonio Salieri occupies no inconsiderable position in operatic history. This is a well-chosen selection of music from his Italian operas, in serious, comic and mixed genres. The purely comic pieces are perhaps the least interesting: his conception of comedy is, in the Italian tradition, quite literal and direct. But among the lighter items are a delightfully spirited little 'rustic' piece from *La finta scema* and a charming minuet from *La grotta di Trofonio*, very sharply and neatly characterised here.

That piece was written for Nancy Storace, the English soprano who created Mozart's Susanna. So is the beautiful slow aria from *La scuola de' gelosi*, preceded by a recitative sung with much feeling by Bartoli; the aria itself is a lament for lost love, deeply felt and affecting. So, too, is the rondo from *La cifra*, written for another Mozart singer, Adriana Ferrarese, the first Fiordiligi, again preceded by a forceful recitative, which is reminiscent of Mozart's 'Per pietà', written for Ferrarese shortly after, and which it surely influenced. This is a noble and powerful piece.

Others that demand to be mentioned here include a couple with spectacular orchestral writing: one from *La fiera di Venezia* with solo parts for flute and oboe, a real virtuoso piece, with lots of top Ds, and another from *La secchia rapita* with its dialogues with oboe and its arresting trumpet interventions.

Bartoli is an enormously accomplished artist: every note plumb in the middle, the words always carefully placed, naturally musical phrasing, and beauty and variety of tone. Musicianly and finely modulated playing from the OAE set off the voice perfectly.

Aulis Sallinen   Finnish b1935

Sallinen was a pupil of Merikanto and Kokkonen at the Helsinki Academy (1955-60), where he returned to teach in 1970. In the late 1960s he began melding

triads with avant-garde techniques; then in the 1970s he turned to opera, drawing on sources as diverse as Shostakovich, Janáček and Orff in The Horseman (1975), The Red Line (1978), The King Goes forth to France (1984) and Kullervo (1992). His concert works include four symphonies, five string quartets and concertos for violin and for cello.
GROVEmusic

Orchestral Works

Variations for Orchestra, Op 8. Violin Concerto, Op 18. Some aspects of Peltoniemi Hintrik's funeral march, Op 19. The nocturnal dances of Don Juanquixote, Op 58
Eeva Koskinen *vn* **Torleif Thedéen** *vc*
Tapiola Sinfonietta / Osmo Vänskä
BIS CD560 (63' · DDD)   Ⓕ

Sallinen's operas and symphonies have stolen the limelight in recent years at the expense of other works fully worthy of attention, as this well-played and well-recorded disc proves. Whereas the Variations (1963) are somewhat anonymous if deftly written, the Violin Concerto (1968) is an altogether maturer work, unusually sombre for so bright a solo instrument, and perhaps the first piece to point to his later stature. His next published work was the Third String Quartet (1969), subtitled *Some aspects of Peltoniemi Hintrik's funeral march*, which, thanks to the Kronos Quartet's advocacy has become one of Sallinen's most heard works This arrangement for string orchestra dates from 1981. *The nocturnal dances of Don Juanquixote* is an extended fantasia for cello and strings, the title being the only parody of Strauss (although a solo violin enters late as Sancho Panza-leporello!). Sallinen is fond of playing games and all is never as it seems: one can almost hear the collective thud of critics' jaws falling open at this Arnold-like spoof.

The King Goes Forth to France

The King Goes Forth to France
Tommi Hakala *bar* Prince **Jyrki Korhonen** *bass* Prime Minister **Riikka Rantanen** *sop* Nice Caroline **Lilli Paasikivi** *mez* Caroline with the Thick Mane **Mari Palo** *sop* Anne who Steals **Laura Nykänen** *contr* Anne who Strips **Jyrki Anttila** *ten* Guide **Herman Wallén** *bar* English Archer **Kirsi Thum** *sop* Queen **Santeri Kinnunen** *spkr* Froissart **Tapiola Chamber Choir; Finnish Philharmonic Choir; Helsinki Philharmonic Orchestra / Okko Kamu**
Ondine ② ODE1066-2D (128' · DDD · S/T/t/N) Ⓕ

The King Goes Forth to France (1980-83) was Sallinen's third opera and is regarded by many commentators as the composer's most problematic. On the contrary, it is the best and most profound, and its impact on Sallinen's subsequent music is incalculable. Subtitled a 'Chronicle for the Music Theatre of the Coming Ice Age', *The King Goes Forth* is a bitingly satirical musical allegory. Sal-

linen has referred to it as a 'fairy-tale for adults' and there are undoubtedly fantastical elements in the storyline, which blends the past, present and one possible future into a dark yet vivid vision of the corruptibility of absolute power.

The premise of the opera, to Paavo Haavikko's libretto based on his own radio play, is this: at some point in the near future, England will be overwhelmed by the advance of a new ice sheet. The Prince, whom the Prime Minister is urging to take a wife (even providing a quartet of nubile candidates: the two Carolines and two Annes), decides instead that the only safe course is to abandon England (and, presumably, the old King) and cross the Channel on a bridge of ice to resettle in France – where he is declared King. Along the way, however, the events of the Hundred Years' War unfold again with the Battle of Crécy and Siege of Calais refought to the same result. In the meantime, the King has married, for political reasons, a German Princess and immediately pawned her (and his crown) to raise funds for his campaign. As Calais falls once more – the tale recorded by a new Froissart – and a storm signals the advance to Paris and the onset of spring, the King instructs his chronicler to omit him from history, abrogating all responsibility, claiming to have been made by Time.

Those familiar with Sallinen's Fourth Symphony, Fifth Quartet or, especially, the orchestral prelude *Shadows* will recognise several strands in the music. Brilliantly scored, the orchestral contribution is crucial, underpinning the foreground action – often with emotional correctives, such as the chirpy march that accompanies the flaying of the Archer – and the word-setting and dramaturgy have the effectiveness of Britten or Henze. The cast is uniformly good, although Tommi Hakala as the King cannot banish memories of Jorma Hynninen in the premiere productions, while Lilli Paasikivi shines as the mentally fragile Caroline with the Thick Mane. Ondine's spectacular sound catches both the quietest ruminations of the four women and the explosive eruptions of the King's great cannon, Parliament. Highly recommended.

Esa-Pekka Salonen   Finnish b1935

As famous as a conductor – he is currently music director of the Los Angeles Philharmonic – Salonen is also a highly regarded composer. His music is imaginative and approachable with a string rhythmic sense and a keen ear for colour.

Orchestral works

Foreign Bodies. Insomnia. Wing on Wing[a]
[a]**Anu Komsi,** [a]**Piia Komsi** *sops* **Finnish Radio Symphony Orchestra / Esa-Pekka Salonen**
DG 477 5375 (67' · DDD)   ⒻⒹ→
The download, available from iTunes, contains a bonus piece, Dichotomie, played by Yefim Bronfman

The immediate sensory impact of these three scores, written between 2001 and 2004, bears out the booklet's claim that for Salonen 'sound first and foremost leads a physical, rather than an intellectual or mental existence'. Would that the densely orchestrated sound and fury which predominates signified something substantial, something truly memorable.

Foreign Bodies, with its governing image of nature under threat, is too amorphous to create a genuinely visceral excitement. The short finale – 'Dance' – works best, with some effective rhythmic cross-cutting, but even this grows clotted in texture: it's too reluctant to expose, juxtapose or superimpose its mechanisms in ways which would bring much-needed light and air to the music.

The 21-minute, single-movement work *Insomnia* displays a similar lack of differentiation, the great washes of sound more effective in keeping a large orchestra busy than in promoting a persuasive musical argument. Finally there's the 26-minute *Wing on Wing*, written for the opening of the LAPO's new base, the Walt Disney Concert Hall, in June 2004. Understatement was clearly not an option, and Salonen's overblown hymn of praise aims to celebrate 'a fusion between instrument and body, nature and technology'. The voice of architect Frank Gehry is electronically treated to produce mysterious, oracular sounds, and a pair of wordless sopranos soar ecstatically above saturated post-Messiaen chorales, in tribute to the imagery of wings and sails which link Gehry's building to the nearby Pacific Ocean.

It seems more than a little ironic that this technically imposing recording should have been made in Helsinki rather than Los Angeles. But the Finnish RSO play magnificently. If you like your music to be 'first and foremost physical', this disc will not disappoint.

Helix[a]. Piano Concerto[b]. Dichotomie[c]
[bc]**Yefim Bronfman** pf [ab]**Los Angeles Philharmonic Orchestra / Esa-Pekka Salonen**
DG 477 8103 (60' · DDD)
Recorded live   ⓕ🔴▷

Esa-Pekka Salonen's Piano Concerto runs for more than half an hour, barely pausing for breath. The turbulence and energy of the music give it a surreal quality, as if the whole history of the Romantic concerto were being feverishly revisited and reshaped in 2007 with a matter-of-life-and-death urgency. You may hear echoes of any number of august historical figures – Scriabin, Rachmaninov, even Respighi – but the aura is always contemporary. While those composers might recognise Salonen's rhythmic vocabulary, and the flamboyant rhetoric of his piano-writing, his harmonic palette is something else.

Recorded live in Los Angeles's Walt Disney Concert Hall, this performance has virtuosity and no-holds-barred exuberance in abundance. On early acquaintance it was hard to find enough shape or sense of purpose within the welter of notes, the sheer density of the solo-orchestra mix. But Salonen the composer certainly has the courage of his convictions. *Helix*, written two years before the concerto and less than a third of its length, is an even more uncompromising demonstration of textural overload, a noisy, relentlessly forceful response to the image of a spiral revolving at increasing speed. Performance and recording are stunning, the audience reaction at the end ecstatic.

Dichotomie (2000) for solo piano provides a useful digest of Salonen's current compositional preoccupations. Its first movement deploys aggressive but constantly shifting rhythmic mechanisms whose origins lie in Prokofiev, while its second seems closer to the flowing spontaneity of the Ligeti *Etudes*. Bronfman's authority in this music is phenomenal and here, at last, you sense a genuine match between medium and message.

Erik Satie   French 1866-1925

Satie entered the Paris Conservatoire in 1879, but his record was undistinguished. After leaving he wrote the triptychs of Sarabandes (1887), Gymnopédies (1888) and Gnossiennes (1890), of which the latter two sets are modal and almost eventless. In the 1890s he began to frequent Montmartre, to play at the café Chat Noir and to involve himself with fringe Christian sects. He also made the acquaintance of Debussy.

From 1905-8 he was a student again, at the Schola Cantorum. At last in 1911 his music began to be noticed, and this seems to have stimulated a large output of small pieces, mostly for solo piano and mostly perpetuating his earlier simplicity in pieces with ironic titles. Sports et divertissements (1914), published with illustrations by Charles Martin, contains 20 miniatures eccentrically and beautifully annotated by Satie. In 1915 he came to the attention of Cocteau, who seized on him as the ideal of the anti-Romantic composer and who facilitated the more ambitious works of his last years: the ballets Parade (1917), Mercure (1924) and Relâche (1924), and the cantata Socrate (1918). These have the same flatness as the smaller pieces and songs, achieved by means of directionless modal harmony, simple rhythm and structures made up through repetition or inconsequential dissimilarity. In different ways the style had an effect on French composers from Debussy and Ravel to Poulenc and Sauguet, as later on Cage. **GROVE**music

Piano Works

Six Gnossiennes. Ogives. Petite ouverture à danser. Sarabandes. Trois Gymnopédies
Reinbert de Leeuw pf
Philips 446 672-2PH (67' · DDD)   ⓕ🔴▷

Tender, solemn, droll, silly and occasionally plain boring, Satie's piano music has certainly proved its appeal for performers and record collectors, judging from the number of recitals devoted to it. But this one is out of the ordinary, for unlike the majority of artists, who offer a mixed bag of pieces, Reinbert de Leeuw has chosen music that's entirely solemn and even hieratic in utterance. He begins with the archaically beautiful *Gnossiennes*, taking the first of them unusually slowly but with compelling concentration. The composer's devotees will be thrilled, though you have to surrender completely to get the message of this repetitive, proto-minimalist music. The four *Ogives* derive their name from church architecture, and their unbarred, diatonically simple music has clear affinities with plainchant although, unlike chant, it's richly harmonised. Monotonous it may be, but that's part of its charm, if that term can apply to such a contemplative style. The very brief *Petite ouverture à danser* is a mere meandering sketch in lazy waltz-time, but all Satie is sacred to the converted and the writer of the booklet-essay accords it four lines, finding in it (as translated here) 'a suggestion of indifference, vacillating between a melancholy melody and indecisive harmony'. (Not exactly Beethoven, one might say.) The two pensively sad triptychs of *Sarabandes* and *Gymnopédies* – here very slow yet tonally most refined – complete this finely played and recorded disc, which offers nothing whatsoever of the bouncier *café-concert* Satie.

Alessandro Scarlatti   Italian 1660-1725

When he was 12 Alessandro Scarlatti was sent to Rome, where he may have studied with Carissimi. He married in 1678 and later that year was appointed maestro di cappella of S Giacomo degli Incurabili (now 'in Augusta'). By then he had already composed at least one opera and a second, Gli equivoci nel sembiante, was a resounding success in 1679. It confirmed Scarlatti in his chosen career as an opera composer and attracted the attention of Queen Christina of Sweden, who made him her maestro di cappella.

In 1684 Scarlatti was appointed maestro di cappella at the vice-regal court of Naples, at the same time as his brother Francesco was made first violinist. It was alleged that they owed their appointments to the intrigues of one of their sisters (apparently Melchiorra) with two court officials, who were dismissed. For the next two decades over half the new operas given at Naples were by Scarlatti. In 1702 he left with his family for Florence, where he hoped to find employment for himself and his son Domenico with Prince Ferdinando de' Medici.

When these hopes failed, Scarlatti accepted the inferior position in Rome of assistant music director at S Maria Maggiore. With a papal ban imposed on public opera, he found an outlet for his talents in oratorio and in writing cantatas for his Roman patrons. In 1706 he was elected to the Arcadian Academy, along with Pasquini and Corelli. The following year he attempted to conquer Venice, the citadel of Italian opera, with

Mitridate Eupatore and Il trionfo della libertà, but they both failed and Scarlatti was subsequently forced to return to Rome, where he was promoted to the senior post at S Maria Maggiore.

Scarlatti found little satisfaction in the life of a church musician, and towards the end of 1708 he accepted an invitation from the new Austrian viceroy to resume his position at Naples, where he remained for the rest of his life, though he maintained close contacts with his Roman patrons. It was probably in 1715 that he received a patent of nobility from Pope Clement XI. His final opera, La Griselda, was written for Rome in 1721, and he seems to have spent the final years of his life in Naples in semi-retirement.

GROVEmusic

Dixit Dominus

Dixit Dominus I. Arsi un tempo e l'ardore. Mori, mi dici. O morte, agli altri fosca, a me serena. O selci, o tigre, o ninfa. Sdegno la fiamma estinse. Magnificat a 5 voci. **Concerto Italiano / Rinaldo Alessandrini**
Naïve OP30350 (59' · DDD · T/t)   Ⓕ

For this setting of *Dixit Dominus* Alessandro Scarlatti harked back to the early 17th century (if not earlier) with some wilfully old-fashioned stile antico. Likewise, the Magnificat featured here is an exquisite polyphonic composition: it opens with long sustained contrapuntal lines, and closes with a flowing 'Amen'. All of the music featured here is simply scored for voices and continuo; choral passages are superbly sung by Concerto Italiano's five singers, and some intimate passages for solo voice accompanied only by theorbo ('Quia respexit humilitatem') require excellent coloratura. Scarlatti's genius as a word-painter and composer for voices is obvious in five superb madrigals.

The two sopranos are infrequently guilty of loose intonation but on the whole Concerto Italiano perform with a commendable juxtaposition of colour and restraint. The close-knit ensemble finely judges sweetly balanced suspensions during *Sdegno la fiamma estinse*. The glorious harmonic unfurling during the opening bars of *O morte, agli altri fosca, a me serena* is worth the price of the disc alone.

Vespers

The Cecilian Vespers. Salve regina. Audi filia, et inclina aurem. Nisi Dominus
Dominique Labelle, Susanne Rydén sops **Ryland Angel** counterten **Michael Slattery** ten **Neal Davies** bass **Philharmonia Chorale and Baroque Orchestra / Nicholas McGegan**
Avie ② CD/SACD AV0048 (131' · DDD/DSD · T/t). Recorded live   Ⓕ➡

Scarlatti's Vespers were composed for a service at the Roman church of Santa Cecilia in Trastevere in 1721. He was in his sixties by then, his music out of fashion, and one can sense that with this friendly commission he was relishing the freedom to be himself, revisiting all his old skills in vocal brilliance, melodic charm, graceful counterpoint and succinctly effective word-setting. There are echoes of Handel and Vivaldi, though given Scarlatti's eminence in his own time it might be more appropriate to think of things the other way round. And if in the end it lacks either Handel's grandeur or Vivaldi's spark, it's palpably the work of a master. The performance is expertly shaped and paced by Nicholas McGegan.

Cain, overo il primo omicidio

Cain, overo il primo omicidio   P
Graciela Oddone, Dorothea Röschmann sops
Bernarda Fink contr **Richard Croft** ten **Antonio Abete** bass **Academy for Ancient Music, Berlin /
René Jacobs** counterten
Harmonia Mundi ② HMC90 1649/50
(138' · DDD · T/t)   Ⓕ**OOO**

This is a stunning performance of a remarkable work. It was classified at the time not as an oratorio but as a *trattenimento sacro* ('sacred entertainment'), which suggests that its first performance, in 1707 in Venice, took place in a private palace rather than a church. But Scarlatti brought to the work, besides his seemingly inexhaustible invention, all the dramatic instinct that had made him famous as a composer of operas (of which he had already written about 40). Anyone charged with extracting a 'highlights' selection from this would find themselves in a quandary, since almost every number could be considered a highlight, from the brilliant opening aria for Adam, to two remorseful arias, with affecting chromaticisms, for Eve, and Lucifer (with excited violins) tempting Cain.

Jacobs has assembled an absolutely outstanding cast whose technical accomplishment, dramatic commitment and stylish ornamentation could scarcely be bettered. Furthermore, the instrumental playing is first class.

Stabat mater

Stabat mater[a]. Flute Concerto No 21[b]
[a]**Emma Kirkby** sop [a]**Daniel Taylor** counterten
Theatre of Early Music ([b]Francis Colpron rec [b]Oliver Brault, [a]Adrian Butterfield, [ab]Hélène Plouffe vns [ab]Susie Napper vc [a]Peter Buckoke, [b]Pierre Cartier, [a]Jeremy Gordon vcs [a]Sylvain Bergeron lte [a]Nicholas Kraemer, [b]Alexander Weimann orgs)
ATMA Baroque ACD22237 (51' · DDD · T/t)   Ⓕ

Alessandro Scarlatti's celebrated *Stabat mater* was commissioned by a confraternity of aristocrats, the Cavalieri della Vergine dei Dolori, for its annual Lenten service at the Franciscan church of San Luigi in Naples. It remained in use until the confraternity commissioned Pergolesi to compose his famous setting to supplant Scarlatti's old-fashioned music. Both Pergolesi and Scarlatti composed for limited resources,

each using two solo voices, two violins and basso continuo. Scarlatti's setting is by no means inferior to Pergolesi's but remains much less familiar, despite several excellent recordings.

This ATMA recording boasts a beautifully captured atmospheric sound, with the perfect amount of reverberation. Daniel Taylor gives an understated and gentle performance. His solos, especially the longest movement, 'Iuxta crucem tecum stare', are the best elements of a performance that is spiritually contemplative rather than dramatic, although the final 'Amen' duet contains dynamic energy.

Although Emma Kirkby's attention to text and style is as admirable as ever, she does not sound at ease and compensates for the loss of clarity by under-singing. Her voice is pinched and vulnerable in some of the divisions during 'Fac ut ardeat'. The Theatre of Early Music excellently capture the contrasts and subtleties in Scarlatti's instrumental parts.

La Griselda

La Griselda
Dorothea Röschmann sop Griselda **Lawrence Zazzo** counterten Gualtiero **Veronica Cangemi** sop Costanza **Bernarda Fink** mez Roberto **Silvia Tro Santafé** mez Ottone **Kobie van Rensburg** ten Corrado **Akademie für Alte Musik Berlin / René Jacobs**
Harmonia Mundi ③ HMC90 1805/7
(182' · DDD · N/T/t)   Ⓕ**O**

The opera *Griselda* was performed only once at Rome's Teatro Capranica in 1721, towards the end of Alessandro Scarlatti's career. It was probably sponsored by Prince Ruspoli, who'd been Handel's major Roman patron 15 years earlier. The libretto, adapted from the *Decameron*, portrays Gualtiero, King of Sicily, relentlessly testing his wife Griselda's fidelity. There's a lot of recitative among the irony, deceptions and intense passions, but the action progresses at a compelling pace, and the concise arias are consistently inventive, unpredictable and attractive. Dorothea Röschmann brings dignified integrity to a dangerously subservient title-role, and Lawrence Zazzo's lyrical singing is both sweet and theatrical as the complex Gualtiero. Veronica Cangemi's steely voice is judiciously cast as Griselda's daughter Costanza, and Bernarda Fink is strong and stylish as her lover Roberto. Silvia Tro Santafé is arrogant and dislikable as Ottone, which is entirely right for the King's malcontent villainous servant. Kobie van Rensburg displays marvellous assured coloratura that flows smoothly, and it's good to hear a tenor of such quality in this repertoire.

If *Griselda* represents one of Scarlatti's finest artistic achievements, it's apt that this recording accordingly shares a similarly privileged status within René Jacobs' discography. The conductor is helped by the alert brilliance of the Akademie für Alte Musik Berlin, which clearly relishes the splendid score. Jacobs paces the drama sensitively, and characterises the arias with intelligence. His only sin is overly fussy decisions about restless recitatives in which the continuo is historically implausible and artistically intrusive. Yet whether you love or loathe Jacobs, this is an immensely important achievement. Handel wasn't the only talented opera composer working in the early 18th century, but at long last we've a genuinely credible comparison on disc. This recording does much to explain why Handel's librettist Charles Jennens slyly remarked that the Saxon regularly pinched musical ideas from Scarlatti.

Domenico Scarlatti   Italian 1685-1757

In 1701 Domenico Scarlatti was appointed organist and composer of the vice-regal court at Naples, where his father Alessandro was maestro di cappella. In 1705 his father sent him to find employment in Venice where he may have first met Handel, with whom he formed a strong attachment. By 1707, however, he was in Rome, assisting his father at S Maria Maggiore, and he remained in Rome for over 12 years, occupying posts as maestro to the dowager Queen of Poland from 1711, to the Marquis de Fontes from 1714, and at St Peter's.

In 1719 Scarlatti resigned his positions in Rome and apparently spent some years in Palermo before taking up his next post, as mestre of the Portuguese court in Lisbon. The Lisbon earthquake of 1755 destroyed documents about his career there, but his duties included giving keyboard lessons to John V's daughter, Maria Barbara, and his younger brother, Don Antonio. When Maria Barbara married the Spanish crown prince in 1729 Scarlatti followed her to Seville and then, in 1733, to Madrid, where he spent the rest of his life. Although he continued to write vocal music, sacred and secular cantatas contain much admirable music. But his fame rightly rests on the hundreds of keyboard sonatas, nearly all in the same binary form, in which he gave free rein to his imagination, stimulated by the new sounds, sights and customs of Iberia and by the astonishing gifts of his royal pupil and patron. In these he explored new worlds of virtuoso technique, putting to new musical ends such devices as hand-crossing, rapidly repeated notes, wide leaps in both hands and countless other means of achieving a devastating brilliance of effect.

GROVEmusic

Keyboard Sonatas

Keyboard Sonatas Kk1, 3, 8, 9, 11, 17, 24, 25, 27, 29, 87, 96, 113, 141, 146, 173, 213, 214, 247, 259, 268, 283, 284, 380, 386, 387, 404, 443, 519, 520, 523
Mikhail Pletnev pf
Virgin Classics ② 561961-2 (140' · DDD)   Ⓑ**OOO**⇨

 Every so often a major pianist reclaims Scarlatti for the piano with an outstanding recording. As Ralph Kirkpatrick put it, Scarlatti's harpsichord, while supremely itself, is continually menacing a transformation into something else. True, the relation of the music to harpsichord sound could hardly be closer, and it wouldn't have been composed the way it is for a different instrument. Scarlatti is marvellous at suggesting imaginary orchestrations and stimulating the imagination. He makes us aware of different vantage points as the music passes before us, of the different tones of voice and rhetorical inflexions – as various in these sonatas as the events in them are unpredictable. There are dances, fiestas and processions here, serenades, laments, and evocations of everything from the rudest folk music to courtly entertainments and churchly polyphony; and as the kaleidoscope turns you marvel at the composer who could embrace such diversity, shape it and put it all on to the keyboard.

Pletnev's playing is strongly individual, and his free-ranging poetic licence may not be to your taste. Not that his spectacular virtuosity is likely to be controversial: this really is *hors de catégorie* and enormously enjoyable. And the evocations of the harpsichord are often very witty, but he doesn't shrink from using the full resources of the piano, sustaining pedal included, and if you baulk at the prospect, he may not be for you. The sustaining pedal is certainly dangerous in music that's almost wholly to do with lines, not washes of colour; it can make us see Scarlatti as if through Mendelssohn's eyes. Yet moments of such falsification are rare. Characterisation is everything, and though he can be coy in the reflective sonatas, he generally goes straight to the heart of the matter. The vigorous, full tone in the quick numbers is a joy, and most admirable is the way he makes sound immediately command character. Superb recorded sound.

Keyboard Sonatas Kk3, 54, 141, 145, 175, 162, 177, 185, 199, 208, 248, 249, 299, 310, 484, 492, 531, 535
Pierre Hantaï hpd
Mirare MIR9918 (68' · DDD)   Ⓟ**OO**

The first track (Kk535) is typical of the quick-moving sonatas that abound in this programme – an astonishing display of dexterity in which the harpsichord he uses (a 1999 copy of an anonymous Thuringian instrument of 1720) and the acoustic help in preserving total clarity. Even at maximum velocity (did Scarlatti and his pupil reach such speeds?) he manages to shape his phrases with micro-second dwellings.

It isn't only the speedy sonatas that are impressive; Kk208 exemplifies his skilful shifts to either side of the pulse in giving the lines a natural 'vocal' quality. It also illuminates Kk185, 310, 199 and 162, in the last of which it's more evident in the playful quicker 'interludes'. The irresistible disc is splendidly annotated by Hantaï and beautifully packaged.

Keyboard Sonatas Kk443, 444, 448, 450, 462, 466, 469, 474, 503, 504, 508, 516, 517, 526, 527, 531, 540, 541, 545, 548
Frédérick Haas hpd
Calliope CAL9330 (78' · DDD)   Ⓕ

This is a stunning recording. There are some tough nuts here but Haas cracks them with ease and a sense of surging virtuosity. He plays on the warmly resonant but clear-sounding French harpsichord last used by Scott Ross. If you want to introduce Scarlatti to someone you couldn't do it better than by playing this disc. This appears to be a one-off recording but it offers strong temptation as a 'supplement' to anyone already embarked on an integral sonata collection.

Keyboard Sonatas, Kk3, 14, 20, 27, 32, 33, 39, 98, 109, 141, 146, 208, 209, 213, 322, 436, 481, 492, 517
Michael Lewin pf
Naxos 8 553067 (76' · DDD)   ⓈⓄ⟿

Michael Lewin is an American pianist as dexterous and assured as he's audacious. Here there's no sense of 'studio' caution but only of liberating and dazzling music-making, live and on the wing. Kk492 in D could hardly provide a more brilliant curtain-raiser, and in Kk3 in A minor (the one where Scarlatti's impish humour offers the musical equivalent of someone slipping on a banana skin) Lewin's playing positively brims over with high spirits. The D major Sonata, Kk33, is all thrumbing guitars and bursts of sunlight and in Kk141, with its cascades of repeated notes, Lewin even gives Martha Argerich a run for her money. There's a no less appealing balm and musical quality in the more restrained numbers such as Kk32 in D minor and Kk208 in A, though the recital comes to a suitably ebullient conclusion with Kk517 in D minor which is here like a river in full spate.

The New York-based recordings are suitably lively. Not even the most persistent lover of Scarlatti on the harpsichord could accuse Michael Lewin of an absence of the necessary glitter, panache and stylistic awareness.

Keyboard Sonatas Kk20, 24, 27, 30, 87, 197, 365, 426, 427, 429, 435, 448, 455, 466, 487, 492, 545
Yevgeny Sudbin pf
BIS BIS-CD1508 (76' · DDD)   ⒻⓄⓄ

This generously packed CD is sheer delight from start to finish. Even with recorded selections available from the likes of Horowitz, Pletnev, Schiff and Pogorelich, the 25-year-old Russian pianist Yevgeny Sudbin makes his solo debut on disc with performances of a superlative vitality and super-fine sensitivity.

His choice of sonatas is richly enterprising, pinpointing their infinite variety, their abrupt changes of mood and direction, so that whether familiar or unfamiliar (and there are many unfamiliar numbers), each offering is a delectable surprise. Free from the nervous tension that can sometimes plague him in the concert hall, Sudbin relishes the way Scarlatti turns convention topsy-turvy, presenting him in both performance and his affectionate accompanying essay as one of music's most ardent and life-affirming adventurers. He's brilliant and incisive in Kk545, and makes every bar of the reflective Kk57 glisten with poetry. What thrumming guitars he evokes in Kk435 and 487, reminding us that Scarlatti forsook his native Italy and later Portugal for a heady addiction to all things Spanish.

There are spicy and witty imitations of changing registrations and some notably rumbustious closes to make every facet of these diamond-like sonatas spark and scintillate as if new-minted. This is, arguably, among the finest, certainly most enjoyable of all Scarlatti recitals. As a crowning touch Sudbin is heard in a beautifully warm and natural acoustic.

Giacinto Scelsi   Italian 1905-1988

Of aristocratic birth, Scelsi had no formal training and ranged over many styles in his earlier works while remaining constant to an ideal of music as a link with the transcendental. That remained his conviction in works after the 1950s, in which he often used microtones, thin textures and extremely slow movement.   GROVEmusic

Choral Music

Complete Choral Works
Three Latin Prayers. Sauh – III; IV. Yliam. TKRDGa. Antifona sul nome Jesu. Tre Canti Populari. Tre Canti Sacri
ᵃ**Alan Thomas** gtr **New London Chamber Choir;** ᵃ**Percussive Rotterdam** (Wilbert Grootenboer, Hans Leenders, Norman van Dartel perc) / **James Wood**
Accord 465 401-2 (72' · DDD)   Ⓜ

The best known music here is the *Tre Canti Sacri*, but just about everything is on a very high level of virtuosity and inspiration. The *Tre Canti Populari* are scarcely less inventive.

Scelsi's mysticism encompasses a fair degree of stylistic variety, but repeated listening tends to bring out what unites rather than the opposite. At the same time, he was capable of assuming strikingly different idioms more or less contemporaneously. The chant-inspired *Three Latin Prayers* and *Antifona* (the former seem like preparatory studies for the latter) both date from 1970, only two years after the *Canti Sacri*. 1968 also saw the composition of *TKRDG*, which incorporates the strongest Eastern influences, the only instrumental interventions (ably supplied by Percussive Rotterdam and guitarist Alan Thomas), and arguably the most radical aesthetic of this collection. The slightly earlier *Yliam* is marginally reminiscent of the choral music of Ligeti (and, indeed Xenakis) from the same period: the treatment of the super-high register is very effective, and admirably dispatched by the sopranos. That adjective describes these performance in the round (with perhaps the exception of the *Three Latin Prayers*, which sound a little tentative).

Scelsi's stature has grown steadily since his death in 1988 and this reissue only adds to his reputation. Within the contemporary choral repertory, it ought to be required listening.

Franz Xaver Scharwenka
Polish-German 1850-1924

Scharwenka studied with Kullak in Berlin. A touring artist from 1874, he became increasingly active as a concert organizer and teacher in Berlin, founding his own conservatory in 1881 (the Klindworth-Scharwenka, with a New York branch in 1891). He was renowned as a Chopin interpreter. Among his best compositions are the Polish Dance op.3 no.1 and the Piano Concerto in B flat minor (1877). His brother Philipp (1847-1917) was a composer and teacher at the Scharwenka Conservatory.

Piano Concerto No 4

F X Scharwenka Concerto for Piano and Orchestra No 4 in F minor, Op. 82 **Sauer** Concerto for Piano and Orchestra No 1 in E minor
Stephen Hough pf **City of Birmingham Symphony Orchestra / Lawrence Foster**
Hyperion CDA66790 (70' · DDD) Ⓕ❍❍❍

 This jewel in the crown in Hyperion's Romantic Piano Concerto series marries flawlessly composer, performance, recording and presentation. Scharwenka's Piano Concerto No 4 is a far cry from his early, ubiquitous success, the E flat minor Polish Dance. Grand, Lisztian ambitions are fulfilled and embellished in writing of the most ferocious intricacy; the tarantella finale in particular throws everything at the pianist, seemingly simultaneously. It's therefore hardly surprising that after early triumphs the Fourth Concerto fell into neglect. At its second performance, given in 1910 with Scharwenka as soloist and Mahler as conductor, it was described as being of a 'truly Dionysian and bewildering brilliancy', a phrase that encapsulates Stephen Hough's astonishing performance. For here is scintillating wit and ebullience. As magisterial as it's ear-tickling and affectionate, his playing glows with warmth in the third movement Lento, and pulses with the most nonchalant glitter in the finale; one guaranteed to strike down less intrepid and fluent spirits with St Vitus's dance.

Emil von Sauer's First Concerto has a style and content to make even the least susceptible listeners' heads nod and feet tap. The Cavatina is as luscious and enchanting as the finale is teasingly brief and light-hearted. Throughout, haunting melodies are embroidered with the finest pianistic tracery. Once again the performance is bewitching. In the Cavatina Hough's caressing, fine-spun tone and long-breathed phrasing are a model for singers as well as pianists, and in the finale there's a lightly deployed virtuosity that epitomizes his aristocratic style.

Though the spotlight falls unashamedly on the soloist in such music, the orchestra has no small part in the proceedings, and Lawrence Foster and the CBSO are superbly resilient and enthusiastic, with strings that sing their hearts out. Sound and balance are exemplary. Stephen Heliotis's accompanying notes deserve separate publication for their wit and perspicacity.

Samuel Scheidt   German 1587-1654

Scheidt was organist of the Moritzkirche, Halle, for several years, and studied with Sweelinck in Amsterdam before becoming Halle court organist in 1609. From 1619-20 he was also court Kapellmeister, but the musical establishment almost disbanded (because of the Thirty Years War) in 1625. In 1627-30 he was director of music in Halle, also composing for the Marktkirche. His duties as court Kapellmeister resumed in 1638. Scheidt was active as an organ expert and a teacher and knew both Schütz and Schein.

Scheidt distinguished himself in both keyboard and sacred vocal music, in which he combined traditional counterpoint with the new Italian concerto style. Contrapuntal chorale settings are important among his c150 keyboard pieces. Some appear in his three-volume Tabulatura nova (1624), the first German publication of keyboard music to be in open score rather than in German organ tablature or in two-staff format; the collection also contains variations and liturgical pieces. Scheidt left some 160 sacred vocal works. His first book, Cantiones sacrae (1620), consists of polychoral motets, some of them based on chorales, and his second (1620) of large concertos with obbligato instrumental parts. Small concertos for few voices make up the four volumes of Geistliche Concerte (1631-40). Scheidt also composed dances, canzonas, sinfonias etc and canons.
GROVEmusic

Ludi Musici

Ludi Musici – Alamande a 4; Canzon ad   Ⓟ
imitationem Bergamas angl a 5; Canzon super
Cantionem Gallicam a 5; Canzon super O Nachbar
Roland a 5; Five Courants a 4; Courant dolorosa a 4;
Two Galliards a 4; Galliard a 5; Galliard battaglia a 5;
Three Paduanas a 4
Hespèrion XX / Jordi Savall viol
Astrée Naïve ES9980 (62' · DDD) Ⓜ

Scheidt's *Ludi Musici* reflects the fusion of English and German traditions in the emergent world of instrumental music in early 17th-century Germany and is a mouth-wateringly diverse and inventive mixture of dance, canzona and variation. These are works which brim over with character and nonchalantly brilliant craftsmanship. Scheidt has that rare knack, for the 1620s and 1630s, of sustaining an instrumental piece for more than two minutes without bombarding us with a new idea every 10 bars; the longer pieces such as the Paduanas and the brilliant Canzon a 5 *ad imitationem Bergamas angl*, with its thrilling close, convey admirable long-term direction amid a concentrated love of ephemeral effect. This is a cocktail which Hespèrion XX relishes.

The Pavans are, as you would expect from Jordi Savall, eventful. There are moments when an indulgence from Savall's treble viol stifles the potential for a more reflective allusion, but the overriding effect is of a performer striving to find a meaningful discourse, not content just to 'let the music play itself'; the colour and shape he brings to line and texture is often beguiling (disarmingly poignant in the stillness of the final Paduana), at times too much of a good thing but always engaging.

Johann Heinrich Schmelzer
Austrian c1620/23-1680

Schmelzer was trained in Vienna and served in the court chapel from the mid-1630s, becoming a member of the orchestra in 1649 and vice-Kapellmeister in 1671. In 1679 he was made Kapellmeister. The leading Austrian composer of instrumental music before Biber, he wrote 150 ballet suites for court dramatic productions and over 100 sonatas. The former each have between two and nine dances, sometimes thematically related; some include elements of folk music. Notable among the sonatas are the six Sonatae unarum fidium (1664), the earliest published set for solo violin and continuo. Schmelzer's prolific output also includes sepolcri and other dramatic pieces, nearly 200 sacred works and some secular vocal music. GROVEmusic

Sonatae unarum fidium

Schmelzer Sonatae unarum fidium[b] **Anonymous** Ⓟ
Scordatura Violin Sonata[a] **Bertali** Chiaconna
John Holloway vn [ab]**Aloysia Assenbaum** org
[a]**Lars Ulrik Mortensen** hpd/org
ECM New Series 465 066-2 (63' · DDD) ⒻⓄⓄⒹ

Johann Heinrich Schmelzer was the first homegrown Kapellmeister to be appointed at the Hapsburg Court in Vienna in 1679, following generations of Italians hired for their *oltremontani* flair and easy command of prevailing fashion. Schmelzer's six sonatas from 1664 are certainly Italianate, and not without freewheeling virtuosity, but they also contain a type of extended lyricism, and, as in the opening of the Fourth Sonata, a sense of no-nonsense progression of comforting expectation. In fact, this work, and that by his dynamic forebear, Antonio

Bertali (whose own *Chiaconna* is quite a party-piece) are typical 17th-century showcases for the violin where intricate and fantastical divisions unfold above a recurring bass pattern. The playing in this technically demanding repertoire is dazzling, and the intonation faultless. Yet equally impressive is John Holloway's measured classicism and subtle poetical restraint. Not every bar of Schmelzer's set is compelling and he opts for a consistent clarity of sound rather than milking every note as if it's of earth-shattering importance; he uses *rubato* discerningly, as in the introspective musings in the Fifth Sonata where the narrative is beautifully and elegantly articulated. The idea of a double continuo of organ and harpsichord is highly effective throughout.

The first recording of *Sonatae unarum* was made by Romanesca (see above), and they too opt for a counterpoint of continuos with organ and theorbo. The sense of a rich consort-like texture can only bring a much-needed breadth to music which might otherwise test the concentration over the course of an hour. To choose between these two fine recordings isn't easy, save to say that Romanesca is more consistently adventurous and theatrical. Holloway and his excellent keyboardists are less extrovert, softer-grained and more inclined to hover with sweet and restrained decorum. Both recordings are exceptional in their way, revealing how much interpretative leeway Schmelzer gives his players.

Franz Schmidt
Austrian 1874-1939

He first performed as an infant prodigy on the piano and continued his studies with Leschetitzky. In 1888 he moved to Vienna, and in 1890 began attending the conservatory of the Gesellschaft der Musikfreunde, where he studied theory and cello. From 1896 to 1911 he was a cellist in the Vienna PO, playing also in the orchestra of the Hofoper from 1896 until 1914. In 1901 he began teaching at the conservatory. After it had been renamed the Hochschule, Schmidt served as both its director (1925-7) and its rector (1927-31). His compositions, which include four symphonies, chamber and organ music and the oratorio Das Buch mit sieben Siegeln (composed 1935-7), show sensitive melodic invention and reveal the influence of Bruckner, Mahler, Reger, Schoenberg and Debussy. Romanticism, expressionism and atonality can all be found in his music.

Concerto for Piano Left-Hand

Concerto for Piano Left-Hand. Konzertante Variationen über ein Thema von Beethoven
Carlo Grante pf
MDR Symphony Orchestra / Fabio Luisi
Querstand VKJK0611 (79' · DDD) Ⓕ

Franz Schmidt's works for piano left-hand and

orchestra have merited even less coverage than his symphonies. Yet of all his commissions, Paul Wittgenstein valued them the most highly; not least because the balance between soloist and orchestra is so painstakingly achieved. Ironic, then, that both works have long been available only in two-hand editions: expertly prepared, but no match for the poise and subtlety of the originals – as Carlo Grante's performances so eloquently attest.

The *Beethoven* Variations (1922) demonstrate Schmidt's innovative approach to a form too frequently dogged by its inherent limitations. The variations (on the *Scherzo* from the *Spring* Sonata), are grouped in sequences whose contrast of pace and variety of mood ensure a cumulative momentum from the slow introduction to the fugal finale – both of which are an active part of the process. Cast in the familiar three movements, the Piano Concerto (1934) might seem defiantly conventional, and Schmidt's ingenuity in building the work from the unassuming melody heard in the initial tutti only gradually becomes clear; notably when the finale's lengthy cadenza recalls the opening material as if setting the seal on the concerto's evolution as a whole.

Grante sets new standards in both works: a noted Busonian, one would expect so keen a response to the elusive coherence of the Variations and revivified classicism of the Concerto. Fabio Luisi displays the same conviction distinguishing his Schmidt symphony cycle with his Leipzig-based orchestra, and the sound is up to Querstand's high standards. Newcomers are in for a real treat.

Symphony No 1

Symphony No 1. Notre Dame – Introduction; Carnival Music; Intermezzo
Malmö Symphony Orchestra / Vassily Sinaisky
Naxos 8 570828 (61' · DDD)   ⓈＢ➤

Despite some celebrated past recordings, Franz Schmidt's symphonies have never quite made it into the musical premier league. It is not through lack of championship nor the quality of the works themselves, which is of the highest order.

The quality of Schmidt's music is demonstrated here by the least of his four symphonies, the prize-winning First (1899). Its four expansive movements play for some 45 minutes, the essential qualities of Schmidt's style evident in every bar: attractive melodies in appealing late-Romantic (but not overdone) harmonies with plentiful contrapuntal interest. If not possessing its successors' structural subtleties, the First is a well made and more satisfying whole than many better-known works. True, there are traces of Brahms, Bruckner and Wagner (and even foreshadowings of Elgarian *nobilmente* in the finale), but Schmidt's own voice shines through.

So it does in the splendid extracts from the first act of his opera *Notre Dame* (1902-04), of which

the Intermezzo shows the lyrical Hungarian side of Schmidt's musical personality to radiant effect. Sinaisky directs searching accounts of the works here and the Malmö players relish the task of tackling repertoire put on the map by the erstwhile director of their Gothenburg rivals along the Swedish coast.For those unfamiliar with Schmidt this newcomer makes a fine introduction.

Das Buch mit sieben Siegeln

Das Buch mit sieben Siegeln
Johannes Chum ten St John **Robert Holl** bass-bar
Voice of the Lord **Sandra Trattnigg** sop **Michelle Breedt** mez **Nikolai Schukoff** ten Manfred Hemm
bass **Robert Kovács** org **Wiener Singverein; North Austrian Tonkünstler Orchestra / Kristjan Järvi**
Chandos ② 🎵 CHSA5061 (114' · DDD · T/t)
Recorded live at the Musikverein, Vienna in 2005ⓂＢ➤

Best known for his work with the left-field Absolute Ensemble, Kristjan Järvi might not be thought a natural exponent but there can be no doubting his conviction. He is abetted by a strong vocal line-up: Johannes Chum is a youthful and forthright St John who, though a little strained in his initial entry, exudes the right impulsiveness and awe; Robert Holl is eloquently authoritative as the Voice of the Lord; and with the remaining quartet well contrasted as soloists and finely balanced in ensemble. The Wiener Singverein lack nothing in either incisiveness or sensitivity, while the Tonkünstler Orchestra, if a mite undernourished in string sound, are more than equal to Schmidt's surprisingly wide-ranging demands.

Surprising in that this is a piece which marks a culmination within the Austro-German choral tradition and yet looks defiantly to its future – an aspect Järvi pointedly emphasises – whether in the stark expressive contrasts as the Seven Seals are opened, the powerful momentum unleashed by the Seven Trumpets, or the climactic 'Hallelujah' chorus whose grandeur is charged with a keen fervency.

More evocative than Franz Welser-Möst (EMI) but less theatrical than Nikolaus Harnoncourt (BMG), Järvi makes it the concert-drama Schmidt surely intended. SACD sound maximises its textural and dynamic extremes, but a pity that applause was retained at the end of disc 1. Even so, this could well be first choice for those new to the work.

Alfred Schnittke   USSR 1934-1998

Schnittke was a pupil of Rakov and Golubev at the Moscow Conservatory (1953-61), where he taught until 1972. His works often use quotations, parodies and stylistic imitations in a highly charged manner, though some are more unified in expression. Textures are rich and complexly varied and string instruments feature prominently in his output, which, apart from four symphonies and various stage works, includes five concerti grossi, four violin concertos, two violin sonatas and chamber music. He was a prolific writer on Russian music. **GROVE**music

Cello Concertos

Cello Concertos – No 1[a]; No 2[b]. Concerto grosso No 2[c]. Cello Sonatas[d] – No 1; No 2
Alexander Ivashkin *vc*
[c]**Tatjana Grindenko** *vn* [d]**Irina Schnittke** *pf*
[ab]**Russian State Symphony Orchestra /**
Valéri Polyansky
Chandos ② CHAN241-39 (153' · DDD) Ⓜ☐➔

Schnittke's Cello Concerto No 1 was written in the months after his first devastating stroke in 1985 and gives a grim portrayal of the composer's psychological terror and disorientation, to the point where you start to empathise. Polystylistic jump-cuts, once the result of political repression, flip inwards as mournful intoning slams against feral, expressionistic orchestral screams. Schnittke lays it on with a trowel, but his genius for building dialectic tension between competing harmonies raises his argument above the vanilla juxtapositions of lesser composers. When Schnittke returned home from hospital he had no memory of sketches he'd already made for his concerto – these narrative disjoints are painfully authentic.

The Concerto No 1 is one of Schnittke's most recorded works, but it would be difficult to imagine a more physically committed performance than Alexander Ivashkin's. The Cello Concerto No 2 was written in 1990 and is less in-your-face. A Viennese waltz that sounds like it's been reharmonised by Berg briefly wanders into focus, hinting at Schnittke's earlier compositional techniques. But 'borrowed' reference-points are now more distilled, and the work spends 40 minutes amplifying and reinvestigating the implications of its opening moments, as the orchestra sits on the soloist's attempts to generate more extended gestures.

Chandos has added Schnittke's two cello sonatas to this reissued pairing of the concertos. The First is archetypal Schnittke, with grave slow opening and closing movements interrupted by the black humour of an intervening *Scherzo*, in this case characterised by dense tone clusters and bizarre *pizzicato* cello figurations. Impetus is turned on its head – progress gets increasingly staggered to create a kind of anti-momentum, a paradox that Ivashkin exploits keenly. The aphoristic Second Sonata is less imposing, and the 'wrong-note' humour of the *Concerto grosso* No 2 is a brand of Schnittke that may be something of an acquired taste, but that's neither here nor there – here's the definitive document of Schnittke's relationship with the cello.

Concerti grossi

Schnittke Concerto grosso No 6[a]. Violin Sonata
Takemitsu Nostalgia **Weill** Concerto for Violin and Wind Orchestra, Op 12
Daniel Hope *vn* [a]**Simon Mulligan** *pf/hpd* **English Symphony Orchestra / William Boughton**
Nimbus NI5582 (73' · DDD) Ⓕ

Full marks to Nimbus for variety. The danger is that three such different composers, combined in a way you'd never expect in a concert, will cancel each other out. Fortunately, the performances are strong enough – even when heard in close succession – to justify the enterprise, and the recordings are no less successful in the way they capture the intimacy of tone characteristics of all four compositions.

A textual point of some interest emerges in the earlier of the Schnittke works, the Sonata. Usually, the harpsichord functions as the violinist's *alter ego* throughout, but Daniel Hope, with Schnittke's agreement, has the keyboardist move from harpsichord to piano from the final stages of the second movement onwards. The desiccated harpsichord sound may be preferable in the third movement, but the change is certainly justified in the finale, and adds an extra dimension to a commendably unexaggerated account of this turbulent score.

The early Weill Violin Concerto can easily sprawl and sound too earnest for its own good. Here there's an appropriate fluency; excessive gravity is avoided. Hope is able to project the required authority, especially in the cadenza, and although some might prefer a more forward placement for the soloist, the excellent qualities of his playing are no less appealing. As for Takemitsu's song of farewell for the film-maker Andrei Tarkovsky, the music is a model of how to balance emotional restraint and expressive warmth, and the performance does it justice.

Piano Quintet

Schnittke Piano Quintet[a] **Shostakovich** String Quartet No 15 in E flat minor, Op 144
[a]**Alexei Lubimov** *pf* **Keller Quartet** (András Keller, János Pilz *vns* Zoltán Gál *va* Judit Szabó *vc*)
ECM New Series 461 815-2 (65' · DDD) Ⓕ

Just as Schnittke's First Symphony picks up the threads from Shostakovich's last, so his Piano Quintet feels like the natural successor to Shostakovich's last string quartet; that makes ECM's coupling of the two chamber works an effective and thought-provoking one, the more so since both performances are of the highest quality.

This music is a good deal harder to bring off than it looks. The textures are emaciated, and the pain of emotional starvation needs to register with unremitting intensity. In Schnittke's solo piano opening, Alexei Lubimov shows the requisite temperament and control of sonority, and both he and the Kellers keep us inside the Quintet's world through the first movement's obsessive, quarter-tone-inflected bell-tolling, through the ghost-train-ride of the film-derived *Tempo di valse*, through the catatonic laments of the two succeeding slow movements, all the way to the anxious transfigurations of the finale.

Curiously, Lubimov goes against the score in the final phrase, where Schnittke asks for pitched notes to fade into the noise of fingertips tapping on the keys, echoing the pedal-knocking at the end of the first movement. But his carefully graded *diminuendo* is effective enough in its own way.

Single-disc versions of Shostakovich's valedictory quartet are surprisingly thin on the ground. Here, too, the Kellers can stand comparison with the very finest. Shostakovich's parched and starved textures can be made to sound even more discomforting, but the Kellers' tonal control brings out its own range of nuance. Recording quality is nicely judged, the players being set in a nicely unobtrusive perspective.

Violin Sonatas

Violin Sonatas – No 1; No 2, 'Quasi una Sonata'; No 3. Gratulations rondo. Stille Nacht. Suite in the Old Style
Francesco d'Orazio *vn* **Giampaolo Nuti** *pf*
Stradivarius STR33675 (75' · DDD)   Ⓕ

Schnittke's music for violin and piano spans most of his composing career, from the early 1960s, when Shostakovich's genius and Soviet ideology both loomed large, to the mid-1990s, a time of freedom and desperate illness. The three sonatas and three other works chart Schnittke's sad but heroic decline, as he confronted head-on the special 20th-century challenge of composing from the heart as well as from a sense of history.

The First Sonata (1963) is probably the best of the six compositions. There's already plenty of that sardonic, to-hell-with-it manner he made his own, but his willingness to grapple with the possibilities of well-made instrumental design and to admit a sense of pathos that didn't exclude touches of understatement, make for a memorable 15 minutes. By comparison, the Second Sonata (1968) is more slapdash, not polystylistic enough to engineer the surreal confrontations of his most powerful exercises in bringing old and new into collision, its climactic bashings-out of a minor triad as dated as they are annoying. In the third sonata (1994) the earlier energy hasn't totally drained away, and the poignancy of a musical voice facing its own imminent extinction still gets through. Hearing this after the winsome pastiche of the *Suite in Old Style*, the po-faced Mozartisms of the *Gratulations rondo*, and the crude but unfailingly shudder-making deconstruction of *Stille Nacht* is moving, with its hints of what might have been had Schnittke lived in more stable times. Francesco d'Orazio, as recorded here, doesn't have the full-bodied tone and blazingly forthright rhetoric of a Russian violinist like Mark Lubotsky, for whom Schnittke composed. But he shapes the sonatas well, and has strong support from Giampaolo Nuti.

Concerto for Choir

Concerto for Choir. Requiem[a]
Prague Philharmonic Choir; [a]members of the
Prague Philharmonia / Jaroslav Brych
Praga Digitals PRD350 044 (66' · DDD)   Ⓕ

Had Alfred Schnittke's Concerto for Choir been written in 1975 rather than '85, it would have necessarily been a different piece. Mikhail Gorbachev took office in 1985 and Schnittke, perhaps sniffing the profound change that was about to sweep his country, thought it was timely to reaffirm a core Russian identity. Consequently his Concerto is that rarest of beasts – a Schnittke work that is unequivocally sincere, and evolves organically rather than through a dialogue of competing styles.

With the Prague Philharmonic Choir you get authentic east European enunciation and those boomy, sonorous low male voices raise the emotional temperature to at least the power 10. Getting the 'right' sound for the Concerto is vital. Schnittke's basic melodic contours and modal harmonies are rooted in his deep understanding of the Orthodox choral tradition, but he loads his piece with intricate complexities and ambiguous shadings: the occasional tart dissonance tells of now, and ebbing-and-flowing chromatic tumbles are strategically balanced against authentic open 'perfect' intervals. The second movement's conclusion may feel like an anticipation of Holy Minimalism, but this bountiful score makes John Tavener and his like sound like intellectual cowards.

Schnittke's Requiem was indeed written in 1975 and is full of trademark incongruous clashes and grotesque theatricals. Rockist electric guitars and, in the *Credo*, a brief input of kit drumming symbolise a spirit of defiance. It's another powerful performance on an unfailingly top-notch disc.

12 Penitential Psalms

12 Penitential Psalms
Swedish Radio Choir / Tõnu Kaljuste
ECM New Series 453 513-2 (53' · DDD · T/t)   ⒻⓄ

Schnittke's 12 *Penitential Psalms* (1988) aren't biblical: Nos 1-11 use 16th-century Russian texts and No 12 is a wordless meditation which encapsulates the spirit and style of what precedes it. Though at times dark and despairing in tone, this is in no sense liturgical music. It's too expansive, and reaches towards the ecstatic too consistently, to qualify as ascetic or austere. Indeed, the warmly euphonious chorale-like textures with which several of the movements end are sumptuous enough for one to imagine a soulful saxophone weaving its way through them. As this suggests, the recording is extremely, and not inappropriately, resonant, and the performance is polished to a fault, the individual lines superbly controlled and the textures balanced with a fine feeling for their weight and diversity. Although some may find this issue a little too refined, it realises the work's expressive world with imposing and irresistible authenticity. In these works, Schnittke seems to be doing penance for the extravagant indulgences of pieces such as *Stille Nacht* and the Viola Concerto, abandoning modernism in general and expressionism in particular. The music nevertheless retains strong links with the images of lament and spiritual aspiration, and there's nothing in the least artificial or contrived about its emotional aura. It's difficult to imagine a more convincing or better recorded account of it than this one.

Othmar Schoeck   Swiss 1886-1957

Schoeck studied at the Zürich Conservatory and with Reger in Leipzig (1907-8), then worked in Zürich and St Gall as a conductor. He was one of the leading Swiss composers of his time. His numerous songs, usually setting German Romantic poetry, establish him among the foremost lieder composers, but he also wrote important operas: the dense and richly scored Penthesilea *(1927) and* Vom Fischer und syner Fru *(1930), which like other works is more folklike. The rest of his output includes choral and orchestral scores and a few chamber pieces.*   GROVEmusic

Cello Concerto

Cello Concerto, Op 61ᵃ. Cello Sonataᵇ. Song Transcriptionsᵇ – Der Reisebecher, Op 60 No 19; Epigramm, Op 31 No 5; 12 Lieder, Op 30 – Nachklang; Winternacht; Nacht. In der Herberge, Op 7 No 3
Christian Poltéra vc ᵇ**Julius Drake** pf
ᵃ**Malmö Symphony Orchestra / Tuomas Ollila**
BIS BIS-CD1597 (62' · DDD)   Ⓕ〇

His output dominated by operas and Lieder, Othmar Schoeck (1886-1957) wrote few large-scale orchestral and chamber works. Of his three concertos, that for cello (1947) is among his last pieces and exudes an autumnal spirit. Its opening *Allegro* is among the composer's most successful sonata movements, generating no mean rhythmic momentum in spite of its predilection for long-breathed melodic lines, and purposefully sustaining its considerable length. The slow movement is the emotional heart – a luminous threnody in which the interplay of cello and strings is particularly felicitous. A brief but animated *Scherzo* and a finale that recalls earlier themes, while maintaining impetus on the way to a decisive conclusion, complete a work that ought to find its way into the still-limited cello canon now the Schumann concerto has become firmly established.

Christian Poltéra taps its ruminative depths unerringly and receives sensitive support from the Malmö Symphony strings under the direc-

tion of Tuomas Ollila. Julius Drake is equally responsive in the remaining pieces. The Cello Sonata remained incomplete at Schoeck's death: if its first movement evinces a certain weariness, the pert *Scherzo* and songful *Andantino* suggest a work likely to become more than the sum of its parts. The song transcriptions (presumably by Poltéra) are idiomatically done; that of the winsome *Nachklang* deserves to be an encore in every cellist's repertoire. Warmly spacious sound and informative booklet-notes round out this desirable debut from a highly promising cellist.

Penthesilea

Penthesilea
Helga Dernesch sop Penthesilea **Jane Marsh** sop Prothoe **Mechtild Gessendorf** sop Meroe **Marjana Lipovšek** mez High Priestess **Gabriele Sima** sop Priestess **Theo Adam** bass-bar Achilles **Horst Hiestermann** ten Diomede **Peter Weber** bass Herold **Austrian Radio Chorus and Symphony Orchestra / Gerd Albrecht**
Orfeo C364941B (80' · ADD · N/T) Recorded live 1982 Ⓕ

Schoeck's one-act opera, *Penthesilea* is an astonishing and masterly score. It seems barely credible that a work so gripping in its dramatic intensity, and so powerful in atmosphere, should be so little known. It has the listener on the edge of the seat throughout its 80 short minutes and, like any great opera, it continues to cast a spell long after the music has ended. In the *Grove Dictionary of Opera*, Ronald Crichton wrote that 'at its most intense, the language of *Penthesilea* surpasses in ferocity Strauss's *Elektra*, a work with which it invites comparison'. In so far as it's a one-act work, set in the Ancient World, highly concentrated in feeling and with strongly delineated characters, it's difficult not to think of Strauss's masterpiece. Yet its sound world is quite distinctive. Though he's a lesser figure, Schoeck similarly renders the familiar language of Straussian opera entirely his own. The vocabulary isn't dissimilar yet the world is different. We are immediately plunged into a vivid and completely individual world, packed with dramatic incident: off-stage war cries and exciting, dissonant trumpet calls. There's an almost symphonic handling of pace, but the sonorities are unusual: for example, there's a strong wind section, some 10 clarinets at various pitches, while there are only a handful of violins; much use is made of two pianos in a way that at times almost anticipates Britten.

This performance emanates from the 1982 Salzburg Festival; Helga Dernesch in the title-role commands the appropriate range of emotions as Penthesilea and the remainder of the cast, including the Achilles of Theo Adam, rise to the occasion. The important choral role and the orchestral playing under Gerd Albrecht are eminently committed and the recording is good. There's a useful essay and libretto, though in German, not English.

Arnold Schoenberg

Austro/Hungarian 1874-1951

Schoenberg began violin lessons when he was eight and almost immediately started composing, though he had no formal training until he was in his late teens, when Zemlinsky became his teacher and friend (in 1910 he married Zemlinsky's sister). His first acknowledged works date from the turn of the century and include the string sextet Verklärte Nacht as well as some songs, all showing influences from Brahms, Wagner and Wolf. In 1901-3 he was in Berlin as a cabaret musician and teacher, and wrote the symphonic poem Pelleas und Melisande, pressing the Straussian model towards denser thematic argument and contrapuntal richness.

He then returned to Vienna and began taking private pupils, Berg and Webern being among the first. He also moved rapidly forwards in his musical style. The large orchestra of Pelleas and the Gurrelieder was replaced by an ensemble of 15 in Chamber Symphony No 1, but with greater harmonic strangeness, formal complexity and contrapuntal density. When atonality arrived in 1908, it was the inevitable outcome of a doomed attempt to accommodate ever more disruptive material. However, he found it possible a quarter-century later to return to something like his tonal style, as in the Suite in G for strings.

That, however, was not possible immediately. The sense of key was left behind as Schoenberg set poems by George in the last two movements of String Quartet No 2 and in the cycle Das Buch der hängenden Gärten, and for the next few years he lived in the new, rarefied musical air. With tonality had gone thematicism and rhythmic constraint; works tended to be short statements of a single extreme musical state, justifying the term 'expressionist' (Five Orchestral Pieces; Three Pieces and Six Little Pieces for piano). The larger pieces of this period have some appropriate dramatic content: the rage and despair of a woman seaching for her lover (Erwartung), the bizarre stories, melancholia and jokes of a distintegrating personality (Pierrot lunaire, for reciter in Sprechgesang with mixed quintet), or the progress of the soul towards union with God (Die Jakobsleiter).

Gradually Schoenberg came to find the means for writing longer instrumental structures, in the 12-note serial method, and in the 1920s he returned to standard forms and genres, notably in the Suite for piano, String Quartet No 3, Orchestral Variations and several choral pieces. He also founded the Society for Private Musical Performances (1919-21), involving his pupils in the presentation of new music under favourable conditions. In 1923 his wife died (he remarried the next year), and in 1925 he moved to Berlin to take a master class at the Prussian Academy of Arts. While there he wrote much of his unfinished opera Moses und Aron which is concerned with the impossibility of communicating truth without some distortion in the telling.

In 1933 he was obliged as a Jew to leave Berlin: he went to Paris, and formally returned to the faith which he had deserted for Lutheranism in 1898. Later the same year he arrived in the USA, and he settled in Los Angeles in 1934. It was there that he returned to tonal composition, while developing seri-

alism to make possible the more complex structures of the Violin Concerto and the String Quartet No 4. In 1936 he began teaching at UCLA and his output dwindled. After a heart attack in 1945, however, he gave up teaching and made some return to expressionism (A Survivor from Warsaw, String Trio), as well as writing religious choruses. **GROVE**music

---

Piano Concerto

Schoenberg Piano Concerto, Op 42ᵃ. Drei Klavierstücke, Op 11. Sechs Klavierstücke, Op 19. **Berg** Sonata for Piano, Op 1. **Webern** Variations, Op 27
Mitsuko Uchida pf
ᵃ**Cleveland Orchestra / Pierre Boulez**
Philips 468 033-2PH (63' · DDD)   Ⓕ**OOO**▷

Uchida's distinctive musical personality and outstanding technique make her Schoenberg, Berg and Webern well worth hearing, however many other version of these works you have in your collection. She brings a marvellous spontaneity and sense of drama to the more overtly romantic compositions here – Berg's Sonata and Schoenberg's Op 11 *Pieces*. This certainly isn't one of those accounts of the Berg where you question the composer's wisdom in marking the first section for repeat. As for the Schoenberg, never has one been more aware of this music's closeness in time and spirit to the cataclysmic world of the monodrama *Erwartung*. Uchida's earlier recording of Op 11 was warmly praised, and this one is no less accomplished. Elsewhere, her relish for strongly juxtaposed contrast risks occasional over-emphasis, as in the third of the Op 19 pieces, and the virtues of more sharply articulated playing in this repertory are demonstrated on Peter Hill's admirable super-bargain-price Naxos disc. His account of Webern's *Variations* is exemplary in its clarity and feeling for line; yet Uchida manages to suggest deeper links with more romantic perspectives without in any way traducing the music's inherent radicalism.

Links with romanticism are even more explicit in the texture and thematic character of Schoenberg's Concerto, and this performance places the work firmly in the tradition of Liszt and Brahms. Not even Pierre Boulez can bring ideal lucidity to the occasionally lumpy orchestral writing, but the performance as a whole, with excellent sound, has an attractive sweep and directness of utterance.

Violin Concerto

Schoenberg Violin Concerto
Sibelius Violin Concerto
Hilary Hahn vn **Swedish Radio Symphony Orchestra / Esa-Pekka Salonen**
DG 477 7346 (63' · DDD)   Ⓕ**OOO**▷

Hilary Hahn's performance of Schoenberg's Concerto is magnificent recording. When the last chord sounds its full stop, the sense of satisfied finality is exhilarating. Hahn has the full of measure of the piece, its gawky lyricism, ethereal filigree and cripplingly difficult cadenzas (awkward chords galore), all rendered seemingly effortless. Wisps of old-world Vienna echo from the *Andante*, whereas in a performance of this calibre the finale's complex acrobatics suddenly have musical meaning. Of course having a first-rate orchestra and conductor helps: Esa-Pekka Salonen's direction is in the very best sense of the term 'slick', a perfect example of musical badinage, alert, crystal-clear and superbly recorded. Which makes the CD mandatory listening both for lovers of the work who crave an appreciative performance and for doubters who still await conversion.

The Sibelius performance is fascinating but less wholly convincing although as with the Schoenberg Hahn weaves a seductive, evenly deployed tone and her technique is impeccable. But while in the Schoenberg you sense a palpable level of emotional engagement Hahn's approach to Sibelius is cool, sphinx-like one might say, the first movement's many solo passages broadly drawn but somehow remote. No violinist currently performing makes a lovelier sound and although time and again one notes some illuminating phrase (not to mention Salonen's immaculately groomed accompaniment) the sum effect is of a strangely cold beauty. But the Schoenberg performance is magnificent.

Violin Concerto, Op 36[a]. Dreimal tausend Jahre, Op 50[ab]. Psalm 130, 'De profundis', Op 50[b]. Ode to Napoleon, Op 41[c]. A Survivor from Warsaw, Op 46[d]. Prelude to Genesis, Op 44[e]
[cd]**David Wilson-Johnson** *spkr*
[a]**Rolf Schulte** *vn* [c]**Jeremy Denk** *pf*
[c]**Fred Sherry Quartet**; [bde]**Simon Joly Chorale**;
[ade]**Philharmonia Orchestra / Robert Craft**
Naxos 8 557528 (71' · DDD) Ⓢ⯈

Hilary Hahn's recording of Schoenberg's Violin Concerto (see above) paraded cool beauty where others could find only sweat and tears. Yes, an overstatement perhaps – Louis Krasner and Israel Baker, for example, are among a few honourable exceptions.

Rolf Schulte and Robert Craft credibly project a work that sounds like an extension of Brahms's language in terms of Schoenberg's treatment of the orchestra and his melodic structures. Schulte's performance reminds one of Huberman's *bon mot* about Brahms setting the violin against the orchestra: it's a gutsy, fiercely intense interpretation with next to nothing of Hahn's centredness about it, though Craft's sane but enthusiastic conducting assures a workable temperature beyond the solo line. It's attractive but the sensation of Hahn holding her poise in the eye of a storm is preferable.

Most of Craft's programme is fervid stuff. Both *A Survivor from Warsaw* and *Ode to Napoleon* are fired-up reactions to the Second World War, the former – a concise and startling music drama magnificently scored for full orchestra – is a chilling slice of narrative about Nazi brutality; the latter – a 15-minute chamber work that waves a clenched fist for the duration – is a bold indictment of totalitarianism, based on a poem by Byron. Both works place English recitations centre-stage, declaimed with clarity and dramatic zeal by David Wilson-Johnson.

Craft's direction is very much 'straight from the hip', and the results are at the very least humbling. The *Genesis Prelude* is terse and powerful, and the two choral works, both at times starkly beautiful, take their prompts from Schoenberg's Jewish roots.

This is not an easy programme to take in at a single sitting, but it's a valuable one; an essential addition to Craft's invaluable Schoenberg series.

Chamber Symphony No 2

Chamber Symphony No 2, Op 38[a].
Wind Quintet, Op 26[b]. Die glückliche Hand, Op 18[c]
[c]**Mark Beesley** *bar* [b]**New York Woodwind Quintet;**
[ac]**Philharmonia Orchestra / Robert Craft**
Naxos 8 557526 (79' · DDD) Ⓢ

This eighth instalment of Robert Craft's Naxos cycle touches the polar opposites of Schoenberg's output. The radiant Chamber Symphony No 2 might be a beloved classic if Schoenberg hadn't so comprehensively queered his pitch elsewhere, while the Wind Quintet represents darkest deepest 'elsewhere', a work to challenge even the most devoted Schoenbergian.

This magisterial recording of the Quintet from the New York Woodwind Quintet marks a new plateau in our understanding of the work. As Craft's notes testify, performances during Schoenberg's life were normally conducted and lasted around an hour. This lithe, quicksilver version clocks in at 38 minutes and, with the right tempi restored, Schoenberg's contrapuntal labyrinth sparks into life. Melodic motifs evolve and morph into new terrain with profound inevitability, while his harmonic daring and recherché timbres now feel holistically connected.

The Chamber Symphony No 2 is another work where intellectual energy equates to a virtuoso instrumental showdown. The Philharmonia are fully engaged and Craft's fastidious approach makes every little detail count: but, as the cumulative impact of the second movement demonstrates, his ear is also focused on the larger picture. The 20-minute melodrama *Die glückliche Hand* sits in the stylistic overlap between Quintet and Symphony. Mark Beesley's small but anchoring role is powerfully executed, while Craft's artful unpicking of the prickly orchestral and choral writing places the listener at the core of Schoenberg's dream-world.

Verklärte Nacht, Op 4

Verklärte Nacht. Pelleas und Melisande, Op 5
Berlin Philharmonic Orchestra / Herbert von Karajan

DG The Originals 457 721-2GOR (74' · ADD)
Recorded 1973-4   Ⓜ●●●➔

🅖 This is a very distinguished coupling, superbly played by the BPO – a truly 'legendary' reissue, quite unsurpassed on record. Karajan never approached contemporary music with the innate radicalism and inside knowledge of a composer-conductor like Boulez; yet he can't be accused of distorting reality by casting a pall of late-Romantic opulence and languor over these works. He's understandably most at home in the expansive and often openly tragic atmosphere of Schoenberg's early tone-poems *Verklärte Nacht* and *Pelleas und Melisande*. The richly blended playing of the BPO provides the ideal medium for Karajan's seamless projection of structure and expression. He remains especially sensitive to the music's lyricism, to the connections that to his ears override the contrasts. Although *Verklärte Nacht* has certainly been heard in performances less redolent of 19th-century tradition, as well as less calculated in its recorded acoustic, this remains a powerfully dramatic reading. One man's view, then: but, given the man, a notably fascinating one.

Schoenberg Verklärte Nacht, Op 4 (orig version) Ⓗ
Schubert String Quintet in C, D956
Alvin Dinkin va **Kurt Reher** vc **Hollywood Quartet**
(Felix Slatkin, Paul Shure vns Paul Robyn va Eleanor Aller vc)
Testament mono SBT1031 (73' · ADD) Recorded
1950-51   Ⓕ●●●

This was the first ever recording of *Verklärte Nacht* in its original sextet form and it remains unsurpassed. When it was first reviewed in *Gramophone*, the late Lionel Salter wrote of it as being 'beautifully played with the most careful attention to details of dynamics and phrasing, with unfailing finesse, with consistently sympathetic tone, and, most important, with a firm sense of the basic structure'. The Schubert too fully deserves its classic status. The tranquillity of the slow movement has never been conveyed with greater nobility or more perfect control.

The Hollywood Quartet made music for the sheer love of it and as a relaxation from their duties in the film-studio orchestras, for which they were conspicuously over-qualified. They have incomparable ensemble and blend; and their impeccable technical address and consummate tonal refinement silence criticism. To add to the pleasure, the transfers could not be better.

Variations for Orchestra, Op 31

Variations for Orchestra. Pelleas und Melisande
Chicago Symphony Orchestra / Pierre Boulez
Erato 2292-45827-2 (62' · DDD)   Ⓕ●●

The two faces of Schoenberg could scarcely be more starkly juxtaposed than they are on this superbly performed and magnificently recorded disc – Boulez and the CSO at their formidable best. *Pelleas und Melisande* can be taken not only as Schoenberg's 'answer' to Debussy's opera (also based on Maeterlinck's play), but as his challenge to Richard Strauss's supremacy as a composer of symphonic poems. It's an intensely symphonic score in Schoenberg's early, late-Romantic vein, with an elaborate single-movement structure and a subtle network of thematic cross-references. Yet none of this is an end in itself, and the music is as gripping and immediate a representation of a tragic love story as anything in the German romantic tradition.

To move from this to the abstraction of the 12-note Variations, Op 31 may threaten extreme anticlimax. Yet from the delicate introduction of the work's shapely theme to the turbulent good humour of the extended finale Schoenberg proves that his new compositional method did not drain his musical language of expressive vitality. The elaborate counterpoint may not make for easy listening, but the combination of exuberance and emotion is irresistible – at least in a performance like this.

String Quartets

No 1 in D minor, Op 7 **No 2** in F sharp minor, Op 10
No 31 Op 30 **No 4** Op 37

String Quartets Nos 1-4
ᵃ**Dawn Upshaw** sop **Arditti Quartet** (Irvine Arditti, David Alberman vns Garth Knox va Rohan de Saram vc)
Auvidis Montaigne ② MO782135 (139' · DDD)   Ⓜ●

These recordings were made in London, in collaboration with the BBC, and the sound is consistently spacious, with a natural clarity and an even balance; the details of Schoenberg's complex counterpoint, as evident in No 1 as in No 4, can be heard with a minimum of stress and strain. Though one occasionally gets the impression that the Arditti is relatively cool in its response to this often fervent music, the mood they create is far from anti-Romantic, and they call on a wide range of dynamics and tone colours. Even if every nuance in Schoenberg's markings isn't followed, this is warmly expressive playing. Dawn Upshaw's contribution to the Second Quartet helps to heighten the drama, although she misses some of that mysterious, ecstatic quality which makes this music so haunting. It's in the Third and Fourth Quartets that the superior sound quality of the Auvidis Montaigne issue pays greatest dividends. Textural clarity is vital here, and although even the Arditti struggles to sustain the necessary lightness in the long second movement of No 4, their wider dynamic range brings you close to the toughly argued, emotionally expansive essence of this music. Yet the performance of No 3 is the finest achievement of the set: clarity of form and emotional conviction combine to create an absorbing account of a modern masterwork. It sets the seal on a most distinguished enterprise.

Choral Works

Friede auf Erden, Op 13. Kol nidre, Op 39. Drei Volkslieder, Op 49. Zwei Kanons – Wenn der schwer Gedrückte klagt; O dass der Sinnen doch so viele sind!. Drei Volkslieder (1929) – Es gingen zwei Gespielen gut; Herzlieblich Lieb, durch Scheiden; Schein uns, du liebe Sonne. Vier Stücke, Op 27. Drei Satiren, Op 28. Sechs Stücke, Op 35. Dreimal tausen Jahre, Op 50. De profundis (Psalm 130), Op 50b. Modern Psalm (Der erste Psalm), Op 50c. A Survivor from Warsaw, Op 46
John Shirley-Quirk, Günter Reich narrs **BBC Singers; BBC Chorus and Symphony Orchestra; London Sinfonietta / Pierre Boulez**
Sony Classical ② SM2K44571 (105' · DDD/ADD · T/t)
Recorded 1976-86　　　　　　　　　　　　Ⓑ〇

This two-disc compilation of choral works includes performances recorded on three separate occasions in 1982, 1984 and 1986, as well as transferring the 1976 recording of *A Survivor from Warsaw*, originally coupled on LP with three purely orchestral works. There's no lack of interpretative consistency in what we hear, however. By 1976 Boulez was a seasoned Wagner conductor, and while it may be simplistic to ascribe the weightiness and spaciousness of these Schoenberg performances to his experiences at Bayreuth, the generally recessed sound perspective strongly suggests a desire to turn the BBC's Maida Vale studios into a much larger and more resonant hall. This distancing is especially evident in John Shirley-Quirk's declamation of the text of *Kol nidre*, one of Schoenberg's later and more substantial sacred compositions. Once you adjust to the balance, the performance itself has an appropriately fervent atmosphere, as do the accounts of the other works involving narrator, chorus and orchestra, the unfinished *Modern Psalm* and *A Survivor from Warsaw*. Both are characteristically intense and exultant, the *Psalm* with some particularly telling orchestral interjections, *A Survivor from Warsaw* with its climactic choral hymn (sung in Hebrew, though the booklet fails to provide transliterations of the Hebrew text both for this and for Psalm 130). Günter Reich's memorably dramatic (but not melodramatic) narration in *A Survivor from Warsaw* benefits from his relatively forward placing.

Most of the music on the discs is for chamber choir, usually unaccompanied. Boulez's expressiveness tends to be fairly generalised, creating and sustaining an overall mood rather than responding to every nuance of the text. The BBC Singers are technically excellent, but the recording magnifies the collective vibrato, the tonal fruitiness which can blur textural definition, especially in the close-knit part-writing of the six pieces for male choir, Op 35. Where the late-Romantic sheen Boulez casts over Schoenberg's harmony works best is in such beautifully turned exercises in nostalgia as the German folk-song arrangements, especially the ravishingly beautiful 'Schein uns, du liebe Sonne'. Fortunately the singers find the necessary incisiveness for the Opp-27 and 28 collections, even if a drier acoustic might have helped to clarify the convoluted lines of the problematic Op 27 No 4, 'Der Wunsch der Liebhabers'. A firm recommendation.

Gurrelieder

Gurrelieder
Karita Mattila sop **Anne Sofie von Otter** mez **Thomas Moser** ten **Philip Langridge** ten **Thomas Quasthoff** bass-bar **Berlin Radio Chorus; MDR Radio Chorus, Leipzig; Ernst Senff Choir; Berlin Philharmonic Orchestra / Sir Simon Rattle**
EMI ② 557303-2 (110' · DDD · T/t)　　Ⓕ〇〇〇〇▷

 Apparently Rattle told the Berlin Philharmonic to play *Gurrelieder* 'as though it were *Daphnis et Chloé*', which sounds crazy until you listen to the result: indeed, the sonorities do rather often sound subtly and delicately French. It also seems obvious from this performance that he means it when he says that *Gurrelieder* is 'the world's largest string quartet'. It's only rarely that the full resources of Schoenberg's gargantuan orchestra are called for (all the more satisfyingly vast when they are). This has an effect on the soloists: none is required to force. Karita Mattila gains from this intimate approach, floating over exquisite orchestral textures in her first song and touching the second very lightly, though in the fourth she can manage both a splendid opening out and an ethereal close. Anne Sofie von Otter has a brighter voice than many exponents of the Wood Dove, better at quieter expressiveness than the wild, gutturally expressed grief of Brigitte Fassbaender, still unrivalled in this role in Riccardo Chailly's recording. Langridge is vividly characterful as Klaus-Narr, Thomas Quasthoff a fine Peasant and a vehement Speaker. The choral singing is first class, the orchestral playing superfine and the recording – a mixture of live and studio performances – both detailed and spacious. There are several fine accounts of *Gurrelieder* in the current catalogue, of which Chailly's has for a long while been a favourite; his soloists are at least as fine as Rattle's, but Rattle's control of *rubato*, his readiness to adopt more relaxed tempos and to allow silences to register are all tangible advantages. He now replaces Chailly at the head of the list.

Gurrelieder
Susan Dunn sop **Brigitte Fassbaender** mez **Siegfried Jerusalem, Peter Haage** tens **Hermann Becht** bass **Hans Hotter** narr **St Hedwig's Cathedral Choir, Berlin; Dusseldorf Musikverin Chorus; Berlin Radio Symphony Orchestra / Riccardo Chailly**
Decca ② 473 728-2DF2 (101' · DDD · T/t)　　Ⓜ〇▷

This vast cantata, a direct descendant of Wagnerian music-drama, was for the turn-of-the-century musical scene the ultimate gorgeous sunset. Schoenberg's forces are, to put it mildly, extravagant. As well as the six soloists and two choruses, the orchestra sports such luxuries as four piccolos, ten horns and a percussion battery that includes iron chains; and so complex are some of the textures that, to achieve a satisfactory balance, a near miracle is required of conductor and recording engineers. Decca has never been mean with miracles where large-scale forces are concerned and this set is no exception.

Chailly gives us a superbly theatrical presentation of the score. The casting of the soloists is near ideal. Susan Dunn's Tove has youth, freshness and purity on her side. So exquisitely does she float her lines that you readily sympathise with King Waldemar's rage at her demise. Siegfried Jerusalem has the occasional rough moment, but few previous Waldemars on disc have possessed his heroic ringing tones and range of expression. And Decca makes sure that its trump card, the inimitable Hans Hotter as the speaker in 'The wild hunt of the summer wind', is so tangibly projected that we miss not one vowel or consonant of his increasing animation and excitement at that final approaching sunrise.

Gurrelieder
Melanie Diener *sop* **Jennifer Lane** *mez* **Stephen O'Mara, Martyn Hill** *tens* **David Wilson-Johnson** *bass* **Ernst Haefliger** *spkr* **Simon Joly Chorale; Philharmonia Orchestra / Robert Craft**
Naxos ② 8 557518/9 (118' · DDD · N)　　Ⓢ**Ⓞ**➛

On the evidence of this superb performance we've quite clearly been underestimating Robert Craft. Precision and finely moulded detail are evident throughout, at least as clearly as in Chailly's and Rattle's accounts, but in Craft's case one is no less often aware of sumptuous richness, passionate eloquence and satisfying orchestral weight. He's also more prepared than rivals to adopt broad tempos and expressive *rubato*. Despite a few tiny reservations it a more thrilling account than either of the rivals mentioned above, and carries something of the excitement of a live performance.

Stephen O'Mara has the sort of voice you associate with Wagner's Siegmund, but with a fine sense of line and sufficient variety of dynamic to open out stirringly at climaxes. There have been more expressive Toves than Melanie Diener, but not many who are so firm-voiced and steady. Jennifer Lane is an excellent Wood Dove, dramatic and expressive, David Wilson-Johnson a grippingly vehement Peasant, while anyone who thinks of Martyn Hill as a typically understating English tenor will be astonished by his Klaus-Narr, which is vividly acted and firm of voice. In his 83rd year Ernst Haefliger is an extraordinarily lively, urgent Speaker. The chorus are inspiritingly full-voiced, singing out like heroes.

Yet most of the memorable moments of this performance are Craft's and the Philharmonia's: the wonderfully glittering chamber textures of the penultimate scene, the passion and savagery of the orchestral interlude that heralds the death of Tove, the tumultuous power of the 'wild hunt'. *Gurrelieder* has been exceptionally fortunate on disc in recent years, but this recording (whose sound is often magnificently full and spacious) need fear none of its rivals.

Pierrot lunaire

Pierrot lunaire, Op 21. Herzgewächse, Op 20. Ode to Napoleon, Op 41
Christine Schäfer *sop* **David Pittman-Jennings** *narr* **Ensemble InterContemporain / Pierre Boulez**
DG 457 630-2GH (53' · DDD · T/t)　　Ⓕ**Ⓞ**➛

Pierre Boulez's third recording of *Pierrot lunaire* is an intense yet intimate reading, in a recording that's positively anti-resonant, and which veers, like the music itself, between harshness and reticence. Boulez's second recording (for Sony Classical), with Yvonne Minton, has long been notorious as the 'sung' *Pierrot*, flouting the composer's specific instructions about recitation. This time Christine Schäfer is more speech-orientated, the few fully sung notes perfectly pitched, and although slidings-away from sustained sounds are on the whole avoided, the effect is superbly dramatic in the work's more expressionistic movements. The work's strange world, half-way between cabaret and concert hall, is admirably caught.

In the *Ode to Napoleon* David Pittman-Jennings has a heavy voice, but he skilfully inflects the sketchily notated dynamics of the vocal part, and the instrumental backing is forceful and well nuanced. The sound may be clinically dry, but this is scarcely a serious drawback when the performance has such expressive immediacy. The disc is completed by the brief, exotic Maeterlinck setting from 1911, whose hugely demanding vocal line deters all but the hardiest. Christine Schäfer copes, while the accompaniment for celesta, harmonium and harp weaves its usual spell. A thoroughly memorable disc.

Songs

2 Balladen, Op 12 – Jane Grey[a]; Der verlorene Haufen[b]. Das Buch der hängenden Gärten, Op 15[a]. Lieder, Op 1 – Dank[b]. Lieder, Op 2[a]. Lieder, Op 3 – Die Aufgeregten[b]; Warnung[b]; Geübtes Herz[b]. Lieder, Op 6 – Lockung[a]; Traumleben[b]
[a]**Sarah Connolly** *mez* [b]**Roderick Williams** *bar* **Iain Burnside** *pf*
Black Box BBM1072 (65' · DDD · T/t)　　Ⓕ**ⓄⓄ**

These performances were originally recorded for BBC Radio 3's regular and imaginative series, *Voices*. Roderick Williams's fine-grained baritone copes well with some of the bigger utterances here; only in the huge and awkward intervals of 'Traumleben' is there any hint of strain, and both baritone and pianist find real power and drama in 'Der verlorene Haufen' and in that quite repulsive (but fascinating) song 'Warnung'. The splendid, Brahmsian (but then distinctly Wagnerian) 'Dank' opens the recital most inspiritingly.

The amount of work that Burnside and Sarah Connolly put into preparing *Das Buch der hängenden Gärten* is obvious throughout, in subtle phrasing and colouring, intimacy of expression and scrupulous attention to Stefan George's often obscure and feverish words. A very fine reading, and Burnside is throughout outstandingly imaginative. All the songs here were recorded in as little as three days, but all three musicians sound as though they had lived with them for months at least. A distinguished and absorbing recital, the recording admirably combining intimacy with space.

Moses und Aron

Moses und Aron

David Pittman-Jennings *narr* Moses **Chris Merritt** *ten* Aron **László Polgár** *bass* Priest **Gabriele Fontana** *sop* Young Girl, First Naked Woman **Yvonne Naef** *mez* Invalid Woman **John Graham Hall** *ten* Young Man, Naked Youth **Per Lindskog** *ten* Youth **Henk de Vries** *bar* Young Man **Siegfried Lorenz** *bar* Another Young Man **Chorus of the Netherlands Opera; Royal Concertgebouw Orchestra / Pierre Boulez**
DG ② 449 174-2GH2 (106' · DDD · T/t)　　Ⓕ**Ⓞ**Ⓓ➔

Moses und Aron is respected rather than loved, with the reputation of being a tough assignment for all concerned. One of the essays in the booklet accompanying this recording calls it a didactic opera. Pierre Boulez, however, is a conductor in whom didacticism is close to a passion, and he's obviously passionate about this opera. We take it for granted that, in any work to which he feels close, every detail will be both accurate and audible. But for Schoenberg *Moses und Aron* was a warning as well as a homily, and as much a confession of faith as either. Boulez, often himself a Moses preaching against anti-modern backsliding, is at one with Schoenberg here.

Some such reason, surely, has led to this being not only a performance of immaculate clarity, but of intense and eloquent beauty and powerful drama too. The recording was made during a run of stage performances, but in the Concertgebouw in Amsterdam, not in the theatre. In the beautiful acoustic of their own hall, the orchestra plays with ample richness and precision, and the sometimes complex textures benefit enormously from a perceptible space around them.

The choral singing matches the orchestral playing in quality: beautiful in tone, eloquently urgent, vividly precise in the difficult spoken passages. The soloists are all admirable, with no weak links. Merritt in particular seems to have all that the hugely taxing role of Aron demands: a fine control of long line, intelligently expressive use of words, where necessary the dangerous demagogue's glamour. Pittman-Jennings is a properly prophetic Moses, grand of voice. This is one of Boulez's finest achievements.

Moses und Aron

Franz Grundheber *bar* Moses **Thomas Moser** *ten* Aron **Ildikó Raimondi** *sop* Young Girl; Naked Woman II **Janina Baechle** *sop* Invalid Woman **Peter Jelosits** *ten* Young Man; Youth **Johann Reinprecht** *ten* Naked Youth **Morten Frank Larsen** *bar* Another Man **Georg Tichy** *bass* Ephraimite **Alexandru Moisiuc** *bass* Priest **Ileana Tonca** *sop* Naked Woman I
Slovak Philharmonic Chorus; Vienna State Opera Chorus; Vienna State Opera Orchestra / Daniele Gatti
Stage director **Reto Nickler**
Video director **Claus Viller**
ArtHaus Musik 📀 101 259 (134' · NTSC · 16:9 · PCM stereo, 5.1 and DTS 5.1 · 0) Recorded live at the Staatsoper, Vienna, in 2006　　　　　　Ⓕ

A student recently asked Milton Babbitt what he made of the plot of *Moses und Aron*. 'Oh I don't know, I'm not really a plot person,' he replied. 'Boy meets Girl, Moses meets Aron...' Of course, there's more than a grain of truth to Babbitt's quip.

The bonus to this appearance of Schoenberg's 'opera fragment' on DVD is a discussion which does not attempt to explain what the piece is 'about' (dread phrase) but throws up some arresting images along the way, not least the suggestion that Moses is a 'Führer des Jüdischen Volks'. It certainly accords with the director Reto Nickler's conception of the work as 'a highly topical psychodrama that represents the thorny path between theory and practice'. Indeed, Schoenberg's absurdly unrealisable stage directions make the last scene of *Les Troyens* pale into insignificance.

Nickler takes an effectively practical tack, abstract but straightforward. Three-dimensional video conjures the miracles of the First Act, staff into serpent and so forth, while in Act 2 it becomes the focus of consumer materialism. Aron dons a natty gold jacket while the chorus wave hankies of the same material, economically symbolising the banality of their demands and theology. The Golden Calf is revealed as a set of letters spelling out ICH BIN GOTT, the counterpart of Moses's tablets of stone.

Such intelligent, dramatic pragmatism lends equal lustre to the musical values. It's good to hear a conductor who is steeped in *verismo* conveying the underestimated sweep of these Biblical declamations, even if it is inevitably at the expense of many of the notes. Both Grundheber and Moser seize every cue for lyrical expression, and the super-size chorus is every bit the collective hero/anti-hero of the piece. The prologue to Act 2 is typically stark and precise, with harsh lighting and tenebrous murk reflecting the sotto voce polyphony of abandonment as the Jewish people sit motionless. Their grim suitcases, their raised clenched fists and mob behaviour, all allude to fresher horrors in Jewish history, until they whip out gold party-frocks and dinner-jackets for the orgy. The Ephraimites become Scaramangas, murdering the true believers to a backdrop of clicking cameraphones and rolling TV coverage – then Z-list celebs totter on as alter egos of the Four Naked Virgins, copulating with the God-letters while Buñuel-esque images of cruelty dominate the giant TV screens. No wonder the Viennese loved it.

ment of the hinterland between art and entertainment where so much American music has been obliged to sit. In Schoenfield's hands, it's art for sure.

Paul Schoenfield   American b1947

Schoenfield studied at Converse College (Spartanburg, South Carolina), Carnegie Mellon University and the University of Arizona. His principal teachers include Ozan Marsh and Rudolf Serkin (piano), and Robert Muczynski (composition). Although he has composed for virtually all media, he has shown a special affinity for solo piano works and chamber music with piano. His brilliant piano writing often requires enormous technical facility on the part of the performer. His interest in folk music stems largely from his desire to explore his own Jewish roots.
GROVEmusic

Piano Concerto, 'Four Parables'

Piano Concerto, 'Four Parables'ᵃ. Cafe Musicᵇ. Four Souvenirsᶜ
ᵇᶜ**James Ehnes** vn ᵇ**Edward Arron** vc **Andrew Russo** pf ᵃ**Prague Philharmonia / JoAnn Falletta**
Black Box BBM1109 (54' · DDD)   Ⓕ

If you turned the radio dials and stumbled across Paul Schoenfield's *Four Parables*, written in 1983, it would be perfectly reasonable to assume the work originated in 1920s New York. Out of a mournful opening, Schoenfield jams his solo pianist into a propulsive Swing Era groove, complete with big-band brass swagger and a drum-kit part that Gene Krupa could have called his own. But listen more carefully and Schoenfield lets slip that he's drawing on a source rather than writing historically authentic music. Chromatic Gershwinisms reach a tipping-point from where they tumble into Thelonious Monk-like clusters. Shaking brass chords leap forward three decades to suggest *West Side Story* or the Dizzy Gillespie big-band. The third-movement 'Elegy' collages gospel tunes and deploys string *glissandi* as a nod towards Charles Ives's activities during the Jazz Age. This is a superior 'genuine fake' – rigorously assembled from its constituent parts and transformed via Schoenfield's idiosyncratic imagination. Andrew Russo's muscular pianism and the Prague Philharmonia's evocative playing help clinch the illusion.

Essentially Schoenfield is building on top of existing structures to reveal simple truths. His *Four Souvenirs* (1989) features archetypal dance forms. A 'Tango' sounds like it's rebounding out of the way-back standard 'Brother, can you spare a dime', while a 'Square Dance' is yee-hah authentic. The piano trio *Café Music* pitches itself between 'high-class dinner music' and 'concert-hall music', a cogent acknowledge-

Franz Schreker   Austrian 1878-1934

Schreker studied with Fuchs at the Vienna Conservatory (1892-1900) and won success with his ballet Der Geburtstag der Infantin (1908) and still more with his opera Der ferne Klang (1912), which established his mastery of a harmonically rich, luxuriantly eventful orchestral style, used to suggest the surreal power of music over the characters. In 1908 he established the Philharmonic Choir, which performed many new works, and in 1912 was invited to teach at the Music Academy in Vienna, from where he moved in 1920 to the directorship of the Berlin Musikhochschule: for the next 10 years his fame was at its peak. Meanwhile the operas Die Gezeichneten (1918) and Der Schatzgräber (1920) had shown a more Wagnerian manner, though he returned to his earlier style, influenced by the more expressionist Strauss, in Irrelohe (1924). Der singende Teufel (1928) and Der Schmied von Gent (1932) are more neo-classical, but continue his abiding concern with the metaphysics of artistic creation (he wrote all his own librettos). Christophorus (1927), unperformed in his lifetime and dedicated to Schoenberg, is the most extraordinary expression of his existential anguish and vision of voluptuousness. His few non-operatic works include a Chamber Symphony (1916) and songs.
GROVEmusic

Overtures and Preludes

Prelude to a Drama. Valse lente. Ekkehard, Op 12. Symphonic Interlude. Nachtstück. Fantastic Overture, Op 15
BBC Philharmonic Orchestra / Vassily Sinaisky
Chandos CHAN9797 (78' · DDD)   ⒻⓄ▸

Sumptuously performed and unflinchingly recorded, this collection will be seized on by Schreker enthusiasts, who will enjoy every massively scored climax, every gorgeously coloured, embroidered and encrusted texture. Those who are only Schreker enthusiasts north-north-west may need to be warned that the climaxes are pretty frequent and that the textures are in constant flux. Listening to this programme uninterrupted is recommended only to addicts; others may wonder whether Schreker isn't repeating himself. All are operatic preludes or entr'actes (from *Die Gezeichneten*, *Der Schatzgräber* and *Der ferne Klang* respectively), and all serve similar functions: to represent in a darkened auditorium erotic acts or emotions that could scarcely be represented on a stage. The *Valse lente* is balletic light music, softly and delicately scored. *Ekkehard* is a tone-poem about a monk who falls in love with a Duchess and goes to war to defend her:

each of these aspects has its own theme, and they're turbulently developed before a peaceful conclusion on Ekkehard's 'monastic' melody over a palpable organ pedal. No programme is stated for the *Fantastic Overture*, but it approaches the three big dramatic pieces in richness. Not many composers demand quite so much of a vast orchestra as Schreker, and Sinaisky and his orchestra amply fulfil those demands.

Der Gerburtstag der Infantin

Der Gerburtstag der Infantin. Die drei Tänze der Zwerges. Die Rose. Der Spiegel. In leichter Bewebung. In wiegender, walzserähn Bewebung. Wie am Anfäng. Valse lente. Festwalzer und Walzerintermezzo. Der Wind. Ein Tanzspiel
Lucerne Symphony Orchestra / John Axelrod
Nimbus NI5753 (71' · DDD)   Ⓕ🅑➔

Bürger Zwei Lieder[a]. Legende. Stille der Nacht.
Krenek Symphony No 1, Op 7 **Schreker** Intermezzo, Scherzo, Op 8
[a]**Dietrich Henschel** bar
Lucerne Symphony Orchestra / John Axelrod
Nimbus NI5808 (72' · DDD) Ⓕ🅑➔

The main work by Franz Schreker on these discs is *The Birthday of the Infanta* (1908), a dance score inspired by an Oscar Wilde novel which later provided the subject for Zemlinsky's engrossing opera *Der Zwerg* ('The Dwarf', 1922). There are only a few anticipations of Schreker's later, hyper-romantic operatic style: most strikingly in a movement called 'The Mirror'. But much of the music here has a lighter touch. *Festwalzer und Walzerintermezzo* is closer to Johann Strauss than to Richard, and the two string pieces on the second disc are accomplished, undemanding trifles. Most characterful is *Der Wind* (1909), a dance score which sounds like music for a silent film, responding with entertaining flexibility to an economical scenario.

The second disc couples Schreker's two string pieces, written in 1900 when he was just 22, with music by two of the many young composers he taught, later on, in Vienna and Berlin. The *Two Songs* (1919) by Julius Bürger have an extravagant Schrekerian opulence in places, and these performances wring every last drop of intensity from their often rather solemn music, Dietrich Henschel coping admirably with Bürger's high-lying phrases. (Nimbus unaccountably fail to provide the texts: a pity, though at least Christopher Hailey's booklet-notes are detailed and informative.)

The main work on the second disc is the very un-Schreker-like Symphony No 1 (1921) by Ernst Krenek. Written when he was 21, it's unashamedly youthful, often sounding like a self-conscious gesture of disrespect to most of what then passed as Germanic tradition. There are signs of the anti-romanticism which was becoming increasingly fashionable, and a wealth

of quirky, brash materials which almost manage to sustain one's interest throughout its not inconsiderable length. On both CDs, the Lucerne Symphony Orchestra perform with energy and spontaneity, and the recordings are particularly effective in revealing the many felicities of Schreker's expert orchestration.

Franz Schubert   Austrian 1797-1828

Schubert, son of a schoolmaster, showed an extraordinary childhood aptitude for music, studying the piano, violin, organ, singing and harmony and, while a chorister in the imperial court chapel, composition with Salieri (1808-13). By 1814 he had produced piano pieces, settings of Schiller and Metastasio, string quartets, his first symphony and a three-act opera. Although family pressure dictated that he teach in his father's school, he continued to compose prolifically; his huge output of 1814-15 includes Gretchen am Spinnrade and Erlkönig (both famous for their text-painting) among numerous songs, besides two more symphonies, three masses and four stage works. From this time he enjoyed the companionship of several friends: frequently gathering for domestic evenings of Schubert's music (later called 'Schubertiads'), this group more than represented the new phenomenon of an educated, musically aware middle class, it gave him an appreciative audience and influential contacts as well as the confidence, in 1818, to break with schoolteaching. More songs poured out, including Der Wanderer and Die Forelle, and instrumental pieces – inventive piano sonatas, some tuneful, Rossinian overtures, the Fifth and Sixth Symphonies – began to show increased harmonic subtlety.

In 1820-21 aristocratic patronage, further introductions and new friendships augured well. Schubert's admirers issued 20 of his songs by private subscription, and he and Schober collaborated on Alfonso und Estrella. Though full of outstanding music, it was rejected. Strained friendships, pressing financial need and serious illness – Schubert almost certainly contracted syphilis in late 1822 – made this a dark period, which however encompassed some remarkable creative work: the epic Wandererfantasie for piano, the passionate, two-movement Eighth Symphony (Unfinished), the exquisite Schöne Müllerin song cycle, Die Verschworenen and the opera Fierabras. In 1824 he turned to instrumental forms, producing the A minor and D minor (Death and the Maiden) string quartets and the lyrically expansive Octet for wind and strings; around this time he at least sketched the Great C major Symphony. With his reputation in Vienna now steadily growing Schubert entered a more assured phase. He wrote mature piano sonatas, notably the one in A minor, some magnificent songs and his last, highly characteristic String Quartet, in G. 1827-8 saw not only the production of Winterreise and two piano trios but a marked increase in press coverage of his music; and he was elected to the Vienna Gesellschaft der Musikfreunde. But though he gave a full-scale public concert in March 1828 and worked diligently to satisfy pub-

lishers – composing some of his greatest music in his last year, despite failing health – appreciation remained limited. At his death, aged 31, he was mourned not only for his achievement but for 'still fairer hopes'. GROVEmusic

Symphonies

No 1 in D, D82; **No 2** in B flat, D125; **No 3** in D, D200; **No 4** in C minor, D417, 'Tragic'; **No 5** in B flat, D485; **No 6** in C, D589; **No 8** in B minor, D759, 'Unfinished'; **No 9** in C, D944, 'Great'

Symphonies Nos 1-6, 8 & 9
Berlin Philharmonic Orchestra / Karl Böhm
DG Collectors Edition ④ 471 307-2GB4 (250' · ADD)
Recorded 1963-71 ⑧

These are marvellous performances: vibrant, clear, characterful and effortlessly well played. The recordings, too, still seem new-minted, even the Ninth, the first of the symphonies to be recorded. The Berliners' art is the art that disguises art. Böhm never feels the need to do anything clever but just quietly sees to it that this superb orchestra plays at its best. Böhm's way with the two late symphonies is, in fact, highly sophisticated. The *Unfinished* begins in what seems to be a leisurely fashion but his performance of the first movement catches Schubert's mix of lyricism and high drama with extraordinary acuity. Conversely, the second movement seems swift but brings the work full circle with an equally extraordinary sense of calm and catharsis in the final pages. The celebrated 1963 Ninth out-Furtwänglers Furtwängler in the myriad means it uses within a single grand design to capture the symphony's sense of danger and derring-do in addition to its lyricism, nobility, and earthy Austrian charm.

In the early symphonies, Böhm's approach is simpler-seeming and more direct. Rhythms are so finely propelled, the pulse so effortlessly sustained, the music always lands on its feet. The zest comes from the stylish Berlin string-playing; melodically, it's the woodwinds (every one a Lieder singer) who catch the beauty of Schubert's melodies and the skirl of the attendant descants. You won't find yourself tiring of Böhm's approach; he doesn't give in to irritating idiosyncrasies (à la Harnoncourt), but ensures that the Schubertian stream is always clear to the eye and sweet to the taste.

Symphonies Nos 1-6, 8 & 9
**Royal Concertgebouw Orchestra /
Nikolaus Harnoncourt**
Teldec ④ 2564-62323-2 (284' · DDD)
Recorded live 1992 ⓂⓄ

Harnoncourt, like Abbado on DG, has examined Schubert's own manuscripts, and corrected many unauthentic amendments that found their way into the printed editions of the symphonies, such

as the eight bars later added to the Fourth Symphony's first movement exposition; but the differences between Harnoncourt's interpretative Schubert and Abbado's are startling. The Ninth's finale, unlike Abbado's, a whirling, spinning *vivace* – is borne aloft on astonishingly precise articulation of its rhythms and accents, and a springy delivery of the triplets. Characteristics one has come to expect from a Harnoncourt performance. Still, what a joy to hear this *Allegro*, and those of most of the earlier symphonies, seized with such bright and light-toned enthusiasm. Here's urgent, virile and vehement playing, never too forceful, overemphatic or burdened with excessive weight. What came as a surprise was the consistent drawing out of these scores' potential for sadness and restlessness. Harnoncourt doesn't set apart the first six symphonies as merely diverting, unlike Abbado: their bittersweet ambiguities and apparent affectations of anxiety here acquire a greater significance, and the cycle, as a whole, a greater continuity.

Up to a point, the darker, more serious Schubert that emerges here, derives from the type of sound Harnoncourt fashions from his orchestra; not least, the lean string tone and incisive brass. And maybe, up to a point, from the corrections: Harnoncourt refers to the manuscripts as often being 'harsher and more abrupt in tone [than the printed editions], juxtaposing extreme dynamic contrasts', though you can't help feeling that contrasts in general have been given a helping hand. Trios are mostly much slower than the urgent minuets/scherzos that frame them (with pauses in between the two). And Schubert's less vigorous moments are very noticeable as such, and are inflected with varying degrees of melancholy. It's uncanny how the string playing, in particular, often suggests a feeling of isolation. The *Unfinished* Symphony's first movement is a stark, harrowing experience (yet it remains a well-tempered musical one: gestures are never exaggerated); the opening is as cold as the grave itself; the second subject knows its song is short-lived. In both movements, the elucidation and balance of texture can only be described as masterly: just listen to the trombones casting shadows in both codas. This, then, is as seriously pondered, coherent and penetrating a view of the complete cycle as we have had. Whether or not you feel Harnoncourt focuses too much on Schubert's darker side, you have to marvel at his ability to realise his vision. The recorded sound offers a blend of the utmost clarity and wide open spaces.

Symphonies Nos 3, 5 & 6 Ⓗ
**Royal Philharmonic Orchestra /
Sir Thomas Beecham**
EMI Great Recordings of the Century 566984-2
(78' · ADD) Recorded 1955-9 Ⓜ❶❷❸❹

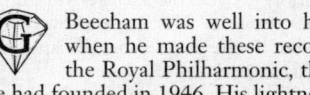 Beecham was well into his seventies when he made these recordings with the Royal Philharmonic, the orchestra he had founded in 1946. His lightness of touch, his delight in the beauty of the sound he was

SCHUBERT SYMPHONY NO 8, 'UNFINISHED' – IN BRIEF

COE / Claudio Abbado
DG 476 2626GRR5   Ⓕ❍❍ᗪ→
Currently only available as part of a conplete Schubert symphony set, Abbado's *Unfinished* combines elegance and energy in equal measure. Stunningly alove playing from the young COE.

Royal Concertgebouw Orchestra / Nikolaus Harnoncourt
Warner Classsics 0927-49813-2   Ⓜ❍ᗪ→
Drawn from his complete symphony cycle, Harnoncourt offers an Unfinished of dark, rich colours. The opening movement is emotionally draining, and everything is donw with immense skill.

Cologne Gürzenich Orchestra / Günter Wand
Testament SBT1364   Ⓕ❍
A master conductor at work early in his career. The sound is good for its age but the performance it contains is touched with greatness. Try and sample first.

Philharmonia Orchestra / Giuseppe Sinopoli
DG 445 514-2GMA   Ⓕ
The recording that put Sinopoli on the musical map. Controversial perhaps, but it's a reading vividly alive to the move from dark to light. The playing of the Philharmonia does him proud.

Hallé Orchestra / Sir John Barbirolli
BBC Legends BBCL4120   Ⓜ
Recorded in the BBC's London studios, Barbirolli's *Unfinished* is a wonderfully humane performance drawing on a lifetime's experience of the work. Good sound.

Vienna PO / Carlos Kleiber
DG 449 745-2GOR   Ⓜ❍ᗪ→
Kleiber's Schubert is not on a level with his Beethoven but is still worth hearing. Taken quite swiftly, this is an *Unfinished* slightly short on poetry but high on drama.

London Classical Players / Sir Roger Norrington
Virgin Classics 562227-2   Ⓜᗪ→
It may not get off to the most auspicious start but once in its stride, Norrington's is a swift, lively affair with an almost jaunty gait. The second movement achieves appealing levels of serenity.

Berlin PO / Karl Böhm
DG 453 664-2GFS   Ⓜᗪ→
Karl Böhm's Schubert is elegant, unforced and beautifully played by a large-sounding Berlin Philharmonic. He doesn't overplay the drama but at the same time he captures the work's darker currents.

summoning, the directness of his approach to melody, and his general high spirits will all dominate our memory of these performances. But listening again, we may be reminded that Beecham could equally well dig deep into the darker moments of these works. Schubert's elation was rarely untroubled and the joy is often compounded by its contrast with pathos – Beecham had that balance off to a tee. It should be noted that he doesn't take all the marked repeats and he doctored some passages he considered over-repetitive. However, these recordings may also serve as a reminder of the wonderful heights of musicianship that his players achieved, as in the trio of the Third.

Symphony No 9, 'Great'
Bamberg Symphony Orchestra / Jonathan Nott
Tudor ⊕ TUDOR7144 (62' · DDD)   Ⓕ❍❍

Relatively unfamiliar conductor, very familiar symphony. But don't let the unfamiliarity of Jonathan Nott allow you to believe that this is yet another version of a much-recorded work. It isn't. On the contrary, Nott offers a performance that hews close to the text (all repeats are also observed) yet is replete with the touches of a thoughtfully considered interpretation. And consideration begins at the beginning: the solo horn theme broadly stated, hairpin accents strong, the tempo picking up almost imperceptibly afterwards but no speeding up to the main *Allegro ma non troppo*, no slowing down for the second subject and no dissipation of tension in the coda. Nott keeps the momentum going to the end.

This literal account may suggest rigidity – which isn't the case. What cannot actually be described is Nott's malleable control of rhythm, the subtle distensions and contractions of phrases, and a feel for orchestral colour and balance that is particularly noticeable in the second movement. The bass here is firmly delineated, wind writing is finely clarified, *fortissimos* don't degenerate into noise. The texture remains clean. Sound and perspective are natural. Though SACD playback could offer improvements in audio quality, it couldn't sharpen Nott's subjective immersion in the many facets of the music, one of which is a lilting impulse that he senses in the finale. Yet the line doesn't go slack. Nott, as always, keeps a tight hold on the reins while expressing his convictions with a conviction that is sure to win you over.

Symphony No 9, 'Great'
Berlin Philharmonic Orchestra / Sir Simon Rattle
EMI 339382-2 (58' · DDD) Recorded live 2005   Ⓕᗪ→

Knowing Sir Simon Rattle has regularly conducted period-instrument orchestras, it may come as a surprise that with his Berlin Philharmonic he takes a relatively free and romantic view of this massive symphony, maybe reflecting that this is a live recording. Not only are his speeds on the broad side, but he allows marked *rallentandi* at the ends of sections, as at the end of the development sections of both the first and last movements.

His moulding of phrases, too, seems to reflect the older traditions of this great orchestra rather than those of Karajan. One key passage comes in the middle of the *Andante con moto* slow movement, where on repeated phrases in *crescendo* Schubert builds up the movement's biggest climax, resolved after a sudden pause on an affectionate cello melody. What emerges from this relatively relaxed approach is an extra sense of joy in Schubert's inspiration, with rhythms lifted infectiously.

Not that Rattle's interpretation lacks bite or precision – quite the opposite: one of its great qualities is the way he brings out the many counter-motifs, notably on cellos or second violins, that in many performances are hidden. That transparency of texture is outstanding: Rattle persuades the orchestra to produce extreme pianissimi, as at the start of the recapitulation in the first movement, where far more than usually one is aware of the score markings.

With full, warm sound, this is a first-rate recommendation. The only slight reservation is that it comes without a coupling, though at 58 minutes for the symphony (even with one of the repeats in the *Scherzo* and that of the exposition in the finale omitted), one cannot really complain of short measure.

Schubert Symphony No 9, 'Great'[cv]   H
Beethoven Fidelio – Overture, Op 72b[a]
Berg Three Scenes from Wozzeck[b]
[b]**Anneliese Kupper** *sop* **Cologne Radio Symphony Orchestra / Erich Kleiber**
Medici Masters mono MM027-2 (76' · ADD)
Recorded live at the Funkhaus, WDR Cologne, on
[bc]November 23, 1953, and [a]January 7, 1956 M

Of various surviving broadcasts featuring Erich Kleiber with the Cologne RSO, the expertly judged Schubert Ninth issued here is perhaps the most distinctive. It's a wonderful performance, one that generously repays repeated listening. Kleiber somehow manages to combine the grandeur and humanity of Furtwängler with the drive of Toscanini, or at least he seems to. Not that this reading is in any way imitative of either maestro, just that its sum effect – acute structure-consciousness, forceful though lyrical projection, well drilled but flexible playing and with key melodies beautifully drawn – is as elevating as anything Furtwängler or Toscanini achieved in this work, at least judging by those performances that have so far come down to us. Even after the passage of over some 55 years Kleiber's performance still sounds remarkably spontaneous.

The buoyant *Fidelio* Overture is taken from a compelling complete broadcast recording of the opera (with Nilsson as Leonore) that is, or has been, available elsewhere; but the most interesting item is the Berg *Wozzeck* sequence, Kleiber having conducted the 1925 premiere of *Wozzeck* at the Berlin Staatsoper – after a total of 137 rehearsals. Kleiber's performance of these 'Three Scenes' is both sensitive to detail, especially in terms of internal balancing, and, from a purely dramatic standpoint, uncompromisingly direct, with Annelies Kupper an emotionally charged Marie. Rarely has there been a *Wozzeck* sequence where the conductor is so entirely under the skin of the music. All in all this is a superb programme with good, well packed mono sound throughout.

Schubert Symphony No 9, 'Great'[c]   H
Cherubini Anacréon – Overture[a]
Cornelius The Barber of Baghdad – Overture[b]
[a]**Royal Philharmonic Orchestra;** [bc]**BBC Symphony Orchestra / Sir Adrian Boult**
BBC Legends/IMG Artists [b]mono BBCL4072-2
(72' · ADD) Recorded live [a]1963; [b]1954, [c]1969   F

Schubert's *Great* C major Symphony was a work close to Boult's heart. He recorded it for the first time in 1934, for the last in 1972, and in between came countless performances. This one was at rather a noisy Prom in 1969, when he returned to the BBC SO from which he had been severed by the mercilessness of BBC bureaucracy.

Among much else, he was a supreme master of the orchestra, attentive to his players without ever losing sight of a work's architecture. In this performance there's his absolute security of tempo, which doesn't mean stiffness. The finale is steady without inflexibility; the *scherzo* drives along brightly; and the *Andante* moves inexorably towards its terrifying climax, with a movingly sad cello aftermath. This is vintage Boult. So, in their own ways, are the two overtures.

Symphony No 10 in D, D936a (realised Newbould).
Symphonic fragments – D, D615; D, D708a (orch Newbould)
Scottish Chamber Orchestra / Sir Charles Mackerras
Hyperion CDA67000 (54' · DDD)   F

Someone will have to find another name for Schubert's *Unfinished* Symphony (the B-minor) before long. In fact there are six unfinished Schubert symphonies: there are two whole movement expositions for D615, torsos of three movements and a nearly complete *Scherzo* for D708a, and enough sketch material for Brian Newbould to attempt a complete conjectural reconstruction of D936a, the symphony Schubert began writing in the last weeks of his life. Inevitably some will ask, why bother? Well, apart from the increase in the sense of wonder at Schubert's sheer productivity, there's some wonderful music here, especially the slow movement of D936a, desolate and warmly consoling by turns. As a whole, D936a suggests that, even at this late stage, Schubert was still thinking in terms of new developments. The concluding third movement, contrapuntally fusing elements of scherzo and finale, is like nothing else in Schubert – or any other

SCHUBERT STRING QUINTET – IN BRIEF

Heinrich Schiff; Hagen Quartet
DG 439 774-2GH (68' ·DDD)　　　Ⓕ**OO**D▸
Coupled with the *Grosse Fuge*, the Hagen Quartet and Heinrich Schiff give a very fine reading, full of detail and sensitivity to texture. It's a performance that maintains a high level of intensity throughout. Very impresive.

Stern; Schneider; Katims; Tortelier; Casals Ⓗ
Sony Classical mono 0746 45899-2 (76' · ADD)
　　　　　　　　　　Ⓜ**OOO**
Ⓖ Recorded in 1952 at Casals' Prades Festival, this is one of the great Schubert Quintets, human, rich, varied and totally spontaneous. The sound is good for the age, but the sheer quality of playing soon sweeps any sonic reservations to one side. (Coupled with Schubert's Fifth Symphony conducted with charm by Casals.)

Douglas Cummings; Lindsay Quartet
ASV CDDCA537 (58' · DDD)　　　　Ⓕ
A fine, natural performance with an appealingly intimate sense of scale. There are some truly heavenly moments in this reading which fills the disc thanks to the first-movement repeat.

Heinrich Schiff; Alban Berg Quartet
EMI 566890-2 (48' · DDD)　　　Ⓜ**OO**D▸
Another recording featuring Heinrich Schiff and something of a modern classic. There is a wonderful ease about the playing that's very appealing. Rather short value though.

Kurt Reher; Hollywood Quartet Ⓗ
Testament mono SBT1031 (73' · ADD)　Ⓕ**O**
A glorious and civilised reading from the 1950s. These musicians really get under the skin of the music and search out its passionate, beating heart. Generously coupled with Schoenberg's *Verklärte Nacht*.

Matt Haimowitz; Miró Quartet
Oxingale OX2006 (79' · DDD)　　　Ⓕ**O**
Coupled with Mendelssohn's last string quartet, this is a very fine modern version from one of the US's most imaginative and charismatic young cellists. Youth certainly does not preclude profundity, and these young musicians deliver a stunning performance.

Villa Musica Ensemble
Naxos 8 550388 (77' · DDD)　　　Ⓜ**O**D▸
A fine, super-budget-price performance coupled with the B flat String Trio that offers some very classy chamber musicianship. Theirs is quite a dramatic reading with plenty of passion.

composer of the classical period. Newbould has had to do some guessing here, but the results are mostly strikingly authoritative. The performances carry conviction and the recordings are atmospheric yet detailed. Altogether a fascinating disc.

Additional recommendation

Complete Symphonies
ASMF / Marriner
Philips Ⓖ 470 886-2PB6 (367' · DDD)　　Ⓑ
　　Marriner's Schubert is light on its feet, full of sprung rhythms and gracefully turned phrases. His set can be confidently recommended if you respond to a more agile, 'modern' (though not authentic) approach.

Complete Symphonies
COE / Abbado
DG Ⓖ 4672626 (334' · DDD)　　　Ⓜ**OO**D▸
　　A radical rethink brings a wonderful freshness to these symphonies with Abbado drawing magical playing from his young COE.

String Quintet in C, D956

Schubert String Quintet
Beethoven Grosse Fuge in B flat, Op 133
Hagen Quartet (Lukas Hagen, Rainer Schmidt *vns* Veronika Hagen *va* Clemens Hagen *vc*) **Heinrich Schiff** *vc*
DG 439 774-2GH (68' · DDD)　　　Ⓕ**OO**D▸

By following Boccherini in using two cellos instead of two violas for his String Quintet, Schubert increased the potential for greater textural contrast. Moreover, the dichotomy between the tragic perspective and Viennese gaiety in the Quintet, so evident in much of Schubert's greatest music, generates an especially potent dramatic force.

The Hagen Quartet's performance of the first movement, which presents remarkably clear textural detail, is broad and expansive. The Hagen include the exposition repeat in a movement that lasts almost 20 minutes. Perhaps as a consequence, they play the *Adagio* second movement at an unusually fast tempo. However, through breathtaking dynamic control in the first section, passionate intensity in the second, and engaging spontaneity of the ornamentation in the final section, the Hagen achieve an expression that's powerfully compelling.

The second half of the Quintet is often treated as a period of emotional relief from the profound concentration of the first two movements. Startlingly, the Hagen maintain the tension with violent textural and dynamic contrast in the *Scherzo*, and distinctively varied registral sonority in the Trio. The finale, in which the Hagen effectively balance the music's charming Hungarian flavour with its more sinister touches, provides an arresting conclusion

The Hagen's account of Beethoven's *Grosse Fuge* is polished and sensitive and it vividly conveys the difference between Beethoven's and Schubert's compositional means. The Hagen's is an outstanding disc, in which exceptional performances, that challenge the finest alternatives, are complemented by superb recording.

String Quintet[a]. Symphony No 5[b]　　　　　　**H**
[a]**Isaac Stern**, [a]**Alexander Schneider** vns [a]**Milton Katims** va [a]**Paul Tortelier** vc [b]**Prades Festival Orchestra / Pablo Casals** [a]vc
Sony Classical Casals Edition mono 0746 45899-2
(76' · ADD) Recorded 1952-3　　　　　　**M〇〇〇**

This should have an in-built fail-safe against hasty consumption, in that their interpretative ingredients are so rich, varied and unpredictable that to experience it all at once is to invite mental and emotional exhaustion. Casals is the lynchpin. A charismatic presence, he embraces everything with the passion of a devoted horticulturist tending his most precious flowers, and that his love extended beyond the realms of music to mankind itself surely enriched his art even further. The most celebrated Prades recording ever is still the Stern/Casals/Tortelier reading of the C major Quintet, a masterful traversal graced with elastic tempos, songful phrasing, appropriate rhetorical emphases (especially in the first and second movements) and fabulous string playing. The coupling is a 'first release' of Schubert's Fifth Symphony, recorded in 1953 – a warm, keenly inflected performance, jaunty in the outer movements and with an adoring, broadly paced *Adagio*. One presumes that it has been held from previous view only because of a few minor executant mishaps. It's certainly well worth hearing. The transfer of the Quintet reveals itself as marginally warmer but occasionally less well-focused than previous incarnations. Still, the original was no sonic blockbuster to start with but this shouldn't deter you from hearing this disc.

Additional recommendations

Alban Berg Quartet with **Heinrich Schiff** vc
EMI Great Recordings of the Century 566890-2
(48' · ADD)　　　　　　**M〇〇〇**
A classic recording that still takes some beating. The music floats effortlessly in the outside sections, and the effect is mesmeric, and in the finale the players find just the right combination of understatement and swagger.

Coupled with: Schoenberg Verklärte Nacht, Op 4　**H**
(orig version) **Hollywood Quartet** (Felix Slatkin, Paul Shure vns Paul Robyn va Eleanor Aller vc) **Alvin Dinkin** va **Kurt Reher** vc
Testament mono SBT1031 (73' · ADD)　　　　**F**
In the 1950s the authors of *The Record Guide* spoke of the Schubert as 'one of the best [LPs] in the discography of chamber music'; and so it remains. The Schoenberg, too, is superb.

Piano Quintet in A, 'Trout', D667

Piano Quintet in A, 'Trout', D667[a].
String Trios – B flat, D581; B flat, D111a
Members of the **Leipzig Quartet** (Andreas Seidel vn Ivo Bauer va Matthias Moosdorf vc) [a]**Christian Zacharias** pf [a]**Christian Ockert** db
Dabringhaus und Grimm MDG307 0625-2
(66' · DDD)　　　　　　**F〇〇**

This *Trout* must surely be one of the very best versions of this much-recorded work – the sound is wonderfully natural, and so is the performance. You get the impression that here was an occasion when everything 'clicked', giving the playing a friendly, relaxed feeling that's just right for this carefree piece. Zacharias has the knack of making even the simplest phrase sound expressive, and the strings, without any exaggeration, produce the most beautiful tonal shadings. All five players, too, have an impressive sense of line; the phrasing and points of emphasis are balanced so that Schubert's expansive designs are projected compellingly. If the *Trout* shows a Schubertian spaciousness, his one completed String Trio is unusually compact. Another distinguished feature is the florid, Spohr-like elegance of much of the violin writing – Andreas Seidel is splendidly stylish and confident. This is another very fine performance, emphasising the predominating gentle lyricism, but with plenty of vigour and panache when required. The String Trio fragment, less than two minutes, continues the same, 'let's hear everything' approach; it's a sketch for what subsequently became the comparatively familiar B flat Quartet, D112.

Schubert Piano Quintet in A, 'Trout'[a]
Mozart Piano Quartet in G minor, K478
Thomas Zehetmair vn **Tabea Zimmermann** va
Richard Duven vc [a]**Peter Riegelbauer** db
Alfred Brendel pf
Philips 446 001-2PH (75' · DDD)　　　　　　**F〇〇D**

Brendel is the lynchpin here, and, as ever, balances heart and mind with innate good taste. Time and again you find yourself overhearing detail that might otherwise have passed for nothing: every modulation tells; every phrase of dialogue has been polished, pondered and carefully considered. And yet it *is* a dialogue, with the loose-limbed Thomas Zehetmair leading his supremely accomplished colleagues through Schubert's delightful five-tier structure. The *Scherzo* and *Allegro giusto* frolic within the bounds of propriety (some will favour an extra shot of animal vigour), whereas the first, second and fourth movements are rich in subtle – as opposed to fussy – observations. The recording, too, is exceedingly warm, with only the occasional want of inner detail to bar unqualified enthusiasm. Philips, as ever, achieves a well-rounded, almost tangible piano tone.

SCHUBERT PIANO QUINTET, 'TROUT' – IN BRIEF

Christian Zacharias; Leipzig Quartet
Dabringhaus und Grimm MDG307 0625-2
(66' · DDD)   Ⓕ**OO**
Beautiful string tone and glistening piano work are just the surface trappings of a fine, musicianly account of Schubert's evergreen masterpiece, caught in excellent sound.

Capuçon; Caussé; Capuçon; Posch; Braley
Virgin Classics 545563-2 (59' · DDD)   Ⓕ**OOOD**
A joyful, youthful Trout from these superb chamber musicians. There's a delightful sense of interplay as they toss the tunes around. The variations themselves are quite enchanting.

Clifford Curzon; members of the Vienna Octet Ⓗ
Decca 417 59-2DM (71' · ADD)   Ⓜ**O**
Curzon's genial piano playing and the sweet-toned playing of Willi Boskovsky and his colleagues ideally complement each other in this classic recording. The dryish mono sound adds to the intimate charm.

Ax; Frank; Young; Ma; Meyer
Sony Classical 0746 46196-4 (65' · DDD)   Ⓕ
A sprightly yet genial performance, bubbling with energy. Though clearly individual players, they evidently enjoy each other's company and working as a team.

András Schiff; Hagen Quartet
Decca Ovation 458 608-2 (75' · DDD)   Ⓜ
After a tension-filled opening, this proves to be another fresh reading, most delightful in the bouncing lightness of the *scherzo*.

Brendel; Zehetmair; Zimmermann; Duven; Riegelbauer
Philips 446 001-2PH (75' · DDD)   Ⓕ**OOD**
Despite a rather languid start, the performance becomes quite forthright – serious rather than relaxed – yet it's also persuasive and engaging.

Jenö Jandó; Kodaly Quartet; Istvan Toth
Naxos 8 550658 (53' · DDD)   Ⓢ**OD**
Though the sound is not quite in the same class as the full-price versions, with the piano a touch prominent at the expense of the strings, this is a charming performance and excellent value at the price.

Clifford Curzon; Amadeus Quartet; James Edward Merrett
BBC Legends BBCL4009-2 (82' · ADD)   Ⓜ
A joyous live performance which, despite one or two slightly rough spots and a moment of premature applause, rises to truly memorable heights. Coupled with an inspired account of the Brahms Piano Quintet.

Mozart's G minor Quartet makes for an unexpected, though instructive, coupling, following the *Trout*. Here again there's much to learn and enjoy, especially in terms of phrasal dovetailing and elegant articulation (Brendel's opening flourish is a model of Mozartian phrase-shaping). Still, you may sometimes crave rather more in the way of *Sturm und Drang* – a fiercer, more muscular attack, most especially in the first movement. Yet there will be times when the conceptual unity and executive refinement of this performance – its articulate musicality – will more than fit the bill. Both works include their respective first movement repeats.

Piano Quintet in A, 'Trout'ᵃ. Litanei, D343. Variations on 'Trockne Blumen', D802
Renaud Capuçon *vn* ᵃ**Gérard Caussé** *va* ᵃ**Gautier Capuçon** *vc* ᵃ**Alois Posch** *db* **Frank Braley** *pf*
Virgin Classics 545563-2 (59' · DDD)   Ⓕ**OOOD**

Ⓖ A memorable account of the *Trout* Quintet. This group may not project the warmth and bonhomie of the famous Curzon/Boskovsky recording, nor does it have the searching quality of the performance led by Alfred Brendel, but for verve and refinement it's hard to beat. The happy, carefree nature of the music is captured perfectly on a beautifully clear recording; it's especially notable how every detail of the double bass's very spirited contribution, is clearly heard yet with no sense that Alois Posch is 'bringing out' his part. Especially enjoyable is the *Scherzo* – a fast tempo, but finely poised, and with a subtle, effective relaxation of the trio – and the Variations. In Variation 2 Renaud Capuçon's figuration is so delicate that the viola melody can create a particularly strong expressive effect, and the following variation is just as magical – Frank Braley's demisemiquavers are quite brilliant, with a lovely, silvery tone, and the bass melody has, for once, nothing elephantine about it.

The elaborate, showy set of variations on 'Trockne Blumen' from *Die schöne Müllerin*, dating from 1824, is an unhackneyed choice of filler. It's curious that the current catalogue lists only two recordings, and one of these, like the present version, substitutes violin for the original flute. It certainly makes a virtuoso violin and piano piece, and played with the precision and delicacy that Capuçon and Braley bring to it is highly effective, though with only occasional touches of the melancholy we expect in late Schubert. After this extravagant music, the touching simplicity of the song arrangement is the more striking.

Piano Quintet in A, 'Trout'ᵃ. Adagio and Rondo concertante in F, D487
Kodály Quartet (Attila Falvay, Tamás Szabo *vns* Gábor Fias *va* János Devich *vc*) ᵃ**IstvánTóth** *db* **Jenö Jandó** *pf*
Naxos 8 550658 (53' · DDD)   Ⓢ**OD**

This disc is further proof of Naxos's impressive ability to produce outstanding recordings at an astonishingly low price. Jenö Jandó's recording of the Trout Quintet, in a version which is based on the first edition of 1829, is buoyant and vigorous. The string support from members of the Kodály Quartet and István Tóth, despite some rough edges, is generally sonorous and appropriate. Balance is good, with the piano agreeably highlighted. The result is a performance which is a most desirable acquisition. Although Schubert wrote no concertos, he did write a concertante work for piano and strings which is also included here. Notwithstanding limitations of thematic invention, the *Adagio and Rondo* makes an attractive coupling. Jandó's sheer enthusiasm for this music provides a compelling alternative to other full-price accounts.

String Quartets

D18 in B flat; **D32** in C; **D36** in B flat; **D46** in C; **D68** in B flat; **D74** in D; **D87** in E flat; **D94** in D; **D103** in C minor (fragment); **D112** in B flat; **D173** in G minor; **D353** in E; **D703** in C minor (Quartettsatz); **D804** in A minor (Rosamunde); **D810** in D minor (Death and the Maiden); **D887** in G

String Quartets D87, D703 & D804
Belcea Quartet (Corina Belcea, Laura Samuel *vns* Krzysztof Chorzelski *va* Alasdair Tait *vc*)
EMI 557419-2 (73' · DDD)   ℗ⓄⓄⓄ➔

Ⓖ 'Schubert's Quartet has been performed, rather slowly in his opinion, but very purely and tenderly,' wrote Moritz von Schwind on the day D804 was premiered by the Schuppanzigh Quartet. The composer may well have reacted similarly on hearing the Belcea's first movement. It's a spacious tempo, certainly, causing some of the more energetic music – the last four bars for instance – to sound slightly ponderous. But purity and tenderness are certainly in evidence. Internal balance and intonation are exemplary, and in the songful melodic writing that dominates the whole work, Corina Belcea and her colleagues seem to have the knack of shaping each long phrase to perfection, knowing just when to intensify the vibrato or give a note extra emphasis, and when to allow the music to flow effortlessly onwards.

These fine qualities persist throughout. There may be more dramatic accounts of D703, but no other group presents its *cantabile* music in a more affecting way. The lesser work, D87, gets a charming, persuasive interpretation, but the profound and subtle way these young players engage with the later, greater music is the most impressive thing this group has done so far.

String Quartets D703[a], D804[b], D810, 'Death and the Maiden'[a] & D887[b]
Quartetto Italiano (Paolo Borciani, Elisa Pegreffi *vns* Piero Farulli *va* Franco Rossi *vc*)

Philips Duo ② 446 163-2PM2 (142' · ADD) Recorded [a]1965, [b]1976-7   Ⓜ

The Italians' playing has freshness, affection, firm control and above all authority to a degree that no relative newcomer can match. It's notable not only for the highest standards of ensemble, intonation and blend, but also for its imaginative insights; these attributes readily apply to the music-making on this Duo reissue, particularly in the slow movements. Indeed, the players' progress through the wonderful set of variations in the *Andante con moto*, which reveals the *Death and the Maiden* Quartet's association with the famous Schubert song of that name, has unforgettable intensity.

The comparable *Andante* of No 13, with its lovely *Rosamunde* theme – which is approached here in a relaxed, leisurely manner – is held together with a similar (almost imperceptible) sureness of touch. When this work was originally issued, the first-movement exposition repeat was cut in order to get the quartet complete on to a single LP side. Here it has been restored.

Finest of all is the great No 15, a work of epic scale. The first movement alone runs to nearly 23 minutes, and the players' masterly grip over the many incidents that make up the *Allegro molto moderato* is effortless. For an encore we're given No 12, a piece on a smaller scale, but here presented with a comparable hushed intensity of feeling. This, like No 14, was recorded in 1965 and the textures are leaner than on the others, with a fractional edge on *fortissimos*. Nevertheless, the ear soon adjusts when the playing is as remarkable as this. The other recordings have more body, and a fine presence. The CD transfers throughout are excellent.

String Quartets – D804 & D810, 'Death and the Maiden'
Takács Quartet (Edward Dusinberre, Károly Schranz *vns* Geraldine Walther *va* András Fejér *vc*)
Hyperion CDA67585 (69' · DDD)   ⓂⓄⓄⓄ

Ⓖ With their Decca Beethoven cycle, the Takács Quartet set a modern-day benchmark. Now, with a new record company and a replacement viola-player, things look set for them to do the same for Schubert's two most popular string quartets. These works were written in 1824, a year of despondency for Schubert who was ill and clearly felt he was living under the shadow of death. Whereas in the *Rosamunde*, the underlying feeling is a tearful nostalgia, in *Death and the Maiden*, there's a black despair that at times gives way to anger.

The Takács have the ability to make you believe that there's no other possible way the music should go, and the strength to overturn preconceptions that comes only with the greatest performers. Tempi are invariably apt – the opening of the *Rosamunde* is wonderfully judged. They also have a way of revealing detail that you'd never previously noticed – in the *Allegro* of

D810, Schubert's sighing figure in the viola is here poignantly brought out.

But though there's plenty of humanity in these recordings, there's nothing sentimental about the playing; they make Schubert sound symphonic, and a sense of drama and tensile strength underlines everything, even a movement as luscious as the *Andante* of the *Rosamunde* Quartet, which is based on the theme that gives this quartet its name.

The recording captures the quartets vividly and realistically and Misha Donat's notes are erudite and stylish.

Octet in F, D803

Octet
Gaudier Ensemble (Richard Hosford *cl* Robin O'Neill *bn* Jonathan Williams *hn* Marieke Blankestijn, Lesley Hatfield *vns* Iris Juda *va* Christoph Marks *vc* Stephen Williams *db*)
Hyperion CDA67339 (60' · DDD)　　Ⓕ ⦿⦿

An intriguing point arises in the second movement. It's meant to be *Adagio* but the Gaudier pace it fairly swiftly, offering a reminder that one edition marks it *Andante un poco mosso*. The Vienna Octet of 1957 followed this instruction, but its 1990 counterpart preferred something slower. The Gaudier, though, are anything but perfunctory. Their line is curvaceous and malleable with a dynamic range that contains many shades of softness. Engineer Tony Faulkner has helped by using the ambience of the Henry Wood Hall to create both a blend and a distinctiveness of timbre. There's a glow to the sound that other versions don't have.

The Gaudier's control over the grading of tonal intensity draws attention to the many passages in this work that are written *piano* or *pianissimo*; and where leavened by hairpin accents, stabbing *sforzandos* and even *fortissimos* they supply necessary impact without being crude. If there's one movement that encapsulates all that's striking about this performance, then it's the fourth – an *Andante* with seven variations. Here's an example of how these musicians balance themselves, and how they've thought about the different facets of the music. Were he alive today, this recording might even persuade Schubert scholar Maurice JE Brown to change his mind about the seventh variation, which he described as 'a distasteful episode'.

Octet, D803ᵃ. Der Hirt auf dem Felsen, D965ᵇ
ᵇ**Ailish Tynan** *sop* ᵃᵇ**Michael Collins** *cl* ᵃ**Robin O'Neill** *bn* ᵃ**Martin Owen** *hn* ᵃ**Isabelle van Keulen**, ᵃ**Peter Brunt** *vns* ᵃ**Lars Anders Tomter** *va* ᵃ**Daniel Müller-Schott** *vc* ᵃ**Peter Riegelbauer** *db* ᵇ**Malcolm Martineau** *pf*
Wigmore Hall Live WHLIVE0017 (74' · DDD)
Recorded live in 2006　　Ⓕ ⦿⦿➔

A hugely enjoyable account of Schubert's Octet. It is a work lasting an hour, which with its many repeats can easily outstay its welcome despite the freshness of Schubert's invention. But Michael Collins and friends give a performance that is wonderfully resilient and imaginative.

The Octet was commissioned by Count Ferdinand Troyer, steward to the clarinet-playing Archduke Rudolph, and that instrument is most regularly brought to the fore. Michael Collins, the most inspired British clarinettist of his generation, fully brings out the beauty of the writing. Schubert also knew that Ignaz Shuppanzigh, leader of the quartet most closely associated with performing Beethoven's later quartets, was to be the first violin, and he, too, was given the limelight. Isabelle van Keulen is the excellent first violin. Others in the brilliant team include the Norwegian viola-player Lars Tomter, double bass-player Peter Riegelbauer of the Berlin Philharmonic, and Robin O'Neill, first bassoon in the Philharmonia.

It would be hard to devise a more distinguished group, and that is reflected in the freshness of the playing. The *Scherzo* third movement is wonderfully bouncy and the following Minuet elegant in its phrasing, with a fine spring in the rhythm and nice interplay between clarinet and violin. The finale swaggers along infectiously. In the lovely song with clarinet obbligato, *Der Hirt auf dem Felsen*, Malcolm Martineau is the sensitive pianist accompanying the bright, fresh soprano of Ailish Tynan. The sense of a live performance in both Octet and song is beautifully caught.

Octet
Mullova Ensemble (Pascal Moraguès *cl* Marco Postinghel *bn* Guido Corti *hn* Viktoria Mullova, Adrian Chamorro *vns* Erich Krüger *va* Manuel Fischer-Dieskau *vc* Klaus Stall *db*)
Onyx ONYX4006 (64' · DDD)　　Ⓕ➔

A spacious performance, enthralling and poetic: it leaves behind the world of happy Viennese music-making. Instead, we have a view of the Octet as one of Schubert's major achievments, sharing much common ground with the other great chamber works of 1824, the A minor and D minor string quartets.

The *Adagio* is taken unusually slowly, but without any feeling of the rhythm sagging – the effect is unexpectedly profound and meditative. The following *Scherzo* is unhurried, too, yet is still full of spirit; it's beautifully poised, with each phrase convincingly shaped. There's only one movement, the Minuet, where the measured approach is maybe overdone; it's marked *Allegretto*, after all, and here the effect is distinctly languid. However, the romantic feeling of the first movement's introductory *Adagio* is perfectly captured, and the corresponding slow introduction to the finale, whose melodrama can sometimes sound like a tongue-in cheek shock tactic, emerges here as one extreme of a multi-faceted yet perfectly unified work.

And the thoughtful shaping of phrases isn't confined to the *Scherzo*; it's present throughout, keeping us constantly aware of the music's expressive power. Even when these inflections seem slightly contentious – in the finale's main theme, for example – they contribute to a constant feeling of lively communication.

Piano Trios

Piano Trios[a] – B flat, D28 (Sonata in one movement); B flat, D898; E flat, D929. Notturno in E flat, D897[b]. String Trios[b] – B flat, D471; B flat, D581
[a]**Beaux Arts Trio** (Menahem Pressler pf Daniel Guilet vn Bernard Greenhouse vc); [b]**Grumiaux Trio** (Arthur Grumiaux vn Georges Janzer va Eva Czako vc)
Philips Duo ② 438 700-2PM2 (127' · ADD) Recorded 1966-9   Ⓜ**Ⓞ**

These performances are polished, yet the many solo contributions from each of the players emerge with a strong personality. The Beaux Arts cellist brings lovely phrasing and a true simplicity of line, so right for Schubert—memorably in the lovely slow movement melody of the Trio No 2 in E flat. In addition to the great piano trios (B flat, D898 and E flat, D929) the set includes the extremely personable, very early Sonata in B flat, D28, where the lyrical line already has the unmistakable character of its young composer.

Also included is the *Notturno*, D897, a raptly emotive short piece played here with a remarkable depth of feeling that recalls the gentle intensity of the glorious slow movement of the String Quintet. The recording is naturally balanced, although a little dry in the treble. Of the two rarer string trios, also early works, the four-movement Trio, D581, is totally infectious, with that quality of innocence that makes Schubert's music stand apart. Such persuasive advocacy and vivid recording can't fail to give the listener great pleasure.

Piano Trio in E flat, D929
Florestan Trio (Anthony Marwood vn Richard Lester vc Susan Tomes pf)
Hyperion CDA67347 (58' · DDD)   Ⓕ**ⓞⓞ**

This profound, yet still often light-hearted, E flat Trio was written in the same month (November) that Schubert completed *Winterreise*. We are instantly reminded of this in the Florestan's eloquent and aptly paced account of the C minor *Andante con moto*, with what Richard Wigmore describes as its 'stoical trudging gait'. Its essential melancholy is gently caught, first by the cellist, Richard Lester, and then equally touchingly by the pianist, Susan Tomes. The dramatically rhythmic opening of the first movement could almost be by Beethoven, but once again these players show themselves to be completely within the Schubertian sensibility and catch perfectly the atmosphere of the more important lyrical motif, first heard on the cello (in bars 15 and 16), which is to dominate the movement alongside the engaging repeated-note figure (so delicately articulated by the piano).

They set a winningly jaunty mood for the finale, which is maintained whenever the main theme reappears, even though, as always with late Schubert, much happens to vary the music's mood and atmosphere. Another superb performance then from the Florestans, penetrating, yet full of spirited spontaneity, and in spite of the moments of sadness, much Schubertian bonhomie. The recording is completely lifelike and very well balanced.

Piano Trios – Sonatensatz, D28; E flat, D929
Kungsbacka Trio (Malin Broman vn Jesper Svedberg vc Simon Crawford Phillips pf)
Naxos 8 555700 (61' · DDD)   Ⓢ**Ⓞ**▶

The opening to this trio appears to take up the gauntlet thrown down by Beethoven's mature piano trios – but how very different a path Schubert takes. It's easy to sound strenuous at the beginning of this movement but it's not a mistake the Kungsbacka Trio make, sounding strong yet never belligerent, and finding almost as many colours as the miraculous Florestan recording (see above). What is particularly impressive is their confidence and sweep: more extrovert than the soul-searching Florestan Trio, they relish the outgoing E flat major (surely Schubert was inspired by the fact that for Beethoven this was the ultimate heroic key). For the second movement, the Kungsbacka choose their trudging tempo carefully, vividly reminding us that this work dates from the same year as *Winterreise*. The remaining movements are similarly impressive: the Minuet/Scherzo hybrid, a tail-chasing canon, is great fun, the Trio stomping but never coarse. Unusually, the Kungsbacka choose the composer's uncut original finale (also offered by the Florestan Trio, as an additional track alongside the shorter version). It's one of those extraordinary Schubert movements that starts unassumingly and yet stretches out to the horizon, seemingly unstoppable. In the hands of the Kungsbacka, there are no longueurs.

The Kungsbacka fill out their disc with the early Sonatensatz, D28, a delightful little *petit four* to complete the feast, elegantly played. This is certainly impressive playing, and a bargain at the price.

Arpeggione Sonata

Schubert Arpeggione Sonata, D821 **Schumann** Adagio and Allegro, Op 70. Drei Fantasiestücke, Op 73. Fünf Stücke im Volkston, Op 102. Märchenbilder, Op 113
Antonio Meneses vc **Gérard Wyss** pf
Avie AV2112 (78' · DDD)   Ⓕ**Ⓟ**▶

Meneses negotiates the *Arpeggione* Sonata's dauntingly high tessitura with no sense of strain, and the other Schumann sets, designed respectively for horn, clarinet and viola, sound like idiomatic cello music. He's a true virtuoso, as the fast passages in the *Arpeggione* and the third of the *Märchenbilder* amply demonstrate, but one never feels that he's presenting himself. The impression is rather that he's inviting us into Schumann's or Schubert's inner world, urbanely drawing attention, by means of subtle emphasis or change of colour, to all the music's incidental beauties.

Gérard Wyss, as an experienced Lieder accompanist, has a similar eye for illustrative detail; his touch is unusually sensitive, with chords always beautifully balanced, and his left hand gives exceptional vitality to the bass-lines. The finale's minor-key episode in Hungarian style bubbles with vitality. Similarly, all the Schumann pieces are performed in an outgoing, friendly way; especially enjoyable is the first of the *Stücke im Volkston*, progressing from a light, playful start to sweeping romantic gestures, and the last of the *Märchenbilder*, sweet and tender, with an almost Mahlerian sense of regret and loss.

Violin and piano works

Violin Sonata, D574. Fantasie, D934.
Rondo brillant, D895
Isabelle Faust *vn* **Alexander Melnikov** *pf*
Harmonia Mundi HMC90 1870 (58' · DDD)   Ⓕ

In nearly every respect this is outstanding. The *Rondo* and the *Fantasie*, both written for the virtuoso duo of Karl von Bocklet and Josef Slawik, can sound as if Schubert were striving for a brilliant, flashy style, foreign to his nature. Both are in places uncomfortable to play (when first published, the *Fantasie*'s violin part was simplified), but you would never guess this from Faust's and Melnikov's performance; they both nonchalantly toss off any problem passages as though child's play.

The *Fantasie*'s finale and the *Rondo* are irresistibly lively and spirited, and this duo's technical finesse extends to more poetic episodes – Melnikov's *tremolo* at the start of the *Fantasie* shimmers delicately, while the filigree passagework in the last of the variations that form the *Fantasie*'s centrepiece have a delightful poise and sense of ease.

The Sonata's more intimate style is captured just as convincingly; in all three performances Faust and Melnikov observe Schubert's often very detailed, careful expression marks, not as a matter of duty, but as a stimulus to the imagination, as a way of entering more deeply into the music.

The one slight reservation concerns Isabelle Faust's manner of expression. She makes the most of any passionate phrases and is equally convincing at cool, mysterious or dreamlike moments. But the lyrical phrases in the *Rondo*'s introduction surely demand a more heartfelt utterance. In the Sonata, too, there are places where one longs for more warmth. This quibble aside, it's a lovely disc, one to listen to over and over again.

Works for Piano Duet

Allegro, 'Lebensstürme', D947. Divertissement à la hongroise, D818. Divertissement, D823. Fantasie,

D940. German Dance with Two Trios and Two Ländler, D618. Grande marche funèbre, D859. Grande marche héroïque, D885. Vier Ländler, D814. Two Marches caractéristiques, D968b. Six Grandes marches, D819. Trois Marches héroïques, D602. Trois Marches militaires, D733. Rondo, D951. Piano Sonata, 'Grand Duo', D812. March, D928
Christoph Eschenbach, Justus Frantz *pf*
Brilliant Classics ④ 92858 (4h 31' · ADD)
From HMV originals, recorded 1978-79   Ⓢ

Throughout his life Schubert was drawn to the piano duet more than any other great composer, partly for practical reasons (there was an insatiable demand for four-hand music in Biedermeier Vienna), partly because he evidently relished the rich, quasi-orchestral sonorities that two players could conjure from one keyboard. In the late 1970s Christoph Eschenbach and Justus Frantz recorded around half of Schubert's four-hand output. Their performances were always unsurpassed for refinement of touch and hyper-sensitive balancing of voices. Reincarnated in a slimline four-CD set they make a terrific bargain.

Even they cannot do much for dull utility pieces like the three *Marches héroïques*. But with playing that mingles fire, grace and a vast range of colour and dynamics (finely caught by the engineers), they rekindle the appetite for the *Marches militaires*, so much more appealing as piano duets than in their more familiar brash orchestral guise. The magnificent *Grand Duo* is dangerously leisurely and flexible in its opening movement. Both rival performances listed strike a better balance between epic sweep and ravishing detail and give the *Scherzo* more of Schubert's prescribed *vivace* – though Eschenbach and Frantz yield to no one in pace and temperament in the Hungarian-tinged finale.

Among the other masterpieces, the A minor *Lebensstürme* receives a thrilling, richly imagined performance, with *pp* and *ppp* playing of ethereal tenderness, while the F minor Fantasie has drama, colour and intense, aching *cantabile*, and surpasses rivals in the *élan* and *delicatezza* of the *Scherzo*. A spellbinding performance, crowning a feast of memorable Schubert playing from one of the great duo partnerships.

Sonata for Piano Duet, 'Grand Duo', D812. Allegro, 'Lebensstürme', D947. Fantasie, D940. Marche militaire, D733 No 1. Marche caractéristique, D968b No 1
Evgeny Kissin, James Levine *pfs*
RCA Red Seal ② 82876 69283-2 (85' · DDD)
Recorded live in 2005   ⓂⓄⓄ▷

On paper it seems an unlikely pairing. On disc, however, it is something of a triumph, a recording that is far more than a mere *souvenir d'occasion* of a memorable night in Carnegie Hall. Intriguingly, it is difficult to detect purely aurally which is the world-famous pianist and which the world-famous conductor. From his familiar sometimes over-insistent tone, we guess it is

Kissin who takes the *primo* part in the F minor *Fantasie* (he plays to the back of the hall, not to the microphone) but elsewhere it is impossible to tell them apart, so well do they blend dynamics, phrasing and ensemble. This is even more remarkable given that the music, written for four hands at one piano, is played on two (beautifully balanced) Hamburg Steinways – less of a squeeze on the piano stool but trickier to coordinate.

The *Fantasie* is the least successful item. Its dramatic elements are energetically characterised but its introspective, questioning discourse goes by the board, leaving the emotions untouched. *Lebensstürme* ('Storms of Life'), written a month after the *Fantasie*, is given a terrific whirlwind of a performance and completes the first short disc (34'05").

The second half features the *Grand Duo* (40'49"), a symphony for piano in all but name. Here Kissin and Levine come into their own with a fiercely argued, compelling account some way removed from the intimacy of a Schubertiad, and the best reason for buying this release. They close with two fast and furious crowd-pleasers bringing as much pleasure to the audience as they so obviously do to the players.

Piano Sonatas

D157 in E; **D279** in C; **D459** in E; **D537** in A minor; **D557** in A flat; **D566** in E minor; **D568** in E flat; **D571** in F sharp minor; **D575** in B; **D613** in C; **D625** in F minor; **D664** in A; **D784** in A minor; **D840** in C (Relique); **D845** in A minor; **D850** in D; **D894** in G; **D958** in C minor; **D959** in A; **D960** in B flat

Piano Sonatas – A minor, D537; E flat, D568; B, D575; A, D664; A minor, D784; C, D840; A minor, D845; D, D850; G, D894; C minor, D958; A, D959; B flat, D960. Moments musicaux, D780. German Dances, D790 & D820. Klavierstücke, D946. Impromptus, D899 & D935.
Mitsuko Uchida *pf*
Philips 475 628-2PB8 (476' · DDD)　　　Ⓜ❍❍🅑➤

While the deletions axe may have removed individual volumes in Uchida's cycle, this collection, competitively priced, is a highly tempting proposition. This is a set that celebrates the music first and foremost: her Schubert is never less than wonderfully finished in pianistic terms. With her exceptional finger technique Uchida takes everything in her stride, yet she never allows physical excitement to become the be-all-and-end-all. She is also extremely good at exposing the light-filled dream world that Schubert so often inhabits as well as guiding us into stark waking reality. The sound throughout the set is very fine indeed.

Piano Sonatas – E, D157; G, D894. Die schöne Müllerin – Der Müller und der Bach (arr Liszt, S565)
Arcadi Volodos *pf*
Sony Classical SK89647 (64' · DDD)　　　Ⓕ❍

Here is irrefutable proof of Arcadi Volodos's genius and versatility. Naturally, lovers of long-cherished recordings by Schubertians of the stature of Schnabel, Kempff, Pollini and Brendel will hesitate, equating Volodos's sheen and perfection with an external glory rather than an interior poetic truth. But such witnesses for the prosecution will find themselves silenced by an empathy with Schubert's spirit so total that it would be extraordinary in a pianist of any age, let alone one still in his twenties.

The jubilant burst of scales and arpeggios that launch the E major Sonata, D157, are given with a deftness and unforced eloquence that are pure Volodos, while the *Andante*'s sighing chromaticism and surprise modulations have a tonal translucence that will make lesser mortals weep with envy. But it's in the G major Sonata, D894, that epitome of Schubertian lyricism, that Volodos erases all possible doubts. His opening has an unforgettable stillness and mystery, his velvet-tipped sonority and seamless *legato* a reminder that Schubert's vocal and instrumental inspiration were for the most part one and the same. For Volodos and for his listeners this is a true dance of the gods. The recordings are as flawless as the playing.

Piano Sonatas – E, D157; A flat, D557; F minor, D664; A minor, D784; A minor, D845; G, D894; C minor, D958; A, D959; B flat, D960. Scherzos, D593. Moments musicaux, D780.
Radu Lupu *pf*
Decca ④ 475 7074DC4 (289' · DDD/ADD)　　Ⓜ❍❍

'A lyricist in a thousand', Lupu has, naturally, placed Schubert at the centre of his repertoire and conjured from a seemingly recalcitrant black-and-white instrument a range of vocal colours and nuances that even a Souzay or Fischer-Dieskau might envy. Heard at his greatest in the sombre A minor Sonata, D845, he recreates a place where even the most outwardly genial phrase is troubled and despairing. Then turn to the A major Sonata's finale (D664) and you hear a pianist who can change from blazing defiance to a delectable lightness and vivacity. In the shorter, less familiar sonatas, too, Lupu makes you aware of Schubert's tirelessly fecund imagination, of his experimenting with ideas and procedures far ahead of his time.

Piano Sonatas – B, D575; F minor, D625; A, D664. Moment musical in C, D780 No 1
Sviatoslav Richter *pf*
BBC Legends BBCL4010-2 (78' · ADD)
Recorded live 1979　　　　　　　　　　Ⓜ❍❍

Richter's Schubert is simply in a class of its own. No pianist did more to overturn the traditional view of the composer as a blithe, unreflecting child of nature. And in this Festival Hall recital three sonatas from 1817-19 unfold with a grandeur of conception, a spirituality

SCHUBERT PIANO SONATA IN B FLAT, D960 – IN BRIEF

Mitsuko Uchida
Philips 456 572-2PH (71' · DDD) Ⓕ**OO**➔
There is a sense of wariness, even apprehension from the start, as if anticipating the ominous bass trill. This is a beautifully nuanced performance, with poignant lyricism and baleful menace revealed as complementary traits. Excellently recorded.

Alfred Brendel
Philips ② 456 573-2PM2 (138' · DDD) Ⓜ
Although in this live recording the listener is initially aware of Brendel's audience (in this respect the sound on the coupled works is better), such is the concentration of his playing that you're quickly absorbed. A truly dramatic account not to be missed.

Stephen Hough
Hyperion CDA67027 (76' · DDD) · Ⓕ**O**
Hough takes relatively slow speeds in his thoughtful and concentrated performance, his sensitivity to phrasing and pianistic colour compelling attention throughout.

Andras Staier
Teldec ② 0630 13143-2 (119' · DDD) Ⓕ
A masterful performance on a fortepiano, whose different registers translate into quasi-orchestral contrasts in colour, so adding a further dimension to Schubert's masterpiece.

Stephen Kovacevich
EMI 562817-2 (72' · DDD) Ⓜ
A straightforward account which underplays the lyricism in favour of structural clarity, bringing the sonata closer to Beethoven in sound. The piano is sometimes a bit clangorous at the bass end.

Clifford Curzon Ⓗ
Decca ④ 475 084-2DC4 (304' · ADD) Ⓜ**O**➔
A musicianly account which cuts to the core of Schubert's inspiration, yet overstates nothing: details are in place, but never at the expense of the overall musical structure.

Wilhelm Kempff
DG ② 459 412-2GTA2 (150' · ADD) Ⓜ**OO**➔
A ravishingly beautiful account, though the sound is quite dated, and can often seem rather shallow. But nothing stands in the way of appreciated such a master at work.

Leif Ove Andsnes
EMI 557901-2 (71' · DDD) Ⓕ**O**➔
A beautifully judged performance that emphasises Schubert's poetry – something highlighted by the coupling of a group of songs in which Andsnes accompanies Ian Bostridge. Nicely recorded, too.

and a stoical timelessness that were unique to Richter. The first two movements of the A major Sonata are, on the face of it, implausibly slow: but with his mesmeric, self-communing intensity Richter convinces you for the duration of the performance that no other way is admissable. Phrases, paragraphs are shaped with calm inevitability, underpinned by the sublime, luminous simplicity of Richter's *cantabile*; and no pianist is more sensitive to Schubert's magical harmonic strokes or understands more surely their place in the larger scheme. As Richter conceives them, the first two movements of the A major, D664, foreshadow the rapt, philosophical contemplation of the late G major and B flat Sonatas, D894 and D960; and even the finale, projected with Richter's characteristic mastery and subtlety of rhythm, has something rarefied in its playfulness. Richter is equally lofty and far-sighted in the two lesser-known sonatas.

The BBC recording, while perhaps a shade bass-light, is warm, and does ample justice to Richter's vast dynamic and tonal palette. A bronchial March audience can intrude at the start of tracks, especially in finales. But no matter. All but those terminally resistant to Richter's uniquely introspective, long-spanned view of the composer should acquire as a matter of urgency these visionary performances by one of the greatest Schubertians of the century.

Piano Sonatas – C, D613; A minor, D784; B flat, D960
Stephen Hough pf
Hyperion CDA67027 (76' · DDD) Ⓕ**O**

Stephen Hough's moving performance of D960 is marked throughout by refined, discerning pianism and an uncommonly subtle ear for texture. In all four movements, he seeks out the music's inwardness and fragility, its ethereal, self-communing remoteness. The opening *Molto moderato*, unfolding in vast, calm spans, has a hypnotic inevitability; there are countless felicities of timing and colour, but always a vital sense of forward motion. Hough adopts a dangerously slow tempo in the *Andante* but sustains it through the breadth and concentration of his line, the subtlety of his tonal palette and his pointing of rhythmic detail. His rarefied grace and delicacy, his gentle probing of the music's vulnerability, are of a piece with his conception of the sonata as a whole.

As usual, Hyperion doesn't stint over playing time, offering another complete sonata in addition to the two-movement fragment, D613. D784, perhaps Schubert's most depressive instrumental work, is magnificently done. Hough distils an immense weight of suffering from the pervasive two-note motif that dominates the first movement like some massive, Wagnerian pendulum; but, typically, the lyrical music is limpidly coloured and poignantly inflected, with an unusually precise observation of Schubert's accents. The *Andante* is flowing and long-arched, with some ravishing soft playing, and he a brings a superb rhythmic impulse to the eerily scudding counterpoint of the main subject and a piercing tenderness to the contrasting F major theme. The fragmentary C major Sonata, D613, one of numerous Schubert torsos from the years 1817-22, is no great shakes: two pleasant but uneventful movements, both incomplete. The recording is of exemplary clarity, warmth and truthfulness.

Piano Sonatas – A minor, D784; D, D850
Alfred Brendel pf
Philips 422 063-2PH (63' · DDD)

There's an extraordinary amount of highly experimental writing in Schubert's piano sonatas. The essence of their structure is the contrasting of big heroic ideas with tender and inner thoughts; the first impresses the listener, the second woos him. The two works on this CD are in some ways on a varying scale. The D major, D850, lasts for 40 minutes, the A minor, D784, for around 23. However, it's the latter that contains the most symphonically inspired writing––it sounds as if it could easily be transposed for orchestra. Alfred Brendel presents the composer not so much as the master of Lieder-writing, but more as a man thinking in large forms. Although there are wonderful quiet moments when intimate asides are conveyed with an imaginative sensitivity one remembers more the urgency and the power behind the notes. The A minor, with its frequently recurring themes, is almost obsessive in character, while the big D major Sonata is rather lighter in its mood, especially in the outer movements. The recorded sound is very faithful to the pianist's tone, while generally avoiding that insistent quality that can mar his loudest playing.

Piano Sonata, 'Sonata oubliée', D916b.
Impromptus, D935. Adagio and Rondo
concertante, D487 (arr Knauer)[a]
Sebastian Knauer pf [a]**Resonanz Ensemble**
Berlin Classics 0016162BC (76' · DDD) Ⓕ

This disc is invaluable on two fronts. First, it introduces us in a first recording to 572 bars of original Schubert with a complementary six bars, all thanks to the sensitive scholarship of Jörg Demus and Roland Solder. Second, it presents a 36-year-old German pianist whose playing is a marvel of robust eloquence and unfaltering mastery, free from all distracting caprice or idiosyncrasy. Entitled by the editors 'The Forgotten Sonata', D916b is a classic instance of Schubert at his most audacious and experimental. Indeed, it is hard to imagine the opening *Allegro*'s taut, quasi-orchestral splendour and poetic inwardness, the central *Allegretto*'s enigma or the finale's *Marcia* as gracing a fireside Schubertiade. The *Adagio and Rondo concertante*, too, which is as close as Schubert got to writing a piano concerto (there are solo and tutti markings in the score), is richly inventive particularly

when presented by both pianist and ensemble with such authority.

Then, on more familiar territory, Knauer, who has studied with András Schiff and Christoph Eschenbach, gives us the second book of Impromptus, at once inviting comparison with even the finest Schubertians. Not for him the nervous telescoping of the A flat Impromptu's rhythm but a truly remarkable poise and insight. The final Impromptu may be taken at a spanking pace but once again the clarity and focus are enviable. All these performances are as disciplined as they are acute.

Piano Sonata No 20, D959. Moments musicaux, D780
Martin Helmchen pf
Pentatone PTC5186 329 (67' · DDD) ⒻⓄ→

Here is musical gold indeed. Martin Helmchen is a 27-year-old German pianist who won the Clara Haskil Competition in 2001 and whose playing in its mastery and unadorned quality has much in common with that great artist. Memorable recordings of Schubert's D959 Sonata and the six *Moments musicaux* are hardly thin on the ground yet such is the strength and poetic commitment of Helmchen's playing that he already makes comparison irrelevant. And if one was to single out one awe-inspiring moment it would be the *Andantino* from the Sonata, naturally paced, enviably poised and focused with a stealthy approach to the central elemental uproar that suggests a young pianist of rare maturity and vision.

All possible longueur, too, in the finale is banished in playing that makes for heavenly rather than interminable length. Again, the last of the *Moments musicaux*, an epic in miniature, is given with an unforgettable inwardness and quite without recourse to sub-normal timing or false sophistication. Just occasionally you could say that Helmchen's tempi are insufficiently integrated with a tendency to relax into lyricism and accelerate into drama. But given his overall command this is little more than a spot on the sun. Pentatone's sound is both clear and natural.

Piano Sonata in B flat, D960. Drei Klavierstücke, D946
Mitsuko Uchida pf
Philips 456 572-2PH (71' · DDD) ⒻⓄ→

Uchida's concentration and inwardness are of a rare order in her absorbed, deeply poetic reading of the B flat Sonata. No pianist makes you so aware how much of the first two movements is marked *pp* or even *ppp*; and none conjures such subtlety of colour in the softest dynamics: listen, for instance, to her playing of the three unearthly C sharp minor chords that usher in the first-movement development, or her timing and colouring of the breathtaking sideslip from C sharp minor to C major in the *Andante*. Other pianists may find a stronger undercurrent of foreboding or desperation in these two movements – though Uchida builds the development of the initial *Molto moderato* superbly to its dramatic climax.

But none probes more hauntingly the music's mysterious contemplative ecstasy or creates such a sense of inspired improvisation. And her limpid *cantabile* sonorities are always ravishing on the ear. She's equally attuned to the less rarefied world of the *Scherzo* and finale, the former a glistening, mercurial dance, *con delicatezza* indeed, the latter graceful and quixotic, with a hint of emotional ambiguity even in its ostensibly cheerful main theme and a tigerish ferocity in its sudden Beethovenian eruptions.

The coupling is generous: the three *Klavierstücke*, D946, composed, like the sonata, in Schubert's final year, 1828, and assembled by Brahms for publication. She brings a wonderfully impassioned sweep, with razor-sharp rhythms, to the opening of the E flat minor, No-1, and mesmerically floats its slow B major episode. She also restores the beguiling barcarolle-like episode in A flat that Schubert excised from his autograph manuscript. The recording finely captures Uchida's subtle, pellucid sound world. A revealing disc from a Schubertian of rare insight and spirituality.

Wandererfantasie, D760

Fantasie in C, D934ᵃ. Fantasy in C,
'Wandererfantasie', D760
ᵃ**Yuuko Shiokawa** *vn* **András Schiff** *pf*
ECM New Series 464 320-2 (50' · DDD)　　Ⓕ🅱️➕

Nearly all Schubert's great instrumental works maintain the Classical four-movement layout: but he did turn occasionally to the fashionable, looser, fantasia-style forms – in the case of the *Wandererfantasie*, one of his most disturbing works, he seems to be using his structural know-how in order to subvert the expectations of Classical form. András Schiff vividly brings out the switches between Classical poise, intensely Romantic mood-painting and near-expressionistic disruption; the key lies in the way he doesn't exaggerate any contrast, but makes each detail tell, so that the full range of the piece can be heard. One shouldn't underestimate the technical achievement – the lead-in to the *adagio* section is a perfect demonstration of a gradual *diminuendo*, of energy falling away, and when the *Adagio* arrives the chordal playing is superb – the melodic line perfectly balanced by the dark, melancholic colours in the bass.

Balance and lack of exaggeration inform the D934 *Fantasie*, too. From the start, when Shiokawa steals in above the piano *tremolando*, there's an air of magic. Her fine, silvery tone only rarely expands to a richer or more dramatic utterance, but her care not to overplay actually adds to the rich impression the performance gives. Whereas Kremer and Afanassiev present the central variation set as a brilliant showpiece, Schiff and Shiokawa paint a noticeably more varied picture – drama and virtuosity alternating with delicacy and touches of lyrical tenderness. In short, these are interpretations of rare penetration and individuality.

Schubert Fantasy in C, 'Wandererfantasie' D760
Schumann Fantasie in C, Op 17
Maurizio Pollini *pf*
DG The Originals 447 451-2GOR (52' · ADD)
Recorded 1973　　Ⓜ🅾️🅾️🅾️🅱️➕

 The cover shows Caspar David Friedrich's familiar *The Wanderer above the Sea of Fog*. Pollini, on the other hand, is a wanderer in a transparent ether or crystalline light, and both these legendary performances, recorded in 1973 and beautifully remastered, are of a transcendental vision and integrity. In the Schubert his magisterial, resolutely unvirtuoso approach allows everything its time and place. Listen to his flawlessly graded triple *piano* approach to the central *Adagio*, to his rock-steady octaves at 5'23" (where Schubert's merciless demand is so often the cause of confusion) or to the way the decorations in the *Adagio* are spun off with such rare finesse, and you may well wonder when you've heard playing of such an unadorned, unalloyed glory. Pollini's Schumann is no less memorable. Doubting Thomases on the alert for alternating touches of imperiousness and sobriety will be disappointed, for, again, Pollini's poise is unfaltering. The opening *Moderato* is *sempre energico*, indeed, its central *Etwas langsamer* is so sensitively and precisely gauged that all possible criticism is silenced. The coda of the central march (that *locus classicus* of the wrong note) is immaculate and in what someone once called the finale's 'shifting sunset vapour' Pollini takes us gently but firmly to the shores of Elysium. Here is a record that should grace every musician's shelf.

Impromptus

Impromptus – D899; D935. Drei Klavierstücke, D946
Allegretto in C minor, D915
Maria João Pires *pf*
DG ② 457 550-2GH2 (108' · DDD)　　Ⓕ🅾️🅾️🅾️🅱️➕

Ⓖ This is something very special. Pires's characteristic impassioned absorption in all she plays – that concentration which makes the listener appear to be eavesdropping on secrets shared between friends – could hardly find a truer soul mate than Schubert. Each *Impromptu* has a rare sense of integrity and entirety, born of acute observation and long-pondered responses.

Pires's instinct for tempo and pacing brings a sense of constant restraint, a true *molto moderato* to the *Allegro* of the C minor work from D899, created by a fusion of right-hand *tenuto* here with momentary left-hand rubato there. Then there's the clarity of contour within the most subtly graded undertones of the G flat major of D899 which re-creates it as a seemingly endless song. Or an *Andante* just slow, just nonchalant enough for the *Rosamunde* theme of the D935 B-flat major to give each variation space and breath enough to sing out its own sharply defined character.

The *Allegretto*, D915 acts as a *Pause* between the two discs, a resting place, as it were, for reflection and inner assessment on this long journey. Its end – which could as well be its beginning – is in the *Drei Klavierstücke*, D946 of 1828. The first draws back from the fiery impetuousness within the *Allegro assai*'s tautly controlled rhythms, to an inner world with its own time scale; the second, more transpired than played, has an almost unbearable poignancy of simplicity. The paradox of these unselfregarding performances is how unmistakably they speak and sing out Pires and her unique musicianship. To draw comparisons here would be not so much odious as to miss the point.

Piano Transcriptions

Schubert/Godowsky Passacaglia. Die schöne Müllerin, D795 – No 8, Morgengruss. Winterreise, D911 – No 1, Gute Nacht **Schubert/Prokofiev** Waltzes Suite **Schubert/Busoni** Overture in the Italian style, D590 **Schubert/Liszt** Erlkönig, D328. Winterreise – No 5, Der Lindenbaum; No 17, Im Dorfe; No 18, Der stürmische Morgen
Antti Siirala pf
Naxos 8 555997 (63' · DDD)　　　⑤●➔

This young Finnish prize-winning pianist makes his recorded début with a challenging and enterprising a programme of Schubert transcriptions by Liszt, Godowsky, Prokofiev and Busoni.

Schubert takes less kindly to arrangement than most; his profound simplicity is easily compromised. True Schubertians might well have winced at what Godowsky does to 'Morgengruss' from *Die schöne Müllerin*, where innocence is turned into experience and a tropical efflorescence. Yet if to some this is sacrilegious, others, will celebrate an act of engaging decadence. Liszt, for all his theatricality, is much more an ardent devotee than mischief-maker, often memorably true to both his own and Schubert's sharply opposed natures, whereas Prokofiev and Busoni's offerings are disappointingly more deferential than genuinely re-creative.

Siirala's performances are masterly and warmly sympathetic throughout, and never more so than in Godowsky's horrendously demanding Passacaglia on Schubert's *Unfinished* Symphony. Even Horowitz balked before this challenge, complaining that you needed six hands to encompass such fearsome difficulties.

Masses

Mass No 6, D950
Susan Gritton sop **Pamela Helen Stephen** mez **James Gilchrist, Mark Padmore** tens **Matthew Rose** bar **Collegium Musicum 90 / Richard Hickox**
Chandos Chaconne ② CHAN0750 (53' · DDD · T/t)

Ⓕ●➔

Long the Cinderella work of Schubert's miraculous final year, the E flat Mass is now acknowledged as a powerful masterpiece that mingles liturgical grandeur with the composer's own subjective Romanticism. The apocalyptic *Sanctus*, with its daring harmonic shifts and heavenstorming crescendi, is a musical counterpart to Turner's molten canvases, while the *Agnus Dei* has a violent, contorted anguish unmatched in a setting of this text. The least personal, and most problematic, sections of the Mass are the monumental set-piece fugues at the end of the *Gloria* and *Credo*, where Schubert ostentatiously displays his contrapuntal credentials, probably with an eye on an official church appointment. At the worthy tempi prevalent 20 and more years ago, these could seem interminable, and were often cut.

Hickox chooses broad tempi, balancing dignity and vitality, and building thrillingly to the climaxes. In the *Kyrie*, at a mobile tempo, he combines gravitas with a Schubertian lyrical ease, and later he manages the tempo fluctuations far more naturally. You hear how this heavenly music should sound, with the three soloists (Mark Padmore, James Gilchrist – an ideally matched tenor pairing – and soprano Susan Gritton) singing with pure tone and wondering tenderness. Hickox scores over most rivals with his extra choral firepower at climaxes, and the wonderfully pungent sonorities of Collegium Musicum 90, whether in the dry, fearful rattle of period timpani in the *Credo*, the lovely 'woody' oboe and clarinet in the 'Et incarnatus est' or the steely, scything trumpets in the *Agnus Dei*.

Part-songs

Psalm 23, D706. Im Gegenwärtigen Vergangenes, D710. Gesang der Geister über den Wassern, D714. Gondelfahrer, D809. Coronach, D836. Nachthelle, D892. Grab und Mond, D893. Nachtgesang im Walde, D913. Ständchen, D920. Die Nacht, D983c. Gott im Ungewitter, D985
Birgit Remmert contr **Werner Güra** ten **Philip Mayers** pf **Scharoun Ensemble; RIAS Chamber Choir, Berlin / Marcus Creed**
Harmonia Mundi HMC90 1669 (59' · DDD · T/t)　Ⓕ●

Most of the part-songs here evoke some aspect of night, whether benevolent, romantic, transfigured or sinister. Between them they give a fair conspectus of Schubert's achievement in the part-song genre, ranging from the mellifluous, Biedermeier *Die Nacht*, forerunner of many a Victorian glee, and the gently sensuous *Gondelfahrer* to the eerie, harmonically visionary *Grab und Mond* and the brooding *Gesang der Geister über den Wassern*. Other highlights here include the alfresco *Nachtgesang*, with its quartet of echoing horns, *Ständchen*, a delicious nocturnal serenade, the austere, bardic Scott setting *Coronach* and the serenely luminous *Nachthelle*.

The RIAS Chamber Choir confirms its credentials as one of Europe's finest, most virtuosic ensembles. It sings with rounded, homogeneous tone, well-nigh perfect intonation and an excitingly wide dynamic range. Characterisation tends to be very vivid, whether in the ecstatic central climax in *Nachthelle*, sharp contrasts in *Gesang der Geister über den Wassern* or the great sense of awe – and palpable feeling for Schubert's strange modulations – in *Grab und Mond*.

Birgit Remmert, the alto soloist in *Ständchen* (sung, incidentally, in the version with women's voices), sings well enough but with insufficient lightness and sense of fun. But Werner Güra negotiates what one of Schubert's friends called 'the damnably high' tenor solo in *Nachthelle* gracefully and with no sense of strain. Philip Mayers is a serviceable rather than specially imaginative pianist, though the delicate, silvery treble of the early 19th-century instrument is enchantingly heard in *Psalm-23* and the shimmering high repeated notes of *Nachthelle*; and the other instrumentalists make their mark – splendid rotund horns in *Nachtgesang im Walde*, sombrely intense strings in *Gesang der Geister*. The recorded sound is clear and warm, with a well-judged vocal-instrumental balance.

Lieder

Abendstern, D806[a]. Amalia, D195[a]. Atys, D585[a]. Auf-dem See, D543[b]. Auflösung, D807[a]. Augenlied, D297[a]. Blumenlied, D431[b]. Die Entzückung an Laura, D390[a]. Gondelfahrer, D808[b]. Die Götter Griechenlands, D677 – Strophe[b]. Die junge Nonne, D828[b]. Der Jüngling am Bache, D30[a]. Der Jüngling und der Tod, D545[c]. Memnon, D541[a]. Der Musensohn, D764[a]. Das Rosenband, D280[b]. Schwestergruss, D762[c]. Sehnsucht, D636[a]. Der Sieg, D805[a]

Dame Janet Baker *mez* [a]**Geoffrey Parsons,** [b]**Graham Johnson,** [c]**Martin Isepp** *pfs*
BBC Legends BBCL4070-2 (73' · ADD) Live broadcasts from [c]1970, [b]1977, [a]1980 Ⓕ🅞

The interpretation of Schubert's Lieder comes no better than this, a recital taken from three different broadcast sources, catching Dame Janet at the absolute peak of her powers. Most of the songs are by poets who moved the composer to his most noble inspiration. As several Schubert specialists have commented, for each he reserved a particular style, in response to their very different manner, and Baker catches the precise meaning of each.

Of the Schiller settings, the operatic expression of *Amalia* and the dreamy rapture of the praise of *Laura* (here the singer achieves one miraculous *pianissimo* effect) are perfectly caught. Best of all is that wonderful song, *Die Götter Griechenlands*, where longing is so movingly expressed. All seven Mayrhofer settings find Baker truly at one with the poet's high-minded self-communing on the meaning of life, and with his underlying fatalism. Most notable are the calm assurance and serenity she brings to *Der Sieg*, the resigned isolation found in *Abendstern*, and the holy fire of *Auflösung*, the last two masterpieces that the singer did so much to make popular.

As Gerald Moore once pointed out, Baker liked the stimulus of the different ideas she received from different pianists. Here Isepp, Parsons and the young Graham Johnson provide just that, completing pleasure in a recital that goes to the heart of the chosen material: as ever one realises that Baker was, above all, a singer of conviction. The absence of any texts or translations is the only blot on a superb issue.

'Goethe-Lieder'
Am Flusse (first version), D160. An den Mond (second version), D296. Auf dem See, D543. Bundeslied, D258. Claudine von Villa Bella, D239 – No 6, Liebe schwärmt auf allen Wegen. Der Fischer, D225. Der Goldschmiedsgesell, D560. Der Gott und die Bajadere, D254. Harfenspieler – D325; D478 (two versions); D479; D480. Liebhaber in allen Gestalten, D558. Nachtgesang, D119. Nähe des Geliebten, D162. Prometheus, D674. Der Sänger, D149. Der Schatzgräber, D256. Schweizerlied, D559. Sehnsucht, D123. Tischlied, D234. Trost in Tränen, D120. Wer kauft Liebesgötter?, D261. Willkommen und Abschied, D767
Wolfgang Holzmair *bar* **Gérard Wyss** *pf*
Tudor TUDOR7110 (77' · DDD · T) Ⓕ

All Holzmair's familiar gifts in Lieder are brought to bear on this absorbing selection of Goethe settings. Nowhere are they more to the fore than in a deeply considered account of the composer's final thoughts on the poet's *Harfenspieler* poems. Each of these masterpieces rends the heart by virtue of the sad, poignant singing. No less impressive, in a quite different fashion, is the biting defiance of *Prometheus*. In this miniature drama Schubert is writing in a prophetic manner way beyond his own time, and Holzmair's delivery of text and music is searing.

The lighter, lyrical side of Schubert's nature is encompassed with equal facility. The tender thoughts of *Nachtgesang* are given a properly palpitating expression; *Der Fischer* is warmly affecting; the longing of *An den Mond* is finely enacted. In the ineffably beautiful *Nähe des Geliebten*, the baritone's colouring of the text is exemplary, as it is in *Am Flusse*. In lighter pieces, such as the folklike *Schweizerlied*, the Papageno-like *Wer kauft Liebesgötter?* and the ever-charming ariette from *Claudine von Villa Bella*, Holzmair lightens his tone and and brings a smile into it. Sensibly these trifles are neatly intermixed with the serious offerings. He does his best to enliven some lesser Schubert – the composer is never quite at his most telling in longish ballad settings – but here, as throughout, he is admirably partnered by Gérard Wyss's lively and perceptive playing. The recording is spacious and well balanced.

'Lieder, Vol 1'
Fahrt zum Hades, D526. Freiwilliges Versinken, D700. Das Weinen, D926. Das Fischers Liebesglück, D933. Der Winterabend, D938. Memnon, D541. Lied eines Schiffers an die Dioskuren, D360. Der Schiffer, D536. Sehnsucht, D636. Der Jüngling am Bache, D638. An Emma, D113. Der Pilgrim, D794. Gruppe aus dem Tartarus, D583. Hoffnung, D295. Grenzen der

Menschenheit, D716
Matthias Goerne *bar* **Elisabeth Leonskaja** *pf*
Harmonia Mundi HMC90 1988 (65' · DDD · T/t)   Ⓕ◗

'Do you know of any happy music?' Schubert once asked a friend. 'I don't.' Those words could stand as an epigraph to Matthias Goerne's opening salvo in a projected 11- or 12-disc survey of Schubert Lieder. Evanescence, elegy and yearning for a transcendent otherness are the keynotes of a programme that encompasses the Attic majesty and *terribilità* of 'Memnon' and 'Gruppe aus dem Tartarus', the disillusioned fatalism of 'Der Pilgrim' and the philosophical grandeur of 'Grenzen der Menschenheit'. In these songs Goerne, with his distinctive dark, velvet timbre, is in his element. An intense, almost tortured concentration of thought and feeling has always been his hallmark, as has an unblemished *legato*. The way he bows Schubert's long lines like a cellist is reminiscent of the great Hans Hotter.

Goerne's rich bass resonances are heard to advantage in a performance of 'Grenzen der Menschenheit' that embraces aching tenderness as well as deep, rolling gravitas. 'Memnon' – a typical Mayrhofer allegory of the artist as tragic outsider – is equally spellbinding, illuminated by telling details like the lingering *portamento* on 'liebend' – 'lovingly' – as dawn's rays break through the mists. And when have the hazardous leaps of another allegorical Mayrhofer song, 'Freiwilliges Versinken been negotiated with such smoothness and hypnotic eloquence.

Where doubts creep in is in the handful of songs where, *pace* Schubert's own words, a certain lightness of tone and spirit is implied, but Goerne's involvement is so palpable and his style so scrupulous. For two-thirds and more of this recital the interpretative rewards are uncommonly rich, with the baritone well complemented by Elisabeth Leonskaja's deep-toned (if on occasion over-pedalled), often orchestrally conceived accompaniments.

Lied eines Schiffers an die Dioskuren, D360.
Nachtstück, D672. Auf der Donau, D553. Abendstern, D806. Auflösung, D807. Geheimes, D719. Versunken, D715. Schäfers Klagelied, D121. An die Entfernte, D765. Am Flusse, D766. Willkommen und Abschied, D767. Die Götter Griechenlands, D677. An die Leier, D737. Am See, D746. Alinde, D904. Wehmut, D772. Über Wildemann, D884. Auf der Riesenkoppe, D611. Sei mir gegrüsst, D741. Dass sie hier gewesen, D775. Der Geistertanz, D116
Ian Bostridge *ten* **Julius Drake** *pf*
EMI 557141-2 (68' · DDD)   Ⓕ◗◗⊕

A truly memorable experience. The first half of the programme is divided between settings of Mayrhofer and Goethe, two poets who drew the very best out of Schubert. Bostridge responds to this inspiration with singing that's worthy of the pieces both in terms of silvery, poised tone and inflection of the text. Such musing songs as *Nachtstück*, *Abendstern*, *Geheimes*, *Versunken* and

An die Entfernte are delivered in that peculiarly plangent tone of the tenor's which causes his audiences to tremble in admiration.

Using vibrato, verbal emphases, *pianissimos* and floated touches to quite magical yet seemingly spontaneous effect, these songs, and many others receive near-ideal performances. Only in the rough-hewn *Willkommen und Abschied* would perhaps a heavier voice, a baritone rather than a tenor, be preferable. Bostridge enthusiasts will lap up this wonderful issue; so ought all lovers of Schubert Lieder. Bostridge need fear no comparison with other great interpreters of these songs. The admirable recording catches voice and piano in ideal balance.

An den Mond, D193. Wandrers Nachtlied I, D224. Der Fischer, D225. Erster Verlust, D226. Heidenröslein, D257. Erlkönig, D328. Litanei auf das Fest Allerseelen, D343. Seligkeit, D433. Ganymed, D544. An die Musik, D547. Die Forelle, D550. Frühlingsglaube, D686. Im Haine, D738. Der Musensohn, D764. Wandrers Nachtlied II, D768. Der Zwerg, D771. Auf dem Wasser zu singen, D774. Du bist die Ruh, D776. Nacht und Träume, D827. Fischerweise, D881. Im Frühling, D882. An Silvia, D891
Ian Bostridge *ten* **Julius Drake** *pf*
EMI 556347-2 (69' · DDD · T/t)   Ⓕ◗◗⊕

Bostridge's devoted admirers will once more wonder at his famed engagement with the text in hand and his innate ability both to sing each piece in an entirely natural manner and at the same time to search out its inner meaning, everything achieved without a vocal or technical mishap within hearing. His gift for finding the right manner for each song is exemplified in the contrast between the easy simplicity he brings to such apparently artless pieces as *Fischerweise*, *Frühlingsglaube* and the less familiar *Im Haine* (this a wondrous performance of a song that's the very epitome of Schubert the melodist) and the depth of feeling found in *Erster Verlust* (a properly intense reading), *Nacht und Traüme*, *Wandrers Nachtlied* I and II, *Du bist die Ruh* (so elevated in tone and style) and *Litanei*.

Bostridge also characterises spine-chillingly the intense, immediate drama of *Erlkönig* and *Der Zwerg*, though here some may prefer the weight of a baritone. In the latter piece Drake is particularly successful at bringing out the originality of the piano part, and in a much simpler song, *An Sylvia*, he gives to the accompaniment a specific lift and lilt that usually goes unheard. In these songs, as in everything else, the ear responds eagerly to the tenor's fresh, silvery tone and his ever-eager response to words. The recording and notes are faultless.

An die Entfernte, D765[a]. Auf dem Wasser zu singen, D774[a]. Du bist die Ruh, D776[b]. Erlkönig, D328[c]. Die Forelle, D550[b]. Heidenröslein, D257[b]. Das Heimweh, D456[a]. Der Jüngling an der Quelle, D300[b]. Der Jüngling und der Tod, D545[a]. Das Lied im

Grünen, D917ᵃ. Litanei auf das Fest aller Seelen, D343ᵃ. Nachtgesang, D314ᵃ. Der Schiffer, D536ᵃ. Sei mir gegrüsst, D741ᵇ. Ständchen, 'Horch! Horch! die Lerch', D889ᵇ. Der Strom, D565ᵃ. Der Tod und das Mädchen, D531ᵃ. Der Wanderer, D649ᵃ. Der Winterabend, D938ᵃ. Das Zügenglöcklein, D871ᵃ. Der zürnende Barde, D785ᵃ

Dietrich Fischer-Dieskau bar **Gerald Moore** pf
EMI Encore 574754-2 (69' · ADD) Recorded 1960/66 Ⓢ

Almost 70 minutes of Fischer-Dieskau singing Schubert in his absolute prime at super-bargain price can't be bad, in spite of the absence of texts. The songs chosen – some outright favourites, others fine pieces the baritone helped to rescue from obscurity – make up a most desirable programme. As regards interpretation, Fischer-Dieskau is at his most soft-grained and persuasive in the lyrical pieces, notably the rarely heard but most beautiful *Nachtgesang*, at his most melodramatic in the more forceful Lieder, culminating in a hair-raising account of *Erlkönig*.

Moore is both sensitive and positive as the great baritone's partner, and contributes meaningfully to all the performances. EMI's recording of the period was wholly successful in catching the full tone of its singers.

'Abendbilder'
Abendbilder, 'Nocturne', D650. Alinde, D904. Am Fenster, D878. Auf der Bruck, D853. Bei dir allein, D866 No 2. Dass sie hier gewesen, D775. Drang in die Ferne, D770. Du bist die Ruh, D776. Des Fischers Liebesglück, D933. Fischerweise, D881. Greisengesang, D778. Himmelsfunken, D651. Im Abendrot, D799. Der Musensohn, D764. Willkommen und Abschied, D767. Der Winterabend, D938. Das Zügenglöcklein, D871

Christian Gerhaher bar **Gerold Huber** pf
RCA Red Seal 82876 77716-2 (70' · DDD · T/t)
Ⓕ ⦿⦿⦿⦿▷

Eschewing the eccentricities and exaggerations of some of his contemporaries, Gerhaher wonderfully exhibits the verities of Schubert interpretation in this well-planned and absorbing programme. Everything he does evolves from the song in hand and so accords with all that is needed in performing some of the composer's greatest Lieder.

The title, 'Abendbilder', is interpreted freely but almost all the pieces have some relevance to the dreams and moods of evening. Gerhaher enters into these nocturnal moods with unerring artistry where line, tone and word-painting are concerned. He is at his very best in the three settings of Rückert. That quirky, equivocal piece *Dass sie hier gewesen*, prophesying the style and harmony of Hugo Wolf, is sung with a full understanding of its inner meaning. *Du bist die Ruh* is delivered with the fine line and intense concentration such a great song deserves, and the thoughts of an elderly man in *Greisengesang* are as meaningful as they should be.

Highly appealing throughout is the melliflu-

ousness and breath control, a feature prominent throughout the recital, of the quietly contemplative *Im Abendrot*, and the appropriate dreaminess brought to the hypnotic barcarolle that is *Des Fischers Liebesglück*. As a nice contrast, Gerhaher brings virile energy to the fierce riding of *Auf der Bruck* – and here Gerold Huber deserves as much praise as his partner for portraying the insistent beat of horse's hooves in the piano part so vividly – and the familiar *Der Musensohn* has just the right verve as does another Goethe setting, the ecstatic *Willkommen und Abschied*, that brings a rewarding recital to an exhilarating close with Huber – as throughout – seconding the singer with his discerning contribution. The recording is ideally balanced.

'Poets of Sensibility, Volume 3'
Abendlied, D499. An den Mond, D193. An die Apfelbäume, D197. An eine Quelle, D530. Auf dem Wasser zu singen, D774. Auf den Tod einer Nachtigall, D201. Auf den Tod einer Nachtigall, D399. Die Frühe Liebe, D430. Klage an den Mond, D436. Klage, D371. Der Leidende (two versions), D432, D432b. Der Liebende, D207. Lied in der Abwesenheit, D416. Minnelied, D429. Die Mutter Erde, D788. Die Nonne (first version), D208. Seligkeit, D433. Seufzer, D198. Stimme der Liebe, D412. Täglich zu singen, D533. Der Tod und das Mädchen, D531. Totengräberlied, D44. Der Traum, D213

Wolfgang Holzmair bar **Ulrich Eisenlohr** fp
Naxos 8 557568 (61' · DDD)   Ⓢ▷

The pre-Romantic poets of Empfindsamkeit ('sensibility'), represented here by Hölty, Claudius and Stolberg, inspired a handful of famous Schubert settings alongside dozens of songs that are still too little known. *Die Mutter Erde*, for instance, written when the composer was suffering from the first symptoms of syphilis, is quintessentially Schubertian in its mingled grandeur, serenity and yearning; *Stimme der Liebe*, dating from 1816 but sounding 10 years later, is one of his most poignant and intense love songs (a reflection of his failed affair with Therese Grob?); *An die Apfelbäume* is a *bel canto* melody of delicious sensuous grace. Elsewhere we have what must be the jolliest song ever about death (*Toten-gräber-lied*), a pair of solemnly archaic hymns, and charming Haydnesque settings of poems in that faintly risqué (and, to us, impossibly coy) vein beloved of the 18th century.

As ever, Wolfgang Holzmair, with his plangent, tenorish (and distinctly Viennese) timbre, is a highly sympathetic Schubertian, scrupulous in enunciation, always sensitive to mood and nuance yet never prone to exaggeration. Where darker, deeper voices make Death in *Der Tod und das Mädchen* a solemn, hieratic figure, Holzmair intones Death's chant with a gentle beneficence. The many songs of pathos or wistful longing – say, *Der Leidende* or the exquisite *Seufzer* – suit Holzmair to perfection. He brings an unforced variety to the successive verses of strophic settings like *Abendlied* (another little-known gem), finds the vocal equivalent of a twinkle in the eye for *Der Traum* (marked to be sung 'flirtatiously'), and even compels you to listen in the potentially absurd ballad *Die Nonne*, in which a nun of fiery Latin temperament turns murderess. Holzmair understands, too, the virtue of simplicity in early Schubert.

Reservations? Well, these days Holzmair sounds a touch strained at high-lying climaxes; and while he can spin a true *legato*, his line can on occasion be slightly bumpy, as in an otherwise touching (and unusually reflective) *Auf dem Wasser zu singen*. But there is nothing to detract seriously from enjoyment of a shrewdly planned recital that begins in the grip of Death and ends with an exuberant affirmation of life's pleasures (*Seligkeit*). Ulrich Eisenlohr is a discerning partner, drawing an array of delicate, evocative sonorities from his 1820s fortepiano, including (in, for instance, *An den Mond*) a hazy *con sordino* (muted) resonance impossible to conjure on a modern grand. Naxos provide texts and translations via their website.

Lieder, Volume 27

Lob der Tränen, D711. Lebensmelodien, D395. Sprache der Liebe, D410. Wiedersehn, D855. Sonett I, D628. Sonett II, D629. Sonett III, D630. Abendröte, D690. Die Berge, D634. Die Vögel, D691. Der Fluss, D693. Der Knabe, D692. Die Rose, D745. Der Schmetterling, D633. Der Wanderer, D649. Das Mädchen, D652. Die Sterne, D684. Die Gebüsche, D646. Blanka, D631. Der Schiffer, D694. Fülle der Liebe, D854. Im Walde, D708
Matthias Goerne *bar* **Christine Schäfer** *sop*
Graham Johnson *pf*
Hyperion CDJ33027 (78' · DDD · T/t)   Ⓕ

Goerne's brief is Schubert's settings of the brothers Schlegel, whose volatile character and life are amply and fascinatingly described in Johnson's introduction to the booklet. As ever in this series, there are songs that we should curse ourselves for neglecting for so long. Among the few settings of August von Schlegel is the interesting *Lebensmelodien*, where the Swan and the Eagle engage in a colloquy – the one all tranquil, the other all disturbed – and are observed by doves on whom Schubert lavishes his most beautiful music. In the formal *Wiedersehn*, as Johnson avers, Schubert imitates the style of a Handelian aria. The second of three Petrarch translations prefigures, arrestingly, the mood of *Winterreise*.

When we come to brother Friedrich and the quasi-cycle *Abendröte* we're in an even more exalted world where *Der Fluss*, another of Schubert's miraculous water songs, *Der Knabe*, above all *Die Rose*, where the fading of the rose is a metaphor for lost virginity (this, movingly done by Schäfer), and *Der Wanderer* show just how willingly Schubert responded to Schlegel's imagery. About Goerne's singing as such, ably assisted by Johnson's playing, there are no reservations, particularly in the visionary *Die Sterne*, but as the CD progresses his interpretations can seem a shade soporific; one wonders if he has

lived long enough with these songs to penetrate to their heart. His easily produced, slightly vibrant and mellifluous baritone and sense of Schubertian style make him a largely rewarding interpreter. The recording is superb.

Abendstern, D806. Abschied von der Harfe, D406. Am Bach im Frühling, D361. Am Flusse first version, D160. An die Laute, D905. An die Musik, D547. An eine Quelle, D530. Am mein Herz, D860. An Mignon, D161. Auf dem See, D543. Auf der Donau, D553. Auflösung, D807. Augenlied, D297. Drang in die Ferne, D770. Du bist die Ruh, D776. Der Fischer, D225. Geheimnis An Franz Schubert, D491. Gondelfahrer, D808. Das Heimweh, D456. Heiss mich nicht reden Mignon I (second version), D877/2. Der Herbstabend, D405. Der Herbstnacht, D404. Der Jüngling und der Tod, D545. Klage, D371. Liebeslauschen, D698. Lied, 'Ins stille Land', D403. Das Lied im Grünen, D917. Liedesend, D473. Nachtstück, D672. Nähe des Geliebten, D162. Nur wer die Sehnsucht kennt (fourth version), D877/4. Rückweg, D476. Der Sänger am Felsen, D482. Der Sieg, D805. Die Sternennächte, D670. Über Wildemann, D884. Der Wanderer, D649. Wer sich der Einsamkeit ergibt Harfenspieler I, D478. Wie Ulfru fischt, D525. Willkommen und Abschied, D767. Wonne der Wehmut, D260
Matthias Goerne *bar*
Eric Schneider, Helmut Deutsch *pfs*
Harmonia Mundi ② HMC90 2004/5
(124' · DDD · T/t)   ⒫Ⓞ▶

Here elegy, fatalism and death-longing predominate and in such repertoire Goerne's mellow, darkly rounded timbre, expressive diction and care – rare in Lieder singers today – for a true, 'bound' line are well nigh ideal. Even at the most anguished *fortissimo*, his tone never grows harsh or hectoring. Perfectionism like Goerne's has inevitably provoked charges of over-calculation. Some might protest at the ultra-slow tempo for *Du bist die Ruh*. Yet Goerne's beauty of tone and phrasing (founded on seemingly superhuman reserves of breath), and a rapt intensity that rises to spiritual radiance in the final verse are mesmerising. At a more conventional tempo, he sings *An die Musik* as a simple, sincere confession of faith, with affectionate touches of *rubato* (and how eloquently Helmut Deutsch's left hand duets with the voice). Elsewhere Goerne's unsentimental tenderness can illuminate little-known songs that seem ordinary on the printed page – *Abschied von der Harfe*, say, or the quasi-operatic lament *Der Sänger am Felsen*. He even appropriates, successfully, two of Mignon's songs, giving one of the most desolate and – in the central section – disturbed performances of *Nur wer die Sehnsucht kennt* you will hear.

True to form, Goerne makes an uncommonly melancholy serenader in *An die Laute* and *Des Mädchens Liebeslauschen*, which never smiles. Yet he can lighten up, as in the story-telling of *Der Fischer* and *Wie Ulfru fischt*. Like Deutsch on the first disc, Eric Schneider fully matches Goerne in acumen and command of colour, not least in a performance of *Nachtstück* of mingled grandeur, mystery and compassionate gentleness.

Schubert Atys, D585. Einsamkeit, D620. Der Fluss, D693. Im Freien, D880. Die Gebüsche, D646. Die-Götter Griechenlands, D677. Sehnsucht, D516 **Hüttenbrenner** Frühlingsliedchen. Der Hügel. Lerchenlied. Die Seefart. Seegras. Spinnerlied. Die-Sterne
Gundula Janowitz *sop* **Irwin Gage pf**
Orfeo C592021B (72' · DDD) Recorded live 1972 Ⓜ**O**

This is an unusual and wholly absorbing recital by a soprano often, mistakenly, considered no more than a singer with a lovely voice. In 1972, at the height of her appreciable powers, Janowitz impressed her Salzburg audience with this, her first recital at the Festival. Her discerning choice comprises some notable songs by Schubert rarely heard in recital and ones by his contemporary Hüttenbrenner, which Janowitz sang from manuscript copies, seldom performed since the composer's day. These are surely their first recordings.

Has there ever been such a lovely, poised account of the great Schiller-inspired song, *Die Götter Griechenlands* or such an ingratiating one of *Sehnsucht*, the Mayrhofer setting? The first offering, *Im Freien*, has its winning cantilena filled with gloriously sustained, long-breathed tone. The programme ends with *Einsamkeit*. This grandly imaginative if slightly impersonal quasi-cantata, to a Mayrhofer text, a composition that Schubert himself thought so highly of, is a kind of a panorama of a life, ending in a wonderfully reposeful final section. Janowitz and her impressive partner perform it with total conviction, sustaining interest throughout.

Although not in Schubert's class – who is? – Hüttenbrenner reveals a talent apparently well able to encompass the meaning of poems in fluent and often imaginative writing. Orfeo provide no texts, let alone translations, but the delightful *Spinnerlied* must be about spinning: it's an artlessly charming song. *Der Hügel* is obviously about more serious matters, and in its sad course comes closes to Schubert in depth of feeling. *Frühlingsliedchen* has a simple, spring-like joy to it, and an appealingly varied, strophic form. Janowitz takes the measure of them all, and adds to a gently vibrant tone many tints and touches of half-voice. They could not have a better advocate.

The recording catches the full glow of the singer's voice. The only drawback, that absence of texts, isn't serious enough to stop acquiring this issue, given that Janowitz virtually tells you in her utterance what the songs are about.

Lieder, Volume 23
Der Tod Oscars, D375. Das Grab, D377ᵃ. Der Entfernten, D350. Pflügerlied, D392. Abschied von der Harfe, D406. Der Jüngling an der Quelle, D300. Abendlied, D382. Stimme der Liebe, D412. Romanze, D144. Geist der Liebe, D414. Klage, D415. Julius an

Theone, D419. Der Leidende, D432. Der Leidende (second version), D432b. Die frühe Liebe, D430. Die Knabenzeit, D400. Edone, D445. Die Liebes-götter, D446. An Chloen, D363. Freude der Kinderjahre, D455. Wer sich der Einsamkeit ergibt, D478. Wer nie sein Brot mit Tränen ass, D480. An die Türen, D479. Der Hirt, D490. Am ersten Maimorgen, D344. Bei dem Grabe meines Vaters, D496. Mailied, D503. Zufriedenheit, D362. Skolie, D507
Christoph Prégardien *ten* ᵃ**London Schubert Chorale; Graham Johnson** *pf*
Hyperion CDJ33023 (78' · DDD · T/t)   Ⓕ

When the Hyperion Schubert Edition is completed, this latest wondrous offering will rank among its most precious jewels. Prégardien is a prince among tenor interpreters of Lieder at present, on a par with Blochwitz in instinctive, natural and inevitably phrased readings. Johnson, besides finding exactly the right performers for these songs, surpasses even his own high standard of playing in this series. Then there's Schubert himself, the Schubert of 1816 by and large, who was, Johnson tentatively suggests in his notes, going through a phase of 'bringing himself under control'. That means, largely but far from entirely, writing gently lyrical strophic songs, most of them of ineffable beauty and simplicity, starkly contrasting with the Harfenspieler settings from *Wilhelm Meister*, two of which were written in 1816, the other in 1822.

In such an outright masterpiece as *Der Jüngling an der Quelle*, Prégardien and Johnson confirm the latter's view that this piece 'makes time stand still'. They emphasise, in *Stimme der Liebe*, how Schubert uses shifting harmonies to indicate romantic obsession. They show in the two similar but subtly different versions of *Der Leidende* ('The suffering one') what Johnson calls 'two sides of the same coin', with the tenor's plangent, tender singing, line and text held in perfect balance. The two Hölty songs that follow, *Die frühe Liebe* and *Die Knabenzeit*, evince a wonderful affinity with thoughts of childhood on the part of poet and composer, again ideally captured here. So is the 'chaste and wistful' mood of Klopstock's *Edone*. The recording is ideally balanced .

Lieder – Gruppe aus dem Tartarus, D583. Litanei auf das Fest Allerseelen, D343. Die Forelle, D550. An die Leier, D737. Lachen und Weinen, D777. Schwanengesang, D957 – Ständchen; Das Fischermädchen; Die Taubenpost. Meerestille, D216. Der Wanderer, D489 (formerly D493). Erlkönig, D328. Der Tod und das Mädchen, D531. Heidenröslein, D257. Wandrers Nachtlied II, D768. An die Musik, D547. Auf der Bruck, D853. Schäfers Klagelied, D121. An Silvia, D891. Du bist die Ruh', D776. An die Laute, D905. Rastlose Liebe, D138. Ganymed, D544. Der Musensohn, D764
Bryn Terfel *bass-bar* **Malcolm Martineau** *pf*
DG 445 294-2GH (69' · DDD · T/t)   Ⓕ**OOO**↦

Terfel's gift is a generous, individual voice, a natural feeling for German and an inborn ability to go to the heart of what he attempts. His singing here is grand in scale – listen to any of the dramatic songs and the point is made – but like Hotter, whom he so often resembles, he's able to reduce his large voice to the needs of a sustained, quiet line, as in *Meerestille*. When the two come together as in *Der Wanderer*, the effect can be truly electrifying, even more so, perhaps, in *Erlkönig* where the four participants are superbly contrasted. Yet this is a voice that can also smile, as in *An die Laute* and 'Die Taubenpost' or express wonder, as in *Ganymed*, a most exhilarating interpretation, or again explode in sheer anger as in the very first song, the strenuous *Gruppe aus dem Tartarus*. Terfel isn't afraid to employ rubato and vibrato to make his points and above all to take us right into his interpretations rather than leave us admiring them, as it were, from afar. Throughout, Martineau's at once vigorous and subtle playing is an apt support: his accompaniment in *Erlkönig* is arrestingly clear and precise.

An die Musik, D547. Im Frühling, D882. Wehmut, ☐
D772. Ganymed, D544. Das Lied im Grünen, D917.
Gretchen am Spinnrade, D118. Nähe des Geliebten,
D162. Die junge Nonne, D828. An Silvia, D891. Auf
dem Wasser zu singen, D774. Nachtviolen, D752. Der
Musensohn, D764. Six moments musicaux, D780ᵃ
Elisabeth Schwarzkopf sop ᵃ**Edwin Fischer** pf
EMI Références mono 567494-2 (67' · ADD) Recorded
ᵃ1950, 1952   Ⓜ❶➡

Many young and not-so-young singers can't abide Schwarkopf's interpretative style, which is strikingly at odds with the straightforward readings so often heard today. Playing devil's advocate, one can understand the nature of the complaints about her interventionist approach, her occasional distortion of vowel sounds and a general approach that William Mann once described as 'verschmuckt' (bejewelled). You may judge such views, for instance, in a song like *Auf dem Wasser*, where not a phrase is left to speak for itself; compare it with the natural and simple reading of her contemporary Irmgard Seefried (Testament), which is so much more appropriate to the song.

That said, the doubters should listen to this recital with Edwin Fischer, one of the greatest ever discs of Schubert singing. As so often in her recitals dating back to Oxford days in 1950, annoyance with the occasional mannerism soon gives way to wonder at such an amazingly eager response to every facet of a song and its setting. And truly inspired by Fischer, she throws caution utterly to the wind and astonishes us in accounts of *Die junge Nonne*, *Ganymed* and *Gretchen am Spinnrade* that have seldom if ever been surpassed for vocal consistency and concentration – though it's a pity the singer makes a break in the final, long phrase of *Ganymed*.

Fischer, one of the noblest Schubert interpreters of his or any time, is obviously a partner in a thousand, and on his own confirms his stature in the legendary 1950 recording of the *Moments*

musicaux better transferred here than ever before – as are the Lieder. So this is a CD no Schubertian can do without.

Lieder, Volume 24
Schäfers Klagelied, D121. An Mignon, D161. Geistes-Gruss, D142 (two versions). Rastlose Liebe, D138. Der Gott und die Bajadere, D254. Tischlied, D234. Der Schatzgräber, D256. Der Rattenfänger, D255. Bundeslied, D258. Erlkönig, D328. Jägers Abendlied, D215. Jägers Abendlied, D368. Wer nie sein Brot mit Tränen ass, D480 (two versions). Nur wer die Sehnsucht kennt, D359. So lasst mich scheinen, D469a & D469b (two fragments). Nur wer die Sehnsucht kennt, D481. Nur wer die Sehnsucht kennt, D656. An Schwager Kronos, D369. Hoffnung, D295. Mahomets Gesang, D549 (cptd R. Van Hoorickx). Ganymed, D544. Der Goldschmiedsgesell, D560. Gesang der Geister über den Wassern, D484 (cptd R Van Hoorickx). Gesang der Geister über den Wassern, D705 (cptd E Asti).
Christine Schäfer sop **John Mark Ainsley** ten **Simon Keenlyside** bar **Michael George** bass **Graham Johnson** pf **London Schubert Chorale / Stephen Layton**
Hyperion CDJ33024 (79' · DDD · T/t)   Ⓕ

Renewed praise first of all for Graham Johnson. This volume is as cogent an example as any of his method, a masterly exposition, in written words and musical performance, of the crucial relationship between Goethe and Schubert upon which Johnson throws a good deal of new light. Not all here is notable Schubert, but the lesser songs serve to place in perspective the greater ones.

The CD begins with one of the latter, *Schäfers Klagelied*, in a finely honed, dramatic performance by Ainsley, who's heard later on the disc always to advantage. Good as Christine Schäfer is in the first version of *An Mignon*, she's better in the sadly neglected *Der Gott und die Bajadere*, as Johnson avers. This is the only song in the genre about prostitution, and a haunting one too, even though, throughout its appreciable length, it relies on just one melody, and Schäfer precisely catches its haunting atmosphere. But the climax of her contribution comes in *Ganymed* – with Johnson providing exactly the right rhythmic lilt at the piano, her voice conveys all the elation of poem and music.

Schäfer is the child in a three-voice rendering of *Erlkönig*, a manner of performing the piece that has the composer's blessing. Johnson has surely never surpassed his account here of the hair-raisingly difficult piano part. George, who perhaps has the least ingratiating songs to perform, sings with feeling and style but sometimes an excess of vibrato. An invaluable addition to the series.

Lieder, Volume 26
Der Einsame, D800. Des Sängers Habe, D832. Lied der Delphine, D857 No 1. Lied des Florio, D857 No 2. Mondenschein, D875. Nur wer die Sehnsucht kennt,

D877 No 1. Heiss mich nicht reden, D877 No-2. So lasst mich scheinen, D877 No 3. Nur wer die Sehnsucht kennt, D877 No 4. Totengräberweise, D869. Das Echo, D990C. An Silvia, D891. Horch, horch! die Lerch', D889. Trinklied, D888. Wiegenlied, D867. Widerspruch, D865. Der Wanderer an den Mond, D870. Grab und Mond, D893. Nachthelle, D892. Abschied von der Erde, D829

Christine Schäfer sop **John Mark Ainsley** ten
Richard Jackson bar **London Schubert Chorale;**
Graham Johnson pf
Hyperion CDJ33026 (76' · DDD · T/t)   Ⓕ**OO**

It's hard to know where to begin in praise of this disc. It has several centres of excellence, the first being Schäfer's beseeching, urgent account of the Mignon settings from Goethe's *Wilhelm Meister* that make plain her pre-eminence today among sopranos in Lieder. Next comes Ainsley's winningly fresh account of *An Silvia*. You may be surprised at how wholly new-minted Ainsley's ardent tones and Johnson's elating piano manage to make of such a hackneyed song. Schäfer and Johnson do the same service for *Horch, horch! die Lerch'*. Then comes the extraordinary discovery of this volume. As a rule, Johnson has excluded unaccompanied vocal pieces from his project; happily, he has made an exception in the case of the astonishingly original Seidl setting *Grab und Mond*, which touches on eternal matters, or rather the permanence of death, a message starkly expressed in typically daring harmony. The London Schubert Chorale gives it a spellbinding interpretation and also contributes positively to a performance of another Seidl setting, the better-known *Nachthelle*, where the high-lying tenor lead provides no problems for Ainsley. There have to be reservations over the work of Richard Jackson; his tone is inadequate to the demands of *Der Einsame*, the unjustly neglected *Totengräberweise* and *Der Wanderer an den Mond*, which call for a richer sound-palette.

Throughout, Johnson's playing is a source of pleasure and enlightenment. The recording is well-nigh faultless.

An den Mond, D193. Suleika I, D720. Im Abendrot, D799. Sei mir gegrüsst, D741. Die Forelle, D550. Heimliches Lieben, D922. Der Sänger am Felsen, D482. Thekla, D595. An die Sonne, D270. Aus Diego Manzanares, D458. Nacht und Träume, D827. Frühlingsglaube, D686. Die Blumensprache, D519. Nähe des Geliebten, D162. An die Nachtigall, D497. Liane, D298. Des Mädchens Klage, D191. Nachtviolen, D752. Marie, D658. Lambertine, D301. Die Männer sind méchant, D866/3

Elizabeth Watts sop **Roger Vignoles** pf
RCA Red Seal 88697 32932-2 (70' · DDD)   Ⓕ

Hailed as a singer to watch after winning the 2006 Kathleen Ferrier Award and the 2007 Cardiff Song Prize, Elizabeth Watts makes her CD debut with this refreshingly unhackneyed Schubert programme. Perennial soprano favourites – *Die Forelle, Nacht und Träume, Frühlingsglaube, Suleika* – are not shunned. But Watts has alighted on

some rarely aired gems. How often in recital do we hear the agitated scena-in-miniature *Aus Diego Manzanares*; or the playfully charming paean to spring *Die Blumensprache*; or the Novalis setting *Marie*, where sacred and profane blur in a song of exquisite, rarefied grace?

A voice in its first, radiant freshness is always to be cherished in Schubert. Watts is a thoughtful interpreter, too, alive to mood and atmosphere, colouring her tone in response to a darkening of the harmony in, say, *Sei mir gegrüsst*. Crucially, she also brings a measure of innocence and simplicity – not quite the same thing as artlessness – to many of these songs, allied to a technical mastery that allows her to spin a rapt, unblemished line in *Nacht und Träume*. Encouraged by Vignoles's buoyant accompaniment, she makes an engaging story-teller in *Die Forelle*, with an unexaggerated touch of indignation at the angler's treachery; and she sings the mildly salacious refrain song *Die Männer sind méchant* with just the right wide-eyed mock-pathos.

Quibbles? Well, in one or two songs, including the opening *An den Mond*, Watts struck me as overly languid. She treats *Nähe des Geliebten* as an elegiac litany, where, say, Janet Baker, choosing a more mobile tempo and finding greater variety from verse to verse, sings it as a passionate avowal of love. Watts also emphasises melancholy over excited anticipation in *Frühlingsglaube* and *Suleika*. Here and elsewhere, Watts under-exploits the expressive potential of German consonants. That said, highlights are lovely performances of *Nachtviolen* – the high tessitura effortlessly negotiated – or the Mozartian barcarolle *Liane*: just two songs among many where the vernal purity of Watts's tone and the grace of her phrasing are priceless assets.

Lieder, Volume 32
An die Sonne, D439. Beitrag zur fünfzigjährigen Jubelfeier des Herrn von Salieri, D407. Das war ich, D174a/D450a. Didone Abbandonata, D510a (both cptd Hoorickx). Der Entfernten, D331. Entzückung, D413. Der Geistertanz, D494. Gott der Weltschöpfer, D986. Gott im Ungewitter, D985. Grablied auf einen Soldaten, D454. Das Grosse Halleluja, D442. Des Mädchens Klage, D389. Licht und Liebe, D352. Naturgenuss, D422. Ritter Toggenburg, D397. Schlachtgesang, D443. Die verfehlte Stunde, D409. Der Wanderer, D489. Zufriedenheit, D501. Zum Punsche, D492

Lynne Dawson, Patricia Rozario, Christine Schäfer
sops **Ann Murray, Catherine Wyn-Rogers** mezzos
**Paul Agnew, John Mark Ainsley, Philip Langridge,
Jamie MacDougall, Daniel Norman, Christoph
Prégardien, Michael Schade, Toby Spence** tens
**Simon Keenlyside, Maarten Koningsberger,
Stephan Loges, Christopher Maltman, Stephen
Varcoe** bars **Neal Davies, Michael George** basses
Graham Johnson pf **London Schubert Chorale /
Stephen Layton**
Hyperion CDJ33032 (78' · DDD · T/t)   Ⓕ**O**

Like the previous Schubertiads in the Edition, this disc mixes solo songs and partsongs, familiar and unfamiliar. The only really famous work here is *Der Wanderer*, that archetypal expression of romantic alienation whose popularity in Schubert's lifetime was eclipsed only by that of *Erlkönig*. Some of the partsongs – *Zum Punsche*, *Naturgenuss* and *Schlachtgesang* – cultivate a vein of Biedermeier heartiness that wears a bit thin today. Nor will Schubert's consciously archaic tribute to his teacher Salieri have you itching for the repeat button – though, like several other numbers, it shows the 19-year-old composer rivalling Mozart in his gift for musical mimicry. To compensate, though, there are partsongs like the sensual *Der Entfernten*, with its delicious languid chromaticisms, and the colourful setting of *Gott im Ungewitter*. The slight but charming setting of *Das war ich* is appealingly done by the light-voiced Daniel Norman, and Ann Murray brings her usual charisma and dramatic conviction to the pathetic Italian scena *Didone Abbandonata*.

Christine Schäfer is equally charismatic in the unjustly neglected *Die verfehlte Stunde* (recorded here for the first time), catching perfectly the song's mingled yearning and ecstasy and negotiating the mercilessly high tessitura with ease. Other happy discoveries include Schubert's virtually unknown third setting of *Des Mädchens Klage*, with its soaring lines, a melancholy tale of courtly love, sung by Christoph Prégardien with as much drama and variety as the music allows, and the surging *Entzückung* ('music for an infant Lohengrin,' as Graham Johnson puts it), for which Toby Spence has both the flexibility and the necessary touch of metal in the tone. Doubts were fleetingly raised by Lynne Dawson's slight tremulousness in *Des Mädchens Klage*, and by Christopher Maltman's prominent vibrato at *forte* and above in an otherwise involving performance of *Der Wanderer*. But, these cavils apart, no complaints about the singing or the vivid accompaniments.

In his guise as a wizard of an impresario, Graham Johnson has gathered together four baritones and one bass-baritone (Neil Davies) to give us a feast of finely wrought, intelligent interpretations. Hampson's rendering of that outsider's lament, *Atys*, is at once an object-lesson in refined singing and a deeply felt outpouring of sorrow. Keenlyside, singing with as much firm, mellow tone and feeling as his American coeval, gives a properly intense, agonised account of the great, Zeus-defying *Prometheus*, magnificently supported by Johnson. Goerne is assigned the seldom-heard Schlegel setting, *Die gefangenen Sänger*, and brings his gently vibrant tone, reminiscent of his noted predecessor Herbert Janssen, and his natural gift for phrasing to bear on this strange but captivating piece. Maltman, growing in stature as a Lieder artist, begins the programme with the extrovert *Der Alpenjäger* and ends it with the introverted *Wandrers Nachtlied* on which he lavishes the hushed concentration due to a page of rapt utterance, a suitable conclusion to the performance of Goethe settings in the whole edition.

Neil Davies erupts into the series with three absorbing interpretations: the declamatory Schiller setting *Der Kampf*, the flowing, glowing *Das Abendrot* and the awe-inspiring *Grenzen der Menschheit*. All three evince his real affinity for the German language and the world of Schubert. He also has the low notes the pieces call for. The one female solo brings back Lipovšek at her most beguiling in the poignant and unforgettable Schlegel setting *Das Mädchen*, already performed just as movingly by Christine Schäfer in Vol 27. This wonderful fare is interspersed with lighter, less demanding material, all done with pleasure by varying groups of singers, plus three tenor solos. Langridge is predictably charming in *Die Einsiedelei*. Hill isn't quite at his best, and Norman's style is etiolated in their offerings. Piano playing both maintain Hyperion's usual high standard.

Lieder, Volume 34
La pastorella al prato, D513[fjpt]. Frohsinn, D520[q]. Der Alpenjäger, D524[r]. Die Einsiedelei, D563[j]. Das Grab, D569[u]. Atys, D585[c]. Der Kampf, D594[s]. Das Dörfchen, D598[fjpt]. Die Gesellschaft, D609[cdgt]. Sing-Übungen, D619[ac] (ed Roblou). Das Abendrot, D627[s]. Abend, D645[h] (ed Brown). Das Mädchen, D652[e]. Cantate zum Geburtstag des Sängers Michael Vogl, D666[blm]. Prometheus, D674[p]. Über allen Zauber Liebe, D682[k] (ed Hoorickx). Die gefangenen Sänger, D712[n]. Grenzen der Menschheit, D716[s]. Wandrers Nachtlied II, D768[r]
[a]**Lorna Anderson**, [b]**Lynne Dawson**, [c]**Patricia Rozario** *sops* [d]**Catherine Denley**, [e]**Marjana Lipovšek** *mezzos* [f]**John Mark Ainsley**, [g]**Ian Bostridge**, [h]**Martyn Hill**, [i]**Philip Langridge**, [j]**Jamie MacDougall**, [k]**Daniel Norman**, [l]**Michael Schade** *tens* [m]**Gerald Finley**, [n]**Matthias Goerne**, [o]**Thomas Hampson**, [p]**Simon Keenlyside**, [q]**Stephan Loges**, [r]**Christopher Maltman** *bars* [s]**Neal Davies** *bass-bar* [t]**Michael George** *bass* [u]**London Schubert Chorale / Stephen Layton**; Graham Johnson *pf*
Hyperion Schubert Edition CDJ33034
(79' · DDD · T/t) Ⓕ●

Lieder, Volume 37
Auf dem Strom, D943[cd]. Herbst, D945[a]. Bei dir allein, D866/2[c]. Irdisches Glück, D866/4[c]. Lebensmut, D937[c]. Schwanengesang, D957 – No 1, Liebesbotschaft[a]; No 2, Kriegers Ahnung[a]; No 3, Frühlingssehnsucht[a]; No 4, Ständchen[a]; No 5, Aufenthalt[a]; No 6, In der Ferne[a]; No 7, Abschied[a]; No 8, Der Atlas[b]; No 9, Ihr Bild[b]; No 10, Das Fischermädchen[b]; No 11, Die Stadt[b]; No 12, Am Meer[b]; No 13, Der Doppelgänger[b]. Die Taubenpost, D965A[b]. Glaube, Hoffnung und Liebe, D955[abc]
[a]**John Mark Ainsley**, [b]**Anthony Rolfe Johnson**, [c]**Michael Schade** *tens* [d]**David Pyatt** *hn* Graham Johnson *pf*
Hyperion Schubert Edition CDJ33037
(80' · DDD · T/t) Ⓕ●

This disc, the last in Hyperion's Schubert Edition, is in large part devoted to the performance of the non-cycle *Schwanengesang*, that extraordinary collection in which Schubert seems more original and more inclined even than in earlier

Lieder to peer into the future. We usually encounter the work transposed for a baritone, though Schreier and Schiff have recorded it memorably for Decca. Johnson has astutely divided the songs between two voices. Ainsley is given the Rellstab settings, Rolfe Johnson the Heine, plus Seidl's *Die Taubenpost*, which so poignantly and airily closes the set.

Ainsley interprets his songs with the tonal beauty, fine-grained phrasing and care for words that are the hallmarks of his appreciable art, even if his voice sometimes lacks a difficult-to-define individuality of timbre. The over-exposed *Ständchen* is given a new spontaneity of utterance by both the singer and Graham Johnson. Anthony Rolfe Johnson brings all the appropriate intensity one would expect from him to the tremendous Heine settings. Sometimes his tone hardens when he's depicting the deserted lover present in so many of these pieces, but that's hardly inappropriate to the depth of feeling being expressed.

Most of the other songs of 1828, which open the recital, are assigned to Schade, who sings them with refined tone and an innate feeling for sharing his enjoyment in performing them, nowhere more so than in the opening *Auf dem Strom*. Ainsley reads his sole offering here, *Bei dir allein*, with just the fiery passion it calls for.

This is a worthy, often inspired conclusion to the series, once more enhanced by Johnson's copious notes. It also has a complete index to the Edition. The recording is faultless.

Song cycles

Die schöne Müllerin, D795. **Schwanengesang**, D957. **Winterreise**, D911

Die schöne Müllerin[a]. Nacht und Träume, D827[b]. Ständchen, D889[b]. Du bist die Ruh, D776[b]. Erlkönig, D328[c]
Dietrich Fischer-Dieskau bar [a]**Jörg Demus**, [bc]**Gerald Moore** pfs
DG 463 502-2GFD (75' · ADD) Recorded 1968, [bc]1970
Ⓜ❍❍▶

You wouldn't think that a recording by Fischer-Dieskau, given his huge Schubert discography, could still offer an exciting revelation – but that's what the 'new' *Die schöne Müllerin* recording offers. Explanations for its suppression vary. The singer seems to think it has something to do with its technical quality: the booklet-note, slightly more credibly, tells us that it was planned before DG decided to include the cycle in its 'complete' Schubert with the baritone and Gerald Moore, which caused this performance to be put on the back burner. Now we can enjoy a reading that's absolutely spontaneous, daring in its dramatic effects – bold extremes of dynamics, for instance – and full of even more subtle detail than in Fischer-Dieskau's other recordings.

This approach owes not a little to Demus's piano. As Alan Newcombe says in his notes: 'Aided by Demus's lightly pedalled, often almost

brusque *staccato* articulation, the result is starker, more elemental, less comfortable [than the reading with Moore], conceived on a larger scale.' To that one should add that the singer is at the absolute height of his powers; tone, line, breath control and intuitive imagination are most remarkable in the strophic songs that, in lesser hands, can seem over-long. Another feature of this is the significant underlining he gives to pertinent words. For instance, in *Pause* note how 'gehängt', 'durchschauert' and 'Nachklang' receive this treatment. It's this unique vision of the German language in music that still marks out this baritone from his many successors. Immediate, unvarnished sound heightens the value of this extraordinary performance.

Die schöne Müllerin, D795

Die schöne Müllerin
Jochen Kupfer bar **Susanne Giesa** pf
Channel Classics CCS18898 (66' · DDD · T/t)

This reading of Schubert's cycle is confirmation, as if that were needed, of Jochen Kupfer's beautiful singing, and even more of his gifts as a Lieder interpreter. Kupfer's voice and style is highly reminiscent of Wolfgang Holzmair's, but his technique is just that shade firmer and his voice more youthful than the older baritone's with Imogen Cooper, recalling rather Holzmair's first (1983) recording on Preiser. Both artists have a tenor-like quality to their voices, coming near to some ideal for the work. Kupfer begins with the basic verities of immaculate line and imaginative phrasing, to which he adds a complete identification with the youthful lover's aspirations and eventual disappointment and tragedy.

This lad sets out with a spring in his heels and a smile in his voice, quite avoiding any sense of despondency from the outset. All is going to be well in his wooing. That's conveyed in the first few songs with fresh immediacy as though the poetic emotions and their setting were new-minted. The arrival of the unwanted and aggressive hunter provokes an almost breathless jealousy and, in that arresting song, 'Die liebe Farbe', an appropriately mesmeric, plaintive approach. From there on the downward curve of emotional feeling, so arrestingly depicted in the words and music, finds in Kupfer and his alert partner an answering mood of despair, the raw and anguished passion in those final three songs fully achieved. All the while you feel the disillusionment and pathos in the texture and verbal acuity of the interpretation.

With a finely balanced recording to add to one's pleasure, this is a performance among baritones to place very near the top of the pile, if not at its apex, and it challenges even the prevailing tenor recommendations, the versions by Ian Bostridge and Werner Güra.

Die schöne Müllerin
Werner Güra ten **Jan Schultsz** pf

Harmonia Mundi HMC90 1708 (63' · DDD · T/t)
ⓕ 〇〇〇

An enthralling account of the cycle on virtually every count that seriously challenges the hegemony of the many desirable versions already available. In the first place Güra must have about the most beautiful voice ever to have recorded the work in the original keys (and that's not to overlook Wunderlich, a far less perceptive interpreter). Its owner has a technique second to none, able to vary his tone, sing a lovely *pianissimo* and/or a long-breathed phrase with perfect control. Then no musical or verbal subtlety seems to escape him at any stage of the young man's disillusioning journey from happiness to misery and death.

The plaintive quality of his voice and its youthful sap are precisely right for conveying the protagonist's vulnerability and, where needed, his self-pity. That great song 'Der Neugierige' encapsulates these virtues, with the final couplet of questioning the brook immaculately done, just as the *pp* at the close of the previous song is given a curious sense of uncertainty on the boy's part. The three strophic songs are finely varied: here, as throughout, the use of *rubato* is natural and inevitable and the integration of singer and pianist, who's happily playing a Bechstein, are at their most compelling.

'Mein' is properly eager, expectant, 'Pause' as plangent as it should be, especially at its end. The frenetic anger of the 14th and 15th songs is as over-heated as it should be, 'Die liebe Farbe' rightly hypnotic. In those great songs, 'Trockne Blumen' and 'Der Müller und der Bach', both artists go to the heart of the matter, and the final lullaby is soft-grained and consoling. Schultsz's contributions are sometimes controversial, always challenging. Güra surpasses even the *Gramophone* Award-winning Bostridge, simply because his voice is under even better control and because his German is more idiomatic. The Harmonia Mundi sound, in spite of some reverberance, catches voice and piano in ideal balance.

Die schöne Müllerin, with a reading of six poems not set by Schubert
Ian Bostridge ten **Dietrich Fischer-Dieskau** narr
Graham Johnson pf
Hyperion CDJ33025 (73' · DDD · T/t) ⓕ 〇〇〇

The 20 songs of *Die schöne Müllerin* portray a Wordsworthian world of heightened emotion in the pantheistic riverside setting of the miller. The poet, Wilhelm Müller, tells of solitary longings, jealousies, fears and hopes as the river rushes by, driving the mill-wheel and refreshing the natural world. Ian Bostridge and Graham Johnson go to the heart of the matter, the young tenor in his aching tones and naturally affecting interpretation, the pianist in his perceptive, wholly apposite playing. The sum of their joint efforts is a deeply satisfying experience.

Bostridge has the right timbre for the protagonist and a straightforward approach, with an instinctive rightness of phrasing. His peculiarly beseeching voice enshrines the vulnerability, tender feeling and obsessive love of the youthful miller, projecting in turn the young lover's thwarted passions, self-delusions and, finally, inner tragedy. Nowhere does he stretch beyond the bounds of the possible, everything expressed in eager then doleful tones. Johnson suggests that 'Ungeduld' mustn't be 'masterful and insistent' or the youth would have won the girl, so that even in this superficially buoyant song the sense of a sensitive, sad, introverted youth is maintained. The daydreaming strophic songs have the smiling, innocent, intimate sound that suits them to perfection, the angry ones the touch of stronger metal that Bostridge can now add to his silver, the tragic ones, before the neutral 'Baches Wiegenlied', an inner intensity that rends the heart as it should. An occasional moment of faulty German accenting matters not at all when the sense of every word is perceived.

As a bonus we have here a recitation of the Prologue and Epilogue and of the Müller poems not set by Schubert: Fischer-Dieskau graces it with his speaking voice. The ideal Hyperion recording catches everything in very present terms. In all musical matters, everything Johnson writes only enhances one's enjoyment, if that's the right word, of a soul-searching interpretation.

Die schöne Müllerin
Dietrich Fischer-Dieskau bar **András Schiff** pf
Video director **Fritz Jurmann**
TDK **DVD** DV-CODSM (83' · 4:3 · PCM stereo · 0).
Recorded live at the Montforthaus, Feldkirch, on June 20, 1991. Includes 1985 interview with Dietrich Fischer-Dieskau ⓕ 〇〇

To celebrate Fischer-Dieskau's 80th birthday Austrian Television issued this film made at the 1991 Schubertiade. It marked the return, after a 20-year break, of the great baritone, aged 66, to Schubert's first cycle. In restudying the work, the singer comments that he tried, really for the first time, to sing these songs 'not so much by feeling as by narrative, not so much concentrating on the vocal line as responding with curiosity and openness to the wealth of colour and expression in the piano part – which calls for a pianist as sensitive as Schiff'.

He's as good as his word, singing the cycle even more off the words than he had in the past, giving his audience a kind of mini-drama, underlined by some movement on the platform and a wealth of facial expression. At this late stage in his career his voice inevitably shows some decline in tonal body, but in almost every other respect he retains the famed qualities of his prime: astonishing breath-control, an arresting command of wide-ranging dynamics and total control in putting his ideas into action. The hypnotic reading reaches its proper moment of epiphany in the two penultimate, tragic songs, delivered with all the varied resources the performers can offer them.

As a bonus there's a 20-minute portrait of the singer, assembled at the 1985 Schubertiade. It includes a couple more valuable examples of his singing and a fascinating interview, in which he tells us a lot about himself and his approach to his art, something invaluable in years to come.

Schwanengesang, D957

Schubert Schwanengesang
Beethoven An die ferne Geliebte
Matthias Goerne bar **Alfred Brendel** pf
Decca 475 6011DH (72' · DDD · T/t)
Recorded live 2003   ⒻOOOⒹ

As Misha Donat reminds us in outstanding booklet essays, *Schwanengesang* divides clearly into eight Rellstab and six Heine settings; 'Herbst' is here added to the Rellstab group, while the Seidl 'Die Taubenpost' is made into the encore of a wonderful recital.

Goerne and Brendel form one of the great Lieder partnerships of the day. The sympathy between them goes beyond skilful ensemble and shared enjoyment of the wealth of illustration in Schubert, into a deep understanding of the poetry as he composed it. It's no surprise that they should produce powerful performances of the most inward-looking Heine songs – the suffering power of 'Der Atlas', the misery from which the harmony allows no escape in 'Die Stadt', the terror of 'Der Doppelgänger'. But the lighter ones are scarcely less affecting. And their mutual understanding completely solves such a difficult song as 'Kriegers Ahnung'.

The Beethoven cycle moves in a steady progress not into the usual triumphant assertion but into a warmth of belief that song may truly join the parted lovers. This is music-making of genius.

Schwanengesang. Wer sich der Einsamkeit ergibt (Harfenspieler I), D478. An die Türen (Harfenspieler III), D479. Ganymed, D544. Geheimes, D719. Der Musensohn, D764. Rastlose Liebe, D138. Schäfers Klagelied, D121. Wandrers Nachtlied II, D768. Wer nie sein Brot mit Tränen ass, D480
Peter Schreier ten **András Schiff** pf
Wigmore Hall Live WHLIVE0006 (79' · DDD · T/t)
Recorded live 1991   ⓂOO

The 1991 recital by Peter Schreier and András Schiff is highly desirable, though the sound is not quite on the same level. Schreier was never the most honeyed of tenors; but in the lighter songs of *Schwanengesang* he compensates for a touch of reediness and a tendency to harden on high notes with the supple grace of his phrasing and his ultra-keen response to the text. *Liebesbotschaft* is eager and volatile, enhanced by Schiff's wonderfully limpid touch and his care to make the piano's singing left hand match the

voice in eloquence (Schubert's original, high, key an advantage, here and elsewhere).

On the downside, *Aufenthalt* is surely too slow and life-weary, weighed down by recurrent submissive *rallentandos*. But *Das Fischermädchen* has a lilting tenderness, Schiff again singing in dulcet partnership with the voice, while in the remaining Heine songs singer and pianist unflinchingly probe the extremes of anguish and bitterness. *Die Stadt* (the swirling, impressionistic arpeggios eerily insubstantial from Schiff) and *Der Doppelgänger* are as desolate and disturbing as any performances on disc, the suggestion of a whine, even a sneer, in Schreier's timbre extraordinarily apt here.

After this we get a sharply characterised Goethe group that encompasses the bleakness of the three Harper's Songs (done with characteristic intense immediacy) and ends with an impulsive, dancing *Der Musensohn* that rightly brings the house down.

Schwanengesang, D957. Abschied, D475. An Schwager Kronos, D369. Geheimnis, D491. Widerschein (second version), D949.
Ian Bostridge ten **Antonio Pappano** pf
EMI 242639-2 (61' · DDD)   ⒻⒹ

Schwanengesang is really no such thing, and there is nothing to prevent a singer omitting the song or changing the order. Bostridge follows the publisher's order and does not flinch before 'Aufenthalt'; and if momentarily he goes under, perhaps it is part of the musical-verbal picture that he should. In any case, all of this is a diversion, almost a frivolity. At the heart of the matter are 'Der Doppelgänger', 'Die Stadt', 'Ihr Bild', 'Am Meer' and, from the Rellstab settings, 'In der Ferne'. Bostridge has, in the pallor of voice and expression, the haunting that pervades these songs. In the first mentioned (the last sung) he is one of the few who can create unease without anticipating the horror, still making those open-mouthed vowels ('starret', 'Schmerzensgewalt', 'so manche Nacht') call out into the night like a wounded animal.

Such rare moments are the singer's own; elsewhere the performance is equally the pianist's. Pappano plays with imagination as verbally attuned as Bostridge's. The rightness of touch is evident in the first additional song, 'Geheimnis', and in the last, the very simple and aptly chosen 'Abschied'. He is also graceful and interesting in the happier songs. There's one misgiving – Bostridge makes so much of the German words, rather as though anxious to communicate with the back rows of a concert-hall full of non-German speakers. Whatever the justification *in situ*, it nags a little on records.

Schwanengesang, D957. Herbst, D945. Die Taubenpost, D965a. Sehnsucht, D879. Am Fenster, D878. Bei Dir allein, D866. Der Wanderer an den Mond, D870. Das Zückenglöcklein, D871. Im Freien, D880

Christoph Prégardien ten **Andreas Staier** fp
Challenge Classics ⊞ CC72302 (72' · DDD · T/t)
Ⓕ**OOↂ**

Planning a CD programme around *Schwanengesang* is always tricky. The vastly experienced duo of Christoph Prégardien and Andreas Staier here come up with a solution as satisfying as any. They preface the quasi-cycle with the bleak, windswept Rellstab setting *Herbst*, which Schubert unaccountably omitted from the Rellstab sequence that opens *Schwanengesang*. Then, at they end, they follow *Die Taubenpost* – always in danger of jarring after the *Weltschmerz* of the Heine group – with other, complementary, Seidl settings, ending with the blissful nocturnal homecoming of *Im Freien*.

Prégardien's dulcet tenor, subtly and gracefully deployed, is heard to advantage both in these Seidl songs and in *Schwanengesang*. Where so many singers seem to 'think' the whole collection in the minor key, as it were, Prégardien is eagerly expectant in 'Liebesbotschaft' and sings a smiling, seductive 'Fischermädchen'. His 'Ständchen', taken at an easy, mobile tempo, is likewise all caressing charm, while 'Abschied' is blithely insouciant, the wistfulness of the final verse lightly touched – and how well the delicate, slightly veiled sonorities of Staier's fortepiano complement the voice, here and elsewhere.

In the anguished Heine songs Prégardien's less extreme style than, say, Peter Schreier, is scarcely less moving, whether in the rhythmically incisive 'Der Atlas' (where the fortepiano's percussive resonance brings uncommon clarity to Schubert's quasi-orchestral textures), or an 'Am Meer' of aching tenderness, the final stab of pain all the more affecting for being understated. 'Die Stadt', taken at an unusually urgent tempo, emerges in a single grim sweep, with the fortepiano's sustaining pedal creating a mysterious haze impossible to replicate on a modern grand. Prégardien occasionally adds discreet, graceful embellishments to his lines, especially apt in 'Ständchen'. While it is absurd to speak of an outright 'winner' in such a crowded field, Prégardien and the ever-illuminating Staier join the roster of indispensable *Schwanenengesang* recordings.

Winterreise, D911

Winterreise　　　　　　　　　　　　　Ⓟ
Christoph Prégardien ten **Andreas Staier** fp
Teldec Das Alte Werk 0630-18824-2 (74' · DDD · T/t)
Ⓜ**OO**

Prégardien and Staier have something new and important to offer. From the very first song, we're in the presence of a sensitive, inward man in fear of his fate. Something is actually happening to this sufferer's soul at the second 'des ganzen Winters Eis'; indeed the whole final verse of the second song expresses the youth's anguish. Just as memorable are the stab of pain in the repeated final line 'Da ist meiner Liebstens Haus' at the end of 'Wasserflut', the introverted misery of the

ice-carving of the loved-one's name in 'Auf dem Flusse' and the almost mesmeric feeling in the final verse as the torrent rages in the protagonist's heart. This is what the singing of this cycle is about: the exposing of raw nerves.

Staier is just as revelatory. Using his fortepiano to maximum effect, he finds so many fresh perceptions in his part, as in the precise weighting at the start of 'Einsamkeit' and, as important, ones that accord perfectly with those of his regular partner. Here you've the sense of performers who have lived together with the cycle and conceived a unified, thought-through vision. For example, listen to the way the pair mesh together to searing effect at the end of 'Irrlicht'. The ineffable sadness of 'Frühlingstraum' (the text ideally articulated, the close properly trance-like), the raw blast of winter in 'Der stürmische Morgen', the tense weariness of 'Der Wegweiser', the weary half-voice of 'Das Wirtshaus' – these and so much else contribute to the impression of a truly great performance. The recording is very finely balanced.

Winterreise
Dietrich Fischer-Dieskau bar **Jörg Demus** pf
DG The Originals 447 421-2GOR (71' · ADD · T/t)
Recorded 1965　　　　　　　　　　Ⓜ**OOↂ**

On the verge of his fifth decade, the singer was in his absolute prime. Listening to his interpretation is like coming home to base after many interesting encounters away from the familiar. Indeed, it's possibly the finest of all in terms of beauty of tone and ease of technique – and how beautiful, how smooth and velvety was the baritone's voice at that time. This is the most interior, unadorned and undemonstrative of his readings, perhaps because Demus, a discerning musician and sure accompanist, is the most reflective of all the singer's many partners in the cycle. Demus never strikes out on his own, is always there unobtrusively and subtly supportive, with the right colour and phrasing, literally in hand.

Given an intimate, slightly dry recording, finely remastered, the whole effect is of a pair communing with each other and stating the sad, distraught message of Schubert's bleak work in terms of a personal message to the listener in the home. A deeply rewarding performance.

Winterreise
Ian Bostridge ten **Julius Drake** pf Stage director **David Alden** Video director **Peter West**
NVC Arts 🖸 8573-83780-2 (124' · Regions 2-6)
Includes documentary on the making of the film Ⓕ**O**

Winterreise lives on its own without any staging. The initially dubious Bostridge and Drake make that point at the start of the feature, their faces filling with dismay as Alden describes his seemingly hare-brained ideas to turn it into a melodrama about a crazed protagonist. It's implied in what follows that singer and pianist gained confidence in what Alden had in mind, while the director came to respect Bostridge's intelligence and dramatic gifts. Indeed, the project would have collapsed had not the tenor the ability to sear the soul as much visually as aurally. His piercing eyes, striking looks and age make him an ideal candidate for such an experiment.

Inspired by a disused mental asylum in north London, Alden and his designer create a huge, empty space, as desolate as the abandoned asylum itself, in which the beginning and end of the cycle are enacted. In between, Bostridge is projected on to a white background, arrestingly so in the case of 'Die Krähe', where the singer is viewed from above by the crow with Bostridge spread-eagled on the floor below, an astonishing image, mirroring the bird's menace. Among the unforgettable shots are the picture of the forlorn shattered figure in 'Die Nebensonnen', which Alden and Bostridge agree has a mystic, religious aura to it, the lone protagonist seen at a distance in 'Das Wirtshaus', the singer seated back to back with the pianist in 'Mut'. Doubts arise only with the introduction during two songs of the unfaithful girl and her family, disturbing the vision of the lonely sufferer.

At the heart of the video lies Bostridge's silvery tone, special, highly individual intensity of utterance and identification with the man's desperate plight. Drake supports him with playing of equal insight. The sound, fairly closely miked, is excellent; the camerawork highly imaginative.

Winterreise
Thomas Quasthoff bar **Daniel Barenboim** pf
Video director **Michael Beyer**
DG **DVD** 073 4049GH (83' · NTSC · 16:9 ·
PCM stereo, 5.1 and DTS 5.1 · 0)   Ⓕ

As we know from his fine CD version, Thomas Quasthoff is a master of this cycle, his command of word and music consistently true and compelling. His interpretation here is once more imbued with sincere empathy with the suffering traveller, suggesting, as he says in the accompanying interview, a man at once at the end of his tether and yet defiant. He is also keen to show that each song could not exist without its being part of the whole, just one aspect of Schubert's genius. The cohesion of his reading is supported with deep acumen by Barenboim's thoughtfully felicitous playing. Some 30 years ago he recorded the cycle with Fischer-Dieskau, and again he manages to underpin his singer's intentions while managing to add his own mite of individuality.

So why do the results rather underwhelm? The direction is too restless and in close-up Quasthoff constantly rocks from side to side; the effect becomes dizzying. For a DVD version Bostridge offers rich rewards, but for those allergic to any visual dimension outside the music as such, this DVD has much to offer purely in musical terms.

Additional recommendation:

Coupled with: 10 Lieder

Hotter bass **Moore** pf
EMI mono 566985-2 (78' · ADD · T/t)   Ⓜ
A classic interpretation b the one of the great Lieder singers: the dark-voiced Hans Hotter. A winter's journey of extraordinary imaginative thrust, beautifully accompanied by Moore.

Ervin Schulhoff   Bohemian 1894-1942

Schulhoff was a pupil of Reger in Leipzig (1908-10) and later in Germany (1919-23) he associated with Klee and the dadaists; back in Prague he was active as a pianist, in jazz and as an exponent of Hába's quarter-tone music. His works include stage pieces, six symphonies and two piano sonatas, displaying diverse styles. He died in a concentration camp.

GROVEmusic

Sextet

Sextet. String Quartet in G, Op 25. Duoᵃ.
Solo Violin Sonataᵇ
Rainer Johannes Kimstedt va **Michael Sanderling**
vc **Petersen Quartet** (ᵇConrad Muck, ᵃGernot
Sussmuth vns Friedemann Weigle va ᵃHans-Jakob
Eschenburg vc)
Capriccio 10 539 (77' · DDD)   Ⓕⓞ

As Schulhoff enthusiasts will have come to expect, the works represented aren't at all uniform in style. The early quartet is prematurely neo-classical. It was conceived in 1918 when the composer was still serving in the Austrian Army. The German group certainly gives it their all. Taut and tough, they seem intent on radicalising the discourse whether through a heightened response to its finer points or a profound understanding of the Beethovenian models that lurk beneath the surface invention. As a result, the Quartet emerges as a witty, substantial piece.

The string Sextet was completed six years later but sounds quite different, its Schoenbergian first movement well integrated with the more eclectic idiom of the rest. Whatever the outward manner, Schulhoff's rhythmic phraseology is metrically conceived. Even if you already know the Sextet the Petersen makes a plausible first choice. The aggressive communication of their playing is emphasised by the bright, not quite top-heavy sound balance.

The Janáček-Bartók-Ravel axis of the *Duo* is equally well served. The Sonata for solo violin (1927) is at least as interesting as similar works by Hindemith. A thoroughly distinguished issue by an ensemble seemingly incapable of giving a dull performance.

String Quartet No 1

Schulhoff String Quartet No 1 **Hindemith** String Quartet No 3, Op 22 **Weill** String Quartet

---

Brandis Quartet (Thomas Brandis, Peter Brem vns
Wilfried Strehle va Wolfgang Boettcher vc)
Nimbus NI5410 (60' · DDD)   Ⓕ

All three works bear witness to a culture that, in terms of tempo and sensation, was in the process of excited transformation. The period covered is 1923-4, the time of rocketing German inflation, the establishment of the USSR, Rilke's *Duino Elegies* as well as major Kafka (who died in 1924), Mann, Musil, Cocteau and Bréton (his Surrealist manifesto). This music is full of it all. Hindemith's bold Third Quartet launches its explorations within a relatively formal framework, certainly in comparison with Schulhoff and Weill. Rich invention is tempered by a sense of outward propriety. Weill's Quartet opens with real expressive warmth, although it soon busies itself with a whole range of interesting ideas (the finale is particularly rich in incident), with a hoot of a *Scherzo* that suddenly swerves to a Reger-like March, then waltzes gently forth in a manner that suggests Shostakovich before embarking on further discursive episodes and scurrying off to a cheeky *diminuendo*. Granted, one feels that Weill is in search of something he never quite finds, but the very act of searching makes for an absorbing adventure.

Even more compelling, however, is Schulhoff's dazzling First Quartet, the last piece in the programme and a highly dramatic musical mystery tour. Urgency rules right from the opening bars, while Schulhoff's tonal palette is both wide-ranging and ingeniously employed: pizzicato, *col legno*, *sul ponticello*, harmonics (wonderfully effective in the finale), dense harmonic computations and a rhythmic vitality that recalls Bartók at full cry. The work's pale, equivocal coda recalls the parallel quartet mysteries of Schulhoff's fellow Holocaust victims Krása and Haas, while the work as a whole is far more than the sum of its restless and endlessly fascinating parts. A fine programme, lustrously recorded.

William Schuman   American 1910-1992

Schuman studied at Columbia University and under Harris at the Juilliard School. He came firmly to public notice with his Symphony no.3 (1941). He taught at Sarah Lawrence College, 1935-45, then became president of the Juilliard School, which he extensively reorganised. He was president of the Lincoln Center, 1962-9. He received many honours and awards. His symphonies (ten up to 1975) are central to his work; they embody vigorous drive, febrile rhythms and expansive musical and orchestral gestures, with a broad melodic line and a generally tonal idiom. Sometimes his music is layered, using different instrumental groups at different speeds. His chamber music includes four string quartets; he also composed, mainly after the mid-1970s, large-scale vocal pieces. GROVEmusic

Violin Concerto

Schuman Violin Concerto[a]. New England Triptych
Ives Variations on 'America' (orch Schuman)
[a]**Philip Quint** vn **Bournemouth Symphony
Orchestra / José Serebrier**
Naxos 8 559083 (57' · DDD)   Ⓢ**Ⓞ**➔

The rediscovery here is the William Schuman Violin Concerto. The work is in two substantial movements both showing Schuman's own kind of exuberant energy with brass and percussion as well as a special mystical stillness in soft music. The soloist plunges in right at the start of the first movement; there's an oasis of calm at and then a sprawling cadenza of nearly three minutes.

The second movement has an aggressive start which clears the way for the delayed entry of the soloist. Again there's lyrical rapture as well as fireworks and – another Schuman fingerprint – a fugato. Philip Quint, the Russian-born American violinist, make his recorded début here. It's a very capable performance in every way – look out for him again.

Schuman's *New England Triptych*, based on three hymns by the first prominent American pioneer-composer, William Billings, is one of his most familiar pieces, well represented on CD. The *Variations on 'America'* – sending up the USA, royalty or both – ensures that this useful Schuman package ends with a good laugh.

Clara Schumann   German 1819-1896

Developed by her father, Friedrich, into a musician of consummate artistry, she won dazzling success as a touring piano virtuoso both before and after she married Robert Schumann (1840), being praised not only for her mastery of a progressive repertory (Chopin, Schumann and Brahms) but also for her thoughtful interpretations and singing tone. She taught privately in Dresden and Düsseldorf and at the conservatories in Leipzig and Frankfurt.
As a composer she showed imagination and control, notably in the Piano Trio, Op 17 and the songs, Op 23, but her ambitions were not serious; she ceased composing in 1854, the year of Robert's collapse. She prepared a complete edition of his music, attended to family duties and maintained a close relationship with Brahms to the end of her life. GROVEmusic

Piano Concerto in A minor, Op 7

Piano Concerto. Piano Trio, Op 17.
Francesco Nicolosi pf
Rodolfo Bonucci vn and **Andrea Noferini** vc
Alma Mahler Sinfonietta / Stefania Rinaldi
Naxos 8 557552 (54' · DDD) Ⓢ

The autograph manuscript of Robert Schumann's Piano Concerto (1845) revealed not only the toil but also the hand of Clara, particularly in the last movement. Eleven years earlier, Robert had orchestrated a *Concertsatz* by the 14-year-old Clara and this became the corresponding movement of her concerto which she soon completed on her own.

The *Concertsatz* is as long as the other movements put together and a shorter finale might have been beneficial. Yet the complete, though imperfect, work is a notable achievement for so young a composer; and the piano part could be seen as a vehicle for virtuosity. All credit therefore to Francesco Nicolosi for not succumbing to temptation. His playing is deep-toned and tractable and, in conjunction with Stefania Rinaldi who eschews strident orchestral attack, finds a vein of melancholy in the music. He also ably balances the implied duality of the *Romanze* in which the marking *con grazia* conflicts somewhat with the additional *La melodia ben marcato e legato*.

'Not a gifted melodist but skilful handling of other elements compensates' is one of biographer Nancy B Reich's verdicts on Clara Schumann. And an element is the assured way modulations are treated in the Piano Trio (1846). Nicolosi adapts his playing to the demands of the genre, and he interacts sympathetically with his fine partners. Perhaps the *Scherzo* (to be played *Tempo di menuetto*) ought to have been bucolic rather than gracious but this doesn't detract from a very communicative performance. The orchestra's cellos and basses are lightweight and the solo violin occasionally squeaky but the sound is otherwise good.

Piano works

'The Complete Works for Piano Solo'
Susanne Grützmann pf
Profil ④ PH07065 (3h 55' · DDD)   Ⓜ

This four-CD album redresses a faulty or at least misunderstood balance. Superbly played and recorded, it prompts a sharp and necessary awareness of the full range of Clara Schumann's gifts. A deeply courageous woman who juggled her roles of wife, mother (to eight children), pianist and composer, she also bore the tragedy of her beloved Robert's collapse into insanity and the added complication of her relationship with Brahms with rare strength and fortitude. Certainly her Op 1 (composed when she was 11) suggests a startling precocity before her skill deepened over the years into music where outward conventions thinly disguise a highly personal and poetic nature. True, she pays loving tribute to her husband's work, but the listener should not be misled. Theirs was clearly a symbiotic relationship, and composing side by side during the early days of their legendary romance, Schumann both marvelled at and feared her gifts. Indeed, there is evidence to show that Clara felt over-shadowed ('I compose, too,' she asserted as she pushed her compositions under Robert's door) while Robert felt threatenend by his wife's celebrity as a pianist

(the Tsar of Russia politely enquired of Clara, 'and is your husband also musical?').

Yet Clara always remained true to her own lights. And even when her veneration for others (to Chopin in the exquisite Nocturne from Op 6), is clear she always maintains her own voice. There are some strange prophecies (Alkan's *En rhythme molassique*, for example, in her *Le ballet des revenants* from Op 5) as well as a capacity to wear her cap and gown with the best of them (the Op 16 Preludes and Fugues) or play her virtuoso trump cards with aplomb (Op 14 and the *Agitato* from Op 21). But whether you turn to the chirpy *Scherzo* from her single Piano Sonata or to the scintillating *volante* close to the Op 8 Variations you will be brilliantly surprised and subtly challenged. This issue is an invaluable addition to the catalogue.

Robert Schumann   German 1810-1856

The son of a bookseller, Schumann early showed ability as a pianist and an interest in composing as well as literary leanings. He was also enthusiastic over the writings of 'Jean Paul' (JPF Richter), girl friends and drinking champagne, tastes he retained. In 1821 he went to Leipzig to study law but instead spent his time in musical, social and literary activities. He wrote some piano music and took lessons from Friedrich Wieck. After a spell in Heidelberg, ostensibly studying law but actually music, he persuaded his family that he should give up law in favour of a pianist's career, and in 1830 he went to live with Wieck at Leipzig. But he soon had trouble with hands (allegedly due to a machine to strengthen his fingers, but more likely through remedies for a syphilitic sore). Composition, however, continued; several piano works date from this period.

In 1834 Schumann founded a music journal, the Neue Zeitschrift für Musik; he was its editor and leading writer for ten years. He was a brilliant and perceptive critic: his writings embody the most progressive aspects of musical thinking in his time, and he drew attention to many promising young composers. Sometimes he wrote under pseudonyms, Eusebius (representing his lyrical, contemplative side) and Florestan (his fiery, impetuous one); he used these in his music, too. His compositions at this time were mainly for piano: they include variations on the name of one on his lady friends, Abegg (the musical notes A-B-E-G-G), the character-pieces Davidsbündlertänze ('Dances of the league of David', an imaginary association of those fighting the Philistines), Carnaval (pieces with literary or other allusive meanings, including one on the notes A-S-C-H after the place another girl friend came from), Phantasiestücke (a collection of poetic pieces depicting moods), Kreisleriana (fantasy pieces around the character of a mad Kapellmeister) and Kinderszenen ('Scenes from Childhood'). Affairs of the heart played a large part in his life. By 1835 he was in love with Wieck's young daughter Clara, but Wieck did his best to separate them. They pledged themselves in 1837 but were much apart and Schumann went through deep depressions. In 1839 they took legal steps to make Wieck's consent unnecessary, and after many further trials they were able to marry in 1840.

Schumann, understandably, turned in that year to song; he wrote c150 songs, including most of his finest, at this time, among them several groups and cycles, the latter including Frauenliebe und -Leben ('A Woman's Love and Life') and Dichterliebe ('A Poet's Love'), which tells (to verse by Heine) a tragic Romantic story of the flowering of love, its failure and poet's exclusion from joy and his longing for death. Schumann, as a pianist composer, made the piano partake fully in the expression of emotion in such songs, often giving it the most telling music when the voice had finished.

In 1841, however, Schumann turned to orchestral music: he wrote symphonies and a beautiful, poetic piece for piano and orchestra for Clara that he later reworked as the first movement of his Piano Concerto. Then in 1842, when Clara was away on a concert tour (he disliked being in her shadow and remained at home), he turned to chamber music, and wrote his three string quartets and three works with piano, of which the Piano Quintet has always been a favourite for the freshness and Romantic warmth of its ideas. After that, in 1843, he turned to choral music, working at a secular oratorio and at setting part of Goethe's Faust. He also took up a teaching post at the new conservatory in Leipzig of which Mendelssohn was director. But he was an ineffectual teacher; and he had limited success as a conductor too. He and Clara moved to Dresden in 1844, but his deep depressions continued, hampering his creativity. Not until 1847-8 was he again productive, writing his opera Genoveva (given in Leipzig in 1850 with moderate success), chamber music and songs. In 1850 he took up a post in Düsseldorf as town musical director. He was at first happy and prolific, writing the eloquent Cello Concerto and the Rhenish Symphony (No 3: one movement depicts his impressions in Cologne Cathedral). But the post worked out badly because of his indifferent conducting. In 1852-3 his health and spirits deteriorated and he realised that he could not continue in his post. In 1854 he began to suffer hallucinations; he attempted suicide (he had always dreaded the possibility of madness) and entered an asylum, where he died in 1856, almost certainly of the effects of syphilis, cared for at the end by Clara and the young Brahms. **GROVE**music

Concertos

Schumann Cello Concerto. Adagio and Allegro in A flat, Op 70. Fantasiestücke, Op 73. Fünf Stücke im Volkston, Op 102. Mass in C minor, Op 147— Offertorium **Bargiel** Adagio in G, Op 38
Steven Isserlis *vc* **Dame Felicity Lott** *sop* **David King** *org* **Deutsche Kammerphilharmonie / Christoph Eschenbach** *pf*
RCA Red Seal 09026 68800-2 (75' · DDD)   Ⓕ

Only two of the works in this forwardly recorded anthology – the *Fünf Stücke im Volkston* of 1840 and the Cello Concerto of a year later – were originally inspired by the cello. But in closely attuned, super-sensitive partnership with Eschenbach as both conductor and pianist, Ste-

ven Isserlis somehow persuades us that no instrument better revealed 'the beloved dreamer whom we know as Schumann', as Tovey once put it. Helped by unhurried tempos and a lovely voiced c1745 Guadagnini cello, Isserlis draws out the rich, nostalgic poetry of the concerto's first two movements with the eloquence of speech. And with his buoyancy of heart and bow he silences all criticism of the finale – even its low-lying cadenza (this he subsequently plays again with the composer's surely less effective flourish for the soloist in the closing bars). The five engaging *Volkston* pieces with piano are vividly characterised and contrasted in mood. And the Op 73 and Op 70 miniatures lose nothing through transfer from clarinet and horn respectively to one of the composer's two optional alternatives.

The *Adagio and Allegro* for horn surely gains in expressive intimacy and vitality when bowed rather than blown. The *Offertorium* is sung by Felicity Lott with heart-easing beauty. The inclusion of a hitherto unrecorded, noble *Adagio* by Clara Schumann's gifted half-brother, Woldemar Bargiel, also helps to make this disc a collector's piece.

Piano Concerto[a]. Cello Concerto[b]. Introduction and Allegro appassionato, Op 92[a].
[a]**Daniel Barenboim** *pf* [b]**Jacqueline du Pré** *vc*
[a]**London Philharmonic Orchestra / Dietrich Fischer-Dieskau;** [b]**New Philharmonia Orchestra / Daniel Barenboim**
EMI Encore 574755-2 (74' · ADD) Recorded [a]1974, [b]1968   Ⓑ⭕

If ever a performance of Schumann's Piano Concerto stressed the principle of dialogue between soloist and conductor, then this is it. True, the Philharmonia's string ensemble isn't as watertight under Fischer-Dieskau as it might have been under some other conductors; and poetry is invested at the premium of relatively low-level drama. Orchestral textures are absolutely right for Schumann – warm yet transparent, full-bodied yet never stodgy – and poetry is a major priority. Add Barenboim's compatible vision and keyboard finesse, and you indeed have a memorable reading. Despite the extensive competition, both Stephen Kovacevich and Leif Ove Andsnes remain the top recommendations for this work (both reviewed under Grieg) though.

The more discursive *Introduction and Allegro appassionato* has plenty of interest, but remembering that this isn't exactly top-drawer Schumann, the performance could be more arresting. The coupling is du Pré's Schumann Cello Concerto, the tear-laden quality in the slow movement more than matching that in her famous Elgar account. A rewarding disc.

Violin Concerto, Op posth

Schumann Violin Concerto **Wieniawski** Légende, Op 17. Violin Concerto No 2 in D minor, Op 22

Juliette Kang *vn* **Vancouver Symphony Orchestra /
Sergiu Comissiona**
CBC Records SMCD5197 (63' · DDD)　　　　Ⓕ●

Juliette Kang here plays with quicksilver brilliance not only in the virtuosic Wieniawski
concerto but in the rugged Schumann work, less
grateful for the player. Yet, though she plays
brilliantly, with dazzlingly clean articulation in
bravura passages, these are comparatively small-
scale readings. Where those virtuosos in the
grand Romantic tradition are balanced relatively
close, Kang is more naturally balanced in a
slightly recessed acoustic. The impression is of a
sweet, silvery violin tone that can't expand so
fully; the orchestral strings, too, sound relatively
small-scale. What matters is that the performances are all very persuasive. The Schumann,
with its bravura double-stopping at the start,
finds Kang fiery and impetuous, making up for
barnstorming power, and when it comes to lyrical passages the poetry is beautifully caught. So
too in the slow movement – introduced in a
tender account of the brief opening cello solo –
while the finale is taken at a speed which allows
a delicious lilt in the dance-rhythms.

Similarly, in the Wieniawski Concerto, Kang
is light and volatile in the rapid passagework,
and relaxes sweetly into the songful beauty of
the motto theme, playing with a natural, unexaggerated lyricism.

Those who insist on display as the first essential may not be completely satisfied, but deeper
qualities amply make up for that. For those who
want this unique coupling, this is a first-class
recommendation.

Symphonies

No 1 in B flat, Op 38, 'Spring' **No 2** in C, Op 61 **No 3**
in E flat, Op 97, 'Rhenish' **No 4** in D minor, Op 120

Symphonies Nos 1-4. Overture, Scherzo and Finale,
Op 52
Staatskapelle Dresden / Wolfgang Sawallisch
EMI Great Recordings of the Century mono
② 567768-2 (148' · ADD) Recorded 1972　　Ⓜ●●Ⓓ↦

Schumann's symphonies come in for criticism
because of his supposed cloudy textures and
unsubtle scoring, but in the hands of a conductor
who's both skilful and sympathetic they're most
engaging works. Sawallisch's recordings, brightly
transferred, are a much admired set. His style,
fresh and unforced, isn't as high powered as some
other conductors but it's sensible, alert and very
pleasing. He achieves great lightness in the First
and Fourth Symphonies – there's always a sense
of classical poise and control but never at the
expense of the overall architecture of the pieces.
The Second and Third Symphonies, larger and
more far-reaching in their scope, again benefit
from Sawallisch's approach. The playing of the
Staatskapelle Dresden is superlative in every
department, with a lovely veiled string sound and

a real sense of ensemble. With the *Overture,
Scherzo and Finale* thrown in for good measure,
this isn't to be missed.

Symphonies Nos 1 & 2
**Bavarian Radio Symphony Orchestra /
Rafael Kubelík**
Sony Classical Essential Classics 07464 48269-2
(74' · ADD)　　　　Ⓑ●

Symphonies Nos 3 & 4. Manfred, Op 115 – Overture
**Bavarian Radio Symphony Orchestra /
Rafael Kubelík**
Sony Classical Essential Classics 07464 48270-2
(76' · ADD) Recorded 1978-9　　　　Ⓑ

It's hard to understand why Kubelík's wonderful
cycle failed to make an impact when it was first
issued. His sensitivity to detail, his refusal to
bully Schumann's vulnerable structures and his
ability to penetrate occasional thickets of
orchestration, make these especially memorable. Just listen to the cheeky bassoon backing
clarinet, 1'44" into the *Spring* Symphony's
fourth movement or the to-ing and fro-ing
between first and second violins in the last
movement of the Second. Only the first movement of the Fourth seems a little heavy-handed,
but then the poetry of the *Romanze* and the exuberance of the finale more than make amends.
First movement repeats are observed and the
playing throughout is rich in felicitous turns of
phrase. The sound, though, is a minor stumbling block: violins are thin, brass a little fuzzy
and the whole production less focused than
Sawallisch's set. But Kubelík's insights are too
varied and meaningful to miss, and there's much
pleasure to be derived from them. What with a
stirring *Manfred* Overture added for good measure, they also constitute exceptional value for
money.

Symphonies Nos 1-3; No 4 (1841 & 1851　　Ⓟ
G minor versions); WoO29, 'Zwickauer'. Overture,
Scherzo and Finale, Op 52. Konzertstück in F, Op 86
**Roger Montgomery, Gavin Edwards, Susan Dent,
Robert Maskell** *hns* **Orchestre Révolutionnaire et
Romantique / Sir John Eliot Gardiner**
Archiv Produktion ③ 457 591-2AH3 (202' · DDD)
　　　　　　　　　　　　　　　　Ⓕ●Ⓓ↦

The first point to note is how much more comprehensive this is than previous cycles, even the
outstanding RCA set of period performances
from Roy Goodman and the Hanover Band.
Gardiner offers both versions of Symphony No
4, 1841 and 1851, and his performances of them
are very well geared to bringing out the contrasts. Still more fascinating is the inclusion of
both the early, incomplete Symphony in G
minor, and the *Konzertstück* of 1849 for four
horns, with the ORR soloists breathtaking in
their virtuosity in the outer movements, using
horns with rotary valves crooked in F. Otherwise,
except in three specified movements, natural

horns are used, braying clearly through orchestration which always used to be condemned as too thick. In his note, Gardiner fairly points out the merits of the 1841 version in transparency and other qualities, suggesting, as others have, that the doublings in the later version make it safer and more commonplace. Paradoxically in performance, Gardiner is if anything even more electrifying in the later, more thickly upholstered version, as ever clarifying textures and building up to a thrilling conclusion. Even the *Zwickauer* Symphony of 1832 emerges as very distinctive of Schumann.

The contrasts between Gardiner and Goodman in their approach to the numbered works aren't as marked as expected, often as much a question of scale and recording quality as of interpretative differences, with Goodman's orchestra more intimate, and with the RCA sound a degree less brightly analytical. Both prefer fast speeds, with Goodman a shade more relaxed and Gardiner more incisive, pressing ahead harder, with syncopations – so important in Schumann – more sharply dramatic. One advantage that Gardiner has in his slightly bigger scale is that he brings out more light and shade, offering a wider dynamic range. Hence the solemn fourth movement of the *Rhenish* Symphony inspired by Cologne Cathedral – as with Goodman taken at a flowing speed – builds up more gradually in a bigger, far longer *crescendo*, in the end the more powerful for being held back at the start. Though the Goodman set still holds its place, Gardiner offers a conspectus of Schumann as symphonist that's all the richer and more illuminating for the inclusion of the extra rarities.

Symphonies Nos 1-4. Manfred, Op 115 – Overture H
Cleveland Orchestra / George Szell
Sony Classical Masterworks Heritage ② 07464 62349-2 (135' · ADD) Recorded 1958-60 Ⓜ

This famous set gives us the heart of George Szell, his feeling for style, for line and for Schumann's warming but fragile symphonic structures. Szell loved the Schumann symphonies, but readers should be warned that he attempts to correct – and here we quote Szell himself – 'minor lapses [in orchestration] due to inexperience' with 'remedies' that range from 'subtle adjustments of dynamic marks to the radical surgery of re-orchestrating whole stretches'. More often than not, the musical results serve Schumann handsomely. Szell sometimes takes *crescendo* to imply *accelerando*, but his insistence on watertight exchanges facilitates a snug fit between various instrumental choirs, the strings especially. Markings such as *Animato* (in the First Symphony's *Allegro molto vivace*) or *piano dolce* (in the same movement) are scrupulously observed, and so are most of Schumann's metronome markings. Playing standards are very high, but the close-set recordings occasionally undermine Szell's painstaking efforts to clarify Schumann's orchestration, the *Rhenish* being the worst offender.

The *Rhenish* again yields high musical dividends, with sensitively shaped central movements, but were we to single out just one track on the whole set, it would have to be the Second Symphony's *Adagio espressivo*, a performance of such warmth, nobility and elasticity (the latter not a quality normally associated with Szell) that it's tempting to grant it the accolade of 'best ever'. The *Manfred* Overture is given a wildly spontaneous performance, with extreme tempos and some brilliant playing. Sometimes you may feel that Szell was being overprotective towards the music and that the same interpretations played live might have thrown caution to the wind. Still, Szell should certainly be granted equal status with his bargain stablemates Kubelík and Sawallisch. Both are perhaps marginally more spontaneous in the First and Third Symphonies, but Szell's loving exegeses underline details in the music that you won't have heard on many other recordings. Transfers and presentation are superb.

Symphonies Nos 1-4
Tonhalle Orchestra, Zurich / David Zinman
Arte Nova ② 82876 57743-2 (123' · DDD) Ⓢ

David Zinman has recorded Schumann's symphonies before, in Baltimore in the late 1980s, a set recently remarketed by Telarc at mid-price. The remake involves a radical change of orchestral sonority, more grainy, notably lighter, with the sort of sharpened dynamic profile and fine-tipped attenuation more associated with period instrument orchestras.

Zinman's second Schumann set also involves some minor textural novelties. Added ornaments and appoggiaturas appear in the *Adagio espressivo* of No 2, for example, and in the first movement of the *Rhenish*. For this latest project Zinman uses period brass and timpani: note the stopped horns for the pivotal four-note motive in the *Spring* Symphony's *Allegro molto vivace*. Tempos are in general swifter than before. The opening of the *Spring*'s *Scherzo*, for example, just about exceeds the prescribed metronome marking, whereas in Baltimore it was marginally slower. More significantly, the third-movement trio in No 4 is now virtually in tempo with the outer sections. Zinman provides a sort of Schumann slimming kit, useful for those who find the symphonies turgid and who crave more air between and around the notes.

Symphony No 1, 'Spring', Op 38. 'Zwickau' Symphony, WoO29 – I. Overture, Scherzo and Finale, Op 52. Die Braut von Messina, Op 100. Genoveva, Op 81 – Overture
Swedish Chamber Orchestra / Thomas Dausgaard
BIS BIS-SACD1569 (78' · DDD/DSD) Ⓕ

To call a performance 'well made' might seem like a half-hearted compliment but in the case of Thomas Dausgaard's account of the *Spring* Symphony it's only part of the story, albeit a very important part. Clarity is a given with this particular band and here the same impressions of transparency, watertight ensemble, dovetailed phrasing and buoyant rhythms pertain. The first movement is kept on its toes and 'in tempo', and likewise the *Scherzo* where the Trios are skilfully integrated into the rest of the movement, the first of them opening, unusually, to a gently brushed *legato*. The *Larghetto* is streamlined without sounding cold, the important horn and *pizzicato* string parts always crystal-clear, whereas the finale's prime virtue is its judicious pacing, especially the idyllic horn passage just after the halfway point, and the symphony's closing pages, which are thrillingly played.

Dausgaard's understanding of tempo relations is even better demonstrated in the *Zwickau* movement of an early G minor symphony. There are reminders of early Schubert and Bruckner in that rays of light are crossed with moments of darkness, for example the unresolved bassoon motif that closes the exposition, very imaginative (and unsettling), and so is the return of the stern introduction towards the end of the movement.

The Mendelssohnian *Overture, Scherzo and Finale* is again beautifully shaped, the introduction unusually pensive, the ensuing *Allegro* full of life, the *Scherzo* crisp but unhurried. The two relatively late overtures again benefit from smaller-than-usual orchestral forces and perceptive direction, Dausgaard generating bags of energy while allowing textures to breathe. So all we need now is an equally compelling *Rhenish* Symphony to round off the cycle. The recorded sound is superb.

Symphonies – No 2, Op 61; No 4, Op 120 (original version, 1841). Szenen aus Goethes Faust – Overture. Julius Cäsar, Op 128
Swedish Chamber Orchestra / Thomas Dausgaard
BIS ⊕ BIS-SACD1519 (76' · DDD/DSD)   Ⓕ

All this talk of Schumann's stodgy orchestral writing…Rubbish! Evidence for the defence is simple: keep the orchestra slim and well balanced, the tempi lively and the textures clear and the calories positively fall away. Thomas Dausgaard, with just 38 players, turns the symphonic Schumann into a thoughtful athlete who burns energy while his mind spins.

Dausgaard opts for the 1841 original version of the Fourth Symphony, with its faltering, even abrupt, transition from an opening *Andante* to a fleet *Allegro*. It leaves a very different impression to the revision. The transition from *Scherzo* to finale is much as it is in the familiar 1851 version but the finale itself contains 'new' material and neither of the outer movements has repeats. All in all, it is less thick-set than its successor: Brahms preferred it.

The Second Symphony is similarly revealing with keen accents and prominent inner voices, the latter half of the slow introduction biting and muscular, the main *Allegro* superbly built. In the *Scherzo* Dausgaard slows and softens the bridge

passage appealingly, accentuating the dizzy flight back to the main subject. In the achingly beautiful *Adagio*, top line and accompaniment seem to lean on each other to ease the pain, and in speeding for the finale's second set Dausgaard intensifies the argument, making fresh sense of it.

BIS's realistic sound quality helps the clarifying process and the timps (with hard sticks) have tremendous presence. A good idea, too, to include Schumann's *Julius Caesar* and *Faust* overtures: strange, relatively late essays, equivocal music, slightly unhinged and played – appropriately enough – with a restless, slightly nervous edge.

Piano Quintet in E flat major, Op 44

Piano Quintet. Andante and Variations, Op 46. Fantasiestücke, Op 73. Märchenbilder, Op 113.
Marie-Luise Neunecker *hn* **Dora Schwarzberg, Lucy Hall** *vns* **Nobuko Imai** *va* **Natalia Gutman, Mischa Maisky** *vcs* **Martha Argerich, Alexandre Rabinovitch** *pf*
EMI 557308-2 (75' · DDD) Recorded live 1994   Ⓕ

After 'one memorable day of rehearsal', as the introductory note puts it, Martha Argerich and a group of friends recorded this programme at a public concert in Holland 'with the enthusiasm and intimate inspiration of a house-party'. The rarity is the *Andante and Variations*, Op 46, here brought up with all the spontaneous freshness of new discovery in a performance as enjoyable for its self-generating continuity as its diversity. Argerich and her fellow pianist, Rabinovitch, divide keyboard responsibilities in the remainder of the programme. Her own major triumph comes in the Quintet (with truly inspirational help from Maisky's cello). Every note tingles with life and colour in an arrestingly imaginative reading of exemplary textural transparency. In none of the more familiar works in the concert is that little extra stimulus of live as opposed to studio recording combined with more finesse and finish than here.

In the smaller pieces Argerich reaffirms herself as an artist of 'temperament', much given to the impulse of the moment. The recording itself is pleasingly natural. And there's heartening audience applause as a further reminder that we're at a live performance.

String Quartets, Op 41

No 1 in A minor **No 2** in F **No 3** in A

String Quartets Nos 1 & 3
Zehetmair Quartet (Thomas Zehetmair, Matthias Metzger *vns* Ruth Killius *va* Françoise Groben *vc*)
ECM New Series 472 169-2 (50' · DDD)   Ⓕ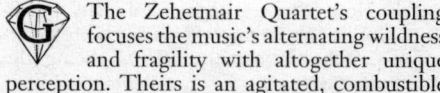

The Zehetmair Quartet's coupling focuses the music's alternating wildness and fragility with altogether unique perception. Theirs is an agitated, combustible and loving view of Schumann, a credible trip into his troubled world that reflects older playing styles not by exaggerating or abandoning vibrato but by constantly varying tone, tempo, bow pressure and modes of attack. Aspects of this trend are usefully exemplified by their handling of the pensive second section of the Third Quartet's third movement, and by the way they negotiate the sudden, bloodless *moderato* passage that forms the coda of the First Quartet's finale. In the less consistent but more challenging First Quartet, minute variations in pulse and emphasis are consistently engaging, ie they enjoy maximum freedom within the law of the page. Contrapuntal passages that other quartets present as dry or self-conscious – at 2'36" into the first movement of No 1, for example, where the viola takes the initial lead – assume newfound meaning.

These aren't comfortable performances. They pass on cosmetic appeal and would rather grate and rail than pander to surface 'gloss'. So be warned. But they're profoundly beautiful in their truthful appropriation of music that can be both poignant and aggressive. Delicate, too, in places (Mendelssohn with added fibre); in fact more comprehensive as musical statements than most of us had previously suspected. That realisation is due almost entirely to the persuasive powers of these supremely accomplished, and realistically recorded, performances.

Additional recommendation

String Quartets, Op 41 – Nos 1-3
Ysaÿe Quartet (Guillaume Sutre, Luc-Marie Aguera vns Miguel da Silva *va* François Salque *vc*)
Aeon AECD0418 (79' · DDD)   Ⓕ

All three quartets are included. And the performance of the Second Quartet is a fine one, stressing the first movement's soaring lyricism, the weird rhythmic dislocations in the *Scherzo*, and bringing out all the finale's fantastical contrasts.

Piano Trios

No 1 in D minor, Op 63 **No 2** in F, Op-80 **No 3** in G minor, Op110

Piano Trios Nos 1 & 2
Florestan Trio (Anthony Marwood *vn* Richard Lester *vc* Susan Tomes *pf*)
Hyperion CDA67063 (57' · DDD)   Ⓕ❶❶❶

 For those who have always thought of Schumann's First Piano Trio as his finest chamber work after the Piano Quintet, the Florestan Trio may encourage you to think again about the Second Trio – a wonderful piece, full of poetic ideas. The artists make vigorous work of the first movement's urgent thematic interrelations but the real surprise is the third movement, a lilting barcarolle awash with significant counterpoint, although

the heart of the Trio is its slow and deeply personal second movement. The differences in the trios are more marked than their similarities. The Second Trio is mellow, loving and conversational, but the First is troubled, tense, even tragic – save, perhaps, for its Mendelssohnian finale. The Florestan Trio realises the music's myriad perspectives, coaxing its arguments rather than confusing them. Marwood employs some subtle *portamento* and varies his use of vibrato, whereas Susan Tomes never forces her tone. Real teamwork, equally in evidence for the gently cantering *Scherzo* and the fine, elegiac slow movement.

Piano Trio No 3. Fantasiestücke, Op 88. Piano Quartet in E flat, Op 47[a]
[a]**Thomas Riebl** *va* **Florestan Trio** (Anthony Marwood *vn* Richard Lester *vc* Susan Tomes *pf*)
Hyperion CDA67175 (71' · DDD)   Ⓕ❶

After their 1999 *Gramophone* Award-winning disc of the first two piano trios, these players champion three works which are less frequently encountered in concert, proving once again how a revelatory interpretation can make us all think again.

The G minor Piano Trio (No 3) of 1851 suffers from over-repetitive, at times perfunctory, rhythmic patterning. But thanks to the mercurial vitality and the spontaneous response to every passing innuendo from all three interwoven voices, not a note here sounds unmotivated. The three fanciful 1842 miniatures for piano trio (revised under the title of *Fantasiestücke* in 1849) have long been criticised for the dominance of the keyboard in all but the third, entitled 'Duet'. Susan Tomes makes no attempt to disguise this.

Last but not least, the Piano Quartet of 1842, long overshadowed by the much-loved Piano Quintet. Misha Donat's appreciative note reminds us that even the loyal Clara waited some seven years before taking it into her repertory. The piano is rarely silent, and mustn't be allowed to dominate; so praise goes to Susan Tomes for a keen ear for balance. The *Scherzo* has a Mendelssohnian, elfin fleetness, and the finale (surely Schumann's *ne plus ultra* in exhilarating contrapuntal ingenuity) an exemplary textural clarity. The slow movement, played with touching simplicity, speaks as eloquently as any of the composer's Clara-inspired lovesongs. Excellently recorded, this welcome disc should win all three works a new lease of life.

Schumann Piano Trio No 1[b]   Ⓗ
Mendelssohn Piano Trio in D minor, Op 94[a]
Alfred Cortot *pf* **Jacques Thibaud** *vn*
Pablo Casals *vc*
Naxos Historical mono 8 110185 (59' · ADD) Recorded 1928/9   ⓈⒹ

Tully Potter's introductory note reminds us that it was in Paris, in their later twenties, that these three legendary artists first made music together

– just for pleasure. But international acclaim after a public début in 1907 soon led to their devoting a regular part of each year to this sphere for just over the next quarter-century. We're told that Schumann's No 1 was always one of their recital favourites. Here it's difficult to evaluate their playing in technical terms such as minute attention to expressive detail without loss of flow, impeccable ensemble, and last but not least, choice of tempo (slower than Schumann's suggestions in the searching *Langsam, mit inniger Empfindung*). The impression is more of intimately shared awareness of, and response to, the music's inner secrets – as if personally communicated to them by the composer himself. In reproduction you're at once aware of difficulty in doing justice to Thibaud's beguiling violin, notably in the higher reaches of Mendelssohn's agitated opening movement. Here it's outweighed by Casals' sumptuously ripe cello and Cortot's multi-voiced keyboard. But the immediacy and freshness of the playing wins the day in a beautifully nuanced *Andante*, a delectably mischievous *Scherzo*, and an unflaggingly urgent finale. Ward Marston's skilful engineering is at its truest and best here.

Cello and piano works

Drei Fantasiestücke, Op 73. Adagio and Allegro, Op 70. Violin Sonata No 3, Op 121 (arr Isserlis). Abendlied, Op 85 No 12 (arr Joachim). Drei Romanzen, Op 94. Fünf Stücke im Volkston, Op 102
Steven Isserlis vc **Dénes Várjon** pf
Hyperion CDA67661 (70' · DDD)   Ⓟ**OO**

Steven Isserlis has long been a stalwart champion of Schumann, through his advocacy of not only the often-maligned Concerto but also the chamber works. For this disc he has had to beg, borrow and steal but the results absolutely justify the means.

In the wrong hands, a work such as the *Fantasiestücke*, Op 73 (which Isserlis plays in its earliest incarnation), can sound a touch seasick, with too much swelling through every phrase, and a loss of the overall shape as a result. But how well Isserlis paces everything; some of his tempi are quite spacious but this gives the music a wonderfully considered and luxuriant aspect; the results never ever sound contrived. That's partly to do with Isserlis's sound (extravagantly he uses not one but two Strads on this recording), which has a very focused centre to it, but also his utterly innate relationship with pianist Dénes Várjon. Perhaps the most ravishing item on the disc is the poignant *Abendlied*, arranged by Joachim from its piano duet form but then further borrowed by Isserlis, playing it down an octave. In his hands it's as moving a wordless Lied as anything you could imagine.

The substantial work here, though, is the Third Violin Sonata. Two of its movements – the Intermezzo and finale – originated in the multi-composer 'FAE' Sonata written for Joachim (for which Brahms famously wrote the

Scherzo). Schumann later added two more movements to form his last large-scale work. It decisively refutes the theory that he had – metaphorically and literally – lost the plot by this stage. While it certainly doesn't conform to standard 19th-century sonata form, in Isserlis's hands it's a work of compelling power, whether in the terrifying scherzo sections of the second movement or the dreamy Intermezzo, a much-needed point of repose in a work of great tumult.

The disc ends with the *Fünf Stücke im Volkston*, and finds Schumann in a more folky idiom. Too often these pieces can sound like an awkward amalgam of styles, but Isserlis again is utterly inside them, revealing Schumann's innovation even at this late stage, from the edginess of the first, via the tender, Brahmsian second one to the spirited fifth piece, where Mendelssohn collides with Bartók.

For all that Isserlis has made many wonderful recordings, not least his seminal Bach Suites, this might just be his finest yet, with warmly detailed sound and a typically acute note from the cellist himself.

Violin Sonatas

No 1 in A minor, Op 105 No 2 in D minor, Op 121 No 3 in A minor

Violin Sonatas Nos 1-3
Carolin Widmann vn **Dénes Várjon** pf
ECM New Series ② 476 6744 (72' · DDD)   Ⓟ**OO**

Schumann's violin-and-piano sonatas have never become favourite staples of the repertoire. Full textures, with the violin mainly confined to its middle and lower registers, often continue uninterrupted for many bars, and a somewhat grey, monotonous effect can be compounded by the composer's obsessive repetition of certain rhythms and motifs. But is this a fair description? You wouldn't think so after hearing Carolin Widmann and Dénes Várjon; their imaginative, wide-ranging variations of tone colour unlock the music's romantic, atmospheric potential, and their command of genuine *rubato* – passionate, unimpeded forward motion followed by lingering backward glances – gives the sonatas an expressive flexibility that's surely authentic.

'With sorrowful expression', writes Schumann at the start of the First Sonata, and the surges of painful emotion in this performance, while sounding quite spontaneous, are rigorously based on the printed expression marks. Similarly, the gripping account of the Second Sonata's slow introduction starts from meticulous observance of Schumann's dynamics, slurs and staccatos, adding to this an entirely convincing rhythmic freedom. The opening page of this sonata's third movement, which creates a remote, almost chilling effect, isn't quite so convincing. Back in 1952, George Enescu, playing with Celiny Chailley-Richez (Opus Kura), gently arpeggiated his plucked chords and, on taking up the bow, found a beautifully intimate, confiding tone – this mood may well be closer to what Schumann intended. Overall, however, Várjon and Widmann are entirely persuasive. Whether or not you know the music well, you'll be enthralled and delighted.

Violin Sonatas Nos 1 & 2; No 3 – Intermezzo
Ilya Kaler *vn* **Boris Slutsky** *pf*
Naxos 8 550870 (51' · DDD)

These performances, powerfully recorded in Indiana by these two young Russian artists, are most enjoyable. The passion of their playing is perhaps not wholly Germanic, but every artist legitimately brings something of himself to the music he performs, and nothing here takes us out of touch with Schumann's world. There's an impressive intensity to this playing, although refinement and tenderness are rightly also present. Kaler and Slutsky mould these melodies well; it's a matter of timing as well as tone and dynamics, as the *Allegretto* of the A minor Sonata shows. The same movement also demonstrates how they follow Schumann naturally through his characteristically rapid changes of mood, while the finale that follows has power and purpose. The single movement from the composite 'FAE Sonata' dedicated to Joseph Joachim, in which Schumann collaborated with the young Brahms and Albert Dietrich, makes a useful bonus in a disc which would otherwise last under 50 minutes. The Naxos disc at super-bargain price represents fine value.

Davidsbündlertänze, Op 6

Davidsbündlertänze. Etudes symphoniques, Op 13 (1852 version). Arabeske in C, Op 18. Blumenstück in D flat, Op 19
András Schiff *pf*
Warner Elatus 0927-49612-2 (76' · DDD)

Schumann was a great rethinker, in Schiff's opinion not always for the better in later life – hence his choice of Schumann's original (1837) conception of the *Davidsbündlertänze* rather than its more usually heard 1851 revision. Except for a touch of mischief (subsequently removed) at the end of No 9, textual differences are slight. But Schiff prefers the fewer repeat markings in the first edition, so that ideas never lose their freshness. More importantly, the exceptional immediacy and vividness of his characterisation reminds us that Schumann initially signed nearly all these 18 'bridal thoughts' with an F (the impetuous Florestan) or an E (the introspective, visionary Eusebius) – or sometimes both – as well as including literary inscriptions (and one or two more colourful expression marks) as a clue to the mood of the moment.

Schiff laughs and teases, storms and yearns, as if the hopes and dreams of the youthful Robert, forbidden all contact with his distant beloved,

were wholly his own – there and then. The impatient Florestan fares particularly well. For the much metamorphosed *Etudes symphoniques* Schiff chooses the generally used late version of 1852 with its admirably tautened finale. Here, his bold, firmly contoured approach reaffirms it as the most magisterially 'classical' work the young Schumann ever wrote. Schiff emphasises its continuity and unity as a whole. Even the five so-called supplementary variations emerge as more purposeful, less ruminative, than often heard. These Schiff wisely offers as an independent group at the end. The recital is completed by the *Arabeske* and *Blumenstück*, again played with a very strong sense of direction, even if Schiff isn't yet Richter's equal in disguising the repetitiveness of the latter. Nothing but praise for the naturalness of the reproduction.

Davidsbündlertänze. Papillons, Op 2. Carnaval, Op 9. Etudes symphoniques, Op 13. Kinderszenen, Op 15. Kreisleriana, Op 16. Fantasie in C, Op 17. Arabeske in C, Op 18. Humoreske in B flat, Op 20. Piano Sonata No 2 in G minor, Op 22. Vier Nachtstücke, Op 23. Drei Romanzen, Op 28. Waldszenen, Op 82. Bunte Blätter, Op 99 – No 9, Novelette
Wilhelm Kempff *pf*
DG Collectors Edition ④ 471 312-2GB4 (297' · ADD)
Recorded 1967-75

A collection that will give great pleasure. Sample it anywhere and there can be no mistaking who this is – you know great pianists by their sound. Kempff was one of the most distinguished German pianists of the last century, blossoming through two decades in the Austro-German repertory after the death of Schnabel and Edwin Fischer, but he never carried the flame quite as they did. Performing bravura pieces didn't interest him, so the Toccata, the *Concert-Studies after Paganini*, Op 10, and the *Abegg* Variations aren't here. Nevertheless it's a good selection, lacking only the Fantasy Pieces, Op 12, to give a rounded picture of the phenomenal explosion of Schumann's creativity for the piano that took place between the ages of 20 and 29.

Kempff's special quality seems to be a songfulness and *cantabile* style which is in danger of becoming a forgotten art nowadays. Listening to him in Schumann, it's as if a wind is blowing through, rising and falling, sweeping incident along and carrying everything forward: song, dance, stories, poems, moods, portraits, parades of characters, visions of landscape, recollections. Few players have matched his infallible touch with the way the music holds together.

As pianism his *Carnaval* may not leave you astonished, but it's immaculately characterised: festive, buoyant, irresistible in movement, the comings and goings of the masked personages and the guest appearances of 'Chopin' and 'Paganini' all spot on. There's no single right way to play this masterpiece, but his is vivid.

When he made the earliest of these recordings he was already 71; the last are from his 78th year. In the later ones you notice more weight on the keys and perhaps a reduced inclination to be volatile; but he has kept his technique in trim, and continues to sound at ease with the instrument. The difficult numbers in the *Davidsbündlertänze* are hard for every pianist, but Kempff doesn't see them as virtuoso challenges to be confronted and dispatched. Always the music is paramount, and beautiful sound, and a control of voices under the fingers that seem to be following Schumann instinctively in the exploration of the piano's potential. The opening of *Kreisleriana* hangs fire as if he were feeling his way into it but the rest is magnificent and thrillingly projected.

When at his best you have the impression his insights aren't only musical but brought to bear on every area of Schumann's imagination. All the big works have this definition and can be counted among the best on record. The *Fantasy* comes high on the list, perhaps top, as does the undervalued *Humoreske*. He's a guide to Schumann you should not be without, authoritative and companionable, balanced and most human.

Additional recommendation

Davidsbündlertänze
 Coupled with: Fantasiestücke, Op 12
Frith *pf*
Naxos 8 550493 (63' · DDD)   ⑤➪
 Frith summons his excellent technique here for some exciting pianism. Recommended not just for the budget-conscious but for those who enjoy youthful pianistic exuberance.

Fantasiestücke, Op 12

Fantasiestücke. Kinderszenen, Op 15. Humoreske, Op 20
Philippe Cassard *pf*
Ambroisie AMB9961 (74' · DDD)   ⑤●

Here's a disc of fine Schumann playing, superbly recorded and on a beautifully voiced piano. To undertake a critical nit-pick of each of the 27 short pieces that make up these three works would seem invidious and, besides, not reflect the spirit in which the music is offered. In the *Fantasiestücke* some might feel that Cassard takes too much pedal here, or takes such-and-such too fast or too slow there; others might justifiably counter by saying that Richter in his famous 1956 selection uses too little pedal, and strives for effect, compared with Cassard's more relaxed approach in infinitely better sound.

Kinderszenen, likewise, is distinguished by its simplicity, its tenderness and unexaggerated rubato, nowhere more apparent than in the final 'Der Dichter spricht'. Perhaps Argerich finds more impish delight in the extrovert titles, but that again must be a matter of personal preference.

Humoreske – 42 pages almost all in B flat major or G minor – is one of Schumann's works that might have been more satisfactory had he let it mature in the cellar for a while before drinking. It's difficult to overcome the problems pre-

sented by a continuous flow of fragments of such varying musical interest. Cassard almost succeeds if only because his mellifluous tone and subtle phrasing are such a pleasure to hear. Both Ashkenazy (1972) and Horowitz (1979) in their very different ways find more character in the details, the latter's pacing of Schumann's meandering 'Conclusion' more convincing than Cassard. But that's quite the wrong note on which to conclude a review of a recital that merits the highest praise.

Kreisleriana, Op 16

Kreisleriana. Humoreske in B flat, Op 20
Kinderszenen, Op 15.
Radu Lupu *pf*
Decca 440 496-2DH (75' · DDD)   ⑤●●➪

As piano playing this disc has an aristocratic distinction reminiscent of Lipatti. As music-making it's underpinned by unselfconscious intuition, making you feel you're discovering the truth of the matter for the first time. It's difficult to recall a more revealing performance of Schumann's *Humoreske*. Lupu captures all the unpredictability of its swift-changing moods while at the same time imparting a sense of inevitability to the sequence as a whole. Florestan's caprice is as piquant as Eusebius's tenderness is melting. Yet there's an underlying unity in the diversity from Lupu, enhanced by most beautifully timed and shaded 'links'. Goodness knows how long this work has been in his repertory. But here it emerges with the keen edge of new love.

Next, *Kinderszenen*: simplicity is its keynote. To begin with (as notably in the opening 'Von fremden Ländern und Menschen') you wonder if, in rejection of sentimentality, he might not be allowing himself enough time for wide-eyed wonderment. But you're soon won over by his limpid tonal palette and the sheer purity of his phrasing. Each piece tells its own magical little tale without the slightest trace of special pleading. Such pristine grace will never pall, however often heard.

Kreisleriana in its turn offers rich contrasts of desperation, dedication and Hoffmannesque drollery. And except, perhaps, in the impetuous No 7 (taken dangerously fast), it brings further reminders that we're in the presence of a master pianist – among so much else able to rejoice in this work's endless dialogues between left hand and right with his opulent bass and gleaming treble. Reproduction is totally faithful throughout.

Kreisleriana. Arabeske, Op 18. Fantasie, Op 17.
Jonathan Biss *pf*
EMI 365391-2 (70' · DDD)   ⑤

In 2006 EMI signed the 25-year old American Jonathan Biss to an exclusive two-year contract. This is the partnership's first fruit and this is Schumann-playing on an exalted level with performances of all three works that bear comparison with the finest. Schumann's youthful declaration of love in the *Fantasie* is echoed by Biss's obvious love for the ardent score. On the technical side, passages such as the treacherous close of the March are seen off with convincing relish.

Biss's musicality and maturity also make for an outstanding *Kreisleriana*. The spirit of Cortot hovers over this reading: try the fugal section of No 7 (*Sehr rasch*), thrillingly attacked by both pianists in a way that quite eludes Pollini and sounds blandly academic in Rubinstein's hands. Biss, for whose grandmother, Raya Garbousova, Barber composed his Cello Concerto, and whose mother is the violinist Miriam Fried, is living proof that musical genes are inherited.

Kreisleriana. Arabeske, Op 18. Davidsbündlertänze, Op 6. Fantasiestücke, Op 12. Frühlingsnacht (arr Liszt). Papillons, Op 2. Waldszenen, Op 82. Widmung (arr Liszt)
Leon McCawley *pf*
Avie ② AV0029 (143' · DDD)   Ⓜ️🅳➔

This two-CD album celebrates a richly inclusive cross-section ranging from Schumann's Opp 2 to 82, from early ardour to later introspection, and *vice versa*. For whatever the opus, Schumann's ultra-Romantic genius – his rapid shifts from pain to solace, from tears to laughter – is paramount. Above all, it's in his wide-eyed wonder, his naivety, that Leon McCawley shines and makes his mark.

True, a certain politeness inhibits him from relishing to the full every shift of the kaleidoscopic imagination in, say, *Papillons*, but elsewhere – in the closing, enchanted reminiscence of *Davidsbündlertänze* or in the 'exquisite bird song in an ominous setting' (the 'Prophet Bird' from Op 82) – he's at his very best. In the *Fantasiestücke* he delights in the cross-accentuation, kittenish by-play of 'Fabel' and provides an attractive alternative to more hectic performances of 'Träumes Wirren'.

The *Arabesque* is another notable success (particularly in the glowing retrospective coda). Most of all, he's finely sensitive to the inner promptings and recesses of *Kreisleriana*: the *sehr langsam* and *Bewegt* of No 4, the central mock-polyphonic whirl of No 7 or the alternately gentle and explosive whimsy of No 8 all testify to his winning ease and sensitivity. Excellent recording, first-class accompanying essay and lavish presentation.

Additional recommendation

Kreisleriana, Op 16
Coupled with: **Bach/Busoni** Chaconne. **Beethoven** Rondo, Op 51 No2 and Rondo capriccio, Op 129
Kissin *pf*
RCA Victor Red Seal 09026 68911-2 (63' · DDD)   🅕🅳➔
The fantastic side of *Kreisleriana* isn't always in focus here. That said, this is still a very enjoyable performance.

Fantasie in C, Op 17

Fantasie in C. Faschingsschwank aus Wien, Op 26. Papillons, Op 2
Sviatoslav Richter *pf*
EMI Encore 575233-2 (67' · ADD/DDD) Recorded 1961-2   Ⓢ🔴🔴🔴

 There can surely be no doubt as to Richter's current status as elder statesman of the piano world. And collectors now have a bewildering array of his recent, mainly live performances and reissues to choose from. Richter's Schumann is unequalled. The *Fantasia* is arguably Schumann's keyboard masterpiece. And Richter plays it better than other pianists. Nobody can phrase as beautifully as he can, or produce those marvellously soft accompaniments beneath quietly singing tunes or toss off the middle movement with such speed and brilliance. There's astonishing poetry in his playing. It almost amounts to a rediscovery of the work.

And the same could be said of *Faschingsschwank aus Wien* and *Papillons*. (The way he plays the main theme of the latter should make you buy this disc if nothing else does – he seems to add stature to the work.) His assets in all these works are, first, an unusually musical sense of phrasing. Secondly, he can reduce an accompaniment to a mere murmur without any loss of evenness so that a tune above it can sing even when it's soft. Thirdly, he uses a great deal of rubato, but always with impeccable taste; his rubato in slow passages has a mesmeric quality only partly due to the fact that he usually plays such passages much slower than other pianists. Fourthly, he has faultless technique. His superiority is apparent throughout. The recording is magnificent for its date. Classic performances which no pianophile should be without.

Piano Sonatas

No 1 in F sharp minor, Op 11 **No 2** in G minor, Op-22
No 3 in F minor, Op 14

Piano Sonatas Nos 1 & 3
Bernd Glemser *pf*
Naxos 8 554275 (65' · DDD)   Ⓢ🔴🔴🅳➔

Bernd Glemser's playing here is an exceptionally arresting experience in its graphic immediacy and freshness. With his prodigious technique, underpinned by exuberant imaginative vitality, it was no surprise to learn that in a wide-ranging repertory, he feels particularly drawn to the later Romantic virtuoso school. Some listeners might well think his approach to Schumann's F sharp minor Sonata (written at the age of 25) too overtly Lisztian in expression to be truly stylish. Sure, the more classically disciplined Clara, for example, would never have allowed herself such extreme changes of tempo in contrasting Florestan's turbulence with Eusebius's

SCHUMANN KINDERSZENEN & KREISLERIANA – IN BRIEF

Radu Lupu
Decca 440 496-2DH (75' · DDD)   Ⓕ🅞🅞🅳➔
Lupu's characteristically limpid and purposeful playing effortlessly holds attention, revealing the character and charm of each vignette in *Kinderszenen*. Just as effortlessly, he hurls his listener into the quite different world of *Kreisleriana*, capturing its emotional turmoil and its dazzling contrasts.

Vladimir Horowitz
Sony 07464 42409-2 (61' · ADD)   Ⓜ🅞
A classic account of *Kreisleriana*, demonstrating profound understanding of Schumann's idiom and projected with extraordinary clarity, most impressively in the final movement where several themes weave together symphonically.

Alfred Cortot   🄷
Music & Arts ② CD858 (131' · ADD)   Ⓕ
Here's a style of piano-playing all but non-existent today, yet one which still compels attention with its combination of rhetoric and limpid musicality. Both as narrator and protagonist, Cortot is an engaging artist, fully identifying with the emotional tenor of Schumann's music.

Martha Argerich
DG 410 653-2GH (52' · DDD)   Ⓕ🅞🅳➔
By turns affectionate and vigorous, these are never tame performances. Argerich's vivid characterisations in *Kinderszenen* may be a bit extreme for some, but will delight those who dislike more salon-friendly performances.

Wilhelm Kempff
DG ④ 471 312-2GB4 (317' · ADD)   Ⓜ🅳➔
Kempff made these recordings in his seventies; though he doesn't, or possibly can't, play up the virtuosity of Kreisleriana, he projects the music compellingly. His laconic style, however, is perhaps not ideal for Schumann's fervid Romanticism.

Maurizio Pollini (*Kreisleriana* only)
DG 471 370-2GH (48' · DDD)   Ⓕ🅞🅞🅳➔
Despite rather close and clangorous sound, Pollini's artistry shines through in a performance which may seen a touch detached from the emotional drama, but has a steady burn that becomes irresistible.

Mitsuko Uchida (*Kreisleriana* only)
Philips 442 777-2PH (67' · DDD)   Ⓕ🅳➔
A virtuoso and brilliantly executed account, that may yet strike some as rather detached from Schumann's drama. Nonetheless the music's sometimes quite strange beauty shines through.

idyllic lyricism in the two spacious outer movements. Yet with his innate musicality Glemser somehow allows the argument to cohere. His challenging rhythm in the *Scherzo* (and the richly savoured burlesque of its trio), like the *senza passione ma espressivo* of the slow movement's intimate song, are all finely judged. The F minor Sonata comes in Schumann's 1853 revision, restoring the second of the two *Scherzo*s omitted when the work was first published 17 years earlier, as a three-movement *Concert sans orchestre*. With Naxos's tonal reproduction at its best, this disc comes recommended as a true 'super-bargain' not to be missed.

Piano works

Allegro, Op 8. Arabeske, Op 18. Blumenstück, Op 19. Acht Fantasiestücke, Op 12. Drei Fantasiestücke, Op 111. Fantasiestücke (additional movement). Humoreske, Op 20. Kinderszenen, Op 15. Drei Romanzen, Op 28. Waldszenen, Op 82
Finghin Collins pf
Claves ② 50-2601/2 (149' · DDD)   Ⓕ

In this young Irish pianist we have an artist of rare poetic empathy, one with an uncanny and moving capacity to arrive at the still centre, the very heart, of Schumann's teeming and frenzied imagination.

Winner of the 1999 Clara Haskil Competition, Collins is here to stay. Indeed, it is no exaggeration to say that he plays in the spirit of Haskil herself, a great artist who while appearing to do so little ended by doing everything. At his finest his playing is enviably clear and transparent yet touched with a subtle and distinctive eloquence, allowing Schumann's voice to shine through. Hear him in the *Waldszenen*, capturing the quizzical melancholy in 'Vogel als Prophet' and the dark and lighter sides of Schumann's schizophrenic nature in the sinister 'Verrufene Stelle' and 'Freundliche Landschaft'.

The storm clouds scud across the sky in the first of the *Fantasiestücke*, Op 111, and the B minor *Allegro*, a souvenir of Schumann's early ambitions as a virtuoso pianist, takes on a new poetic quality and dimension, and never more so than in the glorious sunset coda. *Kinderszenen* glows with an inner warmth and radiance, 'Träumerei' displaying rare musical honesty and 'Rocking Horse' set in realistic cantering rather than jet-propelled motion.

Humoreske, a notably elusive challenge, is again a marvel of interior light, grace and energy, and if Collins's *Fantasiestücke*, Op 12, are less illuminating they include a fascinating final addition, a 'Feurigst' normally excluded. Claves's sound is as natural as the playing.

Additional recommendation

Papillons. Arabeske. Humoreske
Coupled with: Haydn Piano Sonata HobXVI/20

Dal Segno M DSPRCD044 (72 · DDD) Ⓕ
Youthful Schiff from his Denon days, but already demonstrating the poetry and imagination that make him an artist of the top rank.

Szenen aus Goethes Faust

Szenen aus Goethes Faust
Karita Mattila, Barbara Bonney, Brigitte Poschner-Klebel, Susan Graham sops **Iris Vermillion** mez **Endrik Wottrich, Hans-Peter Blochwitz** tens **Bryn Terfel** bass-bar **Jan-Hendrik Rootering, Harry Peeters** basses **Tölz Boys' Choir; Swedish Radio Chorus; Berlin Philharmonic Orch / Claudio Abbado**
Sony Classical ② 07464 66308-2 (115' · DDD · T/t)
Recorded live 1994 ⒻOO

No one before Schumann had ever attempted to set Goethe's mystical closing scene, which he finished in time for the Goethe centenary in 1849. What eventually emerged as his own Parts 1 and 2 (in turn portraits of Gretchen and the by now repentant Faust) followed later, after his move from a Mendelssohn-dominated Leipzig to a Wagner-ruled Dresden, hence the striking difference in style. Nothing Schumann ever wrote is more dramatic than Faust's blinding and death in the course of Part 2.

The Berlin Philharmonic is very forwardly recorded – occasionally perhaps a little too much so for certain voices. But never in the case of Bryn Terfel in the title-role. Any advance fears that he might disappoint were immediately banished not only by the generosity and flow of his warm, round tone but also the total commitment and conviction of his characterisation. Moreover as Dr Marianus in Part 3 he offers some wonderfully sustained *mezza* and *sotto voce*. Karita Mattila's Gretchen is always sympathetically pure-toned, clean-lined and assured. At times, as positioned, the other male soloists seem a little outweighed by the orchestra.

No praise can be too high for the Four Grey Sisters (so tellingly contrasted in vocal colour) led by Barbara Bonney: their midnight encounter with Faust and his eventual blinding is brilliantly done. And there's splendidly characterful choral singing thoughout from both adult and youthful choirs. In the more operatically conceived Parts 1 and 2 and the visionary Part 3, Abbado himself takes the music to heart and what he draws from his orchestra makes nonesense of the charge that Schumann was an inept scorer. This is worth every penny of its full-price.

Das Paradies und die Peri, Op 50

Das Paradies und die Peri, Op 50
Dorothea Röschmann, Malin Hartelius sops **Rebecca Martin, Bernarda Fink** mez **Christoph Strehl, Werner Güra** tens **Christian Gerhaher** bar **Bavarian Radio Chorus and Symphony Orchestra / Nikolaus Harnoncourt**

RCA Red Seal ② 88697 27155-2 (101' · DDD/DSD) ⒻOOⁱ

Initially envisaged as an opera, Schumann's haunting 1843 oratorio *Das Paradies und die Peri* tells of how a Peri – according to Persian mythology, the 'impure' child of a fallen angel and a human female – can enter Paradise only if she arrives at Heaven's gates with a worthy offering. Her first two offerings (a hero's blood and a vision of selfless love) fail the test whereas a third (abstinence inspired by a child at prayer) wins her Heavenly access.

Clara Schumann thought *Das Paradies* her husband's finest work and Nikolaus Harnoncourt calls it a 'splendid' score. So why the neglect? Partly negative political memory, maybe (Goebbels commissioned an arrangement that emphasised sacrificial death), and partly the work's hybrid nature. But it contains music that is at once dramatic, lyrical, ethereal, deeply personal and shot through with sincere human feeling. Mendelssohn's influence is discernible more or less throughout, especially in the choral writing which is very lightly dispatched on this superb 2005 performance from Munich's 'shoebox' Herkulessaal. The dramatic core is vividly exemplified by the chorus 'Doch seine Ströme sind jetzt rot', which reports rivers of human blood, whereas the transition to the tenor solo about the felled hero is meltingly beautiful, Christoph Strehl on excellent form.

Bach is another obvious point of reference, particularly at the point where the mezzo (Bernarda Fink) sings of a plague-inflected youth facing death, 'Verlassner Jüngling', music that's unmistakably reminiscent of Bach's Passion music and where Harnoncourt leans meaningfully on every fourth note of the strings' accompaniment. His Bavarian RSO sound warm, though period awareness on the conductor's part ensures sonorities that are light and pointedly attenuated.

Der Rose Pilgerfahrt, Op 112

Der Rose Pilgerfahrt
Inga Nielsen, Helle Hinz sops **Annemarie Møller, Elizabeth Halling** mezzos **Deon van der Walt** ten **Guido Päevatalu** bar **Christian Christiansen** bass **Danish National Radio Choir and Symphony Orchestra / Gustav Kuhn**
Chandos CHAN9350 (62' · DDD · T) ⒻO

Amidst today's great upsurgence of interest in Schumann's later choral undertakings, the work's long neglect is no doubt due to its all-too-naive tale of a rose who, after an eagerly sought transformation into a maiden to experience human love, chooses to sacrifice herself for her baby. Schumann's own ready response to Moritz Horn's poem can best be explained by its underlying moral message together with a strain of German rusticity then equally close to the composer's heart. Having said that, how grateful Schumann lovers should be to Chandos for at

last introducing the work to the English catalogue in so sympathetic yet discreet a performance from this predominantly Danish cast. All
credit to the conductor, Gustav Kuhn, for
revealing so much fancy in fairyland, so much
brio in peasant merriment, and so much charm
in more tender lyricism without ever making
heavy weather of this essentially *gemütlich*
little score.

No praise can be too high for the Danish
National Radio Choir: such immediacy of
response leaves no doubt as to their professional
status. Nor do the soloists or orchestra disappoint. Tonal reproduction is agreeably natural.

Liederkreis, Op 24

Liederkreis. Myrthen, Op 25 – No 7, Die Lotosblume;
No 21, Was will die einsame Träne?; No 24, Du bist
wie eine Blume. Romanzen und Balladen – Op 45:
No 3, Abends am Strand; Op 49: No 1, Die beiden
Grenadiere; No 2, Die feindlichen Brüder; Op 53:
No 3, Der arme Peter; Op 64: No 3, Tragödie.
Belsazar, Op 57. Lieder und Gesänge, Op 127 –
No 2, Dein Angesicht; No 3, Es leuchtet meine Liebe.
Gesänge, Op 142 – No 2, Lehn deine Wang; No 4,
Mein Wagen rollet langsam
Stephan Genz bar **Christoph Genz** ten
Claar ter Horst pf
Claves CD50-9708 (59' · DDD · T/t) Ⓕ○

This is a recital of promise and fulfilment.
Stephan Genz's voice and style are as wide-
ranging as his mode of expression. He lives
every moment of Op 24, entering into all
aspects of Schumann's settings and Heine's
originals yet never overstepping the mark in his
verbal painting. The other Heine settings
receive no less than their due. The sensuous
and plaintive qualities in Genz's tone are well
suited to the three Heine poems in *Myrthen*. In
contrast he rises to the histrionic challenges of
Die beiden Grenadiere, *Belsatzar* and the rarely
encountered *Die feindlichen Brüder*, performances that are felt as immediately as if at the
moment of composition. In *Abends am Strand*
the voice follows to the full the song's romantic
import. In the third song of Op 64, *Tragödie*,
the baritone is joined by his talented tenor
brother: their voices naturally blend well.
Finally, Genz is inspired by that amazingly
original song, *Mein Wagen rollet langsam*, to
give of his absolute best. Here, as throughout,
Claar ter Horst matches the perceptions of her
partner, and both are caught in an amenable
acoustic.

Frauenliebe und -Leben, Op 42

Frauenliebe und -leben. Sieben Lieder, Op-104.
Gedichte der Königen Maria Stuart, Op 135. Lieder
und Gesänge – I, Op 27:-No 1, Sag an, o lieber
Vogel; No 4, Jasminenstrauch; III, Op 77:-No 3,
Geisternähe; No 4, Stiller Vorwurf; IV, Op 96:-No 4,
Gesungen!; No 5, Himmel und Erde. Romanzen und

Balladen – III, Op 53:-No 1, Blondels Lied; No 2,
Loreley; IV, Op 64:-No 1, Die Soldatenbraut. Die
Kartenlegerin, Op 31 No 2
Juliane Banse sop **Graham Johnson** pf
Hyperion CDJ33103 (74' · DDD · T/t) Includes
readings of 'Traum der eignen Tage' and
'Nachschrift'. Ⓕ○

This offering places Banse and Johnson among
the most thoughtful and convincing of Schumann interpreters in the history of recording
the composer's Lieder. From start to finish, in
well-loved pieces and in others that will be new
discoveries to many, the pair at once work in
close concord and get to the heart of Schumann's very particular genius. The pair wholly
dispel the oft-repeated view that Schumann's
later songs are by and large failures: it's simply
that the older man wrote differently from his
younger, Romantically exuberant self. Thus
the 1852 settings of Mary Stuart unerringly
capture the soul of the troubled Queen's predicaments through the most concise means.
Not a florid or untoward gesture is allowed to
destroy the mood of sustained concentration
and intimate musings. Banse brings to the
songs just the right sense of a person sharing
her innermost thoughts with us, the mezzo-like
warmth of her lower voice gainfully employed,
Johnson's piano communing in consort with
the voice.

Schumann showed himself equally in
sympathy with the poems of Elisabeth
Kulmann (Op 104), a susceptible girl who died
at the age of 17, his writing here simple and
apparently artless. The composer, amazingly,
thinks himself into the thoughts of the imaginative, fanciful young poetess; so does his
interpreter, Banse, here using a lighter, more
palpitating tone.

The faultless recording completes one's
pleasure in a very special issue.

Frauenliebe und -Leben, Op 42. Myrthen, Op 25 –
No 3, Der Nussbaum; No 7, Die Lotosblume. Die
Kartenlegerin, Op 31 No 2. Ständchen, Op 36 No 2.
Das verlassne Mägdlein, Op 64 No 2. Aufträge, Op 77
No 5. Lieder-album für die Jugend, Op 79 – No 13,
Der Sandmann; No 29, Mignon. Lieder, Op 90.
Nachtlied, Op 96 No 1
Bernarda Fink mez **Roger Vignoles** pf
Harmonia Mundi HMC90 1753 (60' · DDD · T/t) Ⓕ○

Bernarda Fink proves conclusively here that she
can be just as compelling in German song as she is
in Baroque works. For a start few accounts of any
of these pieces have been quite so beautifully and
effortlessly sung. Not a note in this recital is ugly
or mishandled; everything is projected on a stream
of perfectly produced, mellow mezzo tone. In
itself, that's almost enough to recommend the
disc. But Fink has so much more to offer. Her
interpretation of the oft-recorded *Frauenliebe*
cycle isn't one with the kind of overwhelming
emotional tug evinced by Baker and von Otter, yet
in her slightly more reticent way Fink conveys just

as much feeling as her rivals. Her sweet, reflective, slightly vibrant tone very much calls to mind Seefried's and Isokoski's equally artless style among soprano versions. With Roger Vignoles as a sympathetic and positive partner, Fink's version deserves to be equated with those of her distinguished predecessors. There's no anti-climax in the other performances.

The very familiar 'Nussbaum' and 'Aufträge' are as delightfully eager and spontaneous as they ought to be. Those ineffably Schumannesque pieces, 'Die Lotosblume' and, in the Op 90 settings of Lenau, 'Meine Rose', receive treatment, in timbre and line and verbal assurance that would be hard to better. The recording has the singer blessedly forward so one catches the true flavour of her voice and words. A joy from start to finish.

Dichterliebe, Op 48

Dichterliebe. Liederkreis, Op 24. Belsatzar, Op-57. Abends am Strand, Op 45 No 3. Die beiden Grenadiere, Op 49 No 1. Lieder und Gesänge, Op-127 – No 2, Dein Angesicht; No 3, Es leuchtet meine Liebe. Vier Gesänge, Op 142 – No 2, Lehn deine Wang; No 4, Mein Wagen rollet langsam
Ian Bostridge ten **Julius Drake** pf
EMI 556575-2 (69' · DDD · T/t)   Ⓕ**OOO**B+

 Bostridge makes you think anew about the music in hand, interpreting all these songs as much through the mind of the poet as that of the composer, and, being youthful himself, getting inside the head of the vulnerable poet in his many moods. Quite apart from his obvious gifts as a singer and musician, that's what raises Bostridge above most of his contemporaries, who so often fail to live the words they're singing. Every one of the magnificent Op-24 songs has some moment of illumination, whether it's the terror conveyed so immediately in 'Schöne Wiege', the breathtaking beauty and sorrow of 'Anfang wollt ich' or the breadth and intensity of 'Mit Myrten und Rosen'. In between the two cycles comes a group of the 1840 Leipzig settings that adumbrates every aspect of Bostridge's attributes, as well as those of his equally perceptive partner.

The vivid word-painting in *Belsatzar* brings the Old Testament scene arrestingly before us. Perhaps best of all is the unjustly neglected *Es leuchtet meine Liebe*, a melodrama here perfectly enacted by both performers. *Mein Wagen rollet langsam* forms a perfect introduction, in its lyrical freedom, to *Dichterliebe*, an interpretation to rank with the best available in terms of the sheer beauty of the singing and acute response to its sustained inspiration. Listen to the wonder brought to the discovery of the flowers and angels in 'Im Rhein', the contained anger of 'Ich grolle nicht', the sense of bereavement in 'Hör ist das Liedchen' and you'll judge this is an interpretation of profundity and emotional identification, the whole cycle crowned by the sensitivity of Drake's playing of the summarising postlude. To

complete one's pleasure EMI has provided an exemplary and forward recording balance.

Dichterliebe. Liederkreis, Op 39
Werner Güra ten **Jan Schultsz** pf
Harmonia Mundi HMC901766 (56' · DDD · T/t)   Ⓕ**OO**

Güra delivers *Dichterliebe* with impeccable line and tone, and in a style following the best traditions of German tenors in the work. Only in 'Ich will meine Seele tauchen' does he stray from grace, choosing an oddly dragging tempo, slower than any other singers in this song. Although Bostridge's singing for EMI is slightly softer-grained, he opts for a more dramatic approach than Güra, distinctly underlining certain words, even syllables, to press home the import of Heine's and Schumann's inspiration. This may be found a shade mannered on repeated hearing. The contrast is most marked in 'Ich hab' im Traum geweinet'. Güra sings this in a dreamy *legato*, as if in a trance; Bostridge often breaks the shape of a phrase in order to give it a more histrionic edge. His very personal approach is underlined by a more intimate recording than Güra receives. Both pianists seem wholly in consort with their respective singer.

Bostridge adds to his disc more Heine, Op 24, and separate songs to texts by the same poet, a consistent policy, and it also has more music over all; but Güra's choice of Op 39 is entirely justified by his quite beautiful rendering of this haunting work. His classically wrought, plangent-voiced reading goes, without too much interpretative intervention, to the heart of Eichendorff, and to Schumann's imaginative response to the poems. Listen to such masterpieces as 'Die Stille', 'Mondnacht' (a perfect *legato* here again) and 'Wehmut' and you'll hear him at his most eloquent, pianist Jan Schultsz adding his own insights to the tenor's reading. This simpler, unsophisticated version goes to the heart of the matter, and deserves a place among the élite.

Dichterliebe. Die Lotosblume, Op 25 No 7. Die Minnesänger, Op 33 No 2. Romanzen und Balladen – II, Op 49: No 1, Die beiden Grenadiere; III, Op 53: No 3, Der arme Peter; IV, Op 64: No 3, Tragödie. Belsatzar, Op 57. Lieder und Gesänge – Op 127: No 2, Dein Angesicht; No 3, Es leuchtet meine Liebe. Gesänge, Op 142 – No 2, Lehn deine Wang; No 4, Mein Wagen rollet langsam **C-Schumann** Lieder, Op 13 – No 1, Ich stand in dunklen Träumen; No 2, Sie liebten sich beide. Loreley. Volkslied
Christopher Maltman bar **Graham Johnson** pf
Hyperion CDJ33105 (77' · DDD · T/t)   Ⓕ**OO**

With this superbly executed recital Maltman leaps in a single bound into the front rank of Lieder interpreters today. Seemingly inspired by the wonderful programme, he executes it with bitingly intense tone and an innate feeling for the German language, his high baritone easily encompassing every test placed on it. There are so many deeply satisfying performances here of mostly familiar songs that it's difficult to know which to alight on for special praise, but the last two groups – the sad, frightening tale of the near-deranged Peter and the great *Dichterliebe* cycle – undoubtedly form the climax of the recital.

Maltman's and Johnson's account of the cycle is reminiscent of the underrated version made long ago by Waechter and Brendel: it has the same immediacy, the same perceptions, with the singer's voice on each occasion being of the ideal weight and tessitura, and in its absolute prime. All the inner melancholy of words and notes, all their variety of texture are adumbrated. And here we have the added advantage of Johnson's inspired exegesis of the work in his accompanying notes.

Johnson also points out the foretaste of Mahler in the third of the Peter songs, a piece Maltman sings with just the right touch of vulnerability. He's just as sensitive in such well-known pieces as *Die Lotusblume* and *Dein Angesicht*, and brings tremendous impulse of drama to the familiar *Die beiden Grenadiere*, here sounding new-minted. The songs by Clara are a pleasing bonus, but the difference between talent and genius is apparent in comparing her setting of 'Es fiel ein Reif' (from Heine's *Volkslied*) with Schumann's. A perfectly balanced recording adds to one's pleasure in listening to this generously filled CD, which is up to the high standard of this series to date.

Dichterliebe. Sechs Gedichte und Requiem. Belsatzar. Die Löwenbraut. Der arme Peter
Christian Gerhaher bar **Gerold Huber** pf
RCA Red Seal 82876 58995-2 (66' · DDD · T/t)
Ⓕ🔘🔘➔

With this recital Christian Gerhaher confirms his pre-eminence in Lieder, and bids fair to equal or surpass his fellow baritones by dint of his attractively warm, firm tone and his complete understanding of the songs. In *Dichterliebe* he fully enters into the melancholic, romantic world of the rejected lover, projecting the love and sorrow in a committed yet unexaggerated manner. It's hard to imagine a reading by a voice of his kind that could possibly surpass his inspired performance – and that includes even the legendary Fischer-Dieskau.

He makes as good a case as possible for the *Six Poems* and *Requiem*, though it's hard to breathe life into the broken-backed ballad that is *Die Löwenbraut*. On the other hand, Gerhaher arrestingly enacts the melodrama of *Belsatzar*, biting consonants to the fore; the sadness of *Der arme Peter* benefits from the same thoughtful approach as *Dichterliebe*. Huber supports his partner with finely honed playing. The recording could not be better balanced or more immediate. This is, in every respect, a winner.

Dichterliebe, Op 48. Belsatzar, Op 57. Vier Gesänge, Op 142 – No 2, Lehn' deine Wang'; No 4, Mein Wagen rollet langsam. Fünf Lieder und Gesänge, Op 127 – No 2, Dein Angesicht; No 3, Es leuchtet meine Liebe. Myrthen, Op 25 – No 7, Die

Lotosblume; No 21, Was will die einsame Träne?; No 24, Du bist wie eine Blume. Abends am Strand, Op 45 No 3. Romanzen und Balladen II, Op 49 – No 1, Die beiden Grenadiere; No 2, Die feindlichen Brüder. Der arme Peter, Op 53 No 3. Tragödie, Op 64 No 3
Gerald Finley bar **Julius Drake** pf
Hyperion CDA67676 (69' · DDD) Ⓕ🔘🔘🔘➔

In close collusion with the ever-sentient Julius Drake, Gerald Finley gives one of the most beautifully sung and intensely experienced performances on disc of Schumann's cycle of rapture, disillusion and tender regret. This is a *Dichterliebe* firmly in the past tense, the poet-lover achingly resigned from the outset. Finley sings the second song, 'Aus meinen Tränen', as if in a trance, and lingers luxuriantly, even masochistically, over the remembered 'Ich liebe dich' in 'Wenn ich' in deine Augen seh". Yet here and elsewhere some dangerously slow tempi are vindicated by the acuity of his verbal and musical responses. Where most singers end 'Im Rhein' in wistful tenderness, Finley infuses his final words with a wry bitterness. The disenchantment of 'Ich grolle nicht' is already glimpsed. In the cycle's latter stages Finley veers between numb reverie and acerbic self-dramatisation. The birds' assuaging response in 'Am leuchtenden Sommermorgen' is magical, barely breathed, the mounting trauma of the funereal dream-song 'Ich hab' im Traum geweinet' chillingly conveyed, the dissolving vision of the penultimate 'Aus alten Märchen' relived with ineffable sadness. Adding a cutting edge to his warm, mahogany baritone, Finley imbues the final song with savage irony, before the rueful, healing close. Throughout, Drake's playing is a model of clarity and acutely observed detail (he is more attentive than most to bass-lines), epitomised in his fluid, exquisitely voiced epilogue.

Singer and pianist are just as compelling in the other Heine settings here. The church acoustic is more resonant than is ideal for Lieder, though that hardly detracts from a glorious Schumann recital.

Schumann Dichterliebe[a] **Schoenberg** Pierrot lunaire[b]
Christine Schäfer sop [a]**Natascha Osterkorn** pf
[b]**Ensemble InterContemporain, Paris / Pierre Boulez** Film director **Oliver Herrmann**
ArtHaus Musik ⓋⒹⓋⒹ 100 330 (126' · 16:9 · 2.0 · 0) Ⓕ🔘

Schäfer's virtuosity as a singing actress is exploited to the full in this highly imaginative double-bill. In the Schumann, work and artists are placed in a new and controversial context, with the production of the film intermingled with the performance of the cycle. In an intimate, sparsely lit nightclub in Berlin-Mitte, re-creating the salon atmosphere of a performance in the composer's time, the cycle is sung by the soprano in a tight-fitting black outfit while moving around the room in sympathy with evocations of each song's mood. The idea is to make the emotions of the work part of everyday life. Schäfer's reading of the songs is at once simple and intense, devoid entirely of sentimentality. She's supported in the performance and rehearsal by the equally fascinating personality of the pianist Natascha Osterkorn.

As far as one can tell, the singer isn't dubbed here. But in the 'staging' of *Pierrot lunaire*, she's undoubtedly miming to her own *Sprechgesang*. With clown-like make-up, Schäfer wanders Kafka-like, through a kaleidoscopic range of situations and venues – including an abattoir, railway station and a medical lecture theatre – vaguely appropriate to the texts. In this, one of the soprano's best-known roles, she excels in declaiming the text with meaning, assisted by that past master of the genre, Pierre Boulez.

As a bonus, there's a 45-minute interview with the singer. This whole issue extends the boundaries of interpreting vocal works on DVD. A riveting experience.

Lieder Recitals

'Melancholie'

Sechs Gedichte, Op 36. Der Einsiedler, Op 83 No 3. Gesänge des Harfners, Op 98a. Liederkreis, Op 39. Spanische Liebeslieder – Tief im Herzen trag ich Pein, Op 138 No 2. Spanisches Liederspiel, Op 74 – No 6 Melancholie

Christian Gerhaher *bar* **Gerold Huber** *pf*
RCA Red Seal 88697 16817-2 (73' · DDD)   Ⓕ

Though the catch-all title 'Melancholie' is slightly misleading, Christian Gerhaher's enterprisingly planned programme provides a conspectus of Schumann's art as a Lieder composer. With his bright, burnished high baritone, expressive diction and alert, unexaggerated response to mood and nuance, Gerhaher confirms his credentials as one of the most probing Lieder singers of the younger generation. While it is virtually impossible for a single voice to do equal justice to all 12 songs of the *Liederkreis*, he succeeds better than most. He beautifully suggests the melancholy and mystery of the opening 'In der Fremde', singing with fine *legato* and a subtly judged use of *rubato*, and brings an impetuous urgency and a chilling final frisson to the Lorelei scene 'Waldesgespräch'. 'Die Stille', a difficult song for a man to bring off, is delicate and wondering without archness; the bardic 'Auf einer Burg' is hypnotically sustained in a numb, blanched tone, devoid of all nuances, while the final 'Frühlingsnacht', which can easily sound flustered, here has an ecstatic sense of finality. Perhaps Gerhaher and the discerning if sometimes over-discreet Gerold Huber slightly miss the tremulous expectation of 'Intermezzo'; and there have been more magical performances of 'Mondnacht', here taken dangerously slowly. But for imaginative depth in the *Liederkreis* Gerhaher can certainly stand alongside the best.

Gerhaher and Huber choose unusually slow tempi for one or two of the other songs, most questionably in the Andersen song 'Der Spielmann', where the village wedding music should surely suggest more feverish wildness than here.

Far more often, though, Gerhaher impresses with his unselfconscious eloquence, whether in the anguished life-weariness of the Harpers' songs, a chillingly timed and coloured 'Der Soldat' or in the potentially mawkish 'Liebesbotschaft', sung with a rapt, *echt* Schumannesque inwardness. Not for the only time in these Reinick songs, Gerhaher makes you 'upgrade' music that can look distinctly homely, even bland, on the printed page. The baritone provides his own thoughtful note, though frustratingly you'll have to go to his website for English translations of the song texts.

Complete Lieder, Volume 1

Das verlassene Mägdlein, Op 64 No 2. Melancholie, Op 74 No 6. Aufträge, Op 77 No 5. Op 79 – No 7a, Zigeunerliedchen I; No 7b, Zigeunerliedchen II; No 23, Er ist's!. Die Blume der Ergebung, Op 83 No 2. Röslein, Röslein!, Op 89 No 6. Sechs Gedichte und Requiem, Op 90. Op 96 – No 1, Nachtlied; No 3 Ihre Stimme. Lieder und Gesänge aus Wilhelm Meister, Op 98a – No 1, Kennst du das Land?; No 3, Nur wer die Sehnsucht kennt; No 5, Heiss' mich nicht reden; No 7, Singet nicht in Trauertönen; No 9, So lasst mich scheinen. Sechs Gesänge, Op 107. Warnung, Op 119 No 2. Die Meerfee, Op 125 No 1. Sängers Trost, Op-127 No 1. Mädchen-Schwermut, Op 142 No 3

Christine Schäfer *sop* **Graham Johnson** *pf*
Hyperion CDJ33101 (75' · DDD · T/t)   Ⓕ ❶❷❸

This disc launches Hyperion's Schumann Lieder project as auspiciously as Dame Janet Baker's recital opened their Complete Schubert Edition. As ever, Graham Johnson shows an unerring gift for matching singer and song. These are almost all late pieces, written between 1849 and 1852 under the shadow of depression and sickness; and their intense chromaticism can all too easily seem tortuous. However, imaginatively supported by Johnson, Christine Schäfer illuminates each of these songs with her pure, lucent timbre, her grace and breadth of phrase and her unselfconscious feeling for verbal meaning and nuance. The voice is an expressive, flexible lyric-coloratura; she can spin a scrupulously even *legato*, integrates the high notes of, say, 'Er ist's' perfectly within the melodic line, and has the breath control to sustain the long phrases of 'Requiem' with apparent ease.

Aided by Johnson's lucid textures and subtle feel for *rubato* and harmonic direction, Schäfer avoids any hint of mawkishness in songs like 'Meine Rose', Op 90 No 2, 'Mädchen-Schwermut' and 'Abendlied. Several songs here have been overshadowed or eclipsed by the settings by Schubert, Wolf or Brahms, and Schäfer and Johnson do much to rehabilitate them.

Schäfer brings an exquisite wondering stillness to the Goethe 'Nachtlied', more disturbed and earthbound than Schubert's sublime setting, but here, at least, scarcely less poignant. She also has the dramatic flair to bring off the difficult Mignon songs, especially the volatile, quasi-operatic 'Heiss' mich nicht reden' and 'Kennst du das Land', where the final verse, evoking Mignon's terrifying passage across the Alps, builds to a climax of desperate, almost demented yearning. At the other end of the emotional spectrum, Schäfer brings a guileful, knowing touch to the first of the *Zigeunerliedchen*; the Mendelssohnian 'Die Meerfee' glistens and glances and 'Aufträge' has a winning eagerness and charm, with a delicious sense of flirtation between voice and keyboard. A delectable, often revelatory recital. The recording is natural and well balanced, while Graham Johnson provides typically searching commentaries.

Complete Lieder, Volume 2
Drei Gedichte, Op 30. Die Löwenbraut, Op 31 No 1. 12 Gedichte, Op 35. Lieder und Gesänge aus Wilhelm Meister, Op 98a – No 2, Ballade des Harfners; No 4, Wer nie sein Brot mit Tränen ass; No 6, Wer sich der Einsamkeit ergibt; No 8, An die Türen will ich schleichen. Vier Husarenlieder, Op 117
Simon Keenlyside *bar* **Graham Johnson** *pf*
Hyperion CDJ33102 (70' · DDD · N/T/t) Ⓕ**OO**

In his notes Graham Johnson says that what we have always lacked is a convincing way of performing late Schumann songs, often spare in texture and elusive in style. Well, he and Keenlyside seem to have found one here in their wholly admirable versions of the very different Opp 98a and 117. The Op 98a settings of the Harper's outpourings from *Wilhelm Meister* have always stood in the shade of those by Schubert and Wolf. This pair show incontrovertibly that there's much to be said for Schumann's versions, capturing the essence of the old man's sad musings, as set by the composer in an imaginative, free way, alert to every nuance in the texts.

The extroverted Lenau *Husarenlieder* could hardly be more different. Keenlyside identifies in turn with the bravado of the first, the cynicism of the second, and the eerie, death-dominated mood of the fourth. The pair enter into the openhearted mood called for by the *Knabenhorn* settings, most of all in the irresistible 'Der Hidalgo'. Keenlyside is just as forthright in *Die Löwenbraut* and in those of Op 35, the well-known Kerner settings, and he brings impressive control to the Eusebius ones, not least the all-enveloping 'Stille Tränen'. The interpretation of this quasi-cycle is convincing and unerringly paced. The recording and Johnson's persuasive playing are superb.

Complete Lieder, Volume 6
Lieder, Op 40ª. Spanisches Liederspiel, Op 74ᵇ. Spanische Liebeslieder, Op 138ᶜ **C Schumann** Lieder aus Jucunde, Op 23ᵈ
ᵇᶜᵈ**Geraldine McGreevy** *sop* ᵇᶜ**Stella Doufexis** *mez*
ᵇᶜ**Adrian Thompson** *ten* ᵃᵇᶜ**Stephan Loges** *bar*
Graham Johnson, ᶜ**Stephen Hough** *pfs*
Hyperion CDJ33106 (76' · DDD · N/T/t) Ⓕ**O**

This disc is a delight from start to finish. Songs and interpretations are on a high level of achievement, in this case all the more welcome

as these groups, for various reasons, don't figure that often in recitals. Both the Spanish sets are of the highest order of composition, though not often acknowledged as such. The Op 74 set is notable for many mood changes and its touches of fantasy, melded with a typically Schumannesque pull on the emotions. Alone or together, all four singers revel in their chances for expressive singing, none more than McGreevy, now a Lieder singer of major calibre, in 'Melancholie'. McGreevy also stands out in the wistful duet 'In der Nacht' with the sensitive Thompson, a poem set quite differently, as are some others, by Wolf later in the century. Loges contributes to concerted pieces with his expected artistry and has fun with 'Die Contrabandiste'.

The Op 138 set is even fuller of variety of mood and composition. All four singers seize their chances eagerly, with faultlessly sculpted readings under the tutelage of Johnson, who's joined here by no less a pianist than Stephen Hough in the two-piano accompaniments. The Andersen settings (Op 40) are fascinating songs delivered by Stephan Loges with refined tone and diction to which he adds a sure insight into their meaning in performances that compel one to place the set among Schumann's masterpieces in the genre. Add the naturally balanced recording and Johnson's extensive notes and this issue is treasure indeed.

Complete Lieder, Volume 7
Myrthen, Op 25ª. Four Duets, Op 34ª. Four Duets, Op 78ª. John Anderson, Op 145 No 4ᵇ
ᵃ**Dorothea Röschmann** *sop* ᵃ**Ian Bostridge** *ten*
Graham Johnson *pf* ᵇ**Polyphony / Stephen Layton**
Hyperion CDJ33107 (78' · DDD) Ⓕ**OO**

Hyperion's Schumann song series has already produced some profoundly satisfying discs, but none quite to equal the pleasures found on this volume. Its centrepiece, *Myrthen* – the cycle of love songs celebrating the union of Clara and Robert – is framed by eight duets to form a wonderfully balanced offering, and one that could hardly be surpassed in execution, through the understanding and skills of the three participants.

If one has to be singled out for particular praise, it must be Dorothea Röschmann. In tones at once fresh, warm and communicative, she sings all her contributions with an ideal balance between word and note. To such a familiar and lovely song as 'Der Nussbaum' she brings a heartfelt sense of anticipated pleasure that bears comparison with any of the heap of noted performances from the past, occasional vibrato used to arresting effect, as in all her readings. And 'Lied der Suleika' has its intensity underlined by the palpitating intimacy of her singing.

Not to be outdone, Bostridge presents deeply considered accounts of all his songs, combining his silvery, lightly tremulous tone with his customary feeling for words, most notably in the song 'Aus den hebräischen Gesängen' and the two Venetian Songs. Even better is his sensitive enactment of the marvellous setting of Heine,

'Was will die einsame Träne', which reveals his complete understanding of the idiom, and of the popular 'Du bist wie eine Blume', where his half-voice is skilfully deployed.

Johnson is on his most alert and empathetic form at the piano throughout. In the two sets of duets, full of Schumann at his most easeful, the voices intertwine effortlessly. Some oldsters will recall the famous, endearingly romantic Lehmann/Melchior recordings of some of these: Röschmann and Bostridge are just as persuasive. With one of Hyperion's best recordings to complement the performances, voices nicely forward, this disc is definitely one to have.

movie music. But there are innocent, Biedermeier delights in assorted duets, sung with bright-eyed eagerness by Felicity Lott and Ann Murray, and in three settings of Emanuel Geibel, beginning with a duet in Schumann's most cosy-comfy vein and ending with a mildly exotic ensemble evoking the gypsy life.

Among a clutch of young singers making cameo appearances, the virginal-toned Lydia Teuscher is true and touching in 'Die Nonne' and in the virtually unknown 'Frühlingsgrüsse', whose shy, halting lyricism is so typical of late Schumann. Collectors of this revelatory series will need no reminder that Johnson writes about the music as discerningly and eloquently as he plays.

Complete Lieder, Volume 10

Liederkreis, Op 39ᵃ. Schön Hedwig, Op 106ᵇ. Zwei Balladen für Deklamation, Op 122ᵇ. Drei Gedichte nach Emanuel Geibel, Op 29ᵇ. Die Nonne, Op 49 No 3ᵈ. Was soll ich sagen, Op 27 No 3ᵉ· Frühlingsgrüsseᶠ. Drei Duette, Op 43ᵍ. Mein Garten, Op 77 No 2ʰ. Sommerruh, WoO 7ⁱ. Mädchenlieder, Op 103j. Bei Schenkung eines Flügels, WoO 26 No 4ᵏ
ᵃ**Kate Royal**, ᵍʰⁱʲ**Felicity Lott**, ᶜᵈᶠᵏ**Lydia Teuscher** sops
ᵍⁱʲ**Ann Murray**, ᶜᵏ**Daniela Lehner** mezzos
ᶜᵉᵏ**Stephan Loges** bar ᵇ**Christoph Bantzer** spkr
Graham Johnson pf with ᶜ**Edith Barlow** sop
ᶜ**Melanie Lang** mez ᶜᵏ**Adrian Ward**, ᶜ**Nicky Spence** tens ᶜ**Lucas Kargl** bar ᵉ**Marcus Gruett** perc
Hyperion CDJ33110 (76' · DDD · N · T/t)   Ⓕ

The prime attraction for many here will be English soprano-of-the-moment Kate Royal in the popular Eichendorff *Liederkreis*. Royal's pure, pellucid tone, free-soaring top notes (gloriously heard in, say, 'Schöne Fremde') and refined musicianship give constant pleasure. In this cycle of dusk and shadows there are two or three songs that always seem to elude a bright, lyric soprano; and for all her beauty of voice and care for phrasing, Royal doesn't quite catch the fear and eeriness of 'Zwielicht' (which here sounds merely melancholy) or the sudden sense of isolation and dread at the end of 'Im Walde'. Other singers, too, have made 'Waldesgespräch' more scary, though Royal does touchingly suggest a human sadness in the spooky woodland drama.

But these are minor quibbles. Abetted by Johnson's ever-sentient keyboard-playing, Royal reveals a true understanding of Schumann's *Innigkeit*, whether in the suppressed passion of the opening 'In der Fremde' (the notorious phrase beginning 'Und über mir rauscht' taken effortlessly in a single breath) and 'Die Stille' (where she avoids the trap of ingénue coyness), the exquisite poise of 'Die Mondnacht' or the tremulous excitement and sense of imminent revelation in 'Schöne Fremde'. In the final 'Frühlingsnacht', often rushed off its feet, she and Johnson catch the elusive mix of secretiveness and ecstasy to perfection.

The remainder of the disc is given over to curiosities and rarities. Despite the eloquent declamation of actor Christoph Bantzer, it's hard to work up much enthusiasm for three 'melodramas' which too easily suggest silent

---

Complete Lieder, Volume 11

Sechs Gesänge, Op 89ᵃ – No 1, Es stürmet am Abendhimmel; No 2, Heimliches Verschwinden; No 3, Herbstlied; No 4, Abschied vom Walde; No 5, Ins Freie. Drei Gesänge, Op 83ᵃ – No 1, Resignation; No 3, Der Einsiedler. Fünf Lieder und Gesänge, Op 127 – No 4, Mein altes Rossᵃ. Drei Gesänge, Op 95ᵇ. Minnespiel, Op 101ᶜᵈ. Sechs Gedichte aus dem Liederbuch eines Malers, Op 36ᵃ. Des Sängers Fluch, Op 139 – No 4, Provenzalisches Liedᵈ; No 7, Balladea. Der Handschuh, Op 87ᵃ
ᵇ**Katherine Broderick**, ᶜ**Geraldine McGreevy** sops
ᶜ**Stella Doufexis** mez ᵈ**Adrian Thompson** ten
ᵃ**Hanno Müller-Brachmann**, ᶜ**Stephan Loges** bars
Graham Johnson pf
Hyperion CDJ33111 (78' · DDD)   ⒻⓄ

Hyperion's Schumann Song Edition ends, as it began 12 years ago, with a recital devoted largely to the problematic late songs of 1849-52. With the odd exception, these have often been castigated, not least by Eric Sams in *The Songs of Robert Schumann*, as the products of a torpid and increasingly sick mind. But though most of the songs on this disc tend to be more understated, less romantically subjective than those of Schumann's great song year, 1840, the best of them are not necessarily inferior to their predecessors, just different.

There are undeniable duds, usually when Schumann is in hearty or heroic vein, alongside touching lyrics like the fragile 'Heimliches Verschwinden', the rapturous 'Liebster, deine Worte stehlen', or 'Provenzalisches Lied', a piquant celebration of courtly love.

The lion's share of the programme, including the six Reinick Songs falls to baritone Hanno Müller-Brachmann, whose singing is more notable for robust directness than subtlety. He exploits his deep bass resonances to good effect in 'Sonntags am Rhein', that quintessential song of pious Biedermeier contentment. In 'Liebesbotschaft, Müller-Brachmann sounds lugubrious, despite the flowing tempo, rather than tenderly devoted. He is at his best in declamatory, dramatic mode, recounting a minstrel's bloody revenge in 'Ballade', or in a powerful and atmospheric performance of another chivalrous ballad, 'Der Handschuh'.

Elsewhere there are welcome cameo appearances from Adrian Thompson (graceful and smiling in 'Provenzalisches Lied'), Geraldine McGreevy and Stella Doufexis, who combine with baritone Stefan Loges in two attractive quartets from the Rückert *Minnespiel*. Katherine Broderick, a Wagnerian soprano of the future, impresses with her vibrant intensity in the three Op 95 songs, though even she and Johnson cannot disguise the bombastic tawdriness of 'Dem Helden'. Whatever the provisos, this disc goes far to vindicating some of Schumann's least-favoured late songs, not least due to Graham Johnson's eloquent advocacy, in print and in performance.

Genoveva, Op 81

Genoveva
Ruth Ziesak sop Genoveva **Deon van der Walt** ten
Golo **Rodney Gilfry** bar Hidulfus **Oliver Widmer** bar
Siegfried **Marjana Lipovšek** mez Margaretha **Thomas
Quasthoff** bar Drago **Hiroyuki Ijichi** bass Balthasar
Josef Krenmair bar Caspar **Arnold Schoenberg
Choir; Chamber Orchestra of Europe / Nikolaus
Harnoncourt**
Teldec ② 0630-13144-2 (129' · DDD · T/t) Recorded live
1996   Ⓕ〇

For most listeners Schumann's only opera is still a relatively unknown quantity, but lovers of his music will celebrate a work that's intimate, thought-provoking and melodious. The libretto (by Schumann himself, after Tieck and Hebbel) deals with secret passion and suspected adultery, while the music mirrors emotional turmoil with great subtlety, and sometimes with astonishing imagination. Copious foretastes are provided in the familiar overture, and thereafter, discoveries abound. Sample, for example, the jagged counter-motif that shudders as Genoveva's husband Siegfried entreats Golo (his own *alter ego*) to guard his wife while he's away at war; or the off-stage forces representing drunken servants; or the almost expressionist writing at 4'00" into track-10, where Golo responds with seething hatred to Genoveva's vengeance. The entreaties of Drago's ghost (track-4, 6'10") aren't too far removed from Siegmund's 'Nothung!' in Act-1 of *Die Walküre*, and Genoveva's singing from 'a desolate, rocky place' (track-5, first minute or so), sounds prophetic of Isolde (who was as yet unborn, so to speak). Harnoncourt suspects that *Genoveva* was a 'counterblast' to Wagner, and though Wagner apparently thought the opera 'bizarre', there remains a vague suspicion of sneaking regard, even a smidgen of influence.

Teldec's balancing is mostly judicious, and the musical direction suggestive of burning conviction. The worthy though relatively conventional Gerd Albrecht (in Orfeo's mellow 1992 recording) only serves to underline the leaner, more inflected and more urgently voiced profile of Harnoncourt's interpretation. As to the two sets of singers, most preferences rest with the latter's line-up. Stage effects are well handled;

the sum effect is of a top-drawer Schumann set within an unexpected structural context.

Heinrich Schütz   German 1585-1672

In 1590 Schütz moved with his family to Weissenfels. In 1598 Landgrave Moritz, impressed by his musical accomplishments, took him to Kassel, where he served as a choirboy and studied music with the court Kapellmeister, Georg Otto. In 1609 Schütz proceeded to the University of Marburg to study law, but Landgrave Moritz advised him to abandon his university studies and to go to Venice as a pupil of G Gabrieli; moreover, the landgrave provided the financial means to do this. Schütz remained in Venice for over three years, returning to Moritz's court at Kassel in 1613. The following year he was seconded to serve for two months at the electoral court in Dresden, and in 1615 the Elector Johann Georg I requested his services for a further two years. Moritz reluctantly agreed, and was obliged, for political reasons, to comply when the elector insisted on retaining Schütz in his permanent employ.

As Kapellmeister at Dresden, Schütz was responsible for providing music for major court ceremonies, whether religious or political. In 1619 Schütz published his first collection of sacred music, the Psalmen Davids, dedicated to the elector.

Schütz was often absent from Dresden on his own or the elector's business, and in 1627 he was at Torgau, where his Dafne (the first German opera) was performed for the wedding of the elector's daughter Sophia Eleonora. Visits to Mühlhausen and possibly Gera were undertaken later in the year. Towards the end of the 1620s economic pressures of the Thirty Years War began to affect the electoral court. Musicians wages fell into arrears, and in 1628 Schütz decided on a second visit to Venice, where he was able to study developments in dramatic music under Monteverdi's guidance. He returned to Dresden in 1629, but two years later Saxony entered the war and musical activities at court soon came to a virtual halt. Schütz then accepted an invitation to direct the music at the wedding of Crown Prince Christian of Denmark. He arrived in Copenhagen in December 1633 and was paid a salary as Kapellmeister by King Christian IV until his return to Dresden in May 1635.

From Michaelmas 1639 Schütz was again absent from Dresden, this time for about 15 months in the service of Georg of Calenberg. On his return he found the Kapelle further depleted and its members living in penury, and for most of 1642-4 he was again employed at the Danish court. After a year in and around Brunswick he went into semi-retirement, spending much of his time in Weissenfels, though he retained the title and responsibilities of Kapellmeister at Dresden. The end of the Thirty Years War had little immediate effect on musical conditions and in 1651 Schütz renewed an earlier plea for release from his duties and the granting of a pension. This and later petitions were ignored and Schütz obtained his release only on the elector's death in 1656. He was far from inactive during his remaining 15 years. He continued to supply music for occasions at Dresden, frequently travelled and worked on the masterpieces of his last years – the Christmas History, the three Passions and the settings of Psalms cxix and c.

Schütz was the greatest German composer of the 17th century and the first of international stature. His output was almost exclusively sacred; he set mainly biblical texts and wrote little chorale-based music. His music, largely to German texts, constitutes the ultimate realisation of Luther's endeavours to establish the vernacular as a literary and liturgical language, and embodies the Protestant and humanistic concept of musica poetica in perhaps its most perfect form. GROVEmusic

Psalms of David

Psalmen Davids sampt etlichen Moteten und Concerten, SWV22-47
Cantus Cölln / Konrad Junghänel
Harmonia Mundi ② HMC90 1652/3
(143' · DDD · T/t) Ⓕ❍

Here's something to get excited about: a new recording, at last, of Schütz's first monumental publication of sacred music. Whether anything can be worth waiting for that long is a moot point, but Cantus Cölln and Concerto Palatino give us an interpretation that's unlikely to be surpassed. With eight singers and no fewer than two dozen instrumentalists, the scale is little short of symphonic. For sheer splendour, who can top *Danket dem Herren* (SWV45) or the next piece in the collection, *Zion spricht*?

It's easy enough to single out the most opulent pieces, but as Peter Wollny remarks in his admirable booklet-notes, the whole point of the *Psalmen Davids* is its variety in the treatment of a medium whose potential for cliché is very great. The musicians respond to Schütz's demands with verve and perception and the sort of confidence that would carry any music aloft in triumph. The sound recording does them full justice. You'll almost certainly listen, enthralled, to the entire collection – nearly two-and-a-half hours – in one sitting.

Symphoniae sacrae

Symphoniae sacrae, tertia pars
Cantus Cölln; Concerto Palatino / Konrad Junghänel
Harmonia Mundi ② HMC90 1850/1
(126' · DDD · T/t) Ⓕ

Twenty years having passed since the Schütz 400th anniversary, it's hard to think of many composers before Bach whose discography has been as uniformly well served in the intervening years. This is the third offering from Konrad Junghänel's ensemble, who team up once again with Concerto Palatino; the result is bound to impress even the casual listener, and will certainly delight those already well acquainted with Schütz's music.

The third and final volume of the *Symphoniae sacrae* was issued in 1650 when Schütz was 65.

One of the pieces in the collection had originally been composed more than 30 years earlier, which suggests a concern to bring together his life's work: he could hardly have foreseen that he would live some 20 years more.

As ever, Schütz puts the biblical texts right at the heart of the music. It is striking just how many of the texts you will be able to recall instantly, such is his knack for their acute characterisation. The same applies to the performances, which capture the aura of the grand statement, juxtaposed with an intimate feeling for detail and psychological observation. This comes across particularly in *Mein Sohn, warum hast Du uns das getan*, the 'dialogue' between the child Jesus and his parents. The parable of the sower is evoked in *Es ging ein Sämann aus*, and Psalm 127 ('Except the Lord build this house') in *Wo der Herr nicht das Haus bauet*.

These count among the most impressive pieces in the collection, alongside the most famous one, *Saul, Saul, was verfolgst du mich*. So persuasive is the architecture of these readings that local niggles are easily dismissed: at times the sound recording favours the voices at the expense of detailed instrumental passagework, and just occasionally intonation goes off the straight and narrow. But never do such details detract from a project whose high ambitions are so consistently realised.

O bone, o dulcis, o benigne Jesu, SWV53. Erbarm dich mein, o Herre Gott, SWV447. Herr, der du bist vormals genädig gewest, SWV461. O Jesu, nomen dulce, SWV308. O misericordissime Jesu, SWV309. Magnificat, SWV468. Ich hebe meine Augen auf, SWV399. Wo der Herr nicht das Haus bauet, SWV400. Hütet euch, dass eure Herzen, SWV413. Herr, wie lang willst du mein so gar vergessen, SWV416
Tanya Aspelmeier, Monique Zanetti sops **Rolf Ehlers** counterten **Henning Kaiser** ten **Markus Flaig** bass **La Chapelle Rhénane / Benoît Haller** ten
K617 K617 191 (69' · DDD) Ⓕ

It would be a shame if the lack of English translations of the sung texts put potential investigators off hearing this enjoyable survey of Schütz's richly expressive music. The sonorous acoustic of the convent where the disc was recorded is ideal for the warm yet stylishly sprung performances. Directed by tenor Benoît Haller, the singers deliver gutsy, assured performances. When all the players and choir combine, with all the stops out, the effect is magnificent: two cornetts and three sackbuts make a tremendous noise when let loose, reinforcing the opulent conclusion to *Herr, der du bist vormals genädig gewest*. But there is also subtly evocative music here, such as the lush continuo configurations in the soprano solo motet *O misericordissime Jesu* or the solemn brass and tenor solo texture in *Erbarm dich mein, o Herre Gott*.

Most recordings of this quality concentrate on one of Schütz's major collections but La Chapelle Rhénane instead pick and mix from *Symphonia sacrae*, *Cantiones sacrae* and the *Kleine geistliche Konzerte*, and throw in a few obscurities, too. The result is a refreshing manifesto from musicians who zealously believe in the music they have chosen to perform. La Chapelle Rhénane's biography claims that the group are 'able to provide original interpretations that are sparkling and flavoursome, in a vision brimming with sensuality and sincerity'. This is one of the rare occasions when we can believe the hype.

Opus ultimum (Schwanengesang)

Opus ultimum (Schwanengesang), SWV482-94
**Ghent Collegium Vocale; Concerto Palatino /
Philippe Herreweghe**
Harmonia Mundi ② HMC90 1895/6 (89' · DDD · T/t)Ⓕ

The beauty of this remarkable performance of Schütz's last work resides principally in Collegium Vocale's blooming cradle of sound and how it unassumingly stakes its claim – with no subtext – on the unique ambitions of Schütz's 'Swansong'. These are founded on the composer's distilled and often austere contemplation of Psalm 119 in 11 double-choir motets, joined by Psalm 150 and the impressive *Deutsches Magnificat*.

If not texturally pared down, this is a journey where the 86-year-old Schütz withdraws from the world in a lexicon of finely drawn plainchants, antique modes, taut contrapuntal and antiphonal exchanges, melodic swathes and quicksilver declamations. Herreweghe illuminates each verse with a considered and gentle ear for the progression from the 'statutes' of faith towards a sense of hope and salvation as we move towards a new Covenant, revealed in the final motet with its assuaging supplications and rock-like assurance. Here we sense, above all, Schütz's mix of defiance and resignation for the gradual passing of a self-contained sacred tradition threatened by radical worldly things (like operas).

Collegium Vocale relish Schütz's introspection and easy exchange between solo and tutti sections, which allow the inspired rhetorical mood-changes to reveal each marked-out image ('when thou shalt enlarge my heart' at the end in the second motet is dealt a moment of special attention as it moves towards a conclusion in rapt homage to Monteverdi). Herreweghe's performances are generally outstanding in their attention to detail: some might quibble that the inner tutti voices occasionally lack focus and energy, but this is a performance where Schütz's seasoned harmonic shifts are treated as pure music and not over-accentuated by rhetorical zeal: the music doesn't need it. Can a greater work have been completed by an octogenarian? This recording urges us, very persuasively, to think perhaps not.

Secular Works

Freue dich des Weibes deiner Jugend, SWV453. Liebster, sagt in süssem Schmerzen, SWV441. Nachdem ich lag in meinem öder Bette, SWV451.

Glück zu dem Helikon, SWV96. Haus und Güter erbat man von Eltern, SWV21. Tugend ist der beste Freund, SWV442. Teutoniam dudum belli atra pericla, SWV338. Wie wenn der Adler, SWV434. Siehe, wie fein und lieblich ists, SWV48. Vier Hirtinnen, gleich jung, gleich schön, SWVAnh1. Lässt Salomon sein Bette nicht umgeben, SWV452. Die Erde trinkt für sich, SWV438. Wohl dem, der ein Tugendsam Weib hat, SWV20. Itzt blicken durch des Himmels Saal, SWV460. Syncharma musicum, SWV49
Weser-Renaissance Bremen / Manfred Cordes
CPO CPO999 518-2 (71' · DDD · T/t)　Ⓜ❍

Here's a discovery of several unrecorded byways of Schütz's miscellaneous secular music. The 17th century being what it is, secular and sacred are deliberately dovetailed into a cultural pea soup: these works are embedded in the literary morality of the age and aren't entirely profane. There's a pleasing lightness of touch from the soloists (especially the soprano) and the instrumental consort doesn't attempt, as is so mistakenly regarded these days as the ideal, to ape the vocal lines at every turn in a wash of homogeneity; there are many distinctive virtuosic commentaries, as in *Tugend ist der beste Freund*, which Cordes (enhanced by the excellent recorded sound) allows to breathe naturally.

Noble intensity and harmonious accord are the order of the day in the splendidly uplifting concerto *Teutoniam dudum*, which through its extraordinary structural clarity immediately delights the listener with a celebration of the cessation of hostilities after the miserable Thirty Years War. Most impressive, though, is the sympathetic and gentle treatment of the words from Weser-Renaissance, beautifully complemented by the soft articulation of the winds, especially in *Siehe, wie fein* and the domestic charm of *Wohl dem, der ein Tugendsam*. This is chamber music-making from the heart, tempered convincingly by the intellect and affectionately delivered.

Cyril Scott　　British 1879-1970

Early musical promise led to study at the Frankfurt Conservatoire, where he encountered 'The Frankfurt Group', Norman O'Neill, Roger Quilter, Balfour Gardiner and Percy Grainger. His early orchestral works received performances in Germany and his Second Symphony was conducted by Henry Wood. A prolific composer, Scott wrote some 400 works including four symphonies, three operas, two piano concertos, four oratorios, concertos for violin, cello, oboe and harpsichord, many vhamber works and innumerable songs.

Orchestral works

Cello Concerto[a]. Symphony No 1
[a]**Paul Watkins** vc
BBC Philharmonic Orchestra / Martyn Brabbins
Chandos CHAN10452 (58' · DDD)　Ⓟ❍▶

This fourth volume in the Chandos Scott series opens not only with a first recording, but a first performance of the Cello Concerto from 1937. By then Scott had become so unfashionable that, along with at least two unperformed operas, this concerto got forgotten. That would be an unjust final judgement. It opens with a 16-minute movement that is virtually a concerto on its own. Right at the start the sustained strings with superimposed celesta create a magical atmosphere. The cello soloist enters with a distinctive rising figure and then Scott's improvisatory instinct takes over. The continuity is close to Delius and some of the scoring is as rich as Ravel.

The second movement is largely an accompanied cadenza, leading to the final rondo where a perky solo bassoon kicks off. There's plenty for the soloist to do but it takes a few hearings for the distinctive qualities of Scott's idiom to sink in. Unlike the Elgar Concerto there's little thematic repetition. Paul Watkins sounds superb and, as before, Martyn Brabbins is an admirable exponent.

The Symphony No 1 (1899) is another curiosity – this is probably only its second performance since the composer withdrew it after the premiere. The first movement is labelled Allegro frivolo and it's not far from Sullivan; the Andante has a baleful cor anglais solo; and, because the first two pages of the score were missing, the *Allegretto* has been completed by Leslie De'Ath, the pianist who has recorded Scott's complete piano works. The finale starts with a modal trombone theme followed by a series of variations and a tentative fugue. A weird touch is the minor-key ending.

Symphony No 4. Piano Concerto No 1ᵃ.
Early One Morning
ᵃ**Howard Shelley** pf **BBC Philharmonic Orchestra /**
Martyn Brabbins
Chandos CHAN10376 (73' · DDD)　　　Ⓕ🠞

Cyril Scott was born in 1879, the same year as Ireland and Bridge, and with CDs like this he can be heard alongside their contributions in both piano and orchestral music. The First Piano Concerto (the Second is on a previous Chandos CD) was premiered by the composer under Beecham in 1915, by which time Scott's reputation in Germany had taken a terminal blow. Lewis Foreman, in the CD booklet, remembers seeing Scott at his 90th birthday concert at the Queen Elizabeth Hall in 1969 when Moura Lympany played the concerto. Reviews were generally condescending – and wrong. This is a wonderfully inventive work, completely imagined in every detail: the core of this music, like that of Delius, is the present sensual moment. If the actual sound is seductive enough it satisfies the ear. Both Scott and Delius, like Messiaen, were fixated on chords decked in luxuriant orchestral textures.

The extraordinary thing about this CD is that both *Early One Morning* (1931) and the Fourth Symphony (1952) are not just first recordings but first performances, too. Scott, neglected to the point of ostracism, continued to compose

when anyone else would have succumbed with clinical depression long before. As his psychic writings show, he was supported by higher powers. The symphony, however courageous, is not as original as either of the piano concertos and the exuberant finale falls somewhere between Debussy's *La mer* and Ravel's *Daphnis*.

Chamber works

Sonata lirica. Elégie, Op 73 No 1. Romance, Op 73 No 2. Valse triste, Op 73 No 3. Tallahassee Suite, Op 73 No 4. Three Little Waltzes, Op 58 W178 – Andante languido. Danse nègre, Op 58 No 5 W89. Two Pieces, Op 47 – Lotus Land. Lullaby, Op 57 No 2. Four Pieces, Op 67 – Intermezzo, W161. Two Preludes. Fantasie Orientale
Clare Howick vn **Sophia Rahman** pf
Dutton Digital Epoch CDLX7200 (76' · DDD)　　Ⓕ

The Scott revival marches on! The *Sonata lirica* (1937) was lost for years and this seems to be its first performance. Hearing it without knowing the composer, one might have guessed Delius. There's the same rhapsodic improvisational approach, if less subtle, where attractive melody is qualified by sumptuous chords. But Scott has his own way of doing this and the violin and piano medium exploits his gift for melody.

The disc contains five transcriptions, of which the most famous is *Lotus Land* (1905), arranged by Kreisler in 1922. It was always a mesmeric piano solo with its oriental inflections but the violin version is ecstatic. Kramer's arrangement of another evergreen, *Danse nègre*, creates some odd exchanges but is catchy and vivid. The lovely melodies of the *Intermezzo* and the *Lullaby*, also a haunting song, work beautifully in this arrangement. The *Tallahassee Suite* (1911) is presumably evocative of the Florida landscape and the final 'Danse nègre' boasts ragtime syncopations.

The whole collection is a most attractive expression of Scott's highly characteristic style, all wonderfully played. Clare Howick and Sophia Rahman are both superb.

'Complete Piano Music, Volume 1 –　　　🄷
Suites and Miniatures'
Leslie De'Ath pf
Dutton Laboratories Epoch ② CDLX7150 (146' ·
DDD) Includes bonus historical recordings performed
by the composer　　　Ⓜ

This admirable recording inaugurates Cyril Scott's complete solo piano music on disc. Scott was a pianist-composer – and he was a capable player, as the bonus historic performances show. The instrument's romantic associations, inherited from Chopin, Scriabin and Debussy, permeate Scott's earlier works. And he was fascinated by harmony, which he employed sensuously to define his idiom: Grainger aptly called him a 'perpendicular' composer.

Like Bridge and Ireland, Scott wrote miniatures for the amateur market but he also made history with the experimental rhythmic and harmonic features of his Piano Sonata No 1 in 1908 and the expansive Suite No 2, dedicated to Debussy, who much admired him. The five movements of this half-hour Suite range from a two-minute Caprice to a substantial theme and variations with a concluding 10-minute Introduction and Fugue. Some of this is rhapsodic and the charm of the salon miniatures, at which De'Ath excels, is not so easily extended. But Scott has his own kind of rhetoric, as the oddly titled *Handelian Rhapsody*, dedicated to Grainger, also shows.

Absolutely fascinating, in clean transfers, are the eight pieces Scott recorded between 1928 and 1930. He plays *Water Wagtail* delicately, a perfect counterpart to the airy skipping motions of these birds. But the perennial favourite *Lotus Land* is played eccentrically, the rapid notes inexplicably rushed to cut almost half a beat at times. There are informative notes from De'Ath but little about the pieces Scott plays. The piano sound is clean but slightly close.

'Complete Piano Music, Volume 3 –
Music for two pianos and piano duet'
Leslie De'Ath with Anya Alexeyev *pfs*
Dutton Digital Epoch ② CDLX7166 (153' · DDD) Ⓜ

The first disc contains works for two pianos or piano duet. In the 1930s Scott had a recital partnership with the pianist Esther Fisher and provided works for them to play. He also made arrangements of Bach, five of which are included here. These are really re-compositions, attractively and sometimes amusingly done – you can't kill Bach – and should be a hit in these sparkling performances.

The first CD opens with one of Scott's catchiest tunes, *Russian Fair*, in its two-piano version, followed by the extended but impressive *Theme and Variations* (1935). The *Three Symphonic Dances* from the turn of the century were arranged by Percy Grainger in 1920. He and Scott were students together at Frankfurt; Scott often dedicated pieces to him, and this is a thoroughly idiomatic exploitation of the two-piano medium.

The piano solo CD contains four unpublished pieces, all worth having, although the Ballade is a Brahmsian student work. There's evidence to support the description of early Scott as 'the English Debussy' and the *Inclination à la danse* (1922) is enticingly Scriabinesque; but Scott developed his own way with melody and harmony that we can now appreciate in more detail than ever before. The two picturesque suites, *Egypt* and *Karma*, are piano solo versions of ballet scores, both with occult connections. Good recording and presentation again: nobody could do better for Scott.

Alexander Scriabin   Russian 1872-1915

Scriabin was a fellow pupil of Rachmaninov's in Zverev's class from 1884 and at the Moscow Con-

servatory (1888-92), where his teachers were Taneyev, Arensky and Safonov. From 1894 his career as a pianist was managed by Belyayev, who arranged his European tours and also published his works: at this stage they were almost exclusively for solo piano, and deeply influenced by Chopin (most are preludes and mazurkas), though in the late 1890s he began to write for orchestra. In 1903 he left Russia and his family to live in western Europe for six years with a young female admirer, and his musical style became more intensely personal, developing a profusion of decoration in harmony becalmed by unresolved dominant chords or whole-tone elements. The major works of this period include the Divine Poem and again numerous piano pieces.

In 1905 he encountered Madame Blavatsky's theosophy, which soon ousted the enthusiasm for Nietschean superhumanism that had underlain the immediately preceding works. The static and ecstatic tendencies in his music were encouraged, being expressed notably in the Poem of Ecstasy and Prometheus, the latter intended to be performed with a play of coloured light. Still more ambitious were the plans for the Mysterium, a quasi-religious act which would have united all the arts, and for the composition of which the exclusively piano works of 1910-15 were intended to be preparatory, this journey into mystical hysteria going along with a voyage beyond tonality to a floating dissonance often based on the 'mystic chord' (C-F sharp-B flat-E-A-D).

GROVEmusic

Piano Concerto

Scriabin Piano Concerto
Tchaikovsky Piano Concerto No 1
Nikolai Demidenko *pf* BBC Symphony Orchestra /
Alexander Lazarev
Helios CDH55304 (65' · DDD)   Ⓕ

The chief attraction here is the unusual coupling which pairs two sharply opposed examples of Russian Romanticism, and although the reasons for the neglect of Scriabin's Piano Concerto aren't hard to fathom (its lyrical and decorative flights are essentially inward-looking), its haunting, bittersweet beauty, particularly in the central *Andante*, is hard to resist. Demidenko's own comments, quoted in the accompanying booklet, are scarcely less intense and individual than his performance: 'in the ambience, phrasing and cadence of his music we meet with a world almost without skin, a world of nerve-ends where the slightest contact can bring pain.' His playing soars quickly to meet the music's early passion head on, and in the first *più mosso scherzando* he accelerates to produce a brilliant lightening of mood. His flashing *fortes* in the *Andante*'s second variation are as volatile as his *pianissimos* are starry and refined in the finale's period reminiscence, and although he might seem more tight-lipped, less expansive than Ashkenazy on Decca, he's arguably more dramatic and characterful. Demidenko's Tchaikovsky, too, finds him ferreting out and sifting through every texture, forever aiming at optimum clarity. While this is hardly among the greatest Tchaikovsky Firsts on record, it's often gripping and mesmeric. The recorded balance isn't always ideal and the piano sound is sometimes uncomfortably taut.

Symphonies / Prometheus

No 1 in E, Op 26 **No 2** in C minor, Op 29 **No 3** in C minor, Op 43 'Divin poème'.

Symphonies – Nos 1ᵃ, 2 & 3. Le poème de l'extase, Op 54ᵇ. Prometheus, Op 60, 'Le poème du feu'ᶜ
ᵃ**Stefania Toczyska** mez ᵃ**Michael Myers** ten ᶜ**Dmitri Alexeev** pf ᵇ**Frank Kaderabek** tpt ᵃ**Westminster Choir;** ᶜ**Philadelphia Choral Arts Society; Philadelphia Orchestra / Riccardo Muti**
Brilliant Classics ③ 92744 (188' · DDD) Ⓢ🔘🔘

There can be few more thrilling sounds on disc (and no more compelling reason for a totally sound-proofed listening room) than the climax to Muti's *Poème de l'extase*. The clamour of bells here (both literal and imitative) reveals an essentially Russian heart at the core of this most cosmopolitan of Russian composers, and the *maestoso* proclamation of the theme of self assertion has the raised Philadelphia horns in crucially sharp focus. As in the corresponding climax in *Prometheus* (at 18'21"), this 'éclat sublime' is filled out with a floor-shaking contribution from the organ. Like the organ, the wordless chorus at this point in *Prometheus* registers more as a device for enriching and exalting the texture, rather than as a striking new presence.

Muti's *Prometheus* is, arguably, the most complete realisation of the mind-boggling demands of this score ever to have been recorded. The inert opening ('Original chaos' – lovely *pp* bass drum!) and mysterious awakening have rarely sounded so atmospheric. Alexeev's first entry isn't as strong willed as some, but he seems to be saving a more imperious attack for the same point in the recapitulation. Muti builds the work superbly: the imposing clash of states in the development (and the changes of tempo) charted with mighty assurance. And thereafter *Prometheus* is airborne, with Alexeev both agile and articulate in the 'Dance of Life'.

Throughout the cycle, the tonal allure of the Philadelphia Orchestra is fully in evidence. Only in the Third Symphony, *Divin poème*, do Muti and the recording team seem to be on less than their indomitable form. Compared with some versions, the tempo relationships in the first movement don't fully convince. However, this cycle is unlikely to be seriously challenged for many a year. As a whole it immeasurably enhances Scriabin's stature as a symphonist and offers the kind of playing and recording which, as recently as two decades ago, Scriabin enthusiasts could only have imagined in their dreams – and it's ridiculously low new price makes it a real bargain!

Etudes

Etude in C sharp minor, Op 2 No 1. 12 Etudes, Op 8. Etudes, Op 42. Etude in E flat, Op 49 No 1. Etude, Op 56 No 4. Three Etudes, Op 65
Piers Lane pf
Hyperion CDA66607 (56' · DDD) Ⓕ🔘

Although Scriabin's *études* do not fall into two neatly packaged sets in the same way as Chopin's celebrated contributions, nevertheless there's a strong feeling of continuity and development running throughout the 26 examples produced between the years 1887 and 1912. This is admirably demonstrated in this excellent issue from Hyperion, which, far from being an indigestible anthology proves to be an intriguing and pleasurable hour's worth of listening charting Scriabin's progression from late-romantic adolescence to harmonically advanced mystical poet. Indeed, although these studies can be counted as amongst the most digitally taxing and hazardous of their kind, Scriabin also saw them as important sketches and studies for his larger works, and as experiments in his gradually evolving harmonic language and mystical vision.

Piers Lane attains the perfect balance of virtuoso display and poetic interpretation. Expressive detail and subtle nuance are finely brought out, and he's more than receptive to Scriabin's sometimes highly idiosyncratic sound world; rarely, for instance, has the famous 'Mosquito' *Etude* (Op 42 No 3) been captured with such delicate fragility as here, and in No 1 of the three fiendishly difficult *Etudes*, Op 65 the tremulous, ghostly flutterings are tellingly delivered with a gossamer-light touch and a sense of eerie mystery. The clear, spacious recording is exemplary.

Mazurkas

10 Mazurkas, Op 3. Nine Mazurkas, Op 25. Two Mazurkas, Op 40
Gordon Fergus-Thompson pf
ASV CDDCA1086 (80' · DDD) Ⓕ🔘

Volume 4 of Gordon Fergus-Thompson's Scriabin series for ASV is of the complete *Mazurkas*. The *Mazurka* remains an intransigently indigenous dance genre, and Chopin's incomparable example is more than a hard act to follow. However, Scriabin was among the few who accepted such a challenge wholeheartedly and, while his gratitude to his beloved Polish master is obvious, so too is the skill with which he takes Chopin's Slavonicism on a journey through bittersweet nostalgia into a more convoluted idiom and, finally, into a pensive and hallucinatory shadowland. The elusive character of these fascinating and neglected works could hardly be presented more vividly and insinuatingly than by Fergus-Thompson.

How well he understands the way Scriabin's momentary high spirits (in, say, No 4) collapse into morbid introspection in No 5 – into a close-knit chromaticism later refined still further by dark and obsessive intervals and patterning. The balletic leaps of No 6 are deftly contrasted with its sinuous central melody, and, however circuitous the route, Fergus-Thompson travels it with a special clarity and romantic fervour. The two confidential Op 40 *Mazurkas* are a notable success, and the recordings are crystalline and immediate.

Preludes

Complete Preludes – Op 2 No 2; Op 9 No 1;
Opp 11, 13, 15-17, 22, 27, 31, 33, 35, 37, 39; Op 45
No 3; Op 48; Op 49 No 2; Op 51 No 2; Op 56 No 1;
Op 59 No 2; Opp 67 & 74
Piers Lane pf
Hyperion ② CDA67057/8 (127' · DDD)   Ⓕ**OO**

Everything about this two-disc set is ideal. Beautifully packaged and recorded, superbly played, there's the added bonus of an outstanding essay by Simon Nicholls, in which acute musical analysis is presented within the wider context of Scriabin's bewildering genius. Nicholls sees Scriabin as 'a musical Fabergé', a composer who contrasted his love of the ambitious epic with an even greater love of miniatures that could be 'short as a sparrow's beak or a bear's tail'. And throughout the extraordinary journey from Op 2 No 2 to Op 74, where the memories of Chopin are subdued by 'scarifying documents of individual and social catastrophe', you're tossed abruptly from a serene or bitter introspection to a crazed violence and exuberance, encouraged by idiosyncratic directions such as *patetico, con stravaganza, vagamente, irato impetuoso, sauvage belliqueux*.

The demands on the pianist are fierce, but it would be hard to imagine a more focused or immaculate reading than that offered by Piers Lane. Few pianists could show more sympathy and affection for such volatile romanticism, or display greater stylistic consistency. He underlines the despondency of the left-hand Prelude, Op 9 No 1 (here separated from its celebrated Nocturne companion); and in, for example, Op 11 No 3 the fleeting melodic outline is always kept intact amid so much whirling activity. The turbulence of No 14 is caught just as surely, and as an instance of how his scrupulousness is combined with the most vivid imagination, he gives us No 16 in an agitated and freely expressive style rather than opting for a more conventional, stricter tempo, creating a novel and nightmarish dimension. He takes No 2 at a true *Allegro* (as marked) and is never tempted into the sort of virtuoso skirmish offered by lesser players. Indeed, his gift for clarifying even the most tortuous utterances with an exemplary poise and assurance is among his finest qualities. The machine-gun fire of Op 31 No 3 and the menacing tread of Op 33 No 4 are fully realised, and Lane ably taps the darkest regions of the imagination in the final Op 74 Preludes.

These discs complement Piers Lane's earlier recording of the complete Scriabin Etudes, and should be in any serious record collection.

Preludes – Op 22; Op 27; Op 31; Op 33; Op 35;
Op 37; Op 39; Op 48; Op 67; Op 74. Prelude in E flat,
Op 45 No 3. Prelude in F, Op 49 No 2. Prelude in
A minor, Op 51 No 2. Prelude in E flat minor, Op 56
No 1. Prelude, Op 59 No 2 **J Scriabin** Prelude in C,
Op 2. Preludes, Op 3 – No 1 in B; No 2. Prelude in
D flat
Evgeny Zarafiants pf
Naxos 8 554145 (65' · DDD)   Ⓢ**O⇨**

With this second volume Evgeny Zarafiants completes his superb survey of Scriabin's 86 Preludes, adding four Preludes by Julian Scriabin, the composer's precociously gifted son, as encores. Listening to music of such morbid and refined intricacy played with the finest musical poise and commitment returns us to Stravinsky's bemused question, 'Scriabin, where does he come from, and who are his followers?' Is the angst and angry convolution of, say, Op 27 No 1 a slavonic memory of Brahms's Op 118 No 1? Does the explosive whimsy of Op 35 No 3 take its cue from the *Scherzo* of Beethoven's Op 26 Sonata? The hair-raising *presto* of Op 67 No 2 recalls the menace and enigma of the finale from Chopin's Op 35 Sonata, while the terse and belligerant Op 33 No 3 looks ahead to Stravinsky's sharpest modernist utterances. Yet if there are countless examples of reflection and prophecy, there are still more of the most startling originality. Scriabin is always Scriabin, and as he journeys from Op 22 to Op 74 into the darkest reaches of the imagination you're reminded that this is hardly music for the faint-hearted.

Once again, Zarafiants is equal to each and every vivid occasion. Whether in the fragrant *grazioso* of Op 22 No 2, where the line twists and turns like so much honeysuckle, in the toppling argument of Op 31 No 3, or in the *sauvage belliqueux* of Op 59 No 2, he's richly responsive, his playing alive with a rare pianistic skill and imaginative brio. The Brandon Hill recordings are resonant and full-blooded.

Complete Piano Sonatas

No 1 in F minor, Op 6 **No 2** in G sharp minor (Sonata-fantasy), Op 19 **No 3** in F sharp minor, Op 23 **No 4** in F sharp, Op 30 **No 5** in F sharp, Op 53 **No 6** in G, Op 62; **No 7** in F sharp (White Mass), Op 64 **No 8** in A, Op 66 **No 9** in F (Black Mass), Op 68 **No 10** in C, Op 70

Piano Sonatas Nos 1-10. Fantasie in B minor, Op 28.
Sonata-fantaisie in G sharp minor
Marc-André Hamelin pf
Hyperion ② CDA67131/2 (146' · DDD)   Ⓕ**OO**

Scriabin was an ambitious composer. A romantic alchemist, he saw his music as a transmuting agent. Through its influence pain would become happiness and hate become love, culminating in a phoenix-like rebirth of the universe. With Shakespearian agility he would change the world's dross into 'something rich and strange'. Not surprisingly, given Scriabin's early prowess as a pianist, the 10 sonatas resonate with exoticism, ranging through the First Sonata's cries of despair, to the Second Sonata's Baltic Sea inspiration, the Third Sonata's 'states of being', the 'flight to a distant star' (No 4) and 'the emergence of mysterious forces' (No 5). Nos 7 and 9 are *White* and *Black Mass* Sonatas respectively, and the final sonatas blaze with trills symbolising an extra-terrestrial joy and incandescence.

Such music makes ferocious demands on the pianist's physical stamina and imaginative resource. However, Marc-André Hamelin takes everything in his stride. Blessed with rapier reflexes he nonchalantly resolves even the most outlandish difficulties. He launches the First Sonata's opening outcry like some gleaming trajectory and, throughout, his whistle-stop virtuosity is seemingly infallible.

You might, however, miss a greater sense of the music's Slavonic intensity, its colour and character; a finer awareness, for example, of the delirious poetry at the heart of the Second Sonata's whirling finale. Hamelin's sonority is most elegantly and precisely gauged but time and again his fluency (admittedly breathtaking) erases too much of the work's originality and regenerative force. However, he shows a greater sense of freedom in the Fifth Sonata, and in the opalescent fantasy of the later sonatas, he responds with more evocative skill to subjective terms, as well as to moments where Scriabin's brooding introspection is lit by sudden flashes of summer lightning.

The recordings are a little tight and airless in the bass and middle register, but the set does includes a superb essay on Scriabin.

Piano Sonatas – No 2, 'Sonata-fantasy'; No 3; No 9, 'Black Mass'. Fantaisie, Op 28. Feuillet d'album, Op 45 No 1. Ironies, Op 56 No 2. Mazurka, Op 24 No 3. Deux morceaux, Op 57. Deux poèmes, Op 32. Prelude, Op 11 No 4. Five Preludes, Op 74
Alexander Melnikov pf
Harmonia Mundi HMN91 1914 (68' · DDD)   Ⓕ

Writing with touching enthusiasm and insight, 33-year-old Alexander Melnikov is clearly lost in wonder over Scriabin's strange and ever-controversial genius. Referring to the composer's 'eclectic mixture of mysticism, theosophy and a hefty dose of megalomaniac ambition', he offers up a richly comprehensive recital ranging from Op 11 to Op 74 – from personal if Chopin-inspired beginnings to the dark, opalescent obsessions of his final years. And never for a moment would you doubt his nationality, his poetic empathy or his superb pianistic mastery.

At the same time Scriabin's idiosyncrasy can rarely have sounded more natural, his music

emerging as if new-minted, improvised, as it were, in the first white heat of inspiration. Whether whipping up a storm in the Second Sonata's tempest-tossed finale or contrasting a clipped, even severe way, with the Third Sonata's opening *Dramatico* with a truly glowing and interior sense of lyricism, he is ideally attuned to Scriabin's volatile imagination. The Op 57 pieces emerge teasingly enigmatic despite their titles (*Désir* and *Caresse dansée*) and the Ninth Sonata can rarely have had its subtitle (*Black Mass*) or instruction (*légendaire*) more acutely observed. More generally, while wholly individual, there is something of Martha Argerich's pace and nervous vitality, her flame-like brilliance, about these performances.

Harmonia Mundi's sound is suitably vivid and immediate. The recital is dedicated to the memory of Vladimir Sofronitsky – for Melnikov and many others the finest performer of Scriabin's music and a pianist who, according to Sviatoslav Richter, 'discovered an elixir of life in Scriabin's upward spiral'.

Piano Sonatas – No 2, 'Sonata-fantasy'; No 5; No 9, 'Black Mass'. Etude, Op 2 No 1. Four Pieces, Op 56 – Nuances. Two Pieces, Op 59 – Poème. Etude, Op 8 No 12. Mazurkas, Op 3 – No 1; No 3; No 4; No 6. Valse, Op 38
Yevgeny Sudbin pf
BIS Ⓢ BIS-SACD1568 (57' · DDD/DSD)   Ⓕ ○○○

Writing in prose as delirious as his playing, Yevgeny Sudbin speaks in his accompanying nine-page essay of the incomprehension that greeted Scriabin's half-crazed genius in both Russia and the West. This is entirely apt and no pianist of any generation has surely captured Scriabin's volatility so vividly as Sudbin.

In his choice of sonatas (ranging through Scriabin's early, middle and late periods), his mix of drama and introspection are positively alchemic and entirely his own. It is as if the music's very nerve ends are exposed to view and rarely has a pianist been prepared to take such risks on record. He takes virtuosity to the very edge at the end of the Fifth Sonata and his daredevil aplomb is at its height in the Ninth, suitably named *Black Mass* Sonata.

How he varies the colour, light and shade in the early D sharp minor Etude so that its familiar heroic octaves sound newly minted and never merely frenetic! His selection of Mazurkas is given with a breathtaking subtlety, making you long to hear him in Chopin, while his response to Scriabin's command in the Fifth Sonata, *presto tumultuoso esaltato*, is like the vortex of a whirlwind. All these performances are flecked with personal touches and brilliances above and beyond even Scriabin's wildest demands.

Finally, BIS captures Sudbin's astonishing range of colours and sonorities, ranging from the utmost delicacy to an enraged uproar, in crystalline demonstration sound. This, put suitably euphorically, is a disc in a million.

Piano Sonatas – No 4, Op 30; No 5, Op 53; No 8, Op 66; No 9, 'Black Mass', Op 68. Deux poèmes – Op 32; Op 69; Op 71. Vers la flamme, Op 72
Andrei Korobeinikov pf
Mirare MIR061 (64' · DDD)   Ⓕ**OO**

Andrei Korobeinikov's recital of music taken from the Scriabin's middle and late periods, alternating light and darkness, exultation and desolation, will surely become a compulsory addition to all lovers of his neurotic and compulsive genius.

At 22 this Russian pianist already ranks among his foremost interpreters. A graduate in law as well as music, won a glittering array of awards and is presently pursuing graduate studies at the Royal College of Music. Such largesse is reflected in playing of an unswerving musical honesty backed by a gargantuan technical command. His tempo for the Fourth Sonata's opening *Andante* may be exceptionally slow but it is sustained with rare poise and concentration; and if the following *Prestissimo volando* is less mercurial than from others it is once again totally convincing in its own ultra-Russian terms.

Korobeinikov goes through the second of the *Deux poèmes*, Op 32, and the Fifth Sonata's final outburst in a blaze of elemental thunder and lightning. And his authority is no less unarguable in the Eighth Sonata's extra-territorial wanderings and in *Vers la flamme* where Scriabin's obsessive patterning receives its ultimate nemesis. Such playing, finely recorded and presented, makes further recordings by this phenomenally gifted young pianist a necessity rather than a probability.

'The Early Scriabin'
Piano Sonata in E flat minor. Sonate-fantaisie. Allegro appassionato, Op 4. Canon in D minor. Etude No 12 in D sharp minor, Op 8. Fugue. Nocturne in A flat. Two Nocturnes, Op 5. Two Pieces for the left hand, Op 9. Mazurkas – in B minor; in F. Valses – Op 1; Op 6, No 1; No 2. Variations on a theme by Mlle Egorova
Stephen Coombs pf
Hyperion CDA67149 (74' · DDD)   Ⓕ

Stephen Coombs's 'The Early Scriabin' is a programme of fascinating rarities played with touching sensitivity and affection. Coombs's booklet essay, a mine of information and research, tells the history of such oddities as the sombre D minor Canon and E minor Fugue (their titles essentially alien to Scriabin's precociously romantic and far-reaching sensibility) or the complex provenance of the masterly E flat minor Sonata. He also tells us that Scriabin's genius received short shrift from the academic *ancien régime*; allowing him to graduate in piano but not in composition.

Coombs's performances are, for the most part, what painters call 'low in tone', and even when you wish for greater voltage in, say, the nightmarish equestrian finale of the Sonata you can hardly wish for more gently persuasive

accounts of the Waltzes or the A flat Nocturne. He's much less dazzling and rhetorical than, for example, Leon Fleisher in the Prelude and Nocturne for the left hand but, conversely his playing suggests a subtly characterful and communing alternative. He does, though, make a full-blooded but finely graded assault on the cadenza just before the return of the principle idea in the *Allegro appassionato*. This record is a most impressive achievement, as beautiful in sound as it's endlessly thought-provoking.

Piano works

Complete Solo Piano Works
Maria Lettberg pf
Capriccio 49 586 (8h 9' · DDD)
Includes bonus DVD, 'Mysterium: The Multimedia Projects'   Ⓢ

Here is a virtually complete recording of Scriabin's piano music (works without opus numbers are omitted). Each disc allows you to journey from his early Romanticism to middle-period idiosyncrasy and finally to the hallucinatory magic of his last years. Reactions to Scriabin's 'creative laboratory' have fluctuated wildly. For some such music was a reminder that 'there are those who think that the air is filled with green monkeys with crimson eyes and sparkling tails, a kind of ecstasy that is sold in Russia at two roubles a bottle' while Stravinsky wondered: 'Scriabin, where does he come from and who are his followers?'.

What is not controversial is the immensity of the challenge facing even the most intrepid pianist compelled on a journey of discovery as fraught as it is dazzling. And while Maria Lettberg, a Swedish pianist who has found fame outside the competition circuit, is not in the same league as, say Horowitz, Richter or Ashkenazy, she is for the most part warmly fluent and sympathetic.

How she relishes the violent moodswings of the Op 11 Preludes, music alternately lost in its own delirium or ablaze with pianistic heroics. She understands ideally the Mazurkas where Chopin is made to speak with an increasingly strong Russian accent and she casts a shimmering haze across the necromancy of the late sonatas where we are ushered into a painfully self-absorbed world. Here obsessive patterns, harmonies and intervals seem to spin in interstellar space, but Lettberg manages to make sense of an instruction such as *très doux et pur* (the Tenth Sonata's opening) when the mood is cloudy and malignant.

An accompanying DVD shows the pianist once more fully attuned to Scriabin's demand in the Fourth Sonata to 'fly towards the blue star', to imply 'the creation of the world' in the Fifth Sonata and, finally, to realise the composer's assumption that he was God. This is an invaluable issue and a formidable achievement finely recorded.

Two Poèmes: Op 32; Op 44; Op 63; Op 69;
Op 71. Poème tragique, Op 34. Poème satanique,
Op 36. Poèmes – Op 41; Op 52 No 1; Op 59 No 1.
Poème ailé, Op 51 No 2. Poème languide, Op 52 No
3. Poème-nocturne, Op 61. Poème 'Vers la flamme',
Op 72. Feuillet d'album, Op 45 No 1; Poème
fantasque, Op 45 No 2. Quasi valse, Op 47. Valse,
Op 38
Pascal Amoyel pf
Calliope CAL9353 (75' · DDD)   Ⓕ

Pascal Amoyel admits he was driven close to
neurosis when preparing his Scriabin recording
and found it difficult to re-emerge into the
world of other composers. Aphoristic or endlessly protracted, seemingly lost in a harmonic
limbo or fiercely to the point, such music is
indeed challenging to both listener and performer. For Amoyel the tirelessly extended
Poème-nocturne is 'phantasmagorical, ill-defined
and confused' (terms he intends as the greatest
compliment) and his playing on what he
describes as a 'rather sombre-sounding Steinway' amply conveys his enthusiasm.

He is acutely sensitive to the dark mystery at the
heart of the Op 41 *Poème*, its final section a decadent memory of Chopin's Op 10 No 6 Etude, and
responds with refinement as well as energy to the
Poème tragique with its demands of *festivamente,
fastoso, irato* and *fiero*. In the *Poème satanique*
(music indelibly associated with Sofronitsky)
light is stalked by darkness in a menacing game of
tag, while the enchanting Op 38 *Valse* is an all-
Russian extension of the world of Liszt's *Valses
oubliées*. The Op 69 No 2 *Poème* is a notably grotesque danse macabre and in the final *Vers la
flamme* Amoyel takes us on a mesmeric journey
from threatening shadows to searing brilliance.

Yet even here he resists virtuoso temptations,
making it odd that he should be described in
France as one of Cziffra's 'spiritual heirs'. Confidentiality and insinuation are his hallmarks
rather than wildness or flamboyance. Calliope's
sound, like Amoyel's instrument, is subdued but
it hardly detracts from an experience that is stifling or exhilarating, according to taste.

Peter Sculthorpe   Australian b1929

*Sculthorpe studied at Melbourne University and
with Rubbra and Wellesz at Oxford (1958-61) and
in 1963 he began teaching at Sydney University. His
music features an expressive brilliance of colour and
vigorous use of ostinato, sometimes reflecting his
interest in Balinese music. His works include the
opera Rites of Passage (1974), orchestral and vocal
pieces (including the series Sun Music) and a sequence
of nine string quartets.*   **GROVE**music

Piano Concerto

Piano Concerto. Little Nourlangie. Music for Japan.
The song of Tailitnama

Kirsti Harms mez **Mark Atkins** didjeridu **Tamara
Anna Cislowska** pf **David Drury** org **Sydney
Symphony Orchestra / Edo de Waart**
ABC Classics 8 770030 (53' · DDD · T)   Ⓕ

Sculthorpe has long been preoccupied with the
music from other countries situated in and
around the Pacific – and Japanese music in particular, elements of which he has incorporated
into other works such as the present Piano Concerto of 1983. Sculthorpe's Piano Concerto is an
imposing creation, less indigenous-sounding
and 'pictorial' than many of his other compositions, including *The song of Tailitnama* (1974).
Conceived for high voice, six cellos and percussion, this haunting piece was in fact written for a
TV documentary.

Little Nourlangie dates from 1990. It takes its
name from a small outcrop of rocks in Australia's Kakadu National Park on which can be
found the Aboriginal Blue Paintings, depicting
fish, boats and ancestral figures and which
inspired the composer. *Little Nourlangie* is a
characteristically striking creation, scored with
much imaginative flair. It shares its diatonic
main theme with that of Sculthorpe's 1989 guitar concerto, *Nourlangie*, and comprises four-
and-a-half minutes of 'straightforward, joyful
music' (to quote the composer). By contrast,
Music for Japan exhibits a much more uncompromising demeanour, and according to annotator Graeme Skinner, is at once 'his most abstract
and modernist orchestral score'.

Edo de Waart presides over a set of performances that exhibit great commitment and exemplary finish. The recording is excellent too.

Cello Dreaming

Irkanda Iᵃ. Irkanda IVᵇᶜ. Lament for stringsᶜ. Sonata for
Strings No 2ᶜ. Cello Dreamingᵇᶜ. Djilileᶜ
ᵇ**Emma-Jane Murphy** vc ᶜ**Australian Chamber
Orchestra / Richard Tognetti** ᵃvn
Chandos CHAN10063 (66' · DDD)   Ⓕ➔

The Australian Chamber Orchestra has consistently championed the music of its countryman
Peter Sculthorpe. *Cello Dreaming*, premiered by
Steven Isserlis and the BBC Philharmonic during the 1998 Manchester Cello Festival, is
inspired by the sights, sounds and diverse cultural mix of Australia's northern coastline. It's
a beguiling evocation, boasting nature music
of imagination and local colour; Emma-Jane
Murphy is an impressive soloist. The Aboriginal
melody known as 'Djilile' was first used by
Sculthorpe as far back as 1950 in his Fourth
String Quartet. This transcription for strings is
one in a series of reworkings of a tune that has
haunted the composer for over 50 years. No less
appealing is the substantial Second String
Sonata (1988), an arrangement of the Ninth
Quartet of 1975.

Shrewd programming frames the threnodic
Irkanda IV for solo violin, strings and percussion
(Sculthorpe's first real breakthrough from 1961,

named after the Aboriginal word for a remote and lonely place) between *Irkanda I* for solo violin from 1955 (a beautifully proportioned essay which provides the first glimpse of the mature composer in its rapt identification with Australia's landscape and wildlife) and the moving 1976 Lament for strings. It isn't hard to detect a kinship, so naturally does each piece emerge from its predecessor.

Three tracks here (*Irkanda IV, Lament* and the Second Sonata) overlap with a rival ABC Classics release featuring these same artists. There's little to choose between the two in terms of performance (those earlier accounts are a degree more restrained), but Chandos's sound has the edge, possessing breathtaking definition and range. A very fine issue.

Earth Cry

Earth Cry[a]. Kakadu. Piano Concerto[b]. Memento Mori.
From Oceania
[a]**William Barton** didg [b]**Tamara Anna Cislowska** pf
New Zealand Symphony Orchestra / James Judd
Naxos 8 557382 (71' · DDD)   ⑤↦

Earth Cry. Kakadu. Mangrove. Songs of Sea and Sky.
From Ubirr
William Barton didg **Queensland Orchestra /
Michael Christie**
ABC Classics ABC476 1921 (71' · DDD)   Ⓕ

Earth Cry (1986), previously recorded in 1989 by Stuart Challender, is one of Sculthorpe's major utterances, music at once approachable and elusive. These aspects are extraordinarily heightened by a recently added didgeridoo part. The two recordings here use this new version sound quite different. Judd revels in a harsher orchestral sound, spotlighting each detail, while Christie conjures a more rounded tone, though edgy and laden with menace. William Barton's haunting didgeridoo playing is quite different on each.

Kakadu (1988), another shared item, finds both Judd and Christie alive to every nervy detail, though Christie responds more naturally to its mercurial changes. It's Challender, however, who finds the sheer joy: his interpretation is unsurpassed. He's also unbeatable in *Mangrove*, another heavyweight score that repays further investigation, though Christie summons a shining performance and shows a fine understanding of every nuance of the intricate orchestration.

Christie's disc includes another work revised to include didgeridoo: *From Ubirr*, which is conceptually and audibly related to *Earth Cry*. Sculthorpe wrote it for Kronos, and Christie has arranged it for larger forces. The orchestra finds greater sonic depth and the didgeridoo emphasises the earthy quality of the music. *Songs of Sea and Sky*, originally for clarinet and piano, also benefits from expansion from its original chamber format.

The mesmerising Piano Concerto, dating from 1983, is one of Sculthorpe's finest creations. Tamara Anna Cislowska has already

recorded it with Edo de Waart, a relaxed performance with 'impressionistic' orchestral sound; this Naxos recording is sharper. Judd also includes a work from Sculthorpe's 'sun music' period, *From Oceania* (1970/2003), more ostentatiously bright and more 'foreign' than later works, as well as the affecting and straightforward *Memento Mori* (1993).

Sculthorpe lovers will want both these recordings, but for a one-disc showcase of his work the programme and performances of the Queensland Orchestra have the edge.

Rodion Shchedrin   Russian b1932

Shchedrin is one of the better-known Russian composers of the later half of the 20th century. He studied at the Moscow Choir School and in 1955 he graduated from the Moscow Conservatory. In 1958 he married the ballerina Mayya Plisetskaya. Between 1965 and 1969 he taught composition at the Moscow Conservatory and since 1969 has worked freelance. From 1973 to 1990 he was Shostakovich's successor as Chairman of the Composers' Union of the Russian Federation. In 1989 he was a member of the Interregional Group of People's Deputies in Support of perestroyka, along with Andrey Sakharov and Boris Yeltsin. Since 1992 he has divided his time between Moscow and Munich. His work is distinguished by diversity of musical genres and by breadth of musical language. His style unifies contrasting elements by means of organic fusion: freely serial procedures and avant-garde techniques such as pointillism, sonoristic and aleatory methods rub shoulders with complex polyphony, collage and, on the other hand, reflections of various types of Russian folk music ranging from peals of bells, lamentations, church music, shepherds' tunes, the chastushka and the style of folk singing.
                                                    GROVEmusic

The Sealed Angel

The Sealed Angel
Marie Macklin, Emma Walshe sops **Nina Canter**
contr **Benedict Hymas** ten **Clare Wills** ob **Gonville
and Caius College Choir, Cambridge / Geoffrey
Webber; King's College Choir, London / David
Trendell**
Delphian DCD34067 (55' · DDD)   ⒻO

The allegorical resonances of *The Sealed Angel* – in which a rural community protects a religious icon – seem obvious and the text is purely religious, the equivalent of a cinematic treatment featuring the icon alone. The nine movements play continuously, the first three a flowing evocation of angels before the atmosphere changes in the freely dissonant fourth, depicting Judas's betrayal. After the great choral screech at its climax, the music calms down with the choir tacet in the fifth; the halting, static sixth is a chordal prayer of repentance and salvation. The vertical and horizontal elements then fuse in a powerful setting of the

Lord's Prayer (section eight) before the quiet reprise of the opening.

Shchedrin provides a detached counterpoint to the voices with a series of oboe solos, free variations not so much on a theme as a way of writing. These top and tail the main choral blocks, punctuating rather than accompanying, nicely played by Clare Wills. The choirs sing splendidly, without producing a Russian sound, yet the composer is aware of the English choral tradition so his music's translation here is fascinating. So is his avoidance of the holy minimalism of many of his compatriots or the consonance of Rautavaara's larger choral works. Caught here in fine sound, this is a splendid disc of a multifaceted, many-layered modern masterpiece.

John Sheppard British c1515-1559/60

Sheppard was at Magdalen College, Oxford, 1543-8, and by 1552 was a Gentleman of the Chapel Royal. Most of his extant music for the Latin rite probably dates from Mary's reign. The six-voice Magnificat, for example with its florid counterpoint and lack of imitation, belongs to the tradition of the Eton Choirbook composers. Among his more modern works are the four-voice Magnificat, the Missa 'Cantate' and the Mass 'The Western Wynde'. He was at his best when writing vigorous counterpoint around a plainchant. The English works, which include 15 anthems and service music, seem to date from Edward's reign. **GROVE**music

Western Wynde Mass

Western Wynde Mass. Gaude, gaude, gaude Maria; Dum transisset Sabbatum I; Spiritus Sanctus procedens II; In manus tuas II; Audivi vocem de coelo; Libera nos, salva nos II; Beata nobis gaudia; Impetum fecerunt unanimes; Sancte Dei preciose; Sacris solemniis; Aeterne Rex altissime; Dum transisset sabbatum II; Hostes Herodes impie; In manus tuas III; Te Deum laudamus.
The Sixteen / Harry Christophers
Hyperion Dyad ② CDD22022 (125' · DDD · T/t) ⓜⓞ

This set centres round one of Sheppard's best-known four-part Masses, *The Western Wynde*. Though largely syllabic in style, in accordance with liturgical prescriptions at a time when taste in church music was turning towards ever greater emphasis on the text, this Mass still has moments that recapture the earlier visionary style in all its wonder. The section 'Et incarnatus est', coming after an amazing cadence at 'descendit de coelis' in the *Credo*, is a case in point. 'Pleni sunt coeli' is another, and also the opening of the *Benedictus*, where the melody unfolds unhurriedly over the delicate counterpoint of the mean and the bass. In such passages The Sixteen is in its element, each singer relating to the others with the intimacy and mutual understanding of performers of chamber music.

The supporting programme includes *alternatim* hymn settings, responsories and a *Te Deum*. In all these the chant is sung with excellent phrasing and a smooth *legato*. Some subtle repercussions in the intonation to *Dum transisset Sabbatum* are particularly pleasing.

In all five pieces, though, the tempo of the chant sections bore little relationship to the polyphony – the least far removed being that of the hymn *Aeterne Rex altissime*, where the individual chant notes had roughly the duration of a half-beat of the polyphony. The English *Magnificat and Nunc dimittis* reveal Sheppard fully conforming to the later syllabic style in a rich and joyful texture. Here, and in the Latin *Te Deum* The Sixteen display to the full their glowing vocal qualities. This is wonderful singing, with a sense of freedom and flow that's almost overpowering.

'Audivi vocem'

Sheppard Gaudete celicole omnes. Beati omnes. Laudate pueri Dominum. Eterne rex, altissime **Tallis** In ieiunio et fletu. Te lucis ante terminum. Audivi vocem. Salvator mundi **Tye** Omnes gentes. Missa sine nomine
The Hilliard Ensemble (David James *countertenor* Rogers Covey-Crump, Steven Harrold *tens* Gordon Jones *bar* Robert Macdonald *bass*)
ECM New Series 476 6353 (72' · DDD) Ⓕ

The Hilliards here return to familiar territory with a programme of Tallis, Tye and Sheppard. While the territory may be familiar, however, not all of its landmarks are, and neither is their disposition – this is an extremely well organised disc, surveying the impact that the musical aspects of the Reformation had in the first instance on English composers (what David Skinner aptly describes as 'that musicologically grey period in the last decades of Henry VIII's reign'). Thus, while all the works by Tallis (*In ieiunio et fletu*, *Te lucis ante terminum*, *Audivi vocem* and *Salvator mundi*, the latter given a particularly beautiful performance) are well known, they are set in the context of much more recondite material.

The rarities from Sheppard include the early *Gaudete celicole omnes*, whose constant flow almost suggests at times a kind of English Gombert, and later, clearly Henrician works, such as the marvellously luminous hymn *Eterne rex, altissime*. The music by Tye includes *Omnes gentes plaudite*, which may perhaps be considered relatively known, but the four sections of the *Missa sine nomine* from the Peterhouse partbooks will probably be unknown even to most connoisseurs of this period, precisely on account of the missing voice. Hopefully these beautifully blended performances will help to change this state of affairs, for it is an extremely impressive work, heralding the new, compact and more declamatory style with consummate skill. An outstanding release.

Dmitry Shostakovich

Russian/USSR 1906-1975

He studied with his mother, a professional pianist, and then with Shteynberg at the Petrograd Conservatory (1919-25): his graduation piece was his Symphony no.1, which brought him early international attention. His creative development, however, was determined more by events at home. Like many Soviet composers of his generation, he tried to reconcile the musical revolutions of his time with the urge to give a voice to revolutionary socialism, most conspicuously in his next two symphonies, no.2 ('To October') and no.3 ('The First of May'), both with choral finales. At the same time he used what he knew of contemporary Western music (perhaps Prokofiev and Krenek mostly) to give a sharp grotesqueness and mechanical movement to his operatic satire The Nose, while expressing a similar keen irony in major works for the ballet (The Age of Gold, The Bolt) and the cinema (New Babylon). But the culminating achievement of these quick-witted, nervy years was his second opera The Lady Macbeth of the Mtsensk District, where high emotion and acid parody are brought together in a score of immense brilliance.

Lady Macbeth was received with acclaim in Russia, western Europe and the USA, and might have seemed to confirm Shostakovich as essentially a dramatic composer: by the time he was 30, in 1936, he was known for two operas and three full-length ballets, besides numerous scores for the theatre and films, whereas only one purely orchestral symphony had been performed, and one string quartet. However, in that same year Lady Macbeth was fiercely attacked in Pravda, and he set aside his completed Symphony no.4 (it was not performed until 1961), no doubt fearing that its Mahlerian intensity and complexity would spur further criticism. Instead he began a new symphony, no.5, much more conventional in its form and tunefulness – though there is a case for hearing the finale as an internal send-up of the heroic style. This was received favourably, by the state and indeed by Shostakovich's international public, and seems to have turned him from the theatre to the concert hall. There were to be no more operas or ballets, excepting a comedy and a revision of Lady Macbeth; instead he devoted himself to symphonies, concertos, quartets and songs (as well as heroic, exhortatory cantatas during the war years).

Of the next four symphonies, no.7 is an epic with an uplifting war-victory programme (it was begun in besieged Leningrad), while the others display more openly a dichotomy between optimism and introspective doubt, expressed with varying shades of irony. It has been easy to explain this in terms of Shostakovich's position as a public artist in the USSR during the age of socialist realism, but the divisions and ironies in his music go back to his earliest works and seem inseparable from the very nature of his harmony, characterised by a severely weakened sense of key. Even so, his position in official Soviet music certainly was difficult. In 1948 he was condemned again, and for five years he wrote little besides patriotic cantatas and private music (quartets, the 24 Preludes and Fugues which constitute his outstanding piano work).

Stalin's death in 1953 opened the way to a less

rigid aesthetic, and Shostakovich returned to the symphony triumphantly with no.10. Nos. 11 and 12 are both programme works on crucial years in revolutionary history (1905 and 1917), but then no.13 was his most outspokenly critical work, incorporating a setting of words that attack anti-semitism. The last two symphonies and the last four quartets, as well as other chamber pieces and songs, belong to a late period of spare texture, slowness and gravity, often used explicitly in images of death: Symphony no.14 is a song cycle on mortality, though no.15 remains more enigmatic in its open quotations from Rossini and Wagner. GROVEmusic

Cello Concertos

No 1 in E flat, Op 107; **No 2** in G, Op 126

Cello Concertos Nos 1 & 2
Daniel Müller-Schott vc **Bavarian Radio Symphony Orchestra / Yakov Kreizberg**
Orfeo C659 081A (67' · DDD)   ⓕ🔘🔘🕭

With roughly a dozen single-disc couplings of the two Shostakovich cello concertos available on CD, a new one needs a sharp profile in order to gain visibility. Müller-Schott and his supporting team have most of the obvious credentials: technique and temperament in abundance, finely judged tempi, and excellent recorded balance and perspective, the soloist placed a little further forward than in some versions, but not distractingly so. They bring dash, drive and discipline to the fast movements, and soulfulness to the slow ones. But the trick with Shostakovich is to combine those things with weight of tone and flashes of personal expression, so that the drama of the individual caught up in the machinations of larger forces gains life-or-death significance.

How that is achieved is a matter for debate and legitimate disagreement. For all Mischa Maisky's special touches of romantic eloquence, he comes up with some bizarre technical fudges in the big cadenzas, while Heinrich Schiff is far more direct but so fast and furious in the first movement of the E flat First Concerto that it loses as much in stoical defiance as it gains in physical excitement. Müller-Schott's tempi and characterisation are more central, and as a modern alternative to Rostropovich they take the lead, also because there are a number of telling passages in Kreizberg's accompaniments.

Cello Concerto No 1ᵃ. Cello Sonataᵇ
Han-Na Chang vc ᵃ**London Symphony Orchestra / Antonio Pappano** ᵇpf
EMI 332422-2 (57' · DDD)   ⓕ🕭

Antonio Pappano belies his reputation for carefully prepared, soft-grained music-making, encouraging the LSO winds to emulate the edginess of Soviet Russian playing styles. True, his cellist has a smaller sound than Rostropovich, something only partly disguised by close miking, yet she plays with such conviction that you feel she too could have been the inspiration for those great composers.

Chang's intense and aggressive style carries its own risks. Adopting in fast music speeds a notch swifter than the norm, Chang combines raw emotion with a structural grip that, in its way, is even more remarkable in one so young. No doubt some will find her playing OTT, her tone too lean, her approach inelegant. And the LSO is right there with her, as deeply attentive in the slow movement as in the composer's astringent, nagging brand of fireworks elsewhere in the piece.

The Cello Sonata is a less passionate utterance, though it too has its (quieter) attractions. This is Shostakovich trying his hand at a purer, relatively neutral idiom even before Stalin's direct intervention in his creative life. With Pappano at the keyboard the performance is sympathetic if less extraordinary than that of the main work, Chang's projection at times unduly vehement. Still in her early twenties, she is none the less a phenomenon.

Piano Concertos

No 1 C minor for Piano, Trumpet and Strings, Op 35;
No 2 in F, Op 102
Piano Concertos Nos 1 & 2. The Unforgettable Year 1919, Op 89 – The assault on beautiful Gorky
Dmitri Alexeev pf **Philip Jones** tpt **English Chamber Orchestra / Jerzy Maksymiuk**
Classics for Pleasure 382234-2 (48' · DDD) Ⓑ⚪

Shostakovich's piano concertos were written under very different circumstances, yet together they contain some of the composer's most cheerful and enlivening music. The First, with its wealth of perky, memorable tunes, has the addition of a brilliantly conceived solo trumpet part (delightfully done here by Philip Jones) that also contributes to the work's characteristic stamp. The Second Concerto was written not long after Shostakovich had released a number of the intense works he had concealed during the depths of the Stalin era. It came as a sharp contrast, reflecting as it did the optimism and sense of freedom that followed the death of the Russian dictator. The beauty of the slow movement is ideally balanced by the vigour of the first, and the madcap high spirits of the last. The poignant movement for piano and orchestra from the Suite from the 1951 film *The Unforgettable Year 1919*, 'The assault on beautiful Gorky', provides an excellent addition to this disc of perceptive and zestful performances by Alexeev. He's most capably supported by the ECO under Maksymiuk, and the engineers have done them proud with a recording of great clarity and finesse. A joyous issue.

Concerto for Piano, Trumpet and Strings, Op 35[a].
Concertino, Op 94[b]. Piano Quintet, Op 57[c]
Martha Argerich pf with [a]**Sergei Nakariakov** tpt
[c]**Renaud Capuçon**, [c]**Alissa Margulis** vns
[c]**Lida Chen** va [c]**Mischa Maisky** vc
[b]**Lilya Zilberstein** pf [a]**Orchestra della**

Svizzera Italiana / Alexander Vedernikov
EMI 504504-2 (66' · DDD) Recorded live in 2006 Ⓟ⚪⚪⚪⚪▷

Argerich's 1994 DG reading of the Concerto for Piano, Trumpet and Strings is already a benchmark version among modern recordings, complementing the composer's own technically fallible yet still indispensable 1958 account. But now there is a more natural flow in the slow movement, some previously slightly forced rubati are smoother, and although the textures are a fraction more richly pedalled, as often needs to be the case for projection to a big audience rather than the microphone, there is no more than an infinitesimal loss of clarity. So if anything Argerich's playing has the tiniest of edges even over her former self. More decisively, Sergei Nakariakov brings an extra dash of wit and soloistic presence to the trumpet part, not to mention an astonishing feat of (circular?) breathing in the slow movement. There is a fraction more flair from orchestra and conductor too, while the recording brings everything further forward, so that the electricity of the playing crackles around the room.

The two-piano Concertino is a little piece of high-quality *Gebrauchsmusik* for the then 16-year-old Maxim Shostakovich son to romp around with; Argerich and Zilberstein give it a wonderfully characterful rendition.

Much of the Piano Quintet also emerges as one has only always dreamt of hearing it – vivid from moment to moment, yet with a long musical line and dramatic overall conception. Occasionally the nervous energy of the playing is too much of a good thing, as in the tricky bridge from Intermezzo to finale – from darkest profundity to deceptive easy-going cheeriness – and as in the piano's first statement of the fugue theme in the second movement. So, recommended alongside the safer Ashkenazy/Fitzwilliam recording rather than above it. As for the disc as a whole: a sure-fire winner.

Violin Concertos

No 1 in A minor, Op 99; **No 2** in C sharp minor, Op 129

Violin Concertos Nos 1 & 2
Lydia Mordkovitch vn
Scottish National Orchestra / Neeme Järvi
Chandos CHAN8820 (69' · DDD) Ⓟ⚪⚪▷

This coupling completely explodes the idea of the Second Violin Concerto being a disappointment after the dramatic originality of No 1. Certainly No 2, completed in 1967, a year after the very comparable Cello Concerto No 2, has never won the allegiance of violin virtuosos as the earlier work has done, but here Lydia Mordkovitch confirms what has become increasingly clear, that the spareness of late Shostakovich marks no diminution of his creative spark, maybe even the opposite. In that she's greatly helped by the equal commitment of Neeme Järvi in drawing such purposeful, warmly expressive playing from the SNO. With such spare textures the first two movements can be difficult to hold together, but here from the start, where Mordkovitch plays the lyrical first theme in a hushed, beautifully withdrawn way, the concentration is consistent.

It isn't just that Mordkovitch has the benefit of far fuller recording and a less close recording balance, but that her playing has an even wider range of colouring and dynamic than Oistrakh's. She conveys more of the mystery of the work and is perfectly matched by the orchestra. As in the First Concerto the principal horn has a vital role, here crowning each of the first two movements with a solo of ecstatic beauty in the coda. The range of the recording helps in the finale, where the *Allegro* has a satisfyingly barbaric bite, while the *scherzando* element is delectably pointed, as it is in the first movement too.

In the First Concerto Mordkovitch is hardly less impressive. As in Concerto No 2 one of her strengths lies in the meditative intensity which she brings to the darkly lyrical writing of the first and third movements. Here, too, she has never sounded quite so full and warm of tone on record before. In the brilliant second and fourth movements she may not play with quite the demonic bravura of Oistrakh, but again there's no lack of power, and in place of demonry she gives rustic jollity to the dance rhythms, faithfully reflecting the title of the finale, *Burlesque*. She's helped by recorded sound far fuller than Oistrakh's. This is a superb disc.

Shostakovich Violin Concertos Nos 1 & 2
Maxim Vengerov *vn*; **London Symphony Orchestra / Mstislav Rostropovich**
Warner Elatus 2564-69452-7 (73' · DDD)   Ⓜ❍❍❍❑➔

Ⓖ There's an astonishing emotional maturity in Vengerov's Shostakovich. He uses Heifetz's bow, but it's to David Oistrakh that he's often compared. His vibrato is wider, his manners less consistently refined, and yet the comparison is well founded. Oistrakh made three commercial recordings of the Shostakovich and one can guess that Vengerov has been listening to those earlier Oistrakh renditions, as there's nothing radically novel about his interpretation. Some may find Vengerov's impassioned climaxes a shade forced by comparison. Yet he achieves a nobility and poise worlds away from the superficial accomplishment of most modern rivals. He can fine down his tone to the barest whisper; nor is he afraid to make a scorching, ugly sound. While his sometimes slashing quality of articulation is particularly appropriate to the faster movements, the brooding, silver-grey 'Nocturne' comes off superbly too, though it seems perverse that the engineers mute the low tam-tam strokes.

Rostropovich has the lower strings dig into the third movement's passacaglia theme with his

usual enthusiasm. Indeed the orchestral playing is very nearly beyond reproach.

This is an exceptionally fine peformance of the Second, the desperate bleakness perfectly realised. There has been no finer account since that of the dedicatee, David Oistrakh (Chant du Monde). With Rostropovich rather than Kondrashin on the podium, tempos are comparatively deliberate in the first two movements, but there's no lack of intensity in the solo playing and rather more in the way of light and shade. In the stratospheric writing of the *Adagio*, Vengerov is technically superb, while the all-pervading atmosphere of desolation has never been more potently conveyed. The finale is more extrovert than some will like, the fireworks irresistible, and yet you do not lose the disquieting sense of a composer at the end of his tether, seemingly contemptuous of his own material. This is an extraordinary disc.

Violin Concertos Nos 1 & 2
Sergey Khachatryan *vn*
French National Orchestra / Kurt Masur
Naïve V5025 (70' ·DDD)   Ⓜ❍❍

Do we need another pairing of the Shostakovich violin concertos? The answer is an unequivocal yes when the playing is as sensational as this. Not just a preternaturally gifted teen, Sergey Khachatryan is a real rival to Maxim Vengerov in this repertoire: the Shostakovich No 1 is his party piece as well. Interpreting it with a less unyielding intensity, he too satisfies its demands as few have done since the great David Oistrakh. Rock-solid intonation is combined with wonderfully sweet tone.

Kurt Masur's accompaniment is characteristic of him. You'll hear the important tam-tam contributions in the first movement, which Rostropovich and/or his sound team fail to clarify, but you shouldn't expect minatory timp thwacks when the third movement passacaglia launches with kapellmeisterish restraint. Masur's lack of theatricality puts the focus on the way the music is put together. One drawback hereabouts is a microphone placement that captures soloistic sniffles, distracting if you do your listening on headphones. The finale is aptly lighter in style, with a dash to the finishing-line perfectly calculated to win prizes and bring the house down.

Authoritative booklet-notes portray the companion concerto as something of an also-ran, an impression the performance perhaps does too little to allay. There are some exquisite effects but Vengerov, Rostropovich and the LSO take us to another, darker place. In Paris the accompaniment has too much politesse and is backwardly balanced. Strongly recommended even so.

Shostakovich Violin Concerto No 1
Prokofiev Violin Concerto No 1
Sarah Chang *vn*
Berlin Philharmonic Orchestra / Sir Simon Rattle
EMI 346053-2 (60' · DDD)   Ⓟ❍❍❑➔

Gone are the days when Shostakovich's First Concerto meant one or other frequently inaccessible David Oistrakh LP. Today's young virtuosi are queuing up to record the piece. In making the transition from wunderkind to mature artist, Sarah Chang and EMI have previously played it safe, setting down lesser known concertos to general acclaim. This live recording from Berlin moves into more demanding territory with results that invite comparison with established classics. The soloist is fortunate to be partnered by Sir Simon Rattle and his Berliners and this is a reminder of his unambiguous excellence as a concerto accompanist. Notwithstanding a sound-stage that feels overstuffed at high decibels, the effect is quite different from those rival accounts where the orchestral part is painted in shades of grey. The sophisticated sense of colour and control of line anchor the performance.

What you might miss is that indefinable factor 'authenticity of experience'. Not that Sarah Chang lacks heart, courage or individuality. She plunges excitedly into climactic passages, determined to give her big dark sound a scorching edge. The technical control is mightily impressive. Chang's deployment of *vibrato*, perhaps a little wide and unvaried for some tastes, is unashamed; ditto the blood-and-guts bowing. Her ability to fine down her tone to a barely audible *pianissimo* is spellbinding in the opening *Nocturne*.

So what if there's a momentary lapse of intonation; this is great playing, perhaps the best she has yet given us. While the Passacaglia third movement is somehow less eloquent, it's well worth sampling a recording which, like Repin's, ensures that the music can actually be heard as variations on a ground.

The Prokofiev goes well, too, positively projected but never over-personalised.

Shostakovich Violin Concerto No 1[a]
Mendelssohn Violin Concerto in E minor, Op 64[b]
Hilary Hahn vn **Oslo Philharmonic Orchestra /**
[b]**Hugh Wolff,** [a]**Marek Janowski**
Sony Classical 50997 08992-1 (64' · DDD) Ⓕ Ⓞ

Years ago the merest mention of Shostakovich's First Violin Concerto brought just two key stylistic templates to mind: David Oistrakh and, a little later, Leonid Kogan. Oistrakh in particular had fashioned such a warm and intimate reading of the piece that it became almost impossible to imagine a credible alternative. And yet the passing years have brought many, not least Perlman, Mullova, Vengerov and Chang, to name some of the best.

Hilary Hahn is certainly in their league, though different again. She's a lean, athletic player, utterly still at the muted centre of the Concerto's first movement, and with elfin agility in the *Scherzo*. Hahn is to be preferred, primarily because her sweetness-and-steel tone, with its expressive but narrow vibrato, lends a fresh perspective to the work but also because of Marek Janowski's fine conducting.

Some might find Hahn's approach a trifle cool, especially in the cadenza. Hahn is a very clean player, colour-conscious but never dangerous in the manner of her most rival, Ilya Gringolts, though she does engage in some active dialogue with individual soloists. Only the finale seems a little short on what one might call ambiguous sparks – where sudden ignition could be taken either as celebration or protest – but as fiddle-playing per se, it really does cut the mustard. Among digital rivals Vengerov and Khachatryan are still tops, though as Hahn is nearer than they are to the honeyed tones of pre-war players some collectors might favour her on that count alone.

As to the coupling, Hahn gives a swift, resilient, bright-toned reading, tender-hearted in the *Andante* and very fast in the finale. Too fast perhaps for true composure. Still, it's a fine display, and this is a thoroughly fine disc, confirming Hilary Hahn as among the most gifted and individual players on the concert circuit.

Symphonies

No 1 in F minor, Op 10; **No 2** in B, Op 14, 'To October'; **No 3** in E flat, Op 20, 'The first of May'; **No 4** in C minor, Op 43; **No 5** in D minor, Op 47; **No 6** in B minor, Op 54; **No 7** in C, Op 60, 'Leningrad'; **No 8** in C minor, Op 65; **No 9** in E-flat, Op 70; **No 10** in E-minor, Op 93; **No 11** in G minor, Op 103, 'The year 1905'; **No 12** in D minor, Op 112, 'The year 1917'; **No 13** in B flat minor, Op 113, 'Babiy Yar'; **No 14**, Op 135; **No 15** in A, Op 141

Symphonies Nos 1-15. October, Op 131. Violin Concerto No 2. The Execution of Stepan Razin, Op 119. The Sun shines on our Motherland, Op 90. **Evgenia Tselovalnik** sop **Evgeny Nesterenko, Vitaly Gromadsky, Artur Eizen** basses **David Oistrakh** vn **Russian State Polyphonic Cappella; Moscow Choral Academy Boys Chorus; Moscow Philharmonic Symphony Orchestra / Kyrill Kondrashin**
Melodiya MELCD1001065 (721 minutes : ADD) Ⓕ Ⓞ Ⓞ

If Kondrashin's name isn't the first listeners associate with the composer these days that has more to do with the spotty availability of his recordings than with their intrinsic quality. Of course the sound is not state-of-the-art, the mid-range tending to be rather crowded and shouty, but the transfers are more than listenable. The Fourth in particular is an enormous improvement on its mono-only predecessor, the Ninth disappointing only in the way the sound cuts out abruptly at the close, probably to disguise wear on the master tape. Both these readings are usually judged 'definitive' and the Russians have added to the attractions of the cycle with extras occupying the same high ground. You'll not find a more compelling account of *The Execution of Stepan Razin* than the one by its onlie begetters and this would seem to be the most 'official' transfer of David Oistrakh's Second Violin Concerto currently doing the rounds.

Black marks, and there had to be some, are earned by the flimsiness of the box containing the 11 sturdy individual cardboard folders and the lack of adequate annotations, texts and translations. This is the textually bowdlerised version of the Thirteenth which weakens the author's personal identification with the fate of the Jewish people. Here the indictment of anti-Semitism becomes less specific to Mother Russia and we are reminded of the latter's 'heroic deed in blocking the way to Fascism'. Not that you'd know it. Neither this nor the Fourteenth make much sense without the words in front of you.

Whatever the case, the Melodiya set is a compulsory purchase for all true lovers of Shostakovich, especially those who feel that most recent recordings speak with a foreign accent or are simply too damn slow! The first complete Shostakovich cycle from one interpreter can still startle with its resilience and panache and the raw tone of the Moscow Philharmonic is part and parcel of the appeal. Over to you.

Additional recommendation

Symphonies Nos 1-15.
Coupled with: Six Poems of Marina Tsvetayeva. From Jewish Folk Poetry
Soloists; Concertgebouw; LPO / Haitink
Decca ⑪ 475 7413 (DDD) ⒷО⮁⮲
  The first Western complete Shostakovich cycle and a very fine achievement indeed. Competitively priced and stunningly recorded, this is well worth considering.

Symphony No 1

Symphonies Nos 1 & 6
Russian National Orchestra / Vladimir Jurowski
Pentatone ⓈⒶ PTC5186 068 (67' · DDD/DSD)   Ⓕ

The Russian National Orchestra's relatively lean, frosty sonority, only partly a product of divided violins, is presented with outstanding fidelity in a spacious acoustic.

While both performances are excellent, the Sixth receives the more remarkable interpretation. Here Shostakovich can be Beethovenian in his allocation of seemingly unworkable metronome marks and most conductors blunt his excesses. Leonard Bernstein, one of the few to give credence to the *Largo*'s broad opening indication of quaver=72, makes the *Scherzo* into something ambivalent and dogged, a more 'logical' transition to the *Presto* finale than the composer seems to intend. Yevgeny Mravinsky, altogether brisker in that *Scherzo*, attempts to articulate its substance at dotted crochet=144 (the dot missing from my score can reasonably be inferred). Only this comes after a first movement incontrovertibly more fluid than quaver=72.

It's Jurowski who proves the most faithful, almost too dour as the argument gets underway, yet potently conveying the near-paralysis at its heart. The second movement is a fierce whirlwind outpacing even Mravinsky, a gambit that only occasionally sounds like a gabble. Perhaps there have been more exhilarating finales but this one has grace as well as the necessary vulgarity. All in all a remarkable achievement.

Symphony No 1
Schleswig-Holstein Music Festival Orchestra / Leonard Bernstein
Medici Arts 📀 207 2158
(85' · NTSC · 4:3 · PCM stereo and DTS 5.1 · 0)
Recorded live on July 16, 1988   Ⓕ

This ties up nicely – Leonard Bernstein performing Shostakovich's First Symphony, written when he was 19, with an orchestra of young music students at the 1988 Schleswig-Holstein Music Festival. Bernstein was a first-rate Shostakovich interpreter and here's the clearest available insight into his concept of how the pathologically enigmatic Russian composer ticked. The DVD opens with a 40-minute rehearsal in which Bernstein cogently describes Shostakovich's 'naughty boy' attitude – 'would you really want to start your first symphony like this?' he asks his amused orchestra, as he sings the jaunty, deadpan introductory bars.

Shostakovich's First was written only two years into Stalin's dictatorship, but Bernstein is right to locate an emerging, self-defensive satirical approach in these opening bars – if Ian MacDonald's *The New Shostakovich* is to be believed, he didn't think much of Lenin either. His description of how the work gradually fills the dimensions of a 'proper' symphony and arrives, symbolically, at a middle section filled with references to Wagner is persuasive. The complete performance, too, accumulates expressive weight as Bernstein holds the satire of the opening at a distance, letting the material tell its own story, before unlocking the magisterial depth of the symphony's middle section and finale.

This version was cut only a month after his 'official' reading with the Chicago SO. Hearing the two versions together demonstrates that this was Bernstein's settled view. And watching him gently coax his young charges – especially an obviously petrified clarinettist – is unexpectedly touching.

Symphony No 4

Shostakovich Symphony No 4
Britten Russian Funeral
City of Birmingham Symphony Orchestra / Sir Simon Rattle
EMI 555476-2 (68' · DDD)   ⒻО

This could just be the most important Western recording of the Fourth since the long-deleted Ormandy and Previn versions. Naturally, it complements rather than replaces Kondrashin's reading (Chant du Monde), taped shortly after the work's belated unveiling in December 1961:

papery strings and lurid brass can't disguise that conductor's unique authority even when Shostakovich's colouristic effects are muted by rudimentary Soviet sound engineering. In his recording, Rattle's approach is more obviously calculated, supremely brilliant but just a little cold. A certain firmness and self-confidence is obvious from the first. The restrained Hindemithian episode is relatively square, the first climax superbly built. The second group unfolds seamlessly with the glorious *espressivo* of the strings not much threatened by the not very mysterious intrusions of harp and bass clarinet. Tension builds again, some way into the development, with the lacerating intensity of the strings' *moto perpetuo fugato* passage.

Six miraculously terraced discords herald the two-faced recapitulation. Kondrashin and Järvi (Chandos) find more emotional inevitability in Shostakovich's destabilising tactics hereabouts. Rattle doesn't quite locate a compensating irony, although his closing bars are convincingly icy, with nicely audible gong. Even in Rattle's experienced hands, the finale isn't all plain sailing. The initial quasi-Mahlerian march is underpinned by disappointingly fuzzy timpani strokes which lose the point of their own lopsidedness. But then the section's mock-solemn climax is simply tremendous (and tremendously loud). The incisive *Allegro* is launched with (deliberate?) abruptness at an unbelievably fast tempo and, even if the music doesn't always make sense at this pace, the results are breathtaking. The denouement is approached with real flair. A superbly characterised trombone solo, hushed expectant strings and the most ambiguous of all Shostakovich perorations is unleashed with devastating force. The coda is mightily impressive too.

After this, the Britten encore risks seeming beside the point; this really is emotional play-acting. Neither Kondrashin's nor Järvi's more direct emotional involvement is easily passed over. On the other hand, Rattle does give us a thrilling example of what a relatively objective, thoroughly 'modern' approach has to offer today. With its huge dynamic range and uncompromising, analytical style, EMI's recording pulls no punches, and the awesome precision of the CBSO's playing makes for an unforgettable experience.

Symphony No 4, Op 43ᵃ. Katarina Izmaylova, Op 114a – selectionᵃ. Festive Overture, Op 96ᵇ
ᵃ**Philharmonia Orchestra;** ᵇ**London Symphony Orchestra / Gennady Rozhdestvensky**
BBC Legends BBCL4220-2 (74' · ADD)
Recorded live in ᵃ1962, ᵇ1985   Ⓕ**OO**

A genuine BBC Legend this. We tend to think of Kyrill Kondrashin as the most 'authentic' pioneer of Shostakovich's long-suppressed Fourth Symphony, except that the recordings of this work by Gennady Rozhdestvensky are no less fine. Where Kondrashin offers total commitment and unremitting intensity, Rozhdestvensky proves peculiarly adept at teasing out the score's strange, subversive elements.

Here, giving the work its first hearing outside the Soviet bloc during a large-scale Shostakovich retrospective at the 1962 Edinburgh Festival, Rozhdestvensky conducts with greater urgency than usual, galvanising the Philharmonia into a coruscating display. Small wonder the piece so wowed contemporary critics. The inclusion of an edited and reordered *Katerina Izmaylova* Suite, performed a few days earlier, reminds us that this was also the period in which Shostakovich at last secured official acceptance of his opera *The Lady Macbeth of Mtsensk*, albeit in bowdlerised form. Western commentators were understandably less kind about the Twelfth Symphony which featured on the same programme.

BBC Legends' festive filler is an LSO relay from 1985, dangerously like a non sequitur in this context. It also betrays a more worrying aspect of the Rozhdestvensky phenomenon. While the rendition has more than enough verve and spirit to delight the audience at London's Barbican Hall, you may find it too sloppy for repeated listening. (Applause is retained.)

Symphony No 5

Symphony No 5. Chamber Symphony, Op. 110a
Vienna Philharmonic Orchestra / Mariss Jansons
EMI 556442-2 (71' · DDD)   Ⓕ**D**

Jansons exercises tight technical control, imparting rather less in the way of inner character. As usual he goes for maximal rhythmic clarity, smooth legato lines and extreme dynamic contrasts. Inevitably, some will feel that the luscious string sound only gets in the way and there are a few agogic touches. Isn't there something unnatural about the shift up a gear in the first-movement development (around 8'00"), the cliff-edge dynamics of the slow movement, the self-conscious pacing of the start of the finale?

More positively, there are some wonderfully sustained *pianissimos* from both strings and winds – try the return of the first movement's second subject (from 12'26"). EMI's recording isn't quite ideal, cavernous and a little occluded in the bass; the presence of an audience is never betrayed, and doesn't seem to have influenced the character of the music-making. The Chamber Symphony is distinguished by its unique atmosphere.

Additional recommendation

London Symphony Orchestra / Previn
RCA 74321 24212-2 (76' · ADD)   Ⓢ
André Previn's classic 1960s recording of the Fifth still figures among the very finest accounts, and at this price it represents a superb bargain.

Symphony No 7

Symphonies Nos 1 & 7
Chicago Symphony Orchestra / Leonard Bernstein

SHOSTAKOVICH SYMPHONY NO 5 – IN BRIEF

Philadelphia Orchestra / Leopold Stokowski Ⓗ
Dutton CDAX 8017 (79' · ADD) Ⓜ
Stokowski's 1939 world premiere recording continues to thrill to the marrow in its searing intensity and overwhelming emotional clout.

Czech PO / Karel Ančerl
Supraphon SU3699-2 (74' · ADD) Ⓜ
There's no missing the tingle-factor on this vintage display from Prague. Ančerl's lucid conception has tremendous sweep and ardour, while the playing of the Czech PO is predictably superb.

Concertgebouw Orchestra / Bernard Haitink
Decca 467 478-2 (76' · DDD) Ⓑ●
In sheer sonic splendour, Haitink's 1981 Decca recording has no equals. The performance unfolds in typically noble, unmannered fashion and won't disappoint this maestro's many admirers.

London SO / André Previn
RCA 82876 55493-2 (76' · ADD) Ⓑ
Previn's much-loved 1965 recording with the LSO has come up as fresh as new paint in its latest remastering. Serebrier's lively account of the suite from Shostakovich's *Hamlet* incidental music makes a generous fill-up.

Royal Scotish National Orchestra / Neeme Järvi
Chandos CHAN8650 (76' · DDD) Ⓕ●
Interpretatively, Järvi doesn't put a foot wrong. Although the RSNO's hard-working strings are not always absolutely secure, this account replicates the buzz of Järvi's Shostakovich in the concert hall.

New York PO / Leonard Bernstein
Sony 509970 94733-2 (77' · DDD) Ⓜ
An no-holds-barred performance from Lenny and his beloved New Yorkers, recorded live on tour in Japan during the summer of 1979.

Vienna PO / Mariss Jansons
EMI 556442-2 (71' · DDD) Ⓕ
Another live recording, this time from January 1997, and Jansons' second recording of the Fifth for EMI. Although not entirely free of self-regarding gesture, it's a painstakingly prepared performance that communicates urgently.

BBC NOW / Mark Wigglesworth
BIS ② BIS-CD973/4 (140' · DDD) Ⓕ●
Wigglesworth is nothing if not individual. Often daringly broad and pungently characterised, this Fifth serves up plenty of ear-tickling observation and sumptuous food for thought.

DG ② 427 632-2GH2 (120' · DDD) Recorded live 1988 Ⓕ●●➾

The *Leningrad* Symphony was composed in haste as the Nazis sieged and bombarded the city (in 1941). It caused an immediate sensation, but posterity has been less enthusiastic. What business has the first movement's unrelated long central 'invasion' episode doing in a symphonic movement? Is the material of the finale really distinctive enough for its protracted treatment? Michael Oliver, in his original *Gramophone* review, wrote that in this performance 'the symphony sounds most convincingly like a symphony, and one needing no programme to justify it'. Added to which the work's epic and cinematic manner has surely never been more powerfully realised. These are live recordings, with occasional noise from the audience (and the conductor), but the Chicago Orchestra has rarely sounded more polished or committed. The strings are superb in the First Symphony, full and weightily present, and Bernstein's manner here is comparably bold and theatrical of gesture. A word of caution: set your volume control carefully for the *Leningrad* Symphony's start; it's scored for six of both trumpets and trombones and no other recording has reproduced them so clearly, and to such devastating effect.

Symphony No 7 in C, 'Leningrad', Op 60
Cologne Radio Symphony Orchestra / Rudolf Barshai
Regis Records RRC1074 (72' · DDD) Recorded live 1992 Ⓑ●

With the variable availability of the Melodiya catalogue (at least in the UK), seekers after truth – or at least some measure of authenticity – in their Shostakovich symphonies will have to look elsewhere. One option is to investigate the recordings made outside Russia by musicians closely associated with the composer. Rudolf Barshai certainly qualifies for inclusion in this select group. Certain musicians seem to have found him more pernickety than inspirational, but Sviatoslav Richter for one praised his honesty and professionalism. Now, belatedly, cult status has arrived, thanks in part to the 'underground' success of a live account of Mahler's Fifth Symphony.

It's idle to pretend that the players of Bernstein's Chicago Symphony need look to their laurels. Nor does Barshai feel the need to go for broke (and bombast?) in the Bernstein manner. That said, his first movement is both 'felt' and fluent, the main material presented with convincing elegance and lucidity at a flowing pace. Barshai's slow movement glows with (rather than oozes) compassion, and it's principally in the finale that the conducting doesn't always succeed in disguising the fact that Shostakovich was, of necessity, composing on automatic pilot. Even here, timps are well tuned, and Barshai's diligence is always readily apparent in the detailed phrasing of his strings. The recorded sound has been well managed too, the crystalline textures obtained by the conductor and the attractively spacious acoustic compensating for a relatively constricted dynamic range and limited bass response.

This disc is a clear winner in its price range: it's vastly superior to Ladislav Slovák's bargain basement alternative on Naxos. Expect a few fluffs and some audience noise and you won't be disappointed.

Symphony No 8

Shostakovich Symphony No 8
Mozart Symphony No 33 in B flat, K319
Leningrad Philharmonic Orchestra /
Evgeny Mravinsky
BBC Legends/IMG Artists ② BBCL4002-2 (82' · ADD)
Recorded live 1960   Ⓜ🔘

There was a time when Mravinsky's greatness had to be taken on trust, such was the paucity of his representation in the record catalogues. The situation has been transformed in recent years; hence this version of the Shostakovich has to find its niche in a market-place documenting the orchestra's prowess in the piece from the 1940s to the 1980s. In a variety of different transfers (and at a variety of different pitches) Mravinsky's March 1982 concert performance is widely known. But in 1960, when the orchestra made an epochal visit to these shores with Rostropovich, Rozhdestvensky and Shostakovich himself in tow, the work had never been heard here and was unavailable on disc. Small wonder the event was such a sensation, with the November 1960 *Gramophone* leading the call for new recordings of the Soviet repertoire played on the tour.

Mravinsky was a conductor in the Karajan mould both in his undemonstrative, albeit politically ratified, exercise of authority and the way in which his interpretations remained broadly consistent from one decade to the next. The authentic timbre of the Leningrad Philharmonic is there for all to hear – the winds tearing into their phrases like scalded cats, the string sound huge and inimitable, dominating the sound-stage and yet never fat or complacent. In almost every respect, Mravinsky's London performance lives up to its legendary status, and the sound has been reprocessed to yield excellent results. Unfortunately the listeners in the hall are surprisingly restless. The first movement is patiently built, stoic, even bleaker than usual from this source, and with only minor technical imperfections: the problem is the barrage of coughing. The power and control of the second and third movements is awesome by any standards and here the audience is less intrusive. In the finale, Mravinsky keeps a tight rein on his players, adopting marginally slower tempos and securing finer results than he did in 1982. The climax is cataclysmic with the paying public at last stunned into silence during the magical coda. Shostakovich dedicated the symphony to Mravinsky, and it's for this work that most people will want to acquire the set.

Symphony No 8
London Symphony Orchestra / André Previn
EMI Encore 509024-2 (61' · DDD)   Ⓑ🔘🔘

André Previn's first, 1973 version of the Eighth sneaks back into contention at budget price. More than a decade after Mravinsky introduced what is now perhaps an over-familiar score to London audiences, EMI undertook this, the first commercial recording to be made in the West. It stands up remarkably well. The first and fourth movements are long-breathed, as deeply felt as any, while the reckless tempo of the second *Scherzo* is probably modelled on early US accounts by Koussevitzky and Rodzinski. Rhythmic flair is a hallmark of the LSO's work in this period and the freshness, colour and spontaneity of the playing cannot be gainsaid. One curious oddity comes with the violin solo leading into the finale's mysterious C-D-C coda. The aberrant ascending line there is also to be found in earlier studio sessions by Haitink *et al*.

Gloomy and spiritless it may be at times, yet this is also young man's music, something that rarely comes across in recent, apparently more idiomatic (and, dare one suggest, more boring?) performances. Shostakovich sceptics in particular should give it a listen.

Symphony No 10

Symphony No 10
Berlin Philharmonic Orchestra /
Herbert von Karajan
DG 4775909 (52' · DDD)   Ⓕ🔘🔘➔

Few works give a deeper insight into the interior landscape of the Russian soul than Shostakovich's 10th, and this is a powerful and gripping account of what's, by general consent, his masterpiece. Karajan has the measure of its dramatic sweep and brooding atmosphere, as well as its desolation and sense of tragedy. Haitink's is nowhere near so intense or, for that matter, so well played, though the recording has impressive transparency of detail. There are many things here (the opening of the finale, for example) which are even more succesful than in Karajan's 1966 recording, though the main body of the finale still feels too fast – however, at crotchet=176, it's what the composer asked for. His earlier account of the first movement is for some more moving – particularly the poignant coda. However, the differences aren't significant and this is hardly less impressive. The CD deserves a strong recommendation.

Symphony No 10
London Philharmonic Orchestra / Bernard Haitink
LPO LPO0034 (55' · ADD). Recorded live at the Royal Albert Hall, London, on August 28, 1986   Ⓜ🔘

The Tenth has never seemed dependent on performers steeped in the Russian tradition and the only drawback of Haitink's well played, expertly recorded studio account (1977) was its over-confident tone in the enigmatic third movement. Attempts to decode that *Allegretto* have gone through several phases since but it remains desirable to convey a mood of wistfulness and frustrated self-assertion.

There's no lack of subtlety in this 1986 Prom relay which also has the advantage of a true sense of euphoria at the end. The applause is earned, frenzied rather than merely respectful though rather abruptly faded. In other respects little has changed. The inexorability and stoicism of the big opening *Moderato* is predictably impressive and there is no hint of restraint in the *Scherzo* which some, Kurt Sanderling among them, have been prepared to accept as a portrait of Stalin himself.

Whatever the truth of this, Haitink's musical priorities always deliver the goods and his admirers will welcome this unexpected reclamation from the archives of BBC Radio 3. The famously resonant acoustic of the Royal Albert Hall gives us the sound from the bottom up, with great weight in the cellos and basses. The booklet-note by Geoffrey Norris appropriately eschews speculative revisionist comment. Is the Tenth Shostakovich's greatest single achievement? Haitink may make you think so.

Symphony No 11

Symphony No 11, 'The Year 1905'
West German Radio Symphony Orchestra, Cologne / Semyon Bychkov
Avie 🎵 AV2062 (59' · DDD/DSD)　　Ⓕ❶❶❶❶➡

Half a century on from its composition and a full century from the events it ostensibly commemorates, the Eleventh Symphony remains a problematic work for conductors, not least because very few of them or their players have direct memories to draw on. Whatever view they take, nothing is going to come across unless the balance between atmosphere and flow is convincingly struck, and in this respect Bychkov has sure instincts.

Now that he has been principal conductor in Cologne for nearly 10 years, it seems that matters of texture, colour and line in Shostakovich have become second nature for his players: Bychkov gives onward momentum its due, and urgency and inevitability are his reward.

Quibbles could be entered. In the second movement, from 12'45" (the scene of the attack of the Tsarist police), the trombone *glissandi* may disappoint those who have heard them given full power. At the heart of the following 'In memoriam' more poignancy would not have gone amiss. But then the climax of that movement is magnificently denunciatory, and the WDR cor anglais laments with eloquence and depth but not a trace of sentimentality. The *attacca* into the finale is ideal in its sudden spit of venom.

Symphony No 11, 'The Year 1905', Op 103
Royal Liverpool Philharmonic Orchestra / Vasily Petrenko
Naxos 8 572082 (58' · DDD)　　Ⓢ🔵➡

Vasily Petrenko has galvanised Liverpool music-making to such an extent that his contract has already been extended until 2012, with a fair chance that the Rattle/Birmingham phenomenon will be replicated on Merseyside. That said, who made the decision to start the new series with No 11? This is a piece which, viewed variously as a conformist artefact of socialist realism, a coded indictment of Soviet tyranny, 'a film score without the film' and/or something more complex, tends to divide the composer's admirers. Mstislav Rostropovich was one of its most individualistic interpreters, extending its playing time to more than 72 minutes in his epic 2002 account (see above). Petrenko has no truck with that kind of self-indulgence, if self-indulgence it be, looking instead to the furious 54-minute precedent of Kyrill Kondrashin in 1973. There's never any feeling of ploughing dutifully through the notes at this kind of lick, although the Naxos recording is not quite ideal. Timps and bells could be more sympathetically miked and more carefully pitched, while brass and upper strings lack the extraordinary weight of Rostropovich's LSO. Still, there's no mistaking the rapid transformation of the RLPO's corporate profile, no want of character, attack or rhythmic definition.

Symphony No 13

Symphony No 13, 'Babi Yar'
Sergei Aleksashkin bass **St Petersburg Philharmonic Choir and Orchestra / Yuri Temirkanov**
RCA Red Seal 88697 02163-2 (58' · DDD)　　Ⓕ🔵🔵

Of the many recent versions of Shostakovich's finest vocal symphony, surprisingly few employ a Russian chorus. And for all that Western choirs can now draw on superb language coaches and emulate the darkness of Slavonic voices, the difference is still decisive. Temirkanov's Petersburg basses speak and speak about their words, unencumbered by the basic need to get them right, and without having to take their expressive cue solely from the conductor. This helps the episodes in the 'Babi Yar' first movement to unfold with an inevitability that few Western recordings can match. Some may even find that the *bel canto* mellifluousness the chorus brings to Yevtushenko's verses compromises the poet's moralising tone, by comparison with the raw passion of performances from nearer the time of composition.

This is Sergei Aleksashkin's fourth CD appearance as soloist in this work, and he has never done it better than here. Apart from his familiar nobility of line, there are many fresh nuances, of a piece with Temirkanov's subtle interpretation. Temirkanov's most conspicuous intervention is to dash through the second movement in record time: pretty disconcerting at first, but he puts across the scalding quality of Shostakovich's take on 'Humour'. And although communicative urgency is again the watchword in the slower surrounding movements, Temir-kanov actually finds a happy medium between Kondrashin (conductor of the fraught 1962 pre-miere) and broader modern accounts. Record-ing quality is straightforward and well balanced. Overall then, this is the preferred modern studio version.

Symphony No 13
Marius Rintzler bass **Concertgebouw Orchestra Choir** (male voices) **Concertgebouw Orchestra / Bernard Haitink**
Decca 425 073-2DM (64' · DDD · T/t)　　Ⓜ️Ⓞ

With one single reservation Haitink's account of *Babiy Yar* is superb. The reservation is that Mar-ius Rintzler, although he has all the necessary blackness and gravity and is in amply sonforous voice, responds to the anger and the irony and the flaming denunciations of Yevtushenko's text with scarcely a trace of the histrionic fervour they cry out for. The excellent chorus, though, is very expressive and it makes up for a lot, as does the powerful and sustained drama of Haitink's direc-tion. He has solved the difficult problems of pac-ing a symphony with three slow movements (one is gripped throughout) and the atmosphere of each movement is vividly evoked, with a particu-lar care for the subtleties of Shostakovich's orchestration. The orchestral sound, indeed, is magnificent: one can readily believe that the huge forces called for in the score were actually pro-vided, but this doesn't necessitate any unnatural focusing on (say) the celeste in order that it shall register. The perspective is very natural through-out, and there's an excellent sense of the perform-ance taking place in a believable space.

Symphony No 13, 'Babi Yar'
Jan-Hendrik Rootering bass
Netherlands Radio Choir and Philharmonic Orchestra / Mark Wigglesworth
BIS 🔊 BIS-SACD1543 (62' · DDD/DSD)　　Ⓕ

If all that mattered in Shostakovich's 13th was the *Babi Yar* setting that first motivated it, then there would be reason to approach Mark Wiggles-worth's recording with caution. That long first movement sags, because he has tipped the bal-ance slightly too far away from frightening imme-diacy in favour of philosophical reflection. The first entries of chorus and soloist feel a bit soggy.

Yet hearing their chillingly full-blooded con-tributions later, it's possible to go back and appreciate that there is profound careworn sad-ness behind their delivery of the opening, rather than mere tentativeness. Their Russian is as plausible as anything heard from non-native speakers. And since the 'voice' behind the solo voice is Shostakovich's as much as Yevtushen-ko's, it's not inappropriate that Jan-Hendrik

Rootering should sound prematurely aged. More than usually, the line 'I feel I am gradually going grey' feels like a key moment.

The Netherlands Radio PO do not have quite the muscle for the biggest climaxes in *Babi Yar* or for the scalding irony of 'Humour'. But they certainly rise to the challenge of the remaining movements, so often anti-climactic but which here make the deepest impression.

Wigglesworth has plenty of ideas about timing and articulation, and they are of a piece with a powerful overall view. In the faster movements, admittedly, he doesn't yet have the knack of showing all this without losing momentum, but in the slower ones his subtle moulding of phrase and texture pays huge dividends. 'In the Store' plumbs depths of sadness and compassion, and even Rootering's less than infallible steadiness of tone feels like part and parcel of the same conception. 'Fears' and 'A Career' seemingly come from somewhere beyond the experiences they describe. This, then, is a performance in which you feel the presence of a lyrical commen-tator throughout, rather than being in the grip of some overwhelming larger force. Soft-grained but marvellously spacious recording.

Symphony No 14

Symphony No 14. Two Pieces for String Quartet (arr Sikorski)
Margareta Haverinen sop **Petteri Salomaa** bass
Tapiola Sinfonietta / Joseph Swensen
Ondine ODE845-2 (59' · DDD · T/t)　　Ⓕ Ⓞ

The multilingual version of the 14th Symphony was sanctioned by the composer but it remains a rarity on disc; some vital and specific tone colour is lost along with the original note values, and the 'three lilies' adorn the grave of 'The Suicide' more elegantly in the Russian. Haitink may not agree. He elected to use the multilingual text in his 1980 recording and now Joseph Swensen presents this compelling alternative. We tend to take sonic excellence for granted these days but this is a true state-of-the-art recording with the soloists more naturally placed than in the rival Decca issue and an orchestral sound combining great clarity with just enough hall resonance. The performance has character too, if lacking the pervasive chill of the earliest Soviet accounts. The conductor secures excellent results from the Tapiola Sinfonietta.

Of the soloists, the bass-baritone Petteri Salo-maa is particularly impressive: his is a voice of rare tonal beauty, a Billy Budd rather than a Boris. His pronunciation is a little odd at times, but you may not see this as a problem. Tempos are perceptibly more 'extreme' than Haitink's, with the opening 'De profundis' dangerously slow in the modern manner and a strikingly well-characterised instrumental contribution to 'A la Santé' ('In the Santé Prison'). The fillers, larger than life, brilliantly dispatched and curiously inappropriate, are based on original quartet pieces which only came to light in the mid-

1980s. The first shares material with *Lady Macbeth of Mtsensk*; the second appears as the polka from *The Age of Gold*! This is nevertheless a more rewarding, more probingly conducted disc than most of the current Shostakovich crop.

Symphony No 15

Symphonies Nos 1 & 15
**Cincinnati Symphony Orchestra /
Jesús López-Cobos**
Telarc CD80572 (77' · DDD)   Ⓕ

These are extremely well played and cleanly recorded performances, and in a field surprisingly lacking in strong contenders they deserve serious consideration. By dint of careful preparation López-Cobos brings exceptional clarity to the First Symphony, forcing you to admire afresh the sheer inventiveness of the teenage Shostakovich's counterpoint. His Cincinnati players are suave, without ever sounding emotionally complacent, and they seem to appreciate better than most Western orchestras the extraordinary depth of feeling at the heart of the finale. That said, there's little of the bite and sheer recklessness that make Kondrashin's interpretation so special, though sadly that classic version is hampered by poor recording quality, and the Moscow Philharmonic's first oboe in the slow movement is excruciating.

López-Cobos's account of Symphony No 15 lacks a fanatical edge in the fast movements, a sense of mystery in the slow ones and of strangeness throughout, but this Cincinnati version is as good as anything currently available, and certainly better than the over-praised Haitink, Rostropovich or Sanderling. López-Cobos plays the symphony straight and keeps the stylistically competing elements in balance. He negotiates the treacherous finale successfully, building the passacaglia to a properly passionate climax.

The Golden Age, Op 22

The Golden Age
**Royal Stockholm Philharmonic Orchestra /
Gennadi Rozhdestvensky**
Chandos ② CHAN9251/2 (134' · DDD)   ⒻⒹ➤

The ballet *The Golden Age* (1930) depicts an industrial exhibition organised in a capitalist country, at which a group of Soviet sportsmen have been invited to compete. The general idea of the music is to differentiate between goodies and baddies by assigning them respectively healthy-folk and decadent-bourgeois idioms. The trouble was that Shostakovich couldn't stop himself enjoying being decadent.

Not all the 37 movements stand up independently of the stage-action. But the finales and the whole of Act 3 are top-notch stuff, at times surprisingly threatening in tone and symphonic in continuity; and there are several movements which could undoubtedly be promoted along-

side the four in the familiar concert suite (the Tap Dance of Act 2 is especially appealing, for instance). Those who know their Shostakovich will be constantly intrigued by foretastes of *Lady Macbeth*, Symphony No 4 and the *Hamlet* music, and by the appearance of Shostakovich's 'Tea for Two' arrangement as an Interlude in Act 2.

This first complete recording is a major coup for Chandos. Admittedly not even their flattering engineering can disguise a certain lack of confidence and idiomatic flair on the part of the Royal Stockholm Philharmonic Orchestra.

But don't let that deter anyone with the least interest in Shostakovich, or ballet music, or Soviet music, or indeed Soviet culture as a whole, from investigating this weird and intermittently wonderful score. A really fascinating disc.

Film Music

Odna, Op 26 – Complete Film Score
Irina Mataeva *sop* **Anna Kiknadze** *mez*
Dmitri Voropaev *ten* **Mark van Tongeren** *voc*
Barbara Buchholz *theremin* **Frankfurt University of
Music and Performing Arts Vocal Ensemble;
Frankfurt Radio Symphony Orchestra /
Mark Fitz-Gerald**
Naxos 8 570316 (80' · DDD)   ⓈⒹ➤

Although long known through various selections, Shostakovich's second film score *Odna* ('Alone') is only now available complete. This 1931 Kozintsev/Trauberg collaboration – in which a young teacher finds herself transferred to the remote Altai region, incurs the wrath of the local peasantry and is left to die in a snowstorm, only to be rescued by a Soviet plane – emerged on the cusp of 'silent' and 'sound' cinema. Lack of suitable venues meant the film received few showings with its soundtrack and, while it received considerable acclaim abroad, it was allowed to fall into obscurity until the 1960s.

Even now, the film – reconstructed after the master was destroyed in wartime Leningrad – is missing its 'snowstorm' reel. Luckily, the score has now been reclaimed in full – due in no small part to Mark Fitz-Gerald, who has assembled it from numerous sources and presented it in live showings around Western Europe. The result is one of Shostakovich's most innovative scores: the ebullience of his early theatre music being combined with music anticipating the emotional intensity of *Lady Macbeth of Mtsensk*, alongside some of his most startling experiments – with cues for overtone singing and a contribution from the theremin (an early electronic instrument).

The brief vocal items are attractively done, and Fitz-Gerald secures playing of exceptional vitality from the Frankfurt orchestra. Vividly recorded, with a detailed note from Russian film expert John Riley, *Odna* is engrossing and pleasurable in purely musical terms. Those wishing to investigate Shostakovich's film music should start here.

Light Music

'The Dance Album'

Moscow-Cheryomushki, Op 105 – concert suite (ed Cornall). The Bolt – ballet suite, Op 27a (1934 version). The Gadfly, Op-97 – Overture; The Cliff; Youth; Box on the Ear; Barrel Organ; Contredanse; Galop; At the Market Place; The Rout; The Passage of Montanelli; Finale; The Austrians; Gemma's Room
Philadelphia Orchestra / Riccardo Chailly
Decca 452 597-2DH (73' · DDD) Ⓕ◗◉➔

Although entitled 'The Dance Album', interestingly only one of the items on this disc (*The Bolt*) is actually derived from music conceived specifically for dance. However, what the disc reveals is that Shostakovich's fondness for dance forms frequently found expression in his other theatrical/film projects.

The world premiere recording of a suite of four episodes from the 1959 operetta *Moscow-Cheryomushki* will be of particular interest to Shostakovich devotees. Despite the somewhat mundane plot, the score produces some surprisingly attractive and entertaining numbers, most notably perhaps the invigorating 'A spin through Moscow' and the 'Waltz'. For the suite from the ballet *The Bolt* Chailly brings us the less frequently heard 1934 version in which the composer dropped two of the eight numbers and changed some of the titles in order to deflect from the story-line of the ballet. Lots of parody and plenty of Shostakovich with his tongue planted firmly in his cheek is what we get, and if this aspect of the composer's output appeals then you'll certainly enjoy Chailly's and his players' spirited and colourfully buoyant performances of this energetic score.

Less familiar light is also shed on the music from the film *The Gadfly* which is heard here in a version which brings together 13 of the score's episodes and preserves Shostakovich's original orchestration, as opposed to the suite prepared and reorchestrated by Levin Atovmyan. All the performances on the disc are superbly delivered and the recorded sound is excellent.

'The Jazz Album'

Jazz Suites Nos 1 & 2. Taiti trot, Op 16. Concerto for Piano, Trumpet and Strings in C minor, Op 35
ᵃ**Peter Masseurs** tpt ᵃ**Ronald Brautigam** pf
Royal Concertgebouw Orchestra / Riccardo Chailly
Decca 433 702-2DH (59' · DDD) Ⓕ◉◗◉➔

Shostakovich's lively and endearing forays into the popular music of his time were just that, and light years away from the work of real jazz masters such as, say Jelly Roll Morton or Duke Ellington And yet they do say something significant about Shostakovich's experience of jazz, as a comparison of these colourful, Chaplinesque *Jazz* Suites with roughly contemporaneous music by Gershwin, Milhaud, Martinu, Roussel and others will prove. Shostakovich engaged in a particularly brittle

almost Mahlerian form of parody – his concert works are full of it – and that's what comes across most powerfully here. Besides, and as annotator Elizabeth Wilson rightly observes, 'real' jazz was treated with suspicion in Soviet Russia and Shostakovich's exposure to it was therefore limited.

The two *Jazz* Suites were composed in the 1930s, the First in response to a competition to 'raise the level of Soviet jazz from popular cafe music to music with a professional status', the Second at the request of the then-newly formed State Orchestra for Jazz (!). The First will make you chuckle, but it's the Second (subtitled 'Suite for Promenade Orchestra') that contains the best music, especially its achingly nostalgic Second *Waltz*. The instrumentation is light (the saxophone and accordion add a touch of spice to a generally bland recipe), while the playing is quite superb. In fact, there's little to be said about Chailly's direction other than that it's good-humoured, affectionate and utterly professional, his Royal Concertgebouw players sound at home in every bar and the recording (Grotezaal, Concertgebouw) is both clean and ambient.

Taiti trot came to life when Nikolai Malko challenged Shostakovich to score Vincent Youmans's *Tea for Two* in an hour, or less – which he did, as a sort of mini-concerto for orchestra, each refrain being dealt to different instrumental forces. Fun that it is, its charm is terminal. Which leaves the Piano Concerto, music that for sophistication and inventive ingenuity is actually closer to what we now think of as jazz than the *Jazz* Suites. (Sample the free-wheeling, improvisatory opening to the last movement, on track 7.)

Ronald Brautigam's instrument is twangy at the bass end, which mightn't seem too inappropriate, but as it was recorded two years before the other items on the disc (1988), I doubt that that was the intention. Still, it's a lively and fairly intense reading, neatly supported by Chailly and trumpeter Peter Masseurs, but ultimately less memorable than Argerich or Jablonski or the composer himself.

Piano Quintet in G minor, Op 57

Piano Quintetᵃ. String Quartets – No 1; No 12
ᵃ**Martin Roscoe** pf **Sorrel Quartet**
(Gina McCormack, Catherine Yates vns Sarah-Jane Bradley va Helen Thatcher vc)
Chandos CHAN10329 (77' · DDD) Ⓕ

Volume 6 of the Sorrel Quartet's Shostakovich series gives us two of his outwardly formulaic works framing one of his most audacious, the Twelfth Quartet. It's a rather peculiar programme, not that this need bother anyone collecting this particular intégrale.

The playing is as idiomatic as you might expect from an ensemble once coached by Rostislav Dubinsky, founder member and first leader of the Borodin Quartet. True, the almost casual opening of the First Quartet is not ideally euphonious and, in the first movement of the Twelfth, there's a momentary lapse of concentration from the viola, whose expressive swoops elsewhere may not be to all tastes. What matters more is the palpable, very human sense of engagement, something you don't always get from glitzier groups.

Given that the best recordings of the Piano Quintet are 20 years old and either tucked away or buried altogether, the present account is not unwelcome, though it is relatively small-scale. It's the subtle intimacy of the final pay-off one remembers, the warmth of the Maltings acoustic masking any thinness of tone.

String Quartets

No 1 in C, Op 49 **No 2** in A, Op 68 **No 3** in F, Op 73 **No 4** in D, Op 83 **No 5** in B flat, Op 92 **No 6** in G, Op 101 **No 7** in F sharp minor, Op 108 **No 8** in C minor, Op 110 **No 9** in E flat, Op 117 **No 10** in A flat, Op 118 **No 11** in F minor, Op 122 **No 12** in D flat, Op 133 **No 13** in B flat minor, Op 138 **No 14** in F sharp minor, Op 142 **No 15** in E flat minor, Op 144

String Quartets Nos 1-15. Two Pieces[b]
Emerson Quartet (Eugene Drucker, Philip Setzer vns Lawrence Dutton va David Finckel vc)
DG ⑤ 475 7407DC5 (360' · DDD)   Ⓕ❋❋❋❋➔

The Emersons have played Shosta-kovich all over the world, and this long-pondered *intégrale* sets the seal on a process that has brought the quartets to the very centre of the repertoire – the ensemble's and ours. While some listeners will miss the intangi-ble element of emotional specificity and sheer Russianness that once lurked behind the notes, the playing is undeniably committed in its cool-ness, exposing nerve endings with cruel clarity. The hard, diamond-like timbre of the two vio-lins (the leader's role is shared democratically) is far removed from the breadth of tone one might associate with a David Oistrakh, just as cellist David Finckel is no Rostropovich. But these recordings reveal surprising new facets of a body of work that isn't going to stand still. The Fourth Quartet is a case in point, more delicate than most rivals with the finale relatively pressed, less insistently Jewish. The Fifth some-times seems closer to Ustvolskaya or American minimalism than the mid-century Soviet sym-phonic utterance we're used to; the Emerson's almost hectoring mode of address and unflu-ctu-ating tempo are maintained for as long as (in)humanly possible. The very vehemence of, say, the finale of the Ninth tends to blunt the harmonic sense of the music, leaving something more visceral and rosiny than the argument can stand. To get the unique feel of this set, sample one of the encore pieces, the 'Polka' from *The Age of Gold*. Little humanity and wit, but can you resist the explosive brilliance of the technique?

DG's recording is exceptionally vivid if some-what airless, the separation of the instruments

being achieved at the expense of tonal blend. Given that all the quartets were taped live with only remedial patching, the audience is com-mendably silent: their enthusiastic applause is retained for Nos 1, 2, 9 and 12 only. This is a Shostakovich cycle for the 21st century.

String Quartets Nos 1-15
Danel Quartet (Marc Danel, Gilles Millet vns Tony Nys va Guy Danel vc)
Fuga Libera ⑤ FUG512 (6h 16' · DDD)   Ⓑ

This is a remarkable set which sells for less than £30 in the UK or around $50 in the States. The recordings, made by Bavarian Radio between 2001 and 2005, are, if anything, classier still, with equally classy annotations by Shostakovich scholars Frans Lemaire and David Fanning. Since fact and speculation are for once carefully defined, you won't see here the incautious revi-sionism of so much Shostakovich commentary.

After securing first prize at the 1993 Interna-tional Dmitri Shostakovich Competition, the Brussels-based Danel Quartet started their on-disc explorations with rarities, mainly French and Belgian, Modernist and Romantic. Meanwhile, Quartet colleagues have worked with members of both the Borodin and Beethoven Quartets, enjoying cordial relations with the composer's widow, Irina. Fascinating then to find that their approach is often unlike that of recent exponents. While many of those groups have brought the quartets to the very centre of the repertoire, theirs and ours, they have tended to make them into big, declamatory statements, public property if you will. This development may have begun gloriously with the post-Dubinsky, Soviet State-sanctioned Borodin line-up, but a quartet like the Emerson (DG) displays a forceful technocratic sensibility that precludes much sense of four musicians playing together for pleasure.

With consistently sweet sounds, pronounced yet carefully matched *vibrato* and lithe, inti-mately drawn interpretations, the Danel offer something else again. Though old hands may take a while to adjust, their Gallic wit and finesse add a new dimension to familiar music. You're never hit with anything more visceral and rosiny than the argument (and the tuning) can stand, but neither is there is any lack of commitment and fire. There is, however, some close-miked sniffing and at times the recorded sound takes on a wiry quality (especially in No 5). In the conventional *intégrale* we would certainly rate them above many bigger names.

Shostakovich String Quartet No 5, Op 92
Beethoven String Quartet No 10, 'Harp', Op 74
Atrium Quartet (Alexey Naumenko, Anton Ilyunin vns Dimitri Pitulko va Anna Gorelova vc)
Zig Zag Territoires ZZT080702 (60' · DDD)   Ⓕ

The Atrium Quartet won first prize in the 2003 London International String Quartet Competi-tion with a gripping account of Shostakovich's

Fifth Quartet – along with the Twelfth, the most wide ranging and powerfully wrought of the cycle, though among the least performed. On their disc, unfazed by its demands, the Atrium steer a propulsive course through the *Allegro* – easily the most persuasively argued of Shostakovich's sonata-form movements – and effect a suspenseful transition into the *Andante*, whose otherworldliness is underlined by the sparing but varied use of vibrato. Nor does the finale disappoint – its initial animation and violent culmination leading to a coda whose bittersweet oblivion is unerringly captured.

This is undoubtedly the finest recording of the Fifth Quartet to have appeared during recent years and if that of Beethoven's *Harp* Quartet is not of the same stature, then the smouldering pathos and visceral excitement that the Atrium draw from its slow movement and *Scherzo* respectively suggest that the Beethoven quartets are territory hardly less ripe for further exploration. The Atrium's Shostakovich, however, is a performance to treasure. Decently recorded, too.

String Quartets Nos 6 & 11
Jerusalem Quartet (Alexander Pavlovsky, Sergei Bresler *vns* Amichai Grosz *va* Kyril Zlotnikov *vc*)
Harmonia Mundi HMC90 1953 (63' · DDD)　Ⓕ〇

The Sixth Quartet is by no means all sweetness and light, yet the Jerusalem are rather too vehement in the first movement development and a touch coy in the ensuing intermezzo. They catch the pathos of the passacaglia third movement to perfection, but the finale is again overwrought. In the Eighth Quartet, the Jerusalem are right not to point up extra-musical associations, but the opening *Largo* is too passive, the *Allegro* too relentless and expressive nuance in the *Allegretto* awkwardly inflected. In the fourth movement they strike the right balance between formal control and expressive candour but the finale fails to clinch the design with real conviction.

It is with the Eleventh Quartet that this disc really comes into its own. A tribute to Vasily Shirinsky (second violin of the Beethoven Quartet), the contrasts between its seven brief movements are less remarkable than the motivic unity evident by the close. A quality fully borne out in a reading that is fully aware of the music's elusive spirit, and wonderfully successful in seeing the work whole. Spacious if neutral sound, and a release that certainly confirms the Jerusalem as one of the most technically assured and tonally responsive quartets of today.

Piano Trios

No 1 in C minor, Op 8 No 2 in E minor, Op 67

Shostakovich Piano Trios Nos 1 & 2
Schnittke Trio
Vienna Piano Trio (Wolfgang Redik *vn* Marcus Trefny Stefan Mendl *pf*)

Nimbus NI5572 (69' · DDD)　Ⓕ〇

Shostakovich's adolescent First Trio's ramshackle structure seems to matter less than its surprisingly Gallic-sounding, passionately late-romantic invention. The Vienna Piano Trio offers a rich-toned and meticulously prepared account. The tricky cello opening to the Second Trio is wonderfully ethereal here, and the even more tricky accumulating tempo over the entire movement is steady and logical, though this and the main tempo for the *Scherzo* are both more reined in than in the composer's own account (once available on Supraphon). The passacaglia and finale are properly intense and none the worse for being kept within the bounds of euphony, though the ideal performance, yet to be realised on CD, would be one which drained bitterer dregs of sorrow and took excitement closer to the point of hyperventilation.

Schnittke's Trio is more than an interesting makeweight. The String Trio original dates from 1985, the fateful year of the composer's first stroke and a period when he seemed to have a direct line to a kind of other-worldly inspiration. True, the two longish movements occasionally seem at a loss, but overall this is one of Schnittke's most economical and restrained scores, and one of his finest. At every turn the Vienna Piano Trio is sensitive to the character and flow of this haunting music. A fine disc, then – imaginative programming, accomplished performances, and rich, well-balanced recording.

---

24 Preludes and Fugues, Op 87

No **1** in C No **2** in A minor No **3** in G No **4** in E minor No **5** in D No **6** in B minor No **7** in A No **8** in F sharp minor No **9** in E No **10** in C sharp minor No **11** in B No **12** in G sharp minor No **13** in F sharp No **14** in E flat minor No **15** in D flat No **16** in B flat minor No **17** in A flat No **18** in F minor No **19** in E flat No **20** in C minor No **21** in B flat No **22** in G minor No **23** in F No **24** in D minor
Preludes and Fugues Nos 1-24
Vladimir Ashkenazy *pf*
Decca ② 466 066-2DH2 (142' · DDD)　Ⓕ〇➔

Here's a Shostakovich Preludes and Fugues cycle to be reckoned with. It starts none too promisingly, with (by the highest standards) a rhythmically stiff, tonally lumpy C-major prelude and some overpedalling in the fugue. However, the neo-Baroque figuration of the A minor prelude and its spiky fugue, on the other hand, presents his true credentials. On form and well prepared, as here, Ashkenazy remains a formidably fluent pianist, and the clarity and energy he brings to the faster, denser pieces is surpassed only by Richter (Philips). The sound itself is quite 'pingy', with a generous ambience behind it. That serves to heighten the impact of the more demonstrative pieces, but makes it difficult for Ashkenazy to sustain the atmosphere of the more meditative ones. Or maybe he simply doesn't feel the music that way. In the final D minor Fugue (No 24), where you can almost hear Shostakovich's 10th Symphony being born, Ashkenazy fails to build the texture as mightily as the early stages lead you to expect. Nikolaieva surpasses him here, and in general she reveals both subtler and grander perspectives, especially in her tauter, more drily recorded 1987 Melodiya set. Even so the balance-sheet for Ashkenazy comes out comfortably in the black. For consistency of pianism, straightforward integrity of interpretation and high quality of recording, his set can be warmly recommended.

Shostakovich Preludes and Fugues Nos 1, 5, 6, 7, 11, 12, 13, 17, 18, 19, 23, 24 in D minor **Bach** The Well-Tempered Clavier, Book I – C minor, C sharp, C sharp minor, E flat minor, E, E minor, F sharp minor, G, G minor, A minor, B flat, B flat minor
Olli Mustonen pf
Ondine ② ODE1033-2D (105' · DDD)   Ⓕ

The first volume of Olli Mustonen's thoughtfully melded sequence of Bach's '48' (Book 1) and Shostakovich's '24' Preludes and Fugues appeared on RCA, the sequence there based on chromatically ascending keys. Here, the pattern is planned according to the circle of fifths, especially fascinating for listeners who are sensitive to the contrasting colours of individual key signatures. Consistent to both is the sometimes bewildering extremism of Mustonen's own playing.

Our first port of call is a winning performance of Shostakovich's C major Prelude, with its light, sensual touch, and gently rhapsodised phrasing. Then in bounces the A minor Prelude from Bach's Book 1, brittle and jabbing with dramatic dynamic oscillations, especially in the succeeding fugue where even at speed individual notes either fade to near-inaudability or virtually poke your eyes out. This seems unlikely to be tolerable for long, but, by the end, one's gripped.

Yes, there are affectations, such as the prettily arpeggiated flourish at the start of Bach's E minor Prelude, and the way the succeeding line bobs like a buoy at sea. But then there are such things as the ravishing delicate arpeggios at the start of Shostakovich's D major Prelude, or the shaded spectres in the beautifully played B minor Fugue.

Two very different views of counterpoint then: Bach the consummate master of abstract patterns, Shostakovich more the dramatic tone poet donning Bachian garb. Whatever the ultimate judgement on Mustonen's interpretations, you can't deny either the brilliance or imagination of his playing, or the consistency of his approach.

From Jewish Folk Poetry, Op 79

From Jewish Folk Poetry, Op 79. The New Babylon – suite (arr Rozhdestvensky)
Tatyana Sharova sop **Ludmila Kuznetsova** mez
Alexei Martynov ten **Russian State Symphony**

Orchestra / Valéry Polyansky
Chandos CHAN9600 (70' · DDD · T/t)   Ⓕ●

This recording of Shostakovich's song cycle *From Jewish Folk Poetry* is first-rate. For a start Polyansky's three vocal soloists are uncommonly well chosen: the light, youthful, slightly vulnerable soprano, the rich, world-weary mezzo and the ardent but unheroic tenor are ideally suited to the texts Shostakovich cunningly chose to convey his solidarity with mass suffering. Polyansky sets spacious tempos which allow every nuance of that suffering to register, and his orchestra is responsive and idiomatic in colouring. The recording, by Russian engineers, feels almost too good to be true in its excessive warmth; otherwise this version is preferable to the rival Rozhdestvensky on RCA.

Polyansky's choice of the first of Shostakovich's 35 or so film scores makes for a more than welcome coupling. Polyansky offers an admirably idiomatic version of the Suite. He's especially adept at choosing timbres to reflect mood and situation. Even if you don't know the storyline the music was designed to accompany, this performance is so vividly characterised it can hardly fail to engage you.

Songs

Complete Songs, Volume 1
Four Monologues on Poems by Alexander Pushkin, Op 91[d]. Spanish Songs, Op 100[c]. Five Romances, 'Songs of Our Days', Op 98[d]. Two Romances to Lyrics by Lermontov, Op 84[b]. Four Songs to Lyrics by Dolmatovsky, Op 86[a]. Four Greek Songs[c]
[a]**Victoria Evtodieva** sop [b]**Natalia Biryukova** mez [c]**Mikhail Lukonin** bar [d]**Fyodor Kuznetsov** bass
Yury Serov pf
Delos DE3304 (71' · DDD · T/t)   Ⓕ●●

Complete Songs, Volume 2
Four Verses of Captain Lebyadkin, Op 146[c]. Seven Romances on Verses by Alexander Blok, Op 127[a]. Six Marina Tsvetayeva Poems, Op 143[b]. Preface to the Complete Edition of my Works and a Brief Reflection apropos of this Preface, Op 123[c]. Five Romances, Op-121[c]
[a]**Victoria Evtodieva** sop [b]**Liubov Sokolova** mez [c]**Fyodor Kuznetsov** bass [a]**Lidia Kovalenko** vn [a]**Irina Molokina** vc **Yury Serov** pf
Delos DE3307 (70' · DDD · T/t)   Ⓕ●●

Here are two CDs dedicated to some of the finest and most under-recorded song repertoire of the 20th century. Yury Serov is the presiding spirit; his sharply characterised piano playing radiating musical and cultural understanding, and his singers are first-rate.

The first volume is dedicated to the 1950s and contains several first recordings; few, if any, of the songs have ever appeared on CD before. Much of his music from this time is marked by various nuances of cheerfulness (tentative, determined, over-stated, but never as brattish as in his first maturity). Often these seem rather to belie his true nature. Indeed, only the four *Pushkin Monologues*, with their topics of suffering, sorrow, imprisonment and resistance, are easily recognisable as the voice of Shostakovich, the Chronicler and Conscience of his Times. Fyodor Kuznetsov is slightly unsteady of voice here, but he still manages to convey a quality of wise, noble weariness that rings absolutely true.

It's to the enormous credit of all four singers that most of the remaining songs come across not as mere sops to authority but as genuine attempts to take on new artistic challenges. Was it still possible to do something worthwhile with the homespun, soft-centred verses of Yevgeny Dolmatovsky? Many of Shostakovich's countrymen certainly thought he had done so, at least in respect of 'The Homeland is Listening' (first of the Op 86 Songs), since this was taken up as a signature tune for All-Union Radio and was actually sung by Yuri Gagarin during the first manned space-flight. Seemingly looking back to the tradition of Tchaikovsky, Rimsky-Korsakov and Rachmaninov, Shostakovich's two *Lermontov Romances* are gorgeously atmospheric and tender. By contrast his earthier *Greek* and *Spanish Songs* reflect his long-standing interest in poetry from other national traditions. Was his heart in them? Again you wouldn't find it hard to think so after hearing these fine performances.

Volume 2 gathers together the cycles from the last decade of Shostakovich's life, with the exception of his massive *Suite on Verses by Michelangelo*. While this repertoire isn't quite so rare as that on Volume 1, the performances are just as fine. In the Blok cycle – surely the finest songs on the disc – Evtodieva may not be the last word in subtlety, but she's still far preferable to the crude hectoring of Natalia Gerasimova on Chant du Monde. Given that the *Four Verses of Captain Lebyadkin* are otherwise unavailable, and the extraordinarily elusive *Six Marina Tsvetayeva Poems* can currently be obtained only in the composer's orchestrated version, this disc is again pretty well self-recommending.

Altogether this enterprise is a winner. The recording quality is good, though there's a slight 'pinginess' to the piano sound.

Four Verses of Captain Lebyadkin, Op 146[a]. Five Satires, Op 109[a]. Five Romances, Op 121[a] (all orch Tishchenko). Suite of Eight Waltzes (from the films The Gadfly, The Golden Hills, The Human Comedy, The Return of Maxim, Michurin, Pirogov, The First Echelon, Unity, 'Song of the Great Rivers'). Preface to the complete edition of my works and a brief reflection apropos of this preface, Op 123 (orch Desyatnikov)[a][b].

[a]**Sergei Leiferkus** bar [b]**Moscow State Chamber Choir; Russian Philharmonic Orchestra / Thomas Sanderling**
DG 477 6111GH (71' · DDD)　　　　Ⓕ Ⓑ→

Satire of various hues is the running theme on this disc devoted mainly to songs from Shosta-

kovich's embittered last 15 years. These have been orchestrated with a faultless grasp of the idiom by Boris Tishchenko, the composer's favourite pupil from the early 1960s, and in the case of the self-pillorying *Preface*, by Leonid Desyatnikov (a nice touch on his part to bring in the chorus just to sing the composer's name). In all of these Sergei Leiferkus bends and shapes his voice to the words and to the musical line so as to administer a double dose of causticity, and Sanderling makes the orchestra spit and curse to properly alarming effect. Recording quality is absolutely outstanding.

Cheryomushki

Cheryomushki (Cherry Town)
Olga Zabotkina sop Lidochka **Vladimir Vasilyev** bar Boris **Marina Khotuntseva** mez Masha **Grigori Bortnikov** bar Sasha **Svetlana Zhivankova** sop Lyusya **Vladimir Zemlyanikin** ten Sergei **Marina Polbentseva** mez Vava **Leningrad Philharmonic Orchestra / Nikolai Rabinovich**
Film director **Gerbert Rappaport**
Decca ⅅⅤⅅ 074 3138DH (87' · NTSC · 4:3 · PCM enhanced mono · 0)　　　　　　　　Ⓕ

Like *The Lady Macbeth of Mtsensk* a quarter of a century earlier, Shostakovich's one and only musical was a hit. Other similarities are hard to find. Unlike its bloody predecessor, *Cheryomushki* did not fall from official grace. In fact such was the breadth of esteem it enjoyed that it was reworked as a feature-film in 1963 – four years after its first staging – and broadcast on Soviet television at intervals for the rest of the composer's life. It was even, as Andrew Huth's helpful essay recalls, released in the US, under the title *Song over Moscow*, albeit it to rather less acclaim than in its homeland.

This anodyne little comedy about rehousing (to Moscow's 'Cherry-trees' suburbs) and petty corruption had enormous resonance for Russians in the Khrushchev and Brezhnev eras. Both the musical and the film were brilliantly engineered pieces of Socialist Realist spin, encouraging good-humoured acceptance of dire social conditions and continued belief in a 'bright future'. There is satire here, but only of the most cautious variety: with a smile, but no teeth.

Of its kind the film is admirably put together, and both audio and video scrub up well in its remastering for DVD. A good deal of innocuous fun is had on the part of the singer-actors, many of whom would have been familiar to Soviet audiences. The squally sopranos and boomy baritones may be an acquired taste, but the direction – both musical and visual – has the sharpness of pacing crucial to the genre.

Yet the film version is in no way a substitute for the musical itself. For one thing, probably little more than a third of the music Shostakovich 'composed' survives the translation of media (though completists should note that he actually added bits for the film as well). For another thing, the re-jigging of the scenario is extensive (but then so it would most likely have been in stage productions). For a full picture of Shostakovich's score we really need also a reissue of the sparky Melodiya LP recording conducted by Grigory Stolyarov. Meanwhile this DVD provides us with a fine document of Soviet culture in the late-Thaw years and some modest entertainment value over and above that.

Lady Macbeth of Mtsensk, Op 29

Lady Macbeth of the Mtsensk District
Galina Vishnevskaya *sop* Katerina Izmailova **Nicolai Gedda** *ten* Sergey Dubrovin **Dimiter Petkov** *bass* Boris Izmailov **Werner Krenn** *ten* Zinovy Borisovich Izmailov **Robert Tear** *ten* Russian peasant **Taru Valjakka** *sop* Aksinya **Martyn Hill** *ten* Teacher **Leonard Mroz** *bass* Priest **Aage Haugland** *bass* Police Sergeant **Birgit Finnila** *mez* Sonyetka **Alexander Malta** *bass* Old convict **Leslie Fyson** *ten* Milhand, Officer **Steven Emmerson** *bass* Porter **John Noble** *bar* Steward **Colin Appleton** *ten* Coachman, First foreman **Alan Byers** *bar* Second foreman **James Lewington** *ten* Third foreman **Oliver Broome** *bass* Policeman **Edgar Fleet** *ten* Drunken Guest **David Beaven** *bass* Sentry **Lynda Richardson** *mez* Female convict **Ambrosian Opera Chorus; London Philharmonic Orchestra / Mstislav Rostropovich**
EMI Great Recordings of the Century ③ 567776-2
(155' · ADD · T/t)   Ⓜ🅞🅑➤

Rostropovich's cast has no weak links to it. More importantly, he gives a full-blooded projection of the poignant lyricism that underlies the opera's brutality. Vishnevskaya's portrayal of Katerina is at times a bit too three-dimensional, you might think, especially when the recording, which favours the singers in any case, seems (because of her bright and forceful tone) to place her rather closer to you than the rest of the cast. But there's no doubt in her performance that Katerina is the opera's heroine, not just its focal character, and in any case Gedda's genially rapacious Sergey, Petkov's grippingly acted Boris, Krenn's weedy Zinovy, Mroz's sonorous Priest, and even Valjakka in the tiny role of Aksinya, all refuse to be upstaged.

The 'minor' parts are luxuriously cast from artists who may not have had the advantage of singing their roles on stage but have clearly relished building them into vivid portraits. The close focusing on the voices and the relative distancing of the orchestra into a warmer, more ample acoustic is a bit more noticeable on CD.

Lady Macbeth of the Mtsensk district
Galina Vishnevskaya *sop* Katerina Izmailova **Nicolai Gedda** *ten* Sergei **Dimiter Petkov** *bass* Boris Izmailov **Werner Krenn** *ten* Zinovi Izmailov **Robert Tear** *ten* Shabby Peasant **Taru Valjakka** *sop* Aksinya **Martyn Hill** *ten* Teacher **Leonard Andrzej Mróz** *bass* Priest **Aage Haugland** *bass* Police Sergeant **Birgit Finnilä** *mez* Sonyetka **Alexander Malta** *bass* Old Convict **Leslie Fyson** *ten* Millhand, Officer **Scott Emerson** *ten* Porter **John Noble** *bar* Steward **Colin**

Appleton *ten* Coachman, Foreman I **Alan Byers** *ten* Foreman II **James Lewington** *ten* Foreman III **Oliver Broome** *bass* Policeman **Edgar Fleet** *ten* Drunken Guest **David Beavan** *bass* Sentry **Linda Richardson** *mez* Woman Convict **Ambrosian Opera Chorus; London Philharmonic Orchestra / Mstislav Rostropovich**
Film director **Petr Weigl**
Carlton Entertainment 📀 ID5655CLDVD
(100' · Region 1)   Ⓕ🅞

Petr Weigl returns to form with this remarkable realisation of Shostakovich's scarifying drama. Filming in his native Czech Republic, as usual with actors lip-synching singers, he nevertheless brings its nasty and brutish setting to vivid life. Only the Siberian trek looks a little milder than traditional depictions, but it's accurate enough. The atmospheric photography of the Izmailov farm's barren, lamplit rooms and bathhouse adds a *verismo* dimension to the music's quasi-expressionist force. You really feel a place like this would breed adultery and impulsive murder. The soundtrack is the classic Rostropovich recording (reviewed left).

Its splendid pace and vivid playing suit the film, as do its lively effects, though it's substantially cut. The generally excellent actors do their best with the limitations of lip-synch, no doubt assisted by Czech's kinship with Russian. The Katerina is youngish, nervy and intense, tragically ripe pickings for Sergei's – and indeed her own – passion, but Vishnevskaya's maturely resonant dramatic soprano sits uneasily on her. The Sergei melds better with Gedda's bright tones to suggest the ruthless predator beneath the boyish charm, and Aksinya, old Izmailov and the Old Convict are splendidly portrayed.

The studio acoustic is too evident to make the outdoor scenes convincing. But they achieve their effect through the music none the less. Highly recommended.

The Lady Macbeth of Mtsensk
Eva-Maria Westbroek *sop* Katerina Izmailova **Christopher Ventris** *ten* Sergei **Vladimir Vaneev** *bass* Boris Izmailov **Ludovít Ludha** *ten* Zinovi Izmailov **Alexander Kravets** *ten* Shabby Peasant **Carole Wilson** *sop* Aksinya; Woman Convict **Valentin Jar** *ten* Teacher **Alexandre Vassiliev** *bass* Priest; Old Convict **Nikita Storojev** *bar* Police Sergeant **Lani Poulson** *contr* Sonyetka **Harry Teeuwen** *bar* Millhand **Netherlands Opera Chorus; Royal Concertgebouw Orchestra, Amsterdam / Mariss Jansons**
Stage director **Martin Kušej**
Opus Arte Ⓕ ② 📀 OA0965D (3h 56' · NTSC · 16:9 · PCM stereo and DTS 5.1 · 0)
Recorded live at Het Muziektheater, Amsterdam, in June 2006
Extra features include 'The Tragedy of Katerina Izmailova' – a documentary film by Reiner E Moritz, Illustrated Synopsis and Cast Gallery

Katerina Izmailova
Galina Vishnevskaya *sop* Katerina Izmailova

V **Tretyak** *ten* Sergei **Alexander Vedernikov** *bass*
Boris Izmailov **V Radziyevsky** *ten* Zinovi Izmailov
S **Strezhnev** *ten* Shabby peasant **V Reka** *contr*
Sonyetka
**Kiev Opera Chorus and Orchestra /
Konstantin Simeonov**
Film director **Mikhail Shapiro**
Decca Ⓕ 🆅 074 3137DH
(112' · NTSC · 2.35:1 · PCM mono · 0)
Filmed in 1966. Extra features include excerpts from
'Cheryomushki' and 'Shostakovich Against Stalin',
and Shostakovich Chronology

Shostakovich's operatic masterpiece is notoriously problematic to stage, especially if directors go back to the 1932 score and try to present the action realistically, as these days they almost all seem hell-bent on doing. In fact a whole book has been written (in Russian) about the absurdities that result, with suggestions offered for combining all three principal versions (the 1935 first published score was already substantially different from the original).

For Netherlands Opera, Martin Kušej comes up with at least one effective ploy, which is to show the seduction scene through stroboscopic lighting. That really does solve a problem and add theatrical frisson, all in one go. Otherwise he produces a dreary, concept-driven, vaguely updated mish-mash. His declared aim is to present 'the entire complex of Eros and sexuality when it is put under pressure from power and dependency structures', as if that theme is not already blindingly and deafeningly obvious. This he does through indulging an apparent obsession with underpants (even the police station scene features them) and by adding absurdities of his own, such as having the Shabby Peasant drag Zinovi's body to the police and telling them that said body is in the Izmailovs' cellar, while we can all see it on his back. Worst of all, having Katerina ultimately lynched by her fellow convicts destroys the glimmer of compassion that is essential to the final scene, as well as making another mockery of the sung text.

There is some good singing and Jansons obtains classy orchestral playing. Visually the casting is poor. The 'documentary film' is nothing more than a tedious retelling of the story through paraphrases from the director and his principal singers, intercut with illustrations from the production.

Mikhail Shapiro's 1966 film uses a cut version of Shostakovich's heavily revised score, prepared over several years but only finalised in 1963 and generally known as *Katerina Izmailova*. This excises the adult-rating sex and violence but otherwise has far more to be said in its favour than most people are inclined to these days. In its own early Brezhnev-era terms, the film itself is really rather fine. Vishnevskaya sings passionately, if unsubtly, and also acts well (her reminiscences of the whole filming process in her autobiography, *Galina*, make for compelling reading). For all the other roles the singing and acting are split, but in every case with superb results. Konstantin Simeonov paces the score

with an acuity that many other conductors, including Jansons, could learn from.

Even given the extra cuts that reduce the opera to feature-film length, and the painfully close miking of Vishnevskaya's in any case somewhat raucous voice, the sense of dramatic truthfulness is more overwhelming than in any staging with the exception of David Pountney's at English National Opera. Oh, for a DVD of that…

Jean Sibelius
Finnish 1865-1957

Sibelius studied in Helsinki from 1886 with Wegelius, also gaining stimulus there from Busoni, though at the same time he fostered ambitions as a violinist. In 1889 he went to Berlin to continue his composition studies with Becker, then after a year to Vienna under Goldmark and Fuchs. He returned to Helsinki in 1891 and immediately made a mark with his choral symphony Kullervo, though it took him another decade to establish a wholly consistent style and to emerge from the powerful influence of Tchaikovsky: important stages on the journey were marked by the Karelia suite, the set of four tone poems on the legendary hero Lemminkäinen (including The Swan of Tuonela), the grandiose Finlandia and the first two symphonies.

As these titles suggest, he was encouraged by the Finnish nationalist movement (until 1917 Finland was a grand duchy in the Russian empire), by his readings of Finnish mythology (Kullervo and Lemminkäinen are both characters from the Kalevala, which was to be the source also for subjects of later symphonic poems) and in some degree by the folk music of Karelia. But the most important stimulus would seem to have been purely musical: a drive towards continuous growth achieved by means of steady thematic transformation, and facilitated by supporting the main line very often with highly diversified ostinato textures instead of counterpoints. The singleness of purpose also has to do with the frequently modal character of Sibelius's harmony.

The Violin Concerto of 1903 was effectively a farewell to 19th-century Romanticism, followed by a pure, classical expression of the new style in the Symphony No 3. This was also a period of change in his personal life. In 1904 he bought a plot of land outside Helsinki and built a house where he spent the rest of his life with his wife and daughters, removed from the city where he had been prone to bouts of heavy drinking. Also, his music gained a large international following, and he visited England (four times in 1905-12) and the USA (1914). Symphony No 4, with its conspicuous use of the tritone and its austere textures, took his music into its darkest areas; No 5 brought a return to the heroic mould, developing the process of continuous change to the extent that the first movement evolves into the scherzo. But that work took him some time to get right (written in 1915, it was revised in 1916 and again in 1919), and after World War I he produced only four major works: the brilliant and elusive Symphony No 6; No 7, which takes continuity to the ultimate in its unbroken unfolding of symphonic

SIBELIUS VIOLIN CONCERTO – IN BRIEF

Ginette Neveu; Philharmonia Orchestra / Walter Susskind
Dutton CDEA5016 (71' · ADD)　　　Ⓢ**OO**
Among the pantheon of great fiddlers who have recorded Sibelius's Concerto, the tragically short-lived Ginette Neveu continues to occupy a special place of honour.

Jascha Heifetz; Chicago SO / Walter Haendl　Ⓗ
RCA 09026 61744-2 (69' · ADD)　　　Ⓜ**O**
As jaw-droppingly brilliant a display as you would expect from this giant of the violin. Heifetz's pioneering 1935 mono recording with Beecham is also definitely worth seeking out.

David Oistrakh; Stockholm PO / Sixten Ehrling
Testament SBT1032 (75' · ADD)　　　Ⓜ
The composer himself professed admiration for Oistrakh's wonderfully poised and serene interpretation. Sibelians and violin fanciers alike needn't hesitate.

Salvatore Accardo; London SO / Sir Colin Davis
Philips ② 446 160-2PM2 (146' · ADD)　　　Ⓜ
Accardo plays with great taste and assurance. Part of an all-Sibelius twofer which includes Sir Colin Davis's magnificent Boston accounts of Symphonies Nos 3, 6 and 7.

Kyung Wha Chung; London SO / André Previn
Decca download 4757734 (66' · ADD)　　Ⓜ**O**➡
Chung was at the outset of her career when she set down this touching, spontaneous-sounding recording, which is balanced to perfection by Decca's Kenneth Wilkinson.

Cho-Liang Lin; Philharmonia Orchestra / Esa-Pekka Salonen
Sony 07464 44548-2 (65' · DDD)　　　Ⓜ**OO**
Lin's immaculate, silk-spun version is second to none, and Salonen conducts with great sympathy both here and in the Nielsen Concerto which acts as a coupling.

Sergey Khachatryan; Sinfonia Varsovia / Emmanuel Krivine
Naive V4959 (70' · DDD)　　　Ⓕ
Armenian Sergey Khachatryan was just 15 when, in 2000, he became the youngest ever winner of the Sibelius Competition. He's already an exceptionally gifted musician, and this, his début concerto recording, has to be be heard.

Lisa Batiashvili; Finnish Radio Symphony Orchestra / Jukka Pekka Saraste
Sony Classical 88697 12936-2 (57' · DDD)　　Ⓕ➡
Enterprisingly coupled with Lindberg's new concerto, here's a Sibelius that emphasises the work's dreamier qualities, elegantly done.

development; the incidental music for *The Tempest*; and the bleak symphonic poem *Tapiola*. He lived for another three decades, but published only a few minor pieces; an eighth symphony may possibly have been completed and destroyed. His reputation, however, continued to grow, and his influence has been profound, especially on Scandinavian, English and American composers, reflecting both the traditionalism and the radical elements in his symphonic thinking.　　　GROVEmusic

---

Violin Concerto in D minor, Op 47

Violin Concerto (original 1903-4 version and final 1905 version)
Leonidas Kavakos vn
Lahti Symphony Orchestra / Osmo Vänskä
BIS BISCD500 (75' · DDD)　　　Ⓕ**OOO**➡

It's difficult to conceive of a masterpiece in any other form than it is. The impression the listener receives from Sibelius's Fifth Symphony – or *The Rite of Spring* or *La mer* – must convey what Schoenberg called the illusion of spontaneous vision. It's as if the artist had caught a glimpse of something that's been going on all the time, and has stretched out and effortlessly captured it. One of Sibelius's letters written to his friend Axel Carpelan in the autumn of 1914 puts it perfectly: 'God opens his door for a moment, and his orchestra is playing Sym 5'. But life isn't like that, and Sibelius worked for seven years (1912-19) before the Fifth Symphony reached its final form. He was nothing if not self-critical, and a number of his works underwent their birthpangs in public. The main theme came to him much earlier than 1903, and he recognised it for what it was, an inspired idea which remained unchanged. After its first performance in Helsinki in 1904 Sibelius decided to overhaul it. He realised the necessity to purify it, to remove unnecessary detail that impedes the realisation of a cogent structure. In its finished form, it was given in Berlin with Karl Halir as soloist and Richard Strauss conducting.

Listening to Sibelius's first thoughts played with great virtuosity and excellent taste by Leonidas Kavakos and the superb Lahti orchestra is an absorbing experience. Although it's a great pity that many interesting details had to go, there's no doubt that the movement gains structural coherence. The fewest changes are in the slow movement, which remains at the same length. As in the case of the Fifth Symphony, where the revision is far more extensive than it is here, the finished work tells us a great deal about the quality of Sibelius's artistic judgement, which is what makes him such a great composer.

This disc offers an invaluable insight ino the workings of Sibelius's mind. Kavakos and the Lahti orchestra play splendidly throughout, and the familiar concerto which was struggling to get out of the 1903-4 version emerges equally safely in their hands. Invaluable.

Sibelius Violin Concerto
Tchaikovsky Violin Concerto in D, Op 35
Kyung-Wha Chung *vn* **London Symphony Orchestra / André Previn**
Decca download 4757734 (66' · ADD)   Ⓕ**O**▶

If the vital test for a recording is that a performance should establish itself as a genuine one, not a mere studio run-through, Chung's remains a disc where both works leap out at you for their concentration and vitality, not just through the soloist's weight and gravity, expressed as though spontaneously, but through the playing of the LSO under Previn at a vintage period. The great melodies of the first two movements of the Sibelius are given an inner heartfelt intensity rarely matched, and with the finale skirting danger with thrilling abandon.

Chung's later Montreal version of the Tchaikovsky (also Decca) is rather fuller-toned with the tiny statutory cuts restored in the finale. Yet the very hint of vulnerability amid daring, a key element in Chung's magnetic, volatile personality, here adds an extra sense of spontaneity. This remains breathtaking playing, and the central slow movement, made to flow without a hint of sentimentality, has an extra poignancy. The Kingsway Hall sound, full and sharply focused, gives a sense of presence to match or outshine today's digital recordings.

Violin Concerto[a]. Symphony No 2 in D, Op 43[b]   Ⓗ
[a]**Ginette Neveu** *vn* [a]**Philharmonia Orchestra / Walter Susskind;** [b]**New York Philharmonic Symphony Orchestra / Sir John Barbirolli**
Dutton mono CDBP9733 (71' · ADD) Recorded 1940-46   Ⓢ**OO**

In Ginette Neveu's fêted account of Sibelius's Violin Concerto, the strength, passion and stamina of the solo playing is particularly admirable, though Walter Susskind's Philharmonia accompaniment is rather foursquare, especially in the finale. Heifetz and Beecham triumph every time. Still, EMI's famous recording is a fine memento of a fiery interpretation, and the solo line comes across with miraculous immediacy in this Dutton transfer – better, in fact, than the orchestra, which tends to retreat under a veil whenever the music quietens.

Barbirolli's impulsive New York recording of the Second Symphony burns bright and fast, but there are countless minor imprecisions that may irritate on repetition. A handful of slow but distant swishes suggests that Dutton's generally excellent refurbishment might have been based on an early LP transfer.

Symphonies

No **1** in E minor, Op 39 No **2** in D, Op 43 No **3** in C, Op 52 No **4** in A minor, Op 63 No **5** in E flat, Op 82 No **6** in D minor, Op 104 No **7** in C, Op 105

Complete Symphonies

Symphonies Nos 1-7. The Oceanides. Kuolema – Scene with cranes. Nightride and Sunrise[a]
City of Birmingham Symphony Orchestra, [a]**Philharmonia Orchestra / Sir Simon Rattle**
EMI ⑤ 764118-2 (267' · DDD)   Ⓜ**O**▶

Simon Rattle's reissued Sibelius cycle is now accommodated on four mid-price CDs (as opposed to five full-priced ones), losing among the fill-ups only Kennedy's well-played account of the concerto. The first movement of Symphony No 1 is impressive; its epic quality is splendidly conveyed. You may be less taken with the slow movement: the rather mannered closing bars, not particularly acceptable in the concert hall, are distinctly worrying on disc. The measured tempo of the *Scherzo* is also a problem: it's slower than the metronome marking and the movement lacks fire. However, *The Oceanides* is the finest on disc. In the Second Symphony, Rattle's first movement is again on the slow side and the Trio section of the *Scherzo* is pulled about. The Fourth and Seventh find him at his finest and the magnificent EMI recording is very richly detailed and well defined. The Fourth distils a powerful atmosphere in its opening pages; one is completely transported to its dark landscape with its seemingly limitless horizons. Only Beecham has surpassed Rattle in the slow movement.

Rattle's version of the Sixth is still among the best around, with tremendous grip and concentration. In both the Third and the Fifth he's equally impressive, although his handling of the celebrated transition in the first movement of the Fifth in his Philharmonia version is preferable (reviewed further on).

However, the inducement of *The Oceanides*, *Nightride and Sunrise* and an evocative account of the 'Scene with cranes' from *Kuolema* tips the scales in Rattle's favour.

Symphonies-Nos 1-7
Philharmonia Orchestra / Vladimir Ashkenazy
Double Decca ② 455 402-2DF2 & ② 455 405-2DF2 (144' & 150' · ADD/DDD) Recorded 1980-86   Ⓜ**OO**

Of all the cycles of Sibelius's symphonies recorded in recent years this is one of the most consistently successful. Ashkenazy so well understands the thought processes that lie behind Sibelius's symphonic composition just as he's aware, and makes us aware, of the development between the Second and Third Symphonies. His attention to tempo is particularly acute and invariably he strikes just the right balance between romantic languor and urgency. The Philharmonia plays for all it's worth and possesses a fine body of sound. The recordings are remarkably consistent in quality and effectively complement the composer's original sound world.

Symphonies – selected

Symphony Nos 1 & 7
Helsinki Philharmonic Orchestra / Leif Segerstam
Ondine ODE1007-2 (59' · DDD)   Ⓕ Ⓞ

This is an issue to rank alongside Segerstam's outstanding Helsinki PO coupling of the *Legends* and *Tapiola* (Ondine) in its pungent character and re-creative spark.

Segerstam's Seventh is well paced and keenly phrased, hitting real heights in the darkly boiling maelstrom beginning at 13 bars before fig L (9'53") and awe-inspiring culmination at fig Z (18'06"). His orchestra responds with zest and no mean poise. In fact, despite what sounds suspiciously like an edit at 15'50", this Seventh is one of the most imposing and highly charged of recent years. Bracing drama and a bold emotional scope are the keynotes to Segerstam's deeply pondered reading of the First Symphony. Assisted by alert and enthusiastic playing from his Helsinki band, he uncovers much illuminating detail within Sibelius' meticulous canvas, yet seldom to the detriment of the grander scheme. You may not agree with every interpretative decision, but Segerstam never sells the music short, revelling in its passion and often daring originality (sample the untamed fury of the *Allegro molto* material in the finale – nature red in tooth and claw). If Segerstam's strikingly pliable account lacks the thrust of, say, Vänskä's exhilarating Lahti SO performance, his Helsinki strings generate greater lyrical breadth.

True, the recording is very good rather than exceptional, but Segerstam is never dull and makes you listen.

Symphonies Nos 1 & 3ª
Hallé Orchestra / Mark Elder
Hallé CDHLL7514 (69' · DDD)
ªRecorded live in 2007   Ⓕ Ⓞ ➔

The rhetorical thrust Sibelius inherited from the music of Tchaikovsky is downplayed in Sir Mark Elder's studio recording of the First Symphony so as to expose those compositional details which make the invention inescapably Sibelian. Throughout Elder looks for significant detail, heightening string sawings more often viewed as accompanimental and even reintroducing touches of portamento redolent of the Barbirolli era. He seems fascinated by the way Sibelius can make his music appear to move at different speeds at different levels of an orchestral texture. What's missing is the adrenalin rush of a speed merchant like Anthony Collins or the über-Romantic throb of Leonard Bernstein.

With the Third Symphony (taped live) Elder is on firmer ground. Sibelius seems to have intended to give the music a self-consciously cool attitude anticipating that defined in 1920 by his friend Ferrucio Busoni as *Junge Klassizität* or the 'New Classicality'. Its freshness has a

studied air but who's to say it shouldn't have? The overall pacing is spacious with the finale fusing its various sections into a convincing proto-minimalist chug.

The back inlay quotes the claim by an unnamed *Guardian* critic (actually Tim Ashley) that the Hallé sound captures the composer's 'quintessential mix of frost and fire better than any other UK orchestra'. That may be pushing it. Still this is a thought-provoking pairing, finely recorded.

Symphonies – Nos 1 & 4
London Symphony Orchestra / Sir Colin Davis
LSO Live 🏵 LSO0601 (78' · DDD/DSD)
Recorded live in 2006 & 2008   Ⓑ Ⓞ ➔

Sir Colin Davis and the LSO pair the First and Fourth Symphonies as once they did for RCA. Davis cleaves to the heavier sound and interpretative subjectivity of an earlier age, fiercely engaged and, to some, a tad over-dressed. The First is archetypal latter-day Davis, vehemently alive and unafraid to slam on the brakes in the interests of heightened expressivity. Sir Colin's third commercial recording of this work is taken from live concerts, with the maestro caught humming along to the second movement's languishing Tchaikovskian melody.

The Fourth is even more impressive in its muscular directness, contemplating barren wastelands without the sugar-coating of Romanticism. Sir Colin's slow movement redefines slow, here with an awesome Brucknerian weight and dignity. His finale solves the dilemma posed by Sibelius's ambiguous request for glocken by doubling up on glockenspiel and tubular bells, an unusual effect that will catch the ears of ardent Sibelians. Davis's Boston version of No 4 for Philips was always highly regarded and, although LSO Live's SACD encoding cannot transform the impactful if rather shallow sound stage of the orchestra's home base, this second remake preserves an extraordinary evening. There are full notes as throughout what has been a distinguished series, well worth its modest asking price.

Symphony No 2ª. Pohjola's Daughterᵇ
London Symphony Orchestra / Sir Colin Davis
LSO Live 🏵 LSO0605 (59' · DDD/DSD)
Recorded live 2005/06   Ⓜ Ⓞ Ⓞ ➔

What Sir Colin Davis has to say about Sibelius's Second Symphony hasn't changed in substance since his first recording with the Boston Symphony (Philips), but the paragraphs now flow with ever more assured cadences. The life-and-death struggle of the second movement is underlined by two alternating tempi which Davis has not contrasted so dramatically before. Strong rhythmic underpinnings in the *Scherzo*, the highly contrasted trio and their eventual assimilation into the mighty onrush towards the finale: these all have a distinctively Beethovenian cast. The finale's jubilations justify their length and splendour, just about, with some generous *portamento* and care over the recitatives of the central, quieter section.

Pohjola's Daughter is an unusual but logical coupling, having its origins in the same Italian trip that brought the birthpangs of the Second Symphony. The tone-poem only saw the light five years after the symphony, however, and you could see it as the Yin to the finale's Yang, moving from the interrupted sonata-form processes of the symphony's first movement into still darker regions of creative despair – the Fourth Symphony looms on the horizon. You can sense this in Davis's conception, which prizes coherence over local colour.

Symphonies Nos 2 & 3
Lahti Symphony Orchestra / Osmo Vänskä
BIS BISCD862 (76' · DDD)   Ⓕ

The first issue in the Sibelius cycle by Osmo Vänskä and the Lahti orchestra (Symphonies Nos 1 and 4) made a strong impression. Indeed it holds its own against the most exalted competition. The present set doesn't disappoint either: these artists are right inside this music.

First, the Second Symphony where competition is stiffest, with Karajan, Barbirolli and Colin Davis leading a field that includes Szell (Philips), Kletzki (EMI) and Ormandy (Sony). Admittedly it would have been preferable if Vänskä had set a slightly brisker tempo at the very opening, though he's not alone in the pace he adopts. Karajan and Sir Colin are equally measured. Kajanus took 8'14" over this movement and Sibelius's first biographer, the scholar-critic Erik Furuhjhelm, records that the composer took it even faster! Perhaps the briskest of all modern performances is Neeme Järvi and the Gothenburg Symphony Orchestra. Vänskä's reading is both powerfully wrought and well thought-out though there are some self-conscious touches. He pulls back a little too much at the *tranquillo* marking in the first movement (track 1, 4'31"), of which one becomes too aware. Elsewhere he makes one think afresh about the score. The F sharp major tune on the strings in the slow movement marked *ppp* is played as a barely audible whisper (track 2, 4'40") and so exaggerated does it seem that the wind four bars later sound (and are) much louder than the marked *pianissimo*. But these are minor matters in a performance marked by feeling and eloquence.

It's good to see the Third Symphony doing so well on record. Vänskä sets the right tempo for the first movement and gets the right atmosphere. The opening bars do not build up as powerfully as they do in the hands of the LSO and Sir Colin, and it's possible to feel a certain want of momentum in the slow movement by their side and in comparison with Kajanus's pioneering set. On the whole, however, this is a very good performance, well paced and full of perceptive touches. The sound is excellent and, exceptionally wide-ranging.

Symphonies Nos 2ª & 5ᵇ
ªRoyal Philharmonic Orchestra;
ᵇHallé Orchestra / Sir John Barbirolli
Testament SBT1418 (77' · ADD). ᵇRecorded live at the Royal Albert Hall, London, on August 9, 1968
Ⓟ ⓞⓞ

In the pantheon of essential Sibelius recordings, Barbirolli's October 1962 account of the Second Symphony with the RPO deservedly occupies a place of honour. Recorded at Walthamstow for Reader's Digest with Charles Gerhardt producing and Decca's legendary Kenneth Wilkinson as balance engineer, it finds Sir John at his inspirational best in a reading which marries outsize but never wilful temperament to edge-of-seat spontaneity and keen poetic instinct. The experience is very much akin to attending a live concert of one's dreams.

The deceptively tricky slow movement is particularly remarkable for its daring flexibility of pulse and line yet never threatens to run aground, while the stirring finale (its big string tune so fervently sung both times round) will have you on your feet long before the end. If you haven't yet made this famous performance's acquaintance, don't hesitate for an instant.

The coupling is a Fifth Symphony with Barbirolli's beloved Hallé from the 1968 Proms which, in strength of personality and palpable depth of feeling, has a lot going for it. As on this team's 1966 EMI recording, the opening pages have exactly the right sense of awe-struck wonder and pregnant growth, and in the second movement it's a joy to hear Sibelius's delicious *pizzicato* writing "speak" with such clarity and eloquence. The first half of the finale has vitality and atmosphere in abundance, but you might crave a greater nobility of utterance in the towering epilogue. A commendably unbronchial audience roars its approval. Despite any minor quibbles, JB's many fans should be well pleased that Testament has salvaged such a typically vibrant display from the BBC vaults.

Symphonies Nos 4 & 7. Kuolema – Valse triste
Berlin Philharmonic Orchestra /
Herbert von Karajan
DG Galleria 439 527-2GGA-(66' · ADD) Recorded 1965-7   Ⓜ ⓞⓞ↝

Karajan recorded the Fourth Symphony three times, once in the 1950s with the Philharmonia and twice with the Berlin Philharmonic. The work obviously meant a great deal to him. He insisted on its inclusion in his very first concert on his appointment at the Berlin Philharmonic in the mid-1950s at a time when Sibelius's cause had few champions in Germany, so keen was he to stake its claim as one of the great symphonies of the day. Karajan's account has withstood the test of time as one of the most searching, profound and concentrated performances of this masterpiece, and its reappearance at mid price was very welcome. The Seventh is finer than his

SIBELIUS'S SYMPHONY NO 5 – IN BRIEF

London SO / Robert Kajanus　　　　　Ⓗ
Koch Historic 37133-2 (62' · ADD)　　　Ⓜ︎Ⓞ
Kajanus was one of the composer's favourite interpreters of his music. What this pioneering 1932 recording may lack in refinement is more than made up for by the subtlety and electric charge of the conductor's purposeful direction.

Boston SO / Serge Koussevitzky
Naxos Historical 8 110170 (71' · ADD)　Ⓢ▶
A performance of boundless integrity and pedigree, notable for its painstaking attention to detail and astonishing depth of string tone. The 1936 recording has impressive body and bloom in this new transfer.

Berlin PO / Herbert von Karajan
DG ② 457 748-2GOR2 (149' · ADD)　Ⓜ︎ⓄⓄ▶
Karajan always had the measure of this great symphony and this famous 1965 recording for DG is by common consent one of the pinnacles of his recorded legacy.

Philharmonia Orchestra / Vladimir Ashkenazy
Decca ② 455 405-2DF2 (150' · DDD)　Ⓜ︎
By no means a first choice artistically, but Decca's Kingsway Hall sound is just stunning. Excellently played, Ashkenazy's fresh-faced performance gives little cause for complaint.

City of Birmingham SO / Sir Simon Rattle
EMI 749717-2 (62' · DDD)　　　　　Ⓕ▶
Rattle's Birmingham remake is fascinatingly different from his 1982 Philharmonia predecessor in its fleeter, more animated manners. Coupled with Rattle's invigorating 1987 account of the Sibelius Concerto with Nigel Kennedy

Lahti SO / Osmo Vänskä
BIS BIS-CD800 (58' · DDD)　　　ⒻⓄⓄⓄ
This BIS issue is a model of rewarding enterprise, coupling the Fifth in the second of its three versions from 1915 with *En Saga* in its original 1892 guise. Exemplary performances and production values.

Iceland SO / Petri Sakari
Naxos 8 554377 (69' · DDD)　　　　Ⓢ▶
If the pennies are in short supply, then this likeable account from Reykjavík should prove just the ticket. Alert and enthusiastic playing from the Iceland SO under Petri Sakari, and very good sound to boot.

Swedish RSO / Sergiu Celibidache
DG 469 069-2GH4 (278' · ADD)　　　Ⓜ︎▶
Celibidache conducts an astounding account from 1971, full of fascinating detail. It comes as part of a four-CD Swedish RSO collection, but you can download selectively.

earlier Philharmonia version but doesn't enjoy quite the same classic status. Karajan's *Valse triste* is wonderfully seductive. Indispensable!

Symphonies Nos 4 & 7[a].　　　　　　Ⓗ
Pelléas et Mélisande, Op 46. Swanwhite, Op 54. The Tempest – Dance of the Nymphs. Tapiola, Op 112
Royal Philharmonic Orchestra / Sir Thomas Beecham
BBC Legends/IMG Artists ② BBCL4041-2 (139' · ADD)
Recorded live [a]1954, 1955. Includes Beecham on Sibelius, broadcast 1955　　　　　　　Ⓜ︎Ⓞ

In a broadcast concert to mark Sibelius's 90th birthday on December 8, 1955, the RPO under Sir Thomas Beecham (one of his doughtiest champions) played to a capacity Royal Festival Hall. The inclusion here of the British and Finnish national anthems, both stirringly done, recreates the necessary sense of occasion. In the delightful, too rarely encountered *Swanwhite* suite, from which Beecham omits the powerfully sombre fifth movement ('The Prince alone'), one may at first miss his characteristic concentration and charisma, but his leisurely, affectionate rendering grows on one. Orchestral discipline takes a dip with the Fourth Symphony, but far more disconcerting is the all-pervading air of loose-limbed impatience: the opening *Tempo molto moderato, quasi adagio* is wayward and fussy. There are glimpses of greatness in the third movement, as well as some effective dynamic emendations in the finale, but overall it's a curiously uninvolving display.

Only in the concert's second half does this legendary partnership really begin to show what it's capable of. The *Pelléas* suite distils a poetic enchantment (try the ineffably touching 'Mélisande') and tingling sense of atmosphere that not only make you forget about the maddeningly bronchial audience, but also act as a timely reminder that these artists' glorious studio recording dates from exactly the same period (EMI – unavailable at present). *Tapiola* is even finer, a performance of giant authority, devastating emotional candour and towering humanity – indeed Beecham's most powerful *Tapiola* currently available. As an encore, the fetching 'Dance of the Nymphs' from *The Tempest* is delectably done. As a substantial bonus there's a radiantly moving Sibelius Seventh from the 1954 Proms, and a personable, at times entertainingly scatty talk on Sibelius and his music by the inimitable maestro recorded for the BBC's Third Programme two weeks before that 90th-birthday concert. A mandatory purchase for the frequently spellbinding contents of disc 2 alone.

Symphony No 5 (original 1915 version). En saga (original 1892 version)
Lahti Symphony Orchestra / Osmo Vänskä
BIS BISCD800 (58' · DDD)　　　　ⒻⓄⓄⓄ

Every so often a CD appears which, by means of some interpretative insight, changes our view of a piece of music. This disc changes our whole perspective in a wholly different sense, for it gives us a glimpse of two familiar masterpieces in the making. Sibelius struggled with the Fifth Symphony for almost seven years from about 1912 until it reached its definitive form in 1919. Although the finished score of the first version doesn't survive, the orchestral material does, so it was not difficult to reconstruct the score.

To study how the two scores differ is to learn something important about the creative process and it's this mystery that makes this disc imperative listening – and not just for Sibelians. The four-movement 1915 score has a more complex harmonic language than the final score and so it provides a missing link, as it were, between the Fourth Symphony and the definitive Fifth. The opening horn motive has yet to emerge, and the finale's coda has yet to acquire its hammer-blow chords. And in between you'll find that the various themes, some distinctly recognisable, others taking off in totally unexpected directions and charting unknown regions.

The version of *En saga* with we're familiar with doesn't come between the *Kullervo* Symphony and the *Karelia* music, but from 1901, between the First and Second Symphonies and was made for Busoni.

The original offers fascinating material for comparison: there's a brief glimpse of Bruckner, whose work he had encountered in Vienna a year or two earlier, and the orchestral writing, though not always as polished as in the later version, still has flair. Praise to the Lahti orchestra and their fine conductor, and the excellent and natural balance.

Symphonies Nos 6 & 7. Tapiola, Op 112
Lahti Symphony Orchestra / Osmo Vänskä
BIS BISCD864 (68' · DDD)   ⓕ**OO**

The Lahti orchestra bring total dedication to these great scores, and Osmo Vänskä is a Sibelian of substance. With this account of the Sixth and Seventh he brings his survey to a triumphant conclusion. Indeed this is every bit as impressive as the First and Fourth. To the Sixth Symphony he brings total concentration: a serene slow movement but a very fast Scherzo and tautly held-together finale. The Seventh is finely conceived and paced and though the Lahti orchestra aren't the equal of the Finnish RSO for Saraste or the Helsinki PO for Berglund (both conductors fine Sibelians), directed by Vänksä they give the more compelling and convincing performances. The *Tapiola* is thrilling: atmospheric and powerfully built up and though it doesn't displace Karajan, Koussevitzky or Beecham, it's a measure of its splendour and power – and the terror it evokes – that it invites only the most exalted comparisons. In the Sixth Symphony one wouldn't want to be without either Sir Colin Davis, the Beecham or any of the Karajan versions, and for the Seventh the roll-call must certainly include Koussevitzky's seminal

account, as well as both Sir Colin's Boston and LSO accounts.

This is an impressive issue.The recorded sound is in the first flight, and there are excellent notes by Andrew Barnett.

Symphonies Nos 6 & 7.
The Tempest – Suite No 2, Op 109
Iceland Symphony Orchestra / Petri Sakari
Naxos 8 554387 (71' · DDD)   Ⓢ➤

A most enjoyable conclusion to Petri Sakari's Sibelius symphony cycle. Sakari's Sixth impresses by dint of its unpretentious honesty and quiet cogency. As on previous instalments within this series, the Icelanders respond with a keen fervour as contagious as it's heartwarming. Their woodwind roster comprises an especially personable bunch, and if the strings inevitably lack that very last ounce of tonal clout and sheer composure provided by, say, Karajan's Berlin Philharmonic or the San Francisco Symphony under Blomstedt – to name but two of the strongest rivals – there's no missing the touching expressive warmth they bring to the work's transcendental closing pages. In Sakari's hands both outer movements develop real fire and purpose, and he uncovers plenty of happy detail along the way – the distinctive colouring of the bass clarinet being one of this performance's chief pleasures.

Sakari's Seventh, too, is very good indeed, patient and imaginative in the manner of Vänskä, or Sanderling's much underrated, irresistibly sinewy 1974 recording with the Berlin Symphony Orchestra. Perhaps the Iceland Symphony's principal trombonist could have been just a touch more assertive for that heroic initial solo six bars after fig C, and the timpanist appears to enter a bar late just before fig E, but the only sizeable niggle concerns Sakari's not-quite-seamless handling of that tricky *Poco a poco affrettando* transition passage into the *Vivacissimo* section beginning at fig J, itself not entirely free of a certain breathless fluster. All this means that Sakari's conception as a whole isn't as thrillingly inevitable an experience as Koussevitzky's, Maazel's or Boult's masterly 1963 concert relay with the RPO. That said, Sakari builds the shattering *Largamente* climax at fig Z superbly, and the closing bars are exceptionally fine. Not a front-runner, perhaps, but no mean achievement all the same. Well worth investigating at Naxos price.

Additional recommendations

Symphony No 7
Coupled with: **Schubert** Symphony No 8. **Bizet** Jeux
d'enfants – excerpts. **Ravel** Daphnis et Chloé
Royal Philharmonic Orchestra / Boult
BBC Music Legends/IMG Artists BBCL4039-2
(75' · ADD)   Ⓜ
    Boult iasn't a conductor you'd immediately
    associate with Sibelius, but this honest reading
    forms part of a highly enticing concert.
Symphonies Nos 1, 2 , 4 & 5

Boston Symphony Orchestra / C Davis
Philips Duo ② 446 157-2PM2 (154' · ADD)   Ⓜ
  Davis's late-1970s Boston Sibelius cycle has many
  admirers, and should entrance a new generation of
  music-lovers in this competitive reissue.

Symphonies Nos 3, 6 & 7
Coupled with: Violin Concerto. Finlandia. Tapiola.
Legends, 'Lemminkaïnen Suite', Op 22
Accardo vn **Boston Symphony Orchestra; London
Symphony Orchestra / C Davis**
Philips Duo 446 160-2PM2 ② (146' · ADD)   Ⓜ
  The second half of the cycle. The symphonies have
  a wonderful sheen and the couplings are
  particularly generous.

Symphony No 2
Coupled with: Romance for Strings
Gothenburg Symphony Orchestra / Järvi
BIS CD252 (DDD)   Ⓕ
  This is a performance full of sinew and fire. Fast
  and vigorous in the first movement, the orchestra
  play with tremendous commitment.

Symphonies Nos 4-7.
Coupled with: The Swan of Tuonela. Tapiola
Berlin Philharmonic Orchestra / Karajan
DG The Originals ② 457 748-2GOR2 (ADD)   Ⓜ

Symphonies Nos 5 & 6
Coupled with: Legends, 'Lemminkaïnen Suite', Op 22
Berlin Philharmonic Orchestra / Karajan
DG Galleria 439 982-2GGA (69' · ADD)   Ⓜ
  Karajan's Sibelius is very compelling and the BPO
  have the full measure of the music

Symphonies Nos 1 & 3
Iceland Symphony Orchestra / Sakari
Naxos 8 554102 (68' · DDD)   Ⓢ
  Well worth considering for those on a budget.
  Good, committed playing from the Iceland SO.

Symphonies Nos 6 & 7
Coupled with: Nightride and Sunrise
Berlin Symphony Orchestra / Sanderling
Berlin Classics 0092 812BC (70' · DDD)   Ⓜ
  A coupling that enjoys quite a following among
  informed Sibelians. By no means mainstream but
  worth exploring.

En saga, Op 9

En saga, Op 9. Night Ride and Sunrise, Op 55. The
Dryad, Op 45 No 1. Dance Intermezzo, Op 45 No 2.
Pohjola's Daughter, Op 49. The Bard, Op 64. The
Oceanides, Op 73
Lahti Symphony Orchestra / Osmo Vänskä
BIS BIS-CD1225 (76' · DDD)   Ⓕ❶❶❶

Ⓖ Anyone who has already encountered
    the Lahti/Vänskä partnership in Sibel-
    ius will know to expect performances of
great vitality and freshness. And the expectation
is fully met – perhaps even surpassed; in these
tone poems he simply allows his profound grasp
of musical inner workings to dictate the course

of events. The trenchant Lahti strings, the
ecstatically floating woodwind and the rasping
brass all play their part. But while their contributions are gripping in their own right, they're
the more impressive for being so precisely
placed at the service of the music's larger-scale
unfolding.
  Each of the longer works feels as though
composer and performers alike have imagined
them in one huge mental breath. Vänskä
knows exactly when and how much to hold
back, when to push on, and, crucially, when
simply to stand back and let the music tick over
to the beat of some higher rhythm. The same
sense of inevitability informs the more compact masterpieces – *The Dryad* and the extraordinarily cryptic *The Bard*. Only the *Dance-
Intermezzo*, companion piece to *The Dryad*, is
in any way negligible.
  All the other tone poems have been recorded
many times over, but rarely with such a consistent feeling of idiomatic rightness. (Vänskä
himself has recorded the 1892 original version
of *En Saga* as well – coupled with the original
Fifth Symphony on a *Gramophone* Award-winning set, reviewed under Symphony No 5 – and
a fascinating contrast it makes with the more
compact 1902 revision offered here.) BIS's
recording is of demonstration quality. An outstanding release.

Additional recommendations

En Saga

Coupled with: Tapiola. The Bard. The Oceanides.
Pohjola's Daughter
Iceland Symphony Orchestra / Sakari
Naxos 8 555299 (70' · DDD)   Ⓢ➔
  En Saga unfolds with enviable naturalness and
  vigour, yet the dusky mystery of the coda is also
  very well conveyed. *Tapiola*, too, receives a
  stimulating interpretation, with a gripping climax
  to its famous storm.

Karelia Suite, Op 11

Karelia Suite. Incidental music – King Christian II;
Pelleas and Melisande (all original versions)
Anna-Lisa Jakobsson mez **Raimo Laukka** bar
Lahti Symphony Orchestra / Osmo Vänskä
BIS CD918 (78' · DDD · T/t)   Ⓕ

Sibelius supplied four numbers for the February
1898 Helsinki premiere of Adolf Paul's historical drama *King Christian II* – the 'Minuet', 'The
Fool's Song', 'Elegy' and 'Musette' – and these
eventually took their place in the five-movement
concert suite alongside the 'Nocturne', 'Serenade' and 'Ballade' which the composer completed the same summer. The street music of the
'Musette' is simply delightful in its original garb
without added strings, and in both the 'Serenade' and 'Ballade' Vänskä uncovers strong
thematic and stylistic links with the almost

exactly contemporaneous First Symphony. The defiant quality these fine artists bring to 'The Fool's Song' (eloquently delivered by Raimo Laukka) is also very likeable. Music-making of refreshing perception and meticulous sensitivity similarly illuminates this first complete recording of Sibelius's original incidental music for a 1905 production of Maeterlinck's symbolist play (the venue was again Helsinki's Swedish Theatre). There are 10 numbers in all.

The performance of the *Karelia Suite* in its original scoring (which acts as a splendid curtain-raiser here) has been compiled from Vänskä's complete recording of the original *Karelia* music. Both outer movements have a real sense of pageantry about them (Vänskä directs with exhilaratingly clean-limbed swagger), though there are certain reservations about his occasional predilection for exaggerated and affected *pianopianissimos*. Thus, at around 3'30" in the central 'Ballade' (track 2), the dynamic level drops almost below the threshold of audibility and has you rushing to boost the volume control (Vänskä repeats this trick twice in the *King Christian II* 'Elegy', and towards the end of the final number in *Pelléas*). For optimum results, therefore, playback needs to be higher than many listeners may think reasonable. That said, the engineering is quite spectacularly truthful throughout and there's no doubt that this is an unusually absorbing collection.

Legends (Lemminkäinen Suite), Op 22

Legends. En Saga, Op 9
**Swedish Radio Symphony Orchestra /
Mikko Franck**
Ondine ODE953-2 (74' · DDD)　　　Ⓕ**ⓞⓞ**🄳▸

Mikko Franck presides over the most intrepidly individual and pungently characterful performance of the Lemminkäinen *Legends* since Leif Segerstam's 1995 Helsinki PO account for this same label. Clocking in at an eyebrow-raising 53'48" overall, Franck's conception evinces an unhurried authority, a generous expressive scope and a richly stocked imagination remarkable in one so young.

Lemminkäinen and the Maidens of the Island unfolds in especially gripping fashion here. Even more than Segerstam, Franck takes an extraordinarily long-breathed, flexible view of this heady tableau, imparting an unashamedly sensual voluptuousness to the secondary material in particular. It's a risky, impulsive approach, but one that pays high dividends in terms of intoxicating sweep, brazen ardour and, well, sheer daring. Both *The Swan of Tuonela* (which, in a refreshing change from the norm these days, Franck places second, according to Sibelius's final wishes) and *Lemminkäinen in Tuonela* combine dark-hued grandeur with tingling atmosphere, the latter's haunting A minor central episode handled with particular perception. True, *Lemminkäinen's Return* lacks something in animal excitement, but its unruffled sense of

SIBELIUS TAPIOLA – IN BRIEF

Helsinki PO / Leif Segerstam
Ondine ODE852-2　　　　　　　Ⓕ**ⓞ**
The Helsinki orchestra have just the perfect sound for Sibelius, and naturally they play with a total grasp of the idiom. Segerstam can be a willful Sibelian, but he unfurls this glorious piece with a winning simplicity.

Royal Philharmonic Orchestra / Sir Thomas 🄷
Beecham
BBC Legends BBCL4041-2　　　　　Ⓕ**ⓞ**
Recorded in 1955 this shows what a great Sibelian Beecham was: this is his finest version of *Tapiola*, an interpretation of colossal emotional weight and scope.

Lahti Symphony Orchestra / Osmo Vänskä
BIS BIS-CD864　　　　　　　　Ⓕ**ⓞⓞ**
Joining the Sixth and Seventh Symphonies, Vanska's *Tapiola* receives an extraordinarily intense performance with fine playing from his loyal Lahti band. Top-class BIS sound.

Philharmonia Orchestra / Vladimir Ashkenazy
Decca 452 576-2DF2　　　　　　Ⓜ**ⓞ**🄱▸
A really tremendous performance that gives this atmospheric work a colossal emotional charge. Ashkenazy has clearly absorbed much of the Finnish spirit oin his many visits to the country and it certainy shows in this powerful vision of *Tapiola*.

Boston SO / Sir Colin Davis
Philips 446 160-2PM2　　　　　　Ⓜ🄱▸
Paired with Symphonies Nos 5 and 6, this is Sibelius playing with a strong and loyal following: the Boston orchestra have a really alluring sound in this music and Davis is totally in his element.

**Berlin Philharmonic Orchestra /
Herbert von Karajan**
DG 457 748-2GOR2　　　　　　Ⓜ**ⓞ**🄱▸
Coupled with Symphonies Nos 4-7 (including a magnificent No 6), this *Tapiola* from the mid-1960s remains for many unsurpassed evoking the mood of the Nordic forests. Glorious, rich tone from the BPO

Gothenburg SO / Neeme Järvi
DG 475 634-2GH　　　　　　　Ⓕ🄱▸
Neeme Järvi is an excellent guide in the music of Sibelius, and with his superb Gothenburg orchestra on fine form, this is an impressive performance.

Iceland Symphony Orchestra / Petri Sakari
Naxos 8 555299　　　　　　　　Ⓢ🄱▸
A fine collection of shorter Sibelius works contains this excellent performance of *Tapiola*, with a particularly gripping account as the storm reaches its powerful climax.

purpose, rhythmic spring and sinewy, clean-cut textures serve up plenty of food for thought none the less.

The Legends are preceded by an uncommonly fresh *En Saga*, brimming with watchful sensitivity and interpretative flair, and once again studded with revelatory detail. Throughout, the Swedish RSO responds with heartwarming application and genuine enthusiasm, audibly galvanised by Franck's fervent, always invigorating direction. The engineering, too, is very good, without perhaps being absolutely in the top flight.

An auspicious recording début, then, from a young artist of clearly prodigious potential.

Lemminkäinen in Tuonela, Op 22 No 3 (reconstructed 1896 version, ed Davis). Humoresque, Op 87 No 1 (first version)[a]. In memoriam, Op 59 (two versions). Two Serious Melodies, Op 77[b]. Three Pieces, Op 96. Presto for Strings
[a]**Jaakko Kuusisto** vn [b]**Marko Ylönen** vc
Lahti Symphony Orchestra / Osmo Vänskä
BIS BIS-CD1485 (78' · DDD)　　　Ⓕ〇

The centrepiece of this fine collection is a reconstruction of *Lemminkäinen in Tuonela* as it sounded at the April 1896 Helsinki premiere. When Sibelius reworked the score in 1939, he excised at least 108 bars, including an impressive 32-bar introduction and a hefty chunk of the ghostly A minor central episode.

Annotator Andrew Barnett tells us that the Op 77 *Two Serious Melodies*, for violin and orchestra, were first heard in March 1916 in Sibelius's arrangement for cello. Soloist Marko Ylönen is a rapt proponent of this headily lovely diptych, while the Lahti SO's leader Jaakko Kuusisto is a model of sensitive agility in the first version (from 1917) of the enchanting *Humoresque* No 1 in D minor.

The *Three Pieces* contain a fetching 18th-century pastiche, 'Autrefois', which incorporates a setting for soprano and contralto of a poem by Hjalmar Procopé. Bookending the programme are the original and revised versions (from 1909 and 1910 respectively) of the funeral march In memoriam, a stark yet noble (and at times intriguingly Mahlerian) processional to remind us that the uncompromising Fourth Symphony was not far off.

Vänskä and his bright-eyed Lahti band are on irreproachable form, and the BIS production crews have come up trumps once again with resplendently natural sound.

Legends. Karelia Suite, Op 11. Finlandia, Op 26
Iceland Symphony Orchestra / Petri Sakari
Naxos 8 554265 (73' · DDD)　　　Ⓢ〇▷

Most impressive. In its keen intelligence, fiery snap and thrust, Petri Sakari's account of the four *Legends* proves more than a match for the finest. The Iceland SO may not be world-beaters, but they respond to their thoughtful young

Finnish maestro's illuminating direction with clean-limbed zest and commitment to the cause (their winds are an especially personable bunch).

Perhaps the highlight of the new set is *Lemminkäinen in Tuonela*, which, like Segerstam and Salonen before him, Sakari places second (reverting to the composer's original scheme), and where he distils a relentless concentration and pin-sharp focus (only Segerstam is more gripping in this brooding essay). No one should miss out on the heady opulence of Ormandy's magnificent Philadelphia strings in those glorious singing lines of *Lemminkäinen and the maidens of the island*, but the Icelanders play their hearts out, and anyway Sakari gives a dramatic reading of bold contrasts and strong symphonic cohesion. No grumbles, either, about *The Swan of Tuonela* or *Lemminkäinen's Homeward Journey* which is firmly controlled, dashingly detailed and genuinely exciting (as opposed to merely excitable).

Sakari's rewarding *Legends* comes very near the top of the heap alongside (though, ultimately, not ahead of) Segerstam, Saraste and Ormandy. In the popular couplings, Sakari's unhackneyed approach once again pays dividends, though his unusually brisk (and ever-so-slightly hectic) tempo for the main portion of the *Karelia* Suite's opening Intermezzo isn't always convincing . None the less, this is quite a bargain. Eminently pleasing sound, too: free of gimmickry and tonally very true.

Legends. Tapiola, Op 112
Helsinki Philharmonic Orchestra / Leif Segerstam
Ondine ODE852-2 (70' · DDD)　　　Ⓕ〇

The four *Legends* first began to surface in Sibelius's mind in 1893, at the same time as he was working on his *Kalevala* opera, *The Building of the Boat*, the prelude to which became *The swan of Tuonela*. It isn't the only thing from the opera that found its way into the *Legends*. The lovely A-minor idea for muted strings in the middle section of *Lemminkäinen in Tuonela* is also among the sketches, where Sibelius scribbled over it the words, 'the Maiden of Death'. In the opera she would have rowed Väinämöinen across the river to Tuonela. In the tone-poem she symbolises the very opposite, the loving mother whose ministrations return Lemminkäinen to life. In 1954 Sibelius reversed the order of the inner movements so that *The swan* preceded *Lemminkäinen in Tuonela*. Segerstam disregards the composer's wishes and places them in the old order; there's a case for this – you otherwise have two highly dramatic pieces (*Lemminkäinen in Tuonela* and *Lemminkäinen's Homeward Journey*) placed alongside each other. Segerstam gets very good results from the Helsinki orchestra, which responds with a keen enthusiasm that's inspiriting. The performance is free from excessive mannerisms, and his account of *Tapiola* is very impressive. He tellingly evokes the chilling terrors and awesome majesty of the Nordic forest.

Finlandia, Op 26

Finlandia, Op 26ª. Karelia Suite, Op 11ª. Tapiola,
Op 112ª. En Sagaª. Luonnotar, Op 70ª. Pohjola's
Daughter, Op 49ᵇ. Nightride and Sunrise, Op 55ᵇ.
Legends, 'Lemminkäinen Suite', Op 22ᵇ
ªPhilharmonia Orchestra / Vladimir Ashkenazy;
ᵇOrchestra de la Suisse Romande / Horst Stein
Double Decca ② 452 576-2DF2 (DDD/ADD)
ªRecorded 1980-85　　　　　　　　　Ⓜ❍

Ashkenazy makes a superb job of *Finlandia*,
which boasts some of the most vibrant, powerful
brass sounds on disc.

More than 30 years separate *En Saga* and *Tapiola*, yet both works are quintessential Sibelius.
The latter is often praised for the way Sibelius
avoided 'exotic' instruments, preferring instead
to draw new and inhuman sounds from the more
standard ones; and the former is, in many ways,
just as striking in the way the orchestration
evokes wind, strange lights, vast expanses and
solitude. Both works suggest a dream-like
journey: *En Saga* non-specific, though derived
from Nordic legend; *Tapiola* more of an airborne nightmare in, above and around the
mighty giants of the Northern forests inhabited
by the Green Man of the Kalevala, the forest god
Tapio (the final amen of slow, bright major
chords brings a blessed release!). Ashkenazy's
judgement of long-term pacing is very acute; the
silences and shadows are as potent here as the
wildest hurricane. And Decca's sound allows
you to visualise both the wood and the trees;
every detail of Sibelius's sound world is caught
with uncanny presence, yet the overall orchestral image is coherent and natural.

Night Ride and Sunrise, Op 55

Night Ride and Sunrise, Op 55. Pan and Echo, Op 53.
Two Pieces, Op 45. Kuolema – Valse triste, Op 44
No 1; Scenes with Cranes, Op 44 No 2. Canzonetta,
Op 62a; Valse romantique, Op 62b. Belshazzar's
Feast, Op 51 – Oriental Procession; Solitude; Night
Music; Khadra's Dance
New Zealand Symphony Orchestra / Pietari
Inkinen
Naxos 8 570763 (65' · DDD)　　　　　　Ⓢ🢂

As on this partnership's previous Sibelius
anthology (see page 1076) the New Zealand SO
respond with conspicuous poise and application
for their Finnish chief. Inkinen's readings, too,
show a real feeling for the idiom: phrases are
shaped – and textures sifted – with fastidiousness
and imagination, and he brings an abundant
recreative flair and cogent grip to the task in
hand, not least in *Night Ride and Sunrise*, whose
elusive structure he binds together with a
sure-footed skill that belies his tender years.
Moreover, Inkinen's luminous account of the
suite from *Belshazzar's Feast* will have you questioning why such an appealing and highly evocative score is so seldom performed.

Elsewhere, rarities such as *Pan and Echo* and
The Dryad emerge with a dewy freshness and
ear-pricking sophistication that prompt a radical
reappraisal. Inkinen even manages to breathe
new life into the Op 44 diptych from the 1903
incidental music for *Kuolema* (the ubiquitous
'Valse triste' and bleakly beautiful 'Scene with
Cranes'), and his alchemy extends to the two
altogether more mundane numbers that Sibelius
added for a 1911 revival of the play.

A disc, then, guaranteed to give pretty much
unbridled pleasure. Naxos's sound combines
helpful transparency with plenty of ambient
glow.

Humoresques, Opp 87 and 89

Humoresques Nos 1-6, Opp 87 & 89. Two Serenades,
Op 69. Two Pieces, Op 77. Overture in E. Ballet scene
Dong-Suk Kang vn **Gothenburg Symphony
Orchestra / Neeme Järvi**
BIS BIS-CD472 (62' · DDD)　　　　　　Ⓕ❍

The music for violin and orchestra here is marvellously rewarding and gloriously played. The
six *Humoresques*, Opp 87 and 89 come from the
same period as the Fifth Symphony, at a time
when Sibelius was toying with the idea of a second violin concerto, and some of the material of
the *Humoresques* was possibly conceived with a
concerto in mind. Sibelius wrote that these radiant pieces convey something of 'the anguish of
existence, fitfully lit up by the sun', and behind
their outward elegance and charm, there's an
all-pervasive sadness. This is even more intense
in the *Serenades*, which are glorious pieces and
quintessential Sibelius. Dong-Suk Kang is an
outstanding player. His impeccable technique
and natural musical instinct serve this repertoire
well and he seems to have established an excellent rapport with Järvi and the Gothenburg
orchestra. The two fill-ups are juvenilia and are
only intermittently characteristic. The Overture
is very much in his *Karelia* idiom, though they're
of undoubted interest to all Sibelians. The
recording up to BIS's usual high quality.

Pelleas and Melisande, Op 46

Cassazione, Op 6. Pelleas and Melisande. Suite
mignonne, Op 98a. Suite champêtre, Op 98b.
Suite caractéristique, Op 100. Presto
Tapiola Sinfonietta / Tuomas Ollila
Ondine ODE952-2 (56' · DDD)　　　　　　Ⓕ

Don't let the low opus number hoodwink you:
Cassazione dates from 1904 and was first given
under Sibelius's baton at the same Helsinki concert as the premiere of the first version of the
Violin Concerto. Revised the following year but
never published, it's well worth hearing, containing as it does echoes of both *Pelleas and
Melisande* and the Second Symphony's finale.
The dashing *Presto* began life as the third movement of Sibelius's Op 4 String Quartet in B flat

of 1889-90, and was subsequently transcribed for string orchestra in 1894. The three suites date from 1921-2. True, the *Suite caractéristique* serves up a pretty thin brew, but both the *Suite mignonne* and *Suite champêtre* contain their fair share of felicities and are delightfully scored.

These performances from Tuomas Ollila and the Tapiola Sinfonietta evince a bracing, unsentimental thrust and high degree of technical finish, though some will crave more in the way of affectionate charm and tingling atmosphere. However, it's in the *Pelleas and Melisande* incidental music that these newcomers truly throw down the gauntlet. There's no hint of the customary portentous grandeur in Ollila's 'At the Castle Gate', a nervy urgency that resurfaces with a vengeance in 'Melisande at the Spinning Wheel' and the ensuing 'Entr'acte'. Elsewhere, those screaming winds and *sul ponticello* strings at the heart of 'At the Seashore' set one's teeth on edge, while textures throughout are uncommonly transparent. What's missing is any real sense of poignancy or pathos: 'The Death of Melisande' is very cool, the characteristically bleached string timbre emphasising the disconcertingly pristine, self-conscious mood. An intriguing and intelligent re-think, then, but not to all tastes (anyone brought up on, say, Beecham will be in for a shock). Crystal-clear, slightly clinical sound.

Scènes historiques – I, Op 25; II, Op 66. King Christian II, Op 27 – Nocturne; Elegie; Musette; Serenade; Ballade; Menuetto
New Zealand Symphony Orchestra / Pietari Inkinen
Naxos 8 570068 (63' · DDD)   Ⓢ**O**➔

Recordings of this entrancing repertoire are always welcome, particularly when they are as polished and involving as this. Pietari Inkinen (*b*1980) has recently taken up the reins as the NZSO's music director and, on this showing, is a talent to watch. Not only does he draw some high-quality, notably zestful playing from his new charges, he directs both sets of *Scènes historiques* with such keen temperament, abundant character and sensitivity to texture and nuance that they come up sounding strikingly newminted. Indeed, his generously expressive and pliable shaping of the ravishing secondary material in 'Festivo' manages to stoke memories of Beecham's indelible RPO rendering from the early 1950s – and that's saying something!

In the *King Christian II* suite, Inkinen and his responsive band easily hold their own against some stiff competition. There's some particularly eloquent string-playing in the achingly wistful 'Elegy' (where Inkinen distils a hushed intimacy that is deeply touching), while the dashing helterskelter ride of the concluding 'Ballade' has both invigorating spring and bite to commend it.

Boasting handsomely true and atmospheric sound, this collection certainly merits the attention of all Sibelians and represents enticing value at bargain price.

Violin Works

Five Pieces, Op 81. Novelette, Op 102. Five Danses champêtres, Op 106. Four Pieces, Op 115. Three Pieces, Op 116
Nils-Erik Sparf *vn* **Bengt Forsberg** *pf*
BIS BIS-CD625 (57' · DDD)   Ⓕ**O**

No one listening to this music would doubt that Sibelius had a special feeling for the violin. Whether he's composing lighter music such as the captivating 'Rondino' from the Op 81 set or the more substantial later pieces, such as the first of the *Danses champêtres*, which comes close to the world of *The Tempest*. Neither the Op 115 nor the Op 116 set contains great music but they're much finer than they have been given credit for. Both 'On the heath' and the 'Ballade', Nos 1 and 2 of Op 115, have an innocence that calls to mind the wonderful *Humoresques* for violin and orchestra. In particular 'The Bells', Op 115 No 4 is a rather cryptic miniature and the 'Scène de danse' of Op 116, with its striking tonal juxtapositions, is a kind of Finnish equivalent of the Bartók *Romanian Dances*. Nils-Erik Sparf and Bengt Forsberg are dedicated and sensitive exponents who make the most of the opportunities this repertoire provides. One small reservation: the piano tone sounds a little thick at the bottom end, and the violin is by no means the dominant partner. Enthusiastically recommended.

Kullervo, Op 7

Kullervo
Lilli Paasikivi *mez* **Raimo Laukka** *bar* **Helsinki University Chorus; Lahti Symphony Orchestra / Osmo Vänskä**
BIS BIS-CD1215 (81' · DDD · T/t)   Ⓕ**OO**

Vänskä is undoubtedly a Sibelian of strong instinct, and his *Kullervo* enshrines an interpretation of extraordinary grandeur and slumbering, runic mystery. After an ideally paced opening *Allegro moderato* (the Lahti strings lacking just a touch in sheer muscle), 'Kullervo's Youth' lasts an eyebrow-raising 19'18", well over three minutes longer than any predecessor. Courageously, Vänskä sticks to his guns, the music's unnervingly tragic portents distilled with mournful gravity. It's in the big central *scena* that BIS's sumptuously realistic and wide-ranging production really comes into its own. Vänskä directs with keen observation and tingling narrative flair, not missing the wondrous poetry of the nature music accompanying the lament of Kullervo's sister. What's more, his soloists and chorus are first-rate, though baritone Raimo Laukka isn't quite as fresh-voiced here as he was for Segerstam's in 1994. Following a splendidly lusty 'Kullervo goes to War', Vänskä crowns proceedings with a thrillingly grim and inevitable 'Kullervo's Death', with eloquent contributions from the men of the Helsinki University

Chorus. As should be clear by now, this recording must feature high on any short list.

Kullervo, Op 7

Soile Isokoski sop **Tommi Hakala** bar
YL Male Voice Choir; Helsinki Philharmonic Orchestra / Leif Segerstam
Ondine ⏁ ODE1122-5 (78' · DDD)　　　Ⓟ**Ⓞ➔**

As a fine Wagner conductor Leif Segerstam knows something about pacing and maintaining a strong rhythmic profile over the longest spans of musical narrative, and for all the composer's vaunted debt to Bruckner in the instrumental movements, a grander, operatic sweep seems more germane to this always intriguing, sui generis hybrid of symphonic poem, symphony and cantata. Segerstam's second cycle of the numbered symphonies has at points such as the Seventh come a cropper with such largesse of gesture and tempo, but like Segerstam's first recording (Chandos – now available as a download only), is refreshingly straightforward with sound and well chosen tempi. Perhaps partly due to a superbly contoured recording, but also the more keenly expressive responses of the Helsinki orchestra, especially its woodwind, the many transitions in the work seem to count for more, and in 'Kullervo's Youth' achieve a Mussorgskian abruptness and intensity.

That first recording was also graced by Soile Isokoski in the part of Kullervo's raped sister, but here she surpasses herself in creating a self-contained scena for her third-movement lament, vibrant and enticing before turning bitterly eloquent over her shame. Tommi Hakala and the YL Choir bring a complementary, sappy youthfulness. If the finale rather goes off the boil, the composer must take some of the blame; Isokoski too, for stealing the show with a contribution to this over-recorded work which deserves to win currency outside connoisseurs of early Sibelius.

Karelia

Incidental Music – Karelia; Kuolema. Valse triste, Op 44 No 1 (1904 versions)
Heikki Laitinen, Taito Hoffren sngrs **Kirsi Tiihonen** sop **Raimo Laukka** bar **Lahti Symphony Orchestra / Osmo Vänskä**
BIS BIS-CD915 (76' · DDD · T/t)　　　Ⓕ

This is a disc which will be of great interest to Sibelians. The original score of the Karelia music was discovered in the conductor Kajanus's library after his death in 1933 and his widow returned it to Sibelius three years later. The music extended to eight tableaux which portrayed various episodes in Karelian history. In the 1940s Sibelius destroyed the score, about which he had had second thoughts since its premiere in 1893, sparing only the overture, the movements familiar from the suite and the first number, 'A Karelian Home – News of War'. Fortunately for posterity, a set of orchestral

parts came to light, albeit incomplete, and were put into shape by Kalevi Kuoso. It was these that the composer Kalevi Aho used in preparing the edition on which this recording is based.

In all there are some 40 minutes of music, over half of which is new. Those familiar with the 'Ballade' from the Op 11 Suite will no doubt be slightly disconcerted to hear the familiar cor anglais melody taken by a baritone and will find the piece too long in its original form. The opening of the fifth tableau, 'Pontus de la Gardie at the gates of Käkisalmi [Kexholm Castle] in 1580', is highly effective and leads into the famous 'Alla marcia'. It's fascinating to hear what the piece is like, and what Sibelius was prepared to lose. Listening to this reaffirms and illumines both the sureness of his artistic judgement and the vitality of his creative imagination. Sibelius's incidental music to Kuolema, the play by his brother-in-law, Arvid Järnefelt, dates from 1903. The most familiar music from it is the Valse triste, which Sibelius revised the following year, adding flute, clarinet, horns and timpani and making it altogether more sophisticated harmonically and melodically. Osmo Vänskä and his Lahti players prove reliable and responsive guides in this atmospheric music and it's hard to imagine their performances being improved on. Wide-ranging and expertly balanced recorded sound.

Everyman, Op 83

Incidental Music – Everyman, Op 83; Belshazzar's Feast, Op 51. The Countess's Portrait, Op posth
Lilli Paasikivi mez **Petri Lehto** ten **Sauli Tiilikainen** bar **Pauli Pietiläinen** org **Leena Saarenpää** pf
Lahti Chamber Choir; Lahti Symphony Orchestra / Osmo Vänskä
BIS BIS-CD735 (65' · DDD · T/t)　　　Ⓟ**Ⓞ**

These are all first recordings, and interest centres on the score Sibelius wrote for Hofmannsthal's morality play, *Jedermann* ('Everyman') in 1916. The final score comprises 16 numbers and runs to some 40 minutes. Some of the music is fragmentary and hardly makes sense out of context, though most is atmospheric and it's all characteristic. The sustained *Largo* section for muted, divided strings (track-11), is among the most searching music Sibelius ever wrote for theatre and, artistically, is fit to keep company with *The Tempest* music. Overall the material doesn't lend itself to being turned into a suite in the same way as *Belshazzar's Feast* but this recording rescues from obscurity some strangely haunting and at times really inspired music – the last 25 minutes are very powerful.

By all accounts Hjalmar Procopé's *Belshazzar's Feast* was a feeble play and when it first appeared, one newspaper cartoon showed the playwright being borne aloft in the composer's arms. There seems little doubt that his name wouldn't be alive if it weren't for Sibelius's music. The latter certainly makes an expert job of creating an effective and (in the case of the 'Notturno') a moving concert suite. *The Countess's Portrait* (1906) is a wistful, pensive and charming piece for strings, which was published only recently. Obviously this is a self-recommending issue of exceptional interest.

The Tempest, Op 109

The Tempest
Kirsi Tiihonen *sop* Lilli Paasikivi *mez* Anssi
Hirvonen, Paavo Kerola *tens* Heikki Keinonen *bar*
Lahti Opera Chorus and Symphony Orchestra /
Osmo Vänskä
BIS BIS-CD581 (68' · DDD · T/t)   Ⓕ●

A first recording of the full score! Sibelius's music for *The Tempest*, his last and greatest work in its genre, was the result of a commission for a particularly lavish production at the Royal Theatre, Copenhagen in 1926. The score is far more extensive than the two suites and consists of 34 musical numbers for soloists, mixed choir, harmonium and large orchestra. Readers will be brought up with a start by the music for the 'Berceuse', the second item, which uses a harmonium rather than the strings we're familiar with from the two suites. Although it's still more magical in the familiar orchestral suite, the original has an other-worldly quality all its own. The music is played in the order in which it was used in the 1927 production of the play and there are ample and excellent explanatory notes. The 'Chorus of the Winds' is also different but no less magical in effect. Taken out of the theatrical context, not everything comes off, but even if the invention isn't consistent in quality, at its best it's quite wonderful. The singers and chorus all rise to the occasion and Osmo Vänskä succeeds in casting a powerful spell in the 'Intermezzo', which opens Act 4. The recording is marvellously atmospheric, though a little recessed. For Sibelians this issue recommends itself.

Additional recommendation

Viljakainen *sop* Groop *mez* Silvasti *ten* Hynninen,
Tilikainen *bars* Finnish Opera Festival Chorus;
Finnish Radio Symphony Orchestra/Saraste
Ondine ODE813-2 (60' · DDD)   Ⓕ
A fine alternative version with idiomatic singing and playing from these Finnish performers.

Songs

King Christian II, Op 27 – Fool's Song of the Spider.
Five Christmas Songs, Op 1. Eight Songs, Op 57.
Hymn to Thaïs. Six Songs, Op 72 – No 3, The kiss;
No 4, The echo nymph; No 5, Der Wanderer und der
Bach; No 6, A hundred ways. Six Songs, Op 86. The
small girls
Monica Groop *mez* Love Derwinger *pf*
BIS BIS-CD657 (66' · DDD · T/t)   Ⓕ

Monica Groop, following her success in the Cardiff Singer of the World Competition, has built up a busy career. Communication is her strength,

and unevenness of line a relative weakness. Sibelius's songs are a rich and still undervalued part of the song repertoire. Still only four or five are really well known, and none of those is included here. Not all are of very special quality: the title is probably the best thing about the 'Fool's Song of the Spider' (from *King Christian II*), and the *Hymn to Thaïs* gains interest through being Sibelius's only song in English rather than through intrinsic merit. Yet there are many delights here, including the closing waltz-song, *The small girls*. The acoustic is perhaps somewhat too reverberant but has plenty of presence.

Songs, Volume 3. Seven Songs, Op 13. Six Songs, Op
50. Six Songs, Op 90. The Wood Nymph. Belshazzar's
Feast – The Jewish Girl's Song. Resemblance. A
Song. Serenade. The Thought[a]
Anne Sofie von Otter, [a]Monica Groop *mezzos*
Bengt Forsberg *pf*
BIS BIS-CD757 (67' · DDD · T/t)   Ⓕ●

The vast majority of Sibelius's songs are in Swedish, the language with which he grew up as a child, and here they're given by a distinguished native Swedish partnership. The *Seven Songs*, Op 13, are all Runeberg settings and come from the composer's early years (1891-2). Best known, perhaps, are 'Spring is flying' and 'The dream', but there are others, such as 'The young hunter', that are no less delightful and characterful. The other Runeberg settings here, the *Six Songs*, Op 90, come towards the end of Sibelius's career as a song composer (1917-18). 'The north', as in all the nature poetry of Runeberg, touches a very special vein of inspiration. Along with 'Die stille Nacht', Op 50 No 5, which is equally affectingly given by these two artists – it's among his finest songs. Interest naturally focuses on the rarities.

The Wood Nymph, not to be confused with the melodrama or the tone-poem, is recorded here for the first time. As well as *A Song*, there are two other early Runeberg settings, the 1888 *Serenade* and *Resemblance*, both of them also premiere recordings. 'The Jewish Girl's Song' will be familiar from the incidental music to *Belshazzar's Feast*, and is affecting in this form – particularly sung as it is here. Given the artistry and insight of this splendid partnership, and the interest and beauty of the repertoire, this is a self-recommending issue.

To evening, Op 17 No 6. Six Songs, Op 36. Five
Songs, Op 37. Six Songs, Op 50. Belshazzar's Feast,
Op 51 – The Jewish Girl's Song. I am a tree, Op 57 No
5. The Elf-King, Op 57 No 8. The North, Op 90 No 1.
Who has brought you here?, Op 90 No 6. Under the
fir-trees, Op 13 No 1. Spring is flying, Op 13 No 4
Katarina Karnéus *mez* Julius Drake *pf*
Hyperion CDA67318 (65' · DDD · T/t)   Ⓕ●

Sibelius's songs have taken a long time to come in from the cold. After all, the few that are relatively well-known (*Black roses* and Op 37 No 5,

'The Tryst') are passionate enough to have come from Italian opera, and others which over the years have found a place in the repertoire have a span of phrase and a melodic surge that encourage the voice to rise thrillingly, as in 'The Tryst's' predecessor, 'Was it a dream?'. The tingle of a Nordic chill in among this is in fact a further excitement of the blood. Given a voice that can combine the sparkle of sunlight on snow with the dark splendour which lies at the heart of those black roses, an entire programme of Sibelius's songs offers not an austere pleasure but almost a rich indulgence.

But from both singer and pianist there must also be a ready supply of imagination. Katarina Karnéus and Julius Drake answer these calls magnificently. The voice is firm and resonant, purest in quality in the upper D-to-F region and of ample range. In Julius Drake she has a pianist who extends the normal field of vision, and the two work together to great effect.

In the opening song, *To evening* ('Illalle'), Karnéus and Drake 'build' the verses with such effective graduations of power and intensity that everything is enhanced – the vocal line, the piano's *tremolando*s, words, mood, the poem-as-painting, the song as miniature epic. In some others – 'Little Lasse' in Op 37 and the remarkable 'Tennis in Trianon' of Op 36 are examples – von Otter and Bengt Forsberg bring a further sophistication, more rightfully placed in the second example than the first. But if you want a single disc of 25 to to represent Sibelius's output of roughly 100 songs then this disc must take first choice.

Luonnotar, Op 70. Arioso, Op 3. Seven Songs, Op 13 – Neath the fir trees; Spring is flying. Seven Songs, Op 17 – And I questioned them no further; The Dragonfly; To Evening; Driftwood. Six Songs, Op 36 – But my Bird; Sigh, Sedges, Sigh; The Diamond on the March Snow. Five Songs, Op 37 – The First Kiss; Sunrise; Was it a Dream?. Five Songs, Op 38 – Autumn Evening; On a balcony by the sea. Eight Songs, Op 57 – Duke Magnus. Six Songs, Op 72 – The Echo Nymph. Swim, Duck, Swim
Soile Isokoski *sop*
Helsinki Philharmonic Orchestra / Leif Segerstam
Ondine 🏆 ODE1080-5 (62' · DDD/DSD ·T/t)   Ⓕ

Sibelius wrote his songs originally for voice and piano and in that form they are most often recorded. Some he later orchestrated, while others were arranged by Jussi Jalas (his son-in-law), Ernest Pingoud, Ivan Hellman and Nils-Eric Forgstadt. All produce good results and none of the songs appear over-dressed. On the contrary, they are, as it were, fulfilled: orchestral textures are so strongly implicit that the full range of instruments brings out their coloration and renders them complete.

Soile Isokoski has recorded a number of the songs previously with piano, part of a fine recital on Finlandia in 1989, which was about the time we first learned of the radiant Finnish soprano who five or six years later would receive the

international acclaim she deserved. The voice then sounded fuller and was entirely pure in tone: today it is a little more worn but still lovely, firm and ample in range. Above all, she has a rare command of the *legato* style which makes her singing a delight to the ears when others, more subtle and expressive, may frustrate the full satisfaction their efforts would otherwise offer. There are limitations even so, some of them technical. *The Dragonfly* ('En slända') cannot really be sung without a genuine trill, and Isokoski's trill is a very sketchy, rudimentary one compared with, say, Elisabeth Söderström's. The popular *Was it a Dream?* ('Var det en dröm?') sounds well enough until Schwarzkopf is produced for comparison, her voice emerging magically out of the dreamy, murmurous introduction and minting afresh developments that are too nearly predictable and routine in Isokoski.

Yet the recital always gives pleasure, and the challenge of *Luonnotar* itself is joyfully met. The orchestra play with full appreciation of the richly coloured scores, and since Flagstad in the 1950s there have been few recordings which provide these genuinely enhancing accompaniments as an alternative to the piano.

Valentin Silvestrov   Ukrainian b1937

Silvestrov was a pupil of Lyatosynsky at the Kiev Conservatory (1958-64). Influenced at first by his teacher and by Shostakovich, he came in the early 1960s to use serialism, aleatory forms and other avant-garde techniques and in the 1970s to work with a plurality of styles, new and old. His works include symphonies, chamber music, piano pieces, songs, characterized by an individual, expressive lyricism.   **GROVE**music

---

Orchestral works

Bagatellen[a]. Der Bote[b]. Zwei Dialoge mit Nachwort[b]. Elegie. Stille Musik. Abschiedsserenade
[a]**Valentin Silvestrov**, [b]**Alexei Lubimov** *pfs*
Munich Chamber Orchestra / Christoph Poppen
ECM New Series 476 6178 (75' · DDD)   Ⓕ

ECM marks Valentin Silvestrov's 70th birthday with a disc that assembles smaller pieces and collections written over the past decade. A disc, moreover, of two distinct halves – the first of which features the composer in his *Bagatelles*: 13 miniatures that do not so much succeed as 'bleed' into each other in a half-hour sequence whose spectral allusions to Romantic pianism and consistently attenuated dynamics (the damper pedal sustained throughout) go some way to defining the essence of Silvestrov's music. Even then, the dissonance on which the final piece evanesces hints at those darker ambiguities which are present in even his seemingly most unequivocal statements.

The second half focuses on music for strings, sensitively rendered by the Munich Chamber Orchestra and Christoph Poppen. If the trio of ethereal dances comprising *Stille Musik* and distanced elegance of the two-part *Abschiedsserenade* are all of a piece with what came before, *Elegie* evinces a more anguished expression. Pianist Alexei Lubimov makes a fastidious contribution to *Der Bote* – a Mozartian rondo of deceptive tranquillity – and the oblique recollections of Wagner and Schubert that inform the serene *Zwei Dialoge mit Nachtwort*. Recording and annotations reflect ECM's customary high standards, and the release can be recommended as an ideal résumé of one aspect – though not necessarily the lighter one – of Silvestrov's creativity.

Requiem for Larissa

Requiem for Larissa
National Choir of Ukraine, 'Dumka'; National Symphony Orchestra of Ukraine / Volodymyr Sirenko
ECM New Series 472 112-2 (53' · DDD · T)　Ⓕ❍�'

Much of Silvestrov's music since the mid-1970s has been a requiem in all but name – a rite of regret and consolation for music and for the hopes and dreams of modern consciousness. So it's no surprise that he should join Schnittke, Denisov, Tishchenko and others of the post-Shostakovich generation in composing a work of that name. The external stimulus was the sudden death in 1996 of his musicologist wife Larissa Bondarenko, his staunch supporter through trials of the kind virtually all modernist composers in the former USSR had to face.

He completed the work three years later, having built into the 'Tuba Mirum' section the fractured but passionate textures of his First Symphony of 1963, and having arranged the second *Agnus Dei* around his Mozartian piano piece, *The Messenger*. At the heart of the Requiem is his Taras Shevchenko setting, 'The Dream', as breathtakingly moving here as in its original place in the cycle *Silent Songs*. Otherwise he fragments the Requiem text and disposes its incomplete phrases across seven mostly slow movements; only the 'Lacrimosa' survives intact. The choir features a *basso profundo* section and three soloists who gently ease in and out of the texture. The classical-size orchestra is augmented by synthesizer, first heard in the celestial harmonies succeeding the first *Agnus Dei*.

Whether or not you know the fragile, haunting sound world of Ukraine's senior composer, this is a disc you should try.

Robert Simpson   British 1921-1997

Simpson, a pupil of Howells (1942-6), worked for the BBC (1951-80). His main achievement was his cycles of nine symphonies and eight string quartets, both begun in 1951 and both displaying a dynamic tonality quite individual in its energy and purposefulness, encouraged more than influenced by his admiration for Beethoven, Bruckner and Nielsen (on whom he published studies).　GROVEmusic

---

Symphonies

Symphonies Nos 3 & 5
Royal Philharmonic Orchestra / Vernon Handley
Hyperion CDA66728 (71' · DDD)　Ⓕ❍❍

The Third Symphony is Simpson's best-known work and Vernon Handley play the symphony like the repertoire piece it deserves to be, and Hyperion's recording reveals a wealth of unsuspected detail and beauty. The Beethovenian impulse still comes across, and the abrasive edge is only slightly softened. But what has been gained is clarity, blend and perspective, plus a sense of dialogue (Simpson's polyphony never ceases to amaze) and an altogether subtler realisation of the luminosity of Simpson's scoring. The long accumulating second movement is absorbingly poetic, witty in its dialogue, and inevitable in its conclusion.

The Fifth Symphony is surely one of Simpson's most vivid pieces. Moods of terror, anger, anxious probing and fierce determination are right on the surface, and there's a feeling of terrific will-power being exerted to transmute those moods into a symphonic experience. This is one of the great symphonies of the post-war era, magnificently realised by all concerned.

Symphonies Nos 6 & 7
Royal Liverpool Philharmonic Orchestra / Vernon Handley
Hyperion CDA66280 (60' · DDD)　Ⓕ

The first performances of these symphonies had shown many characteristic and admirable qualities, but there was a suspicion of some tentativeness a lowering of sights even, after the explosive Fifth Symphony. One should have guessed that closer acquaintance and more expert performance would show this to be more a matter of concentration of ideas and of conscious change of direction. The RLPO and Vernon Handley show the Sixth to be a work of immense inner power, and if the Seventh is a more cryptic statement, this recording certainly brings it into a clearer focus than previously.

Whereas Tippett (in the same year) wrote a birth-to-death symphony (No 4) Simpson's Sixth shifts the process one stage back – from conception to prime of life. Intense expectancy gives way to a memorable downward-stalking unison figure, the fertilised seed which becomes the most active force in the early stages of the work. From here to the irresistible energy of the final pages Simpson's control of musical momentum can only be marvelled at; and if you don't marvel at it, that may be because you're worrying about the apparent restriction on colour and lyricism, and thus missing the point.

As yet the final D major outcome still refuses to register as a natural outcome, although presumably there's any amount of logical justification for it. The neutral, non-triadic conclusion to the Seventh rings truer, though in this work the processes before it are more inscrutable – not in the technical sense, but simply in terms of what the techniques are driving at. But anyone who has puzzled over, and then clicked with, say, Sibelius's Fourth or Shostakovich's 15th, will know how dangerous it is to jump to conclusions. And even if the click never happens, one probable masterpiece is surely enough to be getting on with.

Symphony No 9
Bournemouth Symphony Orchestra / Vernon Handley
Hyperion CDA66299 (68' · DDD) Includes an illustrated talk by the composer Ⓕ**ⓄⓄⓄ**

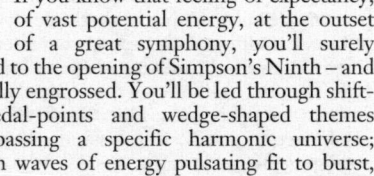 If you know that feeling of expectancy, of vast potential energy, at the outset of a great symphony, you'll surely respond to the opening of Simpson's Ninth – and be wholly engrossed. You'll be led through shifting pedal-points and wedge-shaped themes encompassing a specific harmonic universe; through waves of energy pulsating fit to burst, until burst they do into a titanic scherzo; through slow, disembodied traceries of string lines, through awe-inspiring climaxes to a no less awe-inspiring hushed coda. And as rising scales pass through the coda's pedal-points into the final glacial sonority you'll know that you've heard one of the finest symphonies of the post-war era.

The composer adds an explanatory 18-minute talk. Here are laid bare some of the salient constructional features of the work – the opening's basis in chorale prelude procedures (a fairly cosmic rethinking thereof!), the single underlying pulse of the entire work (a recurrent feature in Simpson's output, but never before applied on this scale), the palindromic variations in the second half, the debts to Bach, Beethoven and Bruckner. To which one might add that the rigorous processes described in this talk suggest a somewhat unlikely kinship with Bartók at his most abstract (as in the first movement of the *Music for strings, percussion and celesta*).

Bartók, it's safe to say, has as little to do with this work's symphonic instincts as any other 'big name' of the last 50 years or so. Simpson stands not at any fixed pole of today's music, but rather at a kind of magnetic north, free from attempts of musical cartographers to pin down his position, spiritually allied to composers of any age and style who have penetrated to the essence of music's motion in time. A totally absorbing symphony and the performance and recording are surely the best possible tribute to all concerned.

String Quartets

String Quartets Nos 7 & 8
Delme Quartet (Galina Solodchin, Jeremy Williams

vns John Underwood va Stephen Orton vc)
Hyperion CDA66117 (51' · AAD) Recorded 1983
Ⓕ**ⓄⓄ**

String Quartet No 9
Delme Quartet
Hyperion CDA66127 (58' · AAD) Recorded 1984 Ⓕ

Quiet music with a sense of purpose and forward-looking destiny; slow music which bears the promise of a controlled release of energy, these are rare and treasurable qualities in music of our time, and they make their presence felt at the beginnings of Simpson's Seventh and Eighth Quartets. How he progresses through subdued scherzo to vehement climax is something to reflect on at length, and with further acquaintance comes the Beethovenian thrill of hearing the music think. But at first these things just steal up on you and take the breath away.

The Seventh Quartet is dedicated to Susi Jeans, widow of astronomer and mathematician Sir James Jeans, the Eighth is dedicated to entomologist David Gillett and his wife. Both works draw on the kind of motion suggested by those areas of scientific enquiry. On the other hand the Ninth calls up what would seem to be the bitterest enemy of forward movement – the palindrome; 32 variations and a fugue, in fact, on the minuet from Haydn's Symphony No 47 and all of them, like the original theme, palindromic. If Simpson's powers of invention falter at any stage in this hour-long tour de force you would be hard pushed to discover where. But then this music so completely absorbing that the necessary critical detachment is difficult to achieve. The only reservation that did register was over recording quality, which for the Ninth Quartet is disappointingly boxy – sensuous appeal isn't what this music is about, but a more ingratiating acoustic wouldn't do it any harm – and to hear the Seventh without the distraction, however faint, of traffic noise would be preferable.

The Delme Quartet's performances are outstandingly dedicated. The Ninth Quartet was composed for their 20th anniversary and they prove themselves entirely worthy of the honour.

Vocal Works

Canzona[a]. Media morte in vita sumus[b]. Tempi[c]. Eppur si muove[d]
[d]**Iain Quinn** org [ab]**Corydon Brass Ensemble;**
[bc]**Corydon Singers / Matthew Best**
Hyperion CDA67016 (68' · DDD · T) Ⓕ**Ⓞ**

Simpson would never have claimed that choral music was his *métier*. Yet for lovers of his music there's something especially revealing about the two pieces recorded here. In *Media morte in vita sumus* ('In the midst of death we are in life') he deliberately reverses the scriptural motto in order to articulate his personal 'anti-pessimist' creed. The musical setting for chorus, brass and timpani is appropriately austere, and Simpson's words are translated into Latin for the sake of universality. *Tempi* for *a cappella* chorus is a *jeu d'esprit*, the text consisting entirely of Italian tempo and character markings. The Corydon Singers offers superbly confident performances, as does the Corydon Brass Ensemble which also shines in the comparatively well-known *Canzona*. It's impossible to avoid comparisons with Nielsen when it comes to the 31-minute *Eppur si muove* ('But it does move') for organ. This 12-minute *ricercare* followed by a 19-minute passacaglia sets its jaw squarely against conventional organ-loft grandiosity. Its intellectual monumentality is clearly in the *Commotio* mould, though it's considerably tougher going than Nielsen's late masterpiece. Iain Quinn joins the long line of dedicated performers who have made Hyperion's Simpson series such a consistent triumph. Recording quality leaves nothing to be desired.

Nikos Skalkottas   Greek 1904-1949

Skalkottas studied as a violinist at the Athens Conservatory and as a composer in Berlin with Juon, Kahn, Jarnach (1925-7), Weill (1928-9) and Schoenberg (1927-31). In 1933 he returned to Athens, where he worked as a back-desk violinist. His Berlin works are relatively compact and high-spirited, being almost exclusively instrumental and following the neo-classicism of his teachers (in 1927 his music became atonal, but not yet serial). But the bulk of his music dates from 1935-45, when the genres remained traditional but the forms were greatly expanded to contain a deep complexity of serial thematic working: major works of this period include the Third Piano Concerto (1939), the Fourth Quartet (1940) and the overture The Return of Odysseus (1943). GROVEmusic

Piano Concerto No 1, AK16

Piano Concerto No 1[a]. The Maiden and Death – Ballet Suite, AK12. Ouvertüre concertante, AK46
[a]**Geoffrey Douglas Madge** pf **Iceland Symphony Orchestra / Nikos Christodoulou**
BIS CD1014 (56' · DDD)   Ⓕ●

BIS's Skalkottas cycle started very well and gets better with each release. The First Piano Concerto's characteristic use of a family of note-rows, rather than just one, may have ignited the rift between the apprentice composer and his teacher, Schoenberg. The neo-classical elements can't have been to the latter's liking, either. Geoffrey Douglas Madge gives a barnstorming performance and the accompaniment is electrifying. The orchestra is heard at its best and in its own right in the suite from the folkballet *The Maiden and Death* (1938). Here Skalkottas's brilliant orchestration shines through in what's much more than a pre-run of *The Mayday Spell*. The idiom is less fragmentary than the latter; indeed, it suggests a Greek *Miraculous Mandarin*, if less overtly spectacular in sound or scandalous in plot.

The disc concludes with a further movement from the unfinished Second Symphonic Suite (1944-5; compare the *Largo sinfonico* on the first disc). This *Ouvertüre concertante* is pretty much what the title leads you to expect it to be, a superbly scored sonata-derivative, employing the composer's note-row-complex manner in a most attractive fashion.

Violin Concerto, AK22

Violin Concerto[a]. Largo Sinfonico, AK4a. Greek Dances, AK11 – Epirotikos; Kretikos; Tsamikos; Thessalikos; Mariori mou-Mariori mou; Arkadikos; Kleftikos (arr cpsr)
[a]**Georgios Demertzis** vn **Malmö Symphony Orchestra / Nikos Christodoulou**
BIS CD904 (78' · DDD)   Ⓕ●

From Skalkottas's earliest works, a personal idiom was clearly in evidence, combining European modernism with the rhythmic dynamism of Greek traditional music, and characterised by a tensile strength and translucency of sound. Like Bartók, Skalkottas wrote 'popular' music without compromise. The *Greek Dances* are ideal encore pieces, not least in these suave arrangements for strings.

The Violin Concerto of 1937 is among his major works, with a solo part that's demanding yet integral to the symphonic nature of the score – something that Georgios Demertzis's vital account readily conveys here. The close of the *Andante* possesses true lyrical repose, before the finale provides fireworks as well as clinching the musical design.

The *Largo Sinfonico*, completed in 1944, embodies some of Skalkottas's most personal music; a seamless fusion of variation and sonata forms, it's as satisfying formally as it is emotionally. Nikos Christodoulou's accompanying notes speak of a private musical universe, yet the plangency of the cello theme and the remorseless tread of the central climaxes betray an unease that must surely be inseparable from the time of composition. The final bars, with the thematic material recast as a series of unearthly chords, feel as much a stoic acceptance of reality as they are a 'harmony of the spheres'. With the Malmö orchestra fully attuned to the idiom, Christodoulou's powerfully shaped reading makes for a compelling experience.

Violin Sonatinas

Violin Sonatinas[a] – No 1, AK46; No 2, AK47; No 3, AK48; No 4, AK49. March of the Little Soldiers, AK53[a]. Rondo, AK54[a]. Nocturne, AK55[a]. Little Chorale and Fugue, AK56[a]. Gavotte, AK57[a]. Scherzo and Menuetto Cantato, AK58[a]. Solo Violin Sonata, AK69
Georgios Demertzis vn [a]**Maria Asteriadou** pf
BIS CD1024 (66' · DDD)   Ⓕ●

Here's a window onto Skalkottas's music for his own instrument, itself a microcosm of his development. There's nothing stylistically tentative about the early Solo Violin Sonata (1925). Written with a Bachian economy of manner, the composer draws in references to jazz and popular music; the finale serves notice of his technical skill with an arching four-part fugue, reaching maximum intensity at the point where it returns to the prelude. The sense of a still-emerging personality is reinforced by the first two *Sonatinas* (both 1929, the *Andantino* is all that survives from No 1). Skalkottas's rhythmic incisiveness owes something to Stravinsky and even Bartók, but the tang of the harmonic writing is his alone. With the Third and Fourth *Sonatinas* (both 1935), the Skalkottas idiom, sinuous and expressive, is in place. The thematic integration of No 3 is breathtaking, as is the variety of tone with which the violin sustains continuity in the *Andante*. If the Fourth *Sonatina* is almost too diverse in mood, its *Adagio* is one of Skalkottas's finest: a threnody unfolding in three waves of mounting intensity, it looks forward to the expansive slow movements of the composer's last decade.

The miniatures are anything but trifles. *March of the Little Soldiers* is a savage take on militarism, while *Nocturne* reinterprets the expressive vocabulary of the 'song without words' for the 20th century. There could be no more sympathetic advocate than Georgios Demertzis. As in his recording of the Violin Concerto (BIS), he gets to the heart of Skalkottas's demanding but deeply felt music, with Maria Asteriadou an attentive partner. Inquiring listeners shouldn't hesitate to acquire this disc.

Piano Works

Musik für Klavier: 32 Piano Pieces, AK70. Suite No 1, AK71. Four Etudes, AK74
Nikolaos Samaltanos pf
BIS ② BIS-CD1133/4 (119' · DDD)   Ⓕ●

Over 60 years after its completion, Skalkottas's *Musik für Klavier* – the overall title of his 32 Piano Pieces – can assume its place among the major piano cycles of the 20th century. Formidably difficult technically, its apparently disparate content – there isn't the conceptual focus of, say, Messiaen's *Vingt regards sur l'enfant Jésus* – may have militated against its wider recognition. So it's a tribute to Nikolaos Samaltanos, in this first complete recording, that he projects the work as an integral entity, and as the compendium of mid-century pianism that the composer intended.

Achieving equal conviction across such diversity is a tall order, given the absence of a performing tradition against which to assess an interpretation. His playing of individual pieces may be open to question but Samaltanos has the measure of the cycle and the way that its groupings of pieces interconnect. The powerful rhetoric of the 'Passacaglia' and sombre poetry of 'Nachtstück', a double-apex on all levels, are impressively wrought, while the relative nonchalance of the closing *divertissement* is dispatched with élan. Other recordings will

surely follow but rivals will be hard pressed to match the scintillating virtuosity of Samaltanos in 'Katastrophe' or the 'Etüde phantastique'.

Wide-ranging sound, lacking only the last degree of clarity in the more heavily chorded pieces, and detailed notes from Christophe Sirodeau. Urgently recommended.

Howard Skempton   British b1947

Skempton was associated from the outset of his career with the English school of experimental music which evolved in the late 1960s out of Satie, Cage, Feldman and others, in which he, in common with Cardew, played a significant part. Webern and La Monte Young, as well as Feldman, were strong formative influences on the development of Skempton's style. Landmarks in what can also be identified as a response to the wider audience his music has gained during this period include Lento for orchestra (1990) and the series of concertos composed during the 1990s. The latter includes a pair of double concertos in which Skempton bestows his characteristic favours on some of the less-favoured members of the Western instrumental pantheon, the hurdy-gurdy in one, the accordion in the other. GROVEmusic

'The Cloths of Heaven'
Missa brevis. Magnificat and Nunc dimittis (Edinburgh Service). Upon my lap my sovereign sits. Locus iste. O Saviour of the World. The Song of Songs. Adam lay y-bounden. Lamentations: How sits this city?; I am the man; The anointed Lord; For oughtest Thou, O Lord. He Wishes for the Cloths of Heaven. Beati quorum via. Emerson Songs. Ave Virgo sanctissima. Ostende nobis Domine. O Life!; Nature's Fire. Recessional.
Exon Singers / Matthew Owens org
Delphian DCD34056 (70' · DDD)   Ⓕ●

Music for piano and accordion may be the 'central nervous system' of his work but recent discs suggest Howard Skempton's chamber and vocal output is hardly less significant. This new disc gives an inclusive overview of his choral music and songs. The former ranges from the austerity of the *Magnificat* and *Nunc dimittis*, through the rhythmic repetition and harmonic accretion of *Locuste iste* and *The Song of Songs*, to the subtle intricacy of *Ostende nobis Domine* and luminous ecstasy found in Yeats's *He Wishes for the Cloths of Heaven* – a miniature masterpiece to be sure. The *Missa brevis* is a composite of these approaches – whether in the inward anxiousness of its *Gloria*, the surging ardour of its *Sanctus* or the plaintive supplication of its *Agnus Dei*. Highlights from among the songs include the formal yet fervent treatment of Burns in *O Life!*, methodical settings from Donne's versification of *Lamentations*, and the harmonic/melodic interplay of the *Emerson Songs*. Two organ pieces round out the programme, with the artless *Recessional* being an apt conclusion.

Music such as this is easy to kill with overstatement or dull with caution, neither of which is true of these performers: notably the mellifluous Bartholomew Lawrence in the *Lamentations*, and the Exon Singers, whose responsiveness is a tribute to Matthew Owens, whether as director or organist. The sound provides an ideal ambience and presentation is on a par with earlier Delphian issues, making for a release in which Skempton admirers and newcomers alike will find much to savour.

Bedřich Smetana   Bohemian 1824-1884

Smetana took music lessons from his father, a keen violinist, and from several local teachers. In his teens he attended the Academic Gymnasium in Prague, but neglected school work to attend concerts (including some by Liszt, with whom he became friendly) and to write string quartets for friends, until his father sent him to the Premonstratensian Gymnasium at Plzen. At first he earned a precarious living as a teacher in Prague until, in January 1884, he was appointed resident piano teacher to Count Leopold Thun's family, which provided him with the means to study harmony, counterpoint and composition with Josef Proksch. When he failed in an attempt to launch a career as a concert pianist in 1847, Smetana decided to found a school of music in Prague. This showed little profit, but he was able to earn something by teaching privately and by playing regularly to the deposed Emperor Ferdinand, and in 1849 he was able to marry Katerina Kolárová, whom he had known since his Plzen days.

Smetana's financial situation improved little in the years that followed, and political uncertainty and domestic tragedy only added to his unrest: three of his four daughters died between 1854 and 1856. When he heard there was an opening for a piano teacher at Göteborg he jumped at the chance. In Sweden his prospects improved, and he was in demand as a pianist, teacher and conductor. Inspired by Liszt's example, he composed his first symphonic poems. His wife's health forced him to return to Bohemia with her in 1859, but she died at Dresden on the way home. After two further summers in Göteborg, between which he found a second wife in Bettina Ferdinandová, Smetana felt the need to return permanently to Prague in order to play an active role in the reawakening of Czech culture that followed the Austrian defeat by Napoleon III at Magenta and Soferino.

He was disappointed to find himself no more successful in Prague than he had been before. It was not until his first opera, The Brandenburgers in Bohemia, was enthusiastically received in January 1866 that his prospects there improved. His second, The Bartered Bride, was speedily put into production and soon found favour, though (as with his other operas) foreign performances long remained rarities. As principal conductor of the Provisional Theatre, 1866-74, Smetana added 42 operas to the repertory, including his own Dalibor (on a heroic national theme) and The Two Widows. Dalibor and Libuše (performed at the opening of the National Theatre in

Prague in 1881) are Smetana's two most nationalistic operas; when completing the latter he also planned a vast orchestral monument to his nation which became the cycle of symphonic poems entitled Má vlast ('My fatherland'), including the evocative and stirring Vltava, a picture of the river that flows through Prague.

In 1874 the first signs of the syphilis appeared that was to result in Smetana's deafness. The String Quartet From my Life (1876) suggests in its last movement the piercing whistling that haunted his every evening, making work almost impossible. He somehow managed to complete two more operas, a second string quartet and several other works, but by 1883 his mental equilibrium was seriously disturbed. In April 1884 he was taken to the Prague lunatic asylum, where he died the following month.

Smetana was the first major nationalist composer of Bohemia. He gave his people a new musical identity and self-confidence by his technical assurance and originality in handling national subjects. In his operas and symphonic poems he drew on his country's legends, history, characters, scenery and ideas, presenting them with a freshness and colour which owe little to indigenous folksong but much to a highly original and essentially dramatic musical style.

GROVEmusic

Má vlast

Má vlast
Czech Philharmonic Orchestra / Rafael Kubelík
Supraphon SU1910-2 (78' · DDD) Recorded live 1990
Ⓕ**OO**

Smetana's great cycle of six tone-poems, *Má vlast*, celebrates the countryside and legendary heroes and heroines of Bohemia. It's a work of immense national significance encapsulating many of the ideals and hopes of that country. What a triumphant occasion it was when Rafael Kubelík returned to his native Czechoslovakia and to his old orchestra after an absence of 42 years and conducted *Má vlast* at the 1990 Prague Spring Festival. Supraphon's disc captures that live performance – not perfectly, since the sound is efficient rather than opulent – but well enough to show off what's arguably the finest performance on record since Talich's early LP set.

You'd never imagine that Kubelík had emerged from five years of retirement and a recent serious illness, such is the power and eloquence of his conducting. He takes a lyrical rather than a dramatic view of the cycle, and if there's strength enough in more heroic sections there's also a refreshing lack of bombast. Kubelík's intimate knowledge of the score shows time and time again in the most subtle touches. Even the weakest parts of the work are most artfully brought to life, and seem of much greater stature than is usually the case. 'Vltava' flows beautifully, with the most imaginative flecks of detail, and in 'From Bohemia's Woods and Fields' there are vivid visions of wide, open spaces. The orchestra rewards its former director with superb playing.

Má vlast **H**
Czech Philharmonic Orchestra / Václav Talich
Supraphon mono SU3826-2 (74' · AAD) Recorded
1954 Ⓕ**OOO**

G Try listening from just before six minutes into 'From Bohemia's Woods and
Fields' and you reach the very heart of
this great performance. The CPO brass lunges
towards the main melody with unconstrained
eagerness, their impact much aided by smiling
glissandos. And as Talich and his players climb
aboard Smetana's homespun melody, everything
assumes a sunny glow: it's almost as if the entire
work thus far had prepared for that one magical
moment. But there are countless additional
splendours: the luminous mobility of 'Vltava', the
grimness of 'Sárka' (so different here to the excitable Kubelík), the sense of foreboding in 'Tábor'
and the chest-swelling patriotism of 'Blaník'. The
strings retain more than a hint of the *portamentos*
that were such a distinctive feature of Talich's
1929 recording, but the woodwinds are notably
superior and the basically excellent sound releases
more of the music's dynamism than was easily
audible on 78s.

The transfer makes a warmer case for the original tapes than did the old LPs, and generally
serves Talich well – except in one maddening
respect. A couple of bars have dropped from
'Tábor', thus utterly ruining the contour of a
major climax. The offending cut was not present
on the original recording. If you can write off the
missing bars as 'historical wear and tear', then
expect a *Má vlast* that's way above average, an
inspired affirmation of national pride by a wonderful people who had only recently escaped one
form of tyranny, and would subsequently fall prey
to another.

Additional recommendation

Má vlast
Czech Philharmonic Orchestra / Mackerras
Supraphon SU3465-2 (76' · DDD) Ⓕ
A live recording from the Rudolfinum in Prague
finds the West's leading Czech music specialist
utterly at home with the music and the orchestra.
The sound is excellent.

Symphonic poems

'Orchestral Works, Vol 1'
Der Fischer, 'Rybář', T103/B138. Hakon Jarl, B118.
Jubel-Ouverture, T46/B63. March for Shakespeare
Festival, T93/B129. Richard III, B106. Venkovanka,
'The Peasant Woman', T123. Wallenstein's Camp,
B111
BBC Philharmonic / Gianandrea Noseda
Chandos CHAN10413 (76' · DDD) Ⓕ**OOꟼ**

This is a superb disc. There have been distinguished collections of Smetana's symphonic
poems but none quite to compare with this in
excitement, richness of detail and, in the case of

**SMETANA MÁ VLAST –
IN BRIEF**

Czech PO / Václav Talich **H**
Supraphon SU3826-2 (74' · ADD) Ⓜ**OOO**
G Infinitely flexible, warm-hearted and
full of chest-swelling pride, the great
Václav Talich's third and final recording
from 1954 has the very stamp of greatness
in every bar. This is the Real Thing –
totally inside the idiom.

Czech PO / Karel Ančerl
Supraphon SU3661-2 (75' · ADD) Ⓜ
Ančerl's 1961 recording sounds far richer
on CD than it ever did on LP. It's an exciting,
always purposeful account, marvellously well
played.

Czech PO / Rafael Kubelík
Supraphon 11 1208-2 (78' · DDD) Ⓕ**OOꟼ**
Returning to his homeland after an absence
of nearly 42 years, Rafael Kubelík launched
the 1990 Prague Spring Festival with this
unforgettable performance of Smetana's
patriotic cycle.

Bavarian RSO / Rafael Kubelík
Orfeo C115842A (77' · DDD) Ⓕ**OO**
Kubelík again, this time at the helm of his
beloved Munich band in arguably the most
spellbinding, subtly moulded version of all.

London Classical Players / Roger Norrington
Virgin 5453012-2 (76' · DDD) Ⓜꟼ
An enjoyable *Má vlast* give period-instrument garb courtesy of one of today's most
questing musicians. Worth hearing.

Vienna Philharmonic / James Levine
DG 459 4182 (124' · DDD) Ⓜꟼ
For sensationally beautiful orchestral playing, Levine's VPO recording is most appealing. It may not have the authentic bite of
Czech PO versions, but it's full of detail, and
the couplings are generous.

Polish National RSO / Antoni Wit
Naxos 8 550931 (80' · DDD) Ⓢꟼ
A distinctive account from Katowice. Wit
opts for unusually lesiurely tempi, but there's
no lack of momentum or atmosphere. Worth
snapping up as a supplement to Talich and
Kubelík.

Czech PO / Sir Charles Mackerras
Supraphon SU3465-2 (74' · DDD) Ⓕ
Another memorable Prague Spring Festival
concert, this time from May 1999 and featuring a maestro whose lifelong experience and
wisdom in Slavonic repertoire require no
further comment. As always the Czech Philharmonic play with an understanding of the
idiom possessed by no other orchestra.

Wallenstein's Camp, sonic spectacle – how well Smetana writes for the brass! Indeed this, *Richard III* and especially *Hakon Jarl* emerge afresh as symphonic poems every bit the equal of those of Liszt. The early *Jubel-Overture* (1848) with its thundering, frantic opening timpani and energetic folksy flavour is a real find. So, too, is the beautiful watery tableau *The Fisherman*, which has a Wagnerian evocation gently reminding one of the moonlight sequence in 'Vltava'.

But the key works are the first three mentioned above, *Wallenstein's Camp* full of vivid military invention, *Richard III* with its atmospheric, doom-laden portrait, including a memorable dominating theme, gently lurching to represent the king's gait. The orchestration is highly evocative, as it is in the even more ambitiously dramatic *Hakon Jarl*. Here the central lyrical section with its falling scalic main theme, introduced by harp and bass clarinet, is all but Tchaikovskian and leads to a superb climax. The Shakespeare March closes the programme boisterously.

Gianandrea Noseda draws wonderfully characterful and spontaneous playing from the BBC Philharmonic, and the Chandos engineers surpass themselves with the realistic vividness of the sound and the naturalness of the balance. Not to be missed.

'Orchestral Works, Vol 2'
The Bartered Bride – Overture; Polka; Furiant; Dance of the Comedians (Skocná). The Brandenburgers in Bohemia, T90/B124 – Prelude; Ballet, Act 1. Dalibor, T96 – Entr'acte. The Devil's Wall, T129 – Overture; Infernal Dance. The Kiss, T115 – Overture. Libuše, T107 – Prelude. The Two Widows, T109 – Overture; Prelude, Act 2; Polka. The Secret, T118 – Overture
BBC Philharmonic Orchestra / Gianandrea Noseda
Chandos CHAN10518 (73' · DDD)   Ⓕ**ⓞⓞ**▷

Brilliant, picturesque and nationalistic, all the music on this superb disc pays colourful tribute to 'the father of Bohemian music'. Even the most familiar pages from *The Bartered Bride* come up fresh as paint, the BBC Philharmonic's immaculate virtuosity as musicianly and refined as it is sparkling. However rapid and propulsive the tempo, nothing is pushed or over-driven. The Polka's grandiose opening leads to music of a courtly charm, enough to set even the least susceptible heads nodding and feet tapping. The Furiant's catchy cross-rhythms lead to a suavely romantic melody and in the Overture to *The Secret* there is a typical Smetana progression from sobriety to lightness and exultance.

The Prelude to *Libuše* was written to celebrate the coronation of the Emperor Franz Josef. But even if Smetana was left in the lurch (the event never took place) his ceremonial fanfares carry all the importance of a promised state occasion. The Entr'acte from *Dalibor* is a special delight, a magical dream-like interlude before a return in *The Two Widows* to hyperactivity. Everything is permeated with a sense of Czech pride and ideals, a mood memorably captured by Noseda. Chandos's sound is exceptional.

String Quartets

String Quartets – No 1, 'From my life'; No 2.
Skampa Quartet (Pavel Fischer, Jana Lukášová *vns* Radim Sedmidubský *va* Lukas Polak *vc*)
Supraphon SU3740-2 (47' · DDD)   Ⓕ

This is music that these Czech players have in their blood, and the variations of tempo which are an essential part of Smetana's idiom seem genuinely improvisatory. Yet the ensemble could not be more polished, with wonderfully clear textures, helped by an excellent, cleanly balanced recording made in Prague's Dvořák Hall.

The Skampa players fully bring out the drama of the First's finale and its spine-chilling tinnitus whistle which the deaf composer included from expperience. No 2 finds them in more relaxed mood, with extreme tempo changes in the first movement, infectious 'oompah' rhythms in the second, and high contrasts in the finale.

The Bartered Bride

The Bartered Bride   Ⓗ
Ada Nordenova *sop* Marenka **Otta Horáková** *sop* Esmeralda **Marie Pixová** *sop* Ludmila **Marta Krásová** *mez* Háta **Valdimir Toms** *ten* Jeník **Jaroslav Gleich** *ten* Vasek **Karel Hruska** *ten* Circus Master **Jan Konstantin** *bar* Krusina **Emil Pollert** *bass* Kecal **Zdenek Otava** *bass* Micha **Václav Marek** *bass* Indian **Prague National Opera Company Chorus; Prague National Opera Company Orchestra/Otakar Ostrčil**
Naxos mono ② 8 110098/9 (118 minutes: ADD)
Recorded 1933   Ⓢ▷

This is the first ever recording of Smetana's most popular opera, performed by a team steeped in the tradition of interpreting the work in Prague. Otakar Ostrčil gives a rhythmically exhilarating, suitably expectant account of the overture, directs the dances with just the right amount of brio tempered by lightness, and gives thoughtful support to his singers. The whole cast is Czech, so the recitative flows with a natural feeling for speech rhythms and accentuation. Nordenova as Mařenka has a sweet, unaffected timbre that's exactly right for her part, and she employs portamento in a way that would not be tolerated today; so much the worse for today. Her Jeník has a plangent tone and intimate delivery nearideal for the role, though some may be surprised at hearing such a light voice in a part now assigned to heavier tenors. The somewhat confined recording has been miraculously restored to obviate most of the drawbacks of the original. At the asking price, anyone interested in the early traditions of interpreting this work will enjoy a welcome bargain.

The Bartered Bride (sung in English)
Susan Gritton *sop* Mařenka **Paul Charles Clarke** *ten* Jeník **Timothy Robinson** *ten* Vašek **Peter Rose** *bass* Kecal **Neal Davies** *bar* Krušina **Diana Montague** *mez* Háta **Geoffrey Moses** *bass* Mícha **Yvette Bonner**

sop Ludmila; Esmeralda **Robin Leggate** ten Circus Master **Kit Hesketh-Harvey** bass Indian **Royal Opera House Chorus, Covent Garden; Philharmonia Orchestra / Sir Charles Mackerras**
Chandos Opera in English ② CHAN3128 (148' · DDD) Ⓜ

By almost any reckoning, this is the most popular of Czech operas, in the repertory of almost every opera house, so it is astonishing how few recordings have appeared in recent years; Košler's Supraphon set of 1981 is the only other digital recording. That well-cast version is in the original Czech; this one comes in a crisp translation by Kit Hesketh-Harvey of cabaret duo Kit and the Widow. Hesketh-Harvey, sporting a cheeky cockney accent, also takes the tiny role of the Indian in the Act 3 Circus scene.

What makes this version so successful? The brilliant conducting of Sir Charles Mackerras, of course, plus the scintillating playing of the Philharmonia; an exceptionally strong team of soloists, too. But it's the extra impact of having the comedy delivered in the vernacular that makes this stand out. Echoes of Gilbert and Sullivan can often be distracting when Donizetti or early Verdi are sung in English, but no so here.

Kecal, the marriage-broker, for example, has many patter numbers, and Peter Rose is agile and crystal clear, establishing himself as the key character in the story. Hesketh-Harvey gives the chorus some rapid tongue-twisters to cope with: the Covent Garden Chorus does so admirably.

The sparkling mood is set at the start, with Mackerras taking the Overture at headlong speed and the Philharmonia strings respond- ing with perfect clarity and precision, vividly caught in the warm, clear, well-balanced Chandos recording. The chorus reinforces the mood, and the duet between the heroine Mařenka and her beloved Jeník instantly has you involved in the complicated story.

Susan Gritton is radiant, producing golden tone and rising superbly to the challenge of the poignant numbers when it seems that Jeník has betrayed her. Paul Charles Clarke as her suitor is less successful: the voice becomes strangulated and uneven under pressure though the characterisation is first-rate. Timothy Robinson as the stuttering simpleton Vašek and Robin Leggate as the Circus Master are superb. Peter Rose as Kecal is wonderfully fluent, matched by the excellent Esmeralda of Yvette Bonner, both defying the tradition of having actors in the roles of the circus artists. Strong casting, too, means the two sets of parents make a considerable impact.

Above all, thanks are due to Mackerras for the emotional warmth as well as highlighting the colour and energy of Smetana's masterpiece.

The Bartered Bride
Gabriela Beňačková sop Mařenka **Peter Dvorský** ten Jeník **Miroslav Kopp** ten Vašek **Richard Novák** bass Kecal **Jindřich Jindrák** bar Krušina **Marie Mrázová** mez Háta **Jaroslav Horáček** bass Mícha **Marie Veselá** sop Ludmila **Jana Jonášová** sop

Esmeralda **Alfréd Hampel** ten Circus Master **Prague Philharmonic Chorus; Prague National Theatre Chorus and Ballet; Czech Philharmonic Orchestra / Zdeněk Košler**
Film director **František Filip**
Supraphon 📀 SU7011-9 (138' · NTSC · 4:3 · 2.0 and 5.1 · 0) Ⓕ

Košler's *Bride* remains a benchmark for a modern recording of Smetana's epochal Czech comedy. Supraphon now makes available on DVD the TV film from which that audio set derived. The overture is given in concert, then, via stock footage of Prague and the Vltava, we fade into a touristy museum/studio set of a 19th-century Czech village. Yes, Czech festivals are a riot of colour and movement – but the clothes don't look as if they're fresh off the costume rail. There's no real production as such, just the soloists giving a concert in costume, with movement and 'action' being provided by the dancers and actors. The result is relentlessly pretty, undramatic and dull.

The vocal performances are almost all distinguished. In camera, Richard Novák's light, laid-back Kecal makes more sense than it did without pictures. Peter Dvorský's passionate, Italianate Jeník does itself justice in acting terms. Film close-ups are not overkind to the two 'young' girls of the cast but both Beňačková and Jonášová's Esmeralda know their business. Košler's fluent conducting avoids what one might call the 'German' side of Smetana, heard clearly on Ostrčil's nonpareil set and Mackerras's recent English version (see above). The sound is fine; the picture quality misty.

Fernando Sor   Spanish 1778-1839

After leaving Spain, Spanish composer and guitarist Fernando Sor lived in Paris (1813-15 and from 1826) and London (1815-26) and visited Russia (1823). He was a famous concert performer and wrote over 60 guitar works (sonatas, studies, variations etc) and an important method (1830). His guitar music is notable for its part-writing. He was also admired for his songs and eight ballets (1821-8); other works include an opera (1797) and chamber and keyboard pieces. GROVEmusic

Guitar Works

Fantaisies – No 12, Op 58; No 13, Op 59, 'Fantaisie élégiaque'. Studies, Op 60
Nicholas Goluses gtr
Naxos 8 553342 (65' · DDD) Ⓢ▶

Sor's guitar music forms a body of work that's perhaps the most consistent in quality, and most manageable in quantity of any major guitar composer of the period. While he was born and died later than Beethoven Sor's language was closer to that of Mozart, barely on the edge of romanticism.

He was a polished, elegant composer, whose works have more quiet emotional content and expressiveness than those of his contemporaries, and though he often calls for technical virtuosity he doesn't lean too heavily on it. The *Fantaisie*, Op 58 isn't one of Sor's more riveting works. Goluses plays it in a somewhat matter-of-fact way. The *Fantaisie élégiaque*, arguably Sor's finest single work, elicits a very different response, a deeply sensitive and dignified reading in which the moments of silent grief are given the breathing-space they call for. Sor devoted five opus numbers to his 97 studies, of which Op 60 was the last. Each has a clear technical and/or musical purpose and even the simplest is lovingly crafted music – which is how Goluses treats it, with lots of care lavished on it.

The guitar of Sor's time differed from today's in construction, stringing and sound, and Sor played without using the right-hand nails. Goluses uses a modern instrument and plays with nails, which inevitably leads to differences in sound and, to some extent, interpretation. Accepting the differences, Goluses sets a benchmark for present-day guitarists.

Grand Sonatas – C, Op 22; C, Op 25. Divertissement, Op 23. Eight Short Pieces, Op 24
Adam Holzman gtr
Naxos 8 553340 (75' · DDD)   ⓢ🅓➔

The major works in Holzman's programme are the two sonatas, each with four movements. Of these Op 25 is by far the finer – and the best work of its kind from the period; the last movement is a Minuet, a final lightening of atmosphere that was not then uncommon. The *Divertissement*, Op 23 contains 10 pieces – *Valses*, *Allegrettos*, *Andantes*, a *Minuetto* and an *Allemande*. With a few exceptions they're more likely to be of interest to guitarists than to the general listener.

Holzman plays very well, with a softer sound than Goluses (see above), and in a tighter acoustic. At slower tempos he exercises a pleasing degree of rubato and commendable dynamic shading; one wishes he had done likewise in the quicker ones, which incline to the metronomic. These are two discs that should, both in their own right and at super-budget price, be irresistible to guitarists.

Introduction and Variations on 'Que ne suis-je la fougère!', Op 26. Introduction and Variations on 'Gentil Housard', Op 27. Introduction and Variations on 'Malbroug', Op 28. 12 Studies, Op 29. Fantaisie et Variations brillantes, Op 30
Jeffrey McFadden gtr
Naxos 8 553451 (62' · DDD)   ⓢ🅞🅞🅓➔

This contribution to Naxos's integral archive of Sor's guitar music consists neatly of the last works he published with Meissonnier, before transferring to Pacini. Sets of variations, whether *per se* or framed in the *Fantaisie*, Op 30,

abound. The *12 Studies*, Op 29 are described as 'Book 2', those of Op 6 being 'Book 1', and are here given as Nos 13-24, as they were in the original edition of 1827. Jeffrey McFadden is a very musical player, with the clear and three-dimensional tone for which his fingers are admirably suited. No composer for the guitar of the time wrote studies that were more truly expressive than those of Sor; McFadden plays them, and everything else here, with humanity and respect. An outstanding disc.

Kaikhosru Sorabji   English 1892–1988

Sorabji was of Spanish-Sicilian-Parsi parentage. Largely self-taught, he became known in the 1920s for luxuriant and polyphonic piano works in a style relatable to Szymanowski and Busoni, and sometimes of enormous duration: the Opus clavicembalisticum (1930) plays for nearly three hours. But soon after writing it he withdrew from public activity and placed an embargo on his music, though he continued to compose immense piano and symphonic works, many incorporating Eastern influences. Only in 1976 did he allow performances to recommence. He was a biting critic of flashing wit, who often praised composers who only later became fashionable; his two books contain many of those essays. **GROVE**music

---

Piano Works

'Legendary Works for Piano'

Fantaisie espagnole. Fantasiettina. Gulistān. Le jardin parfumé. Nocturne. Three Pastiches. Opus clavicembalisticum – Introito and Preludio-Corale. Prelude, Interlude and Fugue. Quaere reliqua hujus materiei inter secretiora. St Bertrand de Comminges, 'He was laughing in the tower'. Two Pieces. Valse-Fantaisie. Fragment for Harold Rutland **Habermann** A la manière de Sorabji: 'Au clair de la lune'
Michael Habermann pf
British Music Society ③ 3-for-the-price-of-2 BMS427/9CD (197' · ADD/DDD)   Ⓕ

The music of Sorabji acquired mythic status long before his death in 1988, not least through the ban on public performances imposed by him in 1938. When the ban was lifted in 1976 Michael Habermann was among the first pianists to take up Sorabji in earnest. The fruits of his devotion – technically and conceptually – to some of the most demanding music yet conceived for piano can be heard on these recordings, made over a 15-year period.

Spanning mainly the period 1918-41, the set covers the first half of Sorabji's career, dominated by the vast *Opus clavicembalisticum*, later championed by John Ogdon and Geoffrey Douglas Madge, and represented here by a swift and eventful rendition of its first two sections. 'In the Hothouse' and *Fantaisie espagnole* will appeal to anyone who enjoys the more demonstrative output of Scriabin or Szymanowski, while the pastiches show that Sorabji's music wasn't without humour.

The second disc comprises a trio of nocturnes: pieces whose rhapsodic unfolding belies their intricacy of construction. If the harmonic profile of *Le jardin parfumé* draws in resonances of Delius and pre-echoes of Messiaen, that of *Djâmî* represents a sublimation of means to wholly original ends – and is the undoubted masterpiece of this collection. Aficionados would no doubt make even greater claims for *Gulistān*, but here the very complexity of texture seems designed to conceal rather than intensify expression.

As to the performances, there can be no doubting the extent of Michael Habermann's sympathies, nor his depth of insight. The release comes with informative notes by Habermann, and can be cordially recommended to those keen to immerse themselves in a composer whose singularity of expression is sometimes matched by the conviction of his achievement.

100 Transcendental Studies

100 Transcendental Studies – Nos 1-25
Fredrik Ullén *pf*
BIS BIS-CD1373 (71' · DDD) Ⓕ

Given the number of recordings now appearing, it was inevitable that Kaikhosru Sorabji's 100 *Transcendental Studies* be tackled, and Swedish pianist Fredrik Ullén has taken up the challenge. Composed in 1940-44, the cycle constitutes the largest known collection of its kind – encompassing brief studies in piano technique and extended pieces amply illuminating the 'parallel universe' that is Sorabji's creativity.

Right from No 1 it is clear that Sorabji's conception of the study is all-embracing. No 3 scatters its melodic content over layers of intricate polyphony, while No 6 is a scintillating study in seconds (with studies for each interval to follow). The febrile whole-tone volleys of No 10 and the delicate interplay of melodic patterns in No 14 touch on different but equally characteristic aspects of Sorabji's pianism – less so the Messiaen-like rhythmic unison writing of No 17. The liquid chains of fifths that inform No 18 and the coolly iridescent textures of No 20 confirm these studies as among the highlights of the cycle so far, with the cumulative rhythmic overlaying of No 23 likely to remain among the most technically demanding. The striding staccato chords of No 25 bring this first quarter of the cycle to a typically quizzical conclusion.

Ullén has the dexterity and finesse to do this music justice without making light of either its innate difficulty or its protean imagination.

Louis Spohr   German 1784-1859

Spohr gained his first important experience as a chamber musician at the Brunswick court, soon becoming a virtuoso violinist and touring throughout Germany; his playing was influenced particularly by his admiration for Rode. As Konzertmeister in Gotha (1805-12) he took up conducting (with a baton) and had some of his own works performed but was most successful as a touring artist (1807-21) with his wife, the harpist Dorette Scheidler. Operatic conducting posts at Vienna (1813-15) and Frankfurt (1817-19) coincided with significant bursts of composing activity, yielding chamber music and the successful operas Faust (1813) and Zemire und Azor (1819).

He settled down as Kapellmeister at Kassel in 1822, where the premières of Jessonda (1823; his greatest operatic success), the oratorio Die letzten Dinge (1826) and the Symphony No 4 (1832) were major achievements; here too he contributed to the cultivation of interest in both Bach and Wagner. A favourite in England, he received international honours and became Generalmusikdirektor at Kassel (1847), but by the 1850s he was an aging, middle-class representative of a rather sober tradition, and after his death his works were largely forgotten. Among his instrumental works (15 violin and 10 other concertos, ten symphonies, virtuoso solo works, scores of chamber works, including a series of double quartets), the four clarinet concertos, the string quartets, the Violin Concerto No 8 ('In the form of a vocal scene') and the Octet and Nonet for wind and strings are noteworthy. His operas anticipate Wagner in being through-composed and in their use of leitmotif. GROVE*music*

Clarinet Concertos

Clarinet Concertos – No 1; No 2. Potpourri on Two Themes from Winter's 'Das Unterbrochene'.
Variations on a Theme from 'Alruna'
Michael Collins *cl* **Swedish Chamber Orchestra / Robin O'Neill**
Hyperion CDA67509 (62' · DDD)   ⒻⓄⓄ

The memorable opening C minor theme of the First Clarinet Concerto (1809) has a Beethovenian contour, yet the solo roulades which follow suggest the minor key is not to be taken too seriously. The work, like its companion, was commissioned by the clarinet virtuoso Johann Hermstedt, who adapted his instrument for the music, adding five extra keys! It is a fine piece with a lovely *Adagio* to remind us that Mozart's Quintet was Spohr's inspiration. The charming finale lollops along engagingly.

The Second Concerto, written a year later, is distinctly galant in the jaunty Hummelian march theme which dominates the first movement. The eloquent *Adagio* is unashamedly operatic, with characteristic turns in the melodic line, but the highlight is the *Polacca* finale, opening neatly with a solo timpani flourish answered by the horns. This gives Michael Collins wonderful opportunities for a spirited bravura display that invites a smile of pleasure, as do his fluid, lyrical line and lovely tone and phrasing throughout.

The *Potpourri* opens invitingly on the horns but is no medley. Instead it centres on two themes, the second with a set of variations, offering more bravura fireworks, clearly relished here. The Variations are very much in the same vein. An outstanding disc, excellently recorded.

Sir John Stainer
British 1840-1901

English organist, scholar and composer Stainer, after appointments at St Michael's College, Tenbury, and Oxford University, became organist at St Paul's Cathedral (1872-88), reforming the musical service there, increasing the number of musicians and expanding the repertory. He soon became a pre-eminent church musician, scholar and composer, helping found the Musical Association, and becoming professor at Oxford University. He was knighted in 1888. As a scholar he made valuable editions of music before Palestrina and Tallis (Early Bodleian Music, 1901). His services and anthems were fashionable during his lifetime and his hymn tunes are still used; his oratorio The Crucifixion (1887) is one of his best-known works. GROVEmusic

The Crucifixion

Martyn Hill *ten* **Michael George** *bass* **BBC Singers; Leith Hill Festival Singers / Brian Kay** with **Margaret Phillips** *org*
Chandos CHAN9551 (71' · DDD · T)　　Ⓕ Ⓞ Ⓓ

Stainer's *Crucifixion* unfolds with a seamless ease, never jolting the listener with gratuitous theatricality or the type of rhetorical intensity which the English find mildly embarrassing. The emotional engagement here is about an unintrusive sobriety, affected by a glowing sentimental identification with the Saviour's plight. One has to admire Stainer for writing a challenging work of sensible length which, without an orchestra, is achievable and satisfying for a capable parish choir: Stainer's *Crucifixion* is a celebration of amateurism, that cherished English virtue. Brian Kay has worked a great deal with committed amateurs, in this case the Leith Hill Festival Singers, the festival of which he's director. There's an underlying freshness of expression here, of singers with eyes and ears on stalks and a real sense of purpose. They are fortified by the excellent BBC Singers. Margaret Phillips's imaginative, genial registrations, not to mention her skilful accompaniment, provide notable support to the fine contributions of the solosits. An unselfregarding and genuine performance.

Sir Charles Villiers Stanford
Irish/British 1852-1924

Stanford was educated at Cambridge (1880-84), where he was appointed organist of Trinity College in 1873 and professor in 1887; from 1883 he also taught at the RCM (his own education had been completed under Reinecke in Leipzig, 1874-5, and Kiel in Berlin, 1876). A demanding and highly influential teacher, he also demanded much of himself in living up to the great tradition, though the weight of academic responsibility could be leavened by his Irish heritage of folksong and mysticism and by his keen feeling for English words. Yet, apart from his Anglican cathedral music, little of his large output (nearly 200 opus numbers) has remained in performance. His works include ten operas (notably Shamus O'Brien, 1896; Much Ado about Nothing, 1901; and The Travelling Companion, given posthumously,1926), a quantity of choral music and songs (his B flat Service of 1879 is still used, and some of his sensitive partsongs are remembered, particularly The Blue Bird), seven symphonies and other orchestral scores (Clarinet Concerto, 1902, and a series of Irish Rhapsodies), eight string quartets, and organ and piano music. GROVEmusic

Concertos

Violin Concerto. Suite for Violin and Orchestra, Op 32
Anthony Marwood *vn* **BBC Scottish Symphony Orchestra / Martyn Brabbins**
Hyperion CDA67208 (67' · DDD)　　Ⓕ Ⓞ

This is a discovery of major importance. Hubert Parry (no mean critic) regarded Stanford's Violin Concerto as one of his finest works, yet it has been played rarely, if at all, since his death in 1924. One preliminary word of warning though: despite Stanford's reputation as a disciple of Brahms, don't listen to this concerto expecting it to sound Brahmsian. Often enough it does, but when it doesn't it isn't because Stanford has failed to match the quality of his 'model'; far more often it's because he's going his own way, speaking with his own and not a derivative voice.

The very opening of the concerto is a case in point: the soloist's melody is accompanied by a beautifully delicate texture of plucked strings and rippling woodwind. There's nothing quite like it in Brahms; nor is Brahms always so generous with his thematic material as Stanford is in this movement. After that 'first subject' and an extensive and varied 'second subject group', a big and dramatic orchestral *tutti* leads not to the expected development but to a new and quite splendid theme. There's plenty of room for virtuosity, but very often the display is modified by a pensive quality, a reticence, that's seemingly Stanford's own, and most attractive.

The slow movement is also notable for its individual scoring (very spare at the outset; a magical return of the melancholy opening melody at the end over murmuring *tremolando* strings) and for its melodic distinction. The sadness of the first theme is again reticent, adding greatly to the eloquence of the heartfelt *tutti* that leads to the finest theme in the entire work, upon which Stanford lavishes rhapsodic figuration of great beauty.

There's not a player better suited to bringing this concerto back to life than Anthony Marwood. He easily surmounts its technical demands, but his distinction as a chamber musician enables him to seek out all its quieter subtleties and pensive asides. The Suite is a lesser but still highly entertaining work, an exercise in neo-Baroque designed as a warmly affectionate tribute to Joseph Joachim. Its sheer ingenuity (the first movement, for example, is a combination of sonata form and two sets of interlocked variations) saves it from being a mere exercise, and its melodic freshness from being a mere makeweight to the masterly concerto. First-class orchestral playing, sympathetically conducted, and a recording that's both clean and spacious.

Cello Concerto[a]. Piano Concerto No 3, Op 171 (orch G Bush)[b]
[a]**Alexander Baillie** vc [b]**Malcolm Binns** pf **Royal Philharmonic Orchestra / Nicholas Braithwaite**
Lyrita SRCD321 (65' · DDD)   Ⓕ Ⓓ➔

Stanford composed nine concertos, only four of which made it into print. The Cello Concerto in D minor is an early work dating from 1879-80. Apart from the slow movement, the concerto was never performed and soon consigned to dusty oblivion by its creator. An endearing effort it proves, too, the solo writing always grateful and assured (the central *Adagio* displays a winsome lyrical charm reminiscent of Dvořák and Sullivan) and deftly scored, above all in the finale which trips along most engagingly. Alexander Baillie's impassioned and stylish advocacy could hardly be improved upon (he also supplies the first-movement cadenza); Nicholas Braithwaite and the RPO provide alert support, though string tone is not as sweet as it might be.

Completed four decades later, the Third Piano Concerto survives in just a two-piano score and was orchestrated for this recording by Geoffrey Bush. Perhaps the imposing opening *Allegro moderato*, like the performance itself, takes a while to get into its stride, but the slow movement has one or two unexpected twists and the exuberant finale is a joy. Malcolm Binns gives an accomplished rendering, but his chosen instrument sounds in less than first-class condition and there's little of the enticing bloom evident on his splendid 1976 Lyrita recording of Stanford's Second Concerto. Musically, however, there's plenty to savour.

Symphonies

Symphony No 1. Clarinet Concerto, Op 80a
[a]**Robert Plane** cl **Bournemouth Symphony Orchestra / David Lloyd-Jones**
Naxos 8 570356 (71' · DDD)   Ⓢ Ⓞ Ⓓ➔

This is the final recording in the Naxos series of Stanford symphonies, featuring an unusual coupling of the early (but by no means juvenile)

First Symphony (1876), without an opus number, and the much later Clarinet Concerto (1903). The sound of these Naxos recordings with an on-form Bournemouth SO has a nice forward quality which, for the rather luminous chamber quality of Stanford's second and third movements (especially the solo string- and wind-writing), gives great clarity to the pointillistic, almost Mendelssohnian orchestration.

As with the other three recordings, Lloyd-Jones shows a real flair for the classical architecture of Stanford's art but at the same time he responds to the underlying and inescapable passion that exudes from the scores. The first movement retains a spaciousness and verve, while the finale has an infectious rhythmical élan reminding us of its foremost influence, Schumann's *Spring* Symphony (in the same key).

Stanford's first (though unpublished) foray into symphonic music deserves to be better known but his Clarinet Concerto, here played by Robert Plane, is frequently given an airing. A fine work, in one continuous movement, written for Robert Mühlfeld (who never played it), it makes masterly use of the instrument's wide register and variety of timbres. Plane's interpretation of the composer's long lyrical lines (in particular the central *Andante*), the climactic peaks, dramatic interjections and tender *pianissimi*, are nothing short of exceptional in their careful grading; clearly, he has a special affinity for this music.

Symphonies – No 2, 'Elegiac'; No 5, 'L'Allegro ed il Penseroso'
Bournemouth Symphony Orchestra / David Lloyd-Jones
Naxos 8 570289 (75' · DDD)   Ⓢ Ⓓ➔

Although labelled *Elegiac* and prefaced with lines from Tennyson's *In memoriam*, Stanford's Second Symphony (1880) wears a largely untroubled demeanour. In fact, it's a thoroughly congenial, skilfully scored creation, with frequent glances of approval towards Mendelssohn, Schumann, Brahms and Dvořák, yet it received just two performances in 1882 and 1883 before falling into oblivion. Vernon Handley revived it with the Ulster Orchestra in 1990 and went on to record it a year later as part of his pioneering Stanford symphony cycle (Chandos). Like Handley, David Lloyd-Jones proves an undisruptive, clear-headed guide, while the playing of the Bournemouth SO has an extra finish, buoyancy and lustre that tip the scales in his favour.

Honours are more evenly divided in the altogether meatier Fifth Symphony of 1894, which derives its subtitle and inspiration from Milton's twinned poems *L'Allegro and Il Penseroso*. Lloyd-Jones's bright-eyed approach is especially effective in the first two movements (the rustic *Scherzo* gambols along most winningly), whereas it's Handley who better captures the more thoughtfully restrained character and inexorable grandeur of the work's second half. More-over, Chandos's 1987 Ulster Hall production has the estimable advantage of an organ *in situ* for the symphony's heady apotheosis (its initial entry on the Naxos disc is too discreet – the sound is otherwise very pleasing). Tiny grumbles aside, Lloyd-Jones's remains a strongly recommendable pairing and should be snapped up without delay.

Symphonies – No 3, 'Irish', Op 28; No 6, 'In memoriam GF Watts', Op 94
Bournemouth Symphony Orchestra /
David Lloyd-Jones
Naxos 8 570355 (80' · DDD)　　　　Ⓢ🅑▸

Completed in 1887, the *Irish* Symphony enjoyed considerable acclaim both at home and abroad (von Bülow and Richter were early champions, and in 1910 Mahler conducted two performances in New York). After a solidly constructed opening *Allegro moderato*, the Irish flavour comes to the fore with a disarming hop, skip and jig of a scherzo, followed by a nobly beautiful lament (of markedly Brahmsian hue and framed by some gorgeous harp-writing) and a finale which deploys two folk tunes and ties up the threads in rousingly effective fashion. Lloyd-Jones's is, in fact, the second recording of this lovable creation we've had from Bournemouth and represents a more dynamic and luminous voyage of discovery than its sturdier 1982 predecessor under Del Mar (EMI). Handley's sprightly 1986 Ulster account (Chandos) is arguably more cogent than either but now sounds a little raw next to this judiciously balanced newcomer.

Written very quickly in the spring of 1905 as a personal response to the recent death and legacy of the esteemed Victorian artist George Frederick Watts (1817-1904), the Sixth Symphony has fared less happily, receiving a mere two performances until its Belfast revival under Handley some 80 years later. A looser-limbed affair than its lengthier bedfellow here, it still affords a sizeable quotient of incidental pleasures (the glowingly sincere slow movement and consolatory closing pages stand out from their garrulous surroundings). Lloyd-Jones masterminds an affectionate, finely disciplined reading, with tensions kept agreeably on the boil throughout, though again it's Handley (Chandos) who better disguises any architectural shortcomings. No matter, it all adds up to another thoroughly desirable (and, at just over 80 minutes, generous) coupling in this useful series.

Further listening
Symphonies Nos 1-7
Ulster Orchestra / Vernon Handley
Chandos ④ CHAN9279　　　　Ⓜ🅞▸
　Wonderfully rich and imaginative late-romantic creations – melodically long-breathed and harmonically engaging. Handley conducts superbly paced and splendidly idiomatic performances. Also available to download singly.

Clarinet Sonata

Clarinet Sonata[a]. Piano Trio No 3, Op 158[b].
Fantasy No 1[c]. Fantasy No 2[c]. Three Intermezzi, Op 13[a]
[a]**Robert Plane** *cl* [a]**Mia Cooper** *vn*
[a]**David Adams** *va* [b]**Gould Piano Trio**
(Lucy Gould *vn* Alice Neary *vc* [a]Benjamin Frith *pf*)
Naxos 8 570416 (74' · DDD)　　　　Ⓢ🅞▸

The Clarinet Sonata is one of Stanford's strongest achievements from his later years, boasting at its heart a powerful *Adagio* ('Caoine' – an Irish lament) which finds Plane wonderfully responsive to the music's raw emotion. Ravishing in tone and exploiting an excitingly wide range of dynamic, Plane forges a commandingly articulate alliance with pianist Benjamin Frith. Indeed, it's hard to imagine more sympathetic music-making – a statement which also holds true for the *Three Intermezzi* (an exceedingly attractive trilogy dating from 1879) and the two substantial, utterly disarming *Fantasies* for clarinet and string quartet, written in 1921-22 for use by students towards the end of Stanford's 40-year stint as professor of composition at the Royal College of Music.

As if all that were not enough, we're also treated to the world premiere recording of the last of Stanford's three piano trios. Completed in 1918, it's a tautly constructed, urgently communicative piece dedicated to the memory of the two sons of Alan Gray, Stanford's successor as organist of Trinity College and conductor of the Cambridge University Music Society. Again, the performance is absolutely first-class and, with sound that is at once intimate and true, this valuable anthology can be welcomed with open arms. Naxos's absurdly modest asking-price is the icing on the cake!

String Quartets

String Quartets – No 1; No 2. Fantasy[a]
RTÉ Vanbrugh Quartet (Gregory Ellis, Keith Pascoe *vns* Simon Aspell *va* Christopher Marwood *vc*) with [a]**Stephen Stirling** *hn*
Hyperion CDA67434 (68' · DDD)　　　　Ⓕ

Stanford wrote the first two of his eight string quartets within just six weeks during the summer of 1891. Cast in four movements and impeccably laid out for the medium, the G major First Quartet launches with an impressive *Allegro assai*, whose considerable intellectual and expressive resource is quarried to the full by the Vanbrughs. Both the *Scherzo* and finale smile as they should, while these fine players bring a rare eloquence to the deeply felt slow movement. Superior craftsmanship is also a trademark of its A minor companion. The first movement's ruminative main theme is developed further still in the *Andante espressivo* slow movement. In between comes a dashing *Prestissimo scherzo*. The work concludes with an irresistible *Allegro molto* (whose cheeky initial idea brings with it more than a whiff of Hungarian paprika).

The A minor Fantasy for horn and string quartet (1922), a companion piece to the Two Fantasy Pieces for clarinet quintet completed not long before, shares that diptych's formal integration (its four sections are interlinked) and technical flair. Stephen Stirling audibly relishes the superbly judged horn writing and generates a most satisfying rapport with the Vanbrughs.

These exemplary first recordings make the best possible case for all this rare material; sound and balance are first-class, too.

Piano Quintet

Piano Quintet[a]. String Quintet No 1[b]
Vanbrugh Quartet (Gregory Ellis, Keith Pascoe vns
Simon Aspell va Christopher Marwood vc) with
[b]**Garth Knox** va [a]**Piers Lane** pf
Hyperion CDA67505 (65' · DDD)   (F)

Boosted by the warm reception afforded to his early sonatas for violin and cello and First Piano Quartet, the 33-year-old Stanford penned what would prove to be his biggest chamber work in the spring of 1886. Lasting some 37 minutes and dedicated to Joseph Joachim, the Piano Quintet in D minor owes much to the example of the Schumann and Brahms quintets (one also wonders whether Elgar ever heard it). In its vaulting ambition, consummate polish and wealth of strong ideas, it's a mightily impressive achievement all round; indeed, such is the music's epic sweep, there are pages in the first and third movements especially which seem to cry out for orchestral garb. It's also full of good tunes, not least in the playful scamper of the *Scherzo* and surgingly energetic and confident finale. A considerable discovery, in sum, which Piers Lane and the Vanbrugh Quartet do absolutely proud.

For the First String Quintet of 1903 the Vanbrugh are joined by violist Garth Knox (formerly of the Arditti Quartet) to give a passionate and stylish rendering of a piece of such beguiling facility and songful grace that one is amazed that it has lain neglected for so long. Of its three movements, the most individual and compelling is the extended concluding *Allegretto*, an entrancing theme-and-variations which not only manages to fuse elements of both scherzo and sonata-form finale but also effectively incorporates material from the work's central *Andante* (an Irish lament in all but name).

The booklet essay by Jeremy Dibble is a model of scholarly research and enthusiasm. Flawless sound and balance, too.

Requiem, Op 63

Requiem. The Veiled Prophet of Khorassan –
Overture; Ballet music No 1; There's a bower of
roses; Ballet music No 2
Virginia Kerr, Frances Lucey sops **Colette
McGahon** mez **Peter Kerr** ten **Nigel Leeson-
Williams** bass-bar **RTÉ Philharmonic Choir and
National Symphony Orchestra of Ireland / Adrian
Leaper, Colman Pearce**
Naxos ② 8 555201/2 (105' · DDD · T)   Ⓢ◗

This resissue of a late-Victorian masterpiece gains the well-deserved chance of wider circulation on the popular Naxos label. The Requiem was written in 1896 in memory of Lord Leighton. Scored for the usual forces of solo quartet, chorus and orchestra, it strikes a familiar balance between grief and condolence; its manner is essentially lyrical, its form determined by that of the Mass and by its well-defined musical climaxes. Yet the composer's individuality is everywhere unobtrusively evident, as is the warmth of his feeling. If these things were indeed too unobtrusive to gain recognition in their own time and the largely unsympathetic century that followed, they should win it now.

The performance is admirable, with good work by all four soloists. A special word of appreciation is due to the delightful soprano, Frances Lucey. The choir needs more presence in the recorded sound, which in general is none too sharply defined. The excerpts from *The Veiled Prophet*, another rarity, provide a well-chosen bonus.

Stabat mater, Op 96

Stabat mater. Te Deum. Six Bible Songs
Ingrid Attrot sop **Pamela Helen Stephen** mez **Nigel
Robson** ten **Stephen Varcoe** bar **Ian Watson** org
**Leeds Philharmonic Chorus; BBC Philharmonic
Orchestra / Richard Hickox**
Chandos CHAN9548 (74' · DDD · T/t)   (F)●

Writing of his old teacher in 1952, Vaughan Williams foretold that his time would come round again: 'With the next generation the inevitable reaction will set in and Stanford will come into his own.' It has taken more than a generation, but at last it does begin to look as though he was right. This recording of a 'symphonic cantata', the *Stabat mater*, strong in ideas, deeply felt and structurally assured, will certainly strengthen the steadily growing appreciation of his worth. The Prelude, impressive as it is, is almost *too* soundly constructed, and the first choral movement, rich in its Verdi-like foreground of soloists, signs off with a slightly self-conscious repetition of the opening words by the soprano. Stanford is never abashed by the prospect of melodic commitment, and the orchestral Intermezzo comes out boldly with what promises to be a good, old-fashioned Grand Tune; but then he seems to remember where he is, and the piece ends with murky explorations that seem not quite to find what they may be seeking. The work itself ends, as Lewis Foreman suggests in his useful notes, in Eternity: 'we seem to reach the crest of a hill only to find the path stretching onward and upward to another.' The performance carries conviction, with Hickox exercising that natural rightness of his so that in a work such as this, without predecessors on record, a listener will feel that this is how it should 'go'.

Fine orchestral playing and choral singing give pleasure throughout. The solo quartet is led by

Ingrid Attrot's colourful but none too evenly produced soprano, and in the *Bible Songs* Stephen Varcoe sings sensitively to the judiciously registered organ accompaniment of Ian Watson. The most tuneful of *Te Deum*s follows, blithe and buoyant in its orchestrated version.

Morning and Evening Services

Morning and Evening Services in B flat, Op 10[a].
Evening Services – A, Op 12[a]; F, Op 36[a]; E flat[b]. Two Anthems, Op 37[b]. Three Motets, Op 38. Pater noster. The Lord is my Shepherd[a]
Winchester Cathedral Choir / David Hill with [a]**Stephen Farr,** [b]**Christopher Monks** org
Hyperion CDA66964 (78' · DDD · T)   Ⓕ❍

The *Magnificat and Nunc dimittis* in E flat major dates back to 1873 isn't with any certainty known even to have been performed. Perhaps this is because both settings are almost indecently tuneful: an apocalyptic 'scattered the proud', a broadly melodious 'to be a light' and a 'Gloria' as catchy as a comic opera. As for the B flat major settings written six years later, these (both Morning and Evening services) have long owed their popularity to a melodic gift that's almost Schubertian and a correspondingly deft mastery of construction.

Winchester Cathedral Choir is surely one of the best in the UK. Under David Hill, the trebles have some of the bright, distinctive tone of the Westminster Cathedral boys. The men are excellent, and all sound as though they're singing for the joy of it. Several of these works involve more than the customary four parts, and the eight-part *Pater noster*, recorded for the first time, has splendid richness, with the choir forming massive pillars of sound in the powerful climax. Stanford's writing for the organ is also a delight, and at times we might wish that the fine playing of both organists had been brought into sharper focus. The choir we hear with rare clarity.

Evening Service in G, Op 81. Services in C, Op 115. Six Short Preludes and Postludes: Set 2, Op 105 – No 3, Prelude in G; No 6, Postlude in D minor. For lo, I raise up, Op 145. Three Motets, Op-38.
St John's College Choir, Cambridge / Christopher Robinson org
Naxos 8 555794 (72' · DDD)   Ⓢ❍➔

The mean old saying, 'Those who can, do, and those who can't, teach', would have withered in the presence of Stanford; and no doubt one of the reasons why he was such a great teacher is that he could and did, and so set an example. His C major services (Morning, Evening and Communion, all included in this programme) are so eminently the works of a master who knows how to get from here to there in one move, to keep always something in reserve for later use but never to write without a good clear melodic idea in the first place. Everything in this programme has freshness and well-founded assurance. It's

music with clarity of purpose: it knows where it's going and doesn't put a foot wrong.

Under Christopher Robinson, the choir has enjoyed a period in which the distinguishing mark has been a renewed vitality of style. It's well caught in this CD. The start of the first track, the C major Te Deum, has it straightaway – the praise carries spirit and conviction. The final track opens still more strikingly. This is *For lo, I will raise up*, for which Stanford, writing in 1914, set his imagination free to bestir the choir-stalls into an almost fiercely dramatic life. The St John's choir bite into the words with relish, while the acoustic and their well-judged tempo reinforce the rhythmic energy of the passage.

Even in the best-stocked collection this would prove a welcome addition, and for those who have as yet nothing of the master, it should provide a lively introduction.

Songs

Tragödie, Op 14 No 5. Op 19 – No 2, A Lullaby; No 5, To the Rose. Windy Nights, Op 30 No 4. Clown's Songs from 'Twelfth Night', Op 65. The Fairy Lough, Op 77 No 2. Songs of the Sea, Op 91. Songs of Faith, Op 97 – No 4, 'To the Soul'; No 6, 'Joy, Shipmate, Joy'. Phoebe, Op 125. A Fire of Turf, Op 139. The Pibroch, Op 157 No 1. For Ever Mine. Tom Lemminn
Stephen Varcoe bar **Clifford Benson** pf
Hyperion CDA67124 (77' · DDD · T/t)   Ⓕ❍

Stanford's *Songs of the Sea* have kept the British baritone afloat for the best part of a century. Drake's hammock and the barnacles of The Old Superb used to be familiar in parlours and drawing-rooms throughout the land. The cries of Captain Keats and his crew ('"Ship ahoy!" a hundred times a day'), the alliterative mysteries of 'Fetter and Faith … Faggot and Father' and the assurance that Drake even now was 'ware and waking' were assimilated almost as the words of folksongs, while the music seemed part of our flesh and blood. They are splendid songs, and the set of five constitutes a small masterpiece. Sceptical readers should try them again in this new recording. Stephen Varcoe and Clifford Benson give a most sensitive performance, not emasculated but treating them thoughtfully. The two quieter songs, 'Outward Bound' and 'Homeward Bound', become more central, better integrated, than usual, and the very fact that this is the solo version, without the male-voice chorus added later, makes it easier to hear them (the whole set) as a personal utterance. With 'Drake's Drum', for instance, Varcoe is very intent upon seeing sense, where others have often sought for little beyond a generalised patriotic earnestness. These, perhaps, are *The Songs of the Sea* as Captain Edward Fairfax Vere might have sung them.

In reviewing the first volume, Michael Oliver wrote of the difficulty of reconciling the Irishman and the Brahmsian in Stanford: the melodic vein of the one seemed at odds with the harmonic language of the other. The occasions here when a dichotomy of style does cause trouble are found in the *Songs of Faith*. Whitman's auto-intoxication incites Stanford to indulge in grandiose gestures that aren't natural to him at all. He's much more at home with Shakespeare and Dekker, or, for that matter, with Quiller-Couch and Winifred M Letts, whose *A Fire of Turf* provides him with poems for some masterly settings. All are beautifully performed by these excellent artists.

Songs of the Fleet. Songs of the Sea. The Revenge: a Ballad of the Fleet
Gerald Finley *bar* **BBC National Chorus and Orchestra of Wales / Richard Hickox**
Chandos ⚛ CHSA5043 (70' · DDD · T) Ⓕ**OOO**→

Two of Stanford's catchiest and most popular settings frame his 1904 *Songs of the Sea* for baritone, male chorus and orchestra: both 'Drake's Drum' and 'The Old Superb' are instantly memorable and have alone justly secured the work's survival. But there's some terrific music tucked away in the three remaining numbers, not least the marvellously serene 'Homeward Bound' with its burnished orchestral palette (Stanford's skilful scoring gives enormous pleasure throughout, in fact), rapt eloquence (nowhere more potent than at the line 'Swiftly the great ship glides') and adventurous harmonic scope.

Six years later, Stanford returned to Henry Newbolt's maritime verse to pen a more reflective sequel entitled *Songs of the Fleet*. Its spacious centrepiece, 'The Middle Watch', evokes a dusky mystery and sense of awe, while the opening 'Sailing at Dawn' is a gloriously assured and noble essay worthy of Elgar himself. In both sets, Gerald Finley's firmly focused, ringing tone is a joy. He doens't possess the salty tang of Benjamin Luxon (a true sea-dog if ever there was one), but the voice is steadier and he sings with unfailing ardour, intelligence and sensitivity. Hickox and his BBC Welsh forces provide exemplary support.

Not so immediately appealing is the 1886 choral ballad *The Revenge*, one of the composer's biggest early successes. Tennyson's poem depicts how Sir Richard Grenville and his Devonian crew aboard Revenge took on – and inflicted terrible damage upon – the Spanish fleet off the Azores in 1591 (one ship against 53 – believe it or not!). Stanford's breezy setting proved a hit with Victorian choral societies up and down the land. Though no forgotten masterpiece, it's most ably served by Hickox and company. Throw in an admirable booklet-essay by Jeremy Dibble and ripe, airy sound from Chandos, and it certainly adds up to a hearty recommendation.

Wilhelm Stenhammar
Swedish 1871-1929

Brought up in a cultivated and musical family, Stenhammar composed from childhood and had little *formal training. His earlier music is in a late Romantic style showing influences from Wagner, Liszt and Brahms, but from 1910 he moved towards a more classical manner, stimulated by contrapuntal studies and a profound concern with Beethoven. Much of his music has a Nordic colour, though he did not use folk material. His works include two symphonies, two piano concertos, cantatas, six string quartets (1894-1916) and songs. An admired pianist, he was also conductor of the Göteborgs Orkesterförening (1906-22).* GROVEmusic

Symphony No 2, Op 34

Excelsior! Symphony No 2
Royal Scottish National Orchestra / Petter Sundkvist
Naxos 8 553888 (58' · DDD) Ⓢ→

This is the first recording of Stenhammar's G minor Symphony to be made by a non-Swedish orchestra; Petter Sundkvist, a young Swedish conductor, draws very good results from the RSNO and conducts with evident feeling.

This symphony grows more glorious with every hearing and this time is no exception. Sundkvist realizes its moments of poetry with a natural ardour and eloquence and without the slightest expressive self-indulgence. He builds up the architecture of the symphony impressively.

The exhilarating *Excelsior!* overture can more than hold its own with any rival, even if the recording doesn't. The acoustic is a shade on the dryish side. Notwithstanding this caveat, the quality of the performance is such as to deserve a strong recommendation.

Piano Sonatas

Piano Sonatas – in G minor (1890); Op 12. Nights of Late Summer, Op 33. Three Fantasies, Op 11
Martin Sturfält *pf*
Hyperion CDA67689 (76' · DDD) Ⓕ

Although Stenhammar's orchestral and *concertante* works are now quite well known, the music he wrote for the piano has, until recently, been unfamiliar. As a recitalist he seemed to value the music of others more than his own. He gave his splendid G minor Sonata (composed at 19) its premiere in May 1891 and then never played it again! Yet it is an ambitious, romantic work with an unforgettable main theme dominating its first movement, and in many ways it is an equivalent in its youthful ardour of the Brahms F minor work.

Stenhammar did, however, take the Three Fantasies, Op 11, of 1895 into his repertoire. They are Brahms-influenced, the first again boldly passionate, but the composer's own personality comes through, notably so in the ingenious *Dolce scherzando* and the closing *Molto espressivo*. The five pieces which make up *Nights of Late Summer* are certainly atmospheric but not overtly descriptive: their feeling is personal and introspective, although the exception is the closing charming *Poco allegretto*, which has almost a whiff of Grieg. But the late A major Sonata (composed in the same year) is a highly individual work balancing serious, even sombre, lyricism with drama and closing with a vibrant unpredictable finale. Martin Sturfält suggests it has an affinity with Beethoven.

He plays all this music with powerful feeling and understanding, and great spontaneity – as at a live recital – and the recording is very real indeed. Well worth exploring.

Rudi Stephan   German 1887-1915

Rudi Stephan (1887-1915) remains one of 20th-century music's most tantalising 'might have beens'. Before his death aged just 28 in the trenches on the Eastern Front, the young German composer had produced an opera, Die ersten Menschen (1910), as well as a clutch of single-movement essays which display a highly developed grasp of organic thought and serve up a heady stylistic cocktail.

Orchestral works

Music for Violin and Orchestra[a]. Music for Orchestra (1910). Music for Orchestra (1912)
[a]**Sergey Stadler** vn **Melbourne Symphony Orchestra / Oleg Caetani**
Chandos ⏤ CHSA5040 (63' · DDD)   Ⓕ🅓➜

The main interest here surrounds the first commercial recording of the 1910 *Music for Orchestra*. Premiered in Munich in January 1911, it's an ambitious and frequently arresting creation. Caetani secures a polished and shapely rendering, though a touch more thrusting purpose might not have come amiss. That observation also holds true for the performance of its eponymous and altogether more tightly knit bedfellow from two years later (both pieces share some thematic material).

In the *Music for Violin and Orchestra* Sergey Stadler plays with admirable precision and sensitivity, though rather greater passion and tonal warmth wouldn't come amiss. This is fascinating and frequently intoxicating repertoire – do to try it. Play 'spot the influence' and you might come up with names as diverse as Wagner, Mahler, Richard Strauss, Debussy, Berg, Reger, Schreker, Hindemith and Szymanowski. The sound is spacious and true.

Die ersten Menschen

Die ersten Menschen
Gabriele Maria Ronge sop Chawa **Hans Aschenbach** ten Chabel **Florian Cerny** bar Kajihn
Siegmund Nimsgern bass Adahm
Berlin Radio Symphony Orchestra / Karl Anton Rickenbacher

CPO ② CPO999 980-2 (112' · DDD · T/t)   Ⓕ

Die ersten Menschen ('The first humans'), the Bible story of Cain and Abel given an erotic, early-20th-century psychological spin by playwright Otto Borngräber, was Stephan's first and only completed opera. The musical language is most akin to that of Richard Strauss, yet, when you start making detailed comparisons with individual works, it's more often the case that the younger composer is anticipating or paralleling the progress of his famous contemporary. The quasi-recitative setting of dialogues recalls strongly Barak and his brothers in *Die Frau ohne Schatten*, while Chawa's (Eve's) big opening number in Act 2, 'Allmachtiger', feels like a first run for Helena's 'Zweite Brautnacht' more than a decade in the future. Occasionally, too, a certain folky tang or Oriental lushness (Stephan invoking the world just post-Garden of Eden) reminds us that *Duke Bluebeard's Castle* was on Bartók's desk at the same period.

The four-handed, two-act drama runs its course excitingly until Abel's murder. If Stephan sometimes is over-faithful to Borngräber's play in the sheer amount of soliloquising he gives his characters (especially Kajihn, his Cain), and is rather too fond of *tremolando* effects, it's a significant and obviously stageable achievement for a first go at the medium. This performance is blessed by fluent, stylish singing, especially from Gabriele Maria Ronge as the (literally) much put-upon Chawa/Eve, but lacks that extra degree of dramatic insight that an interpretation taken from the stage would have brought. Karl Anton Rickenbacher, an expert in rare Strauss, is careful to allow Stephan's often Pfitzner-like lyricism its say alongside more purple passages. The 1998 recording (Deutschland Radio) is clean and true. So far, so good – but once again the wholly incompetent English translations used by CPO render booklet-note and libretto both risible and annoying to non-German readers.

Karlheinz Stockhausen
German 1928-2007

The leading German composer of his generation, he has been a seminal figure of the post-1945 avant garde. A tireless innovator and influential teacher, he largely redefined notions of serial composition, and was a pioneer in electronic music. His seven-part operatic cycle Licht is possibly the most ambitious project ever undertaken by a major composer.
GROVEmusic

Stimmung
Theatre of Voices / Paul Hillier
Harmonia Mundi ⏤ HMU80 7408 (78' · DDD/DSD)
Ⓕ🅞🅞🅓➜

Paul Hillier sang bass in the famous performances of Stockhausen's psychedelic *Stimmung* that Gregory Rose's Singcircle vocal troupe toured during the mid-1980s. Two decades on and Hillier's understanding of this unique piece might even be greater than the composer's own. He has objectivity on his side – a quality that Stockhausen himself squandered many moons ago.

Stimmung is structured around an electronically sustained drone that is sounded throughout the work's duration. Anchored around B flat, the drone contains the complex harmonic overtone series around which Stockhausen constructs his constantly generating sound world of rarefied timbres and ethereal melodies. He provides embryonic melodic cells and fragments of text, arranged in 51 'Models', leaving the singers to embellish this given material during the performance. It's probably more accurate to say that *Stimmung* is 'realised' than 'performed'.

If this all sounds rather academic then the result is actually one of the most gorgeous vocal soundscapes in all 20th-century music. Hillier's Theatre of Voices operate at such a refined level of specialised technique that radically new expressive territory emerges. Standard vocal delivery feels superseded by loops of vocalised harmonics, tactile humming and, as the piece nears its conclusion, a catchy whistled refrain that calmly draws threads together. Stockhausen's flexi-notation blurs the supply and demand chain that usually defines composer and performer relationships. The musicians are licensed to define the micro as they transform and deliberate over the material. They converse and explore, and an enigmatic piece-specific discipline is created. A thrilling and important performance.

Helicopter String Quartet

Helicopter String Quartet
Arditti Quartet (Irvine Arditti, Graeme Jennings *vns* Garth Know *va* Rohan de Saram *vc*)
Video director **Frank Scheffer**
Medici Arts DVD 307 7508 (77' · DDD) Ⓕ

When word went round the contemporary music community that Stockhausen was sending the Arditti Quartet up in helicopters there were some who said he was touched by genius. Others reckoned he was just touched. A decade on, how does Stockhausen's *Helicopter Quartet* really stand up?

Frank Scheffer's gripping documentary follows Stockhausen and the Ardittis as they prepare for the premiere, and his film ends with the complete performance. Stockhausen is on hand throughout to explain himself. If the concept of sending each member of a string quartet up in their own helicopter, where what they play is beamed back into the concert hall and mixed electronically with the sounds of the 'copters seems eccentric, then Stockhausen explains he is simply following the directions of his dreams. From *Gruppen* – his 1957 piece for three spatially distributed orchestras – onwards he was always interested in the idea of sound flying around the heads of his listeners. And here is a supreme realisation of that fantasy.

You could argue that Stockhausen had long since lost touch with reality by the time he conceived and executed this piece. But that's missing the point: although Stockhausen's rock-star ego did lead him to produce some tedious late pieces that relied on the unquestioning faith of his groupies, the *Helicopter String Quartet* has a charm and fascination of its own. As Stockhausen deconstructs his material during rehearsal, singing bits to the players, it becomes clear there is real harmonic depth and melodic direction. Shame about the carbon footprint though.

Alessandro Stradella Italian 1644-1682

Stradella spent most of his career in Rome, where he lived independently but composed many works to commissions from Queen Christina of Sweden, the Colonna family and others. Most of his stage works there were prologues and intermezzos, notably for operas by Cavalli and Cesti revived at the new Tordinona Theatre in 1671-2. His life included many scandals and amorous adventures. He left Rome in 1677 after a dispute, and went by way of Venice and Turin (escaping an attempt on his life) to Genoa (1678). His only comic opera, Il Trespolo tutore, was given there in c 1677; later he presented several other operas, including Il Corispero. He was killed there in 1682, again a consequence of an amorous intrigue.

Stradella was one of the leading composers in Italy in his day and one of the most versatile. His music was widely admired, even as far afield as England. Most of it is clearly tonal, and counterpoint features prominently. His vocal output includes c 30 stage works, several oratorios and Latin church works and some 200 cantatas (most for solo voice). In his operas the orchestra consists of two violin parts and continuo, but some other works, such as the oratorio S Giovanni Battista (1675, Rome), follow the Roman principal of concerto grosso instrumentation. There is a clear differentiation between aria and recitative (which sometimes includes arioso writing), but their succession is still fluid; various aria forms are used. Stradella's 27 surviving instrumental works are mostly of the sonata da chiesa type. **GROVE**music

San Giovanni Battista

San Giovanni Battista
Anke Herrmann, Elena Cecchi Fedi *sops* **Martín Oro** *counterten* **Fredrik Akselberg** *ten* **Antonio Abete** *bass* **Academia Montis Regalis / Alessandro De Marchi**
Hyperion CDA67617 (78' · DDD) Ⓕ●

Stradella's *San Giovanni Battista*, composed for the church of San Giovanni dei Fiorentini in Rome in 1675, is an oratorio that verges on opera. As well as the familiar characters of John the Baptist, Salome, Herod and Herodias, there is an unnamed Counsellor: combined, they form a five-part chorus. The rich string accompaniment is made up of a *concertino* and a *concerto grosso*, which play both separately and together. Alessandro de Marchi makes the most of these forces by inserting short instrumental pieces by two contemporary composers at appropriate points in the story.

The music is delightfully varied, and the performers do it full justice. Martín Oro makes a rich-toned John the Baptist. The action begins with John bidding farewell to pastoral delights with a continuo aria; then, as he leaves to make a nuisance of himself at Herod's court, he embarks on a nautical metaphor aria – winds, sea, billows – with roulades that Oro dispatches with virtuoso precision.

In many of the arias, the instruments accompany the voice rather than simply providing a *ritornello*. When Herod condemns John to prison, the *concerto grosso* plays in the first section, the *concertino* in the second. Antonio Abete rages impressively, his solid bass showing an admirable fleetness. Anke Herrmann's Salome is seductive and wheedling by turns. This is an excellent disc.

Eduard Strauss	Austrian 1835-1916
Johann Strauss I	Austrian 1804-1849
Josef Strauss	Austrian 1827-1870
Johann Strauss II	Austrian 1825-1899

This Austrian family of dance musicians and composers gave the Viennese waltz its classic expression. Johann senior, a violinist in Josef Lanner's dance orchestra, formed a band in 1825 which became famous for its open-air concerts with his original dance music and paraphrases on the symphonic and operatic music of the day, all performed with exquisite precision. He took the band on European tours from 1833, creating a sensation with the fire and finesse of his conducting, violin in hand. His music, its Austrian folk flavour refined by a characteristic rhythmic piquancy (cross-rhythms, syncopations, pauses and rests), includes over 150 sets of waltzes, besides galops, quadrilles (which he introduced to Vienna), marches (notably the Radetzky-Marsch Op-228), polkas and potpourris.

Johann had three sons who were composer-conductors. Johann II, also a violinist and the most eminent member of the family, directed his own orchestra, 1844-9, in rivalry with his father's; after 1849 the two Strauss bands were merged into one. Vienna's imperial-royal music director for balls, 1863-71, and Austria's beat-known ambassador (the 'king of the waltz'), he was acclaimed by swarms of admirers, especially on European tours, 1856-86, and in the USA (1872). In form, his waltzes resemble his father's – slow introduction, five waltzes and coda – but the sections are longer and more organic; the melodies, often inspired, are wide and sweeping, the harmonic and orchestral details richer and more subtle, even Wagnerian in places. Among his most

celebrated waltz masterpieces, dating from the 1860s and early 1870s, are Accellerationen Op 234, Wiener Bonbons Op 307, An die schönen, blauen Donau ('The Blue Danube') Op 314, Wein, Weib und Gesang Op 333 and Wiener Blut Op 354. Of his 17 operettas, the sparkling Die Fledermaus (1874) and the colourful Die Zigeunerbaron (1885) deservedly claim a central place in the repertory.

His brother Josef was a melancholy introvert, shared the direction of the family orchestra in the 1850s and 1860s, and composed waltzes in a more serious, Romantic vein, as well as polkas, quadrilles and marches. The younger brother Eduard, Vienna's imperial-royal music director for balls, 1872-1901, became the best conductor of the family and was much sought after by orchestras throughout Europe.

GROVEmusic

Dance Music

'Ein Straussfest II'
E Strauss Ohne Aufenthalt, Op 112 **Josef Strauss** Plappermäulchen, Op 245. Sphären-Klänge, Op 235. Jockey, Op 278 **J Strauss I** Chinese Galop, Op 20 **J Strauss II** Ägyptischer Marsch, Op 335a. Künstler-Quadrille, Op 71. Kaiser-Walzer, Op 437. Freikugeln, Op 326. Jubelfest-Marsch, Op 396. Tritsch-Tratsch-Polka, Op 214. Geisselhiebe, Op 60. Klipp Klapp, Op 466. Wein, Weib und Gesang, Op 333. Perpetuum mobile, Op 257
Cincinnati Pops Chorale and Orchestra / Erich Kunzel
Telarc CD80314 (68' · DDD)   Ⓕ Ⓞ

This collection sets out to adorn popular Strauss pieces with sound effects to outdo anything one hears at a Vienna New Year Concert. It starts with Eduard Strauss's *Ohne Aufenthalt*, which is accompanied by steam railway effects, has bullets flying mercilessly in the *Freikugeln* Polka, and includes neighing nags and swishing whips in the *Jockey* Polka. The fun is increased by the inclusion of the *Künstler-Quadrille*, a sort of 1850s 'Hooked on Classics' that begins with Mendelssohn's 'Wedding March' and continues through the likes of Mozart's Symphony No 40 and Chopin's 'Funeral March' Sonata to Beethoven's *Ruins of Athens* and *Kreutzer* Sonata. If the Viennese lilt is just a shade lacking in the waltzes, the playing is nevertheless excellent throughout. The Strausses themselves would have approved.

J Strauss II An der schönen, blauen Donau. Furioso. Egyptischer Marsch. Eljen a Magyar! Frühlingsstimmen. Im Sturmschritt. Neue Pizzicato. Nordseebilder. Perpetuum mobile. Tritsch-Tratsch. Die Fledermaus – Overture; Csárdás. Der Zigeunerbaron – Overture
Anima Eterna / Jos van Immerseel
Zig Zag Territoires ZZT020601 (71' · DDD)   Ⓕ

Most of us have got used to period instruments playing Beethoven but 'early music' groups tackling later repertoire still raise eyebrows. Similarly, the suggestion that there is a good composer named Strauss whose first name is not Richard usually invokes derision.

Both of these sniffy attitudes are bravely challenged by Jos van Immerseel, who penitently writes that 'like many musicians I found Strauss's music a bit cheap. This wasn't the case when I began studying music as a 10-year-old and sight-read Strauss waltzes… I liked the music, but the pleasure was short-lived. In the music school where I next studied, it was forbidden to play music by Strauss (or to enjoy anything); Bach and Czerny replaced Strauss on the music desk. The prejudice against Strauss's "unworthy" music made it impossible for me to appreciate even his orchestral scores.'

Aided by a new critical edition published by Bärenreiter, Immerseel's vibrant and ostentatious revisionist approach allows no wilting pretentiousness, but instead the superb Anima Eterna use their period instruments to deliver full-on, gutsy, direct performances that are an unaffected joy.

'New Year's Concert, 2002'
Hellmesberger II Danse diabolique **J Strauss** Beliebte Annen-Polka, Op 137. Radetzky March, Op 228 **J Strauss II** Zivio!, Op 456. Carnevalsbotschafter, Op 270. Künsterleben, Op 316. Die Fledermaus – Overture. Perpetuum mobile, Op 257. Elisen-Polka, Op 151. Wiener Blut, Op 354. Tik-Tak Polka, Op 365. An der schönen blauen Donau, Op 314 **Josef Strauss** Die Schwätzerin, Op 144. Vorwärts!, Op 127. Arm in Arm, Op 215. Aquarellen-Polka, Op 258. Die Libelle, Op 204. Plappermäulchen, Op 245. Im Fluge, Op 230
Vienna Philharmonic Orchestra / Seiji Ozawa
Video director **Brian Large**
TDK Mediactive **DVD** DV-WPNK02 (141' · 16:9 · 2.0, 5.0 & DTS 5.0 · 0)   Ⓕ

What an advantage DVD provides in comparison with the Philips CD of this concert. Quite apart from the bonus of visual presentation, the DVD offers five numbers omitted from the CD – two of them by Josef Strauss celebrating his 175th anniversary, the polkas *Arm in Arm* and *Im Pfluge* and three Johann Strauss numbers, the *Carnevalsbotschafter* waltz, the *Beliebte Annen* polka and *Perpetuum mobile*.

Ozawa is at his most relaxed, naturally idiomatic in his often extreme use of idiomatic pauses and of warm *rubato*, reflected in his decision not to use a baton, relying instead on the inborn expressiveness of the Viennese players to mould in perfect time. In the *Fledermaus* Overture, for example, the switches of tempo and rhythm and the affectionate phrasing are immaculately achieved with a mere flutter of the fingers from the conductor.

Even by the standards of this celebratory occasion this was an unusually warm and happy event thanks to Ozawa. And more than anyone since Karajan in his one New Year concert, Ozawa controls the clapping of the audience, limiting it to the proper passages in the final *Radetzky March*. The direction can't be faulted.

Die Fledermaus

Die Fledermaus
Julia Varady sop Rosalinde **Lucia Popp** sop Adele **Hermann Prey** ten Eisenstein **René Kollo** ten Alfred **Bernd Weikl** bar Doctor Falke **Ivan Rebroff** bass/mez Prince Orlofsky **Benno Kusche** bar Frank **Ferry Gruber** ten Blind **Evi List** sop Ida **Franz Muzeneder** bass Frosch **Bavarian State Opera Chorus and Orchestra / Carlos Kleiber**
DG The Originals ② 457 765-2GOR2 (107' · ADD · T/t) Recorded 1975   ⓂⓄⒶ☞

Twenty-five years after its original release there's still no recording of *Die Fledermaus* that, for many collectors, matches this one for the compelling freshness of its conductor's interpretation – the attention to every nuance of the score and the ability to bring out some new detail, all allied to extreme precision of vocal and instrumental ensemble. The ladies, too, as so often seems to be the case in recordings of *Die Fledermaus*, are quite superlatively good, with ideally characterised and projected singing. If the men are generally less outstandingly good, one can have no more than minor quibbles with the Eisenstein of Hermann Prey or the Alfred of René Kollo. But it's less easy to accept Ivan Rebroff singing the role of Orlofsky falsetto. Some collectors find that his contribution quite ruins the whole set, but most will find it tolerable enough for the glories to be found elsewhere on the recording.

DG remastered the set to make it sound as though it were recorded only yesterday; but it continues to provoke puzzlement by the break between discs, which occurs during the Act 2 finale. If a split into such uneven lengths is to be made, why not have it between Acts 1 and 2? Enough of minor quibbles – this set is a 'must buy'.

Die Fledermaus
Peter Anders ten Gabriel von Eisenstein **Anny Schlemm** sop Rosalinde **Hans Wocke** bar Frank **Anneliese Müller** mez Prince Orlofsky **Helmut Krebs** ten Alfred **Herbert Brauer** bar Dr Falke **Edwin Heyer** ten Dr Blind **Rita Streich** sop Adele **Sylvia Menz** sop Ida **Fritz Hoppe** spkr Frosch
RIAS Chamber Choir and Symphony Orchestra / Ferenc Fricsay
Audite mono ② AUDITE23 411 (114' · ADD) Recorded 1949   Ⓜ

The history of complete *Fledermaus* recordings post-Second World War is generally considered to begin with the 1950 Decca recording with Clemens Krauss conducting the VPO. This Fricsay version, though, predates it, having been recorded for West Berlin Radio at the Titania Palast in November 1949. Its currency is fully deserved. Fricsay was a fine (and prolific) conductor of Johann Strauss, and his roots were, after all, as much on the Danube as Krauss's. If his *Fledermaus* Overture opens more soberly

JOHANN STRAUSS II
DIE FLEDERMAUS – IN BRIEF

Julia Varady *Rosalinde* **Lucia Popp** *Adele*
Hermann Prey *Eisenstein* **Bavarian State Opera
Chorus and Orchestra / Carlos Kleiber**
DG ② 457 765-2GOR2 (107' · ADD)   Ⓜ**OO▷**
Kleiber's mercurial, translucent conducting
and a superb cast make this a marvellous per-
formance – except, sadly, for popular singer
Ivan Rebroff's weird falsetto Orlofsky.

Elisabeth Schwarzkopf *Rosalinde* **Rita Streich** Ⓗ
Adele **Nicolai Gedda** *Eisenstein* **Philharmonia
Chorus and Orchestra / Herbert von Karajan**
EMI ② 567074-2 (110' · AAD)   Ⓜ**OO**
A 1955 mono recording, but with a wonder-
fully idiomatic cast and Karajan's urbane
conducting it still sounds engaging.

Die Fledermaus   Ⓗ
Anny Schlemm *Rosalinde* **Peter Anders**
Eisenstein **Rita Streich** *Adele* **RIAS Chamber
Choir and SO / Ferenc Fricsay**
Audite mono ② AUDITE23 411 (114' · ADD)   Ⓜ
It may date from 1949, it may be in mono but
this is a performance that has a wonderful
youghful zest. Fricsay conducts with terrific
style and panache.

Hilde Gueden *Rosalinde* **Erika Köth** *Adele*
Waldemar Kmentt *Eisenstein* **Vienna State
Opera Chorus, Vienna PO / Herbert von
Karajan**
Decca ② 421 046-2DH2 (143' · ADD)   Ⓕ**O▷**
A 1960 stereo classic, with one of the most
characterfully Viennese casts and Karajan in
almost as fine form. A huge star-studded gala
scene featuring the likes of Del Monaco,
Nilsson and Sutherland will appeal to many.

Hilde Gueden *Rosalinde* **Erika Köth** *Adele*
Waldemar Kmentt *Eisenstein* **Vienna Volksoper
Chorus, Vienna SO / Willi Boskovsky**
HMV ② HMVD573407-2 (110' · ADD)   Ⓢ
A bubbly but pleasantly unexaggerated
performance from the archetypal Viennese
Straussian, with a strikingly distinguished
cast including Dietrich Fischer-Dieskau and
the young Brigitte Fassbaender's marvellous
Orlofsky.

Kiri Te Kanawa *Rosalinde* **Hildegard Heichele**
Adele **Hermann Prey** *Eisenstein* **Chorus and
Orchestra of the Royal Opera House /
Plácido Domingo**
NVC Arts 📀 4509 99216-2 (177')   Ⓕ
Domingo on the podium can't match Kleiber's *Schwung*, but remains lively and serviceable for Covent Garden's splendidly batty
multi-lingual production, in richly authentic
sets with fine principals, including Dennis
O'Neill's hilariously Italianate Alfred, and
authentic Viennoiserie from Josef Meinrad's
beanpole Frosch.

than some other versions, that serves merely to
emphasise the excitement of the final *accelerando*.
Throughout, the inflections that are so essential
to a truly idiomatic *Fledermaus* come utterly
naturally.

Though it will rule out the recording as a first
choice for today, the sound quality is a good deal
fuller than that of the Krauss version. There's
the advantage of dialogue and sound effects too.
Certainly the recording is a must for admirers
not only of Fricsay but also of great vocalists of
the past. It comes, moreover, from an era when
singers knew their place. By contrast with
today's recordings featuring international singers jetting in from around the world, this is
essentially an ensemble production, showcasing
leading Berlin singers of the time as much as the
Krauss recording does Vienna singers. Peter
Anders was a lyric tenor of immense grace, his
career tragically cut short by a car accident in
1954. His Rosalinde is the young Anny Schlemm – only 22 years old, still a soprano, and
wonderfully fresh-voiced. There's the elegant
Helmut Krebs, too, as Alfred. Best of all, perhaps, is Rita Streich, as sprightly an Adele as one
could expect to find.

Even for those already blessed with a collection of *Fledermäuse*, this is not a version to be
ignored.

Die Fledermaus[a]
including Joan Sutherland's farewell to the stage
Bishop Home, sweet home[b]. **Cilea** L'arlesiana[c] – E la
solita storia. **Rossini** Semiramide[d] – Serbami ognor si
fido. **Saint-Saëns** Samson et Dalila[e] – Mon coeur
s'ouvre à ta voix **Verdi** La traviata[f] – Parigi, o cara
[bdf]**Dame Joan Sutherland** *sop* [c]**Luciano Pavarotti**
ten [de]**Marilyn Horne** *mez*

[a]**Nancy Gustafson** *sop* Rosalinde [a]**Judith Howarth**
sop Adele [a]**Louis Otey** *bar* Eisenstein [a]**Bonaventura
Bottone** *ten* Alfred [a]**Anthony Michaels-Moore** *bar*
Doctor Falke [a]**Jochen Kowalski** *counterten* Prince
Orlofsky [a]**Eric Garrett** *bar* Frank [a]**John Dobson** *ten*
Doctor Blind [a]**Glenys Groves** *sop* Ida [a]**John Sessions**
spkr Frosch [a]**Peter Archer** *spkr* Ivan

**Royal Opera House Chorus and Orchestra,
Covent Garden / Richard Bonynge**
Stage director **John Cox**
Video director **Humphrey Burton**
ArtHaus Musik ② 📀 100 134 (197' · Region 2 & 5)
Recorded live 1990   Ⓕ**O**

'Oh, what a night!' sings everybody on stage as
Prince Orlofsky's ballroom takes leave of its
earthly confines and sails for the happy isles
borne on a tide of waltzes and a sea of champagne. It's always a good moment in *Die Fledermaus*, and this particular night was special.
Most of those present at Covent Garden had
seen a few New Year's Eves in their time, but
never a one like this on December 31, 1990.
And never, surely, has a *prima donna* been
treated to such a stage party for her farewell.
Dame Joan Sutherland sang that night for the

last time in the house where she had made her début in 1952. Somebody had a brainwave when they thought of this as the occasion for what might otherwise have been a rather tearful event: Joan and two of her most illustrious partners of many performances would themselves be guests at Orlofsky's party in Act 2. Husband Richard Bonynge would conduct, so the party would therefore be complete. The guests slot in nicely at the moment when the revels are at their height. And there was New Year's Eve to celebrate. If the plan had a drawback it was one that concerned the opera itself. Act 3 of *Fledermaus* is always something of an anticlimax, and, with a celebrity recital thrown in, the middle act could seem to end with chords that cried 'Follow that!'. Happily, the production has a good move in store when, for the Finale, the backdrop for the prison scene goes up to reveal Orlofsky's ballroom aglow and once more ready to receive its guests.

Without in the least dominating, the orchestra here are present with a quite remarkable immediacy and naturalness. The outstanding voices among the cast were (in respect of pure tone) those of Judith Howarth and Anthony Michaels-Moore. Among the three celebrities, gallantly as both ladies sang, it was (and is on the film) Pavarotti whose voice had retained its quality. There's also plenty to watch, and with enjoyment. All on stage, including the chorus, act well. Humphrey Burton has supervised the filming so that the home viewer has the most privileged seat of all.

Der Zigeunerbaron

Der Zigeunerbaron
Pamela Coburn sop Saffi **Herbert Lippert** ten Barinkay **Wolfgang Holzmair** bar Homonay **Rudolf Schasching** ten Zsupán **Christiane Oelze** sop Arsena **Júlia Hamari** mez Czipra **Elisabeth von Magnus** contr Mirabella **Jürgen Flimm** bar Carnero **Robert Florianschutz** bass Pali **Hans-Jürgen Lazar** ten Ottokar **Arnold Schoenberg Choir; Vienna Symphony Orchestra / Nikolaus Harnoncourt**
Teldec ② 4509-94555-2 (150' · DDD · T/t) Ⓕ●

This is an uncommonly interesting and enjoyable release. The extra music comes because Harnoncourt and Johann Strauss specialist Norbert Linke have sought to restore *Der Zigeunerbaron* to the form it had before Strauss made various cuts. The real merits of the set lie elsewhere. Not least, Harnoncourt has stripped away generations of Viennese *Schmaltz* and performing tradition.

This is the first recording to include every number of the published score, and for once the music is sung at its original pitch, without the usual downward transpositions for Zsupán and Homonay. Most particularly Harnoncourt has completely rethought the style of the performance. *Der Zigeunerbaron* is a long work, described as 'Komische Oper' rather than 'Operette', and much of its music is unusually solid for Strauss. Harnoncourt gives the major

numbers their full weight, phrasing them beautifully, and drawing refined singing from the soloists, among whom Herbert Lippert and Pamela Coburn combine beautifully in the duet 'Wer uns getraut?', and Christiane Oelze is a delectably sweet Arsena.

The necessary light relief comes not only from Zsupán (Rudolf Schasching in fine voice) but from usually omitted subsidiary numbers. Elisabeth von Magnus sings Mirabella's 'Just sind es vierundzwanzig Jahre' with exhilarating comic zest, and joins with Jürgen Flimm (more actor than singer) to make the trio 'Nur keusch und rein' an irresistible delight. The live recording comes with some audience laughter and coughs but with the applause suppressed. This deserves to win new admirers both for Harnoncourt and for Strauss's masterly score.

Richard Strauss   German 1864-1949

Strauss's father, a professional horn player, gave him a musical grounding exclusively in the classics, and he composed copiously from the age of six. He went briefly to university, but had no formal tuition in composition. He had several works given in Munich, including a symphony, when he was 17, and the next year a wind serenade in Dresden and a violin concerto in Vienna. At 20, a second symphony was given in New York and he conducted the Meiningen Orchestra in a suite for wind. In 1885 he became conductor of that orchestra, but soon left and visited Italy. He had been influenced by Lisztian and Wagnerian thinking; one result was Aus Italien, which caused controversy on its première in 1887. By then Strauss was a junior conductor at the Munich Opera.

Other tone poems followed: Macbeth, Don Juan and Tod und Verklärung come from the late 1880s. It is Don Juan that, with its orchestral brilliance, its formal command and its vivid evocation of passionate ardour (he was in love with the singer Pauline von Ahna, his future wife), shows his maturity and indeed virtuosity as a composer. With its première, at Weimar (he had moved to a post at the opera house there), he was recognised as the leading progressive composer in Germany. He was ill during 1891-3 but wrote his first opera, Guntram, which was a modest success but a failure later in Munich. His conducting career developed; he directed many major operas, including Wagner at Bayreuth, and returned to Munich in 1896 as chief conductor at the opera. To the late 1890s belong the witty and colourful Till Eulenspiegel, a portrait of a disrespectful rogue with whom Strauss clearly had a good deal of sympathy, the graphic yet also poetic and psychologically subtle Don Quixote (cast respectively in rondo and variation forms) and Ein Heldenleben, 'a hero's life', where Strauss himself is the hero and his adversaries the music critics. There is more autobiography in the Symphonia domestica of 1903; he conducted its première during his first visit to the USA, in 1904.

Strauss was now moving towards opera. His Feuersnot was given in 1901; in 1904 Salome was begun, after Wilde's play. It was given at Dresden in 1905. Regarded as blasphemous and salacious, it ran into censorship trouble but was given at 50 opera houses in the next two years. This and Elektra (given in 1909) follow up the tone poems in their evocation of atmosphere and their thematic structure; both deal with female obsessions of a disordered, macabre kind, with violent climaxes involving gruesome deaths and impassioned dancing, with elements of abnormal sexuality and corruption, exploiting the female voice pressed to dramatic extremes.

Strauss did not pursue that path. After the violence and dissonance of the previous operas, and their harsh psychological realism, Strauss and his librettist Hofmannsthal turned to period comedy, set in the Vienna of Maria Theresa, for Der Rosenkavalier; the score is no less rich in inner detail, but it is applied to the evocation of tenderness, nostalgia and humour, helped by sentimental Viennese waltzes. Again the female voice – but this time its radiance and warmth – is exploited, in the three great roles of the Marschallin, Octavian and Sophie. It was given at Dresden in 1911 with huge success and was soon produced in numerous other opera houses. Strauss followed it with Ariadne auf Naxos, at first linked with a Molière play, later revised as prologue (behind the scenes at a private theatre) and opera, mixing commedia dell'arte and classical tragedy to a delicate, chamber orchestral accompaniment. In 1919 he took up a post as joint director of the Vienna Staatsoper, where his latest collaboration with Hofmannsthal, Die Frau ohne Schatten, was given that year: a work embodying much symbolism and psychology, opulently but finely scored, and regarded by some as one of Strauss's noblest achievements. His last Hofmannsthal opera, Arabella, an appealing re-creation of some of the atmosphere of Rosenkavalier, followed in 1933. Of his remaining operas, Capriccio (1942), a 'conversation-piece' in a single act set in the 18th century and dealing with the amorous and artistic rivalries of a poet and a musician, is the most successful, with its witty, graceful, serene score.

GROVEmusic

Horn Concertos

Horn Concertos Nos 1 & 2. Duett-Concertino, AV147. Serenade, Op 7
David Pyatt hn **Joy Farrall** cl **Julie Andrews** bn
Britten Sinfonia / Nicholas Cleobury
Classics for Pleasure 573 513-2 (66' · DDD) Ⓑ❍❍❍

David Pyatt won the BBC's 'Young Musician of the Year' Competition back in 1988. Since then the fledgling has well and truly flown. This is sensationally good horn playing, with a noble legatoand a beautiful sound, full, even and unclouded. He's sparing with the brassy timbres, holding them in reserve for dramatic effect, for such times as the instrument's well-rounded jocularity must take on a brazen, huntsmen-like air, or rise to shining heroics – like the challenging motto theme of the First Concerto. He shapes the big phrases with ease and authority, but his personality is equally conveyed in the rhythmic articulation: a dashing, Jack-be-nimble mischievousness in Strauss's ath-

letic allegros. Most of all, though – and this is rare – he loves to play really quietly. He's a master of those dreamy, far-away departures – twilit forest-murmurings: mysterious, unreal.

The recording helps with a beautifully integrated balance. The sound of the early Serenade, Op 7, is particularly fine with ripe, euphonious tuttis and room enough for individual personalities to open up. And that's the most remarkable aspect of the piece, the utterly natural way it blends and contrasts across the whole spectrum of wind voices. Two of them take centre-stage in the delightful Duett-Concertino. Joy Farrall's clarinet and Julie Andrews's bassoon are like Octavian and the Baron Ochs in this gentle but spirited opus. This is a spendid disc, then, and sympathetically directed, too.

Additional recommendation

Horn Concertos[a]
Coupled with: **Hindemith** Horn Concerto[b]. Concert Music for Brass and Strings[c]
Brain hn **Philharmonia Orchestra / **[a]**Sawallisch,** [bc]**Hindemith**
EMI Great Recordings of the Century [b]mono 567782-2 (65' · ADD) Recorded 1957-9 Ⓜ❍❍▷

Brain relishes the Straussian bravura in the First Concerto, and the coda is stunning – wonderfully nimble. The frocklicking Rondo finale of the Second is another highlight, played with a deliciously light spiccato by Brain. Sawallisch proves himself a natural Straussian, and his account of the Concert Music for Brass is marvellously played – an outstanding bonus.

Eine Alpensinfonie (An Alpine Symphony)

Eine Alpensinfonie, Op 64. Don Juan, Op 20
Royal Concertgebouw Orchestra, Amsterdam / Mariss Jansons
RCO Live ⚛ RCO08006 (70' · DDD/DSD) Recorded live Ⓜ❍▷

Mariss Jansons opens with a very exciting account of Don Juan, splendidly played, with plenty of impetus, and a touchingly gentle and sensuous account of the seduction scene. His richly expansive shaping of the great horn theme presents Juan as a nobly romantic seducer rather than one carried away by physical passion. But this makes a fine introduction to a truly outstanding account of the Alpine Symphony that ranks alongside Wit's celebrated Naxos version (see below) with the Weimar Staatskapelle, and in some ways is even finer.

Jansons structures the work unerringly and the Concertgebouw sound picture, with extraordinary vividness of detail at every stage of the journey, is remarkable. The entry into the forest is evocative indeed, as are the hunting horns echoing in the woods, while the spectacle of the storm and summit sequences are electrifying; the closing sequence with the Amsterdam deep brass as night falls has a wonderfully rich sonority. The Concertgebouw string-playing has, of course, an eloquent sweep, and if the violins are less sensuously ravishing than at Weimar (partly the effect of closer microphone placing in Amsterdam) they play particularly beautifully in the score's gentler moments.

In short, this magnificent performance, gripping from the opening to the last chord, will be hard to beat.

Eine Alpensinfonie
Staatskapelle Weimar / Antoni Wit
Naxos 8 557811 (54' · DDD) ⓈⓄⓄ↪

This is a magnificent record. The Weimar Staatskapelle are rare visitors to disc, but they are a top-class orchestra, with superb strings which sound overwhelmingly, sensuously beautiful in the opening 'Night' and 'Sunrise' sequences.

The warm and spacious acoustic of the Weimarhalle helps; reminiscent of the Lukaskirche in Dresden, where the Staatskapelle there made their famous analogue Strauss recordings under Kempe. This disc is in that same league of excellence. Indeed, conductor Antoni Wit must take a lion's share of the credit for the success of this mountain-climb.

His tempi are spacious but his pacing is not consistently slow. It is during the vistas that Wit takes his time to overwhelm us with the beauty of what his orchestra are describing, the 'Entry into the Forest', dallying a little 'On the Alpine Pasture' and, most telling of all, the burst of radiance on reaching the summit. Then on the way down there is a storm, thunderously captured, but in the calm before it breaks, Wit creates an almost sinister atmosphere of apprehension. As Strauss's descent nears its end and the music winds down, Wit manages a wonderful feeling of triste, a consciousness of danger experienced and triumphed over, and in that 'Ausklang' the organ steals in magically.

Eine Alpensinfonie
Berlin Philharmonic Orchestra /
Herbert von Karajan
DG Karajan Gold 439 017-2GHS (51' · DDD) ⒻⓄⓄ↪

The *Alpensinfonie* is no longer a rarity on disc, but there are still grounds for preferring the famous Karajan version to subsequent digital rivals, especially in this successful remastering. Karajan's sureness of line is always impressive in Strauss and, while the Berlin Philharmonic Orchestra isn't at its immaculate best, some playing is magnificent here. The sound remains rather fierce, but several passages have been substantially remixed, and the effect is certainly less constricted overall.

Perhaps it doesn't matter that the horn theme that floats in with the (still blinding) 'Sonnenaufgang' isn't quite aligned with the strings. More worrying is the subtle transformation of the opening phrase of 'Der Anstieg': whereas we used to experience it 'from the bottom up' with the balance favouring the basses, we hear more

cellos now – and most of them fluff the B flat! That said, the breadth and majesty of Karajan's conception is indisputable.

Symphonia domestica, Op 53

Symphonia domestica. Josephslegende – Suite
Seattle Symphony Orchestra / Gerard Schwarz
Delos DE3082 (777' · DDD) Ⓕ

Schwarz and his orchestra give an extremely fine account of the *Symphonia domestica*, far finer in fact than Zubin Mehta and the Berlin Philharmonic on Sony. The Berliners may be superior players but the Seattle Symphony sound to be enjoying themselves much more and to be appreciating the wit, fun and sentiment of the music. Schwarz's achievement is that the work becomes a real symphony under his baton. The playing is relaxed and warm and often very tender. At strenuous moments, though, the sound inclines to be a little unflattering to the strings but otherwise it's clear and spacious.

Why don't more orchestras include *Josephslegende* – such a tuneful, colourful score – in their repertoires? Schwarz clearly believes in it, and his excellent orchestra, with a pliant string section and lively woodwind, respond enthusiastically to his lead. Recommended.

Symphonia domestica, Op 53[c]. Burleske, AV85[ac].
Till Eulenspiegels lustige Streiche, Op 28[b]. Don Juan, Op 20[c].
[a]**Alfred Blumen** pf [b]**BBC Symphony Orchestra**;
[c]**Philharmonia Orchestra / Richard Strauss**
Testament mono ② SBT2 1441 (100' · ADD)
Broadcast performances from the Royal Albert Hall,
London, on October 19[a] and [b]29, 1947 ⓂⓄ

'One of my chief pleasures is to hear *Till* and *Don Juan* on the wireless, conducted by yourself. What a difference!' So wrote the 91-year-old George Bernard Shaw to the 83-year-old Richard Strauss shortly before Christmas 1947. Shaw was referring to the two concerts broadcast from the Royal Albert Hall that autumn by the BBC Third Programme during the festival of Strauss's music which the BBC, Sir Thomas Beecham and Strauss's London publishers had jointly sponsored.

In *Till* and briefly in *Domestica* there is audible interference from an adjacent station. Leech also lacked a second machine, which means that, the *Burleske* apart, brief sections of music are missing every four or five minutes. Not that this matters. Such is the fascination of the music-making, the hiatuses are, in Lady Bracknell's word, 'immaterial'.

The transfers of Leech's flawed acetates are by Testament's miracle-worker-in-chief Paul Baily. Examples of what the acetates sounded like before treatment are cheekily offered as an addendum to disc 2. The transformation is astonishing. Perhaps Baily should have a go at Strauss's 1929 Berlin Staatskapelle recording of

RICHARD STRAUSS'S ALSO SPRACH ZARATHUSTRA – IN BRIEF

Chicago SO / Fritz Reiner   H
RCA ⊛ 82876 61389-2 (76' · ADD)   M❶❷❸➔
Reiner's incandescent 1954 account is the stuff of which legends are made. Impossible to believe that the stereo tapes are half a century old. And Reiner draws from his crack Chicago ensemble playing of incredible intensity and concentration.

Berlin PO / Herbert von Karajan
DG 447 441-2GOR (79' · ADD)   M❶❷❸➔
ⓖ Arguably the most imposing of Karajan's three recordings. An interpretation of tremendous stature and aplomb; fabulous playing from the Berliners who have a uniquely dense sound when they played the music of Richard Strauss under Karajan.

Concertgebouw Orchestra / Bernard Haitink
Philips ② 442 281-2PM2 (152' · ADD/DDD)   Ⓜ
Bernard Haitink's distinguished 1973 account appeared at roughly the same time as the above-mentioned Karajan. Some might even prefer it for its extra nobility and opulence.

Vienna PO / Clemens Krauss
Testament SBT1183 (76' · ADD)   Ⓕ
Once you've adjusted to the rather acidulous string timbre, Clemens Krauss's authoritative 1950 reading with the VPO displays a glowing perception that never loosens its hold on the listener.

Staatskapelle Dresden / Rudolf Kempe
EMI 574590-2 (79' · ADD)   Ⓢ❶➔
A somewhat lightweight introduction apart, Kempe secures a performance of treasurable flexibility and comprehensive understanding. What a great Straussian he was!

Zurich Tonhalle Orchestra / David Zinman
Arte Nova 74321 87071-2 (76' · DDD)   Ⓢ
Anyone wanting a bargain-basement *Zarathustra* in realistic, up-to-date sound could do a lot worse than invest in this characterful and sympathetic account=.

Berlin PO / Karl Böhm
DG ③ 463 1902 (176' · ADD)   Ⓢ
Housed in a collection of Strauss tone-poems, Böhm's *Zarathustra* is beautifully shaped and tremendously well played by the BPO. Böhm knew Strauss well so there's added authentic element brought into play.

Staatskapelle Dresden / Herbert Blomstedt
Dal Segno ② DSPRC050 (146' DDD)   Ⓑ❶
This is an excellent performance, recorded with all Denon's usual skill and of course played by the Dresden orchestra with an almost arrogant authority.

Don Juan. Until he does, we are bound to conclude that this live Philharmonia performance is not only fierier and more expressive but far better played.

Strauss had a famously economical beat. Even so, for a man of 83 to conduct a concert of this length at this pitch of intensity – after the three principal works he threw in the *Rosenkavalier* waltzes for good measure – is astonishing. In the opening of *Don Juan* he yields to no one, not even Toscanini, in the brilliance of his attack, yet in the lyric sections there is a yearning loveliness that put me in mind of the fact that in October 1947 the *Four Last Songs* were already gestating. What a crossing of the years is here!

What is true of *Don Juan* is doubly true of this startlingly wonderful performance of *Symphonia domestica*, a work Strauss loved more than some of his public did. This London account communicates fervently his tender and passionate belief in the piece.

The *Till Eulenspiegel*, which he conducted 10 days later during one of Sir Adrian Boult's BBC SO concerts, is less remarkable, too slow and careful. Why, one asks, was the fledgling Philharmonia the more empathetic ensemble, conjuring forth phrasing and nuances the Vienna Philharmonic would have been proud to own? Beecham may be the answer. Many of the Philharmonia's players had worked for the old wizard whose mastery of Strauss's music went back four decades.

The hiring of the gifted and witty but barely remembered Austrian-born Jewish pianist Alfred Blumen was both personal and political. An acquaintance of Strauss, Blumen had spent the war in an internment camp in the north of England. There were reports of disagreements in rehearsal, Strauss telling Blumen to slow down, Blumen muttering how Strauss used to speed through *Burleske*. Neither man hangs about.

Also sprach Zarathustra, Op 30

Also sprach Zarathustra. Ein Heldenleben, Op 40   H
Chicago Symphony Orchestra / Fritz Reiner
RCA Living Stereo ⊛ 82876 61389-2 (76' · ADD)
Recorded 1954   M❶❷➔

It's astonishing that this recording of *Also sprach Zarathustra* was made in 1954, in stereo when Toscanini was still (just) recording in low-fi in New York's Carnegie Hall. The sound may be tonally fierce by current standards, but the balance is fully acceptable, with the first and second violins set close to the listener on either side of the podium, and the basses hard left.

Reiner's *Also sprach* is intense and extrovert. In his second year with the Chicago Symphony Orchestra, the conductor was already getting a thrilling response from the strings, though woodwind intonation could be a problem. Confident and well played as it is, the spectacular opening sunrise inevitably lacks the impact of modern recordings. Instead there's a measure of raw passion and forward thrust unequalled on disc. In the reflective passages, conductor and engineers display some reluctance to achieve a real *pianissimo*, but as the tempo builds Reiner invariably creates great excitement. His reading of *Ein Heldenleben* has humanity as well as virtuosity.

Also sprach Zarathustra. Don Juan, Op 20
Berlin Philharmonic Orchestra / Herbert von Karajan
DG 439 016-2GHS (54' · DDD) Recorded 1983 ⓕⓄ🅓

Also sprach Zarathustra, Op 30. Don Juan, Op 20. Till Eulenspiegels lustige Streiche. Salome – Dance of the Seven Veils
Berlin Philharmonic Orchestra / Herbert von Karajan
DG The Originals 447 441-2GOR (79' · ADD) Recorded 1973 ⓂⓄⓄⓄ🅓

The playing of the Berlin Philharmonic on both sets is as glorious as ever; its virtuosity can be taken for granted along with its sumptuous tonal refinement, and in Strauss Karajan has no peer. As a recording the 1983 disc is very good indeed. The famous opening has greater intensity in the 1973 version, and you may prefer its marginally greater warmth and glow of the strings.

The DG engineers adopt a slightly closer balance on this newcomer, which has greater range and impressive detail, particularly in the bass. Both *Don Juans* are fine performances, too. To sum up, Karajan's classic 1973 account holds sway.

Don Quixote, Op 35

Don Quixote.
Lieder – Morgen, Op 27 No 4;-Der Rosenband, Op 36 No 1; Wiegenlied, Op 41 No 1; Freundliche Vision, Op 48 No 1; Waldseligkeit, Op 49 No 1; Die heiligen drei Könige, Op 56 No 6
Dame Felicity Lott *sop* **André Vauquet** *va* **François Guye** *vc* **Suisse Romande Orchestra / Armin Jordan**
Mediaphon MED72 165 (69' · DDD) Ⓜ Ⓞ

This disc is notable for taking advantage of the superlative acoustic of the Victoria Hall in Geneva, home of the Suisse Romande Orchestra, thus giving us the most impressively recorded *Don Quixote* yet, in sound terms. The detail of the brilliant scoring is clearly delineated, while the whole picture is one of amazing warmth and resplendence. Jordan and his orchestra offer a performance worthy of both the place and the production. Guye brings out all Quixote's endearing and aggravating qualities without a hint of exaggeration, his tone always full and poised.

The songs are more than a makeweight. Lott, the leading Straussian soprano of the day, knows how to make the most of six of the composer's best-loved songs with ethereal, fine-grained tone and line. Jordan presents the music without any

excess of sentiment. So what a great pity, then, that texts and translations aren't provided, the only blot on a disc that's certain to give much pleasure and satisfaction.

R Strauss Don Quixote[a] **Haydn** Cello Concerto No 2, HobVIIb/2[b]
Mstislav Rostropovich *vc* [a]**Harry Danks** *va*
[a]**BBC Symphony Orchestra / Sir Malcolm Sargent,** [b]**London Symphony Orchestra**
BBC Legends mono BBCL4240-2 (66' • ADD)
Recorded live at the [a]Royal Albert Hall, London, on August 25, 1964; [a]Royal Festival Hall, London, on July 1, 1965 Ⓕ

This BBC Legends issue celebrates the playing of Mstislav Rostropovich relatively early in his career. The disc also provides a welcome reminder that, at a time when his reputation has rather fallen back, Malcolm Sargent always produced his best performances at the Proms and that he was always at his best in late Romantic music such as that of Strauss.

Rostropovich's playing is masterly, dominating each performance with its magnetism as well as its resonance. Harry Danks, principal viola in the BBC SO for many years, makes a colourful character out of the faithful Sancho Panza, bringing out the wit of the writing even if his tone is no match for the resonant cello of the principal soloist. Each of the 10 variations is presented in clean separation, with the orchestral players relishing the often spectacular orchestral effects, like the imitation of the bleating of sheep in the second variation, the brilliant percussion-writing in the 'Ride through the Air' and the powerful brass and ominous timpani beats in 'Defeat of Don Quixote'.

That leads up to the most glorious playing of all from Rostropovich in the long epilogue marking the Don's death. He uses a very free vibrato, and yet in the close of his solo his *pianissimo* is breathtaking. For radio recordings of the mid-1960s the sound is excellent and Tully Potter's notes are exemplary.

Ein Heldenleben, Op 40

R Strauss Ein Heldenleben **Beethoven** Symphony No 4
Berlin Philharmonic Orchestra / Herbert von Karajan
Testament SBT1430 (80' · ADD)
Recorded live at the Royal Festival Hall, London, in April 1985 ⒻⓄⓄ

For anyone lucky enough to have secured a ticket few orchestral concerts have remained so vividly in the memory as the one given by Karajan's incomparable Berlin Philharmonic in London's Royal Festival Hall on April 27, 1985. The surprises began with the conductor's own physical frailty. Edging unsteadily towards the rostrum and propping himself up against the railing, he adopted the peculiar posture that enabled him to remain upright and in command notwithstanding a debilitating spinal condition.

In truth the Beethoven was and is a gift to his many detractors. With the maestro unwilling or unable to lift his arms, the band turns in its patented imitation of a gramophone record. Surfaces are immaculate but it's like being trapped in a pudding without air in the texture. Phrases, even whole sections glide by with no intake of breath and the first two movements in particular may induce feelings of claustrophobia in younger listeners. They should persevere.

No superlatives can convey the inevitability, conviction and sweep of Karajan's *Heldenleben* which makes even this notoriously shrill-sounding venue resound in glory. The original BBC sound team of producer Misha Donat and balance engineer John McCulloch capture a paradoxical sonority, rich yet transparent, 'lambent in its beauty, never cloying or opaque' as described by Richard Osborne in his characteristically generous booklet-notes. The battle scene may be slow but was it ever more incisively chronicled? The Strauss at least is indispensable.

Ein Heldenleben. Metamorphosen
West German Radio Symphony Orchestra, Cologne / Semyon Bychkov
Avie AV0017 (75' · DDD)   Ⓕ ⊙ ➡

Semyon Bychkov's Op 40 'Hero' is the sort you could happily live with: he knows his worth but doesn't thrust his exploits in your face. The opening self-portrait more or less says it all, a confident exposition (warm strings, strong brass, crystal-clear timps), well paced, sonorous but never over-forceful. Strauss's cackling adversaries are more chuckled over than caricatured, and violinist Kyoko Shikata makes for an affectionately playful companion, thankfully not the manic cadenza that's sometimes visited on us.

In *Metamorphosen* the line remains fluid but constant, urged on (though never hampered) by genuine warmth of feeling. You sense that the notes and their emotional subtext are being granted an equal footing. Avie's recording has impressive amplitude and, in *Heldenleben*, credible presence. This is a unusual coupling – any rival would need to do a lot to upstage this sympathetic production. Recommended.

Ein Heldenleben. Le bourgeois gentilhomme
Berlin Philharmonic Orchestra / Sir Simon Rattle
EMI 339339-2 (82' · DDD) ªRecorded live 2005   Ⓕ ➡

Ein Heldenleben was always a favourite party-piece of Herbert von Karajan, so the challenge to his successor, Simon Rattle, is all the more formidable. It says much for Rattle's achievement in Berlin that the result in this live recording offers the keenest rivalry to the finest versions already in the catalogue. The heroic opening section already establishes Rattle's approach as a degree more flexible, more warmly expressive than

Karajan's. Karajan is certainly warm, but he generally keeps his expressiveness within steady speeds, where Rattle is a degree freer, with rhythms subtly pointed.

Typically, he treats the violinist, Guy Braunstein, as a genuine soloist, encouraging him to play with the sort of expressive freedom one expects in a concerto, while the equally brilliant Michel Schwalbe for Karajan tends to stay within the set tempo even in the most elaborate sections of the long solo representing the composer's wife. Braunstein is the more individual, and so are the various wind soloists in the piece, including those in the second section representing the composer's enemies, the critics.

What remains a constant is the opulence of the Berlin Philharmonic sound. The 1974 EMI recording of the Karajan version remains impressive for its time but the modern digital recording is richer still, starting with the most resonant E flat in the bass at the very start and covering a formidable dynamic range, bringing out the subtlety of Rattle's control and the refinement of the orchestra's playing. The fine Kempe version dates from rather earlier than Karajan's and, quite apart from the less wide-ranging recording, his is a less forceful, rather more relaxed reading than either Rattle's or Karajan's. In his overall timing Rattle takes a couple of minutes longer than either, with the extra breadth due at least in part to the expressive freedom encouraged in a live performance, something that clearly adds to the magnetism of the finished recording.

The fill-up is a generous one, bringing the overall timing of the disc to an exceptional 82 minutes. The engineers, though working in the Philharmonie as in *Heldenleben*, have rightly balanced the microphones to give a much more intimate result with the chamber ensemble of *Le bourgeois gentilhomme*. This time Rattle's performance is more relaxed than Kempe's, with speeds rather broader, making for a performance that delightfully captures the light-heartedness of this music, with delectable rhythmic pointing in the 18th-century pastiche.

Ein Heldenleben, Op 40. Metamorphosen
Staatskapelle Dresden / Fabio Luisi
Sony Classical 🎵 88697 08471-2 (73' · DDD)   Ⓕ ⊙

Ein Heldenleben and *Metamorphosen*, though written at opposite ends of Strauss's long career, make an ideal coupling, as both were directly inspired by Beethoven's *Eroica* Symphony. The warm strength of the key of E flat is at the root of *Heldenleben* too, while *Metamorphosen*, reflecting Strauss's pain over the wartime destruction of so much he loved in Germany, repeatedly and movingly quotes the *Eroica*'s Funeral March. Aptly too, the orchestra is the Staatskapelle Dresden, Strauss's favourite, responsible for many Strauss performances.

In this new version of *Heldenleben*, Fabio Luisi has opted to go back to what he describes as the original ending. This was Strauss's first idea, never published, of ending the piece pianissimo.

It was only later, realising that the response of audiences would be greater from a loud ending, that he was persuaded to append the now usual ending, adding some two dozen bars with fanfares and a final *fortissimo* chord.

Luisi proves an outstanding Straussian, drawing passionate playing from the orchestra, as flamboyant in *Heldenleben* as anyone would want, and darkly intense in the valedictory paragraphs and complex counterpoint of *Metamorphosen*, though the recording makes it sound as though more than 23 strings are playing. In *Heldenleben* Luisi is excellent in bringing out the massive structure of the work like a gigantic sonata form, quite apart from the programmatic element. Kai Vogler proves an outstanding violin soloist in the role of the Hero's partner, a clear portrait of the volatile Frau Strauss, here played with just the right degree of spontaneous flexibility. The recording is exceptionally full and brilliant, to match the resonant beauty of the playing.

Additional recommendation

Ein Heldenleben
Coupled with: **Strauss** Don Juan   Ⓗ
Wagenaar Cyrano de Bergerac
Concertgebouw Orchestra; New York Philharmonic Symphony Orchestra / Mengelberg
Pearl mono GEMMCD0008 (71' · ADD) Recorded 1928-42   Ⓜ⊙

The perfect set for anyone remotely interested in Strauss or in the history of recording. By the time this disc was made Mengelberg had nearly three decades of the piece under his belt – this is the definitive *Heldenleben*. Given its age, the transfer is little short of miraculous.

Metamorphosen

Metamorphosen. Tod und Verklärung. Four Last Songs[a]
[a]**Gundula Janowitz** *sop* **Berlin Philharmonic Orchestra / Herbert von Karajan**
DG The Originals 4474222 (77' · ADD)   Ⓜ❶❶❶▷

Ⓖ   These are a clear first-choice in all three works. Karajan's *Metamorphosen* has almost unbearable intensity and great emotional urgency – it's a gripping and involving account. The sound is marginally more forward and cleaner than is ideal, though the rich ambience is very appealing. *Tod und Verklärung* isn't as spectacularly recorded as some more modern versions, but it's a greater performance that just about any other. It's electrifying, with superb playing and a life-and-death intensity to the climaxes. It's more vividly recorded than his most recent previous version, and the performance is tauter and more powerful. The quality of the recording gives no cause for reproach. See page 1110 for comments about the Janowitz *Four Last Songs* (in an alternative coupling).

Josephslegende, Op 63

Josephslegende
Budapest Festival Orchestra / Iván Fischer
Channel Classics CCSSA24507
(65' · DDD/DSD)   Ⓕ❶❶❶▷

Ⓖ   Richard Strauss's *Josephslegende* (1914) is a truly extraordinary work. It was written for Diaghilev, who wanted something sensational to follow *The Rite of Spring*. But Nijinsky was unable to take the title-role planned for him, and it was the young Massine as substitute who had to dance what Nijinsky later described as 'undanceable music'. But Nijinsky also had an eccentric hand in the extraordinary scenario which tells of the attempted and unsuccessful seduction of Joseph by Potiphar's wife, her suicide after her failure, the attempt by the suspicious Potiphar to torture the innocent David, and his celestial rescue by an angel who frees him from his bonds.

All this drew from Strauss a richly sensuous score, in many ways an amalgam of his previous successes, predominantly *Salome*, in the voluptuous dances of the veiled and unveiled women near the begining, climaxed by 'Sulamith's dance' of burning desire. But the spectacle of the *Alpine Symphony*, the passion of *Don Juan*, the hyperbole of *Ein Heldenleben*, to say nothing of a touch of *Death and Transfiguration*, are all mixed in. The booklet offers an elaborate cued synopsis of the narrative, so that one can relate Strauss's extraordinary score to what is being described.

Iván Fischer and the enlarged Budapest Festival Orchestra give a magnificent account of the work, readily going over the sensual top when Strauss demands it, but with Fischer ensuring that Strauss's underlying lyrical flow moves seamlessly but erotically onwards to the final climax. This is surely a work for sumptuous surround sound, which is exactly what the Channel Classics recording team provide, and very impressively, too.

Works for winds

Complete Works for Wind Ensemble
Academy Symphonic Wind / Keith Bragg
Royal Academy of Music ② RAM034 (97' · DDD)   Ⓕ

Strauss wrote his Serenade in E flat for 13 instruments in 1881, when he was only 17. It is essentially Mozartian in derivation, yet immediately the ear registers the romantic swing of the melodies and the lusher textures which make the Straussian imprint. Already the young composer's textural blending is masterly, while the sonorities anticipate the future.

The four-movement Suite in B flat (also for 13 instruments) is more diverse and further removed from Mozart, with a tender Romanze (with rich horns), a good-natured Gavotte and a finale which begins in mock darkness before setting off into a jolly, robust fugue.

The two major works date from his last years and show him in full maturity. Extra instruments were added to the Symphony in F – a C clarinet, basset-horn and bass clarinet – and the full sonority is quite luscious, the lines even more melodically complex. The Symphony in E flat dates from 1945 and on its title-page the composer wrote 'To the divine Mozart at the end of a life full of gratitude'. It seems to take off from where the previous symphony finished, the opening glowingly animated and vivacious and – as played here – with exuberant forward thrust. The delicate *Andantino* has appealing classical grace and the Minuet seems good-naturedly bucolic, yet produces an engaging tune for the horns, taken up by the solo clarinet. The finale quotes from *Götterdämerung* but spirits soon lift; the *allegro* sets off with light-hearted lyricism, with swiftly intertwining woodwind, and the music gathers force and momentum to reach its spectacular, life-asserting coda.

It's a magnificent performance, but all four works here are superbly and spontaneously played by eager musicians from the Royal Academy of Music who provide wonderful blending and a splendidly polished, professional ensemble under their fine conductor, Keith Bragg. This new set certainly trumps its rivals.

Piano Quartet

Metamorphosen (version for string septet)[b]. Piano Quartet[a]. Prelude to Capriccio
Nash Ensemble ([a]Marianne Thorsen, Malin Broman vns [a]Lawrence Power, Philip Dukes vas [a]Paul Watkins, Pierre Doumenge vcs [b]Duncan McTier db
[a]Ian Brown pf)
Hyperion CDA67574 (78' · DDD)   (F)

The early and late Strauss on this finely recorded disc are separated by some 60 years: the Piano Quartet was completed in 1884, the year after Wagner's death, while *Metamorphosen* dates from the early months of 1945. Strauss at 20 had abundant promise: Strauss at 80 had managed to avoid lapsing intoer self-parody. The result is full of interest.

The Piano Quartet is invariably labelled 'Brahmsian' and the opening makes that association clear. Yet the piece is too loosely put together, too focused on small-scale harmonic effects, to sound like Brahms for long. Anyone looking for evidence that Strauss's true metier would be programme music and opera need look no further. It's an enjoyable piece for all that, expansively dramatic and genuinely expressive with that touch of spontaneity which signals Strauss at his best.

The Nash Ensemble bring affectionate fervour to the Quartet, without lingering excessively over its creakier transitions. A cooler touch might have been preferable with the *Capriccio* Prelude and *Metamorphosen* – the latter in particular risks overheating, with uniformly high dynamic levels. The status of this version of *Metamorphosen* is ambiguous, since it derives from a draft discovered in 1990. This preceded the final scoring for 23 solo strings, and one wonders if Strauss might not have revised the former in light of the latter had he wished to preserve it – especially the very awkward harmonic switch at the end, which the final version eliminates. A curiosity, then, which inevitably sounds more like a dilution of the familiar score than a genuine alternative.

Violin Sonata in E flat, Op 18

R Strauss Violin Sonata **Bartók** (arr Székely)
Six Romanian Folkdances, Sz56 **Stravinsky** (arr Stravinsky/Dushkin) Divertimento
Vadim Repin vn **Boris Berezovsky** pf
Erato 8573-85769-2 (53' · DDD)   (F)(O)

Stylistically, Strauss's lyrical Op 18 (1887) sits poised somewhere between Brahms's chivalrous song cycle *Die schöne Magelone* and Strauss's own *Don Juan* of the following year. The finale is rich in heroics though not before a seductive 'Improvisation' and the appearance of one of Strauss's loveliest melodies. Anyone familiar with Heifetz's three recordings – his second, the first of two with the late Brooks Smith, is probably the most comprehensively expressive – will have a job adapting to anyone else. No one draws a sweeter, more tender opening phrase, though Vadim Repin, like Gidon Kremer, more or less matches Heifetz in terms of repose.

Repin's feline violin faces leonine support from Boris Berezovsky, whose outsize musical personality draws maximum mileage from Strauss's virtuoso piano writing, though he too is capable of relaxing. His elegant fingerwork is nicely demonstrated in the decorative figurations that dominate the third section of the second movement. Kremer and Oleg Maisenberg are also excellent, but Repin's engagement with the music's lyrical element just about gives him the edge . Heifetz is more 'accompanied' by Brooks Smith than partnered by him.

Echoes of Strauss return for the *Adagio* from Stravinsky's *Fairy's Kiss* re-run, a witty *Divertimento* prepared in collaboration with violinist Samuel Dushkin. Repin's strongest current rival is Perlman, though his reading is perhaps less subtly characterised and, again, Berezovsky's strong-arm pianism strengthens the frame. Bartók's ubiquitous *Romanian Folkdances* are rather less spicy here than you would expect from someone who has fiddled in gypsy style with Lakatos, but Repin's harmonics in the 'Pe loc' third movement are admirably clean and the final dances are suitably dashing. The sound is very well balanced.

Enoch Arden

Enoch Arden, Op 38[a].
Piano Pieces, Op 3 – No 1; No 4

[a]**Patrick Stewart** *spkr* **Emanuel Ax** *pf*
Sony Clasical 88697 09056-2 (62' · DDD)　　　Ⓕ

The traditions of speaking with and over music gained a new lease of life in 19th-century bourgeois drawing rooms, fed especially by Schumann and Liszt, two of Strauss's idols. As he would later with the *Alpine Symphony* and *Die Frau ohne Schatten*, Strauss often tried to surpass his models in scale and ambition, setting (in 1897) a full-on 50 minutes of Tennysonian neuroses about the Victorian male's ever-present fear that he would journey overseas in the service of family and Empire, only to return unrecognised and excluded (in this poem, voluntarily) from hearth and home.

The genius of *Enoch Arden* lies in Strauss's positioning of the actually rather small amount of music: he introduces, interludes and comments on the narrative, but only rarely underpins it. The actor has to take much of the initiative in style and pacing. He must decide whether to remain glowingly neutral, as the veteran Claude Rains does with Glenn Gould (Sony) or pitch in and characterise both the ménage à trois at the centre of the tale and the dramatic locations of the story as does Fischer-Dieskau (DG).

Patrick Stewart has a naturally compelling voice. He opts for a soft Northern burr for Enoch, friend Philip and their girl Annie, and a cunning use of volume and pace for the story's dramatic peaks. Ax, whose spacious, fluent control and use of colours as if lit from behind often remind one of Schnabel, partners perfectly, taking deliberately a more neutral line. The recording is natural and free of trickery. Whoever's idea it was to follow the melodrama with two of the Op 3 piano pieces has provided the ideal wind-down after Strauss's (intentionally) short and unmelodramatic postlude. Hugely recommended.

Choral Works

Deutsche Motette, Op 62[a]. Gesänge, Op 34.
An den Baum Daphne (epilogue to 'Daphne'),
AV137[b]. Die Göttin im Putzzimmer, AV120
[a]**Tina Kiberg**, [b]**Marianne Lund** *sops* [b]**Christian
Lisdorf** *treb* [a]**Randi Stene** *contr* [a]**Gert Henning-
Jensen** *ten* [a]**Ulrik Cold** *bass* [b]**Copenhagen Boys'
Choir; Danish National Radio Choir / Stefan
Parkman**
Chandos CHAN9223 (57' · DDD · T/t)　　Ⓕ●

Under Stefan Parkman the Danish National Radio Choir has established a reputation second to none. Parkman handles his singers as if they were a fully fledged symphony orchestra; which isn't at all inappropriate in this programme by the supreme master of orchestral colour.

From the heart of the 16 chorus parts of the *Deutsche Motette* a further seven are projected by solo voices emerging imperceptibly from the midst of a dense, luxuriant texture. The depth of colour and range of emotions are every bit as extensive in these works as in the great orchestral tone-poems; indeed few orchestral tone-poems evoke dusk and sunset so vividly as 'Der Abend', the first of the 1897 *Zwei Gesänge*. There's a wonderfully luminous soundscape here; a combination of superb compositional skill, sensitive musical direction, superlative choral singing and a warm, full-bodied recording.

Four Last Songs

Four Last Songs. Das Rosenband, Op 36 No 1. Lieder,
Op 68 – Ich wollt ein Sträusslein binden; Säusle, liebe
Myrte; Als mir dein Lied erklang. Befreit, Op 39 No 4.
Lieder, Op 27 – Ruhe, meine Seele!; Morgen. Wiegenlied, Op 41 No 1. Meinem Kinde, Op 37 No 3.
Zueignung, Op 10 No 1. Die heiligen drei Könige aus
Morgenland, Op 56 No 6
Soile Isokoski *sop* **Berlin Radio Symphony
Orchestra / Marek Janowski**
Ondine ODE982-2 (64' · DDD · T/t)　　Ⓕ

Ⓖ Strauss singing doesn't come much better than this. No doubt the composer himself, with his love of the soprano voice, would have been enthralled by Isokoski's glorious singing. He might also have approved of Janowski's straightforward, quite brisk conducting as he was never one to sentimentalise his own music. With a combination of free, unfettered tone, not a hint of strain in high-lying passages, a fine legato and an amazingly long breath, Isokoski fulfils every demand of her chosen songs. To those attributes she adds just a hint of quick vibrato, which she uses unerringly to expressive purpose throughout. Add the depth of feeling she brings to inwardly emotional pieces such as *Befreit*, *Ruhe meine Seele!* and, above all, *Morgen!*, a perfect realisation of this oft-recorded piece, and you have performances to rival any of the greats of the past.

She reminds one most of Lisa della Casa, the first soprano to record the *Four Last Songs*, and Sena Jurinac. She has the same smiling timbre, the same natural style, the same avoidance of wallowing in music that contains its own proportion of sentiment. Try the ecstatic execution of the final verse of 'Beim Schlafengehen' and you'll understand. If, on the other hand, you prefer a more leisurely approach, there are always Janowitz and Karajan.

Janowski is obviously at one with his soprano, not only here but also in *Zueignung*. Refined playing from the Berlin Radio Symphony and an open recording complete the pleasure.

Four Last Songs[a]. Capriccio – Morgen mittag um elf!
… Kein andres[b]. Tod und Verklärung[c]
[ab]**Gundula Janowitz** *sop* [a]**Berlin Philharmonic
Orchestra / Herbert von Karajan**; [b]**Bavarian Radio
Symphony Orchestra**, [c]**Staatskapelle Dresden /
Karl Böhm**
DG Classikon 439 467-2GCL (65' · ADD)
Recorded 1971-2　　　Ⓜ

RICHARD STRAUSS'S FOUR LAST SONGS IN BRIEF

Soile Isokoski; Berlin RSO / Marek Janowski
Ondine ODE982-2 (64' · DDD)　　　Ⓕ**OOO**

💎 Perfectly realised interpretations with which Isokoski proves herself a radiant Straussian yet avoids any trace of sentimentality with relatively brisk tempos. Ideally clean and luminous recording helps.

Gundula Janowitz;
Berlin PO / Herbert von Karajan
DG 439 467-2GCL (65' · ADD)　　　Ⓜ**OO**D→

A more measured, rich-textured approach from a soprano and conductor at one in their pursuit of tonal beauty and sureness of line in 1973. Janowitz's way with the poetry creates an almost liquid stream of sound.

Renée Fleming;
Houston SO / Christoph Eschenbach
RCA 82876 59408-2 (69' · DDD)　　　Ⓜ
Munich Philharmonic Orchestra / Christian Thielemann
Decca 478 0647DH (56' · DDD · T/t)　　Ⓜ**O**D→

Fleming in 1995 and 2008. While both performances take their time, Fleming's richer, burnished tone on the later, Decca version, plus its more interesting couplings, make it the one to go for. Both conductors are sensitive to their singer but the Munich orchestra has a more *echt*-Straussian sound and the live Decca recording is very well managed.

Jessye Norman;
Leipzig Gewandhaus / Kurt Masur
Philips 464 742-2 (48' · DDD)　　　Ⓜ**O**D→

As set down in 1982, the most commanding of all recordings, and probably the slowest. The original disc won the solo vocal category of the 1984 *Gramophone* Record Awards, but Wagner's Wesendonk-Lieder have since replaced the Strauss songs formerly included. Simply glorious even so.

Elisabeth Schwarzkopf;
Berlin RSO / George Szell
EMI 566908-2 (65' · ADD)　　　Ⓜ**OOO**D→

Elisabeth Schwarzkopf's several recordings combine beauty of sound with unequalled feeling for the words. This final version under George Szell, with its very special autumnal quality, has acquired classic status.

Lisa della Casa;
Vienna Philharmonic Orchestra / Karl Böhm
Regis mono RRC1192 (65' · ADD)　　　Ⓢ**OO**

Della Casa's early 1950s version is still full of exquisite singing – coupled with some fascinating *Capriccio* excerpts from 1953. This was the work's first commercial recording and, as so often is the case, has a special magic all of its own.

Here's a feast of glorious Strauss at bargain price, though the performances are anything but bargain in quality. In spite of strong challenges from far and wide, the singing of them by Gundula Janowitz has, arguably, still not been surpassed for Straussian opulence and tenderness – we emphasise 'arguably', for people feel passionately about interpretations of this work! – and Karajan conducts a near-ideal account of the orchestral score. Janowitz, in glorious voice, sings the *Four Last Songs* flowingly. The recording is more hazy than on the other two exemplary performances. The fashion of the moment to denigrate Böhm is incomprehensible when you encounter readings as splendid as his two contributions here, in which he again proves himself an ideal Straussian.

The live account of *Tod und Verklärung* caught at the 1972 Salzburg Festival but not released until 1988 (in memoriam) builds naturally to its various incandescent climaxes, and the music is never allowed to drag or descend into sentimentality. The playing of the Dresden orchestra is lithe and warm. The final scene of *Capriccio* comes from the complete set recorded in Munich in 1971. Once more Böhm judges tempos and texture to a nicety, the music always moving forward in perfect balance to its end.

Four Last Songs. Sechs Lieder, Op 68.
Ariadne auf Naxos, Op 60 – Overture; Dance Scene
Ricarda Merbeth *sop*
Weimar Staatskapelle / Michael Halász
Naxos 8 570283 (60' · DDD)　　　Ⓢ D→

Ricarda Merbeth, a regular Marschallin in Vienna and exponent of other big Strauss roles in Europe, has also been Bayreuth's Elisabeth for the past six years – just as Pauline de Ahna, Strauss's wife and first muse of song, once was. There's something both idiomatic and old-fashioned about these performances. Here is neither the ample, creamy sound of a Jessye Norman nor the studied, polished art of the Schwarzkopf/Legge camp nor the quasi-vocalise of a Janowitz, but rather a welcome, word-conscious directness and emotive agility that is natural and refreshing, and reminiscent of an earlier school of Strauss-singing – Lotte Lehmann, Viorica Ursuleac.

The Op 68 Brentano Lieder of 1918 – never programmed enough – are hair-raisingly difficult for the singer in terms of both tessitura and line in their original piano versions. Given in the complex (and quite weighty) orchestrations to which Strauss devoted much energy in later life, they become even more demanding. 'Lied der Frauen wenn die Männer im Kriege sind' ('Women's Song when the Men are away at War') is eight minutes-plus of high drama in instrumental clothing that deliberately harks back to *Salome*, *Elektra* and *Die Frau ohne Schatten* (it's also highly possible that the events of 1933, the year of this version, impinged on the emotional temperature).

The five other songs in the group become enticing orchestral children of their contemporary operas *Daphne* and *Capriccio*. Merbeth is supremely well prepared and on top of this repertoire, and the Weimar orchestra, cliché to say but true, have the sound of Strauss's music still in their blood. Halász, a regular collaborator of the soprano's, beds down in the tempi of 'Im Abendrot' a little too much but his singer can more than handle that. Natural, unplush sound, aptly matching the music-making.

R Strauss Four Last Songs
Wagner Götterdämmerung – Siegfried's Rhine Journey; Brünnhildes's Immolation. Tristan und Isolde – Prelude; Liebestod
Kirsten Flagstad sop
Philharmonia Orchestra / Wilhelm Furtwängler
Testament mono SBT1410 (67' · ADD)
Recorded live at the Royal Albert Hall, London, on May 22, 1950   Ⓕ 🔴🔴

Here's a live recording of the concert in 1950 when Flagstad gave the premiere of Strauss's *Four Last Songs*, followed by some truly unforgettable Wagner; yet it's the latter that makes the CD so exciting.

Flagstad and Furtwängler had several collaborations in these Wagnerian excerpts, but caught live in very reasonable sound they produce performances that lift one out of one's seat. Furtwängler is in incandescent form in the *Tristan* excerpts, and even more so in the Dawn and Rhine Journey from Act 1 of *Götterdämmerung*. The music whizzes along with the most virtuoso contributions possible from the recently formed Philharmonia, the horns, headed by Dennis and Aubrey Brain, very much to the fore. Flagstad then sings the Immolation with quite wonderful freshness and conviction, and this at the end of a longish programme. The results are to invoke the tingle factor. It is worth mentioning that the pair had just been giving *Ring* cycles at La Scala and seem entirely at one in their readings.

The *Tristan* Prelude and Liebestod offer a similar frisson. Has the Prelude ever sounded so impassioned and urgent as here? Did Flagstad, in her numerous recordings of the Liebestod, ever convey so much tragic passion? Probably not, and she is in much better voice than in the complete 1952 set.

The performance of the Strauss, previously available on the 'grey market', is now heard in improved sound; but Flagstad, for all the richness of her singing, gives a fairly generalised interpretation compared with many that were to follow, and the conductor was never the greatest of Straussians. Still, as a historic document this is an important issue. The whole disc, carefully remastered, is a treasure.

Four Last Songs. Capriccio – Interlude (Moonlight Music); Morgen mittag um elf!ᵇ Salome – Ach, du wolltest mich nicht deinen Mund küssen lassenᵃ
Nina Stemme sop
ᵃ**Liora Grodnikaite** mez ᵃ**Gerhard Siegel** ten
ᵇ**Jeremy White** bass **Royal Opera House**

Orchestra, Covent Garden / Antonio Pappano
EMI Ⓕ 378797-2 (56' · DDD)   Ⓜ🔵▶️

To borrow a phrase from Richard Osborne, mighty tents are already pitched on these fields – for the *Four Last Songs* Schwarzkopf/Szell, Della Casa/Böhm, Norman/Masur; for the *Salome* finale Krauss/Cebotari, Welitsch/Reiner and so on. But the conductor who has already got onto record a newly thought-through *Bohème*, a *Tosca* that can hold its own with de Sabata's, and a modern *Tristan* with Domingo need fear no competition. All the hounds of hell are let loose by the ROH's percussion section to launch a wild, but always intricately shaped and detailed, account of young Princess Salome's sickly Liebestod. Being already a searching, grown-up Isolde, Stemme, like her 1950s forerunners, now really manages to be a teenage Isolde too, by turns sweet, spooky and growing up.

The disc's running order is cunning and effective, and both conductor and soprano are in command of the switch to Madeleine's music-or-words dilemma. In *Capriccio*'s Moonlight Interlude, as in the *Songs*, Pappano achieves richness without overweighting; his *rubato* lingers rather than indulges (like… but let's not compare). Stemme is a more torn and dramatic Countess than, say, Janowitz, Schwarzkopf or Della Casa; this performance harks back to Clemens Krauss and Viorica Ursuleac, emotion shaping the (fine) text, rather than vice-versa.

As if to create a valedictory survey of Strauss, the soprano voice and the orchestra, the start of 'Frühling' aptly seconds the Countess's mood. Michael Tanner's note for the new remastering of Flagstad's creator's performance (see above) remarks how tempi in this work have got slower over the past 50 years. Pappano and his orchestra (what solo playing!), while never hurrying, keep the forward pace of an attentive Lied accompanist – emotional points are made without milking, matching the cool beauty of the soloist's timbre. Stemme has vocal height and weight in equal measure and (again) really uses her text. Finally, the record is produced and engineered with sensitivity to the layout of Strauss's instrumental and vocal textures.

Four Last Songs. Ariadne auf Naxos – Ach! Wo war ich? Tot?; Ein Schönes war: hiess Theseus-Ariadne; Es gibt ein Reich. Die ägyptische Helena – Zweite Brautnacht!. Verführung, Op 33 No 1. Freundliche Vision, Op 48 No 1. Winterweihe, Op 48 No 4. Zueignung, Op 10 No 1
Renée Fleming sop **Munich Philharmonic Orchestra / Christian Thielemann**
Decca 478 0647DH (56' · DDD · T/t)
Recorded live in 2008   Ⓕ🔴▶️

As the penultimate track on this often thrilling recital, Renée Fleming sings Strauss's rethink of *Zueignung*, orchestrated in 1940 as a tribute to the soprano Viorica Ursuleac. Instead of the poet Hermann von Gilm's words, Strauss substituted 'du wunderbare Helena!', referring to Ursuleac's performance in *Die ägyptische Helena*. This soaring, ecstatic phrase is just the sort of thing that Fleming has developed as a speciality, and she caps it with the famous aria from Act 2 of Helena, 'Zweite Brautnacht!' in which Helen of Troy celebrates her reunion with Menelaus. This was famously recorded in the 1960s by Leontyne Price, and to say that Fleming's voice has something of the same richness and sensuality is only a compliment.

The other opera extract, and the best thing on the disc in my opinion, is the big scene from *Ariadne auf Naxos*, and this is surely a part that Fleming must take on stage soon. She has developed her lower register so that the section in which Ariadne anticipates the arrival of Hermes is especially effective. At the end, of course, the great arching phrases of 'Du nimm es von mir' are wonderfully achieved.

As Fleming explains in a note, the *Four Last Songs* has become the work that she has performed most often. She first recorded them with Eschenbach (RCA). At the opening of 'Frühling' the new burnished quality she brings is quite surprising. Throughout the four songs, Fleming not only lavishes every resource of tonal richness at her command, but she seems to be urging all sorts of extra details from the text. This may seem excessive for some tastes, with even the hint of a sob towards the end of 'September'. The sound is stupendous, Fleming's voice complemented by the Munich orchestra, with Thielemann bringing out every detail in Strauss's nostalgic orchestration.

Additional recommendation

Coupled with: **Wagner** Wesendonk Lieder
Norman sop **Leipzig Gewandhaus Orchestra /**
Masur   Ⓜ️Ⓞ↦
Philips 4758507 (48' · DDD)

Norman's glorious performance of Strauss's poignant swansong gained her 1984's *Gramophone* solo vocal award. If you're a Janowitz or Schwarzkopf advocate you'll find it too languorous. For anyone else it's unmissable, despite the short running time.

Songs

Don Juan. Macbeth. Lieder[a] – Morgen; Der Rosenband; Meinem Kinde; Befreit; Wiegenlied; Waldseligkeit; Die heiligen drei Könige aus Morgenland ·
[a]**Anne Schwanewilms** sop
Hallé Orchestra / Mark Elder
Hallé CDHLL7508 (68' · DDD)   Ⓜ️Ⓞ

Anne Schwanewilms, already well-known as an interpreter of Arabella and other Strauss heroines, challenges the likes of Della Casa, Schwarzkopf and Janowitz, and isn't put in the shade by the comparison. Her silvery tone soars easily into the grateful lines of these warm, glowing songs, and she has the gift to fine down

her tone to ravishing *pianissimi*. She catches the rich-hued character of *Waldseligkeit*, the intimacy of *Wiegenlied* and *Meinem Kinde*, the sad serenity of *Morgen* and the inner intensity of *Befreit*, one of Strauss's most profound settings. Just once or twice her approach seems a shade self-regarding but, by and large, these are near-ideal readings, securely supported by Mark Elder and his orchestra.

This is the latest in the series of recordings emanating from the Hallé and does much to confirm their high place in this country's orchestral hierarchy today. There are many masterly accounts of *Don Juan* in the catalogue but this one, nicely timed and richly played, is up among the best. By comparison *Macbeth*, Strauss's first tone-poem and written a year earlier, seems rather an empty piece, successful neither as an evocation of the play nor as a piece in its own right. Elder and the Hallé make as good a case as they can for it and – as a whole – the programme works well, the Lieder sandwiched between the two orchestral works.

The Complete Songs – 1

Acht Gedichte aus Letzte Blätter, Op 10 – No 1, Zueignung; No 4, Die Georgine; No 8, Allerseelen. Sechs Lieder aus Lotusblätter, Op 19 – No 2, Breit über mein Haupt dein schwarzes Haar; No 4, Wie sollten wir geheim sie halten. Sechs Lieder, Op 37 – No 1, Glückes genug; No 2, Ich liebe dich; No 6, Hochzeitlich Lied. Fünf Lieder, Op 39 – No 1, Leises Lied; No 4, Befreit. Fünf Lieder, Op 41 – No 1, Wiegenlied; No 2, In der Campagna. Sechs Lieder, Op 56 – No 5, Frühlingsfeier; No 6, Die heiligen drei Könige aus Morgenland. Gesänge des Orients, Op 77
Christine Brewer sop **Roger Vignoles** pf
Hyperion CDA67488 (61' · DDD · T/t)   Ⓕ Ⓞ Ⓞ

This is the first volume in Hyperion's Richard Strauss edition, something to be devoutly hoped for: he was a great Lieder composer but only a small fraction of his 200-plus songs are at all well known. Admittedly, his taste in poetry wasn't always as elevated as that of his fellow composers, yet his music can transform rather ordinary verses. And the major poets do get a look-in. This disc includes two Heine settings, one of which, 'Frühlingsfeier', came a year after *Salome* and echoes the operatic score. This is where Christine Brewer, whose repertory includes the title-roles in *Ariadne auf Naxos* and *Die ägyptische Helena*, might be expected to be most comfortable: her big, gleaming soprano sweeps through impressively. If at first her voice seems less than ideally flexible as a Lieder instrument, especially in the earlier songs, it would be ungrateful not to marvel at what she does ultimately bring to these performances.

Opening with 'Zueignung', which Strauss never intended to be relegated to encore status, Brewer sounds glorious if a little staid. But she quickly lightens up, catching the palpitations of 'Wie sollten wir geheim sie halten' and the gem-like intimacy of 'Leises Lied'. She positively blazes in the sunlight-evoking 'In der Campagna', where Vignoles's piano captures the splash of a Straussian orchestra. Both artists bring something fresh to the chestnuts 'Allerseelen' and 'Wiegenlied', in which Brewer floats a beautiful line over the rippling accompaniment. Having the high tessitura demanded in the rarely heard *Gesänge des Orients*, she clinches any remaining argument magnificently.

The Complete Songs – 2
Acht Lieder aus Letzte Blätter, Op 10 – No 3, Die Nacht; No 5, Geduld. Mein Herz ist stumm, Op 19 No 6. Schlichte Weisen, Op 21 – No 1, All' mein Gedanken, mein Herz und mein Sinn; No 2, Du meines Herzens Krönelein; No 3, Ach Lieb, ich muss nun scheiden. O wärst du mein, Op 26 No 2. Ruhe, meine Seele, Op 27 No 1. Drei Lieder, Op 29. Vier Lieder, Op 31 – No 1, Blauer Sommer; No 3, Weisser Jasmin. Das Rosenband, Op 36 No 1. Acht Lieder, Op 49 – No 1, Waldseligkeit; No 2, In goldener Fülle; No 3, Wiegenliedchen; No 7, Wer Lieben will; No 8, Ach, was Kummer, Qual und Schmerzen. Drei Lieder der Ophelia, Op 67. Blindenklage, Op 56 No 2
Anne Schwanewilms sop **Roger Vignoles** pf
Hyperion CDA67588 (66' · DDD · T/t)   Ⓕ

Not just for *Salome* did Strauss demand several voices in one: here he ranges from the ditzy skitterings of the *Ophelia Songs* via the full-on operatic scena that is the Schwarzkopf favourite *Blindenklage* to the wandering tonalities of *O wärst du mein!*, not to mention the tricky characterisation of *Ach, was Kummer* (with its repeated 'hm, hm') and the naive playfulness of *Schlagende Herzen*.

It's hard to dispute Roger Vignoles's claim that Anne Schwanewilms is 'a great singing actress'. That's clear in every song, where both the overall *tinta* and the text have not just been scrupulously attended to in the head but are excitingly delivered with the heart. The occasional price to pay is in pitching (coming onto a note from above) and in vocal agility – this is a large voice and it can move through its gears quite slowly – but it's of little significance given the repertoire, the live nature of the takes for which Hyperion opted, and the sheer intensity of the singing.

Schwanewilms achieves the full compass of the testing items noted, finds an appropriately rich skein of tone for *In goldener Fulle* and manages real affection – and a degree of playfulness – in *Wiegenliedchen*. There's a real experience here, knowingly and profoundly communicated. Vignoles is, as always, an equal and fully 'worked-in' team member. As well as being an impressive achievement in itself, this recital is a timely addition to a catalogue currently rather short of female competition in these songs.

The Complete Songs – 3
Acht Lieder aus Letzte Blätter, Op 10 – No 2,

Nichts; No 6, Die Verschwiegenen; No 7, Die Zeitlose. Sechs Lieder, Op 17. Sechs Lieder aus Lotusblättern, Op 19 – No 1, Wozu noch, Mädchen, soll es Frommen; No 3, Schönsind, doch kalt die Himmelssterne; No 5, Hoffen und wieder verzagen. Schlichte Weisen, Op 21 – No 4, Ach weh, mir unglückhaften Mann; No 5, Die Frauen sind oft fromm und still. Heimliche Aufforderung, Op 27 No 3. Fünf Lieder, Op 32. Vier Lieder, Op 36 – No 2, Für fünfzehn Pfennige; No 4, Anbetung. Fünf Lieder, Op 48 – No 1, Freundliche Vision; No 4, Winterweihe; No 5, Winterliebe
Andrew Kennedy ten **Roger Vignoles** pf
Hyperion CDA67602 (63' · DDD · T/t)   Ⓕ

Hyperion is an old hand at programming attractively playable discs that make up complete Lied editions. Kennedy's selection has the earlier material, with the Opp 17 and 32 groups given complete. Strauss's choice of poets at this stage in his Lied career may not have been as sophisticated as it became but he never chose a text that didn't inspire a clear musical portrait. Especially well pointed are two *Des Knaben Wunderhorn* songs ('Himmelsboten' and the droll love-on-the-cheap story of 'Für fünfzehn Pfennige') and the dark, serious 'Sehnsucht'. The better-known 'Ständchen' and what Roger Vignoles's notes call the 'ebullient barnstormer' 'Heimliche Aufforderung' are placed cunningly within the recital order.

Vignoles's playing continues to achieve a maximum of freshness and invention and a chameleon-like closeness to his singer's tone and line. Kennedy's voice is young, sweet, fluent and has what some commentators call 'sap'. Greater naturalness (and especially inwardness) will come in his live and later performances of this repertoire. In the meantime, a lot of work and study has gone into this disc and the readings attain a consistently high standard of beautiful music-making.

The Complete Songs – 4
Fünf Lieder, Op 15[a]. Stiller Gang, Op 31 No 4[a]. Fünf Lieder, Op 39[a] – No 3, Der Arbeitsmann; No 5, Lied an meinen Sohn. Fünf Lieder, Op 41[a] – No 3, Am Ufer; No 5, Leise Lieder. Des Dichters Abendgang, Op 47 No 2[a]. Das Lied des Steinklopfers, Op 49 No 4[a]. Sechs Lieder, Op 56 – No 1, Gefundena; No 3, Im Spätboot[b]; No 4, Mit deinen blauen Augen[a]. Vom künftigen Alter, AV115 Op 87 No 1[b]. Erschaffen und Beleben, Op 87 No 2[b]. Und dann nicht mehr, AV114 Op 87 No 3[b]. Im Sonnenschein, AV121 Op 87 No 4[b]
[a]**Christopher Maltman** bar [b]**Alastair Miles** bass
Roger Vignoles pf
Hyperion CDA67667 (59' · DDD · T/t)   ⒻⓄ

With one possible exception, these are all among Strauss's more rarely performed songs, and quite undeservedly so. Most are highly characteristic and clearly written with affection, while those that may not immediately proclaim the composer's identity ('Das Lied des Steinklopfers' for instance) are among the most interesting. Perhaps that sense of a structured improvisation may (as in the Rückert setting 'Und dann nicht mehr') call for a restraining hand, but more often it is such an appealing personal quality that complaint would be sourly puritanical. Indeed some of the joy arises in just those moments, such as the inspired passage between verses in 'Des Dichters Abendgang', when Strauss the pianist takes over and claims his composer's freedom.

Roger Vignoles captures well the expansiveness and generosity of the writing for piano. He is also a sensitive accompanist in songs where the piano part is relatively simple. "Heimkehr", the last song of Op 15, is one of these, and this is also the exception to the songs' general unfamiliarity. It is well sung, with finely controlled high *pianissimi*, by Christopher Maltman, who has all but the last five songs (mostly Op 81), which are written specifically for bass. It must be said that with the first sound of Alastair Miles, one is immediately aware of a change, not merely in the quality and nature of the voice, but in its production too. Maltman is a valuable artist in many respects, but recording exposes an unevenness of emission which his art is usually able to render inconspicuous 'in the flesh'. Miles impresses deeply, down indeed to the depths of his low D flat.

Opera Arias

Der Rosenkavalier[a] – Da geht er hin; Ach, du bist wieder da!; Die Zeit, die ist ein sonderbar Ding; Ich hab ihn nicht einmal geküsst; Marie Theres!…Hab' mir's gelobt; Ist ein Traum. **Arabella**[b] – Ich danke, Fräulein. **Capriccio**[c] – Interlude; Wo ist mein Bruder?
Renée Fleming *sop* with [ab]**Barbara Bonney** *sop*
[a]**Susan Graham** *mez* [a]**Johannes Chum** *ten* [ac]**Walter Berry** *bass-bar* **Vienna Philharmonic Orchestra /
Christoph Eschenbach**
Decca 466 314-2DH (78' · DDD · T/t) Ⓕ**ⓞⓞ**▷

This is a happily chosen Strauss showcase for Fleming. Her creamy, full-toned, vibrant voice is about the ideal instrument not only for the Marschallin but also for the other parts she attempts here. She has mastered the phraseology and verbal inflexions needed for all three roles, and imparts to them a quick intelligence to second the vocal glories. Sometimes her performance as the Marschallin or Countess Madeleine recalls, almost uncannily, those of Schwarzkopf, leaving one in no doubt that she has studied the readings of her distinguished predecessor. If Schwarzkopf with a slightly slimmer tone has the finer line and quicker responses, her successor provides the richer tone. Fleming need fear no comparisons with more recent interpreters such as Te Kanawa, Tomowa-Sintow and, as Madeleine only, Janowitz. Indeed, Fleming's account of the closing scene of *Capriccio* is just about ideal. Her deluxe team of co-stars includes Susan Graham, who makes an ardent suitor in *Rosenkavalier*'s Act 1 duets; her timbre is so similar to Fleming's that it's hard to

tell them apart, though she isn't as verbally acute as her partner. And Barbara Bonney finally commits an extract of her enchanting Sophie, the best since Lucia Popp's; she also joins Fleming in the Arabella-Zdenka duet. Even the cameo appearances of a lackey at the close of Act 1 of *Der Rosenkavalier*, of Faninal after the Act 3 trio, and the major-domo in the closing scene from *Capriccio*, are filled by the veteran Walter Berry. Under Eschenbach, the VPO plays immaculately – the horn solo in the Moonlight music is pure magic – and the sound quality is outstandingly life-like. A treat for Straussians.

Salome – Ach! du wolltest mich nicht deinen Mund küssen lassen. **Ariadne auf Naxos** – Overture; Ein Schönes war; Es gibt ein Reich. **Die Liebe der Danae** – Wie umgibst du mich mit Frieden; Interlude, Act 3. **Capriccio** – Interlude; Wo ist mein Bruder?; Kein andres, das mir so im Herzen loht[a]
Julia Varady *sop* **Bamberg Symphony Orchestra /
Dietrich Fischer-Dieskau** [a]*bar*
Orfeo C511991A (62' · DDD) Ⓕ**ⓞ**

After giving choice recitals of Verdi and Wagner, Varady turned her attention to Strauss, and once again the results are for the most part rewarding. The final scene of *Salome*, under the watchful eye of Varady's husband, Fischer-Dieskau, has the perfection of pitch and phrase one expects of this singer, as well as an expected acuity for the meaning of the text. Perhaps, away from the theatre in a part she never undertook on stage, the absolute conviction of such great interpreters as Cebotari, Welitsch and Rysanek is absent, but not by much. The two almost consecutive solos of *Ariadne* benefit from shapely, poised singing, ever obedient to the score, although occasionally one misses the creamier tones that Lisa della Casa (DG) and Gundula Janowitz (DG video, and EMI) brought to the part. As Danae, Varady seems a shade tentative and vocally out of sorts. There need be no reservations about the final scene of *Capriccio*, in which she catches ideally Countess Madeleine's emotional perplexity as she tries (unsuccessfully) to choose between her poet and musician admirers. Both her identification with the role and her execution of Strauss's operatic farewell to his beloved soprano voice are near-ideal. Fischer-Dieskau, endearingly, sings the short part of the Haushofmeister. However, his conducting, although sensibly paced, sometimes errs on the side of caution. As a whole, this CD nicely complements Fleming's Strauss concert on Decca, the two discs offering a compendium of the composer's writing for the soprano voice he loved so much.

Arabella

Arabella
Julia Varady *sop* Arabella **Helen Donath** *sop* Zdenka
Dietrich Fischer-Dieskau *bar* Mandryka **Walter Berry** *bass* Waldner **Helga Schmidt** *mez* Adelaide
Elfriede Höbarth *sop* Fiakermilli **Adolf Dallapozza**

ten Matteo **Hermann Winkler** *ten* Elemer **Klaus-Jürgen Küper** *bar* Dominik **Hermann Becht** *bar* Lamoral **Doris Soffel** *mez* Fortune Teller **Arno Lemberg** *spkr* Welko **Bavarian State Opera Chorus; Bavarian State Orchestra / Wolfgang Sawallisch**
Orfeo ② C169882H (144' · DDD · T/t) R   Ⓕ●

Complete except for a brief cut in Matteo's part in Act 3, Sawallisch's 1981 Orfeo recording of *Arabella* has been easily fitted onto two CDs. Sawallisch is the most experienced conductor of Strauss's operas alive today and at his best in this one, his tempos exactly right, his appreciation of its flavour (sometimes sentimental, at others gently ironic and detached) unequalled. Helen Donath's delightful Zdenka is a perfect foil for Varady's Arabella. Varady's singing of the title-role is characterful and intelligent. One should be left with ambivalent feelings about this heroine; is she lovable or a chilling opportunist? Or both? And while Fischer-Dieskau's singing of Mandryka has not the total security of his earlier DG recording of the role with Keilberth, he remains the best Mandryka heard since the war.

Arabella   Ⓗ
Lisa Della Casa *sop* Arabella **Elfride Trötschel** *sop* Zdenka **Hermann Uhde** *bar* Mandryka **Max Proebstl** *bass* Count Waldner **Ira Malaniuk** *mez* Adelaide **Lorenz Fehenberger** *ten* Matteo **Franz Klarwein** *ten* Count Elemer **Karl Hoppe** *bar* Count Dominik **Albrecht Peter** *bass* Count Lamoral **Käthe Nentwig** *sop* Fiakermilli **Chorus and Orchestra of the Bavarian State Opera / Rudolf Kempe**
Testament mono ② SBT2 1367 (147' · ADD)
Broadcast by the BBC from the Royal Opera House, Covent Garden, London 1953   Ⓜ●●

You'd be hard pressed to find a more elating and satisfying interpretation of this work than this live recording, which derives from a BBC Third Programme broadcast, privately taped.

Kempe more or less made his name in London with the visit of the Munich company to the Royal Opera House; it alerted everyone to his great merits as a conductor and particularly as an interpreter of Richard Strauss. In lesser readings the work can seem sprawling, but he makes sure the piece bowls along at an invigorating pace while judging to perfection when to relax in the score's purple passages. In spite of somewhat murky sound, the playing of the company's orchestra, with its then first-hand experience of Strauss himself, only four years gone at the time, brings out all the score's glinting, glowing texture. The results are inspiriting.

Della Casa, in one of the earliest of her many assumptions of the title-part, is in ravishing voice and wholly spontaneous in her immaculately phrased and sung performance. She catches every aspect of the heroine's character, at once firm, warm and positive, and she treats the text with loving care. Her 1958 Salzburg reading may be slightly more confident, but for sheer beauty of sound this one is quite its equal. Her final act of forgiving Mandryka and giving

herself to him is truly heart-warming.

Here, as throughout, Uhde proves himself the most convincing Mandryka on disc. Not only is he the only baritone who seems quite unfazed by the role's high-lying tessitura but he sings it with an exemplary line and tonal breadth. As far as characterisation is concerned he is to the life the wilful country landowner, unused to city ways, and he makes us believe successively in the man's sincerity, jealousy and profound love, while never overdoing the histrionics. He, like his Arabella, seems in inspired form, engaging entirely with the world of Viennese bourgeoisie so unerringly created by librettist and composer.

At that time, there was a strong, experienced ensemble in Munich from which Max Proebstl's endearingly Viennese Waldner, Ira Malaniuk's fussy Adelaide and Lorenz Fehenberger's impassioned Matteo stand out. Elfride Trötschel's Zdenka is not in the class of her Viennese contemporary, Hilde Gueden, but she does project the character's girl/boy dilemma with some conviction. Käthe Nentwig makes the Fiakermilli less of a trial than she can sometimes be.

Mike Ashman puts the performance in its historical perspective in his booklet-note, but you have to go to the web to get a libretto. The remastering of the sound by Paul Baily allows us to hear this historic performance in more-than-tolerable sound. At two for the price of one, this is an issue worth any Straussian's attention.

Arabella   Ⓗ
Lisa della Casa *sop* Arabella **Anneliese Rothenberger** *sop* Zdenka **Dietrich Fischer-Dieskau** *bar* Mandryka **Otto Edelmann** *bass* Count Waldner **Ira Malaniuk** *mez* Adelaide **Eta Köhrer** *sop* Fiakermilli **Kurt Ruesche** *ten* Matteo **Helmut Melchert** *ten* Count Elemer **Georg Stern** *bar* Count Dominik **Karl Weber** *bass* Count Lamoral **Kerstin Meyer** *sop* Fortune-Teller **Vienna State Opera Chorus; Vienna Philharmonic Orchestra / Joseph Keilberth**

Four Last Songs   Ⓗ
Lisa della Casa *sop*
Vienna Philharmonic Orchestra / Karl Böhm
Orfeo d'Or mono ③ C651 053D (178' · ADD · S/N)
Recorded live July 1958   Ⓜ●●

A performance recorded by DG in Munich in 1963 had the same Arabella, Mandryka and conductor. That production originated in 1958 at the Salzburg Festival and it is a broadcast of its auspicious first night that appears here for the first time on disc. That was also the year Decca recorded the work with Della Casa under Solti, so there are interesting comparisons.

What cannot be in dispute is that the part of Arabella might have been written for Della Casa. Excellent as some of her successors may have been, she remains supreme. In 1958 she was at her vocal and interpretative peak: everything she does ravishes the senses. To an even greater extent than in the studio, she inhabits the character from start to finish. Haughty and off-hand with previous lovers, she aurally melts when coming across 'Der Richtige', the right man for her, in the person of Mandryka. The softness and glow of her singing at the end of Act 1 and the start of Act 2 is balm to the ear, as are her ravishing *pianissimi* throughout. Then, when Mandryka unjustly accuses her of infidelity, the tremble suggests all the hurt he is causing her. That's banished when all is cleared up in the ineffably beautiful finale; a memorable climax to a great portrayal.

Fischer-Dieskau on stage was the rough-hewn, impulsive Mandryka to the life. His performance has enormous presence and vitality but he is rather inclined to go into his hectoring mode, with line-breaking over-emphases (George London on Decca may be preferred). The Adelaide and Waldner are common to Orfeo and Decca, both admirable in depicting the Viennese bourgeoisie.

As Zdenka, Hilde Gueden (Decca) is slightly preferable to Rothenberger on Orfeo and DG because of her greater ease on high. Anton Dermota (Decca) is a more fluent Matteo than Karl Ruesche, a tenor unknown to me.

Keilberth lays a lighter, more lyrical hand on the score than Solti but unfortunately makes the common and disfiguring cuts in Act 3. The Decca set enjoys early stereo against Orfeo's mono. But Della Casa, caught on the wing and in freshest voice, is not be missed.

A clinching factor may be the inclusion of the *Four Last Songs*, recorded at Salzburg the night after the *Arabella*. Here she, Böhm and the VPO renew their famous alliance in this work from their classic 1953 recording on Decca. Unlike other interpreters they still start with 'Beim Schlafengehen'. In other respects there are improvements. Speeds overall are a little slower, allowing for subtler shades of colouring, more intensity of feeling, and the voice itself is more rounded. It seems a version that fulfils every one of the work's exigent demands, and surpasses even those by Schwarzkopf, Popp and Janowitz for sheer tonal beauty and sheen, placing it at the top of the pile as the most favoured reading, although it has to be said that the orchestral palette is restricted by modern standards.

 for a small orchestra, demands virtuoso playing from what, in effect, is a group of soloists; the members of the Philharmonia Orchestra rise brilliantly to the occasion. There's a warmth and beauty of tone, a sweep of phrase, that gives lively promise of the wonderful playing we hear throughout the opera. Karajan's genius has never been more apparent than in his treatment of the Bacchus-Ariadne scene, where he makes the score glow with a Dionysiac ardour and in which, at the tremendous climax when Bacchus enters and is greeted by Ariadne as the herald of Death, he gets an ample volume of tone from his players.

Every character is vividly brought to life – Karl Dönch's harassed music master is offset by the cynical dancing master of Hugues Cuénod, and Alfred Neugebauer, in his speaking role, conveys with a superbly calm pomposity his contempt for both sets of artists. The way he enunciates his words is superb. The other small parts, all sung by experienced artists, are wholly in the picture. Rita Streich sings the lyrical phrases of Zerbinetta beautifully. Technical difficulties do not appear to exist for her and all she does is musical. Irmgard Seefried, as the Composer, has less beauty of tone but more variety. The ineffably lovely trio for the Naiad, Dryad and Echo is exquisitely sung by Lisa Otto, Grace Hoffman and Anny Felbermayer, paralleled by the equally beautiful singing of the other trios. They are simply ravishing and, like all the concerted music, have a perfect ensemble. The *commedia dell'arte* characters are all very good, especially Hermann Prey: and their ensembles between themselves and with Zerbinetta are a great delight. After an awkward start, Elisabeth Schwarzkopf, as Ariadne, brings the dark tone that's needed, to Ariadne's sorrows, and gives us much lovely singing thereafter, and also all the rapture called for at the end of her great address to the herald of Death and in her greeting to Bacchus. Rudolf Schock sings the latter with heroic tone and sufficient nuance to make one believe in the youthful god.

The general impression is of a truly magnificent performance and recording in which all concerned have, under Karajan's superb direction, been inspired to give of their best.

Ariadne auf Naxos

Ariadne auf Naxos ⊞
Elisabeth Schwarzkopf *sop* Ariadne **Irmgard Seefried** *sop* Composer **Rita Streich** *sop* Zerbinetta **Rudolf Schock** *ten* Bacchus **Karl Dönch** *bar* Music-Master **Hermann Prey** *bar* Harlequin **Fritz Ollendorff** *bass* Truffaldino **Helmut Krebs** *ten* Brighella **Gerhard Unger** *ten* Scaramuccio **Lisa Otto** *sop* Naiad **Grace Hoffman** *mez* Dryad **Anny Felbermayer** *sop* Echo **Hugues Cuénod** *ten* Dancing Master **Alfred Neugebauer** *spkr* Major-Domo **Philharmonia Orchestra / Herbert von Karajan**
EMI Great Recordings of the Century mono ②
567077-2 (128′ · ADD) Recorded 1954 Ⓜ❶❶❶❶↦

Karajan's *Ariadne* is perfectly cast, magnificently performed, and very well recorded. The scoring,

Ariadne auf Naxos
Emily Magee *sop* Ariadne **Michelle Breedt** *mez* Composer **Elena Mosuc** *sop* Zerbinetta **Roberto Saccà** *ten* Bacchus **Michael Volle** *bar* Music-Master **Sandra Trattnigg** *sop* Echo **Eva Liebau** *sop* Naiad **Irène Friedli** *contr* Dryad **Blagoj Nacoski** *ten* Brighella **Guy de Mey** *ten* Dancing Master **Martin Zysset** *ten* Scaramuccio **Randall Ball** *ten* Officer **Gabriel Bermúdez** *bar* Harlequin **Andrew Ashwin** *bar* Wigmaker **Reinhard Mayr** *bass* Truffaldino **Alexander Pereira** *spkr* Major-Domo **Zurich Opera Chorus and Orchestra / Christoph von Dohnányi**
Stage director **Claus Guth**
Video director **Thomas Grimm**
TDK Ⓕ 📀 DVWW-OPAAN (127′ · NTSC · 16:9 · LPCM stereo, 5.1 and DTS 5.1 · 0)

Recorded live at the Opernhaus, Zurich, in December 2006 ⊙▷

If many productions of this fascinating, but awkward, Strauss/Hofmannsthal hybrid have erred towards the story's comic side – the interruptions of Zerbinetta and her Harlequin troupe – Claus Guth's brave Zurich staging centres markedly on the fate of Ariadne herself. The 'backstage' Prologue plays scenery-less in front of tall curtains which work, of course, as dressing-room doors but also focus on the Composer's frustration at having his opera mounted in such chaos. All the character's despair is played for real here and, despite an obvious attraction to Zerbinetta, the Composer shoots himself, reappearing as a ghost in the opera proper to dance with Zerbinetta or approve Ariadne's dilemma.

The opera proper plays in a smart restaurant where Ariadne, *Brief Encounter*-like with a touch of Joan Crawford, mourns her loss of Theseus. The Harlequins and Nymphs are other diners and waitresses. Ariadne's despair, then her frustrated hope that Bacchus is Theseus, leads her to suicide by overdose. She spends the duet with Bacchus dying. It's amazing how well this concept fits the text sung by the opera's serious pair.

Emily Magee has recently been seen on DVD as Elsa and Ellen Orford, superb in two widely differing operas. This performance (her debut in the role) tops both of those, beginning with the prelude to the opera where her sitting, grieving, at table is the entire action. She can also sing the part gloriously. Roberto Saccà manages this tricky target for his affections well – he becomes a sympathetic assistant to a patient's demise – and has the vocal demands well in control. Michele Breedt is the ultra-intense suicidal Composer, Michael Volle her enigmatic, blind Music-Master. Dohnányi, as always (one may truly say), is a master of Straussian balance and climax. The (very) close-up filming seems to tell Guth's story to perfection. Magee's towering performance must be seen and heard.

Capriccio

Capriccio
Elisabeth Schwarzkopf *sop* The Countess **Eberhard Waechter** *bar* The Count **Nicolai Gedda** *ten* Flamand **Dietrich Fischer-Dieskau** *bar* Olivier **Hans Hotter** *bass-bar* La Roche **Christa Ludwig** *mez* Clairon **Ruldolf Christ** *ten* Monsieur Taupe **Anna Moffo** *sop* Italian Soprano **Dermot Troy** *ten* Italian Tenor **Karl Schmitt-Walter** *bar* Major-domo **Philharmonia Orchestra / Wolfgang Sawallisch**
EMI Great Recordings of the Century mono
② 567394-2 (135' · ADD · T/t) Recorded 1957
Ⓜ⦿❶❶❶▷

Ⓖ Not only is *Capriccio* a source of constant and none-too-demanding delight but its performance and recording, especially in this CD reincarnation, are wellnigh faultless. Walter Legge assembled for the recording in 1957 what was almost his house cast, each singer virtually ideal for his or her part. Some might say that no role she recorded suited Schwarzkopf's particular talents more snugly than Countess Madeleine. Her ability to mould words and music into one can be heard here to absolute advantage. Then the charming, flirtatious, sophisticated, slightly artificial character, with the surface attraction hiding deeper feelings revealed in the closing scene (quite beautifully sung), suit her to the life. She, like her colleagues, is superbly adept at the quick repartee so important an element in this work.

As her brother, the light-hearted, libidinous Count, the young Eberhard Waechter is in his element. So are the equally young Nicolai Gedda as the composer Flamand, the Sonnet so gently yet ardently delivered, and Fischer-Dieskau as the more fiery poet Olivier. Christa Ludwig is nicely intimate, conversational and cynical as the actress Clairon, handling her affairs, waning with Olivier, waxing with the Count, expertly. Above all towers the dominating presence of Hotter as the theatre director La Roche, impassioned in his defence of the theatre's conventions, dismissive of new and untried methods, yet himself not above a trivial flirtation – and how delicately Hotter manages his remarks about his latest protegee as she dances for the assembled company.

Even with so many distinguished singers gathered together, it's the closeness of the ensemble, the sense of a real as distinct from a manufactured performance that's so strongly conveyed. And Legge did not neglect the smaller roles: Rudolf Christ makes an endearingly eccentric Monsieur Taupe, the veteran Schmitt-Walter a concerned Major-domo. Anna Moffo and Dermot Troy sing the music of the Italian soprano and tenor with almost too much sensitivity.

Crowning the performance is the musical direction of Wolfgang Sawallisch, always keeping the score on the move, yet fully aware of its sensuous and its witty qualities: Krauss's amusing libretto has much to do with the work's fascination. Both the extended Prelude and the interludes are gloriously played by the vintage Philharmonia, who are throughout alert to the old wizard's deft scoring, as refined here as in any of his earlier operas. The recording might possibly have given a little more prominence to the instruments; in every other respect, although it's in mono, it hardly shows its age.

Elektra

Elektra
Birgit Nilsson *sop* Elektra **Regina Resnik** *mez* Klytemnestra **Marie Collier** *sop* Chrysothemis **Gerhard Stolze** *ten* Aegisthus **Tom Krause** *bar* Orestes **Pauline Tinsley** *sop* Overseer **Helen Watts** *contr* **Maureen Lehane, Yvonne Minton** *mezzos* **Jane Cook, Felicia Weathers** *sops* First, Second, Third, Fourth and Fifth Maidservants **Tugomir Franc** *bass* Tutor **Vienna Philharmonic Orchestra / Sir Georg Solti**
Decca ② 4758231 (108' · ADD) Recorded 1966-7
Ⓕ⦿❶❶❶▷

Elektra is the most consistently inspired of all Strauss's operas and derives from Greek mythology, with the ghost of Agamemnon, so unerringly delineated in the opening bars, hovering over the whole work. The invention and the intensity of mood are sustained throughout the opera's one-act length, and the characterisation is both subtle and pointed. It's a work peculiarly well suited to Solti's gifts and it's his best recording in the studios. He successfully maintains the nervous tension throughout the unbroken drama and conveys all the power and tension in Strauss's enormously complex score which is, for once, given complete. The recording captures the excellent singers and the Vienna Philharmonic in a warm, spacious acoustic marred only by some questionable electronic effects. Notwithstanding the latter, this is undoubtedly one of the greatest performances on record and sounds even more terrifyingly realistic on this magnificent transfer.

Elektra   Ⓗ
Inge Borkh *sop* Elektra **Jean Madeira** *mez* Klytemnestra **Lisa della Casa** *sop* Chrysothemis **Max Lorenz** *ten* Aegisthus **Kurt Böhme** *bass* Orestes **Alois Pernerstorfer** *bass-bar* Tutor **Anny Felbermayer** *sop* Confidante **Karol Loraine** *mez* Trainbearer **Erich Majkut** *ten* Young Servant **György Littasy** *bass* Old Servant **Audrey Gerber** *sop* Overseer **Kerstin Meyer, Sonja Draksler, Sieglinde Wagner, Marilyn Horne** *mezzos* **Lisa Otto** *sop* First, Second, Third, Fourth and Fifth Maidservants **Vienna State Opera Chorus; Vienna Philharmonic Orchestra / Dimitri Mitropoulos**
Orfeo mono ② C456972I (107' · ADD) Recorded live 1957
Ⓜ**OO**

This is an enthralling performance. Mitropoulos made a speciality of the score, his most important contribution to opera interpretation. Souvenirs exist of his performances at the Met in 1949 and at the Maggio Musicale in Florence in 1950, but his Salzburg reading is the one to have. No other conductor, not even Böhm or Solti in the studio, quite matches the *frisson* of this overwhelming account. And it confirms that Inge Borkh is indeed the most comprehensively equipped soprano for the title-role, vocally secure – high-C apart – and emotionally capable of fulfilling every demand of the strenuous part. In the great scene with Orestes she first expresses ineffably the sorrow at his supposed death, the 'tausendmal' and 'nie wiederkommt' passage done with such a searing sense of loss; then comes the great release of recognition – sung with immense warmth – followed by another almost silvery voice as Elektra recalls her lost beauty. It's a passage of singing to return to repeatedly for its many insights. Chrysothemis finds in della Casa an unusual interpreter, wonderfully ecstatic and pure of voice if not as emotionally involving as some. Madeira is a formidable Klytemnestra, her nightmarish thoughts expressed in a firm voice, accurately deployed. Böhme, a real bass, presents an implacable,

angry Orestes, not as subtle or as sympathetic as Krause for Solti. Lorenz's fading *Heldentenor* is ideal to express Aegisthus's fatuity. And the maids have never, surely, been cast with such secure voices.

Inevitably, cuts are made as is almost always the case in the theatre where, otherwise, Elektra might be left voiceless by the end. If you want the complete score, the famous Solti set will do very nicely. If you want Borkh, you must choose between the Böhm in stereo (DG) or this unique experience.

Elektra
Eva Marton *sop* Elektra **Brigitte Fassbaender** *mez* Klytemnestra **Cheryl Studer** *sop* Chrysothemis **Franz Grundheber** *bar* Orestes **James King** *ten* Aegisthus **Goran Simic** *bass* Tutor **Waltraud Winsauer** *mez* Confidante **Noriko Sasaki** *sop* Trainbearer **Wilfried Gahmlich** *ten* Young Servant **Claudio Otelli** *bass-bar* Old Servant **Gabriele Lechner** *sop* Overseer **Margarita Lilowa, Gabriele Sima, Margareta Hintermeier, Brigitte Poschner-Klebel, Joanna Borowska** Maidservants **Vienna State Opera Chorus and Orchestra / Claudio Abbado**
Stage director **Harry Kupfer**
Video director **Brian Large**
ArtHaus Musik **DVD** 100 048 (109' · DDD) Recorded live 1989   ⒻOO

This is an enjoyable performance, if that's the right word for *Elektra*'s gruesome drama, of Strauss's opera (taken from the first night of a new production at the Vienna State Opera in 1989), still one of the most sensational scores of the last century. Harry Kupfer may have conceived the work in even more lurid terms than its creators Hofmannsthal and Strauss intended, but the principals' psychotic behaviour is so convincingly enacted that we're carried into the soul of all their personal tortures of the mind. Elektra herself is a determined, raddled, single-minded harridan, lording it over sister and mother, a portrayal Eva Marton carries out with a deal of conviction, once one accepts the judder in her voice. Chrysothemis becomes a writhing, overwrought, frustrated figure, at one stage seeming to fake an orgasm, all of which Studer conveys with much emphasis on physical contact with her sister. She sings the taxing role with opulent tone and soaring phraseology.

Physicality is also of the essence in Fassbaender's study of guilt and inner disintegration as a Klytemnestra of intriguing complexity, yet she still somehow manages to suggest the character's feminine attraction. This portrayal alone makes this DVD essential viewing. Grundheber is the avenging Orestes to the life, with savagely piercing eyes and implacable tone. King is a properly futile paramour. In the activity of the extras, and such episodes as the butchering of Aegisthus and Chrysothemis wallowing in his blood-stained cloak, very little is left to the imagination. This is an enclosed world where licence and human sacrifices, unbridled in their

ferocity, have taken over from order and humanity, and that was surely Kupfer's intention, so
that Orestes' arrival has even more of a cleansing
effect than usual.

In the pit, Abbado conducts with a single-
minded intensity, constantly aware of the score's
brutal and tragic aspects, and he procures playing of tremendous concentration from the
Vienna Philharmonic. Although the staging
takes place in Stygian gloom, you can discern
more of its detail in this reincarnation on DVD,
which has the added advantage of containing the
whole opera on a single disc.

This is a version to buy for its absorbing, fully
integrated view of Strauss's masterpiece.

Elektra

Eva Johansson *sop* Elektra **Marjana Lipovšek** *mez*
Klytemnestra **Melanie Diener** *sop* Chrysothemis
Rudolf Schasching *ten* Aegisthus **Alfred Muff** *bar*
Orestes **Reinhard Mayr** *bass* Tutor **Cassandra**
McConnell *sop* Confidante **Christine Zoller** *sop*
Trainbearer **Andreas Winkler** *ten* Young Servant
Morgan Moody *bass* Old Servant **Margaret Chalker**
sop Overseer
Zürich Opera House Chorus and Orchestra /
Christoph von Dohnányi
Stage director **Martin Kušej**
Video director **Felix Breisach**
TDK Ⓕ *DVD* DVWW-OPELEK (102' · NTSC · 16:9 ·
PCM stereo, 5.1 and DTS 5.1 · 0)
Recorded live at the Opernhaus, Zürich, in November
and December 2005   ⒻО

It's a change to see a production of Strauss's and
Hofmannsthal's psychotic masterwork that's
not weighted with greater German gloom, louring Second World War-derived imagery and
cakes of lurid make-up. Martin Kušej directs
people well, and since *Elektra* is largely an opera
of dialogues, his work (all closely derived from
the text) demands attention.

Eva Johansson's Elektra is a hooded tomboy
with definite Asbo leanings; she has to be on
full throttle for this role but both Dohnányi's
orchestra and TDK's engineers are kind to her.
Melanie Diener, a consummate singing actress,
locates the hard, hard role of Chrysothemis
somewhere between Victoria Beckham and
Brechtian alienation: every entry, every new
event is as surprising to her as a goldfish going
round its bowl.

Marjana Lipovšek presents their mother as a
complex of confused identities, eschewing both
in voice and acting any melodramatic harridan
tendencies. As their brother, Alfred Muff survives a dreadful first 'disguise' wig to present a
revenger of quiet, un-neurotic determination.
Equally original is Rudolf Schasching's lecherous groper of an Aegisthus, convincingly
deceived when Elektra plays up to his libido.

The action takes places in a dangerously
uneven, hillock-strewn courtyard, reached by
many doors. There is much cavorting by the
smaller roles: the maids (and one token transvestite) dress up as…maids (French) for Aegis-

thus' pleasure, while action or tension in the
palace (Strauss's 'interludes') is illustrated by
door-to-door crosses by a large troupe of
actors in various states of ecstasy, undress, axe-
carrying, etc. They've not been terribly well
directed and the effect only really works when
the (false) news of Orestes' death sets off Klytemnestra's laugh. At the end, when revenge is
done, the girl extras perform a dance in Las
Vegas-style frillies – weird, but suitably
unnerving.

Dohnányi's old master's approach to the score
goes for a long pay-off rather than whipping up
the tension from the word go, employing a wide
range of tempi and dynamics and stressing the
modernity of the score. Both the Vienna staging
of Harry Kupfer (with Claudio Abbado) and the
studio film of Götz Friedrich (with Karl Böhm
and a veteran stellar cast) remain indispensable.
But, for an alternative vision allied to a close,
human reading of the text, the new performance,
while not quite the sum of its parts, makes for
intelligent viewing.

Die Frau ohne Schatten

Die Frau ohne Schatten
Julia Varady *sop* Empress **Plácido Domingo** *ten*
Emperor **Hildegard Behrens** *sop* Dyer's Wife **José**
van Dam *bar* Barak the Dyer **Reinhild Runkel** *contr*
Nurse **Albert Dohmen** *bar* Spirit-Messenger **Sumi Jo**
sop Voice of the Falcon **Robert Gambill** *ten*
Apparition of a Young Man **Elzbieta Ardam** *mez*
Voice from Above **Eva Lind** *sop* Guardian of the
Threshold **Gottfried Hornik** *bar* One-eyed Brother
Hans Franzen *bass* One-armed Brother **Wilfried**
Gahmlich *ten* Hunchback Brother **Vienna Boys'**
Choir; Vienna State Opera Chorus; Vienna
Philharmonic Orchestra / Sir Georg Solti
Decca ③ 436 243-2DHO3 (195' · DDD · T/t)
                                    Ⓕ ОООО➔

 This was the most ambitious project on
which Strauss and his librettist Hugo
von Hofmannsthal collaborated. It's
both fairy tale and allegory with a score that's
Wagnerian in its scale and breadth. This Solti
version presents the score absolutely complete
in an opulent recording that encompasses every
detail of the work's multi-faceted orchestration.
Nothing escapes his keen eye and ear or that of
the Decca engineers. The cast boasts splendid
exponents of the two soprano roles. Behrens's
vocal acting suggests complete identification
with the unsatisfied plight of the Dyer's Wife
and her singing has a depth of character to compensate for some tonal wear. Varady gives an
intense, poignant account of the Empress's taxing music. The others, though never less tha-
nadequate, leave something to be desired.
Domingo sings the Emperor with vigour and
strength but evinces little sense of the music's
idiom. José van Dam is likewise a vocally impeccable Barak but never penetrates the Dyer's
soul. Runkel is a mean, malign Nurse as she
should be, though she could be a little more

interesting in this part. It benefits from glorious, dedicated playing by the VPO.

Guntram

Guntram
Alan Woodrow ten Guntram **Andrea Martin** bar The Old Duke **Elisabeth Wachutka** sop Freihild **Ivan Konsulov** bar Robert **Hans-Peter Scheidegger** bar Freihold **Enrico Facini** ten The Duke's Fool **Thomas Kaluzny** bar Messenger, Young Man, Minnesinger **Jin-Ho Choi** bar Old Man, Minnesinger **Ute Trekel-Burkhardt** mez Old Woman **Manfred Bittner** ten Young Man, Minnesinger **Matthias Heubusch** voc Minnesinger **Werdenfelser Male Chorus;**
Marchigiana Philharmonic Orchestra /
Gustav Kuhn
Arte Nova Classics ② 74321 61339-2 (100' · DDD · T) Recorded live 1998 ⑤

However much influenced by Wagner this, Strauss's first opera, may have been, it already shows him moving off in his own melodic and harmonic direction. It contains much attractive, well-crafted music, but from the start it was lamed by the composer's own prolix libretto and hesitant dramaturgy. The story of the brave, libertarian knight Guntram's adventures in 13th-century Germany and his love for the heroine Freihild, daughter of the local ruler, whose husband Duke Robert is a sort of villain and opponent of peace, is really one about individual responsibility being more important than religious orthodoxy, something that offended Strauss's strict Catholic mentor, Alexander Ritter. This live performance under the experienced Straussian Gustav Kuhn gives a fair idea of its virtues and defects. His direction is vigorous, forward moving, strongly limned with a proper advocacy of the score's more original features, with resplendent playing from his orchestra. The performance is well served by its two principals. In the title-role, the ENO tenor Alan Woodrow here makes a more-than-passable Heldentenor in the first of many roles for that voice calling for strong, virile, penetrative tone. Woodrow produces just that, plus much of the romantic fervour Guntram's role calls for. Elisabeth Wachutka is reasonably successful as the object of Guntram's desires. Though her tone can be edgy, she rises finely to the challenge of her extended monologue in Act 2. The rest, who don't have much to do, are so-so. The recording is clear and well balanced. At the price, this is worth sampling to hear Strauss's apprentice effort in the operatic field he was so soon to grace with many masterpieces.

Der Rosenkavalier

Der Rosenkavalier ⊞
Elisabeth Schwarzkopf sop Die Feldmarschallin **Christa Ludwig** mez Octavian **Otto Edelmann** bass Baron Ochs **Teresa Stich-Randall** sop Sophie **Eberhard Waechter** bar Faninal **Nicolai Gedda** ten Italian Tenor **Kerstin Meyer** contr Annina **Paul Kuen** ten Valzacchi **Ljuba Welitsch** sop Duenna **Anny Felbermayer** sop Milliner **Harald Pröghlöf** bar Notary **Franz Bierbach** bass Police Commissioner **Erich Majkut** ten Feldmarschallin's Major-domo **Gerhard Unger** ten Faninal's Major-domo, Animal Seller **Karl Friedrich** ten Landlord **Loughton High School for Girls and Bancroft's School Choirs;**
Philharmonia Chorus and Orchestra /
Herbert von Karajan
EMI ③ 3773572 (191' · ADD · T/t) Recorded 1956
⑧❶❶❶⊕

 Der Rosenkavalier concerns the transferring of love of the young headstrong aristocrat Octavian from the older Marschallin (with whom he's having an affair) to the young Sophie, a girl of *nouveau riche* origins who's of his generation. The portrayal of the different levels of passion is masterly and the Marschallin's resigned surrender of her young lover gives opera one of its most cherishable scenes. The comic side of the plot concerns the vulgar machinations of the rustic Baron Ochs and his attempts to seduce the disguised Octavian (girl playing boy playing girl!). The musical richness of the score is almost indescribable, with streams of endless melody, and the final trio which brings the three soprano roles together is the crowning glory of a masterpiece of the 20th century.

This magnificent recording, conducted with genius by Karajan, and with a dream cast, is unlikely to be challenged for many a year. The Philharmonia play like angels, and Schwarzkopf as the Marschallin gives one of her greatest performances. The recording, lovingly remastered, is outstanding.

Der Rosenkavalier
Claire Watson sop Die Feldmarscallin **Brigitte Fassbaender** sop Octavian **Lucia Popp** sop Sophie **Karl Ridderbusch** bass Baron Ochs **Benno Kusche** bar Faninal **Annelie Waas** sop Marianne **David Thaw** ten Valzacchi **Margarethe Bence** mez Annina **Albrecht Peter** bass Police Commissary **Gerhard Unger** ten Italian Singer **Bavarian State Opera Chorus and Orchestra / Carlos Kleiber**
Orfeo d'Or ③ 🔊 C581 083D (178' · ADD)
Recorded live at the Nationaltheater, Bavarian State Opera, Munich, on July 13, 1973 ⑤❶❶

It's taken over 35 years but at last we have a professional audio transfer of Kleiber leading the opera that probably meant more to him than all others. If you're not yet a convert, or a doubter, cut to the chase: go from track 18 of disc 3 (the great Trio) and you'll hear why the Munich Festival audience cannot wait to start clapping some of the most attentively sculpted Strauss conducting, traditional romance mixed with savouring of those still ear-bending harmonies, since, well, Clemens Krauss and a certain Erich Kleiber .

So what is especially magical? The energy, the attention to the stage drama in the music (not least its wit), the pacing – 'fast' compared with Karajan but with a wonderful *rubato* that allows for real pointing and emotion but owes more to Kleiber's natural instincts (and his father's) than Viennese so-called tradition – and the slim textures. Under Kleiber the opera sounds like what its creators sought to do – follow *Elektra* in a different vein, not retreat from it, either musically or dramatically.

In retrospect we might call this Kleiber's first favoured *Rosenkavalier* cast which, like the second (Lott, van Otter, Bonney – DG), was led by its ladies. Long-term Munich resident Claire Watson has done little finer on disc and is well 'aged' in relationship to Fassbaender's *tour de force* Octavian (she makes a good youth throughout and a laugh-aloud Mariandel) and Popp's sweet but never vacant Sophie. But did Kleiber ever find an Ochs to match his girls? As with Ridderbusch here, he tended to trim their traditional excesses but never quite put enough in its place. The so-called 'supporting' roles are energetically taken by an evidently fired-up house ensemble.

Additional recommendation

Crespin Marschallin **Minton** Octavian **Jungwirth** Ochs **Donath** Sophie **Vienna Philharmonic Orchestra / Solti**
Decca 4759988 (200' · DDD)   Ⓜ**ⓄⓄ**Ⓑ⁺
For those craving good sound and a reading of great charm – Crespin's rather Gallic Marschallin is wondrously sung – Solti's 1968 set is worth considering. Many collectors rate this even more highly than the classic Karajan.

Der Rosenkavalier
Nina Stemme *sop* Die Feldmarschallin **Vesselina Kasarova** *sop* Octavian **Alfred Muff** *bass* Baron Ochs **Malin Hartelius** *sop* Sophie **Rolf Haunstein** *bar* Faninal **Boiko Zvetanov** *ten* Italian Tenor **Brigitte Pinter** *contr* Annina **Rudolf Schasching** *ten* Valzacchi **Liuba Chuchrova** *sop* Leitmetzerin **Volker Vogel** *bass* Notary **Günther Groissböck** *bass* Commissioner **Zürich Opera House Chorus and Orchestra / Franz Welser-Möst**
Stage director **Sven-Eric Bechtolf**
Video director **François Duplat**
EMI ⒹⓥⒹ 544258-9 (205' · NTSC · 16:9 · PCM stereo, 5.1 and DTS 5.1 · 0). Recorded live at the Opernhaus, Zürich in July 2004   Ⓕ

This version creates a dilemma. So much that the director does as regards the interplay between the characters – supported in the fascinating performances by the three female singers – is original and interesting, which makes one deeply regret that the settings and much of the detail are so irritating. Acts 1 and 3 are set in some vaguely Eastern-looking, aseptic summer-house, with the skeletons of trees poking through its ceiling. Within them, director Sven-Eric Bechtolf intrudes all kinds of mini-actions not required by the work's scenario, such as an automaton Italian

RICHARD STRAUSS'S DER ROSENKAVALIER – IN BRIEF

Elisabeth Schwarzkopf *Die Feldmarschalin* Ⓗ **Christa Ludwig** *Octavian* **Otto Edelmann** *Baron Ochs* **Philharmonia Chorus and Orchestra / Herbert von Karajan**
EMI ③ 567605-2 (182' · ADD)   Ⓜ**ⓄⓄⓄ**Ⓑ⁺
Taped as long ago as 1956, Karajan tends to linger over the work's purple passages, but, for most commentators, this is *the* classic, thanks not least to the casting of Schwarzkopf, Ludwig and Stich-Randall. Polished yet passionate and often intensely beautiful.

Maria Reining *Die Feldmarschalin* **Sena Jurinac** Ⓗ *Octavian* **Ludwig Weber** *Baron Ochs* **Vienna State Opera Chorus; Vienna PO / Erich Kleiber**
Decca ③ 478 1396 (197' · ADD)   Ⓜ**ⓄⓄ**
Recorded in 1954 in mono only, Kleiber's *echt* Viennese set is still top-rated by connoisseurs who welcome its opening out of the small stage cuts sanctioned by the composer and followed by Karajan.

Yvonne Kenny *Die Feldmarschalin* **Diana Montague** *Octavian* **John Tomlinson** *Baron Ochs* **London PO / David Parry**
Chandos CHAN3022 (80' · DDD)   Ⓜ**Ⓞ**
A delightful highlights disc with several principals familiar from English-language ENO productions, who are at least as distinguished as their counterparts on the more recent original-language recordings.

Kiri Te Kanawa *Die Feldmarschalin* **Anne Sofie von Otter** *Octavian* **Kurt Rydl** *Baron Ochs* **Dresden State Opera Chorus; Staatskapelle Dresden / Bernard Haitink**
EMI ③ 754259-2 (223' · DDD)   Ⓕ**Ⓑ**⁺
Warmly played and sung, Haitink's Dresden recording is the finest audio-only account of the digital era. Te Kanawa's Marschallin is the most beautiful of recent years.

Régine Crespin *Die Feldmarschalin* **Yvonne Minton** *Octavian* **Manfred Jungwirth** *Baron Ochs* **Vienna State Opera Chorus; Vienna PO / Sir Georg Solti**
Decca ③ 4759988 (200' · ADD)   Ⓕ**ⓄⒷ**⁺
Solti's 1968 set has high production values and an all-star casting of minor roles. He avoids the over-affectionate approach, but takes the climactic moments very broadly.

Claire Watson *Die Feldmarschallin* **Brigitte Fassbaender** *Octavian* **Lucia Popp** *Sophie* **Bavarian State Opera Chorus and Orchestra / Carlos Kleiber**
Orfeo d'Or ③ ▨ C581 083D (178' · ADD)   Ⓕ**ⓄⓄ**
The only available audio *Rosenkavalier* from Carlos Kleiber to put alongside his two magnificent videos. This is top-class Strauss singing and conducting!

Tenor and byplay with laundry. Act 2, for some unspecified reason, is set in Faninal's pantry with extras ceaselessly working at pastries for about two-thirds of the act. That severely circumscribes the area needed to portray the act's essential features. Again there are intrusive bits of action conceived for characters unspecified by the libretto. Costumes, in the current cliché, veer between those applicable to 18th-century Vienna and others of more recent provenance.

That is all the more trying given the fact that Bechtolf enlivens the relations between the principals with perceptive insight, helped by an intelligent cast. Vesselina Kasarova's highly impulsive, youthfully impetuous Octavian is a wholly credible lover in Act 1, then falls in love with Sophie in a truly precipitate, love-at-first-sight manner. Kasarova's eyes and body-language constantly reflect Octavian's emotional turmoil. As ever, her singing tries to get more out of the music than is perhaps there, but the voice, in fine shape, makes sense of most of her thought-through, palpitating interpretation.

Nina Stemme's Marschallin seems almost to be feeling what is to follow from the first. Her light-hearted responses to her lover at the start are already tinged with some sadness, which breaks forth into real torment of the soul in the latter portions of Act 1. Her tone, rather darker than we are accustomed to in the part, doesn't 'speak' easily, but its rich colours are more than compensation. Malin Hartelius's Sophie is all eager anxiety, as she prepares to meet her bridegroom, making her shocked recognition of his true nature that much more arresting. When true love strikes, she is pleasantly amazed. Her soaring soprano is fully equal to Strauss's exigent demands upon it. All three, so troubled in their feelings, make the last 25 minutes extraordinrily moving.

Alfred Muff's Baron Ochs is much more traditional in his responses but always a believable character, the role reasonably sung. The lesser roles are mostly well delineated, except when the director interferes, but not exceptionally well sung: the Italian Tenor is a particular trial with his loud, off-centre singing. Welser-Möst's reading is fleet and buoyant, avoiding sentimentality, more lithe and accurate than warm in a Viennese manner. The traditional cuts are observed.

The Kleiber set from Munich – reviewed below – remains in a league of its own, but those partial to a new interpretation will find much to enjoy in the musical side of this vitally sung, well-recorded version.

Der Rosenkavalier
Gwyneth Jones sop Die Feldmarschallin **Brigitte Fassbaender** sop Octavian **Manfred Jungwirth** bass Baron Ochs **Lucia Popp** sop Sophie **Benno Kusche** bar Faninal **Francisco Araiza** ten Italian Tenor **Gudrun Wewezow** contr Annina **David Thaw** ten Valzacchi **Anneliese Waas** sop Leitmetzerin **Susanne Sonnenschein** sop Milliner **Hans Wilbrink** bass Notary **Albrecht Peter** bass Police Commissioner **Georg Paskuda** ten Major-domo **Friedrich Lenz** ten Faninal's Major-domo **Norbert Orth** ten Landlord

Osamu Kobayashi ten Animal Seller **Bavarian State Opera Chorus; Bavarian State Orchestra / Carlos Kleiber**
Stage and video director **Otto Schenk**
DG ② 📀 073 4072GH2 (186' · NTSC · 4:3 · PCM stereo and DTS 5.1 · 0)   Ⓕ ●●●

Although it is 27 years old, this unforgettable performance has lost nothing of its power to delight eye and ear, and is in almost every way superior to Carlos Kleiber's 1994 remake in Vienna. Schenk's direction is finely judged, strong in detail, in Jürgen Rose's handsome, traditional sets. Eschewing fashionable modernities, its has stood the test of time.

Kleiber's reading has that essential mix of warmth and élan the score demands, and a lightness of touch allied to controlled but never effusive sentiment. The Bavarian State Opera Orchestra plays with the brio and confidence gained from long experience of Kleiber's impulsive ways. The shots of the conductor in the pit during the preludes to Acts 1 and 3 show how incisive his beat can be and how much he actually enjoyed conducting the piece.

The instinctive interaction of the principal singers is another indication of the rapport achieved in this wonderful staging. The intimacy of the Act 2 dialogues between the Marschallin and Octavian and between Sophie and Octavian, and the interplay among the three in the closing scene of Act 3, is rewarding and deeply moving. In the name part, Fassbaender acts the ardent, impetuous youth to the life, sensual with the Marschallin in Act 1, lovestruck with Sophie in Act 2 and wittily amusing in the Mariandl disguise, the eyes conveying all the character's changes of mood. Nothing is exaggerated, everything rings true in an ideal assumption.

Popp conveys all the shy charm called for in the Silver Rose scene, indignation at Ochs's boorish behaviour, and in Act 3 confusion as her emotions are torn apart; she sings with the right blend of purity and sensuousness. Dame Gwyneth is in one of her best roles, looks appealing and girlish in Act 1, and then becomes all dignified authority and resignation in Act 3. She is right inside the role, and suggests all the heartbreak at the end, adapting her large voice throughout to the work's conversational style. Jungwirth is a ripely experienced, echt Viennese Ochs, for the most part avoiding excessive boorishness. Kusche is a tetchy old Faninal, Araiza a mellifluous Italian Tenor. The smaller parts are taken by long-serving members of the Munich company.

The picture comes up fresh on DVD and the sound is mostly first-rate, as is the video direction. This is a must-buy.

Salome

Salome
Birgit Nilsson sop Salome **Eberhard Waechter** bar Jokanaan **Gerhard Stolze** ten Herod **Grace Hoffman** mez Herodias **Waldemar Kmentt** ten Narraboth

Josephine Veasey *mez* Page **Tom Krause** *bar* First
Nazarene **Nigel Douglas** *ten* Second Nazarene
Zenon Koznowski *bass* First Soldier **Heinz Holecek**
bass Second Soldier **Theodore Kirschbichler** *bass*
Cappadocian **Vienna Philharmonic Orchestra / Sir
Georg Solti**
Decca The Originals ② 475 7528 (99' · ADD · T/t) Recorded
1961   Ⓜ❍❍❍➾

Solti's *Salome* was one of Decca's notable Sonic-stage successes and still beats
most of its competitors in terms of
sound alone. There's a real sense here of a theatrical performance, as produced by John Culshaw,
with an imaginative use of movement. The vivid,
nervous energy of Strauss has always been Solti's
territory, and this is an overwhelming account of
Strauss's sensual piece, sometimes a little too
hard-hitting: there are places where the tension
might be relaxed just a shade, but throughout,
the VPO answers Solti's extreme demands with
its most aristocratic playing. With only a single
break, the sense of mounting fever is felt all the
more. Birgit Nilsson's account of the title-role is
another towering monument to her tireless
singing. Here, more even than as Brünnhilde,
one notices just how she could fine away her
tone to a sweet and fully supported *pianissimo*,
and her whole interpretation wants nothing of
the erotic suggestiveness of sopranos more
familiar with the role on stage. Gerhard Stolze's
Herod is properly wheedling, worried and, in
the final resort, crazed, but there are times, particularly towards the end of his contribution,
when exaggeration takes over from characterisation. Other interpretations show how effects can
be created without distortion of the vocal line.
Eberhard Waechter is an aggressive rather than
a visionary Jokanaan. Grace Hoffman is a suitably gloating Herodias. Much better than any of
these, Nilsson apart, is Waldemar Kmentt's
wonderfully ardent Narraboth. Hardly any of
the rivals since 1961 has managed a true challenge to this simply outstanding recording.

Salome
Cheryl Studer *sop* Salome **Bryn Terfel** *bar* Jokanaan
Horst Hiestermann *ten* Herod **Leonie Rysanek** *sop*
Herodias **Clemens Bieber** *ten* Narraboth **Marianne
Rørholm** *contr* Page **Friedrich Molsberger** *bass* First
Nazarene **Ralf Lukas** *bass* Second Nazarene **William
Murray** *bass* First Soldier **Bengt Rundgren** *bass*
Second Soldier **Klaus Lang** *bar* Cappadocian
**Orchestra of the Deutsche Oper, Berlin /
Giuseppe Sinopoli**
DG ② 431 810-2GH2 (102' · DDD)   Ⓕ❍❍➾

Strauss's setting of a German translation of
Oscar Wilde's play is original and erotically
explicit. It caused a sensation in its day and even
now stimulates controversy. Sinopoli's recording is a magnificent achievement, mainly
because of Cheryl Studer's representation of the
spoilt Princess who demands and eventually gets
the head of Jokanaan (John the Baptist) on a
platter as a reward for her striptease ('Dance of

the Seven Veils'). Studer, her voice fresh, vibrant
and sensuous, conveys exactly Salome's growing
fascination, infatuation and eventual obsession
with Jokanaan, which ends in the arresting nec-
rophilia of the final scene. She expresses
Salome's wheedling, spoilt nature, strong will
and ecstasy in tones that are apt for every aspect
of the strenuous role.

She's supported to the hilt by Sinopoli's incandescent conducting and by Bryn Terfel's convincing Jokanaan, unflaggingly delivered, by
Hiestermann's neurotic Herod, who makes a
suitably fevered, unhinged sound as the near-
crazed Herod, and Rysanek's wilful Herodias.
The playing is excellent and the recording has
breadth and warmth. This is eminently recommendable. For a newcomer to the work, Studer's superb portrayal may just tip the balance in
favour of Sinopoli, though Solti's famous version is in a class of its own, with a gloriously sung
Salome and the ravishingly beautiful playing of
the Vienna Phil.

Salome
Inga Nielsen *sop* Salome **Robert Hale** *bass-bar*
Jokanaan **Reiner Goldberg** *ten* Herod **Anja Silja** *sop*
Herodias **Deon van der Walt** *ten* Narraboth
Marianne Rørholm *contr* Page **Bent Norup** *bar* First
Nazarene **Morten Frank Larsen** *bar* Second
Nazarene **Per Høyer** *bar* First Soldier **Stephen
Milling** *bass* Second Soldier **Anders Jokobsson** *bass*
Cappadocian **Henriette Bonde Hansen** *sop* Slave
**Danish National Radio Symphony Orchestra /
Michael Schønwandt**
Chandos ② CHAN9611 (99' · DDD · T/t)   Ⓕ❍

Inga Nielsen is a Salome of quite exceptional talent, even inspiration. Better than any of her
predecessors she creates a princess who sounds
credibly teenaged with surely just the pearl-like
yet needle-sharp tone Strauss intended. Nobody
has so convincingly conveyed the impression of a
spoilt, petulant innocent with the will and determination to get her way – and then exploited her
manipulative character to frightening effect as,
sexually awakened, Salome becomes obsessed
with the body of Jokanaan. In a performance
that's vocally stunning from Salome's first
entrance, Nielsen fashions her reading with
supreme intelligence in her response to words
and notes. Throughout she sings keenly, even
maliciously off the text. While still having nothing but praise for Studer's beautifully sung portrayal on the Sinopoli set – her tone is more
refulgent, less narrow than Nielsen's but she isn't
so much inside the role – or for Nilsson's vocally
overwhelming portrayal for Solti, Nielsen simply seems a Salome by nature, made for the part.

Happily Nielsen's riveting interpretation
receives suitable support. Schønwandt yields to
none of his illustrious predecessors in impressing
on us the still-extraordinary originality, fascination and tense horror of Strauss's score. From
start to finish, including an electrifying account of
the Dance, his is a fiercely direct, highly charged
yet never vulgar reading. Hale, who has part-

nered Nielsen in this work at the Brussels Opera, is a noble-sounding, resolute Jokanaan of long experience. Although he doesn't attempt the larger-than-life, tremendous performance of Terfel for Sinopoli, and his tone isn't as steady, his reading is surely more of a piece with the opera as a whole. Goldberg is just right as the degraded, superstitious, lecherous Herod, vocally astute and characterful. Silja is a well-routined, if sometimes over-the-top Herodias.

Chandos provides a recording of extraordinary range and breadth, yet one that makes sure that the singers take stage front. Anyone who already has the highly regarded Sinopoli version will probably not feel the need to invest in this set, but newcomers are urged to hear it. Even though other elements are well taken care of on earlier versions, Nielsen is really unmissable.

Salome

Teresa Stratas sop Salome **Bernd Weikl** bar Jokanaan **Hans Beirer** ten Herod **Astrid Varnay** mez Herodias **Wieslaw Ochman** ten Narraboth **Vienna Philharmonic Orchestra / Karl Böhm**
Film director **Götz Friedrich**
DG 🟥 073 4339GH (101' · NTSC · 4:3 · PCM stereo and DTS 5.1 · 0) Ⓕ

Götz Friedrich's Vienna studio film of Strauss's spooky study of necrophiliac lust (and much else) created quite a stir when it was first shown on TV more than 30 years ago. It has dated badly – largely on account of the porn-shop leather costumes (Jan Skalický), the director's then inexperience in film and penchant for phallic imagery, and Gerd Staub's plexiglass scenery. The 'Carry On Cappadocia' atmosphere is not improved by Salome's clumsily choreographed and over-veiled dance, which Terry Scott would at least have made funny.

At the start of her international career, Teresa Stratas's poor German, aurally evident struggle (even in overdubs) with a part that was in real terms much too heavy for her, and overdone gesturing get in the way of her normally matchless acting. She (and Friedrich) never find the fey terror lurking behind the readings of Welitsch or Cebotari. Weikl sounds well but, when the camera's not looking salaciously at his legs, he seems lost. The star performers here are the veterans who, one suspects, do brilliantly what they've always done: Beirer's unnervingly sympathetic Herod, and Varnay's horrific Herodias (look at her eyes as she watches her daughter dance or backs her demand for Jokanaan's head) – every inch a vicious queen.

Böhm and the orchestra are, of course, ducks to water in this score but their reward is an unexceptional and rather squeezed sound picture. No extras are offered but there is a readable retrospective essay by Friedrich.

Salome

Nadja Michael sop Salome **Michaela Schuster** mez Herodias **Thomas Moser** ten Herod **Joseph Kaiser** ten Narraboth **Michael Volle** bar Jokanaan **Royal Opera House Orchestra, Covent Garden / Philippe Jordan**
Stage director **David McVicar**
Video director **Jonathan Haswell**
Opus Arte ② 🟥 OA0996D (168' · NTSC · 16:9 · PCM stereo and DTS 5.1 · 0). Extra features include documentary 'David McVicar: A work in process'
Ⓕ⊙⊙

For all its nudity and gore Salome ends the evening in a white petticoat red with blood (mostly from the executioner) – this is a conventional production which lays out the story straightforwardly. It is based on Pasolini's film *Salò* which gives us the 1930s setting and 'decadent' extras (who could be much more animated) standing around watching an everyday story of the Herods. Es Devlin's handsome set shows us Herod's banquet in progress upstairs in addition to the main area of the basement, and becomes nicely mobile during a Dance in Seven Rooms (which, according to the accompanying documentary, depicts Salome's abused upbringing). Nadja Michael has become in short order Europe's Number One not-quite-*hochdramatische* choice for physically demanding productions. She is an attractive Salome, moving like a dancer, as physically unafraid as she is vocally – and this tricky sing, with its ferocious tuning, suits her. Michael Volle is an imposing, rich-toned Narraboth, given little to do but emote about Jesus. Both these German artists make a considerable impact through their own voices and physicality – but it is Thomas Moser's weakly human Herod who emerges as the most truly lived-in character. Philippe Jordan seems to have balanced his orchestra extremely well for both house and cast and is especially alert to the most modern twists of Strauss's harmonies. The filming (Jonathan Haswell) is sensitive to David McVicar's work while being much more than merely a static record.

Die schweigsame Frau

Die schweigsame Frau

Kurt Böhme bass Sir Morosus **Martha Mödl** mez Housekeeper **Barry McDaniel** bar Barber **Donald Grobe** ten Henry Morosus **Reri Grist** sop Aminta **Lotte Schädle** sop Isotta **Glenys Loulis** mez Carlotta **Albrecht Peter** bar Morbio **Benno Kusche** bar Vanuzzi **Max Proebstl** bass Farfallo **Bavarian State Opera Chorus and Orchestra / Wolfgang Sawallisch**
Orfeo d'or ② C516992I (126' · ADD) Recorded 1971
Ⓕ

That ardent and devoted Straussian, William Mann, slated this production (in *Opera*) when he saw it at its première in Munich in 1971 because the score was 'cut to ribbons', declaring that it was therefore, in Strauss's home city, 'a national disgrace'. Notwithstanding this objection, all the liveliness and spirit of the Munich event is conveyed in this recording from the archives of Bavarian Radio to the extent that you hear a lot of stage noises. Sawallisch wholly enters into the spirit of the Ben Jonson comedy as adapted for his libretto by Stefan Zweig.

The cast, excellent all round, easily get their collective tongues around the profusion of words. Kurt Böhme, near the end of his long career, is, as he was in the flesh, a magnificently rotund Morosus, with real 'face' in his singing. The then-young American singers, who all spent most of their careers in Germany, cast as Aminta, Henry and the Barber, all possess good German. Grist is a delightfully fresh and pleasing Aminta and Barry McDaniel an inventive Barber, though his rivals on the other sets are even better. As Henry, Grobe isn't quite the equal of Wunderlich – who can be? Mödl enjoys herself hugely as the Housekeeper.

Sawallisch, in 1971 newly appointed Music Director in Munich and destined to do so much there for the cause of Strauss, manages to keep clear all the many strands in Strauss's score.

Further listening

Daphne
Gueden Daphne **King** Apollo **Schoeffler** Peneios
Wunderlich Leukippos
Vienna State Opera Chorus; Vienna Symphony Orchestra / Bohm
DG ② 445 322-2GX2 (94' · ADD)   Ⓜ
Live recording

   Daphne isn't perhaps as involving as Strauss's later operas, but it contains some typically beautiful writing for the soprano voice in the title-role. A fine performance.

Die Liebe der Danae
Kupper Danae **Schöffler** Jupiter **Traxel** Mercury   Ⓗ
Vienna State Opera Chorus, Vienna Philharmonic Orchestra / Krauss
Orfeo mono ③ C292923D (164' · ADD) Live recording
from the Salzburg Festival   Ⓕ
   Despite a number of pages in Strauss's most appealing, late autumnal vein, this is a deeply flawed work, not least because of the wordy and rather empty libretto. For Strauss completists, though, this 1952 recording is the one to have.

Igor Stravinsky
Russian/French/American 1882-1971

Stravinsky was the son of a leading bass at the Mariinsky Theatre in St Petersburg, he studied with Rimsky-Korsakov (1902-8), who was an influence on his early music, though so were Tchaikovsky, Borodin, Glazunov and (from 1907-8) Debussy and Dukas. This colourful mixture of sources lies behind The Firebird (1910), commissioned by Dyagilev for his Ballets Russes. Stravinsky went with the company to Paris in 1910 and spent much of his time in France from then onwards, continuing his association with Dyagilev in Petrushka (1911) and The Rite of Spring (1913).

   These scores show an extraordinary development.

Both use folktunes, but not in any symphonic manner: Stravinsky's forms are additive rather than symphonic, created from placing blocks of material together without disguising the joins. The binding energy is much more rhythmic than harmonic, and the driving pulsations of The Rite marked a crucial change in the nature of Western music. Stravinsky, however, left it to others to use that change in the most obvious manner. He himself, after completing his Chinese opera The Nightingale, turned aside from large resources to concentrate on chamber forces and the piano.

   Partly this was a result of World War I, which disrupted the activities of the Ballets Russes and caused Stravinsky to seek refuge in Switzerland. He was not to return to Russia until 1962, though his works of 1914-18 are almost exclusively concerned with Russian folk tales and songs: they include the choral ballet Les noces ('The Wedding'), the smaller sung and danced fable Renard, a short play doubly formalised with spoken narration and instrumental music (The Soldier's Tale) and several groups of songs. In The Wedding, where block form is geared to highly mechanical rhythm to give an objective ceremonial effect, it took him some while to find an appropriately objective instrumentation; he eventually set it with pianos and percussion. Meanwhile, for the revived Ballets Russes, he produced a startling transformation of 18th-century Italian music (ascribed to Pergolesi) in Pulcinella (1920), which opened the way to a long period of 'neo-classicism', or re-exploring past forms, styles and gestures with the irony of non-developmental material being placed in developmental moulds. The Symphonies of Wind Instruments, an apotheosis of the wartime 'Russian' style, was thus followed by the short number-opera Mavra, the Octet for wind, and three works he wrote to help him earn his living as a pianist: the Piano Concerto, the Sonata and the Serenade in A.

   During this period of the early 1920s he avoided string instruments because of their expressive nuances, preferring the clear articulation of wind, percussion, piano and even pianola. But he returned to the full orchestra to achieve the starkly presented Handel-Verdi imagery of the opera-oratorio Oedipus rex, and then wrote for strings alone in Apollon musagète (1928), the last of his works to be presented by Dyagilev. All this while he was living in France, and Apollon, with its Lullian echoes, suggests an identification with French classicism which also marks the Duo concertant for violin and piano and the stage work on which he collaborated with Gide: Perséphone, a classical rite of spring. However, his Russianness remained deep. He orchestrated pieces by Tchaikovsky, now established as his chosen ancestor, to make the ballet Le baiser de la fée, and in 1926 he rejoined the Orthodox Church. The Symphony of Psalms was the first major work in which his ritual music engaged with the Christian tradition.

   The other important works of the 1930s, apart from Perséphone, are all instrumental, and include the Violin Concerto, the Concerto for two pianos, the post-Brandenburg 'Dumbarton Oaks' Concerto and the Symphony in C, which disrupts diatonic normality on its home ground. It was during the composition of this work, in 1939, that Stravinsky moved to the USA, followed by Vera Sudeikina, whom he had loved since 1921 and who was to be his second wife (his first wife and his mother had both died earlier the same year). In

1940 they settled in Hollywood, which was henceforth their home. Various film projects ensued, though all foundered, perhaps inevitably: the Hollywood cinema of the period demanded grand continuity; Stravinsky's patterned discontinuities were much better suited to dancing. He had a more suitable collaborator in Balanchine, with whom he had worked since Apollon, and for whom in America he composed Orpheus and Agon. Meanwhile music intended for films went into orchestral pieces, including the Symphony in Three Movements (1945).

The later 1940s were devoted to The Rake's Progress, a parable using the conventions of Mozart's mature comedies and composed to a libretto by Auden and Kallman. Early in its composition, in 1948, Stravinsky met Robert Craft, who soon became a member of his household and whose enthusiasm for Schoenberg and Webern (as well as Stravinsky) probably helped make possible the gradual achievement of a highly personal serial style after The Rake. The process was completed in 1953 during the composition of the brilliant, tightly patterned Agon, though most of the serial works are religious or commemorative, being sacred cantatas (Canticum sacrum, Threni, Requiem Canticles) or elegies (In memoriam Dylan Thomas, Elegy for JFK). All these were written after Stravinsky's 70th birthday, and he continued to compose into his mid-80s, also conducting concerts and making many gramophone records of his music. During this period, too, he and Craft published several volumes of conversations. GROVEmusic

Apollon musagète

Apollon musagète (1947 version). ªThe Rite of Spring. The Firebird – Suite. Jeu de cartes. Petrushka.
Royal Concertgebouw Orchestra, ªCleveland Orchestra / Riccardo Chailly
Double Decca ② 473 731-2DF2 (149' · DDD) Ⓜ❶❶⤷

This is a great little set, coupling a ravishing *Apollon musagète* with a truly stunning *Rite of Spring*. The *Petrushka* is equally fine. The fact that Stravinsky's revision of *Apollon* dispensed with 'half the woodwind, two of the three harps, glockenspiel and celesta from the original scoring' hardly constitutes the bleaching process that a less colour-sensitive performance might have allowed. Part of the effect comes from a remarkably fine recording where clarity and tonal bloom are complementary, but Chailly must take the credit for laying all Stravinsky's cards on the table rather than holding this or that detail to his chest. Everything tells, much as it does in the *Scherzo fantastique* – whether the euphonious winds and brass at 3'52", the motorised repeated notes later on or the ornamental swirlings that, in stylistic terms, dance us all the way from Rimsky's Arabian Nights to the unmistakably Russian world of *The Firebird*.

Apollon musagète is something else again, and Chailly takes the lyrical line, pointing without punching and allowing his excellent strings their head. The coda is jaunty, the 'Apothéose' suitably mysterious, and 'Variation d'Apollon' features fine solo work from the orchestra's leader,

Jaap van Zweden. Viable alternatives include leaner, more ascetic readings, but Chailly balances gracefulness with tonal substance and the sound is glorious.

The Firebird – Ballet & Suite

The Firebird (1910 version). Song of the Nightingale.
Flemish Radio Orchestra / Yoel Levi
Glossa ⚛ GCDSA922001 (71' · DDD/DSD) Ⓕ❶

This striking SACD provides remarkably high-calibre recordings: both works sound pretty marvellous played back through normal CD equipment. But if you have a good four-speaker system and set the rear volume level gently and judiciously, the sound is almost unbelievably realistic. Indeed, this Flemish performance of *The Firebird* is one of the finest orchestral recordings of recent years. Stravinsky's vivid scoring lends itself to demonstration sound. Moreover, the music is miraculously well played.

Yoel Levi's totally idiomatic and involving reading, though not lacking drama, is warmly relaxed and evocatively atmospheric, with the Flemish orchestra playing with ravishing sensitivity. Orchestral textures are delectably diaphonous and transluscent: everything seems to be in a magical haze, with iridescent colouring at the 'Appearance of the Firebird', while the music for the 'Enchanted Princesses' is exquisitely tender.

Arguably the *piano-pianissimo* opening is a little too quiet but the ear soon revels in the wide range of playing and sound: the whole progression of infernal music for Kashchei brings some quite astounding sounds. For the great closing rejoicing, the lovely horn melody seemingly appears out of the mist, and the climax builds slowly and magically until the brass enter. Then Levi pulls back a little, creating a spacious, no less involving, climax.

In *Song of the Nightingale*, the orchestra again play with refinement and beauty, especially at the close. The extra dimension of the Glossa recording makes one feel the orchestra really is out there, beyond the speakers.

The Firebird. The Rite of Spring. Perséphone
Stephanie Cosserat narr **Stuart Neill** ten **Ragazzi, The Peninsula Boys Chorus; San Francisco Girl's Chorus; San Francisco Symphony Chorus and Orchestra / Michael Tilson Thomas**
RCA Red Seal (special price) ③ 09026 68898-2 (119' · DDD) Recorded live 1996-8 Ⓜ❶⤷

On the face of it, an odd compilation. Why issue one of Stravinsky's least-known ballets in harness with two of his most popular? The answer lies partly in *Perséphone*'s revisiting, 20 years on, of the theme of *The Rite* (earth and rebirth) with Homer's Greece replacing pagan Russia in a neo-classical piece described by Elliott Carter as 'a humanist *Rite of Spring*'. Rather more difficult to explain is the presence of *The Firebird* (the complete 1910 score plus a piano), but a performance as good as this is its own justification. We have no idea how much post-concert 'patching' there was after the two live recordings (*The Firebird* and *The Rite*), but the playing is superbly 'finished'. Possibly, the ballet's ending was better on that particular night than any of the others; certainly, Tilson Thomas's timing and shading of the last minutes' darkness-to-light is spellbinding, the management of the *crescendo* on the final chord, even more so. Perfumes are distinctly French, with the *Firebird*'s 'supplication' as seductive as any on disc. The general exuberance of the playing in *The Rite* might also be thought French, though the virtuoso delivery and flamboyance are recognisably American. It isn't a *Rite* that investigates the score's radicalism; rather it's one to send you home from the concert hall exhilarated.

You'd be lucky to catch *Perséphone* in the concert hall. Rather baffling given the quality of a piece which shares with *Oedipus Rex* an inspired blend of distancing and direct appeal, and with *Apollo* and *Orpheus*, an archaic beauty and limpidity. The singers rise to that challenge with superb choral work. Stravinsky called *Perséphone* a 'melodrama', referring to the spoken title-role. And as Persephone *is* Spring, RCA has cast an aptly youthful-sounding actress in the part, very good at eagerness, passion and compassion. It may be that the voice is too young for *gravitas*; it may equally be that, as recorded there was no need to project in the same way, and stage projection might have helped create an element of *gravitas*. It's a small point, and her relative immediacy is always appealing. In all other respects, RCA's balance can't be criticised.

Petrushka

Petrushka. The Firebird – Suite. Scherzo à la Russe
Cincinnati Symphony Orchestra / Paavo Järvi
Telarc CD80587 (60' · DDD)   Ⓕ Ⓞ

Paavo Järvi's Telarc coupling of *Petrushka* and *The Firebird* Suite is outstanding in every way. *Petrushka* is so arresting that it invites comparison with the famous pioneering Ansermet account. It should be noted that Ansermet uses the original 1911 score, and Järvi the 1947 version. Switching between the two accounts, the surprise is the closeness of the two interpretations, with Ansermet pressing forward at one moment, Järvi the next, each relishing every detail of Stravinsky's sparkling orchestral palette, yet each completely individual. The more natural concert hall-balance in the superb acoustics of Cincinnati's Music Hall, adds ambient warmth and atmosphere, giving a translucent glow to the woodwind (yet still achieving wonderful detail), a rich patina to the strings, and filling out the brass sonorities without loss of bite. The important piano roulades, too, brilliantly played by Michael Chertock, glitter irridescently. Järvi's reading certainly doesn't lack

histrionic qualities, yet it has added pathos, particularly the scene in the Moor's Room, and at the very end of the ballet. With Ansermet, Petrushka's ghost reappears fiercely, even demonically; Järvi chooses a distanced effect and creates a haunting atmosphere of desolate melancholy.

The Firebird Suite is equally memorable. Again the wonderful Rimskyan colouring is conveyed in lusciously translucent detail, but the spectacular entry of Kashchei will surely make you jump, and the finale expands gloriously. Jack Renner, Telarc's outstanding chief recording engineer, produces the best bass drum in the business, and those thwacks as Järvi builds his final climax are riveting, as is the amplitude of the overall sound.

So this CD not only offers truly memorable performances, splendidly played, but demonstration sound that audiophiles will relish.

Pulcinella

Pulcinella[c]. Danses concertantes[a]. Petrushka[b]. The Rite of Spring[d]. Two Suites[e]
[c]**Yvonne Kenny** *sop* [c]**Robert Tear** *ten* [c]**Robert Lloyd** *bass* [ce]**Academy of St Martin in the Fields;** [a]**Los Angeles Chamber Orchestra / Sir Neville Marriner;** [bd]**Philadelphia Orchestra / Riccardo Muti**
EMI Double Forte ② 574305-2 (136' · DDD/ADD)
Recorded 1968-82   Ⓜ

A very reliable coupling for anyone wanting these six pieces. Marriner's *Pulcinella* is a joy from first bar to last; how the players enjoy the quirkiness of Stravinsky's scoring, and you can almost see jaws dropping as Robert Tear, in the second movement, does precisely what the score asks and sustains a held B flat for 13 seconds. The wit of the two Suites has a deliciously light touch and the good humour as well as the balletic grace of *Danses concertantes* are finely caught. Muti's *Rite of Spring* provokes one or two slight reservations (he over-marks dynamics quite often and his 'Sacrificial Dance' is impressively efficient rather than terrifying or exciting), but the playing is superb – an extraordinarily virtuosic 'Games of the Rival Tribes' – and detail is crystal-clear.

No quibbles about the slightly later *Petrushka*, which is vividly coloured and characterised. All the remasterings sound very well indeed.

The Rite of Spring

Stravinsky The Rite of Spring **Scriabin** Le poème de l'extase
Kirov Orchestra / Valery Gergiev
Philips 468 035-2PH (55' · DDD)   Ⓕ Ⓞ Ⓞ ▷

This is probably the most extraordinary *Rite of Spring* to have been dreamt up since Stravinsky's own final (and finest) 1960 recording. Stravinsky himself said, in so many words, that *The Rite* was born from his unconscious. And although now

STRAVINSKY'S THE RITE OF SPRING – IN BRIEF

Columbia SO / Igor Stravinsky
Sony download 88888 02047-5 (65' · ADD) Ⓜ🅑➔
Stravinsky's own interpretation exhibits an innate musicality, rhythmic bounce and satisfying transparency that really hits the mark. The 1960 recording still packs a pleasing wallop.

Cleveland Orchestra / Pierre Boulez
Sony 07464 64109-2 (69' · ADD) Ⓜ🅞🅑➔
Boulez's 1969 performance remains intensely compelling in its cumulative drive, seismic power and irreproachable precision. Very fine sound, too.

CBSO / Sir Simon Rattle
EMI 749636-2 (65' · DDD) Ⓕ🅞🅞🅑➔
A refreshingly thoughtful, immaculately honed *Rite* from Rattle. Rhythm and ensemble are consistently tight; nor is there any lack of primitivistic fervour.

**Concertgebouw Orchestra /
Sir Colin Davis**
Philips ② 464 744-2PM2 (142' · ADD) Ⓜ
Davis's *Rite* has an irresistible poise, choreographic flair and giddy sense of drama, all captured with unflinching splendour by the Philips engineers.

San Francisco SO / Michael Tilson Thomas
RCA ③ 09026 68898-2 (119' · DDD) Ⓜ
A superbly balanced live recording from Davies Symphony Hall in San Francisco. Thomas's *Rite* is as copiously detailed and exhilarating as any that have appeared in many a moon.

Philadelphia Orchestra / Riccardo Muti
EMI 574581-2 (64' · ADD) Ⓢ
Muti puts his virtuoso Philadelphia band through their paces to flamboyant, often startling effect. As bargain-basement *Rites* go, you won't do better than this.

Philharmonia Orchestra / Igor Markevitch 🄷
Testament SBT1076 (67' · ADD) Ⓕ🅞🅞
Testament allows us the opportunity to compare and contrast Markevitch's 1951 recording and his stereo remake of eight years later. Both are little short of stunning in their immaculate co-ordination and volcanic force.

Kirov Orchestra / Valery Gergiev
Philips 468 035-2PH (55' · DDD) Ⓕ🅞🅞🅑➔
Gergiev has the happy knack of making you listen with fresh ears. Here's a searingly powerful *Rite*, full of elemental fury and fierce abandon.

isn't the time or place to ponder to what extent his – and our – unconscious minds are capable (if at all) of harbouring any memories of pre-Christian ritual, suffice it so say that an exceptional performance of *The Rite* should at least have us thinking about it as a possibility…and about why we respond to *The Rite* in the way that we do.

Among modern interpreters, there isn't anyone better than Gergiev at the important dual roles of showman and shaman. So many of the score's darker workings have a striking profile here – tubas bellowing strange moans, the bass drum sending shock waves around the performance space, the lower strings in 'Spring Rounds' almost 'exhaling' their notes, and, for once, giving a proper foundation to that most significant of quiet chords – the one where the Sage kisses the earth. Indeed, 'Earth' and the 'elemental' seem not so much cultivated in this performance, as an inherent part of it.

Either Gergiev has really pondered the 'sound stuff' of the *Rite*, or it just comes naturally to him and his players. Though whether nature or nurture, the end results make for a marginally more compelling overall listen than all the finest recorded *Rite*s of the last four decades. More controversial is some of the timing of 'events', especially the delay of the ascent to the final chord, though when it arrives, you wonder if its shocking make-up has ever been as effectively exposed. The delaying tactics – theatrical pauses and suspensions – proved a little more problematic in the second half of Scriabin's *Poem of Ecstasy* – along with Gergiev's extremes of tempo in the piece. But should one even be thinking these thoughts when offered a *Poem* which openly embraces the extravagant wonders of the piece as this one does? Better to marvel at all the mysterious curves, the fabulous dark rushes of sound, the celebratory splendours, and the final resolution (dissolution?) into an uncomplicated glory of C major. Here, as in *The Rite*, the recording is superb.

The Rite of Spring (two versions) 🄷
Philharmonia Orchestra / Igor Markevitch
Testament mono/stereo SBT1076
(67' · ADD) Mono version recorded 1951, stereo 1959
Ⓕ🅞🅞

Markevitch's 1959 stereo *Rite* is in a league of its own. This is a model of how to balance the score (and of how to create the illusion of a wide dynamic range within more restricted parameters). Markevitch would have been totally familiar with every note of the piece (in 1949 he sent Stravinsky a list of mistakes he had noticed in the recently revised edition), and by 1959 he clearly knew what it needed in performance, including how to keep its shock-value alive. There are 'improprieties' here, such as the slowing for the 'Evocation of the Ancestors' (making the most of those timpani volleys), but nothing serious. As it happens, Markevitch's 'Introduction' to Part 2 is unusually fast, but he's able to take in the following small marked variations of tempo, providing valuable contrasts. And in any case, the playing is so alive, alert and reactive, whatever the dynamic levels: listen to the incisive clarinets' entry in the 'Mystic Circles' and the *frisson* imparted to the following *pianissimo tremolando* from the strings.

We could fill the rest of the page with similar highlights and other features unique to the performance, but that would be to spoil the fun of discovery (or rediscovery – and what a transfer of the original!). This is a great *Rite* for many reasons, not the least of which is that the sessions were obviously electric. As a fascinating bonus, Testament also offers a 1951 mono recording of a great *Rite* in the making. The differences aren't radical, but enough to justify the idea.

The Rite of Spring. Apollon musagète
**City of Birmingham Symphony Orchestra /
Sir Simon Rattle**
EMI 749636-2 (65' · DDD) Ⓕ**OOⅮ**

Recordings of *The Rite of Spring* are legion, but it's rare to find Stravinsky's most explosive ballet score coupled with *Apollon musagète*, his most serene. The result is a lesson in creative versatility, confirming that Stravinsky could be equally convincing as expressionist and neo-classicist. Yet talk of lessons might suggest that sheer enjoyment is of lesser importance, and it's perfectly possible to relish this disc simply for that personal blend of the authoritative and the enlivening that Simon Rattle's CBSO recordings for EMI so consistently achieve. Rattle never rushes things, and the apparent deliberation of *The Rite*'s concluding 'Sacrificial Dance' may initially surprise, but in this context it proves an entirely appropriate, absolutely convincing conclusion. Rattle sees the work as a whole, without striving for a spurious symphonic integration, and there's never for a moment any hint of a routine reading of what's now a classic of the modern orchestral repertoire.

The account of *Apollon* has comparable depth, with elegance transformed into eloquence and the CBSO strings confirming that they have nothing to fear from comparison with the best in Europe or America. The recordings are faithful to the intensity and expressiveness of Rattle's Stravinsky, interpretations fit to set beside those of the composer himself.

Symphonies

Symphony in Three Movements. Symphony of Psalms[a]. Symphony in C
[a]**Berlin Radio Choir; Berlin Philharmonic Orchestra / Sir Simon Rattle**
EMI 207630-0 (76' · DDD) Ⓜ**OOⅮ**
Recorded live in 2007

The Symphony in Three Movements doesn't so much start as erupt and Sir Simon Rattle's second recording of it has impressive immediacy, richer tonally than his rougher-edged 1980s

recording with the CBSO, but textually warmer and with more refined solos. Interesting points of comparison arise at around 4'00" into the first movement (chamber-like textures involving strings and winds) and the serene passage for strings and harp at 2'08" into the second movement, the relative earnestness of the earlier version replaced here by a true but 'terrible beauty'. In comparison with conductors like Boulez and Gielen, Rattle offers the most polished option, mindful of both mood and structure and beautifully engineered, but don't forget Stravinsky's own 1946 (New York Philharmonic) version, which reflects a new-born masterpiece in the heat of its creation.

Rattle's *Symphony of Psalms* is very sensitively traced, with a rowdy account of the reveille-style 'Laudate Dominum' passage in the last movement. However, the real highlight of this CD is Rattle's pressing but never impatient account of what in my view is Stravinsky's greatest symphony, the terse and poignant Symphony in C, music forged in the wake of illness and death but that only ever suggests anguish, never confesses it. Tchaikovsky's spirit looms large, especially in the first movement, at the onset of the angry central climax where Rattle and his Berliners achieve considerable intensity. Rattle focuses each episode without sounding episodic and shapes the *Larghetto*'s opening most poetically. Stravinsky himself is faster and lighter (especially on his second, stereo, recording) but Rattle gives us both urgency and tonal body. Henceforth, his is a digital front-runner. (And if purchased as a download, a finely observed account of the *Symphonies of Wind Instruments* is thrown in as a generous bonus.)

Symphony in C[c]. Symphony in Three Movements[d]
Octet[a]. Dumbarton Oaks[b].
[a]**Twentieth Century Classics Ensemble**;
[b]**Orchestra of St Luke's**; [cd]**Philharmonia Orchestra / Robert Craft**
Naxos 8 557507 (76' · DDD) Ⓢ

Robert Craft's best rostrum work involves relatively small forces and transparent textures, such as the Octet, which is here given a crisp, dapper performance, biting where needs be and bursting with life. Musical line and clear projection are invariable Craft priorities and both in the Octet and in the post-Baroque *Dumbarton Oaks* Concerto the pulse is kept moving and the musical journey is always clearly directed with generally superb execution from the New York players. All these selections were previously available. An earlier Craft-led version of the Symphony in Three Movements (from 1991) is marginally swifter than this 1999 Philharmonia remake, leaner too with a sharper edge (notably from the brass) but the finale on the new version is very appealing, with the incisive snap of woodwinds against eerily winding strings. The tighter, more astringent language of the Symphony in C suits Craft better, though the outer movements occasionally sound rushed.

In the Symphony in C Craft's approach is all animation and nervous energy. As ever with him, there's the feeling that the mind in charge knows exactly what this music is about, and with generally excellent sound makes for a thoroughly reliable programme, while in the case of the two chamber works the effect is decidedly impressive. Needless to say, Craft's own programme-notes are a mine of relevant information.

L'histoire du soldat

L'histoire du soldat (in English)[a]. Concerto in E flat, 'Dumbarton Oaks'
[a]**David Timson**, [a]**Benjamin Soames**, [a]**Jonathan Keeble** sprks **Northern Chamber Orchestra / Nicholas Ward**
Naxos 8 553662 (76' · DDD)   Ⓢ▶

In this full-length *The Soldier's Tale* (the English translation by Michael Flanders and Kitty Black), the actors have the full measure of their parts, and the musicians, taken as a group, about two-thirds the measure of theirs. The notes are there, but not always the will to make something of them. Perhaps one shouldn't expect violin- and trumpet-playing of the flair and feature of Manoug Parikian and Maurice André in the classic 1962 Markevitch recording (now part of a two-disc set on Philips, and spoken in the original French). On the other hand Nicholas Cox's always fully responsive clarinet-playing on the Naxos recording is a vast improvement on Markevitch's narrow-toned and quavery clarinettist. If Nicholas Cox seems to do a little better out of the Naxos balance than some of his musical colleagues, it's probably because of his more consistent projection of character.

In general, it's a very natural balance that welds the years and miles between the separately recorded actors and musicians into a reasonably convincing illusion of a single-stage whole (with the actors placed in front of the musicians), though it's less convincing than the Markevitch, where the same acoustic was used by both actors and musicians (and where Jean Cocteau's narrator can become almost submerged). The generous bonus here is Stravinsky's modernised 'Brandenburg Concerto', *Dumbarton Oaks*, marginally more presently recorded than the musical contributions to the main work, but with the same mixture of determination to put it across (a wonderful strutting *marcato* at the start of the finale) and lapses into a competent neutral. So, should you be interested at the price? If you only know *The Soldier's Tale* through the Concert Suite (most of the music; none of the words), and can sample before purchasing this complete recording, try two 'low points' – the very opening ('The soldier's march'), and the close ('The devil's triumphal dance') – and if the proceedings don't strike you as tame and lacking vitality, this could be a very rewarding use of a fiver.

Shorter works and ballets

Jeu de cartes[a]. Danses concertantes[b]. Scènes de ballet[c]. Variations[d]. Capriccio[e]
[e]**Mark Wait** pf [b]**Twentieth Century Classics Ensemble**; [ce]**Orchestra of St Luke's**; [d]**London Philharmonic Orchestra**; [a]**Philharmonia Orchestra / Robert Craft**
Naxos 8 557506 (79' · DDD)   Ⓢ▶

This collection of Stravinsky's later ballets represents the composer in lighter mood, making a delightful sequence, very well played and recorded under the authoritative direction of the composer's principal amanuensis. *Jeux de cartes* ('The Card Game') of 1936 points directly forward to Stravinsky's style in his opera *The Rake's Progress*, the piece reflecting his love of the game of poker: the three main sections of the ballet represent first, second and third deals, with the Joker figuring in each. The piece was written for the great choreographer Georges Balanchine. Craft's performance with the Philharmonia has an aptly clean attack, with the chugging rhythms well lifted, very suitable for ballet.

Danses concertantes represents Stravinsky in even lighter mood, the first major work he wrote after his arrival in the United States. It's fun music full of playfulness, ending with a jolly galloping theme in compound time. *Scènes de ballet* of 1944 was commissioned for a Broadway show, but sadly, the bars in 5/4 time were too difficult for the theatre orchestra to play, and it had to be abandoned for its original purpose, only to emerge later as a full concert piece and ballet.

Variations, much the shortest item on the disc, represents Stravinsky using 12-tone technique, an uncompromising, densely packed five minutes which makes for difficult listening, while the *Capriccio* for piano and orchestra of 1929 returns to his jolly and light-hearted mood, the popular rhythms jauntily presented. Mark Wait is an outstanding soloist. Altogether, a delightful collection brilliantly played and recorded.

Scherzo à la russe[a]. Song of the Volga Boatmen[b]. Pastorale, Op 5[c]. Three Pieces for Solo Clarinet[d]. Two Poems of Konstantin Bal'mont[e]. Cats' Cradle Songs[f]. Three Japanese Lyrics[g]. Pribaoutki[h]. L'histoire du soldat – Suite[i]. Renard[j]. Pour Picasso[d]
[eg]**Susan Narucki** sop [fh]**Catherine Ciesinski** mez [j]**John Aler**, [j]**Paul Spears** tens [j]**David Evitts** bar [j]**Wilbur Pauley** bass [j]**Tara O'Connor** picc/fl [ci]**Stephen Taylor** ob/cor ang [c]**Melanie Feld** cor ang [j]**Alan Kay**, [cd]**Charles Neidich**, [i]**William Blount** cls [ci]**Frank Morelli** bn [i]**Daniel Grabois**, [i]**William Purvis** hns [i]**Chris Gekker**, [i]**Louis Hanzlik** tpts [i]**Michael Powell** tbn [i]**Chris Deane** cimb [i]**Gordon Gottlieb** timp [i]**Danny Druckman**, **Thomas Kolor** perc [ci]**Rolf Schulte**, [i]**Jennifer Frautschi**, [i]**David Bowlin** vns [i]**Richard O'Neill** va [i]**Fred Sherry** vc [i]**John Feeney**, [i]**Kurt Muroki** dbs [b]**Philharmonia Orchestra**; [afh]**Orchestra of St Luke's**; [eg]**Twentieth Century Classics Ensemble / Robert Craft**
Naxos 8 557505 (74' · DDD)   Ⓢ▶

Wistful is not a word one expects to use to describe a composition of Stravinsky but the *Pastorale* which opens this collection has just that kind of charm. Written originally as a vocal piece in 1908, it introduces Robert Craft's collection of early works dating from 1911 to 1918, the exception being the audacious arrangement of the *Scherzo à la russe* that Stravinsky made for Paul Whiteman's Band in 1944. The most familiar work here is the *Histoire du soldat* Suite, given a sharply characterised performance. But the opening of *Renard* establishes a similarly dynamic instrumental character, while the dramatic vocal participation is exuberantly full of bawdy wit. It is presented with great accuracy and élan, laced with weird barnyard noises from the orchestra, and is great fun even if one cannot hear all the words (no text is provided).

The two Bal'mont songs are beautiful and the *Three Japanese Lyrics* are sinuously seductive, all exquisitely sung by Susan Narucki. Both sets are provided with translations, but the four *Pribaoutki* are not. Here Catherine Ciesinski brings out their primitive, often robust Russian folk derivation. The four *Cats' Cradle Songs* are equally memorable, slinky morsels with stealthy clarinet colouring. The programme ends with the *Song of the Volga Boatmen*, vulgarly scored but played roisterously by the Philharmonia Orchestra.

All these performances offer superb ensemble playing and spirited, crisply detailed direction from Craft who also provides excellent notes.

Petrushka (version for piano)

Stravinsky Petrushka **Tchaikovsky** The Seasons
Denis Matsuev pf
RCA Red Seal 82876 78861-2 (56' · DDD)　　Ⓕ

Denis Matsuev won the 1998 Tchaikovsky Competition. His brief 'Tribute to Horowitz' disc made a strong impression, even if depth and poetry were sometimes sacrificed at the expense of speed and bedazzlement. This follow-up, though a curiously unsatisfying pairing, confirms him as a major talent. From the opening bars of the *Petrushka* 'Danse russe' you know you are in safe hands, Matsuev's well-oiled mechanism enabling him to gloss over any difficulty – so fluent, in fact, that at times there are the merest hints of complacency. Matsuev's *Petrushka* can hold its own with the best.

His Tchaikovsky is even more appealing. Here, at last, Matsuev reveals himself to be a true poet of the piano. *By the Fireside* (January) and especially *Barcarole* (June) and *Autumn Song* (October) are ineffably touching, played with a quiet introspection and sensitive *rubato* that melt the heart. In the more exuberant numbers, Matsuev does not resort to excessive dynamics or supercharged virtuosity, thereby cleverly retaining their character as part of the cycle of piano miniatures. The only reservation about the whole disc is the microphone placement which (to these ears) has the effect of distancing the listener, resulting in a certain lack of immediacy and engagement.

Les noces

Les noces
Traditional Russian Village Wedding Songs Play, Skomoroshek. River. Trumpet. Cosmas and Demian. The Drinker. Green Forest. God bless, Jesus. My White Peas. Steambath. Berry. Black Beaver. In the House. Bunny with Short Legs. The Bed. Birch Tree
Pokrovsky Ensemble / Dmitri Pokrovsky
Nonesuch 7559-79335-2 (54' · DDD · Eng T)　　Ⓕ

For this Nonesuch recording Dmitri Pokrovsky and the singers in his ensemble travelled to southern and western Russia in search of melodies and texts related to *Les noces*; and they found rich pickings. True, the melodic similarities aren't as tangible as the folk sources for *Petrushka*, but the 15 songs, recorded with immense flair and enjoyment to a variety of instrumental accompaniments, will be a revelation to all listeners. Be prepared for some acerbic sounds. Authentic Russian folk polyphony is an extraordinarily modern-sounding experience, as is authentic open-throated singing. The value of the disc is multiplied by the fact that the singers have carried over the style and expressive content of the folksongs into their performance of *Les noces* itself, bringing it to life in a way that must surely be unprecedented and uniquely illuminating. Not only that, but Pokrovsky had the inspired idea of recreating the instrumental parts on a computer, thus continuing Stravinsky's search for the ideal mechanical realisation.

Les noces[a]. Mass. Cantata on Old English texts[b]
[ab]**Carolyn Sampson** sop [a]**Susan Parry** mez [a]**Vsevolod Grivnov**, [b]**Jan Kobow** tens [a]**Maxim Mikhailov** bass
Berlin Radio Chamber Choir; musikFabrik / Daniel Reuss
Harmonia Mundi ☻ HMC80 1913(67' · DDD · T/t)
　　Ⓕ**OO**

Stravinsky's recording of *Les noces* is famous for its ruthlessness, yet the piece is about a folk wedding, and one feature of most weddings is joy. That, a feeling of rhythmic joy, is what makes this new performance so exhilarating. The rhythms are unrelenting, spellbinding, only pausing for the blessing, the two mothers' lament, and the moment the mother lets her daughter go. The performance is terrific, directed with superb exuberance by Daniel Reuss.

Why is the Mass not better known? Stravinsky, an ardent believer, wrote it for himself and for liturgical use, but it is only really known from recordings. It too has an archaic feeling but it is wonderfully lyrical and inspired. The pungent harmonies give it bite, especially in the thrilling *Sanctus*, and the *Agnus Dei* is haunting in the same way that the 'alleluias' at the end of the *Symphony of Psalms* are unforgettable. The Cantata, too, opens gloriously and is lyrically inspired throughout, using four verses from the *Lyke-Wake Dirge* interspersed with polyphonic Ricercari allotted to solo voices accompanied by celestial flutes, oboe, cor anglais and cello. The music is extraordinarily beautiful – and here is another surprise: it is possible to write serial music worth listening to! The performances are all marvellous: who would have expected to hear Carolyn Sampson singing Stravinsky? This record is not to be missed.

Perséphone

Stravinsky Perséphone[a] **Dukas** Polyeucte[b]
[a]**Nicole Tibbels** sop [a]**Paul Groves** ten [a]**Trinity Boys' Choir**; [a]**Cantate Youth Choir; BBC Symphony** [a]**Chorus and Orchestra /** [a]**Sir Andrew Davis,** [b]**Yan Pascal Tortelier**
Warner Classics 2564 61548-2 (67' · DDD · T/t)
Recorded live 2003   Ⓜ

Stravinsky's recordings of his own music always have a certain indispensable something. But it's surprising what performers under his baton were sometimes allowed to get away with. In his recording of *Perséphone* it's the French language that suffers, notably at the hands of Vera Zorina in the title role, whose French was probably close to Stravinsky's own.

Happily, Nicole Tibbels, Paul Groves and the three choruses employed here have changed all that. Tibbels's narration is particularly impressive. Her French diction is full of variety in speed and tone, and always alive to the drama. Her placing of the narrative in relation to the music is also intelligent. Groves is quite simply one of the best tenors around, and his singing here is clean, powerful and practically faultless in pitching the sometimes awkward melodic lines. The orchestra and choruses live up to these high standards in every respect to produce a treasurable recording of this extraordinarily haunting piece.

The Dukas overture makes an odd coupling, but it's one of the best things he ever wrote, with its Wagnerisms surprisingly well digested for a 26-year-old. Yan Pascal Tortelier produces a more sinewy, contrapuntally aware reading than David Zinman, but also one that breathes more expansively.

Requiem Canticles

Canticum sacrum[a]. Agon. Requiem Canticles[b]
[c]**Stella Doufexis** mez [a]**Christian Elsner** ten [ac]**Rudolf Rosen** bar **South West German Radio** [ab]**Vocal Ensemble and Symphony Orchestra, Baden-Baden and Freiburg / Michael Gielen**
Hänssler Classic CD93 226 (58' · DDD)   ⓈⓄ▶

Rarely has late, gnomic Requiem Canticles sounded so fluent, from the extraordinary prelude (a fast, nervous pulsing with string lines crossing each other), through the taut drama of the 'Dies irae' to the second interlude (so reminiscent of the *Symphonies of Wind Instruments*) and the chiming finale, where ritual bells are enacted by celesta, glockenspiel and vibraphone, a distant recollection of *Les noces*. This was

Stravinsky's last major composition and although it plays for barely a quarter of an hour seems fully to justify that dodecaphonic route that so many at the time had criticised him for taking.

The marginally more expansive and noticeably more austere *Canticum sacrum* marked the composer's return to the Russian Orthodox faith and calls on the unique combination (unique to Stravinsky that is) of flute, three oboes and bassoons, four trumpets and trombones, harp, violas, basses and organ, in addition to the voices. Again Michael Gielen drives a confident course through a work that brooks no compromise and culminates in a harshly oratorical 'Illi autem profectae', one of the most striking episodes in all late Stravinsky.

The ballet *Agon* post-dates *Canticum sacrum*, just, and employs an even wider array of instruments, all of them used with the greatest economy and expressive force, the distinctive and rhythmically alluring interlude/prelude, a recurring motif, connecting a series of brief but terse and mostly outspoken dance movements. *Agon* is pure aural sculpture, angular and uncompromising (with a short-lived fugue in the finale), but in a performance such as this that focuses its every pungent detail makes for an alluring and stimulating listen. The recordings are both airy and admirably clear.

Symphony of Psalms

Symphony of Psalms[a]. Cantata on Old English texts[b]. Mass[c]. Babel[d]. Credo[e]. Pater noster[e]. Ave Maria[e]
[b]**Mary Ann Hart** mez [b]**Thomas Bogdan** ten [d]**David Wilson-Johnson** spkr [b]**Michael Parloff,** [b]**Bart Feller** fls [b]**Stephen Taylor** ob [b]**Melanie Feld** cora [b]**Fred Sherry** vc [bce]**Gregg Smith Singers;** [ad]**Simon Joly Chorale;** [ad]**Philharmonia Orchestra;** [c]**St Luke's Orchestra / Robert Craft**
Naxos 8 557504 (73' · DDD)   ⓈⓄ▶

This superb collection duplicates the aurally fascinating Harmonia Mundi disc (see opposite) in the Cantata and the superb Mass in fine, authoritative performances from Robert Craft. He does not have the advantage of Carolyn Sampson among his soloists but he does have excellent choral singing, and in the glorious *Symphony of Psalms* the Philharmonia Orchestra on top form. This is the highlight of the programme, a superbly structured account, rich in lyrical feeling, building to the frisson-creating 'Alleluias' of the closing section. The Cantata is finely sung and played, with characteristically clear instrumental detail, and the mini-cantata *Babel*, with its spoken narration and choral responses, is also a success.

The programme opens with three brief Russian sacred chorales which are immediately appealing and as idomatic as one can expect from non-Russian singers. The recordings were made over a decade between 1992 and 2002 and are of good quality, with the *Symphony of Psalms* (2001) – made at Abbey Road – standing out on all counts. Craft is obviously uplifted by the music of the composer's supreme vocal masterpiece. As always with Naxos, excellent documentation, with the detailed notes provided by Craft himself. A bargain!

Oedipus Rex

Oedipus Rex. Symphony of Psalms   Ⓗ
Ivo Zídek ten Oedipus **Věra Soukupová** mez Jocasta
Karel Berman bass Créon **Eduard Haken** bass Tiresias **Antonin Zlesák** ten Shepherd **Zdeněk Kroupa** bar Messenger **Jean Desailly** narr **Czech Philharmonic Chorus and Orchestra / Karel Ančerl**
Supraphon Historical SU3674-2 (73' · AAD) Recorded 1964-6   Ⓜ**ⓄⓄ**

Oedipus Rex, to words by Jean Cocteau, is one of Stravinsky's most compelling theatre pieces, a powerful drama that re-enacts the full force of a glorious high spot in ancient culture. The fusion of words and music in *Oedipus* is masterly, and arrests the attention consistently, from the animated severity of the opening narration, through the calculated tension of its musical argument, to the tragic restraint of its closing pages. Karel Ančerl was one of Stravinsky's most committed exponents.

This particular recording was taped in the Dvořák Hall of the House of Artists, Prague, and earned itself at least three major awards. Ančerl traces and intensifies salient points in the tragedy yet maintains a precise, sensitive touch. His vocal collaborators include the noble Karel Berman (Créon) who, like Ančerl himself, suffered considerably during the Nazi occupation of Czechoslovakia. Věra Soukupová is a fine Jocasta and the convincing but occasionally unsteady Ivo Zídek sings the part of Oedipus. Both here and in the *Symphony of Psalms* – one of the most serenely perceptive recorded performances of the work – the Czech Philharmonic Chorus excel, while Supraphon's 1960s engineering (not the DDD suggested on the box) has an appealing brightness.

Le rossignol

Le rossignol
Natalie Dessay sop Nightingale **Hugo Simcic** Child
Marie McLaughlin sop Cook **Violeta Urmana** mez
Death **Vsevolod Grivnov** ten Fisherman **Albert Schagidullin** bar Emperor **Laurent Naouri** bass
Chamberlain **Maxime Mikhailov** bass Bonze
Paris National Opera Chorus and Orchestra / James Conlon
A film by **Christian Chaudet**
Virgin Classics 📀 544242-9 (50' · NTSC · 16:9 · PCM Stereo and 5.1 · 0) Extras include a 'making of' documentary, post-production and audio recording session footage   Ⓕ

Too many mediocre stage productions are being preserved for vocal, not visual, reasons. All the more important, then, is a release like this where

a skilled (and musically literate) film director uses state-of-the-art computer technology to sculpt a multi-dimensional portrait of Stravinsky's gorgeous pre-First World War opera-pantomime.

Christian Chaudet bases it on the well-received EMI recording of 1999, reuniting the major soloists in front of blank blue- and green-screens to act their hearts out to imaginary scenery, effects and people that the computer will supply later. This technique, long used in feature films, has a range and flexibility that might have been created for 20th-century opera.

The film begins with a fairly traditional dream frame: a little boy 'sees' his father's pottery turn into a Chinese landscape introducing all the story's characters and events. Later, the Emperor who so desires the Nightingale's singing is seen to live in a forbidden city made of chinaware. This image of communication via images coming to life is developed to include the presence of mobile phones (with the Nightingale's image and song), webcams and computer screens – a modernisation that works through seamless integration with more traditional references. Relevant instruments of the orchestra are also frequently dropped into view as part of the digital landscape.

Wearing a selection of T-shirts that almost suggest a 1960s Bond girl, Natalie Dessay gives a mesmerising but never indulgent or twee performance as the Nightingale, sometimes with a real bird in the hand. Marie McLaughlin's Cook (who steers the Child through the dream) is equally comfortable and subtle on close-up camera, while Schagidullin, Mikhailov and Naouri exhibit much presence and facial dexterity. From all his players Chaudet has secured that deliberately unemotional and real acting that so distinguishes French (and American) cinema and is such an asset in music-theatre of this genre.

The DVD is of a high visual and sonic quality and (another rarity in opera releases) there are some worthwhile 'extras' not devoted to company promotion. These 'making of' features really show you something of how the film was technically achieved.

On the soundtrack (as we may now call it) James Conlon goes all out for a colour and bite that binds Stravinsky's 1908-09 Debussian Act 1 more closely to the 1913-14, post-*Rite of Spring* final acts than a trenchant, Boulezian approach might have done, although it is not the only way. The singing is first-rate (as was the language-coaching), seeming almost to have been achieved in anticipation of this outstanding film.

The Rake's Progress

The Rake's Progress
Ian Bostridge ten Tom Rakewell **Deborah York** sop
Anne **Bryn Terfel** bass-bar Nick Shadow **Anne Sofie von Otter** mez Baba the Turk **Peter Bronder** ten
Sellem **Anne Howells** mez Mother Goose **Martin Robson** bass Trulove **Julian Clarkson** bass Keeper of the Madhouse **Monteverdi Choir; London**

Symphony Orchestra / Sir John Eliot Gardiner
DG ② 459 648-2GH2 (134' · DDD · T/t)　　Ⓕ🔘🔘➔

Gardiner's *Rake's Progress*, in all but one respect, easily withstands comparison with its five rivals, and in several it surpasses them; if you're happy with Terfel's Nick Shadow, it can be set alongside Stravinsky's own 1964 recording as the finest available. Gardiner is conscious throughout that this is a chamber opera, and the orchestral textures are outstandingly clean and transparent, the rhythmic pointing crisp but airy. This enables his cast to give a fast-moving, conversational account of the text, with every word crystal-clear (including those from the chorus) and no need for any voice to force.

·This benefits the soprano and tenor especially. Deborah York, sounds a very young and touchingly vulnerable Anne; her voice may seem a little pale, but there's pathos as well as brilliance in her Act 1 aria, and the desolation of her reaction to Tom's marriage to Baba the Turk ('I see, then: it was I who was unworthy') is moving. Ian Bostridge is the best Tom Rakewell since Alexander Young in Stravinsky's recording: he too sounds likeably youthful, sings with intelligence and sweetness of tone and acts very well.

Howells is an unexaggerated Mother Goose, and von Otter's economy of comic gesture is a marvel. 'Finish, if you please, whatever business is detaining you with this person' receives the full Lady Bracknell treatment from most mezzos; von Otter gives it the vocal equivalent of a nose wrinkled in well-bred disdain. Terfel often demonstrates that he can fine his big voice down to the subtlety of the other principals, and when he does he's a formidably dangerous, insinuating Shadow. But almost as often he not only lets the voice rip but indulges in histrionics quite uncharacteristic of the performance as a whole. You may not mind: why after all should the Devil restrainedly under-act? At times, though, he sounds bigger than the orchestra. The recording is close but theatrically atmospheric. There are a few sound effects, though some may find the raucous owl in the graveyard scene distracting.

The Rake's Progress　　　　　　　　　　Ⓗ
Hilde Gueden *sop* Anne **Eugene Conley** *ten* Tom
Rakewell **Mack Harrell** *bar* Nick Shadow **Blanche
Thebom** *mez* Baba the Turk **Martha Lipton** *mez*
Mother Goose **Norman Scott** *bass* Trulove **Paul
Franke** *ten* Sellem **Lawrence Davidson** *bass* Keeper
of the Madhouse
**Metropolitan Opera Chorus and Orchestra, New
York / Igor Stravinsky**
Naxos ② 8 111266/7 (146' · ADD · S/N)
Recorded 1953　　　　　　　　　　　Ⓢ🔘➔

In February 1953, 17 months after the world premiere in Venice, *The Rake's Progress* received its first American production, conducted by Fritz Reiner. Less than a month later, this studio recording was made, with the smaller orchestra that Stravinsky envisaged. The cast remained the same, and we can be confident that the per-

formance retains a good deal of Reiner-inspired professionalism. Stravinsky was never a conductor on that level but this version is a viable alternative to his more familiar second recording, made in London in 1964.

Mark Obert-Thorn has done an excellent job of restoration, providing a forward but well-balanced sound. The cast is strong, though with more conventionally operatic qualities than would be favoured today. As Tom, Eugene Conley suggests ease in Verdi and Puccini rather than in Monteverdi, Mozart or Britten. The kind of florid passages that give Philip Langridge or Ian Bostridge no trouble are clearly strange territory for him. But he brings much more than mere fecklessness to the character and makes a strong contribution to those episodes in Act 2 where the dramatic temperature rather falls away.

It takes Baba the Turk and Sellem the Auctioneer to bring the opera back to life, and both performances here are admirable in avoiding excessive caricature. As Nick Shadow, Mack Harrell is almost too benign; his great outburst of rage in Act 3 is less forceful than most. Hilda Gueden, also on unfamiliar territory, manages the lullaby with touching simplicity.

The Rake was Stravinsky's farewell, as the possibilities of the 12-note method beckoned. But, this recording confirms, to dismiss the opera as a tired avowal of the need for fundamental change is grossly unjust.

The Rake's Progress
Laura Claycomb *sop* Anne **Andrew Kennedy** *ten*
Tom Rakewell **William Shimell** *bar* Nick Shadow
Julianne Young *mez* Mother Goose **Dagmar
Pecková** *mez* Baba the Turk **Darren Jeffery** *bass*
Trulove **Donald J Byrne** *ten* Sellem **Shadi Torbey**
bass Keeper of the Madhouse
**Chorus and Symphony Orchestra of La Monnaie –
De Bunt, Brussels / Kazushi Ono**
Stage director **Robert Lepage**
Video director **Benoît Vlietinck**
Opus Arte ② 📀 OA0991D (174' · NTSC · 16:9 ·
PCM stereo and DTS 5.1 · 0) Recorded live at the
Théâtre Royal de la Monnaie, Brussels, in April 2007.
Extra features include Illustrated Synopsis, Cast
Gallery, Interview with Robert Lepage, Insight into
rehearsals, costumes and make-up　　　　Ⓕ🔘🔘

Auden first met Stravinsky to discuss the libretto of *The Rake's Progress* in Hollywood in 1947, and Robert Lepage winds forward his 'clock of fashion' to the time and place of the opera's composition. Hogarth's Gin Alley runs into Easy Street, populated by Vegas hookers, dancers and chancers. The composer-sanctioned division into two halves rather than three acts is a complementary move from the conventions of the opera house to the theater, and what a show we have. Madam, or rather Mother Goose (Julianne Young, bearing a disconcerting resemblance to Julianne Moore), lures the naive Tom onto a heart-shaped satin bed, and the pair literally sink into its folds – before our hero re-emerges, worldly wise and weary, in front of a blow-up

Winnebago, and banishes ennui not with mother's ruin but a line or two of Colombia's finest.

Andrew Kennedy takes all this in his stride, and his always fresh, appealing tenor ensures we retain our sympathy through Tom's piteous downfall from indolence to insanity, far more so than we are likely to for his operatic model, Ferrando. From Nick Shadow's first entrance under the shade of a Dallas derrick to his flame-capped Broadway nemesis, the parallels are not with Dons Alfonso or Giovanni but rather Alberich. This is largely thanks to William Shimell's iron-black baritone and rasping wit, though lines such as 'That man alone is free who chooses what to will and wills his choice as destiny' certainly strike a Wagnerian ring of mania.

The recorded balance is slightly unfavourable to Laura Claycomb in 'I go to him': this is her 'Abscheulicher', but she is no Leonora, and is happiest vocally when she is dramatically downcast. The two crucial scenes, either side of the interval, between her, Tom and Dagmar Pecková's show-stealing Baba are models of ensemble writing and direction, pulling between operatic naturalism and Stravinsky's preferred realism just as Tom is torn between one woman and the other – and all in front of a chorus who change from waltz-time party guests to painfully well observed inhabitants of Bedlam with phenomenal assurance.

Doubtless Kazushi Ono must take credit for some slickly cinematic pacing. This is a show to be seen and, down to the witty, period and silent menu screens, a model of its kind.

Josef Suk · Bohemian 1874-1935

Suk studied at the Prague Conservatory, 1885-92, where he was Dvořák's favourite pupil, and in 1898 married his daughter. Dvořák was, too, the dominant influence on his early music, as in the Serenade for strings (1892) and the Fairy Tale suite (1900); later, most notably in the vast symphony Asrael (1906) – written under the impact of the deaths of his wife and his father-in-law – he developed a more personal style comparable with Mahler's in structural mastery and emotional force. He drew little on folk music. Other works include two published quartets (he was second violinist in the Czech Quartet for most of his life and played in over 4000 concerts), piano pieces (Things lived and Dreamed, 1909) and a group of symphonic poems, A Summer's Tale (1909), The Ripening (1917) and the choral-orchestral Epilog (1929). From 1922 he directed a master class in composition at the Prague Conservatory.
GROVEmusic

Asrael, Op 27

Asrael
Helsinki Philharmonic Orchestra / Vladimir Ashkenazy
Ondine ODE1132-5 (62' · DDD/DSD)　Ⓕ

As Rafael Kubelík's uniquely powerful (and idiomatic) Bavarian Radio tape (see below) is currently elusive, there's certainly room for Ashkenazy's marginally fleeter, cleaner, texturally airier conception. He holds together the sometimes disjunct finale with skill, avoiding any hint of lassitude or bombast; the understated optimism and luminosity of the coda is most moving.

This hybrid SACD, a live recording from which applause has been excised, comes with helpful booklet-notes by Jan Smaczny. Helsinki's Finlandia Hall may look better than it sounds but its acoustic presents no problems to this production team.

Asrael
Bavarian Radio Symphony Orchestra / Rafael Kubelík
Panton 81 1101-2 (64' · ADD) Recorded 1981　ⒻOO

To use large-scale symphonic form for the purging of deep personal grief carries the danger that the result will seriously lack discipline. In 1904-5 Suk's world was shattered by two visits from Asrael (the Angel of Death in Muslim mythology): he lost his father-in-law (and revered teacher) Dvořák, and his beloved wife, Otylka. Forgivably, Suk does perhaps linger a little too long in the fourth movement's gentle, mainly lyrical portrait of Otylka, but elsewhere the progress is as satisfying psychologically as it is symphonically. Much of the music has a concentrated dream-like quality; at the extremes, spectral nightmare visions merge with compensatory surges of lyrical ardour. Set Kubelík's reading alongside any of the other modern versions and one is immediately aware of a wholly compelling imaginative intensity and interpretative flair that betoken a true poet of the rostrum. Kubelík's control throughout is awesome and he conjures up playing of enormous expressive subtlety from his fine Munich orchestra. No other recorded performance – not even Václav Talich's legendary 1952 Supraphon account – succeeds in conveying the intensely personal nature of this music with such devastating emotional candour. Technically, too, one need have no qualms about this Panton disc – the Bavarian Radio engineers secure most truthful results.

Sir Arthur Sullivan · British 1842-1900

Sullivan, a Chapel Royal chorister, became a pupil of Sterndale Bennett at the Royal Academy of Music (1856) and studied at the Leipzig Conservatory (1858-61). The promise shown by his incidental music for The Tempest (1861) and other early concert works led to festival commissions and conducting posts, which he complemented with work as organist, teacher and song and hymn tune writer; from 1866, he also dabbled in comic opera. His increasing success in this last field – with CF Burnand in Cox and Box and then WS Gilbert in Trial by Jury – culminated in the formation by Richard D'Oyly Carte of a company expressly for the performance of Gilbert and Sullivan works. With HMS Pinafore the collaborators became an institution. Their works, produced at the Savoy Theatre from 1881 (the most popular 'Savoy Operas' were The Mikado and The Gondoliers), won a favour with English-speaking audiences that has never waned. Sullivan was knighted in 1883 and continued to conduct, but his serious ouput dwindled. A breach with Gilbert (1890), recurring ill-health and the relative failure of his last works clouded his final years. GROVEmusic

Symphony in E, 'Irish'

Symphony in E, 'Irish'. The Tempest – Suite.
Overture in C, 'In Memoriam'
BBC Philharmonic Orchestra / Richard Hickox
Chandos CHAN9859 (75' · DDD)   ⓅⒹ▸

Plaudits all round to Richard Hickox and his excellent Manchester band (and the Chandos production team) for at last granting Sullivan's *Irish* symphony the first wholly recommendable digital recording it so richly deserves. And what a charmer of a work it is! Mendelssohn (and his *Reformation* Symphony above all) provides the dominant stylistic template, but the work is soundly constructed, effectively scored, and the *scherzo*'s irresistibly perky oboe tune, in particular, already reveals a very real melodic gift. Hickox observes the first-movement repeat, but his direction is highly imaginative and he never allows tensions to sag. What's more, the playing of the BBC Philharmonic ideally combines bright-eyed affection, keen vigour and nimble polish.

Following the symphony's successful March 1866 première under August Manns, Sullivan was asked to provide a work for that same year's Norwich Festival. The sudden death of his father just a few weeks before the festival proper jolted Sullivan into penning the likeable overture, *In Memoriam*. In terms of inventive freshness and orchestral scope it's rather trumped by the astonishingly confident incidental music for Shakespeare's *The Tempest* that Sullivan had written nearly six years earlier while still a student at the Leipzig Conservatory. Again, Hickox and company do plentiful justice to Sullivan's precocious inspiration. A thoroughly enjoyable collection, then, accorded sound of glowing realism in the finest Chandos tradition.

Overtures

Overtures – Cox and Box; The Sorcerer; HMS Pinafore; The Pirates of Penzance; Patience; Iolanthe; Princess Ida; The Mikado; Ruddigore (arr Toye); The Yeomen of the Guard; The Gondoliers; The Grand Duke
Royal Ballet Sinfonia / Andrew Penny
Naxos 8 554165 (70' · DDD)   ⓈⓄ▸

The first thing that sets this apart from other collections of Sullivan overtures is that – for the

first time – it covers the entire Gilbert and Sullivan output. The only works that are missing are *Thespis*, *Trial by Jury* and *Utopia Limited*, none of which had overtures as such. The sensible addition of the overture to *Cox and Box* means that all the Sullivan comic operas likely to be of interest to the general collector are here. An even more intelligent feature is that they're presented in chronological order, so that one can chart the progression of Sullivan's comic opera style from the very French-sounding ending of *Cox and Box* and the equally French-sounding opening of *The Sorcerer* through to more distinctively Sullivanesque sounds of the later pieces.

None of this would count for much if the performances weren't up to scratch. Happily they're models of their kind. Andrew Penny has an agreeably light touch, alternatively reflective and sparkling, and gets graceful phrasing from the Royal Ballet Sinfonia – ideal performers of light music. Nobody wanting a collection of Sullivan's comic opera overtures need look elsewhere.

Pineapple Poll

Pineapple Poll (arr Mackerras). 'Irish' Symphony
Royal Liverpool Philharmonic Orchestra / David Lloyd-Jones
Naxos 8 570351 (78' · DDD)   ⓈⓄ▸

A coupling of these works has never appeared before. Yet Mackerras's medley of Savoy melodies provides an ideal appetiser for Sullivan's *Irish Symphony*, distinguished by delightfully easy-going charm and lightness of touch. Mackerras recorded *Pineapple Poll* complete three times, the versions marked more by progressive improvements in sound quality than by changes in interpretation. If Lloyd-Jones shaves the odd second or two off Mackerras's timings for individual movements, it's due as much as anything to the latter's greater flexibility in allowing the score to unfold. Lloyd-Jones is less successful, too, in drawing out the individual themes of the elaborately woven score.

The Symphony is a different matter. This new version is an improvement both interpretatively and sonically on the pioneering Groves version, one that also lacks the first movement's exposition repeat. More particularly, Lloyd-Jones has the edge on Hickox and the BBC Philharmonic (Chandos – above) in the natural unfolding and emotional contrasts of the work. There's a more inherent urgency to the outer movements and greater attention to instrumental detail throughout. The second movement is especially beautifully done. Even for those who have an earlier version there's a strong case for this inexpensive newcomer. For those who don't, the recommendation is a clear one.

The Gondoliers

The Gondoliers. Overture di ballo (1870 version)
Richard Suart *bar* Duke of Plaza-Toro **Philip Creasey**

ten Luiz **John Rath** bass Don Alhambra **David
Fieldsend** ten Marco **Alan Oke** bar Giuseppe
Tim Morgan bar Antonio **David Cavendish** ten
Francesco **Toby Barrett** bass Giorgio **Jill Pert** contr
Duchess of Plaza-Toro **Elizabeth Woollett** sop
Casilda **Lesley Echo Ross** sop Gianetta **Regina
Hanley** mez Tessa **Yvonne Patrick** sop Fiametta
Pamela Baxter mez Vittoria **Elizabeth Elliott** sop
Giulia **Claire Kelly** contr Inez **D'Oyly Carte Opera
Chorus and Orchestra / John Pryce-Jones**
TER ② CDTER2 1187 (109' · DDD)   Ⓕ

This is one of a series of recordings by the new
D'Oyly Carte Opera Company that offers a
vastly better quality of sound than any of its
ageing competitors. Orchestral detail is the
most immediate beneficiary, and the overture
serves to demonstrate John Pryce-Jones's
lively tempos and lightness of touch. Outstanding among the singers are perhaps John
Rath, who gives Don Alhambra's 'I stole the
prince' and 'There lived a king' real presence,
and Jill Pert, a formidable Duchess of Plaza-
Toro. Richard Suart not only provides the
leading comedy roles with exceptionally clear
articulation and musicality, but also adds considerable character to his portrayals. David
Fieldsend and Alan Oke provide attractive
portrayals of the two gondoliers, and Lesley
Echo Ross and Regina Hanley are also most
agreeable.

Seasoned listeners may note numerous changes
of detail as a result of the purging of the performance material of changes made to the parts
around the time of the 1920s Savoy Theatre
revivals. There's no dialogue, but added value is
provided by Sullivan's sunniest comic opera
score being accompanied by the sparkling *Overture di ballo*, played in its original version with
some traditional cuts opened up.

HMS Pinafore

HMS Pinafore
Richard Suart bass Sir Joseph Porter **Felicity Palmer**
mez Little Buttercup **Rebecca Evans** sop Josephine
Thomas Allen bar Captain Corcoran **Michael Schade**
ten Ralph Rackstraw **Donald Adams** bass Dick
Deadeye **Valerie Seymour** sop Hebe **Richard Van
Allan** bass Bill Bobstay **John King, Philip Lloyd-
Evans** bars Bob Becket **Welsh National Opera
Chorus and Orchestra / Sir Charles Mackerras**
Telarc CD80374 (74' · DDD · N/T)   Ⓕ❂❂

As always, Mackerras keeps the livelier numbers
moving along comfortably without ever a hint of
rushing, while giving full weight to the tender
moments and, above all, caressing all the details
of Sullivan's delicious orchestration.

Right from the overture, with its beautifully
shaped *Andante* section, this is music-making
to perfection. Of the singers, Felicity Palmer's
Buttercup truly oozes plumpness and pleasure,
while Thomas Allen's Captain doesn't just do
the crew of the *Pinafore* proud, but all of us.
If Rebecca Evans's Josephine is a shade lacking

in colour, Mackerras has found in Michael
Schade's Ralph Rackstraw a most elegant addition to his G&S team. As for Richard Suart's
Sir Joseph Porter, this is surely as stylish a demonstration of patter singing as one can find
anywhere on disc, while Donald Adams's Dick
Deadeye is no worse for his 40-odd years singing the role.

Add orchestral playing of refinement, choral
work whose perfection extends from the formal
numbers to the varied inflexions of 'What nevers?', plus a recording that brings out the
instrumental detail to perfection, and one has a
Pinafore that's unadulterated delight from first
note to last.

The Mikado

The Mikado
John Holmes bass The Mikado **John Wakefield** ten
Nanki-Poo **Clive Revill** bar Ko-Ko **Denis Dowling**
bar Pooh-Bah **John Heddle Nash** bar Pish-Tush
Marion Studholme sop Yum-Yum **Patricia Kern** mez
Pitti-Sing **Dorothy Nash** sop Peep-Bo **Jean Allister**
mez Katisha.
Iolanthe – excerpts **Elizabeth Harwood, Elizabeth
Robson, Cynthia Morey** sops **Heather Begg,
Patricia Kern** mezzos **Stanley Bevan** ten **Eric
Shilling, Denis Dowling, Julian Moyle** bars **Leon
Greene** bass **Sadler's Wells Opera Chorus and
Orchestra / Alexander Faris**
Classics for Pleasure ② 5759902 (135' · ADD)
Recorded 1962   Ⓑ❂❂

At the core of these performances are some of
the finest British singers of 30 years ago, who
were all chosen not just for their singing but for
their sense of the theatricality and humour of
Gilbert and Sullivan. Just listen, for instance, to
how John Heddle Nash gives full expression
to every word of Pish-Tush's 'Our great
Mikado'. Here, too, is Marion Studholme's
delicious Yum-Yum and Elizabeth Harwood's
joyous Phyllis.

If one singles out Clive Revill for special
mention, it's because his Ko-Ko is uniquely
well judged and imaginative, combining superb
comic timing, verbal clarity and vocal dexterity. His 'little list' is hilarious, and you can
almost feel your hand gripped at the words
'shake hands with you *like that*'. At the helm in
both works is Alexander Faris who knew
supremely well how to capture the lightness
and sparkle of operetta. The new Overture put
together for *The Mikado* may come as a surprise, but it's apt and cleverly done. The sound
is inevitably dated when compared with more
recent recordings, but it scarcely mars the
enjoyment.

Additional recommendation

Adams The Mikado **Rolfe Johnson** Nanki-Poo **Suart**
Ko-Ko **Van Allen** Pooh-Bah **McLaughlin** Yum-Yum
Howells Pitti-Sing **Palmer** Katisha **Welsh National**

Opera Chorus and Orchestra / Mackerras
Telarc CD80284 (79' · ADD)   Ⓕ
  A delicious Nanki-Poo and a magnificent Katisha.

The Pirates of Penzance

The Pirates of Penzance
Eric Roberts bar Major-General Stanley **Malcolm Rivers** bar Pirate King **Gareth Jones** bar Samuel **Philip Creasy** ten Frederic **Simon Masterton-Smith** bass Sargeant of Police **Marilyn Hill Smith** sop Mabel **Patricia Cameron** sop Edith **Pauline Birchall** mez Kate **Susan Gorton** contr Ruth **D'Oyly Carte Opera Chorus and Orchestra / John Pryce-Jones**
TER ② CDTER2 1177 (85' · DDD)   Ⓕ

The revival of the D'Oyly Carte Opera Company produced the first digital recordings of complete Gilbert and Sullivan scores, and this TER set is a very happy example. Philip Creasy is an engaging and vocally secure Frederic, and Marilyn Hill Smith trips through 'Poor wandering one' with a delectable display of vocal ability and agility. The couple's interplay with the chorus in 'How beautifully blue the sky' is quite enchanting, and their exchanges in 'Stay, Frederic, stay' splendidly convincing. Eric Roberts makes the Major-General a thoroughly engaging personality, and the dotty exchanges between Simon Masterton-Smith's Sargeant of Police and his police force are sheer joy. Even such details as the girls' screams at the appearance of the pirates in Act 1 have a rare effectiveness. John Pryce-Jones keeps the score dancing along. Those who want the dialogue as well as the music must look elsewhere, but this is certainly to be recommended.

The Yeomen of the Guard / Trial by Jury

The Yeomen of the Guard
Peter Savidge bar Sir Richard Cholmondeley **Neill Archer** ten Colonel Fairfax **Donald Adams** bass Sergeant Meryll **Peter Hoare** ten Leonard **Richard Suart** bar Jack Point **Donald Maxwell** bar Shadbolt **Alwyn Mellor** sop Elsie **Pamela Helen Stephen** mez Phoebe **Felicity Palmer** mez Dame Carruthers **Clare O'Neill** sop Kate **Ralph Mason** ten First Yeoman **Peter Lloyd Evans** bar Second Yeoman

Trial by Jury
Rebecca Evans sop Plaintiff **Barry Banks** ten Defendant **Richard Suart** bar Judge **Peter Savidge** bar Counsel **Donald Adams** bass Usher **Gareth Rhys-Davies** bar Foreman **Welsh National Opera Chorus and Orchestra / Sir Charles Mackerras**
Telarc ② CD80404 (121' · DDD · N/T)   ⒻⓄ

Between them, *The Yeomen of the Guard* and *Trial by Jury* contain all that's best in Sullivan's music for the theatre. In the former there's some of his more serious and ambitious writing, in the latter some of his most consistently light-hearted and engaging. All of this is brought out in Telarc's

series of recordings with Welsh National Opera. As always, Sir Charles Mackerras paces the music impeccably, and he has assured contributions from such stalwarts as Donald Adams, Felicity Palmer and Richard Suart. The last-named may be a shade light-voiced compared with some of the more comic performers of Jack Point and the Learned Judge; but in *The Yeomen* it's surely his performance that stands out. His handling of the dialogue after 'Here's a man of jollity' is masterly, and his 'Oh, a private buffoon' is as winning as any, with impeccable clarity of diction and a perfectly judged French accent for 'jests… imported from France'.

  Neill Archer and Alwyn Mellor are admirable as Fairfax and Elsie; but Pamela Helen Stephen could have displayed more of the minx in Phoebe Meryll's personality, while in *Trial by Jury* Barry Banks has too small a voice to convince as the Defendant. Recommended, especially if you want both works on the same set.

Giles Swayne   British b1946

Swayne, with encouragement from his cousin Elizabeth Maconchy, started composing at en early age. At Cambridge he studied with Nicholas Maw, he then won a scholarship to the Academy of Music. He was on the staff at Glyndebourne – working as a répétiteur – in the early 1970s before embarking fulltime as a composer. His huge choral work CRY was premiered in 1980 and has been performed the world over. Since then he has produced a steady stream of work accross all genres to considerable acclaim.

Chamber works

Cello Sonata, Op 103ᵃ. Four Lyrical Pieces, Op 6ᵃ. Suite No 1, Op 111. Canto, Op 31.
Robert Irvine vc ᵃ**Fali Pavrí** pf
Delphian DCD34073 (70' · DDD)   Ⓕ

Superbly played by the Glasgow-based duo of Robert Irvine and Fali Pavrí, this survey of Giles Swayne's compositions for solo cello and cello and piano is recorded with trademark spaciousness and clarity, and has the added appeal of including two of Swayne's most recent large-scale compositions.

  The Cello Sonata (2006) proclaims its ambitions with a 15-minute first movement called 'Turbulence', which challenges the listener's sense of stylistic stability as it explores a welter of conflicting ideas. At once beholden to and resisting tradition, its tone of rhapsodic spontaneity – ironic? celebratory? – involves a protracted tussle with conventional ideas of coherence. But the three remaining movements imaginatively complement all this agitation, and the finale – 'Threnody' – is a richly conceived set of variations that somehow manages to balance out the earlier conflicts without any risk of dumbing down.

Your response to the solo Suite No 1 (2007), will depend on your attitude to its way with historical allusion. It's as if Swayne's response to the august opus number involved prompted him to opt for a whimsical embrace of those musical memories which can never be entirely eliminated, especially in solo cello music: but the piece's jokey scenario seems more than a touch complacent.

Set against this very recent work we have one of Swayne's earliest. *Four Lyrical Pieces* (1970) is a resourceful student effort, occasionally diffuse but showing purposeful engagement with the most potent trends of the time. Finally, *Canto for solo cello* (1981) is a full-on response to Swayne's experience of African musics. Minimalist in some ways, quite complex in others, it projects that positive tone and enquiring spirit which represent this composer at his considerable best.

Choral works

Magnificat, Op 33[e]. Missa Tiburtina[e]. The Coming of Saskia Hawkins, Op 51[c]. The Tiglet, Op 68[ad]. Four Passiontide Motets – Vidit suum dulcem natum[e]; Eia, mater![d]; Fac me cruce custodiri[e]; Dona nobis pacem[e]. A Convocation of Worms[ac]. Winter Solstice Carol[bd]. Midwinter[d]
[a]**Stephen Wallace** *counterten* [b]**Philippa Davies** *fl* [c]**Michael Bonaventure** *org* [d]**Laudibus**; [e]**National Youth Choir of Great Britain / Michael Brewer**
Delphian DCD34033 (79' · DDD · T/t)   Ⓕ

Giles Swayne's *A Convocation of Worms* (1995) is a 20-minute cantata for countertenor and organ setting a thoroughly alarming 15th-century text, adapted from the Coventry miracle plays, in which Death, appearing at Herod's court after the massacre of the innocents, effects instant retribution, declaring that 'where I smite, there is no grace'. This stark mixture of menace and lament is a gift for a composer with Swayne's propensity for questioning received social and religious conventions from the inside, and even if the austerity of the work's central stages risks some loss of impact, the effect of the whole is powerful and memorable. Stephen Wallace and Michael Bonaventure do it proud, and it's recorded, like everything on the disc, in a spacious acoustic which doesn't compromise clarity of texture.

One short, bold organ piece apart, the rest of the music is choral, and includes three of Swayne's most attractive successes: *Magnificat*, *The Tiglet* (that is, Blake's 'The Tyger'), and *Missa Tiburtina*. The National Youth Choir of Great Britain and its offshoot Laudibus tackle this music with enormous energy and skill. There is less to enjoy in *Midwinter* – setting Christina Rossetti's cringingly sentimental verse in 2003 might be thought a touch eccentric – but the *Four Passiontide Motets* include some of Swayne's most cogent musical imagery and abound in imaginative textures. A highly commendable enterprise.

Jan Pieterszoon Sweelinck
Dutch 1562-1621

Sweelinck studied with his father, organist of the Oude Kerk, Amsterdam, succeeding him in or before 1580. He remained in this post all his life, with a few excursions to inspect new organs in other cities. Among the most influential and sought-after teachers of his time, he included Germans among his pupils, notably Scheidt, Jacob Praetorius and Scheidemann. He wrote over 250 vocal works, including a complete French psalter (1604-21), motets (1619), chansons (1594, 1612) and Italian madrigals (1612). But he is best known for his c70 keyboard works, which include monumental fugal fantasias, concise toccatas and well-ordered variation sets. He perfected forms derived from, among others, the English virginalists and greatly influenced 17th-century north German keyboard music, becoming one of the leading composers of his day. His son Dirck (1591-1652), who succeeded him at the Oude Kerk in 1621, edited a popular song collection (1644) and also composed songs and keyboard music.
GROVEmusic

Keyboard Works

Complete Keyboard Works
Freddy Eichelberger, Liuwe Tamminga, Leo van Doeselaar, Pieter van Dijk, Bernard Winsemius, Reinhard Jaud, Stef Tuinstra, Bert Matter, Vincent van de Laar orgs **Glen Wilson, Siebe Henstra, Menno van Delft, Pieter Dirksen, Bob van Asperen, Pieter-Jan Belder** hpds
NM Classics ⑨ NM92119 (10 hours, 29' · DDD)   Ⓑ

The fact that no fewer than 15 musicians (nearly all Sweelinck's countrymen) have contributed to this complete keyboard project in no way lessens the impressiveness of what has been achieved here. Led by Pieter Dirksen and Pieter van Dijk, they get through nearly 90 pieces (some of which are heard more than once on organ and on harpsichord). This complete edition rests on sound and fresh scholarship, and is laid out in an engaging and informative manner. Each artist contributes a recital intended to stand on its own, usually on the same instrument.

Fourteen organs from the 16th and 17th centuries, and three harpsichords, are heard over the course of ten-and-a-half hours. The harpsichords are an original by Johannes Ruckers, and two recent copies of other instruments also by him. But it's the organs that steal the show: spread across three countries, several still close to original condition, their individual characteristics and the acoustics of their respective churches make for endlessly absorbing listening. As an anthology of great early organs this set would be worth recommending. The fact that here they're pressed into serving music of such sustained quality only increases their impact. For there's no doubting Sweelinck's variety, charm and infinite resource. He touched all the significant genres of the keyboard repertory of his day (toccatas, fantasias, dance movements, variation sets, ricercars).

Of all these genres, the fantasia furnishes Sweelinck with perhaps his most congenial medium: simple subjects serve as the basis for wide-ranging explorations, stretching out over many minutes without ever losing the thread – indeed, frequently his conclusions have an awe-inspiring power. Sweelinck needs no advocacy beyond the performances themselves; rather, it's the consistency of these performances that concerns us here. That consistency would be impressive had it originated with a single interpreter, but given the number of participants it's equally remarkable. It's all very impressive. What more could one want?

Esce mars, Sw3 No 3. Fantasia crommatica. Mein junges Leben hat ein Endt. Unter der Linden grune. Pavana lachrimae. Pavana Philippi. Die flichtig Nimphae. Allemand (Gratie). Toccata noni toni, SwWV297. Toccata, C2. Toccata primi toni, d2, SwWV286. Toccata a 3, SwWV289. Toccata secundi toni, g1, SwWV292. Von der Fortuna werd ich getrieben, Sw3 No 2.
Robert Woolley hpd/virg
Chandos CHAN0758 (64' · DDD)

What a fine composer Sweelinck was! This volume drives the point home by presenting several of his best compositions, including the imaginatively patterned variations on *Esce mars* and *Unter der Linden grune*, the weighty and implacable *Fantasia crommatica* (how Bach would surely have admired this piece) and the hauntingly beautiful variations on *Mein junges Leben hat ein Endt*. Other works here include a take on Peter Philips's *Pavana dolorosa*, a lovingly plumped-up version of Dowland's *Lachrymae*, and a handful of improvisatory toccatas. Sweelinck brings together in his music many of the influences current in the first years of the 17th century – Italian flair, north European seriousness, English resonance and melodic grace – and makes of them a rich and rewarding brew, maintaining coherence by the force of his own good taste and sound compositional judgement.

Robert Woolley switches between two marvellous harpsichords – Malcolm Rose's currently much-in-demand copy of the Victoria and Albert Museum's 1579 Theewes claviorganum, and a deep and mellow copy by Derek Adlam of a 1611 Ruckers virginals. His playing, too, covers most bases. Without forcing the pace, he shows brilliant fingerwork in *Esce mars* or a piece like the *Toccata C2*, and achieves clarity and composure in the more melodically driven works. The toccatas occupy a convincing middle ground between the improvisatory and the written-out in feel, and tempi are for the most part expertly judged. In other words, these are pleasingly natural performances. There is not much competition in the world of Sweelinck recordings, but this stands out as an excellent harpsichord release in its own right.

Organ Works

Toccata in C. Ballo del granduca. Ricercar.Malle Sijmen. Mein junges Leben hat ein End'. Aeolian Echo Fantasia. Onder een linde groen. Toccata in A minor I. Erbarm dich mein, o Herre Gott. Poolsche dans
James David Christie org
Naxos 8 550904 (64' · DDD) Played on the C B Fisk Organ, Houghton Chapel, Wellesley College, USA

The Houghton Chapel is nowhere near as resonantly spacious as the Oude Kerk in Amsterdam, but its relative intimacy doesn't rob the organ of its natural resonance and tonal beauty. James David Christie presents what's in effect a most satisfactory re-creation of one of Sweelinck's organ recitals, given daily between 1580 and 1621, for the burghers of Amsterdam. One hopes they were appreciative of the most consistently witty and generous-spirited keyboard music before the era of Buxtehude, Couperin and Bach.

While Christie may not possess the lyricism of a Leonhardt, the humane warmth of a Piet Kee or the mercurial whimsy of a Koopman, he is, in his own right, a bold, stylish, unhasty player, clearly thoroughly versed in early performance practice, with an incisive technique disclosing musical intelligence and common sense. He's particularly successful in the five major variation sets here, relishing the variety of decorative motifs but still conveying an impression of structural coherence and unity. Just occasionally his articulation might have worked better in a somewhat larger acoustic: at times a more obviously singing touch might have suggested greater tenderness in quieter moments and more ample majesty in louder ones.

Nevertheless, with appealing registrations, an almost ideal choice of programme and undistractingly natural recording this is recommended.

Karol Szymanowski   Polish 1882-1937

Szymanowski was born into an artistic family of the Polish landed gentry and began his musical education with his father. At 13, in Vienna, he was powerfully impressed by hearing Wagner for the first time. He then had formal tuition from Zawirski and Noskowski in Warsaw (1901-4), and during the next decade began to make an international reputation for music in the German tradition, relating to Wagner, Strauss and Reger: the main works of this period include the Symphony No 2 (1910), Piano Sonata No 2 (1911) and the opera Hagith (1913).

During these years he visited Italy, Sicily and north Africa he also encountered Pelléas, The Firebird and Petrushka, and all these enriching influences were remembered in his abundant output of 1914-17, when he was confined by the war to Russia. Works of this period are typically classical or oriental in inspiration, and ornately figured in a manner relating to Skryabin or Debussy. They include the choral Sym-

phony No 3 (1916), Violin Concerto No 1 (1916), Myths for violin and piano (1915) and the piano triptychs Metopes (1915) and Masques (1916). He then used this new, highly sensuous language to tackle the theme of The Bacchae in his opera King Roger (1926), set in the orientalised Norman kingdom of Sicily. In 1919 he settled in Warsaw, now the capital of an independent Poland; and he began while completing King Roger to compose in a nationalist style, drawing on folk music in his choral orchestral Stabat mater (1926), ballet Harnasie (1935) and other works. He accepted the directorship of the Warsaw Conservatory (1927-32), but his last years were dogged by ill health, and he wrote nothing after his Violin Concerto No 2 (1933) and a pair of piano mazurkas, adding to a set of 20 dating from 1924-5. Other works include two quartets, songs, folksong arrangements and cantatas. GROVEmusic

Violin Concertos

No 1 Op 35 **No 2** Op 61
Violin Concertos Nos 1 & 2. Three Paganini Caprices, Op 40. Romance in D, Op 23
Thomas Zehetmair vn **Silke Avenhaus** pf
**City of Birmingham Symphony Orchestra /
Sir Simon Rattle**
EMI 503429-2 (65' · DDD)   Ⓕ❶❷❸Ɒ

Ⓖ They make an admirable coupling, the two Szymanowski violin concertos, but a demanding one for the soloist. They are both so beautiful that it must be tempting to embellish both with a similarly glowing tone. They inhabit quite different worlds (they were written 16 years apart) and Zehetmair shows how well they respond to quite different approaches.

In the First, after a rapt solo entry, he uses for the most part a lovely but delicate tone, expanding to athletic incisiveness but not often to lushness. It all fits very well with Rattle's handling of the orchestra: occasionally full and rich but mostly a sequence of exquisitely balanced chamber ensembles. Generous but finely controlled *rubato* from both soloist and conductor allows the concerto's improvisatory fantasy to flower; and the quiet close even has a touch of wit to it.

Zehetmair's sound is immediately less ethereal, more robust, for the opening melody of the Second Concerto. This is the sort of tone, you suspect, that he would use in Bartók's Second Concerto, and it points up a vein of Bartókian strength to this work's longer and firmer lines. Rattle, too, seeks out bolder and more dense colours.

The *Paganini Caprices* were equipped by Szymanowski not with deferential accompaniments but with independent and quite freely composed piano parts. They change Paganini, even where the violin part is unmodified, into a late Romantic virtuoso, with a hint of Lisztian poetry alongside the expertly pointed-up fireworks of the Twenty-Fourth *Caprice*; even here Zehetmair is a listening violinist, not one to upstage his excellent pianist. The *Romance*,

the warmest and most luscious piece here, is beautifully done but with a touch of restraint to prevent it cloying. A first-class coupling, and a recording that makes the most of the superb acoustic of Symphony Hall in Birmingham.

Violin Concertos Nos 1 & 2. Nocturne and Tarantella, Op 28 (orch Fitelberg)
Ilya Kaler vn
Warsaw Philharmonic Orchestra / Antoni Wit
Naxos 8 557981 (60' · DDD)   ⓈⒶƒⒹƐ

Naxos offers an exceptionally clear recording of these three *concertante* works by Szymanowski, not just the two violin concertos but an orchestrated version of the *Nocturne and Tarantella*. Ilya Kaler, as on his other Naxos discs, gives pure, clear readings with flawless intonation and careful use of vibrato. Having a Polish conductor and orchestra as his accompanists adds to the idiomatic feel of each, with the magical orchestral sounds beautifully conjured up, particularly in No 1, the more radical of the two works.

Kaler is a degree warmer with a shade more vibrato than some interpreters, and the Naxos recording brings out the fantasy of the composer's orchestration, particularly in No 1, with wonderful clarity. In the more openly lyrical Second Concerto, Kaler adopts more flowing speeds with lighter results.

Kaler then plays the relatively brief *Nocturne and Tarantella* just as sympathetically, with the *Tarantella* a flamboyant virtuoso vehicle making a splendid climax to an excellent disc. The point which trumps all competition inevitably is that the Naxos issue, beautifully and idiomatically played and brilliantly recorded, comes at such a reasonable price.

Symphonies

No 1 in F minor, Op 15 **No 2** in B flat, Op 19 **No 3** (The Song of the Night), Op 27 **No 4** (Symphonie concertante), Op 60

Symphony No 2 in B flat, Op 19. Concert Overture in E, Op 12. Wordsong, Op 46[a]. Songs of the Infatuated Muezzin, Op 42[a]
[a]**Zofia Kilanowicz** sop **London Philharmonic Orchestra / Leon Botstein**
Telarc CD80567 (68' · DDD)   ⒻⒶ

The *Concert Overture* is a hugely gifted young composer's homage to Richard Strauss, and fully worthy of its model in impetuousness, rich sonority and close-woven polyphony. The Second Symphony is no less rich but more disciplined, with Reger's influence added to (and modifying) that of Strauss, and with Szymanowski's own high colouring, sinuous melody and tonal adventurousness now in their first maturity. The *Infatuated Muezzin* songs are a high point of his middle period, Debussian harmony and florid orientalising arabesques fusing to an aching voluptuousness, colour now applied with the refinement of a miniaturist. Leon Botstein is fully aware of the quite different palettes these pieces use, and the orchestra play splendidly.

Wordsong (Telarc's translation for *Słopiewnie*) is the key to Szymanowski's final phase, a setting of five poems in an artificial language, using Slavonic roots to suggest a sort of 'pre-Polish'. Szymanowski responded to the poems' assonances, rhythms and alliterations (he couldn't resist 'słodzik słowi słowisienkie'), finding for them a fusion of folk elements, archaisms and melodies that retain something of the discarded middle period's exoticism.

You sense the influence of Stravinsky (*Les noces* in particular) and hear already both the folk vigour and the ritual purity of Szymanowski's late style (in the third song, too, there's a startling pre-echo of the slow movement of Górecki's Third). There's a slight, attractive tremor to Kilanowicz's voice, but she has both the almost white purity and the flexible coloratura the songs need. It's very hard to make a single adverse comment about this important addition to the discography.

Symphonies – No 1, Op 15; No 4, 'Symphonie Concertante', Op 60[a]. Etude, Op 4 No 3 (orch Fitelberg). Concert Overture, Op 12
[a]**Jan Krzysztof Broja** pf **Warsaw Philharmonic Orchestra / Antoni Wit**
Naxos 8 570722 (67' · DDD)　　　　　Ⓢ**ⓞ**➔

The early *Concert Overture*, son of *Rosenkavalier* and proud of it, is resplendently played here, only at rare moments craving a more glamorous sound stage. And the over-heated two-movement First Symphony, which the composer himself described as a 'contrapuntal-harmonic-orchestral monstrosity' and withdrew after its premiere, emerges as far more purposeful and less rebarbative than any of the admittedly few rival versions that have come and gone over the years.

As a listening experience the Fourth Symphony is initially somewhat more problematic, in that the opening pages (surely the model for Bartók's Third Piano Concerto) suffer from slight intonation problems between the *concertante* piano and the orchestra. But with a bit of acclimatisation, helped by the firm and affectionate shaping of the performance, this proves to be liveable with. Jan Krzysztof Broda seems to grow in stature through the rhapsodic slow movement, and he never loses the thread in the finale's Ravelian and Prokofievian deviations.

All in all, it would take significantly greater financial outlay to find anything better than this, and even then the differences would be marginal.

Symphonies – No 2; No 3, 'Song of the Night'[a]
[a]**Ryszard Minkiewicz** ten **Warsaw Philharmonic Choir and Orchestra / Antoni Wit**
Naxos 8 570721 (61' · DDD)　　　　　Ⓢ**ⓞ**➔

Antoni Wit conducts his Warsaw forces in exceptionally warm and idiomatic performances of these two exotic symphonies, vividly recorded. They make an important addition to the Naxos catalogue. The more immediately attractive is No 3, subtitled *Song of the Night*, with its tenor solo and chorus adding to its impact. The poem which the tenor sings has the refrain 'Do not sleep friend' and builds to the most powerful climax with Szymanowski's love of exotic orchestral colours exploited to the full. The thrust and passion of Wit's performance, splendidly supported by the clear-voiced tenor and the chorus, is impossible to resist, and leads to a second movement with hints of birdsong followed by a slow finale, a deep meditation.

The performance of No 2 in two movements, an opening *Allegro* followed by an extended set of variations, is equally persuasive. Again the first movement is passionate and thrustful and the variations bring some fascinating contrasts, ending with a powerful fugue. Antoni Wit's performance could not be more idiomatic, with singers and players totally inside the music. An outstanding issue.

String Quartets

Szymanowski String Quartets – No 1, Op 37; No 2, Op 56 **Rózycki** String Quartet, Op 49
Royal Quartet (Izabella Szałaj-Zimak, Elwira Przybyłowska vns Marek Czech va Michał Pepol vc)
Hyperion CDA67684 (70' · DDD)　　　　　Ⓟ**ⓞ**

This is what Szymanowski needs: firm, full-bodied playing, with a wide range of dynamic, colour and attack, and with all the unexpected twists and turns confidently negotiated. The Royal Quartet are as finely tuned to his quirkiness as to his trademark voluptuous post-impressionism and moments of mystic withdrawal or volatile transition. In every way this makes a persuasive bid for best available version.

Ludomir Rózycki was two years younger than Szymanowski, with whom he co-founded the group that came to be known as Young Poland, and he was prominent enough as composer and teacher in Lwów, Warsaw and Katowice to have at least two books written about him. Most highly regarded for his symphonic poems and songs, he wrote his sole string quartet in 1916 during a stay in Paris.

It moves confidently enough within its somewhat impersonal Romantic idiom, occasionally giving off a perfume of Debussy and Ravel, and in the finale even some moments of Bartók. This is a not dissimilar mixture to Szymanowski, in fact, but in far less concentrated form, and at nearly 33 minutes the prospect of a concert-hall breakthrough is rather remote. On CD, however, the piece is more than welcome as a coupling to the Royal's outstanding Szymanowski.

Szymanowski can take a degree more atmosphere in the acoustic than we get here; but the clarity of the recording certain lets the myriad details speak eloquently.

Piano Works

Piano Sonata No 3. Masques. Métopes
Piotr Anderszewski pf
Virgin Classics 545730-2 (68' · DDD)   Ⓕ**OOO**Ɖ⤳

Here Anderszewski turns his attention away from well-tried classics of the repertoire to Szymanowski and to 'an aura of extreme *fin de siècle* opulence' (John Ogdon). Szymanowski's neurotically questing imagination was fired by his travels in Africa and the Mediterranean; and leaving earlier influences of Chopin (the Op 1 Preludes) and a lengthy dalliance with Regèr and Richard Strauss (the Second Piano Sonata) far behind, he turned to impressionism, to Debussy and the glittering, mosaic-like structures he inherited from Scriabin.

Yet despite such influences his music achieves a unique fragrance and character and both *Masques* and *Métopes* shed a new and scintillating light on the myths of ancient Greece. Such music calls for a pianist of unlimited, superfine virtuosity and a complete temperamental affinity for such exoticism, and in Anderszewski it has surely found its ideal champion. Under his astonishing mind and fingers the chains of trills at the climax of 'Schéhérazade' take on an incandescence that transcends their Scriabinesque origins and Anderszewski's razor-sharp clarity and stylistic assurance make you hang on every one of the composer's teeming notes.

Here and in *Métopes* every hyper-nervous fluctuation of mood is judged to an uncanny perfection and in the Third Sonata, where Szymanowski returns from his richly programmatic sources to a more objective if no less intricate utterance, every aspect of the music's refined and energetic life is held in a blazing light from which it is impossible to escape. Visceral and superhuman, all these performances have been superbly recorded.

Piano Sonata No 1 in C minor, Op 8. Mazurkas, Op 50 – No 13, Moderato; No 14, Animato; No 15, Allegretto dolce; No 16, Allegramente – vigoroso. Etudes, Op 33. Four Polish Dances, Op 47. Prelude and Fugue in C sharp minor
Martin Roscoe pf
Naxos 8 553867 (69' · DDD)   Ⓢ**O**

This CD offers a cross-section of Szymanowski's styles as a composer for the keyboard, from the early First Sonata (always described as post-Chopin and post-Scriabin but, Roscoe convincingly demonstrates, no less importantly post-Liszt as well) to the pungent *Mazurkas*, with their flavour of Bartók as well as of late Grieg.

The *Prelude and Fugue* is an interesting link between that early Sonata and the Op 33 *Etudes* which are usually referred to as representing Szymanowski's 'impressionist' phase. Again, Roscoe makes you question this conventional description: yes, the harmonies look rather Debussian but they don't often sound that way. These very brief pieces (just over a minute on average) are studies in the conventional sense, written by one

fine pianist for another, Alfred Cortot, but they're also exercises in harmonic subtlety and rich in Szymanowski's personal fantasy. The *Four Polish Dances* inhabit the same world as the *Mazurkas*, and it's obvious that Roscoe enjoys open fifths and flat sevenths as much as Szymanowski did.

Stabat mater, Op 53

Stabat mater. Litany to the Virgin Mary, Op 59. Symphony No 3, Op 27, 'The song of the night'
Elzbieta Szmytka sop **Florence Quivar** contr
Jon Garrison ten **John Connell bass City of Birmingham Symphony Orchestra and Chorus / Sir Simon Rattle**
EMI 555121-2 (56' · DDD · T/t)   Ⓕ**OOO**Ɖ⤳

 The first impression here is that Rattle is relatively new to Szymanowski. There's a huge enthusiasm here, a missionary quality that bespeaks the recent convert. On the other hand the care over matters of balance, the knowledge of just those points where Szymanowski's complexity needs very careful handling if it isn't simply to blur into opacity, suggest a conductor who has been there before and knows the dangers. You get the feeling that a conscious decision was made to delay recording this music until the circumstances were right.

The CBSO Chorus sound thoroughly at home not only in the music but in the language too. In Elzbieta Szmytka, Rattle has a soprano who might have been born to sing Szymanowski's pure, floated and very high-lying soprano lines. The result is very fine: one of the most beautiful Szymanowski recordings ever made. And yet 'beautiful Szymanowski' isn't all that hard if the orchestra's good enough and the conductor capable. Rattle's insistence that all the music be heard, its urgency and passion as well as its deliquescent loveliness, makes for uncommonly gripping Szymanowski as well. He reminds one of how much more there is to the Third Symphony than voluptuous yearning.

The choice of soloists for the *Stabat mater* is interesting: alongside Szmytka's radiant purity are Quivar's throaty vibrancy and Connell's weighty darkness. Not a matching trio, but the contrast is appealing. Garrison in the symphony is a touch hard and strenuous, less enraptured than one or two of the Polish tenors (and sopranos) who've recorded it, but he's a musicianly and likeable singer. The recording is outstanding: lucid, rich and spacious.

Songs

Complete Songs for Voice and Piano
Juliana Gondek, Iwona Sobotka sops **Urszula Kryger** mez **Piotr Beczala** ten **Reinild Mees** pf
Channel Classics ④ CCS19398 (264' · DDD · T/t)   Ⓜ

This set proposes a kind of luxury musical package-tour for the jet-set age – today expressionist Austria, tomorrow Slavic fantasy, the day after high-romanticism in Germany, and then away for a weekend in the exotic realms of the Near East. The different locales materialise out of thin air, colourful, fully formed, without a moment for the traveller to get bored on the way. Szymanowski's song output is doubly intriguing – first, for those far-flung contrasts of style; second, because it's so little known. Though the Polish language is an issue, this admirable set reminds us that there are also songs in German and even a James Joyce cycle in English.

Four singers take part, one to each disc. Piotr Beczala is a light, poetic young tenor with some passion up his sleeve. He's dreamily captivating in the early Six Songs of Op 2, where Fauré and Rachmaninov seem to be whispering ideas alternately over Szymanowski's shoulders; catches well the change of tone to religious concentration in the *Three Fragments by Jan Kasprowicz*; and brings lyric beauty to the Schoenberg-inspired Op 13 settings.

The voice of soprano Juliana Gondek is a touch brittle for the sultry mood Szymanowski must have had in mind for the *Songs of the Infatuated Muezzin*, and a bit more could be made of the words in the Joyce cycle; yet there's still much to enjoy. The sensitive singing of mezzo Urszula Kryger plunges straight into the swirling Tristan-esque ecstasy of the Wagnerian Op-20 set. The glinting lights of the Orient return in *Des Hafis Liebeslieder*, another set of paraphrases by Hans Bethge to place beside *Das Lied von der Erde*, and the four songs of Op 41 take us forward into more ambiguous and experimental terrain.

The familiar *Songs of the Fairy Princess* promise a magical opening to the fourth disc in a winning performance by young Iwona Sobotka. Here's a pure, steady, light soprano who can flit up into the ledger lines without a hint of shrillness. She's also interesting in the antique Polish songs of the *Słopiewnie*, Op 46, and makes a lively job of the miniature *Children's Rhymes* of Op 49, even if a few go rather a long way.

The pianist, Reinild Mees, exhibits a faultless sense of atmosphere throughout, whether delicately conjuring Oriental mystery or thundering up and down Lisztian octaves. The adventurous traveller need look no further.

Songs of a Fairy-tale Princess[a].
Eight Love Songs of Hafiz[b]. Harnasie[c]
[a]**Iwona Sobotka** sop [b]**Katarina Karnéus** mez
[c]**Timothy Robinson** ten
City of Birmingham Symphony [c]**Chorus and Orchestra / Sir Simon Rattle**
EMI 364435-2 (65' · DDD)　　　Ⓕ ⦿⦿🅑

Here's another sumptuous instalment of Sir Simon Rattle's Szymanowski cycle, showing that his rapport with his former Birmingham colleagues is as productive as ever. The main item is *Harnasie*, a 'ballet-pantomime' which loses nothing in concert performance, at least when that performance is as exciting as this one. It occupied the composer on and off for eight years (1923-31), bridging the gap between the exotic late-

romanticism that reached its apogee in the opera *King Roger* and his final pair of concertos. *Harnasie* has long been acclaimed for demonstrating Szymanowski's ability to move with the times but its use of folk music doesn't mean that it challenges mid-1920s Bartók or Janáček in progressiveness. This tale of romance and mayhem in bandit country is kitschy in the extreme. Yet even when the music evokes Borodin more vividly than Stravinsky it is utterly irresistible.

Timothy Robinson makes a strong contribution to *Harnasie* but it's the solo singing of Katarina Karnéus and Iwona Sobotka in the two song sets that confirms the disc's special appeal. In the *Eight Love Songs of Hafiz* Szymanowski conjures up a sound world of almost Bergian concentration and opulence, with the richly eloquent final lament the crown in this superbly refined account. *The Songs of a Fairy-tale Princess* is a slighter piece and Iwona Sobotka is not ideally flexible in its taxingly florid lines. But Rattle ensures, as he does throughout, that the mesmerising allure and elaborate textual fantasy of the music are always tinglingly immediate. With a recording that projects the often dense orchestral fabric without undue constraint or loss of clarity, this disc is undoubtedly a winner.

Harnasie

Harnasie, Op 55[a]. Mandragora, Op 43[b].
Prince Potemkin, Op 51[c]
[a]**Wiesław Ochman**, [b]**Alexander Pinderak** tens
[c]**Ewa Marciniec** mez [a]**Ewa Marczyk** vn [b]**Kazimierz Koslacz** vc **Warsaw Philharmonic a** **Choir and Orchestra / Antoni Wit**
Naxos 8 570723 (73' · DDD)　　　Ⓢ ⦿⦿🅑

The ballet *Harnasie* is a powerful complement to the opera *King Roger*, giving similarly Dionysian subject-matter a very different dramatic setting. Szymanowski's joyous embrace of folk idioms in *Harnasie*, and his relish for exploring them in ways which retain certain points of contact with his earlier late-romantic opulence, invites comparisons with Bartók and Janáček in the years after the First World War. But *Harnasie* has a very personal, Polish aura to it, well projected in this robust yet technically secure account by Antoni Wit and his Warsaw forces, including brief contributions from the veteran yet still strong-voiced Wiesław Ochman.

The other examples of Szymanowski's theatre music are rarities, and neither quite convinces as a concert work. *Mandragora* was designed for a 1920 Warsaw production of Molière's *Le bourgeois gentilhomme* and depicts, all too episodically, the mugging and mayhem of various attempts to entertain the assembled company – a scenario best known from Strauss's *Ariadne auf Naxos*. The incidental music Szymanowski provided in 1925 for the final act of *Prince Potemkin*, a Polish play about Russian history, was left in manuscript during the composer's lifetime, and he might well have been surprised to learn of its revival apart from its original function. While not entirely lacking in character, it comes across as rather dull, even in a performance as accomplished, committed and decently recorded as this one.

King Roger, Op 46

King Roger
Thomas Hampson bar Roger II **Elzbieta Szmytka** sop Roxana **Ryszard Minkiewicz** ten Shepherd **Robert Gierlach** bar Archbishop **Jadwiga Rappé** contr Deaconess **Philip Langridge** ten Edrisi **City of Birmingham Symphony Youth Chorus; City of Birmingham Symphony Chorus**

Symphony No 4, 'Symphonie concertante', Op 60
Leif Ove Andsnes pf **City of Birmingham Symphony Orchestra / Sir Simon Rattle**
EMI ② 556823-2 (112' · DDD · T/t)   ⑤ⓄⓄⓄ⟶

King Roger is a ravishingly beautiful opera, but a very fragile one. With a shrill soprano or a less than ideally cast tenor it would be fatally flawed. Minkiewicz's Dionysiac Shepherd betrays a slight hardness and a touch of stress in full voice, but he has both the allure and the mystery that the role imperatively demands. Almost his first words are 'My God is as beautiful as I', and he should vocally suggest that he is indeed radiantly beautiful. His voice shades to a croon at times, but he never sounds epicene.

Szmytka is a wonderful Roxana, with beautifully pure high notes and bell-like coloratura. At the end of Act 2 her florid aria is repeated (in Szymanowski's concert version), at just the point where you might well have replayed the earlier track for the pleasure of listening to her again. The use of distinguished singers in the smaller roles is no extravagance: Langridge evokes the exotic strangeness of the Arab sage Edrisi, while Rappé and Gierlach add to the hieratic gravity of the opening scene. Hampson in the central role is in fine voice, easily conveying Roger's authority, his angry but bewildered rejection of the Shepherd's new religion. He's even finer, however, in Act 5, where the King is painfully torn between Dionysus and Apollo. The ambiguity of the final scene remains, as it must. Is Roger accepting the Shepherd in place of Roxana? Or, since Roxana herself immediately succumbs to the Shepherd's glamour, is Roger achieving wholeness by at last acknowledging feminine intuitions within himself?

That these questions remain resonant and provoking at the end of the performance is a tribute both to the work itself, and also to Rattle's handling of it. The orchestral textures are voluptuously rich and subtly coloured, aided by a spacious recording (the vast Byzantine basilica of the opening scene is magnificently evoked) and orchestral playing of a very high order indeed. This is the finest recording of *King Roger* that has so far appeared.

The Fourth Symphony, in Szymanowski's later, folk-derived and harder-edged style, is a huge contrast: quite a shock after the opera's

radiant conclusion. Andsnes's powerfully athletic playing points up the music's affinities with Prokofiev, and both he and Rattle emphasise the new vigour that Szymanowski was drawing from the fiddle music of the Tatra region.

Further recommendation

King Roger
Drabowicz Roger II **Olga Pasiecznik** Roxana **Polish National Opera Chorus and Orchestra / Kaspszyk**
CD Accord ACD131-2 (80' · DDD · T/t)   ⑤
The sound is more vivid than the EMI, allowing these completely idiomatic performers maximum impact. Where Rattle was characteristically high-gloss, Jacek Kaspszyk uses the experience of live performance to dig deep into this ambiguous work.

Toru Takemitsu   Japanese 1930-1996

Takemitsu was a pupil of Kiyose from 1948. Influenced by Webern, Debussy and Messiaen, he has reflected what is most oriental in these composers: a concern with timbre and elegant sound and with the precision of the moment rather than with pattern and development. His music often gives the impression of spatial experience and of materials evolving freely of their own accord; silence is fully organised. Some of his works use Japanese instruments, but most are for Western orchestral and chamber media. Among the best known are Requiem for strings (1957), November Steps for biwa, shakuhachi and orchestra (1967), A Flock Descends into the Pentagonal Garden (1977) and From me flows what you call Time (1990) for percussion quintet and orchestra.
GROVEmusic

I Hear the Water Dreaming

I Hear the Water Dreaming[a]. riverrun[b]. A String around Autumn[c]. A Way A Lone II
[a]**Sharon Bezaly** fl [c]**Philip Dukes** va [b]**Noriko Ogawa** pf **BBC National Orchestra of Wales / Tadaaki Otaka**
BIS BIS-CD1300 (60' · DDD)   ⑤ⓄⓄⓄ

Since Takemitsu's evolution into self-confessed Romantic, virtually every major label has released something by him, so Otaka has stiff competition, notably Patrick Gallois's fine reading of *Water Dreaming*. *A Way A Lone II* is included on Rudolf Werthen's admirable survey of Takemitsu's film and concert music. Aided effectively by the soloists, Otaka's interpretations compare well.

In *riverrun* Takemitsu approached closer to the conventional soloist-ensemble than usual. Noriko Ogawa, who has recorded the complete piano solos for BIS, judges the balance sensitively, preparing the ground for that moment when the orchestra leaves the piano to decorate the silence with a few farewell notes.

riverrun and *A Way A Lone* draw inspiration from *Finnegans Wake*. Leif Hasselgren notes a parallel between the circular structure of Joyce's novel and the way Takemitsu's music seems to 'start from nowhere and disappear into the same nowhere'. For all his acknowledged debt to French Impressionism, and to Japanese traditions, his early interest in electronic music – where sounds appear and fade like headlights on the horizon or plants flowering in a time-lapse film – has undoubtedly had a strong influence.

Sharon Bezaly's flute playing intensifies the feeling that *Water Dreaming* is a perfect crash-course in later Takemitsu, full of references to his influences yet identifiable at any moment as pure, individual and personal Takemitsu, and always bewitching.

A Flock Descends into the Pentagonal Garden

Dreamtime. A Flock Descends into the Pentagonal Garden. Solitude sonore. Spirit Garden. Three Film Scores for String Orchestra
Bournemouth Symphony Orchestra / Marin Alsop
Naxos 8 557760 (63' · DDD) ⑤●▶

Discs of Toru Takemitsu's orchestral music have been numerous these past two decades but this Naxos release has the advantage of providing a chronological overview. What comes through, above all, is the consistency of his musical development during that time. The sound world of *Solitude sonore* (1958) might evoke an Asiatic Messiaen, yet the translucent sonorities and suspended – never merely static – sense of motion denote an already personal voice.

Moving to *A Flock Descends into the Pentagonal Garden* (1977) is to reach the point where all the elements of Takemitsu's mature idiom are in place: the music unfolding as waves of diaphanous textures in which melodies and harmonies are ceaselessly changing. Less sensuous in manner, *Dreamtime* (1981) is possibly the finer piece – its interplay of motifs effortlessly evoking an atmosphere remote yet ethereal. From the output of the composer's last decade, *Spirit Garden* (1994) stands out for its clarity and subtlety of thought – a 'concerto for orchestra' that is emphatically no display piece.

The Bournemouth orchestra are on fine form in what is probably their finest collaboration yet with Marin Alsop. She also includes three pieces for strings drawn from film scores – of which 'Funeral Music' has a baleful intensity rare in Takemitsu's concert music. First rate sound, not too close in perspective, and detailed notes from Andrew Burn complete a worthwhile introduction to this singular composer.

Air

Air[a]. And then I knew 'twas Wind[b]. Bryce[c]. Itinerant[d]. Rain Spell[e]. Rain Tree[f]. Toward the Sea[g]. Voice[h]
New Music Concerts Ensemble ([e]Joaquin Valdepeñas *cl* [e]David Swan *pf* [ce]Robin Engelman *mari/vib* [c]John Wyre, [f]Bob Becker, [f]Russell Hartenberger, [f]Ryan

Scott *percs* [g]Norbert Kraft *gtr* [bce]Erica Goodman, [c]Sanya Eng *hps* [b]Steven Dann *va*) /
[abcdegh]**Robert Aitken** *fl*
Naxos 8 555859 (72' · DDD) ⑤●▶

Takemitsu's work in the final decade of his life was gentle, full of tenderness, sentiment and sighs. But he never entirely discarded the starker beauty of his earlier work. *Air* distills much of the spirit of his music, evoking the French Impressionists, modernist asceticism and the pared-down elegance of Japanese traditional music and gardens. It was written for flautist Aurèle Nicolet and first played in public by Yasukazu Uemura, but it's hard to imagine Robert Aitken's performance being bettered.

Aitken invited Takemitsu to Canada in 1975 and 1983. From these visits grew a special relationship with the musicians featured on this outstanding album. They performed most of these works for the composer, so we can assume that the interpretations bear the hallmark of authenticity: they sound utterly convincing, with their perfect balance of the technical and the emotional. *Itinerant* (1989) is a case in point: Takemitsu pictures a garden where vegetable and mineral, motion and stability mingle in precisely designed harmony, yet each visitor's perspective discovers a fresh view.

The programming is as admirable as the playing, surveying Takemitsu's music for small forces from 1971 (*Voice*, with its references to Noh theatre) to 1995 (*Air*). From the pastoral, slightly eerie trio for flute, viola and harp *And Then I Knew* – devised as a companion-piece to Debussy's 1915 Sonata for the same instruments – and the shimmering, celestial *Rain Tree*, to *Rain Spell*, brooding and turbulent in turns, this is yet another excellent 20th-century showcase from Naxos.

Joby Talbot British b1971

Talbot began his musical career writing for and performing in the group The Divine Comedy. His first piece to receive major attention was the theme music to TV's The League of Gentlemen. Since then, he has written scores and made arrangements for numerous TV programmes and films. In the 'classical' arena he has collaborated with Evelyn Glennie, Tenebrae and The King's Singers. 2004 saw his first Proms commission, Sneaker Wave; the same year he was also appointed Composer in Residence by Classic FM.

Path of Miracles
Tenebrae / Nigel Short
Signum 📀 SIGCD078 (62' · DDD · T/t) ⑤▶

Joby Talbot was in the band that provided music for that divine comedy *Father Ted*. After such beatification by association, the only way would seem to be down, yet he continued to produce works of considerable quality and imagination.

'Roncesvalles', 'Burgos', 'Leon' and 'Santiago', the movements of *Path of Miracles*, are named after four points on the Camino Frances, one of the principal pilgrims' routes to Santiago de Compostela. The vivid libretto was compiled by poet Robert Dickinson from medieval texts (including the *Carmina Burana*), the Psalms and his own original reflections. Those words, and a visit to the main sites along the route, evidently inspired Talbot: this is a work of remarkable range and assurance.

'Roncesvalles' opens with eerie, long-held tones in the bass register, gradually hauled up to a radiant chord in the higher voices. The passage was inspired by a technique used in traditional Taiwanese music but one could just as well imagine it as a synthesis of Ligeti and Pärt. The movement goes on to describe Herod's execution of St James, and the eventual discovery of the body at Compostela, in a rich, agile, vibrant evocation of medieval dances and hymns.

Throughout the work Talbot achieves a similarly fertile accommodation between ancient shapes and contemporary colours, moulding often challenging parts into a luminous and uplifting whole. Let's hope for further collaborations between Talbot and the splendid Tenebrae, whose beauty of sound is matched by clarity of diction.

Thomas Tallis

British c1505-1585

Tallis was organist of the Benedictine Priory of Dover in 1532, then probably organist at St Mary-at-Hill, London (1537-8). About 1538 he moved to Waltham Abbey where, at the dissolution (1540), he was a senior lay clerk. In 1541-2 he was a lay clerk at Canterbury Cathedral, and in 1543 became a Gentleman of the Chapel Royal; he remained in the royal household until his death acting as organist, though he was not so designated until after 1570. In 1575 Elizabeth I granted him a licence, with Byrd, to print and publish music, as a result of which the Cantiones sacrae, an anthology of Latin motets by both composers, appeared later that year.

His earliest surviving works are probably three votive antiphons (Salve intemerata virgo, Ave rosa sine spinis and Ave Dei patris filia) in the traditional structure common up to c1530: division into two halves, with sections in reduced and full textures. Other early works include the Magnificat and another votive antiphon, Sancte Deus, both for men's voices. Two of his most sumptuous works, the six-voice antiphon Gaude gloriosa Dei mater and the seven-voice Mass ' Puer natus est nobis ', date from Mary Tudor's brief reign (1553-8), the former featuring musical imagery and melismatic writing, the latter expert handling of current techniques of structural imitation and choral antiphony. He also composed six Latin responsories and seven Office hymns for the Sarum rite and large-scale Latin psalm motets early in Elizabeth's reign. The 40-voice motet, Spem in alium, an astonishing technical achievement, may have been composed in 1573.

Tallis was one of the first to write for the new Anglican liturgy of 1547-53. Much of this music, including If ye love me and Hear the voice and prayer, is in four parts with clear syllabic word-setting and represents the prototype of the early English anthem. His Dorian Service is in a similar style. Among his Elizabethan vernacular music are nine four-voice psalm tunes (1567) and various English adaptations of Latin motets (e.g. Absterge Domine); the Latin Lamentations and the paired five-voice Magnificat and Nunc dimittis also date from this period. His instrumental works include keyboard arrangements of four partsongs and many cantus firmus settings and a small but distinguished contribution to the repertory of consort music which includes two fine In Nomines. Tallis's early music is relatively undistinguished, with neither Taverner's mastery of the festal style nor Tye's modernisms. But much of his later work is among the finest in Europe, ranging from the artless perfection of his short anthems to the restrained pathos of the Lamentations.

GROVEmusic

Beati immaculati

Beati immaculati. Puer natus est nobis. Mass 'Puer natus est nobis'. Viderunt omnes. Dies sanctificatus. Celeste organum. Viderunt omnes. Suscipe quaeso Dominus. Gaude gloriosa Dei mater
Chapelle du Roi / Alistair Dixon
Signum SIGCD003 (65' · DDD · T/t)   Ⓕ

The illuminating insert-notes place Mary's short reign within the bewilderingly stormy context of the 16th century with a calm understanding that enables the listener to see how this Latin music came to be written. Incidentally, the first piece was originally an English setting of *Beatus vir*. Sandon says it falls naturally into place with its Latin text. But the verses in the booklet don't exactly correspond to what's being sung, which raises an unnecessary question mark. Sandon's edition of the Proper Salisbury chants for the Third Mass of Christmas are performed between the polyphonic items. Meticulously researched, they serve as a foil to the sumptuous settings of the Ordinary.

If only they had been sung with more solemnity and gusto, omitting those irritating little bursts of volume on the high notes! All these chants would have sounded more authentic at a slower tempo with the occasional semi-metrical dactyl: as it is, they comes across rather as a poor relation beside the magnificence of Tallis's seven-part polyphony. The polyphonic singing is exemplary, the clarity of the individual parts and the rhythmic interplay well under control. The singers enter into the spirit of the liturgical texts, in particular in the third section of the *Agnus Dei*. Their interpretation of the final motet, *Gaude gloriosa*, at times almost touches the visionary.

Lamentations of Jeremiah

Lamentations of Jeremiah. Motets – Absterge Domine; Derelinquat impius; Mihi autem nimis;

O sacrum convivium; In jejunio et fletu; O salutaris hostia; In manus tuas; O nata lux de lumine. Salve intemerata virgo
The Tallis Scholars / Peter Phillips
Gimell CDGIM025 (68' · DDD · T/t)　　ⒻⓄⒹ►

This, the third volume of the survey by The Tallis Scholars of the music of the Tudor composer, Thomas Tallis, contains the well-known *Lamentations*, eight motets, and the extended motet *Salve intemerata virgo*. The *Lamentations* and motets are typical of the style of late Renaissance English composers. The overall mood is one of considerable austerity and their simplicity is indicative of the probability of their having been written for the private use of loyal Catholics rather than for formal ritual. *Salve intemerata virgo*, on the other hand, looks back to the glories of the late 15th century. In particular, Tallis's use of the phrygian mode gives the work as a whole a strong sense of the medieval. Despite this disparity of styles the Tallis Scholars acquit themselves, as always, with great distinction. In the *Lamentations* and motets they achieve an appropriate sense of intimacy, while in *Salve intermerata virgo* they rise fully to the challenges of one of the more extended and demanding examples of Tudor choral composition. In addition the formidable challenges which this latter work sets for the conductor, such as the sense of pace, variation of dynamics, and overall architecture of the work, are all extremely well handled by Peter Phillips. The recording is very fine.

Complete Works – 8, Lamentations and Contrafacta
Sing and glorify heaven's high majesty. Lamentations of Jeremiah – I; II. Blessed are those that be undefiled. I call and cry to thee. Wipe away my sins. Forgive me, Lord, my sin. Arise, O Lord, and hear. With all our hearts. O sacred and holy banquet. When Jesus went into Simon the Pharisee's house. Blessed be thy name. O praise the Lord (2nd version)
Chapelle du Roi / Alistair Dixon
Signum Records SIGCD036 (64' · DDD · T/t)　　ⒻⒹ►

Two of the Biblical lessons for Maundy Thursday show Tallis at his most creative and imaginative. 'Incipit lamentatio…' the rising fourth, followed by a descending minor scale, imitated in turn by each of the other voices, sets the tone of sorrowful lamenting. Chapelle du Roi capture this mood with calm perfection. The flowing melodies of the introductory Hebrew letters, the clear articulation of the homophonic sections, each element is performed with understanding, due restraint, and never overdone.

The Latin motets that lie behind the English *contrafacta* have been recorded on Volume 7 of this series. It's remarkable how well the English texts, not necessarily translations or paraphrases, are made to fit the originals. Much interesting research lies behind the notes to Volumes 7 and 8: the identification of the original sources throws additional light on the religious and political struggles of Tallis's working life, and offers glimpses of domesticity. Dixon's choice between two possible groupings of five voices, the lower male-voice group and a higher one to include the ladies of the house, makes perfect sense.

Sing and glorify is a *contrafactum* of Tallis's monumental *Spem in alium*, intended for a joyful royal investiture a quarter of a century after his death. The motet was recast in an entirely different mould: to wish long life to the young Prince of Wales was a far cry from a desperate appeal to God for mercy: even Dixon's faster tempo can't alter that, but what a fine performance his singers give of it.

Additional recommendation

Lamentations of Jeremiah
Coupled with: **Brumel** Lamentations **A Ferrabosco I** De lamentatione Ieremiae prophetae **Palestrina** Lamentations for Holy Saturday **Tallis** Lamentations of Jeremiah **White** Lamentations of Jeremiah
The Tallis Scholars / Phillips
Gimell CDGIM996 (73' · DDD · T/t)　　ⒻⒹ►
A compilation of 16th-century Tenebrae music for Holy Week. The Lamentations texts set are quite different, but all show an intensity and a devotional power that work cumulatively to produce a remarkably satisfying disc.

Spem in alium

Te lucis ante terminum. Salvator mundi. Spem in alium. In jejunio et fletu. O salutaris hostia. Lamentations I & II. Miserere. Mass for four voices
Magnificat / Philip Cave
Linn Records CKD233 (67' · DDD · T/t)　　ⒻⓄⓄⓄⒹ►

Ⓖ This is quite simply the best performance of Tallis's 40-part *Spem in alium* to date. Sung by a constellation of singers, many of them familiar names from other well-established choral groups, it's a gripping realisation. The effect of the slowly moving harmonies is enhanced by a well-conceived and very positive use of dynamics. Precise entries, gently undulating rhythms that are wonderfully supple, and then those firm antiphonal phrases – one group of choirs answered by another at 'Creator coeli et terra' – raise the tension, until we twice almost miss a heart-beat at the well-placed rest before 'Respice …'.

That great motet, so central to the whole programme, is well supported by the four-part Mass and the delightful group of other pieces for various combinations of voices. The hymn *Te lucis* with its alternating chant strophes sounding so very English (almost too perfect for what was, after all, just run-of-the-mill everyday chant!) has the tempo relationship of the chant to the polyphony just right, which is a tremendous plus, rarely achieved.

Spem in alium. Salvator mundi (I, II). Sancte Deus, sancte fortis. Gaude gloriosa Dei mater. Miserere

nostri. Loquebantur variis linguis
The Tallis Scholars / Peter Phillips
Gimell CDGIM006 (43' · DDD) Ⓕ**OO**🡒

For the 1985 quatercentenary of Tallis's death, Peter Phillips and The Tallis Scholars produced this version of *Spem in alium*; in many respects it's clearly the most successful ever recorded. Not only is the choir superb and the interpretation an intelligent one; this is also the only recording in which the eight choirs seem genuinely to sing from different positions in the stereo spread, a technical achievement that leads to some thrilling antiphonal exchanges. Above all, Phillips's reading is a confident and assertive one. The effect is more that of a plea than a prayer, and the overall shaping is most characterful. Inevitably there are problems of balance, both at the top of the texture (several of the trebles are given rather too much prominence) and in the middle, where in full sections the music of the inner voices sometimes blends too readily into rich chords rather than emerging as a complex web of counterpoint. But these are relatively small complaints to be made against an outstanding achievement. This is a *Spem in alium* to be cherished.

Complete Works – 7, Music for Queen Elizabeth
Spem in alium. Absterge Domine. Derelinquat impius. Domine quis habitat. In ieiunio et fletu. In manus tuas. Laudate Dominum. Mihi autem nimis. Miserere nostri. O nata lux de lumine. O sacrum convivium. O salutaris hostia. Salvator mundi, salva nos – I & II
Chapelle du Roi / Alistair Dixon
Signum Records SIGCD029 (63' · DDD · T/t) Ⓕ**OO**🡒

Volume 7 of Chapelle du Roi's complete series of Tallis recordings, is a further witness to the composer's consummate command of his art, in whatever religious or political situation he found himself at each changing period of his life. It might seem puzzling that Elizabeth, in 1575, should sanction the publication of Tallis's and Byrd's *Cantiones sacrae*, but she apparently enjoyed hearing Latin-texted music in her private chapel, and many of the prayers would have been familiar from her childhood.

Dixon makes a number of interesting points. He demonstrates Tallis's use of older material: for example, the Latin *Absterge Domine*, side by side with its later English contrafactum *Discomfort them, O Lord*. He shows how five-voice scoring might be used for an all-male ensemble, or privately in, say, a recusant family situation, with ladies on the top line (*In ieiunio et fletu*). Tallis's craftsmanship is further revealed in his two through-composed psalms, *Domine, quis habitabit* and *Laudate Dominum*, which, while adhering to 16th-century principles of syllabic word-setting, are varied enough to relieve the inevitable tedium. We hear finally, Dixon's masterly interpretation of *Spem in alium* 'in the round' – or 'in horseshoe formation' – possibly the Chapelle's highest achievement to date.

TALLIS SPEM IN ALIUM IN BRIEF

Tallis Scholars / Peter Phillips
Gimell ② CDGIM203 (159' · DDD) Ⓜ**OO**🡒
Gimell CDGIM006 (43' · DDD) Ⓕ**OO**🡒
The punchy, no-holds-barred sonorities and spot-on tuning of The Tallis Scholars make for exhilarating listening. The recording – crucial when it comes to delineating 40 separate lines – doesn't wrap around the listener, but offers a tightly focused experience. It's available both with the original couplings of Latin motets or as the starter for The Scholars' complete recordings of Tallis.

Magnificat / Philip Cave
Linn CKD075 (67' · DDD) Ⓕ**OOO**
Ⓖ Demonstration-quality openness and balance makes this quite spacious version one to treasure. Lots of young British voices bring an unchurchy, dynamic panorama to Tallis's elaborate testament of faith – *My hope is founded in the Lord* – and demonstration of compositional skill.

Clerkes of Oxenford / David Wulstan
Classics for Pleasure 575982-2 (69' · ADD) Ⓑ
A pioneering 'new' early-music choir in the 1970s combining modern scholarship (and female voices) with roots in the English choral tradition. The result is unhurried and effortlessly conveys the scale of Tallis's conception. Fine couplings of church music.

Chapelle du Roi / Alistair Dixon
Signum SIGCD047 (20' · DDD) Ⓑ
If you only want *Spem*, this is the one to have. The second track is the first recording of the English version of the motet, *Sing and glorify*. Carefully sung and balanced.

The Sixteen / Harry Christophers
Coro 🔉 CORSACD16016 / 📀 CO5RDVD1 (72' · DDD) Ⓕ
Spem is literally a surround-sound piece, so this recording, the first to use the latest technology in new audio formats, gets closer than most. The Sixteen (enlarged to the requisite 40) have a suitably festive air for this, their 25th anniversary recording.

Choir of Winchester Cathedral / David Hill
Hyperion CDA66400 (59' · DDD) Ⓕ
A definite first choice for those who want to hear the boys' voices that Tallis would have composed for. A wide, open recording within Winchester's vast space still captures all the intricate detail to touching effect.

Kronos Quartet
Nonesuch 7559 79242-2 (62' · DDD) Ⓕ
For something a bit different: the avant-garde string quartet, multi-tracked with sometimes revelatory clarity.

Tan Dun ·   Chinese/America b1957

Growing up during the Cutural Revolution, Tan Dun received no early musical training. After working as a violinist, at the age of 19 he entered the composition department of Beijing's reopened Central Conservatory of Music. There he encountered Western music and was stimulated by visits of guest composers Goehr, Crumb and Takemitsu. He moved to New York in 1986.   **GROVE**music

The Map

Concerto for Cello, Video and Orchestra, 'The Map' – A multimedia event in rural China[a]. Includes the documentary, 'Rediscovering the Map'[b]
Anssi Karttunen *vc* **Shanghai Symphony Orchestra / Tan Dun** [a]*Aural and visual imaging* **Davey Frankel**
Video directors [a]**Sheng Boji,** [a]**Wang Ping,**
[b]**Uri Gal-Ed**
DG 20/21 **DVD** 073 4009GH (73' · NTSC · 4:3 · PCM stereo, 5.1 & DTS 5.1 · 0)   Ⓕ Ⓞ

The Map is Tan Dun's quest to find the shamanistic 'stone man' he once heard in his youth. Armed with a commission from Yo-Yo Ma and the Boston Symphony Orchestra, he returned to Hunan with a camera crew to document village musical life and the non-Han minority peoples in particular. Once back in New York, he became a sort of Bartók for the media age, spinning ethnic traditional material into an abstract modernism while simultaneously preserving its roots on screen. The results are sprawling, to say the least. At times, such as the polyphonic tongue-singing of a group of Dong women, the orchestra merely frames the film footage. Elsewhere Tan's orchestral writing cheekily adapts the techniques of the village practitioners on a grand scale, such as having the entire percussion section enter into a dialogue with a group of Tujia cymbal players, or the winds and brass playing their reeds and mouthpieces in response to a village leaf-blower. The most creative touch comes in a *feige*, traditionally an antiphonal courtship song sung across mountains and valleys, but here featuring a Miao girl on screen performing with a live cello soloist, transcending entirely new boundaries of time and space.

Grasping the dimensions of this piece in a home format obviously requires a video recording; fortunately Hunan television was on hand when Tan brought the *The Map* to the village that inspired it. That broadcast, carefully edited and remixed here, is paired with a short film documenting that production, as well as Tan's original writing process.

Much of these musical traditions, it must be said, remain as exotic to most Chinese listeners as a Navajo chant would in the West. The most obvious weakness of *The Map* is that sometimes Tan seems all too content to play tourist, filming music that villagers play for outsiders rather than what they perform for themselves. Still,

since his stated goal was not to document those cultures but to bring their rustic vitality into counterpoint with the slick urban world, *The Map* succeeds not in spite of its messiness but because of it.

Sergey Taneyev ·   Russian 1856-1915

At the Moscow Conservatory Taneyev studied with Nikolay Rubinstein (piano) and Tchaikovsky (composition), whose friend he became, giving the Moscow première of Tchaikovsky's Piano Concerto no.1 (1875) and succeeding him as teacher at the conservatory (1878). He eventually became director (1885-9) though it was as a teacher that he had the greater influence (his pupils included Skryabin, Rakhmaninov and Glier). An eclectic and conservative at heart, he was early drawn to the music of Bach and the Renaissance contrapuntists; these studies, allied to his diligence in formal planning, gave him a compositional skill unsurpassed by his Russian contemporaries. His most successful works are the large-scale instrumental pieces, particularly the fluent sonata structures, as in the C minor Symphony (1898) and the First String Quintet (1901), where his craftsmanship and contrapuntalism lend uncommon precision and polish to the musical argument. But his unoriginality and rejection of the indigenous Russian tradition resulted in conventional melodies and wooden musical characterisation, for example in his ambitious opera The Oresteia (1887-94). Apart from the important chamber works (11 string quartets, three quintets), Taneyev wrote choruses and many songs (some in Esperanto); his last work, the cantata At the Reading of a Psalm (1915), was acclaimed and considered by some his masterpiece. He wrote books on counterpoint and on canon.   **GROVE**music

Piano Concerto

Piano Concerto[c]. Andante semplice. Prelude. Lullaby. Theme and Variations. Allegro. Repose Elegy. March. Four Improvisations. The Composer's Birthday (two versions)[a/ab]
Joseph Banowetz, [a]**Adam Wodnicki** *pfs* [b]**Vladimir Ashkenazy** *narr* [c]**Russian Philharmonic of Moscow / Thomas Sanderling**
Toccata Classics TOCC0042 (77' · DDD)   Ⓕ Ⓓ➤

How can it be that the only piano concerto by a pianist-composer of the standing of Taneyev has never previously been recorded? True, it was left incomplete – Taneyev was a harsh self-critic, and adverse comment from Anton Rubinstein, Cui and Rimsky-Korsakov can hardly have helped. True, it was only published in 1957. True, there are times in the 25-minute first movement when it's hard not to wish that the 19-year-old recent graduate from Tchaikovsky's class might have drawn the threads of the structure a little tighter. Yet the very opening bars bring a characteristic touch of nobility, gravitas and subdued enthusiasm. And while it's unlikely that anyone would rank the two movements beside the finest of Taneyev's mature symphonic or chamber works, the fact that the Concerto remained unfinished and unrevised surely robbed us of a work worthy of a place in the great Russian tradition.

The performance never gives off the whiff of dutiful generality that so often accompanies such ventures. Banowetz plays with a natural eloquence and heart, as well as a fine technical address, qualities which ennoble the frankly less distinguished solo pieces too. The rather rambling *Theme and Variations* cannot entirely disguise its origins as a composition exercise, and there are no regrets that the *Allegro* never grew into a complete sonata.

But the end of the disc is a delight. The *Four Improvisations* are a cataloguer's nightmare, since they were jointly composed with Arensky, Glazunov and Rachmaninov, passing round sheets of manuscript paper in a game of musical 'consequences'. Just as quirky is Taneyev's greeting for Tchaikovsky's 52nd birthday, whose whimsical scenario is built around quotations of nine of the latter's major works. The piece is helpfully recorded here once with the accompanying text declaimed (by Ashkenazy, no less), once without.

Less than one fifth of the music on the disc has been previously recorded. All of it is excellently recorded, and serious collectors should flock to snap it up.

Symphonies

Symphonies Nos 1 & 3
Russian State Symphony Orchestra /
Valery Polyansky
Chandos CHAN10390 (64' · DDD)   Ⓕ Ⓑ➔

Taneyev's first composed symphony, in E minor, was the work of a 17-year-old student, dutifully ticking the prescribed boxes for his graduation from Moscow Conservatoire. As so often in the academic Russian tradition, the *Scherzo* is the most striking movement; the finale, by contrast, puts its folksong material through so many harmonic and contrapuntal routines that one almost imagines it crying for mercy.

The Third Symphony, in D minor and dedicated to Arensky, drew Tchaikovsky's praise for its musical content but also his reservations about the 'abstract' (ie non-orchestral) nature of the material. That seems a just assessment. The first movement, like Beethoven's *Eroica*, Schumann's *Rhenish* and Nielsen's *Espansiva*, moves in a liberally cross-accented triple metre (a useful aide-mémoire that these should all be third symphonies). It is in many ways no less ingenious than those works but never achieves lift-off in the way they do; the same goes for the *Scherzo*, whose strategy for integrating the Trio is resourceful but hardly revelatory. The modest Intermezzo is easy to like as a pleasantly relaxing episode, but would be more effective placed in more dramatic surroundings.

Polyansky and the Russian State Symphony have done Taneyev a superb service with these thoroughly prepared, expertly recorded performances. The music itself may be too firmly tied to academic apron-strings to be viable in the concert hall, and the composer's verdict in not releasing them was surely the right one. But these are still need-to-know pieces for anyone interested in the Russian symphonic repertoire.

Symphonies No 2 & 4
Russian State Symphony Orchestra /
Valery Polyansky
Chandos CHAN9998 (75' · DDD)   Ⓕ Ⓑ➔

Polyansky provides a splendidly passionate and invigorating introduction to music that we really should know better in the West. The Fourth Symphony has always been the most popular of Taneyev's symphonies, and with good reason. He writes a powerful opening *Allegro* and a well-built finale, but for all his symphonic skills here, it's in the middle two movements that the most personal music is to be found. The *scherzo* dances along with the vitality that many a Russian composer has brought to comparable movements, and with the rhythmic quirks that he liked so much; but it's in the *Adagio* that something more is discovered. Taneyev has routinely been reproached for lacking melodic distinction, sometimes with reason, but this superb movement comes close to the manner of Bruckner, or sometimes Mahler. For English ears, the sense of 'stately sorrow' serves as a reminder that the phrase was coined of his own music by Elgar.

Conductor and players make of this fine music a tragic statement, and it's here that they're at their most intense. Polyansky also produces a strong case for the Second Symphony, his sense of structure holding the rather oddly organised opening movement together, as a powerful chorale passage has to be integrated with a sonata *Allegro*. He doesn't play down the suggestions of Dvořák, whom Taneyev clearly found sympathetic. This is a striking, and very well-recorded, pair of performances, well worth the attention of lovers of Russian music.

Chamber works

Piano Quintet[a]. Piano Trio, Op 22
Vadim Repin, [a]**Ilya Gringolts** vns [a]**Nobuko Imai** va
Lynn Harrell vc **Mikhail Pletnev** pf
DG 477 5419 (83' · DDD)   Ⓕ ❶❷❸❹➔

Piano Quartet, Op 20[a]. Piano Trio, Op 22
Barbican Piano Trio (James Kirby pf Gaby Lester vn
Robert Max vc) with [a]**James Boyd** va
Dutton Laboratories CDSA6882 (74' · DDD)   Ⓕ

Sergey Taneyev composed his three piano chamber works in the years 1902-11, on either side of his 50th birthday, when his days as director of the Moscow Conservatoire were well behind him but when he still commanded nationwide respect for his gifts as pianist, administrator and craftsman-composer. These pieces were in the first instance vehicles for his own concert performances, and the piano parts are accordingly massive. Compositionally the writing is unfailingly well wrought and resourceful: by no means entirely confined to middle-of-the-road tastefulness, yet rarely, if ever, touched by the kind of distinction evinced by his great pupils, Rachmaninov and Scriabin.

At times, especially in the Piano Quartet, it is like being in the presence of a very large and likeable student, who has never quite found his own voice but who remains intent on getting higher and higher marks for the same type of exercise. Yet at the same time the music has an undeniable sweep, and some of the ideas evidently lodged in the minds of future generations – compare the opening bars of the Quintet with Prokofiev's First Violin Sonata, for instance, or the opening of the Piano Trio with the third movement of Shostakovich's First Violin Concerto. There is a certain Elgarian gruffness here and there, and a liking for fulminating, low-lying textures that may be off-putting at first encounter but which exerts its own particular charm on closer acquaintance.

The Piano Quintet is the latest and grandest of the three works, its structural layout and textures being indebted in just about equal measure to Tchaikovsky and César Franck. The initially consoling second subject is destined for heroic things in a grandstand résumé at the end of the finale, and on repeated hearings it's a pleasure to discover its unassuming beginnings. In between, the *Scherzo* has that touch of fairytale magic that came so naturally to most of the great Russians while the slow movement daringly strips down to a passacaglia theme on the cello before dressing up impressively again. Pletnev and his dream-team string colleagues are passionate advocates, as they are for the more classically conceived (or at least more Schumannesque) Trio.

The strings are placed rather far forward, and the acoustic is a fraction too dry for comfort. It's a tribute to the Barbican Piano Trio that they hardly ever find themselves outdone in crusading passion, or indeed outplayed technically, by their bigger-name rivals. James Kirkby is as sensitive as Pletnev to the oases of calm in the slow movement of the Trio, where the piano holds the stage in moments of quiet rapture. By contrast, the Piano Quartet launches immediately into its ecstatic stride, risking anticlimax but rescuing itself by constant renewed initiatives. Violist James Boyd makes his presence strongly felt in the dark-hued slow movement. The Dutton recording strays a fraction the other side of the ideal from DG by giving us a little too much of the room acoustic of St George's, Brandon Hill, Bristol; but once again it is perfectly serviceable.

String Trios – Op 31; in B minor; in D
Leopold String Trio (Isabelle Van Keulen vn
Lawrence Power va Kate Gould vc)
Hyperion CDA67573 (67' · DDD)   Ⓕ🅞

Given the scarcity of Russian contributions to this traditionally most demanding of chamber media, there is all the more reason to investigate what Russia's greatest master of counterpoint (according to Tchaikovsky and others well placed to comment) does with it.

Hyperion has wisely placed the finest of the three first. The E flat Trio (1910-11) is chronologically second, and apart from Taneyev's usual craftsmanly values, there is a winning freedom of invention. The first movement has the confidence to go down inviting sidetracks, confident that there will be marvels to bring back. One of Taneyev's trademark quick-witted scherzos follows – irresistibly charming – then a gorgeously warm-hearted slow movement, with plentiful florid yet never tasteless elaboration, and a jocund finale. Given that the lowest part of the E flat Trio was conceived and published for the tenor viola (tuned a fourth higher than the cello) there is some justification for Kate Gould's occasional redistribution of the texture; though if anyone can dig out an example of the original instrument it would be fun to compare.

After this the unfinished B minor Trio (1913), partially reconstructed from sketches for its posthumous first publication, is a tougher nut, grainier in its texture and more heavily shadowed in its moods – a sober and impressive footnote to one of the great chamber music composing careers. The D major Trio (1879-80) is a perfectly respectable debut in the medium, checking every step of the way before boldly going where no major Russian composer had gone before.

It would be hard to over-praise the Leopold Trio's performances. Agility and all-round aplomb? Check. Warmth and colour? Check. Structural and idiomatic awareness? Check. Fine recording quality and helpful annotation (Calum MacDonald) too; so no reason not to invest.

Giuseppe Tartini   Italian 1692-1770

After abandoning plans for a monastic career Tartini studied in Assisi and by 1714 had joined the orchestra at Ancona. He later spent time in Venice and Padua, where he settled in 1721 as principal violinist at the basilica of S Antonio. He worked there until 1765 except for a period in Prague (1723-6). Besides performing with success, he founded in 1727-8 a 'school' of violin instruction; his many pupils included JG Graun, Nardini and Naumann.

Tartini was one of the foremost Italian instrumental composers, writing over 400 works: these include violin concertos and sonatas (many with virtuoso solo parts), trio sonatas and sonatas for string ensemble. Most have three movements, ordered slow-fast-fast (sonatas) or fast-slow-fast (concertos). His later works in particular approach Classical structures and display galant features, including regular four-bar melodic phrases. Elaborate cadence formulae are especially characteristic. He also composed some sacred music. Noteworthy among his writings are a work on violin playing and ornamentation, Traité des agré-

ments de la musique – published only in 1771 but thought to have been written earlier (L Mozart, in 1756, is thought to have borrowed from it, but it may be the other way round) – and two treatises on the acoustical foundations of harmony (1754, 1767), in which his discovery of the Difference tone phenomenon is discussed. **GROVE**music

Violin Concertos

Violin Concertos – C, D4[a]; E minor, D56[b]; F, D63[c]; G, D75[d]
[ad]**Federico Guglielmo,** [c]**Carlo Lazari** *vns*
L'Arte dell'Arco / [b]**Giovanni Guglielmo** *vn*
Dynamic CDS220 (64' · DDD) Ⓕ

The works in this fourth volume of Tartini's violin concertos all supposedly belong to the composer's earliest period, the years between *c*1720 and 1735. One of them, in E minor, has long been popular with soloists and has often been recorded. The remaining three, however, are less familiar and, it's claimed, here make their first appearance on disc. The C major piece sounds as if it might be the earliest concerto here, though many of the distinctive hallmarks of Tartini's style are firmly in place – little chromaticisms and short-lived, playful melodic patterns in the outer movements, and wistfully lyrical solo cantilenas in the tenderly expressive slow one. The author of the accompanying note erroneously claims the tonal plan is more imaginative than in Vivaldi's concertos. Tartini simply avails himself of a more advanced pool of stylistic knowledge, in no sense improving on the art of his forebears – especially Vivaldi.

An enjoyable programme with engaging solo contributions from Guglielmo. Listeners will notice the acid quality of the *tutti* playing, and a recorded sound that does little to ameliorate it, though they will quickly adjust to both.

Violin Sonatas

Tartini Violin Sonata in G minor, 'Devil's Trill' (arr Kreisler) **Corelli** Violin Sonata in D minor, 'La Folia', Op 5 No 12 (arr Kreisler) **Nardini** Sonata (arr Flesch) **Vitali** Chaconne (arr David)
Ida Haendel *vn* **Geoffrey Parsons** *pf*
Testament SBT1258 (59' · ADD) Recorded 1970s. Ⓕ●

This is a genuinely great fiddle record, one to place alongside those in which Heifetz, Szigeti or Elman (to name but three) tackle similar repertoire. Indeed, if it's possible to make this music sound so beautiful, why does the 'historic performing' lobby kick up so much noisy opposition? One understands all the counter-arguments; and, yes, these are arrangements – which is different. But to take just one small example, at around 2'02" into the opening *Adagio* of Nardini's Sonata, Haendel suddenly dips from *mezzo-forte* to *piano*, as if she's switching from a serene smile to a questioning glance. The effect is both subtle and dramatic. Corelli's *La Folia* and Tartini's *The Devil's Trill* Sonata are similarly expressive. As for Vitali's *Chaconne*, Haendel admits that she was knocked out when she heard Heifetz play the piece and in some ways her impassioned performance resembles Heifetz's interpretatively spectacular 1950 recording (of Respighi's arrangement; Haendel plays David's more comprehensive alternative). Always there's that ecstatic control of melodic line, holding fast to the harmonic thread – musically, patiently and with the touch of a true craftsman. The recording is superb, and the partnership with Geoffrey Parsons is beautifully balanced. A truly wonderful CD.

Violin Sonatas – G minor, 'Devil's Trill', B:g5; A minor, B:a3. Variations on a Gavotte by Corelli, B: F11 – excerpts. Pastorale in A, B:A16 (all arr Manze)
Andrew Manze *vn*
Harmonia Mundi HMU90 7213 (69' · DDD) Ⓕ●

The romantic connotations of Tartini's Violin Sonata in G minor, the *Devil's Trill*, deriving from the composer's account of an appearance by the devil in a dream, have contributed towards making it one of the great *morceaux favoris* of the 19th and 20th centuries. Furthermore, it's just about the only remaining piece of Baroque music where a piano accompaniment can still be countenanced without raised eyebrows. Some traditions die hard. But Tartini never intended anything of the kind; in fact, he probably never envisaged a keyboard continuo part at all, since none of his surviving autographs contains a figured bass for keyboard realisation. Most include unfigured bass parts, though these were often provided as an afterthought, for reasons of convention. Andrew Manze sees this as a justification for playing all the pieces in his programme without bass accompaniment. On the whole the experiment works well, since the expressive content and structural power of the music lies foremost in Tartini's melodic line. There are moments, however, where harmonic support from the bass is required, and at such times, above all in the *Devil's Trill* Sonata, Manze has had to introduce chords in the violin part to compensate for the absence of a cello. His athletic technique, his musical sensibility and perhaps, too, his engaging sense of fun, ensure fascination and entertainment in equal measure. None will regret the passing of the piano in this context. A stimulating release, beautifully recorded, and rich in fantasy.

Tartini Solo Violin Sonatas – No 2; No 13; No 14; No 17; in A minor, Brainard A3. Solitario bosco ombroso **Rolli** Solitario bosco ombroso[a] **Anonymous** Lieto ti prendo e poi[a]. Depon Clorinda la sue spoglie inteste[a]. Intanto Erminia fra l'ombrose piante
Chiara Banchini *vn* with [a]**Patrizia Bovi** *voc*
Zig-Zag Territoires ZZT080502 (67' · DDD) Ⓕ●Ⓓ➜

Tartini often prefaced movements of his later sonatas with short poetic quotations (usually from Metastasio or Tasso) indicating his expressive intent. An adherent of the fashionable theory that the role of art is to imitate nature, he showed a keen interest in folksong (perceived as closer to nature than art music). In several pieces he quotes the melody of the celebrated 'Aria di Tasso', an anonymous setting of verses from *La Gerusalemme liberata*, sung by Venetian gondoliers, and this forms the starting-point for Banchini's disc, which alternates solo sonatas with some of the popular melodies that inspired the composer.

Patrizia Bovi sings these most convincingly, combining stylish ornamentation with strong projection of line and text. There's a handsome booklet too, with texts of the songs and the poems quoted by Tartini, a little selection of 18th-century writings and paintings, and an interesting essay (by Stefano Aresi).

It's the violin, however, that's the main focus of attention, and Banchini plays elegantly, with great expressive freedom and, in the quicker movements, with considerable force and panache. She also ornaments liberally and imaginatively, obviously inspired by Tartini's own examples and instructions concerning embellishment. Listeners can be assured, however, that the startling dissonances in the opening *Siciliana* of Sonata No 2 (in D minor, not B minor as printed) stem from Tartini's own pen. In the way it allows us to appreciate fully the aesthetic ideals of a bygone age, this is an exceptional issue.

Sir John Tavener
British b1944

Tavener studied with Berkeley and Lumsdaine at the Royal Academy of Music (1961-5). Most of his music is explicitly religious, influenced by late Stravinsky but containing strong, bold images from a variety of other sources; his biblical cantata The Whale (1966) enjoyed a vogue. An early leaning towards Catholic devotion reached a consummation in the Crucifixion meditation Ultimos ritos (1972) and the opera Thérèse (1979). In 1976 he converted to the Russian Orthodox faith, composing in a simpler, luminous style (Liturgy of St John Chrysostom for unaccompanied chorus, 1978; Protecting Veil for cello and orchestra, 1989). GROVEmusic

The Protecting Veil

The Protecting Veil. Wake Up...And Die.
Yo-Yo Ma vc
Baltimore Symphony Orchestra / David Zinman
Sony Classical 07464 62821-2 (67' · DDD) ⓕ**O**▶

This was the third recording of *The Protecting Veil* to appear since Steven Isserlis's *Gramophone* Award-winning premiere recording on Virgin Classics (see below). As expected, Yo-Yo Ma brings us a reading of tremendous stature and technical refinement which is a serious rival to

Isserlis's equally remarkable account. However, whether Isserlis is preferable to Ma or vice versa seems irrelevant; what is essential is that the work continues to live and grow through performance, and with a piece such as *The Protecting Veil* the interpretative scope for the soloist is wide indeed. Ma's version is quite different from Isserlis's in many ways. Isserlis takes the opening of the work ('The Protecting Veil' section) slightly faster and certainly with more passionate phrasing than Ma, whose pacing in the corresponding bars is altogether more static, though he still matches Isserlis in intensity. He is complemented by the strings of the Baltimore Symphony Orchestra under David Zinman. Tavener's comment that 'the strings should act as a vast resonating chamber for the solo cello' is fully realized and the effect is at times quite awesome. Particularly beautiful is Ma's reading of 'The Dormition of the Mother of God' section.

Wake up ... And Die, for cello solo and orchestral cello section, is a 20-minute work in two parts. The Byzantine, chant-like opening section for solo cello has great beauty and the second half of the work, with cello section harmonically supporting the solo cello with its hypnotic repeating episodes, is quite spell-binding. This is a piece that will quickly find admirers who are familiar with Tavener's unique sound world. The recording is vivid and well balanced.

Additional recommendation

The Protecting Veil
Coupled with: The Last Sleep of the Virgin. Choral Music.
Isserlis; LSO / Rozhdestvensky
EMI 20th Century Classics ② 237691-2

or Coupled with: Thrinos. **Britten** Cello Suite No 3
Virgin Classics 503 430-2
The premiere recording and one that has a magic all of its own. Isserlis brings huge amounts of passion and intensity to this now very popular work for cello and orchestra.

Lalishri

Tavener Song for Athene. Dhyana. Lalishri
Vaughan Williams The Lark Ascending
Nicola Benedetti vn **London Philharmonic Orchestra / Andrew Litton**
DG 476 6198GH (64' · DDD) ⓕ**O**▶

The third disc of DG's deal with the former BBC Young Musician amply justifies the company's confidence in this wonderfully pure-toned young violinist. It is an imaginative coupling of three Tavener works – two inspired by Benedetti and a third arranged for her – and the VW work voted the nation's most popular classic.

The choral *Song for Athene* crowned the music at Princess Diana's funeral. This arrangement cannot match that haunting quality although it's beautifully played. Tavener has described Benedetti's playing as 'like a voice…you feel her breathing a line,' and the brief *Dhyana* (Sanskrit for 'meditation') is meant to reflect her contemplative style. *Lalishri* is much more ambitious, almost 40 minutes long, and is inspired by the 14th-century Hindu poet and saint Lalia Yogishwari. The solo violin represents the songs of the poet while the music reflects Tavener's devotion to the Indian raga, meditational depths punctuated by sharp, even frenetic, changes of mood in dance rhythms. Benedetti's fine performance sustains its length well with much double-stopping, *pizzicato* effects, trills and quarter tones. Unlike much of Tavener's music, the work has great vigour with a powerful rather than meditative close.

The Lark Ascending receives a spacious performance, reflective and pure-toned in the fluttering evocations of the lark and powerful in the tuttis, thanks to the weighty accompaniment of Andrew Litton and the LPO, with far bigger dynamic contrasts than usual. A fascinating disc that should have even more listeners magnetised by the music of Tavener as well as of Vaughan Williams.

Lament for Jerusalem

Lament for Jerusalem
Angharad Gruffydd Jones *sop* **Peter Crawford** *counterten* **Choir of London; London Orchestra / Jeremy Summerly**
Naxos 8 557826 (55' · DDD)　　　　Ⓢ🔁

Lament was premiered in Australia in 2003 but this disc features a revised version Tavener prepared for the Choir of London's visit to Jerusalem, Ramallah and Bethlehem in December 2004.

Tavener insists that *Lament* should be seen less as a statement about the current plight of Jerusalem and its inhabitants than as an elegy for humankind's exile from the soul's home, and seeks to remind us what Judaism, Christianity and Islam have in common. Through the purity of his musical gestures he achieves an intensity that can affect listeners regardless of their own religious convictions.

This revision radically reduces the forces needed, both in numbers and range of instrumentation. While some weight is lost, along with the variety of sounds (the brass section comprises just three trumpets, the woodwind two flutes, two bassoons and oboe) this is amply compensated for by increased radiance and clarity.

The premiere recording of the full-scale *Lament* was recorded under Thomas Woods for ABC Classics; and even though it is almost impossible to find in the UK, to a large extent this more transparent version is preferable. The soprano part was originally taken by the marvellous Patricia Rozario but even on this count Summerly's recording need not fear comparison: Angharad Gruffydd Jones has a less distinctive voice but uses it to beautiful effect. Peter Crawford sings well too, less passionate but

sweeter in tone than Christopher Josey, the countertenor on the first recording.

Svyati

God is With Us. Song for Athene. The Lamb. The Tiger. Magnificat and Nunc dimittis. Funeral Ikos. Two Hymns to the Mother of God. Love Bade Me Welcome. As One Who Has Slept. The Lord's Prayer. Svyati[a]
[a]**Tim Hugh** *vc* **St John's College Choir, Cambridge / Christopher Robinson**
Naxos 8 555256 (70' · DDD)　　　　Ⓢ🔁🔁🔁

If John Tavener's reputation were to rest solely on his unaccompanied choral music and nothing else, then his stature as one of the most striking and original composers working today would be just as high. Much of Tavener's creativity is founded on the traditions of his Orthodox faith and of Orthodox chant, and yet curiously, intentionally or unintentionally, he has also, through works such as those presented here, extended the tradition of English choral music. Through their popularity *The Lamb*, *The Tiger* and *Song for Athene* have become immovably imbedded in our choral tradition, but one need only listen to the splendid *Magnificat and Nunc dimittis*, for instance, to find a unique symbiosis of Eastern and Western traditions at work.

Many of the works presented on this CD have enjoyed wide circulation on numerous Tavener-only and compilation discs, but the performances here from the Choir of St John's College, Cambridge, under the direction of Christopher Robinson, have much to recommend them and the super-budget price makes this issue especially desirable for those seeking a survey of Tavener's choral music for the first time.

Svyati for solo cello and choir, with echoes of *The Protecting Veil*, opens a window on Tavener's more overtly Eastern/ Orthodox-inspired music. Tim Hugh's serenely beautiful account of the solo cello part is a winner from beginning to end. The recording, made in St John's College Chapel, is resplendently atmospheric.

Choral Works

As One Who Has Slept. The Bridegroom. Birthday Sleep. Butterfly Dreams. The Second Cominga. Schuon Hymnen. Shûnya. Exhortation and Kohima
Polyphony / Stephen Layton with [a]**Christopher Bowers-Broadbent** *org*
Hyperion CDA67475 (75' · DDD · T/t)　　Ⓕ🔁🔁🔁

 As One Who Has Slept, the earliest work here, represents Tavener's most musically ascetic period, which, by 1996 was drawing to a close. The mesmeric use of drone-like chords behind and beyond the melodic lines reassures and comforts the listener during this portrait of Christ's harrowing of hell. He soon returned to a warmer palette and a wider range of techniques. In *Birthday Sleep* and *The Bridal*

Chamber (1999) hymn-like tunes still predominate, but the voices move more independently, the harmonies are richer.

The 2001 setting of Yeats's *The Second Coming* is full of skilfully realised, dramatically startling gestures, but the mood is quizzical where it should describe fear-threaded apprehension, bombastic where it should be aghast with dismay. Finally, a group of pieces completed in 2003. In *Butterfly Dreams*, a set of miniatures, form and content are better matched. Parts of *Schuon Hymnen*, especially the writing for solo soprano (a glittering, heart-lifting performance by Amy Haworth) suggests music from 1950s sci-fi films: as with those films, it's easy to see how the effects are achieved, yet somehow the magic survives. *Exhortation and Kohima* achieves a Tudoresque splendour, while *Shûnya* adds elements of Buddhist ritual to the mix.

The Veil of the Temple

The Veil of the Temple (short version)
Patricia Rozario *sop* **Simon Wall, Nathan Vale** *tens*
Adrian Peacock, Jeremy Birchall *basses* **Temple Choir / Stephen Layton**
RCA Red Seal ② 82876 66154-2 (149' · DDD/
DSD · T/t)   ⓕ**OO**

Ravi Shankar teases European audiences about their short attention span, condescending to limit improvisations to under an hour rather than the much longer performances expected at an Indian concert. Tavener's original conception for *The Veil of the Temple* was as an all-night vigil, lasting some seven hours. It moves through eight cycles, intensifying in structural complexity and emotional depth, each cycle reflecting the mood of the hour of the night in which it's heard, like a time-specific *rāg*.

Tavener believes that tired audiences are more likely to open up to the deepest spiritual levels of the music. Since the Renaissance Western art has been about promoting artists' individuality. Eastern art is more concerned with tapping into a collective ideal: ikons are to be meditated on, not dissected. He always intended to distil a concert version of *The Veil*, lasting around two-and-a-half hours. This handsomely presented set draws on three of the earliest performances of the complete vigil at the Temple Church in London. Even at around one-third of its full length, *The Veil*, with its rich mix of Orthodox, Indian and English devotional gestures, is a mesmerising experience, a convincing journey from dusk to dawn.

Patricia Rozario is at her heart-stoppingly beautiful best, and there are marvellous contributions from tenor soloists Simon Wall and Nathan Vale and basses Adrian Peacock and Jeremy Birchall. As the ritual moves towards the final revelations, Stephen Layton deftly marshals the swirling chorales and increasingly elemental brass and percussion, keeping everything in sharp focus through to the closing celebratory hymn.

As the piece was devised to be seen as well as heard and, indeed, smelt – live performances incorporate lighting effects, candles and incense – and as the audience should be immersed in the experience, listening to a CD is inevitably a somewhat pale reflection of the whole. However, these recordings do a creditable job of evoking the atmosphere. For those without SACD surround-sound capability, listening on headphones is recommended to get the best impression of positioning and movements.

John Taverner   British c1490-1545

The earliest unequivocal references to Taverner occur in 1524-5, when he was a lay clerk at the collegiate church of Tatershall. In 1526 he accepted the post of instructor of the choristers at Cardinal College (now Christ Church), Oxford, and c1530 became a lay clerk (and probably instructor of the choristers) at the parish church of St Botolph, Boston. By 1537 he had retired from full-time employment as a church musician. Although he was embroiled in an outbreak of Lutheran heresy at Cardinal College (in 1528) there is no evidence, contrary to popular opinion, that his views were seriously in conflict with Catholicism or that he ceased composing on leaving Oxford.

Most of his extant works, which include eight masses, three Magnificats, numerous motets and votive antiphons and a few consort pieces and fragmentary secular partsongs, probably date from the 1520s. The three six-voice masses use cantus firmi, sectional structure, huge spans of melisma and skilful counterpoint; of the smaller-scale masses ' Western Wynde ' is based on a secular tune and in a less expansive, more Lutheran style. Characteristic of his writing is the development of a melodic or rhythmic fragment in imitation or canon or as an ostinato figure. The Magnificats are large-scale, florid works in the English tradition, also using cantus firmi. Two of his antiphons, however, Mater Christi sanctissima and Christe Jesu, pastor bone, clearly show Josquin's influence. His four-voice In Nomine, the prototype of this English genre, is simply a transcription of the 'In nomine Domine' section of his Missa 'Gloria tibi Trinitas'.

Taverner was pre-eminent among English musicians of his day: he enriched and transformed the English florid style by drawing on its best qualities, as well as on some continental techniques, and produced simpler works of great poise and refinement.
                                                   GROVEmusic

Missa Gloria tibi Trinitas

Taverner Missa Gloria tibi Trinitas. Dum transisset Sabbatum I. Mater Christi sanctissima. O Wilhelme, pastor bone **Anonymous** Cantus firmus: Gloria tibi trinitas. Kyrie, 'Deus creator omnium'
Christ Church Cathedral Choir, Oxford / Stephen Darlington
Avie AV2123 (63' · DDD · T/t)   ⓕ**OO**⯈

The Choir of Christ Church could hardly have made a more ambitious return to recording after their valuable but variable series of Nimbus discs. Taverner's Mass is the *chef d'oeuvre* of the greatest composer of his time, yet it has never before been recorded by the kind of liturgical choir which he had in mind; this is a courageous and significant act of reclamation. Courageous, because Taverner's demands of phrase and melodic continuity are more subtle, but no less daunting in their own way, than those presented by Palestrina and Gombert. Performing at written pitch helps.

Stephen Darlington and his choir aren't afraid of a few dirty edges around the sound; this is a world away from the hygienic surfaces of the Gabrieli Consort or from the shapely halo of King's, Cambridge. The Christ Church trebles have a full-frontal attack to a phrase that is more commonly heard from middle-European choirs. That makes it more susceptible to the glare of the microphone, but the recording itself dares to go in closer than Nimbus ever did. The risk largely pays off in tutti passages of startling immediacy, contrasted with more solo verse sections than is usual (to rest tired voices?). Some distended cadences leave you wondering whether they can possibly have the puff to sustain them. Sometimes they can't (at the end of the first paragraph of the *Sanctus*); often they can (the 'Hosanna' at the end of the famous *Benedictus*). The motets are no less individual in concept and execution, including a cheeky but winning slide in *Mater Christi*; like the rest of the disc it will divide opinion, but it demands to be taken seriously.

Missa Mater Christi sanctissima

Hodie nobis caelorum Rex. Mater Christi sanctissima. Magnificat sexti toni. Nesciens mater. Quemadmodum a 6. Missa Mater Christi sanctissima. In nomine a 4
Fretwork (Wendy Gillespie, Richard Campbell *treble viols* Susanna Pell, Julia Hodgson, Richard Boothby *bass viols* William Hunt *great bass viol*) **The Sixteen / Harry Christophers**
Helios CDH55053 (65' · DDD · T/t) Ⓑ⊙

The Sixteen offer an impressive account of Taverner's five-part *Missa Mater Christi sanctissima*, based on his votive anthem of the same name. It's a lively and vigorous work, beautifully crafted, and this performance amply matches its craftsmanship. Harry Christophers attempts no liturgical reconstruction, concentrating instead upon sheer musical quality. Three female sopranos replace the boy trebles. The music is pitched up a tone, which has the effect of adding brilliance to every climax. He demonstrates the good acoustic of St Jude's in Hampstead – an acoustic of space and definition, ideal for the interweaving of the strands of early Tudor polyphony; indeed, clarity and a sense of space are hallmarks of the recording. The supporting programme of the Christmas responsory, *Hodie*, the votive anthem *Mater Christi* and a four-part *Magnificat* is completed – unexpectedly but most delightfully – by two pieces for viols.

Missa Sancti Wilhelmi

Missa Sancti Wilhelmi. Motets – O Wilhelme, pastor bone; Dum transisset Sabbatum; Ex eius tumba
The Sixteen / Harry Christophers
Helios CDH55055 (52' · DDD · T/t) Ⓑ

The *Missa Sancti Wilhelmi* isn't one of Taverner's best known works, but there's no reason why this should be the case. Though it doesn't have the sometimes rather wild melodic beauty of the six-voice Masses, it's nevertheless an impressive work in a more modern imitative style, in keeping with its model *O Wilhelme, pastor bone*. The Sixteen perform with their customary clarity and precision, and convey enthusiasm even in the somewhat syllabic *Gloria* and *Credo* movements of the Mass, something which isn't always easy to do. While both the 'Wilhelm' works and *Dum transisset Sabbatum* are among Taverner's later works, there's no doubt at all that *Ex eius tumba* is one of the earliest. It's firmly late medieval in style, and the intricate tracery of its construction makes a thought-provoking contrast to the pieces in a more 'continental' imitative style. At 15 minutes this is a substantial composition, and one can only be surprised that it's so little known. *Dum transisset Sabbatum* is, however, the high point of the disc, and if The Sixteen do not quite attain the ecstatic heights achieved in the recording by The Tallis Scholars, neither do they fail to rise to Taverner's inspiration.

Pyotr Ilyich Tchaikovsky
Russian 1840-1893

Tchaikovsky began piano studies at five and soon showed remarkable gifts; his childhood was also affected by an abnormal sensitivity. At 10 he was sent to the School of Jurisprudence at St Petersburg, where the family lived for some time. His parting from his mother was painful; further, she died when he was 14 – an event that may have stimulated him to compose. At 19 he took a post at the Ministry of Justice, where he remained for four years despite a long journey to western Europe and increasing involvement in music. In 1863 he entered the Conservatory, also undertaking private teaching. Three years later he moved to Moscow with a professorship of harmony at the new conservatory. Little of his music so far had pleased the conservative musical establishment or the more nationalist group, but his First Symphony had a good public reception when heard in Moscow in 1868.

Rather less successful was his first opera, The Voyevoda, given at the Bol'shoy in Moscow in 1869; Tchaikovsky later abandoned it and re-used material from it in his next, The Oprichnik. A severe critic was Balakirev, who suggested that he wrote a work on Romeo and Juliet: this was the Fantasy-Overture, several times rewritten to meet Balakirev's criticisms; Tchaikovsky's tendency to juxtapose blocks of material rather than provide organic transitions

Tchaikovsky

serves better in this programmatic piece than in a symphony as each theme stands for a character in the drama. Its expressive, well-defined themes and their vigorous treatment produced the first of his works in the regular repertory.

The Oprichnik won some success at St Petersburg in 1874, by when Tchaikovsky had won acclaim with his Second Symphony (which incorporates Ukrainian folktunes); he had also composed two string quartets (the first the source of the famous Andante cantabile), most of his next opera, Vakula the Smith, and of his First Piano Concerto, where contrasts of the heroic and the lyrical, between soloist and orchestra, clearly fired him. Originally intended for Nikolay Rubinstein, the head of Moscow Conservatory, who had much encouraged Tchaikovsky, it was dedicated to Hans von Bülow (who gave its première, in Boston) when Rubinstein rejected it as ill-composed and unplayable (he later recanted and became a distinguished interpreter of it). In 1875 came the carefully written Third Symphony and Swan Lake, commissioned by Moscow Opera. The next year a journey west took in Carmen in Paris, a cure at Vichy and the first complete Ring at Bayreuth; although deeply depressed when he reached home – he could not accept his homosexuality – he wrote the fantasia Francesca da Rimini and (an escape into the 18th century) the Rococo Variations for cello and orchestra. Vakula, which had won a competition, had its première that autumn. At the end of the year he was contacted by a wealthy widow, Nadezhda von Meck, who admired his music and was eager to give him financial security; they corresponded intimately for 14 years but never met.

Tchaikovsky, however, saw marriage as a possible solution to his sexual problems; and when contacted by a young woman who admired his music he offered (after first rejecting her) immediate marriage. It was a disaster: he escaped from her almost at once, in a state of nervous collapse, attempted suicide and went abroad. This was however the time of two of his greatest works, the Fourth Symphony and Eugene Onegin. The symphony embodies a 'fate' motif that recurs at various points, clarifying the structure; the first movement is one of Tchaikovsky's most individual with its hesitant, melancholy waltz-like main theme and its ingenious and appealing combination of this with the secondary ideas; there is a lyrical, intermezzo-like second movement and an ingenious third in which pizzicato strings play a main role, while the finale is impassioned if loose and melodramatic, with a folk theme pressed into service as second subject. Eugene Onegin, after Pushkin, tells of a girl's rejected approach to a man who fascinates her (the parallel with Tchaikovsky's situation is obvious) and his later remorse: the heroine Tatyana is warmly and appealingly drawn, and Onegin's hauteur is deftly conveyed too, all against a rural Russian setting which incorporates spectacular ball scenes, an ironic background to the private tragedies. The brilliant Violin Concerto also comes from the late 1870s.

The period 1878-84, however, represents a creative trough. He resigned from the conservatory and, tortured by his sexuality, could produce no music of real emotional force (the Piano Trio, written on Rubinstein's death, is a single exception). He spent some time abroad. But in 1884, stimulated by Balakirev, he produced his Manfred symphony, after

Byron. He continued to travel widely, and conduct; and he was much honoured. In 1888 the Fifth Symphony, similar in plan to the Fourth (though the motto theme is heard in each movement), was finished; a note of hysteria in the finale was recognised by Tchaikovsky himself. The next three years saw the composition of two ballets, the finely characterised Sleeping Beauty and the more decorative Nutcracker, and the opera The Queen of Spades, with its ingenious atmospheric use of Rococo music (it is set in Catherine the Great's Russia) within a work of high emotional tension. Its theatrical qualities ensured its success when given at St Petersburg in late 1890. The next year Tchaikovsky visited the USA; in 1892 he heard Mahler conduct Eugene Onegin at Hamburg. In 1893 he worked on his Sixth Symphony, to a plan – the first movement was to be concerned with activity and passion; the second, love; the third, disappointment; and the finale, death. It is a profoundly pessimistic work, formally unorthodox, with the finale haunted by descending melodic ideas clothed in anguished harmonies. It was performed on October 28. He died nine days later. **GROVE**music

Piano Concertos

No 1 in B flat minor; No 2 in G, Op 44; No 3 in E flat, Op 75

Complete Works for Piano and Orchestra
Oleg Marshev pf **Aalborg Symphony Orchestra / Owain Arwel Hughes**
Danacord ② DACOCD586/7 (134' · DDD) ⓕⓞ

Marshev returns to top form, all guns blazing, with the three piano concertos (the last two movements of No 3 orchestrated by Taneyev as the Andante and Finale in B flat/E flat, Op 79), the Concert Fantasia in G and Tchaikovsky's rarely heard early Allegro in C minor for piano and strings. The latter dates from his student days (1863-64) and lasts a mere two and a half minutes. It was unearthed only in 1965 and, while hardly significant music, is an interesting sign of things to come. David Fanning's comprehensive essay on the evolution of the six works on these two discs is a further reason to invest.

But to the main fare. The much-thumbed pages of the B flat minor Concerto (No 1) come up as fresh as paint without any startling revelations, a fine account, with all concerned at one with the spirit and the letter. No 2, however, recorded a year later in August 2002, is quite outstanding. The first movement's bracing tempo (a true allegro brillante e molto vivace) allows Marshev to revel in the massive piano-writing to properly heroic effect, the brittle tone that he prefers well pitted against the Aalborg players, especially the enthusiastic brass section. The highlight of the two discs, though, is the slow movement. Played without Ziloti's cuts, it is one of the most affecting accounts on disc. Alexander Zeiher, violin, and Vincent Stadlmaier, cello, are Marshev's partners.

With the Third Concerto (Marshev's first movement comparable with an old favourite –

Gary Graffman and Ormandy) and the *Concert Fantasia* handled in a similar vein, all 134 minutes of music come enthusiastically recommended.

Piano Concerto No 1ª. The Nutcracker – Suite, Op 71a (arr Economou)ᵇ
Martha Argerich, ᵇNicolas Economou pfs ªBerlin Philharmonic Orchestra / Claudio Abbado
DG 449 816-2GH (53' · DDD) Recorded live ᵇ1983

Ⓕ**O**▷

Tchaikovsky's First Concerto has already appeared twice on disc from Martha Argerich in complementary performances: live and helterskelter on Philips with Kondrashin (reviewed under Rachmaninov), studio and magisterial with Dutoit on DG. Now, finely recorded, here's a third, live recording with the BPO and Claudio Abbado surpassing even those earlier and legendary performances. Argerich has never sounded on better terms with the piano, more virtuoso yet engagingly human. Lyrical and insinuating, to a degree her performance seems to be made of the tumultuous elements themselves, of fire and ice, rain and sunshine. The Russians may claim this concerto for themselves, but even they will surely listen in disbelief, awed and – dare one say it – a trifle piqued. Listen to Argerich's *Allegro con spirito*, as the concerto gets under way, where her darting *crescendos* and *diminuendos* make the triplet rhythm speak with the rarest vitality and caprice. Her nervous reaching out towards further pianistic frays in the heart-easing second subject is pure Argerich and so are the octave storms in both the first and third movements that will have everyone, particularly her partners, tightening their seat belts. The cadenza is spun off with a hypnotic brilliance, the central *Prestissimo* from the *Andantino* becomes a true 'scherzo of fireflies', and the finale seems to dance off the page; a far cry from more emphatic Ukranian point-making and brutality.

For encores DG has reissued Argerich's 1983 performance of *The Nutcracker* where she's partnered by Nicolas Economou in his own arrangement, a marvel of scintillating pianistic prowess, imagination and finesse.

Violin Concerto in D, Op 35

Tchaikovsky Violin Concerto **Brahms** (arr Joachim) Hungarian Dances – No 1 in G minor; No 2 in D minor; No 4 in B-minor; No 7 in A
Sarah Chang vn **Jonathan Feldman** pf **London Symphony Orchestra / Sir Colin Davis**
EMI 503433-2 (49' · DDD)

Ⓕ**O**▷

The range of dynamic truthfulness conveyed in Sarah Chang's performance, helped by a clear, full, naturally balanced recording, brings not just momentary delight in individual phrases but cumulative gain, in a reading that strongly hangs together. Not only does she play with exceptionally pure tone, avoiding heavy coloration, but her individual artistry doesn't demand the wayward

---

TCHAIKOVSKY VIOLIN CONCERTO – IN BRIEF

Jascha Heifetz; Chicago SO / Fritz Reiner Ⓗ
RCA 09026 61495-2 (64' · ADD) Ⓜ**O**
A performance of outsize personality from Heifetz and Reiner. Coupled with this same partnership's sovereign account of the Brahms Concerto.

David Oistrakh; Staatskapelle Dresden / Ⓗ
Franz Konwitschny
DG ② 447 427-2GOR2 (142' · ADD) Ⓜ**O**
Oistrakh at his sublimely musical and involving best in a work that stood at the centre of his extensive concerto repertoire. DG's 1954 mono recording retains its remarkable sense of presence.

Leonid Kogan; Paris Conservatoire Orchestra / Constantin Silvestri
EMI Encore 574757-2 (69' · ADD) Ⓢ
Yet another fabulous Russian fiddler, this time Leonid Kogan, who plays with a muscular panache and unruffled security that rivet the attention. Silvestri lends splendidly feisty support.

Julia Fischer; Russian National Orchestra / Yakov Kreizberg
Pentatone PTC5186 095 (68' · DDD) Ⓜ**O**▷
A splendid recording from the hugely impressive young Julia Fischer. There's power and poetry in spades and the orchestra accompany with thrilling commitment.

Kyung Wha Chung; London SO / André Previn
Decca 425 080-2DCS (66' · ADD) Ⓜ**O**
Chung's engagingly svelte and warm-hearted account has barely aged at all. A longstanding favourite, this, with Previn and the LSO also on top form.

Sarah Chang; London SO / Sir Colin Davis
EMI 754753-2 (49' · DDD) Ⓕ**O**▷
For once the hype didn't mislead: soloist Sarah Chang was only 11 when she made this recording, and her vibrant tone and absolute technical security betoken a very special talent.

Vadim Repin; Kirov Orchestra / Valery Gergiev
Philips 473 343-2PM (72' · DDD) Ⓕ▷
Enterprisingly coupled with Miaskovsky's lovely Concerto, Repin's remake of the Tchaikovsky proves even more masterly and engrossing than his Erato predecessor.

Christian Tetzlaff; Russian National Orchestra / Kent Nagano
Pentatone PTC5186022 (68' · DDD) Ⓕ
Tetzlaff and Nagano take a gentler, more restrained approach than is customary, but there's no want of brilliance or brazen intensity.

TCHAIKOVSKY PIANO CONCERTO NO 1 – IN BRIEF

Vladimir Horowitz; NBC SO / Arturo Toscanini Ⓗ
Naxos 8 110671 (74' · ADD) ⓈⓄ
Horowitz's celebrated live 1941 Carnegie Hall recording with his father-in-law Toscanini serves up a potent mix of adrenalin-fuelled vigour and jaw-dropping virtuosity.

Solomon; Philharmonia Orch / Issay Dobrowen Ⓗ
Testament SBT1232 (60' · ADD) Ⓕ
A high-voltage yet nourishing reading from this incomparable British pianist. Definitely one to hear, as is Solomon's earlier 1929 recording with Harty and the Hallé (now refurbished on Naxos 8 110680).

Emil Gilels; Chicago SO / Fritz Reiner Ⓗ
RCA 09026 68530-2 (74' · ADD) Ⓜ
The work with which Gilels made his belated American début in October 1955. Later that same month, RCA shrewdly took the opportunity to preserve his by turns dazzling and poetic interpretation for posterity.

Yevgeny Sudbin pf
São Paulo Symphony Orchestra / John Neschling ⒻⓄ➔
BIS ⬜ BIS-SACD1588 (71' · DDD/DSD)
An astounding new account from the 26-year-old Sudbin who brings a freshness and power to this warhorse. He is particularly good at the mercurial changes of mood.

Martha Argerich; Berlin PO / Claudio Abbado
DG 449 816-2GH (53' · DDD) ⒻⓄ➔
Martha Argerich's smouldering pianism silences criticism and sparks off a hugely eloquent reponse from the Berliners under Claudio Abbado.

Mikhail Pletnev; Philharmonia Orchestra / Vladimir Fedoseyev
Virgin ② 561463-2 (112' · DDD) Ⓢ
Pletnev's imperious account represents tempting value, coming as it does with this same team's laudable survey of all of Tchaikovsky's output for piano and orchestra.

Lang Lang; Chicago SO / Daniel Barenboim
DG 474 291-2GH (59' · DDD) Ⓕ➔
Lang Lang's 2003 Proms performance was a big hit with the public, so this glittering and dapper – and unshowy – studio recording should find a wide, appreciative audience.

Nikolai Lugansky; Russian National Orchestra / Kent Nagano
Pentatone PTC5186022 (68' · DDD) Ⓕ
Lugansky, winner of the 1994 Tchaikovsky Competition, possesses quicksilver reflexes and a dark, burnished tone. A thoughtful performance, but with a passionate edge, too.

pulling-about often found in this work. She's enormously helped by the fresh, bright and dramatic accompaniment of the LSO under Sir Colin Davis. In the outer movements she conveys wit along with the power and poetry, and the intonation is immaculate. Brahms's *Hungarian Dances* are delectable, marked by the sort of naughty pointing of phrase and rhythm that tickles your musical funny-bone just as Kreisler always did. Here's a young artist who really does live up to the claims of the publicists.

Violin Concerto. Piano Concerto No 1
ᵃ**Christian Tetzlaff** vn ᵇ**Nikolai Lugansky** pf
Russian National Orchestra / Kent Nagano
Pentatone CD/SACD ⬜ PTC5186 022 (68' · DDD) Ⓕ

These are stimulating versions of two favourite concertos, which take a fresh interpretative approach. Nikolai Lugansky's conception is spacious, with pianist and conductor taking time to relish the music's puissance. The opening is broad and weighty. Then, although the first subject of the *Allegro* has a vividly Russian rhythmic character, in both the exposition and recapitulation much is made of the beauty of lyrical secondary material and the Romantic link with Tchaikovsky's *Romeo and Juliet*. The exquisitely delicate central *Andantino* is followed by a scintillating *Scherzando*. The finale bursts forth with irrepressible dash and virtuosity. When, near the close, the tempo broadens massively to make a hugely positive climax some forward impetus is lost, but Lugansky's bravura is thrilling.

Tchaikovsky's friendly opening for his Violin Concerto is shaped by Nagano in a mood of disarming simplicity, and the two main themes are invested with lyrical warmth. Tetzlaff bounces his bow with engaging lightness in the key passage (7'03") that Hanslick described as 'beating the violin black and blue', while the cadenza is played with such affectionate detail that it becomes a highlight of the work. Tetzlaff's playing throughout is polished and secure.

In both concertos the recording has the orchestra placed naturally within a warm concert hall acoustic.

Violin Concerto. Souvenir d'un lieu cher, Op 42 (arr Lascae)
Janine Jansen vn
Mahler Chamber Orchestra / Daniel Harding
Decca 478 0651DH (53' · DDD) Ⓕ➔

You can anticipate something individual and special from the way that Janine Jansen insinuates herself into the first subject of the Concerto – shyly confidential at first, building assertiveness with the double-stopped reprise. Everything here is vital, un-hackneyed. And yet Jansen is very much the old-fashioned romantic. Her way with tempo *rubato* and with dynamic contrasts is unashamedly free. She spins sound like an excellent singer, taking it away *subito pianissimo* in true *bel canto* fashion. She does so quite demurely, suggestively, with the second subject of the first movement and again with the second movement canzonetta, which is lovely – and natural.

There's an intimacy about her playing which sits well with the Mahler Chamber Orchestra; not that the introverted elements of the concerto in any way upstage the extrovert. In many ways it's the Cossack-dancing finale that sends this version spinning into the orbit of the very best available. The partnership with Daniel Harding could hardly be tighter. No rhetorical slacking of tempo as Jansen responds to the fiery orchestral introduction – she presses forward with a will. The gritty second theme is very much a coarse folksy baritone against hang-dog bassoon, and come the second round of dancing, Harding has the orchestral *pizzicati* really kicking up dust.

A smashing performance, then, with only marginal disappointment concerning the recorded sound – crisp and immediate, but of a dry ambience without much atmosphere. The supporting piece – *Souvenir d'un lieu cher* – gives us the chance to hear the concerto's original slow movement in a lovely arrangement for violin and strings by the Romanian-Dutch conductor Alexandru Lascae. Again, the sense of Jansen as the first among equals makes for especially telling interplay with her colleagues.

Symphonies

No 1 in G minor (Winter Daydreams), Op 13 **No 2** in C minor (Little Russian), Op 17 **No 3** in D (Polish), Op 29; **No 4** in F minor, Op 36; **No 5** in E minor, Op 64; **No 6** in B minor (Pathétique), Op 74

Complete Symphonies

Symphonies Nos 1-6. Violin Concerto in D, Op 35[a]. Piano Concerto No 1 in B flat minor, Op 23de. 1812 Overture, Op 49. Capriccio italien, Op 45. Eugene Onegin – Polonaise; Waltz. Marche slave, Op 31. The Nutcracker – Suite, Op 71[a]. Romeo and Juliet Fantasy Overture. Serenade in C, Op 48. The Sleeping Beauty – Suite. Swan Lake – Suite. Variations on a Rococo Theme, Op 33[c]
[a]**Christian Ferras**, [b]**Michel Schwalbé** *vns* [c]**Mstislav Rostropovich** *vc* [d]**Sviatoslav Richter** *pf* **Berlin Philharmonic Orchestra**, [e]**Vienna Symphony Orchestra / Herbert von Karajan**
DG Ⓑ 463 774-2GB8 (531' · ADD/DDD) Recorded 1962-80   ⒷⓄⓄ

Karajan was unquestionably a great Tchaikovsky conductor. Yet although he recorded the last three symphonies many times, he did not turn to the first three until the end of the 1970s, and then proved an outstanding advocate. In the Mendelssohnian opening movement of the First, the tempo may be brisk, but the music's full charm is displayed and the melancholy of the Andante is touchingly caught. Again at the opening of the Little Russian (No 2), horn and bassoon capture that special Russian colouring, as they do in the

engaging *Andantino marziale*, and the crisp articulation in the first movement allegro is bracing. The sheer refinement of the orchestral playing in the scherzos of all three symphonies is a delight, and finales have great zest with splendid bite and precision in the fugato passages and a convincing closing peroration.

The so-called *Polish* Symphony (No 3) is the least tractable of the canon, but again Karajan's apt tempos and the precision of ensemble makes the first movement a resounding success. The *Alla tedesca* brings a hint of Brahms, but the Slavic dolour of the *Andante elegiaco* is unmistakeable and its climax blooms rapturously. No doubt the reason these early symphonies sound so fresh is because the Berlin orchestra was not over-familiar with them, and clearly enjoyed playing them. The sound throughout is excellent. It gets noticeably fiercer in the Fourth Symphony, recorded a decade earlier, but is still well balanced. The first movement has a compulsive forward thrust, and the breakneck finale is viscerally thrilling. The slow movement is beautifully played but just a trifle bland. Overall, though, this is impressive and satisfying, especially the riveting close.

DG has chosen the 1965 recording of the Fifth, rather than the mid-'70s version, and they were right to do so. It's marvellously recorded (in the Jesus-Christus Kirche): the sound has all the richness and depth one could ask and the performance too is one of Karajan's very finest. There's some indulgence of the second-subject string melody of the first movement. But the slow movement is gloriously played from the horn solo onwards, and the second re-entry of the Fate theme is so dramatic that it almost makes one jump. The delightful Waltz brings the kind of elegant warmth and detail from the violins that's a BPO speciality, and the finale, while not rushed Mravinsky fashion, still carries all before it and has power and dignity at the close.

The *Pathétique* was a very special work for Karajan (as it was for the Berlin Philharmonic) and his 1964 performance is one of his greatest recordings. The reading as a whole avoids hysteria, yet the resolution of the passionate climax of the first movement sends shivers down the spine, while the finale has a comparable eloquence, and the March/*Scherzo*, with ensemble wonderfully crisp and biting, brings an almost demonic power to the coda. Again the sound is excellent, full-bodied in the strings and with plenty of sonority for the trombones.

The *String Serenade* is digital, brightly recorded in the Philharmonie in 1980, but naturally balanced. Marvellous playing. The Waltz, with a most felicitous control of *rubato*, is the highlight, and the *Elégie* is certainly ardent; and if the first movement could have been more neatly articulated, the finale has tremendous bustle and energy. As for the *concertante* works, the account of the glorious *Rococo* Variations with Rostropovich is another classic of the gramophone, even though it uses the truncated score. The First Piano Concerto is a disappointment, with Richter and Karajan failing to strike sparks as a part-

TCHAIKOVSKY'S SYMPHONIES NOS 4-6 – IN BRIEF

Berlin PO / Herbert von Karajan
DG ② 453 088-2GD2 (139' · ADD) Ⓜ🔘▶
Of Karajan's countless recordings of Tchaikovsky's three last symphonies, this set from the mid-1970s is probably the finest. With excellent playing by the BPO it certainly makes a safe recommendation, neither over-emotional nor cool. (His 1960s set is also available on a budget-price DG set, but it's worth going for this one at much the same price.)

Philharmonia / Vladimir Ashkenazy
Decca ② 443 844-2DF2 (136' · DDD) Ⓜ
Among Ashkenazy's earliest recordings as a conductor, this trilogy demonstrates his effectiveness of the podium. There's a really refreshing feeling here, with the Philharmonia playing superbly.

Leningrad PO / Kurt Sanderling (No 4),
Evgeny Mravinsky
DG mono ② 447 423-2GDO2 (133' · ADD) Ⓜ🔘🔘
Staggering performancs from the great St Petersburg orchestra. Everything is held on a very tight rein, but the passion and intensity comes through with incredible force. The *Pathétique* leaves you absolutely shattered.

Leningrad PO / Evgeny Mravinsky
DG ② 419 745-2GH2 (129' · DDD) Ⓕ🔘🔘🔘▶
Ⓖ Mravinsky re-recorded Nos 5 and 6 when on tour in the UK, and also set down No 4 – in stereo. It may lack the visceral thrill of the mono set but here we're talking high-intensity performances, way above the norm. These are stunning, with playing of astounding virtuosity.

Oslo PO / Mariss Jansons
Chandos CHAN8361, CHAN8351, CHAN8446
(42', 43' & 44' · DDD) Ⓜ🔘🔘▶
The three individual Chandos CDs from Jansons's cycle are included here simply because they are so fine, and deserve to be considered in any discussion of the last three Tchaikovsky symphonies. The Fifth is earth-shattering; the other two scarcely less involving. And, given the extraordinarily high standard of sound Chandos achieved here, these are major performances – it's a shame Chandos has yet to box them up more economically.

Orchestra dell'Accademia Nazionale di Santa
Cecilia (Rome) / Antonio Pappano
EMI ② 353258-2 (127' · DDD) Ⓕ🔘▶
Recorded live in front of a very quiet Rom,an auideinces, these are wonderfully fresh readings, with a nice feeling for Tchaikovsky's *legato*. If they lean towards the vocal rather than the symphonic that's no hardship.

nership. In spite of brilliant solo playing, the first movement lacks supporting tension in the orchestra, and in the finale you can sense Richter wanting to press forward, while Karajan seems to hold back: the coda itself hangs fire in the orchestra. Similarly Ferras was not an ideal choice for the Violin Concerto. Not all will take to his somewhat febrile timbre, with its touches of near-schmaltz. But the performance as a whole works better than the Piano Concerto.

Romeo and Juliet is finely done, passionate and dramatic, if not quite so spontaneously inspired as Karajan's early VPO version for Decca, especially at the opening. But *Marche slave*, ideally paced, is very successful, sombre and exciting by turns. *Capriccio italien* and *1812* are both brilliantly played, and the triptych of ballet suites can be recommended almost without reservation, with the *Sleeping Beauty* suite memorable for some very exciting climaxes.

Even with the reservations about the two concertos, this bargain box is a fine investment, and certainly value for money. The documentation is excellent.

Symphonies – Nos 1-6. Manfred Symphony, Op 58.
Capriccio Italien, Op 45. Serenade in C, Op 48.
The Tempest, Op 18. Romeo and Juliet. Eugene
Onegin – Polonaise
Bournemouth Symphony Orchestra /
Andrew Litton
Virgin Classics ⑥ 561893-2 (420' · DDD) Ⓢ🔘🔘▶

Here's another of those extraordinary Virgin bargain boxes, offered at an astonishingly low price. These Tchaikovsky performances would be highly recommendable if they cost twice as much, while the recordings – realistically set back in a concert hall acoustic – are superb, full-bodied, and wide ranging and brilliant. The playing of the Bournemouth orchestra may not always be quite as polished as, say, the BPO for Karajan, but it's still very, very good indeed: ensemble is as keen as it's passionately responsive. Moreover Litton has a natural ear for Tchaikovskian detail – time and again he draws the listener to revel in those delightful orchestral touches with which Tchaikovsky embroiders his melodies.

Litton gets off to an outstanding start with Nos 1 and 2, where the atmosphere is imbued with bonhomie and high spirits; he readily disguises the structural flaws of the *Polish* Symphony with his geniality and a clever ebb and flow of tempos; in No 4 you're more aware of the slight distancing of the sound, which he matches by his spacious tempo in the first movement; the same broad approach works less well in No 5, where you need more impetus in the outer movements; but he's back on form in No 6. There the phrasing of the first movement's secondary theme is ravishing, and the climax is as powerful as the cumulative peak of the *scherzo*/march. In *Manfred* his emphasis is on its programmatic basis, with tenderly delicate splendidly dramatic moments.

The extra items are all enjoyably spontaneous, the *Capriccio italien* has visceral thrills and panache, the *String Serenade* is warmly romantic; and both *Romeo and Juliet*, matching romantic pathos with passion, and the underrated but masterly Shakespearean *Tempest* are among the highlights. Even if you have much of this repertoire already, this set remains very enticing.

Complete Symphonies. Manfred
BBC Philharmonic Orchestra / Gianandrea Noseda
Chandos Download-only available from www.theclassicalshop.net ⓈⓄⒷ

Originally broadcast as part of BBC Radio 3's Tchaikovsky Experience, these performances are now being offered for download. Movements are available individually for £1 to £2.50 (depending on duration), though if you buy all six symphonies and *Manfred* as a set, the price is a mere £15. A bargain, certainly, though everything's relative in this repertory and Noseda's interpretations are wildly inconsistent. Let's consider each in turn.

No 1: Sloppily played, heavy-handed and shapeless. Tempi in the outer movements are too slow to allow for even a hint of Mendelssohnian lightness, and the *Scherzo* is anything but *giocoso*. The beginning of the slow movement, with its misty, muted strings, is lovely, but after that the playing is strangely tentative.

No 2: The BBC Philharmonic sounds like a different orchestra here: disciplined, fiery. Noseda discovers dark Mussorgskian echoes in the first movement's slow introduction, and the *Allegro* bristles with excitement. With a charmingly perky *Andantino marziale*, an intelligently phrased *Scherzo* and a frolicsome finale, the result is exhilarating music-making from start to finish.

No 3: There's some sensitive, affectionate playing here, especially in the first movement and in the delectably bubbly *Alla tedesca*. But the slow movement seems to meander and both *Scherzo* and finale require far greater thrust.

No 4: If the opening fanfare represents fate, it seems a puny, timid force in this interpretation. Where's the weight and bite? Even the fanfare's surprise recurrence in the finale fails to startle; Muti, for one, makes it overwhelming.

No 5: An impressively taut, coherent and flexible performance. The *scherzando* elements are nicely integrated into the Waltz. If only the finale were wilder.

No 6: Beginning with the shattering chord at the start of the first movement's central development section, Noseda's interpretation takes wing, and the remainder of the movement is scorching in its fervour. There's grief lurking under the second movement's elegant surface and manic energy in the march-like *Scherzo*. As with the Fifth Symphony, the *lamentoso* finale burns at a slightly lower temperature, yet the overall effect is still devastating.

Manfred :There are a few pretty moments here – the *Scherzo*'s Trio is attractively coloured, for example – but Noseda strains to hold the diverse strands of this vast programmatic symphony together. Jansons's incisive and atmospheric account is far more persuasive.

If it's a download of the Tchaikovsky symphonies you're after, note that Jansons's cycle is also available in MP3 format from the same source. It's well worth the additional cost.

Symphonies – selected

Symphony No 1
Oslo Philharmonic Orchestra / Mariss Jansons
Chandos CHAN8402 (44' · DDD) ⒻⓄⒷ

Symphony No 2. Capriccio italien, Op 45
Oslo Philharmonic Orchestra / Mariss Jansons
Chandos CHAN8460 (48' · DDD) ⒻⓄⒷ

The composer gave the work the title *Winter Daydreams*, and also named the first two movements. The opening *Allegro tranquillo* he subtitled 'Dreams of a winter journey', while the *Adagio* bears the inscription 'Land of desolation, land of mists'. A *Scherzo* and finale round off a conventional four-movement symphonic structure. In the slow movement Jansons inspires a performance of expressive warmth and tenderness, while the *Scherzo* is managed with great delicacy and sensitivity. Both the opening movement and finale are invested with vigour and passion, and everywhere the orchestral playing is marvellously confident and disciplined.

Jansons also has the full measure of the Second Symphony. It's a direct performance – the first movement *allegro* is relatively steady, but never sounds too slow, because of crisp rhythmic pointing – and the second movement goes for charm and felicity of colour. The finale is properly exuberant, with the secondary theme full of character, and there's a fine surge of adrenalin at the end. The *Capriccio italien*, a holiday piece in which the composer set out to be entertaining, is also played with great flair and the hint of vulgarity in the Neapolitan tune isn't shirked. Again the closing pages produce a sudden spurt of excitement which is particularly satisfying. The recording here is just short of Chandos's finest – the massed violins could be sweeter on top, but the hall resonance is right for this music.

Symphony No 2, 'Little Russian'. Festival Overture on the Danish National Hymn. The Storm. Overture in F
Gothenburg Symphony Orchestra / Neeme Järvi
BIS BIS-SACD1418 (72'· DDD/DSD) ⒻⓄⓄⒷ

The Gothenburg Symphony Orchestra, under their longtime music director Neeme Järvi, give an outstanding performance of the *Little Russian* Symphony, beautifully played and paced and immaculately recorded, though it lacks a little on felicitous detail.

Järvi's flowing tempo for the long opening *Andante* is reassuring and his free expressiveness is most persuasive, the crisp attack of the *Allegro*, with its Ukrainian themes, bringing echoes of Tchaikovsky's ballet music. Though the *Andantino marziale* is on the brisk side, the rhythmic

lift again is most persuasive. The *Scherzo* is fresh
and light and the opening of the finale has ample
weight to contrast with the lightness of the second subject, its cross-rhythms suggesting Cuban
rhythms. The way Järvi presses forward as the
climaxes build adds to the excitement.

The overture inspired by Ostrovsky's play *The
Storm* is by far the most inspired of the three and
is given a powerful performance. The Overture
in F is a student work whose deft orchestration
points to the mature Tchaikovsky while the one
on the Danish national anthem suffers from its
relatively uninteresting theme. It's not nearly as
striking as the Russian national anthem, with
which it is entwined – rather as the *Marseillaise* is
in the *1812*. Tchaikovsky thought it a much
more successful piece though it is hard to justify
the pompous final repeat of the Danish theme,
fortissimo, even in a performance as well judged
as Järvi's.

Symphony No 4
Oslo Philharmonic Orchestra / Mariss Jansons
Chandos CHAN8361 (42' · DDD)　　　　Ⓕ🔘➡

A high emotional charge runs through Jansons's
performance of the Fourth, yet this rarely seems
to be an end in itself. There's always a balancing
concern for the superb craftsmanship of Tchaikovsky's writing: the shapeliness of the phrasing;
the superb orchestration, scintillating and subtle
by turns; and most of all Tchaikovsky's marvellous sense of dramatic pace. Rarely has the first
movement possessed such a strong sense of
tragic inevitability, or the return of the 'fate'
theme in the finale sounded so logical. The playing of the Oslo Philharmonic Orchestra is first
rate: there are some gorgeous woodwind solos
and the brass achieve a truly Tchaikovskian
intensity. Recordings are excellent.

Symphonies Nos 4-6
**Leningrad Philharmonic Orchestra /
Evgeny Mravinsky**
DG ② 4775911 (129' · ADD) Recorded 1960
　　　　　　　　　　　　　　　　Ⓕ🔘🔘➡

 These recordings are landmarks not
just of Tchaikovsky interpretation but
of recorded orchestral performances in
general. The Leningrad Philharmonic plays like
a wild stallion only just held in check by the
willpower of its master. Every smallest movement is placed with fierce pride; at any moment
it may break into such a frenzied gallop that you
hardly know whether to feel exhilarated or terrified. The whipping up of excitement towards
the fateful outbursts in Symphony No 4 is astonishing – not just for the discipline of the *stringen-
dos* themselves, but for the pull of psychological
forces within them. Symphony No 5 is also mercilessly driven, and pre-echoes of Shostakovichian hysteria are particularly strong in the
coda's knife-edge of triumph and despair. No
less powerfully evoked is the stricken tragedy of

the *Pathétique*. Rarely, if ever, can the prodigious
rhythmical inventiveness of these scores have
been so brilliantly demonstrated.

The fanatical discipline isn't something one
would want to see casually emulated but it's
applied in a way which sees far into the soul of
the music and never violates its spirit. Strictly
speaking there's no real comparison with
Mariss Jansons's Chandos issues, despite the
fact that Jansons had for long been Mravinsky's
assistant in Leningrad. His approach is warmer,
less detailed, more classical, and in its way very
satisfying. Not surprisingly there are deeper
perspectives in the Chandos recordings, but
DG's refurbishing has been most successful,
enhancing the immediacy of sound so appropriate to the lacerating intensity of the interpretations.

Symphony No 5
Oslo Philharmonic Orchestra / Mariss Jansons
Chandos CHAN8351 (43' · DDD)　　　　Ⓕ🔘

With speeds which are fast but never breathless
and with the most vivid recording imaginable,
this is as exciting an account as we have had of
this symphony. In no way does this performance
suggest anything but a metropolitan orchestra,
and Jansons keeps reminding one of his background in Leningrad in the great years of
Mravinsky and the Philharmonic. Nowhere
does the link with Mravinsky emerge more
clearly than in the finale, where he adopts a
tempo very nearly as hectic as Mravinsky's on
his classic DG recording. In the first movement
he resists any temptation to linger, preferring to
press the music on, and the result sounds totally
idiomatic. In the slow movement Jansons again
prefers a steady tempo, but treats the second
theme with delicate rubato and builds the climaxes steadily, not rushing his fences, building
the final one even bigger than the first. In the
finale it's striking that he follows Tchaikovsky's
notated slowings rather than allowing extra *rallentandos* – the bravura of the performance finds
its natural culmination.

The Oslo string ensemble is fresh, bright and
superbly disciplined, while the wind soloists are
generally excellent. The Chandos sound is very
specific and well focused despite a warm reverberation, real-sounding and three-dimensional
with more clarity in *tuttis* than the rivals.

Symphony No 5. Romeo and Juliet
Royal Philharmonic Orchestra / Daniele Gatti
Harmonia Mundi HMU90 7381 (66' · DDD)　　Ⓕ🔘

In Daniele Gatti's performance of Tchaikovsky's Fifth the detail of the wind scoring is
continually and vividly revealed, helped by some
superb playing from the RPO's soloists. Tempos are close to the composer's metronome
markings, somewhat faster than usually heard.
The result in the first movement is invigorating,
the forward thrust carrying from beginning to

end. The primary secondary theme is graceful and Romantic, rather than ardently passionate in a Slavic manner. The great climaxes of the slow movement are spacious but not viscerally overwhelming, and the powerful interruptions of the motto theme are less theatrical than usual. The Abbey Road recording is first class, full-bodied, with resplendent brass, and glowing woodwind and horns. Perhaps the massed violins lack a little weight, but the overall sonority has the necessary depth and amplitude for Tchaikovsky.

Gatti's acount of *Romeo and Juliet* is superbly characterised. It opens chillingly, then introduces the great love theme very gently, followed by the most delicate moonlight sequence. The central climax, with the reintroduction of the Friar Lawrence theme, is terrific, and the love theme blooms gloriously in a great curving sweep of violins. What more can you ask?

Symphony No 5, Op 64. Francesca da Rimini, Op 32
Simón Bolívar Youth Orchestra of Venezuela / Gustavo Dudamel
DG 477 8022GH (74' · DDD)
Recorded live in 2008   ℗ **OO**▸

A sinewy, uninhibited Tchaikovsky Fifth – you'd expect nothing less from this source. Dudamel and his young players feed on one another; the exchange of energy is extraordinary. Tchaikovsky's impulsive changes of tempo feel more naturally impetuous while the phrasing is directly reflected in the sound: just listen to the yearning second theme of the *Allegro con anima* and the way that the sheen on the violin sound intensifies with the release.

But as with their famous Prom a few years back, it's not just the fireworks but the inwardness of this performance that brings the biggest surprises. The great *Andante cantabile* horn theme (so soft and consoling) emerges almost imperceptibly from the somnolent harmonies of the lower strings at the start of the movement. It's like discovering Romeo and Juliet before the unwelcome dawn – the atmosphere is extraordinarily charged. And what sweep the Simón Bolívar string-players lend the second theme, not least in the climactic return. As for the finale – well, there's nothing like headstrong youngsters to reignite an old favourite: the *allegro vivace* comes off the starting-blocks at such a blistering pace as to register a nanosecond of disbelief that such a tempo is even possible.

But the real disbelief is still to come. To better this account of *Francesca da Rimini* you need to go back to Stokowski or Bernstein. As if the descent into Dante's inferno isn't intense enough – Dudamel's pacing of this lengthy introduction is quite masterly – the whirlwind at its core glows white hot with astonishing virtuosity displayed from every department. Then the loveliest of all Tchaikovsky's lyric creations brings a limpid melancholy from the solo clarinet – truly times of happiness recalled in misery. And though Dudamel's tempo *rubato* in the

string-led approach to the climax may not be as abandoned as Bernstein's, it's still pretty brave. Hearing is believing in the coda as the trombones and trumpets tumble into the abyss. Exciting? Deliriously so.

Symphony No 6. Marche slave, Op 31. The Seasons, Op 37b. Six morceaux composés sur un seul thème, Op 21 The Sleeping Beauty (arr Pletnev) – excerpts
Russian National Orchestra / Mikhail Pletnev *pf*
Virgin Classics ② 561636-2 (138' · DDD)   ℗ **OOO**▸

There's no denying that Russian orchestras bring a special intensity to Tchaikovsky, and to this Symphony in particular. But, in the past, we have had to contend with lethal, vibrato-laden brass and variable Soviet engineering. Not any more. Pianist Mikhail Pletnev formed this orchestra in 1990 from the front ranks of the major Soviet orchestras, and the result here is now regarded as a classic. The brass still retain their penetrating power, and an extraordinary richness and solemnity before the Symphony's coda; the woodwind make a very melancholy choir; and the strings possess not only the agility to cope with Pletnev's aptly death-defying speed for the third movement march, but beauty of tone for Tchaikovsky's yearning *cantabiles*. Pletnev exerts the same control over his players as he does over his fingers, to superb effect. The dynamic range is huge and comfortably reproduced with clarity, natural perspectives, a sense of instruments playing in a believable acoustic space, and a necessarily higher volume setting than usual. *Marche slave*'s final blaze of triumph, in the circumstances, seems apt.

Pletnev finds colours and depths in *The Seasons* that few others have found even intermittently. Schumann is revealed as a major influence, not only on the outward features of the style but on the whole expressive mood and manner. And as a display of pianism the whole set is outstanding, all the more so because his brilliance isn't purely egoistic. Even when he does something unmarked – like attaching the hunting fanfares of 'September' to the final unison of 'August' – he's so persuasive that you could believe that this is somehow inherent in the material. This is all exceptional playing, and the recording is ideally attuned to all its moods and colours.

Manfred Symphony, Op 58

Manfred Symphony. The Voyevoda
Royal Liverpool Philharmonic Orchestra / Vasily Petrenko
Naxos 8 570568 (69' · DDD)   ⓈOOO▸

Petrenko's *Manfred* emerges from the gothic greys of the opening wind chorale to vent his heartache in an emotive surge of string sound. And to ensure that we've grasped the measure of his despair, he repeats himself. Petrenko's Byronic petulance makes something really stirring of the self-loathing – Tchaikovsky's as much as that of Byron's anti-hero. But the real miracle of this first movement is the vision of idealised love emerging so tenderly in what one might normally call the development. The palest clarinet against muted *tremolando* strings takes us directly to the heart of the matter, and Petrenko and his orchestra don't disappoint. Likewise in the epic coda, where anguish is again writ large in overreaching horns and trumpets. No superfluous tam-tam, thankfully.

The dazzling apparitions of the second movement's light-catching waterfall are sharply etched, and if Petrenko has a rather leisurely idea of what constitutes *Andante con moto* in the third movement, he can't be blamed for loving this vintage Tchaikovsky melody too much. The playing, again, is lovely. Petrenko also keeps his head in the inferno of the finale, emphasising Tchaikovsky the classicist in the hard-working fugue. The 'phantom' organ, though impressively caught here, gets no better, but is quickly forgotten amid the serenity of the final pages.

The opening pages of *The Voyevoda* seem to suggest a psychological summit meeting between Manfred and Hermann from *The Queen of Spades*. Its galloping obsessiveness ratchets up the torment again. The bass clarinet gives everyone the evil eye; no wonder Tchaikovsky tried to destroy it. This is impressive – and, at Naxos's pricing, not to be missed.

Manfred Symphony
London Philharmonic Orchestra /
Vladimir Jurowski
LPO LPO0009 (59' · DDD) Recorded live 2004   Ⓜ🅑➙

With a work as episodic as the *Manfred Symphony*, particularly in the long first movement, there is much to be said for a live recording, with dramatic tension more readily sustained. Vladimir Jurowski, the LPO's brilliant young principal conductor, directs a powerful performance in which the tension never flags. Recorded live, the sound is clear and well balanced.

In his characteristic manner, Jurowski presses the music hard, generally to impressive effect, except that he goes too far in the second-movement *Scherzo*. At his hectic speed it loses much of its sparkle and gives little idea of the programme which the composer was illustrating – the Alpine Fairy appearing to Byron's hero Manfred. Compared with Pletnev (above) – outstanding and made in the studio – the ensemble is not as crisp though more than acceptable by general standards. The 'live-ness' offers ample compensation, though, making this a strong recommendation at mid-price and a welcome addition to the orchestra's own label.

Swan Lake, Op 20

Swan Lake
Montreal Symphony Orchestra / Charles Dutoit
Decca ② 436 212-2DH2 (154' · DDD)   Ⓕ🅞🅑➙

No one wrote more beautiful and danceable ballet music than Tchaikovsky, and this account of *Swan Lake* is a delight throughout. This isn't only because of the quality of the music, which is here played including additions the composer made after the première, but also thanks to the richly idiomatic playing of Charles Dutoit and his Montreal orchestra in the superb and celebrated location of St Eustache's Church in that city. Maybe some conductors have made the music even more earthily Russian, but the Russian ballet tradition in Tchaikovsky's time was chiefly French and the most influential early production of this ballet, in 1895, was choreographed by the Frenchman Marius Petipa. Indeed, the symbiosis of French and Russian elements in this music (and story) is one of its great strengths, the refinement of the one being superbly allied to the vigour of the other, notably in such music as the 'Russian Dance' with its expressive violin solo. This is a profoundly romantic reading of the score, and the great set pieces such as the Waltz in Act 1 and the marvellous scene of the swans on a moonlit lake that opens Act 2 are wonderfully evocative; yet they do not overshadow the other music, which supports them as gentler hills and valleys might surround and enhance magnificent, awe-inspiring peaks, the one being indispensable to the other. You do not have to be a ballet aficionado to fall under the spell of this wonderful music, which here receives a performance that blends passion with an aristocratic refinement and is glowingly recorded.

Additional recommendation

Swan Lake
Russian State Symphony Orchestra / Yablonsky
Naxos ② 8 555873/4 (148' · DDD)   Ⓢ🅑➙
This complete *Swan Lake* is thoroughly recommendable and most enjoyable, both as a performance and as a recording. The Orchestra is obviously utterly at home, as is their excellent conductor, whose tempi can hardly be faulted. This is an obligatory bargain buy.

The Sleeping Beauty, Op 66

The Sleeping Beauty
Czecho-Slovak State Philharmonic Orchestra /
Andrew Mogrelia
Naxos ③ 8 550490/92 (174' · DDD)   Ⓢ🅞🅑➙

Andrew Mogrelia is clearly a ballet conductor to his fingertips. His account of *The Sleeping Beauty* isn't only dramatic, when called for, but graceful and full of that affectionate warmth and detail which readily conjure up the stage imagery. Moreover, the House of Arts in Košice seems to have just the right acoustics for this work. If the sound is too brilliant the louder passages of Tchaikovsky's score can easily hector the ear; if the effect is too mellow, the result can become bland. Neither happens here – the ear is seduced throughout and Mogrelia leads the listener on from number to number with an easy spontaneity. The woodwind playing is delightful (try track 9 with its 'singing canaries' – so like Delibes in its scoring). At the end of Act 1 the Lilac Fairy's tune is given a spacious, *frisson*-creating apotheosis. The alert Introduction to Acts 2 and 3 brings crisp brass and busy strings on the one hand, arresting hunting horns on the other, and what sparkling zest there is in the strings for the following 'Blind-man's buff' sequence, while the famous Act 2 Waltz has splendid rhythmic lift. Act 3 is essentially a great extended *Divertissement*, with Tchaikovsky's imagination at full stretch through some two dozen characterful dance numbers of every balletic flavour, are all played here with fine style.

Irrespective of price, this is a first choice among current recordings of the score, and you get two and a half hours of music. The value is even more remarkable when the excellent notes clearly relate the ballet's action to each of the 65 separate cues.

The Sleeping Beauty
BBC Symphony Orchestra / Gennadi Rozhdestvensky
BBC Legends/IMG Artists ② BBCL4091-2
(141' · ADD) Recorded live 1979   Ⓜ**OO**🔁

David Brown, Tchaikovsky's eminent biographer, thought that on balance *The Sleeping Beauty* was the finest of the three great ballet scores. But as Diaghilev found to his cost when he mounted it in London in 1921, it's a very extended work and suffers from a storyline in which not a great deal happens. Performing it is as a complete orchestral work in the concert hall is probably not the best way to approach the work but, if it's to be performed in this way, Rozhdestvensky is just the man for it. In this recording he shows just how to hold together Tchaikovsky's remarkably diverse score as a symphonic entity by creating a consistent narrative momentum without ever over-driving.

The very opening is enormously dramatic and arresting, and then the petite Lilac Fairy appears in her delectably delicate orchestral apparel. Rozhdestvensky is a master of this kind of contrast. Sample the daintiness of string texture at the opening of the 'Pas de six' (track 3), the delicious piccolo and *pizzicato*s for the 'Singing canary' (track 8), so reminiscent of Delibes, followed by the sheer energy of track 9 ('Violente').

The ballet ends grandiloquently, but with great majesty, and one is left in wonder: there isn't a single number in which Tchaikovsky's imagination fails him.

Several other versions of this ballet are available on CD, but Rozhdestvensky is even finer, and the BBC recording is remarkably good, with plenty of amplitude, a warm string patina, glowing woodwind and a natural concert-hall balance. Highly recommended.

The Sleeping Beauty, Op 66 – excerpts. The Nutcracker, Op 71 – excerpts. Swan Lake, Op 20 – excerpts
Royal Liverpool Philharmonic Orchestra / Vasily Petrenko
Avie AV2139 (58' · DDD)   Ⓕ**OO**

Vasily Petrenko was a shrewd choice of principal conductor for the Royal Liverpool Philharmonic Orchestra. His promise is clear, his reputation growing. These bonbons from the Tchaikovsky ballets don't offer too many surprises in terms of choice (except perhaps the exclusion of the "Rose Adagio" from *Sleeping Beauty*) but they do clearly demonstrate the difference Petrenko is already making to the quality of the RLPO playing.

Essentially it's a personalisation process where the articulation of the wind voices (listen, for instance, to the "Entrée" from the Bluebird Pas de quatre in *Sleeping Beauty*) takes on a really idiomatic colour and cast and the string-playing sounds freer and fuller. Petrenko's watchwords are shape and purpose and clarity; there is an elegance and inner life to the playing making everything sound freshly minted. The three great waltzes are pivotal, of course, and they glide across Tchaikovsky's imperial ballroom with all due suavity and opulence.

The *Swan Lake* highlights wipe the floor with Gergiev's pale showing in the complete ballet (Decca): the nobility of the horns emblazoned across the opening Scene, the swagger and sophistication of the national dances with a brilliant trumpet solo in the *Danse napolitaine* and a delightfully folksy lilt to the contrasting Trio of the Mazurka.

The climactic modulation of the Lilac Fairy's spellbinding pronouncement that love will redeem all is nailed with all the assurance of a young master, but what is thus far missing if you compare someone like Rostropovich in this music (his *Sleeping Beauty* highlights with the Berlin Philharmonic on DG are simply sensational) is the stamp of real temperament, a daring born of long and intimate familiarity. Give him time. All the signs are favourable.

1812 Overture, Op 49

Tchaikovsky 1812 Overture[a]. Capriccio italien,   Ⓗ
Op 45[b] **Beethoven** Wellingtons Sieg, 'Die Schlacht bei Vittoria', Op 91[c]
[a]**University of Minnesota Brass Band;** [ab]**Minneapolis Symphony Orchestra;** [c]**London Symphony Orchestra / Antál Dorati**
Mercury Living Presence 434 360-2MM (66' · ADD)
Recorded 1955-60. Includes commentary on making the recordings   Ⓜ**OO**

Both battle pieces incorporate cannon fire recorded at West Point, with *Wellington's Vic-*

tory adding antiphonal muskets and *1812*, the University of Minnesota Brass Band and the bells of the Laura Spelman Rockefeller carillon. In a recorded commentary on the *1812* sessions, Deems Taylor explains how, prior to 'battle', roads were blocked and an ambulance crew put on standby. The actual weapons used were chosen both for their historical authenticity (period instruments of destruction) and their sonic impact, the latter proving formidable even today. In fact, the crackle and thunder of *Wellington's Victory* could easily carry a DDD endorsement; perhaps we should, for the occasion, invent a legend of Daring, Deafening and potentially Deadly. Dorati's conducting is brisk, incisive and dramatic. *1812* in particular suggests a rare spontaneity, with a fiery account of the main 'conflict' and a tub-thumping peroration where bells, band, guns and orchestra conspire to produce one of the most riotous key-clashes in gramophone history.

Capriccio italien was recorded some three years earlier (1955, would you believe) and sounds virtually as impressive. Again, the approach is crisp and balletic, whereas the 1960 LSO Beethoven recording triumphs by dint of its energy and orchestral discipline. As 'fun' CDs go, this must be one of the best – provided you can divorce Mercury's aural militia from the terrifying spectre of real conflict. Wilma Cozart Fine has masterminded an astonishingly effective refurbishment, while the documentation – both written and recorded – is very comprehensive.

Francesca da Rimini. Romeo and Juliet. 1812[a].
Eugene Onegin – Waltz[a]; Polonaise
Santa Cecilia Academy [a]Chorus and Orchestra, Rome / Antonio Pappano
EMI 370065-2 (71' · DDD) ⓕ🅞➔

With chorus added in the *1812* as well as the Waltz from *Eugene Onegin*, this is an exceptional Tchaikovsky collection, a fine start for Antonio Pappano's recordings with his Italian orchestra. What is very striking is how refreshing the *1812* is when played with such incisiveness and care for detail, with textures clearly defined. It starts with the chorus singing the opening hymn, expanding thrillingly from an extreme *pianissimo* to a full-throated *fortissimo*.

A women's chorus then comes in very effectively, twice over, for one of the folk-themes, and at the end the full chorus sings the Tsar's Hymn amid the usual percussion and bells, though Pappano avoids extraneous effects, leaving everything in the hands of the orchestral instruments. It is equally refreshing to have the Waltz from *Eugene Onegin* in the full vocal version from the opera, again wonderfully pointed, as is the Polonaise which follows.

What comes out in all the items is the way that Pappano, in his control of flexible *rubato*, is just as persuasive here as he is in Puccini, demonstrating what links there are between these two supreme melodists. So he builds the big melodies into richly emotional climaxes without any hint of

vulgarity, strikingly so in both *Francesca da Rimini* and *Romeo and Juliet*. Pappano is impressive in bringing out the fantasy element in *Francesca*, and in *Romeo* the high dynamic contrasts add to the impact of the performance. There have been many Tchaikovsky collections like this, but with well balanced sound, outstandingly rich and ripe in the brass section, this is among the finest.

Fantasy Overtures

Hamlet, Op 67. The Tempest, Op 18. Romeo and Juliet.
Bamberg Symphony Orchestra / José Serebrier
BIS BIS-CD1073 (62' · DDD) ⓕ🅞🅞➔

What a good idea to couple Tchaikovsky's three fantasy overtures inspired by Shakespeare. José Serebrier writes an illuminating note on the genesis of each of the three, together with an analysis of their structure. He notes that once Tchaikovsky had established his concept of the fantasy overture in the first version of *Romeo and Juliet* in 1869 – slow introduction leading to alternating fast and slow sections, with slow coda – he used it again both in the *1812 Overture* and *Hamlet*. *The Tempest* (1873) has similarly contrasting sections, but begins and ends with a gently evocative seascape, with shimmering arpeggios from strings divided in 13 parts.

It's typical of Serebrier's performance that he makes that effect sound so fresh and original. In many ways, early as it is, this is stylistically the most radical of the three overtures here, with sharp echoes of Berlioz in some of the woodwind effects. The clarity of Serebrier's performance, both in texture and in structure, helps to bring that out, as does a warm and analytical BIS recording.

Hamlet, dating from much later, is treated to a similarly fresh and dramatic reading, with Serebrier bringing out the yearningly Russian flavour of the lovely oboe theme representing Ophelia. He may not quite match the thrusting power of his mentor, Stokowski, but he's not far short, and brings out far more detail.

Serebrier is also meticulous in seeking to observe the dynamic markings in each score. Those in *The Tempest* are nothing if not extravagant – up to a *fortissimo* of five *f*s in the final statement of the love theme – yet Serebrier graduates the extremes with great care. Highly recommended.

Hamlet, Op 67a – Overture and Incidental Music[a].
Romeo and Juliet – Fantasy Overture
[a]**Tatiana Monogarova** *sop* [a]**Maxim Mikhailov** *bass*
Russian National Orchestra / Vladimir Jurowski
Pentatone 🖩 PTC5186 330 (60' · DDD/DSD) ⓕ🅞➔

At first glance this might look like the traditional pairing of Tchaikovsky's two fantasy overtures – but you might have known that Vladimir Jurowski was likely to be more inquisitive than that. In 1891 a complete stage performance of Shakespeare's *Hamlet* took place in St Petersburg with music by Tchaikovsky. His fantasy overture, written for a charity event three years earlier, was heard again, this time filleted to roughly half its original length and reduced in scoring to the requirements of a theatre orchestra. The results are fascinating, not least for the ingenuity of Tchaikovsky's cut-and-paste job, jump-cutting now with renewed urgency. Of course, one misses the symphonic weight of the original. The effect is more muted here, the scale diminished so as not to pre-empt that moment in the actual drama. But Ophelia is more than ever at the heart of the piece, her plaintive oboe melody very much dominating this version and exquisitely played – as is everything – by the Russian National Orchestra, whose refinement has opened a new chapter in Russian orchestral playing. Ophelia's first entrance, incidentally, is none other than the graceful 'Alla tedesca' second movement of Tchaikovsky's Third Symphony, the *Polish*. How's that for recycling? And there's more with the Prelude to Act 4 scene 1, a poignant string elegy turned on wistful arabesques. That is one of the more substantial of the 16 clips and touchingly foreshadows Ophelia's tragedy. She – the lovely Tatiana Monogarova – has a two-part Mad Scene or 'melodrama' where the spoken lines lend a stark reality to her delusions.

Those who know the original 1869 version of the *Romeo and Juliet Fantasy Overture* will be aware that it's another example of how much more interesting, though not necessarily better, a composer's first thoughts can be. Fascinating is the earlier premonition of the great love theme and the way Tchaikovsky quite literally tosses it about in the more radical and certainly more violent development of the fight music: all gone in the revision!

Jurowski savours the differences and makes capital of the anomalies. Very exciting.

Variations on a Rococo Theme, Op 33

Variations on a Rococo Theme. Nocturne No 4, Op 19. (arr Tchaikovsky). Pezzo capriccioso, Op 62. When Jesus Christ was but a child No 5, Op 54. Was I not a little blade of grass? No 7, Op 47 (both orch Tchaikovsky). Andante cantabile, Op 11 (arr Tchaikovsky)
Raphael Wallfisch vc
English Chamber Orchestra / Geoffrey Simon
Chandos CHAN8347 (48' · DDD)   Ⓢ**O**B⃗

This account of the *Rococo* Variations is the one to have: it presents Tchaikovsky's variations as he wrote them, in the order he devised, and including the *allegretto moderato con anima* that the work's first interpreter, 'loathsome Fitzenhagen', so high-handedly jettisoned. (See also the review under Dvořák where Rostropovich uses the published score rather than the original version.) The first advantage is as great as the second: how necessary the brief cadenza and the *andante* that it introduces now seem, as an up-beat to the central sequence of quick variations

(Fitzenhagen moved both cadenza and *andante* to the end). And the other, shorter cadenza now makes a satisfying transition from that sequence to the balancing *andante sostenuto*, from which the long-suppressed eighth variation is an obvious build-up to the coda – why, the piece has a form, after all! Raphael Wallfisch's fine performance keeps the qualifying adjective 'rococo' in mind – it isn't indulgently over-romantic – but it has warmth and beauty of tone in abundance. The shorter pieces are well worth having: the baritone voice of the cello suits the *Andante cantabile* and the Tatyana-like melody of the *Nocturne* surprisingly aptly. The sound is first-class.

Serenade in C, Op 48

Serenade in C. Souvenir de Florence, Op 70
Vienna Chamber Orchestra / Philippe Entremont
Naxos 8 550404 (65' · DDD)   Ⓢ**OO**B⃗

This is one of the many CDs now on the market that dispel the myth once and for all that only full-price recordings contain really outstanding performances. The Naxos label is just about as 'bargain' as you can get, and here they have given us superlative performances of two of Tchaikovsky's most endearing works. The Serenade in C contains a wealth of memorable and haunting music, beautifully and inventively scored and guaranteed to bring immense pleasure and delight to those dipping their toes in to the world of classical music for the first time. Philippe Entremont and the Vienna Chamber Orchestra give a marvellously polished and finely poised performance full of warmth, affection and high spirits, and the famous second movement Waltz in particular is played with much elegance and grace. The *Souvenir de Florence*, originally written for string sextet, makes a welcome appearance here in Tchaikovsky's own arrangement for string orchestra. This is a delightfully sunny performance, full of suavity, exuberance and romantic dash, but always alert to the subtleties of Tchaikovsky's skilful, intricate part-writing. The *Adagio cantabile* is particularly notable for some extremely fine and poetic solo playing from the violin and cello principals of the VPO. The beautifully spacious recording does ample justice to the performances.

Suites

Suite No 2. The Tempest
Detroit Symphony Orchestra / Neeme Järvi
Chandos CHAN9454 (64' · DDD)   ⒻB⃗

Tchaikovsky's elusive blend of instrumental precision and free-flowing thematic fantasy in the Second Suite meets its match in the Detroit/Järvi partnership: the conductor's imagination works alongside the lean, clean Detroit sound with interesting results. The strings aren't always the ideal: the lush chordings and central fugal energy of the opening movement, 'Jeu de sons', cry out for a richer, Russian tone. But the semiquaver patter is beautifully done, the lower lines clear and personable. Keen articulation and driving force go hand-in-glove as Järvi prepares for the entry of the four accordions in the virile 'Rondo-Burlesque', sweeping on to the folk-song of the central section with characteristic aplomb. It's in the Schumannesque phrases and the subtly shifting moods of the most poetic movement, 'Rêves d'enfant', that Järvi really comes into his own; the short-lived, other-worldly radiance at the heart of the movement seems more than ever like a preliminary study for the transformation scenes of *The Nutcracker*, just as the woodwind choruses look forward to that and *Sleeping Beauty*.

The magical haze surrounding Prospero's island in *The Tempest* doesn't quite come off; here it's Pletnev (reviewed above) who surprises us with the true magician's touch, but then his Russian horns, and later his trumpeter, cast their incantations more impressively. Järvi is no more successful than any other conductor in stitching together Tchaikovsky's strong impressions of the play, though a little more forward movement in the love-music might have helped.

Tchaikovsky Suite No 3
Stravinsky Divertimento from 'La baiser de la fée'
Russian National Orchestra / Vladimir Jurowski
Pentatone ⦿ PTC5186 061 (64' · DDD/DSD)　　Ⓕ

Vladimir Jurowski here offers performances that are as near-ideal as one can imagine, the electric tension giving the illusion of live music-making. We have had some impressive recordings from this Moscow-based orchestra in the past but this one is among the finest.

Tchaikovsky's Third Suite, with its final extended set of variations, can seem rather square under some conductors but Jurowski, maybe influenced by conducting opera and ballet, brings out the surging lyricism. So the opening 'Elegie' is warmly moulded without sounding fussy, the phrasing totally idiomatic. The rhythmic second-movement Waltz leads to a dazzling account of the *Scherzo*, taken at a genuine presto yet with no feeling of breathlessness, while the Variations have rarely seemed so attractive in their breadth of ideas, with a thrilling build-up and conclusion.

Stravinsky's Divertimento, its four movements taken from the ballet *The Fairy's Kiss*, may make an unexpected coupling, but it is apt and illuminating. Jurowski steers a nice course between the romantic warmth of the Tchaikovsky sources from which Stravinsky took his material (songs and piano pieces) and his 1920s neo-classicism. The delicate and refined account of the slow first section leads to sharp syncopations in the *Vivace agitato* which follows, and the chugging rhythms on horns in the most memorable section of the second movement show jollity in their springing step, while the pointing of con-

trasts in the final 'Pas de deux' brings yearning warmth in the big lyrical moments and wit in the faster sections. With exceptionally vivid sound, recorded by PentaTone's Dutch engineers in Moscow, this disc cannot be recommended too highly.

Souvenir de Florence, Op 70

Tchaikovsky Souvenir de Florence.
Dvořák String Sextet in A, B80
Sarah Chang, Bernhard Hartog vns **Wolfram Christ, Tanjia Christ** vas **Georg Faust, Olaf Maninger** vcs
EMI 557243-2 (68' · DDD)　　Ⓕ○○⤇

Two of the finest string sextets ever written by Slavonic composers make an excellent coupling, particularly with such a starry line-up of musicians. Sarah Chang's warmly individual artistry is superbly matched by players drawn from the Berlin Philharmonic, past and present. These are players who not only respond to each other's artistry, but do so with the most polished ensemble and a rare clarity of inner texture, not easy with a sextet.

Souvenir de Florence is given the most exuberantly joyful performance. Written just after he had left Florence, having completed his opera, *The Queen of Spades*, Tchaikovsky was prompted to compose one of his happiest works, one which for once gave him enormous pleasure. The opening movement's bouncy rhythms in compound time set the pattern, with the second subject hauntingly seductive in its winning relaxation, a magic moment here (track 1, 1'28").

The *Adagio cantabile* second movement is tenderly beautiful, with the central section sharply contrasted, while the folk-dance rhythms of the last two movements are sprung with sparkling lightness. There are now dozens of versions of this winning work in the catalogue, both for sextet and string orchestra, but none is more delectable than this.

Equally, the subtlety as well as the energy of Dvořák's Sextet is consistently brought out by Chang and her partners, with the players using a huge dynamic range down to the gentlest *pianissimo*. Here, too, it just outshines the competition.

String Quartets

No 1 in D, Op 11 No 2 in F, Op 22 No 3 in E flat minor, Op 30

String Quartets Nos 1-3. Quartet Movement in B-flat. Souvenir de Florence, Op 70
Yuri Yurov va **Mikhail Milman** vc **Borodin Quartet**
(Mikhail Kopelman, Andrei Abramenkov vns Dmitri Shebalin va Valentin Berlinsky vc)
Teldec ② 4509-90422-2 (151' · DDD)　　Ⓕ○○○

Who could fail to recognise the highly characteristic urgency and thematic strength of the F major Quartet's first movement development section, or miss premonitions of later masterpieces in the Third Quartet's *Andante funèbre*? None of these works is 'late' (the last of them predates the Fourth Symphony by a couple of years), yet their rigorous arguments and sweeping melodies anticipate the orchestral masterpieces of Tchaikovsky's full maturity. So why the neglect of all but the First Quartet? The most likely reason is our habitual expectation of orchestral colour in Tchaikovsky, a situation that doesn't really affect our appreciation of the early, almost Schubertian D major Quartet (the one with the *Andante cantabile* that moved Tolstoy to tears). The Second and Third Quartets are noticeably more symphonic and particularly rich in the kinds of harmonic clashes and sequences that Tchaikovsky normally gave to the orchestra. Even minor details, like the quick-fire exchanges near the beginning of No 3's *Allegretto*, instantly suggest 'woodwinds' (you can almost hear oboes, flutes and clarinets jostle in play), while both finales could quite easily have been transposed among the pages of the early symphonies. But if these and other parallels are to register with any conviction, then performers need to locate them, and that's a challenge the Borodins meet with the ease of seasoned Tchaikovskians.

They are natural and spontaneous, most noticeably in the first movement of the exuberant *Souvenir de Florence* sextet, and in that wonderful passage from the Second Quartet's first movement where the lead violin calms from agitated virtuosity to a magical recapitulation of the principal theme – an unforgettable moment, superbly paced here. Additionally we get a 15-minute B flat Quartet movement – an appealing torso imbued with the spirit of Russian folksong.

Piano Trio

Tchaikovsky Piano Trio **Rachmaninov** Trio élégiaque in G minor (1892)
Kempf Trio (Pierre Bensaid *vn* Alexander Chaushian *vc* Freddy Kempf *pf*)
BIS BIS-CD1302 (69' · DDD)   Ⓕ**O**

Understandably, remembering its dedicatee, Nikolai Rubinstein, Tchaikovsky's Trio is dominated by the piano part, which has moments of intrepid (sometimes repetitive) rhetoric, which must ring out triumphantly yet not be allowed to usurp the work's underlying elegiac feeling. In many respects this performance carries all before it. Freddy Kempf leads with great conviction, yet can pull back whenever his colleagues are in the ascendant. The very opening is lyrically seductive, and the closing pages, with a moving reprise of the opening theme at the *Lugubre* finale, are most sensitively managed. But before that the kaleidoscopic variations of the second movement, which begins so serenely, have been presented with sparkling panache: the delightful pianistic roulades of Variation 3 and the exquisite music-box effect of Var 5 both show Kempf as

delectably light-fingered, yet he finds real swagger for Var 7, and a Chopinesque rhythmic delicacy for the *Tempo di mazurka* of Var 10. And in the lovely *Andante flebile* (Var 9) violinist Pierre Bensaid and cellist Alexander Chaushian share a ravishing delicate duet.

While Tchaikovsky's Piano Trio is ambitiously epic in scale; Rachmaninov's, although obviously drawing on the inspiration of the Tchaikovsky model, with the piano still taking a leading role, is in a single movement. Its mood is tinged with melancholy throughout, surging to moments of passion less extrovert than with Tchaikovsky, but with that characteristic ebb and flow of expressive feeling captured most naturally by these players; they find a touching gentleness for the wistfully sad closing bars. The performance comes into competition with that by the superb Borodin Trio on Chandos, whose coupling is more logical (the first *Trio élégiaque*, Op 8); but on performance grounds Kempf and his colleagues are by no means second best.

The recording is very well balanced, and the acoustic seems equally suitable for both works. Altogether this is a splendid disc.

Tchaikovsky Piano Trio **Smetana** Piano Trio, Op 15
Vienna Piano Trio (Wolfgang Redik *vn* Matthias Gredler *vc* Stefan Mendl *pf*)
Dabringhaus und Grimm Ⓕ 🎵 MDG942 1512-6
(74' · DDD)   Ⓕ**OO**

This version of the Tchaikovsky measures up extremely well against its competition; moreover it is (like all chamber recordings from this source) very well balanced. Pianist Stefan Mendl is able to dominate yet become a full member of the partnership throughout. The second movement's variations open gently but soon develop the widest range of style, moving through Tchaikovsky's kaleidoscopic mood-changes like quicksilver and often with elegiac lyrical feeling.

But what makes this disc especially recommendable is the inclusion of Smetana's G minor Piano Trio, which the composer himself premiered in 1855. All three movements are in the home key and thematically linked yet are enticingly diverse, the first with strong contrasts of dynamic and tempo, the second a most engaging scherzo (marked *non agitato* and with slower interludes), while the rondo finale bursts with energy (especially as presented here). All in all a real winner of a disc that can be highly recommended on all counts.

Piano Works

Tchaikovsky 18 Morceaux, Op 72 **Chopin** Nocturne No 20 in C sharp minor, Op posth
Mikhail Pletnev *pf*
DG 477 5378GH (70' · DDD) Recorded live 2004
      Ⓕ**OOO**▷

Mikhail Pletnev's persuasive 1986 recording of Tchaikovsky's *18 Morceaux* for Melodiya was unfortunately hampered by strident sound and an ill-tuned piano. Happily, a state-of-the-art situation prevails in this new live recording for Deutsche Grammophon, extending, of course, to Pletnev's own contributions. His caring, characterful and technically transcendent way with this cycle casts each piece in a three-dimensional perspective that honours the composer's letter and spirit beyond the music's 'salon' reputation, while making the most of its pianistic potential. The results are revelatory, akin to, say, Ignaz Friedman's illuminating re-creations of Mendelssohn's *Songs Without Words*.

The Fifth *Morceau*, 'Meditation', demonstrates the Pletnev-Tchaikovsky chemistry at its most sublime. The melodies are firmly projected yet flexibly arched over the bar-lines, as if emerging from different instruments, culminating in a febrile central climax that gently dissipates into some of the most ravishing trills on record. In No 8, 'Dialogue', Pletnev elevates Tchaikovsky's *quasi parlando* with the type of off-hand skill and pinpoint timing of a master actor who knows just which lines to throw away.

Note, too, the deliciously pointed scales and music-box colorations in No 13, 'Echo rustique'. Shades of Liszt's Third *Liebestraum* seep into No 14, 'Chant élégiaque', in what amounts to a masterclass in how to sustain long melodies against sweeping accompaniments. A stricter basic pulse throughout No 9, 'Un poco di Schumann', might have made the dotted rhythms and two strategically placed *ritenutos* more obviously Schumannesque, yet there's no denying the inner logic the looser treatment communicates.

There's extraordinary virtuosity behind the musical insights. For example, the interlocking octaves in the coda to No 7, 'Polacca de concert', are unleashed with Horowitz-like ferocity and not a trace of banging. The rapid, vertigo-inducing triplet runs in No 10, 'Scherzo-fantaisie', could scarcely be more even and controlled. Pletnev is all over the final, unbuttoned *trepak* in grand style, and he certainly makes the glissandos swing. A fresh, unfettered account of Chopin's C sharp minor Nocturne is offered as an encore to this urgently recommended recital.

Liturgy of St John Chrysostom, Op 41

Liturgy of St John Chrysostom. Nine Sacred Pieces.
An Angel Crying
Corydon Singers / Matthew Best
Hyperion CDA66948 (75' · DDD · T/t)   Ⓕ**O**

Tchaikovsky's liturgical settings have never quite caught the popular imagination which has followed Rachmaninov's (his All-Night Vigil, at any rate). They are generally more inward, less concerned with the drama that marks Orthodox celebration than with the reflective centre which is another aspect. Rachmaninov can invite worship with a blaze of delight, setting 'Pridite';

Tchaikovsky approaches the mystery more quietly. Yet there's a range of emotion which emerges vividly in this admirable record of the Liturgy together with a group of the minor liturgical settings which he made at various times in his life. His ear for timbre never fails him. It's at its most appealing, perhaps, in the lovely 'Da ispravitsya' for female trio and answering choir, beautifully sung here; he can also respond to the Orthodox tradition of rapid vocalisation, as in the Liturgy's Creed and in the final 'Blagosloven grady' (in the West, the Benedictus). Anyone who still supposes that irregular, rapidly shifting rhythms were invented by Stravinsky should give an ear to his Russian sources, in folk poetry and music but also in the music of the Church.

Matthew Best's Corydon Singers are old hands at Orthodox music, and present these beautiful settings with a keen ear for their texture and 'orchestration'. The recording was made in an (unnamed) ecclesiastical acoustic of suitable resonance, and sounds well.

Songs

'Romances'
My genius, my angel, my friend. Six Songs, Op 6 –
No 1, Do not believe, my friend; No 2, Not a word,
O my friend; No 5, Why?; No 6, None but the lonely
heart. Cradle Song, Op 16 No 1. Six Songs, Op 25 –
No 1, Reconciliation; No 2, Over burning ashes.
The Fearful Moment, Op 28 No 6. Six Songs, Op 38 –
No 2, It was in the early spring; No 3, At the Ball.
Seven Songs, Op 47 – No 1, Had I only known; No 6,
Can it be day?; No 7, The Bride's Lament. Children's
Songs, Op 54 – Cuckoo. Twelve Songs, Op 60 – No 7,
Gypsy Song; No 12, The mild stars looked down. The
lights were being dimmed, Op 63 No 5. Six Songs,
Op 73 – No 4, The sun has set; No 6, Again, as
before, alone
Christianne Stotijn *mez* **Julius Drake** *pf*
Onyx Classics ONYX4034 (63' · DDD)   Ⓕ**O**➔

For the most part these are angst-ridden stories of death and lost love. The two best-known songs open proceedings: 'At the Ball', with its reminiscence of unrequited passion to the lilt of a sad waltz, and then 'None but the lonely heart'. Everyone conceivable from Rosa Ponselle to Frank Sinatra has recorded this, but Stotijn loses nothing in comparison with ghosts from the past. Her voice is a full-blooded mezzo but steady and true, without a hint of that vibrato that can often disturb the line in Slavonic singers (Stotijn is from The Netherlands).

The emotional climax of the selection comes with 'The Bride's Lament'. This outpouring of grief can seem over melodramatic but Stotijn and Drake find exactly the right mood. The piano parts are superbly done: in every sense these songs are duets. There are a couple of other light moments – 'Cuckoo', one of 16 children's songs composed in the 1880s, and a 'Gypsy Song' from around the same time. Tchaikovsky's songs are not nearly well enough known and this superb recital should encourage more interest in them. Highly recommended.

The Snow Maiden

The Snow Maiden
Irina Mishura-Lekhtman *mez* **Vladimir Grishko** *ten*
Michigan University Musical Society Choral Union;
Detroit Symphony Orchestra / Neeme Järvi
Chandos CHAN9324 (79' · ADD · T/t)   Ⓕ

Tchaikovsky wrote his incidental music for Ostrovsky's *Snow Maiden* in 1873, and though he accepted it was not his best, he retained an affection for it and was upset when Rimsky-Korsakov came along with his full-length opera on the subject. The tale of love frustrated had its appeal for Tchaikovsky, even though he was not to make as much as Rimsky did of the failed marriage between Man and Nature. But though he did not normally interest himself much in descriptions of the natural world, there are charming pieces that any lover of Tchaikovsky's music will surely be delighted to encounter. A strong sense of a Russian folk celebration, and of the interaction of the natural and supernatural worlds, also comes through, especially in the earlier part of the work. There's a delightful dance and chorus for the birds, and a powerful monologue for Winter; Vladimir Grishko, placed further back, sounds magical.

Natalia Erassova (for Chistiakov's recording on CdM) gets round the rapid enunciation of Lel's second song without much difficulty, but doesn't quite bring the character to life; Mishura-Lekhtman has a brighter sparkle. Chistiakov's Shrove Tuesday procession goes at a much steadier pace than Järvi's, and is thus the more celebratory and ritual where the other is a straightforward piece of merriment. Both performances have much to recommend them, and it isn't by a great deal that Järvi's is preferable. Chandos provides transliteration and an English translation.

Additional recommendation

Arias from The Enchantress, Eugene Onegin, The Maid of Orleans, Mazeppa and Queen of Spades
Varady *sop* **Evangelatos** *mez*
Munich Radio Orchestra / Kofman
Orfeo C540011A (78' · DDD)   Ⓕ

Varady is truly a phenomenon; recording in her 59th year she shows no signs of age and brings to these arias her innate gift for going to the heart of the matter.

Eugene Onegin, Op 24

Dmitri Hvorostovsky *bar* Eugene Onegin **Nuccia Focile** *sop* Tatyana **Neil Shicoff** *ten* Lensky **Sarah Walker** *mez* Larina **Irina Arkhipova** *mez* Filipyevna **Olga Borodina** *contr* Olga **Francis Egerton** *ten*
Triquet **Alexander Anisimov** *bass* Prince Gremin **Hervé Hennequin** *bass* Captain **Sergei Zadvorny** *bass* Zaretsky **Orchestre de Paris; St Petersburg Chamber Choir / Semyon Bychkov**
Philips 473 7017 (141' · DDD · N/t)   Ⓜ**ⓄⓄ**▷

This is a magnificent achievement on all sides. In a recording that is wide in range, the work comes to arresting life under Bychkov's vital direction. Too often of late, on disc and in the theatre, the score has been treated self-indulgently and on too large a scale. Bychkov makes neither mistake, emphasizing the unity of its various scenes, never lingering at slower tempos than Tchaikovsky predicates, yet never moving too fast for his singers.

Focile and Hvorostovsky prove almost ideal interpreters of the central roles. Focile offers keen-edged yet warm tone and total immersion in Tatyana's character. Aware throughout of the part's dynamic demands, she phrases with complete confidence, eagerly catching the girl's dreamy vulnerability and heightened imagination in the Letter Scene, which has that sense of awakened love so essential to it. Then she exhibits Tatyana's new-found dignity on Gremin's arm and finally her desperation when Onegin reappears to rekindle her romantic feelings.

Hvorostovsky is here wholly in his element. His singing has at once the warmth, elegance and refinement Tchaikovsky demands from his antihero. He suggests all Onegin's initial disdain, phrasing his address to the distraught and humiliated Tatyana – Focile so touching here – with distinction, and brings to it just the correct *bon ton*, a kind of detached humanity. He fires to anger with a touch of the heroic in his tone when challenged by Lensky, becomes transformed and single-minded when he catches sight of the 'new' Tatyana at the St Petersburg Ball. Together he, Focile and Bychkov make the finale the tragic climax it should be: indeed here this passage almost unbearably moving in this reading.

Shicoff has refined and expanded his Lensky since he recorded it for Levine. His somewhat lachrymose delivery suits the character of the lovelorn poet, and he gives his big aria a sensitive, Russian profile, full of much subtlety of accent, the voice sounding in excellent shape, but there is a shade too much self-regard when he opens the ensemble at Larin's party with 'Yes, in your house'. Anisimov is a model Gremin, singing his aria with generous tone and phrasing while not making a meal of it. Olga Borodina is a perfect Olga, spirited, a touch sensual, wholly idiomatic with the text – as, of course, is the revered veteran Russian mezzo Arkhipova as Filipievna, an inspired piece of casting. Sarah Walker, Covent Garden's Filipievna, is here a sympathetic Larina. Also from the Royal Opera comes Egerton's lovable Triquet, but whereas Gergiev, in the theatre, dragged out his couplets inordinately, Bychkov once more strikes precisely the right tempo.

There will also be a very special place in the discography of the opera for the vintage Russian versions, but as a recording they are naturally outclassed by the Philips, which now becomes the outright recommendation.

TCHAIKOVSKY'S EUGENE ONEGIN – IN BRIEF

Dmitri Hvorostovsky *Eugene Onegin*
Nuccia Focile *Tatyana* **Neil Shicoff** *Lensky*
St Petersburg Chamber Choir; Orchestre de Paris / Semyon Bychkov
Philips ② 475 7017 (141' · DDD)   **Ⓜ❶❶▶**

A fleetfooted, vividly conducted performance with two highly convincing stars in Dmitri Hvorostovsky's warm-voiced Onegin and Nuccia Focile's Tatyana, fresh and youthful. Neil Shicoff's plangent Lensky heads a fine supporting cast, and the recording is excellent.

Bernd Weikl *Eugene Onegin* **Teresa Kubiak**
Tatyana **Stuart Burrows** *Lensky*
John Alldis Choir; Orchestra of the Royal Opera House / Sir Georg Solti
Decca ② 417 413-2DH2 (143' · ADD)   **Ⓕ**

A polished old warhorse, conducted by Solti with superlative warmth, and international principals. The theatrical energy is there but, despite orchestral gloss and some superb singing, especially Stuart Burrows's Lensky, it never quite attains the idiomatic feeling of more Slavic versions.

(In English) Thomas Hampson *Eugene Onegin*
Kiri Te Kanawa *Tatyana* **Neil Rosenshein** *Lensky*
WNO Chorus and Orchestra / Sir Charles Mackerras
Chandos ② CHAN3042 (142' · DDD)   **Ⓕ**

This English-language recording is not the best, but with Thomas Hampson's strong Onegin and Mackerras's propulsive, atmospheric conducting it's still enjoyable; and for non-Russian listeners the English does make this intimate drama much more immediate.

Panteleimon Nortsov *Eugene Onegin* **Yelena** Ⓗ
Kruglikova *Tatyana* **Ivan Kozlovsky** *Lensky*
Bolshoi Theatre Chorus and Orchestra / Alexander Orlov
Naxos ② 8 110216/7 (136' · AAD)   **Ⓢ❶**

The first Bolshoi version of 1937, in early but reasonable sound and still fascinating, particularly for its principals, Nortsov's resonant Onegin, Kruglikova's sensitive, touching Tatyana, and the great Ivan Koslovsky's plangent Lensky.

Bernd Weikl *Eugene Onegin* **Teresa Kubiak**
Tatyana **Stuart Burrows** *Lensky*
John Alldis Choir; Orchestra of the Royal Opera House / Sir Georg Solti
Decca 📀 071 124-9DH (117')   **Ⓕ**

Enterprising director Petr Weigl has created this cinematic version, using, as he often does, actors miming to a recording, in this case Solti's (see above). It looks marvellous, with lustrous production values; but chunks are cut, especially half the opening scene, and though the actors convince, the lip-sync may not.

Iolanta, Op 69

Iolanta
Galina Gorchakova *sop* Iolanta **Gegam Grigorian** *ten* Vaudémont **Dmitri Hvorostovsky** *bar* Robert **Sergei Alexashkin** *bass* King René **Nikolai Putilin** *bar* Ibn-Hakia **Larissa Diadkova** *mez* Martha **Nikolai Gassiev** *ten* Alméric **Tatiana Kravtsova** *sop* Brigitta **Olga Korzhenskaya** *mez* Laura **Gennadi Bezzubenkov** *bar* Bertrand **Chorus and Orchestra of the Kirov Opera, St Petersburg / Valery Gergiev**
Philips ② 442 796-2PH2 (96' · DDD · N/T/t)   **Ⓕ**

Iolanta, the touching little princess, blind and virginal, into whose darkness and isolation there eventually shines the 'bright angel' of Duke Robert, is delightfully sung by Galina Gorchakova. There's a freshness and sense of vulnerability here, especially in the opening scenes with Martha in the garden as she sings wistfully of something that appears to be lacking in her life: the *Arioso* is done charmingly and without sentimentality. Gegam Grigorian sometimes sounds pinched and under strain, even in the Romance. He's also overshadowed by Hvorostovsky who's at his best here: warm and with a somewhat dusky tone. The King, Provence's 'bon roi René', is benignly if a little throatily sung by Sergei Alexashkin, and he has at hand a sturdy-voiced Ibn-Hakia in Nikolai Putilin. Valery Gergiev conducts a sensitive performance, responding constructively to the unusual scoring, and not overplaying the more demonstrative elements in a score that gains most through some understatement.

The Queen of Spades

The Queen of Spades
Gegam Grigorian *ten* Herman **Maria Gulegina** *sop* Lisa **Irina Arkhipova** *mez* Countess **Nikolai Putilin** *bar* Count Tomsky **Vladimir Chernov** *bar* Prince Yeletsky **Olga Borodina** *mez* Pauline **Vladimir Solodovnikov** *ten* Chekalinsky **Sergei Alexashkin** *bass* Surin **Evgeni Boitsov** *ten* Chaplitsky **Nikolai Gassiev** *ten* Major-domo **Gennadi Bezzubenkov** *bass* Narumov **Ludmila Filatova** *mez* Governess **Tatiana Filimonova** *sop* Masha **Kirov Theatre Chorus and Orchestra / Valery Gergiev**
Philips ③ 438 141-2PH3 (166' · DDD · N/T/t)   **Ⓕ❶**

There are major problems with all the current sets of *The Queen of Spades*, but Valery Gergiev, one of the outstanding Tchaikovskians of the day, here coaxes from a thoroughly Western-sounding Kirov Theatre Orchestra what's surely the most refined account of the score yet recorded, and one that's never lacking energy or full-blooded attack. His isn't so much a compromise approach as one which stresses fatalism and underlying sadness. The recording was made in the Kirov Theatre itself, and there's admittedly some constriction to the orchestral sound picture; but for many the atmosphere of a real stage-venue will be a plus, and the all-important balance between voices and orchestra is just right. If the spine still fails to tingle as often as it should, that's mainly a reflection of the respectable but unexciting singing.

The Queen of Spades
Yuri Marusin *ten* Herman **Nancy Gustafson** *sop* Lisa **Felicity Palmer** *mez* Countess **Sergei Leiferkus** *bar* Count Tomsky **Dimitri Kharitonov** *bar* Prince Yeletsky **Marie-Ange Todorovitch** *contr* Pauline **Graeme Matheson-Bruce** *ten* Chekalinsky **Andrew Slater** *bass* Surin **Robert Burt** *ten* Chaplitsky **Geoffrey Pogson** *ten* Major-Domo **Christopher Thornton-Holmes** *bass* Narumov **Enid Hartle** *mez* Governess **Rachel Tovey** *sop* Masha **Glyndebourne Festival Chorus; London Philharmonic Orchestra / Sir Andrew Davis** *Stage director* **Graham Vick** *Video director* **Peter Maniura**
ArtHaus Musik 🟥 100 272 (170' · 4:3 · 2.0 · 0)   Ⓕ◑

Graham Vick's 1992 staging is worthy of this extraordinary score. He reflects exactly the highly charged emotions and sense of brooding menace pervading the composer's re-enactment of Pushkin's story, thus creating a compelling psycho-drama that compels both eye and ear. Davis catches most, if not all, of the score's romantic sweep and inner, dislocating turbulence, although the impassioned undercurrents are better achieved in the Kirov video, conducted by Gergiev (below). Yuri Marusin is the crazed Herman incarnate. Whether or not you can accept his often off-pitch singing is a personal matter. As his Lisa, Nancy Gustafson, offers a portrayal of an impressionable girl driven to distraction and suicide by the unhinged behaviour of her lover. She sings the part in warm, passionate tones.

Peter Maniura's video direction catches every facial expression of both characters and of Felicity Palmer's electrifying Countess. Sergei Leiferkus is elegant and commanding as the free-loving Tomsky. Dimitri Kharitonov is the soul of rectitude as Yeletsky and brings a bronzed tone to his lovely aria. Marie-Ange Todorovitch is an attractively palpitating Pauline. Picture and sound are exemplary.

Additional recommendation

The Queen of Spades
Grigorian *ten* Hermann **Guleghina** *sop* Lisa **Filatova** *mez* Countess **Leiferkus** *bar* Count Tomsky **Gergalov** *bar* Prince Yeletsky **Borodina** *contr* Pauline **Kirov Opera Chorus and Orchestra / Gergiev** *Stage director* **Temirkanov** *Video director* **Large**
Philips 🟥 070 434-9PH (179' · NTSC · 16:9 · 2.0 & DTS 5.1 · 0)   Ⓕ◑
This production from St Petersburg, and contemporaneous with the Glyndebourne production reviewed above, is a much more conventional but equally valid approach. The staging is always apt, and in terms of cast, the Kirov holds the edge over its rival. The young Guleghina is the intense, vibrant Lisa to the life. The video direction is exemplary, though the sound leaves something to be desired.

Georg Philipp Telemann
German 1681-1767

Telemann was one of the most prolific composers ever. At 10 he could play four instruments and had written arias, motets and instrumental works. His parents discouraged musical studies, but he gravitated back to them. At Leipzig University he founded a collegium musicum; at 21 he became musical director of the Leipzig Opera at 23 he took on a post as church organist. The next year he moved to Z̃ary, as court Kapellmeister, where he wrote French-style dance suites, sometimes tinged by local Polish and Moravian folk music, and cantatas. In 1708 he went in the same capacity to the Eisenach court and in 1712 to Frankfurt as city music director. As Kapellmeister of a church there, he wrote at least five cantata cycles and works for civic occasions, while his duties as director of a collegium musicum drew from him instrumental works and oratorios.

He was offered various other positions, but moved only in 1721, when he was invited to Hamburg as director of music at the five main churches and Kantor at the Johanneum. Here he had to write two cantatas each Sunday, with extra ones for special church and civic occasions, as well as an annual Passion, oratorio and serenata. In his spare time he directed a collegium musicum and wrote for the opera house; the city councillors waived their objections to the latter when he indicated that he would otherwise accept an invitation to Leipzig. He directed the Hamburg Opera from 1722 until its closure in 1738. In 1737 he paid a visit to Paris, appearing at court and the Concert Spirituel. From 1740 he devoted more time to musical theory, but from 1755 he turned to the oratorio. He published much of his music, notably a set of 72 cantatas and the three sets of Musique de table (1733), his best-known works, each including a concerto, a suite and several chamber pieces. He was eager to foster the spread of music and active in publishing several didactic works, for example on figured bass and ornamentation. He was by far the most famous composer in Germany; in a contemporary dictionary he is assigned four times as much space as JS Bach.

Telemann composed in all the forms and styles current in his day; he wrote Italian-style concertos and sonatas, French-style overture-suites and quartets, German fugues, cantatas, Passions and songs. Some of his chamber works, for example the quartets in the Musique de table, are in a conversational, dialogue-like manner that is lucid in texture and elegant in diction. Whatever style he used, Telemann's music is easily recognisable as his own, with its clear periodic structure, its clarity and its ready fluency. Though four years senior to Bach and Handel, he used an idiom more forward-looking than theirs and in several genres can be seen as a forerunner of the Classical style. **GROVE**music

Flute Concertos

Concerto for Flute, Strings and Continuo in D,   **P**,
TWV51:D2. Concerto for Flute, Strings and Continuo
in G, TWV51:G2. Concerto for 2 Flutes, Violone,
Strings and Continuo in A minor, TWV53:A1ª.
Concerto for Flute, Violin, Cello, Strings and
Continuo in A, TWV53:A2. Concerto for Flute, Oboe
d'amore, Viola d'amore, Strings and Continuo in E,
TWV53:E1
Emmanuel Pahud, ªJacques Zoon fls **Berlin
Baroque Soloists** (Wolfram Christ vad Georg Faust
vc Klaus Stoll violone Albrecht Mayer obd) /
Rainer Kussmaul vn
EMI 557397-2 (66' · DDD)   **F○**➔

You'll rarely hear such personality in a Baroque-
concerto soloist as the extraordinary Emmanuel
Pahud exhibits here. Berlin Baroque Soloists
acclimatise effortlessly to an 18th-century palette, and distinguished colleagues they make for
Pahud. The flautist sets out his stall from the
Andante of the succinct G major concerto (completed from a damaged source and therefore
making its recording début) whose startling
resemblance to the slow movement of Bach's F
minor Concerto, BWV1056, seems to inspire
Pahud to a lyricism of understated elegance
which one often hears in the best performances of
the Bach work. Indeed, it's his sensitivity to Telemann's gestural implications and ability to colour
the music at every turn which makes Pahud's
playing so enchanting in all five concertos.
Telemann performance on a modern flute will
inevitably lead to some recoiling, but one never
feels deprived of the gentle and beguiling articulation of a 'period' instrument or its capacity for
soft dynamic and purity of sound. One only has
to hear the lithe performance of the A major
Triple Concerto, from Part 1 of Telemann's
famous banquet publication of 1733, *Tafelmusik*,
where character abounds through Pahud's concern with first principles. Joyous exchange and
textural delights abound in the Triple Concerto
in E major, where Wolfram Christ's viola
d'amore and Albrecht Mayer's oboe d'amore
combine with the flautist in a ravishingly
blended montage. The Flute Concerto in D
confirms everything about Pahud's exquisite
taste and mesmerising sound. A real winner.

Horn Concertos

Concerto for Three Horns, Violin and Orchestra   **P**
in D major. Overture-Suites – C, TWV55:C5, 'La
bouffonne'; F, TWV55:F11, 'Alster Echo'. Concerto in
G, 'Grillen-Symphonie'
Anthony Halstead, Christian Rutherford, Raul Diaz
hns **Collegium Musicum 90 / Simon Standage** vn
Chandos Chaconne CHAN0547 (70' · DDD).   **F○**

This release shows Telemann at his most irrepressibly good-humoured and imaginative.
There's a concerto for three rattling horns and a
solo violin (a splendid sound, with the horns

recorded at what seems like the ideal distance),
and an elegant suite for strings which sounds like
Handel, Bach and a few French composers all
thrown in together. More striking, though, is the
most substantial piece on the disc, the *Alster Echo*
Overture-Suite, a nine-movement work for
strings, oboes and horns full of tricks and surprises occasioned by a host of representative
titles. Thus 'Hamburg Carillons' brings us horns
imitating bells, 'Concerto of Frogs and Crows'
has some mischievously scrunchy wrong notes,
and in 'Alster Echo' there's a complex network of
echoes between oboes and horns. But the show-
stealer is the *Grillen-Symphonie* ('Cricket Symphony'). This is a work for the gloriously silly
scoring of piccolo, alto chalumeau, oboe, violins,
viola, and two double basses, a somewhat Stravinskian combination that you're unlikely to
encounter every day. But it's not just the instrumentation that's irresistibly odd. There's a slow
movement with curious, melancholy woodwind
interventions a little reminiscent of *Harold in
Italy*, and a finale which is quite a hoot.

Overture-Suites

Overture-Suite in G, 'Burlesque de Don Quichotte',
TWV55:G10. Overture-Suite in D minor, WV55:d3.
Overture-Suite in E flat, 'La Lyra', TWV55: Es3
Northern Chamber Orchestra / Nicholas Ward
Naxos 8 554019 (57' · DDD)   **S**➔

Overture-Suite in G, 'Burlesque de Don Quichotte',.
TWV55:G10. Overture-Suite in B minor, TWV55:h1.
Concerto for Two Violins, Bassoon and Strings in D.
Overture-Suite in G.   **P**
Collegium Musicum 90 / Simon Standage
Chandos Chaconne CHAN0700 (66' · DDD)   **F**➔

Telemann is never more irresistible than when
he's in light-hearted pictorial mode, and both
these new releases feature one of the most entertainingly evocative of all his overture-suites for
strings, the *Burlesque de Quixote*. Taking episodes from the Cervantes novel as its inspiration, it provides us with a memorable sequence
of cameos, from the deluded Don tilting at
windmills and sighing with love, to Sancho
Panza tossed high in a blanket, to portrayals of
the pair's respective steeds. Telemann achieves
all this with such humour and descriptive precision that, when you hear it, you'll surely laugh in
delighted recognition. What a good film composer he would have been!
Both performances strike an appropriate
tongue-in-cheek attitude. Northern Chamber
Orchestra show good style and a pleasingly light
and clear texture, unclouded by excessive vibrato
or over-egged string tone. Only at the bass end
does the sound occasionally become a little thick,
but this is really quibbling when what we actually
have is a good demonstration of how to perform
Baroque music on modern strings. It still makes
quite a contrast with Collegium Musicum 90,
however, whose period instruments, recorded
more intimately, sound slighter and sparkier.

Having already recorded so much of Telemann's music, they sound more at home and have that extra ounce of freedom to enjoy themselves.

The couplings of the Chandos disc are more interesting. For all that the NCO offer another attractive string suite, *La Lyra*, containing a typically realistic and beguiling hurdy-gurdy impersonation, the D major Overture isn't especially memorable; CM90 have found more colourful stuff in the strikingly French-accented G major Overture and a thoroughly charming Concerto for two violins, bassoon and strings. A pair of bassoons also makes a delightful appearance in the second Minuet of the Overture in B minor.

Musique de Table / Tafelmusik

Musique de Table, 'Tafelmusik', Part 3 – Concerto . **P** for Two Horns and Strings in E flat; Overture in B flat; Quartet in E minor; Sonata for Oboe and Continuo in G minor; Trio in D; Conclusion in B flat
Orchestra of the Golden Age
Naxos 8 553732 (73' · DDD)   ⑤𝇗

The Orchestra of the Golden Age bring expressive warmth to this evergreen repertoire. The present disc contains the third of the three 'Productions' that make up Telemann's most comprehensive orchestral/instrumental publication. It's the shortest of the three and so can be accommodated comfortably on a single disc. Like its predecessors, the Third consists of an orchestral Suite, Quartet, Concerto, Trio, Sonata for melody instrument with figured bass and an orchestral 'Conclusion'. Telemann had already generously provided for transverse flute, trumpet and solo violins in the previous 'Productions' while maintaining the flute profile (Quartet and Trio) in the third anthology; he gives pride of place to oboe(s) in the Suite, Sonata and Conclusion, and a pair of horns in the Concerto.

One might feel that a slightly augmented string section would have been justified for the orchestral suites and concertos. But, in this instance the players realise the innate nobility of the French overture character with a justly 'occasional' tempo. In the Concerto, which comes over well, if perhaps a shade rigidly in its rhythm, the horn players Roger Montgomery and Gavin Edwards sustain an evenly balanced and tonally secure partnership. That also goes for the lightly articulated flute partnership of Edwina Smith and Felicity Bryson in the Trio. The lovely G minor Oboe Sonata is played with warmth and expressive intimacy by Heather Foxwell. Telemann brings all to a vigorous close with a little three-section orchestral coda, marked *Furioso*. This is a set which makes rather more of Telemann's inflective *délicatesse* than others at twice or even three times the price.

Chamber Works

Sonates Corellisantes – No 1 in F, TWV42:F2.   **P**
Paris Quartets, 'Nouveaux quatuors en Six Suites' –

No 6 in E minor, TWV43:e4. Essercizii Musici – Trio
No 8 in B flat, TWV42:B4. Quartets – A minor, TWV43: a3; G minor, TWV43:g4
Florilegium Ensemble
Channel Classics CCS5093 (53' · DDD)   Ⓕ⊙⊙

The rarity here is the *Sonata Corellisante* for two violins and continuo in which Telemann pays tribute to Corelli. The remaining works are the sixth and perhaps finest of the 1738 *Nouveaux Quatuors* or *Paris Quartets* as they have become known, a little *Quartet* (or *Quadro*) in G minor, a B flat Trio from the *Essercizii Musici* collection (c1739) and a fine Concerto da camera (Quartet) in A minor, very much along the lines of Vivaldi's pieces of the same kind in which each instrument other than the continuo has an obbligato role. The finest work is the *Paris Quartet*, which consists of a Prelude, a sequence of dance-orientated movements and an elegiac Chaconne that lingers long in the memory. The performance is full of vitality and probes beneath the music's superficialities. Throughout the programme there's an intensity and a youthful spontaneity about this playing which has considerable appeal.

Paris Quartets, Volume 2   **P**
Quartets – in D, TWV43: D3; in A minor, TWV43: a2; in G, TWV43: G4. Six Concerts and Six Suites – Suite No 1 in G, TWV42: G4
Florilegium (Ashley Solomon *fl* Kati Debretzini *vn* Reiko Ichise *bvio* Jennifer Morsches *vc* James Johnstone *hpd*)
Channel Classics CD/SACD 🎧 CCSSA20604 (71' · DDD)   Ⓕ

Printed in Paris by Le Clerc without Telemann's permission in 1736 but composed in Hamburg in 1730, the first six of these quartets called 'Quadri' were such a success that the composer himself was able to have printed – through a 'Privilege du Roi' – another six, the *Nouveaux quatours en suites*, in 1738. That set, too, had originated in the German city but also went down a treat with the Parisians.

Both groups are written for flute, violin, viola da gamba (with an alternative part for cello) and basso continuo, and comprise the composer's total output for this set of instruments. But confusingly, he divided 'Quadri' into pairs titled concertos, sonatas and suites; and in Concerto Primo, Florilegium use the cello while sticking with the gamba for the remaining pieces.

As before, James Johnstone is the right sort of continuo player, an inventive and expressive presence, not an intrusion. His colleagues are of a similar persuasion and their responses to both the robustness and delicacy of the music is exemplified in the first movement ('Allègrement') of the A minor quartet and second movement ('Légèrement') of the G major quartet. These interpretations are of very high calibre.

The image is on the close side and the lines are a little crowded; a reduction in volume helps separate them and convey more clearly the nuances in the playing.

Paris Quartets, Volume 3   **P**
Paris Quartets, 'Nouveaux quatuors en six suites',
TWV43 – No 2; No 3; No 4. Six Concerts et Six Suites
– Suite No 3
Florilegium Ensemble (Ashley Solomon *fl* Kati
Debretzeni *vn* Reiko Ichise *viol* Jennifer Morsches *vc*
James Johnstone *hpd*)
Channel Classics ⊛ CCSSA21005 (74' · DDD)   Ⓕ

Florilegium here complete their cycle of Telemann's 'Paris' Quartets – actually a set of six
quartet sonatas composed in Hamburg in 1730
but popular in France after their publication
there, and a second set of six with which the
canny Telemann followed them up while in
Paris in 1738. This release contains three works
from the second set and one from the first.

The quartets have become among the most
popular pieces in the Baroque chamber repertoire, so there is no need to rehearse their qualities
here, save to reiterate that their beguiling, convivial style is about as comfortably civilised as it gets.
Florilegium's performances mix technical and
musical finesse in equal measure and observe
every expressive and rhetorical nuance with a delicious light touch. Theirs is not the chiselled precision and up-front high energy of some modern-
day Baroque chamber groups, but their playing is
unfailingly alive and the details of their elegant
conversation are well captured in a recorded balance in which no instrument is allowed undue
dominance. The chaconne which ends the sixth
quartet, TWV43:e4, is exquisitely drawn out,
there are some charming drone effects here and
there, and overall it is difficult to know what else
to add – only, perhaps, that in their mutual refinement and good taste, Florilegium and Telemann
could have been made for each other.

12 Fantaisies for Violin without Continuo, TWV40:   **P**
14-25. Der getreue Music-Meister – 'Gulliver' Suite in
D, TWV40:108
Andrew Manze, Caroline Balding *vns*
Harmonia Mundi HMU90 7137 (78' · DDD)   Ⓕ

Andrew Manze brings a very distinctive angle to
the 12 *Fantaisies*. We have learnt to take virtuosity for granted with Manze – his remarkable
feats allow the most prejudiced to forget that
he's playing a Baroque fiddle. But without such
an instrument he could barely create such a
biting astringency in the more self-effacing and
tortured moments (*Fantaisie* No 6) or a cultivated assurance and definition in articulation to
the recognisably regular sections, such as *Fantaisie* No 10, where Telemann is working in
established forms – particularly in the latter
works in the set where dance forms predominate. If characterisation is the key, Manze is
arguably more persuasive than any of his rivals.
He grows through phrases in the Gigue of the
Fourth *Fantaisie* in a fashion which gives the
work a peculiarly stoical strength, purrs through
the contrapuntally conceived *Fantaisies* with
nonchalant disdain for their extreme technical
demands and leaves sighs and pauses hanging

with supreme eloquence. With sheer lucidity,
imagination and colour, he most acutely captures the sense of a famous public figure
ensconced in a private world against the backdrop of a musical world in a state of flux. To add
spice to an already outstanding release, we have
the short and delightful *Gulliver* Suite for two
violins.

12 Sonate metodiche   **P**
Barthold Kuijken *fl* **Wieland Kuijken** *va da gamba*
Robert Kohnen *hpd*
Accent ② ACC94104/5D (140' · DDD)   ⒻOO

No, the title is hardly an incentive to part with
your pocket-money. But with Telemann we
should know better than to be taken in by such
packaging details. These are, in fact, 12 skilfully written and entertaining sonatas, published in two sets of six and issued in 1728 and
1732. Telemann seems, right from the start, to
have had two instruments in mind: flute or
violin, and though Barthold Kuijken has
elected to them play all on a Baroque flute, he
does so with such technical mastery that
there's little cause for regret. He savours the
many playful ideas contained in the faster
movements and realises a touching sense of
melancholy in several of the slow ones. Among
the most impressive of the sonatas is that in B
minor, which Kuijken plays with sensitivity
and technical panache. The interpretation is
on a sufficiently elevated level to warrant
unqualified praise. The recorded sound is first
rate.

Die Donner-Ode, TWV6:3

Der Herr ist König, TWV8:6. Die Donner-Ode   **P**
Ann Monoyios, Barbara Schlick *sops* **Axel Köhler**
counterten **Wilfried Jochens** *ten* **Harry van der**
Kamp, Hans-Georg Wimmer, Stephan Schrecken-
berger *basses* **Rheinische Kantorei; Das Kleine**
Konzert / Hermann Max
Capriccio 10 556 (65' · DDD · T/t)   Ⓕ

The *Donner-Ode* was one of Telemann's biggest
public successes during his lifetime and is a striking piece in its own right, a vivid reaction to the
Lisbon earthquake of 1755. The shock caused to
the international community by this dreadful
event (in which some 60,000 people were killed)
was enormous, and in Hamburg a special day of
penitence was the occasion for this 'Thunder
Ode', though it does perhaps suggest a rather
smug satisfaction that such a disaster didn't befall
northern Germany. 'The voice of God makes the
proud mountains collapse', the text proclaims,
'Give thanks to Him in His temple!' The music,
too, both in its mood and in that extraordinarily
up-to-date style of Telemann's later years, frequently conjures the benign, entertainingly song-
like pictorial mood of a Haydn Mass or oratorio.
Entertaining is the word, though, especially in
this energetic performance under Hermann Max.

He's fleet-footed and buoyantly athletic, benefiting from what's becoming his customary excellent team of German soloists.

For the coupling Max chooses another German work, the cheerful cantata *Der Herr ist König*, written much earlier in the composer's life and more Bach-like in character and form (though it's worth pointing out that since it survives partly in Bach's hand, we ought perhaps to conclude that Telemann was the one wielding the influence here). As in the *Ode*, choir, soloists and orchestra are bright, tight-knit and well recorded, making this release an enjoyable one.

Brockes Passion

Brockes Passion, TVWV5:1　　　　　　　　Ⓟ
Lydia Teuscher, Birgit Christensen sops **Marie-Claude Chappuis** mez **Donát Havár, Daniel Behle** tens **Johannes Weisser** bar **RIAS Chamber Choir, Berlin; Akademie für Alte Musik Berlin / René Jacobs**
Harmonia Mundi ② HMC90 2013/14
(140' · DDD)　　　　　　　　　　　　　ⒻⓄ⟿

The Hamburg poet Barthold Heinrich Brockes wrote the Passion oratorio libretto *Der für die Sünde der Welt gemarterte und sterbende Jesus* for Reinhard Keiser to set to music in 1712. Handel composed a setting in London about four years later (probably for Hamburg), and in April 1716 Telemann's version was first performed in Frankfurt. The broody opening Sinfonia makes one think of Haydn's late orchestral writing at its most daring. The Berlin AAM's playing is lean and angular but the 35-strong RIAS Chamber Choir seems overpowering at times, and it would be good to hear this work performed by smaller and more integrated forces.

René Jacobs divides the soprano arias for the Daughter of Zion and the Faithful Soul between Birgitte Christensen and Lydia Teuscher (the booklet fails to indicate what singer performs which arias): 'Was Bärentatzen, Löwenklauen' has snappy percussive horn fanfares, and several contrasting arias during the scene of Christ's scourging are among the highest points of the oratorio. Marie-Claude Chappuis's singing of Judas's guilt-wracked scene, in which the betrayer resolves to commit suicide, is extraordinary. The trio 'O Donnerwort!' crackles with theatrical velocity. Johannes Weisser is a grainy Jesus, but his declamatory singing in the volatile 'Erwäg, ergrimmte Natterbrut' is impressive. Donát Havár does not have a mellifluous timbre but is a good communicator of Peter's texts. Jacobs paces the oratorio as if it is a vivid religious opera: he omits six arias and two recitatives 'for reasons of dramatic coherence'. There are moments of brittle intensity that could have afforded more gentleness, but Jacobs's committed vision provides us with a valuable glimpse of Telemann's brilliant imagination.

Die Hirten an der Krippe zu Bethlehem

Die Hirten an der Krippe zu Bethlehem.　　　Ⓟ
Siehe, ich verkündige Euch, TWV1:1334. Der Herr hat offenbaret, TWV1:262
Constanze Backes sop **Mechthild Georg** contr **Andreas Post** ten **Klaus Mertens** bass **Michaelstein Chamber Choir; Telemann Chamber Orchestra / Ludger Rémy**
CPO CPO999 419-2 (65' · DDD · T/t)　　　　ⒻⓄ

The tenderly expressive and ingenuous character of German Protestant Christmas music of the Baroque seldom fails to exert its magic. Though the greatest achievements in this tradition greatly diminished after Bach, there were exceptions. One of them is Telemann's intimate and imaginative oratorio *Die Hirten an der Krippe zu Bethlehem* ('The Shepherds at the Crib in Bethlehem'). The text is by the Berlin poet, Ramler and though Ramler's taste for classical forms sometimes makes his work stiff and austere, nothing could be further removed from this than his intimate account and celebration of Christ's birth. Certainly, it touched a chord in Telemann, who responded with music of expressive warmth and irresistible charm.

This isn't at all the world of Bach's *Christmas Oratorio*. Indeed, it's only approximately a sixth of the length of Bach's masterpiece. Telemann's concept is one rather of noble simplicity, a sought-after goal in post-Bach church music which, in this respect, at least, provided a perfect foil to Ramler's text. Every reader will recognise the melody of the opening number as belonging to the Latin carol *In dulci jubilo*. Telemann's harmonisation of the 16th-century tune sets the scene concisely and intimately. Thereafter, follows one delight after another. Of outstanding beauty are the 'Shepherd's Song' and the bass aria, 'Hirten aus den goldnen Zeiten'. This is an extremely pleasurable, well-filled, disc with a pervasive charm. The remaining two items are both Christmas cantatas, of 1761 and 1762 respectively, and contain music of enormous appeal. Performances are excellent, with outstanding singing by Klaus Mertens and Mechthild Georg. Both choir and orchestra rise to the occasion under the sensitive and stylish direction of Ludger Rémy. Three hitherto unrecorded pieces in performances of such vitality make this a very strong issue.

Cantatas

Lobet den Herrn, alle seine Heerscharen, TWV1:061. Wer nur den lieben Gott lässt walten, TWV1:593. Der Tod ist verschlungen in den Sieg, TWV1:320
Dorothee Fries sop **Mechthild Georg** contr **Andreas Post** ten **Albert Pöhl** bass **Friedemann Immer Trumpet Consort** (Friedemann Immer, Klaus Osterloh, Ute Hübner tpts Stefan Gawlik timp) **Bach Collegium Vocale, Siegen; Hanover Hofkapelle / Ulrich Stötzel**
Hänssler Classic CD98 179 (56' · DDD · T/t)　　　Ⓕ

While Telemann's concertos, suites, instrumental chamber music and oratorios have been well explored by performers, his large-scale cantatas, comparatively speaking, have not. Part of the problem is that there's a truly daunting number of them. And, it need hardly be said, the quality is variable. But few are utterly devoid of inspiration and the three pieces contained in this programme rise well beyond that category. Until now they have remained very possibly unperformed, but certainly unrecorded. These aren't domestic pieces of the kind which characterise his well-known Hamburg anthology, *Der harmonische Gottes-dienst*, but generously, sometimes colourfully orchestrated works with choruses, recitatives, arias and chorales. The format, in short, is Bach-like, though with nothing remotely comparable to the great opening choral fantasies of which Bach was the master. Telemann usually treats his hymn melodies simply, this approach lending them a distinctive, ingenuous charm.

The three cantatas offer strong contrasts of colour and of mood. The New Year piece, *Lobet den Herrn* has glittering trumpet parts with timpani and Telemann's deployment of them is deft and effective. The Neumeister setting, on the other hand, with an orchestra confined to strings and woodwind, is quietly spoken and more reflective. Performances are stylish, and the director, Ulrich Stötzel, has a lively feeling for Telemann's frequent use of dance rhythms. The soloists are expressive, notably Mechthild Georg, who offers a lyrical account of her aria with oboe in the Easter cantata, *Der Tod ist verschlungen in den Sieg*. In short, this is a release which should interest and delight all readers with a taste for the music of this imaginative, prolific and seemingly indefatigable composer.

Ambroise Thomas   French 1811-1896

Born into a musical family, Thomas was groomed for a career in music and by the age of 10 was accomplished both as a pianist and as a violinist. His father had played in the theatre orchestras of Metz, and in his 20s had been swept up in the post-Revolutionary currents of change which affected the orchestra and opera there no less than elsewhere in France; he subsequently became a respected teacher and published pedagogical works. After years of neglect, Thomas' work has seen a considerable revival in the last two decades of the 20th century, with major performances, at least of Mignon and Hamlet, being mounted in France, Great Britain and the USA. In the context of French opera of the late 19th century Thomas was a figure of considerable importance, an imaginative innovator and a master of musical characterisation.   GROVEmusic

La Cour de Célimène

La Cour de Célimène
Laura Claycomb sop La Comtesse **Joan Rodgers**
sop La Baronne **Alastair Miles** bass-bar Le Commandeur **Sébastien Droy** ten Le Chevalier **Nicole Tibbels** sop Bretonne **Geoffrey Mitchell Choir; Philharmonia Orchestra / Andrew Litton**
Opera Rara ② ORC37 (73' · DDD · S/T/t/N)   Ⓕ◐

La Cour de Célimène was introduced at the Opéra Comique in 1855, a time of mass-production of new operas in Paris, and was dropped after 19 performances. It was probably not so robust in tunefulness or dramatic situation as to make its way through in these circumstances. It was also tagged with the old-fashioned characteristic of an ornate vocal style. Presumably, with its courtly setting in the *ancien régime* it would have appeared to the more serious-minded and left-inclined of Parisians to be reactionary in its nostalgic appeal and trivial in every other respect.

Today the first reaction is likely to be gratitude and delight in the discovery of a score which, if not coming up with 'big' tunes, is unfailingly melodious. We may also be more inclined to credit the comedy with a certain sophistication, the light irony of a raised eyebrow surveying the human scene, as in *Così fan tutte*. The title, with its implied reference to Molière, possibly adds a suggestion or two, for the countess, the central character here, is like Célimène in *Le misantrope* representative of the maddeningly beautiful, frivolous and privileged, and here too the world arranges itself to suit its convenience rather than its virtuous principles.

At least if time rejects it yet again it will not be the fault of this performance. Both sopranos manage the florid work with apparent ease, Laura Claycomb soaring aloft gracefully, Joan Rodgers having the additional warmth to suit the Baroness's more thoughtful nature. Alastair Miles enjoys himself in his role of worldly aristocrat with the attributes of a virtuoso and a *buffo* bass. Sébastien Droy has the right lightness and youth of voice and manner, and, as the only Frenchman, does not show up the efforts of the English in his language. Chorus and orchestra contribute splendidly; Andrew Litton conducts with stylish zest; recorded sound is clear and well balanced.

Sir Michael Tippett   British 1905-1998

Tippett studied with C Wood and Kitson at the RCM (1923-8), then settled in Oxted, Surrey, where he taught, conducted a choir and began to compose. However, dissatisfaction with his technique led him to take further lessons with Morris (1930-32), and he published nothing until he was into his mid-30s. By then he was conducting at Morley College, of which he became music director in 1940; there he performed his oratorio A Child of our Time (1941), which uses a story of Nazi atrocity but draws no simple moral from it, concluding rather that we must recognise within ourselves both good and evil.
A Child of our Time seems further to have released creative energy that went into a series of works – two

more quartets, the cantata for tenor and piano *Boy-hood's End* and the *Symphony No 1 –* leading to the composition of the opera *The Midsummer Marriage* in the years 1946–52. The message is again that of the oratorio: before marriage the central characters must each accept the wedding within their personalities of intellect and carnality. The theme relates to *The Magic Flute*, and Tippett's sources for his own libretto also include Shaw, Yeats and Eliot.

The opera's musical exuberance spilt over into succeeding works, including the *Fantasia concertante on a Theme of Corelli* for strings and the *Piano Concerto*, but then through the *Symphony No 2* (1957) came a clearing and hardening of style towards the vivid block forms and declamatory vocal style of the opera *King Priam*, composed in 1958–61, which concerns the problem of free will. Once more an opera had its off-shoots; notably in the *Piano Sonata No 2* and the *Concerto for Orchestra*, with its distinct gestures and circular formal schemes, but followed by a new, ecstatic continuity in the cantata *The Vision of St Augustine* (1965). In his opera *The Knot Garden* (1970) he concentrates on the emotional substance of clashes of personality and their outcome. His unusually candid if stylised presentation of raw human relationships and of the need to make a success of the seemingly incompatible ones produce a score of lapidary compression, notable for its metallic sonorities, its use of a 12-note theme (though not serial technique) to represent fractured relationships and its revival of blues and boogie-woogie in a manner analogous to his use of spirituals in *A Child of our Time*.

Symphony No 3 continues to explore the seemingly inexhaustible flow of invention stimulated by the 'light' and the 'shadow'. The range of reference is wider in the opera *The Ice Break*, where again the blues stand for human warmth in a time of uncertainty but where the composer alludes to diverse strands of high and popular culture in a work that depicts and transfigures clashes of age, race and milieu. Again, the opera is composed of fragmentary scenes in which archetypal characters confront one another, but now in a context of global discord; the musical style is even more jaggedly kaleidoscopic, as it is also in *Symphony No 4*, which abandons the vocal solution of the Third but finds in purely musical development a metaphor of physical birth, growth and dissolution. Other late works include the oratorio *The Mask of Time* (1982), a grand restatement of Tippett's musical and philosophical concerns, as well as a *Concerto for string trio and orchestra*.

GROVEmusic

Concerto for Double String Orchestra

Concerto for Double String Orchestra. Fantasia concertante on a Theme of Corelli. The Midsummer Marriage – Ritual Dances
BBC Symphony Chorus and Orchestra / Sir Andrew Davis
Warner Apex 8573-89098-2 (64' · DDD) ⓢ↦

Sir Andrew Davis's formidable Tippettian credentials shine through in every bar of this outstanding anthology. Aided by realistic, firmly focused sound, the *Concerto for Double String*

Orchestra sounds glorious here. Davis directs a performance of enormous humanity, intelligence and dedication – even Sir Neville Marriner's excellent EMI remake now seems a little matter-of-fact by comparison. In the slow movement Davis secures a rapt response from his BBC strings (the exquisite closing bars are drawn with ineffable tenderness), while the finale bounds along with irrepressible vigour and fine rhythmic panache. Davis's *Fantasia concertante* is an even more remarkable achievement. This is another inspirational display: sensitive and fervent, yet marvellously lucid and concentrated too. Once again, the BBC strings are on radiant form, and the lyrical intensity of their playing during the central climax has to be heard to be believed. Davis's identification with this sublime music is total. Much the same applies, for that matter, to the committed and incisive account of the 'Ritual Dances' from *The Midsummer Marriage*, a veritable tour de force to which the BBC Symphony Chorus contributes thrillingly in the final dance.

Piano Concerto

Piano Concerto[a]. Fantasia on a Theme of Handel[a].
Four Piano Sonatas
Steven Osborne pf
[a]**BBC Scottish Symphony Orchestra / Martyn Brabbins**
Hyperion ② CDA67461/2 (141' · DDD)　ⓕ🔴🔴🔴

 The young Tippett – magpie and maverick – sought maximum intensity of feeling while shunning what he felt to be the sentimental fervour of Elgar, Bax and Walton. Equally abhorrent were the pastoral pieties of Vaughan Williams. Tippett took his stand with Blake and Yeats rather than Bunyan, and a Blake whose 'bow of burning gold' required something altogether less complacent than Parry's well upholstered jingoism.

The results are plain to hear in Tippett's earliest works for piano, the First Sonata and the *Handel* Fantasia. The slow movement of the sonata may flirt briefly with Hindemith-style counterpoint but the predominant spirit is fiery and spontaneous, with a reinvigorated romanticism embracing those aspects of popular music which Tippett believed to have 'classical' potential.

The road ahead was bumpy and he occasionally lost his way, as in the very long slow movement of the Third Sonata, aspiring to Beethovenian depth but bogged down in overly dense textures. There are also several repetitions too many in the Fourth Sonata, though the final movement's gently poetic sense of resignation more than compensates.

Most powerful of all is the mighty Concerto, starkly and confidently poised between Tippett's still richly potent earlier style and the brave new possibilities explored in its visionary central movement. This recording blends the piano in with the orchestra, acknowledging the work's symphonic attributes, and there is a certain recessed quality to the sound of the piece throughout. Nevertheless, the eloquence and fantasy of what is undoubtedly one of the major works of the 1950s is superbly projected in a performance which need fear no comparison with the best earlier recordings. As for the sonatas, Steven Osborne is at least the equal of Paul Crossley (CRD) in interpretative empathy, and has the advantage of superlative modern recording. There's a further advantage: perceptive and lucid booklet-notes by Ian Kemp, Tippett's friend and biographer, and one of Osborne's mentors. The set is dedicated to him.

Symphonies

Symphonies Nos 1-4. New Year – Suite
Faye Robinson sop
Bournemouth Symphony / Richard Hickox
Chandos ③ CHAN10330 (193' · DDD)　　Ⓜ❶❷➔

The riot of proliferating counterpoint that is Tippett's Symphony No 1 presents enough problems of orchestral balance to give recording teams nightmares. Chandos has managed creditable degrees of containment and clarity, without loss of realism, and the impact, when the last movement finally settles on to its long-prepared harmonic goal, is powerful and convincing. Doubts as to whether initial impetus is sufficient to keep the complex structures on course prove groundless. This is a fine account, well balanced between lively rhythmic articulation and broad melodic sweep.

The balance Hickox achieves between attention to detail and large-scale symphonic sweep is exemplary, and especially impressive in the tricky finale of Symphony No 2, where he conveys the essential ambiguity of an ending which strives to recapture the optimistic *élan* of the work's opening without ever quite managing it. The recording, too, gives us much more of the symphony's contrapuntal detail. The first recording of music from Tippett's opera *New Year*, premiered in 1989, is thoroughly welcome. The music of this suite may seem over-emphatic to anyone who hasn't experienced the opera in the theatre, and the recording relishes the booming electric guitars and wailing saxophones, as well as the taped spaceship effects.

The Third Symphony (1972) is one of Tippett's most complex and highly charged attempts to create a convincing structure from the collision between strongly contrasted musical characteristics. The first two movements (Part 1, as Tippett calls it) remain a considerable technical challenge, especially to the strings, but this performance manages to sustain an appropriate level of tension without sounding merely effortful, and without skimping on the opportunities for eloquence of phrasing. It could well be that Tippett has over-indulged the percussion in the slow movement, but this vivid and well-balanced Chandos recording lets us hear ample detail without exaggerating the bright colours and hyper-resonant textures. The later stages have the advantage of a superbly characterful singer in Faye Robinson who has the power, the edge,

and also the radiance, to make Tippett's progression from idiosyncratic blues to Beethoven-quoting peroration utterly convincing.

It is good to find Richard Hickox and the Bournemouth SO taking on some imposing competition and holding their own so well. Hickox's Fourth Symphony is more broadly conceived than Solti's for Decca, and it's a considerable success, for despite giving even more weight to the work's strong contrasts, as is evident especially in the final stages, Hickox avoids any impression that the work is merely a succession of separate episodes. This well-integrated reading receives a well-rounded recording, and playing which needn't fear comparison with the best Chicago has to offer. (The individual works are also available as downloads.)

String Quartets

String Quartets – Nos 1-5
The Lindsays (Peter Cropper, Ronald Birks *vns* Roger Bigley/Robin Ireland *va* Bernard Gregor-Smith *vc*)
ASV ② CDDCS231 (123' · ADD/DDD) Recorded 1975-92　　Ⓕ❶

Tippett coached the The Lindsays for these recordings of his first three quartets, and wrote the other two for the quartet. In a note written for their 25th anniversary in 1992 he said that in these recordings they were 'concerned to establish good precedents in matters of style, so that succeeding generations of interpreters start at an advantage'. In fact one of the most enjoyable things about these readings is that they're so very characteristic of the The Lindsays. A number of the qualities you might call 'characteristic' are uncommonly well suited to Tippett's earlier quartets: big tone, vigour of attack and an infectious enjoyment of his lithe sprung rhythms. These performances are excellent precedents for later interpreters. They establish a style – big-scaled, urgently communicative – that's presumably 'authentic' and yet they challenge listeners as well as other performers to imagine how else they might be done. They also affirm the aching absence of a quartet between the Third and the Fourth (Tippett intended to write one in the late 1940s or early 1950s but got sidetracked by *The Midsummer Marriage*) and make one wonder what the rejected two movements of the First Quartet might be like. It's wonderful, though, to hear the five as a sequence in such authoritative readings. The recordings sound very well, but have been transferred at an exceptionally high level.

Piano Sonatas

Piano Sonatas Nos 1-3
Peter Donohoe *pf*
Naxos 8 557611 (54' · DDD)　　Ⓕ❶➔

It's a pity that, at 35 minutes-plus, Tippett's Fourth and last piano sonata is too long to join the others on a single CD. Be that as it may, it's good

Naxos is opening up this repertoire, and Peter Donohoe is recorded with pleasing immediacy.

The First Sonata is especially successful – imaginatively characterised, the music's tendency to sprawl in the outer movements kept firmly in check. Despite the derivative aspects of its style, the piece has many distinctive qualities and – at least in Donohoe's performance – it stands up rather better than its successors.

No 2, a single-movement mosaic closely linked to *King Priam* and the Concerto for Orchestra, is in most respects the absolute antithesis of No 1, and the sheer number of repetitions of small thematic units creates a degree of stasis at odds with the free-flowing aspirations of the overall design.

Donohoe is acutely responsive to the broad contrasts and insistent rhythmic patterns of the Third Sonata but his tempo for the first movement is distinctly slower than Paul Crossley's (the Third Sonata's commissioner and first performer).

Choral Works

The Windhover. The Source. Magnificat and Nunc dimittis, 'Collegium Sancti Johannis Cantabrigiense'. Lullaby. Four Songs from the British Isles. Dance, Clarion Air. A Child of Our Time – Five Negro Spirituals. Plebs angelica. The Weeping Babe
Finzi Singers / Paul Spicer
with **Andrew Lumsden** org
Chandos CHAN9265 (55' · DDD · T)　　Ⓕ●🅑➤

The Finzi Singers are eloquent in the Spirituals, and polished in the *British Songs* (especially the beguiling 'Early One Morning'). However, it's especially good to have the works which represent early sightings of Tippett's later, less lusciously lyrical style – the *Lullaby* (with countertenor, reminding us that it was written for the Deller Consort) and the *Magnificat* and *Nunc dimittis*: here not only are the intonation and phrasing of the tricky lines supremely confident, but the accompanying organ is recorded with exemplary naturalness. The vocal sound throughout is generally no less successful. There may be almost too full and rich a texture for the linear intricacies of *Plebs angelica* and *The Weeping Babe* to make their maximum effect, but there's no lack of exuberance in *Dance*, *Clarion Air* and the other secular pieces.

Four Songs from the British Isles. Dance, Clarion Air. Lullaby. Two Madrigals. Magnificat and Nunc dimittis, 'Collegium Sancti Johannis Cantabrigiense'. Five Negro Spirituals from 'A Child of Our Time'. Plebs angelica. The Weeping Babe. Unto the Hills. Over the Sea to Skye
BBC Singers / Stephen Cleobury
with **Ian Farrington** org
Signum SIGCD092 (63' · DDD · T/t)　　Ⓕ🅑➤

Tippett's choral music makes for a heterogeneous collection on disc: just the sort of programme you would never expect to encounter at a live concert. Signum Classics underlines the heterogeneity by cramming the 19 items together with only a few brief seconds between them. This makes for several jarring shifts of tonality, and seems especially careless since the disc plays for under 63 minutes anyway. Constant use of the pause button is the only solution.

Fortunately, the performances compensate. The polish and professionalism of the BBC Singers are everywhere apparent, and they bring an imposing tonal weight to such familiar items as the *Spirituals from 'A Child of Our Time'*. This is a fine account, aided by the lively acoustic of the Temple Church: for once one hardly misses the orchestra in 'Go down, Moses'. For the same reason the absence of boys' voices in the Magnificat and Nunc dimittis for St John's College, Cambridge, and of a plangent solo countertenor in *Lullaby*, for the Deller Consort, are less troubling than they might otherwise be.

Stephen Cleobury and the BBC Singers are especially impressive in the weaving lines and dancing rhythms of the madrigals and motets from the 1940s. Even they can do little to clarify the congested textures of the *Songs from the British Isles*, but there are two previously unrecorded items: an arrangement of 'Over the Sea to Skye' weaves the familiar tune in some appealingly offbeat counterpoints, and a hymn-tune written by the atheist Tippett for the Salvation Army proves to be touchingly sincere.

A Child of our Time

A Child of our Time
Faye Robinson sop **Sarah Walker** mez
Jon Garrison ten **John Cheek** bass **City of Birmingham Symphony Chorus and Orchestra / Sir Michael Tippett**
Naxos 8 557570 (70' · DDD)　　Ⓢ🅑➤

The centenary of Sir Michael Tippett's birth saw a fair amount of critical agonising about whether he was, any longer, a composer for our time, or whether his time had passed. It's difficult to find much substance in that viewpoint when confronted with a work, first performed in 1944, which seems to have more in common with John Adams's much-admired *El Niño* of 2000 than with *Belshazzar's Feast*, or even the *War Requiem*. The starkness of the confrontations in *A Child of our Time* between politics and psychology, between a high-art style rooted in Bach and a more popular, folk-tinged manner (the tango, Negro Spirituals), remains vivid, as does the sense of a composer doggedly carving out a viably personal idiom while not shirking matters of burning social and spiritual relevance. Maybe the focus wavers in places but the accumulated dramatic power, and its double release, first in a magical vision of spring, then in a more anxious, uncertain cry for peace and reconciliation, isn't something a bumbling amateur could have brought off.

Tippett was 87 when this recording was made, and neither its rhythmic momentum nor its textural clarity are ideal. But the composer's own lovingly crafted reading has a special place in the discography of this still-modern masterpiece.

A Child of Our Time
Indra Thomas sop **Mihoko Fujimura** contr
Steve Davislim ten **Matthew Rose** bass
**London Symphony Chorus and Orchestra /
Sir Colin Davis**
LSO Live 🔊 LSO0670 (64' · DDD · T)
Recorded live in 2007　　　　　　　Ⓑ Ⓞ ➭

Four years after his Dresden version of *A Child of Our Time*, recorded live in the Semperoper (Profil, 3/08), Sir Colin Davis returned to the work in the very different environment of London's Barbican Hall. On this occasion the Classic Sound engineers and editors have managed a good blend of the intimate and the intense. Now and again a soloist may seem unduly reticent – perhaps a vocal problem on the day rather than a matter of recorded balance. But is there another recording that surpasses this one in the expressive power with which choral singing and orchestral playing combine to reinforce the timeless message of this most history-conscious work, rooted as it is in events just prior to the years of its composition (1939-41)?

The formidable discipline and sensitivity of the London Symphony Chorus are immediately clear in the well defined dynamic contrasts of Part 1's first movement. While an imposing weight of sonority, as in the Spiritual 'Go Down Moses', can be guaranteed, there is a rare lightness of articulation in the passage beginning 'We are as seed before the wind', which returns in 'Nobody knows the trouble I see'.

Of the soloists, soprano Indra Thomas struggles with foggy vibrato while still managing to float some beautifully unstrained high notes in the final ensemble. Mihoko Fujimura, Steve Davislim and Matthew Rose are all excellent, and it's especially good to have a tenor who sounds young enough to embody the character of Herschel Grynszpan convincingly. Of course, some collectors will not be persuaded that Sir Colin could ever match, let alone outdo, his first, 1975 Philips recording of the work. Nevertheless, the enduring significance of the piece for him is palpable right through to the superbly shaped account of the final Spiritual, 'Deep River'. There are emotional depths here which turn this recording into something very special.

Songs

Tippett Music. Songs for Ariel. Songs for Achilles. Boyhood's End. The Heart's Assurance. **Purcell** If music be the food of love, Z379/2. The Fairy Queen – Thrice happy lovers. The Fatal hour comes on apace, Z421. Bess of Bedlam, Z370. Pausanias – Sweeter than roses

Martyn Hill ten **Craig Ogden** gtr **Andrew Ball** pf
Hyperion CDA66749 (70' · DDD · T)　　　　　Ⓕ Ⓞ

The two longest works – the cantata *Boyhood's End* and song cycle *The Heart's Assurance* – challenge the musicianship and sensitivity of both singer and pianist alike. *Boyhood's End* (1943), a setting of prose that's never prosaic, shows the ecstasy of *Midsummer Marriage* to be already within the system, and the profusion of notes has to be mastered so that the dance shall seem as delicate and natural as graceful improvisation. In *The Heart's Assurance* (1951) the spirit's similar, although the technical accomplishment of all concerned, composer and performers, is heightened. For the singer, in addition to the quite fearsome difficulties of pitch and rhythm, there's also likely to be some problem of tessitura, particularly in the third of the songs, 'Compassion'. For the pianist, concentration has to be divided between the virtuoso writing of his own part and responsiveness to the singer, his notes, words and expression. Martyn Hill and Andrew Ball are wonderfully at one in all this, and the balancing of voice and piano has been finely achieved. The *Songs for Achilles*, with guitar, also convey a real sense of ardent improvisation, and the voice rings out freely. The *Songs for Ariel* here work their natural magic. Tippett's affinities with Purcell are felt at one time or another in most of these compositions, starting with the opening of the programme, the setting of Shelley's *Sleep*. The disc was issued to mark the composer's 90th birthday, and serves as a touching and eloquent tribute.

'Remember Your Lovers'

Tippett Boyhood's End. The Heart's Assurance. Music. Songs for Ariel. **Britten** Canticle No 1 'My beloved is mine' Humfrey A Hymne to God the Father **Purcell** (arr Tippett/Bergmann) An Evening Hymn on a Ground, 'Now that the sun hath veil'd his light'. If music be the food of love. The Fairy Queen – Thrice happy lovers (Epithalamium). The Indian Queen – I attempt from love's sickness. The Mock Marriage – 'Twas within a furlong. Oedipus – Music for a while. Pausanias – Sweeter than roses. Tyrannic Love – Ah! how sweet it is to love. The History of Dioclesian – What shall I do?
John Mark Ainsley ten **Iain Burnside** pf
Signum Classics SIGCD066 (73' · DDD · T)　　Ⓕ ➭

John Mark Ainsley and Iain Burnside make a formidable combination and they are matched here with a formidable programme. Tippett's writing for voice and piano is unremitting in its demands and much less certain in its rewards. The performers' concentration must be absolute: that is fact. Whether the listener will be proportionately moved is a matter for doubtful speculation.

It goes against the grain to say this, because the Tippett of youthful ecstasy (as in *The Midsummer Marriage* and the Concerto for Double String Orchestra) exerts a strong allure. But there's no escaping the fact that *Boyhood's End* and *The Heart's Assurance* exert a slim hold on the memory – only a few specific phrases, particularly of the singer's music, having stuck. That is extraordinary, and it is reinforced by the inclusion here of the *Canticle* by Britten which the mind retains, both in feeling and specific detail.

That work, the setting of Francis Quarles's 'So I my best-beloved's am', presumably has been chosen, as the one item in which Tippett is neither composer nor arranger, because it accords with the line 'Remember your lovers', taken as the title-phrase. I'm not sure it was a good idea, as Britten's mastery suggests just what is so often wanting in Tippett: economy and repose.

The other composer present in force is Purcell and here, curiously, Tippett's self-discipline is impressive, even as against Britten's in his comparable arrangements. Burnside writes in his introductory notes: 'While Britten's dense pianistic approach now jars on ears that have undergone the Early Music revolution, Tippett and [Walter] Bergmann stay light on their feet.'

The recording is fine with excellent presence.

King Priam

King Priam
Rodney Macann *bass* Priam **Sarah Walker** *mez*
Andromache **Howard Haskin** *ten* Paris **Anne Mason**
sop Helen **Janet Price** *sop* Hecuba **Neil Jenkins** *ten*
Achilles **Omar Ebrahim** *bar* Hector **Kent Opera**
Chorus and Orchestra / **Roger Norrington**
Stage director **Nicholas Hytner**
Video director Robin Lough
ArtHaus Musik 📀 102 087
(138' · NTSC · 4:3 · PCM stereo · 0)   Ⓕ❍❍

Many listeners – even or especially those who had been beguiled by *The Midsummer Marriage* – could once take refuge in the harsh assessment of Tippett's biographer, Ian Kemp, that *King Priam* was 'the most didactic and theoretical of his works'. This Kent Opera production proved them wrong. The Royal Opera premiere in Coventry had been overshadowed by the acclaim for Britten's *War Requiem*, first heard the following night, and the big voices and grand, clangorous manner of the fine Decca recording (based on a later Covent Garden production) are fully operatic in scale and projection.

By contrast, Roger Norrington and the young Nicholas Hytner push right into the claustrophobic citadel of the drama to find out, in the composer's words, 'what happens when the psychological balance symbolised by marriage is knocked awry by responsibilities, war and fate'. Acoustic, camera and microphones are close, oppressively and rightly so. We are but a few feet from Rodney Macann's piercing blue eyes as his Priam rebels against the choices that Tippett so relentlessly adumbrates: to smother Paris or love him, to sacrifice Helen or Troy, to confront Achilles or retain his royal dignity – how different from the hopeless determinism of Britten and Owen, where men are 'the foolish toys

of time', to quote Eric Crozier for *St Nicolas*.

Robin Lough's direction for TV uses the tricks of the medium sparingly, and to most telling effect in the blood-lust of the Trojans' vengeance trio at the end of Act 2, answered by Achilles' war-cry with Verdian immediacy. All the principals have the measure of their roles. If Sarah Walker's Andromache, Neil Jenkins's Achilles and Macann's Priam do most to stop us in our tracks, perhaps it is their painfully human heroism that Tippett was most interested in himself. In the brief but demanding role of the boy Paris, Nani Antwi-Nyanin also deserves a special mention: Tippett was not in the habit of writing down for younger performers.

Kent Opera sank in 1989, no longer kept afloat by government subsidy. There could be no more imposing memorial to the power of its work, and to the determination of its artistic director, Norman Platt, who died in 2004.

Boris Tishchenko   Russian b1939

Tishchenko studied at the Leningrad Conservatory and with Shostakovich (1962-5). He is an outstanding representative of a generation that reinvigorated Russian music in the 1960s. His richly inventive works include symphonies, concertos, string quartets, piano sonatas, and children's stage pieces.
                                         GROVEmusic

Symphony No 7, Op 119

Symphony No 7
Moscow Philharmonic Orchestra /
Dmitry Yablonsky
Naxos 8 557013 (53' · DDD)   Ⓢ

Not very much of Boris Tishchenko's substantial list of works has so far appeared on record. It includes ten piano sonatas, five string quartets and a cello concerto for Rostropovich, which Shostakovich himself took the trouble to rescore for more conventional forces than the original. Like so many composers of his generation he's been much influenced by Shostakovich, with whom he studied for a while. The influence shows in this symphony, even though it's for the most part thoroughly absorbed and makes for a quirky but fascinating work.

Tishchenko doesn't give his movements titles or even tempo indications. The first is an unusual but convincing symphonic exposition, based on an obsessive use of a simple figure. The second makes much play with ragtime clichés, merry enough on the face of it though with a deliberately forced atmosphere creeping in. The third is a forlorn, dirge-like piece, with a bleak climax. The fourth begins gracefully enough with what one may perhaps describe as a frightened waltz. Like the other movements, including the finale, it has a restrained lyricism that seems vulnerable to attack, and indeed is attacked by dissonant and alarming orchestral climaxes, after which the music ends on an equivocal note.

Tishchenko scores imaginatively, with chamber music textures and single instruments unusually handled – xylophone, bass clarinet, piano, tom-toms. The Moscow players respond skilfully, and though the recording is sometimes over-anxious to single out individual instrumental contributions, it seems to give a fair representation of the imaginative scoring. This is a piece well worth hearing.

Thomas Tomkins English 1572-1656

Tomkins, from a musical family, claimed Byrd as his teacher. He divided his time between Worcester Cathedral (organist from 1596) and London, becoming a Gentleman in Ordinary of the Chapel Royal by 1620, assistant organist from 1621 and senior organist from 1625; that year he wrote music for Charles I's coronation. He left Worcester in 1654. A prolific and respected successor of Byrd, he composed church music, including over 100 anthems (Musica Deo sacra, 1668), madrigals (1622, among them When David heard, a moving, polyphonic setting of a powerful text), over 50 keyboard pieces and a few highly original fantasias, pavans and galliards for viol consort. His half-brothers John, Giles and Robert and his son Nathaniel were also musicians.

GROVEmusic

Keyboard Works

Barafostus' Dream. Fantasia. Fancy. Fancy for two to play. Fortune my foe. A Ground. A Grounde. In Nomine, 'Gloria tibi Trinitas'. The Lady Folliott's Galliard. Miserere. Pavan. Pavan and Galliard, 'Earl Strafford'. Pavan and Galliard of Three Parts. A sad pavan for these distracted times. Toy, 'Made at Poole Court'. What if a day. Worster Braules
Carole Cerasi *hpd* **James Johnstone** *virg/bhpd*
Metronome METCD1049 (74' · DDD) Ⓕ**OO**

Forming a mental picture of Thomas Tomkins isn't difficult. Most of the pieces here were composed in the 1640s and 50s, yet adopt the style of three or four decades earlier, when composers like Gibbons, Bull and Tomkins's own teacher Byrd were alive. A contemporary of these men, Tomkins had survived them through the execution of Charles I and the destruction during the Civil War of the organ at Worcester Cathedral, where he had presided since 1596. Now, in later life, he had retired to live with his family and quietly compose plainsong settings, variation sets, fancies, grounds and pavans 'for these distracted times'. But though about as fashionable as a 'Welcome home, Walter Raleigh' hat, these pieces have a quality to them – showing by turns something of the exuberance of Bull and the eloquence of Byrd – that's more than enough to maintain their currency today. This disillu-

sioned early version of a *Daily Telegraph* reader was nothing less than the last representative of that great school of keyboard composers known as the English virginalists, and more than 350 years on, it matters not a bean to the listener which decade he was writing in.

Cerasi's selection of about a third of Tomkins's extant keyboard pieces showcases all the genres in which he composed, as well as demonstrating the excellence and range of her own technique. Few listeners will fail to be impressed by the fearless accuracy and panache with which she throws off Tomkins's torrential passagework and finger-breaking double thirds, but she's sensitive, too, in the slower pavans and fancies. Like Leonhardt, she achieves a supreme eloquence in such pieces by the sheer precision and control with which she places each note, and it's a pleasure just to hear her playing. An outstanding disc.

Choral Works

Third Service. O Lord, let me know mine end. O that the salvation were given. Know you not. In Nomine (1648). In Nomine (1652). Voluntaries – G; C; A minor
New College Choir, Oxford / Edward Higginbottom with **David Burchell** *org*
CRD CRD3467 (62' · DDD· T) Ⓕ

This is a well-balanced programme of sacred music by Thomas Tomkins. The four movements of the Third, or Great Service, together with the three anthems are spaced out with five organ pieces – two *In Nomines* and three voluntaries – chosen and arranged in such a way that the resulting key sequence has a satisfying natural flow. After an unassuming beginning, the truly royal *Te Deum* of the Great Service takes off with great verve and vigour, the rich 10-part texture of the full sections contrasting well with the lighter scoring of the verses. This energy and these contrasts are characteristic of the performances as a whole. There's some delightful solo singing in the verse anthems, in particular the alto solo in *O Lord, let me know mine end*. The two solo trebles are kept busy: they have a rather distinctive but complementary tone-quality, which makes up for a slight imbalance in volume. In general, however, the balance is good and the ensemble excellent. The trebles are a confident group with good articulation; they soar up to their top B flats with ease.

'These Distracted Times'

A Fancy. Pavan 'for these distracted times'. Almighty God, the fountain of all wisdom. When David heard. The Fifth Service – Te Deum; Jubilate; Magnificat; Nunc dimittis. The heavens declare. Pavan I (a 4); Pavan VII; Pavan VIII. Hear my prayer, O Lord. O Lord, how manifold. Remember me, O Lord.
My help cometh from the Lord
Fretwork; Alamire; Choir of Sidney Sussex College, Cambridge / David Skinner with **Jamal Sutton** *org*

Obsidian CD702 (67' · DDD)　　　Ⓕ**OOO**

The career of Thomas Tomkins straddled several reigns as well as the Cromwell era and this had an impact on his music, which otherwise reflects the influence of his mentor, William Byrd. Vocal textures are varied, clear and satisfying; the instrumental works, too, exude sanity in what were turbulent times. Tomkins favoured the solo bass voice, which introduces four of the sacred choral works here, though others contain ravishing, if brief, duets for tenors and sopranos. Best known is the lament on the death of Absalom, which with the verse anthem *My help cometh from the Lord* crowns the disc.

In the choral works David Skinner has drawn a beautifully blended sound from his Sidney Sussex Chapel Choir of mixed voices; the solo parts are taken by members of both Alamire (the polished male vocal quartet Skinner founded in 2005) and the choir. Although the organ is present as a solo instrument in the title-track and in *A Fancy* as well as accompanying Alamire in *The heavens declare*, Skinner transcribed the organ parts for the Fifth Service and the closing anthem for viol quartet – a liberty he defends in his engaging booklet-notes and which are so sensitively played by members of the renowned Fretwork.

The viol music and much of the church music date from Tomkins's time as organist of Worcester Cathedral, which came to an abrupt end in 1647; he composed the 'Sad Pavan' for organ just two weeks after the execution of Charles I in 1649. Once also a Gentleman of the King's Chapel Royal, Tomkins had good reason to feel 'distracted'. Cromwell happens to have been a member of Sidney Sussex College.

The college chapel provides a clear and sympathetic acoustic. It's difficult to know whether Tomkins or Cromwell would have been the more surprised. Tomkins would most certainly have been delighted.

Veljo Tormis.　　　Estonian b1930

Tormis is considered by Estonians to be one of their most important composers of the 20th century. His oeuvre is best considered in the context of the strong Estonian choral tradition and the political history of Estonia, both ancient and contemporary, but its appeal has reached far beyond the Baltics. He has taught at the Tallinn Music School and the Tallinn Music High School, and served as a consultant at the Estonian Union of Composers. From 1969 he has supported himself through the purchase of his manuscripts by the Ministry of Culture, by frequent prizes for his choral works, and by numerous sojourns at 'houses of creativity' in the Soviet Union. Although Tormis has written a well-crafted opera and various instrumental pieces (including film scores), his special voice is heard in his choral works.

GROVEmusic

Choral works

An Aboriginal Song[a]. The Bishop and the Pagan. Curse upon Iron[a]. Forging the Sampo[ab]. Double Dedication. Crosswind. Our Shadows. Incantation for a Stormy Sea. Men's Songs – Men's Song; Bundling Song; Betrothal Visiting Song; Song of the Turkish War; Serf's Song; Dancing Song
Svanholm Singers / Sofia Söderberg Eberhard with [a]**Veljo Tormis**, [b]**Stefan Engström** *perc*
Toccata Classics TOCC0073 (68' · DDD · T/t)　　Ⓕ**O**

Livonian Heritage. Singing Aboard Ship. Two Songs to Words by Ernst Enno. Three Estonian Game Songs. Three Songs from the Epic 'Kalev's Son'. Autumn Landscapes. Four Estonian Lullabies. Childhood Memory Herding Calls.
Holst Singers / Stephen Layton
Hyperion CDA67601 (72' · DDD · T/t)　　Ⓕ**OO**

The quality of choral singing in the Baltic region is legendary, and with the 20 male voices of the Svanholm singers – most of them apparently students at Lund University – the legend lives on. Tormis writes that any of his doubts about the 2006 concert they organised in his honour melted with just a few phrases from his 'Double Dedication'. No wonder. Both music and performance of this celebration of two poets who emigrated from Soviet Estonia to Sweden immediately seize the attention, even without knowledge of the poems, the cultural role of the poets or the nature of the composer's tribute to them – all of which only serve to reinforce and deepen the initial impact.

So, which to single out? The phenomenal precision of intonation, tonal focus and communicative urgency in the singing, the high-mindedness and vividness of the poetry, or the music's sheer range of appeal and refusal to recognise boundaries between different kinds of audience? There are rich pickings here, the programme covering a gamut of expression from folk-comic-macho through saga-epic to wondrous-romantic. Tormis himself gives the disc a symbolic imprimatur by playing the shaman drum in 'An Aboriginal Song' and 'Curse upon Iron'. Whistling, sighing, tongue-clicking, falsetto and log drumming add to the tonal palette but the music and singing are seductive enough even without them. Documentation is exemplary, recording quality perfectly judged. Irresistible!

Hard on its heels comes another beautifully prepared and executed compilation. Stephen Layton and his Holst Singers have a well deserved reputation as bold explorers, and their intelligence and dedication are evident here. It seems that the language barrier has not proved greatly inhibiting: they've thrown down the gauntlet to others outside the Baltic region to investigate this superb repertoire.

By comparison with the crack Nordic teams, the English voices are admittedly a degree softer-focused in tone and not quite so high-pressure in expression. The composer's compatriots bring even more electricity to the five marvellous songs that make up *Livonian Heritage*, for example, though the Holst Singers find a subtlety and affection that certainly compensates. In any case, given that there is little very duplication of repertoire with available CDs (and none at all with the superb Svanholmers), and that the quality of Tormis's output is wonderfully consistent, there is really no reason not to invest in both new issues.

Charles Tournemire French 1870-1939

Tournemire was a pupil of Widor at the Paris Conservatoire and of Franck, whose place as organist at Ste Clotilde he inherited in 1898; from 1919 he also taught at the Conservatoire. His works include operas, oratorios and eight symphonies (1900-24), often on religious and esoteric subjects. But he is remembered for the monumental L'orgue mystique (1932), 51 organ masses using plainsong melodies appropriate to a particular Sunday, for the liturgical year, in a mystical style between Franck and Messiaen. GROVEmusic

L'Orgue mystique

L'Orgue mystique – Office 2, Postlude; Office 3, Paraphrase; Office 7, Fantaisie; Office 11, Diptyque; Office 27, Fantaisie paraphrase; Office 29, Alleluia No 1; Office 30, Alleluia No 2; Office 31, Alleluia No 3; Office 32, Alleluia No 4; Office 33, Alleluia No 5; Office 35, Paraphrase and Carillon; Office 43, Choral alleluiatique No 1; Office 51, Fantaisie sur le Te Deum et Guirlandes Alleluiatiques Office 44, Choral alleluiatique No 2; Office 45, Choral alleluiatique No 3; Office 46, Choral alleluiatique No 4; Office 47, Choral alleluiatique No 5
Marie-Bernadette Dufourcet-Hakim *org*
Priory ② PRCD669AB (134' · DDD) Played on the organs of La Sainte Trinité, Paris and La Basilique du Sacré-Cœur de Montmartre, Paris   Ⓕ

This two-CD set makes an excellent introduction to the sprawling, theatrical, sometimes hysterically neo-Gothic and spontaneous world of *L'Orgue mystique*, the magnum opus of Charles Tournemire. Until 1927 his compositional output was directed mostly at secular music, orchestral symphonies, string quartets and opera. Over the next five years he renewed French liturgical organ music, writing 51 suites (one for each Sunday of the year) based on 300 Gregorian plainchants. Dufourcet-Hakim's 17-track selection consists of postludes, 11 of them drawn from the 13 suites for Sundays during Pentecost.

She captures brilliantly the improvisatory fleetingness and impressionistic mysticism inherent in Tournemire's music. She steers committedly and seemingly effortlessly around this often turbulent organistic assault course, helped by the generous acoustics of La Sainte Trinité (Messiaen's church) and, in two tracks, the Basilica of Sacré-Coeur in Montmartre, the latter more out of tune than the former. For

anyone intrigued by the roots of Messiaen's radical organ writing these recordings will provide clear answers. Strongly recommended.

Suite évocatrice, Op 74

Tournemire Suite évocatrice, Op 74
Vierne Symphony No 3, Op 28
Widor Symphonie Gothique, Op 70
Jeremy Filsell *org*
Herald HAVPCD145 (71' · DDD) Played on the Harrison & Harrison organ of Ely Cathedral   ⒻⓄⓄ

Compared with, say, the symphonies of Tchaikovsky or Sibelius the organ symphonies of Widor and his pupil Vierne aren't particularly long. But in terms of organ music they're among the longest single works in the repertory. Within their five-movement form the composers set out to exploit the full expressive range of the organ, and it was no coincidence that the organ symphony developed in turn of the century France. The great French organ builder Aristide Cavaillé-Coll was then producing instruments capable of hitherto undreamt-of colour and expression. Both Widor at St Sulpice and Vierne at Notre Dame had at their disposal the finest instruments in Paris and they indulged themselves fully in their symphonies.

The subtitle of Widor's Ninth (*Gothic*) says it all. The structure is vast, intricately detailed, and almost forbidding in its grandness. Vierne's Third also presents an awesome spectacle, full of complex music and technically demanding writing, while Tournemire's neo-Classical Suite gives a moment almost of light relief in such heavyweight company. Jeremy Filsell is an outstanding virtuoso player with a gift for musical communication, and the Ely Cathedral organ produces the range of the great French instruments, but within an altogether clearer acoustic. These are performances and recordings of exceptional quality.

Donald Tovey. British 1875-1940

Long-time Reid Professor of Music at Edinburgh University, Sir Donald Francis Tovey remains best known for his magnificently readable and insightful Essays in Musical Analysis (OUP: 1935-44). He was also a gifted pianist and composer, completing a Piano Concerto in 1903 and, 10 years later, this earnest and admirably ambitious Symphony in D.

Orchestral works

Cello Concerto, Op 40[ac]. Elegiac Variations, Op 25[ab].
Aria and Variations, Op 11 – Aria (arr P Shore)[c]
[a]**Alice Neary** *vc* [b]**Gretel Dowdeswell** *pf*
[c]**Ulster Orchestra / George Vass**
Toccata Classics TOCC0038 (67' · DDD)   Ⓕ◗➔

With a playing time of nearly 55 minutes, Sir Donald Tovey's Cello Concerto (composed in 1932-33 for Pablo Casals) is almost certainly the longest ever written. Casals gave the world premiere in Edinburgh's Usher Hall in November 1934, with the composer conducting. Two London performances by the dedicatee followed in 1935 and 1937. Plans for a modern recording fell through a decade or so ago; now Toccata Classics has at last delivered the goods.

Readers who know and love their Brahms and Elgar will recognise many a stylistic and temperamental bond in this painstakingly plotted music. However, the protracted opening *Allegro moderato* constitutes something of a stumbling block. Both middle movements do little to dispel the obstinately somnolent mood – although the finale's jocular yet cleverly manipulated antics nearly save the day. If you've enjoyed grappling with Tovey's large-scale Symphony in D, it's worth persevering. Alice Neary performs valiantly, with sympathetic (if at times rather under-energised) support from George Vass and the Ulster Orchestra. Throw in the engaging fill-ups, decent sound and assiduously detailed booklet-notes, and it adds up to yet another intriguing release from this young label.

Symphony, Op 32. The Bride of Dionysus – Prelude
Malmö Opera Orchestra / George Vass
Toccata Classics TOCC0033 (64' · DDD)   Ⓕ🄳➔

Although lasting the best part of an hour and occasionally over-thickly scored, Tovey's Symphony holds the attention, not least due to his keen sense of long-term dialogue and harmonic adventure, allied to a felicitous mastery of counterpoint. Brahms and Reger are the most obvious stylistic templates (the symphony's arrestingly pregnant *pianissimo* opening idea even hints at Nielsen), yet a quiet individuality emerges from the radiant *Canzonetta* slow movement in particular, and the scampering *Scherzo* has a pleasingly mischievous twinkle in its eye.

A very creditable performance, too, from the Malmö Opera Orchestra under George Vass, who also acquit themselves most ably in the noble Prelude to Tovey's 1918 opera *The Bride of Dionysus* which launches proceedings. Good if not perhaps ideally ventilated sound.

Piano Trios

Piano Trios – Op 1; Op 8, 'Style tragique'
London Piano Trio (Robert Atchison vn
Bozidar Vukotic vc Olga Dudnik pf)
Toccata Classics TOCC0068 (65' · DDD)   Ⓕ

Having already given us useful modern recordings of Donald Francis Tovey's Symphony in D and vast Cello Concerto (see above), Toccata Classics now presents this first volume in a series devoted to his chamber music. Both works were composed in 1895, during Tovey's first full calendar year at Balliol College, Oxford.

Inscribed to Parry 'as the first work of a grateful pupil', Tovey's Op 1 is as sizeable as it is thoughtful – a patiently argued creation of remarkable fluency, organisational skill and imagination for one so young. The influence of Brahms dominates, and the German master's kindly presence can also be felt in Op 8 in C minor, which was originally conceived for clarinet, horn and piano. The version performed here was eventually published by Schott in 1912, by which time the trio had also acquired the title *Style tragique*. At its heart is a particularly appealing *Largo* in A flat (thus following the key scheme of Beethoven's Fifth Symphony and *Pathétique* Sonata), which leads without a break into the confidently striding finale.

The London Piano Trio audibly believe in every note, and their dedicated performances are set within a bold sound frame that's somewhat tiring on the ear. The presentation is copiously detailed, as ever from this source. Inquisitive collectors can safely investigate.

Eduard Tubin   Estonian 1905-1982

Tubin was a pupil of Eller at the Tartu Academy (1924-30); in 1944 he moved to Sweden. His music often combines propulsive rhythm with expansive melody, orchestrated in an expressive manner; he wrote ten symphonies (1934-73). GROVEmusic

Symphonies

Symphonies – No 1 in C minor[a]; No 2, 'The Legendary'[b]; No 3 in D minor[c]; No 4 in A, 'Sinfonia lirica'[d]; No 5 in B minor[c]; No 6[c]; No 7[f]; No 8[c]; No 9, 'Sinfonia semplice'[g]; No 10[h]. Kratt – Ballet Suite[e]. Toccata[g]
[abc]**Swedish Radio Symphony Orchestra;** [d]**Bergen Philharmonic Orchestra;** [e]**Bamberg Symphony Orchestra;** [fgh]**Gothenburg Symphony Orchestra / Neeme Järvi**
BIS ⑤ BIS-CD1402/4 (331' · DDD)   Ⓜ🅞🅞

Vividly scored and dynamically expressive, Tubin's symphonies span almost his entire creative career. The First, only his third orchestral score, dates from 1931-4, and the single-movement Tenth from 1973, while at his death nine years later an Eleventh lay unfinished on his desk. Even without the Eleventh, the BIS set has much to commend it. The performances, variable in acoustic, are remarkably consistent in approach and quality of execution.

Järvi's commitment to and understanding of the music is total and its quality shines through in every bar, whether in the early symphonies where Tubin was still moving towards his mature style, or Nos 5 to 8 with their absolute mastery of form. OK, even Järvi can't avoid the Third's peroration sounding like *The Pines of Tallinn*, but there's no doubt of the work's or its creator's stature. Although repackaged from the original issues, BIS avoids laying out the symphonies in chronological sequence. The recordings still sound wonderful, though occasionally perhaps too spacious. Järvi never sounds rushed, allowing the Eighth's opening *Andante quasi Adagio* to build into an impressive-sounding edifice. He's unmatched in the deeply felt finale.

Joaquín Turina   Spanish 1882-1949

Turina trained in Seville, Madrid and Paris (at the Schola Cantorum), and was associated with Falla, with whom he returned to Spain in 1914; he remained there, working as a teacher, critic and composer. His Schola experience gave him a command of the grand scale, moderated by Sevillian grace and wit. His works include operas, orchestral works, chamber music, guitar music, songs and numerous piano pieces, including many colourful and effective character and genre pieces as well as some larger-scale works.   GROVEmusic

Orchestral Works

Sinfoniá sevillana. Danzas fantásticas. Ritmos (Fantasía coreográfica). La procesión del Rocío
Castilla y León Symphony Orchestra / Max Bragado Darman
Naxos Spanish Classics 8 555955 (62' · DDD) ⓢ ⦿ ▶

Turina was a gentle man who, like Segovia, placed high value on beauty and clarity of thought, and responded to 'programmatic' images; the portrayal of profound tragedy had no place in his music. Although he tried harder than his contemporaries to write in the conventional musical forms, his *Sinfonía sevillana* is a poetic and colourful tone poem rather than a symphony, a French-influenced depiction of aspects of the city of his birth.

Ritmos was conceived as a ballet but was never performed as such – present-day choreographers please note! The *Danzas fantásticas* range from the quietly poetic to the energetic, and relate to quotations from José Más's novel *La orgía*. Two dances, the Aragonese *jota* and the Andalusian *farruca*, frame a dream-like evocation of elements of Andalusian melody and dance rhythm of the Basque *zortziko*. More specifically focused is *La procesión del Rocío*, a charming picture of the annual festival procession in the village of El Rocío.

Turina's skill and sensitivity in the art of orchestration shines throughout this programme, as does that of the Castilla y Léon Symphony Orchestra in extracting every good feature the music offers. The recording is clear, with a believably spacious acoustic. There are other recordings of these works, but none that brings them all together – or exceeds the quality of these performances. An outstanding issue.

Mark-Anthony Turnage   British b1960

Turnage studied at the Royal College of Music, with Oliver Knussen and John Lambert. He gained wide attention with his first orchestral score Night Dances (1981) which won the Guinness Prize and revealed the eclectic nature of his style, drawing on a wide range of early 20th-century sources and the inflections of jazz and blues harmonies. An even wider stylistic net informs On All Fours for 13 instruments (1986), in which Baroque dance forms, refracted through the model of Stravinsky's Agon, provide the rhythmic impulsion. Jazz and rock elements are incorporated effectively in Greek and are also particularly evident in such instrumental works as Kai (1989–90) and Your Rockaby (1992–3). Blood on the Floor (1993–6) is his most explicit engagement with the materials of jazz and includes, for the first time, sections of improvisation. In 1995 Turnage was appointed composer-in-association with the ENO. He is also artistic consultant to the ENO Contemporary Opera Studio, under whose auspices he has continued to explore the confrontation of the violent and the lyrical in two dramatically assured works, Twice Through the Heart (1994-6) and a chamber opera, The Country of the Blind (1996-7), both first performed at the 50th Aldeburgh Festival (1997). Turnage has recently been appointed Mead Composer in Residence with the Chicago Symphony Orchestra, 2006-2008, following a similar appointment with the LPO who have recorded a number of his recent works.   GROVEmusic

Orchestral works

Yet Another Set To[a]. Scherzoid[b].
Evening Songs[c]. When I Woke[d]
[d]**Gerald Finley** bar [a]**Christian Lindberg** tbn
London Philharmonic Orchestra / [a]**Marin Alsop,**
[cd]**Vladimir Jurowski,** [b]**Jonathan Nott**
LPO ⏺ LPO0007 (66' · DDD) Ⓜ ▶

Mark-Anthony Turnage has enjoyed associations with the CBSO, BBC SO and now the London Philharmonic, each resulting in a wealth of new music and, fortunately for us, a CD for home listening. A number of ensembles had a hand in commissioning *Scherzoid*, the first work on this latest collection, and its particular propulsive character would seem to have been influenced by the involvement of the New York Philharmonic. Though rhythmically complex and changing its mood as rapidly as the title punningly suggests, the music is easy to assimilate. Its urban bustle and swagger take in minimalist influences alongside the usual Stravinsky-meets-Miles Davis mélange. As if to secure transatlantic approval, at one point there's a distinct whiff of *On the Waterfront*, although, in the event, Lorin Maazel elected not to conduct the first performance. Jonathan Nott does the honours here – and splendidly.

Turnage's subtler, shell-shocked lyricism is more in evidence in the purely orchestral *Evening Songs*. Originating in lullabies for his sons, the calm outer panels enclose an interlude with a more troubled, expressionist melodic line, typically Brittenish at the outset. The Dylan Thomas settings, *When I Woke*, were written for a celebrated singer who did not take them up but it's difficult to feel them in any way problematic in this ardent account. Certainly, the spare accompanying textures create no difficulties for the soloist. *Yet Another Set To* brings back the more boisterous, head-banging Turnage. All is not plain sailing in that the composer here shows us his Boulez-like propensity to reshape and recycle existing music.

Cheekily, the score incorporates not only 2000's *Another Set To* – itself a reworking, previously recorded by Christian Lindberg for Chandos – but also a movement derived from *Blood on the Floor*. It's exhilarating, explosive stuff, even more fun in live performance. Here alone concluding applause is (not inappropriately) retained.

All credit to the LPO for compiling a whole evening of Turnage. You may not always like what he does or how he does it but his instantly recognisable voice is well served by the blunt immediacy of the sound and the obvious flair of the performances.

Chamber works

Two Memorials[a]. An Invention on Solitude[b]. Sleep on[c]. Cortège for Chris[d]. Two Elegies Framing a Shout[e]. Three Farewells[f]. Tune for Toru[g]
Nash Ensemble ([f]Philippa Davies *fl* [bdf]Richard Hosford *cl* [bf]Marianne Thorsen, [bf]Elizabeth Wexler *vns* [bf] Lawrence Power *va* [bcdf]Paul Watkins *vc* [f]Skaila Kanga *hp* [cdeg]Ian Brown *pf* [ce]Richard Hosford *cl* [ae]Martin Robertson *sop sax*)
Black Box BBM1065 (58' · DDD)   Ⓕ

An effective showcase for the composer's small-ensemble music of the 1990s, this album might have been entitled 'Another Side of... Mark-Anthony Turnage'. Where, in some of his major orchestral works, Turnage's idiom has seemed quintessentially urban, indebted (via Tippett and Britten) to Stravinsky and Berg, here we come surprisingly close to the much-derided English pastoral tradition. The jazz element is evident too, as you might expect, but there's little trace of the composer's penchant for rock and raunch; the mood is more wistful than confrontational. Anyone who thinks that contemporary music and memorable melodic writing are somehow incompatible should audition this disc without delay. From the plangent solo sax of the *Two Memorials* to the intensely evocative solo piano version of *Tune for Toru*, there's little to frighten the horses and much that touches the heart. The biggest utterance is the clarinet quintet, *An Invention on Solitude*, composed, like much of this music, during Turnage's work on the score of his opera *The Silver Tassie*. The Nash Ensemble are no strangers to Turnage and their unsentimental playing is well served by the boldly immediate recording.

This Silence[a]. True Life Stories[b]. Slide Stride[c]. Two Baudelaire Songs[d]. Eulogy[e]. Two Vocalises[f]. Cantilena[g]
[d]**Sally Matthews** *sop* **Nash Ensemble** ([d]Philippa Davies *fl* Gareth Hulse [g]*ob*/[e]*cora* [ade]Michael Collins *cl* [a]Ursula Leveaux *bn* [ae]Richard Watkins *hn* [acdeg]Marianne Thorsen, [acdg]Benjamin Nabarro *vns* [acdeg]Lawrence Power *va* [acdfg]Paul Watkins *vc* [ae]Duncan McTier *db* [e]Lucy Wakeford *hp* [bcdef]Ian Brown *pf*) / [d]**Lionel Friend**
Onyx Classics ONYX4005 (79' · DDD · T/t)   Ⓕ Ⓓ➤

Here's yet another disc from the Nash Ensemble devoted to the music of Mark-Anthony Turnage and it is, in a sense, the most representative because it gives a fine indication of his range.

Favourites come from opposite tendencies. *Slide Stride* (2002) is a noisily affirmative piano quintet based on James P Johnson's style of jazz piano and dedicated to Richard Rodney Bennett, whereas *True Life Stories*, unveiled as a group by Leif Ove Andsnes in 2000, are cool piano miniatures. As is usual with Turnage these days, not all the core material is new and the last in the sequence, the haunting tribute to Tōru Takemitsu, cheekily reprises the final item on that Black Box anthology. Ian Brown plays it with more restraint and less pedal this time around – or it could be simply that the sound is not as resonant.

While Turnage demonstrates a continuing ability to straddle disparate musical worlds, his startling fluency begins to look as much a problem as an asset. In *Two Baudelaire Songs* (2004) he sets poems already transmogrified by Debussy and Henri Duparc. Only here *L'invitation au voyage* is deconstructed rather than indulged, a peculiarly dissonant close undercutting the 'Luxe, calme et volupté' of the text. As miked, the soloist Sally Matthews is very much one of the band. Lawrence Power's viola seems rather forwardly placed in the autumnal *Eulogy* (2003), an immediately convincing composition that doesn't strive for novelty.

Turnage's world has dark, claustrophobic qualities, underlined here by the immediate, focused recording masterminded by Chris Craker. Barry Witherden's copious notes are helpful. Not perhaps a disc you would want to digest at one sitting though this generous selection of definitive performances is well worth sampling.

Twice Through the Heart[a]. Hidden Love Song[b]. The Torn Fields[c]
[a]**Sarah Connolly** *mez* [c]**Gerald Finley** *bar* [b]**Martin Robertson** *sax* **London Philharmonic Orchestra / Marin Alsop**
LPO LPO0031 (66' · DDD). [b]Recorded live   Ⓜ

This is the second CD to result from Mark-Anthony Turnage's LPO's residency. The surprise is that two of the three pieces are heard in top-notch studio recordings. *Twice Through the Heart* is a revival of a dramatic song-cycle-cum-scena from as long ago as 1997. The text is drawn from a series of poems originally written for a television film about a woman who stabs her abusive husband. As might be expected it's a pretty bleak affair. Sarah Connolly is a distinguished protagonist, and if listeners feel uncomfortable with the mix of artful delivery and documentary realism, that may be part of the intended effect.

Hidden Love Song, featuring saxophonist Martin Robertson, derives from a live concert with applause retained. This first new composition associated with Turnage's LPO tenure is a wordless offering built from musical ciphers associated with the composer's partner. The characteristic attempts to disrupt the lyrical line are thus carefully rationed and there's no mistaking the professional gleam and twinkle of the results.

Confirming a certain softening of idiom, *The Torn Fields* is equally accessible though weightier thematically. Here Turnage eschews Jackie Kay's down-to-earth phraseology in *Twice Through the Heart*, preferring the sort of poetry that attracted composers of a previous anti-war generation. The music still draws on vernacular bluesy elements but they lie within a smoother, more melodic, high-culture mix. It's difficult to imagine a more ardent exponent than Gerald Finley. While the orchestral writing is spare, Finley's diction is second to none, allied to exceptional beauty of tone. Particularly haunting is the Wilfred Owen setting, the narrative of a soldier who, like the protagonist of *The Silver Tassie*, survives severely maimed only to experience physical and emotional rejection. The gentle treatment of the familiar final poem by Siegfried Sassoon provides a glimpse of the transcendent. Excellent contextual notes plus full texts (including passages not set by the composer).

Blood on the Floor

Blood on the Floor
Martin Robertson *sax* **Peter Erskine** *drums* **John Scofield** *elec gtr* **Ensemble Modern / Peter Rundel**
Video director **Barrie Gavin**
ArtHaus Musik **DVD** 100 430 (92' · NTSC · 4:3 · PCM stereo · 2 & 5) Ⓕ

The title comes from a painting by Francis Bacon, while the music ranges widely in its references and allusions. A decade on, *Blood on the Floor* remains Turnage's magnum 'fusion' opus. With a raw expressive energy fuelled by the loss of his brother to a drugs overdose, the composer's gift for sour melody and guttural sonority has never been deployed to better effect.

The body of this DVD release is a live performance taped in Frankfurt's Alte Oper during the same 1996 premiere tour that yielded a CD recording. The concert was presumably intended for low-fi TV broadcast and consists of the usual series of close-ups of instrumentalists edited to the music. The technique is less irksome here than in many such outings; it highlights the breathtaking artistry of the multifarious musicians involved, genuinely conveying a charged atmosphere.

Sound quality is good if not quite up to the standard of the audio equivalent; there are some

perplexing moments when the camera focuses on an instrument barely audible in the mix. More happily, John Scofield is shown creating something wonderful from the simple melody of 'Elegy for Andy', while Peter Erskine's *sotto voce* drum solos in 'Crackdown' are astonishing.

Extras include an unrevealing introduction shot during rehearsals and the more welcome inclusion of two encores, arrangements of pieces by Erskine and Scofield which prefigure Turnage's recent Scorched project.

Greek

Greek
Quentin Hayes *bar* Eddy **Richard Suart** *bar* Dad;
Cafe Manager; Police Chief **Fiona Kimm** *mez* Wife;
Doreen; Waitress 1; Sphinx 2 **Helen Charnock** *sop*
Mum; Waitress 2; Sphinx 1
Almeida Ensemble
Video directors **Peter Maniura, Jonathan Moore**
ArtHaus **DVD** 102 105
(81' · NTSC · 4:3 · PCM stereo · 0)
Recorded at the Liverpool Warehouse in 1990 Ⓕ

Mark-Anthony Turnage's first opera, his Steven Berkoff treatment *Greek* (1988), packs quite a punch, reminding us of the vehemently oppositional mood of so much cultural production in the Thatcher years. Even if you attribute some of its pugnacious energy to the text's radical mix of the highfalutin and the scatological, Turnage's musical treatment imparts an edginess of its own. There is lyricism of a kind but more late Stravinsky than Britten, Tippett or Vaughan Williams, a balance neatly reversed in *The Silver Tassie* (2000), a less economical, more stylistically conformist successor.

While an audio recording of *Greek* was a jewel in the crown of the Argo label, the ultra-stylised retelling of the Oedipus myth works better in the context of this vintage BBC film chock-full of memorably revolting scenes. Greater chronological distance may be required to give the piece's indictment of 1980s Britain the timeless quality of great art. That may seem a pretentious comment but Berkoff is nothing if not ambitious: '...this is not simply an adaptation of Sophocles but a recreation of the various Oedipus myths which seemed to apply, particularly to a play about what I saw London had become. London equals Thebes and is full of riots, filth, decay, bombings, football mania, mobs at the palace gates, plague madness and post-pub depression.'

The singers are close-miked but opting into the subtitles (available in several languages) helps focus the sense and the warped poetry of the whole. Light entertainment it ain't. The direction by Jonathan Moore and Peter Maniura certainly avoids the cosy naturalism of conventional TV drama. And you may not feel like eating toast for a long time after witnessing the Act 1 breakfast scene. Unusually helpful booklet-notes provide extra context. Strongly recommended.

Erkki-Sven Tüür

Estonia b1959

Drawing on both his immediate classical heritage and aspects of jazz and rock, Tüür came to prominence with the Architectonic series of nine ensemble pieces (1990-93), each with an atmospheric and open-minded approach to instrumental writing. This timbrel sensitivity has been continued in such recent works as the Third Symphony (1997), whose formal subtlety and thematic resource is a promising continuation of the Nordic tradition. GROVEmusic

Symphonies

Symphony No 3. Cello Concerto[a]. Lighthouse
[a]**David Geringas** vc **Vienna Radio Symphony Orchestra / Dennis Russell Davies**
ECM New Series 465 134-2 (64' · DDD) Ⓕ Ⓞ ➡

Among the younger generation of would-be symphonists, Erkki-Sven Tüür is one of the most hope-inspiring. The first movement of his Third Symphony builds impressive momentum from the contrast of two types of music: one dogged and metronomic, the other free and apparently tempo-less. These eventually collide, producing an electrifying climax. The second movement has wildly diffuse elements – from Lutosławskian modernism to quasi-Bachian chorale tune and lush tonal romanticism. This is music of strong personality, integrity and confidence, with warmth as well as acerbity, directness as well as ingenuity. The same could equally be said for the string fantasy *Lighthouse*, and still more for the Cello Concerto, though here the transition from modernism to Romantic lyricism is easier to follow and harder to resist. Also appealing is the vigour of much of the writing, especially for the strings, occasionally recalling the great string works of Tippett. Like the Finnish symphonist Kalevi Aho, Tüür is plainly worth taking very seriously, and it's good to report that the performers on this disc do just that. Excellent recordings too.

Symphony No 4, 'Magma'[a]. Inquiétude du fini[b]. Igavik[c]. The Path and the Traces
[bc]**Estonian Philharmonic Chamber Choir;** [c]**Estonian National Male Choir;** [a]**Evelyn Glennie** perc **Estonian National Symphony Orchestra / Paavo Järvi**
Virgin Classics 385785-2 (66' · DDD) Ⓕ Ⓞ Ⓞ ➡

Estonia's best-known internationally orientated modernist has composed six symphonies, among which the 30-minute single-movement Fourth, dating from 2002 and subtitled *Magma*, is outstanding. Tüür's style is essentially mobile-sculptural: which is to say that shifting sound-masses count for more than expressivity. Sibelius is a distant yet clear affinity, and Lutosławski and the sonorism of the Polish school of the 1960s and '70s supply something of the technical means. At its gentlest – as in the tinkling early

stages of *Magma* – the effect resembles Oliver Knussen; at its toughest, Elliott Carter. Impersonal yet irresistible forces seem to guide the structure, while the orchestra builds up a succession of analogies to unpopulated landscapes and natural forces. Behind the sonic richness and the dazzling surfaces there is an ascetic instinct at work: a refusal to take easy, opportunistic paths and an immensely vimpressive traversal of craggier ones.

Though written for Evelyn Glennie, who takes the solo percussion part with superb aplomb, this really is a symphony rather than a flashy, beefed-up concerto. It stays just on that side of the divide everywhere except in the brief cadenza at approximately the half-way mark.

The other three works on this disc feel similarly substantial and born of inner necessity. *The Path and the Traces* is simply the finest recently composed piece for string orchestra, and each of the choral items is memorable, without sacrificing complexity. Tüür is currently well represented on CD, but this new disc is probably the most rewarding devoted to his music, no doubt partly because performances and recordings are first-class. If the prospect of challenging, granite-hewn musical invention has any appeal, then this is a must.

Crystallisatio

Architectonics VI. Passion. Illusion. Crystallisatio. Requiem
Estonian Philharmonic Chamber Choir; Tallinn Chamber Orchestra / Tõnu Kaljuste
ECM New Series 449 459-2 (64' · DDD · T/t) Ⓕ ➡

Architectonics VI (1992) sounds like one of those titles that are too good to resist, and it's to the credit of Erkki-Sven Tüür that he admits as much in the brief interview in the booklet to this beguiling disc. Tüür's piece isn't especially architectonic in construction, but it's well put together and effective on its own terms. *Passion* and *Illusion*, both for string orchestra and composed in 1993, are closer in spirit to the prevailing 'New Simplicity' of current East Baltic composition. *Passion*, indeed, is occasionally reminiscent of Tüür's better-known compatriot, Arvo Pärt, although the brief *Illusion* has a curiously English feel to it. The title track, *Crystallisatio* (1995), is scored for three flutes, bells, string orchestra and live electronics and is somewhat more demanding in scope. It's here that Tüür's synthesis of minimalism with serial techniques is heard most eloquently; not wholly achieved, perhaps, but fascinating in application. By far the biggest piece is the Requiem (1992-3), in memory of the conductor Peeter Lilje. It's a deeply felt, half-hour-long setting of the Mass for the Dead, and is of markedly different character to the other pieces here. This is a handsomely produced, thought-provoking release. If you want to hear up-to-the-minute new music that won't sear the ears off your head, do try it.

Geirr Tveitt   Norwegian 1908-1981

Tveitt studied at the Leipzig Conservatory and in Vienna and Paris. His often rhythmic, dynamic music derives from Norwegian folk music and he wrote two concertos for the Hardanger fiddle. He was heard as the soloist in his six piano concertos.

GROVEmusic

Hardanger Fiddle Concertos

Hardanger Fiddle Concertos[a] – No 1, Op 163; No 2, 'Three Fjords', Op 252. The Water Sprite, Op 187
[a]**Arve Moen Bergset hard Stavanger Symphony Orchestra / Ole Kristian Ruud**
BIS BIS-CD1207 (65' · DDD)   Ⓕ

The Hardanger fiddle of western Norway probably originated in the mid-17th century, possibly – as Reidar Storaas suggests in his notes – as a hybrid of earlier folk fiddles and the viola d'amore. Its tone is smaller than the violin and, with its four sympathetic strings, sounds not unlike a treble viol. Local boy Geirr Tveitt has produced these two marvellous concertos for the instrument. The First dates from 1955, and its premiere at the Bergen Festival the following year was a triumph for the composer. It isn't hard to hear why: the idiom is Tveitt's best folksy manner, the orchestration expert and bright, with a virtuoso solo part. The opening movement is relatively gentle, succeeded by a wonderfully atmospheric if wistful *Andante* and a lively finale reminiscent of Malcolm Arnold. The Second followed ten years later, and replicates the same basic design, yet is a more personal utterance, the structure more concisely realised, the inspiration drawn from the three fjords of his native region. Arve Moen Bergset is a prize-winning folk player and plays with commendable feeling and technical assurance. He's ably supported by Ruud and the splendid Stavanger orchestra, who also provide an excellent performance of *The Water Sprite* ('Nykken', 1956), a tone-poem relating how the sprite snares a boy by disguising itself as a horse. Beautifully clear as usual from BIS.

Piano Concerto No 4

Piano Concerto No 4, 'Aurora Borealis'. Variations on a Folksong from Hardanger[a]
Håvard Gimse, [a]**Gunilla Süssmann** pfs **Royal Scottish National Orchestra / Bjarte Engeset**
Naxos 8 555761 (61' · DDD)   Ⓢ**OO**

There are many musical depictions of the Northern Lights, but few if any on quite so lush and expansive a scale as Tveitt's Fourth Piano Concerto (1947). A paean to this extraordinary natural phenomenon, it's conceived on a Baxian scale following a seasonal cycle with its kaleidoscopic first movement, 'The Northern Lights awakening above the autumn colours', running

to almost 31 of the whole 51-minute length. The slower central span, 'Glittering in the winter heavens, and…' is more straightforward and the swifter final movement ('Fading away in the bright night of spring') acts as an epilogue. The manuscript of the Fourth Concerto was lost in the calamitous 1970 fire that destroyed Tveitt's home and 80 per cent of his output. Christian Eggen was able to reconstruct it from the orchestral parts and a two-piano reduction, leaving the Third to be issued (Nos 2 and 6 are irretrievably lost). The coupling here is the delightful *Variations on a Folksong from Hardanger* for two pianos and orchestra, written in 1939 for Tveitt to play with his first wife, a highly diverse late-Romantic effusion and a real winner. The performances are superb, Gimse totally in the Tveitt style with exemplary support from the RSNO and Bjarte Engeset; Gunilla Süssmann makes a splendid second soloist in the *Variations*. Excellent sound and a marvellous disc.

A Hundred Hardanger Tunes

A Hundred Hardanger Tunes, Op 151 – Suite No 2, 'Fifteen Mountain Songs'; Suite No 5, 'Troll-tunes'
Royal Scottish National Orchestra / Bjarte Engeset
Naxos 8 555770 (72' · DDD)   Ⓢ**D→**

Only four of Geirr Tveitt's suites from his unique, folk-inspired collection, *A Hundred Hardanger Tunes*, survive. The two presented here exhibit the same principal characteristics as Nos 1 and 4 (also on Naxos), although without the quasi-narrative structure of No 4, *Wedding Suite*. The Second Suite is largely a pastoral affair, though with moments of rugged grandeur befitting its subject, the mountains of Hardanger in western Norway. They are brilliantly orchestrated, as one now expects from Tveitt, the final six exceptionally so. The scoring of the Fifth Suite is richer still, like a kind of concerto for orchestra. The trolls here aren't the moronic ogres of *Harry Potter* or *The Fellowship of the Ring*, nor even the subterranean imps of *Peer Gynt*, but rather all the 'netherworld' peoples, whose music is as dazzling as they were legendarily beguiling.

The Royal Scottish orchestra sound as if they thoroughly enjoyed themselves in this music, as well they should have. A splendid and enjoyable disc, beautifully played and recorded. Strongly recommended.

Edgard Varèse   French/American 1883-1965

Varèse studied with d'Indy at the Schola Cantorum (1903-5) and Widor at the Paris Conservatoire (1905-7), then moved to Berlin, where he met Strauss and Busoni. In 1913 he returned to Paris, but in 1915 he emigrated to New York; nearly all his compositions disappeared at this stage, with the exception of a single published song and an orchestral score, *Bourgogne (1908)*, which he took with him but destroyed towards the end of his life. His creative output therefore effectively begins with *Amériques* for large orchestra (1921), which sets out to discover new worlds of sound: fiercely dissonant chords, rhythmically complex polyphonies for percussion and/or wind, forms in continuous evolution with no large-scale recurrence.

In 1921 he and Carlos Salzedo founded the International Composers Guild, who gave the first performances of several of his works for small ensemble, these prominently featuring wind and percussion, and presenting the innovations of *Amériques* in pure, compact form: *Hyperprism* (1923), *Octandre* (1923) and *Intégrales* (1925). *Arcana* (1927), which returns to the large orchestra and extended form with perfected technique, brought this most productive period to an end.

There followed a long stay in Paris (1928-33), during which he wrote *Ionisation* for percussion orchestra (1931), the first European work to dispense almost entirely with pitched sounds, which enter only in the coda. The flute solo *Density 21. 5* (1936) was then his last completed work for nearly two decades.

During this time he taught sporadically and also made plans for *Espace*, which was to have involved simultaneous radio broadcasts from around the globe; an *Etude pour Espace* for chorus, pianos and percussion was performed in 1947. Then, with electronic music at last a real possibility owing to the development of the tape recorder, he produced *Déserts* for wind, percussion and tape (1954) and a *Poème électronique* (1957-8), devised to be diffused in the Philips pavilion at the Brussels Exposition of 1958. His last years were devoted to projects on themes of night and death, including the unfinished *Nocturnal* for voices and chamber orchestra (1961).

GROVEmusic

Complete Works

Tuning Up. Amériques. Poème électronique. Arcana. Nocturnal. Un grand sommeil noir (orig version/orch Beaumont). Offrandes. Hyperprism. Octandre. Intégrales. Ecuatorial. Ionisation. Densité 21.5. Déserts. Dance for Burgess
Sarah Leonard, Mireille Delunsch sops **Kevin Deas** bass **Jacques Zoon** fl **François Kerdoncuff** pf **Edgard Varèse** electronics **Prague Philharmonic Choir; ASKO Ensemble; Royal Concertgebouw Orchestra / Riccardo Chailly**
Decca ② 460 208-2 (151' · DDD) Ⓜ ❍❍❍▷

Ⓖ This set is announced as 'The Complete Works' of Edgard Varèse. 'Complete' requires clarification. Excluded are *La procession du Vergès*, the electronic interlude from the 1955 film *Around and About Joan Mirò*, as well as the 1947 *Etude* Varèse wrote as preparation for his unrealised *Espace* project.

Works such as *Octandre* and *Intégrales* require scrupulous attention to balance if they're to sound more than crudely aggressive: Chailly secures this without sacrificing physical impact – witness the explosive *Hyperprism*. He brings

out some exquisite harmonic subtleties in *Offrandes*, Sarah Leonard projecting the surreal imagery of the texts with admirable poise. The fugitive opening bars of *Ionisation* sound slightly muted in the recorded ambience, though not the cascading tuned percussion towards the close.

The instrumentational problems of *Ecuatorial* are at last vindicated, allowing Varèse's inspired mix of brass and electronic keyboards to register with awesome power. Chailly opts for the solo bass, but a unison chorus would have heightened the dramatic impact still further. *Amériques*, the true intersection of romanticism and modernism, is performed in the original 1921 version, with its even more extravagant orchestral demands and bizarre reminiscences of *The Rite of Spring* and Schoenberg's *Five Orchestral Pieces*, understandably replaced in the revision. *Arcana* was recorded in 1992, Chailly probing beyond the work's vast dynamic contours more deeply than any other rival on disc.

No one but Varèse has drawn such sustained eloquence from an ensemble of wind and percussion, or invested such emotional power in the primitive electronic medium of the early 1950s. *Déserts* juxtaposes them in a score which marks the culmination of his search for new means of expression. The opening now seems a poignant evocation of humanity in the atomic age, the ending is resigned but not bitter. The tape interludes in Chailly's performance have a startling clarity, as does the *Poème électronique*, Varèse's untypical but exhilarating contribution to the 1958 Brussels World Fair. The unfinished *Nocturnal*, with its vocal stylisations and belated return of string timbre, demonstrates a continuing vitality that only time could extinguish. Varèse has had a significant impact on post-war musical culture, with figures as diverse as Stockhausen, Charlie Parker and Frank Zappa acknowledging his influence. Chailly's recordings demonstrate, in unequivocal terms, why this music will continue to provoke and inspire future generations.

Orchestral works

Amériques. Ecuatorial[a]. Nocturnal[b]. Ionisation. Hyperprism. Densité 21.5[c]. Un grand sommeil noir[d]. Dance for Burgess. Tuning Up
[bd]**Elizabeth Watts** sop [c]**Maria Grochowska** fl [a]**Thomas Bloch** onde [ab]**Camerata Silesia; Polish National Radio Symphony Orchestra / Christopher Lyndon-Gee** [d]pf
Naxos 8 557882 (67' · DDD) ❍❍▷

With Varèse fans still revelling in Riccardo Chailly's groundbreaking 1998 Decca cycle, anybody else approaching this provocative and inflammable music better have something profound to say: Christopher Lyndon-Gee and the Polish National Radio Symphony Orchestra don't let the side down. These Polish musicians are well used to the rough-and-tumble of performing the early textural works of Penderecki and Górecki and that visceral rawness, inherent in their own culture, transmutes powerfully to these seminal Varèse scores.

The standout performance for sure is the original 1921 version of *Amériques*, scored for an orchestra of over 150 musicians and an offstage 'banda'. Lyndon-Gee marshals his charges with a careful ear to balancing this monolithic ensemble: Varèse's emphatically reiterated rhythmic mantras are daintily articulated, but the musicians never sound browbeaten by his attention to detail. The elemental power of the closing moments is feral way beyond the call of duty.

Performances of the trail-blazing percussion ensemble work *Ionisation*, and other classics like *Hyperprism*, *Densité 21.5* and *Ecuatorial*, are cut from the same devoted cloth. And the rest of the album is devoted to curios like *Dance for Burgess* and *Tuning Up*, reconstructed by Varèse's pupil Chou Wen-Chung and recorded for the first time by Chailly. *Tuning Up* was conceived for a 1947 film about Carnegie Hall and incorporates Ives-like illusions to Varèse's own and borrowed music, all ricocheting against repeated As. Inevitably he came to blows with the film-makers, but Lyndon-Gee makes one think the by-product of their collaboration might be a minor masterpiece.

Peteris Vasks
Latvian b1952

Peteris Vasks was born in Aizpute, Latvia, and trained as a double-bass player. In 1970 he joined the Latvian National Opera orchestra, the Latvian Symphony Orchestra and chamber orchestra. In 1978, after graduating from the Latvian State Conservatory's Composition Class, Vasks began his teaching career, and many of his pupils are now noted Latvian composers. His initial compositional forays were noted for their unconventionality but by the 1980s he had found his uniquely Latvian voice in string, brass and piano music. **GROVE**music

Violin Concerto

Vasks Violin Concerto, 'Distant Light'
Weill Violin Concerto
Academy of St Martin in the Fields /
Anthony Marwood vn
Hyperion CDA67496 (57' · DDD)   Ⓕ

This new account of Vasks's *Distant Light* swells the number of recordings it has garnered to five, an amazing statistic for a work premiered as recently as August 1997. Then again, perhaps we shouldn't be too surprised: the Latvian's music speaks without artifice and offers an enticing blend of unspoilt beauty, compassionate heartache and superior compositional craft. Of all the competing versions, Gidon Kremer's pioneering Teldec reading has a charisma, intensity and concentration that are wholly arresting. More's the pity it has been deleted, so head-of-the-pack status must now pass to this excellently engineered newcomer. Anthony Marwood keeps a tight grip

on the structural tiller and plays with exquisite polish and intimacy of feeling; he also secures an exceptionally alert and involving contribution from his Academy forces.

Winds, percussion and double basses assemble for the coupling, Kurt Weill's ambitious early Violin Concerto of 1923-24, which receives as persuasive and vital a performance as any. Marwood and company quarry every ounce of bony lyricism and spooky burlesque from what can initially seem a rather dry, unyielding creation. Again, the sound is vividly realistic (if lacking just a whisker in bite and focus), and the disc as a whole certainly bodes well for Marwood's tenure as artistic director of the Irish CO.

Symphony No 2

Symphony No 2[a] Violin Concerto, 'Distant Light'[b]
[a]**Tampere Philharmonic Orchestra /** [b]**John Storgårds** vn [b]**Ostrobothnian Chamber Orchestra /**
Juha Kangas
Ondine ODE1005-2 (73' · DDD)   ⒻO

Peteris Vasks has been winning himself something of a cult following over the past decade. On the evidence of this blistering premiere recording, his Second Symphony of 1998-9 seems set to repeat the popular and critical success of *Voices*, its hugely effective 1991 predecessor for string orchestra.

A single-movement canvas of nearly 40 minutes' duration, it traverses emotions from bare-faced rage and serene contemplation to icy despair, achieving a vast, uneasy quietude at the close ('a sense of light-filled sorrow,' in the composer's words). Stylistic echoes are plentiful: Shostakovich, Kancheli, Górecki and Pärt; folk-music, birdsong and hymnody are further ingredients in this approachable cocktail. Fortunately, Vasks's compassionate inspiration eschews any hint of New Age pretentiousness or designer chic, conveying instead a strength of conviction, unflinching honesty and profound sense of wonder that easily hold the listener in its thrall. All of which is also testament to the formidable interpretative skills of conductor John Storgårds, who secures exemplary results from the Tampere Philharmonic. The sound is splendidly ample and detailed to match.

For the coupling, Storgårds gives a heartfelt performance of Vasks's Violin Concerto (*Distant Light*). Written in 1996-7 at the behest of Gidon Kremer and his then recently formed Kremerata Baltica, this is another single-movement, readily assimilable essay, though its at times enigmatically disparate elements are here perhaps less convincingly fused into a satisfying whole. Nevertheless, this enterprising release deserves every success.

Choral works

Dona nobis pacem. Pater noster. Missa
Latvian Radio Choir; Riga Sinfonietta /

Sigvards Klava
Ondine ODE1106-2 (58' · DDD)   Ⓕ

In the booklet interview, Peteris Vasks notes that during the Soviet rule in Latvia composition of sacred choral music was heavily discouraged. Personal necessity as well, it seems, also put him off writing the *Pater noster* his Protestant minister father kept asking for. Instrumental music was of greater importance.

When he did write a *Pater noster* (1991), it was in a simpler, more consonant style than much of his earlier work, expressively close to the 'holy minimalism' common to a number of Baltic composers, but Vasks's triadic style – which he feels essential for sacred music – shares little with them. A short, peaceful meditation, it is reverentially performed by the Latvian Radio Choir. So, too, is *Dona nobis pacem* (1996), inhabiting the same evocative sound world.

The *Missa* (2000, rev 2000-05) is a different matter. True, the expressive idiom is the same, but Vasks here invests his ideas in more musically satisfying forms. The use of string orchestral accompaniment is reminiscent in places, the *Sanctus* especially, of English music and sounds a touch like what an early Mass setting by Tippett might have sounded like. There are sympathetic echoes (no doubt coincidental) of Howells in the *Benedictus* and overlong *Agnus Dei*, too.

and orchestra, and then of the *Pastoral Symphony*. At the beginning of the 1920s there followed a group of religious works continuing the visionary manner: the unaccompanied *Mass in G minor*, the Revelation oratorio *Sancta civitas* and the 'pastoral episode' The *Shepherds of the Delectable Mountains*, later incorporated in *The Pilgrim's Progress*. But if the glowing serenity of pastoral and vision were to remain central during the decades of work on that magnum opus, works of the later 1920s show a widening of scope, towards the comedy of the operas *Sir John in Love* (after *The Merry Wives of Windsor*) and *The Poisoned Kiss*, and towards the angularity of Satan's music in *Job* and of the *Fourth Symphony*. The quite different *Fifth Symphony* has more connection with *The Pilgrim's Progress*, and was the central work of a period that also included the cantata *Dona nobis pacem*, the opulent *Serenade to Music* for 16 singers and orchestra, and the A minor string quartet, the finest of Vaughan Williams's rather few chamber works.

A final period opened with the desolate, pessimistic *Sixth Symphony*, after which Vaughan Williams found a focus in the natural world for such bleakness when he was asked to write the music for the film *Scott of the Antarctic* : out of that world came his *Seventh Symphony*, the *Sinfonia antartica*, whose pitched percussion colouring he used more ebulliently in the *Eighth Symphony*, the Ninth returning to the contemplative world of *The Pilgrim's Progress*.

GROVE music

Ralph Vaughan Williams
British 1872-1958

Vaughan Williams studied with Parry, Wood and Stanford at the Royal College of Music and Cambridge, then had further lessons with Bruch in Berlin (1897) and Ravel in Paris (1908). It was only after this that he began to write with sureness in larger forms, even though some songs had had success in the early years of the century. That success, and the ensuing maturity, depended very much on his work with folksong, which he had begun to collect in 1903; this opened the way to the lyrical freshness of the Housman cycle On Wenlock Edge and to the modally inflected tonality of the symphonic cycle that began with A Sea Symphony. But he learnt the same lessons in studying earlier English music in his task as editor of the English Hymnal (1906) – work which bore fruit in his Fantasia on a Theme by Tallis for strings, whose majestic unrelated consonances provided a new sound and a new way into large-scale form. The sound, with its sense of natural objects seen in a transfigured light, placed Vaughan Williams in a powerfully English visionary tradition, and made very plausible his association of his music with Blake (in the ballet Job) and Bunyan (in the opera The Pilgrim's Progress). Meanwhile the new command of form made possible a first symphony, A London Symphony), where characterful detail is worked into the scheme. A first opera, Hugh the Drover, made direct use of folksongs, which Vaughan Williams normally did not do in orchestral works.

His study of folksong, however, certainly facilitated the pastoral tone of The Lark Ascending, for violin

Piano Concerto

Vaughan Williams Piano Concerto in C
Foulds Dynamic Triptych, Op 88
Howard Shelley pf **Royal Philharmonic Orchestra /**
Vernon Handley
Lyrita SRCD211 (57' · DDD)   Ⓕ⬤

There are four unequivocal masterpieces for piano and orchestra in English 20th-century music: Bax's *Winter Legends*, Frank Bridge's *Phantasm* and the two works recorded here. Until the appearance of this recording the VW Concerto had been more frequently presented in its revised 1946 version for two pianos and orchestra – one that did no favours in revealing the masterpiece of his original inspiration. The exceptionally taxing solo part, and the power required by the soloist to project over an extremely large orchestra, almost certainly inhibited the original version's ingress into the repertoire. However, when heard under the guiding hand of a pianist of Howard Shelley's calibre, we're allowed once more to discover the work in its true glory.

It's easy to see why the piece was so admired by Bartók when it received its German premiere under Hermann Scherchen and the concerto's dedicatee Harriet Cohen, for this is surely one of the most cogent and tautly constructed examples of its genre to have emerged from English music of the period. John Fould's *Dynamic Triptych* is scarcely less impressive.

Though it lacks the conciseness of the VW, this is a work and a performance to treasure.

Symphonies

No 1, 'A Sea Symphony'; **No-2**, 'A London Symphony'; **No 3**, 'A Pastoral Symphony'; **No 4** in F minor; **No 5** in D; **No 6** in E minor; **No 7**, 'Sinfonia antartica'; **No 8** in D minor; **No 9** in E minor

Complete Symphonies

Symphonies Nos 1-9   **(H)**
Baillie, Ritchie sops **Cameron** bar **Gielgud** narr **London Philharmonic Choir and Orchestra / Boult**
Decca British Music Collection ⑤ 473 241-2DC5 (353' · ADD) Recorded 1952-8   **(M)**

Music-making of the highest calibre throughout. The mono engineering is always vivid, often stunningly so – especially in *A Sea Symphony* and *Sinfonia antartica*.

Symphonies Nos 1-9
Coupled with: Fantasia on a Theme by Thomas Tallis. The Wasps. Serenade to Music. In the Fen Country. Norfolk Rhapsody No 1. The Lark Ascending. English Folk Song Suite. Fantasia on 'Greensleeves'. Concerto for Two Pianos and Orchestra. Job
Armstrong, Burrowes, Price sops **Case** bar **London Philharmonic Choir and Orchestra; New Philharmonia / Boult; various artists**
EMI ⑤ 573924-2 (534' · ADD)   **(B)**

An ideal supplement to Boult's mono VW cycle for Decca.

Symphonies No 1-9. Tallis Fantasia. In the Fen Country. The Lark Ascending. Norfolk Rhapsody No 1. On Wenlock Edge
Soloists; London Philharmonic Choir and Orchestra / Bernard Haitink
EMI ⑤ 586026-2 (474' · DDD · T)   **(S)**

Haitink's majestic VW symphony cycle was recorded with the LPO over 13 years. His eloquent and illuminatingly intense interpretations serve up a feast of stimulating listening. The fill-ups are mostly marvellous, too; both *On Wenlock Edge* (with Ian Bostridge) and *In the Fen Country* receive sublime advocacy. An outstanding bargain.

Symphonies – selected

Vaughan Williams Symphony No 2 (original version, 1913) **Butterworth** The Banks of Green Willow
London Symphony Orchestra / Richard Hickox
Chandos CHAN9902 (68' · DDD)   Ⓟ**OOO**☞

It was during the summer of 1911 that George Butterworth, whose enchanting 1913 idyll, *The Banks of Green Willow*, comprises the achingly poignant curtain-raiser here, first suggested to Vaughan Williams that he should write a purely orchestral symphony. VW dug out some sketches h'd made for a symphonic poem about London, while at the same time deriving fruitful inspiration from HG Wells's 1908 novel, *Tono-Bungay*. Geoffrey Toye gave the successful Queen's Hall premiere in March 1914, and VW subsequently dedicated the score to Butterworth's memory. Over the next two decades or so, the work underwent three revisions (including much judicious pruning) and was published twice (in 1920 and 1936). In his compelling 1941 recording with the Cincinnati SO, Eugene Goossens employed the 1920 version, which adds about three minutes of music to that definitive 1936 'revised edition'. Now Richard Hickox at long last gives us the chance to hear VW's original, hour-long canvas – and riveting listening it makes too!

Whereas the opening movement is as we know it today, the ensuing, expanded *Lento* acquires an intriguingly mournful, even world-weary demeanour. Unnervingly, the ecstatic full flowering of that glorious E major *Largamente* idea, first heard at fig F in the final revision, never materialises, and the skies glower menacingly thereafter. Towards the end of the *Scherzo* comes a haunting episode that Arnold Bax was particularly sad to see cut ('a mysterious passage of strange and fascinating cacophony' was how he described it). The finale, too, contains a wealth of additional material, most strikingly a liturgical theme of wondrous lyrical beauty, and, in the epilogue, a gripping paragraph that looks back to the work's introduction as well as forward to the first movement of *A Pastoral Symphony*. Sprawling it may be, but this epic conception evinces a prodigal inventiveness, poetry, mystery and vitality that do not pall with repeated hearings. Hickox and the LSO respond with an unquenchable spirit, generous flexibility and tender affection that suit VW's ambitious inspiration to a T, and Chandos's sound is big and bold to match. An essential purchase for anyone remotely interested in British music.

Symphonies Nos 4[a] & 5[b]   **(H)**
[a]**BBC Symphony Orchestra / Ralph Vaughan Williams**; [b]**Hallé Orchestra / Sir John Barbirolli**
Dutton mono CDBP9731 (66' · ADD) Recorded [a]1937, [b]1944   **(S)OOO**

No performance on record of Vaughan Williams's Fourth Symphony has ever quite matched this very first one, recorded under the composer's baton in October 1937. As Michael Kennedy says in his note for this reissue, it's 'taken at a daredevil pace', and more importantly has a bite and energy beyond any rival. If early listeners to this violent work were shocked by the composer's new boldness, here his conducting demonstrates the passionate emotion behind the piece. The remastered sound is so vivid and immediate, so full of presence, that in places one almost has the illusion of stereo before its time.

Barbirolli's premiere recording of the Fifth Symphony, made in February 1944 eight months after the first performance, is hardly less remarkable. This, too, has never been matched since for the stirring passion of the great climaxes in the first and third movements, with Barbirolli in each carefully grading the intensity between exposition and recapitulation. It's also a revelation to find him taking the triple-time of the Passacaglia finale much faster than latter-day rivals, relating it more closely than usual to the great example of the finale of Brahms's Fourth Symphony, making it no pastoral amble but a searing argument. Here again hiss has been virtually eliminated, but that has left the high violins sounding rather papery. Even so, there's no lack of weight in the big climaxes, with brass and wind atmospherically caught.

An outstanding issue for all lovers of this composer's music, not just those who specialise in historic recordings.

Symphony No 5[a]. Valiant for truth[b]. The Pilgrim Pavement[c]. Psalm 23 (arr Churchill)[b]. Hymn-tune Prelude on 'Song 13' by Orlando Gibbons (arr Glatz)[a]. Prelude and Fugue in C minor[a]
[d]**Ian Watson** org [bc]**Richard Hickox Singers;** [a]**London Symphony Orchestra / Richard Hickox**
Chandos CHAN9666 (71' · DDD · T)   Ⓕ**ⓞⓞ▷**

This is an exceptionally powerful yet deeply moving account of the Fifth. Aided by glowing, wide-ranging engineering, Hickox's is an urgently communicative reading. The first and third movements in particular emerge with an effortless architectural splendour and rapt authority, the climaxes built and resolved with mastery. The *Scherzo* is as good a place as any to sample the lustrous refinement of the LSO's response. Hickox ensures that the symphony's concluding bars positively glow with gentle ecstasy: here's a Fifth that can surely hold its own in the most exalted company.

Material from *The Pilgrim's Progress* made its way into the Fifth Symphony and two of the five enterprising couplings here provide further links with John Bunyan's timeless allegory: the 1940 motet for mixed voices with organ, *Valiant-for-truth* and John Churchill's 1953 arrangement for soprano and mixed chorus of Psalm 23 (originally sung by The Voice of a Bird in Act 4 of *The Pilgrim's Progress*). The latter receives its finely prepared recorded début on this occasion, as do both *The Pilgrim Pavement* (a 1934 processional for soprano, chorus and organ) and Helen Glatz's string-orchestra arrangement of the solo-piano *Hymn-tune Prelude on 'Song 13'* by Gibbons. Which just leaves the Prelude and Fugue, originally written for organ in 1921, but heard here in a sumptuous orchestration.

Symphony No 6 in E minor[a]. The Lark Ascending[b]. A Song of Thanksgiving[c]
[c]**Betty Dolemore** sop [c]**Robert Speaight** narr [c]**Harry Grab** org [b]**Jean Pougnet** vn [c]**Luton Choral Society;** [a]**London Symphony Orchestra,** [bc]**London Philharmonic Orchestra / Sir Adrian Boult**

Dutton Laboratories mono CDBP9703 (69' · ADD) Recorded 1949-52   Ⓑ**ⓞⓞ**

Although it was Boult who premiered VW's awesome Sixth Symphony, his white-hot February 1949 account with the LSO wasn't in fact the work's début recording – that honour fell to Stokowski and the New York Philharmonic (who pipped their British counterparts to the post by just two days). The return to the catalogue of Boult's legendary version – last available on an identically programmed Great Recordings of the Century anthology (EMI) – is a cause for celebration, especially in such a vivid transfer (if fractionally hollow in the bass), and so modestly priced to boot. Like Stokowski's scarcely less thrilling realisation, the performance offers us the opportunity to hear VW's original *Scherzo*. This has been allotted a separate track at the end of the symphony, its place taken by the same team's February 1950 recording of the composer's revision (not an ideal arrangement, perhaps). Whether the performance as a whole entirely displaces Sir Adrian's marvellous 1953 Decca version with the LPO (available in a disappointingly rough transfer on Belart) is open to debate, but both interpretations comprehensively outflank Sir Adrian's New Philharmonia stereo remake for EMI in terms of fiery concentration and sheer guts.

Written in response to a commission from the BBC in 1943 for a work to celebrate the defeat of Hitler's Germany, *A Song of Thanksgiving* was first broadcast shortly after VE Day. This commercial recording followed in December 1951. The work (which is scored for soprano, narrator, chorus and orchestra) has a smattering of decent invention (including, from around 4'30", fleeting echoes of the Sixth's second movement), but overall it's hardly representative of VW at his most inspired.

Last, and certainly not least, comes a wholly cherishable account (from October 1952) of *The Lark Ascending*, with Jean Pougnet a wonderfully silky toned, humane soloist. Boult's accompaniment, too, is a model of selfless dedication and intuitive rapture. For some, it remains, quite simply, the most tenderly unaffected and profoundly moving *Lark* on disc, though the string timbre on that earlier EMI restoration is much preferable to this over-processed newcomer. None the less, a most valuable VW reissue.

Symphony No 6. Fantasia on a Theme by Thomas Tallis. The Lark Ascending
Tasmin Little vn **BBC Symphony Orchestra / Sir Andrew Davis**
Warner Apex 0927 49584-2 (62' · DDD)   Ⓢ**ⓞ▷**

Sir Andrew Davis clearly thought long and hard before committing this enigmatic and tragic symphony to disc, and the result is one of the most spontaneous and electrifying accounts of the Sixth Symphony available. The urgency and vigour of the first and third movements is astonishing, leaving one with the impression that the work might have been recorded in one take. His treatment of the second subject's reprise in the closing pages of the first movement is more underplayed and remote than the beautifully sheened approach of some recordings, but is arguably more nostalgic for being so. The feverish, nightmare world of the *Scherzo* is a real tour de force in the hands of an inspired BBC Symphony Orchestra, and the desolate wasteland of the eerie final movement has rarely achieved such quiescence and nadir as here. Davis's searchingly intense *Tallis Fantasia* is finely poised with a beautifully spacious acoustic. The disc concludes on a quietly elevated note with Tasmin Little's serene and gently introspective reading of *The Lark Ascending*. The recording is excellent.

Film Music

The Film Music of Ralph Vaughan Williams, Volume 2
49th Parallel – Suite[a]. The Dim Little Island[b]. The England of Elizabeth – Suite[c]. (all ed Hogger)
[a]**Emily Gray** *sop* [b]**Martin Hindmarsh** *ten* [c]**Chetham's Chamber Choir; BBC Philharmonic Orchestra / Rumon Gamba**
Chandos CHAN10244 (71' · DDD)

Directed by Michael Powell and written by Emeric Pressburger and Rodney Ackland, *49th Parallel* (1941) was the Ministry of Information's only feature film, its plot of five stranded Nazi U-boat crewmen journeying through Canada to the haven of the then neutral United States – designed, in Powell's words, 'to scare the pants off the Americans and bring them into the war'. Vaughan Williams's film score was the first of 11 he wrote between 1941 and 1958.

It was a challenge that evidently stoked his imagination, for inspiration runs high throughout this 39-minute sequence fashioned by Stephen Hogger. The unforgettable, nobly flowing 'Prelude' accompanies both the opening and closing titles, and enthusiasts will enjoy spotting thematic and stylistic links with masterworks to come (including Symphonies Nos 5-7 and Second String Quartet).

The present suite from *The England of Elizabeth* (written in the autumn of 1955 for a British Transport Commission documentary) adds eight minutes to Mathieson's three-movement adaptation (familiar to many from Previn's 1968 LSO account). It is, as annotator Michael Kennedy observes, a splendidly vital and inventive achievement. In the section depicting Tintern Vaughan Williams quotes a theme from his unpublished tone-poem of 1906, *The Solent* (the tune also crops up in his first and last symphonies), and it's soon followed by a haunting passage for choir alone.

Sandwiched between these two is a partial reconstruction of VW's amiable 1949 score for *The Dim Little Island*, a 10-minute short commissioned by the Central Office of Information (which also featured the composer in the role of narrator). It borrows heavily from VW's own *Five Variants of Dives and Lazarus* and even incorporates a verse of that self-same melody sung by a solo tenor.

Rumon Gamba draws a polished and wholehearted response from all involved. The Chandos recording has striking body and lustre; exemplary presentation, too. Very strongly recommended.

String Quartets

String Quartets – No 1 in G minor; No 2 in A minor. Phantasy Quintet[a]
[a]**Garfield Jackson** *va* **Maggini Quartet**
Naxos 8 555300 (66' · DDD)

Why isn't Vaughan Williams's Second Quartet part of the international chamber repertory? Played as eloquently as this it seems unarguably a masterpiece, one specifically of its time: 1942-3. Its first movement and deeply fraught *Scherzo* are as troubled as Shostakovich (whose music at moments, like a sudden stab of violence in that first *allegro*, it passingly resembles), while the misleadingly titled slow 'Romance' is haunted and haunting. It's tranquil but not at peace. It achieves an impassioned nobility and approaches serenity at the end, but something ghostly (it walks again in the Epilogue to the Sixth Symphony) refuses to be exorcised until the beautiful calm finale.

What these players do with the two much earlier pieces is no less remarkable. In them Vaughan Williams's style is audibly emerging from the influences (notably Ravel, briefly his teacher) that helped form it. In the First Quartet's opening movement an arching, lyrical melody that sounds like Vaughan Williams speaking with a French accent (and is it a French lark that ascends a little later?) has shed the accent by its return; something similar happens in the finale. But it was not an immature composer (he was 36, after all) who in the slow movement recognised a kinship with Fauré. And the *Phantasy Quintet* is audibly by the composer of the *Tallis* Fantasia, grateful to Ravel for giving him access to a deft rhythmic flexibility, but exploring his own unmistakable territory in the serenity tinged with poignancy of the slow movement. The Magginis and Garfield Jackson clearly love this music deeply; they play it with great beauty of tone and variety of colour and with passionate expressiveness. The ample recording allows both grand gestures and quiet intimacy.

Dona nobis pacem

Dona nobis pacem[a]. Sancta civitas[b]
[a]**Yvonne Kenny** *sop* [b]**Philip Langridge** *ten* **Bryn Terfel** *bass-bar* [b]**St Paul's Cathedral Choir; London Symphony Chorus and Orchestra / Richard Hickox**
EMI British Composers 754788-2 (63' · DDD · T)

This is a generous and inspiring coupling of two of Vaughan Williams's most important choral utterances. Hickox coaxes magnificent sounds from the LSO throughout: in *Dona nobis pacem*, for example, the sense of orchestral spectacle during 'Beat! Beat! drums!' is riveting in its physical impact. The London Symphony Chorus combines full-throated discipline and sensitivity to nuance, and Hickox's trio of soloists is excellent, with Terfel outstandingly eloquent. *Sancta civitas* is a work whose multi-layered scoring places great demands on both conductor and production team alike: suffice it to report, it's difficult to see Hickox's inspirational account of this still-underrated score being surpassed for years to come. EMI's clean, wide-ranging sound is admirable.

Additional recommendations

Coupled with: Four Hymns. Toward the Unknown Region. O clap your hands. Lord, thou hast been our Refuge
Howarth sop **Ainsley** ten **Allen** bar
Corydon Singers and Orchestra / Best
Helios CDS44321 (76' · DDD)   Ⓑ
   An enticing VW collection enhanced by the late
   Christopher Palmer's typically illuminating notes.

Further listening

Vaughan Williams Magnificat
Coupled with: Song of Thanksgiving, Choral Hymns, Shepherds of the Delectable Mountains, Old 100th
Dawson sop **Wyn-Rogers** contr **Ainsley** ten **Terfel** bar **Corydon Singers, CLS / Best**
Hyperion CDA66569 (73' · DDD)   Ⓕ
   The only version available of the sensuous
   Magnificat.

Mass in G minor

Vaughan Williams Mass in G minor. Te Deum in G
Howells Requiem. Take him, earth, for cherishing
Mary Seers sop **Michael Chance** counterten **Philip Salmon** ten **Jonathan Best** bass **Corydon Singers / Matthew Best** with **Thomas Trotter** org
Hyperion CDA66076 (60' · ADD · T)   ⒻOO

Vaughan Williams's unaccompanied Mass in G minor manages to combine the common manner of Elizabethan liturgical music with those elements of his own folk-music heritage that make his music so distinctive, and in so doing arrives at something individual and new. The work falls into five movements and its mood is one of heartfelt, if restrained, rejoicing. Howells's Requiem dates from 1936, a year after the death of his only son. The work was not released in his lifetime but was reconstructed and published in 1980 from his manuscripts. It's a most hauntingly beautiful work of an intensely personal nature. *Take him, earth, for cherishing* was composed to commemorate the assassination of J F Kennedy. The text is an English translation

of Prudentius's 4th-century poem, *Hymnus circa Exsequias Defuncti*. Again it shows the great strength of Howells's choral writing, with a clear outline and affecting yet unimposing harmonic twists. The Corydon Singers give marvellous performances and the sound is very fine.

Mass in G minor. Lord, thou hast been our refuge. Prayer to the Father of Heaven. O vos omnes. O clap your hands. O taste and see. O how amiable. The Christian Year. Come down, O Love divine
Thomas Fitches org **Elora Festival Singers / Noel Edison**
Naxos 8 554826 (57' · DDD)   ⓈO➔

This fine Canadian choir perform very beautifully in a style which seems natural and right. The Elora Festival Singers have much in common with King's College, Cambridge under Willcocks; relaxed and habituated, they offer the welcome loveliness of a choral tone where the blend and match of voices produce a sound that's eminently 'at unity with itself'. There's no shortage of good recordings of the Mass in G minor, the one that stands out as being open-eyed and adventurous in spirit being the version on Meridian by the Choir of New College, Oxford. They favour a sharper tone, a quicker tempo in the *Credo* and a brighter acoustic. The choice between women's and boys' voices may prove the deciding factor when it comes to which version; the Elora Singers' female voices seem to give this music precisely what's required. Yet more decisive may be the coupling. The two recordings by the college choirs couple music by other composers. The Canadians stay with Vaughan Williams, in a mood which assorts well with the Mass. Particularly apt is *O vos omnes*, also written for Sir Richard Terry and the Choir of Westminster Cathedral. The Skelton setting, *Prayer to the Father of Heaven*, from 1948 – a comparative rarity and sensitively performed – has a chill which is partly medieval, partly perhaps from the Antarctica of VW's Seventh Symphony. *Down Ampney* ('Come down, O Love divine') brings the warmth and cheer of a settled major tonality at the close.

Serenade to Music

Serenade to Music. Flos campi. Five mystical songs[a]. Fantasia on Christmas carols[a]
Elizabeth Connell, Linda Kitchen, Anne Dawson, Amanda Roocroft sops **Sarah Walker, Jean Rigby, Diana Montague** mezzos **Catherine Wyn-Rogers** contr **John Mark Ainsley, Martyn Hill, Arthur Davies, Maldwyn Davies** tens [a]**Thomas Allen, Alan Opie** bars **Gwynne Howell, John Connell** basses **Nobuko Imai** va **Corydon Singers; English Chamber Orchestra / Matthew Best**
Hyperion CDA66420 (68' · DDD · T)   ⒻO

In 1938 Sir Henry Wood celebrated his 50 years as a professional conductor with a concert. Vaughan Williams composed a work for the occasion, the *Serenade to Music*, in which he set words by Shakespeare from Act 5 of *The Merchant of Venice*. Sixteen star vocalists of the age were gathered together for the performance and Vaughan Williams customised the vocal parts to show off the best qualities of the singers. The work turned out to be one of the composer's most sybaritic creations, turning each of its subsequent performances into a special event. Hyperion has gathered stars of our own age for this outstanding issue and Best has perceptively managed to give each their head, while melding them into a cohesive ensemble. A mellow, spacious recording has allowed the work to emerge on disc with a veracity never achieved before.

The coupled vocal pieces are given to equal effect and the disc is completed by Nobuko Imai's tautly poignant account of *Flos campi*, in which the disturbing tension between solo viola and wordless chorus heighten the cryptic nature of the work.

Additional recommendations

Serenade to Music

Coupled with: The Wasps Overture. Symphony No 2. Fantasia on 'Greensleeves'
Sols inc **Baillie, Suddaby** sops **Nash** ten **Henderson** bar **BBC Symphony Orchestra; Queen's Hall Orchestra / Wood**
Dutton Laboratories CDBP9707 (63' · ADD)　　Ⓜ
This performance with the 16 original soloists possesses a very special beauty and atmosphere.

Five Tudor Portraits

Five Tudor Portraits. Five Variants of 'Dives and Lazarus'
Jean Rigby mez **John Shirley-Quirk** bar **London Symphony Chorus and Orchestra / Richard Hickox**
Chandos CHAN9593 (55' · DDD · T)　　ⒻⓄ🅑➔

First heard at the 1936 Norwich Festival, Vaughan Williams's *Five Tudor Portraits* find the composer at his most dazzlingly inventive, the resourceful and witty writing fitting Skelton's words like a glove. Moreover, an irresistible humanity illuminates the most ambitious of the settings, 'Jane Scroop (Her Lament for Philip Sparrow)', which contains music as compassionate as Vaughan Williams ever conceived. It's a life-enhancing creation and well deserving of this first-rate recording. Aided by disciplined orchestral support, the London Symphony Chorus launches itself in lusty fashion into the ale-soaked narrative of 'The Tunning of Elinor Rumming', though the resonant acoustic rather precludes ideal clarity of diction. Hickox is exuberant in this sparkling tableau, while Jean Rigby's characterful contribution should raise a smile. John Shirley-Quirk's is a touching presence in 'My Pretty Bess', and the mordant, black humour of 'Epitaph of John Jayberd of Diss' is effectively captured. Jane Scroop's lament in the

fourth (and surely best) movement finds these fine artists at their most perceptive. How ravishingly Hickox moulds his strings in the hushed passage following 'It was proper and prest!' where the music movingly anticipates the poignancy of the closing section. Listen out, too, for the wealth of exquisitely observed woodwind detail in the enchanting funeral processional. The concluding 'Jolly Rutterkin' goes with a swing, though Shirley-Quirk is a mite unsteady at the top of his range.

The coupling is a heart-warming *Dives and Lazarus*, with the LSO strings producing their most lustrous tone.

A Cotswold Romance

A Cotswold Romance. Death of Tintagiles
Rosa Mannion sop **Thomas Randle** ten **Matthew Brook** bar **London Philharmonic Choir; London Symphony Orchestra / Richard Hickox**
Chandos CHAN9646 (54' · DDD · T)　　Ⓕ🅑➔

A Cotswold Romance is a gift from Vaughan Williams to those who hold the music of *Hugh the Drover* in deep affection but who, under torture, would probably have to admit that the opera itself is less than perfect. *Hugh*, first produced in 1924, enjoyed sufficient immediate success for a set of records to be produced with the original cast. It then had to wait till 1979 for a complete recording on LP (reissued on EMI), and till 1994 for a new one on CD. The adaptation as a dramatic cantata came out in 1951, reducing the two-act opera to 10 numbers and rescoring some of the music to allow a larger part for the chorus. The addition of wordless chorus is delightful, not least when the chorus sings the first part of Hugh's song of the road and re-enters with delicious harmonies at 'All the scented night'. Thomas Randle, who has the voice of a man of the road and a lover, is admirably cast. Rosa Mannion, with a slight hint of turning tremulous under pressure, is otherwise an ideal Mary, and the chorus is excellent. Hickox conducts with brio and with due feeling for the romance.

Death of Tintagiles is incidental music written for a play by Maeterlinck, performed without much success in 1913. In his interesting notes, Stephen Connock associates it with *Riders to the Sea* and the *Sinfonia antartica*; and it's true that there are sternly impressive moments, of menace and darkness. Though it hardly seems viable as an orchestral suite, it's good to have on this disc, nevertheless.

On Wenlock Edge

On Wenlock Edge. Merciless Beauty. Two English Folksongs. Ten Blake Songs. Along the Field
John Mark Ainsley ten **The Nash Ensemble** (Gareth Hulse ob Leo Phillips, Elizabeth Wexler vns Roger Chase va Paul Watkins vc Ian Brown pf)
Hyperion CDA67168 (69' · DDD · T)　　ⒻⓄ

The programme here has an identity of its own and as such is without competitors. Its 'theme' is to collect those of Vaughan Williams's songs which have something other than piano accompaniment. *On Wenlock Edge* (1909) is for voice, piano and string quartet, *Merciless Beauty* (1921) with string trio, *Along the Field* (1927) and *Two English Folksongs* (published 1935 but of earlier date) voice and violin, and the Blake songs (1957) with oboe. Eligible for inclusion might have been *Four Hymns* (1914) with piano and viola, and perhaps *The Willow Whistle* (1939) for voice and pipe. The *Three Vocalises* of 1958, with clarinet, are specifically for soprano, but show the composer's continuing taste for such combinations right into the last year of his life. John Mark Ainsley sings with the sense of a civilised personal utterance, refined and restrained, yet capable of full-bodied tone and a ringing *forte* when needed: the cry 'O noisy bells, be dumb' is as emotional as an operatic climax and all the more effective for the exceptional frankness of its release. These are highly demanding pieces, the voice unremittingly exposed. He brings to them a fine poise, in breathing, phrasing, expression and the even emission of quite beautiful tone. He has also the considerable advantage of exceptional players to work with. Individually admirable, they combine in *On Wenlock Edge* to give an unusually imaginative performance.

Songs of Travel

Vaughan Williams Songs of Travel **Butterworth** Bredon Hill and other songs. A Shropshire Lad **Finzi** Let us garlands bring, Op 18 **Ireland** Sea Fever. The Vagabond. The Bells of San Marie
Bryn Terfel bass-bar **Malcolm Martineau** pf
DG 445 946-2GH (77' · DDD · T)　　　Ⓕ ⓄⓄ▶

There's a touch of genius about Bryn Terfel. To those who've known most of these songs since childhood and heard them well performed innumerable times, it will come not quite as a revelation but more as the fulfilment of a deeply felt wish, instinctive rather than consciously formed. As in all the best Lieder singing, everything is specific: 'Fly away, breath' we recite, thinking nothing of it, but with this singer it's visual – we see it in flight, just as in *Sea Fever* we know in the very tiniest of gaps that in that second he has *heard* 'the seagulls crying'. As in all the best singing of songs, whatever the nationality, there's strong, vivid communication: he'll sometimes sing so softly that if he'd secured anything less than total involvement he'd lose us. There's breadth of phrase, variety of tone, alertness of rhythm. All the musical virtues are there; and yet that seems to go only a little way towards accounting for what's special.One after another, these songs are brought to full life. There's a boldness about Terfel's art that could be perilous, but which, as exercised here, is marvellously well guided by musicianship, intelligence and

the genuine flash of inspiration. Malcolm Martineau's playing is also a delight: his touch is as sure and illuminating as the singer's.

Songs

Seven Songs from 'The Pilgrim's Progress'.
Ten Songs from 'Hugh the Drover'. Sir John in Love – Greensleeves; See the chariot at hand
Sarah Fox sop **Juliette Pochin** mez
Andrew Staples ten **Roderick Williams** bar
Iain Burnside pf
Albion ALB001 (60' · DDD)　　　Ⓕ

According to the booklet, no fewer than 11 world premieres adorn this first release from Albion Records, the RVW Society's own label. The 10 songs from *Hugh the Drover* (the first of VW's six operas, 1911-14) were arranged by the composer in 1924, the same year as its belated first performance under Malcolm Sargent, and make doubly absorbing listening as they offer us a glimpse into the composer's initial thoughts. Particularly heartwarming here are the two extended love duets for Hugh and Mary ('Ah! Love I've found you' and 'Hugh my lover'), the latter a cunning conflation of the most tenderly lyrical music to be found in Act 2 (culminating in the ecstatic 'O the sky shall be our roof').

Next come two numbers from *Sir John in Love*, including the sublime setting of Ben Jonson's 'See the chariot at hand' from Act 4. Seven songs from *The Pilgrim's Progress* make up the remainder and find Roderick Williams and Sarah Fox both ingratiating in tone and pleasingly articulate. In fact, all four singers acquit themselves with credit, while Iain Burnside's accompaniments are past praise in their scrupulous sensitivity.

Beautifully produced and attractively presented, this likeable anthology deserves to do well – and if it fosters further exploration of VW's operatic output, so much the better!

The Pilgrim's Progress

The Pilgrim's Progress
Gerald Finley bar Pilgrim **Peter Coleman-Wright** bar John Bunyan **Jeremy White** bass Evangelist, Envy, Third Shepherd **Donaldson Bell** bar Pontius Pilate **Gidon Saks** bass Apollyon, Lord Hate-Good, Mistrust **Richard Coxon** ten Pliable, Mister By-Ends **Francis Egerton** ten Timorous, Usher **Roderick Williams** bar Obstinate, Watchful, First Shepherd **Adrian Thompson** ten Lord Lechery, Celestial Messenger **Rebecca Evans** sop Madam Wanton, Shining One **Pamela Helen Stephen** mez Madam Bubble, Shining One, Heavenly Being II **Anne-Marie Owens** mez Madam By-Ends, Pickthank **Christopher Keyte** bass Simon Magus **John Kerr** bass Judas Iscariot **Susan Gritton** sop Malice, Bird, Shining One, Heavenly Being I **Neil Gillespie** ten Worldly Glory **Jonathan Fisher** bar Demas **Mark Padmore** ten Interpreter, Superstition, Second Shepherd **Robert**

Hayward *bar* Herald **Mica Penniman** *sop*
Woodcutter's Boy **Chorus and Orchestra of the
Royal Opera House, Covent Garden /
Richard Hickox**
Chandos ② CHAN9625 (130' · DDD · N/T)　ⒻⓄ➔

John Noble was a fine Pilgrim on the old Boult
recording, but Gerald Finley brings not only a
voice that's as good and well suited but also a
dramatic quality that is more colourful and
intense. But Boult's cast is very strong, with
several of the short parts, such as the Herald
(Terence Sharpe) better sung than as here (Robert Hayward). In the Valley of Humiliation the
voice of Apollyon comes as an amplified sound
from off-stage, but on record the trick is to catch
an overpowering terror, and this they managed
better on EMI, partly by virtue of having Robert
Lloyd to strike it, and also by the producer's
decision to bring it closer. Nor, in the comparison, is there any sense of a confrontation of
'bright young feller' and 'grand old fuddy-
duddy'. Boult doesn't *sound* like an old man, any
more than Hickox sounds like a youngster.

Hickox has a big canvas for the recorded
sound, and achieves a clearer texture from EMI.
The newer version also has Gerald Finley, and is
a fine performance anyway.

The Poisoned Kiss

The Poisoned Kiss
Neal Davies *bar* Dipsacus **Janice Watson** *sop*
Tormentilla **Pamela Helen Stephen** *mez* Angelica
James Gilchrist *ten* Amaryllus **Roderick Williams**
bar Gallanthus **Gail Pearson** *sop* First Medium
Helen Williams *sop* Second Medium **Emer
McGilloway** *sop* Third Medium **Anne Collins**
contr Empress Persicaria **John Graham-Hall** *ten* Hob
Richard Suart *bar* Gob **Mark Richardson**
bass Lob **Adrian Partington Singers; BBC
National Orchestra of Wales / Richard Hickox**
Chandos ② CHAN10120; CD/SACD hybrid ◉
CHSA5020 (116' · DDD · N/T)　ⒻⓄ➔

Written in the late 1920s when he was at the
height of his powers, *The Poisoned Kiss* is Vaughan
Williams's forgotten opera: this is the first complete recording. The composer chose his friend
Evelyn Sharp to write a libretto based on a short
story by Richard Garnett about a beautiful princess who lives on poison. But the verse treatment
is deplorable. Though the pair had in mind the
operettas of Gilbert and Sullivan, the result is coy
and self-conscious, never witty or pointed in a
Gilbertian way. Vaughan Williams made revisions in 1936 and 1955, but there are still too
many embarrassingly unfunny lines. This recording helps to rehabilitate the opera by eliminating
virtually all the spoken dialogue.

Neither Vaughan Williams nor Sharp could
work out the right balance between comedy and
the central romance – the love between Prince
Amaryllus and Tormentilla, brought up on poison by her magician father, Dipsacus.

Though planned as a light opera, the music has

substance. The score is rich in ideas; each
number is beautifully tailored, never outstaying
its welcome. At almost two hours of music, it has
to be said that the opera is too long (and it would
be even longer with dialogue), but the inspiration never flags.

Charm predominates, with tender melodies
like that in the Act 1 duet of Amaryllus and Tormentilla, 'Blue larkspur in a garden', and a surging emotional climax in the ensemble which
crowns Act 2, when their love leads to the passionate poisoned kiss. There are direct echoes of
Sullivan in the multi-layered ensembles and patter numbers, which come closest to achieving
the lightness aimed at.

Whatever the shortcomings of the piece, no
lover of Vaughan Williams's music should miss
hearing this wonderful set, with a strong and
characterful cast superbly led by Richard
Hickox, and with atmospheric sound enhancing
the musical delights. Janice Watson as Tormentilla sings with sweetness and warmth, while
giving point to the poisonous side of the character, and James Gilchrist makes an ardent Amaryllus. Pamela Helen Stephen and Roderick
Williams are totally affecting in their love
music, and Neal Davies is firm and strong as the
magician Dipsacus.

Sir John in Love

Sir John in Love
Adrian Thompson *ten* Shallow/Dr Caius **Stephan
Loges** *bar* Shallow/Host **Stephen Varcoe** *bass* Sir
Hugh Evans **Daniel Norman** *ten* Slender **Henry Moss**
ten Peter Simple **Roderick Williams** *bar* Page **Don-
ald Maxwell** *bar* Sir John Falstaff **John Bowen** *ten*
Bardolph **Richard Lloyd-Morgan** *bass* Nym **Brian
Bannatyne-Scott** *bass* Pistol **Susan Gritton** *sop*
Anne Page **Laura Claycomb** *sop* Mrs Page **Sarah
Connolly** *mez* Mrs Ford **Mark Padmore** *ten* Fenton
Mark Richardson *bass* Rugby **Anne-Marie Owens**
mez Mrs Quickly **Matthew Best** *bass* Ford **The Sinfo-
nia Chorus; Northern Sinfonia / Richard Hickox**
Chandos ② CHAN9928 (137' · DDD · N/T)　ⒻⓄ➔

There's no lack of glorious melody in *Sir John
in Love*, and not just folksong cunningly interwoven. Musically, what comes over strongly, more
richly than ever before in this magnificent recording from Richard Hickox, is the way
that the writing anticipates later Vaughan Williams, not just the radiant composer of the Fifth
Symphony and *Serenade to Music*, with key-
changes of heartstopping beauty, but the composer's darker side, with sharply rhythmic writing.

The work's title, *Sir John in Love*, points to
Vaughan Williams's different approach to the
central character. With him Shakespeare's fat
knight isn't just comic but a believable lover,
more genial and expansive than in Boito's portrait, yet hardly a noble figure such as Elgar portrayed in his big symphonic study. Donald Maxwell makes a splendid Falstaff, relishing the
comedy without making it a caricature. Above all,
his full, dark voice is satisfyingly fat-sounding. On

the only previous recording, the vintage EMI set of 1974, Raimund Herincx gave a finely detailed performance, but lacked that important quality. The 1974 set certainly stands the test of time remarkably well, but the extra fullness and richness of the Chandos sound coupled with as keen a concern for the atmospheric beauties of the score, notably in offstage effects, gives the new set an obvious advantage. Interpretatively, Hickox is just as incisive as Meredith Davies on EMI in bringing out the sharper side of the score, though he's more warmly expressive, a degree more affectionate in drawing out the glowing lyricism.

Chandos's casting is satisfyingly consistent, with no weak link. Matthew Best may be rather gruff at times as Ford, but that's very much in character, when, if anything, he's more venomous here than in Verdi, until at the start of Act 3 Vaughan Williams allows a wonderful duet of reconciliation with Mrs Ford, 'Pardon me, wife'.

As Ursula Vaughan Williams has reported, her husband wrote *Sir John in Love* 'entirely for his own enjoyment', because he was in love with the subject. And from first to last this new set reflects that.

Giuseppe Verdi   Italian 1813-1901

Born into a family of small landowners and taverners, at 12 Verdi was studying with the local church organist at the main church in nearby Busseto, whose assistant he became in 1829. In 1832 he was sent to Milan, but was refused a place at the conservatory and studied with Vincenzo Lavigna, composer and former La Scala musician. He returned to Busseto, where he was passed over as maestro di cappella but became town music master in 1836 and married Margherita Barezzi, his patron's daughter (their two children died in infancy).

Verdi had begun an opera, and tried to arrange a performance in Parma or Milan; he was unsuccessful but had some songs published and decided to settle in Milan in 1839, where his Oberto was accepted at La Scala and further operas commissioned. It was well received but his next, Un giorno di regno, failed totally; and his wife died during its composition. Verdi nearly gave up, but was fired by the libretto of Nabucco and in 1842 saw its successful production, which carried his reputation across Italy, Europe and the New World over the next five years. It was followed by another opera also with marked political overtones, I lombardi alla prima crociata, again well received. Verdi's gift for stirring melody and tragic and heroic situations struck a chord in an Italy struggling for freedom and unity, causes with which he was sympathetic; but much opera of this period has political themes and the involvement of Verdi's operas in politics is easily exaggerated.

The period Verdi later called his 'years in the galleys' now began, with a long and demanding series of operas to compose and (usually) direct, in the main Italian centres and abroad: they include Ernani, Macbeth, Luisa Miller and eight others in 1844-50, in Paris and London as well as Rome, Milan, Naples,

Venice, Florence and Trieste (with a pause in 1846 when his health gave way). Features of these works include strong, sombre stories, a vigorous, almost crude orchestral style that gradually grew fuller and richer, forceful vocal writing and above all a seriousness in his determination to convey the full force of the drama.

The 'galley years' have their climax in the three great, popular operas of 1851-3. Rigoletto, produced in Venice (after trouble with the censors, a recurring theme in Verdi), was a huge success, as its richly varied and unprecedentedly dramatic music amply justifies. No less successful, in Rome, was the more direct Il trovatore, at the beginning of 1853; but six weeks later La traviata, the most personal and intimate of Verdi's operas, was a failure in Venice – though with some revisions it was favourably received in 1854 at a different Venetian theatre. Later in 1853 he went – with Giuseppina Strepponi, the soprano with whom he had been living for several years, and whom he married in 1859 – to Paris, to prepare Les vêpres siciliennes for the Opéra, where it was given in 1855 with modest success. Verdi remained there for a time to defend his rights in face of the piracies of the Théâtre des Italiens and to deal with translations of some of his operas. The next new one was the sombre Simon Boccanegra, a drama about love and politics in medieval Genoa, given in Venice. Plans for Un ballo in maschera, about the assassination of a Swedish king, in Naples were called off because of the censors and it was given instead in Rome (1859).

Verdi was involved himself in political activity at this time, as representative of Busseto (where he lived) in the provincial parliament; later, pressed by Cavour, he was elected to the national parliament, and ultimately he was a senator. In 1862 La forza del destino had its premiere at St Petersburg. A revised Macbeth was given in Paris in 1865, but his most important work for the French capital was Don Carlos, a grand opera after Schiller in which personal dramas of love, comradeship and liberty are set against the persecutions of the Inquisition and the Spanish monarchy. It was given in 1867 and several times revised for Italian revivals.

Verdi returned to Italy, to live at Genoa. In 1870 he began work on Aida, given at Cairo Opera House at the end of 1871 to mark the opening of the Suez Canal: again in the grand opera tradition, and more taut in structure than Don Carlos. Verdi was ready to give up opera; his works of 1873 are a string quartet and the vivid, appealing Requiem in honour of the poet Manzoni, given in 1874-5, in Milan, Paris, London and Vienna. In 1879 composer-poet Boito and publisher Ricordi prevailed upon Verdi to write another opera, Otello; Verdi, working slowly and much occupied with revisions of earlier operas, completed it only in 1886. This, his most powerful tragic work, a study in evil and jealousy, had its premiere in Milan in 1887; it is notable for the increasing richness of allusive detail in the orchestral writing and the approach to a more continuous musical texture, though Verdi, with his faith in the expressive force of the human voice, did not abandon the 'set piece' (aria, duet etc) even if he integrated it more fully into its context – above all in his last opera. This was another Shakespeare work, Falstaff, on which he embarked two years later – his first comedy since the beginning of his career, with a score whose wit and lightness betray the hand of a serene master, was given in 1893.

His final work was a set of *Quattro pezzi sacri* (although he was a non-believer). He spent his last years in Milan, rich, authoritarian but charitable, much visited, revered and honoured. For his funeral 28,000 people lined the streets. **GROVE**music

Overtures and Preludes

Overtures and Preludes – Oberto; Un giorno di regno; Nabucco; Ernani; Giovanna d'Arco; Alzira; Attila; I masnadieri; Macbeth; Il corsaro; La battaglia di Legnano; Luisa Miller; Rigoletto; La traviata; I vespri siciliani; Un ballo in maschera; La forza del destino; Aida **Berlin Philharmonic Orchestra /Herbert von Karajan**
DG ② 453 058-2GTA2 (113' · ADD) Recorded 1975
Ⓜ ❶ ▶

Karajan was one of the most adaptable and sensitive of dramatic conductors. His repertoire in the theatre is extraordinarily wide, and he's at home equally in Verdi, Wagner, Richard Strauss and Puccini. In this celebrated 1975 collection of all Verdi's overtures, he gives us some fine insights into the composer's skill as an orchestrator, dramatist and poet. Though Karajan had only recorded *Aida* complete his dramatic instincts bring some fine performances of the lesser-known preludes. The earliest, *Nabucco* from 1842 (the collection is arranged chronologically), already shows a mastercraftsman at work, with a slow introduction promising much. *La traviata* shows a quite different skill – the delicate creation of a sensitive poet working in filigree. The final four preludes are great works fully worthy of this individual presentation. Even the lesser-known preludes are enhanced by Karajan's dramatic instincts. Good recordings, though less than outstanding.

Messa da Requiem

Verdi Messa da Requiem[b]. Overture 'I vespri siciliani'[c]
Schubert Mass No 6 in E flat, D950[a]
[a]**Anne Pashley**, [b]**Amy Shuard** sops [a]**Sybil Michelow**, [b]**Anna Reynolds** mezzos [a]**David Hughes**, [b]**Richard Lewis**, [a]**Duncan Robertson** tens [a]**William McCue**, [b]**David Ward** basses [a]**Scottish Festival Chorus**, [a]**New Philharmonia Orchestra**; Philharmonia [b]**Chorus and** [bc]**Orchestra / Carlo Maria Giulini**
BBC Legends/IMG Artists BBCL4029-2 (153' · ADD) Recorded live [bc]1963, [a]1968
Ⓜ ❶ ❷ ❸

Ⓖ In Great Britain in the 1960s, the art of large-scale choral singing reached what was arguably its apogee with the work of the two choruses featured here: the Philharmonia Chorus, directed by Wilhelm Pitz, and the Edinburgh Festival Chorus, directed by Arthur Oldham. Even allowing for the fact that this Prom performance of the Verdi *Requiem* was given around the time of an intensive period of rehearsal during which the EMI studio recording was also being made, the Philharmo-

nia Chorus's singing is stunningly good: first-rate diction, impeccable intonation, fine dynamic control and absolute involvement in the music as Giulini relays it to them.

In the Schubert Mass the Edinburgh Festival Chorus acquits itself magnificently. Giulini's reading is powerful and reverential, one in which the chorus comes to speak with the single voice of an individual believer.

The Verdi is superbly recorded. The unnamed BBC team working live in the Royal Albert Hall produce sound that's focused yet open, clear but warm. Giulini's reading of the *Requiem*, thrilling yet humane, is precisely the one we hear on EMI's recording, with the Philharmonia Chorus and Orchestra as expert live as they are on record (the orchestral playing is well-nigh flawless). Of the solo singers, the youngest, Anna Reynolds, could have gone straight into the EMI recording, so well does she sing. Richard Lewis, nearing the end of his career, is less gorgeous of voice than EMI's Nicolai Gedda, but the bass, David Ward, here at the height of his powers, is more than a match for the younger Nicolai Ghiaurov. Amy Shuard and EMI's Elisabeth Schwarzkopf are complementary. Shuard is technically fine; very much the real thing dramatically and absolutely right for the live performance. In short, this is an indispensable set.

Messa da Requiem
Violeta Urmana sop **Olga Borodina** mez **Ramón Vargas** ten **Ferruccio Furlanetto** bass **Teatro Regio Choir, Turin; North German Radio Chorus; West German Radio Symphony Chorus and Orchestra, Cologne / Semyon Bychkov**
Profil ② PH08036 (81' · DDD)
Ⓜ ❶ ❷ ❸

On this fine new Cologne recording, Semyon Bychkov deploys two specialist German radio choirs shrewdly intermixed with the chorus of Turin's Teatro Regio. If Bychkov's reading doesn't quite burn white in the *Dies irae* as Fricsay's did, or Toscanini's, it is nonetheless a supremely well directed Requiem, scrupulously observed, meticulously prepared, vivid, lucid, forward-moving. If there's a reservation, it is that the recorded balance occasionally has one straining to hear how good the choral work actually is.

Olga Borodina is an eloquent exponent of the mezzo-soprano role, well matched to her younger colleague, herself an erstwhile mezzo. What Urmana's voice lacks in evenness in *legato* passages is more than made up for by her command of the *spinto* manner, the drama of the text vividly purveyed. Ferruccio Furlanetto, now in his 59th year, has lost none of his mastery of the legato style. He brings an authentically Italianate feel to the music, as does bel canto specialist Ramón Vargas, here at his eloquent best.

Verdi's Requiem can seem a somewhat self-regarding piece, not least when 'great interpreters' get hold of it. This reading, for all its distinction, gives itself no airs.

Messa da Requiem
Angela Gheorghiu *sop* **Daniela Barcellona** *mez*
Roberto Alagna *ten* **Julian Konstantinov** *bass* **Eric**
Ericson Chamber Choir; Swedish Radio Chorus;
Berlin Philharmonic Orchestra / Claudio Abbado
EMI ② 557168-2 (84' · DDD) Recorded live 2001. Also
available on DVD (see page 1208)   Ⓕ☉➔

EMI was quite right to be on hand to record this
performance in Berlin at a time when Abbado had
arisen from his sick-bed to show just how much
this work meant to him in the circumstances. It's
conveyed in spades through the tremendous concentration and emotional thrust felt throughout
this shattering interpretation. This performance
has something extra that you find in Fricsay's live,
1960 account, and both come close to the spiritual
element in the music. Abbado has at his bidding a
superb group of specialist choirs who combine
effortlessly into a cohesive whole, singing with
commendable breadth, accuracy and involvement, few if any better on disc. They find fit
counterparts in the players of the BPO who seem
individually, in solos, and collectively intent on
giving of their appreciable best for their chief. So
all the big choral moments, *Dies Irae, Rex tremendae, Sanctus, Libera me* fugue are superbly achieved.
EMI's recording is wide-ranging and immediate,
the equal of any the work has yet received.

If the solo singing can't be given such an
unqualified encomium, much of it is impressive,
especially that of the young mezzo Daniela Barcellona, even in tone and beseeching in manner.
Gheorghiu does so much so well: she sings
throughout in that rich, warm tone of hers and
offers many long, arching phrases. She's also as
dramatic as one could wish in the *Libera me*, but
she doesn't really do the ethereal moments as
well as many of her predecessors. Alagna has his
uneven moments and can't compare with Pavarotti on Muti's version (reviewed below) for sheer
effulgence, but he sings with a deal of passion
and authority. The disappointment is the youthful Bulgarian bass Julian Konstantinov, whose
singing is lamed by several untidy moments and
by ill-tuned pitching.

In terms of fidelity to Verdi, Toscanini, Serafin, Giulini (in the BBC Legends version), Muti
(though the live EMI recording at La Scala isn't
so successful as this one in Berlin) and Gardiner,
in his individually authentic way, are indispensable, but the new Abbado, given its superlative
sound and special circumstances, is an important
addition to the work's discography.

Messa da Requiem
Cheryl Studer *sop* **Dolora Zajick** *mez* **Luciano**
Pavarotti *ten* **Samuel Ramey** *bass* **Chorus and**
Orchestra of La Scala, Milan / Riccardo Muti
EMI ② 749390-2 (88' · DDD · T/t) Recorded live 1989
                                                    Ⓕ☉➔

Muti's tempos, both in his 1979 EMI version
and here, are substantially faster (*Sanctus*) or
slower (opening *Kyrie*, 'Rex tremendae', 'Lacrymosa') than Verdi indicates and permits far

more *rallentandos* than are marked. Nobody
wants slavish adherence to what may be
accounted only as suggestions on the composer's part, but Muti does sometimes lose the
overall view of a movement by overplaying his
hand as an interpreter. That's the main criticism
of a performance that's certainly positive in
terms of its dramatic strength, deriving from
Muti's close rapport with his Scala forces.

Here he has a very different chorus from the
much smaller professional British group on his
earlier set (on EMI Double Forte). That has
advantages and disadvantages. The sound here
is grander, more specifically operatic in scale
as one would expect, with some arrestingly
histrionic effects such as the bold, black-
browed singing at 'Rex tremendae' and the
awed *senza misura* incantation at the start of
the 'Libera me'. But there isn't quite the
bright, incisive quality found on the former
recording.

The performance starts hesitantly, particularly
where the soloists are concerned. Cheryl Studer
initially seems a shade tentative and over-awed,
but as the evening develops she confirms what a
fine *lirico-spinto* soprano she is. The final phrase
of the 'Offertorio' is perfectly accomplished and
the whole of the 'Libera me' is delivered with
strong, firm tone and a deal of passion. Her
slightly resinous tone blends very well with
Zajick's in the 'Recordare' and the *Agnus Dei*,
one of the set's most successful movements. On
her own Zajick also improves from an anonymous start to reach heights of eloquence at the
start of the 'Lux aeterna'. The dark grain of her
chest register contrasts with a degree of brilliance at the top.

Many will probably buy the recording for
Pavarotti. He's in his best, most persuasive
form, more individual and subtle in utterance
than for Solti (Decca), even if the voice has lost a
little of its old opulence. He's also more considerate of his colleagues in the unaccompanied
passages, which here are as carefully blended as
on any recording, much helped by Ramey's solid
bottom line. Ramey trumps even Pavarotti at
'Hostias' in the 'Domine Jesu', his dolcissimo
singing here full of inward feeling. 'Oro supplex', taken up to Verdi's tempo rather than
being dragged as it can be by heavier basses, is
firmly and securely phrased. Others have sung
the bass part with more character, few – except
Pinza – with such security and musicality.

The recording is rather recessed with the character of the soloists' voices hard to discern.
However, where the chorus and orchestra are
concerned, the newer Muti certainly achieves a
theatrical perspective, catching the atmosphere
of La Scala, and the choral recording obviously
has a bigger range than on his old set.

Messa da Requiem[a] . **Quattro pezzi sacri**[b]
[a]**Luba Orgonášová,** [b]**Donna Brown** *sops* **Anne Sofie**
von Otter *mez* **Luca Canonici** *ten* **Alastair Miles** *bass*
Monteverdi Choir; Orchestre Révolutionnaire et
Romantique / Sir John Eliot Gardiner

Philips ② 442 142-2PH2 (120' · DDD · T/t)   ⓕ⦿➤

Gardiner's Verdi *Requiem* is in a class of its own. His are readings that combine a positive view and interpretative integrity from start to finish, something possible only in the context of the superb professionalism of the (augmented) Monteverdi Choir, which sings with a burnished and steady tone throughout and suggests, rightly, a corporate act of worship. Its contribution is beyond praise.

He might also have been surprised and delighted to ear the soloists' contribution sung with such precision by such a finely integrated quartet, who perform the important unaccompanied passages with special grace and sensitivity. Instead of the usual jostle of vibratos, here the four voices are firm and true. Individually they're also distinguished. Pride of place must go to Orgonášová who gives the performance of her life. The exactly placed high B in the 'Quid sum miser' section of the 'Dies irae', the perfect blending with von Otter at 'Dominum', the whole of the *Andante* section of the 'Libera me', sung with ethereal tone and a long breath, make the heart stop in amazement.

In 'Oro supplex' Gardiner follows Verdi's tempo marking. More often he follows tradition, with slower speeds than those suggested, and he allows more licence than the score, or conductors like Toscanini. But as his liberties all seem so convincing in the context of the whole, who should complain? In the *Pezzi sacri*, Gardiner gives the most thrilling account yet to appear.

The recording, made in Westminster Cathedral, has a huge range which may cause problems in confined spaces. You're liable to be overwhelmed, for instance, by the 'Dies irae'.

Messa da Requiem. Quattro pezzi sacri
Elena Filipova *sop* **Gloria Scalchi** *mez* **César Hernández** *ten* **Carlo Colombara** *bass* **Hungarian State Opera Choir and Orchestra / Pier Giorgio Morandi**
Naxos ② 8 550944/5 (126' · DDD · T/t)   ⓢ⦿➤

Morandi brings to his interpretation a youthful, Italian energy and generosity of expression. Given a judicious choice of young soloists, all up to their exigent tasks, an excellent chorus (a shattering 'Dies irae', an alert, not too drilled *Sanctus*, a disciplined 'Libera me' fugue) and a well-fashioned recording, this set makes a compelling case for recommendation as an alternative to Gardiner's period-performance set. Try track 7, the 'Rex tremendae', where you can hear how Morandi builds a movement unerringly to an appropriately tremendous climax.

The soloists show how involved they are in the work, form a good ensemble and individually exhibit the intelligence to sing quietly as needed. Filipova and Scalchi combine into a rich-toned duo in 'Liber scriptus', spoilt a little by moments of indeterminate pitch from the soprano. Hernández, with his warm, baritonal, Spanish-style tenor, sings a sensitive

'Ingemisco' (a touch of insecurity at the start excepted), succeeded by Colombara's truly magisterial conjuring of the flames of hell at 'Confutatis maledictis'. Filipova's floated entry at 'huic ergo' in the succeeding trio and the sheer intensity of the whole 'Lacrymosa' bring the 'Dies irae' to a fitting close.

The rest of the work's performance is on an equivalent level of achievement, Morandi always judging speeds to a nicety. The fill-up to this large-scale reading is a fine performance of the *Quattro pezzi sacri*.

Messa da Requiem
Angela Gheorghiu *sop* **Daniela Barcellona** *mez* **Roberto Alagna** *ten* **Julian Konstantinov** *bass* **Swedish Radio Chorus; Berlin Philharmonic Orchestra / Claudio Abbado**
Video director **Bob Coles**
EMI ⟐ DVB4 92693-9 (89' · 16:9, · 2.0, 5.1 & DTS 5.1 · 0)   ⓕ⦿

Seeing makes a deal of difference here. Though the CD issue of this performance at the Philharmonie, Berlin, in January 2001 was hugely enjoyable, this DVD enables one actually to see how the recently sick Abbado conducts the work as if it might be the last thing he does (happily not the case). He looks gaunt and tense: that translates into a heaven-seeking, searing account of the work, one to which everyone taking part readily responds. All the singers and players perform as though their lives depended on the outcome, and the results are simply electrifying.

Praise can't be too high for the two professional choirs or for the Berlin Philharmonic who, technically and emotionally, give their all. The soloists also seem on a devotional high, singing with appropriately spiritual fervour so that incidental criticisms seem of no importance. Bob Coles's video direction is always in the right place at the right time, and the sound perspective is as excellent as on the CD.

Messa da Requiem
Leontyne Price *sop* **Fiorenza Cossotto** *mez* **Luciano Pavarotti** *ten* **Nicolai Ghiaurov** *bass* **Chorus and Orchestra of La Scala, Milan / Herbert von Karajan**
Video director **Henri-Georges Clouzot**
DG ⟐ 073 4055GH (83' · NTSC · 4:3 · PCM stereo and DTS 5.1 · 0)   ⓕ⦿⦿

This film of the Verdi Requiem was made under studio conditions, in an empty La Scala before a concert in 1967 in memory of Toscanini's death a decade earlier. In his vision of this work, Henri-Georges Clouzot sees ranks of choristers – from heaven or hell – with Price and Cossotto framed by the sopranos' hands and grey silk wraps beneath like angels' wings, double basses angled heavenwards, Karajan's quiff with a life of its own, his profile at home among all those Roman (and Milanese) noses.

Price is simply magnificent but Karajan colludes with Cossotto (in a lovely black empire-line number) in letting her steal the show, as the two of them warm every line with intimate little touches: the 'Recordare' and 'Lux aeterna' are rapt highlights. Pavarotti, clutching a score like a votive offering, looks out of his depth in such company but he shades the opening phrase of 'Hostias' with all the subtlety at his disposal. Ragged choral work and occasional dead spots notwithstanding – the 'Quam olim' and 'Sanctus' seem handled rather than shaped – Clouzot's and Karajan's achievement has the authentic sniff of pathos. Even Toscanini might have given grudging approval.

Additional recommendations

Milanov *sop* **Thorborg** *mez* **Rosvaenge** *ten*   ⒽMoscona *bass* **BBC Symphony Chorus and Orchestra / Arturo Toscanini**
Testament mono ② SBT21362 (89' · ADD · N/T/t). Recorded live at the Queen's Hall, London, 27 May 1938   Ⓜ

Skilfully remastered from BBC originals, this is a superior performance to Toscanini's familiar RCA version of 1951 simply because he gives the music more time to breathe. He imposes a unified and beseeching style on all his charges, impressing on them his own awe before Verdi's score.

Opera Choruses

Un ballo in maschera – Posa in pace. **Don Carlos** – Spuntato ecco il dì. **Aida** – Gloria all' Egitto. **I Lombardi** – Gerusalem!; O Signore, dal tetto natio. **Macbeth** – Tre volte miagola; Patria oppressa. **I masnadieri** – Le rube, gli stupri. **Nabucco** – Gli arredi festivi giù cadano infranti; Va, pensiero, sull'ali dorate. **Otello** – Fuoco di gioia. **Rigoletto** – Zitti zitti. **La traviata**[a] – Noi siamo zingarelle … Di Madride nio siam mattadori. **Il trovatore** – Vedi! Le fosche notturne spoglie; Squilli, echeggi la tromba guerriera. **Requiem** – Sanctus
[a]**Marsha Waxman** *mez* [a]**David Huneryager**, [a]**Richard Cohn** *basses* **Chicago Symphony Chorus and Orchestra / Sir Georg Solti**
Decca 430 226-2DH (70' · DDD · T)   ⒻⓄ▶

Verdi's opera choruses are invariably red-blooded and usually make a simple dramatic statement with great impact. The arresting 'Chorus of the Hebrew Slaves' from *Nabucco* is probably the best-known and most popular chorus in the entire operatic repertoire, immediately tugging at the heart-strings with its gentle opening cantilena, soon swelling out to a great climax. Solti shows just how to shape the noble melodic line, which soars with firm control, yet retaining the urgency and electricity in every bar. The dramatic contrasts at the opening of 'Gerusalem!' from *I Lombardi* are equally powerfully projected, and the brass again makes a riveting effect in 'Patria oppressa' from *Macbeth*. Bu not all Verdi choruses offer blood and thunder: the volatile

---

VERDI MESSA DA REQUIEM – IN BRIEF

Philharmonia Orchestra / Carlo Maria Giulini
BBC Legends ② BBCL4029-2 (153' · ADD)
   ⓂⓄⓄⓄ

Ⓖ Of the several performances by Giulini currently in circulation, this one arguably has the most atmosphere and the best sound. It's a live relay of a concert he gave at the Royal Albert Hall with British soloists in the run up to his starrier studio recording. ▶

Berlin PO / Claudio Abbado
EMI ② 557168-2 (84' · DDD)   ⒻⓄ▶
A live recording, also available on DVD, to mark the occasion of the 100th anniversary of the composer's death. The conductor's searing intensity reflects his own recent brush with mortality. The soloists, Angela Gheorghiu in particular, are excellent too.

La Scala Chorus and Orchestra / Riccardo Muti
EMI ② 749390-2 (88' · DDD)   ⒻⓄ▶
Muti's second recording is an authentically Italian affair on a big operatic scale, with sometimes histrionic extremes of tempo and Pavarotti in the line-up of soloists. The recorded sound conveys the spaciousness of the venue at some expense of detail.

Orchestre Révolutionnaire et Romantique / Sir John Eliot Gardiner
Philips ② 442 142-2PH2 (120' · DDD)   ⒻⓄ▶
Gardiner's historically aware set has many assets: uncommonly accurate choral singing, a cleaned-up text, the widest dynamic range and traditionally broad tempos. The makeweight is an unbeatable *Four Sacred Pieces*.

Hungarian State Opera / Pier Giorgio Morandi
Naxos ② 8 550944/5 (126' · DDD)   ⓈⓄ▶
A super-budget account with youthful sounding soloists and effective, if not ideally focused choral forces.

Kirov Orchestra / Valery Gergiev
Philips ② 468 079-2 (DDD)   ⒻⓄ▶
Gergiev conducts one of the latest, most theatrical (and certainly the most hyped) account of the *Messa da Requiem* in the current catalogue; his Kirov forces are joined by the 'dream team' line-up of Renée Fleming, Olga Borodina, Andrea Bocelli and Ildebrando d'Arcangelo

NBC SO / Arturo Toscanini
RCA mono ⑪ 8287 667893-2 (141' · ADD)   ⓂⓄ
Toscanini's searingly intense RCA version of 1951 is considered a classic of the gramophone; his singers are Herva Nelli, Fedora Barbieri, Giuseppe di Stefano and Cesare Siepi. Currently only available in an 11-CD set of all of Toscanini's Verdi recordings.

'Fire chorus' from *Otello* flickers with an almost visual fantasy, while the wicked robbers in *I masnadieri* celebrate their excesses gleefully, and with such rhythmic jauntiness that you can't quite take them seriously. The 'Gypsies' chorus' from *La traviata* has a nice touch of elegance, and the scherzo-like 'Sanctus', from the *Requiem* is full of joy. But it's the impact of the dramatic moments that's most memorable, not least the big triumphal scene from *Aida*, complete with the ballet music, to provide a diverse interlude in the middle. The recording is in the demonstration class.

Opera Duets

Aida[a] – La fatal pietra; Morir si pura e bella; O terra addio[b]. **Don Carlo** – E dessa!...Un detto, un sol; Vago sogno m'arrise; Ma lassù ci vedremo. **I Lombardi**[a] – Oh belle, a questa misera; All' armi! **I masnadieri** – Qual mare, qual terra; Qui nel bosco?; Lassù risplendere. **Otello** – Già nella notte densa; Venga la morte!. **Rigoletto** – Ah! veglia, o donna; Signor ne principe; T'amo! T'amo; E il sol dell' anima; Addio, addio[c]. **Simon Boccanegra** – Cielo di stelle orbato; Vieni a mirar la cerula. **La traviata**[a] – Libiamo, ne' lieti calici. **Il trovatore**[a] – Miserere ...Ah, che la morte ognora. **I vespri siciliani** – Pensando a me!
Angela Gheorghiu *sop* **Roberto Alagna** *ten* [bc]**Sara Mingardo** *mez* [c]**Brian Parsons**, [c]**Rodney Gibson** *tens*; **London Voices; Berlin Philharmonic Orchestra / Claudio Abbado**
EMI 556656-2 (70' · DDD)　　　Ⓕ🅾🅾➔

This long, fascinating, highly ambitious recital is nothing less than a conspectus of Verdi's soprano-tenor duets, and is executed with distinction on all sides. Gheorghiu deserves particular plaudits. It seems that nothing in Verdi (and indeed in much else) is beyond her capabilities. Her singing here, especially as Gilda, Aida and Desdemona, is so exquisite, the tone so warm and limpid, the phrasing so shapely as surely to melt any heart. Take, for example, Gilda's touching exchanges with Giovanna, herself sung by the superb mezzo Sara Mingardo, the whole of Aida's solo beginning 'Presago il core', with the soprano's warm lower register coming into play and that ultimate test, Desdemona's poised 'Amen'. Throughout, both musically and interpretatively, she simply can't be faulted.

Neither she nor her husband is backward in coming forward with less hackneyed pieces, those from the early operas – try the section starting 'Ma un' iri di pace' in the *Masnadieri* duet, the two voices in ideal blend, phrases and tone sweetly shaded with the following cabaletta all light eagerness on both sides. Then there's plangent singing on both sides in the sad little piece from *Vespri*, though it's a pity they did not attempt this in the original French. Here and throughout Alagna is his customary self, assured (a few over-pressed high notes, some unwritten, apart), impassioned, thoughtful and accurate in his phraseology, nowhere more so than in the

parts he's unlikely as yet to take on stage – Radames and Otello. Even more important in so many passages, Alagna finds the right *mezzo-piano*, where heavier tenors have to sing forte , notably in the closing phrases where Otello wafts his love of Desdemona on to the night air – a moment of sheer magic.

Abbado and the Berlin Philharmonic Orchestra are at their peak of achievement and the recording catches these voices in their full glory, making this a most desirable issue.

Opera Arias

Un ballo in maschera – Ecco l'orrido campo ... Ma dall'arido stelo divulsa ... Morrò, ma prima in grazia. **La forza del destino** – Pace, pace, mio Dio. **Nabucco** – Ben io t'invenni ... Anch'io dischiuso un giorno. **La traviata** – E strano!... Ah, fors'è lui ... Follie! Sempre libera[a]; Teneste la promessa ... Addio del passato. **Il trovatore** – Tacea la notte placida ... Di tale amor; Timor di me? ... D'amor sull'ali rosee
Julia Varady *sop* [a]**Lothar Odinius** *ten* **Bavarian State Orchestra / Dietrich Fischer-Dieskau**
Orfeo C186951 (51' · DDD)　　　Ⓕ🅾

Varady endows these arias we have heard hundreds of times, and of which we all have our favourite memories and recordings, with renewed life through an art which is fully responsive, highly fastidious, lovely in the quality of its sound and individual in its timbre and inflection. The beauty of tone is evident first of all in its well-preserved purity (and Varady, born in 1941, is of an age when normally allowances have to be made). Hers isn't a full-bodied, rich Ponselle-like voice, but she makes wonderfully effective use of her resources, which include a surprisingly strong lower register and an upward range that (as we hear) easily encompasses the high D flat and has an E flat available. She's dramatic in style yet also thoroughly accomplished in her scales, trills and other fioriture. Her first *Trovatore* aria, for instance, includes the cabaletta with its full complement of technical brilliances. The musical instinct seems almost infallible – a 'wrong' portamento or rubato always irritates and here everything seems just right. A remarkable sensitivity is at work throughout.

The orchestra is conducted by Fischer-Dieskau, Varady's husband, and here too is a fine example of a positive, non-routine collaboration, the pacing and shading of the orchestral parts so frequently having something specific to offer (for example, in the letter passage from *La traviata*). The recording is well balanced.

Aida

Aida　　　　　　　　　　　　　　　　　Ⓗ
Maria Callas *sop* Aida **Fedora Barbieri** *mez* Amneris **Richard Tucker** *ten* Radames **Tito Gobbi** *bar* Amonasro **Giuseppe Modesti** *bass* Ramphis **Nicola Zaccaria** *bass* King of Egypt **Elvira Galassi** *sop*

Priestess **Franco Ricciardi** *ten* Messenger **Chorus and Orchestra of La Scala, Milan / Tullio Serafin**
EMI mono ② 562678-2 or Regis RRC2074 (144' · ADD · T/t) Recorded 1955 Ⓕ/Ⓢ❍❍▶

Callas's Aida is an assumption of total understanding and conviction; the growth from a slave-girl torn between love for her homeland and Radames, to a woman whose feelings transcend life itself represents one of the greatest operatic undertakings ever committed to disc. Alongside her is Fedora Barbieri, an Amneris palpable in her agonised mixture of love and jealousy – proud yet human. Tucker's Radames is powerful and Gobbi's Amonasro quite superb – a portrayal of comparable understanding to set alongside Callas's Aida.

Tullio Serafin's reading is in the central Italian tradition of 50 years ago. That's to say, it's unobtrusively right in matters of tempo, emphasis and phrasing, while occasionally passing indifferent ensemble in the choral and orchestral contribution. Although the recording can't compete with modern versions (it was never, in fact, a model of clarity), nowhere can it dim the brilliance of the creations conjured up by this classic cast.

Aida
Birgit Nilsson *sop* Aida **Grace Bumbry** *mez* Amneris **Franco Corelli** *ten* Radames **Mario Sereni** *bar* Amonasro **Bonaldo Giaiotti** *bass* Ramfis **Ferruccio Mazzoli** *bass* King **Piero de Palma** *ten* Messenger **Mirella Fiorentini** *mez* Priestess **Chorus and Orchestra of Rome Opera / Zubin Mehta**
EMI ② 358645-2 Recorded 1966　　Ⓜ▶

In the 1950s and 1960s EMI made a series of what have become classics with Rome Opera forces that have Verdi in their blood. This *Aida*, greeted with reservations then, now seems like manna from heaven in a world starved of true Verdian voices. Above all there's Corelli's truly *spinto* tenor, a thrilling sound in itself, and used, as Radames (one of the most exciting on disc), with far more sensitivity than is usually allowed for. Nilsson matches Corelli in vocal bite and gets inside the character, even if she's a touch unwieldy at times. As on stage, Bumbry is an imposing, spirited Amneris, Sereni makes an above-average Amonasro and Giaiotti sounds like Pinza as Ramfis – praise can't be higher. The young Zubin Mehta conducts with a deal of dramatic verve. The recording is excellent.

Aida
Anna Tomowa-Sintow *sop* Aida **Brigitte Fassbaender** *mez* Amneris **Plácido Domingo** *ten* Radames **Siegmund Nimsgern** *bar* Amonasro **Robert Lloyd** *bass* Ramfis **Nikolaus Hillebrand** *bass* King **Norbert Orth** *ten* Messenger **Marianne Seibel** *sop* Priestess; **Bavarian State Opera Chorus and Orchestra / Riccardo Muti**
Orfeo d'Or ② C583 022I (143' · ADD · N) Recorded live 1979　　Ⓕ❍

Riccardo Muti's 1974 studio recording on EMI, with Caballé, Cossotto and Domingo, has been one of the steady recommendations for this work on CD. This live account from 1979 in many, but not all ways, surpasses the studio performance. In the first place, Muti's reading has matured to the extent of being less wilful – for instance, his tempo for the closing scene's 'O terra addio' is the better for being more orthodox – and even more persuasive in terms of fulfilling Verdi's exacting demands on all concerned. Seldom can the full panoply and subtlety of the composer's scoring, especially the wonderful wind writing, have been so clearly expounded. The chorus is also commendable in every respect.

Domingo, fine enough on EMI, here gives possibly his most responsive and exciting Radames on disc and that's saying something. In tremendous voice, he produces magic towards the end of 'Celeste Aida' with the triple *pianissimo* Verdi asks for but seldom gets, and throughout he make every effort to fulfil Verdi's demand for *dolce* and *pp* effects. It hardly needs saying that he was at the time at the peak of his amazing powers.

Tomowa-Sintow provides most of the heft combined with sensibility that the title part calls for. Although she can't manage Caballé's many exquisite moments when she floats her tone on high, she has the firmer, stronger voice to ride the orchestra at climactic moments. You don't quite feel the strong identification with the part that Fassbaender undoubtedly gives to her first Amneris. Fassbaender is very much her idiosyncratic, wholly compelling self, rising to heights of music-drama in Amneris's great Act 4 scene, the repeated 'io stessa… lo getta' rending the heart. This is an interpretation to savour.

The recording, although the voices are sometimes a little distanced, catches the high excitement of a first night in the opera house. Applause is never intrusive, scenery change only once so. This is as gripping an account of the piece of any on disc.

Aida
Adina Aaron *sop* Aida **Kate Aldrich** *mez* Amneris **Scott Piper** *ten* Radames **Giuseppe Garra** *bar* Amonasro **Enrico Giuseppe Iori** *bass* Ramfis **Paolo Pecchioli** *bass* King **Stefano Pisani** *ten* Messenger **Micaela Patriarca** *sop* Priestess **Arturo Toscanini Foundation Chorus and Orchestra / Massimiliano Stefanelli**
Stage and video director **Franco Zeffirelli**
TDK ② **DVD** DV-AIDDB (188' · 4:3 · 2.0 & 5.1 · 0) Includes documentary, 'The Making of Aida'　　Ⓕ❍

Who would have imagined that this performance, which took place at Verdi's birthplace, Busseto, in January 2001 to mark the centenary of the composer's death, would carry such an emotional charge and evince such dramatic truthfulness? The performers are young singers gathered together under the auspices of the Toscanini Foundation and under the artistic

VERDI AIDA – IN BRIEF

Anna Tomowa-Sintow *Aida* **Brigitte Fassbaender** *Amneris* **Siegmund Nimsgern** *Amonasro* **Bavarian State Opera Chorus and Orchestra / Riccardo Muti**
Orfeo ② C583022I (143' · ADD)　　Ⓜ◗

Under Riccardo Muti's vivid direction an already special cast gains greatly from the excitement of a live recording, worth the very few flaws in voice and recording.

Maria Callas *Aida* **Fedora Barbieri** *Amneris* **Tito Gobbi** *Amonasro* **Chorus and Orchestra of La Scala, Milan / Tulio Serafin**
EMI ② 556316-2 (144' · AAD)　　Ⓗ Ⓕ◗◗◗▷

Maria Callas's blazing yet vulnerable Aida heads a cast of great names, conducted with real grandeur by Serafin. Only the mono recording is any drawback.

Birgit Nilsson *Aida* **Grace Bumbry** *Amneris* **Mario Sereni** *Amonasro* **Rome Opera Chorus and Orchestra / Zubin Mehta**
EMI ② 358645-2 (141' · ADD)　　Ⓑ◗▷

Nilsson and Corelli are a vocally towering pair of lovers, along with Bumbry's rich Amneris the main attractions of a cast that otherwise ranges from excellent to acceptable.

Leontyne Price *Aida* **Rita Gorr** *Amneris* **Robert Merrill** *Amonasro* **Rome Opera Chorus and Orchestra / Sir Georg Solti**
Decca ② 460 765-2DF2 (152' · ADD)　　Ⓜ▷

Two superlative voices, Leontyne Price a sensuous, dark-toned Aida, and Vickers a steely yet tormented Radames, with strong support from Rita Gorr's Amneris and Robert Merrill's bluff Amonasro. Solti's conducting is electrifyingly dramatic.

Adina Aaron *Aida* **Kate Aldrich** *Amneris* **Giuseppe Garra** *Amonasro* **Arturo Toscanini Foundation Chorus and Orchestra / Massimiliano Stefaneli**
TDK ⊕ DV-AIDDB (188')　　Ⓕ

Aida works unexpectedly well in the smaller scale, in a good-looking 'traditional' staging by Franco Zeffirelli with a non-starry but immensely vital young cast, in the theatre at Verdi's birthplace Busetto.

Aprile Millo *Aida* **Dolora Zajick** *Amneris* **Sherrill Milnes** *Amonasro* **Metropolitan Opera Chorus and Orchestra / James Levine**
DG ⊕ 073 001-9 (158')　　Ⓕ

The Met's staging is on a suitably Pharaonic scale, although the spectacularly authentic sets aren't matched by the rather silly costumes. Domingo, though below his best, is a splendid Radames, and, while local girl Millo isn't as expressive as some, she's still involving. Levine conducts with epic grandeur but too little *brio*.

direction of tenor Carlo Bergonzi, and of Franco Zeffirelli who directs the performance. It took place in the small gem of a 19th-century theatre at Busseto, not the most likely venue for such a grand opera, yet the very confinement of the surroundings forces everyone to re-think the work on a more intimate scale and in doing so they manage to go to the heart of the matter.

Adina Aaron is already a complete Aida. Every gesture, every movement, every note seems to come from the very soul of her being and her naturally shaped singing and sheer beauty of tone bespeak an auspicious future. As moving an Aida in fact since the young Leontyne Price.

Kate Aldrich as Amneris is very nearly as impressive. Possessor of a strikingly beautiful mezzo and the wherewithal to project it, she conveys every facet of the tormented Princess's predicament with total conviction. As Amonasro, Giuseppe Garra discloses a strong, vibrant baritone in the best traditions of his kind and he, like everyone else, acts with complete conviction. If the Radames, Scott Piper, another singer keen to obey Verdi's markings – witness a *pp* high B flat at the end of 'Celeste Aida' – was slightly less impressive, it's only because his voice is at present one size too small for the role. The orchestra plays with every fibre of its collective being for its committed conductor. Zeffirelli directs stage and film alike with all the experience at his command. The sound is a shade boxy, surely due to the small size of the venue. But that shouldn't be enough to stop anyone enjoying this riveting occasion.

Aida
Nina Stemme *sop* Aida **Salvatore Licitra** *ten* Radames **Luciana d'Intino** *mez* Amneris **Juan Pons** *bar* Amonasro **Matti Salminen** *bass* Ramfis **Günther Groissböck** *bass* King **Christiane Kohl** *sop* Priestess **Miroslav Christoff** *ten* Messenger **Zurich Opera House Chorus and Orchestra / Adám Fischer**
Stage director **Nicolas Joël**
Video director **Andy Sommer**
Bel Air Classiques ② ⊞ DVD BAC022
(3h 37' · NTSC · 16:9 · PCM stereo, 5.1 and DTS 5.1 · 0). Extra features include 'The Story of Aida' – a film by Louis Wallecan and an interview with Andy Sommer　　Ⓕ◗◗

This 2006 production from the Zurich Opera is a traditional one by Nicolas Joël in veteran Ezio Frigerio's wonderfully evocative, highly coloured sets. Then Adám Fischer in the pit leads a remarkably strong yet subtle account of the score, which – when played and sung like this – is once more revealed as one of Verdi's greatest masterpieces.

Four of the principals easily surpass their DVD rivals. Stemme offers a deeply considered, expressive and superbly sung Aida, one for whom the work's vocal perils do not seem to exist. Add to that acting that goes to the heart of the matter, and one is left breathless in admiration after so many sopranos not truly fitted to the part. Licitra has done nothing better than his

Radames here. At last fulfilling his potential, he sings the role with an open-hearted sincerity and a heroic voice up to the part's exigent demands. He and Stemme make their Act 3 duet the highlight it should be.

D'Intino, an experienced Amneris, sings her role with intense feeling allied to a mezzo of generous proportions. The demands of her Act 4 scena are fully met, and she storms off to a well earned burst of applause. Stemme and Licitra give the final scene with the utmost sensibility. Salminen remains a force to be reckoned with, but Pons – as Amonasro – no longer is the baritone he once was, although dramatically he is up to the part.

The showpiece close to Act 2 is the one comparative disappointment, not offering the frisson it ought to. And here Andy Sommer's video direction is uncertain, too often dividing the screen into three for no discernible purpose, but he directs the principals with a deal of senstivity. So this is the DVD *Aida* we have long awaited.

Additional recommendation

Aida
Caballé Aida **Domingo** Radames **Cossotto** Amneris
Chorus of the Royal Opera House, Covent Garden; New Philharmonia Orchestra;Trumpeters of the Royal Military School of Music, Kneller Hall / Muti
EMI Great Recordings of the Century ② 567613-2 (148' · ADD)   Ⓜ️🅳

Montserrat Caballé gives her most successful Verdi performance on record, full of those vocal subtleties and beauties that inform her best singing, while Muti gives an impassioned account of the score.

Attila

Attila
Samuel Ramey bass Attila **Cheryl Studer** sop Odabella **Giorgio Zancanaro** bar Ezio **Kaludi Kaludov** ten Foresto **Ernesto Gavazzi** ten Uldino **Mario Luperi** bass Leone **Chorus and Orchestra of La Scala, Milan / Riccardo Muti**
Stage director **Jerome Savary**
Video director **Christopher Swann**
Opus Arte 📀 OALS3010D (118' · NTSC · 4:3 · 2.0 · 0). Recorded live in 1991   Ⓕ

Spectacular and pacy, *Attila* fills the stage with barbarians, gives them good tunes to sing and places them in a busy world where every moment may bring a reversal of fortune. Moreover, the four leading characters are fired with passionate determination which in turn fires their magnificent voices. There is sure to be something to write home about after a good *Attila*. And this is a La Scala performance fully worthy of the great house and its best traditions. It is very much the kind of opera that thrives in Muti's care.

A hard, percussive energy plays off against long elegiac phrases, and the resulting tension, very Italian with its sense of personal suffering in the midst of great public events, permeates the whole

performance. The singers match up to the challenge wonderfully well. Samuel Ramey's iron-fisted voice is the perfect vocal image of the man, a voice with no flab, trained as by an athlete. The limitations are of tonal variety, in the dream sequence; but this is still a triumphant *Attila*. The soprano role of Odabella is as formidable as any in the Verdi canon, and Cheryl Studer masters it with astonishing assurance, and without the usual register-breaks and smudged scales. The tenor Kaludi Kaludov brings a clean, incisive tone and a well-schooled *legato*, and among all these foreigners Giorgio Zancanaro represents his country in its leading national opera house with a welcome infusion of Italian resonance and a reminder (intrusive aspirates apart) of the true vocal method of which Italy was for so long the fount. Moreover, these individual talents come together as a well-disciplined ensemble, and the concerted numbers have the authentic thrill of Italian opera in best working order.

Un ballo in maschera

Un ballo in maschera   🅷
Maria Callas sop Amelia **Giuseppe di Stefano** ten Riccardo **Ettore Bastianini** bar Renato **Eugenia Ratti** sop Oscar **Giulietta Simionato** contr Ulrica **Antonio Cassinelli** bass Sam **Marco Stefanoni** bass Tom **Giuseppe Morresi** bar Silvano **Angelo Mercuriali** ten Judge **La Scala, Milan Chorus and Orchestra / Gianandrea Gavazzeni**
EMI mono ② 567918-2 or Regis RRC2079 (131' · ADD · T/t) Recorded live 1957   Ⓜ️/Ⓢ🅞🅞🅳

This set comes from live performances at La Scala in the mid-1950s when the diva was at the height of her powers. Callas gives here an even more vital performance than on her studio recorded set. It was Callas's particular genius to find exactly the appropriate mode of expression for every role she tackled. Here we have Callas the tormented, guilty wife. But she also gives us a hundred different individual inflections to reflect the emotion of the moment: indeed, as John Steane points out in one of his illuminating notes, it's often a small aside that reveals as much about the character she's portraying s a big set-piece.

The context of an evening in the theatre makes this a more arresting, vivid interpretation on all sides than its studio counterpart of a year earlier, with Gianandrea Gavazzeni galvanising his fine cast to great things. As the late John Ardoin put it in his study of Callas's recordings: 'The La Scala performance is sung with more vivid colours, with accents more etched and a general intensification of Verdi's drama.' Here the sound picture is appreciably superior to that on earlier live sets which capture Callas in other roles at La Scala. The irresistible Di Stefano is the soul of vital declamation as Riccardo. Ettore Bastianini's forthright Renato, the only role he sang in London and one of his best in an all too short career, and Giulietta Simionato's classic Ulrica are also huge assets. Other roles are filled with house singers of the day. An unbeatable set.

Un ballo in maschera
Plácido Domingo *ten* Riccardo **Piero Cappuccilli** *bar*
Renato **Martina Arroyo** *sop* Amelia **Fiorenza
Cossotto** *mez* Ulrica **Reri Grist** *sop* Oscar **Giorgio
Giorgetti** *bass* Silvano **Gwynne Howell** *bass* Samuel
Richard Van Allan *bass* Tom **Kenneth Collins** *ten*
Judge **David Barrett** *bar* Servant **Haberdashers'
Aske's School Girls' Choir; New Philharmonia
Orchestra; Chorus of the Royal Opera House,
Covent Garden / Riccardo Muti**
EMI 566510-2 (127' · ADD · T/t) Recorded 1975 Ⓜ❂➔

This is the *Ballo* which, above all else, glories in
Muti as an exuberant man of the theatre. The
impetus with which he whips up the constituent
parts of an ensemble into the vortex, and the juxtaposition of blasting *tutti* with slim, sweetly phrased
woodwind detail, so typical of this opera, hits the
ear more thrillingly than ever. So does the equally
characteristic tugging undercurrent of the *ballo*
against the intrigue of the *maschera*, activated by
Muti with such acute perception and *élan*.

He provides pliant, springing support for all
his singers too: Domingo, a warm, generous
Riccardo, is every bit as happy with Muti as with
Abbado. The same can't be said of Martina
Arroyo, the weak link on this recording. Dramatically forceful, but curiously cool and
detached from the expressive nuancing of her
part, she has little of the vulnerability of a Ricciarelli (Abbado), or the individuality of a Price
(Solti). But, although this mid-price recording
may not offer the most consistently luxurious
vocal banquet, none the less, with Cossotto's
stentorian Ulrica and Cappuccilli's staunch,
resilient Renato, its strong sense of theatrical
presence and its dramatic integrity will make it
the chosen version for many new collectors.

Un ballo in maschera   Ⓗ
Jon Vickers *ten* Gustavo III **Amy Shuard** *sop* Amelia
Ettore Bastianini *bar* Renato **Regina Resnik** *contr*
Ulrica **Joan Carlyle** *sop* Oscar **Victor Godfrey** *bass*
Cristiano **Michael Langdon** *bass* Horn **David Kelly**
bass Ribbing **Chorus and Orchestra of the Royal
Opera House, Covent Garden / Edward Downes**
Royal Opera House mono ② ROHS009 (122' · ADD).
Recorded live on February 23, 1962   Ⓜ❂

House-habitués know this as the Bastianini
Ballo. It marked the baritone's debut at the Royal
Opera House, to which he never returned. His
photograph is accordingly on the booklet-cover,
and the note-writer, David Patmore, leads on
his notable part in the performance. Notable,
but not outstanding. The recording catches
Bastianini's voice well, a voice of finest quality in
the upper middle notes, a little thick and throaty
lower down, throwing out an exciting high G
('brillava' in 'Eri tu') but giving the impression
that he was not entirely comfortable elsewhere.
And whether it was that he hadn't entirely got
the measure of the house (this has happened to
many eminent newcomers), by the side of the
other principals (except perhaps in the arias) it
was not really a projecting voice.

The great performance is Vickers's. He was
then in best vocal form, and already his intensity
in such music by far exceeded that of any other
tenor of our time. There are moments ('O qual
soave') in the love duet, for instance, where one
might wish for a plainer, less inflected singing
style, but at full power he is thrilling and his
mezza voce could sail freely up to the balcony,
where it was almost as though he was singing
softly in one's ear. His solo scene in Act 3 is
deeply moving: one of the most memorable by
any tenor in any opera.

Amy Shuard also emerges well: a little rigid
and severe in expression at first, but steadily
gaining in freedom and humanity. The power of
Regina Resnik's Ulrica, another artist at the top
of her vocal form at this time, is memorable.
Edward Downes's firm but sensitive conducting
is also very fine. The source of the recording is
not a broadcast but tapes made in-house for
Lord Harewood. It is not flawless but comes out
remarkably well. In any case, there is a saying
with regard to gift-horses.

Un ballo in maschera
Josephine Barstow *sop* Amelia **Plácido Domingo**
ten Gustav **Leo Nucci** *bar* Renato **Sumi Jo** *sop* Oscar
Florence Quivar *contr* Ulrica **Jean-Luc Chaignaud**
bass Christiano **Kurt Rydl** *bass* Horn **Goran Simic**
bar Ribbing **Wolfgang Witte** *ten* Judge **Adolf
Tomaschek** *ten* Servant **Vienna Philharmonic
Orchestra / Sir Georg Solti**
Stage director **John Schlesinger**
Video director **Brian Large**
TDK 📀 DV-CLOPUBIM. (145' · 4:3 · PCM stereo · 0).
Recorded live at the Grosses Festspielhaus, Salzburg,
on July 28, 1990   Ⓕ

1990 was the last year of the ancien régime at the
Salzburg Festival before the revolution brought
about by Gérard Mortier. In many ways it represented the *ne plus ultra* of the Karajan-influenced
era; indeed, this production, first seen in 1989,
should have been conducted by the old maestro
had he not died some months before it was due
to be staged – not, however, before he had had
time to record it for DG.

John Schlesinger's bold, sumptuous production in William Dudley's evocative Swedish
settings underline the mood of each scene.
Gustav's study is a true trompe-l'œil, with a
model theatre (the monarch's pet project) in the
foreground. Ulrica's cave, surrounded by rot-
ten-looking tenements and the eerie gallows for
the start of Act 2, are nicely counterpointed by a
realistic Swedish house for the home of Renato
– though we could have done without the
slightly embarrassing presence of his little boy.
The finale is admittedly well over the top but
succeeds in creating the fever pitch of the
masked ball. Within this breathtaking scenery,
Schlesinger occasionally over-eggs the pudding
with too many extras and intrusive dancers, yet
he cleverly maintains the principals in the foreground so that they are never overawed by the
magnificence of the decor.

Solti, not always one's favoured conductor where Verdi is concerned, gives a carefully crafted and surely paced account of this inspired score, and he is eminently supportive of his distinguished cast. Domingo, in peak form, gives a commanding portrayal of the doomed monarch, by turns lightly insouciant in the early scenes, suitably impassioned with Amelia, tragic as the ruler dies; everything is executed with technical assurance and fine control of dynamics. On this night, after a squally scene in the soothsayer's den, Barstow finds her best Verdian form, pouring her heart and soul into Amelia's predicament in tone and phrasing always apt to the character's circumstance. The Act 3 prayer, 'Morrò, ma prima in grazia', is particularly fine. Her interpretation is a worthy souvenir of her under-recorded art. Nucci is also at his best. He delivers his whole role in exemplary voice, firm, steady in tone to support his supple phrasing: 'Eri tu' is the heart-rending experience it should be.

Florence Quivar also surpasses herself with her sturdy, steady Ulrica and, as the icing on the cake, Sumi Jo is a buoyant, charming, bright-voiced Oscar. With excellent conspirators, the cast is very near ideal.

It is a pity the picture isn't widescreen and that the sound recording is not always ideally balanced, but these minor drawbacks cannot prevent a strong recommendation.

Additional recommendation

Un ballo in maschera
Ricciarelli Amelia **Domingo** Riccardo **Bruson** Renato
Chorus and Orchestra of La Scala, Milan / Abbado
DG ② 453 148-2GTA2 (127' · ADD) Notes included Ⓜ
   A satisfying and unified performance, largely
   because Abbado and his La Scala forces give us the
   sense of a real theatrical experience. Ricciarelli
   and Domingo give involved and expressive
   performances.

Don Carlo / Don Carlos

Don Carlo
Plácido Domingo ten Don Carlo **Montserrat
Caballé** sop Elisabetta di Valois **Shirley Verrett** mez
Eboli **Sherrill Milnes** bar Rodrigo **Ruggero Raimondi**
bass Filippo II **Giovanni Foiani** bass Grand Inquisitor
Simon Estes bass-bar Monk **Delia Wallis** mez
Tebaldo **Ryland Davies** ten Conte di Lerma **John
Noble** bar Herald **Maria-Rosa del Campo** sop Voice
from Heaven **Ambrosian Opera Chorus; Royal
Opera House Orchestra, Covent Garden /Carlo
Maria Giulini**
EMI Great Recordings of the Century ③ 567401-2
(209' · ADD · T/t) Recorded 1970   Ⓜ❶❷❸❹

Ⓖ From the day that Giulini conducted the
now legendary production of *Don Carlo*
at Covent Garden in 1958, a recording
of the opera by him looked a must. In fact, it was
to be 12 years before EMI took the plunge, but

the set was worth waiting for: it's the five-act version in Italian, without the cuts made at the Royal Opera, and well recorded and handsomely cast. Giulini himself had slowed down since the live performances, but the blend of majesty and lyric beauty that he brings to the opera is hard to resist. The music glows warmly in his hands, as befits one of Verdi's most human dramas.

His cast gathers together five of the leading singers of the 1970s. In particular, the trio of Caballé, Domingo and Milnes seemed to be rather predictably the names on almost every Italian opera recording at the time, but how glad we would be to have young singers like them today. Caballé, though occasionally sounding blowsy, is exquisite whenever quiet singing is called for, and Domingo is at his golden best throughout. Their murmured farewells at the monastery of San Giusto in Act 5 have never been surpassed. Verrett is a fiery Eboli (although it's a shame Giulini did not give her more pace in 'O don fatale'), and Milnes provides generous-hearted singing as Rodrigo. It's good to have an Italian bass as Philip II, but Raimondi lacks the black tone and fearsome presence of his notable predecessor in the role, Boris Christoff. Lovers of the opera will want to investigate the four-act version under Santini and also the five-act version in French under Pappano, both on EMI (which has more or less cornered the market for this opera). Otherwise, 30 years on, Giulini's splendid performance is as satisfying as any, probably still the number one recommendation.

Don Carlos (French version)
André Turp ten Don Carlos **Edith Tremblay** sop
Elisabeth de Valois **Robert Savoie** bar Rodrigue
Joseph Rouleau bass Philippe II **Richard Van Allan**
bass Grand Inquisitor **Robert Lloyd** bass Monk
Michèle Vilma mez Eboli
**BBC Singers and Concert Orchestra /
John Matheson**
Opera Rara ④ ORCV305 (3h 51' · ADD · S/T/t/N)
Recorded live in 1972   Ⓕ

This is part of Opera Rara's invaluable issues of first versions of Verdi's operas, broadcast on BBC Radio 3 in the 1970s. It is given by a cast of largely Francophone singers, who make it sound – at last – like the truly French work it is.

Text first: we have the complete Fontainebleau scene, a short solo for Posa at the beginning of scene 2, a longer version of the Posa-Philippe scene in Act 2, the costume-changing of Elisabeth and Eboli, their duet before 'O don fatal' in Act 3, the whole of the ballet, the full Insurrection scene, and the longest version of the finale. That adds up to almost four hours. No wonder Verdi either made or sanctioned cuts. However, this enthralling set makes out the best case for this fullest of all versions, its considerable length quite forgotten on account of John Matheson's thoughtful, vital direction, every detail of the vast canvas given its due and played (and sung) finely by the assembled BBC musicians.

The Carlos, André Turp, often at Covent Garden, he did nothing better than this portrayal of the sorely tested and unhappy Infante. His voice, full of emotional plangency, his well crafted phrasing and the sheer passion of his delivery make him ideal. As the tormented, dictatorial Philippe, Joseph Rouleau also surpasses himself vocally and dramatically, so we are at once angered by his tyrannical ways and saddened by his inner misery. Robert Savoie, the Rodrigue/Posa, does not have quite the vocal resources of his confrères, but he gives an honest, deeply felt account of a taxing part.

Edith Tremblay is a gloriously committed Elisabeth. She does not give a traditionally 'star' performance but one that is ideally aligned with the character. Her singing, especially of her big Act 5 solo, is full of natural, true feeling. The Eboli of Michèle Vilma is also a reading to treasure, replete with all the equivocal feelings of that erring character and sung with gratifying confidence. Richard Van Allan, the sole 'foreigner' in a main part, commands the French language and, with Rouleau as antagonist, makes the scene of the Grand Inquisitor and King, the clash of Church and State, the riveting confrontation it should be.

The recording is well balanced and has plenty of presence but careless digitalisation can lend a rather hard quality to some of the voices, although that is easily forgotten in the dedication of a unique occasion.

Don Carlo   **H**
Jon Vickers *ten* Don Carlo **Gré Brouwenstijn** *sop* Elisabetta di Valois **Fedora Barbieri** *mez* Eboli **Tito Gobbi** *bar* Rodrigo **Boris Christoff** *bass* Filippo II **Michael Langdon** *bass* Grand Inquisitor **Joseph Rouleau** *bass* Monk **Jeannette Sinclair** *sop* Tebaldo **Edgar Evans** *ten* Conte di Lerma **Robert Allman** *ten* Herald **Ava June** *sop* Voice from Heaven
**Royal Opera House Chorus, Covent Garden /
Carlo Maria Giulini**
Royal Opera House Heritage Series mono ③
ROHS003 (3h 22' · ADD · T/t/N)
Recorded live at the Royal Opera House, Covent Garden, London, on May 12, 1958
Includes Lord Harewood in conversation with Roger Beardsley   Ⓜ**OO**

The prestige of conductor Giulini and producer Visconti was of a special type: they were the aristocrats of their kind. And the cast, particularly with Gobbi and Christoff in their already famous roles, was as distinguished as any presented by Covent Garden since the war. This recording brings it back vividly and is so clear and faithful that it recreates in large measure all that was heard in these great performances. Chorus and orchestra must take a generous share of the praise. The recording also compels some adjustment of the remembered credits.

Barbieri's Eboli seemed at that period not quite to rank with the other principals. This was partly because it lay high for her voice and, though she comes through 'O don fatale' to win some of the evening's most enthusiastic applause,

it was done only by omitting some top notes, and the recording suggests (as was probably not evident in the theatre) that at the end she had come very near to the limit of her resources. But, as we can hear now, it really was a magnificent performance of the part as a whole, and in dramatic commitment the intensity of the others is fully matched by her own.

Gobbi, so thoroughly identified with the role of Posa, is neither the most elegant of Verdi baritones nor the most lustrous in his production of the high notes, but his tones are so personal, the expression so warm in humanity, that he remains the great Rodrigo of memory. And Christoff is greatness itself. He too is utterly irreplaceable, so individual is the timbre and so authoritative the utterance. He sets a daunting standard for his fellow basses in the cast, but Langdon (Inquisitor) and Rouleau (monk or Charles V) prove worthy colleagues.

But the opera, after all, is called Don Carlo, and Jon Vickers is its hero. Nothing about this recording is more moving than to hear this extraordinary singer as he was at that time. Nothing, that is, unless to find Gré Brouwenstijn so wonderfully brought back to life. She too was an aristocrat among the artists of her time. The duets of Elisabetta and Carlo are of the opera's essence, almost unbearable in their poignancy.

The omission of the Insurrection scene following Posa's death is regrettable: Lord Harewood explains in an illuminating interview with Roger Beardsley the thinking behind it, and in those days very few in the audience would have missed it, because they didn't know it existed! But this is not an occasion for regrets. Andrew Porter sums it up in his introductory essay: 'It does much to recapture the excitement of being there in 1958 and of demonstrating in a realisation at once scrupulous and impassioned a great opera that had been for too long undervalued.'

Don Carlos (French version)
Roberto Alagna *ten* Don Carlos **Karita Mattila** *sop* Elisabeth de Valois **Waltraud Meier** *mez* Eboli **Thomas Hampson** *bar* Rodrigue **José van Dam** *bass-bar* Philippe II **Eric Halfvarson** *bass-bar* Grand Inquisitor **Csaba Airizer** *bass* Monk **Anat Efraty** *sop* Thibault **Scot Weir** *ten* Comte de Lerme, Herald **Donna Brown** *sop* Voice from Heaven **Chorus of the Théâtre du Châtelet, Paris; Orchestre de Paris /
Antonio Pappano**
Stage director **Luc Bondy**
Video director **Yves André Hubert**
NVC Arts 🄳🅅🄳 0630-16318-2 (211' · 2-6)   Ⓕ**OO**

This performance appeared on VHS back in March 1997. On a new, wide-screen television, it makes a far more arresting effect. The action seems to be happening in the room with you. That's due not only to the format but also to director Luc Bondy's wish to portray the personal relationships, the characters' trials and tribulations in the most intimate manner. In contrast to most stagings of Verdi's epic, this one turns all but the outdoor scenes, mainly the Inquisition, into almost a domestic drama.

For better or worse, the principals seem very modern. José van Dam, a magnificent and moving Philippe II, does sometimes remind one of an out-of-sorts bank manager rather than a ruler of an empire, with his troubled wife, in the attractive person and voice of Mattila, as workaday Queen. Charisma is excluded by this interpretation. The relationship of Carlos and Rodrigue, obviously a very close one, is a touchy-feely affair, one that Alagna, in a sincere, beautifully sung assumption, and a palpitating Thomas Hampson, execute with flair.

As ever, Meier isn't content with conventional acting: her Eboli is a scheming and seductive presence, consoling us with the intensity of her singing with a voice a shade light for her part. Indeed, on re-appraising the musical side of the performance, which was recorded live at the Châtelet in Paris, it strikes you that all the voices are a degree lighter than we're used to in the piece, but that suits the French text, giving an ease and fluidity to the vocal line that is, in truth, its own justification.

Even more impressive on rehearing is Pappano's conducting, alive to every nuance of the long work yet aware of its overall structure. In the new medium the clarity and immediacy of the picture is arresting. The sound, though a shade soft in focus, is a great improvement on its 'ordinary' video counterpart. Owners of DVD players who want to add this unforgettable work to their collection need not hesitate – provided they can see it on a wide screen.

Don Carlo

Luciano Pavarotti *ten* Don Carlo **Daniella Dessì** *sop* Elisabetta di Valois **Luciana d'Intino** *mez* Eboli **Paolo Coni** *bar* Rodrigo **Samuel Ramey** *bass* Filippo II **Alexander Anisimov** *bass* Grand Inquisitor **Andrea Silverstrelli** *bass* Monk **Marilena Laurenza** *sop* Tebaldo **Orfeo Zanetti** *ten* Conte di Lerma **Mario Bolognesi** *ten* Herald **Nuccia Focile** *sop* Voice from Heaven **Chorus and Orchestra of La Scala, Milan / Riccardo Muti**
Stage and video director **Franco Zeffirelli**
EMI 📀 599442-9 (182' · NTSC · 4:3 · PCM Stereo 5.1 & DTS 5.1 · 0) Recorded live at Teatro alla Scala, Milan, December 1992   Ⓕ

If you want the edition of the work revised in Italian by Verdi, first performed in 1884, this is your only choice to date on DVD – and it proves, as it did on VHS, a satisfying experience. The work in this form is tauter and more direct than the five-act French original caught on the DVD of the Châtelet production conducted by Pappano. Those who know Zeffirelli's style won't be surprised by the conventionally lavish production, but it effectively evokes the atmosphere of religious oppression and personal antagonisms Verdi so unerringly depicts.

The dark-hued, threatening setting fits Muti's energetic, rhythmically vital conception. He quickens the emotions in a peculiarly Italianate

way, and throughout evinces a feeling for the colouring of the score. His reading is in turn a good background for some thoughtful and idiomatic singing.

Pavarotti delivers Carlo's music in a typically fervent manner, words ideally placed on the voice and his tone consistently firm and pliable. His girth makes him unconvincing as the small, lean, nervous Carlo of history, but his simple, sincere acting is its own advocate. Daniella Dessì looks the very image of the wronged, sympathetic Elisabetta and sings with feeling and good phrasing. Paolo Coni offers a concerned, upright Rodrigo, sung in warm tones though he sometimes loses focus under pressure.

Zeffirelli's video direction is well fashioned and the sound picture catches the aural ambience of La Scala. As a whole, this is a vivid experience.

Ernani

Ernani   Ⓗ
Mario Del Monaco *ten* Ernani **Anita Cerquetti** *sop* Elvira **Ettore Bastianini** *bar* Don Carlo **Boris Christoff** *bass* De Silva **Luciana Boni** *sop* Giovanna **Athos Cesarini** *ten* Don Riccardo **Aurelian Neagu** *bass* Iago **Maggio Musicale Fiorentino Chorus and Orchestra / Dimitri Mitropoulos**
Bel Canto mono ② BCS5011 (118' · ADD · N) Recorded live 1957   Ⓜ●

This is a performance to delight Verdians, Florence seriously challenging its La Scala rival on EMI. The calibre and strength of the singing is a reminder of how often today we put up with third-best. All four principals not only have voices of essential power but also have Verdian style as part of their interpretative make-up. Furthermore they're led by the legendary Mitropoulos, such a force for good at the Maggio Musicale until his untimely death. He easily encompasses the cut and thrust, the rudimentary fervour of one of Verdi's earliest successes, combining at once rude rhythms with lyrical breadth of phrase in supporting is admirable cast and firmly controlling the many ensembles, and his orchestra responds with eagerness to is positive beat.

Cerquetti, whose brief but distinguished career came to an abrupt end not long after this performance took place, had an evenly projected *spinto* soprano and used it with such command that she was at the time spoken of as Tebaldi's equal. She encompasses with confidence her taxing aria and cabaletta at the beginning of the work and makes the most of what little the composer offers his soprano thereafter, shining particularly in the final trio, where Verdi is at his most inspired. As the eponymous hero, Del Monaco shows conclusively that he was more than the stentorian tenor he was often portrayed as being in his day, combining, in the lovers' brief moment of repose in Act 2, with Cerquetti's Elvira in a quietly reflective way. Where the supposed bandit breathes fire, Del Monaco is there with the appropriately flashing tone that made him so popular.

Verdi gives his baritone, Don Carlo, the meatiest music. Bastianini, then at the height of his powers, sings all his solos with resplendent and keen tone. Although he doesn't provide all the subtleties of line and colour Bruson achieves for Muti, Bastianini touches a real note of eloquence at 'O sommo Carlo' in Act 3. As old Silva, Christoff is his imposing self, rivalling his younger Bulgarian colleague, Ghiaurov, on the version from La Scala: both are excellent, but Christoff makes more of the text.

Mitropoulos sanctions a few regrettable cuts not tolerated by Muti. In other respects there's little to choose between these two live performances. For its age the sound on this 'new' version is remarkably good and well worth investigating at mid-price.

Ernani
Plácido Domingo ten Ernani **Mirella Freni** sop Elvira
Renato Bruson bar Don Carlo **Nicolai Ghiaurov** bass
De Silva **Jolanda Michieli** sop Giovanna **Gianfranco
Manganotti** ten Don Riccardo **Alfredo Giacomotti**
bass Iago **Chorus and Orchestra of La Scala, Milan /
Riccardo Muti**
EMI ② 381884-2 (128' · DDD · T/t) Recorded live 1982.
Ⓜ️▷

Renato Bruson's Don Carlo is an assumption that's as gripping dramatically as it is vocally. In his portrayal more than anywhere, the musical tension of *Ernani* becomes manifest, and everywhere Bruson offers superb Verdi singing. Domingo's Ernani is hardly less impressive and he benefits from being caught live on stage. His opening aria and cabaletta are full of delicate touches and obedience to the dynamic marks. In the last act, his recitative, 'Tutto ora tace d'intorno', has great pathos, and his contributions to the final trio an overwhelming eloquence. Here, too, Freni achieves most, the etching in of 'Il riso del tuo volto fa ch' io veda', a brief utterance of happiness, most affecting, and her desperate appeals to Silva for mercy sung with brio.

In her opening aria and cabaletta, the famous 'Ernani, Ernani', too much is asked of a voice not really meant by nature for this kind of heavy duty, but none can quite match the sorrow and heartbreak of Elvira's predicament that Freni manages in the theatre. Ghiaurov, rusty as his voice had become, creates a great impression of dignity and implacable strength, and many of those qualities are carried over into his singing. 'Infelice' is delivered with mature nobility, 'Ah, io l'amo' is intensely moving. Ghiaurov is denied Silva's probably spurious cabaletta. Otherwise the work is given complete.

Muti conducts the score in exemplary manner. He has learnt when to allow his singers licence to phrase with meaning and when to press on. The La Scala chorus gives us the genuine sound of Italian voices in full flight, sounding much more inside their various assumptions than their

rivals. The audience is occasionally in evidence, as are the on-stage effects, but the atmosphere of being in an opera house and taking part, as it were, in a real occasion has all the advantages over the aseptic feeling of a studio.

Falstaff

Falstaff   Ⓗ
Tito Gobbi bar Falstaff **Rolando Panerai** bar Ford
Elisabeth Schwarzkopf sop Alice Ford **Anna Moffo**
sop Nannetta **Luigi Alva** ten Fenton **Fedora Barbieri**
mez Mistress Quickly **Nan Merriman** mez Meg Page
Tomaso Spataro ten Dr Caius **Renato Ercolani** ten
Bardolph **Nicola Zaccaria** bass Pistol **Philharmonia
Chorus and Orchestra / Herbert von Karajan**
EMI ② 377349-2 (120' · ADD · N/S) Recorded 1956
Ⓑ🅞🅞🅞▷

Ⓖ This *Falstaff* still stands (with Toscanini) peerless in the catalogue. At its centre stands Tito Gobbi, and his is a presence large enough to encompass both the lord and the jester, the sensuous and the sensual, and the deep seriousness as well as the deep absurdity of his vision. Few Falstaffs have such a measure of the simplicity of his first monosyllables in the bustle around him; few find the poise as well as the confusion within his music. Karajan's recording is incomparable in its quartet of merry wives.

Schwarzkopf's Alice radiates both the 'gioia nell'aria' and the 'gioia nel' cor' of Verdi's writing, Fedora Barbieri's redoubtable Mistress Quickly, with her stentorian cries of 'Povera donna!', puts other readings in the shade; Anna Moffo's Nannetta, perfectly matched in timbre and agility with Luigi Alva's Fenton, is a constant delight. Above all, it's their corporate presence that works at such a distinctively higher level. Rolando Panerai is a magnificent Ford; his 'E sogno? o realtà?' is a high point of the performance.

This 1956 recording has been discreetly and skilfully doctored, but a little background hiss does remain. But one doesn't actually end up hearing it. This great recording is a-flutter with pungent solo detail, realising, with Nannetta, that the world is 'tutto deliro, sospiro e riso'. The episodes of the opera, its exits and entrances, its subjects and counter-subjects, pass with the unique sensibility of Verdi's final great exuberant fugue of life.

Falstaff   Ⓗ
Giuseppe Valdengo bar Falstaff **Frank Guarrera** bar
Ford **Herva Nelli** sop Alice Ford **Teresa Stich-
Randall** sop Nannetta **Antonio Madasi** ten Fenton
Cloe Elmo contr Mistress Quickly **Nan Merriman**
mez Meg Page **Gabor Carelli** ten Dr Caius **John
Carmen Rossi** ten Bardolph **Norman Scott** bass
Pistol **Robert Shaw Chorale; NBC Symphony
Orchestra / Arturo Toscanini**
RCA Gold Seal mono ② 74321 72372-2 (117' · ADD ·
T/t) Recorded 1950
Ⓜ️🅞🅞🅞

This *Falstaff* remains, as it always has been, one of the half a dozen greatest opera sets ever recorded. It's a miracle in every respect. How Toscanini loved Verdi and how he strained every sinew to fulfil this amazing score's variety in line, feeling and colour. Whether it's the clarity and discipline of the ensembles, the extraordinary care taken over orchestral detail or the alert control of dynamics, Toscanini is supreme, yet nothing is done for effect's sake; everything seems natural, inevitable, unforced, as though the score was being created anew before us with chamber-music finesse – and the atmosphere of a live performance adds to the feeling of immediacy. Nobody dares, or seems to want, to interrupt the magic being laid before him. Toscanini in his old age is matching the subtlety and vitality of the composer's own Indian summer – or one might be tempted to say spring, so delicate and effervescent does the scoring sound.

If, vocally, the main glory is the wonderful sense of ensemble gained through hours of hard rehearsals, individual contributions are almost all rewarding. Indeed, Valdengo's Falstaff, under Toscanini's tutelage, has not been surpassed on disc even by Gobbi. Flexibility, charm, exactness, refinement inform his beautifully and wisely sung portrayal. He's no less pointed and subtle in his encounter with Frank Guarrera's imposing Ford. Another great joy of the set is the women's ensemble, their contribution to the very epitome of smiling chatter. The Alice, Meg and Nannetta (Stich-Randall – none better), all sound, as they were, fresh and youthful. Herva Nelli is a lively and delightful Alice and Cloe Elmo's Quickly is as rich and ripe of voice and diction as any on disc, though a trifle coarse at times. The Fenton is sweet and Italianate in tone, but not as stylish as others. The smaller roles are all very much part of the team.

This set should certainly be a source of delightful revelation to a new generation of collectors who may have a wrong-headed view of what Toscanini was about. The remastering gives it clearer, more immediate sound than ever heard before from the originals.

Falstaff

Michele Pertusi bar Sir John Falstaff **Carlos Alvarez** bar Ford **Ana Ibarra** sop Alice Ford **Maria José Moreno** sop Nannetta **Bülent Bezdüz** ten Fenton **Jane Henschel** contr Mistress Quickly **Marina Domashenko** mez Meg Page **Alasdair Elliott** ten Dr Caius **Peter Hoare** ten Bardolph **Darren Jeffrey** bass Pistol **London Symphony Chorus and Orchestra / Sir Colin Davis**
LSO Live ② LSO0055 Ⓢ; .⚛. ② LSO0528 (119' · DSD/DDD · T/S/t/N) Recorded live   ⓜ❍❍▷

By all accounts the performances at the Barbican were among the most enjoyable of their kind in London for a long time, and certainly the enjoyment comes across on disc. The 'how' of it isn't so easily defined. It isn't the applause and occasional chuckles, though they help (comedy abhors a vacuum). It isn't even that, despite this being a concert rather than a staged event, the cast are performing entirely in character, and that they're doing so with zest and humorous intelligence. Rather it's as though a spirit of fun is in the air, breathed in by everyone, including the orchestra, who see the score's jokes and respond to its wit with the speed of light. Much of this must emanate from the maestro, who has every right to take pride in a brilliant achievement.

Michele Pertusi as Falstaff may lack Tito Gobbi's expressive resources, but he nevertheless has plenty of variety to offer. The grotesque acolytes and preposterous doctor play up well, and the lovers, Nannetta and Fenton, are a charming couple, convincingly young in voice and lyrical in style. Jane Henschel is a strong Mistress Quickly, better integrated into the ensemble than the riper plum-pudding dames who get the big laughs.

Falstaff has been well served on records ever since Toscanini set the standard high in 1950, but in few versions can the orchestra have played with more evident appreciation of the comedy on stage – it's almost as though the members of the LSO know the libretto by heart. This bids to become a firm favourite.

Falstaff

Ambrogio Maestri bass-bar Falstaff **Roberto Frontali** bar Ford **Barbara Frittoli** sop Alice Ford **Inva Mula** sop Nannetta **Juan Diego Flórez** ten Fenton **Bernadette Manca di Nissa** contr Mistress Quickly **Anna Caterina Antonacci** mez Meg Page **Ernesto Gavazzi** ten Doctor Caius **Paolo Barbacini** ten Bardolph **Luigi Roni** bass Pistol **Chorus and Orchestra of La Scala, Milan / Riccardo Muti**
Stage director **Ruggero Cappuccio**
Video director **Pierre Cavasillas**
TDK Mediactive 🎥 DV-OPFAL (118' · 16:9 · 2.0 & 5.1 · 0)   Ⓕ❍❍

This performance derives from a special production of *Falstaff* at Verdi's birthplace to mark the centenary of his death. It's a replica of staging given in the same theatre, the Teatro Verdi, under Toscanini, in 1913, using facsimiles of the original sets. Some may find the small stage and traditional sets simply old-fashioned, but given a superb cast perceptively directed by Ruggero Cappuccio, what we see and hear is Verdi's masterpiece presented in the most natural, unforced way, with everyone on stage enjoying themselves. The result is a warm-hearted, unforced reading that makes the rival Graham Vick production at Covent Garden look, by its side, forced and contrived, not to mention the inadequacies of the anti-Verdian Aix production also on DVD. Muti's masterly traversal of the score – at once prompt yet relaxed – adds to the pleasure.

The cast is headed by Ambrogio Maestri, 31 at the time, in the title part who in vocal and physical size is Italy's answer to Bryn Terfel, Haitink's Falstaff, and as with Terfel is a youngish man playing the ageing Knight; but Maestri is very much a member of an ensemble, not a star giving his interpretation. He portrays the Fat Knight as still youthful in his outlook and quite nimble afoot. He performs it entirely without Terfel's (or Vick's) attempts at vulgar exaggeration: everything emerges from the text and music, and the singing itself is finely modulated and easy on the ear.

He's surrounded by a group of Merry Wives as ebullient and resourceful as any on audio or video versions. Barbara Frittoli's scheming Alice is nicely set of against Anna Caterina Antonacci's witty Meg, while Bernadette Manca di Nissa sings and acts Quickly truly, without the traditional guying of the part. Roberto Frontali's Ford is much more in character than on the rival version and he parleys perfectly with Maestri's Falstaff. Juan Diego Flórez and Inva Mula as sweetvoiced and handsome-looking lovers and excellent *comprimarios* are all part of this highly recommendable DVD. Video direction and sound picture are exemplary. Don't miss its many delights.

Falstaff
José van Dam bar Falstaff **William Stone** bar-Ford
Barbara Madra sop Alice Ford **Elzbieta Szmytka** sop-Nannetta **Laurence Dale** ten Fenton **Livia Budai** mez Mistress Quickly **Benedetta Pecchioli** mez Meg Page **Mario Luperi** bass Pistol **Ugo Benelli** ten Dr Caius **Théâtre de la Monnaie Chorus and Orchestra, Brussels / Sylvain Cambreling**
Stage director **Lluis Pasqual**
Video director **André Flédérick**
Warner Music Vision/NVC Arts DVD 5050467 4469-2-2 (130' · NTSC · 4:3 · 2.0 · 2-6) Recorded live at the Aix-en-Provence Festival, 1987   Ⓕ

There can seldom have been so wholly satisfactory a traversal of Verdi's closing masterpiece, on both dramatic and musical grounds, as this 1987 staging at Aix. Director Lluis Pasqual goes to the heart of the matter in sets by Fabia Puigserver that are at once minimalist yet highly evocative in terms of milieu, and happily coloured by sepia tints, subtly lit. Within them, Pasqual directs his principals with an eye for natural yet cleverly pointed movement.

He's lucky to have José van Dam, at the height of his powers in 1987. This Falstaff is wholly believable as a mature lover and true knight, one who never plays the fool. At every point Van Dam allows him to arise from the text and the music, which he sings with firm and well-moulded tone. He's surrounded by a cast on a similarly high level, headed by Barbara Madra's lively, quickwitted, beautifully sung Alice. Benedetta Pecchioli makes more of Meg than most mezzos, and also looks her part. Livia Budai is a witty, pert Quickly who sings the role rather than mugging it. William Stone projects Ford's jealousy convincingly on a flood of strong, firm tone. Mario Luperi is a nicely lugubrious Pistol, Ugo Benelli a characterful Dr Caius. The lovers may not be the most fluent ever heard, but they're worthy members of a distinguished ensemble.

Cambreling conducts a scrupulously prepared account of the score. The autumnal colours mean that sometimes the facial expressions aren't as clear as they might be, but by and large

the video direction is excellent, as is the sound. This version is preferable to the admirable Muti one, which suffers from the rather restricting confines of the small theatre at Busseto.

Falstaff
Renato Bruson bar Falstaff **Leo Nucci** bar Ford **Katia Ricciarelli** sop Alice Ford **Barbara Hendricks** sop Nannetta **Dalmacio Gonzales** ten Fenton **Lucia Valentini-Terrani** mez Mistress Quickly **Brenda Boozer** mez Meg Page **John Dobson** ten Doctor Caius **Francis Egerton** ten Bardolph **William Wilderman** bass Pistol **Royal Opera House Chorus and Orchestra, Covent Garden / Carlo Maria Giulini**
Stage director **Robert Eyre**
Video director **Brian Large**
Warner Music Vision/NVC Arts 50 51442 0494-2-8 (137' · NTSC · 4:3 · PCM stereo · 0). Recorded live at the Royal Opera, Covent Garden, London, in July 1982 Ⓕ

This *Falstaff* (it's a pleasure to report) is a delight from start to finish. The box quotes the *Sunday Times* which proclaimed it 'the operatic event of the year'. Generally, though, the enthusiasm was more qualified in some opinions, the main complaint being that Giulini's tempi were too slow. In the theatre that is how it seemed but on video it no longer seems so. This may be because the detail of action onstage can be observed so closely and with so much enjoyment in the rightness and liveliness which seem never to desert the producer and his company.

Bruson is a magnificent Falstaff, whether from the twinkle in his eye or the radiant rotundity of his voice. He has a worthy Bardolph and Pistol too, both with an infallible feel for comedy. The wives are merry as it were from inner delight rather than as dutiful part of an evening's work. Barbara Hendricks (a few low notes apart) makes an enchanting Nannetta, and Dalmacio Gonzales is a honey-toned Fenton. All do well, and although there's now a whole gallery of *Falstaff*s on film (some of them admirable), this will do very well.

Falstaff   Ⓗ
Giuseppe Taddei bar Falstaff **Scipione Colombo** bar Ford **Rosanna Carteri** sop Alice Ford **Anna Moffo** sop Nannetta **Luigi Alva** ten Fenton **Fedora Barbieri** mez Mistress Quickly **Anna Maria Canali** mez Meg Page **Mario Carlin** ten Doctor Caius **Renato Ercolani** ten Bardolph **Franco Calabrese** bass Pistol **RAI Chorus and Orchestra, Milan / Tullio Serafin**
Video director **Herbert Graf**
Video Artists International DVD VAIDVD4333 (118' · 4:3 black and white · PCM mono · 0)   Ⓕ

Vintage 1956, Italian television, black and white, 'the flicks' appropriately named, with an occasional vertical line down the middle, and on the generally vivid soundtrack an occasional 'wow' – but all of this is nothing to the 'wow' of a performance. Splendidly cast, with not a weak link, conducted with benevolent mastery and produced so as to give the composer what he (and not some imposer of a crack-brained concept) wanted. And above all it's a happy *Falstaff* (you'd think that would go without saying, but there have been too many frowning *Falstaffs* making heavy weather amid dutifully rehearsed mirth with no joy in it).

Giuseppe Taddei's smile is at the centre of everything, teeth white as his wig, more emblematic of the man even than his big belly. He sings gloriously, absolutely in his prime (the Karajan recording by which his Falstaff is probably most generally remembered was made 24 years later).

The Ford is also a fine singer, Scipione Colombo, courtly and vulpine in appearance, convincing in his wounded monologue. The merry wives take their centre not so much from the Alice Ford (Rosanna Carteri) as from the Mistress Quickly and the ripe chest notes of Fedora Barbieri. The lovers, Anna Moffo and Luigi Alva, make a good-looking as well as mellifluous pair. The Caius, Mario Carlin, actually sings (most of them peck), and the Bardolph, Renato Ercolani, is a star, a kind of Dudley Moore with a Cyrano nose. We don't at any point see the conductor, but Serafin's presence is real enough nonetheless.

Additional recommendation

Falstaff
Trimarchi Falstaff **Servile** Ford **Faulkner** Alice Ford
Dilbèr Nannetta **Comencini** Fenton **Chorus and
Orchestra of Hungarian State Opera / Humburg**
Naxos ② 8 660050/1 (120' · DDD · T/N)　　　Ⓢ🅓➔

Naxos's set does a good job at challenging the best in the field. Humburg strikes just the right balance between the high spirits and the delicacy in Verdi's score. Trimarchi as Falstaff gives a reading full of ripe understanding; his voice lies, as the role requires, ideally poised between baritone and bass. A very lovable portrait. This is a *Falstaff* to savour and one that will bear repetition.

La forza del destino

La forza del destino　　　　　　　　　　🄷
Maria Caniglia sop Leonora **Galliano Masini** ten Don
Alvaro **Carlo Tagliabue** bar Don Carlo **Tancredi
Pasero** bass Padre Guardiano **Ebe Stignani** mez
Preziosilla **Saturno Meletti** bar Fra Melitone **Ernesto
Dominici** bass Marquis of Calatrava **Giuseppe Nessi**
ten Trabuco **Liana Avogadro** mez Curra **Italian
Broadcasting Authority Chorus and Orchestra /
Gino Marinuzzi**
Naxos Historical mono ③ 8 110206/7(154' · ADD · N)
Recorded 1941　　　　　　　　　　　　Ⓢ🅓➔

This is a fascinating, unmissable set both in historic and musical terms. Marinuzzi, a Toscanini coeval at La Scala, was chosen as conductor, and it's his only complete recording of an opera. The recording took place in May 1941 and was issued on 78rpm discs by Cetra. After the war Parlo-

phone, which was then in charge of Cetra recordings in Britain, issued – in desultory fashion – a few separate discs. Sadly the whole version has never had the currency its great merits deserve, not at least as the first complete set (bar one traditionally cut scene) of the work and one with an entirely Italian cast. Now we have it to enjoy at superbudget price and in admirable transfers from original Cetra pressings, by Ward Marston.

For the recording Marinuzzi had assembled a vintage cast of Italian singers of the day. Caniglia herself rightly considered her Leonora here as one of her finest recordings: one can hear why in her committed, vibrant and often very sensitive singing: she even attempts some of the refined *pianissimo*s that graced the reading of this role by her near-contemporary, Zinka Milanov. It's a performance imbued with spiritual yearning – exactly what's wanted. By her side Masini's Alvaro is obviously a man of action with his blade-like, *spinto* tenor and sense of desperation at Alvaro's plight. If he's occasionally too lachrymose that's only a sign of his empathy with his role. As Alvaro's implacable antagonist, Don Carlo, Tagliabue provides dependable tone and an authentically styled interpretation of a kind seldom heard today. The pair's final and fatal encounter is one of the score's and the set's highlights.

Stignani, in her absolute prime, is a formidable Preziosilla, full in tone and clear in her passagework, exemplary in every way. Marston has made the recording as amenable as is possible. In any case it would be worth suffering much worse sound than this for such a satisfying traversal on all sides of this inspired score.

La forza del destino　　　　　　　　　　🄷
Stella Roman sop Leonora **Frederick Jagel** ten Don
Alvaro **Lawrence Tibbett** bar Don Carlo **Ezio Pinza**
bass Padre Guardiano **Irra Petina** mez Preziosilla
Salvatore Baccaloni bass Melitone **Louis d'Angelo**
bass Marquese **Thelma Votipka** mez Curra **Alessio
de Paolis** ten Trabuco **Lorenzo Alvary** bass Mayor
John Gurney bass Surgeon **Metropolitan Opera
Chorus and Orchestra, New York / Bruno Walter**
Naxos Historical mono ③ 8 110038/40 (168' · AAD)
Recorded live 1943　　　　　　　　　　　　Ⓢ

There has never been quite so electrifying a *Forza* as Walter's vital, brilliantly executed reading, which encapsulates the essence of the forthcoming drama. It confirms what few may know today, that Walter was a superb interpreter of Verdi. Yet this was the first time he had conducted *Forza*, so his lithe, finely honed reading is all the more remarkable. The other revelation is the Leonora of Stella Roman, a greatly underrated soprano brought to the Met in 1941, who yields few points to such notable interpreters of the part as Ponselle, Milanov and Tebaldi. They apart, you would go far to hear a Leonora so well equipped for the role, and so committed to it, one who uses her warm, generous voice to unerring effect in projecting the woman's dire predicament.

Padre Guardiano appears in the guise of Pinza, none better, and sounding, one uncertain high E apart, secure, concerned and authoritative. Jagel as Don Alvaro passes easily the test of the taxing aria of sad recollection at the start of Act 3. Tibbett as Don Carlo compels attention at every entry with his distinctive timbre and faultless style, but truth to tell the glorious tone had dulled since his great days in the 1930s and at times he sounds stretched by the part. Both his arias suffer cuts. Carlo's second (of three) duets with Alvaro is also excised as was then the custom, and strettas throughout are foreshortened. Baccaloni enjoys himself hugely as Melitone and obviously relishes his encounters with his superior, the Padre Guardiano, the two Italians revelling in the text. Petina is a lively but lightweight Preziosilla.

The sound is a bit crackly and restricted but good enough to enjoy an absorbing account of the score. This vivid version has much to commend it at the price.

La forza del destino (original St Petersburg version, 1862)
Martina Arroyo *sop* Leonora **Kenneth Collins** *ten* Don Alvaro **Peter Glossop** *bar* Don Carlo **Don Garrard** *bass* Padre Guardiano **Janet Coster** *mez* Preziosilla **Derek Hammond-Stroud** *bar* Melitone **Roderick Kennedy** *bass* Marquis **Kenneth Bowen** *ten* Trabuco **BBC Singers and Concert Orchestra / John Matheson**
Opera Rara ② ORCV304 (137' · DDD · T/t) Ⓜ Ⓞ

This marks the final offering from Opera Rara's laudable restoration of BBC broadcasts from the 1970s and '80s of Verdi's first thoughts on specific operas, and it is quite up to the standard of the series. It differs only in being given without an audience, and was broadcast two years after the recording.

On disc we know the 1862 original *Forza* from Gergiev's Philips set recorded, appropriately enough, in St Petersburg. That version is by and large finely cast with Russian singers and excitingly conducted, but this one, featuring British artists and one North American, need hardly fear the comparison. John Matheson may be a slightly more measured interpreter than Gergiev but he is perhaps even more adept at disclosing the many subtleties in shaping the slightly sprawling score as a unified whole. His orchestra provides fine playing – special praise for the first clarinet before Alvaro's Act 3 solo – and the BBC Singers nicely characterise their roles.

Alvaro, an even more taxing role than in the better-known revised version for Milan, is superbly sung by Kenneth Collins: Bergonzi and Domingo apart, no other tenor in the late 20th century was as ideal for the part. Collins, a true *spinto*, makes light of the demands, and sings with unstinting strength and an innate sense of Verdian style, a suitable souvenir of a singer so little represented on disc.

Martina Arroyo, also on Gardelli's EMI recording of 12 years earlier, is a profoundly sympathetic, even-voiced Leonora: she really sings her heart out. As the implacable Don Carlo, Peter Glossop remains an appreciable Verdian. His tone had

loosened a little by 1981 but he splendidly conveys the avenging brother's wrath, particularly in his fiery encounter with Alvaro in Act 4.

Like Collins, Don Garrard and Derek Hammond-Stroud were then singing the revised version at the Coliseum. The much-admired Canadian bass sings with depth and authority as Padre Guardiano, and Hammond-Stroud in one of his favourite roles makes Melitone more than a mere *buffo* but rather a hot-headed, obtuse friar, as he should be. Janet Coster fills most of the considerable demands of Preziosilla's role and it is good to be reminded of the stalwart tenor Kenneth Bowen and of Roderick Kennedy's sturdy bass. All sing with exemplary Italian.

The recording has breadth and presence. The booklet is lavish though the skimpy note seriously underestimates the differences between this and the more famous revision, and it is a pity there are no biographies: the singers are hardly well known to most younger Verdi enthusiasts. But these complaints are of little consequence when the performance is so inspiriting and dedicated on all sides.

La forza del destino Ⓗ
Antonietta Stella *sop* Leonora **Giuseppe di Stefano** *ten* Don Alvaro **Ettore Bastianini** *bar* Don Carlo **Walter Kreppel** *bass* Padre Guardiano **Giulietta Simionato** *mez* Preziosilla **Karl Dönch** *bar* Fra Melitone **Ludwig Welter** *bass* Marquis of Calatrava **Hugo Meyer-Welfing** *ten* Trabuco **Harald Pröglhöf** *bass* Mayor **Franz Bierbach** *bass* Surgeon **Vienna State Opera Chorus and Orchestra / Dimitri Mitropoulos**
Orfeo d'Or mono Ⓜ ② C681 062I (151' · ADD · S/N)
Recorded live 1960 Ⓜ Ⓞ

Mitropoulos, who had only weeks to live, directs the work with that combination of sensitivity and drive that marked all his performances. With the Vienna State Opera Orchestra in glowing form, the results are very special. One quirk: rather than playing the Overture at the beginning, Mitropoulos places it after the first scene, a plan Verdi had but eventually abandoned. It works quite well, at least when played with the élan evident here.

Bastianini presents Don Carlo in all his menacing, vengeful fury with that dark-hued, immensely powerful baritone of his. As his antagonist he has Di Stefano as Alvaro in his most eloquent, incisive and appealing form, relishing every word and note. If it's possible, the Leonora and Preziosilla are even better. Stella had a brief period when she was fully the equal of Tebaldi and here she is in the middle of it, singing the role as well as, if not better than any soprano on disc. Tebaldi-like in her full, Italianate tone, Caniglia-like in her identification with Leonora's plight, from start to finish she is magnificent, and she crowns her portrayal with a finely nuanced and felt 'Pace, pace' in the final act. Simionato was always one of the few mezzos who had the range and brio to fulfil the demands of Preziosilla's part, and she too is here at her appreciable best.

The rest of the cast is drawn from resident singers at the Staatsoper. Kreppel is a sound, full-bottomed bass who sings a sympathetic Padre Guardiano, especially fine in the long Act 2 duet with Leonora. But the rest are not half as idiomatic as their Italian counterparts in Florence, with Dönch comic as Melitone but in rather a Viennese way. Another drawback is the traditional cuts then imposed on the score; particularly heinous is the excising of Alvaro/Carlo duet in Act 3.

In this the performance's first official appearance, the sound is by and large excellent. Although there is no libretto, there are interesting notes in the booklet by Gottfried Kraus and Michael Gielen (on Mitropoulos).

La forza del destino   Ⓗ
Renata Tebaldi sop Leonora **Franco Corelli** ten Don Alvaro **Ettore Bastianini** bar Don Carlo **Boris Christoff** bass Padre Guardiano **Oralia Dominguez** mez Preziosilla **Renato Capecchi** bar Fra Melitone **Jorge Algorta** bass Marquis of Calatrava **Mariano Caruso** ten Trabuco **Anna di Stasio** mez Curra **Giuseppe Forgione** bass Mayor **Gianni Bardi** bass Surgeon **Naples San Carlo Opera Chorus and Orchestra / Francesco Molinari-Pradelli**
Hardy Classic Video **DVD** HCD4002 (160' · NTSC · 4:3 · 1.0 · 0) Recorded live at the San Carlo Theatre, Naples 1958 Includes interview with Tebaldi   Ⓕ

Why is it that this performance in low-fi and indifferent black-and-white picture, and in a distinctly old-fashioned staging, has become a legend among collectors of opera on video to the extent of becoming a VHS best-seller? The answer lies in the quality of execution of a once-in-a-lifetime cast, supported by idiomatic conducting and playing at the San Carlo in Naples back in 1958.

Tebaldi had already proved at the Maggio Musicale at Florence in 1953 under Mitropoulos that Leonora was to be among her most successful roles, and here she confirms the fact in spades with her lustrous, effortlessly shaped and eloquent traversal of the role.

By her side she has the incomparable Corelli, singing his first Don Alvaro, and revealing that his brilliant, exciting yet plangent tone is precisely the right instrument to project Alvaro's loves and sorrows. At this stage of his career his thrilling upper register and incisive delivery of the text were at their most potent, as he makes abundantly clear in aria and duet. As his antagonist, Bastianini sings with the kind of Verdian élan seemingly now extinct among his breed. He may not be the most subtle of Verdian baritones, but here his macho approach ideally suits Don Carlo's vengeful imprecations.

If that weren't enough vocal splendour for one occasion, there's Christoff – yet another member of the cast at the peak of his career – intoning Padre Guardiano's dignified utterances in that unique if not always entirely Italianate manner of his. Renato Capecchi for long made the part of Melitone his own: one can see and hear why here in his amusing yet never

overstated sense of the role's comic possibilities. The voices are caught with very little distortion in goodish sound. The original film has suffered some deterioration over the years, but its recent restoration yields far better results than was once the case on dim VHS copies: this DVD derives from RAI's original master copy. Pleasure is completed by the bonus of an interview with Tebaldi.

Additional recommendations

La forza del destino

Price Leonora **Domingo** Don Alvaro **Milnes** Don Carlo **John Alldis Choir; London Symphony Orchestra / Levine**
RCA ③ 74321 39502-2 (171' · DDD · T/t)   Ⓜ
A well-cast set and a strong recommendation. Leontyne Price followers will be tempted no doubt, but note she's past her prime here. The recording is uncut.

Callas Leonora **Tucker** Don Alvaro **Tagliabue** Ⓗ
Don Carlo **Chorus and Orchestra of La Scala, Milan / Serafin**
EMI ③ 556323-2 (164' · ADD · T/t)   ⒻↃ
Callas is superb as Leonora and, Tagliabue aside, the rest of the cast turn in fine performances. Serafin does, however, make some cuts.

I Lombardi alla prima crociata

I Lombardi
June Anderson sop Giselda **Luciano Pavarotti** ten Oronte **Samuel Ramey** bass Pagano **Richard Leech** ten Arvino **Ildebrando d'Arcangelo** bass Pirro **Yanni Yannissis** bass Acciano **Jane Shaulis** mez Sofia **Anthony Dean Griffey** ten Prior **Patricia Racette** mez Viclinda **Chorus and Orchestra of the Metropolitan Opera, New York / James Levine**
Decca ② 455 287-2DHO2 (129' · DDD · T/t)   ⒻↃ

Pavarotti appeared at the Met production of *I Lombardi* in 1993: this recording is the delayed result. He's in good voice and sings Oronte's aria with fine legato, binding the decorative turns of the cabaletta beautifully into the vocal line and throwing in a respectable top C to show us he still can. I Lombardi is a viscerally exciting opera. The first complete recording, conducted by Lamberto Gardelli (Philips), set a good benchmark in 1972, but that need not deter us from welcoming this lively newcomer. The Met Opera Orchestra plays with splendid precision and, as Turks and Crusaders, women of the harem and virgins, the Met Chorus has a high old time on both sides of *I Lombardi*'s war-zone. Levine himself has improved beyond recognition as a Verdian; this studio recording is well paced and has a good sense of theatre. Everything is swift and crisp.

The best role goes to the soprano Giselda, specially tailored for the delicate skills of Erminia Frezzolini. Among the current crop of Verdi sopranos, June Anderson is probably as plausible a modern Frezzolini as any. There's some lovely, pure-toned singing in her big scene at the end of Act 2 and her coloratura is shining bright, both in this cabaletta and later in 'In fondo all' alma'. Samuel Ramey makes a relatively lightweight Pagano, who alone decorates his second verses. In the second tenor role Richard Leech holds his own, although his voice doesn't take well to the microphone. Ildebrando d'Arcangelo proudly represents the younger generation of Italian singers in the small role of Pirro, and Patricia Racette sings brightly as Viclinda.

Gardelli's crusading first recording has a rough Italianate vigour that lovers of early Verdi will enjoy, but Levine and his forces more than hold their ground with pace and brilliance, and a bright, modern recording with on balance a better cast and the voices well forward.

Luisa Miller

Luisa Miller.
Katia Ricciarelli sop Luisa **Plácido Domingo** ten Rodolfo **Renato Bruson** bar Miller **Gwynne Howell** bass Walter **Elena Obraztsova** cont Federica **Wladimiro Ganzarolli** bass Wurm **Audrey Michael** mez Laura **Luigi de Corato** ten Peasant **Chorus and Orchestra of the Royal Opera House, Covent Garden / Lorin Maazel**
DG 459 481-2GTA2 (133' · ADD) Recorded 1980 Ⓜ️🅑➜

The strength of this DG reissue is the singing of the three principals. The production of *Luisa Miller* at the Royal Opera House, Covent Garden, on which the set was based, probably marked the high point of Katia Ricciarelli's career. Maybe the recording caught her just a year too late, when some harsh sounds had started to intrude in her singing at *forte* above the stave, but the soft singing remains beautiful and the character is immensely touching. Domingo sings Rodolfo with a voice of metal as firm and glowing as bronze, even if he does not have the poetry of Bergonzi or the flair of Pavarotti. Bruson is heard in one of the best roles in his repertoire: the sympathetic music of the Miller calls for exactly the long, lyrical lines at which he excels, often spanning two phrases in a single breath where the average Verdi baritone would be left gasping.

Howell makes a stately, but not very incisive Walter. Neither Ganzarolli nor Obraztsova had been in the Royal Opera stage production, and the decision to bring them into the cast solely for the recording was not justified by the results. Obraztsova's thick-voiced Federica is a liability, but the real stumbling-block is Maazel's insensitive conducting. Nevertheless, as a totality, this set remains the equal of any before us at the moment (neither the Cleva/RCA nor Maag/Decca is currently listed).

Macbeth

Macbeth
Piero Cappuccilli bar Macbeth **Shirley Verrett** mez

Lady Macbeth **Nicolai Ghiaurov** bass Banquo **Plácido Domingo** ten Macduff **Antonio Savastano** ten Malcolm **Carlo Zardo** bass Doctor **Giovanni Foiani** bass Servant **Sergio Fontana** bass Herald **Alfredo Mariotti** bass Assassin **Stefania Malagú** mez Lady-in-waiting **Chorus and Orchestra of La Scala, Milan / Claudio Abbado**
DG ② 734380 (154' · ADD · T/t) Recorded 1976 Ⓜ️🅞➜

Verdi's lifelong admiration for Shakespeare resulted in only three operas based on his plays. Macbeth, the first, originally written in 1847, was extensively revised in 1865. Without losing the direct force of the original, Verdi added greater depth to is first ideas. Once derided as being un-Shakespearian, it's now recognised as a masterpiece for its psychological penetration as much as for its subtle melodic inspiration.

Abbado captures perfectly the atmosphere of dark deeds and personal ambition leading to tragedy, projected by Verdi, and his reading holds the opera's disparate elements in the score under firm control, catching its interior tensions. He's well supported by his Scala forces. Shirley Verrett may not be ideally incisive or Italianate in accent as Lady Macbeth, but she peers into the character's soul most convincingly. As ever, truly inspired by Abbado, Cappuccilli is a suitably daunted and introverted Macbeth who sings a secure and unwavering legato. Domingo's upright Macduff and Ghiaurov's doom-laden Banquo are both admirable in their respective roles.

Macbeth
Peter Glossop bar Macbeth **Rita Hunter** sop Lady Macbeth **John Tomlinson** bass Banquo **Kenneth Collins** ten Macduff **Richard Greager** ten Malcolm **Christian du Plessis** bass Doctor **Michael George** bass Servant **Roger Heath** bass Assassin **Ludmilla Andrew** mez Lady-in-Waiting **BBC Singers; BBC Concert Orchestra / John Matheson**
Opera Rara ② ORCV301 (132' · DDD) Recorded 1979 🅕🅞🅞

This recording starts project engendered by the Verdi specialist Julian Budden in the more adventurous days of BBC Radio 3 to perform a number of Verdi operas in their original versions. Although Verdi's revisions of his first Shakespearian opera are mostly improvements, several aspects of the original score are worth reviving. Inevitably it's a more consistent whole, since the later amendments are in a changed and improved style. Lady Macbeth's second aria, 'Trionfai', is more basic and showy than its subtle successor, 'La luce langue'. The cabaletta to Macbeth's Act 3 aria is rousing and unusual, and was dropped in favour of another duet for Macbeth and his Lady. The chorus at the start of Act 4, replaced by a more distinctive piece, is in its own right a fine example of Risorgimento ardour, and the final scene, besides having Macbeth's effective aria as he lies mortally wounded is tauter, if more blatant, than its successor.

What makes this issue most worth while, however, is the superb performance. John

Matheson directs a vital, finely timed and well-integrated account of the score that catches all its astonishing originality. Rita Hunter is as accomplished and appropriate a Lady Macbeth as any on disc, bar the unique Callas for De Sabata. Peter Glossop's Verdian style is faultless, and his understanding of the part complete. Kenneth Collins delivers 'Ah, la paterno mano' in exemplary voice and style. John Tomlinson, then in pristine voice, is an imposing Banquo. Chorus and orchestra are hard to fault. The recording, slightly bass-heavy, has been transferred at rather a low level, but its balance is as good as you'd expect, given its origins. This is definitely an experience convinced Verdians should not miss.

Macbeth
Thomas Hampson bar Macbeth **Paoletta Marrocu** sop Lady Macbeth **Roberto Scandiuzzi** bass Banquo
Luis Lima ten Macduff **Miroslav Christoff** ten Malcolm **Mihály Kálmándi** bass Doctor **Liuba Chuchrova** mez Lady-in-Waiting **Zurich Opera House Chorus and Orchestra / Franz Welser-Möst**
Stage director **David Pountney**
Video director **Thomas Grimm**
TDK Mediactive ② DV-OPMAC (186' · 16:9 · 2.0, 5.1 & DTS 5.1 · 2) Recorded live at the Opera House, Zurich 2001. Includes special feature, 'Macbeth – an Introduction'.   Ⓟ**OO**

Here's yet another challenging and well-executed staging from the Zurich Opera, this one dating from 2001. David Pountney, in at least his third attempt at the work, presents the Shakespearian drama in predictably unorthodox manner, irritating in its overuse of distracting symbols, extras and props, but revelatory in its pointed treatment of the principal pair of characters. The production is at its most bizarre in the Witches' scenes, where a pack of maddened women disport themselves in an orgy of man-hating, but even when the effects are at their most outrageous a sense of a guiding hand is there to lend some sort of dramatic cohesion to the whole.

Pountney bases his concept on the erotic relationship, vividly delineated, between Macbeth and his spouse; their sex-dominated marriage is obviously the spur to their overweening ambition, with she – as ever – leading the way. Paoletta Marrocu, a Sardinian soprano with a growing reputation, throws caution to the winds in her energetic, purposeful, fierce attack on Lady Macbeth. From first to last it's a truly stunning performance both histrionically and vocally. Few sopranos, Callas undoubtedly is one, have sung the part so confidently and incisively in a powerful, lean yet strong voice unflinchingly projected. By her side Hampson's haunted Macbeth is a striking portrait of a man pushed to the limits in the cause of getting to the top. His voice may not be truly Italianate in timbre, but he uses it here with such intelligence and force that one can overlook the want of a certain bite in his tone.

Welser-Möst presides over everything with an acute ear for the work's *tinta* and judges his speeds to a nicety, with admirable support from his own house's chorus and orchestra.

Additional recommendation

Macbeth   Ⓗ
Mascherini Macbeth **Callas** Lady Macbeth **Tajo** Banquo **Chorus and Orchestra of La Scala, Milan / de Sabata**
EMI mono ② 566447-2 (139' · ADD · T/t)
Recorded live   Ⓜ
Callas's portrayal of Lady Macbeth is definitive and Victor de Sabata's conducting electrifying. However, the rest of the cast aren't up to much, and the recorded sound is poor. A set for Callas fans only.

Nabucco

Nabucco
Tito Gobbi bar Nabucco **Bruno Prevedi** ten Ismaele **Carlo Cava** bass Zaccaria **Elena Suliotis** sop Abigaille **Dora Carral** sop Fenena **Anna d'Auria** sop Anna **Giovanni Foiani** bass High Priest of Baal **Walter Krautler** ten Abdallo **Vienna Opera Orchestra; Vienna State Opera Chorus / Lamberto Gardelli**
Decca ② 417 407-2DH2 (121' · ADD · T/t)
Recorded 1965   Ⓕ**O**➔

The years have hardly lessened the excitement of listening to this vigorous, closely knit performance. One realises why we were all amazed by Suliotis's account of the role of Abigaille. Her singing seizes you by the throat through its raw depiction of malice and through its youthful, uninhibited power. With the benefit of hindsight one can ear how a voice treated so carelessly and unstintingly could not last long, and so it was to be; but we should be glad for the brightness of the meteor while it flashed all too briefly through the operatic firmament. As an interpretation, her Abigaille seems a little coarse set beside the refinements shown by Scotto for Muti on EMI. However, Suliotis can manage by nature what Scotto has to conjure up by art, and she's certainly a subtler artist than Dimitrova on the wayward Sinopoli/DG version.

Gobbi, nearing the end of his illustrious career in 1965, remains the most convincing interpreter on record of the crazed king. The voice may have become a shade hard and uningratiating, but his use of Italian and his colouring of his tone, finally his pathos, are certainly not rivalled by Cappuccilli (Sinopoli). Carlo Cava exudes implacable fury as old Zaccaria, but he's inclined to go through his tone at forte . Prevedi is more than adequate as Ismaele, Carral less than adequate as Fenena (here DG score with Valentini Terrani).

One of the main assets of the Decca remains Gardelli's prompt, unfussy, and yet thrillingly delivered interpretation, clearly conveyed to his excellent Viennese forces. It's much more steadily and convincingly paced than Sinopoli's reading. The recording is forward and has plenty of presence, but it now sounds a little boxy beside the greater spaciousness of the DG. But the panache of the Decca enterprise silences criticism (except when the minute cuts in Nabucco's part are conceived). It's a pleasure to hear the bold inspiration of Verdi's first triumph conveyed with such conviction.

Listen to the Act 1 finale and you're sure to be won over to the set as an entity.

Nabucco (sung in English)
Alan Opie bar Nabucco **Leonardo Capalbo** ten Ismael **Alastair Miles** bass Zachariah **Susan Patterson** sop Abigail **Jane Irwin** mez Fenena **Dean Robinson** bass High Priest **Paul Wade** ten Abdullah **Camilla Roberts** sop Anna
Opera North Chorus and Orchestra / David Parry
Chandos Opera in English ② CHAN3136
(126' · DDD · S/T/N) Ⓜ**OO**➩

Opera in English is here fully justified by virtue of an excellent cast all-round who let us hear every word of the old, trusted translation by Norman Tucker and Tom Hammond, pioneers of giving works in the vernacular. But perhaps the most convincing reason for acquiring this set is the superb singing of the Opera North Chorus, who are in a sense this work's heroes. From start to finish they sing wholeheartedly and make the most of the text.

Heading the cast is Alan Opie, perhaps giving his best performance to date on disc. He reveals every facet of the troubled king's character. His early wilfulness, followed by madness and then his conversion to Jehovah, are all depicted with an unerring feeling for every word of the text. Of course the core of the opera comes in the great Act 3 duet with Abigail, then the noble solo 'Lord God of Judah', which Opie sings with proper sorrow and contrition.

In the duet he is partnered by Susan Patterson. She conveys every bit of the anti-heroine's scheming and unforgiving character, sings pretty much all of her taxing part with firm, full tone, then at the close shows suitable remorse in the Act 3 finale. As the one truly upright character, Zachariah, Alastair Miles proves his pre-eminence among British basses today in Verdi: every note of his two solos is sung with strength and a feeling for line, and he is as happy on high as below. Fenena is well served by Jane Irwin's lovely mezzo, shining forth in her Act 3 solo ending with a glorious high A. The one disappointment is the rather feeble Ismael, but he doesn't play a very big part in proceedings.

David Parry makes the most of Verdi's early, rudimentary style, conducting the piece for all its worth, supported finely by the Opera North Orchestra. We have the customary slightly over-reverberant Chandos sound, which at times favours the chorus and band at the expense of the soloists, but that is a minor blemish on a truly exemplary performance.

Nabucco
Leo Nucci bar Nabucco **Fabio Sartori** ten Ismaele **Carlo Colombara** bass Zaccaria **Maria Guleghina** sop Abigaille **Nino Surguladze** sop Fenena **Carlo Striuli** bass High Priest **Carlo Bosi** ten Abdallo **Patrizia Cigna** sop Anna
Verona Arena Chorus and Orchestra / Daniel Oren
Stage director **Denis Krief**
Video director **Tiziano Mancini**
Decca 📀 074 3245DH (141' · NTSC · 16:9 · HD · PCM stereo and DTS 5.1 stereo · 0)
Recorded live in 2007 Ⓕ

There is a good sense here of the fitness of things, and of their grandeur too. As the camera roves and observes the great arena before the show begins, one becomes probably more aware of its size than if one were there in person with the milling crowds trying to find a seat. For a roof there is the spacious firmament on high, and onstage a structure that might have been designed to fill the Tate Modern. Then, as the opera unfolds, Verdi's music fills the auditorium and merely human voices rise to their almost superhuman task.

Vocally, and perhaps dramatically, the opera is dominated by Abigaille, an outsize soprano whose music makes harder demands upon voice and technique than almost any comparable role in opera. Guleghina is the Abigaille of our time: powerful, intense, wide of range, agile in passagework, and when need arises capable of softness. If she were completely steady and if her timbre had an Italianate vibrancy and variety of coloration she would be ideal. As Nabucco, the veteran Nucci comes through with impressive authority and stamina, the middle of his voice still rich and ample. The High Priest, Zaccaria, the third major character, has one of the great bass roles in the Verdi repertoire: finely sung here by Carlo Colombara, firm, sonorous and noble in bearing.

Of the others, Fabio Sartori deserves mention, physically somewhat cumbersome, vocally full-bodied and incisive. Chorus and orchestra do the arena and its 2007 season credit, and the conductor, Daniel Oren, is well in control of his far-flung forces. The production team also wins its way through to grateful acknowledgment, despite the initial ill-will created by the blocks of scaffolding which suggest nothing more biblical than the local Ikea store in its early stages of construction. It has its uses, which include doing duty for the banks of the Euphrates, from which the Israelites sing (most beautifully) their immortal 'Va, pensiero'.

Otello

Otello
Plácido Domingo ten Otello **Cheryl Studer** sop Desdemona **Sergei Leiferkus** bar Iago **Ramón Vargas** ten Cassio **Michael Schade** ten Roderigo **Denyce Graves** mez Emilia **Ildebrando d'Arcangelo** bass Lodovico **Giacomo Prestia** bass Montano **Philippe Duminy** bass Herald **Hauts-de-Seine Maîtrise; Chorus and Orchestra of the Opéra-Bastille, Paris / Myung-Whun Chung**
DG ② 439 805-2GH2 (132' · DDD · T/t) Ⓕ**OO**➩

Just as *Othello* is a difficult play to bring off in the theatre, so *Otello* is a difficult opera to bring off out of it. For some years now, Domingo has been, on stage, the greatest Otello of our age. On record, though, he has had less success. Leiferkus and Domingo have worked closely together in the theatre; and it shows in scene after scene – nowhere more so than in the crucial sequence in Act 2 where Otello so rapidly ingests Iago's lethal poison. By bringing into the recording studio the feel and experience of a stage performance – meticulous study subtly modified by the improvised charge of the moment – both singers help defy the jinx that so often afflicts Otello on record. The skill of Leiferkus's performance is rooted in voice and technique: clear diction, a very disciplined rhythmic sense and a mastery of all ornament down to the most mordant of mordents. Above all, he's always there (usually stage right in this recording), steely-voiced, rabbiting on obsessively. We even hear his crucial interventions in the great Act 3 *concertato*.

Domingo is in superb voice; the sound seems golden as never before. Yet at the same time, it's a voice that's being more astutely deployed. To take that cruellest of all challenges to a studio-bound Otello, the great Act 3 soliloquy 'Dio! mi potevi', Domingo's performance is now simpler, more inward, more intense. It helps that his voice has darkened, winning back some of its russet baritonal colourings.

Chung's conducting is almost disarmingly vital. Verdi's scoring is more Gallic than Germanic. The score sounds very brilliant in the hands of the excellent Opéra-Bastille orchestra, and, in Act 4, very beautiful. Maybe Chung is wary of the emotional depths and, occasionally, the rhythmic infrastructure is muddled and unclear. And yet, the freshness is all gain. He's already a master of the big ensemble and the line of an act. Tension rarely slackens. On the rare occasions when it does, the mixing and matching of takes is probably to blame.

Studer's is a carefully drawn portrait of a chaste and sober-suited lady. Perhaps Verdi had a sweeter-voiced singer in mind for this paragon of 'goodness, resignation, and self-sacrifice' (Verdi's words, not Shakespeare's). Studer's oboe tones keep us at a certain distance, yet you'll look in vain for a better Desdemona. What's more, Studer is a singer who can single-mindedly focus the drama afresh, as she does more than once in Act 3. DG's recording is clear and unfussy and satisfyingly varied; Studer, in particular, is much helped by the beautifully open acoustic the engineers provide for the closing act. This is undoubtedly the best *Otello* on record since the early 1960s. It also happens to be the first time on disc that a great Otello at the height of his powers has been successfully caught in the context of a recording that can itself be generally considered worthy of the event, musically and technically.

Otello [H]
Giovanni Martinelli *ten* Otello **Elisabeth Rethberg** *sop* Desdemona **Lawrence Tibbett** *bar* Iago

Nicholas Massue *ten* Cassio **Giovanni Paltrinieri** *ten* Roderigo **Thelma Votipka** *mez* Emilia **Nicola Moscona** *bass* Lodovico **George Cehanovsky** *bass* Montano **Metropolitan Opera Orchestra and Chorus, New York / Ettore Panizza**
Naxos Historical mono ② 8 111018/9 (150' · ADD). Recorded live in 1938 ⑤▷

Not tall or ideally loud enough, his voice past its prime when (at over 50) he took the role into his repertoire, Giovanni Martinelli's Otello was a somewhat handicapped creation. He nevertheless wrung the heart, as Olin Downes (*New York Times*) put it, by conviction, subtlety and pathos: 'Mr Martinelli was Otello, in facial play and tragic bearing, the suggestion of great uncontrollable force and agony – a figure which never failed to evoke admiration and pity.'

On records he does more: almost every phrase comes to take the impress of his voice and style. The taut concentration of tone matches the emotional intensity; at every point a close and receptive study of the score has yielded its reward. Certainly there are things his voice would not do (take the high A flats at the end of the Love Duet softly, for instance), but it was still an impressive instrument. Walter Legge reported of his singing the role at Covent Garden in 1937 that 'a thread of pure gold runs through his voice', and he added that it was 'unlike any other tenor in the world today' save possibly the young Jüssi Björling, 23 years Martinelli's junior. At its best, as in the monologue, Martinelli's Otello remains finest of all.

The recording was pirated from radio and its transfer now is a triumph of Ward Marston's skill and hard work. He explains in a producer's note that the originals were not available for him to work on, but he has cleaned and restored so that the performance emerges more vividly than ever before. And what a performance!

The conductor Panizza was Toscanini's deputy in earlier years, and something of the master's energy is felt, in company with more flexibility and willingness to accommodate his singers. In Act 1 especially he makes frightening demands upon orchestra and chorus who, it must be said, meet them dauntlessly.

The recording, which places everything in such a bright light, is less than kind to Elisabeth Rethberg. Until recently hers had been a voice of special and most beautiful quality; but too many Aidas seem to have left their mark and the close recording catches an untoward hardness, though there is no mistaking the stylishness and a high degree of surviving mastery.

Tibbett's Iago is superbly caught, the best account of the role on records, not forgetting Gobbi. It is a mercurial portrayal, now genial, now ironic or insinuative, nakedly malignant. Like Martinelli, his response to every phrase is specific and vivid; and his voice resonates richly. It was for him the recording was made. Anyway, he deserves our gratitude twice over – for his own magnificent performance and for this inestimable gift to posterity.

Otello   H

Ramón Vinay ten Otello **Gré Brouwenstijn** sop
Desdemona **Otakar Kraus** bar Iago **John Lanigan**
ten Cassio **Raymond Nilsson** ten Roderigo **Noreen
Berry** mez Emilia **Marian Nowakowski** bass
Lodovico **Michael Langdon** bass Montano **Forbes
Robinson** bass Herald **Royal Opera House Chorus
and Orchestra, Covent Garden / Rafael Kubelík**
Royal Opera House Heritage Series mono ②
ROHS001 (140' · ADD · T/t) Recorded live 1955   M

This *Otello* of 1955, issued at long, long last,
marked Rafael Kubelík's accession as music director and the first staging by the company of Verdi's
tragedy. Excitement and expectation were high,
and the performance was electrifying – after more
than 50 years does it still sound as impressive?

Indeed it does, thanks not least to Kubelík's
superb conducting. Even today he remains
underrated as an opera conductor. Here he
combines the dramatic drive of Toscanini with
the more yielding approach of Serafin. While
never losing an overview of the score, he brings
out the myriad detail with an unerring ear for
what matters: the two big ensembles are nicely
contrasted with the plangent intricacies of
Desdemona's Willow Song and 'Ave Maria'.

Vinay's Moor is an overwhelming interpretation – a terrifying portrayal of love, jealousy
and anguish, sung in that peculiarly pained
tone of his; Vinay's timbre tears at the heart so
that one shares in his pain of the soul. Brouwenstijn is a most womanly and vulnerable Desdemona. In the love duet she is not quite at her
best but in the devastating Act 3 duet she sings
with tremenedous passion, and her Act 4 scena
is notable for sweet tone, musical accuracy and,
in the 'Ave Maria', a lovely *cantabile* and an
exquisitely poised high A flat at its end.

At the time there was disappointment that the
announced Iago, Tito Gobbi, was sacked by
Kubelík because of his failure to turn up for
rehearsals. He was replaced by the estimable
house baritone of the day, Otakar Kraus, who
brings an insinuating tone and plausible manner
based on obedience to the text. From his singing
alone one can almost visualise the bright-eyed,
scheming villain. John Lanigan, the company's
young lyric tenor of the day, provides a debonair
Cassio. The rest are more than adequate.

The mono sound is dim at times and one
would like a broader perspective, but one soon
forgets these limitations in the immediacy of the
performance. As well as any of its successors, it
fulfils the exigent demands Verdi places on his
cast and Vinay here surpasses even his own high
standards. His murder of Desdemona and its
terrible aftermath are truly tragic.

Additional recommendations

Otello

Domingo Otello **Scotto** Desdemona **Milnes** Iago
**National Philharmonic Orchestra; Ambrosian
Opera Chorus / Levine**

RCA ② 88687 44820-2 (134' · ADD)   M O
For some this is the finest of Domingo's several
recorded Otellos. Also, Scotto's Desdemona is one
of the most moving on disc. At mid price this set is
a real winner.

Vickers Otello **Rysanek** Desdemona **Gobbi** Iago
Rome Opera Chorus and Orchestra / Serafin
RCA ② 09026 63180-2 (144' · ADD)   M
Tito Gobbi's Iago remains irreplaceable (except
possibly for Giuseppe Valdengo's for Toscanini),
and Jon Vickers is a superb Otello, more metallic
and heroic than Domingo though not necessarily
more sensitive.

Otello

Plácido Domingo ten Otello **Kiri Te Kanawa** sop
Desdemona **Sergei Leiferkus** bar Iago **Robin
Leggate** ten Cassio
**Chorus and Orchestra of the Royal Opera House,
Covent Garden / Sir Georg Solti**
Stage director **Elijah Moshinsky**
Video director **Brian Large**
Opus Arte 🅿 OAR3102D
(145' · NTSC · 4:3 · PCM stereo and 2.0 · 0)
Recorded live at the Royal Opera House, Covent
Garden, London in 1992   M

At Covent Garden, Elijah Moshinsky's production insists heavily on its religious agenda: Christ
crucified looms at the back, dominant as in the
east window of a cathedral. In the film version
(because the camera roams) it is more a suggestive
presence, less a directional imposition. If the
opening storm is prefigurative, the Byzantine
Christ may have a valid place among the chaos of
images that bewilders the eye in the first few minutes; and though initially it may seem that the
film crew are finding it impossible to capture at
once the detail and the overall picture of the complex stage action, the confusion makes its own
point and of course resolves itself into reassuring
single focus with Otello's entry. The boldness of
pictorial imagination at work here can be appreciated by comparison with the conventional battery
of stage lightning in Graham Vick's production at
La Scala (filmed in 2001 and also with Domingo),
where the chorus is simply a mass embodiment of
terror and awe, unlike Moshinsky's where all are
individuals with a task in hand and up against a
real emergency.

We then look on, helpless, as order turns to
chaos in the unfolding tragedy. Here again film
probes the principal characters. Conventional
operatic gestures and facial expressions will not
do, and it is deeply impressive, and moving, to
see how completely Domingo lives his role. Te
Kanawa too shows herself alive to every suggestion of her music and words (it is utterly wrong
to represent her here as bland or uncomprehending). Leiferkus is a powerful embodiment
of malign will, and, as with the others, his voice,
sure in its bony-hard definition, is the perfect
instrument of his character. As much again
could now be written about Domingo's singing,
and Te Kanawa's, and about Solti's conducting,

but a video demands attention to the visual. Suffice to say that you can have the highest expectation and not be disappointed.

Otello   Ⓗ
Mario Del Monaco *ten* Otello **Rosanna Carteri** *sop*
Desdemona **Renato Capecchi** *bar* Iago **Gino**
Mattera *ten* Cassio **Athos Cesarini** *ten* Roderigo
Luisella Ciaffi *mez* Emilia **Plinio Clabassi** *bass*
Lodovico **Nestore Catalani** *bass* Montano **Bruno**
Cioni *bass* Herald **Chorus and Orchestra of RAI,**
Milan / Tullio Serafin
Film director **Franco Enriquez**
Hardy Classic Video 📀 HCD4004 (136' · NTSC ·
4:3 Black & White · 1.0 · 0 · N) Recorded 1958   Ⓕ

This film of *Otello* isn't to be overlooked, in spite of its age, because of the quality of the performance. It formed part of Italian television's pioneering series of productions employing the top rank of native singers when such a group still existed. On this occasion a well-known opera director, Franco Enriquez, was employed to achieve as much as was possible in terms of dramatic fluidity within the technical restrictions then applicable in the studio. The acting of minor characters may be a bit stilted, but the principals, who come under face-to-face scrutiny, stand up well to Enriquez's methods.

So preserved here is a native account of Verdi's masterpiece that would be hard to equal today. Mario Del Monaco was then at the height of his powers, the reigning Otello of the time, and one of the role's most powerful exponents ever. His portrayal had developed by the late 1950s into a psychological study of some depth and intensity, released on a stream of taut, exciting tone. By his side, Renato Capecchi sings a strongly voiced, highly articulate, intelligently shaped and believable Iago. But perhaps the most compelling performance of all is Rosanna Carteri's Desdemona. Love, fidelity and sincerity are conveyed in her eyes, indeed her whole being, and in her faultless vocal traversal of the role. Over all presides Serafin, conducting an unobtrusively correct and vital performance of a score he knew so well.

There are downsides. The lip-synch, especially in the case of Capecchi, leaves much to be desired. The sound is confined and occasionally wayward, and the film is obviously a shade worn, but all that's easily forgotten when you're caught up in such a convincing performance.

Otello
Plácido Domingo *ten* Otello **Barbara Frittoli** *sop*
Desdemona **Leo Nucci** *bar* Iago **Cesare Catani** *ten*
Cassio **Antonello Ceron** *ten* Roderigo **Rossana**
Rinaldi *mez* Emilia **Giovanni Battista Parodi** *bass*
Lodovico **Cesare Lana** *bass* Montano **Ernesto**
Panariello *bass* Herald **Giuseppe Verdi**
Conservatory Children's Choir, Milan; La Scala
Children's Choir, Chorus and Orchestra, Milan /
Riccardo Muti
Stage director **Graham Vick**
Video director **Carlo Battistoni**

VERDI OTELLO – IN BRIEF

Plácido Domingo *Otello* **Cheryl Studer**
Desdemona **Sergei Leiferkus** *Iago* **Bastille Opera**
Chorus and Orchestra / Myung-Whun Chung
DG ② 439 805-2GH2 (132' · DDD)   ⒻⓄⓄ🅑➔
Chung's high-octane conducting sets the standard for a marvellous set, with Domingo at his peak of vocal power and expression and Sergei Leiferkus a smooth-voiced, subtle Iago.

Jon Vickers *Otello* **Leonie Rysanek** *Desdemona*
Tito Gobbi *Iago* **Rome Opera Chorus and**
Orchestra / Tullio Serafin
RCA ② 09026 63180-2 (144' · ADD)   Ⓜ Ⓞ
Jon Vickers is a heroically anguished Moor in his first recording, with Gobbi a marvellously rich and malevolent Iago, and Rysanek a large-voiced but vulnerable Desdemona. Serafin's conducting is splendidly powerful.

Jon Vickers *Otello* **Mirella Freni** *Desdemona*
Peter Glossop *Iago* **Berlin Deutsche Oper**
Chorus; Berlin PO / Herbert von Karajan
EMI ② 769308-2 (140' · ADD)   Ⓜ🅑➔
Karajan's recording comes up better on his spectacular film version, but since this isn't presently available the CD is still recommendable at mid-price, with Freni's deeply touching Desdemona and Peter Glossop's characterfully nasty Iago.

Otello
Giovanni Martinelli *Otello* **Elisabeth Rethberg**
Desdemona **Lawrence Tibbett** *Iago*
Metropolitan Opera Orchestra and Chorus,
New York / Ettore Panizza
Naxos Historical mono ② 8 111018/9 (150' · ADD).
                                      Ⓢ🅑➔
Recorded live in 1938 this tremendous performance enshrines the magnificent Otello of Giovanni Martinelli: a towering characterisation that demands to be heared. Tibbett's Iago is comparably superb; only Rethberg is slightly under-par.

Plácido Domingo *Otello* **Barbara Frittoli**
Desdemona **Leo Nucci** *Iago* **Chorus and**
Orchestra of La Scala, Milan / Riccardo Muti
TDK 📀 DV-OPOTEL (140')   ⒻⓄ
In this well-staged 2001 recording Domingo is in drier voice than in his younger selves, but still overwhelming. Barbara Frittoli is a deeply felt Desdemona. Muti conducts with spirit.

Plácido Domingo *Otello* **Renée Fleming**
Desdemona **James Morris** *Iago* **Metropolitan**
Opera Chorus and Orchestra / James Levine
DG 📀 073 092-9GH (142')   Ⓕ
A fine 1995 stage version from the Met, with Domingo a commanding Moor, Renée Fleming a beautiful Desdemona and James Morris, though not the most menacing Iago, credible and richly sung. Levine's conducting, while not as lively as Muti's, is still enjoyable.

TDK Mediactive 📀 DV-OPOTEL (140' · 16:9 · PCM
Stereo, 5.1 & DTS 5.1· 0)   Ⓕ🔴🔴

This is one of Graham Vick's most intelligent,
detailed and involving productions housed in
Ezio Frigero's superbly crafted and atmospheric
set and clothed by Franca Squarciapino's traditional, beautifully wrought costumes. Here's
proof, if proof were needed, that setting an
opera in its period still works best provided you
have such sensitive hands in control.

The thoughtful, often revelatory, handling of
the principals often lends a new dimension to
the work, especially with such eloquent singing
actors as Plácido Domingo and Barbara Frittoli;
remarkable is the strength of passion engendered by the fated lovers – blissful in Act 1, desperately tormented in Act 3.

At this late stage in his career Domingo was
able to compensate for a voice that doesn't
always obey his exemplary instincts with a moving portrayal of the Moor. His projection of his
own near-disbelief in his agony and jealousy in
Act 3, and again before the murder, is deeply
affecting. So are Frittoli's facial expressions and
body language, yielding and erotic in Act 1,
making her Act 3 and final disillusion that much
more terrifying to behold. Vocally Domingo
sings with even more variety of dynamic and
timbre than before. His pent-up fury in the big
ensemble is truly frightening. Frittoli sings with
many shades of tone and exquisite phrasing
throughout, not least in her Act 4 solos, which
she enacts with searing emotion. Leo Nucci's
penny-plain, dully sung Iago isn't in the same
league, and the young tenor taking Cassio lacks
the requisite sweetness in the voice. The Emilia
is admirable, as are the two basses. Muti leads
the drama to its dreadful conclusion with his
customary brio and care for incidentals.

The video direction and the sound picture leave
nothing to be desired. This is the only modern-
day DVD of *Otello* worth having at present.

Rigoletto

Rigoletto   Ⓗ
Leonard Warren *bar* Rigoletto **Bidú Sayão** *sop* Gilda
Jussi Björling *ten* Duke **Norman Cordon** *bass*
Sparafucile **Martha Lipton** *contr* Maddalena **William
Hargrave** *bass* Monterone **Thelma Altman** *sop*
Giovanna **Richard Manning** *ten* Borsa **George
Cehanovsky** *bar* Marullo **Maxine Stellman** *mez*
Countess Ceprano **John Baker** *bass* Count Ceprano
**Metropolitan Opera Chorus and Orchestra, New
York / Cesare Sodero**
Naxos Historical ② 8 110051/2 (116' · ADD) Recorded
live 1945   Ⓢ🔴🔴

This performance marked the return of Björling
to the Met after a wartime break of four years
spent mostly in his native Sweden. And what a
return it was: at 34 he was at the absolute peak of
his powers and sings a Duke of Mantua imbued
with supreme confidence and tremendous brio
– just try the start of the Quartet. He and the

house clearly revel in his display of tenor
strength, yet that power is always tempered by
innate artistry. If not a subtle interpreter, he's
always a thoughtful one, and never indulges
himself or his audience.

Similarly, Warren was, at the time, at the zenith
of his career. Vocally he's in total command of the
role and the house. His reading, although slightly
extroverted in some areas, evinces a firm tone, a
secure line and many shades of colour. He's at is
very best in his two duets with Gilda (sadly and
heinously cut about) and no wonder, given the
beautiful, plangent singing of Sayão, whose
'Caro nome' is so delicately phrased, touching
and keenly articulated. 'Tutte le feste' is still better, prompting Paul Jackson (who in general is
unjustifiably hard on the performance in *Saturday Afternoons at the old Met*, Duckworth:1992)
to comment that Sayão's 'lovely, pliant, fully
rounded tones are immediately affecting'.
Indeed, in spite of the merits of the two male
principals, it's her truly memorable interpretation that makes this set essential listening.

All round, there are few recordings that match
this one for vocal distinction – perhaps only the
Serafin-Callas-Gobbi on EMI and the Giulini-
Cotrubas-Cappuccilli on DG. They are much
more expensive but boast superior sound. Björling and Warren both made later studio sets,
but neither matches his live contribution here,
off the stage.

The final virtue of this absorbing experience
is the conducting of the little-known Sodero.
His moderate – but never sluggish – tempos
allow for almost ideal articulation on all sides,
and his insistence on letting us hear the score so
clearly makes one regret even more all those
excisions then common in the opera house and
the studios.

Rigoletto   Ⓗ
Tito Gobbi *bar* Rigoletto **Maria Callas** *sop* Gilda
Giuseppe di Stefano *ten* Duke **Nicola Zaccaria** *bass*
Sparafucile **Adriana Lazzarini** *mez* Maddalena **Plinio
Clabassi** *bass* Monterone **Giuse Gerbino** *mez*
Giovanna **Renato Ercolani** *ten* Borsa **William Dickie**
bar Marullo **Elvira Galassi** *sop* Countess Ceprano
Carlo Forti *bass* Count Ceprano **Chorus and
Orchestra of La Scala, Milan / Tullio Serafin**
EMI mono ② 556327-2 or Regis RRC2076 (118' · ADD
· N/T/t) Recorded 1955   Ⓜ/Ⓢ🔴🔴

That one recording should continue to hold
sway over many other attractive comers after 45
years is simply a tribute to Callas, Gobbi, Serafin
and Walter Legge. Whatever the merits of its
successors, and they are many, no Rigoletto has
surpassed Gobbi in tonal variety, line, projection of character and understanding of what
Rigoletto is about; no Gilda has come anywhere
near Callas in meaningful phrasing – listen to
'Caro nome' or 'Tutte le feste' on any other set
if you're disbelieving – nor achieved such a careful differentiation of timbre before and after
her seduction; no conductor matches Serafin
in judging tempo and instrumental detail on a

nicety; nor benefited from a chorus and orchestra bred in the tradition of La Scala; no producer has equalled Legge in recording voices rather than the space round them. And di Stefano? Well, he may not be so stylish a Duke as some others, but the 'face' he gives his singing, and the sheer physical presence he conveys, not to mention his forward diction, are also unique in this opera. Nothing in this world is perfect, and so there are some small drawbacks here. Serafin sadly makes small cuts in the first Gilda-Rigoletto duet and omits entirely the Duke's cabaletta as used to be practice in the theatre. Gobbi could be said not to have quite the weight of voice ideally called for by a Verdi baritone role. Finally, the recording, although immeasurably improved from previous issues of the set, still has one or two places of distortion obviously present on the original tape. In every other way, this remains the classic performance on record.

Rigoletto

Paolo Gavanelli bar Rigoletto **Christine Schäfer** sop Gilda **Marcelo Álvarez** ten Duke **Eric Halfvarson** bass Sparafucile **Graciela Araya** contr Maddalena **Giovanni Battista Parodi** bass Monterone **Elizabeth Sikora** sop Giovanna **Peter Auty** ten Borsa **Quentin Hayes** bar Marullo **Dervla Ramsay** mez Countess Ceprano **Graeme Broadbent** bass Count Ceprano **Andrea Hazell** mez Page **Nigel Cliffe** bass Usher **Royal Opera House Orchestra and Chorus, Covent Garden / Edward Downes**
Stage director **David McVicar**
Film director **Sue Judd**
Opus Arte Media 📀 OA0829D (169' · 16:9 · 5.1 · 0)   Ⓕ🔵

David McVicar's engrossing 2001 production of *Rigoletto* at Covent Garden caused something of a stir because of the frank licentiousness of the opening scene, including sex of all varieties. It's a bold and sensational beginning to the staging, depicting the Duke of Mantua as a libidinous and strident ruler of his ill-disciplined domain. Given that picture of the court, the contrast of Rigoletto's almost obsessive love for his daughter is all the more poignant.

That's the background to a performance of thrilling commitment on all sides, at whose centre is the arresting portrayal of Rigoletto from Paolo Gavanelli, probably the best acted and most sensitively sung, in terms of variety and colouring of tone, since Tito Gobbi essayed the role in the same house 35 years ago (even if he has an occasional tendency to lose pitch).

By comparison, Christine Schäfer's Gilda is a trifle cool at the start, but once ravished she comes to emotional life and is particularly moving in the final act. Her singing, though not Italianate in colour, is musically shaped and technically flawless. Marcelo Álvarez is the epitome of a selfish, macho ruler, and Eric Halfvarson a suitably sinister Sparafucile. Downes conducts a well-nigh faultless account. The only reservation concerns the sound. Too frequently the voices are too backwardly placed in relation

---

VERDI RIGOLETTO – IN BRIEF

Leonard Warren Rigoletto **Bidù Sayão** Gilda Ⓗ
Jussi Björling Duke **Metropolitan Opera Chorus and Orchestra / Cesare Sodero**
Naxos mono ② 8 110051/2 (116' · AAD) Ⓢ🔵🔵🔵▸
A superb performance live from the New York Met in this bargain-price 1945 set, although the sound wouldn't make it everyone's first choice.

Tito Gobbi Rigoletto **Maria Callas** Gilda Ⓗ
Giuseppe di Stefano Duke **Chorus and Orchestra of La Scala, Milan / Tullio Serafin**
EMI mono ② 556327-2 or Regis RRC2076 (118' · AAD)   Ⓕ🔵🔵▸
Equally historic but in much finer sound, though still mono, this 1955 version has the great trio of principals with Serafin's dynamic conducting; Regis adds a pair of bonus arias.

Renato Bruson Rigoletto **Edita Gruberová** Gilda **Neil Shicoff** Duke **Santa Cecilia Academy Chorus and Orchestra / Giuseppe Sinopoli**
Philips ② 462 158-2PM2 (128' · DDD)   Ⓜ
Renato Bruson and Edita Gruberová head a good cast in a fine modern version, though Neil Shicoff's Duke is sometimes rather forced. Sinopoli's exciting reading is less eccentric in its tempi than usual.

Piero Cappuccilli Rigoletto **Ileana Cortrubas** Gilda **Plácido Domingo** Duke **Vienna State Opera Chorus; Vienna PO / Carlo Maria Giulini**
DG ② 457 753-2GOR2 (128' · DDD)   Ⓜ🔵▸
Giulini's graceful, detailed conducting has plenty of drama, still more so a strong cast headed by Plácido Domingo, Piero Cappuccilli's restrained jester and Ileana Cotrubas's meltingly vulnerable Gilda.

Robert Merrill Rigoletto **Anna Moffo** Gilda **Alfredo Kraus** Duke **RCA Italiana Opera Chorus and Orchestra / Sir Georg Solti**
RCA ② 82876 70785-2 (113' · ADD)   Ⓜ
The 1960s Solti at high voltage may not suit everyone, but this is an exciting and splendidly cast set – Alfredo Kraus in his elegant prime, Anna Moffo a beautifully girlish Gilda, Robert Merrill's rich-voiced jester, uncharacteristically expressive, and for once, among the supporting cast, the commanding Monterone that Verdi required.

Paolo Gavanelli Rigoletto **Christine Schäfer** Gilda **Marcelo Álvarez** Duke **Chorus and Orchestra of the Royal Opera House / Edward Downes**
BBC Opus Arte 📀 OA0829D (169')   Ⓕ
This highly modern but recognisable Covent Garden staging, splendidly conducted by Sir Edward Downes, stands out among DVDs. Paolo Gavanelli is a magnificent jester, Marcello Alvarez a swaggering Duke and Christine Schäfer's clear-voiced Gilda detailed and moving.

to the orchestra, but that shouldn't deter you from being part of a very special occasion.

Simon Boccanegra

Simon Boccanegra
Piero Cappuccilli bar Simon Boccanegra **Mirella Freni** sop Amelia **José Carreras** ten Gabriele **Nicolai Ghiaurov** bass Fiesco **José van Dam** bass-bar Paolo **Giovanni Foiani** bass Pietro **Antonio Savastano** ten Captain **Maria Fausta Gallamini** sop Maid **Chorus and Orchestra of La Scala, Milan / Claudio Abbado**
DG The Originals ② 449 752-2GOR2 (136' · ADD · T/t) Recorded 1977 　　　　Ⓜ🔘🔘▷

This famous recording has become a classic, a studio performance following a series of performances at La Scala in the Strehler staging. The close, slightly claustrophobic recording exactly mirrors the mood of nefarious activities and intrigues following Boccanegra's rise to be Doge of Genoa, he and his lovely daughter victims of the dark deeds round them. In his plebeian being, clement exercise of authority and warm, fatherly love, Simon Boccanegra is made for Cappuccilli, who, under Abbado's tutelage, sings it not only *con amore* but with exemplary, delicately tinted tone and unbelievably long-breathed phrasing. As his daughter Amelia, Freni was just entering her quasi-spinto phase and expands her lyric voice easily into the greater demands of this more dramatic role. Similarly heavier duties hadn't yet tarnished the youthful ardour and sap in the tone of the 30-year-old Carreras. As the implacable Fiesco, Ghiaurov exudes vengeful command, and van Dam evil machinations as the villain Paolo. Over all presides Abbado in what remains one of his greatest recordings, alert to every facet of the wondrous score, timing every scene, in an opera tricky to pace, to near-perfection, and bringing theatrical drama into the home. This set should be essential to any reputable collection of Verdi.

Stiffelio

Stiffelio
José Carreras ten Stiffelio **Catherine Malfitano** sop Lina **Gwynne Howell** bass Jorg **Gregory Yurisich** bar Stankar **Adele Paxton** sop Dorotea **Robin Leggate** ten Raffaele di Leuthold **Lynton Atkinson** ten Federico di Frengel **Chorus and Orchestra of the Royal Opera House, Covent Garden / Edward Downes**
Stage director **Elijah Moshinsky**
Video director **Brian Large**
Opus Arte 📀 OAR3103D (122' · NTSC · 4:3 · 2.0 · 0) Recorded live at the Royal Opera House, Covent Garden, London, on February 2 and 6, 1993 　Ⓕ🔘🔘

In 2007 *Stiffelio* was reported sinking under the weight of a lavish production at the Metropolitan. At Covent Garden, the production team, led by Elijah Moshinsky, had much more the right idea and, in one decision of casting, the visual element is transformed. The opera has only one female among the principals, and, rather as in *Otello*, the action turns on her largely passive character. She is Lina, wife of the minister of a Protestant community where the way of life is simple and biblical law is strictly upheld. At the Met she is played by Sharon Sweet whose ample form and golden curls suggest (however unjustly) an ungodly allowance of worldly pleasure. In her husband's absence she has 'fallen', and Catherine Malfitano (the Lina at Covent Garden) is attractive enough to make that seem plausible while remaining in figure and demeanour one of the devout, and a 'pure' woman at heart.

The other major difference in production is one of scale. At the Metropolitan everything has gone up in the world. The minister's house is palatial, the modest gathering to celebrate his return a full-scale ambassador's dinner party. Lina's father is decked out in full military grandeur, while at Covent Garden he is clad in simple civilian dignity. Covent Garden's graveyard is a matter of plain stones and crosses; the Met's sports elaborate and (surely) abhorred images. In every respect the London production is better, with unostentatious care taken over furnishings and each member of the chorus provided with an identity.

The *Stiffelio* is Carreras in what was probably the finest achievement among roles following his serious illness. Gregory Yurisich sings magnificently as the father. Gwynne Howell is a pillar of sonorous authority, and Robin Leggate, having played Cassio so often, fits in perfectly as his guilty counterpart. Edward Downes conducts with a sure and thoughtful touch.

La traviata

La traviata　　　　　　　　　　　　　　　Ⓗ
Maria Callas sop Violetta Valéry **Alfredo Kraus** ten Alfredo Germont **Mario Sereni** bar Giorgio Germont **Laura Zanini** mez Flora Bervoix **Piero De Palma** ten Gastone **Alvaro Malta** bar Baron Douphol **Maria Cristina de Castro** sop Annina **Alessandro Maddalena** bass Doctor Grenvil **Vito Susca** bass Marquis D'Obigny **Manuel Leitao** ten Messenger **Chorus and Orchestra of the Teatro Nacional de San Carlos, Lisbon / Franco Ghione**
EMI mono ② 556330-2 (123' · ADD · T/t) Recorded live 1958 　　　　　　　　Ⓜ🔘🔘▷

Callas caught live is preferable to Callas recorded in the studio, and Violetta was perhaps her supreme role. The former Covent Garden producer Ande Anderson pointedly commented that, whereas other sopranos made you cry in the final act of *Traviata*, Callas also made you cry in the second, and one hears here what he meant, as Callas's Violetta comes to the stark realisation that she's going to have to give up her one and only true beloved seemingly for ever. The desperation that enters her voice at 'Non sapete' is surpassed only by the sorrow and emptiness in the lead-in to 'Dite alla giovine', then the fatalism of 'morro! la mia memoria', which

John Steane in his note that accompanies this essential CD reissue describes as being sung with such 'fullness of heart and voice'.

The final act is almost unbearable in its poignancy of expression:the reading of the letter so natural in its feeling of emptiness, the realisation that the doctor is lying so truthful, the sense of hollowness at what's possibly the opera's most moving moment, 'Ma se tornando …': 'If in returning you haven't saved my life, then nothing can save it.' All this and so much else suggests that Callas understood better than anyone else what this role is truly about.

But there's more to it even than that. Alfredo Kraus's Alfredo as heard here is as appealing as any on record. His Schipa-like tone at that stage in his career, his refinement of phrasing, especially in the duets with Callas, and his elegant yet ardent manner are exactly what the role requires. Mario Sereni may not quite be in the class of his colleagues but his Germont père is securely, sincerely and often perceptively sung and more acutely characterised than in his account of the part with de los Angeles. Almost as important, contrary to what you may read in some earlier reviews, Franco Ghione is an expert, knowledgeable conductor of this score, yielding to his singers yet prompt and dramatic when need be, and able to draw singing string tone from his excellent orchestra in the two preludes. So are there any drawbacks? Yes indeed; the prompter is all too audible, the audience coughs intrusively, particularly during the recitative at the start of Act 3, and the score is extensively cut in the manner traditional to pre-authentic days. Nevertheless, if it's to be but one *Traviata* in your collection, it must be this one.

La traviata
Angela Gheorghiu *sop* Violetta **Frank Lopardo** *ten* Alfredo **Leo Nucci** *bar* Germont **Leah-Marian Jones** *mez* Flora **Gillian Knight** *mez* Annina **Robin Leggate** *ten* Gaston **Richard Van Allan** *bass* Baron **Roderick Earle** *bass* Marquis **Mark Beesley** *bass* Doctor **Neil Griffiths** *ten* Giuseppe **Bryan Secombe** *bass* Messenger **Rodney Gibson** *ten* Servant **Chorus and Orchestra of the Royal Opera House, Covent Garden / Sir Georg Solti**
Decca ② 448 119-2DHO2 (127' · DDD · T/t) Recorded live 1994　　　　　　　　　　　　　　Ⓕ**Ⓞ**➔

For Angela Gheorghiu, Violetta was the right role at the right time. The whole drama is there in her voice, every expression in the eyes and beat of the heart reflected in the way she shapes and colours Verdi's vocal lines. Her quiet singing is particularly lovely, affording subtle variations of tenderness and inner anxiety. When she does choose to make a point with force, as in her sudden warmth of feeling towards Giorgio Germont at 'Qual figlia m'abbracciate' or her chilling cry of 'Morro!', accompanied by a loud thump on the table, her ideas always hit home. A few moments of vocal weakness are accentuated by the microphone, mainly a tendency to go sharp and some hardness at the top of the voice that

was not troublesome in the theatre. Otherwise she's the most complete and moving Violetta we have had since her compatriot, Ileana Cotrubas.

These live performances were the first time that Sir Georg Solti, at the age of 82, had conducted a staged *La traviata* and he wanted two young singers who were also coming fresh to the opera. What was so spellbinding in the theatre was the touching intimacy they brought to their scenes together. Instead of the duets for Violetta and Alfredo turning into standard Italian operatic bawling, they became lovers' whispers. The effect comes across here in the cadenzas, where Gheorghiu and Frank Lopardo really seem to be listening to each other. Elsewhere, one is more aware than in the theatre that Lopardo's light tenor is far from being an idiomatic Italian voice. His idiosyncratic tone quality and un-Italian vowels can be problematical, as is some ungainly lifting up into notes. Leo Nucci, Decca's resident Verdi baritone at the time, makes a standard Giorgio Germont, not more, and apart from Leah-Marian Jones's energetic Flora, the smaller roles don't say a great deal for the Royal Opera's depth of casting.

Solti insisted that the opera be performed complete. But there's nothing studied about his conducting: the performance is fresh and alive from the first note to the last, the result of a lifetime's experience of how to pace a drama in the opera house . With the increasing number of live opera sets, a recommendation for *La traviata* is likely to be based on whether one is prepared to accept noises-off or not. Decca's recording is well balanced and vivid, dancing feet and banging doors included. Among the live sets, Giulini and Callas at La Scala in 1955 must be *hors concours*, but in rather awful sound. Muti's more recent La Scala set, in which he has to wrestle with Tiziana Fabbricini's wayward talents as Violetta, is the nearest comparison.

La traviata
Norah Amsellem *sop* Violetta **José Bros** *ten* Alfredo **Renato Bruson** *bar* Germont **Itxaro Mentxaka** *mez* Flora **Maria Espada** *sop* Annina **Emilio Sánchez** *ten* Gastone **David Rubiera** *bar* Baron **Marco Moncloa** *bar* Marquis **Chorus and Orchestra of the Teatro Real, Madrid / Jesús López Cobos**
Stage Director **Pier Luigi Pizzi**
Opus Arte ② **DVD** OA0934D (175' · NTSC · 16:9 · PCM stereo and DTS 5.1 · 0) Recorded live at the Teatro Real, Madrid in 2005　　　　　　　　Ⓕ

Pier Luigi Pizzi's updating of *Traviata* to occupied Paris, first seen in 2003 in Madrid, might seem gratuitous, but because of his skill as designer and his experience directing singers, the new milieu hardly ever interferes, after the opening scene, with the central tragedy of Violetta's plight. That owes much to the freshness and immediacy of the portrayal by Norah Amsellem. From Violetta's first fevered entry to her agonising death she is totally absorbed in the role, acting and singing with the most eloquent feeling.

VERDI LA TRAVIATA – IN BRIEF

Maria Callas *Violetta* **Alfredo Kraus** *Alfredo* **Ⓗ**
Mario Sereni *Germont* **San Carlos Theatre**
Lisbon Chorus and Orchestra / Franco Ghione
EMI ② 556330-2 (124' · AAD)   **ⓂOO**
Callas incarnates the doomed Violetta unlike
any rival, with Alfredo Kraus a poised,
plangent Alfredo, even if Ghione is not quite
their equal, the traditional cuts are made and
the live recording is not brilliant.

Ileana Cotrubas *Violetta* **Plácido Domingo**
Alfredo **Sherrill Milnes** *Germont* **Bavarian State**
Opera Chorus and Orchestra / Carlos Kleiber
DG ② 477 7115GOR2 (106' · ADD)   **ⒻO**
Cotrubas makes a more touching heroine than
Callas, vocally glorious and ardently sup-
ported by Domingo's Alfredo and Kleiber's
tautly dramatic conducting. Despite tradi-
tional cuts, a deeply moving performance.

Angela Gheorghiu *Violetta* **Frank Lopardo**
Alfredo **Leo Nucci** *Germont* **Chorus and**
Orchestra of the Royal Opera House /
Sir Georg Solti
Decca ② 448 119-2DHO2 (127' · DDD)   **ⒻOD→**
Decca ⌗ 071 431-9DH (135')   **ⒻO**
The famous performance that marked Gheor-
ghiu's début appearance and one of Solti's
last. Splendidly recorded and alive – but do
consider the DVD. The production is lively
but unexceptional, with a decent supporting
cast, but it's still immensely involving.

Norah Amsellem *Violetta* **José Bros** *Alfredo*
Renato Bruson *Germont* **Chorus and Orchestra**
of the Teatro Real, Madrid / Jesús López Cobos
Opus Arte ② **DVD** OA0934D   **ⒻO**
A wonderfully sensitive updating of La traviata to wartime France. A fine cast acts and
sings magnificently.

Stefania Bonfadelli *Violetta* **Scott Piper** *Alfredo*
Renato Bruson *Germont* **Arturo Toscanini**
Foundation Chorus and Orchestra / Plácido
Domingo
TDK Mediactive **DVD** DV-OPLTR (205')   **Ⓕ**
Franco Zeffirelli brings his long expereince
of this opera to a largely young cast - Stefania
Bonfadelli is a lovely actress as well as a vocal
imaginative Violetta. Scott Piper imbues
Alfredo with considerable ardour. The vet-
eran Renato Bruson is a typically implacable
Germont. Domingo conducts efficiently.

In the first scene we see her entering her soirée from her bedroom, the stage split in two – a
slightly questionable idea – and she becomes
infatuated with Alfredo in their Act 1 duet while
on her lavish bed. It sounds gimmicky but as
played by Amsellem and the sympathetic and
stylishly sung Alfredo of José Bros it is totally
convincing. The act ends with an all-consuming
account of 'Ah! fors e lui', both verses, shaped in
long lines and phrased with unerring conviction
so that one forgives harshness when she presses
on her higher notes.

Act 2 scene 1 is set in the drawing-room of a
1930s-style country villa. Here the central
encounter of Violetta and Germont *père* is the
emotional centre of the work, as it should be,
with Amsellem and Renato Bruson acting and
reacting to each other with rewarding rapport.
Bruson, at 69, sings with all the experience of
his years and few signs of wear, and follows it
with a masterly account of 'Di provenza'. In the
second scene the whole company excels itself
and the heroine is infinitely touching in
'Alfredo, Alfredo'.

In a stark, simple set for Act 3, this Violetta
conveys her sorrow and terrified thoughts with
inward passion. 'Addio del passato', again two
verses, is notable for the length of line and exquisite phrasing Amsellem provides. She and Bros
sing a near-ideal 'Parigi, o cara' before Violetta
dies, a desperately tragic figure. Amsellem's slim
figure and expressive face are notable assets in
achieving her intelligent reading.

López-Cobos conducts an interpretation
notable for yielding support of his singers combined with dramatic dash, and the Madrid
orchestra play as though their lives depended on
the results. No wonder this staging has received
so much praise in Spain. Its preservation on
DVD is welcome.

La traviata
Angela Gheorghiu *sop* Violetta **Natascha Petrinsky**
mez Flora **Ramón Vargas** *ten* Alfredo Germont
Roberto Frontali *bar* Giorgio Germont **Tiziana**
Tramonti *sop* Annina **Enrico Cossutta** *ten* Gastone
Alessandro Paliaga *bar* Barone Douphol **Piero**
Terranova *bass* Marchese d'Obigny **Luigi Roni** *bass*
Doctor Grenvil **Chorus and Orchestra of La Scala,**
Milan / Lorin Maazel
Stage director **Liliana Cavani**
Video director **Paolo Longobardo**
ArtHaus Musik **DVD** 101 343 (134' · NTSC · 16:9 · PCM
stereo, 5.1 and DTS 5.1 · 0)
Recorded live in 2007   **ⒻO**

Nothing is perfect, always some stammer in the
divine speech: we know that. But such blemishes
as occur in the Scala production are incidental to
its general excellence and to the greatness of
Angela Gheorghiu's Violetta. She is a strangely
variable quantity in the musical life of our time
but here she is once again a true artist, the voice
lovely as ever throughout most of its range, the
expressive art in both singing and acting
matured so that this portrayal is intensely mov-

ing and memorable. Here is a Violetta who rises to the great moments but whose every phrase and movement is intelligently guided and deeply felt. The internal argument in the solo of Act 1, for instance, develops with a marvellously subtle conflict of impulses, and though 'pleasure' wins at the end of it there has been just the right degree of forced gaiety to make it no surprise to find in Act 2 that love has prevailed after all.

The Germonts, son and father, are maddeningly stupid characters but decent, honest singers, the one (Ramón Vargas) not imaginative but capable of delicacy, the other (Roberto Frontali) clean-cut in his tone and modestly affecting in his aria. Maazel's conducting is a model of controlled flexibility, and the orchestra respond to him with unfailing precision. Visually, the production is a treat, the chorus handled unfussily as a collection of individuals, with the principal characters and their relationships given thoughtful and sensitive preparation.

To be ranked with the Los Angeles production with Fleming and Villazón (see above): we should count ourselves a favoured generation to have both or the choice of either.

La traviata
Renée Fleming sop Violetta **Rolando Villazón** ten Alfredo Germont **Renato Bruson** bar Giorgio Germont **Daniel Montenegro** ten Gastone **Philip Kraus** bar Baron **Lee Poulis** bass Marquis **James Creswell** bass Doctor **Suzanna Guzmán** mez Flora **Anna Alkhimova** sop Annina **Sal Malaki** ten Giuseppe
Los Angeles Opera Chorus and Orchestra / James Conlon
Stage director **Marta Domingo**
Video director **Brian Large**
DG 🎬 074 3215DH (141' · NTSC · 16:9 · PCM stereo and DTS 5.1 · 0)   Ⓕ

La traviata
Teresa Stratas sop Violetta **Plácido Domingo** ten Alfredo Germont **Cornell MacNeil** bar Giorgio Germont **Maurizio Barbacini** ten Gastone **Allan Monk** bar Baron **Richard Oneto** bass Marquis **Robert Sommer** bass Doctor **Axelle Gall** mez Flora **Pina Cei** sop Annina **Luciano Brizi** ten Giuseppe
Metropolitan Opera Chorus and Orchestra / James Levine
Film director **Franco Zeffirelli**
DG 🎬 073 4364GH (105' · NTSC · 4:3 · PCM stereo and DTS 5.1 · 0)   Ⓕ

'What about all this luxury?' Father Germont wants to know as he looks around him on arrival in Act 2. It's a fair question, and not only concerning the rural love-nest. If 'sumptuous' is (as we are assured) the word for the stage production at Los Angeles, a word has yet to be coined that will do justice to Zeffirelli's film version.

In their different ways both of these are unmissable. The Los Angeles performance is very moving; and the 1982 film has to be seen to be believed – which of course (again) is an equivocal form of recommendation. Each is

committed to its medium, and perhaps some will find that a disqualification. In Los Angeles the audience makes its presence felt with generous and frequent applause, including (in two instances) at the rise of curtain. The film makes it clear from the start that every advantage is to be taken of freedom to roam: 'Look here upon this picture,' it seems to say, 'and on this… and this… and this.'

Both Violettas are distinguished and memorable, Fleming with one of the most lovely voices to be heard in the part, Stratas as one of the best actresses among singers. Fleming's warm, vibrant quality makes its mark from her very first phrase, and again from the start Stratas's face reflects all the shades by which hope and fear, the public image and the inner self may be expressed. Both meet the notoriously disparate vocal demands of the role, though Stratas's voice sounds worn on the high notes. In the last act Stratas's relative slightness of vocal and physical build works to her advantage. Both are fine in the developing emotions of the great duet with Germont père.

For all that Domingo and Villazón may seem to represent a kind of vocal continuum, their identities here are quite distinct, with Villazón the lighter, more volatile Alfredo, and, also, in musical detail sometimes the more refined. The fathers MacNeil and Bruson are quite unalike, MacNeil relatively coarse in character and singing, Bruson well past his prime as a singer but patrician in manner and still refulgent in the centre of his voice. At Los Angeles Conlon conducts levelheadedly: Levine's flair is most evident in vigorous rhythmic passages such as the dances and the card game. In both videos the orchestra is less to the fore than it would be in a sound recording, and in the film is sometimes almost relegated to the status of background music. The film also makes cuts to the score, while the stage performance is complete with cabalettas for father and son and a second verse of 'Addio del passato' for Violetta.

Additional recommendation

La traviata
Bonfadelli Violetta **Piper** Alfredo **Bruson** Germont **Arturo Toscanini Foundation Chorus and Orchestra / Domingo** Stage director **Zeffirelli**
TDK Mediactive 🎬 DV-OPLTR (205' · 16:9 · 2.0, 5.1 & DTS 5.1 · 0) Includes documentary, 'Making of La traviata' and interviews.   Ⓕ

Lovingly directed and designed by the then 78-year-old Zeffirelli. Bonfadelli makes a very fine Violetta – it's a reading that demands to be seen and heard. Sound quality is beyond reproach, and though it may not surpass the López-Cobos DVD (reviewed above) it deserves a recommendation.

Additional recommendations

La traviata
Callas Violetta **di Stefano** Alfredo **Bastianini** 🅷 Germont **Chorus and Orchestra of La Scala, Milan / Giulini**

VERDI IL TROVATORE – IN BRIEF

Giuseppe di Stefano *Manrico* **Maria Callas** 🅷
Leonora **Fedora Barbieri** *Azucena* **Chorus and Orchestra of La Scala, Milan / Herbert von Karajan**
EMI mono ② 556333-2 (129' · AAD) Ⓕ🅞🅞🅟
A 1957 mono recording shouldn't put you off this, with its thrilling combination of Maria Callas and Giuseppe di Stefano in top form. Karajan is at his most dramatic, with the rest of the cast, notably Fedora Barbieri's Azucena, to match.

Plácido Domingo *Manrico* **Leontyne Price** *Leonora* **Fiorenza Cossotto** *Azucena* **Ambrosian Opera Chorus, New Philharmonia Orchestra / Zubin Mehta**
RCA ② 74321 39504-2 (136' · AAD) 🅜🅞
This is probably the best among several excellent modern recordings, with no weak links in its stellar cast. Mehta is more galvanic than usual. A rich, vivid recording.

Franco Corelli *Manrico* **Gabriella Tucci** *Leonora* **Giulietta Simionato** *Azucena* **Rome Opera Chorus and Orchestra / Thomas Schippers**
HMV ② HMVD573413-2 (123' · ADD) Ⓢ
Vivid, fast-moving conducting and a less conventional cast – apart from its stars – give this a real sense of drama.

Jussi Björling *Manrico* **Zinka Milanov** *Leonora* **Fedora Barbieri** *Azucena* **Robert Shaw Chorale, RCA Victor Orchestra / Renato Cellini**
RCA ② GD86643 (107' · AAD) 🅜
A 1952 mono recording that still carries plenty of excitement, with two quite extraordinary voices in Jussi Björling and the Met's great Verdi baritone Leonard Warren. Zinka Milanov is slightly less compelling, but Barbieri is a fine Azucena, and Cellini is more vital than many better-known interpreters.

Plácido Domingo *Manrico* **Rosalind Plowright** *Leonora* **Brigitte Fassbaender** *Azucena* **Santa Cecilia Academy Chorus and Orchestra / Carlo Maria Giulini**
DG ② 479 5915 (140' · DDD) Ⓕ
'The thinking man's *Trovatore*', beautifully judged and detailed in both conducting and singing – yet intensely Italianate, with a cast conceding nothing to other versions.

EMI mono ② 566450-2 (124' · ADD) Recorded 1955 🅜
Surely the most famous recording of *Traviata*, with Callas an incomparable Violetta. The big let down, though, is Bastianini's Germont and the poor recorded sound.

Il trovatore

Il trovatore 🅷
Maria Callas *sop* Leonora **Giuseppe di Stefano** *ten* Manrico **Rolando Panerai** *bar* Count di Luna **Fedora Barbieri** *mez* Azucena **Nicola Zaccaria** *bass* Ferrando **Luisa Villa** *mez* Ines **Renato Ercolani** *ten* Ruiz, Messenger **Giulio Mauri** *bass* Old Gipsy **Chorus and Orchestra of La Scala, Milan / Herbert von Karajan**
EMI ② 377365-2 (129' · ADD · N/S) Recorded 1956.
Ⓑ🅞🅞🅟

Callas and Karajan took the world by the ears in the 1950s with this *Il trovatore*. Leonora was one of Callas's finest stage roles, and this recording is wonderfully intense, with a dark concentrated loveliness of sound in the principal arias that puts one in mind of Muzio or Ponselle at their best. Walter Legge always managed to team Callas with the right conductor for the work in question. Often it was Serafin, but Karajan in *Il trovatore* is utterly compelling. This opera, like Beethoven's Seventh Symphony and Stravinsky's *The Rite of Spring*, is one of music's great essays in sustained rhythmic intensity; dramatically it deals powerfully in human archetypes. All this is realised by the young Karajan with that almost insolent mastery of score and orchestra which made him such a phenomenon at this period of is career. There are some cuts, but, equally, some welcome inclusions (such as the second verse of 'Di quella pira', sung by di Stefano with his own unique kind of *slancio*).

Although the EMI sound is very good, one or two climaxes suggest that in the heat of the moment, the engineer, Robert Beckett, let the needle run into the red and you might care to play the set in mono to restore that peculiar clarity and homogeneity of sound which are the mark of Legge's finest productions of the mono era. But whatever you do don't miss this set.

Il trovatore
Plácido Domingo *ten* Manrico **Leontyne Price** *sop* Leonora **Sherrill Milnes** *bar* Count di Luna **Fiorenza Cossotto** *mez* Azucena **Bonaldo Giaiotti** *bass* Ferrando **Elizabeth Bainbridge** *mez* Ines **Ryland Davies** *ten* Ruiz **Stanley Riley** *bass* Old Gipsy **Neilson Taylor** *bar* Messenger **Ambrosian Opera Chorus; New Philharmonia Orchestra / Zubin Mehta**
RCA Red Seal ② 74321 39504-2 (137' · ADD · T/t) Recorded 1969 🅜🅞

The Leonora of Leontyne Price is the high point of the Mehta recording: her velvety, sensuous articulation of what's certainly an 'immenso, eterno amor' is entirely distinctive and dramatically astute. The New Philharmonia is a no less ardent exponent. Mehta's pacing may be uneven, his accompanying breathless, but he draws robust playing in bold primary colours to which the recording gives vivid presence.

The acoustic serves Manrico less well: he seems to be singing in the bath when we first overhear him. This, though, is a younger, simpler Domingo than the one we encounter elsewhere, and there are passages of wonderfully sustained intensity. Cossotto's Azucena is disappointing. All the vocal tricks and techniques are there, but it's very much a concert performance, and we're never entirely engaged.

Il trovatore   H

Peter Glossop bar Il Conte di Luna **Gwyneth Jones** sop Leonora **Giulietta Simionato** mez Azucena **Bruno Prevedi** ten Manrico **Joseph Rouleau** bass Ferrando **Elizabeth Bainbridge** mez Ines **John Dobson** ten Ruiz **William Clothier** bar Un vecchio zingaro **Handel Owen** ten Un messo **Chorus and Orchestra of the Royal Opera House, Covent Garden / Carlo Maria Giulini**

Royal Opera House Heritage Series mono ②
ROHS011 (127' · ADD)
Recorded live at the Royal Opera House, Covent Garden, on November 26, 1964   Ⓜ

Leontyne Price being expected, prices were raised. When Price did not come and Gwyneth Jones was substituted the cast began to assume a more homely complexion than seemed right for a gala occasion, and absentees from the gallery began to feel complacent. As a result, many never heard Bruno Prevedi's Manrico. His 'Di quella pira' is not one for the book of legends, but the 'Ah si, ben mio' that precedes it deserved its applause, and the final scene is sung as by one inspired.

Gwyneth Jones is in best voice, before the loosening process had made itself evident and when her ample soprano was in its fullest bloom. She is technically in firm control and includes the Act 4 cabaletta, sung with assurance and scrupulous precision. Peter Glossop's performance is particularly moving. If lacking the brazen edge to battle it out with the brass in 'Per me ora fatale', he had all the warmth and generosity of tone to make a human being and not a paste-board villain of di Luna, and he sings his aria with the ease, range, power and beauty of the true Verdi baritone.

By 1964 Simionato's voice was too fragmented to capture with pleasure, but she still gives a performance on the grand lines. Otherwise the vocal heroes are the male chorus. For Giulini, his personal touch is felt more distinctively in the studio recording of 1983, but this performance is truer to the distinctive tensions and excitement of the opera itself.

Il trovatore

Plácido Domingo ten Manrico **Raina Kabaivanska** sop Leonora **Piero Cappuccilli** bar Count di Luna

Fiorenza Cossotto mez Azucena **José van Dam** bass Ferrando **Vienna State Opera Chorus and Orchestra / Herbert von Karajan**
Stage director **Herbert von Karajan**
Video director **Günther Schneider-Siemssen**
TDK ② 🅓🅥🅓 DV-CLOPIT (151' · 4:3 · PCM stereo, 5.1 & DTS 5.1 · 0) Recorded live at the Staatsoper, Vienna, 1 May 1978   ⒻOO

Never available before, this marvellous performance marked Karajan's long-awaited return to the Vienna State Opera in 1978. It was also the notorious occasion when Franco Bonisolli threw a tantrum and walked out of the dress rehearsal. He was replaced at the eleventh hour by Domingo, who thereby completed a cast that has hardly been bettered. Inspired no doubt by the reception he receives on first entering the pit, Karajan is at his most proactive, and the singers react with real conviction to complement their exemplary singing.

The staging, Karajan's own, and the sets are pretty conventional, but who cares when the score is projected with such confidence and the voices are of such rare quality? The youngish Domingo is the feisty troubadour of the title to the life, and he sings Manrico's taxing music as if that were the easiest thing in the world. As his adversary, Count di Luna, Piero Cappuccilli is in firm, supple voice, giving a faultless account of 'Il balen' and fierily dramatic in the ensembles. Fiorenza Cossotto offers her appreciable all to Azucena, a role she made very much her own and one in which she's yet to be surpassed. As Ferrando, José Van Dam launches the opera with tremendous authority. Raina Kabaivanska, the Leonora, may not have had a typically Verdian voice, but what she does with her resources is remarkable, combining a classic style – some beautifully etched phrasing – with a poise as a vocal and dramatic actress that's second to none, except perhaps Callas.

So it's one vocal treat after another, culminating in a superlative Act 4. Sound, picture and direction are exemplary. This absorbing issue is highly recommended to all admirers of Verdi and great singing.

I vespri siciliani

I vespri siciliani   H

Maria Callas sop Elena **Giorgio Kokolios-Bardi** ten Arrigo **Enzo Mascherini** bar Montforte **Boris Christoff** bass Procida **Bruno Carmassi** bass Bethune **Mario Frosini** bass Vaudemont **Mafalda Masini** contr Ninetta **Chorus and Orchestra of the Maggio Musicale, Florence / Erich Kleiber**
Testament mono ② SBT21416 (159' · ADD)
Recorded live at the Teatro Comunale, Florence, on May 26, 1951   Ⓕ

This recording, like Verdi's opera, has attracted mixed reviews over the years. Composed for Paris in 1855, Les Vêpres siciliennes has never enjoyed the affection of critics or public in the way the other 'mid-period' operas (Boccanegra, Ballo and Forza) have.

This revival was one of the productions that helped to spread Maria Callas's fame. At the time, Lord Harewood wrote memorably in *Opera* magazine about the tremendous force he puts into the recitative in Act 1, in which the Duchess Elena encourages the Sicilian population to rebellion with the words 'Il vostro fato e in vostra man' ('Your fate is in your own hands').

Callas is terrific in the Act 1 aria and cabaletta, as well as in the long duet with Arrigo in Act 4, sung by Greek tenor Giorgio Kokolios-Bardi. He had been one of Callas's leading men at the National Opera in Athens, and she particularly requested him for this part. He's no Di Stefano but he gives a good performance, especially of the aria in the Fourth Act, 'Giorno di pianto'. In some ways this opera is dominated by the two low male voices – Boris Christoff is magnificent as the gloomy, unforgiving Procida, while Enzo Mascherini is in his element as the anguished Guido di Montforte, who finds out too late that his opponent is his own son.

Erich Kleiber is not usually associated with the 19th-century Italian repertory but he leads a vigorous performance, although there are quite a few cuts. This tape (made for Walter Legge) does not include the overture, so the opera fits on two CDs. For Callas and Christoff admirers, of course, this is an essential document. Although the sound quality is variable, it is clearer than previous issues. The Testament booklet is excellent, the libretto available to download from the company's website.

Tomás Luis de Victoria

Spanish 1548-1611

Victoria was a choirboy at Avil Cathedral; when his voice broke he was sent to the Jesuit Collegio Germanico, Rome (c1565), where he may have studied under Palestrina. He was a singer and organist at S Maria di Monserrato (1569-at least 1574) and from 1571 to 1576-7 he taught at the Collegio Germanico (maestro from 1575). He became a priest and joined the Oratory of S Filippo Neri. In the 1580s he returned to Spain as chaplain to Philip II's sister the Dowager Empress Maria, at the Descalzas Reales convent, Madrid, from 1587 until her death in 1603; he remained there as organist until his death, apart from a visit to Rome (1592-5), when he attended Palestrina's funeral. The greatest Spanish Renaissance composer, and among the greatest in Europe in his day, he wrote exclusively Latin sacred music. Most was printed in his lifetime; in 1600 a sumptuous collection of 32 of his most popular masses, Magnificats, psalms and motets appeared in Madrid. Though his output ranged widely through the liturgy, he is chiefly remembered for his masses and motets, which include well-known pieces (Missa Ave regina caelorum, Missa pro victoria, O magnum mysterium, O quam gloriosum, O vos omnes). Like Palestrina, he wrote in a serious, devotional style, often responding emotionally to the texts with dra-matic word-painting. Some of his more poignant pieces are characterised by a religious, almost mystical fervour. GROVEmusic

Officium defunctorum

Officium defunctorum
Gabrieli Consort / Paul McCreesh
Archiv Produktion 447 095-2AH (60' · DDD · T/t)
Ⓟ❍❍▶

This is a remarkable recording. In some ways it's like a rediscovery, for here's an approach not too far from Pro Cantione Antiqua at its best and yet that group never recorded the work. The Gabrieli Consort adds chant to the Requiem Mass itself, thus creating more of a context for Victoria's magisterial work.

We have therefore the Epistle and preceding prayer, the Tract, Sequence, Gospel, Preface, Lord's Prayer and Postcommunion in addition to the polyphony; this also means, for example, that the *Kyrie* is sung nine-fold with alternating chant instead of simply three-fold only in polyphony. We can presume that the chant was taken from a suitable Spanish source by Luis Lozano Virumbrales, who's an expert in this field and the author of the insert-notes together with Paul McCreesh.

The performance itself is stately and imposing, with a tremendous homogeneity of sound: the use of an all-male choir, together with the added chant, lends it a tangibly monastic feel, though it would have been a fortunate monastery indeed that had falsettists of this quality. About the performance of the chant there are two points of interest: first, that it's doubled, like the polyphony, by a shawm, common Spanish practice at this period, and second, that McCreesh isn't afraid to have the falsettists singing the chant too.

The pace of the polyphony often seems unhurried, but never feels slow, and Westminster Cathedral Choir is faced with the hugely reverberant acoustics of its home building. From the beginning the singing is involving and incarnate, but the real magic comes nearer the end: from the *Agnus Dei* onwards one feels that the Gabrieli Consort have really got the measure of the music and is allowing it to speak through them. The final great responsory, the 'Libera me', is performed with heart stopping power and conviction. McCreesh's approach shows how the Mass would have fitted into and complemented the liturgical framework without ever losing its own internal power and drama. A revelatory disc.

Masses

Missa O quam gloriosum. Missa Ave maris stella.
Motet – O quam gloriosum
Westminster Cathedral Choir / David Hill
Hyperion CDA66114 (57' · DDD)
Ⓟ❍❍❍

This is likely to become one of your most cherished discs. It's notable for its spacious depth of

G sound, volatile unpredictability of interpretation, and above all the soaring sostenuto of the boy trebles, with their forward and slightly nasal tone quality. With their magnificently controlled legato lines, the Westminster boys treat Victoria's music as though it were some vast plainchant, with a passion that excites and uplifts. The choir is recorded in the exceptionally resonant Westminster Cathedral, at a distance and with great atmosphere.

Ave maris stella isn't one of Victoria's familiar Masses, quite simply because no music publisher has made it available to choirs in a good, cheap edition. To have it rescued from obscurity is laudable in itself, but to have it sung with such poise and sensitivity is an unexpected double treat. Unlike *O quam gloriosum*, this is a work that thrills with echoes of Victoria's Spanish upbringing, of Morales and his predecessors, even of Josquin Desprez, whose own *Ave maris stella* Mass was brought to the cathedrals of the Iberian peninsula earlier in the century. The plainchant melody, familiar through Monteverdi's setting in the 1610 Vespers, completely dominates Victoria's music, for it's placed most often in huge treble lines that wheel high above the general texture. Magnificent as the early parts of the work are, nothing quite matches the final five-part *Agnus Dei*, sung here with admirable support and exquisitely shaped by David Hill. Recommended without reservation.

Missa Gaudeamus. Missa pro Victoria (both ed Dixon). Motets –Cum beatus Ignatius; Descendit angelus Domini; Doctor bonus amicus Dei Andreas; Ecce sacerdos magnus; Estote fortes in bello; Hic vir despiciens mundum; O decus apostolicum; Tu es Petrus; Veni, sponsa Christi (all ed Skinner)
The Cardinall's Musick /Andrew Carwood
ASV Gaudeamus CDGAU198 (78' · DDD · T/t) Ⓕ**OO**

There have been some fine recordings of Victoria's music in recent years, but none finer than this one at its best. The Cardinall's Musick has become known for its CDs of English renaissance polyphony, but its approach, which joint directors Andrew Carwood and David Skinner describe as 'open and soloistic', works extremely well here, too. The two contrasted Mass settings are given the same highly expressive treatment as the motets, which, sung one to a part, have a madrigal quality bringing out beautifully the natural, unforced rhetoric of Victoria's idiom.

The *Missa Gaudeamus*, based on a Morales motet, is scored for six voices. Performed with only two singers on each part, it sounds as rich and dark as the strongest chocolate; the overall blend is superb, clear and strikingly well balanced. With only two female voices on the upper part, the polyphonic texture isn't, as is so often the case, top-heavy; each strand carries equal weight, just as the densely contrapuntal writing demands. The final canonic *Agnus Dei* is sublime, and throughout – even in the longer movements – Carwood's sure-footed pacing allows the polyphony to ebb and flow like the swell of the sea.

The *Missa pro Victoria*, based on Janequin's chanson, *La guerre*, could hardly be more different in its forward-looking polychoral idiom. Here the writing is more condensed, more economical, but nevertheless highly dramatic. The ending of the *Gloria* is breathtaking, as is the magical opening of the Sanctus and the final 'dona nobis pacems' of the *Agnus Dei*. The clarion calls of the second *Kyrie* are equally striking. There are so many high spots on this disc that it's simply impossible to mention them all, and this is perhaps still more to the group's credit given that, as explained in the notes, a bout of flu among the singers can't have made for the easiest of recording sessions.

Missa Dum complerentur. Dum complerentur. Veni Sancte Spiritus. Popule meus. Vexilla Regis. Veni Creator Spiritus. Pange lingua gloriosi. Lauda Sion
Westminster Cathedral Choir /James O'Donnell
with **Joseph Cullen** org
Hyperion CDA66886 (70' · DDD· T/t)   Ⓕ**OO**

Westminster Cathedral Choir here makes a special contribution to the music of Tomás Luis de Victoria. The *Missa Dum complerentur*, for Pentecost, is based on Victoria's own motet; he adds an extra voice in the parody Mass setting and draws much on the opening material of the motet as well as its distinctive 'Alleluia' sections which ring out like a peal of bells – especially in this excellent performance. Indeed, the motet is finely conceived, with Victoria characteristically responding to the imagery of the text with changes of texture and pacing within the essentially contrapuntal idiom: a true master.

The choir, with its full-bodied sound and well-sustained vocal lines, has, over long years of tradition in singing this particular part of the repertory, achieved an almost intuitive feel for the flow of the music, which is perhaps as near as we'll ever get today to the authentic situation of professional church singers in Rome or the Spanish cathedrals in the 16th century. What we'll never know is whether the sonority – in particular the timbre of the boys' voices – resembles anything Victoria might have heard, that distinctive focus and intensity of tone well illustrated by the two Holy Week settings on the disc: the homophonic Popule meus and the hymn *Vexilla Regis*. This, and the two Pentecost hymns, are performed in alternatim with alternate verses in plainchant and polyphony. This is a superb and compelling disc that adds to our knowledge and appreciation of Victoria's art.

Officium Hebdomadae Sanctae

Officium Hebdomadae Sanctae – Dominica in ramis Palmarum; Feria sexta; Sabbato Sancto; Feria quinta. In Coena Domini. In Passione Domini
La Colombina Ensemble; Schola Antiqua /
Juan Carlo Asensio
Glossa ③ GCD922002/3 (3h 17' · DDD)   Ⓕ

Victoria's massive publication of 1585, the *Officium Hebdomadae Sanctae*, was never intended as a self-contained 'work': alongside the famous Tenebrae settings, it includes Lamentations for the three holy days, the Improperia ('Reproaches'), and music for Palm Sunday and for the St John and St Matthew Passions. Given the scale of these liturgies, a full CD re-creation is a practical impossibility.

Josep Cabré, director of La Colombina, therefore steers a pragmatic course, presenting enough of the surrounding plainchant to give a sense of its scale in relation to the polyphony. This sensible strategy works well, reconciling the complete presentation of the publication's contents with a more contextually sensitive approach. To the extent that both aims are fulfilled, this recording takes its place as one of the most significant contributions to Victoria's already impressive discography.

It's worth mentioning Victoria's use of a handful of simple recurring motifs (usually associated with specific words or phrases) that he would no doubt have expected his listeners to recognise. A recording such as this is probably the only way to experience the cumulative effect of such a strategy, now that actual liturgical performances within Holy Week are a thing of the past.

As to the performances, the polyphony is polished and involving in equal measure, although the emotional intensity associated with Victoria seems inversely proportional to the number of singers used. (They respond particularly well to the pieces scored for high voices, surely some of the most memorable music here.) While the inclusion of plainchant is both logical and effective, the manner in which it is sung is nearer to Solesmes than to the metrical approach that has sometimes been urged (and put into practice) for this period. The recording achieves a good presence, however, and enhances the performance's ambient qualities.

Louis Vierne · French 1870-1937

Born mearly blind, Vierne showed extraordinary musical promise. He joins César Franck's organ class at the Conservatoire in Paris; he later became Widor's assistant at St Sulpice. In 1900 he is given post of organist at Notre-Dame. Among his compositions are six organ symphonies as well as numerous songs and a large quantity of chamber music.

Organ works

Symphonies Nos 1-6
Jeremy Filsell *org*
Signum Classics ③ SIGCD063 (3h 24' · DDD)
Played on the Cavaillé-Coll organ of St Ouen de Rouen, France ⓕ

Vierne's six organ symphonies have very uneven representation in the catalogues. Most popular by far is the Third; and for 10 years the only widely available box-set was Ben van Oosten's (Dabringhaus und Grimm). In many ways this set was pretty well ideal, the only drawback being his lack of flair in the big toccata-like movements (such as the finale of No 1). Now Jeremy Filsell has brought just that kind of flair and panache to this set, recorded, interestingly, on the same instrument as Oosten's set.

It sounds quite different, though. The sound engineers have produced an altogether warmer and more all-embracing sound, giving the quieter movements (such as the enchanting Menuet of the Fourth Symphony) plenty of space to reveal their charms, while handling the monumental *pleno* in such a way that it still sends shivers down the spine without ever becoming overwhelming. The music, too, may be the same but Filsell seems to have a better sense of the musical architecture, especially in the later and more remote symphonies. As a result he convinces that the relative neglect, especially of the Fourth Symphony, is unwarranted; it may not be easy to communicate this music but it can be done and Filsell does it wonderfully.

The booklet-notes are exceptionally pretentious but all in all, Filsell has done both Vierne and discerning organ-lovers a great service.

Heitor Villa-Lobos · Brazilian 1887-1959

Villa-Lobos was taught to play the cello by his father, and in his teens he performed with popular musicians in the city. He then travelled widely, returning to Rio in his mid-20s for a few formal lessons. From 1923 to 1930 he was in Paris, where he wrote several works in his Chôros series, giving Brazilian impressions a luxuriant scoring: Messiaen and others were impressed. He returned to Brazil, where he did valuable work in reforming musical education. In 1945 he founded the Brazilian Academy of Music in Rio de Janeiro. Also during this period he produced the cycle of nine Bachianas brasileiras for diverse combinations (1930-45), marrying the spirit of Brazilian folk music with that of Bach; the two for eight cellos (one with soprano) have been especially successful. His gigantic output includes operas, 12 symphonies (1916-57), 17 string quartets (1915-57), numerous songs and much piano music. GROVEmusic

Chôros

Chôros – No 1ª; No 4 ᵇ; No 6ᵈ; No 8ᶜᵈ; No 9ᵈ
ªFabio Zanon *gtr* ᵇDante Yenque,
ᵇOzéas Arantes, ᵇSamuel Hamzem *hn*
ᵇDarren Coleman Milling *bass tbn*
ᶜLinda Bustani, ᵈIlan Rechtman *pfs*
ᵈSão Paulo Symphony Orchestra / John Neschling
BIS BIS-CD1450 (81' · DDD) ⓕⓞⒹ

How many *Chôros* are there? Fourteen numbered examples (with two claimed as "lost"), two *Chôros bis*, a Wind Quintet *en forme de Chôros* and a concluding (!) choral-and-orchestral "Introduction to the *Chôros*", all more or less from the 1920s. No 6 (1926), which opens this second volume of BIS's survey, and No 9 (1929) may not have been written down until 1942 in time for their Rio premieres. Villa-Lobos was unreliable about many details of his work and these would not be unique in his output in being created only when performances finally materialised.

Whenever it was set down, the Sixth is a hugely engaging, if sprawling, orchestral fantasia and like the Eighth (written and premiered between 1925 and 1927) and Ninth, was scored for large orchestra using exotic local percussion instruments. The Eighth is far more barbaric in character, tailored for the fad for primitivism then fashionable in Paris (where it was written), with parts for two pianos. Yet this is no concerto in disguise; although the first is a melodic soloist, the second is deployed as a percussive instrument and both orchestrally. BIS provides a clear balance.

Neschling and the São Paulo SO have the edge in the Ninth, which lies expressively between Nos 6 and 8. Separating these difficult orchestral works come the First for guitar (1920-21) and Fourth for brass (1926). There have been crisper performances of the latter, but Fabio Zanon's of the well known First is really rather good, languid and wistful, the tempi vibrantly elastic. This fine disc augurs well for what will presumably be the final instalment.

Bachianas Brasileiras

Bachianas Brasileiras Nos 2, 4 & 8
Cincinnati Symphony Orchestra / Jesús López-Cobos
Telarc CD80393 (70' · DDD)   Ⓕⓞ

If any parallels existed between Bach and Brazilian idioms, they were largely in Villa-Lobos's mind – even the Fugue in No 8 of these *Bachianas Brasileiras* is totally un-Bach-like; so anyone coming fresh to these exotically coloured, rather sprawling works should not be misled by false expectations. But they're fascinating, indeed haunting, in a highly individual way. In view of the composer's sublime indifference to instrumental practicalities (as, for instance, the feasible length of a trombone glissando), his carelessness over detail in his scores, his Micawber-like trust that problems of balance he had created would be sorted out in performance, the chaotic state of the printed scores and orchestral parts of his music (littered as they are with wrong notes), and numerous misreadings in past performances, the only half-way reliable yardstick for conductors or critics is the composer's own recordings, made in the 1950s.

Compared to them, the present issue shows a number of differences. Chief of these is the warmer, more generalised sound, with less emphasis on clarity of detail. This works reasonably well in the Preludio of No 8, where concentration on the melodic line and the adoption of a

slower tempo aid the movement's lyricism (likewise the more sentimental approach to the Aria of No 2). The Aria of No 8 is unquestionably more poetic and the Dansa of No 4 lighter; but in the most famous movement, the hilarious and ingenious 'Little train of the Caipira' of No 2, the rasps near the start and the clatter of wheels on the track (evoked by the fiendishly difficult piano part) are far too subdued in favour of the 'big tune'.

López-Cobos deals persuasively with knotty questions of balance, such as in the middle section of No 3's Toccata, and brings to the fore the bell-like araponga bird's cry in No 4's Coral, but makes less of that movement's jungle screeches. He makes clear the thematic link between the sections of No 4's Aria, and seeks to overcome the repetitive pattern of its Preludio by taking a faster speed rather than by the wealth of tonal nuance the composer imself introduced. Perhaps such detailed comparisons are superfluous: enjoy, enjoy!

Bachianas Brasileiras – Nos 4, 5, 7 & 9.
Chôros No-10, 'Rasga o coração'
Renée Fleming *sop* **BBC Singers; New World Symphony / Michael Tilson Thomas**
RCA Red Seal 09026 68538-2 (78' · DDD) Ⓟⓞ➔

In his booklet-note, the commentator here calls *Chôros* No 10 the masterpiece of that quintessentially Brazilian series. It's certainly the most ambitious, with very large orchestral and choral forces in a complex mélange of urban street song (a popular schottisch by Medeiros), chattering native Indian chants and bird-song twitterings, of mysterious jungle atmosphere, compulsive ostinato rhythms and virtuoso orchestral effects. The present performance is excellent. The couplings here are illuminating, consisting as they do of more Villa-Lobos – four of his highly individual tributes to Bach's influence. By far the best known of the *Bachianas Brasileiras* is No 5, whose Aria demonstrates the composer's ability to spin a haunting long-flowing melody. Renée Fleming is the sweet-toned soloist with the cello section of this accomplished orchestra of young graduates from American conservatoires: warmly lyrical as she is, however, and brilliantly exact in the dartings of the Dansa, her words aren't very distinct even in the slow-moving Aria.

By his deeply expressive shaping of No 4's Preludio Tilson Thomas avoids any satiety with its extreme monothematicism, and in the second movement secures coherent continuity despite the (rather loud) insistent interventions of the araponga bird's repeated note. He produces a beautifully poetic tranquillity in the brief Prelude of No 9 and complete lucidity and rhythmic buoyancy in its Fugue. If that's the most Bachian of the series, the much more substantial No 7 also has its moments of homage: its first movement has a fine breadth, and its finale is an impressive and serious-minded large-scale fugue that begins quietly and culminates in a grandiose blaze of sound; but the busy Toccata is characteristically and challengingly Brazilian, and the first part of its Giga (before it goes all Hollywood) is delightfully fresh in this invigorating performance.

Solo Piano Works

Prole do bebê No 1. Cirandas. Hommage à Chopin
Sonia Rubinsky pf
Naxos 8 554489 (65' · DDD)   ⑤❶➔

Villa-Lobos's claim that his music was 'the fruit of an immense, ardent and generous land' at once disarms familiar criticism of extravagance and formlessness. To regard such largesse through the blinkered eyes of someone exclusively nurtured on a more restrained and economical diet is unacceptable. There may be tares among the wheat but such strictures hardly apply to the music in this Vol 1 which commences with the enchanting *Prole do bebê*, Book 1 (the Second Book is a tougher, altogether more astringent and percussive experience, while a Third Book is sadly lost). Intimately associated with Artur Rubinstein (who rearranged Villa-Lobos's miniatures, omitting some and ending 'O Polichinelo' with an unmarked rip-roaring *glissando*), *Prole do bebê* is here played complete. Sonia Rubinsky makes light of a teasing rhythmic mix in 'Morenhina' (No 2) and in 'Caboclinha'(No 3) she relishes Villa-Lobos's audacity; his way of making his seductive melody and rhythm surface through a peal of church bells. Again, despite strong competition from Alma Petchersky on ASV in the no less delightful *Cirandas*, Rubinsky scores an unequivocal success, ideally attuned to the central and beguiling melody of 'Terezinha de Jesus' (No 1) with its *forte e canto* instruction, and allowing the fight between the carnation and the rose (No 4) to melt into a delicious love duet. Much celebrated in her native Brazil and also in America, Sonia Rubinsky is excellently recorded.

Guia prático – Vol 1 (excs); Album 10; Album 11.
Ibericarabe. Suite infantil – No 1; No 2. Marqueza de Santos – Gavota-Chôro; Valsinha-Brasileira
Sonia Rubinsky pf
Naxos 8 570504 (79' · DDD)   ⑤❶❶➔

With Volume 8 of the piano music of Villa-Lobos, Sonia Rubinsky reaches a triumphant end to a long, complex and luxuriant journey. And to an even greater extent than in the earlier issues she relishes every twist and turn of Brazil's ever-varied genius, playing with an enviable virtuosity, warmth and affection. And here, in a disc that includes five world-premiere recordings, she illustrates ideally her chosen composer's statement of intent, namely his wish to subsume the widest variety of influences into a grateful sense of national identity and his burning love of his native Brazil. Volume 8 extends Volume 5 by completing the *Guia prático*, a 137-piece tribute to Villa-Lobos's love of children; music where early innocence is recalled through sophisticated adult eyes and ears. How Rubinsky

relishes the alternately spry and gracious waltz of 'Constancia', the charm of 'Ba, Be, Bi, Bo, Bu', or the syncopated dance rhythms, piquantly harmonised, of Nos 95 and 105. The two 'Infantil' Suites elaborate the mix into a near-Scriabinesque etude in 'No Balanco' and a melody peppered with rapid bouncing staccatos in 'Allegretto' (Second Suite, No 3). *Ibericarabe* (transcribed by Lucília Guimarães Villa-Lobos, the composer's first wife) is more familiar territory with sumptuously deployed melody wreathed round in intricate figuration, and there is much, much more to enjoy, ponder over and occasionally reject (Villa-Lobos's vast output led to inevitable unevenness). This is a magnificent conclusion to a formidable undertaking, recorded in ideal sound.

Choral Works

Missa São Sebastião. Bendita sabedoria. Praesepe[a].
Cor dulce, cor amabile. Panis angelicus. Sub tuum praesidium. Ave Maria a 5. Ave Maria a 6. Pater noster. Magnificat-alleluia[b]
[a]**Ansy Boothroyd,** [b]**Elizabeth McCormack** mez
Corydon Singers and Orchestra / Matthew Best
Hyperion CDA66638 (77' · DDD · T/t)   Ⓕ

Asked to identify the composer of all these religious works except the Mass one would be most unlikely to think of Villa-Lobos. That larger-than-life exotic, that extravagantly experimental and boisterous figure, the composer of such chastely restrained music, the sweetly gentle *Cor dulce*, the controlled fervour of the *Pater noster*? Even the impressive and grandiose *Magnificat-alleluia* gives no hint of its country of origin. The one clue here might be that, of the two *Ave Marias*, the (earlier) five-part setting is in Portuguese. It's only the Mass that reveals all. Amid its austere style and purely diatonic, contrapuntal idiom the *Sanctus* suddenly seems to come from a different background: then one remembers that Sebastian is the patron saint of Rio de Janeiro; and looking into the score one finds that the liturgical heading of each movement is followed by a local one, the final *Agnus Dei* bearing the subtitle 'Sebastian, protector of Brazil'.

This programme, all of unaccompanied music except for the *Magnificat-alleluia*, should not be listened to as a continuity if some feeling of sameness is to be avoided: the Corydon Singers are most efficient in all they do, but the outstanding performance is of the Mass.

Antonio Vivaldi   Italian 1678-1741

Vivaldi was the son of a professional violinist who played at St Mark's and may have been involved in operatic management. Vivaldi was trained for the priesthood and ordained in 1703 but soon after his ordination ceased to say Mass; he claimed this was because of his unsure health (he is known to have suffered from chest complaints, possibly asthma or angina). In 1703 he was appointed maestro di violino at the Ospedale della Pietá, one of the Venetian girls' orphanages; he remained there until 1709, and held the post again, 1711-16; he then became maestro de' concerti. Later, when he was away from Venice, he retained his connection with the Pietà. He became maestro di capella, 1735-8; even after then he supplied concertos and directed performances on special occasions. Vivaldi's reputation had begun to grow with his first publications: trio sonatas (probably 1703-5), violin sonatas (1709)and especially his 12 concertos L'estro armonico op. 3 (1711). These, containing some of his finest concertos, were issued in Amsterdam and widely circulated in northern Europe; this prompted visiting musicians to seek him out in Venice and in some cases commission works from him (notably for the Dresden court). Bach transcribed five op. 3 concertos for keyboard, and many German composers imitated his style. He published two further sets of sonatas and seven more of concertos, including 'La stravaganza' op 4 (c1712), Il cimento dell'armonia e dell'inventione (c1725, including 'The Four Seasons') and La cetra (1727).

It is in the concerto that Vivaldi's chief importance lies. He was the first composer to use ritornello form regularly in fast movements, and his use of it became a model; the same is true of his three-movement plan (fast-slow-fast). Vivaldi was an enterprising orchestrator, writing several concertos for unusual combinations like viola d'amore and lute, or for ensembles including chalumeaux, clarinets, horns and other rarities. There are also many solo concertos for bassoon, cello, oboe and flute. Some of his concertos are programmatic, for example 'La tempesta di mare' ((the title of three concertos). Into this category also fall 'The Four Seasons', with their representation of seasonal activities and conditions accommodated within a standard ritornello form – these are described in the appended sonnets, which he may have written himself. Vivaldi was also much engaged in vocal music. He wrote a quantity of sacred works, chiefly for the Pietà girls, using a vigorous style in which the influence of the concerto is often marked. He was also involved in opera and spent much time travelling to promote his works. More than 20 of his operas survive; those that have been revived include music of vitality and imagination as well as more routine items. But Vivaldi's importance lies above all in his concertos, for their boldness and originality and for their central place in the history of concerto form. GROVEmusic

Cello Concertos

Cello Concertos – in C minor, RV401; in B flat, RV423. Violin Concerto in F minor, 'Winter', RV297. Double Concerto in G minor, RV531[g]. Double Concerto, RV540[a]. Gloria, RV589 – Laudamus te[ag]. Juditha Triumphans, RV645[a] – Noli ò cara, te adorantis[b]; Quanto magis generosa[f]. La Fida ninfa, RV714[a] – Così sugl'occhi miei[bde]; Dite oihime[gh]. Il Giustino, RV717 – La gloria del mio sangue[abc] ([a]arr Koopman)
Yo-Yo Ma bqvc with [b]**Alfredo Bernardini**, [c]**Michel Henry** obs [d]**Wouter Verschuren** bn [e]**Margaret Faultless** bqvn [f]**Katherine McGillivray** vad [g]**Jonathan Manson** bqvc [h]**Mike Fentross** lte

Amsterdam Baroque Orchestra / Ton Koopman hpd/org
Sony Classical 509970 90916-2 (68 minutes: DDD) Ⓕ🅑▸

It was only a matter of time before Yo-Yo Ma turned to Vivaldi, the first of the great composers to take the cello seriously as a soloist. Strange to relate, however, in this cheery get-together with Ton Koopman and the Amsterdam Baroque Orchestra only three of its 11 pieces – the Double Concerto RV531, and the two solo concertos RV401 and 423 – were written for the cello. The others are all arrangements, from the appropriation of the slow movement of 'Winter', to the recasting of vocal numbers for colourful combinations of winds and strings, to the transformation of the beautiful Concerto for viola d'amore and lute, RV540, into a slightly less magical concerto for cello and organ.

Koopman, whose arrangements these are, claims that no one in Vivaldi's day would have thought twice about such things. Maybe he's right. RV540 apart, they're perfectly convincing, and you'd have to be a sour old grouch to object to them for long when they are played as expertly, as joyously and as lovingly as they are here. And, superb though Ma is on his 'baroqued' 1712 Stradivarius, each of the musicians, with special mentions going to Katherine McGillivray's exquisite viola d'amore and Jonathan Manson's cello, matching Ma all the way in RV531 and 'Laudamus te'.

An uncomplicated joy all round then, for its music, its performances and its recording, too, save only for the sometimes maddening prominence of the keyboard continuo.

Flute Concertos

Flute Concertos, Op 10. Flute Concerto in C minor, RV441
Nicolaus Esterházy Sinfonia / Béla Drahos fl
Naxos 8 553101 (59' · DDD) Ⓢ🅞▸

Vivaldi's flute concertos have certainly not been neglected on disc, and there's a wide choice of 'authentic' and middle-of-the-road versions played on both transverse flute and recorder; this present selection is in the MOR vein and faces numerous competitors. In the flute concertos Béla Drahos is a superb soloist, as smooth as silk and agile as a kitten, and whose flights of fanciful embellishment might have won Vivaldi's approval. The Esterházy Sinfonia sounds a little beefy at times in its opening statements, but in the presence of the soloist its touch is appropriately light, and the third Largo ('Il sonno'), of Op 10 No 2, 'La notte', is impressively hushed. The outer movements of the bonus concerto, R441, dance on the lightest of feet; the work was originally written for the recorder, but on whichever instrument it's played, you wonder why it has no other currently listed recording. This present one would carry a warm recommendation even if it were not at bargain price.

Six Flute Concertos, Op 10.
Flute Concertos – RV429; RV440
Emmanuel Pahud *fl*
Australian Chamber Orchestra / Richard Tognetti
EMI 347212-2 (66' · DDD)　　　　　ⒻⒹ⊁

Among the first flute concertos ever written, Vivaldi's Op 10 are also among the most imaginative. With vivid descriptive writing and everywhere unmistakably Vivaldian vitality and sparkle, they are surely a must for all flautists Baroque and modern. Taking time off from the Berlin Philharmonic, 'modern' Emmanuel Pahud establishes a mastery of them that blasts out of the water any concerns about what kind of instrument he is using. His tone is light and liquid, his technical command complete and, more importantly, he is utterly at one with the music's character. Where some 'modern' players who dip into Baroque music work too hard, overburdening the music with stiff interpretative detail and resolutely showing off the embellishments they have learned, Pahud's performances are natural and convincing, yet at the same time subtly stylish in matters of ornamentation, articulation and rhythm; the lilting first and second movements of No 5 are superbly poetic matchings of Baroque sensibility and technical control.

Not that he neglects the pictorial; he adds joyous extra bird-trills to *Il gardellino*, and enters deep into the spectral world of *La notte*, emerging from the impressionistic 'sleep' movement into a finale in which we can almost feel the last phantoms of the night flying past our heads. In this he is keenly partnered by his excellent accompanists, and indeed the taut but far from unyielding contribution of the Australian Chamber Orchestra is of the highest order throughout. A disc to give nothing but pleasure.

Oboe Concertos

Double Concerto for Two Oboes and Strings in D 🅿
minor, RV535. Concertos for Multiple Instruments – A, RV552, 'per eco in lontano'; D, RV562; F, RV568; F, RV569; G minor, RV577, 'per l'orchestra di Dresda'
Philharmonia Baroque Orchestra /
Nicholas McGegan
Reference Recordings RRCD77 (72' · DDD)　　Ⓕⓞ

Here is Vivaldi-playing with a commendably light, athletic touch. It's so easy to make a meal out of his orchestral *tuttis* yet these performances inspire the music with expressive delicacy and rhythmic vitality. The programme is a colourful one of concertos for a variety of instruments, wind and strings, in various combinations. Apart from occasional instances of predictable passagework, present above all in some of the wind writing, this music is engaging on many different levels. Slow movements such as the wonderfully free violin fantasy of RV562 reveal the exhilarating flights of fancy of which Vivaldi was capable, while the profusion of alluring inflexions present in fast and slow movements alike makes strong appeal to the

senses. Vivaldi was no stranger to the art of parody and, in the opening movement of RV568, we find him introducing sensuous, sighing quaver motifs present in the finale of the Concerto a due cori per la Santissima Assenzione di Maria Vergine (RV535). This kind of approach to Vivaldi's music greatly enlivens and refreshes its innate character. The disc is superbly recorded, allowing us to revel in every sonorous detail of solo and continuo playing alike.

Recorder Concertos

Recorder Concertos[d] – in C minor, RV441[b];
in F, RV442[a]; in C, RV443[b]; in C, RV444[b]; in A minor, RV445[b]. Chamber Concerto in D, 'La Pastorella', RV95[bc]
[a]**László Czidra,**[b]**László Kecskeméti** *recs* [c]**Béla Horváth** *ob* [d]**István Hartenstein** *bn* [c]**Tamás Zalay** *vn* [c]**György Eder** *vc* [c]**Borbála Dobozy** *hpd* [d]**Nicolaus Esterházy Sinfonia**
Naxos 8 553829 (64' · DDD)　　　　　ⓈⒹ⊁

This is claimed to be a recording of the 'complete' recorder concertos of Vivaldi (RV441-5) and there's no other listed version of RV441 it has that field to itself. Such archival primacy would be of little significance if the performances were sub-standard – but here they're high quality on all counts.

Kecskeméti bears the bulk of the soloist's burden, while Czidra appears only in RV442 (for treble recorder). Kecskeméti acquits himself on the same instrument with no less distinction in RV441 and, with no reflection on Czidra's manifest abilities, he could surely have made a clean sweep. Kecskeméti has the greatest 'showcase' opportunities, and he makes the most of them. His speed and clarity of articulation (as clean as a whistle, as it were) in the flanking movements are breathtaking and in some scale passages his sure-tongued choice of separate articulation gives life and variety – listen to the *Allegro molto* of RV443 and marvel! He adds embellishment where appropriate and in good taste. The basic five concertos alone would leave a disc somewhat under-filled and the choice of RV95, in which the recorder is featured, as a filler is a happy one. The Nicolaus Esterházy Sinfonia's contributions are happily light-footed. Excellent recording quality and bargain price are just extra reasons why this disc is a must-buy.

Vivaldi Recorder Concertos – in C minor, RV441; 🅿
in G, RV443; in C, RV444 **Sammartini** Recorder Concerto in F **Telemann** Suite in A minor, TWV55:a2
Pamela Thorby *recs* **Sonnerie** (Monica Huggett, Emilia Benjamin *vns* Katherine McGillivray *va* Alison McGillivray *vc* Sarah Groser *vion* Mathew Halls *hpd/org*)
Linn Records CKD217 (69' · DDD)　　　ⒻⓞⒹ⊁

Pamela Thorby's work with the Palladian Ensemble has alone been sufficient to establish her as a world class performer, and the reputation of Sonnerie has long been sky-high. Their coming together offers a delightful prospect and though, as any sports-person knows, teams assembled from star players don't always work happily, this one lives up to its promise. Their material has a familiar look but their delivery of it is of rare quality and fully justifies this journey along oft-trodden paths.

The music trips off Thorby's tongue with the utmost fluency, cleanly articulated, and without any trace of the distressing sagging or wavering of pitch on long notes that haunts too many otherwise laudable performances by some others. No less notable is her enhancing embellishment, particularly though not exclusively in the slow movements. Sonnerie provide the perfect substrate for Thorby's excursions: stylish, precise and ideally balanced in the Linn recording.

Throughout, one has the impression of a single mind in control of two 'hands', soloist and *ripieno*. This recording is sheer pleasure and comes highly recommended.

Concertos, Op 3 – L'estro armonico

L'estro armonico   **P**
Europa Galante / Fabio Biondi vn
Virgin Classics Veritas ② 545315-2 (100' · DDD)
       Ⓕ**OO**ᴰ

No other set of Vivaldi's concertos contains the sheer variety on display in *L'estro armonico*. The catalogue has seldom been without a decent recording of these ceaselessly fascinating works, though none begins to approach this version in respect of fantasy and exuberance. Fabio Biondi and his Italian ensemble, Europa Galante, bring something entirely fresh and vital to oft-performed repertoire, illuminating well-trodden paths with affective articulation and eloquently voiced inflexions. Not all of their extravagant, Mediterranean gestures, perhaps, will find favour with listeners; indeed, some of Biondi's own embellishments can be a little inapposite. Tempos are well chosen, by and large, and ensemble is clear-textured and evenly balanced. The continuo group, which includes harpsichord, organ, archlute and Baroque guitar, makes an important contribution to the overall success.

This music is wonderful stuff, rejuvenating and immensely satisfying.

Violin Concertos, Op 4 – La stravaganza

Violin Concertos 'La stravaganza', Op 4 – No 1 in B flat, RV383 a; No 2 in E minor, RV279; No 3 in G, RV301; No 4 in A minor, RV357; No 5 in A, RV347; No 6 in G minor, RV316a
Andrew Watkinson vn **City of London Sinfonia /**
Nicholas Kraemer
Naxos 8 553323 (52' · DDD)   Ⓢᴰ

Violin Concertos, 'La stravaganza', Op 4 – No 7 in C, RV185; No 8 in D minor, RV249; No 9 in F, RV284; No

10 in C minor, RV196; No 11 in D minor, RV204; No 12 in G, RV298
Andrew Watkinson vn **City of London Sinfonia /**
Nicholas Kraemer
Naxos 8 553324 (46' · DDD)   Ⓢᴰ

La stravaganza is the second of the sets of concertos published during Vivaldi's lifetime. It was issued in about 1714 as the composer's Op 4 and, as with the greater number of his printed collections, contains 12 works. They are essentially violin concertos, although, to a much lesser extent than *L'estro armonico*, Vivaldi also provides on occasion solo parts for an additional violin or cello. These concertos have long been favourites, above all, perhaps, for the profusion of lyrically affecting slow movements, of which those belonging to Concertos Nos 1, 4, 5 and 12 are notably fine examples: in this music there's delicate nuance, poetic fantasy and sheer originality lying beneath the immediately recognisable hallmarks of the composer's outward style. Nicholas Kraemer is no stranger to this repertory having already recorded two of Vivaldi's other printed sets, Opp 8 and 9. Those, however, were with his period-instrument Raglan Baroque Players, whereas *La stravaganza* is played on instruments tuned to today's standard pitch. This, paradoxically, may be closer to the pitch which Vivaldi himself used rather than the lower Baroque pitch.

Listening to this music, so full of vitality, invention and expressive tenderness, leaves one feeling exhilarated. Andrew Watkinson plays with virtuosic flair, but senses the highly developed fantasy present in every one of the concertos. His embellishments are tasteful and restrained and his melodic line always clearly articulated. Tempos, for the most part, are effectively judged, though the almost unbearably beautiful *Largo* of the First Concerto, with its emotionally highly charged modulation towards the close, is perhaps a shade too slow.

The strings of the City of London Sinfonia sound tonally bright and unfailingly alert. Only in the *Adagio* of No 8 does the balance of the recording falter; the harpsichord's arpeggios (notably in the *Adagio molto* of 'Autumn') might have been allowed a little more prominence.

Violin Concertos 'La stravaganza', Op 4 – Nos 1-12   **P**
Arte dei Suonatori / Rachel Podger vn
Channel Classics ② CCS19598 (103' · DDD) Also
available on SACD CCSSA19503   Ⓕ**OOO**

 By the standards of the average Vivaldi violin concerto, the *La stravaganza* set is quite extravagant stuff, full of fantasy and experiment – novel sounds, ingenious textures, exploratory melodic lines, original types of figuration, unorthodox forms. It's heady music, and listening to its 12 concertos at a sitting, isn't a mode of listening one would recommend.

Still less so in performances as high in voltage as the present ones. There's a current trend in Baroque performance to get away from the coolness and objectivity which for a long time were supposed (on the whole, mistakenly) to be a part of performing practice of the time, but possibly the pendulum has swung a little wildly the other way. Perhaps here it's intended to reflect Vivaldi's own notorious freedom of performance. But anyone who's admired earlier recordings with period instruments may find these a little extravagant and hard-hitting. And they aren't helped by the resonant acoustic of the church in Poland used for the recording, which produces a full and bright sound but a boomy bass and less clear a texture than might be ideal.

That said, however, these performances by Rachel Podger are crackling with vitality and executed with consistent brilliance as well as a kind of relish in virtuosity that catches the showy spirit, the self-conscious extravagance, of this particular set of works. There are plenty of movements here where her sheer digital dexterity is astonishing – for instance, the finale of No 6, with its scurrying figures, the second movement of No 7 or the finale of No 2 with its repetitive figures and leaping arpeggios. But perhaps even more enjoyable isthe exquisitely fine detail of some of the slow movements. No 8 in D minor is perhapsthe wildest concerto of the lot, with its extraordinary lines in the first movement, the passionate, mysterious outer sections in the second and the powerful and original figuration inthe finale: that one has a performance to leave you breathless.

Another thing Podger is specially good at is the shaping of those numerous passages of Vivaldian sequences, which can be drearily predictable, but aren't so here because she knows just how to control the rhythmic tension and time the climax and resolution with logic and force. This set is certainly recommended as a fine example of a modern view of Baroque performance – and it sounds even better on SACD.

Violin Concertos, Op 8 (incl Four Seasons)

Violin Concertos, Op 8 – Nos 1-4, 'The Four Seasons': No 1 in E, 'Spring', RV269; No 2 in G minor, 'Summer', RV315; No 3 in F, 'Autumn', RV293; No 4 in F minor, 'Winter', RV297; **No 5** in E flat, RV253, **'La tempesta di mare'; No 6** in C, RV180, **'Il piacere'; No 7** in D minor, RV242; **No 8** in G minor, RV332; **No 9** in D minor, RV236; **No 10** in B flat, RV362, **'La caccia'; No 11** in D, RV210; **No 12** in C (two versions, RV178 & RV449)

The Four Seasons.   P
Violin Concertos in E flat, RV257; in B flat, RV376; in D, RV211
Giuliano Carmignola vn
Venice Baroque Orchestra / Andrea Marcon
Sony Classical 82796 90391-2 (72' · DDD)   P**OO**B→

Vivaldi's *Four Seasons*, like nature's, come and go in their various moods and meteorological vicissitudes. We've had ochre sunsets from Louis Kaufmann, Harnoncourt's Breughel-style rustic-

ity and the provocative Nigel Kennedy, to mention but a scant few. Giuliano Carmignola's primary claim on our attentions (this is his second shot at the piece) is, aside from a delightfully woody-sounding Baroque instrument, a keen narrative flair. He knows the musical period, understands principles of embellishment and doesn't hesitate to enrich his performances with added colour and with rhythmic thrust. 'Spring' arrives in rude high spirits, toying with birdsong (slowly at first then speeding up) and with thunder thrashing between violin desks. The violas' 'barking dog' is worryingly prominent (if you don't like dogs) and the finale contrasts a swelling *legato* against sparkly solo passagework. The 'impetuous weather of summer' has power enough to keep the National Grid up and running, and the diverse winds of the multi-faceted opening *Allegro* of 'Autumn' and the way the harpsichord holds its own in the second and third movements are wonderful. The cruel weathers of 'Winter' inspire the expected bursts of virtuosity while the *Largo*'s raindrops unexpectedly seep through to the busy bass line (most versions don't allow for the leak). Varieties of plucked continuo help fill out textures and Carmignola himself plays with immense brilliance. The three additional violin concertos are all said to be first recordings and reveal a rather different aspect of Vivaldi's style. Generally speaking, they sound more formal than the *Four Seasons*, almost pre-classical in RV257's opening *Andante molto e quasi allegro* and with sideways glances at Rameau in the opening of RV211 (which also includes a brief first-movement cadenza). Dance rhythms again predominate.

Great sound, full and forward and with every instrumental strand given its proper due. Thinking in terms only of the *Four Seasons*, good rivals are so plentiful that comparative discussion becomes less a question of 'who gets it right' than how you like your birds and storms. There are countless period-instrument options and almost as many that use modern instruments, but take heed of period performing practice. Up to now, the period favourites have been Il Giardino Armonico (reviewed below) and Harnoncourt's Concentus Musicus Wien, and there's no reason why this new version shouldn't join their hallowed ranks.

The Four Seasons
Janine Jansen vn with **Henk Rubingh, Candida Thompson** vns **Julian Rachlin** va **Maarten Jansen** vc **Stacey Watton** db **Elizabeth Kenny** theo **Jan Jansen** org/hpd
Decca ⏤ 475 6188DSA (39' · DDD)   P B→

There's so much to be said against it on extramusical grounds. The cynicism of the presentation, for a start: the booklet includes seven photographs of the beautiful Miss Jansen in four dresses, one of them a diaphanous décolleté number embroidered with butterflies. Then, opposite a black-and-white version of the latter in soft focus, there's a note by the violinist of numbing and ungrammatical banality. And Decca is charging full price for 39 minutes of music.

So to approach the music in a jaundiced frame of mind is understandable, and first impressions are not good: lush, squeeze-box phrasing in the opening tutti of 'Spring' and a distant harpsichord continuo put me in mind of old recordings by I Musici. Equally unstylish are the gratuitous *pizzicati* in the last movement of 'Autumn', where the frightened game is trying to escape horse and hound.

But the playing grows on you. Oddly enough, the absence of a *ripieno* string group doesn't make the performance small-scale. Janine Jansen and her colleagues play with splendid vigour in the outer movements, and Jansen herself weaves a line of great beauty in the *Largo*s and the *Adagio*. There's a fair amount of *rubato*, especially in the first movement of 'Autumn', which certainly holds the attention. The dialogue between violin and organ continuo in the 'cuckoo' section of 'Summer' is a delight.

Worth begging or borrowing; not stealing, perhaps!

Vivaldi Violin Concertos, 'The Four Seasons', Op 8 Nos 1-4 **Tartini** Violin Sonata, 'Devil's Trill'
Academy of St Martin in the Fields / Joshua Bell vn
Sony Classical Ⓕ 88697 11013-2 (54' · DDD)

A big-name violinist, the Academy of St Martin in the Fields, John Constable tinkling away on a ten-ton Goble – this *Seasons* is a bit like returning to old times. Any Vivaldi-lover will have these iconic concertos in their collection already, probably several times over, but the merest glance at the packaging of this one will tell you that it is not aimed at them anyway. So what will the 'I want a *Four Seasons* but by somebody I've heard of' clientele get for their money? Well, mighty fine playing for certain: Bell has the lightness and quickness of Mercury in passagework, and a smooth and sweet lyricism no less divine in the slower sections. Not a single ugly noise emanates from his instrument, and he is well matched by the ASMF, their sound ample and softly comfortable yet clean and clear. It is doubtful if you will ever hear a more purely beautifully rapt ensemble rendition of the slow movement from *Spring*, for instance.

What is missing amid all this high-class musicianship is the inventive spark of excitement these pieces can provoke in so many players, especially through its descriptive elements. All right, not everyone has to give themselves over entirely to being dying stags, drunken peasants or barking dogs, but these performances would surely benefit from the greater rhythmic and dynamic flexibility a bit more pictorial imagining could bring. The fill-up is a thoughtful choice, however; Tartini's *Devil's Trill* Sonata, adroitly played with extra-romantic, stratospheric cadenza, as if to Bell the Devil were ne'er a foe.

The Four Seasons   Ⓟ
Oboe Concertos, Op 7 – No 1 in B flat, RV465; No 5 in F, RV285*a*

VIVALDI FOUR SEASONS – IN BRIEF

Concerto Italiano / Rinaldo Alessandrini   Ⓟ
Opus 111 ② OP30363 (103' · DDD)   ⒻOO
A stunning new version of the *Four Seasons*, each season granted its own soloist. Theatricality and discipline are ideally combined in this unforgettable performance.

Enrico Onofri; Il Giardino Armonico   Ⓟ
Teldec 4509-96158-2 (61' · DDD)   ⒻOO
Though a relatively small group, Il Giardino Armonico give as much vigour and sonority as you might wish, while allowing telling contributions from their continuo section.

Giuliano Carmignola; Venice Baroque Orchestra / Andrea Marcon   Ⓟ
Sony Classical 82796 90391-2 (72' · DDD)   ⒻOO
A violinist of extraordinary technique and attractive tone and a truly imaginative interpretation. He's aided by the equally inventive playing of the orchestra, and the result is one of the most highly charged performances.

Gottfried von der Goltz; Freiburg Baroque Orchestra, Harp Consort   Ⓟ
Deutsche Harmonia Mundi 05472 77384-2 (66' · DDD)   Ⓕ
An imaginative performance which draws from a rich palette of continuo instruments – lirone, Baroque lute, cittern, archlute, guitar, theorbo, arch-cittern, harp and psaltery, together with harpsichord, organ and regal!

Andrew Manze; Amsterdam Baroque Orchestra / Ton Koopman   Ⓟ
Elatus 0927 46726-2 (57' · DDD)   Ⓕ
An 'authentic' performance for those who don't want their performance too spiced up. A straightforward account with subtle but telling individual touches by Manze.

Anthony Marwood; Scottish CO / Nicholas McGegan
BMG 75605 570452 (67' · DDD)   Ⓜ
An excellent performance on modern instruments, but with the briskness and lightness of Baroque practice. Real thought has gone into the characterisation of each season, and this is easily one of the most invigorating and uplifting accounts you can hope to find.

Anne-Sophie Mutter; Trondheim Soloists
DG 463 2592 (63' · DDD)   ⒻOⒹ→
A nice halfway house between period manners and a more traditional interpretation. Quicksilver fiddling and a orchestra in total sympathy with their starry soloist make this a delight.

Janine Jansen *et al*
Decca 475 6188DSA (39' · DDD)   ⒻⒹ→
A tremendous, small-scale interpretation from the young Janine Jansen and friends. A big hit on iTunes!

Andrew Manze *vn* **Marcel Ponseele** *ob* **Amsterdam Baroque Orchestra / Ton Koopman**
Warner Elatus 0927-46726-2 (56' · DDD)   Ⓜ️Ⓞ

This is a splendid set, valid for a lifetime of pleasure. Little differences in attention to detail soon begin to show, first at 0'17"of the first movement of 'Spring', where the chords that are usually hit hard are here given a happy little squeeze. Amsterdam Baroque (consisting here of 13 instrumentalists) play with the unanimity of one mind and body, with extreme changes of volume that never sound theatrically contrived, as concerned with the fate of every note as with the shaping of each phrase. Manze's bow breathes vocal life into his strings; in the slow movements many notes whisper their way into being, and his *fortissimo* whiplashes have rasp-free edges. There are many delightful little personal touches – his slurred resolution of the sighing appoggiatura at 2'50" in the third movement of 'Spring', and the way he nudges his way up the ladder of trills in the first movement of 'Autumn' are just two.

The remaining works come from Op 7, in the first of which (RV465) the oboe is the soloist; its transcribed role in No 5 (RV285*a*) accords with Baroque practice. Both are charming works with a high level of inspiration.

Violin Concertos – Op 8 No 8, RV332; 'La caccia', Op 8 No 10, RV362; 'Il sospetto', RV199; 'Grosso Mogul', RV208 No 2; 'L'inquietudine', RV234; 'Il riposo', RV270
Academia Montis Regalis / Enrico Onofri *vn*
Naïve OP30417 (55' · DDD) Ⓕ

Enrico Onofri writes that 'when subjected to a profound, subtle and precise reading of the rhetorical formulas that compose them, [Vivaldi's] concertos stand revealed as extremely impassioned works, by turns gently melancholic, impetuous, ironic, dramatic, caricatural, introspective, voluptuous, violent, tender, graceful.' All these characteristics are depicted in Onofri's intensely rhetorical playing. Occasionally he likes to introduce mischievous (perhaps even anarchic) elements into Academia Montis Regalis's performances, as if to insist that we must not regard this music as mere fashionable wallpaper music. The relentlessly tempestuous Concerto RV234, *L'inquietudine*, is not stuff that corporations will use for holding callers on the telephone.

Onofri's rapid flourishes in the extensive cadenza that concludes the *Grosso Mogul* Concerto, RV208, are not only phenomenal from a technical point of view but delivered in such a convincing way that every single note seems to matter. Amid the thwacks and snaps in fast tuttis one wonders if elegance might be an authentic Vivaldian characteristic in danger of becoming overlooked, although there is much more to these performances than shock tactics. Among the finest elements of this kaleidoscopic disc are the quieter slower movements: eloquence, grief, tranquillity and desire all seem to be worn on Onofri's sleeve. The *Adagio* in Concerto RV270, *Il riposo*, is breathtakingly beautiful; *La caccia* is unusually

provocative, rewarding and frequently amazing. Academia Montis Regalis present Vivaldi's concertos as totally compelling and meaningful music that demands full attention and respect.

Violin Concertos – Miscellaneous

Dresden Concertos – D, RV213; D, RV219; D, RV224; D minor, RV240; E flat, RV260; A, RV344; B minor, RV388
Cristiano Rossi *vn*
Accademia I Filarmonici / Alberto Martini
Naxos 8 554310 (67' · DDD)   Ⓢ️Ⓓ➔

The Dresden link was forged by Vivaldi's friend and one-time pupil Johann Georg Pisendel. Pisendel visited Venice in 1716 when he appears to have struck up a warm friendship with Vivaldi, who dedicated several sonatas and concertos to him. The seven violin concertos on this disc have survived in manuscripts preserved in the Dresden Sächsische Landesbibliothek. Much of this music will be entirely new to most collectors. By and large these are pieces which do not wear their hearts on their sleeves. There are few extravagant flourishes and perhaps less than we might expect in the way of extrovert gesture. But there's no lack of brilliance in the solo violin writing – Pisendel's reputation as a virtuoso was hardly less than Vivaldi's –and, as ever, the music contains a profusion of effective rhythmic ideas. The solo violin parts are entrusted to Cristiano Rossi, who often, though not always, discovers the fantasy in Vivaldi's solo writing. The bowing is graceful and relaxed even if intonation is occasionally awry. The A major Concerto, RV344 affords a good instance of soloist and orchestra at their most persuasive. But the lyrically expressive violin melody against a dotted rhythm continuo of the *Largo* of RV224 is unquestionably the most alluring.

The more you hear this music, the more you're likely to be captivated by it. The recorded sound seems a little boxy and confined, but textures come through clearly all the same.

Concertos for Strings – RV111*a*; RV114; RV119; RV121; RV127; RV146; RV152; RV156; RV157; 'Conca', RV163; RV167; RV168
Venice Baroque Orchestra /
Andrea Marcon *hpd/org*
Archiv Produktion 474 5092AH (68' · DDD)   Ⓕ️Ⓞ️Ⓓ➔

This collection draws from Vivaldi's 'Concerti per archi', concertos for strings and continuo without the flamboyant writing for solo instruments found in the majority of the Red Priest's orchestral works. Across 68 minutes Vivaldi seems to have a seemingly inexhaustible arsenal of tricks, but it's never merely superficial. All the music on offer here is unmistakably Vivaldian: although there is common ground in many of these 'concerti per archi', they contain a dazzling kaleidoscope of moods and textures.

Andrea Marcon directs vivid, strongly etched

performances that often reach fiery intensity. Things get off to a sizzling start with the precocious beginning of RV111*a*, and the opening *Allegro* of RV157 is a perfect illustration of Marcon's fondness for wonderfully incisive yet flowing continuo. But there are also notable moments of exquisite beauty, such as a gorgeously played *Largo* from RV127. The *Adagio* in RV121 is an evocative hushed moment graced with lovely theorbo playing. It is easy to notice the athleticism of the Venice Baroque Orchestra's vigorous playing of fast movements, yet it is equally significant that the group perform Vivaldi's slower music with tenderness.

Violin Concertos – 'Grosso Mogul', RV208; 'L'inquietudine', RV234; RV277; RV187. Concerto grosso, RV580 Op 3 No 10.
Viktoria Mullova vn **Il Giardino Armonico / Giovanni Antonini**
Onyx Classics ONYX4001 (54' · DDD)   Ⓕ🅑➔

Viktoria Mullova isn't quite a Baroque violinist – her Strad is fitted with gut strings, she's using a Baroque bow and she plays very stylishly – but there's something about her sound that betrays the modern virtuoso. Her vibrato is modest but it's used in a way that harks back to her conventional Russian training. Much more important than rating her on a scale of authenticity, however, is to note that it's top-class violin playing: the rhythms are lively and poised, all the passagework is beautifully clear and exact.

The programme is excellent, too, in the way it shows the wide range of Vivaldi's imagination. The rarely encountered RV187 is a lovely piece, full of delightful original touches, in contrast to the better known *Grosso Mogul* which, despite its brilliance and its satisfying formal design, is oppressively short of significant ideas.

Il Giardino Armonico provide an immensely spirited accompaniment, four members taking the extra solo roles in Op 3 No 10 with great style. Vivaldi's music needs strong contrasts in performance; it should create a sense of amazement, which these accounts supply in a striking and convincing way. The prevalence of ferocious accents, ultra-short off-the-string bowing, and exaggerated dynamic shading is a little troubling: the strongest, swiftest bow stroke should retain the character of a gesture, rather than a hammer blow. But whether or not you agree, you're likely to enjoy the vigour, colourful variety and sheer expertise of these performances.

Violin Concertos – RV190; RV217; RV303; RV331; RV325
Giuliano Carmignola vn
Venice Baroque Orchestra / Andrea Marcon
Archiv Produktion 477 6005AH (58' · DDD)   Ⓕ🅑➔

Giuliano Carmignola and the Venice Baroque Orchestra here return to the all-Vivaldi format which has so far served them well. Given that the concertos on this release are advertised as world

premiere recordings, that seems sensible enough. The mushrooming of the Vivaldi catalogue means that the excitement of hearing 'new' works can be as immediate as if he were still working among us today; and where we used to know but a handful of (mostly early) concertos, we are now becoming more aware of different stylistic periods, as well as the cross-fertilisation with other areas of his output.

Three of the works here show affinities with vocal works from the 1720s, when the brusque energy of the *L'estro armonico* concertos had been left behind in favour of something more dance-like; the other two are in the expansive, laid-back style of the 1730s. It is a little voyage of discovery, then, with the scenery including much harmonic resource and violinistic devilry.

There are no surprises in the performances though: they are as purringly beautiful as ever from these artists. Carmignola dashes around Vivaldi's scampering passagework and giant leaps with an easy control and consistency of good tone, and the Venice Baroque Orchestra are worthy partners – their surging rivers of sound in the finale of RV325 give a real thrill. Indeed, while one can imagine violinists of the Manze or Biondi kind finding more drama or humour in this music, it is otherwise hard to find anything to fault in these Rolls-Royce performances.

Double Concertos – RV509; RV511; RV514; RV516; RV523; RV524
Giuliano Carmignola, Viktoria Mullova vns
Venice Baroque Orchestra / Andrea Marcon
Archiv Produktion 477 7466AH (59' · DDD)   Ⓕ🅞🅑➔

The Venice Baroque Orchestra have a frill-less way of going about their Vivaldi programming: no mixed running orders, no imaginative fillers, no clever links between different items, just single-minded concentration on one genre. This time the subject is double violin concertos, six of them and nothing else. Surprisingly, this is largely unexplored territory, not least as our performers have eschewed the four published examples of the Op 3 set in favour of works from the 24 surviving in Vivaldi's manuscripts. None is new to the catalogue, but none is exactly well known, and all the more welcome are they for that.

Vivaldi's approach to double-concerto writing was mostly to provide equal music for both soloists, who either play in euphonious parallel or alternate melody and accompaniment in short snatches. For this reason it is not only impossible to separate or differentiate the playing of Viktoria Mullova and Giuliano Carmignola here, but undesirable too. In this music they are as they should be: one living organism, both playing their Baroque violins with gorgeously burnished tone and an agile virtuosity which, freed from the macho pyrotechnics of the solo concertos, gains a relaxed and tender quality that reveals the poet in Vivaldi. And in those rare moments when there really is a difference, when one violin cuts loose with a glorious, yearning stretch of melody while the other accompanies with arpeggios or some such (as occurs in the finales of RV524 and 516), it warms like a sudden surge of blood through the veins.

Andrea Marcon and the VBO play their accompanimental role with their usual expert light touch, and the recording is spacious, clear and neatly balanced. A perfect Vivaldi treat.

'Concertos for the Emperor'
Violin Concertos – in C, RV189; in C minor, RV202; in F, 'Concerto per la solennità di San Lorenzo', RV286; in C, RV183; in E, 'L'amoroso', RV271; in E minor, 'Il favorito', RV277
The English Concert / Andrew Manze vn
Harmonia Mundi HMU90 7332 (79' · DDD)   Ⓕ

Vivaldi published his Op 9 concertos, *La cetra* ('The Lyre'), in 1727. Soon after, he presented Charles VI, the Habsburg emperor, with a manuscript set of concertos, also called *La cetra*. It was long supposed that these were the same concertos until someone looked at them more carefully, and noticed that 11 of the 12 were entirely different works. Vivaldi had simply used the same name again for a set of pieces he thought particularly well suited to the needs of the Viennese court. No one seems to have gathered them together for performance as a group until now. The six presented here show Vivaldi in his grandest and most magnificent vein, and exceptionally varied in mood.

The first item (No 2 of the set) is a dashing C major piece, with vigorous scales to catch the attention, then more contemplative minor-key music with much brilliant high writing for the soloist; there's a quietly eloquent slow movement, again with violin reaching its upper reaches; and in the finale, a lively, playful piece, the cadenza is positively stratospheric.

The second concerto (No 10) is entirely different, soft-toned, with a lovely E major glow, and a tenderness to the musical ideas untypical of Vivaldi. Then comes a big C minor work (No 7) with large gestures in its outer movements; in the finale there's a huge *crescendo* that makes the later Mannheim ones sound tame by comparison, with some elaborate violin coloratura.

The final concerto, in F major (No 4), is a big, ceremonial, stately piece, originally composed 'per la solennità di San Lorenzo', but it serves Charles VI pretty well, too, with a virtuoso finale to round it off. Perhaps the most powerful of the concertos, however, is No 11, full of nervous energy in its first movement, with an improvisatory violin line in its second above soft chords, and a strong reminiscence of the *Four Seasons* (not the only one here) in the finale.

This is an immensely enjoyable disc: the music very characteristic, but much freer of cliché than Vivaldi sometimes is. The violin-playing from Andrew Manze is of an extremely high order: rhythms beautifully springy, articulation clear and precise, intonation perfect, great refinement in the shaping of phrases, and a real command of the logic of the music. The orchestral support is strong and energetic, the recorded quality first-rate. An outstanding CD in every way.

Concertos – 'L'inquietudine', RV234; 'La tempesta di mare', RV253; RV273; RV565. Sonata, 'La folia', RV63. Andromeda liberata – Sovvente il sole[a]
Chamber Orchestra of Europe / Daniel Hope vn
with [a]**Anne Sofie von Otter** mez
DG 477 7463GH (58' · DDD)   ⒻⓄ▷

Three cheers for Daniel Hope for making a high-profile Vivaldi release without recourse to *The Four Seasons*. Not that there is anything wrong with those marvellous pieces of course but the disc he has produced is surely a deeper way of signalling his love and understanding of the Red Priest. Vivaldi lovers will be familiar with some of the works here, but RV234 is not so well known, while real rarities are RV273, a delicious and long-limbed late work, and a spaciously atmospheric aria with obbligato violin from the opera *Andromeda liberata*.

Hope and the COE play them with the clarity and ensemble precision of a top-class Baroque orchestra, and with their spritely bowing and general avoidance of vibrato, perhaps only the occasional sweetening of tone in Hope's top register really gives away that modern instruments are at work. There seems little doubt as to the kind of performances Hope has been influenced by, and the 'Baroque' feel is enhanced by a generous and active continuo section which even runs to a harp and a lirone. What results is Vivaldi that is enjoyable and without quirks, and perhaps all one would wish for is that final ounce of drive and energy the less reined-in playing of a Baroque orchestra can bring to faster movements. On the other hand, Hope's obvious relish for Vivaldi's stiller moments brings memorable results in the rich poetry of RV273 (real summer-night warmth here) and the captivatingly wistful 'Sovvento il sole', in which, though vocally less smooth-running than she has been in the past, guest soloist Anne Sofie von Otter catches the mood superbly. This is a disc made with love and intelligence – a powerful combination.

'The Rise of the North Italian Violin Concerto: 1690-1740'
'Vol 2 – Antonio Vivaldi: Virtuoso Impresario'
Vivaldi Violin Concertos – 'senza cantin', RV243; RV254; RV370. Concerto for Two Cellos and Strings, RV561. Concerto for Strings, RV134. La costanza trionfante degl'amori e de gl'odii, RV706[a] – Sento il cor brillarmi in petto; Hai sete di sangue; Amoroso caro sposo. La fida ninfa, RV714[a] – Dolce fiamma; Alma oppressa
[a]**Mhairi Lawson** sop
La Serenissima / Adrian Chandler vn
Avie AV2128 (77' · DDD · T/t)   Ⓕ

'Antonio Vivaldi: Virtuoso Impresario' examines links between Vivaldi's concertos and operas. Thus, the Concerto RV370 has origins partly in the opera *Ottone in villa*, RV134 was probably once the sinfonia to an oratorio, and RV254 shows signs of having started out life as an entr'acte. It should be said that the links are sometimes tenuous, but who could complain when the snippets of minutely detailed information which Adrian Chandler clearly commands encourage mixed programming so refreshingly different from the Vivaldian norm? It may not always bring us the Red Priest at his most inspired but it certainly shows a few sides to him that we do not always see – enough to confound daft comments about his lack of variety. For this is music brimming with ideas, from the unusual accompanimental texture of the slow movement of RV561, to the E-string-less experiment of RV243 (and the strange, off-beam harmonies of its slow movement), to RV134's excellent fugue. All are played with La Serenissima's customary bright energy and enthusiasm, to which qualities are here added considerable subtlety of detail: listen to the way Chandler picks his way intelligently through the changing textural landscape of the first movement of RV243. Indeed, his playing throughout shows a smooth but vital tone, a fundamental likeability of sound and manner which is matched by soprano Mhairi Lawson in her five contrasted arias, all relative rarities dispatched with no-nonsense skill and aplomb. Here is further proof from this young British group that the Italian orchestras need not think to have Vivaldi to themselves just yet.

Double and Triple Concertos

Concertos – for Two Cellos in G minor, RV531;   P
for Two Violins, Two and Cellos in D, RV564; for
Recorder – A minor, RV108; G, RV436. Trio Sonatas –
D minor, 'La follia', RV63; C minor, RV83
Musica Alta Ripa
Dabringhaus und Grimm MDG309 0927-2 (56' · DDD)
                                              F O

None of the pieces is new to the catalogue, but the playing is of a calibre that might entice readers to consider these alternative versions. The two largest works are the Concerto for two cellos and strings in G minor, and another, in D major, for two violins, two cellos and strings. Both fare well in the hands of sensitive performers such as these, and especially enjoyable is the beautifully inflected playing of the two solo cellists in the G minor work.

Albert Brüggen is an excellent cellist, and here (alongside partner Juris Teichmanis) he fulfils expectation raised by previous discs. Vivaldi wrote two concertos for pairs of solo violins and cellos; the other is RV575 – and both are satisfying pieces with beguiling slow movements. Melodically, this one gives pride of place to a solo violin in its centrally placed Largo, but one should nevertheless be allowed to hear more of the solo cello than is granted by this performance. The rhythmic élan of the finale is quite exhilarating. The two remaining concertos feature a recorder. One, RV436, is scored for transverse flute with strings, though a descant recorder has been substituted here. The other, RV108, is a chamber concerto for treble recorder, two violins and continuo. The soloist in each is Danya Segal, who brings the music to life with fluency and unpretentious elo-

quence. An attractive menu is completed by two strongly contrasting sonatas which, in their quite different ways, demonstrate Vivaldi's craftsmanship and invention in the medium.

This disc makes rewarding listening. The pieces have been chosen with real discernment and are played with virtuosity and an effective understanding of style.

Concerto for Multiple Instruments in C, RV557   P
Double Concertos – 2 Oboes in D minor, RV535;
Oboe and Bassoon in G, RV545; 2 Trumpets in C,
RV537; 2 Horns in F, RV538. Oboe Concerto in A
minor, RV461. Bassoon Concerto in E minor, RV484
Ensemble Zefiro / Alfredo Bernardini
Astrée Naïve E8679 (64' · DDD)   F O O

Ensemble Zefiro is one of the most remarkable Baroque bands to emerge during the last decade or so, though we hear of it less often than it deserves. Its specialised front line is its battery of exceptionally gifted wind players, but the support troops of strings and continuo are no less worthy of commendation. In all technical and musical respects they think, breathe and act as one. Their dynamic range (from sotto voce whisper to as many *f*s as you regard as adding up to 'issimo') is put to vivid and impressive use, whether terraced in *crescendo*s or *diminuendo*s, or in the finely judged squeezing of notes. The Allegros are crisp, animated, joyously propulsive and full of Italian sunshine, and the eloquent music-making of the oboe and bassoon soloists effortlessly conceals Vivaldi's severe technical demands. It's perhaps the slow movements that make the deepest impression: how many times have we heard the same harmonic progressions but marvelled at Vivaldi's ability to invest them with constantly new charm and depth? There are appealing conversations in those of RV545 (oboe and bassoon), RV535 (two oboes), RV557 (two recorders, whose players aren't among the declared personnel in the booklet!) and RV538 (two cellos). They are all marked by stylish embellishment, and the last was an irresistible reminder of the benchmark recording of the two-cello Concerto RV531 by Pleeth and Bylsma with the AAM (L'Oiseau Lyre). Nicholas Anderson has rightly described Alberto Grazzi as 'the poet of the bassoon'; in this recording we have a veritable eisteddfod. This is a faultless and marvellous recording.

Concertos[a] – D, 'L'inquietudine', RV234; E,   P
'Il riposo, per il Santissimo Natale', RV270. Recorder
Concerto No 2 in G minor, 'La notte', RV439[b].
Concerto for 2 Cellos in G minor, RV531[c]. Concertos
for Multiple Instruments – A, 'Per eco in lontano',
RV552; F, 'La tempesta di mare', RV570; B flat,
'Concerto funèbre', RV579
[b]**Lorenzo Cavasanti** *rec* [c]**Maurizio Naddeo,**
[c]**Antonio Fantinuoli** *vcs* **Europa Galante /
Fabio Biondi**[a] *vn*
Virgin Veritas 545424-2 (64' · DDD)   F O

There's a real lickety-split opening to this colourful disc of Vivaldi concertos: the violin concerto *L'inquietudine*, not one of its composer's best-known, really earns its title with a restlessly virtuosic solo part, dispatched with taut, nervous energy by Fabio Biondi. In truth there's some scintillating music here, as well as performances which mix suitable inspiration with scrupulous but unfussy attention to detail. The nearest we get to well-trodden ground here are the vigorous *La tempesta di mare* and the fantastical *La notte* (played here in their later 'flute' revisions, but on recorder), and both are performed with tightly controlled virtuosity, and with plenty of surprises – the giant off-beat accents in both concertos' finales, for instance. Elsewhere we get a creamy account of the charming (but perhaps slightly long) *Concerto per eco in lontano*, a encourage mixed programming so refreshingly different from the Vivaldian norm? It may not always bring us the Red Priest at his most inspired but it certainly shows a few sides to him that we do not always see – enough to confound daft comments about his lack of variety. For this is music brimming with ideas, from the unusual accompanimental texture of the slow movement of RV561, to the E-string-less experiment of RV243 (and the strange, off-beam harmonies of its slow movement), to RV134's excellent fugue.

All are played with La Serenissima's customary bright energy and enthusiasm, to which qualities are here added considerable subtlety of detail: listen to the way Chandler picks his way intelligently through the changing textural landscape strong-boned concerto for two violins, and an exquisite, muted-string Christmas concerto entitled Il riposo. If the sombre *Concerto funèbre* for multiple soloists is a slight disappointment, it's only because Concerto Italiano (for Erato) have recently taken it to another level of dark theatricality. Overall, though, this is another disc to add to the growing pile of wonderfully refreshing and enlightening Vivaldi recordings to have come out of Italy in recent years.

Concertos – for Viola d'amore and Lute in D minor, 🅿 RV540; for Cello in G, RV413; for Flute in G minor, 'La notte', RV439; for Oboe in D minor, RV454; for Two Horns in F, RV539; for Multiple Instruments – in D minor, RV566; in F, 'Il Proteo ò sia il mondo rovescio', RV572. Chamber Concerto in G minor, RV107.
Orchestra of the Age of Enlightenment
Linn Records CKD151 (74' · DDD)   Ⓕ🅾️➔

It's a nice idea for the Orchestra of the Age of Enlightenment to record a disc of such varied Vivaldian fare. The young women of the orchestra which Vivaldi directed at the Ospedale della Pietà in Venice were as renowned for the range of instruments they could wield as for their virtuosity; so it seems neatly apposite that the OAE, so full of capable soloists itself, should use this music to celebrate its members' own star qualities. And the mixture is a wide one: three solo concertos; a rare Concerto for two horns; the deservedly popular Concerto for lute and viola d'amore, two concertos for typically extravagant Vivaldian multiple line-ups; and one of those chamber concertos in which all the players are soloists. The OAE play with great expertise and good taste throughout. Judging by the list in the booklet, they use a relatively large body of strings, but, although this is noticeable, there's no feeling of heaviness, and indeed the use of two double basses gives the sound a substantial foundation which is at the same time deliciously light on its feet. There's a total of 16 soloists listed: among the highlights are David Watkin's habitually assured and intensely musical playing of the Cello Concerto; Lisa Beznosiuk, sensitive as ever in *La notte* (though struggling a bit against the string sound); Andrew Clark and Roger Montgomery, treading securely and confidently through the Concerto for two horns; Anthony Robson, a little under the note sometimes but showing good breath control and phrasing in the Oboe Concerto; and a fairy-light performance of the Concerto for lute and viola d'amore from Elizabeth Kenny and Catherine Mackintosh. The performances are all directorless, and there was the odd place where a guiding hand might have pepped things up (or stopped the theorbo from twiddling so much in the slow movement of the Cello Concerto), but in general this is a relaxed and convivial Vivaldi programme that one can simply sit back and enjoy.

String Concertos

String Concertos – in C, RV110; in C, 'Ripieno', RV115; in C minor, RV118; in D minor, 'Madrigalesco', RV129; in E minor, RV134; in F, RV142; in G, RV145; in G, 'Alla rustica', RV151; in G minor, RV156; in A, 'Ripieno', RV158; in A minor, RV161; in B flat, RV166; in B flat, RV167
Collegium Musicum 90 / Simon Standage vn
Chandos Chaconne CHAN0687 (62' · DDD)   Ⓕ🅾️

This third volume of Collegium Musicum 90's survey of Vivaldi's string concertos offers a varied selection of works which bears testament to their composer's untiring imagination. Vivaldi composed more than 40 of these sparky little miniatures, united by an (almost) uniform adoption of a three-movement format and by the lack anywhere of any kind of soloist; for this reason they're also sometimes known either as 'concertos for orchestra' or 'ripieno concertos'. None lasts longer than eight minutes, and most come in under five.

CM90 perform with accomplished ease, attempting nothing outrageous but maintaining a relaxed bonhomie and clear-cut eloquence entirely suited to the music's modest aspirations. Theirs isn't the taut Vivaldi sound we have become used to hearing from other ensembles, but they have no difficulty serving up lyrical sweetness or joyous energy as required. Realistically and lucidly recorded, the disc leaves little to be desired.

Cello Sonatas

Cello Sonatas – E flat, RV39; E minor, RV40;   Ⓟ
G minor, RV42; A minor, RV44; B flat, RV45; B flat,
RV46
Pieter Wispelwey *vc* **Florilegium Ensemble**
(Elizabeth Kenny, William Carter *ltes/theorboes/gtrs*
Daniel Yeadon *vc* Neal Peres da Costa *hpd/org*)
Channel Classics CCS6294 (66' · DDD)   ⒻⓄ

Vivaldi wrote with great imagination for the
cello, and the sonatas, like the concertos, are
plentifully endowed with affecting melodies –
the third movement of the E minor Sonata is a
superb example –and virtuoso gestures. It would
seem, on the strength of these pieces, that
Vivaldi possessed a rare sensibility to the expressive *cantabile* possibilities in writing for the cello.
Certainly, few Baroque composers other than
Bach and perhaps Geminiani realised the instrument's solo potential better than he. Wispelwey
is a sensitive player who draws a warm if at times
under-assertive sound from his instrument. Fast
movements are clearly articulated, slow ones
lyrically played with some feeling for the poetry
of the music. The performances are thoughtful
and enlightened, with a continuo group that
includes organ, harpsichord, cello, archlutes,
theorboes and guitars in a variety of combinations. The quality of the recorded sound is fine.

Violin Sonatas

12 Violin Sonatas, Op 2 – No 1 in G minor, RV27; No
2 in A, RV31; No 3 in D minor, RV14; No 4 in F, RV20;
No 5 in B minor, RV36; No 6 in C, RV1
Elizabeth Wallfisch *vn* **Richard Tunnicliffe** *vc*
Malcolm Proud *hpd*
Hyperion CDA67467 (59' · DDD)   Ⓕ

Vivaldi's 12 violin sonatas, Op 2 were originally
released in an edition by the Venetian music
publisher Antonio Bortoli in 1709. They were
highly regarded enough for Estienne Roger to
publish his own edition in Amsterdam three
years later, quickly followed by a pirated edition by John Walsh in London. Listening to
this impressive new recording it's easy to
understand why they were so appealing. Each
of the six included here is packed with musical
treasure. Elizabeth Wallfisch's delivery of the
fast movements is dazzling, and her animated
and witty playing in the Giga towards the end of
the second sonata is stunning. More memorable
still is her clean and lyrical expression in the
simpler melodic movements. The slower *Andantes* that introduce each sonata are sensuously
played, and suggest Vivaldi could articulate
emotional depth beyond his Corellian model.
  Richard Tunnicliffe and Malcolm Proud form an
ideally sympathetic continuo section. In Bortoli's
1709 printed edition these sonatas were described
as for violin and cello, without mention of a keyboard instrument. Following this clue, the third
sonata is performed as a fabulous sinewy duet.

This magnificent disc is complemented by an
authoritative essay by Michael Talbot.

Gloria in excelsis Deo, RV588

Gloria, RV588[abcd] Laetatus sum, RV607[d]. Laudate
pueri, RV601[b]. Vestro principi divino, RV633[c]. Jubilate,
o amoeni chori, RV639[abcd]. [a]**Susan Gritton** *sops* [b]**Carolyn
Sampson** *sops* [c]**Nathalie Stutzmann** *contr* [a]**Charles
Daniels** *ten* The King's Consort and [d]**Choir / Robert
King**
Hyperion CDA66819 (69' · DDD · T/t)   Ⓕ

Volume 6 of this series was a *Gramophone* Award
nominee in 2001 and this one is just as good: it
contains some very fine and largely unfamiliar
music, in splendid performances. The principal
work is the 'other' *Gloria* – RV588, not the
popular 589, which, however, by no means outshines it. This setting, in fact, begins particularly
fascinatingly, as the choral climax to a short,
introductory solo motet *Jubilate, o amoeni chori*;
the motet elides, as it were, into the choral *Gloria* in an attractive and lively movement. Then
follows a poetic, choral 'Et in terra pax', rich in
texture and especially in harmony, and several
further movements scarcely less appealing than
their counterparts in RV589.
  The disc starts a shade unpromisingly, with
what seems rather a routine *Laetatus sum*, in
solid block choral writing against orchestral figuration. But the *Laudate pueri* is quite another
matter, a highly demanding solo motet which
Carolyn Sampson sings with great precision and
brilliance – Vivaldi often writes for the solo
voice as if it has the agility of a violin, but this
clearly doesn't disturb her. There's a lot of
original and imaginative writing here.
  The short motet *Vestro principi divino* was probably written for a weak contralto, in which case the
use of Nathalie Stutzmann is an inspired piece of
miscasting: she sings this entertaining piece with
great power and accuracy, and goes on to do the
motet introducing the *Gloria* in virtuoso fashion.
The other soloists, Susan Gritton and Charles
Daniels, have less to sing but do it with no less
distinction. And Robert King directs his choir and
orchestra with sensitive feeling for tempo, nuance
and style. One could hardly ask for more.

Gloria, RV588. Dixit Dominus, RV595. Jubilate o
amoeni chori. Nulla in mundo pax
Jane Archibald, Michele de Boer *sops* **Anita
Krause** *mez* **Peter Mahon** *counterten* **Nils Brown**
ten **Giles Tomkins** *bass-bar* **Aradia Ensemble /
Kevin Mallon**
Naxos 8 557445; 🔊 Ⓜ 6 110064 (69' · DDD · T/t)
                                                ⓈⒹ➤

In 1713 Vivaldi, teacher of the violin at the
school of the Ospedale della Pietà in Venice,
found himself taking on the responsibility for
composing music for the Pietà's all-female
choir. Here, in the first of a new series of recordings of all his sacred music on Naxos, are three

works from around 1715: none is well known, but all are extremely attractive.

Dixit Dominus only came to light in the 1960s. Visitors came from all over Europe to hear the girls' singing and playing, and in 'Tecum principium', for two sopranos and two cellos, we can imagine their delight. The puzzle is how the 'male' parts were sung. Was the bass-line taken at pitch by deep-voiced women, or transposed upwards? The Aradia Chorus goes for the conventional lay-out, with a mixed alto line, and sings with admirable clarity and vigour.

Jane Archibald, who copes fearlessly with the coloratura of 'Dominus a dextris tuis', does equally well in the 'Alleluia' of *Nulla in mundo*, and tastefully decorates the reprise of the *da capo* siciliana with which the motet begins.

The oddity here is Vivaldi's integration of the alto motet, *Jubilate, o amoeni chori*, with a setting of the Gloria, RV588. Anita Krause is up against stiff competition from the throaty contralto of Nathalie Stutzmann on Hyperion, but more than holds her own, especially in the lilting 'Qui sedes'. Kevin Mallon is rather dogged in the Gloria's 'Et in terra pax', but elsewhere he conducts with a sure sense of style.

Gloria in D, RV589

Vivaldi Gloria[b]. Ostro picta, RV642[c]. Nisi Dominus, RV803[d] **Ruggieri** Gloria, RV ANH 23[a]
[ab]**Joanne Lunn, Carolyn Sampson** sops
[ab]**Joyce DiDonato**, [ad]**Tuva Semmingsen** mezs
[abd]**Hilary Summers** contr [a]**Robin Blaze** counterten
The King's Consort Choir; The King's Consort / Robert King
Hyperion CDA66849 (77' · DDD · T/t)   (F)

Robert King had the good fortune that a lost Vivaldi *Nisi Dominus* turned up just as his project to record the composer's complete sacred music reached its 10th and final volume. This is its première recording. As the work's authenticator, Michael Talbot, has pointed out, only Vivaldi would have dared to include solos for chalumeau, violin 'in tromba marina', viola d'amore, organ and cello in a single multi-sectional work. If, as it seems, this is one of the great colouristic experimenter's last sacred compositions, he certainly goes out with a bang. An atmospheric and loving performance gives a perfect start to its new life.

The other major work for this final volume is the famous *Gloria*, a fitting crown to the series. So much is good in it – boldness, brightness, expressive depth, melodic beauty – and it all comes through in this carefully judged interpretation. Carolyn Sampson is excellent in the short solo motet *Ostro picta*, a final reminder that high-quality solo singing has been one of the principal pleasures of this series. But King gives the final word to the members of his choir, who ably sing the stand-out solos in the intriguing *Gloria* by Giovanni Maria Ruggieri from which Vivaldi pinched his own concluding 'Cum Sancto Spiritu' fugue. With its bold strokes of

originality and colour, it's easy to see how it could have impressed Vivaldi.

Psalms

Dixit Dominus in D, RV595[ab]. Domine ad   [P]
adiuvandum me, RV593[a]. Credidi propter quod,
RV605. Beatus vir in B flat, RV598[ab]. Beatus vir in C,
RV597[abc]
[a]**Susan Gritton**, [b]**Catrin Wyn-Davies** sops [b]**Catherine Denley** mez [c]**Charles Daniels** ten [c]**Neal Davies** bass
[c]**Michael George** bass **Choir of The King's Consort; The King's Consort / Robert King**
Hyperion CDA66789 (70' · DDD · T/t)   (F)

Here are two of Vivaldi's most extended and impressive psalm settings. These are the single-choir *Dixit Dominus*, RV595 (Psalm 110), and double-choir *Beatus vir*, RV597 (Psalm 112). Vivaldi set both psalms more than once, and King's programme also includes the single-movement *Beatus vir*, RV598, as well as the response, *Domine ad adiuvandum me*, RV593, and the conservatively styled Vesper psalm, *Credidi propter quod*, RV605. The King's Consort Choir make a lively and warm-textured contribution; the solo line-up is also strong; with Susan Gritton and Catrin Wyn-Davies providing an evenly matched, lightly articulated partnership in their two duets. Neal Davies and Michael George are splendidly robust in their vigorous 'Potens in terra' duet from *Beatus vir* (RV597). Catherine Denley gives an appropriately strongly inflected account of 'Judicabit in nationibus' but is intimate and tender in her beautiful 'De torrente in via bibet' (from *Dixit*). The remaining soloist, Charles Daniels, delivers the virtuoso 'Peccator videbit' (*Beatus vir*, RV597) with lightness and comfortable agility. Although consisting of only three movements, the G major *Domine ad adiuvandum me*, is easily on a level with the larger-scale pieces, its expressive warmth irresistible. This is a rewarding issue, spaciously recorded.

Dixit Dominus in D, RV594

Dixit Dominus in D, RV594[e]. Lauda Jerusalem in   [P]
E minor, RV609[b]. Magnificat in G minor, RV610[a]. Kyrie
in G minor, RV587[c]. Credo in E minor, RV591[d]
[abe]**Susan Gritton**, [abe]**Lisa Milne** sops [ae]**Catherine Denley** mez [ae]**Lynton Atkinson** ten [e]**David Wilson-Johnson** bar **The King's Consort Choristers and Choir; The King's Consort / Robert King**
Hyperion CDA66769 (63' · DDD · T/t)   (F)

King's 'super-group' featuring choristers drawn from seven English cathedral and collegiate choirs sounds better than ever – technically reliable, with a good, full sound – and are a credit to King's vision in bringing them together. This volume has five typically uplifting works, three of which – *Lauda Jerusalem*, *Dixit Dominus* and the G minor *Kyrie* – offer the opulent sound of double choir and orchestra. *Dixit Dominus* is the most substantial, a colourful 23-minute sequence of varied solos and choruses, with trumpets, oboes and two organs all chipping in, most notably in an awe-inspiring depiction of the Day of Judgement. The other two are perhaps less striking, though *Lauda Jerusalem* is certainly charming in its two-soprano interchanges. Highlights of the single-chorus works include another exquisite soprano duet and a fiery 'Fecit potentiam' in the *Magnificat*, and an extraordinary 'Crucifixus' in the *Credo* which departs from the pain-wracked norm by seemingly depicting with lugubrious slow tread Christ's walk to Calvary. King manages very well in capturing the essence of Vivaldi's bold, sometimes disarmingly straightforward style. These tidy performances are driven with just the right amount of springy energy – neither too much nor too little – and are well recorded in the warm resonance of St Jude's Church, Hampstead in London.

Motets

Laudate pueri Dominum, RV600[a]. **P**
Salve Regina, RV616[c]. Sanctorum meritis, RV620[a]. Sum in medio tempestatum, R632[b]. Cur sagittas, cur tela, RV637[c]
[a]**Susan Gritton** sop [b]**Tuva Semmingsen** mez
[c]**Nathalie Stutzmann** contr **The King's Consort /
Robert King**
Hyperion CDA66829 (68' · DDD · T/t) Ⓕ

The best-known item here is the *Salve Regina*, a piece which has been recorded on several occasions before, usually by countertenors. Vivaldi intended it for a woman, however, and here Nathalie Stutzmann is given the chance to show off the depth and dark nobility of her contralto voice. She strikes a suitably reverential tone, one which King's orchestral accompaniment matches perfectly – the opening *ritornelli* of the first and last sections are both exquisitely done.

The psalm *Laudate pueri* presents 23 minutes of attractive music without really doing much to set the pulse racing. More interesting are *Cur sagittas, cur tela* – which shows the soul maintaining stoical faith in the face of attack by 'the soldiers of hell' (with violins exuberantly chucking the arrows of the title), before enjoying the protected world of the believer – and the disc's star find, *Sum in medio tempestatum*. This is a bright, unashamedly operatic number, opening with a classic simile aria comparing the troubled soul to a storm-tossed ship, and going on to depict the safe haven that hoves into view when one has turned to Jesus. The virtuoso vocal writing is negotiated with stunning agility and lightness by mezzo Tuva Semmingsen.

Another well-executed Vivaldi disc, then, from King. The recorded sound is also just right.

In furore iustissimae irae, RV626[a]. Laudate pueri   **P**
Dominum, RV601[ab]. Violin Concerto, 'per la Solennità di San Lorenzo', RV286[c]. Double Concerto for Violin,

Organ and Strings, RV541[cd]. Sinfonia for Strings, 'Sinfonia al Santo Sepolcro', RV169
[a]**Sandrine Piau** sop [b]**Marcello Gatti** fl
[c]**Stefano Montanari** vn **Accademia Bizantina /
Ottavio Dantone** [d]org
Naïve OP30416 (62' · DDD · T/t) Ⓕ

'*In furore* is the ideal score for any soprano who's spoiling for a fight – with herself!' So says Sandrine Piau in the booklet, and she could have added that it also makes a superb opener for any disc. The motet could have been made for a singer of Piau's avian lightness and agility, and sure enough she throws herself into it, bringing to it her usual precision and, with a technique that enables plenty of dazzling extra ornaments, winning personality.

With her energy and imagination, Piau manages to find contrast in the work, not just between its fearful opening movement and more penitential second, but on a local scale as well. In the *Laudate pueri*, an altogether more urbane offering, she sings with poise, expressive sophistication and tonal power. Piau's quickness of mind is matched by the orchestral playing of Accademia Bizantina, whose sound, typically for an Italian group, is deliciously grainy, allowing for an alert and intense approach to interpretative detail. Thus they never fail to enhance the mood of a particular number, a skill which they also put to good use in the disc's three orchestral works.

'Amor sacro'
In furore iustissimae irae, RV626. In turbato mare, RV627. Nulla in mundo pax, RV630. Sum in medio tempestatum, R632
Simone Kermes sop
Venice Baroque Orchestra / Andrea Marcon
Archiv Produktion 477 5980AH (67' · DDD · T/t) Ⓕ🅑➔

Opening with one of the composer's most thrillingly virtuoso motets, *In furore iustissimae irae*, the Venice Baroque Orchestra go on to one of his most beautiful, *Nullo in mundo pax*. And if the other two are less individually striking, they are nevertheless well worth hearing; *In turbato mare* opens with a stomach-churning depiction of those raging seas that are always tossing the soul so, and later conjures dread at mention of the 'horrors of death', while *Sum in medio tempestatum* treats a similar subject with a touch more mid-century leisure and politeness.

The disc is, of course, a vehicle for Simone Kermes, whose bright vocal talents have so far impressed in a number of Baroque operas but here make their solo recording debut. She proves more than a match for Vivaldi's typically athletic vocal demands – indeed adds to them in a number of tessitura-extending cadenzas – and makes much of the music's bold contrasts. Some may look for more innocence in the gentler music, where her mini-vibrato can sound rather knowing, but in general Kermes's performances give nothing but pleasure. The orchestra is forthright and exciting, with a satisfyingly full, organ-enriched sound, marred only by some of the cheesy lute embellishments. A straightforward Vivaldi disc, but one full of the strength of expertise.

Stabat mater in F minor, RV621

Stabat mater[c]. Confitebor tibi   **P**
Domine, RV596[a]. Deus tuorum militum, RV612[b].
In turbato mare, RV627[d]. O qui coeli terraeque
serenitas, RV631[d]. Non in pratis aut in hortis, RV641[e]
[d]**Susan Gritton** sop [abe]**Jean Rigby** mez [c]**Robin Blaze**
counterten [ab]**Charles Daniels** ten [a]**Neal Davies** bass
The King's Consort / Robert King
Hyperion CDA66799 (78' · DDD · T/t)   Ⓕ**O**

This release in Robert King's complete cycle of Vivaldi's church music mainly features works unconnected with the Ospedale della Pietà, including a motet written in Rome and the famous *Stabat mater* composed for a church in Brescia. All are for solo voice or voices and orchestra, and for the most part they all carry the typical Vivaldi trademarks: boisterous energy alongside a tender if angular lyricism; a vivid and excitable responsiveness to verbal imagery; and what the insert-notes describe as 'a shocking radicalism: a willingness to strip music down to its core and reconstitute it from these simplest elements'. The best works on this disc are the first three. *In turbato mare* is a rip-roaring 'simile' motet which makes use of the old operatic device of comparing a troubled soul to a storm-tossed ship finding peace in port. The noble *Non in pratis aut in hortis* is an *introduzione*, a short motet designed to precede a performance of a lost *Miserere*; since it ends on a half-close, it's followed here (with musical if not liturgical logic) by the *Stabat mater*. All are excellently sung; few recordings exist of the first two, but it's hard to imagine the ebulliently virtuosic Susan Gritton and the movingly firm-voiced Jean Rigby being significantly bettered. By contrast, the *Stabat mater* is well-trodden territory, but the warmly mellifluous Robin Blaze easily matches his rivals on disc. The King's Consort is a little raw in the string department, but in general it shows bright and lively form and is well served by an acoustic perfectly suited to the occasion. Under King's direction, too, they capture splendidly the spirit of this uncomplicated but atmospheric music.

Stabat mater. Cessate, omai cessate,   **P**
RV684. Filiae mestae Jerusalem, RV638. String
Concertos – C, RV114; E flat, RV130, 'Sonata al Santo
Sepolcro'
Andreas Scholl counterten
Ensemble 415 / Chiara Banchini vn
Harmonia Mundi HMC90 1571 (52' · DDD · T/t)
   Ⓕ**OOO**

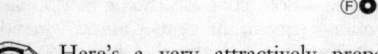

Here's a very attractively prepared menu whose main course is the *Stabat mater* for countertenor and strings. Hors-d'oeuvres and side-dishes consist of a

ripieno concerto (RV114), a chamber cantata for countertenor and strings (RV684), a string sonata in E flat (RV130) and an introductory motet to a lost *Miserere* (RV638). Taken together, the pieces demonstrate something of Vivaldi's diverse style as a composer.

The chamber cantata, if closely related to the two sacred vocal items on the disc in respect of tonal colour, differs from them in character. Conforming with the standard Italian cantata pattern at the time of two pairs of alternating recitative and da capo aria Vivaldi enlivens his pastoral idyll with two particularly affecting arias, the first with a palpitating *pizzicato* violin, the second a virtuoso vocal tour de force illustrating the plight of the forsaken lover. Andreas Scholl brings the whole thing off superbly with only a moment's faulty intonation at the close of the first aria. Unlike settings of the *Stabat mater* by Pergolesi and others, Vivaldi used only the first 10 of the 20 stanzas of the poem. His deeply expressive setting of the poem will be familiar to many readers, but few will have heard such an affecting performance as Scholl achieves here. The lyrical prayer of human yearning for faith contained in the 'Fac ut ardeat' movement is tenderly sung and here, as throughout the programme, sympathetically supported by Ensemble 415 under Chiara Banchini's experienced direction.

Vespers

Vespri Solenni per la Festa dell'Assunzione di Maria
Vergine (ed Alessandrini/Delaméa) – Violin Concerto
in C, RV581[g]; Concerto for 2 Violins and 2 Organs in
F, RV584[h]; Domine ad adiuvandum me festina in G,
RV593[b]; Introduzione al Dixit, RV635[b]; Dixit Dominus
in D, RV594[abdef]; Laudate pueri in C minor, RV600[a];
Laetatus sum, RV607; Nisi Dominus in G minor,
RV608[d]; Lauda Jerusalem in E minor, RV609[ab];
Magnificat in G minor, RV610a[abdef]; Salve Regina in C
minor, RV616[d]; Antiphons[c]
[a]**Gemma Bertagnolli**, [b]**Roberta Invernizzi**, [c]**Anna
Simboli** sops [d]**Sara Mingardo** contr [e]**Gianluca
Ferrarini** ten [f]**Matteo Bellotto** bar [g]**Antonio De
Secondi**, [h]**Mauro Lopes Ferreira**, [h]**Francesca Vicari**
vns [h]**Francesco Moi**, [h]**Ignazio Schifani** orgs
Concerto Italiano / Rinaldo Alessandrini
Opus 111 ③ OP30383 (153' · DDD · T/t)   Ⓕ**OOO**

Ⓖ This isn't the 'Vivaldi Vespers', or even a reconstruction of a specific event, but a kind of 'sacred concert' in Vespers form, of the sort that Venetian churches in Vivaldi's time would mount in the name of worship. Whether he ever supplied all the music for any such occasion isn't clear, but he certainly set plenty of Vespers texts, enough at any rate for Rinaldo Alessandrini and scholar Frédéric Delaméa to put together this rich programme.

So this is music for a Vespers for the Feast of the Assumption as it might have been heard in one of Venice's more important churches, made up of Vivaldi's settings of the five Vespers psalms, a *Magnificat*, a *Salve Regina*, a solo motet

(*Ascende in laeta*) and a couple of orchestral concertos. Unmistakably Vivaldian in almost every bar, these pieces nevertheless show considerable variety; the psalms range from the opulence of *Dixit Dominus* for five soloists, two choirs and two choirs, to the expressive solo settings of *Laudate pueri* and *Nisi Dominus*, to the breezily functional choral treatments of *Laetatus sum* and *Lauda Jerusalem*; *Ascende in laeta* is a virtuoso showpiece for soprano, and the *Salve Regina* a sombre vehicle for contralto. The liturgical thread is supplied by plainchant antiphons, prettily rendered in a fascinating conjectural imitation of the 18th century's 'corrupt' manner, which is to say, with organ accompaniment and unabashed ornamentation.

Alessandrini's reading has an energy which is both forthright and controlled. His solo singers are of high quality; Roberta Invernizzi and Sara Mingardo are from the front rank of Italian Baroque singers, capable of expressive lyricism and thrilling virtuosity, but Gemma Bertagnolli is no less effective. The orchestra plays with inspiriting precision and life, but the choir could be improved on, and is poorly favoured in the recorded balance. Indeed, the recorded sound as a whole is a bit noisy, in places suffering a distant mechanical whir. Still, the overall effect is what counts most in a recording like this: the music has a vital sense of direction, resulting in two and a half hours of invigorating listening.

Chamber Cantatas

Cantatas – Alla caccia, alla caccia, RV670; Care selve amici prati, RV671; Elvira, anima mia, RV654. Chamber Concertos – in F, RV97; in G minor, 'La notte', RV104; in G minor, RV105.
Laura Polverelli *mez* **L'Astrée Ensemble**
Opus 111 OP30358 (55' · DDD · T/t)   Ⓕ〇

Whether Vivaldi wrote these cantatas for an exceptionally talented singer or just decided to give others a mischievously hard time isn't known; the fact remains that they're tough assignments. If Polverelli finds them so, she gives no sign of it. She's a mezzo with a cloudless upper register and a full-throated lower one, a wide and subtly nuanced range of volume, supple and pitch-perfect. These three chamber cantatas deal with various unhappy aspects of love, and she projects them without resorting to 'grand-operatic' excess. These are performances to treasure.

The chamber concertos show Vivaldi at his most happily inventive. All those on this disc have alternative versions, and if RV97 and 105 lack something of the verve of those by Giardino Armonico they're no less infectious.

The recording is clear and very well balanced, and the vocal texts are given in three languages, including English. A thoroughly enjoyable disc.

Alla caccia dell'alme, RV670. Care selve, RV671.

Perfidissimo cor, RV674. Pianti, sospiri, RV676. Qual per ignoto, RV677. Orlando furioso, RV728 – Piangerò sinché l'onda. Tito Manlio, RV778 – Di verde ulivo. Cello Sonata, RV47
Philippe Jaroussky *counterten*
Ensemble Artaserse (Jérémie Papasergio *bn* Emilia Gliozzi *vc* Claire Antonini *theo* Yoko Nakamura *hpd*)
Virgin Classics 545721-2 (68' · DDD · T/t)   Ⓕ🅑►

The countertenor Philippe Jaroussky soars as effortlessly as a bird, with no sense of strain: perhaps – for we can never know for certain – this is how the great castrati of the 18th century sounded. He was certainly convincing in the soprano role of Nero in the Euroarts DVD of Handel's *Agrippina*.

Little is known about the background to these cantatas. Each is in the familiar form of two *da capo* arias, separated and sometimes preceded by a recitative. The themes are equally familiar, generally concerned with the inconstancy or inaccessibility of the beloved, with reference to the storms, bright dawns and shipwrecks of *opera seria*. *Alla caccia dell'alme* describes 'barbarous Cloris' hunting souls and hearts, with predictable consequences for the victim. And there is a delightful surprise: no horn depicting the chase, of course: instead, here and elsewhere, we have the jolly bassoon of Jérémie Papasergio on the bass line.

In fact the composition of the continuo group varies within each cantata and even during a movement: the 'A' section of the first aria in *Pianti, sospiri e dimandar mercede* features bassoon and lute, the 'B' section cello and harpsichord. This is justified by the quality of the playing but to switch from harpsichord to organ in the same piece seems to me fussy.

Philippe Jaroussky is sweet-toned and, as well as singing the divisions with wonderful control, he shows care for the meaning of the words. The aria from *Tito Manlio*, which really was written for contralto, finds him duetting with the cello obbligato of Emilia Gliozzi – superb!

'Concerti e cantate da camera III'
Amor hai vinto, RV683. Lungi dal vago volto, RV680. Vengo a voi, luci adorate, RV682. Chamber Concertos – RV87; 'La tempesta di mare', RV98; RV103
Laura Polverelli *mez*
L'Astrée / Giorgio Tabacco *hpd*
Naïve Opus 111 OP30381 (60' · DDD · T/t)   Ⓕ

Naïve's monumental Vivaldi series continues its sensible policy of mixing chamber cantatas and concertos in this third volume, in which Italian ensemble L'Astrée are joined by mezzo-soprano Laura Polverelli. Polverelli proves an agile artist, as much she needs to be; Vivaldi, as is his wont, challenges her vocal athleticism with the kind of jagged melodic lines and rattling passagework that a kinder composer might have avoided, all in the cause of expressing what seem like the rather subtler shades of Arcadian love.

Happy to say, she triumphs. Despite having a voice whose operatic intensity, dark colouring and low centre of gravity sound at first as if they will be ill-suited to the angular music that Vivaldi-lovers will know lies ahead, when the time comes she negotiates the composer's treacherously scattered notes with languid ease. What is more, she brings a commanding sense of drama to the recitatives and uncommon dignity and moment to the arias. The cantatas themselves are worth the trouble: the two intertwining violins of *Amor hai vinto* ooze amorous disquiet; *Lungi dal vago volto* closes with a gleeful hoedown; and *Vengo a voi, luci adorate* sets out in a mood of modish galant but cannot escape its Vivaldian identity for long.

The instrumental support from L'Astrée is tightly solid throughout (save for a slightly acid violin in *Lungi dal vago volto*) and the three concertos are performed with imagination and spirit. Particularly enjoyable is RV107, where the omission of continuo leaves us with a charming (and in no way incomplete-sounding) trio of recorder, oboe and bassoon. A disc principally for Vivaldi specialists, perhaps, but newcomers who stumble across it will surely find plenty to entertain them too.

Opera arias

'Amor profano'
L'olimpiade – Siam navi all'onde algenti **La fede tradita e vendicata** – Sin nel placido soggiorno **Orlando furioso** – Ah, fuggi rapido **Tito Manlio** – Non m'affligge il tormento di morte; Dopo sì rei disastri; Combatta un gentil cor **Semiramide** – Quegl'occhi luminosi **Il Tigrane** – Squarciami pure il seno **Catone in Utica** – Se in campo armato **Bajazet** – Sinfonia **Griselda** – Agitata da due venti **La verità in cimento** – Amato ben, tu sei la mia speranza **Giustino** – La farfalletta audace s'invola; Or che cinto ho il crin d'alloro
Simone Kermes *sop*
Venice Baroque Orchestra / Andrea Marcon
Archiv Produktion 477 6618AH (71' · DDD) Ⓕ Ⓞ ▶

Simone Kermes has once again teamed up with Andrea Marcon and his Venice Baroque Orchestra for a superbly balanced exploration of opera arias. The level of effort and intelligence in choosing the right repertoire is clearly manifest in this varied and stimulating anthology. There is a tangible variety of dramatic sentiments and instrumental colours: the introduction of solo cello, recorders, trumpets, solo trumpet and horns in occasional arias is perfectly timed to avoid too much textural monotony, and they make the experience livelier and entertaining. Each aria seems to have been meticulously placed in a sequence that pulls the listener through the contrasts in Vivaldi's operatic writing, which also means that the disc tells a story about the repertoire as well as giving Kermes and the Venetian players plenty of opportunities to show how well they can perform it.

Some of Kermes's dizzying cadenzas are perhaps excessive, but such extravagances are never dull. Her delivery of tempestuous coloratura arias is often exhilarating (the opening aria 'Siam navi all'onde algenti'). The Venice Baroque Orchestra's playing is also dazzling, sensitive and lyrical.

Five of the arias here are first recordings, including a robust heroic aria from *Orlando Furioso* – not Vivaldi's famous opera of that title but an earlier setting of the story that also featured music by Ristori – in which Kermes's rapid repeated notes are astonishing. The finest of the rare items is 'Quegl'occhi luminosi' (from *Semiramide*), which reminds us that, notwithstanding the flashy fast stuff, both singer and composer are often at their dramatic finest in ravishing slow music. 'Se in campo armato' (*Catone in Utica*) is tastefully played, with its vivacious trumpet-laden accompaniment excellently juxtaposed with a tender B section (although Kermes perhaps over-eggs the ornaments in the *da capo* repeat). The concluding aria 'Or che cinto ho il crin d'alloro' (*Giustino*) shows the musicians' infectious joy in the music, with an extrovert vocal line, exuberant horns, and snappy strings and continuo.

'Amor profano' is a role model of how a Baroque opera arias recital disc should be put together – with proper research, affection for the composer, and top-notch artistry.

'Arie ritrovate'
Arias from Orlando Furioso, Tito Manlio, La verità in cimento, Teuzzone and Scanderbeg
Sonia Prina *contr* **Stefano Montanari** *vn*
Accademia Bizantina / Ottavio Dantone
Naïve OP30443 (71' · DDD) Ⓕ

Some of these arias are individual pieces in anthologies made by Vivaldi, or long-forgotten alternative opera arias that will not be recorded in the context of their parent work in Naïve's series.

'Con palme ed allori' is one of the few traces to have survived from *Scanderbeg*, an opera written to celebrate the reopening of the Teatro alla Pergola in Florence in June 1718. A martial aria with two trumpets, two oboes and strings, its spectacular boldness arrives just in time to inject some flamboyant theatricality after some less-than-striking alternative arias from *La verità in cimento*. However, all of the music is expertly crafted, and some of it is extraordinary, such as the beautiful 'Tu dormi in tante pene' from *Tito Manlio*. Sonia Prina has a firm grasp on melodic lines and a supple timbre. She reaffirms her status as an outstanding Baroque opera singer, and Ottavio Dantone lends excellent support from Accademia Bizantina.

Juditha triumphans, RV644

Juditha triumphans Ⓟ
Magdalena Kožená *mez* **Anke Herrmann** *sop*

Maria José Trullu, Marina Comparato, Tiziana Carraro *mezs* Coro di Camera Accademia Nazionale di Santa Cecilia; Academia Montis Regalis / Alessandro de Marchi
Opus 111 ② OP30314 (105' · DDD · T/t)　Ⓕ**OO**

Vivaldi's only surviving oratorio, *Juditha triumphans* (1716), with its strongly characterised roles and luxuriant orchestration, is a true Baroque masterpiece. Alessandro de Marchi has departed from other recent interpreters by daring to transpose the tenor and bass choral parts up an octave, as is widely believed was done by Vivaldi himself to accommodate the choir of the Ospedale della Pietà. The effect is breathtaking: the compressed, female choral textures positively gleam. From his superb cast of female soloists, de Marchi coaxes remarkable and dramatically convincing male vocal timbres. Maria José Trullu projects the various sides of Holofernes, who's depicted not merely as a monster but as capable of dignity and charm, even if ultimately incautious; she infuses her tone with a warmth and richness that countertenors might envy.

Magdalena Kožená, the Bethulian widow Judith, casts a spell on those who only hear her: as well as Holofernes. She sings with poise almost throughout, as she enters the enemy camp, meets and seduces Holofernes, reflects on the transitoriness of life and prays for peace and strength before murdering the sleeping Holofernes. Only then, as she carries out her heroic – if horrific – mission does she fully convey her emotion.

The instrumentation offers a treasure trove of unusual and evocative instruments, even for the time: a pair of clarinets to characterise the dissolute Assyrian soldiers, recorders for 'nocturnal breezes' and a quartet of theorbos to depict the preparation of the feast. These and the more common obbligato and continuo instruments of the day are affectingly played by the musicians of the Academia Montis Regalis. At every turn there's ample evidence of the care de Marchi has lavished on this performance, and Robert King's by comparison seems less full-blooded and relatively static. Congratulations all round for an outstanding recording.

Bajazet

Bajazet　　　　　　　　　　　　　　　Ⓟ
Ildebrando D'Arcangelo *bass-bar* Bajazet Patrizia Ciofi *sop* Idaspe David Daniels *counterten* Tamerlano Elina Garanca *mez* Andronico Vivica Genaux *mez* Irene Marijana Mijanovic *mez* Asteria Europa Galante / Fabio Biondi *vn*
Virgin Classics ② 545676-2 (147' · DDD · T/t)
　　　　　　　　　　　　　Ⓕ**OOO**▷

Ⓖ　Vivaldi's *Bajazet*, based on the same libretto as Handel's *Tamerlano*, tells the story of the Tartar emperor Tamerlano and the Ottoman sultan Bajazet whom he's

defeated. Vivaldi responds with sound dramatic sense. His recitatives especially show a conversational realism that allows them to be more than just a functional advancement of the plot; indeed, Bajazet's biggest moment is a powerful accompanied recitative.

Vivaldi works hard at characterisation, if by unusual means: *Bajazet* is partly a *pasticcio*, which is to say that it borrows and adapts arias from other operas written in the fashionable and suave Neapolitan style by composers such as Hasse and Giacomelli, who by the 1730s were beginning to dominate the operatic world. Vivaldi chose well. He'd have appreciated the crowd-pleasing virtuosity of an aria such as 'Qual guerriero in campo armato', originally written for Farinelli by his brother Riccardo Broschi; here it aptly expresses Irene's near-deranged indignation at being dumped by Tamerlano. Clever choices such as this make *Bajazet* a real opera, not just a hotch-potch.

The same can be said for the performers here. The cast has hardly a weak link: David Daniels is in typically beautiful voice as Tamerlano, yet at the same time manages enough hardness to suggest the spiteful anger of the man; Elina Garanca conveys a suitable measure of weakness as the indecisive Andronico; and Marijana Mijanovic's moving and dignified Asteria never looks like losing her moral high ground. Vivica Genaux gives a show-stopping display as Irene, and Patrizia Ciofi proves no less equal to the tough technical challenges set by the role of Andronico's friend Idaspe. Only Ildebrando D'Arcangelo as Bajazet disappoints slightly, failing to reach to the Sultan's defiant heart.

The orchestra's contribution, on the other hand, is a major bonus. Fabio Biondi has never been one to miss details, and he and his players bring out countless nuances in the score with their usual array of interpretative devices ranging from gentle cello chords in recitative to sparky off-beat accents and *pizzicati*, and even some acid *sul ponticello*. There could hardly be a better way to bring this opera to life.

Griselda

Griselda
Marie-Nicole Lemieux *contr* Griselda Veronica Cangemi *sop* Costanza Simone Kermes *sop* Ottone Philippe Jaroussky *counterten* Roberto Stefano Ferrari *ten* Gualtiero Iestyn Davies *counterten* Corrado Ensemble Matheus / Jean-Christophe Spinosi
Naïve ③ OP30419 (155' · DDD · S/T/t/N)
　　　　　　　　　　　　　Ⓕ**O**

Griselda was first performed at Venice's Teatro di San Samuele during spring 1735. Apostolo Zeno's libretto, based on a tale from Boccacio's *Decameron*, was adapted for Vivaldi by Carlo Goldoni: Gualtiero is forced by political unrest and public criticism of his common-born wife Griselda to prove her noble worth by subjecting her to a torrent of cruel tests.

Marie-Nicole Lemieux's passionate performance of the title-role has vivid handling of text and emotive singing. Stefano Ferrari gets around Gualtiero's fiendish coloratura competently, and 'Tu vorresti col tuo pianto' is a rarity among Vivaldi's operas: a bona fide first-class tenor aria of real distinction, beauty and dramatic subtlety. Simone Kermes navigates Ottone's wide leaps in the slow aria 'Vede orgogliosa' with immaculate poise and tenderness, and in 'Dopo un'orrida' gleefully represents Ottone's premature exultation with some outstanding pyrotechnics. Veronica Cangemi provides some relaxed, attractive coloratura. Philippe Jaroussky's arias are consistently gorgeous but he is also surprisingly strong at the tempestuous 'Che legge tiranna'. Iestyn Davies is impressive in the colourful hunting aria 'Alle minaccie'.

Spinosi's pacing of the arias suggests sensible interpretation of Vivaldi's instructions. In extrovert arias one occasionally hears some contrived clattering bows from the strings but there is a substantial problem throughout the performance caused by underwhelming, pale playing from the lower strings. Three cellists and two basses play quietly most of the time, making the hushed *basso continuo* far too thin and rarely giving enough depth and texture to the dynamic width of Vivaldi's harmonic writing. One imagines the stronger musical sense that Alessandrini, Dantone or Sardelli might have brought to Griselda. Despite reservations about the top-heavy instrumental textures, this finely sung recording unveils another inventive opera.

L'Olimpiade

L'Olimpiade, RV725 (ed Alessandrini)   🅿
Sara Mingardo *contr* Licida; **Roberta Invernizzi** *sop* Megacle; **Sonia Prina** *mez* Aristea; **Marianna Kulikova** *mez* Argene; **Laura Giordano** *sop* Aminta; **Riccardo Novaro** *bar* Clistene; **Sergio Foresti** *bass* Alcandro; **Concerto Italiano / Rinaldo Alessandrini**
Opus 111 ③ OP30316 (175' · DDD · T/t)   Ⓕ🅞🅞

More than 50 composers set Pietro Metastasio's libretto *L'Olimpiade* between 1733 and 1815, starting with Caldara and including along the way such names as Pergolesi, Galuppi, Cimarosa, Cherubini and Paisiello. The booklet note for this new recording suggests that Vivaldi was trying to take on the newly fashionable Neapolitan composers at their own game, not only by setting a poem by their favourite librettist, but also by adopting some of their musical mannerisms. Maybe so, but there can be few composers with a more deeply ingrained personal style than our friend the Red Priest, and it's an unmistakably Vivaldian flavour which is the strongest in this thoroughly agreeable work.

Despite the public context – the story is played out against the backdrop of the Olympic Games – this is a drama which focuses on the personal predicaments of the principal characters, each of whom faces an interesting conflict between head and heart somewhere along the line. This is more apparent from Metastasio's words than from Vivaldi's music, to be honest, but that isn't to say that the composer has been unresponsive. The most effective and intimate moments occur in the recitatives, which are fluidly conversational and full of realistic interruptions, questions and exclamations, all of which Vivaldi handles with considerable dramatic skill.

Rinaldo Alessandrini's direction is typically unfussy and to the point, ever alert to the music's dramatic intent but without imposing himself on it unduly. The finest vocal performances come from Sara Mingardo, Roberta Invernizzi and Sonia Prina, but in truth no one is a weak link. The recitatives are effectively done, the arias thrown off with dash and aplomb, and everyone sounds as if they believe in the work.

Orlando finto pazzo

Orlando finto pazzo   🅿
Antonio Abete *bass* Orlando **Gemma Bertagnolli** *sop* Ersilla **Marina Comparato** *mez* Tigrinda **Sonia Prina** *contr* Origille **Manuela Custer** *mez* Argillano **Martín Oro** *counterten* Grifone **Marianna Pizzolato** *mez* Brandimarte **Teatro Regio Chorus, Turin; Academia Montis Regalis / Alessandro de Marchi**
Opus 111 ③ OP30392 (207' · DDD · T/t)   Ⓕ🅞

Orlando finto pazzo ('Orlando feigns madness') was the second of Vivaldi's numerous operas, and his first for the Venetian stage. The story of Orlando's madness is taken not from the usual source, Ariosto's poem *Orlando furioso*, but Boiardo's earlier *Orlando innamorato*, a similarly tragicomic mix of love, intrigue and magic. In Ariosto's poem Orlando's madness is real, but here he pretends it for no obvious reason; in fact it's no more than a couple of episodes in a convoluted and unengaging plot built around a love-pentangle (no less), and further complicated by various disguises and rampant dissembling.

As it happens, Vivaldi doesn't on this evidence appear to have been a natural musical dramatist. Yet what makes this music worth hearing is his evident desire to make an operatic splash at his first major attempt: there's music of irrepressible zest and personality; this early attempt deploys all the fiery and ebullient energy of his concertos and allies it to vocal music of neck-tingling excitement. Like Haydn, Vivaldi may not have been a great opera composer, but he did write operas full of great music.

Alessandro de Marchi's joyous recording brings together a typical Italian Baroque cast for a performance and recording of skill and enthusiasm.

Orlando furioso

Orlando furioso   🅿
Marie-Nicole Lemieux *contr* Orlando **Jennifer Larmore** *mez* Alcina **Veronica Cangemi** *sop* Angelica **Philippe Jaroussky** *counterten* Ruggiero **Lorenzo Regazzo** *bass-bar* Astolfo **Ann Hallenberg**

mez Bradamante **Blandine Staskiewicz** mez Medoro
Les Eléments; Ensemble Matheus / Jean-Christophe Spinosi
Opus 111 ③ OP30393 (183' · DDD · T/t)   Ⓕ**OO**

Vivaldi's opera combines magic, heroism and comedy to tell of a seductive sorceress, a noble knight driven insane by love, a feisty fiancée who disguises herself as a man to rescue her bewitched lover, and a magic ring that helps ensure everything ends happily ever after. This recording bears the fruit of Vivaldi scholar Frédéric Delaméa's painstaking reconstruction of the original 1727 version. Marie-Nicole Lemieux's delivery of Orlando's anguished and often unhinged recitative is astonishingly good, full of conviction, passionate, and vocally brilliant. When his sanity is restored, she achieves a tangible lucidity that makes the drama wholly satisfying. Jennifer Larmore's sorceress Alcina is devious, vivacious, and venomous. Philippe Jaroussky's Ruggerio is adept at both delicacy and heroism and Ann Hallenberg is excellent as his fiancée Bradamante.

Ensemble Matheus provide bright *ritornelli* and intelligent accompaniments. The playing is often abrasive and intentionally percussive in fast music, but the performers also excel at the softer moments. Spinosi's direction is vividly theatrical, and recitatives are declaimed with aplomb, although sometimes it sounds as if characters cannot wait to interrupt their next line.

Vivaldi's score has a dramatic stature greater than most of his other operas. He rarely devoted much attention to accompanied recitatives, but here he composed several that are unusually extensive and adventurous. This is a magnificent achievement: if Vivaldi needed a champion to establish his credentials as an opera composer, then this recording is it.

Ottone in Villa

Ottone in Villa   Ⓟ
Monica Groop mez Ottone **Nancy Argenta** sop
Caio Silio **Susan Gritton** sop Cleonilla **Sophie Daneman** sop Tullia **Mark Padmore** ten Decio
Collegium Musicum 90 / Richard Hickox
Chandos Chaconne ② CHAN0614 (145' · DDD · T/t)
Ⓕ

This, Vivaldi's very first opera, was premièred in Vicenza in 1713 and was an instant hit. The story is a relatively uncomplicated one by the standards of Baroque opera, of amatory pretences and misunderstandings: it has been admirably summarised by Eric Cross (who has edited the work) as a 'light-weight, amoral entertainment in which the flirtatious Cleonilla consistently has the upper hand, and gullible Emperor Ottone (a far from heroic figure) never discovers the truth about the way he has been deceived'. The score proceeds in a succession of secco recitatives (with just a very occasional accompagnato) and da capo arias – which the present cast ornament very stylishly. There are no duets or ensembles except for a

perfunctory final chorus in which the characters merely sing in unison; but there's an abundance of tuneful arias, and when Vivaldi can be bothered to write proper accompaniments to them – he often merely has violins doubling the voice, plus a bass line – he can provide interesting imitative counterpoint. Several arias employ only the upper strings without cello and bass except in ritornellos. The small Vicenza theatre couldn't afford star singers, so only limited opportunities were provided for vocal virtuosity; but the present cast makes the most of its opportunities, both in display and in meditative mood. It isn't always easy to tell the three sopranos apart, but Susan Gritton well suggests the scheming minx Cleonilla; Nancy Argenta with her bright voice has the castrato role that includes several fine arias, and displays a *messa di voce* in an echo aria; and Sophie Daneman, in a breeches role, produces a wide range of colour. Monica Groop slightly undercharacterises Ottone except when roused to dismiss Rome's anxiety at his dalliance. It's quite a relief to ear one male voice, and Mark Padmore is excellent. Richard Hickox keeps a firm rhythmic hand on everything and delivers quite the best and neatest Vivaldi operatic recording yet.

Richard Wagner   German 1813-1883

Wagner went to school in Dresden and then Leipzig; at 15 he wrote a play, at 16 his first compositions. In 1831 he went to Leipzig University, studying music. In 1833 he became chorus master at the Würzburg theatre and wrote the text and music of his first opera, Die Feen; this remained unheard, but his next, Das Liebesverbot, written in 1833, was staged in 1836. By then he had made his début as an opera conductor with a small company which, however, went bankrupt soon after performing his opera. He married the singer Minna Planer in 1836 and went with her to Königsberg, where he became musical director at the theatre, but he soon left and took a similar post in Riga, where he began his next opera, Rienzi, and did much conducting, especially of Beethoven. In 1839 they slipped away from creditors in Riga, by ship to London and then to Paris. He also worked on the text and music of an opera on the 'Flying Dutchman' legend; but in 1842 Rienzi, a large-scale opera with a political theme set in imperial Rome, was accepted for Dresden and Wagner went there for its highly successful première. Die fliegende Holländer ('The Flying Dutchman'), given the next year, was less well received, though a much tauter musical drama, beginning to move away from the 'number opera' tradition and strong in its evocation of atmosphere, especially the supernatural and the raging seas (inspired by the stormy trip from Riga). Wagner was now appointed joint Kapellmeister at the Dresden court.

In 1845 Tannhäuser was completed and performed and Lohengrin begun. In both Wagner moves towards a more continuous texture with semi-melodic narrative and a supporting orchestral fabric helping convey its sense. In 1848 he was caught up in

Wagner

the revolutionary fervour and the next year fled to Weimar (where Liszt helped him)and then Switzerland (there was also a spell in France); politically suspect, he was unable to enter Germany for 11 years. By 1853 the text for this four-night cycle (to be The Nibelung's Ring) was written, printed and read to friends – who included a generous patron, Otto Wesendonck, and his wife Mathilde, who loved him, wrote poems that he set, and inspired Tristan und Isolde – conceived in 1854 and completed five years later, by which time more than half of The Ring was written. In 1855 he conducted in London; tension with Minna led to his going to Paris in 1858-9. In 1863 he gave concerts in Vienna, Russia etc; the next year King Ludwig II invited him to settle in Bavaria, near Munich, discharging his debts and providing him with money.

Wagner did not stay long in Bavaria, because of opposition at Ludwig's court, especially when it was known that he was having an affair with Cosima, the wife of the conductor Hans van Bülow (she was Liszt's daughter); Bülow (who condoned it) directed the Tristan première in 1865. Here Wagner, in depicting every shade of sexual love, developed a style richer and more chromatic than anyone had previously attempted, using dissonance and its urge for resolution in a continuing pattern to build up tension and a sense of profound yearning. The opera was given, under Bülow, in 1868; Wagner had been living at Tribschen, near Lucerne, since 1866, and that year Cosima formally joined him; they had two children when in 1870 they married. The first two Ring operas, Das Rheingold and Die Walküre, were given in Munich, on Ludwig's insistence, in 1869 and 1870; Wagner, however, was anxious to have a special festival opera house for the complete cycle and spent much energy trying to raise money for it. Eventually, when he had almost despaired, Ludwig came to the rescue and in 1874 – the year the fourth opera, Götterdämmerung, was finished – provided the necessary support. The house was built at Bayreuth, designed by Wagner as the home for his concept of the Gesamtkunstwerk ('total art work' – an alliance of music, poetry, the visual arts, dance etc). The first festival, an artistic triumph but a financial disaster – was held there in 1876, when the complete Ring was given.

In 1877 Wagner conducted in London, hoping to recoup Bayreuth losses; later in the year he began a new opera, Parsifal. He continued his musical and polemic writings, concentrating on 'racial purity'. He spent most of 1880 in Italy. Parsifal, a sacred festival drama, was given at the Bayreuth Festival in 1882. He went to Venice for the winter, and died there in February of the heart trouble that had been with him for some years. His life and his music arouse passions like no other composer's. His works are hated as much as they are worshipped; but no-one denies their greatness. GROVEmusic

---

Orchestral Excerpts from Operas

Lohengrin – Prelude. Tannhäuser – Overture. **H** Siegfried Idyll. Götterdämmerung – Siegfried's Rhine Journey; Siegfried's Funeral March
Lucerne Festival Orchestra; Vienna Philharmonic

Orchestra / Wilhelm Furtwängler
Testament mono SBT1141 (61' · ADD) Recorded late 1940s
Ⓕ**O**

This is, as they say, something else. The Lohengrin Act 1 Prelude opens the disc of studio recordings, the only item of five with the Lucerne Festival Orchestra. The way the Swiss brass crescendos on the upbeat to the climactic delivery of the hymn must rate as among the most elating of all Furtwängler moments. Why this and the Tannhäuser Overture have never been issued before remains a mystery, as probably do all the reasons why, in the latter piece, the Vienna Philharmonic sounds on fire for Furtwängler and on duty for, say, Knappertsbusch in 1953 (once available on a Decca LP). Siegfried's Rhine Journey evolves in one seamless sweep, barring the split-second but disconcerting rhythmic hiatus at the moment of take-off (4'51"). And mercifully, Furtwängler doesn't tag on the trite concert ending (as did Reiner and Toscanini), giving a chance to wonder at the uniquely resonant low brass sounds of the VPO. Then on to the Funeral March, every dark sound fully charting the depths, every phrase carrying special import, and, as in the Siegfried Idyll, the occasional passage reminding us of standards of tuning of the day. The latter account, Furtwängler's only recording of the piece, engages rather than diverts and charms, with Vienna string-playing typically sweet and rapturous, and 'Siegfried, Hope of the World' tensely built to an almost delirious climax. Depth, presence and a naturally achieved clarity characterise all these recordings, and 78 sources only occasionally make their presence felt.

Der fliegende Holländer – Overture. Die Meistersinger von Nürnberg – Prelude, Act 1; Prelude, Act 3. Parsifal – Prelude; Good Friday Music. Tristan und Isolde – Prelude; Liebestod[a]
[a]**Anja Kampe** sop **Hallé Orchestra / Mark Elder**
Hallé CDHLL7517 (73' · DDD)
Ⓜ**O**

Conductor, orchestra and recording team have gone to subtle lengths (including the use of two recording venues) to make a Wagner 'bleeding chunks' concert really work on disc. Like Rattle at the Royal Opera House before him, Elder has (re)calculated the crucial silences and the balancing of the brass and wind choirs in the Parsifal items to give them lift and presence outside the acoustic halo of the Bayreuth pit for which they were intended. The Meistersinger Act 3 Prelude makes use of 'period' string portamenti (the score's influence on Elgar's Second Symphony becoming even more apparent), while the same opera's Act 1 Prelude and the Tristan excerpts show clear touches of Elder's work with original instrument bands, eschewing Karajanesque symphonic gloss (and its 'big' 1970s sound) for the sake of increased mobility and presence of important inner part writing.

Anja Kampe is a clear, word-conscious, passionate Isolde, closely in tune with the 'house style' of these interpretations, while the final pages of this Liebestod (after the voice finishes) are attended to with a Boulez-like detail and fascination. Only the *Dutchman* Overture falls somewhat in between two stools – not quite the development of *Der Freischütz* that you might have expected after Elder's cunning reading of that score for ENO, nor the all-out nautical thriller provided in very different ways by Klemperer or Solti.

This is not a disc which blows you away at first hearing but one that repays careful and repeated hearing. The recordings are in every way the handmaid of the performances.

'Wagner/Stokowski Symphonic Syntheses'
Parsifal – Symphonic Synthesis of Act 3.
Das Rheingold – Entrance of the Gods into Valhalla.
Die Walküre – Magic Fire Music; Ride of the Valkyries.
Tristan und Isolde – Symphonic Synthesis
Bournemouth Symphony Orchestra /
José Serebrier
Naxos 8 570293 (74' · DDD)   ⑤→

It would be hard to imagine a more sumptuous disc. Stokowski, in these 'symphonic syntheses', enhances Wagner's already opulent orchestration with shrewdly added instrumental lines and with the vocal parts usually given to the strings. Then at times he thins the orchestration down for more transparent textures. José Serebrier conducts the Bournemouth SO in thrilling performances, passionate in a genuinely Stokowskian manner and treated to orchestral sound of demonstration quality.

Stokowski's aim was to provide more satisfying orchestral items in concerts than the popular 'bleeding chunks'. So in the most ambitious item, on *Tristan*, we have between the Prelude and Liebestod a rich orchestral version of the Love Duet. Where the end of the duet builds up to that chilling interruption from King Marke, Stokowski has it lead seamlessly into the equivalent passage in the Liebestod. It works superbly.

The selection starts excitingly with the Entry of the Gods into Valhalla and it is good to find Serebrier splendidly adding an anvil when Donner brings his hammer down. The *Parsifal* synthesis is limited to music from Act 3, thus ignoring the Good Friday Music. From *Die Walküre* comes the Magic Fire Music and, most excitingly, the Ride of the Valkyries. This is the finest of Naxos's Stokowski discs to date.

Wesendonk Lieder

Wesendonk Lieder. Tristan und Isolde – Prelude, Act 1; Mild und leise. Götterdämmerung – Dawn and Siegfried's Rhine Journey; Starke Scheite
Julia Varady sop **Deutsches Symphony Orchestra, Berlin / Dietrich Fischer-Dieskau**
Orfeo C467981A (71' · DDD · T/t)   ⑤OO

This is a truly riveting recital of Wagner from Varady (magnificent singing) and Fischer-

Dieskau. Varady's reading of the *Wesendonk Lieder* is remarkable, enthralling. There's nothing here of the slow, wallowing approach often favoured today. The feeling of the words is one of very present emotions. Try the final section of 'Stehe still!' starting 'Die Lippe verstummt' or the emphasis on the single word 'Smaragd' in 'Im Treibhaus' or the whole of a most beautifully etched 'Träume'. She's helped here by Fischer-Dieskau's refusal to indulge the music.

There have been few such warmly and intelligently sung versions of the Immolation. Maybe on stage Brünnhilde might have been beyond Varady; here there's not a sign of strain as she rides the orchestra, sympathetically supported by her husband. But what makes it stand out from performances by possibly better-endowed sopranos is her deep understanding of the text: again and again, nowhere more so than at 'Ruhe, ruhe, du Gott', where Varady's vibrating lower register is so effective, you feel the tingle factor coming to the fore. In the more heroic final sections, this Brünnhilde is like a woman transfigured. And transfiguration is a feature of Varady's concentrated, urgent Liebestod, her complete absorption with the text as much as with the music an object-lesson in great Wagner singing. The players of Fischer-Dieskau's Berlin orchestra cover themselves in glory. The recording is exemplary.

Opera Duets

Love Duets
Siegfried – Act 3 scene 3.. Tristan und Isolde[a] – Act 2 scene 2 (concert version from 'O sink hernieder')
Deborah Voigt sop [a]**Violeta Urmana** mez **Plácido Domingo** ten **Royal Opera House Orchestra, Covent Garden / Antonio Pappano**
EMI 557004-2 (57' · DDD · T/t)   ⑤O→

It appears that in 1862, three years before *Tristan and Isolde*'s première, Wagner hoped that the Schnorrs, his original Tristan and Isolde, would give part of the Love duet in a concert performance. This never took place, and nothing was known about the musical preparations Wagner made for the event until 1950; even then it seems the material remained unexamined, and certainly unused, until very recently. Omitting the first 15 minutes or so, the duet was to start at 'O sink hernieder' and continue to the end, including in it the interpolations of Brangäne. The question which forms in the listener's mind as the end approaches is how that's to be managed. This supreme expression of eroticism in music culminates in erotic catastrophe. It's hard to imagine a concert performance ending with the rude abruptness of the score, but worse to think of its possible closure (as in some early recordings) on a glib and alien major chord. However, without giving the game away, the solution constitutes a stroke of genius; it has that kind of simplicity and rightness that evokes a cry of 'But of course!', almost as though one had thought of it oneself – which assuredly one had not. Unfortunately the booklet-notes provide no information on the genesis of this ending. Amazing as it is to relate, Domingo's voice, after all these years and all this unsparing usage, is still the most beautiful – the most richly firm and even – on recordings of this music. He's exact and lyrical in his reading of the music and is largely, if not invariably, imaginative and convincing in his dramatic commitment. Voigt impresses as being less successfully 'in character', especially as the Siegfried Brünnhilde, whose exaltation and wonder lack the majesty of her godly state as they do the excitement of her humanity. The fresh and vibrant tones are good to hear even so, as is the firm-voiced mezzo of Violeta Urmana's Brangäne. The Covent Garden orchestra play for Pappano with fine attentiveness and exhilaration, and he seems to bring a renewing spirit to everything he touches.

Der fliegende Holländer

Der fliegende Holländer
Theo Adam bass-bar Holländer **Anja Silja** sop Senta
Martti Talvela bass Daland **Ernst Kozub** ten Erik
Annelies Burmeister mez Mary **Gerhard Unger** ten
Steuermann **BBC Chorus; New Philharmonia**
Orchestra / Otto Klemperer
EMI Great Recordings of the Century ③ 567408-2
(152' · ADD · T/t) Recorded 1968   Ⓜ Ⓞ ➔

Klemperer's magisterial interpretation of this work was unavailable in any form for far too long so that its reissue was most welcome. As ever, Klemperer by and large justifies some moderate tempos by the way in which he sustains line and emphasises detail. Only once or twice – in the Spinning and Sailors' choruses – do you sense a lack of propulsion. Otherwise throughout there's a blazing intensity to the reading that brooks no denial. The storm and sea music in the Overture and thereafter is given stunning power, and the Dutchman's torture and passion is evoked in the orchestra. Indeed, the playing of the New Philharmonia is a bonus throughout. Klemperer catches as convincingly as anyone the elemental feeling of the work – the sense of the sea, basic passions and the interplay of character unerringly adumbrated.

There have been few baritones before or since Theo Adam who have sustained the line of the Dutchman so well and so intelligently reached the heart of the matter where the text is concerned. Silja's bright, sometimes piercing timbre isn't to everyone's taste, but hers is a most moving portrayal of trust and loyalty and love unto death, the interpretation of an outstanding singing-actress. Martti Talvela, singing magnificently and suggesting a formidable presence, is a bluff, burly Daland. Ernst Kozub's Erik has its clumsy moments, but one admires the shining tone. Gerhard Unger offers an ardent, cleanly articulated Sailor. Annelies Burmeister is a ripe Mary. The overall sound is a shade on the dry side but doesn't detract from the enjoyment.

Der fliegende Holländer
Theo Adam bass-bar Der Holländer **Anja Silja** sop
Senta **Martti Talvela** bass Daland **James King** ten
Erik **Kenneth Macdonald** ten Der Steuermann
Annelies Burmeister mez Mary **BBC Chorus; New**
Philharmonia Orchestra / Otto Klemperer
Testament ② SBT2 1423 (151' · ADD)
Recorded live at the Royal Festival Hall, London, on
March 19, 1968   Ⓕ Ⓞ

Thanks to Testament, we now have the Royal Festival Hall performance, as broadcast by the BBC, to put alongside the Abbey Road recording (above – made by EMI at the same period) which might be justifiably deemed one of two or three great readings of the score on CD.

The two main characters are taken by the same singers, Theo Adam and Anja Silja. Martti Talvela and Annelies Burmeister can also be heard on both sets. The main difference is in the tenor department. James King, rather than Ernst Kozub, would probably have sung Erik in the studio if Decca had been willing to release him, and although this is a notoriously unrewarding part – especially when it has to be acted as well as sung – King's distinctive tonal combination of purity and weight was certainly a bonus in the Festival Hall, just as Kenneth Macdonald makes a fine Steersman. The most remarkable aspect of the performance nevertheless remains the empathy between Klemperer, Silja and Adam. Adam's Act 1 monologue seizes the dramatic high ground, but Silja raises the stakes still further with an electrifying account of Senta's Ballad, and the long duet which ends Act 2 has rarely been as intense and eloquent as it is here.

Live performance always brings risks: there is a split brass note early in Act 1, and Talvela loses his way briefly a little later on. But Klemperer's love of the music's raw edges and robust rhythms is evident throughout. Even at the stately tempo he adopts the Act 3 sailor's dance is so strongly projected that the tension never sags for a moment, and Klemperer's eccentric devotion to the three-act version of the score is far less damaging than it would be in a performance of lower voltage.

The recorded sound also comes up pretty well in this remastering. This extraordinarily 'live' reading of Wagner's windswept score now has the edge, even over the admirable studio alternative.

Der fliegende Holländer   Ⓗ
Hermann Uhde bar Holländer **Ludwig Weber** bass
Daland **Astrid Varnay** sop Senta **Rudolf Lustig** ten
Erik **Elisabeth Schärtel** contr Mary **Josef Traxel** ten
Steuermann
Bayreuth Festival Chorus and Orchestra /
Joseph Keilberth
Testament ② SBT21384 (141' · ADD · S/T/t/N)
Recorded live in 1955   Ⓕ

As with the Ring, Keilberth seemed on high in 1955; once again his reading moves with electrifying concentration from scene to scene. Keilberth achieves great unanimity of approach from his players and absolutely superb singing from the chorus (trained by the remarkable Wilhelm Pitz). The orchestra, perhaps because they knew they were being recorded, play their hearts out to create a fusion of notes and rhythm that is really thrilling from start to finish.

The singers are no less inspired. Uhde gives a supreme interpretation of the tortured, yearning Dutchman. His firm, compact, grainy tone is used with his customary artistry to convey the character's longing for salvation, total elation in the love duet, and desperation when he thinks Senta has betrayed him. Phrase after phrase etches itself in the mind in this unmissable portrayal. Incredibly Varnay, who was also Brünnhilde in 1955, brings to Senta a tireless dedication and vision to match Uhde's hero. She fines her large voice down to the more intimate needs of Senta, and only once or twice do the most taxing passages, as her final outburst, slightly strain her resources.

Ludwig Weber's earthy, experienced Daland is another rewarding interpretation. Lustig, who took over Erik from Windgassen, makes rather a throaty sound in the manner of earlier German Heldentenors, but he has all the notes and conveys the character's understandable frustrations. The Mary is admirable. All seem under the spell of the work and the conductor in a reading that now has the stereo sound it so richly deserves.

Additional recommendation

Hotter Holländer Varnay Senta Glaz Mary   Ⓗ
Haysward Steersman Svanholm Erik Nilsson Daland
Metropolitan Opera Chorus and Orchestra, New
York / Reiner
Naxos Historical mono ② 8 110189/90 (128' · ADD)
Recorded live at the Met, New York 1950. Notes and
synopsis included   Ⓢ Ⓞ

> This performance marked the Met house début of Hans Hotter, and what a début! Varnay and Hotter seem to inspire each other to astonishing feats of musical and dramatic truth. Among historic recordings, this deserves a place up there with the Clemens Krauss.

Lohengrin

Lohengrin
Jess Thomas ten Lohengrin **Elisabeth Grümmer** sop
Elsa **Christa Ludwig** mez Ortrud **Dietrich Fischer-
Dieskau** bar Telramund **Gottlob Frick** bass King
Henry **Otto Wiener** bass Herald V**ienna State Opera
Chorus; Vienna Philharmonic Orchestra / Rudolf
Kempe**
EMI Great Recordings of the Century ③ 567415-2
(217' · ADD · T/t) Recorded 1963-4   Ⓜ Ⓞ Ⓞ ◗

EMI's sound may have less presence and a narrower perspective than other versions, but neither the 'studio' ambience – the recording was made in the Theater an der Wien – nor the occasionally excessive prominence of the voices prevents Kempe's reading from projecting a strongly theatrical quality. However, it's the all-round excellence of the cast, plus the bonus of an uncut Act 3, which makes this the leading mid-price recommendation.

Jess Thomas combines ardour and anguish as well as any, and with Fischer-Dieskau a formidable (but never over-emphatic) antagonist, and Gottlob Frick a majestic King Henry, the drama of the opera's central conflict remains supremely immediate and powerful. As Elsa and Ortrud, Elisabeth Grümmer and Christa Ludwig are ideal opposites, the former radiant yet quite without the simpering overtones that afflict some Elsas, the latter as potent in seductive insinuation as in demonic ferocity. Not even Ludwig can surpass the visceral intensity of Astrid Varnay in the 1953 Bayreuth set under Keilberth, and Keilberth's Telramund and Elsa (Hermann Uhde and Eleanor Steber) are also outstanding: yet Wolfgang Windgassen's Lohengrin isn't as distinguished, nor as distinctive, as Jess Thomas's here. Even more importantly, Keilberth's reading lacks the visionary quality that Kempe finds in the score. Ultimately, it's the power of that vision which raises this performance above its rivals.

Lohengrin
Johan Botha ten Lohengrin **Adrianne Pieczonka**
sop Elsa **Kwangchul Youn** bass King Henry **Falk
Struckmann** bar Telramund **Petra Lang** mez Ortrud
Eike Wilm Schulte bar King's Herald
**North German Radio Chorus; Prague Chamber
Choir; West German Radio Chorus and Symphony
Orchestra, Cologne / Semyon Bychkov**
Profil ③ 💿 PH09004 (3h 34' · DDD · T/t)   Ⓕ

As a studio recording, this new Profil release can claim a degree of rarity value. Also rare is its inclusion of a segment of Lohengrin's 'In fernem Land' monologue which Wagner cut at the time of the premiere, though this has previously appeared in two of the best earlier recordings (from Leinsdorf and Barenboim – see below).

The studio atmosphere means that there are no obvious theatrical effects: no thumps and bumps during fights, for example. But Semyon Bychkov's impassioned conducting ensures that there's no serious loss of theatricality; and even in ordinary stereo the big ensembles sound immensely imposing (the end of Act 2 overwhelming), which compensates to a degree for a wide dynamic range that makes it difficult to set a single suitable volume level throughout.

It can be argued that Wagner never settled on a definitive version of Act 3. He was surely right to cut the anticlimactic episode after Lohengrin reveals his and his father's names, but despite its inclusion here, Profil has failed to include the text in a libretto whose usefulness is already compromised by not having German, French and English in parallel, as well as by a fusty English translation.

Fortunately, there are many positive factors too. Bychkov's reading is admirable, with only occasional exaggerations (including slowing up towards the end of the Act 1 Prayer). Although none of the cast surpasses the work's best exponents elsewhere, all are well worth hearing. Johan Botha is ardent and mellifluous, lacking only that finely spun, silvery thread of tone that distinguished Jess Thomas in the role; nor does Petra Lang – for all her sensitivity to the text – quite set the stage ablaze as Astrid Varnay did. Adrianne Pieczonka is occasionally shrill in more strenuous passages, but there's an attractive tonal brightness that brings extra weight to her Elsa. Underpinning it all are the excellent Cologne forces, with Bychkov in the Act 1 Prelude conveying the 'awesome sweetness' that has to be brought to life if the drama is to work its magic. Not the best Lohengrin ever then, but it's good to have such a well characterised and sumptuously recorded new version.

Lohengrin
Peter Seiffert ten Lohengrin **Emily Magee** sop Elsa
Deborah Polaski sop Ortrud **Falk Struckmann** bar
Telramund **René Pape** bass King Henry **Roman
Trekel** bar Herald **Chorus of the Deutsche Oper,
Berlin; Staatskapelle Berlin / Daniel Barenboim**
Teldec ③ 3984-21484-2 (211' · DDD · T/t)   Ⓕ

This recording is based on the cast with which Barenboim performed the opera at the Berlin State Opera in 1996, although the tenor taking the title-role is different. The chorus, so important in this work, sings with refinement, discipline and enthusiasm in its many roles while all departments of the orchestra play the score to the hilt. Barenboim himself manages to give an overriding unity to a work that can, in lesser hands, sprawl. That's particularly true as regards Act 2, which can test a listener's concentration; not here when the conductor so unerringly weaves the disparate elements into a coherent, forward-moving whole. He's also to be commended for playing Act 3 complete, restoring not only the theatre cuts often made in recording but also the second verse of Lohengrin's Grail narration, cut by Wagner before the first night. In the opera house it's sensibly omitted because it lengthens the act unduly. The only reservation concerns the famous Prelude to Act 3, which seems too brash and too fast. All the singers, with one exception, are regulars at the Berlin State Opera. The exception is Seiffert as Lohengrin, who in tone, phrasing and sheer lyrical ardour makes a near-ideal white knight. His Elsa is Emily Magee, her tone full and refulgent, her interpretation deeply felt. The one worry is that her voice is so much like that of Polaski that they're hard to tell apart in their long confrontation in Act 2. Polaski makes a splendidly forceful and articulate Ortrud, only very occasionally sounding taxed by heavier passages, most worryingly in her closing imprecations. Struckmann's Telramund isn't as tortured as Fischer-Dieskau's in Kempe's set, but these vital, involving interpretations have their own validity. Pape is a model King Henry, pouring out his concerns in golden tone. Trekel is a

strong Herald. The set is enhanced by a perfectly balanced and warm recording.

Lohengrin
Klaus Florian Vogt ten Lohengrin **Solveig
Kringelborn** sop Elsa **Waltraud Meier** mez Ortrud
Tom Fox bar Telramund **Hans-Peter König** bass King
Henry **Roman Trekel** bar
Herald **Lyon National Opera Chorus; Mainz
EuropaChor Akademie; Deutsches Symphony
Orchestra, Berlin / Kent Nagano**
Stage director **Nikolaus Lehnhoff**
Video director **Thomas Grimm**
Opus Arte ③ 🖸 DVD OA0964D (4h 39' · NTSC · 16:9 ·
PCM stereo and DTS 5.1 · 0) Ⓕ
Recorded live at the Festspielhaus, Baden-Baden, in
June 2006. Extra features include 'Never Shall Thou
Ask of Me' – a documentary film by Reiner E Moritz,
Illustrated Synopsis and Cast Gallery

Nikolaus Lehnhoff's new *Lohengrin* is a calculated distillation of both the work's dramatic contents and its production history. The hand of his old master Wieland Wagner lies beneficially over the outer acts' terraced ranks of Brabantine courtiers and Saxon soldiers, as it does on the chessboard movements of the principals around a central disc. (The sets here are by the noted German architect Stephan Braunfels, whose recreation of a giant Svoboda staircase for the Act 2 processions is memorable.) The (swanless) appearance and departure of Lohengrin into a thin, central beam of light recall the imagery of Bayreuth's recent Keith Warner/Stefanos Lazaridis staging, while the promotion of Elsa to a constantly onstage narrator/dreamer continues an idea of Götz Friedrich's in an earlier Bayreuth production.

Yet, although Bettina Walter's costumes are modern-ish – somewhere between Juan Carlos's ceremonial Spain and a Hollywood Prisoner of Zenda – Lehnhoff's direction, as always, remains narrative-based and essentially traditional. Only once, in the bridal chamber scene of Act 3 does this director allow himself a conceit, showing Lohengrin, Wagner-like, at a reversed keyboard piano, composing and playing the wedding march. It's a strange and acute image, revealing at a stroke the hero's narcissistic and chauvinistic self-absorption.

Lehnhoff's accumulation of images is trenchantly delivered onstage by his two leading ladies, both wide-ranging, attention-holding actresses: Kringelborn in her vocal prime, strong, pure, never forcing; Meier in her vocal Indian summer, strong, impure, sometimes forcing, but always wholly in the service of this sexy, brainy Ortrud. Vogt, in his silver-blue zoot suit, is a charismatic enigma (hence ideal for this role), an apparently super-light voice but one with both stamina and sustaining power. The lower male voices also make their mark: Fox creates sympathy for this Macbeth without a brain; Trekel's Herald has power and attitude; König is a subtly eponymous, weak liberal Henry. The chorus(es) sound undernourished, acting better

than they keep together (in the tricky vocal helter-skelter of Lohengrin's arrival) with the pit. It
sounds like early days for Kent Nagano at maintaining pace and flow through the weighty four-
in-a-bar recitative-like passages.

Thomas Grimm gets his cameras in close,
leaving the singers to track reactions to solo
utterances but missing some crucial interplay.
Within a natural sound spectrum, some tweak-
ing has been done to pull out solo lines in
ensemble, but the emotions of Lehnhoff's vision
ring true and will give pleasure.

Die Meistersinger von Nürnberg

Die Meistersinger von Nürnberg
Thomas Stewart bar Hans Sachs **Sándor Kónya** ten
Walther **Gundula Janowitz** sop Eva **Franz Crass**
bass Pogner **Thomas Hemsley** bar Beckmesser
Gerhard Unger ten David **Brigitte Fassbaender**
mez Magdalene **Kieth Engen** bass Kothner **Horst
Wilhelm** ten Vogelgesang **Richard Kogel** bass
Nachtigall **Manfred Schmidt** ten Zorn **Friedrich Lenz**
ten Eisslinger **Peter Baillie** ten Moser **Anton Diakov**
bass Ortel **Karl Christian Kohn** bass Schwartz **Dieter
Slembeck** bass Foltz **Raimund Grumbach** bass
Nightwatchman **Bavarian Radio Chorus and
Symphony Orchestra / Rafael Kubelík**
Calig ④ CAL50971/4 (272' · ADD) Recorded 1967
Ⓕ**OO**

There could be no more fitting memorial to
Kubelík than the appearance of this, probably
the most all-round satisfying *Meistersinger* in the
era of stereo. It was recorded in 1967 by Bavarian Radio to mark the work's centenary the following year. Kubelík conducts an unforced,
loving interpretation, showing a gratifying grasp
of overall structure. As a whole the reading has
an unobtrusive cohesion achieved within flexible
tempos and dynamics. Everything proceeds at
an even, well-judged pace with just the right
surge of emotion at the climaxes. All this is conveyed unerringly to his own Bavarian Radio
Symphony forces.

Stewart's Sachs is certainly his most successful
performance on disc. He offers a finely moulded,
deeply considered reading that relies on firm,
evenly produced, mostly warm tone to create a
darkish, philosophical poet-cobbler. Kónya is
simply the most winning Walther on any set,
superseding Sawallisch's excellent Heppner by
virtue of a greater ardour in his delivery. Kónya
pours out consistently warm, clear tone, his
tenor hovering ideally between the lyric and the
heroic. Nor are there many better Evas than the
young Janowitz, certainly none with a lovelier
voice. Franz Crass, a less pompous Pogner than
some, sings his part effortlessly, with noble feeling. Hemsley, though singing his first
Beckmesser, evinces a close affinity with the
Town Clerk's mean-mindedness, and his German is faultless. Unger is a paragon among
Davids, so eager in his responses and finding just
the right timbre for the role. His Magdalene,
again perfect casting, is the young Fassbaender.

With a characterful Kothner in Engen, the
requirements for a near-ideal *Meistersinger*
ensemble are in place. As the recording doesn't
betray its age this would undoubtedly be the first
choice among stereo versions.

Die Meistersinger von Nürnberg   Ⓗ
Paul Schöffler bass-bar Hans Sachs **Hans Beirer** ten
Walther **Irmgard Seefried** sop Eva **Gottlob Frick**
bass Pogner **Erich Kunz** bass Beckmesser **Murray
Dickie** ten David **Rosette Anday** mez Magdalene
Hans Braun bass Kothner **Karl Terkal** ten
Vogelgesang **Eberhard Waechter** bass Nachtigall
Erich Majkut ten Zorn **Fritz Sperlbauer** ten
Eisslinger **William Wernigk** ten Moser **Harald
Pröglhöf** bass Ortel **Adolf Vogel** bass Schwarz
Ljubomir Pantscheff bass Foltz **Frederick Guthrie**
bass Nightwatchman **Vienna State Opera Chorus
and Orchestra / Fritz Reiner**
Orfeo d'Or mono d C667 054L (4h 18' · ADD)
Recorded live 1955   Ⓕ

The heavily bombed State Opera House in
Vienna reopened on November 5, 1955, with a
performance of *Fidelio*. *Die Meistersinger*, the
Viennese favourite, followed in a new production and was the occasion of some disappointment. Critics blamed the stage production team;
Gottfried Kraus, in an authoritative essay
accompanying this recording, is inclined to
think that the reaction was due rather more to a
shock to the system caused by the transference
of the opera from the relative intimacy of the
Theater an der Wien to the less cosy expansiveness of the new-old house.

As listeners merely, we are hardly affected,
instead experiencing a few disappointments of
our own. First among these must be the singing
of our hero for the evening, the Walther von
Stolzing of Hans Beirer. He is sympathetic and
objectionable almost by alternation, starting in a
warm-toned, naturally colloquial style, then
developing a lumpy, graceless, forced manner of
utterance: an unlikely candidate for any prize in
singing. Reiner's conducting, too, will not be to
all tastes, prosaic in the overture, then given to
marked *rallentandi* and some unusually slow
speeds in Act 3. More generally, the live recording is not entirely even-handed in its balancing
of stage and orchestra, certain areas caught less
clearly than others.

Irmgard Seefried is particularly a victim. Sung
with character in every phrase, her Eva charms
from the first whispered exchanges in church,
throughout the great duets and quintet to the
awarding of the victory-laurels, but seems small-
scale, miniaturised. Of course, as long as they are
on stage alongside Gottlob Frick, most voices
are likely to sound small. He is the magnificent
Pogner of the age, gloriously full and secure, and
dealing with the tessitura of 'Das schöne Fest' as
if (as the shop-girls say) 'No problem'.

Kunz's Beckmesser is familiar, and does not
gain from another hearing. But Paul Schöffler,
the undoubted true hero of the evening, is surely
here giving the performance of a lifetime. It has

all the warmth and understanding we remember from the studio recording but now, with the stage his artistic home and freedom to let movement influence pace, he is newly impressive: in the last act especially, with his deeply moved acknowledgement ('Euch macht ihr's leicht') and the final admonition ('Verrachtet mir'), where he draws on a rich reserve of vocal power and resonance.

This is a recording one would want to have for that alone, though indeed there are other as yet unmentioned attractions such as Murray Dickie's lively, clean-cut David and the sonorous Watchman of Frederick Guthrie. And the flexibility and warmth of Reiner's conducting does have an appeal of its own. Above all, the recording renews joyful contact with the adorable opera. The Viennese of 1955 may have wended their way home a little disappointedly. We, home-listeners half a century later, are likely to retire for the night with a note in our diaries: 'Bounteous *Meistersinger*, and, so to bed, well content'.

Die Meistersinger von Nürnberg
John Tomlinson bass Hans Sachs **Thomas Allen** bar Beckmesser **Gösta Winbergh** ten Walther **Nancy Gustafson** sop Eva **Catherine Wyn-Rogers** mez Magdalene **Herbert Lippert** ten David **Gwynne Howell** bass Pogner
Chorus and Orchestra of the Royal Opera House, Covent Garden / Bernard Haitink
Royal Opera House Heritage Series ④ ROHS008 (265' · DDD). Recorded live on July 7, 1997   Ⓜ

The Mastersingers of Nuremberg
Norman Bailey bass-bar Hans Sachs **Derek Hammond-Stroud** bar Beckmesser **Alberto Remedios** ten Walther **Margaret Curphey** sop Eva **Ann Robson** mez Magdalene **Gregory Dempsey** ten David **Noel Mangin** bass Pogner
Chorus and Orchestra of Sadler's Wells Opera / Reginald Goodall
Chandos ④ CHAN3148 (293' · ADD)
Recorded live on February 10, 1968   Ⓜ

Both these new/old performances, stemming from live broadcasts at key moments in the two major London opera companies' histories, reflect the sense of community ensemble and Shakespearean mix of sacred and profane comedy which has become our particular national gift to Wagner's comedy.

The more recent performance is something of a coronation for Bernard Haitink's embattled but admired music directorship of the old Covent Garden. The performance, his happiest Wagner outing to date on disc, shows him to be a listening accompanist and precise balancer of orchestral textures. The discs too provide a souvenir of a memorable British double-act: John Tomlinson's Sachs (fully engaged as philosophical poet or virile, passionate shoemaker) and Thomas Allen's carefully drawn assumption of Beckmesser – pomposity and pathos founded on a vocal delivery which satisfies both demands for comedy and the stature appropriate to a senior member of the Mastersingers' Guild.

They are ably supported. Gösta Winbergh is a thinking man's knight who, like his bright and beautiful Evchen, Nancy Gustafson, is a great user of text as well as tone. Lippert is a fluent David, Gwynne Howell and Catherine Wyn-Rogers field a Pogner and Magdalene of uncommonly rich shadings – while the Masters' list is a veritable who's who of subtle, musical character actors. The recording has come up with a good sense of theatrical ping – apart from an oddly forward balance for the would-be eloping lovers in their Act 2 asides.

How happy one would be with this set in a competition-less world but other recorded maestros delve more profoundly into the text and theatricality of this score than Haitink chooses to do. One such is Reginald Goodall, whose 1968 Sadler's Wells performance(s) – legendary at least in British memory – has finally reached an official release on Chandos in Sir Peter Moores's Opera in English series. Here is one legend which hits the light of a 2008 day as brightly as it shone 40 years ago. Goodall's understanding of what every beat of this score means, and his successful communication of that to his personally trained cast, is a thing of wonder. Climaxes (end of Act 1, the riot, the quintet etc) are immense; timers may tell us it's slow, but the pulse never flags.

Goodall's Walther, Alberto Remedios, once said that when he played Caruso's records at home he forgot to go out. The same compliment might be paid to this singer when he starts 'Am stillen Herd', or tells Sachs his morning dream in three parts, or delivers the prize song with a dream mixture of Italianate tone and line and German lyrical weight. OK, it's in English, and a rather quaint English – but it has to be heard. So does Norman Bailey's Sachs. He is a noble humanist, free (even in the gulling of Beckmesser) of petty concerns and stirred as opposed merely to being moody in yielding Evchen to Walther. His seamless delivery of the 'Flieder' monologue, natural authority in the 'Ein Kind war geboren' sequence and striking of the right blend of admonishment and advice in 'Verrachtet mir die Meister nicht' all represent work on a Friedrich Schorr/Hans Hotter level. And, together with Goodall, Margaret Curphey makes Eva's predicaments and love always real rather than simply coy.

The plentiful laughter that can be heard is due to both the sharp theatrical pointing of Goodall's conducting and to the Eric Morecambe-like ability of Derek Hammond-Stroud's Beckmesser to be genuinely funny just by appearing. Hammond-Stroud's is a masterly comic performance at the other end of the pole to Allen's – but equally valid.

One can understand non-Anglophone readers smiling whimsically but this Chandos release genuinely becomes one of the miracles of the current Wagner discography.

Die Meistersinger von Nürnberg
Wolfgang Brendel bass-bar Hans Sachs **Gösta Winbergh** ten Walther **Eva Johansson** sop Eva **Victor von Halem** bass Pogner **Elke Wilm Schulte**

bar Beckmesser **Uwe Peper** *ten* David **Ute Walther**
mez Magdalene **Lenus Carlson** *bass* Kothner **David**
Griffith *ten* Vogelgesang **Barry McDaniel** *bar*
Nachtigall **Volker Horn** *ten* Zorn **Peter Maus** *ten*
Eisslinger **Otto Heuer** *ten* Moser **Ivan Sardi** *bass*
Schwarz **Friedrich Molsberger** *bass* Foltz **Peter**
Edelmann *bass* Nightwatchman **Berlin Opera**
Orchestra and Chorus / Rafael Frühbeck de
Burgos
Stage director **Götz Friedrich**
Video director **Brian Large**
Arthaus Musik ⏺DVD⏺ 100 152 (266' · Region 0)   Ⓕ**OO**

This has to be one of the most engrossing and
satisfactory performances of *Die Meistersinger*
in memory. Pleasure derives as much as anything from the sense of a complete intregra-
tion of music and action in a staging that has
been scrupulously rehearsed on all sides. This
is a 1995 revival with the same cast as the 1993
original, and it's clear how keen the response
of the singers to each other is.

The credit for one's profound enjoyment
undoubtedly goes to Götz Friedrich. Renowned
for his handling of characters and their interaction on stage, his skills in that sphere have seldom if ever been more fruitfully displayed. The
action and reaction of the masters in their Act 1
disputations, the subtle relationship between
Sachs and Eva, the ebb and flow of the arguments between Sachs and Beckmesser, and the
friendly interplay between Walther and Sachs,
the disciple eagerly learning from the teacher in
Act 1 scene 3, are all revelatory. In these and
other scenes, more of the characters' humanity
is expressed than has ever been shown before.
This is operatic acting on the highest level of
achievement.

Frühbeck de Burgos enhances the director's
approach with his chamber-like treatment of
the orchestra, allowing the singers' clear enunciation to be heard at all times. He's also to be
commended for the discerning ebb and flow of
his reading as a whole, which is at once lively
and unforced. Wolfgang Brendel presents an
affectionate, sympathetic, somewhat laid-back,
ruminative Sachs, his voice lacking in warmth
only at the bottom of his register, the sound
more baritone than bass-orientated. As we
know from Covent Garden, Winbergh is a
well-nigh ideal Walther, singing his role with
unwonted ease and lyrical breadth, responsive
always to the text's meaning.

Johansson is a knowing, flirtatious Eva, forthcoming in voice and mien; her earthbound start
of the Quintet comes as a disappointment after
her gloriously outgoing 'O Sachs, mein
Freund'. Schulte sings and acts Beckmesser to
perfection, never resorting to caricature in
depicting the self-important, didactic town
clerk and giving the role a wealth of nuance,
always keeping to the notes. Peper is a well-
routined, likeable David, Von Halem an
imposing, properly fatherly Pogner.

As a whole, this is a performance to treasure. It
has admirably balanced sound and perceptive
video direction by the ultra-experienced Brian

WAGNER'S RING CYCLE – IN BRIEF

Birgit Nilsson *Brünnhilde* **Wolfgang Windgassen**
Siegfried **Hans Hotter, George London** *Wotan*
Vienna PO / Sir Georg Solti
Decca ⑭ 455 555-2DMO14 (14 hr 36' · ADD)
                                        Ⓜ**OO**
The first complete cycle is still the most
clearly recommendable. Even if Solti's blazingly dynamic conducting isn't everyone's
ideal, he unites the most consistently superb
casting with John Culshaw's still magnificent
recording. A classic of the recording era.

Jeannine Altmeyer *Brünnhilde* **René Kollo**
Siegfried **Theo Adam** *Wotan*
Staatskapelle Dresden / Marek Janowski
RCA ⑨ 82876 55709-2 (13 hr 59' · DDD)   Ⓑ**OO**
Janowski makes this first digital version fresh,
fast and straightforward, with several fine
voices such as Jessye Norman and Peter Schreier, but also, unfortunately, Adam's now
desiccated Wotan, and a rather studio-bound
recording.

Rita Hunter *Brünnhilde* **Alberto Remedios**
Siegfried **Norman Bailey** *Wotan* **ENO /**
Sir Reginald Goodall
Chandos ⑭ CHAN3038/45/54/60 (16 hr 31' · DDD)
                                        Ⓑ**OO**
Goodall's famously massive reading may
shock some with its slowness, but it's beautifully detailed, with the immediacy of English,
and offers some truly world-class performances. Recorded live, mostly in winter, hence
some obtrusive coughing.

Helga Dernesch *Brünnhilde* **Helge Brilloth**
Siegfried **Dietrich Fischer-Dieskau** *Wotan*
Berlin PO / Herbert von Karajan
DG ⑭ 457 780-2GOR14 (14 hr 58' · ADD)   Ⓑ**O**
An underrated version, largely because
Karajan's emphasis on orchestral and vocal
beauty sometimes sounds mannered, and
encompasses inconsistent and occasionally
inadequate casting – particularly Siegfried.
Nevertheless this is a well recorded and
often magical set.

Astrid Varnay *Brünnhilde* **Bernd Aldenhoff** Ⓗ
Siegfried **Hans Hotter** *Wotan* **Bayreuth Fetival**
Orchestra / Joseph Keilberth
Testament SBT21390, SBT41391, SBT41392,
SBT41392   Ⓕ**OOO**
An astounding cycle, recorded in stereo live
at Bayreuth in 1955, this has leapt to the top
of the pile of historic *Ring*s. Keilberth shows
what a superb Wagnerian he was and his cast
is faultless – dominated by Hotter's amazing;y
complete Wotan and Astrid Varnay as his
wayward daughter. The sound, courtesy of
Decca engineers, is stunning.

Large. Recommended, though it probably bows to the Levine set (below).

Die Meistersinger von Nürnberg
James Morris bass Hans Sachs **Ben Heppner** ten
Walther **Karita Mattila** sop Eva **René Pape**
bass-Pogner **Sir Thomas Allen** bass Beckmesser
Matthew Polenzani ten David **Jill Grove** mez
Magdalene **John Del Carlo** bass Kothner
Metropolitan Opera Chorus and Orchestra,
New York / James Levine
Stage director **Otto Schenk**
Video director **Brian Large**
DG ② **DVD** 0730949-2GH2 (292' · NTSC · 16:9 ·
PCM-stereo, 5.1 & DTS 5.1 · 0)
Recorded live at the Metropolitan Opera,
New York, December 2001. Extras include
picture gallery   Ⓕ**OO**

This most humane and intimate of all Wagner's operas is a natural for DVD, but we haven't yet had a wholly satisfactory version. However, this Met version, superbly recorded in widescreen, boasting a mouthwatering cast, largely fulfils the considerable expectations it raises.

Conducting and staging are solidly uncontroversial. Levine's rich, weighty Wagner style seems to suit *Meistersinger* better than *The Ring*. There are still some unexpected gear changes, but better integrated into a fluent, warm reading. Otto Schenk's production is almost aggressively traditional – lively enough, but one longs for some subtler spark of originality or insight, in the sets especially. A properly bustling Act 3 'Festweise' is welcome, instead of dull grandstands, but the Act 2 brawl is sadly shirked.

The singers are the best on DVD. With his clear, unbaritonal lyric Heldentenor, Ben Heppner is a convincingly poetic Walther; but the bulky face and frame lose credibility in Brian Large's vivid camera direction. Even the beautiful Karita Mattila's girlish antics look less appropriate, but she remains a stunning Eva, dramatic in power but with reserves of crystalline lyricism.

René Pape's Pogner looks no older than his 'daughter', a minor blemish on a finely resonant performance, but a blow to dramatic involvement. Sir Thomas Allen's minutely characterised, acidulous Beckmesser is properly malevolent yet unexpectedly mellifluous, hilarious without vocal distortions.

James Morris's Sachs is warm-hearted, quintessentially American and none the worse for that. His voice is more sinewy now and less steady, losing some of its rich tone and silken *legato*, but gaining in character. He's still not ideally expressive, though, making less of the cobbler-poet's visionary and temperamental side, and more telling as Eva and Walther's genial mentor than in the monologues. His fellow Mastersingers are well portrayed, though John Del Carlo could make more of Kothner, but the chorus and apprentices can't quite match Bayreuth's.

This amiable, large-scale performance is highly recommendable.

Parsifal

Parsifal
Jess Thomas ten Parsifal **George London** bass-bar
Amfortas **Hans Hotter** bass-bar Gurnemanz **Irene**
Dalis mez Kundry **Gustav Neidlinger** bass-bar
Klingsor **Martti Talvela** bass Titurel **Niels Møller** ten
First Knight **Gerd Nienstedt** bass Second Knight
Sona Cervená mez First Squire Sixth Flower Maiden
Ursula Boese mez Second Squire **Gerhard Stolze**
ten Third Squire **Georg Paskuda** ten Fourth Squire
Rita Bartos, Gundula Janowitz, Anja Silja, Elsa-
Margrete Gardelli, Dorothea Siebert sops Flower
Maidens; **Bayreuth Festival Chorus and Orchestra**
/ Hans Knappertsbusch
Philips ④ 4757785 (250' · ADD · T/t) Recorded live
1962   Ⓜ**OOO**▷

This is one of the greatest sets of all time. Every time one returns to it, its inspiration and distinction seem to have been enhanced. There have been many fine recordings of this great Eastertide opera, but none has so magnificently managed to capture the power, the spiritual grandeur, the human frailty and the almost unbearable beauty of the work as Hans Knappertsbusch. This live recording has a cast that has few equals. Hotter is superb, fleshing out Gurnemanz with a depth of insight that has never been surpassed. London's Amfortas captures the frightening sense of impotence and anguish with painful directness, while Thomas's Parsifal grows as the performance progresses and is no mean achievement. Dalis may lack that final degree of sensuousness but she provides a fine interpretation nevertheless. Throughout the work, Knappertsbusch exercises a quite un-equalled control over the proceedings; it's a fine testament to a great conductor. The Bayreuth acoustic is well reproduced, and this record is a profound and moving experience.

Parsifal
Thomas Stewart bar Amfortas **Heinz Hagenau** bass
Titurel **Hans Hotter** bass Gurnemanz **Jon Vickers**
ten Parsifal **Gustav Neidlinger** bass Klingsor **Barbro**
Ericson mez Kundry **Hermann Winkler** ten Knight I
Gerd Nienstedt bass Knight II **Ruth Hesse, Sylvia**
Lindenstrand sops **Dieter Slembeck, Erwin**
Wohlfahrt tens Squires **Anja Silja, Dorothea**
Siebert, Liselotte Rebmann, Rita Bartos, Elsa-
Margrete Gardelli, Sylvia Lindenstrand sops Flower
Maidens **Ruth Hesse** contr Voice from Above
Bayreuth Festival Chorus and Orchestra /
Hans Knappertsbusch
Orfeo d'Or mono ④ C690 074L (4h 10' ·
ADD · S/N). Recorded live on August 13, 1964
                                        Ⓜ**OOO**

The (to date) 11 released recordings of Hans Knappertsbusch's *Parsifal* performances at

Bayreuth between 1951 and 1964 constitute a unique record of one conductor's work on a favoured score in a single theatre. By 1942 'Kna' had logged up over 90 performances in a number of venues of a work he first led when he was 25, but after 1951 he would only conduct it in Bayreuth. Technical gremlins in Bavarian Radio's transmission of the 1964 first night led to its being replaced by a recording of the present performance, the last night of the run. It was not only Kna's last ever *Parsifal*, it was to be his last ever public performance.

Thirteen years of performances saw changes to Knappertsbusch's shaping of the score which were as subtle but as continuous as those taking place in the seminal Wieland Wagner stage production which it accompanied. Compare the original 1951 recording (Decca, now Naxos): if the basic tempi remain slow, the pulse is much more sharply defined and the much-commented weight has been replaced by a colourful plasticity which is almost Debussian. Also, rather like an extended version of *Walküre* Act 1, there is now only one real climax in the whole interpretation. 'Be off with you now and let's have a good Good Friday Spell', the conductor apparently told Hans Hotter in an interval conversation – and they did, with a monumental strike (shattering timpani, shining brass, thrilling precision from Gurnemanz) at the launch of the scene on the holy meadow.

The performance is also vital for its preservation of Jon Vickers's Parsifal. In his second appearance on the Green Hill the Canadian tenor mixes great strength and great beauty of voice to an almost platonic ideal in the tricky Act 2 dialogue with Kundry. Here what can sound like sermonising becomes passionate, convincing rhetoric. Hotter's Gurnemanz, in its range of inflections and illuminating line readings a close cousin of his Wotan, has ripened too since the widely circulated Philips reading of 1962. Thomas Stewart took over Amfortas this year from George London, reaching frightening heights of persecution mania in his last confrontation with the brethren in Act 3.

As with the predecessors in their 'official' Bayreuth series, Orfeo has denied us some of the 'live' atmosphere with its scrubbing and cleaning up of the original radio recording. It is also transferred at rather a low volume. However, forced into a ridiculous choice between 'Kna' *Parsifals*, this stands alongside the 1954 version (Archipel, his return to the Green Hill after an enforced year off) as the ranking interpretations from this maestro.

sops **Anne Howells, Marjorie Biggar** mezs Flower Maidens
Chorus and Orchestra of the Royal Opera House, Covent Garden / Reginald Goodall
Royal Opera House Heritage Series ④ ROHS012 (4h 44' · ADD). Recorded live on May 8, 1971   Ⓜ**ⓄⓄ**

Although Reginald Goodall was thoroughly familiar with Wagner's last opera from sitting in the pit for Hans Knappertsbusch's 1950s Bayreuth performances and from his own coaching work at Covent Garden, he actually made his debut conducting the work with the 1971 run from which this release derives. The planned cast was strong but illness led to four Gurnemanzes and two Klingsors being called upon to keep the curtain up.

By many accounts the opening night (with Gottlob Frick coming out of retirement as Gurnemanz) was a great evening – is there not some test recording of that around? The present performance, with the Belgian Louis Hendrikx returning as a careful, direct Gurnemanz, has passionate, well defined interpretations from Jon Vickers in the title-role, Donald MacIntyre as a rapaciously evil Klingsor (with superb German), Norman Bailey's sorrowful Amfortas and soaring contributions from solo flowers Kiri Te Kanawa and Anne Howells. Amy Shuard also makes her mark in a role especially suited to her dramatic, hard-edged soprano. Goodall's guidance of the music is replete with beautiful apercus of balance and rhythm, not to mention much fine wind-playing. But, on this particular evening, the reading too often hangs fire. As interesting reviews of other Goodall performances have pointed out, the conductor's habits of following (rather than leading) singers he especially trusts, and his taking over of a German, especially Knappertsbusch-like, tradition of marking the end of paragraphs with lengthy, unwritten *Luftpausen* – in a score that already calls for many significant pauses – often elongate his reading to a point where Act 1, in the iconoclastic words of note-writer John Deathridge, 'verges on incoherence'.

In addition, Goodall's textures and instrumental colours here continually stress the work's pain and sadness. But it's not the whole story – there's exciting psychological drama in this score too, of a *Tristan*-like beat and intensity.

Medici and ROH Heritage Series have done fine work in remastering these BBC tapes for release. Admirers of the conductor and collectors of the art of Jon Vickers will find a great deal of consummate music-making and singing here – but, without sounding mealy-mouthed, the story of Sir Reginald Goodall's *Parsifal* should not yet be over.

Parsifal
Norman Bailey bar Amfortas **Michael Langdon** bass Titurel **Louis Hendrikx** bass Gurnemanz **Jon Vickers** ten Parsifal **Donald McIntyre** bass Klingsor **Amy Shuard** sop Kundry **Edgar Evans** ten First Grail Knight **Dennis Wicks** bass Second Grail Knight **Nan Christie** sop **Delia Wallis** mez **David Lennox, John Dobson** tens Four Esquires **Kiri Te Kanawa, Maureen Keetch, Alison Hargan, Anne Pashley**

Parsifal
Peter Hofmann ten Parsifal **José van Dam** bass-bar Amfortas **Kurt Moll** bass Gurnemanz **Dunja Vejzovic** mez Kundry **Siegmund Nimsgern** bass Klingsor **Victor von Halem** bass Titurel **Claes Hakon Ahnsjö** ten First Knight **Kurt Rydl** bass Second Knight

Marjon Lambriks, Anne Gjevang *mezzos* **Heiner Hopfner** *ten* **Georg Tichy** *bass* Squires **Barbara Hendricks, Janet Perry, Inga Nielsen** *sops* **Audrey Michael** *mez* **Doris Soffel, Rohângiz Yachmi Caucig** *contrs* Flower Maidens **Hanna Schwarz** *mez* Voice from above **Berlin Deutsche Opera Chorus; Berlin Philharmonic Orchestra / Herbert von Karajan**
DG ④ 413 347-2GH4 (256' · ADD · T/t) Recorded 1979-80   Ⓕ❶❶❶❿

Karajan's *Parsifal* seems to grow in stature as an interpretation on each rehearing; on its CD transfer it appears to have acquired a new depth, in terms of sound, because of the greater range of the recording and the greater presence of both singers and orchestra. As in practically all cases, CD offers a more immediate experience. Karajan's reading, a trifle stodgy in Act 1, grows in intensity and feeling with the work itself, reaching an almost terrifying force in the Prelude to Act 3 which is sustained to the end of the opera. Moll's Gurnemanz is a deeply expressive, softly moulded performance of notable beauty. Vejzovic, carefully nurtured by Karajan, gives the performance of her life as Kundry. Hofmann's tone isn't at all times as steady as a Parsifal's should be, but he depicts the character's anguish and eventual serenity in his sincere, inward interpretation. Van Dam is a trifle too placid as Amfortas, but his singing exhibits admirable power and fine steadiness. Nimsgern is the epitome of malice as Klingsor. The choral singing doesn't have quite the confidence of the superb orchestral playing, which has both qualities of Keats's imagining of beauty and truth in abundance.

Rienzi

Rienzi
René Kollo *ten* Cola Rienzi **Siv Wennberg** *sop* Irene **Janis Martin** *sop* Adriano **Theo Adam** *bass* Paolo Orsini **Nikolaus Hillebrand** *bass* Steffano Colonna **Siegfried Vogel** *bass* Raimondo **Peter Schreier** *ten* Baroncelli **Günther Leib** *bass* Cecco del Vecchio **Ingeborg Springer** *sop* Messenger of Peace **Leipzig Radio Chorus; Dresden State Opera Chorus; Staatskapelle Dresden / Heinrich Hollreiser**
EMI ③ 567131-2 (225' · ADD· T/t) Recorded 1974-6 Ⓜ

Rienzi is grand opera with a vengeance. Political imperatives count for more than mere human feelings, and politics means ceremony as well as warfare: marches, ballet music and extended choruses are much in evidence in this work, while even the solo arias often have the rhetorical punch of political harangues. It could all be an enormous bore. Yet the young Wagner, basing his work on Bulwer Lytton's story of the tragic Roman tribune, did manage to move beyond mere tub-thumping into a degree of intensity that – for those with ears to hear – prefigures the mature genius to come. In the end, Rienzi himself is more than just a political animal, and the existential anguish of Tannhäuser, Tristan and

even Amfortas can be found glimmering in the distance. This performance isn't ideal in every respect, either musically, or as a recording. But its virtues outweigh its weaknesses by a considerable margin. Siv Wennberg was not in best voice at the time, but the other principals, notably René Kollo and Janis Martin, bring commendable stamina and conviction to their demanding roles. Above all Heinrich Hollreiser prevents the more routine material from sounding merely mechanical, and ensures that *Rienzi* has a truly Wagnerian sweep and fervour.

The Ring – Das Rheingold / Die Walküre

Das Rheingold
John Tomlinson *bass* Wotan **Linda Finnie** *mez* Fricka **Graham Clark** *ten* Loge **Helmut Pampuch** *ten* Mime **Günter von Kannen** *bar* Alberich **Eva Johansson** *sop* Freia **Kurt Schreibmayer** *ten* Froh **Bodo Brinkmann** *bar* Donner **Birgitta Svendén** *mez* Erda **Matthias Hölle** *bass* Fasolt **Philip Kang** *bass* Fafner **Hilde Leidland** *sop* Woglinde **Annette Küttenbaum** *mez* Wellgunde **Jane Turner** *mez* Flosshilde **Bayreuth Festival Orchestra / Daniel Barenboim**
Teldec ③ 4509-91185-2 (149' · DDD · T/t) Recorded live 1991   Ⓕ❶❶

Die Walküre
Poul Elming *ten* Siegmund **Nadine Secunde** *sop* Sieglinde **Anne Evans** *sop* Brünnhilde **John Tomlinson** *bass* Wotan **Linda Finnie** *mez* Fricka, Siegrune **Matthias Hölle** *bass* Hunding **Eva Johansson** *sop* Gerhilde **Eva-Maria Bundschuh** *sop* Helmwige **Ruth Floeren** *sop* Ortlinde **Shirley Close** *mez* Waltraute **Hebe Dijkstra** *mez* Rossweisse **Birgitta Svendén** *mez* Grimgerde **Hitomi Katagiri** *mez* Schwertleite **Bayreuth Festival Orchestra / Daniel Barenboim**
Teldec ④ 4509-91186-2 (233' · DDD) Recorded live 1992   Ⓕ❶❶

These are enthralling performances. Tomlinson's volatile Wotan is the most potent reading here. He manages to sing every word with insistent meaning and forceful declamation while maintaining a firm *legato*. His German is so idiomatic that he might have been speaking the language his whole life and he brings breadth and distinction of phrase to his solos at the close of both operas. Anne Evans as a single, important advantage over other recent Brünnhildes in that her voice is wholly free from wobble and she never makes an ugly sound. Hers is a light, girlish, honest portrayal, sung with unfailing musicality if not with the ultimate insights. Linda Finnie is an articulate, sharp-edged Fricka, and Graham Clark a sparky, incisive Loge. Nadine Secunde's impassioned Sieglinde is matched by the vital, exciting Siegmund of Poul Elming, and Matthias Hölle as both Hunding and Fasolt is another of those black basses of which Germany seems to have an inexhaustible supply. The whole is magnificently conducted by Barenboim, a more expansive Wagnerian than Böhm. By

1991 he had the full measure of its many facets, bringing immense authority and power to building its huge climaxes, yet finding all the lightness of touch for the mercurial and/or diaphanous aspects of the score. He has the inestimable advantage of a Bayreuth orchestra at the peak of its form, surpassing – and this says much – even the Metropolitan orchestra for Levine. Similar qualities inform his interpretation of *Die Walküre*. Barenboim has now learnt how to match the epic stature of Wagner's mature works, how to pace them with an overview of the whole, and there's an incandescent, metaphysical feeling of a Furtwänglerian kind in is treatment of such passages as Wotan's anger and the Valkyrie ride. The orchestra is superb. It's backed by a recording of startling presence and depth, amply capturing the Bayreuth acoustic.

Das Rheingold
Hans Hotter *bass-bar* Wotan **Georgine von Milinkovič** *mez* Fricka **Rudolf Lustig** *ten* Loge **Paul Kuen** *ten* Mime **Gustav Neidlinger** *bass-bar* Alberich **Hertha Wilfert** *sop* Freia **Josef Traxel** *ten* Froh **Toni Blankenheim** *bar* Donner **Maria von Ilosvay** *mez* Erda **Ludwig Weber** *bass* Fasolt **Josef Greindl** *bass* Fafner **Jutta Vulpius** *sop* Woglinde **Elisabeth Schärtel** *mez* Wellgunde **Maria Graf** *mez* Flosshilde **Bayreuth Festival Orchestra / Joseph Keilberth**
Testament ② SBT2 1390 (142' · ADD)
Recorded live at the Festspielhaus, Bayreuth, on July 24, 1955 Ⓕ

Here we are at the start of the revelatory Bayreuth *Ring* of 1955, and from the very first primordial sounds Joseph Keilberth establishes that this is to be a very special cycle. The opening scene is dominated by Gustav Neidlinger's nonpareil of an Alberich, who in the third scene becomes a frightening incarnation of malevolent power. But the Rhinemaidens aren't as steady as one might wish.

Scene 2 brings a kaleidoscope of authoritative interpretations, headed by Hans Hotter's commanding Wotan, a thoughtful portrait of an overweening, troubled figure sung with a Lieder-like attention to verbal detail. Georgine von Milinkovič is a suitably imposing Fricka and a convincing nag. Ludwig Weber's expressive, articulate Fasolt is partnered by Josef Greindl's louring Fafner. Rudolf Lustig's strongly sung Loge – no comprimario tenor he – is not the most fluent piece of singing, but he gives the text real meaning. Among the minor gods Josef Traxel stands out for his beautifully lyric Froh, luxury casting from one of the leading tenors then active in Germany. Maria von Ilosvay as Erda and Paul Kuen as Mime are just as characterful as in in Siegfried. Over all you have once again a sense of a truly experienced ensemble, each member of which plays to the other.

Once again, one is astounded by the ideal capturing of the Bayreuth acoustics and by the superlative playing of the orchestra, stimulated by Keilberth's astutely dramatic conducting.

Das Rheingold
Falk Struckmann *bass-bar*-Wotan **Lioba Braun** *mez*-Fricka **Graham Clark** *ten*-Loge **Francisco Vas** *ten*-Mime **Günter von Kannen** *bar*-Alberich **Elisabete Matos** *sop*-Freia **Jeffrey Dowd** *ten*-Froh **Wolfgang Rauch** *bar*-Donner **Andrea Bönig** *contr*-Erda **Kwangchul Youn** *bass*-Fasolt **Matthias Hölle** *bass*-Fafner **Cristina Obregón** *sop*-Woglinde **Ana Ibarra** *sop*-Wellgunde **Francisca Beaumont** *mez*-Flosshilde **Liceu Grand Theatre Symphony Orchestra, Barcelona / Bertrand de Billy**
Stage director **Harry Kupfer**
Opus Arte ② 𝗗𝗩𝗗 OA0910D (159' · NTSC · 16:9 · PCM stereo & DTS 5.1 · 0) Recorded live at the Gran Teatre del Liceu, Barcelona, 1 & 7 June 2004 Ⓕ●

Harry Kupfer's Bayreuth staging was Teutonically technological and ugly, but despite some dramatic silliness it actually heeded Wagner's stage directions. So does this one, created originally for Berlin, but it's a lot more attractive, and rightly attentive to the *Ring*'s mythological core. Its centrepiece, towering above a black mirrored stage surface, is the massive World-Ash tree, from which we see Wotan tearing his spear, and around whose roots the Rhinemaidens gambol and climb; the action moves up and down the trunk with the aid of the Liceu's splendid new machinery. Sillinesses – recurring suitcases, the gods' premature entrances and over-extended dance finale, the serpent reduced to feeble claws – aren't crippling.

Bertrand de Billy's warm, slowish reading is likeable, but doesn't generate enough shape and dramatic drive. Falk Struckmann's Wotan is a strong-voiced dynamic presence, but his tone is harsh and vibrant, and his characterisation arrogantly unsympathetic. Günter von Kannen is now a rather portly Alberich, and, despite a wonderfully malign glare, short on vocal and dramatic bite. Not so Graham Clark's Loge, incisively sung, even if his character tenor underplays the part's more lyrical side. Lioba Braun, Elisabete Matos and Andrea Bönig are worthy goddesses, Jeffrey Dowd a strong if not ideally mellifluous Froh, and Wolfgang Rauch an unusually impressive Donner. Veteran Matthias Hölle and rising star Kwangchul Youn are excellent Giants, android-like figures more effective than Bayreuth's dehumanised monstrous puppets. That goes, too, for the romantic rather than tarty Rhinemaidens.

So we have a decent modern staging on DVD, recorded in vivid surround-sound and clear if somewhat stygian vision. It does, though, have one infuriating disadvantage: unlike any other *Rheingold* it's spread over two discs; the side-break isn't well chosen, and you have to go through the whole menu rigmarole before the second side.

Die Walküre
Poul Elming *ten* Siegmund **Nadine Secunde** *sop* Sieglinde **Anne Evans** *sop* Brünnhilde **John Tomlinson** *bass* Wotan **Linda Finnie** *mez* Fricka

Matthias Hölle bass Hunding Eva Johansson sop
Gerhilde Eva-Maria Bundschuh sop Helmwige Ruth
Floeren sop Ortlinde Shirley Close mez Waltraute
Hebe Dijkstra mez Rossweisse Linda Finnie mez
Siegrune Birgitta Svendén mez Grimgerde Hitomi
Katagiri contr Schwertleite Bayreuth Festival
Orchestra / Daniel Barenboim
Stage director Harry Kupfer
Video director Horant H Hohlfeld
Warner Classics ② 🟥 2564 62319-2
(3h 57' · NTSC · 16:9 · PCM stereo, 5.1 and
DTS 5.1 · 2/3/4/5)   Ⓕ

Wagner's most violent and personally anguished
drama plays here on designer Hans Schaver-
noch's 'road of history' – a stage so bare that it
makes Wieland Wagner's abstractions of the
1950s look scenically crowded. From his singing
actors director Harry Kupfer has secured performances of unremitting physical and emotional energy. Like Wagner's beloved philosopher Feuerbach, he believes that the gods were
created by humans in their own image. So in this
part of the tetralogy which is, surely, Wagner's
King Lear, John Tomlinson runs, dives, falls
and embraces, living out every part of the tragedy of his Wälsung family (all of them red-
haired). It's an extraordinary tour de force,
thrillingly sung off the text and the action.

This godfather's big dialogues with his wife
(Linda Finnie is his fur-collared, leather-great-
coated double, but all in black) and Erda-
daughter (Anne Evans, costumed likewise but
without fur) are not presented at all as the usual
stand-and-deliver displays of implacable will.
Fricka struggles to psych herself up to be
tough, clutching her still-loved husband in
stress at the sacrifice she is requiring. And in
Act 3, once Brünnhilde explains to her father
that it was the power of Siegmund's love for his
sister/bride that made her disobey his battle
orders, the two plot her punishment with
warm, almost incestuous smiles of complicity.
(Don't be alarmed; it's all in Wagner's text and
music.) Kupfer also has a strong line on Wagner's tricky-to-stage Act 1, showing the instant
attraction between Elming's freedom-fighter
Siegmund and Secunde's subtle psychological
portrait of Sieglinde, and emphatically marking the coming of spring by the disappearance
of the whole of Hunding's house bar the tree
with the sword.

This *Walküre* has made a belated bow on DVD
but its transfer is a visual and sonic success.
Video director Hohlfeld has mixed close-up and
distance well; only the Act 2 fight is confusing at
first view. There are no extras, only a moderately interesting interview with the director as
intellectual matter in the booklet and some
sloppy proofing of the German text in the subtitles.

Die Walküre   🄷
Astrid Varnay sop Brünnhilde Gré Brouwenstijn sop
Sieglinde Hans Hotter bass-bar Wotan Ramón
Vinay ten Siegmund Josef Greindl bass Hunding

Georgine von Milinkovič mez Fricka/Grimgerde
Hertha Wilfert sop Gerhilde Hilde Scheppan sop
Helmwige Elisabeth Schärtel mez Waltraute Maria
von Ilosvay mez Schwertleite Gerda Lammers sop
Ortlinde Jean Watson contr Siegrune Maria Graf
mez Rossweisse Bayreuth Festival Orchestra /
Joseph Keilberth
Testament ④ SBT4 1391 (3h 38' · ADD · T/t)
Recorded 1955   Ⓕ

Very properly, Hans Hotter, as Wotan, dominates this utterly absorbing and exciting account
of *Walküre*, the second instalment of the rediscovered Keilberth Ring at Bayreuth in 1955.
There exist several other incarnations of his
dominant reading but perhaps only that in the
Krauss cycle of 1953 reveals him in such superb
form. Whether arguing the moral toss with von
Milinkovič's harrying Fricka, sunk in deep desolation after his capitulation to his spouse (Wotan's
long narration so full of insights, not for a
moment dull), his fury at Brünnhilde's disobedi-
ence and his final relenting in an unforgettable
account of the Farewell, Hotter commands every
aspect of the role. His sonorous, wide-ranging
voice is matched by his verbal acuity, text and
tone in ideal accord. This, much more than his
portrayal in the Solti cycle, when his voice often
struggles with the part, is the performance to
judge him by.

As ever, his long-standing stage partnership
with the Brünnhilde of Astrid Varnay pays many
dividends. She, too, is in prime form; she, too,
melds words and voice into a well-nigh perfect
unity. Not even a god could fail to response
positively to her appeals to be forgiven, and that
follows a warmly sung and deeply considered
account of the the Todesverkündigung in Act 2.
That wonderfully moving scene also finds
Ramón Vinay's Siegmund in most eloquent
form. As throughout the first two acts, his singing benefits from his attractively plangent tone
and, in Act 1, his tale of his sad plight. That, of
course, turns to ecstasy in the glorious love
music that ends Act 1, where Gré Brouwenstijn's
womanly, vibrant Sieglinde is a fit match. She
properly distraught and guilt-ridden in Act 2 but
– as so many lyrical sopranos have found – the
taxing passages in Act 3 prove a shade beyond
her.

In Act 1, Keilberth's direction takes a while
to catch fire. From the exciting start of Act 2
he is in his most persuasive form, he and his
fine orchestra projecting the manifold events
and changes of mood with a persuasively dramatic drive. The Ride of the Valkyries whizzes
along, Wotan's fury is frightening, the Magic
Fire music elating. Once more, he proves that
this was the year his *Ring* came into its own.

The recording is again amazingly lifelike,
catching the excitement of a notable occasion
on the Green Hill. The stage noises are
hardly ever distracting, nor should one be too
bothered by two or three moments when a
singer forgets his or her words. Altogether we
are here in the highest realm of Wagnerian
interpretation.

The Ring – Siegfried / Götterdämmerung

Siegfried
Heinz Kruse ten Siegfried **John Bröcheler** bass-bar
Wanderer **Jeannine Altmeyer** sop Brünnhilde
Graham Clark ten Mime **Henk Smit** bar Alberich
Anne Gjevang contr Erda **Carsten Stabell** bass
Fafner **Stefan Pangratz** treb Woodbird **Rotterdam
Philharmonic Orchestra / Hartmut Haenchen**
Stage director **Pierre Audi**
Video director **Misjel Vermeiren**
Opus Arte Ⓕ ③ 📀 OA0948D (4h 33' ·
NTSC · 16:9 · PCM stereo and DTS 5.1 · 0)
Recorded live at Het Muziektheater, Amsterdam, in
1999. Extra features include Illustrated Synopsis,
Cast Gallery and Introduction to Siegfried presented
by Michaël Zeeman

Götterdämmerung
Jeannine Altmeyer sop Brünnhilde **Heinz Kruse** ten
Siegfried **Kurt Rydl** bass Hagen **Wolfgang Schöne**
bass-bar Gunther **Eva-Maria Bundschuh** sop
Gutrune **Henk Smit** bass Alberich **Anne Gjevang**
mez Waltraute **Netherlands Philharmonic Orchestra
/ Hartmut Haenchen**
Stage director **Pierre Audi**
Video director **Hans Hulscher**
Opus Arte ③ 📀 OA0949D (4h 29' · NTSC · 16:9 ·
PCM stereo and DTS 5.1 · 0)
Recorded live at Het Muziektheater,
Amsterdam, in 1999. Extra features include Illustrated
Synopsis, Cast Gallery and Introduction to
Götterdämmerung presented by Michaël Zeeman Ⓕ

The Pierre Audi Amsterdam *Ring* wholly justifies
Opus Arte's decision to follow up so soon its
uneven Harry Kupfer/Barcelona cycle. Audi and
designer George Tsypin work with a varying
series of thrillingly lit (Wolfgang Goebbel) acting
areas, Hartmut Haenchen's orchestra(s) constantly visible in a manner reminiscent of Baroque
theatre. There may be reservations about
Haenchen's straight, low-profile interpretation
of the music (given in the new critical edition,
here featuring colourful percussion and sound
effects, and some new brass pitches at the opening
of Act 3 of *Götterdämmerung*), or the harshness of
Eiko Ishioka's far from conventionally beautiful
Japanese theatrical costumes. But there can surely
be few about the freshness of Audi's theatrical
thinking, and his reinvention of 'deconstruction-
ist' effects – Fafner as his own mouth; a fierily lit
and smoked platform to walk into; or the Wanderer's spear presented for Siegfried to break as a
huge, ceiling-high, world ash tree-like totem.
The visible Woodbird (at last, as Wagner wished,
taken by a boy) with his white, waif-like cockade
of hair is also a moving presence, especially at the
violent death of Mime.
Audi has cast and used his singing actors well.
Altmeyer goes from strength to strength, proving how right she was that Brünnhilde was her
role. Clark delivers another variation on his
widely travelled Mime, now older, more worried, perhaps more frightening. Gjevang, a
matchless Erda, then unveils a Waltraute that

for textual understanding, projection and sheer
intensity you'd have to have on a desert island.
Her Act 1 colleagues in *Götterdämmerung* –
Rydl's neurotic, exhibitionist Hagen and the
identical-looking Sebastian/Viola incestuous
Gibichungs of Bundschuh and Schöne – provide
compulsive acting too. And when Siegfried
comes to the rock with the tarnhelm? You'll
have to see (and hear!) for yourself.
   A black mark, though, to Opus Arte for
forgetting (totally) the chorus in *Götterdämmerung* – viewers intrigued by their Cuprinol-
advertisement wooden-puppet look may want to
know who they are. The Netherlands Philharmonic lack, in the final pages of *Götterdämmerung*, the necessary lustrous string tone; in
Siegfried, their Rotterdam colleagues are idiomatically magnificent. If you're buying individually, the Audi *Götterdämmerung* is mandatory.

Götterdämmerung
Astrid Varnay sop Brünnhilde **Bernd Aldenhoff** ten
Siegfried **Ludwig Weber** bass Hagen **Heinrich
Pflanzl** bass Alberich **Hermann Uhde** bar Gunther
Martha Mödl sop Gutrune, Third Norn **Elisabeth
Höngen** mez Waltraute **Elisabeth Schwarzkopf** sop
Woglinde **Hanna Ludwig** sop Wellgunde **Hertha
Töpper** mez Flosshilde **Ruth Siewert** mez First Norn
Ira Malaniuk mez Second Norn **Chorus and
Orchestra of the Bayreuth Festival /
Hans Knappertsbusch**
Testament mono ④ SBT4175
(281' · ADD · T/t) Recorded live 1951   Ⓕ🅞🅞🅞

Testament awakened this sleeping
Brünnhilde after half a century in Decca's vaults, held there because of an
age-old dispute over rights between that company and EMI. This is a fitting memorial, alongside the exactly contemporaneous Parsifal (Teldec), to the phoenix-like reincarnation of
Bayreuth post-war and to Wieland Wagner's
genius as a producer and gatherer of all the talents to the Green Hill. The other hero of the
occasion, as with Parsifal, is Knappertsbusch.
From the first bars of the Prologue he takes us
right into the work, as concerned as three notable Norns (Mödl the most arresting of the three
when prophesying the conflagration to come)
with the inevitability of the tragic events portrayed within. He then takes us from Stygian
gloom to mountain-top ecstasy with a masterly
touch few equal. There we meet Varnay's
youthful, vibrant, womanly heroine. Beside her
is Aldenhoff's not-so-lovely Siegfried, yet once
you become accustomed to his aggrandising,
extrovert moments you hear a Heldentenor in
the old mould, alive to every word and communicating with his audience. Later, arriving at
Gibichung Hall, you meet the most forthright,
articulate Gunther in Uhde. His greeting to
Siegfried, 'Begrüsse froh, O Held', makes one
realise why Uhde is pre-eminent in this role.
Beside him is Weber's louring, gloating, ambitious Hagen. What intelligence there is in every
bar he sings (try 'Ein Weib weiss ich' or the

whole of the Watch). As Gutrune, Mödl isn't your usual sweet-toned milksop but a women not afraid to show her deep emotions. The great mezzo Höngen as Waltraute conveys with amazing immediacy Wotan's despair, and, with a shudder in her tone at 'Da brach sich sein Blick', the tenderness of his thoughts on his beloved Brünnhilde, making one feel it to be the most moving moment in the whole *Ring* and consoling us for occasionally grainy tone.

Throughout Act 2, Knappertsbusch is trenchant in characterising the tremendous conflicts depicted therein. Weber rouses the vassals with vigorous enthusiasm. Varnay is tremendous in her denunciations of Siegfried, Aldenhoff as vivid in his replies. Such immediacy can only be found in the opera house – damn the momentary lapses in ensemble, the few distractions when scenery is being moved or the audience coughs. In Act 3 the Rhine Maidens, led by Schwarzkopf, are too backwardly placed, the sole blot on the sound picture. In Siegfried's Narration, Aldenhoff captures the vitality of his earlier exploits, supported by gloriously rippling strings, and sings a fulsome death-song. Knappertsbusch, eagerly supported by Bayreuth's hand-picked orchestra (all individually named in the accompanying booklet), unleashes all the tremendous import of the Funeral March. Finally Varnay carries all before her, in better voice than later at Bayreuth, in a visionary account of the Immolation that rightly crowns a noble interpretation of her role and the whole work. The recording is superior even to that of the 1951 *Parsifal*, with only a few passages of uncertain balance to fault it, supporting an experience nobody ought to miss.

The Ring – complete

Das Rheingold   H
George London *bass-bar* Wotan **Kirsten Flagstad** *sop* Fricka **Set Svanholm** *ten* Loge **Paul Kuen** *ten* Mime **Gustav Neidlinger** *bass-bar* Alberich **Claire Watson** *sop* Freia **Waldemar Kmentt** *ten* Froh **Eberhard Waechter** *bar* Donner **Jean Madeira** *contr* Erda **Walter Kreppel** *bass* Fasolt **Kurt Böhme** *bass* Fafner **Oda Balsborg** *sop* Woglinde **Hetty Plümacher** *mez* Wellgunde **Ira Malaniuk** *mez* Flosshilde

Die Walküre   H
James King *ten* Siegmund **Régine Crespin** *sop* Sieglinde **Birgit Nilsson** *sop* Brünnhilde; **Hans Hotter** *bass-bar* Wotan **Christa Ludwig** *mez* Fricka **Gottlob Frick** *bass* Hunding **Vera Schlosser** *sop* Gerhilde **Berit Lindholm** *sop* Helmwige **Helga Dernesch** *sop* Ortlinde **Brigitte Fassbaender** *mez* Waltraute **Claudia Hellmann** *sop* Rossweisse **Vera Little** *contr* Siegrune **Marilyn Tyler** *sop* Grimgerde **Helen Watts** *contr* Schwertleite

Siegfried   H
Wolfgang Windgassen *ten* Siegfried **Hans Hotter** *bass-bar* Wanderer **Birgit Nilsson** *sop* Brünnhilde **Gerhard Stolze** *ten* Mime **Gustav Neidlinger** *bass-*

bar Alberich **Marga Höffgen** *contr* Erda **Kurt Böhme** *bass* Fafner **Joan Sutherland** *sop* Woodbird

Götterdämmerung   H
Birgit Nilsson *sop* Brünnhilde **Wolfgang Windgassen** *ten* Siegfried **Gottlob Frick** *bass* Hagen **Gustav Neidlinger** *bass-bar* Alberich **Dietrich Fischer-Dieskau** *bar* Gunther **Claire Watson** *sop* Gutrune **Christa Ludwig** *mez* Waltraute **Gwyneth Jones** *sop* Wellgunde **Lucia Popp** *sop* Woglinde **Maureen Guy** *mez* Flosshilde **Helen Watts** *contr* First Norn **Grace Hoffman** *mez* Second Norn **Anita Välkki** *sop* Third Norn
Vienna State Opera Chorus; Vienna Philharmonic Orchestra / Georg Solti
Decca ⑭ 455 555-2DMO14 (876' · ADD · T/t)
Recorded 1958-65. Also available separately   Ⓜ**OO**

As perspectives on the Solti/Culshaw enterprise lengthen, and critical reactions are kept alert by the regular appearance of new, or newly issued, and very different recordings, it may seem increasingly ironic that of all conductors the ultra-theatrical Solti should have been denied a live performance. There are indeed episodes in this recording that convey more of the mechanics of the studio than of the electricity of the opera house – the opening of *Die Walküre*, Act 2, and the closing scenes of *Siegfried* and *Götterdämmerung*, for example. Yet, in general, dramatic impetus and atmosphere are strongly established and well sustained, sometimes more powerfully than is usually managed in the theatre. As just one example one would instance the superb control with which the intensity of Donner's summoning up of the thunder in *Das Rheingold* is maintained across Froh's greeting to the rainbow bridge into Wotan's own great salutation. At the majestic climax of this scene the power of feeling conveyed by George London's fine performance counts for more than any 'artificiality' in the way the voice is balanced against the orchestra.

Equally memorable in a totally different context is Solti's management of the long transition in *Götterdämmerung* between Hagen's Watch and the appearance of Waltraute. Nothing could be less mannered or unnatural than Solti's grasp of perspective and feeling for the life of each phrase in this music. On CD the clarity of instrumental detail is consistently remarkable, and while not all the singers sound as if they're constantly in danger of being overwhelmed there are some vital episodes, especially those involving Windgassen and Nilsson. Awareness of what these artists achieved in other recordings strengthens the suspicion that they may have been giving more than we actually get here. Windgassen isn't allowed to dominate the sound picture in the way his part demands, and Nilsson can seem all-too relaxed within the comforting cocoon of the orchestral texture.

Factors like these, coupled with those distinctive Soltian confrontations between the hard-driven and the hammily protracted, have prevented the cycle from decisively seeing off its rivals over the years. It's questionable nevertheless whether any studio recording of *The Ring* could reasonably be expected to be more atmospheric, exciting or better performed than this one. The VPO isn't merely prominent, but excellent, and such interpretations as Svanholm's Loge, Neidlinger's Alberich and Frick's Hagen remain very impressive.

Above all, there's Hotter, whose incomparably authoritative, unfailingly alert and responsive Wotan stands up well when compared to his earlier Bayreuth accounts. Nowhere is he more commanding than in *Siegfried*, Act 1, where one even welcomes Stolze's mannerisms as Mime for the sparks they strike off the great bass-baritone. Earlier in this act the interplay of equally balanced instruments and voices in relatively intimate conversational phrases displays the Culshaw concept at its most convincing. He would have been astonished to hear what his successors have achieved in renewing his production through digital remastering. One now realises how much of the original sound was lost on the old pressings. In comparison with the 1980 Janowski/RCA version, the approaches are so different they almost seem like different experiences. Culshaw was intent on creating a theatre on record with all the well-known stage effects; the rival version eschews all such manifestations. In general, Janowski presents a much more intimate view of the work than Solti's.

However many other *Ring*s you may have, though, you'll need this one.

Der Ring des Nibelungen
Casts include **Gré Brouwenstijn, Ilse Hollweg, Gerda Lammers, Paula Lenchner, Astrid Varnay, Lore Wissmann** sops **Maria von Ilosvay, Luisecharlotte Kamps, Jean Madeira, Georgine von Milinkovic, Elisabeth Schärtel** mezs **Paul Kuen, Ludwig Suthaus, Josef Traxel, Wolfgang Windgassen** tens **Alfons Herwig, Hermann Uhde** bars **Hans Hotter, Gustav Neidlinger** bass-bars **Josef Greindl, Arnold Van Mill** basses **Bayreuth Festival Chorus and Orchestra / Hans Knappertsbusch**
Orfeo d'Or mono ⑬ C660 513Y (15h 13' · ADD · N).
Recorded live in 1956   Ⓕ

During the pioneering post-war era at Bayreuth the conducting of the *Ring* was shared among the Ks – Karajan, Krauss, Knappertsbusch, Keilberth and Kempe. These conductors collectively had a knowledge and experience of the cycle not equalled before or since, with the sole exception of their contemporary Furtwängler, who returned after the war only to conduct Beethoven's Ninth.

Although they were brought up in the same, exemplary tradition, the Ks had very different ways of treating the *Ring*, as you can now discover given the availability of so many cycles on CD. Krauss in his superb 1953 cycle went for a lean, dramatic, often electrifying and elating approach. He shared the cycles with Keilberth in 1953 after Karajan refused to return to Bayreuth, and was scheduled to return in 1954. His

sudden death left Keilberth solely in charge in 1954 and '55. We now have the elusive Keilberth cycle of 1955 from Testament, a version recorded by Decca but never issued. This now becomes the first stereo recording.

In 1956 Knappertsbusch, who had shared the 1951 cycles with Karajan returned to give what is generally agreed to be his most successful reading, taken as a whole. Unlike Krauss, Karajan and to a lesser extent Keilberth, the older conductor took a more measured view of the scores overall, one based on his preference for the long paragraph, well defined, almost pawky rhythms, and prominent ritardandi at points not always indicated in the score. At moments he seems to lose focus and let things run their own way where ensemble is concerned but, as a whole, especially in *Rheingold* and *Götterdämmerung*, his epic view of the score is almost unsurpassed. Even in the two middle operas there are moments of alternating quiet reflection and earthy energy that are very special.

He has at his command an ensemble of dedicated singers who had built their characterisations to a peak of achievement by 1956. Practically all are German-speaking and all have the art of acting with their voices in an immediate and communicative way, not to forget that they each had voices of a Wagnerian power too seldom found today.

Throughout *Rheingold* astonishment and delight are responses once more to the frightening power and presence of Gustav Neidlinger's trenchantly sung Alberich and by the detail, feeling and vocal authority of Hans Hotter's unsurpassed Wotan. Beside them an erstwhile Siegfried, Ludwig Suthaus, offers a Loge who gives every word, even syllable a distinctive colour and meaning, while Jean Madeira's Erda emits other-worldly authority. And any *Rheingold* that boasts Josef Traxel, then a leading lyric tenor in Germany, as Froh has a bonus.

Four singers heard in later operas are introduced here. Paul Kuen, another familiar figure, is Mime and provides character without exaggeration. Georgine von Milinkovic introduces us to an imperiously nagging Fricka and comes into her own in the next work. Josef Greindl is a formidable if unsubtle Fasolt, later a granite Hunding and a fearsome Hagen: no wonder, given so much work to do, he sometimes tires a little. Gré Brouwenstijn, a properly worried Freia, then gives us a Sieglinde who develops, in glorious tones, from an introvert to an extrovert when love strikes her. Beside her is Wolfgang Windgassen, standing in at the last moment for an ailing Vinay, and singing a Siegmund who is at once *bel canto* in line yet intensely eloquent. Incredibly, the next evening he is a tirelessly effective Siegfried.

Hotter is magnificent in Wotan's Act 2 monologue, here made to seem at the very heart of the whole cycle, and as ever deeply moving in his Act 3 Farewell, forgiving signs of vocal weariness at the start of the act. By then we have met and admired Astrid Varnay's very womanly yet heroic Brünnhilde. She occasionally overdoes the histrionics but by and large she has the character in her voice and bones in a way few other dramatic sopranos have managed.

In Siegfried Hotter manages ideally the humour of his Act 1 colloquy with Mime, his face-off with Neidlinger's Alberich in Act 2, and his desperation when meeting Madeira's implacable Erda at the start of Act 3. The awakening of Brünnhilde is not one of the conductor's best moments but the lovers give their all in the closing duet.

All the momentous climaxes of the cycle's finale find Kna at his most potent and involved, just as in 1951, and Varnay seconds him with her projection of all Brünnhilde's joy and sorrow. She also – incredibly – took on the Third Norn, at very short notice, Mödl having been taken suddenly ill. Madeira is heard again to advantage as both First Norn and Waltraute – would any singer do both today? Act 2 is simply tremendous. In this work Brouwenstijn returns as a vocally comely Gutrune, and Hermann Uhde, as in all the 1950s cycles, is an unsurpassed Gunther. With the Immolation one rightly feels that the earth has moved and that one has been through a life-enhancing experience, which is as it should be.

Music & Arts issued this cycle in 1998 but this is the first issue with the Bayreuth imprimatur, though the sound quality is only marginally superior here. Orchestral textures are sometimes muted but that has much to do with the opera house's layout. No texts or translations but a good booklet, which quotes one contemporary critic as saying this was undoubtedly the Festival's greatest moment to date. Allegiance to the 1953 Krauss set is not altered but there is much here that remains unsurpassed.

Der Ring des Nibelungen
Chorus and Orchestra of the Metropolitan Opera, New York / James Levine
Stage director **Otto Schenk**
Video director **Brian Large**
DG ⑦ DVD 073 043-9GH7 (941' · 4:3 · 2.0 & 5.1* · 0)
*Dolby digital & dts. Recorded live at the Metropolitan Opera House 1989-90.   Ⓕ
Also available separately as below

Das Rheingold
James Morris bass Wotan **Christa Ludwig** mez Fricka **Siegfried Jerusalem** ten Loge **Heinz Zednik** ten Mime **Ekkehard Wlaschiha** bass Alberich **Mari Anne Häggander** sop Freia **Mark Baker** ten Froh **Alan Held** bar Donner **Birgitta Svendén** mez Erda **Jan-Hendrik Rootering** bass Fasolt **Matti Salminen** bass Fafner **Kaaren Erickson** sop Woglinde **Diane Kesling** mez Wellgunde **Meredith Parsons** contr Flosshilde
DG DVD 073 036-9GH (163')   Ⓕ

Die Walküre
Gary Lakes ten Siegmund **Jessye Norman** sop Sieglinde **Hildegard Behrens** sop Brünnhilde **James Morris** bass Wotan **Christa Ludwig** mez Fricka **Kurt Moll** bass Hunding **Pyramid Sellers** sop Gerhilde **Katarina Ikonomu** sop Helmwige **Martha Thigpen**

sop Ortlinde **Joyce Castle** mez Waltraute **Jacalyn Bower** mez Rossweise **Diane Kesling** mez Siegrune **Wendy Hillhouse** mez Grimgerde **Sondra Kelly** contr Schwertleite
DG ② DVD 073 049-9GH2 (241')   Ⓕ

Siegfried
Siegfried Jerusalem ten Siegfried **James Morris** bass Wanderer **Hildegard Behrens** sop Brünnhilde **Heinz Zednik** ten Mime **Ekkehard Wlaschiha** bass Alberich **Birgitta Svendén** mez Erda **Fritz Hübner** bass Fafner **Dawn Upshaw** sop Woodbird
DG ② DVD 073 037-9GH2 (253')   Ⓕ

Götterdämmerung
Hildegard Behrens sop Brünnhilde **Siegfried Jerusalem** ten Siegfried **Matti Salminen** bass Hagen **Ekkehard Wlaschiha** bass Alberich **Anthony Raffell** bass Gunther **Hanna Lisowska** sop Gutrune **Christa Ludwig** mez Waltraute **Kaaren Erickson** sop Woglinde **Diane Kesling** mez Wellgunde **Meredith Parsons** contr Flosshilde **Gweneth Bean** contr First Norn **Joyce Castle** mez Second Norn **Andrea Gruber** sop Third Norn
DG ② DVD 073 040-9GH2 (281')   ⒻⒶⒶ

None of the four video-recorded versions can be called ideal; but this Met cycle has plenty of strong points. It's the only one Wagner would have recognised – no small consideration. It's frequently assumed these days that he chose myth primarily to convey political allegory, but this is misleading. Myth inspired Wagner as directly as it did, say, Sibelius; and producers who ignore or mock this, like Patrice Chéreau on Pierre Boulez's rival set, miss a vital dimension. Here, Otto Schenk and designer Gunther Schneider-Siemssen preserve the Romantic imagery, often beautifully, as Brian Large's cameras reveal; but also unimaginatively, with too many tired compromises. Some, such as the Rhinemaidens' non-swimming contortions and the feeble dragon, are embarrassing, and the costumes often look poor on screen. Individual performances, too, sometimes don't fit into a satisfactory ensemble.

This set can also claim musical superiority; but again, not conclusively. Boulez mistakes speed for energy, drying out the richness of the score; Levine, with the magnificent Met orchestra, tends to wallow in it, especially in a disappointing *Rheingold*. Matters improve from *Walküre* onward, but he's prone to sudden wheelspinning accelerations, sometimes wrongfooting his singers. Boulez remains invisible at Bayreuth; Levine is too much with us, to the detriment of atmosphere. Nevertheless, his monumental approach does bring out *The Ring*'s sheer beauty and grandeur, where Boulez simply seems glib.

Levine's cast is superior, too, although the pivotal roles are the closest. Both Brünnhildes are splendid, spirited and deeply moving, but Boulez's Gwyneth Jones has the fuller voice; Hildegard Behrens, lithe and nervy, must force an essentially lyric instrument – quite successfully, but the effort shows. James Morris, aspiring to be a *bel canto* Wotan, has a richer voice than Boulez's Donald MacIntyre, but his diction and his acting are less incisive – partly the producer's fault in *Rheingold*; he improves thereafter. Siegfried Jerusalem, though, eclipses Boulez's inadequate Manfred Jung. More lyrical and vocally more heroic, he's a finer musician, less liable to strain and distort the line, and an impressive stage figure.

Jerusalem's surprisingly characterful Loge, despite his galia melon headgear, is probably the best thing in *Rheingold*. It's rewarding to hear the 'Narration' in this kind of voice. Otherwise this is lacklustre. A superb Rhinemaiden trio is left earthbound, writhing unconvincingly round Ekkehard Wlaschiha's buffoonish Alberich, short on menace until the final curse. Christa Ludwig's once definitive Fricka looks and sounds tired. Levine's tempi in *Rheingold* rival those of Reginald Goodall, but without his structure and pacing; the Giants' entrance is marked *molto pesante*, not funereal. They, the Rhinemaidens and the lesser gods – especially Birgitta Svendén's keen-voiced Erda – outclass their betters.

Levine handles *Walküre* more successfully. Act 1, though, isn't a success. Gary Lakes' massive but rather lean-toned Siegmund is ill-matched with Jessye Norman, whose vocally searing Sieglinde is subverted by her *grande dame* manner, robbing the love scenes of any real involvement. Behrens, however, injects Act 2 with life, and though Ludwig's Fricka still sounds tired, Morris begins to make an impact, singing rather than declaiming the Narration. With a ringingly athletic Valkyrie band, Levine rushes the Ride, but brings the act to a moving Farewell.

Siegfried is visually and musically the best, with Levine at his liveliest and a Romantic forest out of Altdorfer or von Schwind. Jerusalem's ardent hero may lack Heldentenor heft, and suffer some constraint at the top, but he carries off the forging and lyrical scenes with credit. The Wanderer often suits basses' range and personae, and Morris's commanding, world-weary god dominates Zednik's veteran Mime (mercifully not Chéreau's cute victim), Wlaschiha's now mordant Alberich; and Svendén's eerie Erda. Levine's protracted 'Awakening' stretches Behrens, but she and Jerusalem infuse the love duet with appealing life.

Levine's expansiveness suits *Götterdämmerung*, which opens with a powerful trio of Norns and a radiant Dawn duet. Chez Gibichung, though, the temperature drops, with Anthony Raffell (a fine Wotan) a miscast, bumbling Gunther, and Gutrune sadly unseductive. Matti Salminen's brutish Hagen, though richly sung, lacks the essential supernatural undertones. Ludwig is much better as Waltraute, but Jerusalem and especially Behrens carry the performance with involving intensity. The Immolation strains her voice, but remains satisfyingly cathartic, aided by appropriate stage spectacle, though Valhalla's downfall is disappointing.

All told, while this set may be less stimulating than the Boulez, it's also less distracting – without, as an eminent colleague once remarked, someone forever shouting in your ear. As well as the original digital stereo, remixed surround-sound tracks convincingly evoke extra ambiance and detail. The image also remasters well, although you may want to turn up the colour.

Der Ring des Nibelungen
Chorus and Orchestra of the Royal Danish Opera / Michael Schønwandt
Stage director **Kasper Bech Holten**
Video director **Uffe Borgwardt**

Das Rheingold
Johan Reuter bass-bar Wotan **Hans Lewaetz** bar Donner **Johnny van Hal** ten Froh **Michael Kristensen** ten Loge **Stephen Milling** bass Fasolt **Christian Christiansen** bar Fafner **Sten Byriel** bar Alberich **Bengt-Ola Morgny** ten Mime **Randi Stene** mez Fricka **Anne Margrethe Dahl** sop Freia **Susanne Resmark** contr Erda **Dijna Mai-Mai** sop Woglinde **Ylva Kihlberg** sop Wellgunde **Hanna Fischer** mez Flosshilde

Die Walküre
Stig Andersen ten Siegmund **Gitta-Maria Sjöberg** sop Sieglinde **James Johnson** bass-bar Wotan **Iréne Theorin** sop Brünnhilde **Stephen Milling** bass Hunding **Randi Stene** mez Fricka **Emma Vetter** sop Helmwige **Carolina Sandgren** sop Ortlinde **Ylva Kihlberg** sop Gerhilde **Hanna Fischer** mez Waltraute **Anna Rydberg** mez Siegrune **Elisabeth Jansson** mez Rossweise **Elisabeth Halling** mez Grimgerde **Ulla Kudsk Jensen** contr Schwertleite

Siegfried
Stig Andersen ten Siegfried **Bengt-Ola Morgny** ten Mime **James Johnson** bass-bar Wotan **Sten Byriel** bar Alberich **Christian Christiansen** bar Fafner **Susanne Resmark** contr Erda **Iréne Theorin** sop Brünnhilde **Giselle Stille** sop Woodbird

Götterdämmerung
Stig Andersen ten Siegfried **Guido Paevatalu** bar Gunther **Peter Klaveness** bass Hagen **Sten Byriel** bar Alberich **Iréne Theorin** sop Brünnhilde **Ylva Kihlberg** sop Gutrune **Anna Bod** mez Waltraute **Susanne Resmark** contr First Norn **Hanna Fischer** mez Second Norn **Anne Margrethe Dahl** sop Third Norn **Djina Mai-Mai** sop Woglinde **Elisabeth Meyer-Topsoe** sop Wellgunde **Ulla Kudsk Jensen** contr Flosshilde

Decca ⑦ **DVD** 074 3264DH7 (15h 20' · NTSC · 16:9 · PCM stereo and DTS 5.1 · 0)   Ⓟ**OOO**

The first of several wonders in this new set, collated from three cycles in the early summer of 2006, is the intuitive performing skill of a genuine house ensemble. Even the 'borrowed' Swedish and Norwegian artists, including the Brünnhilde and Hagen, are regulars in a company which inevitably casts the most demanding repertoire from its own – Copenhagen has achieved a class *Ring* with just one guest, James Johnson's *Walküre/Siegfried* Wotans. Moreover, if Stockholm is the Venice of the north, the Royal Danish Orchestra must be the Vienna Philharmonic of the north with its forward, rich woodwind timbres (a Nielsen sound, wholly suitable for Nibelung music) and cool-sweet string tone, the whole integrated, balanced and paced with a Kempe-like swiftness and attention to rhythmic detail by their chief Michael Schønwandt.

The assembled cut from the filming of the live performances (Uffe Borgwardt is the credited director of photography) is quite radical for a record of live opera. Like the curious spectator, these cameras want to look up the Rhinedaughters' flapper skirts, focus on props or the after-effects of violent action, or wonder how a scene looks from behind, from the wings, or even from beneath stage level in the orchestra pit. So the visual editing is busy, justifying allusions to the hand-held operation rediscovered by Danish art cinema directors. It gives the films a breathless close-up quality, the absolute inverse of the accustomed best-seat-in-the-stalls approach.

Kasper Bech Holten's production doesn't intentionally disturb realism and story-telling. There is a frame story – Brünnhilde is seen researching, in some giant sidestage Valhalla library store, the events of the past from the moment she betrayed Siegfried. But, in principle, this Copenhagen *Ring* follows a linear narrative. It's costumed and situated between (approximately) 1920 and the 1990s, and – through ever-ingenious lateral thinking – finds latter-day equivalents for Wagner's geography, properties and dramatic violence. Thus the Rhinegold itself is a beautiful, golden, naked swimming boy, whose heart is bloodily torn out by a serially drinking, lecherous Alberich when he is rejected by *les girls*. Once captured in Nibelheim, Alberich is chained up in a scary white-tiled torture room, surrendering the ring only when Wotan literally hacks off his entire lower arm. Loge, knowing too much at the end of *Rheingold*, is murdered by Wotan; Erda's life-support is turned off, sorrowfully, by Wotan in *Siegfried*; Alberich, having worn out Hagen, is dispatched at the end of their colloquy in *Götterdämmerung*; and, later in that same act, hostages are executed by Hagen in 'celebration' of Gunther's wedding.

But don't get squeamish at the horror, or sniff at Quentin Tarantino-influenced trendiness. See instead how this director finds more heartbreaking emotion in Wagner's drama than almost any since Patrice Chéreau. In the last scene of *Walküre* Johnson's Wotan – a characterisation admirably unafraid of appearing less than godlike – searches the whole scene for a way out for Theorin's emotionally mobile Brünnhilde but has to end up (at that huge climax between the 'verses' of the Farewell) by tearing off her Valkyrie's black wings. Stig Andersen's Siegfried, sung with lyrical beauty, is seen desperately alone in the 'forest', stroking the bodies of Mime and Fafner whom he has killed and thus left himself stranded. Kasper Bech Holten is astute too at those potentially awkward moments of embarrassment and waiting – watch the superb detail in the playing of his ensemble stars like Andersen (as

both the Walsungs), Theorin, Byriel's unclichéd Alberich, Peter Klaveness's terrifying SS officer of a Hagen (although the voice cannot always equal his dramatic presence), Randi Stene's Fricka (Hillary Clinton with humour) or Guido Paevatalu's multifacetedly lazy, brutal coward of a Gunther.

In addition to the sheer zip of performance and filming, the sound picture is warm, resonant and true, the English subtitles give an unusually revealing and detailed insight into Wagner's text, and, winningly, the 'extra' item consists of a discussion between the stage director and his country's opera-loving head of state. But finally, can these performers, only some of them known on main stages outside Scandinavia, cut the mustard alongside the more international competition on six rival DVD productions? They most certainly can.

The Ring – complete in English

The Rhinegold (sung in English)
Norman Bailey *bar* Wotan **Katherine Pring** *mez* Fricka **Emile Belcourt** *ten* Loge **Gregory Dempsey** *ten* Mime **Derek Hammond-Stroud** *bar* Alberich **Lois McDonall** *sop* Freia **Robert Ferguson** *ten* Froh **Norman Welsby** *bar* Donner **Anne Collins** *contr* Erda **Robert Lloyd** *bass* Fasolt **Clifford Grant** *bass* Fafner **Valerie Masterson** *sop* Woglinde **Shelagh Squires** *mez* Wellgunde **Helen Attfield** *sop* Flosshilde **English National Opera Orchestra / Reginald Goodall**
Chandos Opera in English Series ③ CHAN3054 (174' · ADD · N/t) Recorded live 1975 ⒻⓄ

The Valkyrie (sung in English)
Alberto Remedios *ten* Siegmund **Margaret Curphey** *sop* Sieglinde **Rita Hunter** *sop* Brünnhilde **Norman Bailey** *bar* Wotan **Ann Howard** *contr* Fricka **Clifford Grant** *bass* Hunding **Katie Clarke** *sop* Gerhilde **Anne Evans** *sop* Helmwige **Ann Conoley** *sop* Ortlinde **Elizabeth Connell** *sop* Waltraute **Anne Collins** *contr* Rossweisse **Sarah Walker** *mez* Siegrune **Shelagh Squires** *mez* Grimgerde **Helen Attfield** *sop* Schwertleite **English National Opera Orchestra / Reginald Goodall**
Chandos Opera in English Series ④ CHAN3038 (249' · ADD · N/t) Recorded live 1976 ⒻⓄ

Siegfried (sung in English)
Alberto Remedios *ten* Siegfried **Norman Bailey** *bass-bar* Wanderer **Rita Hunter** *sop* Brünnhilde **Gregory Dempsey** *ten* Mime **Derek Hammond-Stroud** *bar* Alberich **Anne Collins** *contr* Erda **Clifford Grant** *bass* Fafner **Maurine London** *sop* Woodbird **Sadler's Wells Opera Orchestra / Reginald Goodall**
Chandos ④ CHAN3045 (279' · ADD · N/t) Recorded live 1973 ⒻⓄⓄ

Twilight of the Gods (sung in English)
Alberto Remedios *ten* Siegfried **Norman Welsby** *bar* Gunther **Aage Haugland** *bass* Hagen **Derek Hammond-Stroud** *bar* Alberich **Rita Hunter** *sop* Brünnhilde **Margaret Curphey** *sop* Gutrune **Katherine Pring** *mez* Waltraute **Anne Collins** *contr*

First Norn **Gillian Knight** *mez* Second Norn **Anne Evans** *sop* Third Norn **Valerie Masterson** *sop* Woglinde **Shelagh Squires** *mez* Wellgunde **Helen Attfield** *contr* Flosshilde **English National Opera Orchestra and Chorus / Reginald Goodall** Chandos Opera in English CHAN3060 (312′ · ADD · N/t)
Recorded live 1977 ⓟⓞ

Valkyrie: There's something inevitable, even eternal about Goodall's long-breathed, full-toned, often ideally articulated reading. The ENO management's faith in him was handsomely repaid in his ability to convey his lifetime vision to is regular cast and eventually to his audiences. On paper, tempos may look unacceptably slow; in practice there are very few places – perhaps Siegmund's Spring song and Sieglinde's reply – where they seem too tardy. That's largely due to his ability to find the *Hauptstimme* for every paragraph of the music, indeed for a whole act and, perhaps even more, to his ability to persuade players and singers alike to sustain a long line. Listeners familiar only with the Solti cycle will hardly recognise this as the same work.

By 1976 all his singers were entirely inside their respective roles and so able to project a feeling of familiarity with their music that's evident in every bar. Like all the most satisfying sets of the *Ring*, it benefits enormously from being heard live in a theatre acoustic, and here no compromises have to be made, so superb are producer John Mordler's and his team's skills. You seem to be seated in centre stalls imbibing the performance. Rita Hunter bestrides the role of Brünnhilde in a confident manner achieved in relatively modern times only by Birgit Nilsson, whose bright tone and effortless top Hunter's so much resembles. She's also a thoughtful, very human interpreter of the role, keen with her words and investing them with the right import. By her side Bailey confirms that he's as excellent a Wotan as any since Hans Hotter. His reading of the taxing part is virtually tireless and his interpretation combines authority with fatherly concern. Remedios's Siegmund remains one of the most sweetly sung and appealing on disc. If Curphey isn't quite in his class vocally, she offers a deeply felt and sympathetic Sieglinde. Ann Howard is, rightly, a termagant of a Fricka, with a touch of asperity in her tone. Clifford Grant is a sonorous, towering Hunding. The Valkyries, comprising many of the most promising female singers of the day (among them Elizabeth Connell and Anne Evans), acquit themselves very well. All the cast benefit from Andrew Porter's carefully wrought, very singable translation. Overall, a hearty welcome back to a great recording.

Siegfried: That Reginald Goodall idolised Klemperer and Knappertsbusch is evident in every aspect of this weighty, consistently thought-through interpretation; indeed it consoles us for the cycle Klemperer never recorded. The performance is also a reminder of what those then in charge of the ENO – Stephen Arlen, Lord Harewood and Edmund Tracey –

had the sense to realise: that here was a unique opportunity to let a seasoned Wagnerian have his head in terms of the time and trouble to prepare a cycle in his own long time-scale. The results are there for all to hear in the total involvement of every member of the orchestra, the lyrical lines of the singers, the superb enunciation of the faultless translation.

Remedios's fresh, lyrical singing is a joy from start to finish; nobody since has equalled him as Siegfried. Dempsey's Mime is at once subtle, funny yet menacing. Those who so praise Tomlinson as Wotan/Wanderer can't have heard Bailey's better sung, articulate and eloquent assumption, another reading not since surpassed. To crown the performance we have Rita Hunter's glorious Brünnhilde, so luminously and keenly sung, just about on a par with Nilsson in the role. They are all wonderfully supported by Goodall and his players. Only in some of Siegfried's Act 1 forging and his struggle with Fafner might one ask for a shade more physical energy, but that's a small price to pay for such understanding of Wagnerian structure. *Rhinegold* and *Twilight of the Gods* : After more than 25 years, these recordings remain gripping for reasons similar to those applying to the other sections of the English Ring reissued by Chandos. In spite of speeds that in other hands would seem often unreasonably slow, or to an extent because of them, Goodall's interpretation has an unerring sense of lyrical and dramatic concentration, every paragraph, phrase and bar carefully considered and executed with loving care by singers and players alike, all so closely coached by their veteran conductor. Above all there's the refined legato observed by all the singers. And the sense of real-life occasion, the theatre's acoustic clearly felt throughout. Andrew Porter's wonderfully lucid translation is given its full due by all the soloists, who once more sound an utterly convincing team. In *Rhinegold* the main honours are carried off by Emile Belcourt's plausible, witty and articulate Loge, Hammond-Stroud's imposing, strongly sung Alberich, Robert Lloyd's sympathetic Fasolt and Bailey's ever-authoritative Wotan. With a pleasing trio of Rhinemaidens headed by Masterson's gleaming Woglinde, Clifford Grant's gloomy, louring Fafner and Anne Collins's deep-throated Erda, the strength of the ENO roster at the time is there for all to hear. In *Twilight*, Hunter and Remedios excel themselves as a more heroic than tragic pair, their singing steady, keen with words and very much in character following so many performances, by 1977, of the complete cycle. The recently departed Aage Haugland offers a welcome souvenir of his career as a louring Hagen. Welsby uncovers the right touches of weak will for Gunther while Curphey is suitably alluring as sister Gutrune. Pring offers an appropriately urgent and strongly sung Waltraute. The Norns could hardly be more strongly cast.

By and large, the playing of the ENO Orchestra is of an equally consistent nature, responding to Goodall's long-breathed conducting with playing of beauty and strength adding up to a formidable traversal of the score. The recording, masterminded by John Mordler, need not fear comparison with anything more recent. Indeed the absence of unwanted reverberation and excessive sound effects is most welcome. What we get is the music unvarnished and truthful, for which many thanks again to the foresight of the ENO directors of the day and to Peter Moores for providing the wherewithal to execute it. Anyone wanting the work in the vernacular, who hasn't already acquired it in its previous incarnations, need not hesitate.

Tannhäuser

Tannhäuser
Peter Seiffert ten Tannhäuser **Jane Eaglen** sop
Elisabeth **Thomas Hampson** bar Wolfram **Waltraud
Meier** mez Venus **René Pape** bass Hermann **Gunnar
Gudbjörnsson** ten Walther **Hanno Müller-
Brachmann** bass-bar Biterolf **Stephan Rügamer** ten
Heinrich **Alfred Reiter** bass Reinmar **Dorothea
Röschmann** sop Shepherd **Berlin State Opera
Chorus; Berlin Staatskapelle / Daniel Barenboim**
Teldec ④ 8573-88064-2 (195' · DDD · T/t)　　ⒻⓄ

This must be one of the most opulent recordings made of any opera. The truly remarkable range, perspective and balance of the sound is most appropriate for a work conceived on the grandest scale, yet it retains its focus in the more intimate scenes. The achievement of Barenboim's Berlin chorus, so important in this opera, and orchestra could hardly be bettered. The results are, if nothing else, an audio treat, surpassing the DG version's rather hit-and-miss engineering and the now slightly dated feel of the Decca. Indeed it's Konwitschny's 40-year-old set (EMI) that comes closest to the Teldec in terms of sonic breadth.

Domingo recorded Tannhäuser for DG but shied away from it on stage. The title-role, as many tenors admit, is a real killer. Seiffert is probably its most telling exponent: his performance that combines vocal assurance and emotional involvement to create a vivid portrait of the hero torn between sacred and profane love. The objects of Tannhäuser's attention are impressively portrayed by Waltraud Meier and Jane Eaglen. Meier makes the most of the bigger opportunities and brings her customary tense expression to bear on Venus's utterance, while not quite effacing Christa Ludwig's voluptuous reading for Solti. Eaglen launches herself into the Hall of Song with a rather squally 'Dich teure Halle'; thereafter she sings with much of the inner feeling and prayerful dignity predicated by Wagner for his Elisabeth.

Hermann is a gift of a role for most German basses and René Pape takes his chances with his accustomed feeling for notes and text. Thomas Hampson delivers Wolfram's solos with the expected blend of mellifluous tone and verbal acuity, but his manner is a touch set apart and self-conscious, as if he has had to record these at separate sessions. One reservation about this Teldec set: Barenboim's penchant in meditative

passages for very slow speeds. But he paces the Prelude, the huge ensemble at the end of Act 2 and all the Pilgrim's music with unerring skill.

It's unlikely that we shall ever hear a totally convincing account of what was, after all, Wagner's problem child among his mature works, but this new one has about as much going for it as any in recent times. If you want the Dresden version unaltered by later revisions, and there's something to be said for that choice, the Konwitschny has much to offer in terms of its conductor, sound and much of the solo work.

Tannhäuser (Paris version)
Plácido Domingo ten Tannhäuser **Cheryl Studer** sop
Elisabeth **Andreas Schmidt** bar Wolfram **Agnes
Baltsa** mez Venus **Matti Salminen** bass Hermann
William Pell ten Walther **Kurt Rydl** bass Biterolf
Clemens Biber ten Heinrich **Oskar Hillebrandt** bass
Reinmar **Barbara Bonney** sop Shepherd Boy **Chorus
of the Royal Opera House, Covent Garden;
Philharmonia Orchestra / Giuseppe Sinopoli**
DG ③ 427 625-2GH3 (176' · DDD · T/t)　　Ⓕ◗⥁

Domingo's Tannhäuser is a success in almost every respect. He evokes the erotic passion of the Venusberg scene and brings to it just the right touch of nervous energy. This is boldly contrasted with the desperation and bitterness of the Rome Narration after the hero's fruitless visit to the Pope seeking forgiveness:Domingo's description of how Tannhäuser avoided every earthly delight on his pilgrimage is delivered with total conviction. In between he berates the slightly prissy attitude of his fellow knights on the Wartburg with the dangerous conceit of someone who knows a secret delight that they will never enjoy in their measured complacency. His tenor must be the steadiest and most resplendent ever to have tackled the part, although his German is far from idiomatic. Baltsa also has problems with her German, but she has the range and attack for an awkwardly lying part. It's obviously Sinopoli's concern throughout to bring out every last ounce of the drama in the piece, both in terms of orchestral detail and in his awareness in this opera of the longer line, often sustained by the upper strings. The Philharmonia's violins respond with their most eloquent playing. The kind of *frisson* Sinopoli offers is evident in the anticipatory excitement at the start of Act 2 and the iron control he maintains in the big ensemble later in the same act. Cheryl Studer's secure, beautiful voice has no difficulty coping with Sinopoli's deliberate tempos. She takes her part with total conviction, both vocal and interpretative, phrasing with constant intelligence. Andreas Schmidt is a mellifluous, concerned Wolfram, Salminen a rugged, characterful Landgrave and Barbara Bonney an ideally fresh Shepherd Boy.

The Covent Garden Chorus sings with consistent beauty of sound, and has been sensibly balanced with the orchestra. Domingo and Studer make this version a winner.

Tannhäuser   **H**
Wolfgang Windgassen *ten* Tannhäuser
Gré Brouwenstijn *sop* Elisabeth **Dietrich Fischer-
Dieskau** *bar* Wolfram **Herta Wilfert** *mez* Venus **Josef
Greindl** *bass* Hermann **Josef Traxel** *ten* Walther
**Bayreuth Festival Chorus and Orchestra / André
Cluytens**
Orfeo d'Or mono ③ C643043D (198' · ADD)
Recorded live 1955   Ⓜ

This is a revelatory interpretation of a work which isn't easy to bring off. André Cluytens had taken over the musical direction at Bayreuth from Eugen Jochum at short notice, and he seems energised by the challenge. Contemporary reviews spoke of the bright, shining strings and the luminous texture of the orchestra, and of the 'intoxicating magic' of the whole concept – all of which is confirmed by this first release. It comes from the second year of what is still considered one of Wieland Wagner's most elevating productions, and the photos in the booklet show us its moving simplicity and sense of dedication.

Director and conductor seem to have persuaded a fine cast to give of their very best. Wolfgang Windgassen, who also takes the title-role in Wolfgang Sawallisch's 1962 recording from Bayreuth, is here in fresher voice and is even more alternately elated and anguished in his delivery than seven years later. His paean to Venus in Act 1 is as heroically fervent as his narration in Act 3, telling of the Pope's rejection of his appeal for pardon, and expressing his own terrible torment of the spirit.

His true love, Elisabeth, is sung with total commitment and vibrant, outgoing voice by Gré Brouwenstijn. Her radiance in 'Dich teure Halle' and her reverence in her Act 3 Prayer could hardly be better done, equalling if not surpassing Anja Silja's rather different but just as valid approach in 1962. The young Fischer-Dieskau is a model Wolfram with a heart of gold and tone to match, each phrase benefiting from his eloquent approach. Josef Greindl, if you can excuse variable intonation, is an imposing Landgraf. Herta Wilfert, a little-known mezzo, is competent but perhaps a little staid as Venus. Wieland, as later in 1962, opts for the Paris version in Act 1, the Dresden in Act 2. The latter restores Walther's solo, a definite plus when it is sung with such beauty by Josef Traxel. The choral singing is up to the superb standard of Wilhelm Pitz during his long reign as Bayreuth's chorus-master, and Cluytens draws playing of tremendous élan from what sounds like a vintage Bayreuth band. The mono sound is so good that you soon forget any limitations. This set enters the pantheon of great Bayreuth performances on disc.

Tannhäuser
Spas Wenkoff *ten* Tannhäuser **Gwyneth Jones** *sop*
Elizabeth; Venus **Bernd Weikl** *bar* Wolfram **Hans
Sotin** *bass* Hermann **Franz Mazura** *bar* Biterolf
Robert Schunk *ten* Walther **Heinz Feldhoff** *bass*
Reinmar **John Pickering** *ten* Heinrich

**Chorus and Orchestra of the Bayreuth Festival /
Sir Colin Davis**
Stage director **Götz Friedrich**
Video director **Thomas Oloffson**
DG ② **DVD** 073 4446GH2
(3h 8' · NTSC · 4:3 · PCM stereo and DTS 5.1 · 0)
                            Ⓕ**OO**

Tannhäuser (Paris version)
Robert Gambill *ten* Tannhäuser **Camilla Nylund** *sop*
Elisabeth **Waltraud Meier** *sop* Venus **Roman Trekel**
bar Wolfram **Stephen Milling** *bass* Hermann **Tom
Fox** *bar* Biterolf **Marcel Reijans** *ten* Walther **Andreas
Hörl** *bass* Reinmar **Florian Hoffmann** *ten* Heinrich
**Deutsches Symphony Orchestra, Berlin /
Philippe Jordan**
Stage director **Nikolaus Lehnhoff**
Video director **Patrick Buttmann**
ArtHaus Musik ② **DVD** 101 351 (4h 23' · NTSC · 16:9 ·
PCM stereo, 5.1 and DTS 5.1 · 0)   Ⓕ

Thirty years separate these performances of *Tannhäuser*. The original video of the 1978 revival of Götz Friedrich's 1972 production was, we're told, 'the first complete film from Bayreuth', and this is its first DVD release. You're soon aware that it has not had the benefit of the latest technology: the lighting is not always well suited to the action and shifts between relatively close and relatively distant shots can appear awkward and arbitrary. The sound, too, is basic in its fixed focus, giving the voices too much prominence. All of this hardly matters, however, since the performance is electrifying, managing the difficult feat of doing justice to Wagner's inspiration without seeking to gainsay its gloriously hybrid nature.

Jürgen Rose's setting is austere, and one of the work's greatest moments, the astonishingly abrupt transition in Act 1 from the Venusberg to the idyllic countryside near the Wartburg, goes visually for too little. But the combination of Friedrich's tightly focused production and Sir Colin Davis's supremely flexible and energised conducting more than compensates. Davis is particularly in his element in the early stages of Act 2, to which he brings a Berliozian buoyancy, and what can sometimes seem almost comically tedious repetitions in the long processional chorus are anything but.

Adding to the lustre is the central trio of star performances. In 1978 Dame Gwyneth Jones was at her peak, taking time out from her definitive Bayreuth Brünnhilde to show how the roles of Venus and Elisabeth can be equally affecting, given maximum vocal and dramatic conviction. She weeps real tears in the mime that accompanies the Prelude to Act 3, as well she might, realising perhaps that she would never be better than this. Less sympathetically filmed, Spas Wenkoff still scores with the dogged power of his singing and acting, never out of character, never off the note, while Bernd Weikl is caught at his ardent, mellifluous best. With a fine supporting cast and the Bayreuth chorus and orchestra on top form, even those who resist the stylised eroticism of John Neumeier's choreography for the Bacchanale should find this set a memorable and moving experience.

The 2008 Baden-Baden version on ArtHaus Musik is, of course, technically superior as the film of a stage performance. It is not strictly comparable with the DG release anyway, since it offers the full post-Tristan Paris version, with the extended Venusberg music, while Bayreuth uses its own favoured hybrid – the Paris Bacchanale, before the singing starts, then the original Dresden version. Performances of the full Paris version are more likely to use different sopranos for the roles of Venus and Elisabeth, and it is one of the strengths of Baden-Baden 2008 to have two such different but excellent singers in these roles. Finnish soprano Camilla Nylund is new to me, and (like the Danish bass-baritone Stephen Milling, who comes close to upstaging most of his male colleagues as the Landgraf) is clearly a singer-actor of huge potential in this repertoire.

The solo singing is the outstanding feature of this new recording. Robert Gambill might have more of the 'mad axeman' about him than Bayreuth's Spas Wenkoff, but he has immense stamina and the presence to command the stage, especially during the big ensembles. Roman Trekel is a less spontaneous Wolfram than Weikl, his voice recorded with a degree of edginess that reduces its actual lyrical beauty. As with the remastered DG, the ArtHaus sound balance favours the voices at the expense of salient orchestral detail, but this drawback is much less bothersome than certain details of the production. In a setting even more austere than Bayreuth in 1978, Nikolaus Lehnhoff seems determined to drain the work of its Christian iconography and to nudge the audience with such deliberately incongruous props as a (non-functioning) microphone for the contestants in the Hall of Song. The production gets off to a bad start with a robotic, anti-erotic Bacchanale, and it is here that conductor Philippe Jordan's unsteady tempi, replete with pseudo-expressive over-emphases, first become apparent. Though it recurs, this problem is less pervasive than it might be, and Jordan is an alert supporter of his singers. But it is Colin Davis who has the fuller measure of this extraordinary score.

Tristan und Isolde

Tristan und Isolde
Plácido Domingo ten Tristan **Nina Stemme** sop Isolde **Mihoko Fujimura** sop Brangäne **René Pape** bass König Marke **Olaf Bär** bar Kurwenal **Jared Holt** ten Melot **Ian Bostridge** ten Shepherd **Matthew Rose** bar Steersman **Rolando Villazón** ten Young Sailor **Royal Opera House Chorus and Orchestra, Covent Garden / Antonio Pappano**
EMI ③ 558006-2 (3h 46' · DDD · T/t)   Ⓕ❍❍➌

Any major new recording of *Tristan und Isolde* is a big event, and this is bigger than most. As possibly the last studio recording on such a scale, it carries a weight of expectation, something doubled by an assumption which many never believed they'd hear: Plácido Domingo's Tristan. Of course, the 60-something tenor could never tackle this role on stage now, but it is not often one hears quite such a fantasy interpretation being realised on disc; even after Domingo's previous EMI releases of Wagnerian scenes, the idea of him recording this masterpiece in full seemed a little far-fetched. The advantage of the recording studio is that his Tristan never seems to tire and he gives an ardent account, characterised by the almost baritonal warmth of his voice. He may swallow the odd word but this is a committed and communicative performance, and he rises to the heights of Act 3.

Even so, it is the conducting of Antonio Pappano and the Isolde of Nina Stemme that truly put this in the highest league. Right from the start of the Prelude, which sounds languid without being really slow, Pappano draws a performance of glowing warmth. He moulds each detail but is never indulgent, with the result that the long spans all fall naturally into place. There is no need to over-stress Pappano's Italianate credentials, especially not when he conducts such an idiomatic Wagnerian performance, but they show themselves in the way he brings a bel canto quality to this music. This is a work that may have pushed the boundaries of tonality but it also reaches back to the world in which the composer served his operatic apprenticeship. Pappano's experience of *Tristan* in Brussels helps to make this sound like a 'lived-in' performance, and it must be hoped he will conduct it at Covent Garden.

Stemme is everything an Isolde needs to be: singing with radiant grandeur, she is rare in being able to sound sensuous even on the high notes. From her exciting first entry, she captures Isolde's temperament, and her Liebestod is notable for its beauty; her partnership with Domingo makes for a thrilling love duet. It is not often that a Brangäne sounds almost as glamorous, but Mihoko Fujimura sings with a warmly focused and even tone. René Pape is a noble and sonorous Marke, but Olaf Bär is less distinctive and occasionally woolly. As for the cameos, Rolando Villazón's Sailor is much less impressive than Ian Bostridge's ethereal and alert Shepherd. Even if this is not a recording to knock its legendary predecessors off their pedestals, it is an important addition to the discography and a stunning *Tristan* on today's terms. More than that: we'd think ourselves in operatic heaven if a live *Tristan* came close to this today.

Tristan und Isolde   Ⓗ
Lauritz Melchior ten Tristan **Kirsten Flagstad** sop Isolde **Sabine Kalter** contr Brangäne **Emanuel List** bass King Marke **Herbert Janssen** bar Kurwenal **Frank Sale** ten Melot **Octave Dua** ten Shepherd **Leslie Horsman** bar Steersman **Roy Devereux** ten Young Sailor **Royal Opera House Chorus, Covent Garden; London Philharmonic Orchestra / Fritz Reiner**
Naxos Historical mono ③ 8 110068/70 (209' · ADD)
Recorded live 1936   Ⓢ❍➌

This is an improved remastering by Ward Marston of a VAI set which received a warm welcome for preserving the rewarding partnership of Flagstad and Melchior, some would say unsurpassed in their respective roles and here on great form. The soprano, though at the start of her career in the part, is already a fully formed Isolde, and one marvels at Melchior, confirming his stature as the greatest Wagner tenor of all time. The rest of the cast are nothing special. Reiner, after a slow start, provides the right breadth and vitality to the work even when the playing leaves a little to be desired. The thencustomary cuts are made in Acts 2 and 3. At superbargain price (the VAI was at full price) this is an essential purchase for Wagnerians.

Tristan und Isolde
Wolfgang Windgassen ten Tristan **Birgit Nilsson** sop Isolde **Christa Ludwig** mez Brangäne **Martti Talvela** bass King Marke **Eberhard Waechter** bar Kurwenal **Claude Heater** ten Melot **Erwin Wohlfahrt** ten Shepherd **Gerd Nienstedt** bass Helmsman **Peter Schreier** ten Sailor **Bayreuth Festival Chorus and Orchestra / Karl Böhm**
DG The Originals ③ 449 772-2GOR3 (219' · ADD · T/t) Recorded live 1966   Ⓜ❶❶❶❶➾

Siegfried Jerusalem ten Tristan **Waltraud Meier** mez Isolde **Marjana Lipovšek** mez Brangäne **Matti Salminen** bass King Marke **Falk Struckmann** bar Kurwenal **Johan Botha** ten Melot **Peter Maus** ten Shepherd **Roman Trekel** bar Helmsman **Uwe Heilmann** ten Sailor **Berlin State Opera Chorus; Berlin Philharmonic Orchestra / Daniel Barenboim**
Teldec ③ 4509-94568-2 (235' · DDD · T/t) Recorded 1994   Ⓕ❶

Böhm's recording is a live Bayreuth performance of distinction, for on stage are the most admired Tristan and Isolde of their time, and in the pit the 72-year-old conductor directs a performance which is unflagging in its passion and energy. He has a striking way in the Prelude and Liebestod of making the swell of passion seem like the movement of a great sea, sometimes with gentle motion, sometimes with the breaking of the mightiest of waves. Nilsson characterises strongly, and her voice with its cleaving-power can also soften beautifully. Windgassen's heroic performance in Act 3 is in some ways the crown of his achievements on record, even though the voice has dried and aged a little. Christa Ludwig is the ideal Brangäne, Waechter a suitably forthright Kurwenal and Talvela an expressive, noble-voiced Marke. Orchestra and chorus are at their finest.

Over several seasons of conducting the work at Bayreuth, Barenboim has thoroughly mastered the pacing and shaping of the score as a unified entity. Even more important, he has peered into the depths of both its construction and meaning, emerging with answers that satisfy on almost all counts, most tellingly so in the melancholic adumbration of Isolde's thoughts during her narration, in the sadly eloquent counterpoint of

---

WAGNER TRISTAN UND ISOLDE – IN BRIEF

Lauritz Melchior Tristan **Kirsten Flagstad** Isolde **Sabine Kalter** Brangäne **Chorus of the Royal Opera House; London PO / Fritz Reiner** Ⓗ
Naxos ③ 8 110068/70 (209' · AAD)   Ⓢ❶
A 1936 live recording from Covent Garden, chiefly memorable for preserving the classic Melchior/Flagstad team in Reiner's broad reading. Some cuts, and only reasonable sound.

Wolfgang Windgassen Tristan **Birgit Nilsson** Isolde **Christa Ludwig** Brangäne **Bayreuth Festival Chorus and Orchestra / Karl Böhm**
DG ③ 449 772-2GOR3 (219' · ADD)   Ⓜ❶❶❶
💎 A 1966 live recording from Wieland Wagner's legendary Bayreuth production, with Böhm's fast-moving, dramatic conducting and Nilsson's searing, dominant Isolde, Windgassen's restrained Tristan, and Talvela's warm Marke heading a good cast.

Siegfried Jerusalem Tristan **Waltraud Meier** Isolde **Marjana Lipovšek** Brangäne **Berlin State Opera Chorus; Berlin PO / Daniel Barenboim**
Teldec ③ 4509 94568-2 (235' · DDD)   Ⓕ❶
Excellent modern studio recording captures Barenboim's warm, balanced reading and a good cast, with the two lovers less vocally resplendent than most rivals, but younger-sounding and no less committed.

René Kollo Tristan **Margaret Price** Isolde **Brigitte Fassbaender** Brangäne **Leipzig Radio Chorus; Staatskapelle Dresden/ Carlos Kleiber**
DG ③ 477 5355GOR3 (235' · DDD)   Ⓜ➾
Kleiber's quicksilver reading makes full use of studio recording to create a lighter-voiced, less effortful performance, Margaret Price's cut-glass Isolde in particular. Finely cast, very beautiful, but somewhat artificial.

Ludwig Suthaus Tristan **Kirsten Flagstad** Isolde **Blanche Thebom** Brangäne **Chorus of the Royal Opera House; Philharmonia Orchestra / Wilhelm Furtwängler** Ⓗ
EMI ③ 585873-2 (255' · AAD)   Ⓑ❶
Unarguably a classic, with Furtwängler's richly flowing reading, even if Flagstad sounds rather matronly (with a couple of high notes provided by Elisabeth Schwarzkopf) and Suthaus is more dependable than exciting.

Jon Vickers Tristan **Helga Dernesch** Isolde **Christa Ludwig** Brangäne **Berlin Deutsche Oper Chorus; Berlin PO / Herbert von Karajan**
EMI ③ 769319-2 (246' · ADD)   Ⓜ➾
Despite peculiar recorded perspectives, at mid-price Karajan's sleekly beautiful version is worth considering, with a fine cast headed by Vickers's toweringly tragic Tristan and Dernesch's most feminine Isolde.

bass clarinet, lower strings and cor anglais underpinning King Marke's lament, and in the searingly tense support to Tristan's second hallucination. These are but the most salient moments in a reading that thoughtfully and unerringly reveals the inner parts of this astounding score. The obverse of this caring manner is a certain want of spontaneity, and a tendency to become a shade self-regarding. You occasionally miss the overwhelming force of Furtwängler's metaphysical account or the immediacy and excitement of Böhm's famous live Bayreuth reading. But the very mention of those conductors suggests that Barenboim can live in their world and survive the comparisons with his own perfectly valid interpretation. Besides, he has the most gloriously spacious yet well-focused recording so far of this opera, and an orchestra not only familiar with his ways but ready to execute them in a disciplined and sensitive manner. The recording also takes account of spatial questions, in particular the placing of the horns offstage at the start of Act 2.

Salminen delivers a classic account of Marke's anguished reproaches to Tristan, his singing at once sonorous, dignified and reaching to the heart, a reading on a par with that of his fellow countryman Talvela for Böhm. Meier's Isolde is a vitally wrought, verbally alert reading, which catches much of the venom of Act 1, the visceral excitement of Act 2, the lambent utterance of the Liebestod. Nothing she does is unmusical; everything is keenly intelligent, yet possibly her tone is too narrow for the role. Lipovšek's Brangäne tends to slide and swim in an ungainly fashion, sounding at times definitely overparted. Listening to Ludwig (Böhm) only serves to emphasise Lipovšek's deficiencies. Then it's often hard on the newer set to tell Isolde and Brangäne apart, so alike can be their timbre. As with his partner, Jerusalem sings his role with immaculate musicality; indeed, he may be the most accurate Tristan on disc where note values are concerned, one also consistently attentive to dynamics and long-breathed phrasing. On the other hand, although he puts a deal of feeling into his interpretation, he hasn't quite the intensity of utterance of either Windgassen (Böhm) or, even more, Suthaus (Furtwängler). His timbre is dry and occasionally rasping: in vocal terms alone Suthaus is in a class of his own. Yet, even with reservations about the Isolde and Tristan, this is a version that will undoubtedly hold a high place in any survey of this work, for which one performance can never hope to tell the whole story.

Tristan und Isolde
Siegfried Jerusalem *ten* Tristan **Waltraud Meier** *sop* Isolde **Matthias Hölle** *bass* König Marke **Falk Struckmann** *bar* Kurwenal **Poul Elming** *ten* Melot; A Young Sailor **Uta Priew** *sop* Brangäne **Peter Maus** *ten* A Shepherd **Sándor Sólyom-Nagy** *bar* A Helmsman **Chorus and Orchestra of the Bayreuth Festival / Daniel Barenboim**
Stage director **Heiner Müller**

Video director **Horant H Hohlfeld**
DG ② 𝐃𝐕𝐃 073 4439GH2 (3h 55' · NTSC · 16:9 · PCM stereo and DTS 5.1 · 0)   Ⓕ**OO**

Daniel Barenboim's earliest performances of *Tristan* at Bayreuth are documented in a DVD of the 1981 production by Jean-Pierre Ponnelle (filmed in 1983) with René Kollo and Johanna Meier in the title-roles (available from DG). In 1993, when he was vastly more experienced and assured in his handling of this formidable score, Barenboim returned to the work in conjunction with playwright and theatre director Heiner Müller. This recording was made two years later, over seven days during the festival's rehearsal period. One imagines that the acts were filmed (without audiences) on separate days, to great advantage where the singers' stamina is concerned: but one particularly evident edit, at the point of Isolde's long-awaited entrance in Act 3, indicates that this is in some respects a hybrid product, halfway between a live performance and a studio version of a particular staging.

This is a fine and intensely moving account of a supreme masterpiece of musical theatre. It is not perfect, with the setting for Act 2 particularly unappealing, but it is serious in its dramatic, theatrical intent, and (that Act 2 setting apart) accomplished in its realisation. Müller's conception of the work is austere, not expecting setting or acting to get in the way of things which are best left to the music, and on the whole he has managed a difficult assignment with flair and conviction. Nowhere is this clearer than at the end, where Waltraud Meier sings the Liebestod from the front of the stage, with no semaphoring gestures and only facial expression and beautifully graded vocal projection to convey the essence of the drama.

Singers with more opulent voices have undertaken the role, yet Meier's contained, richly nuanced approach to both acting and singing is ideally suited to this production. Her Tristan, Siegfried Jerusalem, is no less impressive, with a poised demeanour avoiding the woodenness that afflicts so many Wagner tenors. Add a marvellously sonorous Marke in Matthias Hölle, no weaknesses in the other roles, and the virtues stack up to something special.

Does Barenboim's very explicit musical moulding actually fit with such a restrained stage production? Or is the whole point in the contrast between the visible and the audible? Such basic questions make one think yet again about the nature and significance of Wagner's most provocative and inexhaustible work for the stage. Something special, indeed.

Tristan und Isolde
Robert Gambill *ten* Tristan **Nina Stemme** *sop* Isolde **Bo Skovhus** *bar* Kurwenal **René Pape** *bass* King Marke **Katarina Karnéus** *mez* Brangäne **Glyndebourne Chorus; London Philharmonic Orchestra / Jiří Bělohlávek**
Stage director **Nikolaus Lehnhoff**

Video director **Thomas Grimm**
Opus Arte ③ 📀 OA0988D (5h 58' · NTSC · 16:9 ·
LPCM stereo and DTS 5.1 · 0) Recorded live at
Glyndebourne in 2007   Ⓕ**OOO**

The filming of each act begins annoyingly with
a *Star Wars* storyline pan-in on the words
'Tristan und Isolde', 'Act 2' etc, using up the
preludes. After that, however, comes a performance realised to Glyndebourne's highest standards – the chorus and stage brass are Bayreuth-
level, the casting immaculate (they can all really
sing these parts), and Bělohlávek's conducting
balanced with a Goodall-like attention to the
filigree detail of Wagner's new-wave scoring.
   Old-style analyses of the music used to talk
about the 'glance' motif. Lehnhoff's staging
deploys a series of heartbreaking glances:
Stemme's Isolde when Karnéus's Brangäne tells
her she's taken the love draught, Stemme again
when Tristan arrives in Act 2, Pape's Marke as
he sees the lovers together and, at *Brokeback
Mountain*-level, Skovhus's Kurwenal as he cra-
dles Gambill's Tristan then breaks away, half in
fear of his lord's death, half in fear of his feelings
for him. In fact, has a Tristan ever been so
deeply loved by his lady and squire as here, or
felt so wretched at betraying his king? And is
Skovhus actually the greatest Kurwenal yet
recorded?
   Roland Aeschlimann provides a geometrically
attractive whorl of a standing set, concentric
wooden circles telescoping towards a constantly
varied horizon: a ship, a spaceship, everywhere,
nowhere – perfect. The lighting (Robin Carter
and Aeschlimann) has a genuine physical presence and seems to reinvent the colour blue. At
the point of Isolde's almost belated arrival in Act
3, a surreal, Ingmar Bergman-like atmosphere
permeates events: she arrives from behind on
high as a figure of death and wraps him in a black
cloak, while Skovhus's poignant Kurwenal gets a
non-realistic, Brechtian centre-stage for his
fights and death.

Sir William Walton   British 1902-1983

*Walton was educated at Oxford, and was a member
of the Sitwells circle from the beginning of the 1920s.
His first important work was Façade, setting poems
by Edith Sitwell for reciter and sextet and evidently
modelled on Pierrot lunaire while looking more to Les
Six in its wit and jazziness. The next works again
showed Parisian connections: with Stravinsky and
Honegger in the overture Portsmouth Point, with
Prokofiev in the Viola Concerto. Then, without losing the vividness of his harmony and orchestration,
he responded to the English Handelian tradition in
Belshazzar's Feast and to Sibelius in his First Symphony, though here Elgar too is invoked, as in much
of his later music. The Violin Concerto (1939) confirmed this homecoming. The next decade was comparatively unproductive, except in film music (Henry
V, Hamlet). At the end of it he married and moved*

*to Ischia, where all his later works were composed.
These include the opera Troilus and Cressida, found
theatrically effective if conservative in approach
when given at Covent Garden in 1954, and his one-
act opera The Bear, a parodistic Chekhovian extravaganza, given at Aldeburgh in 1967. Among the
late orchestral works are a Cello Concerto, cooler and
more serene than the earlier concertos, a Second Symphony and miscellaneous pieces including a finely
worked set of Hindemith Variations, which shows an
improvisatory character typical of his late music.*
                    GROVEmusic

Concertos, Symphonies, etc

Centenary Edition

Cello Concerto[el]. Viola Concerto[dl]. Violin Concerto[d].
Symphonies – No 1 in B flat minor[a]; No-2[bl]. Scapino[fl].
Variations on a Theme by Hindemith[hl]. Crown
Imperial[in]. Orb and Sceptre[k]. Henry V – Suite[m].
Facade Suites[gl] – No 1; No 2. Coronation Te Deum[i].
Belshazzar's Feast[hn]

[n]**Bryn Terfel** *bass-bar* [c]**Tasmin Little** *vn* [d]**Paul
Neubauer** *va* [e]**Robert Cohen** *vc* [f]**Timothy Byram-
Wigfield** *org* [n]**L'inviti**; [in]**Waynflete Singers;**
[i]**Winchester Cathedral Choir; Bournemouth
Symphony Orchestra and** [n]**Chorus** / [l]**Andrew
Litton,** [il]**David Hill**
Decca ④ 470 508-2DC4 (298' · DDD)
Recorded 1992-6   Ⓜ**OO⮕**

Decca's four-disc Walton Edition offers consistently fine versions of all the composer's most
important orchestral works, some of them unsurpassed, in full, brilliant sound. Andrew Litton, the
conductor of all but two minor items, is central to
the success of the whole. Like his compatriot,
André Previn, he's idiomatic, with a natural feeling for the jazzy syncopations at the heart of so
much of Walton's music.
   This issue brings together the three Litton
discs previously issued, with important additions. The third disc was issued separately, and
contains outstanding versions, never previously
released, of the Viola Concerto and *Hindemith
Variations* plus the two *Façade* Suites. Where
most latterday interpreters of the Viola Concerto have taken a very expansive view of the
lyrical first movement, Paul Neubauer comes
nearer than anyone else to the original interpreters on disc, Frederick Riddle and William
Primrose.
   With Neubauer – his tone firm and precise,
clean rather than fruity – the result is more persuasive than other modern versions, with no
suspicion of expressive self-indulgence. The
brisker passages are taken faster than is now
usual; the impact is tauter and stronger without
losing romantic warmth. He relaxes seductively
for the hauntingly beautiful epilogue, using the
widest dynamic range. Litton encourages wide
contrasts in the orchestra, the big *tuttis* bringing
an element of wildness in the brassy syncopations, the ensemble kept crisp and incisive. The
Hindemith Variations also brings a taut and purposeful performance with contrasts in both

dynamic and speed heightened to extremes. *Façade* is predictably fun, though there's some danger of the warm acoustic softening some of the sharpness of these witty parodies.

Two of the other discs remain the same as with their original release, with Tasmin Little's heartfelt reading of the Violin Concerto coupled with Litton's outstanding account of the Second Symphony, the finest digital version yet, as well as *Scapino*, while Robert Cohen's thoughtful reading of the Cello Concerto is coupled with the richly recorded First Symphony. Litton's powerful account of *Belshazzar's Feast* with Bryn Terfel brings fresh, cleanly focused choral sound in an atmospheric acoustic that clearly lets you appreciate the terracing between the different groupings of voices. That aptly comes with the coronation music – and the *Henry V* Suite, with David Hill, chorus-master in *Belshazzar*, ably standing in for Litton in the *Coronation Te Deum* and *Orb and Sceptre*.

Cello Concerto

Cello Concerto[a] Violin Concerto[b]
[a]**Tim Hugh** vc [b]**Dong-Suk Kang** vn
English Northern Philharmonia / Paul Daniel
Naxos 8 554325 (60' · DDD) Ⓢ Ⓞ ▷

Tim Hugh, outstanding in every way, gives a reading of the Concerto that's the most searching yet. More than direct rivals he finds a thoughtfulness, a sense of mystery, of inner meditation in Walton's great lyrical ideas – notably the main themes of the outer movements and the yearning melody of the central section of the second movement Scherzo. Most strikingly his *pianissimos* are more extreme. The openings of both the outer movements are more hushed than ever heard before on disc, with Hugh in inner intensity opting for broader speeds than usual. Not that he dawdles, as the overall timings of each movement make plain, and the bravura writing finds him equally concentrated, always sounding strong and spontaneous in the face of any technical challenges.

In the Violin Concerto Dong-Suk Kang plays immaculately with fresh, clean-cut tone, pure and true above the stave. Many will also applaud the way that Kang opts for speeds rather faster and more flowing than have latterly been favoured. That follows the example of Heifetz as the original interpreter, and Kang similarly relishes the bravura writing, not least in diamond-sharp articulation in the *Scherzo*.

Paul Daniel and the English Northern Philharmonia play with equal flair and sympathy, so that the all-important syncopations always sound idiomatic. But though the recorded textures are commendably clear, the strings are too distantly balanced, lacking weight, so that moments where the violins are required to surge up warmly sound thin – hardly the fault of the players. An excellent coupling, though, with the Cello Concerto offering new depths of insight.

Additional recommendation

Coupled with: **Walton** Passacaglia **Bloch** Solo Cello Suite No 1 **Britten** Solo Cello Suite No 2, Op 80 – Ciaconna **Ligeti** Cello Sonata
Wispelwey vc **Sydney SO / Tate**
Onyx ONYX4042 (66' · DDD) Ⓕ
 The inspired Dutch cellist Peter Wispelwey here couples the Walton Cello Concerto with a sequence of works for unaccompanied cello. As one would expect, his playing is flawless, though in the Walton the fast passages like the central *Scherzo* are more successful in their brilliance than the slow ruminative ones.

Viola Concerto

Viola Concerto. Symphony No 2.
Johannesburg Festival Overture
Lars Anders Tomter va **English Northern Philharmonia / Paul Daniel**
Naxos 8 553402 (61' · DDD) Ⓢ ▷

This disc opens with one of the wittiest, most exuberant performances of the *Johannesburg Festival Overture*: Daniel encourages the orchestra's virtuoso wind and brass soloists to point the jazz rhythms idiomatically, making the music sparkle. The Viola Concerto is just as delectably pointed, the whole performance magnetic. Tomter's tone, with its rapid flicker-vibrato, lacks the warmth of Kennedy's (reviewed below), but the vibrato is only obtrusive in that upper-middle register and his intonation is immaculate, his attack consistently clean, to match the crisp ensemble of the orchestra. Although he adopts relatively measured speeds both for the Scherzo and the jaunty opening theme of the finale, the rhythmic lift brings out the scherzando jollity of the latter all the more.

Daniel's keen observance of dynamic markings is again brought out in the stuttering fanfare theme of the Scherzo, with muted trumpets and trombones for once played *pianissimo* as marked. The close of the slow epilogue has never been recorded with such a profound hush as here, subsiding in darkness, and the recording team is to be complimented on getting such beautiful sound, clean with plenty of bloom. Paul Daniel adopts a relatively broad tempo in the Symphony's first movement, and the flowing tempo for the central slow movement makes for a lighter, less passionate result too. The finale, with its brassy first statement of the Passacaglia theme, brings fine dynamic contrasts, but again Litton and others produce a fatter, weightier sound, which on balance is preferable. Yet Daniel's view is a very valid one, to round off most convincingly an invaluable addition to the Walton discography.

Walton Viola Concerto (original version)[a] **Rubbra** Meditations on a Byzantine Hymn. Viola Concerto[a]
Lawrence Power va
[a]**BBC Scottish Symphony Orchestra / Ilan Volkov**
Hyperion CDA67587 (61' · DDD) Ⓕ

It is good to welcome a modern recording of Walton's Viola Concerto in its original orchestration. When in 1938 Frederick Riddle, principal viola of the LSO, first recorded this seminal work, Walton had yet to slim down the orchestration to make the concerto more accessible. But even dedicated Waltonians may not notice much difference, particularly when in this fine recording the balance marginally favours the solo instrument. Yet as Leo Black suggests in his booklet-notes, the result 'perhaps conveys to a greater extent the freshness and grittiness of Walton's original conception'.

This was in many ways the breakthrough work in Walton's early career; it brought together in full maturity his distinctive mixture of yearning lyricism and jazzily syncopated writing. Lawrence Power serves the work superbly. Riddle's is arguably still the finest version (Dutton Labs), with speeds marginally faster than modern versions, something approved by Walton. Yet Power is not much slower than Riddle in the *Andante comodo* first movement. In the finale differences in timing between Riddle and modern versions is greater, largely because of the final expansive epilogue, which clearly echoes the accompanied cadenzas of Elgar's Violin Concerto.

The two Rubbra items here are welcome. His orchestration in the Concerto is never as clear as Walton's but it suits his musical idiom with its reliance on perfect fourths and other open intervals, as well as plainsong. The *Meditations on a Byzantine Theme*, the first recording in the version for unaccompanied viola, makes an apt extra. All told, a superb disc, much to be welcomed.

Violin Concerto

Violin Concerto. Viola Concerto
Nigel Kennedy vn,va
Royal Philharmonic Orchestra / André Previn
EMI Great Artists of the Century 562813-2 (72' · DDD)
Ⓕ**❂❂**➔

Nigel Kennedy has stepped in, and – with the uniquely expert guidance of André Previn – produced a recording of both works which in this coupling is unlikely to be bettered for a long time. Even next to the finest individual recordings of the two works, differently coupled, Kennedy provides formidable competition. Warmly expressive as Kennedy's mentor Menuhin was in both works, spaciously romantic and characteristically individual in every phrase, he is not a natural Waltonian, even with the composer to guide him. The comparison with Kennedy is fascinating. Not surprisingly, Kennedy's jazz sympathies give his playing a natural bite in the sharply syncopated passages so typical of Walton, matching Previn's similarly jazz-founded understanding.

The most controversial point of both interpretations of the Viola Concerto comes in the speed of the *Andante comodo* first movement. Kennedy is almost as slow as Menuhin and far slower than usual – but his pulse is steadier. The aching melancholy of that lovely opening, the dreamy quality of the second subject (*sognando* the marking) are caught more hauntingly. In the finale Kennedy's natural contrasting of the romantic and the *scherzando* sides of Walton are again most convincing, and the epilogue brings the most magic moment, when the pianissimo return of the first movement main theme is so hushed you hear it as though from the distance.

The marking *sognando* also comes at the opening of the Violin Concerto, and again Kennedy captures it beautifully. You might argue that he is the more dreamy compared with Kyung-Wha Chung on Decca, when his manner is more relaxed, less yearningly intense, a quality which generally makes her performance so magnetic. Kennedy's is a gloriously rich and red-blooded reading of the whole work, bringing ripe playing in the big romantic melodies balanced with formidable bravura in the contrasting passages written with Heifetz in mind.

For a coupling of two of the most beautiful string concertos written this century, this Kennedy record will set standards for many years to come. The recording is full and rounded, well-balanced with the soloist's wide dynamic range fully conveyed.

Symphonies

Symphony No 1
London Symphony Orchestra / Sir Colin Davis
LSO Live LSO0076 (46' · DDD); 🄯 LSO0576.
Recorded live 2005   Ⓢ➔

When Sir Colin Davis conducted Walton's First Symphony at the Barbican it was greeted by ecstatic reviews – and rightly so. It was as though critics had suddenly rediscovered this iconic work, which so tellingly reflects the mood of uncertainty and tension in the 1930s. The recording bears out that response: the hushed opening seems as though the music is only just emerging into human consciousness. The mystery quickly evaporates as the nagging syncopations of the ostinato figure become more insistent, developing into a powerful climax. The clarity of texture and sharpness of attack add to the impact, with Davis at ease with the jazz element and finding more light and shade than is common. The *Scherzo* brings big contrasts too; the slow movement sounds as haunting as the opening and then brings warmly lyrical ideas. The extrovert finale again brings clarity in the contrapuntal writing of successive fugatos, leading to a ripe conclusion.

This new recording, the first version on SACD at a low price, finds a welcome place. Yet it is amazing how well the benchmark recording, André Previn's 1966 reading with the LSO (now contained in a two-CD Walton collection – see below), stands up. The sound is fatter, more punchy than on Davis's disc and Previn, early in his conducting career in the UK, is more biting, in the slow movement conveying a chill that exactly suits Walton's sweet-sour inspiration.

This music may have been inspired by a frustrated love affair rather than anything to do with world politics, but it stands as a symbol of its times, and Previn powerfully conveys that. Meanwhile, this new disc earns a very warm welcome.

Symphony No 1. Partita
English Northern Philharmonia / Paul Daniel
Naxos 8 553180 (64' · DDD) ⑤●●⯈

Daniel demonstrates clearly here his natural affinity with Walton's music. In the sustained paragraphs of the First Symphony he knows unerringly how to build up tension to breaking point, before resolving it, and then building again – a quality vital above all in the first and third movements. He's freer than many in his use of *rubato* too, again often a question of building and resolving tension, as well as in the degree of elbow-room he allows for jazzy syncopations, always idiomatic. This symphony, with its heavy orchestration, would certainly have benefited from rather drier sound, but well-judged microphone balance allows ample detail through. Only occasionally do you feel a slight lack of body in high violin tone, a tiny reservation. Daniel's reading of the *Partita* brings out above all the work's joyfulness. It may not be quite as crisp in its ensemble as that of the dedicatees (Szell and the Cleveland Orchestra), but the degree of wildness, with dissonances underlined, proves a positive advantage in conveying enjoyment. In the slow movement Daniel at a relatively slow speed is markedly more expressive than those brilliant models, again a point which makes the performance more endearing.

Irrespective of price, this is a version of the much-recorded symphony that competes with the finest ever, and outshines most.

Symphony No 1 in B flat minor[a]. Violin Concerto[b].
Viola Concerto[c]. Cello Concerto[d]. Sinfonia
concertante[e]
[b]**Jascha Heifetz** vn [c]**Yuri Bashmet** va [d]**Gregor
Piatigorsky** vc [e]**Kathryn Stott** pf [ac]**London
Symphony Orchestra / [a]André Previn, [c]Neeme
Järvi; [b]Philharmonia Orchestra / William Walton;
[d]Boston Symphony Orchestra / Charles Munch;
[e]Royal Philharmonic Orchestra / Vernon Handley**
RCA Red Seal [b]mono ② 74321 92575-2 (145' · ADD/
[ce]DDD) Recorded [a]1966, [c]1998, [d]1959, [b]1950, [e]1989
  Ⓜ●●

RCA's two-disc collection includes the premiere recording of the Cello Concerto with Piatigorsky – who commissioned the work – and the Boston Symphony under Charles Munch. Here is a high-powered reading, given an upfront recording, commendably full and open for 1959. Similarly Heifetz, who commissioned the Violin Concerto, remains supreme as an interpreter of that work, urgent beyond any rival as well as passionate. Here he plays with the composer conducting the Philharmonia. The 1950 mono recording has been nicely opened up, putting more air around the sound, making the absence of stereo a minimal drawback. The other two concertante works

come in digital versions: Kathryn Stott, originally for Conifer, adventurously going back to the original more elaborate version of the *Sinfonia concertante*, and Yuri Bashmet bringing his yearningly Slavonic temperament and masterly virtuosity to the Viola Concerto.

Bashmet's partners are the ideal combination of Previn and the LSO, and it's Previn's vintage version of the First Symphony with the LSO of an earlier generation that sets the seal on the whole package. Previn has never been matched, let alone surpassed. Also remarkable is the clarity, definition and sense of presence of the 1966 recording, with the stereo spectrum more sharply focused than in the digital recordings.

Symphony No 2[c]. Variations on a Theme by
Hindemith[d]. Partita[c]. Violin Concerto[b]. Johannesburg
Festival Overture[e]. Capriccio burlesco[e]. Belshazzar's
Feast[a]
[a]**Walter Cassel** bar [b]**Zino Francescatti** vn [a]**Rutgers
University Choir; [cd]Cleveland Orchestra / George
Szell; [ab]Philadelphia Orchestra / Eugene Ormandy;
[e]New York Philharmonic Orchestra /
André Kostelanetz**
Sony Classical ② SB2K 89934 (143' · ADD) Recorded
1959-73 Ⓑ

Sony's two-disc Essential Classics collection brings together major offerings from three previous Walton CDs, all of them American. Outstanding are the vintage Szell performances with the Cleveland Orchestra, in sheer brilliance never likely to be outshone. The composer himself was bowled over by Szell's 1961 Second Symphony, a work till then rather discounted, which drew an interpretation not just brilliant but passionate. In Szell's high-powered reading the *Hindemith Variations*, too, hang together superbly, and the *Partita*, a Cleveland commission, is scintillating from first to last.

André Kostelanetz turns the *Capriccio burlesco* into a sparkling comedy overture, a work he was the first to conduct, and the *Johannesburg Festival Overture* is made to sparkle too, arguably the finest of the Walton overtures. Both the Violin Concerto and *Belshazzar's Feast* are given expressive performances by Ormandy conducting the Philadelphia Orchestra. In the Concerto Zino Francescatti is powerful and passionate with his rapid, slightly nervy vibrato, while in *Belshazzar* choir and soloist are as committed as any British performers, even if their pronunciation of 'Isaiah' is pure American, the second syllable rhyming with 'day'. The sound is typically up-front and not as warm as it might be, though with plenty of atmosphere. Buy it for Szell's Second – an account Walton described as 'fantastic and stupendous'.

Spitfire Prelude and Fugue

Spitfire Prelude and Fugue. Sinfonia concertante[e].
Variations on a Theme by Hindemith. March –
The History of the English Speaking Peoples

[a]**Peter Donohoe** *pf*
English Northern Philharmonia / Paul Daniel
Naxos 8 553869 (53' · DDD)   Ⓢ❍❍🅳➤

Naxos opts for the original version of the *Sinfonia concertante* rather than Walton's revision, with piano writing and orchestration slimmed down. Walton himself, before he died, suggested such a return. As soloist Peter Donohoe plays with power and flamboyance, brought home the more when the piano is very forwardly balanced, too much so for a work which doesn't aim to be a full concerto, leaving the orchestra a little pale behind. Even so, hopefully this account, broad in the first movement, flowing in the central *Andante*, will persuade others to take it up, young man's music built on striking, colourful ideas, used with crisp concision.

Paul Daniel is splendid at interpreting the jazzy syncopations with the right degree of freedom, and in the *Spitfire Prelude and Fugue* he adds to the impact by taking the big march tune faster than many, similarly demonstrating that *The History of the English Speaking Peoples March*, buried for rather too long, is a match for Walton's other ceremonial marches. Best of all is the performance of the *Hindemith Variations*, given here with winning panache. The strings of the English Northern Philharmonia may not be as weighty as in some rival versions, but the articulation is brilliant, and the complex textures are all the more transparent. The fire and energy of the performance has never been surpassed on disc.

Façade

Walton Façade – An Entertainment[a]
Lambert Salome – Suite
[a]**Eleanor Bron**, [a]**Richard Stilgoe** *spkrs* **Nash Ensemble** (Paul Watkins *vc*, Philippa Davies *fl*, Richard Hosford *clar*, John Wallace *tpt*, Martin Robertson [a]*sax*, Simon Lembrick *perc*) /
David Lloyd-Jones
Hyperion CDA67239 (72' · DDD · T)   Ⓕ❍

The *Façade* entertainment – poems by Edith Sitwell to music by the then-unknown William Walton – was an amorphous creation, a collection of over 40 poems and settings built up over the years between 1922 and 1928.

Pamela Hunter in her disc on the Koch Discovery label did a marvellous job collecting all the surviving settings, adding recitations of the poems for which the music had been lost. The difference is that, instead of being recited on the disc, the texts of those extra poems are printed in the booklet, with revealing comments. Also, David Lloyd-Jones has devised an order for the 34 items (including the opening fanfare) which is arguably the best yet, avoiding the anticlimactic effect of *Façade 2* being separated. Eleanor Bron and Richard Stilgoe make an excellent pair of reciters, and the recording in a natural acoustic balances them well – not too close. They inflect the words more than Edith Sitwell and early interpreters did, but still keep a stylised

manner, meticulously obeying the rhythms specified in the score. Not everyone will like the way Stilgoe adopts accents – Mummerset for 'Mariner Man' and 'Country Dance', Scots for 'Scotch Rhapsody', and something like southern-state American for the jazz rhythms of 'Old Sir Faulk' – but he's the most fluent *Façade* reciter on disc so far, with phenomenally clear articulation. Eleanor Bron is also meticulous over rhythm, in slower poems adopting a trance-like manner, which is effective and in-style.

Under David Lloyd-Jones the brilliant sextet of players from the Nash Ensemble couldn't be more idiomatic.

Piano Quartet

Piano Quartet[a]. Violin Sonata[b]. Anon in love[c]. Passacaglia[d]. Façade – Valse[e]
[c]**John Mark Ainsley** *ten* [c]**Craig Ogden** *gtr*
[a]**Nash Ensemble** ([b]Marianne Thorsen *vn* Lawrence Power *va* [d]Paul Watkins *vc* [be]Ian Brown *pf*)
Hyperion CDA67340 (76' · DDD · T)   Ⓕ❍❍

This excellent Hyperion issue brings together a wide-ranging group of Walton's chamber works, from his earliest major work, the Piano Quartet, originally written when he was 16, to his last instrumental piece, the *Passacaglia*, which he composed for Rostropovich when he was nearly 80. As a substantial bonus there's the little song cycle for tenor and guitar, *Anon in Love*, as well as the two shorter pieces.

Helped by a spacious recording, the extra lightness and clarity brings an element of fantasy into such a movement as the *Scherzo* of the Piano Quartet and an extra tenderness into the lovely slow movement. Nowhere else does Walton so enthusiastically use modal thematic material, starting with the mysterious opening theme, which the Nash players take very reflectively at a speed much slower than the movement's main tempo, *Allegramente*. It's an astonishingly confident work for so young a composer, with adventurous writing for the strings that belies the fact that Walton was no string-player.

The Violin Sonata, a more elusive work, long underestimated, is given an equally persuasive performance, with Marianne Thorsen, accompanied by Ian Brown, freely expressive. John Mark Ainsley is totally undaunted by the taxing vocal writing of *Anon in Love*, originally designed for Peter Pears. And Craig Ogden is an ideal accompanist, totally idiomatic, adding sparkle to the vigorous songs in this offbeat collection. Though Ian Brown gives a slightly sluggish account of *Façade*'s 'Valse' – in the awkward piano transcription ascribed to Walton himself – cellist Paul Watkins crowns the disc with a fine reading of the solo *Passacaglia*.

String Quartets

Piano Quartet in D minor[a]. String Quartet in A minor
[a]**Peter Donohoe** *pf* **Maggini Quartet** (Laurence

Jackson, David Angel *vns* Martin Outram *va* Michal
Kaznowski *vc*)
Naxos 8 554646 (58' · DDD)　　　　　Ⓢ🅞🅞🅑▷

The Maggini Quartet give refined and powerful
performances in this Naxos release. The opening
of the 1947 String Quartet is presented in hushed
intimacy, making the contrast all the greater
when Walton's richly lyrical writing emerges in
full power. There's a tender, wistful quality here,
which culminates in a rapt, intense account of the
slow movement, where the world of late
Beethoven comes much closer than most interpreters have appreciated. The poignancy of those
two longer movements is then set against the
clean bite of the second movement Scherzo and
the brief hectic finale, with their clear and transparent textures. With Peter Donohoe a powerful
and incisive presence, and the Maggini Quartet
again playing most persuasively, the early Piano
Quartet is also given a performance of high contrasts, enhanced by a refined recording which
conveys genuine pianissimos that are free from
highlighting. If, in the first three movements, the
pentatonic writing gives little idea of the mature
Walton to come, some characteristic rhythmic
and other devices are already apparent. Even the
pentatonicry suggests that the boy had been looking at the Howells Piano Quartet rather than any
Vaughan Williams. It's in the finale that one gets
the strongest Waltonian flavour in vigorously
purposeful argument, though there the echoes
are different, and Stravinsky's *Petrushka* is an
obvious influence. The only reservation is that
the piano is rather too forwardly balanced.

Belshazzar's Feast

Belshazzar's Feast[a]. Coronation Te Deum. Gloria[b]
[b]**Ameral Gunson** *contr*[b]**Neil Mackie** *ten* [a]**Gwynne
Howell,** [b]**Stephen Roberts** *bars* **Bach Choir;
Philharmonia Orchestra / Sir David Willcocks**
Chandos CHAN8760 (62' · DDD · T)　　　　　Ⓟ🅞

With Sir David Willcocks in charge of the choir
which he has directed since 1960, one needn't
fear that the composer's many near-impossible
demands of the chorus in all three of these masterpieces won't be met with elegance and poise.
In *Belshazzar* there's also a predictably fine balance of the forces to ensure that as much detail as
possible is heard from both chorus and orchestra,
even when Walton is bombarding us from all
corners of the universe with extra brass bands
and all manner of clamorous percussion in praise
of pagan gods. Such supremely musical concerns
bring their own rewards in a work that can often
seem vulgar. The revelation here is the sustained
degree of dramatic thrust, exhilaration and what
Herbert Howells called 'animal joy' in the proceedings. How marvellous, too, to hear the work
paced and scaled to avoid the impression of
reduced voltage after the big moments. Gwynne
Howell is the magnificently steady, firm and dark
toned baritone. The *Gloria* and *Coronation Te
Deum* are informed with the same concerns:

accuracy and professional polish are rarely
allowed to hinder these vital contributions to the
British choral tradition. The recording's cathedral-like acoustic is as ideal for the *Te Deum*'s
ethereal antiphonal effects, as it is for *Belshazzar*'s glorious spectacle; and Chandos matches
Willcocks's care for balance, bar by bar.

Belshazzar's Feast[b]. Viola Concerto[a].　　　　Ⓗ
Facade – Suite No 1[c]; Suite No 2[d]
[b]**Dennis Noble** *bar* [a]**Frederick Riddle** *va*
[b]**Huddersfield Choral Society;** [a]**London Symphony
Orchestra;** [b]**Liverpool Philharmonic Orchestra;**
[cd]**London Philharmonic Orchestra / William Walton**
Pearl mono GEM0171 (76' · ADD) Recorded [b]1943,
[c]1936, [d]1938　　　　　　　　　　　Ⓜ🅞🅞

A fine CD transfer of Walton's own premiere
recording of *Belshazzar's Feast* is coupled here
with two other important first recordings of his.
In some ways these have never been surpassed
musically. That applies especially to the *Belshazzar* performance, made with lavish resources
at the height of the war. The recording was
made over two weekends in 1943, in sessions
supervised by Walter Legge. The challenge of a
work then regarded as difficult for an amateur
choir was superbly taken, with Walton's conducting even more electric and impulsive than
in his later stereo version, and with Dennis
Noble unsurpassed as the baritone soloist. The
'writing on the wall' sequence has never
sounded creepier, despite the limitations of
mono sound, and the choral and brass sounds
are full and immediate, with the words of the
chorus commendably clear.

The *Facade Suites* in their orchestral form
stand among the demonstration recordings of
the period, while the premiere recording of the
Viola Concerto just as strikingly makes its
claims against any version recorded since. Even
more than William Primrose in his subsequent
recordings, Riddle brings expressive warmth as
well as tautness.

Additional recommendation

Coupled with: Job
Terfel *bass-bar;* **BBC Singers; BBC Symphony
Orchestra / A Davis**
Warner Apex 0927-44394-2 (78' · DDD)　　　Ⓑ
　Bryn Terfel makes an electrifying soloist in Davis's
　recommendable version of *Belshazzar*, and brings
　the important solo utterances vividly before us.
　Walton's rarely performed ballet is equally fine.

Coronation Te Deum

Coronation Te Deum. A Litany: Drop, drop slow tears.
Magnificat and Nunc Dimittis. Where does the
uttered music go? Jubilate Deo. Henry V – Touch her
soft lips and part; Passacaglia. Cantico del Sole. The
Twelve.Set me as a seal upon thy heart. Antiphon.
Missa brevis

Christopher Whitton *org* St John's College Choir,
Cambridge / Christopher Robinson
Naxos 8 555793 (66' · DDD) ⑤**OO**▷

This latest addition to Naxos's English Church Music series isn't just a first-rate bargain but provides a distinctive alternative to the Finzi Singers in the Chandos Walton Edition, in its use of boy trebles. The presence of boys' voices consistently brings extra freshness to the St John's Choir's performances, giving them the sort of bite one can imagine the composer having in mind, with Waltonian syncopations wonderfully idiomatic in their crisp articulation. Smaller in scale, with the organ set behind the choir, these more intimate readings also convey more clearly the impression of church performances, a clear advantage in the liturgical items above all, not just the delightful *Missa brevis*, but the *Jubilate*, and the *Magnificat and Nunc dimittis*. You might argue that this collegiate choir is on the small side for the big ceremonial *Te Deum* written for the Queen's Coronation in 1953, but there, more than ever, the freshness and bite make for extra clarity hard to achieve with bigger forces. With Robinson and the St John's Choir the words aren't just sharply defined but are given life, with subtle *rubato* and fine shading of dynamic.

Coronation Te Deum[ab]. A Queen's Fanfare[b]. A-Litany (three versions). The Twelve[a]. Set me as a-seal upon thine heart. Magnificat and Nunc Dimittis[a]. Where does the uttered music go? Jubilate Deo[a]. Missa Brevis[a]. Cantico del sole. Make we joy now in this fest. King Herod and the cock. All-this time. What cheer? Antiphon[ab]
[a]James Vivian *org* Polyphony; [b]The Wallace Collection / Stephen Layton
Hyperion CDA67330 (77' · DDD · T/N) Ⓕ**O**

This disc has important bonuses that all Walton devotees will value. The inclusion of The Wallace Collection brings an immediate advantage in the first choral item, the *Coronation Te Deum*, when the extra bite of brass adds greatly to the impact of a piece originally designed for very large forces in Westminster Abbey. Brass also adds to the impact of the final item, *Antiphon*, one of Walton's very last works, setting George Herbert's hymn *Let all the world in every corner sing*. The new disc also includes Walton's four carols, which makes this as comprehensive a collection of Walton's shorter choral pieces as could be imagined. As for the performances and recording, the professional group, Polyphony, with sopranos very boyish, have many of the advantages that the St John's Choir offer on Naxos in bright choral sound set in an ecclesiastical atmosphere. The acoustic of Hereford Cathedral is a little washy in places, and the balance of some of the solo voices is odd at times, yet the merits of these performances far outweigh any slight reservations, with the professional singers a degree more warmly expressive than the all-male St John's Choir.

Troilus and Cressida

Troilus and Cressida
Judith Howarth *sop* Cressida Arthur Davies *ten*
Troilus Clive Bayley *bass* Calkas Nigel Robson *ten*
Pandarus Alan Opie *bar* Diomede James Thornton
bar Antenor David Owen-Lewis *bass* Horaste
Yvonne Howard *mez* Evadne Peter Bodenham *ten*
Priest Keith Mills *ten* Soldier Bruce Budd *bass* First
Watchman Stephen Dowson *bass* Second
Watchman Brian Cookson *ten* Third Watchman
Chorus of Opera North; English Northern
Philharmonia / Richard Hickox
Chandos ② CHAN9370/1 (133' · DDD · N/T)
Ⓕ**OOO**▷

Ⓖ   *Troilus and Cressida* is here powerfully presented as an opera for the central repertory, traditional in its red-blooded treatment of a big classical subject. Few operas since Puccini's have such a rich store of instantly memorable tunes as this. Walton wrote the piece in the wake of the first great operatic success of his rival, Benjamin Britten. What more natural than for Walton, by this time no longer an *enfant terrible* of British music but an Establishment figure, to turn his back on operas devoted like Britten's to offbeat subjects and to go back to an older tradition using a classical love story, based on Chaucer (not Shakespeare). Though he was praised for this by critics in 1954, he was quickly attacked for being old-fashioned. Even in the tautened version of the score offered for the 1976 Covent Garden revival – with the role of the heroine adapted for the mezzo voice of Dame Janet Baker – the piece was described by one critic as a dodo. Yet as Richard Hickox suggests, fashion after 40 years matters little, and the success of the Opera North production in January 1995 indicated that at last the time had come for a big, warmly Romantic, sharply dramatic work to be appreciated on its own terms.

This recording was made under studio conditions during the run of the opera in Leeds. The discs confirm what the live performances suggested, that Walton's tautening of the score, coupled with a restoration of the original soprano register for Cressida, proved entirely successful.

Hickox conducts a performance that's magnetic from beginning to end. The scene is atmospherically set in Act 1 by the chorus, initially off-stage, but then with the incisive Opera North snapping out thrilling cries of 'We are accurs'd!'. The first soloist one hears is the High Priest, Calkas, Cressida's father, about to defect to the Greeks, and the role is superbly taken by the firm, dark-toned Clive Bayley. Troilus's entry and his declaration of love for Cressida bring Waltonian sensuousness and the first statements of the soaring Cressida theme. Arthur Davies isn't afraid of using his head voice for *pianissimos*, so contrasting the more dramatically with the big outbursts and his ringing top notes. This is a young-sounding hero, Italianate of tone. Similarly, Judith Howarth's Cressida is quite girlish, and she brings out the vulnerability of the character along with sweetness and warmth. After Calkas has defected to the Greeks, her cry of 'He has deserted us and Troy!' conveys genuine fear, with her will undermined. All told, although some fine music has been cut, the tautened version is far more effective both musically and dramatically, with no longueurs. The role of Diomede, Cressida's Greek suitor, can seem one-dimensional, but Alan Opie in one of his finest performances on record sharpens the focus, making him a genuine threat, with the element of nobility fully allowed. As Antenor, James Thornton sings strongly but is less steady than the others, while Yvonne Howard is superb in the mezzo role of Evadne, Cressida's treacherous servant and confidante. Not just the chorus but the orchestra of Opera North respond with fervour.

Naturally and idiomatically they observe the Waltonian *rubato* and the lifting of jazzily syncopated rhythms which Hickox as a dedicated Waltonian instils, echoing the composer's own example. As for the recorded sound, the bloom of the acoustic enhances the score, helped by the wide dynamic range.

Peter Warlock
British 1894-1930

Warlock was self-taught, though he was in contact with Delius from 1910, and was a friend of Van Dieren, Moeran and Lambert. Under his original name of Heseltine he wrote on music and edited English works of the Elizabethan era. As Warlock he produced a large output of songs, some dark, desolate and bleakly intense (The Curlew for tenor and sextet, 1922), others rumbustious, amorous or charming, but all informed by an exceptional sensitivity to words and high technical skill. He also wrote choral music and a few instrumental pieces (notably Capriol Suite for strings, 1926, based on 16th-century dances).
GROVEmusic

Choral Works

Warlock A Cornish Carol. I saw a fair maiden. Benedicamus Domino. The Full Heart. The Rich Cavalcade. Corpus Christi. All the flowers of the spring. As Dewe in Aprylle. Bethlehem Down. Cornish Christmas Carol **Moeran** Songs of Springtime. Phyllida and Corydon
Finzi Singers / Paul Spicer
Chandos CHAN9182 (76' · DDD · T) Ⓕ**O**

The Peter Warlock of the evergreen *Capriol Suite* and the boisterous songs seems a world away from the introverted and intense artist of these unaccompanied choral carols. Perhaps Warlock's real genius was an ability to create profound expression in short musical structures, but even the more outgoing pieces – the joyful *Benedicamus Domino* and the *Cornish Christmas Carol*, with its gentle hint at 'The First Nowell' – have an artistic integrity which raises them high above the level of the syrup of modern-day carol settings. Given performances as openly

sincere and sensitive as these, few could be unmoved. In the two Moeran madrigal suites there's an indefinable Englishness – the result of a deep awareness of tradition and love of the countryside. The Finzi Singers' warm-toned, richly expressive voices capture the very essence of this uniquely lovely music.

Songs

The Wind from the West. To the Memory of a F Great Singer. Take, o take those lips away. As ever I saw. The bayley berith the bell away. There is a lady. Lullaby. Sweet content. Late summer. The Singer. Rest sweet nymphs. Sleep. A Sad Song. In an arbour green. Autumn Twilight. I held love's head. Thou gav'st me leave to kiss. Yarmouth Fair. Pretty Ring Time. A Prayer to St Anthony. The Sick Heart. Robin Goodfellow. Jillian of Berry. Fair and True. Ha'nacker Mill. The Night. My Own Country. The First Mercy. The Lover's Maze. Cradle Song. Sigh no more, ladies. Passing by. The Contented Lover. The Fox
John Mark Ainsley ten **Roger Vignoles** pf
Hyperion CDA66736 (69' · DDD · T) Ⓕ**O**

Philip Heseltine, so strangely renamed, didn't facilitate either the singing or the playing of his songs. For the voice they have a way of passing awkwardly between registers, and, though the high notes aren't very high, they tend to be uncomfortably placed. The pianist, caught for long in a pool of chromatics, suddenly finds his hands flying in both directions. Yet, for the singer with the control of breath and command of voice that John Mark Ainsley so splendidly employs, and for a pianist with Roger Vignoles's sureness of touch and insight, they must be wonderfully satisfying, for there's such a love of song implicit in them and they speak with such a personal voice. The programme here is arranged chronologically, 1911-30. Favourite sources are early and Elizabethan poems, and the verse of contemporaries such as Belloc, Symons and Bruce Blunt. Even the earliest setting, *The Wind from the West*, has the characteristic touch of a lyrical impulse, directly responsive to words, and a fastidious avoidance of strophic or harmonic banality. Often a private unease works within the chromaticism, as in the *Cradle Song*, yet nothing could be more wholehearted in gaiety when he's in the mood (*In an arbour green, Robin Goodfellow, Jillian of Berry*). Ainsley sings with fine reserves of power as well as softness; he phrases beautifully, and all the nuance that's so essential for these songs (in 'Sleep', say) is most sensitively judged. Vignoles is entirely at one with singer and composer.

Carl Maria von Weber
German 1786-1826

Weber studied in Salzburg (with Michael Haydn), Munich (JN Kalcher)and Vienna (Abbé Vogler), becoming Kapellmeister at Breslau (1804) and working for a time at Württemberg (1806) and Stuttgart (1807). With help from Franz Danzi, intellectual stimulation from his friends Gänsbacher, Meyerbeer, Gottfried Weber and Alexander von Dusch and the encouragement of concert and operatic successes in Munich (especially Abu Hassan), Prague and Berlin, he settled down as opera director in Prague (1813-16). There he systematically reorganised the theatre's operations and built up the nucleus of a German company, concentrating on works, mostly French, that offered an example for the development of a German operatic tradition. But his searching reforms (extending to scenery, lighting, orchestral seating, rehearsal schedules and salaries) led to resentment. Not until his appointment as Royal Saxon Kapellmeister at Dresden (1817)and the unpre-cedented triumph of Der Freischütz (1821) in Berlin and throughout Germany did his championship of a true German opera win popular support. Official opposition continued, both from the Italian opera establishment in Dresden and from Spontini in Berlin; Weber answered critics with the grand heroic opera Euryanthe (1823, Vienna). His rapidly deteriorating health and his concern to provide for his family induced him to accept the invitation to write an English opera for London; he produced Oberon at Covent Garden in April 1826. Despite an enthusiastic English reception and every care for his health, this last journey hastened his decline; he died from tuberculosis, at 39.

Weber won his widest audience with Freischütz, outwardly a Singspiel celebrating German folklore and country life, using an idiom touched by German folksong. Through his skilful use of motifs and his careful harmonic, visual and instrumental designs notably for the Wolf's Glen scene, the outstanding example in music of the early Romantic treatment of the sinister and the supernatural – he gave this work a new creative status. Euryanthe, despite a weak libretto, further advances the unity of harmonic and formal structures, moving towards continuous, freely composed opera. In Oberon Weber reverted to separate numbers to suit English taste, yet the work retains his characteristically subtle motivic handling and depiction of both natural and supernatural elements. Of his other works, some of the German songs, the colouristic Konzertstück for piano and orchestra, the dramatic clarinet and bassoon concertos and the virtuoso Grand duo concertant for clarinet and piano deserve special mention. **GROVE**music

Clarinet Concertos

Clarinet Concertos – No 1; No 2. Clarinet Concertino. Clarinet Quintet (arr Kantorow)
Martin Fröst cl
Tapiola Sinfonietta / Jean-Jacques Kantorow
BIS ⬚ BIS-SACD1523 (74' · DDD/DSD)   Ⓕ➟

Martin Fröst's style of playing is well suited to Weber: he has a clear, fresh tone and fingers undefeated by even the most sensational of the applause music that ends some of these works. He is not afraid of considerable tempo variations within a movement, as Weber is on record as having wanted.

This all contributes to a charming, eloquent performance of the Concertino. However, the F minor Concerto (No 1) does not need its opening Allegro to be taken quite so fast for it to make its points, and the finale, here sounding like a brisk allegro verging on presto, is actually marked Allegretto, which gives the music more space and freedom. The slow movements of both concertos are played simply, without affectation, and Fröst remembers that the alla polacca of the finale of No 2 is a dance. He takes a bright lead in the Quintet; it is played here as a concerto with full strings, which is a pity but, given the quatuor concertant nature of the work, not as disastrous as it would be with Mozart. This is a fresh, amiable performance that responds to the music's varied nature.

Fröst also plays some cadenzas of his own, rejecting those which were later added by Carl Baermann, son of the much-admired dedicatee of the works, Heinrich Baermann. He further adds a few flourishes: unnecessarily, but there is no need to be too purist here. These are attractive, exhilarating performances, clearly recorded so as to do justice to the orchestral effects which were always part of Weber's exuberant invention.

Additional recommendation

Clarinet Concertos Nos 1 & 2. Clarinet Concertino. Clarinet Quintet
Kriikku cl **New Helsinki Qt**; **Finnish RSO / Oramo**
Ondine ODE895-2 (76' · DDD)   ⒻⒶ➟
The formidable difficulties hold no terrors for Kriikku. He plays the First Concerto as a slightly tense, witty work, giving the Adagio a long-breathed lyricism and the finale humour as well as wit. The Second Concerto is treated as a more lyrical and dramatic work, with an elegant polacca finale, and there's a beautiful length of phrasing in the Andante, as there is in the 'Fantasia' movement of the Quintet. Kriikku neatly touches off the mock-sinister intervention in the Quintet's finale, refusing to take it seriously.

Overtures

Overtures – Euryanthe, J291; Peter Schmoll und seine Nachbarn, J8; Oberon, J306; Der Beherrscher der Geister, J122; Preciosa, J279; Silvana, J87; Abu Hassan, J106; Der Freischütz, J277. Turandot – Overture and Act 2 March, J75. Jubel-Ouvertüre, J245
New Zealand Symphony Orchestra / Antoni Wit
Naxos 8 570296 (76' · DDD)   ⓈⒶ➟

Here are all six opera overtures, plus those for the incidental music to Preciosa and Turandot. The Ruler of the Spirits and Jubel are independent pieces, the latter celebratory and ending with a terrific orchestration of the tune we know as 'God Save the Queen', the former one of Weber's most brilliant pieces, one that really ought to feature more as a concert-opener. Antoni Wit goes at it with a will, and nimbly catches the good humour of the *Abu Hassan* overture, not least thanks to a lively oboe here and in *Peter Schmoll*. The orchestra also boasts a good horn section, very much called for in both *Oberon* and *Der Freischütz*. *Peter Schmoll* and *Silvana* are attractive examples of how early Weber began finding his voice as an orchestrator, in the case of *Schmoll* when still in his teens.

If only the sound were better, this would be an easy record to recommend. But as well as writing beautifully for wind, Weber makes demands on the richness and depth of the full orchestra and, especially in *Euryanthe* and *Oberon*, on the hurtling virtuosity of the strings. A crowded acoustic does not help clarity here, or in the busy figuration at the climax of *Jubel*. The seldom-played *Turandot*, with its quirky little oriental tune that caught Hindemith's ear for his *Weber Metamorphoses*, fares rather better.

Clarinet Quintet

Clarinet Quintet. Trio for Flute, Cello and Piano. Piano Quartet.
Gaudier Ensemble (Richard Hosford *cl* Jaime Martin *fl* Marieke Blankestijn, Lesley Hatfield *vns* Iris Juda *va* Christoph Marks *vc* Susan Tomes *pf*)
Hyperion CDA67464 (73' · DDD)   Ⓕ

Weber's three pieces of chamber music make an attractive record, and the performances here are responsive to the works' particular problems. With the early Piano Quartet, the young virtuoso set himself some tricky tests, especially in the matter of balance. In the complicated middle section of the *Adagio*, for instance, there are leaping violin phrases, *forte*, against soft *piano* chords with a viola murmuring away to itself *pianissimo* in the middle. It works well here. In Susan Tomes's hands, the Trio of the Minuet has a nice waltzing lilt and the finale blazes with energy. The players are willing to take liberties: though there is no warrant for the long *accelerando* in the finale of the Piano Trio, it is not the kind of thing Weber would have objected to, and both the pensive opening and the brooding melancholy of the 'Shepherd's Lament' are very much in the right spirit.

Richard Hosford is excellent in the Clarinet Quintet and is given a nice, clean acoustic for all the brilliant effects. There is, however, an oddity in the *Adagio* with the pairs of chromatic scales: the first, 'as loud as possible', is fine, but the second, pianissimo, is so quiet as to be barely audible, sounding as if it is drawn right away from the microphone. Hosford rounds it all off sensationally in the dazzling final pages. The only regret is that the players use the version, or something near it, prepared by the son of Weber's first performer, Heinrich Baermann. Carl Baermann claimed that this was the performing tradition but the evidence is insecure, and there is a good modern edition that comes closer to what must have been Weber's intentions. All the same, a very enjoyable disc.

Piano Sonatas

Piano Sonatas –No 1 in C, J138; No 2 in A flat, J199. Rondo brillante in E flat, J252, 'La gaité'. Invitation to the Dance, J260
Hamish Milne *pf*
CRD CRD3485 (76' · DDD)   Ⓜ●

Weber's piano music, once played by most pianists, has since suffered neglect and even the famous *Invitation to the Dance* is now more often heard in its orchestral form. Since he was a renowned pianist as well as a major composer, the neglect seems odd, particularly when other pianist composers such as Chopin and Liszt are at the centre of the concert repertory; but part of the trouble may lie in the difficulty of the music, reflecting his own huge hands and his tendency to write what the booklet-essay calls 'chords unplayable by others'. Hamish Milne makes out a real case for this music, and his playing of the two sonatas is idiomatic and resourceful, even if one can't banish the feeling that Weber all too readily used the melodic and harmonic formulae of 18th-century galanterie and simply dressed them up in 19th-century salon virtuosity. From this point of view, a comparison with Chopin's mature sonatas or Liszt's magnificent single essay in the form reveals Weber as a lightweight. A hearing of the first movement in the First Sonata will quickly tell you if this is how you may react, while in its Presto finale you may praise a Mendelssohnian lightness but also note a pomposity foreign to that composer. Leaving aside the musical quality of these sonatas, this is stylish playing which should win them friends. The *Rondo brillante* and *Invitation to the Dance* make no claim to be other than scintillating salon music, and are captivating in Milne's shapely and skilful performances. The recording is truthful and satisfying.

Lieder

Meine Lieder, meine Sänge, J73. Klage, J63. Der Kleine Fritz an seine jungen Freunde, J74. Was zieht zu deinem Zauberkreise, J86. Ich sah ein Röschen am Wege stehn, J67. Er an Sie, J57. Meine Farben, J62. Liebe-Glühen, J140. Über die Berge mit ungestüm, Op 25 No 2. Es stürmt auf der Flur, J161. Minnelied, J160. Reigen, J159. Sind es Schmerzen, J156. Mein Verlangen, J196. Wenn ich ein Vöglein war', J233. Mein Schatzerl ist hübsch, J234. Liebesgruss aus der Ferne, J257. Herzchen, mein Schätzchen, J258. Das Veilchen im Thale, J217. Ich denke dein, J48. Horch'!, Leise horch', Geliebte, J56. Elle était simple et gentilette, J292
Dietrich Fischer-Dieskau *bar* **Hartmut Höll** *pf*
Claves CD50-9118 (52' · DDD · T/t) Recorded 1991   Ⓕ●

'In my opinion the first and most sacred duty of a song-writer is to observe the maximum of fidelity to the prosody of the text that he is setting.' Weber was writing in defence of a number he composed for an obscure play, but his words can stand as an apologia for his 90-odd songs. His contribution to German song has been underrated, for his ideas were different from those of his contemporaries. Fischer-Dieskau used to resist suggestions that he might take up Weber's songs, and it's good that he has now done so, even late in his career. Always sensitive to words, he now responds with the subtlety of understanding that comes from many years of closeness to German poetry. Only very occasionally is there the powerful emphasis on the single expressive word that sometimes used to mar his interpretations, keeping them too near the surface of the poetry. He can still use individual colour marvellously: the tonal painting of 'blue', 'white' and 'brown' in *Meine Farben* is exquisitely done. But more remarkable, here and in other songs, is the manner in which he follows the novel melodic lines which Weber has contrived out of the poetry.

Ein steter Kampf is a masterly example; so is *Was zieht zu deinem Zauberkreise*, one of the few songs in which Weber enters Schubertian territory; so are *Es türmt auf der Flur* and *Liebesgruss aus der Ferne*. Not even Fischer-Dieskau can quite bring off the coy *Der Kleine Fritz* by slightly sending it up (the only hope), and there's something a bit hefty about *Reigen*, a very funny wedding song full of 'Heissa, lustig!' and 'Dudel, didel!', though Hartmut Höll does wonders with the clanking accompaniment. Höll varies his tone so much here from the warmth and depth of his touch elsewhere that one wonders if the engineers did not take a small hand: why not? These are charming, touching, witty, colourful verses, often by minor figures of Weber's circle, and they drew from him music that eightens their point. Fischer-Dieskau's intelligent artistry could not more eloquently support the praise for Weber from Wilhelm Müller, poet of *Die schöne Müllerin* and *Winterreise*, as 'master of German song'.

Der Freischütz

Der Freischütz
Peter Schreier *ten* Max (Hans Jörn Weber) **Gundula Janowitz** *sop* Agathe (Regina Jeske) **Edith Mathis** *sop* Aennchen (Ingrid Hille) **Theo Adam** *bass* Caspar (Gerhard Paul) **Bernd Weikl** *bar* Ottokar (Otto Mellies) **Siegfried Vogel** *bass* Cuno (Gerd Biewer) **Franz Crass** *bass* Hermit **Gerhard Paul** *spkr* Samiel **Günther Leib** *bar* Kilian (Peter Hölzel) **Leipzig Radio Chorus; Staatskapelle Dresden / Carlos Kleiber**
DG The Originals ② 457 736-2GOR2 (130' · ADD · T/t)
Recorded 1973
Ⓕ ❶❷❸

Carlos Kleiber's fine set of *Der Freischütz* earns reissue on CD for a number of reasons. One is the excellence of the actual recorded sound with a score that profits greatly from such attention. Weber's famous attention to details of orchestration is lovingly explored by a conductor who has taken the trouble to go back to the score in manuscript and observe the differences between that and most of the published versions. So not only do we hear the eerie sound of low flute thirds and

the subtle contrast of unmuted viola with four-part muted violins in Agathe's 'Leise, leise', among much else, with a new freshness and point, but all the diabolical effects in the Wolf's Glen come up with a greater sense of depth, down to the grisliest detail. The beginning of the Overture, and the opening of the Wolf's Glen scene, steal upon us out of a primeval silence, as they should. All this would be of little point were the performance itself not of such interest. There's a good deal to argue about but this is because the performance is so interesting. Even if some of Kleiber's tempos are possibly unwise, they spring from a careful, thoughtful and musical mind.

The singing cast is excellent, with Gundula Janowitz an outstanding Agathe to a somewhat reflective Max from Peter Schreier, at his best when the hero is brought low by the devilish machinations; Edith Mathis is a pretty Aennchen, Theo Adam a fine, murky Caspar. The dialogue, spoken by actors, is slightly abbreviated and occasionally amended. Kleiber's reading produces much new insight to a magical old score.

Der Freischütz
Eberhard Waechter *bar* Ottokar **Gundula Janowitz** *sop* Agathe **Renate Holm** *sop* Aennchen **Manfred Jungwirth** *bass* Cuno **Karl Ridderbusch** *bass* Caspar **James King** *ten* Max
Vienna State Opera Chorus and Orchestra / Karl Böhm
Orfeo d'Or ② C732 072I (129' · ADD · S/N)
Recorded live at the Wiener Staatsoper on May 28, 1972
Ⓕ

Karl Böhm's *Freischütz* (1972) that has the natural ease of born kinship. His playing of the overture sets the tone with sounds that breathe the sunlit forests; the Wolf's Glen scene tilts these into the lurking horror that is the dark side of the opera's coin.

The cast also inhabit their parts as if born into them. Gundula Janowitz floats her tone with ravishing effect in Agathe's 'Leise, leise' and in the later prayer, 'Und ob die Wolke'. Renate Holm sparkles alongside her, deliciously sending up the song about the 'ghostly' dog. Karl Ridderbusch is the blackest of Caspars, sinister yet not without a hint of pathos in this self-destroying soul. By the same token James King, much of whose career lay in German-speaking lands, has the heroic ring for Max but also the anxiety that has weakened his character. He earns the sonorous forgiveness of Franz Crass's Hermit. The smaller parts fit no less easily into this village community, Manfred Jungwirth making more than usual of Cuno.

There is a merry set of Bridesmaids, and Huntsmen who rejoice infectiously in the chase, though the Act 3 prelude anticipating their chorus is cut (so, reasonably, is a good deal of the dialogue). In the Wolf's Glen itself, there is too much in the way of shrieking winds and clattering hooves, when the music really does it all; but then this was a stage performance, and the scene meets with somewhat stunned applause. It never fails as a spine-chiller. Böhm handles everything beautifully, and unobtrusively, as if the work can be left to speak for itself, which of course is the art of real experience in the opera house. It is a most attractive performance. (The booklet excludes a text and translation.)

Anton Webern · Austrian 1883-1945

Webern studied at Vienna University under Adler (1902-6), taking the doctorate for work on Isaac; in composition he was one of Schoenberg's first pupils (1904-8), along with Berg. Like Berg, he developed rapidly under Schoenberg's guidance, achieving a fusion of Brahms, Reger and tonal Schoenberg in his orchestral Passacaglia, already highly characteristic in its modest dynamic level and its brevity. But he was closer than Berg in following Schoenberg into atonality, even choosing verses by the same poet, George, to take the step in songs of 1908-9. His other step was into a conducting career which he began with modest provincial engagements before World War I.

After the war he settled close to Schoenberg in Mödling and took charge of the Vienna Workers Symphony Concerts (1922-34). Meanwhile he had continued his atonal style, mostly in songs:the relatively few instrumental pieces of 1909-14 had grown ever shorter, ostensibly because of the lack of any means of formal extension in a language without key or theme. However, the songs of 1910-25 show a reintroduction of traditional formal patterns even before the arrival of serialism (especially canonic patterns, no doubt stimulated, as was the instrumentation of many of these songs, by Pierrot lunaire), to the extent that the eventual adoption of the 12-note method in the Three Traditional Rhymes (1925) seems almost incidental, making little change to a musical style that was already systematised by strict counterpoint. However, Webern soon recognised that the 12-note principle sanctioned a severity and virtuosity of polyphony that he could compare with that of the Renaissance masters he had studied. Unlike Schoenberg, he never again sought to compose in any other way. His use of the series as a source of similar motifs, especially in instrumental works, merely emphasises the almost geometrical perfection of this music, for which he found literary stimulus in Goethe and, more nearly, in the poetry of his friend and neighbour Hildegard Jone, whose words he set exclusively during his last dozen years. With Schoenberg gone, Berg dead and himself deprived of his posts, Webern saw Jone as one of his few allies during World War II. He was shot in error by a soldier after the end of hostilities, leaving a total acknowledged output of about three hours' duration. GROVEmusic

Complete works, Opp 1-31

Passacaglia, Op 1 (**London Symphony Orchestra / Pierre Boulez**). Entflieht auf leichten Kähnen, Op 2 (**John Alldis Choir / Boulez**). Five Songs from 'Der siebente Ring', Op 3. Five Songs, Op 4 (**Heather Harper** *sop* **Charles Rosen** *pf*). Five Movements, Op-5 (**Juilliard Quartet**). Six Pieces, Op 6 (**LSO /**

Boulez). Four Pieces, Op 7 (**Isaac Stern** *vn* **Rosen** *pf*). Two Songs, Op 8 (**Harper** *sop* **chamber ensemble / Boulez**). Six Bagatelles, Op 9 (**Juilliard Qt**). Five Pieces, Op 10 (**LSO / Boulez**). Three Little Pieces, Op 11 (**Gregor Piatigorsky** *vc* **Rosen** *pf*). Four Songs, Op 12 (**Harper** *sop* **Rosen** *pf*). Four Songs, Op 13. Six Songs, Op 14 (**Harper** *sop* **chamber ens / Boulez**). Five Sacred Songs, Op 15. Five Canons on Latin Texts, Op 16 (**Halina Lukomska** *sop* **chamber ens / Boulez**). Three Songs, Op 18 (**Lukomska** *sop* **John Williams** *gtr* **Colin Bradbury** *cl* **/ Boulez**). Two Songs, Op 19 (**John Alldis Ch, members LSO / Boulez**). String Trio, Op 20 (**members Juilliard Qt**). Symphony, Op 21 (**LSO / Boulez**). Quartet, Op 22 (**Robert Marcellus** *cl* **Abraham Weinstein** *sax* **Daniel Majeske** *vn* **Rosen** *pf* **/ Boulez**). Three Songs from 'Viae inviae', Op 23 (**Lukomska** *sop* **Rosen** *pf*). Concerto, Op 24 (**members LSO / Boulez**). Three Songs, Op 25 (**Lukomska** *sop* **Rosen** *pf*). Das Augenlicht, Op 26 (**John Alldis Ch, LSO / Boulez**). Piano Variations, Op 27 (**Rosen** *pf*). String Quartet, Op 28 (**Juilliard Qt**). Cantata No 1, Op 29 (**Lukomska** *sop* **John Alldis Ch; LSO / Boulez**). Variations, Op 30 (**LSO / Boulez**). Cantata No 2, Op 31 (**Lukomska** *sop* **Barry McDaniel** *bar* **John Alldis Ch; LSO / Boulez**). Five Movements, Op 5 – orchestral version (**LSO / Boulez**) **Bach** (orch Webern) Musikalischen Opfer, BWV1079 – Fuga (Ricercata) No 2 (**LSO / Boulez**) **Schubert** (orch Webern) Deutsche Tänze, D820 (**Frankfurt Radio Orchestra / Anton Webern**) (recorded live 1932) **Various artists**
Sony Classical ③ SM3K45845 (223' · ADD · T/t).
Recorded 1967-72 ⓂOOO

 Webern is as 'classic' to Boulez as Mozart or Brahms are to most other conductors, and when he's able to persuade performers to share his view the results can be remarkable – lucid in texture, responsive in expression. There are many sides to Webern, despite his well-nigh exclusive concern with miniature forms, and although this set isn't equally successful in realising them all, it leaves you in no doubt about the music's variety and emotional power, whether the piece is an ingenious canon-by-inversion or a simple, folk-like Lied. From a long list of performers one could single out Heather Harper and the Juilliard Quartet for special commendation; and the smooth confidence of the John Alldis Choir is also notable. The recordings were made over a five-year period, and have the typical CBS dryness of that time. Even so, in the finest performances which Boulez himself directs, that remarkable radiance of spirit so special to Webern is vividly conveyed. It's a fascinating bonus to hear Webern himself conducting his Schubert arrangements – music from another world, yet with an economy and emotional poise that Webern in his own way sought to emulate.

Passacaglia, Op 1

Webern Passacaglia. Five Pieces, Op 5. Six Pieces, Op 6. Im Sommerwind **Bach** (orch Webern) Musikalisches Opfer, BWV1079 –Ricercar a 6

Schubert (orch Webern) Deutsche Tänze, D820
Berlin Philharmonic Orchestra / Pierre Boulez
DG 447 099-2GH (67' · DDD)   Ⓕ**O**Ⓑ

With the exception of the Bach and Schubert arrangements, this is all relatively early, pre-serial Webern, yet Boulez devotes as much care and as much affection to the D minor *Passacaglia* and to the undeniably immature but irresistibly luscious *Im Sommerwind* as to the far more characteristic Op 5 and Op 6 pieces. Boulez doesn't imply that the mature Webern is present here in embryo; but he does perhaps make us ask how much of that later music is, like this, inspired by nature.

To be reminded of Brahms by the *Passacaglia* is no less appropriate. This is a Janus of a piece, looking back not only to Brahms's Fourth Symphony but beyond, and at the same time moving onwards from the delicate chamber passages in *Im Sommerwind* towards the 'orchestral chamber music' of Op 5 and Op 6. Boulez looks both ways too, with rich orchestral amplitude and expressive phrasing (very broad *rubato*) but he also notices Webern's already marked liking for transparent textures, quiet subtleties of string colour and the sound of the muted trumpet. And yes: heard in this context the shorter pieces are a logical progression. They are intensely expressive, with a wide range of emotion often within a few bars; no wonder Boulez prefers the earlier, richer scoring of Op 6. He obviously loves their Mahler-derived dissolution of the boundary between orchestral and chamber music, and encourages the orchestra to play with great tonal beauty. Those qualities recur in the Bach and Schubert arrangements. The recordings are warm and clean.

Five Pieces, Op 5

Webern String Quartet (arr Poppen). Five Pieces, Op 5. **Bach** Musical Offering, BWV1079 – Ricercar a 6 (orch Webern). Cantata No 4, Christ lag in Todes-banden, BWV4[a]
[a]**Hilliard Ensemble; Munich Chamber Orchestra / Christoph Poppen**
ECM New Series 461 912-2 (69' · DDD)   Ⓕ**OOO**Ⓑ

Ⓖ   Symmetry, the cyclic evolution of a musical germ and the idea of birth in the midst of death: all are fundamental to this disc. Webern's motivically determined orchestration of the Ricercar from Bach's late *The Musical Offering*, where single lines change colour by the bar, opens and closes the programme. Christoph Poppen's orchestration of Webern's 1905 String Quartet soars and surges with an ardour that befits this early but significant masterpiece. Like Webern in Bach, Poppen knows how and where to taper his forces, while his players respond with obvious dedication. Bach's Cantata *Christ lag in Todesbanden* grows, as Herbert Glossner reminds us, from a 'primordial cell' of a single semitone motive. Eight stanzas each end with a 'Halleluja', as unalike in shade and meaning as the strands of Webern's 'Ricercar', so magnificent is the young Bach's handling of the

texts. Poppen performs choral Bach with single voices; he also encourages a string playing style that largely dispenses with vibrato, so that when you cross from Webern's Quartet to Bach's BWV4 you could as well be switching to a period performance. The Hilliards sing beautifully, both solo and in ensemble, and the balance between voices and instruments is impeccable.

Some might balk at the sudden eruption of Webern's violent 'Heftig betwegt' on the heels of Bach's closing 'Halleluja', but the musical sense of having five 'symmetrical' Movements for String Quartet fall within the greater symmetry of the programme as a whole overrides any initial discomfort. Again, Poppen's finely tooled reading focuses in precise detail the mood and texture of each miniature so that the eventual return of Bach-Webern is indeed like a profound thought revisited by a changed mind.

Thomas Weelkes   English 1575?-1623

He was one of the most gifted of the madrigalists, and a major composer of English church music. As a vocal composer Weelkes's main deficiencies were a lack of response to the sound of words themselves, and uneven melodic invention. As a madrigalist he could not match Wilbye's ability for making his individual lines grow around the verbal phrase, and he lacked that composer's sensitive ear for the textural variety which may enhance the poetic shadings of the text; nor did he share Gibbons's mastery of vocal declamation. Weelkes's great strength lay in the vivid inventiveness of his very calculated musical imagery, and the commanding brilliance of a fully developed contrapuntal technique whose roots are more English than Italian.   GROVEmusic

O Jonathan. Rejoice in the Lord. All people, clap your hands. Te Deum & Jubilate (Eighth Service). O how amiable are thy dwellings. Christ Rising Again. When David Heard. Laboravi in gemitu meo. Magnificat & Nunc dimittis (Third Service). O vos omnes. Lord, to Thee I make my moan. Give ear, O Lord. Hosanna to the Son of David
Tewkesbury Abbey Schola Cantorum / Benjamin Nicholas
Delphian DCD34070 (60' · DDD)   Ⓕ

There remains an intensity of passionate utterance in the most striking of Weelkes's works, balanced by a sober moderation in much else. He himself, as we learn from contemporary accounts, was not characterised by either moderation or sobriety, at least in his latter years, coming to his choir 'from the Taverne or Ale house' cursing and swearing 'most dreadfully'. You would never guess as much from the decorous verse anthems and evening canticles, but the intensity of the lament *O Jonathan*, which opens the present recital, might suggest a less bridled temperament, as might the concentrated fervour of *Hosanna to the Son of David*, which closes it.

Under Benjamin Nicholas, director of Tewkesbury Abbey's Schola Cantorum, the choir has
developed a strong style, remarkable for its
sense of personal (or corporate) commitment as
for the sonority of its tone and the assurance of
its delivery. The trebles splendidly vindicate the
tradition that places them at the heart of English
cathedral music. The men's voices are also powerful and resonant and the total effect is rich and
forthright. If anything, the 'standard' level of
volume is set too high – it is not until the sixth
item, *O bow amiable are thy dwellings*, that we find
reassurance that the choir can sing quietly. Fine
solo work and neat organ-playing are further
assets, as is the introductory note by Dr Peter
James.

Kurt Weill   German/American 1900-1950

Weill was a pupil of Humperdinck, Busoni and Jar-
nach in Berlin (1918-23); their teaching informed
his early music, including the choral Recordare
(1923) and the Concerto for violin and wind (1924),
the latter also influenced by Stravinsky. But the
deeper influence of Stravinsky, coupled with an
increased consciousness of music as a social force, led
him to a rediscovery in the mid-1920s of tonal and
vernacular elements, notably from jazz, in his can-
tata Der neue Orpheus and one-act stage piece Royal
Palace, written between two collaborations with the
expressionist playwright Georg Kaiser: Der Prota-
gonist and Der Zar lässt sich photographieren. In
1926 he married the singer Lotte Lenya, who was to
be the finest interpreter of his music.

His next collaborator was Brecht, with whom he
worked on The Threepenny Opera (1928), The Rise
and Fall of the City of Mahagonny (1929) and Happy
End (1929), all of which use the corrupted, enfeebled
diatonicism of commercial music as a weapon of social
criticism, though paradoxically they have beome the
epitome of the pre-war culture they sought to despise.
Yet this is done within the context of a new harmonic
consistency and focus. These works have also drawn
attention from the theatre works in which Weill devel-
oped without Brecht during the early 1930s, Die
Bürgschaft and Der Silbersee (with Kaiser again).

In 1933 he left Germany for Paris, where he
worked with Brecht again on the sung ballet The
Seven Deadly Sins. Then in 1935 he moved to the
USA, where he cut loose from the European art-
music tradition and devoted himself wholeheartedly
to composing for the Broadway stage. GROVEmusic

Symphonies

Symphonies No 1 & 2. Lady in the Dark – Symphonic
Nocturne (arr R Russell Bennett)
Bournemouth Symphony Orchestra / Marin Alsop
Naxos 8 557481 (74' · DDD)   ⑤🅑

Weill's Symphony No 2 is one of his most important works but it is not music calculated to cheer
one up. Commissioned by the Princesse de Polig-

nac in 1933, Weill completed it during the
months immediately following his flight from
Germany, after the Nazi seizure of power. Coming just after *Der Silbersee* and *Die sieben Todsünden*,
it has a number of thematic similarities to those
works but also seems to hint at some of Weill's
later music, composed in America. A deeply pessimistic piece in its first two movements, it nevertheless ends on a questioning note that may
express hope, or at least the energy to continue.
The Bournemouth Symphony Orchestra under
Marin Alsop give a satisfying performance.

For those who already possess versions of the
ballet-chanté or the concerto, Alsop's programme
may be more alluring. She achieves quite a triumph with the very early single-movement First
Symphony, a student work never performed in
the composer's lifetime: it's rarely played as
confidently as here. The suite from *Lady In the
Dark* is just a curiosity; without Ira Gershwin's
lyrics the tunes don't sound particularly enticing. At least, though, it lightens the mood after
some pretty relentless gloom. Excellent clear
sound, at Naxos's price an easy recommendation.

Aufsteig und Fall der Stadt Mahagonny

Aufsteig und Fall der Stadt Mahagonny
Dame Gwyneth Jones sop Leokadja Begbick **Roy
Cornelius Smith** ten Fatty **Wilbur Pauley** bass Trinity
Moses **Catherine Malfitano** sop Jenny Smith **Jerry
Hadley** ten Jimmy Mahoney **Udo Holdorf** ten Jake
Schmidt **Dale Duesing** bar Pennybank Bill **Harry
Peeters** bass Alaska Wolf Joe **Toby Spence** ten
Tobby Higgins **Vienna State Opera Chorus; Vienna
Radio Symphony Orchestra / Dennis Russell
Davies**
Stage director **Peter Zadek**
Video director **Brian Large**
ArtHaus Musik 🆅 100 092 (160' · 16:9 · 2.0 · 2, 5)   Ⓕ

Peter Zadek's production of Weill, and Brecht's
largest-scale opera, was much criticised in 1998.
It's possible to see in this DVD version that the
Salzburg stage is really too big for the work, and
that there's rather a lot of unnecessary action,
much coming and going, walking about, and
movement of furniture. However, Brian Large's
filmed production makes such good use of close-
ups that much of this is bypassed.

What makes this unmissable is Jerry Hadley's
performance as Jim. From every point of view,
dramatic, vocal and emotional, he encompasses
the part so completely that you're totally
gripped. The tension in his pose, his burning
eyes, the physical daring of the interpretation
command attention at every turn. At the end of
Act 2, when Jenny sings 'Denn wie man sich bet-
tet', Catherine Malfitano declaims the first verse
as she's carried on Hadley's shoulders. Although
the camera and the microphone are both harsh
where Malfitano is concerned, she too gives
such an involved and committed reading of the
part that one has to forgive everything.

At no moment in her career would Gwyneth

Jones's voice have been suitable for the role of the Widow Begbick, but she too is fascinating to watch, under-playing most of the time, so that when the trial scene arrives, the extra cruel edge she gives to gesture and song tells all the more. The other tremendous performance comes from Wilbur Pauley as a totally repellent Trinity Moses – his pose, Christ-like, after he's killed Joe in the boxing scene is horrific.

Dennis Russell Davies conducts a searing account of the score from the pit. The balance between voices and orchestra is sometimes very echoey, but this is inevitable on a stage as cavernous as Salzburg's.

The Seven Deadly Sins

Die sieben Todsünden[a]. Berlin im Licht[b]. La complainte de la Seine[b]. Es regnet[b]. Nannas Lied, 'Meine Herren, mit siebzehn Jahren'[b]. Youkali[b]. Wie lange noch?[b]
Brigitte Fassbaender mez [a]**Hans Sojer**, [a]**Karl-Heinz Brandt** tens [a]**Hidenori Komatsu** bar [a]**Ivan Urbas** bass [a]**North German Radio Philharmonic Orchestra, Hanover / Cord Garben** [b]pf
Harmonia Mundi HMA195 1420 (55' · DDD)   Ⓢ

Kurt Weill composed *La complainte de la Seine* in 1934, while he was living in France. It was first sung and recorded by Lys Gauty. In the introduction to the first verse, Weill weaves in a quote from the marching theme at the end of *Die sieben Todsünden*. The two are neatly linked here, as Brigitte Fassbaender sings the chanson directly after the *ballet-chanté*. Of all the opera singers who have recorded *The Seven Deadly Sins*, Fassbaender's has always been a favourite. She sings it in the original, higher key, and although some of the tempi chosen by Cord Garben seem a little slow, Fassbaender's luscious mezzo invests the work with a superb sense of world-weariness. All the other songs come from the cache of unpublished work that we first got to know in 1982 through Teresa Stratas's 'The Unknown Kurt Weill' (Nonesuch). Stratas gives the songs more urgency; Fassbaender seems relaxed by comparison, which is not to say that she doesn't extract every last ounce of irony from the lyrics, including one unique contribution from Jean Cocteau (*Es regnet*). The original issue had full texts and translations; here there are merely synopses. Nevertheless, at its modest price, this is highly recommended.

Street Scene

Street Scene
Ashley Putnam sop Anna Maurrant **Marc Embree** bar Frank Maurrant **Teri Hansen** sop Rose Maurrant **Kip Wilborn** ten Sam Kaplan **Claudia Ashley** sop Nursemaid 1 **Muriel Costa-Greenspon** mez Nursemaid 2 **Yvette Bonner** sop Jennie Hildebrand **David Rae Smith** ten Abraham Kaplan **Janice Felty** mez Emma Jones **Heidi Eisenberg** mez Olga Olsen **Anthony Mee** ten Lippo Fiorentino **Ludwigshafen**

Theatre Chorus; Rhineland Palatinate State Philharmonic Orchestra / James Holmes
Stage director **Francesca Zambello**
Film director **José Montes-Baquer**
ArtHaus Musik 📀 100 098 (143' · 16:9 · 2.0 · 2 & 5)
Recorded 1994   Ⓕ

Street Scene was the most ambitious product of Weill's American years. It's a kind of *Porgy and Bess* transferred to the slum tenements of New York during the Depression, mixing genuine operatic writing with unashamedly popular numbers. It's essentially a team opera, with many roles, portraying the ups and downs of urban life, including childbirth and death.

Ashley Putnam is visually too young for the role of Anna, perhaps, but vocally outstanding in her solo numbers. Teri Hansen initially sounds a shade constricted as her daughter Rose, but she's tender enough in her duet with Kip Wilborn as her lover Sam. Marc Embree is suitably menacing as husband Frank, Janice Felty a strong Emma, and Anthony Mee a delightful roly-poly Neapolitan. An undoubted star of the production is designer Adrienne Lobel, against whose magnificently solid and realistic set the action unfolds. Another is James Holmes, who brings out the score's darker, dramatic moments as much as its unashamed romanticism and jazz-inflected numbers.

This production reveals what a wonderful work it is – convincing both for its extended operatic writing and its marvellous tunes.

Mieczysław Weinberg
Polish/Russian 1919-1996

Also known by his Jewish name Moisei Samuilovich Vainberg, he studied at the Warsaw Conservatoire, and after moving to the USSR continued his studies at the coservatoire in Minsk. He wrote a lot of music, including 22 symphonies, 17 string quartets, and seven operas.

Clarinet Concerto, Op 104[a]. Fantasia, Op 52[b]. Flute Concertosc – No 1, Op 75; No 2, Op 148
[c]**Anders Jonhäll** fl [a]**Urban Claesson** cl
[b]**Claes Gunnarsson** vc
Gothenburg Symphony Orchestra / Thord Svedlund
Chandos 🅜 CHSA5064 (79' · DDD)   Ⓕ Ⓞ ➡

Appreciation of the Polish-born Mieczysław Weinberg has increased markedly over recent years. This collection of four concertos covers a fair proportion of the composer's maturity. The Cello Fantasia (1953) is a deftly through-composed design recalling the Myaskovsky Concerto in a melodic directness that yet conceals considerable expressive depths. The flute concertos are both lighter in content though not necessarily in manner: No 1 (1961) places its ruminative passacaglia between movements whose effervescence is often tempered by the ambivalent strains of klezmer, while No 2 (1987) places a brooding

Largo between an *Allegro* that elides, Nielsen-like, between its frequently conflicting ideas and a finale whose valedictory allusions to the music of others are fitting in the context of one of Weinberg's last works.

Yet it is the Clarinet Concerto (1970) that is the real discovery here. On a substantial scale, it allows the soloist subtle dominance against a string orchestra that, in the first movement, evinces a sparseness often redolent of (though not indebted to) late Shostakovich and which, in the Andante, blends austerity with poetry to touching effect – before a finale whose dancing gait prevails in the face of more disruptive elements. The soloists are finely attuned to their respective concertos, and Thord Svedlund secures an incisive response from his Gothenburg forces. Excellent sound and a welcome addition to the Weinberg discography.

Judith Weir   British b1954

Weir studied composition with John Tavener and Robin Holloway before teaching for sxi years at the University of Glasgow and the RSAMD. Her music, at once approachable but never bland, has earned her numerous major commissions that include three operas and symphonic works. From 1995 to 1998 she was the CBSO's Composer in Association; and from 1995 to 2000 she was the Artistic Director of the Spitalfields Festival in London. Weir frequently exploits music's ability to paint a scene or to function as an illustrative backdrop. In an onomatopoeic sense this is deftly achieved in the engaging The Consolations of Scholarship (later incorporated, as a play-within-a-play device, in A Night at the Chinese Opera). At a deeper level Act 2 of Blond Eckbert, in a strategy that follows the example of Janáček and Britten's Peter Grimes, the orchestra's own commentary plays a crucial role in the intensification of the psychological drama.   **GROVE**music

---

Operas

Blond Eckbert
Nicholas Folwell *bar* Blond Eckbert **Nerys Jones**
sop Bird **Anne-Marie Owens** *mez* Berthe
Christopher Ventris *ten* Walther, Hugh, Old Woman
**English National Opera Chorus and Orchestra /
Sian Edwards**
NMC Ancora NMCD106 (65' · DDD · S/T)   Ⓕ

Ludwig Tieck's novella *Der Blonde Eckbert* (1796) is a dark tale of incest and despair made even darker by the ironic framework of a bird's song extolling the peaceful solitude that can be found in nature. Judith Weir, writing her own libretto, has seized on this essential contrast. While her bird sings eloquently, joyfully, her human characters articulate their growing awareness of the horrors that surround them in lines that are questing, often aggressive, though never shorn of the kind of lyricism that best represents vulnerability.

Unfolding over just 65 minutes to an ending suffused with a spirit of tragic radiance, the opera is a gripping, harrowing experience, and admiration of ENO for commissioning it is tempered only by regret at their failure to revive on a regular basis a work of such intense theatricality and musical approachability.

This recording (originally issued by Collins Classics) is not of one of the Coliseum performances but was made for a TV film shown on Channel 4. The balance strongly favours the voices and although most of the pungent, imaginative orchestral details still come across – with the use of brass and woodwind especially telling – the sound highlights a certain lack of nuance in Nicholas Folwell's account of the principal role and conveys little sense of stage movement or action. Nevertheless, Folwell and the rest of the small cast are persuasive, and the music is so immediate in its evocation of pastoral enchantment and menace that any studio-bound quality is far less of a hindrance than would often be the case.

The Consolations of Scholarship[a]. King Harald's Saga[b]. Piano Concerto[c]. Musicians Wrestle Everywhere[d]
[a]**Janice Felty** *mez* [b]**Judith Kellock** *sop* [c]**Xak Bjerken** pf **Ensemble X /** [bcd]**Mark Davis Scatterday,** [a]**Steven Stucky**
Albany TROY803 (65' · DDD · S/N)   Ⓕ

A 'grand opera in three acts' for a single unaccompanied soprano, lasting less than 15 minutes? You expect *King Harald's Saga* to be a joke, and there are indeed moments where the music seems to be echoing celebrated operatic extravagances, like Baba the Turk's cadenzas in Stravinsky's *The Rake's Progress*. But one of Judith Weir's great strengths is that she can combine irony with genuine depth of feeling, and in this early (1979) demonstration of benign iconoclasm she sets out a distinctive and appealing perspective on those alternatives to grand opera which music theatre has been exploring for most of the past century. Judith Kellock gives a finely judged performance.

Written six years later, *The Consolations of Scholarship* turns from Icelandic sagas to 14th-century Chinese plays. Here the singer is supported by a nine-strong instrumental ensemble which relishes the kind of bold, pungent textures that Weir would soon develop in her first 'proper' stage work, *A Night at the Chinese Opera* (1987). Indeed, so powerful is the instrumental writing that the voice's contribution – alternating between speech and song – sometimes has to struggle to cut through. A more forward balance for the otherwise excellent Janice Felty might have helped.

This admirable disc is completed by a pair of instrumental works from the mid-1990s. Appropriately, in view of its title, taken from American poet Emily Dickinson, *Musicians Wrestle Everywhere* reveals Weir at her most streetwise, the shapely modal lines and sharply delineated rhythms, as well as the wind-dominated scoring, suggesting a host of allusions ranging from Copland to John Adams and Louis Andriessen. The Piano Concerto is another exercise in puncturing pretension, making strong points about how both lyrical and brittle textures can interact with folklike idioms in ways where nothing seems diluted or bland. Exemplary performances given resonant recordings, and strongly recommended.

Egon Wellesz
Austrian 1885-1974

Wellesz was a pupil of Schoenberg and Adler like his close friend Webern. Unlike Webern, though, he continued to pursue both creative and scholarly activities, before and after his move to England in 1938, where he lectured at Oxford from 1943. He did important, far-reaching work on Venetian opera, Viennese Baroque music and Byzantine chant, especially notation and hymnography; his compositions cover many genres and extend from a Schoenbergian style towards Bruckner (especially in the nine symphonies 1945-71, his major works in England), BartÜk (in his chamber music, which includes a fine octet, 1949, a Clarinet Quintet, 1959, nine string quartets, 1912-66) or Strauss (in the operas, notably Alkestis, 1924, Die Bakchantinnen, 1931, and Incognita, 1951). GROVE music

Symphonies

Symphonies – No 4, 'Sinfonia Austriaca', Op 70; No 6, Op 95; No 7, 'Contra torrentem', Op 102
Vienna Radio Symphony Orchestra /
Gottfried Rabl
CPO CPO999 808-2 (71' · DDD)   Ⓕ

Like his near-contemporaries Ernst Toch and Havergal Brian, Wellesz came late to the symphony, composing his first (1945), inspired by memories of Austria, at the age of 60. No 4 (1951-53) had similar inspiration and bears the soubriquet *Sinfonia Austriaca*. Although Wellesz used atonality or serialism throughout his life, he also used tonality if he felt it appropriate, mixing the disciplines as his expressive purposes demanded. No 4 is a case in point, essentially a pastoral (albeit vigorously so) tonal symphony employing varying degrees of 'free tonality' throughout, especially in the intense *Adagio*.

Wellesz's later symphonies employ a slow-fast-slow design, the slow outer spans tending to be varied in pulse, encasing vigorous central *scherzi*. No 6 (1965) is perhaps his best known, having been broadcast a few times over the years. A riveting work, it's one of his finest utterances, showcasing his mastery of symphonic cogency, formal construction and orchestration. As in the late symphonies of Vaughan Williams, Wellesz was constantly refining and exploring his sound world: if the harmonic language of the Fourth is the most accessible to general listeners, the orchestration of the terser Seventh

(1967) makes the earlier work seem pallid by comparison. Very strongly recommended.

String Quartets

String Quartets – No 3; No 4; No 6
Artis Quartet (Peter Schuhmayer, Johannes Meissl *vns* Herbert Kefer *va* Othmar Müller *vc*)
Nimbus NI5821 (63' · DDD)   Ⓕ

Viennese composer Egon Wellesz was very much a product of his times. Mahler's conducting was an early influence, while Schoenberg and von Hofmannsthal were influential associates. Once Hitler's hordes had conquered Europe he landed in Oxford where he became a Reader in Byzantine music. For a while the trauma of exile blocked Wellesz's creative impulse but he recovered well, and by the time of his death in 1972 had clocked up an impressively varied output. The quartets cover the length and breadth of Wellesz's career, the earliest here, the Third (1918), reflecting key Romantic and 'Impressionist' influences, the turbulent second movement starting out in the manner of Chausson, the rest more indebted perhaps to Debussy and early Schoenberg. There's also, in the fugal passages of the finale, a hint of Max Reger's playful counterpoint.

The curve of Wellesz's development reflects a trend similar to many of his contemporaries: early romanticism gives way, in the 1920s and beyond, to confrontational modernism eventually leading to a cooler, post-classical style. The Fourth Quartet (1922) is terse, aphoristic and tautly argued, each of its five movements shorter in length than you might expect, its style intense and inscrutable. Calum MacDonald's invaluable note suggests an audible prophecy of Berg's *Lyric Suite* and there some telling similarities to Bartók too.

The Sixth Quartet (1947) opens like a homage to Beethoven's *Coriolan* Overture and the classical axis remains in place more or less throughout, especially in the middle movements. Performance-wise one could hardly ask for more in the way of dedication or perception.

Samuel Sebastian Wesley
British 1810-1876

A grandson of Charles Wesley, the founder of Methodism, SS Wesley is one of the most significant composer of hymns. Between 1832 and his death he was organist at four different cathedrals.

Ascribe unto the Lord. Blessed be the God and Father. Cast me not away from Thy presence. Let us lift up our heart. O give thanks unto the Lord. Thou wilt keep him in perfect peace. Wash me throughly from my wickedness. The Wilderness and the solitary place. O God, whose nature and property
Choir of Clare College, Cambridge /

Christopher Robinson with **James McVinnie** org
Naxos 8 570318 (75' · DDD) ⓢⓞⓞ🅓►

There are few lovelier anthems than Wesley's *Thou wilt keep him in perfect peace*; *Cast me not away* is worthy to stand with Purcell's *Hear my prayer*; and among his larger choral compositions *The Wilderness* retains an enviable place in the service-lists. For those who know *Ascribe unto the Lord* there will be many more for whom its final chorus, 'The Lord hath been mindful of us', is a firm favourite, satisfying in structure, vigorous in counterpoint, and sporting as its main themes two of the best melodies in the chorister's repertoire.

The Choir of Clare College, which many will remember for their fresh and accomplished singing under John Rutter, is here directed by Christopher Robinson, than whom none better. The Robinson touch is manifest in the marvellous phrase 'that the bones which thou hast broken may rejoice' (*Cast me not away*). Poor old Wesley had injured his in a fishing accident: he writes feelingly and the choir are with him. The 'ransomed of the Lord' passage in *The Wilderness* has terrific energy. And the soprano soloist in 'And sorrow and sighing' sings like an angel.

Charles-Marie Widor French 1844-1937

Best known today for the closing Toccata of his Fifth Symphony, Widor was one of the most influential organists and composers for the instrument of the 19th century. In 1869 became the organist at St Sulpice in Paris, where he remained until 1934. In 1890 Widor succeeded Franck as organ professor at the Paris Conservatoire; among his pupils was Albert Schweitzer. He wrote 10 symphonies for all which call for an almost pianistic virtuosity.

Symphonies – No 9, 'Gothic'[a]; No 10, 'Roman'[b]
Jeremy Filsell org
ASV CDDCA1172 (63' · DDD)
Played on the organs of [a]St George's Chapel, Windsor, and [b]Liverpool Metropolitan Cathedral Ⓕ

Jeremy Filsell rounds off ASV's series of the Widor symphonies with the two final and, some would say, most austere symphonies, and the disc is most welcome. Less welcome is the choice of St George's Chapel, Windsor, for No 9. It's a lovely organ and makes a huge noise, and the recording does it full justice. But it is so manifestly not French that it's had to understand why it's been used. Of course great music transcends the limitations of national characteristics but Widor's symphonies are so perfectly tailored to the unique sounds of a Cavaillé-Coll that to chose an instrument which is the very antithesis seems perverse. With the first movement we have the impression of a genial and portly uncle trying, without much success, to sound both stern and angry, while with the charming second movement, the warm, glutinous wash of sound is (like the booklet-notes) so

self-indulgent that it clouds the musical message.

Against this the Liverpool Metropolitan organ (for the Tenth Symphony) comes like a breath of fresh air, and while much of the detail is lost in the swimming-bath-like acoustic, with Filsell's wonderfully focused playing we do have a conclusion to this series which is both musically convincing and a pleasure to listen to.

Henryk Wieniawski Polish 1835-1880

After studying at the Paris Conservatoire Wieniawski embarked on the career of a travelling virtuoso, giving concerts in Russia, Germany, Paris and London. At the bidding of Anton Rubinstein he settled in St Petersburg (1860-72) and exerted a decisive influence on the growth of the Russian violin school. Meanwhile he composed his best works including the demanding Etudes-caprices op.18, the Polonaise brillante op.21 and his masterpiece, the Second Violin Concerto in D minor op.22. Further world travels, notably to the USA and Russia, and a period as violin professor at the Brussels Conservatory (1875-7) contributed to the breakdown of his health. One of the most important violinists of the generation after Paganini, he was known for the emotional quality of his tone. As a composer he combined the technical advances of Paganini with Romantic imagination and Slavonic colouring, showing Polish nationalism in his mazurkas and polonaises. His brother Józef (1837-1912) was an accomplished pianist who taught in Moscow, Warsaw and Brussels; their nephew Adam (1879-1950) was a director of the Chopin Music School in Warsaw. GROVEmusic

Violin Concerto No 1

Wieniawski Violin Concerto No 1 in F sharp minor, Op 14[b] **Beach** Romance, Op 23[a] *Debussy* Préludes – La fille aux cheveux de lin (arr A Hartmann)[a] **Elgar** Chanson de nuit, Op 15 No 1[a] **Kreisler** La Gitana[a] **Poldini** Marionnettes – Poupée valsante (arr Kreisler)[a] **Prokofiev** Tales of an Old Grandmother, Op 31 (arr Milstein)[a] – Andantino; Andante assai
Midori vn [a]**Robert McDonald** pf
[b]**St Louis Symphony Orchestra / Leonard Slatkin**
Sony Classical SK89700 (52' · DDD) Ⓕⓞ🅑►

Wieniawski's First Violin Concerto has never matched No 2 in popularity, but Midori's involving performance makes one wonder why. Put it alongside Perlman's EMI version with the LPO under Ozawa, and – perhaps not surprisingly – her live account sounds more volatile and more freely expressive, with even the conventional passage-work given an extra sparkle. She also chooses a more flowing *Larghetto* for the central 'Preghiera' (Prayer) slow movement, which brings out the songful lyricism more persuasively, with her first entry magically hushed, full of natural gravity. The dotted rhythms of the Rondo finale are then even more playful. The radio recording is full and forwardly balanced, but the range of dynamic and expression in Midori's playing is never compromised.

In the encore pieces, the range of dynamic is again remarkable. She plays the opening item, Hartmann's arrangement of Debussy's 'La fille aux cheveux de lin', with such delicacy she seems simply to be musing to herself, and her simple gravity in Elgar's *Chanson de nuit*, the last item, taken steadily, turns it into a sort of prayer. Such an approach could easily have lapsed into sentimentality, but emphatically not so here. A thoroughly enjoyable disc.

Hugo Wolf
Austrian 1860-1903

Wolf played the violin, piano and organ as a child and studied briefly at the Vienna Conservatory (1875-7, meeting his idol Wagner) but, lacking discipline and direction, he had to rely on friends and cultured benefactors for help and introductions. His first important works, the songs of 1877-8, arose from the effects of his sexual initiation and first romantic attachment. Some are bright, others agonised, reflecting his depression and illness from a syphilitic infection. Though in 1880 this cloud seemed to abate, a pattern of cyclic mood swing and sporadic creativity was already established. Holidays, studies of Wagner and radiant song settings alternated with personal estrangements and a dark, dramatic strain in his music. For three years (1884-6), he wrote trenchant musical criticism for the Wiener Salonblatt, siding with Wagner and against Brahms, meanwhile working on Penthesilea (1883-5) and the D minor Quartet (1878-84)and beginning a secret love affair with Melanie Köchert. Compositional mastery and a sense of purpose came only in the late 1880s, when he turned from subjectivity to imaginative literature as a stimulus. In 1888 Eichendorff's poetry and in particular Mörike's inspired a sudden flowering of song music that in profusion and variety matched Schubert and Schumann. His acclaimed public performances won new converts, and in February 1889 he finished the 51 songs of the Goethe songbook, in April 1890 the 44 Spanish songs. Publication and critical recognition turned his thoughts to opera but from 1891 physical exhaustion and depressive phases stemmed the flow of original music. In 1895 he composed his only completed opera, Der Corregidor, but it was unsuccessful; in 1897 he composed his last songs and had the mental breakdown that led to his terminal illness.

Wolf's strength was the compression of large-scale forms and ideas – the essences of grand opera, tone poem and dramatic symphony – into song. Combining expressive techniques in the piano part with an independent vocal line, and using an array of rhythmic and harmonic devices to depict textual imagery, illustrate mood and create musical structure, he continued and extended the lied tradition of Schubert and Schumann. Yet he was original in his conception of the songbook as the larger dramatic form; each one seems to have been planned in advance to represent a poet or source. Folk music, nature studies, humorous songs and ballads peopled by soldiers, sailors, students or musicians recur in the German settings, while

religious or erotic themes dominate the Spanish and Italian songbooks. GROVEmusic

Goethe Lieder

Goethe Lieder – Harfenspieler: I, Wer sich der **H**
Einsamkeit ergibt; II, An die Türen; III, Wer nie sein
Brot; Cophtisches Lied I & II; Anakreons Grab;
Ob der Koran von Ewigkeit sei?; So lang man
nüchtern ist; Prometheus; Grenzen der Menschheit.
Italienisches Liederbuch – Ein Ständchen Euch
zu bringen; Schon streckt' ich aus; Geselle, woll'n
wir uns in Kutten hüllen. Drei Gedichte von
Michelangelo. Eichendorff Lieder – Der Musikant..
Mörike Lieder – Der Tambour; Nimmersatte Liebe;
Fussreise; Verborgenheit
Hans Hotter bass-bar **Gerald Moore** pf
Testament mono SBT1197 (70' · ADD · T/t) Recorded
1951, 1953 & 1957 Ⓕ**OO**

At last: a reissue of Hotter's 1953 Hugo Wolf recital, which forms the centrepiece of this release, and it's in far better, more immediate sound than on the original LP. Hotter's interpretations of *Prometheus, Grenzen der Menschheit*, the gloomy *Harfenspieler* Lieder and resigned Michelangelo settings – Wolf at his greatest – remain virtually unsurpassed. They were surely written with a bass-baritone of Hotter's calibre in mind and, quite apart from his vocal prowess, his verbal insights are once again remarkable, while the account of the naughty monks' exploits from the *Italian Songbook* remind us of Hotter the humorist. The earlier and later items that complete the CD disclose similar gifts, notably the delightful *Der Tambour* – and *Anakreons Grab*, which, both in 1951 and 1957, matches the *Innigkeit* of Goethe's poem and Wolf's setting. Moore is a masterly partner in music that severely taxes the pianist. This disc is a must for Wolf enthusiasts.

Goethe Lieder – Mignon – I, Heiss mich nicht reden;
II, Nur wer die Sehnsucht kennt; III, So lasst mich
scheinen. Philine. Mignon, 'Kennst du das Land?'.
Gutmann und Gutweib. Epiphanias. St Nepomuks
Vorabend. Der Schäfer. Blumengruss. Gleich und
Gleich. Die Spröde. Die Bekehrte. Frühling übers
Jahr. Anakreons Grab. Dank des Paria. Phänomen.
So lang man nüchtern ist. Hoch beglückt in deiner
Liebe. Als ich auf dem Euphrat schiffte. Nimmer will
ich dich verlieren! Ganymed. Gretchen vor dem
Andachtsbild der Mater Dolorosa. Wanderers
Nachtlied
Geraldine McGreevy sop **Graham Johnson** pf
Hyperion CDA67130 (76' · DDD · T/t) Ⓕ

The first and abiding impression made by this recital is of air and grace. Graham Johnson's piano-playing is delightfully free yet exact. McGreevy's voice has a warmth in its still youthful glow; she also has the art of making it smile. In the first two Mignon songs she intensifies tone and emotion quite movingly; in *Kennst du das Land?* she may be not quite *seeing* the mountain and caves of the third verse or feeling the awesome power of the 'Flut', and in *Philine* she lacks the naughty zest for it. Yet always there are lovely things – as when she catches the expression of the statues as they put to Mignon their piteous question. She's also good (as are they both) at the boisterous *Gutmann und Gutweib*: a rarity that's lucky to find in Johnson so persuasive an advocate.

Italienisches Liederbuch

Italienisches Liederbuch
Christiane Oelze sop **Hans Peter Blochwitz** ten
Rudolf Jansen pf
Berlin Classics 0017482BC (78' · DDD · T) Ⓟ Ⓞ

These three excellent artists sensibly understate rather than overstate the songs' emotional content and where – about midway through the collection – the feelings become more immediate, the performers come forth with just the right amount of added intensity.

Christiane Oelze's fine-grained soprano, spirited readings and incisive diction fulfil just about every side of the songs assigned to her – from mocking, jealousy and anger to true love – and she wholly avoids the archness that afflicts some interpreters. Hans Peter Blochwitz, always a discerning Lieder singer, may have lost a little of his sweet tenor's bloom but compensates with a true understanding of the lyrical impulse that suffuses those wonderful love songs given to the male interpreter, especially the three successive, outright masterpieces beginning with 'Sterb' ich, so hüllt in Blumen'.

Rudolf Jansen deserves a notice to himself for his unravelling of all the intricacies of the often independent piano parts and for his outright mastery in giving the keyboard its due without ever stealing the thunder of the singers; his instrument is ideally balanced with the voices in a truthful recording. These songs are so remarkable that there will never be one definitive way of singing them. On the only other disc featuring a tenor, Schreier is a fuller-voiced, more 'interventionist' interpreter than Blochwitz: that pays huge dividends in some songs, less in others. In the end, the choice depends on a preference for one singer over another: Oelze and Blochwitz are probably favourite.

Mörike Lieder

Mörike Lieder –Der Genesene an die Hoffnung; Ein Stündlein wohl vor Tag; Der Tambour; Nimmersatte Liebe; Fussreise; Verborgenheit; Im Frühling; Auf einer Wanderung; Der Gärtner; In der Frühe; Gebet; Neue Liebe; Wo find' ich Trost?; Frage und Antwort; Lebe wohl; Heimweh; Denk' es, o Seele!; Der Jäger; Storchenbotschaft; Bei einer Trauung; Selbstgeständis; Abschied
Peter Schreier ten **Karl Engel** pf
Orfeo C142981A (60' · DDD · T/t) Ⓟ Ⓞ

Peter Schreier's ever-supple tenor, honed by keen-eyed intelligence and a verbal palate sharp enough to taste and try every last word, makes him a Wolf interpreter of the highest order. In this meticulously shaped programme of 22 of Wolf's eager settings of Mörike, one wonder appears after another. Schreier and his ever-sentient pianist, Karl Engel, move from a gentle awakening of love, which grows in intensity towards the innermost core of songs of doubt and fear, and on through a gallery of wonderfully dry, wry tableaux to the final farewell and the kicking of the critic downstairs. The first song here, *Im Frühling*, epitomises the equilibrium, security and entirety of performances which have grown from long-pondered consideration. The long, drowsy vowels, and Schreier's sensitivity to the high-register placing of crucial words of longing all fuse into the slow-walking movement of cloud, wing, river, breeze, as language becomes expanded and enriched by tone. Schreier's remarkable steadiness of line in *Verborgenheit* reveals the song's secrets only reluctantly: the fierce intensity of sudden illumination is all the more searing. Grotesquerie and poignancy coexist in *Bei einer Trauung*, and we feel every catch of the voice as Schreier turns weird and whimsical tale-teller in Storchenbotschaft.

Mörike Lieder – Der Genesene an die Hoffnung; Er ist's; Begegnung; Fussreise; Verborgenheit; Im Frühling; Auf einer Wanderung; Um Mitternacht; Auf ein altes Bild; In der Frühe; Wo find' ich Trost?; An die Geliebte; Peregrina I; Peregrina II; Lebe wohl; Heimweh; Denk' es, o Seele!; Der Feuerreiter; Die Geister am Mummelsee; Storchenbotschaft; Auftrag; Abschied
Roman Trekel bar **Oliver Pohl** pf
Oehms OC305 (68' · DDD · T) Ⓕ

There can be no better advocate of Hugo Wolf than Roman Trekel, now at the peak of his career as a Lieder interpreter, who presents this deeply satisfying recital of the best of the *Mörike Lieder*. These inspired songs need, above all, the kind of intense expression and intimate, detailed treatment that Trekel brings them. Performed as convincingly as they are here, they offer a particular *frisson* of individual accent that no other composer in the genre, whatever their other merits, quite equals: words and music seem as though they were written at one and the same time
Trekel achieves an ideal fusion of tonal security, sense of line and word-painting. In a comparatively long and complex Lied such as 'Im Frühling', he and the admirable Oliver Pohl traverse all the points of the expressive compass, and all the nuances of dynamics that belong to them. In that surpassingly sincere and beautiful love-song 'An die Geliebte' they build to the climax from 'Von Tiefe dann zu Tiefen' with a confidence that bespeaks long familiarity with the piece. Even better is the heartache they bring to 'Peregrina II' and 'Lebe wohl', where Wolf seems to enter into all the poet's suffering at the hands of a beloved. They also find the inner spirituality of

the religion-inspired settings, such as 'Auf ein altes Bild' and 'Denk' es o Seele', the latter so compelling for saying so much in such a short time. In a quite different vein, they rise marvellously to the frenzied melodrama of 'Der Feuerreiter', always a challenge to singer and pianist and one that's surely met here.

A truthful recording adds to the disc's merits. Not so the notes, which omit any exposition of the songs and also English translations. Even so, this is a recital that ought to convert even Wolf heretics to the cause.

Mörike Lieder
Werner Güra ten **Jan Schultsz** pf
Harmonia Mundi HMC90 1882 (64' · DDD · T/t)   Ⓕ

Just to hear again Wolf's masterful settings of Mörike's beautiful poetry is a source of enormous pleasure: seldom has a composer so fully understood and empathised with a poet. To have these songs presented by two artists so fully able to comprehend the inner meaning of these inspired pieces is an added blessing. Few tenors have interpreted them, but none has surpassed Güra in his understanding of the idiom, and none has had a partner so aware of every nuance in the piano parts as Schultsz.

Together they box the compass of these far-ranging and inspired Lieder, by turns philosophical, love-enchanted, light-footed, dramatic and comic. From the quiet meditation of *Gebet* right at the start through to the cynical humour of *Abschied* right at the end the pair take us through an emotional trail that is ever-absorbing. In terms of vocal acuity Güra offers a wide range of tone, a specially vivid gift where word-painting is concerned, above all the sheer evenness and beauty of the singing.

Just to offer a few examples of the many delights encountered along the way, there is the spring ecstasy at the end of *Er ist's*, the wonder of *Im Frühling*, the plangent tone in the famous *Auf ein altes Bild*, the spontaneous joy of *Auf einer Wanderung*, the erotic excitement of *Begegnung*, the blissful lassitude of *Verborgenheit*, the comic enactment of the drummer-boy's dreams and – perhaps best of all – the inner wonder and broad intensity of the four master-songs about love beginning with *An die Geliebte*. Finally, in the nightmarish melodrama of *Der Feuerreiter* and the coyish humour of *Storchenbotschaft*, Schultsz's virtuoso playing seconds the wide-ranging dynamics of Güra's singing.

This disc cannot be recommended too strongly either to admirers of Wolf or to those who want to know why he can be among the most compelling of composers in the genre.

Lieder

Eichendorff Lieder – Der Musikant; Verschwiegene Liebe; Das Ständchen; Nachtzauber; Seemanns Abschied. Goethe Lieder – Gutmann und Gutweib; Ganymed. Mörike Lieder – Der Genesene an die Hoffnung; Der Knabe und das Immlein; Begegnung; Nimmersatte Liebe; Verborgenheit; Im Frühling; Auf einer Wanderung; Um Mitternacht; Auf ein altes Bild; Gebet; An den Schlaf; An die Geliebte; Peregrina I; Peregrina II; Der Jäger; Lied eines Verliebten; Abschied
Ian Bostridge ten **Antonio Pappano** pf
EMI 342256-2 (72' · DDD · T/t) Ⓕ   ⚫⚫▶

Recordings of Wolf songs are rare today, ones sung by tenors even rarer, yet here comes one to delight the ear. Ian Bostridge's choice of songs is typically fastidious, his interpretation of them full of the intelligence, understanding and musicality we expect from him.

With Antonio Pappano in wonderfully supportive, positive form, they rise to inspired heights in the central group of Mörike settings – *Im Frühling, Auf ein altes Bild, Gebet, An den Schlaf* and *An die Geliebte*. In these contrasting songs of religious insight and deep love, Bostridge performs with a kind of inward concentration and then elatory spirit, coupled with his rapt palpitating tone, that precisely matches with Wolf's masterpieces. He is perhaps even better in the Goethe setting *Ganymed*, which can seldom if ever have received such a rapturous performance, and brings the recital to a satisfying close.

Against these wonders must be set songs where his syllabic emphasis and tendency to *Sprechgesang* lead to performances that sound mincing: *Begegnung, Nimmersatte Liebe* (grossly overdone) and, earlier among the Eichendorff songs, *Nachtzauber*. Here the wish to extract something from every word robs the songs of their natural flow, though among the Eichendorff settings, the over-familiar *Verschwiegene Liebe* receives an unfettered and restorative reading.

Bostridge, with Pappano an always inventive partner, makes you hear the songs – like it or not – anew. One may not always capitulate to the results, but Wolf is a composer who, above all, benefits from two artists willing to live dangerously. They are helped by John Fraser's well balanced and full-bodied recording.

Iannis Xenakis   Greek/French 1922-2001

Xenakis was a French composer of Greek parentage and Romanian birth. In 1932 his family returned to Greece, and he was educated on Spetsai and at the Athens Polytechnic, where he studied engineering. In 1947 he arrived in Paris, where he became a member of Le Corbusier's architectural team, producing his first musical work, Metastasis, only in 1954, based on the design for the surfaces of the Philips pavilion to be built for the Brussels Exposition of 1958. This, with its divided strings and mass effects, had an enormous influence; but in ensuing works he moved on to find mathematical and computer means of handling large numbers of events, drawing on (for example) Gaussian distribution (ST/10, Atrées), Markovian chains (Analogiques) and game theory (Duel, Stratégie). Other interests were in electronic music

(Bohor, 1962), ancient Greek drama (used in several settings) and instrumental virtuosity (Herma for piano, 1964; Nomos alpha for cello, 1966). His later output, chiefly of orchestral and instrumental pieces, is large, many works from the mid-1970s onwards striking back from modernist complexity to ostinatos and modes suggestive of folk music. **GROVE**music

Knephas

A Colone. Nuits. Serment. Knephas. Medea
New London Chamber Choir; Critical Band / James Wood
Hyperion CDA66980 (58' · DDD · T/t) Ⓕ**❍❍❍**

This enterprising release is a great success, showing just how varied – and unintimidating – Xenakis's music can be. The performances are nothing short of phenomenal in their technical assurance and emotional power, and the recording is also something special, giving the singers just the right degree of space and resonance to project the often complex textures with all the necessary precision. The earliest works offer different angles on the composer's ultra-expressionist idiom, with *Nuits* (1967) adopting a very direct way of representing its anguished lament for the martyrs of Greece's struggle for freedom after 1945. *Medea* (also 1967) uses much more text, and its chant-like style has affinities with Stravinsky's *Les noces*, but the overall effect is much harsher, with abrasive yet imaginative instrumental writing. *A Colone* (1977) also has Stravinskian affinities, and the text (Sophocles's description of the delights of Colonus) prompts music which is uninhibitedly exuberant. This warmer, more celebratory side of Xenakis is carried over into *Serment* (1980), a short setting of a text derived from the Hippocratic Oath and not, one suspects, an entirely serious effort, though there's nothing trivial about it either. Finally, the superb *Knephas* ('Darkness') of 1990 begins in an appropriately unsparing manner, but ends with a hymnic apotheosis which recalls Messiaen in its harmonic character and warmth of atmosphere. Here is one of the 20th century's most important musical voices, and this recording does it full justice.

Dmaathen[a]. Kassandra[b]. Komboï[c].
Okho[d]. Oophaa[e]. Persephassa[f].
Pleïades – Métaux[g]; Claviers[h];
Mélanges[h]; Peaux[h]. Psappha[i]. Rebonds[i]
[a]**Jacqueline Leclair** *ob* [b]**Philip Larson** *bar* [c]**Shannon Wettstein**, [e]**John Mark Harris** *hpds* [e]**Greg Stuart**, [g]**Gustavo Aguilar**, [g]**Rob Esler**, [g]**Ross Karre**, [g]**Don Nichols**, [g]**Morris Palter**, [g]**Lisa Tolentino** *perc*
[f,h]**Red Fish Blue Fish** (Patti Cudd, [c]Aiyun Huang, [d]Terry Longshore, [d]Brett Reed, [d]David Shively, Vanessa Tomlinson *perc*) / [a,b]**Steven Schick** *perc*
Mode ③ MODE171/3 (176' · DDD) Ⓕ

All credit to Red Fish Blue Fish and their director Steven Schick for their dedication in realising some of the most visceral and exhilarating music

yet written for percussion. The eight works cover two decades (1969-89) of Xenakis's 45-year career. The earliest, *Persephassa*, takes up the challenge of Varèse and Cage in a sextet whose combining freedom and discipline is only to be expected from one who used mathematical formulae to create music of uninhibited abandon. It is a measure of Xenakis's building on recent tradition that the solo *Psappha* (1975) draws on the example of Stockhausen's *Zyklus* in its pursuing of a methodical yet inherently dynamic trajectory, while *Pleïades* (1978) might be a riposte to Reich's *Drumming* in its systematic working-through of a formal process denoted by specific percussive 'types' – for all that Xenakis's explosive energy is worlds away from Reich's calm incremental change.

In between comes *Dmaathen*, its juxtaposing of percussion and oboe in a tense yet lyrical dialogue anticipating the duets of the 1980s. These comprise two with harpsichord – the bewitching interplay of sonorities in *Komboï*, and restrained rhythmic overlay of *Oophaa* – and one with voice in *Kassandra*, whose plangent declamation is less a prophecy of doom than an abstract evocation of tragedy. The latest works eschew flamboyance, yet the trio *Okho* is an imaginative stylisation of West African drumming, while the two-part solo *Rebonds* (played B-A) acutely balances sound and silence so to compel admiration.

These pieces exist in often several recordings, but this Mode set has a completeness and, above all, a conviction as regards performance. Sound is excellent and Schick's superb booklet essay has a depth of insight to mirror that of the playing. Essential.

Eugene Ysaÿe   Belgian 1858-1931

Ysaÿe studied under Wieniawski at Brussels and Vieuxtemps at Paris, forming close ties with Franck, Chausson, d'Indy, Fauré, Saint-Saëns and Debussy. As professor at the Brussels Conservatory (1887-99) he initiated the Concerts Ysaÿe, appearing as violinist and conductor in contemporary French and Belgian music, meanwhile becoming renowned throughout Europe and in the USA (conductor of the Cincinnati SO, 1918-22); the shift to a conducting career was necessitated by his increasingly unsteady bowing arm. Idolized by a generation of violinists for his intense but poetic playing, he also composed with expertise in a post-Romantic style, notably for the violin (Six Sonatas op.27, eight concertos, Poème élégiaque, Caprice Saint-Saëns). **GROVE**music

Violin Sonatas

Solo Violin Sonatas, Nos 1-6
Thomas Zehetmair *vn*
ECM New Series 472 687-2 (66' · DDD) Ⓕ**❍❍**➔

By tailoring his solo sonatas to fit the styles of six very different violinists Eugène Ysaÿe may have been acting as the ultimate critic, describing his subjects with musical illustrations rather than mere words. For example, there are the winking appoggiaturas in the finale of No 4, dedicated to Kreisler, which Thomas Zehetmair throws off with a mere flick of the wrist, or the rich chord structures of No 1, whose dedicatee, Joseph Szigeti, was a great Bach player. Bach is a particularly strong presence there, the key (G minor) and language so reminiscent of his first solo sonata. Again, the Jacques Thibaud piece, No 2 in A minor, has obsessive repetitions of the Prelude from Bach's E major Partita, played initially by Zehetmair with the lightest touch, though later repetitions gain in intensity. The sinister melding of Bach with the 'Dies irae' chant has to be one of the canniest masterstrokes of the period. There are stylistic parallels between No 2 and No 4, just as there were similarities between the players themselves.

The spicy Sixth Sonata recalls the Spanish fiddler Manuel Quiroga and takes on Latin influences, initially suggesting Ravel's *Tzigane* (composed at around the same time, though the similarity is probably coincidental) before shifting, a little later, to *habañera* mode.

As the ultimate thinking virtuoso, Zehetmair is an ideal interpreter of these pieces, delving between the notes, coaxing a wealth of colour, inflection and dynamic shading from each score, always with acute imagination. He is both explorer and demonstrator, his modes of attack as varied as his tone colouring. This is the best possible showcase for some marvellous if still undervalued music.

Jan Dismas Zelenka

Bohemian 1679-1745

After serving Count Hartig in Prague, Zelenka became a double bass player in the royal orchestra at Dresden in 1710. He studied with Fux in Vienna and Lotti in Venice, 1715-16; from 1719 he remained in Dresden, except for a visit to Prague in 1723. Having gradually taken over the duties of the ailing Kapellmeister, Heinichen, he was made only church music composer (1735); Hasse was the new Kapellmeister. He composed mainly sacred works, among them three oratorios, 12 masses, and many other pieces; his output also includes a festival opera (1723, Prague), six chamber sonatas for oboes (c 1715) and other instrumental pieces. His music, like that of Bach (whom he knew), is notable for its adventurousness, its contrapuntal mastery and its harmonic invention. GROVEmusic

Trio Sonatas

Trio Sonatas –No 2 in G minor, No 5 in F;   Ⓟ
No 6 in C minor
Ensemble Zefiro (Paolo Grazzi, Alfredo Bernardini *obs* Alberto Grazzi *bn* Roberto Sensi *db* Rolf Lislevand *theorbo* Rinaldo Alessandrini *hpd/org*)

Astrée Naïve E8511 (52' · DDD)   Ⓕ●

For sheer élan and spirit the Baroque instrumental players on this disc take some beating. Zelenka's six sonatas for two oboes, bassoon and continuo are among the most rewarding and at times most difficult pieces of Baroque chamber music in the oboe repertory. Indeed, pieces demanding such virtuosity from these instruments were probably without precedent at the time (1715). The writing is often such as to make us wonder if they were destined for friends or for enemies of the composer. Here, then, we're treated to some splendidly invigorating playing of music which offers a great deal beyond face value. The sounds of the solo instruments themselves, together with an effective continuo group of double bass, harpsichord/organ and theorbo are admirably captured in the recording.

The Lamentations of Jeremiah

The Lamentations of Jeremiah   Ⓟ
Michael Chance *counterten* **John Mark Ainsley** *ten* **Michael George** *bass* **Chandos Baroque Players**
Hyperion Helios CDH55106 (73' · DDD · T/t)   Ⓑ

Between the incomparable settings by Thomas Tallis and the extremely austere one by Stravinsky (which he called *Threni*) the *Lamentations of Jeremiah* have attracted surprisingly few composers. Perhaps the predominantly sombre tone, without even the dramatic opportunities presented by the *Dies irae* in a *Requiem*, is off-putting. Be that as it may, Zelenka showed remarkable resourcefulness in his 1722 setting for the electoral chapel at Dresden, where he was Kapellmeister. His musical language is in many ways similar to that of JS Bach but there are also daring turns of phrase which are entirely personal. The six *Lamentations* feature each singer twice; this performance is intimate, slightly spacious in tempo and with a resonant acoustic.

Alexander Zemlinsky

Austrian 1871-1942

Zemlinsky was a pupil of Fuchs at the Vienna Conservatory (1890-92). In 1895 he became a close friend of Schoenberg's; he also had encouragement from Mahler, who presented his opera Es war einmal at the Hofoper in 1900. His orchestral fantasy Die Seejungfrau dates from these years. By this time he was working as a theatre conductor in Vienna his later appointments were at the German theatre in Prague (1911-27) and the Kroll Opera in Berlin (1927-31). In 1933 he fled to Vienna, and then in 1938 to the USA. From the same background as Schoenberg, and similarly influenced by Mahler and Strauss, he developed an impassioned style in such works as his Second Quartet (1914), one-act operas Eine florentinische Tragödie (1917) and Der Zwerg

(1922), and Lyric Symphony (1923). Later works, including the opera Der Kreidekreis (1932), the Sinfonietta (1934) and the Fourth Quartet (1936), are influenced more by Weill and German neo-classicism. GROVEmusic

Eine lyrische Symphonie, Op 18

Lyrische Symphonie
Christine Schäfer *sop* **Matthias Goerne** *bar*
Orchestre de Paris / Christoph Eschenbach
Capriccio ⊚ 71 081 (52' · DDD/DSD · T/t)   Ⓕ

There have been several memorable recordings of Zemlinsky's masterpiece and this one, the first for many years, can be placed in their company. Christoph Eschenbach and his soloists clearly agree that the *Lyric Symphony* is not simply an orchestral song-cycle but a symphonic music-drama: the resulting performance has all the vividness and immediacy of a live event yet – equally importantly – excessive histrionics are avoided. This is music that needs no nudging or special pleading to exercise its power and poignancy.

Matthias Goerne has the combination of vocal heft and lyric mellifluousness necessary to sustain the demanding lines of the work's four odd-numbered episodes. Perhaps the third section, with its particularly sumptuous orchestral backcloth, could have taken a degree or two more of sheer vocal refinement, but overall Goerne does full justice to the heart-rending finale.

Christine Schäfer is especially convincing in the dramatic final stages of the second movement, and also in the expressionistic sixth. Ideally, the fourth movement's gentle lover's plea might be even more rapt, more other-worldly than it is here. But this reading fits well with the interpretation as a whole. The voices are forwardly placed without loss of orchestral detail, and only in the brief, turbulent fifth movement might one feel that the instrumental sound needs more edge. Even so, the orchestral playing throughout is superb.

Der König Kandaules

Der König Kandaules
James O'Neal *ten* König Kandaules **Monte Pederson** *bar* Gyges **Nina Warren** *sop* Nyssia **Klaus Häger** *bass* Phedros **Peter Galliard** *ten* Syphax **Mariusz Kwiecien** *bar* Nicomedes **Kurt Gysen** *bass* Pharnaces **Simon Yang** *bass* Philebos **Ferdinand Seiler** *ten* Sebas **Guido Jentjens** *bar* Archelaos
Hamburg State Philharmonic Orchestra / Gerd Albrecht
Capriccio ② 60 071/2 (128' · DDD · T/t)
Recorded live 1996   Ⓕ

Der König Kandaules, based on a play by André Gide, was Zemlinsky's last opera, written during the Nazis' rise to power and complete in short score when he fled to America in 1938. He showed it to his pupil Artur Bodanzky, then a principal conductor at the Met, who seems to have warned him that the libretto would not be acceptable. It concerns Kandaules, king of Lydia, who befriends Gyges, a fisherman, and persuades him to use a magic ring to become invisible and see his queen, Nyssia, naked. After they spend a night of passion together Nyssia orders Gyges to kill Kandaules and seize power.

Zemlinsky never completed the orchestration but left a large number of indications of scoring. Antony Beaumont's orchestration sounds perfectly convincing. When two excerpts from the score were performed and recorded in 1994 it already looked as though a major work was about to be revealed. And that's the case: a marvellous and quite characteristic score, but in some ways a dismaying one. All the orchestral richness and the voluptuously singing lines are there, but wedded to a plot that seems all too accurately to reflect the disorder and disillusion of the times in which it was written.

The performance is a fine one, O'Neal lacking only the last touch of heroic vocal stature for Kandaules, Warren only a little stretched by the Ariadne-like role of Nyssia, Pederson first class (a moment or two of suspect intonation aside) as Gyges. Albrecht is perfectly at home in this sort of music, the orchestra's admirable richness of tone doesn't obscure detail, and the recording is atmospheric (stage business audible) but clear. Zemlinsky's reputation can only be enhanced by this ravishing, richly complex, disturbing opera.

Further listening

Eine florentinische Tragödie[a]. Eine lyrische Symphonie, Op 18[b]. Symphonische Gesänge[c]
3 Psalms
Vermillion *mez* **Kruse** *ten* **Dohmen** *bar* **Marc** *sop* **Hagegård** *bar* **White** *bass* **Royal Concertgebouw Orchestra / Chailly**
Double Decca ② 473 734-2DF2 (156' · DDD)   ⓂⓄ🔁
A Florentine Tragedy is a disturbing, shocking piece, but to make its fullest impact it also needs to sound ravishingly beautiful. Zemlinsky's sumptuous scoring often demands an orchestra of the Royal Concertgebouw's stature, and in this reading it sounds quite magnificent. The recording leaves nothing to be desired: the colours are rich and clean. (Not currently listed on CD, but downloadable.)

CONDUCTORS

Conductors

'Abbado in Lucerne'
Debussy La mer[a]. Le Martyre de Saint Sébastien –
Suite[b]
[b]**Eteri Gvazava**, [b]**Rachel Harnisch** *sops*
Swiss Chamber Choir; Lucerne Festival Orchestra /
Claudio Abbado *Video director* **Michael Beyer**
Euroarts **DVD** 205 3469 (64' · NTSC · 16:9 · PCM
stereo, 5.1 & DTS 5.1 · 0) [ab]Recorded live at the
Lucerne Festival in 2003. Includes the documentary
'From Toscanini to Abbado' – The History of the
Lucerne Festival Orchestra, written and directed by
Arthur Spirk   Ⓕ**O**

'Sir John Barbirolli in rehearsal and performance'
Haydn Oboe Concerto in C, HobVIIg/C1
Evelyn Rothwell *ob* **Vancouver Symphony**
Orchestra / Sir John Barbirolli
Video Artists International **DVD** VAIDVD4293
(60' · 4:3 b/w · PCM mono · 0)   Ⓕ**O**

'George Szell – One Man's Triumph'
Beethoven Symphony No 5 **Berg** Violin Concerto (in
rehearsal)[a] **Brahms** Academic Festival Overture (in
rehearsal)
[a]**Rafael Druian** *vn* **Cleveland Orchestra / George**
Szell
Video Artists International **DVD** VAIDVD4271
(55' · 4:3 · PCM mono · 0) 1966 Bell Telephone Hour
documentary   Ⓕ**OO**

Fritz Reiner
Bach/Weiner Toccata, Adagio and Fugue in C,
BWV564[b] **Beethoven** Symphony No 2[b] **Debussy**
Petite Suite[a] **Mozart** Symphony No 39[a] **Tchaikovsky**
The Nutcracker – Waltz of the flowers[a]. The Sleeping
Beauty – Valse[a]
Chicago Symphony Orchestra / Fritz Reiner
Video Artists International **DVD** VAIDVD4287
(97' · 4:3 b/w · PCM mono · 0)   Ⓕ**OO**

Stravinsky
featuring interviews and recording sequences of the
Symphony of Psalms
Toronto Festival Singers; CBC Symphony
Orchestra / Igor Stravinsky
Directors **Wolf Koenig, Roman Kroitor**
Video Artists International **DVD** VAIDVD4290 (50' · 4:3
b/w · PCM mono · 0) 1965 documentary   Ⓕ**O**

For some the main attraction of *Abbado in Lucerne*
will be the great Italian maestro conducting
Debussy at the 2003 Lucerne Festival. For others
it's the documentary, with its footage of some of
the last century's greatest conductors in action:
every brief glimpse adds flesh and bones to the
names that adorn the labels of treasured discs by
Ansermet, Fricsay, Kempe, Furtwängler and de
Sabata. The film is confusingly structured, however, and though it confronts admirably Karajan's
ruthless use of Lucerne to reinvent himself after

his denazification, the commentary sounds like
something written by the Swiss Tourist Board.

Barbirolli is filmed in Vancouver rehearsing
the Haydn-attributed Oboe Concerto with his
wife as soloist, who, as in her 1957 recording
with the Hallé, plays her own cadenzas. All eyes
are on JB (indeed, it's some time before we're
aware that the soloist is at the rehearsal at all) but
there is one lovely exchange when Rothwell suggests that they start again from the repeat of the
second subject. 'Well, I don't know what the
second subject is,' retorts her husband. 'That's
for programme annotators.'

George Szell, who died in the same year as Barbirolli (1970), was, by contrast, unpopular and
despotic. The colour film profiles – but does not
explore or question – his extraordinary 24-year
relationship with the Cleveland Orchestra. With
his lupine smile and fearsome presence, he tries to
play the role of regular guy: rehearsal and performance sequences are riveting, with fascinating
footage of him instructing three young conductors (James Levine one of them) on how to kick-
start *Don Juan* and Beethoven's Fifth.

With the hooded eyes of a falcon and his sour
mien, Szell's fellow Hungarian, Fritz Reiner
looks as unpleasant as his reputation conducting
the Chicago Symphony in 1953-4 at the start of
his celebrated nine-year association with the
orchestra. These black-and-white transmissions
(sometimes more black than white) of one of the
truly great conductors are of immense importance, and include one work (the Bach-Weiner)
that Reiner did not record commercially. The
DVD preserves Francis Coughlin's hopelessly
unprepared in-vision linking commentary: every
faultering sentence makes you thank God for
the invention of the autocue.

The Stravinsky documentary features the
famous (and equally toe-curling) encounter
between the young Julian Bream and the elderly
composer. Just as Stravinsky is about to start
recording his *Symphony of Psalms*, Bream is introduced, sits down and plays a pavane on the lute …
all the way through. As a conductor, Stravinsky is
an uninspiring, baton-less time-beater, but the
exchanges filmed simultaneously in the control
room make for an unusually vivid sequence. Most
revealing, though, is Stravinsky's conversation
with his friend Nicholas Nabokov, filmed in
Hamburg over a glass of whisky. Here, one of
music's geniuses appears touchingly vulnerable
and human. VAI may be a no-frills merchant but
such treasure needs no fancy packaging. Its priceless contents speak for themselves.

Sir John Barbirolli

Haydn Symphony No 83 in G minor, 'La Poule'
Lehár Gold und Silber, Op 79 **J Strauss II**
Die Fledermaus – Overture. Kaiser-Walzer, Op 437.
Perpetuum mobile, Op 257. Tritsch-Tratsch-Polka, Op
214 **R Strauss** Der Rosenkavalier Suite
Hallé Orchestra / Sir John Barbirolli
BBC Legends/IMG Artists BBCL4038-2 (76' · ADD)
Recorded live 1969   Ⓜ**OO**

Among all the treasures rediscovered in the BBC archives, this disc of a Barbirolli Prom Concert of 1969 is among the most enticing. He opens with one of his favourite Haydn symphonies, and only Beecham can match his delightful characterisation of *The Hen* which Haydn makes sure we hear several times in the course of a most appealing first movement. As shaped by JB the *Andante* combines an Elysian simplicity with classical beauty of line, and the *Minuet* and finale similarly match grace with exuberance. There's surely no finer performance on disc.

Then comes the Johann Strauss section, with Sir John himself vocalising in the Overture's glorious waltz theme. But the highlight is a richly contoured, magical account of the *Emperor Waltz*, with all the mellow nobility of line one associates with Bruno Walter, plus an added touch of Barbirolli's Italianate sunshine. The reprise is so lovely it would melt the hardest heart. Then follows a fun performance of the *Tritsch-Tratsch-Polka*, with outrageous agogic tempo distortions and sudden pauses which bring a couple of great bursts of laughter from the Promenaders. But the best is yet to come.

With the *Rosenkavalier* suite the Hallé strings and horns surpass themselves. The suite may be no more than a comparatively inept pot-pourri, but Sir John invests each section of the score with such loving detail that you can only regret that he never recorded the whole opera. The Prelude, with its sexy, whooping horns, and a great passionate *tenuto* on the key moment of the lovers' passionate embrace (behind the curtain), then leads on to a wonderful feeling of tenderness as their ardour gently subsides. Later the Presentation of the Rose scene, with exquisite oboe playing, is meltingly beautiful. After the great surge of the Viennese waltz sequence, the closing section and the sensuous duet that sees Octavian and Sophie departing together is wonderfully affectionate, rudely interrupted by the explosive coda.

The encore is Lehár's *Gold and Silver*. Sir John encourages his Promenaders to hum along gently so as not to overwhelm its famous lyrical melody; he even manages to entice them into a *pianississimo* when it's reprised. Prommers in the late 1960s were just as appreciative but more self-disciplined than they are today, and there's no hint of vulgarity and much warmth in their response. Sir John cuts the coda to make time for his own witty little speech in appreciation of their contribution, continuing with a warmly expressed wish to return with his orchestra; this alone is worth the price of an unforgettable disc, recorded with great warmth and atmosphere.

Sir Thomas Beecham

The Beecham Collection – Delius   Ⓗ
An Arabesk[dfh]. A Mass of Life – Part 2 No 3: Prelude[h]. Songs of Sunset – Parts 1-7[bdfh]; Part 8[cegi]. I-Brasil[ah]. Le ciel est pardessus le toit[ei]. Cradle Song[ei]. Irmelin Rose[ei]. Klein Venevil[eh]. The Nightingale[ei]. Twilight Fancies[ei]. The Violet[eh]. The Violet[ei]. Whither[eh]
[a]**Dora Labbette** sop [b]**Olga Haley**, [c]**Nancy Evans**

mezzos [d]**Roy Henderson**, [e]**Redvers Llewellyn** bars [f]**London Select Choir**; [g]**BBC Chorus**; [h]**London Philharmonic Orchestra**; [i]**Royal Philharmonic Orchestra / Sir Thomas Beecham** [i]pf
Somm Recordings mono SOMM-BEECHAM8 (74' · ADD) Recorded 1929-46   Ⓜ●

The Beecham Collection – Handel   Ⓗ
Piano Concerto in A (arr Beecham)[a]. The Gods Go a'Begging[b] – Introduction; Minuet; Hornpipe; Musette; Tambourine; Gavotte; Sarabande; Fugato. The Gods Go a'Begging[c] – Introduction; Larghetto; Gavotte; Allegro; Ensemble; Bourrée The Origin of Design[d]
[a]**Lady Betty Humby Beecham** pf [abd]**London Philharmonic Orchestra**; [c]**Royal Philharmonic Orchestra / Sir Thomas Beecham**
Somm Recordings mono SOMM-BEECHAM7 (75' · ADD) Recorded 1932-49   ●

Thanks to Shirley, Lady Beecham, we have here a splendid range of recordings from Sir Thomas's personal archive, most never issued before. The great treasure is the live recording of Delius's orchestral song-cycle to words by Ernest Dowson, *Songs of Sunset*. The performance has been described as 'achingly beautiful', and that's no exaggeration. Recorded at the Leeds Festival in 1934, it presents a strikingly different view of the work from that of other interpreters on disc. Beecham conveys a virile thrust and energy in the writing, partly opting for faster speeds. Thanks to his magnetism, arguments have a tautness that can otherwise seem to ramble. Both in this, with its seven linked sections, and in the single span of *An Arabesk*, a setting of Jens Peter Jacobsen in Philip Heseltine's translation, the line of the argument is clarified. Roy Henderson is the clean-cut, sensitive baritone soloist in both, sounding very English, with Olga Haley a fresh, bright mezzo soloist in the *Songs of Sunset*. What prevented this inspired reading of the *Songs of Sunset* from being issued before is that the test pressing of the final climactic section is missing. To complete the work, that final ensemble for soloists and chorus together is taken from the studio recording Beecham made for HMV in 1946, but which he rejected. With Nancy Evans and Redvers Llewellyn as soloists, it makes an excellent conclusion, with the chorus more clearly focused than its predecessor in 1934. What matters is that the choral sound in both has ample weight. There's some noise at the ends of 78 sides, but the full-bodied nature of the transfer makes that flaw easy to ignore.

Dora Labbette is the enchanting soprano soloist in all the separate songs, bright and silvery, attacking even the most exposed high notes with astonishing purity and precision, producing magical *pianissimos*. Four of the ten come in the beautiful orchestral versions, with the rest accompanied at the piano by Beecham himself. He may not have been the most accomplished pianist, but his natural magnetism still shines out, not least in the striking early song, longer than the rest, *Twilight Fancies*.

INSTRUMENTALISTS

Piotr Anderszewski _piano_

Bach English Suite No 6 in D minor, BWV811
Beethoven Piano Sonata in D minor No 31, Op 110
Webern Variations, Op 27
Piotr Anderszewski pf
Virgin Classics 545632-2 (61' · DDD)　　ⒻⓄⓄ▸

In an age when great, good, bad and indifferent recordings rub shoulders in a chaotic marketplace, Piotr Anderszewski's playing stands out like a beacon of light and quality. His is the most powerful and distinctive of musical voices, a rare combination of purity and adventure. In Bach's Sixth _English Suite_ his intelligence is as razorsharp as his technique is immaculate. What an endless play of light and shade he brings to the Prelude, what buoyancy to the First Gavotte! His varied registration in the Second Gavotte is central to a deeply imaginative response to Bach; so too is the uncanny stillness he evokes in the Sarabande or the sinister momentum of the final nail-biting, fiercely chromatic Gigue.

In Beethoven's Op 110 he gives us a scrupulously modern equivalent of legendary recordings of the past (by Solomon and Myra Hess, for example), reawakening our sense of the otherworldly, the speculative and mystical in this late masterpiece. His poise and tonal translucency in the opening _Moderato_ are enviable, and so is his explosive sense of contrast in the following _Allegro molto_. And if for some his attention to detail will seem microscopic and over-refined, others will surely rejoice in a concentration and integrity that are at once exhausting and exhilarating.

Exceptionally self-critical, Anderszewski once left the stage during a performance of the Webern Variations at the Leeds Piano Competition, unhappy and disgruntled with his playing. Here, even he must have felt a sense of achievement, with his precise and deeply sensitive performance.

'Piotr Anderszewski at Carnegie Hall'
Bach Partita No 2, BWV826 **Bartók** Hungarian Folksongs from the Csík District, Sz35a **Beethoven** Piano Sonata No 31, Op 110 **Janáček** In the Mists **Schumann** Faschingsschwank aus Wien, Op 26
Piotr Anderszewski pf
Virgin Classics ② 267291-2 (85' · DDD)
Recorded live at the Stern Auditorium, Carnegie Hall, New York City, on December 3, 2008　　ⒻⓄ▸

Some recital, this. Piotr Anderszewski establishes a commanding tone for the opening section of the Second Partita's Ouverture, hopping elegantly through the little march that leads on to a fast, immaculately voiced fugue. He uses the Courante's ornaments to 'lift' the melody line, and the play between a seamless _legato_ and a gentle _staccato_ accompaniment in the following

Sarabande works wonderfully well. The Rondeau is again trippingly elegant, the closing Capriccio assertive in a way that balances it with the opening fugue.

Faschingsschwank aus Wien launches with a flourish: Anderszewski fractionally delays the opening's second chord in authentic Viennese style, while the _Scherzo_ is full of telling though effective emphases, mostly along the lines of 'question and answer'. And yet in the ravishing Intermezzo he seems too aware of the notes (so many to negotiate). The finale works best, a fantastical sojourn dazzlingly negotiated.

Janáček's In the Mists is a given a peach of a performance, a sense of improvisation sitting securely at its heart. Each movement tells its own very personal story, or seems to, the third alternating idyll with searing drama. Anderszewski's mastery of simultaneously varied dynamics comes into play here but in Beethoven's Op 110 he can be just a little over-emphatic on detail – in particular the accompaniment that underpins the first movement's principal theme. Throughout the recital the understandably enthusiastic Carnegie Hall audience is rather too keen to bound in at the end of each piece, a mild distraction on a recording that you hope to play again and again. This is an exceptional recital, and as ever the Carnegie Hall acoustic allows for a luminous piano tone.

Leif Ove Andsnes _piano_

'Horizons'
Albéniz Tango, Op 165 No 2 **Antheil** Toccata No 2 **Bach/Busoni** Ten Chorale Preludes – Ich ruf zu dir, Herr **Chopin** Impromptu No 1, Op 29 **Debussy** Suite bergamasque – Clair de lune **Grieg** Humouresqe, Op 6 No 3. Folksong, Op 73 No 4 **Halvorsen/Andsnes** Chant de Veslemøy **Ibert** Dix Histoires – Le petite âne blanc **Chopin/Liszt** Meine Freuden, S480 No 5 **Liszt** Liebestraum No 3, S541. Valse impromptu, S213 **Mendelssohn** Song Without Words, Op 67 No 2 **Mompou** Cançións i danses I. Paisajes – El lago **C Scott** Lotusland, Op 47 No 1 **Scriabin** Impromptu No 1, Op 14 **Shostakovich** The Golden Age – Polka **Sibelius** Etude, Op 76 No 2 **Smetana** Am Seegestade (Concert Study), B119 **R Strauss/Gieseking** Ständchen, Op 17 No 2 **Trénet/'Mr Nobody'** Coin de rue
Leif Ove Andsnes pf
EMI 341682-2 (68' · DDD)　　ⓂⓄⓄ▸

Andsnes here reveals a hitherto hidden side to his art – the salon charmer. Some of the pieces are favourites from his childhood, though it is not every nine-year-old who has tackled Sibelius's uncharacteristically jolly 'Staccato' Etude or mastered Chopin's First Impromptu with such fluency and grace. Appealing, too, is the drama and sweep he brings to Liszt's _Liebestraum_ No 3 (though it will not suit everyone's taste) and his avoidance of cliché, while the Norwegian's own transcription of Halvorsen's _Chant de Veslemøy_ (originally for violin), Ibert's _Le petit âne blanc_ and Debussy's _Clair de lune_ are played with a beguiling innocence, ravishing tonal finesse and – most important – palpable affection.

Bravura highlights include Gieseking's effulgent transcription of Richard Strauss's *Ständchen* and Smetana's *Am Seegestade* ('By the sea'), reminiscent of Raff's *La fileuse* and a rare example of a concert étude that opens in one key (B major) and closes a tone lower! Enterprisingly, Andsnes has tracked down a score of Charles Trénet's song *Coin de rue* transcribed by the coyly named 'Mr Nobody' whom I have no qualms about outing as none other than Alexis Weissenberg.

The whole recital is superbly recorded. As Andsnes himself says, 'It's great to see people walk away from a concert with a smile on their face'. This disc has the same effect.

'Shadows of Silence'
Dalbavie Piano Concerto **Kurtág** Játékok – selection
Lutosławski Piano Concerto **Sørensen** Lullabies. The Shadows of Silence
Leif Ove Andsnes pf ªBavarian Radio Symphony Orchestra / Franz Welser-Möst
EMI 264182-2 (75' · DDD)   ℗Ⓓ➨

This substantial demonstration of Leif Ove Andsnes's commitment to contemporary composers is framed by two fine Bent Sørensen pieces which underline the programme's governing concern with music that echoes, or shadows, other music. *Lullabies* is brief but its spirit of troubled nostalgia carries over into *The Shadows of Silence* itself. The title may be paradoxical – surely it is sound, not silence, that is being shadowed? – but the music is superbly crafted and powerfully expressive, ranging in mood between fluttering, melancholy reticence and tolling menace.

Sørensen's music is refined even at its most aggressive, and as such it beautifully complements the eight miniatures from Kurtág's *Játékok* ("Games") which need only a few seconds to create complex worlds of starkly delineated yet imaginative allusion. But the meat of Andsnes's double-decker sandwich is provided by two sizeable concertos, both of which acknowledge the apparent impossibility of escaping from the aura of romantic warhorses that, from Beethoven to Rachmaninov, still provide a staple diet for concert audiences (and record buyers).

The Lutosławski – written for Krystian Zimerman and recorded by him with the composer conducting soon after the premiere – is an intricate tapestry referencing virtuoso and poetic concerto traditions in an ironic yet never cynically exploitative fashion, and Andsnes manages to avoid po-faced downplaying of its parodic aspects while not exaggerating them either. After this, Marc-André Dalbavie's concerto is a disappointment, taking far too long to turn time-honoured pianistic conventions into clichés. But Andsnes and Welser-Möst give it their all, and in well-engineered sound this is a disc which, for the most part, can be cherished for being on the side of the angels, where contemporary repertoire is concerned.

Martha Argerich   *piano*

Début Recital
Brahms Two Rhapsodies, Op 79 **Chopin** Scherzo No 3 in C sharp minor, Op 39. Barcarolle in F sharp, Op 60 **Liszt** Hungarian Rhapsody No 6 in D flat. Piano Sonata in B-minor, S178 **Prokofiev** Toccata in D minor, Op 11 **Ravel** Jeux d'eau
Martha Argerich pf
DG The Originals 447 430-2GOR (71' · ADD)
Recorded 1960-71   ⓜ❶❷❸Ⓓ➨

 Here, on this richly filled CD, is a positive cornucopia of musical genius. Martha Argerich's 1961 disc remains among the most spectacular of all recorded débuts, an impression reinforced by an outsize addition and encore: her 1972 Liszt Sonata. True, there are occasional reminders of her pianism at its most fraught and capricious (Chopin's *Barcarolle*) as well as tiny scatterings of inaccuracies, yet her playing always blazes with a unique incandescence and character.

The Brahms *Rhapsodies* are as glowingly interior as they're fleet. No more mercurial Chopin *Scherzo* exists on record and if its savagery becomes flighty and skittish (with the chorale's decorations sounding like manic bursts of laughter), Argerich's fine-toned fluency will make other, lesser pianists weep with envy. Ravel's *Jeux d'eau* is gloriously indolent and scintillating and the Prokofiev *Toccata* is spun off in a manner that understandably provoked Horowitz's awe and enthusiasm. Liszt's Sixth *Hungarian Rhapsody* is a marvel of wit and daring and the B minor Sonata is among the most dazzling ever perpetuated on disc. The recordings have worn remarkably well and the transfers have been expertly done.

'Live from the Lugano Festival 2008'
Arensky Piano Quintet, Op 51ª **Dvořák** Slavonic Dancesᵇ – Op 46 Nos 1 & 7; Op 72 Nos 2 & 4 **Janáček** Concertinoᶜ **Mozart** Andante and Variations, K501ᵈ **Piazzolla** Tre Tanghi (trans E Hubert)ᵉ. Las cuatro estaciones (arr Bragato)ᶠ **Pletnev** Fantasia elveticaᵍ **Rachmaninov** Suite No 1, Op 5ʰ **Ravel** Introduction and Allegroⁱ **Saint-Saëns** Scherzo, Op 87ʲ **Schumann** Violin Sonata No 2, Op 121ᵏ **Shostakovich** Piano Trio No 1, Op 8ˡ
ᶜCorrado Giuffredi cl ᶜVincent Godel bn ᶜZora Slokar hn ᵏRenaud Capuçon, ᵃᶜLucia Hall, ᶜⁱAlissa Margulis, ᵃDora Schwarzberg vns ᵃᶜNora Romanoff-Schwarzberg va ᶠAlexandre Debrus, ᵃMark Drobinsky, ˡMischa Maisky vcs ᶜᵈᵉᵍʰᵏMartha Argerich, ᶠAlexander Gurning, ᵉEduardo Hubert, ᵈStephen Kovacevich, ᵇKarin Lechner, ᵇˡLily Maisky, ᵍAlexander Mogilevsky, ⁱAkane Sakai, ⁱAlessandro Stella, ⁱGiorgia Tomassi, ᵃʰʲLilya Zilberstein pfs ᵍOrchestra della Svizzera Italiana / Mikhail Pletnev
EMI ③ 267051-2 (3h 40' · DDD)   ⓈⒶ❶➨

'The Berlin Recital'
Bartók Violin Sonata No 1, Sz75. Solo Violin Sonata, Sz117 **Kreisler** Liebesleid. Schön Rosmarin

Schumann Kinderszenen, Op 15. Violin Sonata No 2, Op 121
Gidon Kremer vn **Martha Argerich** pf
EMI ② 693399-2 (117' · DDD)　　　Ⓕ**ⓄⒸⒹ**

Anyone seeking evidence of how keenly Martha Argerich can adjust her personality to suit the interpretative preferences of her colleagues need only compare these two versions of Schumann's Second Violin Sonata from Lugano in 2008 and Berlin in 2006. Argerich in Lugano collaborates with Renaud Capuçon, darting about the score as if treading hot coals, nimble, at times breathless, and consistently appreciative of Capuçon's malleable phrasing and warmly brushed tone. The rapport with a more grainy, acerbic-sounding Gidon Kremer (Berlin) is as great but quite different in musical effect, even though the two sets of movement timings match (within seconds) and in both cases Argerich is recognisably herself. But the contrasts in approach are telling and at times fairly subtle. For example, near the start of the Sonata's slow movement, when the violinist switches from *pizzicato* to *arco* – in Gidon Kremer's case a transformation from genial troubadour to ghostly apparition – Argerich anticipates the change by stealthily, almost hesitantly, slowing the tempo. This is Schumann at his most unhinged. While the Capuçon/Argerich partnership goes for colour and volatility, Kremer and Argerich (who recorded the work some years ago for DG), although equally exciting, are more darkly insistent, more appreciative perhaps of the music's troubled soul. Rarely on disc have so many superficial similarities gone hand in hand with as many profound dissimilarities.

Both performances are riveting, and the two very different acoustics (Lugano is far airier) might have something to do with why Argerich projects so differently in each case. Still, when deciding which version to go for, potential purchasers are likely to view the two programming contexts as crucial. The Lugano set, the latest in series devoted to live recordings from the Festival, is full of memorable treats. It closes with a kaleidoscopic half-hour *Fantasia elvetica* by Mikhail Pletnev who also conducts the Svizzera Italiana Orchestra, his two piano soloists for the occasion Argerich and Alexander Mogilevsky. Although stylistically eclectic (Respighi, Sibelius, Saint-Saëns, Poulenc and Shchedrin all came to mind) the Fantasia is delightful; frothy, listener-friendly and packed full of cheeky tunes. Ravel's two-piano transcription of his *Introduction and Allegro* (Giorgia Tomassi, Alessandro Stella) trades a delicate dreamscape for billowing virtuosity: the effect is rather like the piano version of 'Une barque sur l'océan'. There are piano duets or two-piano works by Mozart (*Andante and Variations*, K501), Saint-Saëns (a rather equivocal-sounding *Scherzo*, Op 87), Rachmaninov (Suite No 1 with Argerich and Lilya Zilberstein) and dances by Piazzolla and Dvořák. We're also given Piazzolla's *Four Seasons* arranged for piano trio. Argerich leads a tangy, rhythmically supple account of Janáček's

madcap Concertino, Lily and Mischa Maisky join violinist Alissa Margulis for Shostakovich's 12-minute First Piano Trio and Zilberstein is the pianist in Arensky's richly romantic Piano Quintet in D. A sense of joy reigns throughout: this music-making could happily serve as a corrective whenever some half-hearted studio-bound session dampens your spirits.

The Berlin concert with Argerich and Kremer is equally gripping but quite different. Argerich goes solo for a typically quixotic account of Schumann's *Kinderszenen*, each cameo following swiftly on the heels of the last, the style alert, playful, keenly attentive to inner voices and in the last two pieces appropriately poised. But for me the performances that make this Berlin concert absolutely indispensable are the two Bartók sonatas. The First Sonata's agitated badinage reaches fever pitch in the finale where Kremer swings in on a *glissando* and the two go hell for leather as one racy folk-style motif follows another. The Sonata's close is an absolute riot, so much so that the first encore, Kreisler's *Liebesleid*, limps in like an innocent bystander mistakenly targeted in a fight. True, *Schön Rosmarin* picks up the spirit but even Kreisler's charm cannot quite erase the recent memory of Bartók's unrelenting onslaught.

The first CD concludes with one of the finest ever recorded performances of Bartók's Solo Sonata, Kremer calling on his full repertoire of violinistic devices which include, in addition to the many called for in the score, a mastery of tonal colouring and a rhythmic grip that at times seem to transcend the limitations of the instrument. Kremer doesn't so much play as speak to you through the music and while his tone hasn't the alluring sweetness of, say, a (young) Menuhin, the sheer electricity of his interpretation more than compensates. Not once does the tension even begin to ease. What an artist!

'Evening Talks'
Martha Argerich pf
Medici Arts **DVD** 307 3428　　　　　　Ⓕ

Pin down Martha Argerich's genius and she walks away with the pin. Most magisterially gifted of all pianists, her quixotic personality flashes in and out of the Medici Arts film 'Evening Talks', at once confiding and capricious as she reflects on the nature of her fraught and zigzag career. Camera-shy ('I'm not an exhibitionist like those people on Big Brother; they actually enjoy being filmed!'), she admits that if (heaven forbid) she was 'a Martha Argerich fan, she would love to see this movie'. Above all there is a sense of healing or recovery, a coming-to-terms with her gifts. For years, she confesses, her face clouding with memories, she felt like someone hurled into a swimming pool, unable to swim and with an increasing sense that her instinctive ability was not counterbalanced by reason or understanding. Catapulted into stardom, she travelled incessantly, met few people of her own age and became confused and depressed. And after reading a sizeable amount of Gide and Dostoyevsky (both obsessed with the idea of the outlaw) she decided to 'transgress', to tell her agent that she had injured her hand before cutting her finger to avoid further public appearances.

Happily such harrowing talk is balanced by a growing sense of realism and confidence as depression shades into whimsy and, finally, stability. She confesses to a heavy debt to Friedrich Gulda, with whom she studied and who she idealised ('I never knew anyone so gifted or extraordinary'). From him she learnt about humour in early Beethoven while confessing that the trills in the central outburst of the slow movement of the Fourth Concerto unnerved her ('I could never play that piece'). Under his stern but often playful guidance she achieved a lighter view of life ('In Argentina we only did 'feelings' and *bel canto*'). Gradually forgetting a time when she thought that one wrong note spelt the end of her career, she relished a jazz critic's comment – 'your Bach swings' – and Erroll Garner's response when he was told his jazz was influenced by Debussy ('Who was that dude?'). She accidentally learnt Prokofiev's Third Concerto while asleep, absorbing a neighbour's performance complete with inaccuracies. Today she rejoices in her appearances with a multitude of exceptionally talented musicians, cherishing their artistry and friendship. Her repertoire may have shrunk but this enables her to recreate endlessly her favoured works, to take risks and live dangerously. For her nothing is set in stone and the Schumann Piano Concerto, for example, is 'forever warm and still to be enjoyed'. A portrait of this elusive artist at all stages of her career, 'Evening Talks' comes triumphantly close to revealing the very essence of Martha Argerich.

Vladimir Ashkenazy　　　　　　　*piano*

'Vladimir Ashkenazy: Master Musician'
Film director **Christopher Nupen**
Vladimir Ashkenazy pf/cond
Allegro Films 📀 A09CND (160' · NTSC · 4:3 · 2.0 · 0
　　　　　　　　　　　　　　　　　Ⓕ

Each of the four sections of this DVD is prefaced by one of the director's idiosyncratic chats to us viewers explaining the background to what we are about to see. Though these introductions are nothing if not self-regarding, Nupen has, to be fair, every right to be pleased with his achievements. He is a director in whose cultured and reassuring company musicians feel secure and relaxed.

The results are films of depth and real insight – and already of some historical importance. For instance, in the first one on the present volume, *The Vital Juices Are Russian*, we meet the young Ashkenazy in 1968 in the throes of moving his wife and small children from London to Iceland while fulfilling a hectic schedule of concerts – as a pianist, of course. The conducting phase of his

career is celebrated in the brief second section, a nine-minute montage of four orchestral movements taken from various other Nupen/Ashkenazy films.

More substantial is the previously unpublished film of Ashkenazy's lengthy, thought-provoking introduction to Rachmaninov's *Corelli* Variations, followed by a live performance of the work in Lugano. The DVD ends with the customary Allegro Films makeweight compilation of 33 short extracts from its catalogue.

Sharon Bezaly　　　　　　　　　*flute*

Dutilleux Sonatine **Jolivet** Chant de Linos **Prokofiev**
Flute Sonata, Op 94 **Schubert** 13 Variations on
'Trockne Blumen', D802
Sharon Bezaly fl **Ronald Brautigam** pf
BIS 🔊 BIS-SACD1429 (63' · DDD/DSD)　　　Ⓕ

The glowing richness of Sharon Bezaly's tone is immediately striking. It may be something of an acquired taste compared to the greater coolness of many of her contemporaries but it proves seductive in this enterprising programme. The Schubert Variations take as their theme the tragic 'Trockne Blumen' from *Die schöne Müllerin*. Outwardly this is an unlikely choice for a set of virtuoso variations but it's far from the vapid fripperies beloved of many a third-rate 19th-century composer, with Schubert brilliantly transforming his original, to end in a triumphant blaze of light. Bezaly is most persuasive, avoiding the sense that this is a mere technical showpiece in even the most noteheavy variations.

The Prokofiev Sonata, here reclaimed for the flute, is light and fast on its feet. There are more dramatically contrasted readings around but none that offers more scintillating brilliance. Bezaly is particularly effective in the *Scherzo*, taken at lightning speed, with the upward glissandi impeccably played, while she makes much of the exoticism of the sinuous middle section. In the *Andante* she plays the throaty seductress to perfection. Throughout, Brautigam is an unobtrusively supportive partner.

The Dutilleux Sonatina dates from the same year (1943) and is a tightly knit three-movement structure originally designed as a test piece for the Paris Conservatoire. The composer has long dismissed it but it's easy to hear why it remains so popular among flautists, especially in this intensely felt performance, Bezaly darting from bar to bar in the *animé* finale, as if eluding capture. Jolivet's *Chant de Linos* has a simple beauty in Bezaly's hands. Overall, a fine disc, matched by ideally warm SACD sound.

Dennis Brain　　　　　　　　　*horn*

Beethoven Quintet for Piano and Wind in E flat,　Ⓗ
Op 16ᵃ **Brahms** Trio for Horn, Violin and Piano in
E flat, Op 40ᵇ **Dukas** Villanelleᶜ **Marais** Le Basqueᵈ
(arr hn & pf) **Mozart** Quintet for Horn and Strings in

E flat, K407/K386[e]
Dennis Brain hn [b]**Max Salpeter** vn [cd]**Wilfrid Parry,**
[b]**Cyril Preedy** pfs [a]**Dennis Brain Wind Ensemble;**
[e]**English String Quartet**
BBC Legends/IMG Artists BBCL4048-2 (72' · ADD)
Recorded 1957   Ⓜ **OO**

This is a marvellous record that does the fullest justice to the art of Dennis Brain, whom Boyd Neel called 'the finest Mozart player of his generation on any instrument'. This 1957 recording of the Mozart Horn Quintet surely bears that out. Brain has warm support from the English String Quartet, particularly in the lovely slow movement, but here his playing consistently dominates the ensemble lyrically, while the closing *Rondo* is sheer joy. So is Marais's delectable *Le Basque*. James Galway has subsequently made this piece his own on record, but Brain uses it as a witty encore, without showing off. Needless to say, the performance of the Brahms Horn Trio is very fine indeed. The infinitely sad, withdrawn atmosphere of the slow movement created by Brain's gentle soliloquy is unforgettable; and the infectious hunting-horn whooping of the finale carries all before it. The recording is distanced in a resonant acoustic and isn't ideally clear, but one soon forgets this.

The Dukas *Villanelle* is an arch-Romantic piece which all horn players feature for the want of something better, and Brain's ardour all but convinces us that it's fine music. But the highlight of the programme is the Beethoven piano and wind quintet, in which Brain shows himself the perfect chamber music partner. Without wishing to dominate, he can't help making his mark at every entry. And his colleagues join him to make a superb team. The recording is astonishingly real. The blending is so perfect, and Parry's pianism isn't only the bedrock of the performance – the playing itself is very beautiful indeed. In short, this is the performance against which all others must now be judged.

Julian Bream   *guitar, lute*

'Julian Bream plays Dowland and Bach'
Julian Bream lte/gtr with **The Golden Age Singers /
Margaret Field-Hyde**
DG mono ② 477 7550GOM2 (141' · ADD)   Ⓜ

When, in 1950, a teenage Julian Bream happened upon Peter Warlock's piano arrangements of some of John Dowland's lute pieces, it was love at first sight. For almost the next 30 years, Bream would devote himself to both the lute and the guitar before relinquishing the former in favour of the latter (although he was to return to the lute many years later).

This wonderful two-CD set takes in three LPs originally released by Westminster during the mid-1950s. As Tully Potter mentions in the booklet-notes, the solo Dowland and Bach LPs are especially significant for having been the first, for a plucked-string instrument, to be entirely devoted to a single composer. Also included is a selection of Dowland's ayres for lute and four voices, in which Bream is joined by the Golden Age Singers.

Ideas about what constitutes an authentic approach to early music fluctuate over time, but Art never goes out of fashion. Yes, Bream uses a wholly guitaristic technique on the lute (including the use of nails – but then Baroque lutenists like Piccinini also used them); yes, his phrasing and sense of timbre bear Segovia's influence to an uncommon degree. But Bream's genius transcends all. Whether it's in the astonishing intensity of Dowland's *Melancholy Galliard* and *Forlorn Hope Fancy* or in the finely proportioned sense of pace and drama in Bach's Chaconne, the impression is ultimately of a meeting of equals.

Alfred Brendel   *piano*

Haydn Piano Sonata in E flat, HobXVI/49 **Mozart**
Piano Sonata No 14 in C minor, K457 **Schubert**
Impromptu in G flat, D899 No 3
Alfred Brendel pf
Opus Arte 📀 OA0811D (155' · 16:9 ·
2.0 · 0) Includes documentary 'Man and Mask',
conversations with Sir Simon Rattle and poetry
readings   Ⓕ **O**

The main element in this double-disc tribute is the 70-minute portrait, 'Man and Mask', directed for television by Mark Kidel. This takes the great pianist to many of the haunts of his early life, as well as showing him relaxing at home in Hampstead. His first recital came in Graz in 1948, and received glowing notices, when he concentrated on works with fugues, including the Brahms *Handel Variations* and a sonata of his own which boasted a double-fugue at the end.

In Vienna he recalls making his first recording for Vox, a coupling of Balakirev's *Islamey*, Mussorgsky's *Pictures at an Exhibition* and Stravinsky's *Petrushka* suite. Later, on the day after his début at Queen Elizabeth Hall, he had offers of recording contracts from three major companies. All this is amplified by clips from archive performances and a separate half-hour conversation with Sir Simon Rattle in rehearsal for Beethoven's Piano Concertos Nos 2 and 4, offering fascinating revelations from both pianist and conductor.

On the second disc comes a recital recorded at The Maltings, Snape, crowning this revealing issue with masterly performances of three of Brendel's favourite works.

Renaud & Gautier Capuçon   *violin & cello*

'Inventions'
Bach/Neumann 20 Duos – selection **Bartók** Seven
Hungarian Folkdances (arr Kreaute)[a] **Beffa** Masques I
(Modéré). Masques II (Rythmiquement souple)
Eisler Duo, Op 7 **Klein** Duo **Kreisler** Marche

miniature viennoise **Martinů** Duo No 2, H371
Renaud Capuçon vn **Gautier Capuçon** vc
ªAude Capuçon pf
Virgin Classics 332626-2 (73' · DDD)   Ⓕ⮕

If you're put off by the idea of a whole CD of just violin and cello (Aude Capuçon only joins brothers Renaud and Gautier for the final three minutes), think again! There's an impressive range both in the music, with its central-European theme, and the performances. The Bach transcriptions are splendidly spirited and stylish; one minor fault – difficult to avoid when playing Bach with a modern bow – is a tendency to exaggerate dynamic inflexions and the difference between long and short notes. The Bartók arrangements are wonderfully colourful and evocative; with such short pieces it's crucial to establish the character straight away, and the Capuçons do this every time.

The items by Karol Beffa were written expressly for the brothers. Each starts in meditative mood, with unclouded tonality, developing more complicated formulations as it proceeds, and each makes masterly use of the instruments' sonorities. The Martinů, dating from the year before his death in 1959, sounds remarkably full. The first movement is particularly attractive – if you imagine a mixture of Stravinsky and Dvořák, you'd be close. The Eisler, by contrast, is an early work, full of expressionistic outbursts, realised here with extreme vividness. The unfinished Duo by Gideon Klein (a young Holocaust victim) is rather more sober, intensely chromatic but not especially dissonant, and with powerfully concentrated melancholy expression.

All this music has a strong sense of time and place. Fritz Kreisler nostalgically evokes the Vienna of Johann Strauss, and here again the Capuçons get right into the idiom.

Sophie Cashell   *piano*

Chopin Nocturne No 20, Op posth. Scherzo No 3, Op 39 **Debussy** L'isle joyeuse. Préludes – La cathédrale engloutie; Minstrels **Kapustin** Motive Force, Op 45 **Liszt** Ballades – No 1, S170; No 2, S171. Drei Liebesträume, S541 **P Martin** Two Variations on Irish Airs **Ravel** Pavane pour une infante défunte
Sophie Cashell pf
Universal Classics & Jazz 476 6459 (79' · DDD)   Ⓕ

Sophie Cashell, winner of the BBC's talent show *Classical Star* and still a student at the RAM, has turned in an impressive debut full of promise. Not the least of its attractions are beautifully sculpted, poised performances of all three of Liszt's *Liebesträume* instead of just the evergreen No 3. The last – more in her fingers than the two lesser-known ones – is nicely done.

In addition we have both of Liszt's Ballades: No 1 is rarely performed but Cashell makes a convincing case for it with some compelling flights of bravura; and No 2, if somewhat too fragmentary in the early stages, is played with

real fire in the belly. She will almost certainly get more out of the C sharp minor *Scherzo* and *L'isle joyeuse* in the future, though they are far from negligible achievements. Two further refreshingly different choices round off the recital – Philip Martin's *Two Variations on Irish Airs* and Nikolai Kapustin's *Motive Force*.

The lively, resonant piano sounds rich and natural, though the upper treble floats away in quieter exposed passages, disembodied from the middle and bass registers. Not a big deal. Sophie Cashell, on the other hand, probably is.

Shura Cherkassky   *piano*

Mendelssohn Andante and Rondo capriccioso, Op 14 **Schubert** Piano Sonata No 20, D959 **Schumann** Carnaval, Op 9 **Schumann/Tausig** Der Kontrabandiste, Op 74 No 10 **Tchaikovsky/Rachmaninov** Cradle Songs, Op 16 No 1
Shura Cherkassky pf
BBC Legends BBCL4254-2 (77' · ADD)   Ⓕ
Recorded live at the Queen Elizabeth Hall, London, on November 1, 1970

'The Complete HMV Stereo Recordings'
Bach/Busoni Chaconne, BWV1004 **Beethoven** Bagatelle, Op 119 No 1 **Chasins** Three Chinese Pieces **Chopin** Mazurka No 7, Op 7 No 3. Waltz No 1, Op 18. Nocturne No 8, Op 27 No 2. Ballades – No 2, Op 38; No 3, Op 47 (two recordings) **Gershwin** Three Preludes (two recordings) **Liszt** Hungarian Rhapsody, S244 No 13. Valse de l'opéra Faust (Gounod), S407 **Litolff** Concerto symphonique No 4, Op 102 – Scherzoª **Lyadov** A Musical Snuffbox, Op 32 **Poulenc** Trois pièces – Toccata **Rachmaninov** Preludes, Op 23 – No 2; No 5 **Saint-Saëns/Godowsky** Le carnival des animaux – Le cygne **Schubert** Impromptu, D899 No 4
Shura Cherkassky pf
ªBBC Symphony Orchestra / Sir Malcolm Sargent
First Hand Records Remasters ② FHR04
(119' · AAD) Recorded 1956/58   Ⓑ

The live Queen Elizabeth Hall recital opens with quintessential Cherkassky. A more perfect rendition of Mendelssohn's *Andante and Rondo capriccioso* you are unlikely ever to hear, deftly executed with a bewitching feather-light delicacy. That said, Cherkassky in heavyweight German repertoire was always less clear cut. Here he plays Schubert's late A major Sonata, a work he visited infrequently. While it is the melody rather than the drama that attracts him, it is difficult not to fall under the beguiling spell of what you are hearing. *Carnaval*, too, for all its idiosyncratic moments, offers a masterclass in colouring and touch – who else can produce such a ravishing *pianissimo* or make an apparent *crescendo* and *decrescendo* on a single note? The Rachmaninov transcription (Cherkassky at his most melancholy) is new to the pianist's official discography.

First Hand's classily presented two-disc set of the complete HMV stereo recordings made in 1956 and 1958 is a treasure chest of Cherkassky rarities. Of the 20 works here, all released for the first time in stereo, 12 have never previously appeared on CD, among them the five Chopin titles and the Bach-Busoni Chaconne. While he was generally at his best in front of an audience, these studio recordings have the same vitality and spontaneity as his live performances. The Litolff *Scherzo* is a delicious musical soufflé while the *Hungarian Rhapsody* No 13 and the *Faust* Waltz (especially the stunning coda) are examples of pure pianistic *joie de vivre*. But above all – and this applies to both discs – are the sheer beauty of sound, individuality of conception and musical imagination that Cherkassky brings to whatever takes his fancy. Required listening for all students of the piano.

Stephen Cleobury   *organ*

'The Grand Organ of King's College, Cambridge'
Bach O Mensch, bewein' dein' Sünde gross, BWV622. Prelude and Fugue, BWV532 **Elgar** Chanson de matin, Op 15 No 2 **Gigout** Six Pièces – Grand choeur dialogué **Handel** Solomon, HWV67 – Arrival of the Queen of Sheba (arr Stainton de B Taylor) **Howells** Six Pieces – Master Tallis's Testament **Mendelssohn** Organ Sonata No 3, Op 65 **Reger** Seven Pieces, Op 145 – Weihnachten **Thalben-Ball** Elegy **Walton** Crown Imperial (arr Brewer) **S Wesley** 12 Short Pieces with a Voluntary added – Gavotte; Air
Stephen Cleobury org
Priory ② (**DVD** + CD) PRDVD3
(72' · 16:9 · PCM stereo and 5.1 · 0)   Ⓕ

King's College's Director of Music, Stephen Cleobury, guides us through the 79 stops of this much-enlarged, rebuilt and oft-heard instrument. It is good to be reminded of its capabilities as a solo instrument and not just as an accompanimental accessory to the College Choir. This film (made in May and June 2008) predates the most recent restoration work to the organ (in early 2009).

The filming and sound recording are up to Priory's excellent standards. Richard Knight's camerawork captures all the action, despite the cramped console environment, with plenty of interesting shots of the pedalboard. Interior views of the Chapel are well-lit, varied and appropriate to the accompanying soundtrack. During Elgar's *Chanson de Matin* and Thalben-Ball's *Elegy* the camera travels further afield across The Backs to Grantchester and the American Cemetery at Madingley.

Cleobury's playing is measured, smooth and beautifully synchronised with that tricky and cavernous acoustic. Nothing is overblown: flamboyance is eschewed. Instead, we can simply revel in the plummy weightiness of Reger, the beautiful lightness of The Queen of Sheba's semiquavers and the rolling timelessness of Master Tallis. Murrill's arrangement of Walton's *Crown Imperial* makes a fulsome finale with the tuba stop making its solitary appearance in the recital. The bonus features are also splendid. Particularly enjoyable is Cleobury's explanation of his approach to registration in each piece.

Imogen Cooper   *piano*

Beethoven Piano Sonata No 28, Op 101
Debussy 24 Préludes – Les terrasses des audiences
Mozart Piano Sonata No 8, K310 **Ravel** Miroirs
Imogen Cooper pf
Wigmore Hall Live WHLIVE0018 (78' · DDD)
Recorded live in 2007   Ⓕ

Throughout her live programme Imogen Cooper's poise and overall artistry make a refreshing change from a more overt, less subtle virtuosity. She captures all of Beethoven's speculative beauty at the start of his Op 101 Sonata, and if others are more fiercely energised in the second movement march, with its prophecy of Schumann's obsessive dotted rhythms, few are more stylish and refined. Again, if her view of Mozart's A minor Sonata could be thought sometimes self-consciously beautiful or manicured, there is no denying her calibre, never more so than in her urgent propulsion of the wind-swept finale.

Cooper studied with Kathleen Long in London and Jacques Février in Paris, which gives her Ravel a special distinction. Less animated or razor-sharp than others in 'Alborada del gracioso', she never forces the issue, and there is never a hint of the literalism that is the bane of many French pianists. 'Noctuelles', 'Oiseaux tristes' and 'La vallée des cloches' come beguilingly alive when played with such freedom and fantasy, yet always within a scrupulously true and accurate framework.

For her encore Cooper gives us Debussy's 'Les terraces des audiences', reminding you in every elusive phrase that subtlety and finesse are at the very heart of great French piano writing. The BBC's soft-grained sound is ideally attuned to this never less than beautiful recital.

Alfred Cortot   *piano*

'Encores'   Ⓗ
Albéniz Sous la palmera, Op 232 No 3
Brahms Wiegenlied, Op 49 No 4 **Chopin** Ballade No 1, Op 23. Berceuse, Op 57. Etude, 'Harp Study', Op 25 No 1. Impromptu No 2, Op 36. Waltz No 7, Op 64 No 2 **Handel** Keyboard Suite, Set 1 – No 5, HWV430 **Liszt** 19 Hungarian Rhapsodies, S244 – No 2; No 11. Paraphrase (on Verdi's Rigoletto), S434 **Schubert** Litanei auf das Fest Allerseelen, D343 **Weber** Aufforderung zum Tanze, J260 Op 65
Alfred Cortot pf
Naxos Historical mono 8 111261 (79' · ADD)
Recorded 1925-26   Ⓢ

Here, in recordings dating from 1925-26, is the very essence of Cortot, superbly remastered by Mark Obert-Thorn. A voice from another age, Cortot was addicted to his incomparable recreative art. Every bar and phrase of these performances induces a frenzy or delirium in the listener, setting the mind and senses reeling. Cortot may have 'discovered the opium in Chopin' (Daniel Barenboim) but he also discovered the opium in virtually everything else. His arrangement and playing of Schubert's *Litany* has all the poetic freedom and sumptuous tonal allure of the greatest singers and always you are made aware of his alternating simplicity, richness and intricacy of expression. Hear the cascades close to the end of Chopin's Second Impromptu and you may well agree that you have rarely heard such feline ease and facility. The mechanics (forced out of focus in the heat of the moment) could be erratic but the technique was scintillating in a way known to very few pianists. Cortot's Liszt Rhapsodies, decked out with an array of sly nudges and winks, are as flamboyant as any on record, and time and again you are made aware of his own dictum on music: 'my secret is, I can't have enough of it'. Above all, he reminds you of Liszt's celebrated description of a virtuoso as 'one called upon to make emotion weep, and sing, and sigh. To conjure scent and blossom, and breathe the breath of life'. A wild but enthralling fragment from Chopin's First Ballade is included (a complete version comes later) and there are two versions of both Liszt's 11th Hungarian Rhapsody and Weber's *Invitation to the Dance*.

Jacqueline du Pré   *cello*

Jacqueline du Pré: Les introuvables
Bach Cello Suites – No 1 in G, BWV1007; No 2 in D minor, BWV1008 (rec live 1962) **Beethoven** 12 Variations on Handel's 'See the conqu'ring hero comes', WoO45[i]. Seven Variations in E flat on Mozart's 'Bei Männern, welche Liebe fühlen', WoO46[i]. 12 Variations in F on 'Ein Mädchen oder Weibchen', Op 66[i] (recorded live 1970). Cello Sonatas[c] – No 3 in A, Op 69; No 5 in D, Op 105 No 2 **Bruch** Kol Nidrei, Op 47[a] **Chopin** Cello Sonata, Op 65[i] **Delius** Cello Concerto[e] **Dvořák** Cello Concerto in B minor, B191[g]. Silent woods, B182[g] **Elgar** Cello Concerto in E minor, Op 85[d] **Fauré** Elégie, Op 24[a] **Franck** Violin Sonata in A[i] (arr vc/pf) **Handel** Oboe Concerto in G minor, HWV287[b] (arr vc/pf Slatter. rec live 1961) **Haydn** Cello Concertos – No 1 in C[h]; No 2 in D[d] **Monn** (arr Schoenberg) Cello Concerto in G minor[d] **Saint-Saëns** Cello Concerto No 1 in A minor, Op 33[f] **Schumann** Cello Concerto in A minor, Op 129[f]
Jacqueline du Pré vc [a]**Gerald Moore**, [b]**Ernest Lush**, [c]**Stephen Kovacevich** pfs [d]**London Symphony Orchestra / Sir John Barbirolli**; [e]**Royal Philharmonic Orchestra / Sir Malcolm Sargent**; [f]**New Philharmonia Orchestra**, [g]**Chicago Symphony Orchestra**, [h]**English Chamber Orchestra / Daniel Barenboim** [i]*pf*
EMI ⑥ 568132-2 (857' · ADD)   Ⓑ**OO**

As the title suggests, this fine six-disc retrospective of Jacqueline du Pré's recording career – a mere 10 years long – was masterminded by French EMI. The wonder was that right from the start Jacqueline du Pré was mature in her artistry, and it's good that from the period even before the first official EMI sessions the collection includes three BBC recordings: Bach's Cello Suites Nos 1 and 2 and a Handel sonata arranged from the Oboe Concerto in G minor. Those early BBC recordings are inevitably flawed, but the sheer scale of the artistry is never in doubt. Of the handful of items recorded by EMI in July 1962 with Gerald Moore accompanying, only Bruch's *Kol Nidrei* is included.

The Delius was du Pré's first concerto recording, and she wasn't nearly as much at ease as she came to be later. The CD transfers don't minimise any of the flaws in the original recordings, notably the disappointing sound given to her Chicago recording of the Dvořák Concerto. Not only does the orchestra sound coarse and thin with a lot of background hiss, the cello is balanced far too close. Even so, the wide dynamic range of du Pré's playing is clearly represented, down to a whispered *pianissimo*. It was right to include it and also the cello sonata recordings of Chopin and Franck, the last she ever made, in December 1971. The tone may not have been quite so even, but the fire and warmth are undiminished.

All the concerto recordings are welcome, with the tear-laden quality in the slow movement of the Schumann matching that in the Elgar. It's good that her supreme Beethoven sonata recordings with Stephen Bishop (later Kovacevich) are included, both sparkling and darkly intense. From the Beethoven series recorded at the 1970 Edinburgh Festival by the BBC only the three sets of variations are included. A must for anyone who was ever magnetised by du Pré's playing.

James Ehnes   *violin*

Barber Violin Concerto **Korngold** Violin Concerto **Walton** Violin Concerto
James Ehnes vn **Vancouver Symphony Orchestra / Bramwell Tovey**
Onyx Classics ONYX4016 (79' · DDD)   Ⓕ

It's an inspired coupling, as well as a generous one, to have these three high-romantic concertos together. James Ehnes gives superb performances, bringing out their full emotional thrust without vulgarity or exaggeration. His playing has always been impressive on disc, but here he excels himself in expressive range as well as tonal beauty, with expressive *rubato* perfectly controlled.

The concertos date from the late 1930s and '40s, and though at the time their romanticism might have seemed outdated, the strength and memorability of the musical ideas in each amply justifies the composers' stance. In the Barber, Ehnes more than usually brings out the contrast between the first movement – improbably marked *Allegro* when the impression is of a slowish piece – and the *Andante* slow movement, strengthening the work's impact. The Korngold, drawing its striking main themes from some of the composer's film scores, is just as richly lyrical, prompting from Ehnes some ecstatic playing of the many stratospheric melodies above the stave, using a wide dynamic range with wonderfully delicate half-tones.

The Walton is just as memorable, for unlike most latter-day interpreters Ehnes has taken note of the example of the work's commissioner and dedicatee, Jascha Heifetz. Where the work is generally spread to well over half an hour, Ehnes takes exactly 30 minutes and the result is all the stronger. This is one of Walton's most richly inspired works, and Ehnes brings that out strongly, helped by the powerful playing of the Vancouver orchestra under Bramwell Tovey. Textures are not always as transparent as they might be but the power of the orchestral playing in all three works adds greatly to the impact of the performances. An outstanding disc in every way.

Rudolf Firkušný   *piano*

Chopin Mazurka, Op 63 No 3 **Martinů** Fantaisie et Toccata **Mussorgsky** Pictures at an Exhibition **Schubert** Three Pieces, D946 **Smetana** Furiant. Concert étude
Rudolf Firkušný pf
BBC Legends BBCL 4238-2 (76' · ADD)
Recorded live at the Queen Elizabeth Hall, London, on February 21, 1980   Ⓕ

Those inclined to think of Rudolf Firkušný as a stylish but understated pianist are in for a surprise. True, in Schubert's D946 pieces he remains a master of understatement. Playing with a patrician ease and grace, he none the less finds all of the Second Impromptu's central agitation, and if the quietly pulsing centre at the heart of No 3 sounds oddly diffident, he ends this whimsical caprice in dazzling style. In the Mussorgksy *Pictures* you sit back and listen to the highest musical quality caught, as it were, on the wing, but it is Firkušný's unleashing of power in the final pages of 'The Great Gate of Kiev' that hints at the sort of reserves he had up his sleeve when in his most outgoing mood.

For his Czech items (always at the heart of a Firkušný recital) he throws off Martinů's *Fantaisie* and Toccata with a special authenticity and aplomb, though even here he hardly prepares you for his Smetana encores. Smetana's piano music bristles with every virtuoso challenge, and the sheer excitement of Firkušný's storm though the C major *Concert Study* (taken at a gloriously indiscreet, hair-raising speed) has the audience cheering him to the rafters. Chopin's Op 63 No 3 Mazurka is spun off with the most gentle lift to its phrases, another reminder of a pianist garlanded with honours, particularly in his homeland and in his adopted America. Firkušný was the sort of musician other musicians flocked to hear and since he made relatively few commerical recordings, this thrilling disc, finely mastered, is doubly welcome.

Leon Fleisher   *piano*

Two Hands
Bach Jesu, Joy of Man's desiring (arr Hess). Sheep may safely graze (arr E Petri) **Chopin** Mazurka No 32.

Nocturne No 8, Op 27 No 2 **Debussy** Suite bergamasque – Clair de lune **D Scarlatti** Keyboard Sonata in E, Kk380 **Schubert** Piano Sonata No 21
Leon Fleisher pf
Vanguard Classics ATMCD1551 (74' · DDD)   ⒻⓄⓄ▸

This verges on the unbelievable. Leon Fleisher, now 75, who for more than 35 years couldn't use his right hand because of dystonia (a neurological disease 'characterised by involuntary muscle contractions which force certain parts of the body into abnormal, sometimes painful movements or positions'), recovers fully after treatment with botulinum toxin (more familiarly known as Botox). And he plays as if he'd never been incapacitated. Dexterity and dynamics are effortlessly controlled. Tone is evenly spread; bass lines aren't weak, chords are cleanly articulated and inner voices have their place. Best of all, technique is coupled to an imaginative intellect that portrays the language of each composer in deep terms.

Schubert's sonata is very personal, running a gamut of feelings from resignation to gaiety but Fleisher (who repeats the first-movement exposition) also finds an undercurrent of toughness which he allows to burst forth in the finale. Yet there's a place for ease, for moments of stillness in the transcriptions of Bach; and it''s gratifying to hear Chopin hauntingly dark and shorn of glitter. Perhaps some glitter would have enlivened Scarlatti's sonata but Fleisher finds a contemplative side to the music that is often overlooked.

Good sound, though the piano is close and recorded level is higher in the Schubert. There are also breathing noises.

Karen Geoghegan   *bassoon*

Bitsch Concertino **Boutry** Interférences I **Debussy** Préludes, Book 1 – No 12, Minstrels. Children's Corner – No 5, The Little Shepherd; No 6, Golliwogg's Cakewalk **Dutilleux** Sarabande et Cortège **Fauré** Pièce **Gallon** Recit et Allegro **Grovlez** Sicilienne et Allegro giocoso **Jancourt** Nocturne (d'après John Field), Op 124 **Koechlin** Sonata, Op 71 **Pierné** Solo de concert, Op 35 **Tansman** Sonatine
Karen Geoghegan bn **Philip Fisher** pf
Chandos CHAN10521 (74' · DDD)   ⒻⒹ▸

Here is an exceptional young musician – technically highly accomplished and to whom lyrical, mellifluous playing seems to come as naturally as wit and charm – at long last raising the profile of the orchestra's Cinderella. The instrument's solo literature is comparatively sparse and one supposes that bassoonists are grateful for any morsel (or, in this case, *morceau*) that comes their way. The problem here is that although many of the works are digitally, respiratorily and musically challenging (several written as test pieces for the Paris Conservatoire), not all of them are terribly good. And there is only so much indistinguishable Gallic caprice one can take at a sitting, as the sequence of Boutry, Gallon, Dutilleux and Bitsch items makes plain.

But there are few enough discs on the market that demonstrate the bassoon's expressive range in such an imaginative programme, the rather distant sound focus of the two instruments notwithstanding. Geoghegan is one of those naturally gifted artists who can make a persuasive case for pieces like Grovlez's *Sicilienne et Allegro giocoso*, Tansman's *Sonatine* and Pierné's *Solo de concert*. The Jancourt and three Debussy titles (transcribed by Bronislav Prorvich) are first recordings, the latter proving surprisingly effective encores.

Emil Gilels   *piano*

Debussy Suite bergamasque – Clair de lune.   [H]
Nocturnes – Fêtes (arr Borwick) **Godowsky**
Renaissance, Book 2 – Gigue in E major, after Loeillet
Mendelssohn Scherzo, Op 16 No 2. Songs Without
Words, Book 3, Op 3 – No 18, 'Duetto', Op 38 No 6
Mozart Piano Sonata No 14, K457 **Rameau** Keyboard
Suite in E minor – Le rappel des oiseaux; La
villageoise **Ravel** Le tombeau de Couperin – Prélude;
Forlane; Toccata **Schumann** Toccata, Op 7.
Fantasiestücke, Op 12 – No 7, Traumes Wirren.
Spanisches Liederspiel, Op 74 – No 10, Der
Kontrabandiste (arr Tausig) **Smetana** Czech Dances –
No 2, Polka in A minor; No 3, Polka in F major
Emil Gilels *pf*
Naxos Historical mono 8 111350 (74' · ADD)
Recorded 1935-51   ⑤❂❂

Here, in performance after performance, is the sort of playing that made Rubinstein, on hearing the teenage Gilels in Russia, exclaim, 'if that boy ever comes to America I might as well pack my bags and retire'. Even in dated sound an 'elemental virtuoso gift' and a 'sonority rich in noble metal' are omnipresent. And whether you hear Gilels in his exquisite Rameau, the thunderous brilliance of his Godowsky or in the way his decorations in Smetana's A minor Polka shimmer like the beating of a hummingbird's wings, you will hear a nonpareil pianism. True, in years to come Gilels would find greater depth than his enviably spruce and immaculately turned Mozart conveys, but even here the playing is of an aristocratic distinction and finesse.

All in all these performances is a reminder of this grandest of musical titans. Ward Marston's transfers come up excellently and special thanks go to Judith Rayner for the loan of discs from her priceless collection.

Naji Hakim   *organ*

Boëllmann Suite gothique, Op 25 – Prière à
Notre-Dame **Franck** Trois Chorales – No 3
Grigny Premier livre d'orgue – Récit de tierce en
taille **Hakim** Sakskøbing Preludes. Improvisation
on 'Amazing Grace'. Glenalmond Suite
Langlais Te Deum, Op 5 No 3
Naji Hakim *org*
Signum Classics SIGCD130 (72' · DDD)
Recorded live on the Harrison & Harrison organ

in the Chapel of Glenalmond College, Perth,
Scotland, on June 10, 2007   Ⓕ

From nearly every point of view this disc is a treat. First, it is a historical document, the inaugural recital – no less – of Glenalmond College's new Harrison & Harrison organ. Its 26 stops, spread over two manuals, are comprehensively explored by Naji Hakim, Messiaen's successor at La Trinité in Paris. He opens this Franco-Belgian display with a centenary tribute to his master and friend Jean Langlais before turning the clock back 300 years to de Grigny's affecting *Récit de tierce en taille*. Boëllmann's *Prière* is carefully controlled, eschewing saccharine and providing a tranquil meditation between Franck's A minor Chorale and the specially commissioned *Glenalmond Suite*.

Initially the Franck seems perfunctory, but the dryish acoustic demands a swifter approach than we are accustomed to. Hakim's Suite and the dozen *Sakskøbing Preludes* (2005, based on Danish hymns) are deliciously enjoyable and entertaining. In the latter he weaves fresh and attractive textures from unfamiliar melodic material. The Suite is based on the chime of Glenalmond's clock tower. The excellent programme note explains fully the biblical allusions of the four movements, the last of which romps along in quasi-theatre organ style, hinting at silent movie chase sequences and the tango!

Although billed as a live recording the audience is entirely silent. However, there are more 'noises off' in the concluding Improvisation in which Hakim contrasts 'Amazing Grace' with 'Auld Lang Syne'. This last track slightly outstays its welcome but don't let this caveat put you off. The playing is beautifully polished, the organ sound is natural and engrossing and the booklet full of interest.

Marc-André Hamelin   *piano*

'The Composer-Pianists'
Alkan Esquisses, Op 63 – No 46, Le premier billet-
doux; No 47, Scherzetto **Bach/Feinberg** Kommst du
nun, Jesu, vom Himmel herunter BWV650 **Busoni**
Fantasia after J. S. Bach **Feinberg** Berceuse, Op 19a
Godowsky Toccata in G flat, Op 13 **Hamelin** Etudes
– No 9, 'd'après Rossini'; No 10, 'd'après Chopin';
No-12 (Prelude and Fugue) **Haydn/Alkan** Symphony
No 94 in G, 'Surprise' – Andante **Medtner** Impro-
visation in B flat minor, Op 31 No 1 **Rachmaninov**
Moment musical in E flat minor, Op 16 No 2. Etude-
tableau in E flat, Op 33 No 4 **Scriabin** Poème
tragique in B flat, Op 34. Deux Poèmes, Op 71
Sorabji Pastiche on Hindu Song from Rimsky-
Korsakov's 'Sadko'
Marc-André Hamelin *pf*
Hyperion CDA67050 (68' · DDD)   Ⓕ❂❂

Here is a cunning and potent mix of every conceivable form of pianistic and musical intricacy (it excludes the merely decorative, salon or ephemeral). Everything is of the most absorbing interest; everything is impeccably performed. Hamelin's richly inclusive programme ranges from Godowsky's *Toccata*, music of the most wicked, labyrinthine complexity, to three of his own projected cycle of 12 *Etudes*, among them a ferociously witty and demanding Prelude and Fugue and a reworking of Chopin's Op 10 No 5, full of black thoughts as well as black notes. Then there's Alkan's sinister absorption of the *Andante* from Haydn's *Surprise* Symphony (loyal to Haydn, Alkan's teasing perversity also makes such music peculiarly his own); a *Berceuse* by Samuel Feinberg that prompts Francis Pott, in his brilliantly illuminating notes, to question what sort of child would be lulled by such strangeness; some superb Medtner and Scriabin and a cloudy, profoundly expressive *Fantasia after J. S. Bach* by Busoni. Clearly among the most remarkable pianists of our time, Hamelin makes light of every technical and musical difficulty, easing his way through Godowsky's intricacy with yards to spare, registering every sly modulation of Alkan's 'Le premier billet-doux' and generating a white-hot intensity in Rachmaninov's admirably revised version of his Second *Moment musical*. Here, Hamelin's maintenance of a 'line' set within a hectically whirling complexity is something to marvel at. Taut, sinewy and impassioned, this performance is a worthy successor to Rachmaninov's own legendary disc. Every phrase and note is coolly appraised within its overall context and the results are audacious and immaculate as required. Hyperion's sound is superb.

'In a State of Jazz'
Antheil Jazz Sonata **Gulda** Prelude and Fugue. Play Piano Play – Exercise No 1; Exercise No 4; Exercise No 5 **Kapustin** Piano Sonata No 2 **Weissenberg** Six Arrangements of songs sung by Charles Trenet. Sonate en état de jazz
Marc-André Hamelin *pf*
Hyperion CDA67656 (69' · DDD)   Ⓕ Ⓞ

'In a State of Jazz' presents a form of fusion music where the influence of jazz is grafted onto classical forms. So although Gulda, Kapustin and Weissenberg whirl us into heady jazz idioms, their work is notated rather than improvised. As Marc-André Hamelin tells us in the opening sentence of his brilliant accompanying essay, 'there is no jazz on this recording'.

Again, all three composers, temporarily stifled by classical norms and mores, sought a liberation that would send them soaring into what would once be considered alien territory. Weissenberg, for example, claims his *Sonata in a State of Jazz* is fuelled by 'intoxication, contamination and madness' while 'written in a state of indisputable sobriety'. Gulda, too, loved to escape from the confines of Carnegie Hall to the Birdland club in New York, jamming away into the small hours and claiming that he had left the past to join the vibrant living present and future. All this and much more makes for music that is arguably more brittle and sophisticated than

uplifting, but it is played with such astounding agility and aplomb that you end up mesmerised by virtually every bar. Indeed, it is no exaggeration to say that no other pianist could approach Hamelin in such music. Notes pour and cascade like diamonds from his fingers and he has an inborn flair for the music's wild, free-wheeling melodies and rhythms, for its glittering whimsy and caprice.

Doubting Thomases should try the first movement of Kapustin's Second Sonata for crazed virtuoso exuberance and Trenet's 'Coin de rue' (cunningly arranged by Weissenberg) for teasing nostalgia. Superbly presented and recorded, this is a special addition to Hamelin's towering and unique discography.

Jascha Heifetz   *violin*

'Heifetz the Supreme'   Ⓗ
Bach Violin Partita No 2 in D minor, BWV1004 – Chaconne **Brahms** Violin Concerto in D, Op 77[a] **Bruch** Scottish Fantasy, Op 46[b] **Gershwin** (arr Heifetz) Three Preludes[c] **Glazunov** Violin Concerto in A minor, Op 82[d] **Sibelius** Violin Concerto in D minor, Op 47[e] **Tchaikovsky** Violin Concerto in D, Op 35[f]
Jascha Heifetz *vn* [c]**Brooks Smith** *pf* [aef]**Chicago Symphony Orchestra** / [af]**Fritz Reiner**; [b]**New Symphony Orchestra** / [b]**Sir Malcolm Sargent**; [d]**RCA Victor Symphony Orchestra** / [de]**Walter Hendl**
RCA Red Seal ③ 74321 63470-2 (154' · ADD)
Recorded 1955-65   Ⓜ

For once a record company's hype is totally justified. Heifetz was and is supreme. He plays the Bach 'Chaconne', with an extraordinary range of dynamic and feeling, and a total grip on the structure. The subtlety of his bowing is a thing to marvel at. This is a superb anthology, excellently accompanied. How persuasively Reiner shapes the opening of the Brahms, and Sargent the *Scottish Fantasy*; how tenderly Heifetz plays the 'Canzonetta' of the Tchaikovsky, and then astonishes us with his quicksilver brilliance in the finale. Heifetz's first entry in the Sibelius is quite Elysian, and his tone in the slow movement sends shivers down the spine. He discovered all the romantic charm in the Glazunov concerto, and virtually made it his own. And how good that the selection ends with Gershwin, sparklingly syncopated and bluesy by turns: nothing else here better shows the flexibility of the Heifetz bow arm, even if the microphones are too close.

Christopher Herrick   *organ*

Organ Dreams, Volume 2
Barber (arr Strickland) Adagio, Op 11 **Dubois** In paradisum **Bridge** Adagio in E, H63 No 2 **Elgar** 11 Vesper Voluntaries, Op 14 **Guilmant** Sonata No 7 in F, Op 89 – Rêve **Howells** Siciliano for a High Ceremony **Liszt** Evocation à la Chapelle Sixtine, S658 **Schumann** Study in A flat, Op 56 No 4 **S Wesley** Short Pieces with Voluntary – No 5 in A minor; No 8 in F; No 9 in F; No 11 in D

Christopher Herrick *org*
Hyperion CDA67146 (73' · DDD)   Ⓕ 〇

Following eight highly acclaimed discs of 'Organ Fireworks', the winning combination of Christopher Herrick and Hyperion turn their attention towards the calmer and more reflective repertory grouped under the title 'Organ Dreams'. Volume 2 consists mostly of original organ music spanning the period 1815-1952, all of which fits the instrument in Ripon Cathedral like a well-tailored glove.

Not every title reflects a dream-like state, though the disc's opening track – Dubois' *In paradisum* creates an aura of calm. Frank Bridge's oft-played *Adagio in E* is also smoothly shaped, with its grand climax carefully controlled. Guilmant's 'Rêve' of 1902 is delicious, its impressionistic perfume wafting effortlessly.

With a running time of 19 minutes, Elgar's rarely heard *Vesper Voluntaries* of 1889 form the centrepiece of Herrick's programme. What charmers they are: mostly *mezzopiano* in dynamic, with occasional fuller-bodied outbursts, none of them outstays its welcome. They are followed by Howells' rambling *Siciliano* (the most recent piece on the disc), which Herrick keeps moving. However, he does allow himself plenty of time for William Strickland's convincing arrangement of Barber's *Adagio*.

The Liszt is a shameless piece of kitsch which borrows freely from Allegri's *Miserere* and Mozart's *Ave verum corpus*. More worthwhile are Schumann's *Study* and a quartet of miniatures by Samuel Wesley. The only fault with the whole package is that the portrait purporting to be that of Wesley senior is, in fact, that of his natural son, Samuel Sebastian.

In summary, this thoroughly enjoyable disc is sensitively and affectionately played, and works well at a single hearing.

Vladimir Horowitz   *piano*

The Solo European Recordings, 1930-36,   Ⓗ
Bach/Busoni Nun freut euch, lieben Christen gmein, BWV734 **Beethoven** 32 Variations on an Original Theme in C minor, WoO80 **Chopin** Etudes – C sharp minor, Op 10 No 4; G flat, 'Black Keys', Op 10 No 5; F, Op 10 No 8; F, Op 25 No 3 (recorded 1934). Mazurkas – F minor, Op 7 No 3; E minor, Op 41 No 2; C sharp minor, Op 50 No 3. Scherzo No 4 in E, Op 54. Piano Sonata No 2 in B flat minor, 'Funeral March', Op 35 – Grave … doppio movimento (rec 1936) **Debussy** Etude No 11 'Pour les arpèges composés' **Haydn** Keyboard Sonata in E flat, HobXVI/52 **Liszt** Funérailles, S173 No 7. Piano Sonata in B minor, S178 **Poulenc** Pastourelle. Toccata **Prokofiev** Toccata in D minor, Op 11 (rec 1930) **Rachmaninov** Prelude in G minor, Op 23 No 5 **Rimsky-Korsakov/Rachmaninov** The tale of Tsar Saltan – Flight of the bumble-bee **D Scarlatti** Keyboard Sonatas – B minor, Kk87; G, Kk125 **Schumann** Presto passionato in G minor (rec 1932). Arabeske in C, Op 18. Traumes Wirren, Op 12 No 7. Toccata in C, Op 7 **Stravinsky** Petrushka –

Russian dance (rec 1932)
Vladimir Horowitz *pf*   Ⓑ 〇〇
APR mono ② APR6004 (140' · ADD)

Horowitz's 1930-36 European recordings are beyond price, and so it's more than gratifying to have them permanently enshrined on APR rather than fleetingly available elsewhere. This is notably true of Horowitz's legendary, forever spine-tingling 1932 recording of the Liszt Sonata. Here, once more, is that uniquely teasing and heroic sorcery with octaves and passagework that blaze and skitter with a manic force and projection; an open defiance of all known musical and pianistic convention. Horowitz's virtuosity, particularly in his early days, remains a phenomenon, and hearing, for example, the *vivamente* elaboration of the principal theme or the octave uproar preceding the glassy, retrospective coda is to be reminded of qualities above and beyond the explicable. His way with the Chopin *Mazurkas* unites their outer dance elements and interior poetry with a mercurial brilliance and idiosyncrasy, and who but Horowitz could use his transcendental pianism to conjure a *commedia dell'arte* vision of such wit and caprice in Debussy's *Etude, Pour les arpèges composés*? Of the previously unpublished recordings, the first movement from Chopin's Second Sonata is as macabre and tricky as ever, with a steady, oddly menacing tempo. Prokofiev's *Toccata*, on the other hand, is tossed off at a nail-biting speed, and not even a small but irritating cut, a wild, approximate flailing at the end and an added chord by way of compensation, can qualify the impact of such wizardry. In Rachmaninov's G minor Prelude, however, Horowitz's volatility gets the better of him. If Horowitz, in common with virtually every other pianist, was not equally convincing in every composer and was even 'a master of distortion' for some, he was a Merlin figure of an indelible, necromantic brio for all others.

Though expertly transferred, they do show their age somewhat, but nothing can lessen the impact of Horowitz's early charisma.

'Rediscovered – Carnegie Hall Recital, November 16, 1975'
Chopin Scherzo No 1 in B minor, Op 20. Waltz No 3 in A minor, Op 34 No 2 **Debussy** Children's Corner – Serenade for a doll **Liszt** Au bord d'une source, S160 No 4. Valse oubliées in F sharp, S215 No 1 **Moszkowski** Etincelles, Op 36 No 6 **Rachmaninov** Etudes-tableaux, Op 39 – No 5 in E flat minor; No 9 in D. Prelude in G, Op 32 No 5 **Schumann** Blumenstück in D flat, Op 19. Träumerei, Op 15 No 7. Piano Sonata No 3 in F minor, Op 14
Vladimir Horowitz *pf*
RCA Red Seal ② 82876 50754-2 (87' · ADD)   Ⓜ〇〇〇

Ⓖ Aged 72 at the time of this 1975 Carnegie Hall recital, this musical Merlin plays with all his compulsive, mesmerising magic. Mischievous, egotistical, lavishly tinted and tilted very much towards the performer rather than the composer it may be, but the illusion that theirs is the only possible way still holds in a concert issued on disc for the first time.

Schumann was always at the heart of Horowitz's repertoire, the *Blumenstück* a speciality with which he loved to tease and cajole his audience, its arched and inflected phrases declaring his identity in every coaxing note and nuance. His performance of the Third Sonata, too, is of an astonishing intricacy. Everything is on the wild side, a mix of raging passions and whispered confidences.

Such playing isn't for those who feel that music should be allowed its own voice, that the zenith of artistry lies in the selfless subordination of re-creator to creator. His performance of Chopin's A minor Waltz, for example, is at once outrageous and inimitable, sighing and crooning shamelessly to the gallery.

RCA faithfully capture the sound of Horowitz's piano, its glassy treble and resonating bass making Neville Cardus's description of 'the greatest pianist dead or alive' a vivid and persuasive possibility, rather than mere hyperbole.

Stephen Hough   *piano*

'English Piano Album'
Bantock Song to the Seals (arr Hough) **Bowen**
Rêverie d'amour, Op 20 No 2. Serious Dance Op 51
No 2. The Way to Polden, Op 76 **Bridge** The Dew
Fairy. Heart's Ease **Elgar** In Smyrna **Hough** Valse
énigmatique – No 1; No 2 **Leighton** Study Variations,
Op 56 Rawsthorne Bagatelles **Reynolds** Two Poems
in Homage to Delius. Two Poems in Homage to
Fauré
Stephen Hough *pf*
Hyperion CDA67267 (74' · DDD)   Ⓕ

The very opening item, Rawsthorne's four *Bagatelles*, instantly makes it clear that this latest recital disc from Stephen Hough has a different aim from his previous collections of charmers. Gritty and tough, in Hough's hands sounding wonderfully pianistic, these miniatures are thoughtful and intense, balanced at the end of the disc by the final item, also by far the longest, Kenneth Leighton's *Study Variations*. These do not make for easy listening either, but they inspire Hough to superb pianism over six sharply characterised pieces, at times echoing Bartók in their angry energy, at others full of fantasy. What all these very varied pieces demonstrate is Hough's profound love of keyboard sound and textures, and his rare gift of bringing out the full tonal beauty.

It's evidence, too, of Hough's wizardry that he makes the Elgar piece, *In Smyrna*, sound so magical. In his hands it's like an improvisation with echoes of the lovely solo viola serenade in the overture, *In the South*. The three Bowen works are simple and song-like using an almost cabaret-style of piano writing. In all these pieces Hough's magic is presented in full, clear Hyperion sound. Thoroughly recommended.

Stephen Hough's New Piano Album
Chaminade Autrefois, Op 87 No 4. Pierrette, Op 41
Godowsky Triakontameron – Alt Wien **Hough** Etude
de Concert. Musical Jewellery Box **Kálmán** Was
weiss ein nie geküsster Rosenmund (arr Hough) **Liszt**
Soirée de Vienne-in A minor, S427 No 6 **Moszkowski**
Etincelles, Op 36 No 6 **Pabst** Paraphrase on
'Sleeping Beauty' (arr Hough) **Paderewski** Mélodie
in G flat, Op 16 No 2 **Rachmaninov** Humoresque in
G, Op 10 No 5. Mélodie in E, Op 3 No 3 (1940 vers)
Rodgers Carousel – The Carousel Waltz. The King
and I – Hello, Young Lovers (all arr Hough) **Schubert**
Moment musical in F minor, D780 No 3. Die schöne
Müllerin, D795 – No 8, Morgengruss (all arr
Godowsky) **Tchaikovsky** Dumka, Op 59. Humoresque
in E minor, Op 10 No 2. Swan Lake, Op 20 – Pas de
quatre (arr Wild) **Traditional** The Londonderry Air
(arr Hough)
Stephen Hough *pf*
Hyperion CDA67043 (78' · DDD)   Ⓕ

Stephen Hough fashions a viable programme culled from a bottomless piano bench of transcriptions, encores and other sundry ear-ticklers. Indeed, Hough proves that one can make a well-balanced meal using only desserts. Modern pianists, to be sure, are more calorie conscious than their forebears, and Hough is no exception. It's not his way to emphasise inner voices or linger over juicy modulatory patterns, *à la* Hofmann, Moiseiwitsch, Horowitz, Cortot or Cherkassky. If Hough prefers to bind Godowsky's garish counterpoints with skimmed milk rather than double cream, he's cheeky (and smart!) enough to insert his own *ossias* into Moskowski's *Etincelles*, or to retool the Tchaikovsky/Pabst *Sleeping Beauty* Paraphrase to more brilliant pianistic effect. As in his previous 'Piano Albums', Hough serves up his own Rodgers & Hammerstein transcriptions. If the decorative note-spinning in 'Hello, Young Lovers' distracts from rather than enhances the eloquent original, the pianist's giddy romp through 'The Carousel Waltz' is a tour de force that brilliantly recaptures both the tender and tough-minded qualities inherent in the musical's book. Hough's own *Etude de Concert* gets plenty of finger-twisting mileage out of a rather un-memorable theme, harmonised, however, with clever Gershwinisms. The unadorned Rachmaninov and Tchaikovsky selections are played with heartfelt simplicity and a lean yet singing sonority.

'A Mozart Album'
Cramer Hommage à Mozart **I Friedman** Menuetto
Hough Three Mozart Transformations after Poulenc
Liszt/Busoni Fantasia on Two Themes from Mozart's
'The Marriage of Figaro' **Mozart** Fantasia, K396.
Fantasia, K475. Piano Sonata No 13, K333
Stephen Hough *pf*
Hyperion CDA67598 (70' · DDD)   ⒻⓄ

This is the kind of musical meal that any pianist with the imagination and culinary skills of a good chef should be able to put together. Sadly there are all too few pianists with the equivalent of Hough's three Michelin stars.

Opening with two of Mozart's solo master-pieces, the ear is welcomed into an intimate, pellucid sound world with a sophisticated grading of dynamics. Hough plays with what used to be called 'a quiet hand', particularly effective in the first movement of the B flat major Sonata in which he finds an unexpected melancholy amid the music's basically optimistic character.

After the dramatic second (earlier) C minor Fantasia completed by Stadler, and Cramer's attractive Etude, Op 103 No 6, we seem to be listening to a different pianist who now relishes the delicate, perfumed harmonies of Friedman's Menuetto transcription. In the same vein, but imbued with witty Poulencian devices, Hough the pianist-composer reminds us how important charm is to the pianist's arsenal. Again, the pianist changes. This time we hear a barn-storming virtuoso in the Liszt-Busoni Fantasy on 'Non più andrai' and 'Voi che sapete' from *The Marriage of Figaro*. More fragmentary than the better-known *Don Giovanni* Fantasy and not quite as effective, it nevertheless provides a hair-raising bravura display that deserves to be heard more often. At least, when played like this.

Stephen Hough in Recital
Beethoven Piano Sonata No 32, Op 111
Chabrier Feuillet d'album Leaf **Chopin** Waltzes – No 2, Op 34 No 1; No 7, Op 64 No 2 **Debussy** La plus que lente **Liszt** Mephisto Waltz No 1, 'Der Tanz in der Dorfschenke', S514. 4 Valse oubliées, S215 No 1
Mendelssohn Variations sérieuses, Op 54
Saint-Saëns Valse nonchalante, Op 110
Traditional Waltzing Matilda **Weber** Aufforderung zum Tanze, J260 Op 65
Stephen Hough pf
Hyperion CDA67686 (79' · DDD)   Ⓕ

The menu for this sumptuous banquet, with its tasty hors d'oeuvre, substantial classic dish as the main course followed by a variety of unexpected and nourishing desserts, is perfectly balanced – enough to fill you without being bloated, and nothing that is hard to chew or liable to give you indigestion. But it is the different wines accompanying each course that make this meal special, that is to say the discriminating premier cru tone, touch (what magically hushed *pianissimos*) and masterly pedalling to which the diners are treated, each element adjusted to each composer yet all unmistakably Stephen Hough – vintage Hough at that, for here is a pianist at the height of his powers.

This is the sort of programme and style of playing redolent of the so-called Golden Age of Rachmaninov, Hofmann, Godowsky, Cortot *et al* but which, in this earnest urtext era, is encountered all too infrequently. The Mendelssohn (with some seriously brisk tempi – try variations Nos 8 and 9) and a taut, crisply articulated account of Beethoven's Op 111 explore two aspects of variation form.

The 'second half' is devoted to waltz time, beginning with Weber's pioneering *Invitation*

(1819), the earliest work in this recital. For some unaccountable reason it is rarely heard in its original form these days. Hough's is at his finest – exuberant, seductive and scintillating by turns with the repeats (all are given) subtly varied second time round. After two delectably suave Chopin waltzes, Hough offers three contrasted Gallic takes on 3/4 time, imbuing each with the kind of affection and charm for which Cherkassky was famous. After this he cleverly takes us gently by the ear via Liszt's nostalgic *Valse oubliée* No 1 to the pianistic diablerie of his *Mephisto Waltz* No 1. Rounding off this master-class is Hough's own witty transformation of *Waltzing Matilda* from its normal duple time to triple time. A great piano recording.

Mayuko Kamio   *violin*

Chausson Poème, Op 25 **Stravinsky** Suite italienne (after Pulcinella) **Szymanowski** Mythes, Op 30 **Tchaikovsky** Méditation, Op 42 No 1. Valse-Scherzo, Op 34 **Waxman** Carmen Fantasy
Mayuko Kamio vn **Vadim Gladkov** pf
RCA Red Seal 88697 30100-2 (79' · DDD)   Ⓕ

Mayuko Kamio, born in Osaka, Japan, but who studied also in the USA, won the 1998 Menuhin International Competition. She was the youngest artist to win this award – performing with Menuhin directing – and went on to win the gold medal in the 13th International Tchaikovsky Competition in Moscow. She plays a 1727 Stradivarius once owned by Joachim and creates with it a remarkable range of vividly glowing timbre, playing with infinite subtlety of colour and phrasing. Moreover, she has planned this ambitious recital with skill, offering six shorter concertante works which are beautifully balanced as a whole, with the gentle charm and melancholy of the two Tchaikovsky pieces ideally placed to set off against their companions. She closes the *Méditation* exquisitely so that the sensuous rapture of the Chausson *Poème* follows on perfectly to make the rich musical highlight of the programme, helped by the lovely playing of her excellent partner pianist, Vadim Gladkov.

Szymanowski's shimmering *Mythes* make for another sensuous peak of feeling, full of exotic, lyrical fervour, the finale 'Dryads and Pan' pictorially quite riveting. How clever, too, not to end the recital with Waxman's sparkling *Carmen Fantasy* but to open with it, and immediately show her ability to catch the individual vocal quality of each of Bizet's indelibly folksy tunes. Then she offers Stravinsky's vigorously genial *Pulcinella* arrangement for her finale, another stream of rhythmically catchy melody that violinist and pianist share with gusto. Excellent recording makes this a debut not to be missed.

William Kapell   *piano*

'Kapell Rediscovered – The Australian Broadcasts'
Bach Suite, BWV818 **Chopin** Barcarolle, Op 60.

Nocturne, Op 55 No 2. Scherzo No 1, Op 20
Debussy Suite Bergamasque **Mozart** Piano
Sonata No 16, K570 **Mussorgsky** Pictures at an
Exhibition **Prokofiev** Piano Sonata No 7, Op 83
Rachmaninov Piano Concerto No 3[a] **Traditional** God
Save the Queen
William Kapell pf
[a]**Victorian Symphony Orchestra /
Sir Bernard Heinze**
RCA Red Seal mono ② 82876 68560-2
(151' · ADD). Radio broadcasts live from Town Hall,
Melbourne, in July and October 1953   Ⓜ

William Kapell was killed in a plane crash just
south of San Francisco in October 1953 – the
flight that was taking him home a week after he
had completed a triumphant three-month tour
of Australia. He was 31 years old. Several items
from this final trip have surfaced over the years
(the Rachmaninov, Mussorgsky and Chopin's
Second Sonata), but other rumoured recordings
never materialised – until 2003, when the titles
issued here were identified in a huge collection
of acetate discs recorded off-air by an Australian
music lover.

The surfaces are noisy, sometimes heavily
swishy and the sound is often horribly distorted
despite the best efforts of producer Jōn M Sam-
uels. His apologia notes that, because they did
not make it on to the acetates, a passage in the
final movement of the Rachmaninov had to be
patched (from a 1948 performance), and that the
first movement of the Bach Suite and final pages
of the Mussorgsky are taken from other sources.
You will not need to be told where these 'edits'
occur.

So, is it all worth persevering with? Oh yes.
This is the playing of a sublimely gifted artist.

Edin Karamazov   *lute*

'The Lute is a Song'
Anonymous So Maki Se Rodila **Bach** Toccata and
Fugue, BWV565 **Brouwer** Paisaje cubano con rumba
Domeniconi Koyunbaba, Op 19 **Handel** Saul –
O Lord, whose mercies[a] **Purcell** Dido and Aeneas –
When I am laid in earth[b] **Sting** Alone with my
thoughts this evening[c] **Zamboni** Lute Sonatas, Op 1
– Sonata in C minor
Edin Karamazov gtr/lte with [b]**Renée Fleming** sop
[a]**Andreas Scholl** counterten [c]**Sting** sngr
L'Oiseau-Lyre 478 1077DH (60' · DDD)   Ⓕ

Here's a release that's as unusual and distinctive
as Edin Karamazov's own playing. What other
lutenist would open his disc with Leo Brouwer's
Paisaje cubano con rumba, originally for four guitars but here played on a single, multi-tracked
electric guitar, and follow it by accompanying
Sting on archlute as the latter sings his own
Alone with my thoughts this evening?

Karamazov was always a great player – technically superb, musically imaginative and never
afraid to take risks. But when he and Sting
recorded an album of songs by English Renaissance master John Dowland, he found himself

achieving almost superstar status overnight – no
mean feat for a lutenist. Thus 'The Lute is a
Song' is in many ways designed to appeal to a
broad, albeit relatively sophisticated, audience.

And appeal it should: after all, who can resist a
fabulous, Eastern-sounding lute version of
Bach's Toccata and Fugue in D minor (certainly
not all those Sky fans out there)? Or a lute version of Carlo Domeniconi's Turkish delight
Koyunbaba, normally heard on classical guitar
but here given a mind-bending reappraisal on a
14-course Baroque lute? Purists aren't forgotten
either, a stylish account of Giovanni Zamboni's
Sonata and a superb rendering of Handel's 'Oh
Lord, whose mercies numberless' from *Saul*
with countertenor Andreas Scholl being among
the choicest items in this vein.

Wilhelm Kempff   *piano*

Bach Chromatic Fantasia and Fugue in D minor,
BWV903 **Beethoven** Piano Sonata No 22 in F, Op 54
Schubert Piano Sonata No 12 in F minor, D625. Drei
Klavierstücke, D946. Impromptus, D899 – No 3 in G
flat; No 4 in A flat
Wilhelm Kempff pf
BBC Legends/IMG Artists BBCL4045-2 (77' · ADD)
Recorded live 1969   Ⓜ ⓞⓞⓞ

Ⓖ   Kempff's art was at its apogee at the
        time of his 70th birthday in the autumn
        of 1965; rigour and fantasy held in per-
fect poise. Bryce Morrison, who has provided
the notes for this BBC Legends release, and who
was present at this concert – and indeed many
other legendary recitals, recalls: 'If I were to
single out one musical experience that transcended all others, it would have to be Wilhelm
Kempff's 1969 Queen Elizabeth Hall recital. At
his greatest, as he undoubtedly was on this occasion, Kempff's playing seemed bathed in a
numinous light or halo of sound, his choice of
music by Bach, Beethoven, and Schubert seemingly improvised on the spot.'

Alfred Brendel has said of Kempff, 'he was an
Aeolian harp, ever ready to respond to whatever
interesting wind blew his way'. It's a remark that
applies especially well to Kempff's Schubert. He
has said that in his early years Schubert's music
was a book with seven seals. He played Schubert
Lieder, but it was not until much later, after the
First World War, that he entered the private
world of the piano sonatas. For him, Schubert's
'heavenly length' was never lengthy if seen in
proportion to the larger experience. 'If length
becomes evident as longueur,' Kempff has written, 'the fault lies with the interpreter (I speak
from my own experience …).'

Not here. The reading is wonderfully taut yet
touched with a rare ease of utterance. The enigmatic end is perfectly judged (and well 'heard' by
an audience whose applause merely stutters into
life). After the 'disconsolate lyricism' (BM's
phrase) of the sonata, the *Drei Klavierstücke* offer
more or less unalloyed pleasure, Kempff wing-
ing the music into life. The playing has charm,

dash and magic. He once said of Schubert's piano music: 'It ought not to be subjected to the glaring lights of the concert halls, as it's the confession of an extremely vulnerable spirit. Schubert reveals his innermost secrets to us *piano-pianissimo*.' We hear this wonderfully well in Kempff's playing of the first of his two encores, the Impromptu in G flat, where his fabled *cantabile* comes even more mesmerisingly into its own. An Aeolian harp indeed!

At the start of the recital, Kempff provides a shrewdly voiced and somewhat Mendelssohnian account of Bach's *Chromatic Fantasia and Fugue*. It's a performance to free the fingers and light the way ahead, the great work assuming the role of warm-up man with as good a grace as can be expected.

Garth Knox   *viola da gamba*

'D'Amore'
Ariosti Six Lessons – Lesson I **Huber** ...Plainte...
Hume A Pavin **Knox** Malor me bat **Marais** Variations
on 'Les folies d'Espagne' **Moser** Manners of
Speaking **Traditional** Celtic Dance/I once loved a
lass/Jig
Garth Knox va da gamba **Agnes Vesterman** vc
ECM New Series ② 476 6369 (54' • DDD) Ⓕ

This is quite simply an outstandingly magical disc. From the very first notes one is totally captivated by the fantastic richness of the sound produced by the combination of the viola d'amore and the cello. The viola's sound is precisely described by Paul Griffiths in his notes when he writes of a 'rainbow resonance' – the phrase describes the shimmering harmonic aura created around the music by the freely resonating sympathetic strings. And it traverses, as this recording amply demonstrates, time as well as acoustical space: Knox's transcriptions of Marais and Hume, not to mention of traditional melodies ('Celtic Dance/I once loved a lass/Jig') work marvellously, making the two instruments merge into some kind of enormously expanded viola da gamba.

The contemporary works, with the exception of Knox's own inevitably idiomatic fantasy on 'Malor me bat', might seem initially to work against this resonant universe built on the harmonic series, but in fact they are all carefully written with the instrument's possibilities in mind. Klaus Huber's ...*Plainte*... is dedicated to Luigi Nono, and it transfers something of the Italian's fragmented late sound world very successfully to solo viola d'amore, making use in the process of special tunings (three strings are tuned in third-tones). The stunning sound of this remarkable CD will disappoint nobody.

Patricia Kopatchinskaya   *violin*

Bartók Six Romanian Folk Dances, Sz56
Beethoven Violin Sonata No 9, 'Kreutzer', Op 47
Ravel Violin Sonata **Say** Violin Sonata

Patricia Kopatchinskaja vn **Fazil Say** pf
Naïve V5146 (67' · DDD)   Ⓕ

This is far from being just another recording of the *Kreutzer* Sonata. Patricia Kopatchinskaja and Fazil Say share a radical approach, performing each musical gesture in the most vivid way, with smoothness and tonal beauty a secondary consideration. It's undeniably exciting, especially the first movement which, after all, is quite a wild piece, but the exaggerated shortness of many *staccato* notes can be quite disturbing. And in the finale, which, though it shares something of the first *Presto*'s manic quality, has a joyful aspect, Kopatchinskaja's ultra-short, rather splashy bowing of both main themes fails to project their full melodic élan.

Like the Beethoven, the Bartók is a slightly frustrating mixture of the brilliant and the questionable, but in the Ravel the performance's radical edge is more completely successful. The first movement's out-of-key interjections are sharply characterised and drawn together by a powerful sense of line, and the spirit of the Blues movement is captured wholeheartedly, with some unusual piano sounds and spectacular violin-playing. Not surprisingly, Say's own Sonata is also beautifully played. Most imaginatively written for the two instruments and adopting a direct, uncomplicated style, four short movements chart a progression from romantic melancholy through an area of dark, grotesque struggle to an empty, bleak landscape, with a repeat of the gentle first movement as consolation. Daring, and highly individual playing – it's a CD worth investigating.

Oleg Marshev   *piano*

Chopin Three Waltzes, Op 34. Ballade No 4, Op 52
Liszt Funérailles, S173 No 7. Rhapsodie espagnole,
S254. Etudes d'exécution transcendante, S139 –
No 10 **Scriabin** Mazurkas – Op 25 No 3; Op 40 Nos 1
& 2. Poèmes, Op 32. Preludes, Op 15. Vers la flamme,
Op 72
Oleg Marshev pf
Danacord DACOCD677 (79' · DDD)   Ⓕ

Oleg Marshev's formidable virtuosity is backed by a no less enthralling musicianship. Marshev's earlier record of the Liszt-Tausig *Tasso* will have alerted even the most blasé virtuoso-fancier to exceptional powers and here in the Rhapsodie espagnole he sets all guns blazing, sinking up to his shoulders rather than mere elbows in an engulfing brilliance. His *Funérailles*, too, is hypnotically graphic and threatening, building remorselessly to a ferocious climax, and in the tenth of the *Transcendental Etudes* there is a superb sense of its appassionato F minor turbulence. Such virtuosity is scarcely less visceral in Chopin, with the closing pages of the Fourth Ballade heated to boiling-point, though relaxing in a selection of waltzes into an open-hearted relish of everything the composer has to offer. Poised and patrician in Rubinstein's or Lipatti's sense he may not be, but he makes it impossible to resist such character and liberation, such rich and lavish musical breathing. Marshev is on home ground in Scriabin, memorably attuned to his volatility and introspection, to those startling shifts of mood and emphasis at the heart of his bewildering genius.

This is an astonishing, all-stops-out release, beautifully recorded.

Antonio Meneses   *cello*

'Soirées internationales'
N Boulanger Three Pieces **Guarnieri** Cello Sonata No 1 **Martinů** Cello Sonata No 3 **Villa-Lobos** Bachianas Brasileiras No 2 – O canto do capadócio; O canto da nossa terra; O trenzinho do Caipira. Bachianas Brasileiras No 5 – Aria (Cantilena) (arr W Primrose). O canto do cisne negro
Antonio Meneses *vc* **Celina Szrvinsk** *pf*
Avie ② AV2162 (71' · DDD) Ⓕ

Of the four very different personalities gathered on this highly entertaining Avie release, the most influential is the slightest: Parisian-born Nadia Boulanger, whose incalculable impact as a teacher of composers in the 20th century far outstrips her own music. None the less, the Three Pieces for cello and piano (1915) at the centre of this programme make a charming set.

The five Villa-Lobos miniatures are closest in scale to Boulanger's and show just how different their compositional sensibilities were. *O canto do cisne negro* may be a touch pallid but the three pieces from *Bachianas* No 2 work superbly in the cello and piano format; but then Villa-Lobos was a cellist and the two *Cantos* and *O trenzinho do Caipira* all started life in this form, being recast in 1930 in their familiar orchestral guise. Primrose's arrangement – presumably made for viola and here transposed for cello, although the booklet does not give the full provenance – of No 5's opening Aria is also well laid out.

However, the major works here are the two sonatas. The recording of Martinů's Third (1952) is a fine one. Meneses and Szrvinsk have no rivals in Mozart Camargo Guarnieri's lyrical and vivid First Sonata (1931) but it is hard to imagine the work done better. Recommended.

Arturo Benedetti Michelangeli   *piano*

Chopin Fantasie in F minor, Op 49. Ballade No 1 Ⓗ in G minor, Op 23. Waltz in E flat, Op posth **Debussy** Images – Reflets dans l'eau; Hommage à Rameau; Cloches à travers les feuilles; Et la lune descend sur le temple qui fût **Schumann** Carnaval, Op 9. Faschingsschwank aus Wien, Op 26 **Mompou** Cançons i danses No 6 – Canción
Arturo Benedetti Michelangeli *pf*
Testament mono ② SBT2088 (130' · ADD) Includes a half-hour rehearsal sequence. Recorded live 1957 Ⓕ

Readers who are familiar with Michelangeli's 1971 DG recording of Debussy's *Images* will be astonished at this highly mobile 1957 concert performance of 'Cloches à travers les feuilles', which is almost a full minute faster than its stereo successor; or 'Reflets dans l'eau', which glides across the water's surface with such swiftness and ease that the more considered DG alternative – glorious though it is – sounds studied by comparison. 'Hommage à Rameau' is shaped with the utmost finesse and 'Et la lune descend sur le temple qui fût' coloured by exquisitely graded nuances. The performance of Schumann's *Carnaval* is a choice gallery of aural sculpture, whether in the minutely calculated responses of 'Pierrot', the teasing rubato of 'Coquette', the energy and attack of 'Papillons', the effortless flow of 'Chopin' or the ecstatic lingerings in 'Aveu'. Michelangeli's 'Eusebius' is tender but unsentimental, whereas his 'Florestan' has enough 'reflective' ingredients to suggest that the two characters are closer in spirit than we often think. *Faschingsschwank aus Wien* contrasts muscular assertiveness (the opening *Allegro*) with the most amazing control (in the 'Romanze'), while the 'Intermezzo' promotes a virtually orchestral range of dynamics. Michelangeli's Chopin has a rare nobility, the *Fantasie* especially which, at a rather faster tempo than usual, holds together as a narrative entity. Then there's the imposing First *Ballade* and the encores – a sunny posthumous E flat *Waltz* (a regular extra on Michelangeli's concert programmes) and Mompou's sad but tender 'Canción'. This disc leaves you humbled by, and grateful for, some wonderful piano playing. Michelangeli's art is both rare and elusive, his expressive vocabulary finely distilled and unlikely to impress those who listen only for technical mastery. So it's ironic that those who criticise Michelangeli for 'coldness' or 'aloofness' are often the very commentators who are so dazzled by his virtuosity that they can't hear beyond it. Testament's transfers are superb.

'The Early Recordings 1, 1939-48'   Ⓗ
Albéniz Malagueña, Op 71 No 8 **Bach** Italian Concerto, BWV971 **Bach/Busoni** Chaconne **Brahms** Variations on a Theme by Paganini, Op 35 **Galuppi** Presto in B flat **Granados** Andaluza, Op 37 No 5 **Marescotti** Fantasque **Mompou** Canción y danza No 1 **D Scarlatti** Keyboard Sonatas – Kk9; Kk11; Kk27; Kk96 **Tomeoni** Allegro in G
Arturo Benedetti Michelangeli *pf*
Naxos Historical mono 8 111351 (80' · ADD) Ⓢ☞

Michelangeli ranks among the grandest of all musical autocrats. And when his transcendent mastery is complemented by warmth, wit and charm, such additions are beyond price. Early in his career he possessed a Romantic as well as magisterial charisma, and listening to his performance of Bach's *Italian Concerto* with its wealth of colour, nuance and resilience is to be reminded that a human heart beat beneath that legendary *froideur*. What sparkle, too, in Tomeoni's G major *Allegro* and how he plays the arch-seducer to the manner born in Albéniz's *Malagueña*. Granados's *Andaluza* is heavily but irresistibly personalised, all fun and fancy-free; hardly for lovers of a more 'correct' Spanish style, while Marescotti's *Fantasque* is spun off with a virtuosity as life-enhancing as it is thrilling. Michelangeli's reordering of the Brahms *Paganini* Variations is odd, but his performance remains of classic status. So, too, does his way with the Bach/Busoni Chaconne with his rapid tempi and lean, not-an-ounce-of-fat way with Busoni's *maestoso* instruction. This is an issue that all lovers of great artistry will pounce on, particularly when so enticingly offered on Naxos's bargain label.

Marianne Muller   *viola da gamba*

'Tombeau pour Mr de Sainte Colombe'
Music by Forqueray, D Gaultier, E Gaultier, Marais, Rameau and Sainte-Colombe
Marianne Muller *va da gamba* **Claire Antonini** *theo*
Ensemble Spirale
Zig Zag Territoires ZZT080302 (69' · DDD)   Ⓕ

The title only hints at the disc's riches: it is a veritable 'art gallery' in sound. Marianne Muller and her continuo colleagues in the Ensemble Spirale explore the ways in which 17th- and 18th-century French composers, inspired by the popularity of 'literary portraits', devised self-portraits and hommages in music to their teachers, family and friends.

Composing a tombeau was a uniquely French way of honouring the life and musical legacy of a departed colleague. The lute-playing Gautier cousins (Ennemond and Denis) were early masters of this form; this recording may indeed have been inspired by those Marais composed for his teachers, Lully and Ste Colombe.

There is more to ponder: we find Rameau's evocation of Forqueray and the reverse as well as self-portraits. However, as both Forqueray (father and son) and Rameau were married to musicians, it may be that some of these allude to the ladies. Further *pièces de caractère* by Forqueray complete the CD. That the music of most of these composers is reasonably well known to us helps us today to appreciate the allusions being made.

But there is still more here to excite our interest. Muller has arranged two of Rameau's well known *Pièces de clavecin en concerts*, substituting a second bass viol in the part usually taken by a flute or violin. The result is a slightly lighter, more homogeneous texture that loses none of its sparkle in translation. These are fascinating and eloquent performances.

David Oistrakh   *violin*

Franck Violin Sonata **Ravel** Tzigane **Schumann** (arr Kreisler) Fantasie, Op 131 **Szymanowski** Three Myths, Op 30
David Oistrakh *vn* **Vladimir Yampolsky** *pf*
Testament mono SBT1442 (70' · ADD)   Ⓕ
Here we have a fabulous unpublished pro-

gramme that not only offers us new David Oistrakh repertoire but, in the case of the works we do already have from him, delivers performances that are sufficiently distinctive to warrant the duplication.

Take César Franck's Sonata, where Oistrakh's vibrato is more expressively intense than it often is on disc and where Vladimir Yampolsky transcends his familiar 'accompanist' role to assert an individual musical personality with playing that in its freedom and grandeur at times reminded me of Cortot, no less. Ravel's *Tzigane* is another winner – witty, spontaneous, incisive in its attack and, near the end, dangerously fast. Other available Oistrakh *Tzigane*s also deliver, musically speaking, but none sounds quite so thrillingly off the cuff.

And then there are the newcomers to Oistrakh's discography, all of them fine works. The Szymanowski *Myths* 'Narcissus' and 'Dryads and Pan' extend the experience we already have of Oistrakh in the opening 'Fountain of Arethusa' with seductive tone production, filigree passage-work and a sense of play that perfectly matches Szymanowski's fantastical imagination. The late and rather discursive Schumann Fantasy in C, presented here with Fritz Kreisler's rich piano reduction, is a true tour de force, bittersweet one moment, boldly virtuoso the next and graced by a uniquely rounded musical sensibility that left the world the day David Oistrakh died.

Happily we still have the records, with this 1958 Bucharest recital being one of the finest of all. The sound is fairly good, the balance variable but never skewed. Utterly unmissable.

Ignacy Jan Paderewski   *piano*

'US Victor Recordings, 1914-41'
Beethoven Piano Sonata No 14, 'Moonlight', Op 27 No 2 – I **Schubert** Impromptu, D935 No 3 **Schubert/Liszt** Ständchen, S558 **Chopin** Waltz No 5, Op 42. Nocturne No 5, Op 15 No 2. Mazurkas – No 37, Op 59 No 2; No 38, Op 59 No 3. Etudes, Op 25 – No 7; No 8; No 9 **Mendelssohn** Songs Without Words, Bk 6, Op 67 – No 4, 'Spinnerlied' **Schumann** Fantasiestücke, Op 12 – No 3, 'Warum' **Liszt** La leggierezza, S144 No 2 **Wagner/Liszt** Spinnerlied aus dem Fliegenden Holländer, S440 **Wagner/Schelling** Tristan und Isolde – Prelude **Rachmaninov** Prelude, Op 3 No 2. Preludes, Op 32 – No 12 **Debussy** Préludes, Bk 1 – No 10, 'Minstrels' **Paderewski** Melody, Op 8 No 3. Minuet, Op 14 No 1
Ignacy Jan Paderewski *pf*
Naxos Historical mono 8 112011 (79' · ADD)   Ⓢ

A choice selection of the Polish master's prolific recorded output Despite (and often because of) such old-fashioned devices as the asynchronisation of hands and exaggerated *rubato*, there is playing of incomparable beauty on these 20 discs; many pianists today could learn much from listening to Paderewski's clarity of line, luminous tone and artful use of the pedals. These (mainly) electrical sides were the first to approach capturing successfully the pianist's unique sound (Ward Marston has done the audio restoration here) though the earliest, a 1914 acoustic of Schumann's "Warum?", is astonishingly successful for its time.

Producer Jonathan Summers has chosen short pieces representative of the more than 70 titles Paderewski recorded in America between 1914 and 1931. The most substantial works are Schubert's B flat Impromptu (9'06"), lyrical and heartfelt, and of the Prelude to *Tristan und Isolde* (7'38") arranged by Paderewski's pupil Ernest Schelling. Elsewhere there are the celebrated recordings of the Wagner-Liszt *Spinnerlied* and one of many of the pianist's own ubiquitous Minuet in G; of particular interest are the two Chopin studies and Rachmaninov titles unpublished on 78rpm, the first (and only) movement of the *Moonlight* in which bars 34-42 are played with an *accelerando* and *crescendo* – an interesting idea – and Rachmaninov's famous Prelude the final page of which is executed with surprising ferocity. All in all, much to treasure.

Maurizio Pollini   *piano*

Boulez Piano Sonata No 2 **Prokofiev** Piano Sonata No 7 in B flat, Op 83 **Stravinsky** Petrushka – three movements **Webern** Piano Variations, Op 27
Maurizio Pollini pf
DG The Originals 447 431-2GOR (68' · ADD)
Recorded 1971-6   Ⓜ**OOO**▷

 Perfection needs to be pursued so that you can forget about it. Pollini's *Petrushka* movements are almost inhumanly accurate and fast; but what comes across is an exhilarating sense of abandon, plus an extraordinary cumulative excitement. The Prokofiev Seventh Sonata remains a benchmark recording not only for the athleticism of its outer movements but for the epic remorselessness of the central *Andante*. The Webern Variations are a magical fusion of intellectual passion and poetry, and the Boulez Sonata vividly reminds us why the European avant-garde was such a powerful force in the 1950s. These recordings are a monument to what it's possible for two hands to achieve on one musical instrument. The 'original-image bit-processing' has given a bit more brilliance and presence, as claimed, and another gain is the retention of atmosphere between movements.

Nadia Reisenberg   *piano*

Chopin Allegro de concert, Op 46. Barcarolle,   Ⓗ
Op 60. Berceuse, Op 57. Piano Sonata No 3, Op 58.
Complete Nocturnes and Mazurkas
Nadia Reisenberg pf
Bridge ④ BRIDGE9276A/D (5h 1' · ADD)
From Westminster originals, recorded 1947-57 Ⓜ**OO**

This four-CD reissue of Nadia Reisenberg's Chopin, recorded for Westminster between 1947 and 1957, includes a live and fearless per-

formance of the B minor Sonata, taken live from Carnegie Hall. Subtitled 'A Chopin Treasury', these records are treasure indeed, an Aladdin's cave of performances of such breathtaking pianistic finesse that they are able to achieve an expressive and imaginative freedom known to very few pianists. Reisenberg can be wistful and confiding, her playing most subtly coloured and nuanced in the Nocturnes, the fruit of a deep and abiding affection. Even the finest singer would envy her heart-easing warmth and flexibility in Op 32 No 2 in A flat, and in the Berceuse she gives new, iridescent meaning to James Huneker's loving reference to 'a rain of silvery fire'. The *Allegro de concert* holds no terrors for such a flawlessly equipped pianist and if she is surprisingly robust in the Barcarolle she is less impulsive and tempest-tossed than Argerich. Then there are the complete Mazurkas: once more, Reisenberg is responsive to virtually every facet of these works, in music proudly strutting or sunk in deep-dyed Slavic melancholy. Hear her in Op 17 No 4 in A minor or try the opening of Op 24 No 4 in B flat minor where her *rubato* is at once natural and personal, with its subtle quickening and relaxing of the pulse. Here she strikes gold, as she does too in the great B minor Sonata, flinging all inhibition to the wind and exiting from the stage in a blaze of virtuoso glory. An invaluable, finely remastered album.

Sviatoslav Richter   *piano*

Richter Rediscovered
Chopin Ballade No 3 in A flat, Op 47. Etudes, Op 10 – No 10 in A flat; No 12 in C minor, 'Revolutionary'. Mazurka in C, Op 24 No 2. Scherzo No 4 in E, Op 54 **Debussy** Préludes, Book 1 – No 5, 'Les collines d'Anacapri' **Haydn** Keyboard Sonata No 60 in C, HobXVI/50 **Prokofiev** Gavotte, Op 95 No 2. Piano Sonata No 6, Op 82. Visions fugitives, Op 22 – No 3, Allegretto; No 4, Animato (two recordings); No 5, Molto giocoso; No 6, Con eleganza; No 8, Commodo; No 9, Allegretto tranquillo; No 11, Con vivacità; No 14, Feroce; No 15, Inquieto; No 18, Con una dolce lentezza **Rachmaninov** Preludes – F sharp minor, Op 23 No 1; A, Op 32 No 9; G sharp minor, Op 32 No 12 **Ravel** Jeux d'eau. Miroirs – La vallée des cloches
Sviatoslav Richter pf
RCA Red Seal ② 09026 63844-2 (113' · ADD)
Recorded live 1960   Ⓕ**O**

'Richter Rediscovered' is a two-disc album celebrating a unique pianist in much of his early glory. The producer's note tells us that 'virtually none of the recordings on these CDs have been heard since their actual performance of over 40 years ago.' He also tells us that the reasons for this remain unclear, though knowing Richter's fluctuating attitudes to his own performances, it isn't difficult to deduce why these recitals have remained in limbo for so long. True there are gaucheries and confusions, inaccuracies and memory lapses, but never for a second do you doubt that you're listening to one of the greatest of all pianists. Both recitals date from 1960 and were given with an almost palpable tension, a discomfort that has you on the edge of your seat in both an enthralling and bad sense; the playing is phenomenal at one level, strange and nerve-wracking at another.

He courses his way through the first movement of Haydn's C major Sonata, hiding behind an incontestable but inscrutable mastery, is teasingly whimsical in Chopin's Fourth *Scherzo* and much given to sudden sprints and skirmishes in the Third Ballade (try him at the capricious flight commencing at 4'10"). He chivies Ravel's delicious indolence and sparkle in *Jeux d'eau* virtually out of existence but is unforgettable in the chiming bells of *La vallée des cloches*. He's at his most awe-inspiring on home territory, plumbing the very depths of despair in Rachmaninov's great B minor Prelude before storming through its central carillon of Moscow bells in a style all his own. Prokofiev's Sixth Sonata is launched with a punishing venom and articulacy, its extremes of stillness and hyperactivity miraculously unified, and how he tantalises his adoring audience with his incomparably played selection from the *Visions fugitives*! Chopin's Etude Op 10 No 10 is spun off with a grace and rapidity that must have left all aspiring pianists weak at the knees.

The recordings have come up trumps. All in all, these records create an ever-astonishing portrait of a pianist of bewildering fantasy and caprice, urgency and commitment.

Arthur Rubinstein   *organ*

Beethoven Piano Concerto No 4, Op 58[a]
Chopin Etude, Op 10 No 5[b]. Scherzo No 2, Op 31[c]
Saint-Saëns Piano Concerto No 2, Op 22[d]
Villa-Lobos Prole do bebê, Book I[b] – Moreninha; Pobrezinha; Polichinelle
Arthur Rubinstein pf [d]**BBC Symphony Orchestra / Rudolf Schwarz**; [a]**London Philharmonic Orchestra / Antál Dorati**
BBC Legends [abd]mono BBCL4216-2 (77' · ADD)
Recorded live in [d]1957, [b]1958, [a]1967, [c]1968   (F)

One could hardly call this a disc of novel Rubinstein repertoire. All the works are familiar from his studio recordings and had been under his fingers for many years. Yet there is no better way of hearing this great artist than in front of an audience. All except the Villa-Lobos items and Chopin Etude come from performances in the Royal Festival Hall. We can overlook the less than glamorous sound and forgive the odd clinker here and there (what Rubinstein appearance would be complete without them?), for here is a pianist at the height of his considerable powers.

This performance of Beethoven's Fourth is imbued with a lifetime's experience. The Saint-Saëns, a work Rubinstein had played to the composer nearly 60 years earlier, could hardly be bettered (his second and preferred studio recording with Alfred Wallenstein was made just two months later). As a friend of Villa-

Lobos we have authoritative versions of pieces he first recorded in 1931. The E minor Etude, too, was a special favourite, while the Scherzo, interrupted by applause from those who did not know the piece, is all patrician elegance.

Altogether marvellous – except for the printing of Jeremy Siepmann's thoughtful notes where the typesetter, who enjoys using the smallest possible font, is clearly a stranger to the convention of leaving a space after full stops. Why does this label insist on such unnecessary and irritating practices?

Beethoven Piano Sonata – No 23, 'Appassionata', Op 57 **Brahms** Intermezzo, Op 117 No 2
Chopin Ballade No 1, Op 23. Etude, Op 25 No 5
Liszt Hungarian Rhapsody, S244 No 12
Schumann Carnaval, Op 9 **Villa-Lobos** A prole do bebê – O polichinelo
Arthur Rubinstein pf
Medici Arts MM029-2 (81' · ADD)
Recorded live in Nijmegen, Netherlands, on April 20, 1963   (M)

This live recital has the added frisson of being played in Nijmegen, just a few miles from the German border, a country in which Rubinstein vowed never to play again after the horrors of the Nazi regime. Chris de Souza's excellent booklet reveals that Rubinstein was unusually nervous on the occasion, having decided to play to an audience which he knew might include former Nazis. So, although this is a mere snapshot of a 76-year-old legend, it is a vividly coloured one.

His Beethoven is direct and unmannered, a performance which truly inhabits the sonata's subtitle. Its famous *presto* coda is a real white-knuckle ride that you feel might hurtle out of control any second (it doesn't). By contrast, the Brahms *Intermezzo* casts a warm glow over proceedings – magical, understated, inimitable. *Carnaval*, which follows, was another Rubinstein favourite and though his observation of some dynamics and repeats is cavalier, with playing of such charm and utter conviction it seems invidious to nit-pick. As was said of another pianist, why look for spots on the sun? The Chopin items are imbued with a lifetime's close friendship, and the comparative rarity (for Rubinstein) of Liszt's 12th Hungarian Rhapsody, an account that would turn many pianists half his age green with envy, is the cherry on top.

'The Legendary Moscow Recital'
Chopin Barcarolle, Op 60. Etudes – Op 10 No 4; 'Black Keys', Op 10 No 5; 'Harp Study', Op 25 No 1; Op 25 No 5. Impromptu No 3, Op 51. Nocturne No 8, Op 27 No 2. Piano Sonata No 2, Op 35. Polonaises – No 5, Op 44; No 6, 'Heroic', Op 53
Debussy 24 Préludes – Ondine **Schumann** Des Abends, Op 12 No 1 **Villa-Lobos** Prole do bebê, Book 1 – Polichinelle
Arthur Rubinstein pf
Medici Arts ☒ 307 8548 (97' · NTSC · 4:3 · PCM

mono · 0). Recorded live at the Great Hall of the Moscow Conservatory on October 1, 1964 Ⓕ

Considering his celebrity, longevity and huge studio recording legacy, there is very little film of Rubinstein in concert. Indeed, this is the only full solo recital one can recall and as such is immensely valuable, not least because the printed programme is devoted entirely to the composer with whom he was most closely associated and because, fine as are most of his studio recordings, Rubinstein played with a greater freedom and daring than in front of an audience.

The film of the occasion, preserved in the vaults of the Russian State television archives for nearly 50 years, provides a vivid reminder of this great artist's idiosyncrasies – the dignified, immobile posture, the expressionless face and the little tug at his lapels before the start of each item.

The playing, of course, is heart-warming, the kind that can absorb the odd fluff, though the memory lapse in the *Scherzo* of the Sonata is disconcerting (he has to make an unwritten repeat before ad libbing his way into the Trio). Everything seems so inevitable and right, whether in the caressing phrases of the *Barcarolle* or the bravura of the A flat *Polonaise*, the inevitable trademark conclusion to any Rubinstein recital. Aficionados will relish his only known performance of the *Aeolian Harp* Study, Op 25 No 1. (The bonuses are two short – 1'45" – silent films of excerpts from two *études* shot in slow motion in Canada in 1928.)

Maxim Rysanov *viola*

Brahms Scherzo, 'FAE Sonata', WoO2 (arr Rysanov) **Bridge** Allegro appassionato, H82. Pensiero, H53a **Enescu** Pièce de concert **Franck** Violin Sonata (arr Rysanov) **Glinka** Viola Sonata **Tabakova** Whispered Lullaby
Maxim Rysanov *va* **Evelyn Chang** *pf*
Avie ② AV2111 (69' · DDD) Ⓕ

If you have the initial impression that this is a motley collection of pieces, lacking focus, do think again. For one thing, it makes an effective recital programme, the items setting one another off, leading up to the major work (Franck) and concluding with a perfect encore (Tabakova). And the playing, in its technical command and imaginative grasp, is outstanding. One feels that Maxim Rysanov has a very special relationship with his Guadagnini viola, delighting in bringing out the particular qualities of its different registers – husky lower notes, brilliant high ones which, however, retain weight and intensity. He's well matched by the energy and vitality of Evelyn Chang's playing, strikingly so at the start of the CD (Brahms). On the following tracks (Glinka), she shows very different qualities; sparkling passagework and elegant lyrical expression, and she's equally convincing with the impressionistic sonorities of the Enescu.

Throughout the disc, the attention is constantly grabbed by powerfully expressive duo playing. Rysanov appears as a true virtuoso in the Enescu and in the second of the Bridge pieces, yet he's able to scale down his performance for the intimate, dreamy Tabakova Lullaby, and in the Glinka he brings a subtly individual quality to each melodic phrase. And there's a strong sense that Chang and Rysanov really enjoy playing together.

Kathryn Stott *piano*

'Dance'
Albéniz Tango, Op 165 No 2 **Bartók** Six Romanian Folk Dances, Sz56 **Brahms** 10 Hungarian Dances – No 1 **Chopin** Mazurka No 13, Op 17 No 4 **Dvořák** Dumka, B136 **Fitkin** Old Style **Ginastera** Danza de la moza donosa, Op 2 No 2 **Guarnieri** Dansa negra **Lecuona** La conga de media noche **Piazzolla** Milonga del ángel **Satie** Je te veux **Shostakovich** Three Fantastic Dances, Op 5 **Sibelius** Valse triste, Op 44 No 1 **Stravinsky** Tango **Tchaikovsky** Polka peu dansante, Op 51 No 2 **Villa-Lobos** Valsa da dor
Kathryn Stott *pf*
Chandos CHAN10493 (72' · DDD) ⒻⓄ↦

Notching up her half-century has clearly not quelled the joy of discovery and sense of adventure that's marked the career of this delightful artist. Kathryn Stott decided the best way in which to mark her 50th would be with dance. Sixteen composers contribute to the celebration, with most of the works relatively unfamiliar but all of them having close personal associations.

It seems invidious to trawl through each track one by one, for all are encore-type charmers in one way or another, the one exception being *Valse triste*. Worth the price of the disc alone are *Dansa negra* by Mozart Carmargo Guarnieri (1907-93), Lecuona's *La conga de media noche*, and *Old Style*, the disc's one concession to dance music by a British composer, specially written for Stott by Graham Fitkin (*b*1963). It juxtaposes four dance and playing styles. It certainly gives the pianist a workout. Satie's salon waltz *Je te veux* affords another unexpected find, but it's the final selection, Chopin's Mazurka in A minor (ironically the only dance here that one would really want to sit out), that is the most moving (and, arguably, outstanding) performance on this most enjoyable disc.

Ilona Timchenko *piano*

Brahms Variations on a Theme by Paganini, Op 35 **C Schumann** Preludes and Fugues – in G minor; in B flat; in D minor **R Schumann** Kreisleriana, Op 16
Ilona Timchenko *pf*
Landor LAN286 (68' · DDD) Ⓕ

Cradling Clara Schumann's three *Preludes and Fugues* between two outsize challenges, Ilona Timchenko links three composers closely entwined both personally and professionally. More importantly, her warmth in Clara's Mendelssohnian B flat Prelude and Fugue, where a much-neglected composer doffs her hat to academe, is complemented by an astonishing sense of Robert's ominously schizophrenic fantasy in his *Kreisleriana*. Clara herself feared for her husband with his sudden dive into the darkest regions of Romantic poetry (Intermezzo 2 from section 2) and it is here that Timchenko, with her superb sense of the outgoing and interior sides of Schumann's teeming imagination, reveals herself in total accord with such richness and complexity. Her stealthy view of the final gnomic march, alive with eerie voicing and cross-accentuation, has rarely been equalled; again it is her formidable command and poetic commitment that make such a musical rather than merely athletic experience of Brahms's *Paganini* Variations. Romantically free, even in the theme, she takes nothing on face value.

Potton Hall's sound is rich and full, if a trifle bass-heavy, but this is among the most commanding and musically fascinating of all new and recent piano issues.

Paul Tortelier *cello*

Brahms Double Concerto, Op 102ᵃ **Debussy** Cello Sonataᵇ **Elgar** Cello Concerto, Op 85ᶜ
ᵃ**Yan Pascal Tortelier** vn **Paul Tortelier** vc
ᵇ**Ernest Lush** pf ᵃᶜ**BBC Symphony Orchestra /**
ᶜ**Sir Adrian Boult,** ᵃ**Sir John Pritchard**
BBC Legends BBCL4236-2 (72' · ADD)
Recorded live at the Royal Festival Hall, London on
ᶜNovember 14, 1972; ᵃApril 17, 1974   Ⓕ●

This generous collection of three favourite works provides a fine portrait of the great French cellist Paul Tortelier at the height of his career in the post-war period. It is specially valuable to have his view of the Elgar Cello Concerto, which he recorded commercially at least three times. Here it comes in a live recording which gives an even warmer, more spontaneous-sounding view of the piece in his distinctive interpretation.

Tortelier strongly believed that Elgar's markings should not be exaggerated, in particular the marking *tenuto*, at which many interpreters bring the music practically to a halt. In the second-movement *Scherzo*, for example, the drawing out of the tempo in two key places is markedly less here than in most rival readings. Tortelier also felt that the *portamento* slides should be kept to a minimum in the first movement, something he was able to achieve thanks to his very large hands. Even so, there is no lack of warmth in the dedicated slow movement or the meditative epilogue, which are given their full emotional weight.

The performance of Brahms's Double Concerto has similar qualities, and is important too for demonstrating what a fine violinist Tortelier's son Yan Pascal is. The bright purity of his violin tone contrasts illuminatingly with the richness of his father's cello tone.

The performance of the Debussy Sonata dates from much earlier, a 1959 studio recording, which yet brings out the natural spontaneity with which Tortelier tackled this improvisational work with its many stops and starts. Recording quality is generally good, though in the Elgar the audience is irritatingly bronchial at times.

Ian Tracey *organ*

'Fantaisie triomphale'
Dubois Fantaisie triomphale – Maestoso
Dupré Cortège et litanie, Op 19 **Gigout** Six Pièces –
Grand choeur dialogué **Gounod** Fantaisie sur
l'Hymne National Russe **Guilmant** Allegro, Op 81.
Marche fantaisie sur des chants d'eglise, Op 44.
Méditation sur le Stabat mater, Op 63. Final alla
Schumann sur un Noël languedocien, Op 83 **Saint-
Saëns** Cyprès et lauriers, Op 156
Ian Tracey org
BBC Philharmonic Orchestra / Rumon Gamba
Chandos 🏵 CHSA5048 (72' · DDD)
Recorded on the Willis organ of Liverpool
Anglican Cathedral   Ⓕ

Orchestral music lovers, organ buffs and hi-fi enthusiasts will be well satisfied with the epic sonic splendour of this CD from the combined forces of the BBC Philharmonic and the five-manual, 146-stop Willis organ of Liverpool Anglican Cathedral. Dubois, Gigout and Guilmant may be better known to organists than anyone else but they're capable of composing music which can easily withstand comparison with the works by the more famous Dupré, Gounod and Saint-Saëns.

With all the composers the emphasis is on strong, heroic melodies, adventurous harmonies and key changes, and the fullest exploitation of the ever-increasing resources of the post-Berlioz symphony orchestra and the French Cavaillé-Coll organ. Dubois's, Gigout's and Gounod's pieces are undemanding essays in triumphal march-like compositions; more thoughtful and interesting music with some magical orchestral effects is to be found in the works by Dupré, Guilmant and Saint-Saëns.

Ian Tracey finds suitably Gallic colours from the Willis organ and he, Rumon Gamba and the BBC Phil achieve impeccable ensemble and balance in their fine performances. It's a pity, though, that this CD wasn't recorded in a different venue as in the cathedral there's an uncomfortable contrast between the immediate sound of the orchestra at floor level and the more distant sound of the organ pipes higher up and spread around the building. Despite these obstacles, full marks to Chandos for its excellent engineering.

Simon Trpčeski *piano*

Scriabin Piano Sonata No 5 in F sharp, Op 53
Stravinsky Three movements from Petrushka
Prokofiev Piano Sonata No 6 in A, Op 82

Tchaikovsky The Nutcracker – Suite, Op 71a (arr
Pletnev)
Simon Trpčeski pf
EMI Debut 575202-2 (73' · DDD)   Ⓢ ❍❍❍☒➪

 The minute Trpčeski opens Pletnev's
Concert Suite from Tchaikovsky's
Nutcracker, you hear a master of
rhythmic precision and, later, a capacity to
shoulder fierce challenges with unflinching
aplomb and authority. Everything is musically
and ardently inflected and while Trpčeski's
virtuoso voltage in the final pages of the
Andante maestoso is awe-inspiring, his unfailing musicianship is even more remarkable.
Again, in Scriabin you sense a pianist who, for
all his compelling mastery, sounds still in the
first flush of love for the composer's vividness
and idiosyncrasy. The *accelerando* into the first
Presto con allegrezza is steep and thrilling and
Trpčeski's sense of Scriabin's towering rhetoric at 7'20" is masterly.

In *Petrushka*, Trpčeski rejoices in virtuosity
tailor-made for Artur Rubinstein, but also
remembers the music's balletic origins. Time
and again he fills a score too often treated as a
vehicle for black and white ferocity with a wealth
of colour and character.

There are more pulverising accounts of
Prokofiev's Sixth Sonata (notably from Richter,
Kissin and, most recently, the formidably lean
and articulate François-Frédéric Guy) but few
more musical. Trpčeski's quality is unfailing,
and he has been recorded with a fine mix of clarity and resonance.

Yuja Wang

Chopin Piano Sonata No 2, Op 35 **Ligeti** Etudes,
Book 1 – Fanfares; Book 2 – Der Zauberlehrling **Liszt**
Piano Sonata, S178 **Scriabin** Piano Sonata No 2,
'Sonata-fantasy', Op 19
Yuja Wang pf
DG 477 8140GH (73' · DDD)   Ⓢ ❍❍❍☒➪

Make no mistake, 22-year-old Yuja Wang is a
wondrously gifted pianist whose debut album of
sonatas by Chopin, Liszt and Scriabin, with the
stimulating addition of two Ligeti *Etudes*, suggests a combination of blazing technique and a
rare instinct for poetry. Curtis-trained under
Gary Graffman, Wang tells us in an accompanying DVD of her special love for music of drama
and turbulence and how ever since first hearing
Pollini's recording of the Chopin *Etudes* she
dreamt of recording for DG.

In Scriabin's Second Sonata she is beautifully
sensitive to the moods, whether tranquil and
starlit or tempestuous, reflecting the composer's love of the Baltic Sea. She is fiery but never
reckless in Chopin's Second Sonata, off like the
proverbial greyhound at the first *doppio movimento*, and offers a dramatic bass emphasis at
the climax of the heaven-storming development. Her finale is truly *sotto voce* yet with the
widest variety of touch and expression, and for

the most part her playing, while sharply individual, is free from all distorting idiosyncrasy
or mannerism.

You wont hear anything on the scale of Richter
or Gilels in the Liszt Sonata but on the other
hand Wang is young, wonderfully talented and
trained, superbly recorded and, if this disc is
anything to go by, with the world at her feet. As
a crowning touch her Ligeti *Etudes* are both
musicianly and dazzlingly incisive. In the words
of the publicist, 'a star is born'.

Gillian Weir   *organ*

The Grand Organ of The Royal Albert Hall
Cook Fanfare **Elgar** Variations on an Original Theme,
'Enigma' – Nimrod. Pomp and Circumstance March
No 1 **Howells** Rhapsody, Op 17 No 3 **Lanquetuit**
Toccata **Liszt** Fantasia and Fugue, 'Ad nos, ad
salutarem undam'. St Francis de Paule walking on the
water **Parry** Toccata and Fugue, 'The Wanderer'
Gillian Weir org
Priory PRCD859 (78' · DDD) Played on the grand
organ of the Royal Albert Hall, London   Ⓕ

The sight and sound of the Royal Albert Hall
organ are familiar to Proms-goers, but for those
who regard it as merely a noisy backdrop to the
orchestral works of Elgar, Mahler, Strauss and
others, this CD will come as a revelation.
There's a wealth of colourful quiet registers on
the newly restored instrument which are fully
exploited by Dame Gillian Weir, including a
soft percussion Carillon stop heard during
Liszt's *Ad nos Fantasia*.

She gives this giant composition a truly
authentic 19th-century Romantic-style performance, with an unhurried approach to the slow
middle movement and rhythmic virtuosity in
the rapid outer sections. The vast *tutti* of the
organ makes the C major conclusion even more
glorious than usual and her account of this
piece is one of the most spectacular you'll ever
hear.

The other solo works are equally successful.
Howells's Rhapsody is passionate and eloquent,
and Parry's Toccata and Fugue has a dignified
flow. In comparison, Cook and Lanquetuit's
pieces may seem lightweight, but the former has
some attractive jazzy elements and the latter is as
dazzling a French toccata as you'd hear from
Dupré, Widor *et al.* Meanwhile, the transcriptions of Elgar and Liszt are entirely convincing
thanks to Weir's skill as a colourist.

Priory has done the RAH organ proud with an
excellent recording and a comprehensive booklet. One must salute the endurance of Weir and
engineer Paul Crichton for making this disc
during the hall's only available hours – 1am to
6am. This is an exceptionally fine CD that
should become a landmark recording.

John Scott Whiteley   *organ*

Alain Litanies, Op 79 **Bernard** Scherzo-Caprice,

Op 26 No 2 **Cochereau** Symphonie en improvisation
Dupré Cortège et Litanie, Op 19 No 2 **Pâque** Pièce
pour orgue, Op 80 **Ravel** Ma Mère l'Oye – Petit
Poucet **Verdin** Organetto **Guillaume** Berceuse
marine, Op 24
John Scott Whiteley org
Regent REGCD275 (74' • DDD) Ⓕ
Played on the organ of York Minster
'The Grand Organ of York Minster'
Albinoni/Giazotto Adagio **Cochereau** Improvisation
sur Haec dies **Dubois** Fiat lux **Duruflé** Fugue sur Le
carillon des heures de la Cathédrale de Soissons
Elgar Imperial March **Gigout** Scherzo in E. Toccata
in B minor **Mozart** Fantasia, K608 Mulet Rosace
(Esquisses Byzantines) **Mushel** Toccata **Peraza** Medio
registro alto 1er tono **Thalben-Ball** Variations on a
Theme of Paganini for pedals **Vierne** Suite No 2 –
Toccata **C Wood** Prelude on York Tune
John Scott Whiteley org
Priory 📀 PRDVD2
(74' · NTSC · 16:9 · PCM stereo and 5.1 · 0)   Ⓕ

Volume 15 of Regent's splendid English Cathedral Series takes us to York and the superb artistry of John Scott Whiteley, who has served the
Minster with great distinction since 1976. His
daily contact with this vibrant instrument
ensures a sonic as well as musical treat. Whiteley
is also filmed for Priory's DVD, playing the
Minster's mobile nave console.

Regent's programme opens with a magisterial
account of Alain's ecstatic *Litanies*, followed by
a nicely contrasted *Berceuse marine* by Maurice
Guillaume. Marie Joseph Léon Désiré Pâque's
Pièce ambles along agreeably (if slightly dis-
jointedly) but more satisfactory is Bernard's
delicious *Scherzo-Caprice*. Another highlight is
the Ravel transcription (from *Mother Goose*)
which fits the organ like a glove. Dupré's *Cortège et Litanie* is most beautifully shaped. The
Organetto by Joris Verdin (*b*1952) consists of
seven short movements that parody those
forms of composition possible on the 15th-cen-
tury Italian portative organetto. It's worth
hearing once. The major work is Whiteley's
transcription of Cochereau's *Symphonie en
improvisation* (1963), a strong work, played with
great verve. A thunderous opening movement
and a tremendous *Tarantella* frame an elfin
Scherzo and a meditative *Adagio*. The disc is a
treat for the ear with first-rate notes and documentation.

Priory's DVD programme eschews any music
by York composers, though there is Charles
Wood's charming *Prelude on York* and the briefest
extract from Francis Jackson's Op 5 *Impromptu*.
Instead, the emphasis is on the player's physical
interaction with the manuals and pedalboard.
With reference to the latter, this performance of
Thalben-Ball's *Paganini* Variations should be
compulsory viewing. Views of the Minster's
exquisite stained glass and clocks add flavour,
particularly in Mulet's *Rosace* and Mozart's Fantasia, K608. The Cymbelstern stop adds tingle to
Mushel's fairground-like Toccata.

Although Elgar's Imperial March suffers from
a surfeit of *rubato* there is no shortage of élan in

Cochereau's thrilling Easter plainsong improvisation on *Haec dies*. Appealing too is the authentically Gallic tang to the tuning as the wind
occasionally struggles to cope. Richard Knight's
camerawork is superb and Paul Crichton's
sound beautifully balanced and warm. A delightful production throughout.

**Frank Peter Zimmermann & Heinrich
Schiff**   *violin & cello*

Bach Die Kunst der Fuge, BWV1080 – Canon alla
ottava; Canon alla duodecima in contrapuncto alla
quinta **Honegger** Sonatina, H80 **Martinů** Duo No 1,
H157 **Pintscher** Study I for 'Treatise on the Veil' **Ravel**
Sonata
Frank Peter Zimmermann vn **Heinrich Schiff** vc
ECM New Series 476 3150 (62' · DDD)   Ⓕ

Frank Peter Zimmermann and Heinrich Schiff
have been a musical item for more than two
decades and the fruits of their mutual understanding are audible from the outset of Honegger's Sonatina, which opens a typically wide-
ranging and challenging ECM programme.

Both players have an instinctive feeling for line
which serves Honegger's robust polyphony
well, lifting his melodies off the page. The same
is true in Martinů's First Duo, where a mysterious Preludium is succeeded by a lively, warm-
hearted Rondo in which players catch the Czech
tang through the overlay of French gloss. They
face fierce competition in the one true French
item, Ravel's Sonata. Zimmermann and Schiff
are wonderfully fleet of foot, perhaps a shade too
quick in the *Lent*, but in the faster movements
their impulsion is irresistible.

Between these peaks of early-20th-century
repertoire come two Bach canons from *The Art
of Fugue* and a new commission from Matthias
Pintscher. The Bach canons are delivered with
consummate skill, as one expects, while
Pintscher's ethereal vision, inspired by Cy
Twombly's art, casts a wholly different light on
their musicality. With state-of-the-art sound,
is this the best violin-and-cello duo disc
around?

Collections of pianists

The Recordings
Various Cpsrs Pf Wks **Alexis Weissenberg**
Medici Arts 📀 307 8048   Ⓜ

Chopin. Mozart Pf Wks **Sviatoslav Richter**
Medici Arts 📀 308 5208   Ⓜ

Shostakovich Preludes & Fugues **Tatyana Nikolaieva**
Medici Arts 📀 308 5248   Ⓜ

If you invested in Marc-André Hamelin's recent
CD 'In a State of Jazz' (see page 1328) you will
have heard the eponymous Sonata and five
Charles Trenet song transcriptions by Alexis
Weissenberg. Here is Weissenberg himself

seen first in the innovative black–and–white film of Three Movements from *Petrushka* directed by Åke Falck in 1965 which revived the pianist's flagging career. The print is remarkably crisp and vivid even if, as on the original film, the sound of this high–octane performance is not always in sync. The DVD's bonus features a short interview with the pianist talking about the work.

The rest of the programme has performances that reveal what an uneven player Weissenberg was. His impassive face and economic gestures seem to reflect his disengagement with some of the music (try the Bach–Hess *Jesu, Joy of Man's Desiring* and the slow movement – the only part of the work here – of Chopin's B minor Sonata). On the other hand there's a riveting Prokofiev Third Sonata (complete) and Scriabin Nocturne for the left hand alone. The longest work from the 150 minutes of the disc is Brahms's Second Piano Concerto, a lightweight reading conducted by the amiable Georges Prêtre in 1969.

From the same label comes a 1989 recital from Sviatoslav Richter given in London's Barbican Centre by the light of a 40–watt bulb. Now expressing any criticism of the great man will invite a heap of invective, but when Richter comes on stage conveying the distinct impression that he would rather be anywhere else, it does appear rather graceless. What with that, the anglepoise and reading from the score you wonder if he is in the mood to play Mozart at all. Thank heavens he is. One can put up with any amount of eccentricity to hear K282, K545 (*Sonata facile*) and K310 played like this. Close your eyes – that's the best way of enjoying this, especially as the editing is a real distraction.

The three (black–and–white) bonus tracks from 20 years earlier were broadcast in October 1969. Looking once more as though his cat's just been run over, Richter rampages through Rachmaninov's *Etude–Tableau* Op 9 No 3 and Chopin's *Etudes* Op 10 No 4 (ludicriously fast) and No 12.

Then there is the endearing figure of Tatyana Nikolaieva in her signature work, the 24 Preludes and Fugues of Shostakovich. Filmed in December 1992 just 11 months before her death at the age of 69, the setting for the 150 minutes of the cycle appears to be a capacious Victorian drawing room, the instrument illuminated by an old–fashioned standard lamp (what is it about Russians and electricity?). Talking of which, Nikolaieva, looking every inch the archetypal babushka and clad in clothes that might have been worn by Clara Schumann, lights up these works from within. Here are old and intimate friends. It's doubtful whether we'll hear them better played – unsuprisingly, as she was the composer's inspiration for the cycle (she reveals as much in the brief interview that forms the DVD's bonus). Already, this is a valuable historical document.

Cziffra . Moiseiwitsch . Bolet

Albéniz Iberia – Triana[c] **Bach/Busoni** Prelude and Fugue, BWV532[a] **Chopin** Polonaise No 6, 'Heroic',

Op 53[a]. Berceuse, Op 57[c] **Liszt** Hungarian Rhapsody, S244 No 6[a]. Polonaise, S223 No 2[a]. Grand galop chromatique, S219[a/c] **Rachmaninov** Rhapsody on a Theme of Paganini, Op 43 – Vars 17–24[b] **D Scarlatti** Piano Sonatas[a] – K101; K96 **Schumann** Toccata, Op 7[a]. Kinderszenen, Op 15[b]. Fantasiestücke, Op 12[b] – No 3, Warum?; No 4, Grillen; No 7, Träumes Wirren
[a]**György Cziffra**, [b]**Benno Moiseiwitsch**, [c]**Jorge Bolet** pfs
Medici Arts 📀 308 5288 (107' · NTSC · 4:3 · PCM mono · 0)   Ⓕ

Cziffra's 1962 recital has appeared on DVD before. It's the one that opens with the astonishing 'warm–up', an improvisation that ends with a vertiginous Chopin C major Etude. After a powerful Bach–Busoni Prelude and Fugue in D major and two skittish Scarlatti sonatas, we hear one of the fastest Schumann Toccatas ever recorded, reminding us of Simon Barere who, when asked why he played the piece so fast, replied, 'Because I can'. But you ain't heard nothin' yet until, after scintillating accounts of the *Hungarian Rhapsody* No 6 and the E major *Polonaise*, Cziffra launches into the ne plus ultra of piano circus acts, the *Grand galop chromatique*. Seeing is believing, though in the Chopin Polonaise that follows (from 1963) he seems disengaged, and musically completely misses the point.

After this, Moiseiwitsch seems to be from another age – economically, quietly singing his way through his beloved Schumann. The final eight Rachmaninov *Paganini* Variations, filmed two months before his death, are a ghostly souvenir of one of the composer's greatest interpreters. Finally, the magisterial Jorge Bolet. How wonderful it is to see again that huge torso bent in concentration over the keyboard and the characteristic upward snap of the hands. *Triana*, Chopin's *Berceuse* and a steady, dignified *Grand galop* are all–too–brief reminders of this great artist.

Somewhat irritatingly, the menu does not allow you to view the DVD without interruption. For each of the 18 sections you have to use the remote to select the next part of the programme. It's like having to get up and down to change sides on a 78rpm disc.

ENSEMBLES

Kronos

'Black Angels'

Crumb Black Angels **Tallis** (arr Kronos Qt) Spem in alium **Marta** Doom. A sigh **Ives** (arr Kronos Qt/Geist) They are there! **Shostakovich** String Quartet No 8 in C minor, Op-110
Kronos Quartet (David Harrington, John Sherba *vns* Hank Dutt *va* Joan Jeanrenaud *vc*)
Nonesuch 7559–79242–2 (62' · DDD)   Ⓕ 🔴🔴

This is very much the sort of imaginative programming we've come to expect from this talented young American quartet. With an overall theme of war and persecution the disc opens with George Crumb's *Black Angels*, for electric string quartet. This work was inspired by the Vietnam War and bears two inscriptions to that effect——*in tempore belli* (in time of war) and 'Finished on Friday the 13th of March, 1970', and it's described by Crumb as 'a kind of parable on our troubled contemporary world'. The work is divided into three sections which represent the three stages of the voyage of the soul——fall from grace, spiritual annihilation and redemption.

As with most of his works he calls on his instrumentalists to perform on a variety of instruments other than their own——here that ranges from gongs, maracas and crystal glasses to vocal sounds such as whistling, chanting and whispering. *Doom. A sigh* is the young Hungarian composer István Marta's disturbing portrait of a Romanian village as they desperately fight to retain their sense of identity in the face of dictatorship and persecution.

Marta's atmospheric blend of electronic sound, string quartet and recorded folk–songs leave one with a powerful and moving impression. At first sight Tallis's *Spem in alium* may seem oddly out of place considering the overall theme of this disc, but as the insert–notes point out the text was probably taken from the story of Judith, in which King Nebuchadnezzar's general Holofernes besieged the Jewish fortress of Bethulia. Kronos's own arrangement of this 40–part motet (involving some multi–tracking) certainly makes a fascinating alternative to the original.

A particularly fine account of Shostakovich's Eighth String Quartet (dedicated to the victims of fascism and war) brings this thought–provoking and imaginative recital to a close. Performances throughout are outstanding, and the recording first–class.

The Binchois Consort

'Marriage of England and Burgundy'
Anonymous O pulcherrima mulierum/Girum coeli circuivi. Incomprehensibilia firme/Praeter rerum ordinem **Busnois** Regina coeli I. Regina coeli II **Frye** Missa Sine Nomine. Missa Summe trinitati
The Binchois Consort / Andrew Kirkman
Hyperion CDA67129 (75' · DDD)　　Ⓕ**OO**

This is another disc to derive inspiration from the marriage in 1468 of Charles the Bold, Duke of Burgundy, and Margaret of York, sister of Edward IV and Richard III. The event fascinates performer–scholars because a manuscript of polyphony survives that can be very plausibly linked to these wedding celebrations (it's now kept in the Royal Library of Belgium in Brussels). After the Ferrara Ensemble's CD of mostly secular music came the Clerks' Group's mix of Masses from the manuscript (including Walter Frye's *Flos regalis* and Plummer's three–voice setting) and secular English songs. Now, with last year's Early Music Award–winners, the Binchois

Consort, offering an all–sacred programme, four out of the five so–called 'Brussels' Masses (all in fact by English composers) are now available in fine performances.

It would be easy to insist on the fact that this programme is led by recent research. The attribution to Walter Frye of the anonymous three–voice Mass that opens this recording was made by Andrew Kirkman himself, and those of the two motets that conclude it to Busnois were proposed by Sean Gallagher (*O pulcherrima/ Girum coeli*) and Rob Wegman (*Incomprehensibilia firme/Praeter rerum ordinem*), all young scholars with impeccable credentials. Kirkman's notes are informative and detailed, but he's as concerned as his singers to drive home the music's purely aesthetic, chamber–musical qualities. As to Kirkman's attribution there's no doubt: listen to the sustained duets of the *Sanctus* and *Agnus Dei*, and there can be no doubt that the Mass is by a composer of the first rank; one has to agree that Wegman's attribution of *Incomprehensibilia* cries 'Busnois' out of the speakers: it could hardly be by anyone else. Rightly Kirkman gently expresses doubts concerning *O pulcherrima/ Girum coeli*, – in fact it puts one very firmly in mind of late Dufay, and of his motet *Ave regina coelorum* in particular.

In some these are faultlessly judged and engaging performances. The music's nuances and details are very sensitively rendered, but so is the sense of larger–scale architecture and pacing; and Kirkman's long–standing commit–ment to Frye is particularly evident. The performances of Busnois' motets (both conjecturally attributed and firmly ascribed) are, at their best, equally exciting; but just occasionally there's the hint of strain in the higher voices' upper reaches and in the intricate tracery of *O pulcherrima* and *Incomprehensibilia* (particularly the latter, whose many sections do not quite flow together), and of the singers bracing themselves for the cross-rhythms of *Regina coeli I*. But these are details, and it's difficult to imagine more lucid or elegant performances. In a very short time, the Binchois Consort have established themselves as one of the very finest ensembles in the field.

Brabant Ensemble

'Music from the Chirk Castle Part–Books'
Byrd O God give ear and do apply **Caustun** Yield unto God the mighty Lord **Deane** O Lord, Thou has dealt graciously. The grace of our Lord Jesus Christ **Hooper** Behold it is Christ **Mundy** Te Deum, 'for trebles'. Benedictus, 'for trebles' **R Parsons** Deliver me from mine enemies. 'I am the resurrection and the life saith the Lord', from the Burial Service **W Parsons** The Litany, 'for trebles', 'O God the Father of Heav'n' **Sheppard** Submit yourselves one to another. O God be merciful unto us, and bless us **Tallis** Christ rising again. With all our hearts. Not every one that saith unto me **Tye** Blessed are all they that fear the Lord
Brabant Ensemble / Stephen Rice
Hyperion CDA67695 (71' · DDD · T/t)　　Ⓕ**O**

Here, the Brabant Ensemble turn their attention to English repertory of the same period: the Chirk Castle part–books' chequered history began in Wales, where they were copied for the choral establishment of a rich merchant turned landed gentry. One of the part–books was lost fairly early on, and has been reconstructed. It's been worth the effort, for although much of their repertory is known from other sources, a few significant pieces, here recorded for the first time, are not. These include two works by William Mundy, an English *Te Deum* and a *Benedictus*. Both are described as being 'for trebles' in the source; both are conceived on a large scale, and are undoubtedly significant additions to the repertoire. On that count alone this recording is self–recommending. An even greater name among the new additions is that of Tallis: his *Not every one that saith unto me* is brief indeed, but then how often is the discovery of an unfinished sketch by Mozart or Bach hailed as a 'significant find'?

A new departure it may be but the Brabant Ensemble is not on unfamiliar ground, for this is the repertory on which its singers cut their teeth. The predominant sonority is familiarly clear, transparent and assured, though in the lower range the voices are not quite so well defined as at the top. This soft centre is perhaps attributable to the sound recording, which is rather recessed and slightly unfocused. But for the sake of the new pieces alone, lovers of this repertory will welcome this enthusiastically.

Cambridge Singers

Hail, Gladdening Light
J Amner Come, let's rejoice **Anonymous** Rejoice in the Lord **Bairstow** I sat down under his shadow **Dering** Factum est silentium **Elgar** They are at rest **J-Goss** These are they that follow the lamb **WH-Harris** Bring us, O Lord God **Howells** Nunc dimittis **Morley** Nolo mortem peccatoris **Philips** O-beatum et sacrosanctum diem **Purcell** Remember not, Lord, our offences, Z50 **Rutter** Loving shepherd of Thy sheep **J Sheppard** In manus tuas **Stanford** Justorum animae, Op 38 No 1 **R Stone** The Lord's Prayer **Tallis** O nata lux **Tavener** A hymn to the mother of God. Hymn for the dormition of the mother of God **Taverner** Christe Jesu, pastor bone **Tomkins** When David heard **Vaughan Williams** O-vos omnes **Walton** A litany **C Wood** Hail, gladdening light
Cambridge Singers / John Rutter
Collegium COLCD113 (72' · DDD · T/t)   Ⓕ**O**

This has the subtitle 'Music of the English Church' and it's arranged under four main headings: anthems and introits (these count as one), Latin motets, settings of hymns and other poetry, and prayer–settings. Each of them is well represented in a programme that varies delightfully in period and style, and in performances which are remarkably consistent in quality. Some of the items will come as discoveries to most listeners: for example, the anthem *Come, let's rejoice*, a

splendid, madrigal–like piece written by John Amner, organist from 1610 to 1641 at Ely Cathedral where these recordings were made. Others are equally impressive in their present performance: a deep quietness attends the opening of Richard Dering's *Factum est silentium*, which ends with rhythmic Alleluias set dancing with subdued excitement. Among the hymn–settings is one by a 16–year–old called William Walton. Included in the prayers is the choirmaster's own setting, characteristically made for pleasure, of *Loving shepherd of Thy sheep*. All are unaccompanied, and thus very exactly test the choir's blend of voices, its precision, articulation and feeling for rhythm. In all respects it does exceptionally well; the tone is fresh, the attack unanimous, the expression clear and sensitive, the rhythm on its toes. These are young, gifted singers, formed with disciplined enthusiasm into a choir with a distinctive style – recorded with admirable results by a family firm.

Clare College, Cambridge

Blessed Spirit – Music of the soul's journey
Anonymous Requiem aeternam. Kontakion of the Dead. Domine Jesu Christe. O quanta qualia. In paradisum **Byrd** Iustorum animae **Harris** Faire is the Heaven **Hildegard of Bingen** O felix anima **Holst** The Evening Watch, H159 **Parry** Songs of Farewell – No 4, There is an old belief **Schütz** Selig sind die Toten **Sheppard** Audivi vocem de caelo **Tavener** Funeral Ikos **Tchaikovsky** Blessed are they **Traditional** Steal Away (arr Brown). Deep River (arr Luboff) **Victoria** O quam gloriosum **Walford–Davies** Psalm No 121 and Requiem aeternam
Clare College Choir, Cambridge / Timothy Brown
Collegium COLCD127 (71' · DDD · T/t)   Ⓕ**O**

There can be nothing but praise for the excellence of these performances, for the quality and choice of the music itself and, most of all, for the gorgeous sound quality of these recordings made in Ely Cathedral. Add to this some eminently readable booklet–notes and we have a real winner, even if the overall aural effect bears a striking resemblance to those ubiquitous inoffensive compilation discs played in hotel lobbies the world over.

Within the basic theme of death and the soul's subsequent journey to paradise the music juxtaposes chunks of plainsong and standard cathedral choir repertoire with some rather more esoteric choral pieces. Whether it's the ancient plainchant *In paradisum*, Psalm 121 sung to Walford Davies's fine Anglican chant, William Harris's richly textured anthem *Faire is the Heaven* or the almost erotically indulgent arrangement by Timothy Brown of *Steal Away*, Clare College Choir distinguish it all with finely crafted and beautifully shaped performances that aren't just note–perfect but intensely perceptive as well. There's no hint of the sickliness we sometimes experience when church music is exposed to such slick professionalism on disc – rather a real sense of wonder and awe at the timeless beauty of the programme.

It's difficult to listen to the disc in its entirety without falling into some kind of soporific trance, but taken individually each piece is, in its own way, as dramatic and earth–shaking as the garish blue cover leads us to suspect.

Illumina

Anonymous Lumen ad revelationem **Byrd** O lux, beata Trinitas **Grechaninov** The seven Days of the Passion, Op 58 – O gladsome light **Harris** Bring us, O Lord God **Hildegard of Bingen** O choruscans stellarum **Holst** Nunc dimittis, H127 **Josquin Desprez** Nunc dimittis **Ligeti** Lux aeterna **Palestrina** Christe, qui lux es et dies. Lucis Creator optime **Rachmaninov** Vespers, Op 37 – Nunc dimittis **Rautavaara** Vigilia – Evening Hymn **Rutter** Hymn to the Creator of Light **Tallis** O nata lux de lumine. Te lucis ante terminum **Tchaikovsky** Vesper Service, Op 52 – Hail, gladdening Light **Whyte** Christe, qui lux es et dies **Wood** Hail, gladdening light
Clare College Choir, Cambridge / Timothy Brown
Collegium COLCD125 (76' · DDD · T/t)   Ⓕⓞ

Retrospectively the disc's final item, Ligeti's *Lux aeterna*, dominates the recital. Not only does it make an indelible impression, but it also casts its light over the entire programme and style of singing. To a listener who has not heard it before (a slightly smaller category than might be thought, as the piece was used in the film *2001: A Space Odyssey*) it may even come as the light on the road to Damascus, a blinding revelation of unknown choral sonorities. An extraordinary sound–world is opening up, with long, finely ruled streams of light, a spectrum of colours wide as the distance from heaven to earth, and all mingling eventually within the cavern of a great bell. The challenge to singers (even when assisted by the reverberance of Ely Cathedral's Lady Chapel) is formidable indeed, and these young voices (with lungs and ears involved also) do marvellously well. And so they do throughout. The quality of choral tone here is remarkable: no thready sopranos, none of those bone–dry basses, but a sound that, though strictly disciplined in the matter of vibrato, is still fresh and natural. They achieve wonders of *crescendo*, as in William Harris's *Bring us, O Lord God*, and their opening chords (in Tallis's *O nata lux* for instance) are as if cut by the sharpest slicer ever made. Even so, this smooth, flawless beauty of sound is, in some contexts, like the modern beauty of the face of a heroine in some televised piece of period–drama. Josquin Desprez's *Nunc dimittis* is an example: the singing is extremely beautiful, but conceptually (and not just in the women's voices) seems anachronistic. It's as though they have worked on their programme with the precept 'All choral music aspires to the condition of Ligeti'. A wondrous record, all the same.

Estonian Philharmonic Chamber Choir

'Baltic Voices 3'
Augustinas The Stomping Bride **Bergman** Vier Galgenlieder **Górecki** Five Kurpian Songs **Gudmundsen–Holmgreen** Statements **Martinaitis** Alleluia **Mažulis** The dazzled eye lost its speech **Saariaho** Nuits, adieux (1996 version) **Tüür** Meditatio[a]
Estonian Philharmonic Chamber Choir / Paul Hillier with [a]**Raschèr Saxophone Qt**
Harmonia Mundi HMU90 7391 (79' · DDD · T/t)   Ⓕⓞ

Paul Hillier continues his top–class 'Baltic Voices' series with a compilation that embraces Denmark, Finland, Estonia, Lithuania and Poland. It is an attractive, stylistically wide–ranging programme, one that carefully avoids the obvious in its choice of pieces. The styles range from pseudo–medievalism (Augustinas) through 'sculptural minimalism' (Gudmundsen–Holmgreen) to modernism (Saariaho, with a version of *Nuits, adieux* that transfers its original electronic effects to the choir), by way of 'spiral canon' (Mažulis), elaborated Sprech-stimme (Bergman), new spirituality (Martinaitis), ascetic ritualism (Tüür, whose *Meditatio* strikes me as the intellectually toughest yet most rewarding music on the disc and least deserves having a label pinned on it), and straightforward folksiness (Górecki, in soft–grained but undeni-ably memorable form).

Not all of the works are on an especially exalted level but they are well chosen as vehicles for displaying the versatility and polish of Hilli-er's fine Estonian singers. Harmonia Mundi's recording is unimpeachable and the disc comes with a thoughtful background essay as well as notes on composers and works, all by Hillier, plus texts and translations presented with scru-pulous care. A quality issue this, then, and a high priority, surely, for anyone interested in the contemporary choral repertoire.

Fretwork

'Birds on Fire'
A Bassano Pavan & Galliard No 1 **H Bassano** Fantasia No 1 **L Duarte** Two Sinfonias in 5 Parts **Gough** Birds on Fire **J Lupo** Pavana a 5 **T Lupo** Fantasia in 6 parts – No 1; No 4; No 9; No 11. Fantasia in 4 Parts – No 5. Pavan in 3 Parts – No 26 **S Rossi** Hashkivénu[a]. Shir hamma'alót[a] **Van Wilder** Fantasia
Fretwork (Wendy Gillespie, Asaki Morikawa, Susanna Pell, Richard Boothby, Richard Campbell, Richard Tunnicliffe *viols*) with [a]**Jeremy Avis** *voc*
Harmonia Mundi HMU90 7478 (75' · DDD)   Ⓕⓞⓞ

The title of this recording is a quotation from Aaron Appelfeld's 1939 novel *Badenheim*. The subtitle, 'Jewish Music for Viols', more accurately describes the contents: Fretwork have also recorded consort music by some of the Jewish composers at the Tudor court – the Bassanos and Lupos – along with two contemporaries in Hol-land, Philip van Wilder and Leonara Duarte, illustrating the extent to which they set aside the declamatory music of their forefathers in favour of the imitative polyphonic style prevailing in Northern Europe. Even the Venetian 'Ebreo'

Salamone Rossi borrowed from the Latin motet for his 1622 *Songs of Solomon*, *stilo antico* settings with Hebrew texts sung here by Jeremy Avis.

If you're seeking the exotic, listen to tracks 1, 13 and 24. Orlando Gough, best known for his theatre music, composed *Birds on Fire* in 1997. This is demanding, wonderfully offbeat music inspired by Ashkenazi Klezmers (more cabaret than camera), which Fretwork brings off with a panache that astonishes and delights. Importantly, it demonstrates the extent to which the viol consort has been circumscribed by its historic – largely amateur – repertoire and suggests that it is capable of far more. Each of the three Gough pieces begins with eerie sounds and is characterised by a kaleidoscope of syncopated ostinati, droll *pizzicato* asides and sinewy, modal themes conveyed in parallel octaves. You'll swear you can hear an organ, accordion, clarinet and a saxophone, but you don't. Fascinating, liberating music!

Gabrieli Consort

'A Spotless Rose'
Adès The Fayrfax Carol **Bax** Mater ora filium **Górecki** Totus tuus, Op 60 **Grieg** Ave maris stella, CW156/2 **Howells** A Spotless Rose **Josquin Desprez** Ave Maria, Virgo serena **MacMillan** Seinte Mari moder milde **Mouton** Nesciens mater Virgo virum **Palestrina** Stabat mater **Stravinsky** Ave Maria **Swayne** Magnificat, Op 33 **Tavener** A Hymn to the Mother of God **Traditional** There is no rose of such virtue
Gabrieli Consort / Paul McCreesh
DG 477 7635 (81' · DDD)   ⓕ🔘Ⓓ➔

'My intention was to create a collection of private meditations highlighting the key events of Mary's life,' writes Paul McCreesh, 'Like the *Book of Hours*, it would consist of works intended for metaphysical reflection: for revealing and and commenting on the ineffable.' It's a tremendously rewarding sequence, some 13 items in all spanning no fewer than 600 years, and so cannily programmed that temporal and stylistic boundaries shift and sometimes evaporate altogether: prepare to marvel at the way Josquin's *Ave Maria, Virgo serena* follows on so naturally from Sir John Tavener's ravishing *A Hymn to the Mother of God*.

Tavener is one of five living figures represented, the contributions by Giles Swayne, Thomas Adès and James MacMillan adding a not unwelcome element of astringency to the mix and contrasting boldly with the transcendent diatonic radiance of Górecki's *Totus tuus*. There can be nothing but praise for the breathtaking assurance and responsiveness of McCreesh's singers throughout.

Emanating from the magically apt surroundings of Ely Cathedral's Lady Chapel, the sound is as atmospheric and voluptuous as can be imagined, though the formidable resonance means that the words are not always ideally clear. But that's about the only grumble, for this is indeed a glorious CD.

King's College, Cambridge

Best Loved Hymns
Bain Brother James's Air[a] (arr Johns) **Bourgeois** Praise to the Lord, the Almighty[b] **Gibbons** Drop, drop slow tears **Goss** Praise my soul, the King of Heaven[b] **Handel** Thine be the glory, risen, conquering Son[b] (arr Cleobury) **W Harris** O what their joy and their glory must be[b] **Howells** All my hope on God is founded[bc] **Ireland** My song is love unknown[b] **Luther** A mighty fortress is our God[bc] (arr Rutter) **Miller** When I survey the wondrous cross[b] **Parry** Dear Lord and Father of Mankind[b] **Rutter** Be thou my vision[a] **Scholefield** The day thou gavest, Lord, is ended[b] **Taylor** Glorious things of Thee are spoken[b] **Traditional** All people that on earth do dwell[bc] (arr Vaughan Williams). Morning has broken[a] (arr Rutter). Let all mortal flesh[b] (arr Jackson) **Vaughan Williams** Come down, O Love Divine[b]
[a]**Sioned Williams** *hp* [b]**Benjamin Bayl, Thomas Williamson** *orgs* **King's College Choir, Cambridge;** [c]**The Wallace Collection / Stephen Cleobury**
EMI 557026-2 (69' · DDD)   ⓕ🔘Ⓓ➔

Here is the high art of hymnody. No tentative playover on the stopped diapason while knee–joints crack and fingers fumble for collection money. No intrusive notes from the congregation with members who pride themselves on 'singing seconds' (presumably, as Harvey Grace remarked, because the interval almost exclusively used is that of a third). These are musical performances, as surely as if they were the canticles and anthems featured here, and in some instances the form is indeed that of the hymn–anthem. The hymns themselves, as the title proclaims, are 'best loved', but are presented with elaborations for brass, organ, harp and descanting trebles. Dressed up in Sunday best, they're thrilling in majesty, exquisite in contemplative piety, but very largely cordoned off amid notices that say 'Do not join in.'

The selection probably reflects modern, conservative good taste quite faithfully. At the popular end, *Brother James's Air* and *Morning has broken* are admitted; at the mystical other, *Let all mortal flesh keep silence* preserves the ancient tune but swathed in subtly abrasive harmonies. Of things grandly Victorian, *The day Thou gavest* is in, but *Lead, kindly light* and *Abide with me* are out. Some would have found a place among any 'top 10' chosen 50 years ago – *Dear Lord and Father of Mankind, When I survey the wondrous Cross* and *Praise, my soul, the King of Heaven* for example. Some such as *All my hope on God is founded* and *Be thou my vision* are relatively new to the lists. Two – *A mighty fortress* and the *Old Hundredth* – seem timeless.

The famous choir sing well (though their uncovered 'ee' sounds nag somewhat, as does an oddly unyielding element somewhere in the men's voices). The accompaniments are skilfully played, colourfully arranged and spaciously recorded. Excellent annotations are provided by Alan Luff, who comes up with a fund of information such as the identity of Brother James (a Christian Scientist, James Leith Macbeth Bain) and the origin of the tune *Abbot's Leigh*, which was composed in 1941 when BBC listeners were complaining that *Glorious Things of Thee are Spoken* was still being sung to the old German national anthem.

King's Singers

'Sacred Bridges'
Anonymous Psalm 113, 'Laudate pueri Dominum'
Rossi Hebreo The Songs of Solomon – Psalm 118;
Psalm 124; Psalm 128 **Sweelinck** Pseaumes des
David, Premier livre – Ne vueilles pas, Ô Sire;
Pourquoy font bruit et s'assemblent les gens?;
Troisième livre – Mon Dieu, j'ay toy esperance **Ufkî**ª,
Goudimel Psalm 5.Psalm 9 **Ufkî**ª Psalm 2. Psalm 6
King's Singers; ªSarband
Signum Classics SIGCD065 (72' · DDD · T/t) Ⓕ**OOO**▷

Lately, TV arts/documentary schedules have teemed with films on Islam, mostly over–simplifying history to the point of distortion and suggesting a centuries–old conspiracy to deny the contribution Muslim civilisation made to European culture. Viewers with an interest in early music (and contemporary music, for that matter) may have raised an eyebrow: if Islamic influence has been concealed, it's been hidden in plain sight.

Especially in the context of fears of growing Islamophobia after 9/11 and 7/7, any campaign to foster understanding is commendable. This CD reminds us of the common roots of Judaism, Christianity and Islam, the importance of the Psalms to each religion, and the connections between the music of each. The programme includes Rossi Hebreo's attempts to reconcile Catholic liturgy with the Jewish tradition (from which it ultimately sprang) and works by Ufkî, a Polish Calvinist captive and convert to Islam who recast melodies from the Genevan (Huguenot) Psalter in Turkish modes.

Sarband has collaborated with Concerto Köln in intriguing explorations of the interaction between European classical and Turkish music, while the King's Singers have tackled an eclectic repertoire ranging from Gesualdo to The Beatles, so it's hardly surprising that the groups work well together, meshing Reformation counterpoint with 17th–century Ottoman music, comparing and contrasting the incorporeal sounds of one and the lithe rhythms of the other. They share the pieces by Ufkî, Sarband performs an improvisation inspired by Psalm 2, and the King's Singers take the rest of the tracks. Altogether a fascinating, attractive, beautifully performed album.

Monteverdi Choir

'Santiago a cappella'
Anonymous Mariam matrem Virginem **Cardoso** Non
mortui **Guerrero** Ave virgo sanctissima. Duo
Seraphim **João IV** Crux fidelis **Lobo** Versa est in
luctum. Lamentationes – Ieremiae Prophetae **Rogier**
Salva nos Domine **Victoria** O vos omnes, qui transitis
per viam. O lux et decus Hispaniae

Monteverdi Choir / Sir John Eliot Gardiner
Emarcy 986 7305 (67' · DDD · T/t) Ⓕ**OOO**▷

 This impressive collection is the Monteverdi Choir going back, in a sense, to their roots, or even beyond them. After so many years in which it's concentrated on later styles, that John Eliot Gardiner's choir have their origins in earlier repertoire. They return to it here with gusto, illustrating their habitual superb choral blend, and a sense of pace and drama that the prize–strewn path of Bach and Mozart recordings hasn't in any way dampened.

Among the highlights are the taut rendition of Alonso Lobo's monumental *Lamentations* and the blaze of glory that is the same composer's *Versa est in luctum*, but Gardiner shows himself extremely sensitive to this late Iberian Renaissance style in general.

The only piece that actually has to do with the pilgrim route to Santiago de Compostela is the earliest, the lovely *Maria matrem* from the *Llibre Vermell*. This is mainly an excuse to assemble a marvellous collection of Iberian polyphony from a rather later period, and the collection is outstanding and the programme well conceived. Recommended.

Phantasm

'Four Temperaments'
 Byrd Pavan and Galliard a 6, BE17/15. Mass for four
voices. Prelude and Ground, 'The Queen's
Goodnight' **A Ferrabosco** I In Nomine a 5 – No 1;
No-2; No 3. Fantasia a 4. Fantasia a 6. Pavan a 5
Parsons In Nomine a 5. A Song called Trumpets.
Ut-re-me fa sol la. De la Court. A Song of Mr Robert
Parsons **Tallis** In Nomine a 4 – No 1; No 2. A Solfaing
Song
Phantasm (Laurence Dreyfuss, Wendy Gillespie,
Jonathan Manson, Marrku Luolajan–Mikkola *viols*)
with **Emilia Benjamin, Asako Morikawa** *viols*
Avie AV2054 (72' · DDD) Ⓕ**OOO**▷

 The 'Four Temperaments' of the title refer back to the ancient theory of the four humours, or bodily fluids, responsible for conditions of the body and so, by extension, for personalities. Laurence Dreyfus suggests that each composer represented personifies one of these 'temperaments': Parsons the choleric, Alfonso Ferrabosco the Elder the calm phlegmatic, Tallis the sanguine, and Byrd the passionate melancholic.

Admitting, however, that personalities are far more complex than that, what this recording really demonstrates is the vast variety of colour and mood represented not only by each composer individually but also by the skill and beauty of the consort's interpretation. The stately patterning of the pavans contrasts with the sprightly tossing, by one player to another, of small melodic fragments in other pieces.

The arrangement of the programme, too, is carefully planned: pitches, sometimes even themes, follow naturally one after another. A fine example is Ferrabosco's *In nomine I*, with its theme of a rising minor scale, followed by the same scale in Byrd's *Sanctus*. The ingenious interspersing of movements from Byrd's four–part Mass is justifiable by his description of some of his works as suitable for 'voices or viols', though the plangent descending final phrases of the *Agnus Dei* call for the sung text to fulfil their ultimate purpose.

The players' contribution to the painting and mixing of humours is outstanding. They bring to life the importance of the viol consort in Elizabethan society, in teaching as well as entertainment for old and young. Did Parsons have in mind the children of the Chapel Royal with his *Ut re mi fa sol la*? Or Tallis with his *Solfaing Song*, or in the settings of familiar tunes, both sacred – the Ferrabosco, Tallis or Parsons *In nomine*s – and secular, for example Parsons's brilliant *Song called Trumpets*? For insight as well as enjoyment, this recording is highly recommended.

St Paul's Cathedral Choir

Advent at St Paul's
Anonymous Laudes Regiae. Angelus ad Virginem (arr Willcocks)[a]. O come, O come, Emmanuel (arr Carter)[a]. Rejoice in the Lord alway **Britten** A Hymn of St Columba[a] **Bruckner** Virga Jesse floruit **Byrd** Laetentur coeli **A Carter** Toccata on Veni Emmanuel[b] **Gibbons** This is the record of John[a] **Handl** Ecce concipies[c] **R Lloyd** Drop down, ye heavens[a] **Palestrina** Matins Responsory. Vesper Responsory **Parsons** Ave Maria **Peerson** Blow out the trumpet[a] **Rutter** Hymn to the Creator of Light **Weelkes** Hosanna to the Son of David **Wilby** Echo Carol[a]
St Paul's Cathedral Choir / John Scott [b]org with [a]Andrew Lucas org
Hyperion CDA66994 (71' · DDD · T/t) Ⓕ

As in the seasonal calendar a single window opens first, so in this Advent recital a solo voice sings in the distance; and by the end, all windows alight, the great Cathedral is filled with the organ's *fortissimo* from deepest pedal sub–bass to brightest trumpet and topmost piccolo. The programme begins with some plainsong dating back to the first millennium of the era. The end, more plainsong but not so plain now, has *O come, O come, Emmanuel* audaciously arranged, then to become the subject of an organ toccata with sufficient energy to propel the hymn, the Cathedral and all into the new age. In between comes a satisfying alternation of ancient and modern. Particularly splendid is Martin Peerson's *Blow out the trumpet*, an anthem strong in rhythm and colour. Robert Parsons's five–part *Ave Maria* is also a joy. The modern works include an interesting, deeply felt piece by John Rutter, *Hymn to the Creator of Light*: its first section, less ingratiating (but not therefore less good) than his more characteristic style, is followed by an angular refulgence of praise in preparation for a chorale–melody sung quietly in octaves amid an affectionate interweave of gentle polyphony – the effect is lovely.

The choir is on top form. Britten's *Hymn of St Columba* is especially well performed, probably making the strongest impression of all. Andrew Lucas is the remorselessly exercised organist in this, and John Scott takes over for the Toccata: both are excellent.

The Sixteen

'Renaissance: music of inner peace'
Allegri Miserere mei **Anonymous** Veni creator spiritus. Ubi caritas. Te lucis ante terminum. In paradisum **Barber** Agnus Dei **Blow** Salvator mundi **Bruckner** Locus iste **Byrd** Ave verum corpus. Gradualia, Vol 1/i: Feast of All Saints – Offertory: Iustorum animae. Mass for four voices – Agnus Dei **F Guerrero** Ave virgo sanctissima. Duo Seraphim **G Gabrieli** Exultet jam angelica turba **Gibbons** Hosanna to the Son of David **Górecki** Totus tuus **Josquin** Ave Maria **Lassus** Ave regina coelorum. Timor et tremor **Lotti** Crucifixus a 8 **Melgás** Salve Regina **Monteverdi** Christe, adoramus te **Mouton** Nesciens mater virgo virum **Palestrina** Missa Papae Marcelli – Kyrie. Sicut cervus desiderat **Parsons** Ave Maria **Poulenc** Salve Regina **Purcell** Beati omnes qui timent Dominum. Hear my prayer, O Lord **Sheppard** Libera nos, salva nos I **Tallis** If ye love me. O nata lux de lumine. Salvator mundi Domine. Adesto nunc proprius **Tavener** The Lamb **Tomkins** When David heard **Victoria** Salve regina **Weelkes** Hosanna to the Son of David
The Sixteen / Harry Christophers
UCJ ② 986 6727 (150' · DDD) ⓂⓄⓄ▶

This splendid two–disc set features works from The Sixteen's repertory. Over a quarter of a century, under the direction of Harry Christophers, group has never done anything that wasn't totally compelling in its musicianship and technical assurance.

Even the most casual collector is likely to have at least some of these pieces on disc already, but you'd have to look very hard to find performances to match any here. For example, they give us an electrifying account of Guerrero's *Duo seraphim*, while that great English Tudor classic, Weelkes' *Hosanna to the Son of David* can rarely have been recorded with such fiery zeal. That mainstay of any half–decent church choir's repertoire, *Locus iste*, comes across here as freshly and as intensely moving as it must have sounded in 1869 when Bruckner wrote it. As for modern repertory, the subtlety brought to pieces by Górecki and Tavener elevates these already established choral classics.

For some this pair of discs will serve as conclusive proof that The Sixteen is the finest small choral group in existence. For others this matchless music–making will provide a source of endless satisfaction and enrichment.

'A Mother's Love'
Music for the Virgin Mary by **Anonymous, Britten, Bruckner, Cornysh, Duruflé, Elgar, Fauré, Grieg, Josquin Desprez, Lassus, Liszt, Mendelssohn,**

Obrecht, Palestrina, Rizza and Saint–Saëns
The Sixteen / Harry Christophers
with **Huw Williams** org
UCJ 476 6295 (73' · DDD)　　　　　　　　ⒻⒹ⇨

With its sentimental title, this collection is clearly aimed at the wider market–place. But the programme is perceptively chosen to show how much wonderful music the image of the Virgin Mary has inspired over five centuries. Grieg's opening *Ave maris stella* is immediately inviting: it has a ravishing simplicity but is passionate too and it is followed by rich, lively music by Cornysh and Josquin laced with the special harmonic character of its period. Next comes expansive Bruckner with a thundering organ and then a delightful surprise, Saint–Saëns's delicious *Ave Maria* – a real hit.

The simple beauty of Britten's *A Hymn to the Virgin* captivates the ear, while Mendelssohn's readily melodic and characteristically ambitious *Ave Maria* moves forward with great fervour, splendidly climaxed by Christophers. Other highlights include Margaret Rizza's richly plangent *Ave generosa*, eloquently set to words by Hildegard of Bingen, and the romantically soaring Fauré *Ave Maria*, again using the organ to add background colour, followed by the gentle contrast of Palestrina's *Sicut lilium*.

Liszt wrote his *Ave maris stella* while awaiting ordination as Abbé in the Vatican: its hint of austerity is not entirely banished by a natural exuberance which intensifies the plea 'Loosen the chains of the guilty' with which Liszt no doubt closely identified. The programme ends with the dedicated, passionate serenity of Lassus's *Salve regina*, a most satisfying coda. Performances throughout show this marvellous choir at their most eloquent, beautifully balanced and blended. Highly recommended for sheer pleasure, but also as a way of exploring a wide range of repertoire.

Stile Antico

'Song of Songs'
Anonymous Nigra sum. Tota pulcra es amica mea. Dum esset rex – antiphon. Laeva ejus – antiphon. Speciosa facta es. Iam hiems transiit **Ceballos** Hortus conclusus **Clemens Non Papa** Ego flos campi **Gombert** Quam pulchra es **F Guerrero** Surge propera. Trahe me post te. Ego flos campi **Lassus** Veni dilecte mi **Lhéritier** Nigra sum **Palestrina** Motets, Book 4, 'Canticum canticorum' – Osculetur me; Nigra sum **Victoria** Vidi speciosam. Vadam, et circuibo civitatem. Secunda pars moteci **Vivanco** Veni dilecte mi
Stile Antico
Harmonia Mundi HMU80 7489 (78' · DDD)　　ⒻⓄⒹ⇨

One expectation that such an album may raise in its listeners is an answer to the question of what common and special inspiration might composers have taken from contemplating this most erotic of Biblical texts. The symptoms of their reactions might be sensuous melismas, perhaps, and

anguished suspensions, surging bass–lines and… let us draw a veil there. Such devices and stratagems are in abundance, whether chastely deployed in turn by Clemens and Palestrina or flaunted all at once in the selections of Guerrero and Gombert, though no more so than they would be on a programme of Marian or Lenten devotions; and these are just the opening four tracks.

That unfair calculation ignores the plainchant antiphons between each pair of motets. These interspersions work well – as they must in a genuinely liturgical context, as here, thanks to the quiet good taste and stylistically homogeneous approach of Stile Antico, with an especially winsome unanimity to the female–only *Tota pulchra es*.

Indeed, these are just the sort of performances one would hope to hear in church, which was (one feels) the practical and creative laboratory for what is recorded: full but not strained singing, allowing an advantageous acoustic and the number (12) and freshness of voices to take care of blend and balance, with plenty left in reserve for the longer spans of the two magnificent Victoria anthems, *Vadam et circuibo* and *Vidi speciosam*.

Westminster Abbey Choir

'Mary and Elizabeth at Westminster Abbey'
Byrd Ne irascaris Domine. O Lord make thy servant. Teach me, O Lord **W Mundy** Vox Patris caelestis **Sheppard** Libera nos, salva nos I. Second Service – Magnificat; Nunc dimittis **Tallis** Videte miraculum **Tye** Omnes gentes, plaudite **R White** Exaudiat te Dominus
Westminster Abbey Choir / James O'Donnell
Hyperion CDA67704 (65' · DDD)　　　　　　　Ⓕ

Following the success in the *Gramophone* Awards of the Choir of New College, Oxford, this first–rate survey of old favourites suggests that collegiate institutions such as these continue to enjoy rude health, fears to the contrary notwithstanding. Conceived as a memorial to two royal sisters buried in the Abbey, it includes some wonderfully strong singing from boy trebles. As ever, their tone conforms to the 'house style', clearer and brighter than that of Edward Higginbottom's but with no hint of shrillness.

Undoubtedly the most impressive achievement here is Mundy's *Vox Patris caelestis*, which looks a rather unwieldly, sprawling thing on paper (and sounds it in some performances); here it is convincing formally, and the cohesion of the ensemble forces admiration, as indeed does the trebles' athleticism and stamina. For this alone this disc warrants the strongest recommendation. Also worth singling out is Nicholas Trapp, the treble solo in Byrd's *Teach me, O Lord*, and the choir as a whole in the opening and closing numbers, Tye's *Omnes gentes* and White's *Exaudiat te Dominus*. The different combinations of solo voices, organ and full choir offer sufficient variety to keep the ear fresh. As a showcase for English choral singing at its most charismatic, this deserves to be widely heard.

SINGERS

Victoria de los Angeles   *soprano*

Berlioz Les nuits d'été, Op 7[a] – Villanelle;   H
Le spectre de la rose; L'île inconnue **Brahms** Meine
Liebe ist grün, Op 63 No 5. Nachtigall, Op 97 No 1
Delibes Bonjour, Suzon! **Halffter** Dos Canciones
Handel Judas Maccabaeus, HWV63 – So shall the lute
and harp awake **Nin** Cantos populares españolas –
Montañesa; Paño murciano **Obradors** Chiquitita la
novia **Ravel** Vocalise en forme de habanera **A Scar-
latti** Le Violette **Schubert** Mein!, D795 No 11 **Schu-
mann** Widmung, Op 25 No 1 **Stravinsky** Pastorale
Valverde Clavelitos **Vives** Canciones epigramáticas –
La presumida; El ritrato de Isabela
Victoria de los Angeles sop **Gerald Moore** pf
[a]**BBC Symphony Orchestra / Rudolf Schwarz**
BBC Legends/IMG Artists mono BBCL4101–2
(62' · ADD) Recorded live 1957   Ⓕ**OO**

When Victoria de los Angeles appeared at the
Edinburgh Festival in 1957, she was in her
prime, the voice as supple and sensitive as it was
beautiful. Everything she tackled seemed to be
touched by the magic of her attractive presence
and glorious singing.

Good as her account of Schumann's *Widmung*
may be, it's when she gets to Brahms, perhaps
her favourite composer in this genre, that she's
wholly at home, the wistful sense of pain in *Nachtigall* caught to perfection. In the wordless pieces
by Stravinsky and Ravel she floats that warm yet
ethereal tone of hers with consummate ease, and
the long–breathed phrasing and excellent French
in Duparc's *mélodie* are enhanced by this artist's
innate skill in word–painting. For all that, audiences were always impatient for her to get to the
Spanish part of her programme, for in this field
she was unsurpassed as a singer and interpreter.
Many of these songs were also recorded by her in
the studio, but the live occasion gives these performances an extra *frisson*. The encores are even
better. An account of *Clavelitos* is a superior reading even to those famous ones available elsewhere. That's complemented by a delightfully
insouciant account of the Delibes song that she
didn't attempt on any other recorded occasion.

Gerald Moore, as was his wont, manages to
change idioms with his familiar virtuosity. As a
whole, this is an invaluable addition to the singer's extensive discography.

Songs and Arias by Brahms   H
Falla, Fusté, Granados, Guridi, Handel, Nin, Respighi,
Schumann, Toldrá, Turina, Valverde and Vives
Victoria de los Angeles sop with various artists
Testament mono SBT1087 (75' · ADD) Recorded
1942–53   Ⓕ

The two Respighi songs are magical performances – *Stornellatrice*, with the golden voice at
its richest and *E se un giorno tornasse*, a study in

subtle shading of tone, a dialogue between a
mother and her dying, jilted daughter. For those
two brief items alone, superbly transferred, this
collection is an essential for all admirers of this
singer, but there's much more. Handel's 'O had
I Jubal's lyre' in German rather than English
may be odd, but the performance sparkles and
among the Lieder it's good to have not just 'Der
Nussbaum' – the Schumann song which was
always special to her – but two previously
unpublished, 'Widmung' from the Myrthe
songs and 'Ich grolle nicht' from *Dichterliebe*.

Through the whole collection the superb
transfers capture the full–throated glory of los
Angeles's voice at the beginning of her career.
The 1942 recordings of two Hungarian folk–
songs, previously unpublished, may be rough
and limited – made when the singer was only 18
– but they amply demonstrate that already the
voice was fully developed in its beauty. No fewer
than 18 of the 27 items are of Spanish songs, and
though in one or two instances los Angeles was
destined to make even more idiomatic readings
later with a Spanish accompanist, these ones
with Gerald Moore as her partner have a freshness and brilliance that has rarely been matched
in this repertory. In particular it's good to have
her first recording of the encore number which
she made her own, *Clavelitos*.

Dame Janet Baker   *mezzo–soprano*

'Scottish and English Folksongs'
Arne The Tempest – Where the bee sucks[a]
Beethoven Scottish Songs, Op 108[b] – No 5, The
sweetest lad was Jamie; No 7, Bonnie laddie,
highland laddie; No 20, Faithfu' Johnie; WoO156[b] –
Cease your funning; Polly Stewart **Boyce** Tell me
lovely shepherd[c] **Campion** Third Booke of Ayres[d] – If
thou long'st so much to learne; Never love unlesse
you can; Oft have I sigh'd for him that heares me not.
Fourth Booke of Ayres[d] – Faine would I wed a faire
young man **Dowland** The First Book of Songs or
Ayres – Come againe[d] **Haydn** Scottish Folksong
Arrangements[e] – I'm o'er young to marry yet; John
Anderson; O can ye sew cushions; Sleepy Bodie; Up
in the morning early; The White Cockade; The brisk
young lad; O bonny lass; Duncan Gray; My boy
Tammy; Shepherds, I have lost my love; Green grow
the rashes; Love will find out the way; The birks of
Abergeldie; My ain kind dearie; Cumbernauld House;
Jamie come try me; The Flower of Edinburgh **Monro**
My lovely Celia[c] **Purcell** Lord, what is man?, Z192[c].
Sleep, Adam, sleep and take thy rest, Z195[c]
Dame Janet Baker mez [a]**Douglas Whittaker** fl
[be]**Yehudi Menuhin** vn [b]**Ross Pople** vc [ac]**Ambrose
Gauntlett** vada [d]**Robert Spencer** lte **George
Malcolm** [b]hpd/[e]pf [ac]**Martin Isepp** hpd
Testament SBT1241 (70' · ADD · T/t) Recorded 1967,
                    Ⓕ**OOO**

 'A Pageant of English Song' was Baker's first solo LP for EMI. Side 1, in
which she's accompanied by Martin
Isepp and Robert Spencer, is reissued on this
CD. Side 2, with Gerald Moore at the piano,

can be heard on a double CD on EMI. Dame Janet was at the beginning of the high summer of her career when this was recorded in 1967. Every recital, concert appearance or opera role was an event. In the first song, Dowland's 'Come againe', each word is given the perfect weight, with beautiful touches on the repeated 'I sit, I sigh, I weep, I faint, I die'. The jolly 'Never love unlesse you can', the melancholy 'Oft have I sigh'd' and the coquettish 'Faine would I wed' each has its own 'face', Baker finding just the right expression in her voice. The Scottish songs arranged by Haydn, recorded eight years later, seem rather slight in comparison. Nineteen of these arrangements one after another seem rather too much of a good thing.

The five Beethoven Scottish arrangements are the best part of the 1975 session. 'Fathfu' Johnnie' is a setting to place beside any great song of the same period. The recording seems to favour the instrumentalists somewhat, whereas in the 1967 selections, Baker's voice is always fresh and forward.

im Traüme' in the third song. This cycle belonged to Janet Baker, and with the single exception of Sena Jurinac, there just isn't a singer to equal her in it.

The songs recorded in the studio with Paul Hamburger include two by Wolf, not available anywhere else in Baker's discography. 'Geh' Geliebter' is sung with typical ardour. The two Schubert and Schumann songs are fresh and lively, but it's the Strauss group that has the highest voltage. *Heimliche Aufforderung* doesn't really suit her, with its intoxicated ardour, but *Morgen* is a superb example of that hushed, rapt quality that was one of the characteristic joys of Baker's art. The final song, *Befreit*, achieves a dramatic thrust that suggests the theatre in the best possible sense. Admirers who already possess Baker's other versions of this material shouldn't be deterred – this is a splendid souvenir of her in the full glory of her prime. Newcomers to Baker's singing – there can't be many people under 30 who heard her live – are in for a treat.

Haydn Arianna a Naxos, HobXXVIb/2[a] **Schubert** Der Blinde Knabe, D833[b]. Totengräberweise, D869[b] **Schumann** Frauenliebe und –leben, Op 42[c]. Der Page, Op 30 No 2[b]. Meine Rose, Op 90 No 2[b] **R Strauss** Vier Lieder, Op 27[b] – No 3, Heimliche Aufforderung; No 4, Morgen. Befreit, Op 39 No 4[b] **Wolf** Spanisches Liederbuch[b] – Die ihr schwebet um diese Palmen; Geh' Geliebter
Dame Janet Baker *mez* [a]**John Constable,** [b]**Paul Hamburger,** [c]**Geoffrey Parsons** *pfs*
BBC Music Legends/IMG Artists BBCL4049–2 (80' · ADD) Recorded live [ab]1968, [c]1971   Ⓜ🔾🔾

Although recorded on three separate occasions, and with different accompanists, this programme is fairly typical of the recitals that Dame Janet gave in the late 1960s and early 70s when she was at the absolute peak of her form. She probably wouldn't have opened with the Haydn, reserving it usually as the final item in the first half, an operatic climax to work towards. She recorded it later with Raymond Leppard, but this live version has a wonderful sense of intimacy. The recording is first rate, with marvellous presence; Baker has that ability to invest a simple phrase in the first recitative such as 'la face splenda del nostro amor' with unforgettable poignancy. In the second part, as Ariadne rails against her fate, she allows herself an almost *verismo*–like outburst at 'ei qui lascia in abbandono'. This cantata can sometimes seem a bit heavyweight on a recital programme, but as Baker sings it seems to grows in beauty and intensity.

Frauenliebe und –leben was the work that brought Baker early fame as a recording artist, in her recital for Saga. Later she recorded it again for EMI with Barenboim. This recording from 1968, accompanied by Geoffrey Parsons, finds her in luxurious full voice, revelling in each successive melody. It isn't preferable to the earlier Saga version with Isepp, but here she lets herself go more at certain key moments such as 'O lass

---

Cecilia Bartoli   *mezzo–soprano*

'Maria'
Bellini Norma – Casta diva. I Puritani – O rendetemi la speme…Qui la voce; Vien, diletto. La Sonnambula – Ah! Non credea mirarti; Ah! Non giunge **García** El poeta calculista – Yo que soy contrabandista. La figlia dell'aria – E non lo vedo…Son regina **Halévy** Clari – Come dolce a me favelli **Hummel** Air à la tirolienne avec variations, Op 118 **Malibran** Prendi, per me sei libero. Rataplan **Mendelssohn** Infelice, Op 94 **Pacini** Irene – Se un mio desir…Cedi al duol; Ira del ciel. Dopo tante e tante pene **G Persiani** Ines de Castro – Cari giorni **L Rossi** Amelia, ovvero Otto anni di constanza – Scorrete, o lagrime
Cecilia Bartoli *mez*
with **Celso Albelo** *ten* **Luca Pisaroni** *bass–bar* **Maria Goldschmidt** *fl* **Robert Pickup** *cl* **Elena Vicini** *cast* **Benjamin Forster** *drum* **Maxim Vengerov,** **Ada Pesch** *vns* **Daniel Pezzotti** *vc* **Una Prelle** *hp* **Claudio Mermoud** *gtr* La Scintilla Orchestra, Zurich; International Chamber Soloists / **Adám Fischer**
Decca 475 9077DH (80' · DDD · T/t)   🔾🔾🔾↦

This new recital is a brilliant summation of Bartoli's art and the special contribution it makes. At best, she has brought an individuality and sense of personal commitment to her singing, rare both in kind and degree. Voice and usage have always been fascinating, whatever their limitations. Enthusiasm, the awareness of a remarkable will–power and with it the recognition of an adventurous musical spirit in seeking out new material: all these have further distinguished her. And now she appears to have found a figure on whom she can hang all these gifts while exploring the repertoire that appeals to her most strongly.

Maria Malibran (1808-36) is now remembered for her death almost as much as for her life. In poor health, she sang in a duet which became so competitive that she determined to repeat it, thus vanquishing her rival, even if it killed her. And it did; at least, she died (in Manchester, aged 28) nine days later. The concentration of a scorching will–power is strikingly caught in Bartoli's performances: in the cabaletta of the first item, from Pacini's *Irene*, for instance, the phrase 'mi squarcia il seno' is almost ferociously intense. Gaiety and charm were also at Malibran's command, as they are at Bartoli's in the Spanish song by the father, Manuel García, and in Maria's own *Rataplan*. The quality of her voice is variously reported (at times she was said to be practically voiceless), but there is no doubt about the magical effect of her singing upon her audiences. If it was anything like the spell Bartoli herself casts in the quiet rapture of her 'Casta diva' it must have been memorable indeed.

'The Barcelona Concert'
Balfe The Maid of Artois – Yon moon o'er the mountain **Bellini** La Sonnambula – Ah! non credea mirarti…Ah! non giunge. **García** El poeta calculista – Yo que soy contrabandista. La figlia dell'aria – E non lo vedo…Son regina **Hummel** Air à la tirolienne avec variations, Op 118 **Malibran** Rataplan. Oh dolce incanto (for Donizetti's L'elisir d'amore) **Mendelssohn** Infelice, Op 94. **Persiani** Ines de Castro – Cari giorni **Rossini** La Cenerentola – Nacqui all'affanno…Non più mesta. Otello – Assisa al piè d'un salice…Deh, calma
Cecilia Bartoli *mez* **David Casares** *gtr*
La Scintilla Orchestra, Zurich

Documentary, 'Malibran Rediscovered – The Romantic Revolution'

Film director **Michael Sturminger**
Decca ② **DVD** 074 3252DX2 (147' · NTSC ·16:9 · PCM stereo and DTS 5.1 · 0)   Ⓕ**OO**

No prima donna since Callas and Sutherland has excited such extreme reactions in audiences and critics as Cecilia Bartoli. This pair of DVDs will delight her admirers and perhaps confound some of the detractors. Bartoli's evident, and infectious, enthusiasm and delight in studying the career of Maria Malibran is sketched in Michael Sturminger's documentary, in whichwe follow her to many of the theatres and streets associated with the diva beloved of the Romantic imagination. In libraries and museums we are able to view some of the scores used by Malibran in her brief and stormy progress through the capitals of Europe. From the opening shots of a gondola in Venice passing through the Rio Malibran, to the final glimpse of her tomb in Brussels, one gets some idea of the impact she made on audiences in the 1820s and '30s.

Bartoli's concert, in the spectacular surroundings of Barcelona's Palau de la Música Catalana, includes many of the same arias that were on her CD 'Maria' (see above). With the encouragement of a wildly enthusiastic audience, she surpasses those performances, and in two Rossini items, the Willow Song from *Otello* and the final

Rondo from *La Cenerentola* (neither on the CD), one feels that she is indeed invoking the shade of Manuel García's daughter. 'Nacqui' all'affano' benefits from Bartoli's study of Malibran's own variations for *Cenerentola*. As for the final encore, 'Yo que soy contrabandista' from García's opera *El poeta calculista*, in which Bartoli is accompanied by guitar, castanets, and 'clappers', it has to be heard and seen to be appreciated: serious fun.

Ian Bostridge   *tenor*

The English Songbook
Britten The Salley gardens[a] **WCD Brown** To Gratiana dancing and singing[a] **Delius** Twilight Fancies[a] **Dunhill** The Cloths of Heaven, Op 30 No 3[a] **Finzi** The dance continued, Op 14 No 10[a]. Since we loved, Op 13 No 7[a] **German** Orpheus with his lute[a] **Grainger** Bold William Taylor, BFMS43[a]. Brigg Fair, BFMS7[b] **Gurney** Sleep[a] **Parry** No longer mourn for me[a] **Quilter** Come away, death, Op 6 No 1[a]. I will go with my father a–ploughing[a]. Now sleeps the crimson petal, Op 3 No 2[a] **Somervell** To Lucasta, on going to the wars[a] **Stanford** La belle dame sans merci[a] **Traditional** The death of Queen Jane[a]. The little turtle dove[a]. My love's an arbutus (arr. Stanford)[a] **Vaughan Williams** Linden Lea[a]. Silent Noon[a] **Warlock** Cradle Song[a]. Jillian of Berry[a]. Rest, sweet nymphs[a]
Ian Bostridge *ten* [a]**Julius Drake** *pf* [b]**Polyphony / Stephen Layton**
EMI 556830–2 (69' · DDD · T)   Ⓕ**O**

The recital begins with Keats and ends with Shakespeare: that can't be bad. But it also begins with Stanford and ends with Parry; what would the modernists of their time have thought about that? They would probably not have believed that those two pillars of the old musical establishment would still be standing by in 1999. And in fact how well very nearly all these composers stand! Quilter's mild drawing–room manners might have been expected to doom him, but the three songs here – the affectionate, easy grace of his Tennyson setting, the restrained passion of his 'Come away, death' and the infectious zest of 'I will go with my father a–ploughing' – endear him afresh and demonstrate once again the wisdom of artists who recognise their own small area of 'personal truth' and refuse to betray it in exchange for a more fashionable 'originality'. Likewise Finzi, whose feeling for Hardy's poems is so modestly affirmed in 'The dance continued'. Does that song, incidentally, make deliberate reference, at 'those songs we sang when we went gipsying', to Jillian of Berry by Warlock (whose originality speaks for itself)? Jillian of Berry itself perhaps calls for more full–bodied, less refined tones than Bostridge's. One could do with a ruddier glow and more rotund fruitiness in the voice. Yet for most of the programme he isn't merely a well–suited singer but an artist who brings complete responsiveness to words and music. The haunted desolation of Delius's *Twilight Fancies* is perfectly caught in the pale hue of the voice which can nevertheless give body and intensity to the frank cry of desire, calming then to *pianissimo* for the last phrase amid the dim echoes of hunting horns in the piano part. Julius Drake plays with strength of imagination and technical control to match Bostridge's own.

Measha Brueggergosman   *soprano*

'Surprise'
Bolcom 12 Cabaret Songs[b]: Vol 1 – Song of Black Max (as told by the de Kooning boys); Amor; Toothbrush Time; Surprise!; The Actor; George; Vol 2 – The Total Stranger in the Garden **Satie** La diva de l'empire[a]. L'omnibus automobile[a]. Tendrementa. Je te veux (arr Bolcom)[b]. Trois Mélodies – Daphénéo (arr Caby)[b] **Schoenberg** Cabaret Songs[b] – Galathea; Gigerlette; Der genügsame Liebhaber; Einfältiges Lied; Mahnung; Jedem das Seine; Seit ich so viele Weiber sah (all arr Davin); Der Nachtwandler (arr Schoenberg)
Measha Brueggergosman *sop* [a]**William Bolcom** pf [b]**BBC Symphony Orchestra / David Robertson**
DG 477 6589 (60' · DDD)   Ⓕ🅑➔

William Bolcom's *Cabaret Songs* (there are 28 of them in all) were composed for his wife Joan Morris, who recorded them with the composer at the piano in the 1970s. For Measha Brueggergosman's first solo recording, Bolcom has orchestrated seven of them into a nifty little song–cycle. The mood is generally slightly sinister, from the opening 'Surprise!' ('When she tried to drink iodine from a paper cup'), through a worrying tale of crime and punishment, 'Amor!', to the best–known of the songs, the Weill–style 'Black Max'. This bears the subtitle 'As told by the de Kooning boys', and all the verses by Bolcom's long–time lyricist and librettist Arnold Weinstein have overtones of surrealism and world–weary irony, suitable for one who lived out his days in that seediest of grand hotels, The Chelsea.

It's a brave man who sets out to orchestrate Schoenberg, and Patrick Davin's reworkings of the *Brettl-Lieder* inevitably have a softening effect (just one, 'Der Nachtwandler', has Schoenberg's own orchestration). Brueggergosman deals with them in a straightforward way, without trying to overload them with charm or significance.

The voice is a full soprano, well focused, with a 'snarling' edge used to great effect in the Bolcom songs. In the Schoenberg she employs a more obviously operatic style, with a gentle vibrato. The BBC Symphony Orchestra under David Robertson play with considerable spirit, above all in Bolcom's really gorgeous orchestration of Satie's 'Je te veux'. This and the other chansons composed for Paulette Darty ('Tendrement' and 'La diva de l'empire') go well, but 'L'omnibus automobile' is taken too fast, so that much of the crazy humour of Vincent Hyspa's poem is lost. No matter, there is an enormous amount to enjoy here from a hugely talented singer.

Maria Callas   *soprano*

Bellini Norma – Casta diva **Bizet** Carmen –   Ⓗ L'amour est un oiseau rebelle; Près des remparts de Séville; Les tringles des sistres **Catalani** La Wally – Ebben? … Ne andrò lontana **Donizetti** Lucia di Lammermoor – Spargi d'amaro pianto **Giordano** Andrea Chénier – La mamma morta **Gluck** Orphée et Eurydice – J'ai perdu mon Eurydice **Puccini** Gianni Schicchi – O mio babbino caro. La bohème – Sì, mi chiamano Mimì; Donde lieta usci. Madama Butterfly – Un bel dì vedremo. Tosca – Vissi d'arte **Rossini** Il barbiere di Siviglia – Una voce poco fa **Saint–Saëns** Samson et Dalila – Mon coeur s'ouvre à ta voix **Verdi** La traviata – Ah, fors'è lui; Addio del passato
Maria Callas *sop* with **various artists**
EMI 557050–2 (74' · ADD · T/t)   Ⓕ🅞🅞🅑➔

This single–disc collection comes with the subtitle 'Callas sings film', as half the items have been chosen to link with film soundtracks. It may be interesting to learn that 'Vissi d'arte' was used in a film called *Copycat* or that the Habanera from *Carmen* now has three film credits to its name, but that's unlikely to sway the confirmed opera–lover. The more important factors will be the generous length of the CD at 74 minutes and its full–price tag, which is optimistic for what's in effect a sampler designed to encourage purchasers to investigate Callas's recordings further.

There's nothing cut–price about the performances. The 17 tracks on this disc are taken from recordings that made operatic history in the second half of the 20th century. It's particularly heartening to find items from the 1954 Puccini recital disc that Callas made with Serafin, where the singing is perfectly schooled in every detail. The two extracts from the live performance of *La traviata* in Lisbon are welcome for showing that Callas was as impressive live as on disc, though it's a shame that 'Ah, fors' è lui' is shorn of both its recitative and cabaletta.

Enrico Caruso   *tenor*

Complete Recordings, Volume 5, 1908–1910   Ⓗ **Franchetti** Germania – Studenti udite; Non, non chiuder gli occhi vaghi **Geehl** For you alone **Gounod** Faust – O merveille![a]; Seigneur Dieu, que vois–je![b]; Eh! quoi! toujours seule?[b]; Il se fait tard![c]; O nuit d'amour[c]; Mon coeur est pénétré d'épouvante[c]; Attends! Voici la rue[c]; Que voulez–vous, messieurs?[d]; Alerte! alerte![e] **Leoncavallo** Pagliacci – No, Pagliaccio non son **Mascagni** Cavalleria rusticana[g] – O Lola ch'ai di latti fior di spino **Ponchielli** La Gioconda – Cielo e mar! **Puccini** Madama Butterfly – Amore o grillo; Non ve l'avevo detto?[f] **Tosti** Addio **Verdi** Il trovatore – Mal reggendo[h]; Se m'ami ancor[h]. Aida – Già i sacerdoti[h]; Misero appien mi festi[h]
[bce]**Geraldine Farrar** *sop* [b]**Gabrielle Gilibert** *mez* [h]**Louise Homer** *contr* **Enrico Caruso** *ten* [d]**Antonio Scotti** *bar* [abde]**Marcel Journet** *bass* [g]**Francis Lapitino** hp **Victor Orchestra**
Naxos Historical 8 110720 (79' · AAD) Recorded 1910   Ⓢ

Caruso in Opera, Volume 2 ⊞
Arias – L'Africaine, Andrea Chenier, La bohème
(Leoncavallo and Puccini), Carmen, Cavalleria
rusticana, Don Pasquale, Eugene Onegin, La favorita,
Les Huguenots, Macbeth, Martha, Nero, La reine de
Saba, Rigoletto, Tosca & Il trovatore
Enrico Caruso ten with various artists
Nimbus Prima Voce mono NI7866 (79' · ADD)
Recorded 1905–20   Ⓢ

The 1906 recording of 'M'apparì' from *Martha*
comes first, and it introduces an aspect of Caruso's singing that rarely finds a place in the critical
commentaries: his subtlety. Partly, it's rhythmic.
The move–on and pull–back seems such an
instinctive process that we hardly notice it
(though no doubt a modern conductor would –
and check it immediately). It makes all the difference to the emotional life of the piece, the feeling
of involvement and spontaneous development.
Then there's the phrasing, marvellously achieved
at the melody's reprise. The play of louder and
softer tones, too, has every delicacy of fine graduation; and just as masterly is the more technical
covering and (rare) opening of notes at the *passaggio*. An edition of the score which brought out all
these features of Caruso's singing would be a
densely annotated document. It would, even so,
be a simplification, for accompanying all this is
the dramatic and musical feeling, which defies
analysis – and, of course, the voice.

That voice! You may feel you know all these
records and hardly need to play them, yet there's
scarcely an occasion when the beauty of it
doesn't thrill with a sensation both old and new
(the first 'Ah!' is one of recognition, the second
of fresh wonder). So it is with the items here:
excepting the *Eugene Onegin* aria, which remains
external, and the late *L'Africaine* recording, with
its saddening evidence of deterioration. The
transfers are excellent.

Sarah Connolly   *mezzo–soprano*

'The Exquisite Hour'
Brahms Da unten im Tale, WoO33 No 6. Vier Lieder,
Op 43 – No 1, Von ewiger Liebe; No 2, Die Mainacht.
Alte Liebe, Op 72 No 1. Sechs Lieder, Op 86 – No 2,
Feldeinsamkeit; No 3, Nachtwandler. Ständchen,
Op 106 No 1 **Britten** Tit for Tat **Hahn** A Chloris.
L'enamourée. L'heure exquise. Quand je fus pris au
pavillon. Trois jours de vendage **Haydn** Arianna a
Naxos **Ireland** Three Songs to Poems by Thomas
Hardy – Her Song **Korngold** Gluckwunsch. Alt–
Spanisch. Abschiedslieder, Op 14 – Sterbelied;
Gefasster Abschied **Weill** Lost in Stars – Lost in
the Stars; One Touch of Venus – Speak Low
Sarah Connolly mez **Eugene Asti** pf
Signum Classics SIGCD072 (75' · DDD · T/t) Recorded
live 2005   Ⓕ

Almost seven years ago we went to the Wigmore
Hall expecting to hear a well known soprano
only to find that she had been replaced by a less
well-known mezzo. Sarah Connolly had already
appeared with the English National Opera in

major roles such as Handel's Xerxes and Donizetti's Mary Stuart. Disappointment at missing
the scheduled artist vanished with the completion of the substitute's first phrases. Delight
took its place and increased steadily throughout
the recital. It was a clear, fresh and powerful
voice, used with intelligent assurance, and by the
final groups (Duparc and Falla) she had established with the audience the rapport of a much
more experienced artist. What was true at the
Wigmore holds for this concert at St John's,
Smith Square, where her success with the audience is again unmistakable and fully merited.

Again, her choice of programme contributes to
the success: a judicious mixture of the familiar
and out-of-the-way, and well suited to voice and
style. The Brahms group is particularly satisfying, with *Die Mainacht* broadly phrased, *Nachtwandler* imaginatively hushed and *Von ewiger
Liebe* warmly felt. The Hahn songs are equally
(if contrastingly) delightful, the two pastiche
pieces, *A Chloris* and *Quand je fus pris au pavillon*
charmingly in period. Weill's *Speak Low* and
Ireland's *Her Song* are winning encore pieces.

That leaves Haydn's *Arianna a Naxos*, the
long and demanding concert aria which opens
the programme. Here we find a substantial
achievement and a limitation. The style is
admirably clean and the emotional range well
probed, but the whole remains a little impersonal and one is driven to comparisons. Janet
Baker brings warmer humanity and a more
memorable timbre while Cecilia Bartoli is
more vivid – hear her intense 'Tradita io sono'
for instance, or the pale 'Già più non reggo' or
the furious final 'Barbaro ed infedel'.

That comparison does, however, throw into a
very favourable light Eugene Asti's accompaniment: where András Schiff (for Bartoli) is over-
assertive, Asti is sensitive and keeps proportion.
And indeed he does so throughout: a constant
pleasure and a major contribution to the recital's
undoubted success.

Diana Damrau   *soprano*

'Donna'
No, no che non sei capace, K419. Vorrei spiegarvi,
oh Dio, K418. La clemenza di Tito – S'altro che
lagrime; Ecco il punto…Non più di fiori.
Don Giovanni – Crudele? Ah no, mio bene…Non mi
dir. Die Entführung aus dem Serail – Durch
Zärtlichkeit; Martern aller Arten. La finta semplice –
Senti l'eco, ove t'aggiri. Mitridate, re di Ponto –
Al destin, che la minaccia. Le nozze di Figaro –
E Susanna non vien…Dove sono; Giunse alfin il
momento…Deh, vieni, non tardar. Die Zauberflöte –
Ach, ich fühl's
Diana Damrau sop **Le Cercle de l'Harmonie /
Jérémie Rhorer**
Virgin Classics 212023–2 (73' · DDD)   Ⓕⵔ⟶

The glamorous German soprano, Diana Damrau, now in her mid-thirties, made her international reputation as a sensational Queen of Night
and Zerbinetta. Like Lucia Popp at a similar age,

she has now abandoned the Queen's trapeze act for the more amenable tessitura of her daughter Pamina, singing 'Ach, ich fühl's' as an intensely private, almost dazed, expression of grief. Yet she still sails effortlessly into the ionosphere, whether as Konstanze, Blonde or, most spectacularly of all, in two 'insertion' arias (K418 and 419) Mozart composed for his sister–in–law Aloysia Lange to sing in Anfossi's *Il curioso discreto*. Damrau's pearly, aspirate–free coloratura is immediately on display in Aspasia's opening aria from *Mitridate*. Her fiery, imperious yet never hard–toned 'Martern aller Arten' – sung here with Mozart's cuts opened out – would silence any Pasha. In the same opera, Damrau alternately cajoles and taunts Osmin in a delightful 'Durch Zärtlichkeit' – the feisty Blonde to the life.

Hardly less successful are the double acts from *Figaro*, *La clemenza di Tito* and *Don Giovanni*, each a distinct, individual portrayal. Perhaps Countess Almaviva (which Damrau has yet to sing on stage) is the one role here that ideally calls for a warmer, richer voice. That said, few singers have matched her surge of joyous resolve – or the imagination of her phrasing – in the fast section of 'Dove sono'. Moving from mistress to maid, Damrau sings an enchanting, sensuously caressed 'Deh, vieni'. In *La clemenza di Tito* she has the tonal depth, as well as the grace of line, for Vitellia's aria of remorse, and brings an anxious urgency rather than mere charm to Servilia's minuet song (she is, after all, pleading for her brother's life). The notoriously taxing 'Mi tradì' is sung with technical panache and acute delineation of Elvira's fluctuating emotions; and it is good to hear the coloratura in Anna's 'Non mi dir', so often a trial, despatched with such elegance and delicacy. Here and elsewhere Jérémie Rhorer draws tangy, rhythmically lively playing from his period band.

Plácido Domingo　　　　　　　　　*tenor*

'Pasión Española'
Alonso Suspiros de España **Anta** La Cruz de Mayo
Lacosta Porque te quiero. Cariño verdá **López–Quiroga y Miquel** ¡Ay, Maricruz! Me embrujaste.
Te lo juro yoa. ¡No me quieras tanto! Ojos verdesa
Morales Falsa monedaa. La bien pagá. El día que
nací yo **Morales/Bosch** Antonio Vargas Heredia
Plácido Domingo ten ªJosé María Gallardo del Rey
gtr **Madrid Communidad Orchestra / Miguel Roa**
DG 477 6590GH (54' · DDD)　　　　Ⓕ**ⓄⒹ**

In this selection of coplas and pasodobles, the majority composed in the 1930s and '40s, Domingo uses his voice in a mostly baritonal range. These are the songs, as he writes in the notes, that he heard as a child in Spain, even before his family moved to Mexico: 'Since then I have had them in my mind's ear.'

The mood is for the most part highly emotional, drawing on a sort of fatalistic romanticism. Two of the most famous songs, composed by Juan Mostazo Morales to words by Perelló, 'Falsa moneda' and 'La bien pagá', were associated with Conchita

Piquer, Imperio Argentina and Juan Valderrama, popular idols of the era, performing both before and after the Spanish Civil War. In these, and in more upbeat songs such as '¡Ay, Maricruz!' by Manuel López-Quiroga y Miquel, Domingo brings a fervent commitment to the story-telling. Each song is what he calls a 'mini-opera'.

Although originally they would have been accompanied by solo piano or guitar duettists, once the coplas transferred to the big screen – the huge repertory of popular Spanish musical films remains completely unknown in other centres – the sort of large-scale orchestration heard here became the norm. The Madrid orchestra under Miguel Roa provide elegant and idiomatic accompaniment.

Renée Fleming　　　　　　　　　*soprano*

'I Want Magic'
Barber Vanessa – He has come…Do not utter a
word, Anatol **Bernstein** Candide -- Glitter and be
gay **Floyd** Susannah – Ain't it a pretty night; The
trees on the mountains **Gershwin** Porgy and Bess--
Summertime; My man's gone now **Herrmann**
Wuthering Heights – I have dreamt **Menotti** The
Medium – Monica's Waltz **D Moore** The Ballad of
Baby Doe – The Letter Song **Previn** A Streetcar
Named Desire – I want magic! **Stravinsky** The Rake's
Progress – No word from Tom…I go to him
Renée Fleming sop **Metropolitan Opera
Orchestra, New York / James Levine**
Decca 460 567–2DH (58' · DDD · T/t)　　Ⓕ**ⓄⓄⓄⒹ**

Ⓖ　This survey of operas old and new reinforces the feeling that the current generation of star singers in the USA is making an effort to explore home-grown repertory. Fleming's voice is sumptuous, her lower register especially sounds so warmly resonant that it's reminiscent of Leontyne Price in her glory days. Fleming shows herself equal to every mood; only at the end of 'Glitter and be gay' is there a false moment when she rather overdoes the brittle laughter. What beautiful tunes there are here, including the waltz song from *The Medium* and 'Ain't it a pretty night' from *Susannah*. This was recorded before Fleming took part in the world premiere of André Previn's *A Streetcar Named Desire* in San Francisco and her programme ends with a sneak preview of that. 'I want magic!' is Blanche's philosophy of life, justifying her flights of fancy. Among the other items, Fleming makes the extract from *Wuthering Heights* sound positively Mahleresque, and Anne's great aria from *The Rake's Progress* – 'officially' an American opera, Stravinsky, Auden and Kallman at least all being resident there when it was written – suits her surprisingly well. Levine and the Met Orchestra provide idiomatic accompaniment.

Gerald Finley　　　　　　　　　*baritone*

Ives Memories **Mussorgsky** Songs and Dances of
Death **Rautavaara** Three Sonnets – Shall I compare

thee? **Rorem** War Scenes **Tchaikovsky** Six Songs,
Op 25 – No 2, As o'er the burning ashes. Six Songs,
Op 38 – No 1, Don Juan's Serenade; No 2, It was in
the early spring; No 3, At the ball. Seven Songs,
Op 47 – No 6, Does the day reign?. Twelve Songs,
Op 60 – No 3, If only you knew; No 12, The mild stars
shone for us **W Charles** The Green-Eyed Dragon
Gerald Finley bass–bar **Julius Drake** pf
Wigmore Hall Live WHLIVE0025 (71' · DDD)
Recorded live at the Wigmore Hall, London, on
October 18, 2007   ⓜ

Aided by scrupulous support from Julius Drake,
Gerald Finley lavishes wonderfully rounded
treatment upon the sequence of seven Tchaikovsky songs that open proceedings. Be it in the
ardent swagger of 'Don Juan's Serenade', wistful
glow of 'At the ball' or meltingly lovely 'The
mild stars shone for us', Finley is not found
wanting. Not only do his top notes ring out with
thrilling projection (yet without a hint of hardness), he exhibits a grace, sensitivity and intelligence that ensure that the music never topples
into rampant self-pity.

There's a comparable authority and integrity
about these artists' interpretation of Mussorgsky's *Songs and Dances of Death*. Finley is in complete command of his very considerable resources,
distilling every ounce of pathos from the mother's
desperate pleadings in the opening 'Lullaby' and
conveying in full the grim implacability of 'The
Field-Marshal'. Ned Rorem's similarly declamatory *War Scenes* is also performed with total
understanding, while the last of the three encores,
Wolseley Charles's wickedly amusing *The
Green-Eyed Dragon* (written in 1926 for Stanley
Holloway), predictably brings the house down.
A genuine treat, this, and not to be missed.

Juan Diego Flórez   tenor

'Una furtiva lagrima'
Bellini I Capuleti e i Montecchi[bc] – O, di Capellio
generosi amici; E serbato a questo acciaro; L'amo
tanto e m'è si cara. I Puritani – A te, o cara[abc].
La-sonnambula[a] – Vedi, o madre; Tutto è sciolto;
Pasci il guardo; Ah! perche non posso odiarti
Donizetti Don Pasquale – Povero Ernesto!; Cercherò
lontana terra; Com' è gentil. Elisabetta – Ah non
sogno!; Disperato amante afflitto. L'elisir d'amore –
Una furtiva lagrima. Rita – Allegro io son. La fille du
régiment[b] – Ah! mes amis; Pour mon âme quel
destin!
Juan Diego Flórez ten
[a]**Ermonela Jaho** sop [b]**Nikola Mijalovic** bar
[c]**Nicola Ulivieri** bass **Giuseppe Verdi Chorus and
Symphony Orchestra, Milan / Riccardo Frizza**
Decca 473 440–2DH (64' · DDD · T/t)   ⒻⓄ▶

This is a well-thought-out programme showing
the continuing development in this singer's art.
The opening number, a light-hearted waltz
song from Donizetti's rarely heard one-act comedy *Rita* is balanced by the finale, which is the
by-now celebrated solo for Tonio in *La fille du
régiment* with its nine top Cs that at one time

seemed to be the unique possession of Luciano
Pavarotti. Such convivialities contrast with the
more elegiac mood of Ernesto's 'Cercherò lontana terra' in *Don Pasquale*, and that in turn with
the turbulent excerpt from *Elisabetta*. Items
which call for the participation of other soloists
and/or chorus are well supplied, to most lovely
effect in *I puritani*.

It's altogether an attractive record, introduced
with a lively and informative note by Tom Sutcliffe. A slight cause for regret is the lack of a
sentence or two putting each extract briefly into
dramatic context. As for Flórez, the grace and
accomplishment with which he uses his clear,
resonant voice are beyond praise; the next stage
in his career should see a growth of imagination
and a deepening of feeling.

'Bel Canto Spectacular'
Bellini I Puritani – Fini[!] Me lassa!…Vieni, fra queste
braccia[b] **Donizetti** Don Pasquale – Povero Ernesto!
L'elisir d'amore – Venti scudi[e]; Una furtiva lagrima. La
Favorite – La maîtresse du roi?…Ange si pur. La fille
du régiment – Ah! mes amis (Miei buoni amiche)[f].
Linda di Chamounix – Linda! Linda![a]; Da quel dì
che t'incontra. Lucrezia Borgia – Partir degg'io…
Io vuol Lucrezia; T'amo qual dama un angelo
Rossini Otello – Ah vieni, nel tuo sangue vendicherò
le offese[d]. Il viaggio a Reims – Di che son reo?[c];
D'alma celeste, oh Dio
Juan Diego Flórez ten with [a]**Patricia Ciofi**,
[b]**Anna Netrebko** sops [c]**Daniela Barcellona** mez
[d]**Plácido Domingo** ten [e]**Mariusz Kwiecien**,
[f]**Fernando Piqueras** bars **Cor de la Generalitat
Valenciana; Orquesta de la Comunitat Valenciana /
Daniel Oren**
Decca 478 0315DH (77' · DDD)   Ⓕ
Also available as a special limited edition
with DVD 478 0314

The opening track here is presumably Juan
Diego Flórez's final word on the show–stopping
aria from *La fille du régiment*. Having recorded it
three times in French, he now offers it in Italian,
although it hardly matters what language is
being sung when it gets to the famous sequence
of top Cs. It has become for him what 'Nessun
dorma' was for Pavarotti – the aria every audience expects.

The rest of this attractive canter through the
bel canto repertory finds our hero in robust
form. This is very much a case of 'Flórez and
friends'. Anna Netrebko contributes a touching
Elvira to the great last–act duet from *I Puritani*,
a very full version that culminates in those
stratospheric phrases taking the tenor up to the
high D. This is surely a role Flórez was born to
sing. One could say the same about Carlo in
Linda di Chamounix. Is there any more catchy
Donizetti tune than the duet, 'Da quel dì che
t'incontra'? Flórez and Patricia Ciofi are not
undermined by comparison with Sutherland and
Pavarotti and the lovely solo from the same
opera suits Flórez perfectly.

The two extracts from *L'elisir d'amore* are both
winning, with Mariusz Kwiecien as an excep-

tionally vivid Belcore. Flórez has recorded 'Una furtiva lagrima' before – here he offers some new, attractive variations in the second verse. Rodrigo in Rossini's *Otello* was his first big success at Covent Garden, and a bonus track has him fighting it out with Plácido Domingo as the Moor. Somewhat more attractive is the long duet with Daniella Barcellona from *Il viaggio a Reims*. Flórez brings the CD to a rousing close with the extra aria from *Lucrezia Borgia* that Donizetti composed for Nicolai Ivanoff.

One gets the feeling this disc proved to be not only challenging but fun to record.

Elīna Garanča   *mezzo–soprano*

'Bel canto'
Bellini Adelson e Salvini – Dopo l'oscuro nembo. I Capuleti e i Montecchi[a] – Lieto del dolce incarco; La tremenda ultrice spada **Donizetti** L'assedio di Calais[b] – Al mio core oggetti amati; Io l'udio chiamarmi a nome; La speme un dolce palpito. Dom Sébastien – Sol adoré. Lucrezia Borgia – Il segreto per esser felici (Brindisi). Maria Stuarda[b] – Sì, vuol di Francia il Rege (Elisabetta); Ah! quando all'ara scorgemi; In tal giorno di contento; Ah! dal ciel discenda un raggio. Roberto Devereux – All' afflitto è dolce il pianto **Rossini** Maometto Secondo – In questi estremi istanti. Tancredi – Oh patria!; Di tanti palpiti **Elīna Garanča** *mez* with [b]**Ekaterina Siurina** *sop* [ab]**Matthew Polenzani,** [c]**Adrian Sâmpetrean** *tens* [ac]**Ildebrando d'Arcangelo** *bar* **Teatro Comunale Philharmonic Orchestra, Bologna / Roberto Abbado**
DG 477 7460GH (65' · DDD)   Ⓕ**Ⓞ**Ⓓ➤

Garanča begins with the best-known item, the Brindisi from the last act of *Lucrezia Borgia*, and if her voice is a little soft-grained for the reckless Maffio Orsini, she sings the song well. Strangely she sounds more masculine as Donizetti's Queen Elizabeth I in the entrance aria from *Maria Stuarda*. The gentle songs from *Adelson e Salvini* and *Dom Sébastien* make a nice contrast with the fireworks of 'Di tanti palpiti' from *Tancredi*.

Garanča is joined by Ekaterina Siurina in the spectacular duet from *L'assedio di Calais* – it's worth hearing the disc just for this – and they are aided here by Matthew Polenzani as well as in the trio from *Maometto Secondo*. Roberto Abbado and the Bologna orchestra provide the always sympathetic accompaniment (several of the items are performed 'from the original manuscript'). What of that long *bel canto* line? It is never allowed to overwhelm the dramatic situation of each scene but Garanča seems to find no difficulty in any of this music.

Angela Gheorghiu   *soprano*

'Live from La Scala'
Alessandrescu Sub perdeaua dragei mele **Bellini** Malinconia, ninfa gentile. Vanne o rosa fortunata **Bizet** Chant d'amour **Brediceanu** Floricica

de pe apa. Bade, pentru ochii tai. Vai, badita, dragi ne-avem **Dendrino** Lasati–ma sa cant – Te iubesc **Donizetti** Me voglio fa'na casa **Gheciu** Si daca **Gluck** O del mio dolce ardor **Gounod** Faust – Vous qui faite l'endormie **Lerner/Loewe** I could have danced all night **Martini** Piacer d'amor **Massenet** Elégie **Parisotti** Se tu m'ami **Puccini** Gianni Schicchi – O mio babbino caro **Scarlatti** O cessate di piagarmi **Tosti** A vucchella **Verdi** Stornello. In solitaria stanza. Brindisi II
Angela Gheorghiu *sop* **Jeff Cohen** *pf*
EMI 394420–2 (66' · DDD). Recorded live at Teatro alla Scala, Milan, on April 3, 2006   Ⓕ Ⓓ➤

The audience is clearly out for an orgy of diva–worship, applause after every song, so this is a recital to be enjoyed in the spirit of indulgence. It's a bit odd to hear 'Plaisir d'amour' in Italian right at the start, and although Angela Gheorghiu sings that and the succeeding group of 18th–century songs and arias by Scarlatti, Parisotti and Gluck with plenty of luscious tone, like many singers before her she is using these ancient airs to give the proceedings a gentle start. The songs by Bellini and Donizetti suit her better, but it's the Verdi group that is the heart of the first half. 'In solitaria stanza', with its main theme closely resembling 'Tacea la notte' from *Il trovatore*, must rank as one of the loveliest things she has recorded. This is framed by the coquettish 'Stornello' and the almost raucous 'Brindisi' (nothing to do with *La traviata*).

The second half opens with a French group, the Gounod *Sérénade* and Bizet's 'Chant d'amour' nicely contrasted, love songs in relaxed and urgent moods. It is the Massenet 'Elégie' that benefits from Gheorghiu's operatic experience: here are words and music given equal importance to make a miniature drama. The songs by Romanian composers Alfred Alessandrescu, Diamanti Gheciu and Tiberiu Brediceanu are sung with obvious affection and relish; in these, and throughout the recital, Jeff Cohen provides sensitive and idiomatic accompaniment. Brediceanu's 'Bade, pentru ochii tai' is a particularly haunting melody. To end this group, Gheorghiu sings a classic of Romanian operetta, 'Te iubesc' from Gherase Dendrino's *Lasati-ma sa cant*, a beautiful slow waltz, and another song that suits her perfectly. The encores, including 'I could have danced all night' (no comment), seem to provoke a certain amount of heckling from the audience, to which Gheorghiu responds simply with 'Grazie'. The recording catches the mood; it was obviously a fun evening.

Susan Graham   *mezzo–soprano*

'Un frisson français'
Bachelet Chère nuit **Bizet** Chanson d'avril **Canteloube** Chants d'Auvergne – Brezairola **Caplet** Le corbeau et la renard **Chabrier** Les cigales **Chausson** Les papillons, Op 2 No 3 **Debussy** Fêtes galantes, Set 2 – Colloque sentimental **Duparc** Au pays où se fait la guerre **Fauré** Vocalise–étude

Franck Nocturne **Gounod** Au rossignol **Hahn** A Chloris **Honegger** Trois chansons de la petite sirène, H63 **Lalo** Gitarre, Op 17 No 1 **Messiaen** Trois Mélodies – La fiancée perdue **Paladilhe** Psyché **Poulenc** La dame de Monte–Carlo **Ravel** Histoires naturelles – Le paon **M Rosenthal** Chansons de monsieur Bleu – La Souris d'Angleterre **Roussel** Réponse d'une épouse sage, Op 35 No 2 **Saint–Saëns** Danse macabre **Satie** Trois Mélodies – Le chapelier
Susan Graham mez **Malcolm Martineau** pf
Onyx ONYX4030 (78' · DDD)   Ⓕ

With Susan Graham in radiant form and Malcolm Martineau not just an accompanist but an active partner in the project, 'Un frisson français' offers a unique survey of French *mélodie* from the mid–19th century to the mid–20th: 22 songs…one per composer.

Martineau describes the plan as a 'tasting menu', starting with Gounod, to whom he ascribes the launching of the genre of French *mélodie*. Even Ravel said that Gounod was 'the true founder of the *mélodie* in France' and his song 'Au rossignol' ('To the Nightingale') is included in the first of five sections – 'founding fathers', including Bizet, Franck, Lalo and Saint–Saëns. It is fascinating to hear the original version with piano of 'Danse macabre', Graham marvellously biting.

Martineau describes the sequence as 'loosely chronological', and one beauty of the scheme is that rare and forgotten composers are included, such as Paladilhe and Bachelet who are represented in late–Romantic *mélodies* with night and nature dominating themes. The third group – including Ravel and Debussy – takes us into the 20th century. Especially fascinating is André Caplet's setting of 'Le corbeau et le renard' ('The Crow and the Fox') with elaborate piano accompaniment.

Only rare songs are chosen for each composer and perhaps Martineau chose some of them for the colourful accompaniments, as in Chausson's fluttering accompaniment for his picture of the butterfly in 'Le papillon'. The fourth section has childhood as a common theme and the climactic section has only one song, much the longest, Poulenc's 'La dame de Monte-Carlo', to words by Jean Cocteau. It is like an encapsulated version of the operatic monodrama *La voix humaine* with the singer on the verge of a breakdown.

A rich collection in excellent sound: no one is likely to be disappointed.

Philippe Jaroussky   *countertenor*

'Opium'
Caplet Viens, une flûte invisible soupire[c] **Chausson** Le colibri, Op 2 No 7. Le temps de lilas. Les papillons, Op 2 No 3. Les heures, Op 27 No 1.
Chaminade Sombrero. Mignonne **Debussy** Romance No 2 **D'Indy** Lied maritime, Op 43 **Dukas** Sonnet **Dupont** Les donneurs de sérénade **Fauré** Nell, Op 18 No 1. Automne, Op 18 No 3 **Franck** Nocturne **Hahn** A Chloris. Fêtes galantes (Mandoline). 12

Rondels – No 8, Quand je fus pris au pavillon. Offrande. Chansons grises – No 5, L'heure exquise **Lekeu** Trois Poèmes – No 1, Une tombe **Massenet** Elégie[b]. Nuit d'Espagne **Saint–Saëns** Tournoiement, 'Songe d'opium', Op 26. Violons dans le soir[a]
Philippe Jaroussky counterten
Jérôme Ducros pf with [a]**Renaud Capuçon** vn [b]**Gautier Capuçon** vc [c]**Emmanuel Pahud** fl
Virgin Classics 216621–2 (66' · DDD)   Ⓕ Ⓞ Ⓓ⁺

This is beautiful but it takes a bit of getting used to. Philippe Jaroussky's countertenor (he has often been called a male soprano), so well suited to Vivaldi and Monteverdi, at first seems quite wrong in the repertory of belle époque *mélodies*. The song that gives the disc its title, *Tournoiement, 'Songe d'Opium'* by Saint–Saëns, with its madly whirling accompaniment – splendidly played by Jérôme Ducros – benefits from the other–worldy sounds Jaroussky can produce.

Some of the better–known songs, for instance Chausson's *Le temps des lilas* and Hahn's *Offrande* are so familiar as performed by rich–voiced female singers that hearing just the initial phrases one might suppose that the disc were being played at an exaggeratedly high pitch. However, there is no denying the accomplishment of Jaroussky's vocalism, although the basic tone lacks warmth and variation at several key moments. The selection is certainly adventurous, including rarities such as Dukas's *Sonnet*, d'Indy's *Lied maritime*, and two songs by composers who may be unfamiliar to many listeners: *Sur une tombe*, words and music by Guillaume Lekeu (1870-94), the first of his *Trois Poèmes* of 1892, is a little elegy that begins gently but rises to quite a passionate climax, while Gabriel Dupont's *Les donneurs de sérénades* is yet another setting of Verlaine's *Mandoline* – Jaroussky gives a wonderfully flirtatious performance. The songs that require extra instruments are well served by the trio of guest players, with Gautier Capuçon especially eloquent in Massenet's *Elégie*.

Jonas Kaufmann   *tenor*

'Romantic Arias'
Berlioz La damnation de Faust – Nature immense (Invocation) **Bizet** Carmen – La fleur que tu m'avais jetée **Flotow** Martha – Ach so fromm **Gounod** Faust – Quel trouble inconnu; Salut! demeure chaste et pure **Massenet** Manon – Je suis seul!; Ah! fuyez, douce image. Werther – Pourquoi me réveiller? **Puccini** La bohème – Che gelida manina. Tosca – È lucevan le stelle **Verdi** Don Carlo – Io la vidi; Io l'ho perduta. Rigoletto – Ella mi fu rapita!; Parmi veder le lagrime. La traviata – Lunge da lei; De' miei bollenti spiriti[a]; O mio rimorso! **Wagner** Die Meistersinger von Nürnberg – Morgenlich leuchtend (Prize Song) **Weber** Der Freischütz – Nein! länger trag' ich
Jonas Kaufmann ten with [a]**Jana Sibera** sop
Prague Philharmonic Orchestra / Marco Armiliato
Decca 475 9966DH (65' · DDD)   Ⓕ Ⓞ Ⓓ⁺

The more delicate critical constitutions among us will recoil at the very idea of there being anything so distasteful as a World's Top Tenor, but were such a position available and the title to be competed for, there would probably be no stronger candidate at the present time than Jonas Kaufmann.

Kaufmann's voice, warm and full–bodied in its middle register, has an excitingly brilliant top. It has a Latin richness, and the elements are well integrated. The German component (his home town is Munich, though you might have thought Vienna more likely) accounts for the broader musicianship that shapes his phrases and fashions his tone as an instrument sensitive to modulations of sense and sound. The recital opens with Rodolfo's *La bohème* narrative, and fine as that is, the Flower Song from *Carmen*, which follows, is still better. Deeply touching in the sincerity of its appeal, it is nevertheless offered as song, its lyrical inviolate, the B flat of 'et j'étais une chose à toi', a climax not of volume but of devoted tenderness. And the recorded sound catches him most truly in this. Along with the Rigoletto, Don Carlos and Manon arias, it brings him before us as remembered 'in the flesh', whereas elsewhere some element in the tonal balance (an over–insistence on upper frequencies perhaps) somehow blurred the individuality. The *Traviata* disappoints: too heroic in the recitative, almost completely unsmiling in the aria (he should hear Gigli). For the most part, though, this recital is a triumph.

Dame Emma Kirkby   *soprano*

'The Artistry of Emma Kirkby'
Includes works by Amodei, Ariosti, Bach, Blow, Böddecker, Boësset, Couperin, Danyel, Dowland, Ferrabosco, Graupner, Greene, Handel, d'India, R Johnson, Lalande, Lawes, Moulinié, A Scarlatti, Schimmelpfennig, Schütz, Weldon and J Wilson
Dame Emma Kirkby *sop* with **Agnès Mellon** *sop*
John Abberger *ob* **Lucas Harris, Jakob Lindberg, Anthony Rooley** *ltes* **Lars Ulrik Mortensen** *hpd*
Thomas Georgi *va da gamba* **Mime Yamahiro Brinkmann** *vc* **London Baroque; Royal Academy of Music Baroque Orchestra; Theatre of Early Music**
BIS ④ BIS–CD1734/5 (4h 52' · DDD)   Ⓜ**OO**

Emma Kirkby began her current working relationship with BIS in 1999, so this 60th–birthday tribute represents a period in which the novelty value of her unique vocal timbre had long been augmented in the public's appreciation by what really places her in the front rank of early music singers: deep–set musical intelligence made manifest in perfect clarity of diction, an unerring sense of line (including the most tasteful ornamentation) and pinpoint accuracy of movement. Though she never was a purely 'straight' singer, there are still few on this earth who can evince such pleasure from as simple a thing as a long–held, vibratoless note.

BIS's selection policy deserves much credit. It would have been easy to chuck a few existing CDs into the box with a bit of new packaging, but instead they have shrewdly chosen from across a total of nine Kirkby releases to give a true picture of her latest decade of work. There are some unusual things: Kirkby has rarely sung in French, but here are airs de cours by Boësset and Moulinié; and it is not often that you will hear her offering such characterful play–acting as (egged on by Anthony Rooley's lute) she does in Henry Lawes's *At dead low ebb of night*. There is also an exquisitely pained penitential cantata by Graupner, in a performance not previously released. Elsewhere, there are the expected samplings from lute–song repertory (in which she surely remains unsurpassed), brightly virtuoso Handel motets with London Baroque, and a movingly wise account of two of Couperin's *Leçons de Ténèbres*. Yet it's often in the modest–looking pieces that she's at her most compelling. Robert Johnson's *Full Fathom Five* is 109 seconds of breathtaking stillness and beauty, Böddecker's *Natus est Jesus* a masterclass in how quietly to find variety and meaning in a piece that might have seemed to have little to offer. Artistry indeed, and praise to BIS for recognising how to honour it.

Magadalena Ko12ená   *mezzo–soprano*

'Songs My Mother Taught Me'
Dvořák Gypsy Melodies, Op 55[b]. Evening Songs, Op 3[b]. Moravian Duets, Op 32[ab] **Eben** Lute Songsc **Janáček** Moravian Folk Poetry[b]. Silesian Songs[b]
Martinů Songs on Two Pages[b] **Novák** Fairytale of the Heart, Op 8[b] **Rösler** An die Entfernte[b] **Schulhoff** Folksongs and Dances from Těšin[b] **Traditional** If I were a strawberry plant[b]
Magdalena Ko12ená *mez* [a]**Dorothea Röschmann** *sop* [b]**Malcolm Martineau** *pf* [c]**Michael Freimuth** *gtr*
DG 477 6665GH (70' · DDD)   Ⓕ**OO**

Magdalena Ko12ená's heartwarming new album takes its title from one of the best–loved of all Czech songs, the centrepiece of Dvořák's *Gypsy Melodies*. Her smoothly phrased performance captures the nostalgia of this music, with which she is very much at home.

Singing in a language she really did learn from her mother, Ko12ená sounds at her most relaxed; there is no hint of the strain she has shown in some recent operatic work. She also suggests a fierce connection with these songs, abandoning herself into music that showcases well her glinting top and dusky lower notes. This is rich repertory, and Dvořák is not the earliest composer represented here. That honour goes to Jan Josef Rösler (1771–1813), with a Goethe setting (in German). The programme stretches all the way to the lyrical Lute Songs of Peter Eben, who died in 2008.

Along the way we encounter the sophisticated music of Ervín Schulhoff and a lovely set by Vítězslav Novák. The mezzo opens with an unaccompanied folksong, and elsewhere benefits from the sympathetic partnership of Malcolm Martineau. But her programme is essentially framed with songs (and a couple of duets with Dorothea Röschmann) by Janáček, aptly since Kožená grew up in Brno. Miniatures by Martinů speak directly, as so often with this delightful composer.

Anna Netrebko *soprano*

'Souvenirs'

Arditi Il bacio **Dvořák** Songs my mother taught me, B104 No 4 **G Charpentier** Louise – Depuis le jour **Giménez** La Tempranica – La tarántula é un bich mú malo **Grieg** Peer Gynt, Op 23 – Solveig's Song **Guastavino** La rosa y el sauce **Hahn** L'Enamourée **Heuberger** Der Opernball – Im Chambre separée[c] **Kálmán** Die Csárdásfürstin – Heia, heia, in den Bergen ist mein Heimatland **Lehár** Giuditta – Meine Lippen, sie küssen **Lloyd Webber** Requiem – Pie Jesu **Messager** Fortunio – Lorsque je n'étais qu'une enfant **Offenbach** Les contes d'Hoffmann – Belle nuit, ô nuit d'amour (Barcarolle)[b] **R Strauss** Cäcilie, Op 27 No 2. Wiegenlied, Op 41 No 1 **Rimsky– Korsakov** Not the wind, blowing from the heights, Op 43 No 2. Enslaved by the rose, the nightingale, Op 2 No 2 **Traditional** Schlof sche, mein Vögele
Anna Netrebko *sop* with [a]Andrew Swait *treb* [b]Elina Garanča *mez* [c]Piotr Beczała *ten* Prague Philharmonic Choir; Prague Philharmonia / Emmanuel Villaume
DG 477 7639GH (62' · DDD)   Ⓕ**O**▶

Something for everybody here. Netrebko is nothing if not adventurous in her choice of 'lollipops', and sings in nine languages. Inevitably the Russian items come off best: the lovely little Rimsky–Korsakov song about the wind whispering love into the poet's soul, and then the 'Oriental romance' of the rose and the nightingale. Both of these have been discreetly orchestrated for this disc by Andreas Tarkmann. The Yiddish lullaby *Schlof sche, mein vögele* is done with great tenderness, as is the 'Pie Jesu' from Andrew Lloyd Webber's Requiem. This is one of three duets, Netrebko joined here by the boy soprano Andrew Swait. For the Barcarolle from *Les contes d'Hoffmann* she has Elina Garanča on hand as Niklausse; they make a convincing pair of Venetian serenaders. Even better is 'Im Chambre separée' from Heuberger's *Der Opernball*, heard for once in its authentic form as a duet, taken slowly but done with great style, Piotr Beczała contributing a nice turn as the youthful Henri, eager to learn about the demi-monde.

Of the other operetta items Netrebko's raunchy 'Zapateado' from Giménez's *La Tempranica* is preferable to the rather effortful 'Heia, in den Bergen' from Kálmán's *Die Csárdásfürstin*. Two French opera arias make a neat contrast: 'Depuis le jour' from *Louise*, very dreamy, the words well defined, and with a beautifully executed leap up to the exultant 'Je suis heureuse!' Then there is the little song from Messager's *Fortunio*, a moment of quietness sandwiched between Solveig's Song and *Songs my mother taught me* – this done in Czech, to the apparent delight of the Prague Philharmonie, conducted throughout with gentlemanly care by Emmanuel Villaume. Although the fireworks of Arditi's *Il bacio*

bring the disc to an exuberant finish, the introspective songs fare best.

Anna Netrebko *soprano*
Rolando Villazón *tenor*

'Duets'

Bizet Les pêcheurs de perles – De mon amie…Leïla! Leïla!; Dieu puissant, le violà! **Donizetti** Lucia di Lammermoor – Lucia, perdona…Sulla tomba che rinserra **Gounod** Roméo et Juliette – Va! je t'ai pardonné…Nuit d'hyménée **Massenet** Manon – Toi! Vous!; Oui, c'est moi!…N'est–ce plus ma main **Moreno Torroba** Luisa Fernanda – Cállate corazón **Puccini** La bohème – O soave fanciulla **Tchaikovsky** Iolanta – Iolanta and Vaudémont duet **Verdi** Rigoletto – Giovanna, ho dei rimorsi…E il sol dell'anima
Anna Netrebko *sop* Rolando Villazón *ten* Staatskapelle Dresden / Nicola Luisotti
DG 477 6457GH (71' · DDD)   Ⓕ**O**▶

Netrebko and Villazón have toured with a recital programme in which most of these duets have been included, interspersed with a few solos and orchestral pieces. In London they sang to much cheering but against a general feeling that Villazón's warm tone and eager personality contrasted with Netrebko's rather chilly star–grooming, while the purity of her tone was a little less appealing than it might have been because she sang so much more loudly than she need have done. As recorded, the voices match well in terms of volume, and Netrebko's brightness seems reduced in wattage sufficiently to distribute the lighting more evenly. It's still not the voice of a Mimì (not warm enough) or a Lucia (not vulnerable) but the voice–character becomes better suited after these two, which as it happens are the opening numbers, though in the London recital there was no Donizetti and the Puccini was used for the finale.

It was then spoiled, as it is now, by the offstage notes at the end being sung in octaves and fortissimo instead of in harmony and *pianissimo* as marked. Also Mimì's 'Io t'amo' is marked con abbandono but not *molto ritardando*. Such changes vulgarise a finely calculated score which needs no additional underlining. There is, however, lovely singing by Villazón, who in the Lucia duet phrases his verse of 'Verrano a te' with a breadth matched by the grace of his beautifully lightened tone. The French excerpts go well, the Manon being particularly well characterised. Netrebko is her best self in the Tchaikovsky duet. The voices are well recorded; the Dresden violins caught in rather harsh exposure of the overtones, which are not the things we most want to hear.

Patricia Petibon *soprano*

'Amoureuses'

Arias from **Gluck** Armide; Iphigénie en Tauride **Haydn** L'anima del filosofo; Armida; L'isola

disabitata; Il mondo della luna; Lo Speziale
Mozart Lucio Silla; Le nozze di Figaro; Zaïde;
Die Zauberflöte. Vorrei spiegarvi, oh Dio, K418
Patricia Petibon sop **Concerto Köln / Daniel
Harding**
DG 477 7468GH (69' · DDD)　　　　　Ⓕ**Ⓞ**➔

Here Patricia Petibon presents an attractive
recital of arias by Gluck, Haydn and Mozart.
Five are by Haydn. In her aria from Act 1 of *Il
mondo della luna*, Flaminia sings that reason
must yield to love. Petibon is bright and confident. In Eurydice's dying aria from *L'anima del
filosofo* she finds a quiet intensity; in the concluding aria to Part 1 of *L'isola disabitata* she captures
Silvia's confusion without quite matching Linda
Zoghby's nicely tremulous account for Dorati.
A complete contrast is 'Odio, furor, dispetto'
from *Armida*, where Petibon brilliantly exploits
the breathless short phrases to convey the sorceress's rage.

There are excerpts from Gluck's *Armide*, too,
including a heartfelt air from Act 3. In the last
scene, Petibon is mesmerising in the recitative
– excellent support here, and indeed throughout, from Daniel Harding – before, again, bursting out in fury.

The Mozart numbers are not quite so successful. 'Der Hölle Rache' from *Die Zauberflöte* is
certainly fiery, but Petibon doesn't sound comfortable with the language. In the first aria from
Lucio Silla, a dry run for Konstanze in *Die Entführung*, the coloratura is not quite secure
enough; and having Barbarina's touching little
plaint moving straight into Susanna's 'Deh
vieni' really doesn't work. Overall, though, this
is a considerable success.

Kate Royal　　　　　　　　　　*soprano*

'Midsummer Night'
Arias from **Alwyn** Miss Julie **Barber** Vanessa **Britten**
Peter Grimes. Paul Bunyan. The Turn of the Screw
Dvořák Rusalka **Floyd** Susannah **Herrmann**
Wuthering Heights **Korngold** Die tote Stadt **Lehár**
Die lüstige Witwe **Messager** Monsieur Beaucaire
Stravinsky Le Rossignol **Walton** Troilus and Cressida
Kate Royal sop with **Andrew Staples** ten Sir
Thomas Allen bar **Crouch End Festival Chorus;
English National Opera Orchestra / Edward
Gardner**
EMI 268192–2 (62' · DDD)　　　　　Ⓕ**ⓞⓞ**➔

Here is an interesting, sometimes curious, selection of arias from 20th–century opera and operetta. Maybe, in the age of the iPod, people don't
bother much with the order in which items have
been assembled on such a disc. Even so, it's a bit
of a jolt to move from Britten to Lehár: Ellen
Orford's aria, 'Embroidery in childhood" from
Peter Grimes comes before 'Vilja' from *Die
lüstige Witwe*. Then it's another plunge into
darkness, with 'Do not utter a word' from Barber's *Vanessa*. All the extracts from English and
American works go extremely well; the aria that
gives the disc its title, 'Midsummer Night' from

William Alwyn's *Miss Julie*, is a rarity. This and
'I have dreamt' from Herrmann's *Wuthering
Heights* may be new to some listeners – although
both operas have been recorded complete.

It is surprising that Royal should have chosen
to sing 'Philomel' from Messager's English
comic opera *Monsieur Beaucaire* in its French
translation, as 'Rossignol'. Neither this, nor
'Vilja', seem to suit her particularly, exposing a
beat in the voice and lacking that mysterious
sense of zest and intimacy so essential in operetta. The Tower scene from *The Turn of the
Screw*, with its spooky woodwind and harp
accompaniment, is as good as the *Grimes* scene
– Royal comes into her own in the Britten roles.
Stravinsky and Dvořák – the inevitable 'Song to
the Moon' – add Russian and Czech to the languages chosen, but it is for the arias in English
that one will return. Recording is very clear, the
accompaniments by the ENO Orchestra under
Edward Gardner all well played, although the
concluding Lute song from *Die tote Stadt* seems
awfully slow.

Andreas Scholl　　　　　　　*countertenor*

'Crystal Tears'
Anonymous O Death, rock me asleep Bennet Venus'
birds **Byrd** Though Amaryllis dance in green
Dowland A Fancy. Semper Dowland semper dolens.
The Lady Rich, her Galliard, P43. Now, O now I needs
must part. Go crystal tears. Come, heavy sleep. Go
nightly cares. From silent night. Time stands still.
Sorrow, come! **A Ferrabosco** II Four–Note Pavan
R Johnson II Care–charming sleep. Full fathom five.
Have you seen the bright lily grow? **P Mando** Like as
the day **Mico** Fantasia No 13 **Ward** Seven Fantasias a
6 – No 3; No 4
Andreas Scholl counterten **Concerto di Viole**
Harmonia Mundi HMC90 1993 (80' · DDD)
Includes bonus DVD of Scholl singing 'Venus' birds'
and documentary on the making of the recording　Ⓕ

Inevitably, Andreas Scholl gets the headline
treatment, though the man himself seems very
much a team player. And though there are a few
quibbles with his approach to this repertory, his
interaction with Concerto di Viole and lutenist
Julian Behr carries great conviction. The choice
of Dowland songs holds few surprises. Although
Scholl's technique is unimpeachable, his tone
polished beyond doubt, there's a surprising diffidence. Dowland's melancholy may have been a
genuine personality trait but the Elizabethan
penchant for this most intractable of humours
was also (as Scholl acknowledges) a wider social
phenomenon, a fashionable affectation; and
from an artist of Scholl's accomplishment, a
tauter balance between demure reserve and theatricality would have been welcome. Otherwise,
one runs the risk of a one–dimensional Dowland, and Scholl doesn't entirely avoids it here.
That said, the first track, 'Go crystal tears',
makes for a fine opening, and in 'Go nightly
cares' the dialogue between voice and viols is
very impressive. The whistling in the refrain of

John Bennett's 'Venus' birds' seems the wrong sort of affectation, and the *portamenti* in the refrain of Byrd's 'Though Amaryllis dance in green' are likewise overdone.

The gems here are the pieces by lesser–known composers, in which Scholl's reserve is perhaps less of an issue: Robert Johnson's 'Have you seen the bright lily grow?' is particularly moving, and movingly conveyed, with something of the languor of the *air de cour*. Concerto di Viole's contributions are stylish, and Behr is both a sensitive accompanist and a distinguished soloist (in 'Semper Dowland semper dolens'). On a bonus DVD there's a short documentary that faithfully captures the atmosphere of a recording session, in which Scholl comes across as a down-to-earth, reflective and genuinely charming person.

Dame Joan Sutherland   *soprano*

'The Art of the Prima Donna'
Opera Arias – Artaxerxes, Die Entführung aus dem Serail, Faust, Hamlet, Les Huguenots, Lakmé, Norma^a, Otello, I Puritani, Rigoletto^a, Roméo et Juliette, Samson, Semiramide^a, La sonnambula & La traviata
Dame Joan Sutherland sop ^a**Chorus and Orchestra of the Royal Opera House, Covent Garden / Francesco Molinari–Pradelli**
Decca Legends ② 467 115–2DL2 (109' · ADD · T/t)
Recorded 1960   Ⓜ❶❶❶❶▸

Ⓖ 'The Art of the Prima Donna', hardly out of the catalogue since 1960, is now remastered for Classic Sound. There can't be many admirers who haven't already got this, so for newcomers to Sutherland on disc one can only say – listen and wonder. Her voice, even throughout its range right up to the high-E, always keeping its natural quality, is heard at its early fullness. Perhaps the best tracks of all are 'The soldier tir'd' from *Artaxerxes* and 'Let the bright seraphim' from *Samson*, but every track is beautiful. 'Casta Diva' – her earliest attempt at it – is her most limpid recording of this prayer, 'Bel raggio' from *Semiramide* has sparkling decorations, quite different from the ones she sang on the complete recording six years later, and the whole thing ends with the Jewel Song from *Faust*. It was a big voice and sounded at its best in larger theatres; listening to 'O beau pays' from *Les Huguenots*, you can see Sutherland in your mind's eye, in pale blue silk, as Marguerite de Valois at the Royal Albert Hall in 1968. It's difficult to imagine anyone, coming to it for the first time, being disappointed.

Rolando Villazón   *tenor*

Italian Opera Arias
Cilea L'Arlesiana – E la solita storia (Lamento)
Donizetti Il Duca d'Alba – Inosservato, penetrava; Angelo casto e bel. L'elisir d'amore – Quanto è bella; Una furtiva lagrima. Lucia di Lammermoor – Tombe

degl'avi miei; Fra poco a me ricovero **Mascagni** L'amico Fritz – Ed anchè Beppe amò; O Amore, o bella luce. Nerone – Vergini, Muse; Quando al soave anelito **Puccini** La bohème – Che gelida manina. Tosca – E lucevan le stelle **Verdi** Don Carlo – Io la vidi. I Lombardi – La mia letizia infondere. Macbeth – O-figli, o figli miei!; Ah, la paterna mano. Rigoletto – Ella mi fu rapita!; Parmi veder le lagrime. La donna è mobile. La traviata – Lunge da lei; De' miei bollenti spiriti … O mio rimorso!
Rolando Villazón ten
Munich Radio Orchestra / Marcello Viotti
Virgin Classics 545626–2 (62' · DDD · T/t)   Ⓕ❶❶▸

Here comes the new tenor on the block. Rolando Villazón's first disc on Virgin Classics might have been expected to provide a souvenir snapshot, but it doesn't quite. A voice that sounds slim, lithe, intently focused in the theatre is more resilient here, and comes with a grainy quality that isn't unpleasant, but certainly sets it aside from the purity of any native Italian.

The short aria from *I Lombardi*, briskly dispatched by Viotti, shows the singer's quick reflexes as he deftly catches expressive details on the wing. The *L'elisir d'amore* and *La traviata* arias have some similar nuances, but could do with more. Even in the helpful ambience of Glyndebourne his Rodolfo in *La bohème* only scraped by with just enough depth of tone, but here he sounds made for the role.

This Mexican newcomer has no single knockout gift, but his strengths are many and varied – a healthy, youthful tenor, decent sense of line, and a young man's ardour and energy. He's well served by the recording. The booklet comes with texts and translations, but not a word about the singer himself. Maybe Virgin Classics felt that the best of Villazón's biography lies in the future.

'Cielo e mar'
Boito Mefistofele – Dai campi, dai prati; Giunto sul passo estremo **Cilea** Adriana Lecouvreur – La dolcissima effigie sorridente; L'anima ho stanca **Donizetti** Poliuto – Veleno è l'aura ch'io respiro!; Sfolgorò divino raggioa **Gomes** Fosca – Intenditi con Dio!; Ah! Se tu sei fra gli angeli **Mercadante** Il giuramento – La dea di tutti i cor!; Compita è omai; Fu celeste quel contento **Pietri** Maristella – Io conosco un giardino **Ponchielli** Il figliuol prodigo – Il padre!... Il padre mio!; Tenda natal. La Gioconda – Cielo e mar! **Verdi** Luisa Millera – Oh! fede negar potessi; Quando le sere al placido; L'ara o l'avello apprestami. Simon Boccanegra – O inferno! Amelia qui!; Sento avvampar nell'anima
Rolando Villazón ten with ^a**Gianluca Alfano** bar
Giuseppe Verdi Symphony Chorus and Orchestra, Milan / Daniele Callegari
DG 477 7224GH (57' · DDD)   Ⓕ❶▸

This is a well chosen selection of tenor arias with a few comparative rarities to offset the more obvious favourites. In its way it is a mini-history of a century of Italian opera, from Donizetti's *Poliuto* (1838) to Pietri's *Maristella* (1934). The Donizetti is the longest item and well though

Villazón copes with this, it's hard to imagine him in this part, beloved of *tenore di forza* of the past including Tamagno and Corelli. In fact he has not sung any of these roles on stage yet; in a note he explains that the repertory here is something 'with more spontaneity…without the burden of history'.

Be that as it may, the parts for which he would seem to be destined are Gabriele Adorno in *Simon Boccanegra*, Rodolfo in *Luisa Miller* and Viscardo in *Il giuramento*. Mercadante's opera is based on the same Victor Hugo play as Ponchielli's *La Gioconda*, so it is a good idea to contrast these two very different interpretations of the same character.

The little romanza from Pietri's opera is the only piece by him that we ever get to hear. It was a favourite with Gigli, and several other tenors have recorded it. The aria from Brazilian composer Carlos Gomes's 1873 opera *Fosca* is a high-voltage outpouring of emotion, as is the aria for Azael in Ponchielli's *Il figliuol prodigo*.

Villazón sings them all with admirable intensity, his diction is excellent, and he can float a *pianissimo* when necessary, as in the opening 'Cielo e mar' from *La Gioconda* that gives the disc its title. Recording quality is first–rate, and the accompaniment is always sympathetic.

Various singers

'The NMC Songbook'
Includes songs by J Anderson, Bainbridge, Baker, G Barry, Basford, Bauld, Bawden, D Bedford, L Bedford, M Berkeley, Bingham, Birtwistle, Blake, Bryars, Burrell, Butler, G Carpenter, Cashian, Casken, Causton, J Cole, Cresswell, Crosse, Cutler, PM Davies, T Davies, C Dench, Dennehy, Dillon, Duddell, B Elias, Finnissy, Foskett, Fox, Fujikura, Gilbert, Goehr, Grange, Grant, Grime, Hall, B Harrison, S Harrison, J Harvey, M Hayes, Holloway, Holt, Horne, Howard, Hunt, Keeley, Kindsdottir, Leach, Lefanu, J Lloyd, MacMillan, MacRae, Marsh, PN Martin, C Matthews, D Matthews, Mayo, McCabe, Meredith, Molitor, Montague, Moore, Morley/C Matthews, Musgrave, Northcott, O'Regan, R Panufnik, Payne, Phibbs, J Philips, Poole, Powell, Powers, JD Roberts, Roxburgh, Rushton, Sackman, Sawer, Saxton, J Simpson, Skempton, Stoneham, Swayne, Turnage, Wallen, Watkins, Weir, J White, Wiegold, R Williams, H Wood and Woolrich
Artists include Andrew Swait, Sam Harris *trebs* Elizabeth Atherton, Claire Booth, Ailish Tynan *sops* Susan Bickley, Loré Lixenberg, Jean Rigby *mezs* James Bowman, Michael Chance, Andrew Watts *countertens* Benjamin Hulett, Andrew Kennedy, Daniel Norman *tens* Omar Ebrahim, Richard Jackson, Stephan Loges, George Mosley, David Stout, Roderick Williams *bars* Gerald Barry, Errollyn Wallen *vocs* Andrew Ball, Iain Burnside, Michael Finnissy, Andrew Plant, Jonathan Powell, Huw Watkins, Andrew West *pfs* Jane Chapman *hpd* Lucy Wakeford *hp* Owen Gunnell *perc* Antonis Hatzinikolaou *gtr*
NMC ④ NMCD150 (5h' · DDD · T)   Ⓟ❶❶➔

NMC's 20th anniversary celebrations may or may not 'kick-start a new interest in the genre' (Bayan Northcott) but the initiative gives us a useful snapshot of British Music now, even if certain tendencies are better represented than others.

There are full texts and the imaginative design concept reflects the disparity of the idiomatic options available. Whether tonal, atonal or pseudo-tonal, some of these are found as if by chance and loosely worn, others carefully nurtured and obsessively worked. Britten remains in some ways the key figure in that his example persuades many contributors to stick with conventionally accompanied solo voice(s). That said, his intuitive response to a text is less easily imitated than the externals of his style. Martin Butler's Blake setting upholds the tradition in its best and purest form. Other examples might lead you to conclude that dislocated consonance, high voicing and a certain infuriating feyness constitute the defining features of British song.

There's room for the provocateurs as well. Luke Stoneham gets away with an electronic soundscape while Gerald Barry turns in a gleefully graceless recitation of Oscar Wilde. Jonathan Cole has Roderick Williams perform a sequence of phonemes while guesting on balloon.

Is a song a song at all if its text is merely a jumping-off point, a colour without a context? Morgan Hayes's Dickensian passages, ideally chosen for such a project, are quickly sidelined amid dizzying virtuosity. Chris Dench is still sufficiently hard–core to represent what was once a New Complexity. Few others appear capable of writing fast music even in short bursts, hence perhaps Colin Matthews's decision to break up the sequence with instrumental interludes. In the tradition of Stanford's pseudonymous Karel Drofnatzki he may also be behind the modest haiku setting with its allusions to NMC marketing strategy. Call me old–fashioned but my own favourite items are those in which both the original text and the passion of a composer's response are intelligible in the finished product. In Hugh Wood's George Herbert setting, careful workmanship does not preclude a Tippettian sense of exaltation. There's a similar sense of engagement in Simon Holt's unaccompanied declamation (evoking a real-life incident in rural India) and Brian Elias's more subdued John Clare solo. The way in which the items are juxtaposed can be crucial too; the cooler limpidity of Howard Skempton and Gavin Bryars is doubly welcome in context.

The performers range from good to excellent. The recordings were almost all made in Hall One, Kings Place, an acclaimed venue where instrumental voices are unfailingly well projected. Human ones, less comfortable with its zingy resonance, can become a little hectoring.

But then only a critic or a fool would listen to the entire collection at a sitting. Much better to study at leisure what should prove to be an important cultural document.

THE
GRAMOPHONE
CLASSICAL
MUSIC
GUIDE
2010

INDEX OF COUPLINGS

A

Adams, John
Lollapalooza 455

Addinsell, Richard
Festival 486

Adès, Thomas
Asyla 698
The Fayrfax Carol 1343

Agricola, Alexander
Se congié prens 623

Alain, Jehan (Ariste)
O Salutaris 393
Prière pour nous autres charnels, 'Praise for we 395

Albarti,
Pavan and Galliard 1342

Albéniz, Isaac (Manuel Francisco)
Cantos de España – Op. 232 (excs) 1321
España – Op. 165 (excs) 641, 1315, 1335
Iberia (excs) 288, 488
Navarra 488

Alessandrescu, Alfred
Sub perdeaua dragei mele 1354

Alkan, (Charles–)Valentin
(48) Esquisses – Op. 63 (excs) 1324

Allegri, Gregorio
Miserere mei 1345

Alonso,
(La) Tricotea 623

Alonso, Antonio
Suspiros de España 1352

Amner, John
Come, let's rejoice 1341

Amodei, Cataldo
Cantate a voce sola – Op 2 (excs) 1356

Anonymous,
Alma redemptoris mater 826, 1346
Angelus ad Virginem 1345
Assumpta est Maria in caelum 838
Ballet des fous et des estropiés de la cervelle (excs) . . 228
Ballet des vaillans combattans 228
Belles tenés moy 623
Benedicamus Domino 452
Dami conforto Dio 302
Depon Clorinda le sue spoglie inteste 1153
Desperada (Lumley part books) 1342
Domine Jesu Christe 1341
Entrée des Laquais 228
Fammi cantar l'amor 302
Fantaisie in E minor 709
Galliard (Lumley part books) 1342
Gregorian Responsories for Holy Week 560
(L') homme armé 826
Hosanna filio David 839
Hyer matin a l'enjournee 452
Immittet angelus Domini 826
In paradisum 1341, 1345
Incomprehensibilia firme/Praeter rerum ordinem . . 1340
Intanto Erminia fra l'ombrose piante 1153
Isias cecinit 847
Kontakion of the Dead 1341
Laudes Regiae 1345
L'homme armé 723
Lieto ti prendo e poi 1153
Lumen ad revelationem 1342
Mariam matrem Virginem 1344
Nos esprits libres et contents 228
O death, rock me asleep 1358
O Maria virginei 847
O pulcherrima mulierum/Girum coeli circuivi 1340
O quanta qualia 1341
Pavana (Lumley part books) 1342
Plainchants (excs) 762
Praise to the Lord, the Almighty 1343
Psalm 113, 'Laudate pueri Dominum' 1344
Rejoice in the Lord alway 1341, 1345
Requiem Aeternam 1341
Salve Regina 1346
S'amours dont sui espris 452
Sarum Chant (excs) 1156
Seconda Desperada (Lumley part books) 1342
So Maki Se Rodila 1329
Sonata for Scordatura Violin and Basso Continuo . . 976
Te lucis ante terminum 1345
Terza Desperada (Lumley part books) 1342
Ubi caritas 1345
Veni creator spiritus 847, 1345
Vexilla Regis 723

Anta, Manuel Font de
(La) Cruz de Mayo 1352

Antheil, George (Johann Carl)
Jazz Sonata 1325
(A) Jazz Symphony 455
Toccatas (excs) 1315

Arditi, Luigi
(Il) Bacio 1357

Arensky, Anton Stepanovich
Concerto for Violin and Orchestra in A minor – Op. 54 . 27
Piano Quintet in D – Op. 51 1316

Ariosti, Attilio (Malachia)
(6) Lessons (excs) 1330
Pur al fin gentil Viola 1356

Arne, Thomas (Augustine)
Artaxerxes (excs) 1359
The Tempest (excs) 1347

Astorga, Emanuele (Gioacchino Cesare Rincón) d'
Stabat mater 228

Auber, Daniel–François–Esprit
(La) Muette de Portici (Masaniello) (excs) 192

Augustinas, Vaclovas
The Stomping Bride 1342

B

Bach, Johann Sebastian
2–Part Inventions – BWV772–86 (excs) 1040, 1320
Cantata No. 4, 'Christ lag in Todesbanden' – BWV4 . . 1299
Cantata No. 22, 'Jesus nahm zu sich die Zwölfe' – BWV22 . . . . 27, 227
Cantata No. 61, 'Nun komm, der Heiden Heiland' – BWV61 (excs) 1356
Cantata No. 106, 'Gottes Zeit ist die allerbeste Zeit' – BWV106 642
Cantata No. 136, 'Erforsche mich, Gott' – BWV136 (excs) 27, 227
Cantata No. 147, 'Herz und Mund und Tat und Leben' – BWV147 (excs) . . . 27, 227, 490, 1323, 1338, 1356
Cantata No. 163, 'Nur jedem das Seine' – BWV163 (excs) 27, 227
Cantata No. 167, 'Ihr Menschen, rühmet Gottes' – BWV167 (excs) 27, 227
Cantata No. 208, 'Was mir behagt, ist nur die munt' – BWV208 (excs) 1323
Chorale Preludes – BWV714–40 (excs) 1326
Chromatic Fantasia and Fugue in D minor – BWV903 . . 1329, 1338

Concerto for 2 Violins and Strings in D minor
– BWV1043 1159
Concerto for Violin and Strings in E – BWV1042 (excs).
496, 1159
Concerto for Violin and Strings in A minor – BWV1041
(excs). 496, 1159
Concerto in the Italian style, 'Italian Concerto' in F
– BWV971 1247
English Suites – BWV806–11 (excs) . . . 1040, 1315, 1320
French Suites – BWV812–17 (excs). 1040, 1320
Fugue, 'Jig Fugue' in G – BWV577. 1040
(Die) Kunst der Fuge, 'The Art of Fugue' – BWV1080
(excs). 1338
Magnificat in E flat – BWV243a 672
Magnificat in D – BWV243 87
Musikalisches Opfer, 'Musical Offering' – BWV1079
(excs). 1298, 1299
Orchestral Suites – BWV1066–9 (excs). 27, 227
Orgel–Büchlein – BWV599–644 (excs) 27, 227, 490, 1321
Partita in C minor – BWV997 (excs). 1319
Partitas – BWV825–30 (excs). 163, 490, 1315, 1317, 1338
Prelude in C minor – BWV999 1319
Prelude, Fugue and Allegro in E flat – BWV998 . . . 1319
Preludes and Fugues – BWV531–552 (excs) . . . 928, 1321
Schübler Chorales – BWV645–50 (excs) . . . 27, 227, 1324
Sonata in D minor – BWV964 (excs) 1040
Sonatas and 3 Partitas – BWV1001–06 (excs). . 641, 900,
1027, 1319, 1320, 1325
Sonatas for Flute and Harpsichord – BWV1030–35 (excs)
490
St Matthew Passion – BWV244 (excs). 27, 227
Suite in E minor – BWV996 (excs) 1319
Suites (Sonatas) for Cello – BWV1007–12 (excs)413, 415,
1322
Toccata, Adagio and Fugue in C – BWV564 1311
Toccata and Fugue in D minor – BWV565 (excs) . . . 1329
(Das) Wohltemperierte Klavier, 'The Well–Tempered
Clavier' – BWV846–893 (excs) 1062, 1320

Bacheler, Daniel
The Earl of Essex Galliard – P89. 386
(Une) Jeune Fillette – P93 386

Bachelet, Alfred
Chère nuit 1355

Baermann, Heinrich (Joseph)
Quintet (Septet) in E flat – Op. 23 (excs) 355

Bain, Leith Macbeth
Brother James' Air 1343

Bairstow, Sir Edward C(uthbert)
I sat down under his shadow 1341

Balakirev, Mily Alexeyevich
Islamey. 813, 930

Balfe, Michael William
The Maid of Artois (excs). 1349

Bantock, Granville
Song to the seals 1327

Barber, Samuel
Adagio for Strings – Op. 11 . . . . 99, 101, 347, 1326
Agnus Dei – Op. 11 . . . . 102, 204, 1345
Concerto for Violin and Orchestra – Op. 14 99, 100, 544,
637, 1322, 4713
God's Grandeur 102
Heaven–Haven 102
Knoxville: Summer of 1915 – Op. 24 102
Let down the bars, O Death – Op. 8/2 102
The Monk and his cat. 102
Reincarnation – Op. 16. 102
Sonata for Piano – Op. 26 609
Sure on this shining night 102
Symphony No. 1 – Op. 9 347
To be sung on the water – Op. 42/2 102
Twelfth Night – Op. 42/1 102
Vanessa – Op. 32 (excs) 1352
The Virgin Martyrs – Op. 8/1 102

Barbirolli, John
(An) Elizabethan Suite 421

Bargiel, Woldemar
Adagio in G – Op. 38 1019

Bartók, Béla
Allegro barbaro – Sz49 113
Burlesques – Sz47 (excs) 113
Concerto for Orchestra – Sz116 106
Concerto for Piano and Orchestra No. 2 – Sz95 104
Concerto for Piano and Orchestra No. 3 – Sz119 . . . . . .
105, 861
Concerto for Viola and Orchestra – Sz120 105
Duos – Sz98 112
Easy Pieces – Sz39 (excs) 113
For Children (1945 revision) – Sz42 (excs) 1320
Hungarian folksongs from the Csík district – Sz35a. 1315
Hungarian Folktunes – Sz66 113
Hungarian Peasant Songs – Sz71 (excs). 113
Improvisations on Hungarian Peasant Songs – Sz74
(Op. 20) (excs) 113
Kossuth – Sz21 (excs) 112
Little Pieces – Sz82 (excs). 113
Mikrokosmos – Sz108 (excs). 113
Mikrokosmos, Book 5 – Sz107 (excs). 113
Mikrokosmos, Book 6 – Sz107 (excs). 112, 113
Petite Suite – Sz105 (excs) . . . .
Romanian Folkdances – Sz56. . . . . 1108, 1330, 1335
Rondos on (Slovak) Folktunes – Sz84 112
Sketches – Sz44. 112
Sonata for Solo Violin – Sz117 1317
Sonata for Violin and Piano No. 1 – Sz75. 1317
String Quartet No. 5 – Sz102 110
Suite – Sz62 (Op. 14) 113

Bassano, Augustine
Pavan and Galliard 1342

Bassano, Giovanni
Hodie Christus natus est. 755

Bassano, Jeronimo
Fantasias a 5 (excs) 1342

Bax, Arnold (Edward Trevor)
The Garden of Fand. 421
Mater ora filium 1343
Tintagel. 119

Beach, Amy Marcy (Cheney)
Romance – Op. 23 1304

Beethoven, Ludwig van
Ah! perfido – Op. 65 789
An die ferne Geliebte – Op. 98 . . . . 165, 1014
Bagatelles (excs). 1320
Concerto for Piano and Orchestra No. 1 126
Concerto for Piano and Orchestra No. 2 . . . . . 126, 1317
Concerto for Piano and Orchestra No. 3 126
Concerto for Piano and Orchestra No. 4 126, 1317, 1334
Concerto for Piano and Orchestra No. 5, 'Emperor' 126
Concerto for Violin and Orchestra . . . 131, 132, 289, 290,
732, 1066
Concerto for Violin, Cello, Piano and Orchestra (Triple
Concerto) 133
Coriolan – Op. 62 245
Fidelio – Op. 72 (excs) 991
Grosse Fuge in B flat – Op. 133. 992
Leonore – Op. 72 (excs) 245, 403
Mass in D, 'Missa solemnis' – Op. 123 . . . . 168, 169
Piano Trios (excs) 734
Quintet for Piano and Wind in E flat – Op. 16 143, 1319
Romances 1159
Rondo a capriccio, 'Rage over a lost penny' in G – Op.
129 1027
Rondos – Op. 51 (excs). 1027
Scottish Songs – WoO156 (excs) 1347
Scottish Songs – Op. 108 (excs) 1347
Sonata for Cello and Piano No. 3 in A – Op. 69 . . . 1322
Sonata for Cello and Piano No. 5 in D – Op. 102/2 1322
Sonata for Piano No. 4 in E flat – Op. 7 914
Sonata for Piano No. 8, 'Pathétique' in C minor – Op. 13
160
Sonata for Piano No. 10 in G – Op. 14/2 660
Sonata for Piano No. 11 in B flat – Op. 22 902

Sonata for Piano No. 12 in A flat – Op. 26 914
Sonata for Piano No. 14, 'Moonlight' in C sharp minor
– Op. 27/2 (excs) 238, 1317, 1332
Sonata for Piano No. 15, 'Pastoral' in D – Op. 28 . . . 161
Sonata for Piano No. 19 in G minor – Op. 49/1 660
Sonata for Piano No. 20 in G – Op. 49/2 660
Sonata for Piano No. 22 in F – Op. 54 1329
Sonata for Piano No. 23, 'Appassionata' in F minor – Op.
57 . . . . 160, 161, 1334
Sonata for Piano No. 28 in A – Op. 101 1321
Sonata for Piano No. 31 in A flat – Op. 110 . . . 160, 1315
Sonata for Piano No. 32 in C minor – Op. 111 1328
Sonata for Violin and Piano No. 9, 'Kreutzer' in A – Op.
47 (excs) 1330
String Quartet No. 10, 'Harp' in E flat – Op. 74 . . . 1060
String Quartet No. 16 in F – Op. 135 150
Symphony No. 2 . . . . 248, 1311
Symphony No. 4 1105
Symphony No. 5 1311
Symphony No. 6, 'Pastoral' 141
Symphony No. 7 . . . . 168, 169
Variations and a Fugue on an original theme, 'Eroica' in
E flat – Op. 35 902
Variations in C on a Waltz by Diabelli (Diabelli
Variations) – Op. 120 163
Variations on an Original Theme in C minor – WoO80.
1326
Variations on Mozart's 'Bei Männern' – WoO46 . . . 1322
Variations on Mozart's 'Ein Mädchen oder Weibchen'
– Op. 66 1322
Variations on 'See the conqu'ring hero comes'
– WoO45 1322
Wellingtons Sieg, '(Die) Schlacht bei Vittoria' – Op. 91 .
1167

Beffa, Karol
Masques 1320

Bellini, Vincenzo
Adelson e Salvini (excs) 1354
Ariette da camera (excs) 1354
I Capuleti e i Montecchi (excs) 1353, 1354
Norma (excs) 852, 1348, 1350, 1359
I Puritani (excs) 1348, 1353, 1359
La Sonnambula (excs) 1348, 1349, 1353, 1359

Ben Haim, Paul
Berceuse sfaradite 225
Improvisation and Dance in Op 30 225
Sonata in G 225

Bennet, John
Venus' birds 1358

Berg, Alban (Maria Johannes)
Concerto for Violin and Orchestra . . .181, 182, 290, 732,
1311
Sonata for Piano – Op. 1 . . . . 183, 981
Wozzeck – Op. 7 991

Bergman, Erik (Valdemar)
Gallows Songs (Galgenlieder) – Op. 51b 1342

Berio, Luciano
Folk Songs 188
Recital I for Cathy 188

Berkeley, Lennox (Randall Francis)
String Quartet No 2 – Op 15 189

Berkeley, Michael
Abstract Mirror 189
Magnetic Field 189

Berlioz, (Louis–)Hector
(La) Damnation de Faust – Op. 24 (excs) 1355
King Lear – Op. 4 1313
(Les) Nuits d'été – Op. 7 .198, 199, 721, 916, 1347, 1999
Symphonie fantastique 192
(Les) Troyens, 'The Trojans' (excs) 199

Bernstein, Leonard
Candide – excs 1352
Chichester Psalms 204

Prelude, Fugue and Riffs 455
Symphony No. 2, 'The Age of Anxiety' 203
West Side Story (excs) 1313

Bertali, Antonio
Chiaconna 976

Biber, Heinrich Ignaz Franz von
Sonatae for Violin and Continuo (excs) 210

Binchois, Gilles de Bins dit
Choral works 212

Bingham, Judith
The Darkness Is No Darkness 212
First Light 212
Salt in the Blood 212
The Secret Garden 212
The Snows Descend 212

Bishop, Henry R(owley)
Home, sweet home 1100

Bitsch, Marcel
Concertino 1323

Bizet, Georges (Alexandre César Léopold)
(L')Arlésienne (excs) 900
Carmen (excs) 1350, 1351, 1355
Chanson d'avril 1355
Chant d'amour 1354
Jeux d'enfants, 'Children's Games' (excs) 1071
(Les) Pêcheurs de Perles, 'The Pearl Fishers' (excs) . 1357

Bliss, Arthur (Drummond)
Checkmate – T57 (excs) 223

Bloch, Ernest
Baal Shem 99, 225, 290
Schelomo 414, 415
Suite for solo Cello No. 1 1288
Suite hébraïque 225
Suites for Solo Violin 225

Blow, John
Fugue in G minor 226
Ground in G minor 226
Ground in C minor 226
Mark how the lark and linnet sing 226, 889
Salvator mundi 1345
Sappho to the Goddess of Love 1356
Sonata in A 226
Suite No. 10 in G 226

Boccherini, Luigi
Concertos for Cello and Orchestra . . . 27, 227, 415
Stabat mater – G532 228

Böddecker, Philipp Friedrich
Natus est Jesus 1356

Boëllmann, Léon
Suite gothique – Op. 25 (excs) 1324

Boësset, Antoine (de)
Airs de court 228

Boësset, Jean–Baptiste
Que Philis a l'esprit léger 1356

Boito, Arrigo
Mefistofele (excs) 1359

Bolcom, William (Elden)
Cabaret Songs 1350
Concerto for Piano and Orchestra 203

Boldemann, Laci
Epitaphs – Op 10 230

Borodin, Alexander Porfir'yevich
In the Steppes of Central Asia 930
Prince Igor (excs) 814

Boulanger, Lili
Pie Jesu 434
Psalm 24 434
Psalm 130, 'Du fond de l'abîme' 434

Boulanger, Nadia
Pièces...1331

Boulez, Pierre
Sonata for Piano No. 2.........................1333

Boutry, Roger
Interférences................................1323

Bowen, (Edwin) York
Allegro de concert.............................238
Concerto for Viola and Orchestra in C minor – Op 25 ..
....237
Fantasie Quartet..............................238
Melody for the G string – Op 47................238
Phantasy for Viola and Piano – Op 54...........238
Reverie d'Amour – Op 20/2....................1327
Rhapsody.....................................238
Romance in A.................................238
Romance in D flat.............................238
Serious Dances – Op 51 (excs)............238, 1327
Sonatas for Viola and Piano....................238
String Quartet No 2 in D minor – Op 41.........238
The Way to Polden............................1327

Boyce, William
Tell me lovely shepherd.......................1347

Brahms, Johannes
Academic Festival Overture....................1311
Alto Rhapsody.................................707
Chorale Preludes – Op. 122 (excs)..............260
Concerto for Piano and Orchestra No. 1 . 126, 379, 1000
Concerto for Piano and Orchestra No. 2.........1338
Concerto for Violin and Orchestra ...132, 241, 243, 637,
                                    1159, 1325
Concerto for Violin, Cello and Orchestra (Double
Concerto)....................133, 243, 1336
Deutsche Volkslieder – WoO33 (excs)..........1351
Hungarian Dances (excs) 1159, 1335
Hungarian Dances – WoO 1 (excs) ...245, 258, 1159
Lieder........................1321, 1347, 1351
Pieces – Op. 117 (excs).................1000, 1334
Pieces – Op. 119 (excs)......................1000
Quintet for Piano and Strings in F minor – Op. 34 ..253,
                                    254, 994
Rhapsodies – Op. 79.............654, 664, 665, 1316
Scherzo, 'FAE Sonata' in C minor – WoO2......1335
Serenade No. 1 in D – Op. 11..................250
Sonata for Cello and Piano No. 1 in E minor – Op. 38..
....256
Sonata for Cello and Piano No. 2 in F – Op. 99.....256
Sonata for Clarinet and Piano No. 1 in F minor – Op.
120/1..252
Sonata for Clarinet and Piano No. 2 in E flat – Op.
120/2..252
Sonata for Piano No. 3 in F minor – Op. 5....260, 1000
Sonata for Two Pianos in F minor – Op. 34b......258
Symphony No. 1 ....245, 246, 247, 421
Symphony No. 2 ....245, 248
Symphony No. 3.............................245
Symphony No. 4.............................245
Trio for Clarinet/Viola, Cello and Piano in A minor
– Op. 114....................................255
Trio for Horn/Viola, Violin and Piano in E flat – Op. 40
                                            1319
Variations on a Theme by Haydn, 'St Antoni Chorale
– Op. 56a....................................245
Waltzes – Op. 39 (excs) 258, 490

Brandl, Johann
(Der) Liebe Augustin (excs) 641

Brediceanu, Tiberiu
Bade, pentru ochii tai........................1354
Floricică de pe apă...........................1354
Vai, badita, dragi ne–avem....................1354

Brian, Havergal
Symphony No 6, 'Sinfonia Tragica'.............266
Symphony No 16 266

Briçeño, Luis de
(La) gran chacona.............................228

Bridge, Frank
Allegro appassionato – H82....................1335
Berceuse – H8.................................269
Cradle song – H96.............................269
The Dew Fairy...............................1327
Elegy – H47...................................269
Lyrics – H161 (excs)..........................1327
Meditation – H103a...........................269
Mélodie – H99................................269
Pensiero – H53a..............................1335
Pieces – H63 (excs)..........................1326
Scherzo – H19a...............................269
Serenade – H23...............................269
Sonata for Cello and Piano in D minor – H125.....269
Spring Song – H157...........................269

Britten, (Edward) Benjamin (Lord Britten of Aldeburgh)
Canticle No. 1: My beloved is mine – Op. 40......1184
Concerto for Violin and Orchestra in D minor – Op. 15.
                                            270
Divertimentos................................725
Folk Song Arrangements (excs) 278, 290, 1349
(A) Hymn of St Columba, 'Regis regum rectissimi' . 1345
(A) Hymn to the Virgin 1346
Phantasy – Op. 2.............................274
Russian Funeral..............................1052
Serenade – Op. 31............................278
Sonata for Cello and Piano – Op. 65............269
String Quartet No. 3 – Op. 94.................725
Suite No. 2 – Op. 80 (excs) 1288
Suite No. 3 – Op. 87.........................1154
Symphony for Cello and Orchestra – Op. 68 ... 272, 415
Tit for Tat...................................1351

Brouwer, Leo
Concerto for Guitar and Orchestra No. 5, 'Concerto de
Helsinki'.....................................288
From Yesterday to Penny Lane..................288
Paisaje Cubano con Rumba.....................1329

Browne, William Charles Denis
To Gratiana dancing and singing................1349

Bruch, Max (Karl August)
Concerto for Violin and Orchestra No. 1 in G minor
– Op. 26......................289, 290, 732
Kol Nidrei – Op. 47.....................415, 1322
Scottish Fantasy – Op. 46..................290, 1325

Bruckner, (Joseph) Anton
Locus iste...................................1345
Symphony No. 3..............................292
Symphony No. 6..............................296
Tota pulchra es..............................1346
Virga Jesse floruit..........................1345

Brumel, Antoine
Du tout plongiet/Fors seulement................827
Lamentation: Heth. Cogitavit Dominus 1148
Missa pro defunctis..........................301

Bryars, Gavin
Cadman Requiem.............................302
Glorious Hill................................302
Laudae 22–24, 'Fammi cantar l'amor'............302

Burger, Julius
Lieder 988

Busnois, Antoine
Gaude coelestis Domina.......................827
In hydraulis.................................827
Regina coeli (two settings) 1340

Busoni, Ferruccio (Dante Michelangiolo Benvenuto)
Chorale Preludes (Bach) (excs)................1315
Fantasia, Adagio and Fugue 304
Fantasia after JS Bach – K253 1324
Fantasia contrappuntistica – K255/6 304

Butler, Martin
American Rounds 306

Funérailles 306
Nathaniel's Mobile 306
Sequenza Notturna 306
Siward's River Song 306
Suzanne's River Song 306
Walden Snow 306

Butterworth, George (Sainton Kaye)
The Banks of Green Willow 1198
Bredon Hill and other songs from 'A Shropshire Lad . . .
1203
(A) Shropshire Lad 421, 1203

Byrd, William
Ave verum corpus 1345
Browning a 5 – BE17/10 310
The Carman's Whistle – BK36 487
Deus, venerunt gentes. 1149
Fantasia a 5, C(Canon 2 in 1) – BE17/8 310
Fantasia a 6, G minor No. 2 – BE17/13 310
Fantasia a 6 No. 3 310
Gradualia, Vol 1/i: Feast of All Saints (excs) 1345
In Nomines a 5 – BE17/18–22 (excs). 310
Iustorum animae 1341
Laetentur coeli 1345
Mass for four voices (excs) 1344, 1345
Ne irascaris Domine 1346
O God give ear and do apply 1340
O Lord make thy servant 1346
O lux, beata Trinitas. 1342
Pavan and Galliard a 6, C – BE17/15 1344
Prelude and Ground, 'The Queen's Goodnight' . . . 1344
Teach me, O Lord 1346
Though Amaryllis dance in green 1358

C

Cabezón, Antonio de
Beata viscera Mariae Virginis 762
Tiento sobre el hymno, 'Ave Maris stella' 762

Calandrelli, Jorge
Tango Remembrances 850

Caldara, Antonio
Missa Dolorosa 510

Campion, Thomas
Fourth Booke of Ayres (excs) 1347
Third Booke of Ayres (excs) 1347

Canteloube (de Calaret), (Marie) Joseph
Chants d'Auvergne 319, 1355

Caplet, André
(Le) Corbeau et la renard 1355

Cardoso, Manuel
Non mortui 1344

Carissimi, Giacomo
Exsurge cor meum 728
O dulcissimum Maria nomen 728
Salve Regina 728

Carreño, Innocente
Margariteña 1313

Carter, Andrew
Toccata on Veni Emmanuel. 1345

Carter, Elliott (Cook)
90 + ... 914, 915
Night Fantasies 914, 915
Two Diversions. 914, 915

Castellanos, Evencio
Santa Cruz de Pacairigua 1313

Castelnuovo–Tedesco, Mario
Concerto for Guitar and Orchestra No. 1 in D – Op. 99.
932

Catalani, Alfredo
(La) Wally (excs) 1350

Caustun, Thomas
Yield unto God the mighty Lord 1340

Ceballos, Rodrigo de
O pretiosum et admirabile sacrementum. 762

Cerha, Friedrich
Concerto for Cello and Orchestra 323

Chabrier, (Alexis–)Emmanuel
Album Leaf 1328
(Les) Cigales 1355

Chaminade, Cécile (Louise Stèphanie)
Pièces humoristiques – Op. 87 (excs). 1327
Pierrette – Op. 41 1327

Charpentier, Gustave
Louise (excs) 1357

Charpentier, Marc–Antoine
Ave maris stella – H60 324
Beatus vir – H221 324
Laetatus sum – H216 324
Lauda Jerusalem – H210 324
Laudate pueri – H149. 324
Magnificat – H72 324
Psalmus 126us, 'Nisi Dominus' – H160 324
Salve regina – H24 324

Chasins, Abram
Chinese Pieces – Op 5 1320

Chausson, (Amedée–)Ernest
Chanson perpétuelle – Op. 37 913
Mélodies – Op. 2 (excs) 1355
Piano Trio in G minor – Op. 3 327
Poème 624, 732
Poème de l'amour et de la mer – Op. 19 . . .198, 199, 327,
916
Poème – Op. 25 1328
Symphony in B flat – Op. 20 326

Cherubini, Luigi (Carlo Zanobi Salvadore Maria)
Anacréon (excs) 168, 169, 192, 991

Chopin, Fryderyk Franciszek
Andante spianato and Grande Polonaise in E flat –
Op. 22 662
Ballades (excs) . .341, 1320, 1321, 1330, 1331, 1333, 1334
Barcarolle in F sharp – Op. 60 . . . . 490, 1316, 1334
Berceuse in D flat – Op. 57 . . . . 341, 1321
Concerto for Piano and Orchestra No. 1 .490, 661, 1317
Concerto for Piano and Orchestra No. 2 . . . . . .665, 666
Etudes – Opp. 10, 25 and posth (excs). 341, 476, 490,
1321, 1326, 1332, 1333, 1334, 1338
Fantasie in F minor – Op. 49 1331
Grande Valse Brillante in D – Op. 18 1320
Impromptus (excs). 341, 1315, 1321, 1334
Mazurkas (excs) . 341, 490, 1320, 1322, 1323, 1326, 1332,
1333, 1335
Nocturnes (excs) . . . 243, 290, 341, 490, 902, 1171, 1320,
1323, 1332, 1334, 1338
Polonaises (excs) 341, 1334
Preludes (excs). 340, 341
Scherzos (excs). .341, 1316, 1317, 1320, 1326, 1333, 1334
Sonata for Cello and Piano in G minor – Op. 65 . . . 1322
Sonata for Piano No. 2, 'Funeral March' in B flat minor
– Op. 35 . . . . .334, 914, 1326, 1334, 1337
Sonata for Piano No. 3 in B minor – Op. 58 . . 490, 1338
Waltzes (excs) . . 341, 490, 1320, 1321, 1326, 1328, 1330,
1331, 1332

Cilea, Francesco
Adriana Lecouvreur (excs) 1359
(L')Arlesiana, 'The Girl from Arles' (excs) . . . 1100, 1359

Cima, Giovanni Paolo
Concerti ecclesiastici (excs). 755, 756

Coleridge–Taylor, Samuel
Concerto for Violin and Orchestra in G minor . 343, 344

Compère, Loyset
Scaramella fa la galla. 623

Constantin, Louis
(La) Pacifique 228

Cook, John
Fanfare. 1337

Cooke, Arnold (Atkinson)
Quintet for Clarinet and Strings 595
Symphony No. 3 in D 266

Copland, Aaron
Appalachian Spring. 101, 347
In the Beginning. 204
Lincoln Portrait 347
Motets 204
(El) salón México 347

Corelli, Arcangelo
Sonatas for Violin/Recorder and Continuo – Op. 5 (excs)
453, 1153

Corigliano, John (Paul)
The Red Violin Caprices 350
Sonata for Violin and Piano 350

Cornelius, (Carl August) Peter
(Der) Barbier von Bagdad, 'The Barber of Baghdad (excs)

Cornysh, William
Ave Maria, mater Dei 1346

Couperin, François
Leçons de ténèbres (excs) 709, 1356
Livres de clavecin (excs) 352

Couperin, Louis
Harpsichord Works (excs) 351
Pavane in F sharp minor. 351
Suite in F. 351

Cramer, Johann Baptist
Hommage à Mozart 1327

Crecquillon, Thomas
Andreas Christi famulus 762

Crumb, George (Henry)
Black Angels: 13 Images from the Dark Lands (Image. . .
1149, 1339

Crusell, Bernhard Henrik
Concerto for Clarinet and Orchestra No. 2 in F minor
– Op. 5 355

D

Dalbavie, Marc–André
Concerto for Piano and Orchestra. 1316
Concerto pour flûte 356

Danyel, John
Songs for the Lute, Viol and Voice (excs) 1356

Davies, (Henry) Walford
Psalm 121, 'I will lift up mine eyes' 1341

Deane, William
The grace of our Lord Jesus Christ 1340
O Lord, Thou has dealt graciously 1340

Debussy, (Achille–)Claude
Ballades de François Villon 916
Chansons de Bilitis 199, 916, 1999
Children's Corner (excs). 1323, 1326
(La) Damoiselle élue 721
Danse sacrée et danse profane 916
Etudes (excs) 1326
Fêtes galantes, Set 2 (excs) 1355
Images (excs) 914, 1331
(L') Isle joyeuse 1320
Jeux – L126 360
(La) Mer 360, 361
Petite suite. 1311
(La) Plus que lente 1328
Poèmes de Charles Baudelaire (excs) 327, 916
Prélude à l'après–midi d'un faune 360, 361
Préludes (excs). . . 360, 489, 490, 1304, 1320, 1321, 1323,
1332, 1333, 1334

Decaux, Abel
Clairs de lune 389

Delibes, (Clément Philibert) Léo
Bonjour, Suzon! 1347
Lakmé (excs) 1359
Sylvia 371

Delius, Frederick (Theodore Albert)
Air and Dance – RTVI/21 487
Concerto for Cello and Orchestra – RTVII/7 1322
Concerto for Violin and Orchestra – RTVII/6. 417
(A) Dance Rhapsody No. 1 – RTVI/18 486
Songs from the Norwegian – RTV/9 (excs) 1349
Summer Evening – RTVI/7 1313

Dendrino, Gherase
Lasati–ma sa Cint (Let me Sing) (excs) 1354

Dering, Richard
Cantica sacra (excs) 1341

D'Indy, (Paul Marie Théodore) Vincent
Symphonie sur un chant montagnard français in G – Op.
25 430

Dinicu, Grigoras
Hora Staccato 243

Dohnányi, Ernö
Serenade in C – Op. 10 274
Variations on a Nursery Theme – Op. 25 379

Domeniconi, Carlo
Koyunbaba – Op 19 1329

Donizetti, (Domenico) Gaetano (Maria)
(L') Assedio di Calais (excs) 1354
Dom Sébastien (excs) 1354
Don Pasquale (excs) 1351, 1353
(Il) Duca d'Alba (excs). 1359
Elisabetta, o Il castello di Kenilworth (excs) 1353
(L')Elisir d'amore, 'Elixir of Love' (excs). 1353, 1359
(La) Favorita (excs) 1351, 1353
(La) Fille du régiment, 'Daughter of the Regiment' (excs)
1353
Linda di Chamounix (excs). 1353
Lucia di Lammermoor, 'The Bride of Lammermoor'
(excs). 1350, 1357, 1359
Lucrezia Borgia (excs). 852, 1353, 1354
Maria Stuarda (excs) 1354
Poliuto (excs). 1359
Rita (excs) 1353
Roberto Devereux, ossia Il conte di Essex (excs). . . . 1354
Soirées d'automne à l'Infrascata (excs) 1354

Dowland, John
Almains – P47–54 (excs) 386, 1319
Captayne Pipers Galliard – P88. 386
(A) Fancy. 1358
Fantasies and Other Contrapuntal Pieces – P1–7 (excs). .
386, 1319
The First Book of Songs or Ayres (excs) .487, 1319, 1347,
1358
Fornlorn Hope Fancy. 1319
Frogg galliard – P90 386
Galliards – P19–46 (excs) 386, 1319, 1358
Hasellwoods Galliard – P84 386
Jigs, Corantos, Toys, etc – P55–59 (excs) 386, 1319
The King of Denmark's Galliard. 386, 1319
Lachrimae, or Seaven Teares (excs). 386, 1358
My Lady Hunsdon's Puffe 1319
Pavan: Lachrimae Antiquae 1319
Pavana Doulandi Angli 386
Pavans – P8–18 (excs) 386, 1319
(A) Pilgrimes Solace (excs) 1319, 1356, 1358
The Second Booke of Songs or Ayres (excs) . . 1319, 1356

Decaux, Abel

Delius, Frederick (Theodore Albert)

Premier trio in G 363
Rêverie. 397
Sonata for Cello and Piano in D minor 364, 1336
Sonata for Flute, Viola and Harp. 445
Sonata for Violin and Piano in G minor 445
String Quartet in G minor – Op. 10 . . 362, 363, 913, 914
Suite bergamasque (excs) 1315, 1323

Settings of Ballads and Other Popular Tunes – P61–70
  (excs). 386, 1319
Sir Henry Umpton's Funeral 1319
Sir John Smith, His Almain 386
Sorrow, come! 1358
Squires Galliard. 386
The Third and Last Book of Songs or Aires (excs). .1319,
                                                   1356, 1358

Dowland, Robert
  Almande. 386
  Sir Thomas Monson, his Galliard 386
  Sir Thomas Monson, his Pavin 386

Duarte, Leonora
  Sinfonia No 5 1342
  Sinfonia No 6 (sopra Sol mi fa la sol) 1342

Dubois, Théodore (François Clement)
  Fantaisie Triomphale – Maestoso 1336
  In paradisum 1326

Dufay, Guillaume
  Mass for St Anthony Abbott. 212

Dukas, Paul (Abraham)
  (L')Apprenti sorcier, 'The Sorcerer's Apprentice'. . . . 389
  Polyeucte. 1132
  Sonata for Piano in E flat minor 389
  Villanelle 1319

Dunhill, Thomas Frederick
  The Cloths of Heaven – Op. 30/3 1349

Duparc, (Marie Eugène) Henri
  Mélodies 840, 916, 1355

Duphly, Jacques
  Pièces de clavecin (excs) 352

Dupré, Marcel
  Cortège et litanie – Op. 19. 1336
  (La) France au Calvaire – Op. 49. 393

Duruflé, Maurice
  (4) Motets sur des thèmes grégoriens – Op. 10. .394, 434,
                                                            1346
  Prélude et Fugue sur le nom d'Alain – Op. 7 . . . 394, 434
  Requiem – Op. 9. . . . . 394, 434

Dutilleux, Henri
  Ainsi la Nuit. 362, 363, 913
  Concerto for Violin and Orchestra, '(L')arbre des . . . 395
  Sarabande et cortège. 1323
  Sonatine. 1318
  Sonnets de Jean Cassou 395
  Timbres, espace, mouvement 395

Dvořák, Antonín
  American Suite in A – B190 (Op. 98b) 403
  Concerto for Cello and Orchestra . .397, 398, 414, 1322
  Concerto for Piano and Orchestra 398
  Concerto for Violin and Orchestra 343, 400
  Cypresses – B152 613
  Dumka in C minor – B136 (Op. 12/1). 1335
  Gipsy Melodies, 'Zigeunerlieder' – B104 (Op. 55) . . .840,
                                                            1357
  The Golden Spinning–Wheel – B197 (Op. 109) . . . 1313
  Humoresques – B187 (Op. 101) (excs). 641
  In Folk Tone – B146 (Op. 73) 408
  Love Songs – B160 (Op. 83) 408
  Mass in D – B153 (Op. 86). 407
  Othello – B174 (Op. 93). 400
  Quintet for Piano and Strings in A – B155 (Op. 81) 1000
  Romantic Pieces – B150 (Op. 75) 406
  Rondo in G minor – B171 (Op. 94). 256, 406
  Scherzo capriccioso – B131 (Op. 66) 400
  Silent woods – B173 (Op. 68/5) (excs) . . . .
  Silent woods – B182 (Op. 68/5). 1322
  Slavonic Dances – B78 & B145 (Opp. 46 & 72) (excs). . .
                                                641, 1316, 1317
  Sonatina for Violin and Piano in G – B183 (Op. 100) 406
  Songs – B124 (Op. 2) 408
  String Sextet in A – B80 (Op. 48) 1170
  Symphony No. 5. 400

Symphony No. 6 403
Symphony No. 7 400
Symphony No. 8 400
Symphony No. 9, 'From the New World' in E minor. . .
                                                400, 402, 403

Dyson, George
  Rhapsodies. 595

E

Eben, Petr
  Prague Te Deum 407

Eisler, Hanns
  Duo for Violin and Cello – Op. 7 1320

Elgar, Edward (William)
  Ave Maria – Op. 2/2 1346
  Bavarian Dances – Op. 27 (excs) 421
  Chanson de matin – Op. 15/2 1321
  Chanson de nuit – Op. 15/1. 1304
  Concerto for Cello and Orchestra . .272, 413, 414, 415,
                                                1322, 1336
  Concerto for Violin and Orchestra 415, 417, 732
  The Dream of Gerontius – Op. 38 . . . . 424, 425
  In Smyrna 1327
  Pomp and Circumstance – Op. 39 (excs). 1337
  Sonata for Violin and Piano in E minor – Op. 82. . . . 423
  They are at rest. 1341
  Variations on an Original Theme, 'Enigma' – Op. 36421,
                                                589, 590, 1337
  Vesper Voluntaries – Op. 14 1326

Enescu, George
  Impressions d'enfance – Op. 28 428
  Pièce de concert 1335
  Sonata for Piano No. 2 in D – Op. 24/3 490
  Sonata for Violin and Piano No. 3 in A minor – Op. 25
  428

Eötvös, Peter
  Replica. 105

Esenvalds, Eriks
  Légende de la femme emmurée 302

Estévez, Antonio
  Mediodia en el Llano (Venezuala) 1313

F

Falla (y Matheu), Manuel de
  Canciones populares españolas (excs). 290, 1347
  (La) Vida breve (excs). 243, 641

Fasch, Carl Friedrich Christian
  Concerto for Trumpet, Oboe d'amore, Violin and
    Strings in E 430

Fasch, Johann Friedrich
  Concerto for Oboe and Strings in G minor 430
  Concerto for Trumpet, 2 Oboes and Strings in D . . . 430
  Concerto in C minor 430
  Overture in D minor – FWV K:d4 430

Fauré, Gabriel (Urbain)
  Ave Maria – Op. 93. 1346
  Ballade in F sharp – Op. 19 . . . . 430, 431, 912
  Berceuse – Op. 16. 397
  Cantique de Jean Racine – Op. 11 . . . . 394, 434
  Chanson – Op. 94. 436
  Elégie – Op. 24. . . . . 199, 397, 1322
  En prière 436
  (Les) Jardins clos – Op. 106 436
  Mélodies – Op. 58 (excs) 199
  Messe basse 394, 434
  Pavane – Op. 50 434
  Petite Pièce in G – Op 49 1323
  Piano Trio in D minor – Op. 120 363
  Puisqu'ici–bas – Op. 10/1. 436
  Requiem – Op. 48. . . . . 394, 434, 435, 444

Shylock – Op. 57 (excs). 192
Songs – Op. 46 (excs) 199, 436
String Quartet in E minor – Op. 121 . 363, 444, 913, 914
Vocalise-étude. 1355

Febel, Reinhard
Chorale Arrangements after Johann Sebastian Bach (excs)
260

Feinberg, Samuel
Berceuse – Op. 19a 1324

Fernström, John (Axel)
Wind Quintet – Op. 59 822

Ferrabosco, Alfonso I
Fantasias 1344
In Nomines 1344
(De) lamentatione Ieremiae prophetae 1148
Pavan a 5 1344

Ferrabosco, Alfonso II
Four–Note Pavan 'Hear me O God' 1358
So beauty on the waters stood 1356

Févin, Antoine de
Faulte d'argent 623

Finzi, Gerald (Raphael)
Concerto for Cello and Orchestra in A minor – Op. 40. .
439
Dies natalis – Op. 8. 440
Elegy in F – Op. 22. 423
Intimations of Immortality – Op. 29 441
Let us garlands bring – Op. 18. 1203
Oh fair to see – Op. 13 (excs). 1349
Romance in E flat – Op. 11 440
(A) Young Man's Exhortation – Op. 14 (excs). 1349

Fitkin, Graham
Old Style 1335

Flotow, Friedrich (Adolf Ferdinand) von
Martha (excs). 1351, 1355

Floyd, Carlisle
Susannah (excs) 1352

Forqueray, Antoine
Pièces de viole (excs). 1332

Forsyth, Cecil
Concerto for Viola and Orchestra in G minor 237

Foulds, John
Dynamic Triptych – Op. 88. 1197

Franchetti, Alberto
Germania (excs). 1350

Franck, César (-Auguste-Jean-Guillaume-Hubert)
Chorales (excs) 1324
Nocturne 1355
Quintet for Piano and Strings in F minor 444, 1000
Sonata for Violin and Piano in A . . . 445, 446, 1322, 1332,
1335
String Quartet in D – M9. 444
Symphonic Variations. 430, 444, 964
Symphony in D minor 326, 434, 435, 444, 1314

Frankel, Benjamin
Quintet for Clarinet and Strings – Op. 28 595

French, William Percy
Phil the Fluter's Ball. 726

Frescobaldi, Girolamo
Canzona a due cori 728

Friedman, Ignaz
Menuetto in D 1327

Froberger, Johann Jacob
(Le) Tombeau de Monsieur Blancheroche 351

Frye, Walter
Missa Sine Nomine. 1340
Missa Summe trinitati – unidentified. 1340

Fusté, Ernesto
Háblame de amores 1347

G

Gabrieli, Andrea
Madrigals (excs). 448

Gabrieli, Giovanni
Angelus ad pastores. 755
Audite principes 755
Canzoni (excs). 448
Exultet jam angelica turba 1345
O magnum mysterium 755
Quem vidistis, pastores. 755
Sacri di Giove augei 448
Symphoniae sacrae, liber secundus (excs) 755

Gallon, (Gabbier) Noël
Récit et Allegro. 1323

García, Manuel (del Pópulo Vicente Rodríguez)
(La) Figlia dell'aria (excs) 1348, 1349
(El) Poeta calculista (excs). 1348, 1349

Gaultier, Denis
Suite in B minor in B minor (excs). 1332

Gaultier, Ennemond
(Les) larmes de Monsieur Boisset. 1332

Gautier de Coincy,
Miracles de Nostre–Dame (excs) 452

Geehl, Henry Ernest
For you alone 1350

Gefors, Hans
Lydias sanger, 'Lydia's Songs' 230

Geminiani, Francesco (Xaverio)
(12) Concerti Grossi 453
(6) Sonatas for Cello and Continuo – Op. 5 (excs) . . . 453

Gerle, Hans
Mille regretz 623

German, Edward
Orpheus with his lute 1349

Gershwin, George
(An) American in Paris 455
Concerto for Piano and Orchestra in F. 455, 456
Girl Crazy (excs) 486
Porgy and Bess (excs) 1352
Preludes. 1320, 1325
Rhapsody in Blue 101, 347, 455

Getty, Gordon
Joan and the Bells 1052

Gheciu, Diamandi
Si Dacá. 1354

Gibbons, Orlando
Drop, drop slow tears 1343
Great King of Gods (Lord of Lords). 1149
Hosanna to the Son of David. 1345
O all true faithful hearts 1149
This is the record of John. 1345

Gigout, Eugène
Pièces (excs). 1321, 1336

Giménez (y Bellido), Jerónimo
(La) Tempranica (excs) 1357

Ginastera, Alberto (Evaristo)
Danzas argentinas – Op. 2 (excs) 1335
Estancia – Op. 8a (excs) 1313

Giordano, Umberto
Andrea Chénier (excs). 1350, 1351

Giuliani, Mauro (Giuseppe Sergio Pantaleo)
Concerto for Guitar and Strings No. 1 in A – Op. 30 463

Glazunov, Alexander Konstantinovich
Concerto for Violin and Orchestra in A minor – Op. 82 .
467, 632, 862, 863, 1066, 1325
Spanish Serenade – Op. 20/2 641

Glinka, Mikhail Ivanovich
Ruslan and Lyudmila (excs) 814

Sonata for Viola and Piano................... 1335

Gluck, Christoph Willibald (Ritter von)
Alceste (excs)................................. 470
Armide (excs)................................ 1358
Iphigénie en Aulide (excs)................... 296
Iphigénie en Tauride (excs)................. 1358
Orfeo ed Euridice (excs)..................... 470
Orphée et Eurydice (excs)................... 1350
Paride ed Elena (excs).................. 470, 1354

Godowsky, Leopold
Moment Musical No. 3 (Schubert) in F minor..... 1327
Passacaglia_44 variations, cadenza and fugue on th . 1003
The Schubert songs transcribed for the piano (excs) ...
                                             1327
Studies on the Chopin Etudes (excs) 476
Toccata (Perpetual Motion) in G flat – Op. 13..... 1324
Triakontameron (excs)................... 476, 1327
Waltz in D flat 476

Gombert, Nicolas
Ego sum qui sum............................. 933
Lugebat David Absalon 623

Gomes, (Antonio) Carlos
Fosca 1359

Górecki, Henryk (Mikolaj)
Kurpian Songs – Op 75 1342
Totus tuus – Op. 60 .... 1343, 1345

Goss, John
Praise my soul, the King of Heaven............. 1343
These are they which follow the Lamb 1341

Goudimel, Claude
Psalms (excs)............................... 1344

Gough, Orlando
Birds on Fire 1342

Gounod, Charles (François)
(L')Arithmétique............................ 483
Au printemps................................ 483
Au rossignol................................ 1355
(Le) Banc de Pierre 483
Donne–moi cette fleur 483
D'un coeur qui t'aime 483
Fantaisie sur l'Hymne National Russe........... 1336
Faust (excs)........... 720, 1350, 1355, 1359
Fleur de bois 483
Mélodies (excs)............................. 483
Mignon 483
Mireille (excs)............................. 720
Par une belle nuit 483
Polyeucte (excs)............................ 720
(La) Reine de Saba (excs)............... 720, 1351
Roméo et Juliette, 'Romeo and Juliet' (excs)...720, 1357,
                                             1359
Sérénade................................ 483, 1354
(La) Siesta 483
(Les) Vacances.............................. 483

Grainger, (George) Percy (Aldridge)
Beautiful fresh flower 487
Bold William Taylor – BFMS43 1349
Brigg Fair – BFMS7 1349
Colonial Song – S1 487
Country gardens – BFMS22.................... 487
Crew of the Long Dragon 486
Fantasy on George Gershwin's 'Porgy and Bess' 486
Free Settings of Favourite Melodies (excs) 487
Gershwin Transcriptions (excs) 487
Handel in the Strand – RMTB2 .... 487, 604
Harvest Hymn............................... 487
The Hunter in his career – OEPM4 487
The Immovable Do (or the Ciphering C)......... 604
In a Nutshell Suite (excs) 487
In Dahomey................................. 487
Irish Tune from County Derry (Londonderry Air)
 – BFMS15..........................487, 604
Jutish Medley on Danish folksongs – DFMS8 487
Lullaby.................................... 487
The Merry King – BFMS38..................... 487

Mock Morris – RMTB1.................... 487, 604
Molly on the shore – BFMS19.................. 487
Molly on the shore – BFMS1................... 604
My Robin is to the greenwood gone – OEPM2 .. 604
Paraphrase on the Waltz of the Flowers 487
Rondo 486
Scotch Strathspey and Reel – BFMS37 487
Shallow Brown – SCS3........................ 604
Shepherd's Hey – BFMS4 487
Shepherd's Hey – RMTB3...................... 604
Spoon River – AFMS1 487
Sussex Mummers' Christmas Carol – BFMS17 604
Tiger–Tiger – KS4/JBC9...................... 486
Walking Tune – RMTB3................... 486, 487
Ye banks and braes o' Bonnie Doon – BFMS32 486

Granados (y Campiña), Enrique
Allegro de concierto 488
Danza lenta 488
Danzas españolas – Op. 37.............. 488, 641
Goyescas 488
Tonadillas al estilo antiguo (excs) 1347
Valses poeticos 488

Graupner, (Johann) Christoph
Ach Gott Herr............................. 1356

Grechaninov, Alexandr Tikhonovich
The Seven Days of the Passion – Op. 58 (excs) 1342

Greene, Maurice
Orpheus with his lute 1356

Grieg, Edvard (Hagerup)
Ave maris stella – CW156/2.............. 1343, 1346
Concerto for Piano and Orchestra in A minor – Op. 16 .
                                 489, 490, 491, 1000
Holberg Suite – Op. 40 491
Humoresques – Op. 6 (excs)................. 1315
Lyric Pieces, Book 8 – Op. 65 490
Norwegian peasant dances – Op. 72 (excs) 486
Peer Gynt – Opp. 46 & 55 491
Peer Gynt – Op 23 (excs)................... 1357
Stimmungen – Op. 73 (excs) 1315
String Quartet No. 1 in G minor – Op. 27..... 492
String Quartet No. 2 in F – CW146.......... 492

Grigny, Nicolas de
Organ Works, Book 1 (Premier livre d'orgue) (excs) 1324

Grofé, Ferde
Grand Canyon Suite........................ 455

Grovlez, Gabriel
Sicilienne et Allegro giocoso 1323

Guarnieri, Mozart Camargo
Dansa negra............................... 1335
Sonata for Cello and Piano No 1............ 1331

Guastavino, Carlos
(La) rosa y el sauce 1357

Gubaidulina, Sofia
Concerto for Violin and Orchestra, 'In Tempus Praesens'
                                             496

Gudmundsen-Holmgreen, Pelle
Statements................................ 1342

Guerrero, Francisco
Ave Maria 762
Ave virgo sanctissima 1344, 1345
Dulcissima Maria 762
Duo Seraphim 1344, 1345
Maria Magdalene 671

Guilmant, (Felix) Alexandre
Allegro – Op. 81 1336
Final alla Schumann sur un Noël languedocien – Op. 83.
                                             1336
Marche fantaisie sur des Chants d'Eglise – Op. 44 . . 1336
Meditation sur le Stabat Mater – Op. 63......... 1336
Sonata No. 7 in F – Op. 89 (excs) 1326

Gulda, Friedrich
Play Piano Play (excs)..................... 1325
Prelude and Fugue 1325

Guridi (Bidaola), Jesús
Canciones castellanas (excs) 1347

Gurney, Ivor (Bertie)
I will go with my father a–ploughing. 1349
Sleep 1349

H

Haas, Pavel
String Quartet No. 1 in C sharp minor – Op. 3 . 498, 613
String Quartet No. 2, 'Z opicích hor' – Op. 7 . . 499, 613
String Quartet No. 3 – Op. 15. . . . . 498, 613

Hadley, Patrick (Arthur Sheldon)
The Trees so high, symphonic ballad in A minor. . . . 441

Hahn, Reynaldo
A Chloris 1351, 1355
(L') Enamourée. 1351, 1357
(L') Heure exquise 1351
Quand je fus pris au pavillon 1351
Trois jours de vendage 1351

Hakim, Naji
Glenalmond Suite 1324
Improvisation on 'Amazing Grace' 1324
Sakskøbing Præludier 1324

Halévy, (Jacques–François-)Fromental(-Elie)
Clari (excs). 1348

Halffter, Ernesto
Dos Canciones 1347

Halvorsen, Johan
Veslemöy's song 1315

Hamelin, Marc-André
Etude No. 9 d'après Rossini 1324
Etude No. 10 d'après Chopin 1324
Etude No. 12 (Prelude and Fugue) 1324

Handel, George Frideric
Aci, Galatea e Polifemo, 'Sorge il dì' – HWV72 (excs) . . 1320
Chaconne in G – HWV435. 509
Coelestis dum spirat aura 1356
Concertos for Oboe and Strings 1322
(Il) delirio amoroso, 'Da quel giorno fatale' – HWV99 . . 1320
Dixit Dominus – HWV232 510
German Arias – HWV202-10 (excs) 526
Gloria. 1356
The Great Elopement (excs) 1313
Joshua – HWV64 (excs) 1347
Judas Maccabaeus – HWV63 (excs) 1347
Laudate pueri Dominum – HWV236/7 1356
Lessons (excs) 160
Mi, palpita il cor – HWV132 1320
O qualis de coelo sonus 1356
Salve Regina – HWV241 1356
Samson – HWV57 (excs) 1359
Saul – HWV53 (excs) 1329
Solomon – HWV67 (excs) 1321
Suites for Keyboard, Set I. 160, 509, 1321
Thine be the glory, risen, conquering Son 1343
(Il) Trionfo del Tempo e del Disinganno – HWV46a
(excs). 1247
Water Music – HWV348-50 (excs) 487

Handl, Jacob
Ecce concipes 1345

Hanson, Howard
Symphony No. 2, 'Romantic' – Op. 30 544

Harbison, John H.
Mirabai Songs. 102

Harris, William (Henry)
Bring us, O Lord God 1341, 1342
Faire is the Heaven 1341
O what their joy and their glory must be 1343

Haydn, (Franz) Joseph
(L')Anima del filosofo, ossia Orfeo ed Euridice 1358
Arianna a Naxos – HobXXVIb/2 . . . . 1348, 1351
Armida – HobXXVIII/12 (excs) 1358
Berenice che fai – HobXXIVa/10 789
The birks of Abergeldie 1347
The brisk young lad 1347
Concerto for Cello and Orchestra No. 1 in C
– HobVIIb/1 1322
Concerto for Cello and Orchestra No. 2 in D
– HobVIIb/2 (excs) 415, 1105, 1322
Concerto for Keyboard and Orchestra in D
– HobXVIII/11 990
Concerto for Trumpet and Orchestra in E flat
– HobVIIe/1 549
Cumbernauld House. 1347
Duncan Gray. 1347
(La) Fedeltà premiata – HobXXVIII/10 (excs) 470
The Flower of Edinburgh 1347
Green grow the rashes 1347
I'm o'er young to marry yet – HobXXXIa/30. 1347
(L') isola disabitata – HobXXVIII/9 1358
Jamie come try me 1347
John Anderson. 1347
Love will find out the way 1347
(Il) Mondo della luna – HobXXVIII/7 (excs) . . 470, 1358
My ain kind dearie 1347
My boy Tammy 1347
O bonny lass 1347
O can ye sew cushions – HobXXXIa/48 1347
Orlando Paladino – HobXXVIII/11 (excs) 470
Seven Last Words – Op. 51/HobIII/50-56 560
Shepherds, I have lost my love 1347
Sleepy Bodie – HobXXXIa/31 1347
Sonata for Keyboard No. 37 in E – HobXVI/22 902
Sonata for Keyboard No. 44 in F – HobXVI/29. 562
Sonata for Keyboard No. 59 in E flat – HobXVI/49 1319
Sonata for Keyboard No. 60 in C – HobXVI/50 . . . 1333
Sonata for Keyboard No. 62 in E flat – HobXVI/52 1326
(Lo) Speziale – HobXXVIII/3 1358
String Quartet in D – Op. 42:HobIII/43. 557
String Quartets – Op. 50 (HobIII/44-49) (excs) 555
String Quartets – Op. 33 (HobIII/37-42) (excs) 555
String Quartets, 'Apponyi I' – Op. 71 (HobIII/69-71)
(excs). 555
String Quartets, 'Apponyi II' – Op. 74 (HobIII/72-74)
(excs). 555
String Quartets (Divertimentos) – Op. 1 (HobIII/1-4,6)
(excs). 555
String Quartets (Divertimentos), 'Sun' – Op. 20
(HobIII/31-36) (excs) 555
String Quartets, 'Lobkowitz' – Op. 77 (HobIII/81-82)
(excs). 555
String Quartets, 'Tost II' – Op. 55 (HobIII/60-62) (excs)
555
String Quartets, 'Tost III' – Op. 64 (HobIII/63-68) (excs)
555
Symphony No. 40 in F 1313
Symphony No. 83, 'The Hen' in G minor 1311
Symphony No. 94, 'Surprise' in G (excs). 1324
Symphony No. 102 in B flat. 1313
Up in the morning early – HobXXXIa/28 1347
The White Cockade – HobXXXIa/22. 1347

Heinichen, Johann David
Pastorale in A, 'Per la notte della Nativitate Chr – S242 .
574
Te Deum 574

Hellmesberger, Joseph II
Danse diabolique. 1099

Hely-Hutchinson, (Christian) Victor
The Young Idea: Rhapsody for Piano & Orchestra . . 849

Henze, Hans Werner
Sebastian im Traum 701

Herbert, Victor August
Concerto for Cello and Orchestra No. 2 397

Herrmann, Bernard
Wuthering Heights (excs). 1352

Heuberger, Richard (Franz Joseph)
(Der) Opernball, 'Opera Ball' (excs) 641, 1357

Higdon, Jennifer
Blue Cathedral 347

Hildegard of Bingen, Abbess
O choruscans stellarum. 1342
O felix anima 1341

Hillborg, Anders
...lontana in sonno... 230

Hindemith, Paul
Concerto for Horn and Orchestra 1102
Konzertmusik – Op. 50. 1102
Rag Time (well-tempered) 455
String Quartet No. 4 – Op. 22. . . . . 110, 580, 1017
Trauermusik 105

Hoffstetter, Roman
String Quartets – Op. 3 (excs) 555

Holbrooke, Joseph
Concerto for Piano and Orchestra No. 1, 'The Song' 583
Eilen Shona 595
Quintet for Clarinet and Strings No. 1 in G – Op. 27/1 .
255

Holliger, Heinz
Concerto for Violin and Orchestra 584

Holloway, Robin (Greville)
Fantasy-Pieces on the Heine "Liederkreis" of Schumann
– Op. 16 585
Serenade in C – Op. 41 585

Holst, Gustav(us Theodore von)
The Evening watch – H159 (Op. 43/1) 1341
Lyric Movement – H191 . . . . 589, 590
Nunc dimittis – H127. 1342
The Perfect Fool – H150 (Op. 39) (excs) 590
The Planets – H125 (Op. 32). 421, 589, 590

Honegger, Arthur
Chansons de la Petite Sirène d'Anderson – H63 (excs) . .
1355
Sonatina for Violin and Cello – H80. 1338
Symphony No. 2 in D – H153. 592
Symphony No. 3, 'Liturgique' – H186 592

Hooper, Edmund
Behold it is Christ. 1340

Hough, Stephen
Etude de Concert 1327
Mozart Transformations (after Poulenc) 1327
Musical Jewellery Box. 1327
Valse Enigmatique 1327

Hove, Joachim van den
Pavana Lachrimae. 386

Howells, Herbert (Norman)
All my hope on God is founded 1343
Nunc dimittis 1341
Pieces (excs). 1321
Requiem 596, 1201
Rhapsodic Quintet – Op. 31. 595
Rhapsodies – Op. 17 (excs) 1337
Siciliano for a High Ceremony 1326
(A) Spotless Rose. 1343
String Quartet, 'In Gloucestershire' 595
Take him, earth, for cherishing 596, 1201

Huber, Klaus
...Plainte... 1330

Hughes, Herbert
Down by the Salley Gardens 960
She moved through the fair 960

Hume, Tobias
(A) Pavan 1330

Humfrey, Pelham
(A) Hymne to God the Father, 'Wilt thou forgive th 1184

Hummel, Johann Nepomuk
Air à la tirolienne avec variations – Op. 118 . . 1348, 1349
Concerto for Trumpet and Orchestra in E flat. 549
Sonata for Cello and Piano in A – Op. 104. 598

Humperdinck, Engelbert
Hänsel und Gretel (excs) 296

Hüttenbrenner, Anselm
Frühlingsliedchen 1008
(Der) Hügel. 1008
Lerchenlied 1008
(Die) Seefahrt 1008
Seegras. 1008
Spinnerlied 1008
(Die) Sterne. 1008

I

Ibert, Jacques (François Antoine)
Concerto for Flute and Orchestra 631
Divertissement 748, 7483
Histoires (excs) 1315
Pièce 631

India, Sigismondo d'
Le musiche I (excs) 1356

Ippolitov-Ivanov, Mikhail Mikhailovich
Caucasian Sketches, Suite 1 – Op. 10 633

Ireland, John (Nicholson)
The Bells of San Marie. 1203
The Forgotten Rite. 421
Mai-Dun 421
My song is love unknown 1343
Sea Fever 1203
Songs to Poems by Thomas Hardy (excs) 1351
These Things Shall Be 421
The Vagabond 1203

Isaac, Heinrich
Agnus Dei (Missa Wohlauf gesell von hinnen) (excs) . 623

Ives, Charles E(dward)
Memories. 1353
Sonata for Piano No. 2, 'Concord, Mass.: 1840-60' . . 609
They are there! 1149, 1339
Variations on 'America' 1017

J

Jacquet de Mantua,
Aspice Domine 753

Janácek, Leos
Concertino 1316
From a Fairy Tale. 634
Glagolitic Mass 615
In the mists 1315
Mass in E flat 635
Moravian folk poetry in songs (excs) 408
Our Father. 407
Sinfonietta. 182, 403
String Quartet No. 1, 'The Kreutzer Sonata' . . . 498, 613
String Quartet No. 2, 'Intimate Letters' 499, 613

Jancourt, (Louis Marie) Eugène
Nocturne (d'après John Field) – Op 124 1323

Japart, Jean
Se congié prens 623

Jarrell, Michael
..un temps de silence. 356

John IV, King of Portugal
Crux fidelis 1344

Johnson, Robert II
Care-charming sleep 1358
Full fathom five. 1356, 1358

Have you seen the bright lily grow? 1358

Jolivet, André
Chant de Linos 1318
Concerto for Violin and Orchestra 624

Josquin Desprez,
Absalon fili mi 623
Adieu mes amours 622, 623
Ave Maria 1345
Ave Maria...virgo serena 622, 623, 1343
Bergerette savoyenne 623
(La) Bernardina 622
Cela sans plus 622
Comment peult haver joye 623
De profundis clamavi 623
De tous biens playne 622, 623
(La) déploration de Johannes Ockeghem: Nymphes d 623
Dido (excs) 623
En l'ombre d'un buissonet au matinet 623
Faulte d'argent 623
Fortuna d'un gran tempo 622
Gaude Virgo, Mater Christi 1346
(El) grillo è buon cantore 623
Ile fantazies de Joskin 622
Illibata Dei virgo nutrix/La mi la 827
In te Domine speravi, per trovar pietà 623
Je me complains 623
Je ne me puis tenir d'aimer 623
Memor esto verbi tui 826
Mille regretz 622, 623
Miserere mei, Deus 623
Missa 'D'ung aultre amer' 622
Missa, 'Hercules Dux Ferrarie' 623
Nunc dimittis 1342
Nymphes des bois/Requiem, 'La déploration de Johannes
    Ockeghem' 826
Pater noster/Ave Maria 623
Pauper sum ego (à 3) 623
Petite camusette 623
Plaine de dueil 623
Planxit autem David 622
Qui belles amours 622
Sanctus 'D'ung aultre amer' 622
Scaramella va alla guerra 623
Se congié prens (excs) 623
Se j'ay perdu mon amy 623
Si j'avoys Marion 623
Tu lumen, tu splendor Patris 622
Tu solus qui facis mirabilia 622, 623
Veni, Sancte Spiritus 623
Victimae paschali laudes/D'ung aultre amer 622
(Le) villain 623

K

Kabalevsky, Dmitry Borisovich
Colas Breugnon – Op. 24 (excs) 814
Concerto for Cello and Orchestra No. 2 in G – Op. 77 . .
    414, 415, 625
Rondo in A minor – Op. 59 896

Kálmán, Imre (Emmerich)
(Die) Csárdásfürstin, 'The Gypsy Princess' (excs) . . . 1357
Was weiss ein nie geküsster Rosenmund 1327

Kancheli, Giya Alexandrovich
Styx 628

Kapustin, Nikolai
Moving Force 1320
Sonata for Piano No 2 1325

Khachaturian, Aram Il'yich
Concerto for Cello and Orchestra 625
Concerto for Flute and Orchestra 99, 631
Concerto for Violin and Orchestra in D minor 632, 1066
Gayaneh (excs) 632, 633
Masquerade (excs) 633
Spartacus_Ballet Suite No. 1 (excs) 633
Spartacus_Ballet Suite No. 2 (excs) 633
The Valencian Widow 632

Khachaturian, Karen
Sonata for Violin and Piano – Op. 1 866

Klein, Gideon
Duo 1320
Partita for String 106

Knox, Garth
Malor me bat 1330

Kodály, Zoltán
Háry János – Op. 15 814
Laudes organi 635
Missa Brevis 635
Pieces – Op. 11 (excs) 290
Psalmus Hungaricus – Op. 13 615
Sonata for Cello and Piano – Op. 4 634
Sonata for Solo Cello – Op. 8 634

Koechlin, Charles (Louis Eugène)
Choral sur le nom de Fauré 434
Sonata for Bassoon and Piano – Op. 71 1323

Korngold, Erich Wolfgang
Abschiedslieder – Op. 14 (excs) 1351
Concerto for Violin and Orchestra – Op. 35 99, 100, 636,
    637, 1322, 4713
Devotion (excs) 1351
Much Ado About Nothing (excs) 99, 100, 637, 4713
The Sea Hawk (excs) 1351

Kreisler, Fritz
Aucassin and Nicolette, 'Canzonetta medievale' 641
Berceuse romantique – Op. 9 641
Caprice viennois – Op. 2 641
Chanson Louis XIII and Pavane in the style of Couperin
    641
(La) Gitana 641, 1304
Liebesfreud 641, 900, 901
Liebesleid 641, 900, 901, 1317
Marche miniature viennoise 1320
Polichinelle 641
Précieuse in the style of Couperin 641
Rondino on a Theme by Beethoven 641
Scherzo in the style of Dittersdorf 641
Schön Rosmarin 641, 1317
Slavonic Fantasie 641
Tambourin chinois – Op. 3 641
Viennese Rhapsodic Fantasietta 641
Zigeuner capriccio 641

Krenek, Ernst
Symphony No. 1 – Op. 7 988

Kurtág, György
Játékok (Games), Books 1-8 (excs) 642, 1316
Ligatura – Op. 31b 112
Movement for Viola and Orchestra 105
Transcriptions from Machaut to Bach (excs) 642

Kvandal, Johann
Sacred Folktunes – Op. 23b 822
Wind Quintet – Op. 34 822

L

La Rue, Pierre de
Fors seulement 827
Missa pro defunctis 301

Lalo, Edouard(-Victoire-Antoine)
Aubade 483
Concerto for Cello and Orchestra in D minor 644
Dansons! 483
Guitare – Op. 17/1 1355
Puisqu, ici bas 483
Symphonie espagnole – Op. 21 . . . . 645, 732

Lambert, (Leonard) Constant
Horoscope (excs) 223
Salome 1291

Langlais, Jean
Festival Alleluia 393
Paraphrases grégoriennes – Op. 5 (excs) 1324

Lanquetuit, Marcel
Toccata 1337

Lassus, Orlande de
Ave regina coelorum 1345
Salve regina mater 1346
Timor et tremor 1345

Lawes, Henry
Ayres and Dialogues (excs) .1356
Orpheus's Hymn 1356

Le Jeune, Claude
(La) Bel'aronde 486

Le Roy, Adrian
Tordion 623

Lecuona, Ernesto
(La) Conga de Media Noche 1335

Lehár, Franz
Giuditta (excs) 1357
Gold und Silber, 'Gold and Silver' – Op. 79 1311

Leigh, Walter
Concertino for piano/harpsichord and strings 431

Leighton, Kenneth
Concerto for Cello and Orchestra – Op. 31 439
Fantasy Octet on Themes of Grainger – Op. 87 604
Studies (Study-Variations) – Op 56 1327

Lekeu, Guillaume (Jean Joseph Nicholas)
Fragment 913
Poèmes (excs) 913
Sonata for Cello and Piano .445

Lelasi, Giuseppe
Untitled 961

Leoncavallo, Ruggiero
(La) Bohème, 'Bohemian Life' (excs) 1351
Pagliacci, 'Players' 655, 718, 719, 1350

Liadov (Lyadov), Anatole Konstantinovich
(A) Musical snuffbox – Op. 32 1320

Ligeti, Gyorgy (Sandor)
Ballade and Dance 112
Etudes, Book 1 (excs) 1337
Etudes, Book 2 (excs) 1337
Lux aeterna 1342
Sonata for Cello 1288

Lindberg, Magnus
Concerto for Violin and Orchestra 659, 1066

Liszt, Franz
Années de pèlerinage: année 1 – Suisse – S160 (excs) . . . . .
260, 1326
Années de pèlerinage: année 2 – Italie – S161 (excs) . . . . . .
490, 665, 666
Années de pèlerinage: année 3 – S163 (excs) 113, 665, 666
Ave maris stella – S34/1 1346
Ballade No. 1 in D flat – S170 1320
Ballade No. 2 in B minor – S171 . . . . . 665, 666, 1320
Chants polonais (Chopin) – S480 (excs) . . . 341, 665, 666,
1315
Concert Studies – S145 (excs) 665, 666
Concert Studies – S144 (excs) 260, 665, 666, 1332
Concerto for Piano and Orchestra No. 1 in E flat – S124 . . .
126, 660, 661, 662, 1317
Concerto for Piano and Orchestra No. 2 in A – S125 126,
490, 660, 662
Consolations – S172 (excs) .290
Elegie No. 1 – S130 634
Elegie No. 2 – S131 634
Etudes d'exécution transcendante – S139 (excs) 1330
Evocation à la Chapelle Sixtine (Allegri/Mozart) – S658 . .
1326
Fantasia and Fugue, 'Ad nos, ad salutarem undam' – S259
304, 1337
Fantasia and Fugue in G minor (Bach) – S463 . . 665, 666
Fantasia on Hungarian Folk Themes – S123 . . 490, 662
Fantasia on themes from Mozart's Figaro and Don
Giovanni – S697 1327

Faust (Gounod)_Waltz – S407 1320
(Der) Fliegende Holländer (Wagner) – Spinning Chorus
– S440 . . . . .665, 666, 1332
Frühlingsnacht (Schumann) – S568 . . . . . . 665, 666, 1027
Grandes études de Paganini – S141 (excs) 665, 666
Harmonies poétiques et réligieuses – S173 (excs) 665, 666,
1326, 1330
Hungarian Rhapsodies – S621 (excs) 1317
Hungarian Rhapsodies – S244 (excs) . . 260, 654, 664, 665,
1316, 1320, 1321, 1334
Légendes – S175 (excs) 1337
Liebesträume – S541 . . . . 665, 666, 1315, 1320
Lieder (Mendelssohn) – S547 (excs) 737
Lieder (Schubert) – S558 (excs) 1332
(Die) Loreley – S532 . . . . 665, 666
(La) lugubre gondola – S134 634
Mendelssohn Lieder – S547 (excs) 737
Mephisto Polka – S217 . . . . 665, 666
Mephisto Waltz No. 1, 'Der Tanz in der Dorfschenke
– S514 . . . . .665, 666, 1328
Müllerlieder, 'Mélodies favorites' (Schubert – S565 (excs)
999
Orpheus – S98 1313
Polonaises – S223 (excs) 665, 666
Rapsodie espagnole – S254 .1330
Rigoletto (Verdi)_Paraphrase – S434 . . . . 665, 666, 1321
Soirées de Vienne: 9 Valses caprices d'après Schubert
– S427 (excs) 1327
Sonata for Piano in B minor – S178 . .654, 664, 665, 666,
1316, 1326, 1337
Symphonies (Beethoven) – S464 (excs) 665, 666
Valse impromptu – S213 1315
Valses oubliées – S215 (excs) 665, 666, 1326, 1328
Via crucis – S583 664
Widmung (Schumann) – S566 . . . . 665, 666, 1027

Litolff, Henry (Charles)
Concerto symphonique No. 4 in D minor – Op. 102
(excs) 1320

Llobet, Miguel
Catalan Folksongs 670
(La) Fill del Rei 670
Historical Arrangements 670
Original Compositions 670
(La) Pastoreta 670
(La) Preço de Lleida 670
Preludes 670

Lloyd, Richard
Drop down, ye heavens 1345

Lloyd Webber, Andrew
Requiem (excs) 1357

Lobo, Alonso
Ave Maria 671
Ave Regina caelorum 671
Credo quod Redemptor 671
Lamentations (excs) 1344
Missa Maria Magdalene 671
O quam suavis est, Domine .671
Quam pulchri sunt 671
Versa est in luctum 671, 1344
Vivo ego, dicit Dominus 671

Loewe, Frederick
My Fair Lady (excs) 1354

López-Quiroga y Miquel, Manuel
Ay, Maricruz! 1352
Me embrujaste 1352
Ojos verdes 1352
Te lo juro yo 1352

Lotti, Antonio
Crucifixus a 8 1345
Missa Sapientae in G minor .672

Lully, Jean-Baptiste
Marche pour la cérémonie des Turcs 709

Lupo, Joseph
Pavana a 5 1342

Lupo, Thomas

Fantasies a 4 (excs) 1342
Fantasies a 6 (excs) 1342
Fantasy-airs a 3 (excs) 1342

Luther, Martin
(A) mighty fortress is our God.................... 1343

Lutoslawski, Witold
Concerto for Cello and Orchestra................. 415
Concerto for Piano and Orchestra 1316
Dance Preludes................................... 819
Sonata For Piano 678
Variations on a Theme of Paganini............... 1317

M

Mackenzie, Alexander (Campbell)
Scottish Concerto – Op. 55 682

MacMillan, James
Seinte Mari moder milde....................... 1343

Maconchy, Elizabeth
Quintet for Clarinet and Strings 595

Mahler, Gustav
(Das) Lied von der Erde, 'Song of the Earth'........ 707
(5) Rückert-Lieder 706
Symphony No. 2, 'Resurrection' in C minor 361, 421
Symphony No. 5 in C sharp minor 698
Symphony No. 6 in A minor..................... 701
Symphony No. 7 in E minor..................... 702

Malibran, Maria
Oh dolce incanto (for Donizetti – L'elisir d'amore)... 1349
Prendi, per me sei libero 1348
Rataplan 1348, 1349

Mando, Patrick
Like as the day 1358

Marais, Marin
(Le) Basque 1319
La gamme et autres morceaux de simphonies (excs).... 709
Pièces de viole, Livre 2_Part 2 (excs) 1332
Pièces de viole, Livre 3_Part 2 (excs) 709
Pièces de viole, Livre 4_Parts 2 and 3 (excs)........ 709
Pièces en trio (excs) 1332
Variations on 'Les folies d'Espagne' 709, 1330

Marenzio, Luca
Jubilate Deo (excs) 709
Madrigals, Book 1 (Il primo libro de madrigali) (excs).. 709
Madrigals, Book 2 (Il secondo libro de madrigali) (excs)709, 1247
Madrigals, Book 4 (Il quarto libro de madrigali) (excs) . 709
Madrigals, Book 5 (Il quinto libro de madrigali) (excs) . 709
Madrigals, Book 6 (Il sesto libro de madrigali) (excs) ... 709
Madrigals, Book 7 (Il settimo libro de madrigali) (excs) 709
Madrigals, Book 9 (Il nono libro de madrigali) (excs) .. 709
Nè fero sdegno mai donna mi mosse 709
Satiati Amor ch'a a più doglioso amante............ 709

Márquez, Arturo
Danzón No. 2................................. 1313

Marta, Istvan
Doom 1149, 1339
(A) Sigh 1149, 1339

Martin, Frank
Mass 711
Passacaglia................................... 711

Martin, Philip
Variations on Irish Airs 1320

Martinaitis, Algirdas
Alleluia 1342

Martini, Johann Paul Aegidius
Piacer d'amor 1354

Martinů, Bohuslav (Jan)
Duo for Violin and Cello No. 1 – H157........... 1338
Duo for Violin and Cello No. 2 in D – H371 1320
Fantasie and Toccata – H281 1322
Mélodies pour une amie de mon pays.............. 408

Memorial to Lidice – H296..................... 106
New Anthology – H288........................ 408
New Slovak Songs (excs) 408
Rhapsody-Concerto for Viola and Orchestra – H337 .. 105
Sonata for Cello and Piano No. 3 – H340 1331
Songs on Negro Poetry (excs) 408
Songs on one page – H294 408
Symphony No. 2 – H295....................... 402

Mascagni, Pietro
(L')amico Fritz (excs) 1359
Cavalleria rusticana 655, 718, 719, 1350, 1351
Nerone (excs) 1359

Massenet, Jules (Emile Frédéric)
(Le) Cid (excs) 720
Élégie 1354
Fantaisie 644
Grisélidis (excs).............................. 720
(Le) Mage (excs)............................. 720
Manon (excs)................... 720, 721, 1355, 1357
(Le) Roi de Lahore (excs)...................... 720
Roma (excs)................................. 720
(La) Vierge (excs) 1313
Werther (excs) 720, 1355

Mathias, William (James)
Antiphonies – Op. 88/2 723
Berceuse – Op. 95/3 723
Canzonetta – Op. 78/2 723
Carillon.................................... 723
Chorale.................................... 723
Fanfare.................................... 723
Fanfare for KBL............................. 723
Fantasy – Op. 78............................ 723
Fenestra.................................... 723
Invocations – Op. 35 723
Jubilate – Op. 67/2 723
Partita – Op. 19 723
Postlude 723
Processional 723
Recessional – Op. 96/4........................ 723
Variations on a Hymn Tune (Briant) – Op. 20 723

Matthews, Colin
Pluto – the Renewer........................ 589, 590
Postlude: Monsieur Croche..................... 360

Maw, (John) Nicholas
String Quartet No 3 725

Mayerl, Billy
April's Fool.................................. 726
Beguine Impromptu........................... 726
The Big Top (excs)........................... 726
Canaries' Serenade........................... 726
Carminetta.................................. 726
Chopsticks.................................. 726
Contrasts – Op. 24 (excs)...................... 726
Crystal Clear................................ 726
Fascinating Ditty............................. 726
The Forgotten Forest......................... 726
From a Spanish lattice 726
Funny Peculiar.............................. 726
In my Garden – Autumntime (excs) 726
In my Garden – Summertime (excs) 726
Insect Oddities (excs)......................... 726
Japanese Pictures – Op. 25 (excs) 726
Jasmine – Op. 84............................ 726
Jill all alone................................ 726
Leprechaun's Leap........................... 726
Mignonette................................. 726
Minuet for Pamela 726
Orange Blossom............................. 726
Oriental – Op. 21............................ 726
Pastorale Exotique........................... 726
Penny Whistle.............................. 726
Piano Exaggerations (excs)..................... 726
Piano Transcriptions (excs)..................... 726
Postman's knock............................. 726
Puppets Suite – Op. 77 726
Scallywag................................... 726

Shy Ballerina 726
Siberian lament 726
Song of the Fir-Tree 726
Studies in Syncopation – Op. 55 (excs) 726
Syncopated Rambles (excs) 726
Weeping Willow 726
Wistaria 726

Mazulis, Rytis
The dazzled eye lost its speech 1342

Mazzocchi, Virgilio
Vespro della beata Vergine 728

Medtner, Nikolay Karlovich
Concerto for Piano and Orchestra No. 1 in C minor
– Op. 33 . . . . 729, 1160
Morceaux – Op. 31 (excs) 1324
Songs – Op. 6 (excs) 729, 1160

Méhul, Nicholas Etienne
(Les) deux aveugles de Tolède (excs) 1313

Melgás, Diogo Dias
Salve Regina 1345

Mendelssohn (-Bartholdy), (Jakob Ludwig) Felix
Andante and rondo capriccioso – Op. 14 1320
Caprices – Op. 33 (excs) 737
Concerto for Piano and Orchestra No. 1 in G minor
– Op. 25 1160
Concerto for Violin and Orchestra in E minor – Op. 64 .
131, 132, 290, 732, 1051
Infelice – Op. 94 . . . . 1348, 1349
Lieder – Op. 34 (excs) 737
(A) Midsummer Night's Dream – Opp. 21 and 61 (excs) .
340, 737, 766, 900
Octet for strings in E flat – Op. 20 . . . . 734, 1313
Piano Trio No. 1 in D minor – Op. 49 1023
Preludes – Op. 104a (excs) 737
Rondo capriccioso in E – Op. 14 737
Sacred Pieces – Op. 23 (excs) 1346
Scherzo in E minor in E minor – Op. 16/2 737
(Die) Schöne Melusine – Op. 32 1313
Sonatas for Organ – Op. 65 (excs) 1321
Songs without Words (excs) 737, 1315, 1332
String Quartet No. 2 in A minor – Op. 13 492
String Quartet No. 6 in F minor – Op. 80 . . . . 992, 8550
Studies – Op. 104b (excs) 737
Symphony No. 4, 'Italian' in A – Op. 90 990
Variations sérieuses in D minor – Op. 54 . . . . . 737, 1328

Menotti, Gian Carlo
The Medium (excs) 1352
The Old Maid and the Thief 102

Mercadante, (Giuseppe) Saverio (Raffaele)
(Il) Giuramento (excs) . . . .

Messager, André (Charles Prosper)
Fortunio (excs) 1357

Messiaen, Olivier
Mélodies (excs) 1355
O sacrum convivium! 393

Meyer, Edgar
Concerto for Violin and Orchestra 99, 100

Meyerbeer, Giacomo
(L')Africaine, 'The African Maid' (excs) 1351
(Les) Huguenots (excs) 1351, 1359

Mico, Richard
Fantasia No. 13 1358
Four-part Consorts (excs) 310

Milhaud, Darius
(Le) Boeuf sur le toit, 'The Bull on the Roof' – Op. 58 . .
748, 7483
(La) Création du monde – Op. 81a 455, 748, 7483
String Quartet No. 1 – Op. 5 913

Miller, Edward
When I survey the wondrous cross 1343

Moeran, E(rnest) J(ohn)
Phyllida and Corydon 1294

Songs of Springtime 1294

Molter, Johann Melchior
Concerto for Clarinet and Strings No. 1 in D –
MWV6:36 750
Concerto for Clarinet and Strings No. 3 in G –
MWV6:38 750
Concerto for Clarinet and Strings No. 4 in A –
MWV6:39 750

Mompou, Federico
Cançons i danses (excs) 1315, 1331
Paisajes (excs) 1315

Monn, Matthias Georg
Concerto for Cello and Orchestra in G minor 1322

Monreal-Lacosta,
Cariño verdá 1352
Porque te quiero 1352

Monro, George
My lovely Celia 1347

Monte, Philippus de
Clamavi de tribulatione mea 753
Factum est silentium 753
Miserere mei Domine 753
Missa Aspice Domine 753
O suavitis et dulcedo 753
Pie Jesu, virtus mea 753

Monteverdi, Claudio (Giovanni Antonio)
Christe, adoramus te 1345
Exultent caeli 755
Scherzi musicali (excs) 1247
Vespro della Beata Vergine, 'Vespers' 755, 756

Montsalvatge, Xavier
Divagación 488
Sonatine pour Yvette 488

Moore, Douglas S(tuart)
The Ballad of Baby Doe (excs) 1352

Morales, Cristóbal de
Ave regina caelorum 762
Exaltata est sancta Dei genitrix 762
Missa Benedicta est regina caelorum (excs) 762
Missa Si bona suscepimus 762

Morales, Juan Mostazo
Antonio Vargas Heredia 1352
(La) bien pagá 1352
El día que nací yo 1352
Falsa moneda 1352

Moreno Torroba, Federico
Luisa Fernanda (excs) 1357

Moritz, Landgrave of Hessen-Kassel
Pavan 386

Morley, Thomas
Nolo mortem peccatoris 1341

Moscheles, Ignaz
Melodic-contrapuntal Studies – Op 137 (excs) 598
Sonata for Cello and Piano No 2 in E – Op 121 598

Moser, Roland
Manners of Speaking 1330

Moszkowski, Moritz
Characteristic Pieces – Op. 36 (excs) 1326, 1327

Moulinié, Etienne
Paisible et ténébreuse nuit 1356

Mouton, Jean
Nesciens mater virgo virum 1343, 1345

Mozart, (Johann Georg) Leopold
Cassation, 'Toy Symphony' in G 775, 833

Mozart, Wolfgang Amadeus
Adagio in C – KAnh94/K580a 274
Adagio and Fugue in C minor – K546 . . . . 775, 833
Andante and Variations in G – K501 1316
(La) Clemenza di Tito – K621 (excs) 470
Concerto for 2 Pianos and Orchestra in E flat – K365/

K316a.................................771
Concerto for Clarinet and Orchestra in A – K622 ... 750
Concerto for Horn and Orchestra in E – KAnh98a/
  K494a....................................766
Concerto for Oboe and Orchestra in C – K314/K271k..
  767
Concerto for Piano and Orchestra No. 9 in E flat – K271
  126, 304
Concerto for Piano and Orchestra No. 15 in B flat
  – K450 ....126, 431
Concerto for Piano and Orchestra No. 16 in D – K451..
  104
Concerto for Piano and Orchestra No. 17 in G – K453..
  104
Concerto for Piano and Orchestra No. 21, 'Elvira
  Madigan' in C – K467.....................490
Concerto for Piano and Orchestra No. 23 in A – K488..
  1000
Concerto for Piano and Orchestra No. 24 in C minor
  – K491................................431, 1000
Concerto for Piano and Orchestra No. 27 in B flat
  – K595 771
Concertos for Horn and Orchestra 766
Don Giovanni – K527 (excs) 470
(Die) Entführung aus dem Serail, 'The Abduction from
  the Seraglio' – K384 (excs) 1359
Fantasia in C minor – K396.................1327
Fantasia in C minor – K475.................1327
(La) finta giardiniera – K196 (excs) 470
Lucio Silla – K135 (excs) 470, 1358
Mass No. 18, 'Great' in C minor – K427/K417a 789
(Le) nozze di Figaro, 'The Marriage of Figaro' – K492
  (excs)...........................470, 916, 1358
Quartet for Keyboard, Violin, Viola and Cello in G
  minor – K478........................993, 994
Quartet for Oboe, Violin, Viola and Cello in F – K370/
  368b....................................274
Quintet for Clarinet and Strings in A – K581....... 444
Quintet for Horn and Strings in E flat – K407/K386c...
  1319
Quintet for Keyboard, Oboe, Clarinet, Horn and
  Bassoon in E flat – K452....................143
Rondo in A minor – K511 787
Rondo for Horn and Orchestra, "Concert Rondo" in E
  flat – K371...............................766
Serenade No. 13, "Eine kleine Nachtmusik" in G – K525
  775, 833
Sinfonia concertante in E flat – K297b/KAnh9/C14.01..
  143
Sonata for 2 Keyboards in D – K448/375a 786
Sonata for Piano No. 4 in E flat – K282/K189g.... 1338
Sonata for Piano No. 5 in G – K283/K189h........ 866
Sonata for Piano No. 6 in D – K284/K205b........ 787
Sonata for Piano No. 8 in A minor – K310/K300d ..490,
  1321, 1338
Sonata for Piano No. 13 in B flat – K333/K315c ... 1327
Sonata for Piano No. 14 in C minor – K457....... 1319
Sonata for Piano No. 16 in C – K545 1338
Sonata for Piano No. 17 in B flat – K570 334
String Quartet No. 14 in G – K387.............. 362
Symphony No. 33 in B flat – K319.............. 1055
Symphony No. 35, "Haffner" in D – K385..... 168, 169
Symphony No. 36, "Linz" in C – K425............ 247
Symphony No. 39 in E flat – K543 1311
Symphony No. 41, "Jupiter" in C – K551.......... 702
Variations on 'Ah, vous dirai-je, Maman' in C – K265/
  K300e.................................787
Vorrei spiegarvi, oh Dio – K418 1358
Zaïde – K344/336b (excs)....................1358
(Die) Zauberflöte, 'The Magic Flute' – K620 (excs) ..274,
  1358

Muffat, Georg
  Sonata for Violin and Continuo.................. 210

Mundy, William
  Benedictus, 'for Trebles'..................... 1340
  Te Deum, 'for Trebles' 1340
  Vox patris caelestis 1346

Mussorgsky, Modest Petrovich
  Boris Godunov (excs) 812

The Fair at Sorochintsï, 'Sorochinskaya yarmar (excs) 900
Khovanshchina (excs) 812, 814
(A) Night on the Bare Mountain 812, 814
Pictures at an Exhibition ..106, 811, 812, 813, 814, 1322
The Seamstress 290
Songs and Dances of Death 1353

Myaskovsky, Nikolay
  Concerto for Violin and Orchestra in D minor – Op. 44.
  816, 1159

N

Nardini, Pietro
  Sonata for Violin and Piano.................... 1153

Nebra, José Melchor de
  Tempestad grande amigo....................... 818

Neruda, Johann Baptist Georg
  Concerto for Trumpet and Strings in E flat 549

Nielsen, Carl (August)
  Concerto for Clarinet and Orchestra – FS129 (Op. 57)..
  819
  Concerto for Violin and Orchestra – FS61 (Op. 33) .819,
  1066
  Symphony No. 4, 'The inextinguishable' – FS76 (Op. 29)
  821
  Wind Quintet – FS100 (Op. 43) 822

Nin (y Castellanos), Joaquín
  Cantos populares españolas (excs) 1347

Nivers, Guillaume Gabriel
  Antiphonarium Monasticum (excs) 324

Novák, Vítezslav (Augustín Rudolf)
  Sonata for Cello and Piano – Op 68 634

O

Obradors, Fernando J
  Chiquitita la novia........................... 1347

Obrecht, Jacob
  Humilium decus 827
  Salve regina 826, 1346

Ockeghem, Johannes
  Alma redemptoris mater...................... 826
  Ave Maria 826
  D'un autre amer 622
  Fors seulement l'attente 827
  Intemerata Dei mater 826
  Missa 'Ecce ancilla Domini'.................. 826
  Missa Fors seulement 827
  Missa '(L')homme armé'..................... 826
  Missa prolationum 827
  Requiem 827

Offenbach, Jacques
  (Les) Contes d'Hoffmann, 'The Tales of Hoffmann'
  (excs)...................................1357

Orff, Carl
  Carmina Burana 590

Orto, Marbrianus
  Si j'ay perdu mon amy (à 4) 623

P

Pabst, Paul
  Paraphrase on 'Sleeping Beauty' (Tchaikovsky) 1327

Pachelbel, Johann
  Canon and Gigue in D...................... 775, 833

Pacini, Giovanni
  Dopo tante e tante pene...................... 1348
  Irene, o L'assedio di Messina (excs)............. 1348

Paderewski, Ignacy Jan
  Address at Golden Anniversary of American Debut . 1332
  Chants du Voyageur – Op. 8 (excs) 1332
  Humoresques de concert – Op. 14 (excs) 1332

Miscellanea – Op. 16 (excs) 1327

Paganini, Nicolò
Concerto for Violin and Orchestra No. 1 in E flat – MS21
(Op. 6) 835
Concerto for Violin and Orchestra No. 2 in B minor
– MS48 (Op. 7) (excs) 290

Paisiello, Giovanni
Nina, o sia La pazza per amore (excs) 1313

Paladilhe, Emil
Psyché 1355

Palestrina, Giovanni Pierluigi da
Ardens est cor meum 839
Assumpta est Maria 838
Ave maris stella 728
Christe, qui lux es et dies 1342
Congratulamini mihi omnes 839
Crucem Sanctam Subiit 839
Crux fidelis/Pange lingua 839
Domine Jesus in qua nocte 839
Fratres ego enim accepi 839
Haec Dies 839
Improperia 839
Lamentations for Holy Saturday 1148
Lucis Creator optime 1342
Magnificat III Toni 839
Matins Responsory 1345
Missa Assumpta est Maria 838
Missa Papae Marcelli (excs) 1345
Missa Sicut lilium inter spinas 838
Motets, Book 2 (excs) 839
O Domine, Jesu Christe 839
Popule Meus 839
Pueri Hebraeorum 839
Sicut cervus desiderat 1345
Sicut lilium inter spinas I 838
Sicut lilium inter spinas II 1346
Stabat mater 839, 1343
Terra tremuit 839
Vesper Responsory 1345
Victimae Paschali 839

Palmgren, Selim
Finnish rhythms – Op. 31 (excs) 490, 491
Refrain de Berceau 490, 491

Panufnik, Andrzej
Heroic Overture 840
Landscape 840
Symphony No. 3, `Sinfonia Sacra' 840
Symphony No. 5, 'Sinfonia di sfere' 840

Parkin, Eric
Mayerl Shots, Set 1 726
Mayerl Shots, Set 2 726
Mayerl Shots, Set 3 726

Parry, (Charles) Hubert (Hastings)
Choral Fantasies 841
Chorale Preludes, Set 1 841
Chorale Preludes, Set 2 841
Dear Lord and Father of Mankind 1343
Elégie 841
Elegy in A flat 841
English Lyrics, Set 2 (excs) 1349
Fantasia and Fugue in G 841
I was glad 424, 425
Ode at a Solemn Music, 'Blest Pair of Sirens' . . . 424, 425
Songs of Farewell (excs) 1341
Toccata and Fugue in G (Wanderer) 841, 1337

Parsons, Robert I
Ave Maria 1345
De la Court 1344
Deliver me from mine enemies 1340
'I am the resurrection and the life saith the Lord', from
the Burial Service 1340
In Nomine a 5 1344
(A) Song of Mr Robert Parsons 1344
The Songe called Trumpetts 1344
Ut re me fa sol 1344

Parsons, William
The Litany 'for Trebles' (O God the Father of Heav'n)
1340

Passarani, Marco
Left mouse button doesn' t know what the right mouse
button is doing 961

Peerson, Martin
Blow out the trumpet 1345

Pergolesi, Giovanni Battista
Se tu m'ami 1354

Pérotin
Alleluia, Nativitas 847
Alleluia, Posui adiutorium 847
Beata viscera 847
Dum sigillum summi patris 847
Sederunt principes V. Adiuva 847
Viderunt omnes V. Notum fecit 847

Persiani, Giuseppe
Ines de Castro (excs) 1348, 1349

Petrini, Francesco
Graziello e Nella 818

Philips, Peter
O beatum et sacrosanctum diem 1341
Tirsi, Freno and Cosi moriro 709

Phillips, Montague F(awcett)
Concerto for Piano & Orchestra No. 1 in F sharp minor
849
Concerto for Piano & Orchestra No. 2 in E – Op. 32 849

Piazzolla, Astor
(Las) Cuatro Estaciones porteñas, 'The Four Seasons' . . .
1316
Fugata 850
(Le) Grand Tango 850
Histoire du Tango (excs) 850
Libertango 850, 1317
Milonga del ángel 850, 1335
Minutos con realidad 850
Mumuki 850
Sur: Regreso al amor 850
Tango Suite (excs) 850
Tres Tangos 1316

Pierné, (Henri Constant) Gabriel
Solo de concert – Op 35 1323

Pietri, Giuseppe
Maristella (excs) 1359

Pintscher, Matthias
Study I for 'Treatise on the Veil' 1338
Transir 356

Pizzetti, Ildebrando
Canti ad una giovane fidanzata (excs) 290
De profundis 711
Messa di requiem 711

Pletnev, Mikhail
Fantasia elvetica 1316

Poldini, Ede
Marionnettes (excs) 641, 1304

Pomar, José
Preludio y Fuga ritmicos 929

Ponchielli, Amilcare
(Il) Figliuol prodigo 1359
(La) Gioconda 852, 1350, 1359

Poulenc, Francis (Jean Marcel)
Banalités (excs) 199, 916, 1999
(Les) Biches 748, 7483
Chansons villageoises (excs) 199, 916, 1999
Concerto for Organ, Strings and Timpani in G minor . .
854
(La) Courte paille (excs) 199, 916, 1999
(La) Dame de Monte Carlo 1355
Exultate Deo 394, 434
Litanies à la vierge noire 394, 434
Mass in G 394, 434

Pastourelle. 1326
Pièces (excs). 1320, 1326
Poèmes 199, 916, 1999
Salve Regina 394, 434, 1345
Sonata for Cello and Piano. 364

Previn, André (George)
(A) Streetcar Named Desire (excs). 1352

Prokofiev, Sergey (Sergeyevich)
Alexander Nevsky – Op. 78 1314
Cantata for the 60th Birthday of Stalin, 'Zdravitsa' . 1314
Concerto for Piano and Orchestra No. 1 in D flat – Op.
10 . . . . .105, 661, 861
Concerto for Piano and Orchestra No. 2 in G minor
– Op. 16 862
Concerto for Piano and Orchestra No. 3 in C – Op. 26 .
105, 861, 912, 914, 1317
Concerto for Violin and Orchestra No. 1 in D – Op. 19 .
467, 632, 863, 1050
Concerto for Violin and Orchestra No. 2 in G minor
– Op. 63 . . . . .467, 862, 863, 1066
Lieutenant Kijé – Op. 60 814
The Love for Three Oranges. 403
(4) Pieces – Op. 4 (excs) 340
(10) Pieces – Op. 12 (excs) 562
(3) Pieces from Cinderella – Op. 95 (excs) 1333
(10) Pieces from Romeo and Juliet – Op. 75 (excs). . . 787
Sonata for Flute and Piano in D – Op. 94. . . . . 819, 1318
Sonata for Piano No. 2 in D minor – Op. 14 562
Sonata for Piano No. 3 in A minor – Op. 28 . . 787, 1338
Sonata for Piano No. 4 in C minor – Op. 29 866
Sonata for Piano No. 6 in A – Op. 82 . . . . .334, 562, 914,
1333, 1337
Sonata for Piano No. 7 in B flat – Op. 83 1333
Sonata for Violin and Piano in D – Op. 94a. . . 866
String Quartet No. 2 in F – Op. 92. 580
Symphony No. 5 in B flat – Op. 100 . . . . 864, 8643
The Tales of an old grandmother – Op. 31 (excs) . . 1304
Toccata in D minor – Op. 11. . . . .787, 1316, 1317, 1326
Visions fugitives – Op. 22. . . . . 562, 1333
Waltzes Suite (Schubert) 1003

Puccini, Giacomo (Antonia Domenico Michele Secondo Maria)
(La) Bohème, 'Bohemian Life' (excs). . .1350, 1351, 1355,
1357, 1359
Gianni Schicchi (excs). 1350, 1354
Madama Butterfly (excs). 421, 1350
Tosca (excs). 1350, 1351, 1355, 1359

Pullois, Jean
Flos de spina 827

Purcell, Henry
Beati omnes qui timent Dominum – Z131 1345
Bell Barr, 'I love and I must' – Z382 889
Bess of Bedlam, 'From silent shades' – Z370. 1184
Birthday Ode, 'Celebrate this festival' – Z321 (excs) . 889
Birthday Ode, 'Come ye sons of art away' – Z323 . . . 889
Birthday Ode, 'Love's goddess sure was blind' – Z331 226
The Blessed Virgin's Expostulation, 'Tell me, so – Z196.
889
Bonduca – Z574 (excs) 889
Chaconne – Three parts upon a ground – Z731. 889
(A) Choice Collection of Lessons (excs) 889
Close thine eyes and sleep secure – Z184 889
Dido and Aeneas – Z626 . . . . 889, 1329
(The History of) Dioclesian, or The Prophetess – Z627
(excs). 889, 1184
(The Comical History of) Don Quixote – Z578 (excs) 889
(An) Evening Hymn on a Ground, 'Now that the sun
hath veil'd his light' – Z193 1184
The Fairy Queen – Z629 (excs) 889, 1184
Fantasias – Z732-4 (excs) 889
The Fatal hour comes on apace – Z421. . . . . . 889, 1184
Hear my prayer, O Lord – Z15 1345
Here let my life 226
If ever I more riches did desire – Z544 (excs) 889
If music be the food of love – Z379a. 889, 1184
If music be the food of love – Z379b. 1184
The Indian Queen – Z630 (excs) 889, 1184
King Arthur – Z628 (excs) 889

Lord, what is man? – Z192. 1347
The Mock Marriage – Z605 (excs). 1184
My beloved spake – Z28. 889
Not all my torments can your pity move – Z400 889
Oedipus – Z583 (excs). 226, 889, 1184
Pausanias – Z585 (excs). 889, 1184
Rejoice in the Lord alway – Z49 889
Remember not, Lord, our offences – Z50. 1341
The Second Part of Musick's Hand-maid (excs) 889
Sleep, Adam, sleep and take thy rest – Z195. 1347
Sonata for Violin and Continuo in G minor – Z780 . 889
Sonatas in Four Parts – Z802-11 (excs). 889
St Cecilia's Day Ode, 'Hail, bright Cecilia' – Z328 (excs)
226, 889
St Cecilia's Day Ode, 'Welcome to all the pleasures'
– Z339 (excs) . . . .
Suite. 421
Tyrannic Love – Z613 (excs) 1184

Q

Quijano, Mansilla
Estilo 670
Estilo II 670
Estilo III 670

Quilter, Roger
Shakespeare Songs – Op. 6 (excs). 1349
Songs – Op. 3 (excs) 1349

R

Rachmaninov, Sergey (Vasil'yevich)
Concerto for Piano and Orchestra No. 3 . .896, 897, 963
Concerto for Piano and Orchestra No. 4 . .895, 897, 912
Daisies. 900, 901
Etudes-tableaux – Op. 39 (excs) 866
Etudes-tableaux – Op. 33 900
Etudes-tableaux – Op. 39 900
Etudes-tableaux – Op. 33 (excs) 1324
Etudes-tableaux – Op. 39 (excs) 1326, 1338
Fragments in A flat. 900
Fughetta in F. 900
Lilacs 340, 900, 901
Moments musicaux – Op. 16 (excs) 340, 900, 1324
Morceau de fantaisie in G minor 900
Morceaux de fantaisie – Op. 3 (excs) 900, 1327, 1332
Morceaux de salon – Op. 10. . . . . 900, 1327
Nocturnes 900
Oriental Sketch in B flat. 900
Pièce in D minor. 900
Pièces. 900
Polka de W. R. 900
Prelude in D minor. 900
Prelude in F. 900
Preludes (excs). . . 340, 900, 902, 1320, 1326, 1332, 1333,
1338
Sonata for Piano No. 1 in D minor – Op. 28 900
Sonata for Piano No. 2 in B flat minor – Op. 36 900, 901
Song without words in D minor 900
Songs – Op. 4 (excs) 840
Songs – Op. 21 (excs) 840
Songs – Op. 34 (excs) 625, 840
Suite No. 1, 'Fantaisie-tableaux' – Op. 5 1316
Trio élégiaque in G minor. 1171
Trio élégiaque in D minor – Op. 9 900
Variations on a theme of Chopin – Op. 22 . . . . . 900, 901
Variations on a theme of Corelli – Op. 42 . . . . . 900, 901
Vespers, 'All-Night Vigil' – Op. 37 (excs) 1342
Vocalise – Op. 34/14. 900

Raksin, David
Laura (excs). 455

Rameau, Jean-Philippe
Pièces de clavecin en concerts (excs) 1332

Rautavaara, Einojuhani
Sonnets (excs) 1353
Vigilia 1342

Ravel, (Joseph) Maurice
Boléro 360, 361
Concerto for Piano and Orchestra in G . . .455, 456, 862, 895, 897, 912, 914, 1317
Concerto for Piano (Left-Hand) and Orchestra . 912, 964
Daphnis et Chloé (excs) 360, 361, 1071
Fanfare pour 'L'éventail de Jeanne' 1314
Gaspard de la nuit. 334, 813, 912, 914, 915
Histoires naturelles (excs). 1355
Introduction and Allegro for flute, clarinet, harp 362, 445, 1316
Jeux d'eau 1316, 1333
Ma Mère l'oye, 'Mother Goose'. 421, 1317
Mélodies populaires grecques. 199
Menuet antique. 916
Miroirs (excs). 490, 915, 1321, 1333
Pavane pour une infante défunte 199, 434, 916
Piano Trio in A minor 327, 363
Pièce en forme de habanera 397
Shéhérazade. 199, 327, 916, 1999
Sonata for Violin and Cello 1338
Sonata for Violin and Piano in G (excs) 1330
Sonatine for Piano 914
String Quartet in F 362, 363, 913, 914
(Le) Tombeau de Couperin 916
Tzigane 181, 243, 428, 1332
Vocalise-étude en forme de habanera 1347

Rawsthorne, Alan
Bagatelles. 1327

Reger, (Johann Baptist Joseph) Max(imilian)
Chorale Fantasia on 'Freu' dich sehr, o meine Seel – Op. 30 260
Pieces – Op. 145 (excs) 1321

Respighi, Ottorino
(La) Boutique Fantasque. 928
E se un giorno tornasse 1347
(La) Pentola magica 928
Pieces (excs). 665, 666
Stornellatrice. 1347

Revueltas, Silvestre
Caminando 929
Este era un Rey 929
Homenaje a Federico Garcia Lorca 929
Hora de Junio 929
Little Pieces (excs). 929
Ocho x Radio 929
Planos 929
(El) Renacuajo Paseador 929
Sensemayá 929, 1313

Reynolds, Stephen
Poems in Homage to Delius 1327
Poems in Homage to Fauré 1327

Ribero, Bernardo de
Beata Mater. 762

Rihm, Wolfgang
Gesungene Zeit. 182

Rimbaud (Scanner), Robin
Dawnfire Mix 961

Rimsky-Korsakov, Nikolay Andreyevich
Capriccio espagnol – Op. 34 814
In spring – Op. 43 (excs). 1357
Sadko (excs). 641
Scheherazade – Op. 35 . . . . 814, 930
Songs – Op. 2 (excs) 1357
The Tale of Tsar Saltan (excs) 900, 1326

Ristori, Giovanni
Messa per il santissimo natale di Nostro Signore in D 574
O admirabile mysterium. 574

Rizza, Margaret
Ave generosa 1346

Rodgers, Richard
Carousel (excs) 1327
The King and I (excs) 1327

Rodrigo, Joaquín
Concierto de Aranjuez 932

Rogier, Philippe
Dominus regit me. 933
Heu mihi Domine. 933
Laboravi in gemitu meo 933
Missa Ego sum qui sum 933
Peccavi quid faciam tibi 933
Salva nos Domine 1344
Taedet animam meam 933
Vias tuas. 933

Rolli, Paolo
Solitario bosco ombroso 1153

Romero, Aldemaro
Suite for Strings No. 1 (excs) 1313

Rorem, Ned
War Scenes 1353

Rosenthal, Manuel
Chansons de monsieur Bleu (excs). 1355

Rossi, Lauro
Amelia, ovvero Otto anni di constanza (excs) 1348

Rossi, Salamone
The Songs of Solomon, `Hashrim Asher Lishlomo' (excs) 1342, 1344

Rossini, Gioachino (Antonio)
(Il) Barbiere di Siviglia, 'The Barber of Seville' (excs) 1247, 1350
(La) Cenerentola (excs). 1349
Guillaume Tell (excs) 852
Introduction, Theme and Variations in B flat. 355
Maometto Secondo (excs). 1354
Otello (or Il moro di Venezia) (excs) 1349, 1353
Péchés de vieillesse, Book 9 (excs) 766
Semiramide (excs). 1100, 1359
Tancredi (excs) 1247, 1354
(Il) viaggio a Reims (excs). 1353

Roussel, Albert (Charles Paul Marie)
Poèmes chinois – Op. 35 (excs) 1355

Rózsa, Miklós
Concerto for Violin and Orchestra – Op. 24 636
Tema con variazioni – Op. 29a 636

Rózycki, Ludomir
String Quartet in D minor – Op 49. 1142

Rubbra, (Charles) Edmund
Concerto for Viola and Orchestra in A – Op. 75 . . . 1288
Meditations on a Byzantine Hymn – Op 117 1288

Rubinstein, Anton (Grigor'yevich)
Concerto for Piano and Orchestra No. 4 954
Nero 1351

Ruggieri, Giovanni Maria
Gloria – RV ANH 23 1254

Rutter, John
Be thou my vision 1343
Hymn to the Creator of Light 1342, 1345
Loving Shepherd of Thy Sheep 1341
Traditional Songs 960

Rzewski, Frederic (Anthony)
Attica 961
Coming togheter. 961
Main Drag 961
(Les) Moutons de Panurge 961

S

Saariaho, Kaija
Instants 840
Nuits, Adieux. 1342

Sainte-Colombe,
Concerts à deux violes esgales (excs) 709, 1332
Gavotte de Tendre 709

(Les) Pleurs 709
Prelude (Tournus mss) 1332

Saint-Saëns, (Charles) Camille
Allegro appassionato in B minor – Op. 43 720
Ave Maria in B flat 1346
(Le) Carnaval des animaux, 'Carnival of the Animals'
(excs) 397, 720, 1320
Clair de lune 483
Concerto for Cello and Orchestra No. 1 in A minor
– Op. 33 . . . . .397, 644, 1322
Concerto for Cello and Orchestra No. 2 in D minor
– Op. 119 1334
Concerto for Piano and Orchestra No. 2 in G minor
– Op. 22 . . . . .444, 489, 963, 1334
Concerto for Piano and Orchestra No. 4 in C minor
– Op. 44 964
Concerto for Piano and Orchestra No. 5, 'Egyptian' in F
– Op. 103 444
Cyprès et Lauriers – Op. 156 1336
Dans les coins bleus 483
Danse macabre 1355
(El) Desdichado 483
Etudes – Op. 52 (excs) 964
Henry VIII (excs) 371
Introduction and Rondo capriccioso in A minor – Op. 28
1317
Pastorale 483
Rêverie 483
(Le) Rossignol 483
(Le) Rouet d'Omphale in A – Op. 31 1313
Samson et Dalila (excs) 1100, 1350
Scherzo – Op. 87 1316
(Le) Soir descend sur la colline 483
Symphony No. 3, 'Organ' in C minor – Op. 78 . 389, 854
Valse nonchalante in D flat – Op. 110 1328
Variations on a Theme of Beethoven – Op. 35 258
Viens! 483
Wedding Cake in A flat – Op. 76 720

Salonen, Esa-Pekka
Dichotomie 678
Preludes 678
Yta II 678

**Sammartini, Giuseppe (Francesco Gaspare Melchiorre
Baldassare)**
Concerto for Recorder and Strings in F 1244

Satie, Erik (Alfred Leslie)
(La) Diva de l'Empire 1350
Je te veux 1335, 1350
(3) Mélodies (excs) 1350, 1355
(L') Omnibus automobile 1350
Socrate 664
Tendrement 1350

Sauer, Emil von
Concerto for Piano and Orchestra No. 1 in E minor . 975
Savall, Jordi
Prélude pour M. Vauquelin 709
Say, Fazil
Sonata for Violin and Piano 1330

Scarlatti, (Giuseppe) Domenico
Sonatas for Keyboard Nos. 1-555 (excs) . . .112, 306, 490,
509, 1323, 1326
Stabat mater in C minor (excs) 1247

Scarlatti, (Pietro) Alessandro (Gaspare)
Magnificat à 5 voci (excs) 1247
Non sò qual più m'ingombra 1356
O di Betlemme altera povertà 1356
(Il) Pompeo (excs) 1354
(Le) Violette 1347

Scharwenka, (Franz) Xaver
Concerto for Piano and Orchestra No. 1 in B flat minor
– Op. 32 954
Concerto for Piano and Orchestra No. 4 in F minor – Op.
82 975

Schimmelpfennig, Georg
Madrigale à voce sola (excs) 1356

Schmelzer, Andreas Anton
Sonata "Victory of the Christians over the Turks" in A
minor 210

Schmelzer, Johann Heinrich
Sonatae unarum fidium 976

Schmitt, Florent
In memoriam Gabriel Fauré – Op. 72 (excs) 434

Schnittke, Alfred
Concerto Grosso No. 6 978
Dead Souls suite 1314
Piano Quintet 978
Piano Trio 1061
Sonata for Violin and Chamber Orchestra 978

Schoenberg, Arnold (Franz Walther)
Cabaret Songs (excs) 1350
Concerto for Piano and Orchestra – Op. 42 981
Concerto for Violin and Orchestra – Op. 36 981
Gurrelieder (excs) 198, 199
Klavierstück – Op. 33a 183
Klavierstück – Op. 33b 183
Klavierstücke – Op. 11 . . . . 183, 981
Klavierstücke – Op. 23 183
Klavierstücke – Op. 19 . . . . 183, 981
Pierrot lunaire – Op. 21 1032
Suite – Op. 25 183
Verklärte Nacht – Op. 4 . . . . 983, 992, 993

Scholefield, Clement Cotterill
The Day thou gavest, Lord, is ended 1343

Schreker, Franz
Chamber Symphony 323
Intermezzo – Op. 8 988
Scherzo 988

Schubert, Franz (Peter)
Atys – D585 1008
(Der) Blinde Knabe – D833 1348
Deutsche Tänze – D820 . . . . 1298, 1299
Divertissement – D823 (excs) 786
Einsamkeit – D620 1008
Erlkönig – D328 1003
Fantasie in F minor – D940 . . . . 771, 786
Fantasy, 'Wandererfantasie' in C – D760 1002
(Der) Fluss – D693 1008
(Die) Gebüsche – D646 1008
(Die) Götter Griechenlands – D677 1008
Im Freien – D880 1008
Impromptus (excs) 490, 1000, 1319, 1320, 1329, 1332
Klavierstücke – D946 . . . . 1322, 1329
Litanei auf das Fest Allerseelen – D343 1321
Mass No. 6 in E flat – D950 . . . . 1206, 1209
Overture in the Italian style in D – D590 1003
Quintet for Piano and Strings, 'Trout' in A – D667. .254,
993, 994
Rondo in A – D438 . . . . 290, 732
Rosamunde, Fürstin von Zypern – D797 (excs) . . . 641
(Die) Schöne Müllerin – D795 (excs) . . . 900, 1003, 1347
Schwanengesang, 'Swan Song' – D957 . . . . 165, 1014
Sehnsucht – D516 1008
Sonata for Arpeggione and Piano in A minor – D821 463,
997
Sonata for Piano No. 1 in E – D157 999
Sonata for Piano No. 12 in F minor – D625 1329
Sonata for Piano No. 18 in G – D894 999
Sonata for Piano No. 20 in A – D959 1320
Sonata for Piano No. 21 in B flat – D960 1000, 1323
String Quartet No. 12, 'Quartettsatz' in C minor – D703
362
String Quintet in C – D956 . . . . 983, 992, 993, 8550
Symphony No. 5 in B flat – D485 141
Symphony No. 6 in C – D589 990
Symphony No. 8, 'Unfinished' in B minor – D759 . .990,
1071
Symphony No. 9, 'Great' in C – D944 991
Totengräberweise – D869 1348
Variations on "Trockne Blumen" D802 1318

Winterreise – D911 (excs) 1003

Schulhoff, Ervín
String Quartet No. 1 . . . . 613, 1017

Schuman, William (Howard)
Concerto for Violin and Orchestra 1017
In Praise of Shahn. 99
Mail Order Madrigals. 102
New England Triptych. 1017
Perceptions 102
To thee Old Cause 99

Schumann, Clara (Josephine)
Lieder – Op. 13 (excs). 1031
Lieder aus Jucunde – Op. 23 1034
Loreley 1031
Romances – Op. 22 252
Volkslied 1031

Schumann, Robert (Alexander)
Adagio and Allegro in A flat – Op. 70 . . . . 997, 1019
Arabeske in C – Op. 18. . . . . 1027, 1326
Belsatzar – Op. 57. 1031
Blumenstück in D flat – Op. 19 1326
Carnaval – Op. 9. . . . . 260, 1320, 1331, 1334
Concerto for Cello and Orchestra in A minor – Op. 129.
243, 250, 397, 398, 1019, 1322
Concerto for Piano and Orchestra in A minor – Op. 54 .
126, 398, 489, 490, 491, 1317
Concerto for Violin and Orchestra in A minor – Op. 129
241
Concerto for Violin and Orchestra in D minor – Op.
posth. 241, 243, 1020
Davidsbündlertänze – Op. 6. 1027
Dichterliebe – Op. 48. . . . . 1031, 1032, 1347
Etudes symphoniques, 'Symphonic Studies' – Op. 13 902
Fantasie in C – Op. 17 1002
Fantasie in C – Op. 131 1332
Fantasiestücke – Op. 48 . . . . 997, 1019
Fantasiestücke – Op. 12 . . . . 914, 1027, 1326, 1332, 1334
Faschingsschwank aus Wien – Op. 26 . . . . 1315, 1331
Frauenliebe und -leben – Op. 42 1348
Gedichte – Op. 30 (excs) 1348
Gedichte und Requiem – Op. 90 (excs) 1348
Gesänge – Op. 142 (excs) 1031
Kinderszenen – Op. 15 . . . . 340, 1317, 1326
Kreisleriana – Op. 16 . . . . 915, 1027
Lieder – Op. 40. 1034
Lieder – Op. 33 (excs) 1031
Lieder und Gesänge – Op. 27 (excs) 1031
Liederkreis – Op. 24. 585
Märchenbilder – Op. 113 997
Mass in C minor – Op. 147 1019
Myrthen – Op. 25 (excs) 1031, 1347
Papillons – Op. 2. 1027
Piano Trio No. 1 in D minor – Op. 63 1023
Presto passionato in G minor 1326
Quintet for Piano and Strings in E flat – Op. 44 253
Romanzen – Op. 94 252
Romanzen – Op. 28 (excs) 490, 491
Romanzen und Balladen II – Op. 49 (excs) 1031
Romanzen und Balladen III – Op. 53 (excs) 1031
Romanzen und Balladen IV – Op. 64 (excs) 1031
Sonata for Piano No. 2 in G minor – Op. 22 . . . 654, 664,
665
Sonata for Piano No. 3 in F minor – Op. 14. 1326
Sonata for Violin and Piano No. 2 in D minor – Op. 121
1316, 1317
Spanische Liebeslieder – Op. 138 1034
Spanisches Liederspiel – Op. 74. . . . . 1034, 1320
String Quartet No. 1 in A minor – Op. 41/1 492
String Quartet No. 3 in A – Op. 41/3 557
Stücke im Volkston – Op. 102 . . . . 997, 1019
Studies – Op. 56 (excs) 1326
Symphony No. 1, 'Spring' in B flat – Op. 38 246
Toccata in C – Op. 7 1326
Waldszenen – Op. 82 (excs) 490, 491, 1027

Schürer, Johann Georg
Christus natus est nobis 574
Jesu redemptor omnium. 574

Schütz, Heinrich
Kleiner geistlichen Concerten, Erster Theil – SWV282-
305 (Op. 8) 1356
Selig sind die Toten 1341

Scott, Cyril (Meir)
Ballade in D minor – W38 1040
Chimes – Op 40/3 (W63). 1040
Dances – Op. 22 1040
Dances – W88. 1040
Egypt: Five Impressions – W105 1040
(An) English Waltz – Op 15 (W109) 1040
Handelian Rhapsody – Op 17 (W134). 487
Impressions from the Jungle Book – W150, W151 . . . 1040
Impromptu (A Mountain Brook) – Op 41 (W152) . . 1040
Inclination à la Danse – W157. 1040
Karma Suite – W168 1040
Pieces – Op 47 (excs) 641, 1040, 1315
Prelude – Op 37 bis (W261) 1040
Russian Fair – W303 1040
Studies for Slow Movements – W352 1040
Symphonic Dances 486
Theme and Variations – W373 1040

Scriabin, Alexander
Concerto for Piano and Orchestra 1040, 1160
Impromptus – Op. 14 (excs) 1315
Mazurkas – Op. 40 (excs) 1330
Mazurkas – Op. 25 (excs) 1330
Pieces – Op. 59 (excs) 1042
Pieces – Op. 49 (excs) 1042
Pieces – Op. 45 (excs) 1042
Pieces – Op. 56 (excs) 1042
Pieces – Op. 51 (excs) 1042
Pieces for the left hand – Op. 9 (excs) 1338
(Le) Poème de l'extase – Op. 54. . . . . 1127, 1128
Poème tragique in B flat – Op. 34 1324
Poèmes – Op. 71 1324
Poèmes – Op. 32 (excs) 1330
Preludes – Op. 27 1042
Preludes – Op. 67 1042
Preludes – Op. 35 1042
Preludes – Op. 22 1042
Preludes – Op. 31 1042
Preludes – Op. 33 1042
Preludes – Op. 37 1042
Preludes – Op. 39 1042
Preludes – Op. 48 1042
Preludes – Op. 74 1042
Preludes – Op. 15 (excs) 1330
Sonata for Piano No. 2, 'Sonata-fantasy' 1337
Sonata for Piano No. 5 in F sharp – Op. 53 1337
Sonata for Piano No. 9, 'Black Mass' in F – Op. 68 . . 866
Vers la flamme – Op. 72 1330

Scriabin, Julian
Prelude – Op. 3/2 1042
Prelude in B – Op. 3/1 1042
Prelude in C – Op. 2. 1042
Prelude in D flat 1042

Seger, Josef
Praeludium in C minor 574

Sheppard, John
Audivi vocem de caelo 1341
Beati omnes. 1047
Eterne rex altissime 1047
Gaude, gaude, gaude Maria virgo 1149
Gaudete caelicole omnes 1047
In manus tuas I 1149, 1341
In pace in idipsum. 1149
Laudate pueri Dominium 1047
Laudem dicite Deo. 1149
Libera nos, salva nos I 1345, 1346
O God be merciful unto us, and bless us 1340
Second Service (excs) 1346
Submit yourselves one to another 1340
Verbum caro factum est 1149

Shostakovich, Dmitry (Dmitriyevich)
Concerto for Piano, Trumpet and Strings 661
Concerto for Violin and Orchestra No. 1 . . . 1050, 1051
Fantastic Dances – Op. 5 1335
The Golden Age – Op. 22 (excs) 1315
Piano Trio No. 1 in C minor – Op. 8 . . . . 1061, 1316
Piano Trio No. 2 in E minor – Op. 67 . . . . . . 900, 1061
Preludes and Fugues – Op. 87 (excs) 334, 963, 1062
Sonata for Violin and Piano – Op. 134 446
String Quartet No. 3 in F – Op. 73 557
String Quartet No. 5 in B flat – Op. 92 1060
String Quartet No. 8 in C minor – Op. 110 . . 1149, 1339
String Quartet No. 15 in E flat minor – Op. 144 978
Symphony No. 1 in F minor – Op. 10 1052
Symphony No. 4 in C minor – Op. 43 1052
Symphony No. 6 in B minor – Op. 54 1052
Symphony No. 8 in C minor – Op. 65 1055
Waltzes (excs) 237

Sibelius, Jean (Julius Christian)
Concerto for Violin and Orchestra in D minor – Op. 47.
632, 659, 819, 981, 1066, 1067, 1159, 1325
Finlandia – Op. 26 491
Legends, 'Lemminkäinen Suite' – Op. 22 (excs) 491
Pieces – Op. 76 (excs) 1315
Symphony No. 3 in C – Op. 52 821
Symphony No. 7 in C – Op. 105 1071
Valse triste – Op. 44/1 . . . . 491, 1335

Smetana, Bedrich
Am Seegestade (Concert Study) in G sharp minor – B119
(Op. 17) 1315
Czech Dances – T112 (excs) 1322
From the homeland – T128 (excs) 290
Má vlast (excs) 400
Piano Trio in G minor – B104 (Op. 15) 1171

Somervell, Arthur
Concerto for Violin and Orchestra in G 344
To Lucasta, on going to the Wars 1349

Sorabji, Kaikhosru Shapurji
Pastiche on Hindu Song from Rimsky-Korsakov's
'Sadko' 1324

Sørensen, Bent
Lullabies 1316
Shadows of Silence 1316

Sousa, John Philip
Semper Fidelis 347
The Stars and Stripes Forever 347

Spinacino, Francesco
Adieu mes amours 623

Spohr, Louis
Concerto for Violin and Orchestra No. 8, 'in modo in A
minor – Op. 47 835

Stanford, Charles Villiers
(La) Belle Dame sans merci 1349
Irish Dances – Op. 89 (excs) 487
Motets – Op. 38 (excs) 1341
Songs of Old Ireland (excs) 1349

Sting
Alone with My Thoughts this Evening 1329

Stokowski, Leopold
Traditional Slavic Christmas Music 812

Stone, Robert
The Lord's Prayer 1341

Strauss, Eduard
Ohne Aufenthalt, 'Non-Stop' – Op. 112 1098

Strauss, Johann (Baptist) I
Beliebte Annen – Op. 137 1099
Chinese Galop – Op. 20 1098
Radetzky March – Op. 228 1099

Strauss, Johann (Baptist) II
An der schönen, blauen Donau, 'Blue Danube' – Op. 314
1099

Carnevals-Botschafter, 'Carnival's ambassador' – Op. 270
1099
Egyptischer Marsch, 'Egyptian March' – Op. 335 . . 1098
Elisen, 'Elise' – Op. 151 1099
(Die) Fledermaus, 'The Bat' (excs) 1099, 1100, 1311
Freikugeln, 'Magic bullets' – Op. 326 1098
Geisselhiebe, 'Whiplashes' – Op. 60 1098
Jubelfest-Marsch, 'Joyous Festival March' – Op. 396 1098
Kaiser, 'Emperor' – Op. 437 . . . . 1098, 1311
Klipp Klapp – Op. 466 1098
Künstler-Quadrille, 'Artist's Quadrille' – Op. 71 . . . 1098
Künstlerleben, 'Artist's Life' – Op. 316 1099
Perpetuum mobile, 'Perpetual Motion' – Op. 257 . . 1098,
1099, 1311
Tik-Tak (on motives from 'Die Fledermaus') – Op. 365 .
1099
Tritsch-Tratsch – Op. 214 . . . . 1098, 1311
Wein, Weib und Gesang, 'Wine, Woman and Song'
– Op. 333 1098
Wiener Blut, "Vienna Blood" – Op. 354 1099
Zivio! – Op. 456 1099

Strauss, Josef
Aquarellen-Walzer, 'Water colours Waltz' – Op. 258 . . .
1099
Arm in Arm – Op. 215 1099
Im Fluge, 'In flight' – Op. 230 1099
Jokey, 'Jockey' – Op. 278 1098
(Die) Libelle, 'The Dragonfly' – Op. 204 1099
Plappermäulchen, 'Chatterboxes' – Op. 245 . . 1098, 1099
(Die) Schwätzerin, 'The Gossip' – Op. 144 1099
Sphären-Klänge, 'Music of the Spheres' – Op. 235 . 1098
Vorwärts!, 'Forward!' – Op. 127 1099

Strauss, Richard (Georg)
Also sprach Zarathustra, 'Thus spake Zarathustra' . . 590
Capriccio – Op. 85 (excs) 444, 916
Concerto for Horn and Orchestra No. 1 1102
Concerto for Horn and Orchestra No. 2 1102
Concerto for Oboe and Orchestra in D – AV144 767
Don Quixote – Op. 35 . . . . 414, 415, 1105
(Ein) Heldenleben, '(A) Hero's Life' – Op. 40 1105
Vier Letzte Lieder, '(4) Last Songs' – AV150 (Op. posth)
916, 1110, 1111
Lieder – Op. 27 (excs) 406, 1348, 1357
Lieder – Op. 39 (excs) 1348
Lieder – Op. 41 (excs) 1357
Lieder – Op. 17 (excs) 1315
Romanze in F – AV75 406
(Der) Rosenkavalier – Av112 1311
Sonata for Cello and Piano in F – Op. 6 406
Sonata for Violin and Piano in E flat – Op. 18 1108

Stravinsky, Igor (Fyodorovich)
Ave Maria 1343
Concertino 362
Concerto for Violin and Orchestra in D 181
Concerto in D 592
Divertimento 1108
Divertimento from 'La Biaser de la Fée' 1170
Double Canon 362
Ebony Concerto 455
Etudes – Op. 7 (excs) 340
The Firebird (excs) 290
(Les) Noces, 'The Wedding' 1131
Pastorale 1347
Perséphone 1132
Petrushka 1131, 1326, 1333, 1337, 1338
Pieces 362
The Rake's Progress 102, 1352
The Rite of Spring, '(Le) sacre du printemps' . . . 106, 864,
1127, 1128, 8643
Suite italienne 1328
Tango 1335

Stucky, Steven
Four Album Leaves 678
Little Variations for David 678

Suk, Josef
Ballade in D minor – Op. 3/1 256

Fantastické Scherzo – Op. 25 403
Fantasy in G minor – Op. 24 400
Pieces – Op. 17 243
Serenade in A – Op. 3/2 256
Serenade in E flat – Op. 6 403

Susato, Tielman
Bergeret sans roche (Reprise à 4) 623
Pavan Mille regretz (excs). 623

Swann, Donald
Ill wind. 766

Swayne, Giles (Oliver Cairnes)
Magnificat – Op. 33 1343

Sweelinck, Jan Pieterszoon
Pseaumes des David_Premier livre (excs) 1344
Pseaumes des David_Troisième livre (excs). 1344

Szymanowski, Karol (Maciej)
Myths – Op. 30 . . . . 1328, 1332
Nocturne and Tarantella – Op. 28 (excs) 290
Sonata for Violin and Piano in D minor – Op. 9 866
String Quartet No. 1 in C – Op. 37 1142
String Quartet No. 2 – Op. 56 1142

T

Takemitsu, Toru
Nostalghia 978

Tallis, Thomas
Audivi vocem de caelo 1047
Christ rising again. 1340
Ecce tempus idoneum. 1149
Gaude gloriosa Dei mater. 1149
If ye love me 1345
In jejunio et fletu. 1047
In Nomine a 4 No. 1 1344
In Nomine a 4 No. 2 1344
Lamentations of Jeremiah. 1148
Loquebantur variis linguis 1149
Not every one that saith unto Me 1340
O nata lux de lumine. 1149, 1341, 1342, 1345
Salvator Mundi 1047
Salvator mundi Domine...Adesto nunc proprius. . . . 1345
Sing and glorify heaven's high majesty 1149
Solfaing Song a 5 1344
Spem in alium 1149, 1339
Te Deum 1149
Te lucis ante terminum I 1047, 1342
Videte miraculum 1346
With all our hearts 1340

Taneyev, Sergey Ivanovich
Suite de concert – Op. 28 27

Tansman, Alexandre
Sonatina for Bassoon and Piano 1323

Tartini, Giuseppe
Piccole sonate (excs) 1153
Solitario bosco ombroso 1153
Sonata for Violin and Continuo, 'Devil's Trill' 1153, 1247
Sonatas for Violin (excs) 1153

Tavener, John (Kenneth)
Dhyana 1154
Funeral Ikos. 1341
Hymn for the Dormition of the Mother of God . . . 1341
Hymns to the Mother of God 1341, 1343
Lalishri. 1154
The Lamb, 'Little Lamb, who made thee?'. 1345
The Myrrh-Bearer 628
The Protecting Veil 1154
Song for Athene 1154
Thrinos 1154

Taverner, John
Christe Jesu, pastor bone 1341
Dum transisset Sabbatum I. 1156
Mater Christi sanctissima 1156
Missa Gloria tibi Trinitas 1156
O Wilhelme, pastor bone 1156

Taylor, (Canon) Cyril V.
Glorious things of Thee are spoken. 1343

Tchaikovsky, Pyotr Il'yich
1812 – Op. 49 1167
Andante cantabile – Op. 11 . . . . 414, 415
Capriccio Italien – Op. 45 1167
Concerto for Piano and Orchestra No. 1 – Op. 23. . . . .
729, 896, 897, 1040, 1160
Concerto for Violin and Orchestra in D – Op. 35 . . . . . .
132, 241, 243, 816, 1067, 1159, 1325
Dumka (Russian rustic scene) – Op. 59. 1327
Eugene Onegin (excs). 1351
Iolanta (excs) 1357
Marche slave, 'Slavonic March' – Op. 31 814
Morceaux – Op. 10 (excs). 812, 1327
Morceaux – Op. 51 (excs) 1335
(18) Morceaux – Op. 72 (excs) 1171
Nocturne in D minor – Op. 19/4. . . . . 414, 415
The Nutcracker – Op. 71a (excs). 1311, 1337
Pezzo capriccioso in B minor – Op. 62 397, 398, 414, 415
Piano Trio in A minor – Op. 50 1171
Sacred Pieces (excs). 1341
The Seasons – Op. 37b (excs). 866, 901, 1131
The Sleeping Beauty – Op. 66 (excs). 1311
Songs – Op. 73 (excs) 812
Songs – Op. 16 (excs) 900, 1320
Songs – Op. 38 (excs) 1353
Songs – Op. 25 (excs) 1353
Songs – Op. 47 (excs) 1353
Songs – Op. 60 (excs) 1353
Souvenir de Florence – Op. 70. 1170
Souvenir d'un lieu cher – Op. 42 (excs). . . 290, 862, 1328
String Quartet No. 1 in D – Op. 11 (excs) 641
Suite No. 1 – Op. 43 (excs) 814
Suite No. 3 in G – Op. 55 1170
Swan Lake – Op. 20 1327
Symphony No. 4 in F minor – Op. 36. 811
Valse-scherzo in C – Op. 34. 1328
Variations on a Rococo Theme in A – Op. 33 . . . .
397, 414, 415
Vesper Service – Op. 52 1342

Telemann, Georg Philipp
Musique de table, 'Tafelmusik' (excs) 526
Suite in A minor – TWV55: a 2. 1244

Terzi, Giovanni Antonio
Intavolatura di liutto, libro primo (excs) 709

Thalben-Ball, George (Thomas)
Elegy 1321

Theofanidis, Christopher
Rainbow Body. 347

Thomas, (Charles Louis) Ambroise
Hamlet (excs). 1359

Thompson, Randall
The Testament of Freedom 347

Thomson, Virgil
Ladies 350
Portraits. 350
Portraits 350

Tippett, Michael (Kemp)
Boyhood's End 1184
Concerto for Double String Orchestra 182
The Heart's Assurance 1184
Music. 1184
Songs for Achilles 1184
Songs for Ariel 1184

Tjeknavorian, Loris
Ballet fantastique – Op. 2 632

Toldrá, Eduardo
Canciones (excs) 1347

Tomkins, Thomas
Be strong and of a good courage 1149
Know you not 1149
O God, the heathen are come 1149
When David heard 1341, 1345

Torelli, Giuseppe
Concerto for 2 Trumpets and Strings in D 549

Torrentes, Andrés de
Asperges Me 762

Tosti, (Francesco) Paolo
'A Vucchella 1354
Addio 1350

Tournemire, Charles (Arnould)
Suite évocatrice – Op. 74 1188

Tovey, Donald Francis
Concerto for Piano and Orchestra in A – Op. 15 682

Traditional,
Afton water 960
All people that on earth do dwell 1343
Benedicamus Domino 1294
Bethlehem Down 1294
The bold grenadier 960
Braint 723
Celtic Dance 1330
(A) Cornish Christmas Carol 1294
The cuckoo 960
The Death of Queen Jane 1349
Deep River 1341
Esik esö majd lesz mezö 1347
I know where I'm going 960
I Once Loved a Lass 1330
Il est né, le divin Enfant 436
Jeunes fillettes 709
Jig 1330
The Keel Row 960
The Lark in the clear air 960
Lekaszálták már a rétet 1347
The Little Turtle Dove 1349
The Londonderry air 641, 1327
The Miller of the Dee 960
Morning has broken 1343
No me quieras tanto! 1352
O can ye sew cushions? 960
O come, o come Emmanuel, 'Veni, veni Emmanuel' 1345
Piros piros piros 1347
Russian Village Wedding Songs (excs) 1131
Sag' mir immer wieder 1347
Schlof sche, mein Vögele 1357
She's like the swallow 960
The Sprig of Thyme 960
Steal away to Jesus 1341
There is no rose of such virtue 1343
Waltzing Matilda 1328
Willow song 960
The Willow Tree 960

Trénet, Charles
Coin de rue 1315

Turina, Joaquín
Poema en forma de canciones – Op. 19 (excs) 1347
Saeta en forme de Salve a la Virgen de la Esperanz – Op.
60 1347
Tríptico – Op. 45 (excs) 1347

Tüür, Erkki-Sven
Meditatio 1342

Tye, Christopher
Blessed are all they that fear the Lord 1340
In pace in idipsum 1047
Missa Sine Nomine 1047
Omnes gentes, plaudite 1047, 1346

U

Ufki (Wojsiech Bobowski), Ali
Psalm 2 1344
Psalm 6 1344

V

Vallier, John
Toccatina 340

Valverde, Joaquín
Clavelitos 1347

Various, (composers)
(A) Little Organ Book in Memory of Sir Hubert Parr 841

Vasks, Peteris
Concerto for Violin and String Orchestra, `Distant
Light' 1196
Ziles zina 302

Vaughan Williams, Ralph
Concerto for Piano and Orchestra in C 1197
English Folksongs 960
The English Hymnal (excs) 1343
Fantasia on a Theme by Thomas Tallis 421, 590
Fantasia on 'Greensleeves' 421
The House of Life (excs) 1349
Job 1292
The Lark ascending 415, 1154, 1289
Linden Lea 1349
Mass in G minor 596, 1201
O vos omnes 1341
Songs of Travel 1203
Symphony No. 2, '(A) London Symphony' 1198
Symphony No. 5 in D 119
Te Deum in G 596, 1201

Verdelot, Philippe
Si bona suscepimus 762

Verdi, Giuseppe (Fortunino Francesco)
Aida (excs) 1350
Don Carlo (excs) 1355, 1359
Ernani (excs) 852
(La) forza del destino, 'The force of destiny' (excs) . . 852
(I) Lombardi alla prima crociata (excs) 852, 1359
Luisa Miller (excs) 1359
Macbeth (excs) 1351, 1359
Messa da Requiem 1206, 1209
Otello (excs) 1359
Rigoletto (excs) 1351, 1355, 1357, 1359
Romanze (excs) 1354
Simon Boccanegra (excs) 1359
Stornello 1354
(La) traviata (excs) 1100, 1350, 1355, 1359
(Il) trovatore (excs) 1350, 1351
(I) Vespri siciliani, 'The Sicilian Vespers' (excs) 1206,
1209

Victoria, Tomás Luis de
O lux et decus Hispaniae 1344
O quam gloriosum 1341
O vos omnes, qui transitis per viam 1344
Salve regina 1345

Vierne, Louis
Symphony No. 3 in F sharp minor – Op. 28 1188

Vieuxtemps, Henry
Concerto for Violin and Orchestra No. 5 in A minor – Op.
37 . . . . 290, 645, 732

Villa-Lobos, Heitor
Bachianas brasileiras No. 2 (excs) 1331
Bachianas brasileiras No. 5 . . . . 319, 1331
Bachianas Brasileiras 1331
Chôros No. 2 237
Concerto for Guitar and Orchestra 932
Prole do bebê, Book I (excs) 1334
Song of the Black Swan 1331
Valsa da dor 1335

Vinci, Leonardo
Adónde Fugitivo 818
Cuando infeliz destino 818
Erighetta e Don Chilone 818
Sinfonia per Archi 818
Triste, ausente, en esta selva 818

Vinders, Jheronimus
Lamentatio super morte Josquin des Pres 623

Vitali, Tomaso Antonio

Ciacona in G minor 1153

Vivaldi, Antonio (Lucio)
Concerti for Violin and Strings, '(Il) cimento
dell'armonia e dell'inventione' – Op. 8 (excs) 1247
Concerti grossi, '(L')estro armonico' – Op. 3 (excs) . . . . .
1247
Concerto for Flute/Recorder and Strings in C minor
– RV441 1244
Concerto for Piccolo and Strings in C – RV444 1244
Concerto for Sopranino Recorder and Strings – RV443 .
1244
Gloria in D – RV589 . . . . 87, 1254
Nisi Dominus in A ma – RV803 1254
(L')Olimpiade – RV725 (excs) 1247
Ostro picta – RV642 . . . . 87, 1254
(La) Senna Festeggiante – RV693 (excs) 1247

Vives, Amadeo
Canciones epigramáticas (excs) 1347
(La) Presumida 1347

W

Wagner, (Wilhelm) Richard
Lohengrin (excs) 292
(Die) Meistersinger von Nürnberg, 'The Mastersingers'
(excs) 192, 421, 1355
(Der) Ring des Nibelungen: Part 3, 'Siegfried' (excs) . 247
(Der) Ring des Nibelungen: Part 4, 'Götterdämmerung'
(excs) 1111
Siegfried Idyll 247
Tristan und Isolde (excs) 706, 1110, 1111, 1332
Wesendonck Lieder 706, 1110

Walton, William (Turner)
Belshazzar's Feast 1292
Concerto for Cello and Orchestra 414, 415, 1288
Concerto for Viola and Orchestra in A minor . 270, 1288,
1289
Concerto for Violin and Orchestra in B minor . . 99, 1289,
1322
Crown Imperial 590, 1321
Façade (excs) 223, 278, 1291
Façade 2 1291
Façade 3 (excs) 1291
(A) Litany, 'Drop, drop slow tears' 1341
Passacaglia 1288
Sonata for strings 150, 440
Sonata for Violin and Piano 423
String Quartet in A minor 580

Ward, John
Fantasias a 6 (excs) 1358

Warlock, Peter
All the flowers of the Spring 1294
As dew in Aprylle 1294
(A) Cornish Carol (Kanow Kernow) 1294
Corpus Christi 1294
Cradle Song 1349
The full heart 1294
I saw a fair maiden 1294
Jillian of Berry 1349
Rest, sweet nymphs 1349
The rich cavalcade 1294

Waxman, Franz
Carmen Fantasia 636, 1328

Weber, Carl Maria (Friedrich Ernst) von
Concertino for Clarinet and Orchestra in E flat – J109
(Op. 26) 255, 355
(Der) Freischütz – J277 (excs) 1355
Invitation to the Dance (Aufforderung zum Tanze) in D
flat – J260 (Op. 65) 1321, 1328
Sonata for Piano No. 1 in C – J138 (Op. 24) (excs) . . 340
Sonatas – J99-104 641

Webern, Anton (Friedrich Wilhelm von)
(Das) Augenlicht – Op. 26 1298
Bagatelles – Op. 9 1298

Canons on Latin texts – Op. 16 1298
Cantata No. 1 – Op. 29 1298
Cantata No. 2 – Op. 31 1298
Concerto for Nine Instruments – Op. 24 1298
Entflieht auf leichten Kähnen I – Op. 2 1298
Geistliche Lieder – Op. 15 1298
Im Sommerwind 1299
Lieder – Op. 19 1298
Lieder – Op. 8 1298
Lieder – Op. 18 1298
Lieder – Op. 25 1298
Lieder – Op. 12 1298
Lieder – Op. 13 1298
Lieder – Op. 4 1298
Lieder – Op. 14 1298
Lieder aus 'Der siebente Ring' – Op. 3 1298
Lieder aus 'Viae inviae' 1298
Little Pieces – Op. 11 1298
Movements – Op. 5 1298
Passacaglia – Op. 1 . . . . 1298, 1299
Pieces – Op. 7 1298
Pieces – Op. 10 1298
Pieces – Op. 5 . . . . 1298, 1299
Pieces – Op. 6 . . . . 1298, 1299
Quartet – Op. 22 1298
String Quartet 362
String Quartet – Op. 28 1298
String Quartet 1299
String Trio – Op.20 1298
Symphony – Op. 21 1298
Traditional Rhymes – Op. 17 1298
Variations – Op. 27 . . . . 183, 981, 1298
Variations – Op. 30 1298
Variations – Op. 27 . . . . 1315, 1333

Weelkes, Thomas
Hosanna to the Son of David 1345

Weill, Kurt (Julian)
Concerto for Violin and Wind Orchestra – Op. 12 . . . . .
978, 1196
(Der) Dreigroschenoper, 'The Threepenny Opera' (excs)
188
Happy End (excs) 188
Lost in the Stars (excs) 1351
Marie Galante (excs) 188
One Touch of Venus (excs) 1351
String Quartet – Op. 8 1017

Weissenberg, Alexis
Arrangements of Song sung by Charles Trenet 1325
Sonate en état de jazz 1325

Weldon, John
Stop, O ye waves 1356

Wesley, Samuel
Short Pieces with a Voluntary added (excs) . . . 1321, 1326

Wesley, Samuel Sebastian
Thou wilt keep him in perfect peace 212

White, Robert
Exaudiat te Dominus 1346
Lamentations (6vv) 1148

Whyte, Robert
Christe, qùi lux es et dies 1342

Widor, Charles-Marie(-Jean-Albert)
Symphony No. 9, 'Gothic' in C minor – Op. 70 . . . 1188

Wieniawski, Henryk
Concerto for Violin and Orchestra No. 1 in F sharp
minor – Op. 14 1304
Concerto for Violin and Orchestra No. 2 in D minor
– Op. 22 (excs) 241, 290, 1020
Etudes-Caprices – Op. 18 (excs) 641
Légende – Op. 17 1020
Polonaise No. 1 in D – Op. 4 290

Wilby, Philip
Echo Carol 1345

Wilder, Philip van
Fantasia con e senza pause 1342

Wilson, John
Horace's Odes (excs). 1356

Wolf, Hugo (Filipp Jakob)
Italian Serenade. 362
Spanisches Liederbuch, 'Spanish Songbook' (excs). . 1348

Wolseley, Charles
Green-eyed Dragon 1353

Wood, Charles
Hail, gladdening light. 1341, 1342

Wood, Haydn
Concerto for Piano and Orchestra in D minor. 583

Y

Ysaÿe, Eugène (Auguste)
Rêve d'enfant – Op. 14. 445
Sonata for Cello – Op. 28. 445
Sonatas for Solo Violin – Op. 27 (excs). 584

Z

Zamboni, Giovanni
Sonatas for Lute – Op. 1 (excs) 1329

INDEX TO ARTISTS

A

A Sei Voci 19, 621, 623
Aalborg Symphony Orchestra. 586, 587, 1158
Aarhus Chamber Choir. 375
Aarhus Symphony Orchestra 297, 375, 587
Aarhus University Choir. 375
Abbado, Claudio cond . .126, 131, 135, 183, 185, 187, 218,
219, 243, 245, 248, 250, 261, 361, 368, 404, 467, 580,
656, 661, 689, 690, 699, 701, 703, 733, 734, 772, 808,
814, 815, 816, 863, 865, 912, 913, 914, 941, 942, 990,
1028, 1118, 1159, 1160, 1207, 1208, 1209, 1210, 1215,
1224, 1232, 1311, 5614
Abbado, Roberto cond 381, 1354
Abdrazakov, Ildar bass-bar 937
Abel, Yves cond 722
Abendroth, Hermann cond 249
Abete, Antonio bass 755, 756, 758, 972, 1097
Abramovic, Charles pf 252
Abravanel, Maurice cond 530
Academia Montis Regalis 1097, 1248, 1259, 1260
Academy of Ancient Music . .453, 503, 504, 511, 515, 518,
540, 572, 789, 794, 846, 891
Academy of Ancient Music Chorus 572, 794, 891
Academy of St Martin in the Fields . . .207, 394, 434, 530,
548, 766, 775, 778, 790, 833, 834, 939, 941, 992, 1049,
1127, 1196, 1247
Academy of St Martin in the Fields Chamber Ensemble. .
121, 530, 604
Academy of St Martin in the Fields Chorus .207, 434, 530,
790
Academy Symphonic Wind. 1107
Accademia Bizantina 1255, 1258
Accademia I Filarmonici 1247, 1248
Accardo, Salvatore vn 1066, 1072, 1073
Accentus Chamber Choir 262, 434, 857
Ackermann, Otto cond 490, 491, 651, 769
Acocella, Luciano cond 174
Acosta, Monica voc 753
Ad Libitum Quartet. 428, 913
Adam, Theo bass-bar 790
Adamec, Petr pf 715
Adams, David va 1092
Adams, Peter vc 920
Adeney, Richard fl 530
Adès, Thomas cond. 8, 9, 10
Adès, Thomas hpd 9
Adès, Thomas pf, org 10
Adni, Daniel pf 715, 7153
Adrian Partington Singers. 1204
Ághová, Lívia sop 407
Agnew, Paul ten . .166, 228, 376, 387, 512, 513, 520, 521,
522, 530, 752, 755, 756, 888, 905, 1010
Agrell, Donna bn 766
Agri, Antonio vn 850
Aikin, Laura sop 936
Aimard, Pierre-Laurent dir 767
Aimard, Pierre-Laurent pf . .107, 125, 126, 133, 178, 364,
399, 609, 634, 656, 657, 742, 743, 744, 767, 914, 915,
6573
Ainsley, John Mark ten . .87, 165, 300, 435, 436, 440, 517,
519, 530, 596, 738, 789, 821, 891, 1009, 1010, 1011,
1184, 1201, 1202, 1291, 1294, 1309

Akademie für Alte Musik Berlin 522, 972
Akselberg, Fredrik ten 1097
Alagna, Roberto ten 195, 871, 879, 1207, 1208, 1209,
1210
Alain, Marie-Claire org 195, 742
Alamire. 622, 1187
Alarm Will Sound 925
Alban Berg Quartet 144, 362, 992, 993
Albelo, Celso ten 1348
Albert, Rudolf cond 741
Albert, Donnie Ray bar 607
Albrecht, Gerd cond 409, 583, 980, 1026, 1310
Alden, David dir 1015
Aleksashkin, Sergei bass 1056
Aler, John ten 197, 832, 1130
Alessandrini, Rinaldo cond .709, 755, 756, 757, 971, 1247,
1260
Alessandrini, Rinaldo hpd 709, 757
Alexander, Carlos bar 690
Alexeev, Alexei cond 1049
Alexeev, Dmitri pf 729, 1049
Alexeyev, Anya pf 1040
Alkan Trio 16
(John) Alldis Choir . . .126, 127, 424, 462, 884, 885, 1174,
1223, 1298
Allegri Quartet. 557, 764
Allen, Thomas bar 275, 373, 434, 441, 832, 1201
Alma Mahler Sinfonietta 1017
Almeida, Antonio de cond 319, 430
Almeida Ensemble. 1192
Alphen, Conrad van cond 932
Alsfeld Vocal Ensemble. 93
Alsop, Marin cond . .7, 9, 99, 100, 101, 108, 113, 204, 248,
249, 250, 350, 402, 832, 1146, 1190, 1191, 1300
Alter Ego. 961
Altinoglu, Alain cond 395
Altmann, Volker hn 656
Alwyn, Kenneth cond 8
Alwyn, William cond 21
Amadeus Quartet 254, 255, 444, 994, 994
Amadinda Percussion Group 657
Ambrosian Opera Chorus . . .281, 717, 718, 941, 945, 948,
1064, 1215, 1236
Ambrosian Singers.218, 219, 372, 373, 394, 406, 424, 434,
889
Ameling, Elly sop 530, 690, 692
American Composers Orchestra. 315
Amherst, Nigel vn 507
Amoyel, Pascal pf 1045
Amsterdam Baroque Orchestra. 27, 227, 1243, 1247, 1248
Amsterdam Sinfonietta 150
Amsterdam Stem des Volks Choir 690, 692
Amsterdam Toonkunst Choir. 690, 692
Anastassov, Orlin bass 193
Ančerl, Karel cond . . .290, 400, 403, 441, 732, 1054, 1085,
1133
Anda, Géza dir 104
Anda, Géza pf 104
Anderson, Jay db 477
Anderson, Lorna sop 512, 565, 570, 891, 1011
Anderson, Mark pf 379
Anderson, Valdine sop 10
Anderszewski, Piotr dir 769

Anderszewski, Piotr *pf* 164, 769, 1143, 1315
Andrew, Ludmilla *sop* 730
Andrews, Julie *bn* 1102
Andsnes, Leif Ove *dir* 549
Andsnes, Leif Ove *pf* . .105, 111, 253, 399, 489, 490, 493,
549, 895, 1145, 1315, 1316
Angas, Richard *bass* 1198
Angel, Ryland *alto* 971
Angeles, Victoria de los *sop* 721, 1347
Angeles Quartet. 554
Angelich, Nicholas *pf* 257
Anima Eterna Orchestra 765, 780, 1098
Anissimov, Alexander *cond* 898, 899
Anonymous Conductor *cond* 891
Anonymous Pianist(s) *pf* 1351
Ansermet, Ernest *cond* 199, 231, 916, 1999
Antal, Mátyás *cond* 82, 83
Antonini, Giovanni *cond* 138, 503, 1249
Antonini, Claire *theo* 1332
Anvik, Vebjørn *pf* 269
Anzellotti, Teodoro *accordion* 188
Apekisheva, Katya *pf* 253, 493
Aradia Baroque Ensemble 892
Aradia Ensemble 239, 325, 505, 1253
Araiza, Francisco *ten* 790
Arangi-Lombardi, Giannina *sop* 852
Arantes, Ozéas *bn* 1240
Arcanto Quartet. 110
Archaeus Quartet. 237
Archibald, Jane *sop* 1253
Archibald, Paul *pt* 178
Arditti, Irvine *vn* 377, 378, 437
Arditti Quartet. . . . 10, 213, 187, 377, 378, 437, 983, 1097
Arena, Maurizio *cond* 747
Arfken, Katharina *ob* 82, 766
Argenta, Nancy *sop* 84, 85, 87, 89, 514, 520, 526, 565, 567
Argerich, Martha *pf* . . .105, 131, 329, 331, 333, 334, 339,
654, 661, 664, 665, 861, 896, 912, 914, 1022, 1028,
1049, 1159, 1160, 1316, 1317, 5614
Armenian Philharmonic Orchestra 631, 632, 633
Armiliato, Marco *cond* 1355
Armstrong, Sheila *sop* 693, 832, 1198
Arnhem Philharmonic Orchestra 398
Arnold, Jonathan *bass* 888
Arnold Schoenberg Chorus. 617
Aronowitz, Cecil *va* 444
Aronowitz Ensemble 102
Arrau, Claudio *pf* 665
Arron, Edward *vc* 987
Arroyo, Martina *sop* 690
Ars Antiqua Austria 208
Ars Nova 825
Ars Nova Copenhagen 805
Ars Nova Ensemble. 742
Arte dei Suonatori 1245
(L')Arte dell'Arco 504, 1153
Artemis Quartet. 253, 657
Artis Quartet 1303
(Les) Arts Florissants Chorus 326, 513, 533, 752, 755, 756,
790, 791, 802, 808, 810, 892, 905, 906, 907
(Les) Arts Florissants Instrumental Ensemble . . .376, 458,
755, 756, 890
(Les) Arts Florissants Orchestra . .325, 326, 513, 530, 533,
539, 752, 755, 756, 790, 791, 802, 808, 810, 892, 905,
906, 907
(Les) Arts Florissants Vocal Ensemble 458, 890

Arturo Toscanini Foundation Chorus . .1211, 1212, 1234,
1235
Arturo Toscanini Foundation Orchestra 1211, 1212, 1234,
1235
d'Ascoli, Bernard *pf* 338
Ashkar, Saleem Abboud *pf* 156
Ashkenazy, Vladimir *cond* .241, 625, 898, 908, 1067, 1073,
1075, 1135, 1162
Ashkenazy, Vladimir *dir* 908
Ashkenazy, Vladimir *pf* .107, 154, 159, 257, 334, 337, 339,
625, 861, 894, 895, 908, 1061
Ashton, Caroline *sop* 433, 434
Asko Ensemble 320, 657, 1195
Aspell, Simon *va* 347
Asperen, Bob van *hpd* 1139
Assad, Odair *gtr* 850
Assad, Sérgio *gtr* 850
Assenbaum, Aloysia *org* 209, 210, 976
Asteriadou, Maria *pf* 1082
Asti, Eugene *pf* 1351
(L')Astrée Ensemble 1257
Asturias Symphony Orchestra. 931, 932
Asztalos, Aliz *pf* 642
Atherton, David *cond* 215, 617, 656
Atkins, Mark *didj* 1045
Atkinson, Lynton *ten* 1254
Atlanta Symphony Chorus 466, 477, 581
Atlanta Symphony Orchestra 347, 466, 477, 581, 812, 814
Atrium String Quartet. 1060
Attrot, Ingrid *sop* 929, 1093
Aucante, Vincent *va* 500
Auchincloss, Daniel *ten* 272, 754, 755
Audite Nova Vocal Ensemble 427
Augér, Arleen *sop* 518, 530, 690, 789
Austin, Christopher *cond* 727
Australian Chamber Orchestra 463, 1045
Australian Opera and Ballet Orchestra 538, 720, 874
Australian Opera Chorus. 874
Austrian Chamber Orchestra, Vienna 1244
Austrian Radio Chorus 980
Austrian Radio Symphony Orchestra 980
Austro-Hungarian Haydn Orchestra 553
Auvity, Cyril *counterten* 324, 892, 480
Avenhaus, Silke *pf* 1141
Avis, Jeremy *cantor* 1342
Ax, Emanuel *pf* 242, 254, 563, 782, 994, 1109
Axelrod, John *cond* 988
Azesberger, Kurt *ten* 788
Azoitei, Remus *vn* 428
Azzaretti, Jaël *sop* 325

B

Babin, Victor *pf* 1198
Baborák, Radek *bn* 279
Bach, Mechthild *sop* 85, 86, 87
Bach Choir. 272, 1292
Bach Collegium Japan 85, 89, 90, 92, 93
Backes, Constanze *sop* 1179
Backhouse, Jeremy *cond* 393
Badings, Vera *hp* 359, 361
Badura-Skoda, Paul *pf* 710
Baert, Lieven *vc* 948
Bailey, Simon *bass* 939
Baillie, Alexander *vc* 918, 1091

Baillie, Isobel *sop* 426, 518, 519, 1198
Bair-Ivenz, Monika *sop* 823
Bakels, Kees *cond* 467, 819
Baker, Martin *cond* 358, 684, 838
Baker, Janet *mez* 85, 86, 198, 199, 264, 413, 415, 418, 424, 530, 693, 705, 707, 1004, 1347, 1348
Baldin, Aldo *ten* 407, 690
Baldin, Dileno *bn* 1251
Balding, Caroline *vn* 1178
Balducci, Antonella *sop* 481
Baldy, Colin *bar* 91
Ball, Andrew *pf* 22, 376, 638, 1184
Balleys, Brigitte *mez* 198, 199
Balogh, József *cl* 143
Balsom, Alison *tpt* 549
Balthasar-Neumann Choir 510, 568, 672, 673
Balthasar-Neumann Ensemble 510, 568, 672, 673
Baltimore Symphony Orchestra . . .99, 350, 402, 421, 422, 455, 456, 1154
Baltsa, Agnes *mez* 693
Bamberg Symphony Orchestra .612, 714, 990, 1114, 1168, 1189
Bamert, Matthias *cond* 379, 454, 710
Banchini, Chiara *cond* 1256
Banchini, Chiara *bq vn* 1153
Bancroft's School Choir 601, 1120, 1121
Banfield, Volker *pf* 649
Banks, Barry *ten* 939
Banks, Kevin *cl* 819
Bannatyne-Scott, Brian *bass* 89
Bannister, Phillida *contr* 748
Bannwart, (Father) Roman *cond* 560
Banowetz, Joseph *pf* 1150
Banse, Juliane *sop* 265, 643, 696, 703, 711, 913, 1030
Bär, Olaf *bar* 88, 89
Barber, Graham *org* 595
Barbican Piano Trio 1151
Barbirolli, John *cond* . . .117, 119, 192, 242, 290, 297, 298, 413, 415, 417, 418, 421, 422, 424, 690, 698, 705, 707, 821, 876, 877, 897, 1066, 1069, 1311, 1322
Barboteu, Georges *bn* 742
Barcellona, Daniela *mez* 193, 1207, 1208, 1209
Barcelona Ars Musica 1347
Barcelona Chamber Ensemble 1347
Bardon, Patricia *mez* 738
Barenboim, Daniel *cond* . . .134, 299, 305, 662, 678, 1019, 1160, 1272, 1274, 1282, 1285, 1286, 1322
Barenboim, Daniel *pf* .126, 127, 134, 156, 242, 784, 1016, 1019, 1266, 1322
Barker, Cheryl *sop* 412
Barker, Edwin *db* 850
Barlow, Edith *sop* 1035
Barnes, Paul *pf* 464
Baroque Chamber Orchestra 530
Barrellon, Jean-Paul *ob* 427
Barshai, Rudolf *cond* 1054
Bárta, Jiří *vc* 598, 634
Bartók, Bela *pf* 113
Bartoletti, Bruno *cond* 462, 874, 944
Bartoli, Cecilia *mez* . 470, 530, 793, 938, 968, 1348, 1349
Barton, Fenella *vn* 845
Barton, William *didj* 1046
Bartosz, Bogna *contr* 91
Basel Chamber Orchestra 138, 529
Bashmet, Yuri *va* 107, 271, 1290
Basses Réunies (Les) 447
Basso, Romina *mez* 525

Bate, Jennifer *org* 377, 737, 744, 745
Batiashvili, Lisa *vn* 274, 659, 1066
Bátiz, Enrique *cond* 927, 930
Battle, Kathleen *sop* 690
Bauchau, Nicholas *ten* 325
Baudo, Serge *cond* 319
Bauer, Andrzej *vc* 677
Bäumer, Hermann *cond* 653
Bavarian Festival Chorus. 1270
Bavarian Festival Orchestra. 1270
Bavarian Radio Chorus .299, 381, 407, 651, 690, 692, 790, 832, 941, 942, 1029, 1267
Bavarian Radio Symphony Orchestra. .291, 299, 403, 407, 580, 690, 694, 707, 862, 872, 874, 1020, 1029, 1048, 1085, 1109, 1110, 1135, 1267, 1316
Bavarian State Opera Chorus . .170, 171, 176, 1099, 1100, 1115, 1120, 1121, 1122, 1124, 1211, 1212
Bavarian State Opera Orchestra . . .176, 1099, 1100, 1115, 1120, 1121, 1124
Bavarian State Orchestra .170, 171, 576, 1115, 1122, 1210, 1211, 1212
Bavouzet, Jean-Efflam *pf* 365, 368, 369
Bax, Alessio *pf* 156
Baxtresser, Jeanne *fl* 99
Bayl, Benjamin *org* 1343
Bayley, Clive *bass* 755, 756
Bayo, María *sop* 1247
Bayodi, Hannah *sop* 892
Bayreuth Festival Chorus . . .142, 1264, 1269, 1270, 1275, 1277, 1283, 1285
Bayreuth Festival Orchestra .142, 1264, 1269, 1270, 1272, 1273, 1274, 1275, 1277, 1283, 1285, 1286
Bazola, François *bass* 752
Bazola-Minori, François *bar* 892
BBC Choir. 484
BBC Choral Society 168, 169, 426
BBC Chorus 372, 434, 984, 1264, 1312
BBC Concert Orchestra .24, 236, 237, 343, 454, 640, 645, 725, 849, 1215, 1222, 1224
BBC National Chorus of Wales . .266, 412, 592, 955, 956, 1095
BBC National Orchestra of Wales266, 267, 412, 419, 588, 592, 604, 654, 954, 955, 956, 1054, 1095, 1145, 1204
BBC Northern Orchestra 426
BBC Northern Symphony Orchestra 707, 708
BBC Opera Orchestra. 426
BBC Philharmonic Orchestra . .7, 22, 115, 117, 118, 179, 234, 277, 326, 379, 394, 395, 399, 420, 431, 434, 435, 443, 469, 485, 486, 579, 583, 625, 629, 630, 637, 638, 644, 663, 664, 678, 679, 682, 683, 684, 724, 742, 824, 856, 920, 928, 929, 952, 987, 1039, 1085, 1086, 1093, 1136, 1200, 1336
BBC Scottish Symphony Orchestra27, 202, 237, 265, 270, 271, 344, 546, 583, 596, 615, 670, 679, 682, 686, 727, 729, 919, 954, 964, 1090, 1181, 1288
BBC Singers. . .98, 102, 212, 216, 236, 283, 389, 547, 616, 640, 683, 856, 984, 1090, 1183, 1215, 1222, 1224, 1241, 1292
BBC Symphony Chorus 98, 212, 442, 590, 717, 1132, 1181, 1209, 1292
BBC Symphony Orchestra . . .2, 23, 95, 98, 102, 104, 110, 117, 168, 169, 178, 179, 181, 182, 193, 216, 235, 236, 272, 320, 321, 327, 373, 389, 403, 413, 415, 417, 419, 420, 422, 424, 425, 426, 434, 442, 454, 490, 584, 590, 595, 616, 662, 696, 717, 727, 729, 916, 984, 991, 1040, 1103, 1132, 1167, 1181, 1199, 1209, 1292, 1320, 1334, 1336, 1347, 1350

BBC Theatre Chorus 201
BBC Welsh Chorus. 654
Beale, Matthew *ten* 91, 393
Bean, Hugh *vn* 1198
Beaufort, Sonia de *mez* 234
Beaux Arts Trio 150, 997
Becht, Hermann *bar* 984
Becker, Bob *marimba* 926
Becker, Markus *pf* 922
Becker-Bender, Tanja *vn* 837
Beczala, Piotr *ten* 1143, 1357
Bedford, Steuart *cond* 99, 280, 283, 287
Bedford, Steuart *pf* 591
Bednall, David *org* 654
Beecham, Thomas *cond* 192, 193, 194, 195, 201, 217, 218,
        219, 248, 372, 373, 374, 484, 494, 551, 810, 871, 874,
                989, 1070, 1073, 1312, 1313
Beecham, Betty Humby *pf* 1312
Beecham, Thomas *pf* 1312
Beecham Choral Society 192, 494
Beesley, Mark *bar* 982
Begley, Kim *ten* 97
Beinum, Eduard van *cond* 106, 359, 361, 431, 1000
Beiser, Maya *vc* 926
Belcea Quartet. 10, 108, 109, 273, 362, 363, 913, 995
Belder, Pieter-Jan *hpd* 1139
Belgian National Orchestra. 909
Bell, David *org* 418
Bell, Emma *sop* 520
Bell, Joshua *vn* . . . .
        99, 241, 243, 350, 641, 725, 732, 962, 1247
Bell, Sebastian *fl* 178, 480
Bell, Stephen *hn* 783
Bellezza, Vincenzo *cond* 655
Belohlávek, Jiří *cond* . . .400, 401, 407, 411, 616, 713, 714,
                715, 717, 1287
Ben-Dor, Gisèle *cond* 461
Benacková, Marta *mez* 407
Benda, Christian *cond* 710
Benda, Sebastian *pf* 710
Benedetti, Nicola *vn* 1154
Benelli, Ugo *ten* 474, 747
Benini, Maurizio *cond* 943
Benjamin, George *cond* 178, 546
Bennett, Alan *pf* 317
Bennett, Malcolm *ten* 89
Benson, Clifford *pf* 251, 1094
Berberian, Cathy *mez* 188
Berezovsky, Boris *pf* 262, 476, 581, 900, 1108
Berg, Nathan *bar* 790, 791
Berganza, Teresa *mez* 530
Bergen Philharmonic Orchestra 20, 490, 1189
Berglund, Paavo *cond* 767
Bergonzi, Carlo *ten* 421
Bergset, Arve Moen *hardanger vn* 1194
Berio, Luciano *cond* 188
Berkes, Kálmán *cl* 111
Berki, Sándor *hn* 143
Berkofsky, Martin *pf* 593
Berlin Academy for Ancient Music. 526, 938, 972
Berlin Academy of Early Music 470, 630
Berlin Baroque Soloists. 1176
Berlin Cathedral Boys' Choir 832
Berlin Cathedral Choir 984
Berlin Deutsche Oper Chorus . . .134, 305, 368, 371, 570,
        807, 832, 833, 872, 874, 1229, 1266, 1269, 1272, 1285

Berlin Deutsche Oper Orchestra 807, 832, 833, 1123,
                1269
Berlin Deutsches Symphony Orchestra 285, 296, 624,
                1263, 1266, 1283
Berlin Philharmonic Orchestra. . .105, 106, 107, 113, 126,
        131, 132, 133, 134, 135, 138, 199, 241, 242, 243, 245,
        246, 248, 261, 279, 291, 293, 294, 297, 298, 299, 360,
        361, 368, 371, 389, 397, 401, 467, 489, 490, 491, 570,
        580, 592, 662, 689, 690, 693, 697, 698, 700, 703, 704,
        705, 734, 742, 778, 810, 814, 815, 832, 862, 863, 864,
        872, 874, 895, 896, 912, 914, 917, 983, 984, 989, 990,
        1028, 1050, 1069, 1070, 1072, 1073, 1103, 1104, 1105,
        1106, 1107, 1109, 1110, 1159, 1160, 1161, 1162, 1206,
                1207, 1208, 120
Academy of the Berlin Philharmonic Orchestra 657
Berlin Philharmonic Wind Ensemble. 774
Berlin Radio Chamber Choir 1131
Berlin Radio Children's Choir 581
Berlin Radio Chorus . . .245, 581, 652, 689, 690, 814, 815,
                832, 912, 984
Berlin Radio Symphony Chorus. 582
Berlin Radio Symphony Orchestra. . . .104, 575, 581, 582,
                652, 870, 896, 1096, 1109, 1110
Berlin RIAS Chamber Choir 199, 263, 520, 522, 630, 711,
        738, 795, 799, 800, 856, 857, 938, 1003, 5770
Berlin RIAS Light Orchestra 457
Berlin Scharoun Ensemble 711, 1003
Berlin Staatskapelle 132, 196, 305, 1266, 1282
Berlin State Boys' Choir 832
Berlin State Opera Chorus 1234, 1282, 1285
Berlin State Opera Orchestra 1234
Berlin Symphony Orchestra . . .179, 461, 984, 1026, 1072,
                1099
Bernardini, Alfredo *cond* 430, 507, 1251
Bernardini, Alfredo *ob* 430, 1243, 1251
Bernas, Richard *cond* 1192
Bernays, John *bass* 91
Berne, Harry van *ten* 93
Bernhardt, Louise *contr* 690
Bernius, Frieder *cond* 85, 86, 87
Bernold, Philippe *fl* 363
Bernstein, Leonard *cond* .99, 101, 172, 177, 204, 205, 347,
        455, 607, 662, 693, 695, 698, 702, 707, 780, 1052, 1053,
                1054
Bernstein, Leonard *pf* 101, 347, 455
Béroff, Michel *pf* 742, 912
Berry, Mary *cond* 681
Berry, Walter *bass-bar* 89, 134, 135
                570, 1114
Bertagnolli, Gemma *sop* 1247
Bertini, Gary *cond* 690, 692
Best, Matthew *cond* 165, 197, 204, 300, 328, 440, 596,
                1081, 1172, 1201, 1242
Best, Jonathan *bass* 358, 892, 1201
Beyer, Amandine *vn* 920
Beynon, Emily *fl* 727, 764
Bezaly, Sharon *fl* 496, 765, 1145, 1318
Beznosiuk, Lisa *fl* 1252
Beznosiuk, Pavlo *vn* 210
Bianchi, Luigi Alberto *va, vn* 922
Biccire, Patrizia *sop* 939
Bicket, Harry *cond* 530
Bickley, Susan *mez* . . .89, 90, 95, 178, 228, 412, 442, 501,
                515, 521, 522, 530, 955, 956
Billy, Bertrand de *cond* 801, 872, 874, 1273
Binchois Consort. 212, 388, 1340
Binns, Malcolm *pf* 1091

Biondi, Fabio *va, vn, cond* 709, 1245, 1251, 1259
Birchall, Simon *bass* 530
Biret, Idil *pf* 235, 260
Birkeland, Øystein *vc* 269
Birmingham Contemporary Music Group. 8, 23, 272, 686
Biryukova, Natalia *mez* 1062
Bisengaliev, Marat *vn* 265
Biss, Jonathan *pf* 156
Bittová, Iva *voc* 474
Bjarnason, Finnur *ten* 520
Bjerken, Xak *pf* 1302
Björling, Jussi *ten* 168
Bjørn-Larsen, Jens *tuba* 586
Blacher, Kolja *vn* 580
Black, George *gtr* 487
Blake, Richard *fl, dir* 178
Blasi, Angela Maria *sop* 788, 791
Blaumane, Kristine *vc* 253
Blaze, Robin *alto* .85, 89, 92, 314, 511, 522, 527, 528, 684,
                                        888, 1254, 1256
Blegen, Judith *sop* 693
Blendis, Simon *vn* 306, 445
Bloch, Thomas *ondes martinot* 742, 1195
Blochwitz, Hans-Peter *ten* 733, 1028, 1306
Blomstedt, Herbert *cond* 820, 821
Blount, William *cl* 1130
Blume, Norbert *va d'amore* 580
Blumen, Alfred *pf* 110, 1103
Bocelli, Andrea *ten* 1209
Boer, Michele de *sop* 1253
Boffard, Florent *pf* 188
Bogdan, Thomas *ten* 1132
Böhm, Karl *cond* ..131, 141, 170, 171, 294, 771, 778, 796,
    807, 989, 990, 1109, 1110, 1115, 1124, 1125, 1285, 1297
Bolcom, William *pf* 230, 1350
Boldoczki, Gábor *tpt* 661
Bollani, Stefano *pf* 855
Bologna Teatro Comunale Chorus 938, 943, 1354
Bologna Teatro Comunale Orchestra 530, 938, 943, 1354
Bolshoi Theatre Chorus 815, 816, 1174, 5678
Bolshoi Theatre Orchestra 815, 816, 1174, 5678
Bolton, Ivor *cond* 293, 533, 793
Bonaventure, Michael *org* 745, 1139
Bond, Jonathon *treb* 394, 434
Bonde-Hansen, Henriette *sop* 375, 670
Boni, Marco *cond* 950
Bonitatibus, Anna *sop* 571
Bonizzoni, Fabio *hpd, dir* 524, 525
Bonn Collegium Josephinum Children's Choir. . 690, 692
Bonner, Tessa *sop* 87, 460, 891
Bonney, Barbara *sop* .88, 89, 135, 261, 570, 821, 889, 994,
                                        1028, 1114
Bonucci, Rodolfo *vn* 1017
Bonynge, Richard *cond* ...1, 177, 382, 530, 626, 650, 720,
                                        829, 948, 1100
Booth, Juliet *sop* 300
Boothby, Richard *vc* 349
Borchev, Nikolay *bass* 567
Bordeaux Opera Chorus 722
Bordeaux-Aquitaine National Orchestra 395, 722
Borden, Barbara *sop* 755
Boreyko, Andrey *cond* 842
Borg, Kim *bass* 299, 424
Borgstede, Michael *hpd* 352
Bork, Hanneke van *sop* 690, 692
Borodin Quartet 1170
Borodina, Olga *mez* 1209

Borowski, Daniel *bass* 938
Borst, Danielle *sop* 391
Boskovsky, Willi *cond* 1100
Boston Baroque 473
Boston Pops Orchestra 455, 456
Boston Pro Musica Chorus 275, 276
Boston Symphony Orchestra 106, 132, 181, 242, 275, 276,
    347, 590, 652, 661, 662, 721, 894, 895, 1066, 1072,
                                1073, 1085, 1104, 1290
Bostridge, Ian *ten* ...10, 279, 501, 530, 1005, 1011, 1013,
                1014, 1015, 1031, 1034, 1198, 1307, 1349
Bosworth, Nicholas *pf* 747
Botstein, Leon *cond* 389, 442, 468, 1141
Bott, Catherine *sop* 507, 531, 891
Bottone, Bonaventura *ten* 234
Boughton, William *cond* 439, 978
Boulanger, Nadia *cond* 434
Boulanger, Nadia *pf* 490
Boulez, Pierre *cond* 104, 105, 106, 107, 184, 214, 235,
    236, 297, 368, 370, 617, 656, 690, 741, 742, 911, 912,
    916, 981, 983, 984, 985, 986, 1032, 1128, 1298, 1299
Boulianne, Julie *mez* 917
Boult, Adrian *cond* 117, 119, 222, 415, 417, 418, 419, 421,
    424, 426, 530, 589, 590, 696, 732, 749, 991, 1071, 1198,
                                        1336
Bournemouth Sinfonietta 766, 960, 963
Bournemouth Symphony Chorus 204, 374, 426, 832, 1287
Bournemouth Symphony Orchestra. .7, 20, 108, 113, 114,
    204, 374, 411, 417, 420, 426, 590, 662, 812, 819, 832,
    919, 1017, 1081, 1091, 1092, 1146, 1162, 1182, 1263,
                                        1287, 1300
Bournemouth Symphony Youth Chorus 832
Boutros, Kamel *bar* 5
Bovi, Patrizia *sop* 1153
Bovino, Maria *sop* 474, 747
Bowen, John *ten* 738, 755, 758, 1201
Bowen, Kenneth *ten* 1198
Bowers-Broadbent, Christopher *org* 843, 844, 1155
Bowlin, David *vn* 1130
Bowman, James *alto* 91, 488, 515, 517, 519, 590, 755, 846,
                                        888, 889
Bowman, Robin *pf* 281
Bowyer, Kevin *org* 13, 18
Boyd, Douglas *cond* 140, 697
Boyd, Douglas *ob* 656, 767
Boyd, James *va* 238, 1151
Brabant Ensemble 478, 708, 762, 1340, 7623
Brabbins, Martyn *cond* ...22, 95, 214, 215, 216, 224, 237,
    272, 344, 583, 585, 596, 640, 679, 682, 851, 964, 1039,
                                        1090, 1181
Bradbury, Colin *cl* 1298
Brafield, Mark *org* 376
Bragg, Keith *cond* 1107
Brahim-Djelloul, Amel *sop* 675
Brain, Dennis *hn* 143, 247, 278, 765, 766, 1102, 1319
Brain, Leonard *ob* 765, 766
Braithwaite, Nicholas *cond* 266, 267, 345, 1091
Braley, Frank *harm* 404
Braley, Frank *pf* 404, 734, 794, 965, 994
The Brandenburg Consort 502, 530, 531
Brandis Quartet 1017
Brandt, Karl-Heinz *ten* 1301
Bratislava Chamber Choir 174
Bratislava Children's Choir 616
Bratislava Conservatory Choir 474
Bratislava Radio Symphony Orchestra 631
Braucher, Ernest *va* 1251

Braun, Lioba *mez* 790
Braunstein, Guy *vn* 1106
Braunstein, Mark *va* 1106
Brautigam, Ronald *fp* 162
Brautigam, Ronald *pf* 449, 580, 1059, 1318
Bream, Julian *gtr* 14, 931
Bream, Julian *lute* 1319
Bremen Baroque Orchestra....................... 93
Brendel, Adrian *vc* 153
Brendel, Alfred *pf* .126, 127, 153, 157, 161, 165, 561, 770,
           793, 993, 994, 1000, 1001, 1014, 1319
Brenner, Roger *tbn* 300
Brett, Charles *alto* 87
Brewer, Michael *cond* 1139
Brewer, Christine *sop* 230, 275, 703, 717, 1112
Bridge Quartet................................. 22
Brindisi Quartet............................... 724
British National Opera Company Chorus 718
British National Opera Company Orchestra 718
Britten, Benjamin *cond* ..91, 270, 271, 272, 276, 278, 280,
           281, 282, 284, 285, 287, 397, 398, 771
Britten, Benjamin *pf* 272, 274, 278, 281, 284
Britten Quartet 595
Britten Sinfonia 96, 300, 544, 684, 725, 1102
Britten Singers................................ 277
Brno Janáček Opera Chorus.................... 409
Brno Janáček Opera Orchestra................. 409
Brno Philharmonic Orchestra.................. 716
Brno State Philharmonic Orchestra 408
Broadbent, Peter *cond* 102, 840
Broadway Chorus 205
Broadway Orchestra 205
Broderick, Katherine *sop* 1035
Broderick, Matthew *sngr* 1035
Brodsky Quartet 148, 273, 613
Bronfman, Yefim *pf* 129, 130, 257, 970
Brook, Matthew *bar* 89, 518, 1202
Brooklyn Boys' Choir 690
Brooks, Gerard *org* 460
Brooks, Robert *treb* 518
Brouwer, Leo *cond* 931
Brovtsyn, Boris *vn* 253
Brown, Iona *cond* 778
Brown, Justin *cond* 320, 455
Brown, Timothy *cond* 959, 960, 1341, 1342
Brown, Donna *sop* 197, 566, 568, 1208, 1209
Brown, Edward *bar* 426
Brown, Ian *pf* 121, 585, 855, 965, 966, 1191, 1291
Brown, Jonathan *bass* 888
Brown, Nils *ten* 892, 1253
Brown, Phillip *tbn* 300
Brown, Wilfred *ten* 89
Brownlee, Lawrence *ten* 832
Brua, Claire *mez* 483
Brua, Claire *sop* 199
Brubaker, Robert *ten* 207
Brueggergosman, Measha *sop* 230, 1350
Brüggen, Frans *cond* 133, 551, 734, 904
Brunskill, Muriel *contr* 426
Brunt, Andrew *treb* 394, 434
Brunt, Peter *vn* 996
Brussels Théâtre de la Monnaie Chorus.......... 1220
Brussels Théâtre de la Monnaie Orchestra........ 1220
Brutscher, Markus *ten* 91
Brych, Jaroslav *cond* 979
Brymer, Jack *cl* 764
Bryn-Julson, Phyllis *sop* 236

Buchholz, Barbara *theremin*.................. 1058
Budapest Children's Choir Magnificat............ 634
Budapest Concert Orchestra.................... 953
Budapest Festival Orchestra .106, 107, 396, 397, 401, 634,
           663, 695, 697, 898, 899, 1107
Buet, Alain *bar* 324, 480
Buffalo Philharmonic Orchestra...... 347, 455, 495, 928
Bukac, Vladimir *va* 105
Bullock, Susan *sop* 22, 583
Bumbry, Grace *mez* 530
Burchell, David *org* 1186
Burgess, Russell *cond* 284
Burgess, Russell *ten* 91
Burgess, Sally *mez* 374
Burnside, Iain *pf* ..22, 166, 279, 348, 606, 639, 985, 1184,
                                              1203
Burrowes, Connor *treb* 517, 888
Burrowes, Norma *sop* 1198
Burrowes, Patrick *treb* 239
Busbridge, Judith *va* 956
Busch Chamber Players (USA)................... 145
Busch Quartet 145
Bustani, Linda *pf* 1240
Buswell, James *vn* 99, 100, 851
Butt, John *cond* 89, 518
Butt, Yondani *cond* 633
Butterfield, Peter *ten* 566
Bychkov, Semyon *cond* 247, 1056, 1106, 1174, 1206, 1265
Byers, Alan *ten* 406
Byram-Wigfield, Timothy *org* 745, 1149, 1287

C

Cachemaille, Gilles *bar* 135, 136, 197, 199
Caetani, Oleg *cond* 1096
Caine, Rebecca *sop* 358
Calcara, Tad *cl* 455
Calderón, Javier *gtr* 594
Calicantus Choir 481
Callas, Maria *sop* 881, 1350
Callegari, Daniele *cond* 1359
Calzi, Nelson *fp* 937
Calzolari, Cristina *sop* 818
Cambreling, Sylvain *cond* 196, 643, 1220
Cambreling, Frédérique *hp* 188
Cambridge King's College Choir................ 530
Cambridge Schola Gregoriana 681
Cambridge Singers 180, 433, 434, 960, 1341
Cambridge University Musical Society Chorus...... 426
Camerata Silesia 1195
Camerata Singers............................. 690
Cameron, Alexander *vc* 418
Cameron, John *bar* 1198
Campbell, Colin *bar* 393, 888
Campoli, Alfredo *vn* 418, 732
Canonici, Luca *ten* 1208, 1209
Cantate Domino Chorus....................... 627
Cantate Youth Choir.......................... 1132
Cantelli, Guido *cond* 247, 361, 362
Cantilena 1198
Cantoreggi, Muriel *vn* 498, 711
Cantoria Children's Choir 723
Cantus Cölln 728, 754, 936, 1037
Canzona (La) 226
Canzonetta................................... 22
Capella Augustina 567, 568, 569

Capella Brugensis 948
Cappella Amsterdam 657
Cappella Coloniensis. 530
Cappella de' Turchini 322, 818
Cappella Romana. 388
Capuano, Gianluca *hpd, dir* 451
Capuçon, Aude *pf* 1320
Capuçon, Gautier *vc* 243, 397, 548, 965, 994, 1320
Capuçon, Renaud *vn* 243, 257, 965, 994, 1049, 1316, 1320
The Cardinall's Musick 310, 312, 313, 314, 436, 839, 1239
Carella, Giuliano *cond* 944
Carewe, Mary *sop* 10, 272
Carmignola, Giuliano *vn* 772, 1246, 1247, 1249
Carmina Quartet 560
Carney, Jonathan *vn* 819
Carnovich, Daniele *bass* 755, 756
Carol Case, John *bar* 89, 434, 1198
Carraro, Tiziana *mez* 1259
Carroll, Thomas *vc* 189
Caruso, Enrico *ten* 1350, 1351
Carwood, Andrew *cond, ten* . . . .
. . . . 310, 312, 313, 314, 436, 839, 1239
Carydis, Constantinos *cond* 803
Casa, Lisa della *sop* 790, 1110, 1115
Casadesus, Jean-Claude *cond* 197, 319, 854
Casals, Pablo *vc* 397, 415, 992, 993, 1023
Casazza, Enrico *vn* 1251
Cascioli, Gianluca *pf* 656
Cassard, Philippe *pf* 1026
Cassidy, Jennie *mez* 623
Cassone, Gabriele *tpt* 188, 1251
Castagna, Gabriel *cond* 461, 850
Castagna, Bruna *mez* 168
Castellani, Luisa *sop* 188
Castilla y León Symphony Orchestra. 931, 932, 1190
Castro-Neves, Oscar *gtr* 850
Caton, Frédéric *bass* 196
Caudle, Mark *va d'amore* 889
Causse, Gérard *va* 289, 363, 994
Cavallier, Nicolas *bass* 905
Cavasanti, Lorenzo *rec* 1251
Cave, Philip *cond* 933, 1149
Cavina, Claudio *dir* 757
Cavina, Claudio *alto* 757
CBC Symphony Orchestra 1311
Cech, Jan *pf* 634
Celibidache, Sergiu *cond* 191, 192, 297
Celis, Joop *pf* 238
Cellini, Renato *cond* 718, 1236, 7183
Cencic, Max Emanuel *counterten* 939
Cerasi, Carole *hpd* 1186
Chailly, Riccardo *cond* .241, 242, 462, 580, 742, 881, 896,
937, 938, 943, 945, 949, 984, 1059, 1126, 1195, 1310
Chalabala, Zdenek *cond* 410
Chamayou, Bertrand *pf* 737
Chamber Choir of the Royal Welh College of Music &
Drama 412
Chamber Ensemble. 1298
Chamber Orchestra. 636
Chamber Orchestra of Europe .9, 125, 126, 131, 132, 133,
134, 168, 170, 404, 414, 415, 656, 734, 767, 865, 931,
990, 1036, 1250
Chambers, John *va* 418
Champs-Élysées Orchestra, Paris .168, 198, 199, 434, 435,
444

Chance, Michael *alto* 10, 84, 85, 87, 88, 89, 516, 518, 755,
891, 1201, 1309
Chandler, Adrian *dir, vn* 1250
Chandos Baroque Players 1309
Chang, Evelyn *pf* 1335
Chang, Han-Na *vc* 863, 1048
Chang, Sarah *vn* 399, 645, 1050, 1159, 1170, 1198
Chapelle du Roi 1147, 1148, 1149
La Chapelle Royale Choir. 168, 434, 435, 444
Charbonnet, Jeanne-Michèle *sop* 442
Charlier, Olivier *vn* 395, 644
Chase, Roger *va* 22, 121
Chaushian, Alexander *vc* 268
Cheek, John *bass* 1183
Chen, Lida *va* 1049
Cheng, Gloria *pf* 678
Cherkassky, Shura *pf* 1320
Cherrier, Sophie *fl* 188
Chertock, Michael *pf* 1127
Chetham's Chamber Choir. 7, 568, 569, 1200
Chicago Lyric Opera Chorus 480
Chicago Symphony Chorus 480, 917, 1209
Chicago Symphony Orchestra . . .105, 106, 107, 182, 241,
242, 243, 678, 689, 690, 701, 702, 732, 814, 983, 1053,
1066, 1104, 1159, 1160, 1209, 1311, 1322, 1325
Chijiiwa, Eiichi *vn* 355
Chilcott, Robert *treb* 434
Chilcott, Susan *sop* 277, 348
Children's Choir of the NDR. 739
Chilingirian Quartet 189, 1154
Chistyakova, Irina *contr* 867
Cho, Young-Chang *vc* 715, 7153
Choeur de Chambre de Namur 472
Choeur des Musiciens du Louvre . . . .
471, 510, 533, 538, 675, 828, 829
Choeur Régional Nord, Pas de Calais 197
Choir Of Eltham College 702
Choir of King Edward's School, Birmingham 272
Choir of London 1155
Choir of the Age of Enlightenment 890
Chojnacka, Elisabeth *hpd* 480, 854
Chorus 206, 284, 590, 941, 1100
Chorus of La Monnaie 721, 1134
Chou, Chia *pf* 922
Christ, Tanjia *va* 1170
Christ, Wolfram *va* 399, 580, 1170
Christ Church Cathedral Choir, Dublin 853
Christ Church Cathedral Choir, Oxford . . . .
275, 406, 753, 1156
Christiansen, Christian *bass* 1029
Christie, Michael *cond* 1046
Christie, William *cond* .325, 326, 376, 458, 513, 523, 530,
533, 537, 539, 568, 752, 755, 756, 790, 791, 802, 808,
810, 890, 892, 905, 906, 907
Christie, James David *org* 1140
Christodoulou, Nikos *cond* 1082
Christophers, Harry *cond* . . .308, 511, 514, 517, 529, 891,
1047, 1149, 1157, 1345, 1346
Christophers, Harry *ten* 530
Chum, Johannes *ten* 1114
Chung, Myung-Whun *cond* 243, 742, 820, 967, 1226,
1229
Chung, Kyung-Wha *vn* 107, 289, 290, 445, 732, 965,
1067, 1159
Chung, Locky *bar* 568
Ciesinski, Katherine *mez* 1130

Cikada Ensemble............................... 439
Cillario, Carlo Felice *cond* 881
Cincinnati Pops Chorale...................... 1098
Cincinnati Pops Orchestra 544, 953, 1098
Cincinnati Symphony Orchestra ....
    402, 911, 928, 1058, 1127, 1241
Ciofi, Patrizia *sop* 531
Cislowski, Tamara Anna *pf* 1045, 1046
City of Birmingham Orchestra 426, 442
City of Birmingham Symphony Orchestra...3, 8, 23, 272,
    275, 303, 415, 442, 491, 615, 703, 720, 731, 742, 963,
    975, 1052, 1067, 1070, 1128, 1129, 1141, 1143, 1144,
    1145, 1183, 1282, 1289
City of Birmingham Symphony Orchestra Chorus...135,
    234, 272, 275, 303, 434, 435, 615, 684, 703, 1143, 1144,
    1145, 1183
City of Birmingham Symphony Youth Chorus ....
    442, 684, 703, 1145
City of London Sinfonia ....
    189, 190, 283, 284, 286, 288, 433, 434,
    440, 591, 840, 960, 1201, 1245
Civil, Alan *hn* 766
Claesson, Urban *cl* 1301
Clair, Judith Le *bn* 99
Clare College Chamber Ensemble, Cambridge...... 959
Clare College Choir, Cambridge ....
    502, 959, 960, 1304, 1341, 1342
Clark, Andrew *hn* 9, 1252
Clarke, Adrian *bar* 358
Clarkson, Julian *bass* 520
Clavier, Denis *vn* 499
Clavier Quartet 499
Clayton, Allan *ten* 189
Cleaver, Michael *pf*......................... 645
Clee, Benjamin *alto* 325
Clein, Natalie *vc* 415
Cleobury, Nicholas *cond* 202, 725, 1102
Cleobury, Nicholas *org* 406
Cleobury, Stephen *cond* 9, 511, 530, 902, 1183, 1343
Cleobury, Stephen *org* 394, 434, 1321
Clerch, Joaquín *gtr* 932
Clerck, Paul de *va* 546
The Clerkes of Oxenford 1149
The Clerks' Group 301, 387, 622, 825, 826, 827
Cleveland Orchestra ...130, 131, 133, 241, 242, 243, 404,
    696, 742, 780, 814, 911, 912, 916, 981, 1021, 1126,
    1128, 1311
Cleveland Quartet........................ 149, 255
Clews, Richard *hn* 1111
Cliburn, Van *pf* 896
Cluytens, André *cond* 830, 963, 1283
Coccioli, Lamberto *elec*........................ 23
Cochran, William *ten* 690, 692
Cocset, Bruno *cond* 447
Cohen, Brad *cond* 946
Cohen, Elie *cond* 723
Cohen, Arnaldo *pf* 665, 668
Cohen, Jeff *pf*........................... 391, 1354
Cohen, Robert *vc* 1287
Coin, Christophe *va da gamba* 709
Coin, Christophe *vc* 199
Coker, Paul *pf* 641
Cold, Ulrik *bass* 615, 1109
Coleman Milling, Darrin *hn* 1240
Coleman-Wright, Peter *bar* 374
Colitto, Lorenzo *vn* 1251
Collard, Jean-Philippe *pf* 912

The Collegiate Singers 595
Collegium Cartusianum 91
Collegium Instrumentale Brugense 948
Collegium Musicum 90....15, 16, 87, 167, 504, 507, 518,
    526, 564, 565, 566, 567, 599, 600, 648, 1003, 1176,
    1252, 1261
Collegium Musicum 90 Chorus ...87, 518, 564, 565, 566,
    567, 599, 600
Collegium Musicum Amstelodamense 690, 692
Collegium Novum Ensemble 91
Collegium Vocale .. 83, 168, 434, 435, 444, 806, 807, 888
Collegium Vocale Orchestra................... 83, 888
Collins, Anthony *cond* 278
Collins, Finghin *pf* 1028
Collins, Michael *cl* ..3, 111, 121, 224, 321, 347, 775, 996,
    1089
Collins, Michael *dir* 775
Collon, Nicholas *org* 960
Cologne Chamber Choir 91
Cologne Gürzenich Orchestra 800, 801, 944, 990
Cologne Musica Antiqua....................... 573
Cologne Opera Chorus.................. 800, 801, 944
Cologne Radio Chorus 409, 583, 690, 692, 1265
Cologne Radio Symphony Orchestra..409, 583, 690, 692,
    1106
Cologne Vocal Ensemble 567, 568, 569
Colombara, Carlo *bass* 1208, 1209
(La) Colombina Ensemble 1239
Colonne Orchestra Choir..................... 427
Colpron, Francis *rec* 972
Columbia Jazz Band 455
Columbia Symphony Orchestra 346, 455, 1128
Columbus Boychoir.............. 718, 871, 874, 7183
Comissiona, Sergiu *cond* 1020
Comparato, Marina *mez* 1259
Il Complesso Barocco ..344, 530, 531, 532, 534, 535, 540,
    541, 542, 571
Le Concert des Nations 505, 674, 709
Le Concert des Tuileries....................... 945
Le Concert Spirituel Chorus 324, 892
Le Concert Spirituel Orchestra .. 324, 505, 506, 676, 892
Le Concert Spirituel Vocal Ensemble 324
Concertgebouw Chamber Orchestra 764, 984
Concertgebouw Choir...................... 1052, 1057
(Royal) Concertgebouw Orchestra, Amsterdam .106, 126,
    127, 128, 129, 131, 137, 244, 245, 289, 290, 359, 361,
    399, 402, 403, 431, 551, 552, 580, 645, 690, 692, 696,
    701, 742, 780, 881, 898, 921, 986, 989, 990, 1000, 1052,
    1054, 1057, 1059, 1064, 1104, 1126, 1128, 1195, 1310,
    1317
Concerto Copenhagen 537, 538
Concerto di Viole 1358
Concerto Italiano.... 709, 755, 756, 757, 971, 1247, 1260
Concerto Köln....... 438, 520, 536, 537, 806, 807, 1358
Concerto Palatino 728, 754, 760, 936, 1037, 1038
Concerto Vocale 755, 758, 760
Concordia 314
Conley, Eugene *ten* 690
Conlon, James *cond*......... 800, 801, 877, 1133, 1235
Connell, Elizabeth *sop* 97, 703, 733, 1201
Connell, John *bass* 1143, 1201
Connolly, Sarah *mez* ..267, 426, 522, 529, 639, 789, 985,
    1191, 1351
Conquer, Jeanne-Marie *vn* 188
Conservatoire Concert Society Orchestra 864
Console, Héctor *db* 850
Consort of Musicke........................... 758

Constable, John *pf* 480, 649, 1348
Constant, Marius *cond* 742
Constantine, Andrew *cond* 243
Continuum 354
Coombs, Stephen *pf* 749, 1044
Cooper, Deidre *vc* 465
Cooper, Gary *fp, pf* 785
Cooper, Imogen *pf* 768, 1321
Cooper, Maria *vn* 1092
Coote, Alice *mez* 424
Copenhagen Boys' Choir 615, 821, 1109
Copland, Aaron *cond* 346
Coppola, Anton *cond* 871
Coppola, Lorenzo *cl* 1251
Coppola, W*aluter ten* 407
Cor Vivaldi 576
Corderoy, Bridget *sop* 840
Cordes, Manfred *cond* 1038
Cordier, David *counterten* 10
Cordier, Pierre *vc* 500
Corliss, Frank *pf* 850
Cornwell, Joseph *ten* 755, 756, 892
Coro del Maggio Musicale Fiorentino 383, 804, 1237
Coro del Teatro dell'Opera di Roma 1211, 1212
Coro di Camera Accademia Nazionale di Santa Cecilia ..
1259
Corréas, Jérôme *bass* 199
Cortese, Paul *va* 749
Cortot, Alfred *pf* 68, 335, 368, 964, 1023, 1028, 1321
Corydon Brass Ensemble 1081
Corydon Orchestra 165, 197, 300, 328, 440, 1242
Corydon Singers .165, 197, 204, 300, 328, 440, 596, 1081,
1172, 1201, 1242
Coryn, Franck *db* 948
Cossotto, Fiorenza *mez* 1208
Costa, Paolo *alto* 1247
Cotrubas, Ileana *sop* 690, 692
Coull Quartet 725
Couraud, Marcel *cond* 742
Cousin, Martin *pf* 613
Covey-Crump, Rogers *ten* 684, 754, 888, 889, 891
Cox, Helen *vn* 411
Coxwell, Janet *sop* 1201
Crabtree, Libby *sop* 434, 435, 530, 738, 960
Cracow Chamber Choir 670
Craft, Robert *cond* 982, 985, 1129, 1130, 1132
Craney, Trudy Ellen *sop* 7
Cranmer, Arthur *bar* 426
Crass, Franz *bass* 690
Crawford, Peter *counterten* 1155
Crawford-Phillips, Simon *pf* 238, 253, 580
Crayford, Marcia *vn* 121
Creed, Marcus *cond* 263, 610, 643, 856, 938, 1003
Crespin, Régine *sop* 199, 916, 1999
Creswick, Bradley *vn* 439
Criswell, Kim *sop* 24
Critical Band 1308
Croft, Richard *ten* 521, 523, 538
Crook, Howard *alto* 675
Crook, Howard *ten* 88, 89, 199, 518
Cropper, Peter *vn* 783
Crossley, Paul *pf* 742
Crouch, Ruth *vn* 685
Crouch End Festival Chorus 442
Crowe, Lucy *sop* 412, 520, 528
Cruft, Ben *vn* 1154
Csalog, Gábor *pf* 642

Csapó, Eva *sop* 690
Csenki, Agnes *contr* 89
Cser, Péter *bar* 89
Cullen, Joseph *org* 1239
Cummings, Douglas *vc* 992
Cummings, Laurence *cond* 515, 529
Cummings, Laurence *hpd, spin* 892
Cummings, Laurence *org* 459, 549
Curnyn, Christian *cond* 412, 521, 539
Currie, Colin *perc* 9, 499, 613
Curror, Ian *org* 393
Curtin, Phyllis *sop* 275, 276
Curtis, Alan *cond* ..344, 530, 531, 532, 534, 535, 540, 541,
542, 571
Curtis, Alan *hpd* 531, 534, 541
Curzon, Clifford *pf* 254, 444, 771, 994, 1000
Cyferstein, Serge *pf* 483
Czech Philharmonic Chamber Orchestra 485
Czech Philharmonic Chorus 714
Czech Philharmonic Orchestra ..290, 397, 400, 401, 403,
404, 407, 409, 411, 421, 441, 612, 713, 714, 732, 1054,
1085, 1087, 1133
Czech Radio Symphony Orchestra 105
Czidra, László *rec* 1244
Cziffra, György *pf* 1159

D

Dahlin, Anders J. *ten* 567
Dalberto, Michel *pf* 965
Dallas Symphony Orchestra 455, 607, 636, 894, 895
Dam-Jensen, Inger *sop* 521, 530
Damiens, Alain *cl* 188
Damrau, Diana *sop* 369, 1351
Damrosch, Walter *cond* 249
Danby, Graeme *bass* 10
Danel Quartet 1060
Daneman, Sophie *sop* 166, 376, 513, 752, 905
Daniel, Paul *cond* ...184, 196, 417, 420, 738, 1288, 1290,
1291
Daniel, Nicholas *ob* 223, 783
Daniels, Charles *ten* 92, 515, 518, 754, 755, 888, 889,
1254, 1256
Daniels, David *counterten* 199, 523, 526, 527, 538
Danielson, Glen *hn* 852
Danish National Choir 591
Danish National Girls Choir 591
Danish National Opera Chorus 375, 586
Danish National Radio Choir ...615, 646, 821, 923, 1029,
1109
Danish National Radio Symphony Orchestra ...449, 615,
646, 821, 1029, 1123
Danish National Symphony Orchestra. 449, 591, 819, 821
Danish Quartet 823
Danish Radio Sinfonietta 587, 805
Danks, Harry *va* 1105
Dante Quartet 444, 956
Dantone, Ottavio *cond* 1255, 1258
Danubia Symphony Orchestra 379
Danuscr, Claudio *bar* 481
Danz, Ingeborg *mez* 82, 84, 93, 788
D'Arcangelo, Ildebrando *bass* 1209
Darlington, Stephen *cond* 753, 1156
Darman, Max Bragado *cond* 931, 932, 1190
Dart, Thurston *hpd* 530, 891
Dasch, Annette *sop* 276

Dausgaard, Thomas *cond* 819, 1021, 1022
Davidson, Ilana *sop* 230
Davies, Arthur *ten* 424, 425, 1201
Davies, Gareth *fl* 819
Davies, Iestyn *counterten* 511, 518
Davies, Maldwyn *ten* 512, 566, 1201
Davies, Neal *bar* 395, 518, 738, 1254
Davies, Neal *bass* .141, 511, 512, 520, 522, 568, 569, 789,
                                971, 1010, 1011, 1256
Davies, Paul Edmund *fl* 913
Davies, Philippa *fl, picc* 22, 121, 855, 967, 1139
Davies, Ryland *ten* 530
Davis, Andrew *cond* 185, 216, 272, 373, 394, 416, 417,
      419, 420, 422, 434, 590, 618, 620, 696, 796, 1132, 1175,
                                        1181, 1199, 1292
Davis, Colin *cond* .125, 191, 192, 193, 194, 195, 200, 284,
      286, 399, 403, 417, 418, 490, 518, 551, 552, 662, 683,
      764, 772, 875, 880, 881, 1066, 1068, 1072, 1073, 1110,
                                1128, 1159, 1219, 1289
Davis, Agnes *sop* 394, 434
Davis, Andrew *org* 530
Davis, Michael *vn* 913, 1181
Davis, Richard *fl* 431
Davislim, Steve *ten* 135, 136, 568, 711, 790
Dawson, Anne *sop* 1201
Dawson, Lynne *sop* . .84, 85, 234, 515, 516, 530, 538, 789,
                          888, 955, 1010, 1011, 1201
Dayez, Jean-Michel *pf* 432
Dazeley, William *bar* 639
De Cogan, Dara *vn* 271
De Labyrintho. 623
De Marchi, Alessandro *cond* 1097
Deane, Chris *cimb* 1130
Dearden, Ian *electronics* 216
Dearman, John *gtr* 477
Deas, Kevin *bass* 1195
De'Ath, Leslie *pf* 726, 1039, 1040
Deats, Gareth *vc* 1250
Debussy, Claude *pf* 68, 368
Defontaine, Martial *ten* 234
Degout, Stéphane *bar* 262, 434
Del Mar, Norman *cond* 117, 198, 199, 243, 284, 372, 373,
                          421, 646, 955
Delaigue, Renaud *bass* 758
Delft, Menno van *hpd* 1139
Deliau, Vincent *bar* 199
Deller, Alfred *counterten, cond* 889
Deller Consort. 889
Delmé Quartet. 407, 1081
Delogu, Gaetano *cond* 411
Delunsch, Mireille *sop* 198, 199, 1195
Demarquette, Henri *vc* 934
Demertzis, Georgios *vn* 1082
Demeyere, Ewald *hpd* 948
Demidenko, Nikolai *pf* 665, 666, 729, 1040
Demus, Jörg *pf* 672, 1012, 1015
Denève, Stéphane *cond* 952
Denize, Nadine *mez* 703
Denk, Jeremy *pf* 350, 982
Denley, Catherine *mez* 204, 393, 515, 517, 530, 1011,
                                        1254
Denman, John *cl* 440
Dennis Brain Wind Ensemble 1319
Dent, Susan *hn* 1020
Deplus, Guy *cl* 742
Deppe, François *vc* 546
Dermota, Anton *ten* 790

Dervaux, Pierre *cond* 858
Derwinger, Love *pf* 1078
Desborough School Choir 394, 434
Desenclos, Frédéric *org, cond* 390
Desjardins, Christophe *va* 188
Desmond, Astra *contr* 426
Desormière, Roger *cond* 68, 368
Dessay, Natalie *sop* 523, 720, 1320
Dessì, Daniella *sop* 938
Detroit Symphony Orchestra 347, 1169, 1173
Deubner, Maacha *sop* 628
Deuter, Florian *vn* 530
Deutsch, Helmut *pf* 265, 1007
Deutsche Kammerakademie Neuss 650
Deutsche Kammerphilharmonie, Bremen 549, 1019
Deutsches Symphony Orchestra. 4, 5
Devine, Stephen *cond* 890
Devoyon, Pascal *pf* 432, 962
DeYoung, Michelle *mez* 706
Di Donato, Joyce *mez* 531, 1254
Diaz, Raul *bn* 1176
Dickerson, Bernard *ten* 1198
Dickinson, Meriel *contr* 1198
Dickinson, Scott *va* 238
DiDonato, Joyce *mez* 85, 86, 530, 531
Dieleman, Marianne *contr* 690, 692
Dieltiens, Roel *vc* 734
Diener, Melanie *sop* 985
Dierstein, Christian *perc* 437
Dijk, Pieter van *org* 1139
Dimpho di Kopane Theatre Ensemble. 221
Ding, Lucy *cond* 480
Dinkin, Alvin *va* 983, 992, 993
Dirksen, Pieter *hpd* 1139
Diry, Roland *cl* 926
Divertimenti 595
Divertimenti Ensemble. 724
Dixon, Alistair *cond* 1147, 1148, 1149
Dixon, Peter *vc* 431
Djupsjöbacka, Gustav *pf* 687
Dobber, Andrezej *bar* 479
Dobozy, Borbála *hpd* 1244
Dobroven, Issay *cond* 243, 729, 1160
Dobson, Michael *ob d'amore* 530
Doherty, Niall *balt* 867
Dohnányi, Christoph von *cond*   172, 241, 243, 1116, 1119
Dolton, Geoffrey *bar* 474, 747
Domaine Musicale Orchestra 741, 742
Domingo, Plácido *cond* 1100, 1234, 1235
Domingo, Plácido *ten* 168, 530, 1263, 1352
Dominguez, Rosa *sop* 318
Domus 405, 431, 432
Donath, Helen *sop* 421
Donatis, Fiorenza de *vn* 1251
Donato, Vincenzo Di *ten* 755, 756
Donohoe, Peter *pf* .20, 222, 223, 442, 451, 545, 670, 742,
                          918, 1182, 1291, 1292
Dorati, Antál *cond* 347, 550, 916, 1167, 1334
Dordolo, Luca *ten* 755, 756
Dorey, Sue *vc* 180
Doufexis, Stella *mez* 435, 436, 938, 1034, 1035
Dougan, Eamonn *bass* 518
Doumenge, Pierre *vc* 956
Douse, Stephen *ten* 376
Dowd, Ronald *ten* 194, 195
Dowdeswell, Gretel *pf* 1188
Downer, Jane *rec* 507

Downes, Edward *cond* 420, 1214, 1231, 1232
D'Oyly Carte Opera Chorus. 1137, 1138
D'Oyly Carte Opera Orchestra. 1137, 1138
Drahos, Béla *dir, fl* 1243
Draijer, Jelle *bass* 755
Drake, Julius *pf* .102, 494, 609, 610, 917, 980, 1005, 1015,
. . . . 1031, 1032, 1078, 1172, 1349, 1353
Dresden Instrumental-Concert. 574
Dresden Körnerscher Sing-Verein. 574
Dresden Kreuzchor Children's Voices. 1121
Dresden Singakademie 194
Dresden State Opera Children's Chorus 602
Dresden State Opera Chorus 194, 1121, 1272
Drobinsky, Mark *vc* 1316
Drottningholm Court Theatre Chorus 471
Drottningholm Court Theatre Orchestra 471
Drucker, Stanley *cl* 99
Druckman, Daniel *perc* 1130
Druian, Rafael *vn* 1311
Drummond, David *cond* 358
Drury, David *org* 1045
Drury Byrne, Aisling *vc* 680
Dry, Marion *mez*. 7
Du Brassus Choir 829
Du Pré, Jacqueline *vc* 413, 415, 1019, 1322
Dubow, Marilyn *vn* 354
Duchâble, François-René *pf* 289
René Duclos Choir 218, 968, 1350
Dudamel, Gustavo *cond* 1165, 1313
Dufour, Mathieu *fl* 363
Dufourcet, Marie-Bernadette *org* 1188
Dugardin, Steve *alto* 226
Dukes, Philip *va* 179, 238, 1145
Dumay, Augustin *vn* 256
Dumestre, Vincent *dir* 228, 675
Dun, Tan *cond* 1150
Dune, Catherine *sop* 499
Dunedin Consort. 89, 518
Dunn, Thomas *cond* . . . . .*. 530
Dunn, Susan *sop* 984
Dunnett, David *org* 1154
Duo Amadè 786
Dupin, François *glok* 742
Dupree, Jillon Stoppels *hpd* 464
Durrant, Benjamin *treb* 189
Dussek, Michael *pf* 98, 122, 236, 237, 654, 956, 957
Dussek, Rachel *pf* 957
Düsseldorf Musikverein Chorus. 984
Duthoit, Marie-Louise *sop* 325
Dutoit, Charles *cond* . . .105, 329, 444, 588, 590, 645, 732,
. . . . 861, 965, 1166, 1317
Duven, Richard *vc* 993, 994
Duykers, John *ten* 7

E

Early Opera Company 412, 521, 539
East, Angela *vc* 530
East Suffolk Children's Orchestra 284
Ébène Quartet. 363, 913, 914
Eberhard, Sofia Söderberg *cond* 1187
Ebony Band. 929
Economou, Nicholas *pf* 1159, 1160, 5614
Edelmann, Otto *bass* 142
Eder, György *vc* 1244

Edgar-Wilson, Richard *ten* 239
Edinburgh Festival Chorus. . 135, 615, 693, 738, 804, 943
Edinburgh Quartet 450
Edison, Noel *cond* 1201
Edwardes, Claire *perc* 214
Edwards, John Owen *cond* 206
Edwards, Sian *cond* 1302
Edwards, Gavin *hn* 1020
Egarr, Richard *cond* 503
Egarr, Richard *hpd* 210, 349, 453, 508, 509, 839
Eggen, Christian *cond* 439
Egmond, Max van *bar* 85
Ehnes, James *vn* 399, 416, 773, 987, 1322
Ehrling, Sixten *cond* 1066
Ehwald, Christian *cond* 574
Eiche, Markus *bar* 832
Eichelberger, Freddy *org* 1139
Eichhorn, Kurt *cond* 832
Eisenlohr, Ulrich *fp* 1006
Eizen, Artur *bass* 1051
Elder, Mark *cond* . .170, 171, 178, 283, 303, 360, 361, 381,
. . . . 411, 424, 589, 590, 1068, 1112, 1262
Elgar, Edward *cond* 415, 418, 421
Elision Ensemble. 103
Ellett, Charlotte *sop* 919
Elliott, Paul *ten* 317
Ellis, Gregory *vn* 347
Ellis, Osian *hp* 445
Elora Festival Singers 1201
Elysian Quartet 753
Elysian Singers of London 376
Emerson Quartet. 109, 735, 1060
Emilia Romagna 'Toscanini' Symphony Orchestra. . . 463
Emmanuel Music Orchestra 82
Emperor Quartet. 683
Endellion Quartet 9, 147
Endo, Yoshiko *pf* 920
Enescu, George *cond* 732
Engel, Karl *pf* 263, 1306
Engel, Norman *tpt* 892
Engerer, Brigitte *pf* 262
Engeset, Bjarte *cond* 1194
English, Gerald *ten* 832
English Baroque Soloists.84, 85, 87, 88, 89, 167, 168, 512,
. . . . . . 516, 530, 563, 566, 568, 570, 755, 759, 780, 790, 798,
. . . . 800, 804, 806, 807
English Chamber Orchestra . .91, 104, 233, 270, 271, 272,
. . . . . 280, 283, 290, 319, 355, 397, 398, 407, 530, 646, 650,
. . . . . 732, 764, 766, 767, 768, 769, 771, 891, 1049, 1169,
. . . . 1201, 1322
English Chamber Orchestra Wind Ensemble 300
The English Concert. . .211, 239, 470, 504, 506, 518, 528,
. . . . 530, 542, 566, 773, 776, 780, 1250
The English Concert Choir 518, 530, 566
The English Cornett and Sackbut Ensemble. 448
English National Opera Chorus . .283, 383, 411, 533, 536,
. . . . 537, 618, 1269, 1281, 1302
English National Opera Orchestra. . . .184, 283, 383, 411,
. . . . 533, 536, 537, 618, 1269, 1280, 1281, 1302
English Northern Philharmonia. 222, 223, 645, 1288,
. . . . 1290, 1291, 1293
English Opera Group Chamber Orchestra 280
English Opera Group Chorus. 282, 283
English Opera Group Ensemble. 278
English Opera Group Orchestra. . . . .`. . . 282, 284, 287
English String Orchestra. 439
English String Quartet 1319

English Symphony Orchestra 978
Engström, Stefan *perc* 1187
(Anonymous) Ensemble 925
Ensemble 360 781
Ensemble 415 1256
Ensemble Artaserse 1257
Ensemble Clément Janequin 301
Ensemble Explorations 404, 734
Ensemble InterContemporain . . 235, 236, 656, 985, 1032
Ensemble Jachet de Mantoue 611
Ensemble Matheus 948, 1259, 1261
Ensemble Modern 179, 214, 643, 926, 1192
Ensemble Musica Nova 826
Ensemble New Art 354
Ensemble Oriol 935
Ensemble Sonnerie 502, 507, 1244
Ensemble Spirale 1332
Ensemble Vocal le Motet de Genève 939
Ensemble X 1302
Ensemble Zefiro 430, 507, 1309
Entremont, Philippe *cond* 1169
EntreQuatre Quitar Quartet 931
Eötvös, Peter *cond* 105, 323, 356, 546
Equilbey, Laurence *cond* 262, 434, 857
Equiluz, Kurt *ten* 85, 755
Erben, Frank-Michael *vn* 733
Erez, Arnon *pf* 225
(Eric) Ericson Chamber Choir . 135, 168, 261, 1207, 1208,
1209
Ericsson, Mikael *vc* 613
Erlingsson, Loftur *bar* 653
Ermler, Mark *cond* 815, 816, 5678
Ernst Senff Chorus 245, 248, 693, 984
Ernst-Senff Women's Chorus 693
Erskine, Peter *perc* 1192
Eschenbach, Christoph *cond* 106, 188, 355, 854, 951, 961,
962, 1019, 1110, 1114, 1310
Eschenbach, Christoph *pf* 998, 1019
Eschenburg, Hans-Jakob *vc* 1016
Esswood, Paul *alto* 530
(Nicolaus) Esterházy Sinfonia . . 169, 170, 644, 1243, 1244
Estonian National Male Choir 1193
Estonian National Symphony Orchestra . . 842, 844, 1193
Estonian Philharmonic Chamber Choir . . 844, 1193, 1342
Eugelmi, Nicolò *va* 263
Europa Academy Chorus 803
Europa Galante 227, 1245, 1251, 1259
European Union Childrens Choir 195
European Voices 759
Evangelatos, Daphne *contr* 1173
Evans, Geraint *bar* 89
Evans, Nancy *contr* 1312
Evans, Peter *pf* 685
Evans, Peter *ten* 197
Evans, Rebecca *sop* 167, 374
Evans, Robert *bass* 623, 754, 755, 888
Evans, Wynford *ten* 84, 85, 1198
Evitts, David *bar* 1130
Evreux, Pierre *ten* 324
Evtodieva, Victoria *sop* 1062
Ewing, Alan *bass* 513
Exon Singers 1083

F

Fabre-Garrus, Bernard *cond* 621, 623
Faerber, Jörg *cond* 1317
Fagen, Arthur *cond* 680
(I) Fagiolini 448
Fagius, Hans *org* 393
Failoni Chamber Orchestra, Budapest . . . 82, 83, 940, 941
Failoni Orchestra, Budapest 810
Falkner, Keith *bass* 426
Falletta, JoAnn *cond* 347, 495, 928, 987
Faltl, Fritz *bn* 656
Fantinuoli, Antonio *vc* 1251
Farley, Carole *sop* 230, 649, 936
Farnes, Richard *cond* 114
Farnham Youth Choir 959
Farr, Stephen *org* 1094
Farrall, Joy *cl* 1102
Farrar, Geraldine *sop* 1350
Farrington, Ian *org* 596, 1183
Fasolis, Diego *cond* 328, 481, 535
Fassbaender, Brigitte *mez* 263, 984, 1301
Faultless, Margaret *bq vn* 1243
Faust, Georg *vc* 399, 580, 1170
Faust, Isabelle *vn* 545, 624, 713, 998
Favres Solisten Vereinigung 810
Fedi, Elena Cecchi *sop* 1097
Fedoseyev, Vladimir *cond* 867, 1160
Fedotov, Maxim *vn* 290
Feeney, John *db* 1130
Feinberg, Alan *pf* 123
Feld, Melanie *cor anglais* 1130, 1132
Feldman, Jonathan *pf* 1159
Félix, Thierry *bass* 755, 756
Feller, Bart *fl* 1132
Felty, Janice *mez* 1302
Fenby, Eric *cond* 372, 373
Fenby, Eric *pf* 374
(La) Fenice 309
Fentross, Mike *lute* 1243
Fergus-Thompson, Gordon *pf* 1041
Fernandez, François *vn* 648
Fernandez, Huguette *vn* 742
Fernández, Yetzabel Arias *sop* 525
Ferrari, Elena *sop* 358
Ferrarini, Gianluca *ten* 755, 756, 1247
Ferras, Christian *vn* 1161
Ferrier, Kathleen *contr* 530, 690, 696, 707, 708
Festetics Quartet 557
Fibonacci Sequence 935
Fiedler, Arthur *cond* 455, 456
Figueras, Montserrat *sop* 709
Filipova, Elena *sop* 1208, 1209
Filsell, Jeremy *org* . . 391, 392, 393, 840, 1188, 1240, 1304
Fine Arts Brass Ensemble 212
Fingerhut, Margaret *pf* 117, 121
Fink, Bernarda *contr* . . . .
88, 89, 264, 307, 318, 408, 518, 758, 779, 790, 791, 972,
1029, 1030
Finley, Gerald *bar* 102, 197, 275, 442, 566, 568, 609, 610,
790, 791, 917, 1011, 1032, 1095, 1190, 1191, 1353
Finnie, Linda *mez* 424, 867, 929
Finnilä, Birgit *mez* 421, 690, 692
Finnis, Catherine *viol* 887

Finnis, Jerome *treb* 888
Finnish Opera Festival Chorus................. 1078
Finnish Philharmonic Choir................... 907, 969
Finnish Radio Symphony Orchestra...355, 627, 659, 660,
           969, 1066, 1078, 1295
Finzi Singers 277, 591, 1183, 1294
Fiorentino, Sergio *pf* 666
Firkušny, Rudolf *pf*............................. 1322
Fischer, Adám *cond* 379, 553, 805, 968, 1212, 1348
Fischer, György *cond* 793
Fischer, Iván *cond* .106, 107, 396, 397, 401, 634, 663, 695,
           697, 797, 898, 899, 1107
Fischer, Thierry *cond* 592, 604
Fischer, Edwin *pf* 131, 160, 1009
Fischer, Julia *vn* 242, 243, 632, 736, 1159
Fischer-Dieskau, Dietrich *cond* .. 1019, 1114, 1210, 1263
Fischer-Dieskau, Dietrich *bar* 89, 261, 263, 271, 281, 672,
   690, 694, 707, 832, 833, 1006, 1012, 1013, 1015, 1052,
           1296
Fisher, Gillian *sop* 891
Fisher, Philip *pf* 1323
Fisk, Elliot *gtr* 188
Fistoulari, Anatole *cond* 126, 1000
Fitches, Thomas *org* 1201
Fitz-Gerald, Mark *cond* 1058
Fitzwilliam Quartet.............................. 560
Flagstad, Kirsten *sop* 1111
Fleisher, Leon *pf* 130, 131, 242, 1323
Fleming, Renée *sop* 530, 738, 1110, 1111, 1114, 1209,
           1241, 1329, 1352
Flemish Radio Choir............................. 903
Flemish Radio Orchestra....................... 1126
Fletcher, Lyn *vn* 271
Florence Maggio Musicale Chorus...177, 383, 885, 1217,
           1350
Florence Maggio Musicale Orchestra.177, 383, 885, 1217,
           1350
Florestan Trio 151, 256, 363, 406, 735, 784, 966, 997,
           1023, 4166
Flórez, Juan Diego *ten* 1353
Florilegium Ensemble............... 1177, 1178, 1253
Florio, Antonio *cond* 322, 818
Foccroulle, Bernard *org* 307
Fondazione Orchestra Stabile di Bergamo 'Gatano
   Donizetti' 452
Forck, Bernhard *dir* 470
Ford, Bruce *ten* 474, 747, 938, 939
Ford, Ian *treb* 627
Ford, Nmon *bar* 230
Foresti, Sergio *bass* 1247
Formosa Quartet................................. 362
Forrester, Maureen *contr* 690, 692
Forsberg, Bengt *pf* 238, 494, 1076, 1078
Forster, Benjamin *perc* 1348
Fortin, Olivier *hpd* 905
Foster, Lawrence *cond* 661, 731, 975
Foster, Mark *cond* 427
Fouchécourt, Jean-Paul *ten* 436
Foulkes, Carolyn *sop* 547
Four Nations Ensemble 318
Fournier, Brigitte *sop* 199
Fournier, Pierre *vc* 397
Fowke, Philip *pf* 372
Fowler, Bruce *ten* 938
Fox, Jacqueline *spkr* 565
Fox, Sarah *sop* 228, 1203
Francis, Alun *cond* 848

Franck, Mikko *cond* 909, 1073
Frank, Pamela *vn* 772, 994
Frankfurt Radio Orchestra 1298
Frankfurt Radio Symphony Orchestra 397, 1058
Frankfurt University of Music and Performing Arts Vocal
   Ensemble 1058
Frantz, Caspar *pf* 122
Frantz, Justus *pf* 998
Franz, Helmut *cond* 656
Frasca, Dominic *gtr* 925
Frautschi, Jennifer *vn* 1130
Fredman, Myer *cond* 116, 266
Freiburg Baroque Orchestra..82, 549, 571, 672, 766, 779,
        795, 799, 800, 1247, 5770
Freiburg Philharmonic Orchestra (members) 823
Freiburg Soloists Choir........................... 823
Freire, Nelson *pf* 161, 241, 242, 366, 896, 1317
Frémaux, Louis *cond* 720
French, Stewart *gtr* 959
French Army Chorus.......................... 188, 483
French National Orchestra..200, 218, 220, 368, 370, 434,
        742, 912, 1050
French National Radio Symphony Orchestra ...217, 218,
        219, 1350
French Radio and TV Opera Orchestra........... 192
French Radio Chamber Orchestra 742
French Radio Choir............................. 218, 219
French Radio Chorus 218, 220, 720
French Radio Philharmonic Orchestra........ 356, 720
French Radio Women's Chorus.................... 742
Frenkel, Noa *alto* 823
Fretwork 178, 314, 315, 1157, 1187, 1342
Frey, Paul *ten* 690, 692
Fricsay, Ferenc *cond* 104, 1099
Frideswide Consort............................. 312
Friend, Lionel *cond* 265, 919, 1191
Friend, Rodney *vn* 418
Fries, Dorothee *sop* 1179
Frimmer, Monika *sop* 93
Frith, Benjamin *pf* 120, 437, 438, 731, 736, 744, 1026,
           1092
Frizza, Riccardo *cond* 946, 947, 1353
Fromm, Nancy Wait *sop* 820
Fröst, Martin *cl* 252, 586, 1295
Frühbeck de Burgos, Rafael *cond* 489, 490, 912, 1269
Fuge, Katharine *sop* 83
Fulgoni, Sara *mez* 738
Fullbrook, Charles *bells* 180
Fuller, Andrew *vc* 98, 654
Fuller, Louisa *vn* 591
Fullington, Andrea *voc* 317
Furtwängler, Wilhelm *cond* 131, 132, 142, 245, 799, 1111,
           1262

G

Gabriel, Alain *ten* 199
Gabriel Quartet................................. 500
Gabrieli Consort ... 89, 90, 518, 520, 521, 522, 530, 568,
        569, 789, 860, 1238, 1343
Gabrieli Players .89, 90, 518, 520, 521, 522, 530, 568, 569,
        789, 860
Gabrieli Quartet 251, 764
Gächinger Kantorei, Stuttgart 93, 690
Gadd, Charmian *vn* 715, 7153
Gaeta, Luis *bass* 461

Gaetani, Jan de *mez* 581
Gage, Irwin *pf* 408, 1008
Gagnepain, Xavier *vc* 432
Galicia Symphony Orchestra 947
Galimir Quartet. 181
Gallén, Ricardo *gtr* 931, 932
Galli, Emanuela *sop* 524
Galliera, Alceo *cond* 490, 941, 1350
Gallimaufry Ensemble. 214
Gallois, Pascal *bn* 188
Gallois, Patrick *fl* 820, 907
Galvez Vallejo, Daniel *ten* 197
Gamba, Rumon *cond* .179, 603, 637, 638, 724, 920, 1200,
1336
Gambill, Robert *ten* 649
Gandini, Gerardo *pf* 850
Garanca, Elina *mez* 794, 1354, 1357
Garben, Cord *pf*, *cond* 199, 1301
Gardelli, Lamberto *cond* 874, 1225
Garden, Mary *sop* 68, 368
Gardiner, John Eliot *cond* 84, 85, 87, 88, 89, 131, 135,
136, 139, 166, 167, 168, 192, 197, 199, 201, 261, 262,
323, 368, 371, 414, 415, 472, 473, 512, 516, 530, 563,
566, 568, 570, 651, 734, 755, 759, 780, 790, 798, 800,
804, 806, 807, 927, 931, 1020, 1134, 1208, 1209, 1344
Garrison, Jon *ten* 1143, 1183
Gastinel, Anne *vc* 634
Gáti, Istvan *bar* 82, 83, 89
Gatti, Daniele *cond* 986, 1164
Gaudier Ensemble. 776, 996, 1296
Gauntlett, Ambrose *va d'amore* 1347
Gauvin, Karina *sop* 101
Gavazzeni, Gianandrea *cond* 380, 718, 884, 1213
Gawriloff, Saschko *vn* 656
Gedda, Nicolai *ten* 89, 424
Geidt, James *treb* 189
Gekker, Chris *tpt* 1130
Geneva Grand Theatre Chorus 305, 945
Gens, Véronique *sop* 319, 793, 892
Genz, Christoph *ten* 792
Genz, Stephan *bar* . . . 165, 434, 435, 444, 706, 792, 1030
Geoffrey Mitchell Choir178, 196, 421, 474, 589, 590, 747,
809, 810, 834, 886, 946, 1121, 1180
Geoghegan, Karen *bn* 1323
Georg, Mechthild *contr* 1179
George, Michael *bass* ..239, 511, 514, 515, 517, 519, 526,
789, 888, 889, 891, 1009, 1010, 1011, 1090, 1254, 1309
Georgian, Karine *vc* 251
Gerecz, Arpad *vn* 781
Gergiev, Valery *cond* . . .232, 496, 637, 699, 702, 811, 813,
814, 815, 816, 863, 864, 865, 869, 930, 949, 1127, 1128,
1159, 1174, 1175, 1209
Gerhaher, Christian *bar* .276, 568, 832, 1006, 1029, 1032,
1033
Gerhardt, Alban *vc* 266, 592, 922
Geringas, David *vc* 1193
German Radio Philharmonic Orchestra. 711
Gershon, Grant *cond* 924, 926
Gershwin, George *pf* 455
Gesualdo Consort Amsterdam 457
Ghelardini, Francesco *counterten* 755, 756
Ghent Collegium Vocale 82, 84, 1038
Gheorghiu, Angela *sop* 871, 1207, 1208, 1209, 1210, 1354
Ghiaurov, Nicolai *bass* 1208
Ghione, Franco *cond* 718, 1232, 1234, 1350
Giacometti, Paolo *pf*. 398
(Il) Giardino Armonico Ensemble 503, 1247, 1249

Gibbons, Jack *pf* 456
Gibbs, Peter *vn* 889
Gibbs, Robert *vn* 119
Gibson, Rodney *ten* 1210
Gibson, Alexander *cond* 530
Gielen, Michael *cond* 292, 320, 690, 705, 1132
Giesa, Susanne *pf* 1012
Gieseking, Walter *pf* 143, 364, 366, 793
Gilad, Jonathan *pf*. 736
Gilchrist, James *ten* ..89, 90, 91, 486, 511, 512, 573, 600,
754, 755, 1003
Gilels, Elena *pf* 771
Gilels, Emil *pf* 129, 131, 241, 242, 255, 334, 493, 771,
963, 1160
Giles, Andrew *alto* 406
Gilfry, Rodney *bar* 261, 262, 568
Gilibert, Gabrielle *mez*. 1350
Gililov, Pavel *pf* 406
Gimse, Håvard *pf* 1194
Ginn, Michael *treb* 512
Giordano, Laura *sop* 937
Giuffredi, Corrado *cl* 1316
Giulini, Carlo Maria *cond* .85, 86, 130, 131, 198, 199, 247,
275, 292, 297, 299, 331, 798, 800, 1206, 1209, 1215,
1216, 1220, 1231, 1236, 1237
Glander, Matthias *cl* 784
(Philip) Glass Ensemble 465
Glemser, Bernd *pf* 331, 644, 901, 1027
Glennie, Evelyn *perc* 685, 1193
Glimmerglass Opera Orchestra 180
Globalis Symphony Orchestra 593
Glyndebourne Chorus. .170, 171, 456, 537, 759, 797, 805,
808, 1287
Glyndebourne Festival Chorus . . .370, 474, 618, 620, 796,
800, 807, 940, 1175
Glyndebourne Festival Opera. 170, 171
Glyndebourne Festival Orchestra 620
Gobbi, Tito *bar* 881
Goebel, Reinhard *va, vn, dir* 573
Goehr, Walter *cond* 255, 330
Goerne, Matthias *bar* 88, 89, 165, 1005, 1007, 1014, 1310
Goff, Scott *fl* 852
Goldberg, Rebecca *bn* 919
Golden Age Singers. 1319
Goldner Quartet 225, 268
Goldschmidt, Maria *fl* 1348
Goltz, Gottfried von der *vn* 82, 672, 1247
Goltz, Gottfried von der *cond* 549, 571, 766
Goluses, Nicholas *gtr* 1087
Gomberg, Harold *ob* 99
Gomez, Jill *sop* 755
Gómez-Martínez, Miguel Angel *cond* 941, 942
Gondek, Juliana *sop* 1143
Gonley, Stephanie *vn* 403
Gönnenwein, Wolfgang *cond* 809
Gonville and Caius College Choir, Cambridge 1046
Goodall, Reginald *cond* 1269, 1271, 1280, 1281
Goode, Richard *pf* 155, 769, 770, 771, 787
Goode, Richard *dir* 770
Gooding, Julia *sop* 89, 90
Goodman, Benny *cl* 346
Goodman, James *treb* 888
Goodman, Roy *hpd, dir* 502, 531
Goossens, Eugene *cond* 1159
Gordon, Hannah *spkr* 277
Goritzki, Johannes *cond* 650
Goerne, Matthias *bar* 1007, 1011

Gothenburg Symphony Orchestra 230, 496, 625, 820,
          1072, 1075, 1163, 1189, 1301
Gothic Voices 578
Gothoni, Mark *vn* 650
Gothóni, Ralf *cond* 464
Gottlieb, Gordon *perc* 354, 1130
Gottlieb, Gordon *timp* 1130
Gould, Chris *pf* 501
Gould, Lucy *vn* 120, 1092
Gould, Stephen *ten* 639
Gould Piano Trio 120, 1092
Gower, Jane *bn* 780
Grabois, Daniel *hn* 1130
Gracis, Ettore *cond* 895, 897, 912
Graf, Uta *sop* 690
Graf, Hans *cond* 395
Graffin, Philippe *vn* 343, 964
Graham, Nathan Lee *sngr* 230
Graham, Susan *mez* . . . 196, 198, 199, 327, 500, 609, 916
          935, 1028, 1114, 1355
Granada City Orchestra 950
(La) Grande Ecurie et La Chambre du Roy 480, 532
Grante, Carlo *pf* 976
Gray, Emily *sop* 1200
Grazzi, Alberto *bn* 1251
Grazzi, Paolo *ob* 1247, 1251
Green, Adam *bar* 272
Green, Stuart *va* 411
Greenall, Matthew *cond* 376
Greene, Arthur *pf* 229
Greevy, Bernadette *mez* 245, 246, 434
Gregg Smith Singers 1132
Gregor-Smith, Bernard *vc* 783
Gregory, Julian *treb* 189
Grenoble Chamber Orchestra 830
Grenoble Orchestra 831
Grier, Francis *org* 432, 962
Griffey, Anthony Dean *ten* 275
Griffiths, David *bar* 600
Griffiths, Howard *cond* 439, 927
Grimaud, Hélène *pf* 105, 455, 456
Grimwood, Daniel *pf* 667
Grindenko, Tatjana *vn* 978
Grindlay, Paul *bass-bar* 892
Gringolts, Ilya *vn* 27, 836, 1151
Grinke, Frederick *vn* 605
Grishko, Vladimir *ten* 1173
Gritton, Susan *sop* . 228, 279, 511, 512, 518, 519, 520, 521,
          522, 530, 564, 566, 591, 599, 600, 790, 856, 888, 889,
          1003, 1254, 1255, 1256
Grivnov, Vsevolod *ten* 468, 1131
Grobe, Donald *ten* 690
Grochowska, Maria *fl* 1195
Grodd, Uwe *cond* 600
Grodnikaite, Liora *mez* 1111
Groethuysen, Andreas *pf* 260, 786
Groh, Markus *pf* 260
Gromadsky, Vitaly *bass* 1051
Grondona, Stefano *gtr* 670
Groop, Monica *mez* 495, 1078
Groot, Peter de *alto* 92
Groot Omroepkoor Netherlands Radio Philharmonic
   Orchestra 1314
Gross, Michael *vc* 922

Group For Contemporary Music 438
Groves, Paul *ten* 196, 424, 1132
Groves, Charles *cond* 355
Gruenberg, Erich *vn* 742
Gruett, Marcus *perc* 1035
Gruffydd Jones, Angharad *sop* 959, 1155
Grumiaux, Arthur *vn* 772
Grumiaux Trio 781, 997
Grümmer, Elisabeth *sop* 261
Gruppo Vocale Cantemus 328
Grützmann, Susanne *pf* 1018
Guadagno, Anton *cond* 485
Gudbjörnsson, Gunnar *ten* 653
Guerrier, David *tpt* 965
Guest, George *cond* 272, 394, 434
Guglielmo, Giovanni *vn*, *dir* 504, 1153
Gui, Vittorio *cond* 370, 940
Guieu, Renaud *vc* 500
Guildford Philharmonic Choir 441
Guildford Philharmonic Orchestra 441
Guillon, Damien *counterten* 675
Guittart, Henk *cond* 384
Gulda, Friedrich *pf* 156, 157, 788
Gunn, Nathan *bar* 203
Gunnarsson, Claes *vc* 1301
Gunson, Ameral *mez* 615, 1292
Gunzenhauser, Stephen *cond* 835, 864
Güra, Werner *ten* . . . 1003, 1012, 1029, 1031, 1307, 5770
Gurning, Alexandre *pf* 1316
Gustafsson, Jan-Erik *vc* 909
Gustav Mahler Youth Orchestra 243
Guthrie, Thomas *bass* 210
Gutman, Natalia *vc* 250, 1022
Guy, Barry *db* 498
Guye, François *vc* 1105
Gvazava, Eteri *sop* 361, 1311
Gwinnett Young Singers 477

H

Haage, Peter *ten* 984
Haas, Frédérick *hpd* 974
Haavisto, Varpu *va d'amore* 709
Haberdashers' Aske's School Girls Choir 1214
Hacker, Alan *cl* 439
Hacker, Alan *cond* 215
Hadady, Lazlo *ob* 188
Haddad, Jamie *perc* 477
Haefliger, Andreas *pf* 161
Haefliger, Ernst *ten* 299, 985
Haenchen, Hartmut *cond* 1275
Haendel, Ida *vn* 1153
Haer, Marjan de *hp* 765
Haffner Wind Ensemble 724
Hagegård, Håkan *bar* 832, 1310
Hagen, Clemens *vc* 133, 848
Hagen Quartet 109, 362, 656, 992, 994
Hägganderr, Mari Anne *sop* 690, 692
Hagley, Alison *sop* 521, 530
Hahn, Detlef *vn* 638
Hahn, Hilary *vn* 99, 100, 835, 981, 1051
Haider, Friedrich *cond* 175, 176

Haïm, Emmanuelle *dir* 523, 759, 1320
Haimovitz, Matt *vc* 656, 992, 8550
Haitink, Bernard *cond* . . 113, 126, 127, 128, 129, 131, 138,
    141, 242, 244, 245, 284, 359, 361, 368, 370, 619, 690,
    692, 693, 800, 805, 1052, 1054, 1055, 1057, 1104, 1121,
           1198, 1268, 1317
Hakala, Tommi *bar* 1077
Hakim, Naji *org* 1324
Halász, Michael *cond* 169, 170, 414, 644, 810, 1110
Haley, Olga *mez* 1312
Hall, Carol *sop* 84, 85
Hall, Lucia *vn* 1316
Hall, Lucy *vn* 1022
Hall, Meredith *sop* 892
Hallchurch, Philip *treb* 888
Hallé Choir 245, 246, 282, 421, 424, 426
Hallé Choir (Women's Voices) 589, 590
Hallé Orchestra . . . 117, 192, 245, 246, 271, 282, 297, 298,
    360, 361, 417, 418, 421, 424, 426, 589, 590, 705, 707,
      746, 821, 1068, 1069, 1112, 1262, 1311
Hallenberg, Ann *mez* 567
Haller, Benoît *bar* 480
Haller, Salomé *sop* 480, 481, 758
Haller, Benoît *cond* 1037
Hallgrím's Church Motet Choir 653
Halling, Elizabeth *mez* 1029
Halls, David *org* 502
Halls, Matthew *org* 502
Halls, Matthew *cond* 520
Halstead, Anthony *hn* 1176
Halstead, Anthony *cond* 226
Hamari, Júlia *mez* 690
Hamburg Philharmonic Orchestra 739
Hamburg State Opera Chorus 143, 186
Hamburg State Philharmonic Orchestra 186, 1310
Hamburger, Paul *pf* 264, 1348
Hamelin, Marc-André *pf* . . . 203, 254, 303, 332, 389, 475,
    476, 487, 562, 609, 629, 730, 954, 1042, 1324, 1325
Hamilton, Susan *sop* 89, 518, 888
Hammer, Moshe *vn* 836
Hampson, Thomas *bar* 135, 608, 755, 1011
Hampstead Church Boys' Choir 89
Hamzem, Samuel *hn* 1240
Handel and Haydn Society Orchestra 503
Handley, Vernon *cond* . . . 97, 98, 115, 117, 118, 236, 237,
    302, 372, 415, 418, 439, 440, 441, 475, 596, 727, 1080,
         1081, 1092, 1197, 1290
Hankinson, Michael *cond* 343
Hannoversche Hofkapelle 1179
Hanover Band 239
Hanover Boys' Choir 630
Hanover Radio Philharmonic Orchestra 1301
Hansen, Bo Anker *bar* 821
Hansen, Michael W. *bar* 821
Hanslip, Chloë *vn* 122, 475
Hansmann, Rotraud *sop* 85
Hanson, Howard *cond* 543
Hantaï, Jérôme *fp* 166
Hantaï, Pierre *hpd* 648, 709, 973
Hanzlik, Louis *tpt* 1130
Harada, Hideyo *pf* 901
Harada, Takashi *ondes martinot* 742
Hardenberger, Håkan *tpt* 656
Harding, Daniel *cond* 287, 548, 797, 1160, 1358
Harms, Kirsti *mez* 1045
Harnisch, Rachel *sop* 1311

Harnoncourt, Nikolaus *cond* . . . 85, 88, 89, 125, 126, 131,
    132, 133, 134, 168, 170, 172, 245, 295, 299, 399, 402,
    403, 404, 503, 552, 568, 572, 734, 755, 761, 780, 788,
    790, 791, 793, 829, 889, 989, 990, 1029, 1036, 1101
Harp Consort 452, 1247
Harper, Heather *sop* . . . 91, 274, 275, 518, 690, 692, 1298
Harrell, Lynn *vc* 319, 580, 1151
Harris, John Mark *hpd* 1308
Harris, Michael *cl* 855
Harrold, Steven *ten* 684
Hart, Mary Ann *mez* 1132
Härtelová, Lydie *hp* 407
Hartenstein, István *bn* 1244
Hartley, Jacqueline *vn* 1181
Hartmann-Claverie, Valérie *ondes martinot* 742, 746
Hartog, Bernhard *vn* 1170
Hartwig, Hildegard *contr* 143
Harvard Glee Club 347
Harvey, Peter *bass* 87, 89, 90, 166, 228, 308, 521, 530,
      568, 569, 573, 754, 755, 888, 891, 892
Hasegawa, Yoko *vc* 327
Haslam, David *cond* 437, 438
Hasson, Maurice *vn* 245, 246
Hatfield, Lesley *vn* 842
Hauk, Franz *org* 923
Haukås, Jan-Inge *db* 331
Hauptmann, Cornelius *bass* 88, 89, 168, 790
Hauts-de-Seine Maîtrise 1226, 1229
Haverinen, Margareta *sop* 1057
Haveron, Andrew *vn* 613
Haydn Trio 570
Hayes, Oliver *treb* 627
Hayroudinoff, Rustem *pf* 399, 902
Hayward, Marie *sop* 1198
Hazlewood, Charles *cond* 221
Hegedus, Olga *vc* 300
Hegyi, Ildikó *vn* 143
Heifetz, Jascha *vn* . . . 132, 241, 243, 290, 636, 1066, 1159,
          1290, 1325
Heilmann, Uwe *ten* 788
Héja, Domonkos *cond* 379
Helbich, Wolfgang *cond* 93
Heldwein, Walter *bass* 690
Heller, Marsha *ob* 354
Hellmann, Claudia *mez* 299
Helmchen, Martin *pf* 1001
Helsinki Philharmonic Orchestra 907, 908, 909, 969,
      1068, 1070, 1073, 1074, 1077, 1079, 1135
Helsinki University Chorus 1076
Hemmi, Tomoko *pf* 643
Henck, Herbert *pf* 316, 750
Henderson, Roy *bar* 1312
Hendl, Walter *cond* 636, 1066, 1325
Hendricks, Barbara *sop* 832
Hengelbrock, Thomas *cond* 510, 568, 672, 673
Henry, Didier *bar* 499
Henry, Michel *ob* 1243
Henschel, Dietrich *bar* 85, 86, 88, 89, 179, 188,
          988, 568, 577
Henschel, Jane *contr* 703
Henschel Quartet 735
Henstra, Siebe *hpd* 1139
Heppner, Ben *ten* 690, 692
Herbers, Werner *cond* 929
Hereford Choral Society 426
Herford, Henry *bar* 224, 530
Heringman, Jacob *gtr, lute, viol* 623

Hermann, Roland *bar* 143
Hernandez, Cesar *ten* 1208, 1209
Herreweghe, Philippe *cond* 82, 83, 84, 168, 198, 199, 434,
435, 444, 888, 1038
Herrick, Christopher *org* 1326
Herrmann, Anke *sop* 1097, 1259
Hessian Radio Orchestra, Frankfurt. 364
Hewitt, Angela *pf* 158, 323, 743, 914
Heynis, Aafje *contr* 690, 692
Hickox, Richard *cond* . . .87, 167, 180, 189, 190, 266, 267,
274, 275, 277, 281, 283, 284, 286, 288, 374, 412, 414,
415, 419, 423, 424, 425, 440, 478, 485, 486, 518, 538,
564, 565, 566, 567, 588, 591, 595, 599, 600, 654, 739,
929, 954, 955, 956, 957, 1003, 1093, 1095, 1136, 1182,
1198, 1199, 1200, 1202, 1204, 1261, 1293
(Richard) Hickox Singers 1199
Hicks, Malcolm *org* 497, 1199
Hida, Yoshie *sop* 89, 90
Higginbottom, Edward *cond* 91, 518, 673, 1186
Highcliffe Junior Choir. 590, 832
Highgate School Choir. 272
Hill, David *cond* 96, 212, 278, 590, 1094, 1149, 1238,
1287
Hill, David *org* 703
Hill, Jenny *sop* 85, 86, 91
Hill, Martyn *ten* 274, 275, 277, 395, 512, 985, 1011, 1090,
1184, 1201
Hill, Peter *pf* 183, 744
Hilliard Ensemble 623, 681, 842, 847, 1047, 1299
Hillier, Paul *bass* 843
Hillier, Paul *voc* 317
Hillier, Paul *cond* .317, 623, 681, 825, 843, 844, 847, 926,
1096, 1342
Hindemith, Paul *cond* 1102
Hindmarsh, Martin *ten* 1200
Hinz, Helle *sop* 1029
Hirsch, Rebecca *vn* 271, 842, 919
Hirsch, Peter *cond* 823
Hirvonen, Anssi *ten* 1078
His Majestys Sagbutts and Cornetts. 449, 755
Hockings, David *perc* 480
Hodges, Nicolas *pf* 214, 320
Hodgson, Alfreda *contr* 91, 426, 707, 708, 1198
Hoffmann, Petra *sop* 823
Hoffren, Taito *sngr* 1077
Hofstetter, Michael *cond* 602, 939
Hogwood, Christopher *cond* 449, 503, 515, 540, 572, 713,
789, 794, 846, 891
Hohenfeld, Linda *sop* 230
Holl, Robert *bass* 134, 168
Höll, Hartmut *pf* 1296
Hollander, Lorin *pf* 347
Holliger, Heinz *cond* 584, 635
Hollingworth, Robert *cond* 448
Holloway, John *vn* 209, 210, 309, 976
Hollreiser, Heinrich *cond* 1272
Hollweg, Ilse *sop* 494
Hollweg, Werner *ten* 570
Hollywood Quartet 145, 580, 983, 992, 993
Holmes, Ralph *vn* 372, 374
Holmes, James *cond* 1301
Holst Singers. 488, 1156, 1187
Holten, Bo *cond* 375, 591
Holton, Ruth *sop* 91, 516
Holzmair, Wolfgang *bar* 1004, 1006
Holzman, Adam *gtr* 1088
Homburger, Maya *bqvn* 498

Homer, Louise *contr* 1350
Honda-Rosenberg, Latica *vn* 649
Honeyman, Ian *ten* 324
Hong Kong Philharmonic Orchestra. 304
Höngen, Elisabeth *contr* 142
Honma, Tamami *pf* 727
Honoré, Philippe *vn* 121, 951
Hooten, Florence *vc* 605
Hope, Daniel *vn* 423, 442, 978, 1250
Hopf, Hans *ten* 142
Hoppe, Esther *vn* 965
Horenstein, Jascha *cond* 707, 708
Horne, Marilyn *mez* 530, 1100
Horowitz, Vladimir *pf* 897, 1028, 1326
Horsley, Colin *pf* 765, 766
Horst, Claar ter *pf* 1030
Horváth, Béla *ob* 1244
Hosford, Richard *cl* 256, 656, 855, 965, 966
Hosszu-Legocky, Géza *vn* 1317
Hotter, Hans *bass-bar* 142, 1016, 1305
Hough, Stephen *pf* 253, 256, 334, 446, 599, 731, 751, 894,
895, 963, 975, 1000, 1034, 1327, 1328
Houssart, Robert *org* 358
Houston Symphony Orchestra 1110
Hovhaness, Alan *cond* 593
Howard, Jason *bar* 234
Howard, Leslie *pf* 667, 668, 669
Howard, William *pf* 306, 445
Howarth, Judith *sop* 165, 424
Howarth, Elgar *cond* 213
Howell, Gwynne *bass* . .91, 197, 300, 424, 425, 530, 1201,
1292
Howells, Anne *mez* 690, 692
Howick, Claire *vn* 1039
Høyer Hansen, Helle *sop* 375
Hrusa, Jakub *cond* 403
Huang, Aiyun *perc* 1308
Huber, Gerold *pf* 1006, 1032, 1033
Huberman, Bronislaw *vn* 132
Hübner, Ulrich *hn* 765
Huddersfield Choral Society. . . . 424, 425, 518, 519, 1292
Huelgas-Ensemble 934
Huggett, Monica *vn, dir* 210, 502
Hugh, Tim *vc* . . .141, 222, 226, 244, 253, 271, 588, 1288,
1555
Hughes, David *ten* 1206, 1209
Hughes, Peter *sax* 343
Hughes, Owain Arwel *cond* 586, 587, 1158
Hula, Pavel *vn* 715
Hull, Percy *cond* 426
Hulse, Gareth *ob* 121, 178, 855, 965, 966, 1191
Humburg, Will *cond* 940, 941, 1221
Humphries, Ian *vn* 465
Hungarian Festival Chorus. 89, 810
Hungarian National Philharmonic Orchestra 108
Hungarian Radio Children's Choir 89
Hungarian Radio Choir 695, 870
Hungarian Radio Chorus . 82, 83, 107, 169, 170, 940, 941
Hungarian State Choir 662
Hungarian State Opera Chorus 1208, 1209, 1221
Hungarian State Opera Orchestra . 870, 1208, 1209, 1221
Hungarian State Philharmonic Orchestra 89
Hungarian State Symphony Orchestra. 379
Hunt, Gordon *ob* 586
Hunt Lieberson, Lorraine *mez* 82, 523
Hurford, Peter *org* 965
Huttenlocher, Philippe *bass* 481, 690

Huybrechts, François *cond* 617
Hynninen, Jorma *bar* 703, 1078
Hyökki, Matti *cond* 910

I

(I) Barocchisti 481, 535
I Fagiolini. 314, 448
I Fiamminghi. 627
Ibragimova, Alina *vn* 544
Iceland Symphony Orchestra .603, 653, 1070, 1071, 1072,
1073, 1074, 1082
Ictus 546, 924
Iiyama, Emiko *sop* 85
Ikaia-Purdy, Keith *ten* 194
Il Canto di Orfeo. 451
Ile de France National Orchestra 218
Illing, Rosamund *sop* 720
Ilosfalvy, Róbert *ten* 406
Im, Sunhae *sop* 568, 569
Imai, Nobuko *va* 1022, 1151, 1201
Immer Trumpet Consort (Friedemann). 1179
Immerseel, Jos van *fp* 765, 792
Immerseel, Jos van *pf* 366
Immerseel, Jos van *cond* 765, 780, 1098
Immerseel, Jos van *dir* 765
Inanga, Glen *pf* 585
Ingham, Nick *cond* 466
Inkinen, Pietari *cond* 1075, 1076
Instrumental Ensemble. 319
International Chamber Soloists 1348
Invernizzi, Roberta *sop* 524, 525, 567, 755, 756, 818
(L')Inviti. 1287
Ireland, John *pf* 605
Ireland, Robin *va* 783
Ireland National Symphony Orchestra. . . . .
243, 292, 430, 820, 899
Irvine, Robert *vc* 1138
Isepp, Martin *hpd* 1347
Isepp, Martin *pf* 1004
Isherwood, Nicholas *bass-bar* 354
Isokoski, Soile *sop* 703, 1077, 1079, 1109, 1110
Israel Philharmonic Orchestra 693
Isserlis, Steven *vc* 256, 414, 415, 432, 736, 962, 1019,
1024, 1154
Istomin, Eugene *pf* 130, 131
Italian Broadcasting Authority Chorus. 1221
Italian Broadcasting Authority Orchestra. 1221
Ito, Kanako *vn* 121
Ivashkin, Alexander *vc* 497, 715, 865, 978, 7153
Iven, Christiane *contr* 93

J

Jackson, Garfield *va* 119, 1200
Jackson, Laurence *vn* 120, 268
Jackson, Richard *bar* 1010
Jackson, Stephen *cond* 212
Jacob, Ariane *pf, celeste* 363
Jacob, Francis *org* 83
Jacob, Irène *spkr* 363
Jacobs, René *alto* 87, 972
Jacobs, René *cond* .318, 520, 536, 537, 630, 755, 758, 760,
779, 795, 799, 800, 806, 807, 889, 972, 5770
Jacquet, Alain *xylo* 742
Jaho, Ermonela *sop* 1353

Jakobsson, Anna-Lisa *mez* 1072
James, Cecil *bn* 143, 765, 766
Janál, Roman *bar* 411
Jandó, Jenö *pf* 111, 562, 563, 634, 669, 994
Janes, Paul *pf* 485
Jane's Minstrels 845
Janezic, Ronald *hn* 323
Janicke, Torsten *vn* 574
Janowitz, Gundula *sop* .134, 135, 261, 262, 570, 832, 833,
1008, 1107, 1109, 1110
Janowski, Marek *cond* . . . 250, 575, 582, 1051, 1109, 1110
Jansen, Jan *org* 1246, 1247
Jansen, Jan Willem *hpd* 1246, 1247
Jansen, Janine *vn* 1160, 1246, 1247
Jansen, Maarten *vc* 1246, 1247
Jansen, Rudolf *pf* 1306
Jansons, Mariss *cond* . . .400, 489, 490, 701, 814, 862, 864,
1049, 1053, 1054, 1064, 1162, 1163, 1164
Jaroussky, Philippe *counterten* 1257
Jarred, Mary *contr* 426
Jarrige, Béatrice *alto* 892
Järvi, Neeme *cond* . . .625, 714, 864, 867, 921, 1049, 1054,
1072, 1075, 1163, 1169, 1173, 1189, 1290
Järvi, Paavo *cond* 397, 402, 842, 911, 1127, 1193
Jaud, Reinhard *org* 1139
Jeffers, Gweneth-Ann *sop* 615
Jenkinson, Henry *treb* 518
Jennings, Gloria *contr* 1198
Jennings, Graeme *vn* 377
Jensen, Gert Henning *ten* 1109
Jérôme Hantaï Ensemble 620
Jerusalem, Siegfried *ten* 984
Jerusalem Quartet 1061
Jezierski, Stefan *hn* 263
Jochens, Wilfried *ten* 94, 1178
Jochum, Eugen *cond* . . .241, 242, 291, 299, 551, 832, 833,
1104
Jodelet, Florent *perc* 965
Johannesberg Philharmonic Orchestra. 343
Johnson, Elizabeth Remy *hp* 477
Johnson, Emma *cl* 355
Johnson, Graham *pf* . . .279, 407, 408, 435, 436, 483, 501,
967, 1004, 1007, 1008, 1009, 1010, 1011, 1013, 1030,
1031, 1033, 1034, 1035, 1305
Johnston, Guy *vc* 724
Johnston, James *ten* 518, 519
Johnston, Jennifer *contr* 358
Johnston, Rachel *vc* 497
Johnstone, James *hpd* 1186
Johnstone, James *virg* 1186
Joly, Simon *cond* 98, 646
Jones, Aled *bar* 515
Jones, Della *mez* 474, 487, 518, 591, 747, 955
Jones, Gordon *bar* 684
Jones, Granville *vn* 889
Jones, Karen *fl* 960
Jones, Martin *pf* 439, 639
Jones, Otta *treb* 518
Jones, Parry *ten* 421
Jones, Susan Hemington *sop* 520
Jones, Granville *cond* 530
(Philip) Jones Brass Ensemble. 755
(Philip) Jones Wind Ensemble 755
Jonhäll, Anders *fl* 1301
Jordan, Armin *cond* 602, 859, 916, 1105
Jordan, Philippe *cond* 306, 1124, 1283
Joshua, Rosemary *sop* 515, 520, 521, 1121

Journet, Marcel *bass* 1350
Joyful Company of Singers 102, 190, 588, 591, 840
Juda, Iris *vn* 121
Judd, Roger *org* 841, 1201
Judd, James *cond* 114, 203, 267, 346, 658, 1046
Juilliard Ensemble 188
Juilliard Quartet 109, 362, 852, 913, 1298
Junghänel, Konrad *cond* 728, 754, 936, 1037
Junkin, Jerry *cond* 350
Juntunen, Helena *sop* 141
Jürgensen, Nicola *cl* 936
Jurowski, Michail *cond* 652
Jurowski, Vladimir *cond* 899, 1052, 1166, 1168, 1170,
                                                    1190
Jussila, Kari *org* 909
Jyväskylä Sinfonia 910

K

Kadouch, David *pf* 156
Kaiserslautern Radio Orchestra 944
Kajanus, Robert *cond* 1070
Kakhidze, Jansug *cond* 628
Kaler, Ilya *vn* 243, 835, 1025, 1141
Kaljuste, Tõnu *cond* 843, 844, 979, 1193
Kallisch, Cornelia *contr* 738
Kalmar Chamber Orchestra of London 889
Kamer... 628
Kamio, Mayuko *vn* 1328
Kamp, Harry van der *bass* 1178
Kamp, Harry van der *cond* 457
Kampe, Anja *sop* 1262
Kampen, Christopher van *vc* 121
Kandel, Lucien *cond* 826
Kaneko, Yoko *fp* 765
Kaneko, Yoko *pf* 500
Kang, Dong-Suk *vn* 1075, 1288
Kang, Juliette *vn* 1020
Kanga, Skaila *hp* 121
Kangas, Juha *cond* 765, 1196
Kanka, Michal *vc* 715
Kantiléna Children's Chorus 408
Kantorow, Jean-Jacques *cond* 1295
Karabits, Kirill *cond* 934
Karajan, Herbert von *cond* . . 106, 133, 134, 135, 138, 143,
   218, 245, 246, 261, 262, 294, 296, 360, 361, 368, 371,
   397, 421, 490, 491, 570, 592, 601, 655, 700, 703, 718,
   765, 766, 864, 872, 873, 874, 876, 877, 880, 881, 885,
   983, 1055, 1069, 1070, 1072, 1073, 1100, 1103, 1104,
   1105, 1107, 1109, 1110, 1116, 1120, 1121, 1161, 1162,
   1206, 1208, 1218, 1229, 1236, 1269, 1272, 1285, 5628,
                                                    8643
Karamazov, Edin *gtr, lute* 1329
Karczykowski, Ryszard *ten* 1052
Kargl, Lukas *bar* 1035
Karnéus, Katarina *mez* 141, 494, 1078, 1144
Karni, Gilad *va* 953
Károlyi, Katalin *mez* 657
Karthäuser, Sophie *sop* 567, 568
Karttunen, Anssi *vc* 961, 1150
Kasarova, Vesselina *mez* 196
Kashkashian, Kim *va* 105, 580
Kasík, Martin *pf* 411
Kaspszyk, Jacek *cond* 1145
Katchen, Julius *pf* 258
Katims, Milton *va* 992, 993

Katkus, Donatas *cond* 727
Katona, Peter *gtr* 932
Katona, Zoltán *gtr* 932
Katowice Radio Symphony Orchestra 479
Katsnelson, Jacob *pf* 253
Katz, Martin *pf* 840
Kaufmann, Jonas *ten* 1355
Kaune, Michaela *sop* 575
Kavacos, Leonidas *vn* 837, 1066
Kavakos, Leonidas *vn* 428, 579, 641
Kawai, Noriko *pf* 378
Kay, Alan R. *cl* 1130
Kay, Brian *cond* 1090
Kay Children's Choir (Peter) 874
Kaznowski, Michal *vc* 268
Kecskemét Chlidren's Choir Miraculum 634
Kecskeméti, László *picc* 1244
Kecskeméti, László *rec* 1244
Keeble, Jonathan *spkr* 1130
Keenlyside, Simon *bar* 1009, 1010, 1011, 1034
Keilberth, Joseph *cond* 1115, 1264, 1269, 1273, 1274
Keinonen, Heikki *bar* 1078
Keith, Gillian *sop* 892
Kell, Reginald *cl* 255
Keller, Andras *vn* 112, 643
Keller Quartet 109, 642, 978
Kellock, Judith *sop* 1302
Kelly, Denise *hp* 281
Kelly, Frances *hp* 502
Kelly, John-Edward *sax* 848
Kemenes, András *pf* 642
Kempe, Rudolf *cond* . . 182, 261, 403, 732, 877, 878, 1115,
                                                    1265
Kempen, Paul van *cond* 126
Kempf, Freddy (Frederick) *pf* 813
Kempf Trio 1171
Kempff, Wilhelm *pf* 126, 131, 154, 156, 1000, 1025, 1028,
                                                    1329
Kendall, William *ten* 166, 167, 168, 1154
Kennard, Julie *sop* 596
Kennedy, Andrew *ten* 515, 1113
Kennedy, Mark *treb* 888
Kennedy, Nigel *vn, va* . . . 290, 415, 475, 732, 1070, 1289
Kenny, Elizabeth *lute, arch lute, theorbo* . . . .
                                     892, 1246,1247, 1253
Kenny, Yvonne *sop* 135, 137, 203, 412, 474, 517, 747,
                                     1121, 1127, 1200
Kensington Symphony Orchestra 358
Kent, Fuat *cond* 354
Kent Opera Chorus 1185
Kent Opera Orchestra 1185
Kentner, Louis *pf* 255
Kerdoncuff, François *pf* 1195
Kermes, Simone *sop* 568, 1255
Kerola, Paavo *ten* 1078
Kerr, Alexander *vn* 399
Kerr, Peter *ten* 1093
Kerr, Virginia *sop* 1093
Kersey, Eda *vn* 117
Kershaw, Caroline *rec* 507
Kertesi, Ingrid *sop* 82, 83
Kertész, István *cond* 114, 400, 406, 771
Kesteren, John van *ten* 832
Kettel, Gary *perc* 204
Keulen, Isabelle van *vn* 715, 996, 7153
Keveházi, János *hn* 143
Keveházi, Jenö *hn* 143

Keyte, Christopher *bass* 394, 434, 530, 1198
Khachatryan, Lusine *pf* 446
Khachatryan, Sergey *vn* 446, 632, 1050, 1066
Khaner, Jeffrey *fl* 252
Kiberg, Tina *sop* 615, 1109
Kidon, Klaudia *sop* 591
Kiehr, Maria Cristina *sop* 318, 709, 755, 758
Kiernan, Patrick *vn* 1154
Kiev Opera Chorus 1065
Kiev Opera Orchestra 1065
Kiknadze, Anna *mez* 1058
Kilanowicz, Zofia *sop* 479, 1141
Killebrew, Gwendoline *contr* 690, 692
Kim, Dominique *ondes martinot* 742, 746
Kimstedt, Rainer Johannes *va* 1016
King, Catherine *mez* 451
King, James *ten* 707
King, Malcolm *bass* 615
King, Robert *treb* 394, 434
King, Robert *hpd, org* 889
King, Robert *cond* .228, 512, 515, 517, 519, 573, 754, 755,
                    758, 792, 888, 1254, 1255, 1256
King, Thea *cl* 251, 595, 764
King's College Choir, Cambridge .... .426, 434, 511, 902,
                    1343
The King's Consort.85, 228, 512, 515, 517, 519, 520, 573,
                    754, 755, 758, 792, 888, 1254, 1255, 1256
King's Consort Choir ..228, 512, 515, 517, 519, 573, 754,
                    755, 758, 792, 888, 1254
King's Consort Choristers 519, 1254
The King's Noyse 387
King's Singers 458, 1344
Kipnis, Alexander *bass* 168
Kirchschlager, Angelika *mez* 529
Kirkby, Emma *sop* ...82, 87, 308, 309, 315, 511, 515, 531,
                    578, 754, 789, 846, 972, 1356
Kirkman, Andrew *cond* 388, 1340
Kirov Opera Chorus 232, 813, 815, 869, 1174, 1175, 1209
Kirov Opera Orchestra232, 813, 815, 816, 865, 869, 1159,
                    1174, 1175, 1209
Kirov Orchestra of the Mariinsky Theatre.......... 930
Kiss, Rózsa *sop* 89
Kissin, Evgeny *pf* .125, 129, 131, 259, 323, 334, 336, 998,
                    1027
Kitaenko, Dmitri *cond* 490
Kitchen, Linda *sop* 474, 747, 1201
Kitsopoulos, Maria *vc* 354
Kjekshus, Helge *pf* 492
Kjøller, John *ten* 375
Klas, Eri *cond* 429
Klava, Sigvards *cond* 302, 1197
Kleiber, Carlos *cond* .137, 140, 231, 249, 990, 1099, 1100,
                    1120, 1121, 1122, 1234, 1285, 1297
Kleiber, Erich *cond* 231, 991, 1121, 1237
(Das) Kleine Konzert........................ 94, 1178
Klemperer, Otto *cond* ...89, 126, 127, 139, 142, 169, 170,
                    245, 261, 296, 695, 696, 707, 766, 810, 1264
Kletzki, Paul *cond* 330
Kliegel, Maria *vc* ..152, 154, 243, 331, 414, 432, 634, 644,
                    963
Klier, Manfred *hn* 263
Klinger, Sebastian *vc* 274
Klosinska, Izabella *sop* 846
Kloubová, Zdena *sop* 411
Klukon, Edit *pf* 664
Kluson, Josef *va* 715
Kmentt, Waldemar *ten* 134, 135, 142, 707

Knappertsbusch, Hans *cond* 1270, 1275, 1277
Knauer, Sebastian *pf* 737, 1001
Knebel, Sebastian *org* 574
Kniazev, Alexander *vc* 900
Knox, Garth *va* 1093
Knox, Garth *va da gamba* 614, 1330
Knussen, Oliver *cond* 179, 320, 321, 584, 724
Kobayashi, Mie *vn* 327
Kobow, Jan *ten* 83, 568, 569, 1131
Kocian Quartet 824
Kocsis, Zoltán *cond* 108
Kodály Quartet 362, 555, 558, 559, 994
Koenig, Jan Latham *cond* 855
Kofman, Roman *cond* 1173
Kogan, Leonid *vn* 1159
Koh, Jennifer *vn* 713, 739
Köhler, Axel *alto* 1178
Kohnen, Robert *hpd* 352, 508, 1178
Koivula, Hannu *cond* 587
Kollo, René *ten* 693
Kölner Rundfunk Sinfonie Orchester.............. 991
Kolor, Thomas *perc* 1130
Komatsu, Hidenori *bar* 1301
Komlóssy, Erzsébet *contr* 406
Komsi, Anu *sop* 179, 546, 969
Komsi, Piia *sop* 969
Kondrashin, Kyrill *cond* 660, 662, 896, 1051
Koningsberger, Maarten *bar* 752, 1010
Konstantinov, Julian *bass* 1207, 1208, 1209
Konstantynowicz, Marek *va* 439
Kontarsky, Alfons *pf* 656, 742
Kontarsky, Aloys *pf* 656
Konwitschny, Franz *cond* 126, 1159
Kooij, Peter *bass* 85, 89
Koopman, Ton *hpd* . 27, 227, 308, 508, 1243, 1247, 1248
Koopman, Ton *org* 27, 227, 307, 508, 1243
Koopman, Ton *cond* 27, 227, 1243, 1247, 1248
Kooy, Peter *bass* 82, 84, 90, 93
Kopatchinskaja, Patricia *vn* 1330
Kopp, Peter *cond* 574
Korhonen, Timo *gtr* 288
Korn, Artur *bass* 581, 755
Korpás, Ferenc *bass* 89
Kosárek, Karel *pf* 713
Koskinen, Eeva *vn* 969
Kosler, Zdenek *cond* 411, 1087
Kostecki, Boguslav *vn* 1154
Koussevitzky, Serge *cond* 106, 132, 347, 1104
Kout, Jirí *cond* 411
Kovác, Juraj *vc* 474
Kovacevich, Stephen *pf* . 157, 163, 490, 1000, 1316, 1322
Kovalenko, Lidia *vn* 1062
Köves, Péter *bass* 89
Kozená, Magdalena *mez* 89, 90, 408, 526, 530, 792,
                    824, 1259
Kraemer, Manfred *vn* 309
Kraemer, Nicholas *cond* 527, 1245
Kraft, Norbert *gtr* 836, 932
Kraggerud, Henning *vn* 492
Krakauer, David *cl* 354
Kramer, Miriam *vn* 225
Krasner, Louis *vn* 181
Kraus, Adalbert *ten* 690
Kraus, Otakar *bar* 89
Krause, Anita *mez* 1253
Krause, Tom *bar* 275, 276, 406
Krauss, Clemens *cond* 249, 1104, 1125

Kreisler, Fritz *vn* 641
Kreisler Quartet............................... 641
Kreizberg, Yakov *pf, cond* 242, 243, 632, 1048, 1159
Kremer, Gidon *vn* 107, 131, 132, 271, 628, 1317
Kriikku, Kari *cl, bass cl* 355, 659, 750, 1295
Krimets, Konstantin *cond* 593
Kringelborn, Solveig *sop* 1154
Krips, Josef *cond* 126, 1000
Kristinsson, Bjarni Thor *bass-bar* 653
Krivine, Emmanuel *cond* 632, 1066
Kronos Quartet 477, 925, 1149, 1339
Kruszewski, Adam *bar* 846
Kryger, Urszula *mez* 1143
Ksica, Josef *org* 407
Kubelík, Rafael *cond* ...397, 401, 403, 407, 690, 694, 707,
                    1020, 1085, 1135, 1228, 1267
Kuchar, Theodore *va* 715, 7153
Kuchar, Theodore *cond* 811, 814, 851
Kühmeier, Genia *sop* 568
Kuhn, Gustav *cond* 1029, 1120
Kühn Children's Chorus........................ 716
Kühn Chorus.................................. 408
Kühn Mixed Choir 409, 411, 485, 715
Kuijken, Barthold *fl* 352, 508, 1178
Kuijken, Sigiswald *vn* 847
Kuijken, Wieland *va d'amore* 508, 1178
Kuijken, Sigiswald *cond* 87, 792
Kuijken, Sigiswald *dir* 847
Kulka, Konstanty Andrzej *vn* 580
Kungsbacka Trio............................... 997
Kuntzsch, Matthias *cond* 739
Kunzel, Erich *cond* 544, 953, 1098
Kupfer, Jochen *bar* 1012
Kupper, Anneliese *sop* 991
Kurtág, György *celeste, pf* 642
Kurtág, Márta *pf* 642
Kusnjer, Iván *bar* 411, 714, 715
Kussmaul, Rainer *dir* 1176
Kuusisto, Jaakko *vn* 1074
Kuznetsov, Fyodor *bass* 1062
Kuznetsova, Ludmila *mez* 468, 1062
Kvapil, Radoslav *pf* 824
Kwella, Patrizia *sop* 84, 85, 87, 512
Kynaston, Nicolas *org* 194, 195

L

(L') Astrée 1257
(La) Chapelle Rhénane 1037
La Lauzeta, Children Choir of Toulouse.......... 218
La Scintilla Orchestra, Zurich 761, 1348, 1349
La Serenissima............................... 1250
Laar, Vincent van *org* 1139
Labbette, Dora *sop* 1312
Labé, Thomas *pf* 544
Labelle, Dominique *sop* 971
Labèque, Katia *pf* 742, 786
Labèque, Marielle *pf* 742, 786
Lagrange, Michèle *sop* 197
Lahti Chamber Choir 1077
Lahti Opera Chorus 1078
Lahti Symphony Orchestra. .836, 1066, 1069, 1070, 1071,
                    1072, 1073, 1074, 1076, 1077, 1078
Laitinen, Heikki *sngr* 1077

Lajarrige, Christine *pf* 857
Laki, Krisztina *sop* 690, 692
Lambert, Constant *cond* 222
Lamoureux Orchestra 192
Lamy, Hervé *ten* 675
Lancelot, James *org* 841
Lanchbery, John *cond* 577, 646
Lane, Carys *sop* 1199
Lane, Jennifer *mez* 985
Lane, Piers *pf* 225, 268, 302, 487, 1041, 1042, 1093
Lang, Ellen *mez* 354
Lang, Lang *pf* 156, 1160
Lang, Melanie *mez* 1035
Lang, Petra *mez* 938
Lang, Rosemarie *mez* 689, 690
Langlamet, Marie-Pierre *hp* 263, 965
Langrée, Louis *cond* 326, 794
Langridge, Philip *ten* ..267, 274, 275, 412, 518, 530, 591,
                    755, 984, 1010, 1011, 1200
Lapitino, Francis *hp* 1350
Laporte, Christophe *alto* 758
Laredo, Jaime *va* 782
Laredo, Jaime *vn* 254
Larrocha, Alicia de *pf* 488
Larson, Philip *bar* 1308
Larsson, Anna *contr* 168, 361
LaSalle Quartet 656
Laske, Thomas *bar* 91
Lasla, Anne-Marie *va da gamba* 892
L'Assemblée des Honnestes Curieux 920
Latham-König, Jan *cond* 859
Latry, Olivier *org* 854
Latvian Radio Choir 302, 602, 1197
Latvija State Choir 628
Laudibus 1139
Laukka, Raimo *bar* 1072, 1076, 1077
Laurence, Elisabeth *mez* 236
Laurens, Guillemette *mez* 481
Lausanne Chamber Orchestra 779, 945
Lausanne Opera Chorus 677
Lausanne Pro Arte Choir 829
Lavender, John *pf* 486, 487
Lavoisier, Annie *hp* 546
Lawrence-King, Andrew *hp, dir* 452, 458, 514, 622, 1247
Lawson, Mhairi *sop* 1250
Layer, Friedemann *cond* 575
Layton, Elizabeth *vn* 615
Layton, Stephen *cond* ..277, 300, 488, 501, 511, 674, 684,
            843, 845, 856, 960, 1009, 1010, 1011, 1034, 1155, 1156,
                    1187, 1293, 1349
Lazarev, Alexander *cond* 729, 1040
Lazareva, Tatyana *pf* 865
Lazic, Dejan *pf* 112
(Le) Cercle de l'Harmonie 1351
(Le) Concert d'Astrée 523, 759, 1320
Le Monnier, David *ten* 513
Le Poème Harmonique................... 228, 675
Le Roux, François *bar* 391, 967
Le Roux, Maurice *cond* 741
Lea, Richard *org* 723
Lea-Cox, Graham *cond* 239
Leaper, Adrian *cond* 631, 820, 1093
Leblanc, Suzie *sop* 308
Lechner, Karin *pf* 1316
Leclair, Jacqueline *ob* 1308
Lederlin, Antoine *vc* 500
Ledger, Philip *cond* 426

Leeds Festival Chorus 583
Leeds Philharmonic Chorus . . . . , . . . 1093
Leeson-Williams, Nigel *bass-bar* 1093
Leeuw, Reinbert de *pf* 970
Leeuw, Reinbert de *cond* 213, 657
Lefebvre, Philippe *org* 854
Legay, Aurélia *sop* 192
Lehner, Daniela *mez* 1035
Lehtinen, Markus *cond* 910
Lehtipuu, Topi *ten* 563
Lehto, Petri *ten* 1077
Leiferkus, Sergei *bar* 706, 903, 1063
Leighton Smith, Laurence *cond* 819
Leinsdorf, Erich *cond* 275, 276, 885, 1317
Leipzig Gewandhaus Orchestra . . 241, 242, 290, 733, 734,
1110
Leipzig Quartet 146, 251, 254, 993, 994
Leipzig Radio Chorus . . . 168, 790, 984, 1272, 1285, 1297
Leister, Karl *cl* 251, 921
Leith Hill Festival Singers 1090
Leitner, Ferdinand *cond* 131, 530
Lejeune, Matthieu *vc* 500
Leleux, François *ob* 274
Lemaire, Bertrand *cond* 621
Lemalu, Jonathan *bass-bar* 180, 520
Lemieux, Marie-Nicole *contr* 263
Lemoh, Tonya *pf* 717
Lenaerts, Thibaut *counterten* 324
Lenehan, John *pf* 224, 605
Leningrad Philharmonic Orchestra 864, 1055, 1063, 1162
Leonard, Sarah *sop* 1195
Leonhardt, Gustav *hpd* 889
Leonhardt Baroque Ensemble 889
Leonskaja, Elisabeth *pf* 1005
Leopold String Trio 152, 254, 783, 1152
Leppard, Raymond *cond* 116, 474, 530, 759, 772
Leroy, Anthony *vc* 257
(Les) Arts Florissants ensemble 568
(Les) Eléments 218, 1261
Les Musiciens du Louvre-Grenoble 217, 831
Les Sacqueboutiers 759
(Les) Veilleurs de Nuit 210
Lesne, Gérard *alto, dir* 226, 325
Lester, Richard *vc* 227, 256
Lesueur, Max *va* 781
Letonja, Marko *cond* 624
Letzbor, Gunar *vn, dir* 208
Leveaux, Ursula *bn* 855, 965, 966
Levi, Yoel *cond* 812, 814, 1126
Levin, Robert *fp* 131
Levine, James *pf* 998
Levine, Joanna *viol* 887
Levine, James *cond* 129, 131, 168, 182, 199, 242, 389, 462,
652, 717, 718, 734, 878, 896, 1085, 1212, 1223, 1229,
1235, 1236, 1270, 1278, 1352
Lewin, Michael *pf* 974
Lewis, Keith *ten* 143, 300
Lewis, Paul *pf* 157, 159, 160, 665, 783
Lewis, Richard *ten* 195, 424, 707, 1206, 1209
Lewis, Anthony *cond* 891
Li, Yundi *pf* 665, 862
Liceu Grand Theatre Chorus 722
Liceu Grand Theatre Symphony Orchestra 576, 722, 1273
Lidström, Mats *vc* 625
Liebeck, Jack *vn* 268
Liège Philharmonic Orchestra 326

Liepaja Symphony Orchestra 628
Ligeti, Andras *cond* 662
Ligorio, Daniel *pf* 931
Lika, Peter *bass* 87
Lille National Orchestra 197, 319
Lille Symphony Orchestra 854
Lin, Cho-Liang *vn* 732, 819, 1066
Lindberg, Christian *tbn* 586, 851, 1190
Lindberg, Jakob *lute* 349
Linden, Jaap ter *va d'amore* 309
Linden, Jaap ter *vc* 508
Lindsay Quartet . . . 145, 149, 231, 406, 556, 557, 558, 559,
613, 782, 783, 783, 992,1182
Lines, Timothy *bass cl* 237
Lingas, Alexander *cond* 388
Linos Ensemble 553
Lintu, Hannu *cond* 627, 908
Linz Bruckner Orchestra 639, 640
Linz Mozart Choir 639
Lipatti, Dinu *pf* 341, 490
Lipovsek, Marjana *mez* 168, 245, 690, 692, 1011
Lipton, Martha *contr* 690, 695
Lira Chamber Chorus 480
Lisbon Gulbenkian Foundation Orchestra 661
Lisbon San Carlos National Theatre Chorus . . 1232, 1234
Lisbon San Carlos National Theatre Orchestra 1232,
1234, 1350
Lislevand, Rolf *theo* 709
(Franz) Liszt Academy of Music Orchestra 662
(Franz) Liszt Chamber Orchestra 774
Little, Tasmin *vn* 440, 1199, 1287
Little Church around the Corner Boys' Choir 690
Littlewood, Joe *treb* 91
Litton, Andrew *cond* . .414, 415, 607, 670, 894, 895, 1154,
1162, 1180, 1287
Liverpool Metropolitan Cathedral Choir 203
Liverpool Philharmonic Choir 203, 596
Liverpool Philharmonic Orchestra 417, 424, 425, 518,
519, 1292
Liverpool Welsh Choral 723
Lixenberg, Loré *mez* 686
Llewellyn, Redvers *bar* 1312
Lloyd, Robert *bass* 424, 790, 1127
Lloyd Webber, Julian *vc* 374
Lloyd-Jones, David *cond* 115, 116, 117, 202, 222, 223,
373, 411, 451, 588, 645, 918, 919, 1091, 1092, 1136,
1291
Lochmann, Daniel *treb* 888
Loges, Stephan *bar* 1010, 1011, 1034, 1035
Loges, Stephan *bass* 89, 90
Lombard, Jean-François *ten* 199
London, George *bass-bar* 690
London Classical Players . . .135, 137, 141, 505, 734, 990,
1085
London Festival Orchestra 551
London Handel Choir 515
London Handel Orchestra 515
London King's College Choir 671, 1046
London Mozart Players 597, 598, 710, 768
London Musica Antiqua 623
London Opera Chorus 807
London Oratory Junior Choir 88, 89, 755, 1201
London Orchestra 1155
London Oriana Choir 358
London Philharmonic Choir . . .275, 424, 426, 703, 1052,
1198, 1202

London Philharmonic Orchestra .107, 116, 119, 170, 171, 178, 185, 198, 199, 243, 245, 246, 248, 249, 250, 266, 267, 275, 289, 290, 294, 298, 343, 345, 372, 414, 415, 417, 418, 419, 421, 424, 426, 456, 474, 475, 484, 530, 551, 589, 590, 611, 617, 618, 646, 696, 701, 702, 703, 725, 732, 747, 749, 759, 796, 800, 805, 807, 808, 809, 810, 814, 884, 885, 899, 944, 964, 1019, 1052, 1054, 1055, 1064, 1121, 1130, 1141, 1154, 1166, 1175, 1190, 1191, 1198, 1284, 1285, 1287, 1292, 1312, 1334
London Piano Trio 1189
London Schubert Chorale . . 501, 1008, 1009, 1010, 1011
London Schütz Choir 135, 137
London Select Choir 1312
London Sinfonietta178, 188, 213, 215, 320, 321, 479, 480, 546, 617, 656, 924, 965, 984, 1317
London Sinfonietta Chorus 617
London Sinfonietta Voices 658
London Symphony Chorus (amateur) .193, 194, 195, 200, 231, 274, 275, 281, 284, 286, 412, 423, 424, 425, 591, 683, 703, 832, 1200, 1202, 1219
London Symphony Chorus (pro) .271, 272, 518, 702, 733, 832, 913
London Symphony Orchestra.99, 100, 105, 107, 114, 119, 125, 126, 138, 141, 191, 192, 193, 194, 195, 198, 199, 200, 218, 219, 231, 244, 249, 270, 271, 272, 274, 275, 276, 281, 284, 346, 397, 398, 399, 400, 403, 406, 412, 413, 414, 415, 417, 418, 421, 423, 424, 425, 455, 461, 467, 468, 496, 505, 506, 518, 530, 585, 589, 590, 591, 637, 660, 661, 662, 683, 693, 699, 701, 702, 707, 722, 733, 734, 764, 771, 772, 793, 832, 861, 863, 864, 879, 883, 894, 895, 898, 911, 912, 913, 931, 942, 948, 962, 1000, 104
London Voices 650, 718, 879, 883, 1210
London Winds 775
Long, Kathleen pf 431
Long, Marguerite pf 431
Longfield, Susan sop 1198
Longo, Isabella va 1251
Lonsdale, Michael spkr 611
López-Cobos, Jesús cond . .719, 873, 928, 943, 945, 1058, 1233, 1234, 1241
Lord, Roger ob 530
Lorengar, Pilar sop 406
Lorenz, Siegfried bar 581
Lorenzini, Germaine hp 363
Loriod, Jeanne ondes martinot 741, 742, 746
Loriod, Yvonne pf 741, 742
Lorraine Philharmonic Orchestra. 499
Lortie, Louis pf 443, 912
Los Angeles Chamber Orchestra 1127
Los Angeles Master Chorale. 924, 926
Los Angeles Opera Chorus 1235
Los Angeles Opera Orchestra 1235
Los Angeles Philharmonic Orchestra. .101, 347, 455, 636, 970
Lott, Felicity sop . .373, 426, 435, 436, 483, 501, 530, 566, 703, 706, 859, 916, 1035, 1105, 1198
Loughran, James cond 245, 246, 297
Loughton High School for Girls' Choir. . 601, 1120, 1121
Lubbock, John cond 482
Lubimov, Alexei pf 842, 978, 1079
Lubman, Bradley cond 926
Lubotsky, Mark vn 270
Lucas, Andrew org 843, 1345
Lucerne Festival Chorus 361, 569
Lucerne Festival Orchestra 361, 490, 699, 1262, 1311
Lucerne Symphony Orchestra 988

Lucey, Frances sop 1093
Ludwig, Christa mez 142, 245, 693, 700, 703, 707
Ludwig, Leopold cond 129, 131
Ludwigsburg Festival Choir 809
Ludwigsburg Festival Orchestra 809
Ludwigshafen Theatre Chorus 1301
Lugansky, Nikolai pf 271, 1159, 1160
Luisi, Fabio cond 173, 592, 976, 1106
Luisotti, Nicola cond 1357
Lukomska, Halina sop 1298
Lukonin, Mikhail bar 1062
Lumsden, Andrew org 277, 960, 1183
Lundberg, Gunnar bar 870
Lunn, Joanne sop 563, 1254
Luolajan-Mikkola, Markku va da gamba 709
Lupo, Benedetto pf 950
Lupu, Radu pf 259, 445, 999, 1026, 1028
Lush, Ernest pf 264, 397, 1322, 1336
Luxembourg Philharmonic Orchestra 234
Luxon, Benjamin bar 394, 434
Lyndon-Gee, Christopher pf 1195
Lyndon-Gee, Christopher cond 1195
Lyon National Opera Chorus 1266
Lyon National Orchestra 361, 913, 924
Lyon Opera Chorus . . .196, 200, 305, 368, 371, 382, 830, 831, 858
Lyon Opera Orchestra .196, 199, 200, 289, 305, 368, 371, 382, 472, 830, 831, 858
Lyric Quartet. 301, 466

M

Ma, Yo-Yo vc .27, 134, 227, 254, 440, 466, 782, 850, 994, 1054, 1154, 1243
Maag, Peter cond 734
Maazel, Lorin cond 218, 220, 876, 912, 1224, 1234
McAslan, Lorraine vn 98, 237, 654
McCabe, John pf 727, 920
McCallum, David vn 374
McCawley, Leon pf 450, 1027
McClure, Mac pf 751
Macco, Andreas bass 196
McCormack, Elizabeth mez 1242
McCreesh, Paul cond 89, 90, 518, 520, 521, 522, 530, 568, 569, 789, 860, 1238, 1343
McCue, William bass 1206, 1209
McDaniel, Barry bar 1298
McDermott, Anne-Marie pf 455
McDonald, Hector hn 530
McDonald, Robert pf 1304
MacDonald, Robert bass 754, 755
MacDougall, Jamie ten 570, 739, 1010, 1011
McFadden, Claron sop 213, 215, 512, 515, 892
McFadden, Jeffrey gtr 1088
McFarlane, Claire vn 638
McGahon, Colette mez 1093
McGegan, Nicholas cond 505, 971, 1244, 1247
McGhee, Lorna fl 121
McGillivray, Alison vc 453
McGillivray, Katherine va da gamba 1243
McGreevy, Geraldine sop 224, 435, 436, 1034, 1035, 1305
MacGregor, Joanna pf 214
Macintyre, Stuart bar 547
McKendree-Wright, Zan contr 600
MacKenzie, Neil ten 234
Mackenzie, Philip cond 97

Mackenzie-Wicks, Andrew *ten* 547
Mackerras, Charles *cond* 135, 245, 383, 401, 403, 409,
418, 471, 505, 506, 528, 530, 536, 537, 590, 601, 612,
615, 616, 617, 618, 619, 716, 766, 770, 778, 779, 780,
790, 794, 796, 800, 801, 804, 809, 810, 859, 931, 991,
1085, 1087, 1137, 1138, 1174, 5759
Mackie, Neil *ten* 1292
Mackintosh, Catherine *va* 1252
Mackintosh, Catherine *vn* 349
McLaughlin, Marie *sop* 512
MacLeod, Stephan *bass* 83, 92
MacLoed, Stephan *bass* 92
McMahon, Michael *pf* 263
McMahon, Richard *pf* 639
McMahon, Sarah *vc* 1250
McMillan, Kevin *bar* 820
MacMillan, James *cond* 682, 684, 685
McNair, Sylvia *sop* 434, 530, 568, 689, 690, 693, 790
McNair, Crawford *cond* 426
McTier, Duncan *db* 121
McVinnie, James *org* 959, 1304
Maderna, Bruno *cond* 186
Madge, Geoffrey Douglas *pf* 1082
Mädler, Ulf Dirk *bar* 574
Madrid Comunidad Orchestra 265, 1352
Madrid Real Theatre Chorus 719
Madrid Real Theatre Orchestra 719
Madrid Symphony Chorus 802, 873, 1233, 1234
Madrid Symphony Orchestra . . 734, 802, 873, 1233, 1234
Magdeburg Philharmonic Orchestra 574
Magee, Gary *bar* 939
Maggini Quartet 119, 223, 268, 273, 357, 750, 1292
Maggini Quartet 189, 357, 605, 1200
Maggio-Ormezowski, Franco *vc* 427
Magnificat Choir 933, 1149
Magnus, Elisabeth von *contr* 88, 89
Magnus, Elisabeth von *mez* 788, 791
Maguire, Hugh *vn* 1105
Mahktin, Dmitri *vn* 900
Mahler Chamber Orchestra .131, 192, 250, 287, 548, 617,
797, 808, 946, 1160
Mahon, Peter *counterten* 1253
Mainz EuropaChor Akademie 1266
Maisky, Lily *pf* 1316
Maisky, Mischa *vc* 406, 1022, 1049, 1316
Maistre, Xavier de *hp* 369
Maîtrise d'Antony Childrens Choir 195
Maîtrise de Radio France 218
Maîtrise des Pays de Loire 621, 623
Maîtrise Notre-Dame de Paris 85, 86
Majeske, Daniel *vn* 1298
Maksymiuk, Jerzy *cond* 729, 1049
Malaniuk, Ira *contr* 790
Malanowicz, Evangelista Jaroslaw *org* 846
Malaysian Philharmonic Orchestra. 467
Malcolm, George *hpd* 530, 889, 1347
Malcolm, George *org* 530
Malcolm, George *pf* 1347
Malgoire, Jean-Claude *cond* 480, 532
Mälkki, Susanna *cond* 686
Mallon, Kevin *vn* 892
Mallon, Kevin *cond* 239, 325, 505, 892, 1253
Malmö Chamber Chorus 608
Malmö Symphony Orchestra . . . 224, 608, 958, 980, 1082
Maltman, Christopher *bar* 435, 436, 591, 683, 1010, 1011,
1031, 1113
Malvicino, Horacio *gtr* 850

Mal, Frantisek *pf* 613
Mammel, Hans Jörg *ten* 309
Manahan Thomas, Elin *sop* 960, 1344
Manchester Boys' Choir 282
Manchester Camerata 140, 697
Manchester Chamber Choir 637
Mandolesi, Giorgio *bn* 1251
Manhattan Public School No. 12 Boys' Choir 690
Maninger, Olaf *vc* 1170
Manning, Jane *sop* 215, 656, 845
Manning, Peter *vn* 1111
Mannino, Franco *cond* 1317
Mannion, Rosa *sop* 168, 960, 1202
Mannov, Johannes *bass* 568
Manson, Jonathan *bq vc* 1243
Manson, Jonathan *va da gamba* 904
Manson, Jonathan *vc* 507
Manze, Andrew *vn* 209, 210, 349, 453, 504, 506, 508, 773,
839, 1153, 1178, 1247, 1248, 1250
Manze, Andrew *cond* . . 211, 453, 504, 506, 528, 773, 1250
Marangella, Joel *ob* 715, 7153
Marc, Alessandra *sop* 1310
Marcellus, Robert *cl* 1298
Marchi, Alessandro de *cond* 1259, 1260
Marchigiana Philharmonic Orchestra 1120
Marcon, Andrea *cond* . .526, 530, 1246, 1247, 1248, 1249,
1255
Marconi, Leonardo *pf* 850
Marconi, Nestor *bandoneón* 850
Margalit, Israela *pf* 99
Margiono, Charlotte *sop* 134, 166, 167, 168, 261, 262
Margulis, Alissa *vn* 1049, 1316
Marin-Degor, Sophie *sop* 483, 755, 756
Marinuzzi, Gino *cond* 1221
Markevitch, Igor *cond* 192, 1128
Markiz, Lev *cond* 224, 733
Märkl, Jun *cond* 361, 913
Marks, Benjamin *tbn* 103
Marriner, Neville *vn* 889
Marriner, Neville *cond* .207, 434, 530, 732, 766, 775, 790,
833, 941, 992, 1049, 1127
Marshall, Conrad *fl* 919
Marshall, Margaret *sop* 755
Marshall, Wayne *org* 580, 682
Marshall, Wayne *pf* 682
Marshev, Oleg *pf* 1158, 1330
Martelli, Dominic *treb* 204
Martin, Laurent *pf* 199
Martin, Philip *pf* 481, 482
Martin, Thomas *db* 300
Martin, Ion *cond* 938
Martin, Judy *cond* 853
Martineau, Malcolm *pf* 935, 996, 1008, 1203, 1355
Martínez, Ana María *sop* 207
Martini, Alberto *cond* 1247, 1248
Martinon, Jean *cond* 231, 864
Martins, Marisa *mez* 751, 758
Marty, Jean-Pierre *pf* 258
Martynov, Alexei *ten* 1062
Marwood, Anthony *va* 431
Marwood, Anthony *vn* 256, 344, 1090, 1196, 1247
Marwood, Christopher *vc* 347
Marzana, Luca *tpt* 1251
Marzorati, Arnaud *bass* 376, 481, 675
Mascagni, Pietro *cond* 718
Maskell, Robert *hn* 1020
Masková, Dagmar *sop* 407

Masó, Jordi *pf* 751
Mason, Anne *mez* 474, 747
Masseurs, Peter *tpt* 1059
Masters, Rachel *hp* 204
Masur, Kurt *cond* . . . 275, 290, 403, 733, 734, 1050, 1110
Mata, Eduardo *cond* 832
Matacic, Lovro von *cond* 294
Mataeva, Irina *sop* 1058
Máthé, Gyözö *va* 143
Matheson, John *cond* 1215, 1222, 1224
Mathis, Edith *sop* 263, 299, 407, 569, 690, 693
Matousek, Bohuslav *vn* 713, 715
Matrix Ensemble 215
Matsuev, Denis *pf* 901, 1131
Matter, Bert *org* 1139
Matthews, Sally *sop* 832, 1191
Mattila, Karita *sop* 733, 840, 961, 984, 1028
Maury, Claude *hn* 199
Max, Hermann *cond* 94, 1178
Maxwell, Donald *bar* 590
Maxwell, Melinda *ob* 724
Mayers, Philip *pf* 1003
Mayr, Ingrid *mez* 693
MDR Rundfunkchor Leipzig 361, 913
MDR Symphony Orchestra 976
Mead, Philip *pf* 753
Medici Quartet 1214
Medlyn, Helen *mez* 203
Medtner, Nicolas *pf* 729
Mees, Reinild *pf* 1143
Mehta, Zubin *cond* . . . 181, 690, 804, 875, 884, 885, 1211,
1212, 1236
Mei, Eva *sop* 168
Mei-Loc Wu, Mary *pf* 119
Meier, Waltraud *mez* 689, 690
Melba, Nellie *sop* 1351
Melbourne Symphony Orchestra 478, 1096
Melik-Pashayev, Alexsander *cond* 1174
Melinek, Julia *sop* 739
Melnikov, Alexander *pf* 998, 1043
Melos Ensemble 275, 445
Melville, Alan G. *cond* 233
(Members) of the Philip Glass Ensemble 466
Mena, Carlos *alto* 83
Meneses, Antonio *vc* 997, 1331
Menges, Herbert *cond* 490, 769
Menna, Siân *mez* 98
Menuhin, Yehudi *vn* 131, 132, 421, 732, 1347
Mera, Yoshikazu *alto* 90, 93
Merbeth, Ricarda *sop* 1110
Mermoud, Claudio *gtr* 1348
Merrett, James Edward *db* 254, 994
Merritt, Chris *ten* 474, 747
Mertens, Klaus *bar* 1179
Messenger, Mark *vn* 920
Messiaen, Olivier *org* 742
Messiaen, Olivier *pf* 741
Messthaler, Ulrich *bass* 318
Metropolitan Opera Chorus . 655, 1134, 1212, 1229, 1230,
1231, 1235, 1265, 1270, 1278
Metropolitan Opera Orchestra 655, 1134, 1212, 1229,
1230, 1231, 1235, 1265, 1270, 1278
Mewton-Wood, Noel *pf* 330
Meyer, Edgar *vc* 994
Meyer, Paul *cl* 243, 289, 545, 965
Meyerson, Mitzi *hpd* 229
Micallef, Jennifer *pf* 585

Michaelstein Chamber Choir 1179
Michaelstein Telemann Chamber Orchestra 1179
Michelangeli, Arturo Benedetti *pf* 130, 366, 489, 490, 895,
897, 912, 914, 1331
Micheli, Gabriele *org* 758
Michelow, Sybil *mez* 1206, 1209
Michigan State University Chamber Choir 230
Michigan State University Children's Choir 230
Michigan State University Symphony Orchestra 230
Michigan University Musical Society Choral Union . .230,
1173
Michnik, Ewa *cond* 752
Midgley, Maryetta *sop* 372
Midgley, Vernon *ten* 372
Midori, Miss *vn* 1304
Mields, Dorothee *sop* 82, 568
Mijalovic, Nikola *bar* 1353
Mikhailov, Maxim *bass* 1131
Miki, Mie *acco* 496
Mikkola, Laura *pf* 908, 910
Mikulás, Peter *bass* 407
Milan Chorus 'Giuseppe Verdi' 874, 937
Milan Giuseppe Verdi Chorus 1353
Milan Giuseppe Verdi Symphony Orchestra . . .871, 1353,
1359
Milan La Scala Ballet School 1234
Milan La Scala Children's Chorus 874
Milan La Scala Chorus .174, 177, 380, 384, 655, 718, 852,
853, 873, 874, 876, 877, 878, 881, 882, 884, 885, 941,
949, 1207, 1208, 1209, 1212, 1213, 1215, 1217, 1218,
1219, 1223, 1224, 1229, 1230, 1231, 1232, 1234, 1236,
1243, 1350
Milan La Scala Orchestra . . .174, 177, 380, 384, 655, 718,
852, 853, 873, 874, 876, 877, 878, 879, 881, 882, 884,
885, 941, 949, 1207, 1208, 1209, 1212, 1213, 1215,
1217, 1218, 1219, 1223, 1224, 1225, 1229, 1230, 1231,
1232, 1234, 1236, 1243, 1350
Milan RAI Chorus 462, 1220
Milan RAI Orchestra 462, 1220
Milan Symphony Orchestra 'Guiseppe Verdi' . . . 530, 937
Milanesi, Raffaella *sop* 524
Milanov, Zinka *sop* 168, 169, 1209
Miles, Alastair *bass* 166, 167, 168, 197, 300, 474, 747, 755,
791, 939, 1113, 1208, 1209
Milhofer, Mark *ten* 888
Miller, Cynthia *ondes martinot* 179
Miller, David *lute* 889
Miller, David *theo* 889
Millinger, Andrew *cond* 595
Mills, Bronwen *sop* 474, 747
Milman, Misha *vc* 1170
Milne, Hamish *pf* 304, 583, 598, 679, 1296
Milne, Lisa *sop* 519, 695, 1254
Milner, Howard *ten* 84, 85
Milstein, Nathan *vn* 290
Mingardo, Sara *contr* 523, 563, 755, 756
Mingardo, Sara *mez* 1247
Mingardo, Rafaele *cond* 1210
Minkiewicz, Ryszard *ten* 846
Minkowski, Marc *cond* .192, 217, 471, 510, 530, 533, 537,
538, 542, 675, 803, 828, 829, 830, 831, 945
Minneapolis Symphony Orchestra 1167
Minnesota Chorale 141
Minnesota Orchestra . . .137, 138, 139, 141, 346, 414, 415,
732
Minton, Yvonne *mez* 426, 690
Minty, Shirley *contr* 1198

Miricioiu, Nelly *sop* 939
Miró Quartet 144, 992, 8550
Mishura-Lekhtman, Irina *mez* 1173
Mistry, Jagdish *vn* 926
(Geoffrey) Mitchell Choir . . . 233, 382, 384, 484, 834, 874,
881, 939
Mitchell-Velasco, Gigi *mez* 639
Mitchinson, John *ten* 615, 707, 708
Mitropoulos, Dimitri *cond* 690, 1217, 1222
Mittman, Leopold *pf* 290
Miyata, Mayumi *sho* 643
Moccia, Alessandro *vn* 166
Modeno Teatro Comunale Chorus 463
Mogilevsky, Alexander *pf* 1316
Mogrelia, Andrew *cond* 371, 1166
Moiseiwitsch, Benno *pf* 340, 341, 490, 491
Molajoli, Lorenzo *cond* 852
Molinari, Enrico *bar* 852
Molinari-Pradelli, Francesco *cond* 886, 1223, 1359
Moll, Kurt *bass* 168
Møller, Annemarie *mez* 1029
Molnár, András *ten* 662
Molokina, Irina *vc* 1062
Mongrelia, Andrew *cond* 1166
Monks, Christopher *org* 1094
Monnard, Jean-François *cond* 963
Monoyios, Ann *sop* 88, 89, 755, 1178
Montague, Diana *mez* 199, 474, 530, 747, 790, 1121,
1201
Montague, Stephen *elec* 753
Montague, Stephen *cond* 753
Montanari, Stefano *vn* 1251, 1255, 1258
Monte Carlo Philharmonic Orchestra 427, 827
Monteilhet, Pascal *theo* 210
Monteux, Pierre *cond* 421, 721
Monteverdi Choir . . 84, 85, 87, 88, 89, 131, 135, 136, 166,
167, 168, 197, 201, 261, 262, 472, 473, 512, 516, 530,
563, 566, 568, 570, 755, 790, 798, 800, 804, 806, 807,
1134, 1208, 1209, 1344
Monteverdi Orchestra 755
Montgomery, Roger *bn* 1020, 1252
Montgomery, Roger *cond* 845
Montpellier National Orchestra 395, 575, 602
Montpellier Opera Chorus 395
Montreal Symphony Orchestra . . 105, 329, 588, 590, 732,
861, 965, 1166
Montreal Symphony Orchestra Chorus 588, 590
Moog, Rainer *va* 715, 7153
Moore, Dudley *pf* 962
Moore, Gerald *pf* 397, 766, 1006, 1012, 1016, 1305, 1322,
1347
Moorhouse, Richard *org* 595
Morandi, Pier Giorgio *cond* 870, 1208, 1209
Mordkovitch, Lydia *vn* 1049
Morelli, Frank *bn* 1130
Moretti, Isabelle *hp* 363
Morgan, Darragh *vn* 465
Morgan, Richard Lloyd *bass* 84, 85
Morikawa, Eiko *sop* 643
Morin, Christophe *vc* 500
Morison, Elsie *sop* 690
Mørk, Truls *vc* 272, 415
Mormon Tabernacle Choir. 953
Moroney, Davitt *clav* 310
Moroney, Davitt *hpd* 210, 310
Moroney, Davitt *org* 210, 310
Moroney, Davitt *virg* 310

Morris, Andrea *vn* 892
Morris, Joan *mez* 230
Mortensen, Lars Ulrik *hpd* 209, 210, 309, 976
Mortensen, Lars Ulrik *org* 309, 976
Mortensen, Lars Ulrik *cond* 537, 538
Morton, Richard *ten* 426
Morton, Robert *bass* 406
Mosaïques Quartet 783
Mosalini, Juan José *band* 850
Moscona, Nicola *bass* 168, 169, 1209
Moscow Choral Academy (Boys Chorus) 1051
Moscow Philharmonic Orchestra 896, 1185
Moscow Philharmonic Symphony Orchestra 1051
Moscow Russian Philharmonic 1150
Moscow State Chamber Choir (men) 1063
Moscow Symphony Orchestra 729
Moser, Edda *sop* 693
Moser, Elsbeth *baya* 496
Moser, Thomas *ten* 196, 706, 984
Moses, Geoffrey *bass* 738
Mott, Louise *mez* 233
Moubarak, Sandra *pf* 257
Mozart Anniversary Orchestra 773
Mozart Orchestra 772
Mravinsky, Evgeny *cond* 1055, 1162, 1164
Muck, Conrad *vn* 1016
Mukk, József *ten* 82, 83, 89
Muller, Marianne *va da gamba* 210, 1332
Müller, Rufus *ten* 93
Müller, Thomas *hn* 1251
Müller-Brachmann, Hanno *bass* 93, 568, 569, 1035
Müller-Schott, Daniel *vc* . . . 242, 243, 414, 415, 736, 996,
1048
Mulligan, Simon *pf* 423, 934, 978
Mullova, Viktoria *vn* 1249
Mullova Ensemble 996
Mulroy, Nicholas *ten* 89, 518, 754, 755
Munch, Charles *cond* 721, 964, 1066, 1290
Münchinger, Karl *cond* 126
Munich Chamber Orchestra . . . 496, 498, 545, 1079, 1299
Munich Motet Choir 690
Munich Philharmonic Orchestra 297, 790, 1111
Munich Radio Orchestra . . 381, 832, 941, 942, 1173, 1359
Munich Radio Symphony Orchestra 651
Munro, Matthew *treb* 738
Munrow Recorder Ensemble 755
Murail, Tristan *ondes martinot* 742
Muraro, Roger *pf* 743
Murcell, Raymond *bar* 354
Murgatroyd, Andrew *ten* 755
Muroki, Kurt *db* 1130
Murphy, Emma-Jane *vc* 1045
Murray, Ann *mez* 234, 483, 600, 891, 1010, 1035
Musica Alta Ripa 1251
Musica Contexta 839
Musica Florea 675
(Les) Musiciens du Louvre . . 192, 471, 510, 530, 533, 537,
538, 542, 675, 803, 828, 829, 831
musikFabrik 1131
Muskett, Doreen *hurd* 578
Mustonen, Elina *hpd* 709
Mustonen, Olli *pf* 1062
Muthelet, Béatrice *vn* 243, 965
Muti, Riccardo *cond* . . . 718, 882, 1127, 1207, 1209, 1211,
1212, 1213, 1214, 1217, 1218, 1219, 1229, 1234, 1243
Mutter, Anne-Sophie *vn* 182, 496, 1247
Mutter, Anne-Sophie *dir* 1247

Myers, Philip *hn* 99
Myerscough, Nadia *vn* 920

N

Naddeo, Maurizio *vc* 1251
Nagano, Kent *cond* 179, 196, 230, 271, 282, 285, 289, 296,
    305, 742, 746, 858, 1159, 1160, 1266
Naglia, Sandro *ten* 755
Nagy, Péter *pf* 428, 641
Nakai, R Carlos *fl* 464
Nakariakov, Sergei *tpt* 1049
Namur Chamber Choir. 480
Namur Symphonic Chorus. 234
Nancarrow, Conlon *pf* 817
Naoumenko, Alexandre *ten* 903
Naouri, Laurent *bar* 523
Naples San Carlo Opera Chorus 1223
Naples San Carlo Opera Orchestra 1223
Narucki, Susan *sop* 1130
Nash, Heddle *ten* 424, 425, 426
Nash Ensemble 95, 152, 213, 215, 224, 251, 344, 423, 585,
   734, 855, 965, 966, 1108, 1191, 1291
Nash Ensemble The 1202
Nashville Symphony Chorus 917
Nashville Symphony Orchestra 123, 607, 917
National Academic Choir of Ukraine 'Dumka' . 903, 1080
National Philharmonic Orchestra. 462, 717, 718, 945
National Polish Radio Symphony Orchestra of Katowice.
                106
National Symphony Orchestra 206, 431
National Symphony Orchestra of Ireland . 680, 898, 1093
National Youth Choir of Great Britain 1139
Natoli, Dominic *ten* 939
Navarra, André *vc* 441
Naviglio, Giuseppe *bar* 818
NBC Symphony Orchestra 132, 168, 231, 1209, 1218
Neary, Alice *vc* 120, 605, 1092, 1188
Neary, Martin *cond* 547
Nebolsin, Eldar *pf* 661
Nédélec, Ronan *bar* 324
Nédélec, Ronan *bass* 325
Neel, Boyd *cond* 431
(Boyd) Neel String Orchestra 278, 431
Neeves, Helen *sop* 393
Neidich, Charles *cl* 1130
Neill, Stuart *ten* 1126, 1128
Neilz, Jacques *vc* 742
Nelson, John *cond* . . . 85, 86, 195, 198, 199, 200, 480, 526
Németh, Judit *mez* 82, 83, 89
Nes, Jard van *contr* 693
Neschling, John *cond* 729, 1160, 1240
Nesterenko, Evgeny *bass* 1051
Netherlands Bach Society 92
Netherlands Chamber Choir 87, 755
Netherlands Chamber Orchestra 803, 942
Netherlands Opera Chorus. 803, 942, 986, 1064
Netherlands Philharmonic Orchestra. 242, 243, 330, 1275
Netherlands Radio Chamber Orchestra. 105, 323
Netherlands Radio Choir 1057
Netherlands Radio Chorus 690, 692
Netherlands Radio Philharmonic Orchestra 415, 546,
                1057
Netrebko, Anna *sop* 1357
Neubauer, Paul *va* 1287
Neul-Bit, Ha *pf* 642

Neumann, Peter *cond* 91
Neumann, Václav *cond* 411
Neunecker, Marie Luise *hn* 1022
Nevel, Paul van *cond* 934
Neveu, Ginette *vn* 243, 1066
Neveu, Jean *pf* 243
Neville, Peter *perc* 103
New Budapest Quartet 729
New College Choir, Oxford . . 91, 239, 515, 517, 518, 519,
            673, 888, 1186
New England Conservatory Chorus. 346
New Helsinki Quartet. 613, 1295
New London Chamber Choir 974, 1308
New London Children's Choir. 601, 859, 886
New Philharmonia Chorus 85, 86, 275
New Philharmonia Orchestra . .85, 86, 117, 126, 127, 242,
  271, 275, 296, 346, 394, 417, 422, 424, 426, 434, 440,
   441, 489, 490, 698, 705, 707, 749, 772, 1019, 1198,
   1206, 1209, 1213, 1214, 1236, 1264, 1317, 1322
New Queen's Hall Orchestra 417
New Symphony Orchestra 290, 415, 530, 1325
New World Symphony. 455, 1241
New York Chamber Symphony Orchestra 543
New York Church of the Transfiguration Boys' Choir 695
New York Collegium 211
New York Metropolitan Opera Ballet 176
New York Metropolitan Opera Chorus . . . 176, 878, 1221,
       1223, 1227, 1229, 1236, 1278
New York Metropolitan Opera Orchestra .176, 878, 1221,
      1223, 1227, 1229, 1236, 1278, 1352
New York Philharmonic Orchestra 99, 181, 204, 403, 455,
      607, 690, 695, 702, 1054, 1128
New York Philharmonic Symphony Orchestra . .137, 140,
         290, 690, 897, 1066
New York Philharmonic-Symphony Orchestra 222
New York Schola Cantorum. 695
New York Symphony Orchestra. 249
New York Woodwind Quintet. 982
New Zealand Symphony Orchestra . . .203, 267, 346, 600,
      658, 1046, 1075, 1076, 1295
Newton, Ivor *pf* 1347
Nicholas, Benjamin *cond* 1299
Nicholls, Alison *hp* 121, 951
Nicholls, Rachel *sop* 85, 600
Nichols, Mary *mez* 84, 85
Nicholson, Paul *org* 502, 514
Nickless, David *treb* 888
Nicolitch, Gordan *vn* 244
Nicoll, Harry *ten* 474, 747
Nicolosi, Francesco *pf* 1017
Nielsen, Inga *sop* 1029
Niese, Danielle de *sop* 530
Nieuw Ensemble 377
Nieuw Sinfonietta Amsterdam 733
Nikolaieva, Tatyana *pf* 1338
Nikolic, Gordan *cond* 774
Nikolitch, Gordan *vn* 141
Nilon, Paul *ten* 474, 747
Nimsgern, Siegmund *bass-bar* 394, 434
Niquet, Hervé *cond* 324, 505, 506, 676, 892
Nixon, John Leigh *ten* 530
Noble, Dennis *bar* 424, 425, 1292
Noble, John *bass* 1198
Nodaira, Ichiro *pf* 178
Noferini, Andrea *vc* 1017
Nolte, Raimund *bar* 85, 86, 87
Noone, Michael *cond* 762

Nordmo-Løvberg, Aase *sop* 142
Norman, Daniel *ten* 141, 1010, 1011
Norman, Jessye *sop* 168, 689, 690, 1110
Norrington, Roger *cond* 135, 137, 141, 293, 296, 505, 527, 725, 732, 734, 990, 1085, 1185
Norris, David Owen *pf* 645, 849
Norrköping Symphony Orchestra 848, 851, 950
North, Nigel *lute* 209
North German Radio Chorus. . . 143, 583, 656, 690, 1265
North German Radio Philharmonic Orchestra 649
North German Radio Symphony Orchestra 143, 245, 297, 575, 962
Northern Chamber Orchestra . . . 552, 777, 778, 919, 932, 1130, 1176
Northern Sinfonia 280, 437, 438, 439, 607, 768, 1204
Northern Voices 282
Northwest Chamber Orchestra 464
Norwegian Chamber Orchestra 549
Norwegian Radio Orchestra 439
Noseda, Gianandrea *cond* . . . 399, 629, 630, 663, 664, 928, 1085, 1086
Nott, Jonathan *cond* 612, 657, 990, 1190
Nouvel Orchestre Philharmonique de Radio France. 1317
Novacek, Libor *pf* 259, 667
Novelli, Jean-Francois *ten* 199, 325
Nowacki, Piotr *bass* 846
Nuñez, Antonio *vn* 764
Nuñez, Gustavo *bn* 764
Nuti, Giampaolo *pf* 979

O

Oberfrank, Géza *cond* 89
Oberlin, Russell *counterten* 530
Oborin, Lev *pf* 155
Ochman, Wieslaw *ten* 299, 407
Ockenden, Rebecca *sop* 376
Ockert, Christian *db* 993, 994
O'Connor, Tara Helen *fl* 1130
Octors, Georges-Élie *cond* 546
Oddone, Graciela *sop* 972
Odense Symphony Orchestra 320, 461
O'Dette, Paul *lute* 386, 387
Odinius, Lothar *ten* 1210
O'Donnell, James *org* 278, 711
O'Donnell, James *cond* . . . 312, 711, 838, 840, 1239, 1346
O'Duinn, Prionnsías *cond* 731
O'Dwyer, Eamonn *treb* 888
Oelze, Christiane *sop* 1306
Ogawa, Noriko *pf* 366, 367, 586, 1145
Ogden, Craig *gtr* 855, 1184, 1291
Ogden, Robert *alto* 530
Ogdon, John *pf* 662
Ogrintchouk, Alexei *ob* 764
Oistrakh, David *vn* .133, 155, 243, 866, 1051, 1066, 1159, 1332
Oistrakh, Igor *vn* 1159
Oistrakh, David *dir* 1159
Oliveira, Elmar *vn* 99, 544
Ollila-Hannikainen, Tuomas *cond* . . . 288, 740, 980, 1075
Ollu, Franck *cond* 179
Olsen, Frode *bass* 523
O'Mara, Stephen *ten* 985
O'Neill, Richard *va* 1130
O'Neill, Robin *bn* 996

O'Neill, Robin *cond* 1089
Ono, Kazushi *cond* 1134
Onofri, Enrico *vn* 1247, 1248
Oosten, Ben van *org* 392
Opera Junior Children's Chorus. 602
Opera North Chorus. 385, 1226, 1293
Opera North Orchestra. 114, 385, 1226
Opéra-Comique Choir 721
Opéra-Comique Orchestra 721
Opie, Alan *bar* 1201
Oppens, Ursula *pf* 320
Oramo, Sakari *cond* . . .355, 442, 491, 659, 660, 963, 1066, 1295
Orán, Maria *sop* 742
Orazio, Francesco d' *vn* 979
(Anonymous) Orchestra . . . 221, 255, 466, 852, 964, 1351
Orchestra Academy of the Gran Teatre del Liceu. . . . 801
Orchestra del Maggio Musicale Fiorentino 383, 804, 1237
Orchestra del Teatro dell'Opera di Roma 1211, 1212
Orchestra della Svizzera Italiana. 1049, 1316
Orchestra Internazionale d'Italia 174
Orchestra Of Opera North. 489
Orchestra of Patras 534, 541
Orchestra of the Age of Enlightenment523, 527, 530, 537, 738, 792, 793, 796, 797, 889, 890, 968, 1252
Orchestra of the Eighteenth Century. . 133, 551, 734, 904
Orchestra of the Golden Age 1177
Orchestra of the Opéra-Bastille (Paris) 742
Orchestra of the Renaissance 762
Orchestra Stabile Accademia di Santa Cecilia, Rome . 875
Orchestre de Bretagne. 934
Orchestre de Chambre de Genève 939
Orchestre de la Société des Concerts du Conservatoire . . 1159
Orchestre de Paris 188, 195, 355, 616, 723, 951, 961, 1174, 1216
Orchestre National du Capitole de Toulouse . . . 218, 811
Orchestre Révolutionnaire et Romantique..131, 135, 136, 139, 166, 192, 197, 201, 261, 262, 473, 1020, 1208, 1209
Oren, Daniel *cond* 1226
Orgonasova, Luba *sop* 135, 136, 168, 1208, 1209
Oriana Concert Choir. 889
Oriana Concert Orchestra 889
Orlando Consort 390
Orlov, Alexander *cond* 1174
Ormandy, Eugene *cond* 130, 131, 895, 898, 1054
Oro, Martín *counterten* 1097
Orpheus Chamber Orchestra 769, 770, 771
Orpheus Quartet 147
Orpheus Singers 230
Orrell, James *treb* 723
Orrell, Keith *dir* 723
ORTF Choir. 742
ORTF National Orchestra 741
ORTF Philharmonic Orchestra 742, 1317
Ortiz, Cristina *pf* 965
Orton, Stephen *vc* 766
Osborne, Steven *pf* 270, 366, 668, 682, 743, 744, 902, 1181
Oslo Philharmonic Chorus. 707
Oslo Philharmonic Orchestra 400, 414, 415, 707, 814, 1051, 1162, 1163, 1164
Oslo Quartet 822
Oslo Wind Quintet. 822
Osmond, Cecilia *sop* 89, 515
Osostowicz, Krysia *va* 956
Osostowicz, Krysia *vn* 111, 954, 956, 967

Ossia. 925
Osterkorn, Natascha *pf* 1032
Östman, Arnold *cond* 471
Ostrcil, Otakar *cond* 1086
Ostrobothnian Chamber Orchestra 765, 1196
Otaka, Tadaaki *cond* 1145
Otter, Anne Sofie von *mez* 88, 89, 135, 136, 183, 199,
230, 470, 494, 516, 518, 530, 538, 689, 690, 916, 984,
1078, 1208, 1209
Otter, Anne Sofie von *sop* 1250
Otto, Susanne *contr* 823
Oue, Eiji *cond* 346, 835
Outram, Martin *va* 120, 223, 268
Outram, Rebecca *sop* 515, 754, 755
Ovenden, Jeremy *ten* 520, 758
Over, Simon *pf* 225
Ovrutsky, Mikhail *vn* 931
Owen, Charles *pf* 614
Owen, Martin *hn* 996
Owens, Shabda *elec* 317
Owens, Shabda *voc* 317
Owens, Matthew *cond* 654, 1083
Oxford Bach Choir 725
Oxford Camerata. 459, 549, 826
Oxford Girls' Choir. 578
Oxford Schola Cantorum 647
Oxley, James *ten* 654
Ozawa, Seiji *cond* 181, 218, 636, 661, 862, 894, 895, 1099

P

Paasikivi, Lilli *mez* 1076, 1077, 1078
Pace, Enrico *pf* 304
Pacifica Quartet. 321
Paderewski, Ignace Jan *pf* 1332
Padmore, Mark *ten* .82, 84, 87, 89, 90, 167, 279, 487, 520,
522, 528, 564, 565, 566, 567, 568, 569, 600, 888, 892,
951, 1003
Paëvatalu, Guido *bar* 1029
Page, Christopher *cond* 578
(Les) Pages et les chantres de la Chapelle. 675
Pahud, Emmanuel *fl* 356, 631, 782, 965, 1176, 1244
Pailthorpe, Daniel *fl* 959
Palau de la Música Catalana Chamber Choir. . . . 576, 801
Palloc, Julie *fl* 765
Palm, Siegfried *vc* 657
Palma, Donald *cond* 320
Palmer, Felicity *mez* 755
Palmer, Felicity *sop* 424, 425, 530, 615, 755
Palomares, Joaquín *vn* 749
Palombi, Antonello *ten* 870
Palumbo, Massimo *pf* 950
Palviainen, Eero *lute* 709
Pancík, Josef *cond* 407
Panizza, Ettore *cond* 1227, 1229
Panula, Jorma *cond* 429
Panzarella, Anna Maria *sop* 790, 791
Pape, René *bass* 569
Pappano, Antonio *pf* 863, 879, 1014, 1048, 1307
Pappano, Antonio *cond* .216, 721, 722, 863, 877, 879, 880,
881, 883, 895, 927, 1048, 1111, 1162, 1168, 1216, 1263,
1284
Paris Chorus 723
Paris Conservatoire Orchestra 963, 964
Paris Ensemble Orchestra. 199
Paris Ensemble Orchestral 85, 86, 526

Paris National Opera Chorus 1133
Paris National Opera Orchestra 968, 1133, 1350
Paris Opera Chorus. . ., ... 858
Paris Opera Orchestra. 184, 218, 858
Paris Opéra-Bastille Chorus 967, 1226, 1229
Paris Opéra-Bastille Orchestra 967, 1226, 1229
Paris Opéra-Comique Chorus 830
Paris Opéra-Comique Orchestra 830
Paris Orchestra 877, 1310
Paris Orchestra Chorus. 195
Parker-Smith, Jane *org* 615
Parkin, Eric *pf* 372, 726
Parkman, Stefan *cond* 923, 1109
Parloff, Michael *fl* 1132
Parrott, Andrew *cond* 211, 754, 755
Parry, Susan *mez* 1131
Parry, Wilfrid *pf* 1319
Parry, David *cond* .178, 382, 384, 385, 474, 484, 747, 834,
874, 881, 886, 939, 1121, 1226
Parsons, Brian *ten* 1210
Parsons, Geoffrey *pf* 1004, 1153, 1348
Partridge, Ian *ten* 122, 202, 434, 441, 514, 891, 1198
Pashley, Anne *sop* 1206, 1209
Pasiecznik, Olga *sop* 678
Pasquier, Etienne *vc* 741
Pasquier, Jean *vn* 741
Pasquier, Régis *vn* 713
Pászthy, Júlia *sop* 83
Pásztory-Bartók, Ditta *pf* 113
Pataky, Koloman von *ten* 168, 169
Patanè, Franco *cond* 882
Patanè, Giuseppe *cond* 718
Paterson, Douglas *va* 306
Paton, Iain *ten* 892
Patzak, Julius *ten* 708
Pauk, György *vn* 106, 111
Pauley, Wilbur *bass* 1130
Pavarotti, Luciano *ten* 530, 1100, 1207, 1208, 1209
Pavel Haas Quartet 498, 499, 613
Pavlutskaya, Natalia *vc* 497
Pavrí, Fali *pf* 1138
Payne, Joseph *hpd* 833
Payne, Sally Bruce *mez* 566
Pazmany, Tibor *org* 640
Pearce, Michael *bass* 530
Pearce, Colman *cond* 1093
Pearlman, Martin *cond* 473
Pears, Peter *spkr* 278
Pears, Peter *ten* . . . 85, 86, 89, 91, 271, 272, 275, 278, 281
Pearson, Gail *sop* 521
Pearson, William *bar* 656
Pecková, Dagmar *mez* 408, 715
Pedersen, Lars *ten* 821
Peeters, Harry *bass* 1028
Peinemann, Edith *vn* 182, 1110
Pekinel, Güher *pf* 258
Pekinel, Süher *pf* 258
Pell, Susanna *va da gamba* 889
Pell, Susanna *viol* 887
Pelliccia, Arrigo *va* 772
Pelton, Carmen *sop* 230
Pelucchi, Pierangelo *cond* 452
Pendlebury, Nic *va* 465
Pennicchi, Marinella *sop* 755
Penny, Andrew *cond* 1136
Perahia, Murray *pf* 126, 127, 128, 129, 131, 159, 329, 333,
334, 335, 509, 767, 768, 769, 771

Perahia, Murray *dir* 767, 768, 769, 771
Percussion de Strasbourg 741, 742
Percussive Rotterdam 974
Percy, Neil *perc* 107
Perényi, Miklós *vc* 152, 642
Pérez, Victor Pablo *cond* 722, 802
Pergamenschikov, Boris *vc* 394, 496
Perkin, Helen *pf* 426
Perlman, Itzhak *vn* 131, 134, 154, 181, 257, 290, 837
Perruche, Ingrid *sop* 480
Persson, Miah *sop* 568, 569, 794, 938
Pertusi, Michele *bass* 195, 937, 938
Pesch, Ada *vn* 1348
Pesek, Libor *cond* 824
Peskó, Zoltán *cond* 576
(Jean) Pesneaud Children's Choir. 218
Peter Kay Children's Choir 881, 1121
Petersen, Marlis *sop* 5770
Petersen Quartet 149, 492, 545, 555, 913, 1016
Petibon, Patricia *sop* 513, 1358
Petit, Marie-Madeleine *pf* 742
(La) Petite Bande. 87, 792, 847
Petitjean, Stéphane *pf* 499
(Les) Petits Chanteurs de Versailles 218, 219
Petrenko, Vasily *cond* 661, 1056, 1165, 1167
Petrou, George *cond* 534, 541
Petzold, Martin *ten* 574
Peyer, Gervase de *cl* 444, 742
Pezzotti, Daniel *vc* 1348
Phantasm 310, 459, 620, 621, 648, 887, 1344
Philadelphia Orchestra .106, 130, 131, 580, 854, 895, 898,
1049, 1054, 1059, 1127
Philharmonia Baroque Chorale 971
Philharmonia Baroque Orchestra 971, 1244
Philharmonia Chorus . . .89, 142, 170, 245, 261, 383, 442,
651, 695, 796, 798, 800, 810, 1120, 1121, 1206, 1209,
1218
Philharmonia Hungarica 550
Philharmonia Orchestra . .89, 99, 110, 119, 129, 131, 132,
135, 139, 142, 143, 170, 180, 196, 243, 245, 247, 261,
294, 295, 296, 330, 331, 361, 362, 382, 383, 384, 394,
397, 416, 422, 434, 474, 484, 490, 491, 601, 615, 633,
645, 651, 658, 695, 707, 718, 729, 732, 742, 747, 765,
766, 769, 796, 798, 800, 810, 819, 834, 859, 874, 881,
883, 886, 895, 897, 912, 930, 941, 946, 955, 965, 982,
985, 990, 1053, 1066, 1067, 1071, 1073, 1075, 1087,
1100, 1102, 1103, 1111, 1116, 1117, 1120, 1121, 1128,
1129, 113
Philharmonia Wind Quartet. 143
Phillips, Leo *vn* 224, 855
Phillips, Margaret *org* 1090
Phillips, Tom *ten* 520
Phillips, Peter *cond* 289, 311, 351, 622, 671, 762, 838,
1148, 1149
Philomusica of London 530
Piatigorsky, Gregor *vc* 636, 1290, 1298
Piau, Sandrine *sop* .262, 434, 523, 528, 568, 569, 711, 892,
1255
Piazzolla, Astor *bandoneón* 850
Piccinini, Monica *mez* 755, 756
Pickup, Robert *cl* 1348
Pidò, Evelino *cond* 382, 720
Pidoux, Roland *vc* 500
Pierlot, Philippe *va da gamba* 648
Pierlot, Philippe *dir* 83
Pierot, Alice *vn* 210
Pierotti, Susan *vn* 103

Pierre Robert Ensemble 390
Pierson, Alan *cond* 924, 925
Pieterson, George *cl* 359, 361
Pietiläinen, Pauli *org* 1077
Pillai, Ashan *va* 121
Pilz, János *vn* 112
Pini, Anthony *vc* 255
Pinkas, Jiří *cond* 408, 409
Pinnock, Trevor *hpd* 470, 504, 904
Pinnock, Trevor *org* 530
Pinnock, Trevor *cond* . .239, 517, 518, 530, 542, 566, 776,
780
Pinnock, Trevor *dir* 470, 504, 530
Pintscher, Matthias *cond* 356
Piolino, François *ten* 513, 752, 755, 756
Piqué, Alessandro *ob* 1251
Piquemal, Michel *bar* 857
Pires, Maria João *pf* 256, 338, 1002
Pisaroni, Luca *bass-bar* 1348
Pitts, Antony *cond* 845
Pittsburgh Symphony Orchestra 250
Pizarro, Artur *pf* 749, 933
Plane, Robert *cl* 120, 439, 605, 683, 1092
Planès, Alain *pf* 367
Plasson, Michel *cond* 218, 221, 371, 483, 484
Platt, Ian *bar* 474, 747
Plazas, Mary *sop* 434, 435
Pleeth, William *vc* 444, 742
Pletnev, Mikhail *pf* 164, 665, 973, 1151, 1160, 1165, 1171
Pletnev, Mikhail *cond* 898, 1165, 1316
Plouvier, Jean-Luc *pf* 546
Pochin, Juliette *mez* 1203
Podger, Rachel *bq vn* 785, 904
Podger, Rachel *vn* 785, 1245
Podobedov, Sergei *pf* 593
Pogorelich, Ivo *pf* 334, 340, 914
Pohl, Oliver *pf* 1306
Pöhl, Albert *bass* 1179
Pokrovsky Ensemble 1131
Polianski, Valéri *cond* 978
Polish Festival Orchestra. 329
Polish National Opera Chorus 1145
Polish National Opera Orchestra 1145
Polish National Radio Symphony Orchestra . . . .
403, 479, 677, 678, 742, 835, 1085, 1195
Polish Radio Choir 479
Pollack, Daniel *pf* 101
Pollini, Maurizio *pf* 126, 131, 162, 330, 334, 336, 338,
1002, 1028, 1333
Polo, Asier *vc* 931
Poltéra, Christian *vc* 980
Polverelli, Laura *mez* 1257
Polyansky, Valéry *cond* 233, 468, 1062, 1151
Polyphony .277, 300, 684, 843, 845, 856, 960, 1034, 1155,
1293, 1349
Pondepeyre, Angeline *pf* 499
Pons, Josep *cond* 950
Ponseele, Marcel *ob* 1247, 1248
Pöntinen, Roland *pf* 252, 304, 581, 656, 922
Pooley, Tim *va* 271, 589, 590
Popa, Péter *vn* 143
Popescu, Maria *mez* 903
Pople, Ross *vc* 178, 1347
Pople, Ross *cond* 551
Popp, Lucia *sop* 394, 434, 690, 692, 703, 832
Poppen, Christoph *vn* 782
Poppen, Christoph *cond* . . 496, 498, 545, 711, 1079, 1299

Porter, Kim *contr* 547
Posch, Alois *db* 994
Poschner-Klebel, Brigitte *sop* 1028
Post, Andreas *ten* 1179
Potter, John *ten* 623
Poulton, Robert *bar* 197
Powell, Michael *tbn* 1130
Power, Lawrence *va* . . .237, 238, 253, 274, 580, 604, 773,
1191, 1288
Power, Patrick *ten* 135, 137, 600
Prades Festival Orchestra 992, 993
Prague Chamber Choir 407, 409, 943, 944, 947
Prague Chamber Orchestra 778, 779
Prague Children's Choir 407
Prague National Opera Company Chorus 1086
Prague National Opera Company Orchestra 1086
Prague National Theatre Chorus 410
Prague National Theatre Orchestra 410
Prague Philharmonia 403, 411, 713, 979, 987, 1357
Prague Philharmonic Choir . . 716, 979, 1133, 1195, 1357
Prague Philharmonic Chorus 407, 689, 690, 692, 814, 946,
1087
Prague Philharmonic Orchestra 1355
Prague Quartet 405
Prague Symphony Orchestra 411, 715
Pratt, Lawrence *pf* 605
Preedy, Cyril *pf* 1319
Prégardien, Christoph *ten* 87, 88, 89, 569, 790, 791, 1008,
1010, 1014, 1015
Preiss, James *marimba* 926
Prelle, Una *hp* 1348
Premiere Ensemble 707
Preston, Simon *org* 389
Preston, Simon *cond* 406, 530
Preston Cecilian Choir 426
Prêtre, Georges *cond* 218, 718, 968, 1350
Previn, André *pf* 99, 100, 455, 637, 4713
Previn, André *cond* .99, 100, 414, 415, 455, 637, 832, 860,
861, 894, 898, 1053, 1054, 1067, 1100, 1159, 1289,
1290, 1317, 4713
Previn, André *dir* 455
Prey, Hermann *bar* 690, 692, 693, 832
Price, Edward *bass* 98
Price, Janet *sop* 434
Price, Leontyne *sop* 1208
Price, Margaret *sop* 426, 790, 1198
Prideaux, William *bar* 97
Prina, Sonia *contr* 1258
Prina, Sonia *mez* 1247
Pritchard, John *cond* 808, 916, 1336
Pro Arte Orchestra 505, 506
Pro Arte Quartet 555
Pro Arte Singers 843
Procter, Norma *contr* 272, 690
Prommel, Peter *perc* 546
Proud, Malcolm *hpd* 1253
Provost, Paul *org* 96
Prutsman, Stephen *pf* 680
Pryce-Jones, John *cond* 1137, 1138
Psappha 358
Pujol, Marcos *voc* 538
Purcell Quartet 87, 507
Purcell Quartet 308
The Purcell Simfony 891
The Purcell Simfony Voices 891
Purefoy, William *alto* 239
Purser, David *tbn* 855

Purves, Christopher *bar* 515
Purvis, William *hn* 1130
Putnins, Pauls *bass* 358
Putnins, Kaspars *cond* 302, 903
Pyatt, David *hn* 605, 766, 1011, 1102

Q

Quartetto Borciani 228
Quartetto Italiano 143, 145, 913, 995
Quasthoff, Thomas *bar* 261, 530, 571, 984, 1016
Quator Diotima 614
Quattrocchi, Fernand *cond* 499
Quatuor Schumann 706
Queensland Symphony Orchestra (Brisbane) 1046
Queyras, Jean-Guihen *vc* . . . 274, 356, 364, 395, 656, 782
Quinn, Iain *org* 1081
Quinney, Robert *org* 312, 358
Quint, Philippe *vn* 350, 1017
Quintiliani, Barbara *sop* 495
Quivar, Florence *contr* 690, 692, 693, 1143

R

Rabinovich, Nikolai *cond* 1063
Rabinowitch, Alexander *pf* 1022
Rabl, Gottfried *cond* 1303
Rachlin, Julian *va* 1246, 1247
Rachmaninov, Sergey *pf* 895
Rácz, Ottó *ob* 143
Radcliffe Choral Society 721
Rademann, Hans-Christoph *cond* 738
Radio France Chorus 200, 218, 368, 370
Radio Svizzera Choir, Lugano 481
Raekallio, Matti *pf* 740
Ragazzi, The Peninsula Boys Chorus 1126, 1128
Rahman, Sophia *pf* 605, 1039
RAI National Symphony Orchestra 304, 356
Rakowski, Maciej *vn* 1154
Ramey, Samuel *bass* 1207, 1209
Ramselaar, Bas *bass* 92
Ranallo, Philippe *tpt* 546
Rancourt, Stéphane *ob* 918
Randle, Thomas *ten* 832, 1202
Ránki, Dezsö *pf* 664
Rännäli, Mika *pf* 686
Ranzani, Stefano *cond* 463
Raphael Ensemble 251, 267
Rappé, Jadwiga *contr* 846
Raschèr Saxophone Quartet 465, 1342
Raskin, Judith *sop* 696
Rastatt Vocal Ensemble 175
Rattle, Simon *cond* 126, 127, 135, 207, 261, 272, 275, 279,
360, 361, 415, 456, 615, 694, 697, 698, 703, 704, 705,
742, 792, 832, 917, 984, 990, 1050, 1052, 1067, 1070,
1106, 1128, 1129, 1141, 1143, 1144, 1145, 1282, 1289
Raucheisen, Michael *pf* 641
Ravens, Simon *cond* 839
Raybould, Clarence *cond* 426, 484
Razumovsky Sinfonia 371
RCA Italiana Opera Chorus 1231

RCA Italiana Opera Orchestra 1231
RCA Victor Chamber Orchestra 931
RCA Victor Chorus. 871, 874
RCA Victor Orchestra. 718, 871, 874, 1236, 7183
RCA Victor Symphony Orchestra 636, 1066, 1325
Reach, Edward *ten* 426
Recherche Ensemble. 437, 823
Rechtman, Ilan *pf* 1240
Red Byrd 460
Red Fish Blue Fish. 1308
Rees-Jones, David *bass* 840
Regensburg Cathedral Choir (Boys' Voices) 690
Reher, Kurt *vc* 983, 992, 993
Reich, Steve *pf* 925
Reich, Steve *dir* 925
(Steve) Reich Ensemble. 926
Reid, Andrew *org* 684
Reiner, Fritz *cond* . . .106, 107, 241, 243, 814, 1104, 1159,
1160, 1265, 1267, 1284, 1285, 1311, 1325
Reinis, Aigars *org* 302
Relyea, John *bass* 703
Remmert, Birgit *contr* 134, 135, 136, 168, 695, 703, 1003
Rémy, Ludger *org* 1179
Rémy, Ludger *dir* 1179
Rensburg, Kobie van *ten* 758
Repin, Vadim *vn* 816, 1108, 1151, 1159
Resonanz Ensemble. 1001
Reuss, Daniel *cond* 522, 711, 857, 1131
Reuter, Johan *bar* 375
Reyghere, Greta de *sop* 87
Reynish, Timothy *cond* 486
Reynolds, Anna *mez* 407, 530, 1206, 1209
Rheinische Kantorei 94, 1178
Rheinland-Pfalz State Philharmonic Orchestra 175
Rhine Opera Chorus. 859
Rhineland Palatinate State Philharmonic Orchestra . 1301
Rhorer, Jérémie *cond* 1351
Rhys-Davies, Jennifer *sop* 1121
Rial, Nuria *sop* 525, 529
Rice, Christine *mez* 794, 927
Rice, Stephen *cond* 478, 708, 762, 1340, 7623
Ricercar Consort 83
Richter, Sviatoslav *pf* . .133, 270, 562, 660, 662, 866, 902,
999, 1027, 1161, 1333, 1338
Richter, Caspar *cond* 639, 640
Rickenbacher, Karl Anton *cond* 1096
Riddell, Duncan *vn* 411
Ridderbusch, Karl *bass* 299
Riddle, Frederick *va* 193, 1292
Riebl, Thomas *va* 1023
Riegel, Kenneth *ten* 662, 693
Riegelbauer, Peter *db* 993, 994, 996
Rieger, Wolfram *pf* 913
Riesman, Michael *pf* 466
Riesman, Michael *cond* 466
Riga Sinfonietta. 1197
Rigby, Cormac *spkr* 277
Rigby, Jean *mez* . .117, 122, 165, 197, 300, 374, 412, 707,
1201, 1202, 1256
Riley, Terry *voc* 317
Rilling, Helmuth *cond* 93, 276, 670, 690, 738
Rime, Noémi *sop* 905
Rimmer, Nicholas *org* 960
Rinaldi, Stefania *cond* 1017
Rintzler, Marius *bass* 1052, 1057
Ripley, Gladys *contr* 424, 425, 518, 519
Rippon, Michael *bass* 755

Risonanza (La). 524, 525
Ritchie, Margaret *sop* 1198
Ritchie, Neil *treb* 406
Rivenq, Nicolas *bar* 905
Riverside Symphony Orchestra. 958
Rivinius, Gustav *vc* 411
Rizzi, Carlo *cond* 484, 619
Roa, Miguel *cond* 265, 1352
Robbin, Catherine *mez* 166, 167, 168, 199, 789
Robert Shaw Chorale 718, 7183
Roberts, Helen *va* 920
Roberts, Stephen *bar* 412, 426, 739, 955, 1292
Roberts, Timothy *hpd* 460
Roberts, Timothy *org* 449
Roberts Trio (Bernard). 268
Robertson, Duncan *ten* 1206, 1209
Robertson, Karen *sop* 640
Robertson, Martin *sax* 1191, 1192
Robertson, David *cond* 924, 1350
Robertson, Stewart *cond* 180, 594
Robinson, Christopher *org* 654, 957, 1094
Robinson, Dean *bar* 939
Robinson, Faye *sop* 1182, 1183
Robinson, Joseph *ob* 99
Robinson, Olivia *sop* 98
Robinson, Timothy *ten* . . . 407, 434, 435, 789, 790, 1144
Robinson, Christopher *cond* .189, 278, 596, 654, 841, 957,
1293, 1304, 1555
Robinson, Christopher *dir* 957, 1094
Robinson, Stanford *cond* 426
Robles, Marisa *hp* 272
Roblou, David *hpd* 210
Robson, Anthony *ob* 1252
Robson, Christopher *alto* 518
Robson, Nigel *ten* 374, 516, 530, 755, 1093
Rodgers, Joan *sop* 300, 374, 518, 903
Rogé, Denise-Françoise *pf* 914, 915
Rogé, Pascal *pf* 327, 369, 445, 914, 915, 965
Rogers, Catherine *contr* 790
Rogers, Jane *va* 892
Rogers, Nigel *ten* 754
Rolfe Johnson, Anthony *ten* 87, 88, 89, 135, 136, 168,
372, 483, 515, 530, 570, 790, 1011
Rolla, János *vn* 774
Rolla, János *dir* 774
Rolland, Sophie *vc* 644
Rolton, Julian *pf* 120
Romanesca. 209
Romanoff-Schwarzberg, Nora *va* 1316
Rome Opera Chorus. 885, 1212, 1228, 1229
Rome Opera Orchestra. 421, 885, 1212, 1228, 1229
Ronald, Landon *cond* 415, 418, 964
Roocroft, Amanda *sop* 1198, 1201
Rooley, Anthony *lute* 758
Rooley, Anthony *dir* 758
Rootering, Jan-Hendrik *bass* 689, 690, 1028, 1057
Rophé, Pascal *cond* 356
Rorem, Ned *pf* 936
Rosamunde Quartet 708
Rosamunde Quartet 560
Rosand, Aaron *vn* 467
Röschmann, Dorothea *sop* 88, 89, 261, 518, 526, 568, 972,
1029, 1034
Roscoe, Martin *pf* 222, 268, 347, 379, 433, 743, 823,
1059, 1143
Rose, Leonard *vc* 130, 131
Rose, Matthew *bar* 1003

Rose, Peter *bass* 790
Rose, Barry *cond* 530
Rose Consort of Viols 460
Rosen, Charles *pf* 1298
Rosenberger, Carol *pf* 543
Rosenfeld, Jayn *fl* 354
Rosenthal, Manuel *cond* 827
Roskilde Cathedral Boys' Choir & Congregation 860
Rosman, Carl *cl* 103
Ross, Alastair *hpd* 530
Rössel-Majdan, Hilde *mez* 134, 135
Rossi, Cristiano *vn* 1247, 1248
Rössl-Majdan, Hilde *mez* 695
Rost, Andrea *sop* 689, 690
Rostropovich, Mstislav *vc* . . .133, 256, 271, 274, 397, 398,
548, 1105, 1161
Rostropovich, Mstislav *cond* . . . 270, 467, 863, 1064, 1105
Rosvaenge, Helge *ten* 1209
Roth, Detlef *bar* 135, 136
Roth, Detlef *bass* 135
Rothman, George *cond* 958
Rothwell, Evelyn *ob* 1311
Rotterdam Chamber Orchestra 932
Rotterdam Philharmonic Orchestra 1275
Rouland, Sébastien *cond* 831
Rousset, Christophe *hpd* 952
Rousset, Christophe *cond* . . . 472, 528, 531, 624, 677, 712
Rowlands, Alan *pf* 605
Royal, Kate *sop* 697, 1035
Royal Academy of Music Chamber Ensemble 214
Royal Albert Hall Orchestra 421
Royal Ballet Sinfonia 202, 728, 1136
Royal Danish Opera Chorus 958, 959, 1279
Royal Danish Orchestra 958, 959, 1279
Royal Liverpool Philharmonic Choir 203, 590
Royal Liverpool Philharmonic Orchestra . .203, 415, 439,
590, 593, 596, 661, 916, 1056, 1080, 1136, 1165, 1167
Royal Military School of Music Band, Kneller Hall . 1213
Royal Northern College of Music Wind Orchestra. . . 486
Royal Opera House Chorus, Covent Garden. . . .169, 170,
172, 216, 272, 284, 285, 286, 372, 381, 382, 471, 800,
801, 874, 875, 877, 878, 880, 881, 1087, 1100, 1204,
1213, 1214, 1216, 1220, 1224, 1228, 1231, 1232, 1233,
1234, 1237, 1268, 1271, 1282, 1284, 1285, 1359
Royal Opera House Orchestra, Covent Garden .169, 170,
172, 198, 199, 216, 222, 272, 284, 285, 286, 381, 382,
471, 530, 577, 619, 800, 801, 874, 875, 877, 878, 880,
881, 1100, 1111, 1124, 1174, 1204, 1214, 1215, 1216,
1220, 1224, 1228, 1231, 1232, 1233, 1234, 1237, 1263,
1268, 1271, 1284, 1359
Royal Philharmonic Chorus 195
Royal Philharmonic Orchestra97, 117, 192, 193, 194, 195,
201, 217, 243, 248, 302, 319, 370, 372, 373, 374, 414,
421, 440, 474, 494, 551, 646, 732, 747, 807, 916, 927,
940, 965, 989, 991, 1070, 1071, 1073, 1080, 1091, 1159,
1164, 1197, 1289, 1290, 1312, 1313, 1322
Royal Scottish National Chorus 867
Royal Scottish National Orchestra .99, 100, 101, 115, 116,
117, 222, 223, 291, 294, 297, 373, 439, 451, 467, 588,
594, 864, 867, 908, 918, 934, 952, 1049, 1054, 1095,
1194
Royal String Quartet 1142
Royal Swedish Opera Orchestra 187
Rozario, Patricia *sop* 591, 1010, 1011, 1156
Rozhdestvensky, Gennady *cond* . . .646, 1053, 1058, 1154,
1167, 1314
RTBF Symphony Orchestra 1053, 1054

RTE Philharmonic Choir 1093
RTE Sinfonietta 202, 731
Rubens, Sibylla *sop* 93, 790
Rubingh, Henk *vn* 1246, 1247
Rubinsky, Sonia *pf* 1242
Rubinstein, Artur *pf* . . .331, 332, 334, 336, 337, 338, 341,
1334
Rudner, Ola *cond* 123, 958
Ruffer, Nancy *fl* 753
Rundel, Peter *cond* 926, 1192
Rundell, Clark *cond* 486
Runnicles, Donald *cond* 640
Rupp, Franz *pf* 641
Ruske, Eric *hn* 766
Russcher, Tristan *org* 853
Russell Davies, Dennis *cond* 315, 465, 593, 628, 1193,
1300
Russian Federation Academic Symphony Orchestra . . 816
Russian Federation State Symphony Orchestra 816
Russian National Chorus 1168
Russian National Orchestra . .632, 898, 1052, 1159, 1160,
1165, 1168, 1170
Russian Philharmonic Orchestra 290, 1063
Russian State Polyphonic Cappella 1051
Russian State Symphonic Cappella 233, 468
Russian State Symphony Orchestra . .468, 816, 978, 1062,
1151, 1166
Russill, Patrick *org* 310, 314
Russo, Andrew *pf* 987
Ruth, Peter 'Madcat' *harc* 230
Rutheford, James *bass-bar* 434, 435, 592
Rutherford, Christian *hn* 1176
Rutter, Clare *sop* 832
Rutter, John *cond* 180, 433, 434, 960, 1341
Ruud, Ole Kristian *cond* 950, 1194
Ruzicka, Peter *cond* 575
Ryan, Kwamé *cond* 823
Rybarská, Lubica *sop* 715
Rydén, Susanne *sop* 971
Rysanov, Maxim *va* 253, 628, 1335
Ryumina, Irina *pf* 836

S

Saarbrücken Radio Symphony Orchestra 299, 848
Saarenpää, Leena *pf* 1077
Sabata, Victor de *cond* 879, 881, 1225, 1350
Sabbatini, Giuseppe *ten* 195, 938
Sachs, Joel *cond, pf* 354
Sächsische Staatskapelle Dresden 194, 602
(Les) Sacqueboutiers de Toulouse 755, 756
Sadlers Wells Orchestra 1137
Saint Paul Chamber Orchestra 99, 100
Sakai, Atsushi *vc* 1316
Sakari, Petri *cond* 1070, 1071, 1072, 1073, 1074
Saks, Gidon *bass* 520, 538
Saksala, Janne *db* 965
Sakurada, Makoto *ten* 89, 90, 481
Salaman, Clare *vn* 308
Salisbury Cathedral Boys' Choir 755
Salle, Lise de la *pf* 661, 787
Salmon, Jane *vc* 306
Salmon, Philip *ten* 1201
Salo, Per *org* 615
Salomaa, Petteri *bass* 135, 137, 892, 1057
Salonen, Esa-Pekka *cond* . . . .

658, 742, 819, 969, 970, 981, 1066

Salpeter, Max *vn* 1319
Salque, François *vc* 445
Salzburg Camerata 732, 794
Salzburg Mozarteum Camerata Academica 775
Salzburg Mozarteum Orchestra 293
Samaltanos, Nikolaos *pf* 1083
Sammons, Albert *vn* 417, 605
Sampson, Carolyn *sop* .82, 84, 85, 512, 520, 522, 527, 573,
754, 755, 792, 892, 1131, 1254
San Francisco Girl's Chorus 608, 1126, 1128
San Francisco Opera Ballet................... 747
San Francisco Opera Chorus 747
San Francisco Opera Orchestra 747, 860
San Francisco Symphony Chorus... 608, 706, 1126, 1128
San Francisco Symphony Orchestra ..346, 347, 608, 699,
704, 706, 820, 821, 1126, 1128
San Sebastian People's Choral Society............ 196
Sanderling, Michael *vc* 1016
Sanderling, Kurt *cond* 244, 245, 1072, 1162
Sanderling, Thomas *cond* 1063, 1150
Sandmann, Marcus *bass* 93
Santa Cecilia Academy Chorus, Rome 875, 877, 1168,
1231
Santa Cecilia Academy Orchestra, Rome ...875, 877, 927,
1162, 1168, 1231
Sante, Sophia van *mez* 1314
Santi, Nello *cond* 941
São Paulo Symphony Orchestra 729, 1160, 1240
Saram, Rohan de *vc* 377
Saraste, Jukka-Pekka *cond* 685, 1078
Sarband 1344
Sargent, Malcolm *cond* .243, 290, 417, 424, 425, 426, 518,
519, 1105, 1320, 1322, 1325
Sari, Atakan *pf* 593
Saroglou, Dimitris *pf* 499
Saulière, Aki *vn* 243
Saunders, Antony *pf* 102
Saunders, Dominic *pf* 845
Savall, Jordi *va da gamba* 597, 709
Savall, Jordi *cond* 505, 674, 709
Savchuck, Yevhen *cond* 903
Savidge, Peter *bar* 530
Sawallisch, Wolfgang *pf* 263
Sawallisch, Wolfgang *cond* 137, 576, 580, 1020, 1102,
1115, 1117, 1124
Say, Fazil *pf* 1330
Scalchi, Gloria *mez* 938, 1208, 1209
Scatterday, Mark Davis *cond* 1302
Schade, Michael *ten* ... 88, 89, 568, 670, 738, 1010, 1011
Schäfer, Christine *sop* ..88, 89, 235, 738, 788, 790, 791,
985, 1007, 1009, 1010, 1032, 1033, 1310
Schäfer, Markus *ten* 88, 89
Schaffer, Frank *vc* 749
Schasching, Rudolf *ten* 134
Scherbakov, Konstantin *pf* 729, 927
Schermerhorn, Kenneth *cond* 123, 607
Schiavo, Maria Grazia *sop* 525
Schick, Steven *perc* 1308
Schiff, András *pf* ...152, 159, 793, 994, 1002, 1013, 1014,
1025
Schiff, Heinrich *vc* 323, 992, 993, 1338
Schiml, Marga *mez* 299, 407
Schirmer, Ulf *cond* 651, 821
Schleiermacher, Steffen *pf* 316
Schleswig-Holstein Music Festival Orchestra 1052
Schlichtig, Hariolf *va* 782

Schlick, Barbara *sop* 94, 1178
Schmid, Benjamin *vn* 636, 848
Schmidl, Peter *cl* 656
Schmidt, Andreas *bar* 88, 89, 265, 570, 670, 790
Schmidt, Trudeliese *mez* 703, 790
Schmithüsen, Ingrid *sop* 90
Schmolck, Jan Peter *vn* 638
Schnabel, Artur *pf* 156, 157
Schnaut, Gabriele *contr* 690
Schneebeli, Olivier *cond* 675
Schneider, Alexander *vn* 992, 993
Schneider, Eric *pf* 1007
Schneiderhan, Wolfgang *vn* 154
Schnittke, Irina *pf* 978
(Arnold) Schoenberg Choir....88, 89, 133, 134, 168, 170,
568, 689, 690, 746, 755, 788, 790, 791, 808, 1036, 1101
Schofrin, Fabian *alto* 755, 756
Schola Antiqua 1239
Schola Cantorum...................... 653, 690
Schola Cantorum Basiliensis Instrumental Ensemble . 318
Schola Romana Lucernensis.................. 560
Scholl, Andreas *alto* ....
318, 520, 521, 530, 755, 1256, 1329, 1358
Schöne, Wolfgang *bass* 690, 738
Schöneberg Boys' Choir 832, 833, 872, 874
Schønwandt, Michael *cond* 821, 958, 1123, 1279
Schoonderwoerd, Arthur *pf* 199
Schreckenbach, Gabriele *mez* 690
Schreckenberger, Stephan *bass* 93, 94, 1178
Schreier, Peter *ten* 263, 690, 1014, 1306
Schreier, Peter *cond* 569, 790
Schröder, Wolfgang *vn* 922
Schröder, Kurt *cond* 364
Schröter, Hans *pf* 990
Schubert, Claudia *contr* 94
Schubert Ensemble of London 306, 445, 638, 724
Schuch, Herbert *pf* 915
Schulte, Rolf *vn* 320, 958, 982, 1130
Schultsz, Jan *pf* 1012, 1031, 1307
Schulz, Wolfgang *fl* 656
Schwalbé, Michel *vn* 1161
Schwanewilms, Anne *sop* 1112, 1113
Schwartz, Felix *va* 784
Schwarz, Britta *contr* 574
Schwarz, Gerard *cond* 203, 347, 543, 593, 852, 1103
Schwarz, Rudolf *cond* 1334, 1347
Schwarzberg, Dora *vn* 1022, 1316
Schwarzkopf, Elisabeth *sop* ...89, 142, 261, 695, 707, 793,
1009, 1110
Scimone, Claudio *cond* 946
Scofield, John *egtr* 1192
Scott, Cyril *pf* 1039
Scott, John *org* 300, 433, 434, 683, 1201, 1345
Scott, John *cond* 1345
Scotti, Antonio *bar* 1350
Scottish Chamber Chorus................. 790, 800
Scottish Chamber Orchestra.135, 226, 245, 505, 528, 530,
569, 682, 685, 766, 769, 770, 780, 790, 794, 800, 804,
943, 991, 1247
Scottish Chamber Orchestra Brass................ 682
Scottish Ensemble....................... 440
Scottish Festival Chorus 1206, 1209
Scottish Opera Chorus 942
Scottish Orchestra Chorus (Royal)............ 867
Scotto, Renata *sop* 421
Sears, Nicholas *bar* 604
Sears, Nicholas *ten* 1247

Seaton, Katherine *sop* 840
Seattle Symphony Chorale 543, 852
Seattle Symphony Orchestra 347, 543, 593, 852, 1103
Seefried, Irmgard *sop* 690
Seers, Mary *sop* 1201
Segerstam, Leif *cond* . 187, 848, 907, 908, 909, 1068, 1073,
1074, 1077, 1079
Seibel, Klauspeter *cond* 649
Seiffert, Peter *ten* 689, 690
Sejna, Karel *cond* 404
Selby, Kathryn *pf* 715, 7153
Selig, Franz-Josef *bass* 168, 788
Seltzer, Cheryl *hpd, pf* 354
(Il) Seminario Musicale 325
Semkow, Jerzy *cond* 296
Semmingsen, Tuva *mez* 1254, 1255
Sempé, Skip *hpd* 351, 905
Semple, Helen *sop* 840
Sepec, Daniel *vn* 155
Serafin, Tullio *cond* . . . 174, 383, 655, 718, 878, 885, 1212,
1220, 1223, 1228, 1229, 1230, 1231, 1350
Serebrier, José *cond* 467, 812, 934, 1017, 1053, 1054,
1168, 1263
Serkin, Rudolf *pf* 163, 242, 256
Serov, Yury *pf* 1062
Serviarian-Kuhn, Dora *pf* 631
Sexton, Sarah *vn* 892
Shaguch, Marina *sop* 706
Shaham, Gil *vn* 99, 100, 243, 637, 866, 4713
Shaham, Hagai *vn* 225, 596, 597
Shaham, Orli *pf* 866
Shallon, David *cond* 580
Shammash, Elizabeth *mez* 207
Shanghai Quartet 492
Shanghai Symphony Orchestra 1150
Shao, En *cond* 653
Shapiro, Lois *fp* 154
Sharova, Tatyana *sop* 1062
Shave, Jaqueline *vn* 1154
Shaw, Robert *cond* 466, 581, 1218
(Robert) Shaw Chorale 1218, 1236
Sheen, Colin *tbn* 300
Sheen, Graham *bn* 422
Sheffield Philharmonic Chorus 424
Shelley, Howard *pf* 342, 379, 478, 489, 578, 595, 597,
598, 679, 742, 763, 768, 900, 903, 956, 1039, 1197
Shelley, Howard *cond* 489, 578, 597, 598, 763, 768
Shelton, Lucy *sop* 958
Sherratt, Brindley *bass* 521, 563
Sherry, Fred *vc* 320, 982, 1130, 1132
Shiokawa, Yuuko *vn* 1002
Shiraga, Fumiko *pf* 331
Shirley-Quirk, John *bar* . . . 85, 86, 91, 274, 275, 407, 424,
426, 518, 530, 755, 1202
Shkosa, Enkelejda *mez* 195, 939
Shore, Andrew *bar* 1121
Short, Nigel *alto* 888
Short, Nigel *cond* 1146
Shuard, Amy *sop* 1206, 1209
(Jean) Sibelius Quartet 909
Sibera, Jana *sop* 1355
Siebens, Etienne *cond* 358
Siegel, Gerhard *ten* 1111
Siegen Bach Chorus Collegium Vocale 1179
Siepi, Cesare *bass* 790
Sigurdsson, Reynir *vib* 653
Siirala, Antti *pf* 259, 1003

Silesian Philharmonic Choir 479
Sillito, Kenneth *vn* 766
Silvasti, Jorma *ten* 1078
Silvestri, Constantin *cond* 662, 1159
Silvestrov, Valentin *pf* 1079
Simas, Jerome *cl* 455
Simboli, Anna *mez* 755, 756, 1247
Simcock, Iain *hbel* 1154
Siméonoff, Konstantin *cond* 1065
Simmonds, Paul *clav* 94
Simon, Geoffrey *cond* 1169
Simón Bolívar Youth Orchestra 1165, 1313
Simon Joly Chorale 982, 985, 1132
Simpson, Marietta *mez* 230
Sinaisky, Vassily *cond* 469, 679, 987
Sinclair, Andrew *ten* 513
Sinclair, James *cond* 607, 608
Sinfonia 21 547
Sinfonia Chorus 1204
Sinfonia Varsovia 296, 632, 1066
Sinfonye 578
Sinopoli, Giuseppe *cond* 696, 990, 1110, 1123, 1231, 1282
Siren Ensemble 384
Sirenko, Vladimir *cond* 1080
Sirmais, Maris *cond* 628
Sitkovetsky, Dimitry *cond* 203
Sivelöv, Niklas *pf* 429
The Sixteen . . . 308, 511, 514, 517, 891, 1047, 1149, 1157,
1345, 1346
Sjöberg, Gitta-Maria *sop* 646
Skampa Quartet 411, 1086
Skelton, Stuart *ten* 135, 442
Skinner, David *cond* 622, 1187
Skrowaczewski, Stanislaw *cond* 299
Slaars, Laurent *bar* 376
Slagter, Jacob *hn* 764
Slatford, Rodney *db* 1214
Slatkin, Leonard *cond* 99, 102, 230, 544, 732, 1304
Slattery, Michael *ten* 520, 971
Slovak Philharmonic Chorus 626, 814, 815, 816, 986
Slovak Philharmonic Male Chorus 631
Slovak Philharmonic Orchestra 864
Slovak Radio Symphony Orchestra 626, 927
Slovak State Philharmonic Orchestra, Kosiče . . 475, 1166
Sluchin, Benny *tbn* 188
Sluk Chamber Choir of Bratislava 106, 107
Slutsky, Boris *pf* 1025
Small, Michael *treb* 203
Smallens, Alexander *cond* 457
Smart, Alison *sop* 547
Smetana Trio 406
Smissen, Robert *va* 766
Smith, Andrew-John *org* 966
Smith, Angus *ten* 515, 520, 522
Smith, Brooks *pf* 1325
Smith, Carol *mez* 721
Smith, Hopkinson *lute* 386
Smith, Jennifer *sop* 435, 436, 512, 530
Smith, Craig *cond* 82
Smith, Julian *cond* 874
Smolij, Mariusz *cond* 953
Smythe, Russell *bar* 474, 747
Snellings, Dirk *bass* 307
Soames, Benjamin *spkr* 1130
Sobotka, Iwona *sop* 1143, 1144
Sodero, Cesare *cond* 1230, 1231
Söderström, Elisabeth *sop* 275, 916, 1052, 1073, 1075

Sojer, Hans *ten* 1301
Sokhiev, Tugan *cond* 811
Sokolov, Grigory *pf* 339
Sokolova, Liubov *mez* 1062
Sol, Tom *bass* 91
Solamente Naturali 474
Sólbergsson, Björn Steinar *org* 653
(I) Solisti Veneti. 946
Solomon *pf* 157, 162, 222, 260, 490. 769, 1160
Solti, Georg *cond* .106, 107, 231, 417, 418, 690, 702, 800,
      807, 810, 1117, 1119, 1123, 1174, 1209, 1212, 1214,
                  1228, 1231, 1233, 1234, 1269, 1276
Solymon, Stefan *cond* 546
Sommerville, James *hn* 656
Søndergård, Thomas *cond* 959
Sonnerie 210, 782
Sonntag, Ulrike *sop* 581
Sørensen, Jesper Juul *tbn* 591
Soroka, Solomia *vn* 229, 715, 7153
Sorrel Quartet 273, 1059
Sotgiù, Antonia *voc* 939
Sotin, Hans *bass* 690, 692, 703
Souquet, Marie-Bénénedicte *sop* 199
Sousa Band. 753
South German Radio Symphony Orchestra. 1132
South West German Radio Orchestra 1132
South West German Radio Symphony Orchestra. . . .292,
                                                  320, 705
      South West German Radio Symphony Orchestra, Baden-
      Baden and Freiburg (members) 823
      South West German Radio Symphony Orchestra, Baden-
      Baden and Freiburg 584, 643, 690
South West German Radio Vokalensemble. 610
Southend Boys' Choir 718
Southern Voices 374
Souza, Luciana *voc* 477
Spägele, Mona *sop* 93
Spagnoli, Pietro *bar* 755, 756
Spanjaard, Ed *cond* 377
Spano, Robert *cond* 347, 477
Sparf, Nils-Erik *vn* 1076
Spears, Paul *ten* 1130
Speculum Musicae. 958
Spence, Nicky *ten* 1035
Spence, Patricia *mez* 474, 747
Spence, Toby *ten* 98, 224, 440, 518, 568, 585, 1010
Spencer, Robert *lute* 1347
Spering, Andreas *cond* 567, 568, 569
Spicer, Paul *cond* 277, 591, 1183, 1294
Spierer, Leon *vn* 1105
Spinosi, Jean-Christophe *cond* 948, 1259, 1261
Spogis, Raimonds *bass* 325
Spoleto Festival Choir. 739
Spoleto Festival Orchestra 739
Spooner, Joseph *vc* 303
Spoorenberg, Erna *sop* 690
Springuel, France *va* 627
St Anthony Singers 891
St Christopher Chamber Orchestra 727
St Clement Danes School Choir. 832
St George's Chapel Choir, Windsor Castle. 841
St Hedwig's Cathedral Choir, Berlin 261
St John, Scott *vn* 836, 837
St John's College Choir, Cambridge . . .96, 189, 272, 278,
            394, 434, 596, 654, 957, 1094, 1293, 1555
St John's Smith Square Orchestra 482
St Louis Symphony Orchestra 99, 544, 1304

St Luke's Orchestra. 102, 1129, 1130, 1132
St Luke's Orchestra (members). 1130
St Margaret's Westminster (Singers and Congregation). .
                                                       957
St Margaret's Westminster Singers 957
St Paul's Cathedral Choir 197, 1200, 1345
St Paul's Cathedral Choir (Boys' Voices) . . . 274, 275, 832
St Paul's Cathedral Orchestra. 99, 100
St Petersburg Chamber Choir 1174
St Petersburg Kirov Orchestra 1127, 1128
St Petersburg Maryinsky Theatre Orchestra 949
St Petersburg Philharmonic Orchestra. 1056
St Willibrord and Pius X Children's Choir 690, 692
St Willibrord's Boys' Choir 690, 692
Staatskapelle Dresden . .126, 194, 244, 245, 530, 696, 790,
      1020, 1106, 1109, 1110, 1121, 1159, 1272, 1285, 1297,
                                                      1357
Staatskapelle Weimar 1103, 1110
Stacey, Martin *org* 737
Stade, Frederica von *mez* 319, 689, 690, 696
Stader, Maria *sop* 299
Stadler, Sergei *vn* 1096
Staier, Andreas *fp* 342, 438, 549, 1000, 1014, 1015
Staier, Andreas *pf* 155, 254, 1014
Stam, Caroline *sop* 92
Stan, Eduard *pf* 428
Standage, Simon *vn* 504, 507, 648, 1176
Standage, Simon *cond* 504, 526, 1176, 1252
Staples, Andrew *ten* 358, 1203
Starker, János *vc* 593
Starobin, David *cond* 958
Stavanger Symphony Orchestra 1194
Steele-Perkins, Crispian *tpt* 87, 654
Steen, Jac van *cond* 415
Steen-Nøkleberg, Einar *pf* 492
Stefanelli, Massimiliano *cond* 1211, 1212
Stefanovich, Tamara *pf* 107
Stefanowicz, Artur *alto* 755, 756
Stein, Horst *cond* 1073, 1075
Steinberg, Mark *vn* 354
Steinberg, William *cond* 132, 590, 690
Stemme, Nina *sop* 1111
Stene, Randi *mez* 615, 1109
Stenz, Markus *cond* 480, 577
Stepanovich, Dmitri *bass* 867
Stepansky, Alan *vc* 99
Stephen, Pamela Helen *mez* 167, 277, 434, 435, 564, 565,
                        566, 567, 600, 1003, 1093
Stern, Isaac *vn* 99, 130, 131, 254, 782, 992, 993, 1298
Stern, Michael *cond* 954
Stevens, Horace *bass* 426
Stewart, Patrick *spkr* 1109
Stignani, Ebe *mez* 852
Stilgoe, Richard *spkr* 1291
Sting *spkr* 865
Sting *sngr* 1329
Stinton, Jennifer *fl* 99
Stirling, Stephen *hn* 256, 1092
Stockholm Festival Orchestra. 1066
(Royal) Stockholm Philharmonic Orchestra 1058
Stockholm Royal Opera Chorus. 199
Stokowski, Leopold *cond* 421, 690, 895, 1054, 1314
Stoltzman, Richard *cl* 819
Stolze, Gerhard *ten* 832, 833
Stone, William *bar* 581
Storey, Martin *vc* 121
Storgårds, John *vn* 1196

Storgårds, John *cond* 304, 750, 840, 1196
Stotijn, Christianne *mez* 1172
Stott, Kathryn *pf* 431, 433, 625, 850, 1290, 1335
Stötzel, Ulrich *cond* 1179
Stoyanova, Krassimira *sop* 938
Strasbourg Philharmonic Orchestra 859
Strauss, Richard *cond* 110, 1103
Stravinsky, Igor *cond* 1128, 1134, 1311
Streit, Kurt *ten* 135, 790, 791
Stringer, Mark *cond* 234
Stryncl, Marek *cond* 474
Stuart, Greg *perc* 1308
Stubbs, Stephen *cond* 760
Stucky, Steven *cond* 1302
Studer, Cheryl *sop* 168, 689, 690, 1110, 1207, 1209
Sturrock, Kathron *pf* 224
Stuttgart Bach Collegium 93, 690, 738
Stuttgart Baroque Orchestra 85, 86, 87
Stuttgart Chamber Choir 85, 86, 87
Stuttgart Chamber Orchestra 126, 465
Stuttgart Ensemble 276
Stuttgart Gächinger Kantorei 670, 738
Stuttgart Radio Symphony Orchestra . . 231, 287, 293, 296,
                        299, 421, 465, 635, 670, 842
Stuttgart School of Music Chorus 421
Stuttgart State Opera Chorus 882
Stuttgart State Opera Orchestra 882
Stuttgart Südfunkchor 421, 690, 692
Stuttgart Vocal Ensemble 643, 1132
Stutzmann, Nathalie *contr* 790, 791, 1255
Suart, Richard *bass* 766, 891
Sudbin, Yevgeny *pf* 729, 901, 974, 1043, 1160
Suddaby, Elsie *sop* 374, 426
Sugawara, Yukiko *pf* 643
Suisse Romande Orchestra . . 126, 199, 231, 444, 592, 829,
                        859, 916, 1073, 1075, 1105, 1999
Suisse Romande Radio Chorus 829
Suk, Josef *vn* 290, 400, 441, 732
Sulzen, Donald *pf* 936
Summerhayes, Adam *va* 303
Summerhayes, Adam *vn* 303
Summerhayes, Catherine *pf* 303
Summerly, Jeremy *cond* 459, 549, 647, 826, 1155
Summers, Hilary *contr* 179, 236, 521, 573, 1254
Summers, Jonathan *bar* 1198
Summers, Patrick *cond* 176
Sundkvist, Petter *cond* 1095
Suovanen, Gabriel *bar* 687
Susskind, Walter *cond* 397, 490, 1066
Süssman, Gunilla *pf* 1194
Sussmuth, Gernot *vn* 1016
Sutcliffe, Sidney *ob* 143
Sutherland, Joan *sop* 515, 530, 1100, 1359
Sutherland, Gavin *cond* 202, 849
Sutre, Guillaume *vn* 445
Sutton, Jamal *org* 1187
Suzuki, Masaaki *hpd, org* 89
Suzuki, Masaaki *cond* 89, 90, 92, 93
Suzuki, Midori *sop* 89, 92
Svanholm, Set *ten* 690
Svanholm Singers 1187
Svedlund, Thord *cond* 1301
Svenheden, Joakim *vn* 814
Svensson, Peter *ten* 615
Svetlanov, Evgeni *cond* 198, 199, 397, 398, 816
Svizzera Italiana Orchestra 710
Swedish Chamber Orchestra 123, 1021, 1022

(Royal) Swedish Chamber Orchestra 1089
Swedish Opera Chorus 187
Swedish Radio Choir 135, 261, 843, 979
Swedish Radio Chorus 168, 1028, 1207, 1208, 1209
Swedish Radio Symphony Orchestra . . 819, 835, 843, 981,
                        1066, 1073, 1189
Sweeney, Donald *bass* 1154
Swensen, Joseph *cond* 682, 1057
Swete, Alexander *gtr* 354
Swiss Chamber Choir 130, 135, 136, 168, 1311
Swiss Radio Chorus 535
Swiss-Italian Radio Chorus 328
Swiss-Italian Radio Orchestra 328
Sydney Symphony Orchestra 1045, 1288
Sykes, Belinda *contr* 623
Symphony of Harmony and Invention . 308, 514, 529, 891
Symphony Orchestra 68, 368, 372, 484
Symphony Orchestra of La Monnaie 721, 1134
Synergy Vocals 924
Szabó, Peter *vc* 143
Szell, George *cond* 130, 131, 132, 133, 242, 397, 404, 696,
                        707, 780, 793, 814, 1021, 1110, 1311
Szidon, Roberto *pf* 668
Szmytka, Elzbieta *sop* 1143
Szrvinsk, Celina *pf* 1331
Szymanski, Morgan *gtr* 951

T

Tafelmusik 676
Tafelmusik Chamber Choir 676
Tagliavini, Franco *ten* 194, 195
Takács Quartet 109, 110, 144, 145, 146, 147,
                        148, 253, 995
Takahashi, Yuji *prep pf* 317
Takenouchi, Hiroaki *pf* 378
Tal, Yaara *pf* 260, 786
(Les) Talens Lyriques 472, 528, 531, 624, 677, 712
Talich, Václav *cond* 1085
Talich Quartet 144, 145, 148, 149, 613
Talla Vocal Ensemble 910
Tallinn Chamber Orchestra 844, 1193
Tallis Scholars . . . 289, 311, 351, 622, 671, 762, 838, 1148,
                        1149
Tamminga, Liuwe *org* 1139
Tampere Philharmonic Orchestra 288, 429, 627, 740, 840,
                        1196
Tan, Margaret Leng *toy pf* 315
Tan, Melvyn *fp* 736
Tan, Melvyn *pf* 793
Tanglewood Festival Chorus 662
Tanski, Claudius *pf* 848
Tapani, Esa *hn* 627, 660
Tapiola Chamber Choir 969
Tapiola Sinfonietta 750, 969, 1057, 1075, 1295
Tarver, Kenneth *ten* 193
Tasmanian Symphony Orchestra 578, 763
Tate, Jeffrey *cond* 290, 319, 732, 764, 916, 1288
Taverner Choir 754, 755
Taverner Consort 754, 755
Taverner Players 754, 755
Taylor, Alexander *pf* 233
Taylor, Daniel *alto* 85, 86, 87
Taylor, Daniel *counterten* 972
Taylor, James *ten* 93, 168
Taylor, Kendall *pf* 605

Taylor, Stephen *ob* 1130, 1132
Tbilisi Symphony Orchestra. 628
Tchaikovsky Symphony Orchestra. 867
Tchistjakova, Irina *mez* 867
Te Kanawa, Kiri *sop* 319, 394, 434, 530, 916
Tear, Robert *ten* 91, 275, 412, 707, 755, 1127
Tees, Stephen *va* 766
Temirkanov, Yuri *cond* 1056
Temple Church Choir 1156
Tena, Lucero *cast*. 932
Tenebrae 1146
Tennant, Scott *gtr* 477
Tennstedt, Klaus *cond* 289, 290, 294, 298, 690, 701,
        702, 703
Terfel, Bryn *bass-bar* . .261, 374, 424, 518, 528, 530, 689,
    690, 738, 755, 794, 1008, 1028, 1200, 1201, 1203, 1287,
        1292
Terroni, Raphael *pf* 748
Tesarowicz, Romuald *bass* 846
Testolin, Walter *cond* 623
Tetzlaff, Christian *vn* 111, 131, 686, 1159, 1160
Tetzlaff, Christian *dir* 686
Teuffel, Gunter *va* 922
Teuscher, Lydia *sop* 1035
Tewkesbury Abbey Schola Cantorum 1299
Texier, Vincent le *bar* 234
Teyte, Maggie *sop* 68, 368
Tharaud, Alexandre *pf* 352, 364
The Clerks. 923
Théâtre du Châtelet Chorus, Paris. 201, 1216
Theatre of Early Music 972
Theatre of Voices 317, 843, 926, 1096
Thedéen, Torleif *vc* 199, 224, 252, 496, 969
Theuns, Frank *fl* 765
Thibaud, Jacques *vn* 1023
Thibaudet, Jean-Yves *pf* 365, 366, 444, 742, 914
Thielemann, Christian *cond* 790, 1111
Thiollier, François-Joël *pf* 430
Thomas, David *bass* 87, 515, 789
Thomas, David Porter *bass* 754
Thomas, Jacqueline *vc* 613
Thomas, Marjorie *contr* 374, 690
Thomas, Mary *sop* 656
Thomas, Nigel *perc* 107
Thompson, Adrian *ten* 91, 615, 1034, 1035, 1201
Thompson, Candida *vn* 1246, 1247
Thompson, Curt *vn* 609
Thompson, Michael *hn, dir* 766
Thomsen, Janne *fl* 713
Thomson, Bryden *cond* 439
Thorborg, Kerstin *mez* 168, 169, 1209
Thorby, Pamela *rec* 509, 1244
Thorby, Philip *dir* 623
Thornhill, Siri *sop* 888
Thorsen, Marianne *vn* 1291
Thwaites, Penelope *pf* 486, 487
Thyssens-Valentin, Germaine *pf* 433
Tibbels, Nicole *sop* 643, 1132
Tiberghien, Cédric *pf* 164, 713
Tichman, Nina *pf* 152, 154, 432
Tiffin Children's Choir. 880, 881
Tiffin School Boys' Choir. 275, 281, 284, 703, 883
Tiihonen, Kirsi *sop* 1077, 1078
Tiilikainen, Sauli *bar* 1077
Tilikainen, Sauli *bar* 1078
Tilkin, Michel *tbn* 398
Tilling, Camilla *sop* 789

Tilney, Colin *hpd* 530
Tilson Thomas, Michael *pf* 455, 608
Tilson Thomas, Michael *cond* . . .346, 347, 455, 585, 608,
        699, 704, 706, 732, 962, 1126, 1128, 1241
Timson, David *spkr* 1130
Tinney, Hugh *pf* 731
Tintner, Georg *cond* 291, 292, 294, 297
Tippett, Michael *cond* 889, 1183
Tipping, Christopher *alto* 530
Tirimo, Martino *pf* 366, 367
Tiso, Elisabetta *sop* 1247
Titus, Graham *bar* 690, 692
Tjeknavorian, Loris *cond* 631, 632, 633
Tobin, John *ten* 91
Tognetti, Richard *vn* 1045
Tognetti, Richard *cond* 1045, 1244
Tokyo Little Singers 690, 692
Tokyo Quartet. 109, 144, 146
Toll, John *hpd* 459
Toll, John *org* 459
Tölz Boys' Choir . 196, 689, 690, 755, 814, 815, 832, 1028
Tölzer Knabenchor. 693
Tomassi, Giorgia *pf* 1316
Tomes, Susan *pf* 111, 256
Tomkins, Giles *bass-bar* 1253
Tomlinson, John *bass* 518, 530, 1121
Tomter, Lars Anders *va* 996, 1288
Tongeren, Mark van *voc* 1058
Tonus Peregrinus 845
Tormis, Veljo *perc* 1187
Toronto Children's Choir. 703
Torres, Victor *bar* 755, 758
Tortelier, Paul *vc* 418, 424, 425, 720, 992, 993, 1336
Tortelier, Yan Pascal *vn* 1336
Tortelier, Yan Pascal *cond* . .234, 326, 327, 394, 395, 431,
    434, 435, 443, 579, 583, 629, 644, 678, 742, 748, 856,
        916, 952, 1132, 7483
Toscanini, Arturo *cond* 132, 137, 140, 168, 169, 245,
        1209, 1218
Tóth, István *db* 143, 994
Toulouse Capitole Chorus 221, 371, 483, 484
Toulouse Capitole Orchestra 221, 371, 483, 484
Toulouse Saqueboutiers 301
Tourel, Jennie *mez* 695
Tovey, Bramwell *cond* 1322
TOWER Voices New Zealand. 600
Tozer, Geoffrey *pf* 730
Tracey, Ian *org* 1336
Tragicomedia. 210, 760
Trekel, Roman *bar* 1306
Trendell, David *cond* 671, 1046
Trevor, Kirk *cond* 475
Trinity Boys' Choir. 442, 717, 1132
Trinity Church Boys' Choir (New York). 690
Trinity College Choir, Cambridge. 511, 674, 856
Trondheim Soloists. 496, 1247
Trost, Rainer *ten* 168
Trotter, Thomas *org* 101, 204, 212, 423, 596
Trpceski, Simon *pf* 332, 334, 368, 1337
Trullu, Maria José *mez* 1259
Tselovalnik, Evgenia *sop* 1051
Tubéry, Jean *cond* 309
Tübingen Festival Band 944
Tucker, Mark *ten* 755
Tuckwell, Barry *hn* 272, 766
Tuckwell, Barry *dir* 766
Tuinstra, Stef *org* 1139

Tuma, Jaroslav *org* 411
Tunnicliffe, Richard *va d'amore* 210
Tunnicliffe, Richard *vc* 1253
Turetschek, Gerhard *ob* 656
Turin RAI Chorus.................................. 883
Turin RAI Orchestra.................... 191, 192, 883
Turin Teatro Regio Chorus 1260
Turin Teatro Regio Filarmonica '900 Orchestra..... 855
Türk, Gerd *ten* 85, 89, 90, 92, 93, 318
Turku Philharmonic Orchestra 429
Turner, John *rec* 919
Tuxen, Erik *cond* 707
Twentieth Century Classics Ensemble....... 1129, 1130
Tynan, Ailish *sop* 996
Tyson, Robin *alto* 314

U

Uchida, Mitsuko *pf* 787, 981, 999, 1000, 1001
Ukraine National Symphony Orchestra....811, 814, 851,
                                              1080
Ulivieri, Nicola *bass* 1353
Ullén, Fredrik *pf* 1089
Ullmann, Marcus *ten* 85, 86, 87, 93
Ulster Orchestra 203, 545, 748, 842, 918, 954, 1092, 1188,
                                              7483
University of Texas Wind Ensemble 350
Upshaw, Dawn *sop* 102, 477, 479, 480, 523, 983
Urano, Chiyuki *bass* 89, 90
Urano, Chiyuki *bass-bar* 92
Urbas, Ivan *bass* 1301
Uria-Monzon, Béatrice *mez* 197
Urmana, Violeta *mez* 1263
USSR State Symphony Orchestra 397, 398
USSR Symphony Orchestra 816
Utah Symphony Orchestra 530

V

Vacellier, André *cl* 741
Vajda, József *bn* 143
Valade, Pierre-André *cond* 214
Valdés, Maximiano *cond* 931, 932
Válek, Vladimir *cond* 105
Valent, Milos *va* 474
Valent, Milos *vn* 474
Vallina, Mauricio *pf* 1317
Van Bockstal, Piet *ob* 546
Van Dam, George *vn* 546
Van Dam, José *bass-bar* 165, 196, 261, 262, 693
Van der Gucht, Jan *ten* 372
Van der Zwart, Teunis *bn* 766
Van Doeselaar, Leo *org* 580, 1139
Van Veldhoven, Jos *cond* 92
Vanbrugh Quartet............... 347, 379, 1092, 1093
Vanbrugh Quartet................................ 227
Vancouver Symphony Orchestra 1020, 1311, 1322
Vandernoot, André *cond* 1159
Vänskä, Osmo *cond* ...137, 138, 139, 141, 836, 969, 1066,
     1069, 1070, 1071, 1072, 1073, 1074, 1076, 1077, 1078
Varady, Julia *sop* ..690, 692, 870, 1052, 1114, 1173, 1210,
                                              1263
Varcoe, Stephen *bar* ..84, 85, 87, 167, 277, 433, 434, 435,
     436, 487, 501, 512, 516, 564, 565, 566, 567, 600, 1010,
                                        1093, 1094

Varcoe, Stephen *bass* 530, 564
Varèse, Edgard *elec* 1195
Varga, Gilbert *cond* 644
Várjon, Dénes *pf* 1024
Vartolo, Sergio *hpd, org* 447
Varviso, Silvio *cond* 807
Vasari Singers 393
Vass, George *cond* 1188
Vaughan, Elizabeth *mez* 1121
Vaughan, Johnny *org* 189
Vauquet, André *va* 1105
Vedernikov, Alexander *cond* 1052
Végh, Sándor *cond* 775
Vele, Ludek *bass* 407
(La) Venexiana...................... 603, 756, 757
Vengerov, Maxim *vn* 270, 290, 467, 773, 863, 1348
Vengerov, Maxim *dir* 773
Venice Baroque Orchestra ...526, 530, 1246, 1247, 1248,
                                        1249, 1255
Venice La Fenice Chorus 938
Venice La Fenice Orchestra 938
Venuti, Maria *sop* 690, 692
Venzago, Mario *cond* 496
Verbier Festival Chamber Orchestra 773
Verbruggen, Marion *fl, rec* 508
Verdernikov, Alexander *cond* 1049
Verebits, Ibolya *sop* 89
Vermillion, Iris *mez* 670, 1028
Vernet, Isabelle *sop* 199
Vernizzi, Fulvio *cond* 883
Verona Arena Chorus............................ 1226
Verona Arena Orchestra 1226
Veronesi, Alberto *cond* 875
Versalle, Richard *ten* 703
Verschuren, Wouter *bn* 1243
Verzier, Alix *vc* 166
Vesna Children's Choir.......................... 867
Vesterman, Agnes *vc* 1330
Viala, Jean-Luc *ten* 197
Vicini, Elena *cast* 1348
Victor Orchestra 1350
Victoria State Orchestra 646
Victorian Opera Chorus 97
Victorian Opera Orchestra 97
Vienna Boys' Choir...85, 88, 89, 185, 218, 689, 690, 693,
                                  810, 816, 885, 1119
Vienna Chamber Orchestra 793, 1169
Vienna Concentus Musicus.85, 88, 89, 503, 552, 568, 572,
                           755, 788, 790, 791, 793, 889
Vienna Hofmusikkapelle Choir 755
Vienna Opera Chorus............................ 1121
Vienna Piano Trio.............................. 1061
Vienna Philharmonic Orchestra..126, 127, 131, 132, 135,
     137, 140, 141, 168, 183, 185, 218, 242, 245, 249, 294,
     295, 296, 297, 299, 323, 368, 421, 577, 616, 617, 618,
     619, 636, 637, 640, 651, 656, 689, 690, 693, 698, 704,
     707, 708, 734, 771, 780, 790, 799, 810, 811, 814, 876,
     877, 881, 885, 927, 990, 1053, 1054, 1085, 1099, 1100,
     1104, 1114, 1115, 1117, 1119, 1121, 1123, 1124, 1125,
     1161, 1214, 1231, 1262, 1265, 1269, 1276, 5628
Vienna Philharmonic Quartet..................... 1000
Vienna Piano Trio.......................... 561, 1171
Vienna Radio Symphony Orchestra ....
                           465, 628, 1193, 1300, 1303
Vienna Singakademie Chorus..................... 173
Vienna Singverein 134, 135, 261, 262, 693

Vienna State Opera Chorus .172, 185, 187, 218, 220, 368, 616, 617, 618, 619, 640, 689, 690, 799, 816, 876, 877, 881, 885, 886, 986, 1100, 1115, 1118, 1119, 1125, 1222, 1225, 1231, 1237, 1265, 1267, 1269, 1276, 1297, 5628
Vienna State Opera Concert Choir . . .577, 693, 790, 810, 1300
Vienna State Opera Orchestra . . .172, 187, 220, 816, 886, 986, 1118, 1222, 1225, 1237, 1267, 1297
Vienna Symphony Orchestra . .130, 173, 292, 1100, 1101, 1125, 1159
Vienna Volksoper Chorus. 1100
Viennensis Chorus. 85
Vignoles, Roger pf 165, 264, 408, 495, 500, 706, 938, 1010, 1030, 1112, 1113, 1294
Viljakainen, Raili sop 1078
Villa Musica Ensemble 992
Villars, Jon ten 703
Villaume, Emmanuel cond 1357
Villazón, Rolando ten 530, 720, 1357, 1359
Viotti, Marcello cond 530, 870, 1359
Virgilio, Nicolas di ten 275, 276
Virtanen, Otto bn 627
(I) Virtuosi Italiani. 950
Vis, Lucas cond 437
Vishnevskaya, Galina sop 272
Visse, Dominique cond 301
Vitale, Salvo bass 524
Vittorio, Giuseppe de ten 818
Vivian, James org 530, 684
Vlach Quartet 405, 613, 913
Vlachova, Jana vn 613
Voces Intimae Trio 599
Vogel, Siegfried bass 690, 692
Vogler Quartet 921
Vogt, Lars pf 141, 580
Voigt, Deborah sop 1263
Volkov, Ilan cond 27, 270, 546, 615, 686, 1288
Volodos, Arcadi pf 896, 999
Voorhees, Donald cond 636
Voropaev, Dmitri ten 1058
Vorster, Len pf 202
Votto, Antonino cond 384, 853
Vronsky, Vitya pf 1198
Vyvyan, Jennifer sop 272

W

Waart, Edo de cond 414, 415, 1045
Waddington, Henry bass 520
Waechter, Eberhard bar 261
Wagemans, Michel pf 749
Wagner, Jan cond 461
Wait, Mark pf 1130
Wakefield, John ten 518
Wakeford, Lucy hp 98
Walden, Timothy vc 411
Walker, Kim bn 95
Walker, Norman bass 424, 425, 518, 519
Walker, Sarah mez 135, 137, 373, 530, 1183, 1201
Wallace, John tpt 214, 855
Wallace, Stephen counterten 521, 1139
Wallace Collection 960, 1293, 1343
Wallenstein, Alfred cond 636
Wallfisch, Elizabeth vn 349, 1253
Wallfisch, Raphael vc 231, 302, 439, 445, 1169
Wallin, Ulf vn 581, 922

Walmsley-Clark, Penelope sop 178, 546
Walt, Deon van der ten 791, 1029
Walter, Bruno cond 690, 704, 707, 708, 790, 1221
Walton, Bernard cl 143
Walton, Sam perc 214
Walton, William cond 1290, 1292
Wand, Günter cond . . . 143, 245, 293, 294, 297, 298, 990
Wandsworth School Boys' Choir . .91, 194, 195, 275, 281, 284, 530, 884, 885
Wang, Jian vc 243, 256
Wang, Yuja pf 1337
Ward, Adrian ten 1035
Ward, David bass 1206, 1209
Ward, Nicholas cond 552, 777, 778, 932, 1130, 1176
Warren-Green, Christopher vn 633
Warsaw Boys' Choir 846
Warsaw National Philharmonic Orchestra 846
Warsaw Philharmonia Orchestra 1142
Warsaw Philharmonic Choir 846, 1142, 1144
Warsaw Philharmonic Orchestra . . .819, 846, 1141, 1142, 1144
Washington Choral Arts Society 702
Waskiewicz, Danusha va 772
Wass, Ashley pf 114, 120, 121, 268
Waterman, David vc 432
Waters, Rodney pf 609
Waters, Stephen cl 765, 766
Waters, Susannah sop 892
Watkin, David vc 453, 1252
Watkins, Paul vc 180, 215, 855, 1181, 1191, 1291
Watkins, Richard hn 855
Watkinson, Andrew vn 1245
Watkinson, Carolyn contr 566, 790
Watson, Christopher ten 515
Watson, Ian org 564, 1093, 1199
Watson, Janice sop 135, 165, 565, 590, 856
(George) Watson College Boys' Chorus 218, 219
Watton, Stacey db 1246, 1247
Watts, Andrew alto 239
Watts, Elizabeth sop 1010, 1195
Watts, Helen contr 85, 89, 424, 518
Waynflete Singers 374, 590, 1287
WDR Symphony Orchestra 1206, 1265
Webber, Aaron treb 888
Webber, Geoffrey cond 1046
Webern, Anton cond 181, 1298
Weigl, François pf 742
Weigle, Sebastian cond 530
Weimann, Alexander hpd 457
Weir, Gillian org 745, 1337
Weiss, Catherine vn 349
Weissenberg, Alexis pf 1338
Wells Cathedral Choir 654
Welser-Möst, Franz cond 284, 286, 1121, 1225, 1316
Welsh National Opera Chorus . . .368, 370, 462, 484, 619, 1137, 1138, 1174, 5759
Welsh National Opera Orchestra. 368, 370, 484, 619, 1137, 1138, 1174, 5759
Wenkel, Ortrun contr 1052
Werba, Markus bar 568
Werdenfelser Male Chorus. 1120
Werthen, Rudolf cond 627
Weser-Renaissance (Bremen) 1038
West German Radio Chorus 690
West German Radio Symphony Orchestra 247, 1054, 1056
Westminster Abbey Choir 312, 530, 1346

Westminster Abbey Orchestra 530
Westminster Cathedral Choir . . .278, 285, 358, 635, 684,
711, 838, 840, 1238, 1239
Westminster Cathedral Choir (Boys' Voices) 358
Westminster Choir 168, 690
Wettstein, Shannon *hpd* 1308
Wexler, Elizabeth *vn* 121
White, Jeremy *bass* 1111
White, Robert *bagpipe* 578
White, Willard *bar* 1310
White, Willard *bass* 196
Whittaker, Douglas *fl* 1347
Whitton, Christopher *org* 654, 1293
Whitworth, John *alto* 889
Wickham, Edward *cond* 301, 387, 622, 825, 826, 827, 923
Widdop, Walter *ten* 426
Widmann, Carolin *vn* 1024
Widmer, Oliver *bass* 88, 89, 788
Wieczorek, Maryseult *sop* 752, 755, 756
Wiener Tschuschenkapelle. 651
Wiens, Edith *sop* 143, 703
Wigglesworth, Mark *cond* 707, 1054, 1057
Wilbraham, John *tpt* 530
Wilbrink, Hans *bar* 275
Wild, Earl *pf* 455, 456, 665, 666
Wilkie, Matthew *bn* 656
Wilkinson, Clare *contr* 89, 518, 622
Willcocks, David *cond* 434, 1292
Williams, Camilla *sop* 690
Williams, Jeremy Huw *bar* 959
Williams, John *gtr* 463, 1298
Williams, Louise *va* 145, 231, 782
Williams, Roderick *bar* 96, 98, 412, 606, 985, 1203
Williams, Sioned *hp* 278, 1343
Williamson, Thomas *org* 1343
Willis, Alastair *cond* 917
Willison, John *vn* 418
Willoughby Quartet 255
Wills, Clare *ob* 1046
Wilson, Christopher *lute* 387
Wilson, Glen *hpd* 1139
Wilson, Malcolm *pf* 272
Wilson, Miranda *vc* 497
Wilson, John *cond* 343, 454
Wilson-Johnson, David bass-*bar* . . . .
195, 522, 566, 703, 985, 1254
Wilson-Johnson, David *spkr* 982, 1132
Wimmer, Hans-Georg *bass* 1178
Wincenc, Carol *fl* 495
Winchester Cathedral Choir 789, 1094, 1149, 1154, 1287
Winchester Quiristers. 789, 1149
Winchester Vocal Arts 1149
Wind Ensemble. 505, 506
Winsemius, Bernard *org* 1139
Winter, Louise *mez* 564
Wirth, Christian *alto sax* 188
Wishart, Stevie *cond* 578
Wispelwey, Pieter *vc* 154, 396, 397, 415, 1253, 1288
Wit, Antoni *cond* .106, 403, 479, 677, 678, 742, 846, 1085,
1103, 1141, 1142, 1144, 1295
Witcomb, Nicholas *treb* 888
Wodnicki, Adam *pf* 1150
Wolff, Christine *sop* 574
Wolff, Hugh *cond* 99, 100, 1051
Wolfram, William *pf* 350
Wong, Samuel *cond* 304
Wood, Henry *cond* 417

Wood, James *cond* 974, 1308
Woolley, Robert *hpd* 349, 1140
Woolley, Robert *org* 349
Woolley, Robert *virg* 1140
Wordsworth, Barry *cond* 343, 611, 645, 646, 728
Wörle, Robert *ten* 581
Worrall, Peter *vc* 271
Wosner, Shai *pf* 156
Wottrich, Erich *ten* 1028
Woytowicz, Stefania *sop* 275
Wright, Adam *tpt* 214
Wright, Gavin *vn* 1154
Wright, Patricia *sop* 600
Wright, Simon *cond* 426
Wroclaw Opera Chorus 752
Wroclaw Opera Orchestra 752
Wu, Mia *vn* 354
Wulstan, David *cond* 1149
Wunderlich, Fritz *ten* 530, 707
Wunrow, Theresa Elder *hp* 852
Württemberg Chamber Orchestra. 690, 1317
Württemberg Philharmonic Orchestra 850
Wustman, John *pf* 199, 916, 1999
Wyn-Davies, Catrin *sop* 1254
Wyn-Rogers, Catherine *contr* 300, 1201
Wyn-Rogers, Catherine *mez* 98, 135, 442, 1010
Wynberg, Simon *gtr* 836, 837
Wyss, Gérard *pf* 997, 1004

Y

Yablonsky, Dmitry *cond* 290, 1166, 1185
Yakar, Rachel *sop* 742
Yampolsky, Vladimir *pf* 866, 1332
Yang, Wen-Sinn *vc* 934
Yates, Sophie *hpd* 353, 509, 905
Yates, Sophie *virg* 314
Yeend, Frances *sop* 690
Yenque, Dante *hn* 1240
Yggdrasil Quartet 331
YL Male Voice Choir 910, 1077
Ylönen, Marko *vc* 627, 1074
York, Deborah *sop* 89, 90, 1247
York, John *pf* 445
Yoshida, Mika *marimba* 925
Young, Alexander *ten* 426
Young, Richard *va* 994
Young, Thomas *ten* 230
Ysaÿe, Eugène *cond* 1023
Ysaÿe Quartet 445, 1023
Yuasa, Takuo *cond* 271, 545, 842, 918, 954
Yurlov State Capella 867
Yurov, Yuri *va* 1170
Yvonne Gouverné Choir. 68, 368

Z

Zacharias, Christian *pf* 779, 788, 993, 994
Zacharias, Christian *cond* 779
Zacher, Gerd *org* 656
Zagrosek, Lothar *cond* 581
Zajick, Dolora *mez* 1207, 1209
Zalay, Tamás *vn* 1244

Zalupe, Rihards *perc* 628
Zanasi, Furio *bar* 755, 756
Zander, Benjamin *cond* 295
Zank, Gerhard *vc* 936
Zanon, Fabio *gtr* 1240
Zarafiants, Evgeny *pf* 1042
Zaremba, Eléna *mez* 814
Zazzo, Lawrence *alto* 520, 529
Zedda, Alberto *cond* 942, 944, 948
Zeffiri, Mario *ten* 758
Zefiro 507, 1251
Zehetmair, Thomas *vn* . . . 133, 584, 993, 994, 1141, 1308
Zehetmair Quartet 110, 1022
Zeijst, Martin van der *alto* 888
Zelles, Allison *voc* 317
Zeppenfeld, George *bass* 790
Zeumer, Gerti *sop* 693
Ziesak, Ruth *sop* 85, 86, 135, 136
Zilberstein, Lilya *pf* 1049, 1316
Zimerman, Krystian *pf* . 105, 329, 365, 366, 661, 894, 895, 911, 912

Zimerman, Krystian *dir* 329
Zimmermann, Frank Peter *vn* 304, 657, 1338
Zimmermann, Tabea *va* 123, 152, 192, 580, 993, 994
Zinman, David *cond* 99, 102, 129, 130, 131, 135, 136, 137, 168, 421, 422, 455, 456, 479, 480, 631, 772, 1021, 1104, 1154
Ziva, Vladimir *cond* 729
Zlotnikov, Kyril *vc* 784
Znaider, Nikolaj *vn* 257, 637, 784, 862
Zöller, Karlheinz *fl* 742
Zomer, Johannette *sop* 434, 435, 444
Zoon, Jacques *fl* 656, 1176, 1195
Zurich Opera House Chorus 172, 284, 286, 306, 829, 941, 1116, 1119, 1121, 1212, 1225
Zurich Opera House Orchestra . . 172, 284, 286, 306, 829, 941, 1116, 1119, 1121, 1212, 1225
Zurich Symphony Orchestra 330
Zurich Tonhalle Orchestra . . 129, 130, 131, 135, 136, 137, 168, 490, 631, 772, 1021, 1104